Peterson's Graduate & Professional Programs

An Overview

2010

PETERSON'S
A nelnet COMPANY

PETERSON'S
A nelnet COMPANY

About Peterson's
To succeed on your lifelong educational journey, you will need accurate, dependable, and practical tools and resources. That is why Peterson's is everywhere education happens. Because whenever and however you need education content delivered, you can rely on Peterson's to provide the information, know-how, and guidance to help you reach your goals. Tools to match the right students with the right school. It's here. Personalized resources and expert guidance. It's here. Comprehensive and dependable education content—delivered whenever and however you need it. It's all here.

For more information, contact Peterson's, 2000 Lenox Drive, Lawrenceville, NJ 08648; 800-338-3282; or find us on the World Wide Web at www.petersons.com/about.

Stephen Clemente, President; Bernadette Webster, Director of Publishing; Jill C. Schwartz, Editor; Ken Britschge, Research Project Manager; Courtney Foust, Amy L. Weber, Research Associates; Phyllis Johnson, Programmer; Ray Golaszewski, Manufacturing Manager; Linda M. Williams, Composition Manager; Justin Freid, Janet Garwo, Mimi Kaufman, Karen Mount, Danielle Vreeland, Shannon White, Client Relations Representatives

ISSN 1520-4359
ISBN-13: 978-0-7689-2708-5
ISBN-10: 0-7689-2708-0

Printed in the United States of America

10 9 8 7 6 5 4 3 2 1   12 11 10

Forty-fourth Edition

By producing this book on recycled paper (40% post consumer waste) 151 trees were saved.

CONTENTS

A Note from the Peterson's Editors

The six volumes of *Peterson's Graduate and Professional Programs*, the only annually updated reference work of its kind, provide wide-ranging information on the graduate and professional programs offered by accredited colleges and universities in the United States, U.S. territories, and Canada and by those institutions outside the United States that are accredited by U.S. accrediting bodies. More than 44,000 individual academic and professional programs at more than 2,300 institutions are listed. *Peterson's Graduate and Professional Programs* have been used for more than forty years by prospective graduate and professional students, placement counselors, faculty advisers, and all others interested in postbaccalaureate education.

Graduate & Professional Programs: An Overview contains information on institutions as a whole, while the other books in the series are devoted to specific academic and professional fields:

Graduate Programs in the Humanities, Arts & Social Sciences
Graduate Programs in the Biological Sciences
Graduate Programs in the Physical Sciences, Mathematics, Agricultural Sciences, the Environment & Natural Resources
Graduate Programs in Engineering & Applied Sciences
Graduate Programs in Business, Education, Health, Information Studies, Law & Social Work

The books may be used individually or as a set. For example, if you have chosen a field of study but do not know what institution you want to attend or if you have a college or university in mind but have not chosen an academic field of study, it is best to begin with the Overview guide.

Graduate & Professional Programs: An Overview presents several directories to help you identify programs of study that might interest you; you can then research those programs further in the other books in the series by using the Directory of Graduate and Professional Programs by Field, which lists 500 fields and gives the names of those institutions that offer graduate degree programs in each.

For geographical or financial reasons, you may be interested in attending a particular institution and will want to know what it has to offer. You should turn to the Directory of Institutions and Their Offerings, which lists the degree programs available at each institution. As in the Directory of Graduate and Professional Programs by Field, the level of degrees offered is also indicated.

All books in the series include advice on graduate education, including topics such as admissions tests, financial aid, and accreditation. **The Graduate Adviser** includes two essays and information about accreditation. The first essay, "The Admissions Process," discusses general admission requirements, admission tests, factors to consider when selecting a graduate school or program, when and how to apply, and how admission decisions are made. Special information for international students and tips for minority students are also included. The second essay, "Financial Support," is an overview of the broad range of support available at the graduate level. Fellowships, scholarships, and grants; assistantships and internships; federal and private loan programs, as well as Federal Work-Study; and the GI bill are detailed. This essay concludes with advice on applying for need-based financial aid. "Accreditation and Accrediting Agencies" gives information on accreditation and its purpose and lists institutional accrediting agencies first and then specialized accrediting agencies relevant to each volume's specific fields of study.

With information on more than 44,000 graduate programs in 500 disciplines, *Peterson's Graduate and Professional Programs* give you all the information you need about the programs that are of interest to you in three formats: **Profiles** (capsule summaries of basic information), **Announcements** (information that an institution or program wants to emphasize, written by administrators), and **Close-Ups** (also written by administrators, with more expansive information than the **Profiles**, emphasizing different aspects of the programs). By using these various formats of program information, coupled with **Appendixes** and **Indexes** covering directories and subject areas for all six books, you will find that these guides provide the most comprehensive, accurate, and up-to-date graduate study information available.

Peterson's publishes a full line of resources with information you need to guide you through the graduate admissions process. Peterson's publications can be found at your local bookstore or library—or visit us on the Web at www.petersons.com.

Colleges and universities will be pleased to know that Peterson's helped you in your selection. Admissions staff members are more than happy to answer questions, address specific problems, and help in any way they can. The editors at Peterson's wish you great success in your graduate program search!

THE GRADUATE ADVISER

The Admissions Process

Generalizations about graduate admissions practices are not always helpful because each institution has its own set of guidelines and procedures. Nevertheless, some broad statements can be made about the admissions process that may help you plan your strategy.

Factors Involved in Selecting a Graduate School or Program

Selecting a graduate school and a specific program of study is a complex matter. Quality of the faculty; program and course offerings; the nature, size, and location of the institution; admission requirements; cost; and the availability of financial assistance are among the many factors that affect one's choice of institution. Other considerations are job placement and achievements of the program's graduates and the institution's resources, such as libraries, laboratories, and computer facilities. If you are to make the best possible choice, you need to learn as much as you can about the schools and programs you are considering before you apply.

The following steps may help you narrow your choices.

- Talk to alumni of the programs or institutions you are considering to get their impressions of how well they were prepared for work in their fields of study.
- Remember that graduate school requirements change, so be sure to get the most up-to-date information possible.
- Talk to department faculty members and the graduate adviser at your undergraduate institution. They often have information about programs of study at other institutions.
- Visit the Web sites of the graduate schools in which you are interested to request a graduate catalog. Contact the department chair in your chosen field of study for additional information about the department and the field.
- Visit as many campuses as possible. Call ahead for an appointment with the graduate adviser in your field of interest and be sure to check out the facilities and talk to students.

General Requirements

Graduate schools and departments have requirements that applicants for admission must meet. Typically, these requirements include undergraduate transcripts (which provide information about undergraduate grade point average and course work applied toward a major), admission test scores, and letters of recommendation. Most graduate programs also ask for an essay or personal statement that describes your personal reasons for seeking graduate study. In some fields, such as art and music, portfolios or auditions may be required in addition to other evidence of talent. Some institutions require that the applicant have an undergraduate degree in the same subject as the intended graduate major.

Most institutions evaluate each applicant on the basis of the applicant's total record, and the weight accorded any given factor varies widely from institution to institution and from program to program.

The Application Process

You should begin the application process at least one year before you expect to begin your graduate study. Find out the application deadline for each institution (many are provided in the **Profile** section of this guide). Go to the institution's Web site and find out if you can apply online. If not, request a paper application form. Fill out this form thoroughly and neatly. Assume that the school needs all the information it is requesting and that the admissions officer will be sensitive to the neatness and overall quality of what you submit. Do not supply more information than the school requires.

The institution may ask at least one question that will require a three- or four-paragraph answer. Compose your response on the assumption that the admissions officer is interested in both what you think and how you express yourself. Keep your statement brief and to the point, but, at the same time, include all pertinent information about your past experiences and your educational goals. Individual statements vary greatly in style and content, which helps admissions officers differentiate among applicants. Many graduate departments give considerable weight to the statement in making their admissions decisions, so be sure to take the time to prepare a thoughtful and concise statement.

If recommendations are a part of the admissions requirements, carefully choose the individuals you ask to write them. It is generally best to ask current or former professors to write the recommendations, provided they are able to attest to your intellectual ability and motivation for doing the work required of a graduate student. It is advisable to provide stamped, preaddressed envelopes to people being asked to submit recommendations on your behalf.

Completed applications, including references, transcripts, and admission test scores, should be received at the institution by the specified date.

Be advised that institutions do not usually make admissions decisions until all materials have been received. Enclose a self-addressed postcard with your application, requesting confirmation of receipt. Allow at least 10 days for the return of the postcard before making further inquiries.

If you plan to apply for financial support, it is imperative that you file your application early.

ADMISSION TESTS

The major testing program used in graduate admissions is the Graduate Record Examinations (GRE) testing program, sponsored by the GRE Board and administered by Educational Testing Service, Princeton, New Jersey.

The Graduate Record Examinations testing program consists of a General Test and eight Subject Tests. The General Test measures critical thinking, verbal reasoning, quantitative reasoning, and analytical writing skills. It is offered as an Internet-based test (iBT) in the United States, Canada, and many other countries.

The typical computer-based General Test consists of one 30-minute verbal reasoning section, one 45-minute quantitative reasoning sections, one 45-minute issue analysis (writing) section, and one 30-minute argument analysis (writing) section. In addition, an unidentified verbal or quantitative section that doesn't count toward a score may be included and an identified research section that is not scored may also be included.

The Subject Tests measure achievement and assume undergraduate majors or extensive background in the following eight disciplines:

- Biochemistry, Cell and Molecular Biology
- Biology
- Chemistry
- Computer Science
- Literature in English
- Mathematics
- Physics
- Psychology

The Subject Tests are available three times per year as paper-based administrations around the world. Testing time is approximately 2 hours and 50 minutes. You can obtain more information about the GRE by visiting the ETS Web site at www.ets.org or consulting the *GRE Information and Registration Bulletin.* The *Bulletin* can be obtained at many undergraduate colleges. You can also download it from the ETS Web site or obtain it by contacting Graduate Record Examinations, Educational Testing Service, PO Box 6000, Princeton, NJ 08541-6000; phone: 1-609-771-7670.

If you expect to apply for admission to a program that requires any of the GRE tests, you should select a test date well in advance of the application deadline. Scores on the computer-based General Test are reported within ten to fifteen days; scores on the paper-based Subject Tests are reported within six weeks.

Another testing program, the Miller Analogies Test (MAT), is administered at more than 500 Controlled Testing Centers, licensed by Harcourt Assessment, Inc., in the United States, Canada, and other countries. The MAT computer-based test is now available. Testing time is 60 minutes. The test consists of 120 partial analogies. You can obtain the *Candidate Information Booklet,* which contains a list of test centers and instructions for taking the test, from http://www.milleranalogies.com or by calling 1-800-622-3231.

Check the specific requirements of the programs to which you are applying.

How Admission Decisions Are Made

The program you apply to is directly involved in the admissions process. Although the final decision is usually made by the graduate dean (or an associate) or the faculty admissions committee, recommendations from faculty members in your intended field are important. At some institutions, an interview is incorporated into the decision process.

A Special Note for International Students

In addition to the steps already described, there are some special considerations for international students who intend to apply for graduate study in the United States. All graduate schools require an indication of competence in English. The purpose of the Test of English as a Foreign Language (TOEFL) is to evaluate the English proficiency of people who are nonnative speakers of English and want to study at colleges and universities where English is the language of instruction. The TOEFL is administered by Educational Testing Service (ETS) under the general direction of a policy board established by the College Board and the Graduate Record Examinations Board.

The TOEFL iBT assesses the four basic language skills: listening, reading, writing, and speaking. It was administered for the first time in September 2005, and ETS continues to introduce the TOEFL iBT in selected cities. The Internet-based test is administered at secure, official test centers. The testing time is approximately 4 hours. Because the TOEFL iBT includes a speaking section, the Test of Spoken English (TSE) is no longer needed.

The TOEFL is also offered in the paper-based format in areas of the world where Internet-based testing is not available. The paper-based TOEFL consists of three sections—listening comprehension, structure and written expression, and reading comprehension. The testing time is approximately 3 hours. The Test of Written English (TWE) is also given. The TWE is a 30-minute essay that measures the examinee's ability to compose in English. Examinees receive a TWE score separate from their TOEFL score. The *Information Bulletin* contains information on local fees and registration procedures.

Additional information and registration materials are available from TOEFL Services, Educational Testing Service, P.O. Box 6151, Princeton, New Jersey 08541-6151. Telephone: 1-609-771-7100. Web site: www.toefl.org.

International students should apply especially early because of the number of steps required to complete the admissions process. Furthermore, many United States graduate schools have a limited number of spaces for international students, and many more students apply than the schools can accommodate.

International students may find financial assistance from institutions very limited. The U.S. government requires international applicants to submit a certification of support, which is a statement attesting to the applicant's financial resources. In addition, international students *must* have health insurance coverage.

Tips for Minority Students

Indicators of a university's values in terms of diversity are found both in its recruitment programs and its resources directed to student success. Important questions: Does the institution vigorously recruit minorities for its graduate programs? Is there funding available to help with the costs associated with visiting the school? Are minorities represented in the institution's brochures or Web site or on their faculty rolls? What campus-based resources or services (including assistance in locating housing or career counseling and placement) are available? Is funding available to members of underrepresented groups?

At the program level, it is particularly important for minority students to investigate the "climate" of a program under consideration. How many minority students are enrolled and how many have graduated? What opportunities are there to work with diverse faculty and mentors whose research interests match yours? How are conflicts resolved or concerns addressed? How interested are faculty in building strong and supportive relations with students? "Climate" concerns should be addressed by posing questions to various individuals, including faculty members, current students, and alumni.

Information is also available through various organizations, such as the Hispanic Association of Colleges & Universities (HACU), and publications such as *Diverse Issues in Higher Education* and *Hispanic Outlook* magazine. There are also books devoted to this topic, such as *The Multicultural Student's Guide to Colleges* by Robert Mitchell.

Financial Support

The range of financial support at the graduate level is very broad. The following descriptions will give you a general idea of what you might expect and what will be expected of you as a financial support recipient.

Fellowships, Scholarships, and Grants

These are usually outright awards of a few hundred to many thousands of dollars with no service to the institution required in return. Fellowships and scholarships are usually awarded on the basis of merit and are highly competitive. Grants are made on the basis of financial need or special talent in a field of study. Many fellowships, scholarships, and grants not only cover tuition, fees, and supplies but also include stipends for living expenses with allowances for dependents. However, the terms of each should be examined because some do not permit recipients to supplement their income with outside work. Fellowships, scholarships, and grants may vary in the number of years for which they are awarded.

In addition to the availability of these funds at the university or program level, many excellent fellowship programs are available at the national level and may be applied for before and during enrollment in a graduate program. A listing of many of these programs can be found at the Council of Graduate Schools' Web site: http://www.cgsnet.org. There is a wealth of information in the "Programs" and "Awards" sections.

Assistantships and Internships

Many graduate students receive financial support through assistantships, particularly involving teaching or research duties. It is important to recognize that such appointments should not be viewed simply as employment relationships but rather should constitute an integral and important part of a student's graduate education. As such, the appointments should be accompanied by strong faculty mentoring and increasingly responsible apprenticeship experiences. The specific nature of these appointments in a given program should be considered in selecting that graduate program.

TEACHING ASSISTANTSHIPS

These usually provide a salary and full or partial tuition remission and may also provide health benefits. Unlike fellowships, scholarships, and grants, which require no service to the institution, teaching assistantships require recipients to provide the institution with a specific amount of undergraduate teaching, ideally related to the student's field of study. Some teaching assistants are limited to grading papers, compiling bibliographies, taking notes, or monitoring laboratories. At some graduate schools, teaching assistants must carry lighter course loads than regular full-time students.

RESEARCH ASSISTANTSHIPS

These are very similar to teaching assistantships in the manner in which financial assistance is provided. The difference is that recipients are given basic research assignments in their disciplines rather than teaching responsibilities. The work required is normally related to the student's field of study; in most instances, the assistantship supports the student's thesis or dissertation research.

ADMINISTRATIVE INTERNSHIPS

These are similar to assistantships in application of financial assistance funds, but the student is given an assignment on a part-time basis, usually as a special assistant with one of the university's administrative offices. The assignment may not necessarily be directly related to the recipient's discipline.

RESIDENCE HALL AND COUNSELING ASSISTANTSHIPS

These assistantships are frequently assigned to graduate students in psychology, counseling, and social work, but they may be offered to students in other disciplines, especially if the student has worked in this capacity during his or her undergraduate years. Duties can vary from being available in a dean's office for a specific number of hours for consultation with undergraduates to living in campus residences and being responsible for both counseling and administrative tasks or advising student activity groups. Residence hall assistantships often include a room and board allowance and, in some cases, tuition assistance and stipends. Contact the Housing and Student Life Office for more information.

Health Insurance

The availability and affordability of health insurance is an important issue and one that should be considered in an applicant's choice of institution and program. While often included with assistantships and fellowships, this is not always the case and, even if provided, the benefits may be limited. It is important to note that the U.S. government requires international students to have health insurance.

The GI Bill

This provides financial assistance for students who are veterans of the United States armed forces. If you are a veteran, contact your local Veterans Administration office to determine your eligibility and to get full details about benefits. There are a number of programs that offer educational benefits to current military enlistees. Some states have tuition assistance programs for members of the National Guard. Contact the VA office at the college for more information.

Federal Work-Study Program (FWS)

Employment is another way some students finance their graduate studies. The federally funded Federal Work-Study Program provides eligible students with employment opportunities, usually in public and private nonprofit organizations. Federal funds pay up to 75 percent of the wages, with the remainder paid by the employing agency. FWS is available to graduate students who demonstrate financial need. Not all schools have these funds, and some only award them to undergraduates. Each school sets its application deadline and work-study earnings limits. Wages vary and are related to the type of work done. You must file the Free Application for Federal Student Aid (FAFSA) to be eligible for this program.

Loans

Many graduate students borrow to finance their graduate programs when other sources of assistance (which do not have to be repaid) prove insufficient. You should always read and understand the terms of any loan program before submitting your application.

FEDERAL LOANS

Federal Stafford Loans. The Federal Stafford Loan Program offers government-sponsored, low-interest loans to students through a private lender such as a bank, credit union, or savings and loan association.

There are two components of the Federal Stafford Loan program. Under the *subsidized* component of the program, the federal government pays the interest on the loan while you are enrolled in graduate school on at least a half-time basis during the six-month grace period after you drop below half-time enrollment, as well as during any period of deferment. Under the *unsubsidized* component of the program, you pay the interest on the loan from the day proceeds are issued. Eligibility for the federal subsidy is based on demonstrated financial need as determined by the financial aid office from the information you provide on the FAFSA. A cosigner is not required, since the loan is not based on creditworthiness.

Although *unsubsidized* Federal Stafford Loans may not be as desirable as *subsidized* Federal Stafford Loans from the student's perspective, they are a useful source of support for those who may not qualify for the subsidized loans or who need additional financial assistance.

Graduate students may borrow up to $20,500 per year through the Stafford Loan Program, up to a cumulative maximum of $138,500, including undergraduate borrowing. This may include up to $8500 in *subsidized* Stafford Loans annually, depending on eligibility, up to a cumulative maximum of $65,500, including undergraduate borrowing. The amount of the loan borrowed through the *unsubsidized* Stafford Program equals the total amount of the loan (as much as $20,500) minus your eligibility for a *subsidized* Stafford Loan (as much as $8500). You may borrow up to the cost of attendance at the school in which you are enrolled or will attend, minus estimated financial assistance from other federal, state, and private sources, up to a maximum of $20,500.

Stafford Loans made on or after July 1, 2006, carry a fixed interest rate of 6.8% both for in-school and in-repayment borrowers.

Two fees may be deducted from the loan proceeds upon disbursement: a Federal Default Fee of 1 percent, which is deposited in an insurance pool to ensure repayment to the lender if the borrower defaults, and a federally mandated 0.5 percent origination fee, for loans made after July 1, 2009, which is used to offset the administrative cost of the Federal Stafford Loan Program. A few lenders may offer reduced-fee or "zero fee" loans. The origination fees are scheduled to be eliminated by July 1, 2010.

Under the *subsidized* Federal Stafford Loan Program, repayment begins six months after your last date of enrollment on at least a half-time basis. Under the *unsubsidized* program, repayment of interest begins within thirty days from disbursement of the loan proceeds, and repayment of the principal begins six months after your last enrollment on at least a half-time basis. Some borrowers may choose to defer interest payments while they are in school. The accrued interest is added to the loan balance when the borrower begins repayment. There are several repayment options.

Federal Direct Loans. Some schools participate in the Department of Education's William D. Ford Direct Loan Program instead of the Federal Stafford Loan Program. The two programs are essentially the same except that with the Direct Loans, schools themselves provide the loans with funds from the federal government. Terms and interest rates are virtually the same except that there are a few additional repayment options with Federal Direct Loans.

Federal Perkins Loans. The Federal Perkins Loan is available to students demonstrating financial need and is administered directly by the school. Not all schools have these funds, and some may award them to undergraduates only. Eligibility is determined from the information you provide on the FAFSA. The school will notify you of your eligibility.

Eligible graduate students may borrow up to $6000 per year, up to a maximum of $40,000, including undergraduate borrowing (even if your previous Perkins Loans have been repaid). The interest rate for Federal Perkins Loans is 5 percent, and no interest accrues while you remain in school at least half-time. There are no guarantee, loan, or disbursement fees. Repayment begins nine months after your last date of enrollment on at least a half-time basis and may extend over a maximum of ten years with no prepayment penalty.

Federal Graduate PLUS Loans. Effective July 1, 2006, graduate and professional students are eligible for Graduate PLUS loans. This program allows students to borrow up to the cost of attendance, less any other aid received. These loans have a fixed interest rate of 8.5% (7.9% for the Federal Direct PLUS), and interest begins to accrue at the time of disbursement. The PLUS loans do involve a credit check; a PLUS borrower may obtain a loan with a cosigner if his or her credit is not good enough. Grad PLUS loans may be deferred while a student in school and for the six months following a drop below half-time enrollment. For more information, contact your FFELP lender or your college financial aid office.

Deferring Your Federal Loan Repayments. If you borrowed under the Federal Stafford Loan Program, Federal Direct Loan Program, or the Federal Perkins Loan Program for previous undergraduate or graduate study, your repayments may be deferred when you return to graduate school, depending on when you borrowed and under which program.

There are other deferment options available if you are temporarily unable to repay your loan. Information about these deferments is provided at your entrance and exit interviews. If you believe you are eligible for a deferment of your loan repayments, you must contact your lender to request a deferment form. The deferment must be filed prior to the time your repayment is due, and it must be refiled when it expires if you remain eligible for deferment at that time.

SUPPLEMENTAL (PRIVATE) LOANS

Many lending institutions offer supplemental loan programs and other financing plans, such as the ones described here, to students seeking additional assistance in meeting their education expenses. Some loan programs target all types of graduate students; others are designed specifically for business, law, or medical students. In addition, you can use private loans not specifically designed for education to help finance your graduate degree.

If you are considering borrowing through a supplemental or private loan program, you should carefully consider the terms and be sure to "read the fine print." Check with the program sponsor for the most current terms that will be applicable to the amounts you intend to borrow for graduate study. Most supplemental loan programs for graduate study offer unsubsidized, credit-based loans. In general, a credit-ready borrower is one who has a satisfactory credit history or no credit history at all. A creditworthy borrower generally must pass a credit test to be eligible to borrow or act as a cosigner for the loan funds.

Many supplemental loan programs have minimum and maximum annual loan limits. Some offer amounts equal to the cost of attendance minus any other aid you will receive for graduate study. If you are planning to borrow for several years of graduate study, consider whether there is a cumulative or aggregate limit on the amount you may borrow. Often this cumulative or aggregate limit will include any amounts you borrowed and have not repaid for undergraduate or previous graduate study.

The combination of the annual interest rate, loan fees, and the repayment terms you choose will determine how much you will repay over time. Compare these features in combination before you decide which loan program to use. Some loans offer interest rates that are adjusted monthly, some quarterly, some annually. Some offer interest rates that are lower during the in-school, grace, and deferment periods and then increase when you begin repayment. Some programs include a loan "origination" fee, which is usually deducted from the principal amount you receive when the loan is disbursed and must be repaid along with the interest and other principal when you graduate, withdraw from school, or drop below half-time study. Sometimes the loan fees are reduced if you borrow with a qualified cosigner. Some programs allow you to defer interest and/or principal payments while you are enrolled in graduate school. Many programs allow you to capitalize your interest payments; the interest due on your loan is added to the outstanding balance of your loan, so you don't have to repay immediately, but this increases the amount you owe. Other programs allow you to pay the interest as you go, which reduces the amount you later have to repay.

Some examples of supplemental programs follow. The private loan market is very competitive, and your financial aid office can help you evaluate these and other programs.

CitiAssist® Graduate Loans. Offered by Citibank, these loans help graduate students fill the gap between the financial aid they receive and the money they need for school. Note that there is a one-time minimum loan amount of $1,000. No minimum loan amount is required on subsequent CitiAssist loans. Visit www.studentloan.com for more loan information from Citibank.

Chase Select℠ Private Student Loans. Offered by Chase, these loans are subject to credit approval, receipt of a completed and signed Application/Promissory Note, verification of application information including enrollment at a participating school, and verification that the requested loan amount does not exceed the student's actual cost of attendance. For more information, visit www.chasestudentloans.com.

Graduate Access Loans. Sponsored by the Access Group, this is for graduate students enrolled at least half-time. The Web site is www.accessgroup.com.

Smart Option Student Loans. Sponsored by Sallie Mae, this loan program is for graduate students who are enrolled at least half-time. Visit www.salliemae.com for more information.

Applying for Need-Based Financial Aid

Schools that award federal and institutional financial assistance based on need will require you to complete the FAFSA and, in some cases, an institutional financial aid application.

If you are applying for federal student assistance, you **must** complete the FAFSA. A service of the U.S. Department of Education, the FAFSA is free to all applicants. Most applicants apply online at www.fafsa.ed.gov. Paper applications are available at the financial aid office of your local college.

After your FAFSA information has been processed, you will receive a Student Aid Report (SAR). If you provided an e-mail address on the FAFSA, this will be sent to you electronically; otherwise, it will be mailed to your home address.

Follow the instructions on the SAR if you need to correct information reported on your original application. If your situation changes after you file your FAFSA, contact your financial aid officer to discuss amending your information. You can also appeal your financial aid award if you have extenuating circumstances.

If you would like more information on federal student financial aid, visit the FAFSA Web site or download the most recent version of *Funding Education Beyond High School: The Guide to Federal Student Aid* at http://studentaid.ed.gov/students/publications/student_guide/index.html. This guide is also available in Spanish.

The U.S. Department of Education also has a toll-free number for questions concerning federal student aid programs. The number is 1-800-4-FED AID (1-800-433-3243). If you are hearing impaired, call toll-free, 1-800-730-8913.

Summary

Remember that these are generalized statements about financial assistance at the graduate level. Because each institution allots its aid differently, you should communicate directly with the school and the specific department of interest to you. It is not unusual, for example, to find that an endowment vested within a specific department supports one or more fellowships. You may fit its requirements and specifications precisely.

Accreditation and Accrediting Agencies

Colleges and universities in the United States, and their individual academic and professional programs, are accredited by nongovernmental agencies concerned with monitoring the quality of education in this country. Agencies with both regional and national jurisdictions grant accreditation to institutions as a whole, while specialized bodies acting on a nationwide basis—often national professional associations—grant accreditation to departments and programs in specific fields.

Institutional and specialized accrediting agencies share the same basic concerns: the purpose an academic unit—whether university or program—has set for itself and how well it fulfills that purpose, the adequacy of its financial and other resources, the quality of its academic offerings, and the level of services it provides. Agencies that grant institutional accreditation take a broader view, of course, and examine university-wide or college-wide services with which a specialized agency may not concern itself.

Both types of agencies follow the same general procedures when considering an application for accreditation. The academic unit prepares a self-evaluation, focusing on the concerns mentioned above and usually including an assessment of both its strengths and weaknesses; a team of representatives of the accrediting body reviews this evaluation, visits the campus, and makes its own report; and finally, the accrediting body makes a decision on the application. Often, even when accreditation is granted, the agency makes a recommendation regarding how the institution or program can improve. All institutions and programs are also reviewed every few years to determine whether they continue to meet established standards; if they do not, they may lose their accreditation.

Accrediting agencies themselves are reviewed and evaluated periodically by the U.S. Department of Education and the Council for Higher Education Accreditation (CHEA). Recognized agencies adhere to certain standards and practices, and their authority in matters of accreditation is widely accepted in the educational community.

This does not mean, however, that accreditation is a simple matter, either for schools wishing to become accredited or for students deciding where to apply. Indeed, in certain fields the very meaning and methods of accreditation are the subject of a good deal of debate. For their part, those applying to graduate school should be aware of the safeguards provided by regional accreditation, especially in terms of degree acceptance and institutional longevity. Beyond this, applicants should understand the role that specialized accreditation plays in their field, as this varies considerably from one discipline to another. In certain professional fields, it is necessary to have graduated from a program that is accredited in order to be eligible for a license to practice, and in some fields the federal government also makes this a hiring requirement. In other disciplines, however, accreditation is not as essential, and there can be excellent programs that are not accredited. In fact, some programs choose not to seek accreditation, although most do.

Institutions and programs that present themselves for accreditation are sometimes granted the status of candidate for accreditation, or what is known as "preaccreditation." This may happen, for example, when an academic unit is too new to have met all the requirements for accreditation. Such status signifies initial recognition and indicates that the school or program in question is working to fulfill all requirements; it does not, however, guarantee that accreditation will be granted.

Institutional Accrediting Agencies—Regional

MIDDLE STATES ASSOCIATION OF COLLEGES AND SCHOOLS
Accredits institutions in Delaware, District of Columbia, Maryland, New Jersey, New York, Pennsylvania, Puerto Rico, and the Virgin Islands.
Jean Avnet Morse, President
Middle States Commission on Higher Education
3624 Market Street, Second Floor Annex
Philadelphia, Pennsylvania 19104
Phone: 267-284-5000
Fax: 215-662-5501
E-mail: info@msche.org
Web: www.msche.org

NEW ENGLAND ASSOCIATION OF SCHOOLS AND COLLEGES
Accredits institutions in Connecticut, Maine, Massachusetts, New Hampshire, Rhode Island, and Vermont.
Barbara E. Brittingham, Director
Commission on Institutions of Higher Education
209 Burlington Road, Suite 201
Bedford, Massachusetts 01730-1433
Phone: 781-271-0022
Fax: 781-271-0950
E-mail: CIHE@neasc.org
Web: www.neasc.org

NORTH CENTRAL ASSOCIATION OF COLLEGES AND SCHOOLS
Accredits institutions in Arizona, Arkansas, Colorado, Illinois, Indiana, Iowa, Kansas, Michigan, Minnesota, Missouri, Nebraska, New Mexico, North Dakota, Ohio, Oklahoma, South Dakota, West Virginia, Wisconsin, and Wyoming.
Sylvia Manning, President
The Higher Learning Commission
30 North LaSalle Street, Suite 2400
Chicago, Illinois 60602
Phone: 312-263-0456
Fax: 312-263-7462
E-mail: smanning@hlcommission.org
Web: www.ncahigherlearningcommission.org

NORTHWEST COMMISSION ON COLLEGES AND UNIVERSITIES
Accredits institutions in Alaska, Idaho, Montana, Nevada, Oregon, Utah, and Washington.
Sandra E. Elman, President
8060 165th Avenue, NE, Suite 100
Redmond, Washington 98052
Phone: 425-558-4224
Fax: 425-376-0596
E-mail: selman@nwccu.org
Web: www.nwccu.org

SOUTHERN ASSOCIATION OF COLLEGES AND SCHOOLS
Accredits institutions in Alabama, Florida, Georgia, Kentucky, Louisiana, Mississippi, North Carolina, South Carolina, Tennessee, Texas, and Virginia.
Belle S. Wheelan, President
Commission on Colleges
1866 Southern Lane
Decatur, Georgia 30033-4097
Phone: 404-679-4512
Fax: 404-679-4528
E-mail: bwheelan@sacscoc.org
Web: www.sacsoc.org

WESTERN ASSOCIATION OF SCHOOLS AND COLLEGES
Accredits institutions in California, Guam, and Hawaii.
Ralph A. Wolff, President and Executive Director
Accrediting Commission for Senior Colleges and Universities
985 Atlantic Avenue, Suite 100
Alameda, California 94501
Phone: 510-748-9001
Fax: 510-748-9797
E-mail: wascsr@wascsenior.org
Web: www.wascweb.org

Institutional Accrediting Agencies—Other

ACCREDITING COUNCIL FOR INDEPENDENT COLLEGES AND SCHOOLS
Albert C. Gray, Ph.D., Executive Director and CEO
750 First Street, NE, Suite 980
Washington, DC 20002-4242
Phone: 202-336-6780
Fax: 202-842-2593
E-mail: info@acics.org
Web: www.acics.org

DISTANCE EDUCATION AND TRAINING COUNCIL (DETC)
Accrediting Commission
Michael P. Lambert, Executive Director
1601 18th Street, NW, Suite 2
Washington, DC 20009
Phone: 202-234-5100
Fax: 202-332-1386
E-mail: detc@detc.org
Web: www.detc.org

Specialized Accrediting Agencies

[Only *Graduate & Professional Programs: An Overview* of *Peterson's Graduate and Professional Programs* Series includes the complete list of specialized accrediting groups recognized by the U.S. Department of Education and the Council on Higher Education Accreditation (CHEA). The lists in all other five books are abridged.]

ACUPUNCTURE AND ORIENTAL MEDICINE
Dort S. Bigg, J.D., Executive Director
Accreditation Commission for Acupuncture and Oriental Medicine
Maryland Trade Center #3
7501 Greenway Center Drive, Suite 760
Greenbelt, Maryland 20770
Phone: 301-313-0855
Fax: 301-313-0912
E-mail: coordinator@acaom.org
Web: www.acaom.org

ART AND DESIGN
Samuel Hope, Executive Director
Karen P. Moynahan, Associate Director
National Association of Schools of Art and Design (NASAD)
Commission on Accreditation
11250 Roger Bacon Drive, Suite 21
Reston, Virginia 20190-5243
Phone: 703-437-0700
Fax: 703-437-6312
E-mail: info@arts-accredit.org
Web: www.arts-accredit.org

BUSINESS
Jerry Trapnell, Executive Vice President/Chief Accreditation Officer
AACSB International--The Association to Advance Collegiate Schools of Business
777 South Harbour Island Boulevard, Suite 700
Tampa, Florida 33602
Phone: 813-769-6500
Fax: 813-769-6559
E-mail: jerryt@aacsb.edu
Web: www.aacsb.edu

CHIROPRACTIC
G. Lansing Bradshaw, Interim Executive Director
Council on Chiropractic Education (CCE)
8049 North 85th Way
Scottsdale, Arizona 85258-4321
Phone: 480-443-8877
Fax: 480-483-7333
E-mail: cce@cce-usa.org
Web: www.cce-usa.org

CLINICAL LABORATORY SCIENCES
Dianne M. Cearlock, Ph.D., Chief Executive Officer
National Accrediting Agency for Clinical Laboratory Sciences
5600 N. River Road, Suite 720
Rosemont, Illinois 60018-5119
Phone: 773-714-8880
Fax: 773-714-8886
E-mail: infonaacls.org
Web: www.naacls.org

CLINICAL PASTORAL EDUCATION
Teresa E. Snorton, Executive Director
Accreditation Commission
Association for Clinical Pastoral Education, Inc.
1549 Claremont Road, Suite 103
Decatur, Georgia 30033-4611
Phone: 404-320-1472
Fax: 404-320-0849
E-mail: acpe@acpe.edu
Web: www.acpe.edu

DANCE
Samuel Hope, Executive Director
Karen P. Moynahan, Associate Director
National Association of Schools of Dance (NASD)
Commission on Accreditation
11250 Roger Bacon Drive, Suite 21
Reston, Virginia 20190-5248
Phone: 703-437-0700
Fax: 703-437-6312
E-mail: info@arts-accredit.org
Web: www.arts-accredit.org

DENTISTRY
Anthony Ziebert, Director
Commission on Dental Accreditation
American Dental Association
211 East Chicago Avenue, Suite 1900
Chicago, Illinois 60611
Phone: 312-440-4643
E-mail: accreditation@ada.org
Web: www.ada.org

DIETETICS
Ulric K. Chung, Ph.D., Senior Director
American Dietetic Association
Commission on Accreditation for Dietetics Education (CADE-ADA)
120 South Riverside Plaza, Suite 2000
Chicago, Illinois 60606-6995
Phone: 800-877-1600
Fax: 312-899-4817
E-mail: cade@eatright.org
Web: www.eatright.org/cade

ENGINEERING
Michael Milligan, Ph.D., PE, Executive Director
Accreditation Board for Engineering and Technology, Inc. (ABET)
111 Market Place, Suite 1050
Baltimore, Maryland 21202
Phone: 410-347-7700
Fax: 410-625-2238
E-mail: info@abet.org
Web: www.abet.org

FORESTRY
Terrance Clark
Associate Director of Science and Education
Society of American Foresters (SAF)
5400 Grosvenor Lane
Bethesda, Maryland 20814-2198
Phone: 301-897-8720 Ext. 123
Fax: 301-897-3690
E-mail: clarkt@safnet.org
Web: www.safnet.org

HEALTH SERVICES ADMINISTRATION
Commission on Accreditation of Healthcare Management Education (CAHME)
John S. Lloyd, President and CEO
2000 14th Street North, Suite 780
Arlington, Virginia 22201
Phone: 703-894-0960
Fax: 703-894-0941
E-mail: info@cahme.org
Web: www.cahme.org

INTERIOR DESIGN
Holly Mattson, Executive Director
Council for Interior Design Accreditation
206 Grandview Avenue, Suite 350
Grand Rapids, Michigan 49503
Phone: 616-458-0400
Fax: 616-458-0460
E-mail: info@accredit-id.org
Web: www.accredit-id.org

JOURNALISM AND MASS COMMUNICATIONS
Susanne Shaw, Executive Director
Accrediting Council on Education in Journalism and Mass Communications (ACEJMC)
School of Journalism
Stauffer-Flint Hall
University of Kansas
1435 Jayhawk Boulevard
Lawrence, Kansas 66045-7575
Phone: 785-864-3986
Fax: 785-864-5225
E-mail: sshaw@ku.edu
Web: www2.ku.edu/~acejmc

LANDSCAPE ARCHITECTURE
Ronald C. Leighton, Executive Director
Landscape Architectural Accreditation Board
American Society of Landscape Architects
636 Eye Street, NW
Washington, DC 20001-3736
Phone: 202-898-2444
Fax: 202-898-1185
E-mail: info@asla.org
Web: www.asla.org

LAW
Hulett H. Askew, Consultant on Legal Education
American Bar Association
321 North Clark Street, 21st Floor
Chicago, Illinois 60654
Phone: 312-988-6738
Fax: 312-988-5681
E-mail: askewh@staff.abanet.org
Web: www.abanet.org/legaled/

LIBRARY
Karen O'Brien, Director
Office for Accreditation
American Library Association
50 East Huron Street
Chicago, Illinois 60611
Phone: 800-545-2433 Ext. 2432
Fax: 312-280-2433
E-mail: accred@ala.org
Web: www.ala.org/accreditation/

MARRIAGE AND FAMILY THERAPY
Jeff S. Harmon, Director of Accreditation Services
Commission on Accreditation for Marriage and Family Therapy Education
American Association for Marriage and Family Therapy
112 South Alfred Street
Alexandria, Virginia 22314-3061
Phone: 703-838-9808
Fax: 703-838-9805
E-mail: coamfle@aamft.org
Web: www.aamft.org

MEDICAL ILLUSTRATION
Commission on Accreditation of Allied Health Education Programs (CAAHEP)
Kathleen Megivern, Executive Director
1361 Park Street
Clearwater, Florida 33756
Phone: 727-210-2350
Fax: 727-210-2354
E-mail: mail@caahep.org
Web: www.caahep.org

MEDICINE
Liaison Committee on Medical Education (LCME)
In odd-numbered years beginning each July 1, contact:
Barbara Barzansky, Ph.D., LCME Secretary
American Medical Association
Council on Medical Education
515 North State Street
Chicago, Illinois 60654
Phone: 312-464-4933
Fax: 312-464-5830
E-mail: cme@aamc.org
Web: www.ama-assn.org
In even-numbered years beginning each July 1, contact:
Dan Hunt, M.D., LCME Secretary
Association of American Medical Colleges
2450 N Street, NW
Washington, DC 20037
Phone: 202-828-0596
Fax: 202-828-1125
E-mail: dhunt@aamc.org
Web: www.lcme.org

MUSIC
Samuel Hope, Executive Director
Karen P. Moynahan, Associate Director
National Association of Schools of Music (NASM)
Commission on Accreditation
11250 Roger Bacon Drive, Suite 21
Reston, Virginia 20190-5248
Phone: 703-437-0700
Fax: 703-437-6312
E-mail: info@arts-accredit.org
Web: www.arts-accredit.org

NATUROPATHIC MEDICINE
Daniel Seitz, J.D., Ed.D., Executive Director
Council on Naturopathic Medical Education
P.O. Box 178
Great Barrington, Massachusetts 01230
Phone: 413-528-8877
Fax: 413-528-8880
E-mail: staff@cnme.org
Web: www.cnme.org

NURSE ANESTHESIA
Francis R. Gerbasi, Executive Director
Council on Accreditation of Nurse Anesthesia Educational Programs
American Association of Nurse Anesthetists
222 South Prospect Avenue, Suite 304
Park Ridge, Illinois 60068
Phone: 847-692-7050 Ext. 1154
Fax: 847-692-6968
E-mail: fgerbasi@aana.com
Web: www.aana.com

NURSE EDUCATION
Jennifer L. Butlin, Director
Commission on Collegiate Nursing Education (CCNE)
One Dupont Circle, NW, Suite 530
Washington, DC 20036-1120
Phone: 202-887-6791

Fax: 202-887-8476
E-mail: jbutlin@aacn.nche.edu
Web: www.aacn.nche.edu/accreditation

NURSE MIDWIFERY
Mary Brucker, Chair
Accreditation Commission for Midwifery Education
American College of Nurse-Midwives
Nurse-Midwifery Program
8403 Colesville Road, Suite 1550
Silver Spring, Maryland 20910
Phone: 240-485-1800
Fax: 240-485-1818
E-mail: mary_brucker@baylor.edu
Web: www.midwife.org/acme.cfm

Jo Anne Myers-Ciecko, Executive Director
Midwifery Education Accreditation Council
P.O. Box 984
La Conner, Washington 98257
Phone: 360-466-2080
Fax: 480-907-2936
E-mail: executivedirector@meacschools.org
Web: www.meacschools.org

NURSE PRACTITIONER
Susan Wysocki, President
National Association of Nurse Practitioners in Women's Health
Council on Accreditation
505 C Street, NE
Washington, DC 20002
Phone: 202-543-9693
Fax: 202-543-9858
E-mail: info@npwh.org
Web: www.npwh.org

NURSING
Sharon J. Tanner, Ed.D., RN, Executive Director
National League for Nursing Accrediting Commission (NLNAC)
3343 Peachtree Road, NE, Suite 500
Atlanta, Georgia 30326
Phone: 404-975-5000
Fax: 404-975-5020
E-mail: sjtanner@nlnac.org
Web: www.nlnac.org

OCCUPATIONAL THERAPY
Neil Harvison, Ph.D., OTR/L
Director of Accreditation and Academic Affairs
The American Occupational Therapy Association
4720 Montgomery Lane
P.O. Box 31220
Bethesda, Maryland 20824-1220
Phone: 301-652-2682 Ext. 2914
Fax: 301-652-7711
E-mail: accred@aota.org
Web: www.aota.org

OPTOMETRY
Joyce L. Urbeck, Administrative Director
Accreditation Council on Optometric Education
American Optometric Association (AOA)
243 North Lindbergh Boulevard
St. Louis, Missouri 63141
Phone: 800-365-2219
Fax: 314-991-4101
E-mail: ACOE@aoa.org
Web: www.theacoe.org

OSTEOPATHIC MEDICINE
Konrad C. Miskowicz-Retz, Ph.D., CAE
Director, Department of Accreditation
Commission on Osteopathic College Accreditation
American Osteopathic Association
142 East Ontario Street
Chicago, Illinois 60611
Phone: 312-202-8048
Fax: 312-202-8202
E-mail: kretz@osteopathic.org
Web: www.osteopathic.org

PHARMACY
Peter H. Vlasses, Executive Director
Accreditation Council for Pharmacy Education
20 North Clark Street, Suite 2500
Chicago, Illinois 60602-5109
Phone: 312-664-3575
Fax: 312-664-4652
E-mail: info@acpe-accredit.org
Web: www.acpe-accredit.org

PHYSICAL THERAPY
Mary Jane Harris, Director
Commission on Accreditation in Physical Therapy Education (CAPTE)
American Physical Therapy Association (APTA)
1111 North Fairfax Street
Alexandria, Virginia 22314
Phone: 703-706-3245
Fax: 703-706-3387
E-mail: accreditation@apta.org
Web: www.capteonline.org

PHYSICIAN ASSISTANT STUDIES
John E. McCarty, Executive Director
Accreditation Review Commission on Education for the Physician Assistant, Inc. (ARC-PA)
12000 Findley Road, Suite 240
Duluth, Georgia 30097
Phone: 770-476-1224
Fax: 770-476-1738
E-mail: arc-pa@arc-pa.org
Web: www.arc-pa.org

PLANNING
Shonagh Merits, Executive Director
American Institute of Certified Planners/Association of Collegiate Schools of Planning/American Planning Association
Planning Accreditation Board (PAB)
122 South Michigan Avenue, Suite 1600
Chicago, Illinois 60603
Phone: 312-334-1271
Fax: 312-334-1273
E-mail: pab@planning.org
Web: www.planningaccreditationboard.org

PODIATRIC MEDICINE
Alan R. Tinkleman, Director
Council on Podiatric Medical Education (CPME)
American Podiatric Medical Association
9312 Old Georgetown Road
Bethesda, Maryland 20814-1621
Phone: 301-571-9200
Fax: 301-571-4903
E-mail: artinkleman@apma.org
Web: www.cpme.org

PSYCHOLOGY AND COUNSELING
Susan Zlotlow, Executive Director
Office of Program Consultation and Accreditation
American Psychological Association
750 First Street, NE
Washington, DC 20002-4242
Phone: 202-336-5979
Fax: 202-336-5978
E-mail: apaaccred@apa.org
Web: www.apa.org/ed/accreditation

Carol L. Bobby, Executive Director
Council for Accreditation of Counseling and Related Educational Programs (CACREP)
1001 North Fairfax Street, Suite 510
Alexandria, Virginia 22314
Phone: 703-535-5990

Fax: 703-739-6209
E-mail: cacrep@cacrep.org
Web: www.cacrep.org

PUBLIC AFFAIRS AND ADMINISTRATION
Crystal Calarusse, Executive Director
Commission on Peer Review and Accreditation
National Association of Schools of Public Affairs and Administration
1120 G Street, NW, Suite 730
Washington, DC 20005
Phone: 202-628-8965
Fax: 202-626-4978
E-mail: calarusse@naspaa.org
Web: www.naspaa.org

PUBLIC HEALTH
Laura Rasar King, M.P.H., CHES, Executive Director
Council on Education for Public Health
800 Eye Street, NW, Suite 202
Washington, DC 20001-3710
Phone: 202-789-1050
Fax: 202-789-1895
E-mail: Lking@ceph.org
Web: www.ceph.org

REHABILITATION EDUCATION
Marvin D. Kuehn, Executive Director
Council on Rehabilitation Education (CORE)
Commission on Standards and Accreditation
300 North Martingale Road, Suite 460
Schaumburg, Illinois 60173
Phone: 847-944-1345
Fax: 847-944-1324
E-mail: mkuehn@emporia.edu
Web: www.core-rehab.org

SOCIAL WORK
Judith Bremner, Interim Director of Accreditation
Commission on Accreditation
Council on Social Work Education
1725 Duke Street, Suite 500
Alexandria, Virginia 22314
Phone: 703-519-2044
Fax: 703-683-8099
E-mail: jbermner@cswe.org
Web: www.cswe.org

SPEECH-LANGUAGE PATHOLOGY AND AUDIOLOGY
Patrima L. Tice, Director of Accreditation
American Speech-Language-Hearing Association
2200 Research Boulevard
Rockville, Maryland 20850-3289
Phone: 301-897-5700
Fax: 301-296-8750
E-mail: ptice@asha.org
Web: www.asha.org/about/credentialing/accreditation

TEACHER EDUCATION
James G. Cibulka, President
National Council for Accreditation of Teacher Education
2010 Massachusetts Avenue, NW, Suite 500
Washington, DC 20036-1023
Phone: 202-466-7496
Fax: 202-296-6620
E-mail: ncate@ncate.org
Web: www.ncate.org

Frank B. Murray, President
Teacher Education Accreditation Council (TEAC)
Accreditation Committee
One Dupont Circle, Suite 320
Washington, DC 20036-0110
Phone: 202-831-0400
Fax: 202-831-3013
E-mail: teac@teac.org
Web: www.teac.org

TECHNOLOGY
Elise Scanlon, Executive Director
Accrediting Commission of Career Schools and Colleges of Technology
2101 Wilson Boulevard, Suite 302
Arlington, Virginia 22201
Phone: 703-247-4212
Fax: 703-247-4533
E-mail: escanlon@accsct.org
Web: www.accsct.org

THEATER
Samuel Hope, Executive Director
Karen P. Moynahan, Associate Director
National Association of Schools of Theatre
Commission on Accreditation
11250 Roger Bacon Drive, Suite 21
Reston, Virginia 20190
Phone: 703-437-0700
Fax: 703-437-6312
E-mail: info@arts-accredit.org
Web: www.arts-accredit.org

THEOLOGY
Bernard Fryshman, Executive Vice President
Association of Advanced Rabbinical and Talmudic Schools (AARTS)
Accreditation Commission
11 Broadway, Suite 405
New York, New York 10004
Phone: 212-363-1991
Fax: 212-533-5335

Daniel O. Aleshire, Executive Director
Association of Theological Schools in the United States and Canada (ATS)
Commission on Accrediting
10 Summit Park Drive
Pittsburgh, Pennsylvania 15275-1103
Phone: 412-788-6505
Fax: 412-788-6510
E-mail: ats@ats.edu
Web: www.ats.edu

Russell Guy Fitzgerald, Executive Director
Transnational Association of Christian Colleges and Schools (TRACS)
Accreditation Commission
P.O. Box 328
Forest, Virginia 24551
Phone: 434-525-9539
Fax: 434-525-9538
E-mail: info@tracs.org
Web: www.tracs.org

VETERINARY MEDICINE
Dr. David Granstrom, Director
Education and Research Division
American Veterinary Medical Association (AVMA)
Council on Education
1931 North Meacham Road, Suite 100
Schaumburg, Illinois 60173
Phone: 847-925-8070
Fax: 847-925-1329
E-mail: avmainfo@avma.org
Web: www.avma.org

How to Use This Guide

As you identify the particular programs and institutions that interest you, you can use both the ***Graduate & Professional Programs: An Overview*** volume and the specialized volumes to obtain detailed information--***Graduate & Professional Programs: An Overview*** for information on the institutions overall and the specialized volumes for details about the individual graduate units and their degree programs.

Directory of Graduate and Professional Programs by Field

This directory lists the 500 fields covered in ***Peterson's Graduate and Professional Programs***, with an alphabetical listing of each of the institutions offering graduate or professional work in that field. Institutions in the United States and U.S. territories and those in Canada, Mexico, Europe, and Africa that are accredited by U.S. accrediting bodies are included. The directory enables readers who are interested in a particular academic area to quickly identify the colleges and universities that they might wish to attend. In each field, degree levels are given if an institution provided the information in response to *Peterson's Annual Survey of Graduate and Professional Institutions.* An *M* indicates that a master's degree program is offered; a *D* indicates that a doctoral program is offered; a *P* indicates that the first professional degree is offered; and an *O* signifies that other advanced degrees (e.g., certificates and specialist degrees) are offered. If no degree is listed, the school offers a degree in a subdiscipline of the field, not in the field itself.

All of the programs listed in this directory are profiled, and many are described in detail in **Close-Ups** or outlined briefly in **Announcements** in the specialized volumes. These **Announcements** or **Displays** and **Close-Ups** are indicated in the directory listings by an asterisk, and their page numbers may be found by consulting the indexes of the specialized volumes. The **Profiles, Announcements**, and **Close-Ups Index** at the back of this book indicate the institutions that chose to place a **Close-Up** or an **Announcement** in this volume.

Directory of Institutions and Their Offerings

This directory contains information identical to that in the **Directory of Graduate and Professional Programs by Field** but conversely presented. Accredited institutions in the United States and U.S. territories and those in Canada, Mexico, Europe, and Africa that are accredited by U.S. accrediting bodies are given here, with an alphabetical listing of which programs they offer out of the selected fields that are covered in the guides. The directory will be of value to readers who are interested in the range of programs at particular institutions, as well as those who wish to compare programs and degree levels. The degree levels are shown if the institution provided information in response to *Peterson's Annual Survey of Graduate and Professional Institutions*; the degree levels included are master's, doctorate, first professional, and other advanced degrees (e.g., certificates and specialist degrees), included as *M, D, P*, and *O*, respectively.

All of the programs listed in this directory are profiled, and many are described in detail in **Close-Ups** or outlined briefly in **Announcements** or **Displays** in the specialized volumes. A note at the end of each institution's listing refers the reader to the specific page number if an **Announcement** or **Close-Up** appears in this book. If there is such information in the specialized volumes, an asterisk appears in the column that lists the degree level offered. The reader should then refer to the **Close-Ups and Announcements Index** in the appropriate volume.

Profiles of Institutions Offering Graduate and Professional Work

This section presents profiles of accredited colleges and universities in the United States and U.S. territories and those in Canada, Mexico, Europe, and Africa that are accredited by U.S. accrediting bodies. Together with the other sections of this book, it is both a basic reference source and a foundation for the specialized volumes of ***Peterson's Graduate and Professional Programs***. (The specialized volumes provide descriptions of graduate programs in the humanities, arts, and social sciences; the biological sciences; the physical sciences, mathematics, agricultural sciences, the environment, and natural resources; engineering and applied sciences; and business, education, health, information studies, law, and social work, respectively.) The profiles in this section include the data on graduate and professional units that were submitted in 2009 by each institution in response to *Peterson's Annual Survey of Graduate and Professional Institutions.* If an institution provided all of the information requested, the profile includes all of the items listed below. A number of graduate school administrators have written brief **Announcements** or **Displays**, which follow their profiles. In these, readers will find information an institution wants to emphasize. In addition, bolded reference lines at the end of a profile indicate the page number on which the reader will find a **Close-Up**, if the institution has chosen to submit one. The absence of an **Announcement** or **Close-Up** does not reflect any type of editorial judgment on the part of Peterson's.

General Information

Type. An institution's control is indicated as independent (private nonprofit), independent with religious affiliation, proprietary (private profit-making), or state-supported or state-related (public). Whether an institution is coeducational or primarily for men or women is indicated. A few schools are designated as undergraduate: women (or men) only; graduate: coed. Institutional type is given as university, comprehensive, graduate only, or upper level.

CGS Membership. Membership in the Council of Graduate Schools in the United States and in Canada is indicated here.

Enrollment. Enrollment figures include total matriculated students (graduate, professional, and undergraduate), total full- and part-time matriculated graduate and professional students, and the number of women in each category.

Enrollment by Degree Level. Figures include the total number of students enrolled at each degree level--master's, doctoral, first-professional, and other advanced degrees.

Graduate Faculty. The numbers of full-time and part-time/adjunct faculty members actively involved with graduate students through teaching or research are given, followed by numbers of women.

Graduate Expenses. Tuition and fees for the overall institution for 2009–10 are indicated on a full-time (per academic year, semester, quarter, etc.) and/or a part-time (per credit, semester hour, quarter hour, course, etc.) basis. In-state and out-of-state figures are supplied where applicable. For exact costs at any given time, contact the schools and programs directly. Keep in mind that the tuition of Canadian institutions is usually given in Canadian dollars.

Graduate Housing. Institutions were asked to indicate whether housing for single and married students is guaranteed or available on a first-come, first-served basis and whether that includes board and to indicate the typical cost per year.

Student Services. Each institution was asked which of the following services are available to graduate and professional students: campus employment opportunities, campus safety program, career counseling, child day-care facilities, disabled student services, exercise/

wellness program, free psychological counseling, grant writing training, international student services, low-cost health insurance, multicultural affairs office, teacher training, and writing training.

Library Facilities. The main library name and the number of additional on-campus libraries, if any, are provided. Also provided are online resources, such as library catalog, Web page, and other libraries' catalogs, and numbers of titles, current serial subscriptions, and audiovisual materials.

Research Affiliations. Institutions were asked to name up to six independent research centers, laboratories, or institutes with which they maintain formal arrangements providing extra research or study opportunities for graduate students.

Computer Facilities

Institutions were asked to provide the total number of PCs and/or terminals available for student use, whether a campuswide network is available, and whether Internet access and/or online class registration is available. The institution's Web site also appears here if that information was supplied.

General Application Contact

The name, title, phone number, fax number, and e-mail address of the person to contact for further information about applying to graduate and professional programs appear here.

Graduate Units

Each major graduate and professional unit within the institution (school, college, institute, center, etc.) is listed below the general information. These units are arranged to show the hierarchical structure of the institution. Those units offering advanced degree programs through the graduate school are listed immediately beneath it. Professional schools not connected with the graduate school are listed separately.

Enrollment. The number of full- and part-time matriculated students and the number of women, minority-group members, and international students are given. Average age is indicated, followed by the number of applicants, percentage accepted, and the number enrolled.

Faculty. Full-time and part-time/adjunct figures are given, and the number of women is indicated.

Expenses. For individual program expenses, readers are advised to contact the institution.

Financial Support. Information is given on the number of fellowships and assistantships awarded in 2008–09 and the availability of other types of aid. The financial aid application deadline is also indicated.

Degree Program Information. The number of degrees awarded in calendar year 2008 is given, broken down by degree level, followed by the availability of part-time and evening/weekend programs. Degree programs offered through the subunits and the specific degrees awarded are listed. Special degree information is also included, such as that a degree is offered jointly with another university.

Applying. The application deadline (for domestic and international students) and application fee are given, followed by a person to contact and a phone number, fax number, and e-mail address (if provided).

Head. The head of the unit and his or her title are indicated, along with a phone number, fax number, and e-mail address (if provided).

Close-Ups of Institutions Offering Graduate and Professional Work

The **Close-Ups** in this section present an overview of accredited graduate and professional schools in the United States and U.S. territories and institutions in Canada, Mexico, Europe, and Africa that are accredited by U.S. accrediting bodies. Critical information sought by all prospective graduate students--regardless of their intended field of study--has been supplied by the schools themselves.

In addition to listing the degree programs available, each entry gives valuable information on research facilities, financial aid opportunities, tuition rates, living and housing costs, students, the faculty, location, the university, and application criteria--in short, facts that all prospective graduate students need to know about an institution when selecting a graduate program.

After using the **Close-Ups** and the other sections of this volume to identify those universities that are appropriate to your needs, refer to the specialized volumes for specific program information. Graduate and professional schools and colleges within the institutions represented in this book are considered in detail in the specialized volumes, which cover the humanities, arts, and social sciences; the biological sciences; the physical sciences, mathematics, agricultural sciences, the environment, and natural resources; engineering and applied sciences; and business, education, health, information studies, law, and social work, respectively.

Appendixes

This section contains two appendixes. The first, *Institutional Changes Since the 2009 Edition,* lists institutions that have closed, moved, merged, or changed their name or status since the last edition of the guides. The second, *Abbreviations Used in the Guides,* gives abbreviations of degree names, along with what those abbreviations stand for. These appendixes are identical in all six volumes of *Peterson's Graduate and Professional Programs.*

Indexes

There are two indexes in this section. The first, **Profiles, Announcements, and Close-Ups,** gives page references for all information on all graduate and professional schools in this volume. Location of the institution's **Profile** is indicated in normal type. An *italic* page number indicates that an **Announcement** follows the institution's **Profile**. A **boldface** page number indicates the location of an institution's **Close-Up**. The second, **Directories and Subject Areas in the Specialized Volumes**, gives references to the directories in other volumes of this set and also includes cross-references for subject area names not used in the directory structure, for example, "Arabic (*see* Near and Middle Eastern Languages)."

Data Collection Procedures

The information published in the directories and **Profiles** of all the books is collected through *Peterson's Annual Survey of Graduate and Professional Institutions.* The survey is sent each spring to more than 2,300 institutions offering postbaccalaureate degree programs, including accredited institutions in the United States, U.S. territories, and Canada and those institutions outside the United States that are accredited by U.S. accrediting bodies. Deans and other administrators complete these surveys, providing information on programs in the 500 academic and professional fields covered in the guides as well as overall institutional information. While every effort has been made to ensure the accuracy and completeness of the data, information is sometimes unavailable or changes occur after publication deadlines. All usable information received in time for publication has been included. The omission of any particular item from a directory or **Profile** signifies either that the item is not applicable to the institution or program or that information was not available. **Profiles** of programs scheduled to begin during the 2009–10 academic year cannot, obviously, include statistics on enrollment or, in many cases, the number of faculty members. If no usable data were submitted by an institution, its name, address, and program name appear in order to indicate the availability of graduate work.

Criteria for Inclusion in This Guide

To be included in this guide, an institution must have full accreditation or be a candidate for accreditation (preaccreditation) status by an institutional or specialized accrediting body recognized by the U.S. Department of Education or the Council for Higher Education Accreditation (CHEA). Institutional accrediting bodies, which review each institution as a whole, include the six regional associations of schools and colleges (Middle States, New England, North Central, Northwest, Southern, and Western), each of which is responsible for a specified portion of the United States and its territories. Other institutional accrediting bodies are national in scope and accredit specific kinds of institutions (e.g., Bible colleges, independent colleges, and rabbinical and Talmudic schools). Program registration by the New York State Board of Regents is considered to be the equivalent of institutional accreditation, since the board requires that all programs offered by an institution meet its standards before recognition is granted. A Canadian institution must be chartered and authorized to grant degrees by the provincial government, affiliated with a chartered institution, or accredited by a recognized U.S. accrediting body. This guide also includes institutions outside the United States that are accredited by these U.S. accrediting bodies. There are recognized specialized or professional accrediting bodies in more than fifty different fields, each of which is authorized to accredit institutions or specific programs in its particular field. For specialized institutions that offer programs in one field only, we designate this to be the equivalent of institutional accreditation. A full explanation of the accrediting process and complete information on recognized institutional (regional and national) and specialized accrediting bodies can be found online at www.chea.org or at www.ed.gov/admins/finaid/accred/index.html.

DIRECTORY OF GRADUATE AND PROFESSIONAL PROGRAMS BY FIELD

ACCOUNTING

Abilene Christian University	M
Adelphi University	M*
Alabama State University	M
American InterContinental University Buckhead Campus	M
American InterContinental University Online	M
American InterContinental University South Florida	M
American International College	M
American University	M*
Anderson University (IN)	M,D
Andrews University	M
Angelo State University	M
Appalachian State University	M
Argosy University, Atlanta	M,D*
Argosy University, Chicago	M,D*
Argosy University, Dallas	M,O*
Argosy University, Denver	M,D*
Argosy University, Hawai'i	M,D,O*
Argosy University, Inland Empire	M,D*
Argosy University, Los Angeles	M,D*
Argosy University, Nashville	M,D*
Argosy University, Orange County	M,D,O*
Argosy University, Phoenix	M,D*
Argosy University, Salt Lake City	M,D*
Argosy University, San Diego	M,D*
Argosy University, San Francisco Bay Area	M,D*
Argosy University, Sarasota	M,D,O*
Argosy University, Schaumburg	M,D,O*
Argosy University, Seattle	M,D*
Argosy University, Tampa	M,D*
Argosy University, Twin Cities	M,D*
Argosy University, Washington DC	M,D,O*
Arizona State University	M,D
Arizona State University at the West campus	M,O
Arkansas State University	M
Assumption College	M,O
Auburn University	M*
Avila University	M
Babson College	M
Baker College Center for Graduate Studies	M
Baldwin-Wallace College	M
Ball State University	M*
Barry University	M*
Bayamón Central University	M
Baylor University	M
Benedictine University	M
Bentley University	M,D
Bernard M. Baruch College of the City University of New York	M,D
Bob Jones University	P,M,D,O
Boise State University	M
Boston College	M*
Boston University	M,D,O*
Bowling Green State University	M*
Bradley University	M
Brenau University	M
Bridgewater State College	M
Brigham Young University	M*
Brock University	M
Brooklyn College of the City University of New York	M
Bryant University	M
Caldwell College	M
California State University, East Bay	M
California State University, Fresno	M
California State University, Fullerton	M
California State University, Los Angeles	M
California State University, Sacramento	M
California Western School of Law	P,M
Canisius College	M
Capella University	M,D,O
Carnegie Mellon University	D*
Case Western Reserve University	M,D*
Centenary College	M
Central Michigan University	M
Central Washington University	M
Charleston Southern University	M
Chatham University	M
City University of Seattle	M,O
Clark Atlanta University	M
Clark University	M
Cleary University	M,O
Clemson University	M
Cleveland State University	M
Coastal Carolina University	M
The College at Brockport, State University of New York	M
College of Charleston	M*
The College of Saint Rose	M*
The College of William and Mary	M
Colorado State University	M*
Colorado Technical University Colorado Springs	M,D
Colorado Technical University Denver	M
Columbia University	M,D*
Concordia University (Canada)	M,D,O
Cornell University	D*
Dallas Baptist University	M
Davenport University	M
Davenport University	M
Davenport University	M
Delta State University	M
DePaul University	M*
DeSales University	M
DeVry University	M*
Dominican University	M
Drexel University	M,D,O*
Duquesne University	M*
East Carolina University	M
Eastern Illinois University	M,O
Eastern Michigan University	M
East Tennessee State University	M
Edgewood College	M
Elmhurst College	M
Emory University	M,D*
Everest University	M
Everest University	M
Fairfield University	M,O*
Fairleigh Dickinson University, College at Florham	M*
Fairleigh Dickinson University, Metropolitan Campus	M,O*
Fitchburg State College	M
Florida Agricultural and Mechanical University	M
Florida Atlantic University	M,D
Florida Gulf Coast University	M
Florida Institute of Technology	M*
Florida International University	M*
Florida Southern College	M
Florida State University	M,D*
Fontbonne University	M
Fordham University	M*
Freed-Hardeman University	M
Gannon University	O
George Mason University	M*
The George Washington University	M,D*
Georgia College & State University	M
Georgia Institute of Technology	M,D,O*
Georgian Court University	M,O
Georgia Southern University	M
Georgia State University	M,D,O
Golden Gate University	M,D,O
Gonzaga University	M
Governors State University	M
Graduate School and University Center of the City University of New York	D*
Grand Canyon University	M*
Grand Valley State University	M
Harding University	M
Harvard University	D*
Hawai'i Pacific University	M*
HEC Montreal	M,O
Hendrix College	M
Hofstra University	M*
Hood College	M
Houston Baptist University	M
Howard University	M
Hunter College of the City University of New York	M
Illinois State University	M
Indiana Tech	M
Indiana University Northwest	M,O
Indiana University–Purdue University Indianapolis	M*
Indiana University South Bend	M
Indiana Wesleyan University	M
Inter American University of Puerto Rico, Barranquitas Campus	M
Inter American University of Puerto Rico, Metropolitan Campus	M
Inter American University of Puerto Rico, Ponce Campus	M
Inter American University of Puerto Rico, San Germán Campus	M,D
Iowa State University of Science and Technology	M*
Ithaca College	M
Jackson State University	M
James Madison University	M
John Carroll University	M
Johnson & Wales University	M
Jones International University	M
Kansas State University	M*
Kean University	M
Kennesaw State University	M
Kent State University	M,D*
Kentucky State University	M
Lakeland College	M
Lamar University	M
La Sierra University	M,O
Lehigh University	M
Lehman College of the City University of New York	M
Lenoir-Rhyne University	M
Lewis University	M
Lincoln University (MO)	M
Lindenwood University	M
Lipscomb University	M
Long Island University, Brooklyn Campus	M
Long Island University, C.W. Post Campus	M,O
Louisiana State University and Agricultural and Mechanical College	M,D
Louisiana Tech University	M,D
Loyola University Chicago	M*
Loyola University Maryland	M*
Maharishi University of Management	M,D
Marquette University	M
Maryville University of Saint Louis	M,O
McGill University	M,D,O*
McNeese State University	M
Mercer University	M
Mercy College	M
Miami University	M*
Michigan State University	M,D*
Middle Tennessee State University	M
Millsaps College	M
Minnesota State University Mankato	M
Mississippi College	M,O
Mississippi State University	M,D
Missouri State University	M*
Monmouth University	M,O
Montana State University	M
Montclair State University	M,O*
Murray State University	M
National University	M
New Jersey City University	M
New Mexico State University	M
New York Institute of Technology	M,O
New York University	M,D*
North Carolina State University	M*
Northeastern Illinois University	M
Northeastern State University	M
Northeastern University	M,O*
Northern Illinois University	M
Northern Kentucky University	M,O
Northwestern University	D*
Northwest Missouri State University	M
Notre Dame College (OH)	M,O
Nova Southeastern University	M,D*
Nyack College	M
Oakland University	M,O
The Ohio State University	M*
Oklahoma City University	M
Oklahoma State University	M,D*
Old Dominion University	M
Oral Roberts University	M
Our Lady of the Lake University of San Antonio	M
Pace University	M*
Pacific States University	M,D
Pittsburg State University	M
Pontifical Catholic University of Puerto Rico	M
Prairie View A&M University	M
Providence College	M*
Purdue University Calumet	M
Queens College of the City University of New York	M
Quinnipiac University	M*
Regis University	M,O
Rhode Island College	M,O
Rhodes College	M
Rider University	M*

Robert Morris College	M
Rochester Institute of Technology	M
Roosevelt University	M
Rutgers, The State University of New Jersey, Newark	M,D,O*
St. Ambrose University	M
St. Bonaventure University	M
St. Edward's University	M,O
St. John's University (NY)	M,O
St. Joseph's College, Long Island Campus	M
St. Joseph's College, New York	M
Saint Joseph's University	M
Saint Leo University	M
Saint Louis University	M
St. Mary's University (United States)	M
Saint Peter's College	M
St. Thomas University	M,O
Salisbury University	M
Sam Houston State University	M
San Diego State University	M*
San Jose State University	M
Seattle University	M
Seton Hall University	M*
Southeastern University	M
Southeast Missouri State University	M
Southern Adventist University	M
Southern Illinois University Carbondale	M,D*
Southern Illinois University Edwardsville	M
Southern Methodist University	M*
Southern New Hampshire University	M,D,O*
Southern Polytechnic State University	M,O
Southern Utah University	M
Southwestern Adventist University	M
State University of New York at Binghamton	M,D*
State University of New York at Fredonia	M
State University of New York at New Paltz	M
State University of New York College at Geneseo	M
State University of New York College at Old Westbury	M
State University of New York Institute of Technology	M
Stephen F. Austin State University	M
Stetson University	M
Stratford University	M
Strayer University	M
Suffolk University	M,O*
Swedish Institute, College of Health Sciences	M
Syracuse University	M,D*
Tabor College	M
Tarleton State University	M
Temple University	M,D*
Texas A&M International University	M
Texas A&M University	M,D*
Texas A&M University–Corpus Christi	M
Texas A&M University–Texarkana	M
Texas Christian University	M
Texas State University–San Marcos	M*
Texas Tech University	M,D
Towson University	M
Trinity University	M
Truman State University	M
Universidad del Este	M
Universidad del Turabo	M
Universidad Metropolitana	M,O
Universidad Nacional Pedro Henriquez Urena	P,M,D
Université de Sherbrooke	M
Université du Québec à Montréal	M,O
Université du Québec à Trois-Rivières	M
Université du Québec en Outaouais	M,O
Université Laval	M,O
University at Albany, State University of New York	M*
University at Buffalo, the State University of New York	M,D,O*
The University of Akron	M
The University of Alabama	M,D
The University of Alabama at Birmingham	M*
The University of Alabama in Huntsville	M,O
University of Alberta	D*
The University of Arizona	M*
University of Arkansas	M
University of Arkansas at Little Rock	M,O
University of Baltimore	M,O
The University of British Columbia	D
University of California, Berkeley	D*
University of Central Arkansas	M
University of Central Florida	M*
University of Central Missouri	M
University of Charleston	
University of Cincinnati	M,D
University of Colorado at Boulder	M,D*
University of Colorado at Colorado Springs	M
University of Colorado Denver	M*
University of Connecticut	M,D*
University of Dallas	M
University of Dayton	M
University of Delaware	M*
University of Denver	M*
University of Florida	M,D*
University of Georgia	M*
University of Hartford	M,O*
University of Hawaii at Manoa	M,D*
University of Houston	M,D*
University of Houston–Clear Lake	M
University of Houston–Victoria	M
University of Idaho	M
University of Illinois at Chicago	M*
University of Illinois at Springfield	M
University of Illinois at Urbana–Champaign	M,D*
The University of Iowa	M,D*
The University of Kansas	M*
University of Kentucky	M
University of La Verne	M
University of Lethbridge	M,D
University of Louisville	M
University of Maine	M*
University of Mary Hardin-Baylor	M
University of Maryland University College	M,O
University of Massachusetts Amherst	M*
University of Massachusetts Dartmouth	M,O
University of Memphis	M,D
University of Miami	M*
University of Michigan–Dearborn	M*
University of Minnesota, Twin Cities Campus	M,D*
University of Mississippi	M,D
University of Missouri–Columbia	M,D*
University of Missouri–Kansas City	M,D*
University of Missouri–St. Louis	M,O
The University of Montana	M
University of Nebraska at Omaha	M
University of Nebraska–Lincoln	M,D*
University of Nevada, Las Vegas	M
University of Nevada, Reno	M*
University of New Hampshire	M*
University of New Haven	M*
University of New Orleans	M
The University of North Carolina at Chapel Hill	M,D*
The University of North Carolina at Charlotte	M*
The University of North Carolina at Greensboro	M,O
The University of North Carolina Wilmington	M
University of North Dakota	M
University of Northern Iowa	M
University of North Florida	M
University of North Texas	M,D
University of Notre Dame	M*
University of Oklahoma	M*
University of Oregon	M,D*
University of Pennsylvania	M,D*
University of Phoenix	M
University of Phoenix–Atlanta Campus	M
University of Phoenix–Augusta Campus	M
University of Phoenix–Austin Campus	M
University of Phoenix–Bay Area Campus	M
University of Phoenix–Birmingham Campus	M
University of Phoenix–Central Florida Campus	M
University of Phoenix–Central Valley Campus	M
University of Phoenix–Charlotte Campus	M
University of Phoenix–Chattanooga Campus	M
University of Phoenix–Cincinnati Campus	M
University of Phoenix–Cleveland Campus	M
University of Phoenix–Columbus Georgia Campus	M
University of Phoenix–Columbus Ohio Campus	M
University of Phoenix–Dallas Campus	M
University of Phoenix–Denver Campus	M
University of Phoenix–Des Moines Campus	M
University of Phoenix–Eastern Washington Campus	M
University of Phoenix–Harrisburg Campus	M
University of Phoenix–Hawaii Campus	M
University of Phoenix–Houston Campus	M
University of Phoenix–Idaho Campus	M
University of Phoenix–Indianapolis Campus	M
University of Phoenix–Jersey City Campus	M
University of Phoenix–Kansas City Campus	M
University of Phoenix–Las Vegas Campus	M
University of Phoenix–Louisiana Campus	M
University of Phoenix–Madison Campus	M
University of Phoenix–Maryland Campus	M
University of Phoenix–Memphis Campus	M
University of Phoenix–Metro Detroit Campus	M
University of Phoenix–Minneapolis/St. Louis Park Campus	M
University of Phoenix–New Mexico Campus	M
University of Phoenix–Northern Nevada Campus	M
University of Phoenix–Northern Virginia Campus	M
University of Phoenix–North Florida Campus	M
University of Phoenix–Northwest Arkansas Campus	M
University of Phoenix–Oklahoma City Campus	M
University of Phoenix–Omaha Campus	M
University of Phoenix–Oregon Campus	M
University of Phoenix–Philadelphia Campus	M
University of Phoenix–Phoenix Campus	M
University of Phoenix–Pittsburgh Campus	M
University of Phoenix–Puerto Rico Campus	M
University of Phoenix–Raleigh Campus	M
University of Phoenix–Renton Learning Center	M
University of Phoenix–Richmond Campus	M
University of Phoenix–Sacramento Valley Campus	M
University of Phoenix–St. Louis Campus	M
University of Phoenix–San Antonio Campus	M
University of Phoenix–San Diego Campus	M
University of Phoenix–Savannah Campus	M
University of Phoenix–Southern Arizona Campus	M
University of Phoenix–Southern California Campus	M
University of Phoenix–Southern Colorado Campus	M
University of Phoenix–South Florida Campus	M
University of Phoenix–Springfield Campus	M
University of Phoenix–Tulsa Campus	M
University of Phoenix–Utah Campus	M
University of Phoenix–Vancouver Campus	M
University of Phoenix–West Florida Campus	M
University of Phoenix–West Michigan Campus	M
University of Phoenix–Wisconsin Campus	M
University of Pittsburgh	M,D*
University of Puerto Rico, Río Piedras	M,D

*M—master's degree; P—first professional degree; D—doctorate; O—other advanced degree; *—Close-Up and/or Announcement or Display in one of the other books in this series*

University of Rhode Island	M
University of St. Thomas (MN)	M*
University of San Diego	M,O
University of Saskatchewan	M
The University of Scranton	M
University of South Africa	M,D
University of South Alabama	M*
University of South Carolina	M
The University of South Dakota	M
University of Southern California	M*
University of Southern Indiana	M
University of Southern Maine	M
University of Southern Mississippi	M
University of South Florida	M*
The University of Tampa	M
The University of Tennessee	M,D
The University of Tennessee at Chattanooga	M
The University of Texas at Arlington	M,D*
The University of Texas at Austin	M,D
The University of Texas at Dallas	M,D*
The University of Texas at El Paso	M
The University of Texas at San Antonio	M,D*
The University of Texas of the Permian Basin	M
The University of Texas–Pan American	M
University of the Incarnate Word	M
University of the Sacred Heart	M
The University of Toledo	M
University of Toronto	M,D
University of Tulsa	M*
University of Utah	M,D*
University of Vermont	M*
University of Virginia	M
University of Washington	M,D*
University of Washington, Tacoma	M
University of Waterloo	M,D
University of West Florida	M
University of West Georgia	M
University of Wisconsin–Madison	D*
University of Wisconsin–Whitewater	M*
University of Wyoming	M
Upper Iowa University	M
Utah State University	M
Utica College	M
Villanova University	M*
Virginia Commonwealth University	M,D
Virginia Polytechnic Institute and State University	M,D*
Wagner College	M
Wake Forest University	M*
Walden University	M,D
Walsh College of Accountancy and Business Administration	M
Washington State University	M,D*
Washington University in St. Louis	M*
Wayne State University	M,D*
Webber International University	M*
Weber State University	M
Western Carolina University	M
Western Connecticut State University	M
Western Illinois University	M
Western Michigan University	M*
Western New England College	M
West Texas A&M University	M
West Virginia University	M
Wheeling Jesuit University	M
Wichita State University	M*
Widener University	M*
Wilkes University	M
Worcester State College	M
Wright State University	M
Yale University	D*
Yeshiva University	M
York University	M,D
Youngstown State University	M

ACOUSTICS

Penn State University Park	M,D*
University of Massachusetts Dartmouth	M,D,O

ACTUARIAL SCIENCE

Ball State University	M*
Boston University	M*
Central Connecticut State University	M,O
Columbia University	M*
Georgia State University	M
Maryville University of Saint Louis	M
Roosevelt University	M
St. John's University (NY)	M
Simon Fraser University	M,D
Temple University	M*
Université du Québec à Montréal	O
University of Central Florida	M,O*
University of Connecticut	M,D*
University of Illinois at Urbana–Champaign	M,D*
The University of Iowa	M,D*
University of Nebraska–Lincoln	M*
The University of Texas at Austin	M,D
University of Waterloo	M,D
University of Wisconsin–Madison	M*

ACUPUNCTURE AND ORIENTAL MEDICINE

Academy of Chinese Culture and Health Sciences	M
Academy of Oriental Medicine at Austin	M
Acupuncture & Integrative Medicine College, Berkeley	M
Acupuncture and Massage College	M
American College of Acupuncture and Oriental Medicine	M
American College of Traditional Chinese Medicine	M,D,O
Atlantic Institute of Oriental Medicine	M
Bastyr University	M,D,O*
Canadian Memorial Chiropractic College	O
Colorado School of Traditional Chinese Medicine	M
Dongguk Royal University	M
East West College of Natural Medicine	M
Emperor's College of Traditional Oriental Medicine	M,D
Five Branches University: Graduate School of Traditional Chinese Medicine	M
Florida College of Integrative Medicine	M
Institute of Clinical Acupuncture and Oriental Medicine	M
Midwest College of Oriental Medicine	M,O
National College of Natural Medicine	M
National University of Health Sciences	P,M,D*
New England School of Acupuncture	M
New York Chiropractic College	M*
New York College of Health Professions	M
New York College of Traditional Chinese Medicine	M
Northwestern Health Sciences University	M
Oregon College of Oriental Medicine	M,D
Pacific College of Oriental Medicine	M,D
Pacific College of Oriental Medicine-Chicago	M
Pacific College of Oriental Medicine-New York	M
Samra University of Oriental Medicine	M,D
Seattle Institute of Oriental Medicine	M
South Baylo University	M
Southern California University of Health Sciences	M
Southwest Acupuncture College	M
Swedish Institute, College of Health Sciences	M
Tai Sophia Institute	M,O
Texas College of Traditional Chinese Medicine	M
Touro College	M,D
Traditional Chinese Medical College of Hawaii	M
Tri State College of Acupuncture	M,O
University of Bridgeport	M
World Medicine Institute: College of Acupuncture and Herbal Medicine	M
Yo San University of Traditional Chinese Medicine	M

ACUTE CARE/CRITICAL CARE NURSING

Allen College	M
Barry University	M,O*
Case Western Reserve University	M,D*
The College of New Rochelle	M,O
Columbia University	M,O*
Duke University	M,D,O*
Duquesne University	O*
Georgetown University	M
Indiana University–Purdue University Indianapolis	M,D*
Inter American University of Puerto Rico, Arecibo Campus	M
The Johns Hopkins University	M,O*
Loyola University Chicago	M,O*
Medical College of Georgia	M
New York University	M,O*
Northeastern University	M,O*
Rush University	M,D,O
Seton Hall University	M*
Texas Tech University Health Sciences Center	M,D,O
Texas Woman's University	M,D
Universidad de Iberoamerica	P,M
Université de Montréal	O
University at Buffalo, the State University of New York	M,D,O*
The University of Alabama in Huntsville	M,D,O
University of Cincinnati	M,D
University of Guelph	M,D,O
University of Illinois at Chicago	M*
University of Massachusetts Worcester	M,D,O
University of Miami	M,D*
University of Michigan	M*
University of Pennsylvania	M*
University of Pittsburgh	M,D*
University of Puerto Rico, Medical Sciences Campus	M
University of Rochester	M,D,O*
University of South Africa	M,D
University of South Carolina	M,O
University of Virginia	M,D
Vanderbilt University	M,D*
Virginia Polytechnic Institute and State University	M,D*
Wayne State University	M*
Wright State University	M

ADDICTIONS/SUBSTANCE ABUSE COUNSELING

Adler School of Professional Psychology	M,D,O*
Alliant International University–Los Angeles	M*
Argosy University, Hawai'i	O*
Cambridge College	M,O
Capella University	M,D,O
Cleveland State University	M,O
The College of New Jersey	M,O
College of St. Joseph	M
The College of William and Mary	M,D
Coppin State University	M
East Carolina University	M
Eastern Michigan University	M,O
Governors State University	M
Grand Canyon University	M*
Hazelden Graduate School of Addiction Studies	M,O
Indiana University–Purdue University Indianapolis	M,D*
Indiana Wesleyan University	M
The Johns Hopkins University	M,D*
Kean University	M
Lewis & Clark College	M
Maryville University of Saint Louis	M
Marywood University	M
McNeese State University	M
Mercy College	M,O
Monmouth University	M,O
Montclair State University	M,D,O*
National-Louis University	M,O
Pace University	M*
Palm Beach Atlantic University	M

St. Mary's University (United States)	M,D,O
Shippensburg University of Pennsylvania	M,O
Southern New Hampshire University	M,O*
Springfield College	M
Stony Brook University, State University of New York	M
Universidad Central del Caribe	M
University of Arkansas at Pine Bluff	M
University of Central Florida	M,O*
University of Central Oklahoma	M
University of Detroit Mercy	M,O
University of Illinois at Springfield	M
University of Lethbridge	M,D
University of Louisiana at Monroe	M
University of Louisville	M,D,O
University of Mary	M
University of Nevada, Las Vegas	M,O
University of New England	M,O
Wayne State University	O*

ADULT EDUCATION

Alverno College	M
Argosy University, Hawai'i	M,D*
Armstrong Atlantic State University	M
Athabasca University	M*
Auburn University	M,D,O*
Ball State University	M,D*
Buffalo State College, State University of New York	M,O
Capella University	M,D,O
Central Michigan University	M
Cheyney University of Pennsylvania	M
Cleveland State University	M,O
Colorado State University	M,D*
Concordia University (Canada)	M,O
Coppin State University	M
Cornell University	M,D*
Defiance College	M
Delaware State University	M
DePaul University	M*
Drake University	M*
East Carolina University	M,O
Eastern Washington University	M
Florida Agricultural and Mechanical University	M,D
Florida Atlantic University	M,D,O
Florida International University	M,D*
Fordham University	M,D,O*
Grand Valley State University	M,O
Indiana University of Pennsylvania	M,D
Indiana University–Purdue University Indianapolis	M*
The Johns Hopkins University	M,O*
Jones International University	M
Kansas State University	M,D*
Kean University	M
Marshall University	M
Memorial University of Newfoundland	M,D,O
Michigan State University	M,D,O*
Montana State University	M,D,O
Morehead State University	M,O
Mount Saint Vincent University	M
National-Louis University	M,D,O
North Carolina Agricultural and Technical State University	M,D
North Carolina State University	M,D*
North Dakota State University	M,D,O
Northern Illinois University	M,D
Northwestern State University of Louisiana	M
Nova Southeastern University	D*
Oregon State University	M*
Penn State University Park	M,D*
Portland State University	M,D
Regis University	M,O
St. Francis Xavier University	M
Saint Joseph's University	M,O
San Francisco State University	M,O
Seattle University	M,O
Suffolk University	M,O*
Syracuse University	M,D*
Teachers College, Columbia University	M,D
Texas A&M University–Kingsville	M
Texas A&M University–Texarkana	M
Troy University	M
TUI University	M
Tusculum College	M
Universidad del Este	M
Université du Québec en Outaouais	O
University of Alaska Anchorage	M
University of Alberta	M,D,O*
University of Arkansas at Little Rock	M
The University of British Columbia	M,D
University of Central Oklahoma	M
University of Cincinnati	M,D,O
University of Connecticut	M,D*
University of Denver	M,D,O*
University of Georgia	M,D,O*
University of Idaho	M,D,O
University of Manitoba	M
University of Memphis	M,D
University of Minnesota, Twin Cities Campus	M,D,O*
University of Missouri–Columbia	M,D,O*
University of Missouri–St. Louis	M,D,O
University of Nebraska–Lincoln	M,D,O*
The University of North Carolina at Charlotte	D*
The University of North Carolina at Greensboro	M,D,O
University of Oklahoma	M,D*
University of Phoenix	M
University of Phoenix–Bay Area Campus	M
University of Phoenix–Metro Detroit Campus	M
University of Phoenix–Omaha Campus	M
University of Phoenix–Phoenix Campus	M
University of Phoenix–Sacramento Valley Campus	M,O
University of Phoenix–Southern Arizona Campus	M,O
University of Phoenix–Southern California Campus	M
University of Regina	M
University of Rhode Island	M
University of South Africa	M,D
University of Southern Maine	M,O
University of Southern Mississippi	M,D,O
University of South Florida	M,D,O*
The University of Tennessee	M,D
The University of Texas at San Antonio	M,D,O*
University of the Incarnate Word	M,D,O
The University of West Alabama	M
University of Wisconsin–Milwaukee	D
University of Wisconsin–Platteville	M
University of Wyoming	M,D,O
Virginia Commonwealth University	M
Virginia Polytechnic Institute and State University	M,D*
Walden University	M,D,O
Wayne State University	M,D,O*
Western Washington University	M
Widener University	M,D*
Wright State University	O

ADULT NURSING

Angelo State University	M
Bloomsburg University of Pennsylvania	M
Boston College	M,D*
California State University, Long Beach	M
Case Western Reserve University	M,D*
The Catholic University of America	M,D,O
Clarkson College	M,O
College of Mount Saint Vincent	M,O
College of Staten Island of the City University of New York	M,O
Columbia University	M,O*
Daemen College	M,O
DeSales University	M
Duke University	M,D,O*
Eastern Michigan University	M,O
Emory University	M*
Felician College	M,O*
The George Washington University	M,D,O*
Georgia College & State University	M
Georgia State University	M,D,O
Goldfarb School of Nursing at Barnes-Jewish College	M
Grand Canyon University	M*
Gwynedd-Mercy College	M
Hampton University	M
Hunter College of the City University of New York	M
Indiana University–Purdue University Fort Wayne	M,O
Indiana University–Purdue University Indianapolis	M,D*
Inter American University of Puerto Rico, Arecibo Campus	M
The Johns Hopkins University	M,O*
Kent State University	M,D*
Lehman College of the City University of New York	M
Lewis University	M
Loma Linda University	M
Long Island University, Brooklyn Campus	M,O
Louisiana State University Health Sciences Center	M,D*
Loyola University Chicago	M,O*
Loyola University New Orleans	M
Madonna University	M
Marian University (WI)	M
Marquette University	M,D,O
Maryville University of Saint Louis	M
Medical College of Georgia	M
Medical University of South Carolina	M
Molloy College	M,O
Mount Carmel College of Nursing	M*
Mount Saint Mary College	M
New Mexico State University	M
New York University	M,O*
North Park University	M
Oakland University	M
Otterbein College	M,O
Quinnipiac University	M,O*
Radford University	M
Rush University	M,D,O
Rutgers, The State University of New Jersey, Newark	M*
Sage Graduate School	M,O
Saint Peter's College	M
Saint Xavier University	M,O
Seattle Pacific University	M,O
Seton Hall University	M*
Southern Adventist University	M
Spalding University	M
State University of New York Institute of Technology	M,O
Stony Brook University, State University of New York	M,O
Texas Christian University	M,D
Texas Woman's University	M,D
Universidad del Turabo	M
University at Buffalo, the State University of New York	M,D,O*
University of Central Florida	M,D,O*
University of Cincinnati	M,D
University of Colorado at Colorado Springs	M,D
University of Delaware	M,O*
University of Hawaii at Manoa	M,D,O*
University of Illinois at Chicago	M*
University of Louisville	M,D
University of Massachusetts Dartmouth	M,D,O
University of Massachusetts Worcester	M,D,O
University of Medicine and Dentistry of New Jersey	M,D,O*
University of Miami	M,D*
University of Michigan	M,O*
University of Minnesota, Twin Cities Campus	M*
University of Missouri–Kansas City	M,D*
The University of North Carolina at Chapel Hill	M,D,O*
The University of North Carolina at Charlotte	M*
The University of North Carolina at Greensboro	M,D,O
University of Pennsylvania	M*
University of Pittsburgh	M,D*
University of Rochester	M,D,O*
University of St. Francis (IL)	M,D
University of San Diego	M,D
The University of Scranton	M,O
University of South Alabama	M,D*

*M—master's degree; P—first professional degree; D—doctorate; O—other advanced degree; *—Close-Up and/or Announcement or Display in one of the other books in this series*

University of South Carolina M
University of Southern Maine M,O
University of Southern Mississippi M,D
The University of Tampa M
The University of Tennessee at Chattanooga M,O
The University of Texas–Pan American M
The University of Toledo M,O
University of Wisconsin–Oshkosh M
Vanderbilt University M,D*
Villanova University M,D,O*
Virginia Commonwealth University M,D,O
Wayne State University M*
Western Connecticut State University M
Wilmington University M
Winona State University M,D,O
Wright State University M

ADVERTISING AND PUBLIC RELATIONS

Academy of Art University M
Ball State University M*
Boston University M*
California State University, Fullerton M
Central Connecticut State University M,O
Colorado State University M,D*
DePaul University M*
Emerson College M
Georgetown University M,D
Golden Gate University M,D,O
Hult International Business School (United States) M
Iona College M*
Lasell College M,O
La Sierra University M
Marquette University M
Michigan State University M,D*
Mississippi College M
Monmouth University M,O
Montana State University–Billings M
Montclair State University M*
New York University M*
Northwestern University M*
Quinnipiac University M*
Rowan University M
Royal Roads University O
San Diego State University M*
Savannah College of Art and Design M*
Seton Hall University M*
Suffolk University M*
Syracuse University M*
Texas Christian University M
Towson University O
Universidad Autonoma de Guadalajara M,D
Universidad Iberoamericana P,M
Université Laval O
The University of Alabama M
University of Denver M*
University of Florida M*
University of Houston M*
University of Illinois at Urbana–Champaign M*
University of Maryland, College Park M,D*
University of Miami M,D*
University of Nebraska–Lincoln M,D*
University of New Haven M*
University of Oklahoma M*
University of Southern California M*
University of Southern Mississippi M,D
The University of Tennessee M,D
The University of Texas at Austin M,D
University of the Sacred Heart M
University of Wisconsin–Stevens Point M
Virginia Commonwealth University M
Wayne State University M,D*
Webster University M

AEROSPACE/AERONAUTICAL ENGINEERING

Air Force Institute of Technology M,D
Arizona State University M,D
Arizona State University at the Polytechnic Campus M
Auburn University M,D*
California Institute of Technology M,D,O*
California Polytechnic State University, San Luis Obispo M
California State University, Long Beach M
Carleton University M,D
Case Western Reserve University M,D*
Concordia University (Canada) M
Cornell University M,D*
École Polytechnique de Montréal M,D,O
Embry-Riddle Aeronautical University (FL) M
Embry-Riddle Aeronautical University Worldwide M
Florida Institute of Technology M,D*
The George Washington University M,D,O*
Georgia Institute of Technology M,D*
Illinois Institute of Technology M,D*
Iowa State University of Science and Technology M,D*
Massachusetts Institute of Technology M,D,O*
McGill University M,D*
Middle Tennessee State University M
Mississippi State University M,D
Missouri University of Science and Technology M,D
Naval Postgraduate School M
North Carolina State University M,D*
The Ohio State University M,D*
Old Dominion University M,D
Penn State University Park M,D*
Polytechnic Institute of NYU, Long Island Graduate Center M,D
Princeton University M,D*
Purdue University M,D
Rensselaer Polytechnic Institute M,D
Rutgers, The State University of New Jersey, New Brunswick M,D*
San Diego State University M,D*
San Jose State University M
Stanford University M,D,O*
Stevens Institute of Technology M,O
Syracuse University M,D*
Texas A&M University M,D*
Université Laval M
University at Buffalo, the State University of New York M,D*
The University of Alabama M,D
The University of Alabama in Huntsville M,D
The University of Arizona M,D*
University of California, Davis M,D,O*
University of California, Irvine M,D*
University of California, Los Angeles M,D*
University of California, San Diego M,D*
University of Central Florida M*
University of Cincinnati M,D
University of Colorado at Boulder M,D*
University of Colorado at Colorado Springs M
University of Dayton M,D
University of Florida M,D,O*
University of Houston M,D*
University of Illinois at Urbana–Champaign M,D*
The University of Kansas M,D*
University of Maryland, College Park M,D,O*
University of Miami M,D*
University of Michigan M,D*
University of Minnesota, Twin Cities Campus M,D*
University of Missouri–Columbia M,D*
University of Nevada, Las Vegas M,D
University of Notre Dame M,D*
University of Oklahoma M,D*
University of Ottawa M,D*
University of Southern California M,D,O*
The University of Tennessee M,D
The University of Tennessee Space Institute M,D*
The University of Texas at Arlington M,D*
The University of Texas at Austin M,D
University of Toronto M,D
University of Virginia M,D
University of Washington M,D*
Utah State University M,D
Virginia Polytechnic Institute and State University M,D*
Washington University in St. Louis M,D*
Webster University M,D
West Virginia University M,D
Wichita State University M,D*

AFRICAN-AMERICAN STUDIES

Boston University M*
Carnegie Mellon University M,D*
Clark Atlanta University M,D
Columbia University M*
Cornell University M,D*
Eastern Michigan University O
Florida Agricultural and Mechanical University M
Harvard University D*
Indiana University Bloomington M*
Michigan State University M,D*
Morgan State University M,D
North Carolina Agricultural and Technical State University M
The Ohio State University M*
Rutgers, The State University of New Jersey, New Brunswick D*
Syracuse University M*
Temple University M,D*
University at Albany, State University of New York M*
University of California, Berkeley D*
University of California, Los Angeles M*
The University of Iowa M*
The University of Kansas M,O*
University of Louisville M
University of Massachusetts Amherst M,D*
University of Wisconsin–Madison M*
West Virginia University M,D
Yale University D*

AFRICAN STUDIES

Boston University M,O*
California State University, Long Beach M
Carnegie Mellon University M,D*
Claremont Graduate University M,D,O*
Columbia University O*
Cornell University M,D*
Florida International University M*
Harvard University D*
Howard University M,D
Indiana University Bloomington M*
Michigan State University M,D*
New York University M,D,O*
Northwestern University O*
The Ohio State University M*
Ohio University M*
Rutgers, The State University of New Jersey, New Brunswick D*
St. John's University (NY) M,O
Stony Brook University, State University of New York M
Syracuse University M*
University at Albany, State University of New York M*
University of California, Los Angeles M*
University of Connecticut M*
University of Florida O*
University of Illinois at Urbana–Champaign M*
The University of Kansas M,O*
University of Louisville M
University of Pittsburgh O*
University of South Florida M*
The University of Texas at Austin M,D
University of Wisconsin–Madison M,D*
University of Wisconsin–Milwaukee D
West Virginia University M,D
Yale University M*

AGRICULTURAL ECONOMICS AND AGRIBUSINESS

Alabama Agricultural and Mechanical University M
Alcorn State University M
American University of Beirut M
Arizona State University M,D
Arizona State University at the Polytechnic Campus M
Auburn University M,D*
California Polytechnic State University, San Luis Obispo M
Colorado State University M,D*
Cornell University M,D*
Delaware Valley College M
Florida Agricultural and Mechanical University M
Illinois State University M
Instituto Centroamericano de Administración de Empresas M

Iowa State University of Science and Technology	M,D*
Kansas State University	M,D*
Louisiana State University and Agricultural and Mechanical College	M,D
McGill University	M*
Michigan State University	M,D*
Mississippi State University	M
New Mexico State University	M,D
North Carolina Agricultural and Technical State University	M
North Carolina State University	M*
North Dakota State University	M
Northwest Missouri State University	M
The Ohio State University	M,D*
Oklahoma State University	M,D*
Oregon State University	M,D*
Penn State University Park	M,D*
Prairie View A&M University	M
Purdue University	M,D
Rutgers, The State University of New Jersey, New Brunswick	M*
South Carolina State University	M
Southern Illinois University Carbondale	M*
Texas A&M University	M,D*
Texas A&M University–Kingsville	M
Texas Tech University	M,D
Tropical Agriculture Research and Higher Education Center	M,D
Tuskegee University	M
Universidad del Este	M
Université Laval	M
University of Alberta	M,D*
The University of Arizona	M*
University of Arkansas	M
The University of British Columbia	M
University of California, Berkeley	D*
University of California, Davis	M,D*
University of California, Santa Barbara	M,D
University of Connecticut	M,D*
University of Delaware	M*
University of Florida	M,D*
University of Georgia	M,D*
University of Guelph	M,D
University of Idaho	M
University of Illinois at Urbana–Champaign	M,D*
University of Kentucky	M,D
University of Maine	M*
University of Manitoba	M,D
University of Maryland, College Park	M,D*
University of Massachusetts Amherst	M,D*
University of Missouri–Columbia	M,D*
University of Nevada, Reno	M,D*
University of Puerto Rico, Mayagüez Campus	M
University of Saskatchewan	M,D
University of Vermont	M*
University of Wisconsin–Madison	M,D*
University of Wyoming	M
Virginia Polytechnic Institute and State University	M,D*
Washington State University	M,D,O*
West Texas A&M University	M
West Virginia University	M
William Woods University	M,O

AGRICULTURAL EDUCATION

Alcorn State University	M,O
Arkansas State University	M,D,O
Clemson University	M
Cornell University	M,D*
Eastern Kentucky University	M
Iowa State University of Science and Technology	M,D*
Louisiana State University and Agricultural and Mechanical College	M,D
Mississippi State University	M,D,O
Missouri State University	M*
Montana State University	M
Murray State University	M
New Mexico State University	M
North Carolina Agricultural and Technical State University	M
North Carolina State University	M,O*
North Dakota State University	M
Northwest Missouri State University	M
The Ohio State University	M,D*
Oklahoma State University	M,D*
Oregon State University	M*
Penn State University Park	M,D*
Purdue University	M,D,O
State University of New York at Oswego	M
Stephen F. Austin State University	M
Tarleton State University	M
Texas A&M University	M,D*
Texas A&M University–Commerce	M
Texas A&M University–Kingsville	M
Texas State University–San Marcos	M*
Texas Tech University	M,D
The University of Arizona	M*
University of Arkansas	M
University of Connecticut	M,D,O*
University of Delaware	M*
University of Florida	M,D*
University of Georgia	M*
University of Idaho	M
University of Illinois at Urbana–Champaign	M,D*
University of Minnesota, Twin Cities Campus	M,D*
University of Missouri–Columbia	M,D,O*
University of Nebraska–Lincoln	M*
University of Puerto Rico, Mayagüez Campus	M
The University of Tennessee	M
University of Wisconsin–River Falls	M
Utah State University	M
Virginia Polytechnic Institute and State University	M,D*
West Virginia University	M,D

AGRICULTURAL ENGINEERING

Cornell University	M,D*
Dalhousie University	M,D
Illinois Institute of Technology	M,D*
Instituto Tecnológico y de Estudios Superiores de Monterrey, Campus Monterrey	M,D
Iowa State University of Science and Technology	M,D*
Kansas State University	M,D*
Louisiana State University and Agricultural and Mechanical College	M,D
McGill University	M,D*
New York University	M,D*
North Carolina State University	M,D,O*
North Dakota State University	M,D
The Ohio State University	M,D*
Oklahoma State University	M,D*
Penn State Great Valley	M
Penn State University Park	M,D*
Purdue University	M,D
South Dakota State University	M,D
Texas A&M University	M,D*
Université Laval	M
The University of Arizona	M,D*
University of Arkansas	M,D
University of Dayton	M
University of Florida	M,D,O*
University of Georgia	M,D*
University of Idaho	M,D
University of Illinois at Urbana–Champaign	M,D*
University of Kentucky	M,D
University of Missouri–Columbia	M,D*
University of Nebraska–Lincoln	M,D*
University of Saskatchewan	M,D
The University of Tennessee	M
University of Wisconsin–Madison	M,D*
Utah State University	M,D
Virginia Polytechnic Institute and State University	M,D*
Washington State University	M,D*

AGRICULTURAL SCIENCES—GENERAL

Alabama Agricultural and Mechanical University	M,D
Alcorn State University	M
Angelo State University	M
Arkansas State University	M,D,O
Auburn University	M,D*
Brigham Young University	M,D*
California Polytechnic State University, San Luis Obispo	M
California State Polytechnic University, Pomona	M
Clemson University	M,D
Colorado State University	M,D*
Dalhousie University	M
Florida Agricultural and Mechanical University	M
Illinois State University	M
Instituto Tecnológico y de Estudios Superiores de Monterrey, Campus Monterrey	M,D
Iowa State University of Science and Technology	M,D*
Kansas State University	M,D*
Louisiana State University and Agricultural and Mechanical College	M,D
McGill University	M,D,O*
McNeese State University	M
Michigan State University	M,D*
Mississippi State University	M,D,O
Missouri State University	M*
Montana State University	M,D
Murray State University	M
New Mexico State University	M
North Carolina Agricultural and Technical State University	M
North Carolina State University	M,D,O*
North Dakota State University	M,D
Northwest Missouri State University	M
Nova Scotia Agricultural College	M
The Ohio State University	M,D*
Oklahoma State University	M,D*
Oregon State University	M,D*
Penn State University Park	M,D*
Prairie View A&M University	M
Purdue University	M,D
Sam Houston State University	M
South Dakota State University	M,D
Southern Arkansas University–Magnolia	M
Southern Illinois University Carbondale	M*
Southern University and Agricultural and Mechanical College	M
Tarleton State University	M
Tennessee State University	M
Texas A&M University	M,D*
Texas A&M University–Commerce	M
Texas A&M University–Kingsville	M,D
Texas Tech University	M,D
Tropical Agriculture Research and Higher Education Center	M,D
Tuskegee University	M
Université Laval	M,D
University of Alberta	M,D*
The University of Arizona	M,D*
University of Arkansas	M,D
The University of British Columbia	M,D
University of California, Davis	M*
University of Connecticut	M,D*
University of Delaware	M,D*
University of Florida	M,D*
University of Georgia	M,D*
University of Guelph	M,D,O
University of Hawaii at Manoa	M,D*
University of Illinois at Urbana–Champaign	M,D*
University of Kentucky	M,D
University of Lethbridge	M,D
University of Maine	M,D*
University of Manitoba	M,D
University of Maryland, College Park	P,M,D*
University of Maryland Eastern Shore	M,D*
University of Minnesota, Twin Cities Campus	M,D*
University of Missouri–Columbia	M,D*
University of Nebraska–Lincoln	M,D*
University of Nevada, Reno	M,D*
University of Puerto Rico, Mayagüez Campus	M
University of Saskatchewan	M,D
University of South Africa	M,D
The University of Tennessee	M,D
The University of Tennessee at Martin	M
University of Vermont	M,D*
University of Wisconsin–Madison	M,D*

*M—master's degree; P—first professional degree; D—doctorate; O—other advanced degree; *—Close-Up and/or Announcement or Display in one of the other books in this series*

University of Wisconsin–River Falls	M
University of Wyoming	M,D
Utah State University	M,D
Virginia Polytechnic Institute and State University	M,D*
Virginia State University	M
Washington State University	M*
Western Kentucky University	M
West Texas A&M University	M,D
West Virginia University	M,D

AGRONOMY AND SOIL SCIENCES

Alabama Agricultural and Mechanical University	M,D
Alcorn State University	M
American University of Beirut	M
Auburn University	M,D*
Colorado State University	M,D*
Cornell University	M,D*
Iowa State University of Science and Technology	M,D*
Kansas State University	M,D*
Louisiana State University and Agricultural and Mechanical College	M,D
McGill University	M,D*
Michigan State University	M,D*
Mississippi State University	M,D
North Carolina Agricultural and Technical State University	M
North Carolina State University	M,D*
North Dakota State University	M,D
Nova Scotia Agricultural College	M
The Ohio State University	M,D*
Oklahoma State University	M,D*
Oregon State University	M,D*
Penn State University Park	M,D*
Prairie View A&M University	M
Purdue University	M,D
South Dakota State University	M,D
Southern Illinois University Carbondale	M*
Texas A&M University	M,D*
Texas A&M University–Kingsville	M,D
Texas Tech University	M,D
Tuskegee University	M
Université Laval	M,D
University of Alberta	M,D*
The University of Arizona	M,D*
University of Arkansas	M,D
The University of British Columbia	M,D
University of California, Davis	M,D*
University of California, Riverside	M,D*
University of Connecticut	M,D*
University of Delaware	M,D*
University of Florida	M,D*
University of Georgia	M,D*
University of Guelph	M,D
University of Idaho	M,D
University of Illinois at Urbana–Champaign	M,D*
University of Kentucky	M,D
University of Maine	M,D*
University of Manitoba	M,D
University of Maryland, College Park	M,D*
University of Massachusetts Amherst	M,D*
University of Minnesota, Twin Cities Campus	M,D*
University of Missouri–Columbia	M,D*
University of Nebraska–Lincoln	M,D*
University of New Hampshire	M*
University of Puerto Rico, Mayagüez Campus	M
University of Saskatchewan	M,D
University of Vermont	M,D*
University of Wisconsin–Madison	M,D*
University of Wyoming	M,D
Utah State University	M,D
Virginia Polytechnic Institute and State University	M,D*
Washington State University	M,D*
West Virginia University	D

ALLIED HEALTH—GENERAL

Alabama State University	D
Andrews University	M
Athabasca University	M,O*
A.T. Still University of Health Sciences	M,D
Australasian College of Health Sciences	M
Baylor University	M,D
Belmont University	P,M,D
Bennington College	O
Boston University	M,D,O*
Brock University	M
Chatham University	M
Cleveland State University	M
Creighton University	P,M,D*
Dominican College	M,D
Drexel University	M,D,O*
Duquesne University	M,D*
East Carolina University	M,D
Eastern Kentucky University	M
East Tennessee State University	M,D,O
Emory University	M,D*
Ferris State University	M
Florida Agricultural and Mechanical University	M
Florida Gulf Coast University	M,D
Georgia Southern University	M,D,O
Georgia State University	M,D,O
Grand Valley State University	M,D
Idaho State University	M,D,O
Ithaca College	M,D
Loma Linda University	M,D
Long Island University, C.W. Post Campus	M,O
Louisiana State University Health Sciences Center	M*
Marymount University	M,D,O
Maryville University of Saint Louis	M,D
Medical College of Georgia	M
Medical University of South Carolina	M,D
Mercy College	M,D,O
MGH Institute of Health Professions	M,D,O*
Midwestern University, Downers Grove Campus	M,D*
Midwestern University, Glendale Campus	P,M,D,O*
Minnesota State University Mankato	M,D,O
Misericordia University	M,D
Moravian College	M
Mountain State University	M*
New Jersey City University	M
Northeastern University	P,M,D,O*
Northern Arizona University	M,D
Nova Southeastern University	M,D*
Oakland University	M,D,O
The Ohio State University	M*
Old Dominion University	M,D
Quinnipiac University	M,D,O*
Regis University	P,M,D,O
Rosalind Franklin University of Medicine and Science	M,D,O*
Saint Louis University	M,D,O
Seton Hall University	M,D*
Shenandoah University	M,D,O
South Carolina State University	M
Southwestern Oklahoma State University	M
Temple University	M,D*
Tennessee State University	M,D
Texas Christian University	M,D
Texas State University–San Marcos	M,D*
Texas Tech University Health Sciences Center	M,D
Texas Woman's University	M,D
Towson University	M
University at Buffalo, the State University of New York	M,D,O*
The University of Alabama at Birmingham	M,D,O*
University of Arkansas at Little Rock	M
University of Connecticut	M*
University of Detroit Mercy	M,O
University of Florida	M,D*
University of Illinois at Chicago	M,D*
The University of Kansas	M,D,O*
University of Kentucky	M,D
University of Massachusetts Lowell	M,D,O
University of Medicine and Dentistry of New Jersey	M,D,O*
University of Mississippi Medical Center	M*
University of Nebraska Medical Center	M,D,O*
University of Nevada, Las Vegas	M,D
The University of North Carolina at Chapel Hill	M,D*
University of North Florida	M,O
University of Oklahoma Health Sciences Center	M,D,O
University of Phoenix–Charlotte Campus	M
University of Phoenix–Las Vegas Campus	M
University of Puerto Rico, Medical Sciences Campus	M,D,O
University of St. Francis (IL)	M,D
University of Saint Francis (IN)	M
University of South Alabama	M,D*
The University of South Dakota	M,D
The University of Tennessee Health Science Center	M,D*
The University of Texas at El Paso	D
The University of Texas Medical Branch	M,D*
University of Vermont	M,D*
University of Wisconsin–Milwaukee	M,D,O
Virginia Commonwealth University	D
Washington University in St. Louis	M,D,O*
Western University of Health Sciences	M,D
Wichita State University	M*

ALLOPATHIC MEDICINE

Albany Medical College	P
Albert Einstein College of Medicine	P
American University of Beirut	P,M
Baylor College of Medicine	P*
Boston University	P*
Brown University	P*
Case Western Reserve University	P*
Charles R. Drew University of Medicine and Science	P
Columbia University	P*
Creighton University	P*
Dalhousie University	P,M,D
Dartmouth College	P*
Drexel University	P*
Duke University	P*
East Carolina University	P
Eastern Virginia Medical School	P
East Tennessee State University	P
Emory University	P*
Georgetown University	P
The George Washington University	P*
Harvard University	P,D*
Howard University	P,D
Indiana University–Purdue University Indianapolis	P,M,D*
Instituto Tecnologico de Santo Domingo	P,M
The Johns Hopkins University	P*
Loma Linda University	P,M,D
Louisiana State University Health Sciences Center	P,M*
Louisiana State University Health Sciences Center at Shreveport	P*
Loyola University Chicago	P*
Marshall University	P
Mayo Medical School	P
McGill University	M,D*
Medical College of Georgia	P
Medical College of Wisconsin	P*
Medical University of South Carolina	P
Meharry Medical College	P
Mercer University	P,M
Michigan State University	P*
Morehouse School of Medicine	P*
Mount Sinai School of Medicine of New York University	P
New York Medical College	P*
New York University	P*
Northeastern Ohio Universities College of Medicine and Pharmacy	P
Northwestern University	*
The Ohio State University	P*
Oregon Health & Science University	P*
Penn State Hershey Medical Center	P,M,D
Ponce School of Medicine	P
Pontificia Universidad Catolica Madre y Maestra	P
Queen's University at Kingston	P
Rosalind Franklin University of Medicine and Science	P*
Rush University	P
Saint Louis University	P
San Juan Bautista School of Medicine	P
Stanford University	P*

State University of New York Downstate Medical Center	P,M*
State University of New York Upstate Medical University	P
Stony Brook University, State University of New York	P
Temple University	P*
Texas Tech University Health Sciences Center	P
Thomas Jefferson University	P*
Tufts University	P*
Tulane University	P
Uniformed Services University of the Health Sciences	P*
Universidad Autonoma de Guadalajara	P
Universidad Central del Caribe	P,M
Universidad Central del Este	P
Universidad de Ciencias Medicas	P,M,O
Universidad de Iberoamerica	P,M
Universidad Iberoamericana	P
Universidad Nacional Pedro Henriquez Urena	P
Université de Montréal	P,O
Université de Sherbrooke	P
Université Laval	P,O
University at Buffalo, the State University of New York	P*
The University of Alabama at Birmingham	P,M,D*
The University of Arizona	P*
The University of British Columbia	P,M
University of Calgary	P
University of California, Berkeley	*
University of California, Davis	P*
University of California, Irvine	P*
University of California, Los Angeles	P*
University of California, San Diego	P*
University of California, San Francisco	P
University of Chicago	P*
University of Cincinnati	P,M
University of Colorado Denver	P*
University of Connecticut Health Center	P*
University of Florida	P*
University of Hawaii at Manoa	P*
University of Illinois at Chicago	P*
University of Illinois at Urbana–Champaign	*
The University of Iowa	P*
The University of Kansas	P,M,D*
University of Kentucky	P
University of Louisville	P
University of Maryland, Baltimore	P*
University of Massachusetts Worcester	P
University of Medicine and Dentistry of New Jersey	P*
University of Miami	P*
University of Michigan	P*
University of Minnesota, Duluth	P
University of Minnesota, Twin Cities Campus	P*
University of Mississippi Medical Center	P*
University of Missouri–Columbia	P*
University of Missouri–Kansas City	P*
University of Nebraska Medical Center	P,O*
University of New Mexico	P*
The University of North Carolina at Chapel Hill	P*
University of North Dakota	P
University of Oklahoma Health Sciences Center	P
University of Ottawa	P,M,D*
University of Pennsylvania	P*
University of Pittsburgh	P*
University of Puerto Rico, Medical Sciences Campus	P
University of Rochester	P*
University of Saskatchewan	P
University of South Alabama	P*
University of South Carolina	P
The University of South Dakota	P
University of Southern California	P*
The University of Tennessee Health Science Center	P,M,D*
The University of Texas Health Science Center at Houston	P
The University of Texas Health Science Center at San Antonio	P,M
The University of Texas Medical Branch	P*
The University of Texas Southwestern Medical Center at Dallas	P*
University of Toronto	P,M,D
University of Utah	P*
University of Vermont	P*
University of Virginia	P,M,D
University of Washington	P*
The University of Western Ontario	P,M
University of Wisconsin–Madison	P*
Vanderbilt University	M,D*
Virginia Commonwealth University	P
Wake Forest University	P*
Washington University in St. Louis	P*
Wayne State University	P*
West Virginia University	P
Wright State University	P
Yale University	P*

AMERICAN INDIAN/NATIVE AMERICAN STUDIES

Central Michigan University	M
Montana State University	M
Trent University	M,D
The University of Arizona	M,D*
University of California, Davis	M,D*
University of California, Los Angeles	M*
The University of Kansas	M*
University of Lethbridge	M,D
University of Manitoba	M
University of Oklahoma	M*
University of Regina	M

AMERICAN STUDIES

American University	M,D,O*
Appalachian State University	M
Baylor University	M
Boston University	D*
Bowling Green State University	M,D*
Brown University	M,D*
California State University, Fullerton	M
California State University, Long Beach	M
The Catholic University of America	M,D
Central Michigan University	M,D,O
Claremont Graduate University	M,D,O*
Clark University	D
The College at Brockport, State University of New York	M
The College of William and Mary	M,D
Columbia University	M*
Cornell University	M,D*
Drake University	M*
East Carolina University	M
Eastern Michigan University	M,O
Emory & Henry College	M
Fairfield University	M*
Florida State University	M,O*
Georgetown University	M,D
The George Washington University	M,D*
Harvard University	D*
Lehigh University	M
Lindenwood University	M
Michigan State University	M,D*
Mississippi State University	M,D
New Mexico Highlands University	M
New York University	M,D*
Northeastern State University	M
Penn State Harrisburg	M,D
Pepperdine University	M
Providence College	M*
Purdue University	M,D
Rutgers, The State University of New Jersey, Newark	M,D*
Saint Louis University	M,D
State University of New York College at Cortland	O
Trinity College	M
Universidad de las Américas–Puebla	M
University at Buffalo, the State University of New York	M,D*
The University of Alabama	M
University of Central Oklahoma	M
University of Dallas	M
University of Delaware	M*
University of Hawaii at Manoa	M,D,O*
The University of Iowa	M,D*
The University of Kansas	M,D*
University of Louisiana at Lafayette	D*
University of Maryland, College Park	M,D*
University of Massachusetts Boston	M
University of Michigan	M,D*
University of Michigan–Flint	M*
University of Minnesota, Twin Cities Campus	D*
University of Mississippi	M
University of New Mexico	M,D*
University of Southern California	D*
University of Southern Maine	M
University of South Florida	M*
The University of Texas at Austin	M,D
University of Utah	M,D*
University of Wisconsin–Madison	M,D*
University of Wyoming	M
Utah State University	M
Washington State University	M,D*
West Virginia University	M,D
Wheaton College	M
Yale University	D*

ANALYTICAL CHEMISTRY

Auburn University	M,D*
Brigham Young University	M,D*
California State University, Los Angeles	M
Clarkson University	M,D*
Cleveland State University	M,D
Cornell University	D*
Florida State University	M,D*
Georgetown University	D
The George Washington University	M,D*
Governors State University	M
Howard University	M,D
Illinois Institute of Technology	M,D*
Indiana University Bloomington	M,D*
Kansas State University	M,D*
Kent State University	M,D*
Laurentian University	M
Marquette University	M,D
McMaster University	M,D
Miami University	M,D*
Northeastern University	M,D*
Old Dominion University	M,D
Oregon State University	M,D*
Purdue University	M,D
Rensselaer Polytechnic Institute	M,D
Rutgers, The State University of New Jersey, Newark	M,D*
Seton Hall University	M,D*
Southern University and Agricultural and Mechanical College	M
State University of New York at Binghamton	M,D*
Stevens Institute of Technology	M,D,O
Tufts University	M,D*
University of Calgary	M,D
University of Cincinnati	M,D
University of Georgia	M,D*
University of Louisville	M,D
University of Maryland, College Park	M,D*
University of Massachusetts Lowell	M,D
University of Michigan	D*
University of Missouri–Columbia	M,D*
University of Missouri–Kansas City	M,D*
The University of Montana	M,D
University of Nebraska–Lincoln	M,D*
University of Regina	M,D
University of Southern Mississippi	M,D
University of South Florida	M,D*
The University of Tennessee	M,D
The University of Texas at Austin	M,D
The University of Toledo	M,D
Vanderbilt University	M,D*
Virginia Commonwealth University	M,D
Wake Forest University	M,D*
West Virginia University	M,D
Youngstown State University	M

ANATOMY

Albert Einstein College of Medicine	D
Auburn University	M,D*
Barry University	M*

*M—master's degree; P—first professional degree; D—doctorate; O—other advanced degree; *—Close-Up and/or Announcement or Display in one of the other books in this series*

Boston University M,D*
Case Western Reserve University M*
Columbia University M,D*
Cornell University M,D*
Creighton University M*
Dalhousie University M,D
Duke University D*
East Carolina University D
East Tennessee State University M,D
Howard University M,D
Indiana University–Purdue University Indianapolis M,D*
The Johns Hopkins University D*
Kansas State University M,D*
Loma Linda University M,D
Louisiana State University Health Sciences Center M,D*
Louisiana State University Health Sciences Center at Shreveport M,D*
Loyola University Chicago M,D*
McGill University M,D*
Medical College of Georgia D
New York Chiropractic College M*
New York Medical College M,D*
The Ohio State University M,D*
Palmer College of Chiropractic M
Penn State Hershey Medical Center M,D
Purdue University M,D
Queen's University at Kingston M,D
Rush University M,D
Saint Louis University M,D
State University of New York Upstate Medical University M,D
Stony Brook University, State University of New York D
Temple University M,D*
Texas A&M University M,D*
Universidad Central del Caribe M
Universidad de Ciencias Medicas P,M,O
Université Laval M,D,O
University at Buffalo, the State University of New York M,D*
The University of Arizona D*
University of Arkansas for Medical Sciences M,D
The University of British Columbia M,D
University of California, Irvine M,D*
University of California, Los Angeles D*
University of California, San Francisco D
University of Chicago D*
University of Georgia M*
University of Guelph M,D
University of Illinois at Chicago D*
The University of Iowa D*
The University of Kansas M,D*
University of Kentucky D
University of Louisville M,D
University of Manitoba M,D
University of Mississippi Medical Center M,D*
University of Missouri–Columbia M*
University of Nebraska Medical Center M,D*
University of North Dakota M,D
University of North Texas Health Science Center at Fort Worth M,D
University of Prince Edward Island M,D
University of Puerto Rico, Medical Sciences Campus M,D
University of Rochester M,D*
University of Saskatchewan M,D
University of South Florida M,D*
The University of Tennessee M,D
The University of Tennessee Health Science Center D*
University of Utah D*
The University of Western Ontario M,D
Virginia Commonwealth University D,O
Wake Forest University D*
Wayne State University M,D*
Wright State University M
Youngstown State University M

ANESTHESIOLOGIST ASSISTANT STUDIES

Case Western Reserve University M*
Emory University M*
South University (GA) M*
Université Laval O
University of Guelph M,D,O

ANIMAL BEHAVIOR

Bucknell University M
Cornell University D*
Emory University D*
Illinois State University M,D
University of California, Davis D*
University of Colorado at Boulder M,D*
University of Minnesota, Twin Cities Campus M,D*
University of Missouri–St. Louis M,D,O
The University of Montana M,D,O
The University of Tennessee M,D
The University of Texas at Austin M,D
University of Washington D*

ANIMAL SCIENCES

Alabama Agricultural and Mechanical University M,D
Alcorn State University M
American University of Beirut M
Angelo State University M
Auburn University M,D*
Boise State University M
Brigham Young University M,D*
California State University, Fresno M
Clemson University M,D
Colorado State University M,D*
Cornell University M,D*
Florida Agricultural and Mechanical University M
Fort Valley State University M
Iowa State University of Science and Technology M,D*
Kansas State University M,D*
Louisiana State University and Agricultural and Mechanical College M,D
McGill University M,D*
Michigan State University M,D*
Mississippi State University M,D
Montana State University M,D
New Mexico State University M,D
North Carolina Agricultural and Technical State University M
North Carolina State University M,D*
North Dakota State University M,D
Nova Scotia Agricultural College M
The Ohio State University M,D*
Oklahoma State University M,D*
Oregon State University M,D*
Penn State University Park M,D*
Prairie View A&M University M
Purdue University M,D
Rutgers, The State University of New Jersey, New Brunswick M,D*
South Dakota State University M,D
Southern Illinois University Carbondale M*
Sul Ross State University M*
Texas A&M University M,D*
Texas A&M University–Kingsville M
Texas Tech University M,D
Tuskegee University M
Universidad Nacional Pedro Henriquez Urena P,M,D
Université Laval M,D
The University of Arizona M,D*
University of Arkansas M,D
The University of British Columbia M,D
University of California, Davis M,D*
University of Connecticut M,D*
University of Delaware M,D*
University of Florida M,D*
University of Georgia M,D*
University of Guelph M,D
University of Hawaii at Manoa M*
University of Idaho M,D
University of Illinois at Urbana–Champaign M,D*
University of Kentucky M,D
University of Maine M*
University of Manitoba M,D
University of Maryland, College Park M,D*
University of Massachusetts Amherst M,D*
University of Minnesota, Twin Cities Campus M,D*
University of Missouri–Columbia M,D*
University of Nebraska–Lincoln M,D*
University of Nevada, Reno M*
University of New Hampshire M,D*
University of Puerto Rico, Mayagüez Campus M
University of Rhode Island M,D
University of Saskatchewan M,D
The University of Tennessee M,D
University of Vermont M,D*
University of Wisconsin–Madison M,D*
University of Wyoming M,D
Utah State University M,D
Virginia Polytechnic Institute and State University M,D*
Washington State University M,D*
West Texas A&M University M
West Virginia University M,D

ANTHROPOLOGY

American University M,D,O*
The American University in Cairo M
American University of Beirut M
Arizona State University M,D
Ball State University M*
Boston University M,D*
Brandeis University M,D
Brigham Young University M*
Brown University M,D*
California Institute of Integral Studies M,D*
California State University, Bakersfield M
California State University, Chico M
California State University, East Bay M
California State University, Fullerton M
California State University, Long Beach M
California State University, Los Angeles M
California State University, Northridge M
California State University, Sacramento M
Carleton University M
Case Western Reserve University M,D*
The Catholic University of America M
Central European University M,D*
The College of William and Mary M,D
Colorado State University M*
Columbia University M,D*
Concordia University (Canada) M
Cornell University D*
Dalhousie University M,D
Duke University D*
East Carolina University M
Eastern New Mexico University M
Emory University D*
Florida Atlantic University M
Florida State University M,D*
George Mason University M,D*
The George Washington University M,D*
Georgia State University M
Graduate School and University Center of the City University of New York D*
Harvard University M,D*
Hunter College of the City University of New York M
Idaho State University M
Indiana University Bloomington M,D*
Iowa State University of Science and Technology M*
The Johns Hopkins University D*
Kent State University M*
Louisiana State University and Agricultural and Mechanical College M,D
McGill University M,D*
McMaster University M,D
Memorial University of Newfoundland M,D
Michigan State University M,D*
Minnesota State University Mankato M
Mississippi State University M
New Mexico Highlands University M
New Mexico State University M
The New School: A University M,D*
New York University M,D*
North Carolina State University M*

Northern Arizona University	M
Northern Illinois University	M
Northwestern University	D*
The Ohio State University	M,D*
Oregon State University	M*
Penn State University Park	M,D*
Portland State University	M,D,O
Princeton University	D*
Purdue University	M,D
Rice University	M,D
Roosevelt University	M
Rutgers, The State University of New Jersey, New Brunswick	M,D*
San Diego State University	M*
San Francisco State University	M
San Jose State University	M
Simon Fraser University	M,D
Sonoma State University	M
Southern Illinois University Carbondale	M,D*
Southern Methodist University	M,D*
Stanford University	M,D*
State University of New York at Binghamton	M,D*
Stony Brook University, State University of New York	M,D
Syracuse University	M,D*
Teachers College, Columbia University	M,D
Temple University	D*
Texas A&M University	M,D*
Texas State University–San Marcos	M*
Texas Tech University	M
Trent University	M
Tulane University	M,D
Universidad de las Américas–Puebla	M
Université de Montréal	M,D
Université Laval	M,D
University at Albany, State University of New York	M,D*
University at Buffalo, the State University of New York	M,D*
The University of Alabama	M,D
The University of Alabama at Birmingham	M*
University of Alaska Anchorage	M
University of Alaska Fairbanks	M,D
University of Alberta	M,D*
The University of Arizona	M,D*
University of Arkansas	M,D
The University of British Columbia	M,D
University of Calgary	M,D
University of California, Berkeley	D*
University of California, Davis	M,D*
University of California, Irvine	M,D*
University of California, Los Angeles	M,D*
University of California, Riverside	M,D*
University of California, San Diego	D*
University of California, San Francisco	D
University of California, Santa Barbara	M,D
University of California, Santa Cruz	D*
University of Central Florida	M*
University of Chicago	M,D*
University of Cincinnati	M
University of Colorado at Boulder	M,D*
University of Colorado Denver	M*
University of Connecticut	M,D*
University of Denver	M*
University of Florida	M,D*
University of Georgia	M,D*
University of Guelph	M,D
University of Hawaii at Manoa	M,D*
University of Houston	M*
University of Idaho	M
University of Illinois at Chicago	M,D*
University of Illinois at Urbana–Champaign	M,D*
The University of Iowa	M,D*
The University of Kansas	M,D*
University of Kentucky	M,D
University of Lethbridge	M,D
University of Manitoba	M,D
University of Maryland, College Park	M*
University of Massachusetts Amherst	M,D*
University of Memphis	M
University of Michigan	D*
University of Minnesota, Duluth	M*
University of Minnesota, Twin Cities Campus	M,D*
University of Mississippi	M
University of Missouri–Columbia	M,D*
The University of Montana	M,D
University of Nebraska–Lincoln	M*
University of Nevada, Las Vegas	M,D
University of Nevada, Reno	M,D*
University of New Brunswick Fredericton	M
University of New Mexico	M,D*
The University of North Carolina at Chapel Hill	M,D*
University of North Texas	M
University of Oklahoma	M,D*
University of Oregon	M,D*
University of Ottawa	M*
University of Pennsylvania	M,D*
University of Pittsburgh	M,D*
University of Regina	M
University of Saskatchewan	M
University of South Africa	M,D
University of South Carolina	M,D
University of Southern Mississippi	M
University of South Florida	M,D*
The University of Tennessee	M,D
The University of Texas at Arlington	M*
The University of Texas at Austin	M,D
The University of Texas at San Antonio	M,D*
University of Toronto	M,D
University of Tulsa	M*
University of Utah	M,D*
University of Victoria	M
University of Virginia	M,D
University of Washington	M,D*
University of Waterloo	M
The University of Western Ontario	M,D
University of West Florida	M
University of Wisconsin–Madison	D*
University of Wisconsin–Milwaukee	M,D,O
University of Wyoming	M,D
Vanderbilt University	M,D*
Washington State University	M,D*
Washington University in St. Louis	D*
Wayne State University	M,D*
West Chester University of Pennsylvania	M,O
Western Kentucky University	M
Western Michigan University	M*
Western Washington University	M
Wichita State University	M*
Yale University	M,D*
York University	M,D

APPLIED ARTS AND DESIGN—GENERAL

Academy of Art University	M
Alfred University	M*
Arizona State University	M
Art Center College of Design	M*
Bowling Green State University	M*
Bradley University	M*
California College of the Arts	M*
California Institute of the Arts	M,O
California State University, Fresno	M
California State University, Fullerton	M
California State University, Los Angeles	M
Cardinal Stritch University	M
Carnegie Mellon University	D*
Concordia University (Canada)	O
Cranbrook Academy of Art	M*
Drexel University	M*
Emily Carr Institute of Art + Design	M
Fashion Institute of Technology	M*
Ferris State University	M
Florida Atlantic University	M
Howard University	M
Illinois Institute of Technology	M,D*
Indiana University–Purdue University Indianapolis	M*
Iowa State University of Science and Technology	M*
Lamar University	M
Louisiana State University and Agricultural and Mechanical College	M
Louisiana Tech University	M
Massachusetts College of Art and Design	M
Memphis College of Art	M*
Minneapolis College of Art and Design	M
New Mexico State University	M
The New School: A University	M*
New York University	M*
North Carolina State University	M,D*
NSCAD University	M
Oklahoma State University	M,D*
Pratt Institute	M,O*
Purdue University	M
Rhode Island School of Design	M
Rutgers, The State University of New Jersey, New Brunswick	M*
San Diego State University	M*
San Francisco Art Institute	M,O*
San Jose State University	M
Savannah College of Art and Design	M*
School of the Art Institute of Chicago	M*
School of Visual Arts	M
Southern Illinois University Carbondale	M*
Stephen F. Austin State University	M
Suffolk University	M*
Sul Ross State University	M*
Syracuse University	M*
University of Alberta	M*
University of Baltimore	M
University of California, Berkeley	M*
University of California, Los Angeles	M*
University of Central Oklahoma	M
University of Cincinnati	M
University of Delaware	M*
University of Idaho	M
University of Illinois at Urbana–Champaign	M,D*
The University of Kansas	M*
University of Kentucky	M
University of Massachusetts Dartmouth	M
University of Michigan	M*
University of Minnesota, Twin Cities Campus	M,D,O*
University of North Texas	M*
University of Notre Dame	M*
University of Oklahoma	M*
The University of Texas at Austin	M
University of Washington	M*
University of Wisconsin–Madison	M,D*
Virginia Commonwealth University	M
Virginia Polytechnic Institute and State University	M,D*
Wayne State University	M*
Western Carolina University	M
Western Michigan University	M*
Yale University	M*
York University	M

APPLIED ECONOMICS

American University	M,D,O*
Auburn University	M,D*
Buffalo State College, State University of New York	M
Clemson University	M,D
Cornell University	D*
Eastern Michigan University	M
Georgia Southern University	M
HEC Montreal	M
The Johns Hopkins University	M*
Mississippi State University	M,D
New York University	M,D,O*
North Carolina Agricultural and Technical State University	M
Northeastern University	M,D*
Ohio University	M*
Old Dominion University	M
Portland State University	M,D
Roosevelt University	M
St. Cloud State University	M
San Jose State University	M
Southern Methodist University	M,D*
Texas Tech University	M,D
University of California, Santa Cruz	M*
University of Georgia	M,D*
University of Idaho	M
University of Michigan	M*
University of Minnesota, Twin Cities Campus	M,D*
University of Nevada, Reno	M,D*
University of New Brunswick Fredericton	M

*M—master's degree; P—first professional degree; D—doctorate; O—other advanced degree; *—Close-Up and/or Announcement or Display in one of the other books in this series*

The University of North Carolina at Greensboro	M
University of North Dakota	M
University of North Texas	M
University of Pennsylvania	D*
University of Vermont	M*
University of Wisconsin–Madison	M,D*
University of Wyoming	M
Utah State University	M
Virginia Polytechnic Institute and State University	M,D*
Washington State University	M,D,O*
Western Michigan University	M,D*
Wright State University	M

APPLIED MATHEMATICS

Acadia University	M
Air Force Institute of Technology	M,D
Arizona State University	M,D
Auburn University	M,D*
Bowie State University	M
Brown University	M,D*
California Institute of Technology	M,D*
California State Polytechnic University, Pomona	M
California State University, Fullerton	M
California State University, Long Beach	M,D
California State University, Los Angeles	M
California State University, Northridge	M
Carnegie Mellon University	M,D*
Case Western Reserve University	M,D*
Central European University	M,D*
Claremont Graduate University	M,D*
Clemson University	M,D
Columbia University	M,D,O*
Cornell University	M,D*
Dalhousie University	M,D
Delaware State University	M,D
DePaul University	M,O*
East Carolina University	M
École Polytechnique de Montréal	M,D,O
Florida Atlantic University	M,D
Florida Institute of Technology	M,D*
Florida State University	M,D*
The George Washington University	M,D*
Georgia Institute of Technology	M,D*
Hampton University	M
Harvard University	M,D*
Hofstra University	M*
Howard University	M,D
Hunter College of the City University of New York	M
Illinois Institute of Technology	M,D*
Indiana University Bloomington	M,D*
Indiana University of Pennsylvania	M
Indiana University–Purdue University Fort Wayne	M,O
Indiana University–Purdue University Indianapolis	M,D*
Indiana University South Bend	M
Inter American University of Puerto Rico, San Germán Campus	M
Iowa State University of Science and Technology	M,D*
The Johns Hopkins University	M,D,O*
Kent State University	M,D*
Lehigh University	M,D
Long Island University, C.W. Post Campus	M
McGill University	M,D*
Michigan State University	M,D*
Missouri University of Science and Technology	M,D
Montclair State University	M,D,O*
Naval Postgraduate School	M,D
New Jersey Institute of Technology	M
New Mexico Institute of Mining and Technology	M,D
North Carolina Central University	M
North Carolina State University	M,D*
North Dakota State University	M,D
Northeastern University	M,D*
Northwestern University	M,D*
Oakland University	M,D
Oklahoma State University	M,D*
Penn State University Park	M,D*
Princeton University	D*
Rensselaer Polytechnic Institute	M
Rice University	M,D
Rochester Institute of Technology	M
Rutgers, The State University of New Jersey, New Brunswick	M,D*
St. John's University (NY)	M
San Diego State University	M*
San Jose State University	M
Santa Clara University	M
Simon Fraser University	M,D
Southern Methodist University	M,D*
Stevens Institute of Technology	M
Stony Brook University, State University of New York	M,D
Temple University	M,D*
Texas A&M University–Corpus Christi	M
Texas State University–San Marcos	M*
Towson University	M
Tulane University	M,D
The University of Akron	M,D
The University of Alabama	M,D
The University of Alabama at Birmingham	M,D*
The University of Alabama in Huntsville	M,D
University of Alberta	M,D,O*
The University of Arizona	M,D*
University of Arkansas at Little Rock	M,O
The University of British Columbia	M,D
University of California, Berkeley	D*
University of California, Davis	M,D*
University of California, San Diego	M,D*
University of California, Santa Barbara	M,D
University of California, Santa Cruz	M,D*
University of Central Arkansas	M
University of Central Florida	M,D,O*
University of Central Missouri	M
University of Central Oklahoma	M
University of Chicago	M,D*
University of Cincinnati	M,D
University of Colorado at Boulder	M,D*
University of Colorado at Colorado Springs	M
University of Colorado Denver	M,D*
University of Connecticut	M*
University of Dayton	M
University of Delaware	M,D*
University of Denver	M,D*
University of Georgia	M,D*
University of Guelph	M,D
University of Illinois at Chicago	M,D*
University of Illinois at Urbana–Champaign	M,D*
The University of Iowa	D*
University of Kentucky	M,D
University of Louisville	M,D
University of Maryland, Baltimore County	M,D*
University of Maryland, College Park	M,D*
University of Massachusetts Amherst	M*
University of Massachusetts Lowell	M,D
University of Memphis	M,D
University of Michigan–Dearborn	M*
University of Minnesota, Duluth	M*
University of Missouri–Columbia	M*
University of Missouri–St. Louis	M,D
University of New Hampshire	M,D,O*
The University of North Carolina at Charlotte	M,D*
University of Notre Dame	M,D*
University of Pennsylvania	D*
University of Pittsburgh	M,D*
University of Puerto Rico, Mayagüez Campus	M
University of Rhode Island	M,D,O
University of Southern California	M,D*
The University of Tennessee	M,D
The University of Tennessee Space Institute	M*
The University of Texas at Austin	M,D
The University of Texas at Dallas	M,D*
The University of Texas at El Paso	M
The University of Texas at San Antonio	M*
The University of Toledo	M,D
University of Washington	M,D*
University of Waterloo	M,D
The University of Western Ontario	M,D
University of West Georgia	M
Utah State University	M,D
Virginia Commonwealth University	M,O
Virginia Polytechnic Institute and State University	M,D*
Washington State University	M,D*
Wayne State University	M,D*
Western Illinois University	M,O
Western Michigan University	M*
West Virginia University	M,D
Wichita State University	M,D*
Worcester Polytechnic Institute	M,D,O*
Wright State University	M
Yale University	M,D*
York University	M,D
Youngstown State University	M

APPLIED PHYSICS

Air Force Institute of Technology	M,D
Alabama Agricultural and Mechanical University	M,D
Brooklyn College of the City University of New York	M,D
California Institute of Technology	M,D*
California State University, Long Beach	M
Carnegie Mellon University	M,D*
Christopher Newport University	M
Colorado School of Mines	M,D
Columbia University	M,D,O*
Cornell University	M,D*
DePaul University	M*
George Mason University	M*
Harvard University	M,D*
Idaho State University	M,D
Iowa State University of Science and Technology	M,D*
The Johns Hopkins University	M,O*
Laurentian University	M
Mississippi State University	M,D
Naval Postgraduate School	M,D
New Jersey Institute of Technology	M,D
Northern Arizona University	M
Oregon State University	M,D*
Pittsburg State University	M
Princeton University	M,D*
Rensselaer Polytechnic Institute	M,D
Rice University	M,D
Rutgers, The State University of New Jersey, Newark	M,D*
Southern Illinois University Carbondale	M,D*
Stanford University	M,D*
State University of New York at Binghamton	M*
Texas A&M University	M,D*
Texas Tech University	M,D
The University of Arizona	M*
University of Arkansas	M
University of California, San Diego	M,D*
University of Denver	M,D*
University of Maryland, Baltimore County	M,D*
University of Massachusetts Boston	M
University of Massachusetts Lowell	M,D
University of Michigan	D*
University of Missouri–St. Louis	M,D
The University of North Carolina at Charlotte	M,D*
University of South Florida	M,D*
The University of Texas at Austin	M,D
University of Washington	M,D*
Virginia Commonwealth University	M
Virginia Polytechnic Institute and State University	M,D*
West Virginia University	M,D
Yale University	M,D*

APPLIED SCIENCE AND TECHNOLOGY

American University	M*

The College of William and Mary	M,D
Colorado State University–Pueblo	M
Harvard University	M,O*
James Madison University	M
Louisiana State University and Agricultural and Mechanical College	M
Missouri State University	M*
Naval Postgraduate School	M
Oklahoma State University	M,D*
Rensselaer Polytechnic Institute	M
Southeastern Louisiana University	M
Southern Methodist University	M,D*
Thomas Edison State College	O
University of Arkansas at Little Rock	M,D
University of California, Berkeley	D*
University of California, Davis	M,D*
University of Colorado Denver	M*
University of Mississippi	M,D

APPLIED SOCIAL RESEARCH

American University	M,O*
California State University, Dominguez Hills	M,O
Hofstra University	M*
Hunter College of the City University of New York	M
Laurentian University	M
The New School: A University	M,D*
Portland State University	M,D
University of California, Los Angeles	M,D*
Virginia Commonwealth University	M,O
West Virginia University	M

APPLIED STATISTICS

American University	M,O*
Bowling Green State University	M,D*
Brigham Young University	M*
California State University, East Bay	M
California State University, Long Beach	M
Cornell University	M,D*
DePaul University	M,O*
Eastern Michigan University	M
Florida State University	M,D*
Indiana University–Purdue University Fort Wayne	M,O
Indiana University–Purdue University Indianapolis	M*
Instituto Tecnológico y de Estudios Superiores de Monterrey, Campus Monterrey	M,D
Kennesaw State University	M
Louisiana State University and Agricultural and Mechanical College	M
Loyola University Chicago	M*
McMaster University	M
Michigan State University	M,D*
Montclair State University	M,O*
New Jersey Institute of Technology	M
North Dakota State University	M,D,O
Oakland University	M
Penn State University Park	M,D*
Rochester Institute of Technology	M,O
Rutgers, The State University of New Jersey, New Brunswick	M,D*
St. Cloud State University	M
Stevens Institute of Technology	O
Syracuse University	M*
The University of Alabama	M,D
University of Arkansas at Little Rock	M,O
University of California, Riverside	M,D*
University of California, Santa Barbara	M,D
University of Guelph	M,D
University of Illinois at Urbana–Champaign	M,D*
University of Memphis	M,D
University of Michigan	M,D*
University of Northern Colorado	M,D
University of Pittsburgh	M,D*
University of South Carolina	M,D,O
The University of Texas at San Antonio	M,D*
Villanova University	M*
Washington State University	M*
West Chester University of Pennsylvania	M,O
Western Michigan University	M*
Worcester Polytechnic Institute	M,D,O*
Wright State University	M

AQUACULTURE

American University of Beirut	M
Auburn University	M,D*
Clemson University	M,D
Kentucky State University	M
Memorial University of Newfoundland	M
Nova Scotia Agricultural College	M
Purdue University	M,D
Texas A&M University–Corpus Christi	M
University of Arkansas at Pine Bluff	M
University of Florida	M,D*
University of Guelph	M
University of Rhode Island	M,D

ARCHAEOLOGY

American University of Beirut	M
Boston University	M,D*
Brown University	M,D*
Bryn Mawr College	M,D*
California State University, Northridge	M
Columbia University	M,D*
Cornell University	M,D*
Florida State University	M,D*
Gordon-Conwell Theological Seminary	P,M,D
Graduate School and University Center of the City University of New York	D*
Harvard University	M,D*
Illinois State University	M
Massachusetts Institute of Technology	M,D,O*
Memorial University of Newfoundland	M,D
Michigan Technological University	M,D
Midwestern Baptist Theological Seminary	P,M,D,O
New York University	M,D*
Northern Arizona University	M
Northwestern State University of Louisiana	M
Princeton University	D*
St. Cloud State University	M
Simon Fraser University	M,D
Temple Baptist Seminary	P,M,D
Trinity International University	P,M,D,O
Tufts University	M*
Universidad de las Américas–Puebla	M
Université Laval	M,D
University of Alberta	M,D*
The University of British Columbia	M,D
University of Calgary	M,D
University of California, Berkeley	M,D*
University of California, Los Angeles	M,D*
University of California, Santa Barbara	M,D
University of California, Santa Cruz	D*
University of Chicago	M,D*
University of Georgia	M,D*
University of Lethbridge	M,D
University of Massachusetts Boston	M
University of Memphis	M,O
University of Michigan	D*
University of Minnesota, Twin Cities Campus	M,D*
University of Missouri–Columbia	M,D*
University of Nebraska–Lincoln	M,D*
The University of North Carolina at Chapel Hill	M,D*
University of Pennsylvania	M,D*
University of Saskatchewan	M,D
University of South Africa	M,D
The University of Tennessee	M,D
The University of Texas at Austin	M,D
University of Virginia	M,D
University of West Florida	M
University of Wisconsin–Madison	D*
Washington State University	M,D*
Washington University in St. Louis	M,D*
Wheaton College	M
Wilfrid Laurier University	M
Yale University	M,D*

ARCHITECTURAL ENGINEERING

Carnegie Mellon University	M,D*
Drexel University	M,D*
Illinois Institute of Technology	M,D*
Kansas State University	M*
Penn State University Park	M,D*
University of Colorado at Boulder	M,D*
University of Detroit Mercy	M
The University of Kansas	M*
University of Louisiana at Lafayette	M*
University of Miami	M,D*
University of Nebraska–Lincoln	M,D*
The University of Texas at Austin	M

ARCHITECTURAL HISTORY

Arizona State University	D
Cornell University	M,D*
Graduate School and University Center of the City University of New York	D*
Harvard University	D*
Massachusetts Institute of Technology	M,D*
Savannah College of Art and Design	M*
University of California, Berkeley	M,D*
University of Pittsburgh	M,D*
The University of Texas at Austin	M,D
University of Virginia	M,D
Virginia Commonwealth University	M,D

ARCHITECTURE

Academy of Art University	M
Andrews University	M
Arizona State University	M
Auburn University	M*
Ball State University	M*
Boston Architectural College	M
California College of the Arts	M*
California Polytechnic State University, San Luis Obispo	M
California State Polytechnic University, Pomona	M
Carleton University	M
Carnegie Mellon University	M,D*
The Catholic University of America	M
City College of the City University of New York	M*
Clemson University	M
Columbia College Chicago	M
Columbia University	M,D*
Cooper Union for the Advancement of Science and Art	M
Cornell University	M,D*
Cranbrook Academy of Art	M*
Dalhousie University	M
Florida Agricultural and Mechanical University	M
Florida International University	M*
Frank Lloyd Wright School of Architecture	M
Georgia Institute of Technology	M,D*
Harvard University	M,D*
Illinois Institute of Technology	M,D*
Instituto Tecnológico y de Estudios Superiores de Monterrey, Campus Estado de México	M,D
Instituto Tecnológico y de Estudios Superiores de Monterrey, Campus Irapuato	M,D
Iowa State University of Science and Technology	M*
Judson University	M
Kansas State University	M*
Kent State University	M,O*
Lawrence Technological University	M
Louisiana State University and Agricultural and Mechanical College	M
Marywood University	M
Massachusetts College of Art and Design	M
Massachusetts Institute of Technology	M,D*
McGill University	M,D,O*
Miami University	M*
Mississippi State University	M
Montana State University	M
Morgan State University	M
New Jersey Institute of Technology	M
The New School: A University	M*
Newschool of Architecture & Design	M

*M—master's degree; P—first professional degree; D—doctorate; O—other advanced degree; *—Close-Up and/or Announcement or Display in one of the other books in this series*

New York Institute of Technology	M
North Carolina State University	M*
Northeastern University	M*
The Ohio State University	M*
Penn State University Park	M*
Philadelphia University	M
Pontificia Universidad Catolica Madre y Maestra	M
Prairie View A&M University	M
Pratt Institute	M*
Princeton University	M,D*
Rensselaer Polytechnic Institute	M,D
Rhode Island School of Design	M
Rice University	M,D
Roger Williams University	M*
Savannah College of Art and Design	M*
School of the Art Institute of Chicago	M*
Southern California Institute of Architecture	M
Southern Illinois University Carbondale	M*
Syracuse University	M*
Texas A&M University	M,D*
Texas Tech University	M
Tulane University	M
Universidad Autonoma de Guadalajara	M,D
Universidad Nacional Pedro Henriquez Urena	P,M,D
Université Laval	M
University at Buffalo, the State University of New York	M*
The University of Arizona	M*
The University of British Columbia	M
University of Calgary	M,D
University of California, Berkeley	M,D*
University of California, Los Angeles	M,D*
University of Cincinnati	M
University of Colorado Denver	M*
University of Florida	M,D*
University of Hartford	M*
University of Hawaii at Manoa	D*
University of Houston	M*
University of Idaho	M
University of Illinois at Chicago	M*
University of Illinois at Urbana–Champaign	M,D*
The University of Kansas	M,D,O*
University of Kentucky	M
University of Manitoba	M
University of Maryland, College Park	M*
University of Massachusetts Amherst	M*
University of Memphis	M
University of Miami	M*
University of Michigan	M,D*
University of Minnesota, Twin Cities Campus	M*
University of Missouri–Columbia	M*
University of Nebraska–Lincoln	M,D*
University of Nevada, Las Vegas	M
University of New Mexico	M*
The University of North Carolina at Charlotte	M*
The University of North Carolina at Greensboro	M,O
University of Notre Dame	M*
University of Oklahoma	M*
University of Oregon	M*
University of Pennsylvania	M,D,O*
University of Puerto Rico, Río Piedras	M
University of Southern California	M,D*
University of South Florida	M*
The University of Tennessee	M
The University of Texas at Arlington	M*
The University of Texas at Austin	M,D
The University of Texas at San Antonio	M,O*
University of Toronto	M
University of Utah	M*
University of Virginia	M*
University of Washington	M,D,O*
University of Waterloo	M
University of Wisconsin–Milwaukee	M,D,O
Virginia Polytechnic Institute and State University	M,D*
Washington State University	M*
Washington State University Spokane	M,D
Washington University in St. Louis	M*
Woodbury University	M
Yale University	M*

ART/FINE ARTS

Academy of Art University	M
Adams State College	M
Adelphi University	M*
Alfred University	M,D*
American University	M*
Anna Maria College	M,O
Antioch University McGregor	M
Arizona State University	M,D
Arkansas State University	M
Arkansas Tech University	M
Art Center College of Design	M*
The Art Institute of Boston at Lesley University	M*
The Art Institute of California–San Francisco	M
Atlantic University	M
Azusa Pacific University	M
Ball State University	M*
Bard College	M*
Barry University	M*
Bob Jones University	P,M,D,O
Boise State University	M
Boston University	M*
Bowling Green State University	M*
Bradley University	M
Brandeis University	O
Brigham Young University	M*
Brooklyn College of the City University of New York	M,D
California College of the Arts	M*
California Institute of the Arts	M,O
California State University, Chico	M
California State University, Fresno	M
California State University, Fullerton	M
California State University, Long Beach	M
California State University, Los Angeles	M
California State University, Northridge	M
California State University, Sacramento	M
California State University, San Bernardino	M
California State University, Stanislaus	O
Carnegie Mellon University	M*
Central Washington University	M
City College of the City University of New York	M*
Claremont Graduate University	M*
Clemson University	M
Cleveland State University	M
The College at Brockport, State University of New York	M
The College of New Rochelle	M
Colorado State University	M*
Columbia University	M*
Concordia University (Canada)	M
Cornell University	M*
Cranbrook Academy of Art	M*
Drake University	M*
Drury University	M
Duke University	D*
East Carolina University	M
Eastern Illinois University	M
Eastern Michigan University	M
East Tennessee State University	M
Edinboro University of Pennsylvania	M
Emily Carr Institute of Art + Design	M
Fairleigh Dickinson University, Metropolitan Campus	M*
Ferris State University	M
Florida Atlantic University	M
Florida International University	M*
Florida State University	M*
Fontbonne University	M
Fort Hays State University	M
Framingham State College	M
The George Washington University	M*
Georgia Southern University	M
Georgia State University	M
Governors State University	M
Hofstra University	M*
Hollins University	M,O
Hood College	M,O
Howard University	M
Hunter College of the City University of New York	M
Idaho State University	M
Illinois State University	M
Indiana State University	M
Indiana University Bloomington	M,D*
Indiana University of Pennsylvania	M
Indiana University–Purdue University Indianapolis	M*
Inter American University of Puerto Rico, San Germán Campus	M
James Madison University	M
John F. Kennedy University	M
Johnson State College	M
Kansas State University	M*
Kean University	M
Kent State University	M*
Laguna College of Art & Design	M
Lamar University	M
Lehman College of the City University of New York	M
Lesley University	M*
Lindenwood University	M
Long Island University, C.W. Post Campus	M
Louisiana State University and Agricultural and Mechanical College	M
Louisiana Tech University	M
Maine College of Art	M
Marshall University	M
Maryland Institute College of Art	M,O
Marywood University	M
Massachusetts College of Art and Design	M
Memphis College of Art	M*
Miami International University of Art & Design	M*
Miami University	M*
Michigan State University	M*
Mills College	M
Minneapolis College of Art and Design	M,O
Minnesota State University Mankato	M
Mississippi College	M
Missouri State University	M*
Montana State University	M
Montclair State University	M,O*
Morehead State University	M
National University	M
New Jersey City University	M
New Mexico State University	M
The New School: A University	M*
New York Academy of Art	M
New York Studio School of Drawing, Painting and Sculpture	M,O
New York University	M,D*
Norfolk State University	M
Northern Illinois University	M
Northwestern State University of Louisiana	M
Northwestern University	M*
NSCAD University	M
The Ohio State University	M*
Ohio University	M*
Oklahoma City University	M
Otis College of Art and Design	M
Penn State University Park	M,D*
Pennsylvania Academy of the Fine Arts	M,O
Pittsburg State University	M
Portland State University	M
Pratt Institute	M*
Purchase College, State University of New York	M
Purdue University	M
Queens College of the City University of New York	M
Radford University	M
Regis University	M,O
Rensselaer Polytechnic Institute	M,D
Rhode Island College	M
Rhode Island School of Design	M
Rochester Institute of Technology	M
Rutgers, The State University of New Jersey, New Brunswick	M*
San Diego State University	M*
San Francisco Art Institute	M,O*
San Francisco State University	M
San Jose State University	M
Savannah College of Art and Design	M*
School of the Art Institute of Chicago	M*
School of the Museum of Fine Arts, Boston	M
School of Visual Arts	M
Seton Hall University	M*

Southern Illinois University Carbondale M*
Southern Illinois University Edwardsville M
Southern Methodist University M*
Stanford University M,D*
State University of New York at New Paltz M
State University of New York at Oswego M
Stephen F. Austin State University M
Stony Brook University, State University of New York M
Sul Ross State University M*
Syracuse University M*
Temple University M*
Texas A&M University–Commerce M
Texas A&M University–Corpus Christi M
Texas A&M University–Kingsville M
Texas Christian University M
Texas Southern University M
Texas Tech University M,D
Texas Woman's University M
Towson University M
Troy University M
Tufts University M*
Tulane University M
United Theological Seminary of the Twin Cities P,M,D,O
Universidad del Turabo M
Université du Québec à Chicoutimi M
Université du Québec à Montréal M
Université Laval M
University at Albany, State University of New York M*
University at Buffalo, the State University of New York M,O*
The University of Alabama M
University of Alaska Fairbanks M
University of Alberta M*
The University of Arizona M*
University of Arkansas M
University of Arkansas at Little Rock M
The University of British Columbia M,D,O
University of Calgary M
University of California, Berkeley M*
University of California, Davis M*
University of California, Irvine M*
University of California, Los Angeles M*
University of California, Riverside M*
University of California, San Diego M,D*
University of California, Santa Barbara M,D
University of California, Santa Cruz M*
University of Central Florida M*
University of Chicago M*
University of Cincinnati M
University of Colorado at Boulder M*
University of Connecticut M*
University of Dallas M
University of Delaware M*
University of Denver M*
University of Florida M,D*
University of Georgia M*
University of Guam M
University of Guelph M
University of Hartford M*
University of Hawaii at Manoa M*
University of Houston M*
University of Idaho M
University of Illinois at Chicago M*
University of Illinois at Urbana–Champaign M*
University of Indianapolis M
The University of Iowa M*
The University of Kansas M*
University of Kentucky M
University of Lethbridge M,D
University of Louisville M
University of Maryland, Baltimore County M*
University of Maryland, College Park M*
University of Massachusetts Amherst M*
University of Massachusetts Dartmouth M,O
University of Memphis M,O
University of Miami M*
University of Michigan M*
University of Minnesota, Duluth M
University of Minnesota, Twin Cities Campus M*
University of Mississippi M
University of Missouri–Columbia M*
University of Missouri–Kansas City M,D*
The University of Montana M
University of Nebraska–Lincoln M*
University of Nevada, Las Vegas M
University of Nevada, Reno M*
University of New Hampshire M*
University of New Mexico M*
University of New Orleans M
The University of North Carolina at Chapel Hill M*
The University of North Carolina at Greensboro M
University of North Dakota M
University of Northern Colorado M
University of Northern Iowa M
University of North Texas M
University of Notre Dame M*
University of Oklahoma M*
University of Oregon M*
University of Pennsylvania M*
University of Regina M*
University of Rochester M,D*
University of Saint Francis (IN) M
University of Saskatchewan M
University of South Carolina M
The University of South Dakota M
University of Southern California M,D,O*
University of South Florida M*
The University of Tennessee M
The University of Texas at Arlington M*
The University of Texas at Austin M
The University of Texas at El Paso M
The University of Texas at San Antonio M*
The University of Texas at Tyler M
The University of Texas–Pan American M
The University of the Arts M*
University of Toronto M,D
University of Tulsa M*
University of Utah M*
University of Victoria M*
University of Washington M*
University of Waterloo M
University of Windsor M
University of Wisconsin–Madison M*
University of Wisconsin–Milwaukee M
University of Wisconsin–River Falls M
University of Wisconsin–Superior M
Utah State University M
Virginia Commonwealth University M,D
Washington State University M*
Washington University in St. Louis M*
Wayne State University M*
Webster University M
Western Carolina University M
Western Connecticut State University M
West Texas A&M University M
West Virginia University M
Wichita State University M*
William Paterson University of New Jersey M*
Winthrop University M*
Yale University M*
York University M,D

ART EDUCATION

Adelphi University M*
American University of Puerto Rico M
Anna Maria College M
Arcadia University M,D,O
Art Academy of Cincinnati M
Austin College M
Averett University M
Ball State University M*
Bennington College M
Boise State University M
Boston University M*
Bowling Green State University M*
Bridgewater State College M
Brigham Young University M*
Brooklyn College of the City University of New York M,O
Buffalo State College, State University of New York M
California State University, Long Beach M
California State University, Los Angeles M
California State University, Northridge M
Cambridge College M,D,O
Cape Breton University O
Carlow University M
Carthage College M,O
Case Western Reserve University M*
Central Connecticut State University M,O
Chatham University M
Christopher Newport University M
Cleveland State University M
College of Mount St. Joseph M
The College of New Rochelle M
The College of Saint Rose M,O*
The Colorado College M
Colorado State University–Pueblo M
Columbus State University M
Concordia University (Canada) M,D
Concordia University Wisconsin M
Converse College M,O
Corcoran College of Art and Design M
Delaware State University M
Eastern Illinois University M
Eastern Kentucky University M
Eastern Michigan University M
East Tennessee State University M
Endicott College M
Fitchburg State College M,O
Florida Atlantic University M
Florida International University M,D*
Florida State University M,D,O*
George Mason University M*
Georgia Southern University M
Georgia State University M,D,O
Harding University M,O
Harvard University M*
Hofstra University M*
Indiana University Bloomington M,D,O*
Indiana University–Purdue University Indianapolis M*
Indiana University South Bend M
James Madison University M
Kean University M
Kent State University M*
Kutztown University of Pennsylvania M,O
Lesley University M,D,O*
Long Island University, C.W. Post Campus M
Manhattanville College M*
Mansfield University of Pennsylvania M
Maryland Institute College of Art M
Maryville University of Saint Louis M,D
Marywood University M
Massachusetts College of Art and Design M
Memphis College of Art M*
Miami University M*
Millersville University of Pennsylvania M
Mills College M,D
Minnesota State University Mankato M
Mississippi College M,D,O
Missouri State University M*
Montclair State University M,O*
Morehead State University M
Nazareth College of Rochester M
New Jersey City University M
New York University M,D*
North Carolina Agricultural and Technical State University M
North Georgia College & State University M,O
Nova Southeastern University M,O*
The Ohio State University M,D*
Penn State University Park M,D*
Pittsburg State University M
Pratt Institute M,O*
Purdue University M,D,O
Queens College of the City University of New York M,O
Rhode Island College M
Rhode Island School of Design M
Rochester Institute of Technology M
Sage Graduate School M
Saint Michael's College M,O

*M—master's degree; P—first professional degree; D—doctorate; O—other advanced degree; *—Close-Up and/or Announcement or Display in one of the other books in this series*

Salem State College	M
San Jose State University	M
School of the Art Institute of Chicago	M*
School of Visual Arts	M
Simon Fraser University	M,D
Southern Connecticut State University	M
Southern Illinois University Edwardsville	M
Southwestern Oklahoma State University	M
Stanford University	M,D*
State University of New York at New Paltz	M
State University of New York at Oswego	M
Sul Ross State University	M*
Syracuse University	M,O*
Teachers College, Columbia University	M,D
Temple University	M*
Texas Tech University	M,D
Towson University	M,O
The University of Alabama at Birmingham	M*
The University of Arizona	M*
University of Arkansas at Little Rock	M
The University of British Columbia	M,D
University of Central Florida	M*
University of Cincinnati	M
University of Dayton	M
University of Florida	M,D*
University of Georgia	M,D,O*
University of Houston	M,D*
University of Idaho	M
University of Illinois at Urbana–Champaign	M,D*
University of Indianapolis	M
The University of Iowa	M,D*
The University of Kansas	M*
University of Kentucky	M
University of Louisville	M
University of Massachusetts Dartmouth	M
University of Minnesota, Twin Cities Campus	M,D,O*
University of Mississippi	M
University of Missouri–Columbia	M,D,O*
University of Nebraska at Kearney	M
University of New Mexico	M*
The University of North Carolina at Charlotte	M*
The University of North Carolina at Pembroke	M
University of Northern Iowa	M
University of North Texas	M,D,O
University of Rio Grande	M
University of South Carolina	M,D
University of Southern Mississippi	M
The University of Tennessee	M,D,O
The University of Texas at Austin	M
The University of Texas at El Paso	M
The University of the Arts	M*
The University of Toledo	M
University of Utah	M*
University of Victoria	M,D
University of West Georgia	M
University of Wisconsin–Madison	M,D*
University of Wisconsin–Milwaukee	M
University of Wisconsin–Superior	M
Ursuline College	M
Virginia Commonwealth University	M
Wayne State University	M,D,O*
Western Kentucky University	M
Western Michigan University	M*
West Virginia University	M
Wichita State University	M*
William Carey University	M,O
Winthrop University	M

ART HISTORY

American University	M*
American University of Puerto Rico	M
Bard College	M,D
Bard Graduate Center for Studies in the Decorative Arts, Design, and Culture	M,D*
Boston University	M,D,O*
Bowling Green State University	M*
Brigham Young University	M*
Brooklyn College of the City University of New York	M,D
Brown University	M,D*
Bryn Mawr College	M,D*
California State University, Chico	M
California State University, Fullerton	M
California State University, Long Beach	M
California State University, Los Angeles	M
California State University, Northridge	M
Caribbean University	M,D
Carleton University	M
Case Western Reserve University	M,D*
Christie's Education	M
City College of the City University of New York	M*
Cleveland State University	M
Columbia University	M,D*
Concordia University (Canada)	M,D
Cornell University	D*
Duke University	D*
East Tennessee State University	M
Emory University	D*
Fashion Institute of Technology	M*
Florida State University	M,D,O*
George Mason University	M*
The George Washington University	M*
Georgia State University	M
Graduate School and University Center of the City University of New York	D*
Graduate Theological Union	M,D,O
Harvard University	D*
Howard University	M
Hunter College of the City University of New York	M
Illinois State University	M
Indiana University Bloomington	M,D*
James Madison University	M
The Johns Hopkins University	M,D*
Kent State University	M*
Lamar University	M
Louisiana State University and Agricultural and Mechanical College	M
Massachusetts Institute of Technology	M,D*
McGill University	M,D*
Montclair State University	M,O*
New Mexico State University	M
New York University	M,D*
Northwestern University	D*
The Ohio State University	M,D*
Ohio University	M*
Penn State University Park	M,D*
Pratt Institute	M*
Purchase College, State University of New York	M
Queens College of the City University of New York	M
Richmond, The American International University in London	M
Rutgers, The State University of New Jersey, New Brunswick	M,D,O*
San Diego State University	M*
San Francisco Art Institute	M*
San Francisco State University	M
San Jose State University	M
Savannah College of Art and Design	M*
School of the Art Institute of Chicago	M,O*
Southern Methodist University	M*
State University of New York at Binghamton	M,D*
Stony Brook University, State University of New York	M,D
Sul Ross State University	M*
Syracuse University	M*
Temple University	M,D*
Texas A&M University–Commerce	M
Texas Christian University	M
Tufts University	M*
Tulane University	M
Université de Montréal	M,D
Université du Québec à Montréal	M,D
Université Laval	M,D
University at Buffalo, the State University of New York	M,O*
The University of Alabama	M
The University of Alabama at Birmingham	M*
University of Alberta	M*
The University of Arizona	M,D*
University of Arkansas at Little Rock	M
The University of British Columbia	M,D,O
University of California, Berkeley	D*
University of California, Davis	M*
University of California, Irvine	M,D*
University of California, Los Angeles	M,D*
University of California, Riverside	M*
University of California, Santa Barbara	D
University of Chicago	M,D*
University of Cincinnati	M
University of Colorado at Boulder	M*
University of Connecticut	M*
University of Delaware	M,D*
University of Denver	M*
University of Florida	M,D*
University of Georgia	M*
University of Hawaii at Manoa	M*
University of Illinois at Chicago	M,D*
University of Illinois at Urbana–Champaign	M,D*
The University of Iowa	M,D*
The University of Kansas	M,D*
University of Kentucky	M
University of Louisville	M,D
University of Maryland, College Park	M,D*
University of Massachusetts Amherst	M*
University of Memphis	M,O
University of Miami	M*
University of Michigan	D*
University of Minnesota, Twin Cities Campus	M,D*
University of Mississippi	M
University of Missouri–Columbia	M,D*
University of Missouri–Kansas City	M,D*
University of Nebraska–Lincoln	M*
University of New Mexico	M,D*
The University of North Carolina at Chapel Hill	M,D*
University of North Texas	M,D,O
University of Notre Dame	M*
University of Oklahoma	M*
University of Oregon	M,D*
University of Pennsylvania	M,D*
University of Pittsburgh	M,D*
University of Rochester	M,D*
University of St. Thomas (MN)	M*
University of South Africa	M,D
University of South Carolina	M
University of Southern California	M,D,O*
University of South Florida	M*
The University of Texas at Austin	M,D
The University of Texas at San Antonio	M*
The University of Texas at Tyler	M
University of Toronto	M,D
University of Utah	M*
University of Victoria	M,D
University of Virginia	M,D
University of Washington	M,D*
University of Wisconsin–Madison	M,D*
University of Wisconsin–Milwaukee	M,O
University of Wisconsin–Superior	M
Virginia Commonwealth University	M,D
Washington University in St. Louis	M,D*
Wayne State University	M*
West Virginia University	M
Williams College	M
Yale University	D*
York University	M,D

ARTIFICIAL INTELLIGENCE/ ROBOTICS

California State University, Northridge	M
Carnegie Mellon University	M,D*
Cornell University	M,D*
Eastern Michigan University	M,O
Indiana University–Purdue University Indianapolis	M,D*
Instituto Tecnológico y de Estudios Superiores de Monterrey, Campus Monterrey	M,D
Portland State University	M,D,O
University of California, Irvine	M*
University of California, Riverside	M,D*

University of California, San Diego M,D*
University of Georgia M*
University of Pittsburgh D*
University of Southern California M,D*
The University of Tennessee M,D
Villanova University M,O*
Worcester Polytechnic Institute M,D,O*

ARTS ADMINISTRATION

American University M,O*
Boston University M,O*
Carnegie Mellon University M*
Claremont Graduate University M*
The College at Brockport, State University of New York M,O
College of Charleston M,O*
Columbia College Chicago M
Drexel University M*
Eastern Michigan University M
Fashion Institute of Technology M*
Florida State University M,D*
George Mason University M*
Goucher College M
HEC Montreal O
Montclair State University M*
New York University M*
The Ohio State University M*
Pratt Institute M*
Regis University M,O
Rhode Island College M
Ryerson University M
Saint Mary's University of Minnesota M
St. Thomas University M
Savannah College of Art and Design M*
School of the Art Institute of Chicago M*
Shenandoah University M,D,O
Southern Methodist University *
Southern Utah University M
Teachers College, Columbia University M
Temple University M,D*
Universidad del Turabo M
The University of Akron M
University of Cincinnati M,D
University of Florida M*
University of New Orleans M
University of Oregon M*
University of Southern California M*
University of Wisconsin–Madison M*
University of Wisconsin–Superior M
Virginia Polytechnic Institute and State University M*
Webster University M
Winthrop University M

ARTS JOURNALISM

School of the Art Institute of Chicago M*
Syracuse University M*

ART THERAPY

Adler School of Professional Psychology M,D,O*
Albertus Magnus College M
Athabasca University M,O*
Caldwell College M
California Institute of Integral Studies M,D*
California State University, Los Angeles M
The College of New Rochelle M
Concordia University (Canada) M
Drexel University M,O*
Eastern Virginia Medical School M
Emporia State University M
The George Washington University M*
Hofstra University M*
Lesley University M,D,O*
Long Island University, C.W. Post Campus M
Marylhurst University M,O
Marywood University M,O
Mount Mary College M
Naropa University M*
Nazareth College of Rochester M
New York University M*
Notre Dame de Namur University M
Ottawa University M
Pratt Institute M*
Prescott College M
Saint Mary-of-the-Woods College M,O
Salve Regina University M,O
School of the Art Institute of Chicago M*
School of Visual Arts M
Seton Hill University M,O
Southern Illinois University Edwardsville M
Southwestern College (NM) M*
Springfield College M,O
University of Maryland, College Park M,D,O*
University of Wisconsin–Superior M
Ursuline College M

ASIAN-AMERICAN STUDIES

California State University, Long Beach M,O
San Francisco State University M
University of California, Los Angeles M*

ASIAN LANGUAGES

Columbia University M,D*
Cornell University M,D*
Harvard University M,D*
Indiana University Bloomington M,D*
Naropa University M*
The Ohio State University M,D*
St. John's College (NM) M
Seton Hall University M*
University of California, Berkeley M,D*
University of California, Irvine M,D*
University of California, Los Angeles M,D*
University of California, Santa Barbara M,D
University of Chicago M,D*
University of Hawaii at Manoa M,D*
University of Illinois at Urbana–Champaign M,D*
The University of Kansas M*
University of Michigan M,D*
University of Minnesota, Twin Cities Campus D*
University of Oregon M,D*
University of Southern California M,D*
The University of Texas at Austin M,D
University of Washington M,D*
University of Wisconsin–Madison M,D*
Washington University in St. Louis M,D*
Yale University D*

ASIAN STUDIES

California Institute of Integral Studies M,D*
California State University, Long Beach M,O
Columbia University M,D,O*
Cornell University M,D*
Duke University M,O*
Florida International University M*
Florida State University M*
The George Washington University M*
Harvard University M,D*
Indiana University Bloomington M,D*
The Johns Hopkins University M,D,O*
Maharishi University of Management M,D
McGill University M,D*
New York University M,D*
Ohio University M*
Princeton University D*
Rutgers, The State University of New Jersey, New Brunswick D*
St. John's College (NM) M
St. John's University (NY) M,O
San Diego State University M*
Seton Hall University M*
Stanford University M*
United Theological Seminary of the Twin Cities P,M,D,O
University of Alberta M*
The University of Arizona M,D*
The University of British Columbia M,D
University of California, Berkeley M,D*
University of California, Los Angeles M,D*
University of California, Riverside M*
University of California, Santa Barbara M,D
University of Chicago M,D*
University of Colorado at Boulder M,D*
University of Hawaii at Manoa O*
University of Illinois at Urbana–Champaign M,D*
The University of Iowa M*
The University of Kansas M*
University of Michigan M,D,O*
University of Minnesota, Twin Cities Campus D*
University of Oregon M*
University of Pennsylvania M,D*
University of Pittsburgh M,O*
University of San Francisco M
University of Southern California M,D*
The University of Texas at Austin M,D
University of Toronto M,D
University of Utah M*
University of Victoria M
University of Virginia M
University of Washington M,D*
University of Wisconsin–Madison M,D*
Valparaiso University M
Washington State University M,D*
Washington University in St. Louis M*
West Virginia University M,D
Yale University M*

ASTRONOMY

Boston University M,D*
Brigham Young University M,D*
California Institute of Technology D*
Case Western Reserve University M,D*
Clemson University M,D
Columbia University M,D*
Cornell University D*
Dartmouth College M,D*
Georgia State University D
Harvard University D*
Indiana University Bloomington M,D*
Iowa State University of Science and Technology M,D*
The Johns Hopkins University D*
Louisiana State University and Agricultural and Mechanical College M,D
Michigan State University M,D*
Minnesota State University Mankato M
New Mexico State University M,D
Northwestern University M,D*
The Ohio State University M,D*
Ohio University M,D*
Penn State University Park M,D*
Princeton University D*
Rice University M,D
Rutgers, The State University of New Jersey, New Brunswick M,D*
Saint Mary's University (Canada) M,D
San Diego State University M*
Stony Brook University, State University of New York D
Université de Moncton M
The University of Arizona M,D*
The University of British Columbia M,D
University of Calgary M,D
University of California, Los Angeles M,D*
University of California, Santa Cruz D*
University of Chicago M,D*
University of Delaware M,D*
University of Denver M,D*
University of Florida M,D*
University of Georgia M,D*
University of Hawaii at Manoa M,D*
University of Illinois at Urbana–Champaign M,D*
The University of Iowa M*
The University of Kansas M,D*
University of Kentucky M,D
University of Maryland, College Park M,D*
University of Massachusetts Amherst M,D*
University of Michigan D*
University of Minnesota, Twin Cities Campus M,D*
University of Missouri–Columbia M,D*
University of Nebraska–Lincoln M,D*
University of Nevada, Las Vegas M,D
The University of North Carolina at Chapel Hill M,D*
University of Rochester M,D*
University of South Carolina M,D
The University of Texas at Austin M,D
University of Toronto M,D
University of Victoria M,D
University of Virginia M,D
University of Washington M,D*

*M—master's degree; P—first professional degree; D—doctorate; O—other advanced degree; *—Close-Up and/or Announcement or Display in one of the other books in this series*

The University of Western Ontario M,D
University of Wisconsin–Madison D*
Vanderbilt University M,D*
Wesleyan University M*
West Chester University of Pennsylvania M,O
Yale University M,D*
York University M,D

ASTROPHYSICS

Air Force Institute of Technology M,D
Arizona State University M,D
Clemson University M,D
Cornell University D*
Harvard University D*
ICR Graduate School M
Indiana University Bloomington M,D*
Iowa State University of Science and Technology M,D*
Louisiana State University and Agricultural and Mechanical College M,D
McMaster University D
Michigan State University M,D*
New Mexico Institute of Mining and Technology M,D
Northwestern University M,D*
Penn State University Park M,D*
Princeton University D*
Rensselaer Polytechnic Institute M,D
Rochester Institute of Technology M,D
Texas Christian University M,D
University of Alaska Fairbanks M,D
University of Alberta M,D*
University of California, Berkeley D*
University of California, Los Angeles M,D*
University of California, Santa Cruz D*
University of Chicago M,D*
University of Colorado at Boulder M,D*
University of Maryland, Baltimore County M,D*
University of Michigan D*
University of Minnesota, Twin Cities Campus M,D*
University of Missouri–St. Louis M,D
The University of North Carolina at Chapel Hill M,D*
University of Oklahoma M,D*
University of Pennsylvania M,D*
University of Toronto M,D
University of Victoria M,D
Yale University M,D*

ATHLETIC TRAINING AND SPORTS MEDICINE

Armstrong Atlantic State University M
A.T. Still University of Health Sciences M,D
Barry University M*
Bloomsburg University of Pennsylvania M
Boston University D*
Brigham Young University M,D*
California Baptist University M
California State University, Long Beach M
California University of Pennsylvania M
Eastern Michigan University M,O
Florida International University M*
Georgia State University M
Humboldt State University M
Indiana State University M
Indiana University Bloomington M,D*
Inter American University of Puerto Rico, Metropolitan Campus M
Kent State University M*
Lenoir-Rhyne University M
Long Island University, Brooklyn Campus M
Montana State University–Billings M
Ohio University M*
Old Dominion University M
Plymouth State University M
Saint Louis University M,D
Seton Hall University M*
Shenandoah University M
Springfield College M,D
Stephen F. Austin State University M
Texas State University–San Marcos M*
Texas Tech University Health Sciences Center M
United States Sports Academy M
Universidad del Turabo M
The University of Findlay M
University of Florida M,D*
University of Miami M*
The University of North Carolina at Chapel Hill M*
University of Pittsburgh M*
The University of Tennessee M,D
The University of West Alabama M
University of Wisconsin–La Crosse M
Virginia Commonwealth University M
Weber State University M
Western Michigan University M*
West Virginia University M,D

ATMOSPHERIC SCIENCES

City College of the City University of New York M,D*
Clemson University M,D
Colorado State University M,D*
Columbia University M,D*
Cornell University M,D*
Creighton University M*
George Mason University D*
Georgia Institute of Technology M,D*
Hampton University M,D
Howard University M,D
Massachusetts Institute of Technology M,D*
McGill University M,D*
Michigan Technological University D
New Mexico Institute of Mining and Technology M,D
North Carolina State University M,D*
The Ohio State University M,D*
Oregon State University M,D*
Princeton University D*
Purdue University M,D
Rutgers, The State University of New Jersey, New Brunswick M,D*
South Dakota School of Mines and Technology M,D*
Stony Brook University, State University of New York M,D
Texas Tech University M,D
Université du Québec à Montréal M,D,O
University at Albany, State University of New York M,D*
The University of Alabama in Huntsville M,D
University of Alaska Fairbanks M,D
The University of Arizona M,D*
The University of British Columbia M,D
University of California, Davis M,D*
University of California, Los Angeles M,D*
University of Chicago M,D*
University of Colorado at Boulder M,D*
University of Delaware M,D*
University of Guelph M,D
University of Illinois at Urbana–Champaign M,D*
University of Maryland, Baltimore County M,D*
University of Massachusetts Lowell M,D
University of Michigan M,D*
University of Missouri–Columbia M,D*
University of Nevada, Reno M,D*
The University of North Carolina at Chapel Hill M,D*
University of North Dakota M,D
University of Utah M,D*
University of Washington M,D*
University of Wisconsin–Madison M,D*
University of Wyoming M,D
Washington State University Tri-Cities M,D
Yale University D*

AUTOMOTIVE ENGINEERING

Central Michigan University M,O
Clemson University M,D
Kettering University M
Lawrence Technological University M,D
Minnesota State University Mankato M
Old Dominion University M
University of Michigan M*
University of Michigan–Dearborn M,D*

AVIATION

Everglades University M
Lewis University M
Southeastern Oklahoma State University M
University of Central Missouri M
University of Illinois at Urbana–Champaign M*
University of North Dakota M
The University of Tennessee M
The University of Tennessee Space Institute M*

AVIATION MANAGEMENT

Concordia University (Canada) M,D,O
Daniel Webster College M
Delta State University M
Dowling College M,O
Embry-Riddle Aeronautical University (FL) M
Embry-Riddle Aeronautical University Worldwide M,O
Lynn University M,D
Middle Tennessee State University M
Southeastern Oklahoma State University M
Vaughn College of Aeronautics and Technology M

BACTERIOLOGY

Illinois State University M,D
The University of Iowa M,D*
University of Prince Edward Island M,D
The University of Texas Medical Branch D*
University of Washington D*
University of Wisconsin–Madison M*

BIOCHEMICAL ENGINEERING

Cornell University M,D*
Dartmouth College M,D*
Drexel University M*
Rutgers, The State University of New Jersey, New Brunswick M,D*
University of California, Irvine M,D*
The University of Iowa M,D*
University of Maryland, Baltimore County M,D,O*
The University of Western Ontario M,D

BIOCHEMISTRY

Albert Einstein College of Medicine D
American University of Beirut P,M
Arizona State University M,D
Auburn University M,D*
Baylor College of Medicine D*
Boston College D*
Boston University M,D*
Brandeis University M,D
Brigham Young University M,D*
Brown University M,D*
California Institute of Technology M,D*
California Polytechnic State University, San Luis Obispo M
California State University, East Bay M
California State University, Long Beach M
California State University, Los Angeles M
California State University, Northridge M
Carnegie Mellon University M,D*
Case Western Reserve University M,D*
Central Connecticut State University M
City College of the City University of New York M,D*
Clemson University M,D
Colorado State University M,D*
Colorado State University–Pueblo M
Columbia University M,D*
Cornell University D*
Cornell University, Joan and Sanford I. Weill Medical College and Graduate School of Medical Sciences M,D
Dalhousie University M,D
Dartmouth College D*
DePaul University M*
Drexel University M,D*
Duke University D,O*
Duquesne University M,D*
East Carolina University D
East Tennessee State University M,D
Emory University D*
Florida State University M,D*
Georgetown University M,D
The George Washington University M,D*
Georgia Institute of Technology M,D*

Georgia State University	M,D
Graduate School and University Center of the City University of New York	D*
Harvard University	D*
Howard University	M,D
Hunter College of the City University of New York	M,D
Illinois State University	M,D
Indiana University Bloomington	M,D*
Indiana University–Purdue University Indianapolis	D*
Iowa State University of Science and Technology	M,D*
The Johns Hopkins University	M,D*
Kansas State University	M,D*
Kent State University	M,D*
Laurentian University	M
Lehigh University	M,D
Loma Linda University	M,D
Louisiana State University and Agricultural and Mechanical College	M,D
Louisiana State University Health Sciences Center at Shreveport	M,D*
Loyola University Chicago	M,D*
Massachusetts Institute of Technology	D*
Mayo Graduate School	D*
McGill University	M,D*
McMaster University	M,D
Medical College of Georgia	D
Medical College of Wisconsin	D*
Medical University of South Carolina	M,D
Memorial University of Newfoundland	M,D
Miami University	M,D*
Michigan State University	M,D*
Mississippi College	M
Mississippi State University	M,D
Montana State University	M,D
Montclair State University	M*
New Mexico Institute of Mining and Technology	M,D
New Mexico State University	M,D
New York Medical College	M,D*
North Carolina State University	D*
North Dakota State University	M,D
Northeastern University	M,D*
Northern Arizona University	M
Northwestern University	D*
OGI School of Science & Engineering at Oregon Health & Science University	M,D
The Ohio State University	M*
Ohio University	M,D*
Oklahoma State University	M,D*
Old Dominion University	M,D
Oregon Health & Science University	M,D*
Oregon State University	M,D*
Penn State Hershey Medical Center	M,D
Penn State University Park	M,D*
Purdue University	M,D
Queens College of the City University of New York	M
Queen's University at Kingston	M,D
Rensselaer Polytechnic Institute	M,D
Rice University	M,D
Rush University	D
Rutgers, The State University of New Jersey, Newark	M,D*
Rutgers, The State University of New Jersey, New Brunswick	M,D*
Saint Joseph College	M
Saint Louis University	D
San Francisco State University	M
Seton Hall University	M,D*
Simon Fraser University	M,D
Southern Illinois University Carbondale	M,D*
Southern University and Agricultural and Mechanical College	M
Stanford University	D*
State University of New York College of Environmental Science and Forestry	M,D
State University of New York Upstate Medical University	M,D
Stevens Institute of Technology	M,D,O
Stony Brook University, State University of New York	D
Syracuse University	D*
Temple University	M,D*
Texas A&M University	M,D*
Texas State University–San Marcos	M*
Texas Tech University Health Sciences Center	M,D
Thomas Jefferson University	D*
Tufts University	D*
Tulane University	M,D
Université de Moncton	M
Université de Montréal	M,D,O
Université de Sherbrooke	M,D
Université Laval	M,D,O
University at Albany, State University of New York	M,D*
University at Buffalo, the State University of New York	M,D*
The University of Alabama at Birmingham	M,D*
University of Alaska Fairbanks	M,D
University of Alberta	M,D*
The University of Arizona	M,D*
University of Arkansas for Medical Sciences	M,D
The University of British Columbia	M,D
University of Calgary	M,D
University of California, Berkeley	D*
University of California, Davis	M,D*
University of California, Irvine	M,D*
University of California, Los Angeles	M,D*
University of California, Riverside	M,D*
University of California, San Diego	M,D*
University of California, San Francisco	D
University of California, Santa Barbara	M,D
University of California, Santa Cruz	M,D*
University of Chicago	D*
University of Cincinnati	M,D
University of Colorado at Boulder	M,D*
University of Colorado Denver	D*
University of Connecticut	M,D*
University of Connecticut Health Center	D*
University of Delaware	M,D*
University of Detroit Mercy	M
University of Florida	M,D*
University of Georgia	M,D*
University of Guelph	M,D
University of Houston	M,D*
University of Idaho	M,D
University of Illinois at Chicago	D*
University of Illinois at Urbana–Champaign	M,D*
The University of Iowa	M,D*
The University of Kansas	M,D*
University of Kentucky	D
University of Lethbridge	M,D
University of Louisville	M,D
University of Maine	M,D*
University of Manitoba	M,D
University of Maryland, Baltimore	M,D*
University of Maryland, Baltimore County	M,D*
University of Maryland, College Park	M,D*
University of Massachusetts Amherst	M,D*
University of Massachusetts Lowell	M,D
University of Massachusetts Worcester	D
University of Medicine and Dentistry of New Jersey	M,D*
University of Miami	D*
University of Michigan	D*
University of Minnesota, Duluth	M,D
University of Minnesota, Twin Cities Campus	D*
University of Mississippi Medical Center	M,D*
University of Missouri–Columbia	M,D*
University of Missouri–Kansas City	D*
University of Missouri–St. Louis	M,D,O
The University of Montana	M,D
University of Nebraska–Lincoln	M,D*
University of Nebraska Medical Center	M,D*
University of Nevada, Las Vegas	M,D
University of Nevada, Reno	M,D*
University of New Hampshire	M,D*
University of New Mexico	M,D*
The University of North Carolina at Chapel Hill	M,D*
The University of North Carolina at Greensboro	M
University of North Dakota	M,D
University of North Texas	M,D
University of North Texas Health Science Center at Fort Worth	M,D
University of Notre Dame	M,D*
University of Oklahoma	M,D*
University of Oklahoma Health Sciences Center	M,D
University of Oregon	M,D*
University of Ottawa	M,D*
University of Pennsylvania	D*
University of Pittsburgh	M,D*
University of Puerto Rico, Medical Sciences Campus	M,D
University of Regina	M,D
University of Rhode Island	M,D
University of Rochester	M,D*
University of Saskatchewan	M,D
The University of Scranton	M
University of South Alabama	D*
University of South Carolina	M,D
University of Southern California	M,D*
University of Southern Mississippi	M,D
University of South Florida	M,D*
The University of Tennessee	M,D
The University of Texas at Austin	M,D
The University of Texas Health Science Center at Houston	M,D
The University of Texas Health Science Center at San Antonio	M,D
The University of Texas Medical Branch	D*
The University of Texas Southwestern Medical Center at Dallas	D*
University of the Sciences in Philadelphia	M,D*
The University of Toledo	M,D
University of Toronto	M,D
University of Tulsa	M*
University of Utah	M,D*
University of Vermont	M,D*
University of Victoria	M,D
University of Virginia	D
University of Washington	D*
University of Waterloo	M,D
The University of Western Ontario	M,D
University of West Florida	M
University of Windsor	M,D
University of Wisconsin–Madison	M,D*
University of Wisconsin–Milwaukee	M,D
Utah State University	M,D
Vanderbilt University	M,D*
Virginia Commonwealth University	M,D,O
Virginia Polytechnic Institute and State University	M,D*
Wake Forest University	D*
Washington State University	M,D*
Washington University in St. Louis	D*
Wayne State University	M,D*
Wesleyan University	M,D*
West Virginia University	M,D
Worcester Polytechnic Institute	M,D*
Wright State University	M
Yale University	D*
Youngstown State University	M

BIOENGINEERING

Alfred University	M,D*
Arizona State University	M,D
Baylor College of Medicine	D*
California Institute of Technology	M,D*
Carnegie Mellon University	M,D*
Clemson University	M,D
Cornell University	M,D*
Dalhousie University	M,D
Georgia Institute of Technology	M,D*
Illinois Institute of Technology	M,D*
Iowa State University of Science and Technology	M,D*
The Johns Hopkins University	M,D*
Kansas State University	M,D*
Lehigh University	M,D
Louisiana State University and Agricultural and Mechanical College	M,D
Massachusetts Institute of Technology	M,D*
McGill University	M,D*

*M—master's degree; P—first professional degree; D—doctorate; O—other advanced degree; *—Close-Up and/or Announcement or Display in one of the other books in this series*

Mississippi State University M,D
North Carolina State University M,D,O*
The Ohio State University M,D*
Oklahoma State University M,D*
Oregon State University M,D*
Penn State Hershey Medical Center M,D
Penn State University Park M,D*
Rensselaer Polytechnic Institute M,D
Rice University M,D
South Dakota School of Mines and Technology M,D*
Stanford University M,D*
Syracuse University M,D*
Texas A&M University M,D*
Tufts University M,D,O*
University at Buffalo, the State University of New York M,D*
University of Arkansas M
University of California, Berkeley D*
University of California, Davis M,D*
University of California, Riverside M,D*
University of California, San Diego M,D*
University of California, San Francisco D
University of Denver M,D*
University of Florida M,D,O*
University of Georgia M,D*
University of Guelph M,D
University of Hawaii at Manoa M*
University of Idaho M,D
University of Illinois at Chicago M,D*
University of Illinois at Urbana–Champaign M,D*
The University of Kansas M,D*
University of Maine M*
University of Maryland, College Park M,D*
University of Missouri–Columbia M,D*
University of Nebraska–Lincoln M,D*
University of Notre Dame M,D*
University of Oklahoma M,D*
University of Pennsylvania M,D*
University of Pittsburgh M,D*
The University of Texas at Arlington M,D*
The University of Toledo M,D
University of Utah M,D*
University of Washington M,D*
University of Wisconsin–Madison M,D*
Virginia Commonwealth University M,D
Virginia Polytechnic Institute and State University M,D*
Washington State University M,D*

BIOETHICS

Albany Medical College M,O
Boston University M*
Case Western Reserve University M*
Cleveland State University M,O
Drew University M,D,O
Duquesne University M,D,O*
Indiana University–Purdue University Indianapolis M,O*
The Johns Hopkins University M,D*
Kansas City University of Medicine and Biosciences M
Loma Linda University M,O
Loyola Marymount University M
McGill University M,D,O*
Medical College of Wisconsin M*
Michigan State University M*
Midwestern University, Glendale Campus M,O*
Mount Sinai School of Medicine of New York University M
New York University M*
Rush University M,O
Saint Louis University D,O
Trinity International University M
Union Graduate College M
Université de Montréal M,O
University of Pittsburgh M*
The University of Tennessee M,D
University of Toronto M,D
University of Virginia M
University of Washington M*

BIOINFORMATICS

Arizona State University M,D
Boston University M,D*
Brandeis University M,O
California State University Channel Islands M
California State University, Dominguez Hills M
The Catholic University of America M,D
Dalhousie University M,D
Duke University D*
Eastern Michigan University M,O
George Mason University M,D,O*
Georgetown University M
The George Washington University M*
Georgia Institute of Technology M,D*
Grand Valley State University M
Indiana University Bloomington M,D*
Iowa State University of Science and Technology D*
The Johns Hopkins University M,D,O*
Marquette University M,D
McGill University M,D*
Medical College of Wisconsin M*
Medical University of South Carolina M,D
Mississippi Valley State University M
Morgan State University M
New Jersey Institute of Technology M,D
North Carolina State University M,D*
North Dakota State University M,D
Northeastern University M*
Northwestern University M*
Oregon Health & Science University M,D,O*
Polytechnic Institute of NYU M
Rochester Institute of Technology M
Stevens Institute of Technology M,D,O
Texas Tech University M,D
University of Arkansas at Little Rock M,D
University of California, Riverside D*
University of California, San Diego D*
University of California, Santa Cruz M,D*
University of Cincinnati D
University of Colorado Denver D*
University of Idaho M,D
University of Illinois at Urbana–Champaign M,D,O*
University of Medicine and Dentistry of New Jersey M,D*
University of Michigan M,D*
University of Missouri–Columbia D*
University of Missouri–Kansas City M,D*
University of Nebraska–Lincoln M,D*
University of Pittsburgh M,D,O*
University of Southern California M,D*
University of South Florida M,D*
The University of Texas at El Paso M
The University of Texas Medical Branch D*
University of the Sciences in Philadelphia M*
The University of Toledo M,O
University of Utah M,D,O*
University of Washington M,D*
Vanderbilt University M,D*
Virginia Commonwealth University M
Virginia Polytechnic Institute and State University D*
Yale University D*

BIOLOGICAL AND BIOMEDICAL SCIENCES—GENERAL

Acadia University M
Adelphi University M*
Alabama Agricultural and Mechanical University M
Alabama State University M
Albany Medical College M,D
Albert Einstein College of Medicine D
Alcorn State University M
American University M*
The American University of Athens M
American University of Beirut M
Andrews University M
Angelo State University M
Appalachian State University M
Arizona State University M,D
Arizona State University at the Polytechnic Campus M
Arkansas State University M,O
A.T. Still University of Health Sciences P,M
Auburn University M,D*
Austin Peay State University M
Ball State University M,D*
Barry University M*
Baylor College of Medicine M,D*
Baylor University M,D
Bemidji State University M
Bloomsburg University of Pennsylvania M
Boise State University M
Boston College D*
Boston University M,D*
Bowling Green State University M,D*
Bradley University M
Brandeis University O
Brigham Young University M,D*
Brock University M,D
Brooklyn College of the City University of New York M,D
Brown University M,D*
Bucknell University M
Buffalo State College, State University of New York M
California Institute of Technology M,D*
California Polytechnic State University, San Luis Obispo M
California State Polytechnic University, Pomona M
California State University, Bakersfield M
California State University, Chico M
California State University, Dominguez Hills M
California State University, East Bay M
California State University, Fresno M
California State University, Fullerton M
California State University, Long Beach M
California State University, Los Angeles M
California State University, Northridge M
California State University, Sacramento M
California State University, San Bernardino M
California State University, San Marcos M
California State University, Stanislaus M
Carleton University M,D
Carnegie Mellon University M,D*
Case Western Reserve University M,D*
The Catholic University of America M,D
Cedars-Sinai Medical Center D
Central Connecticut State University M,O
Central Michigan University M
Central Washington University M
Chatham University M
Chicago State University M
The Citadel, The Military College of South Carolina M
City College of the City University of New York M,D*
City of Hope National Medical Center/Beckman Research Institute D
Clarion University of Pennsylvania M
Clark Atlanta University M,D
Clark University M,D
Clemson University M,D
Cleveland State University M,D
Cold Spring Harbor Laboratory, Watson School of Biological Sciences D*
The College at Brockport, State University of New York M
College of Staten Island of the City University of New York M
The College of William and Mary M
Colorado State University M,D*
Colorado State University–Pueblo M
Columbia University P,M,D,O*
Concordia University (Canada) M,D,O
Cornell University M,D*
Cornell University, Joan and Sanford I. Weill Medical College and Graduate School of Medical Sciences M,D

Creighton University	M,D*
Dalhousie University	M,D
Dartmouth College	D*
Delaware State University	M
Delta State University	M
DePaul University	M*
Dominican University of California	M
Drexel University	M,D,O*
Duke University	D,O*
Duquesne University	M,D*
East Carolina University	M,D
Eastern Illinois University	M
Eastern Kentucky University	M
Eastern Michigan University	M
Eastern New Mexico University	M
Eastern Virginia Medical School	M,D
Eastern Washington University	M
East Stroudsburg University of Pennsylvania	M
East Tennessee State University	M,D
Edinboro University of Pennsylvania	M
Elizabeth City State University	M
Emory University	D*
Emporia State University	M
Fairleigh Dickinson University, College at Florham	M*
Fairleigh Dickinson University, Metropolitan Campus	M*
Fayetteville State University	M
Fisk University	M
Fitchburg State College	M
Florida Agricultural and Mechanical University	M
Florida Atlantic University	M,D
Florida Institute of Technology	M,D*
Florida International University	M,D*
Florida State University	P,M,D*
Fordham University	M,D*
Fort Hays State University	M
Frostburg State University	M
George Mason University	M,D,O*
Georgetown University	M,D
The George Washington University	M,D*
Georgia Campus–Philadelphia College of Osteopathic Medicine	M,O
Georgia College & State University	M
Georgia Institute of Technology	M,D*
Georgian Court University	M,O
Georgia Southern University	M
Georgia State University	M,D
Gerstner Sloan-Kettering Graduate School of Biomedical Sciences	D*
Goucher College	O
Graduate School and University Center of the City University of New York	D*
Grand Valley State University	M
Hampton University	M
Harvard University	M,D,O*
Heritage University	M
Hofstra University	M*
Hood College	M,O
Howard University	M,D
Humboldt State University	M
Hunter College of the City University of New York	M,D
ICR Graduate School	M
Idaho State University	M,D
Illinois Institute of Technology	M,D*
Illinois State University	M,D
Indiana State University	M,D
Indiana University Bloomington	M,D*
Indiana University of Pennsylvania	M
Indiana University–Purdue University Fort Wayne	M
Indiana University–Purdue University Indianapolis	M,D*
Iowa State University of Science and Technology	M,D*
Jackson State University	M,D
Jacksonville State University	M
James Madison University	M
John Carroll University	M
The Johns Hopkins University	M,D*
Kansas City University of Medicine and Biosciences	M
Kansas State University	M,D*
Keck Graduate Institute of Applied Life Sciences	M,D,O
Kent State University	M,D*
Lake Erie College of Osteopathic Medicine	P,M,O
Lakehead University	M
Lamar University	M
Laurentian University	M,D
Lehigh University	M,D
Lehman College of the City University of New York	M
Loma Linda University	M,D
Long Island University, Brooklyn Campus	M
Long Island University, C.W. Post Campus	M
Louisiana State University and Agricultural and Mechanical College	M,D
Louisiana State University Health Sciences Center	M,D*
Louisiana State University Health Sciences Center at Shreveport	M,D*
Louisiana Tech University	M
Loyola University Chicago	M*
Marquette University	M,D
Marshall University	M,D
Massachusetts Institute of Technology	P,M,D*
Mayo Graduate School	D*
McGill University	M,D*
McMaster University	M,D
McNeese State University	M
Medical College of Georgia	M,D,O
Medical College of Wisconsin	M,D,O*
Medical University of South Carolina	M,D
Meharry Medical College	D
Memorial University of Newfoundland	M,D,O
Michigan State University	M,D*
Michigan Technological University	M,D
Middle Tennessee State University	M
Midwestern State University	M
Midwestern University, Downers Grove Campus	M*
Midwestern University, Glendale Campus	M*
Millersville University of Pennsylvania	M
Mills College	O
Minnesota State University Mankato	M
Mississippi College	M
Mississippi State University	M,D
Missouri State University	M*
Missouri University of Science and Technology	M
Montana State University	M,D
Montclair State University	M,O*
Morehead State University	M
Morehouse School of Medicine	M,D*
Morgan State University	M,D
Mount Allison University	M
Mount Sinai School of Medicine of New York University	M,D
Murray State University	M,D
New Jersey Institute of Technology	M,D
New Mexico Institute of Mining and Technology	M
New Mexico State University	M,D
New York Medical College	M,D*
New York University	M,D*
North Carolina Agricultural and Technical State University	M
North Carolina Central University	M
North Carolina State University	M,D,O*
North Dakota State University	M,D
Northeastern Illinois University	M
Northeastern University	M,D*
Northern Arizona University	M,D
Northern Illinois University	M,D
Northern Michigan University	M
Northwestern University	D*
Northwest Missouri State University	M
Notre Dame de Namur University	O
Nova Southeastern University	M*
Oakland University	M,D
Occidental College	M
The Ohio State University	M,D*
Ohio University	M,D*
Oklahoma State University Center for Health Sciences	M,D
Old Dominion University	M,D
Oregon Health & Science University	M,D,O*
Penn State Hershey Medical Center	M,D
Penn State University Park	M,D*
Philadelphia College of Osteopathic Medicine	M,O*
Pittsburg State University	M
Point Loma Nazarene University	M
Polytechnic Institute of NYU, Long Island Graduate Center	M,D,O
Ponce School of Medicine	D
Pontifical Catholic University of Puerto Rico	M
Portland State University	M,D
Prairie View A&M University	M
Purdue University	M,D
Purdue University Calumet	M
Queens College of the City University of New York	M
Queen's University at Kingston	M,D
Quinnipiac University	M*
Rensselaer Polytechnic Institute	M,D
Rhode Island College	M
Rochester Institute of Technology	M
The Rockefeller University	D*
Rosalind Franklin University of Medicine and Science	M,D*
Rutgers, The State University of New Jersey, Camden	M
Rutgers, The State University of New Jersey, Newark	M,D*
Rutgers, The State University of New Jersey, New Brunswick	D*
St. Cloud State University	M
Saint Francis University	M
St. Francis Xavier University	M
St. John's University (NY)	M,D
Saint Joseph College	M
Saint Joseph's University	M
Saint Louis University	M,D
Sam Houston State University	M
San Diego State University	M,D*
San Francisco State University	M
San Jose State University	M
Seton Hall University	M,D*
Shippensburg University of Pennsylvania	M
Simon Fraser University	M,D
Smith College	M
Sonoma State University	M
South Dakota State University	M,D
Southeastern Louisiana University	M
Southeast Missouri State University	M
Southern Connecticut State University	M
Southern Illinois University Carbondale	M,D*
Southern Illinois University Edwardsville	M
Southern Methodist University	M,D*
Southern University and Agricultural and Mechanical College	M
Stanford University	M,D*
State University of New York at Binghamton	M,D*
State University of New York at Fredonia	M
State University of New York at New Paltz	M
State University of New York College at Oneonta	M
State University of New York Downstate Medical Center	M,D*
State University of New York Upstate Medical University	M,D
Stephen F. Austin State University	M
Stony Brook University, State University of New York	D
Sul Ross State University	M*
Syracuse University	M,D*
Tarleton State University	M
Temple University	M,D*
Tennessee State University	M,D
Tennessee Technological University	M*
Texas A&M Health Science Center	M,D
Texas A&M International University	M

*M—master's degree; P—first professional degree; D—doctorate; O—other advanced degree; *—Close-Up and/or Announcement or Display in one of the other books in this series*

Texas A&M University	M,D*
Texas A&M University–Commerce	M
Texas A&M University–Corpus Christi	M
Texas A&M University–Kingsville	M
Texas Christian University	M
Texas Southern University	M
Texas State University–San Marcos	M*
Texas Tech University	M,D
Texas Tech University Health Sciences Center	M,D
Texas Woman's University	M,D
Thomas Jefferson University	M,D,O*
Towson University	M
Trent University	M,D
Truman State University	M
Tufts University	M,D*
Tulane University	M,D
Tuskegee University	M,D
Uniformed Services University of the Health Sciences	M,D*
Universidad Adventista de las Antillas	M
Universidad Central del Caribe	M
Universidad de Ciencias Medicas	P,M,O
Université de Moncton	M
Université de Montréal	M,D
Université de Sherbrooke	M,D,O
Université du Québec à Montréal	M,D
Université du Québec en Abitibi-Témiscamingue	M,D
Université du Québec, Institut National de la Recherche Scientifique	M,D
Université Laval	M,D,O
University at Albany, State University of New York	M,D*
University at Buffalo, the State University of New York	M,D*
The University of Akron	M,D
The University of Alabama	M,D
The University of Alabama at Birmingham	M,D*
The University of Alabama in Huntsville	M
University of Alaska Anchorage	M
University of Alaska Fairbanks	M,D
University of Alberta	P,M,D*
The University of Arizona	M,D*
University of Arkansas	M,D
University of Arkansas at Little Rock	M
University of Arkansas for Medical Sciences	M,D
University of Calgary	M,D
University of California, Berkeley	D*
University of California, Irvine	M,D*
University of California, Los Angeles	M,D*
University of California, Riverside	M,D*
University of California, San Diego	M,D*
University of California, San Francisco	D
University of Central Arkansas	M
University of Central Florida	M,D,O*
University of Central Missouri	M
University of Central Oklahoma	M
University of Chicago	D*
University of Cincinnati	M,D
University of Colorado at Colorado Springs	M
University of Colorado Denver	M,D*
University of Connecticut	M,D*
University of Connecticut Health Center	D*
University of Dayton	M,D
University of Delaware	M,D*
University of Denver	M,D*
University of Florida	D*
University of Georgia	D*
University of Guam	M
University of Guelph	M,D
University of Hartford	M*
University of Hawaii at Manoa	M,D*
University of Houston	M,D*
University of Houston–Clear Lake	M
University of Idaho	M,D
University of Illinois at Chicago	M,D*
University of Illinois at Springfield	M
University of Illinois at Urbana–Champaign	M,D*
University of Indianapolis	M
The University of Iowa	M,D*
The University of Kansas	M,D*
University of Kentucky	M,D
University of Lethbridge	M,D
University of Louisiana at Lafayette	M,D*
University of Louisiana at Monroe	M
University of Louisville	M
University of Maine	D*
University of Manitoba	M,D,O
University of Maryland, Baltimore	M,D*
University of Maryland, Baltimore County	M,D*
University of Maryland, College Park	M,D*
University of Massachusetts Amherst	M,D*
University of Massachusetts Boston	M
University of Massachusetts Dartmouth	M
University of Massachusetts Lowell	M
University of Massachusetts Worcester	D
University of Medicine and Dentistry of New Jersey	M,D,O*
University of Memphis	M,D
University of Miami	M,D
University of Michigan	D*
University of Michigan–Flint	M*
University of Minnesota, Duluth	M,D
University of Minnesota, Twin Cities Campus	M,D*
University of Mississippi	M,D
University of Mississippi Medical Center	M,D*
University of Missouri–Columbia	M,D*
University of Missouri–Kansas City	M,D*
University of Missouri–St. Louis	M,D,O
The University of Montana	M,D
University of Nebraska at Kearney	M
University of Nebraska at Omaha	M
University of Nebraska–Lincoln	M,D*
University of Nebraska Medical Center	M,D*
University of Nevada, Las Vegas	M,D
University of Nevada, Reno	M*
University of New Brunswick Fredericton	M,D
University of New Brunswick Saint John	M,D
University of New England	M
University of New Hampshire	M,D*
University of New Mexico	M,D*
University of New Orleans	M,D
The University of North Carolina at Chapel Hill	M,D*
The University of North Carolina at Charlotte	M,D*
The University of North Carolina at Greensboro	M
The University of North Carolina Wilmington	M,D
University of North Dakota	M,D
University of Northern Colorado	M
University of Northern Iowa	M
University of North Florida	M
University of North Texas	M,D
University of North Texas Health Science Center at Fort Worth	M,D
University of Notre Dame	M,D*
University of Oklahoma Health Sciences Center	M,D
University of Oregon	M,D*
University of Ottawa	M,D*
University of Pennsylvania	M,D*
University of Pittsburgh	D*
University of Prince Edward Island	M
University of Puerto Rico, Mayagüez Campus	M
University of Puerto Rico, Medical Sciences Campus	M,D
University of Puerto Rico, Río Piedras	M,D
University of Regina	M,D
University of Rhode Island	M,D
University of Rochester	M,D*
University of San Francisco	M
University of Saskatchewan	M,D,O
University of South Alabama	M,D*
University of South Carolina	M,D,O
The University of South Dakota	M,D
University of Southern California	M,D*
University of Southern Maine	M
University of Southern Mississippi	M,D
University of South Florida	M,D*
The University of Tennessee	M,D
The University of Tennessee Health Science Center	M,D*
The University of Tennessee–Oak Ridge National Laboratory Graduate School of Genome Science and Technology	M,D
The University of Texas at Arlington	M,D*
The University of Texas at Austin	M,D
The University of Texas at Brownsville	M
The University of Texas at Dallas	M,D*
The University of Texas at El Paso	M,D
The University of Texas at San Antonio	M,D*
The University of Texas at Tyler	M
The University of Texas Health Science Center at Houston	M,D
The University of Texas Health Science Center at San Antonio	M,D
The University of Texas Medical Branch	M,D*
The University of Texas of the Permian Basin	M
The University of Texas–Pan American	M
The University of Texas Southwestern Medical Center at Dallas	M,D*
University of the Incarnate Word	M
University of the Pacific	M
The University of Toledo	M,D,O
University of Toronto	M,D
University of Tulsa	M,D*
University of Utah	M,D,O*
University of Vermont	M,D*
University of Victoria	M,D
University of Virginia	M,D
University of Washington	M,D*
University of Waterloo	M,D
University of West Florida	M
University of West Georgia	M
University of Windsor	M,D
University of Wisconsin–La Crosse	M
University of Wisconsin–Madison	M,D*
University of Wisconsin–Milwaukee	M,D
University of Wisconsin–Oshkosh	M
Utah State University	M,D
Vanderbilt University	M,D*
Vassar College	M
Villanova University	M*
Virginia Commonwealth University	M,D,O
Virginia Polytechnic Institute and State University	M,D*
Virginia State University	M
Wagner College	M
Wake Forest University	M,D*
Walla Walla University	M
Washington State University	M*
Washington State University Tri-Cities	M
Washington University in St. Louis	D*
Wayne State University	M,D*
Wesleyan University	D*
West Chester University of Pennsylvania	M,O
Western Carolina University	M
Western Connecticut State University	M
Western Illinois University	M,O
Western Kentucky University	M
Western Michigan University	M,D*
Western Washington University	M
West Texas A&M University	M
West Virginia University	M,D
Wichita State University	M*
Wilfrid Laurier University	M*
William Paterson University of New Jersey	M*
Winthrop University	M
Worcester Polytechnic Institute	M,D*
Wright State University	M,D
Yale University	D*
York University	M,D

Youngstown State University M

BIOLOGICAL ANTHROPOLOGY

Duke University D*
Kent State University D*
Mercyhurst College M

BIOMATHEMATICS

North Carolina State University M,D*
University of California, Los Angeles M,D*
The University of Texas Health Science Center at Houston M,D

BIOMEDICAL ENGINEERING

Baylor College of Medicine D*
Baylor University M
Boston University M,D*
Brown University M,D*
Carleton University M
Carnegie Mellon University M,D*
Case Western Reserve University M,D*
The Catholic University of America M,D
City College of the City University of New York M,D*
Cleveland State University D
Colorado State University M,D*
Columbia University M,D*
Cornell University M,D*
Dalhousie University M,D
Drexel University M,D*
Duke University M,D*
École Polytechnique de Montréal M,D,O
Emory University D*
Florida Agricultural and Mechanical University M,D
Florida International University M,D*
Florida State University M,D*
Georgia Institute of Technology D*
Graduate School and University Center of the City University of New York D*
Harvard University M,D*
Illinois Institute of Technology D*
Indiana University–Purdue University Indianapolis M,D,O*
The Johns Hopkins University M,D,O*
Louisiana Tech University M,D
Marquette University M,D
Massachusetts Institute of Technology M,D*
Mayo Graduate School D*
McGill University M,D*
Mercer University M
Michigan Technological University D
Mississippi State University M,D
New Jersey Institute of Technology M,D
North Carolina State University M,D*
Northwestern University M,D*
OGI School of Science & Engineering at Oregon Health & Science University M,D
The Ohio State University M,D*
Ohio University M*
Oregon Health & Science University M,D*
Penn State University Park M,D*
Polytechnic Institute of NYU M,D
Polytechnic Institute of NYU, Long Island Graduate Center M,D,O
Purdue University M,D
Rensselaer Polytechnic Institute M,D
Rice University M,D
Rose-Hulman Institute of Technology M*
Rutgers, The State University of New Jersey, New Brunswick M,D*
St. Cloud State University M
Saint Louis University M,D
South Dakota School of Mines and Technology M,D*
Southern Illinois University Carbondale M*
Stanford University M*
State University of New York Downstate Medical Center M,D*
Stevens Institute of Technology M,O
Stony Brook University, State University of New York M,D,O
Texas A&M University M,D*
Thomas Jefferson University D*
Tufts University M,D*
Tulane University M,D
Université de Montréal M,D,O
The University of Akron M,D
The University of Alabama at Birmingham M,D*
University of Alberta M,D*
The University of Arizona M,D*
University of Arkansas M
University of Calgary M,D
University of California, Davis M,D*
University of California, Irvine M,D*
University of California, Los Angeles M,D*
University of Cincinnati D
University of Connecticut M,D*
University of Florida M,D,O*
University of Houston M,D*
The University of Iowa M,D*
University of Kentucky M,D
University of Massachusetts Dartmouth D
University of Massachusetts Worcester D
University of Medicine and Dentistry of New Jersey M,D,O*
University of Memphis M,D
University of Miami M,D*
University of Michigan M,D*
University of Minnesota, Twin Cities Campus M,D*
University of Nevada, Las Vegas M,D
University of Nevada, Reno M,D*
The University of North Carolina at Chapel Hill M,D*
University of Ottawa M*
University of Rhode Island M,D
University of Rochester M,D*
University of Saskatchewan M,D
University of Southern California M,D*
University of South Florida M,D*
The University of Tennessee M,D
The University of Tennessee Health Science Center M,D*
The University of Texas at Austin M,D
The University of Texas at San Antonio M,D*
The University of Texas Southwestern Medical Center at Dallas M,D*
The University of Toledo D
University of Toronto M,D
University of Vermont M*
University of Virginia M,D
University of Wisconsin–Madison M,D*
Vanderbilt University M,D*
Virginia Commonwealth University M,D
Virginia Polytechnic Institute and State University M,D*
Wake Forest University M,D*
Washington University in St. Louis M,D*
Wayne State University M,D*
Worcester Polytechnic Institute M,D,O*
Wright State University M
Yale University M,D*

BIOMETRY

Cornell University M,D*
San Diego State University M*
University of California, Los Angeles M,D*
University of Southern California M*
University of Wisconsin–Madison M*

BIOPHYSICS

Albert Einstein College of Medicine D
Baylor College of Medicine D*
Boston University D*
Brandeis University M,D
California Institute of Technology D*
Carnegie Mellon University M,D*
Case Western Reserve University M,D*
Clemson University M,D
Columbia University M,D*
Cornell University D*
Cornell University, Joan and Sanford I. Weill Medical College and Graduate School of Medical Sciences M,D
Dalhousie University M,D
East Carolina University M,D
East Tennessee State University M,D
Emory University D*
Georgetown University M,D
Harvard University D*
Howard University D
Illinois State University M,D
Iowa State University of Science and Technology M,D*
The Johns Hopkins University D*
Medical College of Wisconsin D*
Northwestern University D*
The Ohio State University M,D*
Oregon State University M,D*
Purdue University M,D
Rensselaer Polytechnic Institute M,D
Simon Fraser University M,D
Stanford University D*
Stony Brook University, State University of New York D
Syracuse University D*
Texas A&M University M,D*
Thomas Jefferson University D*
Université de Montréal M,D,O
Université de Sherbrooke M,D
Université du Québec à Trois-Rivières M,D
University at Buffalo, the State University of New York M,D*
The University of Alabama at Birmingham D*
University of Arkansas for Medical Sciences M,D
University of California, Berkeley D*
University of California, Davis M,D*
University of California, Irvine D*
University of California, San Diego M,D*
University of California, San Francisco D
University of Chicago D*
University of Cincinnati D
University of Colorado Denver M,D*
University of Connecticut M,D*
University of Guelph M,D
University of Illinois at Chicago M,D*
University of Illinois at Urbana–Champaign M,D*
The University of Iowa D*
The University of Kansas M,D*
University of Louisville M,D
University of Miami D*
University of Michigan D*
University of Minnesota, Duluth M,D
University of Minnesota, Twin Cities Campus M,D*
University of Mississippi Medical Center M,D*
University of Missouri–Kansas City D*
University of New Mexico M,D*
The University of North Carolina at Chapel Hill M,D*
University of Rochester M,D*
University of Southern California M,D*
University of South Florida M,D*
The University of Texas Medical Branch D*
University of Toronto M,D
University of Vermont M,D*
University of Virginia M,D
University of Washington D*
The University of Western Ontario M,D
University of Wisconsin–Madison D*
Vanderbilt University M,D*
Washington State University M,D*
Wright State University M
Yale University D*

BIOPSYCHOLOGY

American University M*
Argosy University, Atlanta M,D,O*
Argosy University, Twin Cities M,D,O*
Brown University D*
Carnegie Mellon University D*
Columbia University M,D*
Cornell University D*
Drexel University M,D*
Duke University D*
George Mason University M,D*
Graduate School and University Center of the City University of New York D*
Harvard University D*
Howard University M,D
Hunter College of the City University of New York M
Indiana University–Purdue University Indianapolis M,D*

*M—master's degree; P—first professional degree; D—doctorate; O—other advanced degree; *—Close-Up and/or Announcement or Display in one of the other books in this series*

Louisiana State University and Agricultural and Mechanical College	M,D
Memorial University of Newfoundland	M,D
Northwestern University	D*
Oregon Health & Science University	M,D*
Palo Alto University	D*
Penn State University Park	M,D*
Rutgers, The State University of New Jersey, Newark	D*
Rutgers, The State University of New Jersey, New Brunswick	D*
State University of New York at Binghamton	M,D*
Stony Brook University, State University of New York	D
Texas A&M University	M,D*
University at Albany, State University of New York	M,D,O*
The University of British Columbia	M,D
University of Connecticut	M,D,O*
University of Michigan	D*
University of Minnesota, Twin Cities Campus	D*
University of Nebraska at Omaha	M,D,O
University of Nebraska–Lincoln	M,D*
University of Oklahoma Health Sciences Center	M,D
University of Oregon	M,D*
The University of Texas at Austin	D
The University of Toledo	M,D
University of Windsor	M,D
University of Wisconsin–Madison	D*
Wayne State University	M*

BIOSTATISTICS

American University of Beirut	M
Boston University	M,D*
Brown University	M,D*
California State University, East Bay	M
Case Western Reserve University	M,D*
Columbia University	M,D*
Drexel University	M,D,O*
Emory University	M,D*
Florida International University	M,D*
Florida State University	M,D*
George Mason University	M,D,O*
Georgetown University	M
The George Washington University	M,D*
Georgia Southern University	M,D
Grand Valley State University	M
Harvard University	M,D*
Hunter College of the City University of New York	M
Iowa State University of Science and Technology	D*
The Johns Hopkins University	M,D*
Loma Linda University	M,D,O
Louisiana State University Health Sciences Center	M,D*
McGill University	M,D,O*
Medical College of Georgia	M,D
Medical College of Wisconsin	D*
Medical University of South Carolina	M,D
Middle Tennessee State University	M
New Jersey Institute of Technology	M
New York Medical College	M,D*
The Ohio State University	D*
Oregon Health & Science University	M*
Rice University	M,D
Rutgers, The State University of New Jersey, New Brunswick	M,D*
San Diego State University	M,D*
Tufts University	M,D*
Tulane University	M,D
University at Albany, State University of New York	M,D*
University at Buffalo, the State University of New York	M,D*
The University of Alabama at Birmingham	M,D*
University of Alberta	M,D,O*
The University of Arizona	M,D*
University of California, Berkeley	M,D*
University of California, Davis	M,D*
University of California, Los Angeles	M,D*
University of Cincinnati	M,D
University of Colorado Denver	M,D*
University of Florida	M*
University of Illinois at Chicago	M,D*
The University of Iowa	M,D*
University of Louisville	M,D
University of Maryland, Baltimore	M,D*
University of Maryland, Baltimore County	M,D*
University of Maryland, College Park	M,D*
University of Medicine and Dentistry of New Jersey	M,D,O*
University of Michigan	M,D*
University of Minnesota, Twin Cities Campus	M,D*
The University of North Carolina at Chapel Hill	M,D*
University of North Texas Health Science Center at Fort Worth	M,D
University of Oklahoma Health Sciences Center	M,D
University of Pennsylvania	M,D*
University of Pittsburgh	M,D*
University of Puerto Rico, Medical Sciences Campus	M
University of Rochester	M,D*
University of South Carolina	M,D
University of Southern California	M,D*
University of Southern Mississippi	M
University of South Florida	M,D*
The University of Texas Health Science Center at Houston	M,D
The University of Toledo	M,O
University of Utah	M,D*
University of Vermont	M*
University of Washington	M,D*
University of Waterloo	M,D
The University of Western Ontario	M,D
Virginia Commonwealth University	M,D
Yale University	M,D*

BIOSYSTEMS ENGINEERING

Clemson University	M,D
Iowa State University of Science and Technology	M,D*
Michigan State University	M,D*
North Dakota State University	M,D
South Dakota State University	M,D
The University of Arizona	M,D*
University of Manitoba	M,D
University of Minnesota, Twin Cities Campus	M,D*
The University of Tennessee	M,D

BIOTECHNOLOGY

The American University in Cairo	M
Arizona State University	P,M
Brigham Young University	M,D*
Brock University	M,D
Brown University	M,D*
Cabrini College	M,O
California State University Channel Islands	M
Carnegie Mellon University	M,D*
Claflin University	M
Concordia University (Canada)	M,D,O
Dartmouth College	M,D*
Duquesne University	M*
East Carolina University	M
Florida Institute of Technology	M,D*
The George Washington University	M*
Harvard University	M,O*
Hood College	M,O
Howard University	M,D
Illinois State University	M
Indiana University Bloomington	M,D*
Instituto Tecnológico y de Estudios Superiores de Monterrey, Campus Monterrey	M,D
The Johns Hopkins University	M*
Kean University	M
Marywood University	M
McGill University	M,D,O*
Middle Tennessee State University	M
North Carolina State University	M*
Northeastern University	M,D*
Northwestern University	D*
Oklahoma State University	M,D*
Penn State University Park	M,D*
Polytechnic Institute of NYU	M
Polytechnic Institute of NYU, Long Island Graduate Center	M,D,O
Purdue University Calumet	M
Regis College (MA)	M
Roosevelt University	M
St. John's University (NY)	M
Simon Fraser University	M,D
Southern Illinois University Edwardsville	M
Stephen F. Austin State University	M
Texas Tech University	M
Texas Tech University Health Sciences Center	M
Thomas Jefferson University	D*
Tufts University	O*
Universidad de las Américas–Puebla	M
Université de Sherbrooke	P,M,D,O
University at Buffalo, the State University of New York	M*
The University of Alabama in Huntsville	D
University of Alberta	M,D*
University of Calgary	M
University of California, Irvine	M*
University of Central Florida	M*
University of Connecticut	M*
University of Delaware	M,D*
University of Guelph	M,D
University of Houston–Clear Lake	M
University of Illinois at Chicago	D*
The University of Kansas	M*
University of Maryland, Baltimore County	O*
University of Maryland University College	M,O
University of Massachusetts Amherst	M,D*
University of Massachusetts Boston	M
University of Massachusetts Dartmouth	D
University of Massachusetts Lowell	M,D
University of Minnesota, Twin Cities Campus	M*
University of Missouri–St. Louis	M,D,O
University of Nevada, Reno	M*
University of North Texas Health Science Center at Fort Worth	M,D
University of Pennsylvania	M*
University of Rhode Island	M
University of Saskatchewan	M
The University of Texas at Dallas	M,D*
The University of Texas at San Antonio	M,D*
University of the Sciences in Philadelphia	M,D*
University of Utah	M*
University of Washington	D*
University of West Florida	M
University of Wyoming	D
Western Michigan University	M,D*
West Virginia State University	M
William Paterson University of New Jersey	M*
Worcester Polytechnic Institute	M,D*
Worcester State College	M

BOTANY

Auburn University	M,D*
California State University, Chico	M
Claremont Graduate University	M,D*
Colorado State University	M,D*
Connecticut College	M
Emporia State University	M
Illinois State University	M,D
Miami University	M,D*
North Carolina State University	M,D*
North Dakota State University	M,D
Nova Scotia Agricultural College	M
Oklahoma State University	M,D*
Oregon State University	M,D*
Purdue University	M,D
Texas A&M University	M,D*
University of Alaska Fairbanks	M,D
The University of British Columbia	M,D
University of California, Riverside	M,D*
University of Connecticut	M,D*
University of Florida	M,D*
University of Guelph	M,D
University of Hawaii at Manoa	M,D*
The University of Kansas	M,D*
University of Maine	M*
University of Manitoba	M,D

University of Missouri–St. Louis	M,D,O
The University of North Carolina at Chapel Hill	M,D*
University of North Dakota	M,D
University of Oklahoma	M,D*
University of Wisconsin–Madison	M,D*
University of Wisconsin–Oshkosh	M
University of Wyoming	M,D
Virginia Polytechnic Institute and State University	M,D*
Washington State University	M,D*

BROADCAST JOURNALISM

American University	M*
The American University in Cairo	M
Boston University	M*
Emerson College	M
Northwestern University	M*
Syracuse University	M*
University of Maryland, College Park	M,D*
University of Miami	M,D*
University of Southern California	M*

BUILDING SCIENCE

Arizona State University	M
Auburn University	M*
Carnegie Mellon University	M,D*
Cornell University	M,D*
Georgia Institute of Technology	M,D*
University of California, Berkeley	M,D*
University of Florida	M,D*

BUSINESS ADMINISTRATION AND MANAGEMENT—GENERAL

Adelphi University	M*
Adler Graduate School	M,O
Alabama Agricultural and Mechanical University	M
Alabama State University	M
Alaska Pacific University	M
Albany State University	M
Albertus Magnus College	M
Alcorn State University	M
Alfred University	M*
Alliant International University–Los Angeles	D*
Alliant International University–México City	M*
Alliant International University–San Diego	M,D*
Alliant International University–San Francisco	M*
Alvernia University	M
Alverno College	M
Amberton University	M
The American College	M
American College of Thessaloniki	M,O
American Graduate University	M,O
American InterContinental University (TX)	M
American InterContinental University Buckhead Campus	M
American InterContinental University–London	M
American InterContinental University Online	M
American InterContinental University South Florida	M
American International College	M
American Jewish University	M
American Public University System	M
American Sentinel University	M
American University	M,D,O*
The American University in Cairo	M,O
The American University in Dubai	M
The American University of Athens	M
American University of Beirut	M
American University of Sharjah	M
Anderson University (IN)	M,D
Anderson University (SC)	M
Andrew Jackson University	M
Andrews University	M
Angelo State University	M
Anna Maria College	M,O
Antioch University Los Angeles	M
Antioch University McGregor	M
Antioch University New England	M*
Antioch University Seattle	M
Appalachian State University	M
Aquinas College	M
Arcadia University	M
Argosy University, Atlanta	M,D*
Argosy University, Chicago	M,D*
Argosy University, Dallas	M,O*
Argosy University, Denver	M,D*
Argosy University, Hawai'i	M,D,O*
Argosy University, Inland Empire	M,D*
Argosy University, Los Angeles	M,D*
Argosy University, Nashville	M,D*
Argosy University, Orange County	M,D,O*
Argosy University, Phoenix	M,D*
Argosy University, Salt Lake City	M,D*
Argosy University, San Diego	M,D*
Argosy University, San Francisco Bay Area	M,D*
Argosy University, Sarasota	M,D,O*
Argosy University, Schaumburg	M,D,O*
Argosy University, Seattle	M,D*
Argosy University, Tampa	M,D*
Argosy University, Twin Cities	M,D*
Argosy University, Washington DC	M,D,O*
Arizona State University	M,D
Arizona State University at the West campus	M
Arkansas State University	M,O
Ashland University	M
Aspen University	M,O
Assumption College	M,O
Athabasca University	M,O*
Auburn University	M,D*
Auburn University Montgomery	M
Augsburg College	M
Augusta State University	M
Aurora University	M
Austin Peay State University	M
Averett University	M
Avila University	M
Azusa Pacific University	M
Babson College	M
Baker College Center for Graduate Studies	M
Baker University	M
Bakke Graduate University	M,D
Baldwin-Wallace College	M
Ball State University	M*
Barry University	M,O*
Bayamón Central University	M
Baylor University	M
Belhaven College (MS)	M
Bellarmine University	M
Bellevue University	M,D
Belmont University	M
Benedictine College	M
Benedictine University	M
Bentley University	M,D,O
Bernard M. Baruch College of the City University of New York	M,D,O
Berry College	M
Bethel College (IN)	M
Bethel University	M
Biola University	M
Birmingham-Southern College	M
Black Hills State University	M
Bloomsburg University of Pennsylvania	M
Bluffton University	M
Bob Jones University	P,M,D,O
Boise State University	M
Boston College	M*
Boston University	M,D,O*
Bowie State University	M
Bowling Green State University	M*
Bradley University	M
Brandeis University	M
Brenau University	M
Brescia University	M
Bridgewater State College	M
Briercrest Seminary	M
Brigham Young University	M*
British American College London	M
Brock University	M
Bryant University	M
Butler University	M
Caldwell College	M
California Baptist University	M
California Coast University	M
California Intercontinental University	M,D
California International Business University	M,D
California Lutheran University	M,O
California National University for Advanced Studies	M
California Polytechnic State University, San Luis Obispo	M
California State Polytechnic University, Pomona	M
California State University, Bakersfield	M
California State University Channel Islands	M
California State University, Chico	M
California State University, Dominguez Hills	M
California State University, East Bay	M
California State University, Fresno	M
California State University, Fullerton	M
California State University, Long Beach	M
California State University, Los Angeles	M
California State University, Monterey Bay	M
California State University, Northridge	M
California State University, Sacramento	M
California State University, San Bernardino	M
California State University, San Marcos	M
California State University, Stanislaus	M
California University of Pennsylvania	M
Cambridge College	M
Cameron University	M
Campbellsville University	M
Campbell University	M
Canisius College	M
Cape Breton University	M
Capella University	M,D,O
Capital University	M
Capitol College	M
Cardinal Stritch University	M
Carleton University	M,D
Carlos Albizu University, Miami Campus	M,D
Carlow University	M
Carnegie Mellon University	M,D*
Case Western Reserve University	M,D*
The Catholic University of America	M
Centenary College	M
Centenary College of Louisiana	M
Central Connecticut State University	M,O
Central European University	M*
Central Michigan University	M,O
Chadron State College	M
Chaminade University of Honolulu	M
Chancellor University	M
Chapman University	M
Charleston Southern University	M
Chatham University	M
Christian Brothers University	M,O
The Citadel, The Military College of South Carolina	M
City University of Seattle	M,O
Claflin University	M
Claremont Graduate University	M,D,O*
Clarion University of Pennsylvania	M
Clark Atlanta University	M
Clarke College	M
Clarkson University	M*
Clark University	M
Clayton State University	M
Cleary University	M,O
Clemson University	M
Cleveland State University	M,D
Coastal Carolina University	M
College of Charleston	M*
College of Notre Dame of Maryland	M
College of Saint Elizabeth	M
College of St. Joseph	M
The College of Saint Rose	M*
The College of St. Scholastica	M,O
College of Santa Fe	M
College of Staten Island of the City University of New York	M
The College of William and Mary	M
Colorado Christian University	M
Colorado State University	M*

*M—master's degree; P—first professional degree; D—doctorate; O—other advanced degree; *—Close-Up and/or Announcement or Display in one of the other books in this series*

Colorado State University–Pueblo M
Colorado Technical University Colorado Springs M,D
Colorado Technical University Denver M
Colorado Technical University Sioux Falls M
Columbia College (MO) M
Columbia Southern University M,D
Columbia Union College M
Columbia University M,D*
Columbus State University M
Concordia University (CA) M
Concordia University (OR) M
Concordia University (Canada) M,D,O
Concordia University Chicago M
Concordia University, St. Paul M
Concordia University Wisconsin M
Cornell University M,D*
Cornerstone University M,O
Creighton University M*
Cumberland University M
Curry College M,O
Daemen College M
Dalhousie University M,O
Dallas Baptist University M
Daniel Webster College M
Daniel Webster College–Portsmouth Campus M
Dartmouth College M*
Davenport University M
Davenport University M
Davenport University M
Defiance College M
Delaware State University M
Delaware Valley College M
Delta State University M
DePaul University M*
DeSales University M
DeVry University (IL) M*
DeVry University (MD) M,O
DeVry University (MO) M,O
DeVry University (NC) M,O
DeVry University (NV) M,O
DeVry University (OR) M,O
DeVry University (PA) M,O
DeVry University (TX) M,O
DeVry University (UT) M,O
DeVry University (VA) M,O
DeVry University (WA) M,O
DeVry University (WI) M,O
Doane College M
Dominican College M
Dominican University M
Dominican University of California M
Dowling College M,O
Drake University M*
Drexel University M,D,O*
Drury University M
Duke University M,D*
Duquesne University M*
D'Youville College M*
East Carolina University M,D,O
Eastern Illinois University M,O
Eastern Kentucky University M
Eastern Mennonite University M
Eastern Michigan University M,O
Eastern New Mexico University M
Eastern University M
Eastern Washington University M
East Tennessee State University M,O
Edgewood College M
Elmhurst College M
Elon University M
Embry-Riddle Aeronautical University (FL) M
Emmanuel College M,O
Emory University M,D*
Emporia State University M
Endicott College M
Everest University, Clearwater M
Everest University, Jacksonville M
Everest University, Melbourne M
Everest University, Orlando M
Everest University, Pompano Beach M
Everest University, Tampa M
Everglades University M
Excelsior College M
Fairfield University M,O*
Fairleigh Dickinson University, College at Florham M,O*
Fairleigh Dickinson University, Metropolitan Campus M,O*
Fairmont State University M
Fashion Institute of Technology M*
Fayetteville State University M
Felician College M*
Ferris State University M
Fitchburg State College M
Florida Agricultural and Mechanical University M
Florida Atlantic University M,D,O
Florida Gulf Coast University M
Florida Institute of Technology M*
Florida International University M,D*
Florida Southern College M
Florida State University M,D*
Fontbonne University M
Fordham University M*
Fort Hays State University M
Framingham State College M
Franciscan University of Steubenville M
Francis Marion University M
Franklin Pierce University M,D,O
Franklin University M
Freed-Hardeman University M
Fresno Pacific University M
Friends University M
Frostburg State University M
Full Sail University M*
Gannon University M,O
Gardner-Webb University M
Geneva College M
George Fox University M,D*
George Mason University M*
Georgetown University M*
The George Washington University M,D,O*
Georgia College & State University M
Georgia Institute of Technology M,D,O*
Georgian Court University M,O
Georgia Southern University M
Georgia Southwestern State University M
Georgia State University M,D
Goddard College M
Golden Gate University M,D,O
Goldey-Beacom College M
Gonzaga University M
Governors State University M
Graduate School and University Center of the City University of New York D*
Grand Canyon University M*
Grand Valley State University M
Grand View University M
Grantham University M
Green Mountain College M
Gwynedd-Mercy College M
Hamline University M,D
Hampton University M
Harding University M
Hardin-Simmons University M
Harvard University M,D,O*
Hawai'i Pacific University M*
HEC Montreal M,D,O
Heidelberg University M
Henderson State University M
High Point University M
Hodges University M
Hofstra University M*
Holy Family University M
Holy Names University M
Hood College M
Hope International University M
Houston Baptist University M
Howard University M
Hult International Business School (United States) M
Humboldt State University M
Husson University M
Idaho State University M,O
Illinois Institute of Technology M,D*
Illinois State University M
IMCA–International Management Centres Association M
Independence University M
Indiana State University M
Indiana Tech M
Indiana University Bloomington M,D*
Indiana University Kokomo M
Indiana University Northwest M,O
Indiana University of Pennsylvania M
Indiana University–Purdue University Fort Wayne M
Indiana University–Purdue University Indianapolis M*
Indiana University South Bend M
Indiana University Southeast M
Indiana Wesleyan University M
Instituto Centroamericano de Administración de Empresas M
Instituto Tecnologico de Santo Domingo M
Instituto Tecnológico y de Estudios Superiores de Monterrey, Campus Central de Veracruz M
Instituto Tecnológico y de Estudios Superiores de Monterrey, Campus Ciudad de México M,D
Instituto Tecnológico y de Estudios Superiores de Monterrey, Campus Ciudad Juárez M
Instituto Tecnológico y de Estudios Superiores de Monterrey, Campus Ciudad Obregón M
Instituto Tecnológico y de Estudios Superiores de Monterrey, Campus Cuernavaca M
Instituto Tecnológico y de Estudios Superiores de Monterrey, Campus Estado de México M,D
Instituto Tecnológico y de Estudios Superiores de Monterrey, Campus Guadalajara M
Instituto Tecnológico y de Estudios Superiores de Monterrey, Campus Irapuato M,D
Instituto Tecnológico y de Estudios Superiores de Monterrey, Campus Laguna M
Instituto Tecnológico y de Estudios Superiores de Monterrey, Campus León M
Instituto Tecnológico y de Estudios Superiores de Monterrey, Campus Monterrey M,D
Instituto Tecnológico y de Estudios Superiores de Monterrey, Campus Querétaro M
Instituto Tecnológico y de Estudios Superiores de Monterrey, Campus Sonora Norte M
Instituto Tecnológico y de Estudios Superiores de Monterrey, Campus Toluca M
Inter American University of Puerto Rico, Aguadilla Campus M
Inter American University of Puerto Rico, Barranquitas Campus M
Inter American University of Puerto Rico, Metropolitan Campus M
Inter American University of Puerto Rico, San Germán Campus M,D
International College of the Cayman Islands M
International Technological University M
International University in Geneva M
The International University of Monaco M
Iona College M,O*
Iowa State University of Science and Technology M*
Ithaca College M
ITT Technical Institute (IN) M
Jackson State University M,D
Jacksonville State University M
Jacksonville University M
James Madison University M
John Brown University M
John Carroll University M
John F. Kennedy University M,O
The Johns Hopkins University M,O*
Jones International University M
Kansas State University M*
Kansas Wesleyan University M
Kaplan University–Davenport Campus M
Kean University M
Keiser University M
Keller Graduate School of Management M,O
Keller Graduate School of Management M
Kennesaw State University M
Kent State University M*
Kent State University, Stark Campus M
Kentucky State University M
Kettering University M
Keuka College M
King College M
King's College M

Kutztown University of Pennsylvania	M
Lake Erie College	M
Lake Forest Graduate School of Management	M
Lakeland College	M
Lamar University	M
La Salle University	M,O
Lasell College	M,O
La Sierra University	M,O
Laurentian University	M
Lawrence Technological University	M,D
Lebanese American University	M
Lebanon Valley College	M
Lehigh University	M,D,O
Le Moyne College	M
Lenoir-Rhyne University	M
LeTourneau University	M
Lewis University	M
Liberty University	M
LIM College	M
Lincoln Memorial University	M
Lincoln University (CA)	M
Lincoln University (MO)	M
Lincoln University (PA)	M
Lindenwood University	M,O
Lipscomb University	M
Long Island University, Brooklyn Campus	M
Long Island University, C.W. Post Campus	M,O
Long Island University, Rockland Graduate Campus	M,O
Long Island University, Westchester Graduate Campus	M
Longwood University	M
Louisiana State University and Agricultural and Mechanical College	M,D
Louisiana State University in Shreveport	M
Louisiana Tech University	M,D
Loyola Marymount University	M
Loyola University Chicago	M*
Loyola University Maryland	M*
Loyola University New Orleans	M
Lynchburg College	M
Lynn University	M,D
Madonna University	M
Maharishi University of Management	M,D
Malone University	M
Marian University (WI)	M
Marist College	M,O
Marlboro College	M
Marquette University	M
Marshall University	M,D,O
Marylhurst University	M
Marymount University	M,O
Maryville University of Saint Louis	M,O
Marywood University	M
Massachusetts Institute of Technology	M,D*
McGill University	M,D,O*
McKendree University	M
McMaster University	M,D
McNeese State University	M
Medaille College	M
Memorial University of Newfoundland	M
Mercer University	M
Mercy College	M
Meredith College	M
Meritus University	M
Mesa State College	M
Methodist University	M
Metropolitan College of New York	M
Metropolitan State University	M,O
Miami University	M*
Michigan State University	M,D*
Michigan Technological University	M
MidAmerica Nazarene University	M
Middle Tennessee State University	M
Midwestern State University	M
Milligan College	M
Millikin University	M
Millsaps College	M
Mills College	M
Milwaukee School of Engineering	M*
Minnesota State University Mankato	M
Minot State University	M
Misericordia University	M
Mississippi College	M,O
Mississippi State University	M,D
Missouri Baptist University	M,O
Missouri Southern State University	M
Missouri State University	M*
Monmouth University	M,O
Monroe College	M
Montclair State University	M,O*
Monterey Institute of International Studies	M*
Montreat College	M
Moravian College	M
Morehead State University	M
Morgan State University	D
Morrison University	M
Mount Marty College	M
Mount Mary College	M
Mount Saint Mary College	M
Mount St. Mary's College	M
Mount St. Mary's University	M
Mount Vernon Nazarene University	M
Murray State University	M
National American University	M
The National Graduate School of Quality Management	M
National-Louis University	M
National University	M
Naval Postgraduate School	M
Nazareth College of Rochester	M
New England College	M
New Jersey City University	M
New Jersey Institute of Technology	M
Newman University	M
New Mexico Highlands University	M
New Mexico State University	M,D
New York Institute of Technology	M,O
New York University	P,M,D,O*
Niagara University	M
Nicholls State University	M
Nichols College	M
North Carolina Agricultural and Technical State University	M,D
North Carolina Central University	M
North Carolina State University	M*
North Central College	M
Northcentral University	M,D,O
North Dakota State University	M
Northeastern Illinois University	M
Northeastern State University	M
Northeastern University	M,O*
Northern Arizona University	M
Northern Illinois University	M
Northern Kentucky University	M,O
North Greenville University	M
North Park University	M
Northwest Christian University	M
Northwestern Polytechnic University	M
Northwestern University	M*
Northwest Missouri State University	M
Northwest Nazarene University	M
Northwest University	M
Northwood University	M
Norwich University	M
Notre Dame College (OH)	M,O
Notre Dame de Namur University	M
Nova Southeastern University	M,D*
Nyack College	M
Oakland City University	M
Oakland University	M,O
OGI School of Science & Engineering at Oregon Health & Science University	M,O
Oglala Lakota College	M
Ohio Dominican University	M
The Ohio State University	M,D*
Ohio University	M*
Oklahoma City University	M
Oklahoma State University	M,D*
Old Dominion University	M,D
Olivet Nazarene University	M
Oral Roberts University	M
Oregon State University	M,O*
Ottawa University	M
Otterbein College	M
Our Lady of the Lake University of San Antonio	M
Pace University	M,D,O*
Pacific Lutheran University	M
Pacific States University	M,D
Palm Beach Atlantic University	M
Park University	M
Penn State Erie, The Behrend College	M
Penn State Great Valley	M
Penn State Harrisburg	M
Penn State University Park	M,D*
Pepperdine University	M
Pepperdine University	M
Pfeiffer University	M
Philadelphia University	M
Phillips Theological Seminary	P,M,D
Piedmont College	M
Pittsburg State University	M
Plymouth State University	M
Point Loma Nazarene University	M
Point Park University	M*
Polytechnic Institute of NYU	M,D
Polytechnic Institute of NYU, Long Island Graduate Center	M,O
Polytechnic Institute of NYU, Westchester Graduate Center	M
Polytechnic University of Puerto Rico	M
Polytechnic University of the Americas–Miami Campus	M
Polytechnic University of the Americas–Orlando Campus	M
Pontifical Catholic University of Puerto Rico	M,D
Pontificia Universidad Catolica Madre y Maestra	M
Portland State University	M,D,O
Prairie View A&M University	M
Providence College	M*
Purdue University	M,D
Purdue University Calumet	M
Queen's University at Kingston	M
Queens University of Charlotte	M
Quincy University	M
Quinnipiac University	M*
Radford University	M
Regent University	M,D,O
Regis College (MA)	M
Regis University	M,O
Reinhardt College	M
Rensselaer at Hartford	M
Rensselaer Polytechnic Institute	M,D
Rice University	M
The Richard Stockton College of New Jersey	M
Rider University	M*
Rivier College	M
Robert Morris College	M
Robert Morris University	M
Roberts Wesleyan College	M,O
Rochester Institute of Technology	M
Rockford College	M
Rockhurst University	M
Rollins College	M
Roosevelt University	M
Rosemont College	M
Rowan University	M
Royal Military College of Canada	M
Royal Roads University	M,O
Rutgers, The State University of New Jersey, Camden	M
Rutgers, The State University of New Jersey, Newark	M,D,O*
Sacred Heart University	M
Sage Graduate School	M
Saginaw Valley State University	M
St. Ambrose University	M,D
St. Bonaventure University	M
St. Cloud State University	M
St. Edward's University	M,O
Saint Francis University	M
St. John Fisher College	M
St. John's University (NY)	M,O
Saint Joseph College	M
St. Joseph's College, Long Island Campus	M,O
St. Joseph's College, New York	M
Saint Joseph's College of Maine	M
Saint Joseph's University	M,O
Saint Leo University	M
Saint Louis University	M
Saint Martin's University	M
Saint Mary's College of California	M
Saint Mary's University (Canada)	M,D
St. Mary's University (United States)	M
Saint Mary's University of Minnesota	M
Saint Michael's College	M,O
Saint Peter's College	M
St. Thomas Aquinas College	M*
St. Thomas University	M,O
Saint Xavier University	M,O
Salem International University	M
Salem State College	M
Salisbury University	M
Salve Regina University	M,O

*M—master's degree; P—first professional degree; D—doctorate; O—other advanced degree; *—Close-Up and/or Announcement or Display in one of the other books in this series*

Samford University	M
Sam Houston State University	M
San Diego State University	M*
San Francisco State University	M
San Jose State University	M
Santa Clara University	M
Savannah State University	M
Schiller International University (United States)	M
Schiller International University (Germany)	M
Schiller International University	M
Schiller International University (Spain)	M
Schiller International University	M
Seattle Pacific University	M
Seattle University	M,O
Seton Hall University	M,O*
Seton Hill University	M
Shenandoah University	M,O
Shippensburg University of Pennsylvania	M,O
Shorter College	M
Silver Lake College	M
Simmons College	M,O
Simon Fraser University	M,D
SIT Graduate Institute	M
Sonoma State University	M
Southeastern Louisiana University	M
Southeastern Oklahoma State University	M
Southeastern University	M
Southeast Missouri State University	M
Southern Adventist University	M
Southern Arkansas University–Magnolia	M
Southern Connecticut State University	M
Southern Illinois University Carbondale	M,D*
Southern Illinois University Edwardsville	M
Southern Methodist University	M*
Southern Nazarene University	M
Southern New Hampshire University	M,D,O*
Southern Oregon University	M
Southern Polytechnic State University	M,O
Southern University and Agricultural and Mechanical College	M
Southern Utah University	M
Southern Wesleyan University	M
South University (SC)	M*
South University (GA)	M*
South University (AL)	M*
South University (FL)	M*
Southwest Baptist University	M
Southwestern Adventist University	M
Southwestern College (KS)	M
Southwestern College (KS)	M
Southwestern Oklahoma State University	M
Southwest Minnesota State University	M
Spalding University	M
Spring Arbor University	M
Spring Hill College	M
Stanford University	M,D*
State University of New York at Binghamton	M,D*
State University of New York at Fredonia	M
State University of New York at New Paltz	M
State University of New York at Oswego	M
State University of New York College at Geneseo	M
State University of New York Empire State College	M
State University of New York Institute of Technology	M
Stephen F. Austin State University	M
Stephens College	M
Stetson University	M
Stevens Institute of Technology	M
Stony Brook University, State University of New York	M,O
Stratford University	M
Strayer University	M
Suffolk University	M,O*
Sullivan University	P,M
Sul Ross State University	M*
Syracuse University	M,D*
Tabor College	M
Tarleton State University	M
Taylor University	M
Temple University	M,D*
Tennessee State University	M
Tennessee Technological University	M*
Texas A&M International University	M
Texas A&M University	M,D*
Texas A&M University–Commerce	M
Texas A&M University–Corpus Christi	M
Texas A&M University–Kingsville	M
Texas A&M University–Texarkana	M
Texas Christian University	M,D
Texas Southern University	M
Texas State University–San Marcos	M*
Texas Tech University	M,D
Texas Wesleyan University	M
Texas Woman's University	M
Thomas College	M
Thomas Edison State College	M
Thomas More College	M
Thomas University	M
Thunderbird School of Global Management	M
Tiffin University	M
Towson University	M
Trevecca Nazarene University	M
Trinity International University	P,M,D,O
Trinity University	M
Trinity (Washington) University	M
Trinity Western University	M
Troy University	M
TUI University	M,D
Tulane University	M,D
Union Graduate College	M,O
Union University	M
United States International University	M
Universidad Autonoma de Guadalajara	M,D
Universidad Central del Este	M,D
Universidad de las Americas, A.C.	M
Universidad de las Américas–Puebla	M
Universidad del Este	M
Universidad del Turabo	M,D
Universidad Metropolitana	M,O
Universidad Nacional Pedro Henriquez Urena	P,M,D
Université de Moncton	M
Université de Sherbrooke	P,M,D,O
Université du Québec à Chicoutimi	M
Université du Québec à Montréal	M,D,O
Université du Québec à Rimouski	M,O
Université du Québec à Trois-Rivières	M,D
Université du Québec en Abitibi-Témiscamingue	M
Université Laval	M,D,O
University at Albany, State University of New York	M*
University at Buffalo, the State University of New York	M,D,O*
The University of Akron	M
The University of Alabama	M,D
The University of Alabama at Birmingham	M,D*
The University of Alabama in Huntsville	M,O
University of Alaska Anchorage	M
University of Alaska Fairbanks	M
University of Alaska Southeast	M
University of Alberta	M,D*
The University of Arizona	M,D*
University of Arkansas	M,D
University of Arkansas at Little Rock	M,O
University of Baltimore	M,O
University of Bridgeport	M
The University of British Columbia	M,D
University of Calgary	M,D
University of California, Berkeley	M,D*
University of California, Davis	M*
University of California, Irvine	M,D*
University of California, Los Angeles	M,D*
University of California, Riverside	M*
University of California, San Diego	M*
University of Central Arkansas	M
University of Central Florida	M,D,O*
University of Central Missouri	M
University of Central Oklahoma	M
University of Charleston	M
University of Chicago	M,D*
University of Cincinnati	M,D
University of Colorado at Boulder	M*
University of Colorado at Colorado Springs	M
University of Colorado Denver	M*
University of Connecticut	M,D*
University of Dallas	M
University of Dayton	M
University of Delaware	M,D*
University of Denver	M,O*
University of Detroit Mercy	M,O
University of Dubuque	M
University of Evansville	M
The University of Findlay	M
University of Florida	M,D,O*
University of Georgia	M,D*
University of Guam	M
University of Guelph	M,D
University of Hartford	M*
University of Hawaii at Manoa	M*
University of Houston	M,D*
University of Houston–Clear Lake	M
University of Houston–Victoria	M
University of Idaho	M
University of Illinois at Chicago	M,D*
University of Illinois at Springfield	M
University of Illinois at Urbana–Champaign	M,D*
University of Indianapolis	M,O
The University of Iowa	M,D*
The University of Kansas	M,D*
University of Kentucky	M,D
University of La Verne	M,O
University of Lethbridge	M,D
University of Louisiana at Lafayette	M*
University of Louisiana at Monroe	M
University of Louisville	M
University of Maine	M*
University of Management and Technology	M,D,O
University of Manitoba	M,D
University of Mary	M
University of Mary Hardin-Baylor	M
University of Maryland, College Park	M,D*
University of Maryland University College	M,D,O
University of Mary Washington	M
University of Massachusetts Amherst	M,D*
University of Massachusetts Boston	M
University of Massachusetts Dartmouth	M,O
University of Massachusetts Lowell	M,O
University of Memphis	M,D
University of Miami	M*
University of Michigan	D*
University of Michigan–Dearborn	M*
University of Michigan–Flint	M*
University of Minnesota, Duluth	M
University of Minnesota, Twin Cities Campus	M,D*
University of Mississippi	M,D
University of Missouri–Columbia	M,D*
University of Missouri–Kansas City	M,D*
University of Missouri–St. Louis	M,O
University of Mobile	M
The University of Montana	M
University of Nebraska at Kearney	M
University of Nebraska at Omaha	M
University of Nebraska–Lincoln	M,D*
University of Nevada, Las Vegas	M
University of Nevada, Reno	M*
University of New Brunswick Fredericton	M
University of New Brunswick Saint John	M
University of New Hampshire	M,O*
University of New Haven	M*
University of New Mexico	M*
University of New Orleans	M

University of North Alabama	M
The University of North Carolina at Chapel Hill	M,D*
The University of North Carolina at Charlotte	M,D*
The University of North Carolina at Greensboro	M,O
The University of North Carolina at Pembroke	M
The University of North Carolina Wilmington	M
University of North Dakota	M
University of Northern Iowa	M
University of North Florida	M
University of North Texas	M,D
University of Notre Dame	M*
University of Oklahoma	M,D*
University of Oregon	M,D*
University of Ottawa	M*
University of Pennsylvania	M,D*
University of Phoenix	M,D
University of Phoenix–Atlanta Campus	M
University of Phoenix–Augusta Campus	M
University of Phoenix–Austin Campus	M
University of Phoenix–Bay Area Campus	M
University of Phoenix–Birmingham Campus	M
University of Phoenix–Boston Campus	M
University of Phoenix–Central Florida Campus	M
University of Phoenix–Central Massachusetts Campus	M
University of Phoenix–Central Valley Campus	M
University of Phoenix–Charlotte Campus	M
University of Phoenix–Chattanooga Campus	M
University of Phoenix–Cheyenne Campus	M
University of Phoenix–Chicago Campus	M
University of Phoenix–Cincinnati Campus	M
University of Phoenix–Cleveland Campus	M
University of Phoenix–Columbia Campus	M
University of Phoenix–Columbus Georgia Campus	M
University of Phoenix–Columbus Ohio Campus	M
University of Phoenix–Dallas Campus	M
University of Phoenix–Denver Campus	M
University of Phoenix–Des Moines Campus	M
University of Phoenix–Eastern Washington Campus	M
University of Phoenix–Fairfield County	M
University of Phoenix–Harrisburg Campus	M
University of Phoenix–Hawaii Campus	M
University of Phoenix–Houston Campus	M
University of Phoenix–Idaho Campus	M
University of Phoenix–Indianapolis Campus	M
University of Phoenix–Jersey City Campus	M
University of Phoenix–Kansas City Campus	M
University of Phoenix–Las Vegas Campus	M
University of Phoenix–Little Rock Campus	M
University of Phoenix–Louisiana Campus	M
University of Phoenix–Louisville Campus	M
University of Phoenix–Madison Campus	M
University of Phoenix–Maryland Campus	M
University of Phoenix–Memphis Campus	M
University of Phoenix–Metro Detroit Campus	M
University of Phoenix–Minneapolis/St. Louis Park Campus	M
University of Phoenix–Nashville Campus	M
University of Phoenix–New Mexico Campus	M
University of Phoenix–Northern Nevada Campus	M
University of Phoenix–Northern Virginia Campus	M
University of Phoenix–North Florida Campus	M
University of Phoenix–Northwest Arkansas Campus	M
University of Phoenix–Oklahoma City Campus	M
University of Phoenix–Omaha Campus	M
University of Phoenix–Oregon Campus	M
University of Phoenix–Philadelphia Campus	M
University of Phoenix–Phoenix Campus	M
University of Phoenix–Pittsburgh Campus	M
University of Phoenix–Puerto Rico Campus	M
University of Phoenix–Raleigh Campus	M
University of Phoenix–Renton Learning Center	M
University of Phoenix–Richmond Campus	M
University of Phoenix–Sacramento Valley Campus	M
University of Phoenix–St. Louis Campus	M
University of Phoenix–San Antonio Campus	M
University of Phoenix–San Diego Campus	M
University of Phoenix–Savannah Campus	M
University of Phoenix–Southern Arizona Campus	M
University of Phoenix–Southern California Campus	M
University of Phoenix–Southern Colorado Campus	M
University of Phoenix–South Florida Campus	M
University of Phoenix–Springfield Campus	M
University of Phoenix–Tulsa Campus	M
University of Phoenix–Utah Campus	M
University of Phoenix–Vancouver Campus	M
University of Phoenix–West Florida Campus	M
University of Phoenix–West Michigan Campus	M
University of Phoenix–Wichita Campus	M
University of Phoenix–Wisconsin Campus	M
University of Pittsburgh	M,D*
University of Portland	M
University of Puerto Rico, Mayagüez Campus	M
University of Puerto Rico, Río Piedras	M,D
University of Redlands	M
University of Regina	M,O
University of Rhode Island	M,D
University of Richmond	M
University of Rochester	M,D*
University of St. Francis (IL)	M
University of Saint Francis (IN)	M
University of Saint Mary	M
University of St. Thomas (TX)	M
University of St. Thomas (MN)	M*
University of San Diego	M,O
University of San Francisco	M
University of Saskatchewan	M
The University of Scranton	M
University of Sioux Falls	M
University of South Africa	M,D
University of South Alabama	M*
University of South Carolina	M,D
The University of South Dakota	M
University of Southern California	M,D*
University of Southern Indiana	M
University of Southern Maine	M
University of Southern Mississippi	M
University of Southern Nevada	M
University of South Florida	M,D*
The University of Tampa	M
The University of Tennessee	M,D
The University of Tennessee at Chattanooga	M
The University of Tennessee at Martin	M
The University of Texas at Arlington	M,D*
The University of Texas at Austin	M,D
The University of Texas at Brownsville	M
The University of Texas at Dallas	M,D*
The University of Texas at El Paso	M
The University of Texas at San Antonio	M,D*
The University of Texas at Tyler	M
The University of Texas of the Permian Basin	M
The University of Texas–Pan American	M,D
University of the District of Columbia	M
University of the Incarnate Word	M,O
University of the Pacific	M
University of the Sacred Heart	M
University of the Southwest	M
University of the Virgin Islands	M
University of the West	M
The University of Toledo	M,D
University of Toronto	M,D
University of Tulsa	M*
University of Utah	M,D*
University of Vermont	M*
University of Victoria	M
University of Virginia	M,D
University of Washington	M,D*
University of Washington, Bothell	M
University of Waterloo	M
The University of Western Ontario	M,D
University of West Florida	M
University of West Georgia	M
University of Windsor	M
University of Wisconsin–Eau Claire	M
University of Wisconsin–Green Bay	M
University of Wisconsin–La Crosse	M
University of Wisconsin–Madison	M*
University of Wisconsin–Milwaukee	M,D,O
University of Wisconsin–Oshkosh	M
University of Wisconsin–Parkside	M
University of Wisconsin–River Falls	M
University of Wisconsin–Stevens Point	M
University of Wisconsin–Whitewater	M*
University of Wyoming	M
Upper Iowa University	M
Urbana University	M
Ursuline College	M
Utah State University	M
Valdosta State University	M
Valparaiso University	M,O
Vancouver Island University	M
Vanderbilt University	M,D*
Vanguard University of Southern California	M
Villanova University	M*
Virginia College at Birmingham	M
Virginia Commonwealth University	M,O
Virginia International University	M
Virginia Polytechnic Institute and State University	M,D*
Viterbo University	M
Wagner College	M
Wake Forest University	M*
Walden University	M,D
Walsh College of Accountancy and Business Administration	M
Walsh University	M
Warner Pacific College	M
Warner University	M
Washburn University	M
Washington State University	M,D*
Washington State University Tri-Cities	M*
Washington State University Vancouver	M
Washington University in St. Louis	M,D*
Wayland Baptist University	M
Waynesburg University	M,D
Wayne State College	M
Wayne State University	M,D*
Webber International University	M*
Weber State University	M
Webster University	M,D
Wesleyan College	M
Wesley College	M
West Chester University of Pennsylvania	M,O

*M—master's degree; P—first professional degree; D—doctorate; O—other advanced degree; *—Close-Up and/or Announcement or Display in one of the other books in this series*

Western Carolina University	M
Western Connecticut State University	M
Western Governors University	M
Western Illinois University	M
Western International University	M
Western Kentucky University	M
Western Michigan University	M*
Western New England College	M
Western New Mexico University	M
Western Washington University	M
Westminster College (UT)	M,O
West Texas A&M University	M
West Virginia University	M
West Virginia Wesleyan College	M
Wheeling Jesuit University	M
Whitworth University	M
Wichita State University	M*
Widener University	M*
Wilfrid Laurier University	M,D
Wilkes University	M
Willamette University	M
William Carey University	M
William Paterson University of New Jersey	M*
Wilmington University	M
Wingate University	M
Winston-Salem State University	M
Winthrop University	M
Woodbury University	M
Worcester Polytechnic Institute	M,O*
Worcester State College	M
Wright State University	M
Xavier University	M*
Yale University	M,D*
York College of Pennsylvania	M
York University	M,D
Youngstown State University	M,O

BUSINESS EDUCATION

Arkansas State University	M,O
Armstrong Atlantic State University	M
Auburn University	M,D,O*
Ball State University	M*
Bloomsburg University of Pennsylvania	M
Bowling Green State University	M*
Buffalo State College, State University of New York	M
Central Connecticut State University	M,O
Chadron State College	M,O
The College of Saint Rose	M,O*
Drake University	M*
Eastern Kentucky University	M
Emporia State University	M
Florida Agricultural and Mechanical University	M
Georgia Southern University	M
Hofstra University	M*
Inter American University of Puerto Rico, San Germán Campus	M
International College of the Cayman Islands	M
Lehman College of the City University of New York	M
Louisiana State University and Agricultural and Mechanical College	M,D
Louisiana Tech University	M,D
Maryville University of Saint Louis	M,O
Middle Tennessee State University	M
Mississippi College	M,D,O
Nazareth College of Rochester	M
New York University	M,O*
North Carolina State University	M*
Northwestern State University of Louisiana	M
Old Dominion University	M,D
Penn State Harrisburg	M,D
Pontifical Catholic University of Puerto Rico	M,D
Rider University	O*
Robert Morris University	M,D,O
South Carolina State University	M
Southern New Hampshire University	M,O*
State University of New York at Oswego	M
Thomas College	M
The University of British Columbia	M,D
University of Delaware	M,D*
University of Minnesota, Twin Cities Campus	M,D*
University of Missouri–Columbia	M,D,O*
University of South Carolina	M,D
The University of Toledo	M
University of Washington	M,D*
University of West Georgia	M,O
University of Wisconsin–Whitewater	M*
Utah State University	M,D
Wayne State College	M
Wayne State University	M,D,O*
Western Kentucky University	M,O
Wright State University	M

CANADIAN STUDIES

Carleton University	M,D
Collège universitaire de Saint-Boniface	M
Queen's University at Kingston	M,D
Saint Mary's University (Canada)	M
Trent University	M,D
Université de Sherbrooke	M,D
Université du Québec à Chicoutimi	M
University of Lethbridge	M,D
University of Manitoba	M
University of Ottawa	D*
University of Regina	M,D
University of Saskatchewan	M,D

CANCER BIOLOGY/ONCOLOGY

Baylor College of Medicine	D*
Brown University	M,D*
Case Western Reserve University	D*
Dartmouth College	D*
Duke University	D*
Gerstner Sloan-Kettering Graduate School of Biomedical Sciences	D*
Mayo Graduate School	D*
McMaster University	M,D
Medical University of South Carolina	M,D
Meharry Medical College	D
Memorial University of Newfoundland	M,D
New York University	P,M,D*
Northwestern University	D*
Queen's University at Kingston	M,D
Stanford University	D*
State University of New York Upstate Medical University	
Université de Montréal	O
Université Laval	O
University at Buffalo, the State University of New York	D*
University of Alberta	M,D*
The University of Arizona	D*
University of Calgary	M,D
University of California, San Diego	D*
University of Chicago	D*
University of Cincinnati	D
University of Colorado Denver	D*
University of Delaware	M,D*
University of Manitoba	M
University of Maryland, Baltimore	M,D*
University of Massachusetts Worcester	D
University of Miami	D*
University of Minnesota, Twin Cities Campus	D*
University of Nebraska Medical Center	D*
University of Pennsylvania	D*
University of South Florida	D*
The University of Texas Health Science Center at Houston	M,D
The University of Toledo	M,D
University of Utah	M,D*
University of Wisconsin–Madison	D*
Vanderbilt University	M,D*
Wake Forest University	D*
Wayne State University	M,D*
West Virginia University	M,D
Yale University	D*

CARDIOVASCULAR SCIENCES

Albany Medical College	M,D
Baylor College of Medicine	D*
Dartmouth College	D*
Long Island University, C.W. Post Campus	M
Loyola University Chicago	M,O*
McMaster University	M,D
Medical College of Georgia	D
Medical University of South Carolina	M,D
Memorial University of Newfoundland	M,D
Midwestern University, Glendale Campus	M*
Milwaukee School of Engineering	M*
The Ohio State University	M*
Queen's University at Kingston	M,D
Quinnipiac University	M*
State University of New York Upstate Medical University	
Université Laval	O
University of Calgary	M,D
University of California, San Diego	D*
University of Guelph	M,D,O
University of Medicine and Dentistry of New Jersey	M,D*
The University of South Dakota	M,D
The University of Toledo	M,D

CELL BIOLOGY

Albany Medical College	M,D
Albert Einstein College of Medicine	D
Appalachian State University	M
Arizona State University	M,D
Auburn University	M,D*
Baylor College of Medicine	D*
Boston University	M,D*
Brandeis University	M,D
Brown University	M,D*
California Institute of Technology	D*
Carnegie Mellon University	M,D*
Case Western Reserve University	M,D*
The Catholic University of America	M,D
Colorado State University	M,D*
Columbia University	M,D*
Cornell University	M,D*
Cornell University, Joan and Sanford I. Weill Medical College and Graduate School of Medical Sciences	M,D
Dartmouth College	D*
Drexel University	M,D*
Duke University	D,O*
East Carolina University	D
Eastern Michigan University	M
Emory University	D*
Emporia State University	M
Florida Institute of Technology	M,D*
Florida State University	M,D*
George Mason University	M,D,O*
Georgetown University	D
Georgia State University	M,D
Grand Valley State University	M
Harvard University	D*
Illinois State University	M,D
Indiana University Bloomington	M,D*
Indiana University–Purdue University Indianapolis	M,D*
Iowa State University of Science and Technology	M,D*
The Johns Hopkins University	D*
Kent State University	M,D*
Louisiana State University Health Sciences Center	M,D*
Louisiana State University Health Sciences Center at Shreveport	M,D*
Loyola University Chicago	M,D*
Marquette University	M,D
Massachusetts Institute of Technology	D*
Mayo Graduate School	D*
McGill University	M,D*
McMaster University	M,D
Medical College of Georgia	D
Medical College of Wisconsin	D*
Medical University of South Carolina	M,D
Michigan State University	M,D*
Missouri State University	M*
New York Medical College	M,D*
New York University	P,M,D*
North Carolina State University	M,D*
North Dakota State University	M,D
Northwestern University	D*
The Ohio State University	M,D*
Ohio University	M,D*
Oregon Health & Science University	D*
Oregon State University	M,D*
Penn State Hershey Medical Center	M,D

Penn State University Park	M,D*
Purdue University	M,D
Queen's University at Kingston	M,D
Quinnipiac University	M*
Rensselaer Polytechnic Institute	M,D
Rice University	M,D
Rush University	M,D
Rutgers, The State University of New Jersey, New Brunswick	M,D*
San Diego State University	M,D
San Francisco State University	M
State University of New York Downstate Medical Center	D*
State University of New York Upstate Medical University	M,D
Stony Brook University, State University of New York	M,D
Temple University	M,D*
Texas A&M Health Science Center	D
Texas A&M University	M,D*
Texas Tech University Health Sciences Center	M,D
Thomas Jefferson University	D*
Tufts University	D*
Tulane University	M,D
Uniformed Services University of the Health Sciences	D*
Universidad Central del Caribe	M
Université de Montréal	M,D
Université de Sherbrooke	M,D
Université Laval	M,D
University at Albany, State University of New York	M,D*
University at Buffalo, the State University of New York	D*
The University of Alabama at Birmingham	D*
University of Alberta	M,D*
The University of Arizona	M,D*
University of Arkansas	M,D
The University of British Columbia	M,D
University of California, Berkeley	D*
University of California, Davis	M,D*
University of California, Irvine	M,D*
University of California, Los Angeles	D*
University of California, Riverside	M,D*
University of California, San Diego	D*
University of California, San Francisco	D
University of California, Santa Barbara	M,D
University of California, Santa Cruz	M,D*
University of Chicago	D*
University of Cincinnati	D
University of Colorado at Boulder	M,D*
University of Colorado Denver	D*
University of Connecticut	M,D*
University of Connecticut Health Center	D*
University of Delaware	M,D*
University of Florida	M,D*
University of Georgia	M,D*
University of Guelph	M,D
University of Illinois at Chicago	D*
University of Illinois at Urbana–Champaign	D*
The University of Iowa	M,D*
The University of Kansas	M,D*
University of Maryland, Baltimore	M,D*
University of Maryland, Baltimore County	D*
University of Maryland, College Park	M,D*
University of Massachusetts Amherst	D*
University of Massachusetts Boston	D
University of Massachusetts Worcester	D
University of Medicine and Dentistry of New Jersey	M,D*
University of Miami	D*
University of Michigan	M,D*
University of Minnesota, Twin Cities Campus	M,D*
University of Missouri–Columbia	M,D*
University of Missouri–Kansas City	D*
University of Missouri–St. Louis	M,D,O
University of Nebraska Medical Center	M,D*
University of Nevada, Reno	M,D*
University of New Haven	M*
University of New Mexico	M,D*
The University of North Carolina at Chapel Hill	D*
University of Notre Dame	M,D*
University of Oklahoma Health Sciences Center	M,D
University of Ottawa	M,D*
University of Pennsylvania	D*
University of Pittsburgh	M,D*
University of Rhode Island	M,D
University of Saskatchewan	M,D
University of South Alabama	D*
University of South Carolina	M,D
The University of South Dakota	M,D
University of Southern California	M,D*
University of South Florida	M,D*
The University of Texas at Austin	D
The University of Texas at Dallas	M,D*
The University of Texas at San Antonio	M,D*
The University of Texas Health Science Center at Houston	M,D
The University of Texas Health Science Center at San Antonio	M,D
The University of Texas Medical Branch	D*
The University of Texas Southwestern Medical Center at Dallas	D*
University of the Sciences in Philadelphia	M,D*
University of Toronto	M,D
University of Vermont	M,D*
University of Virginia	D
University of Washington	D*
The University of Western Ontario	M,D
University of Wisconsin–La Crosse	M
University of Wisconsin–Madison	D*
University of Wyoming	D
Vanderbilt University	M,D*
Washington State University	M,D*
Washington University in St. Louis	D*
Wesleyan University	D*
West Virginia University	M,D
Yale University	D*

CELTIC LANGUAGES

Harvard University	D*

CERAMIC SCIENCES AND ENGINEERING

Alfred University	M,D*
Case Western Reserve University	M,D*
Missouri University of Science and Technology	M,D
Rensselaer Polytechnic Institute	M,D
University of Cincinnati	M,D

CHEMICAL ENGINEERING

American University of Sharjah	M
Arizona State University	M,D
Auburn University	M,D*
Brigham Young University	M,D*
Brown University	M,D*
Bucknell University	M
California Institute of Technology	M,D*
Carnegie Mellon University	M,D*
Case Western Reserve University	M,D*
City College of the City University of New York	M,D*
Clarkson University	M,D*
Clemson University	M,D
Cleveland State University	M,D
Colorado School of Mines	M,D
Colorado State University	M,D*
Columbia University	M,D*
Cooper Union for the Advancement of Science and Art	M
Cornell University	M,D*
Dalhousie University	M,D
Drexel University	M,D*
École Polytechnique de Montréal	M,D,O
Fairleigh Dickinson University, College at Florham	M,O*
Florida Agricultural and Mechanical University	M,D
Florida Institute of Technology	M,D*
Florida State University	M,D*
Georgia Institute of Technology	M,D*
Graduate School and University Center of the City University of New York	D*
Howard University	M
Illinois Institute of Technology	M,D*
Instituto Tecnológico y de Estudios Superiores de Monterrey, Campus Monterrey	M,D
Iowa State University of Science and Technology	M,D*
The Johns Hopkins University	M,D*
Kansas State University	M,D*
Lamar University	M,D
Lehigh University	M,D
Louisiana State University and Agricultural and Mechanical College	M,D
Louisiana Tech University	M,D
Manhattan College	M
Massachusetts Institute of Technology	M,D*
McGill University	M,D*
McMaster University	M,D
McNeese State University	M
Michigan State University	M,D*
Michigan Technological University	M,D
Mississippi State University	M,D
Missouri University of Science and Technology	M,D
Montana State University	M,D
New Jersey Institute of Technology	M,D
New Mexico State University	M,D
North Carolina Agricultural and Technical State University	M,D
North Carolina State University	M,D*
Northeastern University	M,D*
Northwestern University	M,D*
The Ohio State University	M,D*
Ohio University	M,D*
Oklahoma State University	M,D*
Oregon State University	M,D*
Penn State University Park	M,D*
Polytechnic Institute of NYU	M,D
Polytechnic Institute of NYU, Long Island Graduate Center	M,D
Polytechnic Institute of NYU, Westchester Graduate Center	M
Princeton University	M,D*
Purdue University	M,D
Queen's University at Kingston	M,D
Rensselaer Polytechnic Institute	M,D
Rice University	M,D
Rose-Hulman Institute of Technology	M*
Royal Military College of Canada	M,D
Rutgers, The State University of New Jersey, New Brunswick	M,D*
San Jose State University	M
South Dakota School of Mines and Technology	M*
Stanford University	M,D,O*
Stevens Institute of Technology	M,D,O
Syracuse University	M*
Tennessee Technological University	M,D*
Texas A&M University	M,D*
Texas A&M University–Kingsville	M
Texas Tech University	M,D
Tufts University	M,D*
Tulane University	D
Universidad de las Américas–Puebla	M
Université de Sherbrooke	M,D
Université Laval	M,D
University at Buffalo, the State University of New York	M,D*
The University of Akron	M,D
The University of Alabama	M,D
The University of Alabama in Huntsville	M
University of Alberta	M,D*
The University of Arizona	M,D*
University of Arkansas	M,D*
The University of British Columbia	M,D
University of Calgary	M,D
University of California, Berkeley	M,D*
University of California, Davis	M,D*
University of California, Irvine	M,D*
University of California, Los Angeles	M,D*
University of California, Riverside	M,D*

*M—master's degree; P—first professional degree; D—doctorate; O—other advanced degree; *—Close-Up and/or Announcement or Display in one of the other books in this series*

University of California, San Diego	M,D*
University of California, Santa Barbara	M,D
University of Cincinnati	M,D
University of Colorado at Boulder	M,D*
University of Connecticut	M,D*
University of Dayton	M
University of Delaware	M,D*
University of Florida	M,D*
University of Houston	M,D*
University of Idaho	M,D
University of Illinois at Chicago	M,D*
University of Illinois at Urbana–Champaign	M,D*
The University of Iowa	M,D*
The University of Kansas	M,D*
University of Kentucky	M,D
University of Louisiana at Lafayette	M*
University of Louisville	M,D
University of Maine	M,D*
University of Maryland, Baltimore County	M,D,O*
University of Maryland, College Park	M,D,O*
University of Massachusetts Amherst	M,D*
University of Massachusetts Lowell	M,D
University of Michigan	M,D,O*
University of Minnesota, Twin Cities Campus	M,D*
University of Missouri–Columbia	M,D*
University of Nebraska–Lincoln	M,D*
University of Nevada, Reno	M,D*
University of New Brunswick Fredericton	M,D
University of New Hampshire	M,D*
University of New Mexico	M,D*
University of North Dakota	M
University of Notre Dame	M,D*
University of Oklahoma	M,D*
University of Ottawa	M,D*
University of Pennsylvania	M,D*
University of Pittsburgh	M,D*
University of Puerto Rico, Mayagüez Campus	M,D
University of Rhode Island	M,D
University of Rochester	M,D*
University of Saskatchewan	M,D
University of South Africa	M
University of South Alabama	M*
University of South Carolina	M,D
University of Southern California	M,D,O*
University of South Florida	M,D*
The University of Tennessee	M,D
The University of Tennessee at Chattanooga	M
The University of Texas at Austin	M,D
The University of Toledo	M,D
University of Toronto	M,D
University of Tulsa	M,D*
University of Utah	M,D*
University of Virginia	M,D
University of Washington	M,D*
University of Waterloo	M,D
The University of Western Ontario	M,D
University of Wisconsin–Madison	M,D*
University of Wyoming	M,D
Vanderbilt University	M,D*
Villanova University	M*
Virginia Commonwealth University	M,D
Virginia Polytechnic Institute and State University	M,D*
Washington State University	M,D*
Washington University in St. Louis	M,D*
Wayne State University	M,D*
Western Michigan University	M,D*
West Virginia University	M,D
Widener University	M*
Worcester Polytechnic Institute	M,D*
Yale University	M,D*

CHEMICAL PHYSICS

Columbia University	M,D*
Cornell University	D*
Harvard University	D*
Kent State University	M,D*
Marquette University	M,D
McMaster University	M,D
Michigan State University	M,D*
The Ohio State University	M,D*
Simon Fraser University	M,D
University of Colorado at Boulder	M,D*
University of Illinois at Urbana–Champaign	M,D*
University of Louisville	M,D
University of Maryland, College Park	M,D*
University of Nevada, Reno	D*
University of Southern California	D*
The University of Tennessee	M,D
University of Utah	M,D*
Virginia Commonwealth University	M,D
Wesleyan University	M,D*
West Virginia University	M,D

CHEMISTRY

Acadia University	M
American University	M*
American University of Beirut	M
Arizona State University	M,D
Arkansas State University	M,O
Auburn University	M,D*
Ball State University	M*
Baylor University	M,D
Boston College	M,D*
Boston University	M,D*
Bowling Green State University	M,D*
Bradley University	M
Brandeis University	M,D
Brigham Young University	M,D*
Brock University	M,D
Brooklyn College of the City University of New York	M,D
Brown University	M,D*
Bryn Mawr College	M,D
Bucknell University	M
Buffalo State College, State University of New York	M
California Institute of Technology	M,D*
California Polytechnic State University, San Luis Obispo	M
California State Polytechnic University, Pomona	M
California State University, East Bay	M
California State University, Fresno	M
California State University, Fullerton	M
California State University, Long Beach	M
California State University, Los Angeles	M
California State University, Northridge	M
California State University, Sacramento	M
California State University, San Bernardino	M
Carleton University	M,D
Carnegie Mellon University	M,D*
Case Western Reserve University	M,D*
The Catholic University of America	M
Central Connecticut State University	M
Central Michigan University	M
Central Washington University	M
City College of the City University of New York	M,D*
Clark Atlanta University	M,D
Clarkson University	M,D*
Clark University	M,D
Clemson University	M,D
Cleveland State University	M,D
The College of William and Mary	M
Colorado School of Mines	M,D
Colorado State University	M,D*
Colorado State University–Pueblo	M
Columbia University	M,D*
Concordia University (Canada)	M,D
Cornell University	D*
Dalhousie University	M,D
Dartmouth College	D*
Delaware State University	M
DePaul University	M*
Drexel University	M,D*
Duke University	D*
Duquesne University	M,D*
East Carolina University	M
Eastern Illinois University	M
Eastern Kentucky University	M
Eastern Michigan University	M
Eastern New Mexico University	M
East Tennessee State University	M
Emory University	D*
Fairleigh Dickinson University, College at Florham	M*
Fairleigh Dickinson University, Metropolitan Campus	M*
Fisk University	M
Florida Agricultural and Mechanical University	M
Florida Atlantic University	M,D
Florida Institute of Technology	M,D*
Florida International University	M,D*
Florida State University	M,D*
Furman University	M
George Mason University	M*
Georgetown University	D
The George Washington University	M,D*
Georgia Institute of Technology	M,D*
Georgia State University	M,D
Graduate School and University Center of the City University of New York	D*
Hampton University	M
Harvard University	D*
Howard University	M,D
Hunter College of the City University of New York	M,D
Idaho State University	M
Illinois Institute of Technology	M,D*
Illinois State University	M
Indiana University Bloomington	M,D*
Indiana University of Pennsylvania	M
Indiana University–Purdue University Indianapolis	M,D*
Instituto Tecnológico y de Estudios Superiores de Monterrey, Campus Monterrey	M,D
Iowa State University of Science and Technology	M,D*
Jackson State University	M,D
The Johns Hopkins University	D*
Kansas State University	M,D*
Kent State University	M,D*
Lakehead University	M
Lamar University	M
Laurentian University	M
Lehigh University	M,D
Long Island University, Brooklyn Campus	M
Louisiana State University and Agricultural and Mechanical College	M,D
Louisiana Tech University	M
Loyola University Chicago	M,D*
Marquette University	M,D
Marshall University	M
Massachusetts College of Pharmacy and Health Sciences	M,D*
Massachusetts Institute of Technology	D*
McGill University	M,D*
McMaster University	M,D
McNeese State University	M
Memorial University of Newfoundland	M,D
Miami University	M,D*
Michigan State University	M,D*
Michigan Technological University	M,D
Middle Tennessee State University	M,D
Mississippi College	M
Mississippi State University	M,D
Missouri State University	M*
Missouri University of Science and Technology	M,D
Montana State University	M,D
Montclair State University	M*
Morgan State University	M
Mount Allison University	M
Murray State University	M
New Jersey Institute of Technology	M,D
New Mexico Highlands University	M
New Mexico Institute of Mining and Technology	M,D
New Mexico State University	M,D
New York University	M,D*
North Carolina Agricultural and Technical State University	M
North Carolina Central University	M
North Carolina State University	M,D*
North Dakota State University	M,D
Northeastern Illinois University	M
Northeastern University	M,D*
Northern Arizona University	M
Northern Illinois University	M,D
Northwestern University	D*
Oakland University	M,D
The Ohio State University	M,D*
Oklahoma State University	M,D*
Old Dominion University	M,D

Oregon State University	M,D*
Penn State University Park	M,D*
Pittsburg State University	M
Polytechnic Institute of NYU	M,D
Polytechnic Institute of NYU, Long Island Graduate Center	M,D
Polytechnic Institute of NYU, Westchester Graduate Center	M
Pontifical Catholic University of Puerto Rico	M
Portland State University	M,D
Prairie View A&M University	M
Princeton University	M,D*
Purdue University	M,D
Queens College of the City University of New York	M
Queen's University at Kingston	M,D
Rensselaer Polytechnic Institute	M,D
Rice University	M,D
Rochester Institute of Technology	M
Roosevelt University	M
Royal Military College of Canada	M,D
Rutgers, The State University of New Jersey, Camden	M
Rutgers, The State University of New Jersey, Newark	M,D*
Rutgers, The State University of New Jersey, New Brunswick	M,D*
Sacred Heart University	M
St. Francis Xavier University	M
St. John's University (NY)	M
Saint Joseph College	M
Saint Louis University	M,D
Sam Houston State University	M
San Diego State University	M,D*
San Francisco State University	M
San Jose State University	M
Seton Hall University	M,D*
Simon Fraser University	M,D
Smith College	M
South Dakota School of Mines and Technology	M*
South Dakota State University	M,D
Southeast Missouri State University	M
Southern Connecticut State University	M
Southern Illinois University Carbondale	M,D*
Southern Illinois University Edwardsville	M
Southern Methodist University	M,D*
Southern University and Agricultural and Mechanical College	M
Stanford University	D*
State University of New York at Binghamton	M,D*
State University of New York at Fredonia	M
State University of New York at Oswego	M
State University of New York College of Environmental Science and Forestry	M,D
Stephen F. Austin State University	M
Stevens Institute of Technology	M,D,O
Stony Brook University, State University of New York	M,D
Syracuse University	M,D*
Temple University	M,D*
Tennessee State University	M
Tennessee Technological University	M*
Texas A&M University	M,D*
Texas A&M University–Commerce	M
Texas A&M University–Kingsville	M
Texas Christian University	M,D
Texas Southern University	M
Texas State University–San Marcos	M*
Texas Tech University	M,D
Texas Woman's University	M
Trent University	M
Tufts University	M,D*
Tulane University	M,D
Tuskegee University	M
Université de Moncton	M
Université de Montréal	M,D
Université de Sherbrooke	M,D,O
Université du Québec à Montréal	M,D
Université du Québec à Trois-Rivières	M
Université Laval	M,D
University at Albany, State University of New York	M,D*
University at Buffalo, the State University of New York	M,D*
The University of Akron	M,D
The University of Alabama	M,D
The University of Alabama at Birmingham	M,D*
The University of Alabama in Huntsville	M
University of Alaska Fairbanks	M,D
University of Alberta	M,D*
The University of Arizona	M,D*
University of Arkansas	M,D
University of Arkansas at Little Rock	M
The University of British Columbia	M,D
University of Calgary	M,D
University of California, Berkeley	D*
University of California, Davis	M,D*
University of California, Irvine	M,D*
University of California, Los Angeles	M,D*
University of California, Riverside	M,D*
University of California, San Diego	M,D*
University of California, San Francisco	D
University of California, Santa Barbara	M,D
University of California, Santa Cruz	M,D*
University of Central Florida	M,D,O*
University of Central Oklahoma	M
University of Chicago	D*
University of Cincinnati	M,D
University of Colorado at Boulder	M,D*
University of Colorado at Colorado Springs	M
University of Colorado Denver	M*
University of Connecticut	M,D*
University of Dayton	M
University of Delaware	M,D*
University of Denver	M,D*
University of Detroit Mercy	M
University of Florida	M,D*
University of Georgia	M,D*
University of Guelph	M,D
University of Hawaii at Manoa	M,D*
University of Houston	M,D*
University of Houston–Clear Lake	M
University of Idaho	M,D
University of Illinois at Chicago	M,D*
University of Illinois at Urbana–Champaign	M,D*
The University of Iowa	M,D*
The University of Kansas	M,D*
University of Kentucky	M,D
University of Lethbridge	M,D
University of Louisville	M,D
University of Maine	M,D*
University of Manitoba	M,D
University of Maryland, Baltimore County	M,D*
University of Maryland, College Park	M,D*
University of Massachusetts Amherst	M,D*
University of Massachusetts Boston	M
University of Massachusetts Dartmouth	M,D
University of Massachusetts Lowell	M,D
University of Memphis	M,D
University of Miami	M,D*
University of Michigan	D*
University of Minnesota, Duluth	M
University of Minnesota, Twin Cities Campus	M,D*
University of Mississippi	M,D
University of Missouri–Columbia	M,D*
University of Missouri–Kansas City	M,D*
University of Missouri–St. Louis	M,D
The University of Montana	M,D
University of Nebraska–Lincoln	M,D*
University of Nevada, Las Vegas	M,D
University of Nevada, Reno	M,D*
University of New Brunswick Fredericton	M,D
University of New Hampshire	M,D*
University of New Mexico	M,D*
University of New Orleans	M,D
The University of North Carolina at Chapel Hill	M,D*
The University of North Carolina at Charlotte	M*
The University of North Carolina at Greensboro	M
The University of North Carolina Wilmington	M
University of North Dakota	M,D
University of Northern Colorado	M,D
University of Northern Iowa	M
University of North Texas	M,D
University of Notre Dame	M,D*
University of Oklahoma	M,D*
University of Oregon	M,D*
University of Ottawa	M,D*
University of Pennsylvania	M,D*
University of Pittsburgh	M,D*
University of Prince Edward Island	M
University of Puerto Rico, Mayagüez Campus	M,D
University of Puerto Rico, Río Piedras	M,D
University of Regina	M,D
University of Rhode Island	M,D
University of Rochester	M,D*
University of San Francisco	M
University of Saskatchewan	M,D
The University of Scranton	M
University of South Carolina	M,D
The University of South Dakota	M,D
University of Southern California	M,D*
University of Southern Mississippi	M,D
University of South Florida	M,D*
The University of Tennessee	M,D
The University of Texas at Arlington	M,D*
The University of Texas at Austin	M,D
The University of Texas at Dallas	M,D*
The University of Texas at El Paso	M,D
The University of Texas at San Antonio	M,D*
The University of Texas–Pan American	M
University of the Sciences in Philadelphia	M,D*
The University of Toledo	M,D
University of Toronto	M,D
University of Tulsa	M,D*
University of Utah	M,D*
University of Vermont	M,D*
University of Victoria	M,D
University of Virginia	M,D
University of Washington	M,D*
University of Waterloo	M,D
The University of Western Ontario	M,D
University of Windsor	M,D
University of Wisconsin–Madison	M,D*
University of Wisconsin–Milwaukee	M,D
University of Wyoming	M,D
Utah State University	M,D
Vanderbilt University	M,D*
Vassar College	M
Villanova University	M*
Virginia Commonwealth University	M,D
Virginia Polytechnic Institute and State University	M,D*
Wake Forest University	M,D*
Washington State University	M,D*
Washington State University Tri-Cities	M
Washington University in St. Louis	D*
Wayne State University	M,D*
Wesleyan University	M,D*
West Chester University of Pennsylvania	M
Western Carolina University	M
Western Illinois University	M
Western Kentucky University	M
Western Michigan University	M,D*
Western Washington University	M
West Texas A&M University	M
West Virginia University	M,D
Wichita State University	M,D*
Wilfrid Laurier University	M
Worcester Polytechnic Institute	M,D*
Wright State University	M
Yale University	D*

*M—master's degree; P—first professional degree; D—doctorate; O—other advanced degree; *—Close-Up and/or Announcement or Display in one of the other books in this series*

York University M,D
Youngstown State University M

CHILD AND FAMILY STUDIES

Arizona State University M,D
Assumption College M,O
Auburn University M,D*
Bank Street College of Education M*
Bowling Green State University M*
Brandeis University M,D
Brigham Young University M,D*
Brock University M
California State University, Los Angeles M
Capella University M,D,O
Central Michigan University M,O
Central Washington University M
Colorado State University M*
Concordia University (Canada) M
Concordia University, St. Paul M,O
Concordia University Wisconsin M
Cornell University D*
East Carolina University M
Eastern Michigan University M,O
Florida State University M,D*
Indiana University Bloomington M,D*
Indiana University–Purdue University Indianapolis M*
Iowa State University of Science and Technology M,D*
Kansas State University M,D*
Loma Linda University M,D,O
Miami University M*
Michigan State University M,D*
Middle Tennessee State University M
Missouri State University M*
Mount Saint Vincent University M
North Dakota State University M,D
Northern Illinois University M
Nova Southeastern University M,D*
The Ohio State University M,D*
Ohio University M*
Oklahoma State University M,D*
Oregon State University M,D*
Oxford Graduate School M,D
Penn State University Park M,D*
Purdue University M,D
Roberts Wesleyan College M
Sage Graduate School M
St. Cloud State University M
Saint Joseph College M
San Diego State University M*
San Jose State University M
South Carolina State University M
Spring Arbor University M
Stanford University D*
State University of New York at Oswego M
Syracuse University M,D*
Texas State University–San Marcos M*
Texas Tech University M,D
Texas Woman's University M,D
Towson University O
Tufts University M,D,O*
The University of Akron M
The University of Alabama M
The University of Arizona M,D*
University of California, Santa Barbara M,D
University of Central Florida M,O*
University of Connecticut M,D,O*
University of Delaware M,D*
University of Denver M,D,O*
University of Georgia M,D,O*
University of Guelph M,D
University of Illinois at Springfield M
University of Kentucky M,D
University of La Verne M
University of Manitoba M
University of Maryland, College Park M,D*
University of Massachusetts Amherst M,D,O*
University of Minnesota, Twin Cities Campus M,D*
University of Missouri–Columbia M,D*
University of Nevada, Reno M*
University of New Hampshire M*
University of New Mexico M,D*
The University of North Carolina at Greensboro M,D
University of North Texas M,O
University of Rhode Island M
University of Southern California M,D*
University of Southern Mississippi M
The University of Tennessee M,D
The University of Tennessee at Martin M
The University of Texas at Austin M,D
The University of Texas at Dallas M,D*
University of Utah M*
University of Victoria M,D
University of Wisconsin–Madison M,D*
University of Wisconsin–Stout M
Utah State University M,D
Vanderbilt University M*
Virginia Polytechnic Institute and State University M,D*
Walden University M,D
Wayne State University O*
West Virginia University M
Wheelock College M

CHILD DEVELOPMENT

American International College M,D,O
Appalachian State University M
Arcadia University M,D,O
California State University, Los Angeles M
California State University, San Bernardino M
California State University, Stanislaus M,O
East Carolina University M
Erikson Institute M
Michigan State University M,D*
Middle Tennessee State University M
North Dakota State University M,D
Ohio University M*
Purdue University M,D
Rutgers, The State University of New Jersey, Camden M,D
San Diego State University M*
Sarah Lawrence College M*
Southern New Hampshire University M,O*
Texas Woman's University M,D
Tufts University M,D,O*
The University of Akron M
University of California, Davis M*
University of La Verne M
University of Minnesota, Twin Cities Campus M,D*
University of Nebraska–Lincoln M,D*
The University of North Carolina at Charlotte M,D*
The University of Tennessee at Martin M
The University of Texas at Austin M,D
University of Wyoming M
Virginia Polytechnic Institute and State University M,D*
Whittier College M

CHINESE

Arizona State University M
Cornell University M,D*
Harvard University D*
Indiana University Bloomington M,D*
Middlebury College M
The Ohio State University M,D*
San Francisco State University M
Seton Hall University M*
Stanford University M,D*
University of Alberta M*
University of California, Berkeley D*
University of California, Irvine M,D*
University of Colorado at Boulder M,D*
University of Hawaii at Manoa M,D,O*
University of Massachusetts Amherst M*
University of Oregon M,D*
University of Washington M,D*
University of Wisconsin–Madison M,D*
Washington University in St. Louis M,D*

CHIROPRACTIC

Canadian Memorial Chiropractic College P,O
Cleveland Chiropractic College–Kansas City Campus P*
Cleveland Chiropractic College–Los Angeles Campus P*
D'Youville College P*
Institut Franco-Européen de Chiropratique P
Life Chiropractic College West P
Life University P
Logan University–College of Chiropractic P,M
National University of Health Sciences P,M,D*
New York Chiropractic College P*
Northwestern Health Sciences University P
Palmer College of Chiropractic P
Parker College of Chiropractic P
Sherman College of Straight Chiropractic P
Southern California University of Health Sciences P
Texas Chiropractic College P
Université du Québec à Trois-Rivières P
University of Bridgeport P
Western States Chiropractic College P

CIVIL ENGINEERING

American University of Beirut M,D
American University of Sharjah M
Arizona State University M,D
Auburn University M,D*
Boise State University M
Bradley University M
Brigham Young University M,D*
Bucknell University M
California Institute of Technology M,D,O*
California Polytechnic State University, San Luis Obispo M
California State Polytechnic University, Pomona M
California State University, Fresno M
California State University, Fullerton M
California State University, Long Beach M
California State University, Los Angeles M
California State University, Northridge M
California State University, Sacramento M
Carleton University M,D
Case Western Reserve University M,D*
The Catholic University of America M,D,O
City College of the City University of New York M,D*
Clarkson University M,D*
Clemson University M,D
Cleveland State University M,D
Colorado State University M,D*
Columbia University M,D,O*
Concordia University (Canada) M,D,O
Cooper Union for the Advancement of Science and Art M
Cornell University M,D*
Dalhousie University M,D
Drexel University M,D*
Duke University M,D*
École Polytechnique de Montréal M,D,O
Florida Agricultural and Mechanical University M,D
Florida Atlantic University M
Florida Institute of Technology M,D*
Florida International University M,D*
Florida State University M,D*
George Mason University M*
The George Washington University M,D,O*
Georgia Institute of Technology M,D*
Graduate School and University Center of the City University of New York D*
Howard University M
Idaho State University M
Illinois Institute of Technology M,D*
Instituto Tecnológico y de Estudios Superiores de Monterrey, Campus Monterrey M,D
Iowa State University of Science and Technology M,D*
The Johns Hopkins University M,D*
Kansas State University M,D*

Lamar University M,D
Lawrence Technological University M,D
Lehigh University M,D
Louisiana State University and Agricultural and Mechanical College M,D
Louisiana Tech University M,D
Loyola Marymount University M
Manhattan College M
Marquette University M,D
Massachusetts Institute of Technology M,D,O*
McGill University M,D*
McMaster University M,D
McNeese State University M
Memorial University of Newfoundland M,D
Michigan State University M,D*
Michigan Technological University M,D
Mississippi State University M,D
Missouri University of Science and Technology M,D
Montana State University M,D
Morgan State University M,D
New Jersey Institute of Technology M,D
New Mexico State University M,D
North Carolina Agricultural and Technical State University M
North Carolina State University M,D*
North Dakota State University M,D
Northeastern University M,D*
Northern Arizona University M
Northwestern University M,D*
Norwich University M
The Ohio State University M,D*
Ohio University M,D*
Oklahoma State University M,D*
Old Dominion University M,D
Oregon State University M,D*
Penn State University Park M,D*
Polytechnic Institute of NYU M,D
Polytechnic Institute of NYU, Long Island Graduate Center M,D
Polytechnic University of Puerto Rico M
Polytechnic University of the Americas–Orlando Campus M
Portland State University M,D,O
Princeton University M,D*
Purdue University M,D
Queen's University at Kingston M,D
Rensselaer Polytechnic Institute M,D
Rice University M,D
Rose-Hulman Institute of Technology M*
Royal Military College of Canada M,D
Rutgers, The State University of New Jersey, New Brunswick M,D*
Saint Martin's University M
San Diego State University M*
San Jose State University M
Santa Clara University M
South Carolina State University M
South Dakota School of Mines and Technology M*
South Dakota State University M
Southern Illinois University Carbondale M*
Southern Illinois University Edwardsville M
Southern Methodist University M,D*
Stanford University M,D,O*
Stevens Institute of Technology M,D,O
Syracuse University M,D*
Temple University M*
Tennessee Technological University M,D*
Texas A&M University M,D*
Texas A&M University–Kingsville M
Texas Tech University M,D
Trine University M
Tufts University M,D*
Université de Moncton M
Université de Sherbrooke M,D
Université Laval M,D,O
University at Buffalo, the State University of New York M,D*
The University of Akron M,D
The University of Alabama M,D
The University of Alabama at Birmingham M,D*
The University of Alabama in Huntsville M,D
University of Alaska Anchorage M,O
University of Alaska Fairbanks M,D
University of Alberta M,D*
The University of Arizona M,D*
University of Arkansas M,D
The University of British Columbia M,D
University of Calgary M,D
University of California, Berkeley M,D*
University of California, Davis M,D,O*
University of California, Irvine M,D*
University of California, Los Angeles M,D*
University of Central Florida M,D,O*
University of Cincinnati M,D
University of Colorado at Boulder M,D*
University of Colorado Denver M,D*
University of Connecticut M,D*
University of Dayton M
University of Delaware M,D*
University of Detroit Mercy M,D
University of Florida M,D,O*
University of Hawaii at Manoa M,D*
University of Houston M,D*
University of Idaho M,D
University of Illinois at Chicago M,D*
University of Illinois at Urbana–Champaign M,D*
The University of Iowa M,D*
The University of Kansas M,D*
University of Kentucky M,D
University of Louisiana at Lafayette M*
University of Louisville M,D
University of Maine M,D*
University of Manitoba M,D
University of Maryland, Baltimore County M,D*
University of Maryland, College Park M,D,O*
University of Massachusetts Amherst M,D*
University of Massachusetts Dartmouth M
University of Massachusetts Lowell M,D,O
University of Memphis M,D
University of Miami M,D*
University of Michigan M,D,O*
University of Minnesota, Twin Cities Campus M,D*
University of Missouri–Columbia M,D*
University of Missouri–Kansas City M,D*
University of Nebraska–Lincoln M,D*
University of Nevada, Las Vegas M,D
University of Nevada, Reno M,D*
University of New Brunswick Fredericton M,D
University of New Hampshire M,D*
University of New Mexico M,D*
The University of North Carolina at Charlotte M,D*
University of North Dakota M
University of Notre Dame M,D*
University of Oklahoma M,D*
University of Ottawa M,D*
University of Pittsburgh M,D*
University of Puerto Rico, Mayagüez Campus M,D
University of Rhode Island M,D
University of Saskatchewan M,D
University of South Alabama M*
University of South Carolina M,D
University of Southern California M,D,O*
University of South Florida M,D*
The University of Tennessee M,D
The University of Tennessee at Chattanooga M
The University of Texas at Arlington M,D*
The University of Texas at Austin M,D
The University of Texas at El Paso M,D
The University of Texas at San Antonio M,D*
The University of Texas at Tyler M
The University of Toledo M,D
University of Toronto M,D
University of Utah M,D*
University of Vermont M,D*
University of Virginia M,D
University of Washington M,D*
University of Waterloo M,D
The University of Western Ontario M,D
University of Windsor M,D
University of Wisconsin–Madison M,D*
University of Wisconsin–Milwaukee M,D,O
University of Wyoming M,D
Utah State University M,D,O
Vanderbilt University M,D*
Villanova University M*
Virginia Polytechnic Institute and State University M,D*
Washington State University M,D*
Wayne State University M,D*
Western Michigan University M*
West Virginia University M,D
Widener University M*
Woods Hole Oceanographic Institution M,D,O
Worcester Polytechnic Institute M,D,O*
Youngstown State University M

CLASSICS

Boston College M*
Boston University M,D*
Brandeis University M,O
Brock University M
Brown University M,D*
Bryn Mawr College M,D*
The Catholic University of America M,D
Columbia University M,D*
Cornell University D*
Dalhousie University M,D
Duke University D*
Florida State University M,D*
Fordham University M,D*
Graduate School and University Center of the City University of New York M,D*
Harvard University D*
Heritage Christian University M
Hunter College of the City University of New York M
Indiana University Bloomington M,D*
The Johns Hopkins University D*
Kent State University M,D*
Marshall University M
McMaster University M,D
Memorial University of Newfoundland M
New York University M,D,O*
The Ohio State University M,D*
Princeton University D*
Queen's University at Kingston M
Rutgers, The State University of New Jersey, New Brunswick M,D*
San Francisco State University M
Stanford University M,D*
Texas Tech University M
Tufts University M*
Tulane University M
University at Buffalo, the State University of New York M,D*
University of Alberta M,D*
The University of Arizona M*
The University of British Columbia M,D
University of Calgary M,D
University of California, Berkeley M,D*
University of California, Irvine M,D*
University of California, Los Angeles M,D*
University of California, Riverside D*
University of California, Santa Barbara M,D
University of Chicago M,D*
University of Cincinnati M,D
University of Colorado at Boulder M,D*
University of Florida M,D*
University of Georgia M*
University of Illinois at Urbana–Champaign M,D*
The University of Iowa M,D*
The University of Kansas M*
University of Kentucky M
University of Manitoba M
University of Maryland, College Park M*
University of Massachusetts Amherst M*
University of Michigan M,D,O*
University of Minnesota, Twin Cities Campus M,D*
University of Mississippi M
University of Missouri–Columbia M,D*
University of Nebraska–Lincoln M*
University of New Brunswick Fredericton M

*M—master's degree; P—first professional degree; D—doctorate; O—other advanced degree; *—Close-Up and/or Announcement or Display in one of the other books in this series*

The University of North Carolina at Chapel Hill M,D*
The University of North Carolina at Greensboro M
University of Oregon M*
University of Ottawa M,D*
University of Pennsylvania M,D*
University of Pittsburgh M,D*
University of South Africa M,D
University of Southern California M,D*
University of South Florida M*
The University of Texas at Austin M,D
University of Toronto M,D
University of Vermont M*
University of Victoria M,D
University of Virginia M,D
University of Washington M,D*
The University of Western Ontario M
University of Wisconsin–Madison M,D*
University of Wisconsin–Milwaukee M,O
Vanderbilt University M*
Washington University in St. Louis M*
Wayne State University M*
West Chester University of Pennsylvania M,O
Wilfrid Laurier University M
Yale University M,D*

CLINICAL LABORATORY SCIENCES/MEDICAL TECHNOLOGY

Austin Peay State University M
Baylor College of Medicine M,D*
The Catholic University of America M,D
Duke University M*
Emory University M,D*
Fairleigh Dickinson University, Metropolitan Campus M*
Inter American University of Puerto Rico, Metropolitan Campus M
Long Island University, C.W. Post Campus M
Medical College of Wisconsin M*
Michigan State University M*
Milwaukee School of Engineering M*
Pontifical Catholic University of Puerto Rico O
Quinnipiac University M*
Rochester Institute of Technology M
Rosalind Franklin University of Medicine and Science M*
Rush University M
San Francisco State University M
State University of New York Upstate Medical University M
Thomas Jefferson University M*
Universidad de las Américas–Puebla M
Université de Montréal O
Université de Sherbrooke M,D
University at Buffalo, the State University of New York M*
University of Alberta M,D*
University of Colorado Denver M,D*
University of Kentucky M,D
University of Maryland, Baltimore M*
University of Massachusetts Lowell M,O
University of Medicine and Dentistry of New Jersey M,D*
University of Mississippi Medical Center M,D*
University of Nebraska Medical Center M,O*
University of New Mexico M*
University of North Dakota M
University of Pittsburgh M,D,O*
University of Puerto Rico, Medical Sciences Campus M,O
University of Rhode Island M
University of Southern Mississippi M
The University of Texas Health Science Center at San Antonio M
The University of Texas Medical Branch M,D*
University of Utah M*
University of Vermont M,D*
University of Washington M*
University of Wisconsin–Milwaukee M
Virginia Commonwealth University M,D
Wayne State University M,O*

CLINICAL PSYCHOLOGY

Abilene Christian University M
Acadia University M
Adelphi University D*
Adler School of Professional Psychology M,D,O*
Alabama Agricultural and Mechanical University M,O
Alliant International University–Fresno D*
Alliant International University–Los Angeles D*
Alliant International University–Sacramento D*
Alliant International University–San Diego M,D*
Alliant International University–San Francisco D,O*
American International College M
American University D*
Antioch University Los Angeles M
Antioch University New England M,D*
Antioch University Santa Barbara D
Appalachian State University M,O
Argosy University, Atlanta M,D,O*
Argosy University, Chicago M,D*
Argosy University, Dallas M,D*
Argosy University, Denver M,D*
Argosy University, Hawai'i M,D,O*
Argosy University, Inland Empire M,D*
Argosy University, Los Angeles M,D*
Argosy University, Orange County M,D*
Argosy University, Phoenix M,D*
Argosy University, San Diego M,D*
Argosy University, San Francisco Bay Area M,D*
Argosy University, Schaumburg M,D,O*
Argosy University, Seattle M,D,O*
Argosy University, Tampa M,D*
Argosy University, Twin Cities M,D,O*
Argosy University, Washington DC M,D*
Arizona State University D
Azusa Pacific University M,D
Ball State University M*
Barry University M,O*
Baylor University M,D
Benedictine University M
Bethany University M
Bowling Green State University M,D*
Brigham Young University M,D*
Bryn Mawr College D*
California Institute of Integral Studies M,D*
California Lutheran University M
California State University, Dominguez Hills M
California State University, Fullerton M
California State University, Northridge M
California State University, San Bernardino M
Capella University M,D,O
Cardinal Stritch University M
Carlos Albizu University M,D
Carlos Albizu University, Miami Campus M,D
Case Western Reserve University D*
The Catholic University of America M,D
Central Michigan University M,D
Chestnut Hill College M,D,O
The Chicago School of Professional Psychology M,D,O
The Chicago School of Professional Psychology: Downtown Los Angeles Campus M,D
The Chicago School of Professional Psychology: Grayslake Campus M
The Chicago School of Professional Psychology: Irvine Campus M
The Chicago School of Professional Psychology: Westwood Campus M
City College of the City University of New York M,D*
Clark University D
Cleveland State University M,D,O
College of St. Joseph M
The College of William and Mary M,D
Concordia University (Canada) M,D,O
Dalhousie University M,D
DePaul University M,D*
Drexel University D*
Duke University D*
Duquesne University D*
East Carolina University M
Eastern Illinois University M,O
Eastern Kentucky University M,O
Eastern Michigan University M,D
Eastern Virginia Medical School D
Eastern Washington University M
East Tennessee State University M
Edinboro University of Pennsylvania M
Emory University D*
Emporia State University M
Evangel University M
Fairleigh Dickinson University, Metropolitan Campus M,D*
Fielding Graduate University M,D,O*
Fisk University M
Florida Institute of Technology M,D*
Florida State University D*
Fordham University D*
Francis Marion University M
Fuller Theological Seminary D
Gallaudet University D
George Fox University M,D*
George Mason University M,D*
The George Washington University D*
Graduate School and University Center of the City University of New York D*
Hofstra University M,D*
Howard University M,D
Idaho State University D
Illinois Institute of Technology M,D*
Illinois State University M,D,O
Immaculata University M,D,O
Indiana State University M,D
Indiana University of Pennsylvania D
Indiana University–Purdue University Indianapolis M,D*
Institute of Transpersonal Psychology M,D
Jackson State University D
James Madison University D
The Johns Hopkins University M,D*
Kean University D
Kent State University M,D*
Lakehead University M,D
Lamar University M
La Salle University M,D
Lesley University M,D,O*
Long Island University, Brooklyn Campus D
Long Island University, C.W. Post Campus D
Louisiana State University and Agricultural and Mechanical College M,D
Loyola University Chicago M,D*
Loyola University Maryland M,D,O*
Madonna University M
Marquette University M,D
Marshall University M,D
Marywood University M,D
Massachusetts School of Professional Psychology M,D,O
McGill University M,D*
Miami University D*
Michigan School of Professional Psychology M,D
Middle Tennessee State University M,O
Midwestern University, Downers Grove Campus M,D*
Midwestern University, Glendale Campus D*
Millersville University of Pennsylvania M
Minnesota State University Mankato M,D
Mississippi State University M,D
Missouri State University M*
Montclair State University M,O*
Morehead State University M
Murray State University M
Naropa University M*
New Mexico Highlands University M
The New School: A University M,D*
Norfolk State University M
North Dakota State University M,D
Northern Arizona University M
Northwestern State University of Louisiana M
Northwestern University D*
Notre Dame de Namur University M

Nova Southeastern University	D,O*
The Ohio State University	M,D*
Ohio University	D*
Oklahoma State University	M,D*
Old Dominion University	D
Pacifica Graduate Institute	M,D
Palo Alto University	D*
Penn State Harrisburg	M,D
Penn State University Park	M,D*
Pepperdine University	M,D
Pepperdine University	M
Philadelphia College of Osteopathic Medicine	M,D,O*
Phillips Graduate Institute	D
Ponce School of Medicine	D
Pontifical Catholic University of Puerto Rico	M,D
Prairie View A&M University	M,D
Queens College of the City University of New York	M
Queen's University at Kingston	M,D
Radford University	M,D,O
Regent University	M,D,O
Roosevelt University	M,D
Rutgers, The State University of New Jersey, New Brunswick	M,D*
St. John's University (NY)	M,D*
Saint Louis University	M,D
St. Mary's University (United States)	M
Saint Michael's College	M
Sam Houston State University	M,D
San Diego State University	M,D*
San Jose State University	M
Saybrook Graduate School and Research Center	M,D
The School of Professional Psychology at Forest Institute	M,D,O
Seattle Pacific University	D
Southern Illinois University Carbondale	M,D*
Southern Illinois University Edwardsville	M
Southern Methodist University	D*
Southern New Hampshire University	M,O*
Spalding University	M,D
State University of New York at Binghamton	M,D*
Stony Brook University, State University of New York	D
Suffolk University	D*
Syracuse University	D*
Teachers College, Columbia University	D
Temple University	D*
Texas A&M University	M,D
Texas Tech University	M,D
Towson University	M
Troy University	M
Uniformed Services University of the Health Sciences	D*
Union College (KY)	M
Union Institute & University	D
Universidad de Iberoamerica	P,M
Université Laval	D
University at Albany, State University of New York	M,D,O*
University at Buffalo, the State University of New York	M,D*
The University of Alabama	D
University of Alaska Anchorage	M,D
University of Alaska Fairbanks	D
The University of British Columbia	M,D
University of Calgary	M,D
University of California, San Diego	D*
University of California, Santa Barbara	M,D
University of Central Florida	M,D*
University of Cincinnati	D
University of Colorado Denver	D*
University of Connecticut	M,D,O*
University of Dayton	M
University of Delaware	D*
University of Denver	M,D*
University of Detroit Mercy	M,D
University of Florida	D*
University of Guelph	M,D
University of Hartford	M,D*
University of Hawaii at Manoa	M,D,O*
University of Houston	M,D*
University of Houston–Clear Lake	M
University of Indianapolis	M,D
The University of Kansas	M,D*
University of Kentucky	M,D
University of La Verne	D
University of Louisville	M,D
University of Maine	M,D*
University of Manitoba	M,D
University of Maryland, College Park	M,D*
University of Massachusetts Amherst	M,D*
University of Massachusetts Boston	D
University of Massachusetts Dartmouth	M,O
University of Memphis	M,D
University of Miami	M,D*
University of Michigan	D*
University of Michigan–Dearborn	M*
University of Minnesota, Twin Cities Campus	D*
University of Mississippi	M,D
University of Missouri–Kansas City	M,D*
University of Missouri–St. Louis	M,D,O
The University of Montana	M,D,O
University of Nebraska–Lincoln	M,D*
University of Nevada, Reno	M,D*
University of New Brunswick Saint John	M,D
University of New Mexico	M,D*
The University of North Carolina at Chapel Hill	D*
The University of North Carolina at Charlotte	M*
The University of North Carolina at Greensboro	M,D
University of North Dakota	M,D
University of North Texas	M,D
University of Oregon	D*
University of Puerto Rico, Río Piedras	M,D
University of Regina	M,D
University of Rhode Island	M,D
University of Rochester	M,D*
University of South Africa	M,D
University of South Carolina	M,D
University of South Carolina Aiken	M
The University of South Dakota	M,D
University of Southern California	M,D*
University of Southern Mississippi	M,D
University of South Florida	M,D*
The University of Tennessee	M,D
The University of Texas at El Paso	M,D
The University of Texas at Tyler	M
The University of Texas of the Permian Basin	M
The University of Texas–Pan American	M
The University of Texas Southwestern Medical Center at Dallas	D*
University of the District of Columbia	M
The University of Toledo	M,D
University of Tulsa	M,D*
University of Utah	D*
University of Vermont	D*
University of Victoria	M,D
University of Virginia	M,D,O
University of Washington	D*
University of Windsor	M,D
University of Wisconsin–Madison	D*
University of Wisconsin–Milwaukee	M,D
Utah State University	M,D
Valdosta State University	M,O
Valparaiso University	M,O
Vanguard University of Southern California	M
Virginia Commonwealth University	D
Virginia Polytechnic Institute and State University	M,D*
Virginia State University	M,D*
Walden University	M,D,O
Washburn University	M
Washington State University	M,D*
Washington University in St. Louis	D*
Wayne State University	M,D,O*
West Chester University of Pennsylvania	M,O
Western Illinois University	M,O
Western Michigan University	M,D*
West Virginia University	M,D
Wheaton College	M,D
Wichita State University	M,D*
Widener University	D*
William Paterson University of New Jersey	M*
Wisconsin School of Professional Psychology	M,D
Wright Institute	D
Wright State University	D
Xavier University	M,D*
Yale University	D*
Yeshiva University	D

CLINICAL RESEARCH

Case Western Reserve University	M*
Duke University	M*
Eastern Michigan University	M,O
Emory University	M*
The Johns Hopkins University	M,D*
Medical College of Georgia	M,O
Medical University of South Carolina	M,D
Memorial University of Newfoundland	M
Morehouse School of Medicine	M*
Mount Sinai School of Medicine of New York University	M,D
New York University	P,M,D*
Northwestern University	M,O*
Palmer College of Chiropractic	M
Thomas Jefferson University	O*
Tufts University	M,D*
TUI University	M,D,O
University of California, Davis	M*
University of California, Los Angeles	M*
University of California, San Diego	M*
University of Connecticut	M*
University of Connecticut Health Center	M*
University of Florida	M*
The University of Iowa	M,D*
University of Louisville	M,O
University of Maryland, Baltimore	M,D*
University of Massachusetts Worcester	M,D
University of Michigan	M*
University of Minnesota, Twin Cities Campus	M*
University of Pittsburgh	M,D,O*
University of Puerto Rico, Medical Sciences Campus	M,O
University of Southern California	M,D,O*
University of South Florida	M,D*
University of Virginia	M
University of Washington	M,D*
University of Wisconsin–Madison	M,D*
Vanderbilt University	M*
Walden University	M,D
Washington University in St. Louis	M*

CLOTHING AND TEXTILES

Academy of Art University	M
Auburn University	M*
Central Michigan University	M,O
Cornell University	M,D*
Eastern Michigan University	M
Fashion Institute of Technology	M*
Iowa State University of Science and Technology	M,D*
Kansas State University	M,D*
North Carolina State University	D*
The Ohio State University	M,D*
Oklahoma State University	M,D*
Oregon State University	M,D*
Philadelphia University	M
Purdue University	M,D
South Dakota State University	M
The University of Akron	M
The University of Alabama	M
University of Alberta	M,D*
University of California, Davis	M*
University of Georgia	M,D*
University of Kentucky	M
University of Manitoba	M
University of Minnesota, Twin Cities Campus	M,D,O*
University of Missouri–Columbia	M*
University of North Texas	M
University of Rhode Island	M
The University of Tennessee	M,D
Virginia Polytechnic Institute and State University	M,D*
Washington State University	M,D*

COGNITIVE SCIENCES

Arizona State University	D
Ball State University	M*
Boston University	M,D*

*M—master's degree; P—first professional degree; D—doctorate; O—other advanced degree; *—Close-Up and/or Announcement or Display in one of the other books in this series*

- Brandeis University M,D
- Brown University M,D*
- Carleton University D
- Carnegie Mellon University D*
- Case Western Reserve University M*
- Claremont Graduate University M,D,O*
- Cornell University D*
- Dartmouth College D*
- Duke University D*
- Emory University D*
- Florida State University D*
- The George Washington University D*
- Graduate School and University Center of the City University of New York D*
- Harvard University M,D*
- Hunter College of the City University of New York M
- Indiana University Bloomington M,D*
- Iowa State University of Science and Technology D*
- The Johns Hopkins University D*
- Louisiana State University and Agricultural and Mechanical College M,D
- Loyola University Chicago M*
- Massachusetts Institute of Technology D*
- Mississippi State University M,D
- New York University M,D,O*
- North Dakota State University M,D
- Northwestern University D*
- The Ohio State University M,D*
- Penn State University Park M,D*
- Queen's University at Kingston M,D
- Rensselaer Polytechnic Institute D
- Rice University M,D
- Rutgers, The State University of New Jersey, Newark D*
- Rutgers, The State University of New Jersey, New Brunswick D*
- State University of New York at Binghamton M,D*
- Temple University D*
- Texas A&M University M,D*
- Texas A&M University–Commerce M,D
- University at Buffalo, the State University of New York M,D*
- The University of Akron M,D
- The University of British Columbia M,D
- University of California, San Diego D*
- University of California, Santa Barbara M,D
- University of Connecticut M,D,O*
- University of Delaware D*
- University of Florida M,D*
- University of Guelph M,D
- The University of Kansas M,D*
- University of Louisiana at Lafayette D*
- University of Maryland, Baltimore County D*
- University of Maryland, College Park D*
- University of Massachusetts Amherst M,D*
- University of Minnesota, Twin Cities Campus D*
- University of Nebraska–Lincoln M,D,O*
- University of Nevada, Reno M,D*
- The University of North Carolina at Chapel Hill D*
- The University of North Carolina at Greensboro M,D
- University of Notre Dame D*
- University of Oregon M,D*
- University of Pittsburgh D*
- University of Rochester M,D*
- University of Southern California M,D*
- University of South Florida M,D*
- The University of Texas at Austin M,D
- The University of Texas at Dallas M,D*
- The University of Toledo M,D
- University of Washington D*
- University of Wisconsin–Madison D*
- Wayne State University M,D*
- Wilfrid Laurier University M,D
- Yale University D*

COMMUNICATION—GENERAL

- Abilene Christian University M
- American University M*
- The American University in Cairo M
- The American University of Paris M
- Andrews University M
- Angelo State University M
- Arizona State University M,D
- Arizona State University at the West campus M
- Arkansas State University M,O
- Arkansas Tech University M
- Auburn University M*
- Austin Peay State University M
- Ball State University M*
- Barry University M,O*
- Baylor University M
- Bellarmine University M
- Bethel University M,O
- Boise State University M
- Boston University M*
- Bowling Green State University M,D*
- Brandeis University M,O
- Brigham Young University M*
- California State University, Chico M
- California State University, East Bay M
- California State University, Fresno M
- California State University, Fullerton M
- California State University, Long Beach M
- California State University, Los Angeles M
- California State University, Northridge M
- California State University, Sacramento M
- California State University, San Bernardino M
- Carleton University M,D
- Carnegie Mellon University M,D*
- Central Connecticut State University M,O
- Central Michigan University M
- Clarion University of Pennsylvania M
- Clark University M
- Clemson University M,D
- Cleveland State University M,O
- The College at Brockport, State University of New York M
- College of Charleston M*
- The College of New Rochelle M,O
- College of Notre Dame of Maryland M
- Columbia University M,D*
- Concordia University (Canada) M,D,O
- Cornell University M,D*
- DePaul University M*
- DeVry University M*
- Drake University M*
- Drexel University M*
- Drury University M
- Duquesne University M,D*
- Eastern Michigan University M
- Eastern New Mexico University M
- Eastern Washington University M
- East Tennessee State University M
- Edinboro University of Pennsylvania M
- Emerson College M
- Fairfield University M*
- Fairleigh Dickinson University, Metropolitan Campus M*
- Fitchburg State College M,O
- Florida Atlantic University M,O
- Florida Institute of Technology M*
- Florida State University M,D*
- Fordham University M*
- Fort Hays State University M
- George Mason University M,D*
- Georgetown University M
- The George Washington University M*
- Georgia State University M,D
- Gonzaga University M
- Governors State University M
- Grand Valley State University M
- Harvard University M,O*
- Hawai'i Pacific University M*
- Hofstra University M*
- Howard University M,D
- Illinois Institute of Technology M,D*
- Illinois State University M
- Indiana State University M
- Indiana University Bloomington M,D*
- Indiana University of Pennsylvania M,D
- Indiana University–Purdue University Fort Wayne M
- Instituto Tecnológico y de Estudios Superiores de Monterrey, Campus Ciudad Obregón M
- Instituto Tecnológico y de Estudios Superiores de Monterrey, Campus Monterrey M,D
- International University in Geneva M
- Ithaca College M
- The Johns Hopkins University M*
- Kansas State University M*
- Kean University M
- Kent State University M,D*
- Lasell College M,O
- La Sierra University M
- Liberty University M
- Lindenwood University M,O
- Louisiana State University and Agricultural and Mechanical College M,D
- Marquette University M
- Marshall University M
- Marywood University M,O
- McGill University M,D*
- Miami University M*
- Michigan State University M,D*
- Mississippi College M
- Missouri State University M*
- Monmouth University M,O
- Montana State University–Billings M
- Montclair State University M*
- Morehead State University M
- National University M
- New Mexico State University M
- The New School: A University M*
- New York Institute of Technology M
- New York University M,D*
- Norfolk State University M
- North Carolina State University M*
- North Dakota State University M,D
- Northeastern State University M
- Northern Arizona University M
- Northern Illinois University M
- Northern Kentucky University M
- Northwestern University M,D*
- The Ohio State University M,D*
- Ohio University M,D*
- Our Lady of the Lake University of San Antonio M
- Penn State University Park M,D*
- Pepperdine University M
- Pittsburg State University M
- Point Park University M*
- Polytechnic Institute of NYU O
- Purdue University M,D
- Purdue University Calumet M
- Queen's University at Kingston M,D
- Quinnipiac University M*
- Regent University M,D
- Regis University M,O
- Rensselaer Polytechnic Institute M,D
- Rochester Institute of Technology M
- Roosevelt University M
- Rutgers, The State University of New Jersey, New Brunswick D*
- Saginaw Valley State University M
- St. John's University (NY) M,D,O
- Saint Louis University M
- St. Mary's University (United States) M
- St. Thomas University M,D,O
- San Diego State University M*
- San Jose State University M
- Seton Hall University M*
- Shippensburg University of Pennsylvania M
- Simon Fraser University M,D
- South Dakota State University M
- Southeastern Louisiana University M
- Southern Illinois University Carbondale M,D*
- Southern Methodist University M*
- Southern Polytechnic State University M,O
- Southern Utah University M
- Spalding University M
- Spring Arbor University M
- Stanford University M,D*
- State University of New York College at Potsdam M
- State University of New York College of

Environmental Science and Forestry	M,D
Stephen F. Austin State University	M
Stevens Institute of Technology	M,D,O
Suffolk University	M*
Syracuse University	M,D*
Teachers College, Columbia University	M,D
Temple University	M,D*
Texas A&M University	M,D*
Texas Southern University	M
Texas State University–San Marcos	M*
Texas Tech University	M
Towson University	M,O
Trinity International University	M
Trinity (Washington) University	M
Troy University	M
Université de Montréal	M,D,O
Université du Québec à Montréal	M,D
Université du Québec à Trois-Rivières	M,O
University at Albany, State University of New York	M,D*
University at Buffalo, the State University of New York	M,D*
The University of Akron	M
The University of Alabama	M,D
The University of Alabama at Birmingham	M*
University of Alaska Fairbanks	M
University of Alberta	M*
The University of Arizona	M,D*
University of Arkansas	M
University of Calgary	M,D
University of California, Davis	M*
University of California, San Diego	M,D*
University of California, Santa Barbara	D
University of California, Santa Cruz	O*
University of Central Florida	M*
University of Central Missouri	M
University of Cincinnati	M
University of Colorado at Boulder	M,D*
University of Colorado at Colorado Springs	M
University of Colorado Denver	M*
University of Connecticut	M,D*
University of Dayton	M
University of Delaware	M*
University of Denver	M,D,O*
University of Dubuque	M
University of Florida	M,D*
University of Georgia	M,D*
University of Hartford	M*
University of Hawaii at Manoa	M,O*
University of Houston	M*
University of Illinois at Chicago	M,D*
University of Illinois at Springfield	M
University of Illinois at Urbana–Champaign	M,D*
The University of Iowa	M,D*
The University of Kansas	M,D*
University of Kentucky	M,D
University of Louisiana at Lafayette	M*
University of Louisiana at Monroe	M
University of Maine	M*
University of Maryland, Baltimore County	M*
University of Maryland, College Park	M,D*
University of Massachusetts Amherst	M,D*
University of Memphis	M,D
University of Miami	M,D*
University of Michigan	D*
University of Minnesota, Twin Cities Campus	M,D,O*
University of Missouri–Columbia	M,D*
University of Missouri–St. Louis	M
The University of Montana	M
University of Nebraska at Omaha	M
University of Nebraska–Lincoln	M,D*
University of Nevada, Las Vegas	M
University of New Mexico	M,D*
The University of North Carolina at Chapel Hill	M,D*
The University of North Carolina at Charlotte	M*
The University of North Carolina at Greensboro	M
University of North Dakota	M,D
University of Northern Colorado	M
University of Northern Iowa	M
University of North Texas	M
University of Oklahoma	M,D*
University of Oregon	M,D*
University of Ottawa	M,D*
University of Pennsylvania	D*
University of Pittsburgh	M,D*
University of Portland	M
University of Rhode Island	M
University of South Africa	M,D
University of South Alabama	M*
The University of South Dakota	M
University of Southern California	M,D*
University of South Florida	M,D*
The University of Tennessee	M,D
The University of Texas at Arlington	M*
The University of Texas at Austin	M,D
The University of Texas at Dallas	M,D*
The University of Texas at El Paso	M
The University of Texas at San Antonio	M*
The University of Texas at Tyler	M
The University of Texas–Pan American	M
University of the Incarnate Word	M,O
University of the Pacific	M
University of the Sacred Heart	M
The University of Toledo	O
University of Utah	M,D*
University of Vermont	M*
University of Washington	M,D*
University of West Florida	M
University of Windsor	M
University of Wisconsin–Madison	M,D*
University of Wisconsin–Milwaukee	M,D,O
University of Wisconsin–Stevens Point	M
University of Wisconsin–Superior	M
University of Wisconsin–Whitewater	M*
University of Wyoming	M
Utah State University	M
Villanova University	M*
Virginia Commonwealth University	D
Virginia Polytechnic Institute and State University	M*
Wake Forest University	M*
Washington State University	M,D*
Wayne State College	M
Wayne State University	M,D*
Webster University	M
West Chester University of Pennsylvania	M
Western Illinois University	M
Western Kentucky University	M
Western Michigan University	M*
Westminster College (UT)	M
West Texas A&M University	M
West Virginia University	M,D
Wichita State University	M*
Wilfrid Laurier University	M
William Paterson University of New Jersey	M*
York University	M,D

COMMUNICATION DISORDERS

Abilene Christian University	M
Adelphi University	M,D*
Alabama Agricultural and Mechanical University	M
Appalachian State University	M
Arizona State University	M,D
Arkansas State University	M
Armstrong Atlantic State University	M
A.T. Still University of Health Sciences	M,D
Auburn University	M,D*
Ball State University	M,D*
Barry University	M*
Baylor University	M
Bloomsburg University of Pennsylvania	M,D
Boston University	M,D,O*
Bowling Green State University	M,D*
Brigham Young University	M*
Brooklyn College of the City University of New York	M,D
Buffalo State College, State University of New York	M
California State University, Chico	M
California State University, East Bay	M
California State University, Fresno	M
California State University, Fullerton	M
California State University, Long Beach	M
California State University, Los Angeles	M
California State University, Northridge	M
California State University, Sacramento	M
California University of Pennsylvania	M
Canisius College	M
Carlos Albizu University	M,D
Case Western Reserve University	M,D*
Central Michigan University	M,D
Chapman University	M
Clarion University of Pennsylvania	M
Cleveland State University	M
The College of New Jersey	M
The College of Saint Rose	M*
Dalhousie University	M,D
Duquesne University	M,D*
East Carolina University	M,D
Eastern Illinois University	M
Eastern Kentucky University	M
Eastern Michigan University	M
Eastern New Mexico University	M
Eastern Washington University	M
East Stroudsburg University of Pennsylvania	M
East Tennessee State University	M,D
Edinboro University of Pennsylvania	M
Elms College	O
Emerson College	M
Florida Atlantic University	M
Florida International University	M*
Florida State University	M,D*
Fontbonne University	M
Fort Hays State University	M
Gallaudet University	M,D,O
The George Washington University	M*
Georgia State University	M
Governors State University	M
Graduate School and University Center of the City University of New York	D*
Hampton University	M
Harding University	M
Harvard University	D*
Hofstra University	M,D*
Howard University	M,D
Hunter College of the City University of New York	M
Idaho State University	M,D,O
Illinois State University	M
Indiana University Bloomington	M,D*
Indiana University of Pennsylvania	M
Indiana University–Purdue University Fort Wayne	M
Ithaca College	M
Jackson State University	M
James Madison University	M,D
Kean University	M
Kent State University	M,D*
Lamar University	M,D
La Salle University	M
Lehman College of the City University of New York	M
Lewis & Clark College	M
Loma Linda University	M
Long Island University, Brooklyn Campus	M
Long Island University, C.W. Post Campus	M
Longwood University	M
Louisiana State University and Agricultural and Mechanical College	M,D
Louisiana State University Health Sciences Center	M,D*
Louisiana Tech University	M
Loyola University Maryland	M,O*
Marquette University	M
Marshall University	M
Marywood University	M
Massachusetts Institute of Technology	D*
McGill University	M,D*
Mercy College	M
MGH Institute of Health Professions	M,O*
Miami University	M*
Michigan State University	M,D*

*M—master's degree; P—first professional degree; D—doctorate; O—other advanced degree; *—Close-Up and/or Announcement or Display in one of the other books in this series*

Minnesota State University Mankato	M
Minnesota State University Moorhead	M
Minot State University	M
Misericordia University	M
Mississippi University for Women	M,O
Missouri State University	M,D*
Montclair State University	M,D*
Murray State University	M
National University	M
Nazareth College of Rochester	M
New Mexico State University	M,D
New York Medical College	M*
New York University	M,D*
North Carolina Central University	M
Northeastern State University	M
Northeastern University	M,D*
Northern Arizona University	M
Northern Illinois University	M,D
Northwestern University	M,D*
Nova Southeastern University	M,D*
The Ohio State University	M,D*
Ohio University	M,D*
Oklahoma State University	M*
Old Dominion University	M
Our Lady of the Lake University of San Antonio	M
Penn State University Park	M,D*
Portland State University	M
Purdue University	M,D
Queens College of the City University of New York	M
Radford University	M
Rockhurst University	M
Rush University	M,D
St. Cloud State University	M
Saint Louis University	M
Saint Xavier University	M
Salus University	M,D,O
San Diego State University	M,D*
San Francisco State University	M
San Jose State University	M
Seton Hall University	M*
South Carolina State University	M
Southeastern Louisiana University	M
Southeast Missouri State University	M
Southern Connecticut State University	M
Southern Illinois University Carbondale	M*
Southern Illinois University Edwardsville	M
State University of New York at Fredonia	M
State University of New York at New Paltz	M
State University of New York at Plattsburgh	M
State University of New York College at Geneseo	M
Stephen F. Austin State University	M
Syracuse University	M,D*
Teachers College, Columbia University	M,D
Temple University	M*
Tennessee State University	M
Texas A&M University–Kingsville	M
Texas Christian University	M
Texas State University–San Marcos	M*
Texas Tech University Health Sciences Center	M,D
Texas Woman's University	M
Touro College	M,D
Towson University	M,D
Truman State University	M
Universidad del Turabo	M
Université de Montréal	M
Université Laval	M
University at Buffalo, the State University of New York	M,D*
The University of Akron	M,D
The University of Alabama	M
University of Alberta	M,D*
The University of Arizona	M,D*
University of Arkansas	M
University of Arkansas for Medical Sciences	M,D
The University of British Columbia	M,D
University of California, San Diego	D*
University of Central Arkansas	M,D
University of Central Florida	M,D,O*
University of Central Missouri	M
University of Central Oklahoma	M
University of Cincinnati	M,D,O
University of Colorado at Boulder	M,D*
University of Connecticut	M,D*
University of Florida	M,D*
University of Georgia	M,D,O*
University of Hawaii at Manoa	M*
University of Houston	M*
University of Illinois at Urbana–Champaign	M,D*
The University of Iowa	M,D*
The University of Kansas	M,D*
University of Kentucky	M
University of Louisiana at Lafayette	M,D*
University of Louisiana at Monroe	M
University of Louisville	M,D
University of Maine	M*
University of Maryland, College Park	M,D*
University of Massachusetts Amherst	M,D*
University of Memphis	M,D
University of Minnesota, Duluth	M
University of Minnesota, Twin Cities Campus	M,D*
University of Mississippi	M
University of Missouri–Columbia	M*
University of Montevallo	M
University of Nebraska at Kearney	M
University of Nebraska at Omaha	M
University of Nebraska–Lincoln	M,D*
University of Nevada, Reno	M,D*
University of New Hampshire	M,O*
University of New Mexico	M*
The University of North Carolina at Chapel Hill	M,D*
The University of North Carolina at Greensboro	M,D
University of North Dakota	M,D
University of Northern Colorado	M,D
University of Northern Iowa	M
University of North Florida	M
University of North Texas	M,D
University of Oklahoma Health Sciences Center	M,D,O
University of Ottawa	M*
University of Pittsburgh	M,D*
University of Puerto Rico, Medical Sciences Campus	M,D
University of Redlands	M
University of Rhode Island	M,D
University of South Alabama	M,D*
University of South Carolina	M,D
The University of South Dakota	M,D
University of Southern Mississippi	M,D
University of South Florida	M,D*
The University of Tennessee	M,D,O
The University of Texas at Austin	M,D
The University of Texas at Dallas	M,D*
The University of Texas at El Paso	M
The University of Texas Health Science Center at San Antonio	M
The University of Texas–Pan American	M
University of the District of Columbia	M
University of the Pacific	M
The University of Toledo	M
University of Toronto	M,D
University of Tulsa	M*
University of Utah	M,D*
University of Virginia	M
University of Washington	M,D*
The University of Western Ontario	M
University of West Georgia	M,O
University of Wisconsin–Eau Claire	M
University of Wisconsin–Madison	M,D*
University of Wisconsin–Milwaukee	M,O
University of Wisconsin–River Falls	M
University of Wisconsin–Stevens Point	M,D
University of Wisconsin–Whitewater	M*
University of Wyoming	M
Utah State University	M,D,O
Vanderbilt University	M,D*
Washington State University Spokane	M
Washington University in St. Louis	M,D*
Wayne State University	M,D*
West Chester University of Pennsylvania	M,O
Western Carolina University	M
Western Illinois University	M
Western Kentucky University	M
Western Michigan University	M,D*
Western Washington University	M
West Texas A&M University	M
West Virginia University	M,D
Wichita State University	M,D*
William Paterson University of New Jersey	M*
Worcester State College	M

COMMUNITY COLLEGE EDUCATION

Argosy University, Chicago	M,D,O*
Argosy University, Denver	M,D*
Argosy University, Inland Empire	M,D*
Argosy University, Los Angeles	M,D*
Argosy University, Orange County	M,D*
Argosy University, Phoenix	M,D,O*
Argosy University, San Diego	M,D*
Argosy University, San Francisco Bay Area	M,D*
Argosy University, Schaumburg	M,D,O*
Argosy University, Seattle	M,D*
Argosy University, Tampa	M,D,O*
Argosy University, Washington DC	M,D,O*
Arkansas State University	M,D,O
California State University, Stanislaus	M,D
Central Michigan University	M
Colorado State University	M,D*
George Mason University	M,D,O*
Mississippi State University	M,D,O
Morgan State University	D
North Carolina State University	M,D*
Northern Arizona University	M,D
Old Dominion University	M,D
Pittsburg State University	O
University of Central Florida	M,D,O*
University of South Florida	M,D,O*
Walden University	M,D,O
Western Carolina University	M

COMMUNITY HEALTH

Adelphi University	M,O*
Arcadia University	M
Arizona State University at the Downtown Phoenix Campus	M,D,O
Austin Peay State University	M
Bloomsburg University of Pennsylvania	M
Brooklyn College of the City University of New York	M
Brown University	M,D*
The Catholic University of America	M,D,O
The College at Brockport, State University of New York	M
Columbia University	M,D*
Dalhousie University	M
Duquesne University	M*
Eastern Kentucky University	M
East Stroudsburg University of Pennsylvania	M
East Tennessee State University	M,O
George Mason University	M,O*
The George Washington University	M*
Georgia Southern University	M,D
Hofstra University	M*
Hunter College of the City University of New York	M
Idaho State University	O
Independence University	M
Indiana State University	M
The Johns Hopkins University	M,D*
Kean University	
Long Island University, Brooklyn Campus	M
McGill University	M,D,O*
Medical College of Wisconsin	M,D,O*
Meharry Medical College	M
Memorial University of Newfoundland	M,D,O
Minnesota State University Mankato	M

Mount Sinai School of Medicine of New York University	M,D
New Jersey City University	M
New Mexico State University	M
Old Dominion University	M
Sage Graduate School	M
Saint Louis University	M
Simon Fraser University	M
Southern Illinois University Carbondale	M*
Southern New Hampshire University	M,O*
State University of New York Downstate Medical Center	M*
Stony Brook University, State University of New York	M,D
Temple University	M*
Texas Woman's University	M,D
Université de Montréal	M,D,O
Université Laval	M,D,O
University at Buffalo, the State University of New York	M,D*
The University of Alabama	M*
University of Alberta	M,D*
University of Calgary	M,D,O
University of California, Los Angeles	M,D*
University of Illinois at Chicago	M,D*
University of Illinois at Urbana–Champaign	M,D*
The University of Iowa	M,D*
University of Manitoba	M,D,O
University of Minnesota, Twin Cities Campus	M*
University of Nevada, Las Vegas	M,O
The University of North Carolina at Greensboro	M,D
University of Northern British Columbia	M,D,O
University of Northern Iowa	M,D
University of North Florida	M,O
University of North Texas	M,D
University of North Texas Health Science Center at Fort Worth	M,D
University of Ottawa	M,D,O*
University of Phoenix	M
University of Phoenix–Birmingham Campus	M
University of Phoenix–Central Valley Campus	M
University of Phoenix–Chattanooga Campus	M
University of Phoenix–Hawaii Campus	M
University of Pittsburgh	M,D,O*
University of Saskatchewan	M,D
University of South Florida	M,D*
The University of Tennessee	M,D
The University of Texas Medical Branch	M,D*
University of Virginia	M,D
University of Washington	M,D*
University of Wisconsin–La Crosse	M
University of Wyoming	M,D
Virginia Commonwealth University	D
Virginia State University	M,D
Walden University	M,D
Wayne State University	M,O*
West Virginia University	M

COMMUNITY HEALTH NURSING

Arizona State University at the Downtown Phoenix Campus	M,D,O
Augsburg College	M
Augustana College	M
Boston College	M,D*
Case Western Reserve University	M*
The Catholic University of America	M,D,O
Cleveland State University	M
D'Youville College	M,O*
Georgia Southern University	M,D,O
Hampton University	M
Hawai'i Pacific University	M*
Holy Family University	M
Holy Names University	M,O
Hunter College of the City University of New York	M
Husson University	M,O
Independence University	M
Indiana University–Purdue University Indianapolis	M,D*
Indiana Wesleyan University	M,O
Inter American University of Puerto Rico, Arecibo Campus	M
The Johns Hopkins University	M*
Kean University	M
Louisiana State University Health Sciences Center	M,D*
New Mexico State University	M
Oregon Health & Science University	M,O*
Rush University	M,D,O
Rutgers, The State University of New Jersey, Newark	M*
Sage Graduate School	M
Saint Xavier University	M,O
Seattle University	M
University of Cincinnati	M,D
University of Colorado at Colorado Springs	M,D
University of Hartford	M*
University of Hawaii at Manoa	M,D,O*
University of Illinois at Chicago	M*
The University of Kansas	M,D,O*
University of Maryland, Baltimore	M*
University of Massachusetts Dartmouth	M,D,O
University of Michigan	M,O*
University of Minnesota, Twin Cities Campus	M*
The University of North Carolina at Chapel Hill	M*
University of Puerto Rico, Medical Sciences Campus	M
University of South Alabama	M,D*
University of South Carolina	M
University of Southern Mississippi	M,D
The University of Texas at Brownsville	M
Wayne State University	M*
Worcester State College	M
Wright State University	M

COMPARATIVE AND INTERDISCIPLINARY ARTS

Bradley University	M
Brigham Young University	M*
Columbia College Chicago	M
Florida Atlantic University	D
Goddard College	M
John F. Kennedy University	M
Ohio University	D*
Simon Fraser University	M

COMPARATIVE LITERATURE

American University	M*
The American University in Cairo	M
Antioch University McGregor	M
Arizona State University	M,D
Brigham Young University	M*
Brock University	M
Brown University	D*
California State University, Fullerton	M
California State University, Northridge	M
Carleton University	D
Carnegie Mellon University	M,D*
Case Western Reserve University	M*
The Catholic University of America	M
Claremont Graduate University	M,D*
College of the Humanities and Sciences, Harrison Middleton University	M,D
Columbia University	M,D*
Cornell University	D*
Dartmouth College	M*
Duke University	D*
Emory University	D,O*
Fairleigh Dickinson University, Metropolitan Campus	M*
Florida Atlantic University	M
Georgetown University	M,D
Graduate School and University Center of the City University of New York	M,D*
Harvard University	D*
Hofstra University	M*
Indiana State University	M
Indiana University Bloomington	M,D*
The Johns Hopkins University	D*
Kent State University	M,D*
Long Island University, Brooklyn Campus	M
Louisiana State University and Agricultural and Mechanical College	M,D
New York University	M,D*
Northwestern University	M,D,O*
Oklahoma City University	M
Penn State University Park	M,D*
Princeton University	D*
Purdue University	M,D
Rutgers, The State University of New Jersey, New Brunswick	M,D*
San Francisco State University	M
San Jose State University	M,O
Stanford University	D*
State University of New York at Binghamton	M,D*
Stony Brook University, State University of New York	M,D
Université de Montréal	M,D
Université de Sherbrooke	M,D
Université du Québec à Chicoutimi	M
Université du Québec à Montréal	M,D
Université du Québec à Rimouski	M,D
Université du Québec à Trois-Rivières	M
Université Laval	M,D
University at Buffalo, the State University of New York	M,D*
University of Arkansas	M,D
University of California, Berkeley	D*
University of California, Davis	D*
University of California, Irvine	M,D*
University of California, Los Angeles	M,D*
University of California, Riverside	M,D*
University of California, San Diego	M,D*
University of California, Santa Barbara	D
University of California, Santa Cruz	M,D*
University of Chicago	M,D*
University of Colorado at Boulder	M,D*
University of Connecticut	M,D*
University of Dallas	D
University of Georgia	M,D*
University of Guelph	D
University of Illinois at Urbana–Champaign	M,D*
The University of Iowa	M,D*
University of Maryland, College Park	M,D*
University of Massachusetts Amherst	M,D*
University of Michigan	D*
University of Minnesota, Twin Cities Campus	D*
University of Missouri–Columbia	M,D*
University of Nebraska–Lincoln	M,D*
University of New Hampshire	M,D*
University of New Mexico	M,D*
The University of North Carolina at Chapel Hill	M,D*
University of Notre Dame	D*
University of Oregon	M,D*
University of Pennsylvania	M,D*
University of Puerto Rico, Río Piedras	M
University of South Carolina	M,D
University of Southern California	M,D*
The University of Texas at Austin	M,D
The University of Texas at Dallas	M,D*
University of Toronto	M,D
University of Utah	M,D*
University of Washington	M,D*
The University of Western Ontario	M,D
University of Wisconsin–Madison	M,D*
University of Wisconsin–Milwaukee	M,D,O
Washington University in St. Louis	M,D*
Wayne State University	M*
Western Kentucky University	M
Yale University	D*

COMPUTATIONAL BIOLOGY

Arizona State University	M
Baylor College of Medicine	D*
Carnegie Mellon University	M,D*
Claremont Graduate University	M,D*
Cornell University	D*
Florida State University	D*
George Mason University	M,D,O*
Iowa State University of Science and Technology	D*
Keck Graduate Institute of Applied Life Sciences	M,D,O
Massachusetts Institute of Technology	D*

*M—master's degree; P—first professional degree; D—doctorate; O—other advanced degree; *—Close-Up and/or Announcement or Display in one of the other books in this series*

...ute of M
...ity D*
...ersity M*
...ity D*
Rutgers, The State University of New Jersey, Newark M*
Rutgers, The State University of New Jersey, New Brunswick D*
University of Idaho M,D
University of Illinois at Urbana–Champaign M,D*
The University of Iowa M,D,O*
University of Pennsylvania D*
University of Pittsburgh D*
University of Rochester M,D*
University of Southern California M,D*
The University of Texas Medical Branch D*
University of Wyoming D
Virginia Polytechnic Institute and State University D*
Washington University in St. Louis D*
Yale University D*

COMPUTATIONAL SCIENCES

California Institute of Technology M,D*
Carnegie Mellon University M,D*
Claremont Graduate University M,D*
Clemson University M,D
The College at Brockport, State University of New York M
The College of William and Mary M
Cornell University M,D*
George Mason University M,D,O*
Hampton University M
Kean University M
Lehigh University M,D
Louisiana Tech University M,D
Marquette University M,D
Massachusetts Institute of Technology M*
McGill University M,D*
Memorial University of Newfoundland M
Michigan Technological University D
Northwestern University M*
Princeton University D*
Rice University M,D
Sam Houston State University M
San Diego State University M,D*
Simon Fraser University M,D
South Dakota State University M,D
Southern Methodist University M,D*
Stanford University M,D*
Temple University M,D*
University of Alaska Fairbanks M,D
University of California, Santa Barbara M,D
University of Central Florida M,D*
The University of Iowa D*
The University of Kansas M,D*
University of Lethbridge M,D
University of Manitoba M
University of Massachusetts Lowell M,D
University of Michigan–Dearborn M*
University of Minnesota, Duluth M
University of Minnesota, Twin Cities Campus M,D*
University of Mississippi M,D
University of New Mexico O*
University of Pennsylvania D*
University of Puerto Rico, Mayagüez Campus M
The University of South Dakota M,D
University of Southern Mississippi M,D
University of South Florida M,D*
The University of Tennessee at Chattanooga M,D
The University of Texas at Austin M,D
University of Utah M*
University of Washington M,D*
Western Michigan University M*

COMPUTER AND INFORMATION SYSTEMS SECURITY

American InterContinental University Online M
American InterContinental University South Florida M
Benedictine University M
Brandeis University M,O
Capella University M,D,O
Capitol College M
Carnegie Mellon University M*
The Catholic University of America M,D
City University of Seattle M,O
Colorado Technical University Colorado Springs M,D
Colorado Technical University Denver M
Colorado Technical University Sioux Falls M
Concordia University (Canada) M,O
Davenport University M
Davenport University M
Davenport University M
DePaul University M,D*
Eastern Illinois University M,O
Eastern Michigan University M,O
Florida State University M,D*
George Mason University M,D,O*
Georgia Institute of Technology M,D*
The Johns Hopkins University M,O*
Jones International University M
Kaplan University–Davenport Campus M
Kentucky State University M
Lewis University M
Marymount University M,O
Mercy College M
Northern Kentucky University M,O
Nova Southeastern University M,D*
Our Lady of the Lake University of San Antonio M
Polytechnic Institute of NYU O
Purdue University M
Regis University M,O
Robert Morris University M,D
Rochester Institute of Technology M,O
Sacred Heart University M,O
Saint Leo University M
Salem International University M
Southern Polytechnic State University M,O
Stevens Institute of Technology M,D,O
Strayer University M
Syracuse University O*
Towson University D,O
TUI University M,D
Universidad del Este M
University of Advancing Technology M
University of Minnesota, Twin Cities Campus M*
University of St. Thomas (MN) M,O*
University of Southern California M,D*
The University of Texas at Dallas M*
University of Wisconsin–Madison M*
West Chester University of Pennsylvania M,O
Western Governors University M
Wilmington University M
Worcester Polytechnic Institute M,O*

COMPUTER ART AND DESIGN

Academy of Art University M
Alfred University M*
Arizona State University M
Art Center College of Design M*
Bowling Green State University M*
Carnegie Mellon University M,D*
The Catholic University of America M
Chatham University M
Claremont Graduate University M*
Clemson University M
Concordia University (Canada) O
Cornell University M,D*
DePaul University M,D*
Digital Media Arts College M
Drexel University M*
East Tennessee State University M
Emily Carr Institute of Art + Design M
Florida Atlantic University M
Georgia Institute of Technology M,D*
Indiana University Bloomington M,D*
International Technological University M
Long Island University, Brooklyn Campus M
Long Island University, C.W. Post Campus M
Memphis College of Art M*
Miami International University of Art & Design M*
Minneapolis College of Art and Design O
Mississippi State University M
National University M
The New School: A University M*
New York University M*
North Carolina State University D*
Philadelphia University M
Regent University M,D
Rensselaer Polytechnic Institute M,D
Rhode Island School of Design M
Rochester Institute of Technology M
St. Edward's University M
San Jose State University M
Savannah College of Art and Design M*
School of Visual Arts M
Stevens Institute of Technology M,D,O
Syracuse University M*
Texas State University–San Marcos M*
Universidad de las Américas–Puebla M
University of Alaska Fairbanks M
University of Baltimore M,D
University of California, Santa Cruz M*
University of Central Arkansas M
University of Central Florida M*
University of Denver M*
University of Florida M,D*
The University of Kansas M*
University of Massachusetts Dartmouth M
University of Missouri–Columbia M*
University of Pennsylvania M*
University of Southern California M*
University of Victoria M
Washington State University M*

COMPUTER EDUCATION

Arcadia University M,D,O
California State University, Dominguez Hills M,O
Canadian Southern Baptist Seminary P,M
Cardinal Stritch University M
Christopher Newport University M
DeSales University M
Eastern Washington University M
Florida Institute of Technology M,D,O*
Fontbonne University M
Indiana University–Purdue University Indianapolis M,O*
Jacksonville University M
Kean University M
Lesley University M,D,O*
Long Island University, C.W. Post Campus M
Marlboro College M
Mississippi College M,D,O
Nova Southeastern University M,D,O*
Ohio University M,D*
Southern New Hampshire University M,O*
Stanford University M,D*
State University of New York College at Potsdam M
Stony Brook University, State University of New York M
Teachers College, Columbia University M
Thomas College M
University of Bridgeport M,O
University of Central Oklahoma M
University of Detroit Mercy M
University of Michigan M,D*
University of North Texas M,D
University of Phoenix M
University of Phoenix–Central Florida Campus M
University of Phoenix–Central Valley Campus M
University of Phoenix–North Florida Campus M
University of Phoenix–Omaha Campus M

University of Phoenix–Phoenix Campus	M
University of Phoenix–San Diego Campus	M
University of Phoenix–South Florida Campus	M
University of Phoenix–Springfield Campus	M
University of Phoenix–Vancouver Campus	M
University of Phoenix–West Florida Campus	M
Wilkes University	M,D
Wright State University	M

COMPUTER ENGINEERING

Air Force Institute of Technology	M,D
American University of Beirut	M,D
American University of Sharjah	M
Arizona State University at the Polytechnic Campus	M
Auburn University	M,D*
Baylor University	M
Boise State University	M,D
Boston University	M,D*
Brown University	M,D*
California State University, Chico	M
California State University, East Bay	M
California State University, Long Beach	M
Carnegie Mellon University	M,D*
Case Western Reserve University	M,D*
Clarkson University	M,D*
Clemson University	M,D
Colorado Technical University Colorado Springs	M
Colorado Technical University Denver	M
Columbia University	M,D,O*
Concordia University (Canada)	M,D
Cornell University	M,D*
Dalhousie University	M,D
Dartmouth College	M,D*
Drexel University	M*
Duke University	M,D*
École Polytechnique de Montréal	M,D,O
Fairfield University	M*
Fairleigh Dickinson University, Metropolitan Campus	M*
Florida Atlantic University	M,D
Florida Institute of Technology	M,D*
Florida International University	M*
George Mason University	M,D,O*
The George Washington University	M,D*
Georgia Institute of Technology	M,D*
Grand Valley State University	M
Illinois Institute of Technology	M,D*
Indiana State University	M
Indiana University–Purdue University Fort Wayne	M
Indiana University–Purdue University Indianapolis	M,D*
Instituto Tecnológico y de Estudios Superiores de Monterrey, Campus Chihuahua	M,O
International Technological University	M
Iowa State University of Science and Technology	M,D*
The Johns Hopkins University	M,D,O*
Kansas State University	M,D*
Kettering University	M
Lakehead University	M
Lawrence Technological University	M,D
Lehigh University	M,D
Louisiana State University and Agricultural and Mechanical College	M,D
Manhattan College	M
Marquette University	M,D
McGill University	M,D*
Memorial University of Newfoundland	M,D
Mercer University	M
Michigan Technological University	D
Mississippi State University	M,D
Missouri University of Science and Technology	M,D
Montana State University	M,D
Naval Postgraduate School	M,D,O
New Jersey Institute of Technology	M,D
New Mexico State University	M,D
New York Institute of Technology	M
Norfolk State University	M
North Carolina Agricultural and Technical State University	M,D
North Carolina State University	M,D*
North Dakota State University	M,D
Northeastern University	M,D*
Northwestern Polytechnic University	M
Northwestern University	M,D,O*
Oakland University	M
OGI School of Science & Engineering at Oregon Health & Science University	M,D
The Ohio State University	M,D*
Oklahoma State University	M,D*
Old Dominion University	M,D
Oregon Health & Science University	M,D*
Oregon State University	M,D*
Penn State University Park	M,D*
Polytechnic Institute of NYU	M,O
Polytechnic Institute of NYU, Long Island Graduate Center	M
Polytechnic Institute of NYU, Westchester Graduate Center	M
Polytechnic University of the Americas–Orlando Campus	M
Portland State University	M,D
Purdue University	M,D
Purdue University Calumet	M
Queen's University at Kingston	M,D
Rensselaer at Hartford	M
Rensselaer Polytechnic Institute	M,D
Rice University	M,D
Rochester Institute of Technology	M
Royal Military College of Canada	M,D
Rutgers, The State University of New Jersey, New Brunswick	M,D*
St. Mary's University (United States)	M
San Jose State University	M
Santa Clara University	M,D,O
Southern Illinois University Carbondale	M,D*
Southern Methodist University	M,D*
Southern Polytechnic State University	M
State University of New York at New Paltz	M
Stevens Institute of Technology	M,D,O
Stony Brook University, State University of New York	M,D,O
Syracuse University	M,D*
Temple University	M*
Texas A&M University	M,D*
The University of Akron	M,D
The University of Alabama	M,D
The University of Alabama at Birmingham	D*
The University of Alabama in Huntsville	M,D
University of Alaska Fairbanks	M,D
University of Alberta	M,D*
The University of Arizona	M,D*
University of Arkansas	M,D
University of Bridgeport	M,D
The University of British Columbia	M,D
University of Calgary	M,D
University of California, Davis	M,D*
University of California, Riverside	M,D*
University of California, San Diego	M,D*
University of California, Santa Barbara	M,D
University of California, Santa Cruz	M,D*
University of Central Florida	M,D*
University of Cincinnati	M,D
University of Colorado at Boulder	M,D*
University of Colorado Denver	M,D*
University of Dayton	M,D
University of Delaware	M,D*
University of Denver	M*
University of Detroit Mercy	M,D
University of Florida	M,D,O*
University of Houston	M,D*
University of Houston–Clear Lake	M
University of Idaho	M
University of Illinois at Chicago	M,D*
University of Illinois at Urbana–Champaign	M,D*
The University of Iowa	M,D*
The University of Kansas	M*
University of Louisiana at Lafayette	M,D*
University of Louisville	M,D
University of Maine	M,D*
University of Manitoba	M,D
University of Maryland, Baltimore County	M,D*
University of Maryland, College Park	M,D*
University of Massachusetts Amherst	M,D*
University of Massachusetts Dartmouth	M,D,O
University of Massachusetts Lowell	M
University of Memphis	M,D
University of Miami	M,D*
University of Michigan	M,D*
University of Michigan–Dearborn	M*
University of Minnesota, Duluth	M
University of Minnesota, Twin Cities Campus	M,D*
University of Missouri–Kansas City	M,D*
University of Nebraska–Lincoln	M,D*
University of Nevada, Las Vegas	M,D
University of Nevada, Reno	M,D*
University of New Brunswick Fredericton	M,D
University of New Mexico	M,D*
The University of North Carolina at Charlotte	M,D*
University of North Texas	M,D
University of Notre Dame	M,D*
University of Oklahoma	M,D*
University of Ottawa	M,D*
University of Puerto Rico, Mayagüez Campus	M
University of Regina	M,D
University of Rhode Island	M,D
University of Rochester	M,D*
University of South Carolina	M,D
University of Southern California	M,D,O*
University of South Florida	M,D*
The University of Tennessee	M,D
The University of Texas at Arlington	M,D*
The University of Texas at Austin	M,D
The University of Texas at Dallas	M,D*
The University of Texas at El Paso	M,D
The University of Texas at San Antonio	M,D*
University of Toronto	M,D
University of Victoria	M,D
University of Virginia	M,D
University of Washington, Tacoma	M
University of Waterloo	M,D
The University of Western Ontario	M,D
University of Wisconsin–Milwaukee	M,D,O
Villanova University	M,O*
Virginia Polytechnic Institute and State University	M,D*
Washington State University	M,D*
Washington State University Tri-Cities	M,D
Washington University in St. Louis	M,D*
Wayne State University	M,D*
Western Michigan University	M,D*
West Virginia University	D
Widener University	M*
Worcester Polytechnic Institute	M,D,O*
Wright State University	M,D
Youngstown State University	M

COMPUTER SCIENCE

Acadia University	M
Air Force Institute of Technology	M,D
Alabama Agricultural and Mechanical University	M
Alcorn State University	M
American Sentinel University	M
American University	M,O*
The American University in Cairo	M
The American University of Athens	M
American University of Beirut	M
Appalachian State University	M

*M—master's degree; P—first professional degree; D—doctorate; O—other advanced degree; *—Close-Up and/or Announcement or Display in one of the other books in this series*

Arizona State University	M,D
Arizona State University at the Polytechnic Campus	M
Arkansas State University	M
Armstrong Atlantic State University	M
Auburn University	M,D*
Ball State University	M*
Baylor University	M
Boise State University	M
Boston University	M,D*
Bowie State University	M,D
Bowling Green State University	M*
Bradley University	M
Brandeis University	M,D,O
Bridgewater State College	M
Brigham Young University	M,D*
Brock University	M
Brooklyn College of the City University of New York	M,D,O
Brown University	M,D*
California Institute of Technology	M,D*
California Polytechnic State University, San Luis Obispo	M
California State Polytechnic University, Pomona	M
California State University Channel Islands	M
California State University, Chico	M
California State University, Dominguez Hills	M
California State University, East Bay	M
California State University, Fresno	M
California State University, Fullerton	M
California State University, Long Beach	M
California State University, Los Angeles	M
California State University, Northridge	M
California State University, Sacramento	M
California State University, San Bernardino	M
California State University, San Marcos	M
Capitol College	M
Carleton University	M,D
Carnegie Mellon University	M,D*
Case Western Reserve University	M,D*
The Catholic University of America	M,D
Central Connecticut State University	M
Central Michigan University	M
Chicago State University	M
Christopher Newport University	M
The Citadel, The Military College of South Carolina	M
City College of the City University of New York	M,D*
Clark Atlanta University	M
Clarkson University	M*
Clemson University	M,D
Cleveland State University	M,D
College of Charleston	M*
The College of Saint Rose	M*
College of Staten Island of the City University of New York	M
The College of William and Mary	M,D
Colorado School of Mines	M,D
Colorado State University	M,D*
Colorado Technical University Colorado Springs	M,D
Colorado Technical University Denver	M
Colorado Technical University Sioux Falls	M
Columbia University	M,D,O*
Columbus State University	M
Concordia University (Canada)	M,D,O
Cornell University	M,D*
Dalhousie University	M,D
Dartmouth College	M,D*
DePaul University	M,D*
DigiPen Institute of Technology	M
Drexel University	M,D*
Duke University	M,D*
East Carolina University	M,D,O
Eastern Illinois University	M,O
Eastern Michigan University	M,O
Eastern Washington University	M
East Stroudsburg University of Pennsylvania	M
East Tennessee State University	M
École Polytechnique de Montréal	M,D,O
Elmhurst College	M
Emory University	M,D*
Fairleigh Dickinson University, Metropolitan Campus	M*
Ferris State University	M
Fitchburg State College	M
Florida Atlantic University	M,D
Florida Gulf Coast University	M
Florida Institute of Technology	M,D*
Florida International University	M,D*
Florida State University	M,D*
Fordham University	M*
Franklin University	M
Frostburg State University	M
Gannon University	M
George Mason University	M,D*
Georgetown University	M
The George Washington University	M,D*
Georgia Institute of Technology	M,D*
Georgia Southwestern State University	M
Georgia State University	M,D
Governors State University	M
Graduate School and University Center of the City University of New York	D*
Grand Valley State University	M
Hampton University	M
Harvard University	M,D*
Hofstra University	M*
Hood College	M
Howard University	M
Illinois Institute of Technology	M,D*
Indiana State University	M
Indiana University Bloomington	M,D*
Indiana University–Purdue University Fort Wayne	M
Indiana University–Purdue University Indianapolis	M,D*
Indiana University South Bend	M
Instituto Tecnológico y de Estudios Superiores de Monterrey, Campus Central de Veracruz	M
Instituto Tecnológico y de Estudios Superiores de Monterrey, Campus Ciudad de México	M,D
Instituto Tecnológico y de Estudios Superiores de Monterrey, Campus Cuernavaca	M,D
Instituto Tecnológico y de Estudios Superiores de Monterrey, Campus Estado de México	M,D
Instituto Tecnológico y de Estudios Superiores de Monterrey, Campus Irapuato	M,D
Instituto Tecnológico y de Estudios Superiores de Monterrey, Campus Monterrey	M,D
Inter American University of Puerto Rico, Metropolitan Campus	M
International Technological University	M
Iona College	M*
Iowa State University of Science and Technology	M,D*
Jackson State University	M
Jacksonville State University	M
James Madison University	M
The Johns Hopkins University	M,D,O*
Kansas State University	M,D*
Kennesaw State University	M
Kent State University	M,D*
Kentucky State University	M
Knowledge Systems Institute	M
Kutztown University of Pennsylvania	M
Lakehead University	M
Lamar University	M
La Salle University	M
Lawrence Technological University	M
Lebanese American University	M
Lehigh University	M,D
Lehman College of the City University of New York	M
Long Island University, Brooklyn Campus	M
Long Island University, C.W. Post Campus	M
Louisiana State University and Agricultural and Mechanical College	M,D
Louisiana State University in Shreveport	M
Louisiana Tech University	M
Loyola Marymount University	M
Loyola University Chicago	M*
Loyola University Maryland	M*
Maharishi University of Management	M
Marist College	M,O
Marquette University	M,D
Massachusetts Institute of Technology	M,D,O*
McGill University	M,D*
McMaster University	M,D
McNeese State University	M
Memorial University of Newfoundland	M,D
Metropolitan State University	M
Michigan State University	M,D*
Michigan Technological University	M,D
Middle Tennessee State University	M
Midwestern State University	M
Mills College	M,O
Minnesota State University Mankato	M,O
Mississippi College	M
Mississippi State University	M,D
Missouri State University	M*
Missouri University of Science and Technology	M,D
Monmouth University	M
Montana State University	M,D
Montclair State University	M,D,O*
National University	M
Naval Postgraduate School	M,D
New Jersey Institute of Technology	M,D
New Mexico Highlands University	M
New Mexico Institute of Mining and Technology	M,D
New Mexico State University	M,D
New York Institute of Technology	M
New York University	M,D*
Nicholls State University	M
Norfolk State University	M
North Carolina Agricultural and Technical State University	M
North Carolina State University	M,D*
North Central College	M
North Dakota State University	M,D,O
Northeastern Illinois University	M
Northeastern University	M,D*
Northern Arizona University	M
Northern Illinois University	M
Northern Kentucky University	M,O
Northwestern Polytechnic University	M
Northwestern University	M,D,O*
Northwest Missouri State University	M,O
Nova Southeastern University	M,D*
Oakland University	M
OGI School of Science & Engineering at Oregon Health & Science University	M,D
The Ohio State University	M,D*
Ohio University	M,D*
Oklahoma City University	M
Oklahoma State University	M,D*
Old Dominion University	M,D
Oregon Health & Science University	M,D*
Oregon State University	M,D*
Pace University	M,D,O*
Pacific States University	M
Penn State Harrisburg	M
Penn State University Park	M,D*
Polytechnic Institute of NYU	M,D
Polytechnic Institute of NYU, Long Island Graduate Center	M,D
Polytechnic Institute of NYU, Westchester Graduate Center	M,D
Portland State University	M,D
Prairie View A&M University	M,D
Princeton University	M,D*
Purdue University	M,D
Queens College of the City University of New York	M

Queen's University at Kingston	M,D
Regis University	M,O
Rensselaer at Hartford	M
Rensselaer Polytechnic Institute	M,D
Rice University	M,D
Rivier College	M
Rochester Institute of Technology	M,D,O
Roosevelt University	M
Royal Military College of Canada	M
Rutgers, The State University of New Jersey, Camden	M
Rutgers, The State University of New Jersey, New Brunswick	M,D*
Sacred Heart University	M,O
St. Cloud State University	M
St. Francis Xavier University	M
St. John's University (NY)	M
Saint Joseph's University	M,O
St. Mary's University (United States)	M
Saint Xavier University	M
Sam Houston State University	M
San Diego State University	M*
San Francisco State University	M
San Jose State University	M
Santa Clara University	M,D,O
Shippensburg University of Pennsylvania	M
Simon Fraser University	M,D
South Dakota School of Mines and Technology	M*
Southeastern University	M
Southern Arkansas University–Magnolia	M
Southern Connecticut State University	M
Southern Illinois University Carbondale	M,D*
Southern Illinois University Edwardsville	M
Southern Methodist University	M,D*
Southern Oregon University	M
Southern Polytechnic State University	M,O
Southern University and Agricultural and Mechanical College	M
Stanford University	M,D*
State University of New York at Binghamton	M,D*
State University of New York at New Paltz	M
State University of New York Institute of Technology	M
Stephen F. Austin State University	M
Stevens Institute of Technology	M,D,O
Stony Brook University, State University of New York	M,D,O
Suffolk University	M*
Télé-université	M,D
Temple University	M,D*
Tennessee Technological University	M*
Texas A&M University	M,D*
Texas A&M University–Commerce	M
Texas A&M University–Corpus Christi	M
Texas A&M University–Kingsville	M
Texas Southern University	M
Texas State University–San Marcos	M*
Texas Tech University	M,D
Towson University	M
Trent University	M
Troy University	M
Tufts University	M,D,O*
Union Graduate College	M
Universidad Autonoma de Guadalajara	M,D
Universidad de las Américas–Puebla	M,D
Université de Moncton	M,O
Université de Montréal	M,D
Université du Québec à Trois-Rivières	M
Université du Québec en Outaouais	M,D
Université Laval	M,D
University at Albany, State University of New York	M,D*
University at Buffalo, the State University of New York	M,D*
University of Advancing Technology	M
The University of Akron	M
The University of Alabama	M,D
The University of Alabama at Birmingham	M,D*
The University of Alabama in Huntsville	M,D,O
University of Alaska Fairbanks	M
University of Alberta	M,D*
The University of Arizona	M,D*
University of Arkansas	M,D
University of Arkansas at Little Rock	M
University of Bridgeport	M,D
The University of British Columbia	M,D
University of Calgary	M,D
University of California, Berkeley	M,D*
University of California, Davis	M,D*
University of California, Irvine	M,D*
University of California, Los Angeles	M,D*
University of California, Riverside	M,D*
University of California, San Diego	M,D*
University of California, Santa Barbara	M,D
University of California, Santa Cruz	M,D*
University of Central Arkansas	M
University of Central Florida	M,D*
University of Central Oklahoma	M
University of Chicago	M*
University of Cincinnati	M,D
University of Colorado at Boulder	M,D*
University of Colorado at Colorado Springs	M,D
University of Colorado Denver	M,D*
University of Connecticut	M,D*
University of Dayton	M
University of Delaware	M,D*
University of Denver	M,D,O*
University of Detroit Mercy	M
University of Evansville	M
University of Florida	M,D*
University of Georgia	M,D*
University of Guelph	M,D
University of Hawaii at Manoa	M,D,O*
University of Houston	M,D*
University of Houston–Clear Lake	M
University of Houston–Victoria	M
University of Idaho	M,D
University of Illinois at Chicago	M,D*
University of Illinois at Springfield	M
University of Illinois at Urbana–Champaign	M,D*
The University of Iowa	M,D*
The University of Kansas	M,D*
University of Kentucky	M,D
University of Lethbridge	M,D
University of Louisiana at Lafayette	M,D*
University of Louisville	M,D
University of Maine	M,D*
University of Management and Technology	M,O
University of Manitoba	M,D
University of Maryland, Baltimore County	M,D*
University of Maryland, College Park	M,D*
University of Maryland Eastern Shore	M*
University of Massachusetts Amherst	M,D*
University of Massachusetts Boston	M,D
University of Massachusetts Dartmouth	M,O
University of Massachusetts Lowell	M,D
University of Memphis	M,D
University of Miami	M,D*
University of Michigan	M,D*
University of Michigan–Dearborn	M*
University of Michigan–Flint	M*
University of Minnesota, Duluth	M
University of Minnesota, Twin Cities Campus	M,D*
University of Missouri–Columbia	M,D*
University of Missouri–Kansas City	M,D*
University of Missouri–St. Louis	M,D
The University of Montana	M
University of Nebraska at Omaha	M
University of Nebraska–Lincoln	M,D*
University of Nevada, Las Vegas	M,D
University of Nevada, Reno	M,D*
University of New Brunswick Fredericton	M,D
University of New Hampshire	M,D*
University of New Haven	M*
University of New Mexico	M,D*
University of New Orleans	M
The University of North Carolina at Chapel Hill	M,D*
The University of North Carolina at Charlotte	M*
The University of North Carolina at Greensboro	M
The University of North Carolina Wilmington	M
University of North Dakota	M
University of Northern British Columbia	M,D,O
University of Northern Iowa	M
University of North Florida	M
University of North Texas	M,D
University of Notre Dame	M,D*
University of Oklahoma	M,D*
University of Oregon	M,D*
University of Ottawa	M,D*
University of Pennsylvania	M,D*
University of Pittsburgh	M,D*
University of Regina	M,D
University of Rhode Island	M,D,O
University of Rochester	M,D*
University of San Francisco	M
University of Saskatchewan	M,D
University of South Alabama	M*
University of South Carolina	M,D
The University of South Dakota	M,D
University of Southern California	M,D*
University of Southern Maine	M
University of Southern Mississippi	M,D
University of South Florida	M,D*
The University of Tennessee	M,D
The University of Tennessee at Chattanooga	M,O
The University of Tennessee Space Institute	M,D*
The University of Texas at Arlington	M,D*
The University of Texas at Austin	M,D
The University of Texas at Dallas	M,D*
The University of Texas at El Paso	M,D
The University of Texas at San Antonio	M,D*
The University of Texas at Tyler	M
The University of Texas of the Permian Basin	M
The University of Texas–Pan American	M
The University of Toledo	M,D
University of Toronto	M,D
University of Tulsa	M,D*
University of Utah	M,D*
University of Vermont	M,D*
University of Victoria	M,D
University of Virginia	M,D
University of Washington	M,D*
University of Waterloo	M,D
The University of Western Ontario	M,D
University of West Florida	M
University of West Georgia	M,O
University of Windsor	M,D
University of Wisconsin–Madison	M,D*
University of Wisconsin–Milwaukee	M,D
University of Wisconsin–Parkside	M
University of Wisconsin–Platteville	M
University of Wyoming	M,D
Utah State University	M,D
Vanderbilt University	M,D*
Villanova University	M,O*
Virginia Commonwealth University	M,D,O
Virginia International University	M
Virginia Polytechnic Institute and State University	M,D*
Virginia State University	M
Wake Forest University	M*
Washington State University	M,D*
Washington State University Tri-Cities	M,D
Washington State University Vancouver	M

*M—master's degree; P—first professional degree; D—doctorate; O—other advanced degree; *—Close-Up and/or Announcement or Display in one of the other books in this series*

Washington University in St. Louis M,D*
Wayne State University M,D,O*
Webster University M,O
West Chester University of Pennsylvania M,O
Western Carolina University M
Western Illinois University M
Western Kentucky University M
Western Michigan University M,D*
Western Washington University M
West Virginia University M,D
Wichita State University M*
Winston-Salem State University M
Worcester Polytechnic Institute M,D,O*
Wright State University M,D
Yale University M,D*
York University M,D
Youngstown State University M

CONDENSED MATTER PHYSICS

Cleveland State University M
Emory University D*
Iowa State University of Science and Technology M,D*
Memorial University of Newfoundland M,D
Rutgers, The State University of New Jersey, New Brunswick M,D*
University of Alberta M,D*
University of Victoria M,D
West Virginia University M,D

CONFLICT RESOLUTION AND MEDIATION/PEACE STUDIES

Abilene Christian University M,O
American Public University System M
American University M,D,O*
The American University of Paris M
Antioch University McGregor M
Arcadia University M
Associated Mennonite Biblical Seminary P,M,O
Baker University M
Bethany Theological Seminary P,M,O
Brandeis University M
California State University, Dominguez Hills M
Cambridge College M
Carleton University M,O
Chaminade University of Honolulu M
Colorado Technical University Colorado Springs M,D
Colorado Technical University Denver M
Columbia College (SC) M,O
Columbia University M*
Cornell University M,D*
Creighton University M,O*
Dallas Baptist University M
Duquesne University M,O*
Eastern Mennonite University M,O
Florida International University O*
Fresno Pacific University M
George Mason University M,D*
Georgetown University M
Hult International Business School (United States) M
Jones International University M
Kennesaw State University M
Lipscomb University M,O
Montclair State University M,O*
National Defense University M
National University M
Norwich University M
Nova Southeastern University M,D*
Old Dominion University M,D
Pepperdine University M
Portland State University M
Regis University M,O
Royal Roads University M,O
St. Edward's University M,O
Saint Paul University M
SIT Graduate Institute M
Southern Methodist University M,O*
Sullivan University P,M
Syracuse University *
Tufts University M,D*
TUI University M,D
United Theological Seminary of the Twin Cities P,M,D,O
Université de Sherbrooke P,M,D,O
University of Arkansas at Little Rock O
University of Baltimore M
University of Bridgeport M
University of Denver M*
University of Hawaii at Manoa O*
University of Massachusetts Amherst M,D*
University of Massachusetts Boston M,O
University of Missouri–Columbia M*
University of Missouri–St. Louis M
University of New Brunswick Fredericton M
The University of North Carolina at Greensboro M,O
University of Notre Dame M,D*
University of Pittsburgh M*
University of San Diego M
University of the Sacred Heart M
University of Victoria M,D
University of Wisconsin–Milwaukee M,O
Walden University M,D,O
Wayne State University M,O*

CONSERVATION BIOLOGY

Antioch University New England M*
Central Michigan University M
Colorado State University M,D*
Columbia University M,D,O*
Frostburg State University M
Illinois State University M,D
North Dakota State University M,D
San Francisco State University M
State University of New York College of Environmental Science and Forestry M,D
Texas State University–San Marcos M*
Tropical Agriculture Research and Higher Education Center M,D
University at Albany, State University of New York M*
University of Alberta M,D*
University of Central Florida M,D,O*
University of Hawaii at Manoa M,D*
University of Illinois at Urbana–Champaign M,D*
University of Maryland, College Park M*
University of Michigan M,D*
University of Minnesota, Twin Cities Campus M,D*
University of Missouri–St. Louis M,D,O
University of Nevada, Reno D*
University of South Florida M,D*
University of Wisconsin–Madison M*

CONSTRUCTION ENGINEERING

The American University in Cairo M
Arizona State University M
Auburn University M,D*
Bradley University M
Columbia University M,D,O*
Concordia University (Canada) M,D,O
Illinois Institute of Technology M,D*
Iowa State University of Science and Technology M,D*
Lawrence Technological University M,D
Massachusetts Institute of Technology M,D,O*
Missouri University of Science and Technology M,D
Montana State University M,D
Ohio University M,D*
Oregon State University M,D*
Pontificia Universidad Catolica Madre y Maestra M
Stevens Institute of Technology M,O
Texas A&M University M,D*
Universidad Nacional Pedro Henriquez Urena P,M,D
The University of Alabama M,D
University of Alberta M,D*
University of Central Florida M,D,O*
University of Colorado at Boulder M,D*
University of Florida M,D*
University of Michigan M,D,O*
University of New Brunswick Fredericton M,D
University of Southern Mississippi M
University of Washington M,D*
Virginia Polytechnic Institute and State University M*
Western Michigan University M*

CONSTRUCTION MANAGEMENT

The American University in Dubai M
Arizona State University M
Auburn University M*
Bowling Green State University M*
Brigham Young University M*
Carnegie Mellon University M,D*
The Catholic University of America M,D,O
Central Connecticut State University M,O
Clemson University M
Colorado State University M*
Columbia University M,D,O*
Eastern Michigan University M
Florida International University M*
Marquette University M,D
Michigan State University M,D*
Missouri State University M*
New York University M,O*
North Carolina Agricultural and Technical State University M
North Dakota State University M
Philadelphia University M
Polytechnic Institute of NYU M
Roger Williams University M*
Southern Polytechnic State University M
State University of New York College of Environmental Science and Forestry M,D
Stevens Institute of Technology M,O
Texas A&M University M,D*
Universidad de las Américas–Puebla M
University of Arkansas at Little Rock M,O
University of Denver M*
University of Houston M*
The University of Kansas M*
University of Nevada, Las Vegas M
University of New Mexico M*
University of Southern California M,D,O*
University of Southern Mississippi M
University of Washington M*
Western Carolina University M
Western Michigan University M*
Worcester Polytechnic Institute M,D,O*

CONSUMER ECONOMICS

California State University, Long Beach M
Colorado State University M*
Cornell University M,D*
Eastern Illinois University M
Indiana State University M
Iowa State University of Science and Technology M,D*
Montana State University M
North Dakota State University M,D
The Ohio State University M,D*
Oklahoma State University M,D*
Purdue University M,D
State University of New York at Oswego M
Texas Tech University M,D
Université Laval O
The University of Alabama M
The University of Arizona M,D*
University of Georgia M,D*
University of Guelph M
University of Idaho M
University of Illinois at Urbana–Champaign M,D*
University of Missouri–Columbia M*
University of South Carolina M
The University of Tennessee M,D
University of Utah M*
University of Wisconsin–Madison M,D*
University of Wyoming M
Utah State University M
Virginia Polytechnic Institute and State University M,D*

CORPORATE AND ORGANIZATIONAL COMMUNICATION

The American University of Athens M
Antioch University Seattle M
Barry University M,O*

Bernard M. Baruch College of the City University of New York	M
Bowie State University	M,O
California State University, San Bernardino	M
Canisius College	M
Carnegie Mellon University	M*
Central Connecticut State University	M,O
Central Michigan University	M,O
College of Charleston	O*
Columbia University	M*
Concordia University Wisconsin	M
Dallas Baptist University	M
DePaul University	M*
Drexel University	M*
Emerson College	M
Fairleigh Dickinson University, College at Florham	M*
Florida State University	M,D*
Fordham University	M*
Franklin University	M
HEC Montreal	O
Howard University	M,D
Illinois Institute of Technology	M*
Iowa State University of Science and Technology	M,D*
John Carroll University	M
Jones International University	M
La Salle University	M
Lasell College	M,O
Loyola University Chicago	M*
Marietta College	M
Marist College	M
Marywood University	M,O
Metropolitan College of New York	M
Mississippi College	M
Monmouth University	M,O
Montclair State University	M*
Murray State University	M
National University	M
New Mexico State University	M,D
New York University	M*
Northwestern University	M*
Oklahoma City University	M
Queens University of Charlotte	M
Radford University	M
Regis College (MA)	M
Roosevelt University	M
Schiller International University (United Kingdom)	M
Seton Hall University	M*
Simmons College	M
Southern Illinois University Edwardsville	O
Southern Polytechnic State University	M,O
Spalding University	M
Stevens Institute of Technology	O
Suffolk University	M*
Temple University	M,D*
Towson University	M
Universidad Autonoma de Guadalajara	M,D
University of Alaska Fairbanks	M
University of Central Florida	M*
University of Connecticut	M,D*
University of Nebraska–Lincoln	M,D*
University of Portland	M
University of St. Thomas (MN)	M*
University of Southern California	M,D*
University of Wisconsin–Stevens Point	M
University of Wisconsin–Whitewater	M*
Washington State University	M,D*
Wayne State University	M,D*
Webster University	M
Western Michigan University	M*
West Virginia University	M,D

COUNSELING PSYCHOLOGY

Abilene Christian University	M
Adelphi University	M*
Adler Graduate School	M,O
Adler School of Professional Psychology	M,D,O*
Alabama Agricultural and Mechanical University	M,O
Alaska Pacific University	M
Alliant International University–México City	M*
Amberton University	M
Amridge University	P,M,D
Andrews University	D
Angelo State University	M
Anna Maria College	M
Antioch University McGregor	M
Antioch University New England	M*
Argosy University, Chicago	D*
Argosy University, Denver	M,D*
Argosy University, Hawai'i	D*
Argosy University, Inland Empire	M,D*
Argosy University, Los Angeles	M,D*
Argosy University, Nashville	M,D*
Argosy University, Orange County	M,D*
Argosy University, Phoenix	M*
Argosy University, Salt Lake City	M,D*
Argosy University, San Diego	M,D*
Argosy University, San Francisco Bay Area	M,D*
Argosy University, Sarasota	M,D,O*
Argosy University, Schaumburg	M,D,O*
Argosy University, Seattle	M,D*
Argosy University, Tampa	M,D*
Argosy University, Washington DC	M,D*
Arizona State University	D
Assumption College	M,O
Athabasca University	M,O*
Auburn University	M,D,O*
Avila University	M
Ball State University	M,D*
Bemidji State University	M
Bethel University	M,O
Boston College	M,D*
Boston Graduate School of Psychoanalysis	M
Boston University	D*
Bowie State University	M
Bowling Green State University	M*
Brigham Young University	M,D,O*
Brooklyn College of the City University of New York	M,D,O
Caldwell College	M
California Baptist University	M
California Institute of Integral Studies	M,D*
California State University, Bakersfield	M
California State University, Sacramento	M
California State University, San Bernardino	M
Cambridge College	M,O
Capella University	M,D,O
Carlos Albizu University, Miami Campus	M,D
Carlow University	M
Centenary College	M
Central Michigan University	M,D,O
Central Washington University	M
Chaminade University of Honolulu	M
Chatham University	M,D
Chestnut Hill College	M,O
The Chicago School of Professional Psychology	M,D,O
City College of the City University of New York	M*
City University of Seattle	M
Cleveland State University	M,D,O
The College at Brockport, State University of New York	M,O
The College of New Rochelle	M,O
College of Saint Elizabeth	M,O
College of St. Joseph	M
College of Staten Island of the City University of New York	M
Colorado Christian University	M
Columbus State University	M,O
Concordia University Chicago	M
Concordia University Wisconsin	M
Dallas Baptist University	M
Dominican University of California	M
Eastern Nazarene College	M
Eastern University	M,O
Eastern Washington University	M
Emporia State University	M
Evangel University	M
Fairleigh Dickinson University, College at Florham	M*
Felician College	M*
Fitchburg State College	M,O
Florida Atlantic University	M,D,O
Florida International University	M*
Florida State University	M,D,O*
Fordham University	M,D,O*
Fort Valley State University	M
Franciscan University of Steubenville	M
Frostburg State University	M
Gallaudet University	M
Gannon University	D
Gardner-Webb University	M
Geneva College	M
George Fox University	M,O*
Georgian Court University	M,O
Georgia State University	M,D,O
Goddard College	M
Gonzaga University	M
Governors State University	M
Grace College	M
Grace University	M
Harding University	M
Heidelberg University	M
Hofstra University	M,O*
Holy Family University	M
Holy Names University	M,O
Houston Baptist University	M
Howard University	M,D,O
Humboldt State University	M
Husson University	M
Idaho State University	M,D,O
Illinois State University	M,D,O
Immaculata University	M,D,O
Indiana State University	M,D,O
Indiana University Bloomington	M,D,O*
Indiana Wesleyan University	M
Institute of Transpersonal Psychology	M,D
Inter American University of Puerto Rico, Aguadilla Campus	M
Inter American University of Puerto Rico, San Germán Campus	M,D
Iona College	M*
Iowa State University of Science and Technology	D*
James Madison University	M,O
John Carroll University	M,O
John F. Kennedy University	M
Kean University	M
Kent State University	M*
Kutztown University of Pennsylvania	M
La Salle University	M
Leadership Institute of Seattle	M
Lee University	M
Lehigh University	M,D,O
Lesley University	M*
Lewis & Clark College	M,O
Lewis University	M
Liberty University	M,D
Lindenwood University	M,D,O
Lindsey Wilson College	M
Lipscomb University	M,O
Long Island University, Brentwood Campus	M
Long Island University, Rockland Graduate Campus	M
Long Island University, Westchester Graduate Campus	M
Louisiana State University in Shreveport	M
Louisiana Tech University	M,D
Loyola University Chicago	D*
Loyola University Maryland	M,O*
Marist College	M,O
Mars Hill Graduate School	M
Marylhurst University	M,O
Marymount University	M,O
Marywood University	M
Massachusetts School of Professional Psychology	M,D,O
McGill University	M,D,O*
McKendree University	M
McNeese State University	M
Medaille College	M
Mercy College	M,O
Michigan Theological Seminary	P,M,O
MidAmerica Nazarene University	M,O
Middle Tennessee State University	M,O
Mississippi College	M,O
Monmouth University	M,O
Montclair State University	M,D,O*
Morehead State University	M
Mount St. Mary's College	M
Naropa University	M*
National University	M
New England College	M
New Jersey City University	M
New Mexico State University	M,D,O
New York Institute of Technology	M
New York University	M,D,O*
Nicholls State University	M,O
Northeastern State University	M
Northeastern University	M,D,O*
Northern Arizona University	D

*M—master's degree; P—first professional degree; D—doctorate; O—other advanced degree; *—Close-Up and/or Announcement or Display in one of the other books in this series*

Northwestern Oklahoma State University M
Northwestern University M*
Northwest University M
Nova Southeastern University M*
Oakland University M,D,O
Ottawa University M
Our Lady of the Lake University of San Antonio M,D
Pace University M*
Pacifica Graduate Institute M,D
Palm Beach Atlantic University M
Penn State University Park M,D*
Philadelphia College of Osteopathic Medicine M,D,O*
Prescott College M
Providence College and Theological Seminary P,M,D,O
Purdue University Calumet M
Radford University M,D,O
Regent University M,D,O
Regis University M,O
Richmont Graduate University M
Rivier College M,D,O
Rosemont College M
Rowan University M
Rutgers, The State University of New Jersey, New Brunswick M*
St. Bonaventure University M,O
St. Edward's University M,O
St. John Fisher College M
Saint Joseph College M
Saint Martin's University M
St. Mary's University (United States) M
Saint Mary's University of Minnesota M,D
Saint Paul University M
St. Thomas University M
Saint Xavier University M,O
Salem State College M
Salve Regina University M,O
San Francisco State University M
Santa Clara University M
The School of Professional Psychology at Forest Institute M,D,O
Seton Hall University M,D*
Shippensburg University of Pennsylvania M,O
Sonoma State University M
Southeast Missouri State University M,O
Southern Adventist University M
Southern Arkansas University–Magnolia M
Southern California Seminary P,M,D
Southern Illinois University Carbondale M,D*
Southern Nazarene University M
South University (SC) M*
South University (GA) M*
South University (AL) M*
South University (FL) M*
Southwestern Assemblies of God University M
Southwestern College (NM) M,O*
Spring Arbor University M
Springfield College M,O
Stanford University D*
State University of New York at New Paltz M
State University of New York at Oswego M,O
Stephens College M
Suffolk University M,O*
Tarleton State University M,O
Teachers College, Columbia University M,D
Temple University M,D*
Tennessee State University M,D
Texas A&M International University M
Texas A&M University M,D*
Texas A&M University–Commerce M,D
Texas A&M University–Texarkana M
Texas Tech University M,D
Texas Wesleyan University M
Texas Woman's University M,D,O
Towson University O
Trevecca Nazarene University M
Trinity International University P,M,D,O
Trinity International University, South Florida Campus M
Trinity Western University M
Union College (KY) M
Union Institute & University M
United States International University M
Universidad del Turabo M
University at Albany, State University of New York M,D,O*
University at Buffalo, the State University of New York M,D,O*
The University of Akron M,D
University of Alberta M,D*
University of Baltimore M
The University of British Columbia M,D,O
University of Calgary M,D
University of California, Santa Barbara M,D
University of Central Arkansas M
University of Central Oklahoma M
University of Colorado Denver M*
University of Connecticut M,D,O*
University of Denver M,D,O*
University of Florida M,D*
University of Great Falls M
University of Houston M,D*
University of Houston–Victoria M
University of Indianapolis M,D
The University of Iowa M,D,O*
The University of Kansas M,D*
University of Kentucky M,D,O
University of La Verne M
University of Lethbridge M,D
University of Mary Hardin-Baylor M
University of Maryland, College Park M,D,O*
University of Massachusetts Boston M,O
University of Medicine and Dentistry of New Jersey M,D,O*
University of Memphis M,D
University of Miami D*
University of Minnesota, Twin Cities Campus D*
University of Missouri–Columbia M,D,O*
University of Missouri–Kansas City M,D,O*
The University of Montana M,D,O
University of Nebraska–Lincoln M,D,O*
The University of North Carolina at Greensboro M,D,O
University of North Dakota M
University of Northern Colorado D
University of North Florida M
University of North Texas M,D,O
University of Notre Dame D*
University of Oklahoma D*
University of Pennsylvania M,D*
University of Phoenix–Las Vegas Campus M
University of Phoenix–Puerto Rico Campus M
University of Phoenix–Sacramento Valley Campus M
University of Phoenix–Utah Campus M
University of Puget Sound M
University of Rhode Island M
University of Saint Francis (IN) M
University of St. Thomas (MN) M,D,O*
University of San Diego M
University of San Francisco M,D
The University of Scranton M,O
University of South Africa M,D
University of Southern Mississippi M,D
The University of Tennessee M,D
The University of Texas at Austin M,D
The University of Texas at Tyler M
University of the District of Columbia M
University of Utah M,D*
University of Vermont M*
University of Victoria M,D
The University of Western Ontario M
University of West Florida M
University of Wisconsin–Madison D*
University of Wisconsin–Milwaukee M,D
University of Wisconsin–Stout M
Utah State University M,D
Valdosta State University M,O
Valparaiso University M,O
Virginia Commonwealth University M,D,O
Walden University M,D,O
Walla Walla University M
Walsh University M
Washington State University M,D,O*
Wayland Baptist University M
Waynesburg University M,D
Webster University M
Western Michigan University M,D*
Western Washington University M
Westfield State College M
Westminster College (UT) M
West Virginia University D
William Carey University M
William Paterson University of New Jersey M*
Wright Institute M
Yeshiva University M
Youngstown State University M

COUNSELOR EDUCATION

Acadia University M
Adams State College M
Adler Graduate School M,O
Alabama Agricultural and Mechanical University M,O
Alabama State University M,O
Albany State University M
Alcorn State University M,O
Alfred University M,D,O*
Angelo State University M
Appalachian State University M
Argosy University, Atlanta M,D,O*
Argosy University, Chicago D*
Argosy University, Denver M,D*
Argosy University, Nashville M,D*
Argosy University, Sarasota M,D,O*
Argosy University, Schaumburg M,D,O*
Argosy University, Tampa M,D*
Argosy University, Washington DC M,D*
Arizona State University M
Arkansas State University M,O
Athabasca University M,O*
Auburn University M,D,O*
Auburn University Montgomery M,O
Augusta State University M
Austin Peay State University M,O
Azusa Pacific University M
Baptist Bible College of Pennsylvania M
Barry University M,D,O*
Bayamón Central University M
Bellevue University M,D
Bloomsburg University of Pennsylvania M
Bob Jones University P,M,D,O
Boise State University M
Boston University M,O*
Bowie State University M
Bowling Green State University M*
Bradley University M
Brandon University M,O
Bridgewater State College M,O
Brooklyn College of the City University of New York M,O
Bucknell University M
Buena Vista University M
Butler University M
Caldwell College M
California Baptist University M
California Lutheran University M
California State University, Bakersfield M
California State University, Dominguez Hills M
California State University, East Bay M
California State University, Fresno M
California State University, Fullerton M
California State University, Long Beach M
California State University, Los Angeles M,D
California State University, Northridge M
California State University, Sacramento M
California State University, San Bernardino M
California State University, Stanislaus M,D,O
California University of Pennsylvania M
Cambridge College M,D,O
Campbell University M
Canisius College M
Cape Breton University O
Carlow University M
Carson-Newman College M
Carthage College M,O
Central Connecticut State University M,O
Central Methodist University M
Central Michigan University M
Central Washington University M
Chadron State College M,O
Chapman University M

The Chicago School of Professional Psychology	M,D,O
Chicago State University	M
The Citadel, The Military College of South Carolina	M
Clark Atlanta University	M
Clemson University	M
Cleveland State University	M,D,O
The College at Brockport, State University of New York	M,O
The College of New Jersey	M
College of St. Joseph	M
The College of Saint Rose	M*
College of Santa Fe	M
The College of William and Mary	M,D
Colorado State University	M,D*
Columbia International University	M,D,O
Columbus State University	M,O
Concordia University Chicago	M,O
Concordia University Wisconsin	M
Creighton University	M*
Dallas Baptist University	M
Delta State University	M,D
DePaul University	M,D*
Doane College	M
Drake University	M*
Duquesne University	M,D*
East Carolina University	M,O
East Central University	M
Eastern Illinois University	M
Eastern Kentucky University	M
Eastern Michigan University	M,O
Eastern New Mexico University	M
Eastern University	M,O
Eastern Washington University	M
East Tennessee State University	M
Edinboro University of Pennsylvania	M,O
Emporia State University	M
Evangel University	M
Fairfield University	M,O*
Fitchburg State College	M,O
Florida Agricultural and Mechanical University	M,D
Florida Atlantic University	M,D,O
Florida Gulf Coast University	M
Florida International University	M*
Florida State University	M,D,O*
Fordham University	M,D,O*
Fort Hays State University	M
Fort Valley State University	M,O
Freed-Hardeman University	M,O
Fresno Pacific University	M
Frostburg State University	M
Gallaudet University	M
Gannon University	M,O
Geneva College	M
George Fox University	M,O*
George Mason University	M*
The George Washington University	M,D,O*
Georgia Southern University	M,O
Georgia State University	M,D,O
Grambling State University	M,D
Grand Canyon University	M*
Gwynedd-Mercy College	M
Hampton University	M
Harding University	M,O
Hardin-Simmons University	M
Henderson State University	M
Heritage University	M
Hofstra University	M,O*
Houston Baptist University	M
Howard University	M,O
Hunter College of the City University of New York	M
Husson University	M
Idaho State University	M,D,O
Immaculata University	M,D,O
Indiana State University	M,D,O
Indiana University Bloomington	M,D,O*
Indiana University of Pennsylvania	M
Indiana University–Purdue University Fort Wayne	M
Indiana University–Purdue University Indianapolis	M,O*
Indiana University South Bend	M
Indiana University Southeast	M
Indiana Wesleyan University	M
Inter American University of Puerto Rico, Arecibo Campus	M
Inter American University of Puerto Rico, San Germán Campus	M,D
Iowa State University of Science and Technology	M,D*
Jackson State University	M,O
Jacksonville State University	M
John Brown University	M
John Carroll University	M,O
The Johns Hopkins University	M,O*
Johnson State College	M
Kansas State University	M,D*
Kean University	M
Kent State University	M,D,O*
Kutztown University of Pennsylvania	M
Lakeland College	M
Lamar University	M,D,O
Lancaster Bible College	M
La Sierra University	M,O
Lee University	M
Lehigh University	M,D,O
Lehman College of the City University of New York	M
Lenoir-Rhyne University	M
Lewis University	M
Liberty University	M,D,O
Lincoln Memorial University	M,O
Lincoln University (MO)	M,O
Loma Linda University	M,D,O
Long Island University at Riverhead	M,O
Long Island University, Brentwood Campus	M
Long Island University, Brooklyn Campus	M,O
Long Island University, C.W. Post Campus	M
Long Island University, Rockland Graduate Campus	M
Long Island University, Westchester Graduate Campus	M
Longwood University	M
Louisiana State University and Agricultural and Mechanical College	M,D,O
Louisiana Tech University	M,D
Loyola Marymount University	M
Loyola University Chicago	M,O*
Loyola University Maryland	M,O*
Loyola University New Orleans	M
Lynchburg College	M
Lyndon State College	M
Malone University	M
Manhattan College	M,O
Marshall University	M,O
Marymount University	M
Marywood University	M,O
McDaniel College	M
McNeese State University	M
Mercy College	M,O
Michigan State University	M,D,O*
Middle Tennessee State University	M,O
Midwestern State University	M
Minnesota State University Mankato	M,D,O
Minnesota State University Moorhead	M
Mississippi College	M,O
Mississippi State University	M,D,O
Missouri Baptist University	M,O
Missouri State University	M*
Montana State University	M,O
Montana State University–Billings	M
Montana State University–Northern	M
Montclair State University	M,D,O*
Morehead State University	M,O
Mount Mary College	M
Multnomah University	M
Murray State University	M,O
Naropa University	M*
National-Louis University	M,O
National University	M
New Mexico Highlands University	M
New Mexico State University	M,D,O
New York Institute of Technology	M
New York University	M,D,O*
Niagara University	M,O
Nicholls State University	M
North Carolina Agricultural and Technical State University	M,D
North Carolina Central University	M
North Carolina State University	M,D*
North Dakota State University	M,D
Northeastern Illinois University	M
Northeastern State University	M
Northeastern University	M*
Northern Arizona University	M
Northern Illinois University	M,D
Northern Kentucky University	M,O
Northern Michigan University	M
Northern State University	M
Northwest Christian University	M
Northwestern Oklahoma State University	M
Northwestern State University of Louisiana	M,O
Northwest Missouri State University	M
Northwest Nazarene University	M
Nova Southeastern University	M*
Ohio University	M,D*
Old Dominion University	M,D,O
Oregon State University	M,D*
Ottawa University	M
Our Lady of Holy Cross College	M
Our Lady of the Lake University of San Antonio	M
Palm Beach Atlantic University	M
Penn State University Park	M,D*
Phillips Graduate Institute	M
Pittsburg State University	M
Plymouth State University	M
Pontifical Catholic University of Puerto Rico	M
Portland State University	M,D
Prairie View A&M University	M,D
Prescott College	M,D
Providence College	M*
Purdue University	M,D,O
Purdue University Calumet	M
Queens College of the City University of New York	M
Quincy University	M
Radford University	M
Regent University	M,D,O
Rhode Island College	M,O
Rider University	M,O*
Rivier College	M,D,O
Roberts Wesleyan College	M
Rollins College	M
Roosevelt University	M
Rosemont College	M
Rowan University	M
Sage Graduate School	M,O
St. Bonaventure University	M,O
St. Cloud State University	M
St. John's University (NY)	M,O
Saint Joseph College	M
St. Lawrence University	M,O
Saint Louis University	M,D,O
Saint Martin's University	M
Saint Mary's College of California	M
St. Mary's University (United States)	D
St. Thomas University	M,O
Saint Xavier University	M
Salem State College	M
Sam Houston State University	M,D
San Diego State University	M*
San Jose State University	M
Santa Clara University	M
Seattle Pacific University	M,D,O
Seattle University	M,O
Shippensburg University of Pennsylvania	M,O
Simmons College	M,D,O
Simon Fraser University	M
Slippery Rock University of Pennsylvania	M
Sonoma State University	M
South Carolina State University	M
South Dakota State University	M
Southeastern Louisiana University	M
Southeastern Oklahoma State University	M
Southeast Missouri State University	M,O
Southern Adventist University	M
Southern Arkansas University–Magnolia	M
Southern Connecticut State University	M,O
Southern Illinois University Carbondale	M,D*
Southern Methodist University	M,O*
Southern Oregon University	M
Southern University and Agricultural and Mechanical College	M
Southwestern Oklahoma State University	M
Spalding University	M
Springfield College	M,O
State University of New York at New Paltz	M

*M—master's degree; P—first professional degree; D—doctorate; O—other advanced degree; *—Close-Up and/or Announcement or Display in one of the other books in this series*

State University of New York at Plattsburgh	M,O
State University of New York College at Oneonta	M,O
Stephen F. Austin State University	M
Stephens College	M
Stetson University	M
Suffolk University	M,O*
Sul Ross State University	M*
Syracuse University	M,D*
Tarleton State University	M,O
Tennessee State University	M,D
Texas A&M International University	M
Texas A&M University	M,D*
Texas A&M University–Commerce	M,D
Texas A&M University–Corpus Christi	M,D
Texas A&M University–Kingsville	M
Texas Christian University	M,O
Texas Southern University	M,D
Texas State University–San Marcos	M*
Texas Tech University	M,D
Texas Wesleyan University	M
Texas Woman's University	M,D
Trevecca Nazarene University	M,D
Trinity (Washington) University	M
Troy University	M,O
Universidad del Turabo	M
Université de Moncton	M
Université Laval	M,D
University at Albany, State University of New York	M,D,O*
University at Buffalo, the State University of New York	M,D,O*
The University of Akron	M,D
The University of Alabama	M,D,O
The University of Alabama at Birmingham	M*
University of Alaska Anchorage	M
University of Alaska Fairbanks	M
University of Alberta	M,D*
University of Arkansas	M,D,O
University of Arkansas at Little Rock	M
University of Central Arkansas	M
University of Central Florida	M,D,O*
University of Central Missouri	M,O
University of Central Oklahoma	M
University of Cincinnati	M,D,O
University of Colorado at Colorado Springs	M,D
University of Colorado Denver	M*
University of Connecticut	M,D,O*
University of Dayton	M,O
University of Detroit Mercy	M
University of Florida	M,D,O*
University of Georgia	M,D,O*
University of Guam	M
University of Hartford	M,O*
University of Houston–Clear Lake	M
University of Houston–Victoria	M
University of Idaho	M,D,O
University of Illinois at Urbana–Champaign	M,D,O*
The University of Iowa	M,D*
University of La Verne	M,O
University of Louisiana at Lafayette	M*
University of Louisiana at Monroe	M
University of Louisville	M,D
University of Maine	M,D,O*
University of Manitoba	M
University of Mary Hardin-Baylor	M
University of Maryland, College Park	M,D,O*
University of Maryland Eastern Shore	M*
University of Massachusetts Amherst	M,D,O*
University of Massachusetts Boston	M,O
University of Memphis	M,D
University of Miami	M,O*
University of Minnesota, Twin Cities Campus	M,D,O*
University of Mississippi	M,D,O
University of Missouri–St. Louis	M,D
The University of Montana	M,D,O
University of Montevallo	M
University of Nebraska at Kearney	M,O
University of Nebraska at Omaha	M
University of Nevada, Las Vegas	M,O
University of Nevada, Reno	M,D,O*
University of New Hampshire	M,O*
University of New Mexico	M,D*
University of New Orleans	M,D,O
University of North Alabama	M
The University of North Carolina at Chapel Hill	M*
The University of North Carolina at Charlotte	M,D*
The University of North Carolina at Greensboro	M,D,O
The University of North Carolina at Pembroke	M
University of Northern Colorado	M,D
University of Northern Iowa	M,D
University of North Florida	M
University of North Texas	M,D,O
University of Oklahoma	M*
University of Phoenix–New Mexico Campus	M
University of Phoenix–Southern Arizona Campus	M,O
University of Puerto Rico, Río Piedras	M,D
University of Puget Sound	M
University of Saint Francis (IN)	M
University of San Diego	M
University of San Francisco	M,D
The University of Scranton	M
University of South Africa	M,D
University of South Alabama	M,D*
University of South Carolina	D,O
The University of South Dakota	M,D,O
University of Southern California	M*
University of Southern Maine	M,O
University of South Florida	M,D,O*
The University of Tennessee	M,D,O
The University of Tennessee at Chattanooga	M,O
The University of Tennessee at Martin	M
The University of Texas at Austin	M,D
The University of Texas at Brownsville	M
The University of Texas at El Paso	M
The University of Texas at San Antonio	M,D,O*
The University of Texas of the Permian Basin	M
The University of Texas–Pan American	M
University of the District of Columbia	M
University of the Southwest	M
The University of Toledo	M,D,O
University of Utah	M,D*
University of Vermont	M*
University of Victoria	M,D
University of Virginia	M,D,O
The University of West Alabama	M
University of West Florida	M
University of West Georgia	M,O
University of Wisconsin–Madison	M*
University of Wisconsin–Milwaukee	M,D
University of Wisconsin–Oshkosh	M
University of Wisconsin–Platteville	M
University of Wisconsin–River Falls	M,O
University of Wisconsin–Stevens Point	M
University of Wisconsin–Superior	M
University of Wisconsin–Whitewater	M*
University of Wyoming	M,D
Utah State University	M,D
Valdosta State University	M,O
Vanderbilt University	M*
Villanova University	M*
Virginia Commonwealth University	M
Virginia Polytechnic Institute and State University	M,D,O*
Wake Forest University	M*
Walsh University	M
Washington State University Tri-Cities	M,D
Wayne State College	M
Wayne State University	M,D,O*
West Chester University of Pennsylvania	M,O
Western Carolina University	M
Western Connecticut State University	M
Western Illinois University	M
Western Kentucky University	M,O
Western Michigan University	M,D*
Western New Mexico University	M
Western Washington University	M
Westfield State College	M
Westminster College (PA)	M,O
West Texas A&M University	M
West Virginia University	M
Whitworth University	M
Wichita State University	M,D,O*
Widener University	M,D*
William Paterson University of New Jersey	M*
Wilmington University	M
Winona State University	M
Winthrop University	M
Wright State University	M
Xavier University	M*
Xavier University of Louisiana	M
Youngstown State University	M

CRIMINAL JUSTICE AND CRIMINOLOGY

Albany State University	M
American Public University System	M
American University	M,D*
American University of Puerto Rico	M
Anderson University (SC)	M
Andrew Jackson University	M
Anna Maria College	M
Appalachian State University	M
Arizona State University at the West campus	M,D
Arkansas State University	M,O
Armstrong Atlantic State University	M
Auburn University Montgomery	M
Bayamón Central University	M
Bellevue University	M,D
Boise State University	M
Boston University	M*
Bowling Green State University	M*
Bridgewater State College	M
Buffalo State College, State University of New York	M
California State University, Fresno	M
California State University, Long Beach	M
California State University, Los Angeles	M
California State University, Sacramento	M
California State University, San Bernardino	M
California State University, Stanislaus	M
California University of Pennsylvania	M
Calumet College of Saint Joseph	M
Capella University	M,D,O
Caribbean University	M,D
Carnegie Mellon University	M*
Central Connecticut State University	M
Chaminade University of Honolulu	M,O
Charleston Southern University	M
Chicago State University	M
Clark Atlanta University	M
Colorado Technical University Colorado Springs	M
Colorado Technical University Denver	M
Colorado Technical University Sioux Falls	M
Columbia College (MO)	M
Columbia Southern University	M
Columbus State University	M
Concordia University, St. Paul	M
Coppin State University	M
Curry College	M
Dallas Baptist University	M
Defiance College	M
Delta State University	M
DeSales University	M
Drury University	M
East Carolina University	M
East Central University	M
Eastern Kentucky University	M

Eastern Michigan University	M,O
East Tennessee State University	M
Everest University	M
Everest University	M
Everest University	M
Everest University	M
Fairmont State University	M
Fayetteville State University	M
Ferris State University	M
Fitchburg State College	M
Florida Agricultural and Mechanical University	M
Florida Atlantic University	M
Florida Gulf Coast University	M
Florida International University	M*
Florida State University	M,D*
George Mason University	M,D*
The George Washington University	M*
Georgia College & State University	M
Georgia State University	M,D,O
Graduate School and University Center of the City University of New York	D*
Grambling State University	M
Grand Valley State University	M
Hodges University	M
Holy Family University	M
Husson University	M
Illinois State University	M
Indiana State University	M
Indiana University Bloomington	M,D*
Indiana University Northwest	M,O
Indiana University of Pennsylvania	M,D
Indiana University–Purdue University Indianapolis	M*
Inter American University of Puerto Rico, Aguadilla Campus	M
Inter American University of Puerto Rico, Metropolitan Campus	M
Inter American University of Puerto Rico, Ponce Campus	M
Iona College	M*
Jackson State University	M
Jacksonville State University	M
John Jay College of Criminal Justice of the City University of New York	M,D
The Johns Hopkins University	M*
Kaplan University–Davenport Campus	M
Kean University	M
Keiser University	M
Kent State University	M*
Keuka College	M
Lamar University	M
Lewis University	M
Lincoln University (MO)	M
Lindenwood University	M,O
Long Island University, Brentwood Campus	M
Long Island University, C.W. Post Campus	M
Longwood University	M
Loyola University Chicago	M*
Loyola University New Orleans	M
Lynn University	M,O
Madonna University	M
Marshall University	M
Marywood University	M
Mercyhurst College	M,O
Methodist University	M
Michigan State University	M,D*
Middle Tennessee State University	M
Midwestern State University	M
Minot State University	M
Mississippi College	M,O
Mississippi Valley State University	M
Missouri Southern State University	M
Missouri State University	M*
Monmouth University	M,O
Morehead State University	M
Mountain State University	M*
Mount Aloysius College	M
National University	M
New Jersey City University	M
New Mexico State University	M
Niagara University	M
Nichols College	M
Norfolk State University	M
North Carolina Central University	M
North Dakota State University	M,D
Northeastern State University	M
Northeastern University	M,D*
Northern Arizona University	M,O
Northern Michigan University	M
Norwich University	M
Nova Southeastern University	M*
Oklahoma City University	M
Old Dominion University	D
Penn State Harrisburg	M,D
Penn State University Park	M,D*
Point Park University	M*
Polytechnic Institute of NYU	M,D,O
Pontifical Catholic University of Puerto Rico	M
Pontificia Universidad Catolica Madre y Maestra	M
Portland State University	M,D
Radford University	M
Regis University	M,O
The Richard Stockton College of New Jersey	M
Roger Williams University	M*
Rowan University	M
Rutgers, The State University of New Jersey, Camden	M
Rutgers, The State University of New Jersey, Newark	D*
Sacred Heart University	M
Sage Graduate School	M,O
St. Ambrose University	M
St. Cloud State University	M
St. John's University (NY)	M
Saint Joseph's University	M,O
Saint Leo University	M
Saint Mary's University (Canada)	M
St. Thomas University	M,O
Salem State College	M
Salve Regina University	M
Sam Houston State University	M,D
San Diego State University	M*
San Jose State University	M
Seattle University	M
Shippensburg University of Pennsylvania	M
Simon Fraser University	M,D
Southeast Missouri State University	M
Southern Illinois University Carbondale	M*
Southern University and Agricultural and Mechanical College	M
Southwestern College (KS)	M
Suffolk University	M*
Sul Ross State University	M*
Tarleton State University	M
Temple University	M,D*
Tennessee State University	M
Texas A&M International University	M
Texas Southern University	M,D
Texas State University–San Marcos	M*
Tiffin University	M
Trine University	M
Troy University	M
TUI University	M,D
Universidad del Este	M
Universidad del Turabo	M
Université de Montréal	M,D
University at Albany, State University of New York	M,D*
The University of Alabama	M
The University of Alabama at Birmingham	M*
The University of Alabama in Huntsville	O
University of Alaska Fairbanks	M
University of Alberta	M,D*
University of Arkansas at Little Rock	M
University of Baltimore	M
University of California, Irvine	M,D*
University of Central Florida	M,O*
University of Central Missouri	M,O
University of Central Oklahoma	M
University of Cincinnati	M,D
University of Colorado at Colorado Springs	M
University of Colorado Denver	M*
University of Delaware	M,D*
University of Denver	M,O*
University of Detroit Mercy	M
University of Florida	M,D*
University of Great Falls	M
University of Guelph	M,D
University of Houston–Clear Lake	M
University of Houston–Downtown	M
University of Illinois at Chicago	M,D*
University of Louisiana at Monroe	M
University of Louisville	M
University of Management and Technology	M
University of Maryland, College Park	M,D*
University of Maryland Eastern Shore	M*
University of Massachusetts Lowell	M
University of Memphis	M
University of Minnesota, Duluth	M
University of Missouri–Kansas City	M*
University of Missouri–St. Louis	M,D
The University of Montana	M
University of Nebraska at Omaha	M,D
University of Nevada, Las Vegas	M
University of Nevada, Reno	M*
University of New Haven	M*
University of North Alabama	M
The University of North Carolina at Charlotte	M*
The University of North Carolina at Greensboro	M
The University of North Carolina Wilmington	M
University of North Dakota	D
University of Northern Iowa	M
University of North Florida	M
University of North Texas	M
University of Ottawa	M,D*
University of Pennsylvania	M,D*
University of Phoenix	M
University of Phoenix–Atlanta Campus	M
University of Phoenix–Augusta Campus	M
University of Phoenix–Austin Campus	M
University of Phoenix–Bay Area Campus	M
University of Phoenix–Birmingham Campus	M
University of Phoenix–Chattanooga Campus	M
University of Phoenix–Cheyenne Campus	M
University of Phoenix–Cincinnati Campus	M
University of Phoenix–Cleveland Campus	M
University of Phoenix–Columbus Georgia Campus	M
University of Phoenix–Columbus Ohio Campus	M
University of Phoenix–Dallas Campus	M
University of Phoenix–Denver Campus	M
University of Phoenix–Des Moines Campus	M
University of Phoenix–Harrisburg Campus	M
University of Phoenix–Hawaii Campus	M
University of Phoenix–Houston Campus	M
University of Phoenix–Idaho Campus	M
University of Phoenix–Indianapolis Campus	M
University of Phoenix–Jersey City Campus	M
University of Phoenix–Kansas City Campus	M
University of Phoenix–Las Vegas Campus	M
University of Phoenix–Louisiana Campus	M
University of Phoenix–Maryland Campus	M
University of Phoenix–Memphis Campus	M
University of Phoenix–Metro Detroit Campus	M
University of Phoenix–New Mexico Campus	M
University of Phoenix–Northern Nevada Campus	M
University of Phoenix–Northern Virginia Campus	M
University of Phoenix–Northwest Arkansas Campus	M
University of Phoenix–Oklahoma City Campus	M
University of Phoenix–Omaha Campus	M

*M—master's degree; P—first professional degree; D—doctorate; O—other advanced degree; *—Close-Up and/or Announcement or Display in one of the other books in this series*

University of Phoenix–Oregon Campus M
University of Phoenix–Philadelphia Campus M
University of Phoenix–Pittsburgh Campus M
University of Phoenix–Renton Learning Center M
University of Phoenix–Richmond Campus M
University of Phoenix–Sacramento Valley Campus M
University of Phoenix–St. Louis Campus M
University of Phoenix–San Antonio Campus M
University of Phoenix–San Diego Campus M
University of Phoenix–Savannah Campus M
University of Phoenix–Southern Arizona Campus M,O
University of Phoenix–Southern California Campus M,O
University of Phoenix–Southern Colorado Campus M
University of Phoenix–Springfield Campus M
University of Phoenix–Tulsa Campus M
University of Pittsburgh M,D*
University of Regina M
University of South Africa M,D
University of South Carolina M,D
University of Southern Mississippi M,D
University of South Florida M,D*
The University of Tennessee M,D
The University of Tennessee at Chattanooga M
The University of Texas at Arlington M*
The University of Texas at Dallas M,D*
The University of Texas at San Antonio M*
The University of Texas at Tyler M
The University of Texas of the Permian Basin M
The University of Texas–Pan American M
University of the Fraser Valley M
University of the Pacific P,M,D
The University of Toledo M,O
University of Toronto M,D
University of West Florida M
University of West Georgia M
University of Windsor M,D
University of Wisconsin–Milwaukee M
University of Wisconsin–Platteville M
Upper Iowa University M
Utica College M
Valdosta State University M
Villanova University M*
Virginia College at Birmingham M
Virginia Commonwealth University M,O
Walden University M,D,O
Washburn University M
Washington State University M,D*
Washington State University Spokane M,D
Wayland Baptist University M
Wayne State University M*
Webber International University M*
Webster University M,D
West Chester University of Pennsylvania M
Western Connecticut State University M
Western Illinois University M,O
Western Oregon University M
Westfield State College M
West Texas A&M University M
Wichita State University M*
Widener University M*
Wilmington University M
Wright State University M
Xavier University M*
Youngstown State University M

CULTURAL STUDIES

Ambrose University College P,M,O
American University M,D,O*
Appalachian State University M
Arizona State University M
Assemblies of God Theological Seminary P,M,D
Athabasca University M*
Baptist Bible College P,M
Biola University M,D,O
Brandeis University M
Brock University M
Carnegie Mellon University M,D*
The Catholic University of America M
Central Michigan University M
Chapman University D
Claremont Graduate University M,D,O*
Columbia International University P,M,D,O
Cornell University M,D*
Eastern Michigan University M
George Mason University D*
Grace Theological Seminary P,M,D,O
Graduate Theological Union M,D,O
Lewis & Clark College M,O
Maranatha Baptist Bible College M
McMaster University M,D
New York University M,D,O*
St. Francis Xavier University M
San Francisco State University M
Simmons College M
Simpson University P,M
Southern Illinois University Carbondale M*
State University of New York at Binghamton M,D*
Stony Brook University, State University of New York M,D
Taylor College and Seminary P,M,O
Trent University D
Union Institute & University M
Union University M
University of Alaska Fairbanks M
University of California, Davis M,D*
University of Houston–Clear Lake M
University of Minnesota, Twin Cities Campus D*
University of Pittsburgh M,D*
The University of Texas at San Antonio M,D*
University of the Sacred Heart M
Washington State University M,D*
Wheaton College M,O
Wilfrid Laurier University M

CURRICULUM AND INSTRUCTION

Abilene Christian University M
Acadia University M
American InterContinental University Online M
American University M,O*
Andrews University M,D,O
Angelo State University M
Appalachian State University M
Arizona State University M,D
Arizona State University at the Polytechnic Campus M,D
Arkansas State University M,D,O
Arkansas Tech University M,O
Armstrong Atlantic State University M
Ashland University M
Auburn University M,D,O*
Augusta State University M
Aurora University M,D
Austin Peay State University M,O
Averett University M
Azusa Pacific University M
Ball State University M,O*
Barry University D,O*
Baylor University M,D,O
Benedictine University M
Berry College O
Black Hills State University M
Bloomsburg University of Pennsylvania M
Bob Jones University P,M,D,O
Boise State University D
Boston College M,D,O*
Boston University M,D,O*
Bowling Green State University M*
Bradley University M,O
Brandon University M,O
Brescia University M
Bucknell University M
Buena Vista University M
Caldwell College M*
California Baptist University M
California Coast University M
California State University, Bakersfield M
California State University, Chico M
California State University, Dominguez Hills M
California State University, East Bay M
California State University, Fresno M
California State University, Northridge M
California State University, Sacramento M
California State University, San Bernardino M
California State University, Stanislaus M,O
Calvin College M
Cambridge College M,D,O
Campbellsville University M
Capella University M,D,O
Caribbean University M,D
Carson-Newman College M
Castleton State College M
The Catholic University of America M,D,O
Centenary College of Louisiana M
Central Michigan University M,D,O
Chapman University M,D
Christian Brothers University M
City University of Seattle M,O
Clarion University of Pennsylvania M
Clark Atlanta University M
Clemson University D
The College at Brockport, State University of New York M
The College of Saint Rose M,O*
College of Santa Fe M
The College of William and Mary M,D
Colorado Christian University M
Columbia International University M,D,O
Concordia University (CA) M
Concordia University (OR) M
Concordia University Chicago M
Concordia University, St. Paul M,O
Concordia University Wisconsin M
Converse College O
Coppin State University M
Cornell University M,D*
Dakota Wesleyan University M
Dallas Baptist University M
Delaware State University M
DePaul University D*
Doane College M
Dominican University M
Drexel University M*
Duquesne University M,D,O*
East Carolina University M
Eastern Kentucky University M
Eastern Michigan University M
Eastern Washington University M
East Tennessee State University M
Emporia State University M
Fairleigh Dickinson University, Metropolitan Campus M*
Ferris State University M
Fitchburg State College M
Florida Atlantic University M,D,O
Florida Gulf Coast University M
Florida International University M,D,O*
Fordham University M,D,O*
Framingham State College M
Franciscan University of Steubenville M
Freed-Hardeman University M,O
Fresno Pacific University M
Frostburg State University M
Furman University M
Gannon University M
Gardner-Webb University D
George Fox University M,D,O*
The George Washington University M,D,O*
Georgia College & State University M,O
Georgia Southern University D
Grambling State University M,D
Grand Canyon University M,D*
Harvard University M*
Henderson State University M
Hood College M
Houston Baptist University M
Idaho State University M,O
Illinois State University M,D
Indiana State University M,D
Indiana University Bloomington M,D,O*

Indiana University of Pennsylvania	M,D
Indiana University–Purdue University Indianapolis	M,O*
Indiana Wesleyan University	M
Inter American University of Puerto Rico, Arecibo Campus	M
Inter American University of Puerto Rico, Barranquitas Campus	M
Inter American University of Puerto Rico, Metropolitan Campus	D
Inter American University of Puerto Rico, San Germán Campus	D
Iowa State University of Science and Technology	M,D*
The Johns Hopkins University	M,O*
Johnson State College	M
Jones International University	M
Kansas State University	M,D*
Kean University	M
Keene State College	M,O
Kent State University	M,D,O*
Kutztown University of Pennsylvania	M,O
LaGrange College	M
Lake Erie College	M
Lander University	M
La Sierra University	M,D,O
Lesley University	M,D,O*
Lewis University	M
Liberty University	M,D,O
Lincoln Memorial University	M,O
Lipscomb University	M
Louisiana State University in Shreveport	M
Louisiana Tech University	M,D
Loyola University Chicago	M,D*
Loyola University Maryland	M,O*
Lynchburg College	M
Lyndon State College	M
Malone University	M
Massachusetts College of Liberal Arts	M
McDaniel College	M
McGill University	M,D,O*
McNeese State University	M
Medaille College	M
Memorial University of Newfoundland	M,D,O
Mercer University	M,D,O
Miami University	M*
Michigan State University	M,D,O*
Middle Tennessee State University	M,O
Midwestern State University	M
Mills College	M,D
Minnesota State University Mankato	M,O
Minnesota State University Moorhead	M
Misericordia University	M
Mississippi College	M,D,O
Mississippi State University	M,D,O
Mississippi University for Women	M
Missouri State University	M*
Montana State University	M,D,O
Montana State University–Billings	M
Montclair State University	M,D,O*
Morehead State University	M,O
Mount Saint Vincent University	M
National-Louis University	M,D,O
Newman University	M
New Mexico Highlands University	M
New Mexico State University	M,D,O
Nicholls State University	M
North Carolina Central University	M
North Carolina State University	M,D*
North Central College	M
Northern Arizona University	D
Northern Illinois University	M,D
Northwestern State University of Louisiana	M
Northwest Nazarene University	M
Nova Southeastern University	M,O*
Ohio University	M,D*
Oklahoma State University	M,D*
Old Dominion University	M,D
Olivet Nazarene University	M
Oral Roberts University	M,D
Ottawa University	M
Our Lady of Holy Cross College	M
Our Lady of the Lake University of San Antonio	M
Pace University	M,O*
Pacific Lutheran University	M
Penn State Great Valley	M
Penn State Harrisburg	M,D
Penn State University Park	M,D*
Peru State College	M
Philadelphia Biblical University	M
Piedmont College	M,O
Point Park University	M*
Pontifical Catholic University of Puerto Rico	M,D
Portland State University	M,D
Prairie View A&M University	M
Purdue University	M,D,O
Regis University	M,O
Rider University	M,O*
Rivier College	M,D,O
Rosemont College	M
Rowan University	M
St. Bonaventure University	M,O
St. Cloud State University	M
St. Francis Xavier University	M
Saint Leo University	M
Saint Louis University	M,D
Saint Mary's College of California	M
Saint Mary's University of Minnesota	M,O
Saint Michael's College	M,O
Saint Peter's College	M,O
Saint Vincent College	M
Saint Xavier University	M,O
Salem International University	M
Sam Houston State University	M
San Diego State University	M*
Seattle Pacific University	M
Seattle University	M,O
Shaw University	M
Shepherd University	M
Shippensburg University of Pennsylvania	M
Simon Fraser University	M,D
Sonoma State University	M
South Dakota State University	M
Southeastern Louisiana University	M
Southern Adventist University	M
Southern Illinois University Carbondale	M,D*
Southern Illinois University Edwardsville	M
Southern Nazarene University	M
Southern New Hampshire University	M,O*
Southwestern Adventist University	M
Southwestern Assemblies of God University	M
Southwestern College (KS)	M
Stanford University	M,D*
State University of New York at Plattsburgh	M
State University of New York College at Potsdam	M
Stephens College	M
Syracuse University	M,D,O*
Tarleton State University	M
Teachers College, Columbia University	M,D
Tennessee State University	M,D
Tennessee Technological University	M,O*
Tennessee Temple University	M
Texas A&M International University	M,D
Texas A&M University	M,D*
Texas A&M University–Commerce	M,D
Texas A&M University–Corpus Christi	M,D
Texas A&M University–Texarkana	M
Texas Christian University	M
Texas Southern University	M,D
Texas Tech University	M,D
Texas Woman's University	M,D
Trevecca Nazarene University	M
Trinity (Washington) University	M
Universidad Adventista de las Antillas	M
Universidad del Turabo	M,D
Universidad Metropolitana	M
Université de Montréal	M,D,O
Université Laval	M,D
University at Albany, State University of New York	M,D,O*
University of Alaska Fairbanks	M,D,O
University of Arkansas	D
The University of British Columbia	M,D
University of Calgary	M,D,O
University of California, Davis	M,D*
University of California, Riverside	M,D*
University of Central Florida	M,D,O*
University of Central Missouri	M,O
University of Cincinnati	M,D
University of Colorado at Boulder	M,D*
University of Colorado at Colorado Springs	M,D
University of Colorado Denver	M*
University of Delaware	M,D,O*
University of Denver	M,D,O*
University of Detroit Mercy	M
University of Florida	M,D,O*
University of Hawaii at Manoa	M,D*
University of Houston	M,D*
University of Houston–Clear Lake	M
University of Houston–Downtown	M
University of Houston–Victoria	M
University of Idaho	M,D
University of Illinois at Chicago	M,D*
University of Illinois at Urbana–Champaign	M,D,O*
University of Indianapolis	M
The University of Iowa	M,D*
The University of Kansas	M,D*
University of Kentucky	M,D
University of Louisiana at Lafayette	M*
University of Louisiana at Monroe	M,D
University of Louisville	D
University of Maine	M*
University of Manitoba	M
University of Mary	M
University of Maryland, Baltimore County	M,O*
University of Maryland, College Park	M,D,O*
University of Massachusetts Boston	M
University of Massachusetts Lowell	M,D,O
University of Memphis	M,D
University of Michigan	M,D*
University of Minnesota, Twin Cities Campus	M,D,O*
University of Mississippi	M,D,O
University of Missouri–Columbia	M,D,O*
University of Missouri–Kansas City	M,D,O*
University of Missouri–St. Louis	M,O
The University of Montana	M,D
University of Nebraska at Kearney	M
University of Nebraska–Lincoln	M,D,O*
University of Nevada, Las Vegas	M,D
University of Nevada, Reno	D*
University of New Orleans	M,D,O
The University of North Carolina at Chapel Hill	M,D*
The University of North Carolina at Charlotte	M,D,O*
The University of North Carolina at Greensboro	M,D,O
The University of North Carolina Wilmington	M
University of Northern Iowa	M,D
University of North Texas	M,D
University of Oklahoma	M,D,O*
University of Phoenix	M
University of Phoenix–Austin Campus	M
University of Phoenix–Bay Area Campus	M
University of Phoenix–Central Florida Campus	M
University of Phoenix–Central Valley Campus	M
University of Phoenix–Chattanooga Campus	M
University of Phoenix–Dallas Campus	M
University of Phoenix–Denver Campus	M
University of Phoenix–Hawaii Campus	M
University of Phoenix–Houston Campus	M
University of Phoenix–Idaho Campus	M
University of Phoenix–Las Vegas Campus	M
University of Phoenix–Louisiana Campus	M
University of Phoenix–Memphis Campus	M
University of Phoenix–Metro Detroit Campus	M
University of Phoenix–Nashville Campus	M
University of Phoenix–New Mexico Campus	M

*M—master's degree; P—first professional degree; D—doctorate; O—other advanced degree; *—Close-Up and/or Announcement or Display in one of the other books in this series*

University of Phoenix–Northern Nevada Campus	M
University of Phoenix–North Florida Campus	M
University of Phoenix–Omaha Campus	M
University of Phoenix–Oregon Campus	M
University of Phoenix–Phoenix Campus	M
University of Phoenix–Richmond Campus	M
University of Phoenix–Sacramento Valley Campus	M,O
University of Phoenix–San Antonio Campus	M
University of Phoenix–San Diego Campus	M
University of Phoenix–Southern Arizona Campus	M,O
University of Phoenix–Southern California Campus	M
University of Phoenix–Southern Colorado Campus	M,O
University of Phoenix–South Florida Campus	M
University of Phoenix–Springfield Campus	M
University of Phoenix–Utah Campus	M
University of Phoenix–Vancouver Campus	M
University of Phoenix–West Florida Campus	M
University of Phoenix–West Michigan Campus	M
University of Puerto Rico, Río Piedras	M,D
University of Regina	M
University of St. Francis (IL)	M
University of Saint Mary	M
University of St. Thomas (MN)	M,D,O*
University of San Diego	M
University of San Francisco	M,D
University of Saskatchewan	M,D,O
The University of Scranton	M
University of South Africa	M,D
University of South Carolina	D
The University of South Dakota	M,D,O
University of Southern Mississippi	M,D,O
The University of Tampa	M
The University of Tennessee	M,D,O
The University of Texas at Arlington	M,D*
The University of Texas at Austin	M,D
The University of Texas at Brownsville	M
The University of Texas at El Paso	M,D
The University of Texas at San Antonio	M*
University of the Pacific	M,D
University of the Southwest	M
The University of Toledo	M,D,O
University of Vermont	M*
University of Victoria	M,D
University of Virginia	M,D,O
University of Washington	M,D*
The University of Western Ontario	M
University of West Florida	D,O
University of Wisconsin–Madison	M,D*
University of Wisconsin–Milwaukee	M,D
University of Wisconsin–Oshkosh	M
University of Wisconsin–Superior	M
University of Wisconsin–Whitewater	M*
University of Wyoming	M,D
Utah State University	D
Virginia Commonwealth University	M,O
Virginia Polytechnic Institute and State University	M,D,O*
Walden University	M,D,O
Walla Walla University	M
Washburn University	M
Washington State University	M,D*
Wayne State College	M
Wayne State University	M,D,O*
Weber State University	M
Western Connecticut State University	M
West Texas A&M University	M
West Virginia University	M,D
Wichita State University	M*
William Woods University	M,O
Wright State University	M,O
Xavier University of Louisiana	M
Youngstown State University	M

DANCE

Arizona State University	M
Bennington College	M
California Institute of the Arts	M,O
California State University, Fullerton	M
California State University, Long Beach	M
California State University, Sacramento	M
Case Western Reserve University	M*
The College at Brockport, State University of New York	M
Florida State University	M*
George Mason University	M*
Hollins University	M
Mills College	M
New York University	M,D*
Northern Illinois University	M
The Ohio State University	D*
Oklahoma City University	M
Purchase College, State University of New York	M
Sam Houston State University	M
Sarah Lawrence College	M*
Shenandoah University	M,D,O
Smith College	M
Southern Methodist University	M*
Temple University	M,D*
Texas Tech University	M,D
Texas Woman's University	M,D
Tufts University	M,D*
Tulane University	M
Université du Québec à Montréal	M
University of California, Irvine	M*
University of California, Los Angeles	M,D*
University of California, Riverside	M,D*
University of Colorado at Boulder	M,D*
University of Hawaii at Manoa	M,D*
University of Illinois at Urbana–Champaign	M*
The University of Iowa	M*
University of Maryland, College Park	M*
University of Michigan	M*
University of Minnesota, Twin Cities Campus	M,D*
University of New Mexico	M*
The University of North Carolina at Charlotte	M*
The University of North Carolina at Greensboro	M
University of Oklahoma	M*
University of Oregon	M*
The University of Texas at Austin	M,D
University of Utah	M*
University of Washington	M*
University of Wisconsin–Milwaukee	M
York University	M

DATABASE SYSTEMS

Colorado Technical University Colorado Springs	M,D
Colorado Technical University Denver	M
Ferris State University	M
George Mason University	M,D,O*
Minnesota State University Mankato	M,O
National University	M
New York University	M,O*
Regis University	M,O
Rochester Institute of Technology	M,O
Sacred Heart University	M,O
Stevens Institute of Technology	M,D,O
Towson University	D,O

DECORATIVE ARTS

Bard College	M,D
Bard Graduate Center for Studies in the Decorative Arts, Design, and Culture	M,D*
Corcoran College of Art and Design	M
The New School: A University	M*

DEMOGRAPHY AND POPULATION STUDIES

The American University in Cairo	M,O
Bowling Green State University	M,D*
Cornell University	M,D*
Emory University	M*
Florida State University	M,O*
Harvard University	M,D*
The Johns Hopkins University	M,D*
Penn State University Park	M,D*
Princeton University	D,O*
Université de Montréal	M,D
Université du Québec, Institut National de la Recherche Scientifique	M,D
University at Albany, State University of New York	M,D,O*
University of Alberta	M,D*
University of California, Berkeley	M,D*
University of California, Irvine	M*
University of Guelph	M,D
University of Hawaii at Manoa	O*
University of Pennsylvania	M,D*
University of Puerto Rico, Medical Sciences Campus	M
The University of Texas at San Antonio	D*
University of Washington	M,D*
Washington State University	M,D*

DENTAL HYGIENE

Boston University	P,M,D,O*
Eastern Washington University	M
Idaho State University	M
Missouri Southern State University	M
Old Dominion University	M
Texas A&M Health Science Center	M
Université de Montréal	O
University of Alberta	O*
University of Bridgeport	M
University of Maryland, Baltimore	M*
University of Michigan	M*
University of Missouri–Kansas City	P,M,D,O*
University of New Mexico	M*
The University of North Carolina at Chapel Hill	M,D*
The University of Texas Health Science Center at San Antonio	M

DENTISTRY

Boston University	P,M,D,O*
Case Western Reserve University	P*
Columbia University	P*
Creighton University	P*
Harvard University	P,M,D,O*
Howard University	P,O
Idaho State University	O
Indiana University–Purdue University Indianapolis	P,M,D,O*
Loma Linda University	P,M,O
Louisiana State University Health Sciences Center	P*
Marquette University	P
McGill University	P,M,D,O*
Medical College of Georgia	P
Medical University of South Carolina	P
Meharry Medical College	P
Midwestern University, Glendale Campus	P*
New York University	P*
Nova Southeastern University	P,M*
The Ohio State University	P,M*
Oregon Health & Science University	P,O*
Saint Louis University	M
Southern Illinois University Edwardsville	P
Stony Brook University, State University of New York	P,O
Temple University	P*
Texas A&M Health Science Center	P
Tufts University	P*
Universidad Iberoamericana	P,M
Universidad Nacional Pedro Henriquez Urena	P
Université Laval	P
University at Buffalo, the State University of New York	P,M,D,O*
The University of Alabama at Birmingham	P*
University of Alberta	P*
The University of British Columbia	P
University of California, Los Angeles	P,O*
University of California, San Francisco	P
University of Colorado Denver	P*
University of Connecticut Health Center	P,O*

University of Detroit Mercy P
University of Florida P,O*
University of Illinois at Chicago P*
The University of Iowa P,M,D,O*
University of Kentucky P,M
University of Louisville P
University of Manitoba P
University of Maryland, Baltimore P,M,O*
University of Medicine and Dentistry of New Jersey P,M,O*
University of Michigan P*
University of Minnesota, Twin Cities Campus P*
University of Mississippi Medical Center P,M,D*
University of Missouri–Kansas City P,M,D,O*
University of Nebraska Medical Center P,M,D,O*
The University of North Carolina at Chapel Hill P*
University of Oklahoma Health Sciences Center P,O
University of Pennsylvania P*
University of Pittsburgh P,M,O*
University of Puerto Rico, Medical Sciences Campus P
University of Saskatchewan P
University of Southern California P*
The University of Tennessee Health Science Center P,M,O*
The University of Texas Health Science Center at Houston P,M
The University of Texas Health Science Center at San Antonio P,M,O
University of the Pacific P,M,O
University of Toronto P
University of Washington P*
The University of Western Ontario P
Virginia Commonwealth University P,M
Western University of Health Sciences P
West Virginia University P

DEVELOPMENTAL BIOLOGY

Albert Einstein College of Medicine D
Baylor College of Medicine D*
Brigham Young University M,D*
Brown University M,D*
California Institute of Technology D*
Carnegie Mellon University M,D*
Columbia University M,D*
Cornell University M,D*
Duke University D,O*
Emory University D*
Illinois State University M,D
Iowa State University of Science and Technology M,D*
The Johns Hopkins University D*
Louisiana State University Health Sciences Center M,D*
Marquette University M,D
Massachusetts Institute of Technology D*
Medical College of Wisconsin D*
Medical University of South Carolina M,D
New York University M,D*
Northwestern University D*
The Ohio State University M,D*
Oregon Health & Science University D*
Penn State University Park M,D*
Purdue University M,D
Rensselaer Polytechnic Institute M,D
Rutgers, The State University of New Jersey, New Brunswick M,D*
Stanford University D*
Stony Brook University, State University of New York M,D
Thomas Jefferson University M,D*
Tufts University D*
University at Albany, State University of New York M,D*
University of California, Davis M,D*
University of California, Irvine M,D*
University of California, Los Angeles D*
University of California, Riverside M,D*
University of California, San Diego D*
University of California, San Francisco D
University of California, Santa Barbara M,D
University of California, Santa Cruz M,D*
University of Chicago D*
University of Cincinnati D
University of Colorado at Boulder M,D*
University of Colorado Denver D*
University of Connecticut M,D*
University of Connecticut Health Center D*
University of Delaware M,D*
University of Illinois at Urbana–Champaign D*
The University of Kansas M,D*
University of Massachusetts Amherst D*
University of Miami D*
University of Michigan M,D*
University of Minnesota, Twin Cities Campus M,D*
University of Missouri–St. Louis M,D,O
The University of North Carolina at Chapel Hill M,D*
University of Pennsylvania D*
University of Pittsburgh D*
University of South Carolina M,D
The University of Texas Health Science Center at Houston M,D
The University of Texas Southwestern Medical Center at Dallas D*
Virginia Polytechnic Institute and State University M,D*
Washington University in St. Louis D*
Wesleyan University D*
West Virginia University M,D
Yale University D*

DEVELOPMENTAL EDUCATION

Eastern Michigan University M,O
Edinboro University of Pennsylvania M,O
Ferris State University M
Grambling State University M,D
Instituto Tecnológico y de Estudios Superiores de Monterrey, Campus Ciudad Obregón M
National-Louis University M,O
North Carolina State University M,D,O*
Rutgers, The State University of New Jersey, New Brunswick M*
Texas State University–San Marcos M,D*
University of California, Berkeley *
The University of Iowa M,D*

DEVELOPMENTAL PSYCHOLOGY

Andrews University M,D
Arizona State University D
Boston College M,D*
Bowling Green State University M,D*
Brandeis University M,D
Brown University D*
Bryn Mawr College D*
Capella University M,D,O
Carnegie Mellon University D*
Chatham University M,D
Claremont Graduate University M,D,O*
Clark University D
Cornell University D*
Duke University D*
Emory University D*
Erikson Institute M,O
Florida State University D*
Fordham University D*
Gallaudet University M,O
George Mason University M,D*
Graduate School and University Center of the City University of New York D*
Harvard University D*
Howard University M,D
Illinois State University M,D,O
Indiana University Bloomington M,D*
Louisiana State University and Agricultural and Mechanical College M,D
Loyola University Chicago M,D*
McGill University M,D,O*
New York University M,D*
North Carolina State University D*
The Ohio State University M,D*
Penn State University Park M,D*
Queen's University at Kingston M,D
Stanford University D*
Teachers College, Columbia University M,D
Temple University D*
Texas A&M University M,D*
Université de Montréal M,D,O
The University of British Columbia M,D
University of California, Santa Barbara M,D
University of Connecticut M,D,O*
University of Florida M,D*
The University of Kansas M,D*
University of Maine M,D*
University of Maryland, Baltimore County D*
University of Maryland, College Park M,D*
University of Massachusetts Amherst M,D*
University of Miami M,D*
University of Michigan D*
The University of Montana M,D,O
University of Nebraska at Omaha M,D,O
University of Nebraska–Lincoln M,D,O*
The University of North Carolina at Chapel Hill D*
The University of North Carolina at Greensboro M,D
University of Notre Dame D*
University of Oregon M,D*
University of Pittsburgh M,D*
University of Rochester M,D*
University of Southern California M,D*
University of Victoria M,D
University of Washington D*
University of Wisconsin–Madison D*
University of Wisconsin–Milwaukee M,D
Virginia Polytechnic Institute and State University M,D*
Walden University M,D,O
Wayne State University M,D*
West Virginia University M,D
Wilfrid Laurier University M,D
Yale University D*

DISABILITY STUDIES

Brandeis University D
Brock University M,O
Chapman University D
New York Medical College M*
Syracuse University O*
University of Hawaii at Manoa O*
University of Illinois at Chicago M,D*
University of Manitoba M
University of Northern British Columbia M,D,O
University of Pittsburgh O*
Utah State University M,D,O
York University M,D

DISTANCE EDUCATION DEVELOPMENT

Athabasca University M,O*
Barry University O*
Endicott College M
Fairmont State University M
Florida State University M,D,O*
Jones International University M
New York Institute of Technology M,O
Nova Southeastern University M,D*
Saginaw Valley State University M
Télé-université M,D
Thomas Edison State College O
University of Maryland, Baltimore County M,O*
University of Maryland University College M,O
University of Nebraska–Lincoln M*
University of Wyoming M,D,O
Western Illinois University M,O

EARLY CHILDHOOD EDUCATION

Adelphi University M,O*
Alabama Agricultural and Mechanical University M,O
Alabama State University M,O
Albany State University M
Albright College M
American University M,O*
Anna Maria College M,O
Antioch University New England M*
Arcadia University M,D,O
Arkansas State University M,O
Armstrong Atlantic State University M
Auburn University M,D,O*
Auburn University Montgomery M,O
Austin Peay State University M,O
Bank Street College of Education M*
Barry University M,D,O*

*M—master's degree; P—first professional degree; D—doctorate; O—other advanced degree; *—Close-Up and/or Announcement or Display in one of the other books in this series*

Bayamón Central University	M
Bellarmine University	M
Belmont University	M
Bennington College	M
Berry College	M
Bloomsburg University of Pennsylvania	M
Boise State University	M
Boston College	M*
Boston University	M,D,O*
Bowling Green State University	M*
Brenau University	M,O
Bridgewater State College	M
Brooklyn College of the City University of New York	M
Buffalo State College, State University of New York	M
California State University, Bakersfield	M
California State University, Fresno	M
California State University, Northridge	M
California State University, Sacramento	M
Cambridge College	M,D,O
Canisius College	M
Caribbean University	M,D
Carlow University	M
Central Connecticut State University	M
Central Michigan University	M,O
Chatham University	M
Chestnut Hill College	M
Cheyney University of Pennsylvania	O
Chicago State University	M
City College of the City University of New York	M*
Clarion University of Pennsylvania	M
Clarke College	M
Cleveland State University	M
Coastal Carolina University	M
College of Charleston	M*
College of Mount St. Joseph	M
The College of New Jersey	M
The College of New Rochelle	M
The College of Saint Rose	M,O*
Columbia International University	M,D,O
Columbus State University	M,O
Concordia University Chicago	M,D
Concordia University, Nebraska	M
Concordia University, St. Paul	M,O
Concordia University Wisconsin	M
Converse College	M,O
Daemen College	M
Dominican University	M
Duquesne University	M*
Eastern Connecticut State University	M
Eastern Illinois University	M
Eastern Michigan University	M
Eastern Nazarene College	M,O
Eastern Washington University	M
East Tennessee State University	M
Edinboro University of Pennsylvania	M,O
Elms College	M,O
Emporia State University	M
Endicott College	M
Erikson Institute	M,D
Fitchburg State College	M
Five Towns College	M
Florida Agricultural and Mechanical University	M
Florida Atlantic University	M,D,O
Florida Gulf Coast University	M
Florida International University	M,D*
Florida State University	M,D,O*
Fordham University	M,D,O*
Framingham State College	M
Francis Marion University	M
Furman University	M
Gallaudet University	M,D,O
Gannon University	M
George Mason University	M,O*
The George Washington University	M*
Georgia College & State University	M,O
Georgia Southern University	M
Georgia Southwestern State University	M,O
Georgia State University	M,D,O
Golden Gate Baptist Theological Seminary	P,M,D,O
Governors State University	M
Grand Valley State University	M,O
Hampton University	M
Harding University	M,O
Hebrew College	M,O
Henderson State University	M
Hofstra University	M,O*
Hood College	M
Howard University	M,O
Hunter College of the City University of New York	M,O
Indiana State University	M
Indiana University–Purdue University Indianapolis	M,O*
Inter American University of Puerto Rico, Guayama Campus	M
Jackson State University	M,D,O
Jacksonville State University	M
Jacksonville University	M,O
James Madison University	M
John Carroll University	M
The Johns Hopkins University	M,D,O*
Kean University	M
Kennesaw State University	M
Kent State University	M*
Keuka College	M
Kutztown University of Pennsylvania	M,O
Lehman College of the City University of New York	M
Le Moyne College	M,O
Lenoir-Rhyne University	M
Lesley University	M,D,O*
Lewis & Clark College	M
Liberty University	M,D,O
Lincoln University (PA)	M
Long Island University at Riverhead	M
Long Island University, Brentwood Campus	M
Long Island University, C.W. Post Campus	M
Long Island University, Rockland Graduate Campus	M
Long Island University, Westchester Graduate Campus	M,O
Loyola Marymount University	M
Loyola University Maryland	M,O*
Manhattan College	M
Manhattanville College	M*
Marshall University	M
Maryville University of Saint Louis	M,D
Marywood University	M
McNeese State University	M
Mercer University	M,D,O
Mercy College	M
Miami University	M*
Middle Tennessee State University	M,O
Millersville University of Pennsylvania	M
Mills College	M,D
Minnesota State University Mankato	M
Minot State University	M
Missouri Southern State University	M
Missouri State University	M*
Montana State University–Billings	M
Montclair State University	M,O*
Mount Saint Mary College	M
Murray State University	M
National-Louis University	M,O
Nazareth College of Rochester	M
New Jersey City University	M
New York University	M,D,O*
Niagara University	M,O
Norfolk State University	M
Northeastern State University	M
Northern Arizona University	M
Northern Illinois University	M,D
North Georgia College & State University	M,O
Northwestern State University of Louisiana	M
Northwest Missouri State University	M
Nova Southeastern University	M,O*
Oakland University	M,D,O
Oberlin College	M
Oglethorpe University	M
The Ohio State University at Lima	M
The Ohio State University at Marion	M,D
The Ohio State University–Mansfield Campus	M
The Ohio State University–Newark Campus	M
Ohio University	M*
Oklahoma City University	M
Old Dominion University	M,D
Ottawa University	M
Our Lady of the Lake University of San Antonio	M
Pacific University	M
Penn State University Park	M,D*
Piedmont College	M,O
Pittsburg State University	M
Portland State University	M,D
Prescott College	M,D
Queens College of the City University of New York	M,O
Regis University	M,O
Reinhardt College	M
Rhode Island College	M
Rivier College	M,D,O
Roberts Wesleyan College	M,O
Roosevelt University	M
Rutgers, The State University of New Jersey, New Brunswick	M,D*
Saginaw Valley State University	M
St. John's University (NY)	M
St. Joseph's College, Long Island Campus	M
St. Joseph's College, New York	M
Saint Mary's College of California	M
Saint Xavier University	M,O
Salem College	M
Salem State College	M
Samford University	M,D,O
San Francisco State University	M
Shippensburg University of Pennsylvania	M
Siena Heights University	M
South Carolina State University	M
Southern Oregon University	M
Southwestern Oklahoma State University	M
Springfield College	M
Spring Hill College	M
State University of New York at Binghamton	M*
State University of New York at New Paltz	M
State University of New York College at Cortland	M
State University of New York College at Geneseo	M
State University of New York College at Potsdam	M
Stephen F. Austin State University	M
Syracuse University	M*
Teachers College, Columbia University	M,D
Temple University	M,D*
Tennessee Technological University	M,O*
Texas A&M International University	M,D
Texas A&M University–Commerce	M,D
Texas A&M University–Corpus Christi	M,D
Texas A&M University–Kingsville	M
Texas State University–San Marcos	M*
Texas Woman's University	M,D
Towson University	M,O
Trinity (Washington) University	M
Troy University	M,O
Tufts University	M,D,O*
TUI University	M
Universidad del Turabo	M
Universidad Metropolitana	M
University at Buffalo, the State University of New York	M,D,O*
The University of Alabama at Birmingham	M,D*
University of Alaska Anchorage	M,O
University of Alaska Southeast	M
University of Arkansas	M
University of Arkansas at Little Rock	M
University of Bridgeport	M,O
The University of British Columbia	M,D
University of Central Arkansas	M
University of Central Florida	M*
University of Central Oklahoma	M
University of Cincinnati	M
University of Dayton	M
The University of Findlay	M
University of Florida	M,D,O*

University of Georgia	M,D,O*
University of Hartford	M*
University of Hawaii at Manoa	M*
University of Houston	M,D*
University of Houston–Clear Lake	M
The University of Iowa	M,D*
University of Kentucky	M,D
University of Louisville	M
University of Mary	M
University of Maryland, Baltimore County	M*
University of Maryland, College Park	M,D*
University of Massachusetts Amherst	M,D,O*
University of Memphis	M,D
University of Miami	M,O*
University of Michigan	M,D*
University of Michigan–Flint	M*
University of Minnesota, Twin Cities Campus	M,D,O*
University of Missouri–Columbia	M,D,O*
University of Missouri–St. Louis	M,O
University of Nebraska–Lincoln	M,D*
University of Nevada, Las Vegas	M,D,O
University of New Hampshire	M*
The University of North Carolina at Chapel Hill	M,D*
The University of North Carolina at Greensboro	M,D,O
University of North Dakota	M
University of Northern Colorado	M,D
University of Northern Iowa	M
University of North Texas	M,D,O
University of Oklahoma	M,D,O*
University of Phoenix	M
University of Phoenix–Central Florida Campus	M
University of Phoenix–Louisiana Campus	M
University of Phoenix–North Florida Campus	M
University of Phoenix–Oregon Campus	M
University of Phoenix–Phoenix Campus	M
University of Phoenix–Puerto Rico Campus	M
University of Phoenix–South Florida Campus	M
University of Phoenix–West Florida Campus	M
University of Pittsburgh	M*
University of Puerto Rico, Río Piedras	M
The University of Scranton	M
University of South Alabama	M,O*
University of South Carolina	M,D
University of South Carolina Upstate	M
University of Southern Mississippi	M,D,O
University of South Florida	M,D,O*
The University of Tennessee	M,D,O
The University of Texas at Brownsville	M
The University of Texas at San Antonio	M*
The University of Texas at Tyler	M
The University of Texas of the Permian Basin	M
The University of Texas–Pan American	M
University of the Cumberlands	M
University of the District of Columbia	M
University of the Incarnate Word	M,D
University of the Sacred Heart	M
University of the Southwest	M
The University of Toledo	M,O
University of Utah	M,D*
University of Victoria	M,D
University of Virginia	M,D
The University of West Alabama	M
University of West Florida	M
University of West Georgia	M,O
University of Wisconsin–Milwaukee	M
University of Wisconsin–Oshkosh	M
Ursuline College	M
Valdosta State University	M,O
Virginia Commonwealth University	M,O
Wagner College	M
Walden University	M,D,O
Wayne State College	M
Wayne State University	M,D,O*
Webster University	M
Wesleyan College	M
West Chester University of Pennsylvania	M,O
Western Kentucky University	M
Western Oregon University	M
Westfield State College	M
West Virginia University	M,D
Wheelock College	M
Widener University	M,D*
Worcester State College	M
Wright State University	M
Xavier University	M*
Youngstown State University	M

EAST EUROPEAN AND RUSSIAN STUDIES

Boston College	M*
Brown University	M,D*
Carleton University	M,O
Columbia University	M,O*
Cornell University	M,D*
Florida State University	M*
Georgetown University	M
The George Washington University	M*
Harvard University	M*
Indiana University Bloomington	M,O*
La Salle University	M
The Ohio State University	M*
Stanford University	M*
University of Alberta	M,D*
The University of British Columbia	M,D
University of Illinois at Urbana–Champaign	M*
The University of Kansas	M*
University of Michigan	M,O*
The University of North Carolina at Chapel Hill	M*
University of Pittsburgh	O*
University of Saskatchewan	M
The University of Texas at Austin	M
University of Toronto	M
University of Washington	M*
Yale University	M,D*

ECOLOGY

Brown University	D*
California State University, Stanislaus	M
Clemson University	M,D
Colorado State University	M,D*
Columbia University	D,O*
Cornell University	M,D*
Dartmouth College	D*
Duke University	M,D,O*
Eastern Kentucky University	M
Eastern Michigan University	M
Emory University	D*
Florida Institute of Technology	M*
Florida State University	M,D*
Frostburg State University	M
Illinois State University	M,D
Indiana State University	M,D
Indiana University Bloomington	M,D*
Iowa State University of Science and Technology	M,D*
Kent State University	M,D*
Laurentian University	M,D
Lesley University	M,D,O*
Marquette University	M,D
Michigan State University	D*
Michigan Technological University	M
Montana State University	M,D
North Dakota State University	M,D
Nova Scotia Agricultural College	M
The Ohio State University	M,D*
Ohio University	M,D*
Old Dominion University	D
Penn State University Park	M,D*
Princeton University	D*
Purdue University	M,D
Rice University	M,D
Rutgers, The State University of New Jersey, New Brunswick	M,D*
San Diego State University	M,D*
San Francisco State University	M
San Jose State University	M
State University of New York College of Environmental Science and Forestry	M,D
Stony Brook University, State University of New York	M,D
Texas Christian University	M
Tulane University	M,D
University at Albany, State University of New York	M,D*
University at Buffalo, the State University of New York	M,D,O*
University of Alberta	M,D*
The University of Arizona	M,D*
University of California, Davis	M,D*
University of California, Irvine	M,D*
University of California, Los Angeles	M,D*
University of California, San Diego	D*
University of California, Santa Barbara	M,D
University of California, Santa Cruz	M,D*
University of Chicago	D*
University of Colorado at Boulder	M,D*
University of Connecticut	M,D,O*
University of Delaware	M,D*
University of Florida	M,D*
University of Georgia	M,D*
University of Guelph	M,D
University of Hawaii at Manoa	M,D*
University of Illinois at Urbana–Champaign	M,D*
The University of Kansas	M,D*
University of Maine	M,D*
University of Manitoba	M,D
University of Maryland, College Park	M,D*
University of Michigan	M,D*
University of Minnesota, Twin Cities Campus	M,D*
University of Missouri–Columbia	M,D*
University of Missouri–St. Louis	M,D,O
The University of Montana	M,D
University of Nevada, Reno	D*
The University of North Carolina at Chapel Hill	M,D*
University of North Dakota	M,D
University of Notre Dame	M,D*
University of Oklahoma	D*
University of Oregon	M,D*
University of Pittsburgh	D*
University of South Carolina	M,D
The University of Tennessee	M,D
The University of Texas at Austin	M,D
The University of Toledo	M,D
University of Toronto	M,D
University of Washington	M,D*
University of Wisconsin–Madison	M*
University of Wyoming	M,D
Utah State University	M,D
Virginia Polytechnic Institute and State University	M,D*
Washington University in St. Louis	D*
William Paterson University of New Jersey	M*
Yale University	D*

ECONOMIC DEVELOPMENT

Albany State University	M
Boston University	M*
Cape Breton University	M
Chicago State University	M
Claremont Graduate University	M,D,O*
Cleveland State University	M,D,O
Concordia University (Canada)	O
Cornell University	M,D*
Eastern Michigan University	M
Eastern University	M
East Tennessee State University	M
Florida Atlantic University	M,O
Fordham University	M,O*
Georgetown University	D
Georgia Institute of Technology	M,D*
Georgia State University	M,D,O
New Mexico State University	M,D
Southern New Hampshire University	M,D*
University of Central Arkansas	M
University of Houston–Victoria	M
University of Massachusetts Lowell	M,O
University of Miami	M,D*
University of Minnesota, Twin Cities Campus	M*
The University of North Carolina at Greensboro	M,D,O
University of Southern California	M,D*
University of Southern Mississippi	M,D
University of Waterloo	M
Vanderbilt University	M,D*
Virginia Polytechnic Institute and State University	M,D*
Wayne State University	O*

*M—master's degree; P—first professional degree; D—doctorate; O—other advanced degree; *—Close-Up and/or Announcement or Display in one of the other books in this series*

West Virginia University	M,D
Yale University	M*

ECONOMICS

Albany State University	M
American University	M,D,O*
The American University in Cairo	M
American University of Beirut	M
Andrews University	M
Arizona State University	M,D
Assumption College	M,O
Auburn University	M*
Baylor University	M
Bernard M. Baruch College of the City University of New York	M
Boston College	D*
Boston University	M,D*
Bowling Green State University	M*
Brandeis University	M,D
Brock University	M
Brooklyn College of the City University of New York	M
Brown University	D*
Buffalo State College, State University of New York	M
California State Polytechnic University, Pomona	M
California State University, East Bay	M
California State University, Fullerton	M
California State University, Long Beach	M
California State University, Los Angeles	M
Carleton University	M,D
Carnegie Mellon University	D*
Case Western Reserve University	M*
The Catholic University of America	M
Central European University	M,D*
Central Michigan University	M
Chapman University	P,M
City College of the City University of New York	M*
Claremont Graduate University	M,D,O*
Clark Atlanta University	M
Clark University	D
Clemson University	M,D
Cleveland State University	M,D,O
Colorado State University	M,D*
Columbia University	M,D*
Concordia University (Canada)	M,D,O
Cornell University	M,D*
Dalhousie University	M,D
DePaul University	M*
Drexel University	M,D,O*
Duke University	M,D*
East Carolina University	M
Eastern Illinois University	M
Eastern Michigan University	M
East Tennessee State University	M
Emory University	D*
Florida Agricultural and Mechanical University	M
Florida Atlantic University	M
Florida International University	M,D*
Florida State University	M,D*
Fordham University	M,D,O*
Georgetown University	D
The George Washington University	M,D*
Georgia Institute of Technology	M*
Georgia State University	M,D
Graduate School and University Center of the City University of New York	D*
Harvard University	D*
Hawai'i Pacific University	M*
Howard University	M,D
Hunter College of the City University of New York	M
Illinois State University	M
Indiana University Bloomington	M,D*
Indiana University–Purdue University Indianapolis	M*
Instituto Centroamericano de Administración de Empresas	M
Instituto Tecnológico y de Estudios Superiores de Monterrey, Campus Ciudad de México	M,D
Iowa State University of Science and Technology	M,D*
The Johns Hopkins University	D*
Kansas State University	M,D*
Kent State University	M*
Lakehead University	M
Lehigh University	M,D
Long Island University, Brooklyn Campus	M
Louisiana State University and Agricultural and Mechanical College	M,D
Louisiana Tech University	M,D
Marquette University	M
Massachusetts Institute of Technology	M,D*
McGill University	M,D*
McMaster University	M,D
Memorial University of Newfoundland	M
Miami University	M*
Michigan State University	M,D*
Middle Tennessee State University	M,D
Mississippi State University	M,D
Montclair State University	M*
Morgan State University	M
Murray State University	M
National University	M
New Mexico State University	M,D
The New School: A University	M,D*
New York University	M,D,O*
North Carolina State University	M,D*
Northeastern University	M,D*
Northern Illinois University	M,D*
Northwestern University	M,D*
Oakland University	O
The Ohio State University	M,D*
Ohio University	M*
Oklahoma State University	M,D*
Old Dominion University	M
Oregon State University	M,D*
Pace University	M*
Penn State University Park	M,D*
Pepperdine University	M
Peru State College	M
Portland State University	M,D,O
Princeton University	D,O*
Providence College	M*
Purdue University	D
Regent University	M
Rensselaer Polytechnic Institute	M
Rice University	M,D
Roosevelt University	M
Rutgers, The State University of New Jersey, Newark	M*
Rutgers, The State University of New Jersey, New Brunswick	M,D*
St. Cloud State University	M
San Diego State University	M*
San Francisco State University	M
San Jose State University	M
Simon Fraser University	M,D
South Dakota State University	M
Southern Illinois University Carbondale	M,D*
Southern Illinois University Edwardsville	M
Southern Methodist University	M,D*
Stanford University	D*
State University of New York at Binghamton	M,D*
Stony Brook University, State University of New York	M,D
Suffolk University	M,D*
Syracuse University	M,D*
Tarleton State University	M
Teachers College, Columbia University	M,D
Texas A&M University	M,D*
Texas A&M University–Commerce	M
Texas Tech University	M,D
Trinity College	M
Tufts University	M*
Tulane University	M,D
Universidad de las Américas–Puebla	M
Universidad Nacional Pedro Henriquez Urena	P,M,D
Université de Moncton	M
Université de Montréal	M,D
Université de Sherbrooke	M
Université du Québec à Montréal	M,D
Université Laval	M,D
University at Albany, State University of New York	M,D,O*
University at Buffalo, the State University of New York	M,D,O*
The University of Akron	M
The University of Alabama	M,D
University of Alaska Fairbanks	M
University of Alberta	M,D*
The University of Arizona	M,D*
University of Arkansas	M,D
The University of British Columbia	M,D
University of Calgary	M,D
University of California, Berkeley	D*
University of California, Davis	M,D*
University of California, Irvine	M,D*
University of California, Los Angeles	M,D*
University of California, Riverside	M,D*
University of California, San Diego	M,D*
University of California, Santa Barbara	M,D
University of California, Santa Cruz	D*
University of Central Arkansas	M
University of Central Florida	M,D*
University of Chicago	D*
University of Cincinnati	M
University of Colorado at Boulder	M,D*
University of Colorado Denver	M*
University of Connecticut	M,D*
University of Delaware	M,D*
University of Denver	M*
University of Florida	M,D*
University of Georgia	M,D*
University of Guelph	M,D
University of Hawaii at Manoa	M,D*
University of Houston	M,D*
University of Illinois at Chicago	M,D*
University of Illinois at Urbana–Champaign	M,D*
The University of Iowa	D*
The University of Kansas	M,D*
University of Kentucky	M,D
University of Lethbridge	M,D
University of Maine	M*
University of Manitoba	M,D
University of Maryland, Baltimore County	M*
University of Maryland, College Park	M,D*
University of Massachusetts Amherst	M,D*
University of Massachusetts Lowell	M,O
University of Memphis	M,D
University of Miami	M,D*
University of Michigan	M,D*
University of Minnesota, Twin Cities Campus	D*
University of Mississippi	M,D
University of Missouri–Columbia	M,D*
University of Missouri–Kansas City	M,D*
University of Missouri–St. Louis	M,O
The University of Montana	M
University of Nebraska at Omaha	M
University of Nebraska–Lincoln	M,D*
University of Nevada, Las Vegas	M
University of Nevada, Reno	M*
University of New Brunswick Fredericton	M
University of New Hampshire	M,D*
University of New Mexico	M,D*
University of New Orleans	D
The University of North Carolina at Chapel Hill	M,D*
The University of North Carolina at Charlotte	M*
The University of North Carolina at Greensboro	D
University of North Texas	M
University of Notre Dame	M,D*
University of Oklahoma	M,D*
University of Oregon	M,D*
University of Ottawa	M,D*
University of Pennsylvania	M,D*
University of Pittsburgh	M,D*
University of Puerto Rico, Río Piedras	M
University of Regina	M,D,O
University of Rhode Island	M,D
University of Rochester	M,D*
University of San Francisco	M
University of Saskatchewan	M
University of South Africa	M,D
University of South Carolina	M,D
University of Southern California	M,D*
University of Southern Mississippi	M,D
University of South Florida	M,D*
The University of Tampa	M
The University of Tennessee	M,D
The University of Texas at Arlington	M*

The University of Texas at Austin	M,D
The University of Texas at Dallas	M,D*
The University of Texas at El Paso	M
The University of Texas at San Antonio	M*
The University of Texas–Pan American	D
The University of Toledo	M
University of Toronto	M,D
University of Utah	M,D*
University of Victoria	M,D
University of Virginia	M,D
University of Washington	M,D*
University of Waterloo	M,D
The University of Western Ontario	M,D
University of Windsor	M
University of Wisconsin–Madison	D*
University of Wisconsin–Milwaukee	M,D
University of Wyoming	M,D
Utah State University	M,D
Vanderbilt University	P,M,D*
Virginia Commonwealth University	M
Virginia Polytechnic Institute and State University	M,D*
Virginia State University	M
Walsh College of Accountancy and Business Administration	M
Washington State University	M,D,O*
Washington University in St. Louis	D*
Wayne State University	M,D,O*
West Chester University of Pennsylvania	M
Western Illinois University	M,O
Western Michigan University	M,D*
West Texas A&M University	M
West Virginia University	M,D
Wichita State University	M*
Wilfrid Laurier University	M
Wright State University	M
Yale University	M,D*
York University	M,D
Youngstown State University	M

EDUCATION—GENERAL

Abilene Christian University	M
Acadia University	M
Adams State College	M
Adelphi University	M,D,O*
Alabama Agricultural and Mechanical University	M,O
Alabama State University	M,D,O
Alaska Pacific University	M
Albany State University	M,O
Albright College	M
Alcorn State University	M,O
Alfred University	M*
Alliant International University–Fresno	M*
Alliant International University–Irvine	M,O*
Alliant International University–Los Angeles	M*
Alliant International University–México City	M*
Alliant International University–Sacramento	M*
Alliant International University–San Diego	M,O*
Alliant International University–San Francisco	M,O*
Alvernia University	M
Alverno College	M
American InterContinental University Online	M
American International College	M,D,O
American Jewish University	M
American University	M,O*
American University of Beirut	M
American University of Puerto Rico	M
Anderson University (IN)	M
Anderson University (SC)	M
Andrews University	M,D,O
Angelo State University	M
Anna Maria College	M,O
Antioch University Los Angeles	M
Antioch University McGregor	M
Antioch University New England	M*
Antioch University Santa Barbara	M
Antioch University Seattle	M
Aquinas College	M
Arcadia University	M,D,O
Argosy University, Atlanta	M,D,O*
Argosy University, Chicago	M,D,O*
Argosy University, Dallas	M*
Argosy University, Denver	M,D*
Argosy University, Hawai'i	M,D*
Argosy University, Inland Empire	M,D*
Argosy University, Los Angeles	M,D*
Argosy University, Nashville	M,D,O*
Argosy University, Orange County	M,D*
Argosy University, Phoenix	M,D,O*
Argosy University, Salt Lake City	M,D*
Argosy University, San Diego	M,D*
Argosy University, San Francisco Bay Area	M,D*
Argosy University, Sarasota	M,D,O*
Argosy University, Schaumburg	M,D,O*
Argosy University, Seattle	M,D*
Argosy University, Tampa	M,D,O*
Argosy University, Twin Cities	M,D,O*
Argosy University, Washington DC	M,D,O*
Arizona State University	M,D
Arizona State University at the Polytechnic Campus	M,D
Arizona State University at the West campus	M,D,O
Arkansas State University	M,D,O
Arkansas Tech University	M,O
Armstrong Atlantic State University	M
Ashland University	M,D
Athabasca University	M,O*
Atlantic Union College	M
Auburn University	M,D,O*
Auburn University Montgomery	M,O
Augsburg College	M
Augustana College	M
Augusta State University	M,O
Aurora University	M,D
Austin College	M
Austin Peay State University	M,O
Averett University	M
Avila University	M,O
Azusa Pacific University	M,D
Baker University	M,D
Baldwin-Wallace College	M
Ball State University	M,D,O*
Bank Street College of Education	M*
Bard College	M
Barry University	M,D,O*
Bayamón Central University	M
Baylor University	M,D,O
Belhaven College (MS)	M
Bellarmine University	M
Belmont University	M
Bemidji State University	M
Benedictine University	M
Bennington College	M
Berry College	M,O
Bethany University	M
Bethel College (IN)	M
Bethel College (TN)	M
Bethel University	M,D,O
Biola University	M
Bishop's University	M,O
Black Hills State University	M
Bloomsburg University of Pennsylvania	M
Bluffton University	M
Boise State University	M,D
Boston College	M,D,O*
Boston University	M,D,O*
Bowie State University	M
Bradley University	M,D,O
Brandon University	M,O
Brenau University	M,O
Briar Cliff University	M
Bridgewater State College	M,O
Brigham Young University	M,D,O*
Brock University	M,D
Brooklyn College of the City University of New York	M,O
Brown University	M*
Bucknell University	M
Buena Vista University	M
Butler University	M
Cabrini College	M,O
California Baptist University	M
California Coast University	M
California Lutheran University	M,D
California Polytechnic State University, San Luis Obispo	M
California State Polytechnic University, Pomona	M
California State University, Bakersfield	M,O
California State University, Chico	M
California State University, Dominguez Hills	M,O
California State University, East Bay	M
California State University, Fresno	M,D
California State University, Fullerton	M
California State University, Long Beach	M,D
California State University, Los Angeles	M,D
California State University, Monterey Bay	M
California State University, Northridge	M,D
California State University, Sacramento	M
California State University, San Bernardino	M,D
California State University, San Marcos	M
California State University, Stanislaus	M,D,O
California University of Pennsylvania	M
Calvin College	M
Cambridge College	M,D,O
Cameron University	M
Campbellsville University	M
Campbell University	M
Canisius College	M
Cape Breton University	O
Capella University	M,D,O
Cardinal Stritch University	M,D
Caribbean University	M,D
Carlow University	M
Carnegie Mellon University	M,D*
Carroll University	M
Carson-Newman College	M
Carthage College	M,O
Castleton State College	M,O
Catawba College	M
The Catholic University of America	M,D,O
Cedar Crest College	M
Cedarville University	M
Centenary College	M
Centenary College of Louisiana	M
Central Connecticut State University	M,D,O
Central Methodist University	M
Central Michigan University	M,D,O
Central State University	M
Central Washington University	M
Chadron State College	M,O
Chaminade University of Honolulu	M
Chapman University	M,D,O
Charleston Southern University	M
Chatham University	M
Chestnut Hill College	M
Cheyney University of Pennsylvania	M,O
Chicago State University	M,D
Christian Brothers University	M
Christopher Newport University	M
The Citadel, The Military College of South Carolina	M,O
City College of the City University of New York	M,O*
City University of Seattle	M,O
Claflin University	M
Claremont Graduate University	M,D,O*
Clarion University of Pennsylvania	M,O
Clark Atlanta University	M,D,O
Clarke College	M
Clark University	M
Clayton State University	M
Clemson University	M,D,O
Cleveland State University	M,D,O
Coastal Carolina University	M
Coe College	M
The College at Brockport, State University of New York	M,O
College of Charleston	M,O*
The College of Idaho	M
College of Mount St. Joseph	M
College of Mount Saint Vincent	M,O
The College of New Jersey	M,O
The College of New Rochelle	M,O
College of Notre Dame of Maryland	M
College of Saint Elizabeth	M,D,O
College of St. Joseph	M
The College of Saint Rose	M,O*
The College of St. Scholastica	M,O
College of Santa Fe	M
College of Staten Island of the City University of New York	M,O
College of the Humanities and Sciences, Harrison Middleton University	M,D

*M—master's degree; P—first professional degree; D—doctorate; O—other advanced degree; *—Close-Up and/or Announcement or Display in one of the other books in this series*

The College of William and Mary	M,D,O
Collège universitaire de Saint-Boniface	M
Colorado Christian University	M
The Colorado College	M
Colorado State University	M,D*
Colorado State University–Pueblo	M
Columbia College (MO)	M
Columbia College (SC)	M
Columbia College Chicago	M
Columbia International University	M,D,O
Columbus State University	M,O
Concordia University (CA)	M
Concordia University (OR)	M
Concordia University (Canada)	M,D,O
Concordia University Chicago	M
Concordia University, Nebraska	M
Concordia University, St. Paul	M,O
Concordia University Texas	M
Concordia University Wisconsin	M
Converse College	M,O
Coppin State University	M
Cornell University	M,D*
Cornerstone University	M,O
Covenant College	M
Creighton University	M*
Cumberland University	M
Curry College	M,O
Daemen College	M
Dakota State University	M*
Dakota Wesleyan University	M
Dallas Baptist University	M
Defiance College	M
Delaware State University	M,D
Delta State University	M,D,O
DePaul University	M,D*
DeSales University	M
Doane College	M
Dominican College	M
Dominican University	M
Dominican University of California	M,O
Dordt College	M
Dowling College	M,D,O
Drake University	M,D,O*
Drexel University	M,D,O*
Drury University	M
Duke University	M*
Duquesne University	M,D,O*
D'Youville College	M,O*
Earlham College	M
East Carolina University	M,D,O
East Central University	M
Eastern Connecticut State University	M
Eastern Illinois University	M,O
Eastern Kentucky University	M
Eastern Mennonite University	M
Eastern Michigan University	M,D,O
Eastern Nazarene College	M,O
Eastern New Mexico University	M
Eastern Oregon University	M
Eastern University	M,O
Eastern Washington University	M
East Stroudsburg University of Pennsylvania	M
East Tennessee State University	M,D,O
Edgewood College	M,D,O
Edinboro University of Pennsylvania	M,O
Elizabeth City State University	M
Elms College	M,O
Elon University	M
Embry-Riddle Aeronautical University Worldwide	M,O
Emmanuel College	M,O
Emory & Henry College	M
Emory University	M,D,O*
Emporia State University	M,O
Evangel University	M
The Evergreen State College	M
Fairfield University	M,O*
Fairleigh Dickinson University, College at Florham	M,O*
Fairleigh Dickinson University, Metropolitan Campus	M,O*
Fairmont State University	M
Felician College	M*
Ferris State University	M
Florida Agricultural and Mechanical University	M,D
Florida Atlantic University	M,D,O
Florida Gulf Coast University	M
Florida International University	M,D,O*
Florida Southern College	M
Florida State University	M,D,O*
Fontbonne University	M
Fordham University	M,D,O*
Fort Hays State University	M,O
Franciscan University of Steubenville	M
Francis Marion University	M
Franklin Pierce University	M,D,O
Freed-Hardeman University	M,O
Fresno Pacific University	M
Friends University	M
Frostburg State University	M
Furman University	M
Gannon University	M,D,O
Gardner-Webb University	M,D
Geneva College	M
George Fox University	M,D,O*
George Mason University	M,D,O*
Georgetown College	M
The George Washington University	M,D,O*
Georgia College & State University	M,O
Georgian Court University	M
Georgia Southern University	M,D,O
Georgia Southwestern State University	M,O
Georgia State University	M,D,O
Goddard College	M
Gonzaga University	M
Gordon College	M
Goucher College	M
Governors State University	M
Graceland University (IA)	M
Grambling State University	M,D
Grand Canyon University	M,D*
Grand Valley State University	M,O
Grand View University	M
Gratz College	M
Greensboro College	M
Greenville College	M
Gwynedd-Mercy College	M
Hamline University	M,D
Hampton University	M
Harding University	M,O
Hardin-Simmons University	M
Harvard University	M,D*
Hastings College	M
Hebrew College	M,O
Hebrew Union College–Jewish Institute of Religion (CA)	M,D,O
Hebrew Union College–Jewish Institute of Religion (NY)	M
Heidelberg University	M
Henderson State University	M,O
Heritage University	M
Hodges University	M
Hofstra University	M,D,O*
Hollins University	M
Holy Family University	M
Holy Names University	M,O
Hood College	M
Hope International University	M
Houston Baptist University	M
Howard University	M,D,O
Humboldt State University	M
Hunter College of the City University of New York	M,O
Huntington University	M
Idaho State University	M,D,O
Illinois State University	M,D
Indiana State University	M,D,O
Indiana University Bloomington	M,D,O*
Indiana University East	M
Indiana University Kokomo	M
Indiana University Northwest	M
Indiana University of Pennsylvania	M,D,O
Indiana University–Purdue University Fort Wayne	M,O
Indiana University–Purdue University Indianapolis	M,O*
Indiana University South Bend	M
Indiana University Southeast	M
Indiana Wesleyan University	M
Institute for Christian Studies	M,D
Instituto Tecnologico de Santo Domingo	M
Instituto Tecnológico y de Estudios Superiores de Monterrey, Campus Central de Veracruz	M
Instituto Tecnológico y de Estudios Superiores de Monterrey, Campus Ciudad de México	M,D
Instituto Tecnológico y de Estudios Superiores de Monterrey, Campus Ciudad Juárez	M
Instituto Tecnológico y de Estudios Superiores de Monterrey, Campus Ciudad Obregón	M
Instituto Tecnológico y de Estudios Superiores de Monterrey, Campus Estado de México	M
Instituto Tecnológico y de Estudios Superiores de Monterrey, Campus Irapuato	M,D
Instituto Tecnológico y de Estudios Superiores de Monterrey, Campus Sonora Norte	M
Inter American University of Puerto Rico, Arecibo Campus	M
Inter American University of Puerto Rico, Barranquitas Campus	M
Inter American University of Puerto Rico, Metropolitan Campus	D
Iona College	M*
Jackson State University	M,D,O
Jacksonville State University	M,O
Jacksonville University	M,O
John Carroll University	M
John F. Kennedy University	M
The Johns Hopkins University	M,D,O*
Johnson & Wales University	M
Johnson Bible College	M
Johnson State College	M,O
Jones International University	M
Judson University	M
Kansas State University	M,D*
Kaplan University–Davenport Campus	M
Kean University	M
Keene State College	M,O
Keiser University	M
Kennesaw State University	M,D,O
Kent State University	M,D,O*
Kutztown University of Pennsylvania	M,O
LaGrange College	M
Lake Erie College	M
Lakehead University	M,D
Lakeland College	M
Lamar University	M,D,O
Lander University	M
Langston University	M
La Salle University	M
La Sierra University	M,D,O
Lee University	M,O
Lehigh University	M,D,O
Lehman College of the City University of New York	M
Le Moyne College	M,O
Lenoir-Rhyne University	M
Lesley University	M,D,O*
Lewis & Clark College	M
Lewis University	M,D,O
Liberty University	M,D,O
Lincoln Memorial University	M,O
Lincoln University (MO)	M,O
Lindenwood University	M,D,O
Lipscomb University	M
Lock Haven University of Pennsylvania	M
Long Island University at Riverhead	M,O
Long Island University, Brentwood Campus	M
Long Island University, Brooklyn Campus	M,O
Long Island University, C.W. Post Campus	M,O
Long Island University, Westchester Graduate Campus	M
Longwood University	M
Louisiana State University and Agricultural and Mechanical College	M,D,O
Louisiana State University in Shreveport	M
Louisiana Tech University	M,D
Lourdes College	M
Loyola Marymount University	M,D
Loyola University Chicago	M,D,O*
Loyola University Maryland	M,O*
Lynchburg College	M
Lyndon State College	M
Madonna University	M
Maharishi University of Management	M
Malone University	M
Manhattan College	M,O
Manhattanville College	M*
Mansfield University of Pennsylvania	M
Marian University (IN)	M
Marian University (WI)	M,D
Marietta College	M
Marist College	M,O
Marlboro College	M
Marquette University	M,D,O

Marshall University	M,D,O
Mary Baldwin College	M
Marygrove College	M
Marylhurst University	M
Marymount University	M
Maryville University of Saint Louis	M,D
Marywood University	M
Massachusetts College of Art and Design	M
Massachusetts College of Liberal Arts	M
McGill University	M,D,O*
McKendree University	M
McNeese State University	M
Medaille College	M
Memorial University of Newfoundland	M,D,O
Mercer University	M,D,O
Mercy College	M,O
Meredith College	M
Merrimack College	M
Mesa State College	M
Miami University	M,D,O*
Michigan State University	M,D,O*
MidAmerica Nazarene University	M
Middle Tennessee State University	M,D,O
Midwestern State University	M
Millersville University of Pennsylvania	M
Milligan College	M
Mills College	M,D
Minnesota State University Mankato	M,D,O
Minnesota State University Moorhead	M,O
Misericordia University	M
Mississippi College	M,D,O
Mississippi State University	M,D,O
Mississippi University for Women	M
Mississippi Valley State University	M
Missouri Baptist University	M,O
Missouri Southern State University	M
Monmouth University	M,O
Montana State University	M,D,O
Montana State University–Billings	M,O
Montana State University–Northern	M
Montclair State University	M,D,O*
Montreat College	M
Morehead State University	M,O
Morgan State University	M,D
Morningside College	M
Mount Mary College	M
Mount Saint Mary College	M
Mount St. Mary's College	M
Mount St. Mary's University	M
Mount Saint Vincent University	M
Mount Vernon Nazarene University	M
Multnomah University	M
Murray State University	M,D,O
Muskingum University	M
Naropa University	M*
National-Louis University	M,D,O
National University	M
Nazareth College of Rochester	M
Neumann University	M,D
New England College	M
Newman University	M
New Mexico Highlands University	M
New Mexico State University	M,D,O
New York Institute of Technology	M,O
New York University	M,D,O*
Niagara University	M,O
Nicholls State University	M
Nipissing University	M,O
Norfolk State University	M
North Carolina Agricultural and Technical State University	M
North Carolina Central University	M
North Carolina State University	M,D,O*
North Central College	M
Northcentral University	M,D,O
North Dakota State University	M,D,O
Northeastern Illinois University	M
Northeastern State University	M
Northern Arizona University	M,D,O
Northern Illinois University	M,D,O
Northern Kentucky University	M,D,O
Northern Michigan University	M,O
Northern State University	M
North Georgia College & State University	M,O
North Park University	M
Northwest Christian University	M
Northwestern Oklahoma State University	M
Northwestern State University of Louisiana	M,O
Northwestern University	M,D*
Northwest Missouri State University	M,O
Northwest Nazarene University	M
Northwest University	M
Notre Dame College (OH)	M,O
Notre Dame de Namur University	M,O
Nova Southeastern University	M,D,O*
Nyack College	M
Oakland City University	M,D
Oakland University	M,D,O
Oberlin College	M
Occidental College	M
Oglethorpe University	M
Ohio Dominican University	M
The Ohio State University	M,D*
The Ohio State University at Lima	M
The Ohio State University at Marion	M,D
The Ohio State University–Newark Campus	M
Ohio University	M,D*
Oklahoma City University	M
Oklahoma State University	M,D,O*
Old Dominion University	M,D,O
Olivet College	M
Olivet Nazarene University	M
Oral Roberts University	M,D
Oregon State University	M,D*
Oregon State University–Cascades	M
Ottawa University	M
Otterbein College	M
Our Lady of Holy Cross College	M
Our Lady of the Lake University of San Antonio	M,D
Pace University	M,O*
Pacific Lutheran University	M
Pacific Union College	M
Pacific University	M
Palm Beach Atlantic University	M
Park University	M
Penn State Great Valley	M
Penn State Harrisburg	M,D
Penn State University Park	M,D*
Pepperdine University	M,D
Peru State College	M
Pfeiffer University	M
Philadelphia Biblical University	M
Piedmont College	M,O
Pittsburg State University	M,O
Plymouth State University	O
Point Loma Nazarene University	M,O
Point Park University	M*
Pontifical Catholic University of Puerto Rico	M,D
Portland State University	M,D
Prairie View A&M University	M,D
Prescott College	M,D
Providence College	M*
Purdue University	M,D,O
Purdue University Calumet	M
Purdue University North Central	M
Queens College of the City University of New York	M,O
Queen's University at Kingston	M,D
Queens University of Charlotte	M
Quincy University	M
Quinnipiac University	M*
Radford University	M
Regent University	M,D,O
Regis College (MA)	M
Regis University	M,O
Reinhardt College	M
Rhode Island College	D
Rice University	M
The Richard Stockton College of New Jersey	M
Rider University	M,O*
Rivier College	M,D,O
Robert Morris University	M,D,O
Roberts Wesleyan College	M,O
Rockford College	M
Rockhurst University	M
Roger Williams University	M*
Rollins College	M
Roosevelt University	M,D
Rowan University	M,D,O
Rutgers, The State University of New Jersey, New Brunswick	M,D*
Sacred Heart University	M,O
Sage Graduate School	M,D,O
Saginaw Valley State University	M,O
St. Ambrose University	M
St. Bonaventure University	M,O
St. Catherine University	M
St. Cloud State University	M,D,O
St. Edward's University	M,O
Saint Francis University	M
St. Francis Xavier University	M
St. John Fisher College	M,D,O
St. John's University (NY)	M,D,O
Saint Joseph College	M
St. Joseph's College, New York	M
Saint Joseph's College of Maine	M
Saint Joseph's University	M,D
St. Lawrence University	M,O
Saint Leo University	M
Saint Louis University	M,D
Saint Martin's University	M
Saint Mary's College of California	M,D
St. Mary's University (United States)	M,O
Saint Mary's University of Minnesota	M,O
Saint Michael's College	M,O
St. Norbert College	M
Saint Peter's College	M,O
St. Thomas Aquinas College	M,O*
St. Thomas University	M,D,O
Saint Vincent College	M
Saint Xavier University	M,O
Salem College	M
Salem International University	M
Salem State College	M
Salisbury University	M
Samford University	M,D,O
Sam Houston State University	M,D
San Diego State University	M,D*
San Francisco State University	M,D,O
San Jose State University	M,O
Santa Clara University	M,O
Sarah Lawrence College	M*
Savannah College of Art and Design	M*
Schreiner University	M
Seattle University	M,D,O
Seton Hall University	M,D,O*
Seton Hill University	M
Shenandoah University	M,D,O
Shippensburg University of Pennsylvania	M,O
Siena Heights University	M
Sierra Nevada College	M
Silver Lake College	M
Simmons College	M,D,O
Simon Fraser University	M,D
Simpson University	M
Sinte Gleska University	M
SIT Graduate Institute	M
Slippery Rock University of Pennsylvania	M
Smith College	M
Sonoma State University	M
South Carolina State University	M
South Dakota State University	M
Southeastern Louisiana University	M,D
Southeastern Oklahoma State University	M
Southern Adventist University	M
Southern Arkansas University–Magnolia	M
Southern Connecticut State University	M,D,O
Southern Illinois University Carbondale	M,D*
Southern Illinois University Edwardsville	M,O
Southern Methodist University	M,D,O*
Southern Nazarene University	M
Southern New Hampshire University	M,O*
Southern Oregon University	M
Southern University and Agricultural and Mechanical College	M,D
Southern Utah University	M
Southern Wesleyan University	M
Southwest Baptist University	M,O
Southwestern Adventist University	M
Southwestern Assemblies of God University	M
Southwestern College (KS)	M
Southwestern Oklahoma State University	M
Southwest Minnesota State University	M
Spalding University	M,D
Spring Arbor University	M
Springfield College	M
Spring Hill College	M
Stanford University	M,D*
State University of New York at Binghamton	M,D*

*M—master's degree; P—first professional degree; D—doctorate; O—other advanced degree; *—Close-Up and/or Announcement or Display in one of the other books in this series*

State University of New York at Fredonia	M,O
State University of New York at New Paltz	M,O
State University of New York at Oswego	M,O
State University of New York College at Cortland	M,O
State University of New York College at Geneseo	M
State University of New York College at Oneonta	M,O
State University of New York Empire State College	M
Stephen F. Austin State University	M,D
Stetson University	M
Strayer University	M
Suffolk University	M,O*
Sul Ross State University	M*
Sweet Briar College	M
Syracuse University	M,D,O*
Tarleton State University	M,D,O
Teachers College, Columbia University	M,D,O
Temple University	M,D*
Tennessee State University	M,D,O
Tennessee Technological University	M,D,O*
Tennessee Temple University	M
Texas A&M International University	M,D
Texas A&M University	M,D*
Texas A&M University–Commerce	M,D
Texas A&M University–Corpus Christi	M,D
Texas A&M University–Kingsville	M,D
Texas A&M University–Texarkana	M
Texas Christian University	M,D,O
Texas Southern University	M,D
Texas State University–San Marcos	M,D*
Texas Tech University	M,D
Texas Wesleyan University	M
Texas Woman's University	M,D
Thomas More College	M
Thomas University	M
Touro University	P,M
Towson University	M
Trevecca Nazarene University	M,D
Trinity Baptist College	M
Trinity International University	M
Trinity University	M
Trinity (Washington) University	M
Troy University	M
Truman State University	M
Tufts University	M,D,O*
TUI University	M,D
Tusculum College	M
Union College (KY)	M
Union Graduate College	M
Union Institute & University	M,D,O
Union University	M,D,O
Universidad Adventista de las Antillas	M
Universidad Autonoma de Guadalajara	M,D
Universidad de las Americas, A.C.	M
Universidad de las Américas–Puebla	M
Universidad del Turabo	M,D
Universidad Metropolitana	M
Universidad Nacional Pedro Henriquez Urena	P,M,D
Université de Moncton	M
Université de Montréal	M,D,O
Université de Sherbrooke	M,O
Université du Québec à Chicoutimi	M,D
Université du Québec à Montréal	M,D,O
Université du Québec à Rimouski	M,D,O
Université du Québec à Trois-Rivières	M,D
Université du Québec en Abitibi-Témiscamingue	M,D,O
Université du Québec en Outaouais	M,D,O
Université Laval	M,D,O
University at Albany, State University of New York	M,D,O*
University at Buffalo, the State University of New York	M,D,O*
The University of Akron	M,D
The University of Alabama at Birmingham	M,D,O*
University of Alaska Anchorage	M,O
University of Alaska Fairbanks	M,D,O
University of Alaska Southeast	M
The University of Arizona	M,D,O*
University of Arkansas	M,D,O
University of Arkansas at Little Rock	M,D,O
University of Arkansas at Monticello	M
University of Arkansas at Pine Bluff	M
University of Bridgeport	M,D,O
The University of British Columbia	M,D,O
University of California, Berkeley	M,D*
University of California, Davis	M,D*
University of California, Irvine	M,D*
University of California, Los Angeles	M,D*
University of California, Riverside	M,D*
University of California, San Diego	M,D
University of California, Santa Barbara	M,D
University of California, Santa Cruz	M,D*
University of Central Arkansas	M,O
University of Central Florida	M,D,O*
University of Central Missouri	M,D,O
University of Central Oklahoma	M
University of Cincinnati	M,D,O
University of Colorado at Boulder	M,D*
University of Colorado at Colorado Springs	M,D
University of Colorado Denver	M,D,O*
University of Connecticut	M,D,O*
University of Dayton	M,D,O
University of Delaware	M,D,O*
University of Denver	M,D,O*
University of Detroit Mercy	M
University of Evansville	M,D
The University of Findlay	M
University of Florida	M,D,O*
University of Georgia	M,D,O*
University of Great Falls	M
University of Guam	M
University of Hartford	M,D,O*
University of Hawaii at Manoa	M,D,O*
University of Houston	M,D*
University of Houston–Clear Lake	M,D
University of Houston–Victoria	M
University of Idaho	M,D,O
University of Illinois at Chicago	M,D*
University of Illinois at Springfield	M
University of Illinois at Urbana–Champaign	M,D,O*
University of Indianapolis	M
The University of Iowa	M,D,O*
The University of Kansas	M,D,O*
University of Kentucky	M,D,O
University of La Verne	M,O
University of Lethbridge	M,D
University of Louisiana at Lafayette	M,D*
University of Louisiana at Monroe	M,D,O
University of Louisville	M,D,O
University of Maine	M,D,O*
University of Maine at Farmington	M
University of Manitoba	M,D
University of Mary	M
University of Mary Hardin-Baylor	M,D
University of Maryland, Baltimore County	M,O*
University of Maryland, College Park	M,D,O*
University of Maryland Eastern Shore	M*
University of Maryland University College	M
University of Mary Washington	M
University of Massachusetts Amherst	M,D,O*
University of Massachusetts Boston	M,D,O
University of Massachusetts Dartmouth	M,O
University of Massachusetts Lowell	M,D,O
University of Memphis	M,D,O
University of Miami	M,D,O*
University of Michigan	M,D*
University of Michigan–Dearborn	M*
University of Michigan–Flint	M*
University of Minnesota, Duluth	D
University of Minnesota, Twin Cities Campus	M,D,O*
University of Mississippi	M,D,O
University of Missouri–Columbia	M,D,O*
University of Missouri–Kansas City	M,D,O*
University of Missouri–St. Louis	M,D,O
University of Mobile	M
The University of Montana	M,D,O
University of Montevallo	M,O
University of Nebraska at Kearney	M,O
University of Nebraska at Omaha	M,D,O
University of Nevada, Las Vegas	M,D,O
University of Nevada, Reno	M,D,O*
University of New Brunswick Fredericton	M,D
University of New England	M
University of New Hampshire	M,D,O*
University of New Haven	M*
University of New Mexico	M,O*
University of New Orleans	M,D,O
University of North Alabama	M,O
The University of North Carolina at Chapel Hill	M,D*
The University of North Carolina at Charlotte	M*
The University of North Carolina at Greensboro	M,D,O
The University of North Carolina at Pembroke	M
The University of North Carolina Wilmington	M,D
University of North Dakota	M,D,O
University of Northern British Columbia	M,D,O
University of Northern Colorado	M,D,O
University of Northern Iowa	M,D,O
University of North Florida	M,D
University of North Texas	M,D,O
University of Notre Dame	M*
University of Oklahoma	M,D,O*
University of Oregon	M,D*
University of Ottawa	M,D,O*
University of Pennsylvania	M,D*
University of Phoenix	M,D
University of Phoenix–Austin Campus	M
University of Phoenix–Bay Area Campus	M
University of Phoenix–Central Florida Campus	M
University of Phoenix–Central Massachusetts Campus	M
University of Phoenix–Central Valley Campus	M
University of Phoenix–Chattanooga Campus	M
University of Phoenix–Dallas Campus	M
University of Phoenix–Denver Campus	M
University of Phoenix–Hawaii Campus	M
University of Phoenix–Houston Campus	M
University of Phoenix–Idaho Campus	M
University of Phoenix–Indianapolis Campus	M
University of Phoenix–Kansas City Campus	M
University of Phoenix–Las Vegas Campus	M
University of Phoenix–Louisiana Campus	M
University of Phoenix–Memphis Campus	M
University of Phoenix–Metro Detroit Campus	M
University of Phoenix–Nashville Campus	M
University of Phoenix–New Mexico Campus	M
University of Phoenix–Northern Nevada Campus	M
University of Phoenix–Northern Virginia Campus	M
University of Phoenix–North Florida Campus	M
University of Phoenix–Omaha Campus	M
University of Phoenix–Oregon Campus	M
University of Phoenix–Phoenix Campus	M
University of Phoenix–Puerto Rico Campus	M
University of Phoenix–Sacramento Valley Campus	M,O
University of Phoenix–San Diego Campus	M
University of Phoenix–Southern Arizona Campus	M,O
University of Phoenix–Southern California Campus	M
University of Phoenix–Southern Colorado Campus	M,O

University of Phoenix–South Florida Campus	M
University of Phoenix–Springfield Campus	M
University of Phoenix–Utah Campus	M
University of Phoenix–Vancouver Campus	M
University of Phoenix–West Florida Campus	M
University of Phoenix–West Michigan Campus	M
University of Pittsburgh	M,D*
University of Portland	M
University of Prince Edward Island	M
University of Puerto Rico, Río Piedras	M,D
University of Puget Sound	M
University of Redlands	M,D,O
University of Regina	M,D
University of Rhode Island	M,D
University of Rio Grande	M
University of Rochester	M,D*
University of St. Francis (IL)	M
University of Saint Francis (IN)	M
University of Saint Mary	M
University of St. Thomas (MN)	M,O*
University of St. Thomas (TX)	M
University of San Diego	M,D,O
University of San Francisco	M,D
University of Saskatchewan	M,D,O
The University of Scranton	M
University of Sioux Falls	M,O
University of South Africa	M,D
University of South Alabama	M,D,O*
University of South Carolina	M,D,O
University of South Carolina Aiken	M
University of South Carolina Upstate	M
The University of South Dakota	M,D,O
University of Southern Indiana	M
University of Southern Maine	M,D,O
University of Southern Mississippi	M,D,O
University of South Florida	M,D,O*
The University of Tampa	M
The University of Tennessee	M,D,O
The University of Tennessee at Chattanooga	M,D,O
The University of Tennessee at Martin	M
The University of Texas at Arlington	M,D*
The University of Texas at Austin	M,D
The University of Texas at Brownsville	M
The University of Texas at El Paso	M,D
The University of Texas at San Antonio	M,D,O*
The University of Texas of the Permian Basin	M
The University of Texas–Pan American	M,D
University of the Cumberlands	M,O
University of the District of Columbia	M
University of the Incarnate Word	M,D
University of the Pacific	M,D,O
University of the Sacred Heart	M
University of the Southwest	M
University of the Virgin Islands	M
The University of Toledo	M,D,O
University of Toronto	M,D
University of Tulsa	M*
University of Utah	M,D*
University of Vermont	M,D*
University of Victoria	M,D
University of Virginia	M,D,O
University of Washington	M,D,O*
University of Washington, Bothell	M
University of Washington, Tacoma	M
The University of West Alabama	M
The University of Western Ontario	M
University of West Georgia	M,D,O
University of Windsor	M,D
University of Wisconsin–Eau Claire	M
University of Wisconsin–Green Bay	M
University of Wisconsin–La Crosse	M
University of Wisconsin–Madison	M,D,O*
University of Wisconsin–Milwaukee	M,D,O
University of Wisconsin–Oshkosh	M
University of Wisconsin–Platteville	M
University of Wisconsin–River Falls	M
University of Wisconsin–Stevens Point	M
University of Wisconsin–Stout	M,O
University of Wisconsin–Superior	M
University of Wisconsin–Whitewater	M*
Urbana University	M
Ursuline College	M
Utah State University	M,D,O
Utah Valley University	M
Utica College	M,O
Valparaiso University	M
Vanderbilt University	M,D*
Vanguard University of Southern California	M
Villanova University	M*
Virginia Commonwealth University	M,D,O
Virginia State University	M,O
Viterbo University	M
Wagner College	M,O
Wake Forest University	M*
Walden University	M,D,O
Walla Walla University	M
Walsh University	M
Warner Pacific College	M
Warner University	M
Washburn University	M
Washington State University	M,D,O*
Washington State University Spokane	M,O
Washington State University Tri-Cities	M,D
Washington State University Vancouver	M,D
Washington University in St. Louis	M,D*
Wayland Baptist University	M
Waynesburg University	M,D
Wayne State College	M,O
Wayne State University	M,D,O*
Weber State University	M
Webster University	M,O
Wesleyan College	M
Wesley College	M
West Chester University of Pennsylvania	M,O
Western Carolina University	M,D,O
Western Connecticut State University	M,D
Western Governors University	M,O
Western Illinois University	M,D,O
Western Michigan University	M,D,O*
Western New Mexico University	M
Western Oregon University	M
Western Washington University	M
Westfield State College	M,O
West Liberty State University	M
Westminster College (PA)	M,O
Westminster College (UT)	M
West Texas A&M University	M
West Virginia University	M,D
Wheaton College	M
Wheelock College	M
Whittier College	M
Whitworth University	M
Wichita State University	M,D,O*
Widener University	M,D*
Wilkes University	M,D
Willamette University	M
William Carey University	M,O
William Howard Taft University	M
William Paterson University of New Jersey	M*
Wilmington College	M
Wilmington University	M
Wingate University	M
Winona State University	M
Winthrop University	M
Wittenberg University	M
Worcester State College	M,O
Wright State University	M,O
Xavier University	M*
Xavier University of Louisiana	M
York College of Pennsylvania	M
York University	M,D
Youngstown State University	M,D

EDUCATIONAL LEADERSHIP AND ADMINISTRATION

Abilene Christian University	M
Acadia University	M
Adelphi University	M,O*
Alabama Agricultural and Mechanical University	M,O
Alabama State University	M,D,O
Albany State University	M,O
Alliant International University–Fresno	D*
Alliant International University–Irvine	M,D,O*
Alliant International University–Los Angeles	M,D,O*
Alliant International University–San Diego	M,D,O*
Alliant International University–San Francisco	M,D,O*
Alverno College	M
American InterContinental University Online	M
American International College	M,D,O
Andrews University	M,D,O
Angelo State University	M
Antioch University McGregor	M
Antioch University New England	M*
Appalachian State University	M,D,O
Arcadia University	M,D,O
Argosy University, Atlanta	M,D,O*
Argosy University, Chicago	M,D,O*
Argosy University, Dallas	M*
Argosy University, Denver	M,D*
Argosy University, Hawai'i	M,D*
Argosy University, Inland Empire	M,D*
Argosy University, Los Angeles	M,D*
Argosy University, Nashville	M,D,O*
Argosy University, Orange County	M,D*
Argosy University, Phoenix	M,D,O*
Argosy University, Salt Lake City	M,D*
Argosy University, San Diego	M,D*
Argosy University, San Francisco Bay Area	M,D*
Argosy University, Sarasota	M,D,O*
Argosy University, Schaumburg	M,D,O*
Argosy University, Seattle	M,D*
Argosy University, Tampa	M,D,O*
Argosy University, Twin Cities	M,D,O*
Argosy University, Washington DC	M,D,O*
Arizona State University	M,D
Arizona State University at the Polytechnic Campus	M,D
Arizona State University at the West campus	M,D,O
Arkansas State University	M,D,O
Arkansas Tech University	M,O
Ashland University	M,D
Auburn University	M,D,O*
Auburn University Montgomery	M,O
Augusta State University	M,O
Aurora University	M,D
Austin Peay State University	M,O
Azusa Pacific University	M,D
Baldwin-Wallace College	M
Ball State University	M,D,O*
Bank Street College of Education	M*
Barry University	M,D,O*
Bayamón Central University	M
Baylor University	M,O
Bellarmine University	M
Benedictine College	M
Benedictine University	M,D
Bernard M. Baruch College of the City University of New York	M,O
Berry College	O
Bethany University	M
Bethel College (TN)	M
Bethel University	M,D,O
Bob Jones University	P,M,D,O
Boise State University	M,D
Boston College	M,D,O*
Boston University	M,O*
Bowie State University	M,D
Bowling Green State University	M,D,O*
Bradley University	M
Brandon University	M,O
Bridgewater State College	M,O
Brigham Young University	M,D*
Brooklyn College of the City University of New York	M
Bucknell University	M
Buffalo State College, State University of New York	O
Butler University	M
Caldwell College	M
California Baptist University	M
California Coast University	M
California Lutheran University	M,D

*M—master's degree; P—first professional degree; D—doctorate; O—other advanced degree; *—Close-Up and/or Announcement or Display in one of the other books in this series*

California State University, Bakersfield M
California State University Channel Islands M
California State University, Dominguez Hills M
California State University, East Bay M
California State University, Fresno M,D
California State University, Fullerton M,D
California State University, Northridge M,D
California State University, Sacramento M
California State University, San Bernardino M,D
California State University, Stanislaus M,D
California University of Pennsylvania M
Calumet College of Saint Joseph M
Calvin College M
Cambridge College M,D,O
Cameron University M
Campbell University M
Canisius College M
Capella University M,D,O
Cardinal Stritch University M,D
Caribbean University M,D
Carlow University M
Carthage College M,O
Castleton State College M,O
The Catholic University of America P,M,D,O
Centenary College M
Centenary College of Louisiana M
Central Connecticut State University M,D,O
Central Michigan University M,D,O
Chadron State College M,O
Chapman University M
Charleston Southern University M
Chestnut Hill College M
Cheyney University of Pennsylvania M,O
Chicago State University M,D
Christian Brothers University M
The Citadel, The Military College of South Carolina M,O
City College of the City University of New York M,O*
City University of Seattle M,O
Claremont Graduate University M,D,O*
Clark Atlanta University M,D,O
Clarke College M
Clearwater Christian College M
Clemson University M,D,O
Cleveland State University M,D,O
The College at Brockport, State University of New York O
College of Mount St. Joseph M
The College of New Jersey M,O
The College of New Rochelle M,O
College of Notre Dame of Maryland M,D
College of Saint Elizabeth M,D,O
The College of Saint Rose M,O*
College of Santa Fe M
College of Staten Island of the City University of New York O
The College of William and Mary M,D
Colorado State University M,D*
Columbia International University M,D,O
Columbus State University M,O
Concordia University (CA) M
Concordia University (MI) M
Concordia University (OR) M
Concordia University Chicago M,D,O
Concordia University, Nebraska M
Concordia University, St. Paul M,O
Concordia University Wisconsin M
Converse College M,O
Creighton University M*
Curry College M,O
Dakota Wesleyan University M
Dallas Baptist University M
Delaware State University M,D
Delaware Valley College M
Delta State University M,D,O
DePaul University D*
Doane College M
Dominican University M
Dowling College M,D,O
Drake University M,D,O*
Drexel University M,D*
Duquesne University M,D,O*
D'Youville College D*
East Carolina University M,D,O
Eastern Illinois University M,O
Eastern Kentucky University M
Eastern Michigan University M,D,O
Eastern Nazarene College M,O
Eastern Washington University M
East Tennessee State University M,D,O
Edgewood College M,D,O
Edinboro University of Pennsylvania M,O
Elizabeth City State University M
Elmhurst College M
Emmanuel College M,O
Emporia State University M
Evangel University M
Fairleigh Dickinson University, College at Florham M*
Fairleigh Dickinson University, Metropolitan Campus M*
Fairmont State University M
Fayetteville State University M,D
Felician College M*
Ferris State University M
Fielding Graduate University M,D,O*
Fitchburg State College M
Florida Agricultural and Mechanical University M,D
Florida Atlantic University M,D,O
Florida Gulf Coast University M
Florida International University M,D,O*
Florida State University M,D,O*
Fordham University M,D,O*
Fort Hays State University M,O
Framingham State College M
Franciscan University of Steubenville M
Freed-Hardeman University M,O
Fresno Pacific University M
Frostburg State University M
Furman University M
Gallaudet University M,D,O
Gannon University M,D,O
Gardner-Webb University M,D
Geneva College M
George Fox University M,D,O*
George Mason University M,O*
The George Washington University M,D,O*
Georgia College & State University M,O
Georgian Court University M,O
Georgia Southern University M,D,O
Georgia State University M,D,O
Golden Gate Baptist Theological Seminary P,M,D,O
Gonzaga University M,D
Governors State University M
Graceland University (IA) M
Grambling State University M,D
Grand Canyon University M,D*
Grand Valley State University M,O
Gwynedd-Mercy College M
Harding University M,O
Harvard University M,D*
Henderson State University M
Heritage University M
High Point University M
Hofstra University M,D,O*
Holy Family University M
Hood College M
Hope International University M
Houston Baptist University M
Howard University M,D,O
Hunter College of the City University of New York O
Idaho State University M,D,O
Illinois State University M,D
Immaculata University M,D,O
Indiana State University M,D,O
Indiana University Bloomington M,D,O*
Indiana University of Pennsylvania M,D,O
Indiana University–Purdue University Fort Wayne M
Indiana University–Purdue University Indianapolis M,O*
Instituto Tecnológico y de Estudios Superiores de Monterrey, Campus Central de Veracruz M
Instituto Tecnológico y de Estudios Superiores de Monterrey, Campus Ciudad Juárez M
Instituto Tecnológico y de Estudios Superiores de Monterrey, Campus Estado de México M,D
Instituto Tecnológico y de Estudios Superiores de Monterrey, Campus Irapuato M,D
Inter American University of Puerto Rico, Aguadilla Campus M
Inter American University of Puerto Rico, Arecibo Campus M
Inter American University of Puerto Rico, Barranquitas Campus M
Inter American University of Puerto Rico, Metropolitan Campus D
Inter American University of Puerto Rico, San Germán Campus M,D
Iona College M*
Iowa State University of Science and Technology M,D*
Jackson State University M,D,O
Jacksonville State University M,O
James Madison University M
John Carroll University M
The Johns Hopkins University M,D,O*
Johnson & Wales University D
Jones International University M
Kansas State University M,D*
Kaplan University–Davenport Campus M
Kean University M,D
Keene State College M,O
Keiser University M
Kennesaw State University M,D,O
Kent State University M,D,O*
Kutztown University of Pennsylvania M
Lake Erie College M
Lamar University M,D,O
La Sierra University M,D,O
Lee University M,O
Lehigh University M,D,O
Le Moyne College M,O
Lewis & Clark College M,D
Lewis University M,D,O
Liberty University M,D,O
Lincoln Memorial University M,O
Lincoln University (MO) M,O
Lindenwood University M,D,O
Lipscomb University M
Long Island University, Brooklyn Campus M
Long Island University, C.W. Post Campus M,O
Long Island University, Rockland Graduate Campus M,O
Longwood University M
Loras College M
Louisiana State University and Agricultural and Mechanical College M,D,O
Louisiana State University in Shreveport M
Louisiana Tech University M,D
Loyola Marymount University M,D
Loyola University Chicago M,D,O*
Loyola University Maryland M,O*
Lynchburg College M
Lynn University M,D
Madonna University M
Manhattan College M
Manhattanville College M*
Marian University (WI) M,D
Marshall University M,D,O
Marygrove College M
Marymount University M,O
Maryville University of Saint Louis M,D
Marywood University M,D
Massachusetts College of Liberal Arts M
McDaniel College M
McGill University M,D,O*
McKendree University M
McNeese State University M,O
Memorial University of Newfoundland M,D,O
Mercer University M,D,O
Mercy College M,O
Mercyhurst College M,O
Miami University M,D*
Michigan State University M,D,O*
Middle Tennessee State University M,O
Midwestern State University M
Mills College M,D
Minnesota State University Mankato M,O
Minnesota State University Moorhead M,O
Mississippi College M,D,O
Mississippi State University M,D,O
Missouri Baptist University M,O
Missouri State University M,O*
Monmouth University M,O*
Montana State University M,D,O
Montclair State University M,D,O*

Morehead State University	M,O
Morgan State University	M,D
Mount St. Mary's College	M
Murray State University	M,O
National-Louis University	M,D,O
National University	M
New England College	M
New Jersey City University	M
Newman Theological College	M,O
Newman University	M
New Mexico Highlands University	M
New Mexico State University	M,D
New York Institute of Technology	O
New York University	M,D,O*
Niagara University	M,O
Nicholls State University	M
Norfolk State University	M
North Carolina Agricultural and Technical State University	M,D
North Carolina Central University	M
North Carolina State University	M,D*
North Central College	M
North Dakota State University	M,O
Northeastern Illinois University	M
Northeastern State University	M
Northern Arizona University	M,D
Northern Illinois University	M,D,O
Northern Kentucky University	M,D,O
Northern Michigan University	M,O
Northern State University	M
North Georgia College & State University	M,O
Northwestern State University of Louisiana	M,O
Northwest Missouri State University	M,O
Northwest Nazarene University	M
Notre Dame de Namur University	M,O
Nova Southeastern University	M,D,O*
Oakland City University	M,D
Oakland University	M,D,O
Oglala Lakota College	M
The Ohio State University	M,D*
Ohio University	M,D*
Oklahoma State University	M,D*
Old Dominion University	M,D,O
Olivet Nazarene University	M
Oral Roberts University	M,D
Oregon State University	M*
Ottawa University	M
Our Lady of Holy Cross College	M
Our Lady of the Lake University of San Antonio	M
Pace University	M,O*
Pacific Lutheran University	M
Park University	M
Penn State Great Valley	M
Penn State University Park	M,D*
Pepperdine University	M,D
Philadelphia Biblical University	M
Pittsburg State University	M
Plymouth State University	M
Point Park University	M*
Pontifical Catholic University of Puerto Rico	D
Portland State University	M,D
Prairie View A&M University	M,D
Prescott College	M,D
Providence College	M*
Purdue University	M,D,O
Purdue University Calumet	M
Queens College of the City University of New York	O
Queens University of Charlotte	M
Radford University	M
Regent University	M,D,O
Regis University	M,O
Rhode Island College	M,O
Rider University	M,O*
Rivier College	M,D,O
Robert Morris University	M,D,O
Roosevelt University	M
Rowan University	M,D
Rutgers, The State University of New Jersey, Camden	M
Rutgers, The State University of New Jersey, New Brunswick	M,D*
Sacred Heart University	M,O
Sage Graduate School	D
Saginaw Valley State University	M,O
St. Ambrose University	M
St. Bonaventure University	M,O
St. Cloud State University	M,D
St. Edward's University	M,O
Saint Francis University	M
St. Francis Xavier University	M
St. John Fisher College	M,D
St. John's University (NY)	M,D,O
Saint Joseph's University	M,D
St. Lawrence University	M,O
Saint Leo University	M
Saint Louis University	M,D,O
Saint Martin's University	M
Saint Mary's College of California	M,D
St. Mary's University (United States)	M,O
Saint Mary's University of Minnesota	M,D,O
Saint Michael's College	M,O
Saint Peter's College	M,O
St. Thomas Aquinas College	M,O*
St. Thomas University	M,D,O
Saint Vincent College	M
Saint Xavier University	M,O
Salem International University	M
Salem State College	M
Salisbury University	M
Samford University	M,D,O
Sam Houston State University	M,D
San Diego State University	M*
San Francisco State University	M,O
San Jose State University	M,O
Santa Clara University	M
Seattle Pacific University	M,D,O
Seattle University	M,D,O
Seton Hall University	D,O*
Shasta Bible College	M
Shenandoah University	M,D,O
Shippensburg University of Pennsylvania	M
Siena Heights University	M
Silver Lake College	M
Simmons College	M,O
Simon Fraser University	M,D
Simpson University	M
Slippery Rock University of Pennsylvania	M
Sonoma State University	M
South Carolina State University	D,O
South Dakota State University	M
Southeastern Louisiana University	M,D
Southeastern Oklahoma State University	M
Southeast Missouri State University	M,O
Southern Adventist University	M
Southern Arkansas University–Magnolia	M
Southern Connecticut State University	M,D,O
Southern Illinois University Carbondale	M,D*
Southern Illinois University Edwardsville	M,O
Southern Nazarene University	M
Southern New Hampshire University	M,O*
Southern Oregon University	M
Southern University and Agricultural and Mechanical College	M
Southwest Baptist University	M,O
Southwestern Adventist University	M
Southwestern Assemblies of God University	M
Southwestern Oklahoma State University	M
Spalding University	M,D
Springfield College	M
Stanford University	M,D*
State University of New York at Fredonia	O
State University of New York at New Paltz	M,O
State University of New York at Oswego	O
State University of New York at Plattsburgh	O
State University of New York College at Cortland	O
Stephen F. Austin State University	M,D
Stetson University	M
Stony Brook University, State University of New York	M,O
Suffolk University	M,O*
Sul Ross State University	M*
Syracuse University	M,D,O*
Tarleton State University	M,D,O
Teachers College, Columbia University	M,D
Temple University	M,D*
Tennessee State University	M,D,O
Tennessee Technological University	M,O*
Tennessee Temple University	M
Texas A&M International University	M
Texas A&M University	M,D*
Texas A&M University–Commerce	M,D
Texas A&M University–Corpus Christi	M,D
Texas A&M University–Kingsville	M,D
Texas A&M University–Texarkana	M
Texas Christian University	M
Texas Southern University	M,D
Texas State University–San Marcos	M*
Texas Tech University	M,D
Texas Woman's University	M,D
Thomas Edison State College	M
Trevecca Nazarene University	M,D
Trinity Baptist College	M
Trinity International University	M
Trinity University	M
Trinity (Washington) University	M
Trinity Western University	M,O
Troy University	M,O
TUI University	M,D
Union College (KY)	M
Union Institute & University	D
Union University	M,D,O
Universidad Adventista de las Antillas	M
Universidad del Turabo	M,D
Universidad Iberoamericana	P,M
Universidad Metropolitana	M
Université de Moncton	M
Université de Montréal	M,D,O
Université de Sherbrooke	M
Université du Québec à Trois-Rivières	O
Université Laval	M,D,O
University at Albany, State University of New York	M,D,O*
University at Buffalo, the State University of New York	M,D,O*
The University of Akron	M,D
The University of Alabama	M,D,O
The University of Alabama at Birmingham	M,D,O*
University of Alaska Anchorage	M,O
University of Alberta	M,D,O*
The University of Arizona	M,D,O*
University of Arkansas	M,D,O
University of Arkansas at Little Rock	M,D,O
University of Arkansas at Monticello	M
University of Bridgeport	D,O
The University of British Columbia	M,D
University of Calgary	M,D,O
University of California, Berkeley	M,D*
University of California, Irvine	M,D*
University of California, Los Angeles	D*
University of California, Riverside	M,D*
University of California, Santa Barbara	M,D
University of Central Arkansas	M,O
University of Central Florida	M,D,O*
University of Central Missouri	M,O
University of Central Oklahoma	M
University of Cincinnati	M,D,O
University of Colorado at Colorado Springs	M,D
University of Colorado Denver	M,D,O*
University of Connecticut	D,O*
University of Dayton	M,D,O
University of Delaware	M,D,O*
University of Denver	M,D,O*
University of Detroit Mercy	M
The University of Findlay	M
University of Florida	M,D,O*
University of Georgia	M,D,O*
University of Guam	M
University of Hartford	D,O*
University of Hawaii at Manoa	M,D*
University of Houston	M,D*
University of Houston–Clear Lake	M,D
University of Houston–Victoria	M
University of Idaho	M,D,O
University of Illinois at Chicago	M,D*
University of Illinois at Springfield	M

*M—master's degree; P—first professional degree; D—doctorate; O—other advanced degree; *—Close-Up and/or Announcement or Display in one of the other books in this series*

University of Illinois at Urbana–Champaign	M,D,O*
University of Indianapolis	M
The University of Iowa	M,D,O*
The University of Kansas	M,D*
University of Kentucky	M,D,O
University of La Verne	M,D,O
University of Lethbridge	M,D
University of Louisiana at Lafayette	M,D*
University of Louisiana at Monroe	M,D
University of Louisville	M,D,O
University of Maine	M,D,O*
University of Maine at Farmington	M
University of Manitoba	M
University of Mary	M
University of Mary Hardin-Baylor	M,D
University of Maryland, College Park	M,D,O*
University of Maryland Eastern Shore	D*
University of Massachusetts Amherst	M,D,O*
University of Massachusetts Boston	M,D,O
University of Massachusetts Lowell	M,D,O
University of Memphis	M,D
University of Miami	M,D,O*
University of Michigan	M,D*
University of Minnesota, Twin Cities Campus	M,D,O*
University of Mississippi	M,D,O
University of Missouri–Columbia	M,D,O*
University of Missouri–Kansas City	M,D,O*
University of Missouri–St. Louis	M,D,O
The University of Montana	M,D,O
University of Montevallo	M,O
University of Nebraska at Kearney	M,O
University of Nebraska at Omaha	M,D,O
University of Nebraska–Lincoln	M,D,O*
University of Nevada, Las Vegas	M,D
University of Nevada, Reno	M,D,O*
University of New England	O
University of New Hampshire	M,O*
University of New Mexico	M,D,O*
University of New Orleans	M,D,O
University of North Alabama	O
The University of North Carolina at Chapel Hill	M,D*
The University of North Carolina at Charlotte	M,D,O*
The University of North Carolina at Greensboro	M,D,O
The University of North Carolina at Pembroke	M
The University of North Carolina Wilmington	M,D
University of North Dakota	M,D,O
University of Northern Colorado	M,D,O
University of Northern Iowa	M,D
University of North Florida	M,D
University of North Texas	M,D
University of Oklahoma	M,D*
University of Pennsylvania	M,D*
University of Phoenix	M
University of Phoenix–Central Florida Campus	M
University of Phoenix–Chattanooga Campus	M
University of Phoenix–Denver Campus	M
University of Phoenix–Hawaii Campus	M
University of Phoenix–Idaho Campus	M
University of Phoenix–Kansas City Campus	M
University of Phoenix–Las Vegas Campus	M
University of Phoenix–Memphis Campus	M
University of Phoenix–Metro Detroit Campus	M
University of Phoenix–Nashville Campus	M
University of Phoenix–New Mexico Campus	M
University of Phoenix–Northern Nevada Campus	M
University of Phoenix–Northern Virginia Campus	M
University of Phoenix–North Florida Campus	M
University of Phoenix–Omaha Campus	M
University of Phoenix–Phoenix Campus	M
University of Phoenix–Puerto Rico Campus	M
University of Phoenix–Richmond Campus	M
University of Phoenix–Southern Arizona Campus	M,O
University of Phoenix–Southern Colorado Campus	M,O
University of Phoenix–South Florida Campus	M
University of Phoenix–Springfield Campus	M
University of Phoenix–Utah Campus	M
University of Phoenix–Vancouver Campus	M
University of Phoenix–West Florida Campus	M
University of Phoenix–West Michigan Campus	M
University of Pittsburgh	M,D*
University of Prince Edward Island	M
University of Puerto Rico, Río Piedras	M,D
University of Regina	M,D
University of St. Francis (IL)	M
University of St. Thomas (MN)	M,D,O*
University of San Diego	M,D,O
University of San Francisco	M,D
University of Saskatchewan	M,D,O
The University of Scranton	M
University of Sioux Falls	M,O
University of South Africa	M,D
University of South Alabama	M,O*
University of South Carolina	M,D,O
The University of South Dakota	M,D,O
University of Southern California	D*
University of Southern Maine	M,O
University of Southern Mississippi	M,D,O
University of South Florida	M,D,O*
The University of Tennessee	M,D,O
The University of Tennessee at Chattanooga	M,D,O
The University of Tennessee at Martin	M
The University of Texas at Arlington	M,D*
The University of Texas at Austin	M,D
The University of Texas at Brownsville	M
The University of Texas at El Paso	M,D
The University of Texas at San Antonio	M,D*
The University of Texas at Tyler	M
The University of Texas of the Permian Basin	M
The University of Texas–Pan American	M,D
University of the Cumberlands	M
University of the Incarnate Word	M,D
University of the Pacific	M,D
University of the Southwest	M
The University of Toledo	M,D,O
University of Utah	M,D*
University of Vermont	M,D*
University of Victoria	M,D
University of Virginia	M,D,O
University of Washington	M,D*
University of Washington, Tacoma	M
The University of West Alabama	M
University of West Florida	M,O
University of West Georgia	M,O
University of Wisconsin–Madison	M,D,O*
University of Wisconsin–Milwaukee	M,D,O
University of Wisconsin–Oshkosh	M
University of Wisconsin–Stevens Point	M
University of Wisconsin–Superior	M,O
University of Wisconsin–Whitewater	M*
University of Wyoming	M,D,O
Ursuline College	M
Valdosta State University	M,D,O
Vanderbilt University	M,D*
Villanova University	M*
Virginia Commonwealth University	D
Virginia Polytechnic Institute and State University	D,O*
Virginia State University	M
Wagner College	O
Walden University	M,D,O
Walla Walla University	M
Washburn University	M
Washington State University	M,D*
Washington State University Spokane	M,O
Washington State University Tri-Cities	M,D
Wayne State College	M,O
Wayne State University	M,D,O*
Webster University	M,O
Western Carolina University	M,D,O
Western Connecticut State University	D
Western Governors University	M,O
Western Illinois University	M,D,O
Western Kentucky University	M,O
Western Michigan University	M,D,O*
Western New Mexico University	M
Western Washington University	M
Westfield State College	M,O
Westminster College (PA)	M,O
West Texas A&M University	M
West Virginia University	M,D
Wheelock College	M
Whittier College	M
Whitworth University	M
Wichita State University	M,D,O*
Widener University	M,D*
Wilkes University	M,D
William Paterson University of New Jersey	M*
William Woods University	M,O
Wilmington University	M,D
Wingate University	M
Winona State University	M,O
Winthrop University	M
Worcester State College	M,O
Wright State University	M,O
Xavier University	M*
Xavier University of Louisiana	M
Yeshiva University	M,D,O
Youngstown State University	M,D

EDUCATIONAL MEASUREMENT AND EVALUATION

American InterContinental University Online	M
Angelo State University	M
Arkansas State University	M,O
Boston College	M,D*
Bucknell University	M
Cambridge College	M,D,O
Claremont Graduate University	M,D,O*
Curry College	M,O
Eastern Michigan University	M,O
Florida State University	M,D,O*
Gallaudet University	M,O
George Mason University	M*
Georgia State University	M,D
Harvard University	D*
Houston Baptist University	M
Indiana University Bloomington	M,D,O*
Iowa State University of Science and Technology	M,D*
Kent State University	M,D*
Louisiana State University and Agricultural and Mechanical College	M,D,O
Loyola University Chicago	M,D*
Michigan State University	M,D,O*
North Carolina State University	D*
Ohio University	M,D*
Rutgers, The State University of New Jersey, New Brunswick	M*
Southern Connecticut State University	M
Southern Illinois University Carbondale	M,D*
Southwestern Oklahoma State University	M
Stanford University	M,D*
Sul Ross State University	M*
Syracuse University	M,D,O*
Teachers College, Columbia University	M,D
Texas A&M University	M,D*
Université Laval	M,D,O
University at Albany, State University of New York	M,D,O*
University of Arkansas	M,D
The University of British Columbia	M,D,O
University of Calgary	M,D,O
University of California, Berkeley	M,D*
University of California, Santa Barbara	M,D
University of Colorado at Boulder	D*
University of Connecticut	M,D,O*
University of Denver	M,D,O*
University of Florida	M,D,O*
The University of Iowa	M,D,O*
The University of Kansas	M,D*

University of Kentucky	M,D
University of Louisiana at Monroe	M,D
University of Maryland, College Park	M,D*
University of Massachusetts Amherst	M,D,O*
University of Memphis	M,D
University of Miami	M,D*
University of Michigan	M,D*
University of Michigan–Dearborn	M,O*
University of Minnesota, Twin Cities Campus	M,D*
University of Missouri–St. Louis	M,D,O
University of Nebraska–Lincoln	M,D,O*
University of New England	M
The University of North Carolina at Chapel Hill	M,D*
The University of North Carolina at Greensboro	D
University of North Dakota	D
University of Northern Colorado	M,D
University of North Texas	D
University of Pennsylvania	M,D*
University of Pittsburgh	M,D*
University of Puerto Rico, Río Piedras	M
University of South Carolina	M,D
University of South Florida	M,D,O*
The University of Tennessee	M,D,O
The University of Texas at El Paso	M
The University of Texas–Pan American	M
University of the Southwest	M
The University of Toledo	M,D
University of Victoria	M,D
University of Virginia	M,D,O
University of Washington	M,D*
University of West Georgia	D
University of Wisconsin–Milwaukee	M,D
Utah State University	M,D
Vanderbilt University	M,D*
Virginia Commonwealth University	D
Virginia Polytechnic Institute and State University	D*
Washington University in St. Louis	D*
Wayne State University	M,D,O*
West Chester University of Pennsylvania	M,O
Western Governors University	M,O
Western Michigan University	M,D,O*
West Texas A&M University	M
Wilkes University	M,D

EDUCATIONAL MEDIA/ INSTRUCTIONAL TECHNOLOGY

Acadia University	M
Adelphi University	M,O*
Alabama State University	M,O
Alliant International University–Irvine	M,O*
Alverno College	M
American InterContinental University Online	M
American InterContinental University South Florida	M
Appalachian State University	M,O
Arcadia University	M,D,O
Argosy University, Denver	M,D*
Argosy University, Nashville	M,D,O*
Argosy University, Orange County	M,D*
Argosy University, Sarasota	M,D,O*
Argosy University, Seattle	M,D*
Arizona State University	M,D
Auburn University	M,D,O*
Azusa Pacific University	M
Baldwin-Wallace College	M
Barry University	M,D,O*
Bellevue University	M,D
Bloomsburg University of Pennsylvania	M
Boise State University	M
Boston University	M,D,O*
Bowling Green State University	M*
Bridgewater State College	M
Brigham Young University	M,D*
Buffalo State College, State University of New York	M
Cabrini College	M,O
California Baptist University	M
California State University, Bakersfield	M
California State University, East Bay	M
California State University, Fullerton	M
California State University, Monterey Bay	M
California State University, Northridge	M
California State University, San Bernardino	M
California State University, Stanislaus	M,D
Cambridge College	M,D,O
Cape Breton University	O
Capella University	M,D,O
Cardinal Stritch University	M
Carlow University	M
Central Connecticut State University	M
Central Michigan University	M,D,O
Chestnut Hill College	M,O
Chicago State University	M
City University of Seattle	M,O
Clarke College	M
College of Mount Saint Vincent	M,O
The College of New Jersey	M
College of Saint Elizabeth	M,D,O
The College of Saint Rose	M,O*
The College of St. Scholastica	M
The College of William and Mary	M,D
Colorado State University–Pueblo	M
Columbia International University	M,D,O
Concordia University (Canada)	M,D,O
Dakota State University	M*
Dowling College	M,D,O
Drexel University	M,D*
Drury University	M
Duquesne University	M,D*
East Carolina University	M,O
Eastern Connecticut State University	M
Eastern Michigan University	M,O
Eastern Washington University	M
East Stroudsburg University of Pennsylvania	M
East Tennessee State University	M
Emporia State University	M
Fairfield University	M,O*
Fairleigh Dickinson University, College at Florham	M,O*
Fairleigh Dickinson University, Metropolitan Campus	M,O*
Ferris State University	M
Fielding Graduate University	M,D,O*
Fitchburg State College	M,O
Florida Gulf Coast University	M
Florida International University	M,D,O*
Florida State University	M,D,O*
Fort Hays State University	M
Framingham State College	M
Fresno Pacific University	M
Frostburg State University	M
Full Sail University	M*
Gannon University	M,O
George Fox University	M,D,O*
George Mason University	M,O*
The George Washington University	M*
Georgia College & State University	M,O
Georgia Southern University	M
Georgia State University	M,D,O
Governors State University	M
Graceland University (IA)	M
Grambling State University	M,D
Grand Valley State University	M,O
Harrisburg University of Science and Technology	M
Harvard University	M,O*
Hofstra University	M,O*
Idaho State University	M,D,O
Indiana State University	M,D
Indiana University Bloomington	M,D,O*
Indiana University of Pennsylvania	M,D
Instituto Tecnológico y de Estudios Superiores de Monterrey, Campus Central de Veracruz	M
Instituto Tecnológico y de Estudios Superiores de Monterrey, Campus Ciudad de México	M,D
Instituto Tecnológico y de Estudios Superiores de Monterrey, Campus Ciudad Juárez	M,D
Instituto Tecnológico y de Estudios Superiores de Monterrey, Campus Estado de México	M,D
Instituto Tecnológico y de Estudios Superiores de Monterrey, Campus Irapuato	M,D
Inter American University of Puerto Rico, Metropolitan Campus	M
Iona College	M,O*
Iowa State University of Science and Technology	M,D*
Jackson State University	M,D,O
Jacksonville State University	M
Jacksonville University	M
The Johns Hopkins University	M,D,O*
Johnson Bible College	M
Jones International University	M
Kaplan University–Davenport Campus	M
Kennesaw State University	M
Kent State University	M*
Kutztown University of Pennsylvania	M,O
Lamar University	M,D,O
La Salle University	M
Lawrence Technological University	M
Lehigh University	M,D,O
Lewis University	M
Lindenwood University	M,D,O
Long Island University, Brooklyn Campus	M
Long Island University, C.W. Post Campus	M
Longwood University	M
Louisiana State University and Agricultural and Mechanical College	M,D,O
Lourdes College	M
Loyola University Chicago	M*
Loyola University Maryland	M*
Malone University	M
McDaniel College	M
McNeese State University	M,O
Memorial University of Newfoundland	M,D,O
Michigan State University	M,D,O*
MidAmerica Nazarene University	M
Middle Tennessee State University	M,O
Midwestern State University	M
Minnesota State University Mankato	M,O
Mississippi State University	M,D,O
Missouri Southern State University	M
Missouri State University	M*
Montana State University–Billings	M
Montclair State University	M,O*
National-Louis University	M,O
National University	M
Nazareth College of Rochester	M
New Jersey City University	M
New York Institute of Technology	M,O
New York University	M,D,O*
North Carolina Agricultural and Technical State University	M
North Carolina Central University	M
North Carolina State University	M,D*
Northeastern State University	M
Northern Arizona University	M,O
Northern Illinois University	M,D
Northern State University	M
Northwestern State University of Louisiana	M,O
Northwestern University	M,D*
Northwest Missouri State University	M
Nova Southeastern University	M,D,O*
Oakland University	O
Ohio University	M,D*
Old Dominion University	M,D
Ottawa University	M
Our Lady of the Lake University of San Antonio	M
Penn State Great Valley	M
Penn State University Park	M,D*
Pepperdine University	M,D
Pittsburg State University	M
Portland State University	M,D
Pratt Institute	M,O*
Purdue University	M,D,O
Purdue University Calumet	M

*M—master's degree; P—first professional degree; D—doctorate; O—other advanced degree; *—Close-Up and/or Announcement or Display in one of the other books in this series*

Ramapo College of New Jersey	M
Regis University	M,O
The Richard Stockton College of New Jersey	M
Sacred Heart University	M,O
Saginaw Valley State University	M
St. Cloud State University	M
St. Edward's University	M,O
Saint Joseph's University	M,D
Saint Leo University	M
Saint Michael's College	M,O
St. Thomas University	M,D,O
Saint Vincent College	M
Salem State College	M
Sam Houston State University	M
San Diego State University	M,D*
San Francisco State University	M,O
San Jose State University	M,O
Seton Hall University	M*
Simmons College	M,D,O
Simon Fraser University	M,D
Southeastern Louisiana University	M,D
Southern Illinois University Edwardsville	M,O
Southern Polytechnic State University	M,O
Southern University and Agricultural and Mechanical College	M
State University of New York College at Potsdam	M
Stony Brook University, State University of New York	M,O
Strayer University	M
Syracuse University	M,O*
Teachers College, Columbia University	M,D
Texas A&M University	M,D*
Texas A&M University–Commerce	M,D
Texas A&M University–Corpus Christi	M,D
Texas A&M University–Texarkana	M
Texas Tech University	M,D
Thomas Edison State College	O
Towson University	M,D
TUI University	M,D
Université Laval	M,D
University at Albany, State University of New York	M,D,O*
University of Alaska Southeast	M
University of Alberta	M,D*
University of Arkansas	M
University of Arkansas at Little Rock	M
University of Calgary	M,D,O
University of Central Arkansas	M
University of Central Florida	M,D,O*
University of Central Missouri	M,O
University of Central Oklahoma	M
University of Colorado Denver	M*
University of Connecticut	M,D,O*
University of Dayton	M
The University of Findlay	M
University of Georgia	M,D,O*
University of Hartford	M*
University of Hawaii at Manoa	M,D*
University of Houston–Clear Lake	M
University of Kentucky	M,D
University of Louisville	M
University of Maine	M*
University of Maine at Farmington	M
University of Maryland, Baltimore County	M,O*
University of Maryland, College Park	M,D,O*
University of Massachusetts Amherst	M,D,O*
University of Memphis	M,D
University of Michigan	M,D*
University of Michigan–Flint	M*
University of Minnesota, Twin Cities Campus	M,D,O*
University of Missouri–Columbia	M,D,O*
University of Nebraska at Kearney	M
University of Nebraska at Omaha	M,O
University of Nevada, Las Vegas	M,D,O
University of New Mexico	M,D,O*
The University of North Carolina at Charlotte	M,D,O*
The University of North Carolina at Greensboro	M,D,O
The University of North Carolina Wilmington	M
University of North Dakota	M
University of Northern Colorado	M,D
University of Northern Iowa	M
University of North Texas	D
University of Pennsylvania	M*
University of Phoenix	M
University of Phoenix–West Florida Campus	M
University of St. Thomas (MN)	M,D,O*
University of San Francisco	M,D
University of Sioux Falls	M,D
University of South Africa	M,D
University of South Alabama	M,D*
University of South Carolina	M
University of South Carolina Aiken	M
The University of South Dakota	M,O
University of Southern California	M*
University of South Florida	M,D,O*
The University of Tennessee	M,D,O
The University of Tennessee at Chattanooga	O
The University of Texas at Brownsville	M
The University of Texas at San Antonio	M*
University of the Incarnate Word	M,D,O
University of the Sacred Heart	M
The University of Toledo	M,D,O
University of Virginia	M,D,O
University of Washington	M,D*
The University of West Alabama	M
University of West Florida	M
University of West Georgia	M,O
University of Wisconsin–Milwaukee	D
University of Wyoming	M,D,O
Utah State University	M,D,O
Virginia Polytechnic Institute and State University	M,D,O*
Walden University	M,D,O
Waynesburg University	M,D
Wayne State University	M,D,O*
Webster University	M,O
West Chester University of Pennsylvania	M,O
Western Connecticut State University	M
Western Governors University	M,O
Western Illinois University	M,O
Western Kentucky University	M
Western Michigan University	M,D,O*
Western Oregon University	M
Westfield State College	M
West Texas A&M University	M
West Virginia University	M,D
Widener University	M,D*
Wilkes University	M,D
Wilmington University	M
Youngstown State University	M

EDUCATIONAL POLICY

Alabama State University	M,D,O
The College of William and Mary	M,D
Florida State University	M,D,O*
The George Washington University	M,D*
Georgia State University	M,D,O
Harvard University	M*
Illinois State University	M,D
Indiana University Bloomington	M,D,O*
Loyola University Chicago	M,D*
Michigan State University	D*
New York University	M,D*
The Ohio State University	M,D*
Portland State University	M,D
Rutgers, The State University of New Jersey, Camden	M
Rutgers, The State University of New Jersey, New Brunswick	D*
Universidad Central del Este	M,D
University of Alberta	M,D,O*
University of Arkansas	D
The University of British Columbia	M,D
University of California, Riverside	M,D*
University of California, Santa Cruz	M,D*
University of Georgia	M,D,O*
University of Hawaii at Manoa	D*
University of Illinois at Chicago	M,D*
University of Illinois at Urbana–Champaign	M,D*
The University of Iowa	M,D,O*
The University of Kansas	D*
University of Kentucky	M,D
University of Maryland, College Park	M,D*
University of Massachusetts Amherst	M,D,O*
University of Minnesota, Twin Cities Campus	M,D,O*
University of St. Thomas (MN)	M,D,O*
University of Southern California	D*
University of Washington	M,D*
The University of Western Ontario	M
University of Wisconsin–Madison	M,D,O*
Vanderbilt University	M,D*
Virginia Commonwealth University	D
Wayne State University	M,D,O*

EDUCATIONAL PSYCHOLOGY

Alliant International University–Irvine	M,D,O*
Alliant International University–Los Angeles	M,D,O*
Alliant International University–San Diego	M,D,O*
Alliant International University–San Francisco	M,D,O*
American International College	M,D,O
Andrews University	M,D
Arcadia University	M,D,O
Arizona State University	M,D
Auburn University	M,D,O*
Ball State University	M,D,O*
Baylor University	M,D,O
Boston College	M,D*
Brigham Young University	M,D
California State University, Northridge	M
Capella University	M,D,O
The Catholic University of America	M,D,O
Chapman University	M,O
Clark Atlanta University	M
The College of Saint Rose	M,O*
Eastern Michigan University	M,O
Edinboro University of Pennsylvania	M,O
Florida State University	M,D,O*
Fordham University	M,D,O*
George Mason University	M*
Georgian Court University	M,O
Georgia State University	M,D
Graduate School and University Center of the City University of New York	D*
Harvard University	M*
Holy Names University	M,O
Howard University	M,D,O
Illinois State University	M,D,O
Indiana University Bloomington	M,D,O*
Indiana University of Pennsylvania	M,O
John Carroll University	M
The Johns Hopkins University	M,O*
Johnson State College	M
Kean University	M
Kent State University	M,D*
La Sierra University	M,D
Long Island University, Westchester Graduate Campus	M
Loyola University Chicago	M*
Marist College	M,O
Maryville University of Saint Louis	M,D
McGill University	M,D,O*
Memorial University of Newfoundland	M,D
Miami University	M,O*
Michigan School of Professional Psychology	M,D
Michigan State University	M,D,O*
Mississippi State University	M,D,O
Montclair State University	M,O*
Mount Saint Vincent University	M
National-Louis University	M,D,O
New Jersey City University	M,O
New York University	M,D*
Northeastern University	M*
Northern Arizona University	D
Northern Illinois University	M,D,O
Oklahoma City University	M
Oklahoma State University	M,D,O*
Penn State University Park	M,D*
Pontifical Catholic University of Puerto Rico	M

Purdue University M,D,O
Rutgers, The State University of New Jersey, New Brunswick M,D*
Simon Fraser University M,D
Southern Illinois University Carbondale M,D*
Stanford University D*
State University of New York College at Oneonta M,O
Teachers College, Columbia University M,D
Temple University M,D*
Tennessee Technological University M,O*
Texas A&M University M,D*
Texas Christian University M,O
Texas Tech University M,D
Universidad de Iberoamerica P,M
Université de Moncton M
Université de Montréal M,D,O
Université du Québec à Trois-Rivières M,D
Université du Québec en Outaouais M
Université Laval M,D
University at Albany, State University of New York M,D,O*
University at Buffalo, the State University of New York M,D,O*
University of Alberta M,D*
The University of Arizona M,D,O*
University of Calgary M,D
University of California, Davis M,D*
University of California, Riverside M,D*
University of Colorado at Boulder M,D*
University of Connecticut M,D,O*
University of Denver M,D,O*
University of Florida M,D,O*
University of Georgia M,D,O*
University of Hawaii at Manoa M,D*
University of Houston M,D*
University of Illinois at Chicago D*
University of Illinois at Urbana–Champaign M,D,O*
The University of Iowa M,D,O*
The University of Kansas M,D*
University of Kentucky M,D,O
University of Louisville M,D
University of Manitoba M
University of Mary Hardin-Baylor M,D
University of Maryland, College Park M,D*
University of Memphis M,D
University of Minnesota, Twin Cities Campus M,D,O*
University of Missouri–Columbia M,D,O*
University of Missouri–St. Louis D,O
University of Nebraska at Omaha M,D,O
University of Nebraska–Lincoln M,D,O*
University of Nevada, Las Vegas M,D,O
University of Nevada, Reno M,D,O*
University of New Mexico M,D*
The University of North Carolina at Chapel Hill M,D*
University of Northern Colorado M,D
University of Northern Iowa M,O
University of North Texas M
University of Oklahoma M,D*
University of Pennsylvania M,D*
University of Phoenix–Southern Arizona Campus M,O
University of Regina M
University of Saskatchewan M,D,O
University of South Africa M,D
University of South Carolina M,D
The University of South Dakota M,D,O
University of Southern California M,D*
University of Southern Maine M,O
The University of Tennessee M,D,O
The University of Texas at Austin M,D
The University of Texas at El Paso M
The University of Texas–Pan American M
University of the Pacific M,D,O
The University of Toledo M,D
University of Utah M,D*
University of Victoria M,D
University of Virginia M,D,O
University of Washington M,D*
The University of Western Ontario M
University of Wisconsin–Madison M,D*
University of Wisconsin–Milwaukee M,D
Virginia Commonwealth University D
Virginia Polytechnic Institute and State University M,D,O*
Washington State University M,D,O*
Wayne State University M,D,O*
Western Kentucky University M,O
West Virginia University M
Wichita State University M,D,O*
Widener University M,D*

EDUCATION OF THE GIFTED

Arkansas State University M,D,O
Arkansas Tech University M,O
Ashland University M
Barry University M,D,O*
Bowling Green State University M*
Carlos Albizu University, Miami Campus M,D
Carthage College M,O
The College of New Rochelle M,O
The College of William and Mary M
Converse College M
Drury University M
Elon University M
Emporia State University M
George Mason University M,O*
Hardin-Simmons University M
Hofstra University M,O*
The Johns Hopkins University M,D,O*
Johnson State College M
Kent State University M*
Liberty University M,D,O
Lynn University M,D
Maryville University of Saint Louis M,D
Millersville University of Pennsylvania M
Minnesota State University Mankato M,O
Mississippi University for Women M
Northeastern Illinois University M
Nova Southeastern University M,O*
Purdue University M,D,O
Saint Leo University M
Saint Mary's University of Minnesota M,O
St. Thomas University M,D,O
Samford University M,D,O
Southern Methodist University M,D,O*
Teachers College, Columbia University M,D
Tennessee Technological University D*
Texas A&M University M,D*
The University of Alabama M,D,O
The University of Arizona M,D,O*
University of Arkansas at Little Rock M
University of Calgary M,D,O
University of Central Florida M,D,O*
University of Connecticut M,D,O*
University of Houston M,D*
University of Louisiana at Lafayette M*
University of Louisiana at Monroe M,D
University of Minnesota, Twin Cities Campus M,D,O*
University of Missouri–Columbia M,D*
The University of North Carolina at Charlotte M,D*
University of St. Thomas (MN) M,D,O*
University of Southern Mississippi M,D,O
University of South Florida M,D,O*
The University of Texas–Pan American M
The University of Toledo D,O
University of Virginia M,D,O
Western Washington University M
West Virginia University M,D
Whitworth University M
William Carey University M,O
Wilmington University M
Wright State University M
Youngstown State University M

EDUCATION OF THE MULTIPLY HANDICAPPED

Cleveland State University M
Fresno Pacific University M
Gallaudet University M,D,O
Georgia State University M
Hunter College of the City University of New York M
Minot State University M
Montclair State University M,O*
Norfolk State University M
Syracuse University M*
Teachers College, Columbia University M
University of Illinois at Urbana–Champaign M,D,O*
West Virginia University M,D

ELECTRICAL ENGINEERING

Air Force Institute of Technology M,D
Alfred University M,D*
American University of Beirut M,D
American University of Sharjah M
Arizona State University M,D
Arizona State University at the Polytechnic Campus M
Auburn University M,D*
Baylor University M
Boise State University M,D
Boston University M,D*
Bradley University M
Brigham Young University M,D*
Brown University M,D*
Bucknell University M
California Institute of Technology M,D,O*
California Polytechnic State University, San Luis Obispo M
California State Polytechnic University, Pomona M
California State University, Chico M
California State University, Fresno M
California State University, Fullerton M
California State University, Long Beach M
California State University, Los Angeles M
California State University, Northridge M
California State University, Sacramento M*
Capitol College M
Carleton University M,D
Carnegie Mellon University M,D*
Case Western Reserve University M,D*
The Catholic University of America M,D
City College of the City University of New York M,D*
Clarkson University M,D*
Clemson University M,D
Cleveland State University M,D
Colorado State University M,D*
Colorado Technical University Colorado Springs M
Colorado Technical University Denver M
Columbia University M,D,O*
Concordia University (Canada) M,D
Cooper Union for the Advancement of Science and Art M
Cornell University M,D*
Dalhousie University M,D
Dartmouth College M,D*
Drexel University M*
Duke University M,D*
École Polytechnique de Montréal M,D,O
Fairfield University M*
Fairleigh Dickinson University, Metropolitan Campus M*
Florida Agricultural and Mechanical University M,D
Florida Atlantic University M,D
Florida Institute of Technology M,D*
Florida International University M,D*
Florida State University M,D*
Gannon University M
George Mason University M,D,O*
The George Washington University M,D*
Georgia Institute of Technology M,D*
Georgia Southern University M
Graduate School and University Center of the City University of New York D*
Grand Valley State University M
Howard University M,D
Illinois Institute of Technology M,D*
Indiana University–Purdue University Fort Wayne M

*M—master's degree; P—first professional degree; D—doctorate; O—other advanced degree; *—Close-Up and/or Announcement or Display in one of the other books in this series*

Indiana University–Purdue University Indianapolis	M,D*
Instituto Tecnológico y de Estudios Superiores de Monterrey, Campus Chihuahua	M,O
Instituto Tecnológico y de Estudios Superiores de Monterrey, Campus Monterrey	M,D
International Technological University	M,D
Iowa State University of Science and Technology	M,D*
The Johns Hopkins University	M,D,O*
Kansas State University	M,D*
Kettering University	M
Lakehead University	M,D
Lamar University	M,D
Lawrence Technological University	M,D
Lehigh University	M,D
Louisiana State University and Agricultural and Mechanical College	M,D
Louisiana Tech University	M,D
Loyola Marymount University	M
Manhattan College	M
Marquette University	M,D
Massachusetts Institute of Technology	M,D,O*
McGill University	M,D*
McMaster University	M,D
McNeese State University	M
Memorial University of Newfoundland	M,D
Mercer University	M
Michigan State University	M,D*
Michigan Technological University	M,D
Minnesota State University Mankato	M
Mississippi State University	M,D
Missouri University of Science and Technology	M,D
Montana State University	M,D
Montana Tech of The University of Montana	M
Morgan State University	M,D
Naval Postgraduate School	M,D,O
New Jersey Institute of Technology	M,D
New Mexico Institute of Mining and Technology	M
New Mexico State University	M,D
New York Institute of Technology	M
Norfolk State University	M
North Carolina Agricultural and Technical State University	M,D
North Carolina State University	M,D*
North Dakota State University	M,D
Northeastern University	M,D*
Northern Arizona University	M
Northern Illinois University	M
Northwestern Polytechnic University	M
Northwestern University	M,D,O*
Oakland University	M
OGI School of Science & Engineering at Oregon Health & Science University	M,D
The Ohio State University	M,D*
Ohio University	M,D*
Oklahoma State University	M,D*
Old Dominion University	M,D
Oregon Health & Science University	M,D*
Oregon State University	M,D*
Penn State Harrisburg	M
Penn State University Park	M,D*
Polytechnic Institute of NYU	M,D
Polytechnic Institute of NYU, Long Island Graduate Center	M,D
Polytechnic Institute of NYU, Westchester Graduate Center	M,D
Polytechnic University of Puerto Rico	M
Polytechnic University of the Americas–Orlando Campus	M
Portland State University	M,D
Prairie View A&M University	M,D
Princeton University	M,D*
Purdue University	M,D
Purdue University Calumet	M
Queen's University at Kingston	M,D
Rensselaer at Hartford	M
Rensselaer Polytechnic Institute	M,D
Rice University	M,D
Rochester Institute of Technology	M
Rose-Hulman Institute of Technology	M*
Royal Military College of Canada	M,D
Rutgers, The State University of New Jersey, New Brunswick	M,D*
St. Cloud State University	M
St. Mary's University (United States)	M
San Diego State University	M*
San Jose State University	M
Santa Clara University	M,D,O
South Dakota School of Mines and Technology	M*
South Dakota State University	M,D
Southern Illinois University Carbondale	M,D*
Southern Illinois University Edwardsville	M
Southern Methodist University	M,D*
Southern Polytechnic State University	M
Stanford University	M,D,O*
State University of New York at Binghamton	M,D*
State University of New York at New Paltz	M
Stevens Institute of Technology	M,D,O
Stony Brook University, State University of New York	M,D
Syracuse University	M,D*
Temple University	M*
Tennessee Technological University	M,D*
Texas A&M University	M,D*
Texas A&M University–Kingsville	M
Texas Tech University	M,D
Tufts University	M,D,O*
Tuskegee University	M
Union Graduate College	M
Universidad de las Américas–Puebla	M
Université de Moncton	M
Université de Sherbrooke	M,D
Université du Québec à Trois-Rivières	M,D
Université Laval	M,D
University at Buffalo, the State University of New York	M,D*
The University of Akron	M,D
The University of Alabama	M,D
The University of Alabama at Birmingham	M*
The University of Alabama in Huntsville	M,D
University of Alaska Fairbanks	M,D
University of Alberta	M,D*
The University of Arizona	M,D*
University of Arkansas	M,D
University of Bridgeport	M
The University of British Columbia	M,D
University of Calgary	M,D
University of California, Berkeley	M,D*
University of California, Davis	M,D*
University of California, Irvine	M,D*
University of California, Los Angeles	M,D*
University of California, Riverside	M,D
University of California, San Diego	M,D*
University of California, Santa Barbara	M,D
University of California, Santa Cruz	M,D*
University of Central Florida	M,D,O*
University of Cincinnati	M,D
University of Colorado at Boulder	M,D*
University of Colorado at Colorado Springs	M,D
University of Colorado Denver	M*
University of Connecticut	M,D*
University of Dayton	M,D
University of Delaware	M,D*
University of Denver	M*
University of Detroit Mercy	M,D
University of Evansville	M
University of Florida	M,D,O*
University of Hawaii at Manoa	M,D*
University of Houston	M,D*
University of Idaho	M,D
University of Illinois at Chicago	M,D*
University of Illinois at Urbana–Champaign	M,D*
The University of Iowa	M,D*
The University of Kansas	M,D*
University of Kentucky	M,D
University of Louisville	M,D
University of Maine	M,D*
University of Manitoba	M,D
University of Maryland, Baltimore County	M,D*
University of Maryland, College Park	M,D,O*
University of Massachusetts Amherst	M,D*
University of Massachusetts Dartmouth	M,D,O
University of Massachusetts Lowell	M,D
University of Memphis	M,D
University of Miami	M,D*
University of Michigan	M,D*
University of Michigan–Dearborn	M*
University of Minnesota, Duluth	M
University of Minnesota, Twin Cities Campus	M,D*
University of Missouri–Columbia	M,D*
University of Missouri–Kansas City	M,D*
University of Nebraska–Lincoln	M,D*
University of Nevada, Las Vegas	M,D
University of Nevada, Reno	M,D*
University of New Brunswick Fredericton	M,D
University of New Hampshire	M,D*
University of New Haven	M*
University of New Mexico	M,D*
The University of North Carolina at Charlotte	M,D*
University of North Dakota	M
University of North Texas	M
University of Notre Dame	M,D*
University of Oklahoma	M,D*
University of Ottawa	M,D*
University of Pennsylvania	M,D*
University of Pittsburgh	M,D*
University of Puerto Rico, Mayagüez Campus	M
University of Rhode Island	M,D
University of Rochester	M,D*
University of Saskatchewan	M,D
University of South Alabama	M*
University of South Carolina	M,D
University of Southern California	M,D,O*
University of South Florida	M,D*
The University of Tennessee	M,D
The University of Tennessee at Chattanooga	M
The University of Tennessee Space Institute	M,D*
The University of Texas at Arlington	M,D*
The University of Texas at Austin	M,D
The University of Texas at Dallas	M,D*
The University of Texas at El Paso	M,D
The University of Texas at San Antonio	M,D*
The University of Texas at Tyler	M
The University of Texas–Pan American	M
The University of Toledo	M,D
University of Toronto	M,D
University of Tulsa	M*
University of Utah	M,D,O*
University of Vermont	M,D*
University of Victoria	M,D
University of Virginia	M,D
University of Washington	M,D*
University of Waterloo	M,D
The University of Western Ontario	M,D
University of Windsor	M,D
University of Wisconsin–Madison	M,D*
University of Wisconsin–Milwaukee	M,D,O
University of Wyoming	M,D
Utah State University	M,D
Vanderbilt University	M,D*
Villanova University	M,O*
Virginia Commonwealth University	M,D
Virginia Polytechnic Institute and State University	M,D*
Washington State University	M,D*
Washington State University Tri-Cities	M,D
Washington University in St. Louis	M,D*
Wayne State University	M,D*
Western Michigan University	M,D*
Western New England College	M
West Virginia University	M,D
Wichita State University	M,D*
Wilkes University	M

Woods Hole Oceanographic Institution	M,D,O
Worcester Polytechnic Institute	M,D,O*
Wright State University	M
Yale University	M,D*
Youngstown State University	M

ELECTRONIC COMMERCE

Adelphi University	M*
Arkansas State University	M
Boston University	M*
California State University, East Bay	M
California State University, Fullerton	M
Carnegie Mellon University	M*
Claremont Graduate University	M,D,O*
Columbia Southern University	M
Dalhousie University	M,D
Dallas Baptist University	M
DePaul University	M,D*
Eastern Michigan University	M,O
Fairleigh Dickinson University, Metropolitan Campus	M*
Ferris State University	M
Florida Institute of Technology	M*
George Mason University	M,D,O*
Georgia Institute of Technology	M,O*
Hawai'i Pacific University	M*
HEC Montreal	M,O
Instituto Tecnológico y de Estudios Superiores de Monterrey, Campus Central de Veracruz	M
Instituto Tecnológico y de Estudios Superiores de Monterrey, Campus Ciudad Juárez	M
Instituto Tecnológico y de Estudios Superiores de Monterrey, Campus Estado de México	M,D
Instituto Tecnológico y de Estudios Superiores de Monterrey, Campus Irapuato	M,D
Inter American University of Puerto Rico, Bayamón Campus	M
Lewis University	M
Maryville University of Saint Louis	M,O
Marywood University	M,O
Mercy College	M
The National Graduate School of Quality Management	M
National University	M
Northwestern University	M*
Regis University	M,O
Saint Xavier University	M,O
Stevens Institute of Technology	M,O
Université Laval	M,O
University at Buffalo, the State University of New York	M,D,O*
The University of Akron	M
University of Dayton	M
University of Denver	M*
University of Florida	M*
University of Massachusetts Dartmouth	M,O
University of New Brunswick Saint John	M
University of Ottawa	M,D,O*
University of Phoenix	M
University of Phoenix–Austin Campus	M
University of Phoenix–Bay Area Campus	M
University of Phoenix–Chicago Campus	M
University of Phoenix–Cincinnati Campus	M
University of Phoenix–Columbus Georgia Campus	M
University of Phoenix–Dallas Campus	M
University of Phoenix–Denver Campus	M
University of Phoenix–Houston Campus	M
University of Phoenix–Louisville Campus	M
University of Phoenix–Madison Campus	M
University of Phoenix–Maryland Campus	M
University of Phoenix–Memphis Campus	M
University of Phoenix–New Mexico Campus	M
University of Phoenix–Northern Virginia Campus	M
University of Phoenix–Oklahoma City Campus	M
University of Phoenix–Pittsburgh Campus	M
University of Phoenix–Raleigh Campus	M
University of Phoenix–San Antonio Campus	M
University of Phoenix–West Michigan Campus	M
University of San Francisco	M
The University of Texas at Dallas	M*
Xavier University	M*

ELECTRONIC MATERIALS

Colorado School of Mines	M,D
Massachusetts Institute of Technology	M,D,O*
Northwestern University	M,D,O*
Princeton University	D*
University of Arkansas	M,D

ELEMENTARY EDUCATION

Adelphi University	M*
Alabama Agricultural and Mechanical University	M,O
Alabama State University	M,O
Alaska Pacific University	M
Albright College	M
Alcorn State University	M,O
American International College	M,D,O
American University	M,O*
American University of Puerto Rico	M
Andrews University	M,D,O
Anna Maria College	M,O
Antioch University New England	M*
Appalachian State University	M
Arcadia University	M,D,O
Argosy University, Atlanta	M,D,O*
Argosy University, Chicago	M,D,O*
Argosy University, Denver	M,D*
Argosy University, Hawai'i	M,D*
Argosy University, Inland Empire	M,D*
Argosy University, Los Angeles	M,D*
Argosy University, Nashville	M,D,O*
Argosy University, Orange County	M,D*
Argosy University, Phoenix	M,D,O*
Argosy University, San Diego	M,D*
Argosy University, San Francisco Bay Area	M,D*
Argosy University, Sarasota	M,D,O*
Argosy University, Schaumburg	M,D,O*
Argosy University, Seattle	M,D*
Argosy University, Tampa	M,D,O*
Argosy University, Twin Cities	M,D,O*
Argosy University, Washington DC	M,D,O*
Arizona State University at the West campus	M,D,O
Arkansas State University	M,D,O
Armstrong Atlantic State University	M
Auburn University	M,D,O*
Auburn University Montgomery	M,O
Augustana College	M
Austin College	M
Austin Peay State University	M,O
Averett University	M
Ball State University	M,D*
Bank Street College of Education	M*
Barry University	M,D,O*
Bayamón Central University	M
Belhaven College (MS)	M
Belmont University	M
Benedictine University	M
Bennington College	M
Bethel College (TN)	M
Bloomsburg University of Pennsylvania	M
Bob Jones University	P,M,D,O
Boston College	M*
Boston University	M*
Bowie State University	M
Brandeis University	M
Bridgewater State College	M
Brooklyn College of the City University of New York	M
Brown University	M*
Buffalo State College, State University of New York	M
Butler University	M
California Lutheran University	M,D
California State University, Fullerton	M
California State University, Los Angeles	M
California State University, Northridge	M
California State University, San Bernardino	M
California State University, Stanislaus	M,O
California University of Pennsylvania	M
Cambridge College	M,D,O
Campbell University	M
Canisius College	M
Capella University	M,D,O
Caribbean University	M,D
Carlow University	M
Carson-Newman College	M
Catawba College	M
Centenary College of Louisiana	M
Central Connecticut State University	M,O
Central Michigan University	M,O
Chadron State College	M,O
Chapman University	M
Charleston Southern University	M
Chatham University	M
Chestnut Hill College	M
Cheyney University of Pennsylvania	M
Chicago State University	M
Christopher Newport University	M
The Citadel, The Military College of South Carolina	M
City University of Seattle	M,O
Clarion University of Pennsylvania	M
Clemson University	M
Coastal Carolina University	M
College of Charleston	M*
The College of New Jersey	M
The College of New Rochelle	M
College of St. Joseph	M
The College of Saint Rose	M,O*
College of Staten Island of the City University of New York	M
The College of William and Mary	M
The Colorado College	M
Columbia College (SC)	M
Columbia College Chicago	M
Columbia International University	M,D,O
Concordia University (OR)	M
Concordia University Chicago	M
Concordia University, Nebraska	M
Converse College	M
Creighton University	M*
Curry College	M,O
Dallas Baptist University	M
Delta State University	M,D,O
DePaul University	M,D*
DeSales University	M
Dominican College	M
Dominican University	M
Drake University	M*
Drury University	M
Duquesne University	M*
D'Youville College	M,O*
East Carolina University	M
Eastern Connecticut State University	M
Eastern Illinois University	M
Eastern Kentucky University	M
Eastern Michigan University	M
Eastern Nazarene College	M,O
Eastern Oregon University	M
Eastern Washington University	M
East Stroudsburg University of Pennsylvania	M
East Tennessee State University	M
Edinboro University of Pennsylvania	M,O
Elizabeth City State University	M
Elms College	M,O
Elon University	M
Emmanuel College	M,O
Emporia State University	M
Endicott College	M
Fairfield University	M,O*
Fayetteville State University	M
Felician College	M*
Ferris State University	M
Fitchburg State College	M
Florida Agricultural and Mechanical University	M
Florida Atlantic University	M
Florida Gulf Coast University	M
Florida Institute of Technology	M,D,O*

*M—master's degree; P—first professional degree; D—doctorate; O—other advanced degree; *—Close-Up and/or Announcement or Display in one of the other books in this series*

Florida International University	M,D*
Florida State University	M,D,O*
Fordham University	M,D,O*
Framingham State College	M
Francis Marion University	M
Fresno Pacific University	M
Friends University	M
Frostburg State University	M
Gallaudet University	M,D,O
Gardner-Webb University	M
The George Washington University	M*
Georgia Southern University	M
Grand Canyon University	M,D*
Grand Valley State University	M,O
Greensboro College	M
Greenville College	M
Hampton University	M
Harding University	M,O
High Point University	M
Hofstra University	M,O*
Holy Family University	M
Hood College	M
Howard University	M
Hunter College of the City University of New York	M
Idaho State University	M,O
Immaculata University	M,D,O
Indiana State University	M
Indiana University Bloomington	M,D,O*
Indiana University Kokomo	M
Indiana University Northwest	M
Indiana University of Pennsylvania	M
Indiana University–Purdue University Fort Wayne	M,O
Indiana University South Bend	M
Indiana University Southeast	M
Inter American University of Puerto Rico, Aguadilla Campus	M
Inter American University of Puerto Rico, Arecibo Campus	M
Inter American University of Puerto Rico, Barranquitas Campus	M
Inter American University of Puerto Rico, Guayama Campus	M
Inter American University of Puerto Rico, Metropolitan Campus	M
Inter American University of Puerto Rico, Ponce Campus	M
Inter American University of Puerto Rico, San Germán Campus	M
Iowa State University of Science and Technology	M,D*
Ithaca College	M
Jackson State University	M,D,O
Jacksonville State University	M
Jacksonville University	M
James Madison University	M
The Johns Hopkins University	M,O*
Jones International University	M
Kennesaw State University	M
Kent State University	M,D,O*
Kutztown University of Pennsylvania	M,O
Lander University	M
Langston University	M
Lee University	M,O
Lehigh University	M,D,O
Lehman College of the City University of New York	M
Le Moyne College	M,O
Lesley University	M,D,O*
Lewis & Clark College	M
Lewis University	M
Liberty University	M,D,O
Lincoln University (MO)	M,O
Lincoln University (PA)	M
Lock Haven University of Pennsylvania	M
Long Island University at Riverhead	M
Long Island University, Brooklyn Campus	M
Long Island University, C.W. Post Campus	M
Long Island University, Rockland Graduate Campus	M
Long Island University, Westchester Graduate Campus	M,O
Longwood University	M
Louisiana State University and Agricultural and Mechanical College	M,D,O
Loyola Marymount University	M
Loyola University Chicago	M*
Maharishi University of Management	M
Manhattanville College	M*
Mansfield University of Pennsylvania	M
Marshall University	M
Mary Baldwin College	M
Marygrove College	M
Marymount University	M
Maryville University of Saint Louis	M,D
Marywood University	M
McDaniel College	M
McNeese State University	M
Medaille College	M
Mercy College	M
Metropolitan College of New York	M
Miami University	M*
Middle Tennessee State University	M,O
Millersville University of Pennsylvania	M
Mills College	M,D
Minnesota State University Mankato	M
Minot State University	M
Mississippi College	M,D,O
Mississippi State University	M,D,O
Mississippi Valley State University	M
Missouri State University	M,O*
Monmouth University	M,O
Montclair State University	M,O*
Montreat College	M
Morehead State University	M,O
Morgan State University	M,O
Mount Saint Mary College	M
Mount St. Mary's College	M
Mount Saint Vincent University	M
Murray State University	M,O
National-Louis University	M
Nazareth College of Rochester	M
New Jersey City University	M
New York Institute of Technology	M,O
New York University	M,D,O*
Niagara University	M,O
North Carolina Agricultural and Technical State University	M
North Carolina Central University	M
North Carolina State University	M*
Northern Arizona University	M
Northern Illinois University	M,D
Northern Michigan University	M
Northern State University	M
Northwestern Oklahoma State University	M
Northwestern State University of Louisiana	M,O
Northwestern University	M*
Northwest Missouri State University	M,O
Nova Southeastern University	M,O*
Nyack College	M
Occidental College	M
Oklahoma City University	M
Old Dominion University	M
Olivet Nazarene University	M
Oregon State University	M*
Ottawa University	M
Our Lady of the Lake University of San Antonio	M
Pacific University	M
Penn State University Park	M,D*
Pfeiffer University	M
Pittsburg State University	M
Plymouth State University	M
Portland State University	M,D
Prescott College	M,D
Providence College	M*
Purdue University	M,D,O
Purdue University North Central	M
Queens College of the City University of New York	M,O
Queens University of Charlotte	M
Quinnipiac University	M*
Regent University	M,D,O
Regis University	M,O
Rhode Island College	M
Rider University	O*
Rivier College	M,D,O
Rockford College	M
Roger Williams University	M*
Rollins College	M
Roosevelt University	M
Rosemont College	M
Rowan University	M
Rutgers, The State University of New Jersey, New Brunswick	M,D*
Sacred Heart University	M,O
Sage Graduate School	M
Saginaw Valley State University	M
St. John Fisher College	M
St. John's University (NY)	M
Saint Joseph's University	M,D
Saint Mary's University of Minnesota	M,O
Saint Peter's College	M,O
St. Thomas Aquinas College	M,O*
St. Thomas University	M,D,O
Saint Xavier University	M,O
Salem College	M
Salem State College	M
Samford University	M,D,O
San Diego State University	M*
San Francisco State University	M
San Jose State University	M,O
Seton Hill University	M,O
Shenandoah University	M,D,O
Shippensburg University of Pennsylvania	M
Siena Heights University	M
Sierra Nevada College	M
Simmons College	M,O
Sinte Gleska University	M
Slippery Rock University of Pennsylvania	M
Smith College	M
Sonoma State University	M
South Carolina State University	M
Southeastern Louisiana University	M
Southeastern Oklahoma State University	M
Southeast Missouri State University	M
Southern Arkansas University–Magnolia	M
Southern Connecticut State University	M,O
Southern New Hampshire University	M,O*
Southern Oregon University	M
Southern University and Agricultural and Mechanical College	M
Southwestern Oklahoma State University	M
Spalding University	M
Springfield College	M
Spring Hill College	M
State University of New York at Fredonia	M
State University of New York at New Paltz	M
State University of New York at Oswego	M
State University of New York at Plattsburgh	M
State University of New York College at Geneseo	M
State University of New York College at Oneonta	M
State University of New York College at Potsdam	M
Stephen F. Austin State University	M
Sul Ross State University	M*
Teachers College, Columbia University	M
Temple University	M,D*
Tennessee State University	M,D
Tennessee Technological University	M,O*
Texas A&M University–Commerce	M,D
Texas A&M University–Corpus Christi	M
Texas A&M University–Kingsville	M
Texas Christian University	M,O
Texas State University–San Marcos	M*
Texas Tech University	M,D
Texas Woman's University	M,D
Towson University	M
Trevecca Nazarene University	M
Trinity (Washington) University	M
Troy University	M,O
Union College (KY)	M
Universidad del Este	M
Université de Sherbrooke	M,O
University at Buffalo, the State University of New York	M,D,O*
The University of Akron	M,D
The University of Alabama	M,D,O
The University of Alabama at Birmingham	M*
University of Alaska Fairbanks	M,D,O
University of Alaska Southeast	M
University of Alberta	M,D*
The University of Arizona	M,D*
University of Arkansas	M,O
University of Arkansas at Pine Bluff	M
University of Bridgeport	M,O

University of California, Irvine M,D*
University of Central Florida M,D*
University of Central Missouri M,O
University of Central Oklahoma M
University of Cincinnati M
University of Connecticut M,D,O*
The University of Findlay M
University of Florida M,D,O*
University of Georgia M,D,O*
University of Hartford M*
University of Houston M,D*
University of Houston–Downtown M
University of Illinois at Chicago M,D*
University of Indianapolis M
The University of Iowa M,D*
University of Louisiana at Monroe M,D
University of Louisville M
University of Maine M,O*
University of Maryland, Baltimore County M*
University of Massachusetts Amherst M,D,O*
University of Massachusetts Boston M,D,O
University of Massachusetts Dartmouth M,O
University of Memphis M,D
University of Miami M*
University of Michigan–Flint M*
University of Minnesota, Twin Cities Campus M,D,O*
University of Missouri–Columbia M,D,O*
University of Missouri–St. Louis M,O
University of Montevallo M
University of Nebraska at Omaha M
University of Nevada, Reno M*
University of New Hampshire M*
University of New Mexico M,O*
University of North Alabama M,O
The University of North Carolina at Charlotte M*
The University of North Carolina at Greensboro D
The University of North Carolina at Pembroke M
The University of North Carolina Wilmington M
University of North Dakota M,D
University of Northern Iowa M
University of North Florida M
University of Oklahoma M,D,O*
University of Pennsylvania M*
University of Phoenix M
University of Phoenix–Bay Area Campus M
University of Phoenix–Central Florida Campus M
University of Phoenix–Central Valley Campus M
University of Phoenix–Chattanooga Campus M
University of Phoenix–Denver Campus M
University of Phoenix–Hawaii Campus M
University of Phoenix–Idaho Campus M
University of Phoenix–Indianapolis Campus M
University of Phoenix–Las Vegas Campus M
University of Phoenix–Memphis Campus M
University of Phoenix–Metro Detroit Campus M
University of Phoenix–Nashville Campus M
University of Phoenix–New Mexico Campus M
University of Phoenix–Northern Nevada Campus M
University of Phoenix–North Florida Campus M
University of Phoenix–Omaha Campus M
University of Phoenix–Oregon Campus M
University of Phoenix–Phoenix Campus M
University of Phoenix–Sacramento Valley Campus M,O
University of Phoenix–San Diego Campus M
University of Phoenix–Southern Arizona Campus M,O
University of Phoenix–Southern California Campus M
University of Phoenix–Southern Colorado Campus M,O
University of Phoenix–South Florida Campus M
University of Phoenix–Utah Campus M
University of Phoenix–West Florida Campus M
University of Pittsburgh M*
University of Puget Sound M
University of Rhode Island M
University of St. Francis (IL) M
University of St. Thomas (MN) M,O*
The University of Scranton M
University of South Alabama M,O*
University of South Carolina M,D
University of South Carolina Aiken M
University of South Carolina Upstate M
The University of South Dakota M
University of Southern Indiana M
University of Southern Mississippi M,D,O
University of South Florida M,D,O*
The University of Tennessee M,D,O
The University of Tennessee at Chattanooga M,O
The University of Tennessee at Martin M
The University of Texas–Pan American M
University of the Cumberlands M
University of the Incarnate Word M
The University of Toledo D,O
University of Utah M,D*
University of Virginia M,D,O
The University of West Alabama M
University of West Florida M
University of Wisconsin–Eau Claire M
University of Wisconsin–La Crosse M
University of Wisconsin–Milwaukee M
University of Wisconsin–Platteville M
University of Wisconsin–River Falls M
University of Wisconsin–Stevens Point M
Utah State University M
Vanderbilt University M*
Villanova University M*
Wagner College M
Walden University M,D,O
Washington State University M,D*
Washington University in St. Louis M*
Wayne State College M
Wayne State University M,D,O*
West Chester University of Pennsylvania M,O
Western Illinois University M
Western Kentucky University M,O
Western New England College M
Western New Mexico University M
Western Washington University M
Westfield State College M
West Virginia University M
Wheaton College M
Wheelock College M
Whittier College M
Whitworth University M
Widener University M,D*
Wilkes University M,D
William Carey University M,O
William Paterson University of New Jersey M*
William Woods University M,O
Wilmington University M
Wingate University M
Winston-Salem State University M
Worcester State College M
Wright State University M
Xavier University M*

EMERGENCY MANAGEMENT

Adelphi University O*
American Public University System M
Anna Maria College M,O
Arkansas Tech University M
Benedictine University M
California State University, Long Beach M
Capella University M,D
Drexel University M*
The George Washington University M,D,O*
Georgia State University M,D,O
Indiana University of Pennsylvania M
Jacksonville State University M
The Johns Hopkins University M,O*
Lynn University M,O
Massachusetts Maritime Academy M
Millersville University of Pennsylvania M
New Jersey Institute of Technology M,D
North Dakota State University M,D
Oklahoma State University M,D*
Park University M
Philadelphia University M
Royal Roads University M,O
San Diego State University M,D*
TUI University M,D,O
Université de Montréal O
University of Central Florida M,O*
University of Hawaii at Manoa O*
University of Nevada, Las Vegas M,D,O
University of Pittsburgh M,D,O*
University of Rochester M,D,O*
Virginia Commonwealth University M,O
West Chester University of Pennsylvania M,O
York University M

EMERGENCY MEDICAL SERVICES

Baylor University D
Drexel University M*
San Diego State University M,D*
Université Laval O
University of Guelph M,D,O

ENERGY AND POWER ENGINEERING

New Jersey Institute of Technology M
New York Institute of Technology M,O
North Carolina Agricultural and Technical State University M,D
Pontificia Universidad Catolica Madre y Maestra M
Rensselaer Polytechnic Institute M,D
Southern Illinois University Carbondale D*
Universidad Autonoma de Guadalajara M,D
University of Alberta M,D*
University of Massachusetts Lowell M,D
University of Memphis M,D
University of Wisconsin–Madison M,D*
Worcester Polytechnic Institute M,D*

ENERGY MANAGEMENT AND POLICY

Holy Names University M
New York Institute of Technology M,O
Université du Québec, Institut National de la Recherche Scientifique M,D
University of California, Berkeley M,D*
University of Delaware M,D*
University of Tulsa M*
University of Washington M,D*

ENGINEERING AND APPLIED SCIENCES—GENERAL

Air Force Institute of Technology M,D
Alabama Agricultural and Mechanical University M
Alfred University M,D*
The American University of Athens M
American University of Beirut M,D
Andrews University M
Arizona State University M,D
Arizona State University at the Polytechnic Campus M
Arkansas State University M
Arkansas Tech University M
Auburn University M,D*
Baylor University M
Boise State University M,D
Boston University M,D*
Bradley University M
Brigham Young University M,D*
Brown University M,D*
Bucknell University M
California Institute of Technology M,D,O*
California National University for Advanced Studies M

*M—master's degree; P—first professional degree; D—doctorate; O—other advanced degree; *—Close-Up and/or Announcement or Display in one of the other books in this series*

California Polytechnic State University, San Luis Obispo	M
California State Polytechnic University, Pomona	M
California State University, Chico	M
California State University, Fresno	M
California State University, Fullerton	M
California State University, Los Angeles	M
California State University, Northridge	M
California State University, Sacramento	M
Carleton University	M,D
Case Western Reserve University	M,D*
The Catholic University of America	M,D,O
Central Connecticut State University	M
Central Michigan University	M
Central Washington University	M
Christian Brothers University	M
City College of the City University of New York	M,D*
Clarkson University	M,D*
Clemson University	M,D
Cleveland State University	M,D
Colorado School of Mines	M,D,O
Colorado State University	M,D*
Colorado State University–Pueblo	M
Columbia University	M,D,O*
Concordia University (Canada)	M,D,O
Cooper Union for the Advancement of Science and Art	M
Cornell University	M,D*
Dalhousie University	M,D
Dartmouth College	M,D*
Drexel University	M,D,O*
Duke University	M,D*
Eastern Illinois University	M,O
Eastern Michigan University	M
École Polytechnique de Montréal	M,D,O
Fairfield University	M*
Fairleigh Dickinson University, Metropolitan Campus	M*
Florida Agricultural and Mechanical University	M,D
Florida Atlantic University	M,D
Florida Institute of Technology	M,D*
Florida International University	M,D*
Florida State University	M,D*
George Mason University	M,D,O*
The George Washington University	M,D,O*
Georgia Institute of Technology	M,D*
Graduate School and University Center of the City University of New York	D*
Grand Valley State University	M
Harvard University	M,D*
Howard University	M,D
Idaho State University	M,D,O
Illinois Institute of Technology	M,D*
Indiana State University	M
Indiana University–Purdue University Fort Wayne	M
Instituto Tecnologico de Santo Domingo	M
Instituto Tecnológico y de Estudios Superiores de Monterrey, Campus Ciudad Obregón	M
Instituto Tecnológico y de Estudios Superiores de Monterrey, Campus Monterrey	M,D
Iowa State University of Science and Technology	M,D*
The Johns Hopkins University	M,D,O*
Kansas State University	M,D*
Kent State University	M*
Lakehead University	M
Lamar University	M,D
Laurentian University	M,D
Lawrence Technological University	M,D
Lehigh University	M,D
Louisiana State University and Agricultural and Mechanical College	M,D
Louisiana Tech University	M,D
Manhattan College	M
Marquette University	M,D
Marshall University	M
Massachusetts Institute of Technology	M,D,O*
McGill University	M,D,O*
McMaster University	M,D
McNeese State University	M
Memorial University of Newfoundland	M,D
Mercer University	M
Miami University	M,O*
Michigan State University	M,D*
Michigan Technological University	M,D
Milwaukee School of Engineering	M*
Mississippi State University	M,D
Missouri University of Science and Technology	M,D
Montana State University	M,D
Montana Tech of The University of Montana	M
Morgan State University	M,D
National University	M
New Jersey Institute of Technology	M,D,O
New Mexico State University	M,D
New York Institute of Technology	M,O
North Carolina Agricultural and Technical State University	M,D
North Carolina State University	M,D*
North Dakota State University	M,D
Northeastern University	M,D,O*
Northern Arizona University	M,D
Northern Illinois University	M
Northwestern Polytechnic University	M
Northwestern University	M,D,O*
Oakland University	M,D
The Ohio State University	M,D*
Ohio University	M,D*
Oklahoma State University	M,D*
Old Dominion University	M,D
Oregon State University	M,D*
Penn State Harrisburg	M
Penn State University Park	M,D*
Pittsburg State University	M
Portland State University	M,D,O
Prairie View A&M University	M,D
Purdue University	M,D,O
Purdue University Calumet	M
Queen's University at Kingston	M,D
Rensselaer at Hartford	M
Rensselaer Polytechnic Institute	M,D
Rice University	M,D
Robert Morris University	M
Rochester Institute of Technology	M,D,O
Rose-Hulman Institute of Technology	M*
Rowan University	M
Royal Military College of Canada	M,D
St. Cloud State University	M
St. Mary's University (United States)	M
San Diego State University	M,D*
San Francisco State University	M
San Jose State University	M
Santa Clara University	M,D,O
Seattle University	M
Simon Fraser University	M,D
South Dakota School of Mines and Technology	M,D*
South Dakota State University	M,D
Southern Illinois University Carbondale	M,D*
Southern Illinois University Edwardsville	M
Southern Methodist University	M,D*
Southern Polytechnic State University	M,O
Southern University and Agricultural and Mechanical College	M
Stanford University	M,D,O*
State University of New York at Binghamton	M,D*
State University of New York Institute of Technology	M
Stevens Institute of Technology	M,D,O
Stony Brook University, State University of New York	M,D,O
Syracuse University	M,D,O*
Temple University	M,D*
Tennessee State University	M
Tennessee Technological University	M,D*
Texas A&M University	M,D*
Texas A&M University–Kingsville	M,D
Texas Tech University	M,D
Trine University	M
Tufts University	M,D*
Tuskegee University	M,D
Union Graduate College	M
Universidad de las Américas–Puebla	M,D
Université de Moncton	M
Université de Sherbrooke	M,D,O
Université du Québec à Chicoutimi	M,D
Université du Québec à Rimouski	M
Université du Québec, École de technologie supérieure	M,D,O
Université du Québec en Abitibi-Témiscamingue	M,D
Université Laval	M,D,O
University at Buffalo, the State University of New York	M,D*
The University of Akron	M,D
The University of Alabama	M,D
The University of Alabama at Birmingham	M,D*
The University of Alabama in Huntsville	M,D
University of Alaska Anchorage	M,O
University of Alaska Fairbanks	M,D
The University of Arizona	M,D,O*
University of Arkansas	M,D
University of Bridgeport	M,D
The University of British Columbia	M,D
University of Calgary	M,D
University of California, Berkeley	M,D*
University of California, Davis	M,D,O*
University of California, Irvine	M,D*
University of California, Los Angeles	M,D*
University of California, Santa Barbara	M,D
University of California, Santa Cruz	M,D*
University of Central Florida	M,D,O*
University of Central Oklahoma	M
University of Cincinnati	M,D
University of Colorado at Boulder	M,D*
University of Colorado at Colorado Springs	M,D
University of Connecticut	M,D*
University of Dayton	M,D
University of Delaware	M,D*
University of Detroit Mercy	M,D
University of Evansville	M
University of Florida	M,D,O*
University of Guelph	M,D
University of Hartford	M*
University of Hawaii at Manoa	M,D,O*
University of Houston	M,D*
University of Idaho	M,D
University of Illinois at Chicago	M,D*
University of Illinois at Urbana–Champaign	M,D*
The University of Iowa	M,D*
The University of Kansas	M,D*
University of Kentucky	M,D*
University of Louisville	M,D
University of Maine	M,D*
University of Manitoba	M,D
University of Maryland, Baltimore County	M,D,O*
University of Maryland, College Park	M*
University of Massachusetts Amherst	M,D*
University of Massachusetts Dartmouth	M,D,O
University of Massachusetts Lowell	M,D,O
University of Memphis	M,D
University of Miami	M,D*
University of Michigan	M,D,O*
University of Michigan–Dearborn	M,D*
University of Minnesota, Twin Cities Campus	M,D*
University of Mississippi	M,D
University of Missouri–Columbia	M,D*
University of Missouri–Kansas City	M,D*
University of Nebraska–Lincoln	M,D*
University of Nevada, Las Vegas	M,D
University of Nevada, Reno	M,D*
University of New Brunswick Fredericton	M,D,O
University of New Haven	M,O*
University of New Mexico	M,D*
University of New Orleans	M,D,O
The University of North Carolina at Charlotte	M,D*
University of North Dakota	D
University of North Texas	M
University of Notre Dame	M,D*
University of Oklahoma	M,D*

- University of Ottawa M,D,O*
- University of Pennsylvania M,D,O*
- University of Pittsburgh M,D*
- University of Portland M
- University of Puerto Rico, Mayagüez Campus M,D
- University of Regina M,D
- University of Rhode Island M,D
- University of Rochester M,D*
- University of St. Thomas (MN) M,O*
- University of Saskatchewan M,D,O
- University of South Africa M
- University of South Alabama M*
- University of South Carolina M,D
- University of Southern California M,D,O*
- University of Southern Indiana M
- University of Southern Mississippi M,D
- University of South Florida M,D*
- The University of Tennessee M,D
- The University of Tennessee at Chattanooga M,D,O
- The University of Tennessee Space Institute M,D*
- The University of Texas at Arlington M,D*
- The University of Texas at Austin M,D
- The University of Texas at Dallas M,D*
- The University of Texas at El Paso M,D
- The University of Texas at San Antonio M,D*
- The University of Toledo M
- University of Toronto M,D
- University of Tulsa M,D*
- University of Utah M,D,O*
- University of Vermont M,D*
- University of Victoria M,D
- University of Virginia M,D
- University of Waterloo M,D
- The University of Western Ontario M,D
- University of Windsor M,D
- University of Wisconsin–Madison M,D,O*
- University of Wisconsin–Milwaukee M,D,O
- University of Wisconsin–Platteville M
- University of Wyoming M,D
- Utah State University M,D,O
- Vanderbilt University M,D*
- Villanova University M,D,O*
- Virginia Commonwealth University M,D,O
- Virginia Polytechnic Institute and State University M,D*
- Walden University M,O
- Washington State University M,D*
- Washington State University Tri-Cities M,D
- Washington State University Vancouver M
- Washington University in St. Louis M,D*
- Wayne State University M,D,O*
- Western Michigan University M,D*
- Western New England College M
- West Texas A&M University M
- West Virginia University M,D
- West Virginia University Institute of Technology M
- Wichita State University M,D*
- Widener University M*
- Wilkes University M
- Worcester Polytechnic Institute M,D,O*
- Wright State University M,D
- Yale University M,D*
- Youngstown State University M

ENGINEERING DESIGN

- Kettering University M
- Northwestern University M*
- Polytechnic Institute of NYU, Long Island Graduate Center M
- Rochester Institute of Technology M
- San Diego State University M,D*
- Santa Clara University M,D,O
- Stanford University M*
- Stevens Institute of Technology M
- University of Central Florida M,D,O*
- University of New Haven M,O*
- Worcester Polytechnic Institute M,O*

ENGINEERING MANAGEMENT

- Air Force Institute of Technology M
- American University of Beirut M,D
- California National University for Advanced Studies M
- California State Polytechnic University, Pomona M
- California State University, East Bay M
- California State University, Long Beach M,D
- California State University, Northridge M
- Case Western Reserve University M*
- The Catholic University of America M,O
- Clarkson University M*
- Colorado School of Mines M,D
- Columbia University M,D,O*
- Cornell University M,D*
- Dallas Baptist University M
- Dartmouth College M*
- Drexel University M,O*
- Duke University M*
- Eastern Michigan University M
- Florida Institute of Technology M*
- Gannon University M
- The George Washington University M,D,O*
- Instituto Tecnológico y de Estudios Superiores de Monterrey, Campus Chihuahua M,O
- International Technological University M
- Kansas State University M,D*
- Kettering University M
- Lamar University M,D
- Lawrence Technological University M,D
- Long Island University, C.W. Post Campus M
- Loyola Marymount University M
- Marquette University M,D
- Marshall University M
- Massachusetts Institute of Technology M,D*
- McNeese State University M
- Mercer University M
- Milwaukee School of Engineering M*
- Missouri University of Science and Technology M,D
- National University M
- New Jersey Institute of Technology M
- New Mexico Institute of Mining and Technology M
- Northeastern University M,D*
- Northwestern University M*
- Oakland University M
- Old Dominion University M,D
- Penn State Great Valley M
- Penn State Harrisburg M
- Point Park University M*
- Polytechnic University of Puerto Rico M
- Polytechnic University of the Americas–Miami Campus M
- Polytechnic University of the Americas–Orlando Campus M
- Portland State University M,D,O
- Rensselaer Polytechnic Institute M,D
- Robert Morris University M
- Rochester Institute of Technology M
- Rose-Hulman Institute of Technology M*
- Rowan University M
- St. Cloud State University M
- Saint Martin's University M
- St. Mary's University (United States) M
- Santa Clara University M
- Southern Methodist University M,D*
- Stanford University M,D*
- Stevens Institute of Technology M,D
- Syracuse University M*
- Texas Tech University M,D
- Tufts University M*
- Union Graduate College M
- Université de Sherbrooke M,O
- The University of Akron M
- The University of Alabama in Huntsville M,D
- University of Alaska Anchorage M
- University of Alaska Fairbanks M,D
- University of Alberta M,D*
- University of California, Berkeley M,D*
- University of Central Florida M,D,O*
- University of Colorado at Boulder M*
- University of Colorado at Colorado Springs M
- University of Dayton M
- University of Detroit Mercy M
- University of Idaho M
- The University of Kansas M*
- University of Louisiana at Lafayette M*
- University of Louisville M
- University of Maryland, Baltimore County M,O*
- University of Massachusetts Amherst *
- University of Michigan–Dearborn M,D*
- University of Minnesota, Duluth M
- University of Nebraska–Lincoln M,D*
- University of New Haven M*
- University of New Orleans M,O
- The University of North Carolina at Charlotte M*
- University of Ottawa M,O*
- University of St. Thomas (MN) M,O*
- University of Southern California M,D,O*
- University of South Florida M,D*
- The University of Tennessee
- The University of Tennessee at Chattanooga
- The University of Tennessee Space Institute M,D*
- University of Waterloo M,D
- University of Wisconsin–Madison M*
- University of Wisconsin–Milwaukee M,D,O
- Valparaiso University M,O
- Virginia Polytechnic Institute and State University M,D*
- Walden University M,D,O
- Washington State University Spokane M
- Wayne State University M*
- Webster University M
- Western Michigan University M*
- Widener University M*

ENGINEERING PHYSICS

- Air Force Institute of Technology M,D
- Appalachian State University M
- Cornell University M,D*
- Dartmouth College M,D*
- École Polytechnique de Montréal M,D,O
- Embry-Riddle Aeronautical University (FL) M
- George Mason University M*
- McMaster University M,D
- Michigan Technological University D
- The Ohio State University M,D*
- Polytechnic Institute of NYU M
- Polytechnic Institute of NYU, Long Island Graduate Center M
- Rensselaer Polytechnic Institute M,D
- Stevens Institute of Technology M,D,O
- The University of British Columbia M
- University of California, San Diego M,D*
- University of Maine M*
- University of Oklahoma M,D*
- University of Saskatchewan M,D
- University of Tulsa M*
- University of Virginia M,D
- University of Wisconsin–Madison M,D*
- Yale University M,D*

ENGLISH

- Abilene Christian University M
- Acadia University M
- The American University in Cairo M
- American University of Beirut M
- Andrews University M
- Angelo State University M
- Appalachian State University M
- Arcadia University M
- Arizona State University M,D
- Arkansas State University M,O
- Arkansas Tech University M
- Asbury College M,O
- Auburn University M,D*
- Austin Peay State University M
- Ball State University M,D*
- Baylor University M,D
- Belmont University M

*M—master's degree; P—first professional degree; D—doctorate; O—other advanced degree; *—Close-Up and/or Announcement or Display in one of the other books in this series*

Bemidji State University	M
Bennington College	M
Bob Jones University	P,M,D,O
Boise State University	M
Boston College	M,D*
Boston University	M,D*
Bowie State University	M
Bowling Green State University	M,D*
Bradley University	M
Brandeis University	M,D
Bridgewater State College	M
Brigham Young University	M*
Brock University	M
Brooklyn College of the City University of New York	M,D
Brown University	M,D*
Bucknell University	M
Buffalo State College, State University of New York	M
Butler University	M
California Baptist University	M
California Polytechnic State University, San Luis Obispo	M
California State Polytechnic University, Pomona	M
California State University, Bakersfield	M
California State University, Chico	M
California State University, Dominguez Hills	M,O
California State University, East Bay	M
California State University, Fresno	M
California State University, Fullerton	M
California State University, Long Beach	M
California State University, Los Angeles	M
California State University, Northridge	M
California State University, Sacramento	M
California State University, San Bernardino	M
California State University, San Marcos	M
California State University, Stanislaus	M,O
Carleton University	M,D
Carnegie Mellon University	M,D*
Case Western Reserve University	M,D*
The Catholic University of America	M,D
Central Connecticut State University	M,O
Central Michigan University	M
Central Washington University	M
Chapman University	M
Chicago State University	M
The Citadel, The Military College of South Carolina	M
City College of the City University of New York	M*
Claremont Graduate University	M,D*
Clarion University of Pennsylvania	M
Clark Atlanta University	M,D
Clark University	M
Clemson University	M,D
Cleveland State University	M
The College at Brockport, State University of New York	M
College of Charleston	M*
The College of New Jersey	M
The College of Saint Rose	M*
College of Staten Island of the City University of New York	M
Columbia University	M,D*
Concordia University (Canada)	M
Converse College	M
Cornell University	M,D*
Creighton University	M*
Dalhousie University	M,D
DePaul University	M*
Drew University	M,D
Duke University	D*
Duquesne University	M,D*
East Carolina University	M
Eastern Illinois University	M
Eastern Kentucky University	M
Eastern Michigan University	M,O
Eastern New Mexico University	M
Eastern Washington University	M
East Tennessee State University	M
Elmhurst College	M
Emory University	D,O*
Emporia State University	M
Fairleigh Dickinson University, Metropolitan Campus	M*
Fayetteville State University	M
Fitchburg State College	M,O
Florida Atlantic University	M
Florida Gulf Coast University	M
Florida International University	M*
Florida State University	M,D*
Fordham University	M,D*
Fort Hays State University	M
Gannon University	M
Gardner-Webb University	M
Georgetown University	M
The George Washington University	M,D*
Georgia College & State University	M
Georgia Southern University	M
Georgia State University	M,D
Governors State University	M
Graduate School and University Center of the City University of New York	D*
Grambling State University	M,D
Grand Valley State University	M
Hardin-Simmons University	M
Harvard University	M,D,O*
Heritage University	M
Hofstra University	M*
Hollins University	M
Howard University	M,D
Humboldt State University	M
Hunter College of the City University of New York	M
Idaho State University	M,D,O
Illinois State University	M,D
Indiana State University	M
Indiana University Bloomington	M,D*
Indiana University of Pennsylvania	M,D
Indiana University–Purdue University Fort Wayne	M,O
Indiana University–Purdue University Indianapolis	M*
Indiana University South Bend	M
Inter American University of Puerto Rico, Metropolitan Campus	M
Iona College	M*
Iowa State University of Science and Technology	M,D*
Jackson State University	M
Jacksonville State University	M
James Madison University	M
John Carroll University	M
The Johns Hopkins University	D*
Kansas State University	M*
Kent State University	M,D*
Kutztown University of Pennsylvania	M
Lakehead University	M
Lamar University	M
La Sierra University	M
Lehigh University	M,D
Lehman College of the City University of New York	M
Long Island University, Brooklyn Campus	M
Long Island University, C.W. Post Campus	M
Longwood University	M
Louisiana State University and Agricultural and Mechanical College	M,D
Louisiana Tech University	M
Loyola Marymount University	M
Loyola University Chicago	M,D*
Lynchburg College	M
Marquette University	M,D
Marshall University	M
Mary Baldwin College	M
Marygrove College	M
Marymount University	M
McGill University	M,D*
McMaster University	M,D
McNeese State University	M
Memorial University of Newfoundland	M,D
Mercy College	M
Miami University	M,D*
Michigan State University	M,D*
Middlebury College	M
Middle Tennessee State University	M,D
Midwestern State University	M
Millersville University of Pennsylvania	M
Mills College	M
Minnesota State University Mankato	M,O
Mississippi College	M
Mississippi State University	M
Missouri State University	M*
Monmouth University	M
Montana State University	M
Montclair State University	M,O*
Morehead State University	M
Morgan State University	M,D
Mount Mary College	M
Murray State University	M
National University	M
New Mexico Highlands University	M
New Mexico State University	M,D
New York University	M,D*
North Carolina Agricultural and Technical State University	M
North Carolina Central University	M
North Carolina State University	M*
North Dakota State University	M
Northeastern Illinois University	M
Northeastern State University	M
Northeastern University	M,D,O*
Northern Arizona University	M
Northern Illinois University	M,D
Northern Kentucky University	M,O
Northern Michigan University	M
Northwestern State University of Louisiana	M
Northwestern University	M,D*
Northwest Missouri State University	M
Notre Dame de Namur University	M,O
Oakland University	M
The Ohio State University	M,D*
Ohio University	M,D*
Oklahoma State University	M,D*
Old Dominion University	M,D
Oregon State University	M*
Our Lady of the Lake University of San Antonio	M
Penn State University Park	M,D*
Pittsburg State University	M
Portland State University	M
Prairie View A&M University	M
Princeton University	D*
Purdue University	M,D
Purdue University Calumet	M
Queens College of the City University of New York	M
Queen's University at Kingston	M,D
Radford University	M
Rhode Island College	M
Rice University	M,D
Rivier College	M
Roosevelt University	M
Rosemont College	M
Rutgers, The State University of New Jersey, Camden	M
Rutgers, The State University of New Jersey, Newark	M*
Rutgers, The State University of New Jersey, New Brunswick	D*
St. Bonaventure University	M
St. Cloud State University	M
St. John's University (NY)	M,D
Saint Louis University	M,D
Saint Louis University–Madrid Campus	M*
St. Mary's University (United States)	M
Saint Xavier University	M,O
Salem State College	M
Salisbury University	M
Sam Houston State University	M
San Diego State University	M*
San Francisco State University	M,O
San Jose State University	M,O
Seton Hall University	M*
Sewanee: The University of the South	M
Simmons College	M
Simon Fraser University	M,D
Slippery Rock University of Pennsylvania	M
Sonoma State University	M
South Dakota State University	M
Southeastern Louisiana University	M
Southeast Missouri State University	M
Southern Connecticut State University	M

Southern Illinois University Carbondale	M,D*
Southern Illinois University Edwardsville	M,O
Southern Methodist University	M,D*
Stanford University	M,D*
State University of New York at Binghamton	M,D*
State University of New York at Fredonia	M
State University of New York at New Paltz	M
State University of New York at Oswego	M
State University of New York College at Cortland	M
State University of New York College at Potsdam	M
Stephen F. Austin State University	M
Stetson University	M
Stony Brook University, State University of New York	M,D,O
Sul Ross State University	M*
Syracuse University	M,D*
Tarleton State University	M
Temple University	M,D*
Tennessee State University	M
Tennessee Technological University	M*
Texas A&M International University	M,D
Texas A&M University	M,D*
Texas A&M University–Commerce	M,D
Texas A&M University–Corpus Christi	M
Texas A&M University–Kingsville	M
Texas A&M University–Texarkana	M
Texas Christian University	M,D
Texas Southern University	M
Texas State University–San Marcos	M*
Texas Tech University	M,D
Texas Woman's University	M,D
Trinity College	M
Trinity Western University	M
Truman State University	M
Tufts University	M,D*
Tulane University	M,D
Universidad de las Américas–Puebla	M
Université de Montréal	M,D
Université Laval	M,D
University at Albany, State University of New York	M,D*
University at Buffalo, the State University of New York	M,D*
The University of Akron	M
The University of Alabama	M,D
The University of Alabama at Birmingham	M*
The University of Alabama in Huntsville	M,O
University of Alaska Anchorage	M
University of Alaska Fairbanks	M
University of Alberta	M,D*
The University of Arizona	M,D*
University of Arkansas	M,D
The University of British Columbia	M,D
University of Calgary	M,D
University of California, Berkeley	D*
University of California, Davis	M,D*
University of California, Irvine	M,D*
University of California, Los Angeles	M,D*
University of California, Riverside	M,D*
University of California, San Diego	M*
University of California, Santa Barbara	D
University of California, Santa Cruz	M,D*
University of Central Arkansas	M
University of Central Florida	M*
University of Central Missouri	M
University of Central Oklahoma	M
University of Chicago	M,D*
University of Cincinnati	M,D
University of Colorado at Boulder	M,D*
University of Colorado Denver	M,O*
University of Connecticut	M,D*
University of Dallas	M
University of Dayton	M
University of Delaware	M,D*
University of Denver	M,D*
University of Florida	M,D*
University of Georgia	M,D*
University of Guam	M
University of Guelph	M
University of Hawaii at Manoa	M,D*
University of Houston	M,D*
University of Houston–Clear Lake	M
University of Houston–Downtown	M
University of Idaho	M
University of Illinois at Chicago	M,D*
University of Illinois at Springfield	M
University of Illinois at Urbana–Champaign	M,D*
University of Indianapolis	M
The University of Iowa	M,D*
The University of Kansas	M,D*
University of Kentucky	M,D
University of Lethbridge	M,D
University of Louisiana at Lafayette	M,D*
University of Louisiana at Monroe	M
University of Louisville	M,D
University of Maine	M*
University of Manitoba	M,D
University of Maryland, College Park	M,D*
University of Massachusetts Amherst	M,D*
University of Massachusetts Boston	M
University of Memphis	M,D,O
University of Miami	M,D*
University of Michigan	M,D,O*
University of Michigan–Flint	M*
University of Minnesota, Duluth	M
University of Minnesota, Twin Cities Campus	M,D*
University of Mississippi	M,D
University of Missouri–Columbia	M,D*
University of Missouri–Kansas City	M,D*
University of Missouri–St. Louis	M,O
The University of Montana	M
University of Montevallo	M
University of Nebraska at Kearney	M
University of Nebraska at Omaha	M,O
University of Nebraska–Lincoln	M,D*
University of Nevada, Las Vegas	M,D
University of Nevada, Reno	M,D*
University of New Brunswick Fredericton	M,D
University of New Hampshire	M,D*
University of New Mexico	M,D*
University of New Orleans	M
University of North Alabama	M
The University of North Carolina at Chapel Hill	M,D*
The University of North Carolina at Charlotte	M*
The University of North Carolina at Greensboro	M,D
The University of North Carolina Wilmington	M
University of North Dakota	M,D
University of Northern Colorado	M
University of Northern Iowa	M
University of North Florida	M
University of North Texas	M,D
University of Notre Dame	M,D*
University of Oklahoma	M,D*
University of Oregon	M,D*
University of Ottawa	M,D*
University of Pennsylvania	M,D*
University of Pittsburgh	M,D*
University of Puerto Rico, Mayagüez Campus	M
University of Puerto Rico, Río Piedras	M,D
University of Regina	M,D
University of Rhode Island	M,D
University of Rochester	M,D*
University of St. Thomas (MN)	M*
University of Saskatchewan	M,D
University of South Africa	M,D
University of South Alabama	M*
University of South Carolina	M,D
The University of South Dakota	M,D
University of Southern California	M,D*
University of Southern Mississippi	M,D
University of South Florida	M,D*
The University of Tennessee	M,D
The University of Tennessee at Chattanooga	M
The University of Texas at Arlington	M,D*
The University of Texas at Austin	M,D
The University of Texas at Brownsville	M
The University of Texas at El Paso	M,D
The University of Texas at San Antonio	M,D,O*
The University of Texas at Tyler	M
The University of Texas of the Permian Basin	M
The University of Texas–Pan American	M
University of the District of Columbia	M
The University of Toledo	M,O
University of Toronto	M,D
University of Tulsa	M,D*
University of Utah	M,D*
University of Vermont	M*
University of Victoria	M,D
University of Virginia	M,D,O
University of Washington	M,D*
University of Waterloo	M,D
The University of Western Ontario	M,D
University of West Florida	M
University of West Georgia	M
University of Windsor	M
University of Wisconsin–Eau Claire	M
University of Wisconsin–Madison	M,D*
University of Wisconsin–Milwaukee	M,D,O
University of Wisconsin–Oshkosh	M
University of Wisconsin–Stevens Point	M
University of Wyoming	M
Utah State University	M
Valdosta State University	M
Valparaiso University	M,O
Vanderbilt University	M,D*
Villanova University	M*
Virginia Commonwealth University	M
Virginia Polytechnic Institute and State University	M,D*
Virginia State University	M
Wake Forest University	M*
Washington College	M
Washington State University	M,D*
Washington University in St. Louis	M,D*
Wayne State University	M,D*
Weber State University	M
West Chester University of Pennsylvania	M,O
Western Carolina University	M
Western Connecticut State University	M
Western Illinois University	M,O
Western Kentucky University	M
Western Michigan University	M,D*
Western Washington University	M
Westfield State College	M
West Texas A&M University	M
West Virginia University	M,D
Wichita State University	M*
Wilfrid Laurier University	M,D
William Paterson University of New Jersey	M*
Winona State University	M
Winthrop University	M
Wright State University	M
Xavier University	M*
Yale University	M,D*
York University	M,D
Youngstown State University	M

ENGLISH AS A SECOND LANGUAGE

Adelphi University	M,O*
Albright College	M
Alliant International University–Fresno	M,D,O*
Alliant International University–Irvine	M,D*
Alliant International University–San Diego	M,D,O*
American University	M,O*
The American University in Cairo	M,O
American University of Sharjah	M
Andrews University	M,D,O
Arizona State University	M,D
Arkansas Tech University	M,O
Asbury College	M,O
Avila University	M,O
Azusa Pacific University	M
Ball State University	M,D*
Barry University	M,D,O*
Biola University	M,D,O
Bishop's University	M,O
Boston University	M,O*

*M—master's degree; P—first professional degree; D—doctorate; O—other advanced degree; *—Close-Up and/or Announcement or Display in one of the other books in this series*

Brigham Young University	M,O*
Brock University	M
Buena Vista University	M
California Baptist University	M
California State University, Dominguez Hills	M,O
California State University, Fresno	M
California State University, Fullerton	M
California State University, Long Beach	M
California State University, Sacramento	M
California State University, San Bernardino	M,D
California State University, Stanislaus	M,O
Cambridge College	M,D,O
Cardinal Stritch University	M
Carlos Albizu University, Miami Campus	M,D
Carson-Newman College	M
Central Connecticut State University	M,O
Central Michigan University	M
Central Washington University	M
Cleveland State University	M
College of Charleston	O*
The College of New Jersey	M,O
The College of New Rochelle	M,O
College of Notre Dame of Maryland	M
Columbia International University	M,D,O
Concordia University (Canada)	M,O
Cornerstone University	M,O
Dallas Baptist University	M
DeSales University	M
Dominican University	M
Drexel University	M,D,O*
Duquesne University	M,D*
Eastern Michigan University	M,O
Eastern Nazarene College	M,O
Eastern Washington University	M
Elms College	M,O
Emporia State University	M
Erikson Institute	M,O
The Evergreen State College	M
Fairfield University	M,O*
Florida Atlantic University	M,D,O
Florida International University	M,D,O*
Fordham University	M,D,O*
Framingham State College	M
Fresno Pacific University	M
Furman University	M
Gannon University	O
George Fox University	M,D,O*
George Mason University	M,O*
Georgetown University	M,D,O
Georgia State University	M,D,O
Gonzaga University	M
Grand Valley State University	M,O
Greensboro College	M
Harding University	M,O
Hawai'i Pacific University	M*
Heritage University	M
Hofstra University	M,O*
Holy Names University	M,O
Houston Baptist University	M
Hunter College of the City University of New York	M
Indiana State University	M,O
Indiana University Bloomington	M,D*
Indiana University of Pennsylvania	M,D
Indiana University–Purdue University Fort Wayne	M,O
Indiana University–Purdue University Indianapolis	M,O*
Inter American University of Puerto Rico, Arecibo Campus	M
Inter American University of Puerto Rico, Metropolitan Campus	M
Inter American University of Puerto Rico, Ponce Campus	M
Inter American University of Puerto Rico, San Germán Campus	M
The Johns Hopkins University	M,O*
Kean University	M
Kennesaw State University	M
Kent State University	M,D*
Langston University	M
Lehigh University	M,O
Lehman College of the City University of New York	M
Lewis University	M
Lipscomb University	M
Long Island University, Brooklyn Campus	M
Long Island University, C.W. Post Campus	M
Long Island University, Westchester Graduate Campus	M,O
Loyola Marymount University	M
Madonna University	M
Manhattanville College	M*
Marymount University	M
Mercy College	M
Michigan State University	M,D*
MidAmerica Nazarene University	M
Middle Tennessee State University	M,O
Midwest University	P,M,D
Millersville University of Pennsylvania	M
Minnesota State University Mankato	M,O
Mississippi College	M
Montclair State University	M,O*
Monterey Institute of International Studies	M*
Mount Saint Vincent University	M
Murray State University	M
Nazareth College of Rochester	M
New Jersey City University	M
Newman University	M
The New School: A University	M*
New York University	M,D,O*
Northern Arizona University	M,D,O
Northwest Missouri State University	M,O
Notre Dame de Namur University	M,O
Nova Southeastern University	M,O*
Oakland University	M,O
Ohio Dominican University	M
Ohio University	M*
Oklahoma City University	M
Oral Roberts University	M,D
Our Lady of the Lake University of San Antonio	M
Pontifical Catholic University of Puerto Rico	M
Portland State University	M
Prescott College	M,D
Providence College and Theological Seminary	P,M,D,O
Queens College of the City University of New York	M
Regent University	M,D,O
Regis University	M,O
Rhode Island College	M
Rider University	O*
Rutgers, The State University of New Jersey, New Brunswick	M,D*
St. Cloud State University	M
St. John's University (NY)	M
Saint Martin's University	M
Saint Michael's College	M,O
St. Thomas University	M,D,O
Salem College	M
Salem State College	M
Salisbury University	M
San Diego State University	M,O*
San Francisco State University	M
San Jose State University	M,O
Seattle Pacific University	M
Seattle University	M,O
Shenandoah University	M,D,O
Simmons College	M,O
Simon Fraser University	M
SIT Graduate Institute	M
Southeast Missouri State University	M
Southern Connecticut State University	M
Southern Illinois University Carbondale	M*
Southern Illinois University Edwardsville	M,O
Southern New Hampshire University	M,O*
State University of New York at Fredonia	M
State University of New York at New Paltz	M
State University of New York College at Cortland	M
Stony Brook University, State University of New York	M
Syracuse University	M*
Teachers College, Columbia University	M,D
Temple University	M,D*
Texas A&M University–Commerce	M,D
Texas A&M University–Kingsville	M
Trevecca Nazarene University	M
Trinity (Washington) University	M
Trinity Western University	M
Universidad Adventista de las Antillas	M
Universidad del Este	M
Universidad del Turabo	M
University at Buffalo, the State University of New York	M,D,O*
The University of Alabama	M,D
The University of Alabama in Huntsville	M,O
University of Alberta	M,D*
The University of Arizona	D*
The University of British Columbia	M,D
University of Calgary	M,D,O
University of California, Los Angeles	M,D,O*
University of Central Florida	M,O*
University of Central Missouri	M
University of Central Oklahoma	M
University of Cincinnati	M,D,O
University of Colorado Denver	M,O*
University of Delaware	M,D,O*
The University of Findlay	M
University of Florida	M,D,O*
University of Guam	M
University of Hawaii at Manoa	M,D,O*
University of Houston	M,D*
University of Idaho	M
University of Illinois at Chicago	M*
University of Illinois at Urbana–Champaign	M,D*
University of Manitoba	M
University of Maryland, Baltimore County	M,O*
University of Maryland, College Park	M,D,O*
University of Massachusetts Amherst	M,D,O*
University of Massachusetts Boston	M
University of Miami	M*
University of Michigan	M,D*
University of Minnesota, Twin Cities Campus	M*
University of Missouri–St. Louis	M,O
University of Nebraska at Omaha	M,O
University of Nevada, Reno	M*
The University of North Carolina at Charlotte	M*
The University of North Carolina at Greensboro	M,D,O
University of Northern Iowa	M
University of Pennsylvania	M,D*
University of Phoenix	M
University of Phoenix–Omaha Campus	M
University of Phoenix–Phoenix Campus	M
University of Phoenix–San Diego Campus	M
University of Phoenix–Springfield Campus	M
University of Pittsburgh	O*
University of Puerto Rico, Río Piedras	M
University of San Francisco	M,D
The University of Scranton	M
University of South Africa	M,D
University of South Carolina	M,D,O
University of Southern California	M*
University of Southern Maine	M,O
University of South Florida	M*
The University of Tennessee	M,D,O
The University of Texas at Arlington	M*
The University of Texas at Brownsville	M
The University of Texas at San Antonio	M,D*
The University of Texas of the Permian Basin	M
The University of Texas–Pan American	M
The University of Toledo	M,O
University of Washington	M,D*
University of West Florida	M
University of Wisconsin–River Falls	M
Valparaiso University	M,O
Wayne State College	M
Webster University	M
West Chester University of Pennsylvania	M,O
Western Carolina University	M

Western Connecticut State University M
Western Kentucky University M
Western New Mexico University M
West Virginia University M
Wheaton College M,O
Wright State University M

ENGLISH EDUCATION

Agnes Scott College M*
Alabama State University M,O
Albany State University M
Andrews University M,D,O
Anna Maria College M,O
Appalachian State University M
Arcadia University M,D,O
Arkansas State University M,O
Arkansas Tech University M,O
Armstrong Atlantic State University M
Auburn University M,D,O*
Averett University M
Belmont University M
Bennington College M
Bethel College (TN) M
Bob Jones University P,M,D,O
Boston College M*
Boston University M,O*
Brooklyn College of the City University of New York M,O
Brown University M*
Buffalo State College, State University of New York M
California Baptist University M
California State University, Northridge M
California State University, San Bernardino M,D
Campbell University M
Caribbean University M,D
Carthage College M,O
Chadron State College M,O
Chatham University M
Christopher Newport University M
The Citadel, The Military College of South Carolina M
City College of the City University of New York M,O*
Clarion University of Pennsylvania M
Clayton State University M
Clemson University M
The College at Brockport, State University of New York M
College of St. Joseph M
The College of William and Mary M
The Colorado College M
Columbia College Chicago M
Columbus State University M,O
Converse College M
Delta State University M
Drake University M*
Duquesne University M*
East Carolina University M
Eastern Kentucky University M
Eastern Michigan University M,O
Elms College M,O
Fitchburg State College M,O
Florida Agricultural and Mechanical University M
Florida Atlantic University M
Florida Gulf Coast University M
Florida International University M,D*
Florida State University M,D,O*
Framingham State College M
Gardner-Webb University M
Georgia Southern University M
Georgia State University M,D,O
Grand Valley State University M
Harding University M,O
Hofstra University M*
Humboldt State University M
Hunter College of the City University of New York M
Indiana State University M
Indiana University of Pennsylvania M,D
Indiana University–Purdue University Fort Wayne M,O
Indiana University–Purdue University Indianapolis M*
Iona College M*
Ithaca College M
Jackson State University M
The Johns Hopkins University M,O*
Kennesaw State University M
Kent State University M,D*
Kutztown University of Pennsylvania M,O
Lehman College of the City University of New York M
Lincoln Memorial University M,O
Long Island University, Brooklyn Campus M
Long Island University, C.W. Post Campus M
Longwood University M
Louisiana Tech University M,D
Lynchburg College M
Manhattanville College M*
Maryville University of Saint Louis M,D
Miami University M,D*
Millersville University of Pennsylvania M
Mills College M,D
Minnesota State University Mankato M,O
Mississippi College M,D,O
Montclair State University M,O*
National-Louis University M,O
New York University M,D,O*
North Carolina Agricultural and Technical State University M
North Carolina State University M*
Northeastern Illinois University M
Northern Arizona University M
Northern State University M
North Georgia College & State University M,O
Northwestern State University of Louisiana M
Northwest Missouri State University M
Nova Southeastern University M,O*
Occidental College M
Our Lady of the Lake University of San Antonio M
Penn State University Park M,D*
Plymouth State University M
Purdue University M,D,O
Queens College of the City University of New York M,O
Quinnipiac University M*
Rhode Island College M
Rider University O*
Rollins College M
Rutgers, The State University of New Jersey, New Brunswick M*
Sage Graduate School M
St. John Fisher College M
Salem State College M
San Francisco State University M,O
San Jose State University M,O
Shippensburg University of Pennsylvania M
Smith College M
South Carolina State University M
Southern Illinois University Edwardsville M,O
Southwestern Oklahoma State University M
Stanford University M,D*
State University of New York at Binghamton M*
State University of New York at New Paltz M
State University of New York at Plattsburgh M
State University of New York College at Cortland M
Stony Brook University, State University of New York M,D,O
Syracuse University M,D*
Teachers College, Columbia University M,D
Temple University M,D*
Texas A&M University M,D*
Texas A&M University–Commerce M,D
Texas Tech University M,D
Trinity (Washington) University M
Union Graduate College M
University at Buffalo, the State University of New York M,D,O*
University of Alaska Fairbanks M,D,O
The University of Arizona D*
University of Central Florida M*
University of Colorado Denver M,O*
University of Connecticut M,D,O*
University of Florida M,D,O*
University of Georgia M,D,O*
University of Illinois at Chicago M,D*
University of Indianapolis M
The University of Iowa M,D*
University of Manitoba M
University of Michigan M,D*
University of Minnesota, Twin Cities Campus M*
University of Missouri–Columbia M,D,O*
The University of Montana M
University of New Hampshire M,D*
University of New Orleans M
The University of North Carolina at Chapel Hill M*
The University of North Carolina at Charlotte M*
The University of North Carolina at Greensboro M,D
The University of North Carolina at Pembroke M
University of Oklahoma M,D,O*
University of Phoenix M
University of Phoenix–Omaha Campus M
University of Phoenix–Phoenix Campus M
University of Phoenix–Springfield Campus M
University of Pittsburgh M,D*
University of Puerto Rico, Mayagüez Campus M
University of Puerto Rico, Río Piedras M,D
University of St. Francis (IL) M
University of South Carolina M,D
University of South Florida M,D,O*
The University of Tennessee M,D,O
The University of Texas at El Paso M,D
The University of Toledo M
University of Victoria M,D
University of Virginia M,D
University of Washington M,D*
The University of West Alabama M
University of West Georgia M,O
University of Wisconsin–Eau Claire M
Vanderbilt University M*
Virginia Polytechnic Institute and State University M,D,O*
Washington State University M,D*
Wayne State College M
Wayne State University M,D,O*
Western Carolina University M
Western Connecticut State University M
Western Governors University M,O
Western Kentucky University M
Western Michigan University M,D*
Western New England College M
Widener University M,D*
Wilkes University M,D
William Carey University M,O
Worcester State College M

ENTERTAINMENT MANAGEMENT

California Intercontinental University M
Carnegie Mellon University M*
Columbia College Chicago M
Full Sail University M
Hofstra University M*
University of Dallas M
University of South Carolina M

ENTOMOLOGY

Auburn University M,D*
Clemson University M,D
Colorado State University M,D*
Cornell University M,D*
Florida Agricultural and Mechanical University M
Illinois State University M,D
Iowa State University of Science and Technology M,D*
Kansas State University M,D*
Louisiana State University and Agricultural and Mechanical College M,D
McGill University M,D*
Michigan State University M,D*
Mississippi State University M,D
New Mexico State University M
North Carolina State University M,D*
North Dakota State University M,D
The Ohio State University M,D*
Oklahoma State University M,D*
Penn State University Park M,D*

*M—master's degree; P—first professional degree; D—doctorate; O—other advanced degree; *—Close-Up and/or Announcement or Display in one of the other books in this series*

Purdue University	M,D
Rutgers, The State University of New Jersey, New Brunswick	M,D*
Simon Fraser University	M,D
State University of New York College of Environmental Science and Forestry	M,D
Texas A&M University	M,D*
Texas Tech University	M,D
The University of Arizona	M,D*
University of Arkansas	M,D
University of California, Davis	M,D*
University of California, Riverside	M,D*
University of Connecticut	M,D*
University of Delaware	M,D*
University of Florida	M,D*
University of Georgia	M,D*
University of Guelph	M,D
University of Hawaii at Manoa	M,D*
University of Idaho	M,D
University of Illinois at Urbana–Champaign	M,D*
The University of Kansas	M,D*
University of Kentucky	M,D
University of Maine	M*
University of Manitoba	M,D
University of Maryland, College Park	M,D*
University of Massachusetts Amherst	M,D*
University of Minnesota, Twin Cities Campus	M,D*
University of Missouri–Columbia	M,D*
University of Nebraska–Lincoln	M,D*
University of North Dakota	M,D
University of Rhode Island	M,D
The University of Tennessee	M,D
University of Wisconsin–Madison	M,D*
University of Wyoming	M,D
Virginia Polytechnic Institute and State University	M,D*
Washington State University	M,D*
West Virginia University	M,D

ENTREPRENEURSHIP

American College of Thessaloniki	M,O
American University	M*
Andrew Jackson University	M
Babson College	M
Bakke Graduate University	M,D
Baldwin-Wallace College	M
Bay Path College	M
Benedictine University	M
Bernard M. Baruch College of the City University of New York	M,D
Boston University	M,O*
California Intercontinental University	M,D
California Lutheran University	M,O
California State University, East Bay	M
California State University, Fullerton	M
Cambridge College	M
Cameron University	M
Carlos Albizu University, Miami Campus	M,D
Carnegie Mellon University	D*
Clarkson University	M*
Columbia University	M*
Dallas Baptist University	M
DePaul University	M*
Eastern Michigan University	M,O
Fairleigh Dickinson University, College at Florham	M,O*
Fairleigh Dickinson University, Metropolitan Campus	M,O*
Felician College	M*
Florida Atlantic University	M,D
Georgia Institute of Technology	M,O*
Georgia State University	M,D
Hult International Business School (United States)	M
Inter American University of Puerto Rico, San Germán Campus	D
The International University of Monaco	M
Jones International University	M
Kaplan University–Davenport Campus	M
Lamar University	M
Lenoir-Rhyne University	M
LIM College	M
Lincoln University (MO)	M
Lindenwood University	M
Marquette University	O
McGill University	M,D,O*
North Carolina State University	M*
Northeastern University	M*
Northern Kentucky University	M,O
Nova Southeastern University	M*
Oakland University	M,O
Oral Roberts University	M
Park University	M
Penn State Great Valley	M
Peru State College	M
Polytechnic Institute of NYU	M
Polytechnic Institute of NYU, Long Island Graduate Center	M,D,O
Providence College	M*
Queen's University at Kingston	M
Regent University	M,D,O
Rensselaer Polytechnic Institute	M,D
St. Edward's University	M,O
San Diego State University	M*
Simmons College	M,O
SIT Graduate Institute	M
South Carolina State University	M
Southeast Missouri State University	M
Southern Methodist University	M*
Stevens Institute of Technology	M,O
Suffolk University	M,O*
Syracuse University	M*
Temple University	D*
Texas Tech University	M
Université Laval	M,O
The University of Akron	M
University of Central Florida	M,O*
University of Colorado at Boulder	M,D*
University of Dallas	M
University of Dayton	M
University of Delaware	M,D*
University of Florida	M,D,O*
University of Hawaii at Manoa	M*
University of Houston	D*
University of Houston–Victoria	M
The University of Iowa	M*
University of Louisville	M,D
University of Massachusetts Lowell	M,O
University of Minnesota, Twin Cities Campus	M*
University of Missouri–Kansas City	M,D*
University of San Francisco	M
University of South Florida	M,O*
The University of Tampa	M
The University of Texas at Austin	M
The University of Texas at Dallas	M*
University of the Incarnate Word	M,D
University of Waterloo	M
The University of Western Ontario	M,D
University of Wisconsin–Madison	M*
Wake Forest University	M*
Walden University	M,D
West Chester University of Pennsylvania	M,O
Western Carolina University	M
Wilkes University	M

ENVIRONMENTAL AND OCCUPATIONAL HEALTH

American University of Beirut	M
Anna Maria College	M
Boston University	M,D*
California State University, Northridge	M
Capella University	M,D
Colorado State University	M,D*
Columbia Southern University	M
Columbia University	M,D*
Duke University	M,D,O*
East Carolina University	M
Eastern Kentucky University	M
East Tennessee State University	M
Emory University	M*
Florida International University	M,D*
Fort Valley State University	M
Gannon University	O
The George Washington University	M,D*
Georgia Southern University	M,D
Harvard University	M,D*
Hunter College of the City University of New York	M
Illinois Institute of Technology	M*
Indiana State University	M
Indiana University of Pennsylvania	M
The Johns Hopkins University	M,D*
Lewis University	M
Loma Linda University	M
Loyola University Chicago	M,O*
McGill University	M,D,O*
Medical College of Wisconsin	M*
Meharry Medical College	M
Mississippi Valley State University	M
Montclair State University	M,D,O*
Murray State University	M
New York Medical College	M*
New York University	M,D*
North Carolina Agricultural and Technical State University	M
Oakland University	M
OGI School of Science & Engineering at Oregon Health & Science University	M,D
Old Dominion University	M
Oregon State University	M*
Saint Joseph's University	M,O
Saint Mary's University of Minnesota	M
San Diego State University	M,D*
Stony Brook University, State University of New York	M,O
Temple University	M*
Texas A&M Health Science Center	M
Towson University	D
Tufts University	M,D*
TUI University	M,D,O
Tulane University	M,D
Uniformed Services University of the Health Sciences	M,D*
Universidad Autonoma de Guadalajara	M,D
Universidad de Ciencias Medicas	P,M,O
Université de Montréal	M,O
Université du Québec à Montréal	O
Université Laval	O
University at Albany, State University of New York	M,D*
The University of Alabama at Birmingham	D*
University of Alberta	M,D*
University of Arkansas for Medical Sciences	M
The University of British Columbia	M,D
University of California, Berkeley	M,D*
University of California, Los Angeles	M,D*
University of Central Missouri	M,O
University of Cincinnati	M,D
University of Connecticut	M*
University of Florida	M*
University of Georgia	M,D*
University of Illinois at Chicago	M,D*
The University of Iowa	M,D,O*
University of Louisville	M,D
University of Maryland, College Park	M,D*
University of Miami	M*
University of Michigan	M,D*
University of Minnesota, Twin Cities Campus	M,D,O*
University of Nevada, Las Vegas	M
University of Nevada, Reno	M,D*
University of New Haven	M*
The University of North Carolina at Chapel Hill	M,D*
University of North Texas Health Science Center at Fort Worth	M,D
University of Oklahoma	M,D*
University of Oklahoma Health Sciences Center	M,D
University of Pittsburgh	M*
University of Puerto Rico, Medical Sciences Campus	M,D
University of South Alabama	M*
University of South Carolina	M,D
University of Southern Mississippi	M
University of South Florida	M,D*
University of the Sacred Heart	M
The University of Toledo	M,O
University of Washington	M,D*

University of Wisconsin–Whitewater	M*
Virginia Commonwealth University	M
Washington State University Tri-Cities	M,D
Wayne State University	M,O*
West Virginia University	D
Yale University	M,D*

ENVIRONMENTAL BIOLOGY

Baylor University	M,D
Chatham University	M
Emporia State University	M
Georgia State University	M,D
Governors State University	M
Hampton University	M
Hood College	M
Inter American University of Puerto Rico, San Germán Campus	M
Massachusetts Institute of Technology	M,D,O*
Missouri University of Science and Technology	M
Morgan State University	D
Nicholls State University	M
Nova Scotia Agricultural College	M
Ohio University	M,D*
Rutgers, The State University of New Jersey, New Brunswick	M,D*
Sonoma State University	M
State University of New York College of Environmental Science and Forestry	M,D
Tennessee Technological University	M*
University of Alberta	M,D*
University of California, Santa Cruz	M,D*
University of Guelph	M,D
University of Louisiana at Lafayette	M,D*
University of Louisville	D
University of Massachusetts Amherst	M,D*
University of Massachusetts Boston	D
University of North Dakota	M,D
University of Southern Mississippi	M,D
University of West Florida	M
University of Wisconsin–Madison	M,D*
Washington University in St. Louis	D*
West Virginia University	M,D
Youngstown State University	M

ENVIRONMENTAL DESIGN

Arizona State University	D
Art Center College of Design	M*
Clemson University	D
Columbia University	M*
Cornell University	M*
Florida Atlantic University	M,O
Michigan State University	M,D*
San Diego State University	M*
Texas Tech University	M,D
Université de Montréal	M,D,O
University of Calgary	M,D
University of California, Berkeley	M*
University of Georgia	M*
University of Missouri–Columbia	M*
Virginia Polytechnic Institute and State University	D*
Yale University	M*

ENVIRONMENTAL EDUCATION

Alaska Pacific University	M
Antioch University New England	M*
Arcadia University	M,D,O
Brooklyn College of the City University of New York	M
California State University, San Bernardino	M
Chatham University	M
Concordia University Wisconsin	M
Florida Atlantic University	M
Florida Institute of Technology	M,D,O*
Gannon University	M
Lesley University	M,D,O*
Maryville University of Saint Louis	M,D
New York University	M*
Nova Southeastern University	M,O*
Prescott College	M,D
Royal Roads University	M,O
Saint Vincent College	M
Slippery Rock University of Pennsylvania	M
Southern Connecticut State University	M,O
Southern Oregon University	M
Universidad Metropolitana	M
Université du Québec à Montréal	M,D,O
University of Minnesota, Twin Cities Campus	M,D,O*
University of New Hampshire	M*
The University of North Carolina Wilmington	M
University of South Africa	M,D
University of Victoria	M,D
Western Washington University	M
West Virginia University	M,D

ENVIRONMENTAL ENGINEERING

Air Force Institute of Technology	M
Arizona State University	M,D
Auburn University	M,D*
California Institute of Technology	M,D*
California Polytechnic State University, San Luis Obispo	M
Carleton University	M,D
Carnegie Mellon University	M,D*
The Catholic University of America	M,D,O
Clarkson University	M,D*
Clemson University	M,D
Cleveland State University	M,D
Colorado School of Mines	M,D
Columbia University	M,D,O*
Concordia University (Canada)	M,D,O
Cornell University	M,D*
Dalhousie University	M,D
Drexel University	M,D*
Duke University	M,D*
École Polytechnique de Montréal	M,D,O
Florida Agricultural and Mechanical University	M,D
Florida International University	M*
Florida State University	M,D*
Gannon University	M
The George Washington University	M,D,O*
Georgia Institute of Technology	M,D*
Idaho State University	M
Illinois Institute of Technology	M,D*
Instituto Tecnologico de Santo Domingo	M
Instituto Tecnológico y de Estudios Superiores de Monterrey, Campus Ciudad de México	M,D
Instituto Tecnológico y de Estudios Superiores de Monterrey, Campus Monterrey	M,D
Iowa State University of Science and Technology	M,D*
The Johns Hopkins University	M,D,O*
Lakehead University	M
Lamar University	M,D
Lehigh University	M,D
Louisiana State University and Agricultural and Mechanical College	M,D
Loyola Marymount University	M
Manhattan College	M
Marquette University	M,D
Marshall University	M
Massachusetts Institute of Technology	M,D,O*
McGill University	M,D*
Memorial University of Newfoundland	M
Mercer University	M
Michigan State University	M,D*
Michigan Technological University	M,D
Milwaukee School of Engineering	M*
Missouri University of Science and Technology	M,D
Montana State University	M,D
Montana Tech of The University of Montana	M
National University	M
New Jersey Institute of Technology	M,D
New Mexico Institute of Mining and Technology	M
New Mexico State University	M,D
New York Institute of Technology	M
North Dakota State University	M,D
Northeastern University	M,D*
Northern Arizona University	M
Northwestern University	M,D*
OGI School of Science & Engineering at Oregon Health & Science University	M,D
Ohio University	M,D*
Oklahoma State University	M,D*
Old Dominion University	M,D
Oregon Health & Science University	M,D*
Oregon State University	M,D*
Penn State Harrisburg	M
Penn State University Park	M,D*
Polytechnic Institute of NYU	M
Polytechnic Institute of NYU, Long Island Graduate Center	M
Pontificia Universidad Catolica Madre y Maestra	M
Portland State University	M,D
Princeton University	M,D*
Rensselaer Polytechnic Institute	M,D
Rice University	M,D
Rose-Hulman Institute of Technology	M*
Royal Military College of Canada	M,D
Rutgers, The State University of New Jersey, New Brunswick	M,D*
Southern Methodist University	M,D*
Stanford University	M,D,O*
State University of New York College of Environmental Science and Forestry	M,D
Stevens Institute of Technology	M,D,O
Syracuse University	M*
Texas A&M University	M,D*
Texas A&M University–Kingsville	M,D
Texas Tech University	M,D
Tufts University	M,D*
Universidad Central del Este	M,D
Universidad Nacional Pedro Henriquez Urena	P,M,D
Université de Sherbrooke	M
Université Laval	M,D
University at Buffalo, the State University of New York	M,D*
The University of Alabama	M,D
The University of Alabama at Birmingham	D*
The University of Alabama in Huntsville	M,D
University of Alaska Anchorage	M
University of Alaska Fairbanks	M,D
University of Alberta	M,D*
The University of Arizona	M,D*
University of Arkansas	M
University of California, Berkeley	M,D*
University of California, Davis	M,D,O*
University of California, Irvine	M,D*
University of California, Los Angeles	M,D*
University of California, Riverside	M,D*
University of Central Florida	M,D*
University of Cincinnati	M,D
University of Colorado at Boulder	M,D*
University of Connecticut	M,D*
University of Dayton	M
University of Delaware	M,D*
University of Detroit Mercy	M,D
University of Florida	M,D,O*
University of Guelph	M,D
University of Hawaii at Manoa	M,D*
University of Houston	M,D*
University of Idaho	M
University of Illinois at Urbana–Champaign	M,D*
The University of Iowa	M,D*
The University of Kansas	M,D*
University of Louisville	M,D
University of Maine	M,D*
University of Maryland, Baltimore County	M,D*
University of Maryland, College Park	M,D*
University of Massachusetts Amherst	M*
University of Massachusetts Dartmouth	M
University of Massachusetts Lowell	M,D,O
University of Memphis	M,D
University of Michigan	M,D,O*
University of Missouri–Columbia	M,D*
University of Nebraska–Lincoln	M,D*
University of New Brunswick Fredericton	M,D

*M—master's degree; P—first professional degree; D—doctorate; O—other advanced degree; *—Close-Up and/or Announcement or Display in one of the other books in this series*

University of New Haven M,O*
The University of North Carolina at Chapel Hill M,D*
The University of North Carolina at Charlotte D*
University of North Dakota M
University of Notre Dame M,D*
University of Oklahoma M,D*
University of Pittsburgh M,D*
University of Regina M,D
University of Rhode Island M
University of Saskatchewan M,D,O
University of Southern California M,D,O*
University of South Florida M,D*
The University of Tennessee M
The University of Texas at Austin M,D
The University of Texas at El Paso M,D
The University of Texas at San Antonio M,D*
University of Utah M,D*
University of Vermont M,D*
University of Washington M,D*
University of Waterloo M,D
The University of Western Ontario M,D
University of Windsor M,D
University of Wisconsin–Madison M,D*
University of Wyoming M
Utah State University M,D,O
Vanderbilt University M,D*
Villanova University M*
Virginia Polytechnic Institute and State University M,D*
Washington State University M*
Washington University in St. Louis M,D*
West Virginia University M,D
Worcester Polytechnic Institute M,D,O*
Yale University M,D*
Youngstown State University M

ENVIRONMENTAL LAW

Chapman University P,M
Golden Gate University P,M,D
Lewis & Clark College P,M
Pace University P,M,D*
University of Calgary M,O
University of Florida P,M,D*
University of Pittsburgh M,O*
University of Tulsa P,M,O*
Vermont Law School M

ENVIRONMENTAL MANAGEMENT AND POLICY

Adelphi University M*
Air Force Institute of Technology M
American Public University System M
American University M,D,O*
American University of Beirut M
Antioch University New England M,D*
Antioch University Seattle M
Arizona State University at the Polytechnic Campus M
Bard College M,O
Baylor University M
Bemidji State University M
Boise State University M
Boston University M,D,O*
Brown University M*
California State University, Fullerton M
The Catholic University of America M,D,O
Central European University M,D*
Clarkson University M*
Clark University M
Clemson University M,D
Cleveland State University M,O
College of the Atlantic M
Columbia University M*
Concordia University (Canada) M,O
Cornell University M,D*
Dalhousie University M
Drexel University M*
Duke University M,D*
Duquesne University M,O*
The Evergreen State College M
Florida Atlantic University M,O
Florida Gulf Coast University M
Florida Institute of Technology M,D*
Florida International University M*
The George Washington University M,D*
Georgia Institute of Technology M,D*
Goddard College M
Green Mountain College M
Hardin-Simmons University M
Harvard University M,O*
Humboldt State University M
Illinois Institute of Technology M*
Indiana University–Purdue University Indianapolis M*
Instituto Tecnológico y de Estudios Superiores de Monterrey, Campus Estado de México M,D
Instituto Tecnológico y de Estudios Superiores de Monterrey, Campus Irapuato M,D
Inter American University of Puerto Rico, Metropolitan Campus M
The Johns Hopkins University M,O*
Kean University M
Lamar University M,D
Lehigh University M
Long Island University, C.W. Post Campus M
Louisiana State University and Agricultural and Mechanical College M
McGill University M,D*
Michigan Technological University M
Missouri State University M*
Montclair State University M,D*
Monterey Institute of International Studies M*
Morehead State University M
Naropa University M*
New Jersey Institute of Technology M
New York Institute of Technology M,O
New York University M*
Northeastern Illinois University M
Northern Arizona University M
Nova Scotia Agricultural College M
Ohio University M*
Penn State University Park M*
Plymouth State University M
Polytechnic University of Puerto Rico M
Pontificia Universidad Catolica Madre y Maestra M
Portland State University M,D
Prescott College M
Princeton University M,D*
Purdue University M,D
Rensselaer Polytechnic Institute M,D
Rice University M
Rochester Institute of Technology M
Royal Roads University M,O
St. Cloud State University M
Saint Mary-of-the-Woods College M
Samford University M
San Francisco State University M
San Jose State University M
Shippensburg University of Pennsylvania M
Simon Fraser University M,D
Slippery Rock University of Pennsylvania M
Southeast Missouri State University M
Southern Illinois University Edwardsville M
Stanford University M*
State University of New York College of Environmental Science and Forestry M,D
Stony Brook University, State University of New York M,O
Texas State University–San Marcos M*
Texas Tech University D
Towson University M
Trent University M,D
Tropical Agriculture Research and Higher Education Center M,D
Troy University M
Tufts University M,D,O*
Universidad Autonoma de Guadalajara M,D
Universidad del Turabo M
Universidad Metropolitana M
Université de Montréal O
Université du Québec à Chicoutimi M
Université du Québec, Institut National de la Recherche Scientifique M,D
Université Laval M,D,O
University at Albany, State University of New York M*
University of Alaska Fairbanks M,D
University of Alberta M,D*
University of Calgary M,D,O
University of California, Berkeley M,D*
University of California, Santa Barbara M,D
University of California, Santa Cruz D*
University of Chicago M,D*
University of Colorado at Boulder M,D*
University of Dayton M,D
University of Delaware M,D*
University of Denver M,O*
The University of Findlay M
University of Guelph M,D
University of Hawaii at Manoa M,D,O*
University of Houston–Clear Lake M
University of Illinois at Springfield M
University of Maryland, Baltimore County M,D*
University of Maryland University College M,O
University of Massachusetts Dartmouth M,O
University of Massachusetts Lowell M,D,O
University of Miami M,D*
University of Michigan M,D*
University of Minnesota, Twin Cities Campus M*
University of Missouri–St. Louis M,D,O
The University of Montana M
University of Nevada, Reno M*
University of New Brunswick Fredericton M,D
University of New Hampshire M*
The University of North Carolina at Chapel Hill M,D*
The University of North Carolina Wilmington M
University of Northern British Columbia M,D,O
University of Oregon M,D*
University of Pennsylvania M*
University of Pittsburgh M,O*
University of Rhode Island M,D
University of South Africa M,D
University of South Carolina M
University of South Florida M*
The University of Tennessee M,D
University of Washington M,D*
University of Waterloo M
University of Wisconsin–Green Bay M
Utah State University M,D
Vanderbilt University M,D*
Vermont Law School M
Virginia Commonwealth University M
Virginia Polytechnic Institute and State University M,D*
Webster University M,D
Wesley College M
West Virginia University M,D
Yale University M,D*
York University M,D
Youngstown State University M,O

ENVIRONMENTAL SCIENCES

Alabama Agricultural and Mechanical University M,D
Alaska Pacific University M
American University M*
American University of Beirut M,D
Antioch University New England M,D*
Arizona State University M,D
Arkansas State University M,D
Brigham Young University M,D*
California State Polytechnic University, Pomona M
California State University, Chico M
California State University, East Bay M
California State University, Fullerton M
California State University, Northridge M
California State University, San Bernardino M
Christopher Newport University M
City College of the City University of New York M,D*
Clarkson University M,D*
Clemson University M,D
Cleveland State University M,D
The College at Brockport, State University of New York M
College of Charleston M*

College of Staten Island of the City University of New York M
Colorado School of Mines M,D
Columbia University M*
Columbus State University M
Cornell University M,D*
Drexel University M,D*
Duke University M,D*
Duquesne University M,O*
Florida Agricultural and Mechanical University M,D
Florida Atlantic University M
Florida Gulf Coast University M
Florida Institute of Technology M,D*
Florida International University M*
Gannon University M,O
George Mason University M,D*
Georgia Institute of Technology M,D*
Graduate School and University Center of the City University of New York D*
Harvard University M*
Howard University M,D
Humboldt State University M
Hunter College of the City University of New York M,O
Idaho State University M
Indiana University Bloomington M,D*
Indiana University Northwest M,O
Instituto Tecnologico de Santo Domingo M
Instituto Tecnológico y de Estudios Superiores de Monterrey, Campus Ciudad de México M,D
Inter American University of Puerto Rico, San Germán Campus M
Iowa State University of Science and Technology M,D*
Jackson State University M,D
The Johns Hopkins University M*
Laurentian University M
Lehigh University M,D
Louisiana State University and Agricultural and Mechanical College M,D
Loyola Marymount University M
Marshall University M
Massachusetts Institute of Technology M,D,O*
McNeese State University M
Memorial University of Newfoundland M
Mercer University M
Miami University M*
Michigan State University M,D*
Minnesota State University Mankato M
Montana State University M,D
Montclair State University M,D,O*
Murray State University M
New Jersey Institute of Technology M,D
New Mexico Institute of Mining and Technology M,D
New Mexico State University M,D
North Carolina Agricultural and Technical State University M
North Dakota State University M,D
Northern Arizona University M
Nova Scotia Agricultural College M
Nova Southeastern University M*
Oakland University M,D
OGI School of Science & Engineering at Oregon Health & Science University M,D
The Ohio State University M,D*
Oklahoma State University M,D*
Oregon Health & Science University M,D*
Oregon State University M,D*
Pace University M*
Penn State Harrisburg M
Penn State University Park M*
Polytechnic Institute of NYU M
Pontifical Catholic University of Puerto Rico M
Portland State University M,D
Queens College of the City University of New York M
Rensselaer Polytechnic Institute M,D
Rice University M,D
Rochester Institute of Technology M
Royal Military College of Canada M,D
Rutgers, The State University of New Jersey, Newark M,D*
Rutgers, The State University of New Jersey, New Brunswick M,D*
South Dakota School of Mines and Technology D*
Southern Illinois University Carbondale D*
Southern Illinois University Edwardsville M
Southern Methodist University M,D*
Southern University and Agricultural and Mechanical College M
Stanford University M,D,O*
State University of New York College of Environmental Science and Forestry M,D
Stephen F. Austin State University M
Tarleton State University M
Taylor University M
Tennessee Technological University D*
Texas A&M University–Corpus Christi M
Texas Christian University M
Texas Tech University M,D
Towson University M,O
Tufts University M,D*
Tulane University M,D
Tuskegee University M
Universidad del Turabo M,D
Université de Sherbrooke M,O
Université du Québec à Montréal M,D,O
Université du Québec à Trois-Rivières M,D
Université du Québec en Abitibi-Témiscamingue M,D
Université Laval M,D
University at Albany, State University of New York M*
The University of Alabama in Huntsville M,D
University of Alaska Anchorage M
University of Alaska Fairbanks M,D
University of Alberta M,D*
The University of Arizona M,D*
University of California, Berkeley M,D*
University of California, Davis M,D*
University of California, Los Angeles M,D*
University of California, Santa Barbara M,D
University of Chicago M,D*
University of Cincinnati M,D
University of Colorado at Colorado Springs M
University of Colorado Denver M*
University of Guam M
University of Guelph M,D
University of Houston–Clear Lake M
University of Idaho M,D
University of Illinois at Springfield M
University of Illinois at Urbana–Champaign M,D*
The University of Kansas M,D*
University of Lethbridge M,D
University of Maine M,D*
University of Manitoba M,D
University of Maryland, Baltimore M,D*
University of Maryland, Baltimore County M,D*
University of Maryland, College Park M,D*
University of Maryland Eastern Shore M,D*
University of Massachusetts Boston D
University of Massachusetts Lowell M,D,O
University of Medicine and Dentistry of New Jersey D*
University of Michigan M,D*
University of Michigan–Dearborn M*
The University of Montana M
University of Nevada, Las Vegas M,D
University of Nevada, Reno M,D*
University of New Haven M*
University of New Orleans M
The University of North Carolina at Chapel Hill M,D*
University of Northern Iowa M
University of North Texas M,D
University of Oklahoma M,D*
University of Pennsylvania M,D*
University of Rhode Island M,D
University of South Africa M,D
University of South Florida M,D*
The University of Tennessee at Chattanooga M
The University of Texas at Arlington M,D*
The University of Texas at El Paso D
The University of Texas at San Antonio M,D*
University of the Virgin Islands M
The University of Toledo M,D
University of Utah M*
University of Virginia M,D
The University of Western Ontario M,D
University of West Florida M
University of Windsor M,D
University of Wisconsin–Green Bay M
University of Wisconsin–Madison M,D*
Vanderbilt University M*
Virginia Commonwealth University M
Virginia Polytechnic Institute and State University M,D*
Washington State University M,D*
Washington State University Tri-Cities M,D
Washington State University Vancouver M
Wesleyan University M*
Western Connecticut State University M
Western Washington University M
West Texas A&M University M
Wichita State University M*
Wright State University M,D
Yale University M,D*

EPIDEMIOLOGY

American University of Beirut M
Boston University M,D*
Brown University M,D*
Case Western Reserve University M,D*
Columbia University M,D*
Cornell University M,D*
Cornell University, Joan and Sanford I. Weill Medical College and Graduate School of Medical Sciences M
Dalhousie University M
Drexel University M,D,O*
East Tennessee State University M,O
Emory University M,D*
Florida International University M,D*
George Mason University M,D,O*
Georgetown University M
The George Washington University M,D*
Georgia Southern University M,D
Harvard University M,D*
Hunter College of the City University of New York M
Indiana University–Purdue University Indianapolis M*
The Johns Hopkins University M,D*
Loma Linda University M,D,O
McGill University M,D,O*
Medical College of Wisconsin M*
Medical University of South Carolina M,D
Memorial University of Newfoundland M,D,O
Michigan State University M,D*
New York Medical College M,D*
New York University M,D*
North Carolina State University M,D*
Oregon Health & Science University M*
Purdue University M,D
Queen's University at Kingston M,D
San Diego State University M,D*
Stanford University M,D*
Temple University M*
Texas A&M Health Science Center M
Texas A&M University M,D*
Thomas Edison State College O
Tufts University M,D,O*
Tulane University M,D
Université Laval M,D
University at Albany, State University of New York M,D*
University at Buffalo, the State University of New York M,D*
The University of Alabama at Birmingham D*

*M—master's degree; P—first professional degree; D—doctorate; O—other advanced degree; *—Close-Up and/or Announcement or Display in one of the other books in this series*

University of Alberta	M,D*
The University of Arizona	M,D*
The University of British Columbia	M,D
University of Calgary	M,D
University of California, Berkeley	M,D*
University of California, Davis	M,D*
University of California, Irvine	M,D*
University of California, Los Angeles	M,D*
University of California, San Diego	D*
University of Cincinnati	M,D
University of Colorado Denver	D*
University of Florida	M*
University of Guelph	M,D
University of Hawaii at Manoa	M,D,O*
University of Illinois at Chicago	M,D*
The University of Iowa	M,D*
University of Louisville	M,D
University of Maryland, Baltimore	M,D*
University of Maryland, Baltimore County	M,O*
University of Maryland, College Park	M,D*
University of Massachusetts Lowell	M,D,O
University of Massachusetts Worcester	D
University of Medicine and Dentistry of New Jersey	M,D,O*
University of Miami	D*
University of Michigan	M,D*
University of Minnesota, Twin Cities Campus	M,D*
The University of North Carolina at Chapel Hill	M,D*
University of North Texas Health Science Center at Fort Worth	M,D
University of Oklahoma Health Sciences Center	M,D
University of Ottawa	M*
University of Pennsylvania	M,D*
University of Pittsburgh	M,D*
University of Prince Edward Island	M,D
University of Puerto Rico, Medical Sciences Campus	M
University of Rochester	M,D*
University of Saskatchewan	M,D
University of South Carolina	M,D
University of Southern California	M,D*
University of Southern Mississippi	M
University of South Florida	M,D*
The University of Toledo	M,O
University of Washington	M,D*
The University of Western Ontario	M,D
University of Wisconsin–Madison	M,D*
Virginia Commonwealth University	D
Walden University	M,D
Yale University	M,D*

ERGONOMICS AND HUMAN FACTORS

Bentley University	M
California State University, Long Beach	M
California State University, Northridge	M
The Catholic University of America	M,D
Clemson University	D
Cornell University	M*
Embry-Riddle Aeronautical University (FL)	M
Florida Institute of Technology	M*
Georgia Institute of Technology	M,D*
Indiana University Bloomington	M,D*
New York University	M,D*
North Carolina State University	D*
Old Dominion University	D
San Jose State University	M
Tufts University	M,D*
Université de Montréal	O
Université du Québec à Montréal	O
The University of Alabama	M
University of Central Florida	M,D,O*
University of Cincinnati	M,D
University of Illinois at Urbana–Champaign	M*
The University of Iowa	M,D*
University of Massachusetts Lowell	M,D,O
University of Miami	M*
The University of Tennessee	M,D
University of Wisconsin–Milwaukee	M,O
Wright State University	M,D

ETHICS

American University	M,D,O*
Azusa Pacific University	M
Biola University	P,M,D
Chicago Theological Seminary	P,M,D
Claremont Graduate University	M,D*
Drew University	M,D
Duquesne University	M*
Emory University	P,M,D*
Fordham University	M,O*
Freed-Hardeman University	M
Georgetown University	M,D
Graduate Theological Union	M,D,O
Lutheran Theological Seminary	P,M,D
Marquette University	M,D
Oregon State University	M*
Phillips Theological Seminary	P,M,D
St. Edward's University	M
Southeastern Baptist Theological Seminary	P,M,D
Suffolk University	M*
Université de Sherbrooke	M,D,O
Université du Québec à Chicoutimi	O
Université du Québec à Rimouski	M,O
Université Laval	O
University of Baltimore	M
University of Nevada, Las Vegas	M
University of North Florida	M,O
University of Pennsylvania	M,D*
University of South Africa	M,D
Valparaiso University	M,O
Warner Pacific College	M
West Chester University of Pennsylvania	M,O
Wilfrid Laurier University	P,M,D,O

ETHNIC STUDIES

Cornell University	M,D*
Minnesota State University Mankato	M
San Francisco State University	M
United Theological Seminary of the Twin Cities	P,M,D,O
Université Laval	M,D
University of California, Berkeley	D*
University of California, Riverside	D*
University of California, San Diego	M,D*
Washington State University	M,D*

EVOLUTIONARY BIOLOGY

Brown University	D*
Clemson University	M,D
Columbia University	D,O*
Cornell University	D*
Dartmouth College	D*
Emory University	D*
Florida State University	M,D*
George Mason University	M,D,O*
Harvard University	D*
Illinois State University	M,D
Indiana University Bloomington	M,D*
Iowa State University of Science and Technology	M,D*
The Johns Hopkins University	D*
Marquette University	M,D
Michigan State University	D*
Northwestern University	D*
The Ohio State University	M,D*
Ohio University	M,D*
Penn State University Park	M,D*
Princeton University	D*
Purdue University	M,D
Rice University	M,D
Rutgers, The State University of New Jersey, New Brunswick	M,D*
Stony Brook University, State University of New York	M,D
Tulane University	M,D
University at Albany, State University of New York	M,D*
University at Buffalo, the State University of New York	M,D,O*
University of Alberta	M,D*
The University of Arizona	M,D*
University of California, Davis	D*
University of California, Irvine	M,D*
University of California, Los Angeles	M,D*
University of California, Riverside	M,D*
University of California, San Diego	D*
University of California, Santa Barbara	M,D
University of California, Santa Cruz	M,D*
University of Chicago	D*
University of Colorado at Boulder	M,D*
University of Delaware	M,D*
University of Guelph	M,D
University of Hawaii at Manoa	M,D*
University of Illinois at Urbana–Champaign	M,D*
The University of Iowa	M,D*
The University of Kansas	M,D*
University of Louisiana at Lafayette	M,D*
University of Maryland, College Park	M,D*
University of Massachusetts Amherst	M,D*
University of Miami	M,D*
University of Michigan	M,D*
University of Minnesota, Twin Cities Campus	M,D*
University of Missouri–Columbia	M,D*
University of Missouri–St. Louis	M,D,O
University of Nevada, Reno	D*
The University of North Carolina at Chapel Hill	M,D*
University of Notre Dame	M,D*
University of Oklahoma	D*
University of Oregon	M,D*
University of Pittsburgh	D*
University of South Carolina	M,D
University of Southern California	M,D*
The University of Tennessee	M,D
The University of Texas at Austin	M,D
University of Toronto	M,D
Virginia Polytechnic Institute and State University	M,D*
Washington University in St. Louis	D*
Wesleyan University	D*
West Virginia University	M,D
Yale University	D*

EXERCISE AND SPORTS SCIENCE

American University	M*
Appalachian State University	M
Arizona State University at the Polytechnic Campus	M,D
Arkansas State University	M,O
Armstrong Atlantic State University	M
Ashland University	M
Auburn University	M,D,O*
Austin Peay State University	M
Ball State University	D*
Barry University	M*
Baylor University	M,D
Bemidji State University	M
Benedictine University	M
Bloomsburg University of Pennsylvania	M
Boise State University	M
Brigham Young University	M,D*
Brooklyn College of the City University of New York	M
California State University, Fresno	M
California State University, Long Beach	M
California University of Pennsylvania	M
Central Connecticut State University	M,O
Central Michigan University	M
Cleveland State University	M
The College of St. Scholastica	M
Colorado State University	M,D*
Concordia University (Canada)	M
Concordia University Chicago	M
Delaware State University	M
East Carolina University	M,D
Eastern Michigan University	M
Eastern Washington University	M
East Stroudsburg University of Pennsylvania	M
East Tennessee State University	M
Florida Atlantic University	M

Florida International University M*
Florida State University M,D*
Gardner-Webb University M
George Mason University M*
The George Washington University M*
Georgia State University M
High Point University M
Howard University M
Humboldt State University M
Indiana State University M
Indiana University Bloomington M,D*
Indiana University of Pennsylvania M
Inter American University of Puerto Rico, Metropolitan Campus M
Ithaca College M
Kean University M
Kennesaw State University M
Kent State University M,D*
Lakehead University M
Life University M
Long Island University, Brooklyn Campus M
Louisiana Tech University M
Manhattanville College M*
Marshall University M
Marywood University M
McNeese State University M
Memorial University of Newfoundland M
Miami University M*
Middle Tennessee State University M,D
Mississippi State University M
Montana State University M
Montclair State University M,O*
Morehead State University M
Murray State University M
New Mexico Highlands University M
North Dakota State University M
Northeastern University M*
Northern Michigan University M
Oakland University M,O
Ohio University M,D*
Old Dominion University M
Oregon State University M,D*
Purdue University M,D
Queens College of the City University of New York M
Queen's University at Kingston M,D
Sacred Heart University M,D
St. Cloud State University M
San Diego State University M*
Smith College M
Southeast Missouri State University M
Southern Connecticut State University M
Southern Utah University M
Springfield College M,D
State University of New York College at Cortland M
Syracuse University M*
Tennessee State University M
Texas A&M University–Commerce M,D
Texas Tech University M
Texas Woman's University M
United States Sports Academy M
University at Buffalo, the State University of New York M,D*
The University of Akron M
The University of Alabama M,D
University of Alberta M,D*
University of Calgary M,D
University of California, Davis M*
University of Central Florida M*
University of Central Missouri M
University of Connecticut M,D*
University of Dayton M,D
University of Delaware M*
University of Florida M,D*
University of Houston M,D*
University of Houston–Clear Lake M
The University of Iowa M,D*
University of Kentucky M,D
University of Lethbridge M,D
University of Louisiana at Monroe M
University of Louisville M
University of Mary Hardin-Baylor M,D
University of Memphis M,D
University of Miami M,D*
University of Minnesota, Twin Cities Campus M,D,O*
University of Mississippi M,D
University of Missouri–Columbia M,D*
The University of Montana M
University of Nebraska at Kearney M
University of Nebraska–Lincoln M,D*
University of Nevada, Las Vegas M
University of New Brunswick Fredericton M
University of New Mexico D*
The University of North Carolina at Chapel Hill M*
The University of North Carolina at Charlotte M*
The University of North Carolina at Greensboro M,D
University of Northern Colorado M,D
University of Oklahoma M,D*
University of Pittsburgh M,D*
University of Puerto Rico, Río Piedras M
University of Rhode Island M,D
University of South Alabama M*
University of South Carolina M,D
University of Southern Mississippi M,D
The University of Tennessee M,D,O
The University of Texas at Arlington M,D*
University of the Pacific M
The University of Toledo M,D
University of Utah M,D*
University of West Florida M
University of Wisconsin–La Crosse M
Virginia Commonwealth University M
Wake Forest University M*
Washington State University M,D*
Washington State University Spokane M,O
Wayne State College M
West Chester University of Pennsylvania M,O
Western Michigan University M*
Western Washington University M
West Texas A&M University M
West Virginia University M,D
Wichita State University M*

EXPERIMENTAL PSYCHOLOGY

American University M*
Appalachian State University M,O
Auburn University M,D*
Bowling Green State University M,D*
Brooklyn College of the City University of New York M,D
California State University, Northridge M
California State University, San Bernardino M
Case Western Reserve University D*
The Catholic University of America M,D
Central Michigan University M,D
Central Washington University M
City College of the City University of New York M,D*
Cleveland State University M,D,O
The College of William and Mary M,D
Columbia University M,D*
Cornell University D*
Dallas Baptist University M
DePaul University M,D*
Duke University D*
Eastern Washington University M
Fairleigh Dickinson University, Metropolitan Campus M,O*
Georgia Institute of Technology M,D*
Graduate School and University Center of the City University of New York D*
Harvard University D*
Howard University M,D
Illinois State University M,D,O
Iona College M*
Kent State University M,D*
Lakehead University M,D
Laurentian University M
McGill University M,D*
McNeese State University M
Memorial University of Newfoundland M,D
Miami University D*
Mississippi State University M,D
Missouri State University M*
Morehead State University M
North Carolina State University D*
Northeastern University M,D*
Ohio University D*
Old Dominion University D
Radford University M,D,O
St. John's University (NY) M,D
Saint Louis University M,D
San Jose State University M
Seton Hall University M*
Southern Illinois University Carbondale M,D*
Stony Brook University, State University of New York D
Syracuse University D*
Texas Tech University M,D
University at Albany, State University of New York M,D,O*
The University of Alabama D
University of Central Florida M,D*
University of Cincinnati D
University of Connecticut M,D,O*
University of Hartford M*
University of Kentucky M,D
University of Louisiana at Monroe M
University of Louisville D
University of Maine M,D*
University of Maryland, College Park M,D*
University of Memphis M,D
University of Michigan D*
University of Mississippi M,D
The University of Montana M,D,O
University of New Brunswick Saint John M,D
The University of North Carolina at Chapel Hill D*
University of North Dakota M,D
University of North Texas M,D
University of Regina M,D
University of South Carolina M,D
University of Southern Mississippi M,D
The University of Tennessee M,D
The University of Tennessee at Chattanooga M
The University of Texas at Arlington M,D*
The University of Texas at El Paso M,D
The University of Texas of the Permian Basin M
The University of Texas–Pan American M
The University of Toledo M,D
University of Victoria M,D
University of Wisconsin–Oshkosh M
Washington State University M,D*
Washington University in St. Louis D*
Western Michigan University M,D*
Western Washington University M
Xavier University M,D*

FACILITIES MANAGEMENT

Cornell University M*
Indiana University of Pennsylvania M
Massachusetts Maritime Academy M
Pratt Institute M*
Southern Methodist University M,D*
Université Laval M,O
The University of Kansas M,D,O*

FAMILY AND CONSUMER SCIENCES-GENERAL

Alabama Agricultural and Mechanical University M,D
Appalachian State University M
Ball State University M*
Bowling Green State University M*
California State University, Fresno M
California State University, Long Beach M
California State University, Northridge M
Central Michigan University M,O
Central Washington University M
Cornell University M,D*
Eastern Illinois University M
Florida State University M,D*
Fontbonne University M
Illinois State University M
Indiana State University M
Iowa State University of Science and Technology M*
Kansas State University M,D*
Kent State University M*
Lamar University M,O
Louisiana State University and Agricultural and Mechanical College M,D
Louisiana Tech University M

*M—master's degree; P—first professional degree; D—doctorate; O—other advanced degree; *—Close-Up and/or Announcement or Display in one of the other books in this series*

- Marshall University M
- Missouri State University M*
- New Mexico State University M
- North Carolina Central University M
- North Dakota State University M
- The Ohio State University M*
- Ohio University M*
- Oklahoma State University M,D*
- Oregon State University M*
- Prairie View A&M University M
- Purdue University M,D
- Queens College of the City University of New York M
- Sam Houston State University M
- San Francisco State University M
- South Carolina State University M
- South Dakota State University M
- State University of New York College at Oneonta M
- Stephen F. Austin State University M
- Tennessee State University M
- Texas A&M University–Kingsville M
- Texas Southern University M
- Texas Tech University M,D
- Tufts University M,D,O*
- The University of Akron M
- The University of Alabama M,D
- University of Alberta M,D*
- The University of Arizona M,D*
- University of Arkansas M
- University of Central Arkansas M
- University of Central Oklahoma M
- University of Florida M*
- University of Georgia M,D*
- University of Houston M*
- University of Louisiana at Lafayette M*
- University of Manitoba M
- University of Maryland, College Park M,D*
- University of Memphis M
- University of Mississippi M
- University of Missouri–Columbia M,D*
- University of Nebraska–Lincoln M,D*
- The University of North Carolina at Greensboro M,D,O
- University of Puerto Rico, Río Piedras M
- University of South Africa M,D
- The University of Tennessee D
- The University of Tennessee at Martin M
- The University of Texas at Austin M,D
- University of Wisconsin–Madison M,D*
- University of Wisconsin–Stevens Point M
- Utah State University M,D
- Western Michigan University M*

FAMILY NURSE PRACTITIONER STUDIES

- Abilene Christian University M,O
- Allen College M
- Austin Peay State University M
- Barry University M,O*
- Baylor University M
- Bellarmine University M,D
- Bloomsburg University of Pennsylvania M
- Bowie State University M
- Brenau University M
- Brigham Young University M*
- California State University, Fresno M
- Carlow University M,D
- Carson-Newman College M
- Case Western Reserve University M,D*
- The Catholic University of America M,D,O
- Clarke College M,O
- Clarkson College M,O
- College of Mount Saint Vincent M,O
- The College of New Rochelle M,O
- Columbia University M,O*
- Concordia University Wisconsin M
- Coppin State University M
- Delta State University M
- DeSales University M
- Dominican College M
- Duke University M,D,O*
- Duquesne University M,O*
- D'Youville College M,O*
- Eastern Kentucky University M
- Edinboro University of Pennsylvania M
- Emory University M*
- Fairfield University M,O*
- Felician College M,O*
- Florida State University M,O*
- Frontier School of Midwifery and Family Nursing M,O
- Gannon University M,O
- George Mason University M,D,O*
- Georgetown University M
- The George Washington University M,D,O*
- Georgia College & State University M
- Georgia Southern University M,O
- Georgia State University M,D,O
- Graceland University (IA) M,O
- Grambling State University M,O
- Grand Canyon University M*
- Gwynedd-Mercy College M
- Hardin-Simmons University M
- Hawai'i Pacific University M*
- Holy Names University M,O
- Howard University M,O
- Husson University M,O
- Illinois State University M,D,O
- Indiana University–Purdue University Indianapolis M,D*
- The Johns Hopkins University M,O*
- Kent State University M,D*
- Lincoln Memorial University M
- Long Island University, C.W. Post Campus M,O
- Loyola University Chicago M,O*
- Loyola University New Orleans M
- Malone University M
- Marymount University M,O
- Maryville University of Saint Louis M
- McGill University M,D,O*
- McNeese State University M
- Medical College of Georgia M
- Medical University of South Carolina M,D
- Middle Tennessee State University M,O
- Midwestern State University M
- Minnesota State University Mankato M,D
- Missouri State University M*
- Molloy College M,O
- Montana State University M,O
- Mountain State University M,O*
- Murray State University M
- Northern Arizona University M
- Northern Kentucky University M,O
- North Georgia College & State University M
- Oakland University M,O
- Old Dominion University M
- Oregon Health & Science University M,O*
- Otterbein College M,O
- Pace University M,D,O*
- Pacific Lutheran University M
- Prairie View A&M University M
- Queen's University at Kingston M,D,O
- Quinnipiac University M,O*
- Radford University M
- Regis College (MA) M,O
- Regis University P,M,D,O
- Research College of Nursing M
- Rivier College M
- Rush University M,D,O
- Rutgers, The State University of New Jersey, Newark M*
- Sacred Heart University M
- Sage Graduate School M,O
- Saginaw Valley State University M
- St. John Fisher College M,O
- Saint Joseph College M,O
- Saint Xavier University M,O
- Samford University M,D
- Samuel Merritt University M,O
- San Francisco State University M
- Seattle Pacific University M,O
- Shenandoah University M,O
- Sonoma State University M
- Southern Adventist University M
- Southern Illinois University Edwardsville M,O
- Southern University and Agricultural and Mechanical College M,D,O
- Spalding University M
- State University of New York Downstate Medical Center M,O*
- State University of New York Institute of Technology M,O
- State University of New York Upstate Medical University M,O
- Stony Brook University, State University of New York M,O
- Tennessee State University M
- Texas A&M University–Corpus Christi M
- Texas Tech University Health Sciences Center M,D,O
- Texas Woman's University M,D
- Uniformed Services University of the Health Sciences M*
- Union University M,D,O
- Universidad del Turabo M,O
- University at Buffalo, the State University of New York M,D,O*
- The University of Alabama in Huntsville M,D,O
- University of Alaska Anchorage M,O
- The University of Arizona M,D,O*
- University of Central Arkansas M
- University of Central Florida M,D,O*
- University of Colorado at Colorado Springs M,D
- University of Delaware M,O*
- University of Detroit Mercy M,O
- University of Hawaii at Manoa M,D,O*
- University of Illinois at Chicago M*
- The University of Kansas M,D,O*
- University of Louisville M,D
- University of Mary M
- University of Massachusetts Lowell M
- University of Massachusetts Worcester M,D,O
- University of Medicine and Dentistry of New Jersey M,D,O*
- University of Miami M,D*
- University of Michigan M,O*
- University of Minnesota, Twin Cities Campus M*
- University of Missouri–Kansas City M,D*
- University of Missouri–St. Louis M,D,O
- University of Nevada, Las Vegas M,D,O
- The University of North Carolina at Chapel Hill M,D,O*
- The University of North Carolina Wilmington M
- University of Northern Colorado M,D
- University of Pennsylvania M,O*
- University of Phoenix M
- University of Phoenix–Bay Area Campus M
- University of Phoenix–Hawaii Campus M
- University of Phoenix–Minneapolis/St. Louis Park Campus M
- University of Phoenix–Phoenix Campus M,O
- University of Phoenix–Sacramento Valley Campus M
- University of Phoenix–Southern Arizona Campus M,O
- University of Phoenix–Southern California Campus M,O
- University of Pittsburgh M,D*
- University of Puerto Rico, Medical Sciences Campus M
- University of Rhode Island M,D
- University of Rochester M,D,O*
- University of St. Francis (IL) M,D
- University of San Diego M,D
- University of San Francisco D
- The University of Scranton M,O
- University of South Carolina M
- University of Southern Maine M,O
- University of Southern Mississippi M,D
- The University of Tampa M
- The University of Tennessee at Chattanooga M,O
- The University of Texas at Arlington M,D*
- The University of Texas at El Paso M,O
- The University of Texas at Tyler M,D
- The University of Texas–Pan American M
- The University of Toledo M,O
- University of Victoria M,D

University of Wisconsin–Milwaukee	M,D,O
University of Wisconsin–Oshkosh	M
Vanderbilt University	M,D*
Virginia Commonwealth University	M,O
Wagner College	O
Western University of Health Sciences	M
Westminster College (UT)	M
Wichita State University	M*
Wilmington University	M
Winona State University	M,D,O
Wright State University	M

FILM, TELEVISION, AND VIDEO PRODUCTION

Academy of Art University	M
American Film Institute Conservatory	M
American University	M*
Antioch University McGregor	M
Arizona State University	M
Art Center College of Design	M*
The Art Institute of California–San Francisco	M
Bob Jones University	P,M,D,O
Boston University	M*
Bowling Green State University	M,D*
Brigham Young University	M*
Brooklyn College of the City University of New York	M
California College of the Arts	M*
California Institute of the Arts	M,O
California State University, Fullerton	M
California State University, Los Angeles	M
California State University, Northridge	M
Carleton University	M
Carnegie Mellon University	M*
Central Michigan University	M
Chapman University	M
Chatham University	M
Columbia College Chicago	M
Columbia University	M*
Concordia University (Canada)	M
Drexel University	M*
Florida Atlantic University	M,O
Florida State University	M*
George Mason University	M*
Georgia State University	M,D
Hofstra University	M*
Hollins University	M
Howard University	M
Humboldt State University	M
Loyola Marymount University	M
Marywood University	M,O
Massachusetts College of Art and Design	M
Miami International University of Art & Design	M*
Minneapolis College of Art and Design	M
Montana State University	M
New York Film Academy	M
New York University	M*
Northwestern University	M,D*
Ohio University	M*
Polytechnic Institute of NYU	O
Regent University	M,D
Rochester Institute of Technology	M
St. Thomas University	M
San Diego State University	M*
San Francisco Art Institute	M,O*
San Francisco State University	M
San Jose State University	M
Savannah College of Art and Design	M*
School of the Art Institute of Chicago	M*
School of Visual Arts	M
Southern Methodist University	M*
Syracuse University	M*
Temple University	M*
The University of Alabama	M
The University of British Columbia	M,O
University of California, Los Angeles	M,D,O*
University of California, Santa Barbara	D
University of Central Arkansas	M
University of Central Florida	M*
University of Denver	M*
The University of Iowa	M*
University of Memphis	M,D
University of Miami	M,D*
University of Nevada, Las Vegas	M
University of New Orleans	M
The University of North Carolina at Greensboro	M
University of North Carolina School of the Arts	M
University of North Texas	M
University of Oklahoma	M*
University of Southern California	M,O*
The University of Texas at Austin	M,D
University of the Sacred Heart	M
University of Utah	M*
University of Victoria	M
University of Wisconsin–Milwaukee	M
York University	M,D

FILM, TELEVISION, AND VIDEO THEORY AND CRITICISM

Boston University	M*
California College of the Arts	M*
Central Michigan University	M
Claremont Graduate University	M,D*
College of Staten Island of the City University of New York	M
Concordia University (Canada)	M
Emory University	M,D,O*
Florida Atlantic University	M,O
Hollins University	M
Indiana University Bloomington	M,D*
New York University	M,D*
The Ohio State University	M*
Ohio University	M*
San Francisco State University	M
Savannah College of Art and Design	M*
Syracuse University	M*
Université de Montréal	M,D
Université Laval	M,D
The University of British Columbia	M,O
University of Chicago	M,D*
The University of Iowa	M,D*
The University of Kansas	M,D*
University of Miami	M,D*
University of Michigan	D,O*
University of Southern California	M,D*
University of Wisconsin–Madison	M,D*
Wilfrid Laurier University	M,D
Yale University	D*

FINANCE AND BANKING

Adelphi University	M*
Alliant International University–San Diego	M,D*
The American College	M
American College of Thessaloniki	M,O
American InterContinental University Buckhead Campus	M
American InterContinental University Online	M
American InterContinental University South Florida	M
American International College	M
American University	M,D,O*
The American University in Dubai	M
The American University of Paris	M
Andrew Jackson University	M
Andrews University	M
Argosy University, Atlanta	M,D*
Argosy University, Chicago	M,D*
Argosy University, Dallas	M,O*
Argosy University, Denver	M,D*
Argosy University, Hawai'i	M,D,O*
Argosy University, Inland Empire	M,D*
Argosy University, Los Angeles	M,D*
Argosy University, Nashville	M,D*
Argosy University, Orange County	M,D,O*
Argosy University, Phoenix	M,D*
Argosy University, Salt Lake City	M,D*
Argosy University, San Diego	M,D*
Argosy University, San Francisco Bay Area	M,D*
Argosy University, Sarasota	M,D,O*
Argosy University, Schaumburg	M,D,O*
Argosy University, Seattle	M,D*
Argosy University, Tampa	M,D*
Argosy University, Twin Cities	M,D*
Argosy University, Washington DC	M,D,O*
Arizona State University	M,D
Aspen University	M,O
Assumption College	M,O
Auburn University	M*
Avila University	M
Baker College Center for Graduate Studies	M
Barry University	O*
Bayamón Central University	M
Benedictine University	M
Bentley University	M
Bernard M. Baruch College of the City University of New York	M,D
Boston College	M,D*
Boston University	P,M,D,O*
Brandeis University	M,D
Bridgewater State College	M
British American College London	M
California College of the Arts	M*
California Intercontinental University	M,D
California Lutheran University	M,O
California State University, East Bay	M
California State University, Fullerton	M
California State University, Los Angeles	M
California State University, Stanislaus	M
Capella University	M,D,O
Carnegie Mellon University	D*
Case Western Reserve University	M,D*
Central European University	M*
Central Michigan University	M
Charleston Southern University	M
Christian Brothers University	M,O
City University of Seattle	M,O
Clark University	M
Cleary University	M,O
Cleveland State University	M,D,O
College for Financial Planning	M
College of Santa Fe	M
Colorado Technical University Colorado Springs	M,D
Colorado Technical University Denver	M
Columbia Southern University	M
Columbia University	M,D*
Concordia University Wisconsin	M
Cornell University	D*
Curry College	M,O
Dalhousie University	M
Dallas Baptist University	M
Davenport University	M
Davenport University	M
Davenport University	M
DePaul University	M,O*
DeSales University	M
DeVry University	M*
Dowling College	M,O
Drexel University	M,D,O*
Eastern Michigan University	M,O
East Tennessee State University	M
Emory University	M,D*
Fairfield University	M,O*
Fairleigh Dickinson University, College at Florham	M,O*
Fairleigh Dickinson University, Metropolitan Campus	M,O*
Florida Agricultural and Mechanical University	M
Florida Atlantic University	M,D
Florida Institute of Technology	M*
Florida International University	M*
Florida State University	M,D*
Fordham University	M*
Gannon University	O
Georgetown University	D
The George Washington University	M,D*
Georgia Institute of Technology	M,D,O*
Georgia State University	M,D,O
Golden Gate University	M,D,O
Goldey-Beacom College	M
Graduate School and University Center of the City University of New York	D*
Grand Canyon University	M*
Hawai'i Pacific University	M*
HEC Montreal	M,O
Hofstra University	M*
Holy Family University	M

*M—master's degree; P—first professional degree; D—doctorate; O—other advanced degree; *—Close-Up and/or Announcement or Display in one of the other books in this series*

Holy Names University	M
Hood College	M
Howard University	M
Hult International Business School (United States)	M
Illinois Institute of Technology	P,M*
Indiana University Southeast	M
Instituto Centroamericano de Administración de Empresas	M
Instituto Tecnologico de Santo Domingo	M
Instituto Tecnológico y de Estudios Superiores de Monterrey, Campus Central de Veracruz	M
Instituto Tecnológico y de Estudios Superiores de Monterrey, Campus Ciudad de México	M,D
Instituto Tecnológico y de Estudios Superiores de Monterrey, Campus Ciudad Obregón	M
Instituto Tecnológico y de Estudios Superiores de Monterrey, Campus Cuernavaca	M
Instituto Tecnológico y de Estudios Superiores de Monterrey, Campus Estado de México	M,D
Instituto Tecnológico y de Estudios Superiores de Monterrey, Campus Guadalajara	M
Instituto Tecnológico y de Estudios Superiores de Monterrey, Campus Irapuato	M,D
Instituto Tecnológico y de Estudios Superiores de Monterrey, Campus Monterrey	M
Inter American University of Puerto Rico, Barranquitas Campus	M
Inter American University of Puerto Rico, Metropolitan Campus	M
Inter American University of Puerto Rico, Ponce Campus	M
Inter American University of Puerto Rico, San Germán Campus	M,D
International University in Geneva	M
The International University of Monaco	M
Iona College	M,O*
The Johns Hopkins University	M,O*
Johnson & Wales University	M,O
Jones International University	M
Kaplan University–Davenport Campus	M
Kent State University	D*
Kentucky State University	M
Lakeland College	M
Lamar University	M
La Sierra University	M,O
Lehigh University	M
Lewis University	M
Lincoln University (CA)	M
Lincoln University (PA)	M
Lindenwood University	M
Lipscomb University	M
Long Island University, C.W. Post Campus	M,O
Louisiana State University and Agricultural and Mechanical College	M,D
Louisiana Tech University	M,D
Loyola University Chicago	M*
Loyola University Maryland	M*
Manhattanville College	M*
Marylhurst University	M
Marywood University	M
McGill University	M,D,O*
Miami University	M*
Michigan State University	M,D*
MidAmerica Nazarene University	M
Minnesota State University Mankato	M
Mississippi College	M,O
Mississippi State University	M,D
Montclair State University	M,O*
Mount Saint Mary College	M
National University	M
New Jersey City University	M
The New School: A University	M*
New York Institute of Technology	M,O
New York University	M,D,O*
Northeastern Illinois University	M
Northeastern State University	M
Northeastern University	M*
Northern Kentucky University	M,O
Northwestern University	D*
Notre Dame College (OH)	M,O
Notre Dame de Namur University	M
Nova Southeastern University	M,D*
Oakland University	M,O
The Ohio State University	M,D*
Ohio University	M*
Oklahoma City University	M
Oklahoma State University	M,D*
Old Dominion University	M,D
Oral Roberts University	M
Ottawa University	M
Our Lady of the Lake University of San Antonio	M
Pace University	M*
Pacific States University	M,D
Pepperdine University	M*
Philadelphia University	M
Polytechnic Institute of NYU	M,O
Polytechnic Institute of NYU, Westchester Graduate Center	M,O
Pontifical Catholic University of Puerto Rico	M
Pontificia Universidad Catolica Madre y Maestra	M
Portland State University	M
Princeton University	M*
Providence College	M*
Purdue University	M
Queen's University at Kingston	M
Quinnipiac University	M*
Regis University	M,O
Rhode Island College	M,O
Robert Morris College	M
Rochester Institute of Technology	M
Rutgers, The State University of New Jersey, Newark	M,D,O*
Sage Graduate School	M
St. Bonaventure University	M
St. Cloud State University	M
St. Edward's University	M,O
St. John's University (NY)	M,O
Saint Joseph's University	M
Saint Louis University	M
Saint Mary's University (Canada)	M,D
St. Mary's University (United States)	M
Saint Peter's College	M
St. Thomas Aquinas College	M*
Saint Xavier University	M,O
Sam Houston State University	M
San Diego State University	M*
Schiller International University (United States)	M
Seattle University	M,O
Seton Hall University	M*
Simon Fraser University	M,D
Southeastern University	M
Southeast Missouri State University	M
Southern Adventist University	M
Southern Illinois University Edwardsville	M
Southern Methodist University	M*
Southern New Hampshire University	M,D,O*
Southwestern Adventist University	M
State University of New York at Binghamton	M,D*
Stevens Institute of Technology	M
Stony Brook University, State University of New York	M,O
Strayer University	M
Suffolk University	M,O*
Syracuse University	M,D*
Tarleton State University	M
Télé-université	M,D
Temple University	M,D*
Texas A&M International University	M
Texas A&M University	M,D*
Texas Tech University	M,D
TUI University	M,D
Union Graduate College	M,O
United States International University	M
Universidad Central del Este	M,D
Universidad de las Americas, A.C.	M
Universidad de las Américas–Puebla	M
Universidad Metropolitana	M
Université de Sherbrooke	M
Université du Québec à Montréal	O
Université du Québec à Trois-Rivières	O
Université du Québec en Outaouais	M,O
Université Laval	M,O
University at Albany, State University of New York	M*
University at Buffalo, the State University of New York	M,D,O*
The University of Akron	M
The University of Alabama	M,D
The University of Alabama in Huntsville	M,O
University of Alaska Fairbanks	M
University of Alberta	M,D*
The University of Arizona	M,D*
University of Baltimore	M
The University of British Columbia	D
University of California, Berkeley	D*
University of California, Santa Cruz	M*
University of Central Florida	D*
University of Cincinnati	D
University of Colorado at Boulder	M,D*
University of Colorado at Colorado Springs	M
University of Colorado Denver	M*
University of Connecticut	M,D,O*
University of Dallas	M
University of Dayton	M
University of Delaware	M*
University of Denver	M*
The University of Findlay	M
University of Florida	M,D,O*
University of Hawaii at Manoa	M,D*
University of Houston	M*
University of Houston–Clear Lake	M
University of Houston–Victoria	M
University of Illinois at Urbana–Champaign	M,D*
The University of Iowa	M,D*
University of La Verne	M
University of Lethbridge	M,D
University of Maryland University College	M,O
University of Massachusetts Dartmouth	M,O
University of Memphis	M,D
University of Miami	M*
University of Michigan–Dearborn	M*
University of Minnesota, Twin Cities Campus	M,D*
University of Missouri–St. Louis	M,O
University of Nebraska–Lincoln	M,D*
University of Nevada, Reno	M*
University of New Haven	M*
University of New Orleans	M,D
The University of North Carolina at Chapel Hill	D*
The University of North Carolina at Greensboro	M,O
University of North Texas	M,D
University of Oregon	D*
University of Ottawa	D,O*
University of Pennsylvania	M,D*
University of Pittsburgh	M,D*
University of Puerto Rico, Mayagüez Campus	M
University of Puerto Rico, Río Piedras	M,D
University of Rhode Island	D
University of San Francisco	M
University of Saskatchewan	M
The University of Scranton	M
University of South Florida	M*
The University of Tampa	M
The University of Tennessee	M,D
The University of Texas at Arlington	M,D*
The University of Texas at Austin	D
The University of Texas at Dallas	M,D*
The University of Texas at San Antonio	M,D*
The University of Texas–Pan American	D
University of the West	M
The University of Toledo	M
University of Tulsa	M*
University of Utah	M,D*
University of Virginia	M
University of Washington	M,D*
University of Washington, Tacoma	M
University of Waterloo	M,D
The University of Western Ontario	M,D

University of Wisconsin–Madison M,D*
University of Wisconsin–Whitewater M*
University of Wyoming M
Upper Iowa University M
Vanderbilt University M,D*
Villanova University M*
Virginia Commonwealth University M
Virginia Polytechnic Institute and State University M,D*
Wagner College M
Wake Forest University M*
Walden University M,D
Walsh College of Accountancy and Business Administration M
Washington State University M,D*
Washington University in St. Louis M*
Webster University M
Western International University M
Western Michigan University M*
West Texas A&M University M
Wilkes University M
Wilmington University M
Wright State University M
Xavier University M*
Yale University D*
York University M,D
Youngstown State University M

FINANCIAL ENGINEERING

Claremont Graduate University M*
Columbia University M,D,O*
HEC Montréal M
The International University of Monaco M
Kent State University M*
North Carolina State University M*
Polytechnic Institute of NYU M,O
Polytechnic Institute of NYU, Long Island Graduate Center M,O
Polytechnic Institute of NYU, Westchester Graduate Center M,O
Princeton University M,D*
Rensselaer Polytechnic Institute M,D
Stevens Institute of Technology M
Temple University M*
University of California, Berkeley M*
University of Hawaii at Manoa M*
University of Michigan M*
University of Tulsa M*

FIRE PROTECTION ENGINEERING

American Public University System M
Anna Maria College M
Oklahoma State University M,D*
University of Central Missouri M,O
University of Maryland, College Park M,O*
University of New Haven M*
Worcester Polytechnic Institute M,D,O*

FISH, GAME, AND WILDLIFE MANAGEMENT

Arkansas Tech University M
Auburn University M,D*
Brigham Young University M,D*
Clemson University M,D
Colorado State University M,D*
Cornell University M,D*
Frostburg State University M
Humboldt State University M
Iowa State University of Science and Technology M,D*
Louisiana State University and Agricultural and Mechanical College M,D
McGill University M,D*
Memorial University of Newfoundland M,O
Michigan State University M,D*
Mississippi State University M,D
Montana State University M,D
New Mexico Highlands University M
New Mexico State University M
North Carolina State University M,D*
Oregon State University M,D*
Penn State University Park M,D*
Purdue University M,D
South Dakota State University M,D
State University of New York College of Environmental Science and Forestry M,D
Sul Ross State University M*
Tennessee Technological University M*
Texas A&M University M,D*
Texas A&M University–Kingsville M,D
Texas State University–San Marcos M*
Texas Tech University M,D
Université du Québec à Rimouski M,D,O
University of Alaska Fairbanks M,D
The University of Arizona M,D*
University of Arkansas at Pine Bluff M
University of Delaware M,D*
University of Florida M,D*
University of Idaho M
University of Maine M,D*
University of Massachusetts Amherst M,D*
University of Miami M,D*
University of Missouri–Columbia M,D*
The University of Montana M,D
University of New Hampshire M*
University of North Dakota M,D
University of Rhode Island M,D
The University of Tennessee M
University of Washington M,D*
University of Wisconsin–Madison M,D*
Utah State University M,D
Virginia Polytechnic Institute and State University M,D*
West Virginia University M

FOLKLORE

George Mason University M*
The George Washington University M,D*
Indiana University Bloomington M,D*
Memorial University of Newfoundland M,D
University of Alberta M,D*
University of California, Berkeley M*
University of Louisiana at Lafayette M,D*
The University of North Carolina at Chapel Hill M*
University of Oregon M*
The University of Texas at Austin M,D
University of Wisconsin–Madison M,D*
Utah State University M

FOOD SCIENCE AND TECHNOLOGY

Alabama Agricultural and Mechanical University M,D
American University of Beirut M
Auburn University M,D*
Boston University M*
Brigham Young University M*
California State University, Fresno M
California State University, Long Beach M
Chapman University M
Clemson University M,D
Colorado State University M,D*
Cornell University M,D*
Dalhousie University M,D
Florida Agricultural and Mechanical University M
Florida State University M,D*
Framingham State College M
Illinois Institute of Technology M*
Iowa State University of Science and Technology M,D*
Kansas State University M,D*
Louisiana State University and Agricultural and Mechanical College M,D
McGill University M,D*
Memorial University of Newfoundland M,D
Michigan State University M,D*
Middle Tennessee State University M
Mississippi State University M,D
Montclair State University M,O*
New York University M,D*
North Carolina State University M,D*
North Dakota State University M,D
Nova Scotia Agricultural College M
The Ohio State University M,D*
Oklahoma State University M,D*
Oregon State University M,D*
Penn State University Park M,D*
Purdue University M,D
Rutgers, The State University of New Jersey, New Brunswick M,D*
South Dakota State University M
Texas A&M University M,D*
Texas Tech University M,D
Texas Woman's University M,D
Tuskegee University M
Universidad de las Américas–Puebla M
Université de Moncton M
Université Laval M,D
University of Arkansas M,D
The University of British Columbia M,D
University of California, Davis M,D*
University of Delaware M,D*
University of Florida M,D*
University of Georgia M,D*
University of Guelph M,D
University of Hawaii at Manoa M*
University of Idaho M,D
University of Illinois at Urbana–Champaign M,D*
University of Maine M,D*
University of Manitoba M,D
University of Maryland, College Park M,D*
University of Maryland Eastern Shore M,D*
University of Massachusetts Amherst M,D*
University of Minnesota, Twin Cities Campus M,D*
University of Missouri–Columbia M,D*
University of Nebraska–Lincoln M,D*
University of Puerto Rico, Mayagüez Campus M
University of Rhode Island M,D
University of Saskatchewan M,D
University of Southern California M,D,O*
University of Southern Mississippi M,D
The University of Tennessee M,D
The University of Tennessee at Martin M
University of Vermont D*
University of Wisconsin–Madison M,D*
University of Wisconsin–Stout M
University of Wyoming M
Utah State University M,D
Virginia Polytechnic Institute and State University M,D*
Washington State University M,D*
Wayne State University M,D*
West Virginia University M,D

FOREIGN LANGUAGES EDUCATION

The American University in Cairo M
Andrews University M,D,O
Appalachian State University M
Auburn University M,D,O*
Bennington College M
Boston College M*
Boston University M*
Bowling Green State University M*
Brigham Young University M*
Brooklyn College of the City University of New York M,O
California State University, Chico M
California State University, Sacramento M
Caribbean University M,D
Central Connecticut State University M,O
Christopher Newport University M
Cleveland State University M
The College at Brockport, State University of New York M,O
College of Charleston M*
The College of New Jersey M
The College of William and Mary M
The Colorado College M
Colorado State University M*
Colorado State University–Pueblo M
Cornell University M,D*
Delaware State University M
Duquesne University M*
Eastern Washington University M
Elms College M,O
Florida International University M,D,O*
Framingham State College M

*M—master's degree; P—first professional degree; D—doctorate; O—other advanced degree; *—Close-Up and/or Announcement or Display in one of the other books in this series*

George Mason University	M*
Georgia Southern University	M
Harding University	M,O
Hofstra University	M*
Hunter College of the City University of New York	M
Indiana University Bloomington	M,D*
Indiana University–Purdue University Indianapolis	M,O*
Inter American University of Puerto Rico, Arecibo Campus	M
Iona College	M*
Ithaca College	M
The Johns Hopkins University	M,O*
Kean University	M
Kent State University	M,D*
Long Island University, C.W. Post Campus	M
Louisiana Tech University	M,D
Manhattanville College	M*
Marquette University	M
McGill University	M,D,O*
Michigan State University	D*
Middle Tennessee State University	M
Mills College	M,D
Mississippi State University	M
Missouri State University	M*
Monterey Institute of International Studies	M*
New York University	M,D,O*
Northern Arizona University	M
Occidental College	M
Oregon State University	M*
Portland State University	M
Purdue University	M,D,O
Queens College of the City University of New York	M,O
Quinnipiac University	M*
Rhode Island College	M
Rider University	O*
Rivier College	M
Rutgers, The State University of New Jersey, New Brunswick	M,D*
St. John Fisher College	M
Shippensburg University of Pennsylvania	M
SIT Graduate Institute	M
Smith College	M
Southern Illinois University Edwardsville	M
Stanford University	M*
State University of New York at Binghamton	M*
State University of New York at Plattsburgh	M
State University of New York College at Cortland	M
Stony Brook University, State University of New York	M,O
Teachers College, Columbia University	M,D
Temple University	M,D*
Texas A&M International University	M,D
Texas A&M University–Kingsville	M
Union Graduate College	M
Universidad del Este	M
University at Buffalo, the State University of New York	M,D,O*
University of Arkansas at Little Rock	M
University of Calgary	M,D,O
University of California, Irvine	M,D*
University of Central Arkansas	M
University of Connecticut	M,D,O*
University of Delaware	M*
University of Georgia	M,D,O*
University of Hawaii at Manoa	M,D,O*
University of Illinois at Urbana–Champaign	M,D*
University of Indianapolis	M
The University of Iowa	M,D*
University of Kentucky	M
University of Maine	M*
University of Maryland, College Park	M,D*
University of Massachusetts Amherst	M*
University of Massachusetts Boston	M
University of Michigan	M,D*
University of Minnesota, Twin Cities Campus	M*
University of Missouri–Columbia	M,D,O*
University of Nebraska at Kearney	M
University of Nebraska at Omaha	M
University of Nevada, Reno	M*
The University of North Carolina at Chapel Hill	M*
The University of North Carolina at Charlotte	M*
The University of North Carolina at Greensboro	M,D,O
University of Northern Colorado	M
University of Pittsburgh	M,D*
University of Puerto Rico, Río Piedras	M,D
University of San Diego	M
University of South Carolina	M,D
University of Southern Mississippi	M
University of South Florida	M,D,O*
The University of Tennessee	M,D,O
The University of Texas at Austin	M,D
The University of Toledo	M
University of Utah	M,D*
University of Vermont	M*
University of Victoria	M
University of Virginia	M,D,O
University of West Georgia	M,O
University of Wisconsin–Madison	M,D*
Vanderbilt University	M,D*
Virginia Polytechnic Institute and State University	M*
Washington State University	M*
Wayne State University	M,D,O*
West Chester University of Pennsylvania	M,O
Worcester State College	M

FORENSIC NURSING

Boston College	M,D*
Cleveland State University	M
Duquesne University	M,O*
Fitchburg State College	M,O
University of Colorado at Colorado Springs	M,D
Vanderbilt University	M,D*

FORENSIC PSYCHOLOGY

Alliant International University–Fresno	D*
Alliant International University–Irvine	D*
Alliant International University–Los Angeles	D*
American International College	M
Argosy University, Chicago	D*
Argosy University, Denver	M,D*
Argosy University, Inland Empire	M,D*
Argosy University, Orange County	M*
Argosy University, Phoenix	M*
Argosy University, San Francisco Bay Area	M*
Argosy University, Sarasota	M,D,O*
Argosy University, Schaumburg	M,D,O*
Argosy University, Twin Cities	M,D,O*
Argosy University, Washington DC	M,D*
California Baptist University	M
Cambridge College	M,O
Castleton State College	M
The Chicago School of Professional Psychology	M,D
The Chicago School of Professional Psychology: Downtown Los Angeles Campus	D
The Chicago School of Professional Psychology: Online	M,O
College of Saint Elizabeth	M,O
Drexel University	D*
Fairleigh Dickinson University, Metropolitan Campus	M*
Holy Names University	M,O
John Jay College of Criminal Justice of the City University of New York	M,D
Marymount University	M
Massachusetts School of Professional Psychology	M,D,O
Oklahoma State University Center for Health Sciences	M,O
Prairie View A&M University	M,D
Roger Williams University	M*
Sage Graduate School	M,O
Tiffin University	M
Universidad de Iberoamerica	P,M
University of Massachusetts Boston	M,O
University of North Dakota	M,D
Walden University	M,D,O

FORENSIC SCIENCES

Alliant International University–Irvine	D*
Arcadia University	M
Cedar Crest College	M
Chaminade University of Honolulu	M
Duquesne University	M*
Florida Gulf Coast University	M
Florida International University	M*
George Mason University	M,D,O*
The George Washington University	M*
John Jay College of Criminal Justice of the City University of New York	M,D
McGill University	M,D,O*
Mercyhurst College	M
Michigan State University	M,D*
National University	M
Nebraska Wesleyan University	M
Oklahoma State University Center for Health Sciences	M,O
Pace University	M*
Philadelphia College of Osteopathic Medicine	M*
Sam Houston State University	M,D
Southeast Missouri State University	M
Southern Utah University	M
Stevenson University	M
Syracuse University	M*
Towson University	M
Universidad del Turabo	M
University at Albany, State University of New York	M,D*
The University of Alabama at Birmingham	M*
University of California, Davis	M*
University of Central Florida	M,D,O*
University of Florida	M,O*
University of Illinois at Chicago	M*
University of Nevada, Las Vegas	M,O
University of New Haven	M*
University of North Texas Health Science Center at Fort Worth	M,D
University of Rhode Island	M,D,O
Virginia Commonwealth University	M
West Virginia University	M,D

FORESTRY

Auburn University	M,D*
California Polytechnic State University, San Luis Obispo	M
Clemson University	M,D
Colorado State University	M,D*
Cornell University	M,D*
Duke University	M*
Harvard University	M*
Humboldt State University	M
Iowa State University of Science and Technology	M,D*
Lakehead University	M,D
Louisiana State University and Agricultural and Mechanical College	M,D
McGill University	M,D*
Michigan State University	M,D*
Michigan Technological University	M,D
Mississippi State University	M,D
North Carolina State University	M,D*
Northern Arizona University	M,D
Oklahoma State University	M,D*
Oregon State University	M,D*
Penn State University Park	M,D*
Purdue University	M,D
Southern Illinois University Carbondale	M*
Southern University and Agricultural and Mechanical College	M
State University of New York College of Environmental Science and Forestry	M,D
Stephen F. Austin State University	M,D
Texas A&M University	M,D*
Tropical Agriculture Research and Higher Education Center	M,D
Université du Québec en Abitibi-Témiscamingue	M,D
Université Laval	M,D
University of Alberta	M,D*
The University of Arizona	M,D*
University of Arkansas at Monticello	M

The University of British Columbia	M,D
University of California, Berkeley	M,D*
University of Florida	M,D*
University of Georgia	M,D*
University of Idaho	M
University of Kentucky	M
University of Maine	M,D*
University of Massachusetts Amherst	M,D*
University of Michigan	M,D,O*
University of Missouri–Columbia	M,D*
The University of Montana	M,D
University of New Brunswick Fredericton	M,D
University of New Hampshire	M*
The University of Tennessee	M
University of Toronto	M,D
University of Vermont	M,D*
University of Washington	M,D*
University of Wisconsin–Madison	M,D*
Utah State University	M,D
Virginia Polytechnic Institute and State University	M,D*
West Virginia University	M,D
Yale University	M,D*

FOUNDATIONS AND PHILOSOPHY OF EDUCATION

Antioch University New England	M*
Arizona State University	M
Arkansas State University	M,D,O
Ashland University	M
Ball State University	D*
Bank Street College of Education	M*
Brigham Young University	M,D*
Central Connecticut State University	M
Chicago State University	M
Curry College	M,O
Duquesne University	M*
Eastern Michigan University	M
Eastern Washington University	M
Fairfield University	M,O*
Fairleigh Dickinson University, Metropolitan Campus	M*
Florida Atlantic University	M
Florida State University	M,D,O*
George Fox University	M,D,O*
Georgia State University	M,D
Harvard University	M,O*
Hofstra University	M,O*
Indiana University Bloomington	M,D,O*
Iowa State University of Science and Technology	M,D*
Kent State University	M,D*
McGill University	M,D,O*
Millersville University of Pennsylvania	M
Montclair State University	M,D,O*
Mount Saint Vincent University	M
New York University	M,D*
Niagara University	M
Northeastern State University	M
Northern Arizona University	M,D
Northern Illinois University	M,D,O
Oakland University	M
Penn State University Park	M,D*
Purdue University	M,D,O
Regis University	M,O
Rutgers, The State University of New Jersey, New Brunswick	M,D*
Saint Louis University	M,D
Simon Fraser University	M,D
Southeast Missouri State University	M
Southern Connecticut State University	O
Southern Illinois University Edwardsville	M
Stanford University	M,D*
State University of New York at Binghamton	D*
Suffolk University	M,O*
Syracuse University	M,D*
Teachers College, Columbia University	M,D
Texas A&M University	M,D*
The University of British Columbia	M,D
University of Calgary	M,D,O
University of California, Berkeley	M,D*
University of Cincinnati	M,D
University of Connecticut	D*
University of Florida	M,D,O*
University of Georgia	M,D,O*
University of Hawaii at Manoa	M,D*
University of Houston	M,D*
University of Houston–Clear Lake	M
The University of Iowa	M,D,O*
The University of Kansas	D*
University of Manitoba	M
University of Maryland, College Park	M,D,O*
University of Michigan	M,D*
University of Minnesota, Twin Cities Campus	M,D,O*
University of New Mexico	M,D*
University of Oklahoma	M,D*
University of Pittsburgh	M,D*
University of Saskatchewan	M,D,O
University of South Africa	M,D
University of South Carolina	D
The University of Tennessee	M,D,O
The University of Texas of the Permian Basin	M
The University of Toledo	M,D
University of Utah	M,D*
University of Victoria	M,D
University of Virginia	M,D
University of Washington	M,D*
The University of West Alabama	M
University of Wisconsin–Milwaukee	M,D
Wayne State University	M,D,O*
Western Illinois University	M
Widener University	M,D*
Wilfrid Laurier University	M
Youngstown State University	M,D

FRENCH

American University	O*
Arizona State University	M,D
Asbury College	M,O
Bennington College	M
Boston College	M,D*
Boston University	M,D*
Bowling Green State University	M*
Brigham Young University	M*
Brooklyn College of the City University of New York	M,D
Brown University	D*
Bryn Mawr College	M,D*
California State University, Fullerton	M
California State University, Long Beach	M
California State University, Los Angeles	M
California State University, Sacramento	M
Carleton University	M
Case Western Reserve University	M*
Central Connecticut State University	M,O
Cleveland State University	M
Columbia University	M,D*
Concordia University (Canada)	M,O
Cornell University	D*
Dalhousie University	M,D
Duke University	D*
Eastern Michigan University	M,O
Emory University	D,O*
Florida Atlantic University	M
Florida State University	M,D*
Georgia State University	M,O
Graduate School and University Center of the City University of New York	D*
Harvard University	M,D*
Hofstra University	M*
Howard University	M
Hunter College of the City University of New York	M
Illinois State University	M
Indiana University Bloomington	M,D*
The Johns Hopkins University	D*
Kansas State University	M*
Kent State University	M,D*
Louisiana State University and Agricultural and Mechanical College	M,D
McGill University	M,D*
McMaster University	M
Memorial University of Newfoundland	M
Miami University	M*
Michigan State University	M,D*
Middlebury College	M,D
Millersville University of Pennsylvania	M
Minnesota State University Mankato	M
Mississippi State University	M
Missouri State University	M*
Montclair State University	M,O*
New York University	M,D,O*
North Carolina State University	M*
Northern Illinois University	M
Northwestern University	D,O*
The Ohio State University	M,D*
Ohio University	M*
Penn State University Park	M,D*
Portland State University	M
Princeton University	D*
Purdue University	M,D
Queens College of the City University of New York	M
Queen's University at Kingston	M,D
Rice University	M,D
Rider University	O*
Rutgers, The State University of New Jersey, New Brunswick	M,D*
Saint Louis University	M
San Francisco State University	M
San Jose State University	M
Simon Fraser University	M
Smith College	M
Stanford University	M,D*
State University of New York at Binghamton	M*
Stony Brook University, State University of New York	M
Syracuse University	M*
Texas Tech University	M
Tufts University	M*
Tulane University	M,D
Université de Moncton	M,D
Université de Montréal	M,D
Université de Sherbrooke	M,D
Université du Québec à Chicoutimi	O
University at Albany, State University of New York	M,D*
University at Buffalo, the State University of New York	M,D*
The University of Alabama	M,D
University of Alberta	M,D*
The University of Arizona	M*
University of Arkansas	M
The University of British Columbia	M,D
University of California, Berkeley	D*
University of California, Davis	D*
University of California, Irvine	M,D*
University of California, Los Angeles	M,D*
University of California, San Diego	M*
University of California, Santa Barbara	M,D
University of Chicago	M,D*
University of Cincinnati	M,D
University of Colorado at Boulder	M,D*
University of Connecticut	M,D*
University of Delaware	M*
University of Florida	M,D*
University of Georgia	M*
University of Guelph	M
University of Hawaii at Manoa	M*
University of Houston	M,D*
University of Illinois at Chicago	M*
University of Illinois at Urbana–Champaign	M,D*
The University of Iowa	M,D*
The University of Kansas	M,D*
University of Kentucky	M
University of Lethbridge	M,D
University of Louisiana at Lafayette	M,D*
University of Louisville	M
University of Maine	M*
University of Manitoba	M,D
University of Maryland, College Park	M,D*
University of Massachusetts Amherst	M*
University of Memphis	M
University of Miami	D*
University of Michigan	D*
University of Minnesota, Twin Cities Campus	M,D*
University of Mississippi	M
University of Missouri–Columbia	M,D*
The University of Montana	M
University of Nebraska–Lincoln	M,D*
University of Nevada, Reno	M*
University of New Mexico	M,D*
The University of North Carolina at Chapel Hill	M,D*
The University of North Carolina at Greensboro	M
University of Northern Iowa	M
University of North Texas	M
University of Notre Dame	M*
University of Oklahoma	M,D*
University of Oregon	M*
University of Ottawa	M,D*
University of Pennsylvania	M,D*
University of Pittsburgh	M,D*
University of Regina	M
University of Saskatchewan	M
University of South Africa	M,D

*M—master's degree; P—first professional degree; D—doctorate; O—other advanced degree; *—Close-Up and/or Announcement or Display in one of the other books in this series*

University of South Carolina	M,D
University of South Florida	M*
The University of Tennessee	M,D
The University of Texas at Arlington	M*
The University of Texas at Austin	M,D
The University of Toledo	M
University of Toronto	M,D
University of Utah	M,D*
University of Vermont	M*
University of Victoria	M
University of Virginia	M,D
University of Washington	M,D*
University of Waterloo	M,D
The University of Western Ontario	M,D
University of Wisconsin–Madison	M,D,O*
University of Wisconsin–Milwaukee	M,O
University of Wyoming	M
Vanderbilt University	M,D*
Washington University in St. Louis	M,D*
Wayne State University	M*
West Chester University of Pennsylvania	M,O
West Virginia University	M
Yale University	M,D*
York University	M

GENDER STUDIES

The American University in Cairo	M,O
Arizona State University	D
Brandeis University	M
Carnegie Mellon University	M,D*
Central European University	M,D*
Central Michigan University	M
Cornell University	M,D*
Eastern Michigan University	M
George Mason University	M*
Indiana University Bloomington	D*
Indiana University–Purdue University Indianapolis	M*
Memorial University of Newfoundland	M,D
Northwestern University	*
Queen's University at Kingston	M,D
Roosevelt University	M,O
Rutgers, The State University of New Jersey, New Brunswick	M,D*
Simmons College	M
University of Florida	M,O*
The University of North Carolina at Greensboro	M,O
University of Northern British Columbia	M,D,O
University of Northern Iowa	M
University of Saskatchewan	M,D
Virginia Commonwealth University	O

GENETIC COUNSELING

Arcadia University	M
Brandeis University	M
California State University, Stanislaus	M
Case Western Reserve University	M*
The Johns Hopkins University	M,D*
McGill University	M,D*
Mount Sinai School of Medicine of New York University	M,D
Northwestern University	M*
Sarah Lawrence College	M*
University of Arkansas for Medical Sciences	M
The University of British Columbia	M
University of California, Irvine	M*
University of Cincinnati	M
University of Colorado Denver	M*
University of Minnesota, Twin Cities Campus	M,D*
The University of North Carolina at Greensboro	M
University of Oklahoma Health Sciences Center	M
University of Pittsburgh	M*
University of South Carolina	M
The University of Texas Health Science Center at Houston	M
University of Toronto	M,D
University of Wisconsin–Madison	M*

GENETICS

Albert Einstein College of Medicine	D
Baylor College of Medicine	D*
Brandeis University	M,D
California Institute of Technology	D*
Carnegie Mellon University	M,D*
Case Western Reserve University	D*
Clemson University	M,D
Columbia University	M,D*
Cornell University	D*
Dartmouth College	D*
Drexel University	M,D*
Duke University	D*
Emory University	D*
Florida State University	M,D*
The George Washington University	D*
Harvard University	D*
Illinois State University	M,D
Indiana University Bloomington	M,D*
Iowa State University of Science and Technology	M,D*
The Johns Hopkins University	M,D*
Kansas State University	M,D*
Marquette University	M,D
Massachusetts Institute of Technology	D*
Mayo Graduate School	D*
McMaster University	M,D
Medical University of South Carolina	M,D
Michigan State University	M,D*
Mississippi State University	M,D
New York University	M,D*
North Carolina State University	M,D*
Northwestern University	D*
The Ohio State University	M,D*
Oregon Health & Science University	D*
Oregon State University	M,D*
Penn State Hershey Medical Center	M,D
Penn State University Park	M,D*
Purdue University	M,D
Rutgers, The State University of New Jersey, New Brunswick	M,D*
Stanford University	D*
Stony Brook University, State University of New York	D
Temple University	D*
Texas A&M University	M,D*
Thomas Jefferson University	D*
Tufts University	D*
Université de Montréal	O
Université du Québec à Chicoutimi	M
University at Albany, State University of New York	M,D*
The University of Alabama at Birmingham	D*
University of Alberta	M,D*
The University of Arizona	M,D*
The University of British Columbia	M,D
University of California, Davis	M,D*
University of California, Irvine	D*
University of California, Riverside	D*
University of California, San Diego	D*
University of California, San Francisco	D
University of Chicago	D*
University of Colorado at Boulder	M,D*
University of Colorado Denver	M,D*
University of Connecticut	M,D*
University of Connecticut Health Center	D*
University of Delaware	M,D*
University of Florida	D*
University of Georgia	M,D*
University of Hawaii at Manoa	M,D*
University of Illinois at Chicago	D*
The University of Iowa	M,D*
University of Miami	M,D*
University of Minnesota, Twin Cities Campus	M,D*
University of Missouri–Columbia	M,D*
University of Missouri–St. Louis	M,D,O
University of Nebraska Medical Center	M,D*
University of New Hampshire	M,D*
University of New Mexico	M,D*
The University of North Carolina at Chapel Hill	M,D*
University of North Dakota	M,D
University of North Texas Health Science Center at Fort Worth	M,D
University of Notre Dame	M,D*
University of Oregon	M,D*
University of Pennsylvania	D*
University of Rochester	M,D*
University of Southern California	M,D*
The University of Tennessee	M,D
The University of Texas Health Science Center at Houston	M,D
The University of Texas Medical Branch	D*
The University of Texas Southwestern Medical Center at Dallas	D*
University of Toronto	M,D
University of Washington	M,D*
University of Wisconsin–Madison	M,D*
University of Wyoming	D
Virginia Commonwealth University	M,D
Virginia Polytechnic Institute and State University	M,D*
Washington State University	M,D*
Washington University in St. Louis	M,D,O*
Wayne State University	M,D*
Wesleyan University	D*
West Virginia University	M,D
Yale University	D*

GENOMIC SCIENCES

Albert Einstein College of Medicine	D
Case Western Reserve University	D*
Concordia University (Canada)	M,D,O
The George Washington University	M*
Harvard University	D*
Medical College of Georgia	D
North Carolina State University	M,D*
North Dakota State University	M,D
Texas Tech University	M
University of California, Riverside	D*
University of California, San Francisco	D
University of Chicago	D*
University of Cincinnati	M,D
University of Connecticut	M*
University of Florida	D*
University of Pennsylvania	D*
The University of Tennessee	M,D
The University of Tennessee–Oak Ridge National Laboratory Graduate School of Genome Science and Technology	M,D
The University of Toledo	M,O
University of Washington	D*
Wake Forest University	D*
West Virginia University	M,D
Yale University	D*

GEOCHEMISTRY

California Institute of Technology	M,D*
California State University, Fullerton	M
Colorado School of Mines	M,D
Columbia University	M,D*
Cornell University	M,D*
Georgia Institute of Technology	M,D*
Indiana University Bloomington	M,D*
Massachusetts Institute of Technology	M,D*
McMaster University	M,D
Missouri University of Science and Technology	M,D
Montana Tech of The University of Montana	M
New Mexico Institute of Mining and Technology	M,D
Ohio University	M*
Penn State University Park	M,D*
Rensselaer Polytechnic Institute	M,D
University of California, Los Angeles	M,D
University of Hawaii at Manoa	M,D*
University of Michigan	M,D*
University of Nevada, Reno	M,D*
University of New Hampshire	M*
The University of Texas at Dallas	M,D*
University of Wisconsin–Milwaukee	M,D
Woods Hole Oceanographic Institution	M,D,O
Yale University	D*

GEODETIC SCIENCES

Columbia University	M,D*
George Mason University	M,D,O*
The Ohio State University	M,D*
Université Laval	M,D
University of New Brunswick Fredericton	M,D,O

GEOGRAPHIC INFORMATION SYSTEMS

Acadia University	M
Appalachian State University	M
Arizona State University	M,D
Boston University	M,D*
Clark University	M
Cleveland State University	M,D,O
Eastern Michigan University	M,O
Florida State University	M,D*
George Mason University	M,D,O*
Georgia Institute of Technology	M,D*
Georgia State University	O
Hunter College of the City University of New York	M,O
Idaho State University	M,O
Indiana University–Purdue University Indianapolis	M,O*
Montclair State University	M,D,O*
North Carolina State University	M,D*
Northern Arizona University	M,O
Northwest Missouri State University	M,O
Saint Louis University	M,D,O
Saint Mary's University of Minnesota	M,O
Salisbury University	M
San Jose State University	M,O
Texas State University–San Marcos	M,D*
Université du Québec à Montréal	O
Université Laval	M,O
University at Albany, State University of New York	M,O*
University at Buffalo, the State University of New York	M,D,O*
The University of Akron	M
University of Central Arkansas	M,O
University of Colorado Denver	M,D*
University of Connecticut	M,D,O*
University of Denver	M,O*
University of Lethbridge	M,D
University of Maryland, Baltimore County	M,O*
University of Minnesota, Twin Cities Campus	M*
The University of Montana	M
The University of North Carolina at Greensboro	M,D,O
University of Pittsburgh	M,D*
University of Redlands	M
University of Southern California	M,O*
The University of Texas at Dallas	M,D*
The University of Toledo	M,O
University of West Georgia	O
University of Wisconsin–Madison	M,D,O*
University of Wisconsin–Milwaukee	M,O
Virginia Commonwealth University	O
West Chester University of Pennsylvania	M,O
Western Illinois University	M,O
West Virginia University	M,D

GEOGRAPHY

Appalachian State University	M
Arizona State University	M,D
Auburn University	M*
Boston University	M,D*
Brigham Young University	M*
Brock University	M
California State University, Chico	M
California State University, East Bay	M
California State University, Fullerton	M
California State University, Long Beach	M
California State University, Los Angeles	M
California State University, Northridge	M
Carleton University	M,D
Central Connecticut State University	M
Chicago State University	M
Clark University	M,D
Concordia University (Canada)	M,D,O
East Carolina University	M
Eastern Michigan University	M,O
Florida Atlantic University	M
Florida State University	M,D*
Fort Hays State University	M
George Mason University	M*
The George Washington University	M*
Georgia State University	M
Hunter College of the City University of New York	M,O
Indiana State University	M,D
Indiana University Bloomington	M,D*
Indiana University of Pennsylvania	M
The Johns Hopkins University	M,D*
Kansas State University	M,D*
Kent State University	M,D*
Louisiana State University and Agricultural and Mechanical College	M,D
Marshall University	M
McGill University	M,D*
McMaster University	M,D
Memorial University of Newfoundland	M,D
Miami University	M*
Michigan State University	M,D*
Minnesota State University Mankato	M
Missouri State University	M*
New Mexico State University	M
Northeastern Illinois University	M
Northern Arizona University	M,O
Northern Illinois University	M
Northwest Missouri State University	M,O
The Ohio State University	M,D*
Ohio University	M*
Oklahoma State University	M,D*
Oregon State University	M,D*
Portland State University	M,D
Queen's University at Kingston	M,D
Rutgers, The State University of New Jersey, New Brunswick	M,D*
St. Cloud State University	M
Salem State College	M
San Diego State University	M,D*
San Francisco State University	M
San Jose State University	M,O
Shippensburg University of Pennsylvania	M
Simon Fraser University	M,D
South Dakota State University	M
Southern Illinois University Carbondale	M,D*
Southern Illinois University Edwardsville	M
State University of New York at Binghamton	M*
Syracuse University	M,D*
Temple University	M*
Texas A&M University	M,D*
Texas State University–San Marcos	M,D*
Towson University	M
Trent University	M,D
Université de Montréal	M,D,O
Université de Sherbrooke	M,D
Université du Québec à Montréal	M
Université Laval	M,D
University at Albany, State University of New York	M,O*
University at Buffalo, the State University of New York	M,D,O*
The University of Akron	M
The University of Alabama	M
The University of Arizona	M,D*
University of Arkansas	M
The University of British Columbia	M,D
University of Calgary	M,D
University of California, Berkeley	D*
University of California, Davis	M,D*
University of California, Los Angeles	M,D*
University of California, Santa Barbara	M,D
University of Central Arkansas	M,O
University of Cincinnati	M,D
University of Colorado at Boulder	M,D*
University of Colorado at Colorado Springs	M
University of Connecticut	M,D,O*
University of Delaware	M,D*
University of Denver	M,D*
University of Florida	M,D*
University of Georgia	M,D*
University of Guelph	M,D
University of Hawaii at Manoa	M,D,O*
University of Idaho	M,D
University of Illinois at Chicago	M*
University of Illinois at Urbana–Champaign	M,D*
The University of Iowa	M,D*
The University of Kansas	M,D*
University of Kentucky	M,D
University of Lethbridge	M,D
University of Manitoba	M,D
University of Maryland, Baltimore County	M,D*
University of Maryland, College Park	M,D*
University of Massachusetts Amherst	M*
University of Miami	M*
University of Minnesota, Twin Cities Campus	M,D*
University of Missouri–Columbia	M*
The University of Montana	M
University of Nebraska at Omaha	M,O
University of Nebraska–Lincoln	M,D*
University of Nevada, Reno	M,D*
University of New Mexico	M*
University of New Orleans	M
The University of North Carolina at Chapel Hill	M,D*
The University of North Carolina at Charlotte	M,D*
The University of North Carolina at Greensboro	M,D,O
University of North Dakota	M
University of Northern Iowa	M
University of North Texas	M
University of Oklahoma	M,D*
University of Oregon	M,D*
University of Ottawa	M,D*
University of Prince Edward Island	M
University of Regina	M,D
University of Saskatchewan	M,D
University of South Africa	M,D
University of South Carolina	M,D
University of Southern California	M,O*
University of Southern Mississippi	M,D
University of South Florida	M,D*
The University of Tennessee	M,D
The University of Texas at Austin	M,D
The University of Toledo	M,O
University of Toronto	M,D
University of Utah	M,D*
University of Victoria	M,D
University of Washington	M,D*
University of Waterloo	M,D
The University of Western Ontario	M,D
University of Wisconsin–Madison	M,D,O*
University of Wisconsin–Milwaukee	M,D
University of Wyoming	M
Utah State University	M,D
Virginia Polytechnic Institute and State University	M,D*
Wayne State University	M*
West Chester University of Pennsylvania	M,O
Western Illinois University	M,O
Western Kentucky University	M
Western Michigan University	M*
Western Washington University	M
West Virginia University	M,D
Wilfrid Laurier University	M,D
York University	M,D

GEOLOGICAL ENGINEERING

Arizona State University	M,D
Colorado School of Mines	M,D
Michigan Technological University	M,D
Missouri University of Science and Technology	M,D
Montana Tech of The University of Montana	M
South Dakota School of Mines and Technology	M,D*
University of Alaska Anchorage	M
University of Alaska Fairbanks	M,D
The University of Arizona	M,D,O*
The University of British Columbia	M,D
University of Hawaii at Manoa	M,D*
University of Idaho	M
University of Minnesota, Twin Cities Campus	M,D*
University of Nevada, Reno	M,D*
University of North Dakota	M

*M—master's degree; P—first professional degree; D—doctorate; O—other advanced degree; *—Close-Up and/or Announcement or Display in one of the other books in this series*

University of Oklahoma M,D*
University of Utah M,D*
University of Wisconsin–Madison M,D*

GEOLOGY

Acadia University M
American University of Beirut M
Arizona State University M,D
Auburn University M*
Ball State University M*
Baylor University M,D
Boise State University M,D
Boston College M*
Bowling Green State University M*
Brigham Young University M*
Brooklyn College of the City University of New York M,D
California Institute of Technology M,D*
California State University, Bakersfield M
California State University, Chico M
California State University, East Bay M
California State University, Fresno M
California State University, Fullerton M
California State University, Long Beach M
California State University, Los Angeles M
California State University, Northridge M
Case Western Reserve University M,D*
Central Washington University M
Colorado School of Mines M,D
Cornell University M,D*
Duke University M,D*
East Carolina University M
Eastern Kentucky University M,D
Florida Atlantic University M
Florida State University M,D*
Fort Hays State University M
Georgia State University M
Humboldt State University M
ICR Graduate School M
Idaho State University M,O
Indiana University Bloomington M,D*
Indiana University–Purdue University Indianapolis M*
Iowa State University of Science and Technology M,D*
Kansas State University M*
Kent State University M,D*
Lakehead University M
Laurentian University M,D
Lehigh University M,D
Louisiana State University and Agricultural and Mechanical College M,D
Massachusetts Institute of Technology M,D*
McMaster University M,D
Memorial University of Newfoundland M,D
Miami University M,D*
Michigan Technological University M,D
Missouri State University M*
Missouri University of Science and Technology M,D
Montana Tech of The University of Montana M
New Mexico Institute of Mining and Technology M,D
New Mexico State University M
Northern Arizona University M
Northern Illinois University M,D
Northwestern University M,D*
The Ohio State University M,D*
Ohio University M*
Oklahoma State University M,D*
Oregon State University M,D*
Portland State University M,D
Queens College of the City University of New York M
Queen's University at Kingston M,D
Rensselaer Polytechnic Institute M,D
Rutgers, The State University of New Jersey, Newark M*
Rutgers, The State University of New Jersey, New Brunswick M,D*
St. Francis Xavier University M
San Diego State University M*
San Jose State University M
South Dakota School of Mines and Technology M,D*
Southern Illinois University Carbondale M,D*
Southern Methodist University M,D*
State University of New York at Binghamton M,D*
Stephen F. Austin State University M
Sul Ross State University M*
Syracuse University M,D*
Temple University M*
Texas A&M University M,D*
Texas A&M University–Kingsville M
Texas Christian University M
Tulane University M,D
Université du Québec à Montréal M,D,O
Université Laval M,D
University at Albany, State University of New York M,D*
University at Buffalo, the State University of New York M,D*
The University of Akron M
The University of Alabama M,D
University of Alaska Fairbanks M,D
University of Arkansas M
The University of British Columbia M,D
University of Calgary M,D
University of California, Berkeley M,D*
University of California, Davis M,D*
University of California, Los Angeles M,D*
University of California, Riverside M,D*
University of California, Santa Barbara M,D
University of Cincinnati M,D
University of Colorado at Boulder M,D*
University of Connecticut M,D*
University of Florida M,D*
University of Georgia M,D*
University of Hawaii at Manoa M,D*
University of Houston M,D*
University of Idaho M,D
University of Illinois at Chicago M,D*
University of Illinois at Urbana–Champaign M,D*
The University of Kansas M,D*
University of Kentucky M,D
University of Louisiana at Lafayette M*
University of Maine M,D*
University of Manitoba M,D
University of Maryland, College Park M,D*
University of Memphis M,D,O
University of Michigan M,D*
University of Minnesota, Duluth M,D
University of Minnesota, Twin Cities Campus M,D*
University of Missouri–Columbia M,D*
University of Missouri–Kansas City M,D*
The University of Montana M,D
University of Nevada, Reno M,D*
University of New Brunswick Fredericton M,D
University of New Hampshire M*
The University of North Carolina at Chapel Hill M,D*
The University of North Carolina Wilmington M
University of North Dakota M,D
University of Oklahoma M,D*
University of Oregon M,D*
University of Pittsburgh M,D*
University of Puerto Rico, Mayagüez Campus M
University of Regina M,D
University of Rochester M,D*
University of Saskatchewan M,D,O
University of South Carolina M,D
University of Southern Mississippi M,D
University of South Florida M,D*
The University of Tennessee M,D
The University of Texas at Arlington M,D*
The University of Texas at Austin M,D
The University of Texas at El Paso M,D
The University of Texas at San Antonio M*
The University of Texas of the Permian Basin M
The University of Toledo M,D
University of Toronto M,D
University of Utah M,D*
University of Vermont M*
University of Washington M,D*
The University of Western Ontario M,D
University of Wisconsin–Madison M,D*
University of Wisconsin–Milwaukee M,D
University of Wyoming M,D
Utah State University M
Virginia Polytechnic Institute and State University M,D*
Washington State University M,D*
Wayne State University M*
West Chester University of Pennsylvania M,O
Western Kentucky University M
Western Washington University M
West Virginia University M,D
Wichita State University M*
Wright State University M
Yale University D*

GEOPHYSICS

Boise State University M,D
Boston College M*
Bowling Green State University M*
California Institute of Technology M,D*
California State University, Long Beach M
Colorado School of Mines M,D
Columbia University M,D*
Cornell University M,D*
Florida State University D*
Georgia Institute of Technology M,D*
ICR Graduate School M
Idaho State University M,O
Indiana University Bloomington M,D*
Louisiana State University and Agricultural and Mechanical College M,D
Massachusetts Institute of Technology M,D*
Memorial University of Newfoundland M,D
Michigan Technological University M
Missouri University of Science and Technology M,D
New Mexico Institute of Mining and Technology M,D
Ohio University M*
Oregon State University M,D*
Rensselaer Polytechnic Institute M,D
Rice University M
Saint Louis University M,D
Southern Methodist University M,D*
Stanford University M,D*
Texas A&M University M,D*
The University of Akron M
University of Alaska Fairbanks M,D
University of Alberta M,D*
The University of British Columbia M,D
University of Calgary M,D
University of California, Berkeley M,D*
University of California, Los Angeles M,D*
University of California, Santa Barbara M,D
University of Chicago M,D*
University of Colorado at Boulder M,D*
University of Hawaii at Manoa M,D*
University of Houston M,D*
University of Manitoba M,D
University of Miami M,D*
University of Minnesota, Twin Cities Campus M,D*
University of Nevada, Reno M,D*
University of Oklahoma M*
The University of Texas at Dallas M,D*
The University of Texas at El Paso M,D
University of Utah M,D*
University of Victoria M,D*
University of Washington M,D*
The University of Western Ontario M,D
University of Wisconsin–Madison M,D*
University of Wyoming M,D
Virginia Polytechnic Institute and State University M,D*
West Virginia University M,D
Woods Hole Oceanographic Institution M,D,O
Wright State University M
Yale University D*

GEOSCIENCES

Arizona State University M,D
Ball State University M*
Baylor University M,D
Boise State University M
Boston University M,D*
Brock University M

Brooklyn College of the City University of New York M
Brown University M,D*
California State University, Chico M
Carleton University M,D
Case Western Reserve University M,D*
Central Connecticut State University M,O
City College of the City University of New York M,D*
Colorado State University M,D*
Columbia University M,D*
Cornell University M,D*
Dalhousie University M,D
Dartmouth College M,D*
Eastern Michigan University M
Emporia State University M,O
Florida International University M,D*
Fort Hays State University M
Georgia Institute of Technology M,D*
Georgia State University M,O
Graduate School and University Center of the City University of New York D*
Harvard University M,D*
Hunter College of the City University of New York M,O
Idaho State University M,O
Indiana University Bloomington M,D*
Iowa State University of Science and Technology M,D*
The Johns Hopkins University M,D*
Lehigh University M,D
Loma Linda University M,D
Long Island University, C.W. Post Campus M
Massachusetts Institute of Technology M,D*
McGill University M,D*
McMaster University M,D
Memorial University of Newfoundland M,D
Michigan State University M,D*
Middle Tennessee State University O
Mississippi State University M
Missouri State University M*
Montana State University M,D
Montana Tech of The University of Montana M
Montclair State University M,D,O*
Murray State University M
New Mexico Institute of Mining and Technology M,D
North Carolina Central University M
North Carolina State University M,D*
Northeastern Illinois University M
Northern Arizona University M
Northwestern University M,D*
Oregon State University M,D*
Penn State University Park M,D*
Princeton University D*
Purdue University M,D
Rensselaer Polytechnic Institute M,D
Rice University M,D
St. Francis Xavier University M
Saint Louis University M,D
St. Thomas University M,D,O
San Francisco State University M
Simon Fraser University M,D
South Dakota State University M,D
Stanford University M,D,O*
State University of New York College at Oneonta M
Stony Brook University, State University of New York M,D
Texas A&M University–Commerce M
Texas Christian University M
Texas Tech University M,D
Tulane University M,D
Université du Québec à Chicoutimi M
Université du Québec à Montréal M,D,O
Université du Québec, Institut National de la Recherche Scientifique M,D
Université Laval M,D
University at Albany, State University of New York M,D*
The University of Akron M
University of Alberta M,D*
The University of Arizona M,D*
University of Arkansas at Little Rock O
University of California, Irvine M,D*
University of California, Los Angeles M,D*
University of California, San Diego M,D*
University of California, Santa Barbara M,D
University of California, Santa Cruz M,D*
University of Chicago M,D*
University of Florida M,D*
University of Illinois at Chicago M,D*
University of Illinois at Urbana–Champaign M,D*
The University of Iowa M,D*
University of Maine M,D*
University of Massachusetts Amherst M,D*
University of Missouri–Kansas City M,D*
The University of Montana M,D
University of Nebraska–Lincoln M,D*
University of Nevada, Las Vegas M,D
University of New Hampshire M*
University of New Mexico M,D*
University of New Orleans M
The University of North Carolina at Charlotte M*
The University of North Carolina Wilmington M
University of North Dakota M,D
University of Northern Colorado M
University of Notre Dame M,D*
University of Ottawa M,D*
University of Pennsylvania M,D*
University of Rhode Island M,D
University of Rochester M,D*
University of South Carolina M,D
University of Southern California M,D*
The University of Texas at Austin M,D
The University of Texas at Dallas M,D*
The University of Toledo M,D*
University of Tulsa M,D*
University of Victoria M,D
University of Waterloo M,D
The University of Western Ontario M,D
University of Windsor M,D
Virginia Polytechnic Institute and State University M,D*
Washington State University M,D*
Washington State University Tri-Cities M,D
Washington University in St. Louis M,D*
Wesleyan University M*
Western Connecticut State University M
Western Michigan University M,D*
Yale University D*
York University M,D

GEOTECHNICAL ENGINEERING

Auburn University M,D*
The Catholic University of America M,D,O
Cornell University M,D*
Drexel University M,D*
École Polytechnique de Montréal M,D,O
Illinois Institute of Technology M,D*
Iowa State University of Science and Technology M,D*
Louisiana State University and Agricultural and Mechanical College M,D
Marquette University M,D
Massachusetts Institute of Technology M,D,O*
McGill University M,D*
Missouri University of Science and Technology M,D
Northwestern University M,D*
Ohio University M,D*
Oregon State University M,D*
Rensselaer Polytechnic Institute M,D
Texas A&M University M,D*
Tufts University M,D*
The University of Alabama in Huntsville M,D
University of Alberta M,D*
University of Calgary M,D
University of California, Berkeley M,D*
University of Colorado at Boulder M,D*
University of Delaware M,D*
University of Maine M,D*
University of Missouri–Columbia M,D*
University of New Brunswick Fredericton M,D
University of Oklahoma M,D*
University of Rhode Island M,D
The University of Texas at Austin M,D
University of Washington M,D*

GERMAN

Arizona State University M
Bowling Green State University M*
Brigham Young University M*
Brown University D*
California State University, Fullerton M
California State University, Long Beach M
California State University, Sacramento M
Columbia University M,D*
Cornell University M,D*
Dalhousie University M
Duke University D*
Eastern Michigan University M,O
Florida State University M*
Georgetown University M,D
Georgia State University M,O
Graduate School and University Center of the City University of New York M,D*
Harvard University D*
Hofstra University
Illinois State University
Indiana University Bloomington M,D*
The Johns Hopkins University D*
Kansas State University M*
Kent State University M,D*
McGill University M,D*
Memorial University of Newfoundland M
Michigan State University M,D*
Middlebury College M,D
Millersville University of Pennsylvania M
Mississippi State University M
Missouri State University M*
New York University M,D*
Northwestern University D*
The Ohio State University M,D*
Penn State University Park M,D*
Portland State University M
Princeton University D*
Purdue University M,D
Queen's University at Kingston M,D
Rider University O*
Rutgers, The State University of New Jersey, New Brunswick M,D*
San Francisco State University M
Stanford University M,D*
Texas Tech University M
Tufts University M*
Université de Montréal M
The University of Alabama M,D
University of Alberta M,D*
The University of Arizona M*
University of Arkansas M
The University of British Columbia M,D
University of Calgary M
University of California, Berkeley D*
University of California, Davis M,D*
University of California, Irvine M,D*
University of California, Los Angeles M,D*
University of California, San Diego M*
University of California, Santa Barbara M,D
University of Chicago M,D*
University of Cincinnati M,D
University of Colorado at Boulder M*
University of Connecticut M,D*
University of Delaware M*
University of Florida M,D*
University of Georgia M*
University of Illinois at Chicago M,D*
University of Illinois at Urbana–Champaign M,D*
The University of Iowa M,D*
The University of Kansas M,D*
University of Kentucky M
University of Lethbridge M,D
University of Manitoba M
University of Maryland, College Park M,D*
University of Massachusetts Amherst M,D*
University of Michigan M,D*
University of Minnesota, Twin Cities Campus M,D*
University of Mississippi M
University of Missouri–Columbia M*
The University of Montana M
University of Nebraska–Lincoln M,D*
University of Nevada, Reno M*

*M—master's degree; P—first professional degree; D—doctorate; O—other advanced degree; *—Close-Up and/or Announcement or Display in one of the other books in this series*

[illegible]o	M,D*
[illegible]	M,D*
[illegible]	M
[illegible]	M*
[illegible]	M,D*
[illegible]nia	M,D*
Universi[illegible]	M,D*
University of Saskatchewan	M
University of South Africa	M,D
University of South Carolina	M,D
The University of Tennessee	M,D
The University of Texas at Austin	M,D
The University of Toledo	M
University of Toronto	M,D
University of Utah	M,D*
University of Vermont	M*
University of Victoria	M
University of Virginia	M,D
University of Washington	M,D*
University of Waterloo	M,D
University of Wisconsin–Madison	M,D*
University of Wisconsin–Milwaukee	M,O
University of Wyoming	M
Vanderbilt University	M,D*
Washington University in St. Louis	M,D*
Wayne State University	M,D*
West Chester University of Pennsylvania	M,O
Yale University	D*

GERONTOLOGICAL NURSING

Boston College	M,D*
Caribbean University	M,D
Case Western Reserve University	M,D*
The Catholic University of America	M,D,O
College of Mount Saint Vincent	M,O
College of Staten Island of the City University of New York	M,O
Columbia University	M,O*
Concordia University Wisconsin	M
Duke University	M,D,O*
Emory University	M*
Gwynedd-Mercy College	M
Hampton University	M
Hunter College of the City University of New York	M
Independence University	M
Kent State University	M,D*
Lehman College of the City University of New York	M
Loma Linda University	M
Marquette University	M,D,O
MGH Institute of Health Professions	M,D,O*
Nazareth College of Rochester	M
New York University	M,O*
Oakland University	M,O
Oregon Health & Science University	O*
Rush University	M,D,O
Rutgers, The State University of New Jersey, Newark	M*
Sage Graduate School	M,D,O
San Jose State University	M,O
Seattle Pacific University	M,O
Seton Hall University	M*
Southern University and Agricultural and Mechanical College	M,D,O
State University of New York Institute of Technology	M,O
Texas Tech University Health Sciences Center	M,D,O
University at Buffalo, the State University of New York	M,D,O*
University of Colorado at Colorado Springs	M,D
University of Delaware	M,O*
University of Illinois at Chicago	M*
University of Maryland, Baltimore	M*
University of Massachusetts Lowell	M,O
University of Massachusetts Worcester	M,D,O
University of Michigan	M*
University of Minnesota, Twin Cities Campus	M*
The University of North Carolina at Greensboro	M,D,O
University of Rhode Island	M,D
University of Utah	M,O*
Vanderbilt University	M,D*
Villanova University	M,D,O*

GERONTOLOGY

Abilene Christian University	M,O
Adelphi University	M,O*
Adler School of Professional Psychology	M,D,O*
Alliant International University–Los Angeles	M*
Appalachian State University	M
Arizona State University at the West campus	M,O
Arkansas State University	M,D,O
A.T. Still University of Health Sciences	M,D
Ball State University	M*
Bethel University	M
California State University, Fullerton	M
California State University, Long Beach	M
California State University, Stanislaus	O
Capella University	M,D
Chestnut Hill College	M,O
Cleveland State University	M,D,O
The College of New Rochelle	M,O
Concordia University Chicago	M
Dominican University of California	M
Eastern Illinois University	M
Eastern Michigan University	M,O
East Tennessee State University	M,O
Emory University	M*
Gannon University	O
Georgia State University	M,O
Hofstra University	M,O*
Kent State University	M*
Lakehead University	M,D
Lindenwood University	M,O
Long Island University, C.W. Post Campus	M,O
Long Island University, Rockland Graduate Campus	M,O
Marywood University	M,O
Miami University	M*
Middle Tennessee State University	O
Minnesota State University Mankato	M,O
Morehead State University	M
Mount Saint Vincent University	M
National-Louis University	M,O
North Dakota State University	M,D
Northeastern Illinois University	M
Notre Dame de Namur University	M,O
Oregon Health & Science University	M,O*
Oregon State University	M*
Portland State University	O
Rochester Institute of Technology	M,O
Sacred Heart University	M
Sage Graduate School	M,O
St. Cloud State University	M
Saint Joseph College	M,O
Saint Joseph's University	M,O
San Diego State University	M*
San Francisco State University	M
San Jose State University	M,O
Shippensburg University of Pennsylvania	M,O
Simon Fraser University	M,D
Texas A&M University–Kingsville	M
Texas Tech University	M,D
Towson University	M,O
Université de Montréal	O
Université de Sherbrooke	M
Université Laval	O
University of Arkansas at Little Rock	O
University of Central Florida	M,O*
University of Central Missouri	M
University of Central Oklahoma	M
University of Georgia	O*
University of Illinois at Springfield	M
University of Indianapolis	M,O
The University of Kansas	M,D,O*
University of Kentucky	D
University of La Verne	M,O
University of Louisiana at Monroe	M,O
University of Louisville	M,D,O
University of Maryland, Baltimore	M,D*
University of Maryland, Baltimore County	D*
University of Massachusetts Boston	M,D,O
University of Missouri–St. Louis	M,O
University of Nebraska at Omaha	M,O
University of Nebraska–Lincoln	M,D*
University of New England	M,O
The University of North Carolina at Charlotte	M*
The University of North Carolina at Greensboro	M,O
The University of North Carolina Wilmington	M
University of Northern Colorado	M
University of North Florida	M,O
University of North Texas	M,D,O
University of Phoenix	M
University of Phoenix–Birmingham Campus	M
University of Phoenix–Central Valley Campus	M
University of Phoenix–Chattanooga Campus	M
University of Phoenix–Hawaii Campus	M
University of Phoenix–Phoenix Campus	M,O
University of Phoenix–Southern Colorado Campus	M
University of Pittsburgh	M,D,O*
University of Puerto Rico, Medical Sciences Campus	M,O
University of Regina	M
University of Rhode Island	M,D
University of South Alabama	O*
University of South Carolina	O
University of Southern California	M,D,O*
University of South Florida	M,D*
The University of Tennessee	M
The University of Toledo	O
University of Utah	M,O*
University of Wisconsin–Milwaukee	M,D,O
Valparaiso University	M,O
Virginia Commonwealth University	M,D,O
Virginia Polytechnic Institute and State University	M,D*
Wayne State University	O*
Webster University	M
West Chester University of Pennsylvania	M,O
Wichita State University	M*
Wilmington University	M

GRAPHIC DESIGN

Academy of Art University	M
Atlantic College	M
Bob Jones University	P,M,D,O
Boston University	M*
Bowling Green State University	M*
California Institute of the Arts	M,O
California State University, Los Angeles	M
Cardinal Stritch University	M
City College of the City University of New York	M*
The College of New Rochelle	M
Cranbrook Academy of Art	M*
Digital Media Arts College	M
Florida Atlantic University	M
George Mason University	M*
Illinois State University	M
Indiana State University	M
Iowa State University of Science and Technology	M*
Kean University	M
Kent State University	M*
Louisiana State University and Agricultural and Mechanical College	M
Louisiana Tech University	M
Maryland Institute College of Art	M
Marywood University	M
Miami International University of Art & Design	M*
Minneapolis College of Art and Design	M
New York University	M*
North Carolina State University	M*
Ohio University	M*
Otis College of Art and Design	M
Pittsburg State University	M,O
Pratt Institute	M*
Rhode Island School of Design	M
Rochester Institute of Technology	M
San Diego State University	M*
Savannah College of Art and Design	M*
School of the Art Institute of Chicago	M*

- Southern Polytechnic State University — M,O
- Suffolk University — M*
- Temple University — M*
- Texas State University–San Marcos — M*
- Université Laval — M
- University of Baltimore — M,D
- University of Cincinnati — M
- University of Florida — M,D*
- University of Guam — M
- University of Illinois at Chicago — M*
- University of Illinois at Urbana–Champaign — M*
- University of Massachusetts Dartmouth — M
- University of Memphis — M,O
- University of Miami — M*
- University of Minnesota, Duluth — M
- University of Notre Dame — M*
- The University of Tennessee — M
- University of Utah — M*
- Western Illinois University — M,O
- Western Michigan University — M*
- West Virginia University — M
- Yale University — M*

HAZARDOUS MATERIALS MANAGEMENT

- Humboldt State University — M
- Idaho State University — M
- New Mexico Institute of Mining and Technology — M
- Rutgers, The State University of New Jersey, New Brunswick — M,D*
- Southern Methodist University — M,D*
- Stony Brook University, State University of New York — M,O
- Tufts University — M,D*
- University of Oklahoma — M,D*
- University of South Carolina — M,D
- Wayne State University — M,O*

HEALTH COMMUNICATION

- Boston University — M*
- Chapman University — M
- Cleveland State University — M,O
- East Carolina University — M
- Emerson College — M
- The George Washington University — M*
- The Johns Hopkins University — M,D*
- Marquette University — M
- Marywood University — M,O
- Michigan State University — M*
- Tufts University — M*
- Tulane University — M
- University of Florida — M,D,O*
- University of Southern California — M*
- Washington State University — M,D*

HEALTH EDUCATION

- Adelphi University — M,O*
- Alabama State University — M
- Albany State University — M
- Alcorn State University — M,O
- Allen College — M
- American University — M,O*
- American University of Beirut — M
- Arcadia University — M
- A.T. Still University of Health Sciences — M,D
- Auburn University — M,D,O*
- Augusta State University — M
- Austin Peay State University — M
- Averett University — M
- Ball State University — M*
- Baylor University — M,D
- Benedictine University — M
- Boston University — M,O*
- Brandeis University — D
- Brigham Young University — M*
- Brooklyn College of the City University of New York — M,O
- California State University, Dominguez Hills — M
- California State University, Long Beach — M
- California State University, Los Angeles — M
- California State University, San Bernardino — M
- Cambridge College — M,D,O
- Central Washington University — M
- The Citadel, The Military College of South Carolina — M
- Cleveland State University — M
- The College at Brockport, State University of New York — M
- The College of New Jersey — M
- Colorado State University–Pueblo — M
- Dalhousie University — M
- D'Youville College — D*
- East Carolina University — M
- Eastern Kentucky University — M
- Eastern Michigan University — M
- Eastern University — M
- East Stroudsburg University of Pennsylvania — M
- Emory University — M*
- Felician College — M,O*
- Florida Agricultural and Mechanical University — M
- Florida State University — M,D*
- Fort Hays State University — M
- Framingham State College — M
- Georgia College & State University — M
- Georgia Southern University — M,D
- Georgia Southwestern State University — M,O
- Georgia State University — M
- Harding University — M,O
- Hofstra University — M*
- Howard University — M
- Idaho State University — M
- Illinois State University — M
- Indiana State University — M
- Indiana University Bloomington — M,D*
- Indiana University of Pennsylvania — M
- Indiana University–Purdue University Indianapolis — M,D*
- Inter American University of Puerto Rico, Metropolitan Campus — M
- Ithaca College — M
- Jackson State University — M
- Jacksonville State University — M
- James Madison University — M
- John F. Kennedy University — M
- The Johns Hopkins University — M,D*
- Kent State University — M,D*
- Lake Erie College of Osteopathic Medicine — P,M,O
- Lehman College of the City University of New York — M
- Loma Linda University — M,D
- Long Island University, Brooklyn Campus — M
- Louisiana Tech University — M,D
- Marshall University — M
- Marywood University — D
- Middle Tennessee State University — M
- Midwestern University, Glendale Campus — M*
- Mills College — M,D
- Minnesota State University Mankato — M
- Mississippi University for Women — M
- Montclair State University — M,O*
- Morehead State University — M
- Mount Mary College — M
- New Jersey City University — M
- New Mexico Highlands University — M
- New Mexico State University — M
- New York University — M,D*
- North Carolina Agricultural and Technical State University — M
- Northeastern State University — M
- Northern State University — M
- Northwestern State University of Louisiana — M
- Northwest Missouri State University — M
- Nova Southeastern University — M,D*
- Oklahoma State University — M,D,O*
- Penn State Harrisburg — M,D
- Plymouth State University — M
- Portland State University — M,O
- Prairie View A&M University — M
- Regis University — P,M,D,O
- Rhode Island College — M,O
- Rosalind Franklin University of Medicine and Science — M*
- Sage Graduate School — M
- Saint Francis University — M
- Saint Joseph's University — M,O
- San Francisco State University — M
- San Jose State University — M,O
- Simmons College — M,D,O
- South Dakota State University — M
- Southeastern Louisiana University — M
- Southern Connecticut State University — M
- Southern Illinois University Carbondale — M,D*
- Southern Illinois University Edwardsville — M,O
- Springfield College — M,D,O
- State University of New York College at Cortland — M
- Suffolk University — M*
- Teachers College, Columbia University — M,D
- Temple University — M*
- Tennessee Technological University — M*
- Texas A&M Health Science Center — M
- Texas A&M University — M,D*
- Texas A&M University–Commerce — M,D
- Texas A&M University–Kingsville — M
- Texas Southern University — M
- Texas State University–San Marcos — M*
- Texas Woman's University — M,D
- TUI University — M,D,O
- Tulane University — M
- Union College (KY) — M
- The University of Alabama — M,D
- The University of Alabama at Birmingham — M,D*
- University of Arkansas — M,D
- University of Calgary — M,D
- University of California, Berkeley — M*
- University of Central Arkansas — M
- University of Central Oklahoma — M
- University of Cincinnati — M,D
- University of Colorado Denver — D*
- University of Florida — M,D,O*
- University of Georgia — M,D*
- University of Houston — M,D*
- University of Illinois at Chicago — M*
- The University of Kansas — M,D,O*
- University of Louisville — M,D
- University of Maryland, Baltimore County — M,O*
- University of Maryland, College Park — M,D*
- University of Medicine and Dentistry of New Jersey — M,D*
- University of Michigan–Flint — M*
- University of Missouri–Columbia — M,D,O*
- The University of Montana — M
- University of Nebraska at Omaha — M
- University of Nebraska–Lincoln — M*
- University of New Mexico — M*
- The University of North Carolina at Chapel Hill — M,D*
- University of Northern Colorado — M
- University of Northern Iowa — M,D
- University of Oklahoma Health Sciences Center — D
- University of Phoenix–Phoenix Campus — M,O
- University of Phoenix–Southern Colorado Campus — M
- University of Pittsburgh — M,D,O*
- University of Puerto Rico, Medical Sciences Campus — M
- University of Rhode Island — M,D
- University of Rochester — M,D,O*
- University of South Africa — M,D
- University of South Alabama — M*
- University of South Carolina — M,D,O
- The University of South Dakota — M
- University of Southern Mississippi — M
- The University of Tennessee — M
- The University of Texas at Austin — M,D
- The University of Texas at El Paso — M
- The University of Texas at San Antonio — M*
- The University of Texas at Tyler — M
- The University of Toledo — M,D
- University of Utah — M,D*
- University of Virginia — M,D
- University of Waterloo — M,D
- University of West Florida — M
- University of Wisconsin–La Crosse — M
- University of Wisconsin–Milwaukee — M,D,O
- University of Wyoming — M
- Utah State University — M
- Virginia Polytechnic Institute and State University — M,D,O*
- Virginia State University — M,D

*M—master's degree; P—first professional degree; D—doctorate; O—other advanced degree; *—Close-Up and/or Announcement or Display in one of the other books in this series*

Wayne State University M,D,O*
West Chester University of Pennsylvania M,O
Western Illinois University M,O
Western Oregon University M
Western University of Health Sciences M
West Virginia University M,D
Widener University M,D*
Worcester State College M
Wright State University M

HEALTH INFORMATICS

American Sentinel University M
Barry University O*
Benedictine University M
Claremont Graduate University M,D,O*
The College of St. Scholastica M,O
Emory University M,D*
Indiana University Bloomington M,D*
The Johns Hopkins University M*
Medical College of Georgia M
Northeastern University M,D*
Northern Kentucky University M,O
Saint Joseph's University M,O
Stevens Institute of Technology M,D,O
TUI University M,D,O
The University of Alabama at Birmingham M*
University of Illinois at Chicago M*
University of Illinois at Urbana–Champaign M,D,O*
The University of Iowa M,D,O*
University of La Verne M
University of Maryland University College M,O
University of Massachusetts Lowell M,O
University of Minnesota, Twin Cities Campus M,D*
University of Missouri–Columbia M*
University of Phoenix M
University of Phoenix–Birmingham Campus M
University of Phoenix–Phoenix Campus M,O
University of Pittsburgh M*
University of Puerto Rico, Medical Sciences Campus M
The University of Texas Health Science Center at Houston M,D,O
University of Victoria M
University of Virginia M
University of Washington M,D*
University of Wisconsin–Milwaukee M,O

HEALTH LAW

Boston University M*
DePaul University P,M,O*
Georgetown University P,M,D
Loyola University Chicago P,M,D*
Nova Southeastern University M*
Quinnipiac University P,M*
Southern Illinois University Carbondale M*
Suffolk University P,M*
Université de Sherbrooke P,M,D,O
University of California, San Diego M*
University of Pittsburgh M,O*
University of Tulsa P,M,O*
Widener University P,M,D*
Xavier University M*

HEALTH PHYSICS/ RADIOLOGICAL HEALTH

Bloomsburg University of Pennsylvania M
Emory University D*
Georgetown University M
Georgia Institute of Technology M,D*
Idaho State University M,D
Illinois Institute of Technology M,D*
McMaster University M,D
Midwestern State University M
New York Chiropractic College M*
Oregon State University M,D*
Quinnipiac University M*
San Diego State University M*
Texas A&M University M,D*
Université de Montréal O
Université Laval O
University of Alberta M,D*
University of Cincinnati M
University of Kentucky M
University of Massachusetts Lowell M
University of Medicine and Dentistry of New Jersey M*
University of Michigan M,D,O*
University of Missouri–Columbia M,D*
University of Nevada, Las Vegas M
University of Oklahoma Health Sciences Center M,D
The University of Toledo M
Virginia Commonwealth University D
Wayne State University M,D*

HEALTH PROMOTION

Auburn University M,D,O*
Ball State University M*
Benedictine University M
Boston University M,D*
Bridgewater State College M
Brigham Young University M,D*
California State University, Fresno M
Canisius College M
Chatham University M
Eastern Kentucky University M
Eastern Michigan University M,O
Emory University M*
Florida Atlantic University M
Florida International University M,D*
George Mason University M*
Georgetown University M,D
The George Washington University M*
Georgia College & State University M
Georgia State University M,D,O
Goddard College M
Harvard University M,D*
Independence University M
Indiana State University M
Indiana University Bloomington M,D*
Lehman College of the City University of New York M
Loma Linda University M,D
Marymount University M
McNeese State University M
Mississippi State University M,D
Missouri State University M*
Montana State University M
Nebraska Methodist College M
New York Medical College M,D*
New York University M,D,O*
Oakland University O
Old Dominion University M
Oregon State University M,D*
Portland State University M,O
Purdue University M,D
San Diego State University M,D*
Simmons College M,O
Springfield College M,D
Texas A&M University–Commerce M,D
Union Institute & University M
Universidad del Turabo M
The University of Alabama M,D
The University of Alabama at Birmingham D*
University of Alberta M,O*
University of Chicago M,D*
University of Delaware M*
University of Georgia M,D*
University of Kentucky M,D
University of Louisville M,D
University of Massachusetts Lowell D
University of Memphis M
University of Michigan M,D*
The University of Montana M
University of Nebraska–Lincoln M,D*
University of Nevada, Las Vegas M
The University of North Carolina at Chapel Hill M*
University of Oklahoma Health Sciences Center M,D
University of Pittsburgh M,D,O*
University of Rochester M,D,O*
University of South Carolina M,D,O
University of Southern California M*
The University of Tennessee M
The University of Texas at El Paso M
The University of Texas at San Antonio M*
University of the Incarnate Word M
University of Utah M,D*
University of Wisconsin–Stevens Point M
Virginia Polytechnic Institute and State University M,D,O*
Walden University M,D
West Virginia University M,D
Wright State University M

HEALTH PSYCHOLOGY

American University of Beirut M
Appalachian State University M,O
Argosy University, Atlanta M,D,O*
Argosy University, Chicago D*
Argosy University, Schaumburg M,D,O*
Argosy University, Twin Cities M,D,O*
Argosy University, Washington DC M,D*
Bastyr University M*
California Institute of Integral Studies M,D*
Central Connecticut State University M
Chatham University M,D
Claremont Graduate University M,D,O*
Drexel University D*
Duke University D*
East Carolina University D
The George Washington University D*
John F. Kennedy University M
Lesley University M*
National-Louis University M,O
North Dakota State University M,D
Northern Arizona University M
Northern Kentucky University M,O
Philadelphia College of Osteopathic Medicine M,D,O*
Prescott College M
Rutgers, The State University of New Jersey, New Brunswick D*
San Diego State University M,D*
Saybrook Graduate School and Research Center M,D
Southwestern College (NM) O*
Stony Brook University, State University of New York D
Texas State University–San Marcos M*
The University of British Columbia M,D
University of Colorado Denver D*
University of Connecticut M,D,O*
University of Florida D*
University of Michigan–Dearborn M*
The University of North Carolina at Charlotte D*
University of North Texas M,D
The University of Texas at Arlington M,D*
University of the Sciences in Philadelphia M*
Virginia State University M,D
Walden University M,D,O
West Chester University of Pennsylvania M,O
Yeshiva University D

HEALTH SERVICES MANAGEMENT AND HOSPITAL ADMINISTRATION

Alaska Pacific University M
Albany State University M
American InterContinental University Online M
American Sentinel University M
The American University in Dubai M
Andrew Jackson University M
Aquinas Institute of Theology P,M,D,O
Argosy University, Atlanta M,D*
Argosy University, Chicago M,D*
Argosy University, Dallas M,O*
Argosy University, Denver M,D*
Argosy University, Hawai'i M,D,O*
Argosy University, Inland Empire M,D*
Argosy University, Los Angeles M,D*
Argosy University, Nashville M,D*
Argosy University, Orange County M,D,O*
Argosy University, Phoenix M,D*
Argosy University, Salt Lake City M,D*
Argosy University, San Francisco Bay Area M,D*
Argosy University, Sarasota M,D,O*
Argosy University, Schaumburg M,D,O*
Argosy University, Seattle M,D*
Argosy University, Tampa M,D,O*
Argosy University, Twin Cities M,D*

Argosy University, Washington DC	M,D,O*
Arizona State University	M,D
Armstrong Atlantic State University	M
A.T. Still University of Health Sciences	M,D
Avila University	M
Baker College Center for Graduate Studies	M
Baldwin-Wallace College	M
Barry University	M,O*
Baylor University	M
Bellevue University	M
Benedictine University	M
Bernard M. Baruch College of the City University of New York	M
Boston University	M,D,O*
Brandeis University	M
Brenau University	M
Brooklyn College of the City University of New York	M
California Intercontinental University	M,D
California State University, Bakersfield	M
California State University, Chico	M
California State University, East Bay	M
California State University, Fresno	M
California State University, Long Beach	M,O
California State University, Los Angeles	M
California State University, Northridge	M
California State University, San Bernardino	M
Cambridge College	M
Capella University	M,D,O
Carnegie Mellon University	M*
Central Michigan University	M,D,O
Charleston Southern University	M
Clark University	M
Clayton State University	M
Cleveland State University	M
The College at Brockport, State University of New York	M,O
College of Saint Elizabeth	M
Colorado Technical University Sioux Falls	M
Columbia Southern University	M
Columbia University	M*
Columbus State University	M
Concordia University (Canada)	M,D,O
Concordia University Wisconsin	M
Cornell University	M,D*
Dalhousie University	M,D
Dallas Baptist University	M
Dartmouth College	M,D*
Davenport University	M
Davenport University	M
Davenport University	M
Defiance College	M
Delta State University	M
DePaul University	M,O*
DeSales University	M
Des Moines University	M
Duke University	O*
Duquesne University	M,D*
D'Youville College	M,D,O*
Eastern Kentucky University	M
Eastern Michigan University	M,O
Eastern University	M
East Tennessee State University	M,D,O
Emory University	M,D*
Fairfield University	M,O*
Fairleigh Dickinson University, College at Florham	M*
Fairleigh Dickinson University, Metropolitan Campus	M*
Florida Institute of Technology	M*
Florida International University	M,D*
Framingham State College	M
Francis Marion University	M
Franklin Pierce University	M,D,O
Friends University	M
The George Washington University	M,D,O*
Georgia Institute of Technology	M*
Georgia Southern University	M,D
Georgia State University	M
Goldfarb School of Nursing at Barnes-Jewish College	M
Governors State University	M
Grambling State University	M
Grand Canyon University	M*
Grand Valley State University	M,D
Harding University	M
Harvard University	M,D*
Hofstra University	M*
Holy Family University	M
Houston Baptist University	M
Hunter College of the City University of New York	M
Husson University	M
Independence University	M
Indiana Tech	M
Indiana University Northwest	M,O
Indiana University–Purdue University Indianapolis	M*
Indiana University South Bend	M,O
Institute of Public Administration	M,O
Iona College	M,O*
The Johns Hopkins University	M,D,O*
Jones International University	M
Kaplan University–Davenport Campus	M,O
Kean University	M
Kennesaw State University	M
King's College	M
Lake Erie College	M
Lakeland College	M
Lamar University	M
Lewis University	M
Lindenwood University	M,O
Lipscomb University	M
Loma Linda University	M
Long Island University, Brooklyn Campus	M
Long Island University, C.W. Post Campus	M,O
Long Island University, Rockland Graduate Campus	M,O
Louisiana State University in Shreveport	M
Loyola University Chicago	M,O*
Loyola University New Orleans	M
Madonna University	M
Marlboro College	M
Marshall University	M,D
Marylhurst University	M
Marymount University	M,O
Marywood University	M
Massachusetts College of Pharmacy and Health Sciences	M*
McGill University	M,D,O*
Medical University of South Carolina	M,D
Meharry Medical College	M
Mercy College	M
Middle Tennessee State University	O
Midwestern State University	M
Mississippi College	M
Missouri State University	M*
Monmouth University	M,O
Montana State University–Billings	M
Mount Aloysius College	M
National University	M
Nebraska Methodist College	M
New England College	M
New Jersey City University	M
The New School: A University	M,O*
New York Medical College	M,D*
New York University	M,O*
Northeastern University	M,O*
Northwest Missouri State University	M
OGI School of Science & Engineering at Oregon Health & Science University	M,O
The Ohio State University	M,D*
Ohio University	M*
Oklahoma City University	M
Old Dominion University	M
Oregon State University	M,D*
Our Lady of the Lake University of San Antonio	M
Pace University	M*
Park University	M
Penn State Great Valley	M
Penn State Harrisburg	M,D
Penn State University Park	M,D*
Pfeiffer University	M
Philadelphia University	M
Portland State University	M
Queen's University at Kingston	M,D
Quinnipiac University	M*
Regent University	M
Regis University	P,M,D,O
Roberts Wesleyan College	M
Rochester Institute of Technology	M,O
Rosalind Franklin University of Medicine and Science	M,O*
Royal Roads University	O
Rush University	M,D
Rutgers, The State University of New Jersey, Newark	M,D*
Sage Graduate School	M,D,O
Saginaw Valley State University	M
St. Ambrose University	M,D
St. Joseph's College, Long Island Campus	M,O
Saint Joseph's College of Maine	M
Saint Joseph's University	M,O
Saint Leo University	M
Saint Louis University	M,D
Saint Mary's University of Minnesota	M
St. Thomas University	M,O
Saint Xavier University	M,O
Salve Regina University	M,O
San Diego State University	M,D*
Seton Hall University	M,O*
Shenandoah University	M,O
Simmons College	M,O
Southeastern University	M
Southeast Missouri State University	M
Southern Adventist University	M
Southern Illinois University Carbondale	M*
South University (SC)	M*
South University (AL)	M*
South University (FL)	M*
Southwest Baptist University	M
Springfield College	M
State University of New York at Binghamton	M,D*
State University of New York Institute of Technology	M
Stony Brook University, State University of New York	M,D,O
Strayer University	M
Suffolk University	M,O*
Syracuse University	O*
Temple University	M*
Texas A&M Health Science Center	M
Texas A&M University–Corpus Christi	M
Texas State University–San Marcos	M*
Texas Tech University	M
Texas Tech University Health Sciences Center	M
Texas Wesleyan University	M
Texas Woman's University	M,D
Towson University	O
Trinity University	M
Trinity Western University	M,O
Troy University	M
TUI University	M,D,O
Tulane University	M,D
Union Graduate College	M,O
Universidad de Ciencias Medicas	P,M,O
Universidad de Iberoamerica	P,M
Universidad Nacional Pedro Henriquez Urena	P,M,D
Université de Montréal	M,O
University at Albany, State University of New York	M*
The University of Akron	M
The University of Alabama at Birmingham	M,D*
The University of Alabama in Huntsville	M,D,O
University of Alberta	M,D*
University of Baltimore	M
The University of British Columbia	M,D
University of California, Berkeley	M,D*
University of California, Los Angeles	M,D*
University of California, San Diego	M*
University of Central Florida	M,O*
University of Colorado at Colorado Springs	M
University of Colorado Denver	M*
University of Connecticut	M,D*
University of Dallas	M
University of Detroit Mercy	M
University of Evansville	M
University of Florida	M,D*
University of Houston–Clear Lake	M
University of Illinois at Chicago	M,D*
The University of Iowa	M,D*
The University of Kansas	M*
University of Kentucky	M
University of La Verne	M,O
University of Louisiana at Lafayette	M*
University of Louisville	M,D
University of Mary	M

*M—master's degree; P—first professional degree; D—doctorate; O—other advanced degree; *—Close-Up and/or Announcement or Display in one of the other books in this series*

University of Maryland, Baltimore County M,O*
University of Maryland, College Park M,D*
University of Maryland University College M,O
University of Massachusetts Boston M,D,O
University of Massachusetts Lowell M,O
University of Medicine and Dentistry of New Jersey M*
University of Memphis M
University of Michigan M,D*
University of Minnesota, Twin Cities Campus M,D*
University of Missouri–Columbia M*
University of Missouri–St. Louis M,O
University of Nevada, Las Vegas M
University of New Haven M*
University of New Orleans M
The University of North Carolina at Chapel Hill M,D*
The University of North Carolina at Charlotte M*
University of North Florida M,O
University of North Texas Health Science Center at Fort Worth M,D
University of Oklahoma M*
University of Oklahoma Health Sciences Center M,D
University of Ottawa M*
University of Pennsylvania M,D*
University of Phoenix M,D
University of Phoenix–Atlanta Campus M
University of Phoenix–Augusta Campus M
University of Phoenix–Austin Campus M
University of Phoenix–Bay Area Campus M
University of Phoenix–Birmingham Campus M
University of Phoenix–Central Florida Campus M
University of Phoenix–Central Valley Campus M
University of Phoenix–Chattanooga Campus M
University of Phoenix–Cheyenne Campus M
University of Phoenix–Cincinnati Campus M
University of Phoenix–Cleveland Campus M
University of Phoenix–Columbus Georgia Campus M
University of Phoenix–Columbus Ohio Campus M
University of Phoenix–Dallas Campus M
University of Phoenix–Denver Campus M
University of Phoenix–Des Moines Campus M
University of Phoenix–Eastern Washington Campus M
University of Phoenix–Harrisburg Campus M
University of Phoenix–Hawaii Campus M
University of Phoenix–Houston Campus M
University of Phoenix–Idaho Campus M
University of Phoenix–Indianapolis Campus M
University of Phoenix–Jersey City Campus M
University of Phoenix–Kansas City Campus M
University of Phoenix–Las Vegas Campus M
University of Phoenix–Louisiana Campus M
University of Phoenix–Louisville Campus M
University of Phoenix–Madison Campus M
University of Phoenix–Maryland Campus M
University of Phoenix–Memphis Campus M
University of Phoenix–Metro Detroit Campus M
University of Phoenix–Minneapolis/St. Louis Park Campus M
University of Phoenix–Nashville Campus M
University of Phoenix–New Mexico Campus M
University of Phoenix–Northern Nevada Campus M
University of Phoenix–Northern Virginia Campus M
University of Phoenix–North Florida Campus M
University of Phoenix–Northwest Arkansas Campus M
University of Phoenix–Oklahoma City Campus M
University of Phoenix–Omaha Campus M
University of Phoenix–Oregon Campus M
University of Phoenix–Philadelphia Campus M
University of Phoenix–Phoenix Campus M,O
University of Phoenix–Pittsburgh Campus M
University of Phoenix–Puerto Rico Campus M
University of Phoenix–Raleigh Campus M
University of Phoenix–Renton Learning Center M
University of Phoenix–Richmond Campus M
University of Phoenix–Sacramento Valley Campus M
University of Phoenix–St. Louis Campus M
University of Phoenix–San Antonio Campus M
University of Phoenix–San Diego Campus M
University of Phoenix–Savannah Campus M
University of Phoenix–Southern Arizona Campus M,O
University of Phoenix–Southern California Campus M,O
University of Phoenix–Southern Colorado Campus M
University of Phoenix–South Florida Campus M
University of Phoenix–Springfield Campus M
University of Phoenix–Tulsa Campus M
University of Phoenix–Utah Campus M
University of Phoenix–Vancouver Campus M
University of Phoenix–West Florida Campus M
University of Phoenix–West Michigan Campus M
University of Phoenix–Wisconsin Campus M
University of Pittsburgh M,D,O*
University of Puerto Rico, Medical Sciences Campus M
University of St. Francis (IL) M
University of St. Thomas (MN) M*
University of San Francisco M
University of Saskatchewan M
The University of Scranton M
University of South Africa M,D
University of South Carolina M,D
University of Southern California M*
University of Southern Indiana M
University of Southern Maine M,O
University of Southern Mississippi M
University of South Florida M,D*
The University of Tennessee M
The University of Texas at Arlington M*
The University of Texas at Dallas M*
The University of Texas at El Paso M,O
The University of Texas at Tyler M
University of the Incarnate Word M,O
University of the Sciences in Philadelphia M,D*
The University of Toledo M,O
University of Virginia M
University of Washington M*
The University of Western Ontario M,D
University of Wisconsin–Oshkosh M
Utica College M
Villanova University M,D,O*
Virginia Commonwealth University M,D
Wagner College M
Wake Forest University M*
Walden University M,D,O
Washington State University M*
Washington State University Spokane M
Wayland Baptist University M
Weber State University M
Webster University M,D
West Chester University of Pennsylvania M,O
Western Carolina University M
Western Connecticut State University M
Western Illinois University M,O
Western Kentucky University M
Western Michigan University M,D,O*
Widener University M*
William Woods University M,O
Wilmington University M
Worcester State College M
Wright State University M
Xavier University M*
Yale University M,D*
Youngstown State University M

HEALTH SERVICES RESEARCH

Brown University M,D*
Case Western Reserve University M,D*
Cornell University, Joan and Sanford I. Weill Medical College and Graduate School of Medical Sciences M
Dartmouth College M,D*
Emory University M,D*
The George Washington University M,D,O*
The Johns Hopkins University M,D*
Lakehead University M
McMaster University M,D
Medical University of South Carolina M
Old Dominion University D
Penn State Hershey Medical Center M
Stanford University M*
Texas State University–San Marcos M*
Thomas Jefferson University O*
University of Alberta M,D*
University of Arkansas for Medical Sciences D
University of Colorado Denver D*
University of Florida M,D*
University of Illinois at Chicago M,D*
University of La Verne M
University of Maryland, Baltimore M,D*
University of Massachusetts Worcester D
University of Minnesota, Twin Cities Campus M,D*
University of New Brunswick Fredericton M
The University of North Carolina at Charlotte D*
University of North Florida M,O
University of Ottawa D,O*
University of Puerto Rico, Medical Sciences Campus M
University of Rochester M,D,O*
University of Southern California D*
University of Virginia M
University of Washington M,D*
University of Wisconsin–Madison M,D*
Virginia Commonwealth University D
Wake Forest University M*

HIGHER EDUCATION

Abilene Christian University M
Alliant International University–Irvine M,D,O*
Alliant International University–Los Angeles M,D,O*
Alliant International University–San Diego M,D,O*
Alliant International University–San Francisco M,D,O*
Angelo State University M
Appalachian State University M,O
Argosy University, Atlanta M,D,O*
Argosy University, Chicago M,D,O*
Argosy University, Denver M,D*
Argosy University, Hawai'i M,D*
Argosy University, Inland Empire M,D*
Argosy University, Los Angeles M,D*
Argosy University, Nashville M,D,O*
Argosy University, Orange County M,D*
Argosy University, Phoenix M,D,O*
Argosy University, San Diego M,D*
Argosy University, San Francisco Bay Area M,D*
Argosy University, Sarasota M,D,O*

Argosy University, Schaumburg M,D,O*
Argosy University, Seattle M,D*
Argosy University, Tampa M,D,O*
Argosy University, Twin Cities M,D,O*
Argosy University, Washington DC M,D,O*
Arizona State University M
Auburn University M,D,O*
Azusa Pacific University M,D
Ball State University M,D*
Barry University M,D*
Benedictine University D
Bernard M. Baruch College of the City University of New York M
Bethel University M,O
Boston College M,D*
Bowling Green State University D*
California Lutheran University M,D
California State University, Long Beach M,D
Capella University M,D,O
Central Michigan University M,D,O
Chicago State University M,D
Claremont Graduate University M,D,O*
College of Saint Elizabeth M,O
Columbia International University M,D,O
Dallas Baptist University M
Delta State University D
Drexel University M*
Eastern Kentucky University M
Fitchburg State College M,O
Florida Atlantic University M,D,O
Florida International University D*
Florida State University M,D,O*
Geneva College M
George Fox University M,D,O*
George Mason University M,D,O*
The George Washington University M,D,O*
Georgia Southern University M
Grambling State University M,D
Grand Valley State University M,O
Harvard University D*
Illinois State University M,D
Indiana State University M,D,O
Indiana University Bloomington M,D,O*
Indiana University of Pennsylvania M
Indiana University–Purdue University Indianapolis M,O*
Inter American University of Puerto Rico, Metropolitan Campus M
Iowa State University of Science and Technology M,D*
John Brown University M
Jones International University M
Kaplan University–Davenport Campus M
Kent State University M*
Louisiana State University and Agricultural and Mechanical College M,D,O
Loyola University Chicago M,D*
Marywood University M,D
Michigan State University M,D,O*
Minnesota State University Mankato M,D,O
Mississippi College M,D,O
Montana State University M,D,O
Morehead State University M,O
Morgan State University D
New York University M,D*
North Carolina State University M,D*
Northeastern State University M
Northern Arizona University M,D
Northern Illinois University M,D
Northwestern University M*
Northwest Missouri State University M,O
Nova Southeastern University D*
Oakland University M,D,O
The Ohio State University M*
Ohio University M,D*
Oklahoma State University M,D*
Old Dominion University M,D,O
Oral Roberts University M,D
Penn State University Park M,D*
Phillips Theological Seminary P,M,D
Pittsburg State University M,O
Portland State University M,D
Purdue University M,D,O
Rowan University M
St. Cloud State University M,D
Saint Louis University M,D,O
Salem State College M
San Diego State University M*
San Jose State University M,O
Seton Hall University D*
Shippensburg University of Pennsylvania M
Southeast Missouri State University M,O
Southern Illinois University Carbondale M*
Stanford University M,D*
Syracuse University M,D*
Taylor University M
Teachers College, Columbia University M,D
Texas A&M University–Commerce M,D
Texas A&M University–Kingsville D
Texas Southern University M,D
Texas Tech University M,D
TUI University M,D
Union Institute & University D
Union University M,D,O
Universidad Central del Este M,D
Universidad Iberoamericana P,M
Université de Sherbrooke M,O
University at Buffalo, the State University of New York M,D,O*
The University of Akron M
The University of Alabama M,D
The University of Arizona M,D*
University of Arkansas M,D,O
University of Arkansas at Little Rock D
The University of British Columbia M,D
University of Calgary M,D,O
University of California, Riverside M,D*
University of Central Florida M,D,O*
University of Central Oklahoma M
University of Connecticut M*
University of Delaware M,D,O*
University of Denver M,D,O*
University of Florida M,D,O*
University of Georgia D*
University of Houston M,D*
University of Illinois at Urbana–Champaign M,D,O*
The University of Iowa M,D,O*
The University of Kansas M,D*
University of Kentucky M,D
University of Louisville M
University of Maine M,D,O*
University of Manitoba M
University of Mary M
University of Maryland, College Park M,D*
University of Massachusetts Amherst M,D,O*
University of Massachusetts Boston M,D,O
University of Memphis M,D,O
University of Miami M,D,O*
University of Michigan M,D*
University of Minnesota, Twin Cities Campus M,D*
University of Mississippi M,D,O
University of Missouri–Columbia M,D,O*
University of Missouri–St. Louis M,D,O
University of New Hampshire M*
The University of North Carolina at Greensboro D
University of Northern Colorado D
University of Northern Iowa M
University of North Texas M,D,O
University of Oklahoma M,D*
University of Pittsburgh M,D*
University of San Diego M,D,O
University of South Carolina M
University of Southern California D*
University of Southern Mississippi M,D,O
University of South Florida M,D,O*
The University of Texas at San Antonio M,D,O*
University of the Incarnate Word M,D
The University of Toledo M,D
University of Virginia M,D,O
University of Washington M,D*
University of Wisconsin–Whitewater M*
Vanderbilt University M,D*
Villanova University M*
Virginia Polytechnic Institute and State University M,D,O*
Walden University M,D,O
Washington State University M,D,O*
Wayne State University M,D,O*
Western Carolina University M
Western Governors University M,O
Western Washington University M
West Virginia University M,D
Wilkes University M,D
Wright State University M,O

HISPANIC STUDIES

Brown University M,D*
California State University, Los Angeles M
California State University, Northridge M
Eastern Michigan University M,O
La Salle University M
Louisiana State University and Agricultural and Mechanical College M
McGill University M,D*
Michigan State University M,D*
New York University M,D*
Oregon State University M*
Pontifical Catholic University of Puerto Rico M,O
Queen's University at Kingston M
St. Thomas University M,O
San Jose State University M
Stony Brook University, State University of New York M,D
Texas A&M International University M,D
Université de Montréal M,D
University of Alberta M,D*
The University of British Columbia M,D
University of California, Berkeley D*
University of California, Los Angeles D*
University of California, Riverside M,D*
University of California, Santa Barbara M,D
University of Illinois at Chicago M,D*
University of Kentucky M,D
University of Nevada, Las Vegas M,O
The University of North Carolina at Greensboro M,O
The University of North Carolina Wilmington M,O
University of Pittsburgh M,D*
University of Puerto Rico, Mayagüez Campus M
University of Puerto Rico, Río Piedras M,D
The University of Texas at Austin M
University of Victoria M
University of Washington M*
Villanova University M*

HISTORIC PRESERVATION

Arkansas State University M,D
Ball State University M*
Boston University M*
Buffalo State College, State University of New York M,O
Clemson University M
College of Charleston M*
Columbia University M,O*
Cornell University M,D*
Delaware State University M
Eastern Michigan University M,O
The George Washington University M*
Georgia State University M,O
Goucher College M
Kent State University M,O*
Michigan Technological University D
New York University *
Northwestern State University of Louisiana M
Pratt Institute M*
Rutgers, The State University of New Jersey, New Brunswick M,D,O*
St. Cloud State University M
Savannah College of Art and Design M*
School of the Art Institute of Chicago M*
Texas Tech University M
Universidad Nacional Pedro Henriquez Urena P,M,D
University of California, Riverside M,D*
University of Delaware M,D*
University of Georgia M*
University of Hawaii at Manoa O*
University of Kentucky M
University of Maryland, College Park M,O*
University of New Mexico O*
The University of North Carolina at Greensboro M,O
University of Oregon M*
University of Pennsylvania M,O*
University of South Carolina M,O
The University of Texas at Austin M,D

*M—master's degree; P—first professional degree; D—doctorate; O—other advanced degree; *—Close-Up and/or Announcement or Display in one of the other books in this series*

The University of Texas at San Antonio	M,O*
University of Vermont	M*
University of Washington	O*
University of West Florida	M
University of Wisconsin–Milwaukee	M,D,O
Ursuline College	M
Virginia Commonwealth University	O

HISTORY

Adams State College	M
American Public University System	M
American University	M,D*
American University of Beirut	M
Andrews University	M
Angelo State University	M
Appalachian State University	M
Arizona State University	M,D
Arkansas State University	M,O
Arkansas Tech University	M
Armstrong Atlantic State University	M
Ashland Theological Seminary	P,M,D,O
Ashland University	M
Auburn University	M,D*
Ball State University	M*
Baylor University	M
Bob Jones University	P,M,D,O
Boise State University	M
Boston College	M,D*
Boston University	M,D*
Bowling Green State University	M,D*
Brandeis University	M,D
Brock University	M
Brooklyn College of the City University of New York	M,D
Brown University	M,D*
Buffalo State College, State University of New York	M
Butler University	M
California Polytechnic State University, San Luis Obispo	M
California State Polytechnic University, Pomona	M
California State University, Bakersfield	M
California State University, Chico	M
California State University, East Bay	M
California State University, Fresno	M
California State University, Fullerton	M
California State University, Long Beach	M
California State University, Los Angeles	M
California State University, Northridge	M
California State University, Stanislaus	M
Cardinal Stritch University	M
Carleton University	M,D
Carnegie Mellon University	M,D*
Case Western Reserve University	M,D*
The Catholic University of America	M,D
Central Connecticut State University	M,O
Central European University	M,D*
Central Michigan University	M,D,O
Central Washington University	M
Centro de Estudios Avanzados de Puerto Rico y el Caribe	M,D
Chicago State University	M
Christopher Newport University	M
The Citadel, The Military College of South Carolina	M
City College of the City University of New York	M*
Claremont Graduate University	M,D,O*
Clark Atlanta University	M,D
Clark University	M,D,O
Clemson University	M
Cleveland State University	M
The College at Brockport, State University of New York	M
College of Charleston	M*
The College of Saint Rose	M*
College of Staten Island of the City University of New York	M
The College of William and Mary	M,D
Colorado State University	M*
Columbia University	M,D*
Concordia University (Canada)	M,D
Converse College	M
Cornell University	M,D*
Dalhousie University	M,D
DePaul University	M*
Drake University	M*
Drew University	M,D
Duke University	M,D*
Duquesne University	M*
East Carolina University	M
Eastern Illinois University	M
Eastern Kentucky University	M
Eastern Michigan University	M,O
Eastern Washington University	M
East Stroudsburg University of Pennsylvania	M
East Tennessee State University	M
Emory & Henry College	M
Emory University	D*
Emporia State University	M
Fairleigh Dickinson University, Metropolitan Campus	M*
Fayetteville State University	M
Fitchburg State College	M,O
Florida Agricultural and Mechanical University	M
Florida Atlantic University	M,O
Florida Gulf Coast University	M
Florida International University	M,D*
Florida State University	M,D*
Fordham University	M,D*
Fort Hays State University	M
George Mason University	M,D,O*
Georgetown University	M,D
The George Washington University	M,D*
Georgia College & State University	M
Georgia Southern University	M
Georgia State University	M,D
Graduate School and University Center of the City University of New York	D*
Hardin-Simmons University	M
Harvard University	D*
High Point University	M
Howard University	M,D
Hunter College of the City University of New York	M
Idaho State University	M
Illinois State University	M
Indiana State University	M
Indiana University Bloomington	M,D*
Indiana University of Pennsylvania	M
Indiana University–Purdue University Indianapolis	M*
Inter American University of Puerto Rico, Metropolitan Campus	M
Iona College	M*
Iowa State University of Science and Technology	M,D*
Jackson State University	M
Jacksonville State University	M
James Madison University	M
John Carroll University	M
The Johns Hopkins University	D*
Kansas State University	M,D*
Kent State University	M,D*
Lakehead University	M
Lamar University	M
La Salle University	M
Laurentian University	M
Lehigh University	M,D
Lehman College of the City University of New York	M
Lincoln University (MO)	M
Long Island University, Brooklyn Campus	M,O
Long Island University, C.W. Post Campus	M
Louisiana State University and Agricultural and Mechanical College	M,D
Louisiana Tech University	M
Loyola University Chicago	M,D*
Lynchburg College	M
Marquette University	M,D
Marshall University	M
McGill University	M,D*
McMaster University	M,D
Memorial University of Newfoundland	M,D
Miami University	M,D*
Michigan State University	M,D*
Middle Tennessee State University	M
Midwestern State University	M
Millersville University of Pennsylvania	M
Minnesota State University Mankato	M
Mississippi College	M,O
Mississippi State University	M,D
Missouri State University	M*
Monmouth University	M
Montana State University	M,D
Montclair State University	M,O*
Morgan State University	M,D
Murray State University	M
National University	M
Nebraska Wesleyan University	M
New Jersey Institute of Technology	M
New Mexico State University	M
The New School: A University	M,D*
New York University	M,D,O*
North Carolina Central University	M
North Carolina State University	M*
North Dakota State University	M,D
Northeastern Illinois University	M
Northeastern University	M,D*
Northern Arizona University	M,D
Northern Illinois University	M,D
Northwestern University	D*
Northwest Missouri State University	M
Oakland University	M
The Ohio State University	M,D*
Ohio University	M,D*
Oklahoma State University	M,D*
Old Dominion University	M
Oregon State University	M,D*
Penn State University Park	M,D*
Pepperdine University	M
Pittsburg State University	M
Pontifical Catholic University of Puerto Rico	M
Portland State University	M
Princeton University	D*
Providence College	M*
Purdue University	M,D
Purdue University Calumet	M
Queens College of the City University of New York	M
Rhode Island College	M
Rice University	M,D
Roosevelt University	M
Rutgers, The State University of New Jersey, Camden	M
Rutgers, The State University of New Jersey, Newark	M*
Rutgers, The State University of New Jersey, New Brunswick	D*
St. Cloud State University	M
St. John's University (NY)	M,D
Saint Louis University	M,D
Saint Mary's University (Canada)	M
Salem State College	M
Salisbury University	M
Sam Houston State University	M
San Diego State University	M*
San Francisco State University	M
San Jose State University	M
Sarah Lawrence College	M*
Seton Hall University	M*
Shippensburg University of Pennsylvania	M,O
Simon Fraser University	M,D
Slippery Rock University of Pennsylvania	M
Smith College	M
Sonoma State University	M
Southeastern Louisiana University	M
Southeast Missouri State University	M
Southern Connecticut State University	M
Southern Illinois University Carbondale	M,D*
Southern Illinois University Edwardsville	M
Southern Methodist University	M,D*
Southern University and Agricultural and Mechanical College	M
Southwestern Assemblies of God University	M
Stanford University	M,D*
State University of New York at Binghamton	M,D*
State University of New York at Oswego	M
State University of New York College at Cortland	M
Stephen F. Austin State University	M

Stony Brook University, State University of New York	M,D
Sul Ross State University	M*
Syracuse University	M,D*
Tarleton State University	M
Teachers College, Columbia University	M,D
Temple University	M,D*
Texas A&M International University	M
Texas A&M University	M,D*
Texas A&M University–Commerce	M
Texas A&M University–Corpus Christi	M
Texas A&M University–Kingsville	M
Texas A&M University–Texarkana	M
Texas Christian University	M,D
Texas Southern University	M
Texas State University–San Marcos	M*
Texas Tech University	M,D
Texas Woman's University	M
Trinity Western University	M
Tufts University	M,D*
Tulane University	M,D
Union Institute & University	M
Universidad Adventista de las Antillas	M
Université de Moncton	M
Université de Montréal	M,D
Université de Sherbrooke	M
Université du Québec à Montréal	M,D
Université Laval	M,D
University at Albany, State University of New York	M,D,O*
University at Buffalo, the State University of New York	M,D*
The University of Akron	M,D
The University of Alabama	M,D
The University of Alabama at Birmingham	M*
The University of Alabama in Huntsville	M
University of Alaska Fairbanks	M
University of Alberta	M,D*
The University of Arizona	M,D*
University of Arkansas	M,D
The University of British Columbia	M,D
University of Calgary	M,D
University of California, Berkeley	M,D*
University of California, Davis	M,D*
University of California, Irvine	M,D*
University of California, Los Angeles	M,D*
University of California, Riverside	M,D*
University of California, San Diego	M,D*
University of California, Santa Barbara	D
University of California, Santa Cruz	M,D*
University of Central Arkansas	M
University of Central Florida	M*
University of Central Missouri	M
University of Central Oklahoma	M
University of Chicago	D*
University of Cincinnati	M,D
University of Colorado at Boulder	M,D*
University of Colorado at Colorado Springs	M
University of Colorado Denver	M*
University of Connecticut	M,D*
University of Delaware	M,D*
University of Florida	M,D*
University of Georgia	M,D*
University of Guelph	M,D
University of Hawaii at Manoa	M,D*
University of Houston	M,D*
University of Houston–Clear Lake	M
University of Idaho	M,D
University of Illinois at Chicago	M,D*
University of Illinois at Springfield	M
University of Illinois at Urbana–Champaign	M,D*
University of Indianapolis	M
The University of Iowa	M,D*
The University of Kansas	M,D*
University of Kentucky	M,D
University of Lethbridge	M,D
University of Louisiana at Lafayette	M*
University of Louisiana at Monroe	M
University of Louisville	M
University of Maine	M,D*
University of Manitoba	M,D
University of Maryland, Baltimore County	M*
University of Maryland, College Park	M,D*
University of Massachusetts Amherst	M,D*
University of Massachusetts Boston	M
University of Memphis	M,D
University of Miami	M,D*
University of Michigan	D,O*
University of Minnesota, Twin Cities Campus	M,D*
University of Mississippi	M,D
University of Missouri–Columbia	M,D*
University of Missouri–Kansas City	M,D*
The University of Montana	M,D
University of Nebraska at Kearney	M
University of Nebraska at Omaha	M
University of Nebraska–Lincoln	M,D*
University of Nevada, Las Vegas	M,D
University of Nevada, Reno	M,D*
University of New Brunswick Fredericton	M,D
University of New Hampshire	M,D*
University of New Mexico	M,D*
University of New Orleans	M
University of North Alabama	M
The University of North Carolina at Chapel Hill	M,D*
The University of North Carolina at Charlotte	M*
The University of North Carolina at Greensboro	M,D,O
The University of North Carolina Wilmington	M
University of North Dakota	M,D
University of Northern British Columbia	M,D,O
University of Northern Colorado	M
University of Northern Iowa	M
University of North Florida	M
University of North Texas	M,D
University of Notre Dame	M,D*
University of Oklahoma	M,D*
University of Oregon	M,D*
University of Ottawa	M,D*
University of Pennsylvania	M,D*
University of Pittsburgh	M,D*
University of Puerto Rico, Río Piedras	M,D
University of Regina	M,D
University of Rhode Island	M
University of Rochester	M,D*
University of San Diego	M
University of Saskatchewan	M,D
The University of Scranton	M
University of South Africa	M,D
University of South Alabama	M*
University of South Carolina	M,D,O
The University of South Dakota	M
University of Southern California	D*
University of Southern Mississippi	M,D
University of South Florida	M,D*
The University of Tennessee	M,D
The University of Texas at Arlington	M,D*
The University of Texas at Austin	M,D
The University of Texas at Brownsville	M
The University of Texas at El Paso	M,D
The University of Texas at San Antonio	M*
The University of Texas at Tyler	M
The University of Texas of the Permian Basin	M
The University of Texas–Pan American	M
The University of Toledo	M,D
University of Toronto	M,D
University of Tulsa	M*
University of Utah	M,D*
University of Vermont	M*
University of Victoria	M,D
University of Virginia	M,D
University of Washington	M,D*
University of Waterloo	M,D
The University of Western Ontario	M,D
University of West Florida	M
University of West Georgia	M
University of Windsor	M
The University of Winnipeg	M
University of Wisconsin–Eau Claire	M
University of Wisconsin–Madison	M,D*
University of Wisconsin–Milwaukee	M,D
University of Wisconsin–Stevens Point	M
University of Wyoming	M
Utah State University	M
Valdosta State University	M
Valparaiso University	M,O
Vanderbilt University	M,D*
Villanova University	M*
Virginia Commonwealth University	M,D
Virginia Polytechnic Institute and State University	M*
Virginia State University	M
Washington College	M
Washington State University	M,D*
Washington State University Vancouver	M
Washington University in St. Louis	M,D*
Wayne State University	M,D*
West Chester University of Pennsylvania	M,O
Western Carolina University	M
Western Connecticut State University	M
Western Illinois University	M
Western Kentucky University	M
Western Michigan University	M,D*
Western Washington University	M
Westfield State College	M
West Texas A&M University	M
West Virginia University	M,D
Wichita State University	M*
Wilfrid Laurier University	M,D
William Paterson University of New Jersey	M*
Winthrop University	M
Worcester State College	M
Wright State University	M
Yale University	M,D*
York University	M,D
Youngstown State University	M

HISTORY OF MEDICINE

Duke University	*
McGill University	M,D*
Rutgers, The State University of New Jersey, New Brunswick	D*
Uniformed Services University of the Health Sciences	M*
University of Minnesota, Twin Cities Campus	M,D*
Yale University	M,D*

HISTORY OF SCIENCE AND TECHNOLOGY

Carnegie Mellon University	M,D*
Cornell University	M,D*
Drexel University	M*
Georgia Institute of Technology	M,D*
Harvard University	M,D*
Indiana University Bloomington	M,D*
Iowa State University of Science and Technology	M,D*
The Johns Hopkins University	M,D*
Massachusetts Institute of Technology	D*
Oregon State University	M,D*
Polytechnic Institute of NYU	M
Princeton University	D*
Rensselaer Polytechnic Institute	M,D
Rutgers, The State University of New Jersey, New Brunswick	D*
Uniformed Services University of the Health Sciences	M,D*
University of California, Berkeley	D*
University of California, San Diego	M,D*
University of California, San Francisco	M,D
University of Delaware	M,D*
University of Massachusetts Amherst	M,D*
University of Minnesota, Twin Cities Campus	M,D*
University of Notre Dame	M,D*
University of Oklahoma	M,D*
University of Pennsylvania	M,D*
University of Pittsburgh	M,D*
University of Toronto	M,D
University of Wisconsin–Madison	M,D*

*M—master's degree; P—first professional degree; D—doctorate; O—other advanced degree; *—Close-Up and/or Announcement or Display in one of the other books in this series*

Virginia Polytechnic Institute and State University M,D*
West Virginia University M,D*
Yale University M,D*

HIV/AIDS NURSING

Duke University M,D,O*
University of Delaware M,O*

HOLOCAUST STUDIES

Clark University D
Drew University M,D,O
Gratz College M,O
Kean University M
Laura and Alvin Siegal College of Judaic Studies M
The Richard Stockton College of New Jersey M
Seton Hall University M*
Seton Hill University O
West Chester University of Pennsylvania M,O

HOME ECONOMICS EDUCATION

Appalachian State University M
Cambridge College M,D,O
Central Washington University M
Eastern Kentucky University M
Harding University M,O
Indiana State University M
Iowa State University of Science and Technology M,D*
Louisiana State University and Agricultural and Mechanical College M,D
Montana State University M
Montclair State University M,O*
Northwestern State University of Louisiana M
The Ohio State University M*
Purdue University M,D,O
Queens College of the City University of New York M
South Carolina State University M
State University of New York College at Oneonta M
Texas Tech University M,D
The University of British Columbia M,D
University of Central Oklahoma M
University of Nebraska–Lincoln M,D*
Utah State University M
Wayne State College M

HOMELAND SECURITY

American Public University System M
Arkansas Tech University M
Chaminade University of Honolulu M,O
Fairleigh Dickinson University, Metropolitan Campus M*
George Mason University M,D*
The Johns Hopkins University M,O*
Long Island University at Riverhead M,O
National Defense University M
National University M
Regent University M
Saint Joseph's University M,O
Salve Regina University M,O
Texas A&M University M,O*
Thomas Edison State College M,O
Tiffin University M
Towson University M,O
University of Central Florida M,O*
University of Connecticut M*
The University of Toledo M,O
Upper Iowa University M
Virginia Commonwealth University M,O
Walden University M,D,O
Wayland Baptist University M
Wilmington University M

HORTICULTURE

Auburn University M,D*
Colorado State University M,D*
Cornell University M,D*
Iowa State University of Science and Technology M,D*
Kansas State University M,D*
Louisiana State University and Agricultural and Mechanical College M,D
Michigan State University M,D*
Mississippi State University M,D
New Mexico State University M,D
North Carolina State University M,D,O*
Nova Scotia Agricultural College M
The Ohio State University M,D*
Oklahoma State University M,D*
Oregon State University M,D*
Penn State University Park M,D*
Purdue University M,D
Rutgers, The State University of New Jersey, New Brunswick M,D*
Southern Illinois University Carbondale M*
Texas A&M University M,D*
Texas Tech University M,D
Universidad Nacional Pedro Henriquez Urena P,M,D
University of Arkansas M
University of California, Davis M*
University of Delaware M*
University of Florida M,D*
University of Georgia M,D*
University of Guelph M,D
University of Hawaii at Manoa M,D*
University of Maine M*
University of Manitoba M,D
University of Maryland, College Park D*
University of Missouri–Columbia M,D*
University of Nebraska–Lincoln M,D*
University of Puerto Rico, Mayagüez Campus M
University of South Africa M,D
University of Vermont M,D*
University of Washington M,D*
University of Wisconsin–Madison M,D*
Virginia Polytechnic Institute and State University M,D*
Washington State University M,D*
West Virginia University M,D

HOSPICE NURSING

Madonna University M

HOSPITALITY MANAGEMENT

Andrew Jackson University M
California State University, Northridge M
Central Michigan University M
Columbia Southern University M
Cornell University M,D*
Eastern Michigan University M,O
East Stroudsburg University of Pennsylvania M
Fairleigh Dickinson University, College at Florham M*
Fairleigh Dickinson University, Metropolitan Campus M*
Florida International University M*
The George Washington University M,O*
Iowa State University of Science and Technology M,D*
Johnson & Wales University M,O
Kansas State University M,D*
Lynn University M,D
Michigan State University M*
New York University M,D,O*
The Ohio State University M,D*
Oklahoma State University M,D*
Penn State University Park M,D*
Purdue University M,D
Rochester Institute of Technology M
Roosevelt University M
Royal Roads University M,O
Schiller International University (United States) M
Schiller International University (United Kingdom) M
South Dakota State University M
Southern New Hampshire University M,D,O*
Strayer University M
Temple University M,D*
Texas Tech University M,D
The University of Alabama M
University of Central Florida M*
University of Delaware M*
University of Guelph M
University of Houston M*
University of Kentucky M
University of Massachusetts Amherst M*
University of Missouri–Columbia M,D*
University of Nevada, Las Vegas M,D,O
University of New Orleans M
University of North Texas M
University of South Carolina M
The University of Tennessee M
Virginia Polytechnic Institute and State University M,D*

HUMAN-COMPUTER INTERACTION

Carnegie Mellon University M,D*
Cornell University D*
Dalhousie University M
DePaul University M,D*
Georgia Institute of Technology M*
Indiana University Bloomington M,D*
Iowa State University of Science and Technology M,D*
Naval Postgraduate School M,D
Old Dominion University M,D
Rensselaer Polytechnic Institute M
Rochester Institute of Technology M
State University of New York at Oswego M
Tufts University O*
University of Baltimore M,D
University of Illinois at Urbana–Champaign M,D,O*
University of Michigan M,D*

HUMAN DEVELOPMENT

Argosy University, Chicago D*
Arizona State University M,D
Auburn University M,D*
Boston University M,D,O*
Bowling Green State University M*
Bradley University M
Brigham Young University M,D*
Brock University M,D
California State University, San Bernardino M
Central Michigan University M,O
Claremont Graduate University M,D,O*
Clemson University M
Colorado State University M*
Cornell University D*
DePaul University M,D*
Dowling College M,D,O
Duke University D*
East Tennessee State University M
Erikson Institute M,O
Fielding Graduate University M,D,O*
The George Washington University M*
Harvard University M,D*
Hofstra University M,D,O*
Hood College M,O
Howard University M
Indiana University Bloomington M,D*
Iowa State University of Science and Technology M,D*
Kansas State University D*
Kent State University M,D*
Laurentian University M
Lehigh University M,D
Lindsey Wilson College M
Marywood University D
Montana State University M
National-Louis University M,D,O
New York Institute of Technology M
New York University M,D,O*
North Dakota State University D
Northwestern University D*
The Ohio State University M,D*
Oklahoma State University M,D*
Oregon State University M,D*
Our Lady of the Lake University of San Antonio M
Pacific Oaks College M
Penn State University Park M,D*
Purdue University M,D
Saint Joseph College M,O
St. Lawrence University M,O
Saint Louis University M,D,O
Saint Mary's University of Minnesota M
South Dakota State University M
Southern Illinois University Carbondale M,D*
Texas A&M University M,D*
Texas Tech University M,D
The University of Alabama M
The University of Arizona M,D*

The University of British Columbia M,D,O
University of Calgary M,D
University of California, Berkeley M,D*
University of California, Davis D*
University of California, Santa Barbara D
University of Central Oklahoma M
University of Chicago D*
University of Connecticut M,D,O*
University of Dayton M,O
University of Delaware M,D*
University of Guelph M,D
University of Houston M*
University of Illinois at Chicago M,D*
University of Illinois at Springfield M
University of Illinois at Urbana–Champaign M,D*
University of Maine M*
University of Maryland, College Park M,D*
University of Missouri–Columbia M,D*
University of Nebraska–Lincoln M,D,O*
University of Nevada, Reno M*
The University of North Carolina at Greensboro M,D
University of North Texas M,O
University of Pennsylvania M,D*
University of St. Thomas (MN) M,D,O*
University of South Africa M,D
The University of Texas at Austin M,D
University of Utah M*
University of Victoria M,D
University of Washington M,D*
University of Wisconsin–Madison M,D*
University of Wisconsin–Stevens Point M
University of Wisconsin–Stout M
Utah State University M,D
Vanderbilt University M*
Virginia Polytechnic Institute and State University M,D*
Washington State University M*
Wayne State University M*
West Virginia University M,D
Wheelock College M

HUMAN GENETICS

Baylor College of Medicine D*
Case Western Reserve University D*
The Johns Hopkins University D*
Louisiana State University Health Sciences Center M,D*
McGill University M,D*
Memorial University of Newfoundland M,D
Sarah Lawrence College M*
Tulane University M,D
University of California, Los Angeles M,D*
University of Chicago D*
University of Manitoba M,D
University of Maryland, Baltimore M,D*
University of Michigan M,D*
University of Pittsburgh M,D,O*
The University of Texas Health Science Center at Houston M,D
University of Utah M,D*
Vanderbilt University D*
Virginia Commonwealth University M,D,O
Wake Forest University D*
West Virginia University M,D

HUMANITIES

American Public University System M
Arcadia University M
Brigham Young University M*
California Institute of Integral Studies M,D*
California State University, Dominguez Hills M
Carlow University M
Central European University M,D*
Central Michigan University M
Claremont Graduate University M,D,O*
College of the Humanities and Sciences, Harrison Middleton University M,D
Concordia University (Canada) D
Dominican University of California M
Drew University M,D,O
Duke University M*
Florida State University M,D,O*
Georgetown University M,D
Hofstra University M*
Hollins University M,O
Hood College M
Instituto Tecnológico y de Estudios Superiores de Monterrey, Campus Central de Veracruz M
Instituto Tecnológico y de Estudios Superiores de Monterrey, Campus Ciudad de México M,D
Instituto Tecnológico y de Estudios Superiores de Monterrey, Campus Ciudad Juárez M
Instituto Tecnológico y de Estudios Superiores de Monterrey, Campus Estado de México M,D
Instituto Tecnológico y de Estudios Superiores de Monterrey, Campus Irapuato M,D
John Carroll University M
Laura and Alvin Siegal College of Judaic Studies M
Laurentian University M
Marshall University M
Marymount University M
Massachusetts Institute of Technology M*
Memorial University of Newfoundland M
Michigan State University M*
Mount St. Mary's College M
National University M
New York University M,O*
Nova Southeastern University M,O*
Old Dominion University M
Penn State Harrisburg M,D
Pepperdine University M
Polytechnic Institute of NYU M,O
Prescott College M
St. Edward's University M,O
Salve Regina University M,D,O
Sam Houston State University M,D
San Francisco State University M
Stanford University M*
Texas Tech University M,D
Tiffin University M
Towson University M
Trinity Western University M
Universidad Nacional Pedro Henriquez Urena P,M,D
University of California, Santa Cruz D*
University of Chicago M*
University of Colorado Denver M*
University of Dallas M
University of Houston–Clear Lake M
University of Louisville M,D
The University of Texas at Arlington M*
The University of Texas at Dallas M,D*
The University of Texas Medical Branch M,D*
University of Utah M*
University of West Florida M
Villanova University M*
Virginia Commonwealth University M,D,O
Wright State University M
York University M,D

HUMAN RESOURCES DEVELOPMENT

Abilene Christian University M
Amberton University M
American International College M
Antioch University Los Angeles M
Azusa Pacific University M
Barry University M,D*
Bowie State University M
California State University, Sacramento M
Claremont Graduate University M,D,O*
Clemson University M
The College of New Rochelle M
Florida International University M,D*
Florida State University M,D,O*
Friends University M
The George Washington University M,D,O*
Illinois Institute of Technology M,D*
Indiana State University M
Indiana Tech M
Indiana University of Pennsylvania M
Inter American University of Puerto Rico, Metropolitan Campus M
Inter American University of Puerto Rico, San Germán Campus M,D
Iowa State University of Science and Technology M,D*
John F. Kennedy University M,O
The Johns Hopkins University M,O*
Johnson & Wales University O
Kentucky State University M
Louisiana State University and Agricultural and Mechanical College M,D
Manhattanville College M*
Marquette University M
McDaniel College M
Midwestern State University M
Mississippi State University M,D,O
Moravian College M
National-Louis University M
Naval Postgraduate School M
The New School: A University M,O*
New York University M,O*
North Carolina Agricultural and Technical State University M,D
North Carolina State University M*
Northeastern Illinois University M
Oakland University M
Ottawa University M
Penn State University Park M*
Pittsburg State University M
Rochester Institute of Technology M
Rollins College M
Roosevelt University M
St. John Fisher College M
Salve Regina University M,O
South Dakota State University M
Southern New Hampshire University M,O*
Suffolk University M,O*
Syracuse University D*
Texas A&M University M,D*
Towson University M
Universidad Central del Este M,D
Universidad Iberoamericana P,M
University of Bridgeport M
University of Connecticut M*
University of Illinois at Urbana–Champaign M,D,O*
University of Louisville M
University of Minnesota, Twin Cities Campus M,D,O*
University of Missouri–St. Louis M,O
University of Regina M
The University of Scranton M
University of South Africa M,D
The University of Tennessee M
The University of Texas at Tyler M,D
University of Wisconsin–Milwaukee M,O
University of Wisconsin–Stout M
Vanderbilt University M,D*
Villanova University M*
Virginia Commonwealth University M
Virginia Polytechnic Institute and State University M,D*
Webster University M,D
Western Carolina University M
Western Michigan University M,D,O*
Western Seminary M,O
William Woods University M,O
Xavier University M*

HUMAN RESOURCES MANAGEMENT

Adelphi University M,O*
Alabama Agricultural and Mechanical University M,O
Albany State University M
Amberton University M
American InterContinental University Online M
American InterContinental University South Florida M
Andrew Jackson University M
Assumption College M,O
Auburn University M,D*
Baker College Center for Graduate Studies M
Baldwin-Wallace College M
Barry University O*
Benedictine University M
Bernard M. Baruch College of the City University of New York M,D

*M—master's degree; P—first professional degree; D—doctorate; O—other advanced degree; *—Close-Up and/or Announcement or Display in one of the other books in this series*

Boston University	M,O*
Briar Cliff University	M
British American College London	M
Buffalo State College, State University of New York	M,O
California Coast University	M
California Intercontinental University	M,D
California State University, East Bay	M
California State University, Sacramento	M
Capella University	M,D,O
Caribbean University	M,D
Case Western Reserve University	M*
The Catholic University of America	M
Central Michigan University	M,O
Claremont Graduate University	M*
Cleveland State University	M
College of Santa Fe	M
Colorado Technical University Colorado Springs	M,D
Colorado Technical University Denver	M
Colorado Technical University Sioux Falls	M
Columbia Southern University	M
Columbia University	M*
Concordia University, St. Paul	M
Concordia University Wisconsin	M
Cornell University	M,D*
Cumberland University	M
Dallas Baptist University	M
Davenport University	M
Davenport University	M
Davenport University	M
DePaul University	M*
DeVry University	M*
East Central University	M
Eastern Michigan University	M,O
Emmanuel College	M,O
Everest University	M
Everest University	M
Fairfield University	M,O*
Fairleigh Dickinson University, College at Florham	M*
Fairleigh Dickinson University, Metropolitan Campus	M,O*
Fitchburg State College	M
Florida Institute of Technology	M*
Florida International University	M*
Fordham University	M,D,O*
Framingham State College	M
Franklin Pierce University	M,D,O
Gannon University	O
George Mason University	M*
Georgetown University	M,D
The George Washington University	M,D*
Georgia State University	M,D
Golden Gate University	M,D,O
Goldey-Beacom College	M
Grambling State University	M
Hawai'i Pacific University	M*
HEC Montreal	M
Hofstra University	M*
Holy Family University	M
Hood College	M
Houston Baptist University	M
Howard University	M
Indiana Tech	M
Indiana Wesleyan University	M
Instituto Tecnologico de Santo Domingo	M
Instituto Tecnológico y de Estudios Superiores de Monterrey, Campus Cuernavaca	M
Inter American University of Puerto Rico, Bayamón Campus	M
Inter American University of Puerto Rico, Metropolitan Campus	M
Inter American University of Puerto Rico, Ponce Campus	M
Inter American University of Puerto Rico, San Germán Campus	M,D
International College of the Cayman Islands	M
Iona College	M,O*
Kaplan University–Davenport Campus	M
La Roche College	M,O
Lasell College	M,O
La Sierra University	M,O
Lewis University	M
Lincoln University (CA)	M
Lincoln University (PA)	M
Lindenwood University	M,O
Long Island University, Brooklyn Campus	M
Loyola University Chicago	M*
Marquette University	M
Marshall University	M
Marygrove College	M
Marymount University	M,O
McKendree University	M
McMaster University	M,D
Mercy College	M,O
Michigan State University	M,D*
Moravian College	M
National-Louis University	M
National University	M
Nazareth College of Rochester	M
New Mexico Highlands University	M
New York Institute of Technology	M,O
New York University	M,D,O*
Notre Dame de Namur University	M
Nova Southeastern University	M,D*
Oakland University	M,O
The Ohio State University	M,D*
Ottawa University	M
Pontifical Catholic University of Puerto Rico	M
Pontificia Universidad Catolica Madre y Maestra	M
Portland State University	M*
Purdue University	M,D
Regis University	M,O
Robert Morris College	M
Robert Morris University	M
Rollins College	M
Roosevelt University	M
Royal Roads University	M,O
Rutgers, The State University of New Jersey, Newark	M,D*
Rutgers, The State University of New Jersey, New Brunswick	M,D*
Sage Graduate School	M
St. Ambrose University	M,D
St. Edward's University	M,O
Saint Francis University	M
St. Joseph's College, Long Island Campus	M,O
Saint Joseph's University	M
Saint Leo University	M
Saint Mary's University of Minnesota	M
St. Thomas University	M,O
Salve Regina University	M,O
San Diego State University	M*
Southern Adventist University	M
Southern New Hampshire University	M,D,O*
Stevens Institute of Technology	M
Stony Brook University, State University of New York	M,O
Strayer University	M
Tarleton State University	M
Temple University	M,D*
Texas A&M University	M,D*
Thomas College	M
Thomas Edison State College	M,O
Trinity (Washington) University	M
Troy University	M
TUI University	M,D
Union Graduate College	M,O
Universidad del Este	M
Universidad del Turabo	M
Universidad Metropolitana	M
University at Albany, State University of New York	M*
University at Buffalo, the State University of New York	M,D,O*
The University of Akron	M
The University of Alabama in Huntsville	M,O
University of Central Florida	M,O*
University of Connecticut	M*
University of Dallas	M
University of Denver	M,O*
The University of Findlay	M
University of Florida	M*
University of Georgia	M,D,O*
University of Hawaii at Manoa	M*
University of Houston–Clear Lake	M
University of Illinois at Urbana–Champaign	M,D*
University of Lethbridge	M,D
University of Louisville	M
University of Mary	M
University of Minnesota, Twin Cities Campus	M,D*
University of Missouri–St. Louis	M,O
University of New Haven	M*
University of New Mexico	M*
University of Phoenix	M
University of Phoenix–Atlanta Campus	M
University of Phoenix–Augusta Campus	M
University of Phoenix–Austin Campus	M
University of Phoenix–Bay Area Campus	M
University of Phoenix–Birmingham Campus	M
University of Phoenix–Central Florida Campus	M
University of Phoenix–Central Valley Campus	M
University of Phoenix–Chattanooga Campus	M
University of Phoenix–Cheyenne Campus	M
University of Phoenix–Chicago Campus	M
University of Phoenix–Cincinnati Campus	M
University of Phoenix–Cleveland Campus	M
University of Phoenix–Columbus Georgia Campus	M
University of Phoenix–Columbus Ohio Campus	M
University of Phoenix–Dallas Campus	M
University of Phoenix–Denver Campus	M
University of Phoenix–Des Moines Campus	M
University of Phoenix–Eastern Washington Campus	M
University of Phoenix–Harrisburg Campus	M
University of Phoenix–Hawaii Campus	M
University of Phoenix–Houston Campus	M
University of Phoenix–Idaho Campus	M
University of Phoenix–Indianapolis Campus	M
University of Phoenix–Jersey City Campus	M
University of Phoenix–Kansas City Campus	M
University of Phoenix–Las Vegas Campus	M
University of Phoenix–Louisiana Campus	M
University of Phoenix–Madison Campus	M
University of Phoenix–Maryland Campus	M
University of Phoenix–Memphis Campus	M
University of Phoenix–Metro Detroit Campus	M
University of Phoenix–Minneapolis/St. Louis Park Campus	M
University of Phoenix–Nashville Campus	M
University of Phoenix–New Mexico Campus	M
University of Phoenix–Northern Nevada Campus	M
University of Phoenix–Northern Virginia Campus	M
University of Phoenix–North Florida Campus	M
University of Phoenix–Northwest Arkansas Campus	M
University of Phoenix–Oklahoma City Campus	M
University of Phoenix–Omaha Campus	M
University of Phoenix–Oregon Campus	M
University of Phoenix–Philadelphia Campus	M
University of Phoenix–Phoenix Campus	M
University of Phoenix–Pittsburgh Campus	M
University of Phoenix–Puerto Rico Campus	M
University of Phoenix–Raleigh Campus	M
University of Phoenix–Renton Learning Center	M
University of Phoenix–Richmond Campus	M
University of Phoenix–Sacramento Valley Campus	M
University of Phoenix–St. Louis Campus	M
University of Phoenix–San Antonio Campus	M
University of Phoenix–San Diego Campus	M
University of Phoenix–Savannah Campus	M
University of Phoenix–Southern Arizona Campus	M

University of Phoenix–Southern California Campus	M
University of Phoenix–Southern Colorado Campus	M
University of Phoenix–South Florida Campus	M
University of Phoenix–Springfield Campus	M
University of Phoenix–Tulsa Campus	M
University of Phoenix–Utah Campus	M
University of Phoenix–Vancouver Campus	M
University of Phoenix–West Florida Campus	M
University of Phoenix–West Michigan Campus	M
University of Phoenix–Wisconsin Campus	M
University of Pittsburgh	M,D*
University of Puerto Rico, Mayagüez Campus	M
University of Puerto Rico, Río Piedras	M,D
University of Regina	M,O
University of Rhode Island	M
University of St. Thomas (MN)	M,D,O*
The University of Scranton	M
University of South Carolina	M
The University of Texas at Arlington	M*
University of the Sacred Heart	M
The University of Toledo	M
University of Toronto	M,D
University of Wisconsin–Madison	M,D*
University of Wisconsin–Whitewater	M*
Upper Iowa University	M
Utah State University	M
Walden University	M,D
Wayland Baptist University	M
Webster University	M,D
West Chester University of Pennsylvania	M,O
Widener University	M*
Wilkes University	M
Wilmington University	M
York University	M,D

HUMAN SERVICES

Abilene Christian University	M,O
Andrews University	M
Bellevue University	M
Boricua College	M
Brandeis University	M
California State University, Sacramento	M
Capella University	M,D,O
Chestnut Hill College	M,O
Concordia University Chicago	M
Concordia University Wisconsin	M,D
Coppin State University	M
DePaul University	M,D*
Drury University	M
Eastern Michigan University	M,O
Eastern New Mexico University	M
Fairfield University	M,O*
Fairmont State University	M
Ferris State University	M
Georgia State University	M
Indiana University Northwest	M,O
Kansas State University	M*
Kent State University	M,D,O*
Lehigh University	M,D,O
Lincoln University (PA)	M
Louisiana State University in Shreveport	M
McDaniel College	M
Minnesota State University Mankato	M
Minnesota State University Moorhead	M,O
Montana State University–Billings	M
Murray State University	M
National-Louis University	M,O
National University	M
New England College	M
Nova Southeastern University	M,D*
Pontifical Catholic University of Puerto Rico	M,D
Purdue University Calumet	M
Roberts Wesleyan College	M
Rosemont College	M
St. Edward's University	M,O
Saint Joseph's University	M,O
St. Mary's University (United States)	M,D,O
Sojourner-Douglass College	M
South Carolina State University	M
Southern Oregon University	M
Springfield College	M
State University of New York at Oswego	M
Texas Southern University	M
Thomas University	M
Universidad del Turabo	M
Université de Montréal	D
University of Baltimore	M
University of Bridgeport	M
University of Central Missouri	M,O
University of Colorado at Colorado Springs	M,D
University of Great Falls	M
University of Illinois at Springfield	M
University of Maryland, Baltimore County	M,D*
University of Massachusetts Boston	M
University of Oklahoma	M*
University of Phoenix–Maryland Campus	M
University of Phoenix–Richmond Campus	M
Upper Iowa University	M
Walden University	M,D
Wayne State University	O*
West Virginia University	M
Wichita State University	M*
Wilmington University	M
Youngstown State University	M

HYDRAULICS

Auburn University	M,D*
Drexel University	M,D*
École Polytechnique de Montréal	M,D,O
McGill University	M,D*
Missouri University of Science and Technology	M,D

HYDROGEOLOGY

California State University, Chico	M
Clemson University	M
Georgia State University	M,O
Illinois State University	M
Indiana University Bloomington	M,D*
Montana Tech of The University of Montana	M
Ohio University	M*
Rensselaer Polytechnic Institute	M,D
University of Hawaii at Manoa	M,D*
University of Nevada, Reno	M,D*
The University of Texas at Dallas	M,D*
West Virginia University	M,D

HYDROLOGY

Auburn University	M,D*
California State University, Bakersfield	M
California State University, Chico	M
Colorado State University	M,D*
Cornell University	M,D*
Drexel University	M,D*
Georgia Institute of Technology	M,D*
Idaho State University	M,O
Illinois State University	M
Massachusetts Institute of Technology	M,D,O*
Missouri University of Science and Technology	M,D
Murray State University	M
New Mexico Institute of Mining and Technology	M,D
State University of New York College of Environmental Science and Forestry	M,D
Stevens Institute of Technology	M,D,O
Université du Québec, Institut National de la Recherche Scientifique	M,D
The University of Arizona	M,D*
University of California, Davis	M,D*
University of Idaho	M
University of Nevada, Reno	M,D*
University of New Brunswick Fredericton	M,D
University of New Hampshire	M*
University of Southern Mississippi	M,D
University of Washington	M,D*

ILLUSTRATION

Academy of Art University	M
Bob Jones University	P,M,D,O
Bradley University	M
Fashion Institute of Technology	M*
Kent State University	M*
Marywood University	M
Mills College	M
Minneapolis College of Art and Design	M
Savannah College of Art and Design	M*
School of Visual Arts	M
Syracuse University	M*
University of California, Santa Cruz	O*
University of Massachusetts Dartmouth	M
Western Connecticut State University	M

IMMUNOLOGY

Albany Medical College	M,D
Albert Einstein College of Medicine	D
Baylor College of Medicine	D*
Boston University	D*
Brown University	M,D*
California Institute of Technology	D*
Case Western Reserve University	M,D*
Colorado State University	M,D*
Cornell University	M,D*
Cornell University, Joan and Sanford I. Weill Medical College and Graduate School of Medical Sciences	M,D
Creighton University	M,D*
Dalhousie University	M,D
Dartmouth College	D*
Drexel University	M,D*
Duke University	D*
East Carolina University	D
Emory University	D*
Georgetown University	M,D
The George Washington University	D*
Harvard University	D*
Hood College	M,O
Illinois State University	M,D
Indiana University–Purdue University Indianapolis	M,D*
Iowa State University of Science and Technology	M,D*
The Johns Hopkins University	M,D*
Long Island University, C.W. Post Campus	M
Louisiana State University Health Sciences Center	M,D*
Louisiana State University Health Sciences Center at Shreveport	M,D*
Loyola University Chicago	M,D*
Massachusetts Institute of Technology	D*
Mayo Graduate School	D*
McGill University	M,D*
McMaster University	M,D
Medical University of South Carolina	M,D
Meharry Medical College	D
Memorial University of Newfoundland	M,D
New York Medical College	M,D*
New York University	P,M,D*
North Carolina State University	M,D*
Northwestern University	D*
The Ohio State University	M,D*
Oregon Health & Science University	D*
Penn State Hershey Medical Center	M,D
Penn State University Park	M,D*
Purdue University	M,D
Queen's University at Kingston	M,D
Rosalind Franklin University of Medicine and Science	M,D*
Rush University	M,D
Rutgers, The State University of New Jersey, New Brunswick	M,D*
Saint Louis University	D
Stanford University	D*
State University of New York Upstate Medical University	M,D
Stony Brook University, State University of New York	M,D
Temple University	M,D*
Texas A&M Health Science Center	D
Thomas Jefferson University	D*
Tufts University	D*
Tulane University	M,D
Uniformed Services University of the Health Sciences	D*
Universidad Central del Caribe	M
Université de Montréal	M,D
Université de Sherbrooke	M,D
Université du Québec, Institut National de la Recherche Scientifique	M,D
Université Laval	M,D

*M—master's degree; P—first professional degree; D—doctorate; O—other advanced degree; *—Close-Up and/or Announcement or Display in one of the other books in this series*

University at Albany, State University of New York	M,D*
University at Buffalo, the State University of New York	M,D*
University of Alberta	M,D*
The University of Arizona	M,D*
University of Arkansas for Medical Sciences	M,D
The University of British Columbia	M,D
University of Calgary	M,D
University of California, Berkeley	D*
University of California, Davis	M,D*
University of California, Los Angeles	M,D*
University of California, San Diego	D*
University of California, San Francisco	D
University of Chicago	D*
University of Cincinnati	M,D
University of Colorado Denver	D*
University of Connecticut Health Center	D*
University of Florida	D*
University of Guelph	M,D,O
University of Illinois at Chicago	D*
The University of Iowa	M,D*
The University of Kansas	D*
University of Louisville	M,D
University of Manitoba	M,D
University of Maryland, Baltimore	D*
University of Massachusetts Worcester	D
University of Medicine and Dentistry of New Jersey	M,D*
University of Miami	D*
University of Michigan	D*
University of Minnesota, Duluth	M,D
University of Minnesota, Twin Cities Campus	D*
University of Missouri–Columbia	M,D*
The University of North Carolina at Chapel Hill	M,D*
University of North Dakota	M,D
University of North Texas Health Science Center at Fort Worth	M,D
University of Oklahoma Health Sciences Center	M,D
University of Ottawa	M,D*
University of Pennsylvania	D*
University of Pittsburgh	M,D*
University of Prince Edward Island	M,D
University of Rochester	M,D*
University of Saskatchewan	M,D
University of South Alabama	D*
The University of South Dakota	M,D
University of Southern California	M,D*
University of Southern Maine	M
University of South Florida	M,D*
The University of Texas Health Science Center at Houston	M,D
The University of Texas Health Science Center at San Antonio	D
The University of Texas Medical Branch	M,D*
The University of Texas Southwestern Medical Center at Dallas	D*
The University of Toledo	M,D
University of Toronto	M,D
University of Virginia	D
University of Washington	M,D*
The University of Western Ontario	M,D
Vanderbilt University	M,D*
Virginia Commonwealth University	M,D
Wake Forest University	D*
Washington University in St. Louis	D*
Wayne State University	M,D*
West Virginia University	M,D
Wright State University	M
Yale University	D*

INDUSTRIAL/MANAGEMENT ENGINEERING

Arizona State University	M,D
Auburn University	M,D*
Bradley University	M
Buffalo State College, State University of New York	M
California Polytechnic State University, San Luis Obispo	M
California State University, Fresno	M
California State University, Northridge	M
Central Washington University	M
Clemson University	M,D
Cleveland State University	M,D
Colorado State University–Pueblo	M
Columbia University	M,D,O*
Concordia University (Canada)	M,D,O
Cornell University	M,D*
Dalhousie University	M,D
East Carolina University	M,D,O
Eastern Kentucky University	M
École Polytechnique de Montréal	M,D,O
Florida Agricultural and Mechanical University	M,D
Florida State University	M,D*
Georgia Institute of Technology	M,D*
Illinois State University	M
Indiana State University	M
Indiana University–Purdue University Fort Wayne	M
Instituto Tecnologico de Santo Domingo	M
Instituto Tecnológico y de Estudios Superiores de Monterrey, Campus Chihuahua	M,O
Instituto Tecnológico y de Estudios Superiores de Monterrey, Campus Ciudad de México	M,D
Instituto Tecnológico y de Estudios Superiores de Monterrey, Campus Laguna	M
Instituto Tecnológico y de Estudios Superiores de Monterrey, Campus Monterrey	M,D
Iowa State University of Science and Technology	M,D*
Kansas State University	M,D*
Lamar University	M,D
Lehigh University	M,D
Louisiana State University and Agricultural and Mechanical College	M,D
Louisiana Tech University	M
Mississippi State University	M,D
Montana State University	M,D
Montana Tech of The University of Montana	M
Morehead State University	M
Morgan State University	M,D
New Jersey Institute of Technology	M,D
New Mexico State University	M,D
North Carolina Agricultural and Technical State University	M,D
North Carolina State University	M,D*
North Dakota State University	M,D
Northeastern University	M,D*
Northern Illinois University	M
Northwestern University	M,D*
The Ohio State University	M,D*
Ohio University	M,D*
Oklahoma State University	M,D*
Oregon State University	M,D*
Penn State University Park	M,D*
Polytechnic Institute of NYU	M
Polytechnic Institute of NYU, Long Island Graduate Center	M,D
Purdue University	M,D
Rensselaer Polytechnic Institute	M,D
Rochester Institute of Technology	M
Rutgers, The State University of New Jersey, New Brunswick	M,D*
St. Mary's University (United States)	M
Sam Houston State University	M
San Jose State University	M
South Dakota State University	M
Southern Illinois University Edwardsville	M
Southern Polytechnic State University	M,O
Stanford University	M,D*
State University of New York at Binghamton	M,D*
Texas A&M University	M,D*
Texas A&M University–Commerce	M
Texas A&M University–Kingsville	M
Texas Southern University	M
Texas State University–San Marcos	M*
Texas Tech University	M,D
Universidad de las Américas–Puebla	M
Université de Moncton	M
Université du Québec à Trois-Rivières	M,O
Université Laval	O
University at Buffalo, the State University of New York	M,D*
The University of Alabama	M
The University of Alabama in Huntsville	M,D
The University of Arizona	M,D*
University of Arkansas	M,D
University of California, Berkeley	M,D*
University of Central Florida	M,D,O*
University of Central Missouri	M
University of Cincinnati	M,D
University of Florida	M,D,O*
University of Houston	M,D*
University of Illinois at Chicago	M,D*
University of Illinois at Urbana–Champaign	M,D*
The University of Iowa	M,D*
University of Louisville	M,D
University of Manitoba	M,D
University of Massachusetts Amherst	M,D*
University of Massachusetts Lowell	M,D,O
University of Memphis	M
University of Miami	M,D*
University of Michigan	M,D*
University of Michigan–Dearborn	M,D*
University of Minnesota, Twin Cities Campus	M,D*
University of Missouri–Columbia	M,D*
University of Nebraska–Lincoln	M,D*
University of New Haven	M,O*
University of Oklahoma	M,D*
University of Pittsburgh	M,D*
University of Puerto Rico, Mayagüez Campus	M
University of Regina	M,D
University of Rhode Island	D
University of Southern California	M,D,O*
University of South Florida	M,D*
The University of Tennessee	M,D
The University of Tennessee at Chattanooga	M
The University of Texas at Arlington	M*
The University of Texas at Austin	M,D
The University of Texas at El Paso	M
The University of Toledo	M,D
University of Toronto	M,D
University of Washington	M,D*
University of Windsor	M,D
University of Wisconsin–Madison	M,D*
University of Wisconsin–Milwaukee	M,D,O
University of Wisconsin–Stout	M
Virginia Polytechnic Institute and State University	M,D*
Wayne State University	M,D*
Western Carolina University	M
Western Michigan University	M*
Western New England College	M
West Virginia University	M,D
Wichita State University	M,D*
Youngstown State University	M

INDUSTRIAL AND LABOR RELATIONS

Bernard M. Baruch College of the City University of New York	M
Carnegie Mellon University	M,D*
Case Western Reserve University	M*
Cleveland State University	P,M
Cornell University	M,D*
Georgetown University	D
Indiana University of Pennsylvania	M
Inter American University of Puerto Rico, Metropolitan Campus	M,D
Inter American University of Puerto Rico, San Germán Campus	M,D
Loyola University Chicago	M*
McMaster University	M
Memorial University of Newfoundland	M
Michigan State University	M,D*
New York Institute of Technology	M,O
The Ohio State University	M,D*
Penn State University Park	M*

Pontificia Universidad Catolica Madre y Maestra	M
Queen's University at Kingston	M
Rutgers, The State University of New Jersey, New Brunswick	M,D*
State University of New York Empire State College	M
Université de Montréal	M,D,O
Université du Québec à Trois-Rivières	O
Université du Québec en Outaouais	M,D,O
Université Laval	M,D
University of Alberta	D*
University of California, Berkeley	D*
University of Cincinnati	M
University of Illinois at Urbana–Champaign	M,D*
University of Massachusetts Amherst	M*
University of Minnesota, Twin Cities Campus	M,D*
University of New Haven	M*
University of North Texas	M
University of Rhode Island	M
University of Saskatchewan	M
University of Toronto	M,D
University of Wisconsin–Milwaukee	M,O
Wayne State University	M*
West Virginia University	M
York University	M,D

INDUSTRIAL AND MANUFACTURING MANAGEMENT

American InterContinental University Online	M
Boston University	D*
California Polytechnic State University, San Luis Obispo	M
California State University, East Bay	M
Carnegie Mellon University	M,D*
Case Western Reserve University	M,D*
Central Michigan University	M
Cleveland State University	D
Colorado Technical University Colorado Springs	M,D
Colorado Technical University Denver	M
DePaul University	M*
Florida Institute of Technology	M*
Friends University	M
Georgetown University	D
Harvard University	D*
HEC Montreal	M
Illinois Institute of Technology	M*
Instituto Tecnológico y de Estudios Superiores de Monterrey, Campus Estado de México	M,D
Instituto Tecnológico y de Estudios Superiores de Monterrey, Campus Irapuato	M,D
Inter American University of Puerto Rico, Metropolitan Campus	M
International Technological University	M
Kettering University	M
Lawrence Technological University	M,D
Marist College	M,O
McGill University	M,D,O*
Milwaukee School of Engineering	M*
Northeastern State University	M
Northern Illinois University	M
Nova Southeastern University	D*
Oakland University	M,O
Penn State University Park	M*
Polytechnic University of Puerto Rico	M
Portland State University	M,D
Purdue University	M
Regis University	M,O
Rochester Institute of Technology	M
San Diego State University	M*
San Jose State University	M
Southeastern Oklahoma State University	M
Southeast Missouri State University	M
Stevens Institute of Technology	M
Syracuse University	D*
Texas A&M University	M,D*
Texas Tech University	M,D
Universidad de las Américas–Puebla	M
University of Arkansas	M
University of Central Missouri	M
University of Cincinnati	D
University of Dayton	M
The University of Iowa	M*
University of Minnesota, Twin Cities Campus	M,D*
University of Missouri–St. Louis	M,O
University of Puerto Rico, Mayagüez Campus	M
University of Puerto Rico, Río Piedras	M,D
University of Rhode Island	M,D
University of St. Thomas (MN)	M,O*
University of Southern Indiana	M
The University of Tennessee	M,D
The University of Texas at Austin	D
The University of Texas at Tyler	M,D
The University of Toledo	M,D
Wake Forest University	M*
Washington State University	M,D*
York University	M,D

INDUSTRIAL AND ORGANIZATIONAL PSYCHOLOGY

Adler Graduate School	M,O
Adler School of Professional Psychology	M,D,O*
Alliant International University–Fresno	M,D*
Alliant International University–Los Angeles	M,D*
Alliant International University–Sacramento	D*
Alliant International University–San Diego	M,D*
Alliant International University–San Francisco	M,D*
American InterContinental University Online	M
Angelo State University	M
Antioch University Seattle	M
Appalachian State University	M,O
Auburn University	M,D*
Bernard M. Baruch College of the City University of New York	M,D,O
Bowling Green State University	M,D*
Brooklyn College of the City University of New York	M
California State University, San Bernardino	M
Capella University	M,D,O
Carlos Albizu University	M,D
Carlos Albizu University, Miami Campus	M,D
Central Michigan University	M,D
Chatham University	M,D
The Chicago School of Professional Psychology	M
The Chicago School of Professional Psychology: Downtown Los Angeles Campus	M
The Chicago School of Professional Psychology: Online	M,D,O
Claremont Graduate University	M,D,O*
Clemson University	D
Cleveland State University	M,D,O
DePaul University	M,D*
Eastern Kentucky University	M,O
Elmhurst College	M
Emporia State University	M
Fairfield University	M,O*
Fairleigh Dickinson University, College at Florham	M*
Florida Institute of Technology	M,D*
George Mason University	M,D*
The George Washington University	M,D*
Georgia Institute of Technology	M,D*
Goddard College	M
Graduate School and University Center of the City University of New York	D*
Hofstra University	M,D*
Illinois Institute of Technology	M,D*
Illinois State University	M,D,O
Indiana University–Purdue University Indianapolis	M*
Inter American University of Puerto Rico, Metropolitan Campus	M,D
Iona College	M*
John F. Kennedy University	M,O
Kean University	M
Lamar University	M
Louisiana State University and Agricultural and Mechanical College	M,D
Louisiana Tech University	M,D
Marshall University	M,D
Massachusetts School of Professional Psychology	M,D,O
Middle Tennessee State University	M,O
Minnesota State University Mankato	M,D
Missouri State University	M*
Montclair State University	M,O*
National-Louis University	M,O
New York University	M,D,O*
North Carolina State University	D*
Northern Kentucky University	M,O
Ohio University	D*
Old Dominion University	D
Penn State University Park	M,D*
Philadelphia College of Osteopathic Medicine	M,D,O*
Pontifical Catholic University of Puerto Rico	M,D
Radford University	M,D,O
Rice University	M,D
Roosevelt University	M
Rutgers, The State University of New Jersey, New Brunswick	M,D*
St. Cloud State University	M
Saint Joseph's University	M,O
Saint Louis University	M,D
Saint Mary's University (Canada)	M,D
St. Mary's University (United States)	M
San Diego State University	M,D*
San Jose State University	M
Seattle Pacific University	M,D
Southern Illinois University Edwardsville	M
Springfield College	M,O
Teachers College, Columbia University	M,D
Temple University	M*
Texas A&M University	M,D*
University at Albany, State University of New York	M,D,O*
The University of Akron	M,D
University of Baltimore	M
University of Central Florida	M,D*
University of Connecticut	M,D,O*
University of Detroit Mercy	M
University of Guelph	M,D
University of Houston	M,D*
University of Maryland, College Park	M,D*
University of Minnesota, Twin Cities Campus	D*
University of Missouri–St. Louis	M,D,O
University of Nebraska at Omaha	M,D,O
University of New Haven	M,O*
The University of North Carolina at Charlotte	M,D*
University of Puerto Rico, Río Piedras	M,D
University of South Africa	M,D
University of South Florida	M,D*
The University of Tennessee	D
The University of Tennessee at Chattanooga	M
The University of Texas at Arlington	M,D*
University of Tulsa	M,D*
University of West Florida	M
University of Wisconsin–Oshkosh	M
Valdosta State University	M,O
Virginia Polytechnic Institute and State University	M,D*
Walden University	M,D,O
Wayne State University	M,D*
West Chester University of Pennsylvania	M,O
Western Michigan University	M,D*
Wright State University	M,D
Xavier University	M,D*

INDUSTRIAL DESIGN

Academy of Art University	M
Arizona State University	M
Art Center College of Design	M*
Auburn University	M*
Brigham Young University	M*
Carleton University	M
North Carolina State University	M*
The Ohio State University	M*
Pratt Institute	M*
Rhode Island School of Design	M
Rochester Institute of Technology	M

*M—master's degree; P—first professional degree; D—doctorate; O—other advanced degree; *—Close-Up and/or Announcement or Display in one of the other books in this series*

San Francisco State University M
Savannah College of Art and Design M*
University of Cincinnati M
University of Illinois at Chicago M*
University of Illinois at Urbana–Champaign M*
University of Notre Dame M*
The University of the Arts M*
University of Washington M*

INDUSTRIAL HYGIENE

California State University, Northridge M
Montana Tech of The University of Montana M
Murray State University M
University of Central Missouri M,O
University of Cincinnati M,D
University of Massachusetts Lowell M,D,O
University of Michigan M,D*
University of Minnesota, Twin Cities Campus M,D*
University of New Haven M*
The University of North Carolina at Chapel Hill M,D*
University of Puerto Rico, Medical Sciences Campus M
University of South Carolina M,D
University of Wisconsin–Stout M
West Virginia University M

INFECTIOUS DISEASES

Cornell University M,D*
Georgetown University M,D
The George Washington University M*
Harvard University D*
The Johns Hopkins University M,D*
Loyola University Chicago M,O*
North Carolina State University M,D*
State University of New York Upstate Medical University M
Tulane University M,D,O
Uniformed Services University of the Health Sciences D*
Université de Montréal O
Université Laval O
University of Calgary M,D
University of California, Berkeley M,D*
University of Georgia M,D*
University of Guelph M,D,O
University of Minnesota, Twin Cities Campus M,D*
The University of Montana D
University of Pittsburgh M,D,O*
University of South Florida M,D*
The University of Texas Medical Branch D*
Yale University D*

INFORMATION SCIENCE

Alcorn State University M
American InterContinental University Dunwoody Campus M
American InterContinental University Online M
American InterContinental University South Florida M
Arizona State University at the Polytechnic Campus M
Arkansas Tech University M
Aspen University M,O
Athabasca University M*
Ball State University M*
Barry University M*
Bellevue University M
Bentley University M
Bradley University M
Brigham Young University M*
Brooklyn College of the City University of New York M,D,O
California State University, Fullerton M
Capitol College M
Carleton University M,D
Carnegie Mellon University M,D*
Case Western Reserve University M,D*
The Citadel, The Military College of South Carolina M
Claremont Graduate University M,D,O*
Clark Atlanta University M
Clarkson University M*
Clark University M
Cleveland State University M,D
Coleman College M
The College of Saint Rose M*
Cornell University D*
Dakota State University M,D*
DePaul University M,D*
DeSales University M
Drexel University M,D*
East Carolina University M
East Tennessee State University M
Everglades University M
Florida Gulf Coast University M
Florida Institute of Technology M*
Florida International University M,D*
Gannon University M
George Mason University M,D,O*
Georgia Southwestern State University M
Georgia State University M
Grand Valley State University M
Harvard University M,D,O*
Hood College M
Indiana University Bloomington M,D,O*
Indiana University–Purdue University Fort Wayne M
Indiana University–Purdue University Indianapolis M,D*
Instituto Tecnológico y de Estudios Superiores de Monterrey, Campus Cuernavaca M,D
Instituto Tecnológico y de Estudios Superiores de Monterrey, Campus Estado de México M,D
Instituto Tecnológico y de Estudios Superiores de Monterrey, Campus Irapuato M,D
Instituto Tecnológico y de Estudios Superiores de Monterrey, Campus Monterrey M,D
Instituto Tecnológico y de Estudios Superiores de Monterrey, Campus Sonora Norte M
Iowa State University of Science and Technology M*
The Johns Hopkins University M*
Kansas State University M,D*
Kennesaw State University M
Kent State University M*
Kentucky State University M
Kettering University M
Knowledge Systems Institute M
Lamar University M
Lehigh University M
Long Island University, C.W. Post Campus M
Loyola University Chicago M*
Marlboro College M
Marshall University M
Marywood University M
Massachusetts Institute of Technology M,D,O*
Missouri University of Science and Technology M
Montclair State University M,O*
National University M
Naval Postgraduate School M,O
New Jersey Institute of Technology M,D
Northeastern University M,D,O*
Northern Kentucky University M,O
Northwestern University M*
Nova Southeastern University M,D*
The Ohio State University M,D*
Oklahoma State University M,D*
Old Dominion University D
Pace University M,D,O*
Penn State Great Valley M
Polytechnic Institute of NYU, Westchester Graduate Center M
Regis University M,O
Rensselaer at Hartford M
Rensselaer Polytechnic Institute M
Robert Morris University M,D
Rochester Institute of Technology M,D
Sacred Heart University M,O
St. Mary's University (United States) M
Saint Xavier University M
Sam Houston State University M
Simon Fraser University M,D
Southern Methodist University M,D*
Southern Polytechnic State University M,O
State University of New York Institute of Technology M
Stevens Institute of Technology M,O
Stevenson University M
Strayer University M
Syracuse University D*
Temple University M,D*
Towson University M,D,O
Trevecca Nazarene University M
Université de Sherbrooke M,D
University at Albany, State University of New York M,D,O*
The University of Alabama at Birmingham M,D*
University of Arkansas at Little Rock M
University of Baltimore M,D
University of California, Irvine M,D*
University of Colorado at Colorado Springs M,D
University of Colorado Denver D*
University of Delaware M,D*
University of Detroit Mercy M
University of Florida M,D*
University of Hawaii at Manoa M,D*
University of Houston M,D*
University of Houston–Clear Lake M
University of Illinois at Urbana–Champaign M,D,O*
The University of Iowa M,D,O*
University of Management and Technology M,O
University of Maryland, Baltimore County M,D*
University of Maryland University College M,O
University of Michigan M,D*
University of Michigan–Dearborn M,D*
University of Michigan–Flint M*
University of Minnesota, Twin Cities Campus M,D*
University of Nebraska at Omaha M,D,O
University of Nebraska–Lincoln M,D*
University of Nevada, Las Vegas M,D
University of New Haven M*
The University of North Carolina at Charlotte M,D*
University of North Florida M
University of Oregon M,D*
University of Ottawa M,O*
University of Pennsylvania M,D*
University of Phoenix–Cincinnati Campus M
University of Phoenix–Phoenix Campus M
University of Pittsburgh M,D,O*
University of Puerto Rico, Mayagüez Campus D
University of South Africa M,D
University of South Alabama M*
The University of Tennessee M,D
The University of Texas at El Paso M,D
The University of Texas at San Antonio M,D*
University of Washington M,D*
University of Waterloo M,D
University of Wisconsin–Parkside M
University of Wisconsin–Stout M
Virginia Polytechnic Institute and State University M*
Youngstown State University M

INFORMATION STUDIES

The Catholic University of America M
Central Connecticut State University M
Claremont Graduate University M,D,O*
Columbia University M*
Cornell University D*
Dalhousie University M
Dominican University M,O
Drexel University M*
Emporia State University M,D,O
Florida State University M,D,O*
Indiana University Bloomington M,D,O*
Long Island University, C.W. Post Campus M,D,O
Long Island University, Westchester Graduate Campus M
Louisiana State University and Agricultural and Mechanical College M,O
Mansfield University of Pennsylvania M
McGill University M,D,O*
Metropolitan State University M,O
North Carolina Central University M
Pratt Institute M,O*
Queens College of the City University of New York M,O
Queen's University at Kingston M,D

Rutgers, The State University of New Jersey, New Brunswick	M,D*
St. Catherine University	M
St. John's University (NY)	M,O
San Jose State University	M,D
Simmons College	M,D,O
Southern Connecticut State University	M,O
Syracuse University	M*
Universidad del Turabo	M
Université de Montréal	M,D
University at Albany, State University of New York	M,O*
University at Buffalo, the State University of New York	M,O*
The University of Alabama	M,D
University of Alberta	M*
The University of Arizona	M,D*
The University of British Columbia	M,D
University of California, Berkeley	M,D*
University of California, Los Angeles	M,D,O*
University of Central Missouri	M,O
University of Denver	M,O*
University of Hawaii at Manoa	M,O*
University of Illinois at Urbana–Champaign	M,D,O*
The University of Iowa	M*
University of Maryland, College Park	M,D*
University of Michigan	M,D*
University of Missouri–Columbia	M,D,O*
The University of North Carolina at Chapel Hill	M,D,O*
The University of North Carolina at Greensboro	M
University of North Texas	M,D
University of Oklahoma	M,O*
University of Pittsburgh	M,D,O*
University of Puerto Rico, Río Piedras	M,O
University of Rhode Island	M
University of South Carolina	M,D,O
University of South Florida	M*
The University of Texas at Austin	M,D
University of Toronto	M,D,O
The University of Western Ontario	M,D
University of Wisconsin–Madison	M,D*
University of Wisconsin–Milwaukee	M,D,O
Valdosta State University	M
Wayne State University	M,O*

INORGANIC CHEMISTRY

Auburn University	M,D*
Boston College	M,D*
Brandeis University	M,D
California State University, Los Angeles	M
Carnegie Mellon University	M,D*
Clarkson University	M,D*
Cleveland State University	M,D
Columbia University	M,D*
Cornell University	D*
Florida State University	M,D*
Georgetown University	D
The George Washington University	M,D*
Harvard University	D*
Howard University	M,D
Indiana University Bloomington	M,D*
Kansas State University	M,D*
Kent State University	M,D*
Marquette University	M,D
Massachusetts Institute of Technology	D*
McMaster University	M,D
Miami University	M,D*
Northeastern University	M,D*
Oregon State University	M,D*
Purdue University	M,D
Rensselaer Polytechnic Institute	M,D
Rice University	M,D
Rutgers, The State University of New Jersey, Newark	M,D*
Rutgers, The State University of New Jersey, New Brunswick	M,D*
Seton Hall University	M,D*
Southern University and Agricultural and Mechanical College	M
State University of New York at Binghamton	M,D*
Tufts University	M,D*
University of Calgary	M,D
University of Cincinnati	M,D
University of Georgia	M,D*
University of Louisville	M,D
University of Maryland, College Park	M,D*
University of Massachusetts Lowell	M,D
University of Miami	M,D*
University of Michigan	D*
University of Missouri–Columbia	M,D*
University of Missouri–Kansas City	M,D*
University of Missouri–St. Louis	M,D
The University of Montana	M,D
University of Nebraska–Lincoln	M,D*
University of Notre Dame	M,D*
University of Regina	M,D
University of Southern Mississippi	M,D
University of South Florida	M,D*
The University of Tennessee	M,D
The University of Texas at Austin	M,D
The University of Toledo	M,D
Vanderbilt University	M,D*
Virginia Commonwealth University	M,D
Wake Forest University	M,D*
Wesleyan University	M,D*
West Virginia University	M,D
Yale University	D*
Youngstown State University	M

INSURANCE

Florida State University	M,D*
Georgia State University	M,D,O
St. John's University (NY)	M
Temple University	D*
University of Florida	M,D,O*
University of Pennsylvania	M,D*
University of Wisconsin–Madison	M,D*
Virginia Commonwealth University	M
Washington State University	D*

INTERDISCIPLINARY STUDIES

Alaska Pacific University	M
Amberton University	M
American University	M*
Angelo State University	M
Antioch University New England	M*
Arizona State University at the West campus	M
Athabasca University	M*
Baylor University	M,D
Boise State University	M
Boston University	M*
Bowling Green State University	M,D*
Buffalo State College, State University of New York	M
California State University, Bakersfield	M
California State University, Chico	M
California State University, East Bay	M,O
California State University, Long Beach	M
California State University, Monterey Bay	M
California State University, Northridge	M
California State University, San Bernardino	M
California State University, Stanislaus	M
Cambridge College	M,D,O
Campbell University	M
Central Washington University	M
College of the Humanities and Sciences, Harrison Middleton University	M,D
Columbia University	M*
Dalhousie University	D
Dallas Baptist University	M
DePaul University	M*
Drew University	M,D,O
Eastern Washington University	M
Emory University	D*
Fitchburg State College	O
Florida Gulf Coast University	M
Franklin Pierce University	M,D,O
Fresno Pacific University	M
Frostburg State University	M
Georgetown University	M,D
Goddard College	M
Graduate School and University Center of the City University of New York	M,D*
Hodges University	M
Hofstra University	M*
Hollins University	M,O
Idaho State University	M
Iowa State University of Science and Technology	M*
John F. Kennedy University	M
Lesley University	M*
Long Island University, C.W. Post Campus	M
Marquette University	M,D
Marylhurst University	M
Marywood University	M,O
Mills College	M,O
Minnesota State University Mankato	M
Montana State University–Billings	M
Montana Tech of The University of Montana	M
Mountain State University	M*
New Mexico State University	M,D
New York University	M*
Niagara University	M
Nova Southeastern University	M,O*
The Ohio State University	M,D*
Oregon State University	M*
Regis University	M,O
Rensselaer Polytechnic Institute	M,D
Rochester Institute of Technology	M
Rosalind Franklin University of Medicine and Science	D*
Rutgers, The State University of New Jersey, New Brunswick	D*
San Diego State University	M*
San Jose State University	M
Sarah Lawrence College	M*
Sonoma State University	M
Stanford University	M,D*
State University of New York at Fredonia	M
State University of New York at New Paltz	M
Stephen F. Austin State University	M
Teachers College, Columbia University	M,D
Texas A&M University–Texarkana	M
Texas State University–San Marcos	M*
Texas Tech University	M
Trinity Western University	M
Tulane University	D
Union Institute & University	M,D
The University of Alabama in Huntsville	M,D,O
University of Alaska Anchorage	M
University of Alaska Fairbanks	M,D
The University of Arizona	M,D*
University of Arkansas	M,D
University of Central Florida	M*
University of Chicago	D*
University of Cincinnati	D
University of Houston–Victoria	M
University of Idaho	M
University of Illinois at Springfield	M
The University of Kansas	M,D*
University of Louisville	M
University of Maine	D*
University of Manitoba	M,D
University of Medicine and Dentistry of New Jersey	M,D*
University of Minnesota, Twin Cities Campus	D*
University of Missouri–Kansas City	D*
The University of Montana	M,D
University of New Brunswick Fredericton	M,D
University of Northern British Columbia	M,D,O
University of North Texas	M
University of Oklahoma	M,D*
University of Oregon	M*
University of Ottawa	D,O*
University of Pittsburgh	D*
The University of South Dakota	M
The University of Texas at Arlington	M*
The University of Texas at Brownsville	M
The University of Texas at Dallas	M*
The University of Texas at El Paso	M
The University of Texas at San Antonio	M*
The University of Texas at Tyler	M
The University of Texas–Pan American	M
University of the Incarnate Word	M
University of Virginia	M,D
University of Washington, Tacoma	M
The University of Western Ontario	M,D
University of Wisconsin–Milwaukee	D

*M—master's degree; P—first professional degree; D—doctorate; O—other advanced degree; *—Close-Up and/or Announcement or Display in one of the other books in this series*

...alth M
M,D,O*
...rsity M
Washington State University D*
Wayland Baptist University M
Western Kentucky University M
Western New Mexico University M
West Texas A&M University M
Worcester Polytechnic Institute M,D,O*
Wright State University M
York University M

INTERIOR DESIGN

Academy of Art University M
Arizona State University M
Boston Architectural College M
Brenau University M
Chatham University M
Columbia College Chicago M
Corcoran College of Art and Design M
Cornell University M*
Drexel University M*
Eastern Michigan University M
Florida International University M*
Florida State University M*
The George Washington University M*
Iowa State University of Science and Technology M*
Lawrence Technological University M
Louisiana Tech University M
Marymount University M
Marywood University M
Miami International University of Art & Design M*
Michigan State University M,D*
Missouri State University M*
The New School: A University M*
New York School of Interior Design M*
The Ohio State University M*
Pontificia Universidad Catolica Madre y Maestra M
Pratt Institute M*
Rhode Island School of Design M
San Diego State University M*
Savannah College of Art and Design M*
School of the Art Institute of Chicago M*
South Dakota State University M
Suffolk University M*
Texas Tech University M,D
The University of Alabama M
University of Central Oklahoma M
University of Cincinnati M
University of Florida M,D*
University of Georgia M,D*
University of Houston M*
University of Kentucky M
University of Manitoba M
University of Massachusetts Amherst M*
University of Memphis M,O
University of Minnesota, Twin Cities Campus M,D,O*
University of Nebraska–Lincoln M,D*

The University of North Carolina at Greensboro M,O
University of Oregon M*
Utah State University M
Virginia Commonwealth University M
Virginia Polytechnic Institute and State University M,D*
Washington State University M,D*
Washington State University Spokane M,D

INTERNATIONAL AFFAIRS

Alliant International University–México City M*
Alliant International University–San Diego M*
American Graduate School of International Relations and Diplomacy M,D
American Public University System M
American University M,D,O*
The American University of Paris M
Appalachian State University M
Arcadia University M
Baylor University M,D
Boston University M,D,O*
Brandeis University M,D
British American College London M
Brock University M
Brooklyn College of the City University of New York M,D
California State University, Fresno M
California State University, Sacramento M
California State University, Stanislaus M
Carleton University M,D
The Catholic University of America M,D
Central Connecticut State University M
Central European University M,D*
Central Michigan University M,O
Chapman University M
City College of the City University of New York M*
Claremont Graduate University M,D*
Colorado School of Mines M,O
Columbia University M*
Concordia University (CA) M
Cornell University D*
Creighton University M*
East Carolina University M
Fairleigh Dickinson University, Metropolitan Campus M*
Florida Agricultural and Mechanical University M
Florida International University M,D*
Florida State University M*
Fordham University M,O*
George Mason University M*
Georgetown University P,M,D
The George Washington University M*
Georgia Institute of Technology M,D*
Harvard University P,D*
Hult International Business School (United States) M
Instituto Tecnológico y de Estudios Superiores de Monterrey, Campus Ciudad Obregón M
The Johns Hopkins University M,D,O*

Kansas State University M*
Kentucky State University M
Lebanese American University M
Lesley University M,O*
Long Island University, Brooklyn Campus M,O
Long Island University, C.W. Post Campus M
Marquette University M
McMaster University M,D
Michigan State University M*
Missouri State University M*
Monterey Institute of International Studies M*
Morgan State University M
Naval Postgraduate School M
The New School: A University M*
New York University M,D,O*
North Carolina State University M*
Northeastern University M,D,O*
Northwestern University P,M,O*
Norwich University M
Ohio University M*
Old Dominion University M,D
Pepperdine University M
Princeton University M,D*
Queen's University at Kingston M,D
Rutgers, The State University of New Jersey, Camden M
Rutgers, The State University of New Jersey, Newark M,D*
Rutgers, The State University of New Jersey, New Brunswick D*
St. John Fisher College M
St. Mary's University (United States) M
Salve Regina University M,O
San Francisco State University M
Schiller International University (United Kingdom) M
Schiller International University M
Seton Hall University M*
SIT Graduate Institute M
Stanford University M*
Syracuse University M*
Texas A&M University M,O*
Texas State University–San Marcos M*
Troy University M
Tufts University M,D*
United States International University M
Universidad de las Americas, A.C. M
Universidad Nacional Pedro Henriquez Urena P,M,D
Université Laval M,D
University of Bridgeport M
The University of British Columbia M
University of California, Berkeley M*
University of California, San Diego M,D*
University of California, Santa Barbara M,D
University of California, Santa Cruz D*
University of Central Florida M*
University of Central Oklahoma M
University of Chicago M*
University of Colorado at Boulder M,D*
University of Connecticut M*
University of Delaware M,D*
University of Denver M,D*

University of Florida M*
University of Indianapolis M
The University of Kansas M*
University of Kentucky M
University of Miami M,D*
University of Northern British Columbia M,D,O
University of Oklahoma M*
University of Oregon M*
University of Pennsylvania M*
University of Pittsburgh M,D,O*
University of Rhode Island M,O
University of San Diego M
University of San Francisco M
University of South Carolina M,D
University of Southern California M,D*
University of Southern Mississippi M,D
University of South Florida M,D*
University of the Pacific P,M,D
University of Utah M*
University of Virginia M,D
University of Washington M*
University of Waterloo M,D
University of Wyoming M
Virginia Polytechnic Institute and State University M,D*
Walden University M,D,O
Washington State University M,D*
Webster University M
West Virginia University M,D
Wilfrid Laurier University M,D
Yale University M,O*
York University M

INTERNATIONAL AND COMPARATIVE EDUCATION

American University M*
Boston University M*
Bowling Green State University M*
California State University, Dominguez Hills M
The College of New Jersey M,O
Drexel University M*
Florida International University M,D*
Florida State University M,D,O*
Gallaudet University M,O
The George Washington University M*
Harvard University M*
Indiana University Bloomington M,D,O*
Lehigh University M,O
Louisiana State University and Agricultural and Mechanical College M,D
Lynn University M,D
Morehead State University M,O
New York University M,D,O*
SIT Graduate Institute M
Stanford University M,D*
Teachers College, Columbia University M,D
Tufts University M,D*
University of Bridgeport M,O
University of California, Santa Barbara M,D
University of Central Florida M,D,O*
University of Maryland, College Park M,D*
University of Massachusetts Amherst M,D,O*
University of Minnesota, Twin Cities Campus M,D*
University of North Texas M,D
University of Pennsylvania M,D*
University of Pittsburgh M,D*
University of San Francisco M,D
University of South Africa M,D

Vanderbilt University	M,D*
Wright State University	M

INTERNATIONAL BUSINESS

Alliant International University–México City	M*
Alliant International University–San Diego	M,D*
American InterContinental University Dunwoody Campus	M
American InterContinental University–London	M
American InterContinental University Online	M
American InterContinental University South Florida	M
American International College	M
American University	M,O*
The American University in Dubai	M
Andrew Jackson University	M
Argosy University, Atlanta	M,D*
Argosy University, Chicago	M,D*
Argosy University, Dallas	M,O*
Argosy University, Denver	M,D*
Argosy University, Hawai'i	M,D,O*
Argosy University, Inland Empire	M,D*
Argosy University, Los Angeles	M,D*
Argosy University, Nashville	M,D*
Argosy University, Orange County	M,D,O*
Argosy University, Phoenix	M,D*
Argosy University, Salt Lake City	M,D*
Argosy University, San Diego	M,D*
Argosy University, San Francisco Bay Area	M,D*
Argosy University, Sarasota	M,D,O*
Argosy University, Schaumburg	M,D,O*
Argosy University, Seattle	M,D*
Argosy University, Tampa	M,D*
Argosy University, Twin Cities	M,D*
Argosy University, Washington DC	M,D,O*
Assumption College	M,O
Avila University	M
Azusa Pacific University	M
Baldwin-Wallace College	M
Barry University	O*
Baylor University	M
Benedictine University	M
Bernard M. Baruch College of the City University of New York	M
Boston University	M,O*
Brandeis University	M,D
British American College London	M
California Intercontinental University	M,D
California Lutheran University	M,O
California State University, East Bay	M
California State University, Fullerton	M
California State University, Los Angeles	M
California State University, Stanislaus	M
Central European University	M,D*
Central Michigan University	M,O
City University of Seattle	M,O
Clarkson University	M*
Clark University	M
Cleveland State University	M,D,O
Columbia Southern University	M
Columbia University	M*
Concordia University Wisconsin	M
Daemen College	M
Dallas Baptist University	M
DePaul University	M*
Dominican University of California	M
D'Youville College	M*
Eastern Michigan University	M,O
Emerson College	M
Everest University	M
Everest University	M
Fairfield University	M,O*
Fairleigh Dickinson University, College at Florham	M,O*
Fairleigh Dickinson University, Metropolitan Campus	M*
Florida Atlantic University	M,D
Florida International University	M*
Florida Southern College	M
Georgetown University	P,M,D
The George Washington University	M,D*
Georgia Institute of Technology	M,O*
Georgia State University	M
Golden Gate University	M,D,O
Harding University	M
Hawai'i Pacific University	M*
HEC Montreal	M
Hofstra University	M*
Hope International University	M
Howard University	M
Hult International Business School (United States)	M
Instituto Tecnológico y de Estudios Superiores de Monterrey, Campus Central de Veracruz	M
Instituto Tecnológico y de Estudios Superiores de Monterrey, Campus Chihuahua	M,O
Instituto Tecnológico y de Estudios Superiores de Monterrey, Campus Ciudad de México	M,D
Instituto Tecnológico y de Estudios Superiores de Monterrey, Campus Cuernavaca	M
Instituto Tecnológico y de Estudios Superiores de Monterrey, Campus Irapuato	M,D
Instituto Tecnológico y de Estudios Superiores de Monterrey, Campus Monterrey	M
Inter American University of Puerto Rico, Metropolitan Campus	M
Inter American University of Puerto Rico, San Germán Campus	M,D
International University in Geneva	M
The International University of Monaco	M
Iona College	M,O*
John Brown University	M
John Marshall Law School	P,M
Johnson & Wales University	M
Kaplan University–Davenport Campus	M
Kean University	M
Keiser University	M
Lewis University	M
Lincoln University (CA)	M
Lindenwood University	M
Long Island University, C.W. Post Campus	M,O
Loyola University Maryland	M*
Lynn University	M,D
Madonna University	M
Maine Maritime Academy	M,O
Manhattanville College	M*
McGill University	M,D,O*
McKendree University	M
MidAmerica Nazarene University	M
Milwaukee School of Engineering	M*
Minnesota State University Mankato	M
Montclair State University	M,O*
Monterey Institute of International Studies	M*
National University	M
Newman University	M
New Mexico Highlands University	M
The New School: A University	M*
New York Institute of Technology	M,O
New York University	M,D*
Northern Kentucky University	M,O
Norwich University	M
Nova Southeastern University	M,D*
Oakland University	M,O
Oklahoma City University	M
Old Dominion University	M
Oral Roberts University	M
Pace University	M*
Pacific States University	M,D
Park University	M
Pepperdine University	M
Pepperdine University	M
Philadelphia University	M
Polytechnic University of Puerto Rico	M
Pontifical Catholic University of Puerto Rico	M
Pontificia Universidad Catolica Madre y Maestra	M
Portland State University	M
Providence College	M*
Purdue University	M
Quinnipiac University	M*
Regis University	M,O
Rochester Institute of Technology	M
Roosevelt University	M
Rutgers, The State University of New Jersey, Newark	M,D*
St. Bonaventure University	M
St. Edward's University	M,O
St. John's University (NY)	M,O
Saint Joseph's University	M
Saint Louis University	M,D
St. Mary's University (United States)	M
Saint Mary's University of Minnesota	M
Saint Peter's College	M
St. Thomas University	M,O
Salem International University	M
San Diego State University	M*
Schiller International University (United States)	M
Schiller International University (Germany)	M
Schiller International University (United Kingdom)	M
Schiller International University	M
Schiller International University (Spain)	M
Schiller International University	M
Seton Hall University	M,O*
Simon Fraser University	M,D
SIT Graduate Institute	M
Southeastern University	M
Southeast Missouri State University	M
Southern New Hampshire University	M,D,O*
Stevens Institute of Technology	M
Suffolk University	M,D,O*
Taylor University	M
Temple University	M,D*
Texas A&M International University	M
Texas A&M University–Corpus Christi	M
Texas Christian University	M
Texas Tech University	M
Thunderbird School of Global Management	M
Trinity Western University	M
Tufts University	M,D*
TUI University	M,D
Universidad Autonoma de Guadalajara	M,D
Universidad Metropolitana	M
Université de Sherbrooke	M
Université du Québec, École nationale d'administration publique	M,O
Université Laval	M,O
The University of Akron	M
University of Alberta	M*
The University of British Columbia	D
University of Chicago	M*
University of Colorado at Colorado Springs	M
University of Colorado Denver	M*
University of Dallas	M
University of Dayton	M
University of Denver	M*
The University of Findlay	M
University of Florida	P,M,D*
University of Hawaii at Manoa	M,D*
University of Houston–Victoria	M
University of Kentucky	M
University of La Verne	M
University of Lethbridge	M,D
University of Maryland University College	M,O
University of Memphis	M,D
University of Miami	M*
University of Minnesota, Twin Cities Campus	M*
University of New Brunswick Saint John	M
University of New Haven	M*
University of New Mexico	M*
University of Oklahoma	M*
University of Pennsylvania	M*
University of Phoenix–Atlanta Campus	M
University of Phoenix–Augusta Campus	M
University of Phoenix–Austin Campus	M
University of Phoenix–Bay Area Campus	M
University of Phoenix–Birmingham Campus	M
University of Phoenix–Boston Campus	M
University of Phoenix–Central Florida Campus	M
University of Phoenix–Central Valley Campus	M
University of Phoenix–Charlotte Campus	M
University of Phoenix–Chattanooga Campus	M
University of Phoenix–Cheyenne Campus	M

*M—master's degree; P—first professional degree; D—doctorate; O—other advanced degree; *—Close-Up and/or Announcement or Display in one of the other books in this series*

University of Phoenix–Chicago Campus	M
University of Phoenix–Cincinnati Campus	M
University of Phoenix–Cleveland Campus	M
University of Phoenix–Columbus Georgia Campus	M
University of Phoenix–Columbus Ohio Campus	M
University of Phoenix–Dallas Campus	M
University of Phoenix–Denver Campus	M
University of Phoenix–Des Moines Campus	M
University of Phoenix–Harrisburg Campus	M
University of Phoenix–Hawaii Campus	M
University of Phoenix–Houston Campus	M
University of Phoenix–Idaho Campus	M
University of Phoenix–Indianapolis Campus	M
University of Phoenix–Jersey City Campus	M
University of Phoenix–Kansas City Campus	M
University of Phoenix–Las Vegas Campus	M
University of Phoenix–Louisiana Campus	M
University of Phoenix–Madison Campus	M
University of Phoenix–Maryland Campus	M
University of Phoenix–Memphis Campus	M
University of Phoenix–Metro Detroit Campus	M
University of Phoenix–Minneapolis/St. Louis Park Campus	M
University of Phoenix–New Mexico Campus	M
University of Phoenix–Northern Nevada Campus	M
University of Phoenix–Northern Virginia Campus	M
University of Phoenix–North Florida Campus	M
University of Phoenix–Northwest Arkansas Campus	M
University of Phoenix–Oklahoma City Campus	M
University of Phoenix–Omaha Campus	M
University of Phoenix–Oregon Campus	M
University of Phoenix–Philadelphia Campus	M
University of Phoenix–Phoenix Campus	M
University of Phoenix–Pittsburgh Campus	M
University of Phoenix–Puerto Rico Campus	M
University of Phoenix–Raleigh Campus	M
University of Phoenix–Renton Learning Center	M
University of Phoenix–Richmond Campus	M
University of Phoenix–Sacramento Valley Campus	M
University of Phoenix–St. Louis Campus	M
University of Phoenix–San Antonio Campus	M
University of Phoenix–San Diego Campus	M
University of Phoenix–Savannah Campus	M
University of Phoenix–Southern Arizona Campus	M
University of Phoenix–Southern California Campus	M
University of Phoenix–Southern Colorado Campus	M
University of Phoenix–South Florida Campus	M
University of Phoenix–Springfield Campus	M
University of Phoenix–Tulsa Campus	M
University of Phoenix–Utah Campus	M
University of Phoenix–Vancouver Campus	M
University of Phoenix–West Florida Campus	M
University of Phoenix–West Michigan Campus	M
University of Phoenix–Wisconsin Campus	M
University of Pittsburgh	M*
University of Puerto Rico, Río Piedras	M,D
University of Regina	M,O
University of Rhode Island	M,D
University of San Francisco	M
University of Saskatchewan	M
The University of Scranton	M
University of South Carolina	M
The University of Tampa	M
The University of Texas at Dallas	M,D*
The University of Texas at San Antonio	M,D*
The University of Texas–Pan American	D
University of the Incarnate Word	M,O
University of the West	M
The University of Toledo	M
University of Tulsa	M*
University of Washington	M,D,O*
The University of Western Ontario	M,D
University of Wisconsin–Milwaukee	M,O
University of Wisconsin–Oshkosh	M
University of Wisconsin–Whitewater	M*
Upper Iowa University	M
Valparaiso University	M
Villanova University	M*
Wagner College	M
Walden University	M,D
Washington State University	M,D,O*
Wayland Baptist University	M
Webster University	M
Western International University	M
Whitworth University	M
Wilkes University	M
Wright State University	M
Xavier University	M*
York University	M,D

INTERNATIONAL DEVELOPMENT

American University	M,D,O*
Andrews University	M
Athabasca University	M*
Brandeis University	M
Clark University	M
Cornell University	M*
Dalhousie University	M
Duke University	M,O*
Eastern University	M
Fordham University	M,O*
The George Washington University	M*
Harvard University	M*
Hope International University	M
The Johns Hopkins University	M,D,O*
McGill University	M,D,O*
The New School: A University	M*
Ohio University	M*
Rutgers, The State University of New Jersey, Camden	M
Saint Mary's University (Canada)	M
Texas A&M University	M,O*
Tufts University	M,D*
Tulane University	M,D
University of Florida	M,D,O*
University of Guelph	M,D
University of Ottawa	M*
University of Pittsburgh	M,O*
University of San Francisco	M
University of Southern Mississippi	M,D
Virginia Polytechnic Institute and State University	M,D*

INTERNATIONAL ECONOMICS

Claremont Graduate University	M,D,O*
Eastern Michigan University	M
Fordham University	M,O*
The Johns Hopkins University	M,D,O*
Regent University	M
University of Miami	M,D*
Virginia Polytechnic Institute and State University	M,D*
West Virginia University	M,D
Yale University	M*

INTERNATIONAL HEALTH

Boston University	M,D,O*
Brandeis University	M
The Catholic University of America	M,D,O
Duke University	M*
Emory University	M*
George Mason University	M,O*
Georgetown University	P,M,D
The George Washington University	M,D*
Harvard University	M,D*
The Johns Hopkins University	M,D*
Loma Linda University	M
New York Medical College	M*
New York University	M,D*
San Diego State University	M,D*
Tufts University	M,D*
TUI University	M,D,O
Tulane University	M,D
Uniformed Services University of the Health Sciences	M,D*
University of Alberta	M,D*
University of Michigan	M,D*
University of Minnesota, Twin Cities Campus	M,D*
University of Southern California	M*
University of South Florida	M,D*
The University of Toledo	M,O
University of Washington	M,D*
Yale University	M*

INTERNATIONAL TRADE POLICY

The George Washington University	M*
Monterey Institute of International Studies	M*

INTERNET AND INTERACTIVE MULTIMEDIA

Academy of Art University	M
Alfred University	M*
Brooklyn College of the City University of New York	M,O
California State University, East Bay	M
Concordia University (Canada)	M,O
DePaul University	M,D*
Duquesne University	M,O*
Elon University	M
Full Sail University	M
Georgetown University	M
Georgia Institute of Technology	M,D*
Indiana University–Purdue University Indianapolis	M,D*
Long Island University, C.W. Post Campus	M
Marlboro College	M
National University	M
New Mexico Highlands University	M
New York University	M*
Polytechnic Institute of NYU	M,O
Pratt Institute	M*
Quinnipiac University	M*
Robert Morris University	M,D
Rochester Institute of Technology	M,O
Sacred Heart University	M,O
San Diego State University	M*
Savannah College of Art and Design	M*
School of Visual Arts	M
Simon Fraser University	M,D
Southern Polytechnic State University	M,O
Stevens Institute of Technology	M,D,O
Towson University	D,O
Universidad Autonoma de Guadalajara	M,D
University of Advancing Technology	M
University of Central Florida	M*
University of Florida	M,D*
University of Georgia	M*
University of Miami	M*
University of Phoenix–Madison Campus	M
University of San Francisco	M
University of Southern California	M,D,O*
Virginia Commonwealth University	M
Western Illinois University	M,O
Wilmington University	M

INTERNET ENGINEERING

New Jersey Institute of Technology	M
University of Georgia	M*
University of San Francisco	M
Wilmington University	M

INVESTMENT MANAGEMENT

Alaska Pacific University	M,O
Arizona State University at the West campus	M,O
Boston University	M*
Concordia University (Canada)	M,D,O
Gannon University	O
The George Washington University	M,D*
International University in Geneva	M
The Johns Hopkins University	M,O*

Lincoln University (CA)	M
Lynn University	M,D
Marywood University	M
Pace University	M*
Quinnipiac University	M*
The University of Iowa	M*
University of San Francisco	M
University of Tulsa	M*
University of Wisconsin–Madison	D*

ITALIAN

Boston College	M,D*
Brown University	D*
Central Connecticut State University	M,O
Columbia University	M,D*
Cornell University	D*
Florida State University	M*
Graduate School and University Center of the City University of New York	M,D*
Harvard University	M,D*
Hunter College of the City University of New York	M
Indiana University Bloomington	M,D*
Iona College	M*
The Johns Hopkins University	D*
McGill University	M,D*
Middlebury College	M,D
Montclair State University	M,O*
New York University	M,D*
Northwestern University	D,O*
The Ohio State University	M,D*
Queens College of the City University of New York	M
Rutgers, The State University of New Jersey, New Brunswick	M,D*
San Francisco State University	M
Stanford University	M,D*
State University of New York at Binghamton	M*
Stony Brook University, State University of New York	M
University at Albany, State University of New York	M*
University of Alberta	M,D*
University of California, Berkeley	D*
University of California, Los Angeles	M,D*
University of Chicago	M,D*
University of Connecticut	M,D*
University of Illinois at Urbana–Champaign	M,D*
University of Massachusetts Amherst	M*
The University of North Carolina at Chapel Hill	M,D*
University of Notre Dame	M*
University of Oregon	M*
University of Pennsylvania	M,D*
University of Pittsburgh	M*
University of South Africa	M,D
The University of Tennessee	D
The University of Texas at Austin	M,D
University of Toronto	M,D
University of Victoria	M
University of Virginia	M
University of Washington	M,D*
University of Wisconsin–Madison	M,D*
University of Wisconsin–Milwaukee	M,O
Wayne State University	M*
Yale University	D*

JAPANESE

Arizona State University	M
Cornell University	M,D*
Eastern Michigan University	M,O
Harvard University	D*
Indiana University Bloomington	M,D*
Kent State University	M,D*
The Ohio State University	M,D*
Portland State University	M
San Francisco State University	M
Stanford University	M,D*
University at Buffalo, the State University of New York	M,D,O*
University of Alberta	M*
University of California, Berkeley	D*
University of California, Irvine	M,D*
University of Colorado at Boulder	M,D*
University of Hawaii at Manoa	M,D,O*
University of Maryland, College Park	M,D*
University of Massachusetts Amherst	M*
University of Oregon	M,D*
University of Washington	M,D*
University of Wisconsin–Madison	M,D*
Washington University in St. Louis	M,D*

JEWISH STUDIES

American Jewish University	M
Baltimore Hebrew University	M,D
Brandeis University	M,D
Brooklyn College of the City University of New York	M
Brown University	D*
Columbia University	M,D*
Concordia University (Canada)	M
Cornell University	M,D*
The Criswell College	P,M
Emory University	M*
Graduate Theological Union	M,D,O
Gratz College	M,O
Harvard University	M,D*
Hebrew College	M,O
Hebrew Union College–Jewish Institute of Religion (CA)	M,D
Hebrew Union College–Jewish Institute of Religion (NY)	M
Hebrew Union College–Jewish Institute of Religion (OH)	P,M,D
The Jewish Theological Seminary	M,D*
Jewish University of America	P,D
Laura and Alvin Siegal College of Judaic Studies	M
McGill University	M*
New York University	M,D,O*
St. Petersburg Theological Seminary	P,M,D
Seton Hall University	M*
Southern Evangelical Seminary	M,D,O
Spertus Institute of Jewish Studies	M,D
Telshe Yeshiva–Chicago	O
Touro College	M
University of California, Berkeley	D*
University of California, San Diego	M,D*
University of Connecticut	M*
University of Maryland, College Park	M*
University of Michigan	M,D,O*
The University of Montana	M
University of St. Michael's College	P,M,D,O
University of Wisconsin–Madison	M,D*
University of Wisconsin–Milwaukee	M,O
Yeshiva University	M,D

JOURNALISM

American University	M*
The American University in Cairo	M
Angelo State University	M
Arizona State University at the Downtown Phoenix Campus	M
Arkansas State University	M
Arkansas Tech University	M
Ball State University	M*
Baylor University	M
Bob Jones University	P,M,D,O
Boston University	M*
California State University, Fresno	M
California State University, Fullerton	M
California State University, Northridge	M
Carleton University	M,D
Columbia College Chicago	M
Columbia University	M,D*
Concordia University (Canada)	O
CUNY Graduate School of Journalism	M*
DePaul University	M*
Drake University	M*
Drexel University	M*
Emerson College	M
Florida Agricultural and Mechanical University	M
Florida Atlantic University	M,O
Georgetown University	M,D
Harvard University	M,O*
Hofstra University	M*
Indiana University Bloomington	M,D*
Iona College	M*
Iowa State University of Science and Technology	M*
Kent State University	M*
Marquette University	M
Marshall University	M
Michigan State University	M*
New York University	M,D,O*
Northeastern University	M*
Northwestern University	M*
The Ohio State University	M*
Ohio University	M,D*
Point Park University	M*
Polytechnic Institute of NYU	M
Quinnipiac University	M*
Regent University	M,D
Roosevelt University	M
School of the Art Institute of Chicago	M*
South Dakota State University	M
Southern Illinois University Carbondale	D*
Stanford University	M,D*
Syracuse University	M*
Temple University	M*
Texas Christian University	M
Université Laval	O
The University of Alabama	M
University of Arkansas	M
University of Arkansas at Little Rock	M
The University of British Columbia	M
University of California, Berkeley	M*
University of Colorado at Boulder	M,D*
University of Florida	M*
University of Georgia	M,D*
University of Illinois at Springfield	M
University of Illinois at Urbana–Champaign	M*
The University of Iowa	M*
The University of Kansas	M*
University of Maryland, College Park	M,D*
University of Memphis	M
University of Miami	M,D*
University of Mississippi	M
University of Missouri–Columbia	M,D*
The University of Montana	M
University of Nebraska–Lincoln	M*
University of Nevada, Las Vegas	M
University of Nevada, Reno	M*
University of North Texas	M,O
University of Oklahoma	M*
University of Oregon	M,D*
University of South Carolina	M,D
University of Southern California	M*
The University of Tennessee	M,D
The University of Texas at Austin	M,D
The University of Western Ontario	M
University of Wisconsin–Madison	M,D*
Virginia Commonwealth University	M
West Virginia University	M

KINESIOLOGY AND MOVEMENT STUDIES

Acadia University	M
Angelo State University	M
Arizona State University	D
A.T. Still University of Health Sciences	M,D
Auburn University	M,D,O*
Barry University	M*
Bowling Green State University	M*
California Baptist University	M
California Polytechnic State University, San Luis Obispo	M
California State Polytechnic University, Pomona	M
California State University, Chico	M
California State University, Fresno	M
California State University, Long Beach	M
California State University, Los Angeles	M
California State University, Northridge	M
California State University, San Bernardino	M
Columbia University	M,D*
Dalhousie University	M
Dallas Baptist University	M
Eastern Michigan University	M
Fresno Pacific University	M
Georgia Southern University	M
Georgia State University	D

*M—master's degree; P—first professional degree; D—doctorate; O—other advanced degree; *—Close-Up and/or Announcement or Display in one of the other books in this series*

Hardin-Simmons University	M
Humboldt State University	M
Indiana University Bloomington	M,D*
Inter American University of Puerto Rico, San Germán Campus	M
Iowa State University of Science and Technology	M,D*
James Madison University	M
Kansas State University	M*
Lakehead University	M
Lamar University	M
Louisiana State University and Agricultural and Mechanical College	M,D
McGill University	M,D,O*
McMaster University	M,D
Memorial University of Newfoundland	M
Michigan State University	M,D*
Midwestern State University	M
Mississippi College	M
Mississippi State University	M
New York University	M,D,O*
Northwestern University	D*
Old Dominion University	D
Oregon State University	M*
Penn State University Park	M,D*
Saint Mary's College of California	M
Sam Houston State University	M
San Diego State University	M*
San Francisco State University	M
San Jose State University	M
Simon Fraser University	M,D
Sonoma State University	M
Southeastern Louisiana University	M
Southern Arkansas University–Magnolia	M
Southern Illinois University Edwardsville	M,O
Southwestern Oklahoma State University	M
Stephen F. Austin State University	M
Teachers College, Columbia University	M,D
Temple University	M,D*
Tennessee Technological University	M*
Texas A&M University	M,D*
Texas A&M University–Commerce	M,D
Texas A&M University–Corpus Christi	M,D
Texas A&M University–Kingsville	M
Texas Christian University	M
Texas Woman's University	M,D
Towson University	M
Université de Montréal	M,D,O
Université de Sherbrooke	M,O
Université du Québec à Montréal	M
Université Laval	M,D
The University of Alabama	M,D
University of Arkansas	M,D
The University of British Columbia	M,D
University of Calgary	M,D
University of Central Arkansas	M
University of Colorado at Boulder	M,D*
University of Delaware	M,D*
University of Florida	M,D*
University of Georgia	M,D*
University of Hawaii at Manoa	M,D*
University of Houston	M,D*
University of Illinois at Chicago	M,D*
University of Illinois at Urbana–Champaign	M,D*
University of Kentucky	M,D
University of Lethbridge	M,D
University of Maine	M*
University of Manitoba	M
University of Maryland, College Park	M,D*
University of Massachusetts Amherst	M,D*
University of Medicine and Dentistry of New Jersey	M,D*
University of Michigan	M,D*
University of Minnesota, Twin Cities Campus	M,D*
University of Nevada, Las Vegas	M
University of New Hampshire	M*
The University of North Carolina at Chapel Hill	M,D*
The University of North Carolina at Charlotte	M*
University of North Dakota	M
University of North Texas	M
University of Ottawa	M*
University of Regina	M,D
University of Saskatchewan	M,D,O
University of Southern California	M,D*
The University of Tennessee	M,D
The University of Texas at Austin	M,D
The University of Texas at El Paso	M
The University of Texas at San Antonio	M*
The University of Texas at Tyler	M
The University of Texas of the Permian Basin	M
The University of Texas–Pan American	M
University of the Incarnate Word	M,D
University of Victoria	M
University of Virginia	M,D
University of Waterloo	M,D
The University of Western Ontario	M,D
University of Windsor	M
University of Wisconsin–Madison	M,D*
University of Wisconsin–Milwaukee	M
Washington University in St. Louis	D*
Wayne State University	M*
West Chester University of Pennsylvania	M,O
Western Illinois University	M
Wilfrid Laurier University	M
York University	M,D

LANDSCAPE ARCHITECTURE

Arizona State University	M
Auburn University	M*
Ball State University	M*
California State Polytechnic University, Pomona	M
Chatham University	M
City College of the City University of New York	M,O*
Clemson University	M
Columbia University	M*
Conway School of Landscape Design	M
Cornell University	M*
Florida Agricultural and Mechanical University	M
Florida International University	M*
Harvard University	M,D*
Illinois Institute of Technology	M,D*
Iowa State University of Science and Technology	M*
Kansas State University	M*
Louisiana State University and Agricultural and Mechanical College	M
Mississippi State University	M
Morgan State University	M
North Carolina State University	M*
The Ohio State University	M*
Oklahoma State University	M,D*
Penn State University Park	M*
Rhode Island School of Design	M
State University of New York College of Environmental Science and Forestry	M
Texas A&M University	M,D*
Texas Tech University	M
The University of Arizona	M*
The University of British Columbia	M
University of California, Berkeley	M*
University of Colorado Denver	M*
University of Florida	M,D*
University of Georgia	M*
University of Guelph	M
University of Idaho	M
University of Illinois at Urbana–Champaign	M,D*
University of Manitoba	M
University of Massachusetts Amherst	M*
University of Michigan	M,D*
University of Minnesota, Twin Cities Campus	M*
University of New Mexico	M*
University of Oklahoma	M*
University of Oregon	M*
University of Pennsylvania	M,O*
The University of Tennessee	M
The University of Texas at Arlington	M*
The University of Texas at Austin	M,D
University of Virginia	M*
University of Washington	M*
University of Wisconsin–Madison	M*
Utah State University	M
Virginia Polytechnic Institute and State University	M,D*
Washington State University	M,D*
Washington State University Spokane	M,D

LATIN AMERICAN STUDIES

American University	M,O*
Arizona State University	M,D
Boricua College	M
Brown University	M,D*
California State University, Long Beach	M
California State University, Los Angeles	M
Centro de Estudios Avanzados de Puerto Rico y el Caribe	M,D
Cleveland State University	M
Columbia University	M,O*
Cornell University	M,D*
Duke University	M,D,O*
Florida International University	M*
Fordham University	M,O*
Georgetown University	M
The George Washington University	M*
Georgia State University	M,D,O
Indiana University Bloomington	M*
La Salle University	M
Michigan State University	D*
New York University	M,D,O*
Ohio University	M*
San Diego State University	M*
Simon Fraser University	M
Tulane University	M,D
University at Albany, State University of New York	M,O*
The University of Arizona	M*
University of California, Berkeley	M*
University of California, Los Angeles	M*
University of California, San Diego	M*
University of California, Santa Barbara	M,D
University of Central Florida	M,D,O*
University of Chicago	M*
University of Connecticut	M*
University of Florida	M,O*
University of Illinois at Urbana–Champaign	M*
The University of Kansas	M,O*
University of Massachusetts Dartmouth	M,D
University of Miami	M*
University of New Mexico	M,D*
The University of North Carolina at Chapel Hill	M,D,O*
The University of North Carolina at Charlotte	M*
University of Notre Dame	M*
University of Pittsburgh	O*
University of South Florida	M,D,O*
The University of Texas at Austin	M,D
University of Wisconsin–Madison	M,D*
Vanderbilt University	M*
West Virginia University	M,D
Yale University	D*

LAW

Albany Law School	P,M
American University	P,M,O*
Appalachian School of Law	P
Arizona State University	P,M
Atlanta's John Marshall Law School	P
Ave Maria School of Law	P
Barry University	P*
Baylor University	P
Boston College	P*
Boston University	P,M*
Brigham Young University	P,M*
Brooklyn Law School	P
California Western School of Law	P,M
Campbell University	P
Capital University	P,M
Case Western Reserve University	P,M*
The Catholic University of America	P
Central European University	M,D*
Chapman University	P,M
Charlotte School of Law	P
City University of New York School of Law at Queens College	P
Cleveland State University	P,M
The College of William and Mary	P,M
Columbia University	P,M,D*
Concord Law School	P
Cornell University	P,M,D*
Creighton University	P,M,O*
Dalhousie University	M,D
DePaul University	P,M*

Drake University	P*
Duke University	P,M,D*
Duquesne University	P,M*
Elon University	P
Emory University	P,M,O*
Facultad de derecho Eugenio María de Hostos	P
Faulkner University	P
Florida Agricultural and Mechanical University	P
Florida Coastal School of Law	P
Florida International University	P*
Florida State University	P,M*
Fordham University	P,M*
Franklin Pierce Law Center	P,M,O
Friends University	M
George Mason University	P,M*
Georgetown University	P,M,D
The George Washington University	P,M,D*
Georgia State University	P
Golden Gate University	P,M,D
Gonzaga University	P
Hamline University	P,M
Harvard University	P,M,D*
Hodges University	M
Hofstra University	P,M*
Howard University	P,M
Humphreys College	P
Illinois Institute of Technology	P,M*
Indiana University Bloomington	P,M,D,O*
Indiana University–Purdue University Indianapolis	P,M,D*
Instituto Tecnológico y de Estudios Superiores de Monterrey, Campus Ciudad de México	P
Inter American University of Puerto Rico School of Law	P
John F. Kennedy University	P
John Marshall Law School	P,M
The Judge Advocate General's School, U.S. Army	M
Kaplan University–Davenport Campus	M
Lewis & Clark College	P,M
Liberty University	P
Louisiana State University and Agricultural and Mechanical College	M
Loyola Marymount University	P,M
Loyola University Chicago	P,M,D*
Loyola University New Orleans	P,M
Marquette University	P
Massachusetts School of Law at Andover	P
McGill University	P,M,D,O*
Mercer University	P
Michigan State University College of Law	P,M
Mississippi College	P,O
New England School of Law	P,M
New York Law School	P,M
New York University	P,M,D,O*
North Carolina Central University	P
Northeastern University	P*
Northern Illinois University	P
Northern Kentucky University	P
Northwestern University	P,M,O*
Nova Southeastern University	P,M,O*
Ohio Northern University	P,M
The Ohio State University	P,M*
Oklahoma City University	P
Pace University	P,M,D*
Park University	M
Penn State Dickinson School of Law	P,M
Pepperdine University	P
Pontifical Catholic University of Puerto Rico	P
Pontificia Universidad Catolica Madre y Maestra	M
Queen's University at Kingston	P,M
Quinnipiac University	P,M*
Regent University	P,M
Roger Williams University	P*
Rutgers, The State University of New Jersey, Camden	P
Rutgers, The State University of New Jersey, Newark	P*
St. John's University (NY)	P
Saint Joseph's University	M,O
Saint Louis University	P,M
St. Mary's University (United States)	P
St. Thomas University	P,M
Samford University	P,M
San Joaquin College of Law	P
Santa Clara University	P,M,O
Seattle University	P,O
Seton Hall University	P,M*
Southern Illinois University Carbondale	P,M*
Southern Methodist University	P,M,D*
Southern New England School of Law	P
Southern University and Agricultural and Mechanical College	P
South Texas College of Law	P
Southwestern Law School	P,M
Stanford University	P,M,D*
Stetson University	P,M
Suffolk University	P,M*
Syracuse University	P*
Temple University	P,M,D*
Texas Southern University	P
Texas Tech University	P
Texas Wesleyan University	P
Thomas Jefferson School of Law	P
Thomas M. Cooley Law School	P,M
Touro College	P,M
Trinity International University	P
Tulane University	P,M,D
Universidad Autonoma de Guadalajara	M,D
Universidad Central del Este	P
Universidad Iberoamericana	P,M
Université de Moncton	P,M,O
Université de Montréal	P,M,D,O
Université de Sherbrooke	P,M,D,O
Université du Québec à Montréal	O
Université Laval	M,D,O
University at Buffalo, the State University of New York	P,M*
The University of Akron	P
The University of Alabama	P,M
University of Alberta	P,M*
The University of Arizona	P,M*
University of Arkansas	P,M
University of Arkansas at Little Rock	P
University of Baltimore	M
The University of British Columbia	M,D
University of Calgary	P,M,O
University of California, Berkeley	P,M,D*
University of California, Davis	P,M*
University of California, Hastings College of the Law	P,M
University of California, Los Angeles	P,M,D*
University of California, San Diego	M*
University of Chicago	P,M,D*
University of Cincinnati	P
University of Colorado at Boulder	P*
University of Connecticut	P*
University of Dayton	P,M
University of Denver	P,M*
University of Detroit Mercy	P
University of Florida	P,M,D*
University of Georgia	P,M*
University of Hawaii at Manoa	P,M,O*
University of Houston	P,M*
University of Idaho	P
University of Illinois at Urbana–Champaign	P,M,D*
The University of Iowa	P,M*
The University of Kansas	P*
University of Kentucky	P
University of La Verne	P
University of Louisville	P
University of Manitoba	M
University of Maryland, Baltimore	P*
University of Maryland, College Park	*
University of Memphis	P
University of Miami	P,M*
University of Michigan	P,M,D*
University of Minnesota, Twin Cities Campus	P,M*
University of Mississippi	P
University of Missouri–Columbia	P,M*
University of Missouri–Kansas City	P,M*
The University of Montana	P
University of Nebraska–Lincoln	P,M*
University of Nevada, Las Vegas	P
University of New Brunswick Fredericton	P
University of New Mexico	P*
The University of North Carolina at Chapel Hill	P*
University of North Dakota	P
University of Notre Dame	P,M,D*
University of Oklahoma	P*
University of Oregon	P,M*
University of Ottawa	M,D*
University of Pennsylvania	P,M,D*
University of Pittsburgh	P,M,O*
University of Puerto Rico, Río Piedras	P,M
University of Richmond	P
University of St. Thomas (MN)	P*
University of San Diego	P,M,O
University of San Francisco	P,M
University of Saskatchewan	P,M
University of South Africa	M,D
University of South Carolina	P
The University of South Dakota	P
University of Southern Maine	P
The University of Tennessee	P
The University of Texas at Austin	P,M
University of the District of Columbia	P
University of the Pacific	P,M,D
The University of Toledo	P
University of Toronto	P,M,D
University of Tulsa	P,M,O*
University of Utah	P,M*
University of Victoria	P,M,D
University of Virginia	P,M,D,O
University of Washington	P,M,D*
The University of Western Ontario	P,M,O
University of Wisconsin–Madison	P,M,D*
University of Wyoming	P
Valparaiso University	P,M
Vanderbilt University	P,M,D*
Vermont Law School	P
Villanova University	P*
Wake Forest University	P,M,D*
Walden University	M,D,O
Washburn University	P
Washington and Lee University	P,M
Washington University in St. Louis	P,M,D*
Wayne State University	P,M,D*
Western New England College	P,M
Western State University College of Law	P
West Virginia University	P
Whittier College	P,M
Widener University	P,M,D*
Willamette University	P,M
William Howard Taft University	P,M
William Mitchell College of Law	P
Yale University	P,M,D*
Yeshiva University	P,M
York University	P,M,D

LEGAL AND JUSTICE STUDIES

American University	M,D,O*
Arizona State University	P,M,D
Arizona State University at the West campus	M
Boston University	M*
Brock University	M
California University of Pennsylvania	M
Capital University	M
Carleton University	M,O
Case Western Reserve University	P,M*
The Catholic University of America	D,O
Central European University	M,D*
College of Charleston	M,O*
College of the Humanities and Sciences, Harrison Middleton University	M,D
Eastern Michigan University	O
Georgetown University	P,M,D
The George Washington University	M,O*
Golden Gate University	P,M,D
Governors State University	M
Harvard University	P*
Hofstra University	P,M*
Hollins University	M,O
John Jay College of Criminal Justice of the City University of New York	M,D
John Marshall Law School	P,M
Kaplan University–Davenport Campus	M,O
Marygrove College	M
Marymount University	M,O
Michigan State University College of Law	P,M
Mississippi College	M,O
Montclair State University	M,O*
New York University	M,D*
Northeastern University	M,D*
Nova Southeastern University	M,O*
Pace University	P,M,D*
Prairie View A&M University	M,D

*M—master's degree; P—first professional degree; D—doctorate; O—other advanced degree; *—Close-Up and/or Announcement or Display in one of the other books in this series*

Queen's University at Kingston	M,D
Regent University	P,M
Regis University	M,O
The Richard Stockton College of New Jersey	O
Rutgers, The State University of New Jersey, New Brunswick	D*
St. John's University (NY)	M
Salve Regina University	M
San Francisco State University	M,O
Southern Illinois University Carbondale	M*
State University of New York at Binghamton	M,D*
Temple University	P,M,D*
Texas State University–San Marcos	M*
TUI University	M,D,O
Université Laval	O
University of Baltimore	M
University of Calgary	M,O
University of California, Berkeley	D*
University of California, San Diego	M*
University of Charleston	M
University of Denver	M,O*
University of Illinois at Springfield	M
University of Mississippi	M
University of Nebraska–Lincoln	M*
University of Nevada, Reno	M,D*
University of New Hampshire	M*
University of Pennsylvania	M,D*
University of Pittsburgh	M,O*
University of San Diego	P,M,O
University of the Pacific	P,M,D
University of the Sacred Heart	M
University of Washington	P,M,D*
University of Windsor	M
University of Wisconsin–Madison	M,D*
Vermont Law School	M
Weber State University	M
Webster University	M
West Virginia University	M
Whittier College	P,M
William Howard Taft University	P,M

LEISURE STUDIES

Aurora University	M
Bowling Green State University	M*
California State University, Long Beach	M
Central Michigan University	M
The College at Brockport, State University of New York	M
Dalhousie University	M
East Carolina University	M
Florida International University	M*
Gallaudet University	M
Howard University	M
Indiana University Bloomington	M,D,O*
Kent State University	M*
Murray State University	M
Penn State University Park	M,D*
Prescott College	M
San Francisco State University	M
Southeast Missouri State University	M
Southern Connecticut State University	M
Temple University	M*
Texas State University–San Marcos	M*
Universidad Metropolitana	M
Université du Québec à Trois-Rivières	M,O
University of Connecticut	M,D*
University of Georgia	M,D,O*
University of Illinois at Urbana–Champaign	M,D*
The University of Iowa	M*
University of Memphis	M
University of Minnesota, Twin Cities Campus	M,D*
University of Mississippi	M,D
University of Nevada, Las Vegas	M
The University of North Carolina at Chapel Hill	M*
University of Northern Iowa	M,D
University of North Texas	M,O
University of South Alabama	M*
University of Southern Mississippi	M,D
The University of Tennessee	M,D
The University of Toledo	M
University of Utah	M,D*
University of Victoria	M
University of Waterloo	M,D
University of West Florida	M

LIBERAL STUDIES

Abilene Christian University	M
Alaska Pacific University	M
Albertus Magnus College	M
Alvernia University	M
Antioch University McGregor	M
Armstrong Atlantic State University	M
Auburn University Montgomery	M
Baker University	M
Barry University	M*
Boston University	M*
Bradley University	M
Brooklyn College of the City University of New York	M
California State University, Sacramento	M
Cardinal Stritch University	M
Clark University	M
Clayton State University	M
The College at Brockport, State University of New York	M
College of Notre Dame of Maryland	M
College of Staten Island of the City University of New York	M
Columbia University	M*
Concordia University Chicago	M
Converse College	M
Creighton University	M*
Dallas Baptist University	M
Dartmouth College	M*
Dowling College	M
Duke University	M*
Duquesne University	M*
East Tennessee State University	M
Excelsior College	M
Florida Atlantic University	M
Florida International University	M*
Fordham University	M*
Fort Hays State University	M
Georgetown University	M,D
Graduate School and University Center of the City University of New York	M*
Hamline University	M,O
Harvard University	M,O*
Henderson State University	M
Hollins University	M,O
Houston Baptist University	M
Indiana University Kokomo	M
Indiana University–Purdue University Fort Wayne	M
Indiana University–Purdue University Indianapolis	M,D,O*
Indiana University South Bend	M
Indiana University Southeast	M
Jacksonville State University	M
The Johns Hopkins University	M,O*
Kean University	M
Kent State University	M*
Lake Forest College	M
Lock Haven University of Pennsylvania	M
Louisiana State University and Agricultural and Mechanical College	M
Louisiana State University in Shreveport	M
Loyola University Maryland	M*
Madonna University	M
Manhattanville College	M*
McDaniel College	M
Metropolitan State University	M
Minnesota State University Moorhead	M
Mississippi College	M
Monmouth University	M
Nazareth College of Rochester	M
The New School: A University	M*
North Carolina State University	M*
North Central College	M
Northern Arizona University	M
Northern Kentucky University	M,O
Northwestern University	M*
Oakland University	M
Occidental College	M
Ohio Dominican University	M
Oklahoma City University	M
Queens College of the City University of New York	M
Ramapo College of New Jersey	M
Reed College	M
Rollins College	M
Rutgers, The State University of New Jersey, Camden	M
Rutgers, The State University of New Jersey, Newark	M*
St. Edward's University	M,O
St. John's College (MD)	M
St. John's College (NM)	M
St. John's University (NY)	M
Saint Mary's College of California	M
St. Norbert College	M
San Diego State University	M*
Simon Fraser University	M
Skidmore College	M
Spring Hill College	M
State University of New York at Plattsburgh	M
State University of New York Empire State College	M
Stony Brook University, State University of New York	M,O
Tarleton State University	M
Temple University	M*
Texas Christian University	M
Thomas Edison State College	M
Towson University	M
Tulane University	M
University at Albany, State University of New York	M*
University of Arkansas at Little Rock	M
University of Delaware	M*
University of Denver	M,O*
University of Detroit Mercy	M
The University of Findlay	M
University of Maine	M*
University of Memphis	M
University of Miami	M*
University of Michigan–Dearborn	M*
University of Minnesota, Duluth	M
University of New Hampshire	M*
The University of North Carolina at Asheville	M
The University of North Carolina at Charlotte	M*
The University of North Carolina at Greensboro	M
The University of North Carolina Wilmington	M
University of Oklahoma	M*
University of Pennsylvania	M*
University of St. Thomas (TX)	M
University of Southern Indiana	M
University of South Florida	M*
The University of Toledo	M
University of Wisconsin–Milwaukee	M
Ursuline College	M
Utica College	M
Valparaiso University	M,O
Vanderbilt University	M*
Villanova University	M*
Wake Forest University	M*
Washburn University	M
Wesleyan University	M,O*
Western Illinois University	M
West Virginia University	M
Wichita State University	M*
Widener University	M*
Winthrop University	M

LIBRARY SCIENCE

Appalachian State University	M,O
Azusa Pacific University	M
The Catholic University of America	M
Chicago State University	M
Clarion University of Pennsylvania	M,O
Dalhousie University	M
Dominican University	M,O
Drexel University	M,D,O*
East Carolina University	M,O
Eastern Kentucky University	M
Emporia State University	M,D,O
Florida State University	M,D,O*
George Mason University	M,O*
Indiana University Bloomington	M,D,O*
Indiana University–Purdue University Indianapolis	M*
Instituto Tecnológico y de Estudios Superiores de Monterrey, Campus Irapuato	M,D
Inter American University of Puerto Rico, Barranquitas Campus	M
Inter American University of Puerto Rico, San Germán Campus	M

Kent State University M*
Kutztown University of Pennsylvania M,O
Long Island University, C.W. Post Campus M,D,O
Long Island University, Westchester Graduate Campus M
Louisiana State University and Agricultural and Mechanical College M,O
Mansfield University of Pennsylvania M
Marywood University M,O
McDaniel College M
McGill University M,D,O*
North Carolina Central University M
Old Dominion University M
Olivet Nazarene University M
Pratt Institute M,O*
Queens College of the City University of New York M,O
Rowan University M
Rutgers, The State University of New Jersey, New Brunswick M,D*
St. Catherine University M
St. John's University (NY) M,O
Sam Houston State University M
San Jose State University M,D
Simmons College M,D,O
Southern Arkansas University–Magnolia M
Southern Connecticut State University M,O
Syracuse University M,O*
Tennessee Technological University M,O*
Texas Woman's University M,D
Trevecca Nazarene University M
Universidad del Turabo M
Université de Montréal M,D
University at Buffalo, the State University of New York M,O*
The University of Alabama M,D
University of Alberta M*
The University of Arizona M,D*
The University of British Columbia M,D
University of California, Los Angeles M,D,O*
University of Central Arkansas M
University of Central Missouri M,O
University of Denver M,D,O*
University of Hawaii at Manoa M,O*
University of Houston–Clear Lake M
University of Illinois at Urbana–Champaign M,D,O*
The University of Iowa M*
University of Kentucky M
University of Maryland, College Park *
University of Michigan M,D*
University of Missouri–Columbia M,D,O*
The University of North Carolina at Chapel Hill M,D,O*
The University of North Carolina at Greensboro M
University of Northern Colorado M
University of North Texas M,D
University of Oklahoma M,O*
University of Pittsburgh M,D,O*
University of Puerto Rico, Río Piedras M,O
University of Rhode Island M
University of South Carolina M,D,O
University of Southern Mississippi M,O
University of South Florida M*
University of Toronto M,D,O
University of Washington M,D*
The University of Western Ontario M,D
University of Wisconsin–Madison M,D*
University of Wisconsin–Milwaukee M,D,O
Valdosta State University M
Wayne State University M,O*
Wright State University M

LIGHTING DESIGN

The New School: A University M*
Rensselaer Polytechnic Institute M
University of Washington M,D,O*

LIMNOLOGY

Baylor University M,D
Cornell University D*
University of Alaska Fairbanks M,D
University of Florida M,D*
University of Wisconsin–Madison M,D*
William Peterson University of New Jersey M*

LINGUISTICS

Arizona State University M,D
Ball State University D*
Biola University M,D,O
Boston College M*
Boston University M,D*
Brandeis University M
Brigham Young University M,O*
Brown University M,D*
California State University, Fresno M
California State University, Fullerton M
California State University, Long Beach M
California State University, Northridge M
Carleton University M
Carnegie Mellon University D*
Case Western Reserve University M*
Cleveland State University M
Concordia University (Canada) M,O
Cornell University M,D*
Eastern Michigan University M
Florida Atlantic University M
Florida International University M*
Gallaudet University M,D
George Mason University M,O*
Georgetown University M,D,O
Georgia State University M,D
Graduate Institute of Applied Linguistics M,O
Graduate School and University Center of the City University of New York M,D*
Harvard University D*
Hofstra University M,D,O*
Indiana State University M,O
Indiana University Bloomington M,D*
Indiana University of Pennsylvania M,D
Instituto Tecnologico de Santo Domingo M
Louisiana State University and Agricultural and Mechanical College M,D
Massachusetts Institute of Technology D*
McGill University M,D*
Memorial University of Newfoundland M,D
Michigan State University M,D*
Midwestern Baptist Theological Seminary P,M,D,O
Montclair State University M,O*
New York University M,D*
Northeastern Illinois University M
Northern Arizona University M,D,O
Northwestern University M,D*
Oakland University M,O
The Ohio State University M,D*
Ohio University M*
Old Dominion University M
Purdue University M,D
Queens College of the City University of New York M
Rice University M,D
Rutgers, The State University of New Jersey, New Brunswick D*
San Diego State University M,O*
San Francisco State University M
San Jose State University M,O
Simon Fraser University M,D
Southern Illinois University Carbondale M*
Stanford University M,D*
Stony Brook University, State University of New York M,D
Syracuse University M*
Teachers College, Columbia University M,D
Temple University M*
Texas Tech University M
Trinity Western University M
Universidad de las Américas–Puebla M
Université de Montréal M,D,O
Université de Sherbrooke M,D
Université du Québec à Chicoutimi M
Université du Québec à Montréal M,D
Université Laval M,D
University at Buffalo, the State University of New York M,D*
University of Alaska Fairbanks M
University of Alberta M,D*
The University of Arizona M,D*
The University of British Columbia M,D
University of Calgary M,D
University of California, Berkeley D*
University of California, Davis M,D*
University of California, Los Angeles M,D*
University of California, San Diego D*
University of California, Santa Barbara M,D
University of California, Santa Cruz M,D*
University of Chicago M,D*
University of Colorado at Boulder M,D*
University of Colorado Denver M,O*
University of Connecticut M,D*
University of Delaware M,D*
University of Florida M,D,O*
University of Georgia M,D*
University of Hawaii at Manoa M,D*
University of Houston M,D*
University of Illinois at Chicago
University of Illinois at Urbana–Champaign M,[illegible]
The University of Iowa M,D*
The University of Kansas M,D*
University of Manitoba M,D
University of Maryland, Baltimore County M*
University of Maryland, College Park M,D*
University of Massachusetts Amherst M,D*
University of Massachusetts Boston M
University of Michigan D*
University of Minnesota, Twin Cities Campus M,D*
University of Missouri–St. Louis M,O
The University of Montana M,D
University of New Hampshire M,D*
University of New Mexico M,D*
The University of North Carolina at Chapel Hill M,D*
University of North Dakota M
University of Oregon M,D*
University of Ottawa M,D*
University of Pennsylvania M,D*
University of Pittsburgh M,D*
University of Puerto Rico, Río Piedras M
University of Regina M
University of South Africa M,D
University of South Carolina M,D,O
University of Southern California M,D*
University of South Florida M*
The University of Tennessee D
The University of Texas at Arlington M,D*
The University of Texas at Austin M,D
The University of Texas at El Paso M
University of Toronto M,D
University of Utah M,D*
University of Victoria M,D
University of Virginia M
University of Washington M,D*
University of Wisconsin–Madison M,D*
University of Wisconsin–Milwaukee M,D,O
Wayne State University M*
West Virginia University M
Yale University D*
York University M,D

LOGISTICS

Air Force Institute of Technology M,D
American Public University System M
Benedictine University M
Case Western Reserve University M,D*
Colorado Technical University Colorado Springs M,D
East Carolina University M,D,O
Florida Institute of Technology M*
George Mason University M*
Georgia College & State University M
HEC Montreal M
Kaplan University–Davenport Campus M
Maine Maritime Academy M,O
Massachusetts Institute of Technology M,D*
North Dakota State University M,D
The Ohio State University M*

*M—master's degree; P—first professional degree; D—doctorate; O—other advanced degree; *—Close-Up and/or Announcement or Display in one of the other books in this series*

	M
	M,D,O
	M,D
	M
State University of New York	M,D,O*
The University of Alabama in Huntsville	M,O
University of Alaska Anchorage	M,O
University of Dallas	M
University of Houston	M*
University of Minnesota, Twin Cities Campus	M,D*
University of Missouri–St. Louis	M,D,O
University of New Hampshire	M,D*
University of New Haven	M,O*
University of South Africa	M,D
The University of Tennessee	M,D
The University of Texas at Arlington	M*
University of Washington	O*
Virginia Polytechnic Institute and State University	M,D*
Wilmington University	M
Wright State University	M

MANAGEMENT INFORMATION SYSTEMS

Adelphi University	M*
Air Force Institute of Technology	M
Alliant International University–San Diego	M,D*
American InterContinental University Dunwoody Campus	M
American InterContinental University–London	M
American Sentinel University	M
American University	M,O*
Argosy University, Atlanta	M,D*
Argosy University, Chicago	M,D*
Argosy University, Dallas	M,O*
Argosy University, Denver	M,D*
Argosy University, Hawai'i	M,D,O*
Argosy University, Inland Empire	M,D*
Argosy University, Los Angeles	M,D*
Argosy University, Nashville	M,D*
Argosy University, Orange County	M,D,O*
Argosy University, Phoenix	M,D*
Argosy University, Salt Lake City	M,D*
Argosy University, San Diego	M,D*
Argosy University, San Francisco Bay Area	M,D*
Argosy University, Sarasota	M,D,O*
Argosy University, Schaumburg	M,D,O*
Argosy University, Seattle	M,D*
Argosy University, Tampa	M,D*
Argosy University, Twin Cities	M,D*
Argosy University, Washington DC	M,D,O*
Arizona State University	M,D
Arizona State University at the Polytechnic Campus	M
Arkansas State University	M
Aspen University	M,O
Auburn University	M,D*
Avila University	M
Baker College Center for Graduate Studies	M
Barry University	O*
Baylor University	M
Bay Path College	M
Bellarmine University	M
Bellevue University	M
Benedictine University	M
Bernard M. Baruch College of the City University of New York	M,D
Boise State University	M
Boston University	D*
Bowie State University	M,O
Brandeis University	M,O
Brigham Young University	M*
British American College London	M
California Intercontinental University	M,D
California Lutheran University	M,O
California State University, Fullerton	M
California State University, Los Angeles	M
California State University, Monterey Bay	M
California State University, Sacramento	M
Capella University	M,D,O
Capitol College	M
Carnegie Mellon University	M,D*
Case Western Reserve University	M,D*
Central European University	M*
Central Michigan University	M,O
Charleston Southern University	M
City University of Seattle	M,O
Claremont Graduate University	M,D,O*
Clark University	M
Cleveland State University	M,D
College of Charleston	M*
The College of St. Scholastica	M,O
Colorado State University	M*
Colorado Technical University Sioux Falls	M
Concordia University Wisconsin	M
Creighton University	M*
Dalhousie University	M
Dallas Baptist University	M
DePaul University	M,D*
DeSales University	M
DeVry University (IL)	M*
Dominican University	M
Duquesne University	M*
East Carolina University	M,D,O
Eastern Michigan University	M,O
Emory University	M,D*
Endicott College	M
Fairfield University	M,O*
Fairleigh Dickinson University, Metropolitan Campus	M,O*
Ferris State University	M
Florida Agricultural and Mechanical University	M
Florida Atlantic University	M
Florida Institute of Technology	M*
Florida International University	M*
Florida State University	M,D*
Fordham University	M*
Franklin Pierce University	M,D,O
Friends University	M
George Mason University	M,D,O*
The George Washington University	M,D*
Georgia College & State University	M
Georgia Institute of Technology	M,D,O*
Georgia State University	M,D
Golden Gate University	M,D,O
Goldey-Beacom College	M
Governors State University	M
Graduate School and University Center of the City University of New York	D*
Grand Canyon University	M*
Grand Valley State University	M
Grantham University	M
Harding University	M
Hawai'i Pacific University	M*
HEC Montreal	M
Hodges University	M
Hofstra University	M*
Holy Family University	M
Hood College	M
Howard University	M
Idaho State University	M,O
Illinois Institute of Technology	M,D*
Illinois State University	M
Indiana University South Bend	M
Instituto Tecnológico y de Estudios Superiores de Monterrey, Campus Central de Veracruz	M
Instituto Tecnológico y de Estudios Superiores de Monterrey, Campus Ciudad de México	M,D
Instituto Tecnológico y de Estudios Superiores de Monterrey, Campus Ciudad Juárez	M
Instituto Tecnológico y de Estudios Superiores de Monterrey, Campus Ciudad Obregón	M
Instituto Tecnológico y de Estudios Superiores de Monterrey, Campus Estado de México	M,D
Instituto Tecnológico y de Estudios Superiores de Monterrey, Campus Irapuato	M,D
Instituto Tecnológico y de Estudios Superiores de Monterrey, Campus Laguna	M
Inter American University of Puerto Rico, Metropolitan Campus	M
Inter American University of Puerto Rico, San Germán Campus	M,D
Iowa State University of Science and Technology	M*
John Marshall Law School	P,M
The Johns Hopkins University	M,O*
Kaplan University–Davenport Campus	M
Kean University	M
Kent State University	D*
Kentucky State University	M
Lawrence Technological University	M,D
Lewis University	M
Lincoln University (CA)	M
Lindenwood University	M,O
Long Island University, C.W. Post Campus	M,O
Louisiana State University and Agricultural and Mechanical College	M,D
Loyola University Chicago	M*
Loyola University Maryland	M*
Marist College	M,O
Marymount University	M,O
Marywood University	M
McGill University	M,D,O*
McMaster University	D
Metropolitan State University	M,O
Miami University	M*
Michigan State University	M,D*
Middle Tennessee State University	M
Minnesota State University Mankato	M,O
Minot State University	M
Mississippi State University	M,D
Missouri State University	M*
Montclair State University	M,O*
Morehead State University	M
National University	M
Naval Postgraduate School	M,O
New Jersey Institute of Technology	M,D
Newman University	M
New Mexico Highlands University	M
New York Institute of Technology	M,O
New York University	M,D,O*
North Central College	M
Northeastern University	M,D*
Northern Illinois University	M
Northwestern University	M*
Northwest Missouri State University	M
Norwich University	M
Notre Dame College (OH)	M,O
Nova Southeastern University	M,D*
Oakland University	M,O
The Ohio State University	M,D*
Oklahoma City University	M
Oklahoma State University	M,D*
Old Dominion University	M
Our Lady of the Lake University of San Antonio	M
Pace University	M*
Pacific States University	M,D
Park University	M
Penn State Great Valley	M
Penn State Harrisburg	M
Polytechnic Institute of NYU, Westchester Graduate Center	M,O
Pontifical Catholic University of Puerto Rico	M
Prairie View A&M University	M,D
Quinnipiac University	M*
Regis University	M,O
Rivier College	M
Robert Morris College	M
Robert Morris University	M,D
Rochester Institute of Technology	M
Roosevelt University	M
Rutgers, The State University of New Jersey, Newark	M,D*
Sacred Heart University	M,O
St. Edward's University	M,O
St. John's University (NY)	M,O
Saint Peter's College	M
San Diego State University	M*
San Jose State University	M
Santa Clara University	M
Schiller International University (United States)	M
Schiller International University (Germany)	M
Schiller International University (United Kingdom)	M
Seattle Pacific University	M

Seton Hall University M*
Shenandoah University M,O
Southeastern University M
Southern Illinois University Edwardsville M
Southern Methodist University M*
Southern New Hampshire University M,D,O*
State University of New York College at Potsdam M
Stevens Institute of Technology M,D,O
Stony Brook University, State University of New York M,D,O
Stratford University M
Strayer University M
Sullivan University P,M
Syracuse University M,D,O*
Tarleton State University M
Temple University M,D*
Texas A&M International University M
Texas A&M University M,D*
Texas Southern University M
Texas State University–San Marcos M*
Texas Tech University M,D
Towson University D,O
Troy University M
TUI University M,D,O
United States International University M
Universidad del Este M
Universidad del Turabo M,D
Université de Sherbrooke M,O
Université du Québec à Montréal M
Université Laval M,O
University at Buffalo, the State University of New York M,D,O*
The University of Akron M
The University of Alabama at Birmingham M*
The University of Alabama in Huntsville M,O
The University of Arizona M*
University of Arkansas M
University of Arkansas at Little Rock M,O
University of Baltimore M,O
The University of British Columbia D
University of Central Florida M*
University of Central Missouri M
University of Cincinnati M,D
University of Colorado at Boulder M,D*
University of Colorado at Colorado Springs M
University of Colorado Denver M,D*
University of Dallas M
University of Dayton M
University of Delaware M*
University of Denver M*
University of Detroit Mercy M
University of Florida M,D*
University of Hawaii at Manoa M,D,O*
University of Houston–Clear Lake M
University of Illinois at Chicago M,D*
University of Illinois at Springfield M
The University of Iowa M*
The University of Kansas M*
University of La Verne M
University of Lethbridge M,D
University of Maine M*
University of Management and Technology M,O
University of Mary Hardin-Baylor M
University of Maryland University College M,O
University of Mary Washington M
University of Memphis M,D
University of Miami M*
University of Minnesota, Twin Cities Campus M,D*
University of Mississippi M,D
University of Missouri–St. Louis M,D
University of Nebraska at Omaha M,D,O
University of Nebraska–Lincoln M*
University of Nevada, Las Vegas M
University of Nevada, Reno M*
University of New Haven M*
University of New Mexico M*
The University of North Carolina at Chapel Hill D*
The University of North Carolina at Greensboro M,D,O
University of North Texas M,D
University of Oklahoma M*
University of Oregon M*
University of Pennsylvania M,D*
University of Phoenix M
University of Phoenix–Atlanta Campus M
University of Phoenix–Augusta Campus M
University of Phoenix–Austin Campus M
University of Phoenix–Bay Area Campus M
University of Phoenix–Birmingham Campus M
University of Phoenix–Boston Campus M
University of Phoenix–Central Florida Campus M
University of Phoenix–Central Valley Campus M
University of Phoenix–Charlotte Campus M
University of Phoenix–Chattanooga Campus M
University of Phoenix–Cheyenne Campus M
University of Phoenix–Chicago Campus M
University of Phoenix–Cincinnati Campus M
University of Phoenix–Cleveland Campus M
University of Phoenix–Columbus Georgia Campus M
University of Phoenix–Columbus Ohio Campus M
University of Phoenix–Dallas Campus M
University of Phoenix–Denver Campus M
University of Phoenix–Des Moines Campus M
University of Phoenix–Eastern Washington Campus M
University of Phoenix–Harrisburg Campus M
University of Phoenix–Hawaii Campus M
University of Phoenix–Houston Campus M
University of Phoenix–Idaho Campus M
University of Phoenix–Indianapolis Campus M
University of Phoenix–Jersey City Campus M
University of Phoenix–Las Vegas Campus M
University of Phoenix–Louisiana Campus M
University of Phoenix–Madison Campus M
University of Phoenix–Maryland Campus M
University of Phoenix–Memphis Campus M
University of Phoenix–Metro Detroit Campus M
University of Phoenix–Nashville Campus M
University of Phoenix–New Mexico Campus M
University of Phoenix–Northern Nevada Campus M
University of Phoenix–Northern Virginia Campus M
University of Phoenix–North Florida Campus M
University of Phoenix–Northwest Arkansas Campus M
University of Phoenix–Oklahoma City Campus M
University of Phoenix–Omaha Campus M
University of Phoenix–Oregon Campus M
University of Phoenix–Philadelphia Campus M
University of Phoenix–Pittsburgh Campus M
University of Phoenix–Raleigh Campus M
University of Phoenix–Renton Learning Center M
University of Phoenix–Richmond Campus M
University of Phoenix–Sacramento Valley Campus M
University of Phoenix–St. Louis Campus M
University of Phoenix–San Antonio Campus M
University of Phoenix–San Diego Campus M
University of Phoenix–Savannah Campus M
University of Phoenix–Southern Arizona Campus M
University of Phoenix–Southern California Campus M
University of Phoenix–Southern Colorado Campus M
University of Phoenix–South Florida Campus M
University of Phoenix–Springfield Campus M
University of Phoenix–Tulsa Campus M
University of Phoenix–Utah Campus M
University of Phoenix–Vancouver Campus M
University of Phoenix–West Florida Campus M
University of Phoenix–West Michigan Campus M
University of Phoenix–Wisconsin Campus M
University of Pittsburgh M*
University of Redlands M
University of Rhode Island D
University of St. Thomas (MN) M,O*
University of San Francisco M
The University of Scranton M
University of South Africa M
University of South Alabama M*
University of Southern Mississippi M
University of South Florida M*
The University of Tampa M
The University of Texas at Arlington M,D*
The University of Texas at Austin D
The University of Texas at Dallas M,D*
The University of Texas at San Antonio M,D*
The University of Texas–Pan American D
University of the Sacred Heart M
University of the West M
The University of Toledo M
University of Tulsa M*
University of Virginia M
University of Wisconsin–Madison D*
Utah State University M,D
Valparaiso University M
Villanova University M*
Virginia Commonwealth University M,D
Virginia International University M
Virginia Polytechnic Institute and State University M,D*
Walden University M,D
Walsh College of Accountancy and Business Administration M
Washington State University M,D*
Wayland Baptist University M
Webster University M,D,O
West Chester University of Pennsylvania M,O
Western Governors University M
Western International University M
Wilmington University M
Winston-Salem State University M
Worcester Polytechnic Institute M,D,O*
Wright State University M
Xavier University M*
York University M,D

MANAGEMENT OF TECHNOLOGY

Air Force Institute of Technology M,D
Alliant International University–San Diego M,D*
Athabasca University M,O*
Boston University M*
California Lutheran University M,O
California State University, Los Angeles M
Cambridge College M
Capella University M,D,O
Carleton University M
Carnegie Mellon University M,D*
Central Connecticut State University M,O
Champlain College M
City University of Seattle M,O
Coleman College M
Colorado School of Mines M,D
Colorado Technical University Colorado Springs M,D
Colorado Technical University Denver M
Colorado Technical University Sioux Falls M
Columbia University M*
Dallas Baptist University M

*M—master's degree; P—first professional degree; D—doctorate; O—other advanced degree; *—Close-Up and/or Announcement or Display in one of the other books in this series*

DePaul University	M,D*
East Carolina University	M,D,O
Eastern Michigan University	M,D
École Polytechnique de Montréal	M,D,O
Embry-Riddle Aeronautical University Worldwide	M,O
Fairfield University	M*
Fairleigh Dickinson University, College at Florham	M,O*
George Mason University	M,D*
The George Washington University	M,D*
Georgia Institute of Technology	M,O*
Golden Gate University	M,D,O
Grantham University	M
Harvard University	D*
Hodges University	M
Idaho State University	M
Illinois State University	M
Indiana State University	D
Instituto Tecnológico y de Estudios Superiores de Monterrey, Campus Central de Veracruz	M
Instituto Tecnológico y de Estudios Superiores de Monterrey, Campus Cuernavaca	M,D
Instituto Tecnológico y de Estudios Superiores de Monterrey, Campus Irapuato	M,D
Iona College	M,O*
The Johns Hopkins University	M,O*
Jones International University	M
La Salle University	M
Lawrence Technological University	M,D
Lewis University	M
Marist College	M,O
Marquette University	M,D
Marshall University	M
Mercer University	M
Moravian College	M
Murray State University	M
National University	M
New Jersey Institute of Technology	M
North Carolina Agricultural and Technical State University	M,D
North Carolina State University	D*
Notre Dame de Namur University	M
OGI School of Science & Engineering at Oregon Health & Science University	M,O
Old Dominion University	M
Oregon Health & Science University	M*
Pacific Lutheran University	M
Pacific States University	M,D
Polytechnic Institute of NYU	M,D
Polytechnic Institute of NYU, Westchester Graduate Center	M
Polytechnic University of Puerto Rico	M
Portland State University	M,D
Regis University	M,O
St. Ambrose University	M
Simon Fraser University	M,D
South Dakota School of Mines and Technology	M*
Southeast Missouri State University	M
State University of New York Institute of Technology	M
Stevens Institute of Technology	M,D,O
Stevenson University	M
Stony Brook University, State University of New York	M
Sullivan University	P,M
Texas A&M University–Commerce	M
Texas State University–San Marcos	M*
University at Albany, State University of New York	M*
University of Advancing Technology	M
The University of Akron	M
University of Arkansas at Little Rock	M,O
University of Bridgeport	M
University of Colorado at Colorado Springs	M
University of Dallas	M
University of Delaware	M*
University of Denver	M,O*
University of Illinois at Urbana–Champaign	M,D*
University of Maryland University College	M,O
University of Miami	M,D*
University of Minnesota, Twin Cities Campus	M*
University of New Hampshire	M,O*
University of New Haven	M*
University of New Mexico	M*
University of Pennsylvania	M*
University of Phoenix	M
University of Phoenix–Atlanta Campus	M
University of Phoenix–Augusta Campus	M
University of Phoenix–Austin Campus	M
University of Phoenix–Bay Area Campus	M
University of Phoenix–Birmingham Campus	M
University of Phoenix–Boston Campus	M
University of Phoenix–Central Florida Campus	M
University of Phoenix–Central Massachusetts Campus	M
University of Phoenix–Central Valley Campus	M
University of Phoenix–Charlotte Campus	M
University of Phoenix–Chattanooga Campus	M
University of Phoenix–Cheyenne Campus	M
University of Phoenix–Chicago Campus	M
University of Phoenix–Cincinnati Campus	M
University of Phoenix–Cleveland Campus	M
University of Phoenix–Columbia Campus	M
University of Phoenix–Columbus Georgia Campus	M
University of Phoenix–Columbus Ohio Campus	M
University of Phoenix–Dallas Campus	M
University of Phoenix–Denver Campus	M
University of Phoenix–Des Moines Campus	M
University of Phoenix–Eastern Washington Campus	M
University of Phoenix–Harrisburg Campus	M
University of Phoenix–Hawaii Campus	M
University of Phoenix–Houston Campus	M
University of Phoenix–Idaho Campus	M
University of Phoenix–Indianapolis Campus	M
University of Phoenix–Jersey City Campus	M
University of Phoenix–Kansas City Campus	M
University of Phoenix–Las Vegas Campus	M
University of Phoenix–Louisiana Campus	M
University of Phoenix–Louisville Campus	M
University of Phoenix–Madison Campus	M
University of Phoenix–Maryland Campus	M
University of Phoenix–Memphis Campus	M
University of Phoenix–Metro Detroit Campus	M
University of Phoenix–Minneapolis/St. Louis Park Campus	M
University of Phoenix–Nashville Campus	M
University of Phoenix–New Mexico Campus	M
University of Phoenix–Northern Nevada Campus	M
University of Phoenix–Northern Virginia Campus	M
University of Phoenix–Northwest Arkansas Campus	M
University of Phoenix–Oklahoma City Campus	M
University of Phoenix–Omaha Campus	M
University of Phoenix–Oregon Campus	M
University of Phoenix–Philadelphia Campus	M
University of Phoenix–Phoenix Campus	M
University of Phoenix–Pittsburgh Campus	M
University of Phoenix–Puerto Rico Campus	M
University of Phoenix–Raleigh Campus	M
University of Phoenix–Renton Learning Center	M
University of Phoenix–Richmond Campus	M
University of Phoenix–Sacramento Valley Campus	M
University of Phoenix–San Antonio Campus	M
University of Phoenix–San Diego Campus	M
University of Phoenix–Savannah Campus	M
University of Phoenix–Southern Arizona Campus	M
University of Phoenix–Southern California Campus	M
University of Phoenix–Southern Colorado Campus	M
University of Phoenix–Springfield Campus	M
University of Phoenix–Tulsa Campus	M
University of Phoenix–Utah Campus	M
University of Phoenix–Vancouver Campus	M
University of Phoenix–West Florida Campus	M
University of Phoenix–West Michigan Campus	M
University of Phoenix–Wisconsin Campus	M
University of St. Thomas (MN)	M,O*
University of Washington	M,D*
University of Waterloo	M,D
University of Wisconsin–Madison	M*
University of Wisconsin–Stout	M
University of Wisconsin–Whitewater	M*
Walden University	M,D,O
West Chester University of Pennsylvania	M
Westminster College (UT)	M,O

MANAGEMENT STRATEGY AND POLICY

Alliant International University–San Diego	M,D*
Azusa Pacific University	M
Bernard M. Baruch College of the City University of New York	M,D
Boston University	M,O*
California State University, East Bay	M
Case Western Reserve University	M*
Claremont Graduate University	M,D,O*
Davenport University	M
Davenport University	M
Defiance College	M
DePaul University	M*
Dominican University of California	M
Drexel University	M,D,O*
Duquesne University	M*
Franklin Pierce University	M,D,O
Freed-Hardeman University	M
The George Washington University	M,D*
Georgia Institute of Technology	M,D,O*
Georgia State University	M,D
Harvard University	D*
HEC Montreal	M
Lamar University	M
Manhattanville College	M*
McGill University	M,D,O*
Middle Tennessee State University	M
Mountain State University	M*
Neumann University	M
New York University	M,D,O*
Northwestern University	D*
Pace University	M*
Regent University	M,D,O
Roberts Wesleyan College	M,O
Rutgers, The State University of New Jersey, Newark	M*
Sage Graduate School	M
Saint Joseph's University	M
Saint Mary-of-the-Woods College	M
Southern Methodist University	M*
Stevens Institute of Technology	M
Suffolk University	M,O*
Syracuse University	D*
Taylor University	M
Temple University	D*
Tennessee Technological University	M*
Towson University	O
Tufts University	O*
United States International University	M
Universidad del Este	M
The University of Arizona	D*

The University of British Columbia	D
University of Calgary	M,D
University of Dallas	M
University of Dayton	M
University of Denver	M,O*
University of Florida	M*
The University of Iowa	M*
University of Lethbridge	M,D
University of Mary	M
University of Minnesota, Twin Cities Campus	M,D*
University of New Haven	M*
University of New Mexico	M*
The University of North Carolina at Chapel Hill	D*
University of Oklahoma	M*
University of Pittsburgh	M*
The University of Texas at Dallas	M*
The University of Western Ontario	M,D
University of Wisconsin–Madison	M*
Western Governors University	M
Western International University	M
York University	M,D

MANUFACTURING ENGINEERING

Arizona State University	M,D
Arizona State University at the Polytechnic Campus	M
Bowling Green State University	M*
Bradley University	M
California State University, Northridge	M
Clemson University	M
Cornell University	M,D*
Dartmouth College	M,D*
East Carolina University	M,D,O
Eastern Kentucky University	M
East Tennessee State University	M
Florida State University	M,D*
Grand Valley State University	M
Illinois Institute of Technology	M,D*
Instituto Tecnológico y de Estudios Superiores de Monterrey, Campus Monterrey	M,D
Kansas State University	M,D*
Kettering University	M
Lawrence Technological University	M,D
Lehigh University	M
Marquette University	M,D
Massachusetts Institute of Technology	M,D,O*
Michigan State University	M,D*
Minnesota State University Mankato	M
Missouri University of Science and Technology	M,D
New Jersey Institute of Technology	M
North Carolina State University	M*
North Dakota State University	M,D
Northeastern University	M,D*
Northwestern University	M*
Ohio University	M,D*
Old Dominion University	M,D
Oregon State University	M,D*
Penn State University Park	M,D*
Polytechnic Institute of NYU	M
Polytechnic Institute of NYU, Long Island Graduate Center	M,D
Polytechnic University of Puerto Rico	M
Portland State University	M
Rochester Institute of Technology	M
Southern Illinois University Carbondale	M*
Southern Methodist University	M,D*
Stevens Institute of Technology	M
Texas A&M University	M*
Texas Tech University	M,D
Tufts University	O*
Universidad Autonoma de Guadalajara	M,D
Universidad de las Américas–Puebla	M
University of Calgary	M,D
University of California, Los Angeles	M*
University of Central Florida	M,D,O*
University of Colorado at Colorado Springs	M
The University of Iowa	M,D*
University of Kentucky	M
University of Manitoba	M,D
University of Maryland, College Park	M,D*
University of Memphis	M
University of Michigan	M,D*
University of Michigan–Dearborn	M,D*
University of Missouri–Columbia	M,D*
University of Nebraska–Lincoln	M,D*
University of New Mexico	M*
University of Regina	M
University of Rhode Island	M
University of St. Thomas (MN)	M,O*
University of Southern California	M,D,O*
University of Southern Maine	M
The University of Tennessee	M,D
The University of Texas at El Paso	M
The University of Texas–Pan American	M
University of Windsor	M,D
University of Wisconsin–Madison	M*
University of Wisconsin–Milwaukee	M,D,O
University of Wisconsin–Stout	M
Villanova University	M,O*
Wayne State University	M*
Western Illinois University	M
Western Michigan University	M*
Western New England College	M
Wichita State University	M,D*
Worcester Polytechnic Institute	M,D,O*

MARINE AFFAIRS

Dalhousie University	M
Duke University	M*
East Carolina University	D
Florida Institute of Technology	M,D*
Louisiana State University and Agricultural and Mechanical College	M,D
Memorial University of Newfoundland	M,D,O
Nova Southeastern University	M*
Old Dominion University	M
Oregon State University	M*
Stevens Institute of Technology	M
Université du Québec à Rimouski	M,O
University of Delaware	M,D*
University of Maine	M*
University of Miami	M*
University of Rhode Island	M,D
University of San Diego	M
University of Washington	M,O*
University of West Florida	M

MARINE BIOLOGY

College of Charleston	M*
Florida Institute of Technology	M*
Memorial University of Newfoundland	M,D
Nicholls State University	M
Northeastern University	M,D*
Nova Southeastern University	M,D*
Princeton University	D*
Rutgers, The State University of New Jersey, New Brunswick	M,D*
San Francisco State University	M
Texas A&M University at Galveston	M,D
Texas State University–San Marcos	M,D*
University of Alaska Fairbanks	M,D
University of California, San Diego	M,D*
University of California, Santa Barbara	M,D
University of Colorado at Boulder	M,D*
University of Guam	M
University of Hawaii at Manoa	M,D*
University of Maine	M,D*
University of Massachusetts Dartmouth	M
University of Miami	M,D*
The University of North Carolina Wilmington	M,D
University of Oregon	M,D*
University of Southern California	M,D*
University of Southern Mississippi	M,D
University of South Florida	M,D*
Western Illinois University	M,O
Woods Hole Oceanographic Institution	M,D,O

MARINE GEOLOGY

Cornell University	M,D*
Massachusetts Institute of Technology	M,D*
University of Delaware	M,D*
University of Hawaii at Manoa	M,D*
University of Miami	M,D*
University of Michigan	M,D*
University of Washington	M,D*
Woods Hole Oceanographic Institution	M,D,O

MARINE SCIENCES

American University	M*
California State University, East Bay	M
California State University, Fresno	M
California State University, Monterey Bay	M
California State University, Sacramento	M
California State University, Stanislaus	M
Coastal Carolina University	M
The College of William and Mary	M,D
Cornell University	M,D*
Duke University	M*
Florida Institute of Technology	M,D*
Hawai'i Pacific University	M*
Medical University of South Carolina	M,D
Memorial University of Newfoundland	M,O
North Carolina State University	M,D*
Nova Southeastern University	M*
Oregon State University	M*
San Francisco State University	M
San Jose State University	M
Savannah State University	M
Stony Brook University, State University of New York	M,D
Texas A&M University at Galveston	M
Texas A&M University–Corpus Christi	D
University of Alaska Fairbanks	M,D
The University of British Columbia	M,D
University of California, San Diego	M*
University of California, Santa Barbara	M,D
University of California, Santa Cruz	M,D*
University of Connecticut	M,D*
University of Delaware	M,D*
University of Florida	M,D*
University of Georgia	M,D*
University of Hawaii at Manoa	O*
University of Maine	M,D*
University of Maryland, Baltimore	M,D*
University of Maryland, Baltimore County	M,D*
University of Maryland, College Park	M,D*
University of Maryland Eastern Shore	M,D*
University of Massachusetts Amherst	M*
University of Massachusetts Boston	D
University of Massachusetts Dartmouth	M,D
University of Miami	M,D*
University of Michigan	M,D*
University of New England	M
The University of North Carolina at Chapel Hill	M,D*
The University of North Carolina Wilmington	M,D
University of Puerto Rico, Mayagüez Campus	M,D
University of Rhode Island	M,D
University of San Diego	M
University of South Alabama	M,D*
University of South Carolina	M,D
University of Southern California	M,D*
University of Southern Mississippi	M,D
University of South Florida	M,D*
The University of Texas at Austin	M,D
University of the Virgin Islands	M
University of Wisconsin–La Crosse	M
University of Wisconsin–Madison	M,D*
Western Washington University	M

*M—master's degree; P—first professional degree; D—doctorate; O—other advanced degree; *—Close-Up and/or Announcement or Display in one of the other books in this series*

MARKETING

Adelphi University	M*
Alabama Agricultural and Mechanical University	M
Alliant International University–San Diego	M,D*
American College of Thessaloniki	M,O
American InterContinental University Buckhead Campus	M
American InterContinental University Online	M
American InterContinental University South Florida	M
American International College	M
American University	M*
The American University in Dubai	M
Andrew Jackson University	M
Andrews University	M
Argosy University, Atlanta	M,D*
Argosy University, Chicago	M,D*
Argosy University, Dallas	M,O*
Argosy University, Denver	M,D*
Argosy University, Hawai'i	M,D,O*
Argosy University, Inland Empire	M,D*
Argosy University, Los Angeles	M,D*
Argosy University, Nashville	M,D*
Argosy University, Orange County	M,D,O*
Argosy University, Phoenix	M,D*
Argosy University, Salt Lake City	M,D*
Argosy University, San Diego	M,D*
Argosy University, San Francisco Bay Area	M,D*
Argosy University, Sarasota	M,D,O*
Argosy University, Schaumburg	M,D,O*
Argosy University, Seattle	M,D*
Argosy University, Tampa	M,D*
Argosy University, Twin Cities	M,D*
Argosy University, Washington DC	M,D,O*
Arizona State University	M,D
Assumption College	M,O
Avila University	M
Baker College Center for Graduate Studies	M
Barry University	O*
Bayamón Central University	M
Benedictine University	M
Bentley University	M
Bernard M. Baruch College of the City University of New York	M,D
Boston University	M,D,O*
British American College London	M
California Intercontinental University	M,D
California Lutheran University	M,O
California State University, East Bay	M
California State University, Fullerton	M
California State University, Los Angeles	M
Canisius College	M
Capella University	M,D,O
Carnegie Mellon University	D*
Case Western Reserve University	M,D*
Central European University	M*
Central Michigan University	M
City University of Seattle	M,O
Clark University	M
Clemson University	M
Cleveland State University	M,D,O
Colorado Technical University Colorado Springs	M,D
Colorado Technical University Denver	M
Columbia Southern University	M
Columbia University	M,D*
Concordia University Wisconsin	M
Cornell University	D*
Dallas Baptist University	M
Davenport University	M
Delta State University	M
DePaul University	M*
DeSales University	M
Drexel University	M,D,O*
Eastern Michigan University	M
Emerson College	M
Emory University	M,D*
Fairfield University	M,O*
Fairleigh Dickinson University, College at Florham	M,O*
Fairleigh Dickinson University, Metropolitan Campus	M,O*
Fashion Institute of Technology	M*
Florida Agricultural and Mechanical University	M
Florida Institute of Technology	M*
Florida State University	M,D*
Fordham University	M*
Franklin University	M
Full Sail University	M*
Gannon University	O
The George Washington University	M,D*
Georgia Institute of Technology	M,D,O*
Georgia State University	M,D
Golden Gate University	M,D,O
Goldey-Beacom College	M
Grand Canyon University	M*
Harvard University	D*
Hawai'i Pacific University	M*
HEC Montreal	M
Hofstra University	M*
Holy Names University	M
Hood College	M
Howard University	M
Hult International Business School (United States)	M
Illinois Institute of Technology	M*
Indiana Tech	M
Instituto Tecnológico y de Estudios Superiores de Monterrey, Campus Central de Veracruz	M
Instituto Tecnológico y de Estudios Superiores de Monterrey, Campus Ciudad Obregón	M
Instituto Tecnológico y de Estudios Superiores de Monterrey, Campus Cuernavaca	M
Instituto Tecnológico y de Estudios Superiores de Monterrey, Campus Estado de México	M,D
Instituto Tecnológico y de Estudios Superiores de Monterrey, Campus Monterrey	M
Inter American University of Puerto Rico, Aguadilla Campus	M
Inter American University of Puerto Rico, Metropolitan Campus	M
Inter American University of Puerto Rico, Ponce Campus	M
Inter American University of Puerto Rico, San Germán Campus	M,D
International University in Geneva	M
The International University of Monaco	M
Iona College	M,O*
The Johns Hopkins University	M*
Johnson & Wales University	M
Kaplan University–Davenport Campus	M
Keiser University	M
Kent State University	D*
Kentucky State University	M
Lasell College	M,O
La Sierra University	M,O
Lewis University	M
Lindenwood University	M,O
Long Island University, C.W. Post Campus	M,O
Louisiana State University and Agricultural and Mechanical College	D
Louisiana Tech University	M,D
Loyola University Chicago	M*
Loyola University Maryland	M*
Lynn University	M,D
Manhattanville College	M*
Marylhurst University	M
Maryville University of Saint Louis	M,O
McGill University	M,D,O*
Miami University	M*
Michigan State University	M,D*
Middle Tennessee State University	M
Milwaukee School of Engineering	M*
Minnesota State University Mankato	M
Mississippi State University	D
Montclair State University	M,O*
National University	M
New Mexico State University	D
New York Institute of Technology	M,O
New York University	M,D,O*
Northeastern Illinois University	M
Northern Kentucky University	M,O
Northwestern University	M,D*
Notre Dame de Namur University	M
Oakland University	M,O
Oklahoma City University	M
Oklahoma State University	M,D*
Old Dominion University	D
Oral Roberts University	M
Ottawa University	M
Pace University	M*
Philadelphia University	M
Pontifical Catholic University of Puerto Rico	M
Pontificia Universidad Catolica Madre y Maestra	M
Providence College	M*
Queen's University at Kingston	M
Quinnipiac University	M*
Regis University	M,O
Roberts Wesleyan College	M,O
Rutgers, The State University of New Jersey, Newark	M,D*
Sage Graduate School	M
St. Bonaventure University	M
St. Cloud State University	M
St. Edward's University	M,O
St. John's University (NY)	M,O
Saint Joseph's University	M,O
Saint Peter's College	M
St. Thomas Aquinas College	M*
Saint Xavier University	M,O
San Diego State University	M*
Seton Hall University	M*
Southeastern University	M
Southern Adventist University	M
Southern Methodist University	M*
Southern New Hampshire University	M,D,O*
Stephen F. Austin State University	M
Stony Brook University, State University of New York	M,O
Strayer University	M
Suffolk University	M,O*
Syracuse University	M,D*
Temple University	M,D*
Texas A&M University	M,D*
Texas Tech University	M,D
TUI University	M,D
United States International University	M
Universidad del Turabo	M
Universidad Iberoamericana	P,M
Universidad Metropolitana	M
Université de Sherbrooke	M
Université Laval	M,O
University at Albany, State University of New York	M*
The University of Akron	M
The University of Alabama	M,D
The University of Alabama in Huntsville	M,O
University of Alberta	D*
The University of Arizona	M,D*
University of Baltimore	M
The University of British Columbia	D
University of California, Berkeley	D*
University of Central Florida	D*
University of Cincinnati	M,D
University of Colorado at Boulder	M,D*
University of Colorado at Colorado Springs	M
University of Colorado Denver	M*
University of Connecticut	M,D*
University of Dallas	M
University of Dayton	M
University of Denver	M*
The University of Findlay	M
University of Florida	M,D*
University of Hawaii at Manoa	M,D*
University of Houston	D*
University of Houston–Victoria	M
The University of Iowa	M,D*
University of La Verne	M
University of Massachusetts Dartmouth	M,O
University of Memphis	M,D
University of Miami	M*
University of Minnesota, Twin Cities Campus	M,D*
University of Missouri–St. Louis	M,O

University of Nebraska–Lincoln	M,D*
University of New Brunswick Fredericton	M,D
University of New Haven	M*
The University of North Carolina at Chapel Hill	D*
The University of North Carolina at Charlotte	M*
The University of North Carolina at Greensboro	M,D
University of North Texas	D
University of Oregon	D*
University of Pennsylvania	M,D*
University of Phoenix	M
University of Phoenix–Atlanta Campus	M
University of Phoenix–Augusta Campus	M
University of Phoenix–Austin Campus	M
University of Phoenix–Bay Area Campus	M
University of Phoenix–Birmingham Campus	M
University of Phoenix–Central Florida Campus	M
University of Phoenix–Central Valley Campus	M
University of Phoenix–Chattanooga Campus	M
University of Phoenix–Cheyenne Campus	M
University of Phoenix–Cincinnati Campus	M
University of Phoenix–Cleveland Campus	M
University of Phoenix–Columbus Georgia Campus	M
University of Phoenix–Columbus Ohio Campus	M
University of Phoenix–Dallas Campus	M
University of Phoenix–Denver Campus	M
University of Phoenix–Des Moines Campus	M
University of Phoenix–Eastern Washington Campus	M
University of Phoenix–Harrisburg Campus	M
University of Phoenix–Hawaii Campus	M
University of Phoenix–Houston Campus	M
University of Phoenix–Idaho Campus	M
University of Phoenix–Indianapolis Campus	M
University of Phoenix–Jersey City Campus	M
University of Phoenix–Kansas City Campus	M
University of Phoenix–Las Vegas Campus	M
University of Phoenix–Louisiana Campus	M
University of Phoenix–Madison Campus	M
University of Phoenix–Maryland Campus	M
University of Phoenix–Memphis Campus	M
University of Phoenix–Metro Detroit Campus	M
University of Phoenix–Minneapolis/St. Louis Park Campus	M
University of Phoenix–New Mexico Campus	M
University of Phoenix–Northern Nevada Campus	M
University of Phoenix–Northern Virginia Campus	M
University of Phoenix–North Florida Campus	M
University of Phoenix–Northwest Arkansas Campus	M
University of Phoenix–Oklahoma City Campus	M
University of Phoenix–Omaha Campus	M
University of Phoenix–Oregon Campus	M
University of Phoenix–Philadelphia Campus	M
University of Phoenix–Phoenix Campus	M
University of Phoenix–Pittsburgh Campus	M
University of Phoenix–Puerto Rico Campus	M
University of Phoenix–Raleigh Campus	M
University of Phoenix–Renton Learning Center	M
University of Phoenix–Richmond Campus	M
University of Phoenix–Sacramento Valley Campus	M
University of Phoenix–St. Louis Campus	M
University of Phoenix–San Antonio Campus	M
University of Phoenix–San Diego Campus	M
University of Phoenix–Savannah Campus	M
University of Phoenix–Southern Arizona Campus	M
University of Phoenix–Southern California Campus	M
University of Phoenix–Southern Colorado Campus	M
University of Phoenix–South Florida Campus	M
University of Phoenix–Springfield Campus	M
University of Phoenix–Tulsa Campus	M
University of Phoenix–Utah Campus	M
University of Phoenix–Vancouver Campus	M
University of Phoenix–West Florida Campus	M
University of Phoenix–Wisconsin Campus	M
University of Pittsburgh	M,D*
University of Puerto Rico, Río Piedras	M,D
University of Rhode Island	D
University of San Francisco	M
University of Saskatchewan	M
The University of Scranton	M
University of South Africa	M,D
The University of Tampa	M
The University of Tennessee	M,D
The University of Texas at Arlington	M,D*
The University of Texas at Austin	D
The University of Texas at Dallas	D*
The University of Texas at San Antonio	M,D*
The University of Texas–Pan American	D
University of the Sacred Heart	M
The University of Toledo	M
University of Virginia	M
The University of Western Ontario	M,D
University of Wisconsin–Madison	D*
University of Wisconsin–Whitewater	M*
Vanderbilt University	D*
Villanova University	M*
Virginia Commonwealth University	O
Virginia Polytechnic Institute and State University	M,D*
Wagner College	M
Wake Forest University	M*
Walden University	M,D
Washington State University	M,D*
Webster University	M,D
West Chester University of Pennsylvania	M
Western International University	M
West Virginia University	M
Wilkes University	M
Worcester Polytechnic Institute	M,O*
Wright State University	M
Xavier University	M*
Yale University	D*
York University	M,D
Youngstown State University	M

MARKETING RESEARCH

American University	M*
Arizona State University at the West campus	M,O
Hofstra University	M*
Instituto Tecnológico y de Estudios Superiores de Monterrey, Campus Irapuato	M,D
Pace University	M*
Southern Illinois University Edwardsville	M
Universidad Autonoma de Guadalajara	M,D
Universidad de las Americas, A.C.	M
University of Georgia	M*
The University of Texas at Arlington	M*
University of Wisconsin–Madison	M*

MARRIAGE AND FAMILY THERAPY

Abilene Christian University	M
Adler Graduate School	M,O
Adler School of Professional Psychology	M,D,O*
Alliant International University–Irvine	M,D*
Alliant International University–Los Angeles	M*
Alliant International University–Sacramento	M*
Alliant International University–San Diego	M,D*
Amridge University	P,M,D
Antioch University New England	M,D*
Appalachian State University	M
Argosy University, Atlanta	M,D,O*
Argosy University, Chicago	D*
Argosy University, Denver	M,D*
Argosy University, Hawai'i	M*
Argosy University, Inland Empire	M,D*
Argosy University, Los Angeles	M,D*
Argosy University, Orange County	M,D*
Argosy University, Salt Lake City	M,D*
Argosy University, San Diego	M,D*
Argosy University, Sarasota	M,D,O*
Argosy University, Schaumburg	M,D,O*
Argosy University, Tampa	M,D*
Argosy University, Twin Cities	M,D,O*
Argosy University, Washington DC	M,D*
Arizona State University	M,D
Azusa Pacific University	M,D
Barry University	M,O*
Bethel Seminary	P,M,D,O
Briercrest Seminary	M
Brigham Young University	M,D*
California Lutheran University	M
California State University, Chico	M
California State University, Dominguez Hills	M
California State University, Fresno	M
California State University, Long Beach	M
California State University, Northridge	M
Cambridge College	M,O
Capella University	M,D,O
Carlos Albizu University, Miami Campus	M,D
Central Connecticut State University	M,O
Chapman University	M
Chatham University	M,D
The Chicago School of Professional Psychology: Downtown Los Angeles Campus	M,D
The Chicago School of Professional Psychology: Irvine Campus	M,D
The Chicago School of Professional Psychology: Westwood Campus	M,D
Christian Theological Seminary	P,M,D
The College of New Jersey	O
The College of William and Mary	M,D
Converse College	O
Denver Seminary	P,M,D,O
Dominican University of California	M
Drexel University	M,D*
East Carolina University	M
Eastern Nazarene College	M
Eastern University	D
East Tennessee State University	M
Edgewood College	M
Fairfield University	M*
Fitchburg State College	M
Florida Atlantic University	M,D,O
Florida State University	M,D*
Friends University	M
Fuller Theological Seminary	M,O
Geneva College	M
George Fox University	M,O*
Harding University	M
Hardin-Simmons University	M
Hofstra University	M*
Hope International University	M
Idaho State University	M,D,O
Indiana Wesleyan University	M
Iona College	M,O*
John Brown University	M
Johnson Bible College	M
Kansas State University	D*
Kean University	O
Kutztown University of Pennsylvania	M

*M—master's degree; P—first professional degree; D—doctorate; O—other advanced degree; *—Close-Up and/or Announcement or Display in one of the other books in this series*

La Salle University D
Lewis & Clark College M
Loyola Marymount University M
Maryville University of Saint Louis M
Mennonite Brethren Biblical Seminary M,O
Mercy College M
Michigan State University M,D*
Minnesota State University Mankato M,D,O
Mississippi College M,O
Montclair State University M,O*
North Dakota State University M,D
Northwestern University M*
Northwest Nazarene University M
Notre Dame de Namur University M
Nova Southeastern University M,D,O*
Oral Roberts University P,M,D
Ottawa University M
Our Lady of Holy Cross College M
Our Lady of the Lake University of San Antonio M,D
Pacific Lutheran University M
Pacific Oaks College M
Palm Beach Atlantic University M
Pepperdine University M,D
Phillips Graduate Institute M,D
Purdue University M,D
Purdue University Calumet M
Reformed Theological Seminary–Jackson Campus P,M,D,O
Regis University M,O
Richmond Graduate University M
St. Cloud State University M
Saint Joseph College M
Saint Louis University M,D,O
Saint Mary's College of California M
St. Mary's University (United States) M,D
Saint Mary's University of Minnesota M,O
Saint Paul University M
St. Thomas University M,O
San Francisco State University M
Saybrook Graduate School and Research Center M,D
The School of Professional Psychology at Forest Institute M,D,O
Seattle Pacific University M,O
Seton Hall University M,D,O*
Seton Hill University M
Shippensburg University of Pennsylvania M,O
Sioux Falls Seminary M
Sonoma State University M
Southern Connecticut State University M
Southern Nazarene University M
Springfield College M,O
Stephens College M
Stetson University M
Syracuse University M,D*
Texas Tech University M,D
Texas Woman's University M,D
Thomas Jefferson University M*
Trevecca Nazarene University M
Universidad de las Americas, A.C. M
The University of Akron M
University of Arkansas at Little Rock O
University of Central Florida M,O*
University of Florida M,D,O*
University of Guelph M,D
University of Houston–Clear Lake M
University of La Verne M
University of Louisiana at Monroe M,D
University of Louisville M,D,O
University of Mary Hardin-Baylor M
University of Maryland, College Park M,D*
University of Massachusetts Boston M,O
University of Miami M,O*
University of Minnesota, Twin Cities Campus M,D*
University of Mobile M
University of Montevallo M
University of Nebraska–Lincoln M,D*
University of Nevada, Las Vegas M,O
University of New Hampshire M*
The University of North Carolina at Greensboro M,D,O
University of North Texas M,D,O
University of Phoenix M
University of Phoenix–Bay Area Campus M
University of Phoenix–Central Valley Campus M
University of Phoenix–Denver Campus M
University of Phoenix–Hawaii Campus M
University of Phoenix–Las Vegas Campus M
University of Phoenix–New Mexico Campus M
University of Phoenix–Northern Nevada Campus M
University of Phoenix–Phoenix Campus M,O
University of Phoenix–Puerto Rico Campus M
University of Phoenix–Sacramento Valley Campus M
University of Phoenix–San Diego Campus M
University of Phoenix–Southern Arizona Campus M,O
University of Phoenix–Southern California Campus M,O
University of Phoenix–Southern Colorado Campus M
University of Rochester M*
University of St. Thomas (MN) M,D,O*
University of San Diego M
University of San Francisco M,D
University of Southern California M*
University of Southern Mississippi M
The University of Texas at Tyler M
The University of Winnipeg P,M,O
University of Wisconsin–Milwaukee M,D,O
University of Wisconsin–Stout M
Utah State University M,D
Valdosta State University M
Virginia Polytechnic Institute and State University M,D*
Wesley Biblical Seminary P,M
Western Michigan University M,D*
Western Seminary–Sacramento Campus P,M
Western Seminary–San Jose Campus P,M

MASS COMMUNICATION

American University M,D,O*
The American University in Cairo M
Arizona State University at the Downtown Phoenix Campus M
Auburn University M*
Boston University M*
Brigham Young University M*
California State University, Fresno M
California State University, Northridge M
Central Michigan University M
The College of Saint Rose M*
Colorado State University M,D*
Drexel University M*
Florida International University M*
Florida State University M,D*
Fordham University M*
The George Washington University M*
Georgia State University M,D
Grambling State University M
Howard University M,D
Indiana University Bloomington M,D*
Iona College M*
Iowa State University of Science and Technology M*
Jackson State University M
Kansas State University M*
Kent State University M*
Louisiana State University and Agricultural and Mechanical College M,D
Lynn University M,D
Marquette University M
Marshall University M
Miami University M*
Middle Tennessee State University M
Murray State University M
The New School: A University M*
North Dakota State University M,D
Oklahoma City University M
Oklahoma State University M*
Point Park University M*
St. Cloud State University M
San Jose State University M
Southern Illinois University Carbondale M*
Southern Illinois University Edwardsville M
Southern University and Agricultural and Mechanical College M
Stephen F. Austin State University M
Syracuse University M,D*
Temple University D*
Texas State University–San Marcos M*
Texas Tech University M,D
Université Laval M,D
The University of Alabama D
University of Arkansas at Little Rock M
University of Central Florida M*
University of Central Missouri M
University of Colorado at Boulder M,D*
University of Denver M*
University of Florida M,D*
University of Georgia M,D*
University of Houston M*
The University of Iowa M,D*
University of Louisiana at Lafayette M*
University of Michigan D*
University of Minnesota, Twin Cities Campus M,D*
University of Nebraska–Lincoln M*
The University of North Carolina at Chapel Hill M,D*
University of Oklahoma M*
University of Puerto Rico, Río Piedras M
University of Southern California M,D*
University of Southern Mississippi M,D
University of South Florida M*
University of Wisconsin–Madison M,D*
University of Wisconsin–Stevens Point M
University of Wisconsin–Superior M
University of Wisconsin–Whitewater M*
Virginia Commonwealth University M

MATERIALS ENGINEERING

Arizona State University M,D
Auburn University M,D*
Boise State University M
Boston University M,D*
California State University, Northridge M
Carleton University M,D
Carnegie Mellon University M,D*
Case Western Reserve University M,D*
Clemson University M,D
Colorado School of Mines M,D
Columbia University M,D,O*
Cornell University M,D*
Dalhousie University M,D
Dartmouth College M,D*
Drexel University M,D*
Florida International University M,D*
Georgia Institute of Technology M,D*
Illinois Institute of Technology M,D*
Instituto Tecnológico y de Estudios Superiores de Monterrey, Campus Estado de México M,D
Iowa State University of Science and Technology M,D*
The Johns Hopkins University M,D*
Lehigh University M,D
Massachusetts Institute of Technology M,D,O*
McGill University M,D,O*
McMaster University M,D
Michigan State University M,D*
Michigan Technological University M,D
New Jersey Institute of Technology M,D
New Mexico Institute of Mining and Technology M,D
North Carolina State University M,D*
Northwestern University M,D,O*
The Ohio State University M,D*
Penn State University Park M,D*
Purdue University M,D
Rensselaer Polytechnic Institute M,D
Rochester Institute of Technology M
Rutgers, The State University of New Jersey, New Brunswick M,D*

San Jose State University	M
Santa Clara University	M,D,O
South Dakota School of Mines and Technology	M,D*
Stanford University	M,D,O*
State University of New York at Binghamton	M,D*
Stevens Institute of Technology	M,D
Stony Brook University, State University of New York	M,D
Texas A&M University	M,D*
Tuskegee University	D
The University of Alabama	M,D
The University of Alabama at Birmingham	M,D*
University of Alberta	M,D*
The University of Arizona	M,D*
The University of British Columbia	M,D
University of California, Berkeley	M,D*
University of California, Davis	M,D*
University of California, Irvine	M,D*
University of California, Los Angeles	M,D*
University of California, Santa Barbara	M,D
University of Central Florida	M,D*
University of Cincinnati	M,D
University of Connecticut	M,D*
University of Dayton	M,D
University of Delaware	M,D*
University of Denver	M,D*
University of Florida	M,D,O*
University of Houston	M,D*
University of Idaho	M,D
University of Illinois at Chicago	M,D*
University of Illinois at Urbana–Champaign	M,D*
University of Maryland, College Park	M,D,O*
University of Massachusetts Lowell	M,D,O
University of Michigan	M,D*
University of Minnesota, Twin Cities Campus	M,D*
University of Nebraska–Lincoln	M,D*
University of Nevada, Las Vegas	M,D
University of Pennsylvania	M,D*
University of Southern California	M,D,O*
The University of Tennessee	M,D
The University of Tennessee Space Institute	M*
The University of Texas at Arlington	M,D*
The University of Texas at Austin	M,D
The University of Texas at Dallas	M,D*
The University of Texas at El Paso	D
University of Toronto	M,D
University of Utah	M,D*
University of Washington	M,D*
The University of Western Ontario	M,D
University of Windsor	M,D
University of Wisconsin–Madison	M,D*
University of Wisconsin–Milwaukee	M,D,O
Virginia Polytechnic Institute and State University	M,D*
Washington State University	M*
Wayne State University	M,D,O*
Worcester Polytechnic Institute	M,D,O*
Wright State University	M

MATERIALS SCIENCES

Air Force Institute of Technology	M,D
Alabama Agricultural and Mechanical University	M,D
Alfred University	M,D*
Arizona State University	M,D
Boston University	M,D*
Brown University	M,D*
California Institute of Technology	M,D*
Carnegie Mellon University	M,D*
Case Western Reserve University	M,D*
Central Michigan University	D
Clemson University	M,D
Colorado School of Mines	M,D
Columbia University	M,D,O*
Cornell University	M,D*
Dartmouth College	M,D*
Duke University	M,D*
Florida State University	M*
Georgetown University	D
The George Washington University	M,D*
Illinois Institute of Technology	M,D*
Instituto Tecnológico y de Estudios Superiores de Monterrey, Campus Estado de México	M,D
Iowa State University of Science and Technology	M,D*
Jackson State University	M
The Johns Hopkins University	M,D*
Lehigh University	M,D
Massachusetts Institute of Technology	M,D,O*
McMaster University	M,D
Michigan State University	M,D*
Missouri State University	M*
New Jersey Institute of Technology	M,D
Norfolk State University	M
North Carolina State University	M,D*
North Dakota State University	D
Northwestern University	M,D,O*
The Ohio State University	M,D*
Oregon State University	M,D*
Penn State University Park	M,D*
Polytechnic Institute of NYU	M
Polytechnic Institute of NYU, Long Island Graduate Center	M,D
Polytechnic Institute of NYU, Westchester Graduate Center	D
Princeton University	D*
Rensselaer Polytechnic Institute	M,D
Rice University	M,D
Rochester Institute of Technology	M
Royal Military College of Canada	M,D
Rutgers, The State University of New Jersey, New Brunswick	M,D*
School of the Art Institute of Chicago	M*
South Dakota School of Mines and Technology	M,D*
Stanford University	M,D,O*
State University of New York at Binghamton	M,D*
Stony Brook University, State University of New York	M,D
Texas A&M Health Science Center	M
Trent University	M
Université du Québec, Institut National de la Recherche Scientifique	M,D
University at Buffalo, the State University of New York	M*
The University of Alabama	D
The University of Alabama at Birmingham	D*
The University of Alabama in Huntsville	M,D
The University of Arizona	M,D*
The University of British Columbia	M,D
University of California, Berkeley	M,D*
University of California, Davis	M,D*
University of California, Irvine	M,D*
University of California, Los Angeles	M,D*
University of California, San Diego	M,D*
University of California, Santa Barbara	M,D
University of Central Florida	M,D*
University of Cincinnati	M,D
University of Connecticut	M,D*
University of Delaware	M,D*
University of Florida	M,D,O*
University of Idaho	M,D
University of Illinois at Urbana–Champaign	M,D*
University of Kentucky	M,D
University of Maryland, College Park	M,D,O*
University of Michigan	M,D*
University of Minnesota, Twin Cities Campus	M,D*
University of Nebraska–Lincoln	M,D*
University of New Brunswick Fredericton	M,D
University of New Hampshire	M,D*
The University of North Carolina at Chapel Hill	M,D*
University of North Texas	M,D
University of Pennsylvania	M,D*
University of Pittsburgh	M,D*
University of Rochester	M,D*
University of Southern California	M,D,O*
University of South Florida	M*
The University of Tennessee	M,D
The University of Tennessee Space Institute	M*
The University of Texas at Arlington	M,D*
The University of Texas at Austin	M,D
The University of Texas at Dallas	M,D*
The University of Texas at El Paso	D
University of Toronto	M,D
University of Utah	M,D*
University of Vermont	M,D*
University of Virginia	M,D
University of Washington	M,D*
University of Wisconsin–Madison	M,D*
Vanderbilt University	M,D*
Virginia Polytechnic Institute and State University	M,D*
Washington State University	M,D*
Wayne State University	M,D,O*
Worcester Polytechnic Institute	M,D,O*
Wright State University	M

MATERNAL AND CHILD/ NEONATAL NURSING

Baylor University	M
Boston College	M,D*
Case Western Reserve University	M,D*
Columbia University	M,O*
Duke University	M,D,O*
Goldfarb School of Nursing at Barnes-Jewish College	M
Hardin-Simmons University	M
Indiana University–Purdue University Indianapolis	M,D*
Lehman College of the City University of New York	M
Marquette University	M,D,O
Medical University of South Carolina	M
Northeastern University	M,O*
Regis University	P,M,D,O
Rush University	M,D,O
Rutgers, The State University of New Jersey, Newark	M*
Stony Brook University, State University of New York	M,O
Université de Montréal	O
University at Buffalo, the State University of New York	M,D,O*
University of Alberta	P*
University of Cincinnati	M,D
University of Colorado at Colorado Springs	M,D
University of Delaware	M,O*
University of Illinois at Chicago	M*
University of Louisville	M,D
University of Maryland, Baltimore	M*
University of Missouri–Kansas City	M,D*
University of Pennsylvania	M,O*
University of Rochester	M,D,O*
University of South Africa	M,D
University of South Alabama	M,D*
University of Southern Mississippi	M,D
Vanderbilt University	M,D*
Wayne State University	M,O*

MATERNAL AND CHILD HEALTH

Bank Street College of Education	M*
Boston University	M,D*
Columbia University	M*
The George Washington University	M*
Oakland University	M,D,O
Tulane University	M,D
University of California, Berkeley	M*
University of California, Davis	M*
University of Maryland, College Park	M,D*
University of Minnesota, Twin Cities Campus	M*
University of Mississippi Medical Center	M*
The University of North Carolina at Chapel Hill	M,D*
University of Puerto Rico, Medical Sciences Campus	M
University of Washington	M,D*

*M—master's degree; P—first professional degree; D—doctorate; O—other advanced degree; *—Close-Up and/or Announcement or Display in one of the other books in this series*

MATHEMATICAL AND COMPUTATIONAL FINANCE

Bernard M. Baruch College of the City University of New York	M
Boston University	M,D*
Carnegie Mellon University	M,D*
DePaul University	M,D*
Florida State University	M,D*
Georgia Institute of Technology	M,D*
Illinois Institute of Technology	M*
The Johns Hopkins University	M,D*
New York University	M,D*
North Carolina State University	M*
Polytechnic Institute of NYU	M,O
Polytechnic Institute of NYU, Westchester Graduate Center	M,O
Rice University	M,D
Stanford University	M,D*
University of Alberta	M,D,O*
University of California, Santa Barbara	M,D
University of Chicago	M*
University of Connecticut	M*
University of Dayton	M
University of Illinois at Chicago	M,D*
The University of North Carolina at Charlotte	M*
University of Pittsburgh	M,D*

MATHEMATICAL PHYSICS

New Mexico Institute of Mining and Technology	M,D
University of Alberta	M,D,O*
University of Colorado at Boulder	M,D*
Virginia Polytechnic Institute and State University	M,D*

MATHEMATICS

Alabama State University	M,O
American University	M*
American University of Beirut	M
Andrews University	M
Appalachian State University	M
Arizona State University	M,D
Arkansas State University	M
Auburn University	M,D*
Aurora University	M
Ball State University	M*
Baylor University	M,D
Boston College	M*
Boston University	M,D*
Bowling Green State University	M,D*
Brandeis University	M,D,O
Brigham Young University	M,D*
Brock University	M
Brooklyn College of the City University of New York	M,D
Brown University	M,D*
Bryn Mawr College	M,D*
Bucknell University	M
California Institute of Technology	D*
California Polytechnic State University, San Luis Obispo	M
California State Polytechnic University, Pomona	M
California State University Channel Islands	M
California State University, East Bay	M
California State University, Fresno	M
California State University, Fullerton	M
California State University, Long Beach	M
California State University, Los Angeles	M
California State University, Northridge	M
California State University, Sacramento	M
California State University, San Bernardino	M
California State University, San Marcos	M
Carleton University	M,D
Carnegie Mellon University	M,D*
Case Western Reserve University	M,D*
Central Connecticut State University	M,O
Central Michigan University	M,D
Central Washington University	M
Chicago State University	M
City College of the City University of New York	M*
Claremont Graduate University	M,D*
Clark Atlanta University	M
Clarkson University	M,D*
Clemson University	M,D
Cleveland State University	M
The College at Brockport, State University of New York	M
College of Charleston	M,O*
Colorado School of Mines	M,D
Colorado State University	M,D*
Columbia University	M,D*
Concordia University (Canada)	M,D
Cornell University	D*
Dalhousie University	M,D
Dartmouth College	D*
Delaware State University	M
DePaul University	M,O*
Dowling College	M
Drexel University	M,D*
Duke University	D*
Duquesne University	M*
East Carolina University	M
Eastern Illinois University	M
Eastern Kentucky University	M
Eastern Michigan University	M
Eastern New Mexico University	M
Eastern Washington University	M
East Tennessee State University	M
Elizabeth City State University	M
Emory University	M,D*
Emporia State University	M
Fairfield University	M*
Fairleigh Dickinson University, Metropolitan Campus	M*
Fayetteville State University	M
Florida Atlantic University	M,D
Florida International University	M*
Florida State University	M,D*
George Mason University	M,D*
Georgetown University	M
The George Washington University	M,D*
Georgia Institute of Technology	M,D*
Georgian Court University	M,O
Georgia Southern University	M
Georgia State University	M,D
Graduate School and University Center of the City University of New York	D*
Hardin-Simmons University	M,D
Harvard University	D*
Hofstra University	M*
Howard University	M,D
Hunter College of the City University of New York	M
Idaho State University	M,D
Illinois State University	M
Indiana State University	M
Indiana University Bloomington	M,D*
Indiana University of Pennsylvania	M
Indiana University–Purdue University Fort Wayne	M,O
Indiana University–Purdue University Indianapolis	M,D*
Iowa State University of Science and Technology	M,D*
Jackson State University	M
Jacksonville State University	M
James Madison University	M
John Carroll University	M
The Johns Hopkins University	D*
Kansas State University	M,D*
Kean University	M
Kent State University	M,D*
Lakehead University	M
Lamar University	M
Lehigh University	M,D
Lehman College of the City University of New York	M
Long Island University, C.W. Post Campus	M
Louisiana State University and Agricultural and Mechanical College	M,D
Louisiana Tech University	M
Loyola University Chicago	M*
Marquette University	M,D
Marshall University	M
Massachusetts Institute of Technology	D*
McGill University	M,D*
McMaster University	M,D
McNeese State University	M
Memorial University of Newfoundland	M,D
Miami University	M*
Michigan State University	M,D*
Michigan Technological University	M,D
Middle Tennessee State University	M
Minnesota State University Mankato	M
Mississippi College	M
Mississippi State University	M,D
Missouri State University	M*
Missouri University of Science and Technology	M,D
Montana State University	M,D
Montclair State University	M,D,O*
Morgan State University	M
Murray State University	M
Naval Postgraduate School	M,D
New Jersey Institute of Technology	D
New Mexico Institute of Mining and Technology	M,D
New Mexico State University	M,D
New York University	M,D*
Nicholls State University	M
North Carolina Central University	M
North Carolina State University	M,D*
North Dakota State University	M,D
Northeastern Illinois University	M
Northeastern University	M,D*
Northern Arizona University	M
Northern Illinois University	M,D
Northwestern University	D*
Oakland University	M
The Ohio State University	M,D*
Ohio University	M,D*
Oklahoma State University	M,D*
Old Dominion University	M,D
Oregon State University	M,D*
Penn State University Park	M,D*
Pittsburg State University	M
Polytechnic Institute of NYU	M,D
Portland State University	M,D,O
Prairie View A&M University	M
Princeton University	D*
Purdue University	M,D
Purdue University Calumet	M
Queens College of the City University of New York	M
Queen's University at Kingston	M,D
Rensselaer Polytechnic Institute	M,D
Rhode Island College	M
Rice University	M,D
Rivier College	M
Roosevelt University	M
Rowan University	M
Royal Military College of Canada	M
Rutgers, The State University of New Jersey, Camden	M
Rutgers, The State University of New Jersey, Newark	D*
Rutgers, The State University of New Jersey, New Brunswick	M,D*
St. Cloud State University	M
St. John's University (NY)	M
Saint Joseph's University	M,O
Saint Louis University	M,D
Saint Xavier University	M
Salem State College	M
Sam Houston State University	M
San Diego State University	M,D*
San Francisco State University	M
San Jose State University	M
Simon Fraser University	M,D
Smith College	O
South Dakota State University	M,D
Southeast Missouri State University	M
Southern Connecticut State University	M
Southern Illinois University Carbondale	M,D*
Southern Illinois University Edwardsville	M
Southern Methodist University	M,D*
Southern Oregon University	M
Southern University and Agricultural and Mechanical College	M
Stanford University	M,D*
State University of New York at Binghamton	M,D*
State University of New York at Fredonia	M
State University of New York College at Cortland	M

State University of New York College at Potsdam M
Stephen F. Austin State University M
Stevens Institute of Technology M,D
Stony Brook University, State University of New York M,D
Syracuse University M,D*
Tarleton State University M
Temple University M,D*
Tennessee State University M
Tennessee Technological University M*
Texas A&M International University M
Texas A&M University M,D*
Texas A&M University–Commerce M
Texas A&M University–Corpus Christi M
Texas A&M University–Kingsville M
Texas Christian University M
Texas Southern University M
Texas State University–San Marcos M,D*
Texas Tech University M,D
Texas Woman's University M
Tufts University M,D*
Tulane University M,D
Université de Moncton M
Université de Montréal M,D
Université de Sherbrooke M,D
Université du Québec à Montréal M,D
Université du Québec à Trois-Rivières M
Université Laval M,D
University at Albany, State University of New York M,D*
University at Buffalo, the State University of New York M,D*
The University of Akron M
The University of Alabama M,D
The University of Alabama at Birmingham M,D*
The University of Alabama in Huntsville M,D
University of Alaska Fairbanks M,D
University of Alberta M,D,O*
The University of Arizona M,D*
University of Arkansas M,D
University of Arkansas at Little Rock M,O
The University of British Columbia M,D
University of Calgary M,D
University of California, Berkeley M,D*
University of California, Davis M,D*
University of California, Irvine M,D*
University of California, Los Angeles M,D*
University of California, Riverside M,D*
University of California, San Diego M,D*
University of California, Santa Barbara M,D
University of California, Santa Cruz M,D*
University of Central Arkansas M
University of Central Florida M,D,O*
University of Central Missouri M
University of Central Oklahoma M
University of Chicago M,D*
University of Cincinnati M,D
University of Colorado at Boulder M,D*
University of Colorado at Colorado Springs M
University of Colorado Denver M*
University of Connecticut M,D*
University of Delaware M,D*
University of Denver M,D*
University of Florida M,D*
University of Georgia M,D*
University of Guelph M,D
University of Hawaii at Manoa M,D*
University of Houston M,D*
University of Houston–Clear Lake M
University of Idaho M,D
University of Illinois at Chicago M,D*
University of Illinois at Urbana–Champaign M,D*
The University of Iowa M,D*
The University of Kansas M,D*
University of Kentucky M,D
University of Lethbridge M,D
University of Louisiana at Lafayette M,D*
University of Louisville M,D
University of Maine M*
University of Manitoba M,D
University of Maryland, College Park M,D*
University of Massachusetts Amherst M,D*
University of Massachusetts Lowell M,D
University of Memphis M,D
University of Miami M,D*
University of Michigan M,D*
University of Minnesota, Twin Cities Campus M,D*
University of Mississippi M,D
University of Missouri–Columbia M,D*
University of Missouri–Kansas City M,D*
University of Missouri–St. Louis M,D
The University of Montana M,D
University of Nebraska at Omaha M
University of Nebraska–Lincoln M,D*
University of Nevada, Las Vegas M,D
University of Nevada, Reno M*
University of New Brunswick Fredericton M,D
University of New Hampshire M,D,O*
University of New Mexico M,D*
University of New Orleans M
The University of North Carolina at Chapel Hill M,D*
The University of North Carolina at Charlotte M,D*
The University of North Carolina at Greensboro M,D
The University of North Carolina Wilmington M
University of North Dakota M
University of Northern British Columbia M,D,O
University of Northern Colorado M,D
University of Northern Iowa M
University of North Florida M
University of North Texas M,D
University of Notre Dame M,D*
University of Oklahoma M,D*
University of Oregon M,D*
University of Ottawa M,D*
University of Pennsylvania M,D*
University of Pittsburgh M,D*
University of Puerto Rico, Mayagüez Campus M
University of Puerto Rico, Río Piedras M,D
University of Regina M,D
University of Rhode Island M,D
University of Rochester M,D*
University of Saskatchewan M,D
University of South Alabama M*
University of South Carolina M,D
The University of South Dakota M
University of Southern California M,D*
University of Southern Mississippi M,D
University of South Florida M,D,O*
The University of Tennessee M,D
The University of Texas at Arlington M,D*
The University of Texas at Austin M,D
The University of Texas at Brownsville M
The University of Texas at Dallas M,D*
The University of Texas at El Paso M
The University of Texas at San Antonio M*
The University of Texas at Tyler M
The University of Texas–Pan American M
University of the Incarnate Word M
The University of Toledo M,D
University of Toronto M,D
University of Tulsa M*
University of Utah M,D*
University of Vermont M,D*
University of Victoria M,D
University of Virginia M,D
University of Washington M,D*
University of Waterloo M,D
The University of Western Ontario M,D
University of West Florida M
University of West Georgia M
University of Windsor M,D
University of Wisconsin–Madison D*
University of Wisconsin–Milwaukee M,D
University of Wyoming M,D
Utah State University M,D
Vanderbilt University M,D*
Villanova University M*
Virginia Commonwealth University M,O
Virginia Polytechnic Institute and State University M,D*
Virginia State University M
Wake Forest University M*
Washington State University M,D*
Washington University in St. Louis M,D*
Wayne State University M,D*
Wesleyan University M,D*
West Chester University of Pennsylvania M,O
Western Carolina University M
Western Connecticut State University M
Western Illinois University M,O
Western Kentucky University M
Western Michigan University M,D*
Western Washington University M
West Texas A&M University M
West Virginia University M,D
Wichita State University M,D*
Wilfrid Laurier University M
Wilkes University M
Worcester Polytechnic Institute M,D,O*
Wright State University M
Yale University M,D*
York University M,D
Youngstown State University M

MATHEMATICS EDUCATION

Acadia University M
Agnes Scott College M*
Alabama State University M,O
Albany State University M
Alfred University M*
Appalachian State University M
Arcadia University M,D,O
Arkansas State University M
Arkansas Tech University M
Armstrong Atlantic State University M
Asbury College M,O
Auburn University M,D,O*
Averett University M
Ball State University M*
Bank Street College of Education M*
Belmont University M
Bemidji State University M
Bennington College M
Bob Jones University P,M,D,O
Boston College M*
Boston University M,D,O*
Bowling Green State University M,D*
Bridgewater State College M
Brigham Young University M*
Brooklyn College of the City University of New York M,O
Buffalo State College, State University of New York M
California State University, Bakersfield M
California State University, Chico M
California State University, Dominguez Hills M
California State University, Fresno M
California State University, Fullerton M
California State University, Long Beach M
California State University, Northridge M
California State University, San Bernardino M
Cambridge College M,D,O
Campbell University M
Caribbean University M,D
Central Michigan University M,D
Chatham University M
Christopher Newport University M
The Citadel, The Military College of South Carolina M
City College of the City University of New York M,O*
Clayton State University M
Clemson University M
Cleveland State University M
The College at Brockport, State University of New York M
College of Charleston M*
The College of William and Mary M
The Colorado College M
Columbus State University M,O
Concordia University (Canada) M,D

*M—master's degree; P—first professional degree; D—doctorate; O—other advanced degree; *—Close-Up and/or Announcement or Display in one of the other books in this series*

Converse College	M
Cornell University	M,D*
Delaware State University	M
Delta State University	M
DePaul University	M,O*
DeSales University	M
Drake University	M*
Drury University	M
Duquesne University	M*
East Carolina University	M
Eastern Illinois University	M
Eastern Kentucky University	M
Eastern Michigan University	M
Eastern Washington University	M
The Evergreen State College	M
Florida Agricultural and Mechanical University	M
Florida Institute of Technology	M,D,O*
Florida International University	M,D*
Florida State University	M,D,O*
Framingham State College	M
Fresno Pacific University	M
George Mason University	M,O*
Georgia Southern University	M
Georgia State University	M,D,O
Grambling State University	M,D
Harding University	M,O
Harvard University	M,O*
Hofstra University	M*
Hood College	M,O
Hunter College of the City University of New York	M
Idaho State University	M,D
Illinois Institute of Technology	M,D*
Illinois State University	D
Indiana State University	M
Indiana University Bloomington	M,D,O*
Indiana University of Pennsylvania	M
Indiana University–Purdue University Indianapolis	M*
Instituto Tecnológico y de Estudios Superiores de Monterrey, Campus Ciudad Obregón	M
Inter American University of Puerto Rico, Arecibo Campus	M
Inter American University of Puerto Rico, Metropolitan Campus	M
Inter American University of Puerto Rico, Ponce Campus	M
Iona College	M*
Iowa State University of Science and Technology	M,D*
Ithaca College	M
Jackson State University	M
Jacksonville University	M
The Johns Hopkins University	M,O*
Kaplan University–Davenport Campus	M
Kean University	M
Kennesaw State University	M
Kutztown University of Pennsylvania	M,O
Lehman College of the City University of New York	M
Lewis University	M
Long Island University, Brooklyn Campus	M
Long Island University, C.W. Post Campus	M
Louisiana Tech University	M,D
Loyola Marymount University	M
Manhattanville College	M*
Marquette University	M,D
Miami University	M*
Michigan State University	M,D*
Middle Tennessee State University	M
Millersville University of Pennsylvania	M
Mills College	M,D
Minnesota State University Mankato	M
Minot State University	M
Mississippi College	M,D,O
Missouri University of Science and Technology	M,D
Montana State University	M,D
Montclair State University	M,D,O*
Morgan State University	M,D
National-Louis University	M,O
New Jersey City University	M
New York University	M*
Nicholls State University	M
North Carolina Agricultural and Technical State University	M
North Carolina Central University	M
North Carolina State University	M,D*
North Dakota State University	M,D,O
Northeastern Illinois University	M
Northeastern State University	M
Northern Arizona University	M
North Georgia College & State University	M,O
Northwestern State University of Louisiana	M
Northwest Missouri State University	M
Nova Southeastern University	M,O*
Oakland University	M,D,O
Occidental College	M
Ohio University	M,D*
Oklahoma State University	M,D*
Oregon State University	M,D*
Our Lady of the Lake University of San Antonio	M
Penn State University Park	M,D*
Plymouth State University	M
Portland State University	M,D
Providence College	M*
Purdue University	M,D,O
Purdue University Calumet	M
Queens College of the City University of New York	M,O
Quinnipiac University	M*
Regent University	M,D,O
Rhode Island College	M
Rider University	O*
Rollins College	M
Rutgers, The State University of New Jersey, New Brunswick	M,D*
Sage Graduate School	M
St. John Fisher College	M
Salem State College	M
Salisbury University	M
San Diego State University	M,D*
San Francisco State University	M
San Jose State University	M
Shippensburg University of Pennsylvania	M
Siena Heights University	M
Simon Fraser University	M,D
Slippery Rock University of Pennsylvania	M
Smith College	M
South Carolina State University	M
Southeastern Oklahoma State University	M
Southern Illinois University Edwardsville	M
Southern University and Agricultural and Mechanical College	D
Southwestern Oklahoma State University	M
Stanford University	M,D*
State University of New York at Binghamton	M*
State University of New York at Plattsburgh	M
State University of New York College at Cortland	M
State University of New York College at Potsdam	M
Stephen F. Austin State University	M
Stony Brook University, State University of New York	M,O
Syracuse University	M,D*
Teachers College, Columbia University	M,D
Temple University	M,D*
Texas A&M University	M,D*
Texas A&M University–Corpus Christi	M
Texas State University–San Marcos	M,D*
Texas Woman's University	M
Towson University	M
Union Graduate College	M
Universidad Autonoma de Guadalajara	M,D
University at Albany, State University of New York	M,D*
University at Buffalo, the State University of New York	M,D,O*
University of Arkansas	M
The University of British Columbia	M,D
University of California, Berkeley	M,D*
University of California, San Diego	D*
University of California, Santa Cruz	M,D*
University of Central Arkansas	M
University of Central Florida	M,D,O*
University of Central Oklahoma	M
University of Cincinnati	M,D
University of Connecticut	M,D,O*
University of Detroit Mercy	M
University of Florida	M,D,O*
University of Georgia	M,D,O*
University of Houston	M,D*
University of Illinois at Chicago	M*
University of Illinois at Urbana–Champaign	M,D*
University of Indianapolis	M
The University of Iowa	M,D*
University of Maryland, Baltimore County	M,O*
University of Massachusetts Lowell	M,D,O
University of Miami	D*
University of Michigan	M,D*
University of Minnesota, Twin Cities Campus	M*
University of Missouri–Columbia	M,D,O*
The University of Montana	M,D
University of Nevada, Reno	M*
University of New Hampshire	M,D,O*
The University of North Carolina at Chapel Hill	M*
The University of North Carolina at Charlotte	M*
The University of North Carolina at Greensboro	M,D,O
The University of North Carolina at Pembroke	M
University of Northern Colorado	M,D
University of Northern Iowa	M
University of Oklahoma	M,D,O*
University of Phoenix	M
University of Phoenix–Central Florida Campus	M
University of Phoenix–North Florida Campus	M
University of Phoenix–Omaha Campus	M
University of Phoenix–Phoenix Campus	M
University of Phoenix–South Florida Campus	M
University of Phoenix–Springfield Campus	M
University of Phoenix–West Florida Campus	M
University of Pittsburgh	M,D*
University of Puerto Rico, Río Piedras	M,D
University of Rio Grande	M
University of St. Francis (IL)	M
University of San Diego	M
University of South Africa	M,D
University of South Carolina	M,D
University of Southern Mississippi	M,D
University of South Florida	M,D,O*
The University of Tampa	M
The University of Tennessee	M,D,O
The University of Texas at Austin	M,D
The University of Texas at Dallas	M*
The University of Texas–Pan American	M
University of the District of Columbia	M
University of the Incarnate Word	M,D
University of the Virgin Islands	M
The University of Toledo	M
University of Tulsa	M*
University of Vermont	M,D*
University of Victoria	M,D
University of Virginia	M,D,O
University of Washington	M,D*
The University of West Alabama	M
University of West Georgia	M,O
University of Wisconsin–Eau Claire	M
University of Wisconsin–Madison	M,D*
University of Wisconsin–Oshkosh	M
University of Wisconsin–River Falls	M
University of Wyoming	M,D
Ursuline College	M
Virginia Polytechnic Institute and State University	M,D,O*
Virginia State University	M
Walden University	M,D,O
Washington State University	M,D*
Wayne State College	M
Wayne State University	M,D,O*
Webster University	M,O

Wesleyan College	M
Western Carolina University	M
Western Connecticut State University	M
Western Governors University	M,O
Western Michigan University	M,D*
Western New England College	M
Western Oregon University	M
West Virginia University	M,D
Widener University	M,D*
Wilkes University	M
Wright State University	M
Youngstown State University	M

MECHANICAL ENGINEERING

Alfred University	M,D*
American University of Beirut	M,D
American University of Sharjah	M
Arizona State University	M,D
Arizona State University at the Polytechnic Campus	M
Auburn University	M,D*
Baylor University	M
Boise State University	M
Boston University	M,D*
Bradley University	M
Brigham Young University	M,D*
Brown University	M,D*
Bucknell University	M
California Institute of Technology	M,D,O*
California Polytechnic State University, San Luis Obispo	M
California State Polytechnic University, Pomona	M
California State University, Fresno	M
California State University, Fullerton	M
California State University, Long Beach	M,D
California State University, Los Angeles	M
California State University, Northridge	M
California State University, Sacramento	M
Carleton University	M,D
Carnegie Mellon University	M,D*
Case Western Reserve University	M,D*
The Catholic University of America	M,D
City College of the City University of New York	M,D*
Clarkson University	M,D*
Clemson University	M,D
Cleveland State University	M,D
Colorado State University	M,D*
Columbia University	M,D,O*
Concordia University (Canada)	M,D,O
Cooper Union for the Advancement of Science and Art	M
Cornell University	M,D*
Dalhousie University	M,D
Dartmouth College	M,D*
Drexel University	M,D*
Duke University	M,D*
École Polytechnique de Montréal	M,D,O
Embry-Riddle Aeronautical University (FL)	M
Fairfield University	M*
Florida Agricultural and Mechanical University	M,D
Florida Atlantic University	M,D
Florida Institute of Technology	M,D*
Florida International University	M,D*
Florida State University	M,D*
Gannon University	M
The George Washington University	M,D,O*
Georgia Institute of Technology	M,D*
Georgia Southern University	M
Graduate School and University Center of the City University of New York	D*
Grand Valley State University	M
Howard University	M,D
Idaho State University	M
Illinois Institute of Technology	M,D*
Indiana University–Purdue University Fort Wayne	M
Indiana University–Purdue University Indianapolis	M,D,O*
Instituto Tecnológico y de Estudios Superiores de Monterrey, Campus Chihuahua	M,O
Instituto Tecnológico y de Estudios Superiores de Monterrey, Campus Monterrey	M,D
Iowa State University of Science and Technology	M,D*
The Johns Hopkins University	M,D*
Kansas State University	M,D*
Kettering University	M
Lamar University	M,D
Lawrence Technological University	M,D
Lehigh University	M,D
Louisiana State University and Agricultural and Mechanical College	M,D
Louisiana Tech University	M,D
Loyola Marymount University	M
Manhattan College	M
Marquette University	M,D
Massachusetts Institute of Technology	M,D,O*
McGill University	M,D*
McMaster University	M,D
McNeese State University	M
Memorial University of Newfoundland	M,D
Mercer University	M
Michigan State University	M,D*
Michigan Technological University	M,D
Mississippi State University	M,D
Missouri University of Science and Technology	M,D
Montana State University	M,D
Naval Postgraduate School	M,D,O
New Jersey Institute of Technology	M,D,O
New Mexico State University	M,D
North Carolina Agricultural and Technical State University	M,D
North Carolina State University	M,D*
North Dakota State University	M,D
Northeastern University	M,D*
Northern Arizona University	M
Northern Illinois University	M
Northwestern University	M,D*
Oakland University	M,D
The Ohio State University	M,D*
Ohio University	M,D*
Oklahoma State University	M,D*
Old Dominion University	M,D
Oregon State University	M,D*
Penn State University Park	M,D*
Polytechnic Institute of NYU	M,D
Polytechnic Institute of NYU, Long Island Graduate Center	M,D
Portland State University	M,D,O
Princeton University	M,D*
Purdue University	M,D,O
Purdue University Calumet	M
Queen's University at Kingston	M,D
Rensselaer at Hartford	M
Rensselaer Polytechnic Institute	M,D
Rice University	M,D
Rochester Institute of Technology	M
Rose-Hulman Institute of Technology	M*
Royal Military College of Canada	M,D
Rutgers, The State University of New Jersey, New Brunswick	M,D*
St. Cloud State University	M
San Diego State University	M,D*
San Jose State University	M
Santa Clara University	M,D,O
South Carolina State University	M
South Dakota School of Mines and Technology	M*
South Dakota State University	M
Southern Illinois University Carbondale	M*
Southern Illinois University Edwardsville	M
Southern Methodist University	M,D*
Stanford University	M,D,O*
State University of New York at Binghamton	M,D*
Stevens Institute of Technology	M,D,O
Stony Brook University, State University of New York	M,D
Syracuse University	M,D*
Temple University	M*
Tennessee Technological University	M,D*
Texas A&M University	M,D*
Texas A&M University–Kingsville	M
Texas Tech University	M,D
Trine University	M
Tufts University	M,D*
Tuskegee University	M
Union Graduate College	M
Université de Moncton	M
Université de Sherbrooke	M,D
Université Laval	M,D
University at Buffalo, the State University of New York	M,D*
The University of Akron	M,D
The University of Alabama	M,D
The University of Alabama at Birmingham	M,D*
The University of Alabama in Huntsville	M,D
University of Alaska Fairbanks	M,D
University of Alberta	M,D*
The University of Arizona	M,D*
University of Arkansas	M,D
University of Bridgeport	M
The University of British Columbia	M,D
University of Calgary	M,D
University of California, Berkeley	M,D*
University of California, Davis	M,D,O*
University of California, Irvine	M,D*
University of California, Los Angeles	M,D*
University of California, Riverside	M,D*
University of California, San Diego	M,D*
University of California, Santa Barbara	M,D
University of Central Florida	M,D,O*
University of Cincinnati	M,D
University of Colorado at Boulder	M,D*
University of Colorado at Colorado Springs	M
University of Colorado Denver	M*
University of Connecticut	M,D*
University of Dayton	M,D
University of Delaware	M,D*
University of Denver	M,D*
University of Detroit Mercy	M,D
University of Florida	M,D,O*
University of Hawaii at Manoa	M,D*
University of Houston	M,D*
University of Idaho	M,D
University of Illinois at Chicago	M,D*
University of Illinois at Urbana–Champaign	M,D*
The University of Iowa	M,D*
The University of Kansas	M,D*
University of Kentucky	M,D
University of Louisiana at Lafayette	M*
University of Louisville	M
University of Maine	M,D*
University of Manitoba	M,D
University of Maryland, College Park	M,D,O*
University of Massachusetts Amherst	M,D*
University of Massachusetts Dartmouth	M
University of Massachusetts Lowell	M,D
University of Memphis	M,D
University of Miami	M,D*
University of Michigan	M,D*
University of Michigan–Dearborn	M*
University of Minnesota, Twin Cities Campus	M,D*
University of Missouri–Columbia	M,D*
University of Missouri–Kansas City	M,D*
University of Nebraska–Lincoln	M,D*
University of Nevada, Las Vegas	M,D
University of Nevada, Reno	M,D*
University of New Brunswick Fredericton	M,D
University of New Hampshire	M,D*
University of New Haven	M*
University of New Mexico	M,D*
University of New Orleans	M
The University of North Carolina at Charlotte	M,D*
University of North Dakota	M
University of Notre Dame	M,D*
University of Oklahoma	M,D*
University of Ottawa	M,D*
University of Pennsylvania	M,D*
University of Pittsburgh	M,D*
University of Puerto Rico, Mayagüez Campus	M
University of Rhode Island	M,D
University of Rochester	M,D*

*M—master's degree; P—first professional degree; D—doctorate; O—other advanced degree; *—Close-Up and/or Announcement or Display in one of the other books in this series*

University of Saskatchewan M,D
University of South Alabama M*
University of South Carolina M,D
University of Southern California M,D,O*
University of South Florida M,D*
The University of Tennessee M,D
The University of Tennessee at Chattanooga M
The University of Tennessee Space Institute M,D*
The University of Texas at Arlington M,D*
The University of Texas at Austin M,D
The University of Texas at Dallas M*
The University of Texas at El Paso M
The University of Texas at San Antonio M*
The University of Texas at Tyler M
The University of Texas–Pan American M
The University of Toledo M,D
University of Toronto M,D
University of Tulsa M,D*
University of Utah M,D*
University of Vermont M,D*
University of Victoria M,D
University of Virginia M,D
University of Washington M,D*
University of Waterloo M,D
The University of Western Ontario M,D
University of Windsor M,D
University of Wisconsin–Madison M,D*
University of Wisconsin–Milwaukee M,D,O
University of Wyoming M,D
Utah State University M,D
Vanderbilt University M,D*
Villanova University M,O*
Virginia Commonwealth University M,D
Virginia Polytechnic Institute and State University M,D*
Washington State University M,D*
Washington State University Tri-Cities M,D
Washington State University Vancouver M
Washington University in St. Louis M,D*
Wayne State University M,D*
Western Michigan University M,D*
Western New England College M
West Virginia University M,D
Wichita State University M,D*
Widener University M*
Woods Hole Oceanographic Institution M,D,O
Worcester Polytechnic Institute M,D,O*
Wright State University M
Yale University M,D*
Youngstown State University M

MECHANICS

Brown University M,D*
California Institute of Technology M,D*
California State University, Fullerton M
Case Western Reserve University M,D*
The Catholic University of America M,D,O
Columbia University M,D,O*
Cornell University M,D*
Drexel University M,D*
École Polytechnique de Montréal M,D,O
Georgia Institute of Technology M,D*
Iowa State University of Science and Technology M,D*
The Johns Hopkins University M*
Lehigh University M,D
Louisiana State University and Agricultural and Mechanical College M,D
McGill University M,D*
Michigan State University M,D*
Michigan Technological University M
Missouri University of Science and Technology M,D
Montana State University M,D
New Mexico Institute of Mining and Technology M
North Dakota State University M,D
Northwestern University M,D*
The Ohio State University M,D*
Penn State University Park M,D*
Rutgers, The State University of New Jersey, New Brunswick M,D*
San Diego State University M,D*
Southern Illinois University Carbondale M,D*
The University of Alabama M,D
The University of Arizona M,D*
University of California, Berkeley M,D*
University of California, San Diego M,D*
University of Cincinnati M,D
University of Dayton M
University of Illinois at Urbana–Champaign M,D*
University of Maryland, College Park M,D*
University of Massachusetts Lowell M,D
University of Minnesota, Twin Cities Campus M,D*
University of Nebraska–Lincoln M,D*
University of New Brunswick Fredericton M,D
University of Pennsylvania M,D*
University of Rhode Island M,D
University of Southern California M,D,O*
The University of Tennessee M,D
The University of Tennessee Space Institute M,D*
The University of Texas at Austin M,D
University of Wisconsin–Madison M,D*
University of Wisconsin–Milwaukee M,D,O
Virginia Polytechnic Institute and State University M,D*
Worcester Polytechnic Institute M,D,O*

MEDIA STUDIES

American University M*
Arizona State University M
Arkansas State University M
Bob Jones University P,M,D,O
Boston University M*
California State University, Fullerton M
Carnegie Mellon University M*
Central Michigan University M
City College of the City University of New York M*
Claremont Graduate University M,D,O*
College of Staten Island of the City University of New York M
Columbia College Chicago M
Concordia University (Canada) M,D,O
Dallas Theological Seminary M,D,O
DePaul University M*
Digital Media Arts College M
Drexel University M*
Edinboro University of Pennsylvania M
Emerson College M
Fairleigh Dickinson University, Metropolitan Campus M*
Florida State University M,D*
Fordham University M*
Full Sail University M*
Georgetown University M,D
Governors State University M
Howard University M,D
Hunter College of the City University of New York M
Indiana State University M
Indiana University Bloomington M,D*
Indiana University of Pennsylvania M,D
International University in Geneva M
Kutztown University of Pennsylvania M
Louisiana State University and Agricultural and Mechanical College M,D
Lynn University M,D
Marquette University M
Marywood University M,O
Massachusetts Institute of Technology M,D*
Metropolitan College of New York M
Michigan State University M,D*
Monmouth University M,O
National University M
New Mexico Highlands University M
The New School: A University M*
New York University M,D*
Norfolk State University M
Northwestern University M,D*
Ohio University M,D*
Rochester Institute of Technology M
Saginaw Valley State University M
San Diego State University M*
San Francisco State University M
Savannah College of Art and Design M*
Southern Illinois University Carbondale M*
Southern Illinois University Edwardsville O
Syracuse University M*
Temple University M,D*
University at Buffalo, the State University of New York M,O*
The University of Alabama M
The University of Arizona M*
University of California, Santa Barbara M,D
University of Chicago M,D*
University of Colorado at Boulder D*
University of Denver M*
University of Florida M*
University of Illinois at Urbana–Champaign D*
The University of Iowa M,D*
University of Lethbridge M,D
University of Maryland, College Park M,D*
University of Michigan M*
University of Nevada, Las Vegas M
The University of North Carolina at Greensboro M
University of South Carolina M
University of Southern California M,D*
The University of Tennessee M,D
The University of Texas at Austin M,D
The University of Western Ontario M,D
University of Wisconsin–Madison M,D*
University of Wisconsin–Milwaukee M,O
Virginia Commonwealth University D
Washington State University M,D*
Wayne State University M,D*
Webster University M
West Virginia State University M
William Paterson University of New Jersey M*

MEDICAL/SURGICAL NURSING

Angelo State University M
Boston College M,D*
Case Western Reserve University M,D*
Columbia University M,O*
Daemen College M,O
Eastern Virginia Medical School O
Emory University M*
Gannon University M,O
Inter American University of Puerto Rico, Arecibo Campus M
New Mexico State University M
Pontifical Catholic University of Puerto Rico M
Rush University M,D,O
Saint Francis Medical Center College of Nursing M,O
State University of New York Downstate Medical Center M,O*
Uniformed Services University of the Health Sciences M*
University of Maryland, Baltimore M*
University of Massachusetts Lowell M,D,O
University of Michigan M*
University of South Africa M,D
University of South Carolina M
University of Southern Maine M,O
Ursuline College M
Vanderbilt University M,D*

MEDICAL ILLUSTRATION

The Johns Hopkins University M*
Medical College of Georgia M

Rochester Institute of Technology	M
University of Illinois at Chicago	M*
The University of Texas Southwestern Medical Center at Dallas	M*

MEDICAL IMAGING

The Catholic University of America	M,D
Cleveland State University	M
Illinois Institute of Technology	M,D*
MGH Institute of Health Professions	O*
University of Cincinnati	D
University of Florida	M,D*
University of Guelph	M,D,O
University of Medicine and Dentistry of New Jersey	M*
University of Southern California	M,D*

MEDICAL INFORMATICS

Arizona State University	M,D
Cambridge College	M
Columbia University	M,D,O*
Dalhousie University	M,D
Drexel University	M,D,O*
Excelsior College	O
Grand Valley State University	M
Harvard University	M*
Marymount University	M,O
Massachusetts Institute of Technology	M*
Medical College of Wisconsin	M*
Middle Tennessee State University	M
Milwaukee School of Engineering	M*
Oregon Health & Science University	M,D,O*
Stanford University	M,D*
The University of Arizona	M,D,O*
University of California, Davis	M*
University of California, San Francisco	D
University of Illinois at Urbana–Champaign	M,D,O*
The University of Kansas	M,D,O*
University of Medicine and Dentistry of New Jersey	M,D,O*
University of Washington	M,D*
University of Wisconsin–Milwaukee	D

MEDICAL MICROBIOLOGY

Creighton University	M,D*
Idaho State University	M,D
Rutgers, The State University of New Jersey, New Brunswick	M,D*
Texas Tech University Health Sciences Center	M,D
Université du Québec, Institut National de la Recherche Scientifique	M,D
University of Alberta	M,D*
University of Hawaii at Manoa	M,D*
University of Manitoba	M,D
University of Minnesota, Duluth	M,D
University of South Florida	M,D*
University of Wisconsin–La Crosse	M
University of Wisconsin–Madison	D*

MEDICAL PHYSICS

Cleveland State University	M
Columbia University	M,D,O*
East Carolina University	M,D
Georgia Institute of Technology	M,D*
Hampton University	M,D
Harvard University	D*
Louisiana State University and Agricultural and Mechanical College	M,D
Massachusetts Institute of Technology	D*
McGill University	M,D*
McMaster University	M,D
Oakland University	M,D
Rosalind Franklin University of Medicine and Science	M*
Rush University	M,D
Stony Brook University, State University of New York	M,D
University of Alberta	M,D*
University of California, Los Angeles	M,D*
University of Central Arkansas	M
University of Chicago	D*
University of Cincinnati	M
University of Colorado at Boulder	M,D*
University of Kentucky	M
University of Massachusetts Worcester	D
University of Minnesota, Twin Cities Campus	M,D*
University of Missouri–Columbia	M,D*
University of Oklahoma Health Sciences Center	M,D
University of Pennsylvania	M,D*
The University of Texas Health Science Center at Houston	M,D
The University of Texas Health Science Center at San Antonio	M,D
The University of Toledo	M
University of Utah	D*
University of Victoria	M,D
University of Wisconsin–Madison	M,D*
Vanderbilt University	M*
Virginia Commonwealth University	M,D
Wayne State University	M,D*
Wright State University	M

MEDICINAL AND PHARMACEUTICAL CHEMISTRY

Duquesne University	M,D*
Florida Agricultural and Mechanical University	M,D
Idaho State University	M,D
Long Island University, C.W. Post Campus	M
The Ohio State University	M,D*
Purdue University	M,D
Rutgers, The State University of New Jersey, New Brunswick	M,D*
Temple University	M,D*
University at Buffalo, the State University of New York	M,D*
University of California, San Francisco	D
University of Connecticut	M,D*
University of Florida	P,M,D*
The University of Kansas	M,D*
University of Michigan	D*
University of Minnesota, Twin Cities Campus	M,D*
University of Mississippi	M,D
University of Rhode Island	M,D
University of the Sciences in Philadelphia	M,D*
The University of Toledo	M,D
University of Utah	M,D*
University of Washington	D*
Wayne State University	P,M,D*
West Virginia University	M,D

MEDIEVAL AND RENAISSANCE STUDIES

California State University, Long Beach	M
The Catholic University of America	M,D,O
Central European University	M,D*
Columbia University	M*
Cornell University	M,D*
Duke University	O*
Fordham University	M,O*
Georgetown University	M,D
Graduate School and University Center of the City University of New York	M,D*
Harvard University	D*
Indiana University Bloomington	M,D*
Marquette University	M,D
Rutgers, The State University of New Jersey, New Brunswick	D*
Southern Methodist University	M*
University of California, Santa Barbara	M,D
University of Colorado at Boulder	M,D*
University of Connecticut	M,D*
University of Guelph	D
University of Michigan	O*
University of Minnesota, Twin Cities Campus	M,D*
University of Notre Dame	M,D*
University of Toronto	M,D
Western Michigan University	M*
Yale University	M,D*

METALLURGICAL ENGINEERING AND METALLURGY

Colorado School of Mines	M,D
Columbia University	M,D,O*
Massachusetts Institute of Technology	M,D,O*
Michigan Technological University	M,D
Missouri University of Science and Technology	M,D
Montana Tech of The University of Montana	M
The Ohio State University	M,D*
Rensselaer Polytechnic Institute	M,D
South Dakota School of Mines and Technology	M*
Université Laval	M,D
The University of Alabama	M,D
The University of British Columbia	M,D
University of Cincinnati	M,D
University of Connecticut	M,D*
University of Idaho	M,D
University of Nebraska–Lincoln	M,D*
The University of Texas at El Paso	M
University of Utah	M,D*
Wayne State University	M,D,O*

METEOROLOGY

Columbia University	M*
Florida Institute of Technology	M,D*
Florida State University	M,D*
Iowa State University of Science and Technology	M,D*
McGill University	M,D*
Naval Postgraduate School	M,D
North Carolina State University	M,D*
Penn State University Park	M,D*
Plymouth State University	M
Saint Louis University	M,D
San Jose State University	M
Texas A&M University	M,D*
Université du Québec à Montréal	M,D,O
University of Hawaii at Manoa	M,D*
University of Maryland, College Park	M,D*
University of Miami	M,D*
University of Oklahoma	M,D*
Utah State University	M,D
Yale University	D*

MICROBIOLOGY

Albany Medical College	M,D
Albert Einstein College of Medicine	D
American University of Beirut	P,M
Arizona State University	M,D
Auburn University	M,D*
Baylor College of Medicine	D*
Boston University	M,D*
Brandeis University	M,D
Brigham Young University	M,D*
Brown University	M,D*
California State University, Long Beach	M
Case Western Reserve University	D*
The Catholic University of America	M,D
Clemson University	M,D
Colorado State University	M,D*
Columbia University	M,D*
Cornell University	D*
Dalhousie University	M,D
Dartmouth College	D*
Drexel University	M,D*
Duke University	D*
East Carolina University	D
East Tennessee State University	M,D
Emory University	D*
Emporia State University	M
George Mason University	M,D,O*
Georgetown University	M,D
The George Washington University	M,D,O*
Georgia State University	M,D
Harvard University	D*
Hood College	M,O
Howard University	D
Idaho State University	M,D
Illinois State University	M,D
Indiana State University	M,D
Indiana University Bloomington	M,D*
Indiana University–Purdue University Indianapolis	M,D*
Inter American University of Puerto Rico, Metropolitan Campus	M
Iowa State University of Science and Technology	M,D*
The Johns Hopkins University	M,D*
Kansas State University	D*
Loma Linda University	M,D
Long Island University, C.W. Post Campus	M
Louisiana State University Health Sciences Center	M,D*
Louisiana State University Health Sciences Center at Shreveport	M,D*
Loyola University Chicago	M,D*
Marquette University	M,D
Massachusetts Institute of Technology	D*
McGill University	M,D*

*M—master's degree; P—first professional degree; D—doctorate; O—other advanced degree; *—Close-Up and/or Announcement or Display in one of the other books in this series*

Medical College of Wisconsin	M,D*
Medical University of South Carolina	M,D
Meharry Medical College	D
Miami University	M,D*
Michigan State University	M,D*
Montana State University	M,D
New York Medical College	M,D*
New York University	P,M,D*
North Carolina State University	M,D*
North Dakota State University	M,D
Northwestern University	D*
The Ohio State University	M,D*
Ohio University	M,D*
Oklahoma State University	M,D*
Oregon Health & Science University	D*
Oregon State University	M,D*
Penn State Hershey Medical Center	M,D
Penn State University Park	M,D*
Purdue University	M,D
Queen's University at Kingston	M,D
Quinnipiac University	M*
Rensselaer Polytechnic Institute	M,D
Rosalind Franklin University of Medicine and Science	M,D*
Rush University	M,D
Rutgers, The State University of New Jersey, New Brunswick	M,D*
Saint Louis University	D
San Diego State University	M*
San Francisco State University	M
San Jose State University	M
Seton Hall University	M,D*
South Dakota State University	M,D
Southern Illinois University Carbondale	M,D*
Southwestern Oklahoma State University	M
Stanford University	D*
State University of New York Upstate Medical University	M,D
Stony Brook University, State University of New York	D
Temple University	M,D*
Texas A&M Health Science Center	D
Texas A&M University	M,D*
Texas Tech University	M,D
Thomas Jefferson University	M,D*
Tufts University	D*
Tulane University	M,D
Uniformed Services University of the Health Sciences	D*
Universidad Central del Caribe	M
Université de Montréal	M,D,O
Université de Sherbrooke	M,D
Université du Québec, Institut National de la Recherche Scientifique	M,D
Université Laval	M,D
University at Buffalo, the State University of New York	M,D*
The University of Alabama at Birmingham	D*
University of Alberta	M,D*
The University of Arizona	M,D*
University of Arkansas for Medical Sciences	M,D
The University of British Columbia	M,D
University of Calgary	M,D
University of California, Berkeley	D*
University of California, Davis	M,D*
University of California, Irvine	M,D*
University of California, Los Angeles	M,D*
University of California, Riverside	M,D*
University of California, San Diego	D*
University of California, San Francisco	D
University of Central Florida	M*
University of Chicago	D*
University of Cincinnati	M,D
University of Colorado at Boulder	M,D*
University of Colorado Denver	D*
University of Connecticut	M,D*
University of Delaware	M,D*
University of Florida	M,D*
University of Georgia	M,D*
University of Guelph	M,D
University of Hawaii at Manoa	M,D*
University of Idaho	M,D
University of Illinois at Chicago	D*
University of Illinois at Urbana–Champaign	M,D*
The University of Iowa	M,D*
The University of Kansas	M,D*
University of Kentucky	D
University of Louisville	M,D
University of Maine	M,D*
University of Manitoba	M,D
University of Maryland, Baltimore	D*
University of Massachusetts Amherst	M,D*
University of Massachusetts Worcester	D
University of Medicine and Dentistry of New Jersey	M,D*
University of Miami	D*
University of Michigan	D*
University of Minnesota, Twin Cities Campus	D*
University of Mississippi Medical Center	M,D*
University of Missouri–Columbia	M,D*
The University of Montana	M,D
University of Nebraska Medical Center	M,D*
University of New Hampshire	M,D*
University of New Mexico	M,D*
The University of North Carolina at Chapel Hill	M,D*
University of North Dakota	M,D
University of North Texas Health Science Center at Fort Worth	M,D
University of Oklahoma	M,D*
University of Oklahoma Health Sciences Center	M,D
University of Ottawa	M,D*
University of Pennsylvania	D*
University of Pittsburgh	M,D,O*
University of Puerto Rico, Medical Sciences Campus	M,D
University of Rhode Island	M,D
University of Rochester	M,D*
University of Saskatchewan	M,D
University of South Alabama	D*
The University of South Dakota	M,D
University of Southern California	M,D*
University of Southern Mississippi	M,D
The University of Tennessee	M,D
The University of Texas at Austin	D
The University of Texas Health Science Center at Houston	M,D
The University of Texas Health Science Center at San Antonio	D
The University of Texas Medical Branch	M,D*
The University of Texas Southwestern Medical Center at Dallas	D*
University of Vermont	M,D*
University of Victoria	M,D
University of Virginia	D
University of Washington	D*
The University of Western Ontario	M,D
University of Wisconsin–La Crosse	M
University of Wisconsin–Madison	D*
University of Wisconsin–Oshkosh	M
University of Wyoming	D
Utah State University	M,D
Vanderbilt University	M,D*
Virginia Commonwealth University	M,D,O
Virginia Polytechnic Institute and State University	M,D*
Wagner College	M
Wake Forest University	D*
Washington State University	M,D*
Washington University in St. Louis	D*
Wayne State University	M,D*
Western Michigan University	M,D*
West Virginia University	M,D
Wright State University	M
Yale University	D*
Youngstown State University	M

MIDDLE SCHOOL EDUCATION

Alaska Pacific University	M
Albany State University	M
Appalachian State University	M
Arkansas State University	M,O
Armstrong Atlantic State University	M
Austin College	M
Bank Street College of Education	M*
Bellarmine University	M
Belmont University	M
Berry College	M
Brenau University	M,O
Brooklyn College of the City University of New York	M
California Lutheran University	M,D
California State University, Bakersfield	M
California State University, Fullerton	M
California State University, Stanislaus	M,O
Cambridge College	M,D,O
Campbell University	M
Canisius College	M
Capella University	M,D,O
Central Michigan University	M
Chicago State University	M
City College of the City University of New York	M,O*
Clemson University	M
Cleveland State University	M
The College at Brockport, State University of New York	M
College of Mount St. Joseph	M
College of Mount Saint Vincent	M,O
Columbus State University	M,O
Daemen College	M
Drury University	M
East Carolina University	M
Eastern Illinois University	M
Eastern Michigan University	M
Eastern Nazarene College	M,O
Emory University	M,D,O*
Fayetteville State University	M
Fitchburg State College	M
Fresno Pacific University	M
Gardner-Webb University	M
Georgia College & State University	M,O
Georgia Southern University	M
Georgia Southwestern State University	M,O
Georgia State University	M,O
Grand Valley State University	M,O
Hampton University	M
Hebrew College	M,O
Henderson State University	M
Hofstra University	O*
Hood College	M,O
James Madison University	M
John Carroll University	M
Kennesaw State University	M
Kent State University	M*
LaGrange College	M
Le Moyne College	M,O
Lesley University	M,D,O*
Lewis & Clark College	M
Long Island University, C.W. Post Campus	M
Manhattanville College	M*
Mary Baldwin College	M
Maryville University of Saint Louis	M,D
Mercer University	M,D,O
Mercy College	M
Middle Tennessee State University	M,O
Montclair State University	M,D,O*
Morehead State University	M,O
Morgan State University	M
Mount Saint Mary College	M
Mount Saint Vincent University	M
Murray State University	M,O
Nazareth College of Rochester	M
Niagara University	M,O
North Carolina Central University	M
North Carolina State University	M*
North Georgia College & State University	M,O
Northwestern State University of Louisiana	M
Northwest Missouri State University	M
Oberlin College	M
The Ohio State University at Lima	M
The Ohio State University at Marion	M,D
The Ohio State University–Mansfield Campus	M
The Ohio State University–Newark Campus	M
Ohio University	M,D*
Old Dominion University	M

Our Lady of the Lake University of San Antonio	M
Pacific University	M
Park University	M
Plymouth State University	M
Quinnipiac University	M*
Roberts Wesleyan College	M,O
Saginaw Valley State University	M
St. John Fisher College	M
St. Thomas Aquinas College	M,O*
Salem College	M
Salem State College	M
Shenandoah University	M,D,O
Shippensburg University of Pennsylvania	M
Siena Heights University	M
Simmons College	M,O
Smith College	M
Southeast Missouri State University	M
Spalding University	M
State University of New York College at Oneonta	M
State University of New York College at Potsdam	M
Suffolk University	M,O*
Texas Christian University	M
Tufts University	M,D*
Union College (KY)	M
University at Buffalo, the State University of New York	M,D,O*
University of Arkansas	M,D,O
University of Arkansas at Little Rock	M
University of Central Florida	M*
University of Dayton	M
University of Georgia	M,D,O*
University of Kentucky	M,D
University of Louisiana at Monroe	M
University of Louisville	M
University of Massachusetts Dartmouth	M,O
University of Memphis	M,D
University of Missouri–St. Louis	M,O
The University of North Carolina at Charlotte	M*
The University of North Carolina at Greensboro	M,D,O
The University of North Carolina at Pembroke	M
The University of North Carolina Wilmington	M
University of Northern Iowa	M
University of Phoenix–Oregon Campus	M
University of Southern Maine	M,O
University of South Florida	M,D,O*
University of the Cumberlands	M
The University of Toledo	M
University of West Florida	M
University of West Georgia	M,O
University of Wisconsin–Milwaukee	M
University of Wisconsin–Platteville	M
Ursuline College	M
Valdosta State University	M,O
Virginia Commonwealth University	M,O
Wagner College	M
Walden University	M,D,O
Wesleyan College	M
Western Kentucky University	M,O
Widener University	M,D*
Winthrop University	M
Worcester State College	M
Wright State University	M
Youngstown State University	M

MILITARY AND DEFENSE STUDIES

American Public University System	M
Austin Peay State University	M
The George Washington University	M*
Hawai'i Pacific University	M*
The Institute of World Politics	M,O*
The Johns Hopkins University	M*
Joint Military Intelligence College	M
The Judge Advocate General's School, U.S. Army	M
Missouri State University	M*
National Defense University	M
Naval Postgraduate School	M,D
Norwich University	M
Royal Military College of Canada	M,D
School of Advanced Air and Space Studies	M
United States Army Command and General Staff College	M
University of Calgary	M,D
University of Detroit Mercy	M
University of Pittsburgh	M*
The University of Texas at El Paso	M

MINERAL/MINING ENGINEERING

Colorado School of Mines	M,D
Columbia University	M,D,O*
Dalhousie University	M,D
Laurentian University	M,D
McGill University	M,D,O*
Michigan Technological University	M,D
Missouri University of Science and Technology	M,D
Montana Tech of The University of Montana	M
New Mexico Institute of Mining and Technology	M
Queen's University at Kingston	M,D
Southern Illinois University Carbondale	M*
Université du Québec en Abitibi-Témiscamingue	M,O
Université Laval	M,D
University of Alaska Fairbanks	M
University of Alberta	M,D*
The University of Arizona	M,O*
The University of British Columbia	M,D
University of Idaho	M,D
University of Kentucky	M,D
University of Nevada, Reno	M*
University of North Dakota	M
The University of Texas at Austin	M
University of Utah	M,D*
Virginia Polytechnic Institute and State University	M,D*
West Virginia University	M,D

MINERAL ECONOMICS

Colorado School of Mines	M,D
Michigan Technological University	M
The University of Texas at Austin	M

MINERALOGY

Cornell University	M,D*
Indiana University Bloomington	M,D*
Université du Québec à Chicoutimi	D
Université du Québec à Montréal	M,D,O

MISSIONS AND MISSIOLOGY

Abilene Christian University	M
Alliance Theological Seminary	P,M
Ambrose University College	P,M,O
Anderson University (IN)	P,M,D
Asbury Theological Seminary	M,D,O
Assemblies of God Theological Seminary	P,M,D
Associated Mennonite Biblical Seminary	P,M,O
Baptist Bible College of Pennsylvania	P,M,D
Bethel Seminary	P,M,D,O
Biblical Theological Seminary	P,M,D,O
Biola University	M,D,O
Briercrest Seminary	M
Calvin Theological Seminary	P,M,D
Catholic Theological Union at Chicago	P,M,D,O
Central Baptist Theological Seminary	P,M,O
Columbia International University	P,M,D,O
Dallas Baptist University	M
Dallas Theological Seminary	M,D,O
Eastern University	D
Emmanuel School of Religion	P,M,D
Fuller Theological Seminary	P,M,D
Gardner-Webb University	P,D
George Fox University	P,M,D,O*
Global University	P,M
Gordon-Conwell Theological Seminary	P,M,D
Grace Theological Seminary	P,M,D,O
Grand Rapids Theological Seminary of Cornerstone University	P,M
Hope International University	M
Knox Theological Seminary	M
Luther Rice University	P,M,D
Mennonite Brethren Biblical Seminary	M
Midwestern Baptist Theological Seminary	P,M,D,O
Nazarene Theological Seminary	P,M,D
Northern Baptist Theological Seminary	P,M,D
Northwest Nazarene University	P,M
Oral Roberts University	P,M,D
Phillips Theological Seminary	P,M,D
Providence College and Theological Seminary	P,M,D,O
Reformed Theological Seminary–Jackson Campus	P,M,D,O
Regent University	P,M,D
Saint Paul University	M
Simpson University	P,M
Southeastern Baptist Theological Seminary	P,M,D
Southern Adventist University	M
Southern Baptist Theological Seminary	P,M,D
Southern Evangelical Seminary	P,M,O
Southwestern Assemblies of God University	P,M
Southwestern Christian University	M
Taylor College and Seminary	P,M,O
Trinity Episcopal School for Ministry	P,M,D,O
Trinity International University	P,M,D,O
Tyndale University College & Seminary	P,M,O
University of South Africa	M,D
Wesley Biblical Seminary	P,M
Western Seminary	M,O
Westminster Theological Seminary	P,M,D,O
Wheaton College	M,O

MOLECULAR BIOLOGY

Albany Medical College	M,D
Albert Einstein College of Medicine	D
Appalachian State University	M
Arizona State University	M,D
Arkansas State University	D
Auburn University	M,D*
Baylor College of Medicine	D*
Boston University	M,D*
Brandeis University	M,D
Brigham Young University	M,D*
Brown University	M,D*
California Institute of Technology	D*
Carnegie Mellon University	M,D*
Case Western Reserve University	D*
Central Connecticut State University	M
Clemson University	M,D
Colorado State University	M,D*
Columbia University	M,D*
Cornell University	D*
Cornell University, Joan and Sanford I. Weill Medical College and Graduate School of Medical Sciences	M,D
Dartmouth College	D*
Drexel University	M,D*
Duke University	D,O*
East Carolina University	M,D
Eastern Michigan University	M
Emory University	D*
Florida Institute of Technology	M,D*
Florida State University	M,D*
George Mason University	M,D,O*
Georgetown University	M,D
The George Washington University	M,D*
Georgia State University	M,D
Grand Valley State University	M
Harvard University	D*
Hood College	M,O
Howard University	M,D
Illinois Institute of Technology	M,D*
Illinois State University	M,D
Indiana University Bloomington	M,D*
Indiana University–Purdue University Indianapolis	D*
Inter American University of Puerto Rico, Metropolitan Campus	M
Iowa State University of Science and Technology	M,D*
The Johns Hopkins University	M,D*
Kent State University	M,D*
Lehigh University	M,D

*M—master's degree; P—first professional degree; D—doctorate; O—other advanced degree; *—Close-Up and/or Announcement or Display in one of the other books in this series*

Louisiana State University Health Sciences Center at Shreveport M,D*
Loyola University Chicago D*
Marquette University M,D
Massachusetts Institute of Technology D*
Mayo Graduate School D*
McMaster University M,D
Medical College of Georgia D
Medical University of South Carolina M,D
Michigan State University M,D*
Mississippi State University M,D
Missouri State University M*
Montana State University M,D
Montclair State University M,O*
New Mexico State University M,D
New York Medical College M,D*
New York University P,M,D*
North Dakota State University M,D
Northwestern University D*
OGI School of Science & Engineering at Oregon Health & Science University M,D
The Ohio State University M,D*
Ohio University M,D*
Oklahoma State University M,D*
Oklahoma State University Center for Health Sciences M,O
Oregon Health & Science University M,D*
Oregon State University M,D*
Penn State Hershey Medical Center M,D
Penn State University Park M,D*
Princeton University D*
Purdue University M,D
Queen's University at Kingston M,D
Quinnipiac University M*
Rensselaer Polytechnic Institute M,D
Rutgers, The State University of New Jersey, New Brunswick M,D*
Saint Louis University D
San Diego State University M,D*
San Francisco State University M
San Jose State University M
Seton Hall University M,D*
Simon Fraser University M,D
Southern Illinois University Carbondale M,D*
State University of New York Downstate Medical Center D*
State University of New York Upstate Medical University M,D
Stony Brook University, State University of New York M,D
Temple University D*
Texas A&M Health Science Center D
Texas Woman's University M,D
Thomas Jefferson University D*
Tufts University D*
Tulane University M,D
Uniformed Services University of the Health Sciences D*
Université de Montréal M,D
Université Laval M,D
University at Albany, State University of New York M,D*
University at Buffalo, the State University of New York D*
The University of Alabama at Birmingham D*
University of Alberta M,D*
The University of Arizona M,D*
University of Arkansas M,D
University of Arkansas for Medical Sciences M,D
The University of British Columbia M,D
University of Calgary M,D
University of California, Berkeley D*
University of California, Davis M,D*
University of California, Irvine M,D*
University of California, Los Angeles M,D*
University of California, Riverside M,D*
University of California, San Diego D*
University of California, San Francisco D
University of California, Santa Barbara M,D
University of California, Santa Cruz M,D*
University of Central Florida M*
University of Chicago D*
University of Cincinnati M,D
University of Colorado at Boulder M,D*
University of Colorado Denver D*
University of Connecticut M*
University of Connecticut Health Center D*
University of Delaware M,D*
University of Florida M,D*
University of Georgia M,D*
University of Guelph M,D
University of Hawaii at Manoa M,D*
University of Idaho M,D
University of Illinois at Chicago D*
The University of Iowa D*
The University of Kansas M,D*
University of Lethbridge M,D
University of Louisville M,D
University of Maine M,D*
University of Maryland, Baltimore M,D*
University of Maryland, Baltimore County M,D*
University of Maryland, College Park D*
University of Massachusetts Boston D
University of Medicine and Dentistry of New Jersey M,D*
University of Miami D*
University of Michigan M,D*
University of Minnesota, Duluth M,D
University of Minnesota, Twin Cities Campus M,D*
University of Missouri–Kansas City D*
University of Missouri–St. Louis M,D,O
University of Nebraska Medical Center M,D*
University of Nevada, Reno M,D*
University of New Haven M*
University of New Mexico M,D*
The University of North Carolina at Chapel Hill M,D*
University of North Texas M,D
University of North Texas Health Science Center at Fort Worth M,D
University of Notre Dame M,D*
University of Oklahoma Health Sciences Center M,D
University of Oregon M,D*
University of Ottawa M,D*
University of Pennsylvania D*
University of Pittsburgh D*
University of Rhode Island M,D
University of South Alabama D*
University of South Carolina M,D
The University of South Dakota M,D
University of Southern California M,D*
University of Southern Maine M
University of Southern Mississippi M,D
University of South Florida M,D*
The University of Texas at Austin D
The University of Texas at Dallas M,D*
The University of Texas at San Antonio M,D*
The University of Texas Health Science Center at Houston M,D
The University of Toledo M
University of Utah D*
University of Vermont M,D*
University of Washington D*
The University of Western Ontario M,D
University of Wisconsin–La Crosse M
University of Wisconsin–Madison D*
University of Wisconsin–Parkside M
University of Wyoming M,D
Utah State University M,D
Vanderbilt University M,D*
Virginia Commonwealth University M,D
Wake Forest University D*
Washington State University M,D*
Washington University in St. Louis D*
Wayne State University M,D*
Wesleyan University D*
West Virginia University M,D
William Paterson University of New Jersey M*
Wright State University M
Yale University D*
Youngstown State University M

MOLECULAR BIOPHYSICS

Baylor College of Medicine D*
California Institute of Technology M,D*
Carnegie Mellon University D*
Duke University O*
Florida State University D*
Illinois Institute of Technology M,D*
The Johns Hopkins University M,D*
Rutgers, The State University of New Jersey, New Brunswick D*
Texas Tech University Health Sciences Center M,D
University of Massachusetts Amherst D*
University of Pennsylvania D*
University of Pittsburgh D*
The University of Texas Medical Branch M,D*
The University of Texas Southwestern Medical Center at Dallas D*
Washington University in St. Louis D*
Yale University D*

MOLECULAR GENETICS

Albert Einstein College of Medicine D
Duke University D*
Emory University D*
The George Washington University D*
Georgia State University M,D
Harvard University D*
Illinois State University M,D
Indiana University–Purdue University Indianapolis M,D*
Medical College of Wisconsin M,D*
Michigan State University M,D*
New York University M,D*
The Ohio State University M,D*
Oklahoma State University M,D*
Rutgers, The State University of New Jersey, New Brunswick M,D*
Stony Brook University, State University of New York D
Texas Tech University Health Sciences Center M,D
The University of Alabama at Birmingham D*
University of California, Irvine M,D*
University of California, Los Angeles M,D*
University of California, Riverside D*
University of Cincinnati M,D
University of Colorado Denver D*
University of Florida M,D*
University of Guelph M,D
University of Illinois at Chicago D*
The University of Kansas D*
University of Maryland, College Park M,D*
University of Massachusetts Worcester D
University of Medicine and Dentistry of New Jersey M,D*
University of Pittsburgh M,D*
University of Rhode Island M,D
The University of Texas Health Science Center at Houston M,D
University of Vermont M,D*
University of Virginia D
Wake Forest University D*
Washington University in St. Louis D*

MOLECULAR MEDICINE

Baylor College of Medicine D*
Boston University D*
Case Western Reserve University D*
Cleveland State University M,D
Cornell University M,D*
Dartmouth College D*
The George Washington University D*
The Johns Hopkins University D*
Medical College of Georgia D
North Shore–LIJ Graduate School of Molecular Medicine D
Penn State Hershey Medical Center M,D
Penn State University Park M,D*
Queen's University at Kingston M,D

- Texas A&M Health Science Center — D
- University of Cincinnati — D
- University of Maryland, Baltimore — M,D*
- University of Medicine and Dentistry of New Jersey — D*
- University of South Florida — M,D*
- The University of Texas Health Science Center at San Antonio — M,D
- University of Washington — D*
- Wake Forest University — M,D*
- Yale University — D*

MOLECULAR PATHOGENESIS

- Dartmouth College — D*
- Emory University — D*
- Massachusetts Institute of Technology — M,D*
- North Dakota State University — M,D
- Texas A&M Health Science Center — D
- University at Albany, State University of New York — M,D*
- Washington University in St. Louis — D*

MOLECULAR PATHOLOGY

- Texas Tech University Health Sciences Center — M
- University of California, San Diego — D*
- University of Medicine and Dentistry of New Jersey — D*
- University of Michigan — D*
- University of Pittsburgh — M,D*
- The University of Texas Health Science Center at Houston — M,D
- Yale University — D*

MOLECULAR PHARMACOLOGY

- Albert Einstein College of Medicine — D
- Brown University — M,D*
- Dartmouth College — D*
- Harvard University — D*
- Massachusetts Institute of Technology — M,D*
- Mayo Graduate School — D*
- Medical University of South Carolina — M,D
- New York University — D*
- Purdue University — M,D
- Rosalind Franklin University of Medicine and Science — M,D*
- Rutgers, The State University of New Jersey, New Brunswick — D*
- Stanford University — D*
- Thomas Jefferson University — D*
- University at Buffalo, the State University of New York — D*
- University of Connecticut Health Center — D*
- University of Massachusetts Worcester — D
- University of Medicine and Dentistry of New Jersey — M,D*
- University of Nevada, Reno — D*
- University of Pittsburgh — D*
- University of Southern California — M,D*
- University of South Florida — M,D*

MOLECULAR PHYSIOLOGY

- Baylor College of Medicine — D*
- Case Western Reserve University — M,D*
- Loyola University Chicago — M,D*
- Stony Brook University, State University of New York — D
- Texas Tech University Health Sciences Center — M,D
- Thomas Jefferson University — D*
- Tufts University — D*
- The University of Alabama at Birmingham — M,D*
- University of Chicago — D*
- University of Illinois at Urbana–Champaign — M,D*
- University of Massachusetts Worcester — D
- The University of North Carolina at Chapel Hill — D*
- University of Pittsburgh — M,D*
- University of Vermont — M,D*
- University of Virginia — M,D
- Vanderbilt University — M,D*
- Yale University — D*

MOLECULAR TOXICOLOGY

- Massachusetts Institute of Technology — M,D*
- New York University — M,D*
- North Carolina State University — M,D*
- Oregon State University — M,D*
- Penn State Hershey Medical Center — M,D
- University of California, Berkeley — D*
- University of California, Los Angeles — D*
- University of Cincinnati — M,D

MULTILINGUAL AND MULTICULTURAL EDUCATION

- Alliant International University–Irvine — M,O*
- Alliant International University–San Francisco — M,O*
- Azusa Pacific University — M
- Bank Street College of Education — M*
- Belhaven College (MS) — M
- Bennington College — M
- Boston University — M,O*
- Brooklyn College of the City University of New York — M
- Brown University — M,D*
- Buffalo State College, State University of New York — M
- California Baptist University — M
- California State University, Bakersfield — M
- California State University, Chico — M
- California State University, Dominguez Hills — M
- California State University, Fullerton — M
- California State University, Northridge — M
- California State University, Sacramento — M
- California State University, San Bernardino — M
- California State University, Stanislaus — M,O
- Capella University — M,D,O
- Chicago State University — M
- City College of the City University of New York — M*
- The College at Brockport, State University of New York — M,O
- College of Mount St. Joseph — M
- College of Mount Saint Vincent — M,O
- The College of New Rochelle — M,O
- The College of Saint Rose — M,O*
- College of Santa Fe — M
- Columbia College Chicago — M
- Columbia International University — M,D,O
- DePaul University — M,D*
- Eastern Michigan University — M,D,O
- Eastern University — M
- Fairfield University — M,O*
- Fairleigh Dickinson University, Metropolitan Campus — M*
- Florida Atlantic University — M,D,O
- Fordham University — M,D,O*
- Fresno Pacific University — M
- George Fox University — M,D,O*
- Georgetown University — M,D,O
- Graduate Institute of Applied Linguistics — M,O
- Harvard University — D*
- Heritage University — M
- Hofstra University — M,O*
- Howard University — M,D
- Hunter College of the City University of New York — M
- Immaculata University — M
- Indiana State University — M,O
- Indiana University Bloomington — M,D*
- Kean University — M
- Langston University — M
- Lehman College of the City University of New York — M
- Long Island University, Brooklyn Campus — M
- Long Island University, C.W. Post Campus — M
- Long Island University, Westchester Graduate Campus — M,O
- Loyola Marymount University — M
- Mercy College — M,O
- Mercyhurst College — M,O
- Minnesota State University Mankato — M
- National University — M
- New Jersey City University — M
- New York University — M,D,O*
- Northeastern Illinois University — M
- Northern Arizona University — M
- Nova Southeastern University — M,O*
- Ohio University — M,D*
- Our Lady of the Lake University of San Antonio — M
- Park University — M
- Penn State University Park — M,D*
- Prescott College — M,D
- Queens College of the City University of New York — M,O
- Rutgers, The State University of New Jersey, New Brunswick — M,D*
- St. John's University (NY) — M,O
- Salem State College — M
- San Diego State University — M,D*
- Seton Hall University — O*
- Southern Connecticut State University — M
- Southern Methodist University — M,D,O*
- State University of New York at New Paltz — M
- State University of New York College at Geneseo — M
- Sul Ross State University — M*
- Teachers College, Columbia University — M
- Texas A&M International University — M,D
- Texas A&M University — M,D*
- Texas A&M University–Commerce — M,D
- Texas A&M University–Kingsville — M,D
- Texas Southern University — M,D
- Texas State University–San Marcos — M*
- Texas Tech University — M,D
- Universidad del Este — M
- Universidad del Turabo — M
- University at Buffalo, the State University of New York — M,D,O*
- University of Alaska Fairbanks — M,D,O
- University of Alberta — M*
- The University of Arizona — M,D,O*
- University of California, Berkeley — M,D*
- University of Colorado at Boulder — M,D*
- University of Connecticut — M,D,O*
- University of Delaware — M,D,O*
- The University of Findlay — M
- University of Florida — M,D,O*
- University of Houston — M,D*
- University of Houston–Clear Lake — M
- University of Houston–Downtown — M
- University of Illinois at Chicago — M,D*
- University of La Verne — O
- University of Maryland, Baltimore County — M,D*
- University of Massachusetts Amherst — M,D,O*
- University of Massachusetts Boston — M
- University of Miami — D*
- University of Michigan — M,D*
- University of Minnesota, Twin Cities Campus — M*
- University of New Mexico — D,O*
- The University of North Carolina at Greensboro — M,D,O
- University of Oklahoma — M,D,O*
- University of Pennsylvania — M,D*
- University of St. Thomas (MN) — M,O*
- University of San Francisco — M,D
- University of Southern California — D*
- The University of Tennessee — M,D,O
- The University of Texas at Brownsville — M
- The University of Texas at San Antonio — M,D*
- The University of Texas–Pan American — M
- University of the Incarnate Word — M,D
- University of Washington — M,D*
- University of Wisconsin–Milwaukee — D
- Utah State University — M
- Vanderbilt University — M,D*
- Washington State University — M,D*
- Wayne State University — M,D,O*
- Western New Mexico University — M
- Western Oregon University — M
- Xavier University — M*

*M—master's degree; P—first professional degree; D—doctorate; O—other advanced degree; *—Close-Up and/or Announcement or Display in one of the other books in this series*

MUSEUM EDUCATION

Bank Street College of Education	M*
The George Washington University	M*
Seton Hall University	M*
The University of the Arts	M*

MUSEUM STUDIES

Arizona State University	M,D
Bank Street College of Education	M*
Bard College	M
Baylor University	M
Boston University	M,D,O*
Brown University	M,D*
California College of the Arts	M*
California State University, Chico	M
Caribbean University	M,D
Case Western Reserve University	M,D*
Christie's Education	M
City College of the City University of New York	M*
Claremont Graduate University	M,D,O*
Cleveland State University	M,D
Duquesne University	M*
Fashion Institute of Technology	M*
Florida State University	M,D,O*
The George Washington University	M,O*
Harvard University	M,O*
Indiana University–Purdue University Indianapolis	M,O*
John F. Kennedy University	M,O
The Johns Hopkins University	M*
New York University	M,D,O*
San Francisco Art Institute	M*
San Francisco State University	M
Seton Hall University	M*
Southern Illinois University Edwardsville	O
State University of New York College at Oneonta	M
Syracuse University	M*
Texas Tech University	M
Tufts University	O*
Université de Montréal	M
Université du Québec à Montréal	M
Université Laval	O
University at Buffalo, the State University of New York	M,O*
The University of British Columbia	M,D,O
University of California, Riverside	M,D*
University of Central Oklahoma	M
University of Colorado at Boulder	M*
University of Denver	M*
University of Florida	M,D*
University of Hawaii at Manoa	O*
The University of Kansas	M,O*
University of Louisville	M,D
University of Manitoba	M,D
University of Missouri–St. Louis	M,O
University of New Hampshire	M,D*
The University of North Carolina at Greensboro	M,D,O
University of North Texas	M,D,O
University of Oklahoma	M*
University of South Carolina	M,O
The University of the Arts	M*
University of Toronto	M,D
University of Washington	M*
University of West Georgia	O
University of Wisconsin–Milwaukee	M,D,O
Virginia Commonwealth University	M,D
Western Illinois University	M

MUSIC

Alabama Agricultural and Mechanical University	M
Alabama State University	M
Andrews University	M
Appalachian State University	M
Arizona State University	M,D
Arkansas State University	M,O
Austin Peay State University	M
Azusa Pacific University	M
Bard College	M
Baylor University	M
Belmont University	M
Bennington College	M
Bethesda Christian University	P,M
Birmingham-Southern College	M
Bob Jones University	P,M,D,O
Boise State University	M
The Boston Conservatory	M,O
Boston University	M,D,O*
Bowling Green State University	M,D*
Brandeis University	M,D
Brandon University	M
Brigham Young University	M*
Brooklyn College of the City University of New York	M,D,O
Brown University	D*
Butler University	M
California Baptist University	M
California Institute of the Arts	M,O
California State University, Chico	M
California State University, East Bay	M
California State University, Fresno	M
California State University, Fullerton	M
California State University, Long Beach	M
California State University, Los Angeles	M
California State University, Northridge	M
California State University, Sacramento	M
Campbellsville University	M
Capital University	M
Cardinal Stritch University	M
Carleton University	M
Carnegie Mellon University	M*
Case Western Reserve University	M,D*
The Catholic University of America	M,D,O
Central Michigan University	M
Central Washington University	M
City College of the City University of New York	M*
Claremont Graduate University	M,D*
Cleveland Institute of Music	M,D,O
Cleveland State University	M
The College of Saint Rose	M*
Colorado State University	M*
Columbia University	M,D*
Concordia University (Canada)	O
Concordia University Chicago	M
Concordia University Wisconsin	M
Conservatorio de Musica	O
Converse College	M
Cornell University	M,D*
The Curtis Institute of Music	M
Dalhousie University	M
Dartmouth College	M*
DePaul University	M,O*
Duke University	M,D*
Duquesne University	M,O*
East Carolina University	M
Eastern Illinois University	M
Eastern Kentucky University	M
Eastern Michigan University	M
Eastern Washington University	M
Emory University	M*
Emporia State University	M
Five Towns College	M,D
Florida Atlantic University	M
Florida International University	M*
Florida State University	M,D*
Fuller Theological Seminary	P,M,D
Garrett-Evangelical Theological Seminary	P,M,D
George Mason University	M,O*
Georgia Southern University	M
Georgia State University	M
Graduate School and University Center of the City University of New York	D*
Gratz College	M,O
Hardin-Simmons University	M
Harvard University	M,D*
Hebrew College	M,O
Hebrew Union College–Jewish Institute of Religion (NY)	M
Hofstra University	M*
Hollins University	M,O
Holy Names University	M,O
Hope International University	M
Houghton College	M
Howard University	M
Hunter College of the City University of New York	M
Illinois State University	M
Indiana State University	M
Indiana University Bloomington	M,D,O*
Indiana University of Pennsylvania	M
Indiana University–Purdue University Indianapolis	M*
Indiana University South Bend	M
Ithaca College	M
Jacksonville State University	M
James Madison University	D
The Jewish Theological Seminary	M*
The Johns Hopkins University	M,D,O*
The Juilliard School	M,D,O
Kansas State University	M*
Kent State University	M,D*
Lamar University	M
Lee University	M
Long Island University, C.W. Post Campus	M
Longy School of Music	M,O
Louisiana State University and Agricultural and Mechanical College	M,D
Loyola University New Orleans	M
Lynchburg College	M
Lynn University	M,O
Manhattan School of Music	M,D,O
Mansfield University of Pennsylvania	M
Marshall University	M
McGill University	M,D*
Memorial University of Newfoundland	M,D
Mercer University	M
Meredith College	M
Miami University	M*
Michigan State University	M,D*
Middle Tennessee State University	M
Midwestern Baptist Theological Seminary	P,M,D,O
Mills College	M
Minnesota State University Mankato	M
Mississippi College	M
Missouri State University	M*
Montclair State University	M,O*
Morehead State University	M
Morgan State University	M
Murray State University	M
New England Conservatory of Music	M,D,O
New Jersey City University	M
New Mexico State University	M
New Orleans Baptist Theological Seminary	M,D
The New School: A University	M,O*
New York University	M,D,O*
The Nigerian Baptist Theological Seminary	P,M,D,O
Norfolk State University	M
North Carolina Central University	M
North Dakota State University	M,D
Northeastern Illinois University	M
Northern Arizona University	M
Northern Illinois University	M,O
Northwestern State University of Louisiana	M
Northwestern University	M,D,O*
Notre Dame de Namur University	M
Oakland University	M,D
Oberlin College	M,O
The Ohio State University	M,D*
Ohio University	M,O*
Oklahoma City University	M
Oklahoma State University	M*
Penn State University Park	M,D*
Phillips Theological Seminary	P,M,D
Pittsburg State University	M
Point Park University	M*
Portland State University	M
Princeton University	D*
Purchase College, State University of New York	M
Queens College of the City University of New York	M
Radford University	M
Regis University	M,O
Reinhardt College	M
Rice University	M,D
Roosevelt University	M,O
Rowan University	M
Rutgers, The State University of New Jersey, Newark	M*
Rutgers, The State University of New Jersey, New Brunswick	M,D,O*
St. Cloud State University	M
Saint John's University (MN)	P,M

Saint Joseph's College M,O
St. Vladimir's Orthodox Theological Seminary P,M,D
Samford University M
Sam Houston State University M
San Diego State University M*
San Francisco Conservatory of Music M
San Francisco State University M
San Jose State University M
Santa Clara University M
Savannah College of Art and Design M*
School of the Art Institute of Chicago M*
Seabury-Western Theological Seminary P,M,D,O
Shenandoah University M,D,O
Southeastern Baptist Theological Seminary P,M,D
Southeastern Louisiana University M
Southern Baptist Theological Seminary P,M,D
Southern Illinois University Carbondale M*
Southern Illinois University Edwardsville M
Southern Methodist University M,O*
Southern Oregon University M
Southwestern Baptist Theological Seminary M,D,O
Southwestern Oklahoma State University M
Stanford University M,D*
State University of New York at Binghamton M*
State University of New York at Fredonia M
State University of New York at New Paltz M
State University of New York College at Potsdam M
Stephen F. Austin State University M
Stony Brook University, State University of New York M,D
Syracuse University M*
Temple University M,D*
Texas A&M University–Commerce M
Texas Christian University M,O
Texas Southern University M
Texas State University–San Marcos M*
Texas Tech University M,D
Texas Woman's University M
Towson University M
Trinity Lutheran Seminary P,M
Truman State University M
Tufts University M*
Tulane University M
Université de Montréal M,D,O
Université Laval M,D
University at Buffalo, the State University of New York M,D*
The University of Akron M
The University of Alabama M,D
University of Alaska Fairbanks M
University of Alberta M,D*
The University of Arizona M,D*
University of Arkansas M
The University of British Columbia M,D
University of Calgary M,D
University of California, Berkeley D*
University of California, Davis M,D*
University of California, Irvine M*
University of California, Los Angeles M,D*
University of California, Riverside M,D*
University of California, San Diego M,D*
University of California, Santa Barbara M,D
University of California, Santa Cruz M,D*
University of Central Arkansas M
University of Central Florida M*
University of Central Missouri M
University of Central Oklahoma M
University of Chicago M,D*
University of Cincinnati M,D,O
University of Colorado at Boulder M,D*
University of Colorado Denver M*
University of Connecticut M,D,O*
University of Delaware M*
University of Denver M,O*
University of Florida M,D*
University of Georgia M,D*
University of Hartford M,D,O*
University of Hawaii at Manoa M,D*
University of Houston M,D*
University of Idaho M
University of Illinois at Urbana–Champaign M,D,O*
The University of Iowa M,D*
The University of Kansas M,D*
University of Kentucky M,D
University of Lethbridge M,D
University of Louisiana at Lafayette M*
University of Louisiana at Monroe M
University of Louisville M,D
University of Maine M*
University of Manitoba M
University of Maryland, Baltimore County O*
University of Maryland, College Park M,D*
University of Massachusetts Amherst M,D*
University of Massachusetts Lowell M
University of Memphis M,D
University of Miami M,D,O*
University of Michigan M,D,O*
University of Minnesota, Duluth M
University of Minnesota, Twin Cities Campus M,D*
University of Mississippi M,D
University of Missouri–Columbia M*
University of Missouri–Kansas City M,D*
The University of Montana M
University of Nebraska at Omaha M
University of Nebraska–Lincoln M,D*
University of Nevada, Las Vegas M,D
University of Nevada, Reno M*
University of New Hampshire M*
University of New Mexico M*
University of New Orleans M
The University of North Carolina at Chapel Hill M,D*
The University of North Carolina at Greensboro M,D
University of North Carolina School of the Arts M
University of North Dakota M,D
University of Northern Colorado M,D
University of Northern Iowa M
University of North Texas M,D
University of Oklahoma M,D*
University of Oregon M,D*
University of Ottawa M,O*
University of Pennsylvania M,D*
University of Pittsburgh M,D*
University of Portland M
University of Redlands M
University of Regina M,D
University of Rhode Island M
University of Rochester M,D*
University of Saskatchewan M
University of South Africa M,D
University of South Carolina M,D,O
The University of South Dakota M
University of Southern California M,D*
University of Southern Maine M
University of Southern Mississippi M,D
University of South Florida M,D*
The University of Tennessee M
The University of Tennessee at Chattanooga M
The University of Texas at Arlington M*
The University of Texas at Austin M,D
The University of Texas at El Paso M
The University of Texas at San Antonio M,O*
The University of Texas–Pan American M
The University of the Arts M*
University of the Pacific M
The University of Toledo M
University of Toronto M,D
University of Trinity College P,M,D,O
University of Utah M,D*
University of Victoria M,D
University of Virginia M,D
University of Washington M,D*
The University of Western Ontario M,D
University of West Georgia M
University of Wisconsin–Madison M,D*
University of Wisconsin–Milwaukee M,O
University of Wyoming M
Virginia Commonwealth University M
Washington State University M*
Washington University in St. Louis M,D*
Wayne State University M,O*
Webster University M
Wesleyan University M,D*
West Chester University of Pennsylvania M,O
Western Carolina University M
Western Illinois University M
Western Michigan University M*
Western Oregon University M
Western Washington University M
Westminster Choir College of Rider University M*
West Texas A&M University M
West Virginia University M,D
Wichita State University M*
William Paterson University of New Jersey M*
Winthrop University M
Wright State University M
Yale University M,D,O*
York University M,D
Youngstown State University M

MUSIC EDUCATION

Alabama Agricultural and Mechanical University M
Albany State University M
Appalachian State University M
Arcadia University M,D,O
Arizona State University M,D
Arkansas State University M,O
Auburn University M,D,O*
Austin College M
Austin Peay State University M
Azusa Pacific University M
Ball State University M,D*
Belmont University M
Bennington College M
Bob Jones University P,M,D,O
Boise State University M
The Boston Conservatory M,O
Boston University M,D*
Bowling Green State University M,D*
Brandon University M
Brigham Young University M*
Brooklyn College of the City University of New York M,D,O
Butler University M
California Baptist University M
California State University, Fresno M
California State University, Fullerton M
California State University, Los Angeles M
California State University, Northridge M
Campbellsville University M
Capital University M
Carnegie Mellon University M*
Case Western Reserve University M,D*
The Catholic University of America M,D,O
Central Connecticut State University M,O
Central Michigan University M
Christopher Newport University M
Cleveland State University M
College of Charleston M*
College of Mount St. Joseph M
The College of Saint Rose M,O*
The Colorado College M
Colorado State University–Pueblo M
Columbus State University M
Conservatorio de Musica M
Converse College M
DePaul University M,O*
Duquesne University M,O*
East Carolina University M
Eastern Kentucky University M
Eastern Michigan University M
Eastern Washington University M
Emporia State University M
Five Towns College M,D
Florida International University M*
Florida State University M,D*
George Mason University M,O*

*M—master's degree; P—first professional degree; D—doctorate; O—other advanced degree; *—Close-Up and/or Announcement or Display in one of the other books in this series*

Georgia College & State University	M
Georgia State University	M,D,O
Gordon College	M
Hampton University	M
Hardin-Simmons University	M
Hebrew College	M,O
Hofstra University	M*
Holy Names University	M,O
Howard University	M
Hunter College of the City University of New York	M
Indiana University of Pennsylvania	M
Inter American University of Puerto Rico, Metropolitan Campus	M
Inter American University of Puerto Rico, San Germán Campus	M
Ithaca College	M
Jackson State University	M
Jacksonville University	M
James Madison University	M,D
Kansas State University	M*
Kent State University	M,D*
Kutztown University of Pennsylvania	O
Lamar University	M
Lebanon Valley College	M
Lee University	M
Lehman College of the City University of New York	M
Long Island University, C.W. Post Campus	M
Louisiana State University and Agricultural and Mechanical College	M,D
Manhattanville College	M*
Marywood University	M
McGill University	M,D*
McKendree University	M
McNeese State University	M
Miami University	M*
Michigan State University	M,D*
Minot State University	M
Mississippi College	M
Missouri State University	M*
Montclair State University	M,O*
Morehead State University	M
Murray State University	M
Nazareth College of Rochester	M
New Jersey City University	M
New Mexico State University	M
New York University	M,D,O*
Norfolk State University	M
North Dakota State University	M,D,O
Northern Arizona University	M
Northwestern University	M,D*
Northwest Missouri State University	M
Notre Dame de Namur University	M
Oakland University	M,D
Ohio University	M,O*
Oklahoma State University	M*
Old Dominion University	M
Oregon State University	M*
Penn State University Park	M,D*
Pittsburg State University	M
Portland State University	M
Queens College of the City University of New York	M,O
Radford University	M
Reinhardt College	M
Rhode Island College	M
Rollins College	M
Roosevelt University	M,O
Rutgers, The State University of New Jersey, New Brunswick	M,D,O*
St. Cloud State University	M
Samford University	M
Sam Houston State University	M
San Diego State University	M*
San Francisco State University	M
Shenandoah University	M,D,O
Silver Lake College	M
Southeast Missouri State University	M
Southern Illinois University Carbondale	M*
Southern Illinois University Edwardsville	M,O
Southern Methodist University	M,O*
Southwestern Oklahoma State University	M
State University of New York at Fredonia	M
State University of New York College at Potsdam	M
Syracuse University	M*
Tarleton State University	M
Teachers College, Columbia University	M,D
Temple University	M,D*
Tennessee State University	M
Texas A&M University–Commerce	M
Texas A&M University–Kingsville	M
Texas Christian University	M,O
Texas State University–San Marcos	M*
Texas Tech University	M,D
Towson University	M,O
Union College (KY)	M
Université Laval	M,D
University at Buffalo, the State University of New York	M,D,O*
The University of Akron	M
The University of Alabama	M,D,O
University of Alaska Fairbanks	M
The University of Arizona	M,D*
The University of British Columbia	M,D
University of Central Arkansas	M
University of Central Oklahoma	M
University of Cincinnati	M
University of Colorado at Boulder	M,D*
University of Connecticut	M,D,O*
University of Dayton	M
University of Delaware	M*
University of Denver	M,O*
University of Florida	M,D*
University of Georgia	M,D,O*
University of Hartford	M,D,O*
University of Houston	M,D*
University of Illinois at Urbana–Champaign	M,D,O*
The University of Iowa	M,D*
The University of Kansas	M,D*
University of Kentucky	M,D
University of Louisiana at Lafayette	M*
University of Louisville	M
University of Maryland, College Park	M,D*
University of Massachusetts Lowell	M
University of Memphis	M,D
University of Miami	M,D,O*
University of Michigan	M,D,O*
University of Minnesota, Duluth	M
University of Missouri–Columbia	M,D,O*
University of Missouri–Kansas City	M,D*
University of Missouri–St. Louis	M
The University of Montana	M
University of Nebraska at Kearney	M
University of Nebraska–Lincoln	M,D*
University of New Hampshire	M*
The University of North Carolina at Chapel Hill	M*
The University of North Carolina at Charlotte	M*
The University of North Carolina at Greensboro	M,D
The University of North Carolina at Pembroke	M
University of North Dakota	M,D
University of Northern Colorado	M,D
University of Northern Iowa	M
University of North Texas	M,D
University of Oklahoma	M,D*
University of Oregon	M,D*
University of Ottawa	M,O*
University of Rhode Island	M,D
University of Rochester	M,D*
University of St. Thomas (MN)	M*
University of South Carolina	M,D,O
University of Southern California	M,D*
University of Southern Mississippi	M,D
University of South Florida	M,D*
The University of Tennessee	M
The University of Texas at Arlington	M*
The University of Texas at El Paso	M
The University of Texas–Pan American	M
The University of the Arts	M*
University of the Pacific	M
The University of Toledo	M
University of Toronto	M,D
University of Victoria	M,D
University of Washington	M,D*
University of West Georgia	M
University of Wisconsin–Madison	M,D*
University of Wisconsin–Milwaukee	M,O
University of Wisconsin–Stevens Point	M
University of Wyoming	M
VanderCook College of Music	M
Virginia Commonwealth University	M
Washington State University	M*
Wayne State College	M
Wayne State University	M,O*
Webster University	M
West Chester University of Pennsylvania	M,O
Western Connecticut State University	M
Western Kentucky University	M
Western Michigan University	M*
Westminster Choir College of Rider University	M*
West Virginia University	M,D
Wichita State University	M*
Winthrop University	M
Wright State University	M
Youngstown State University	M

NANOTECHNOLOGY

Arizona State University	M,D
George Mason University	M,D,O*
The Johns Hopkins University	M*
North Dakota State University	D
Oregon State University	M,D*
South Dakota School of Mines and Technology	D*
University at Albany, State University of New York	M,D*
University of Alberta	M,D*
University of New Mexico	M,D*
University of Washington	M,D*
Western Michigan University	M,D*

NATIONAL SECURITY

American Public University System	M
California State University, San Bernardino	M
Hult International Business School (United States)	M
The Institute of World Politics	M,O*
Kansas State University	M,D*
National Defense University	M
Naval Postgraduate School	M
Naval War College	M
New York University	M*
Texas A&M University	M,O*
Trinity (Washington) University	M
Troy University	M
University of New Haven	M*
University of Pittsburgh	M*
The University of Texas at El Paso	M

NATURAL RESOURCES

American University	M,D,O*
Auburn University	M,D*
Ball State University	M*
California Polytechnic State University, San Luis Obispo	M
Central Washington University	M
Colorado State University	M,D*
Cornell University	M,D*
Dalhousie University	M
Delaware State University	M
Duke University	M,D*
East Carolina University	D
Georgia Institute of Technology	M,D*
Humboldt State University	M
Iowa State University of Science and Technology	M,D*
Laurentian University	M,D
Louisiana State University and Agricultural and Mechanical College	M,D
McGill University	M,D*
Michigan State University	M,D*
Missouri State University	M*
Montana State University	M
North Carolina State University	M,D*
North Dakota State University	M,D
The Ohio State University	M,D*
Oklahoma State University	M,D*
Penn State University Park	M,D*
Purdue University	M,D
San Francisco State University	M
State University of New York College of Environmental Science and Forestry	M,D
Texas A&M University	M,D*
Texas Tech University	M,D

- Universidad Metropolitana M
- Universidad Nacional Pedro Henriquez Urena P,M,D
- Université du Québec à Montréal M,D,O
- Université du Québec en Abitibi-Témiscamingue M,D
- University of Alaska Fairbanks M
- University of Alberta M,D*
- University of Arkansas at Monticello M
- The University of British Columbia M,D
- University of California, Berkeley M,D*
- University of Connecticut M,D*
- University of Florida M,D*
- University of Georgia M,D*
- University of Guelph M,D
- University of Hawaii at Manoa M,D*
- University of Idaho M,D
- University of Illinois at Urbana–Champaign M,D*
- University of Maine M,D*
- University of Manitoba M,D
- University of Maryland, College Park M,D*
- University of Michigan M,D*
- University of Minnesota, Twin Cities Campus M,D*
- University of Missouri–Columbia M*
- The University of Montana M,D
- University of Nebraska–Lincoln M,D*
- University of New Brunswick Saint John M
- University of New Hampshire M,D*
- University of Northern British Columbia M,D,O
- University of Oklahoma M,D*
- University of Rhode Island M,D
- University of San Francisco M
- University of South Africa M,D
- The University of Texas at Austin M
- University of Vermont M,D*
- University of Washington M,D*
- University of Wisconsin–Madison M,D*
- University of Wisconsin–Stevens Point M
- University of Wyoming M,D
- Utah State University M
- Virginia Polytechnic Institute and State University M*
- Washington State University M,D*
- West Virginia University M,D

NATUROPATHIC MEDICINE

- Bastyr University D,O*
- Canadian College of Naturopathic Medicine D*
- National College of Natural Medicine D
- National University of Health Sciences P,M,D*
- Southwest College of Naturopathic Medicine and Health Sciences D*
- University of Bridgeport D

NEAR AND MIDDLE EASTERN LANGUAGES

- The American University in Cairo M,O
- American University of Beirut M
- Brandeis University M,D
- The Catholic University of America M,D
- Columbia University M,D*
- Georgetown University M,D
- Harvard University M,D*
- Hebrew Union College–Jewish Institute of Religion (NY) D
- Indiana University Bloomington M,D*
- The Ohio State University M,D*
- Oral Roberts University P,M,D
- University of California, Los Angeles M,D*
- University of Chicago M,D*
- University of Maryland, College Park M,O*
- University of Michigan M,D*
- University of South Africa M,D
- The University of Texas at Austin M,D
- University of Utah M,D*
- University of Wisconsin–Madison M,D*
- Yale University M,D*

NEAR AND MIDDLE EASTERN STUDIES

- The American University in Cairo M,O
- American University of Beirut M
- The American University of Paris M
- Brandeis University M,D
- California State University, Long Beach M
- The Catholic University of America M,D
- Columbia University M,D,O*
- Cornell University M,D*
- Drew University M,D
- Emory University D,O*
- Georgetown University M,D,O
- The George Washington University M*
- Harvard University M,D*
- Hebrew Union College–Jewish Institute of Religion (OH) M,D
- The Johns Hopkins University D*
- McGill University M,D,O*
- New York University M,D,O*
- Princeton University M,D*
- Regent University M
- SIT Graduate Institute M
- Southern Evangelical Seminary M,D,O
- The University of Arizona M,D*
- University of California, Berkeley M,D*
- University of California, Los Angeles M,D*
- University of Chicago M,D*
- The University of Kansas M*
- University of Michigan M,D*
- University of Pennsylvania M,D*
- University of South Africa M,D
- The University of Texas at Austin M,D
- University of Toronto M,D
- University of Utah M,D*
- University of Washington M,D*
- University of Waterloo M
- University of Wisconsin–Madison M,D*
- Wayne State University M*
- Yale University M,D*

NEUROBIOLOGY

- Albert Einstein College of Medicine D
- Brandeis University M,D
- California Institute of Technology D*
- Carnegie Mellon University M,D*
- Case Western Reserve University D*
- Columbia University D*
- Cornell University D*
- Dalhousie University M,D
- Duke University D*
- Georgia State University M,D
- Harvard University D*
- Illinois State University M,D
- Louisiana State University Health Sciences Center M,D*
- Loyola University Chicago M,D*
- Marquette University M,D
- Massachusetts Institute of Technology D*
- New York University M,D*
- Northwestern University M,D*
- Purdue University M,D
- Queen's University at Kingston M,D
- Université Laval M,D
- University at Albany, State University of New York M,D*
- The University of Alabama at Birmingham D*
- University of Arkansas for Medical Sciences M,D
- University of California, Irvine M,D*
- University of California, Los Angeles D*
- University of California, San Diego D*
- University of Chicago D*
- University of Colorado at Boulder M,D*
- University of Connecticut M,D*
- University of Illinois at Chicago D*
- The University of Iowa M,D*
- University of Kentucky D
- University of Louisville M,D
- University of Maryland, Baltimore D*
- University of Minnesota, Twin Cities Campus M,D*
- University of Missouri–Columbia M,D*
- The University of North Carolina at Chapel Hill D*
- University of Oklahoma D*
- University of Pittsburgh D*
- University of Rochester M,D*
- University of Southern California M,D*
- The University of Tennessee Health Science Center D*
- The University of Texas at Austin D
- The University of Texas at San Antonio M,D*
- University of Utah D*
- University of Washington D*
- University of Wisconsin–Madison D*
- Virginia Commonwealth University D
- Wake Forest University D*
- Wayne State University D*
- Wesleyan University D*
- West Virginia University M,D
- Yale University D*

NEUROSCIENCE

- Albany Medical College M,D
- American University D*
- American University of Beirut P,M
- Argosy University, Tampa M,D*
- Arizona State University M,D
- Baylor College of Medicine D*
- Baylor University M,D
- Boston University M,D*
- Brandeis University M,D
- Brigham Young University M,D*
- Brock University M,D
- Brown University D*
- California Institute of Technology M,D*
- Carleton University M,D
- Carnegie Mellon University D*
- Case Western Reserve University D*
- Central Michigan University M,D
- College of Staten Island of the City University of New York M
- Colorado State University D*
- Cornell University, Joan and Sanford I. Weill Medical College and Graduate School of Medical Sciences M,D
- Dalhousie University M,D
- Dartmouth College D*
- Delaware State University M,D
- Drexel University M,D*
- Duke University D,O*
- Emory University D*
- Florida Atlantic University D
- Florida State University D*
- George Mason University M,D,O*
- Georgetown University D
- Graduate School and University Center of the City University of New York D*
- Harvard University D*
- Illinois State University M,D
- Indiana University Bloomington D*
- Iowa State University of Science and Technology M,D*
- The Johns Hopkins University D*
- Kent State University M,D*
- Lehigh University M,D
- Louisiana State University Health Sciences Center M,D*
- Loyola University Chicago M,D*
- Massachusetts Institute of Technology D*
- Mayo Graduate School D*
- McGill University M,D*
- McMaster University M,D
- Medical College of Georgia D
- Medical College of Wisconsin D*
- Medical University of South Carolina M,D
- Meharry Medical College D
- Memorial University of Newfoundland M,D
- Michigan State University M,D*
- Montana State University M,D
- Mount Sinai School of Medicine of New York University M,D
- New York Medical College M,D*
- New York University P,M,D*
- Northwestern University D*
- The Ohio State University M,D*
- Ohio University M,D*
- Oregon Health & Science University M,D*
- Penn State Hershey Medical Center M,D
- Penn State University Park M,D*
- Princeton University D*
- Queen's University at Kingston M,D
- Rosalind Franklin University of Medicine and Science D*
- Rush University M,D
- Rutgers, The State University of New Jersey, Newark D*
- Rutgers, The State University of New Jersey, New Brunswick D*
- Seton Hall University M,D*
- Stanford University D*

*M—master's degree; P—first professional degree; D—doctorate; O—other advanced degree; *—Close-Up and/or Announcement or Display in one of the other books in this series*

State University of New York Downstate Medical Center	D*
State University of New York Upstate Medical University	D
Stony Brook University, State University of New York	D
Teachers College, Columbia University	M,D
Temple University	M,D*
Texas A&M Health Science Center	D
Texas A&M University	M,D*
Texas Tech University Health Sciences Center	M,D
Thomas Jefferson University	D*
Tufts University	D*
Tulane University	M,D
Uniformed Services University of the Health Sciences	D*
Université de Montréal	M,D
University at Albany, State University of New York	M,D*
University at Buffalo, the State University of New York	M,D*
The University of Alabama at Birmingham	D*
University of Alberta	M,D*
The University of Arizona	D*
The University of British Columbia	M,D
University of Calgary	M,D
University of California, Berkeley	D*
University of California, Davis	D*
University of California, Los Angeles	D*
University of California, Riverside	D*
University of California, San Diego	D*
University of California, San Francisco	D
University of Chicago	D*
University of Cincinnati	D
University of Colorado Denver	D*
University of Connecticut	M,D,O*
University of Connecticut Health Center	D*
University of Delaware	D*
University of Florida	M,D*
University of Georgia	D*
University of Guelph	M,D,O
University of Hartford	M*
University of Idaho	M,D
University of Illinois at Chicago	D*
University of Illinois at Urbana–Champaign	D*
The University of Iowa	D*
The University of Kansas	M,D*
University of Lethbridge	M,D
University of Maryland, Baltimore	D*
University of Maryland, Baltimore County	D*
University of Maryland, College Park	M,D*
University of Massachusetts Amherst	M,D*
University of Massachusetts Worcester	D
University of Medicine and Dentistry of New Jersey	M,D*
University of Miami	M,D*
University of Michigan	D*
University of Minnesota, Twin Cities Campus	M,D*
University of Missouri–Columbia	M,D*
University of Missouri–St. Louis	M,D,O
The University of Montana	M,D
University of Nebraska Medical Center	M,D*
University of New Mexico	M,D*
University of Oklahoma Health Sciences Center	M,D
University of Oregon	M,D*
University of Pennsylvania	D*
University of Pittsburgh	D*
University of Rochester	M,D*
University of South Alabama	D*
The University of South Dakota	M,D
University of Southern California	M,D*
University of South Florida	M,D*
The University of Texas at Austin	D
The University of Texas at Dallas	M,D*
The University of Texas Health Science Center at Houston	M,D
The University of Texas Medical Branch	D*
The University of Texas Southwestern Medical Center at Dallas	D*
The University of Toledo	M,D
University of Utah	D*
University of Vermont	D*
University of Virginia	D
The University of Western Ontario	M,D
University of Wisconsin–Madison	D*
Vanderbilt University	D*
Virginia Commonwealth University	M,D
Wake Forest University	D*
Washington State University	M,D*
Washington University in St. Louis	D*
West Virginia University	D
Yale University	D*

NONPROFIT MANAGEMENT

American International College	M
American Jewish University	M
American University	M,D,O*
Arizona State University	M,D
Assumption College	M,O
Azusa Pacific University	M
Bernard M. Baruch College of the City University of New York	M
Boston University	M,O*
Brandeis University	M
Cambridge College	M
Capella University	M,D,O
Carlos Albizu University, Miami Campus	M,D
Carlow University	M
Case Western Reserve University	M,O*
Cleary University	M
Cleveland State University	M,D,O
The College at Brockport, State University of New York	M,O
College of Notre Dame of Maryland	M
The College of Saint Rose	O*
Columbia University	M*
Dallas Baptist University	M
DePaul University	M,O*
Eastern Michigan University	M,O
Eastern University	M
Fairleigh Dickinson University, Metropolitan Campus	M,O*
Florida Atlantic University	M
The George Washington University	M*
Georgia State University	M,D,O
Hamline University	M,D
High Point University	M
Hope International University	M
Husson University	M
Illinois Institute of Technology	M*
Indiana University Bloomington	M,D,O*
Indiana University Northwest	M,O
Indiana University–Purdue University Indianapolis	M*
Indiana University South Bend	M,O
John Carroll University	M
Kean University	M
Kentucky State University	M
Lasell College	M,O
Lipscomb University	M
Long Island University, C.W. Post Campus	M,O
Marylhurst University	M
Metropolitan State University	M,O
MidAmerica Nazarene University	M
New England College	M
New Mexico Highlands University	M
The New School: A University	M*
New York University	M,D,O*
North Carolina State University	M,D,O*
North Central College	M
Northern Kentucky University	M,O
Oral Roberts University	M
Our Lady of the Lake University of San Antonio	M
Pace University	M*
Park University	M
Providence College	M*
Regis College (MA)	M,O
Regis University	M,O
Robert Morris University	M
Roberts Wesleyan College	M,O
St. Cloud State University	M
Saint Xavier University	M,O
San Francisco State University	M
Seattle University	M
Seton Hall University	M,O*
Southern New Hampshire University	M,D,O*
Spertus Institute of Jewish Studies	M
Suffolk University	M,O*
Texas A&M University	M,O*
Trinity (Washington) University	M
Trinity Western University	M,O
Troy University	M
Tufts University	O*
University of Arkansas at Little Rock	O
University of Central Florida	M,O*
University of Connecticut	M,O*
University of Dallas	M
University of Delaware	M,D*
University of Georgia	M,O*
The University of Iowa	M*
University of La Verne	M,O
University of Louisville	M
University of Maryland, Baltimore County	M,O*
University of Memphis	M
University of Michigan–Dearborn	M,O*
University of Missouri–St. Louis	M,O
University of Nevada, Las Vegas	M,D,O
The University of North Carolina at Greensboro	M,O
University of Northern Iowa	M
University of Notre Dame	M*
University of Pittsburgh	M*
University of San Diego	M,D,O
University of San Francisco	M
University of Southern Maine	M,O
The University of Tampa	M
University of the Sacred Heart	M
University of the West	M
University of Wisconsin–Milwaukee	M,D,O
Virginia Commonwealth University	O
Walden University	M,D,O
West Chester University of Pennsylvania	M,O
Western Illinois University	M,O
Western Michigan University	M,D,O*
Worcester State College	M

NORTHERN STUDIES

University of Alaska Fairbanks	M
University of Manitoba	M

NUCLEAR ENGINEERING

Air Force Institute of Technology	M,D
Colorado School of Mines	M,D
Cornell University	M,D*
École Polytechnique de Montréal	M,D,O
Georgia Institute of Technology	M,D*
Idaho State University	M,D,O
Kansas State University	M,D*
Massachusetts Institute of Technology	M,D,O*
McMaster University	M,D
Missouri University of Science and Technology	M,D
North Carolina State University	M,D*
The Ohio State University	M,D*
Oregon State University	M,D*
Penn State University Park	M,D*
Purdue University	M,D
Rensselaer Polytechnic Institute	M,D
Royal Military College of Canada	M,D
Texas A&M University	M,D*
University of California, Berkeley	M,D*
University of Cincinnati	M,D
University of Florida	M,D,O*
University of Idaho	M,D
University of Illinois at Urbana–Champaign	M,D*
University of Maryland, College Park	M,D*
University of Massachusetts Lowell	M,D
University of Michigan	M,D,O*
University of Missouri–Columbia	M,D*
University of Nevada, Las Vegas	M,D
University of New Mexico	M,D*
University of South Carolina	M,D
The University of Tennessee	M,D
University of Utah	M,D*
University of Wisconsin–Madison	M,D*
Virginia Commonwealth University	M

NURSE ANESTHESIA

Albany Medical College	M
Arkansas State University	M
Barry University	M*
Baylor College of Medicine	M*
Boston College	M,D*
Bradley University	M
Case Western Reserve University	M*
Central Connecticut State University	M,O
Columbia University	M,O*
DePaul University	M*
Drexel University	M*
Duke University	M,D,O*
Emory University	M,D*
Fairfield University	M,O*
Florida Hospital College of Health Sciences	M
Gannon University	M,O
Georgetown University	M
Goldfarb School of Nursing at Barnes-Jewish College	M
Gonzaga University	M
Gooding Institute of Nurse Anesthesia	M
Inter American University of Puerto Rico, Arecibo Campus	M
La Roche College	M
Lincoln Memorial University	M
Louisiana State University Health Sciences Center	M,D*
Mayo School of Health Sciences	M
Medical College of Georgia	M
Medical University of South Carolina	M
Middle Tennessee School of Anesthesia	M
Midwestern University, Glendale Campus	M*
Missouri State University	M*
Mountain State University	M,O*
Mount Marty College	M
Murray State University	M
Newman University	M
Northeastern University	M,O*
Oakland University	M,O
Old Dominion University	M
Oregon Health & Science University	M*
Rosalind Franklin University of Medicine and Science	M*
Rush University	M,D,O
Saint Joseph's University	M,O
Saint Mary's University of Minnesota	M
Saint Vincent College	M
Samford University	M,D
Samuel Merritt University	M,O
Southern Illinois University Edwardsville	M,O
State University of New York Downstate Medical Center	M*
Texas Christian University	M
Texas Wesleyan University	M,D
Uniformed Services University of the Health Sciences	M*
Union University	M,D,O
Université de Montréal	O
University at Buffalo, the State University of New York	M,D,O*
The University of Alabama at Birmingham	M*
The University of British Columbia	M,D
University of Cincinnati	M,D
University of Detroit Mercy	M
The University of Kansas	M*
University of Medicine and Dentistry of New Jersey	M,D,O*
University of Miami	M,D*
University of Michigan–Flint	M*
University of Minnesota, Twin Cities Campus	M*
University of New England	M
The University of North Carolina at Charlotte	M*
The University of North Carolina at Greensboro	M,D,O
University of Pennsylvania	M*
University of Pittsburgh	M*
University of Puerto Rico, Medical Sciences Campus	M
The University of Scranton	M,O
University of South Carolina	M
The University of Tennessee at Chattanooga	M,O
University of Wisconsin–La Crosse	M
Villanova University	M,D,O*
Virginia Commonwealth University	M,D
Wayne State University	M,O*
Webster University	M
Westminster College (UT)	M

NURSE MIDWIFERY

Bastyr University	D,O*
Case Western Reserve University	M,D*
Columbia University	M*
DeSales University	M
Emory University	M*
Frontier School of Midwifery and Family Nursing	M,O
Georgetown University	M
Marquette University	M,D,O
National College of Midwifery	M,D
New York University	M,O*
Old Dominion University	M
Oregon Health & Science University	M,O*
Philadelphia University	M,O
Shenandoah University	M,O
State University of New York Downstate Medical Center	M,O*
Stony Brook University, State University of New York	M,O
University of Cincinnati	M,D
University of Illinois at Chicago	M*
University of Indianapolis	M
The University of Kansas	M,D,O*
University of Maryland, Baltimore	M*
University of Medicine and Dentistry of New Jersey	M,O*
University of Miami	M,D*
University of Michigan	M,O*
University of Minnesota, Twin Cities Campus	M*
University of Pennsylvania	M*
University of Puerto Rico, Medical Sciences Campus	M,O
University of South Africa	M,D
Vanderbilt University	M,D*
Wichita State University	M*

NURSING—GENERAL

Abilene Christian University	M,O
Adelphi University	M,D,O*
Albany State University	M
Alcorn State University	M
Allen College	M
Alverno College	M
American International College	M
American Sentinel University	M
American University of Beirut	M
Andrews University	M
Arizona State University at the Downtown Phoenix Campus	M,D,O
Arkansas State University	M
Arkansas Tech University	M
Armstrong Atlantic State University	M
Athabasca University	M,O*
Augsburg College	M
Augustana College	M
Austin Peay State University	M
Azusa Pacific University	M,D
Ball State University	M*
Barry University	M,D,O*
Baylor University	M
Bellarmine University	M,D
Belmont University	M
Bethel College (IN)	M
Bethel University	M,O
Blessing-Rieman College of Nursing	M
Bloomsburg University of Pennsylvania	M
Boston College	M,D*
Bowie State University	M
Bradley University	M
Briar Cliff University	M
Brigham Young University	M*
California Baptist University	M
California State University, Bakersfield	M
California State University, Chico	M
California State University, Dominguez Hills	M
California State University, Fresno	M
California State University, Fullerton	M
California State University, Long Beach	M
California State University, Los Angeles	M
California State University, Sacramento	M
California State University, San Bernardino	M
Capital University	M
Cardinal Stritch University	M
Carlow University	M,D
Carson-Newman College	M
Case Western Reserve University	M,D*
The Catholic University of America	M,D,O
Central Methodist University	M
Chatham University	M,D
Clarion University of Pennsylvania	M
Clarke College	M,O
Clarkson College	M,O
Clayton State University	M
Clemson University	M
Cleveland State University	M
College of Mount St. Joseph	M
College of Mount Saint Vincent	M,O
The College of New Jersey	M,O
The College of New Rochelle	M,O
College of Saint Elizabeth	M
The College of St. Scholastica	M,O
College of Staten Island of the City University of New York	M,O
Colorado State University–Pueblo	M
Columbia Union College	M
Columbia University	M,D,O*
Concordia University Wisconsin	M
Coppin State University	M,O
Creighton University	M,D*
Daemen College	M,O
Dalhousie University	M,D
Delaware State University	M
Delta State University	M
DePaul University	M*
DeSales University	M
Dominican College	M
Dominican University of California	M
Drexel University	M*
Duke University	D*
Duquesne University	M,D,O*
D'Youville College	M,O*
East Carolina University	M,D
Eastern Kentucky University	M
Eastern Washington University	M
East Tennessee State University	M,D,O
Edgewood College	M
Edinboro University of Pennsylvania	M
Elmhurst College	M
Elms College	M
Emory University	M,D*
Excelsior College	M
Fairfield University	M,O*
Fairleigh Dickinson University, Metropolitan Campus	M,D,O*
Fairmont State University	M
Felician College	M,O*
Ferris State University	M
Florida Agricultural and Mechanical University	M
Florida Atlantic University	M,D,O
Florida Gulf Coast University	M
Florida International University	M,D*
Florida Southern College	M
Florida State University	M,O*
Fort Hays State University	M
Framingham State College	M
Franciscan University of Steubenville	M
Franklin Pierce University	M,D,O
Frontier School of Midwifery and Family Nursing	M,O
Gannon University	M,O
Gardner-Webb University	M,O
George Mason University	M,D,O*
Georgetown University	M
The George Washington University	M,D,O*
Georgia College & State University	M
Georgia Southern University	M,D,O
Georgia State University	M,D,O
Goldfarb School of Nursing at Barnes-Jewish College	M
Gonzaga University	M
Governors State University	M
Graceland University (IA)	M,O
Graduate School and University Center of the City University of New York	D*
Grambling State University	M,O
Grand Canyon University	M*
Grand Valley State University	M,D
Grand View University	M
Gwynedd-Mercy College	M
Hampton University	M

*M—master's degree; P—first professional degree; D—doctorate; O—other advanced degree; *—Close-Up and/or Announcement or Display in one of the other books in this series*

Hardin-Simmons University	M
Hawai'i Pacific University	M*
Holy Family University	M
Holy Names University	M,O
Howard University	M,O
Hunter College of the City University of New York	M,O
Husson University	M,O
Idaho State University	M,O
Illinois State University	M,D,O
Immaculata University	M
Independence University	M
Indiana State University	M
Indiana University of Pennsylvania	M
Indiana University–Purdue University Fort Wayne	M,O
Indiana University–Purdue University Indianapolis	M,D*
Indiana Wesleyan University	M,O
Inter American University of Puerto Rico, Arecibo Campus	M
Jacksonville State University	M
Jacksonville University	M
James Madison University	M
Jefferson College of Health Sciences	M
The Johns Hopkins University	M,D,O*
Kaplan University–Davenport Campus	M
Kean University	M
Kennesaw State University	M
Kent State University	M,D*
Lamar University	M
La Roche College	M
La Salle University	M,O
Laurentian University	M
Lehman College of the City University of New York	M
Le Moyne College	M,O
Lewis University	M
Liberty University	M,D
Lincoln Memorial University	M
Loma Linda University	M
Long Island University, Brooklyn Campus	M,O
Long Island University, C.W. Post Campus	M,O
Louisiana State University Health Sciences Center	M,D*
Loyola University Chicago	M,D*
Loyola University New Orleans	M
Madonna University	M
Malone University	M
Mansfield University of Pennsylvania	M
Marian University (WI)	M
Marquette University	M,D,O
Marshall University	M
Marymount University	M,O
Maryville University of Saint Louis	M
McGill University	M,D,O*
McKendree University	M
McMaster University	M,D
McNeese State University	M
Medical College of Georgia	D
Medical University of South Carolina	D
Memorial University of Newfoundland	M,O
Mercer University	M,D,O
Mercy College	M
Metropolitan State University	M,D
MGH Institute of Health Professions	M,D,O*
Michigan State University	M,D*
Middle Tennessee State University	M,O
Midwestern State University	M
Millersville University of Pennsylvania	M
Millikin University	M
Milwaukee School of Engineering	M*
Minnesota State University Mankato	M,D
Minnesota State University Moorhead	M,O
Misericordia University	M
Mississippi University for Women	M,O
Missouri Southern State University	M
Missouri State University	M*
Molloy College	M,O
Monmouth University	M,O
Montana State University	M,O
Morgan State University	M,D
Mountain State University	M,O*
Mount Carmel College of Nursing	M*
Mount Saint Mary College	M
Mount St. Mary's College	M
Murray State University	M
Nazareth College of Rochester	M
Nebraska Methodist College	M
Nebraska Wesleyan University	M
Neumann University	M
New Mexico State University	M
New York University	M,O*
North Dakota State University	M,D
Northeastern University	M,O*
Northern Arizona University	M
Northern Illinois University	M
Northern Kentucky University	M,O
Northern Michigan University	M
North Park University	M
Northwestern State University of Louisiana	M
Nova Southeastern University	M,D*
Oakland University	M,D,O
The Ohio State University	M,D*
The Ohio State University at Marion	M,D
Oklahoma City University	M,D
Old Dominion University	M,D
Oregon Health & Science University	M,D,O*
Otterbein College	M,O
Pace University	M,D,O*
Pacific Lutheran University	M
Penn State University Park	M,D*
Pittsburg State University	M
Point Loma Nazarene University	M
Pontifical Catholic University of Puerto Rico	M
Prairie View A&M University	M
Purdue University Calumet	M
Queen's University at Kingston	M,D,O
Queens University of Charlotte	M
Quinnipiac University	M,O*
Radford University	M
Ramapo College of New Jersey	M
Regis College (MA)	M,O
Regis University	P,M,D,O
Research College of Nursing	M
Rhode Island College	M
The Richard Stockton College of New Jersey	M
Rivier College	M
Robert Morris University	M,D
Roberts Wesleyan College	M
Rush University	M,D,O
Rutgers, The State University of New Jersey, Newark	M*
Sacred Heart University	M
Sage Graduate School	M,D,O
Saginaw Valley State University	M
St. Ambrose University	M
St. Catherine University	M,D
Saint Francis Medical Center College of Nursing	M,O
St. John Fisher College	M,D,O
Saint Joseph College	M,O
St. Joseph's College, Long Island Campus	M
St. Joseph's College, New York	M
Saint Joseph's College of Maine	M,O
Saint Louis University	M,D,O
Saint Peter's College	M
Saint Xavier University	M,O
Salem State College	M
Salisbury University	M
Samford University	M,D
Samuel Merritt University	M,O
San Diego State University	M*
San Francisco State University	M
San Jose State University	M,O
Seattle Pacific University	M
Seattle University	M
Seton Hall University	M,D*
Shenandoah University	M,O
Simmons College	M,D,O
South Dakota State University	M,D
Southeastern Louisiana University	M
Southeast Missouri State University	M
Southern Adventist University	M
Southern Connecticut State University	M
Southern Illinois University Edwardsville	M,O
Southern Nazarene University	M
Southern University and Agricultural and Mechanical College	M,D,O
Spalding University	M
Spring Arbor University	M
Spring Hill College	M
State University of New York at Binghamton	M,D,O*
State University of New York Downstate Medical Center	M,O*
State University of New York Institute of Technology	M,O
State University of New York Upstate Medical University	M,O
Stony Brook University, State University of New York	M,D,O
Temple University	M*
Tennessee State University	M
Tennessee Technological University	M*
Texas A&M International University	M
Texas A&M University–Corpus Christi	M
Texas Christian University	M,D
Texas Tech University Health Sciences Center	M,D,O
Texas Woman's University	M,D
Thomas Edison State College	M
Thomas Jefferson University	M*
Thomas University	M
Towson University	M,O
Troy University	M
Uniformed Services University of the Health Sciences	M*
Union University	M,D,O
Universidad del Turabo	M
Université de Montréal	M,D,O
Université du Québec à Rimouski	M,O
Université du Québec à Trois-Rivières	M,O
Université du Québec en Outaouais	M,O
Université Laval	M,D,O
University at Buffalo, the State University of New York	M,D,O*
The University of Akron	M,D
The University of Alabama	M,D
The University of Alabama at Birmingham	M,D*
The University of Alabama in Huntsville	M,D,O
University of Alaska Anchorage	M,O
University of Alberta	M,D*
The University of Arizona	M,D,O*
University of Arkansas	M
University of Arkansas for Medical Sciences	D
The University of British Columbia	M,D
University of Calgary	M,D,O
University of California, Los Angeles	M,D*
University of California, San Francisco	M,D
University of Central Arkansas	M
University of Central Florida	M,D,O*
University of Central Missouri	M
University of Cincinnati	M,D
University of Colorado at Colorado Springs	M,D
University of Colorado Denver	D*
University of Connecticut	M,D,O*
University of Delaware	M,O*
University of Evansville	M
University of Florida	M,D*
University of Hartford	M*
University of Hawaii at Manoa	M,D,O*
University of Houston–Victoria	M
University of Illinois at Chicago	M,D*
University of Indianapolis	M
The University of Iowa	M,D*
The University of Kansas	M,D,O*
University of Kentucky	M,D
University of Lethbridge	M,D
University of Louisiana at Lafayette	M*
University of Louisville	M,D
University of Maine	M,O*
University of Manitoba	M
University of Mary	M
University of Mary Hardin-Baylor	M
University of Maryland, Baltimore	M,D*
University of Massachusetts Amherst	M,D*
University of Massachusetts Boston	M,D

University of Massachusetts Dartmouth	M,D,O
University of Massachusetts Lowell	M,D,O
University of Massachusetts Worcester	M,D,O
University of Medicine and Dentistry of New Jersey	M,O*
University of Memphis	M,O
University of Miami	M,D*
University of Michigan	M,D,O*
University of Michigan–Flint	D*
University of Minnesota, Twin Cities Campus	M,D*
University of Mississippi Medical Center	M,D*
University of Missouri–Columbia	M,D*
University of Missouri–Kansas City	M,D*
University of Missouri–St. Louis	M,D,O
University of Mobile	M
University of Nebraska Medical Center	M,D*
University of Nevada, Las Vegas	M,D,O
University of Nevada, Reno	M*
University of New Brunswick Fredericton	M
University of New Hampshire	M,O*
University of New Mexico	M,D*
University of North Alabama	M
The University of North Carolina at Chapel Hill	M,D,O*
The University of North Carolina at Charlotte	M*
The University of North Carolina at Greensboro	M,D,O
The University of North Carolina Wilmington	M
University of North Dakota	M,D
University of Northern Colorado	M,D
University of North Florida	M,O
University of Oklahoma Health Sciences Center	M
University of Ottawa	M,D,O*
University of Pennsylvania	M,D,O*
University of Phoenix	M
University of Phoenix–Atlanta Campus	M
University of Phoenix–Augusta Campus	M
University of Phoenix–Bay Area Campus	M
University of Phoenix–Birmingham Campus	M
University of Phoenix–Central Florida Campus	M
University of Phoenix–Central Valley Campus	M
University of Phoenix–Charlotte Campus	M
University of Phoenix–Cheyenne Campus	M
University of Phoenix–Cincinnati Campus	M
University of Phoenix–Cleveland Campus	M
University of Phoenix–Columbus Georgia Campus	M
University of Phoenix–Columbus Ohio Campus	M
University of Phoenix–Denver Campus	M
University of Phoenix–Harrisburg Campus	M
University of Phoenix–Hawaii Campus	M
University of Phoenix–Idaho Campus	M
University of Phoenix–Indianapolis Campus	M
University of Phoenix–Kansas City Campus	M
University of Phoenix–Las Vegas Campus	M
University of Phoenix–Louisiana Campus	M
University of Phoenix–Maryland Campus	M
University of Phoenix–Metro Detroit Campus	M
University of Phoenix–Minneapolis/St. Louis Park Campus	M
University of Phoenix–New Mexico Campus	M
University of Phoenix–Northern Nevada Campus	M
University of Phoenix–Northern Virginia Campus	M
University of Phoenix–North Florida Campus	M
University of Phoenix–Northwest Arkansas Campus	M
University of Phoenix–Oklahoma City Campus	M
University of Phoenix–Philadelphia Campus	M
University of Phoenix–Phoenix Campus	M,O
University of Phoenix–Renton Learning Center	M
University of Phoenix–Richmond Campus	M
University of Phoenix–Sacramento Valley Campus	M
University of Phoenix–St. Louis Campus	M
University of Phoenix–San Diego Campus	M
University of Phoenix–Savannah Campus	M
University of Phoenix–Southern California Campus	M,O
University of Phoenix–Southern Colorado Campus	M
University of Phoenix–South Florida Campus	M
University of Phoenix–Springfield Campus	M
University of Phoenix–Tulsa Campus	M
University of Phoenix–Utah Campus	M
University of Phoenix–Vancouver Campus	M
University of Phoenix–West Florida Campus	M
University of Phoenix–West Michigan Campus	M
University of Pittsburgh	M*
University of Portland	M,D
University of Puerto Rico, Medical Sciences Campus	M
University of Rhode Island	M,D
University of Rochester	M,D,O*
University of St. Francis (IL)	M,D
University of Saint Francis (IN)	M
University of San Diego	M,D
University of San Francisco	M,D
University of Saskatchewan	M
The University of Scranton	M,O
University of South Alabama	M,D*
University of South Carolina	M,O
University of Southern Indiana	M,D
University of Southern Maine	M,O
University of Southern Mississippi	M,D
University of South Florida	M,D*
The University of Tampa	M
The University of Tennessee	M,D
The University of Tennessee at Chattanooga	M,O
The University of Tennessee Health Science Center	M,D*
The University of Texas at Arlington	M,D*
The University of Texas at Austin	M,D
The University of Texas at El Paso	M,O
The University of Texas at Tyler	M,D
The University of Texas Health Science Center at Houston	M,D
The University of Texas Health Science Center at San Antonio	M,D
The University of Texas Medical Branch	M,D*
The University of Texas–Pan American	M
University of the Incarnate Word	M
The University of Toledo	M,O
University of Toronto	M,D
University of Utah	M,D*
University of Vermont	M*
University of Victoria	M,D
University of Virginia	M,D
University of Washington	M,D,O*
University of Washington, Bothell	M
University of Washington, Tacoma	M
The University of Western Ontario	M,D
University of West Georgia	M
University of Windsor	M
University of Wisconsin–Eau Claire	M
University of Wisconsin–Madison	D*
University of Wisconsin–Milwaukee	M,D,O
University of Wisconsin–Oshkosh	M
University of Wyoming	M
Ursuline College	M
Utah Valley University	M
Valparaiso University	M,O
Vanderbilt University	M,D*
Villanova University	M,D,O*
Virginia Commonwealth University	M,D,O
Viterbo University	M
Wagner College	M
Walden University	M,O
Washington State University Spokane	M
Washington State University Tri-Cities	M
Washington State University Vancouver	M
Waynesburg University	M,D
Wayne State University	D*
Webster University	M
Wesley College	M
West Chester University of Pennsylvania	M,O
Western Carolina University	M
Western Connecticut State University	M
Western Kentucky University	M
Western University of Health Sciences	M
Westminster College (UT)	M
West Texas A&M University	M
West Virginia University	M,D,O
Wheeling Jesuit University	M
Wichita State University	M*
Widener University	M,D,O*
Wilkes University	M
William Carey University	M
William Paterson University of New Jersey	M*
Wilmington University	M
Winona State University	M,D,O
Winston-Salem State University	M
Wright State University	M
Xavier University	M*
Yale University	M,D,O*
York College of Pennsylvania	M
York University	M
Youngstown State University	M

NURSING AND HEALTHCARE ADMINISTRATION

Abilene Christian University	M,O
Allen College	M
Athabasca University	M,O*
Austin Peay State University	M
Barry University	M,D,O*
Baylor University	M
Bellarmine University	M,D
Bloomsburg University of Pennsylvania	M
Bowie State University	M
Bradley University	M
Brenau University	M
California State University, Long Beach	M,O
Capital University	M
Carlow University	M,D
Central Methodist University	M
Chatham University	M,D
Clarke College	M,O
Clarkson College	M,O
College of Mount Saint Vincent	M,O
The College of New Rochelle	M,O
Columbia Union College	M
Daemen College	M,O
Duke University	M,D,O*
D'Youville College	M,O*
Eastern Michigan University	M,O
Emory University	M*
Excelsior College	O
Fairfield University	M,O*
Fairmont State University	M
Ferris State University	M
Florida Agricultural and Mechanical University	M
Framingham State College	M
Gannon University	M,O
George Mason University	M,D,O*
The George Washington University	M,D,O*
Georgia College & State University	M
Graceland University (IA)	M,O
Grand Canyon University	M*
Grand Valley State University	M,D
Holy Family University	M
Holy Names University	M,O
Independence University	M
Indiana University–Purdue University Fort Wayne	M,O
Indiana Wesleyan University	M,O
Jefferson College of Health Sciences	M

*M—master's degree; P—first professional degree; D—doctorate; O—other advanced degree; *—Close-Up and/or Announcement or Display in one of the other books in this series*

The Johns Hopkins University	M*
Kaplan University–Davenport Campus	M
Kean University	M
Kent State University	M,D*
Lamar University	M
La Roche College	M
Le Moyne College	M,O
Lewis University	M
Loma Linda University	M
Long Island University, Brooklyn Campus	M
Loyola University Chicago	M,O*
Madonna University	M
Marywood University	M
McKendree University	M
McNeese State University	M
Medical College of Georgia	M
Medical University of South Carolina	M
Mercy College	M
Millikin University	M
Minnesota State University Mankato	M,D
Molloy College	M,O
Moravian College	M
Mountain State University	M,O*
Mount Carmel College of Nursing	M*
Mount Saint Mary College	M
New Mexico State University	M
Northeastern University	M*
North Park University	M
Norwich University	M
Otterbein College	M,O
Pacific Lutheran University	M
Prairie View A&M University	M
Queens University of Charlotte	M
Regis University	P,M,D,O
Roberts Wesleyan College	M
Sacred Heart University	M
Sage Graduate School	M,D,O
Saginaw Valley State University	M
Saint Joseph's College of Maine	M,O
Saint Peter's College	M
Saint Vincent College	M
Saint Xavier University	M,O
Samford University	M,D
Samuel Merritt University	M,O
San Francisco State University	M
San Jose State University	M,O
Seattle Pacific University	M
Seattle University	M
Seton Hall University	M*
Southern Adventist University	M
Southern Connecticut State University	M
Southern Illinois University Edwardsville	M,O
Southern Nazarene University	M
Southern University and Agricultural and Mechanical College	M,D,O
Spalding University	M
State University of New York Institute of Technology	M,O
Teachers College, Columbia University	M,D
Texas A&M University–Corpus Christi	M
Texas Tech University Health Sciences Center	M,D,O
TUI University	M,D,O
Union University	M,D,O
University of Central Florida	M,D,O*
University of Cincinnati	M,D
University of Colorado at Colorado Springs	M,D
University of Delaware	M,O*
University of Hawaii at Manoa	M,D,O*
University of Illinois at Chicago	M*
University of Indianapolis	M
University of Mary	M
University of Maryland, Baltimore	M*
University of Massachusetts Lowell	D
University of Michigan	M*
University of Minnesota, Twin Cities Campus	M*
University of Missouri–Kansas City	M,D*
The University of North Carolina at Chapel Hill	M,D,O*
The University of North Carolina at Greensboro	M,D,O
University of Pennsylvania	M,D*
University of Pittsburgh	M*
University of Rhode Island	M,D
University of Rochester	M,D,O*
University of San Diego	M,D
University of San Francisco	D
University of South Carolina	M
University of Southern Mississippi	M,D
The University of Tennessee at Chattanooga	M,O
The University of Texas at Arlington	M,D*
The University of Texas at Dallas	M*
The University of Texas at El Paso	M,O
The University of Texas at Tyler	M,D
University of Victoria	M,D
University of Virginia	M,D
University of West Florida	M
Ursuline College	M
Vanderbilt University	M,D*
Villanova University	M,D,O*
Virginia Commonwealth University	M,D,O
Walden University	M,O
Wichita State University	M*
Winona State University	M,D,O
Wright State University	M
Xavier University	M*

NURSING EDUCATION

Abilene Christian University	M,O
Angelo State University	M
Arizona State University at the Downtown Phoenix Campus	M,D,O
Austin Peay State University	M
Azusa Pacific University	M,D
Barry University	M,O*
Bellarmine University	M,D
Bethel University	M,O
Bowie State University	M
Brenau University	M
California State University, Fresno	M
Capella University	M,D
The Catholic University of America	M,D,O
Chatham University	M,D
Clarke College	M,O
Clarkson College	M,O
Cleveland State University	M
College of Mount Saint Vincent	M,O
The College of New Rochelle	M,O
College of Staten Island of the City University of New York	O
Concordia University Wisconsin	M
Daemen College	M,O
Delta State University	M
DeSales University	M
Dominican University of California	M
Duke University	M,D,O*
Duquesne University	M*
D'Youville College	M,O*
Eastern Michigan University	M,O
Eastern Washington University	M
Fairmont State University	M
Felician College	M,O*
Ferris State University	M
Florida State University	M,O*
Framingham State College	M
George Mason University	M,D,O*
Georgetown University	M
Goldfarb School of Nursing at Barnes-Jewish College	M
Graceland University (IA)	M,O
Grambling State University	M,O
Grand Canyon University	M*
Grand Valley State University	M,D
Holy Family University	M
Holy Names University	M,O
Indiana University–Purdue University Fort Wayne	M,O
Indiana Wesleyan University	M,O
Jefferson College of Health Sciences	M
Kaplan University–Davenport Campus	M
Lamar University	M
La Roche College	M
Le Moyne College	M,O
Lewis University	M
Marian University (WI)	M
Marymount University	M,O
Maryville University of Saint Louis	M
McKendree University	M
McNeese State University	M
Medical University of South Carolina	M
Mercy College	M
MGH Institute of Health Professions	M,D,O*
Midwestern State University	M
Millikin University	M
Minnesota State University Mankato	M,D
Minnesota State University Moorhead	M
Missouri State University	M*
Molloy College	M,O
Montana State University	M,O
Moravian College	M
Mountain State University	M,O*
Mount Carmel College of Nursing	M*
Mount Saint Mary College	M
New York University	M,O*
Northern Arizona University	M
North Georgia College & State University	M
Oakland University	M,O
Old Dominion University	M
Oregon Health & Science University	M,O*
Pace University	M,D,O*
Prairie View A&M University	M
Ramapo College of New Jersey	M
Regis College (MA)	M,O
Research College of Nursing	M
Rivier College	M
Roberts Wesleyan College	M
Sage Graduate School	D
Saint Francis Medical Center College of Nursing	M,O
St. John Fisher College	M,O
Saint Joseph's College of Maine	M,O
Samford University	M,D
San Francisco State University	M
San Jose State University	M,O
Seattle Pacific University	M
Seton Hall University	M*
Southern Connecticut State University	M
Southern Illinois University Edwardsville	M,O
Southern Nazarene University	M
Southern University and Agricultural and Mechanical College	M,D,O
State University of New York Institute of Technology	M,O
Teachers College, Columbia University	M,D
Texas Tech University Health Sciences Center	M,D,O
Texas Woman's University	M,D
Thomas Edison State College	O
Towson University	M,O
Union University	M,D,O
The University of Alabama in Huntsville	M,D,O
University of Alaska Anchorage	M,O
University of Central Florida	M,D,O*
University of Hartford	M*
University of Indianapolis	M
University of Mary	M
University of Maryland, Baltimore	M*
University of Massachusetts Lowell	M,D,O
University of Massachusetts Worcester	M,D,O
University of Missouri–Kansas City	M,D*
University of Nevada, Las Vegas	M,D,O
University of New Brunswick Fredericton	M
The University of North Carolina at Greensboro	M,D,O
The University of North Carolina Wilmington	M
University of Northern Colorado	M,D
University of Phoenix	M
University of Phoenix–Atlanta Campus	M
University of Phoenix–Augusta Campus	M
University of Phoenix–Bay Area Campus	M
University of Phoenix–Birmingham Campus	M
University of Phoenix–Central Florida Campus	M
University of Phoenix–Cheyenne Campus	M
University of Phoenix–Harrisburg Campus	M
University of Phoenix–Hawaii Campus	M
University of Phoenix–Idaho Campus	M
University of Phoenix–Indianapolis Campus	M
University of Phoenix–Las Vegas Campus	M
University of Phoenix–Maryland Campus	M
University of Phoenix–Metro Detroit Campus	M

University of Phoenix–Minneapolis/St. Louis Park Campus	M
University of Phoenix–New Mexico Campus	M
University of Phoenix–Northern Nevada Campus	M
University of Phoenix–North Florida Campus	M
University of Phoenix–Northwest Arkansas Campus	M
University of Phoenix–Philadelphia Campus	M
University of Phoenix–Phoenix Campus	M,O
University of Phoenix–Pittsburgh Campus	M
University of Phoenix–Renton Learning Center	M
University of Phoenix–Richmond Campus	M
University of Phoenix–Sacramento Valley Campus	M
University of Phoenix–San Diego Campus	M
University of Phoenix–Savannah Campus	M
University of Phoenix–Southern California Campus	M,O
University of Phoenix–South Florida Campus	M
University of Phoenix–Utah Campus	M
University of Phoenix–West Florida Campus	M
University of Pittsburgh	M*
University of Rhode Island	M,D
The University of Tennessee at Chattanooga	M,O
The University of Texas at Arlington	M,D*
The University of Texas at El Paso	M,O
The University of Texas at Tyler	M,D
The University of Toledo	M,O
University of Victoria	M,D
Ursuline College	M
Valparaiso University	M,O
Villanova University	M,D,O*
Walden University	M,O
Wayne State University	M,O*
West Chester University of Pennsylvania	M,O
Westminster College (UT)	M
Winona State University	M,D,O

NURSING INFORMATICS

Austin Peay State University	M
Case Western Reserve University	M*
Duke University	M,D,O*
Ferris State University	M
Loyola University Chicago	M,O*
Molloy College	M,O
New York University	M,O*
Seattle Pacific University	M
Tennessee State University	M
University of Medicine and Dentistry of New Jersey	M*
Vanderbilt University	M,D*
Walden University	M,O

NUTRITION

American University of Beirut	M
Andrews University	M
Appalachian State University	M
Arizona State University at the Polytechnic Campus	M
Auburn University	M,D*
Bastyr University	M*
Baylor University	M,D
Benedictine University	M
Boston University	M*
Bowling Green State University	M*
Brigham Young University	M*
Brooklyn College of the City University of New York	M
California State University, Chico	M
California State University, Long Beach	M
California State University, Los Angeles	M
Case Western Reserve University	M,D*
Central Michigan University	M,O
Central Washington University	M
Chapman University	M
Clemson University	M
College of Saint Elizabeth	M,O
Colorado State University	M,D*
Columbia University	M,D*
Cornell University	M,D*
Drexel University	M*
D'Youville College	M*
East Carolina University	M
Eastern Illinois University	M
Eastern Kentucky University	M
Eastern Michigan University	M
East Tennessee State University	M
Emory University	M,D*
Florida International University	M,D*
Florida State University	M,D*
Framingham State College	M
George Mason University	M,O*
Georgia State University	M
Harvard University	D*
Howard University	M,D
Hunter College of the City University of New York	M
Huntington College of Health Sciences	M
Idaho State University	M,O
Immaculata University	M
Indiana State University	M
Indiana University Bloomington	M,D*
Indiana University of Pennsylvania	M
Indiana University–Purdue University Indianapolis	M,D*
Iowa State University of Science and Technology	M,D*
The Johns Hopkins University	M,D*
Kansas State University	M,D*
Kent State University	M*
Lehman College of the City University of New York	M
Loma Linda University	M,D
Long Island University, C.W. Post Campus	M,O
Louisiana Tech University	M
Marshall University	M
Marywood University	M,O
McGill University	M,D,O*
McMaster University	M,D
McNeese State University	M
Meredith College	M
Michigan State University	M,D*
Middle Tennessee State University	M
Mississippi State University	M,D
Montana State University	M
Montclair State University	M,O*
Mount Mary College	M
Mount Saint Vincent University	M
New York Chiropractic College	M*
New York Institute of Technology	M
New York University	M,D*
North Carolina Agricultural and Technical State University	M
North Carolina State University	M,D*
North Dakota State University	M
Northern Illinois University	M
The Ohio State University	M,D*
Ohio University	M*
Oklahoma State University	M,D*
Oregon Health & Science University	M*
Oregon State University	M,D*
Penn State University Park	M,D*
Purdue University	M,D
Rosalind Franklin University of Medicine and Science	M*
Rush University	M
Rutgers, The State University of New Jersey, New Brunswick	M,D*
Sacred Heart University	M,D
Sage Graduate School	M,O
Saint Joseph College	M
Saint Louis University	M
Sam Houston State University	M
San Diego State University	M*
San Jose State University	M
Simmons College	M,O
South Carolina State University	M
South Dakota State University	M
Southeast Missouri State University	M
Southern Illinois University Carbondale	M*
State University of New York College at Oneonta	M
Syracuse University	M*
Teachers College, Columbia University	M,D
Texas State University–San Marcos	M*
Texas Tech University	M,D
Texas Woman's University	M,D
Tufts University	M,D*
Tulane University	M
Tuskegee University	M
Université de Moncton	M
Université de Montréal	M,D,O
Université Laval	M,D
University at Buffalo, the State University of New York	M,D*
The University of Akron	M
The University of Alabama	M
The University of Alabama at Birmingham	M,D,O*
University of Alaska Fairbanks	M,D
The University of Arizona	M,D*
University of Arkansas for Medical Sciences	M
University of Bridgeport	M
The University of British Columbia	M,D
University of California, Berkeley	M,D*
University of California, Davis	M,D*
University of Central Oklahoma	M
University of Chicago	D*
University of Cincinnati	M
University of Connecticut	*
University of Delaware	M*
University of Florida	M,D*
University of Georgia	M,D*
University of Guelph	M,D
University of Hawaii at Manoa	M,D*
University of Illinois at Chicago	M,D*
University of Illinois at Urbana–Champaign	M,D*
The University of Kansas	M,O*
University of Kentucky	M,D
University of Maine	M,D*
University of Manitoba	M,D
University of Maryland, College Park	M,D
University of Massachusetts Amherst	M,D*
University of Massachusetts Lowell	M,O
University of Medicine and Dentistry of New Jersey	M,D,O*
University of Memphis	M
University of Michigan	M,D*
University of Minnesota, Twin Cities Campus	M,D*
University of Missouri–Columbia	M,D*
University of Nebraska–Lincoln	M,D*
University of Nebraska Medical Center	O*
University of Nevada, Reno	M*
University of New Hampshire	M,D*
University of New Haven	M*
University of New Mexico	M*
The University of North Carolina at Chapel Hill	M,D*
The University of North Carolina at Greensboro	M,D
University of North Florida	M,O
University of Oklahoma Health Sciences Center	M
University of Pittsburgh	M*
University of Puerto Rico, Medical Sciences Campus	M,D,O
University of Puerto Rico, Río Piedras	M
University of Rhode Island	M,D
University of Southern Mississippi	M,D
The University of Tennessee	M
The University of Tennessee at Martin	M
The University of Texas at Austin	M,D
University of the Incarnate Word	M,O
University of Toronto	M,D
University of Utah	M*
University of Vermont	M,D*
University of Washington	M,D*
University of Wisconsin–Madison	M,D*
University of Wisconsin–Stevens Point	M
University of Wisconsin–Stout	M
University of Wyoming	M
Utah State University	M,D
Vanderbilt University	M,D*
Virginia Polytechnic Institute and State University	M,D*
Washington State University	M,D*

*M—master's degree; P—first professional degree; D—doctorate; O—other advanced degree; *—Close-Up and/or Announcement or Display in one of the other books in this series*

Wayne State University M,D*
West Virginia University M
Winthrop University M

OCCUPATIONAL HEALTH NURSING

University of Cincinnati M,D
University of Illinois at Chicago M*
University of Medicine and Dentistry of New Jersey M,D,O*
University of Michigan M,O*
University of Minnesota, Twin Cities Campus M,D*
The University of North Carolina at Chapel Hill M*
University of Pennsylvania M*
University of the Sacred Heart M

OCCUPATIONAL THERAPY

Alvernia University M
American International College M
A.T. Still University of Health Sciences M,D
Baker College Center for Graduate Studies M
Barry University M*
Bay Path College M
Belmont University M,D
Boston University M,D*
Brenau University M
California State University, Dominguez Hills M
Chatham University M,D
Cleveland State University M
The College of St. Scholastica M
Colorado State University M*
Columbia University M,D*
Concordia University Wisconsin M
Creighton University D*
Dalhousie University M
Dominican College M
Dominican University of California M
Duquesne University M,D*
D'Youville College M*
East Carolina University M
Eastern Kentucky University M
Eastern Michigan University M
Eastern Washington University M
Florida Gulf Coast University M
Florida International University M*
Gannon University M
Governors State University M
Grand Valley State University M
Husson University M
Idaho State University M
Indiana University–Purdue University Indianapolis M,D*
Ithaca College M
James Madison University M
Jefferson College of Health Sciences M
Kean University M
Keuka College M
Lenoir-Rhyne University M
Loma Linda University M,D
Louisiana State University Health Sciences Center M*
Maryville University of Saint Louis M
McMaster University M
Medical University of South Carolina M
Mercy College M
Midwestern University, Downers Grove Campus M*
Midwestern University, Glendale Campus M*
Milligan College M
Misericordia University M,D
Mount Mary College M
New York Institute of Technology M
New York University M,D*
Nova Southeastern University M,D*
The Ohio State University M*
Pacific University M
Philadelphia University M
Queen's University at Kingston M,D
Quinnipiac University M*
The Richard Stockton College of New Jersey M
Rockhurst University M
Rush University M
Sacred Heart University M
Sage Graduate School M
Saginaw Valley State University M
St. Ambrose University M
St. Catherine University M
Saint Francis University M
Saint Louis University M
Salem State College M
Samuel Merritt University M
San Jose State University M
Seton Hall University M*
Shenandoah University M
Spalding University M
Springfield College M,O
Stony Brook University, State University of New York M,D,O
Temple University M*
Texas Tech University Health Sciences Center M
Texas Woman's University M,D
Thomas Jefferson University M*
Touro College M
Towson University M
Tufts University M,D,O*
University at Buffalo, the State University of New York M*
The University of Alabama at Birmingham M*
University of Alberta M,D*
The University of British Columbia M
University of Central Arkansas M
The University of Findlay M
University of Florida M*
University of Illinois at Chicago M,D*
University of Indianapolis M,D
The University of Kansas M,D*
University of Manitoba M,D
University of Mary M
University of Mississippi Medical Center M*
University of Missouri–Columbia M*
University of New England M
University of New Hampshire M,O*
University of New Mexico M*
The University of North Carolina at Chapel Hill M,D*
University of North Dakota M
University of Oklahoma Health Sciences Center M
University of Pittsburgh M*
University of Puerto Rico, Medical Sciences Campus M
University of Puget Sound M
University of St. Augustine for Health Sciences M,D
The University of Scranton M
University of South Alabama M*
The University of South Dakota M
University of Southern California M,D*
University of Southern Indiana M
University of Southern Maine M
The University of Texas at El Paso M
The University of Texas Health Science Center at San Antonio M
The University of Texas Medical Branch M*
The University of Texas–Pan American M
The University of Toledo D
University of Utah M*
University of Washington M,D*
The University of Western Ontario M
University of Wisconsin–La Crosse M
University of Wisconsin–Madison M,D*
University of Wisconsin–Milwaukee M,O
Utica College M
Virginia Commonwealth University M,D
Washington University in St. Louis M,D*
Wayne State University M*
Western Michigan University M*
West Virginia University M
Winston-Salem State University M
Worcester State College M
Xavier University M*

OCEAN ENGINEERING

Florida Atlantic University M,D
Florida Institute of Technology M,D*
Georgia Institute of Technology M,D*
Massachusetts Institute of Technology M,D,O*
Memorial University of Newfoundland M,D
OGI School of Science & Engineering at Oregon Health & Science University M,D
Oregon State University M,D*
Princeton University D*
Stevens Institute of Technology M,D
Texas A&M University M,D*
University of Alaska Anchorage M,O
University of California, San Diego M,D*
University of Delaware M,D*
University of Florida M,D,O*
University of Hawaii at Manoa M,D*
University of Michigan M,D,O*
University of New Hampshire M,D,O*
University of Rhode Island M,D
Virginia Polytechnic Institute and State University M,D*
Woods Hole Oceanographic Institution M,D,O

OCEANOGRAPHY

Columbia University M,D*
Cornell University D*
Dalhousie University M,D
Florida Institute of Technology M,D*
Florida State University M,D*
Louisiana State University and Agricultural and Mechanical College M,D
Massachusetts Institute of Technology M,D,O*
McGill University M,D*
Memorial University of Newfoundland M,D
Naval Postgraduate School M,D
North Carolina State University M,D*
Nova Southeastern University M,D*
Old Dominion University M,D
Oregon State University M,D*
Princeton University D*
Rutgers, The State University of New Jersey, New Brunswick M,D*
Texas A&M University M,D*
Université du Québec à Rimouski M,D
Université Laval D
University of Alaska Fairbanks M,D
The University of British Columbia M,D
University of California, San Diego M,D*
University of Colorado at Boulder M,D*
University of Connecticut M,D*
University of Delaware M,D*
University of Georgia M,D*
University of Hawaii at Manoa M,D*
University of Maine M,D*
University of Maryland, College Park M,D*
University of Miami M,D*
University of Michigan M,D*
University of New Hampshire M,D,O*
University of Rhode Island M,D
University of South Florida M,D*
University of Victoria M,D
University of Washington M,D*
University of Wisconsin–Madison M,D*
Woods Hole Oceanographic Institution M,D,O
Yale University D*

ONCOLOGY NURSING

Columbia University M,O*
Duke University M,D,O*
Emory University M*
Goldfarb School of Nursing at Barnes-Jewish College M
Gwynedd-Mercy College M
Loyola University Chicago M,O*
University of Delaware M,O*
University of Pennsylvania M*

OPERATIONS RESEARCH

Air Force Institute of Technology M,D
Bowling Green State University M*
California State University, East Bay M
Carnegie Mellon University D*
Case Western Reserve University M*
Claremont Graduate University M,D*
Clemson University M,D
The College of William and Mary M
Columbia University M,D,O*
Cornell University M,D*
École Polytechnique de Montréal M,D,O

Florida Institute of Technology	M,D*
George Mason University	M*
Georgia Institute of Technology	M,D*
Georgia State University	M,D
Idaho State University	M
Indiana University–Purdue University Fort Wayne	M,O
Iowa State University of Science and Technology	M,D*
The Johns Hopkins University	M,D*
Kansas State University	M,D*
Massachusetts Institute of Technology	M,D*
Miami University	M*
Naval Postgraduate School	M,D
New Mexico Institute of Mining and Technology	M,D
North Carolina State University	M,D*
North Dakota State University	M,D,O
Northeastern University	M,D*
Northwestern University	M,D*
Oregon State University	M,D*
Penn State University Park	M,D*
Princeton University	M,D*
Rutgers, The State University of New Jersey, New Brunswick	D*
St. Mary's University (United States)	M
Southern Methodist University	M,D*
The University of Alabama in Huntsville	M
University of Arkansas	M
The University of British Columbia	M
University of California, Berkeley	M,D*
University of Central Florida	M,D,O*
University of Colorado at Boulder	M*
University of Delaware	M,D*
University of Illinois at Chicago	D*
The University of Iowa	M,D*
University of Massachusetts Amherst	M,D*
University of Michigan	M,D*
The University of North Carolina at Chapel Hill	M,D*
University of Southern California	M,D,O*
The University of Texas at Austin	M,D
University of Waterloo	M,D
Virginia Commonwealth University	M,O
Virginia Polytechnic Institute and State University	M,D*

OPTICAL SCIENCES

Air Force Institute of Technology	M,D
Alabama Agricultural and Mechanical University	M,D
The Catholic University of America	M,D
Cleveland State University	M
Delaware State University	M,D
École Polytechnique de Montréal	M,D,O
Norfolk State University	M
North Carolina Agricultural and Technical State University	M,D
The Ohio State University	M,D*
Rochester Institute of Technology	M,D
Rose-Hulman Institute of Technology	M*
The University of Alabama in Huntsville	M,D
The University of Arizona	M,D*
University of Central Florida	M,D*
University of Colorado at Boulder	M,D*
University of Dayton	M,D
University of Maryland, Baltimore County	M,D*
University of Massachusetts Lowell	M,D
University of New Mexico	M,D*
The University of North Carolina at Charlotte	M,D*
University of Rochester	M,D*

OPTOMETRY

Ferris State University	P
Illinois College of Optometry	P
Indiana University Bloomington	P,M,D*
Inter American University of Puerto Rico School of Optometry	P
The New England College of Optometry	P,M
Northeastern State University	P
Nova Southeastern University	P,M*
The Ohio State University	P*
Salus University	P
Southern California College of Optometry	P
Southern College of Optometry	P
State University of New York College of Optometry	P
Université de Montréal	P,O
The University of Alabama at Birmingham	P*
University of California, Berkeley	P,O*
University of Houston	P*
University of Missouri–St. Louis	P
University of the Incarnate Word	P
University of Waterloo	M,D
Western University of Health Sciences	P

ORAL AND DENTAL SCIENCES

A.T. Still University of Health Sciences	P,O
Boston University	P,M,D,O*
Case Western Reserve University	M,O*
Columbia University	M,D,O*
Dalhousie University	
Harvard University	M,D,O*
Howard University	P,O
Idaho State University	O
Jacksonville University	O
Loma Linda University	M,O
Marquette University	M
McGill University	M,D,O*
Medical College of Georgia	M,D
New York University	M,D,O*
The Ohio State University	D*
Oregon Health & Science University	P,M,O*
Saint Louis University	M
Stony Brook University, State University of New York	P,M,D,O
Temple University	M,O*
Texas A&M Health Science Center	P,M,D,O
Tufts University	M,O*
Université de Montréal	M,O
Université Laval	M,O
University at Buffalo, the State University of New York	M,D,O*
The University of Alabama at Birmingham	M*
University of Alberta	M,D*
The University of British Columbia	M,D,O
University of California, Los Angeles	M,D*
University of California, San Francisco	M,D
University of Connecticut	M*
University of Connecticut Health Center	M,D*
University of Detroit Mercy	M,O
University of Florida	M,D,O*
University of Illinois at Chicago	M,D*
The University of Iowa	M,D,O*
University of Kentucky	M
University of Louisville	M
University of Manitoba	M,D
University of Maryland, Baltimore	P,M,D,O*
University of Medicine and Dentistry of New Jersey	P,M,O*
University of Michigan	M,D*
University of Minnesota, Twin Cities Campus	M,D,O*
University of Mississippi Medical Center	M,D*
University of Missouri–Kansas City	P,M,D,O*
The University of North Carolina at Chapel Hill	M,D*
University of Oklahoma Health Sciences Center	M
University of Pittsburgh	M,O*
University of Puerto Rico, Medical Sciences Campus	M,O
University of Rochester	M*
University of Southern California	M,D,O*
The University of Tennessee Health Science Center	P,M,O*
The University of Texas Health Science Center at San Antonio	M,O
University of the Pacific	M,O
The University of Toledo	M
University of Toronto	M,D
University of Washington	P,M,O*
The University of Western Ontario	M
West Virginia University	M

ORGANIC CHEMISTRY

Auburn University	M,D*
Boston College	M,D*
Brandeis University	M,D
California State University, Los Angeles	M
Carnegie Mellon University	M,D*
Clarkson University	M,D*
Cleveland State University	M,D
Columbia University	M,D*
Cornell University	D*
Florida State University	M,D*
Georgetown University	D
The George Washington University	M,D*
Harvard University	D*
Howard University	M,D
Instituto Tecnológico y de Estudios Superiores de Monterrey, Campus Monterrey	M,D
Kansas State University	M,D*
Kent State University	M,D*
Laurentian University	M
Marquette University	M,D
Massachusetts College of Pharmacy and Health Sciences	M*
Massachusetts Institute of Technology	M,D,O*
McMaster University	M,D
Miami University	M,D*
Northeastern University	M,D*
Old Dominion University	M,D
Oregon State University	M,D*
Purdue University	M,D
Rensselaer Polytechnic Institute	M,D
Rice University	M,D
Rutgers, The State University of New Jersey, Newark	M,D*
Rutgers, The State University of New Jersey, New Brunswick	M,D*
Seton Hall University	M,D*
Southern University and Agricultural and Mechanical College	M
State University of New York at Binghamton	M,D*
State University of New York College of Environmental Science and Forestry	M,D
Stevens Institute of Technology	M,D,O
Tufts University	M,D*
University of Calgary	M,D
University of Cincinnati	M,D
University of Georgia	M,D*
University of Louisville	M,D
University of Maryland, College Park	M,D*
University of Massachusetts Lowell	M,D
University of Miami	M,D*
University of Michigan	D*
University of Missouri–Columbia	M,D*
University of Missouri–Kansas City	M,D*
University of Missouri–St. Louis	M,D
The University of Montana	M,D
University of Nebraska–Lincoln	M,D*
University of Notre Dame	M,D*
University of Regina	M,D
University of Southern Mississippi	M,D
University of South Florida	M,D*
The University of Tennessee	M,D
The University of Texas at Austin	M,D
The University of Toledo	M,D
Vanderbilt University	M,D*
Virginia Commonwealth University	M,D
Wake Forest University	M,D*
Wesleyan University	M,D*
West Virginia University	M,D
Yale University	D*
Youngstown State University	M

ORGANIZATIONAL BEHAVIOR

Amridge University	P,M,D
Benedictine University	M
Bernard M. Baruch College of the City University of New York	M,D
Boston College	D*
Boston University	D*
California Lutheran University	M,O
Carnegie Mellon University	D*
Case Western Reserve University	M*
Columbia College (SC)	M,O
Cornell University	M,D*
Drexel University	M,D,O*
Fairleigh Dickinson University, College at Florham	M,O*

*M—master's degree; P—first professional degree; D—doctorate; O—other advanced degree; *—Close-Up and/or Announcement or Display in one of the other books in this series*

Georgia Institute of Technology	M,D,O*
Graduate School and University Center of the City University of New York	D*
Harvard University	D*
John Jay College of Criminal Justice of the City University of New York	M,D
Leadership Institute of Seattle	M
Marylhurst University	M
New York University	M,D*
Northwestern University	M,D*
Oral Roberts University	M
Phillips Graduate Institute	M,D
Polytechnic Institute of NYU	M
Purdue University	D
Saybrook Graduate School and Research Center	M,D
Silver Lake College	M
Suffolk University	M,O*
Syracuse University	D*
Towson University	O
Universidad de las Americas, A.C.	M
Université de Sherbrooke	M
The University of British Columbia	D
University of California, Berkeley	D*
University of Hartford	M*
University of Hawaii at Manoa	M*
The University of North Carolina at Chapel Hill	D*
University of Oklahoma	M*
University of Pennsylvania	M*
University of Pittsburgh	M,D*
University of Saskatchewan	M
York University	M,D

ORGANIZATIONAL MANAGEMENT

Adler Graduate School	M,O
Alvernia University	D
The American College	M
American International College	M
American University	M*
Amridge University	P,M,D
Antioch University Los Angeles	M
Antioch University New England	M,O*
Antioch University Santa Barbara	M
Antioch University Seattle	M
Argosy University, Chicago	D*
Argosy University, Denver	M,D*
Argosy University, Hawai'i	D*
Argosy University, Los Angeles	M,D*
Argosy University, Orange County	D*
Argosy University, San Francisco Bay Area	M,D*
Argosy University, Sarasota	M,D,O*
Argosy University, Schaumburg	M,D,O*
Argosy University, Tampa	M,D*
Argosy University, Twin Cities	M,D,O*
Argosy University, Washington DC	M,D*
Athabasca University	M*
Augsburg College	M
Avila University	M,O
Azusa Pacific University	M
Beacon University	P,M
Benedictine University	M,D
Bernard M. Baruch College of the City University of New York	M,D
Bethel University	M
Biola University	M
Bluffton University	M
Boston College	D*
Bowling Green State University	M*
Brenau University	M
Briercrest Seminary	M
Cabrini College	M,O
California College of the Arts	M*
California Intercontinental University	M,D
Cambridge College	M
Capella University	M,D,O
Carlos Albizu University, Miami Campus	M,D
Carlow University	M
Charleston Southern University	M
City University of Seattle	M,O
Cleary University	M,O
College of Mount St. Joseph	M
Colorado State University	M*
Colorado Technical University Sioux Falls	M
Concordia University (MI)	M
Concordia University (Canada)	M
Concordia University, St. Paul	M
Cumberland University	M
Dominican University	M
Duquesne University	M*
Eastern Connecticut State University	M
Eastern Michigan University	M
Eastern University	M,D
Emory University	M,D*
Endicott College	M
Evangel University	M
Fairleigh Dickinson University, College at Florham	M,O*
Fielding Graduate University	M,D,O*
Gannon University	D
Geneva College	M
George Mason University	M*
The George Washington University	M,D*
Georgia State University	M,D
Gonzaga University	M
Grand Canyon University	M,D*
Grand View University	M
Harding University	M
Hawai'i Pacific University	M*
Immaculata University	M
Indiana Tech	M
Indiana University–Purdue University Fort Wayne	M
Indiana Wesleyan University	D
John F. Kennedy University	M,O
Johnson & Wales University	M
Jones International University	M
Judson University	M
Kaplan University–Davenport Campus	M
LaGrange College	M
Leadership Institute of Seattle	M
Lewis University	M
Lourdes College	M
Manhattanville College	M*
Marian University (WI)	M
Marymount University	M,O
Medaille College	M
Mercy College	M
Mercyhurst College	M,O
MidAmerica Nazarene University	M
Misericordia University	M
National University	M
New England College	M
Newman University	M
The New School: A University	M*
New York University	M,D*
North Carolina Agricultural and Technical State University	M,D
Northern Kentucky University	M
Northwestern University	M,D*
Norwich University	M
Nova Southeastern University	D*
Nyack College	M
Olivet Nazarene University	M
Our Lady of the Lake University of San Antonio	M,D
Oxford Graduate School	M,D
Palm Beach Atlantic University	M
Pepperdine University	M
Peru State College	M
Pfeiffer University	M
Philadelphia Biblical University	M
Point Park University	M*
Regent University	M,D,O
Regis College (MA)	M
Regis University	M,O
Rider University	M*
Rivier College	M
Robert Morris University	M,D
Roosevelt University	M,D
Rutgers, The State University of New Jersey, Newark	D*
Sage Graduate School	M
St. Ambrose University	M
St. Catherine University	M
St. Edward's University	M
St. Joseph's College, Long Island Campus	M,O
Saint Joseph's University	M,D,O
Saint Louis University	M,D,O
Saint Mary's University of Minnesota	M
Saybrook Graduate School and Research Center	M,D
Seattle University	M,O
Shippensburg University of Pennsylvania	M
SIT Graduate Institute	M
Southern New Hampshire University	M,D,O*
Southwestern College (KS)	M
Spring Arbor University	M
Springfield College	M
State University of New York College at Potsdam	M
Suffolk University	M,O*
Thomas Edison State College	O
Trevecca Nazarene University	M
Trinity (Washington) University	M
Trinity Western University	M,O
Tusculum College	M
Université Laval	M,O
University of Alberta	D*
University of Cincinnati	M
University of Colorado at Boulder	M,D*
University of Dallas	M
University of Denver	M,O*
University of Guelph	M
University of Hawaii at Manoa	M,D*
The University of Kansas	M,D,O*
University of La Verne	M,D,O
University of Maryland Eastern Shore	D*
University of Massachusetts Dartmouth	M,O
University of New Mexico	M*
University of Pennsylvania	M*
University of Phoenix	D
University of St. Thomas (MN)	M,D,O*
University of San Francisco	M
The University of Scranton	M
University of Southern California	M*
The University of Texas at San Antonio	M,D*
University of the Incarnate Word	M,D,O
Upper Iowa University	M
Vanderbilt University	M,D*
Walden University	M,D,O
Warner Pacific College	M
Wayland Baptist University	M
Wayne State College	M
Webster University	M
Western International University	M
Wheeling Jesuit University	M
Wilmington University	M
Woodbury University	M
Worcester Polytechnic Institute	M,O*
Worcester State College	M

OSTEOPATHIC MEDICINE

A.T. Still University of Health Sciences	P,M
Des Moines University	P
Edward Via Virginia College of Osteopathic Medicine	P
Georgia Campus–Philadelphia College of Osteopathic Medicine	P
Kansas City University of Medicine and Biosciences	P
Lake Erie College of Osteopathic Medicine	P,M,O
Lincoln Memorial University	P
Michigan State University	P*
Midwestern University, Downers Grove Campus	P*
Midwestern University, Glendale Campus	P*
New York Institute of Technology	P
Nova Southeastern University	P,M*
Ohio University	P*
Oklahoma State University Center for Health Sciences	P
Philadelphia College of Osteopathic Medicine	P*
Pikeville College	P
Touro University	P,M
University of Medicine and Dentistry of New Jersey	P*
University of New England	P
University of North Texas Health Science Center at Fort Worth	P,M
Western University of Health Sciences	P
West Virginia School of Osteopathic Medicine	P

PACIFIC AREA/PACIFIC RIM STUDIES

University of California, San Diego	M,D*
University of Guam	M
University of Hawaii at Manoa	M,O*

University of San Francisco	M
University of Victoria	M

PALEONTOLOGY

Cornell University	M,D*
Duke University	D*
South Dakota School of Mines and Technology	M*
University of Chicago	M,D*
The University of Texas at Dallas	M,D*
West Virginia University	M,D
Yale University	D*

PAPER AND PULP ENGINEERING

Miami University	M*
North Carolina State University	M,D*
Oregon State University	M,D*
State University of New York College of Environmental Science and Forestry	M,D
Western Michigan University	M,D*

PARASITOLOGY

Illinois State University	M,D
Louisiana State University Health Sciences Center	M,D*
McGill University	M,D,O*
New York University	P,M,D*
Texas A&M University	M,D*
Tulane University	M,D,O
University of Notre Dame	M,D*
University of Pennsylvania	D*
University of Prince Edward Island	M,D
University of Washington	D*
Yale University	D*

PASTORAL MINISTRY AND COUNSELING

Abilene Christian University	M,D
Alliance Theological Seminary	P,M
Ambrose University College	P,M,O
American Baptist Seminary of the West	P,M
Amridge University	P,M,D
Anderson University (SC)	M
Andrews University	P,M,D,O
Anna Maria College	M
Aquinas Institute of Theology	P,M,D,O
Argosy University, Sarasota	M,D,O*
Asbury Theological Seminary	M,D,O
Ashland Theological Seminary	P,M,D,O
Assemblies of God Theological Seminary	P,M,D
The Athenaeum of Ohio	P,M,O
Austin Presbyterian Theological Seminary	P,M,D
Ave Maria University	M,D
Azusa Pacific University	P,M
Bakke Graduate University	M,D
Baptist Bible College	P,M
Baptist Bible College of Pennsylvania	P,M,D
Baptist Theological Seminary at Richmond	P,D
Barry University	M,D*
Beacon University	P,M
Bethany Theological Seminary	P,M,O
Bethel College (IN)	M
Bethel Seminary	P,M,D,O
Biblical Theological Seminary	P,M,D,O
Bob Jones University	P,M,D,O
Boston College	P,M,D,O*
Briercrest Seminary	P,M
Caldwell College	M
California Baptist University	M
Calvary Bible College and Theological Seminary	P,M
Capital Bible Seminary	P,M,O
Cardinal Stritch University	M
Catholic Theological Union at Chicago	P,M,D,O
The Catholic University of America	P,M,D,O
Chaminade University of Honolulu	M
Chicago Theological Seminary	P,M,D
Christian Theological Seminary	P,M,D
Christ the King Seminary	P,M,O
Church of God Theological Seminary	P,M,D
Cincinnati Christian University	M
Claremont School of Theology	D
College of Mount St. Joseph	M
Columbia International University	P,M,D,O
Concordia University, Nebraska	M
Concordia University, St. Paul	M,O
The Criswell College	P,M
Dallas Baptist University	M
Dallas Theological Seminary	M,D,O
Denver Seminary	P,M,D,O
Eastern Mennonite University	P,M,O
Eastern University	D
Ecumenical Theological Seminary	D
Emmanuel School of Religion	P,M,D
Faith Baptist Bible College and Theological Seminary	P,M
Fordham University	M,D,O*
Freed-Hardeman University	M
Fuller Theological Seminary	P,M,D
Gannon University	M,O
Gardner-Webb University	P,D
Garrett-Evangelical Theological Seminary	P,M,D
General Theological Seminary	P,M,D,O
George Fox University	P,M,D,O*
Georgian Court University	M,O
Golden Gate Baptist Theological Seminary	P,M,D,O
Gonzaga University	M
Gordon-Conwell Theological Seminary	P,M,D
Graceland University (IA)	M
Grace Theological Seminary	P,M,D,O
Grace University	M
Grand Rapids Theological Seminary of Cornerstone University	P,M
Greenville College	M
Hampton University	M
Harding University	M
Harding University Graduate School of Religion	P,M,D
Hardin-Simmons University	M
Hartford Seminary	M,D,O
Heritage Baptist College and Heritage Theological Seminary	P,M,D,O
Heritage Christian University	M
Hillsdale Free Will Baptist College	M
Holmes Institute	M
Holy Names University	M,O
Houston Baptist University	M
Houston Graduate School of Theology	P,M,D
Huntington University	M
Iliff School of Theology	P,M,D
Indiana Wesleyan University	M
Inter American University of Puerto Rico, Metropolitan Campus	D
International Baptist College	M,D
Iona College	M,O*
Jewish University of America	M,D
John Brown University	M
Knox Theological Seminary	D
Lancaster Bible College	M
La Salle University	M
La Sierra University	P,M
Liberty University	M,D
Lincoln Christian Seminary	P,M,D
Loma Linda University	M,O
Loras College	M
Loyola Marymount University	M
Loyola University Chicago	M,O*
Loyola University Maryland	M,D,O*
Lutheran School of Theology at Chicago	P,M,D
Lutheran Theological Seminary	P,M,D
Lutheran Theological Seminary at Gettysburg	P,M,D
The Lutheran Theological Seminary at Philadelphia	P,M,D,O
Luther Rice University	P,M,D
Madonna University	M
Malone University	M
Maple Springs Baptist Bible College and Seminary	P,M,D,O
Maranatha Baptist Bible College	M
Martin University	M
Marymount University	M,O
The Master's College and Seminary	P,M,D
McCormick Theological Seminary	P,M,D,O
McMaster University	P,M,D,O
Meadville Lombard Theological School	P,M,D
Mennonite Brethren Biblical Seminary	M
Midwestern Baptist Theological Seminary	P,M,D,O
Missouri Baptist University	M,O
Moody Bible Institute	P,M,O
Mount Marty College	M
Neumann University	M,O
New Brunswick Theological Seminary	D
New Orleans Baptist Theological Seminary	P,M,D
The Nigerian Baptist Theological Seminary	P,M,D,O
Northern Baptist Theological Seminary	P,M,D
North Greenville University	M
North Park Theological Seminary	M,O
Northwest Nazarene University	P,M
Notre Dame College (OH)	M,O
Oakwood University	M
Oblate School of Theology	P,M,D,O
Oklahoma Christian University	P,M
Oral Roberts University	P,M,D
Ottawa University	M
Philadelphia Biblical University	M
Phillips Theological Seminary	D
Providence College and Theological Seminary	P,M,D,O
Reformed Theological Seminary–Charlotte Campus	P,M,D
Reformed Theological Seminary–Jackson Campus	P,M,D,O
Reformed Theological Seminary–Orlando Campus	P,M,D
Regent University	P,M,D
Regis College (Canada)	P,M,D,O
Roberts Wesleyan College	M
Sacred Heart Major Seminary	P,M
St. Ambrose University	M
St. Augustine's Seminary of Toronto	P,M,O
Saint Bernard's School of Theology and Ministry	P,M,O
Saint Francis Seminary	P,M
St. John's Seminary (CA)	P,M
Saint John's University (MN)	P,M
St. John's University (NY)	P,M,O
Saint Leo University	M
Saint Mary-of-the-Woods College	M,O
St. Mary's University (United States)	M
Saint Mary's University of Minnesota	M,O
Saint Paul University	M,D,O
St. Petersburg Theological Seminary	P,M,D
Saints Cyril and Methodius Seminary	P,M
St. Stephen's College	M,D
St. Thomas University	M,D,O
Santa Clara University	M
Seattle University	M
Seminary of the Immaculate Conception	P,M,D,O
Seminary of the Southwest	P,M,O
Seton Hall University	P,M*
Shasta Bible College	M
Simpson University	P,M
Sioux Falls Seminary	P,M
Southern Baptist Theological Seminary	P,M,D
Southern Evangelical Seminary	P,M,O
Southern Wesleyan University	M
Southwestern Assemblies of God University	P,M
Southwestern Christian University	M
Southwestern College (KS)	M
Spring Arbor University	M
Trinity Baptist College	M
Trinity Episcopal School for Ministry	P,M,D,O
Trinity International University	P,M,D,O
Trinity Western University	P,M,D
Tyndale University College & Seminary	P,M,O
Union University	M,D
United Theological Seminary of the Twin Cities	P,M,D,O
University of Dallas	M
University of Dayton	M,D
University of Portland	M
University of Puget Sound	M
University of Saint Francis (IN)	M
University of St. Michael's College	P,M,D,O

*M—master's degree; P—first professional degree; D—doctorate; O—other advanced degree; *—Close-Up and/or Announcement or Display in one of the other books in this series*

University of St. Thomas (MN) M*
University of South Africa M,D
University of Trinity College P,M,D,O
Warner Pacific College M
Wayland Baptist University M
Wesley Biblical Seminary P,M
Western Seminary P,M,D,O
Western Seminary–Sacramento Campus P,M
Western Seminary–San Jose Campus P,M
Westminster Theological Seminary P,M,D,O
Wheaton College M,D
Wilfrid Laurier University P,M,D,O
Xavier University of Louisiana M

PATHOBIOLOGY

Auburn University M,D*
Brown University M,D*
Columbia University M,D*
Drexel University M,D*
The Johns Hopkins University D*
Kansas State University M,D*
Medical University of South Carolina M,D
Michigan State University M,D*
New York University P,M,D*
The Ohio State University M,D*
Penn State University Park D*
Purdue University M,D
Texas A&M University M,D*
The University of Arizona M,D*
University of Cincinnati D
University of Connecticut M,D*
University of Illinois at Urbana–Champaign M,D*
University of Missouri–Columbia M,D*
University of Southern California M,D*
University of Toronto M,D
University of Washington D*
University of Wyoming M
Wake Forest University M,D*
Yale University D*

PATHOLOGY

Albert Einstein College of Medicine D
Baylor College of Medicine D*
Brown University M,D*
Case Western Reserve University M,D*
Colorado State University M,D*
Columbia University M,D*
Dalhousie University M,D
Duke University M,D*
East Carolina University D
Georgetown University M,D
Harvard University D*
Indiana University–Purdue University Indianapolis M,D*
Iowa State University of Science and Technology M,D*
The Johns Hopkins University D*
Loma Linda University M,D
Louisiana State University Health Sciences Center M,D*
McGill University M,D*
Medical College of Wisconsin M,D*
Medical University of South Carolina M,D
Michigan State University M,D*
New York Medical College M,D*
North Carolina State University M,D*
North Dakota State University M,D
The Ohio State University M*
Purdue University M,D
Queen's University at Kingston M,D
Quinnipiac University M*
Rosalind Franklin University of Medicine and Science M*
Saint Louis University D
Stony Brook University, State University of New York M,D
Temple University D*
Texas A&M University M,D*
Université de Montréal M,D
Université Laval O
University at Buffalo, the State University of New York M,D*
The University of Alabama at Birmingham D*
University of Alberta M,D*
University of Arkansas for Medical Sciences M
The University of British Columbia M,D
University of California, Davis M,D*
University of California, Los Angeles M,D*
University of California, San Francisco D
University of Chicago D*
University of Cincinnati D
University of Colorado Denver D*
University of Florida D*
University of Georgia M,D*
University of Guelph M,D,O
The University of Iowa M*
The University of Kansas M,D*
University of Manitoba M
University of Maryland, Baltimore M*
University of Massachusetts Lowell M,O
University of Medicine and Dentistry of New Jersey D*
University of Michigan D*
University of Mississippi Medical Center M,D*
University of Missouri–Columbia M*
University of Nebraska Medical Center M,D*
University of New Mexico M,D*
The University of North Carolina at Chapel Hill D*
University of Oklahoma Health Sciences Center D
University of Pittsburgh M,D*
University of Prince Edward Island M,D
University of Rochester M,D*
University of Saskatchewan M,D
University of Southern California M,D*
University of South Florida M,D*
The University of Texas Medical Branch D*
The University of Toledo O
University of Utah M,D*
University of Vermont M*
University of Virginia D
University of Washington D*
The University of Western Ontario M,D
University of Wisconsin–Madison D*
Vanderbilt University D*
Virginia Commonwealth University M,D
Wayne State University M,D*
Yale University M,D*

PEDIATRIC NURSING

Caribbean University M,D
Case Western Reserve University M,D*
The Catholic University of America M,D,O
Columbia University M,O*
Duke University M,D,O*
Emory University M*
Georgia State University M,D,O
Gwynedd-Mercy College M
Hampton University M
Indiana University–Purdue University Indianapolis M,D*
The Johns Hopkins University M,O*
Kent State University M,D*
Lehman College of the City University of New York M
Loma Linda University M
Marquette University M,D,O
Medical College of Georgia M
MGH Institute of Health Professions M,D,O*
Molloy College M,O
New York University M,O*
Queen's University at Kingston M,D,O
Rush University M,D,O
Seton Hall University M*
Spalding University M
Stony Brook University, State University of New York M,O
Texas Tech University Health Sciences Center M,D,O
Texas Woman's University M,D
University at Buffalo, the State University of New York M,D,O*
University of Central Florida M,D,O*
University of Cincinnati M,D
University of Colorado Denver M*
University of Delaware M,O*
University of Illinois at Chicago M*
University of Maryland, Baltimore M*
University of Michigan M,O*
University of Minnesota, Twin Cities Campus M*
University of Missouri–Kansas City M,D*
The University of North Carolina at Chapel Hill M,D,O*
University of Pennsylvania M*
University of Pittsburgh M,D*
University of Rochester M,D,O*
University of San Diego M,D
University of South Carolina M
The University of Texas–Pan American M
The University of Toledo M,O
Vanderbilt University M,D*
Villanova University M,D,O*
Virginia Commonwealth University M,D,O
Wayne State University M,O*
Wright State University M

PERFUSION

Long Island University, C.W. Post Campus M
Milwaukee School of Engineering M*
Quinnipiac University M*
The University of Arizona M,D*
University of Nebraska Medical Center M*

PETROLEUM ENGINEERING

Colorado School of Mines M,D
Louisiana State University and Agricultural and Mechanical College M,D
Missouri University of Science and Technology M,D
Montana Tech of The University of Montana M
New Mexico Institute of Mining and Technology M,D
Stanford University M,D,O*
Texas A&M University M,D*
Texas A&M University–Kingsville M
Texas Tech University M,D
University of Alaska Fairbanks M,D
University of Alberta M,D*
University of Calgary M,D
University of Houston M,D*
The University of Kansas M,D*
University of Louisiana at Lafayette M*
University of Oklahoma M,D*
University of Pittsburgh M,D*
University of Regina M,D
University of Southern California M,D,O*
The University of Texas at Austin M,D
University of Tulsa M,D*
University of Wyoming M,D
West Virginia University M,D

PHARMACEUTICAL ADMINISTRATION

Duquesne University M*
Fairleigh Dickinson University, Metropolitan Campus M,O*
Florida Agricultural and Mechanical University M,D
Idaho State University P,M,D
Long Island University, Brooklyn Campus M
The Ohio State University M,D*
Purdue University M,D,O
St. John's University (NY) M
San Diego State University M*
Seton Hall University M*
Temple University M*
University of Arkansas for Medical Sciences M
University of Florida M,D*
University of Houston P,M,D*
University of Illinois at Chicago M,D*
University of Maryland, Baltimore M,D*
University of Michigan D*
University of Minnesota, Twin Cities Campus M,D*
University of Mississippi M,D
University of the Sciences in Philadelphia M*
The University of Toledo M
University of West Florida M
University of Wisconsin–Madison M,D*
Wayne State University P,M,D,O*
West Virginia University M,D

PHARMACEUTICAL ENGINEERING

New Jersey Institute of Technology M
University of Michigan M*

PHARMACEUTICAL SCIENCES

Auburn University M,D*
Boston University M,D*
Butler University P,M
Campbell University P,M
Creighton University M,D*
Dartmouth College D*
Drake University P*
Duquesne University M,D*
Florida Agricultural and Mechanical University M,D
Idaho State University M,D
The Johns Hopkins University M*

Long Island University, Brooklyn Campus	M,D
Long Island University, Rockland Graduate Campus	M
Massachusetts College of Pharmacy and Health Sciences	M,D*
Medical University of South Carolina	D
Memorial University of Newfoundland	M,D
Mercer University	P,M,D
North Dakota State University	M,D
Northeastern University	P,M,D*
The Ohio State University	M,D*
Oregon State University	P,M,D*
Purdue University	M,D
Queen's University at Kingston	M,D
Rush University	M,D
Rutgers, The State University of New Jersey, New Brunswick	M,D*
St. John's University (NY)	M,D
South Dakota State University	M,D
Stevens Institute of Technology	M,O
Temple University	M,D*
Texas Tech University Health Sciences Center	M,D
Université de Montréal	M,D,O
Université Laval	M,D,O
University at Buffalo, the State University of New York	M,D*
University of Alberta	M,D*
The University of Arizona	M,D*
University of Arkansas for Medical Sciences	M
The University of British Columbia	P,M,D
University of California, San Francisco	D
University of Cincinnati	M,D
University of Colorado Denver	P*
University of Connecticut	M,D*
University of Florida	D*
University of Georgia	M,D,O*
University of Houston	P,M,D*
University of Illinois at Chicago	M,D*
The University of Kansas	M*
University of Kentucky	M,D
University of Louisiana at Monroe	M
University of Manitoba	M,D
University of Maryland, Baltimore	D*
University of Michigan	D*
University of Minnesota, Twin Cities Campus	M,D*
University of Mississippi	M,D
University of Missouri–Kansas City	P,M,D*
The University of Montana	M,D
University of Nebraska Medical Center	M,D*
University of New Mexico	M,D*
The University of North Carolina at Chapel Hill	M,D*
University of Oklahoma Health Sciences Center	M,D
University of Pittsburgh	M,D*
University of Puerto Rico, Medical Sciences Campus	P,M
University of Rhode Island	M,D
University of Saskatchewan	M,D
University of South Carolina	M,D
University of Southern California	M,D*
The University of Tennessee Health Science Center	M,D*
The University of Texas at Austin	M,D
University of the Pacific	M,D
University of the Sciences in Philadelphia	M,D*
The University of Toledo	M
University of Toronto	M,D
University of Utah	M*
University of Washington	M,D*
University of Wisconsin–Madison	M,D*
Virginia Commonwealth University	P,M,D
Wayne State University	P,M,D,O*
Western University of Health Sciences	M
West Virginia University	M,D

PHARMACOLOGY

Albany Medical College	M,D
Alliant International University–San Francisco	M*
American University of Beirut	P,M
Argosy University, Hawai'i	M,O*
Auburn University	M,D*
Baylor College of Medicine	D*
Boston University	M,D*
Case Western Reserve University	D*
Columbia University	M,D*
Cornell University	M,D*
Cornell University, Joan and Sanford I. Weill Medical College and Graduate School of Medical Sciences	M,D
Creighton University	M,D*
Dalhousie University	M,D
Dartmouth College	D*
Drexel University	M,D*
Duke University	D*
Duquesne University	M,D*
East Carolina University	D
East Tennessee State University	M,D
Emory University	D*
Fairleigh Dickinson University, College at Florham	M,O*
Florida Agricultural and Mechanical University	M,D
Georgetown University	M,D
Howard University	M,D
Idaho State University	M,D
Indiana University–Purdue University Indianapolis	M,D*
The Johns Hopkins University	D*
Kent State University	M,D*
Loma Linda University	M,D
Long Island University, Brooklyn Campus	M,D
Louisiana State University Health Sciences Center	M,D*
Louisiana State University Health Sciences Center at Shreveport	D*
Loyola University Chicago	M,D*
Massachusetts College of Pharmacy and Health Sciences	M,D*
McGill University	M,D*
McMaster University	M,D
Medical College of Georgia	D
Medical College of Wisconsin	D*
Meharry Medical College	D
Michigan State University	M,D*
New York Medical College	M,D*
New York University	P,M,D*
North Carolina State University	M,D*
Northeastern University	M,D*
Northwestern University	D*
Nova Southeastern University	M*
The Ohio State University	M,D*
Oregon Health & Science University	D*
Penn State Hershey Medical Center	M,D
Purdue University	M,D
Queen's University at Kingston	M,D
Rush University	M,D
Saint Louis University	D
Southern Illinois University Carbondale	M,D*
State University of New York Upstate Medical University	D
Stony Brook University, State University of New York	D
Temple University	M,D*
Texas Tech University Health Sciences Center	M,D
Thomas Jefferson University	M*
Tufts University	D*
Tulane University	M,D
Universidad Central del Caribe	M
Université de Montréal	M,D
Université de Sherbrooke	M,D
University at Buffalo, the State University of New York	M,D*
The University of Alabama at Birmingham	D*
University of Alberta	M,D*
The University of Arizona	M,D*
University of Arkansas for Medical Sciences	M,D
The University of British Columbia	M,D
University of California, Davis	M,D*
University of California, Irvine	M,D*
University of California, Los Angeles	D*
University of California, San Diego	D*
University of California, San Francisco	D
University of Chicago	D*
University of Cincinnati	D
University of Colorado Denver	D*
University of Connecticut	M,D*
University of Florida	M,D*
University of Georgia	M,D*
University of Guelph	M,D
University of Houston	P,M,D*
University of Illinois at Chicago	D*
The University of Iowa	M,D*
The University of Kansas	M,D*
University of Kentucky	D
University of Louisville	M,D
University of Manitoba	M,D
University of Maryland, Baltimore	M,D*
University of Medicine and Dentistry of New Jersey	D*
University of Miami	D*
University of Michigan	D*
University of Minnesota, Duluth	M,D
University of Minnesota, Twin Cities Campus	M,D*
University of Mississippi	M,D
University of Mississippi Medical Center	M,D*
University of Missouri–Columbia	M,D*
University of Nebraska Medical Center	M,D*
The University of North Carolina at Chapel Hill	D*
University of North Dakota	M,D
University of North Texas Health Science Center at Fort Worth	M,D
University of Pennsylvania	D*
University of Prince Edward Island	M,D
University of Puerto Rico, Medical Sciences Campus	M,D
University of Rhode Island	M,D
University of Rochester	M,D*
University of Saskatchewan	M,D
University of South Alabama	D*
The University of South Dakota	M,D
University of South Florida	M,D*
The University of Texas Health Science Center at San Antonio	D
The University of Texas Medical Branch	M,D*
University of the Sciences in Philadelphia	M,D*
The University of Toledo	M
University of Toronto	M,D
University of Utah	D*
University of Vermont	M,D*
University of Virginia	D
University of Washington	D*
University of Wisconsin–Madison	D*
Vanderbilt University	D*
Virginia Commonwealth University	M,D,O
Wake Forest University	D*
Washington State University	M,D*
Wayne State University	P,M,D*
West Virginia University	M,D
Wright State University	M
Yale University	D*

PHARMACY

Albany College of Pharmacy and Health Sciences	P,M
Auburn University	P*
Belmont University	P
Butler University	P,M
Campbell University	P,M
Creighton University	P*
Drake University	P*
Duquesne University	P*
Ferris State University	P
Florida Agricultural and Mechanical University	P,D
Harding University	P
Howard University	P
Idaho State University	P,M,D
Lake Erie College of Osteopathic Medicine	P,M,O
Lebanese American University	P
Lipscomb University	P
Loma Linda University	P
Massachusetts College of Pharmacy and Health Sciences	P*
Medical University of South Carolina	P
Mercer University	P,M,D
Midwestern University, Downers Grove Campus	P*
Midwestern University, Glendale Campus	P*
Northeastern Ohio Universities College of Medicine and Pharmacy	P
Nova Southeastern University	P*
Ohio Northern University	P
The Ohio State University	P*
Oregon State University	P,M,D*
Pacific University	P
Palm Beach Atlantic University	P

*M—master's degree; P—first professional degree; D—doctorate; O—other advanced degree; *—Close-Up and/or Announcement or Display in one of the other books in this series*

Purdue University	P
Regis University	P,M,D,O
Rutgers, The State University of New Jersey, New Brunswick	P,M,D*
St. John Fisher College	P
St. John's University (NY)	P
St. Louis College of Pharmacy	P
Samford University	P
Shenandoah University	P
South Dakota State University	P
Southern Illinois University Edwardsville	P
South University (GA)	P*
Southwestern Oklahoma State University	P
Temple University	P*
Texas Southern University	P,M,D
Thomas Jefferson University	P*
Touro University	P,M
Universidad de Ciencias Medicas	P,M,O
University at Buffalo, the State University of New York	P*
University of Alberta	M,D*
The University of Arizona	P*
University of Arkansas for Medical Sciences	P,M
The University of British Columbia	P,M,D
University of California, San Diego	P*
University of California, San Francisco	P
University of Charleston	P
University of Cincinnati	P
University of Colorado Denver	P,D*
University of Connecticut	P*
The University of Findlay	P
University of Florida	P*
University of Georgia	P*
University of Houston	P,M,D*
University of Illinois at Chicago	P,D*
The University of Iowa	M,D*
University of Kentucky	P
University of Louisiana at Monroe	P,D
University of Maryland, Baltimore	P,M,D*
University of Michigan	P*
University of Minnesota, Twin Cities Campus	P,M,D*
University of Mississippi	P
University of Missouri–Kansas City	P,M,D*
The University of Montana	P,M,D
University of Nebraska Medical Center	P*
University of New Mexico	P*
University of Oklahoma Health Sciences Center	P
University of Pittsburgh	P*
University of Puerto Rico, Medical Sciences Campus	P,M
University of Rhode Island	M,D
University of South Carolina	P
University of Southern California	P*
University of Southern Nevada	P
The University of Tennessee Health Science Center	P,M,D*
The University of Texas at Austin	P
University of the Incarnate Word	P
University of the Pacific	P
University of Utah	P*
University of Washington	P,M,D*
University of Wisconsin–Madison	P*
University of Wyoming	P
Virginia Commonwealth University	P
Washington State University	P*
Washington State University Spokane	P
Wayne State University	P,M,D,O*
Western University of Health Sciences	P
West Virginia University	P,M,D
Wilkes University	P
Wingate University	P
Xavier University of Louisiana	P

PHILANTHROPIC STUDIES

Indiana University–Purdue University Indianapolis	M,D*
Saint Mary's University of Minnesota	M

PHILOSOPHY

American University	M*
American University of Beirut	M
Arizona State University	M,D
Baylor University	M,D
Boston College	M,D*
Boston University	M,D*
Bowling Green State University	M,D*
Brandeis University	M
Brock University	M
Brown University	M,D*
California Institute of Integral Studies	M,D*
California State University, Long Beach	M
California State University, Los Angeles	M
Carleton University	M
Carnegie Mellon University	M,D*
The Catholic University of America	M,D,O
Central European University	M,D*
Claremont Graduate University	M,D*
Cleveland State University	M,O
Collège Dominicain de Philosophie et de Théologie	M,D
College of the Humanities and Sciences, Harrison Middleton University	M,D
Colorado State University	M*
Columbia University	M,D*
Concordia University (Canada)	M
Cornell University	D*
Dalhousie University	M,D
DePaul University	M,D*
Dominican School of Philosophy and Theology	M
Duke University	M,D*
Duquesne University	M,D*
Emory University	D,O*
Florida State University	M,D*
Fordham University	M,D*
Franciscan University of Steubenville	M
George Mason University	M*
Georgetown University	M,D
The George Washington University	M,D*
Georgia State University	M
Gonzaga University	M
Graduate School and University Center of the City University of New York	M,D*
Harvard University	M,D*
Howard University	M
Indiana University Bloomington	M,D*
Indiana University–Purdue University Indianapolis	M,O*
Institute for Christian Studies	M,D
The Johns Hopkins University	M,D*
Kent State University	M*
Louisiana State University and Agricultural and Mechanical College	M
Loyola Marymount University	M
Loyola University Chicago	M,D*
Marquette University	M,D
Massachusetts Institute of Technology	D*
McGill University	M,D*
McMaster University	M,D
Memorial University of Newfoundland	M
Miami University	M*
Michigan State University	M,D*
Montclair State University	M,D,O*
The New School: A University	M,D*
New York University	M,D*
Northern Illinois University	M
Northwestern University	D*
The Ohio State University	M,D*
Ohio University	M*
Oklahoma City University	M
Oklahoma State University	M*
Oregon State University	M*
Penn State University Park	M,D*
Princeton University	D*
Purdue University	M,D
Queen's University at Kingston	M,D
Rice University	M,D
Rutgers, The State University of New Jersey, New Brunswick	D*
St. John's University (NY)	M
Saint Louis University	M,D
Saint Mary's University (Canada)	M
San Diego State University	M*
San Francisco State University	M,O
San Jose State University	M,O
Simon Fraser University	M,D
Southeastern Baptist Theological Seminary	P,M,D
Southern Baptist Theological Seminary	P,M,D
Southern Evangelical Seminary	M,D,O
Southern Illinois University Carbondale	M,D*
Stanford University	M,D*
State University of New York at Binghamton	M,D*
Stony Brook University, State University of New York	M,D
Syracuse University	M,D*
Temple University	M,D*
Texas A&M University	M,D*
Texas Tech University	M
Trinity Western University	M
Tufts University	M*
Tulane University	M,D
Universidad Autonoma de Guadalajara	M,D
Université de Montréal	M,D
Université de Sherbrooke	M,D,O
Université du Québec à Montréal	M,D
Université du Québec à Trois-Rivières	M,D
Université Laval	M,D
University at Albany, State University of New York	M,D*
University at Buffalo, the State University of New York	M,D*
University of Alberta	M,D*
The University of Arizona	M,D*
University of Arkansas	M,D
The University of British Columbia	M,D
University of Calgary	M,D
University of California, Berkeley	D*
University of California, Davis	M,D*
University of California, Irvine	M,D*
University of California, Los Angeles	M,D*
University of California, Riverside	M,D*
University of California, San Diego	D*
University of California, Santa Barbara	D
University of California, Santa Cruz	M,D*
University of Chicago	M,D*
University of Cincinnati	M,D
University of Colorado at Boulder	M,D*
University of Connecticut	M,D*
University of Dallas	M,D
University of Florida	M,D*
University of Georgia	M,D
University of Guelph	M,D
University of Hawaii at Manoa	M,D*
University of Houston	M*
University of Illinois at Chicago	M,D*
University of Illinois at Urbana–Champaign	M,D*
The University of Iowa	M,D*
The University of Kansas	M,D*
University of Kentucky	M,D
University of Lethbridge	M,D
University of Louisville	M
University of Manitoba	M
University of Maryland, College Park	M,D*
University of Massachusetts Amherst	M,D*
University of Memphis	M,D
University of Miami	M,D*
University of Michigan	M,D*
University of Minnesota, Twin Cities Campus	M,D*
University of Mississippi	M
University of Missouri–Columbia	M,D*
University of Missouri–St. Louis	M
The University of Montana	M
University of Nebraska–Lincoln	M,D*
University of Nevada, Reno	M*
University of New Brunswick Fredericton	M
University of New Mexico	M,D*
The University of North Carolina at Chapel Hill	M,D*
University of North Florida	M,O
University of North Texas	M,D
University of Notre Dame	D*
University of Oklahoma	M,D*
University of Oregon	M,D*
University of Ottawa	M,D*
University of Pennsylvania	M,D*
University of Pittsburgh	M,D*
University of Puerto Rico, Río Piedras	M
University of Regina	M
University of Rochester	M,D*
University of St. Thomas (TX)	M,D
University of Saskatchewan	M
University of South Africa	M,D

University of South Carolina	M,D
University of Southern California	M,D*
University of Southern Mississippi	M
University of South Florida	M,D*
The University of Tennessee	M,D
The University of Texas at Austin	D
The University of Toledo	M
University of Toronto	M,D
University of Utah	M,D*
University of Victoria	M
University of Virginia	M,D
University of Washington	M,D*
University of Waterloo	M,D
The University of Western Ontario	M,D
University of Windsor	M
University of Wisconsin–Madison	M,D*
University of Wisconsin–Milwaukee	M
University of Wyoming	M
Vanderbilt University	M,D*
Villanova University	D*
Virginia Polytechnic Institute and State University	M*
Washington State University	M*
Washington University in St. Louis	M,D*
Wayne State University	M,D*
West Chester University of Pennsylvania	M,O
Western Michigan University	M*
Wilfrid Laurier University	M
Yale University	D*
York University	M,D

PHOTOGRAPHY

Academy of Art University	M
Bard College	M
Barry University	M*
Bradley University	M
Brooklyn College of the City University of New York	M,D
Brooks Institute	M
California College of the Arts	M*
California Institute of the Arts	M,O
California State University, Fullerton	M
California State University, Los Angeles	M
Claremont Graduate University	M*
Columbia College Chicago	M
Columbia University	M*
Cornell University	M*
Cranbrook Academy of Art	M*
The George Washington University	M*
Georgia State University	M,D
Howard University	M
Illinois State University	M
Indiana State University	M
Inter American University of Puerto Rico, San Germán Campus	M
James Madison University	M
Lamar University	M
Louisiana State University and Agricultural and Mechanical College	M
Louisiana Tech University	M
Maryland Institute College of Art	M
Marywood University	M
Massachusetts College of Art and Design	M
Memphis College of Art	M*
Mills College	M
Minneapolis College of Art and Design	M
New Mexico State University	M
The New School: A University	M*
The Ohio State University	M*
Ohio University	M*
Otis College of Art and Design	M
Penn State University Park	M,D*
Pratt Institute	M*
Rhode Island School of Design	M
Rochester Institute of Technology	M
San Francisco Art Institute	M,O*
San Jose State University	M
Savannah College of Art and Design	M*
School of the Art Institute of Chicago	M*
School of Visual Arts	M
Southern Methodist University	M*
Syracuse University	M*
Temple University	M*
The University of Alabama	M
University of Alaska Fairbanks	M
University of Colorado at Boulder	M*
University of Florida	M,D*
University of Houston	M*
University of Illinois at Chicago	M*
University of Illinois at Urbana–Champaign	M*
University of Massachusetts Dartmouth	M
University of Memphis	M,O
University of Miami	M*
University of Notre Dame	M*
University of Oklahoma	M*
The University of Tennessee	M
University of Utah	M*
University of Victoria	M
University of Washington	M*
Virginia Commonwealth University	M
Washington State University	M*
Yale University	M*

PHOTONICS

Boston University	M,D*
Lehigh University	M,D
Oklahoma State University	M,D*
Princeton University	D*
Stevens Institute of Technology	M,D,O
The University of Alabama in Huntsville	M,D
University of Arkansas	M,D
University of California, San Diego	M,D*
University of Central Florida	M,D*

PHYSICAL CHEMISTRY

Auburn University	M,D*
Boston College	M,D*
Brandeis University	M,D
California State University, Los Angeles	M
Clarkson University	M,D*
Cleveland State University	M,D
Cornell University	D*
Florida State University	M,D*
Georgetown University	D
The George Washington University	M,D*
Harvard University	D*
Howard University	M,D
Indiana University Bloomington	M,D*
Kansas State University	M,D*
Kent State University	M,D*
Laurentian University	M
Marquette University	M,D
Massachusetts Institute of Technology	D*
McMaster University	M,D
Miami University	M,D*
Northeastern University	M,D*
Old Dominion University	M,D
Oregon State University	M,D*
Purdue University	M,D
Rensselaer Polytechnic Institute	M,D
Rice University	M,D
Rutgers, The State University of New Jersey, Newark	M,D*
Rutgers, The State University of New Jersey, New Brunswick	M,D*
Seton Hall University	M,D*
Southern University and Agricultural and Mechanical College	M
State University of New York at Binghamton	M,D*
Stevens Institute of Technology	M,D,O
Tufts University	M,D*
University of Calgary	M,D
University of Cincinnati	M,D
University of Georgia	M,D*
University of Louisville	M,D
University of Maryland, College Park	M,D*
University of Miami	M,D*
University of Michigan	D*
University of Missouri–Columbia	M,D*
University of Missouri–Kansas City	M,D*
University of Missouri–St. Louis	M,D
The University of Montana	M,D
University of Nebraska–Lincoln	M,D*
University of Notre Dame	M,D*
University of Puerto Rico, Río Piedras	M,D
University of Regina	M,D
University of Southern Mississippi	M,D
University of South Florida	M,D*
The University of Tennessee	M,D
The University of Texas at Austin	M,D
The University of Toledo	M,D
Vanderbilt University	M,D*
Virginia Commonwealth University	M,D
Wake Forest University	M,D*
West Virginia University	M,D
Yale University	D*
Youngstown State University	M

PHYSICAL EDUCATION

Adams State College	M
Adelphi University	M,O*
Alabama Agricultural and Mechanical University	M
Alabama State University	M
Albany State University	M
Alcorn State University	M,O
American University of Puerto Rico	M
Arizona State University at the Polytechnic Campus	M,D
Arkansas State University	M,O
Ashland University	M
Auburn University	M,D,O*
Auburn University Montgomery	M,O
Augusta State University	M
Austin College	M
Averett University	M
Azusa Pacific University	M
Ball State University	M,D*
Bayamón Central University	M
Baylor University	M,D
Bethel College (TN)	M
Boston University	M,D,O*
Bridgewater State College	M
Brooklyn College of the City University of New York	M,O
California Baptist University	M
California State University, Dominguez Hills	M
California State University, East Bay	M
California State University, Fullerton	M
California State University, Long Beach	M
California State University, Los Angeles	M
California State University, Sacramento	M
California State University, Stanislaus	M
Campbell University	M
Canisius College	M
Caribbean University	M,D
Central Connecticut State University	M,O
Central Michigan University	M
Central Washington University	M
Chicago State University	M
The Citadel, The Military College of South Carolina	M
Cleveland State University	M
The College at Brockport, State University of New York	M
The College of New Jersey	M
Colorado State University–Pueblo	M
Columbus State University	M,O
Concordia University (CA)	M
Defiance College	M
Delta State University	M
DePaul University	M,D*
Eastern Illinois University	M
Eastern Kentucky University	M
Eastern Michigan University	M
Eastern New Mexico University	M
Eastern Washington University	M
East Stroudsburg University of Pennsylvania	M
East Tennessee State University	M
Emporia State University	M
Florida Agricultural and Mechanical University	M
Florida International University	M,D,O*
Florida State University	M,D,O*
Fort Hays State University	M
Gardner-Webb University	M
George Mason University	M,O*
Georgia College & State University	M
Georgia Southern University	M
Georgia Southwestern State University	M,O
Georgia State University	M
Henderson State University	M
Hofstra University	M,D,O*
Howard University	M
Humboldt State University	M

*M—master's degree; P—first professional degree; D—doctorate; O—other advanced degree; *—Close-Up and/or Announcement or Display in one of the other books in this series*

Idaho State University M
Illinois State University M
Indiana State University M
Indiana University Bloomington M,D*
Indiana University of Pennsylvania M
Indiana University–Purdue University Indianapolis M*
Inter American University of Puerto Rico, Metropolitan Campus M
Inter American University of Puerto Rico, San Germán Campus M
Ithaca College M
Jackson State University M
Jacksonville State University M
Kent State University M,D*
Long Island University, Brooklyn Campus M
Louisiana Tech University M,D
McDaniel College M
McGill University M,D,O*
Memorial University of Newfoundland M
Middle Tennessee State University M
Minnesota State University Mankato M,O
Mississippi State University M
Missouri State University M*
Montana State University–Billings M
Montclair State University M,O*
Morehead State University M
Murray State University M,O
North Carolina Agricultural and Technical State University M
North Carolina Central University M
North Dakota State University M
Northern Illinois University M
Northern State University M
North Georgia College & State University M,O
Northwest Missouri State University M
The Ohio State University M,D*
Ohio University M*
Old Dominion University M
Oregon State University M*
Pittsburg State University M
Prairie View A&M University M
Purdue University M,D
Rhode Island College M,O
Saginaw Valley State University M
St. Cloud State University M
Salem State College M
San Diego State University M*
Slippery Rock University of Pennsylvania M
South Dakota State University M
Southern Connecticut State University M
Southern Illinois University Carbondale M*
Springfield College M,D,O
State University of New York College at Cortland M
Stony Brook University, State University of New York M,O
Sul Ross State University M*
Tarleton State University M
Teachers College, Columbia University M,D
Temple University M,D*
Tennessee State University M
Tennessee Technological University M*
Texas A&M University M,D*
Texas A&M University–Commerce M,D
Texas Southern University M
Texas State University–San Marcos M*
Union College (KY) M
United States Sports Academy M
Universidad del Turabo M
Universidad Metropolitana M
Université de Montréal M,D,O
Université de Sherbrooke M,O
Université du Québec à Trois-Rivières M
The University of Akron M
The University of Alabama M,D
The University of Alabama at Birmingham M*
University of Alberta M,D*
University of Arkansas M
University of Arkansas at Pine Bluff M
The University of British Columbia M,D
University of California, Berkeley M,D*
University of Central Florida M*
University of Central Missouri M
University of Dayton M,D
University of Florida M,D*
University of Georgia M,D*
University of Houston M,D*
University of Idaho M,D
University of Indianapolis M
The University of Iowa M,D*
The University of Kansas M,D*
University of Louisville M
University of Maine M*
University of Manitoba M
University of Memphis M
University of Minnesota, Twin Cities Campus M,D,O*
The University of Montana M
University of Nebraska at Kearney M
University of Nebraska at Omaha M
University of Nevada, Las Vegas M,D
University of New Brunswick Fredericton M
University of New Mexico M,D,O*
The University of North Carolina at Chapel Hill M*
The University of North Carolina at Pembroke M
University of Northern Colorado M,D
University of Northern Iowa M
University of Rhode Island M,D
University of South Alabama M*
University of South Carolina M,D
The University of South Dakota M
University of Southern Mississippi M,D
University of South Florida M*
The University of Tennessee at Chattanooga M
The University of Texas at Arlington M,D*
University of the Incarnate Word M,O
The University of Toledo M
University of Toronto M,D
University of Victoria M
University of Virginia M,D
University of Washington M,D*
The University of West Alabama M
University of West Florida M
University of West Georgia M
University of Wisconsin–La Crosse M
University of Wyoming M
Utah State University M
Virginia Commonwealth University M,D
Virginia Polytechnic Institute and State University M,D,O*
Wayne State College M
Wayne State University M*
West Chester University of Pennsylvania M,O
Western Carolina University M
Western Kentucky University M
Western Michigan University M*
Western Washington University M
Westfield State College M
West Virginia University M,D
Wichita State University M*
Wilfrid Laurier University M
William Woods University M,O
Wingate University M
Winthrop University M
Wright State University M

PHYSICAL THERAPY

Alabama State University D
American International College D
Andrews University D
Angelo State University D
Arcadia University D
Arkansas State University M,D,O
Armstrong Atlantic State University D
A.T. Still University of Health Sciences M,D
Azusa Pacific University D
Baylor University M,D
Bellarmine University M,D
Belmont University D
Boston University D*
Bradley University D
California State University, Fresno M,D
California State University, Long Beach M
California State University, Northridge M
Carroll University M,D
Central Michigan University M,D
Chapman University D
Chatham University D
Clarke College D
Clarkson University D*
Cleveland State University D
College of Mount St. Joseph M,D
The College of St. Scholastica D
Columbia University D*
Concordia University Wisconsin M,D
Creighton University D*
Daemen College D,O
Dalhousie University M
Des Moines University D
Dominican College M,D
Drexel University M,D,O*
Duke University D*
Duquesne University M,D*
D'Youville College M,D,O*
East Carolina University M,D
Eastern Washington University D
East Tennessee State University D
Elon University D
Emory University D*
Florida Agricultural and Mechanical University M
Florida Gulf Coast University M,D
Florida International University D*
Franklin Pierce University M,D,O
Gannon University D
The George Washington University D*
Georgia State University D
Governors State University M,D
Graduate School and University Center of the City University of New York D*
Grand Valley State University D
Hampton University D
Hardin-Simmons University D
Humboldt State University M
Husson University D
Idaho State University D
Indiana University–Purdue University Indianapolis M,D*
Ithaca College M,D
Langston University D
Lebanon Valley College D
Loma Linda University M,D
Long Island University, Brooklyn Campus D
Louisiana State University Health Sciences Center D*
Marquette University D
Marymount University D
Maryville University of Saint Louis D
Mayo School of Health Sciences D
McMaster University M
Medical University of South Carolina D
Mercy College M,D
MGH Institute of Health Professions M,D,O*
Midwestern University, Downers Grove Campus D*
Misericordia University M,D
Missouri State University D*
Mount St. Mary's College D
Nazareth College of Rochester M,D
Neumann University D
New York Institute of Technology M,D
New York Medical College D*
New York University M,D,O*
Northern Arizona University D
Northern Illinois University M
North Georgia College & State University D
Northwestern University D*
Nova Southeastern University D*
Oakland University M,D,O
The Ohio State University M*
Ohio University D*
Old Dominion University D
Pacific University D
Queen's University at Kingston M,D
Quinnipiac University M,D*
Regis University P,M,D,O
The Richard Stockton College of New Jersey D
Rockhurst University D
Rosalind Franklin University of Medicine and Science M,D*
Rutgers, The State University of New Jersey, Camden D
Sacred Heart University M,D

Sage Graduate School	D
St. Ambrose University	D
St. Catherine University	D
Saint Francis University	D
Saint Louis University	M,D
Samuel Merritt University	D
San Francisco State University	M,D
Seton Hall University	D*
Shenandoah University	D
Simmons College	D
Slippery Rock University of Pennsylvania	D
Southwest Baptist University	D
Springfield College	D
State University of New York Upstate Medical University	D
Stony Brook University, State University of New York	M,D,O
Temple University	D*
Tennessee State University	M,D
Texas State University–San Marcos	D*
Texas Tech University Health Sciences Center	M,D
Texas Woman's University	M,D
Thomas Jefferson University	M,D*
Touro College	M,D
Université de Montréal	O
University at Buffalo, the State University of New York	D*
The University of Alabama at Birmingham	D*
University of Alberta	M,D*
University of California, San Francisco	M,D
University of Central Arkansas	D
University of Central Florida	D*
University of Colorado Denver	D*
University of Connecticut	D*
University of Dayton	M,D
University of Delaware	D*
University of Evansville	D
The University of Findlay	M
University of Florida	D*
University of Hartford	M,D*
University of Illinois at Chicago	M,D*
University of Indianapolis	M,D
The University of Iowa	D*
The University of Kansas	D*
University of Kentucky	M
University of Manitoba	M,D
University of Mary	D
University of Maryland, Baltimore	D*
University of Maryland Eastern Shore	D*
University of Massachusetts Lowell	D
University of Medicine and Dentistry of New Jersey	M,D*
University of Miami	D*
University of Michigan–Flint	D*
University of Minnesota, Twin Cities Campus	D*
University of Mississippi Medical Center	M*
University of Missouri–Columbia	M*
The University of Montana	D
University of Nebraska Medical Center	D*
University of Nevada, Las Vegas	D
University of New England	D
University of New Mexico	M*
The University of North Carolina at Chapel Hill	M,D*
University of North Dakota	M,D
University of North Florida	M
University of Oklahoma Health Sciences Center	M
University of Pittsburgh	M,D*
University of Puerto Rico, Medical Sciences Campus	M
University of Puget Sound	D
University of Rhode Island	D
University of St. Augustine for Health Sciences	M,D,O
The University of Scranton	M,D
University of South Alabama	D*
The University of South Dakota	D
University of Southern California	D*
University of South Florida	M,D*
The University of Tennessee at Chattanooga	D
The University of Tennessee Health Science Center	M,D*
The University of Texas at El Paso	M
The University of Texas Health Science Center at San Antonio	M
The University of Texas Medical Branch	M,D*
The University of Texas Southwestern Medical Center at Dallas	D*
University of the Pacific	M,D
The University of Toledo	M,D
University of Utah	D,O*
University of Vermont	D*
University of Washington	M,D*
The University of Western Ontario	M,O
University of Wisconsin–La Crosse	M,D
University of Wisconsin–Milwaukee	D
Utica College	D
Virginia Commonwealth University	M,D
Walsh University	D
Washington University in St. Louis	D,O*
Wayne State University	M*
Western Carolina University	M
Western University of Health Sciences	D
West Virginia University	D
Wheeling Jesuit University	D
Wichita State University	M*
Widener University	M,D*
Winston-Salem State University	M
Youngstown State University	D

PHYSICIAN ASSISTANT STUDIES

Albany Medical College	M
Alderson-Broaddus College	M
A.T. Still University of Health Sciences	M,D
Augsburg College	M
Barry University	M*
Baylor College of Medicine	M*
Butler University	P,M
California State University, Dominguez Hills	M
Central Michigan University	M,D
Chatham University	M
Cleveland State University	M,D
Daemen College	M
DeSales University	M
Des Moines University	M
Drexel University	M*
Duke University	M*
Duquesne University	M,D*
D'Youville College	M*
East Carolina University	M
Eastern Virginia Medical School	M
Emory University	M*
Gannon University	M
The George Washington University	M*
Grand Valley State University	M
Harding University	M
Idaho State University	M
James Madison University	M
Jefferson College of Health Sciences	M
King's College	M
Le Moyne College	M
Lock Haven University of Pennsylvania	M
Loma Linda University	M
Marietta College	M
Marquette University	M
Marywood University	M
Massachusetts College of Pharmacy and Health Sciences	M*
Medical University of South Carolina	M
Mercy College	M
Methodist University	M
Midwestern University, Downers Grove Campus	M*
Midwestern University, Glendale Campus	M*
Missouri State University	M*
Mountain State University	M*
New York Institute of Technology	M
Northeastern University	M*
Nova Southeastern University	M*
Pace University	M*
Pacific University	M
Philadelphia College of Osteopathic Medicine	M*
Philadelphia University	M
Quinnipiac University	M*
Regis University	P,M,D,O
Rosalind Franklin University of Medicine and Science	M*
Saint Francis University	M
Saint Louis University	M
Samuel Merritt University	M
Seton Hall University	M*
Seton Hill University	M
Shenandoah University	M
Southern Illinois University Carbondale	M*
South University (GA)	M*
Springfield College	M
Stony Brook University, State University of New York	M,D,O
Texas Tech University Health Sciences Center	M
Touro University	P,M
Towson University	M
Trevecca Nazarene University	M
Union College (NE)	M
The University of Alabama at Birmingham	M*
University of Detroit Mercy	M
University of Florida	M*
The University of Iowa	M*
University of Kentucky	M
University of Medicine and Dentistry of New Jersey	M*
University of Nebraska Medical Center	M*
University of New England	M
University of North Dakota	M
University of North Texas Health Science Center at Fort Worth	M
University of St. Francis (IL)	M,D
University of Saint Francis (IN)	M
University of South Alabama	M*
The University of South Dakota	M
University of Southern California	M*
The University of Texas Health Science Center at San Antonio	M
The University of Texas Medical Branch	M*
The University of Texas Southwestern Medical Center at Dallas	M*
The University of Toledo	M
University of Utah	M*
University of Wisconsin–La Crosse	M
Wagner College	M
Wayne State University	M*
Western Michigan University	M*
Western University of Health Sciences	M
Yale University	M,O*

PHYSICS

Adelphi University	M*
Alabama Agricultural and Mechanical University	M,D
American University of Beirut	M
Arizona State University	M,D
Auburn University	M,D*
Ball State University	M*
Baylor University	M,D
Boston College	M,D*
Boston University	M,D*
Bowling Green State University	M*
Brandeis University	M,D
Brigham Young University	M,D*
Brock University	M
Brooklyn College of the City University of New York	M,D
Brown University	M,D*
Bryn Mawr College	M,D*
California Institute of Technology	D*
California State University, Fresno	M
California State University, Fullerton	M
California State University, Long Beach	M
California State University, Los Angeles	M
California State University, Northridge	M
Carleton University	M,D
Carnegie Mellon University	M,D*
Case Western Reserve University	M,D*
The Catholic University of America	M,D
Central Connecticut State University	M,O
Central Michigan University	M,D
Christopher Newport University	M
City College of the City University of New York	M,D*
Clark Atlanta University	M
Clarkson University	M,D*
Clark University	M,D
Clemson University	M,D
Cleveland State University	M
The College of William and Mary	M,D
Colorado School of Mines	M,D
Colorado State University	M,D*

*M—master's degree; P—first professional degree; D—doctorate; O—other advanced degree; *—Close-Up and/or Announcement or Display in one of the other books in this series*

Columbia University	M,D*
Concordia University (Canada)	M,D
Cornell University	M,D*
Creighton University	M*
Dalhousie University	M,D
Dartmouth College	M,D*
Delaware State University	M,D
DePaul University	M*
Drexel University	M,D*
Duke University	M,D*
East Carolina University	M,D
Eastern Michigan University	M
Emory University	D*
Fisk University	M
Florida Agricultural and Mechanical University	M,D
Florida Atlantic University	M,D
Florida Institute of Technology	M,D*
Florida International University	M,D*
Florida State University	M,D*
George Mason University	M*
The George Washington University	M,D*
Georgia Institute of Technology	M,D*
Georgia State University	M,D
Graduate School and University Center of the City University of New York	D*
Hampton University	M,D
Harvard University	D*
Howard University	M,D
Hunter College of the City University of New York	M,D
Idaho State University	M,D
Illinois Institute of Technology	M,D*
Indiana University Bloomington	M,D*
Indiana University of Pennsylvania	M
Indiana University–Purdue University Indianapolis	M,D*
Iowa State University of Science and Technology	M,D*
The Johns Hopkins University	D*
Kent State University	M,D*
Lakehead University	M
Lehigh University	M,D
Louisiana State University and Agricultural and Mechanical College	M,D
Louisiana Tech University	M,D
Marshall University	M
Massachusetts Institute of Technology	M,D*
McGill University	M,D*
McMaster University	D
Memorial University of Newfoundland	M,D
Miami University	M*
Michigan State University	M,D*
Michigan Technological University	M,D
Minnesota State University Mankato	M
Mississippi State University	M,D
Missouri University of Science and Technology	M,D
Montana State University	M,D
Naval Postgraduate School	M,D
New Mexico Institute of Mining and Technology	M,D
New Mexico State University	M,D
New York University	M,D*
North Carolina Central University	M
North Carolina State University	M,D*
North Dakota State University	M,D
Northeastern University	M,D*
Northern Arizona University	M
Northern Illinois University	M,D
Northwestern University	M,D*
Oakland University	M,D
The Ohio State University	M,D*
Ohio University	M,D*
Oklahoma State University	M,D*
Old Dominion University	M,D
Oregon State University	M,D*
Penn State University Park	M,D*
Pittsburg State University	M
Polytechnic Institute of NYU	M,D
Portland State University	M,D
Princeton University	D*
Purdue University	M,D
Queens College of the City University of New York	M,D
Queen's University at Kingston	M,D
Rensselaer Polytechnic Institute	M,D
Rice University	M,D
Royal Military College of Canada	M
Rutgers, The State University of New Jersey, New Brunswick	M,D*
St. Francis Xavier University	M
San Diego State University	M*
San Francisco State University	M
San Jose State University	M
Simon Fraser University	M,D
South Dakota School of Mines and Technology	M*
South Dakota State University	M
Southern Illinois University Carbondale	M,D*
Southern Illinois University Edwardsville	M
Southern Methodist University	M,D*
Southern University and Agricultural and Mechanical College	M
Stanford University	D*
State University of New York at Binghamton	M*
Stephen F. Austin State University	M
Stevens Institute of Technology	M,D,O
Stony Brook University, State University of New York	M,D
Syracuse University	M,D*
Temple University	M,D*
Texas A&M International University	M
Texas A&M University	M,D*
Texas A&M University–Commerce	M
Texas Christian University	M,D
Texas State University–San Marcos	M*
Texas Tech University	M,D
Trent University	M
Tufts University	M,D*
Tulane University	D
Université de Moncton	M
Université de Montréal	M,D
Université de Sherbrooke	M,D
Université du Québec à Trois-Rivières	M,D
Université Laval	M,D
University at Albany, State University of New York	M,D*
University at Buffalo, the State University of New York	M,D*
The University of Akron	M
The University of Alabama	M,D
The University of Alabama at Birmingham	M,D*
The University of Alabama in Huntsville	M,D
University of Alaska Fairbanks	M,D
University of Alberta	M,D*
The University of Arizona	M,D*
University of Arkansas	M,D
The University of British Columbia	M,D
University of Calgary	M,D
University of California, Berkeley	D*
University of California, Davis	M,D*
University of California, Irvine	M,D*
University of California, Los Angeles	M,D*
University of California, Riverside	M,D*
University of California, San Diego	M,D*
University of California, Santa Barbara	D
University of California, Santa Cruz	M,D*
University of Central Florida	M,D*
University of Central Oklahoma	M
University of Chicago	M,D*
University of Cincinnati	M,D
University of Colorado at Boulder	M,D*
University of Colorado at Colorado Springs	M
University of Connecticut	M,D*
University of Delaware	M,D*
University of Denver	M,D*
University of Florida	M,D*
University of Georgia	M,D*
University of Guelph	M,D
University of Hawaii at Manoa	M,D*
University of Houston	M,D*
University of Houston–Clear Lake	M
University of Idaho	M,D
University of Illinois at Chicago	M,D*
University of Illinois at Urbana–Champaign	M,D*
The University of Iowa	M,D*
The University of Kansas	M,D*
University of Kentucky	M,D
University of Lethbridge	M,D
University of Louisiana at Lafayette	M*
University of Louisville	M,D
University of Maine	M,D*
University of Manitoba	M,D
University of Maryland, Baltimore County	M,D*
University of Maryland, College Park	M,D*
University of Massachusetts Amherst	M,D*
University of Massachusetts Dartmouth	M
University of Massachusetts Lowell	M,D
University of Memphis	M
University of Miami	M,D*
University of Michigan	M,D*
University of Minnesota, Duluth	M
University of Minnesota, Twin Cities Campus	M,D*
University of Mississippi	M,D
University of Missouri–Columbia	M,D*
University of Missouri–Kansas City	M,D*
University of Missouri–St. Louis	M,D
University of Nebraska–Lincoln	M,D*
University of Nevada, Las Vegas	M,D
University of Nevada, Reno	M,D*
University of New Brunswick Fredericton	M,D
University of New Hampshire	M,D*
University of New Mexico	M,D*
University of New Orleans	M,D
The University of North Carolina at Chapel Hill	M,D*
University of North Dakota	M,D
University of Northern Iowa	M
University of North Texas	M,D
University of Notre Dame	M,D*
University of Oklahoma	M,D*
University of Oregon	M,D*
University of Ottawa	M,D*
University of Pennsylvania	M,D*
University of Pittsburgh	M,D*
University of Puerto Rico, Mayagüez Campus	M
University of Puerto Rico, Río Piedras	M,D
University of Regina	M,D
University of Rhode Island	M,D
University of Rochester	M,D*
University of Saskatchewan	M,D
University of South Carolina	M,D
University of Southern California	M,D*
University of Southern Mississippi	M,D
University of South Florida	M,D*
The University of Tennessee	M,D
The University of Tennessee Space Institute	M,D*
The University of Texas at Arlington	M,D*
The University of Texas at Austin	M,D
The University of Texas at Brownsville	M
The University of Texas at Dallas	M,D*
The University of Texas at El Paso	M
The University of Texas at San Antonio	M,D*
The University of Toledo	M,D
University of Toronto	M,D
University of Tulsa	M*
University of Utah	M,D*
University of Vermont	M*
University of Victoria	M,D
University of Virginia	M,D
University of Washington	M,D*
University of Waterloo	M,D
The University of Western Ontario	M,D
University of Windsor	M,D
University of Wisconsin–Madison	M,D*
University of Wisconsin–Milwaukee	M,D
Utah State University	M,D
Vanderbilt University	M,D*
Virginia Commonwealth University	M
Virginia Polytechnic Institute and State University	M,D*
Virginia State University	M
Wake Forest University	M,D*

Washington State University	M,D*
Washington University in St. Louis	D*
Wayne State University	M,D*
Wesleyan University	M,D*
Western Illinois University	M
Western Michigan University	M,D*
West Virginia University	M,D
Wichita State University	M*
Worcester Polytechnic Institute	M,D*
Wright State University	M
Yale University	D*
York University	M,D

PHYSIOLOGY

Albert Einstein College of Medicine	D
American University of Beirut	P,M
Ball State University	M*
Boston University	M,D*
Brigham Young University	M,D*
Brown University	M,D*
Case Western Reserve University	M,D*
Columbia University	M,D*
Cornell University	M,D*
Cornell University, Joan and Sanford I. Weill Medical College and Graduate School of Medical Sciences	M,D
Dalhousie University	M,D
Dartmouth College	D*
East Carolina University	D
Eastern Michigan University	M
East Tennessee State University	M,D
Georgetown University	M,D
Georgia Institute of Technology	M*
Georgia State University	M,D
Harvard University	M,D*
Howard University	D
Illinois State University	M,D
Indiana State University	M,D
The Johns Hopkins University	M,D*
Kansas State University	M,D*
Kent State University	M,D*
Loma Linda University	M,D
Louisiana State University Health Sciences Center	M,D*
Louisiana State University Health Sciences Center at Shreveport	M,D*
Marquette University	M,D
McGill University	M,D*
McMaster University	M,D
Medical College of Georgia	D
Medical College of Wisconsin	M,D*
Michigan State University	M,D*
New York Medical College	M,D*
New York University	P,M,D*
North Carolina State University	M,D*
Northwestern University	M*
Nova Scotia Agricultural College	M
The Ohio State University	M,D*
Ohio University	M,D*
Oregon Health & Science University	D*
Penn State Hershey Medical Center	M,D
Penn State University Park	M,D*
Purdue University	M,D
Queen's University at Kingston	M,D
Rush University	D
Saint Louis University	D
Salisbury University	M
San Francisco State University	M
San Jose State University	M
Southern Illinois University Carbondale	M,D*
Stanford University	D*
State University of New York Upstate Medical University	M,D
Stony Brook University, State University of New York	D
Temple University	D*
Texas A&M University	M,D*
Tufts University	D*
Tulane University	M,D
Universidad Central del Caribe	M
Université de Montréal	M,D,O
Université de Sherbrooke	M,D
Université Laval	M,D
University at Buffalo, the State University of New York	M,D*
The University of Alabama at Birmingham	D*
University of Alberta	M,D*
The University of Arizona	M,D*
University of Arkansas for Medical Sciences	M,D
The University of British Columbia	M,D
University of California, Berkeley	M,D*
University of California, Davis	M,D*
University of California, Irvine	D*
University of California, Los Angeles	M,D*
University of California, San Diego	D*
University of California, San Francisco	D
University of Chicago	D*
University of Cincinnati	D
University of Colorado at Boulder	M,D*
University of Colorado Denver	D*
University of Connecticut	M,D*
University of Delaware	M,D*
University of Florida	M,D*
University of Georgia	M,D*
University of Guelph	M,D
University of Hawaii at Manoa	M,D*
University of Illinois at Chicago	M,D*
University of Illinois at Urbana–Champaign	M,D*
The University of Iowa	D*
The University of Kansas	M,D*
University of Kentucky	M,D
University of Louisville	M,D
University of Manitoba	M,D
University of Massachusetts Worcester	D
University of Medicine and Dentistry of New Jersey	M,D*
University of Miami	D*
University of Michigan	D*
University of Minnesota, Duluth	M,D
University of Minnesota, Twin Cities Campus	D*
University of Mississippi Medical Center	M,D*
University of Missouri–Columbia	M,D*
University of Missouri–St. Louis	M,D,O
University of Nebraska Medical Center	M,D*
University of Nevada, Reno	D*
University of New Mexico	M,D*
University of North Dakota	M,D
University of North Texas Health Science Center at Fort Worth	M,D
University of Notre Dame	M,D*
University of Oklahoma Health Sciences Center	M,D
University of Oregon	M,D*
University of Pennsylvania	D*
University of Prince Edward Island	M,D
University of Puerto Rico, Medical Sciences Campus	M,D
University of Rochester	M,D*
University of Saskatchewan	M,D
University of South Alabama	D*
The University of South Dakota	M,D
University of Southern California	M,D*
University of South Florida	M,D*
The University of Tennessee	M,D
The University of Texas Health Science Center at San Antonio	M,D
The University of Texas Medical Branch	M,D*
University of Toronto	M,D*
University of Utah	D*
University of Virginia	D
University of Washington	D*
The University of Western Ontario	M,D
University of Wisconsin–La Crosse	M
University of Wisconsin–Madison	M,D*
University of Wyoming	M,D
Virginia Commonwealth University	M,D,O
Wake Forest University	D*
Washington State University Spokane	M,O
Wayne State University	M,D*
Wesleyan University	D*
Western Michigan University	M*
West Virginia University	M,D
William Paterson University of New Jersey	M*
Wright State University	M
Yale University	D*
Youngstown State University	M

PLANETARY AND SPACE SCIENCES

Air Force Institute of Technology	M,D
California Institute of Technology	M,D*
Columbia University	M,D*
Cornell University	D*
Embry-Riddle Aeronautical University (FL)	M
Florida Institute of Technology	M,D*
Harvard University	M,D*
Massachusetts Institute of Technology	M,D*
McGill University	M,D*
St. Thomas University	M,D,O
The University of Arizona	M,D*
University of Arkansas	M,D
University of California, Los Angeles	M,D*
University of California, Santa Cruz	M,D*
University of Chicago	M,D*
University of Hawaii at Manoa	M,D*
University of Michigan	M,D*
University of New Mexico	M,D*
University of North Dakota	M
University of Pittsburgh	M,D*
Washington University in St. Louis	M,D*
West Chester University of Pennsylvania	M,O
Western Connecticut State University	M
Yale University	M,D*
York University	M,D

PLANT BIOLOGY

Arizona State University	M,D
Clemson University	M,D
Cornell University	M,D*
Illinois State University	M,D
Indiana University Bloomington	M,D*
Iowa State University of Science and Technology	M,D*
Miami University	M,D*
Michigan State University	M,D*
New York University	M,D*
North Carolina State University	M,D*
The Ohio State University	M,D*
Ohio University	M,D*
Rutgers, The State University of New Jersey, New Brunswick	M,D*
Southern Illinois University Carbondale	M,D*
Texas A&M University	M,D*
Université Laval	M,D
University of Alberta	M,D*
University of California, Berkeley	D*
University of California, Davis	M,D*
University of California, Riverside	M,D*
University of California, San Diego	D*
University of Connecticut	M,D*
University of Florida	M,D*
University of Georgia	M,D*
University of Illinois at Urbana–Champaign	M,D*
The University of Iowa	M,D*
University of Maine	M,D*
University of Maryland, College Park	M,D*
University of Massachusetts Amherst	M,D*
University of Minnesota, Twin Cities Campus	M,D*
University of Missouri–Columbia	M,D*
University of New Hampshire	M,D*
The University of Texas at Austin	M,D
University of Vermont	M,D*
The University of Western Ontario	M,D
Washington University in St. Louis	D*
Yale University	D*

PLANT MOLECULAR BIOLOGY

Cornell University	M,D*
Illinois State University	M,D
Michigan Technological University	M,D
Rutgers, The State University of New Jersey, New Brunswick	M,D*
University of California, San Diego	D*
University of Connecticut	M,D*
University of Florida	M,D*
University of Massachusetts Amherst	M,D*
Washington State University	M,D*

PLANT PATHOLOGY

Auburn University	M,D*
Colorado State University	M,D*
Cornell University	M,D*

*M—master's degree; P—first professional degree; D—doctorate; O—other advanced degree; *—Close-Up and/or Announcement or Display in one of the other books in this series*

Iowa State University of Science and Technology	M,D*
Kansas State University	M,D*
Louisiana State University and Agricultural and Mechanical College	M,D
Michigan State University	M,D*
Mississippi State University	M,D
Montana State University	M,D
New Mexico State University	M
North Carolina State University	M,D*
North Dakota State University	M,D
Nova Scotia Agricultural College	M
The Ohio State University	M,D*
Oklahoma State University	M,D*
Oregon State University	M,D*
Penn State University Park	M,D*
Purdue University	M,D
Rutgers, The State University of New Jersey, New Brunswick	M,D*
State University of New York College of Environmental Science and Forestry	M,D
Texas A&M University	M,D*
The University of Arizona	M,D*
University of Arkansas	M
University of California, Davis	M,D*
University of California, Riverside	M,D*
University of Florida	M,D*
University of Georgia	M,D*
University of Guelph	M,D
University of Hawaii at Manoa	M,D*
University of Kentucky	M,D
University of Maine	M*
University of Minnesota, Twin Cities Campus	M,D*
University of Missouri–Columbia	M,D*
The University of Tennessee	M,D
University of Wisconsin–Madison	M,D*
Virginia Polytechnic Institute and State University	M,D*
Washington State University	M,D*
West Virginia University	M,D

PLANT PHYSIOLOGY

Cornell University	M,D*
Nova Scotia Agricultural College	M
Oregon State University	M,D*
Penn State University Park	M,D*
Purdue University	M,D
University of Kentucky	D
University of Manitoba	M,D
University of Massachusetts Amherst	M,D*
The University of Tennessee	M,D
Virginia Polytechnic Institute and State University	M,D*

PLANT SCIENCES

Alabama Agricultural and Mechanical University	M,D
American University of Beirut	M
Brigham Young University	M,D*
California State University, Fresno	M
Clemson University	M,D
Colorado State University	M,D*
Cornell University	M,D*
Delaware State University	M
Florida Agricultural and Mechanical University	M
Illinois State University	M,D
Lehman College of the City University of New York	D
McGill University	M,D,O*
Miami University	M,D*
Michigan State University	M,D*
Mississippi State University	M,D
Missouri State University	M*
Montana State University	M,D
New Mexico State University	M,D
North Carolina Agricultural and Technical State University	M
North Dakota State University	M,D
Oklahoma State University	M,D*
South Dakota State University	M,D
Southern Illinois University Carbondale	M*
State University of New York College of Environmental Science and Forestry	M,D
Texas A&M University	M,D*
Texas A&M University–Kingsville	M,D
Texas Tech University	M,D
Tuskegee University	M
The University of Arizona	M,D*
University of Arkansas	D
The University of British Columbia	M,D
University of California, Riverside	M,D*
University of Connecticut	M,D*
University of Delaware	M,D*
University of Florida	D*
University of Hawaii at Manoa	M,D*
University of Idaho	M,D
University of Kentucky	M
University of Maine	M,D*
University of Manitoba	M,D
University of Massachusetts Amherst	M,D*
University of Minnesota, Twin Cities Campus	M,D*
University of Missouri–Columbia	M,D*
University of Rhode Island	M,D
University of Saskatchewan	M,D
The University of Tennessee	M
University of Vermont	M,D*
The University of Western Ontario	M,D
University of Wisconsin–Madison	M,D*
Utah State University	M,D
Virginia State University	M
West Texas A&M University	M
West Virginia University	D

PLASMA PHYSICS

Princeton University	D*
University of Colorado at Boulder	M,D*
West Virginia University	M,D

PODIATRIC MEDICINE

Barry University	P*
California School of Podiatric Medicine at Samuel Merritt College	P
Des Moines University	P
Midwestern University, Glendale Campus	P*
New York College of Podiatric Medicine	P
Ohio College of Podiatric Medicine	P
Rosalind Franklin University of Medicine and Science	P*
Temple University	P*

POLITICAL SCIENCE

Acadia University	M
American Public University System	M
American University	M,D,O*
The American University in Cairo	M
The American University of Athens	M
American University of Beirut	M
Appalachian State University	M
Arizona State University	M,D
Arkansas State University	M,O
Ashland University	M
Auburn University	M,D*
Auburn University Montgomery	M,D
Augusta State University	M
Ball State University	M*
Baylor University	M,D
Boston College	M,D*
Boston University	M,D*
Bowling Green State University	*
Brandeis University	M,D
Brigham Young University	M*
Brock University	M
Brooklyn College of the City University of New York	M,D
Brown University	D*
California Polytechnic State University, San Luis Obispo	M
California State University, Chico	M
California State University, Fullerton	M
California State University, Long Beach	M
California State University, Los Angeles	M
California State University, Northridge	M
California State University, Sacramento	M
Carleton University	M,D
Case Western Reserve University	M,D*
The Catholic University of America	M,D
Central European University	M,D*
Central Michigan University	M,O
Claremont Graduate University	M,D*
Clark Atlanta University	M,D
The College of Saint Rose	M*
Colorado State University	M,D*
Columbia University	M,D*
Concordia University (Canada)	M,D
Converse College	M
Cornell University	D*
Dalhousie University	M,D
Duke University	M,D*
East Carolina University	M
Eastern Illinois University	M
Eastern Kentucky University	M
Eastern Michigan University	M
East Stroudsburg University of Pennsylvania	M
Emory University	D*
Fairleigh Dickinson University, Metropolitan Campus	M*
Fayetteville State University	M
Florida Agricultural and Mechanical University	M
Florida Atlantic University	M
Florida International University	M,D*
Florida State University	M,D*
Fordham University	M*
George Mason University	M,D*
Georgetown University	M,D
The George Washington University	M,D*
Georgia State University	M,D
Governors State University	M
Graduate School and University Center of the City University of New York	M,D*
Grambling State University	M
Harvard University	M,D*
Howard University	M,D
Hult International Business School (United States)	M
Idaho State University	M,D
Illinois State University	M
Indiana State University	M
Indiana University Bloomington	M,D*
Indiana University of Pennsylvania	M
Indiana University–Purdue University Indianapolis	M,O*
Institute for Christian Studies	M,D
The Institute of World Politics	M,O*
Iowa State University of Science and Technology	M*
Jackson State University	M
Jacksonville State University	M
James Madison University	M
The Johns Hopkins University	M,D,O*
Kansas State University	M*
Kaplan University–Davenport Campus	M,O
Kean University	M
Kent State University	M,D*
Lamar University	M
Lehigh University	M
Lincoln University (MO)	M
Long Island University, Brooklyn Campus	M
Long Island University, C.W. Post Campus	M
Louisiana State University and Agricultural and Mechanical College	M,D
Loyola University Chicago	M,D*
Marquette University	M
Marshall University	M
Massachusetts Institute of Technology	M,D*
McGill University	M,D*
McMaster University	M,D
Memorial University of Newfoundland	M
Miami University	M,D*
Michigan State University	M,D*
Midwestern State University	M
Mississippi College	M,O
Mississippi State University	M,D
Missouri State University	M*
Naval Postgraduate School	M

New Mexico State University M
The New School: A University M,D*
New York University M,D*
Northeastern Illinois University M
Northeastern University M,D,O*
Northern Arizona University M,D,O
Northern Illinois University M,D
Northwestern University M,D*
The Ohio State University M,D*
Ohio University M*
Oklahoma State University M,D*
Penn State University Park M,D*
Pepperdine University M
Portland State University M,D
Princeton University D*
Purdue University M,D
Queen's University at Kingston M,D
Regent University M
Rice University M,D
Roosevelt University M
Rutgers, The State University of New Jersey, Newark M*
Rutgers, The State University of New Jersey, New Brunswick D*
St. John's University (NY) M,O
Saint Louis University M
St. Mary's University (United States) M
Sam Houston State University M
San Diego State University M*
San Francisco State University M
Simon Fraser University M,D
Sonoma State University M
Southern Connecticut State University M
Southern Illinois University Carbondale M,D*
Southern University and Agricultural and Mechanical College M
Stanford University M,D*
State University of New York at Binghamton M,D*
Stony Brook University, State University of New York M,D
Suffolk University M,O*
Sul Ross State University M*
Syracuse University M,D*
Tarleton State University M
Teachers College, Columbia University M,D
Temple University M,D*
Texas A&M International University M
Texas A&M University M,D*
Texas A&M University–Kingsville M
Texas State University–San Marcos M*
Texas Tech University M,D
Texas Woman's University M
Tulane University M,D
Université de Montréal M,D
Université du Québec à Montréal M,D
Université Laval M,D
University at Albany, State University of New York M,D*
University at Buffalo, the State University of New York M,D*
The University of Akron M
The University of Alabama M,D
University of Alberta M,D*
The University of Arizona M,D*
University of Arkansas M
The University of British Columbia M,D
University of Calgary M,D
University of California, Berkeley D*
University of California, Davis M,D*
University of California, Irvine D*
University of California, Los Angeles M,D*
University of California, Riverside M,D*
University of California, San Diego M,D*
University of California, Santa Barbara M,D
University of California, Santa Cruz D*
University of Central Florida M*
University of Central Oklahoma M
University of Chicago D*
University of Cincinnati M,D
University of Colorado at Boulder M,D*
University of Colorado Denver M*
University of Connecticut M,D*
University of Dallas M,D
University of Delaware M,D*
University of Florida M,D,O*
University of Georgia M,D*
University of Guelph M
University of Hawaii at Manoa M,D*
University of Houston M,D*
University of Idaho M,D
University of Illinois at Chicago M,D*
University of Illinois at Springfield M
University of Illinois at Urbana–Champaign M,D*
The University of Iowa M,D*
The University of Kansas M,D*
University of Kentucky M,D
University of Lethbridge M,D
University of Louisville M
University of Manitoba M
University of Maryland, College Park D*
University of Massachusetts Amherst M,D*
University of Massachusetts Boston M,D,O
University of Memphis M
University of Miami M*
University of Michigan M,D*
University of Minnesota, Twin Cities Campus D*
University of Mississippi M,D
University of Missouri–Columbia M,D*
University of Missouri–Kansas City M,D*
University of Missouri–St. Louis M,D
The University of Montana M
University of Nebraska at Omaha M
University of Nevada, Las Vegas M,D
University of Nevada, Reno M,D*
University of New Brunswick Fredericton M
University of New Hampshire M*
University of New Mexico M,D*
University of New Orleans M,D
The University of North Carolina at Chapel Hill M,D*
The University of North Carolina at Greensboro M,O
University of Northern British Columbia M,D,O
University of Northern Iowa M
University of North Texas M,D
University of Notre Dame D*
University of Oklahoma M,D*
University of Oregon M,D*
University of Ottawa M,D*
University of Pennsylvania M,D*
University of Pittsburgh M,D*
University of Regina M
University of Rhode Island M,O
University of Rochester M,D*
University of Saskatchewan M
University of South Africa M,D
University of South Carolina M,D
The University of South Dakota M,D
University of Southern California M,D*
University of Southern Mississippi M,D
University of South Florida M,D*
The University of Tennessee M,D
The University of Texas at Arlington M*
The University of Texas at Austin D
The University of Texas at Brownsville M
The University of Texas at Dallas M,D*
The University of Texas at El Paso M
The University of Texas at San Antonio M*
The University of Texas at Tyler M
The University of Texas of the Permian Basin M
The University of Toledo M
University of Toronto M,D
University of Utah M,D*
University of Victoria M,D
University of Virginia M,D
University of Washington M,D*
University of Waterloo M,D
The University of Western Ontario M,D
University of West Florida M
University of Windsor M
University of Wisconsin–Madison D*
University of Wisconsin–Milwaukee M,D
University of Wyoming M
Utah State University M
Vanderbilt University M,D*
Villanova University M*
Virginia Commonwealth University M,D,O
Virginia Polytechnic Institute and State University M*
Washington State University M,D*
Washington University in St. Louis M,D*
Wayne State University M,D*
West Chester University of Pennsylvania M,O
Western Illinois University M,O
Western Kentucky University M
Western Michigan University M,D*
Western Washington University M
West Texas A&M University M
West Virginia University M,D
Wichita State University M*
Wilfrid Laurier University M
Yale University D*
York University M,D

POLYMER SCIENCE AND ENGINEERING

California Polytechnic State University, San Luis Obispo M
Carnegie Mellon University M,D*
Case Western Reserve University M,D*
Clemson University M,D
Cornell University M,D*
DePaul University M*
Eastern Michigan University M
Florida State University M*
Georgia Institute of Technology M,D*
Lehigh University M,D
Massachusetts Institute of Technology M,D,O*
North Carolina State University D*
North Dakota State University M,D
Polytechnic Institute of NYU M
Rensselaer Polytechnic Institute M,D
Stevens Institute of Technology M,D,O
The University of Akron M,D
University of Cincinnati M,D
University of Connecticut M,D*
University of Massachusetts Amherst M,D*
University of Massachusetts Lowell M,D,O
University of Missouri–Kansas City M,D*
University of Southern Mississippi M,D
University of South Florida M,D*
The University of Tennessee M,D
University of Wisconsin–Madison M,D*
Wayne State University M,D,O*

PORTUGUESE

Brigham Young University M*
Emory University D,O*
Harvard University M,D*
Indiana University Bloomington M,D*
Michigan State University M,D*
New York University M,D*
The Ohio State University M,D*
Princeton University D*
Tulane University M,D
University of California, Los Angeles M*
University of California, Santa Barbara M,D
University of Illinois at Urbana–Champaign M,D*
University of Maryland, College Park M,D*
University of Massachusetts Amherst M,D*
University of Massachusetts Dartmouth M,D
University of Minnesota, Twin Cities Campus M,D*
University of New Mexico M,D*
The University of North Carolina at Chapel Hill M,D*
University of South Africa M,D
The University of Tennessee D
The University of Texas at Austin M,D
University of Toronto M,D
University of Washington M*
University of Wisconsin–Madison M,D*
Vanderbilt University M,D*
Yale University D*

*M—master's degree; P—first professional degree; D—doctorate; O—other advanced degree; *—Close-Up and/or Announcement or Display in one of the other books in this series*

PROJECT MANAGEMENT

American Graduate University M,O
American InterContinental University Online M
Aspen University M,O
Athabasca University M,O*
Avila University M,O
Boston University M*
Brandeis University M,O
Brenau University M
California Intercontinental University M,D
Capella University M,D,O
Christian Brothers University M,O
City University of Seattle M,O
Colorado Technical University Colorado Springs M,D
Colorado Technical University Denver M
Colorado Technical University Sioux Falls M
Dallas Baptist University M
DePaul University M,D*
DeSales University M
DeVry University M*
Embry-Riddle Aeronautical University Worldwide M
The George Washington University M,D*
Grantham University M
Harrisburg University of Science and Technology M
Jones International University M
Kaplan University–Davenport Campus M
Lakeland College M
Lasell College M,O
Lehigh University M,D,O
Lewis University M
Marymount University M,O
Metropolitan State University M,O
Mississippi State University M,D
Missouri State University M*
Montana Tech of The University of Montana M
Northern Kentucky University M,O
Northwestern University M*
Notre Dame de Namur University M
Penn State Erie, The Behrend College M
Queen's University at Kingston M
Regis University M,O
Robert Morris University M,D
Royal Roads University O
St. Edward's University M
Saint Mary's University of Minnesota M,O
Southern Illinois University Edwardsville M
Southern New Hampshire University M,D,O*
Stevens Institute of Technology M,O
TUI University M,D
Universidad del Turabo M
Universidad Nacional Pedro Henriquez Urena P,M,D
Université du Québec à Chicoutimi M
Université du Québec à Montréal M,O
Université du Québec à Rimouski M,O
Université du Québec en Abitibi-Témiscamingue M,O
Université du Québec en Outaouais M,O
The University of Alabama in Huntsville M,O
University of Alaska Anchorage M
University of Dallas M
University of Denver M,O*
University of Management and Technology M,D,O
University of Mary M
University of Ottawa M,O*
University of San Francisco M
The University of Texas at Dallas M*
University of the Incarnate Word M,O
University of Wisconsin–Platteville M
Walden University M,D,O
Western Carolina University M
Winthrop University M,O
Wright State University M

PSYCHIATRIC NURSING

Allen College M
Arizona State University at the Downtown Phoenix Campus M,D,O
Boston College M,D*
Case Western Reserve University M,D*
The Catholic University of America M,D,O
Columbia University M,O*
Fairfield University M,O*
Georgia State University M,D,O
Hampton University M
Hunter College of the City University of New York M,O
Husson University M,O
Indiana University–Purdue University Indianapolis M,D*
Kent State University M,D*
MGH Institute of Health Professions M,D,O*
Molloy College M,O
New Mexico State University M
New York University M,O*
Northeastern University M,O*
Oregon Health & Science University M,O*
Pontifical Catholic University of Puerto Rico M
Rush University M,D,O
Rutgers, The State University of New Jersey, Newark M*
Sage Graduate School M,O
Saint Xavier University M,O
Seattle University M
Shenandoah University M,O
Stony Brook University, State University of New York M,O
University at Buffalo, the State University of New York M,D,O*
University of Alaska Anchorage M,O
University of Cincinnati M,D
University of Delaware M,O*
University of Illinois at Chicago M*
The University of Kansas M,D,O*
University of Louisville M,D
University of Maryland, Baltimore M*
University of Massachusetts Lowell M,O
University of Michigan M*
University of Minnesota, Twin Cities Campus M*
The University of North Carolina at Chapel Hill M,D,O*
University of Pennsylvania M*
University of Pittsburgh M,D*
University of Puerto Rico, Medical Sciences Campus M
University of Rhode Island M,D
University of Rochester M,D,O*
University of South Carolina M,O
University of Southern Maine M,O
University of Southern Mississippi M,D
University of Virginia M,D
Vanderbilt University M,D*
Virginia Commonwealth University M,D,O
Wayne State University M,O*

PSYCHOANALYSIS AND PSYCHOTHERAPY

Adler Graduate School M,O
Argosy University, Chicago D*
Boston Graduate School of Psychoanalysis M,D,O
Naropa University M*
New York University M,D,O*
Prescott College M

PSYCHOLOGY—GENERAL

Abilene Christian University M
Acadia University M
Adelphi University M,D*
Adler School of Professional Psychology M,D,O*
Alabama Agricultural and Mechanical University M,O
Alliant International University–Fresno D*
Alliant International University–Los Angeles M,D*
Alliant International University–Sacramento M,D*
Alliant International University–San Diego M,D*
Alliant International University–San Francisco M,D,O*
American International College M,D
American University D*
American University of Beirut M
Andrews University M,D,O
Angelo State University M
Antioch University Los Angeles M
Antioch University McGregor M
Antioch University New England M,D,O*
Antioch University Santa Barbara M
Antioch University Seattle M,D
Appalachian State University M,O
Arcadia University M,D,O
Argosy University, Atlanta M,D,O*
Argosy University, Chicago M,D*
Argosy University, Dallas M,D*
Argosy University, Denver M,D*
Argosy University, Hawai'i M,D,O*
Argosy University, Inland Empire M,D*
Argosy University, Los Angeles M,D*
Argosy University, Nashville M,D*
Argosy University, Orange County M,D,O*
Argosy University, Phoenix M,D*
Argosy University, Salt Lake City M,D*
Argosy University, San Diego M,D*
Argosy University, San Francisco Bay Area M,D*
Argosy University, Sarasota M,D,O*
Argosy University, Schaumburg M,D,O*
Argosy University, Seattle M,D,O*
Argosy University, Tampa M,D*
Argosy University, Twin Cities M,D,O*
Argosy University, Washington DC M,D*
Arizona State University D
Arizona State University at the Polytechnic Campus M
Assumption College M,O
Athabasca University M,O*
Auburn University M,D*
Auburn University Montgomery M
Augusta State University M
Austin Peay State University M
Avila University M
Azusa Pacific University M,D
Ball State University M*
Barry University M,O*
Bayamón Central University M
Baylor University M,D
Biola University M,D
Boston College M,D*
Boston Graduate School of Psychoanalysis M
Boston University M,D*
Bowling Green State University M,D*
Brandeis University M,D
Brenau University M
Bridgewater State College M
Brigham Young University M,D*
Brock University M,D
Brooklyn College of the City University of New York M,D
Brown University D*
Bryn Mawr College D*
Bucknell University M
Caldwell College M
California Coast University M
California Institute of Integral Studies M,D*
California Lutheran University M
California Polytechnic State University, San Luis Obispo M
California State Polytechnic University, Pomona M
California State University, Bakersfield M
California State University, Chico M
California State University, Dominguez Hills M
California State University, Fresno M
California State University, Fullerton M
California State University, Long Beach M
California State University, Los Angeles M
California State University, Northridge M
California State University, Sacramento M
California State University, San Bernardino M
California State University, San Marcos M
California State University, Stanislaus M,O
Cambridge College M,O
Cameron University M
Capella University M,D,O
Cardinal Stritch University M

Carleton University	M,D
Carlos Albizu University	M,D
Carlos Albizu University, Miami Campus	M,D
Carnegie Mellon University	D*
Case Western Reserve University	D*
Castleton State College	M
The Catholic University of America	M,D
Central Connecticut State University	M
Central Michigan University	M,D,O
Central Washington University	M
Chestnut Hill College	M,D,O
The Chicago School of Professional Psychology	M,D,O
The Chicago School of Professional Psychology: Downtown Los Angeles Campus	M,D
The Chicago School of Professional Psychology: Irvine Campus	D
The Chicago School of Professional Psychology: Online	M,D
The Chicago School of Professional Psychology: Westwood Campus	D
The Citadel, The Military College of South Carolina	M
City College of the City University of New York	M,D*
Claremont Graduate University	M,D,O*
Clark University	D
Clemson University	M,D
Cleveland State University	M,D,O
The College at Brockport, State University of New York	M
College of Saint Elizabeth	M,O
College of St. Joseph	M
The College of William and Mary	M,D
Colorado State University	M,D*
Columbia University	M,D*
Concordia University (Canada)	M,D
Concordia University Chicago	M
Concordia University Wisconsin	M
Connecticut College	M
Cornell University	D*
Dalhousie University	M,D
Dartmouth College	D*
DePaul University	M,D*
Drexel University	M,D*
Duke University	D*
Duquesne University	D*
East Carolina University	M
East Central University	M
Eastern Illinois University	M,O
Eastern Kentucky University	M,O
Eastern Michigan University	M,D
Eastern Washington University	M
East Tennessee State University	M
Edinboro University of Pennsylvania	M
Emory University	D*
Emporia State University	M
Evangel University	M
Fairfield University	M,O*
Fairleigh Dickinson University, College at Florham	M,O*
Fairleigh Dickinson University, Metropolitan Campus	M,D,O*
Fayetteville State University	M
Fielding Graduate University	M,D,O*
Fisk University	M
Florida Agricultural and Mechanical University	M
Florida Atlantic University	M,D
Florida Institute of Technology	M,D*
Florida International University	M,D*
Florida State University	M,D*
Fordham University	D*
Fort Hays State University	M,O
Framingham State College	M
Francis Marion University	M
Frostburg State University	M
Fuller Theological Seminary	M,D,O
Gallaudet University	M,D,O
Gardner-Webb University	M
Geneva College	M
George Fox University	M,D*
Georgetown University	D
The George Washington University	D*
Georgia Institute of Technology	M,D*
Georgia Southern University	M,D
Georgia State University	M,D
Golden Gate University	M,D,O
Governors State University	M
Graduate School and University Center of the City University of New York	D*
Hardin-Simmons University	M
Harvard University	D*
Hodges University	M
Hofstra University	M,D,O*
Hood College	M,O
Houston Baptist University	M
Howard University	M,D
Humboldt State University	M
Hunter College of the City University of New York	M
Idaho State University	M,D
Illinois Institute of Technology	M,D*
Illinois State University	M,D,O
Immaculata University	M,D,O
Indiana State University	M,D
Indiana University Bloomington	M,D*
Indiana University of Pennsylvania	M,D
Indiana University–Purdue University Indianapolis	M,D*
Indiana University South Bend	M
Institute of Transpersonal Psychology	M,D,O
Instituto Tecnologico de Santo Domingo	M
Inter American University of Puerto Rico, Metropolitan Campus	M,D
Inter American University of Puerto Rico, San Germán Campus	M,D
Iona College	M*
Iowa State University of Science and Technology	D*
Jackson State University	D
Jacksonville State University	M
James Madison University	M,D,O
John F. Kennedy University	M,D,O
The Johns Hopkins University	D*
Kansas State University	M,D*
Kean University	M
Kent State University	M,D*
Lakehead University	M,D
Lamar University	M
La Salle University	D
Laurentian University	M
Leadership Institute of Seattle	M
Lehigh University	M,D
Lesley University	M,D,O*
Lewis & Clark College	M,O
Lipscomb University	M,O
Loma Linda University	D
Long Island University, Brooklyn Campus	M,D
Long Island University, C.W. Post Campus	M,D
Loras College	M
Louisiana State University and Agricultural and Mechanical College	M,D
Louisiana Tech University	M,D
Loyola University Chicago	M,D*
Loyola University Maryland	M,D,O*
Lynn University	M,O
Madonna University	M
Marietta College	M
Marist College	M,O
Marquette University	M,D
Marshall University	M,D
Martin University	M
Marywood University	M
Massachusetts School of Professional Psychology	M,D,O
McGill University	M,D*
McMaster University	M,D
McNeese State University	M
Medaille College	M
Memorial University of Newfoundland	M,D
Mercy College	M
Metropolitan State University	M
Miami University	D*
Michigan School of Professional Psychology	M,D
Michigan State University	M,D*
Middle Tennessee State University	M
Midwestern State University	M
Millersville University of Pennsylvania	M
Minnesota State University Mankato	M,D
Mississippi State University	M,D
Missouri State University	M*
Monmouth University	M,O
Montana State University	M
Montana State University–Billings	M
Montclair State University	M,O*
Morehead State University	M
Morgan State University	M,D
Mount Aloysius College	M
Mount Holyoke College	M
Murray State University	M
National-Louis University	M,O
National University	M
New Jersey City University	M,O
New Mexico Highlands University	M
New Mexico State University	M,D
The New School: A University	M,D*
New York University	M,D,O*
Norfolk State University	M,D
North Carolina Central University	M
North Carolina State University	D*
Northcentral University	M,D,O
North Dakota State University	M,D
Northeastern State University	M
Northeastern University	M,D,O*
Northern Arizona University	M
Northern Illinois University	M,D
Northern Michigan University	M
Northwestern State University of Louisiana	M
Northwestern University	D*
Northwest Missouri State University	M
Northwest University	M
Notre Dame de Namur University	M,O
Nova Southeastern University	M,D,O*
The Ohio State University	M,D*
Ohio University	D*
Oklahoma State University	M,D*
Old Dominion University	M,D
Our Lady of the Lake University of San Antonio	M,D
Pace University	M*
Pacifica Graduate Institute	M,D
Pacific University	M,D
Palo Alto University	M,D*
Penn State Harrisburg	M,D
Penn State University Park	M,D*
Pepperdine University	M,D
Pepperdine University	M
Philadelphia College of Osteopathic Medicine	M,D,O*
Pittsburg State University	M
Polytechnic Institute of NYU	M
Pontifical Catholic University of Puerto Rico	M,D
Portland State University	M,D,O
Princeton University	D*
Purdue University	D
Queens College of the City University of New York	M
Queen's University at Kingston	M,D
Radford University	M,D,O
Regis University	M,O
Rhode Island College	M
Rice University	M,D
Richmont Graduate University	M
Rochester Institute of Technology	M
Roosevelt University	D
Rosalind Franklin University of Medicine and Science	M,D*
Rowan University	M
Rutgers, The State University of New Jersey, Camden	M
Rutgers, The State University of New Jersey, Newark	D*
Rutgers, The State University of New Jersey, New Brunswick	M,D*
Sage Graduate School	M,O
St. Cloud State University	M
St. John's University (NY)	M,D
Saint Joseph's University	M,O
Saint Louis University	M,D
Saint Mary's University (Canada)	M,D
St. Mary's University (United States)	M
Saint Xavier University	M,O
Salem State College	M
Sam Houston State University	M,D
San Diego State University	M,D*

*M—master's degree; P—first professional degree; D—doctorate; O—other advanced degree; *—Close-Up and/or Announcement or Display in one of the other books in this series*

San Francisco State University M
San Jose State University M
Saybrook Graduate School and Research Center M,D
The School of Professional Psychology at Forest Institute M,D,O
Seattle University M
Seton Hall University M,D,O*
Shippensburg University of Pennsylvania M
Simon Fraser University M,D
Southeastern Baptist Theological Seminary P,M,D
Southeastern Louisiana University M
Southern Adventist University M
Southern California Seminary P,M,D
Southern Connecticut State University M
Southern Illinois University Carbondale M,D*
Southern Illinois University Edwardsville M,O
Southern Methodist University D*
Southern Nazarene University M
Southern New Hampshire University M,O*
Southern Oregon University M
Southern University and Agricultural and Mechanical College M
Southwestern College (NM) O*
Spalding University M,D
Stanford University D*
State University of New York at Binghamton M,D*
State University of New York at New Paltz M
State University of New York at Plattsburgh M,O
Stephen F. Austin State University M
Stony Brook University, State University of New York D
Suffolk University D*
Sul Ross State University M*
Temple University D*
Tennessee State University M,D
Texas A&M International University M
Texas A&M University M,D*
Texas A&M University–Commerce M,D
Texas A&M University–Corpus Christi M
Texas A&M University–Kingsville M
Texas A&M University–Texarkana M
Texas Christian University M,D
Texas Southern University M
Texas State University–San Marcos M*
Texas Tech University M,D
Texas Woman's University M,D,O
Trevecca Nazarene University M,D
Tufts University M,D*
Tulane University M,D
Uniformed Services University of the Health Sciences D*
Union College (KY) M
Union Institute & University M
Universidad de las Americas, A.C. M
Universidad de las Américas–Puebla M
Université de Montréal M,D
Université de Sherbrooke M
Université du Québec à Montréal D
Université du Québec à Trois-Rivières D,O
Université Laval D
University at Albany, State University of New York M,D,O*
University at Buffalo, the State University of New York M,D*
The University of Akron M,D
The University of Alabama D
The University of Alabama at Birmingham M,D*
The University of Alabama in Huntsville M
University of Alaska Anchorage M,D
University of Alaska Fairbanks D
University of Alberta M,D*
The University of Arizona M,D*
University of Arkansas M,D
University of Arkansas at Little Rock M
University of Baltimore M
The University of British Columbia M,D
University of Calgary M,D
University of California, Berkeley D*
University of California, Davis D*
University of California, Irvine D*
University of California, Los Angeles M,D*
University of California, Riverside M,D*
University of California, San Diego D*
University of California, Santa Barbara M,D
University of California, Santa Cruz D*
University of Central Arkansas M,D
University of Central Florida M,D*
University of Central Missouri M
University of Central Oklahoma M
University of Chicago D*
University of Cincinnati D
University of Colorado at Boulder M,D*
University of Colorado at Colorado Springs M,D
University of Colorado Denver D*
University of Connecticut M,D,O*
University of Dallas M
University of Dayton M
University of Delaware D*
University of Denver M,D*
University of Detroit Mercy M,D,O
University of Florida M,D*
University of Georgia M,D*
University of Guelph M,D
University of Hartford M,D*
University of Hawaii at Manoa M,D,O*
University of Houston M,D*
University of Houston–Clear Lake M
University of Houston–Victoria M
University of Idaho M
University of Illinois at Chicago D*
University of Illinois at Urbana–Champaign M,D*
University of Indianapolis M,D
The University of Iowa M,D,O*
The University of Kansas M,D*
University of Kentucky M,D
University of La Verne M,D
University of Lethbridge M,D
University of Louisiana at Lafayette M*
University of Louisiana at Monroe M,O
University of Louisville M,D
University of Maine M,D*
University of Manitoba M,D
University of Mary Hardin-Baylor M
University of Maryland, Baltimore County M,D*
University of Maryland, College Park M,D*
University of Massachusetts Amherst M,D*
University of Massachusetts Dartmouth M,O
University of Massachusetts Lowell M
University of Memphis M,D
University of Miami M,D*
University of Michigan D,O*
University of Minnesota, Twin Cities Campus D*
University of Mississippi M,D
University of Missouri–Columbia M,D*
University of Missouri–Kansas City M,D*
University of Missouri–St. Louis M,D,O
The University of Montana M,D,O
University of Nebraska at Omaha M,D,O
University of Nebraska–Lincoln M,D*
University of Nevada, Las Vegas D
University of Nevada, Reno M,D*
University of New Brunswick Fredericton M,D
University of New Brunswick Saint John M,D
University of New Hampshire D*
University of New Mexico M,D*
University of New Orleans M,D
The University of North Carolina at Chapel Hill D*
The University of North Carolina at Charlotte M,D*
The University of North Carolina at Greensboro M,D
The University of North Carolina Wilmington M
University of North Dakota M,D
University of Northern British Columbia M,D,O
University of Northern Colorado M,D
University of Northern Iowa M
University of North Florida M
University of North Texas M,D
University of Notre Dame D*
University of Oklahoma M,D*
University of Oregon M,D*
University of Ottawa D*
University of Pennsylvania D*
University of Phoenix M
University of Phoenix–Austin Campus M
University of Phoenix–Birmingham Campus M
University of Phoenix–Chattanooga Campus M
University of Phoenix–Cheyenne Campus M
University of Phoenix–Cincinnati Campus M
University of Phoenix–Cleveland Campus M
University of Phoenix–Columbus Ohio Campus M
University of Phoenix–Dallas Campus M
University of Phoenix–Denver Campus M
University of Phoenix–Harrisburg Campus M
University of Phoenix–Hawaii Campus M
University of Phoenix–Houston Campus M
University of Phoenix–Idaho Campus M
University of Phoenix–Indianapolis Campus M
University of Phoenix–Jersey City Campus M
University of Phoenix–Las Vegas Campus M
University of Phoenix–Louisiana Campus M
University of Phoenix–Maryland Campus M
University of Phoenix–New Mexico Campus M
University of Phoenix–Northern Nevada Campus M
University of Phoenix–Oklahoma City Campus M
University of Phoenix–Oregon Campus M
University of Phoenix–Philadelphia Campus M
University of Phoenix–Phoenix Campus M,O
University of Phoenix–Pittsburgh Campus M
University of Phoenix–Richmond Campus M
University of Phoenix–Sacramento Valley Campus M
University of Phoenix–San Antonio Campus M
University of Phoenix–Southern Arizona Campus M,O
University of Phoenix–Southern California Campus M,O
University of Phoenix–Southern Colorado Campus M
University of Phoenix–Tulsa Campus M
University of Pittsburgh M,D*
University of Puerto Rico, Río Piedras M,D
University of Regina M,D
University of Rhode Island D
University of Rochester M,D*
University of Saint Francis (IN) M
University of Saint Mary M
University of St. Thomas (MN) M,D,O*
University of Saskatchewan M,D
University of South Africa M,D
University of South Alabama M*
University of South Carolina M,D
The University of South Dakota M,D
University of Southern California M,D*
University of Southern Mississippi M,D
University of South Florida M,D*
The University of Tennessee M,D

The University of Tennessee at Chattanooga	M
The University of Texas at Arlington	M,D*
The University of Texas at Austin	D
The University of Texas at Brownsville	M
The University of Texas at Dallas	M,D*
The University of Texas at El Paso	M,D
The University of Texas at San Antonio	M*
The University of Texas at Tyler	M
The University of Texas of the Permian Basin	M
The University of Texas–Pan American	M
University of the Pacific	M
The University of Toledo	M,D
University of Toronto	M,D
University of Tulsa	M,D*
University of Utah	D*
University of Vermont	D*
University of Victoria	M,D
University of Virginia	M,D
University of Washington	D*
University of Waterloo	M,D
The University of Western Ontario	M,D
University of West Florida	M
University of West Georgia	M,D
University of Windsor	M,D
University of Wisconsin–Eau Claire	M,O
University of Wisconsin–La Crosse	M,O
University of Wisconsin–Madison	D*
University of Wisconsin–Milwaukee	M,D
University of Wisconsin–Oshkosh	M
University of Wisconsin–Stout	M
University of Wisconsin–Whitewater	M,O*
University of Wyoming	M,D
Utah State University	M,D
Valdosta State University	M,O
Valparaiso University	M,O
Vanderbilt University	M,D*
Villanova University	M*
Virginia Commonwealth University	D
Virginia Polytechnic Institute and State University	M,D*
Virginia State University	M,D
Wake Forest University	M*
Walden University	M,D,O
Washburn University	M
Washington College	M
Washington State University	M,D*
Washington University in St. Louis	D*
Wayne State University	M,D*
Wesleyan University	M*
West Chester University of Pennsylvania	M,O
Western Carolina University	M
Western Illinois University	M,O
Western Kentucky University	M,O
Western Michigan University	M,D*
Western New England College	D
Western Washington University	M
Westfield State College	M
West Texas A&M University	M
West Virginia University	M,D
Wheaton College	M,D
Wichita State University	M,D*
Widener University	*
Wilfrid Laurier University	M,D
William Carey University	M
Winthrop University	M,O
Wisconsin School of Professional Psychology	M,D
Wright Institute	D
Wright State University	M,D
Xavier University	M,D*
Yale University	D*
Yeshiva University	M,D
York University	M,D
Youngstown State University	M

PUBLIC ADMINISTRATION

Adelphi University	O*
Albany State University	M
American International College	M
American Public University System	M
American University	M,D,O*
The American University in Cairo	M,O
American University of Beirut	M
The American University of Paris	M
American University of Sharjah	M
Andrew Jackson University	M
Angelo State University	M
Anna Maria College	M
Appalachian State University	M
Argosy University, Dallas	M,O*
Argosy University, Orange County	M,D,O*
Argosy University, Salt Lake City	M,D*
Argosy University, Tampa	M,D*
Arkansas State University	M,O
Auburn University	M,D*
Auburn University Montgomery	M,D
Ball State University	M*
Barry University	M*
Baylor University	M,D
Belhaven College (MS)	M
Bellevue University	M,D
Bernard M. Baruch College of the City University of New York	M
Birmingham-Southern College	M
Boise State University	M
Boston University	M,O*
Bowie State University	M
Bowling Green State University	M*
Bridgewater State College	M
Brigham Young University	M*
Brock University	M
California Baptist University	M
California Lutheran University	M
California State Polytechnic University, Pomona	M
California State University, Bakersfield	M
California State University, Chico	M
California State University, Dominguez Hills	M
California State University, East Bay	M
California State University, Fresno	M
California State University, Fullerton	M
California State University, Long Beach	M
California State University, Los Angeles	M
California State University, Northridge	M
California State University, Sacramento	M
California State University, San Bernardino	M
California State University, Stanislaus	M
Capella University	M,D
Carleton University	M,D
Carnegie Mellon University	M*
Central Michigan University	M,O
Cheyney University of Pennsylvania	M
City College of the City University of New York	M,D*
Clark Atlanta University	M
Clark University	M,O
Clemson University	M,D
Cleveland State University	M,O
The College at Brockport, State University of New York	M,O
College of Charleston	M*
Columbia University	M*
Columbus State University	M
Concordia University (Canada)	M,D
Concordia University Wisconsin	M
Cumberland University	M
Dalhousie University	M,O
DePaul University	M,O*
DeVry University	M*
Drake University	M*
Duquesne University	M,O*
East Carolina University	M
Eastern Kentucky University	M
Eastern Michigan University	M,O
Eastern Washington University	M
The Evergreen State College	M
Fairleigh Dickinson University, College at Florham	M*
Fairleigh Dickinson University, Metropolitan Campus	M,O*
Florida Agricultural and Mechanical University	M
Florida Atlantic University	M,D
Florida Gulf Coast University	M
Florida Institute of Technology	M*
Florida International University	M,D*
Florida State University	M,D,O*
Framingham State College	M
Gannon University	M,O
The George Washington University	M,D*
Georgia College & State University	M
Georgia Southern University	M
Georgia State University	M,D,O
Governors State University	M
Grambling State University	M
Grand Valley State University	M
Hamline University	M,D
Harvard University	M*
Hodges University	M
Hood College	M
Howard University	M
Idaho State University	M
Illinois Institute of Technology	M*
Indiana State University	M
Indiana University Bloomington	M,D,O*
Indiana University Kokomo	M,O
Indiana University Northwest	M,O
Indiana University–Purdue University Indianapolis	M*
Indiana University South Bend	M,O
Institute of Public Administration	M,O
Instituto Tecnológico y de Estudios Superiores de Monterrey, Campus Ciudad Juárez	M
Iowa State University of Science and Technology	M*
Jackson State University	M,D
James Madison University	M
John Jay College of Criminal Justice of the City University of New York	M
Kansas State University	M*
Kean University	M
Kennesaw State University	M
Kent State University	M*
Kentucky State University	M
Kutztown University of Pennsylvania	M
Lamar University	M
Lewis University	M
Lincoln University (MO)	M
Lindenwood University	M
Long Island University, Brooklyn Campus	M
Long Island University, C.W. Post Campus	M,O
Long Island University, Rockland Graduate Campus	M,O
Louisiana State University and Agricultural and Mechanical College	M,D
Marist College	M
Marquette University	M
Marywood University	M
McMaster University	M,D
Metropolitan College of New York	M
Metropolitan State University	M,O
Midwestern State University	M
Minnesota State University Mankato	M
Minnesota State University Moorhead	M
Mississippi State University	M,D
Missouri State University	M*
Montana State University	M
Montana State University–Billings	M
Monterey Institute of International Studies	M*
Morehead State University	M
National University	M
National University of Singapore	M,D
New York University	M,D,O*
North Carolina Central University	M
North Carolina State University	M,D*
Northeastern University	M,O*
Northern Arizona University	M,D,O
Northern Illinois University	M
Northern Kentucky University	M,O
Northern Michigan University	M
North Georgia College & State University	M
Norwich University	M
Notre Dame de Namur University	M

*M—master's degree; P—first professional degree; D—doctorate; O—other advanced degree; *—Close-Up and/or Announcement or Display in one of the other books in this series*

Nova Southeastern University	M*
Oakland University	M
Ohio University	M*
Old Dominion University	M,D
Pace University	M*
Park University	M
Penn State Harrisburg	M,D
Pepperdine University	M
Pontifical Catholic University of Puerto Rico	M
Portland State University	M,D
Regent University	M
Regis College (MA)	M,O
Rhode Island College	M
Roger Williams University	M*
Roosevelt University	M
Rutgers, The State University of New Jersey, Camden	M
Rutgers, The State University of New Jersey, Newark	M,D*
Sage Graduate School	M
Saginaw Valley State University	M
St. Edward's University	M,O
Saint Louis University	M,D,O
St. Mary's University (United States)	M
St. Thomas University	M,O
Salisbury University	M
Sam Houston State University	M
San Diego State University	M*
San Francisco State University	M
San Jose State University	M
Savannah State University	M
Seattle University	M
Seton Hall University	M,O*
Shenandoah University	M,D,O
Shippensburg University of Pennsylvania	M
Sojourner-Douglass College	M
Sonoma State University	M
Southeastern University	M
Southeast Missouri State University	M
Southern Arkansas University–Magnolia	M
Southern Illinois University Carbondale	M*
Southern Illinois University Edwardsville	M
Southern University and Agricultural and Mechanical College	M
Southern Utah University	M
State University of New York at Binghamton	M*
Stephen F. Austin State University	M
Strayer University	M
Suffolk University	M,O*
Sul Ross State University	M*
Syracuse University	M,D,O*
Tennessee State University	M,D
Texas A&M International University	M
Texas A&M University	M,O*
Texas A&M University–Corpus Christi	M
Texas Southern University	M
Texas State University–San Marcos	M*
Texas Tech University	M,D
Thomas Edison State College	O
Troy University	M
Tufts University	O*
TUI University	M,D
Universidad Nacional Pedro Henriquez Urena	P,M,D
Université de Moncton	M
Université du Québec à Montréal	M
Université du Québec, École nationale d'administration publique	D,O
University at Albany, State University of New York	M,D,O*
The University of Akron	M
The University of Alabama	M,D
The University of Alabama at Birmingham	M*
University of Alaska Anchorage	M
University of Alaska Southeast	M
The University of Arizona	M,D*
University of Arkansas	M
University of Arkansas at Little Rock	M
University of Baltimore	M,D
University of Central Florida	M,O*
University of Colorado at Colorado Springs	M
University of Colorado Denver	M*
University of Connecticut	M,O*
University of Dayton	M
University of Delaware	M*
University of Evansville	M
The University of Findlay	M
University of Georgia	M,D*
University of Guam	M
University of Guelph	M
University of Hawaii at Manoa	M,O*
University of Idaho	M
University of Illinois at Chicago	M,D*
University of Illinois at Springfield	M,D
The University of Kansas	M,D*
University of Kentucky	M,D
University of La Verne	M,D,O
University of Louisville	M
University of Maine	M,D*
University of Management and Technology	M,O
University of Manitoba	M
University of Maryland, College Park	M*
University of Massachusetts Amherst	M*
University of Memphis	M
University of Michigan–Dearborn	M,O*
University of Michigan–Flint	M*
University of Missouri–Kansas City	M,D*
University of Missouri–St. Louis	M,D,O
The University of Montana	M
University of Nebraska at Omaha	M,D,O
University of Nevada, Las Vegas	M,D,O
University of Nevada, Reno	M*
University of New Brunswick Fredericton	M
University of New Hampshire	M,O*
University of New Haven	M*
University of New Mexico	M*
University of New Orleans	M
The University of North Carolina at Chapel Hill	M*
The University of North Carolina at Charlotte	M*
The University of North Carolina at Pembroke	M
The University of North Carolina Wilmington	M
University of North Dakota	M
University of North Florida	M
University of North Texas	M,D
University of Oklahoma	M*
University of Ottawa	D,O*
University of Pennsylvania	M*
University of Phoenix	M
University of Phoenix–Atlanta Campus	M
University of Phoenix–Augusta Campus	M
University of Phoenix–Austin Campus	M
University of Phoenix–Bay Area Campus	M
University of Phoenix–Birmingham Campus	M
University of Phoenix–Central Florida Campus	M
University of Phoenix–Central Valley Campus	M
University of Phoenix–Chattanooga Campus	M
University of Phoenix–Cheyenne Campus	M
University of Phoenix–Cincinnati Campus	M
University of Phoenix–Cleveland Campus	M
University of Phoenix–Columbus Georgia Campus	M
University of Phoenix–Columbus Ohio Campus	M
University of Phoenix–Dallas Campus	M
University of Phoenix–Denver Campus	M
University of Phoenix–Des Moines Campus	M
University of Phoenix–Eastern Washington Campus	M
University of Phoenix–Harrisburg Campus	M
University of Phoenix–Hawaii Campus	M
University of Phoenix–Houston Campus	M
University of Phoenix–Idaho Campus	M
University of Phoenix–Indianapolis Campus	M
University of Phoenix–Jersey City Campus	M
University of Phoenix–Kansas City Campus	M
University of Phoenix–Las Vegas Campus	M
University of Phoenix–Louisiana Campus	M
University of Phoenix–Madison Campus	M
University of Phoenix–Maryland Campus	M
University of Phoenix–Memphis Campus	M
University of Phoenix–Minneapolis/St. Louis Park Campus	M
University of Phoenix–Northern Nevada Campus	M
University of Phoenix–Northern Virginia Campus	M
University of Phoenix–North Florida Campus	M
University of Phoenix–Northwest Arkansas Campus	M
University of Phoenix–Omaha Campus	M
University of Phoenix–Oregon Campus	M
University of Phoenix–Philadelphia Campus	M
University of Phoenix–Pittsburgh Campus	M
University of Phoenix–Renton Learning Center	M
University of Phoenix–Richmond Campus	M
University of Phoenix–Sacramento Valley Campus	M
University of Phoenix–St. Louis Campus	M
University of Phoenix–San Antonio Campus	M
University of Phoenix–San Diego Campus	M
University of Phoenix–Savannah Campus	M
University of Phoenix–Southern California Campus	M
University of Phoenix–Southern Colorado Campus	M
University of Phoenix–South Florida Campus	M
University of Phoenix–Springfield Campus	M
University of Phoenix–West Florida Campus	M
University of Phoenix–Wisconsin Campus	M
University of Pittsburgh	M,D,O*
University of Puerto Rico, Río Piedras	M
University of Regina	M,D,O
University of Rhode Island	M,O
University of San Francisco	M
University of South Africa	M,D
University of South Alabama	M*
University of South Carolina	M
The University of South Dakota	M,D
University of Southern California	M*
University of Southern Indiana	M
University of South Florida	M*
The University of Tennessee	M
The University of Tennessee at Chattanooga	M,O
The University of Texas at Arlington	M*
The University of Texas at Brownsville	M
The University of Texas at El Paso	M
The University of Texas at San Antonio	M*
The University of Texas at Tyler	M
The University of Texas–Pan American	M
University of the District of Columbia	M
University of the Virgin Islands	M
The University of Toledo	M,O
University of Utah	M*
University of Vermont	M*
University of Victoria	M,D
University of Washington	M,D*
University of West Florida	M
University of West Georgia	M,O
The University of Winnipeg	M
University of Wisconsin–Milwaukee	M
University of Wisconsin–Oshkosh	M
University of Wyoming	M
Upper Iowa University	M
Villanova University	M*
Virginia Commonwealth University	M,O

Virginia Polytechnic Institute and State University M,D,O*
Walden University M,D,O
Wayland Baptist University M
Wayne State University M*
Webster University M,D
West Chester University of Pennsylvania M,O
Western Illinois University M,O
Western International University M
Western Michigan University M,D,O*
West Virginia University M
Wichita State University M*
Widener University M*
Wilmington University M
Wright State University M
York University M,D

PUBLIC AFFAIRS

American University M*
Arizona State University M,D
Concordia University (Canada) O
Cornell University M*
DePaul University M,O*
George Mason University M,D*
The George Washington University M*
Indiana University Bloomington M,D,O*
Indiana University Northwest M,O
Indiana University of Pennsylvania M
Indiana University–Purdue University Fort Wayne M,O
Indiana University–Purdue University Indianapolis M*
Indiana University South Bend M,O
The Institute of World Politics M,O*
Jackson State University M
McMaster University M,D
Murray State University M
National University of Singapore M,D
New Mexico Highlands University M
Northeastern University M,D,O*
Notre Dame de Namur University M
The Ohio State University M,D*
Park University M
Princeton University M,D,O*
Texas A&M University M,O*
The University of Alabama in Huntsville M
University of Arkansas at Little Rock M,O
University of Central Florida D*
University of Colorado at Colorado Springs M
University of Colorado Denver D*
University of Florida M,D,O*
University of Idaho M,D
University of Louisville D
University of Massachusetts Boston M
University of Minnesota, Twin Cities Campus M*
University of Missouri–Columbia M*
University of Missouri–Kansas City M,D*
University of Nevada, Las Vegas M,D,O
The University of North Carolina at Greensboro M,O
The University of Texas at Arlington D*
The University of Texas at Austin M,D
The University of Texas at Dallas M,D*
University of Washington M,D*
University of Waterloo M
University of Wisconsin–Madison M*
Virginia Commonwealth University M,D,O
Virginia Polytechnic Institute and State University M,D*
Washington State University Vancouver M
West Chester University of Pennsylvania M,O
Western Carolina University M
Western Michigan University M,D,O*
York University M

PUBLIC HEALTH—GENERAL

Adelphi University O*
American Public University System M
American University of Beirut M
Arizona State University at the Downtown Phoenix Campus M,D,O
Armstrong Atlantic State University M
A.T. Still University of Health Sciences M,D
Austin Peay State University M
Barry University M*
Bellevue University M,D
Benedictine University M
Boise State University M
Boston University P,M,D,O*
Bowling Green State University M*
Brooklyn College of the City University of New York M
Brown University M*
California State University, Fresno M
California State University, Fullerton M
California State University, Northridge M
California State University, San Bernardino M
Case Western Reserve University M*
Charles R. Drew University of Medicine and Science M
Cleveland State University M
Columbia University M,D*
Dartmouth College M*
Davenport University M
Davenport University M
Davenport University M
Des Moines University M
Dominican University of California M
Drexel University M,D,O*
East Carolina University M
Eastern Virginia Medical School M
East Stroudsburg University of Pennsylvania M
East Tennessee State University M,O
Emory University M,D,O*
Florida Agricultural and Mechanical University M
Florida International University M,D*
Florida State University M*
Fort Valley State University M
Georgetown University M,D
The George Washington University M,D,O*
Georgia Southern University M,D
Georgia State University M,D,O
Graduate School and University Center of the City University of New York D*
Harvard University M,D*
Howard University M
Hunter College of the City University of New York M
Idaho State University M,O
Independence University M
Indiana University Bloomington M,D*
Indiana University–Purdue University Indianapolis M*
The Johns Hopkins University M,D*
Kansas State University M*
Kent State University M*
Laurentian University D
Loma Linda University M,D,O
Medical College of Wisconsin M,D,O*
Michigan State University M*
Missouri State University M*
Morehouse School of Medicine M*
Morgan State University M,D
New Mexico State University M
New York Medical College M,D*
Northern Arizona University M
Northern Illinois University M
Northwestern University M*
Nova Southeastern University M*
The Ohio State University M,D*
Old Dominion University M
Oregon State University M,D*
Penn State Hershey Medical Center M
Ponce School of Medicine M
Portland State University M,O
Purdue University M,D
Queen's University at Kingston M,D
Rutgers, The State University of New Jersey, New Brunswick M,D*
St. Catherine University M
Saint Louis University M,D
Saint Xavier University M,O
San Diego State University M,D*
San Francisco State University M
San Jose State University M,O
Sarah Lawrence College M*
Simon Fraser University M
Southern Connecticut State University M
State University of New York Downstate Medical Center M*
Stony Brook University, State University of New York M
Temple University M,D*
Texas A&M Health Science Center M
Texas A&M University M,D*
Thomas Jefferson University M*
Touro University P,M
Trinity (Washington) University M
Tufts University M*
TUI University M,D,O
Tulane University M,D,O
Uniformed Services University of the Health Sciences M,D*
Universidad Central del Este M,D
Université de Montréal M,D,O
University at Albany, State University of New York M,D*
University at Buffalo, the State University of New York M,D*
The University of Akron M,D
The University of Alabama at Birmingham M,D*
University of Alaska Anchorage M
University of Alberta M,D*
The University of Arizona M,D*
The University of British Columbia M,D
University of California, Berkeley M,D*
University of California, Los Angeles M,D*
University of California, San Diego D*
University of Colorado Denver M,D*
University of Connecticut M*
University of Connecticut Health Center M*
University of Florida M*
University of Hawaii at Manoa M,D,O*
University of Illinois at Chicago M,D*
University of Illinois at Springfield M
University of Illinois at Urbana–Champaign M,D*
The University of Iowa M,D,O*
The University of Kansas M*
University of Kentucky M
University of Louisville M,D
University of Maryland, College Park M,D*
University of Massachusetts Amherst M,D*
University of Massachusetts Lowell M,O
University of Medicine and Dentistry of New Jersey M,D,O*
University of Memphis M
University of Miami M*
University of Michigan M,D*
University of Minnesota, Twin Cities Campus M,D,O*
University of Missouri–Columbia M*
The University of Montana M,O
University of Nebraska at Omaha M
University of Nebraska Medical Center M*
University of Nevada, Reno M,D*
University of New England M,O
University of New Hampshire M,O*
University of New Mexico M*
The University of North Carolina at Chapel Hill M,D*
The University of North Carolina at Charlotte M*
University of Northern Colorado M
University of North Florida M,O
University of North Texas Health Science Center at Fort Worth M,D
University of Oklahoma Health Sciences Center M,D
University of Ottawa D*
University of Pittsburgh M,D,O*
University of Puerto Rico, Medical Sciences Campus M
University of Rochester M*
University of South Africa M,D
University of South Carolina M
University of Southern California M*
University of Southern Mississippi M

*M—master's degree; P—first professional degree; D—doctorate; O—other advanced degree; *—Close-Up and/or Announcement or Display in one of the other books in this series*

University of South Florida M,D*
The University of Tennessee M
The University of Texas at El Paso M
The University of Texas Health Science Center at Houston M,D,O
The University of Texas Medical Branch M*
University of the Sciences in Philadelphia M,D*
The University of Toledo M,O
University of Toronto M,D
University of Utah M,D*
University of Virginia M,D
University of Waterloo M
University of West Florida M
University of Wisconsin–La Crosse M
University of Wisconsin–Milwaukee M,D,O
Vanderbilt University M*
Walden University M,D
Washington University in St. Louis M,D*
Wayne State University M,O*
West Chester University of Pennsylvania M,O
Western Kentucky University M
Westminster College (UT) M
West Virginia University M
Wichita State University M*
Wright State University M
Yale University M,D*

PUBLIC HISTORY

Appalachian State University M
Arizona State University M,D
California State University, Sacramento M
Eastern Illinois University M
Florida State University M,D*
Georgia College & State University M
Indiana University–Purdue University Indianapolis M*
Loyola University Chicago M,D*
Middle Tennessee State University M,D
New York University M,D,O*
North Carolina State University M*
Northeastern University M,D*
Rutgers, The State University of New Jersey, Camden M
Shippensburg University of Pennsylvania M,O
Simmons College
Sonoma State University M
University at Albany, State University of New York M,D,O*
University of Arkansas at Little Rock M
The University of British Columbia M,D
University of Central Florida M*
University of Houston M,D*
University of Illinois at Springfield M
University of Massachusetts Amherst M,D*
University of Massachusetts Boston M
University of South Carolina M,O
The University of Texas at Austin M,D
University of West Florida M
Washington State University M,D*

PUBLIC POLICY

Albany State University M
American University M*
The American University in Cairo M,O
Arizona State University P,M
Baylor University M,D
Boise State University M
Brandeis University M
Brigham Young University M*
Brooklyn College of the City University of New York M,D
Brown University M*
California Lutheran University M
California State University, Long Beach M
California State University, Monterey Bay M
California State University, Sacramento M
Carleton University M,D
Carnegie Mellon University M,D*
Central European University M,D*
Claremont Graduate University M,D,O*
Clemson University M,D
The College of William and Mary M
Columbia University M*
Concordia University (Canada) M,D
Cornell University M,D*
DePaul University M,O*
Duke University M,D,O*
Duquesne University M,O*
Eastern Michigan University M,O
Florida State University M,D,O*
Frederick S. Pardee RAND Graduate School D
George Mason University M,D*
Georgetown University M,D
The George Washington University M,D*
Georgia Institute of Technology M,D*
Georgia State University M,D,O
Graduate School and University Center of the City University of New York M,D*
Harvard University M,D*
Indiana University Bloomington M,D,O*
Indiana University–Purdue University Indianapolis M*
The Institute of World Politics M,O*
Jackson State University M,D
John Jay College of Criminal Justice of the City University of New York M,D
The Johns Hopkins University M*
Kent State University M,D*
Lincoln University (MO) M
Loyola University Chicago M,D*
McMaster University M,D
Mills College M
Mississippi State University M,D
Monmouth University M
National University of Singapore M,D
New England College M
The New School: A University D*
Northeastern University M,D*
Northwestern University D*
Pepperdine University M
Princeton University M,D*
Queen's University at Kingston M
Regent University M
Regis College (MA) M,O
Rochester Institute of Technology M
Rutgers, The State University of New Jersey, Camden M
Rutgers, The State University of New Jersey, Newark M,D*
Rutgers, The State University of New Jersey, New Brunswick M,D*
Saint Louis University M,D,O
San Francisco State University M
Seton Hall University M,O*
Simon Fraser University M
Southern New Hampshire University M,D*
Southern University and Agricultural and Mechanical College D
State University of New York at Binghamton M,D*
State University of New York Empire State College M
Stony Brook University, State University of New York M,D
Suffolk University M*
Texas A&M University M,O*
Trinity College M
Tufts University M*
Universidad Central del Este M,D
Universidad del Este M
University at Albany, State University of New York M,D,O*
The University of Arizona M,D*
University of Arkansas D
University of California, Berkeley M,D*
University of California, Los Angeles M*
University of Chicago M,D*
University of Colorado at Boulder M,D*
University of Delaware M,D*
University of Denver M*
University of Georgia M,D*
University of Guelph M
University of Hawaii at Manoa O*
University of Louisville M
University of Maryland, Baltimore County M,D*
University of Maryland, College Park M,D*
University of Massachusetts Amherst M*
University of Massachusetts Boston D
University of Massachusetts Dartmouth M,O
University of Memphis M
University of Michigan M,D*
University of Michigan–Dearborn M*
University of Minnesota, Twin Cities Campus M*
University of Missouri–St. Louis M,D,O
University of Nebraska–Lincoln M,D,O*
University of Nevada, Las Vegas M
University of New Brunswick Fredericton M
The University of North Carolina at Chapel Hill D*
The University of North Carolina at Charlotte D*
University of Northern Iowa M
University of Oregon M*
University of Pennsylvania M,D*
University of Pittsburgh M,D,O*
University of Regina M,D,O
University of Rhode Island M,O
University of Southern California M*
University of Southern Maine M,D,O
The University of Texas at Austin M,D
The University of Texas at Brownsville M
The University of Texas at Dallas M,D*
The University of Texas at El Paso M
University of the Pacific P,M,D
University of Utah M*
University of Virginia M
University of Washington M,D*
University of Washington, Bothell M
Vanderbilt University M,D*
Virginia Commonwealth University D
Virginia Polytechnic Institute and State University M,D,O*
Walden University M,D,O
Washington State University M,D*
Washington University in St. Louis M*
West Virginia University M,D
Wilfrid Laurier University M
William Paterson University of New Jersey M*
York University M

PUBLISHING

Carnegie Mellon University M*
DePaul University M*
Drexel University M*
Emerson College M
The George Washington University M*
New York University M*
Northwestern University M*
Pace University M*
Rosemont College M
Simon Fraser University M
University of Baltimore M

QUALITY MANAGEMENT

California Intercontinental University M,D
California State University, Dominguez Hills M
Calumet College of Saint Joseph M
Case Western Reserve University M,D*
Dowling College M,O
Eastern Michigan University M,O
Ferris State University M
Florida Institute of Technology M*
Hofstra University M*
Instituto Tecnológico y de Estudios Superiores de Monterrey, Campus Ciudad de México M,D
Instituto Tecnológico y de Estudios Superiores de Monterrey, Campus Ciudad Juárez M
Instituto Tecnológico y de Estudios Superiores de Monterrey, Campus Estado de México M,D
Instituto Tecnológico y de Estudios Superiores de Monterrey, Campus Irapuato M,D
Madonna University M

Marian University (WI) M
The National Graduate School of Quality Management M
Northwest Missouri State University M,O
Penn State University Park M*
Regis College (MA) M
Rutgers, The State University of New Jersey, New Brunswick M,D*
Saint Joseph's College of Maine M
San Jose State University M
Southern Polytechnic State University M,O
Stevens Institute of Technology M,O
TUI University M,D,O
Universidad de las Americas, A.C. M
Universidad del Turabo M
The University of Alabama M
Upper Iowa University M
Webster University M,D

QUANTITATIVE ANALYSIS

Bernard M. Baruch College of the City University of New York M
Drexel University M,D,O*
Georgia State University M,D
Lehigh University M
Michigan State University D*
New York University M,D,O*
Oklahoma State University M,D*
Providence College M*
St. John's University (NY) M,O
Syracuse University D*
Texas Tech University M,D
The University of British Columbia M,D
University of California, Santa Barbara M,D
University of Cincinnati M,D
University of Connecticut M,O*
University of Florida M*
University of Illinois at Chicago M,D*
University of Missouri–St. Louis M,O
University of North Texas M,D
University of Oregon M*
University of Pittsburgh D*
University of Puerto Rico, Río Piedras M,D
University of South Africa M,D
University of Southern California M,D*
The University of Texas at Arlington M,D*
Virginia Commonwealth University M
Walden University M,D

RADIATION BIOLOGY

Auburn University M,D*
Austin Peay State University M
Colorado State University M,D*
Georgetown University M
Université de Sherbrooke M,D
The University of Iowa M,D*
University of Oklahoma Health Sciences Center M,D
The University of Texas Southwestern Medical Center at Dallas M,D*

RANGE SCIENCE

Colorado State University M,D*
Kansas State University M,D*
Montana State University M,D
New Mexico State University M,D
North Dakota State University M,D
Oregon State University M,D*
Sul Ross State University M*
Texas A&M University–Kingsville M
Texas Tech University M,D
The University of Arizona M,D*
University of California, Berkeley M*
University of Idaho M,D
University of Wyoming M,D
Utah State University M,D

READING EDUCATION

Adelphi University M*
Alfred University M*
Alverno College M
American International College M,D,O
Andrews University M
Angelo State University M
Appalachian State University M
Arcadia University M,D,O
Arkansas State University M,O
Asbury College M,O
Ashland University M
Auburn University M,D,O*
Auburn University Montgomery M,O
Aurora University M,D
Austin Peay State University M,O
Averett University M
Avila University M,O
Baldwin-Wallace College M
Bank Street College of Education M*
Barry University M,D,O*
Bellarmine University M
Benedictine University M
Berry College M
Bethel University M,D,O
Bloomsburg University of Pennsylvania M
Boise State University M
Boston College M,O*
Boston University M,D,O*
Bowie State University M
Bowling Green State University M,O*
Bridgewater State College M,O
Brigham Young University M*
Bucknell University M
Buffalo State College, State University of New York M
Butler University M
California Baptist University M
California Lutheran University M
California State University, Bakersfield M,O
California State University, Chico M
California State University, Fresno M
California State University, Fullerton M
California State University, Los Angeles M
California State University, Northridge M
California State University, Sacramento M
California State University, San Bernardino M
California State University, Stanislaus M,O
California University of Pennsylvania M
Calvin College M
Cambridge College M,D,O
Canisius College M
Capella University M,D,O
Cardinal Stritch University M
Carthage College M,O
Castleton State College M,O
Central Connecticut State University M,O
Central Michigan University M,O
Central Washington University M
Chapman University M
Chicago State University M
The Citadel, The Military College of South Carolina M
City College of the City University of New York M*
City University of Seattle M,O
Clarion University of Pennsylvania M
Clarke College M
Clemson University M
The College at Brockport, State University of New York M
College of Mount St. Joseph M
The College of New Jersey M,O
The College of New Rochelle M
College of St. Joseph M
The College of Saint Rose M,O*
The College of William and Mary M
Concordia University Chicago M
Concordia University, Nebraska M
Concordia University Wisconsin M
Coppin State University M
Curry College M,O
Dallas Baptist University M
Delaware State University M
DePaul University M,D*
Dominican University M
Dowling College M,D,O
Drury University M
Duquesne University M*
East Carolina University M
Eastern Connecticut State University M
Eastern Michigan University M
Eastern Nazarene College M,O
Eastern Washington University M
East Stroudsburg University of Pennsylvania M
East Tennessee State University M
Edinboro University of Pennsylvania M,O
Elms College M,O
Emory & Henry College M
Emporia State University M
Endicott College M
Evangel University M
Fairleigh Dickinson University, College at Florham M,O*
Fairleigh Dickinson University, Metropolitan Campus M,O*
Fairmont State University M
Fayetteville State University M
Ferris State University M
Florida Atlantic University M
Florida Gulf Coast University M
Florida International University M,D*
Florida State University M,D,O*
Fordham University M,D,O*
Framingham State College M
Fresno Pacific University M
Frostburg State University M
Furman University M
Gannon University M,O
George Fox University M,D,O*
George Mason University M,O*
Georgia Southern University M
Georgia Southwestern State University M,O
Georgia State University M,D,O
Gonzaga University M
Governors State University M
Grambling State University M,D
Grand Valley State University M
Gwynedd-Mercy College M
Harding University M,O
Hardin-Simmons University M
Harvard University M*
Henderson State University M
Heritage University M
Hofstra University M,D,O*
Holy Family University M
Hood College M
Houston Baptist University M
Howard University M,O
Hunter College of the City University of New York M,O
Idaho State University M,O
Illinois State University M
Indiana University Bloomington M,D,O*
Indiana University of Pennsylvania M
Indiana University–Purdue University Indianapolis M,O*
Iona College M*
Jacksonville State University M
Jacksonville University M
James Madison University M
The Johns Hopkins University M,D,O*
Johnson State College M
Judson University M
Kaplan University–Davenport Campus M
Kean University M
Kent State University M*
King's College M
Kutztown University of Pennsylvania M
Lake Erie College M
Lehman College of the City University of New York M
Lesley University M,D,O*
Lewis University M
Liberty University M,D,O
Lincoln University (PA) M
Long Island University at Riverhead M
Long Island University, Brentwood Campus M
Long Island University, Brooklyn Campus M
Long Island University, C.W. Post Campus M
Long Island University, Rockland Graduate Campus M
Long Island University, Westchester Graduate Campus M,O
Longwood University M
Loyola Marymount University M
Loyola University Chicago M*
Loyola University Maryland M,O*
Lynchburg College M
Lyndon State College M
Madonna University M
Malone University M
Manhattanville College M*
Marshall University M,O
Marygrove College M

*M—master's degree; P—first professional degree; D—doctorate; O—other advanced degree; *—Close-Up and/or Announcement or Display in one of the other books in this series*

Maryville University of Saint Louis M,D
Marywood University M
Massachusetts College of Liberal Arts M
McDaniel College M
Medaille College M
Mercer University M,D,O
Mercy College M
MGH Institute of Health Professions M,O*
Miami University M*
Michigan State University M*
Middle Tennessee State University M,D
Midwestern State University M
Millersville University of Pennsylvania M
Minnesota State University Moorhead M
Missouri State University M*
Monmouth University M,O
Montana State University–Billings M
Montclair State University M,O*
Morehead State University M,O
Mount Saint Mary College M
Mount Saint Vincent University M
Murray State University M,O
National-Louis University M,D,O
Nazareth College of Rochester M
New Jersey City University M
New York University M*
Niagara University M
North Carolina Agricultural and Technical State University M
Northeastern Illinois University M
Northeastern State University M
Northern Illinois University M,D
Northern Michigan University M,O
Northern State University M
Northwestern Oklahoma State University M
Northwestern State University of Louisiana M,O
Northwest Missouri State University M
Northwest Nazarene University M
Notre Dame College (OH) M,O
Notre Dame de Namur University M,O
Nova Southeastern University M,O*
Oakland University M,D,O
Ohio University M,D*
Old Dominion University M,D
Olivet Nazarene University M
Oregon State University M*
Our Lady of the Lake University of San Antonio M
Penn State Harrisburg M,D
Penn State University Park M,D*
Pittsburg State University M
Plymouth State University M
Portland State University M,D
Providence College M*
Purdue University M,D,O
Queens College of the City University of New York M
Queens University of Charlotte M
Radford University M
Regis University M,O
Rhode Island College M
Rider University M,O*
Rivier College M,D,O
Roberts Wesleyan College M,O
Rockford College M
Roger Williams University M*
Roosevelt University M
Rowan University M
Rutgers, The State University of New Jersey, New Brunswick M,D*
Sacred Heart University M,O
Sage Graduate School M
Saginaw Valley State University M
St. Bonaventure University M
Saint Francis University M
St. John Fisher College M
St. John's University (NY) M,D
St. Joseph's College, Long Island Campus M
St. Joseph's College, New York M
Saint Joseph's University M,D
Saint Leo University M
Saint Martin's University M
Saint Mary's College of California M
St. Mary's University (United States) M
Saint Mary's University of Minnesota M,O
Saint Michael's College M,O
Saint Peter's College M
St. Thomas Aquinas College M,O*
St. Thomas University M,D,O
Saint Xavier University M,O
Salem College M
Salem State College M,O
Salisbury University M
Sam Houston State University M,D
San Diego State University M*
San Francisco State University M,O
Seattle Pacific University M
Seattle University M,O
Shippensburg University of Pennsylvania M
Siena Heights University M
Slippery Rock University of Pennsylvania M
Sojourner-Douglass College M
Southeastern Oklahoma State University M
Southern Adventist University M
Southern Connecticut State University M,O
Southern Illinois University Edwardsville M,O
Southern Oregon University M
Southwestern Adventist University M
State University of New York at Binghamton M*
State University of New York at Fredonia M
State University of New York at New Paltz M
State University of New York at Oswego M
State University of New York at Plattsburgh M
State University of New York College at Cortland M
State University of New York College at Geneseo M
State University of New York College at Oneonta M
State University of New York College at Potsdam M
Stetson University M
Sul Ross State University M*
Syracuse University M,D*
Teachers College, Columbia University M
Temple University M,D*
Tennessee Technological University M,O*
Texas A&M International University M,D
Texas A&M University M,D*
Texas A&M University–Commerce M,D
Texas A&M University–Corpus Christi M,D
Texas A&M University–Kingsville M
Texas State University–San Marcos M*
Texas Tech University M,D
Texas Woman's University M,D
Towson University M,O
Trevecca Nazarene University M
Trinity (Washington) University M
TUI University M
Union College (KY) M
University at Albany, State University of New York M,D,O*
University at Buffalo, the State University of New York M,D,O*
University of Alaska Fairbanks M,D,O
The University of Arizona M,D,O*
University of Arkansas at Little Rock M,O
University of Bridgeport M,O
The University of British Columbia M
University of California, Berkeley M,D*
University of California, Riverside M,D*
University of California, Santa Cruz M,D*
University of Central Arkansas M
University of Central Florida M,O*
University of Central Missouri M,O
University of Central Oklahoma M
University of Cincinnati M,D
University of Connecticut M,D,O*
University of Dayton M
University of Florida M,D,O*
University of Georgia M,D,O*
University of Guam M
University of Houston M,D*
University of Houston–Clear Lake M
University of Illinois at Chicago M,D*
University of La Verne M,O
University of Louisiana at Monroe M,D
University of Louisville M
University of Maine M,D,O*
University of Maine at Farmington M
University of Mary M
University of Mary Hardin-Baylor M,D
University of Maryland, College Park M,D,O*
University of Massachusetts Amherst M,D,O*
University of Massachusetts Lowell M,D,O
University of Memphis M,D
University of Miami M,D,O*
University of Michigan M,D*
University of Michigan–Flint M*
University of Minnesota, Twin Cities Campus M,D,O*
University of Missouri–Columbia M,D,O*
University of Missouri–Kansas City M,D,O*
University of Missouri–St. Louis M,O
University of Nebraska at Kearney M
University of Nebraska at Omaha M
University of Nevada, Reno M,D*
University of New England M
University of New Hampshire M*
The University of North Carolina at Chapel Hill M,D*
The University of North Carolina at Charlotte M*
The University of North Carolina at Greensboro M,D,O
The University of North Carolina at Pembroke M
The University of North Carolina Wilmington M
University of North Dakota M
University of Northern Colorado M
University of Northern Iowa M
University of North Texas M,D
University of Oklahoma M,D,O*
University of Pennsylvania M,D*
University of Pittsburgh M,D*
University of Rhode Island M
University of Rio Grande M
University of St. Francis (IL) M
University of St. Thomas (MN) M,D,O*
University of San Diego M
University of San Francisco M,D
The University of Scranton M
University of Sioux Falls M,O
University of South Alabama M,O*
University of South Carolina M,D
University of Southern Maine M,O
University of Southern Mississippi M,D,O
University of South Florida M,D*
The University of Tennessee M,D,O
The University of Texas at Brownsville M
The University of Texas at El Paso M,D
The University of Texas at San Antonio M*
The University of Texas at Tyler M
The University of Texas of the Permian Basin M
The University of Texas–Pan American M
University of the Cumberlands M
University of the Incarnate Word M,D
University of Vermont M*
University of Victoria M,D
University of Virginia M,D,O
University of Washington M,D*
University of West Florida M
University of West Georgia M
University of Wisconsin–Eau Claire M
University of Wisconsin–La Crosse M
University of Wisconsin–Milwaukee M
University of Wisconsin–Oshkosh M
University of Wisconsin–River Falls M
University of Wisconsin–Stevens Point M

University of Wisconsin–Superior M
University of Wisconsin–Whitewater M*
Ursuline College M
Valdosta State University M,O
Vanderbilt University M*
Virginia Commonwealth University M
Wagner College M
Walden University M,D,O
Walla Walla University M
Washburn University M
Washington State University M,D*
Washington State University Tri-Cities M,D
Wayne State University M,D,O*
West Chester University of Pennsylvania M,O
Western Connecticut State University M
Western Illinois University M
Western Kentucky University M
Western New Mexico University M
Westfield State College M
Westminster College (PA) M,O
West Texas A&M University M
West Virginia University M
Wheelock College M
Widener University M,D*
William Paterson University of New Jersey M*
Wilmington College M
Wilmington University M
Winthrop University M
Worcester State College M,O
Xavier University M*
Youngstown State University M

REAL ESTATE

American University M*
California State University, Sacramento M
Central European University M*
Clemson University M
Cleveland State University M,D,O
Columbia University M*
Cornell University M*
DePaul University M*
Florida International University M*
Georgetown University M,D
The George Washington University M*
Georgia State University M,D,O
Hofstra University M*
John Marshall Law School P,M
The Johns Hopkins University M*
Marylhurst University M
Massachusetts Institute of Technology M*
New York University M,O*
Nova Southeastern University M*
Pacific States University M,D
Roosevelt University M,O
Texas A&M University M*
University of California, Berkeley D*
University of Denver M*
University of Florida M,D,O*
University of Hawaii at Manoa M*
University of Illinois at Chicago M*
University of Maryland, College Park M*
University of Memphis M,D
University of Michigan M,O*
University of North Texas M,D
University of Pennsylvania M,D*
University of St. Thomas (MN) M*
University of South Africa M,D
University of Southern California M*
The University of Texas at Arlington M,D*
University of Wisconsin–Madison M,D*
Virginia Commonwealth University M,O
Washington State University D*
Woodbury University M

RECREATION AND PARK MANAGEMENT

Acadia University M
Arizona State University M,D
Bowling Green State University M*
Brigham Young University M*
California State University, Chico M
California State University, Long Beach M
California State University, Northridge M
California State University, Sacramento M
Central Michigan University M,O
Clemson University M,D
The College at Brockport, State University of New York M
Colorado State University M,D*
Delta State University M
East Carolina University M
Eastern Kentucky University M
Florida Agricultural and Mechanical University M
Florida International University M*
Florida State University M,D,O*
Frostburg State University M
Georgia College & State University M
Georgia Southern University M
Hardin-Simmons University M
Indiana University Bloomington M,D,O*
Kent State University M*
Lehman College of the City University of New York M
Michigan State University M,D*
Middle Tennessee State University M
Naropa University M*
North Carolina Central University M
North Carolina State University M,D*
Northwest Missouri State University M
Ohio University M*
Old Dominion University M
Penn State University Park M,D*
San Francisco State University M
San Jose State University M
South Dakota State University M
Southern Connecticut State University M
Southern Illinois University Carbondale M*
Southern University and Agricultural and Mechanical College M
Southwestern Oklahoma State University M
Springfield College M
State University of New York College at Cortland M
State University of New York College of Environmental Science and Forestry M,D
Temple University M*
Texas A&M University M,D*
Texas State University–San Marcos M*
Universidad Metropolitana M
University of Alberta M,D*
University of Arkansas M,D
University of Florida M,D*
University of Idaho M
The University of Iowa M*
University of Manitoba M
University of Minnesota, Twin Cities Campus M,D*
University of Mississippi M,D
University of Missouri–Columbia M*
The University of Montana M,D
University of Nebraska at Omaha M
University of New Brunswick Fredericton M
University of New Hampshire M*
The University of North Carolina at Chapel Hill M*
The University of North Carolina at Greensboro M
University of North Texas M,O
University of Rhode Island M,D
University of South Alabama M*
University of Southern Mississippi M,D
The University of Tennessee M,D
University of Utah M,D*
University of Waterloo M,D
University of Wisconsin–La Crosse M
University of Wisconsin–Milwaukee M,O
Utah State University M,D
Virginia Commonwealth University M
Virginia Polytechnic Institute and State University M,D*
Wayne State University M*
Western Illinois University M
Western Kentucky University M
West Virginia University M
Winona State University M,O
Wright State University M

REHABILITATION COUNSELING

Arkansas State University M,O
Assumption College M,O
Auburn University M,D*
Barry University M,O*
Bayamón Central University M
Bowling Green State University M*
California State University, Fresno M
California State University, Los Angeles M,D
California State University, San Bernardino M
Central Connecticut State University M,O
Coppin State University M
Drake University M*
East Carolina University M
East Central University M
Edinboro University of Pennsylvania M,O
Emporia State University M
Florida Atlantic University M,D,O
Florida International University M*
Florida State University M,D,O*
Fort Valley State University M
The George Washington University M*
Georgia State University M
Hofstra University M,O*
Hunter College of the City University of New York M
Illinois Institute of Technology M,D*
Indiana University–Purdue University Indianapolis M,D*
Jackson State University M,O
Kent State University M,O*
Langston University M
La Salle University D
Louisiana State University Health Sciences Center M*
Maryville University of Saint Louis M
Michigan State University M,D,O*
Minnesota State University Mankato M
Montana State University–Billings M
North Carolina Agricultural and Technical State University M,D
Northeastern University M*
Ohio University M,D*
Pontifical Catholic University of Puerto Rico M
St. Cloud State University M
St. John's University (NY) M,D,O
Salve Regina University M,O
San Diego State University M*
San Francisco State University M
South Carolina State University M
Southern Illinois University Carbondale M,D*
Southern University and Agricultural and Mechanical College M
Springfield College M
Syracuse University M*
Texas Tech University Health Sciences Center M
Thomas University M
Troy University M,O
Université de Montréal O
University at Albany, State University of New York M*
University at Buffalo, the State University of New York M,D,O*
The University of Arizona M,D*
University of Arkansas M,D
University of Arkansas at Little Rock M,O
University of Florida M*
The University of Iowa M,D*
University of Kentucky M,D
University of Louisiana at Lafayette M*
University of Maryland, College Park M,D,O*
University of Maryland Eastern Shore M*
University of Massachusetts Boston M,O
University of Medicine and Dentistry of New Jersey M,D*
University of Memphis M,D
University of Nevada, Las Vegas M,O
The University of North Carolina at Chapel Hill M,D*
University of Northern Colorado M,D
University of North Florida M,O
University of North Texas M
University of Pittsburgh M*
University of Puerto Rico, Río Piedras M
The University of Scranton M

*M—master's degree; P—first professional degree; D—doctorate; O—other advanced degree; *—Close-Up and/or Announcement or Display in one of the other books in this series*

University of South Alabama M,D*
University of South Carolina M,O
University of South Florida M*
The University of Tennessee M,D
The University of Texas–Pan American M
The University of Texas Southwestern Medical Center at Dallas M*
University of Wisconsin–Madison M,D*
University of Wisconsin–Stout M
Utah State University M
Virginia Commonwealth University M,O
Wayne State University M,D,O*
Western Michigan University M*
Western Oregon University M
Western Washington University M
West Virginia University M
Winston-Salem State University M
Wright State University M

REHABILITATION SCIENCES

Boston University D*
California University of Pennsylvania M
Canisius College M
Central Michigan University M,D
Clarion University of Pennsylvania M
Concordia University Wisconsin M
Drake University M,D,O*
East Carolina University M
East Stroudsburg University of Pennsylvania M
Indiana University–Purdue University Indianapolis M,D*
McGill University M,D,O*
McMaster University M,D
Medical University of South Carolina D
Northwestern Health Sciences University O
Northwestern University D*
Queen's University at Kingston M,D
Salus University M,D,O
Texas Tech University Health Sciences Center D
University at Buffalo, the State University of New York M,D,O*
The University of Alabama at Birmingham O*
University of Alberta D*
The University of British Columbia M,D
University of Cincinnati D
University of Florida D*
University of Illinois at Urbana–Champaign M,D*
The University of Iowa D*
The University of Kansas M,D*
University of Kentucky D
University of Manitoba M,D
University of Maryland, Baltimore D*
University of Maryland Eastern Shore M*
University of Northern Iowa M,D
University of North Texas M
University of Oklahoma Health Sciences Center M
University of Ottawa M*
University of Pittsburgh M,D,O*
University of South Carolina M,O
University of Toronto M,D
University of Washington M,D*
University of Wisconsin–La Crosse M
University of Wisconsin–Madison M*
Virginia Commonwealth University D
Wayne State University M,O*

RELIABILITY ENGINEERING

Arizona State University M
The University of Arizona M*
University of Maryland, College Park M,D,O*

RELIGION

Amridge University P,M,D
Arizona State University M,D
Azusa Pacific University M
Baptist Bible College of Pennsylvania P,M,D
Baptist Theological Seminary at Richmond P,D
Baylor University M,D
Bellarmine University M
Bethany Theological Seminary P,M,O
Bethesda Christian University P,M
Beulah Heights University M
Biola University P,M,D
Bob Jones University P,M,D,O
Boston University M,D*
Briercrest Seminary P,M
Brown University D*
Bryn Athyn College of the New Church P,M
California Institute of Integral Studies M,D*
California State University, Long Beach M
Cardinal Stritch University M
The Catholic University of America P,M,D,O
Chestnut Hill College M,O
Chicago Theological Seminary P,M,D
Christian Brothers University M
Christian Theological Seminary P,M,D
Cincinnati Christian University P,M
Claremont Graduate University M,D*
Claremont School of Theology M,D
College of the Humanities and Sciences, Harrison Middleton University M,D
Columbia Union College M
Columbia University M,D*
Concordia University (Canada) M,D
Concordia University Chicago M
Cornell University D*
Denver Seminary P,M,D,O
Drew University M,D
Duke University M,D*
Earlham School of Religion P,M
Eastern Mennonite University P,M,O
Edgewood College M
Elms College M
Emmanuel School of Religion P,M,D
Emory University D,O*
Faith Baptist Bible College and Theological Seminary P,M
Florida International University M*
Florida State University M,D*
Fordham University M,D,O*
General Theological Seminary P,M,D,O
George Fox University P,M,D,O*
George Mason University M*
Georgetown University M,D
The George Washington University M*
Georgia State University M
Gonzaga University M
Gordon-Conwell Theological Seminary P,M,D
Graceland University (IA) M
Graduate Theological Union M,D,O
Grand Rapids Theological Seminary of Cornerstone University P,M
Harding University Graduate School of Religion P,M,D
Hardin-Simmons University M
Hartford Seminary M,D,O
Harvard University D*
Hebrew Union College–Jewish Institute of Religion (OH) M,D
Heritage Christian University M
Holy Names University M,O
Hope International University M
Iliff School of Theology P,M,D
Indiana University Bloomington M,D*
The Jewish Theological Seminary M,D*
John Carroll University M
Kentucky Christian University M
Knox Theological Seminary M
La Salle University M
La Sierra University P,M
Lee University M
Liberty University P,M,D
Lipscomb University P,M
Loma Linda University M
Louisville Presbyterian Theological Seminary P,M,D
Loyola University Chicago P,M,O*
Lutheran Theological Seminary P,M,D
Lutheran Theological Seminary at Gettysburg P,M,D
The Lutheran Theological Seminary at Philadelphia P,M,D,O
Mars Hill Graduate School M
McGill University M,D*
McMaster University M,D
Memorial University of Newfoundland M
Miami University M*
Michigan Theological Seminary P,M,O
Midwestern Baptist Theological Seminary P,M,D,O
Missouri State University M*
Mount St. Mary's College M
Naropa University M*
New Life Theological Seminary M
New York University M,O*
Northwest Nazarene University P,M
Oblate School of Theology P,M,D,O
Oklahoma City University M
Olivet Nazarene University M
Oxford Graduate School M,D
Pacific School of Religion P,M,D,O
Pepperdine University P,M
Point Loma Nazarene University M
Princeton Theological Seminary P,M,D
Princeton University D*
Providence College M*
Queen's University at Kingston M
Reformed Theological Seminary–Charlotte Campus P,M,D
Reformed Theological Seminary–Washington D.C. P,M
Rice University D
Sacred Heart University M
St. Charles Borromeo Seminary, Overbrook M
Saint John's Seminary (MA) P,M
Santa Clara University M
Seminary of the Southwest P,M,O
Seton Hall University M*
Simpson University P,M
Sioux Falls Seminary M
Southern Adventist University M
Southern Baptist Theological Seminary P,M,D
Southern California Seminary P,M,D
Southern Evangelical Seminary P,M,D,O
Southern Methodist University M,D*
Southern Nazarene University M
Southwestern Assemblies of God University P,M
Stanford University M,D*
Syracuse University M,D*
Taylor University M
Temple Baptist Seminary P,M,D
Temple University M,D*
Trevecca Nazarene University M
Trinity Episcopal School for Ministry P,M,D,O
Trinity International University, South Florida Campus M,O
Union University M,D
United Theological Seminary of the Twin Cities P,M,D,O
Université de Sherbrooke M,D,O
Université du Québec à Montréal M,D
Université Laval M,D
The University of British Columbia M,D
University of Calgary M,D
University of California, Berkeley D*
University of California, Santa Barbara M,D
University of Chicago P,M,D*
University of Colorado at Boulder M*
University of Denver M,D*
University of Detroit Mercy M
University of Florida M,D*
University of Georgia M*
University of Hawaii at Manoa M*
The University of Iowa M,D*
The University of Kansas M*
University of Lethbridge M,D
University of Manitoba M,D
University of Michigan M,D*
University of Minnesota, Twin Cities Campus M,D*
University of Missouri–Columbia M*
University of Mobile M
The University of North Carolina at Chapel Hill M,D*
The University of North Carolina at Charlotte M*
University of North Texas M,D
University of Notre Dame M*
University of Ottawa M,D*

University of Pennsylvania	D*
University of Pittsburgh	M,D*
University of Regina	M,D
University of St. Thomas (MN)	M*
University of Saskatchewan	M
University of South Africa	M,D
University of South Carolina	M
University of South Florida	M*
The University of Tennessee	M,D
University of the Incarnate Word	M
University of the West	M,D
University of Toronto	M,D
University of Virginia	M,D
University of Washington	M,D*
University of Waterloo	D
The University of Winnipeg	M
Vanderbilt University	M,D*
Vanguard University of Southern California	M
Virginia University of Lynchburg	P
Wake Forest University	M*
Warner Pacific College	M
Wayland Baptist University	M
Western Michigan University	M*
Western Seminary	M,O
Westminster Seminary California	P,M
Westminster Theological Seminary	P,M,D,O
Wheaton College	M
Wilfrid Laurier University	M,D
Wycliffe College	P,M,D,O
Yale University	D*

RELIGIOUS EDUCATION

Ambrose University College	P,M,O
Andover Newton Theological School	P,M,D
Andrews University	M,D,O
Asbury Theological Seminary	M,D,O
Azusa Pacific University	M
Baptist Bible College of Pennsylvania	P,M,D
Baptist Theological Seminary at Richmond	P,D
Bethel Seminary	P,M,D,O
Biola University	P,M,D
Boston College	P,M,D,O*
Brandeis University	M
Brigham Young University	M*
Calvin Theological Seminary	P,M,D
Campbell University	P,M,D
The Catholic University of America	P,M,D,O
Claremont School of Theology	M,D
Columbia International University	P,M,D,O
Concordia University Chicago	M
Concordia University, Nebraska	M
Concordia University, St. Paul	M,O
Dallas Baptist University	M
Dallas Theological Seminary	M,D,O
Emmanuel School of Religion	P,M,D
Felician College	M,O*
Fordham University	M,D,O*
Gardner-Webb University	P,D
Garrett-Evangelical Theological Seminary	P,M,D
Georgian Court University	M,O
Global University	P,M
Grand Rapids Theological Seminary of Cornerstone University	P,M
Gratz College	M,D,O
Hebrew College	M,O
Hebrew Union College–Jewish Institute of Religion (CA)	M,D,O
Hebrew Union College–Jewish Institute of Religion (NY)	M
Inter American University of Puerto Rico, Metropolitan Campus	D
The Jewish Theological Seminary	M,D*
Jewish University of America	M,D
La Sierra University	P,M
Laura and Alvin Siegal College of Judaic Studies	M
Loyola Marymount University	M
Loyola University Chicago	M*
Luther Rice University	P,M,D
Maple Springs Baptist Bible College and Seminary	P,M,D,O
Michigan Theological Seminary	P,M,O
Midwestern Baptist Theological Seminary	P,M,D,O
Nazarene Theological Seminary	P,M,D
Newman Theological College	M,O
New Orleans Baptist Theological Seminary	P,M,D
The Nigerian Baptist Theological Seminary	P,M,D,O
Oral Roberts University	P,M,D
Pfeiffer University	M
Phillips Theological Seminary	P,M,D
Pontifical Catholic University of Puerto Rico	M
Providence College and Theological Seminary	P,M,D,O
Reformed Theological Seminary–Jackson Campus	P,M,D,O
Regent University	P,M,D,O
St. Augustine's Seminary of Toronto	P,M,O
St. Petersburg Theological Seminary	P,M,D
Saints Cyril and Methodius Seminary	P,M
St. Vladimir's Orthodox Theological Seminary	P,M,D
Shasta Bible College	M
Southeastern Baptist Theological Seminary	P,M,D
Southern Adventist University	M
Southern Baptist Theological Seminary	P,M,D
Southern Evangelical Seminary	P,M,O
Southwestern Assemblies of God University	M
Southwestern Baptist Theological Seminary	M,D,O
Spertus Institute of Jewish Studies	M
Teachers College, Columbia University	M,D
Temple Baptist Seminary	P,M,D
Trinity Baptist College	M
Trinity International University	P,M,D,O
Union Theological Seminary and Presbyterian School of Christian Education	M
University of St. Michael's College	P,M,D,O
University of St. Thomas (MN)	M*
University of San Francisco	M,D
Wesley Biblical Seminary	P,M
Western Seminary	D
Wheaton College	M
Yeshiva University	M,D,O

REPRODUCTIVE BIOLOGY

Cornell University	M,D*
Eastern Virginia Medical School	M
Northwestern University	D*
Queen's University at Kingston	M,D
The University of British Columbia	M,D
University of Colorado Denver	D*
University of Saskatchewan	M,D
University of Wyoming	M,D
West Virginia University	M,D

RHETORIC

Abilene Christian University	M
Ball State University	M*
Bob Jones University	P,M,D,O
Bowling Green State University	M,D*
California State University, Dominguez Hills	M,O
California State University, Northridge	M
California State University, Stanislaus	M,O
Carnegie Mellon University	M,D*
The Catholic University of America	M,D
Clemson University	D
Duquesne University	M,D*
Eastern Washington University	M
Florida State University	M,D*
Georgia State University	M,D
Hofstra University	M*
Idaho State University	M
Indiana University Bloomington	M,D*
Indiana University of Pennsylvania	M,D
Iowa State University of Science and Technology	M,D*
Kansas State University	M*
Kent State University	M,D*
Miami University	M,D*
Michigan State University	M,D*
Michigan Technological University	M,D
New Mexico Highlands University	M
New Mexico State University	M,D
North Carolina State University	D*
Rensselaer Polytechnic Institute	M,D
San Diego State University	M*
Southern Illinois University Carbondale	M,D*
Syracuse University	M,D*
Texas State University–San Marcos	M*
Texas Tech University	M,D
Texas Woman's University	M,D
The University of Alabama	M,D
The University of Arizona	D*
University of Arkansas at Little Rock	M
University of California, Berkeley	D*
The University of Iowa	M,D*
University of Louisiana at Lafayette	M,D*
University of Louisville	M,D
University of Nebraska–Lincoln	M,D*
The University of North Carolina at Greensboro	M,D
The University of Texas at El Paso	M,D
University of Utah	M,D*
University of Wisconsin–Madison	M,D*
University of Wisconsin–Milwaukee	M,D,O
Virginia Commonwealth University	M
Wright State University	M

ROMANCE LANGUAGES

Appalachian State University	M
Boston University	M,D*
Clark Atlanta University	M,D
Columbia University	M,D*
Cornell University	M,D*
Hunter College of the City University of New York	M
The Johns Hopkins University	D*
Michigan State University	M,D*
New York University	M,D*
Northern Illinois University	M
Queens College of the City University of New York	M
San Diego State University	M*
Stony Brook University, State University of New York	M
Texas Tech University	M,D
University at Buffalo, the State University of New York	M,D*
The University of Alabama	M,D
University of California, Berkeley	D*
University of Chicago	M,D*
University of Cincinnati	M,D
University of Georgia	M,D*
University of Miami	D*
University of Michigan	D*
University of Missouri–Columbia	M,D*
University of Missouri–Kansas City	M*
University of New Orleans	M
The University of North Carolina at Chapel Hill	M,D*
University of Notre Dame	M*
University of Oregon	M,D*
University of Pennsylvania	M,D*
University of South Africa	M,D
The University of Texas at Austin	M,D
University of Virginia	M,D
University of Washington	M,D*
Washington University in St. Louis	M,D*

RURAL PLANNING AND STUDIES

Brandon University	M,O
California State University, Chico	M
Concordia University (Canada)	M,D,O
Cornell University	M*
Dalhousie University	M
Iowa State University of Science and Technology	M,D*
Université Laval	O
University of Alaska Fairbanks	M
University of Guelph	M,D
The University of Montana	M

*M—master's degree; P—first professional degree; D—doctorate; O—other advanced degree; *—Close-Up and/or Announcement or Display in one of the other books in this series*

University of West Georgia	M
University of Wyoming	M
Virginia Polytechnic Institute and State University	M,D*

RURAL SOCIOLOGY

Auburn University	M*
Cornell University	M,D*
Iowa State University of Science and Technology	M,D*
The Ohio State University	M,D*
Penn State University Park	M,D*
South Dakota State University	M,D
University of Alberta	M,D*
University of Missouri–Columbia	M,D*
The University of Montana	M
University of Wisconsin–Madison	M,D*

RUSSIAN

American University	O*
Boston College	M*
Brown University	M,D*
Bryn Mawr College	M,D*
Columbia University	M,D*
Harvard University	D*
Hofstra University	M*
Kent State University	M,D*
McGill University	M,D*
Middlebury College	M,D
New York University	M*
Penn State University Park	M,D*
Princeton University	D*
Stanford University	M,D*
University at Albany, State University of New York	M,O*
The University of Arizona	M*
University of California, Berkeley	D*
University of Michigan	M,D*
The University of North Carolina at Chapel Hill	M,D*
University of Oregon	M*
University of South Africa	M,D
The University of Tennessee	D
University of Washington	M,D*
University of Waterloo	M,D
Wayne State University	M,D*
Yale University	D*

SAFETY ENGINEERING

Embry-Riddle Aeronautical University (AZ)	M
Indiana University Bloomington	M,D*
Murray State University	M
National University	M
New Jersey Institute of Technology	M
University of Minnesota, Duluth	M
University of Southern California	M,D,O*
West Virginia University	M

SCANDINAVIAN LANGUAGES

Cornell University	M,D*
Harvard University	D*
University of California, Berkeley	D*
University of California, Los Angeles	M*
University of Massachusetts Amherst	M,D*
University of Minnesota, Twin Cities Campus	M,D*
University of Washington	M,D*
University of Wisconsin–Madison	M,D*

SCHOOL NURSING

Cambridge College	M,D,O
Eastern University	M,O
Kean University	M
Kutztown University of Pennsylvania	M,O
Monmouth University	M,O
Saint Joseph's University	M,O
Seton Hall University	M*
University of Illinois at Chicago	M*
West Chester University of Pennsylvania	M,O
Wright State University	M

SCHOOL PSYCHOLOGY

Abilene Christian University	M
Adelphi University	M*
Alabama Agricultural and Mechanical University	M,O
Alfred University	M,D,O*
Alliant International University–Irvine	M,D,O*
Alliant International University–Los Angeles	M,D,O*
Alliant International University–San Diego	M,D,O*
Alliant International University–San Francisco	M,D,O*
Andrews University	M,O
Appalachian State University	M
Arcadia University	M
Argosy University, Hawai'i	M*
Argosy University, Phoenix	M,D*
Argosy University, Sarasota	M,D,O*
Arkansas State University	M,O
Assumption College	M,O
Auburn University	M,D,O*
Azusa Pacific University	M
Ball State University	M,D,O*
Barry University	M,O*
Bowling Green State University	M,O*
Brigham Young University	M,D,O*
Brooklyn College of the City University of New York	M,O
Bucknell University	M
California Baptist University	M
California State University, Los Angeles	M,D
California State University, Northridge	M
California State University, Sacramento	M
California University of Pennsylvania	M
Canisius College	M
Capella University	M,D,O
Carlos Albizu University, Miami Campus	M,D
Central Connecticut State University	M,O
Central Michigan University	D,O
Central Washington University	M
Chapman University	M,D,O
The Chicago School of Professional Psychology	O
The Chicago School of Professional Psychology: Grayslake Campus	O
The Citadel, The Military College of South Carolina	M,O
City University of Seattle	M,O
Cleveland State University	M,D,O
The College of New Rochelle	M
College of St. Joseph	M
The College of Saint Rose	M,O*
The College of William and Mary	M,O
Duquesne University	M,D,O*
East Carolina University	
Eastern Illinois University	M,O
Eastern Kentucky University	M,O
Eastern University	M,O
Eastern Washington University	M
Edinboro University of Pennsylvania	M,O
Emporia State University	M,O
Evangel University	M
Fairfield University	M,O*
Fairleigh Dickinson University, Metropolitan Campus	M,D*
Florida Agricultural and Mechanical University	M
Florida International University	M,O*
Florida State University	M,O*
Fordham University	M,D,O*
Fort Hays State University	O
Francis Marion University	M
Fresno Pacific University	M
Gallaudet University	M,O
Gardner-Webb University	M
George Fox University	M,O*
George Mason University	M*
Georgia Southern University	M,O
Georgia State University	M,D,O
Grand Valley State University	M
Hofstra University	M,D,O*
Howard University	M,D,O
Humboldt State University	M
Idaho State University	M,D,O
Illinois State University	D,O
Immaculata University	M,D,O
Indiana State University	M,D,O
Indiana University Bloomington	M,D,O*
Indiana University of Pennsylvania	D,O
Inter American University of Puerto Rico, Metropolitan Campus	M,D
Inter American University of Puerto Rico, San Germán Campus	M,D
Iona College	M*
James Madison University	M,D,O
The Johns Hopkins University	M,O*
Kean University	D,O
Kent State University	M,D,O*
La Sierra University	M,O
Lehigh University	M,D,O
Lenoir-Rhyne University	M
Lesley University	M*
Lewis & Clark College	M,O
Lindenwood University	M,D,O
Long Island University, Brooklyn Campus	M
Long Island University, Westchester Graduate Campus	M
Louisiana State University and Agricultural and Mechanical College	M,D
Louisiana State University in Shreveport	O
Loyola Marymount University	M
Loyola University Chicago	M,D,O*
Marist College	M,O
Marshall University	O
Marywood University	M,O
Massachusetts School of Professional Psychology	M,D,O
McGill University	M,D,O*
McNeese State University	M
Mercy College	M
Miami University	M,O*
Michigan State University	M,D,O*
Middle Tennessee State University	M,O
Millersville University of Pennsylvania	M
Minnesota State University Mankato	M,D
Minnesota State University Moorhead	M,O
Minot State University	O
Mississippi State University	M,D,O
Montana State University	M,D,O
Montclair State University	M,O*
Mount Saint Vincent University	M
National-Louis University	M,D,O
National University	M
New Jersey City University	M,O
New Mexico Highlands University	M
New Mexico State University	M,D,O
Niagara University	M,O
Nicholls State University	M,O
North Carolina State University	D*
Northeastern University	M,D,O*
Northern Arizona University	M,D
Northwest Nazarene University	M
Nova Southeastern University	O*
Oregon State University–Cascades	M
Ottawa University	M
Our Lady of the Lake University of San Antonio	M,D
Penn State University Park	M,D*
Philadelphia College of Osteopathic Medicine	M,D,O*
Pittsburg State University	O
Purdue University Calumet	M
Queens College of the City University of New York	M,O
Radford University	M,D,O
Rider University	O*
Roberts Wesleyan College	M
Rochester Institute of Technology	M,O
Rowan University	M,O
Rutgers, The State University of New Jersey, New Brunswick	M,D*
St. John's University (NY)	M,D
San Diego State University	M*
Seattle University	M,O
Seton Hall University	O*
Southeast Missouri State University	M,O
Southern Connecticut State University	M,O
Southern Illinois University Edwardsville	O
Southwestern Oklahoma State University	M
State University of New York at Oswego	M,O
State University of New York at Plattsburgh	M,O
Stephen F. Austin State University	M
Syracuse University	M,D,O*
Tarleton State University	M,O
Teachers College, Columbia University	M,D
Temple University	M,D*
Tennessee State University	M,D
Texas A&M University	M,D*
Texas State University–San Marcos	M*
Texas Woman's University	M,D,O
Towson University	O

Trinity University M
Troy University M
Tufts University M,O*
Union College (KY) M
Universidad del Turabo M
University at Albany, State University of New York M,D,O*
University at Buffalo, the State University of New York M,D,O*
The University of Akron M
University of Alberta M,D*
The University of Arizona M,D,O*
The University of British Columbia M,D,O
University of Calgary M,D
University of California, Berkeley *
University of California, Riverside M,D*
University of California, Santa Barbara M,D
University of Central Arkansas M,D
University of Central Florida O*
University of Cincinnati D,O
University of Connecticut M,D,O*
University of Dayton M,O
University of Delaware M,D,O*
University of Denver M,D,O*
University of Detroit Mercy O
University of Florida M,D,O*
University of Hartford M*
University of Houston–Clear Lake M
University of Houston–Victoria M
University of Idaho O
The University of Iowa M,D,O*
The University of Kansas D,O*
University of Kentucky M,D,O
University of Louisiana at Monroe M,O
University of Manitoba M,D
University of Mary M
University of Mary Hardin-Baylor M
University of Maryland, College Park M,D,O*
University of Massachusetts Amherst D*
University of Massachusetts Boston M,O
University of Memphis M,D
University of Minnesota, Twin Cities Campus M,D,O*
University of Missouri–Columbia M,D,O*
University of Missouri–St. Louis D,O
The University of Montana M,D,O
University of Nebraska at Kearney M,O
University of Nebraska at Omaha M,D,O
University of Nebraska–Lincoln M,D,O*
The University of North Carolina at Chapel Hill M,D*
The University of North Carolina at Greensboro M,D,O
University of Northern Colorado D,O
University of Northern Iowa M,O
University of North Texas M
University of Oklahoma M,D*
University of Phoenix–Denver Campus M
University of Phoenix–Las Vegas Campus M
University of Phoenix–Northern Nevada Campus M
University of Phoenix–Puerto Rico Campus M
University of Phoenix–Southern Colorado Campus M,O
University of Phoenix–Utah Campus M
University of Rhode Island M,D
University of South Alabama M,D*
University of South Carolina D
University of Southern Maine M,D
University of Southern Mississippi M,D
University of South Florida M,D,O*
The University of Tennessee M,D,O
The University of Tennessee at Chattanooga O
The University of Texas at Austin M,D
The University of Texas at Tyler M
The University of Texas–Pan American M
University of the Pacific M,D,O
The University of Toledo M,D,O
University of Utah M,D*
University of Virginia M,D,O
University of Washington M,D*
University of Wisconsin–Eau Claire M,O
University of Wisconsin–La Crosse M,O
University of Wisconsin–Milwaukee D,O
University of Wisconsin–River Falls M,O
University of Wisconsin–Stout M,O
University of Wisconsin–Whitewater M,O*
Utah State University M,D
Valdosta State University M,O
Valparaiso University
Walden University M,D,O
Washington State University M,D,O*
Wayne State University M,D,O*
Western Carolina University M
Western Illinois University M,O
Western Kentucky University M,O
Western New Mexico University M
Wichita State University M,D,O*
Worcester State College M,O
Yeshiva University D
Youngstown State University M

SCIENCE EDUCATION

Acadia University M
Agnes Scott College M*
Alabama State University M,O
Albany State University M
Alverno College M
American University of Puerto Rico M
Andrews University M,D,O
Antioch University New England M*
Arcadia University M,D,O
Arkansas State University M,O
Armstrong Atlantic State University M
Asbury College M,O
Auburn University M,D,O*
Averett University M
Ball State University M,D*
Belmont University M
Bemidji State University M
Benedictine University M
Bennington College M
Bethel College (TN) M
Bloomsburg University of Pennsylvania M
Boise State University M,D
Boston College M,D*
Boston University M,D,O*
Bowling Green State University M*
Bridgewater State College M
Brigham Young University M,D*
Brooklyn College of the City University of New York M,O
Brown University M*
Buffalo State College, State University of New York M
California State University, Chico M
California State University, Fullerton M
California State University, Northridge M
California State University, San Bernardino M
Cambridge College M,D,O
Caribbean University M,D
Carthage College M,O
Central Michigan University M
Chatham University M
Christopher Newport University M
The Citadel, The Military College of South Carolina M
City College of the City University of New York M*
Clarion University of Pennsylvania M
Clemson University M
Cleveland State University M
The College at Brockport, State University of New York M
College of Charleston M*
College of the Humanities and Sciences, Harrison Middleton University M,D
The College of William and Mary M
The Colorado College M
Columbia University M,D,O*
Columbus State University M,O
Converse College M
Cornell University M,D*
Delaware State University M,D
Delta State University M
Drake University M*
Duquesne University M*
East Carolina University M
Eastern Connecticut State University M
Eastern Kentucky University M
Eastern Michigan University M
East Stroudsburg University of Pennsylvania M
Elms College M,O
Fairleigh Dickinson University, Metropolitan Campus M*
Fitchburg State College M
Florida Agricultural and Mechanical University M
Florida Institute of Technology M,D,O*
Florida International University M,D*
Florida State University M,D,O*
Fresno Pacific University M
Gannon University M
George Mason University M,O*
Georgia Southern University M
Georgia State University M,D,O
Grambling State University M,D,O
Harding University M,O
Hardin-Simmons University M,D
Harvard University M*
Heritage University M
Hofstra University M*
Hood College M
Hunter College of the City University of New York M,O
ICR Graduate School M
Illinois Institute of Technology M,D*
Indiana State University M,D
Indiana Tech M
Indiana University Bloomington M,D,O*
Instituto Tecnológico y de Estudios Superiores de Monterrey, Campus Monterrey M,D
Inter American University of Puerto Rico, Arecibo Campus M
Inter American University of Puerto Rico, Metropolitan Campus M
Inter American University of Puerto Rico, Ponce Campus M
Inter American University of Puerto Rico, San Germán Campus M
Iona College M*
Ithaca College M
Jackson State University M,D
John Carroll University M
The Johns Hopkins University M,O*
Johnson State College M
Kaplan University–Davenport Campus M
Kean University M
Kutztown University of Pennsylvania M,O
Laurentian University O
Lawrence Technological University M
Lebanon Valley College M
Lehman College of the City University of New York M
Lesley University M,D,O*
Lewis University M
Long Island University, C.W. Post Campus M
Louisiana Tech University M,D
Loyola University Chicago M*
Lynchburg College M
Lyndon State College M
Manhattanville College M*
McNeese State University M
Michigan State University M*
Michigan Technological University M
Middle Tennessee State University M
Mills College M,D
Minnesota State University Mankato M
Minot State University M
Mississippi College M,D,O
Missouri State University M*
Montclair State University M,D,O*
Morgan State University M,D
National-Louis University M,O
New Mexico Institute of Mining and Technology M
New York University M*
North Carolina Agricultural and Technical State University M
North Carolina State University M,D*
North Dakota State University M,D,O
Northeastern State University M

*M—master's degree; P—first professional degree; D—doctorate; O—other advanced degree; *—Close-Up and/or Announcement or Display in one of the other books in this series*

Northern Arizona University	M
Northern Michigan University	M
North Georgia College & State University	M,O
Northwestern State University of Louisiana	M
Northwest Missouri State University	M
Nova Southeastern University	M,O*
Occidental College	M
Ohio University	M*
Old Dominion University	M
Oregon State University	M,D*
Our Lady of the Lake University of San Antonio	M
Penn State Great Valley	M
Penn State University Park	M,D*
Plymouth State University	M
Portland State University	M,D
Purdue University	M,D,O
Purdue University Calumet	M
Queens College of the City University of New York	M,O
Quinnipiac University	M*
Regis University	M,O
Rensselaer Polytechnic Institute	M
Rider University	O*
Rutgers, The State University of New Jersey, New Brunswick	M,D*
Saginaw Valley State University	M
St. John Fisher College	M
Salem State College	M
San Diego State University	M,D*
Shippensburg University of Pennsylvania	M
Slippery Rock University of Pennsylvania	M
Smith College	M
South Carolina State University	M
Southeast Missouri State University	M
Southern Connecticut State University	M,O
Southern Illinois University Edwardsville	M
Southern University and Agricultural and Mechanical College	D
Southwestern Oklahoma State University	M
Stanford University	M,D*
State University of New York at Binghamton	M*
State University of New York at Fredonia	M
State University of New York at New Paltz	M
State University of New York at Plattsburgh	M
State University of New York College at Cortland	M
State University of New York College at Potsdam	M
Stony Brook University, State University of New York	M,D,O
Syracuse University	M,D*
Teachers College, Columbia University	M,D
Temple University	M,D*
Texas A&M University	M,D*
Texas Christian University	M,D
Texas State University–San Marcos	M*
Texas Woman's University	M,D
Towson University	M
Union Graduate College	M
University at Albany, State University of New York	M,D*
University at Buffalo, the State University of New York	M,D,O*
The University of Alabama in Huntsville	M,D
University of Arkansas at Pine Bluff	M
The University of British Columbia	M,D
University of California, Berkeley	M,D*
University of California, Los Angeles	M,D*
University of California, San Diego	D*
University of California, Santa Cruz	M,D*
University of Central Florida	M,D,O*
University of Chicago	D*
University of Cincinnati	M,D,O
University of Connecticut	M,D,O*
University of Florida	M,D,O*
University of Georgia	M,D,O*
University of Houston	M,D*
University of Idaho	M,D
University of Illinois at Urbana–Champaign	M,D*
University of Indianapolis	M
The University of Iowa	M,D*
University of Maine	M,O*
University of Maryland, Baltimore County	M,O*
University of Massachusetts Lowell	M,D,O
University of Miami	D*
University of Michigan	M,D*
University of Michigan–Dearborn	M*
University of Minnesota, Twin Cities Campus	M*
University of Missouri–Columbia	M,D,O*
University of Nebraska at Kearney	M
University of New Hampshire	M,D*
The University of North Carolina at Chapel Hill	M*
The University of North Carolina at Greensboro	M,D,O
The University of North Carolina at Pembroke	M
University of Northern Colorado	M,D
University of Northern Iowa	M
University of North Texas Health Science Center at Fort Worth	M
University of Oklahoma	M,D,O*
University of Pittsburgh	M,D*
University of Puerto Rico, Río Piedras	M,D
University of St. Francis (IL)	M
University of San Diego	M
University of South Africa	M,D
University of South Alabama	M,O*
University of South Carolina	M,D
University of Southern Mississippi	M,D
University of South Florida	M,D,O*
The University of Tampa	M
The University of Tennessee	M,D,O
The University of Texas at Austin	M,D
The University of Texas at Dallas	M*
University of the Incarnate Word	M
The University of Toledo	M
University of Tulsa	M*
University of Utah	M,D*
University of Vermont	M,D*
University of Victoria	M,D
University of Virginia	M,D,O
University of Washington	M,D*
University of Washington, Tacoma	M
The University of West Alabama	M
University of West Florida	M
University of West Georgia	M,O
University of Wisconsin–Madison	M,D*
University of Wisconsin–River Falls	M
University of Wisconsin–Stevens Point	M
University of Wyoming	M
Ursuline College	M
Vanderbilt University	M,D*
Walden University	M,D,O
Wayne State College	M
Wayne State University	M,D,O*
Wesleyan College	M
West Chester University of Pennsylvania	M,O
Western Carolina University	M
Western Governors University	M,O
Western Kentucky University	M
Western Michigan University	D*
Western Oregon University	M
Western Washington University	M
Widener University	M,D*
Wilkes University	M,D
Wright State University	M
Youngstown State University	M

SECONDARY EDUCATION

Adelphi University	M*
Alabama Agricultural and Mechanical University	M,O
Alabama State University	M,O
Alcorn State University	M,O
American International College	M,D,O
American University	M,O*
Andrews University	M,D,O
Arcadia University	M,D,O
Argosy University, Atlanta	M,D,O*
Argosy University, Chicago	M,D,O*
Argosy University, Hawai'i	M,D*
Argosy University, Inland Empire	M,D*
Argosy University, Los Angeles	M,D*
Argosy University, Nashville	M,D,O*
Argosy University, Orange County	M,D*
Argosy University, Phoenix	M,D,O*
Argosy University, San Diego	M,D*
Argosy University, San Francisco Bay Area	M,D*
Argosy University, Sarasota	M,D,O*
Argosy University, Schaumburg	M,D,O*
Argosy University, Seattle	M,D*
Argosy University, Tampa	M,D,O*
Argosy University, Twin Cities	M,D,O*
Argosy University, Washington DC	M,D,O*
Arizona State University at the West campus	M,D,O
Arkansas State University	M,D,O
Arkansas Tech University	M,O
Armstrong Atlantic State University	M
Auburn University	M,D,O*
Auburn University Montgomery	M,O
Augustana College	M
Augusta State University	M,O
Austin College	M
Austin Peay State University	M,O
Ball State University	M*
Belhaven College (MS)	M
Bellarmine University	M
Belmont University	M
Benedictine University	M
Bennington College	M
Berry College	M
Bethel University	M,D,O
Bob Jones University	P,M,D,O
Boston College	M*
Bowie State University	M
Brandeis University	M
Brenau University	M,O
Bridgewater State College	M
Brooklyn College of the City University of New York	M,O
Brown University	M*
Butler University	M
California State University, Bakersfield	M
California State University, Fullerton	M
California State University, Long Beach	M
California State University, Los Angeles	M
California State University, Northridge	M
California State University, San Bernardino	M
California State University, Stanislaus	M,O
California University of Pennsylvania	M
Campbell University	M
Canisius College	M
Carlow University	M
Carson-Newman College	M
The Catholic University of America	M,D,O
Centenary College of Louisiana	M
Central Connecticut State University	M
Central Michigan University	M,O
Chadron State College	M,O
Chapman University	M
Charleston Southern University	M
Chatham University	M
Chestnut Hill College	M
Chicago State University	M
The Citadel, The Military College of South Carolina	M
City College of the City University of New York	M,O*
Clemson University	M
Coastal Carolina University	M
Colgate University	M
College of Mount St. Joseph	M
The College of New Jersey	M
College of St. Joseph	M
The College of Saint Rose	M,O*
College of Staten Island of the City University of New York	M
The College of William and Mary	M
The Colorado College	M
Columbus State University	M,O
Concordia University (OR)	M
Concordia University Chicago	M
Concordia University, Nebraska	M
Converse College	M

Creighton University M*
Dakota Wesleyan University M
Dallas Baptist University M
Defiance College M
Delta State University M,O
DePaul University M,D*
Dowling College M,D,O
Drake University M*
Drury University M
Duquesne University M*
D'Youville College M,O*
Eastern Connecticut State University M
Eastern Kentucky University M
Eastern Michigan University M
Eastern Nazarene College M,O
Eastern Oregon University M
East Stroudsburg University of Pennsylvania M
East Tennessee State University M
Elms College M,O
Emmanuel College M,O
Emory University M,D,O*
Emporia State University M
Evangel University M
Fairfield University M,O*
Fayetteville State University M
Fitchburg State College M
Florida Agricultural and Mechanical University M
Fordham University M,D,O*
Francis Marion University M
Fresno Pacific University M
Friends University M
Frostburg State University M
Gallaudet University M,D,O
George Fox University M,D,O*
George Mason University M,O*
The George Washington University M*
Georgia College & State University M,O
Georgia Southern University M
Georgia Southwestern State University M,O
Georgia State University M,D,O
Grand Canyon University M,D*
Grand Valley State University M,O
Greenville College M
Hampton University M
Harding University M,O
Hawai'i Pacific University M*
Hofstra University M,O*
Holy Family University M
Hood College M,O
Howard University M,O
Hunter College of the City University of New York M
Idaho State University M,O
Immaculata University M,D,O
Indiana University Bloomington M,D,O*
Indiana University Northwest M
Indiana University–Purdue University Fort Wayne M,O
Indiana University South Bend M
Indiana University Southeast M
Ithaca College M
Jackson State University M,D,O
Jacksonville State University M
James Madison University M
John Carroll University M
The Johns Hopkins University M,O*
Johnson State College M,O
Jones International University M
Kaplan University–Davenport Campus M
Kennesaw State University M
Kent State University M*
Kutztown University of Pennsylvania M,O
LaGrange College M
Lee University M,O
Lehigh University M,D,O
Le Moyne College M,O
Lewis & Clark College M
Lewis University M
Liberty University M,D,O
Lincoln University (MO) M,O
Long Island University, C.W. Post Campus M
Long Island University, Rockland Graduate Campus M
Long Island University, Westchester Graduate Campus M,O
Longwood University M
Louisiana State University and Agricultural and Mechanical College M,D,O
Louisiana Tech University M,D
Loyola Marymount University M
Loyola University Chicago M*
Maharishi University of Management M
Manhattanville College M*
Mansfield University of Pennsylvania M
Marshall University M
Marygrove College M
Marymount University M
Maryville University of Saint Louis M,D
Marywood University M
McDaniel College M
McNeese State University M
Mercer University M,D,O
Mercy College M
Miami University M*
Middle Tennessee State University M,O
Mills College M,D
Minnesota State University Mankato M,O
Mississippi College M,D,O
Mississippi State University M,D,O
Missouri State University M,O*
Montana State University–Billings M
Morehead State University M,O
Morgan State University M
Mount Saint Mary College M
Mount St. Mary's College M
Murray State University M,O
National-Louis University M
New Jersey City University M
Niagara University M,O
Norfolk State University M
North Carolina State University M*
Northern Arizona University M
Northern Illinois University M,D
Northern Michigan University M
Northern State University M
North Georgia College & State University M,O
Northwestern Oklahoma State University M
Northwestern State University of Louisiana M,O
Northwestern University M*
Northwest Missouri State University M,O
Nova Southeastern University M,O*
Oakland University M
Occidental College M
Ohio University M,D*
Old Dominion University M
Olivet Nazarene University M
Our Lady of the Lake University of San Antonio M
Pacific University M
Park University M
Piedmont College M,O
Pittsburg State University M
Plymouth State University M
Portland State University M,D
Prescott College M,D
Providence College M*
Queens College of the City University of New York M,O
Quinnipiac University M*
Regis University M,O
Rhode Island College M
Roberts Wesleyan College M,O
Rochester Institute of Technology M
Rockford College M
Rollins College M
Roosevelt University M
Rowan University M
Sacred Heart University M,O
Saginaw Valley State University M
St. John's University (NY) M
Saint Joseph's University M,D
Saint Mary's University of Minnesota M,O
St. Thomas Aquinas College M,O*
Saint Xavier University M,O
Salem College M
Salem State College M
Samford University M,D,O
San Diego State University M*
San Francisco State University M
San Jose State University M,O
Seattle Pacific University M,O
Shenandoah University M,D,O
Siena Heights University M
Sierra Nevada College M
Simmons College M,O
Slippery Rock University of Pennsylvania M
Smith College M
South Carolina State University M
Southeast Missouri State University M
Southern Arkansas University–Magnolia M
Southern Illinois University Edwardsville M
Southern New Hampshire University M,O*
Southern Oregon University M
Southern University and Agricultural and Mechanical College M
Southwestern Assemblies of God University M
Southwestern Oklahoma State University M
Spalding University M
Springfield College M
Spring Hill College M
State University of New York at Binghamton M*
State University of New York at Fredonia M
State University of New York at New Paltz M
State University of New York at Oswego M
State University of New York at Plattsburgh M
State University of New York College at Cortland M
State University of New York College at Geneseo M
State University of New York College at Oneonta M
State University of New York College at Potsdam M
Stephen F. Austin State University M,D
Suffolk University M,O*
Sul Ross State University M*
Tarleton State University M,O
Tennessee Technological University M,O*
Texas A&M University–Commerce M,D
Texas A&M University–Corpus Christi M
Texas A&M University–Kingsville M
Texas Christian University M
Texas Southern University M,D
Texas State University–San Marcos M*
Texas Tech University M,D
Towson University M
Trevecca Nazarene University M
Trinity (Washington) University M
Troy University M,O
Tufts University M,D*
Union College (KY) M
Universidad Adventista de las Antillas M
The University of Akron M,D
The University of Alabama M,D,O
The University of Alabama at Birmingham M*
University of Alaska Fairbanks M,D,O
University of Alaska Southeast M
University of Alberta M,D*
The University of Arizona M,D*
University of Arkansas M,O
University of Arkansas at Little Rock M
University of Arkansas at Pine Bluff M
University of Bridgeport M,O
University of California, Irvine M,D*
University of Central Missouri M,O
University of Central Oklahoma M
University of Cincinnati M
University of Connecticut M,D,O*
University of Dayton M
University of Great Falls M
University of Guam M
University of Houston M,D*
University of Houston–Downtown M
University of Illinois at Chicago M,D*
University of Indianapolis M
The University of Iowa M,D*
University of Louisiana at Monroe M
University of Louisville M
University of Maine M,O*
University of Maryland, Baltimore County M*
University of Maryland, College Park M,D,O*
University of Massachusetts Amherst M,D,O*
University of Massachusetts Boston M,D,O
University of Massachusetts Dartmouth M,O
University of Memphis M,D
University of Missouri–St. Louis M,O
University of Montevallo M
University of Nebraska at Omaha M
University of Nevada, Reno M*

*M—master's degree; P—first professional degree; D—doctorate; O—other advanced degree; *—Close-Up and/or Announcement or Display in one of the other books in this series*

University of New Hampshire M*
University of New Mexico M,O*
University of North Alabama M
The University of North Carolina at Chapel Hill M*
The University of North Carolina at Charlotte M*
University of North Dakota D
University of North Florida M
University of North Texas M,O
University of Oklahoma M,D,O*
University of Pennsylvania M*
University of Phoenix M
University of Phoenix–Bay Area Campus M
University of Phoenix–Central Florida Campus M
University of Phoenix–Central Valley Campus M
University of Phoenix–Chattanooga Campus M
University of Phoenix–Denver Campus M
University of Phoenix–Hawaii Campus M
University of Phoenix–Idaho Campus M
University of Phoenix–Indianapolis Campus M
University of Phoenix–Memphis Campus M
University of Phoenix–Nashville Campus M
University of Phoenix–New Mexico Campus M
University of Phoenix–Northern Nevada Campus M
University of Phoenix–North Florida Campus M
University of Phoenix–Omaha Campus M
University of Phoenix–Oregon Campus M
University of Phoenix–Phoenix Campus M
University of Phoenix–Sacramento Valley Campus M,O
University of Phoenix–San Diego Campus M
University of Phoenix–Southern Arizona Campus M,O
University of Phoenix–Southern California Campus M
University of Phoenix–Southern Colorado Campus M,O
University of Phoenix–South Florida Campus M
University of Phoenix–Utah Campus M
University of Phoenix–West Florida Campus M
University of Pittsburgh M,D*
University of Puerto Rico, Río Piedras M,D
University of Puget Sound M
University of Rhode Island M
University of St. Francis (IL) M
University of St. Thomas (MN) M,O*
The University of Scranton M
University of South Alabama M,O*
University of South Carolina M,D
The University of South Dakota M
University of Southern Indiana M
University of Southern Mississippi M,D,O
University of South Florida M,D,O*
The University of Tennessee M,D,O
The University of Tennessee at Chattanooga M,O
The University of Tennessee at Martin M
The University of Texas–Pan American M
University of the Cumberlands M
University of the Incarnate Word M
The University of Toledo M,D,O
University of Utah M,D*
University of Washington, Tacoma M
The University of West Alabama M
University of West Florida M
University of West Georgia M,O
University of Wisconsin–Eau Claire M
University of Wisconsin–La Crosse M
University of Wisconsin–Milwaukee M
University of Wisconsin–Platteville M
University of Wisconsin–Whitewater M*
Utah State University M
Valdosta State University M,O
Vanderbilt University M*
Villanova University M*
Virginia Commonwealth University M,O
Wagner College M
Wake Forest University M*
Washington State University M,D*
Washington State University Tri-Cities M,D
Washington University in St. Louis M*
Wayne State University M,D,O*
West Chester University of Pennsylvania M,O
Western Kentucky University M,O
Western New Mexico University M
Western Oregon University M
Western Washington University M
Westfield State College M
West Virginia University M,D
Wheaton College M
Whittier College M
Whitworth University M
Wilkes University M,D
William Carey University M,O
William Woods University M,O
Wilmington University M
Winthrop University M
Worcester State College M
Wright State University M
Xavier University M*
Youngstown State University M

SLAVIC LANGUAGES

Boston College M*
Brown University M,D*
Columbia University M,D*
Cornell University M,D*
Duke University M*
Florida State University M*
Harvard University D*
Indiana University Bloomington M,D*
New York University M*
Northwestern University D*
The Ohio State University M,D*
Princeton University D*
Stanford University M,D*
University of Alberta M,D*
University of California, Berkeley D*
University of California, Los Angeles M,D*
University of Chicago M,D*
University of Illinois at Urbana–Champaign M,D*
The University of Kansas M,D*
University of Manitoba M
University of Michigan M,D*
The University of North Carolina at Chapel Hill M,D*
University of Pittsburgh M,D*
University of Southern California M,D*
The University of Texas at Austin M,D
University of Toronto M,D
University of Virginia M,D
University of Washington M,D*
University of Wisconsin–Madison M,D*
University of Wisconsin–Milwaukee M,O
Yale University D*

SOCIAL PSYCHOLOGY

Alvernia University M
American University M*
Andrews University M
Appalachian State University M
Arcadia University M
Argosy University, Atlanta M,D,O*
Argosy University, Chicago M,D*
Argosy University, Dallas M*
Argosy University, Denver M,D*
Argosy University, Sarasota M,D,O*
Argosy University, Schaumburg M,D,O*
Argosy University, Washington DC M,D*
Arizona State University D
Auburn University M,D,O*
Ball State University M*
Bowling Green State University M,D*
Brandeis University M,D
Brigham Young University M,D*
Brock University M,D
Brooklyn College of the City University of New York M,D
Brown University D*
California Institute of Integral Studies M,D*
California State University, Fullerton M
Canisius College M
Carnegie Mellon University D*
Central Connecticut State University M
Claremont Graduate University M,D,O*
Clark University D
The College of New Rochelle M
College of St. Joseph M
Columbia University M,D*
Cornell University M,D*
Creighton University M*
DePaul University M,D*
Eastern Michigan University M,O
Eastern University M,O
Florida Agricultural and Mechanical University M
Florida State University D*
Francis Marion University M
The George Washington University M,D*
Graduate School and University Center of the City University of New York D*
Harvard University D*
Henderson State University M
Hofstra University M,D,O*
Howard University M,D
Hunter College of the City University of New York M
Indiana University Bloomington M,D*
Indiana Wesleyan University M
Iowa State University of Science and Technology D*
Lamar University M
Lenoir-Rhyne University M
Lesley University M,D,O*
Lewis & Clark College M
Loyola University Chicago M,D*
Lynchburg College M
Martin University M
Marymount University
Memorial University of Newfoundland M,D
Miami University D*
Minnesota State University Mankato M,D,O
Missouri State University M*
Montclair State University M,D,O*
Naropa University M*
National-Louis University M,O
New York University M,D,O*
Norfolk State University M
North Carolina Central University M
North Carolina State University M*
North Dakota State University M,D
Northern Arizona University M
Northern Kentucky University M,O
North Georgia College & State University M
Northwestern University D*
Northwest Nazarene University M
The Ohio State University M,D*
Oregon State University–Cascades M
Penn State Harrisburg M,D
Penn State University Park M,D*
Pittsburg State University M
Queen's University at Kingston M,D
Regent University M,D,O
Regis University M,O
Rutgers, The State University of New Jersey, Newark D*
Rutgers, The State University of New Jersey, New Brunswick D*
Sage Graduate School M
St. Cloud State University M
Saint Joseph College M
Saint Martin's University M
St. Mary's University (United States) M
Shippensburg University of Pennsylvania M,O
Southeastern Oklahoma State University M
Southwestern College (NM) O*
Springfield College M
Stony Brook University, State University of New York D
Syracuse University M,D*
Teachers College, Columbia University M,D
Temple University D*
Texas A&M University M,D*
Thomas University M
Université du Québec à Rimouski M
Université Laval D

University at Albany, State University of New York M,D,O*
University at Buffalo, the State University of New York M,D*
University of Alaska Anchorage M,D
University of Alaska Fairbanks M,D
The University of British Columbia M,D
University of Central Arkansas M
University of Connecticut M,D,O*
University of Dayton M,O
University of Delaware D*
University of Florida M,D*
University of Guelph M,D
University of Hawaii at Manoa M,D,O*
University of Houston M,D*
University of La Verne D
University of Maine M,D*
University of Mary M
University of Mary Hardin-Baylor M
University of Maryland, College Park M,D*
University of Massachusetts Amherst M,D*
University of Massachusetts Lowell M
University of Michigan D*
University of Minnesota, Twin Cities Campus D*
University of Missouri–Kansas City M,D*
University of Missouri–St. Louis M,D,O
University of Montevallo M
University of Nebraska–Lincoln M,D*
University of Nevada, Reno D*
University of New Haven M,O*
The University of North Carolina at Chapel Hill D*
The University of North Carolina at Charlotte M*
The University of North Carolina at Greensboro M,D
University of North Texas M,D,O
University of Oklahoma M*
University of Oregon M,D*
University of Phoenix M
University of Phoenix–Denver Campus M
University of Phoenix–Hawaii Campus M
University of Phoenix–Kansas City Campus M
University of Phoenix–Minneapolis/St. Louis Park Campus M
University of Phoenix–Phoenix Campus M,O
University of Phoenix–Southern Colorado Campus M
University of Rochester M,D*
The University of Scranton M
University of South Carolina M,D
University of Southern California M,D*
The University of Tennessee at Martin M
The University of Toledo M,D,O
University of Victoria M,D
University of Washington D*
University of Windsor M,D
University of Wisconsin–Madison D*
University of Wisconsin–Milwaukee M,D
University of Wisconsin–Superior M
University of Wisconsin–Whitewater M*
Walden University M,D,O
Washington State University M,D*
Washington University in St. Louis D*
Western Carolina University M
Western Connecticut State University M
Western Illinois University M,O
Wichita State University M,D*
Wilfrid Laurier University M,D
Wilmington University M
Yale University D*

SOCIAL SCIENCES

Arizona State University M,D
Arkansas Tech University M
Ball State University M*
California Institute of Technology M,D*
California State University, Chico M
California State University, San Bernardino M
California University of Pennsylvania M
Campbellsville University M
Carnegie Mellon University D*
Central European University M,D*
The Citadel, The Military College of South Carolina M
College of the Humanities and Sciences, Harrison Middleton University M,D
Columbia University M*
Eastern Michigan University M,O
Edinboro University of Pennsylvania M
Florida Agricultural and Mechanical University M
George Mason University M,D,O*
Graduate Theological Union M,D,O
Hollins University M,O
Humboldt State University M
Indiana University Bloomington P,M,D,O*
The Johns Hopkins University M,D*
Lincoln University (MO) M
Long Island University, Brooklyn Campus M,O
Long Island University, C.W. Post Campus M
Massachusetts Institute of Technology D*
Michigan State University M*
Middle Tennessee State University M
Mississippi College M,O
Montclair State University M,O*
The New School: A University M,D*
New York University M,O*
North Dakota State University M,D
Northwestern University M,O*
Nova Southeastern University M,O*
Nyack College M
Ohio University M*
Queens College of the City University of New York M
Regis University M,O
St. Edward's University M,O
Southern Oregon University M
Southern University and Agricultural and Mechanical College M
Stony Brook University, State University of New York M,O
Syracuse University M,D*
Texas A&M International University M
Texas A&M University–Commerce M
Towson University M
Universidad Nacional Pedro Henriquez Urena P,M,D
University of California, Irvine M,D*
University of California, Santa Cruz D*
University of Chicago M,D*
University of Colorado Denver M*
University of Florida M*
University of Idaho M
University of Illinois at Springfield M
The University of Kansas M,D*
University of Lethbridge M,D
University of Maryland, Baltimore County D*
University of Michigan D*
University of Michigan–Flint M*
University of Northern Iowa M
University of Regina M,D
The University of Texas at Tyler M
University of Washington M,D*
University of Wisconsin–Madison D*
Worcester Polytechnic Institute M,D,O*
Yale University M,D*
York University M

SOCIAL SCIENCES EDUCATION

Acadia University M
Alabama State University M,O
Andrews University M,D,O
Appalachian State University M
Arcadia University M,D,O
Arkansas State University M,O
Arkansas Tech University M
Armstrong Atlantic State University M
Asbury College M,O
Auburn University M,D,O*
Averett University M
Belmont University M
Bennington College M
Bethel College (TN) M
Bob Jones University P,M,D,O
Boston College M*
Boston University M,D,O*
Bridgewater State College M
Brooklyn College of the City University of New York M,O
Brown University M*
Buffalo State College, State University of New York M
California State University, Chico M
California State University, Fresno M
California State University, San Bernardino M,D
Cambridge College M,D,O
Campbell University M
Caribbean University M,D
Carthage College M,O
Chadron State College M,O
Chaminade University of Honolulu M
Chatham University M
Christopher Newport University M
The Citadel, The Military College of South Carolina M
City College of the City University of New York M,O*
Clarion University of Pennsylvania M
The College at Brockport, State University of New York M
College of St. Joseph M
The College of William and Mary M
The Colorado College M
Columbus State University M,O
Converse College M
Delta State University M
Drake University M*
Duquesne University M*
East Carolina University M
Eastern Kentucky University M
East Stroudsburg University of Pennsylvania M
Emporia State University M
Fayetteville State University M
Fitchburg State College M,O
Florida Agricultural and Mechanical University M
Florida International University M,D*
Florida State University M,D,O*
Framingham State College M
Georgia Southern University M
Georgia State University M,D,O
Grambling State University M
Harding University M,O
Hofstra University M*
Hunter College of the City University of New York M
Indiana University Bloomington M,D,O*
Instituto Tecnologico de Santo Domingo M
Inter American University of Puerto Rico, Arecibo Campus M
Inter American University of Puerto Rico, Ponce Campus M
Iona College M*
Ithaca College M
The Johns Hopkins University M,O*
Kutztown University of Pennsylvania M,O
Lehman College of the City University of New York M
Lewis University M
Louisiana Tech University M,D
Manhattanville College M*
Miami University M*
Michigan State University M,D*
Mills College M,D
Minnesota State University Mankato M
Mississippi College M,D,O
Missouri State University M*
Montclair State University M,O*
New York University M,D,O*
North Carolina Agricultural and Technical State University M
North Carolina State University M*
North Dakota State University M,D,O
North Georgia College & State University M,O
Northwestern State University of Louisiana M
Northwest Missouri State University M
Nova Southeastern University M,O*

*M—master's degree; P—first professional degree; D—doctorate; O—other advanced degree; *—Close-Up and/or Announcement or Display in one of the other books in this series*

Occidental College M
Ohio University M,D*
Penn State University Park M,D*
Portland State University M
Purdue University M,D,O
Queens College of the City University of New York M,O
Quinnipiac University M*
Rhode Island College M
Rider University O*
Rivier College M
Rutgers, The State University of New Jersey, New Brunswick M,D*
Sage Graduate School M
St. John Fisher College M
Smith College M
South Carolina State University M
Southern Illinois University Edwardsville M
Southwestern Oklahoma State University M
Stanford University M,D*
State University of New York at Binghamton M*
State University of New York at New Paltz M
State University of New York at Plattsburgh M
State University of New York College at Cortland M
State University of New York College at Potsdam M
Stony Brook University, State University of New York M,O
Syracuse University M*
Teachers College, Columbia University M,D
Texas A&M University–Commerce M
Texas State University–San Marcos D*
Trinity (Washington) University M
Union Graduate College M
University at Buffalo, the State University of New York M,D,O*
The University of Alabama in Huntsville M
University of Arkansas at Pine Bluff M
The University of British Columbia M,D
University of California, Santa Cruz M*
University of Central Florida M,D*
University of Cincinnati M,D,O
University of Connecticut M,D,O*
University of Florida M,D,O*
University of Georgia M,D,O*
University of Houston M,D*
University of Indianapolis M
The University of Iowa M,D*
University of Maine M,O*
University of Michigan M,D*
University of Minnesota, Twin Cities Campus M*
University of Missouri–Columbia M,D,O*
University of New Orleans M
The University of North Carolina at Chapel Hill M*
The University of North Carolina at Greensboro M,D,O
The University of North Carolina at Pembroke M
University of Oklahoma M,D,O*
University of Pittsburgh M,D*
University of Puerto Rico, Río Piedras M,D
University of St. Francis (IL) M
University of South Carolina M,D
University of Southern Mississippi M,D,O
University of South Florida M,D,O*
The University of Tampa M
The University of Tennessee M,D,O
The University of Toledo M
University of Victoria M,D
University of Virginia M,D,O
University of Washington M,D*
The University of West Alabama M
University of West Georgia M,O
University of Wisconsin–Eau Claire M
University of Wisconsin–River Falls M
Ursuline College M
Virginia Commonwealth University M,O
Wayne State College M
Wayne State University M,D,O*
Webster University M,O
West Chester University of Pennsylvania M,O
Western Oregon University M
Widener University M,D*
Wilkes University M,D
William Carey University M,O
Worcester State College M

SOCIAL WORK

Abilene Christian University M
Adelphi University M,D*
Alabama Agricultural and Mechanical University M
American Jewish University M
Andrews University M
Appalachian State University M
Arizona State University M,D
Arizona State University at the West campus M
Arkansas State University M
Augsburg College M
Aurora University M
Barry University M,D*
Baylor University M
Boise State University M
Boston College M,D*
Boston University M,D*
Bridgewater State College M
Brigham Young University M*
Bryn Mawr College M,D*
California State University, Bakersfield M
California State University, Chico M
California State University, Dominguez Hills M
California State University, East Bay M
California State University, Fresno M
California State University, Fullerton M
California State University, Long Beach M
California State University, Los Angeles M
California State University, Northridge M
California State University, Sacramento M
California State University, San Bernardino M
California State University, Stanislaus M
California University of Pennsylvania M
Campbellsville University M
Carleton University M
Case Western Reserve University M,D*
The Catholic University of America M,D
Chicago State University M
Clark Atlanta University M,D
Cleveland State University M
The College at Brockport, State University of New York M
Colorado State University M*
Columbia University M,D*
Cornell University M,D*
Dalhousie University M
Delaware State University M
Dominican University M
East Carolina University M
Eastern Michigan University M,O
Eastern Washington University M
East Tennessee State University M
Edinboro University of Pennsylvania M
Fayetteville State University M
Florida Agricultural and Mechanical University M
Florida Atlantic University M
Florida Gulf Coast University M
Florida International University M,D*
Florida State University M,D*
Fordham University M,D*
Gallaudet University M
George Mason University M*
Georgia State University M
Governors State University M
Graduate School and University Center of the City University of New York D*
Grambling State University M
Grand Valley State University M
Gratz College M,O
Hawai'i Pacific University M*
Hebrew Union College–Jewish Institute of Religion (CA) M,O
Howard University M,D
Humboldt State University M
Hunter College of the City University of New York M,D
Illinois State University M
Indiana University East M
Indiana University Northwest M
Indiana University–Purdue University Indianapolis M,D,O*
Indiana University South Bend M
Institute for Clinical Social Work D
Inter American University of Puerto Rico, Metropolitan Campus M
Jackson State University M,D
Kean University M
Kennesaw State University M
Kutztown University of Pennsylvania M
Lakehead University M
Laurentian University M
Loma Linda University M,D
Long Island University, C.W. Post Campus M
Louisiana State University and Agricultural and Mechanical College M,D
Marywood University M,D
McGill University M,D,O*
McMaster University M
Memorial University of Newfoundland M
Michigan State University M,D*
Middle Tennessee State University M
Millersville University of Pennsylvania M
Missouri State University M*
Monmouth University M
Morgan State University M,D
Nazareth College of Rochester M
Newman University M
New Mexico Highlands University M
New Mexico State University M
New York University M,D*
Norfolk State University M,D
North Carolina Agricultural and Technical State University M
North Carolina State University M*
Northwest Nazarene University M
The Ohio State University M,D*
The Ohio State University at Lima M
The Ohio State University at Marion M,D
The Ohio State University–Mansfield Campus M
The Ohio State University–Newark Campus M
Ohio University M*
Our Lady of the Lake University of San Antonio M
Phillips Theological Seminary P,M,D
Pontifical Catholic University of Puerto Rico M
Portland State University M,D
Radford University M
Rhode Island College M
Roberts Wesleyan College M
Rutgers, The State University of New Jersey, New Brunswick M,D*
St. Ambrose University M
St. Catherine University M
St. Cloud State University M
Saint Louis University M
Salem State College M
Salisbury University M
San Diego State University M*
San Francisco State University M
San Jose State University M,O
Savannah State University M
Shippensburg University of Pennsylvania M,O
Simmons College M,D
Smith College M,D
Southern Connecticut State University M
Southern Illinois University Carbondale M*
Southern Illinois University Edwardsville M
Southern University at New Orleans M
Spalding University M
Springfield College M
State University of New York at Binghamton M*
Stephen F. Austin State University M
Stony Brook University, State University of New York M,D
Syracuse University M*
Temple University M*

Texas A&M University–Commerce	M
Texas State University–San Marcos	M*
Tulane University	M
Universidad del Este	M
Université de Moncton	M
Université de Montréal	O
Université de Sherbrooke	M
Université du Québec à Montréal	M
Université du Québec en Abitibi-Témiscamingue	M
Université du Québec en Outaouais	M
Université Laval	M,D
University at Albany, State University of New York	M,D*
University at Buffalo, the State University of New York	M,D*
The University of Akron	M
The University of Alabama	M,D
University of Alaska Anchorage	M,O
University of Arkansas	M
University of Arkansas at Little Rock	M
The University of British Columbia	M,D
University of Calgary	M,D,O
University of California, Berkeley	M,D*
University of California, Los Angeles	M,D*
University of Central Florida	M,O*
University of Chicago	M,D*
University of Cincinnati	M
University of Denver	M,D,O*
University of Georgia	M,D,O*
University of Guam	M
University of Hawaii at Manoa	M,D*
University of Houston	M,D*
University of Illinois at Chicago	M,D*
University of Illinois at Urbana–Champaign	M,D*
The University of Iowa	M,D*
University of Kentucky	M,D
University of Louisville	M,D,O
University of Maine	M*
University of Manitoba	M,D
University of Maryland, Baltimore	M,D*
University of Maryland, College Park	*
University of Michigan	M,D*
University of Minnesota, Duluth	M
University of Minnesota, Twin Cities Campus	M,D*
University of Missouri–Columbia	M*
University of Missouri–Kansas City	M*
University of Missouri–St. Louis	M,O
The University of Montana	M
University of Nebraska at Omaha	M
University of Nevada, Las Vegas	M,O
University of Nevada, Reno	M*
University of New England	M,O
University of New Hampshire	M,O*
The University of North Carolina at Chapel Hill	M,D*
The University of North Carolina at Charlotte	M*
The University of North Carolina at Greensboro	M
The University of North Carolina Wilmington	M
University of North Dakota	M
University of Northern British Columbia	M,D,O
University of Northern Iowa	M
University of Oklahoma	M*
University of Ottawa	M*
University of Pennsylvania	M,D*
University of Pittsburgh	M,D,O*
University of Puerto Rico, Río Piedras	M,D
University of Regina	M,D
University of St. Francis (IL)	M
University of St. Thomas (MN)	M*
University of South Africa	M,D
University of South Carolina	M,D
University of Southern Indiana	M
University of Southern Maine	M
University of Southern Mississippi	M
University of South Florida	M,D*
The University of Tennessee	M,D
The University of Texas at Arlington	M,D*
The University of Texas at Austin	M,D
The University of Texas at San Antonio	M*
The University of Texas–Pan American	M
The University of Toledo	M
University of Toronto	M,D
University of Utah	M,D*
University of Vermont	M*
University of Victoria	M
University of Washington	M,D*
University of Washington, Tacoma	M
University of West Florida	M
University of Windsor	M
University of Wisconsin–Green Bay	M
University of Wisconsin–Madison	M,D*
University of Wisconsin–Milwaukee	M,D,O
University of Wisconsin–Oshkosh	M
University of Wyoming	M
Valdosta State University	M
Virginia Commonwealth University	M,D
Walden University	M,D
Walla Walla University	M
Washburn University	M
Washington University in St. Louis	M,D*
Wayne State University	M,D,O*
West Chester University of Pennsylvania	M
Western Carolina University	M
Western Kentucky University	M
Western Michigan University	M*
West Virginia University	M
Wheelock College	M
Wichita State University	M*
Widener University	M,D*
Wilfrid Laurier University	M,D
Winthrop University	M
Yeshiva University	M,D
York University	M,D

SOCIOLOGY

Acadia University	M
American University	M,O*
The American University in Cairo	M
American University of Beirut	M
Arizona State University	M,D
Arkansas State University	M,O
Auburn University	M*
Ball State University	M*
Baylor University	M,D
Boston College	M,D*
Boston University	M,D*
Bowling Green State University	M,D*
Brandeis University	M,D
Brigham Young University	M*
Brooklyn College of the City University of New York	M,D
Brown University	M,D*
California State University, Bakersfield	M
California State University, Dominguez Hills	M,O
California State University, East Bay	M
California State University, Fullerton	M
California State University, Los Angeles	M
California State University, Northridge	M
California State University, Sacramento	M
California State University, San Marcos	M
Carleton University	M,D
Case Western Reserve University	M,D*
The Catholic University of America	M
Central European University	M,D*
City College of the City University of New York	M*
Clark Atlanta University	M
Clemson University	M
Cleveland State University	M
Colorado State University	M,D*
Columbia University	M,D*
Concordia University (Canada)	M
Cornell University	M,D*
Dalhousie University	M,D
DePaul University	M*
Drake University	M*
Duke University	M,D*
East Carolina University	M
Eastern Michigan University	M
East Tennessee State University	M
Emory University	M,D*
Fayetteville State University	M
Florida Agricultural and Mechanical University	M
Florida Atlantic University	M
Florida International University	M,D*
Florida State University	M,D*
Fordham University	M*
The George Washington University	M*
Georgia Southern University	M
Georgia State University	M,D
Graduate School and University Center of the City University of New York	D*
Harvard University	D*
Hofstra University	M*
Howard University	M,D
Humboldt State University	M
Hunter College of the City University of New York	M
Idaho State University	M
Illinois State University	M
Indiana University Bloomington	M,D*
Indiana University of Pennsylvania	M
Indiana University–Purdue University Fort Wayne	M
Indiana University–Purdue University Indianapolis	M*
Iowa State University of Science and Technology	M,D*
Jackson State University	M
The Johns Hopkins University	D*
Kansas State University	M,D*
Kean University	M
Kent State University	M,D*
Lakehead University	M
Laurentian University	M
Lehigh University	M
Lincoln University (MO)	M
Louisiana State University and Agricultural and Mechanical College	M,D
Loyola University Chicago	M,D*
Marshall University	M
McGill University	M,D,O*
McMaster University	M,D
Memorial University of Newfoundland	M,D
Michigan State University	M,D*
Middle Tennessee State University	M
Minnesota State University Mankato	M
Mississippi State University	M,D
Montclair State University	M*
Morehead State University	M
Morgan State University	M
New Mexico Highlands University	M
New Mexico State University	M
The New School: A University	M,D*
New York University	M,D*
Norfolk State University	M
North Carolina Central University	M
North Carolina State University	M,D*
North Dakota State University	M,D
Northeastern University	M,D*
Northern Arizona University	M
Northern Illinois University	M
Northwestern University	D*
The Ohio State University	M,D*
Ohio University	M*
Oklahoma State University	M,D*
Old Dominion University	M
Penn State University Park	M,D*
Portland State University	M,D,O
Prairie View A&M University	M
Princeton University	D,O*
Purdue University	M,D
Queens College of the City University of New York	M
Queen's University at Kingston	M,D
Roosevelt University	M
Rutgers, The State University of New Jersey, New Brunswick	M,D*
Sage Graduate School	M,O
St. John's University (NY)	M
Sam Houston State University	M
San Diego State University	M*
San Jose State University	M
Shippensburg University of Pennsylvania	M
Simon Fraser University	M,D
Southeastern Louisiana University	M
Southern Connecticut State University	M

*M—master's degree; P—first professional degree; D—doctorate; O—other advanced degree; *—Close-Up and/or Announcement or Display in one of the other books in this series*

Southern Illinois University Carbondale	M,D*
Southern Illinois University Edwardsville	M
Stanford University	D*
State University of New York at Binghamton	M,D*
State University of New York Institute of Technology	M
Stony Brook University, State University of New York	M,D
Syracuse University	M,D*
Teachers College, Columbia University	M,D
Temple University	M,D*
Texas A&M International University	M
Texas A&M University	M,D*
Texas A&M University–Commerce	M
Texas A&M University–Kingsville	M
Texas Southern University	M
Texas State University–San Marcos	M*
Texas Tech University	M
Texas Woman's University	M,D
Tulane University	M,D
Université de Montréal	M,D
Université du Québec à Montréal	M,D
Université Laval	M,D
University at Albany, State University of New York	M,D,O*
University at Buffalo, the State University of New York	M,D*
The University of Akron	M,D
The University of Alabama at Birmingham	M,D*
University of Alberta	M,D*
The University of Arizona	D*
University of Arkansas	M
The University of British Columbia	M,D
University of Calgary	M,D
University of California, Berkeley	M,D*
University of California, Davis	M,D*
University of California, Irvine	M,D*
University of California, Los Angeles	M,D*
University of California, Riverside	M,D*
University of California, San Diego	D*
University of California, San Francisco	D
University of California, Santa Barbara	D
University of California, Santa Cruz	D*
University of Central Florida	M,D,O*
University of Central Missouri	M
University of Chicago	D*
University of Cincinnati	M,D
University of Colorado at Boulder	D*
University of Colorado at Colorado Springs	M
University of Colorado Denver	M*
University of Connecticut	M,D*
University of Delaware	M,D*
University of Florida	M,D*
University of Georgia	M,D*
University of Guelph	M,D
University of Hawaii at Manoa	M,D*
University of Houston	M*
University of Houston–Clear Lake	M
University of Illinois at Chicago	M,D*
University of Illinois at Urbana–Champaign	M,D*
University of Indianapolis	M
The University of Iowa	M,D*
The University of Kansas	M,D*
University of Kentucky	M,D
University of Lethbridge	M,D
University of Louisville	M
University of Manitoba	M,D
University of Maryland, Baltimore County	M,O*
University of Maryland, College Park	M,D*
University of Massachusetts Amherst	M,D*
University of Massachusetts Boston	M
University of Massachusetts Lowell	M,O
University of Memphis	M
University of Miami	M,D*
University of Michigan	D,O*
University of Minnesota, Duluth	M
University of Minnesota, Twin Cities Campus	M,D*
University of Mississippi	M
University of Missouri–Columbia	M,D*
University of Missouri–Kansas City	M,D*
University of Missouri–St. Louis	M
The University of Montana	M
University of Nebraska–Lincoln	M,D*
University of Nevada, Las Vegas	M,D
University of Nevada, Reno	M*
University of New Brunswick Fredericton	M,D
University of New Hampshire	M,D*
University of New Mexico	M,D*
University of New Orleans	M
The University of North Carolina at Chapel Hill	M,D*
The University of North Carolina at Charlotte	M*
The University of North Carolina at Greensboro	M
The University of North Carolina Wilmington	M
University of North Dakota	M
University of Northern Colorado	M
University of Northern Iowa	M
University of North Florida	M
University of North Texas	M,D
University of Notre Dame	D*
University of Oklahoma	M,D*
University of Oregon	M,D*
University of Ottawa	M*
University of Pennsylvania	M,D*
University of Pittsburgh	M,D*
University of Puerto Rico, Río Piedras	M
University of Regina	M,D
University of Saskatchewan	M,D
University of South Africa	M,D
University of South Alabama	M*
University of South Carolina	M,D
University of Southern California	D*
University of South Florida	M,D*
The University of Tennessee	M,D
The University of Texas at Arlington	M*
The University of Texas at Austin	M,D
The University of Texas at Dallas	M*
The University of Texas at El Paso	M
The University of Texas at San Antonio	M*
The University of Texas at Tyler	M
The University of Texas–Pan American	M
The University of Toledo	M
University of Toronto	M,D
University of Utah	M,D*
University of Victoria	M,D
University of Virginia	M,D
University of Washington	M,D*
University of Waterloo	M,D
The University of Western Ontario	M,D
University of West Georgia	M
University of Windsor	M,D
University of Wisconsin–Madison	M,D*
University of Wisconsin–Milwaukee	M
University of Wyoming	M
Utah State University	M,D
Valdosta State University	M
Vanderbilt University	M,D*
Virginia Commonwealth University	M
Virginia Polytechnic Institute and State University	M,D*
Washington State University	M,D*
Wayne State University	M,D*
West Chester University of Pennsylvania	M,O
Western Illinois University	M
Western Kentucky University	M
Western Michigan University	M,D*
West Virginia University	M
Wichita State University	M*
Wilfrid Laurier University	M
William Paterson University of New Jersey	M*
Yale University	D*
York University	M,D

SOFTWARE ENGINEERING

Andrews University	M
Arizona State University	M
Auburn University	M,D*
Bowling Green State University	M*
Brandeis University	M,O
California State University, East Bay	M
California State University, Fullerton	M
California State University, Northridge	M
California State University, Sacramento	M
Carnegie Mellon University	M,D*
Carroll University	M
Cleveland State University	M,D
Colorado Technical University Colorado Springs	M,D
Colorado Technical University Denver	M
Colorado Technical University Sioux Falls	M
Concordia University (Canada)	M,D,O
DePaul University	M,D*
Drexel University	M,D,O*
East Tennessee State University	M
Embry-Riddle Aeronautical University (FL)	M
Fairfield University	M*
Florida Agricultural and Mechanical University	M
Florida Institute of Technology	M,D*
Florida State University	M,D*
Gannon University	M
George Mason University	M,D,O*
Grand Valley State University	M
Hawai'i Pacific University	M*
Illinois Institute of Technology	M,D*
International Technological University	M,D
Jacksonville State University	M
Kansas State University	M,D*
Loyola University Chicago	M*
Loyola University Maryland	M*
Marist College	M,O*
McMaster University	M,D
Mercer University	M
Miami University	M,O*
Monmouth University	M,O
National University	M
Naval Postgraduate School	M,D
New Jersey Institute of Technology	M,D
North Dakota State University	M,D,O
Northern Kentucky University	M,O
Oakland University	M
Penn State Great Valley	M
Polytechnic Institute of NYU	O
Polytechnic Institute of NYU, Long Island Graduate Center	M
Portland State University	M,D
Regis University	M,O
Rochester Institute of Technology	M
Royal Military College of Canada	M,D
St. Mary's University (United States)	M
San Francisco State University	M
San Jose State University	M
Santa Clara University	M,D,O
Seattle University	M
Southern Methodist University	M,D*
Southern Polytechnic State University	M,O
Stevens Institute of Technology	M,D,O
Stony Brook University, State University of New York	M,D,O
Stratford University	M
Strayer University	M
Texas State University–San Marcos	M*
Texas Tech University	M,D
Towson University	D,O
Université du Québec en Outaouais	O
Université Laval	O
The University of Alabama in Huntsville	M,D,O
University of Alaska Fairbanks	M
The University of British Columbia	M
University of Calgary	M,D
University of Colorado at Colorado Springs	M
University of Connecticut	M,D*
University of Detroit Mercy	M
University of Houston–Clear Lake	M
University of Management and Technology	M,O

University of Massachusetts Dartmouth	M,O
University of Michigan–Dearborn	M*
University of Missouri–Kansas City	M,D*
University of New Haven	M*
University of St. Thomas (MN)	M,O*
The University of Scranton	M
University of South Carolina	M,D
University of Southern California	M,D*
The University of Texas at Arlington	M,D*
The University of Texas at Dallas	M,D*
University of Washington, Tacoma	M
University of Waterloo	M,D
University of West Florida	M
University of West Georgia	M,O
University of Wisconsin–La Crosse	M
Villanova University	M*
Walden University	M,O
West Virginia University	M
Widener University	M*
Winthrop University	M,O

SPANISH

American University	M,O*
Arizona State University	M,D
Arkansas Tech University	M
Asbury College	M,O
Auburn University	M*
Baylor University	M
Bennington College	M
Boston College	M,D*
Boston University	M,D*
Bowling Green State University	M*
Brigham Young University	M*
Brooklyn College of the City University of New York	M,D
California State University, Bakersfield	M
California State University, Fresno	M
California State University, Fullerton	M
California State University, Long Beach	M
California State University, Los Angeles	M
California State University, Northridge	M
California State University, Sacramento	M
California State University, San Bernardino	M
California State University, San Marcos	M
The Catholic University of America	M,D
Central Connecticut State University	M,O
Central Michigan University	M
City College of the City University of New York	M*
Cleveland State University	M
The College of New Jersey	M
Columbia University	M,D*
Cornell University	D*
Duke University	D*
Eastern Michigan University	M,O
Emory University	D,O*
Florida Atlantic University	M
Florida International University	M,D*
Florida State University	M,D*
Framingham State College	M
Georgetown University	M,D
Georgia Southern University	M
Georgia State University	M,O
Graduate School and University Center of the City University of New York	D*
Harvard University	M,D*
Hofstra University	M*
Howard University	M
Hunter College of the City University of New York	M
Illinois State University	M
Indiana University Bloomington	M,D*
Inter American University of Puerto Rico, Metropolitan Campus	M
Inter American University of Puerto Rico, Ponce Campus	M
Iona College	M*
The Johns Hopkins University	D*
Kansas State University	M*
Kean University	M
Kent State University	M,D*
Lehman College of the City University of New York	M
Long Island University, C.W. Post Campus	M
Loyola University Chicago	M*
Marquette University	M
Marshall University	M
Miami University	M*
Michigan State University	M,D*
Middlebury College	M,D
Millersville University of Pennsylvania	M
Minnesota State University Mankato	M
Mississippi State University	M
Missouri State University	M*
Montclair State University	M,O*
New Mexico State University	M
New York University	M,D*
North Carolina State University	M*
Northern Illinois University	M
Nova Southeastern University	M,O*
The Ohio State University	M,D*
Ohio University	M*
Penn State University Park	M,D*
Pontifical Catholic University of Puerto Rico	M,O
Portland State University	M
Princeton University	D*
Purdue University	M,D
Queens College of the City University of New York	M
Queen's University at Kingston	M
Rice University	M
Rider University	O*
Roosevelt University	M
Rutgers, The State University of New Jersey, New Brunswick	M,D*
St. John's University (NY)	M,O
Saint Louis University	M
Saint Louis University–Madrid Campus	M*
Salem State College	M
San Diego State University	M*
San Francisco State University	M
San Jose State University	M
Simmons College	M
Stanford University	M,D*
State University of New York at Binghamton	M,O*
Syracuse University	M*
Temple University	M,D*
Texas A&M International University	M,D
Texas A&M University	M,D*
Texas A&M University–Commerce	M,D
Texas A&M University–Kingsville	M
Texas State University–San Marcos	M*
Texas Tech University	M,D
Tulane University	M,D
Universidad Adventista de las Antillas	M
Universidad Autonoma de Guadalajara	M,D
Université de Montréal	M
Université Laval	M,D
University at Albany, State University of New York	M,D*
University at Buffalo, the State University of New York	M,D*
The University of Akron	M
The University of Alabama	M,D
The University of Arizona	M,D*
University of Arkansas	M
University of California, Berkeley	D*
University of California, Davis	M,D*
University of California, Irvine	M,D*
University of California, Los Angeles	M*
University of California, Riverside	M,D*
University of California, San Diego	M*
University of California, Santa Barbara	M,D
University of Central Florida	M*
University of Chicago	M,D*
University of Cincinnati	M,D
University of Colorado at Boulder	M,D*
University of Colorado Denver	M*
University of Connecticut	M,D*
University of Delaware	M*
University of Florida	M,D*
University of Georgia	M*
University of Hawaii at Manoa	M*
University of Houston	M,D*
University of Illinois at Chicago	M,D*
University of Illinois at Urbana–Champaign	M,D*
The University of Iowa	M,D*
The University of Kansas	M,D*
University of Lethbridge	M,D
University of Louisville	M
University of Maryland, College Park	M,D*
University of Massachusetts Amherst	M,D*
University of Memphis	M
University of Miami	M,D*
University of Michigan	D*
University of Minnesota, Twin Cities Campus	M,D*
University of Mississippi	M
University of Missouri–Columbia	M,D*
The University of Montana	M
University of Nebraska–Lincoln	M,D*
University of Nevada, Las Vegas	M,O
University of Nevada, Reno	M*
University of New Hampshire	M*
University of New Mexico	M,D*
The University of North Carolina at Chapel Hill	M,D*
The University of North Carolina at Charlotte	M*
The University of North Carolina at Greensboro	M,O
University of Northern Colorado	M
University of Northern Iowa	M
University of North Texas	M
University of Notre Dame	M*
University of Oklahoma	M,D*
University of Oregon	M*
University of Ottawa	M,D*
University of Pennsylvania	M,D*
University of Pittsburgh	M,D*
University of Rhode Island	M
University of South Africa	M,D
University of South Carolina	M,D
University of South Florida	M*
The University of Tennessee	M,D
The University of Texas at Arlington	M*
The University of Texas at Austin	M,D
The University of Texas at Brownsville	M
The University of Texas at El Paso	M
The University of Texas at San Antonio	M,O*
The University of Texas of the Permian Basin	M
The University of Texas–Pan American	M
The University of Toledo	M
University of Toronto	M,D
University of Utah	M,D*
University of Virginia	M,D
University of Washington	M*
The University of Western Ontario	M,D
University of Wisconsin–Madison	M,D*
University of Wisconsin–Milwaukee	M,O
University of Wyoming	M
Vanderbilt University	M,D*
Washington State University	M*
Washington University in St. Louis	M,D*
Wayne State University	M*
West Chester University of Pennsylvania	M,O
Western Michigan University	M,D*
West Virginia University	M
Wichita State University	M*
Winthrop University	M
Worcester State College	M
Yale University	D*

SPECIAL EDUCATION

Abilene Christian University	M
Acadia University	M
Adams State College	M
Adelphi University	M,O*
Alabama Agricultural and Mechanical University	M,O
Alabama State University	M
Albany State University	M
Albright College	M
Alcorn State University	M,O
Alliant International University–Irvine	M,O*
Alliant International University–San Francisco	M,O*
American International College	M,D,O
American University	M*
American University of Puerto Rico	M
Andrews University	M,D,O
Appalachian State University	M

*M—master's degree; P—first professional degree; D—doctorate; O—other advanced degree; *—Close-Up and/or Announcement or Display in one of the other books in this series*

Arcadia University	M,D,O
Arizona State University	M
Arizona State University at the West campus	M,D,O
Arkansas State University	M,D,O
Armstrong Atlantic State University	M
Asbury College	M,O
Ashland University	M
Assumption College	M
Auburn University	M,D*
Auburn University Montgomery	M,O
Augusta State University	M,O
Austin Peay State University	M,O
Averett University	M
Azusa Pacific University	M
Baldwin-Wallace College	M
Ball State University	M,D,O*
Bank Street College of Education	M*
Barry University	M,D,O*
Bayamón Central University	M
Bellarmine University	M
Belmont University	M
Bemidji State University	M
Benedictine University	M
Bethel College (TN)	M
Bethel University	M,D,O
Bloomsburg University of Pennsylvania	M
Bob Jones University	P,M,D,O
Boise State University	M
Boston College	M,O*
Boston University	M,D,O*
Bowie State University	M
Bowling Green State University	M*
Brandon University	M,O
Brenau University	M,O
Bridgewater State College	M
Brigham Young University	M,D,O*
Brooklyn College of the City University of New York	M
Buffalo State College, State University of New York	M
Butler University	M
Caldwell College	M
California Baptist University	M
California Lutheran University	M
California State University, Bakersfield	M
California State University, Chico	M
California State University, Dominguez Hills	M
California State University, East Bay	M
California State University, Fresno	M
California State University, Fullerton	M
California State University, Long Beach	M
California State University, Los Angeles	M,D
California State University, Northridge	M
California State University, Sacramento	M
California State University, San Bernardino	M
California State University, Stanislaus	M,D
California University of Pennsylvania	M
Calvin College	M
Cambridge College	M,D,O
Campbellsville University	M
Canisius College	M
Cardinal Stritch University	M
Caribbean University	M,D
Carlos Albizu University, Miami Campus	M,D
Carlow University	M
Castleton State College	M,O
The Catholic University of America	M,D,O
Centenary College	M
Central Connecticut State University	M,O
Central Michigan University	M
Central Washington University	M
Chapman University	M
Chatham University	M
Cheyney University of Pennsylvania	M
Chicago State University	M
City College of the City University of New York	M*
City University of Seattle	M,O
Claremont Graduate University	M,D,O*
Clarion University of Pennsylvania	M
Clarke College	M
Clemson University	M
Cleveland State University	M
College of Charleston	M*
The College of New Jersey	M,O
The College of New Rochelle	M
College of St. Joseph	M
The College of Saint Rose	M,O*
College of Santa Fe	M
College of Staten Island of the City University of New York	M
The College of William and Mary	M
Colorado State University–Pueblo	M
Columbia International University	M,D,O
Columbus State University	M,O
Concordia University, St. Paul	M,O
Concordia University Wisconsin	M
Converse College	M
Coppin State University	M
Creighton University	M*
Curry College	M,O
Daemen College	M
Defiance College	M
Delaware State University	M
Delta State University	M
DePaul University	M,D*
DeSales University	M
Dominican College	M
Dominican University	M
Dominican University of California	O
Dowling College	M,D,O
Drake University	M*
Drury University	M
Duquesne University	M*
D'Youville College	M,O*
East Carolina University	M
Eastern Illinois University	M
Eastern Kentucky University	M
Eastern Michigan University	M,O
Eastern Nazarene College	M,O
Eastern New Mexico University	M
Eastern Washington University	M
East Stroudsburg University of Pennsylvania	M
East Tennessee State University	M,D
Edgewood College	M,D,O
Edinboro University of Pennsylvania	M,O
Elmhurst College	M
Elms College	M,O
Elon University	M
Emporia State University	M
Endicott College	M
Fairfield University	M,O*
Fairleigh Dickinson University, Metropolitan Campus	M*
Fairmont State University	M
Felician College	M*
Ferris State University	M
Fitchburg State College	M
Florida Atlantic University	M,D
Florida Gulf Coast University	M
Florida International University	M,D,O*
Florida State University	M,D,O*
Fontbonne University	M
Fordham University	M,D,O*
Fort Hays State University	M
Framingham State College	M
Francis Marion University	M
Freed-Hardeman University	M,O
Fresno Pacific University	M
Frostburg State University	M
Furman University	M
Gallaudet University	M,D,O
Geneva College	M
George Mason University	M,O*
The George Washington University	M,D,O*
Georgia College & State University	M
Georgia Southern University	M
Georgia Southwestern State University	M,O
Georgia State University	M,D
Gonzaga University	M
Governors State University	M
Graceland University (IA)	M
Grand Canyon University	M,D*
Grand Valley State University	M
Greensboro College	M
Gwynedd-Mercy College	M
Hampton University	M
Harding University	M,O
Hebrew College	M,O
Henderson State University	M
Heritage University	M
High Point University	M
Hofstra University	M,D,O*
Holy Family University	M
Holy Names University	M,O
Hood College	M
Howard University	M,O
Hunter College of the City University of New York	M
Idaho State University	M,D,O
Illinois State University	M,D
Immaculata University	M,D,O
Indiana University Bloomington	M,D,O*
Indiana University of Pennsylvania	M
Indiana University–Purdue University Fort Wayne	M
Indiana University–Purdue University Indianapolis	M,O*
Indiana University South Bend	M
Inter American University of Puerto Rico, Metropolitan Campus	M
Inter American University of Puerto Rico, San Germán Campus	M
Iowa State University of Science and Technology	M,D*
Jackson State University	M,O
Jacksonville State University	M
James Madison University	M
The Johns Hopkins University	M,D,O*
Johnson State College	M
Kansas State University	M,D*
Kaplan University–Davenport Campus	M
Kean University	M
Keene State College	M,O
Kennesaw State University	M
Kent State University	M,D,O*
Kentucky State University	M
Kutztown University of Pennsylvania	M,O
Lamar University	M,D
Lancaster Bible College	M
Lee University	M,O
Lehigh University	M,D,O
Lehman College of the City University of New York	M
Le Moyne College	M,O
Lesley University	M,D,O*
Lewis & Clark College	M
Lewis University	M
Liberty University	M,D,O
Lincoln University (MO)	M,O
Lipscomb University	M
Long Island University at Riverhead	M
Long Island University, Brentwood Campus	M
Long Island University, Brooklyn Campus	M
Long Island University, C.W. Post Campus	M
Long Island University, Rockland Graduate Campus	M
Long Island University, Westchester Graduate Campus	M,O
Longwood University	M
Loras College	M
Louisiana Tech University	M,D
Loyola Marymount University	M
Loyola University Chicago	M*
Loyola University Maryland	M,O*
Lynchburg College	M
Lyndon State College	M
Lynn University	M,D
Madonna University	M
Malone University	M
Manhattan College	M
Manhattanville College	M*
Marshall University	M
Marymount University	M
Marywood University	M
Massachusetts College of Liberal Arts	M
McDaniel College	M
McKendree University	M
McNeese State University	M
Medaille College	M
Mercy College	M,O
Mercyhurst College	M,O
Miami University	M*
Michigan State University	M,D,O*
MidAmerica Nazarene University	M
Middle Tennessee State University	M,O
Midwestern State University	M
Millersville University of Pennsylvania	M
Minnesota State University Mankato	M,O
Minnesota State University Moorhead	M
Minot State University	M
Mississippi College	M,D,O
Mississippi State University	M,D,O
Missouri State University	M,D*

Monmouth University	M,O
Montana State University–Billings	M
Montclair State University	M,O*
Morehead State University	M,O
Morningside College	M
Mount Saint Mary College	M
Mount St. Mary's College	M
Mount Saint Vincent University	M
Murray State University	M
National-Louis University	M,O
National University	M
New England College	M
New Jersey City University	M
New Mexico Highlands University	M
New Mexico State University	M,D
New York University	M*
Niagara University	M,O
Norfolk State University	M
North Carolina Central University	M
North Carolina State University	M*
Northeastern Illinois University	M
Northeastern University	M,D,O*
Northern Arizona University	M
Northern Illinois University	M,D
Northern Kentucky University	M,O
Northern Michigan University	M
Northern State University	M
North Georgia College & State University	M,O
Northwestern State University of Louisiana	M,O
Northwestern University	M,D*
Northwest Missouri State University	M
Northwest Nazarene University	M
Notre Dame College (OH)	M,O
Notre Dame de Namur University	M,O
Nova Southeastern University	M,D,O*
Nyack College	M
Oakland University	M,O
Ohio University	M,D*
Old Dominion University	M,D
Ottawa University	M
Our Lady of the Lake University of San Antonio	M
Pacific University	M
Park University	M
Penn State Great Valley	M
Penn State University Park	M,D*
Pittsburg State University	M
Plymouth State University	M,O
Portland State University	M,D
Prairie View A&M University	M
Pratt Institute	M*
Prescott College	M,D
Providence College	M*
Purdue University	M,D,O
Purdue University Calumet	M
Queens College of the City University of New York	M
Radford University	M
Regent University	M,D,O
Regis University	M,O
Rhode Island College	M,O
Rider University	M,O*
Rivier College	M,D,O
Roberts Wesleyan College	M,O
Rochester Institute of Technology	M
Rockford College	M
Roosevelt University	M
Rowan University	M
Rutgers, The State University of New Jersey, New Brunswick	M,D*
Sage Graduate School	M
Saginaw Valley State University	M
St. Ambrose University	M
St. Cloud State University	M
St. John Fisher College	M,O
St. John's University (NY)	M
Saint Joseph College	M
St. Joseph's College, Long Island Campus	M
St. Joseph's College, New York	M
Saint Joseph's University	M,D
Saint Louis University	M,D
Saint Martin's University	M
Saint Mary's College of California	M
Saint Mary's University of Minnesota	M,O
Saint Michael's College	M,O
Saint Peter's College	M
St. Thomas Aquinas College	M,O*
St. Thomas University	M,D,O
Saint Vincent College	M
Saint Xavier University	M,O
Salem College	M
Salem State College	M
Salus University	M,D,O
Sam Houston State University	M,D
San Diego State University	M*
San Francisco State University	M,D,O
San Jose State University	M,O
Santa Clara University	M,O
Seattle University	M,O
Seton Hill University	M,O
Shippensburg University of Pennsylvania	M
Silver Lake College	M
Simmons College	M,D,O
Slippery Rock University of Pennsylvania	M
Smith College	M
Sonoma State University	M
South Carolina State University	M
Southeastern Louisiana University	M
Southeast Missouri State University	M
Southern Connecticut State University	M,O
Southern Illinois University Carbondale	M*
Southern Illinois University Edwardsville	M,O
Southern New Hampshire University	M,O*
Southern Oregon University	M
Southern University and Agricultural and Mechanical College	M,D
Southwestern College (KS)	M
Southwestern Oklahoma State University	M
Southwest Minnesota State University	M
Spalding University	M
Spring Arbor University	M
Springfield College	M
State University of New York at Binghamton	M*
State University of New York at New Paltz	M
State University of New York at Oswego	M
State University of New York at Plattsburgh	M
State University of New York College at Cortland	M
State University of New York College at Potsdam	M
Stephen F. Austin State University	M
Syracuse University	M,D*
Tarleton State University	M,O
Teachers College, Columbia University	M,D,O
Temple University	M,D*
Tennessee State University	M,D
Tennessee Technological University	M,O*
Texas A&M International University	M
Texas A&M University	M,D*
Texas A&M University–Commerce	M,D
Texas A&M University–Corpus Christi	M
Texas A&M University–Kingsville	M
Texas A&M University–Texarkana	M
Texas Christian University	M
Texas State University–San Marcos	M*
Texas Tech University	M,D
Texas Woman's University	M,D
Towson University	M
Trinity Baptist College	M
Trinity (Washington) University	M
Union College (KY)	M
Universidad del Este	M
Universidad del Turabo	M
Universidad Iberoamericana	P,M
Universidad Metropolitana	M
Université de Sherbrooke	M,O
University at Albany, State University of New York	M*
University at Buffalo, the State University of New York	M,D,O*
The University of Akron	M
The University of Alabama	M,D,O
The University of Alabama at Birmingham	M*
University of Alaska Anchorage	M,O
University of Alberta	M,D*
The University of Arizona	M,D,O*
University of Arkansas	M
University of Arkansas at Little Rock	M,O
The University of British Columbia	M,D,O
University of Calgary	M,D
University of California, Berkeley	D*
University of California, Los Angeles	D*
University of California, Riverside	M,D*
University of California, Santa Barbara	M,D
University of Central Arkansas	M
University of Central Florida	M,D*
University of Central Missouri	M,O
University of Central Oklahoma	M
University of Cincinnati	M,D
University of Colorado at Colorado Springs	M,D
University of Connecticut	M,D,O*
University of Dayton	M
University of Detroit Mercy	M
The University of Findlay	M
University of Florida	M,D,O*
University of Georgia	M,D,O*
University of Guam	M
University of Hawaii at Manoa	M,D*
University of Houston	M,D*
University of Houston–Victoria	M
University of Idaho	M,O
University of Illinois at Chicago	M,D*
University of Illinois at Urbana–Champaign	M,D,O*
The University of Iowa	M,D*
The University of Kansas	M,D*
University of Kentucky	M,D
University of La Verne	M
University of Louisville	M
University of Maine	M,O*
University of Manitoba	M
University of Mary	M
University of Maryland, College Park	M,D,O*
University of Maryland Eastern Shore	M*
University of Massachusetts Amherst	M,D,O*
University of Massachusetts Boston	M
University of Memphis	M,D
University of Miami	M,D,O*
University of Michigan–Dearborn	M*
University of Michigan–Flint	M*
University of Minnesota, Twin Cities Campus	M,D,O*
University of Missouri–Columbia	M,D*
University of Missouri–Kansas City	M,D,O*
University of Missouri–St. Louis	M,O
University of Nebraska at Kearney	M
University of Nebraska at Omaha	M
University of Nebraska–Lincoln	M,D,O*
University of Nevada, Las Vegas	M,D,O
University of Nevada, Reno	M,D*
University of New Hampshire	M,O*
University of New Mexico	M,D,O*
University of New Orleans	M,D,O
University of North Alabama	M
The University of North Carolina at Charlotte	M,D*
The University of North Carolina at Greensboro	M,D,O
University of North Dakota	M,D
University of Northern Colorado	M,D
University of Northern Iowa	M,D
University of North Florida	M
University of North Texas	M,D,O
University of Oklahoma	M,D*
University of Oklahoma Health Sciences Center	M,D,O
University of Phoenix	M
University of Phoenix–Hawaii Campus	M
University of Phoenix–Metro Detroit Campus	M
University of Phoenix–Omaha Campus	M
University of Phoenix–Phoenix Campus	M
University of Phoenix–Southern Arizona Campus	M,O
University of Phoenix–Utah Campus	M
University of Pittsburgh	M,D*
University of Puerto Rico, Medical Sciences Campus	O
University of Puerto Rico, Río Piedras	M
University of Rio Grande	M

*M—master's degree; P—first professional degree; D—doctorate; O—other advanced degree; *—Close-Up and/or Announcement or Display in one of the other books in this series*

University of St. Francis (IL) M
University of Saint Francis (IN) M
University of Saint Mary M
University of St. Thomas (MN) M,O*
University of San Diego M
University of Saskatchewan M,D,O
The University of Scranton M
University of South Alabama M,O*
University of South Carolina M,D
University of South Carolina Upstate M
The University of South Dakota M
University of Southern Maine M
University of Southern Mississippi M,D,O
University of South Florida M,D,O*
The University of Tennessee M,D,O
The University of Tennessee at Chattanooga M,O
The University of Texas at Austin M,D
The University of Texas at Brownsville M
The University of Texas at El Paso M
The University of Texas at San Antonio M*
The University of Texas at Tyler M
The University of Texas of the Permian Basin M
The University of Texas–Pan American M
University of the Cumberlands M
University of the District of Columbia M
University of the Incarnate Word M,D
University of the Pacific M,D
University of the Southwest M
The University of Toledo M,D,O
University of Utah M,D*
University of Vermont M*
University of Victoria M,D
University of Virginia M,D,O
University of Washington M,D*
University of Washington, Tacoma M
The University of West Alabama M
The University of Western Ontario M
University of West Florida M
University of West Georgia M,O
University of Wisconsin–Eau Claire M
University of Wisconsin–La Crosse M
University of Wisconsin–Madison M,D*
University of Wisconsin–Milwaukee M,D,O
University of Wisconsin–Oshkosh M
University of Wisconsin–Stevens Point M
University of Wisconsin–Superior M
University of Wisconsin–Whitewater M*
University of Wyoming M,D,O
Ursuline College M
Utah State University M,D,O
Valdosta State University M,O
Vanderbilt University M,D*
Virginia Commonwealth University M,D
Virginia Polytechnic Institute and State University D,O*
Walden University M,D,O
Walla Walla University M
Washburn University M
Washington University in St. Louis M,D*
Waynesburg University M,D
Wayne State College M
Wayne State University M,D,O*
Webster University M,O
West Chester University of Pennsylvania M,O
Western Connecticut State University M
Western Illinois University M
Western Kentucky University M
Western New Mexico University M
Western Oregon University M
Western Seminary M,O
Westfield State College M
West Texas A&M University M
West Virginia University M,D
Wheelock College M
Whitworth University M
Wichita State University M*
Widener University M,D*
Wilkes University M,D
William Carey University M,O
William Paterson University of New Jersey M*
William Woods University M,O
Wilmington College M
Wilmington University M
Winona State University M
Winthrop University M
Worcester State College M
Wright State University M
Xavier University M*
Youngstown State University M

SPEECH AND INTERPERSONAL COMMUNICATION

Arizona State University M,D
Arkansas State University M,O
Ball State University M*
Bob Jones University P,M,D,O
Bowling Green State University M,D*
Brooklyn College of the City University of New York M,D
California State University, Fullerton M
California State University, Los Angeles M
California State University, Northridge M
Central Michigan University M
Colorado State University M*
Drake University M*
Eastern Illinois University M
Florida State University M,D*
Georgia State University M,D
Hofstra University M*
Idaho State University M
Indiana University Bloomington M,D*
Kansas State University M*
Louisiana Tech University M*
Marquette University M
Miami University M*
Minnesota State University Mankato M
Montclair State University M*
New York University M,D*
North Dakota State University M,D
Northeastern Illinois University M
Northeastern University D*
Northwestern University M,D*
Ohio University D*
Portland State University M,O
Rensselaer Polytechnic Institute M,D
San Francisco State University M
San Jose State University M
Seton Hall University M*
Southern Illinois University Carbondale M,D*
Southern Illinois University Edwardsville M
Texas A&M University–Commerce M
Texas Christian University M
The University of Alabama M
University of Arkansas at Little Rock M
University of California, Santa Barbara D
University of Central Florida M*
University of Central Missouri M
University of Denver M,D*
University of Georgia M,D*
University of Hawaii at Manoa M*
University of Houston M*
University of Maryland, College Park M,D*
University of Nebraska–Lincoln M,D*
University of Nevada, Reno M*
University of South Carolina M,D
University of Southern California M,D*
University of Southern Mississippi M,D
The University of Tennessee M,D
University of Wisconsin–Madison M,D*
University of Wisconsin–Stevens Point M
University of Wisconsin–Superior M
Wake Forest University M*
Washington University in St. Louis M,D*
Wayne State University M,D*

SPORT PSYCHOLOGY

Argosy University, Orange County M*
Argosy University, Phoenix M,D*
Barry University M*
California State University, Fresno M
California State University, Long Beach M
California University of Pennsylvania M
Capella University M,D,O
Chatham University M,D
Cleveland State University M
Eastern Washington University M
Florida State University M,D,O*
John F. Kennedy University M
Memorial University of Newfoundland M
Purdue University M,D
Queen's University at Kingston M,D
Southern Connecticut State University M
Springfield College M,D,O
University of Florida M,D*
The University of Iowa M,D*
University of Rhode Island M,D
The University of Texas at Austin M,D
West Virginia University M,D

SPORTS MANAGEMENT

American Public University System M
Ashland University M
Barry University M*
Belmont University M
Boise State University M
Bowling Green State University M*
Brooklyn College of the City University of New York M
California Baptist University M
California State University, Long Beach M
California University of Pennsylvania M
Canisius College M
Cardinal Stritch University M
Central Michigan University M,O
The Citadel, The Military College of South Carolina M
Cleveland State University M
The College at Brockport, State University of New York M
Columbia University M*
Concordia University (CA) M
Concordia University (Canada) M,D,O
Concordia University, St. Paul M,O
Duquesne University M*
Eastern Kentucky University M
Eastern Michigan University M
Eastern Washington University M
East Stroudsburg University of Pennsylvania M
East Tennessee State University M
Endicott College M
Fairleigh Dickinson University, Metropolitan Campus M*
Florida International University M*
Florida State University M,D,O*
Franklin Pierce University M,D,O
Georgetown University M,D
The George Washington University M,O*
Georgia Southern University M
Georgia State University M
Gonzaga University M
Grambling State University M
Henderson State University M
Hofstra University M*
Holy Names University M
Howard University M
Indiana State University M
Indiana University Bloomington M,D,O*
Indiana University of Pennsylvania M
Ithaca College M
Kansas Wesleyan University M
Kent State University M*
Lindenwood University M
Lynn University M,D
Manhattanville College M*
Marshall University M
Millersville University of Pennsylvania M
Mississippi State University M
Missouri State University M*
Montana State University–Billings M
Montclair State University M,O*

Morehead State University	M
Neumann University	M
New Mexico Highlands University	M
New York University	M,O*
Nichols College	M
North Carolina Central University	M
North Carolina State University	M,D*
North Dakota State University	M
Northern Illinois University	M
Nova Southeastern University	M,O*
Ohio University	M*
Old Dominion University	M
St. Cloud State University	M
St. Edward's University	M,O
St. John's University (NY)	M
Saint Leo University	M
St. Thomas University	M,O
San Diego State University	M*
Seattle University	M
Seton Hall University	M*
Slippery Rock University of Pennsylvania	M
Southeast Missouri State University	M
Southern New Hampshire University	M,D,O*
Springfield College	M,D,O
State University of New York College at Cortland	M
Temple University	M,D*
Tiffin University	M
Troy University	M
United States Sports Academy	M,D
The University of Alabama	M,D
University of Alberta	M*
University of Central Florida	M,O*
University of Dallas	M
University of Florida	M,D*
The University of Iowa	M*
University of Louisville	M
University of Massachusetts Amherst	M,D*
University of Miami	M*
University of Michigan	M,D*
University of Minnesota, Twin Cities Campus	M,D,O*
University of Nevada, Las Vegas	M,D
University of New Brunswick Fredericton	M*
University of New Haven	M*
The University of North Carolina at Chapel Hill	M*
The University of North Carolina at Charlotte	M*
University of Northern Colorado	M,D
University of Northern Iowa	M,D
University of Rhode Island	M,D
University of San Francisco	M
University of South Carolina	M
University of Southern Maine	M,O
University of Southern Mississippi	M,D
The University of Tennessee	M,D
University of the Incarnate Word	M,O
University of Wisconsin–La Crosse	M
Valparaiso University	M
Washington State University	M,D,O*
Wayne State College	M
Wayne State University	M*
Webber International University	M*
West Chester University of Pennsylvania	M,O
Western Carolina University	M
Western Illinois University	M
Western Michigan University	M*
Western New England College	M
West Virginia University	M,D
Wichita State University	M*
Wingate University	M
Winona State University	M,O
Xavier University	M*

STATISTICS

Acadia University	M
American University	M,O*
American University of Beirut	M
Arizona State University	M,D
Auburn University	M,D*
Ball State University	M*
Baylor University	M,D
Bernard M. Baruch College of the City University of New York	M
Bowling Green State University	M,D*
Brigham Young University	M*
Brock University	M
California State University, East Bay	M
California State University, Sacramento	M
Carnegie Mellon University	M,D*
Case Western Reserve University	M,D*
Central Connecticut State University	M,O
Claremont Graduate University	M,D*
Clemson University	M,D
Colorado State University	M,D*
Columbia University	M,D*
Cornell University	M,D*
Dalhousie University	M,D
Duke University	D*
Florida Atlantic University	M,D
Florida International University	M*
Florida State University	M,D,O*
George Mason University	M,D,O*
Georgetown University	M
The George Washington University	M,D,O*
Georgia Institute of Technology	M,D*
Georgia State University	M,D
Hampton University	M
Harvard University	M,D*
Indiana University Bloomington	M,D*
Iowa State University of Science and Technology	M,D*
James Madison University	M
The Johns Hopkins University	M,D*
Kansas State University	M,D*
Kean University	M
Lehigh University	M,D
Louisiana State University and Agricultural and Mechanical College	M
Louisiana Tech University	M
Loyola University Chicago	M*
McGill University	M,D,O*
McMaster University	M
McNeese State University	M
Memorial University of Newfoundland	M,D
Miami University	M*
Michigan State University	M,D*
Minnesota State University Mankato	M
Mississippi State University	M,D
Missouri University of Science and Technology	M,D
Montana State University	M,D
Montclair State University	M,D,O*
Murray State University	M
New Mexico State University	M,D
New York University	M,D*
North Carolina State University	M,D*
North Dakota State University	M,D,O
Northern Arizona University	M
Northern Illinois University	M
Northwestern University	M,D*
Oakland University	O
The Ohio State University	M,D*
Oklahoma State University	M,D*
Oregon State University	M,D*
Penn State University Park	M,D*
Portland State University	M,D
Purdue University	M,D,O
Queen's University at Kingston	M,D
Rice University	M,D
Rochester Institute of Technology	M,O
Rutgers, The State University of New Jersey, New Brunswick	M,D*
St. John's University (NY)	M
Sam Houston State University	M
San Diego State University	M*
San Jose State University	M
Simon Fraser University	M,D
South Dakota State University	M,D
Southern Illinois University Carbondale	M,D*
Southern Methodist University	M,D*
Stanford University	M,D*
State University of New York at Binghamton	M,D*
Stephen F. Austin State University	M
Stevens Institute of Technology	M,O
Stony Brook University, State University of New York	M,D
Temple University	M,D*
Texas A&M University	M,D*
Texas Tech University	M
Tulane University	M,D
Université de Montréal	M,D
Université Laval	M
University at Albany, State University of New York	M,D,O*
The University of Akron	M
University of Alaska Fairbanks	M,D
University of Alberta	M,D,O*
The University of Arizona	M,D*
University of Arkansas	M
The University of British Columbia	M,D
University of Calgary	M,D
University of California, Berkeley	M,D*
University of California, Davis	M,D*
University of California, Los Angeles	M,D*
University of California, Riverside	M,D*
University of California, San Diego	M,D*
University of California, Santa Barbara	M,D
University of California, Santa Cruz	M,D*
University of Central Florida	M,O*
University of Central Oklahoma	M
University of Chicago	M,D*
University of Cincinnati	M,D
University of Connecticut	M,D*
University of Delaware	M*
University of Denver	M*
University of Florida	M,D*
University of Georgia	M,D*
University of Guelph	M,D
University of Houston–Clear Lake	M
University of Idaho	M
University of Illinois at Chicago	M,D*
University of Illinois at Urbana–Champaign	M,D*
The University of Iowa	M,D,O*
University of Kentucky	M,D
University of Manitoba	M,D
University of Maryland, Baltimore County	M,D*
University of Maryland, College Park	M,D*
University of Massachusetts Amherst	M,D*
University of Memphis	M,D
University of Michigan	M,D*
University of Minnesota, Twin Cities Campus	M,D*
University of Missouri–Columbia	M,D*
University of Missouri–Kansas City	M,D*
University of Nebraska–Lincoln	M,D*
University of New Brunswick Fredericton	M,D
University of New Hampshire	M,D,O*
University of New Mexico	M,D*
The University of North Carolina at Chapel Hill	M,D*
University of North Florida	M
University of Ottawa	M,D*
University of Pennsylvania	M,D*
University of Pittsburgh	M,D*
University of Puerto Rico, Mayagüez Campus	M
University of Regina	M,D
University of Rhode Island	M,D,O
University of Rochester	M,D*
University of Saskatchewan	M,D
University of South Africa	M,D
University of South Carolina	M,D,O
The University of South Dakota	M,D
University of Southern California	M,D*
University of Southern Maine	M
University of South Florida	M,D,O*
The University of Tennessee	M,D
The University of Texas at Austin	M
The University of Texas at Dallas	M,D*
The University of Texas at El Paso	M
The University of Texas at San Antonio	M,D*
University of the Incarnate Word	M
The University of Toledo	M,D
University of Toronto	M,D
University of Utah	M,D*
University of Vermont	M*
University of Victoria	M,D
University of Virginia	M,D
University of Washington	M,D*
University of Waterloo	M,D
The University of Western Ontario	M,D
University of Windsor	M,D
University of Wisconsin–Madison	M,D*

*M—master's degree; P—first professional degree; D—doctorate; O—other advanced degree; *—Close-Up and/or Announcement or Display in one of the other books in this series*

University of Wyoming	M,D
Utah State University	M,D
Virginia Commonwealth University	M,O
Virginia Polytechnic Institute and State University	M,D*
Washington State University	M*
Washington University in St. Louis	M,D*
Wayne State University	M,D*
Western Michigan University	M,D*
West Virginia University	M,D
Wichita State University	M,D*
Yale University	M,D*
York University	M,D
Youngstown State University	M

STRUCTURAL BIOLOGY

Baylor College of Medicine	D*
Brandeis University	M,D
Carnegie Mellon University	D*
Cornell University	M,D*
Cornell University, Joan and Sanford I. Weill Medical College and Graduate School of Medical Sciences	M,D
Duke University	O*
Florida State University	D*
Harvard University	D*
Illinois State University	M,D
Iowa State University of Science and Technology	D*
Massachusetts Institute of Technology	D*
Mayo Graduate School	D*
Medical University of South Carolina	M,D
Michigan State University	D*
New York University	P,M,D*
Northwestern University	D*
Stanford University	D*
Stony Brook University, State University of New York	D
Syracuse University	D*
Thomas Jefferson University	D*
Tulane University	M,D
University at Albany, State University of New York	M,D*
University at Buffalo, the State University of New York	M,D*
University of California, San Diego	D*
University of Connecticut	M,D*
University of Minnesota, Twin Cities Campus	D*
University of Pittsburgh	D*
The University of Texas Health Science Center at San Antonio	M,D
The University of Texas Medical Branch	D*
University of Washington	D*
Yale University	D*

STRUCTURAL ENGINEERING

Auburn University	M,D*
California State University, Northridge	M
The Catholic University of America	M,D,O
Cornell University	M,D*
Drexel University	M,D*
École Polytechnique de Montréal	M,D,O
Illinois Institute of Technology	M,D*
Instituto Tecnologico de Santo Domingo	M
Iowa State University of Science and Technology	M,D*
Lehigh University	M,D
Louisiana State University and Agricultural and Mechanical College	M,D
Marquette University	M,D
Massachusetts Institute of Technology	M,D,O*
McGill University	M,D*
Milwaukee School of Engineering	M*
Northwestern University	M,D*
Ohio University	M,D*
Oregon State University	M,D*
Penn State University Park	M,D*
Princeton University	M,D*
Rensselaer Polytechnic Institute	M,D
Stevens Institute of Technology	M,D,O
Texas A&M University	M,D*
Tufts University	M,D*
University at Buffalo, the State University of New York	M,D*
The University of Alabama in Huntsville	M,D
University of Alberta	M,D*
University of California, Berkeley	M,D*
University of California, San Diego	M,D*
University of Central Florida	M,D,O*
University of Colorado at Boulder	M,D*
University of Dayton	M
University of Delaware	M,D*
University of Maine	M,D*
University of Memphis	M,D
University of Michigan	M,D,O*
University of Missouri–Columbia	M,D*
University of New Brunswick Fredericton	M,D
University of North Dakota	M
University of Oklahoma	M,D*
University of Rhode Island	M,D*
University of Washington	M,D*
Washington University in St. Louis	M,D*
Western Michigan University	M*
Worcester Polytechnic Institute	M,D,O*

STUDENT AFFAIRS

Alliant International University–Los Angeles	M,D,O*
Alliant International University–San Diego	M,D,O*
Arkansas State University	M,O
Arkansas Tech University	M,O
Ashland University	M
Azusa Pacific University	M
Bloomsburg University of Pennsylvania	M
Bob Jones University	P,M,D,O
Bowling Green State University	M*
Buffalo State College, State University of New York	M
California State University, Bakersfield	M
California State University, Long Beach	M,D
Canisius College	M
Central Michigan University	M,D,O
The Citadel, The Military College of South Carolina	M
Claremont Graduate University	M,D,O*
Cleveland State University	M,O
College of Saint Elizabeth	M,O
The College of Saint Rose	M,O*
Colorado State University	M,D*
Concordia University Wisconsin	M
Creighton University	M*
Eastern Illinois University	M
Fresno Pacific University	M
Grambling State University	M,D
Hampton University	M
Illinois State University	M
Indiana State University	M,D,O
Indiana University–Purdue University Indianapolis	M,O*
Kansas State University	M,D*
Kaplan University–Davenport Campus	M
Kent State University	M*
Lewis University	M
Miami University	M*
Minnesota State University Mankato	M,D,O
Mississippi State University	M,D,O
Missouri State University	M*
New York University	M,D*
Northeastern University	M*
Northern Arizona University	M
Northern Kentucky University	M,O
Northwestern State University of Louisiana	M,O
Nova Southeastern University	M,O*
The Ohio State University	M*
Ohio University	M,D*
Oregon State University	M*
Penn State University Park	M,D*
Providence College and Theological Seminary	P,M,D,O
Radford University	M
Regent University	M,D,O
St. Cloud State University	M
St. Edward's University	M
Saint Louis University	M,D,O
San Jose State University	M
Seton Hall University	M*
Shippensburg University of Pennsylvania	M,O
Slippery Rock University of Pennsylvania	M
Springfield College	M,O
Syracuse University	M*
Teachers College, Columbia University	M,D
Tennessee Technological University	M,O*
University of Bridgeport	M
University of Central Arkansas	M
University of Central Florida	M,D,O*
University of Central Missouri	M
University of Dayton	M,O
University of Florida	M,D,O*
University of Georgia	M,D,O*
The University of Iowa	M,D*
University of Maryland, College Park	M,D,O*
University of Memphis	M,D
University of Miami	M,D,O*
University of Minnesota, Twin Cities Campus	M,D,O*
University of Mississippi	M,D,O
University of Northern Colorado	D
University of Northern Iowa	M
University of Rhode Island	M
University of St. Thomas (MN)	M,D,O*
University of South Carolina	M
University of Southern California	M*
University of South Florida	M,D,O*
The University of Tennessee	M
University of Virginia	M,D,O
University of West Florida	M
University of Wisconsin–La Crosse	M
University of Wyoming	M,D
Washington State University	M,D,O*
Western Illinois University	M
Western Kentucky University	M,O

SUPPLY CHAIN MANAGEMENT

American University	M*
Arizona State University	M,D
California State University, East Bay	M
Case Western Reserve University	M*
Clarkson University	M*
Eastern Michigan University	M,O
Elmhurst College	M
HEC Montreal	O
Howard University	M
Kaplan University–Davenport Campus	M
Lehigh University	M,D,O
Maine Maritime Academy	M,O
Michigan State University	M,D*
Moravian College	M
North Carolina State University	M*
Penn State University Park	M,D*
Rutgers, The State University of New Jersey, Newark	D*
Strayer University	M
Syracuse University	M,D*
The University of Akron	M
The University of Alabama in Huntsville	M,O
University of Dallas	M
University of Florida	M,D*
University of La Verne	M
University of Massachusetts Dartmouth	M,O
University of Memphis	M,D
University of Michigan	M,D*
University of Minnesota, Twin Cities Campus	M*
University of Missouri–St. Louis	M,D,O
The University of North Carolina at Greensboro	M,D,O
University of San Diego	M,O
University of Southern California	M,D,O*
The University of Texas at Austin	D
The University of Texas at Dallas	M*
University of Wisconsin–Madison	M*
University of Wisconsin–Whitewater	M*
Walden University	M,D
Wright State University	M

SURVEYING SCIENCE AND ENGINEERING

The Ohio State University	M,D*
University of New Brunswick Fredericton	M,D,O

SURVEY METHODOLOGY

University of Maryland, College Park	M,D*

University of Michigan	M,D,O*
University of Nebraska–Lincoln	M,D*

SUSTAINABILITY MANAGEMENT

Alliant International University–San Diego	M,D*
Alliant International University–San Francisco	M*
Antioch University New England	M*
Argosy University, Dallas	M,O*
Argosy University, Salt Lake City	M,D*
City University of Seattle	M,O
Colorado State University	M*
Dominican University of California	M
Duquesne University	M*
Goddard College	M
Illinois Institute of Technology	M*
Lipscomb University	M
Maharishi University of Management	M,D
Marlboro College	M
Michigan Technological University	O
Rochester Institute of Technology	D
University of Maine	M*
Walden University	M,D

SUSTAINABLE DEVELOPMENT

American University	M,D,O*
Appalachian State University	M
Arizona State University	M,D
Brandeis University	M
California State University, Stanislaus	M
Clark University	M
Columbia University	M,D*
Dominican University of California	M
Florida Atlantic University	M,O
Hawai'i Pacific University	M*
HEC Montreal	O
Instituto Centroamericano de Administración de Empresas	M
Iowa State University of Science and Technology	M,D*
Lesley University	M*
Michigan Technological University	O
Minneapolis College of Art and Design	O
Northern Arizona University	M
Philadelphia University	M
Rochester Institute of Technology	D
SIT Graduate Institute	M
Slippery Rock University of Pennsylvania	M
University of Connecticut	M*
University of Georgia	M,D*
University of Maryland, College Park	M*
University of Massachusetts Lowell	M,D,O
University of Michigan	M,D*
University of New Brunswick Fredericton	M
University of Southern California	M,D,O*
University of Washington	P,M,D*
The University of Western Ontario	M,D
University of Wisconsin–Madison	M*
Walden University	M,D,O
Western Illinois University	M,O
West Virginia University	D

SYSTEMS BIOLOGY

Cornell University, Joan and Sanford I. Weill Medical College and Graduate School of Medical Sciences	M,D
Dartmouth College	D*
Harvard University	D*
Massachusetts Institute of Technology	D*
Michigan State University	D*
Rutgers, The State University of New Jersey, New Brunswick	D*
Texas A&M Health Science Center	D
University of California, San Diego	D*
University of Chicago	D*
University of Southern California	D*
University of Toronto	M,D
Virginia Commonwealth University	D

SYSTEMS ENGINEERING

Air Force Institute of Technology	M,D
The American University of Athens	M
Arizona State University	M
Auburn University	M,D*
Boston University	M,D*
California Institute of Technology	M,D*
California State University, Fullerton	M
California State University, Northridge	M
Carleton University	M,D
Carnegie Mellon University	M*
Case Western Reserve University	M,D*
The Catholic University of America	M,D,O
Colorado School of Mines	M,D
Colorado State University–Pueblo	M
Colorado Technical University Colorado Springs	M
Colorado Technical University Denver	M
Concordia University (Canada)	M,O
Cornell University	M*
Embry-Riddle Aeronautical University (FL)	M
Florida Institute of Technology	M*
George Mason University	M*
The George Washington University	M,D,O*
Georgia Institute of Technology	M,D*
Indiana University–Purdue University Fort Wayne	M
Instituto Tecnológico y de Estudios Superiores de Monterrey, Campus Chihuahua	M,O
Instituto Tecnológico y de Estudios Superiores de Monterrey, Campus Monterrey	M,D
Iowa State University of Science and Technology	M*
The Johns Hopkins University	M,O*
Lehigh University	M,D
Loyola Marymount University	M
Massachusetts Institute of Technology	M,D*
Mississippi State University	M,D
Missouri University of Science and Technology	M,D
National University	M
Naval Postgraduate School	M,D,O
North Carolina Agricultural and Technical State University	M,D
Northeastern University	M*
Oakland University	M,D
The Ohio State University	M,D*
Ohio University	M*
Old Dominion University	M,D
Oregon State University	M,D*
Polytechnic Institute of NYU	M
Polytechnic Institute of NYU, Long Island Graduate Center	M
Portland State University	M,O
Regis University	M,O
Rensselaer Polytechnic Institute	M,D
Rochester Institute of Technology	M,D
Rutgers, The State University of New Jersey, New Brunswick	M,D*
San Jose State University	M
Southern Methodist University	M,D*
Southern Polytechnic State University	M,O
Stevens Institute of Technology	M,D,O
Stony Brook University, State University of New York	M,D,O
Texas Tech University	M,D
The University of Alabama in Huntsville	M,D
University of Alberta	M,D*
The University of Arizona	M,D*
University of Arkansas at Little Rock	O
University of Central Florida	M,D,O*
University of Florida	M,D,O*
University of Houston	M,D*
University of Houston–Clear Lake	M
University of Idaho	M
University of Illinois at Urbana–Champaign	M,D*
University of Maryland, Baltimore County	M,O*
University of Maryland, College Park	M,O*
University of Michigan	M,D*
University of Michigan–Dearborn	M,D*
University of Minnesota, Twin Cities Campus	M*
The University of North Carolina at Charlotte	D*
University of Pennsylvania	M,D*
University of Regina	M,D
University of Rhode Island	M,D
University of St. Thomas (MN)	M,O*
University of Southern California	M,D,O*
The University of Texas at Arlington	M*
University of Virginia	M,D
University of Waterloo	M,D
University of Wisconsin–Madison	M,D*
Virginia Polytechnic Institute and State University	M,O*
Walden University	M,O
Western International University	M
West Virginia University Institute of Technology	M
Worcester Polytechnic Institute	M,D,O*

SYSTEMS SCIENCE

Arizona State University	M
Arkansas Tech University	M
Carleton University	M,D
Claremont Graduate University	M,D,O*
Eastern Illinois University	M,O
Fairleigh Dickinson University, Metropolitan Campus	M*
Florida Institute of Technology	M*
Hood College	M
Louisiana State University and Agricultural and Mechanical College	M,D
Louisiana State University in Shreveport	M
Miami University	M*
Oakland University	M
Portland State University	M,D,O
Rensselaer at Hartford	M
Southern Methodist University	M,D*
State University of New York at Binghamton	M,D*
Stevens Institute of Technology	M,D
Strayer University	M
Universidad Autonoma de Guadalajara	M,D
University of Michigan–Dearborn	M,D*
The University of North Carolina at Charlotte	M,D*
The University of North Carolina Wilmington	M
University of Ottawa	M,D,O*
Washington University in St. Louis	M,D*
Worcester Polytechnic Institute	M,D,O*

TAXATION

American International College	M
American University	M,O*
Bentley University	M
Bernard M. Baruch College of the City University of New York	M
Boise State University	M
Boston University	P,M*
Bryant University	M
California Polytechnic State University, San Luis Obispo	M
California State University, East Bay	M
California State University, Fullerton	M
California State University, Los Angeles	M
California State University, Northridge	M
Capital University	M
Chapman University	P,M
Cleveland State University	M
DePaul University	M*
Fairfield University	M,O*
Fairleigh Dickinson University, College at Florham	M,O*
Fairleigh Dickinson University, Metropolitan Campus	M*
Florida Atlantic University	M
Florida Gulf Coast University	M
Florida International University	M*

*M—master's degree; P—first professional degree; D—doctorate; O—other advanced degree; *—Close-Up and/or Announcement or Display in one of the other books in this series*

Florida State University M,D*
Fontbonne University M
Fordham University M*
Georgetown University P,M,D
Georgia State University M
Golden Gate University P,M,D,O
Grand Valley State University M
HEC Montreal M,O
Hofstra University M*
Illinois Institute of Technology P,M*
John Marshall Law School P,M
Long Island University, Brooklyn Campus M
Long Island University, C.W. Post Campus M,O
Loyola Marymount University P,M
Mississippi State University M
New York Law School P,M
New York University P,M,D,O*
Northeastern University M,O*
Northern Illinois University M
Northern Kentucky University M,O
Northwestern University P,M*
Nova Southeastern University M*
Pace University M*
Philadelphia University M
Robert Morris University M
Rutgers, The State University of New Jersey, Newark M*
St. John's University (NY) M,O
St. Mary's University (United States) M
St. Thomas University P,M
San Jose State University M
Seton Hall University M*
Southern Methodist University P,M,D*
Southern New Hampshire University M,D,O*
State University of New York College at Old Westbury M
Strayer University M
Suffolk University M,O*
Temple University P,M,D*
Texas Tech University M,D
Thomas M. Cooley Law School P,M
Universidad del Turabo M
University at Albany, State University of New York M*
The University of Akron M
The University of Alabama M,D
The University of Alabama in Huntsville M,O
University of Arkansas at Little Rock M,O
University of Baltimore P,M
University of Central Florida M*
University of Denver M*
University of Florida P,M,D*
University of Hartford M,O*
University of Hawaii at Manoa M*
University of Illinois at Urbana–Champaign M,D*
University of Memphis M
University of Miami M*
University of Michigan P,M,D*
University of Minnesota, Twin Cities Campus M*
University of Mississippi M,D
University of Missouri–Kansas City P,M*
University of New Haven M*
University of New Mexico M*
University of New Orleans M
The University of North Carolina at Greensboro M,O
University of North Texas M,D
University of San Diego P,M,O
University of Southern California M*
The University of Texas at Arlington M*
The University of Texas at Dallas M*
The University of Texas at San Antonio M,D*
University of the Pacific P,M,D
University of the Sacred Heart M
University of Tulsa M*
University of Washington P,M,D*
University of Waterloo M,D
Villanova University M*
Virginia Commonwealth University M
Wake Forest University M*
Walsh College of Accountancy and Business Administration M
Washington State University M*
Wayne State University M,D*
Widener University M*
William Howard Taft University P,M

TECHNICAL COMMUNICATION

Boise State University M
Bowling Green State University M,D*
Colorado State University M,D*
Drexel University M*
Eastern Michigan University M,O
Eastern Washington University M
Harvard University M*
Lawrence Technological University M
Michigan Technological University M,D
Minnesota State University Mankato M,O
Montana Tech of The University of Montana M
New Jersey Institute of Technology M
North Carolina State University M*
Polytechnic Institute of NYU O
Rensselaer Polytechnic Institute M
Rochester Institute of Technology O
Southern Polytechnic State University M,O
Texas State University–San Marcos M*
University of Colorado Denver M*
University of Houston–Downtown M
University of Nebraska at Omaha M,O
University of Washington M,D*

TECHNICAL WRITING

Carnegie Mellon University M*
Colorado State University M,D*
Drexel University M*
Fitchburg State College M,O
Illinois Institute of Technology M,D*
James Madison University M
The Johns Hopkins University M*
Laurentian University O
Massachusetts Institute of Technology M*
Metropolitan State University M
Miami University M*
Northern Arizona University M
Polytechnic Institute of NYU M
Regis University M,O
Texas Tech University M,D
The University of Alabama in Huntsville M,O
University of Arkansas at Little Rock M
University of California, Santa Cruz O*
University of Central Florida M,D,O*
The University of North Carolina at Greensboro M,D,O
University of the Sciences in Philadelphia M,O*
University of Waterloo M,D

TECHNOLOGY AND PUBLIC POLICY

Carnegie Mellon University M,D*
Eastern Michigan University M
The George Washington University M*
Massachusetts Institute of Technology M,D*
Rensselaer Polytechnic Institute M,D
Rochester Institute of Technology M
St. Cloud State University M
Stony Brook University, State University of New York M,D,O
University of Minnesota, Twin Cities Campus M*
University of South Africa M,D
The University of Texas at Austin M
Western Illinois University M

TELECOMMUNICATIONS

The American University of Athens M
Ball State University M*
Boston University M*
California State University, East Bay M
The Catholic University of America M,D
Claremont Graduate University M,D,O*
DePaul University M,D*
Drexel University M*
Florida International University M*
Franklin Pierce University M,D,O
George Mason University M,D,O*
The George Washington University M,D*
Illinois Institute of Technology M,D*
Indiana University Bloomington M*
Instituto Tecnologico de Santo Domingo M
Iona College M,O*
The Johns Hopkins University M,O*
Michigan State University M*
National University M
Ohio University M*
Pace University M,D,O*
Polytechnic Institute of NYU M
Polytechnic Institute of NYU, Long Island Graduate Center M
Polytechnic Institute of NYU, Westchester Graduate Center M
Rochester Institute of Technology M
Roosevelt University M
Saint Mary's University of Minnesota M
Southern Methodist University M,D*
State University of New York Institute of Technology M
Stevens Institute of Technology M,D,O
Syracuse University M*
Universidad del Turabo M
Université du Québec, Institut National de la Recherche Scientifique M,D
University of Alberta M,D*
University of Arkansas M
University of California, San Diego M,D*
University of California, Santa Cruz M,D*
University of Colorado at Boulder M*
University of Denver M,O*
University of Hawaii at Manoa O*
University of Houston M*
University of Louisiana at Lafayette M*
University of Maryland, College Park M*
University of Massachusetts Dartmouth M,D,O
University of Missouri–Kansas City M,D*
University of Oklahoma M*
University of Pennsylvania M*
University of Pittsburgh M,D,O*
University of Southern California M,D,O*
The University of Texas at Dallas M,D*
Widener University M*

TELECOMMUNICATIONS MANAGEMENT

Alaska Pacific University M
Capitol College M
Carnegie Mellon University M*
Concordia University (Canada) M,O
Hawai'i Pacific University M*
Instituto Tecnológico y de Estudios Superiores de Monterrey, Campus Ciudad de México M
Instituto Tecnológico y de Estudios Superiores de Monterrey, Campus Ciudad Obregón M
Instituto Tecnológico y de Estudios Superiores de Monterrey, Campus Estado de México M,D
Instituto Tecnológico y de Estudios Superiores de Monterrey, Campus Irapuato M,D
Morgan State University M
Murray State University M
Northeastern University M,D*
Oklahoma State University M,D*
Polytechnic Institute of NYU M
San Diego State University M*
Santa Clara University M,D,O
Stevens Institute of Technology M,D,O
Strayer University M
Syracuse University M,O*
University of Colorado at Boulder M*
University of Denver M,O*
University of Pennsylvania M*
University of San Francisco M
University of South Africa M,D

University of Wisconsin–Stout M
Webster University M,D

TERATOLOGY

West Virginia University M,D

TEXTILE DESIGN

Academy of Art University M
California College of the Arts M*
California State University, Los Angeles M
Cornell University M,D*
Cranbrook Academy of Art M*
Drexel University M*
Illinois State University M
James Madison University M
Kent State University M*
LIM College M
Marywood University M
Massachusetts College of Art and Design M
Missouri State University M*
Philadelphia University M
Rhode Island School of Design M
Savannah College of Art and Design M*
School of the Art Institute of Chicago M,O*
Sul Ross State University M*
Syracuse University M*
Temple University M*
University of California, Davis M*
University of Cincinnati M
University of Massachusetts Dartmouth M,O
University of Minnesota, Twin Cities Campus M,D,O*
The University of North Carolina at Greensboro M,D

TEXTILE SCIENCES AND ENGINEERING

Auburn University D*
Clemson University M,D
Cornell University M,D*
Georgia Institute of Technology M,D*
North Carolina State University M,D*
Philadelphia University M,D
University of Massachusetts Dartmouth M
The University of Texas at Austin M

THANATOLOGY

Brooklyn College of the City University of New York M
Hood College M,O
Southwestern College (NM) M,O*

THEATER

American Conservatory Theater M,O
Antioch University McGregor M
Arcadia University M,D,O
Arizona State University M,D
Arkansas State University M,O
Austin College M
Baylor University M
Bob Jones University P,M,D,O
The Boston Conservatory M
Boston University M,O*
Bowling Green State University M,D*
Brandeis University M
Brigham Young University M*
Brooklyn College of the City University of New York M,D
Brown University M,D*
California Institute of the Arts M,O
California State University, Fullerton M
California State University, Long Beach M
California State University, Los Angeles M
California State University, Northridge M
California State University, Sacramento M
California State University, San Bernardino M
Carnegie Mellon University M*
Case Western Reserve University M*
The Catholic University of America M
Central Washington University M
Christopher Newport University M
Columbia University M,D*
Cornell University D*
Dell'Arte School of Physical Theatre M
DePaul University M*
Drake University M*
Eastern Michigan University M
Emerson College M
Florida Atlantic University M
Florida State University M,D*
Fontbonne University M
The George Washington University M*
Graduate School and University Center of the City University of New York D*
Hollins University M
Humboldt State University M
Hunter College of the City University of New York M
Idaho State University M
Illinois State University M
Indiana University Bloomington M,D*
Kansas State University M*
Kent State University M*
Lamar University M
Lindenwood University M
Long Island University, C.W. Post Campus M
Louisiana State University and Agricultural and Mechanical College M,D
Mary Baldwin College M
Massachusetts College of Art and Design M
Miami University M*
Michigan State University M*
Minnesota State University Mankato M
Missouri State University M*
Montclair State University M*
Naropa University M*
National Theatre Conservatory M,O
The New School: A University M*
New York University M,D,O*
Northern Illinois University M
Northwestern University M,D*
The Ohio State University M,D*
Ohio University M*
Oklahoma City University M
Oklahoma State University M*
Pace University M*
Penn State University Park M*
Pittsburg State University M
Point Park University M*
Portland State University M
Purchase College, State University of New York M
Purdue University M
Regent University M,D
Rhode Island College M
Roosevelt University M
Rowan University M
Rutgers, The State University of New Jersey, New Brunswick M*
St. John's University (NY) M,D,O
San Diego State University M*
San Francisco State University M
San Jose State University M
Sarah Lawrence College M*
Savannah College of Art and Design M*
Smith College M
Southern Illinois University Carbondale M,D*
Southern Methodist University M*
Stanford University D*
State University of New York at Binghamton M*
Stony Brook University, State University of New York M
Temple University M*
Texas A&M University–Commerce M
Texas State University–San Marcos M*
Texas Tech University M,D
Texas Woman's University M
Towson University M
Tufts University M,D*
Tulane University M
Université de Sherbrooke M,D
Université Laval M,D
University at Albany, State University of New York M*
The University of Akron M
The University of Alabama M
University of Alberta M*
The University of Arizona M*
University of Arkansas M
The University of British Columbia M,D
University of Calgary M
University of California, Berkeley D*
University of California, Davis M,D*
University of California, Irvine M,D*
University of California, Los Angeles M,D*
University of California, San Diego M,D*
University of California, Santa Barbara M,D
University of California, Santa Cruz O*
University of Central Florida M*
University of Central Missouri M
University of Cincinnati M,D
University of Colorado at Boulder M,D*
University of Connecticut M*
University of Delaware M*
University of Florida M*
University of Georgia M,D*
University of Guelph M
University of Hawaii at Manoa M,D*
University of Houston M*
University of Idaho M
University of Illinois at Urbana–Champaign M,D*
The University of Iowa M*
The University of Kansas M,D*
University of Kentucky M
University of Lethbridge M,D
University of Louisville M
University of Maryland, College Park M,D*
University of Massachusetts Amherst M*
University of Memphis M
University of Michigan M,D*
University of Minnesota, Twin Cities Campus M,D*
University of Missouri–Columbia M,D*
University of Missouri–Kansas City M*
The University of Montana M
University of Nebraska at Omaha M
University of Nebraska–Lincoln M*
University of Nevada, Las Vegas M
University of New Mexico M*
University of New Orleans M
The University of North Carolina at Chapel Hill M*
The University of North Carolina at Charlotte M*
The University of North Carolina at Greensboro M
University of North Carolina School of the Arts M
University of North Dakota M
University of Oklahoma M*
University of Oregon M,D*
University of Ottawa M
University of Pittsburgh M,D*
University of Portland M
University of San Diego M
University of Saskatchewan M
University of South Carolina M,D
The University of South Dakota M
University of Southern California M*
University of Southern Mississippi M
The University of Tennessee M
The University of Texas at Austin M,D
The University of Texas–Pan American M
University of Toronto M,D
University of Victoria M
University of Virginia M
University of Washington M,D*
University of Wisconsin–Madison M,D*
University of Wisconsin–Milwaukee M
University of Wisconsin–Superior M
Utah State University M
Villanova University M*
Virginia Commonwealth University M
Virginia Polytechnic Institute and State University M*
Wayne State University M,D*
Western Illinois University M
West Virginia University M
Yale University M,D,O*
York University M,D

THEOLOGY

Abilene Christian University P,M
Acadia University P,M,D
Alliance Theological Seminary P,M
Ambrose University College P,M,O

*M—master's degree; P—first professional degree; D—doctorate; O—other advanced degree; *—Close-Up and/or Announcement or Display in one of the other books in this series*

American Baptist Seminary of the West	P,M
American Jewish University	M
Amridge University	P,M,D
Anderson University (IN)	P,M,D
Andover Newton Theological School	P,M,D
Andrews University	P,M,D,O
Apex School of Theology	P,M
Aquinas Institute of Theology	P,M,D,O
Asbury Theological Seminary	M,D,O
Ashland Theological Seminary	P,M,D,O
Assemblies of God Theological Seminary	P,M,D
Associated Mennonite Biblical Seminary	P,M,O
The Athenaeum of Ohio	P,M,O
Atlantic School of Theology	P,M,O
Austin Graduate School of Theology	M
Austin Presbyterian Theological Seminary	P,M,D
Ave Maria University	M,D
Azusa Pacific University	M,D
Bangor Theological Seminary	P,M,D
Baptist Bible College	P,M
Baptist Bible College of Pennsylvania	P,M,D
Baptist Missionary Association Theological Seminary	P,M
Baptist Theological Seminary at Richmond	P,D
Barry University	M,D*
Baylor University	P,M,D
Beacon University	P,M
Bethany Theological Seminary	P,M,O
Beth Benjamin Academy of Connecticut	
Bethel College (IN)	M
Bethel Seminary	P,M,D,O
Bethesda Christian University	P,M
Beth HaMedrash Shaarei Yosher Institute	
Beth Hatalmud Rabbinical College	
Beth Medrash Govoha	
Bethune-Cookman University	M
Bexley Hall Episcopal Seminary	P,M
Biblical Theological Seminary	P,M,D,O
Biola University	P,M,D
Blessed John XXIII National Seminary	P
Bob Jones University	P,M,D,O
Boston College	P,M,D,O*
Boston University	P,M,D*
Briercrest Seminary	P,M
Bryn Athyn College of the New Church	P,M
California Institute of Integral Studies	M,D*
Calvary Bible College and Theological Seminary	P,M
Calvin Theological Seminary	P,M,D
Campbellsville University	M
Campbell University	P,M,D
Canadian Southern Baptist Seminary	P,M
Capital Bible Seminary	P,M,O
Carey Theological College	M,D
The Catholic Distance University	M
Catholic Theological Union at Chicago	P,M,D,O
The Catholic University of America	P,M,D,O
Central Baptist Theological Seminary	P,M,O
Central Baptist Theological Seminary of Virginia Beach	P,M
Central Yeshiva Tomchei Tmimim-Lubavitch	
Chaminade University of Honolulu	M
Chicago Theological Seminary	P,M,D
Christendom College	M
Christian Theological Seminary	P,M,D
Christ the King Seminary	P,M,O
Church Divinity School of the Pacific	P,M,D,O
Church of God Theological Seminary	P,M,D
Cincinnati Christian University	P,M
Claremont Graduate University	M,D*
Claremont School of Theology	P,M,D
Colgate Rochester Crozer Divinity School	P,M,D,O
Collège Dominicain de Philosophie et de Théologie	M,D,O
College of Emmanuel and St. Chad	P,M
College of Mount St. Joseph	M
College of Saint Elizabeth	M
Columbia International University	P,M,D,O
Columbia Theological Seminary	P,M,D
Concordia Lutheran Seminary	P,O
Concordia Seminary	P,M,D,O
Concordia Theological Seminary	P,M,D
Concordia University (CA)	M
Concordia University (Canada)	M
Concordia University, St. Paul	M,O
Covenant Theological Seminary	P,M,D,O
Creighton University	M*
The Criswell College	P,M
Crown College	M
Dallas Theological Seminary	M,D,O
Darkei Noam Rabbinical College	
Denver Seminary	P,M,D,O
Dominican House of Studies, Pontifical Faculty of the Immaculate Conception	P,M,O
Dominican School of Philosophy and Theology	P,O
Drew University	P,M,D,O
Duke University	P,M,D*
Duquesne University	M,D*
Earlham School of Religion	P,M
Eastern Mennonite University	P,M,O
Eastern University	P,M,D
Ecumenical Theological Seminary	P
Eden Theological Seminary	P,M,D
Emmanuel School of Religion	P,M,D
Emory University	P,M,D*
Episcopal Divinity School	P,M,D,O
Erskine Theological Seminary	P,M,D
Evangelical Seminary of Puerto Rico	P,M,D
Faith Baptist Bible College and Theological Seminary	P,M
Faith Evangelical Lutheran Seminary	P,M,D
Fordham University	M,D*
Franciscan School of Theology	P,M
Franciscan University of Steubenville	M
Freed-Hardeman University	P,M
Friends University	M
Fuller Theological Seminary	P,M,D
Gardner-Webb University	P,D
Garrett-Evangelical Theological Seminary	P,M,D
General Theological Seminary	P,M,D,O
George Fox University	P,M,D,O*
Georgetown University	D
Georgian Court University	M,O
Global University	P,M
Golden Gate Baptist Theological Seminary	P,M,D,O
Gordon-Conwell Theological Seminary	P,M,D
Grace Theological Seminary	P,M,D,O
Grace University	M
Graduate Theological Union	M,D,O
Grand Rapids Theological Seminary of Cornerstone University	P,M
Harding University Graduate School of Religion	P,M,D
Hardin-Simmons University	P,M
Hartford Seminary	M,D,O
Harvard University	P,M,D*
Hebrew College	M
Hebrew Theological College	O
Hebrew Union College–Jewish Institute of Religion (CA)	P
Hebrew Union College–Jewish Institute of Religion (NY)	P,D
Hebrew Union College–Jewish Institute of Religion (OH)	P
Heritage Baptist College and Heritage Theological Seminary	P,M,D,O
Holy Apostles College and Seminary	P,M,O
Holy Cross Greek Orthodox School of Theology	P,M
Hood Theological Seminary	P,M,D
Houston Baptist University	M
Houston Graduate School of Theology	P,M,D
Howard University	P,M,D
Iliff School of Theology	P,M,D
Indiana Wesleyan University	P,M
Institute for Christian Studies	M,D
Inter American University of Puerto Rico, Metropolitan Campus	D
Interdenominational Theological Center	P,M,D
International Baptist College	M
Jesuit School of Theology at Berkeley	P,M,D,O
The Jewish Theological Seminary	M,D,O*
Johnson Bible College	M
Kehilath Yakov Rabbinical Seminary	
Kenrick-Glennon Seminary	P,M
Kentucky Christian University	M
Knox College	P,M,D
Knox Theological Seminary	P,M,O
Kol Yaakov Torah Center	O
Lakeland College	M
Lancaster Bible College	M
Lancaster Theological Seminary	P,M,D,O
La Salle University	M
Lee University	M
Lexington Theological Seminary	P,M,D
Liberty University	P,M,D
Lincoln Christian Seminary	P,M,D
Lipscomb University	P,M
Logos Evangelical Seminary	P,M,D
Loras College	M
Louisville Presbyterian Theological Seminary	P,M,D
Loyola Marymount University	M
Loyola University Chicago	P,M,D,O*
Loyola University New Orleans	M,O
Lubbock Christian University	M
Lutheran School of Theology at Chicago	P,M,D
Lutheran Theological Seminary	P,M,D
Lutheran Theological Seminary at Gettysburg	P,M,D
The Lutheran Theological Seminary at Philadelphia	P,M,D,O
Lutheran Theological Southern Seminary	P,M,D
Luther Rice University	P,M,D
Luther Seminary	P,M,D
Machzikei Hadath Rabbinical College	O
Madonna University	M
Malone University	M
Maple Springs Baptist Bible College and Seminary	P,M,D,O
Maranatha Baptist Bible College	M
Marquette University	M,D
Mars Hill Graduate School	M
Marylhurst University	P,M
The Master's College and Seminary	P,M,D
McCormick Theological Seminary	P,M,D,O
McGill University	M,D*
McMaster University	P,M,D,O
Meadville Lombard Theological School	P,M,D
Memphis Theological Seminary	P,M,D
Mennonite Brethren Biblical Seminary	P,M
Mercer University	P,M,D
Mesivta of Eastern Parkway–Yeshiva Zichron Meilech	
Mesivta Tifereth Jerusalem of America	
Mesivta Torah Vodaath Rabbinical Seminary	
Methodist Theological School in Ohio	P,M,D
Michigan Theological Seminary	P,M,O
Mid-America Baptist Theological Seminary	P,M,D
Mid-America Baptist Theological Seminary Northeast Branch	P
Mid-America Reformed Seminary	P,M
Midwestern Baptist Theological Seminary	P,M,D,O
Midwest University	P,M,D
Mirrer Yeshiva	
Moody Bible Institute	P,M,O
Moravian Theological Seminary	P,M
Mount Angel Seminary	P,M

Mount St. Mary's University	P,M
Mount Vernon Nazarene University	M
Naropa University	P*
Nashotah House	P,M,O
Nazarene Theological Seminary	P,M,D
Ner Israel Rabbinical College	M,D,O
Ner Israel Yeshiva College of Toronto	
New Brunswick Theological Seminary	P,M,D
Newman Theological College	P,M
New Orleans Baptist Theological Seminary	P,M,D
New York Theological Seminary	P,M,D
The Nigerian Baptist Theological Seminary	P,M,D,O
Northeastern Seminary at Roberts Wesleyan College	P,M,D
Northern Baptist Theological Seminary	P,M,D
North Park Theological Seminary	P,M,D
Northwest Baptist Seminary	P,M,D,O
Notre Dame Seminary	P,M
Oakland City University	P,D
Oblate School of Theology	P,M,D,O
Ohio Dominican University	M
Ohr Hameir Theological Seminary	
Oklahoma Christian University	P,M
Olivet Nazarene University	M
Oral Roberts University	P,M,D
Pacific Lutheran Theological Seminary	P,M,D,O
Pacific School of Religion	P,M,D,O
Payne Theological Seminary	P
Philadelphia Biblical University	P,M
Phillips Theological Seminary	P,M,D
Piedmont Baptist College and Graduate School	M,D
Pittsburgh Theological Seminary	P,M,D
Pontifical Catholic University of Puerto Rico	P
Pontifical College Josephinum	P,M
Princeton Theological Seminary	P,M,D
The Protestant Episcopal Theological Seminary in Virginia	P,M,D
Providence College	M*
Providence College and Theological Seminary	P,M,D,O
Queen's University at Kingston	P,M,O
Quincy University	M
Rabbi Isaac Elchanan Theological Seminary	O
Rabbinical Academy Mesivta Rabbi Chaim Berlin	O
Rabbinical College Beth Shraga	
Rabbinical College Bobover Yeshiva B'nei Zion	
Rabbinical College Ch'san Sofer	
Rabbinical College of Long Island	
Rabbinical Seminary M'kor Chaim	
Rabbinical Seminary of America	
Reconstructionist Rabbinical College	P,M,D,O
Reformed Presbyterian Theological Seminary	P,M,D
Reformed Theological Seminary–Charlotte Campus	P,M,D
Reformed Theological Seminary–Jackson Campus	P,M,D,O
Reformed Theological Seminary–Orlando Campus	P,M,D
Reformed Theological Seminary–Washington D.C.	P,M
Regent College	P,M,O
Regent University	P,M,D
Regis College (Canada)	P,M,D,O
Sacred Heart Major Seminary	P,M
Sacred Heart School of Theology	P,M
St. Andrew's College in Winnipeg	P
St. Augustine's Seminary of Toronto	P,M,O
Saint Bernard's School of Theology and Ministry	P,M,O
St. Bonaventure University	M,O
St. Catherine University	M
St. Charles Borromeo Seminary, Overbrook	P,M
Saint Francis Seminary	P,M
St. John's Seminary (CA)	P,M
Saint John's Seminary (MA)	P,M
Saint John's University (MN)	P,M
St. John's University (NY)	P,M,O
St. Joseph's Seminary	P,M
Saint Louis University	M,D
Saint Mary-of-the-Woods College	M,O
Saint Mary Seminary and Graduate School of Theology	P,M,D
St. Mary's Seminary and University	P,M,D,O*
St. Mary's University (United States)	M
Saint Meinrad School of Theology	P,M
Saint Michael's College	M,O
St. Norbert College	M
St. Patrick's Seminary & University	P,M
Saint Paul School of Theology	P,M
Saint Paul University	M,D,O
St. Petersburg Theological Seminary	P,M,D
St. Peter's Seminary	P,M
Saints Cyril and Methodius Seminary	P,M
St. Stephen's College	M,D
St. Thomas University	M,D,O
St. Tikhon's Orthodox Theological Seminary	P
Saint Vincent de Paul Regional Seminary	P,M
Saint Vincent Seminary	P,M
St. Vladimir's Orthodox Theological Seminary	P,M,D
Samford University	P,M,D
San Francisco Theological Seminary	P,M,D
Seabury-Western Theological Seminary	P,M,D,O
Seattle University	P,M,O
Seminary of the Immaculate Conception	P,M,D,O
Seminary of the Southwest	P,M,O
Seton Hall University	P,M*
Sewanee: The University of the South	P,M,D
Shaw University	P,M
Sh'or Yoshuv Rabbinical College	
Sioux Falls Seminary	M,D,O
Southeastern Baptist Theological Seminary	P,M,D
Southern Adventist University	M
Southern Baptist Theological Seminary	P,M,D
Southern California Seminary	P,M,D
Southern Evangelical Seminary	P,M,D,O
Southern Methodist University	P,M,D*
Southern Nazarene University	M
Southwestern Assemblies of God University	P,M
Southwestern Baptist Theological Seminary	P,M,D,O
Spring Arbor University	M
Spring Hill College	M
Starr King School for the Ministry	P
Talmudic College of Florida	M,D
Taylor College and Seminary	P,M,O
Temple Baptist Seminary	P,M,D
Toronto School of Theology	P,M,D
Trevecca Nazarene University	M
Trinity Episcopal School for Ministry	P,M,D,O
Trinity International University	P,M,D,O
Trinity Lutheran Seminary	P,M
Trinity Western University	P,M,D
Tyndale University College & Seminary	P,M,O
Unification Theological Seminary	P,M,D
Union Theological Seminary and Presbyterian School of Christian Education	P,M,D
Union Theological Seminary in the City of New York	P,M,D
United Talmudical Seminary	
United Theological Seminary	P,M,D
United Theological Seminary of the Twin Cities	P,M,D,O
Université de Montréal	M,D,O
Université de Sherbrooke	M,D,O
Université du Québec à Chicoutimi	M,D
Université Laval	M,D
University of Chicago	P,M,D*
University of Dallas	M
University of Dayton	M,D
University of Denver	D*
University of Dubuque	P,M,D
University of Mobile	M
University of Notre Dame	P,M,D*
University of Saint Mary of the Lake–Mundelein Seminary	P,M,D,O
University of St. Michael's College	P,M,D,O
University of St. Thomas (MN)	P,M*
University of St. Thomas (TX)	P,M
University of San Francisco	M
The University of Scranton	M
University of South Africa	M,D
University of Trinity College	P,M,D,O
The University of Winnipeg	P,M,O
Ursuline College	M
Valparaiso University	M,O
Vancouver School of Theology	P,M,O
Vanderbilt University	P,M*
Vanguard University of Southern California	M
Victoria University	P,M,D,O
Villanova University	M*
Virginia Union University	P,D
Walsh University	M
Warner Pacific College	M
Wartburg Theological Seminary	P,M
Washington Theological Union	P,M,D
Wesley Biblical Seminary	P,M
Wesley Theological Seminary	P,M,D
Western Seminary	M,O
Western Seminary–Sacramento Campus	P,M
Western Seminary–San Jose Campus	P,M
Western Theological Seminary	P,M,D
Westminster Seminary California	P,M
Westminster Theological Seminary	P,M,D,O
Wheaton College	M,D
Wilfrid Laurier University	P,M,D,O
Winebrenner Theological Seminary	P,M,D
Wycliffe College	P,M,D,O
Xavier University	M*
Xavier University of Louisiana	M
Yale University	P,M*
Yeshiva Beth Moshe	O
Yeshiva Karlin Stolin Rabbinical Institute	O
Yeshiva of Nitra Rabbinical College	
Yeshiva Shaar Hatorah Talmudic Research Institute	
Yeshivath Zichron Moshe	O
Yeshiva Toras Chaim Talmudical Seminary	

THEORETICAL CHEMISTRY

Carnegie Mellon University	M,D*
Cornell University	D*
Georgetown University	D
Laurentian University	M
University of Calgary	M,D
The University of Tennessee	M,D
Vanderbilt University	M,D*
Wesleyan University	M,D*
West Virginia University	M,D
Yale University	D*

THEORETICAL PHYSICS

Cornell University	M,D*
Delaware State University	D
Harvard University	D*
Rutgers, The State University of New Jersey, New Brunswick	M,D*
University of Victoria	M,D
West Virginia University	M,D

THERAPIES—DANCE, DRAMA, AND MUSIC

Antioch University New England	M*
Appalachian State University	M
Arizona State University	M,D
California Institute of Integral Studies	M,D*
Columbia College Chicago	M,O
Drexel University	M,O*
East Carolina University	M
Florida State University	M,D*
Georgia College & State University	M
Immaculata University	M
Lesley University	M,D,O*

*M—master's degree; P—first professional degree; D—doctorate; O—other advanced degree; *—Close-Up and/or Announcement or Display in one of the other books in this series*

Loyola University New Orleans M
Maryville University of Saint Louis M
Marywood University M,O
Michigan State University M,D*
Montclair State University M,O*
Naropa University M*
Nazareth College of Rochester M
New York University M*
Ohio University M,O*
Pratt Institute M*
Radford University M
Saint Mary-of-the-Woods College M
Shenandoah University M,D,O
State University of New York at New Paltz M
Temple University M,D*
The University of Kansas M*
University of Miami M,D,O*
University of the Pacific M
Western Michigan University M*
Wilfrid Laurier University M

TOXICOLOGY

American University M*
Brown University M,D*
Columbia University M,D*
Cornell University M,D*
Dartmouth College D*
Duke University D,O*
Florida Agricultural and Mechanical University M,D
The George Washington University M*
Indiana University–Purdue University Indianapolis M,D*
Iowa State University of Science and Technology M,D*
The Johns Hopkins University M,D*
Long Island University, Brooklyn Campus M,D
Louisiana State University and Agricultural and Mechanical College M
Massachusetts Institute of Technology M,D*
Medical College of Wisconsin D*
Michigan State University M,D*
New York University M,D*
North Carolina State University M,D*
Northeastern University M*
Northwestern University D*
The Ohio State University M,D*
Oklahoma State University Center for Health Sciences M,O
Oregon State University M,D*
Purdue University M,D
Queen's University at Kingston M,D
Rutgers, The State University of New Jersey, New Brunswick M,D*
St. John's University (NY) M
San Diego State University M,D*
Simon Fraser University M,D
Texas A&M University M,D*
Texas Southern University M,D
Texas Tech University M,D
Université de Montréal O
University at Albany, State University of New York M,D*
University at Buffalo, the State University of New York M,D*
The University of Alabama at Birmingham M,D*
University of Arkansas for Medical Sciences M,D
University of California, Davis M,D*
University of California, Irvine M,D*
University of California, Los Angeles D*
University of California, Riverside M,D*
University of California, Santa Cruz M,D*
University of Colorado Denver D*
University of Connecticut M,D*
University of Florida M,D,O*
University of Georgia M,D*
University of Guelph M,D
The University of Iowa M,D*
The University of Kansas M,D*
University of Kentucky M,D
University of Louisville M,D
University of Maryland, Baltimore M,D*
University of Maryland Eastern Shore M,D*
University of Michigan M,D*
University of Minnesota, Duluth M,D
University of Minnesota, Twin Cities Campus M,D*
University of Mississippi Medical Center M,D*
The University of Montana M,D
University of Nebraska–Lincoln M,D*
University of Nebraska Medical Center M,D*
University of New Mexico M,D*
The University of North Carolina at Chapel Hill M,D*
University of Prince Edward Island M,D
University of Puerto Rico, Medical Sciences Campus M,D
University of Rhode Island M,D
University of Rochester M,D*
University of Saskatchewan M,D,O
University of South Alabama M*
University of Southern California M,D*
The University of Texas Medical Branch M,D*
University of the Sciences in Philadelphia M,D*
University of Toronto M,D
University of Utah D*
University of Washington M,D*
University of Wisconsin–Madison M,D*
Utah State University M,D
Virginia Commonwealth University M,D
Washington State University M,D*
Washington State University Tri-Cities M,D
Wayne State University M,D*
West Virginia University M,D
Wright State University M

TRANSCULTURAL NURSING

Augsburg College M
University of Medicine and Dentistry of New Jersey D*

TRANSLATIONAL BIOLOGY

Baylor College of Medicine D*
Cedars-Sinai Medical Center D
Texas A&M Health Science Center D
The University of Iowa M,D*

TRANSLATION AND INTERPRETATION

American University M,O*
American University of Sharjah M
Babel University School of Translation M
College of Charleston O*
Concordia University (Canada) M,O
Georgia State University O
Kent State University M,D*
Marygrove College O
Montclair State University M,O*
Monterey Institute of International Studies M*
New York University M,D*
Rutgers, The State University of New Jersey, New Brunswick M,D*
State University of New York at Binghamton M,O*
Universidad Autonoma de Guadalajara M,D
Université de Montréal M,D,O
Université Laval M,O
University at Albany, State University of New York M,O*
University of Arkansas M
University of Denver M,O*
The University of Iowa M*
University of Nevada, Las Vegas M,O
University of Ottawa M,D*
University of Puerto Rico, Río Piedras M,O
The University of Texas at San Antonio M,O*
University of Wisconsin–Milwaukee M,O
York University M

TRANSPERSONAL AND HUMANISTIC PSYCHOLOGY

Atlantic University M
Institute of Transpersonal Psychology M,D,O
John F. Kennedy University M
Michigan School of Professional Psychology M,D
Naropa University M*
Saybrook Graduate School and Research Center M,D
Seattle University M

TRANSPORTATION AND HIGHWAY ENGINEERING

Auburn University M,D*
Cornell University M,D*
École Polytechnique de Montréal M,D,O
Illinois Institute of Technology M,D*
Iowa State University of Science and Technology M,D*
Louisiana State University and Agricultural and Mechanical College M,D
Marquette University M,D
Massachusetts Institute of Technology M,D,O*
Morgan State University M
New Jersey Institute of Technology M,D
Northwestern University M,D*
Ohio University M,D*
Oregon State University M,D*
Penn State University Park M,D*
Polytechnic Institute of NYU M,D
Polytechnic Institute of NYU, Long Island Graduate Center M
Rensselaer Polytechnic Institute M,D
South Carolina State University M
Texas A&M University M,D*
Texas Southern University M
The University of Alabama in Huntsville M,D
University of Arkansas M
University of California, Berkeley M,D*
University of California, Davis M,D*
University of California, Irvine M,D*
University of Central Florida M,D,O*
University of Dayton M
University of Delaware M,D*
University of Memphis M,D
University of Missouri–Columbia M,D*
University of Nevada, Las Vegas M,D
University of New Brunswick Fredericton M,D
University of Rhode Island M
University of Southern California M,D,O*
University of Washington M,D*
Villanova University M*
Western Michigan University M*

TRANSPORTATION MANAGEMENT

American Public University System M
Arizona State University O
Arizona State University at the Polytechnic Campus M
Concordia University (Canada) M,D,O
Florida Institute of Technology M*
George Mason University M*
Iowa State University of Science and Technology M*
Maine Maritime Academy M,O
McGill University M,D*
Morgan State University M
New Jersey Institute of Technology M,D
North Dakota State University M,D
Polytechnic Institute of NYU M
San Jose State University M
State University of New York Maritime College M
Texas Southern University M
University at Buffalo, the State University of New York M,D,O*
The University of British Columbia D
University of California, Davis M,D*
University of California, Santa Barbara M,D
University of Central Missouri M,O
University of Denver M*
The University of Tennessee M,D
University of Washington O*
Wilmington University M

TRAVEL AND TOURISM

Arizona State University M,D
Boston University M*
California State University, Fullerton M
California State University, Northridge M
Clemson University M,D
Eastern Michigan University M,O
East Stroudsburg University of Pennsylvania M
Florida Atlantic University M,O

The George Washington University M,O*
Hawai'i Pacific University M*
Indiana University Bloomington M,D,O*
New York University M,O*
North Carolina State University M,D*
Old Dominion University M
Purdue University M,D
Rochester Institute of Technology M
Royal Roads University M,O
Saint Xavier University M,O
Schiller International University (United States) M
Schiller International University (United Kingdom) M
Strayer University M
Temple University M*
Université du Québec à Trois-Rivières M,O
University of Central Florida M*
University of Hawaii at Manoa M*
University of Massachusetts Amherst M*
University of New Orleans M
University of South Africa M,D
University of South Carolina M
The University of Tennessee M
University of Waterloo M
Virginia Polytechnic Institute and State University M,D*
Western Illinois University M

URBAN AND REGIONAL PLANNING

Alabama Agricultural and Mechanical University M
American University of Beirut M,D
American University of Sharjah M
Arizona State University M,D
Auburn University M*
Ball State University M*
Boston University M*
California Polytechnic State University, San Luis Obispo M
California State Polytechnic University, Pomona M
California State University, Chico M
The Catholic University of America M
Clark University M
Clemson University M
Cleveland State University M,O
Columbia University M,D*
Concordia University (Canada) O
Cornell University M,D*
Dalhousie University M
Delta State University M
DePaul University M,O*
Eastern Kentucky University M
Eastern Michigan University M,O
Eastern University M
Eastern Washington University M
East Tennessee State University M
Florida Atlantic University M,O
Florida State University M,D*
Georgia Institute of Technology M,D*
Georgia State University M,D,O
Harvard University M,D*
Hunter College of the City University of New York M
Iowa State University of Science and Technology M*
Jackson State University M
Kansas State University M*
Lesley University M*
Massachusetts Institute of Technology M,D*
McGill University M,D*
Michigan State University M,D*
Minnesota State University Mankato M,O
Missouri State University M*
Morgan State University M
New York University M,O*
The Ohio State University M,D*
Portland State University M
Pratt Institute M*
Queen's University at Kingston M
Rutgers, The State University of New Jersey, New Brunswick M,D*
San Diego State University M*
San Jose State University M,O
State University of New York College of Environmental Science and Forestry M,D
Temple University M*
Texas A&M University M,D*
Texas Southern University M,D
Tufts University M*
Université du Québec à Rimouski M,D,O
Université du Québec en Outaouais M
Université Laval M,D
University at Albany, State University of New York M*
University at Buffalo, the State University of New York M*
The University of Akron M
The University of Arizona M*
The University of British Columbia M,D
University of California, Berkeley M,D*
University of California, Davis M*
University of California, Irvine M,D*
University of California, Los Angeles M,D*
University of Central Florida M,O*
University of Cincinnati M
University of Colorado Denver M,D*
University of Florida M,D*
University of Hawaii at Manoa M,D,O*
University of Idaho M
University of Illinois at Chicago M,D*
University of Illinois at Urbana–Champaign M,D*
The University of Iowa M*
The University of Kansas M*
University of Louisville M
University of Manitoba M
University of Maryland, College Park M,D*
University of Massachusetts Amherst M,D*
University of Memphis M
University of Michigan M,D,O*
University of Minnesota, Twin Cities Campus M*
University of Nebraska–Lincoln M,D*
University of New Mexico M*
University of New Orleans M
The University of North Carolina at Chapel Hill M,D*
University of Oklahoma M*
University of Oregon M*
University of Pennsylvania M,D,O*
University of Pittsburgh M,O*
University of Puerto Rico, Río Piedras M
University of Southern California D*
University of Southern Maine M,O
The University of Texas at Arlington M*
The University of Texas at Austin M,D
The University of Texas at San Antonio M,O*
The University of Toledo M,O
University of Toronto M,D
University of Utah M,D*
University of Virginia M,O
University of Washington M,D*
University of Waterloo M,D
University of Wisconsin–Madison M,D*
University of Wisconsin–Milwaukee M,O
Utah State University M,D
Vanderbilt University M*
Virginia Commonwealth University M,O
Virginia Polytechnic Institute and State University M,D*
Wayne State University M*
West Chester University of Pennsylvania M,O
West Virginia University M,D

URBAN DESIGN

American University of Beirut M,D
Arizona State University M
Ball State University M*
Carnegie Mellon University M,D*
The Catholic University of America M
City College of the City University of New York M*
Cleveland State University M,O
Cornell University M,D*
Georgia Institute of Technology M,D*
Harvard University M*
Kent State University M,O*
New York Institute of Technology M
Prairie View A&M University M
Pratt Institute M*
Rice University M,D
Savannah College of Art and Design M*
State University of New York College of Environmental Science and Forestry M
University at Buffalo, the State University of New York M*
University of California, Berkeley M,D*
University of California, Los Angeles M,D*
University of Colorado Denver M*
University of Miami M*
University of Michigan M*
University of New Mexico O*
University of Pennsylvania D*
The University of Texas at Austin M,D
University of Toronto M,D
University of Washington M,D,O*
Washington University in St. Louis M*

URBAN EDUCATION

Alvernia University M
Cardinal Stritch University M,D
Claremont Graduate University M,D,O*
Cleveland State University D
College of Mount Saint Vincent M,O
Columbia College Chicago M
DePaul University M,D*
Florida International University M*
Graduate School and University Center of the City University of New York D*
Harvard University D*
Holy Names University M,O
The Johns Hopkins University M,O*
Kean University D
Langston University M
Loyola Marymount University M
Marygrove College M
Mercy College M
Morgan State University M,D
New Jersey City University M
Norfolk State University M
Northeastern Illinois University M
Nova Southeastern University M,O*
Roberts Wesleyan College M,O
Simmons College M,O
Sojourner-Douglass College M
Temple University M,D*
Texas A&M University M,D*
University of Central Florida M,D,O*
University of Houston–Downtown M
University of Illinois at Chicago M,D*
University of Massachusetts Boston M,D,O
University of Nebraska at Omaha M,O
University of Southern California D*
University of Wisconsin–Milwaukee M,D
Vanderbilt University M*
Virginia Commonwealth University D

URBAN STUDIES

Boston University M*
Brooklyn College of the City University of New York M,D
Cleveland State University M,D,O
Concordia University (Canada) M,O
Eastern University M
East Tennessee State University M
Fordham University M*
Graduate School and University Center of the City University of New York M,D*
Hunter College of the City University of New York M
Long Island University, Brooklyn Campus M
Massachusetts Institute of Technology M,D*
Minnesota State University Mankato M,O
Moody Bible Institute P,M,O
New Jersey City University M
New Jersey Institute of Technology D
The New School: A University M*
Norfolk State University M
Northeastern University M,O*

*M—master's degree; P—first professional degree; D—doctorate; O—other advanced degree; *—Close-Up and/or Announcement or Display in one of the other books in this series*

Old Dominion University	D
Portland State University	M,D
Queens College of the City University of New York	M
Rutgers, The State University of New Jersey, Newark	M,D*
Saint Louis University	M,D,O
San Francisco Art Institute	M*
Savannah State University	M
Simon Fraser University	M,O
Southern Connecticut State University	M
Temple University	M*
Tufts University	M*
Université du Québec à Montréal	M,D
Université du Québec, École nationale d'administration publique	M
Université du Québec, Institut National de la Recherche Scientifique	M,D
University at Albany, State University of New York	M,D,O*
The University of Akron	M,D
University of California, Irvine	M,D*
University of Central Oklahoma	M
University of Delaware	M,D*
University of Lethbridge	M,D
University of Louisville	D
University of New Orleans	M,D
University of Wisconsin–Milwaukee	M,D
Virginia Polytechnic Institute and State University	M,D*
Wright State University	M

VETERINARY MEDICINE

Auburn University	P*
Colorado State University	P*
Cornell University	P*
Iowa State University of Science and Technology	P,M*
Kansas State University	P*
Louisiana State University and Agricultural and Mechanical College	P
Michigan State University	P*
Mississippi State University	P
North Carolina State University	P,M*
The Ohio State University	P*
Oklahoma State University	P*
Oregon State University	P*
Purdue University	P
Texas A&M University	P,M*
Tufts University	P*
Tuskegee University	P,M
Universidad Nacional Pedro Henriquez Urena	P,M,D
Université de Montréal	P
University of California, Davis	P*
University of Florida	P*
University of Georgia	P*
University of Guelph	M,D,O
University of Illinois at Urbana–Champaign	P*
University of Maryland, College Park	P*
University of Minnesota, Twin Cities Campus	P*
University of Missouri–Columbia	P*
University of Pennsylvania	P*
University of Prince Edward Island	P
University of Saskatchewan	P,M,D
The University of Tennessee	P
University of Wisconsin–Madison	P*
Virginia Polytechnic Institute and State University	P*
Washington State University	P,M,D*
Western University of Health Sciences	P

VETERINARY SCIENCES

Auburn University	M,D*
Clemson University	M,D
Colorado State University	M,D*
Drexel University	M*
Iowa State University of Science and Technology	M,D*
Kansas State University	M*
Louisiana State University and Agricultural and Mechanical College	M,D
Michigan State University	M,D*
Mississippi State University	M,D
Montana State University	M,D
North Carolina State University	M,D*
North Dakota State University	M,D
The Ohio State University	M,D*
Oklahoma State University	M,D*
Oregon State University	D*
Penn State Hershey Medical Center	M
Penn State University Park	D*
Purdue University	M,D
South Dakota State University	M,D
Texas A&M University	M*
Tufts University	M,D*
Tuskegee University	P,M
Université de Montréal	M,D,O
University of California, Davis	M,O*
University of Florida	M,D,O*
University of Georgia	M,D*
University of Guelph	M,D,O
University of Idaho	M,D
University of Illinois at Urbana–Champaign	M,D*
University of Kentucky	M,D
University of Maryland, College Park	M,D*
University of Minnesota, Twin Cities Campus	M,D*
University of Missouri–Columbia	M,D*
University of Nebraska–Lincoln	M,D*
University of Prince Edward Island	M,D
University of Saskatchewan	M,D
University of Washington	M*
University of Wisconsin–Madison	M,D*
Utah State University	M,D
Virginia Polytechnic Institute and State University	M,D*
Washington State University	M,D*

VIROLOGY

Baylor College of Medicine	D*
Case Western Reserve University	D*
Mayo Graduate School	D*
McMaster University	M,D
The Ohio State University	M,D*
Penn State Hershey Medical Center	M,D
Purdue University	M,D
Rush University	M,D
Rutgers, The State University of New Jersey, New Brunswick	M,D*
Texas A&M Health Science Center	D
Université de Montréal	D
Université du Québec, Institut National de la Recherche Scientifique	M,D
University of California, San Diego	D*
The University of Iowa	M,D*
University of Massachusetts Worcester	D
University of Minnesota, Twin Cities Campus	D*
University of Pennsylvania	D*
University of Pittsburgh	M,D*
University of Prince Edward Island	M,D
The University of Texas Health Science Center at Houston	M,D
The University of Texas Medical Branch	D*
Yale University	D*

VISION SCIENCES

Eastern Virginia Medical School	O
Emory University	M*
The New England College of Optometry	P,M
Nova Southeastern University	P,M*
Salus University	M,D,O
State University of New York College of Optometry	M,D
Université de Montréal	M,O
The University of Alabama at Birmingham	M,D*
The University of Alabama in Huntsville	M,D
University of Alberta	M,D*
University of California, Berkeley	M,D*
University of Chicago	D*
University of Guelph	M,D,O
University of Houston	M,D*
University of Missouri–St. Louis	M,D
University of Waterloo	M,D

VITICULTURE AND ENOLOGY

California State University, Fresno	M
University of California, Davis	M,D*

VOCATIONAL AND TECHNICAL EDUCATION

Alabama Agricultural and Mechanical University	M
Alcorn State University	M,O
Appalachian State University	M
Ball State University	M*
Bemidji State University	M
Bowling Green State University	M*
Buffalo State College, State University of New York	M
California Baptist University	M
California State University, Long Beach	M
California State University, Sacramento	M
California State University, San Bernardino	M
California University of Pennsylvania	M
Cambridge College	M,D,O
Central Connecticut State University	M,O
Chicago State University	M
Clarion University of Pennsylvania	M
Colorado State University	M,D*
East Carolina University	M
Eastern Kentucky University	M
Eastern Michigan University	M
East Tennessee State University	M
Fitchburg State College	M
Florida Agricultural and Mechanical University	M
Georgia Southern University	M
Idaho State University	M
Indiana State University	M
Inter American University of Puerto Rico, Metropolitan Campus	M
Iowa State University of Science and Technology	M,D*
Jackson State University	M
James Madison University	M
Kent State University	M,O*
Louisiana State University and Agricultural and Mechanical College	M,D
Marshall University	M
Middle Tennessee State University	M
Millersville University of Pennsylvania	M
Mississippi State University	M,D,O
Murray State University	M
North Carolina Agricultural and Technical State University	M,D
North Dakota State University	M,D,O
Northern Arizona University	M
Nova Southeastern University	D*
The Ohio State University	D*
Old Dominion University	M,D
Our Lady of the Lake University of San Antonio	M
Penn State University Park	M,D*
Pittsburg State University	M,O
Purdue University	M,D,O
Rhode Island College	M
Saint Martin's University	M
South Carolina State University	M
Southern Illinois University Carbondale	M,D*
Southern New Hampshire University	M,O*
State University of New York at Oswego	M
Temple University	M,D*
Texas State University–San Marcos	M*
Trevecca Nazarene University	M
The University of Akron	M
University of Arkansas	M,D
The University of British Columbia	M,D
University of Calgary	M,D,O
University of Central Florida	M*
University of Central Missouri	M,O
University of Georgia	M,D,O*
University of Idaho	M,D,O
University of Illinois at Urbana–Champaign	M,D,O*
University of Kentucky	M
University of Maryland Eastern Shore	M*
University of Minnesota, Twin Cities Campus	M,D,O*
University of Missouri–Columbia	M,D,O*
University of Nebraska–Lincoln	M,D,O*

University of Northern Iowa M,D
University of North Texas M,D
University of South Africa M,D
University of Southern Mississippi M
University of South Florida M,D,O*
The University of Texas at Tyler M,D
The University of Toledo M,O
University of Victoria M,D
University of West Florida M
University of Wisconsin–Platteville M
University of Wisconsin–Stout M,O
Utah State University M
Virginia Polytechnic Institute and State University M,D,O*
Virginia State University M,O
Wayne State College M
Wayne State University M,D,O*
Western Michigan University M*
Westfield State College M,O
Wilmington University M
Wright State University M

WATER RESOURCES

Albany State University M
California State University, Monterey Bay M
Colorado State University M,D*
Duke University M*
Eastern Michigan University M,O
Humboldt State University M
Inter American University of Puerto Rico, San Germán Campus M
Missouri University of Science and Technology M,D
Montclair State University M,D,O*
Nova Scotia Agricultural College M
Rutgers, The State University of New Jersey, New Brunswick M,D*
State University of New York College of Environmental Science and Forestry M,D
Tropical Agriculture Research and Higher Education Center M,D
University of Alaska Fairbanks M,D
The University of Arizona M,D*
University of California, Riverside M,D*
University of Florida M,D*
University of Idaho M,D
The University of Kansas M*
University of Minnesota, Twin Cities Campus M,D*
University of Nevada, Las Vegas M
University of New Brunswick Fredericton M,D
University of New Hampshire M*
University of New Mexico M*
University of Oklahoma M,D*
University of the Pacific P,M,D
University of Wisconsin–Madison M*
University of Wyoming M,D
Utah State University M,D
Washington State University Tri-Cities M,D

WATER RESOURCES ENGINEERING

American University of Beirut M,D
Cornell University M,D*
Louisiana State University and Agricultural and Mechanical College M,D
Marquette University M,D
McGill University M,D*
New Mexico Institute of Mining and Technology M
Ohio University M,D*
Oregon State University M,D*
Penn State University Park M,D*
Princeton University M,D*
Stevens Institute of Technology M,D,O
Texas A&M University M,D*
Tufts University M,D*
The University of Alabama in Huntsville M,D
University of Alberta M,D*
University of California, Berkeley M,D*
University of Colorado at Boulder M,D*
University of Dayton M
University of Delaware M,D*
University of Guelph M,D
University of Memphis M,D
University of Missouri–Columbia M,D*
The University of Texas at Austin M,D
University of Washington M,D*
Utah State University M,D
Villanova University M*

WESTERN EUROPEAN STUDIES

American University M,D,O*
Boston College M,D*
Brown University M,D*
California State University, Long Beach M
Carleton University M,O
The Catholic University of America M,D
Central Michigan University M,D,O
Claremont Graduate University M,D,O*
Columbia University M,O*
Cornell University M,D*
East Carolina University M
Georgetown University M
The George Washington University M*
Indiana University Bloomington M*
Mississippi State University M,D
New York University M*
San Diego State University M*
The University of British Columbia M
University of Connecticut M*
University of Guelph M
University of Nevada, Reno D*
University of Pittsburgh O*
Washington State University M,D*

WOMEN'S HEALTH NURSING

Case Western Reserve University M,D*
Columbia University O*
Emory University M*
Frontier School of Midwifery and Family Nursing M,O
Georgia Southern University M,D,O
Georgia State University M,D,O
Hampton University M
Indiana University–Purdue University Fort Wayne M,O
Indiana University–Purdue University Indianapolis M,D*
The Johns Hopkins University M,O*
Kent State University M,D*
Loyola University Chicago M*
MGH Institute of Health Professions M,D,O*
Old Dominion University M
Queen's University at Kingston M,D,O
Rosalind Franklin University of Medicine and Science M,D,O*
Seton Hall University M*
Stony Brook University, State University of New York M,O
Texas Woman's University M,D
University at Buffalo, the State University of New York M,D,O*
University of Cincinnati M,D
University of Colorado at Colorado Springs M,D
University of Delaware M,O*
University of Illinois at Chicago M*
University of Medicine and Dentistry of New Jersey M,D,O*
University of Minnesota, Twin Cities Campus M*
University of Missouri–Kansas City M,D*
The University of North Carolina at Chapel Hill M,D,O*
University of Pennsylvania M*
University of South Carolina M
The University of Texas at El Paso M,O
Vanderbilt University M,D*
Virginia Commonwealth University M,D,O
Wilmington University M

WOMEN'S STUDIES

The American University in Cairo M,O
Assemblies of God Theological Seminary P,M,D
Brandeis University M
California Institute of Integral Studies M,D*
Claremont Graduate University M,D*
Clark Atlanta University M,D
Cornell University M,D*
Drew University M
Duke University O*
Eastern Michigan University M
Emory University D,O*
Florida Atlantic University M,O
George Mason University M*
The George Washington University M,D,O*
Georgia State University M,O
Graduate School and University Center of the City University of New York M,D*
Institute of Transpersonal Psychology M,D
Lakehead University M,D
Lesley University M*
Memorial University of Newfoundland M
Minnesota State University Mankato M,O
Mount Saint Vincent University M
The Ohio State University M,D*
Old Dominion University M,D
Queen's University at Kingston M,D
Roosevelt University M,O
Rutgers, The State University of New Jersey, New Brunswick M,D*
Saint Mary's University (Canada) M
San Diego State University M*
San Francisco State University M
Sarah Lawrence College M*
Simon Fraser University M,D
Southeastern Baptist Theological Seminary P,M,D
Southern Connecticut State University M
Suffolk University M*
Texas Woman's University M
Towson University M,O
United Theological Seminary of the Twin Cities P,M,D,O
Université Laval O
University at Albany, State University of New York M,D*
The University of Alabama M
The University of Arizona M,D*
University of California, Los Angeles M,D*
University of California, Santa Barbara M,D
University of Cincinnati M,O
University of Florida M,O*
University of Georgia O*
University of Hawaii at Manoa O*
The University of Iowa D*
University of Lethbridge M,D
University of Louisville M,O
University of Maryland, Baltimore County O*
University of Maryland, College Park M,D*
University of Massachusetts Boston M,D,O
University of Michigan D,O*
University of Minnesota, Twin Cities Campus D*
University of Nevada, Las Vegas O
University of New Mexico O*
The University of North Carolina at Greensboro M,D,O
University of Northern Iowa M
University of Ottawa M*
University of Pittsburgh O*
University of Regina M
University of Saskatchewan M,D
University of South Carolina O
University of South Florida M*
University of Washington D*
University of Wisconsin–Madison M,D*
Washington State University M,D*
West Chester University of Pennsylvania M,O
Western Seminary M,O
York University M,D

WRITING

Abilene Christian University M
Adelphi University M*
American University M*
Antioch University Los Angeles M,O
Antioch University McGregor M
Arizona State University M
Asbury College M,O
Ashland University M
Ball State University M,D*
Belmont University M
Bennington College M
Boise State University M
Boston University M,D*
Bowling Green State University M,D*

M—master's degree; P—first professional degree; D—doctorate; O—other advanced degree; *—Close-Up and/or Announcement or Display in one of the other books in this series

Brooklyn College of the City University of New York	M
Brown University	M*
California College of the Arts	M*
California Institute of the Arts	M,O
California State University, Fresno	M
California State University, Long Beach	M
California State University, Northridge	M
California State University, Sacramento	M
California State University, San Bernardino	M
California State University, San Marcos	M
California State University, Stanislaus	M,O
Carlow University	M
Carnegie Mellon University	M*
Central Michigan University	M
Chapman University	M
Chatham University	M
Chicago State University	M
City College of the City University of New York	M*
Claremont Graduate University	M,D*
Clemson University	M
Cleveland State University	M
The College at Brockport, State University of New York	M
Colorado State University	M*
Columbia College Chicago	M
Columbia University	M*
Concordia University (Canada)	M
Cornell University	M,D*
Creighton University	M*
DePaul University	M*
Eastern Kentucky University	M
Eastern Michigan University	M,O
Eastern Washington University	M
Emerson College	M
Fairfield University	M*
Fairleigh Dickinson University, College at Florham	M*
Florida Atlantic University	M
Florida International University	M*
Florida State University	M,D*
George Mason University	M*
Georgia College & State University	M
Georgia State University	M,D
Goddard College	M
Goucher College	M
Hofstra University	M*
Hollins University	M
Hunter College of the City University of New York	M
Illinois State University	M
Indiana State University	M
Indiana University Bloomington	M,D*
Indiana University of Pennsylvania	M,D
The Johns Hopkins University	M*
Kennesaw State University	M
Kent State University	M,D*
La Sierra University	M
Lesley University	M*
Lindenwood University	M,O
Long Island University, Brooklyn Campus	M
Longwood University	M
Louisiana State University and Agricultural and Mechanical College	M,D
Loyola Marymount University	M
Manhattanville College	M*
Massachusetts Institute of Technology	M*
McNeese State University	M
Miami University	M,D*
Michigan State University	M,D*
Mills College	M
Minnesota State University Mankato	M,O
Minnesota State University Moorhead	M
Murray State University	M
Naropa University	M*
National-Louis University	M
National University	M
New England College	M
New Mexico Highlands University	M
New Mexico State University	M,D
The New School: A University	M*
New York University	M,D*
North Carolina State University	M*
Northeastern Illinois University	M
Northern Arizona University	M
Northern Michigan University	M
Northwestern University	M*
Oklahoma City University	M
Oklahoma State University	M,D*
Old Dominion University	M
Otis College of Art and Design	M
Our Lady of the Lake University of San Antonio	M
Pacific Lutheran University	M
Penn State University Park	M,D*
Purdue University	M,D
Queens College of the City University of New York	M
Queens University of Charlotte	M
Rhode Island College	M
Rivier College	M
Roosevelt University	M
Rosemont College	M
Rowan University	M
Rutgers, The State University of New Jersey, Camden	M
Rutgers, The State University of New Jersey, Newark	M*
Rutgers, The State University of New Jersey, New Brunswick	M*
Saint Joseph's University	M
Saint Mary's College of California	M
Saint Xavier University	M,O
Salisbury University	M
San Diego State University	M*
San Francisco State University	M
San Jose State University	M,O
Sarah Lawrence College	M*
Savannah College of Art and Design	M*
School of the Art Institute of Chicago	M,O*
Seattle Pacific University	M
Seton Hall University	M*
Seton Hill University	M
Sewanee: The University of the South	M
Slippery Rock University of Pennsylvania	M
Sonoma State University	M
Southern Illinois University Carbondale	M*
Southern Illinois University Edwardsville	M
Southern New Hampshire University	M,O*
Spalding University	M
Stony Brook University, State University of New York	M
Syracuse University	M,D*
Temple University	M*
Texas State University–San Marcos	M*
Towson University	M
Union Institute & University	M
The University of Akron	M
The University of Alabama	M,D
University of Alaska Anchorage	M
University of Alaska Fairbanks	M
The University of Arizona	M*
University of Arkansas	M
University of Arkansas at Little Rock	M
University of Baltimore	M
The University of British Columbia	M,O
University of California, Davis	M,D*
University of California, Irvine	M*
University of California, Riverside	M*
University of California, Santa Cruz	M*
University of Central Florida	M*
University of Central Oklahoma	M
University of Colorado at Boulder	M,D*
University of Florida	M,D*
University of Georgia	M,D*
University of Houston	M,D*
University of Houston–Downtown	M
University of Idaho	M
University of Illinois at Chicago	M,D*
University of Illinois at Urbana–Champaign	M,D*
The University of Iowa	M,D*
The University of Kansas	M,D*
University of Louisiana at Lafayette	M,D*
University of Louisville	M
University of Maryland, College Park	M,D*
University of Massachusetts Amherst	M,D*
University of Massachusetts Dartmouth	M,O
University of Memphis	M,D,O
University of Miami	M,D*
University of Michigan	M*
University of Missouri–St. Louis	M,O
The University of Montana	M
University of Nebraska at Kearney	M
University of Nebraska at Omaha	M,O
University of Nebraska–Lincoln	M,D*
University of Nevada, Las Vegas	M,D
University of New Hampshire	M,D*
University of New Mexico	M,D*
The University of North Carolina at Greensboro	M
The University of North Carolina Wilmington	M
University of North Florida	M
University of North Texas	M,D
University of Notre Dame	M*
University of Oklahoma	M*
University of Oregon	M*
University of Pennsylvania	M,D*
University of Pittsburgh	M,D*
University of San Francisco	M
University of South Carolina	M,D
University of Southern California	M,D*
University of Southern Maine	M
The University of Texas at Austin	M,D
The University of Texas at El Paso	M,D
The University of Texas at San Antonio	M,D,O*
University of the Sacred Heart	M
The University of Toledo	M,O
University of Utah	M,D*
University of Victoria	M
University of Virginia	M
University of Washington	M,D*
University of West Florida	M
University of Windsor	M
University of Wisconsin–Madison	M,D*
University of Wisconsin–Milwaukee	M,D,O
University of Wyoming	M
Utah State University	M
Vanderbilt University	M*
Virginia Commonwealth University	M
Warren Wilson College	M
Washington University in St. Louis	M*
Wayne State University	M,D*
Western Connecticut State University	M
Western Kentucky University	M
Western Michigan University	M,D*
Westminster College (UT)	M
West Virginia University	M
Wichita State University	M*
Wilkes University	M
Wright State University	M

ZOOLOGY

Auburn University	M,D*
Colorado State University	M,D*
Cornell University	M,D*
Emporia State University	M
Illinois State University	M,D
Indiana University Bloomington	M,D*
Miami University	M,D*
Michigan State University	M,D*
Montana State University	M,D
North Carolina State University	M,D*
North Dakota State University	M,D
Oklahoma State University	M,D*
Oregon State University	M,D*
Southern Illinois University Carbondale	M,D*
Texas A&M University	M,D*
Texas Tech University	M,D
Uniformed Services University of the Health Sciences	M,D*
University of Alaska Fairbanks	M,D
The University of British Columbia	M,D
University of California, Davis	M*
University of Chicago	D*
University of Connecticut	M,D*

University of Florida	M,D*
University of Guelph	M,D
University of Hawaii at Manoa	M,D*
University of Illinois at Urbana–Champaign	M,D*
University of Maine	M,D*
University of Manitoba	M,D
The University of Montana	M,D
University of New Hampshire	M,D*
University of North Dakota	M,D
University of Oklahoma	M,D*
The University of Western Ontario	M,D
University of Wisconsin–Madison	M,D*
University of Wisconsin–Oshkosh	M
University of Wyoming	M,D
Virginia Polytechnic Institute and State University	M,D*
Washington State University	M,D*
Western Illinois University	M,O

*M—master's degree; P—first professional degree; D—doctorate; O—other advanced degree; *—Close-Up and/or Announcement or Display in one of the other books in this series*

DIRECTORY OF INSTITUTIONS AND THEIR OFFERINGS

ABILENE CHRISTIAN UNIVERSITY

Accounting	M
Clinical Psychology	M
Communication Disorders	M
Communication—General	M
Conflict Resolution and Mediation/Peace Studies	M,O
Counseling Psychology	M
Curriculum and Instruction	M
Education—General	M
Educational Leadership and Administration	M
English	M
Family Nurse Practitioner Studies	M,O
Gerontology	M,O
Higher Education	M
Human Resources Development	M
Human Services	M,O
Liberal Studies	M
Marriage and Family Therapy	M
Missions and Missiology	M
Nursing and Healthcare Administration	M,O
Nursing Education	M,O
Nursing—General	M,O
Pastoral Ministry and Counseling	M,D
Psychology—General	M
Rhetoric	M
School Psychology	M
Social Work	M
Special Education	M
Theology	P,M
Writing	M

ACADEMY OF ART UNIVERSITY

Advertising and Public Relations	M
Applied Arts and Design—General	M
Architecture	M
Art/Fine Arts	M
Clothing and Textiles	M
Computer Art and Design	M
Film, Television, and Video Production	M
Graphic Design	M
Illustration	M
Industrial Design	M
Interior Design	M
Internet and Interactive Multimedia	M
Photography	M
Textile Design	M

ACADEMY OF CHINESE CULTURE AND HEALTH SCIENCES

Acupuncture and Oriental Medicine	M

ACADEMY OF ORIENTAL MEDICINE AT AUSTIN

Acupuncture and Oriental Medicine	M

ACADIA UNIVERSITY

Applied Mathematics	M
Biological and Biomedical Sciences—General	M
Chemistry	M
Clinical Psychology	M
Computer Science	M
Counselor Education	M
Curriculum and Instruction	M
Education—General	M
Educational Leadership and Administration	M
Educational Media/Instructional Technology	M
English	M
Geographic Information Systems	M
Geology	M
Kinesiology and Movement Studies	M
Mathematics Education	M
Political Science	M
Psychology—General	M
Recreation and Park Management	M
Science Education	M
Social Sciences Education	M
Sociology	M
Special Education	M
Statistics	M
Theology	P,M,D

ACUPUNCTURE & INTEGRATIVE MEDICINE COLLEGE, BERKELEY

Acupuncture and Oriental Medicine	M

ACUPUNCTURE AND MASSAGE COLLEGE

Acupuncture and Oriental Medicine	M

ADAMS STATE COLLEGE

Art/Fine Arts	M
Counselor Education	M
Education—General	M
History	M
Physical Education	M
Special Education	M

ADELPHI UNIVERSITY

Accounting	M
Art Education	M
Art/Fine Arts	M*
Biological and Biomedical Sciences—General	M*
Business Administration and Management—General	M
Clinical Psychology	D
Communication Disorders	M,D
Community Health	M,O
Counseling Psychology	M
Early Childhood Education	M,O
Education—General	M,D,O*
Educational Leadership and Administration	M,O
Educational Media/Instructional Technology	M,O
Electronic Commerce	M
Elementary Education	M
Emergency Management	O
English as a Second Language	M,O
Environmental Management and Policy	M*
Finance and Banking	M
Gerontology	M,O
Health Education	M,O
Human Resources Management	M,O
Management Information Systems	M
Marketing	M
Nursing—General	M,D,O*
Physical Education	M,O
Physics	M
Psychology—General	M,D*
Public Administration	O
Public Health—General	O
Reading Education	M
School Psychology	M
Secondary Education	M
Social Work	M,D*
Special Education	M,O
Writing	M*

ADLER GRADUATE SCHOOL

Business Administration and Management—General	M,O
Counseling Psychology	M,O
Counselor Education	M,O
Industrial and Organizational Psychology	M,O
Marriage and Family Therapy	M,O
Organizational Management	M,O
Psychoanalysis and Psychotherapy	M,O

ADLER SCHOOL OF PROFESSIONAL PSYCHOLOGY

Addictions/Substance Abuse Counseling	M,D,O
Art Therapy	M,D,O
Clinical Psychology	M,D,O
Counseling Psychology	M,D,O
Gerontology	M,D,O
Industrial and Organizational Psychology	M,D,O
Marriage and Family Therapy	M,D,O
Psychology—General	M,D,O*

AGNES SCOTT COLLEGE

English Education	M*
Mathematics Education	M*
Science Education	M

AIR FORCE INSTITUTE OF TECHNOLOGY

Aerospace/Aeronautical Engineering	M,D
Applied Mathematics	M,D
Applied Physics	M,D
Astrophysics	M,D
Computer Engineering	M,D
Computer Science	M,D
Electrical Engineering	M,D
Engineering and Applied Sciences—General	M,D
Engineering Management	M
Engineering Physics	M,D
Environmental Engineering	M
Environmental Management and Policy	M
Logistics	M,D
Management Information Systems	M
Management of Technology	M,D
Materials Sciences	M,D
Nuclear Engineering	M,D
Operations Research	M,D
Optical Sciences	M,D
Planetary and Space Sciences	M,D
Systems Engineering	M,D

ALABAMA AGRICULTURAL AND MECHANICAL UNIVERSITY

Agricultural Economics and Agribusiness	M
Agricultural Sciences—General	M,D
Agronomy and Soil Sciences	M,D
Animal Sciences	M,D
Applied Physics	M,D
Biological and Biomedical Sciences—General	M
Business Administration and Management—General	M
Clinical Psychology	M,O
Communication Disorders	M
Computer Science	M
Counseling Psychology	M,O
Counselor Education	M,O
Early Childhood Education	M,O
Education—General	M,O
Educational Leadership and Administration	M,O
Elementary Education	M,O
Engineering and Applied Sciences—General	M
Environmental Sciences	M,D
Family and Consumer Sciences-General	M,D
Food Science and Technology	M,D
Human Resources Management	M,O
Marketing	M
Materials Sciences	M,D
Music Education	M
Music	M
Optical Sciences	M,D
Physical Education	M
Physics	M,D
Plant Sciences	M,D
Psychology—General	M,O
School Psychology	M,O
Secondary Education	M,O
Social Work	M
Special Education	M,O
Urban and Regional Planning	M
Vocational and Technical Education	M

ALABAMA STATE UNIVERSITY

Accounting	M
Allied Health—General	D
Biological and Biomedical Sciences—General	M
Business Administration and Management—General	M
Counselor Education	M,O
Early Childhood Education	M,O
Education—General	M,D,O
Educational Leadership and Administration	M,D,O
Educational Media/Instructional Technology	M,O
Educational Policy	M,D,O
Elementary Education	M,O
English Education	M,O
Health Education	M
Mathematics Education	M,O
Mathematics	M,O
Music	M
Physical Education	M
Physical Therapy	D
Science Education	M,O
Secondary Education	M,O
Social Sciences Education	M,O
Special Education	M

ALASKA PACIFIC UNIVERSITY

Business Administration and Management—General	M
Counseling Psychology	M
Education—General	M
Elementary Education	M
Environmental Education	M
Environmental Sciences	M
Health Services Management and Hospital Administration	M
Interdisciplinary Studies	M
Investment Management	M,O
Liberal Studies	M
Middle School Education	M
Telecommunications Management	M

ALBANY COLLEGE OF PHARMACY AND HEALTH SCIENCES

Pharmacy P,M

ALBANY LAW SCHOOL

Law P,M

ALBANY MEDICAL COLLEGE

Allopathic Medicine P
Bioethics M,O
Biological and Biomedical Sciences—General M,D
Cardiovascular Sciences M,D
Cell Biology M,D
Immunology M,D
Microbiology M,D
Molecular Biology M,D
Neuroscience M,D
Nurse Anesthesia M
Pharmacology M,D
Physician Assistant Studies M

ALBANY STATE UNIVERSITY

Business Administration and Management—General M
Counselor Education M
Criminal Justice and Criminology M
Early Childhood Education M
Economic Development M
Economics M
Education—General M,O
Educational Leadership and Administration M,O
English Education M
Health Education M
Health Services Management and Hospital Administration M
Human Resources Management M
Mathematics Education M
Middle School Education M
Music Education M
Nursing—General M
Physical Education M
Public Administration M
Public Policy M
Science Education M
Special Education M
Water Resources M

ALBERT EINSTEIN COLLEGE OF MEDICINE

Allopathic Medicine P
Anatomy D
Biochemistry D
Biological and Biomedical Sciences—General D
Biophysics D
Cell Biology D
Developmental Biology D
Genetics D
Genomic Sciences D
Immunology D
Microbiology D
Molecular Biology D
Molecular Genetics D
Molecular Pharmacology D
Neurobiology D
Pathology D
Physiology D

ALBERTUS MAGNUS COLLEGE

Art Therapy M
Business Administration and Management—General M
Liberal Studies M

ALBRIGHT COLLEGE

Early Childhood Education M
Education—General M
Elementary Education M
English as a Second Language M
Special Education M

ALCORN STATE UNIVERSITY

Agricultural Economics and Agribusiness M
Agricultural Education M,O
Agricultural Sciences—General M
Agronomy and Soil Sciences M
Animal Sciences M
Biological and Biomedical Sciences—General M
Business Administration and Management—General M
Computer Science M
Counselor Education M,O
Education—General M,O
Elementary Education M,O
Health Education M,O
Information Science M
Nursing—General M
Physical Education M,O
Secondary Education M,O
Special Education M,O
Vocational and Technical Education M,O

ALDERSON-BROADDUS COLLEGE

Physician Assistant Studies M

ALFRED UNIVERSITY

Applied Arts and Design—General M
Art/Fine Arts M,D
Bioengineering M,D
Business Administration and Management—General M
Ceramic Sciences and Engineering M,D
Computer Art and Design M
Counselor Education M,D,O
Education—General M
Electrical Engineering M,D
Engineering and Applied Sciences—General M,D
Internet and Interactive Multimedia M
Materials Sciences M,D
Mathematics Education M,D
Mechanical Engineering M,D
Reading Education M
School Psychology M,D,O*

ALLEN COLLEGE

Acute Care/Critical Care Nursing M
Family Nurse Practitioner Studies M
Health Education M
Nursing and Healthcare Administration M
Nursing—General M
Psychiatric Nursing M

ALLIANCE THEOLOGICAL SEMINARY

Missions and Missiology P,M
Pastoral Ministry and Counseling P,M
Theology P,M

ALLIANT INTERNATIONAL UNIVERSITY–FRESNO

Clinical Psychology D*
Education—General M*
Educational Leadership and Administration D*
English as a Second Language M,D,O*
Forensic Psychology D*
Industrial and Organizational Psychology M,D
Psychology—General D

ALLIANT INTERNATIONAL UNIVERSITY–IRVINE

Education—General M,O*
Educational Leadership and Administration M,D,O*
Educational Media/Instructional Technology M,O
Educational Psychology M,D,O*
English as a Second Language M,D*
Forensic Psychology D*
Forensic Sciences D
Higher Education M,D,O
Marriage and Family Therapy M,D*
Multilingual and Multicultural Education M,O
School Psychology M,D,O
Special Education M,O

ALLIANT INTERNATIONAL UNIVERSITY–LOS ANGELES

Addictions/Substance Abuse Counseling M
Business Administration and Management—General D
Clinical Psychology D*
Education—General M*
Educational Leadership and Administration M,D,O*
Educational Psychology M,D,O*
Forensic Psychology D*
Gerontology M
Higher Education M,D,O
Industrial and Organizational Psychology M,D
Marriage and Family Therapy M*
Psychology—General M,D
School Psychology M,D,O
Student Affairs M,D,O

ALLIANT INTERNATIONAL UNIVERSITY–MÉXICO CITY

Business Administration and Management—General M
Counseling Psychology M
Education—General M*
International Affairs M
International Business M

ALLIANT INTERNATIONAL UNIVERSITY–SACRAMENTO

Clinical Psychology D*
Education—General M*
Industrial and Organizational Psychology D
Marriage and Family Therapy M*
Psychology—General M,D

ALLIANT INTERNATIONAL UNIVERSITY–SAN DIEGO

Business Administration and Management—General M,D
Clinical Psychology M,D*
Education—General M,O*
Educational Leadership and Administration M,D,O*
Educational Psychology M,D,O*
English as a Second Language M,D,O*
Finance and Banking M,D
Higher Education M,D,O
Industrial and Organizational Psychology M,D
International Affairs M
International Business M,D
Management Information Systems M,D
Management of Technology M,D
Management Strategy and Policy M,D
Marketing M,D
Marriage and Family Therapy M,D*
Psychology—General M,D
School Psychology M,D,O
Student Affairs M,D,O
Sustainability Management M,D

ALLIANT INTERNATIONAL UNIVERSITY–SAN FRANCISCO

Business Administration and Management—General M
Clinical Psychology D,O*
Education—General M,O*
Educational Leadership and Administration M,D,O*
Educational Psychology M,D,O*
Higher Education M,D,O
Industrial and Organizational Psychology M,D
Multilingual and Multicultural Education M,O
Pharmacology M
Psychology—General M,D,O
School Psychology M,D,O
Special Education M,O
Sustainability Management M

ALVERNIA UNIVERSITY

Business Administration and Management—General M
Education—General M
Liberal Studies M
Occupational Therapy M
Organizational Management D
Social Psychology M
Urban Education M

ALVERNO COLLEGE

Adult Education M
Business Administration and Management—General M
Education—General M
Educational Leadership and Administration M
Educational Media/Instructional Technology M
Nursing—General M
Reading Education M
Science Education M

AMBERTON UNIVERSITY

Business Administration and Management—General M
Counseling Psychology M
Human Resources Development M

*M—master's degree; P—first professional degree; D—doctorate; O—other advanced degree; *—Close-Up and/or Announcement or Display in one of the other books in this series*

Human Resources Management	M
Interdisciplinary Studies	M

AMBROSE UNIVERSITY COLLEGE

Cultural Studies	P,M,O
Missions and Missiology	P,M,O
Pastoral Ministry and Counseling	P,M,O
Religious Education	P,M,O
Theology	P,M,O

AMERICAN BAPTIST SEMINARY OF THE WEST

Pastoral Ministry and Counseling	P,M
Theology	P,M

THE AMERICAN COLLEGE

Business Administration and Management—General	M
Finance and Banking	M
Organizational Management	M

AMERICAN COLLEGE OF ACUPUNCTURE AND ORIENTAL MEDICINE

Acupuncture and Oriental Medicine	M

AMERICAN COLLEGE OF THESSALONIKI

Business Administration and Management—General	M,O
Entrepreneurship	M,O
Finance and Banking	M,O
Marketing	M,O

AMERICAN COLLEGE OF TRADITIONAL CHINESE MEDICINE

Acupuncture and Oriental Medicine	M,D,O

AMERICAN CONSERVATORY THEATER

Theater	M,O

AMERICAN FILM INSTITUTE CONSERVATORY

Film, Television, and Video Production	M

AMERICAN GRADUATE SCHOOL OF INTERNATIONAL RELATIONS AND DIPLOMACY

International Affairs	M,D

AMERICAN GRADUATE UNIVERSITY

Business Administration and Management—General	M,O
Project Management	M,O

AMERICAN INTERCONTINENTAL UNIVERSITY (TX)

Business Administration and Management—General	M

AMERICAN INTERCONTINENTAL UNIVERSITY BUCKHEAD CAMPUS

Accounting	M
Business Administration and Management—General	M
Finance and Banking	M
Marketing	M

AMERICAN INTERCONTINENTAL UNIVERSITY DUNWOODY CAMPUS

Information Science	M
International Business	M
Management Information Systems	M

AMERICAN INTERCONTINENTAL UNIVERSITY–LONDON

Business Administration and Management—General	M
International Business	M
Management Information Systems	M

AMERICAN INTERCONTINENTAL UNIVERSITY ONLINE

Accounting	M
Business Administration and Management—General	M
Computer and Information Systems Security	M
Curriculum and Instruction	M
Education—General	M
Educational Leadership and Administration	M
Educational Measurement and Evaluation	M
Educational Media/Instructional Technology	M
Finance and Banking	M
Health Services Management and Hospital Administration	M
Human Resources Management	M
Industrial and Manufacturing Management	M
Industrial and Organizational Psychology	M
Information Science	M
International Business	M
Marketing	M
Project Management	M

AMERICAN INTERCONTINENTAL UNIVERSITY SOUTH FLORIDA

Accounting	M
Business Administration and Management—General	M
Computer and Information Systems Security	M
Educational Media/Instructional Technology	M
Finance and Banking	M
Human Resources Management	M
Information Science	M
International Business	M
Marketing	M

AMERICAN INTERNATIONAL COLLEGE

Accounting	M
Business Administration and Management—General	M
Child Development	M,D,O
Clinical Psychology	M
Education—General	M,D,O
Educational Leadership and Administration	M,D,O
Educational Psychology	M,D,O
Elementary Education	M,D,O
Finance and Banking	M
Forensic Psychology	M
Human Resources Development	M
International Business	M
Marketing	M
Nonprofit Management	M
Nursing—General	M
Occupational Therapy	M
Organizational Management	M
Physical Therapy	D
Psychology—General	M,D
Public Administration	M
Reading Education	M,D,O
Secondary Education	M,D,O
Special Education	M,D,O
Taxation	M

AMERICAN JEWISH UNIVERSITY

Business Administration and Management—General	M
Education—General	M
Jewish Studies	M
Nonprofit Management	M
Social Work	M
Theology	M

AMERICAN PUBLIC UNIVERSITY SYSTEM

Business Administration and Management—General	M
Conflict Resolution and Mediation/Peace Studies	M
Criminal Justice and Criminology	M
Emergency Management	M
Environmental Management and Policy	M
Fire Protection Engineering	M
History	M
Homeland Security	M
Humanities	M
International Affairs	M
Logistics	M
Military and Defense Studies	M
National Security	M
Political Science	M
Public Administration	M
Public Health—General	M
Sports Management	M
Transportation Management	M

AMERICAN SENTINEL UNIVERSITY

Business Administration and Management—General	M
Computer Science	M
Health Informatics	M
Health Services Management and Hospital Administration	M
Management Information Systems	M
Nursing—General	M

AMERICAN UNIVERSITY

Accounting	M
American Studies	M,D,O
Anthropology	M,D,O
Applied Economics	M,D,O
Applied Science and Technology	M
Applied Social Research	M,O
Applied Statistics	M,O
Art History	M
Art/Fine Arts	M
Arts Administration	M,O
Biological and Biomedical Sciences—General	M
Biopsychology	M
Broadcast Journalism	M
Business Administration and Management—General	M,D,O
Chemistry	M
Clinical Psychology	D
Communication—General	M*
Comparative Literature	M
Computer Science	M,O
Conflict Resolution and Mediation/Peace Studies	M,D,O
Criminal Justice and Criminology	M,D
Cultural Studies	M,D,O
Curriculum and Instruction	M,O
Early Childhood Education	M,O
Economics	M,D,O
Education—General	M,O
Elementary Education	M,O
English as a Second Language	M,O
Entrepreneurship	M
Environmental Management and Policy	M,D,O
Environmental Sciences	M
Ethics	M,D,O
Exercise and Sports Science	M
Experimental Psychology	M
Film, Television, and Video Production	M
Finance and Banking	M,D,O
French	O
Health Education	M,O
History	M,D
Interdisciplinary Studies	M
International Affairs	M,D,O*
International and Comparative Education	M
International Business	M,O
International Development	M,D,O
Journalism	M
Latin American Studies	M,O
Law	P,M,O
Legal and Justice Studies	M,D,O
Management Information Systems	M,O
Marine Sciences	M
Marketing Research	M
Marketing	M
Mass Communication	M,D,O
Mathematics	M
Media Studies	M
Natural Resources	M,D,O
Neuroscience	D
Nonprofit Management	M,D,O
Organizational Management	M
Philosophy	M
Political Science	M,D,O
Psychology—General	D
Public Administration	M,D,O
Public Affairs	M
Public Policy	M
Real Estate	M
Russian	O
Secondary Education	M,O
Social Psychology	M
Sociology	M,O
Spanish	M,O
Special Education	M
Statistics	M,O
Supply Chain Management	M
Sustainable Development	M,D,O
Taxation	M,O
Toxicology	M
Translation and Interpretation	M,O
Western European Studies	M,D,O
Writing	M

THE AMERICAN UNIVERSITY IN CAIRO

Anthropology	M
Biotechnology	M
Broadcast Journalism	M

Business Administration and Management—General	M,O
Communication—General	M
Comparative Literature	M
Computer Science	M
Construction Engineering	M
Demography and Population Studies	M,O
Economics	M
English as a Second Language	M,O
English	M
Foreign Languages Education	M
Gender Studies	M,O
Journalism	M
Mass Communication	M
Near and Middle Eastern Languages	M,O
Near and Middle Eastern Studies	M,O
Political Science	M
Public Administration	M,O
Public Policy	M,O
Sociology	M
Women's Studies	M,O

THE AMERICAN UNIVERSITY IN DUBAI

Business Administration and Management—General	M
Construction Management	M
Finance and Banking	M
Health Services Management and Hospital Administration	M
International Business	M
Marketing	M

THE AMERICAN UNIVERSITY OF ATHENS

Biological and Biomedical Sciences—General	M
Business Administration and Management—General	M
Computer Science	M
Corporate and Organizational Communication	M
Engineering and Applied Sciences—General	M
Political Science	M
Systems Engineering	M
Telecommunications	M

AMERICAN UNIVERSITY OF BEIRUT

Agricultural Economics and Agribusiness	M
Agronomy and Soil Sciences	M
Allopathic Medicine	P,M
Animal Sciences	M
Anthropology	M
Aquaculture	M
Archaeology	M
Biochemistry	P,M
Biological and Biomedical Sciences—General	M
Biostatistics	M
Business Administration and Management—General	M
Chemistry	M
Civil Engineering	M,D
Computer Engineering	M,D
Computer Science	M
Economics	M
Education—General	M
Electrical Engineering	M,D
Engineering and Applied Sciences—General	M,D
Engineering Management	M,D
English	M
Environmental and Occupational Health	M
Environmental Management and Policy	M
Environmental Sciences	M,D
Epidemiology	M
Food Science and Technology	M
Geology	M
Health Education	M
Health Psychology	M
History	M
Mathematics	M
Mechanical Engineering	M,D
Microbiology	P,M
Near and Middle Eastern Languages	M
Near and Middle Eastern Studies	M
Neuroscience	P,M
Nursing—General	M
Nutrition	M
Pharmacology	P,M
Philosophy	M
Physics	M
Physiology	P,M
Plant Sciences	M
Political Science	M
Psychology—General	M
Public Administration	M
Public Health—General*	M
Sociology	M
Statistics	M
Urban and Regional Planning	M,D
Urban Design	M,D
Water Resources Engineering	M,D

THE AMERICAN UNIVERSITY OF PARIS

Communication—General	M
Conflict Resolution and Mediation/Peace Studies	M
Finance and Banking	M
International Affairs	M
Near and Middle Eastern Studies	M
Public Administration	M

AMERICAN UNIVERSITY OF PUERTO RICO

Art Education	M
Art History	M
Criminal Justice and Criminology	M
Education—General	M
Elementary Education	M
Physical Education	M
Science Education	M
Special Education	M

AMERICAN UNIVERSITY OF SHARJAH

Business Administration and Management—General	M
Chemical Engineering	M
Civil Engineering	M
Computer Engineering	M
Electrical Engineering	M
English as a Second Language	M
Mechanical Engineering	M
Public Administration	M
Translation and Interpretation	M
Urban and Regional Planning	M

AMRIDGE UNIVERSITY

Counseling Psychology	P,M,D
Marriage and Family Therapy	P,M,D
Organizational Behavior	P,M,D
Organizational Management	P,M,D
Pastoral Ministry and Counseling	P,M,D
Religion	P,M,D
Theology	P,M,D

ANDERSON UNIVERSITY (IN)

Accounting	M,D
Business Administration and Management—General	M,D
Education—General	M
Missions and Missiology	P,M,D
Theology	P,M,D

ANDERSON UNIVERSITY (SC)

Business Administration and Management—General	M
Criminal Justice and Criminology	M
Education—General	M
Pastoral Ministry and Counseling	M

ANDOVER NEWTON THEOLOGICAL SCHOOL

Religious Education	P,M,D
Theology	P,M,D

ANDREW JACKSON UNIVERSITY

Business Administration and Management—General	M
Criminal Justice and Criminology	M
Entrepreneurship	M
Finance and Banking	M
Health Services Management and Hospital Administration	M
Hospitality Management	M
Human Resources Management	M
International Business	M
Marketing	M
Public Administration	M

ANDREWS UNIVERSITY

Accounting	M
Allied Health—General	M
Architecture	M
Biological and Biomedical Sciences—General	M
Business Administration and Management—General	M
Communication—General	M
Counseling Psychology	D
Curriculum and Instruction	M,D,O
Developmental Psychology	M,D
Economics	M
Education—General	M,D,O
Educational Leadership and Administration	M,D,O
Educational Psychology	M,D
Elementary Education	M,D,O
Engineering and Applied Sciences—General	M
English as a Second Language	M,D,O
English Education	M,D,O
English	M
Finance and Banking	M
Foreign Languages Education	M,D,O
History	M
Human Services	M
International Development	M
Marketing	M
Mathematics	M
Music	M
Nursing—General	M
Nutrition	M
Pastoral Ministry and Counseling	P,M,D,O
Physical Therapy	D
Psychology—General	M,D,O
Reading Education	M
Religious Education	M,D,O
School Psychology	M,O
Science Education	M,D,O
Secondary Education	M,D,O
Social Psychology	M
Social Sciences Education	M,D,O
Social Work	M
Software Engineering	M
Special Education	M,D,O
Theology	P,M,D,O

ANGELO STATE UNIVERSITY

Accounting	M
Adult Nursing	M
Agricultural Sciences—General	M
Animal Sciences	M
Biological and Biomedical Sciences—General	M
Business Administration and Management—General	M
Communication—General	M
Counseling Psychology	M
Counselor Education	M
Curriculum and Instruction	M
Education—General	M
Educational Leadership and Administration	M
Educational Measurement and Evaluation	M
English	M
Higher Education	M
History	M
Industrial and Organizational Psychology	M
Interdisciplinary Studies	M
Journalism	M
Kinesiology and Movement Studies	M
Medical/Surgical Nursing	M
Nursing Education	M
Physical Therapy	D
Psychology—General	M
Public Administration	M
Reading Education	M

ANNA MARIA COLLEGE

Art Education	M
Art/Fine Arts	M,O
Business Administration and Management—General	M,O
Counseling Psychology	M
Criminal Justice and Criminology	M
Early Childhood Education	M,O
Education—General	M,O
Elementary Education	M,O
Emergency Management	M,O
English Education	M,O
Environmental and Occupational Health	M
Fire Protection Engineering	M
Pastoral Ministry and Counseling	M
Public Administration	M

ANTIOCH UNIVERSITY LOS ANGELES

Business Administration and Management—General	M
Clinical Psychology	M
Education—General	M
Human Resources Development	M
Organizational Management	M
Psychology—General	M
Writing	M,O

*M—master's degree; P—first professional degree; D—doctorate; O—other advanced degree; *—Close-Up and/or Announcement or Display in one of the other books in this series*

ANTIOCH UNIVERSITY MCGREGOR

Art/Fine Arts M
Business Administration and Management—General M
Comparative Literature M
Conflict Resolution and Mediation/Peace Studies M
Counseling Psychology M
Education—General M
Educational Leadership and Administration M
Film, Television, and Video Production M
Liberal Studies M
Psychology—General M
Theater M
Writing M

ANTIOCH UNIVERSITY NEW ENGLAND

Business Administration and Management—General M*
Clinical Psychology M,D
Conservation Biology M
Counseling Psychology M
Early Childhood Education M
Education—General M
Educational Leadership and Administration M
Elementary Education M*
Environmental Education M*
Environmental Management and Policy M,D*
Environmental Sciences M,D
Foundations and Philosophy of Education M
Interdisciplinary Studies M
Marriage and Family Therapy M,D*
Organizational Management M,O
Psychology—General M,D,O
Science Education M
Sustainability Management M
Therapies—Dance, Drama, and Music M

ANTIOCH UNIVERSITY SANTA BARBARA

Clinical Psychology D
Education—General M
Organizational Management M
Psychology—General M

ANTIOCH UNIVERSITY SEATTLE

Business Administration and Management—General M
Corporate and Organizational Communication M
Education—General M
Environmental Management and Policy M
Industrial and Organizational Psychology M
Organizational Management M
Psychology—General M,D

APEX SCHOOL OF THEOLOGY

Theology P,M

APPALACHIAN SCHOOL OF LAW

Law P

APPALACHIAN STATE UNIVERSITY

Accounting M
American Studies M
Biological and Biomedical Sciences—General M
Business Administration and Management—General M
Cell Biology M
Child Development M
Clinical Psychology M,O
Communication Disorders M
Computer Science M
Counselor Education M
Criminal Justice and Criminology M
Cultural Studies M
Curriculum and Instruction M
Educational Leadership and Administration M,D,O
Educational Media/Instructional Technology M,O
Elementary Education M
Engineering Physics M
English Education M
English M
Exercise and Sports Science M
Experimental Psychology M,O
Family and Consumer Sciences-General M
Foreign Languages Education M
Geographic Information Systems M
Geography M
Gerontology M
Health Psychology M,O
Higher Education M,O
History M
Home Economics Education M
Industrial and Organizational Psychology M,O
International Affairs M
Library Science M,O
Marriage and Family Therapy M
Mathematics Education M
Mathematics M
Middle School Education M
Molecular Biology M
Music Education M
Music M
Nutrition M
Political Science M
Psychology—General M,O
Public Administration M
Public History M
Reading Education M
Romance Languages M
School Psychology M
Social Psychology M
Social Sciences Education M
Social Work M
Special Education M
Sustainable Development M
Therapies—Dance, Drama, and Music M
Vocational and Technical Education M

AQUINAS COLLEGE

Business Administration and Management—General M
Education—General M

AQUINAS INSTITUTE OF THEOLOGY

Health Services Management and Hospital Administration P,M,D,O
Pastoral Ministry and Counseling P,M,D,O
Theology P,M,D,O

ARCADIA UNIVERSITY

Art Education M,D,O
Business Administration and Management—General M
Child Development M,D,O
Community Health M
Computer Education M,D,O
Conflict Resolution and Mediation/Peace Studies M
Early Childhood Education M,D,O
Education—General M,D,O
Educational Leadership and Administration M,D,O
Educational Media/Instructional Technology M,D,O
Educational Psychology M,D,O
Elementary Education M,D,O
English Education M,D,O
English M
Environmental Education M,D,O
Forensic Sciences M
Genetic Counseling M
Health Education M
Humanities M
International Affairs M
Mathematics Education M,D,O
Music Education M,D,O
Physical Therapy D
Psychology—General M,D,O
Reading Education M,D,O
School Psychology M
Science Education M,D,O
Secondary Education M,D,O
Social Psychology M
Social Sciences Education M,D,O
Special Education M,D,O
Theater M,D,O

ARGOSY UNIVERSITY, ATLANTA

Accounting M,D
Biopsychology M,D,O
Business Administration and Management—General M,D*
Clinical Psychology M,D,O
Counselor Education M,D,O
Education—General M,D,O
Educational Leadership and Administration M,D,O
Elementary Education M,D,O
Finance and Banking M,D
Health Psychology M,D,O
Health Services Management and Hospital Administration M,D
Higher Education M,D,O
International Business M,D
Management Information Systems M,D
Marketing M,D
Marriage and Family Therapy M,D,O
Psychology—General M,D,O*
Secondary Education M,D,O
Social Psychology M,D,O

ARGOSY UNIVERSITY, CHICAGO

Accounting M,D
Business Administration and Management—General M,D*
Clinical Psychology M,D*
Community College Education M,D,O
Counseling Psychology D
Counselor Education D
Education—General M,D,O*
Educational Leadership and Administration M,D,O
Elementary Education M,D,O
Finance and Banking M,D
Forensic Psychology D
Health Psychology D
Health Services Management and Hospital Administration M,D
Higher Education M,D,O
Human Development D
International Business M,D
Management Information Systems M,D
Marketing M,D
Marriage and Family Therapy D
Organizational Management D
Psychoanalysis and Psychotherapy D
Psychology—General M,D
Secondary Education M,D,O
Social Psychology M,D

ARGOSY UNIVERSITY, DALLAS

Accounting M,O
Business Administration and Management—General M,O*
Clinical Psychology M,D*
Education—General M*
Educational Leadership and Administration M
Finance and Banking M,O
Health Services Management and Hospital Administration M,O
International Business M,O
Management Information Systems M,O
Marketing M,O
Psychology—General M,D
Public Administration M,O
Social Psychology M
Sustainability Management M,O

ARGOSY UNIVERSITY, DENVER

Accounting M,D
Business Administration and Management—General M,D*
Clinical Psychology M,D
Community College Education M,D
Counseling Psychology M,D
Counselor Education M,D
Education—General M,D*
Educational Leadership and Administration M,D
Educational Media/Instructional Technology M,D
Elementary Education M,D
Finance and Banking M,D
Forensic Psychology M,D
Health Services Management and Hospital Administration M,D
Higher Education M,D
International Business M,D
Management Information Systems M,D
Marketing M,D
Marriage and Family Therapy M,D
Organizational Management M,D
Psychology—General M,D
Social Psychology M,D*

ARGOSY UNIVERSITY, HAWAI'I

Accounting M,D,O
Addictions/Substance Abuse Counseling O
Adult Education M,D
Business Administration and Management—General M,D,O*
Clinical Psychology M,D,O

Counseling Psychology	D
Education—General	M,D*
Educational Leadership and Administration	M,D
Elementary Education	M,D
Finance and Banking	M,D,O
Health Services Management and Hospital Administration	M,D,O
Higher Education	M,D
International Business	M,D,O
Management Information Systems	M,D,O
Marketing	M,D,O
Marriage and Family Therapy	M
Organizational Management	D
Pharmacology	M,O
Psychology—General	M,D,O*
School Psychology	M
Secondary Education	M,D

ARGOSY UNIVERSITY, INLAND EMPIRE

Accounting	M,D
Business Administration and Management—General	M,D*
Clinical Psychology	M,D
Community College Education	M,D
Counseling Psychology	M,D*
Education—General	M,D
Educational Leadership and Administration	M,D*
Elementary Education	M,D
Finance and Banking	M,D
Forensic Psychology	M,D
Health Services Management and Hospital Administration	M,D
Higher Education	M,D
International Business	M,D
Management Information Systems	M,D
Marketing	M,D
Marriage and Family Therapy	M,D
Psychology—General	M,D
Secondary Education	M,D

ARGOSY UNIVERSITY, LOS ANGELES

Accounting	M,D
Business Administration and Management—General	M,D*
Clinical Psychology	M,D*
Community College Education	M,D
Counseling Psychology	M,D
Education—General	M,D*
Educational Leadership and Administration	M,D
Elementary Education	M,D
Finance and Banking	M,D
Health Services Management and Hospital Administration	M,D
Higher Education	M,D
International Business	M,D
Management Information Systems	M,D
Marketing	M,D
Marriage and Family Therapy	M,D
Organizational Management	M,D
Psychology—General	M,D
Secondary Education	M,D

ARGOSY UNIVERSITY, NASHVILLE

Accounting	M,D
Business Administration and Management—General	M,D*
Counseling Psychology	M,D*
Counselor Education	M,D
Education—General	M,D,O
Educational Leadership and Administration	M,D,O*
Educational Media/Instructional Technology	M,D,O
Elementary Education	M,D,O
Finance and Banking	M,D
Health Services Management and Hospital Administration	M,D
Higher Education	M,D,O
International Business	M,D
Management Information Systems	M,D
Marketing	M,D
Psychology—General	M,D
Secondary Education	M,D,O

ARGOSY UNIVERSITY, ORANGE COUNTY

Accounting	M,D,O
Business Administration and Management—General	M,D,O*
Clinical Psychology	M,D
Community College Education	M,D
Counseling Psychology	M,D
Education—General	M,D*
Educational Leadership and Administration	M,D
Educational Media/Instructional Technology	M,D
Elementary Education	M,D
Finance and Banking	M,D,O
Forensic Psychology	M
Health Services Management and Hospital Administration	M,D,O
Higher Education	M,D
International Business	M,D,O
Management Information Systems	M,D,O
Marketing	M,D,O
Marriage and Family Therapy	M,D
Organizational Management	D
Psychology—General	M,D,O*
Public Administration	M,D,O
Secondary Education	M,D
Sport Psychology	M

ARGOSY UNIVERSITY, PHOENIX

Accounting	M,D
Business Administration and Management—General	M,D*
Clinical Psychology	M,D
Community College Education	M,D,O
Counseling Psychology	M
Education—General	M,D,O*
Educational Leadership and Administration	M,D,O
Elementary Education	M,D,O
Finance and Banking	M,D
Forensic Psychology	M
Health Services Management and Hospital Administration	M,D
Higher Education	M,D,O
International Business	M,D
Management Information Systems	M,D
Marketing	M,D
Psychology—General	M,D*
School Psychology	M,D
Secondary Education	M,D,O
Sport Psychology	M,D

ARGOSY UNIVERSITY, SALT LAKE CITY

Accounting	M,D
Business Administration and Management—General	M,D*
Counseling Psychology	M,D
Education—General	M,D*
Educational Leadership and Administration	M,D
Finance and Banking	M,D
Health Services Management and Hospital Administration	M,D
International Business	M,D
Management Information Systems	M,D
Marketing	M,D
Marriage and Family Therapy	M,D
Psychology—General	M,D*
Public Administration	M,D
Sustainability Management	M,D

ARGOSY UNIVERSITY, SAN DIEGO

Accounting	M,D
Business Administration and Management—General	M,D*
Clinical Psychology	M,D
Community College Education	M,D
Counseling Psychology	M,D*
Education—General	M,D*
Educational Leadership and Administration	M,D
Elementary Education	M,D
Finance and Banking	M,D
Higher Education	M,D
International Business	M,D
Management Information Systems	M,D
Marketing	M,D
Marriage and Family Therapy	M,D
Psychology—General	M,D
Secondary Education	M,D

ARGOSY UNIVERSITY, SAN FRANCISCO BAY AREA

Accounting	M,D
Business Administration and Management—General	M,D*
Clinical Psychology	M,D
Community College Education	M,D
Counseling Psychology	M,D
Education—General	M,D*
Educational Leadership and Administration	M,D
Elementary Education	M,D
Finance and Banking	M,D
Forensic Psychology	M
Health Services Management and Hospital Administration	M,D
Higher Education	M,D
International Business	M,D
Management Information Systems	M,D
Marketing	M,D
Organizational Management	M,D
Psychology—General	M,D*
Secondary Education	M,D

ARGOSY UNIVERSITY, SARASOTA

Accounting	M,D,O
Business Administration and Management—General	M,D,O*
Counseling Psychology	M,D,O
Counselor Education	M,D,O
Education—General	M,D,O*
Educational Leadership and Administration	M,D,O
Educational Media/Instructional Technology	M,D,O
Elementary Education	M,D,O
Finance and Banking	M,D,O
Forensic Psychology	M,D,O
Health Services Management and Hospital Administration	M,D,O
Higher Education	M,D,O
International Business	M,D,O
Management Information Systems	M,D,O
Marketing	M,D,O
Marriage and Family Therapy	M,D,O
Organizational Management	M,D,O
Pastoral Ministry and Counseling	M,D,O
Psychology—General	M,D,O*
School Psychology	M,D,O
Secondary Education	M,D,O
Social Psychology	M,D,O

ARGOSY UNIVERSITY, SCHAUMBURG

Accounting	M,D,O
Business Administration and Management—General	M,D,O*
Clinical Psychology	M,D,O*
Community College Education	M,D,O
Counseling Psychology	M,D,O
Counselor Education	M,D,O
Education—General	M,D,O*
Educational Leadership and Administration	M,D,O
Elementary Education	M,D,O
Finance and Banking	M,D,O
Forensic Psychology	M,D,O
Health Psychology	M,D,O
Health Services Management and Hospital Administration	M,D,O
Higher Education	M,D,O
International Business	M,D,O
Management Information Systems	M,D,O
Marketing	M,D,O
Marriage and Family Therapy	M,D,O
Organizational Management	M,D,O
Psychology—General	M,D,O
Secondary Education	M,D,O
Social Psychology	M,D,O

ARGOSY UNIVERSITY, SEATTLE

Accounting	M,D
Business Administration and Management—General	M,D*
Clinical Psychology	M,D,O*
Community College Education	M,D
Counseling Psychology	M,D
Education—General	M,D*
Educational Leadership and Administration	M,D
Educational Media/Instructional Technology	M,D
Elementary Education	M,D
Finance and Banking	M,D
Health Services Management and Hospital Administration	M,D
Higher Education	M,D
International Business	M,D
Management Information Systems	M,D

*M—master's degree; P—first professional degree; D—doctorate; O—other advanced degree; *—Close-Up and/or Announcement or* ***Display*** *in one of the other books in this series*

Marketing M,D
Psychology—General M,D,O
Secondary Education M,D

ARGOSY UNIVERSITY, TAMPA

Accounting M,D
Business Administration and Management—General M,D*
Clinical Psychology M,D
Community College Education M,D,O
Counseling Psychology M,D
Counselor Education M,D
Education—General M,D,O*
Educational Leadership and Administration M,D,O
Elementary Education M,D,O
Finance and Banking M,D
Health Services Management and Hospital Administration M,D,O
Higher Education M,D,O
International Business M,D
Management Information Systems M,D
Marketing M,D
Marriage and Family Therapy M,D
Neuroscience M,D
Organizational Management M,D
Psychology—General M,D*
Public Administration M,D
Secondary Education M,D,O

ARGOSY UNIVERSITY, TWIN CITIES

Accounting M,D
Biopsychology M,D,O
Business Administration and Management—General M,D*
Clinical Psychology M,D,O
Education—General M,D,O*
Educational Leadership and Administration M,D,O
Elementary Education M,D,O
Finance and Banking M,D
Forensic Psychology M,D,O
Health Psychology M,D,O
Health Services Management and Hospital Administration M,D
Higher Education M,D,O
International Business M,D
Management Information Systems M,D
Marketing M,D
Marriage and Family Therapy M,D,O
Organizational Management M,D,O
Psychology—General M,D,O*
Secondary Education M,D,O

ARGOSY UNIVERSITY, WASHINGTON DC

Accounting M,D,O
Business Administration and Management—General M,D,O*
Clinical Psychology M,D*
Community College Education M,D,O
Counseling Psychology M,D
Counselor Education M,D
Education—General M,D,O*
Educational Leadership and Administration M,D,O
Elementary Education M,D,O
Finance and Banking M,D,O
Forensic Psychology M,D
Health Psychology M,D
Health Services Management and Hospital Administration M,D,O
Higher Education M,D,O
International Business M,D,O
Management Information Systems M,D,O
Marketing M,D,O
Marriage and Family Therapy M,D
Organizational Management M,D
Psychology—General M,D
Secondary Education M,D,O
Social Psychology M,D

ARIZONA STATE UNIVERSITY

Accounting M,D
Aerospace/Aeronautical Engineering M,D
Agricultural Economics and Agribusiness M,D
Anthropology M,D
Applied Arts and Design—General M
Applied Mathematics M,D
Architectural History D
Architecture M
Art/Fine Arts M,D
Astrophysics M,D
Biochemistry M,D
Bioengineering M,D
Bioinformatics M,D
Biological and Biomedical Sciences—General M,D
Biotechnology P,M
Building Science M
Business Administration and Management—General M,D
Cell Biology M,D
Chemical Engineering M,D
Chemistry M,D
Child and Family Studies M,D
Chinese M
Civil Engineering M,D
Clinical Psychology D
Cognitive Sciences D
Communication Disorders M,D
Communication—General M,D
Comparative Literature M,D
Computational Biology M
Computer Art and Design M
Computer Science M,D
Construction Engineering M
Construction Management M
Counseling Psychology D
Counselor Education M
Cultural Studies M
Curriculum and Instruction M,D
Dance M
Developmental Psychology D
Economics M,D
Education—General M,D
Educational Leadership and Administration M,D
Educational Media/Instructional Technology M,D
Educational Psychology M,D
Electrical Engineering M,D
Engineering and Applied Sciences—General M,D
English as a Second Language M,D
English M,D
Environmental Design D
Environmental Engineering M,D
Environmental Sciences M,D
Film, Television, and Video Production M
Finance and Banking M,D
Foundations and Philosophy of Education M
French M
Gender Studies D
Geographic Information Systems M,D
Geography M,D
Geological Engineering M,D
Geology M,D
Geosciences M,D
German M
Health Services Management and Hospital Administration M,D
Higher Education M
History M,D
Human Development M,D
Industrial Design M
Industrial/Management Engineering M,D
Interior Design M
Japanese M
Kinesiology and Movement Studies D
Landscape Architecture M
Latin American Studies M,D
Law P,M
Legal and Justice Studies P,M,D
Linguistics M,D
Management Information Systems M,D
Manufacturing Engineering M,D
Marketing M,D
Marriage and Family Therapy M,D
Materials Engineering M,D
Materials Sciences M,D
Mathematics M,D
Mechanical Engineering M,D
Media Studies M,D
Medical Informatics M,D
Microbiology M,D
Molecular Biology M,D
Museum Studies M,D
Music Education M,D
Music M,D
Nanotechnology M,D
Neuroscience M,D
Nonprofit Management M,D
Philosophy M,D
Physics M,D
Plant Biology M,D
Political Science M,D
Psychology—General D
Public Affairs M,D
Public History M,D
Public Policy P,M
Recreation and Park Management M,D
Reliability Engineering M
Religion M,D
Social Psychology D
Social Sciences M,D
Social Work M,D
Sociology M,D
Software Engineering M
Spanish M,D
Special Education M
Speech and Interpersonal Communication M,D
Statistics M,D
Supply Chain Management M,D
Sustainable Development M,D
Systems Engineering M
Systems Science M
Theater M,D
Therapies—Dance, Drama, and Music M,D
Transportation Management O
Travel and Tourism M,D
Urban and Regional Planning M,D
Urban Design M
Writing M

ARIZONA STATE UNIVERSITY AT THE DOWNTOWN PHOENIX CAMPUS

Community Health Nursing M,D,O
Community Health M,D,O
Journalism M
Mass Communication M
Nursing Education M,D,O
Nursing—General M,D,O
Psychiatric Nursing M,D,O
Public Health—General M,D,O

ARIZONA STATE UNIVERSITY AT THE POLYTECHNIC CAMPUS

Aerospace/Aeronautical Engineering M
Agricultural Economics and Agribusiness M
Biological and Biomedical Sciences—General M
Computer Engineering M
Computer Science M
Curriculum and Instruction M,D
Education—General M,D
Educational Leadership and Administration M,D
Electrical Engineering M
Engineering and Applied Sciences—General M
Environmental Management and Policy M
Exercise and Sports Science M,D
Information Science M
Management Information Systems M
Manufacturing Engineering M
Mechanical Engineering M
Nutrition M
Physical Education M,D
Psychology—General M
Transportation Management M

ARIZONA STATE UNIVERSITY AT THE WEST CAMPUS

Accounting M,O
Business Administration and Management—General M
Communication—General M
Criminal Justice and Criminology M,D
Education—General M,D,O
Educational Leadership and Administration M,D,O
Elementary Education M,D,O
Gerontology M,O
Interdisciplinary Studies M
Investment Management M,O
Legal and Justice Studies M
Marketing Research M,O
Secondary Education M,D,O
Social Work M
Special Education M,D,O

ARKANSAS STATE UNIVERSITY

Accounting M
Agricultural Education M,D,O
Agricultural Sciences—General M,D,O
Art/Fine Arts M
Biological and Biomedical Sciences—General M,O
Business Administration and Management—General M,O
Business Education M,O
Chemistry M,O
Communication Disorders M
Communication—General M,O
Community College Education M,D,O
Computer Science M
Counselor Education M,O
Criminal Justice and Criminology M,O
Curriculum and Instruction M,D,O
Early Childhood Education M,O
Education of the Gifted M,D,O
Education—General M,D,O
Educational Leadership and Administration M,D,O
Educational Measurement and Evaluation M,O
Electronic Commerce M

Elementary Education	M,D,O
Engineering and Applied Sciences—General	M
English Education	M,O
English	M,O
Environmental Sciences	M,D
Exercise and Sports Science	M,O
Foundations and Philosophy of Education	M,D,O
Gerontology	M,D,O
Historic Preservation	M,D
History	M,O
Journalism	M
Management Information Systems	M
Mathematics Education	M
Mathematics	M
Media Studies	M
Middle School Education	M,O
Molecular Biology	D
Music Education	M,O
Music	M,O
Nurse Anesthesia	M
Nursing—General	M
Physical Education	M,O
Physical Therapy	M,D,O
Political Science	M,O
Public Administration	M,O
Reading Education	M,O
Rehabilitation Counseling	M,O
School Psychology	M,O
Science Education	M,O
Secondary Education	M,D,O
Social Sciences Education	M,O
Social Work	M
Sociology	M,O
Special Education	M,D,O
Speech and Interpersonal Communication	M,O
Student Affairs	M,O
Theater	M,O

ARKANSAS TECH UNIVERSITY

Art/Fine Arts	M
Communication—General	M
Curriculum and Instruction	M,O
Education of the Gifted	M,O
Education—General	M,O
Educational Leadership and Administration	M,O
Emergency Management	M
Engineering and Applied Sciences—General	M
English as a Second Language	M
English Education	M,O
English	M
Fish, Game, and Wildlife Management	M
History	M
Homeland Security	M
Information Science	M
Journalism	M
Mathematics Education	M
Nursing—General	M
Secondary Education	M,O
Social Sciences Education	M
Social Sciences	M
Spanish	M
Student Affairs	M,O
Systems Science	M

ARMSTRONG ATLANTIC STATE UNIVERSITY

Adult Education	M
Athletic Training and Sports Medicine	M
Business Education	M
Communication Disorders	M
Computer Science	M
Criminal Justice and Criminology	M
Curriculum and Instruction	M
Early Childhood Education	M
Education—General	M
Elementary Education	M
English Education	M
Exercise and Sports Science	M
Health Services Management and Hospital Administration	M
History	M
Liberal Studies	M
Mathematics Education	M
Middle School Education	M
Nursing—General	M
Physical Therapy	D
Public Health—General	M
Science Education	M
Secondary Education	M
Social Sciences Education	M
Special Education	M

ART ACADEMY OF CINCINNATI

Art Education	M

ART CENTER COLLEGE OF DESIGN

Applied Arts and Design—General	M*
Art/Fine Arts	M
Computer Art and Design	M
Environmental Design	M
Film, Television, and Video Production	M
Industrial Design	M

THE ART INSTITUTE OF BOSTON AT LESLEY UNIVERSITY

Art/Fine Arts	M*

THE ART INSTITUTE OF CALIFORNIA–SAN FRANCISCO

Art/Fine Arts	M
Film, Television, and Video Production	M

ASBURY COLLEGE

English as a Second Language	M,O
English	M,O
French	M,O
Mathematics Education	M,O
Reading Education	M,O
Science Education	M,O
Social Sciences Education	M,O
Spanish	M,O
Special Education	M,O
Writing	M,O

ASBURY THEOLOGICAL SEMINARY

Missions and Missiology	M,D,O
Pastoral Ministry and Counseling	M,D,O
Religious Education	M,D,O
Theology	M,D,O

ASHLAND THEOLOGICAL SEMINARY

History	P,M,D,O
Pastoral Ministry and Counseling	P,M,D,O
Theology	P,M,D,O

ASHLAND UNIVERSITY

Business Administration and Management—General	M
Curriculum and Instruction	M
Education of the Gifted	M
Education—General	M,D
Educational Leadership and Administration	M,D
Exercise and Sports Science	M
Foundations and Philosophy of Education	M
History	M
Physical Education	M
Political Science	M
Reading Education	M
Special Education	M
Sports Management	M
Student Affairs	M
Writing	M

ASPEN UNIVERSITY

Business Administration and Management—General	M,O
Finance and Banking	M,O
Information Science	M,O
Management Information Systems	M,O
Project Management	M,O

ASSEMBLIES OF GOD THEOLOGICAL SEMINARY

Cultural Studies	P,M,D
Missions and Missiology	P,M,D
Pastoral Ministry and Counseling	P,M,D
Theology	P,M,D
Women's Studies	P,M,D

ASSOCIATED MENNONITE BIBLICAL SEMINARY

Conflict Resolution and Mediation/Peace Studies	P,M,O
Missions and Missiology	P,M,O
Theology	P,M,O

ASSUMPTION COLLEGE

Accounting	M,O
Business Administration and Management—General	M,O
Child and Family Studies	M,O
Counseling Psychology	M,O
Economics	M,O
Finance and Banking	M,O
Human Resources Management	M,O
International Business	M,O
Marketing	M,O
Nonprofit Management	M,O
Psychology—General	M,O
Rehabilitation Counseling	M,O
School Psychology	M,O
Special Education	M

ATHABASCA UNIVERSITY

Adult Education	M
Allied Health—General	M,O
Art Therapy	M,O
Business Administration and Management—General	M,O*
Counseling Psychology	M,O
Counselor Education	M,O
Cultural Studies	M
Distance Education Development	M,O
Education—General	M,O
Information Science	M
Interdisciplinary Studies	M
International Development	M
Management of Technology	M,O
Nursing and Healthcare Administration	M,O
Nursing—General	M,O
Organizational Management	M
Project Management	M,O
Psychology—General	M,O

THE ATHENAEUM OF OHIO

Pastoral Ministry and Counseling	P,M,O
Theology	P,M,O

ATLANTA'S JOHN MARSHALL LAW SCHOOL

Law	P

ATLANTIC COLLEGE

Graphic Design	M

ATLANTIC INSTITUTE OF ORIENTAL MEDICINE

Acupuncture and Oriental Medicine	M

ATLANTIC SCHOOL OF THEOLOGY

Theology	P,M,O

ATLANTIC UNION COLLEGE

Education—General	M

ATLANTIC UNIVERSITY

Art/Fine Arts	M
Transpersonal and Humanistic Psychology	M

A.T. STILL UNIVERSITY OF HEALTH SCIENCES

Allied Health—General	M,D
Athletic Training and Sports Medicine	M,D
Biological and Biomedical Sciences—General	P,M
Communication Disorders	M,D
Gerontology	M,D
Health Education	M,D
Health Services Management and Hospital Administration	M,D
Kinesiology and Movement Studies	M,D
Occupational Therapy	M,D
Oral and Dental Sciences	P,O
Osteopathic Medicine	P,M
Physical Therapy	M,D
Physician Assistant Studies	M,D
Public Health—General	M,D

AUBURN UNIVERSITY

Accounting	M
Adult Education	M,D,O
Aerospace/Aeronautical Engineering	M,D
Agricultural Economics and Agribusiness	M,D
Agricultural Sciences—General	M,D
Agronomy and Soil Sciences	M,D
Analytical Chemistry	M,D
Anatomy	M,D
Animal Sciences	M,D
Applied Economics	M,D
Applied Mathematics	M,D
Aquaculture	M,D
Architecture	M
Biochemistry	M,D
Biological and Biomedical Sciences—General	M,D
Botany	M,D
Building Science	M
Business Administration and Management—General	M,D
Business Education	M,D,O
Cell Biology	M,D
Chemical Engineering	M,D
Chemistry	M,D
Child and Family Studies	M,D

*M—master's degree; P—first professional degree; D—doctorate; O—other advanced degree; *—Close-Up and/or Announcement or Display in one of the other books in this series*

Civil Engineering	M,D
Clothing and Textiles	M
Communication Disorders	M,D
Communication—General	M
Computer Engineering	M,D
Computer Science	M,D
Construction Engineering	M,D
Construction Management	M
Counseling Psychology	M,D,O
Counselor Education	M,D,O
Curriculum and Instruction	M,D,O
Early Childhood Education	M,D,O
Economics	M
Education—General	M,D,O
Educational Leadership and Administration	M,D,O
Educational Media/ Instructional Technology	M,D,O
Educational Psychology	M,D,O
Electrical Engineering	M,D
Elementary Education	M,D,O
Engineering and Applied Sciences—General	M,D
English Education	M,D,O
English	M,D*
Entomology	M,D
Environmental Engineering	M,D
Exercise and Sports Science	M,D,O
Experimental Psychology	M,D
Finance and Banking	M
Fish, Game, and Wildlife Management	M,D
Food Science and Technology	M,D
Foreign Languages Education	M,D,O
Forestry	M,D
Geography	M
Geology	M*
Geotechnical Engineering	M,D
Health Education	M,D,O
Health Promotion	M,D,O
Higher Education	M,D,O
History	M,D
Horticulture	M,D
Human Development	M,D
Human Resources Management	M,D
Hydraulics	M,D
Hydrology	M,D
Industrial and Organizational Psychology	M,D
Industrial Design	M
Industrial/Management Engineering	M,D
Inorganic Chemistry	M,D
Kinesiology and Movement Studies	M,D,O
Landscape Architecture	M
Management Information Systems	M,D
Mass Communication	M
Materials Engineering	M,D
Mathematics Education	M,D,O
Mathematics	M,D
Mechanical Engineering	M,D
Microbiology	M,D
Molecular Biology	M,D
Music Education	M,D,O
Natural Resources	M,D
Nutrition	M,D
Organic Chemistry	M,D
Pathobiology	M,D
Pharmaceutical Sciences	M,D
Pharmacology	M,D
Pharmacy	P
Physical Chemistry	M,D
Physical Education	M,D,O
Physics	M,D*
Plant Pathology	M,D
Political Science	M,D
Psychology—General	M,D
Public Administration	M,D*
Radiation Biology	M,D
Reading Education	M,D,O
Rehabilitation Counseling	M,D
Rural Sociology	M
School Psychology	M,D,O
Science Education	M,D,O
Secondary Education	M,D,O
Social Psychology	M,D,O
Social Sciences Education	M,D,O
Sociology	M
Software Engineering	M,D
Spanish	M
Special Education	M,D
Statistics	M,D
Structural Engineering	M,D
Systems Engineering	M,D
Textile Sciences and Engineering	D
Transportation and Highway Engineering	M,D
Urban and Regional Planning	M
Veterinary Medicine	P
Veterinary Sciences	M,D
Zoology	M,D

AUBURN UNIVERSITY MONTGOMERY

Business Administration and Management—General	M
Counselor Education	M,O
Criminal Justice and Criminology	M
Early Childhood Education	M,O
Education—General	M,O
Educational Leadership and Administration	M,O
Elementary Education	M,O
Liberal Studies	M
Physical Education	M,O
Political Science	M,D
Psychology—General	M
Public Administration	M,D
Reading Education	M,O
Secondary Education	M,O
Special Education	M,O

AUGSBURG COLLEGE

Business Administration and Management—General	M
Community Health Nursing	M
Education—General	M
Nursing—General	M
Organizational Management	M
Physician Assistant Studies	M
Social Work	M
Transcultural Nursing	M

AUGUSTANA COLLEGE

Community Health Nursing	M
Education—General	M
Elementary Education	M
Nursing—General	M
Secondary Education	M

AUGUSTA STATE UNIVERSITY

Business Administration and Management—General	M
Counselor Education	M
Curriculum and Instruction	M
Education—General	M,O
Educational Leadership and Administration	M,O
Health Education	M
Physical Education	M
Political Science	M
Psychology—General	M
Secondary Education	M,O
Special Education	M,O

AURORA UNIVERSITY

Business Administration and Management—General	M
Curriculum and Instruction	M,D
Education—General	M,D
Educational Leadership and Administration	M,D
Leisure Studies	M
Mathematics	M
Reading Education	M,D
Social Work	M

AUSTIN COLLEGE

Art Education	M
Education—General	M
Elementary Education	M
Middle School Education	M
Music Education	M
Physical Education	M
Secondary Education	M
Theater	M

AUSTIN GRADUATE SCHOOL OF THEOLOGY

Theology	M

AUSTIN PEAY STATE UNIVERSITY

Biological and Biomedical Sciences—General	M
Business Administration and Management—General	M
Clinical Laboratory Sciences/Medical Technology	M*
Communication—General	M
Community Health	M
Counselor Education	M,O
Curriculum and Instruction	M,O
Early Childhood Education	M,O
Education—General	M,O
Educational Leadership and Administration	M,O
Elementary Education	M,O
English	M
Exercise and Sports Science	M
Family Nurse Practitioner Studies	M
Health Education	M
Military and Defense Studies	M
Music Education	M
Music	M
Nursing and Healthcare Administration	M
Nursing Education	M
Nursing Informatics	M
Nursing—General	M
Psychology—General	M
Public Health—General	M
Radiation Biology	M
Reading Education	M,O
Secondary Education	M,O
Special Education	M,O

AUSTIN PRESBYTERIAN THEOLOGICAL SEMINARY

Pastoral Ministry and Counseling	P,M,D
Theology	P,M,D

AUSTRALASIAN COLLEGE OF HEALTH SCIENCES

Allied Health—General	M

AVE MARIA SCHOOL OF LAW

Law	P

AVE MARIA UNIVERSITY

Pastoral Ministry and Counseling	M,D
Theology	M,D

AVERETT UNIVERSITY

Art Education	M
Business Administration and Management—General	M
Curriculum and Instruction	M
Education—General	M
Elementary Education	M
English Education	M
Health Education	M
Mathematics Education	M
Physical Education	M
Reading Education	M
Science Education	M
Social Sciences Education	M
Special Education	M

AVILA UNIVERSITY

Accounting	M
Business Administration and Management—General	M
Counseling Psychology	M
Education—General	M,O
English as a Second Language	M,O
Finance and Banking	M
Health Services Management and Hospital Administration	M
International Business	M
Management Information Systems	M
Marketing	M
Organizational Management	M,O
Project Management	M,O
Psychology—General	M
Reading Education	M,O

AZUSA PACIFIC UNIVERSITY

Art/Fine Arts	M
Business Administration and Management—General	M
Clinical Psychology	M,D
Counselor Education	M
Curriculum and Instruction	M
Education—General	M,D
Educational Leadership and Administration	M,D
Educational Media/ Instructional Technology	M
English as a Second Language	M
Ethics	M
Higher Education	M,D
Human Resources Development	M
International Business	M
Library Science	M
Management Strategy and Policy	M
Marriage and Family Therapy	M,D
Multilingual and Multicultural Education	M
Music Education	M
Music	M
Nonprofit Management	M
Nursing Education	M,D
Nursing—General	M,D
Organizational Management	M
Pastoral Ministry and Counseling	P,M
Physical Education	M
Physical Therapy	D
Psychology—General	M,D
Religion	M

Religious Education M
School Psychology M
Special Education M
Student Affairs M
Theology M,D

BABEL UNIVERSITY SCHOOL OF TRANSLATION

Translation and Interpretation M

BABSON COLLEGE

Accounting M
Business Administration and Management—General M
Entrepreneurship M

BAKER COLLEGE CENTER FOR GRADUATE STUDIES

Accounting M
Business Administration and Management—General M
Finance and Banking M
Health Services Management and Hospital Administration M
Human Resources Management M
Management Information Systems M
Marketing M
Occupational Therapy M

BAKER UNIVERSITY

Business Administration and Management—General M
Conflict Resolution and Mediation/Peace Studies M
Education—General M,D
Liberal Studies M

BAKKE GRADUATE UNIVERSITY

Business Administration and Management—General M,D
Entrepreneurship M,D
Pastoral Ministry and Counseling M,D

BALDWIN-WALLACE COLLEGE

Accounting M
Business Administration and Management—General M
Education—General M
Educational Leadership and Administration M
Educational Media/Instructional Technology M
Entrepreneurship M
Health Services Management and Hospital Administration M
Human Resources Management M
International Business M
Reading Education M
Special Education M

BALL STATE UNIVERSITY

Accounting M
Actuarial Science M
Adult Education M,D
Advertising and Public Relations M
Anthropology M
Architecture M
Art Education M
Art/Fine Arts M
Biological and Biomedical Sciences—General M,D
Business Administration and Management—General M
Business Education M
Chemistry M
Clinical Psychology M
Cognitive Sciences M
Communication Disorders M,D
Communication—General M
Computer Science M
Counseling Psychology M,D
Curriculum and Instruction M,O
Education—General M,D,O
Educational Leadership and Administration M,D,O
Educational Psychology M,D,O
Elementary Education M,D
English as a Second Language M,D
English M,D
Exercise and Sports Science D
Family and Consumer Sciences-General M
Foundations and Philosophy of Education D
Geology M
Geosciences M
Gerontology M
Health Education M
Health Promotion M
Higher Education M,D
Historic Preservation M
History M
Information Science M
Journalism M
Landscape Architecture M
Linguistics D
Mathematics Education M
Mathematics M
Music Education M,D
Natural Resources M
Nursing—General M
Physical Education M,D
Physics M
Physiology M
Political Science M
Psychology—General M
Public Administration M
Rhetoric M
School Psychology M,D,O
Science Education M,D
Secondary Education M
Social Psychology M
Social Sciences M
Sociology M
Special Education M,D,O
Speech and Interpersonal Communication M
Statistics M
Telecommunications M
Urban and Regional Planning M*
Urban Design M
Vocational and Technical Education M
Writing M,D

BALTIMORE HEBREW UNIVERSITY

Jewish Studies M,D

BANGOR THEOLOGICAL SEMINARY

Theology P,M,D

BANK STREET COLLEGE OF EDUCATION

Child and Family Studies M
Early Childhood Education M
Education—General M*
Educational Leadership and Administration M
Elementary Education M
Foundations and Philosophy of Education M
Maternal and Child Health M
Mathematics Education M
Middle School Education M
Multilingual and Multicultural Education M
Museum Education M
Museum Studies M
Reading Education M
Special Education M

BAPTIST BIBLE COLLEGE

Cultural Studies P,M
Pastoral Ministry and Counseling P,M
Theology P,M

BAPTIST BIBLE COLLEGE OF PENNSYLVANIA

Counselor Education M
Missions and Missiology P,M,D
Pastoral Ministry and Counseling P,M,D
Religion P,M,D
Religious Education P,M,D
Theology P,M,D

BAPTIST MISSIONARY ASSOCIATION THEOLOGICAL SEMINARY

Theology P,M

BAPTIST THEOLOGICAL SEMINARY AT RICHMOND

Pastoral Ministry and Counseling P,D
Religion P,D
Religious Education P,D
Theology P,D

BARD COLLEGE

Art History M,D
Art/Fine Arts M
Decorative Arts M,D
Education—General M
Environmental Management and Policy M,O
Museum Studies M
Music M
Photography M

BARD GRADUATE CENTER FOR STUDIES IN THE DECORATIVE ARTS, DESIGN, AND CULTURE

Art History M,D*
Decorative Arts M,D

BARRY UNIVERSITY

Accounting M
Acute Care/Critical Care Nursing M,O
Anatomy M
Art/Fine Arts M
Athletic Training and Sports Medicine M
Biological and Biomedical Sciences—General M
Business Administration and Management—General M,O
Clinical Psychology M,O
Communication Disorders M
Communication—General M,O
Corporate and Organizational Communication M,O
Counselor Education M,D,O
Curriculum and Instruction D,O
Distance Education Development O
Early Childhood Education M,D,O
Education of the Gifted M,D,O
Education—General M,D,O
Educational Leadership and Administration M,D,O
Educational Media/Instructional Technology M,D,O
Elementary Education M,D,O
English as a Second Language M,D,O
Exercise and Sports Science M
Family Nurse Practitioner Studies M,O
Finance and Banking O
Health Informatics O
Health Services Management and Hospital Administration M,O
Higher Education M,D
Human Resources Development M,D
Human Resources Management O
Information Science M
International Business O
Kinesiology and Movement Studies M
Law P
Liberal Studies M
Management Information Systems O
Marketing O
Marriage and Family Therapy M,O
Nurse Anesthesia M
Nursing and Healthcare Administration M,D,O
Nursing Education M,O
Nursing—General M,D,O
Occupational Therapy M
Pastoral Ministry and Counseling M,D
Photography M
Physician Assistant Studies M
Podiatric Medicine P
Psychology—General M,O*
Public Administration M
Public Health—General M
Reading Education M,D,O
Rehabilitation Counseling M,O
School Psychology M,O
Social Work M,D
Special Education M,D,O
Sport Psychology M
Sports Management M
Theology M,D

BASTYR UNIVERSITY

Acupuncture and Oriental Medicine M,D,O*
Health Psychology M
Naturopathic Medicine D,O*
Nurse Midwifery D,O
Nutrition M*

BAYAMÓN CENTRAL UNIVERSITY

Accounting M
Business Administration and Management—General M
Counselor Education M
Criminal Justice and Criminology M
Early Childhood Education M
Education—General M
Educational Leadership and Administration M
Elementary Education M
Finance and Banking M
Marketing M
Physical Education M
Psychology—General M
Rehabilitation Counseling M
Special Education M

BAYLOR COLLEGE OF MEDICINE

Allopathic Medicine P
Biochemistry D*

*M—master's degree; P—first professional degree; D—doctorate; O—other advanced degree; *—Close-Up and/or Announcement or Display in one of the other books in this series*

- Bioengineering D
- Biological and Biomedical Sciences—General M,D*
- Biomedical Engineering D
- Biophysics D
- Cancer Biology/Oncology D
- Cardiovascular Sciences D
- Cell Biology D*
- Clinical Laboratory Sciences/Medical Technology M,D
- Computational Biology D
- Developmental Biology D*
- Genetics D*
- Human Genetics D
- Immunology D*
- Microbiology D
- Molecular Biology D
- Molecular Biophysics D
- Molecular Medicine D
- Molecular Physiology D*
- Neuroscience D*
- Nurse Anesthesia M
- Pathology D
- Pharmacology D
- Physician Assistant Studies M
- Structural Biology D
- Translational Biology D*
- Virology D

BAYLOR UNIVERSITY

- Accounting M
- Allied Health—General M,D
- American Studies M
- Biological and Biomedical Sciences—General M,D
- Biomedical Engineering M
- Business Administration and Management—General M
- Chemistry M,D
- Clinical Psychology M,D
- Communication Disorders M
- Communication—General M
- Computer Engineering M
- Computer Science M
- Curriculum and Instruction M,D,O
- Economics M
- Education—General M,D,O
- Educational Leadership and Administration M,O
- Educational Psychology M,D,O
- Electrical Engineering M
- Emergency Medical Services D
- Engineering and Applied Sciences—General M
- English M,D
- Environmental Biology M,D
- Environmental Management and Policy M
- Exercise and Sports Science M,D
- Family Nurse Practitioner Studies M
- Geology M,D
- Geosciences M,D
- Health Education M,D
- Health Services Management and Hospital Administration M
- History M
- Interdisciplinary Studies M,D
- International Affairs M,D
- International Business M
- Journalism M
- Law P
- Limnology M,D
- Management Information Systems M
- Maternal and Child/Neonatal Nursing M
- Mathematics M,D
- Mechanical Engineering M
- Museum Studies M
- Music M
- Neuroscience M,D
- Nursing and Healthcare Administration M
- Nursing—General M
- Nutrition M,D
- Philosophy M,D
- Physical Education M,D
- Physical Therapy M,D
- Physics M,D
- Political Science M,D
- Psychology—General M,D
- Public Administration M,D
- Public Policy M,D
- Religion M,D
- Social Work M
- Sociology M,D
- Spanish M
- Statistics M,D
- Theater M
- Theology P,M,D

BAY PATH COLLEGE

- Entrepreneurship M
- Management Information Systems M
- Occupational Therapy M

BEACON UNIVERSITY

- Organizational Management P,M
- Pastoral Ministry and Counseling P,M
- Theology P,M

BELHAVEN COLLEGE (MS)

- Business Administration and Management—General M
- Education—General M
- Elementary Education M
- Multilingual and Multicultural Education M
- Public Administration M
- Secondary Education M

BELLARMINE UNIVERSITY

- Business Administration and Management—General M
- Communication—General M
- Early Childhood Education M
- Education—General M
- Educational Leadership and Administration M
- Family Nurse Practitioner Studies M,D
- Management Information Systems M
- Middle School Education M
- Nursing and Healthcare Administration M,D
- Nursing Education M,D
- Nursing—General M,D
- Physical Therapy M,D
- Reading Education M
- Religion M
- Secondary Education M
- Special Education M

BELLEVUE UNIVERSITY

- Business Administration and Management—General M,D
- Counselor Education M,D
- Criminal Justice and Criminology M,D
- Educational Media/Instructional Technology M,D
- Health Services Management and Hospital Administration M
- Human Services M
- Information Science M
- Management Information Systems M
- Public Administration M,D
- Public Health—General M,D

BELMONT UNIVERSITY

- Allied Health—General P,M,D
- Business Administration and Management—General M
- Early Childhood Education M
- Education—General M
- Elementary Education M
- English Education M
- English M
- Mathematics Education M
- Middle School Education M
- Music Education M
- Music M
- Nursing—General M
- Occupational Therapy M,D
- Pharmacy P
- Physical Therapy D
- Science Education M
- Secondary Education M
- Social Sciences Education M
- Special Education M
- Sports Management M
- Writing M

BEMIDJI STATE UNIVERSITY

- Biological and Biomedical Sciences—General M
- Counseling Psychology M
- Education—General M
- English M
- Environmental Management and Policy M
- Exercise and Sports Science M
- Mathematics Education M
- Science Education M
- Special Education M
- Vocational and Technical Education M

BENEDICTINE COLLEGE

- Business Administration and Management—General M
- Educational Leadership and Administration M

BENEDICTINE UNIVERSITY

- Accounting M
- Business Administration and Management—General M
- Clinical Psychology M
- Computer and Information Systems Security M
- Curriculum and Instruction M
- Education—General M
- Educational Leadership and Administration M,D
- Elementary Education M
- Emergency Management M
- Entrepreneurship M
- Exercise and Sports Science M
- Finance and Banking M
- Health Education M
- Health Informatics M
- Health Promotion M
- Health Services Management and Hospital Administration M
- Higher Education D
- Human Resources Management M
- International Business M
- Logistics M
- Management Information Systems M
- Marketing M
- Nutrition M
- Organizational Behavior M
- Organizational Management M,D
- Public Health—General M
- Reading Education M
- Science Education M
- Secondary Education M
- Special Education M

BENNINGTON COLLEGE

- Allied Health—General O
- Art Education M
- Dance M
- Early Childhood Education M
- Education—General M
- Elementary Education M
- English Education M
- English M
- Foreign Languages Education M
- French M
- Mathematics Education M
- Multilingual and Multicultural Education M
- Music Education M
- Music M
- Science Education M
- Secondary Education M
- Social Sciences Education M
- Spanish M
- Writing M

BENTLEY UNIVERSITY

- Accounting M,D
- Business Administration and Management—General M,D,O
- Ergonomics and Human Factors M
- Finance and Banking M
- Information Science M
- Marketing M
- Taxation M

BERNARD M. BARUCH COLLEGE OF THE CITY UNIVERSITY OF NEW YORK

- Accounting M,D
- Business Administration and Management—General M,D,O
- Corporate and Organizational Communication M
- Economics M
- Educational Leadership and Administration M,O
- Entrepreneurship M,D
- Finance and Banking M,D
- Health Services Management and Hospital Administration M
- Higher Education M
- Human Resources Management M,D
- Industrial and Labor Relations M
- Industrial and Organizational Psychology M,D,O
- International Business M
- Management Information Systems M,D
- Management Strategy and Policy M,D
- Marketing M,D
- Mathematical and Computational Finance M
- Nonprofit Management M
- Organizational Behavior M,D
- Organizational Management M,D
- Public Administration M
- Quantitative Analysis M
- Statistics M
- Taxation M

BERRY COLLEGE

- Business Administration and Management—General M

Curriculum and Instruction	O
Early Childhood Education	M
Education—General	M,O
Educational Leadership and Administration	O
Middle School Education	M
Reading Education	M
Secondary Education	M

BETHANY THEOLOGICAL SEMINARY

Conflict Resolution and Mediation/Peace Studies	P,M,O
Pastoral Ministry and Counseling	P,M,O
Religion	P,M,O
Theology	P,M,O

BETHANY UNIVERSITY

Clinical Psychology	M
Education—General	M
Educational Leadership and Administration	M

BETH BENJAMIN ACADEMY OF CONNECTICUT

Theology	

BETHEL COLLEGE (IN)

Business Administration and Management—General	M
Education—General	M
Nursing—General	M
Pastoral Ministry and Counseling	M
Theology	M

BETHEL COLLEGE (TN)

Education—General	M
Educational Leadership and Administration	M
Elementary Education	M
English Education	M
Physical Education	M
Science Education	M
Social Sciences Education	M
Special Education	M

BETHEL SEMINARY

Marriage and Family Therapy	P,M,D,O
Missions and Missiology	P,M,D,O
Pastoral Ministry and Counseling	P,M,D,O
Religious Education	P,M,D,O
Theology	P,M,D,O

BETHEL UNIVERSITY

Business Administration and Management—General	M
Communication—General	M,O
Counseling Psychology	M,O
Education—General	M,D,O
Educational Leadership and Administration	M,D,O
Gerontology	M
Higher Education	M,O
Nursing Education	M,O
Nursing—General	M,O
Organizational Management	M
Reading Education	M,D,O
Secondary Education	M,D,O
Special Education	M,D,O

BETHESDA CHRISTIAN UNIVERSITY

Music	P,M
Religion	P,M
Theology	P,M

BETH HAMEDRASH SHAAREI YOSHER INSTITUTE

Theology	

BETH HATALMUD RABBINICAL COLLEGE

Theology	

BETH MEDRASH GOVOHA

Theology	

BETHUNE-COOKMAN UNIVERSITY

Theology	M

BEULAH HEIGHTS UNIVERSITY

Religion	M

BEXLEY HALL EPISCOPAL SEMINARY

Theology	P,M

BIBLICAL THEOLOGICAL SEMINARY

Missions and Missiology	P,M,D,O
Pastoral Ministry and Counseling	P,M,D,O
Theology	P,M,D,O

BIOLA UNIVERSITY

Business Administration and Management—General	M
Cultural Studies	M,D,O
Education—General	M
English as a Second Language	M,D,O
Ethics	P,M,D
Linguistics	M,D,O
Missions and Missiology	M,D,O
Organizational Management	M
Psychology—General	M,D
Religion	P,M,D
Religious Education	P,M,D
Theology	P,M,D

BIRMINGHAM-SOUTHERN COLLEGE

Business Administration and Management—General	M
Music	M
Public Administration	M

BISHOP'S UNIVERSITY

Education—General	M,O
English as a Second Language	M,O

BLACK HILLS STATE UNIVERSITY

Business Administration and Management—General	M
Curriculum and Instruction	M
Education—General	M

BLESSED JOHN XXIII NATIONAL SEMINARY

Theology	P

BLESSING-RIEMAN COLLEGE OF NURSING

Nursing—General	M

BLOOMSBURG UNIVERSITY OF PENNSYLVANIA

Adult Nursing	M
Athletic Training and Sports Medicine	M
Biological and Biomedical Sciences—General	M
Business Administration and Management—General	M
Business Education	M
Communication Disorders	M,D
Community Health	M
Counselor Education	M
Curriculum and Instruction	M
Early Childhood Education	M
Education—General	M
Educational Media/Instructional Technology	M
Elementary Education	M
Exercise and Sports Science	M
Family Nurse Practitioner Studies	M
Health Physics/Radiological Health	M
Nursing and Healthcare Administration	M
Nursing—General	M
Reading Education	M
Science Education	M
Special Education	M
Student Affairs	M

BLUFFTON UNIVERSITY

Business Administration and Management—General	M
Education—General	M
Organizational Management	M

BOB JONES UNIVERSITY

Accounting	P,M,D,O
Art/Fine Arts	P,M,D,O
Business Administration and Management—General	P,M,D,O
Counselor Education	P,M,D,O
Curriculum and Instruction	P,M,D,O
Educational Leadership and Administration	P,M,D,O
Elementary Education	P,M,D,O
English Education	P,M,D,O
English	P,M,D,O
Film, Television, and Video Production	P,M,D,O
Graphic Design	P,M,D,O
History	P,M,D,O
Illustration	P,M,D,O
Journalism	P,M,D,O
Mathematics Education	P,M,D,O
Media Studies	P,M,D,O
Music Education	P,M,D,O
Music	P,M,D,O
Pastoral Ministry and Counseling	P,M,D,O
Religion	P,M,D,O
Rhetoric	P,M,D,O
Secondary Education	P,M,D,O
Social Sciences Education	P,M,D,O
Special Education	P,M,D,O
Speech and Interpersonal Communication	P,M,D,O
Student Affairs	P,M,D,O
Theater	P,M,D,O
Theology	P,M,D,O

BOISE STATE UNIVERSITY

Accounting	M
Animal Sciences	M
Art Education	M
Art/Fine Arts	M
Biological and Biomedical Sciences—General	M
Business Administration and Management—General	M
Civil Engineering	M
Communication—General	M
Computer Engineering	M,D
Computer Science	M
Counselor Education	M
Criminal Justice and Criminology	M
Curriculum and Instruction	D
Early Childhood Education	M
Education—General	M,D
Educational Leadership and Administration	M,D
Educational Media/Instructional Technology	M
Electrical Engineering	M,D
Engineering and Applied Sciences—General	M,D
English	M
Environmental Management and Policy	M
Exercise and Sports Science	M
Geology	M,D
Geophysics	M,D
Geosciences	M
History	M
Interdisciplinary Studies	M
Management Information Systems	M
Materials Engineering	M
Mechanical Engineering	M
Music Education	M
Music	M
Public Administration	M
Public Health—General	M
Public Policy	M
Reading Education	M
Science Education	M,D
Social Work	M
Special Education	M
Sports Management	M
Taxation	M
Technical Communication	M
Writing	M

BORICUA COLLEGE

Human Services	M
Latin American Studies	M

BOSTON ARCHITECTURAL COLLEGE

Architecture	M
Interior Design	M

BOSTON COLLEGE

Accounting	M
Adult Nursing	M,D
Biochemistry	D
Biological and Biomedical Sciences—General	D*
Business Administration and Management—General	M
Chemistry	M,D
Classics	M
Community Health Nursing	M,D
Counseling Psychology	M,D
Curriculum and Instruction	M,D,O
Developmental Psychology	M,D
Early Childhood Education	M
East European and Russian Studies	M
Economics	D
Education—General	M,D,O*
Educational Leadership and Administration	M,D,O
Educational Measurement and Evaluation	M,D
Educational Psychology	M,D
Elementary Education	M
English Education	M
English	M,D
Finance and Banking	M,D
Foreign Languages Education	M

*M—master's degree; P—first professional degree; D—doctorate; O—other advanced degree; *—Close-Up and/or Announcement or* **Display** *in one of the other books in this series*

Forensic Nursing	M,D
French	M,D*
Geology	M*
Geophysics	M
Gerontological Nursing	M,D
Higher Education	M,D
History	M,D
Inorganic Chemistry	M,D
Italian	M,D
Law	P
Linguistics	M
Maternal and Child/Neonatal Nursing	M,D
Mathematics Education	M
Mathematics	M*
Medical/Surgical Nursing	M,D
Nurse Anesthesia	M,D
Nursing—General	M,D
Organic Chemistry	M,D
Organizational Behavior	D
Organizational Management	D
Pastoral Ministry and Counseling	P,M,D,O
Philosophy	M,D
Physical Chemistry	M,D
Physics	M,D*
Political Science	M,D
Psychiatric Nursing	M,D
Psychology—General	M,D
Reading Education	M,O
Religious Education	P,M,D,O
Russian	M
Science Education	M,D
Secondary Education	M
Slavic Languages	M
Social Sciences Education	M
Social Work	M,D
Sociology	M,D
Spanish	M,D
Special Education	M,O
Theology	P,M,D,O
Western European Studies	M,D

THE BOSTON CONSERVATORY

Music Education	M,O
Music	M,O
Theater	M

BOSTON GRADUATE SCHOOL OF PSYCHOANALYSIS

Counseling Psychology	M
Psychoanalysis and Psychotherapy	M,D,O
Psychology—General	M

BOSTON UNIVERSITY

Accounting	M,D,O
Actuarial Science	M
Advertising and Public Relations	M
African Studies	M,O
African-American Studies	M
Allied Health—General	M,D,O
Allopathic Medicine	P
American Studies	D
Anatomy	M,D
Anthropology	M,D
Archaeology	M,D
Art Education	M
Art History	M,D,O
Art/Fine Arts	M
Arts Administration	M,O
Astronomy	M,D
Athletic Training and Sports Medicine	D
Biochemistry	M,D*
Bioethics	M
Bioinformatics	M,D
Biological and Biomedical Sciences—General	M,D
Biomedical Engineering	M,D
Biophysics	D
Biostatistics	M,D
Broadcast Journalism	M
Business Administration and Management—General	M,D,O
Cell Biology	M,D*
Chemistry	M,D
Classics	M,D
Cognitive Sciences	M,D
Communication Disorders	M,D,O
Communication—General	M*
Computer Engineering	M,D
Computer Science	M,D
Counseling Psychology	D
Counselor Education	M,O
Criminal Justice and Criminology	M
Curriculum and Instruction	M,D,O
Dental Hygiene	P,M,D,O
Dentistry	P,M,D,O
Early Childhood Education	M,D,O
Economic Development	M
Economics	M,D
Education—General	M,D,O*
Educational Leadership and Administration	M,O
Educational Media/Instructional Technology	M,D,O
Electrical Engineering	M,D
Electronic Commerce	M
Elementary Education	M
Engineering and Applied Sciences—General	M,D
English as a Second Language	M,O
English Education	M,O
English	M,D
Entrepreneurship	M,O
Environmental and Occupational Health	M,D
Environmental Management and Policy	M,D,O
Epidemiology	M,D
Film, Television, and Video Production	M
Film, Television, and Video Theory and Criticism	M
Finance and Banking	P,M,D,O
Food Science and Technology	M
Foreign Languages Education	M
French	M,D
Geographic Information Systems	M,D
Geography	M,D
Geosciences	M,D
Graphic Design	M
Health Communication	M
Health Education	M,O
Health Law	M
Health Promotion	M,D
Health Services Management and Hospital Administration	M,D,O
Historic Preservation	M
History	M,D
Human Development	M,D,O
Human Resources Management	M,O
Immunology	D*
Industrial and Manufacturing Management	D
Interdisciplinary Studies	M
International Affairs	M,D,O
International and Comparative Education	M
International Business	M,O
International Health	M,D,O
Investment Management	M
Journalism	M
Law	P,M
Legal and Justice Studies	M
Liberal Studies	M
Linguistics	M,D
Management Information Systems	D
Management of Technology	M
Management Strategy and Policy	M,O
Marketing	M,D,O
Mass Communication	M
Materials Engineering	M,D
Materials Sciences	M,D
Maternal and Child Health	M,D
Mathematical and Computational Finance	M,D
Mathematics Education	M,D,O
Mathematics	M,D
Mechanical Engineering	M,D
Media Studies	M
Microbiology	M,D*
Molecular Biology	M,D
Molecular Medicine	D*
Multilingual and Multicultural Education	M,O
Museum Studies	M,D,O
Music Education	M,D
Music	M,D,O
Neuroscience	M,D*
Nonprofit Management	M,O
Nutrition	M
Occupational Therapy	M,D
Oral and Dental Sciences	P,M,D,O*
Organizational Behavior	D
Pharmaceutical Sciences	M,D
Pharmacology	M,D*
Philosophy	M,D
Photonics	M,D
Physical Education	M,D,O
Physical Therapy	D
Physics	M,D*
Physiology	M,D
Political Science	M,D
Project Management	M
Psychology—General	M,D
Public Administration	M,O
Public Health—General	P,M,D,O
Reading Education	M,D,O
Rehabilitation Sciences	D
Religion	M,D
Romance Languages	M,D
Science Education	M,D,O
Social Sciences Education	M,D,O
Social Work	M,D
Sociology	M,D
Spanish	M,D
Special Education	M,D,O
Systems Engineering	M,D
Taxation	P,M
Telecommunications	M
Theater	M,O
Theology	P,M,D
Travel and Tourism	M
Urban and Regional Planning	M
Urban Studies	M
Writing	M,D

BOWIE STATE UNIVERSITY

Applied Mathematics	M
Business Administration and Management—General	M
Computer Science	M,D
Corporate and Organizational Communication	M,O
Counseling Psychology	M
Counselor Education	M
Education—General	M
Educational Leadership and Administration	M,D
Elementary Education	M
English	M
Family Nurse Practitioner Studies	M
Human Resources Development	M
Management Information Systems	M,O
Nursing and Healthcare Administration	M
Nursing Education	M
Nursing—General	M
Public Administration	M
Reading Education	M
Secondary Education	M
Special Education	M

BOWLING GREEN STATE UNIVERSITY

Accounting	M
American Studies	M,D
Applied Arts and Design—General	M
Applied Statistics	M,D
Art Education	M
Art History	M
Art/Fine Arts	M
Biological and Biomedical Sciences—General	M,D*
Business Administration and Management—General	M
Business Education	M
Chemistry	M,D
Child and Family Studies	M
Clinical Psychology	M,D
Communication Disorders	M,D
Communication—General	M,D
Computer Art and Design	M
Computer Science	M
Construction Management	M
Counseling Psychology	M
Counselor Education	M
Criminal Justice and Criminology	M
Curriculum and Instruction	M
Demography and Population Studies	M,D
Developmental Psychology	M,D
Early Childhood Education	M
Economics	M
Education of the Gifted	M
Educational Leadership and Administration	M,D,O
Educational Media/Instructional Technology	M
English	M,D
Experimental Psychology	M,D
Family and Consumer Sciences-General	M
Film, Television, and Video Production	M,D
Foreign Languages Education	M
French	M
Geology	M
Geophysics	M
German	M
Graphic Design	M
Higher Education	D
History	M,D
Human Development	M
Industrial and Organizational Psychology	M,D
Interdisciplinary Studies	M,D
International and Comparative Education	M
Kinesiology and Movement Studies	M
Leisure Studies	M
Manufacturing Engineering	M
Mathematics Education	M,D
Mathematics	M,D
Music Education	M,D
Music	M,D
Nutrition	M
Operations Research	M
Organizational Management	M
Philosophy	M,D
Physics	M
Political Science	M
Psychology—General	M,D
Public Administration	M
Public Health—General	M
Reading Education	M,O
Recreation and Park Management	M
Rehabilitation Counseling	M

Rhetoric	M,D
School Psychology	M,O
Science Education	M
Social Psychology	M,D
Sociology	M,D
Software Engineering	M
Spanish	M
Special Education	M
Speech and Interpersonal Communication	M,D
Sports Management	M
Statistics	M,D
Student Affairs	M
Technical Communication	M,D
Theater	M,D
Vocational and Technical Education	M
Writing	M,D

BRADLEY UNIVERSITY

Accounting	M
Applied Arts and Design—General	M
Art/Fine Arts	M
Biological and Biomedical Sciences—General	M
Business Administration and Management—General	M
Chemistry	M
Civil Engineering	M
Comparative and Interdisciplinary Arts	M
Computer Science	M
Construction Engineering	M
Counselor Education	M
Curriculum and Instruction	M,O
Education—General	M,D,O
Educational Leadership and Administration	M
Electrical Engineering	M
Engineering and Applied Sciences—General	M
English	M
Human Development	M
Illustration	M
Industrial/Management Engineering	M
Information Science	M
Liberal Studies	M
Manufacturing Engineering	M
Mechanical Engineering	M
Nurse Anesthesia	M
Nursing and Healthcare Administration	M
Nursing—General	M
Photography	M
Physical Therapy	D

BRANDEIS UNIVERSITY

Anthropology	M,D
Art/Fine Arts	O
Biochemistry	M,D
Bioinformatics	M,O
Biological and Biomedical Sciences—General	O
Biophysics	M,D
Business Administration and Management—General	M
Cell Biology	M,D
Chemistry	M,D
Child and Family Studies	M,D
Classics	M,O
Cognitive Sciences	M,D
Communication—General	M,O
Computer and Information Systems Security	M,O
Computer Science	M,D,O
Conflict Resolution and Mediation/Peace Studies	M
Cultural Studies	M
Developmental Psychology	M,D
Disability Studies	D
Economics	M,D
Elementary Education	M
English	M,D
Finance and Banking	M,D
Gender Studies	M
Genetic Counseling	M
Genetics	M,D
Health Education	D
Health Services Management and Hospital Administration	M
History	M,D
Human Services	M
Inorganic Chemistry	M,D
International Affairs	M,D
International Business	M,D
International Development	M
International Health	M
Jewish Studies	M,D
Linguistics	M
Management Information Systems	M,O
Mathematics	M,D,O
Microbiology	M,D
Molecular Biology	M,D
Music	M,D
Near and Middle Eastern Languages	M,D
Near and Middle Eastern Studies	M,D
Neurobiology	M,D
Neuroscience	M,D
Nonprofit Management	M
Organic Chemistry	M,D
Philosophy	M
Physical Chemistry	M,D
Physics	M,D
Political Science	M,D
Project Management	M,O
Psychology—General	M,D
Public Policy	M
Religious Education	M
Secondary Education	M
Social Psychology	M,D
Sociology	M,D
Software Engineering	M,O
Structural Biology	M,D
Sustainable Development	M
Theater	M
Women's Studies	M

BRANDON UNIVERSITY

Counselor Education	M,O
Curriculum and Instruction	M,O
Education—General	M,O
Educational Leadership and Administration	M,O
Music Education	M
Music	M
Rural Planning and Studies	M,O
Special Education	M,O

BRENAU UNIVERSITY

Accounting	M
Business Administration and Management—General	M
Early Childhood Education	M,O
Education—General	M,O
Family Nurse Practitioner Studies	M
Health Services Management and Hospital Administration	M
Interior Design	M
Middle School Education	M,O
Nursing and Healthcare Administration	M
Nursing Education	M
Occupational Therapy	M
Organizational Management	M
Project Management	M
Psychology—General	M
Secondary Education	M,O
Special Education	M,O

BRESCIA UNIVERSITY

Business Administration and Management—General	M
Curriculum and Instruction	M

BRIAR CLIFF UNIVERSITY

Education—General	M
Human Resources Management	M
Nursing—General	M

BRIDGEWATER STATE COLLEGE

Accounting	M
Art Education	M
Business Administration and Management—General	M
Computer Science	M
Counselor Education	M,O
Criminal Justice and Criminology	M
Early Childhood Education	M
Education—General	M,O
Educational Leadership and Administration	M,O
Educational Media/Instructional Technology	M
Elementary Education	M
English	M
Finance and Banking	M
Health Promotion	M
Mathematics Education	M
Physical Education	M
Psychology—General	M
Public Administration	M
Reading Education	M,O
Science Education	M
Secondary Education	M
Social Sciences Education	M
Social Work	M
Special Education	M

BRIERCREST SEMINARY

Business Administration and Management—General	M
Marriage and Family Therapy	M
Missions and Missiology	M
Organizational Management	M
Pastoral Ministry and Counseling	P,M
Religion	P,M
Theology	P,M

BRIGHAM YOUNG UNIVERSITY

Accounting	M
Agricultural Sciences—General	M,D
Analytical Chemistry	M,D
Animal Sciences	M,D
Anthropology	M
Applied Statistics	M
Art Education	M
Art History	M
Art/Fine Arts	M
Astronomy	M,D
Athletic Training and Sports Medicine	M,D
Biochemistry	M,D
Biological and Biomedical Sciences—General	M,D
Biotechnology	M,D
Business Administration and Management—General	M
Chemical Engineering	M,D
Chemistry	M,D*
Child and Family Studies	M,D
Civil Engineering	M,D
Clinical Psychology	M,D
Communication Disorders	M
Communication—General	M
Comparative and Interdisciplinary Arts	M
Comparative Literature	M
Computer Science	M,D
Construction Management	M
Counseling Psychology	M,D,O
Developmental Biology	M,D
Education—General	M,D,O
Educational Leadership and Administration	M,D
Educational Media/Instructional Technology	M,D
Educational Psychology	M,D
Electrical Engineering	M,D
Engineering and Applied Sciences—General	M,D
English as a Second Language	M,O
English	M
Environmental Sciences	M,D
Exercise and Sports Science	M,D
Family Nurse Practitioner Studies	M
Film, Television, and Video Production	M
Fish, Game, and Wildlife Management	M,D
Food Science and Technology	M
Foreign Languages Education	M
Foundations and Philosophy of Education	M,D
French	M
Geography	M
Geology	M
German	M
Health Education	M
Health Promotion	M,D
Human Development	M,D
Humanities	M
Industrial Design	M
Information Science	M
Law	P,M
Linguistics	M,O
Management Information Systems	M
Marriage and Family Therapy	M,D
Mass Communication	M
Mathematics Education	M
Mathematics	M,D
Mechanical Engineering	M,D
Microbiology	M,D
Molecular Biology	M,D
Music Education	M
Music	M
Neuroscience	M,D
Nursing—General	M*
Nutrition	M
Physics	M,D
Physiology	M,D
Plant Sciences	M,D
Political Science	M
Portuguese	M
Psychology—General	M,D
Public Administration	M
Public Policy	M
Reading Education	M
Recreation and Park Management	M
Religious Education	M
School Psychology	M,D,O
Science Education	M,D
Social Psychology	M,D
Social Work	M
Sociology	M
Spanish	M
Special Education	M,D,O

*M—master's degree; P—first professional degree; D—doctorate; O—other advanced degree; *—Close-Up and/or Announcement or Display in one of the other books in this series*

Statistics M
Theater M

BRITISH AMERICAN COLLEGE LONDON

Business Administration and Management—General M
Finance and Banking M
Human Resources Management M
International Affairs M
International Business M
Management Information Systems M
Marketing M

BROCK UNIVERSITY

Accounting M
Allied Health—General M
Biological and Biomedical Sciences—General M,D
Biotechnology M,D
Business Administration and Management—General M
Chemistry M,D
Child and Family Studies M
Classics M
Comparative Literature M
Computer Science M
Cultural Studies M
Disability Studies M,O
Economics M
Education—General M,D
English as a Second Language M
English M
Geography M
Geosciences M
History M
Human Development M,D
International Affairs M
Legal and Justice Studies M
Mathematics M
Neuroscience M,D
Philosophy M
Physics M
Political Science M
Psychology—General M,D
Public Administration M
Social Psychology M,D
Statistics M

BROOKLYN COLLEGE OF THE CITY UNIVERSITY OF NEW YORK

Accounting M
Applied Physics M,D
Art Education M,O
Art History M,D
Art/Fine Arts M,D
Biological and Biomedical Sciences—General M,D
Chemistry M,D
Communication Disorders M,D
Community Health M
Computer Science M,D,O
Counseling Psychology M,D,O
Counselor Education M,O
Early Childhood Education M
Economics M
Education—General M,O
Educational Leadership and Administration M
Elementary Education M
English Education M,O
English M,D
Environmental Education M
Exercise and Sports Science M
Experimental Psychology M,D
Film, Television, and Video Production M
Foreign Languages Education M,O
French M,D
Geology M,D
Geosciences M
Health Education M,O
Health Services Management and Hospital Administration M
History M,D
Industrial and Organizational Psychology M
Information Science M,D,O
International Affairs M,D
Internet and Interactive Multimedia M,O
Jewish Studies M
Liberal Studies M
Mathematics Education M,O
Mathematics M,D
Middle School Education M,O
Multilingual and Multicultural Education M
Music Education M,D,O
Music M,D,O
Nutrition M
Photography M,D
Physical Education M,O
Physics M,D
Political Science M,D
Psychology—General M,D
Public Health—General M
Public Policy M,D
School Psychology M,O
Science Education M,O
Secondary Education M,O
Social Psychology M,D
Social Sciences Education M,O
Sociology M,D
Spanish M,D
Special Education M
Speech and Interpersonal Communication M,D
Sports Management M
Thanatology M
Theater M,D
Urban Studies M,D
Writing M

BROOKLYN LAW SCHOOL

Law P

BROOKS INSTITUTE

Photography M

BROWN UNIVERSITY

Allopathic Medicine P
American Studies M,D
Anthropology M,D
Applied Mathematics M,D*
Archaeology M,D
Art History M,D
Biochemistry M,D
Biological and Biomedical Sciences—General M,D
Biomedical Engineering M,D
Biopsychology D
Biostatistics M,D
Biotechnology M,D
Cancer Biology/Oncology M,D
Cell Biology M,D
Chemical Engineering M,D
Chemistry M,D
Classics M,D
Cognitive Sciences M,D
Community Health M,D
Comparative Literature D
Computer Engineering M,D
Computer Science M,D
Developmental Biology M,D
Developmental Psychology D
East European and Russian Studies M,D
Ecology D
Economics D
Education—General M
Electrical Engineering M,D
Elementary Education M
Engineering and Applied Sciences—General M,D
English Education M
English M,D
Environmental Management and Policy M
Epidemiology M,D
Evolutionary Biology D
French D
Geosciences M,D
German D
Health Services Research M,D
Hispanic Studies M,D
History M,D
Immunology M,D
Italian D
Jewish Studies D
Latin American Studies M,D*
Linguistics M,D
Materials Sciences M,D
Mathematics M,D
Mechanical Engineering M,D
Mechanics M,D
Microbiology M,D
Molecular Biology M,D*
Molecular Pharmacology M,D
Multilingual and Multicultural Education M,D
Museum Studies M,D
Music D
Neuroscience D
Pathobiology M,D
Pathology M,D
Philosophy M,D
Physics M,D
Physiology M,D
Political Science D
Psychology—General D
Public Health—General M
Public Policy M
Religion D
Russian M,D
Science Education M
Secondary Education M
Slavic Languages M,D
Social Psychology D
Social Sciences Education M
Sociology M,D
Theater M,D
Toxicology M,D
Western European Studies M,D
Writing M

BRYANT UNIVERSITY

Accounting M
Business Administration and Management—General M
Taxation M

BRYN ATHYN COLLEGE OF THE NEW CHURCH

Religion P,M
Theology P,M

BRYN MAWR COLLEGE

Archaeology M,D*
Art History M,D*
Chemistry M,D
Classics M,D*
Clinical Psychology D
Developmental Psychology D
French M,D
Mathematics M,D
Physics M,D
Psychology—General D
Russian M,D
Social Work M,D

BUCKNELL UNIVERSITY

Animal Behavior M
Biological and Biomedical Sciences—General M
Chemical Engineering M
Chemistry M
Civil Engineering M
Counselor Education M
Curriculum and Instruction M
Education—General M
Educational Leadership and Administration M
Educational Measurement and Evaluation M
Electrical Engineering M
Engineering and Applied Sciences—General M
English M
Mathematics M
Mechanical Engineering M
Psychology—General M
Reading Education M
School Psychology M

BUENA VISTA UNIVERSITY

Counselor Education M
Curriculum and Instruction M
Education—General M
English as a Second Language M

BUFFALO STATE COLLEGE, STATE UNIVERSITY OF NEW YORK

Adult Education M,O
Applied Economics M
Art Education M
Biological and Biomedical Sciences—General M
Business Education M
Chemistry M
Communication Disorders M
Criminal Justice and Criminology M
Early Childhood Education M
Economics M
Educational Leadership and Administration O
Educational Media/Instructional Technology M
Elementary Education M
English Education M
English M
Historic Preservation M,O
History M
Human Resources Management M,O
Industrial/Management Engineering M
Interdisciplinary Studies M
Mathematics Education M
Multilingual and Multicultural Education M
Reading Education M
Science Education M
Social Sciences Education M
Special Education M
Student Affairs M
Vocational and Technical Education M

BUTLER UNIVERSITY

Business Administration and Management—General M
Counselor Education M
Education—General M
Educational Leadership and Administration M
Elementary Education M
English M
History M
Music Education M
Music M
Pharmaceutical Sciences P,M
Pharmacy P,M
Physician Assistant Studies P,M

Reading Education	M
Secondary Education	M
Special Education	M

CABRINI COLLEGE

Biotechnology	M,O
Education—General	M,O
Educational Media/ Instructional Technology	M,O
Organizational Management	M,O

CALDWELL COLLEGE

Accounting	M
Art Therapy	M
Business Administration and Management—General	M
Counseling Psychology	M
Counselor Education	M
Curriculum and Instruction	M
Educational Leadership and Administration	M
Pastoral Ministry and Counseling	M
Psychology—General	M
Special Education	M

CALIFORNIA BAPTIST UNIVERSITY

Athletic Training and Sports Medicine	M
Business Administration and Management—General	M
Counseling Psychology	M
Counselor Education	M
Curriculum and Instruction	M
Education—General	M
Educational Leadership and Administration	M
Educational Media/ Instructional Technology	M
English as a Second Language	M
English Education	M
English	M
Forensic Psychology	M
Kinesiology and Movement Studies	M
Multilingual and Multicultural Education	M
Music Education	M
Music	M
Nursing—General	M
Pastoral Ministry and Counseling	M
Physical Education	M
Public Administration	M
Reading Education	M
School Psychology	M
Special Education	M
Sports Management	M
Vocational and Technical Education	M

CALIFORNIA COAST UNIVERSITY

Business Administration and Management—General	M
Curriculum and Instruction	M
Education—General	M
Educational Leadership and Administration	M
Human Resources Management	M
Psychology—General	M

CALIFORNIA COLLEGE OF THE ARTS

Applied Arts and Design—General	M
Architecture	M
Art/Fine Arts	M*
Film, Television, and Video Production	M
Film, Television, and Video Theory and Criticism	M
Finance and Banking	M
Museum Studies	M
Organizational Management	M
Photography	M
Textile Design	M
Writing	M

CALIFORNIA INSTITUTE OF INTEGRAL STUDIES

Anthropology	M,D
Art Therapy	M,D
Asian Studies	M,D
Clinical Psychology	M,D
Counseling Psychology	M,D
Health Psychology	M,D
Humanities	M,D*
Philosophy	M,D
Psychology—General	M,D*
Religion	M,D
Social Psychology	M,D
Theology	M,D
Therapies—Dance, Drama, and Music	M,D
Women's Studies	M,D

CALIFORNIA INSTITUTE OF TECHNOLOGY

Aerospace/Aeronautical Engineering	M,D,O
Applied Mathematics	M,D
Applied Physics	M,D
Astronomy	D
Biochemistry	M,D
Bioengineering	M,D
Biological and Biomedical Sciences—General	M,D*
Biophysics	D
Cell Biology	D
Chemical Engineering	M,D
Chemistry	M,D
Civil Engineering	M,D,O
Computational Sciences	M,D
Computer Science	M,D
Developmental Biology	D
Electrical Engineering	M,D,O
Engineering and Applied Sciences—General	M,D,O
Environmental Engineering	M,D
Genetics	D
Geochemistry	M,D
Geology	M,D
Geophysics	M,D
Immunology	D
Materials Sciences	M,D
Mathematics	D
Mechanical Engineering	M,D,O
Mechanics	M,D
Molecular Biology	D
Molecular Biophysics	M,D
Neurobiology	D
Neuroscience	M,D
Physics	D
Planetary and Space Sciences	M,D
Social Sciences	M,D
Systems Engineering	M,D

CALIFORNIA INSTITUTE OF THE ARTS

Applied Arts and Design—General	M,O
Art/Fine Arts	M,O
Dance	M,O
Film, Television, and Video Production	M,O
Graphic Design	M,O
Music	M,O
Photography	M,O
Theater	M,O
Writing	M,O

CALIFORNIA INTERCONTINENTAL UNIVERSITY

Business Administration and Management—General	M,D
Entertainment Management	M
Entrepreneurship	M,D
Finance and Banking	M,D
Health Services Management and Hospital Administration	M,D
Human Resources Management	M,D
International Business	M,D
Management Information Systems	M,D
Marketing	M,D
Organizational Management	M,D
Project Management	M,D
Quality Management	M,D

CALIFORNIA INTERNATIONAL BUSINESS UNIVERSITY

Business Administration and Management—General	M,D

CALIFORNIA LUTHERAN UNIVERSITY

Business Administration and Management—General	M,O
Clinical Psychology	M
Counselor Education	M
Education—General	M,D
Educational Leadership and Administration	M,D
Elementary Education	M,D
Entrepreneurship	M,O
Finance and Banking	M,O
Higher Education	M,D
International Business	M,O
Management Information Systems	M,O
Management of Technology	M,O
Marketing	M,O
Marriage and Family Therapy	M
Middle School Education	M,D
Organizational Behavior	M,O
Psychology—General	M
Public Administration	M
Public Policy	M
Reading Education	M
Special Education	M

CALIFORNIA NATIONAL UNIVERSITY FOR ADVANCED STUDIES

Business Administration and Management—General	M
Engineering and Applied Sciences—General	M
Engineering Management	M

CALIFORNIA POLYTECHNIC STATE UNIVERSITY, SAN LUIS OBISPO

Aerospace/Aeronautical Engineering	M
Agricultural Economics and Agribusiness	M
Agricultural Sciences—General	M
Architecture	M
Biochemistry	M
Biological and Biomedical Sciences—General	M
Business Administration and Management—General	M
Chemistry	M
Civil Engineering	M
Computer Science	M
Education—General	M
Electrical Engineering	M
Engineering and Applied Sciences—General	M
English	M
Environmental Engineering	M
Forestry	M
History	M
Industrial and Manufacturing Management	M
Industrial/Management Engineering	M
Kinesiology and Movement Studies	M
Mathematics	M
Mechanical Engineering	M
Natural Resources	M
Political Science	M
Polymer Science and Engineering	M
Psychology—General	M
Taxation	M
Urban and Regional Planning	M

CALIFORNIA SCHOOL OF PODIATRIC MEDICINE AT SAMUEL MERRITT COLLEGE

Podiatric Medicine	P

CALIFORNIA STATE POLYTECHNIC UNIVERSITY, POMONA

Agricultural Sciences—General	M
Applied Mathematics	M
Architecture	M
Biological and Biomedical Sciences—General	M
Business Administration and Management—General	M
Chemistry	M
Civil Engineering	M
Computer Science	M
Economics	M
Education—General	M
Electrical Engineering	M
Engineering and Applied Sciences—General	M
Engineering Management	M
English	M
Environmental Sciences	M
History	M
Kinesiology and Movement Studies	M
Landscape Architecture	M
Mathematics	M
Mechanical Engineering	M
Psychology—General	M
Public Administration	M
Urban and Regional Planning	M

CALIFORNIA STATE UNIVERSITY, BAKERSFIELD

Anthropology	M
Biological and Biomedical Sciences—General	M
Business Administration and Management—General	M
Counseling Psychology	M
Counselor Education	M
Curriculum and Instruction	M
Early Childhood Education	M
Education—General	M,O
Educational Leadership and Administration	M
Educational Media/ Instructional Technology	M
English	M

*M—master's degree; P—first professional degree; D—doctorate; O—other advanced degree; *—Close-Up and/or Announcement or Display in one of the other books in this series*

Geology	M
Health Services Management and Hospital Administration	M
History	M
Hydrology	M
Interdisciplinary Studies	M
Mathematics Education	M
Middle School Education	M
Multilingual and Multicultural Education	M
Nursing—General	M
Psychology—General	M
Public Administration	M
Reading Education	M,O
Secondary Education	M
Social Work	M
Sociology	M
Spanish	M
Special Education	M
Student Affairs	M

CALIFORNIA STATE UNIVERSITY CHANNEL ISLANDS

Bioinformatics	M
Biotechnology	M
Business Administration and Management—General	M
Computer Science	M
Educational Leadership and Administration	M
Mathematics	M

CALIFORNIA STATE UNIVERSITY, CHICO

Anthropology	M
Art History	M
Art/Fine Arts	M
Biological and Biomedical Sciences—General	M
Botany	M
Business Administration and Management—General	M
Communication Disorders	M
Communication—General	M
Computer Engineering	M
Computer Science	M
Curriculum and Instruction	M
Education—General	M
Electrical Engineering	M
Engineering and Applied Sciences—General	M
English	M
Environmental Sciences	M
Foreign Languages Education	M
Geography	M
Geology	M
Geosciences	M
Health Services Management and Hospital Administration	M
History	M
Hydrogeology	M
Hydrology	M
Interdisciplinary Studies	M
Kinesiology and Movement Studies	M
Marriage and Family Therapy	M
Mathematics Education	M
Multilingual and Multicultural Education	M
Museum Studies	M
Music	M
Nursing—General	M
Nutrition	M
Political Science	M
Psychology—General	M
Public Administration	M
Reading Education	M
Recreation and Park Management	M
Rural Planning and Studies	M
Science Education	M
Social Sciences Education	M
Social Sciences	M
Social Work	M
Special Education	M
Urban and Regional Planning	M

CALIFORNIA STATE UNIVERSITY, DOMINGUEZ HILLS

Applied Social Research	M,O
Bioinformatics	M
Biological and Biomedical Sciences—General	M
Business Administration and Management—General	M
Clinical Psychology	M
Computer Education	M,O
Computer Science	M
Conflict Resolution and Mediation/Peace Studies	M
Counselor Education	M
Curriculum and Instruction	M
Education—General	M,O
Educational Leadership and Administration	M
English as a Second Language	M,O
English	M,O
Health Education	M
Humanities	M
International and Comparative Education	M
Marriage and Family Therapy	M
Mathematics Education	M
Multilingual and Multicultural Education	M
Nursing—General	M
Occupational Therapy	M
Physical Education	M
Physician Assistant Studies	M
Psychology—General	M
Public Administration	M
Quality Management	M
Rhetoric	M,O
Social Work	M
Sociology	M,O
Special Education	M

CALIFORNIA STATE UNIVERSITY, EAST BAY

Accounting	M
Anthropology	M
Applied Statistics	M
Biochemistry	M
Biological and Biomedical Sciences—General	M
Biostatistics	M
Business Administration and Management—General	M
Chemistry	M
Communication Disorders	M
Communication—General	M
Computer Engineering	M
Computer Science	M
Counselor Education	M
Curriculum and Instruction	M
Economics	M
Education—General	M
Educational Leadership and Administration	M
Educational Media/Instructional Technology	M
Electronic Commerce	M
Engineering Management	M
English	M
Entrepreneurship	M
Environmental Sciences	M
Finance and Banking	M
Geography	M
Geology	M
Health Services Management and Hospital Administration	M
History	M
Human Resources Management	M
Industrial and Manufacturing Management	M
Interdisciplinary Studies	M,O
International Business	M
Internet and Interactive Multimedia	M
Management Strategy and Policy	M
Marine Sciences	M
Marketing	M
Mathematics	M
Music	M
Operations Research	M
Physical Education	M
Public Administration	M
Social Work	M
Sociology	M
Software Engineering	M
Special Education	M
Statistics	M
Supply Chain Management	M
Taxation	M
Telecommunications	M

CALIFORNIA STATE UNIVERSITY, FRESNO

Accounting	M
Animal Sciences	M
Applied Arts and Design—General	M
Art/Fine Arts	M
Biological and Biomedical Sciences—General	M
Business Administration and Management—General	M
Chemistry	M
Civil Engineering	M
Communication Disorders	M
Communication—General	M
Computer Science	M
Counselor Education	M
Criminal Justice and Criminology	M
Curriculum and Instruction	M
Early Childhood Education	M
Education—General	M,D
Educational Leadership and Administration	M,D
Electrical Engineering	M
Engineering and Applied Sciences—General	M
English as a Second Language	M
English	M
Exercise and Sports Science	M
Family and Consumer Sciences-General	M
Family Nurse Practitioner Studies	M
Food Science and Technology	M
Geology	M
Health Promotion	M
Health Services Management and Hospital Administration	M
History	M
Industrial/Management Engineering	M
International Affairs	M
Journalism	M
Kinesiology and Movement Studies	M
Linguistics	M
Marine Sciences	M
Marriage and Family Therapy	M
Mass Communication	M
Mathematics Education	M
Mathematics	M
Mechanical Engineering	M
Music Education	M
Music	M
Nursing Education	M
Nursing—General	M
Physical Therapy	M,D
Physics	M
Plant Sciences	M
Psychology—General	M
Public Administration	M
Public Health—General	M
Reading Education	M
Rehabilitation Counseling	M
Social Sciences Education	M
Social Work	M
Spanish	M
Special Education	M
Sport Psychology	M
Viticulture and Enology	M
Writing	M

CALIFORNIA STATE UNIVERSITY, FULLERTON

Accounting	M
Advertising and Public Relations	M
American Studies	M
Anthropology	M
Applied Arts and Design—General	M
Applied Mathematics	M
Art History	M
Art/Fine Arts	M
Biological and Biomedical Sciences—General	M
Business Administration and Management—General	M
Chemistry	M
Civil Engineering	M
Clinical Psychology	M
Communication Disorders	M
Communication—General	M
Comparative Literature	M
Computer Science	M
Counselor Education	M
Dance	M
Economics	M
Education—General	M
Educational Leadership and Administration	M,D
Educational Media/Instructional Technology	M
Electrical Engineering	M
Electronic Commerce	M
Elementary Education	M
Engineering and Applied Sciences—General	M
English as a Second Language	M
English	M
Entrepreneurship	M
Environmental Management and Policy	M
Environmental Sciences	M
Film, Television, and Video Production	M
Finance and Banking	M
French	M
Geochemistry	M
Geography	M
Geology	M
German	M
Gerontology	M
History	M
Information Science	M
International Business	M
Journalism	M
Linguistics	M
Management Information Systems	M
Marketing	M
Mathematics Education	M
Mathematics	M
Mechanical Engineering	M
Mechanics	M
Media Studies	M
Middle School Education	M
Multilingual and Multicultural Education	M
Music Education	M
Music	M

Nursing—General	M
Photography	M
Physical Education	M
Physics	M
Political Science	M
Psychology—General	M
Public Administration	M
Public Health—General	M
Reading Education	M
Science Education	M
Secondary Education	M
Social Psychology	M
Social Work	M
Sociology	M
Software Engineering	M
Spanish	M
Special Education	M
Speech and Interpersonal Communication	M
Systems Engineering	M
Taxation	M
Theater	M
Travel and Tourism	M

CALIFORNIA STATE UNIVERSITY, LONG BEACH

Adult Nursing	M
Aerospace/Aeronautical Engineering	M
African Studies	M
American Studies	M
Anthropology	M
Applied Mathematics	M,D
Applied Physics	M
Applied Statistics	M
Art Education	M
Art History	M
Art/Fine Arts	M
Asian Studies	M,O
Asian-American Studies	M,O
Athletic Training and Sports Medicine	M
Biochemistry	M
Biological and Biomedical Sciences—General	M
Business Administration and Management—General	M
Chemistry	M
Civil Engineering	M
Communication Disorders	M
Communication—General	M
Computer Engineering	M
Computer Science	M
Consumer Economics	M
Counselor Education	M
Criminal Justice and Criminology	M
Dance	M
Economics	M
Education—General	M,D
Electrical Engineering	M
Emergency Management	M
Engineering Management	M,D
English as a Second Language	M
English	M
Ergonomics and Human Factors	M
Exercise and Sports Science	M
Family and Consumer Sciences-General	M
Food Science and Technology	M
French	M
Geography	M
Geology	M
Geophysics	M
German	M
Gerontology	M
Health Education	M
Health Services Management and Hospital Administration	M,O
Higher Education	M,D
History	M
Interdisciplinary Studies	M
Kinesiology and Movement Studies	M
Latin American Studies	M
Leisure Studies	M
Linguistics	M
Marriage and Family Therapy	M
Mathematics Education	M
Mathematics	M
Mechanical Engineering	M,D
Medieval and Renaissance Studies	M
Microbiology	M
Music	M
Near and Middle Eastern Studies	M
Nursing and Healthcare Administration	M,O
Nursing—General	M
Nutrition	M
Philosophy	M
Physical Education	M
Physical Therapy	M
Physics	M
Political Science	M
Psychology—General	M
Public Administration	M
Public Policy	M
Recreation and Park Management	M
Religion	M
Secondary Education	M
Social Work	M
Spanish	M
Special Education	M
Sport Psychology	M
Sports Management	M
Student Affairs	M,D
Theater	M
Vocational and Technical Education	M
Western European Studies	M
Writing	M

CALIFORNIA STATE UNIVERSITY, LOS ANGELES

Accounting	M
Analytical Chemistry	M
Anthropology	M
Applied Arts and Design—General	M
Applied Mathematics	M
Art Education	M
Art History	M
Art Therapy	M
Art/Fine Arts	M
Biochemistry	M
Biological and Biomedical Sciences—General	M
Business Administration and Management—General	M
Chemistry	M
Child and Family Studies	M
Child Development	M
Civil Engineering	M
Communication Disorders	M
Communication—General	M
Computer Science	M
Counselor Education	M,D
Criminal Justice and Criminology	M
Economics	M
Education—General	M,D
Electrical Engineering	M
Elementary Education	M
Engineering and Applied Sciences—General	M
English	M
Film, Television, and Video Production	M
Finance and Banking	M
French	M
Geography	M
Geology	M
Graphic Design	M
Health Education	M
Health Services Management and Hospital Administration	M
Hispanic Studies	M
History	M
Inorganic Chemistry	M
International Business	M
Kinesiology and Movement Studies	M
Latin American Studies	M
Management Information Systems	M
Management of Technology	M
Marketing	M
Mathematics	M
Mechanical Engineering	M
Music Education	M
Music	M
Nursing—General	M
Nutrition	M
Organic Chemistry	M
Philosophy	M
Photography	M
Physical Chemistry	M
Physical Education	M
Physics	M
Political Science	M
Psychology—General	M
Public Administration	M
Reading Education	M
Rehabilitation Counseling	M,D
School Psychology	M,D
Secondary Education	M
Social Work	M
Sociology	M
Spanish	M
Special Education	M,D
Speech and Interpersonal Communication	M
Taxation	M
Textile Design	M
Theater	M

CALIFORNIA STATE UNIVERSITY, MONTEREY BAY

Business Administration and Management—General	M
Education—General	M
Educational Media/Instructional Technology	M
Interdisciplinary Studies	M
Management Information Systems	M
Marine Sciences	M
Public Policy	M
Water Resources	M

CALIFORNIA STATE UNIVERSITY, NORTHRIDGE

Anthropology	M
Applied Mathematics	M
Archaeology	M
Art Education	M
Art History	M
Art/Fine Arts	M
Artificial Intelligence/Robotics	M
Biochemistry	M
Biological and Biomedical Sciences—General	M
Business Administration and Management—General	M
Chemistry	M
Civil Engineering	M
Clinical Psychology	M
Communication Disorders	M
Communication—General	M
Comparative Literature	M
Computer Science	M
Counselor Education	M
Curriculum and Instruction	M
Early Childhood Education	M
Education—General	M,D
Educational Leadership and Administration	M,D
Educational Media/Instructional Technology	M
Educational Psychology	M
Electrical Engineering	M
Elementary Education	M
Engineering and Applied Sciences—General	M
Engineering Management	M
English Education	M
English	M
Environmental and Occupational Health	M
Environmental Sciences	M
Ergonomics and Human Factors	M
Experimental Psychology	M
Family and Consumer Sciences-General	M
Film, Television, and Video Production	M
Geography	M
Geology	M
Health Services Management and Hospital Administration	M
Hispanic Studies	M
History	M
Hospitality Management	M
Industrial Hygiene	M
Industrial/Management Engineering	M
Interdisciplinary Studies	M
Journalism	M
Kinesiology and Movement Studies	M
Linguistics	M
Manufacturing Engineering	M
Marriage and Family Therapy	M
Mass Communication	M
Materials Engineering	M
Mathematics Education	M
Mathematics	M
Mechanical Engineering	M
Multilingual and Multicultural Education	M
Music Education	M
Music	M
Physical Therapy	M
Physics	M
Political Science	M
Psychology—General	M
Public Administration	M
Public Health—General	M
Reading Education	M
Recreation and Park Management	M
Rhetoric	M
School Psychology	M
Science Education	M
Secondary Education	M
Social Work	M
Sociology	M
Software Engineering	M
Spanish	M
Special Education	M
Speech and Interpersonal Communication	M
Structural Engineering	M
Systems Engineering	M
Taxation	M
Theater	M
Travel and Tourism	M
Writing	M

CALIFORNIA STATE UNIVERSITY, SACRAMENTO

Accounting	M
Anthropology	M
Art/Fine Arts	M
Biological and Biomedical Sciences—General	M
Business Administration and Management—General	M
Chemistry	M
Civil Engineering	M
Communication Disorders	M
Communication—General	M

*M—master's degree; P—first professional degree; D—doctorate; O—other advanced degree; *—Close-Up and/or Announcement* **or Display** *in one of the other books in this series*

Computer Science	M
Counseling Psychology	M
Counselor Education	M
Criminal Justice and Criminology	M
Curriculum and Instruction	M
Dance	M
Early Childhood Education	M
Education—General	M
Educational Leadership and Administration	M
Electrical Engineering	M
Engineering and Applied Sciences—General	M
English as a Second Language	M
English	M
Foreign Languages Education	M
French	M
German	M
Human Resources Development	M
Human Resources Management	M
Human Services	M
International Affairs	M
Liberal Studies	M
Management Information Systems	M
Marine Sciences	M
Mathematics	M
Mechanical Engineering	M
Multilingual and Multicultural Education	M
Music	M
Nursing—General	M
Physical Education	M
Political Science	M
Psychology—General	M
Public Administration	M
Public History	M
Public Policy	M
Reading Education	M
Real Estate	M
Recreation and Park Management	M
School Psychology	M
Social Work	M
Sociology	M
Software Engineering	M
Spanish	M
Special Education	M
Statistics	M
Theater	M
Vocational and Technical Education	M
Writing	M

CALIFORNIA STATE UNIVERSITY, SAN BERNARDINO

Art/Fine Arts	M
Biological and Biomedical Sciences—General	M
Business Administration and Management—General	M
Chemistry	M
Child Development	M
Clinical Psychology	M
Communication—General	M
Computer Science	M
Corporate and Organizational Communication	M
Counseling Psychology	M
Counselor Education	M
Criminal Justice and Criminology	M
Curriculum and Instruction	M
Education—General	M,D
Educational Leadership and Administration	M,D
Educational Media/Instructional Technology	M
Elementary Education	M
English as a Second Language	M,D
English Education	M,D
English	M
Environmental Education	M
Environmental Sciences	M
Experimental Psychology	M
Health Education	M
Health Services Management and Hospital Administration	M
Human Development	M
Industrial and Organizational Psychology	M
Interdisciplinary Studies	M
Kinesiology and Movement Studies	M
Mathematics Education	M
Mathematics	M
Multilingual and Multicultural Education	M
National Security	M
Nursing—General	M
Psychology—General	M
Public Administration	M
Public Health—General	M
Reading Education	M
Rehabilitation Counseling	M
Science Education	M
Secondary Education	M
Social Sciences Education	M,D
Social Sciences	M
Social Work	M
Spanish	M
Special Education	M
Theater	M
Vocational and Technical Education	M
Writing	M

CALIFORNIA STATE UNIVERSITY, SAN MARCOS

Biological and Biomedical Sciences—General	M
Business Administration and Management—General	M
Computer Science	M
Education—General	M
English	M
Mathematics	M
Psychology—General	M
Sociology	M
Spanish	M
Writing	M

CALIFORNIA STATE UNIVERSITY, STANISLAUS

Art/Fine Arts	O
Biological and Biomedical Sciences—General	M
Business Administration and Management—General	M
Child Development	M,O
Community College Education	M,D
Counselor Education	M,D,O
Criminal Justice and Criminology	M
Curriculum and Instruction	M,O
Ecology	M
Education—General	M,D,O
Educational Leadership and Administration	M,D
Educational Media/Instructional Technology	M,D
Elementary Education	M,O
English as a Second Language	M,O
English	M,O
Finance and Banking	M
Genetic Counseling	M
Gerontology	O
History	M
Interdisciplinary Studies	M
International Affairs	M
International Business	M
Marine Sciences	M
Middle School Education	M,O
Multilingual and Multicultural Education	M,O
Physical Education	M
Psychology—General	M,O
Public Administration	M
Reading Education	M,O
Rhetoric	M,O
Secondary Education	M,O
Social Work	M
Special Education	M,D
Sustainable Development	M
Writing	M,O

CALIFORNIA UNIVERSITY OF PENNSYLVANIA

Athletic Training and Sports Medicine	M
Business Administration and Management—General	M
Communication Disorders	M
Counselor Education	M
Criminal Justice and Criminology	M
Education—General	M
Educational Leadership and Administration	M
Elementary Education	M
Exercise and Sports Science	M
Legal and Justice Studies	M
Reading Education	M
Rehabilitation Sciences	M
School Psychology	M
Secondary Education	M
Social Sciences	M
Social Work	M
Special Education	M
Sport Psychology	M
Sports Management	M
Vocational and Technical Education	M

CALIFORNIA WESTERN SCHOOL OF LAW

Accounting	P,M
Law	P,M

CALUMET COLLEGE OF SAINT JOSEPH

Criminal Justice and Criminology	M
Educational Leadership and Administration	M
Quality Management	M

CALVARY BIBLE COLLEGE AND THEOLOGICAL SEMINARY

Pastoral Ministry and Counseling	P,M
Theology	P,M

CALVIN COLLEGE

Curriculum and Instruction	M
Education—General	M
Educational Leadership and Administration	M
Reading Education	M
Special Education	M

CALVIN THEOLOGICAL SEMINARY

Missions and Missiology	P,M,D
Religious Education	P,M,D
Theology	P,M,D

CAMBRIDGE COLLEGE

Addictions/Substance Abuse Counseling	M,O
Art Education	M,D,O
Business Administration and Management—General	M
Conflict Resolution and Mediation/Peace Studies	M
Counseling Psychology	M,O
Counselor Education	M,D,O
Curriculum and Instruction	M,D,O
Early Childhood Education	M,D,O
Education—General	M,D,O
Educational Leadership and Administration	M,D,O
Educational Measurement and Evaluation	M,D,O
Educational Media/Instructional Technology	M,D,O
Elementary Education	M,D,O
English as a Second Language	M,D,O
Entrepreneurship	M
Forensic Psychology	M,O
Health Education	M,D,O
Health Services Management and Hospital Administration	M
Home Economics Education	M,D,O
Interdisciplinary Studies	M,D,O
Management of Technology	M
Marriage and Family Therapy	M,O
Mathematics Education	M,D,O
Medical Informatics	M
Middle School Education	M,D,O
Nonprofit Management	M
Organizational Management	M
Psychology—General	M,O
Reading Education	M,D,O
School Nursing	M,D,O
Science Education	M,D,O
Social Sciences Education	M,D,O
Special Education	M,D,O
Vocational and Technical Education	M,D,O

CAMERON UNIVERSITY

Business Administration and Management—General	M
Education—General	M
Educational Leadership and Administration	M
Entrepreneurship	M
Psychology—General	M

CAMPBELLSVILLE UNIVERSITY

Business Administration and Management—General	M
Curriculum and Instruction	M
Education—General	M
Music Education	M
Music	M
Social Sciences	M
Social Work	M
Special Education	M
Theology	M

CAMPBELL UNIVERSITY

Business Administration and Management—General	M
Counselor Education	M
Education—General	M
Educational Leadership and Administration	M
Elementary Education	M
English Education	M
Interdisciplinary Studies	M
Law	P
Mathematics Education	M
Middle School Education	M
Pharmaceutical Sciences	P,M
Pharmacy	P,M
Physical Education	M
Religious Education	P,M,D
Secondary Education	M

Social Sciences Education M
Theology P,M,D

CANADIAN COLLEGE OF NATUROPATHIC MEDICINE
Naturopathic Medicine D*

CANADIAN MEMORIAL CHIROPRACTIC COLLEGE
Acupuncture and Oriental Medicine O
Chiropractic P,O

CANADIAN SOUTHERN BAPTIST SEMINARY
Computer Education P,M
Theology P,M

CANISIUS COLLEGE
Accounting M
Business Administration and Management—General M
Communication Disorders M
Corporate and Organizational Communication M
Counselor Education M
Early Childhood Education M
Education—General M
Educational Leadership and Administration M
Elementary Education M
Health Promotion M
Marketing M
Middle School Education M
Physical Education M
Reading Education M
Rehabilitation Sciences M
School Psychology M
Secondary Education M
Social Psychology M
Special Education M
Sports Management M
Student Affairs M

CAPE BRETON UNIVERSITY
Art Education O
Business Administration and Management—General M
Counselor Education O
Economic Development M
Education—General O
Educational Media/Instructional Technology O

CAPELLA UNIVERSITY
Accounting M,D,O
Addictions/Substance Abuse Counseling M,D,O
Adult Education M,D,O
Business Administration and Management—General M,D,O
Child and Family Studies M,D,O
Clinical Psychology M,D,O
Computer and Information Systems Security M,D,O
Counseling Psychology M,D,O
Criminal Justice and Criminology M,D,O
Curriculum and Instruction M,D,O
Developmental Psychology M,D,O
Education—General M,D,O
Educational Leadership and Administration M,D,O
Educational Media/Instructional Technology M,D,O
Educational Psychology M,D,O
Elementary Education M,D,O
Emergency Management M,D
Environmental and Occupational Health M,D
Finance and Banking M,D,O
Gerontology M,D
Health Services Management and Hospital Administration M,D,O
Higher Education M,D,O
Human Resources Management M,D,O
Human Services M,D,O
Industrial and Organizational Psychology M,D,O
Management Information Systems M,D,O
Management of Technology M,D,O
Marketing M,D,O
Marriage and Family Therapy M,D,O
Middle School Education M,D,O
Multilingual and Multicultural Education M,D,O
Nonprofit Management M,D,O
Nursing Education M,D
Organizational Management M,D,O
Project Management M,D,O
Psychology—General M,D,O
Public Administration M,D
Reading Education M,D,O
School Psychology M,D,O
Sport Psychology M,D,O

CAPITAL BIBLE SEMINARY
Pastoral Ministry and Counseling P,M,O
Theology P,M,O

CAPITAL UNIVERSITY
Business Administration and Management—General M
Law P,M
Legal and Justice Studies M
Music Education M
Music M
Nursing and Healthcare Administration M
Nursing—General M
Taxation M

CAPITOL COLLEGE
Business Administration and Management—General M
Computer and Information Systems Security M
Computer Science M
Electrical Engineering M
Information Science M
Management Information Systems M
Telecommunications Management M

CARDINAL STRITCH UNIVERSITY
Applied Arts and Design—General M
Business Administration and Management—General M
Clinical Psychology M
Computer Education M
Education—General M,D
Educational Leadership and Administration M,D
Educational Media/Instructional Technology M
English as a Second Language M
Graphic Design M
History M
Liberal Studies M
Music M
Nursing—General M
Pastoral Ministry and Counseling M
Psychology—General M
Reading Education M
Religion M
Special Education M
Sports Management M
Urban Education M,D

CAREY THEOLOGICAL COLLEGE
Theology M,D

CARIBBEAN UNIVERSITY
Art History M,D
Criminal Justice and Criminology M,D
Curriculum and Instruction M,D
Early Childhood Education M,D
Education—General M,D
Educational Leadership and Administration M,D
Elementary Education M,D
English Education M,D
Foreign Languages Education M,D
Gerontological Nursing M,D
Human Resources Management M,D
Mathematics Education M,D
Museum Studies M,D
Pediatric Nursing M,D
Physical Education M,D
Science Education M,D
Social Sciences Education M,D
Special Education M,D

CARLETON UNIVERSITY
Aerospace/Aeronautical Engineering M,D
Anthropology M
Architecture M
Art History M
Biological and Biomedical Sciences—General M,D
Biomedical Engineering M
Business Administration and Management—General M,D
Canadian Studies M,D
Chemistry M,D
Civil Engineering M,D
Cognitive Sciences D
Communication—General M,D
Comparative Literature D
Computer Science M,D
Conflict Resolution and Mediation/Peace Studies M,O
East European and Russian Studies M,O
Economics M,D
Electrical Engineering M,D
Engineering and Applied Sciences—General M,D
English M,D
Environmental Engineering M,D
Film, Television, and Video Production M
French M
Geography M,D
Geosciences M,D
History M,D
Industrial Design M
Information Science M,D
International Affairs M,D
Journalism M,D
Legal and Justice Studies M,O
Linguistics M
Management of Technology M
Materials Engineering M,D
Mathematics M,D
Mechanical Engineering M,D
Music M
Neuroscience M,D
Philosophy M
Physics M,D
Political Science M,D
Psychology—General M,D
Public Administration M,D
Public Policy M,D
Social Work M
Sociology M,D
Systems Engineering M,D
Systems Science M,D
Western European Studies M,O

CARLOS ALBIZU UNIVERSITY
Clinical Psychology M,D
Communication Disorders M,D
Industrial and Organizational Psychology M,D
Psychology—General M,D

CARLOS ALBIZU UNIVERSITY, MIAMI CAMPUS
Business Administration and Management—General M,D
Clinical Psychology M,D
Counseling Psychology M,D
Education of the Gifted M,D
English as a Second Language M,D
Entrepreneurship M,D
Industrial and Organizational Psychology M,D
Marriage and Family Therapy M,D
Nonprofit Management M,D
Organizational Management M,D
Psychology—General M,D
School Psychology M,D
Special Education M,D

CARLOW UNIVERSITY
Art Education M
Business Administration and Management—General M
Counseling Psychology M
Counselor Education M
Early Childhood Education M
Education—General M
Educational Leadership and Administration M
Educational Media/Instructional Technology M
Elementary Education M
Family Nurse Practitioner Studies M,D
Humanities M
Nonprofit Management M
Nursing and Healthcare Administration M,D
Nursing—General M,D
Organizational Management M
Secondary Education M
Special Education M
Writing M

CARNEGIE MELLON UNIVERSITY
Accounting D
African Studies M,D
African-American Studies M,D
Applied Arts and Design—General D
Applied Mathematics M,D
Applied Physics M,D
Architectural Engineering M,D
Architecture M,D
Art/Fine Arts M
Artificial Intelligence/Robotics M,D*
Arts Administration M
Biochemistry M,D

*M—master's degree; P—first professional degree; D—doctorate; O—other advanced degree; *—Close-Up and/or Announcement or Display in one of the other books in this series*

Bioengineering M,D
Biological and Biomedical Sciences—General M,D
Biomedical Engineering M,D
Biophysics M,D
Biopsychology D
Biotechnology M,D
Building Science M,D
Business Administration and Management—General M,D
Cell Biology M,D
Chemical Engineering M,D
Chemistry M,D
Cognitive Sciences D
Communication—General M,D
Comparative Literature M,D
Computational Biology M,D
Computational Sciences M,D
Computer and Information Systems Security M
Computer Art and Design M,D
Computer Engineering M,D*
Computer Science M,D*
Construction Management M,D
Corporate and Organizational Communication M
Criminal Justice and Criminology M
Cultural Studies M,D
Developmental Biology M,D
Developmental Psychology D
Economics D
Education—General M,D
Electrical Engineering M,D
Electronic Commerce M
English M,D
Entertainment Management M
Entrepreneurship D
Environmental Engineering M,D
Film, Television, and Video Production M
Finance and Banking D
Gender Studies M,D
Genetics M,D
Health Services Management and Hospital Administration M
History of Science and Technology M,D
History M,D
Human-Computer Interaction M,D
Industrial and Labor Relations M,D
Industrial and Manufacturing Management M,D
Information Science M,D
Inorganic Chemistry M,D
Linguistics D
Management Information Systems M,D
Management of Technology M,D
Marketing D
Materials Engineering M,D
Materials Sciences M,D*
Mathematical and Computational Finance M,D
Mathematics M,D
Mechanical Engineering M,D
Media Studies M
Molecular Biology M,D
Molecular Biophysics D
Music Education M
Music M
Neurobiology M,D
Neuroscience D
Operations Research D
Organic Chemistry M,D
Organizational Behavior D
Philosophy M,D
Physics M,D
Polymer Science and Engineering M,D
Psychology—General D
Public Administration M
Public Policy M,D
Publishing M
Rhetoric M,D
Social Psychology D
Social Sciences D
Software Engineering M,D*
Statistics M,D
Structural Biology D
Systems Engineering M
Technical Writing M
Technology and Public Policy M,D*
Telecommunications Management M
Theater M
Theoretical Chemistry M,D
Urban Design M,D
Writing M*

CARROLL UNIVERSITY

Education—General M
Physical Therapy M,D
Software Engineering M

CARSON-NEWMAN COLLEGE

Counselor Education M
Curriculum and Instruction M
Education—General M
Elementary Education M
English as a Second Language M
Family Nurse Practitioner Studies M
Nursing—General M
Secondary Education M

CARTHAGE COLLEGE

Art Education M,O
Counselor Education M,O
Education of the Gifted M,O
Education—General M,O
Educational Leadership and Administration M,O
English Education M,O
Reading Education M,O
Science Education M,O
Social Sciences Education M,O

CASE WESTERN RESERVE UNIVERSITY

Accounting M,D
Acute Care/Critical Care Nursing M,D
Adult Nursing M,D
Aerospace/Aeronautical Engineering M,D
Allopathic Medicine P
Anatomy M
Anesthesiologist Assistant Studies M
Anthropology M,D
Applied Mathematics M,D
Art Education M
Art History M,D
Astronomy M,D
Biochemistry M,D
Bioethics M
Biological and Biomedical Sciences—General M,D*
Biomedical Engineering M,D*
Biophysics M,D
Biostatistics M,D
Business Administration and Management—General M,D
Cancer Biology/Oncology D
Cell Biology M,D
Ceramic Sciences and Engineering M,D
Chemical Engineering M,D
Chemistry M,D
Civil Engineering M,D
Clinical Psychology D
Clinical Research M
Cognitive Sciences M
Communication Disorders M,D
Community Health Nursing M
Comparative Literature M
Computer Engineering M,D
Computer Science M,D
Dance M
Dentistry P
Economics M
Electrical Engineering M,D
Engineering and Applied Sciences—General M,D
Engineering Management M
English M,D
Epidemiology M,D
Experimental Psychology D
Family Nurse Practitioner Studies M,D
Finance and Banking M,D
French M
Genetic Counseling M
Genetics D
Genomic Sciences D*
Geology M,D
Geosciences M,D
Gerontological Nursing M,D
Health Services Research M,D
History M,D
Human Genetics D
Human Resources Management M
Immunology M,D
Industrial and Labor Relations M
Industrial and Manufacturing Management M,D
Information Science M,D
Law P,M
Legal and Justice Studies P,M
Linguistics M
Logistics M,D
Management Information Systems M,D
Management Strategy and Policy M
Marketing M,D
Materials Engineering M,D
Materials Sciences M,D
Maternal and Child/Neonatal Nursing M,D
Mathematics M,D
Mechanical Engineering M,D
Mechanics M,D
Medical/Surgical Nursing M,D
Microbiology D
Molecular Biology D
Molecular Medicine D
Molecular Physiology M,D
Museum Studies M,D
Music Education M,D
Music M,D
Neurobiology D
Neuroscience D
Nonprofit Management M,O*
Nurse Anesthesia M
Nurse Midwifery M
Nursing Informatics M
Nursing—General M,D
Nutrition M,D*
Operations Research M
Oral and Dental Sciences M,O
Organizational Behavior M
Pathology M,D
Pediatric Nursing M,D
Pharmacology D
Physics M,D
Physiology M,D*
Political Science M,D
Polymer Science and Engineering M,D
Psychiatric Nursing M,D
Psychology—General D
Public Health—General M
Quality Management M,D
Social Work M,D
Sociology M,D
Statistics M,D
Supply Chain Management M
Systems Engineering M,D
Theater M
Virology D
Women's Health Nursing M,D*

CASTLETON STATE COLLEGE

Curriculum and Instruction M
Education—General M,O
Educational Leadership and Administration M,O
Forensic Psychology M
Psychology—General M
Reading Education M,O
Special Education M,O

CATAWBA COLLEGE

Education—General M
Elementary Education M

THE CATHOLIC DISTANCE UNIVERSITY

Theology M

CATHOLIC THEOLOGICAL UNION AT CHICAGO

Missions and Missiology P,M,D,O
Pastoral Ministry and Counseling P,M,D,O
Theology P,M,D,O

THE CATHOLIC UNIVERSITY OF AMERICA

Adult Nursing M,D,O
American Studies M,D
Anthropology M
Architecture M
Bioinformatics M,D
Biological and Biomedical Sciences—General M,D
Biomedical Engineering M,D
Business Administration and Management—General M
Cell Biology M,D
Chemistry M
Civil Engineering M,D,O
Classics M,D
Clinical Laboratory Sciences/Medical Technology M,D
Clinical Psychology M,D
Community Health Nursing M,D,O
Community Health M,D,O
Comparative Literature M
Computer and Information Systems Security M,D
Computer Art and Design M
Computer Science M,D
Construction Management M,D,O
Cultural Studies M
Curriculum and Instruction M,D,O
Economics M
Education—General M,D,O
Educational Leadership and Administration P,M,D,O
Educational Psychology M,D,O
Electrical Engineering M,D
Engineering and Applied Sciences—General M,D,O
Engineering Management M,O
English M,D
Environmental Engineering M,D,O
Environmental Management and Policy M,D,O

Ergonomics and Human Factors	M,D
Experimental Psychology	M,D
Family Nurse Practitioner Studies	M,D,O
Geotechnical Engineering	M,D,O
Gerontological Nursing	M,D,O
History	M,D
Human Resources Management	M
Information Studies	M
International Affairs	M,D
International Health	M,D,O
Law	P
Legal and Justice Studies	D,O
Library Science	M
Mechanical Engineering	M,D
Mechanics	M,D,O
Medical Imaging	M,D
Medieval and Renaissance Studies	M,D,O
Microbiology	M,D
Music Education	M,D,O
Music	M,D,O
Near and Middle Eastern Languages	M,D
Near and Middle Eastern Studies	M,D
Nursing Education	M,D,O
Nursing—General	M,D,O
Optical Sciences	M,D
Pastoral Ministry and Counseling	P,M,D,O
Pediatric Nursing	M,D,O
Philosophy	M,D,O
Physics	M,D
Political Science	M,D
Psychiatric Nursing	M,D,O
Psychology—General	M,D
Religion	P,M,D,O
Religious Education	P,M,D,O
Rhetoric	M,D
Secondary Education	M,D,O
Social Work	M,D
Sociology	M
Spanish	M,D
Special Education	M,D,O
Structural Engineering	M,D,O
Systems Engineering	M,D,O
Telecommunications	M,D
Theater	M
Theology	P,M,D,O
Urban and Regional Planning	M
Urban Design	M
Western European Studies	M,D

CEDAR CREST COLLEGE

Education—General	M
Forensic Sciences	M

CEDARS-SINAI MEDICAL CENTER

Biological and Biomedical Sciences—General	D
Translational Biology	D

CEDARVILLE UNIVERSITY

Education—General	M

CENTENARY COLLEGE

Accounting	M
Business Administration and Management—General	M
Counseling Psychology	M
Education—General	M
Educational Leadership and Administration	M
Special Education	M

CENTENARY COLLEGE OF LOUISIANA

Business Administration and Management—General	M
Curriculum and Instruction	M
Education—General	M
Educational Leadership and Administration	M
Elementary Education	M
Secondary Education	M

CENTRAL BAPTIST THEOLOGICAL SEMINARY

Missions and Missiology	P,M,O
Theology	P,M,O

CENTRAL BAPTIST THEOLOGICAL SEMINARY OF VIRGINIA BEACH

Theology	P,M

CENTRAL CONNECTICUT STATE UNIVERSITY

Actuarial Science	M,O
Advertising and Public Relations	M,O
Art Education	M,O
Biochemistry	M
Biological and Biomedical Sciences—General	M,O
Business Administration and Management—General	M,O
Business Education	M,O
Chemistry	M
Communication—General	M,O
Computer Science	M
Construction Management	M,O
Corporate and Organizational Communication	M,O
Counselor Education	M,O
Criminal Justice and Criminology	M
Early Childhood Education	M
Education—General	M,D,O
Educational Leadership and Administration	M,D,O
Educational Media/Instructional Technology	M
Elementary Education	M,O
Engineering and Applied Sciences—General	M
English as a Second Language	M,O
English	M,O
Exercise and Sports Science	M,O
Foreign Languages Education	M,O
Foundations and Philosophy of Education	M
French	M,O
Geography	M
Geosciences	M,O
Health Psychology	M
History	M,O
Information Studies	M
International Affairs	M
Italian	M,O
Management of Technology	M,O
Marriage and Family Therapy	M,O
Mathematics	M,O
Molecular Biology	M
Music Education	M,O
Nurse Anesthesia	M,O
Physical Education	M,O
Physics	M,O
Psychology—General	M
Reading Education	M,O
Rehabilitation Counseling	M,O
School Psychology	M,O
Secondary Education	M
Social Psychology	M
Spanish	M,O
Special Education	M,O
Statistics	M,O
Vocational and Technical Education	M,O

CENTRAL EUROPEAN UNIVERSITY

Anthropology	M,D
Applied Mathematics	M,D
Business Administration and Management—General	M
Economics	M,D
Environmental Management and Policy	M,D
Finance and Banking	M
Gender Studies	M,D
History	M,D
Humanities	M,D*
International Affairs	M,D
International Business	M,D
Law	M,D
Legal and Justice Studies	M,D
Management Information Systems	M
Marketing	M
Medieval and Renaissance Studies	M,D
Philosophy	M,D
Political Science	M,D
Public Policy	M,D
Real Estate	M
Social Sciences	M,D
Sociology	M,D

CENTRAL METHODIST UNIVERSITY

Counselor Education	M
Education—General	M
Nursing and Healthcare Administration	M
Nursing—General	M

CENTRAL MICHIGAN UNIVERSITY

Accounting	M
Adult Education	M
American Indian/Native American Studies	M
American Studies	M,D,O
Automotive Engineering	M,O
Biological and Biomedical Sciences—General	M
Business Administration and Management—General	M,O
Chemistry	M
Child and Family Studies	M,O
Clinical Psychology	M,D
Clothing and Textiles	M,O
Communication Disorders	M,D
Communication—General	M
Community College Education	M
Computer Science	M
Conservation Biology	M
Corporate and Organizational Communication	M,O
Counseling Psychology	M,D,O
Counselor Education	M
Cultural Studies	M
Curriculum and Instruction	M,D,O
Early Childhood Education	M,O
Economics	M
Education—General	M,D,O
Educational Leadership and Administration	M,D,O
Educational Media/Instructional Technology	M,D,O
Elementary Education	M,O
Engineering and Applied Sciences—General	M
English as a Second Language	M
English	M
Exercise and Sports Science	M
Experimental Psychology	M,D
Family and Consumer Sciences-General	M,O
Film, Television, and Video Production	M
Film, Television, and Video Theory and Criticism	M
Finance and Banking	M
Gender Studies	M
Health Services Management and Hospital Administration	M,D,O
Higher Education	M,D,O
History	M,D,O
Hospitality Management	M
Human Development	M,O
Human Resources Management	M,O
Humanities	M
Industrial and Manufacturing Management	M
Industrial and Organizational Psychology	M,D
International Affairs	M,O
International Business	M,O
Leisure Studies	M
Management Information Systems	M,O
Marketing	M
Mass Communication	M
Materials Sciences	D
Mathematics Education	M,D
Mathematics	M,D
Media Studies	M
Middle School Education	M
Music Education	M
Music	M
Neuroscience	M,D
Nutrition	M,O
Physical Education	M
Physical Therapy	M,D
Physician Assistant Studies	M,D
Physics	M,D
Political Science	M,O
Psychology—General	M,D,O
Public Administration	M,O
Reading Education	M,O
Recreation and Park Management	M,O
Rehabilitation Sciences	M,D
School Psychology	D,O
Science Education	M
Secondary Education	M,O
Spanish	M
Special Education	M
Speech and Interpersonal Communication	M
Sports Management	M,O
Student Affairs	M,D,O
Western European Studies	M,D,O
Writing	M

CENTRAL STATE UNIVERSITY

Education—General	M

CENTRAL WASHINGTON UNIVERSITY

Accounting	M
Art/Fine Arts	M
Biological and Biomedical Sciences—General	M
Chemistry	M
Child and Family Studies	M
Counseling Psychology	M
Counselor Education	M
Education—General	M
Engineering and Applied Sciences—General	M
English as a Second Language	M
English	M

*M—master's degree; P—first professional degree; D—doctorate; O—other advanced degree; *—Close-Up and/or Announcement or Display in one of the other books in this series*

Experimental Psychology	M
Family and Consumer Sciences-General	M
Geology	M
Health Education	M
History	M
Home Economics Education	M
Industrial/Management Engineering	M
Interdisciplinary Studies	M
Mathematics	M
Music	M
Natural Resources	M
Nutrition	M
Physical Education	M
Psychology—General	M
Reading Education	M
School Psychology	M
Special Education	M
Theater	M

CENTRAL YESHIVA TOMCHEI TMIMIM-LUBAVITCH

Theology	

CENTRO DE ESTUDIOS AVANZADOS DE PUERTO RICO Y EL CARIBE

History	M,D
Latin American Studies	M,D

CHADRON STATE COLLEGE

Business Administration and Management—General	M
Business Education	M,O
Counselor Education	M,O
Education—General	M,O
Educational Leadership and Administration	M,O
Elementary Education	M,O
English Education	M,O
Secondary Education	M,O
Social Sciences Education	M,O

CHAMINADE UNIVERSITY OF HONOLULU

Business Administration and Management—General	M
Conflict Resolution and Mediation/Peace Studies	M
Counseling Psychology	M
Criminal Justice and Criminology	M,O
Education—General	M
Forensic Sciences	M
Homeland Security	M,O
Pastoral Ministry and Counseling	M
Social Sciences Education	M
Theology	M

CHAMPLAIN COLLEGE

Management of Technology	M

CHANCELLOR UNIVERSITY

Business Administration and Management—General	M

CHAPMAN UNIVERSITY

Business Administration and Management—General	M
Communication Disorders	M
Counselor Education	M
Cultural Studies	D
Curriculum and Instruction	M,D
Disability Studies	D
Economics	P,M
Education—General	M,D,O
Educational Leadership and Administration	M
Educational Psychology	M,O
Elementary Education	M
English	M
Environmental Law	P,M
Film, Television, and Video Production	M
Food Science and Technology	M
Health Communication	M
International Affairs	M
Law	P,M
Marriage and Family Therapy	M
Nutrition	M
Physical Therapy	D
Reading Education	M
School Psychology	M,D,O
Secondary Education	M
Special Education	M
Taxation	P,M
Writing	M

CHARLES R. DREW UNIVERSITY OF MEDICINE AND SCIENCE

Allopathic Medicine	P
Public Health—General	M

CHARLESTON SOUTHERN UNIVERSITY

Accounting	M
Business Administration and Management—General	M
Criminal Justice and Criminology	M
Education—General	M
Educational Leadership and Administration	M
Elementary Education	M
Finance and Banking	M
Health Services Management and Hospital Administration	M
Management Information Systems	M
Organizational Management	M
Secondary Education	M

CHARLOTTE SCHOOL OF LAW

Law	P

CHATHAM UNIVERSITY

Accounting	M
Allied Health—General	M
Art Education	M
Biological and Biomedical Sciences—General	M
Business Administration and Management—General	M
Computer Art and Design	M
Counseling Psychology	M,D
Developmental Psychology	M,D
Early Childhood Education	M
Education—General	M
Elementary Education	M
English Education	M
Environmental Biology	M
Environmental Education	M
Film, Television, and Video Production	M
Health Promotion	M
Health Psychology	M,D
Industrial and Organizational Psychology	M,D
Interior Design	M
Landscape Architecture	M
Marriage and Family Therapy	M,D
Mathematics Education	M
Nursing and Healthcare Administration	M,D
Nursing Education	M,D
Nursing—General	M,D
Occupational Therapy	M,D
Physical Therapy	D
Physician Assistant Studies	M
Science Education	M
Secondary Education	M
Social Sciences Education	M
Special Education	M
Sport Psychology	M,D
Writing	M

CHESTNUT HILL COLLEGE

Clinical Psychology	M,D,O
Counseling Psychology	M,O
Early Childhood Education	M
Education—General	M
Educational Leadership and Administration	M
Educational Media/ Instructional Technology	M,O
Elementary Education	M
Gerontology	M,O
Human Services	M,O
Psychology—General	M,D,O
Religion	M,O
Secondary Education	M

CHEYNEY UNIVERSITY OF PENNSYLVANIA

Adult Education	M
Early Childhood Education	O
Education—General	M,O
Educational Leadership and Administration	M,O
Elementary Education	M
Public Administration	M
Special Education	M

THE CHICAGO SCHOOL OF PROFESSIONAL PSYCHOLOGY

Clinical Psychology	M,D,O
Counseling Psychology	M,D,O
Counselor Education	M,D,O
Forensic Psychology	M,D
Industrial and Organizational Psychology	M
Psychology—General	M,D,O
School Psychology	O

THE CHICAGO SCHOOL OF PROFESSIONAL PSYCHOLOGY: DOWNTOWN LOS ANGELES CAMPUS

Clinical Psychology	M,D
Forensic Psychology	D
Industrial and Organizational Psychology	M
Marriage and Family Therapy	M,D
Psychology—General	M,D

THE CHICAGO SCHOOL OF PROFESSIONAL PSYCHOLOGY: GRAYSLAKE CAMPUS

Clinical Psychology	M
School Psychology	O

THE CHICAGO SCHOOL OF PROFESSIONAL PSYCHOLOGY: IRVINE CAMPUS

Clinical Psychology	M
Marriage and Family Therapy	M,D
Psychology—General	D

THE CHICAGO SCHOOL OF PROFESSIONAL PSYCHOLOGY: ONLINE

Forensic Psychology	M,O
Industrial and Organizational Psychology	M,D,O
Psychology—General	M,D

THE CHICAGO SCHOOL OF PROFESSIONAL PSYCHOLOGY: WESTWOOD CAMPUS

Clinical Psychology	M
Marriage and Family Therapy	M,D
Psychology—General	D

CHICAGO STATE UNIVERSITY

Biological and Biomedical Sciences—General	M
Computer Science	M
Counselor Education	M
Criminal Justice and Criminology	M
Early Childhood Education	M
Economic Development	M
Education—General	M,D
Educational Leadership and Administration	M,D
Educational Media/ Instructional Technology	M
Elementary Education	M
English	M
Foundations and Philosophy of Education	M
Geography	M
Higher Education	M,D
History	M
Library Science	M
Mathematics	M
Middle School Education	M
Multilingual and Multicultural Education	M
Physical Education	M
Reading Education	M
Secondary Education	M
Social Work	M
Special Education	M
Vocational and Technical Education	M
Writing	M

CHICAGO THEOLOGICAL SEMINARY

Ethics	P,M,D
Pastoral Ministry and Counseling	P,M,D
Religion	P,M,D
Theology	P,M,D

CHRISTENDOM COLLEGE

Theology	M

CHRISTIAN BROTHERS UNIVERSITY

Business Administration and Management—General	M,O
Curriculum and Instruction	M
Education—General	M
Educational Leadership and Administration	M
Engineering and Applied Sciences—General	M
Finance and Banking	M,O
Project Management	M,O
Religion	M

CHRISTIAN THEOLOGICAL SEMINARY

Marriage and Family Therapy	P,M,D

Pastoral Ministry and Counseling	P,M,D
Religion	P,M,D
Theology	P,M,D

CHRISTIE'S EDUCATION

Art History	M
Museum Studies	M

CHRISTOPHER NEWPORT UNIVERSITY

Applied Physics	M
Art Education	M
Computer Education	M
Computer Science	M
Education—General	M
Elementary Education	M
English Education	M
Environmental Sciences	M
Foreign Languages Education	M
History	M
Mathematics Education	M
Music Education	M
Physics	M
Science Education	M
Social Sciences Education	M
Theater	M

CHRIST THE KING SEMINARY

Pastoral Ministry and Counseling	P,M,O
Theology	P,M,O

CHURCH DIVINITY SCHOOL OF THE PACIFIC

Theology	P,M,D,O

CHURCH OF GOD THEOLOGICAL SEMINARY

Pastoral Ministry and Counseling	P,M,D
Theology	P,M,D

CINCINNATI CHRISTIAN UNIVERSITY

Pastoral Ministry and Counseling	M
Religion	P,M
Theology	P,M

THE CITADEL, THE MILITARY COLLEGE OF SOUTH CAROLINA

Biological and Biomedical Sciences—General	M
Business Administration and Management—General	M
Computer Science	M
Counselor Education	M
Education—General	M,O
Educational Leadership and Administration	M,O
Elementary Education	M
English Education	M
English	M
Health Education	M
History	M
Information Science	M
Mathematics Education	M
Physical Education	M
Psychology—General	M
Reading Education	M
School Psychology	M,O
Science Education	M
Secondary Education	M
Social Sciences Education	M
Social Sciences	M
Sports Management	M
Student Affairs	M

CITY COLLEGE OF THE CITY UNIVERSITY OF NEW YORK

Architecture	M
Art History	M
Art/Fine Arts	M
Atmospheric Sciences	M,D
Biochemistry	M,D
Biological and Biomedical Sciences—General	M,D
Biomedical Engineering	M,D
Chemical Engineering	M,D
Chemistry	M,D
Civil Engineering	M,D
Clinical Psychology	M,D
Computer Science	M,D
Counseling Psychology	M
Early Childhood Education	M
Economics	M
Education—General	M,O
Educational Leadership and Administration	M,O
Electrical Engineering	M,D
Engineering and Applied Sciences—General	M,D*
English Education	M,O
English	M
Environmental Sciences	M,D
Experimental Psychology	M,D
Geosciences	M,D
Graphic Design	M
History	M
International Affairs	M
Landscape Architecture	M,O
Mathematics Education	M,O
Mathematics	M
Mechanical Engineering	M,D
Media Studies	M
Middle School Education	M,O
Multilingual and Multicultural Education	M
Museum Studies	M
Music	M
Physics	M,D*
Psychology—General	M,D
Public Administration	M,D
Reading Education	M
Science Education	M
Secondary Education	M,O
Social Sciences Education	M,O
Sociology	M
Spanish	M
Special Education	M
Urban Design	M
Writing	M

CITY OF HOPE NATIONAL MEDICAL CENTER/BECKMAN RESEARCH INSTITUTE

Biological and Biomedical Sciences—General	D

CITY UNIVERSITY OF NEW YORK SCHOOL OF LAW AT QUEENS COLLEGE

Law	P

CITY UNIVERSITY OF SEATTLE

Accounting	M,O
Business Administration and Management—General	M,O
Computer and Information Systems Security	M,O
Counseling Psychology	M
Curriculum and Instruction	M,O
Education—General	M,O
Educational Leadership and Administration	M,O
Educational Media/Instructional Technology	M,O
Elementary Education	M,O
Finance and Banking	M,O
International Business	M,O
Management Information Systems	M,O
Management of Technology	M,O
Marketing	M,O
Organizational Management	M,O
Project Management	M,O
Reading Education	M,O
School Psychology	M,O
Special Education	M,O
Sustainability Management	M,O

CLAFLIN UNIVERSITY

Biotechnology	M
Business Administration and Management—General	M
Education—General	M

CLAREMONT GRADUATE UNIVERSITY

African Studies	M,D,O
American Studies	M,D,O
Applied Mathematics	M,D
Art/Fine Arts	M
Arts Administration	M
Botany	M,D
Business Administration and Management—General	M,D,O
Cognitive Sciences	M,D,O
Comparative Literature	M,D
Computational Biology	M,D
Computational Sciences	M,D
Computer Art and Design	M
Cultural Studies	M,D,O
Developmental Psychology	M,D,O
Economic Development	M,D,O
Economics	M,D,O
Education—General	M,D,O
Educational Leadership and Administration	M,D,O
Educational Measurement and Evaluation	M,D,O
Electronic Commerce	M,D,O
English	M,D
Ethics	M,D
Film, Television, and Video Theory and Criticism	M,D
Financial Engineering	M*
Health Informatics	M,D,O
Health Psychology	M,D,O
Higher Education	M,D,O
History	M,D,O
Human Development	M,D,O
Human Resources Development	M,D,O
Human Resources Management	M
Humanities	M,D,O
Industrial and Organizational Psychology	M,D,O
Information Science	M,D,O
Information Studies	M,D,O
International Affairs	M,D
International Economics	M,D,O
Management Information Systems	M,D,O
Management Strategy and Policy	M,D,O
Mathematics	M,D
Media Studies	M,D,O
Museum Studies	M,D,O
Music	M,D
Operations Research	M,D
Philosophy	M,D
Photography	M
Political Science	M,D
Psychology—General	M,D,O
Public Policy	M,D,O
Religion	M,D
Social Psychology	M,D,O
Special Education	M,D,O
Statistics	M,D
Student Affairs	M,D,O
Systems Science	M,D,O
Telecommunications	M,D,O
Theology	M,D
Urban Education	M,D,O
Western European Studies	M,D,O
Women's Studies	M,D
Writing	M,D

CLAREMONT SCHOOL OF THEOLOGY

Pastoral Ministry and Counseling	D
Religion	M,D
Religious Education	M,D
Theology	P,M,D

CLARION UNIVERSITY OF PENNSYLVANIA

Biological and Biomedical Sciences—General	M
Business Administration and Management—General	M
Communication Disorders	M
Communication—General	M
Curriculum and Instruction	M
Early Childhood Education	M
Education—General	M,O
Elementary Education	M
English Education	M
English	M
Library Science	M,O
Nursing—General	M
Reading Education	M
Rehabilitation Sciences	M
Science Education	M
Social Sciences Education	M
Special Education	M
Vocational and Technical Education	M

CLARK ATLANTA UNIVERSITY

Accounting	M
African-American Studies	M,D
Biological and Biomedical Sciences—General	M,D
Business Administration and Management—General	M
Chemistry	M,D
Computer Science	M
Counselor Education	M
Criminal Justice and Criminology	M
Curriculum and Instruction	M
Economics	M
Education—General	M,D,O
Educational Leadership and Administration	M,D,O
Educational Psychology	M
English	M,D
History	M,D
Information Science	M
Mathematics	M
Physics	M
Political Science	M,D
Public Administration	M
Romance Languages	M,D
Social Work	M,D
Sociology	M
Women's Studies	M,D

CLARKE COLLEGE

Business Administration and Management—General	M
Early Childhood Education	M
Education—General	M
Educational Leadership and Administration	M
Educational Media/Instructional Technology	M
Family Nurse Practitioner Studies	M,O

*M—master's degree; P—first professional degree; D—doctorate; O—other advanced degree; *—Close-Up and/or Announcement or Display in one of the other books in this series*

Nursing and Healthcare Administration	M,O
Nursing Education	M,O
Nursing—General	M,O
Physical Therapy	D
Reading Education	M
Special Education	M

CLARKSON COLLEGE

Adult Nursing	M,O
Family Nurse Practitioner Studies	M,O
Nursing and Healthcare Administration	M,O
Nursing Education	M,O
Nursing—General	M,O

CLARKSON UNIVERSITY

Analytical Chemistry	M,D
Business Administration and Management—General	M
Chemical Engineering	M,D
Chemistry	M,D
Civil Engineering	M,D
Computer Engineering	M,D
Computer Science	M
Electrical Engineering	M,D
Engineering and Applied Sciences—General	M,D*
Engineering Management	M
Entrepreneurship	M
Environmental Engineering	M,D
Environmental Management and Policy	M
Environmental Sciences	M,D
Information Science	M*
Inorganic Chemistry	M,D
International Business	M
Mathematics	M,D
Mechanical Engineering	M,D
Organic Chemistry	M,D
Physical Chemistry	M,D
Physical Therapy	D
Physics	M,D
Supply Chain Management	M

CLARK UNIVERSITY

Accounting	M
American Studies	D
Biological and Biomedical Sciences—General	M,D
Business Administration and Management—General	M
Chemistry	M,D
Clinical Psychology	D
Communication—General	M
Developmental Psychology	D
Economics	D
Education—General	M
English	M
Environmental Management and Policy	M
Finance and Banking	M
Geographic Information Systems	M
Geography	M,D
Health Services Management and Hospital Administration	M
History	M,D,O
Holocaust Studies	D
Information Science	M
International Business	M
International Development	M
Liberal Studies	M
Management Information Systems	M
Marketing	M
Physics	M,D
Psychology—General	D
Public Administration	M,O
Social Psychology	D
Sustainable Development	M
Urban and Regional Planning	M

CLAYTON STATE UNIVERSITY

Business Administration and Management—General	M
Education—General	M
English Education	M
Health Services Management and Hospital Administration	M
Liberal Studies	M
Mathematics Education	M
Nursing—General	M

CLEARWATER CHRISTIAN COLLEGE

Educational Leadership and Administration	M

CLEARY UNIVERSITY

Accounting	M,O
Business Administration and Management—General	M,O
Finance and Banking	M,O
Nonprofit Management	M,O
Organizational Management	M,O

CLEMSON UNIVERSITY

Accounting	M
Agricultural Education	M
Agricultural Sciences—General	M,D
Animal Sciences	M,D
Applied Economics	M,D
Applied Mathematics	M,D
Aquaculture	M,D
Architecture	M
Art/Fine Arts	M
Astronomy	M,D
Astrophysics	M,D
Atmospheric Sciences	M,D
Automotive Engineering	M,D
Biochemistry	M,D
Bioengineering	M,D
Biological and Biomedical Sciences—General	M,D
Biophysics	M,D
Biosystems Engineering	M,D
Business Administration and Management—General	M
Chemical Engineering	M,D
Chemistry	M,D
Civil Engineering	M,D
Communication—General	M,D
Computational Sciences	M,D
Computer Art and Design	M
Computer Engineering	M,D
Computer Science	M,D
Construction Management	M
Counselor Education	M
Curriculum and Instruction	D
Ecology	M,D
Economics	M,D
Education—General	M,D,O
Educational Leadership and Administration	M,D,O
Electrical Engineering	M,D
Elementary Education	M
Engineering and Applied Sciences—General	M,D
English Education	M
English	M,D
Entomology	M,D
Environmental Design	D
Environmental Engineering	M,D
Environmental Management and Policy	M,D
Environmental Sciences	M,D
Ergonomics and Human Factors	D
Evolutionary Biology	M,D
Fish, Game, and Wildlife Management	M,D
Food Science and Technology	M,D
Forestry	M,D
Genetics	M,D
Historic Preservation	M
History	M
Human Development	M
Human Resources Development	M
Hydrogeology	M
Industrial and Organizational Psychology	D
Industrial/Management Engineering	M,D
Landscape Architecture	M
Manufacturing Engineering	M
Marketing	M
Materials Engineering	M,D
Materials Sciences	M,D
Mathematics Education	M
Mathematics	M,D
Mechanical Engineering	M,D
Microbiology	M,D
Middle School Education	M
Molecular Biology	M,D
Nursing—General	M
Nutrition	M
Operations Research	M,D
Physics	M,D
Plant Biology	M,D
Plant Sciences	M,D
Polymer Science and Engineering	M,D
Psychology—General	M,D
Public Administration	M,D
Public Policy	M,D
Reading Education	M
Real Estate	M
Recreation and Park Management	M,D
Rhetoric	D
Science Education	M
Secondary Education	M
Sociology	M
Special Education	M
Statistics	M,D
Textile Sciences and Engineering	M,D
Travel and Tourism	M,D
Urban and Regional Planning	M
Veterinary Sciences	M,D
Writing	M

CLEVELAND CHIROPRACTIC COLLEGE–KANSAS CITY CAMPUS

Chiropractic	P*

CLEVELAND CHIROPRACTIC COLLEGE–LOS ANGELES CAMPUS

Chiropractic	P*

CLEVELAND INSTITUTE OF MUSIC

Music	M,D,O

CLEVELAND STATE UNIVERSITY

Accounting	M
Addictions/Substance Abuse Counseling	M,O
Adult Education	M,O
Allied Health—General	M
Analytical Chemistry	M,D
Art Education	M
Art History	M
Art/Fine Arts	M
Bioethics	M,O
Biological and Biomedical Sciences—General	M,D
Biomedical Engineering	D
Business Administration and Management—General	M,D
Chemical Engineering	M,D
Chemistry	M,D
Civil Engineering	M,D
Clinical Psychology	M,D,O
Communication Disorders	M
Communication—General	M,O
Community Health Nursing	M
Computer Science	M,D
Condensed Matter Physics	M
Counseling Psychology	M,D,O
Counselor Education	M,D,O
Early Childhood Education	M
Economic Development	M,D,O
Economics	M,D,O
Education of the Multiply Handicapped	M
Education—General	M,D,O
Educational Leadership and Administration	M,D,O
Electrical Engineering	M,D
Engineering and Applied Sciences—General	M,D
English as a Second Language	M
English	M
Environmental Engineering	M,D
Environmental Management and Policy	M,O
Environmental Sciences	M,D
Exercise and Sports Science	M
Experimental Psychology	M,D,O
Finance and Banking	M,D,O
Foreign Languages Education	M
Forensic Nursing	M
French	M
Geographic Information Systems	M,D,O
Gerontology	M,D,O
Health Communication	M,O
Health Education	M
Health Services Management and Hospital Administration	M
History	M
Human Resources Management	M
Industrial and Labor Relations	P,M
Industrial and Manufacturing Management	D
Industrial and Organizational Psychology	M,D,O
Industrial/Management Engineering	M,D
Information Science	M,D
Inorganic Chemistry	M,D
International Business	M,D,O
Latin American Studies	M
Law	P,M
Linguistics	M
Management Information Systems	M,D
Marketing	M,D,O
Mathematics Education	M
Mathematics	M
Mechanical Engineering	M,D
Medical Imaging	M
Medical Physics	M
Middle School Education	M
Molecular Medicine	M,D
Museum Studies	M,D
Music Education	M
Music	M
Nonprofit Management	M,D,O
Nursing Education	M
Nursing—General	M
Occupational Therapy	M
Optical Sciences	M
Organic Chemistry	M,D

Philosophy M,O
Physical Chemistry M,D
Physical Education M
Physical Therapy D
Physician Assistant Studies M,D
Physics M
Psychology—General M,D,O
Public Administration M,O
Public Health—General M
Real Estate M,D,O
School Psychology M,D,O
Science Education M
Social Work M
Sociology M
Software Engineering M,D
Spanish M
Special Education M
Sport Psychology M
Sports Management M
Student Affairs M,O
Taxation M
Urban and Regional Planning M,O
Urban Design M,O
Urban Education D
Urban Studies M,D,O
Writing M

COASTAL CAROLINA UNIVERSITY

Accounting M
Business Administration and Management—General M
Early Childhood Education M
Education—General M
Elementary Education M
Marine Sciences M
Secondary Education M

COE COLLEGE

Education—General M

COLD SPRING HARBOR LABORATORY, WATSON SCHOOL OF BIOLOGICAL SCIENCES

Biological and Biomedical Sciences—General D*

COLEMAN COLLEGE

Information Science M
Management of Technology M

COLGATE ROCHESTER CROZER DIVINITY SCHOOL

Theology P,M,D,O

COLGATE UNIVERSITY

Secondary Education M

THE COLLEGE AT BROCKPORT, STATE UNIVERSITY OF NEW YORK

Accounting M
American Studies M
Art/Fine Arts M
Arts Administration M,O
Biological and Biomedical Sciences—General M
Communication—General M
Community Health M
Computational Sciences M
Counseling Psychology M,O
Counselor Education M,O
Curriculum and Instruction M
Dance M
Education—General M,O
Educational Leadership and Administration O
English Education M
English M
Environmental Sciences M
Foreign Languages Education M,O
Health Education M
Health Services Management and Hospital Administration M,O
History M
Leisure Studies M
Liberal Studies M
Mathematics Education M
Mathematics M
Middle School Education M
Multilingual and Multicultural Education M,O
Nonprofit Management M,O
Physical Education M
Psychology—General M
Public Administration M,O
Reading Education M
Recreation and Park Management M
Science Education M
Social Sciences Education M
Social Work M
Sports Management M
Writing M

COLLÈGE DOMINICAIN DE PHILOSOPHIE ET DE THÉOLOGIE

Philosophy M,D
Theology M,D,O

COLLEGE FOR FINANCIAL PLANNING

Finance and Banking M

COLLEGE OF CHARLESTON

Accounting M
Arts Administration M,O
Business Administration and Management—General M
Communication—General M
Computer Science M
Corporate and Organizational Communication O
Early Childhood Education M
Education—General M,O
Elementary Education M
English as a Second Language O
English M
Environmental Sciences M*
Foreign Languages Education M
Historic Preservation M
History M
Legal and Justice Studies M,O
Management Information Systems M
Marine Biology M*
Mathematics Education M
Mathematics M,O
Music Education M
Public Administration M
Science Education M
Special Education M
Translation and Interpretation O

COLLEGE OF EMMANUEL AND ST. CHAD

Theology P,M

THE COLLEGE OF IDAHO

Education—General M

COLLEGE OF MOUNT ST. JOSEPH

Art Education M
Early Childhood Education M
Education—General M
Educational Leadership and Administration M
Middle School Education M
Multilingual and Multicultural Education M
Music Education M
Nursing—General M
Organizational Management M
Pastoral Ministry and Counseling M
Physical Therapy M,D
Reading Education M
Secondary Education M
Theology M

COLLEGE OF MOUNT SAINT VINCENT

Adult Nursing M,O
Education—General M,O
Educational Media/Instructional Technology M,O
Family Nurse Practitioner Studies M,O
Gerontological Nursing M,O
Middle School Education M,O
Multilingual and Multicultural Education M,O
Nursing and Healthcare Administration M,O
Nursing Education M,O
Nursing—General M,O
Urban Education M,O

THE COLLEGE OF NEW JERSEY

Addictions/Substance Abuse Counseling M,O
Communication Disorders M
Counselor Education M
Early Childhood Education M
Education—General M,O
Educational Leadership and Administration M,O
Educational Media/Instructional Technology M
Elementary Education M
English as a Second Language M,O
English M
Foreign Languages Education M
Health Education M
International and Comparative Education M,O
Marriage and Family Therapy O
Nursing—General M,O
Physical Education M
Reading Education M,O
Secondary Education M
Spanish M
Special Education M,O

THE COLLEGE OF NEW ROCHELLE

Acute Care/Critical Care Nursing M,O
Art Education M
Art Therapy M
Art/Fine Arts M
Communication—General M,O
Counseling Psychology M,O
Early Childhood Education M
Education of the Gifted M,O
Education—General M,O
Educational Leadership and Administration M,O
Elementary Education M
English as a Second Language M,O
Family Nurse Practitioner Studies M,O
Gerontology M,O
Graphic Design M
Human Resources Development M
Multilingual and Multicultural Education M,O
Nursing and Healthcare Administration M,O
Nursing Education M,O
Nursing—General M,O
Reading Education M
School Psychology M
Social Psychology M
Special Education M

COLLEGE OF NOTRE DAME OF MARYLAND

Business Administration and Management—General M
Communication—General M
Education—General M
Educational Leadership and Administration M,D
English as a Second Language M
Liberal Studies M
Nonprofit Management M

COLLEGE OF SAINT ELIZABETH

Business Administration and Management—General M
Counseling Psychology M,O
Education—General M,D,O
Educational Leadership and Administration M,D,O
Educational Media/Instructional Technology M,D,O
Forensic Psychology M,O
Health Services Management and Hospital Administration M
Higher Education M,O
Nursing—General M
Nutrition M,O
Psychology—General M,O
Student Affairs M,O
Theology M

COLLEGE OF ST. JOSEPH

Addictions/Substance Abuse Counseling M
Business Administration and Management—General M
Clinical Psychology M
Counseling Psychology M
Counselor Education M
Education—General M
Elementary Education M
English Education M
Psychology—General M
Reading Education M
School Psychology M
Secondary Education M
Social Psychology M
Social Sciences Education M
Special Education M

THE COLLEGE OF SAINT ROSE

Accounting M
Art Education M,O
Business Administration and Management—General M
Business Education M,O
Communication Disorders M
Computer Science M
Counselor Education M
Curriculum and Instruction M,O
Early Childhood Education M,O
Education—General M,O*
Educational Leadership and Administration M,O
Educational Media/Instructional Technology M,O
Educational Psychology M,O
Elementary Education M,O
English M
History M

*M—master's degree; P—first professional degree; D—doctorate; O—other advanced degree; *—Close-Up and/or Announcement or Display in one of the other books in this series*

Information Science M
Mass Communication M
Multilingual and Multicultural Education M,O
Music Education M,O
Music M
Nonprofit Management O
Political Science M
Reading Education M,O
School Psychology M,O
Secondary Education M,O
Special Education M,O
Student Affairs M,O

THE COLLEGE OF ST. SCHOLASTICA

Business Administration and Management—General M,O
Education—General M,O
Educational Media/Instructional Technology M
Exercise and Sports Science M
Health Informatics M,O
Management Information Systems M,O
Nursing—General M,O
Occupational Therapy M
Physical Therapy D

COLLEGE OF SANTA FE

Business Administration and Management—General M
Counselor Education M
Curriculum and Instruction M
Education—General M
Educational Leadership and Administration M
Finance and Banking M
Human Resources Management M
Multilingual and Multicultural Education M
Special Education M

COLLEGE OF STATEN ISLAND OF THE CITY UNIVERSITY OF NEW YORK

Adult Nursing M,O
Biological and Biomedical Sciences—General M
Business Administration and Management—General M
Computer Science M
Counseling Psychology M
Education—General M,O
Educational Leadership and Administration O
Elementary Education M
English M
Environmental Sciences M
Film, Television, and Video Theory and Criticism M
Gerontological Nursing M,O
History M
Liberal Studies M
Media Studies M
Neuroscience M
Nursing Education O
Nursing—General M,O
Secondary Education M
Special Education M

COLLEGE OF THE ATLANTIC

Environmental Management and Policy M

COLLEGE OF THE HUMANITIES AND SCIENCES, HARRISON MIDDLETON UNIVERSITY

Comparative Literature M,D
Education—General M,D
Humanities M,D
Interdisciplinary Studies M,D
Legal and Justice Studies M,D
Philosophy M,D
Religion M,D
Science Education M,D
Social Sciences M,D

THE COLLEGE OF WILLIAM AND MARY

Accounting M
Addictions/Substance Abuse Counseling M,D
American Studies M,D
Anthropology M,D
Applied Science and Technology M,D
Biological and Biomedical Sciences—General M
Business Administration and Management—General M
Chemistry M
Clinical Psychology M,D
Computational Sciences M
Computer Science M,D
Counselor Education M,D
Curriculum and Instruction M,D
Education of the Gifted M
Education—General M,D,O
Educational Leadership and Administration M,D
Educational Media/Instructional Technology M,D
Educational Policy M,D
Elementary Education M
English Education M
Experimental Psychology M,D
Foreign Languages Education M
History M,D
Law P,M
Marine Sciences M,D
Marriage and Family Therapy M,D
Mathematics Education M
Operations Research M
Physics M,D
Psychology—General M,D
Public Policy M
Reading Education M
School Psychology M,O
Science Education M
Secondary Education M
Social Sciences Education M
Special Education M

COLLÈGE UNIVERSITAIRE DE SAINT-BONIFACE

Canadian Studies M
Education—General M

COLORADO CHRISTIAN UNIVERSITY

Business Administration and Management—General M
Counseling Psychology M
Curriculum and Instruction M
Education—General M

THE COLORADO COLLEGE

Art Education M
Education—General M
Elementary Education M
English Education M
Foreign Languages Education M
Mathematics Education M
Music Education M
Science Education M
Secondary Education M
Social Sciences Education M

COLORADO SCHOOL OF MINES

Applied Physics M,D
Chemical Engineering M,D
Chemistry M,D
Computer Science M,D
Electronic Materials M,D
Engineering and Applied Sciences—General M,D,O
Engineering Management M,D
Environmental Engineering M,D
Environmental Sciences M,D
Geochemistry M,D
Geological Engineering M,D
Geology M,D
Geophysics M,D
International Affairs M,O
Management of Technology M,D
Materials Engineering M,D
Materials Sciences M,D
Mathematics M,D
Metallurgical Engineering and Metallurgy M,D
Mineral Economics M,D
Mineral/Mining Engineering M,D
Nuclear Engineering M,D
Petroleum Engineering M,D
Physics M,D
Systems Engineering M,D

COLORADO SCHOOL OF TRADITIONAL CHINESE MEDICINE

Acupuncture and Oriental Medicine M

COLORADO STATE UNIVERSITY

Accounting M
Adult Education M,D
Advertising and Public Relations M,D
Agricultural Economics and Agribusiness M,D
Agricultural Sciences—General M,D
Agronomy and Soil Sciences M,D
Animal Sciences M,D
Anthropology M
Art/Fine Arts M
Atmospheric Sciences M,D
Biochemistry M,D
Biological and Biomedical Sciences—General M,D
Biomedical Engineering M,D
Botany M,D
Business Administration and Management—General M
Cell Biology M,D
Chemical Engineering M,D
Chemistry M,D
Child and Family Studies M
Civil Engineering M,D
Community College Education M,D
Computer Science M,D
Conservation Biology M,D
Construction Management M
Consumer Economics M
Counselor Education M,D
Ecology M,D
Economics M,D
Education—General M,D
Educational Leadership and Administration M,D
Electrical Engineering M,D
Engineering and Applied Sciences—General M,D
Entomology M,D
Environmental and Occupational Health M,D
Exercise and Sports Science M,D
Fish, Game, and Wildlife Management M,D
Food Science and Technology M,D
Foreign Languages Education M
Forestry M,D
Geosciences M,D
History M
Horticulture M,D
Human Development M
Hydrology M,D
Immunology M,D
Management Information Systems M
Mass Communication M,D
Mathematics M,D
Mechanical Engineering M,D
Microbiology M,D*
Molecular Biology M,D
Music M
Natural Resources M,D
Neuroscience D
Nutrition M,D
Occupational Therapy M
Organizational Management M
Pathology M,D
Philosophy M
Physics M,D
Plant Pathology M,D
Plant Sciences M,D
Political Science M,D
Psychology—General M,D
Radiation Biology M,D
Range Science M,D
Recreation and Park Management M,D
Social Work M
Sociology M,D
Speech and Interpersonal Communication M
Statistics M,D
Student Affairs M,D
Sustainability Management M
Technical Communication M,D
Technical Writing M,D
Veterinary Medicine P
Veterinary Sciences M,D
Vocational and Technical Education M,D
Water Resources M,D
Writing M
Zoology M,D

COLORADO STATE UNIVERSITY–PUEBLO

Applied Science and Technology M
Art Education M
Biochemistry M
Biological and Biomedical Sciences—General M
Business Administration and Management—General M
Chemistry M
Education—General M
Educational Media/Instructional Technology M
Engineering and Applied Sciences—General M
Foreign Languages Education M
Health Education M
Industrial/Management Engineering M
Music Education M
Nursing—General M
Physical Education M
Special Education M
Systems Engineering M

COLORADO TECHNICAL UNIVERSITY COLORADO SPRINGS

Accounting M,D
Business Administration and Management—General M,D

Computer and Information Systems Security	M,D
Computer Engineering	M
Computer Science	M,D
Conflict Resolution and Mediation/Peace Studies	M,D
Criminal Justice and Criminology	M
Database Systems	M,D
Electrical Engineering	M
Finance and Banking	M,D
Human Resources Management	M,D
Industrial and Manufacturing Management	M,D
Logistics	M,D
Management of Technology	M,D
Marketing	M,D
Project Management	M,D
Software Engineering	M,D
Systems Engineering	M

COLORADO TECHNICAL UNIVERSITY DENVER

Accounting	M
Business Administration and Management—General	M
Computer and Information Systems Security	M
Computer Engineering	M
Computer Science	M
Conflict Resolution and Mediation/Peace Studies	M
Criminal Justice and Criminology	M
Database Systems	M
Electrical Engineering	M
Finance and Banking	M
Human Resources Management	M
Industrial and Manufacturing Management	M
Management of Technology	M
Marketing	M
Project Management	M
Software Engineering	M
Systems Engineering	M

COLORADO TECHNICAL UNIVERSITY SIOUX FALLS

Business Administration and Management—General	M
Computer and Information Systems Security	M
Computer Science	M
Criminal Justice and Criminology	M
Health Services Management and Hospital Administration	M
Human Resources Management	M
Management Information Systems	M
Management of Technology	M
Organizational Management	M
Project Management	M
Software Engineering	M

COLUMBIA COLLEGE (MO)

Business Administration and Management—General	M
Criminal Justice and Criminology	M
Education—General	M

COLUMBIA COLLEGE (SC)

Conflict Resolution and Mediation/Peace Studies	M,O
Education—General	M
Elementary Education	M
Organizational Behavior	M,O

COLUMBIA COLLEGE CHICAGO

Architecture	M
Arts Administration	M
Comparative and Interdisciplinary Arts	M
Education—General	M
Elementary Education	M
English Education	M
Entertainment Management	M
Film, Television, and Video Production	M
Interior Design	M
Journalism	M
Media Studies	M
Multilingual and Multicultural Education	M
Photography	M
Therapies—Dance, Drama, and Music	M,O
Urban Education	M
Writing	M

COLUMBIA INTERNATIONAL UNIVERSITY

Counselor Education	M,D,O
Cultural Studies	P,M,D,O
Curriculum and Instruction	M,D,O
Early Childhood Education	M,D,O
Education—General	M,D,O
Educational Leadership and Administration	M,D,O
Educational Media/Instructional Technology	M,D,O
Elementary Education	M,D,O
English as a Second Language	M,D,O
Higher Education	M,D,O
Missions and Missiology	P,M,D,O
Multilingual and Multicultural Education	M,D,O
Pastoral Ministry and Counseling	P,M,D,O
Religious Education	P,M,D,O
Special Education	M,D,O
Theology	P,M,D,O

COLUMBIA SOUTHERN UNIVERSITY

Business Administration and Management—General	M,D
Criminal Justice and Criminology	M
Electronic Commerce	M
Environmental and Occupational Health	M
Finance and Banking	M
Health Services Management and Hospital Administration	M
Hospitality Management	M
Human Resources Management	M
International Business	M
Marketing	M

COLUMBIA THEOLOGICAL SEMINARY

Theology	P,M,D

COLUMBIA UNION COLLEGE

Business Administration and Management—General	M
Nursing and Healthcare Administration	M
Nursing—General	M
Religion	M

COLUMBIA UNIVERSITY

Accounting	M,D
Actuarial Science	M
Acute Care/Critical Care Nursing	M,O
Adult Nursing	M,O
African Studies	O
African-American Studies	M
Allopathic Medicine	P
American Studies	M
Anatomy	M,D
Anthropology	M,D
Applied Mathematics	M,D,O
Applied Physics	M,D,O*
Archaeology	M,D
Architecture	M,D
Art History	M,D
Art/Fine Arts	M
Asian Languages	M,D
Asian Studies	M,D,O
Astronomy	M,D
Atmospheric Sciences	M,D*
Biochemistry	M,D
Biological and Biomedical Sciences—General	P,M,D,O*
Biomedical Engineering	M,D*
Biophysics	M,D
Biopsychology	M,D
Biostatistics	M,D
Business Administration and Management—General	M,D
Cell Biology	M,D
Chemical Engineering	M,D
Chemical Physics	M,D
Chemistry	M,D
Civil Engineering	M,D,O
Classics	M,D
Communication—General	M,D
Community Health	M,D
Comparative Literature	M,D
Computer Engineering	M,D,O
Computer Science	M,D,O*
Conflict Resolution and Mediation/Peace Studies	M
Conservation Biology	M,D,O*
Construction Engineering	M,D,O
Construction Management	M,D,O
Corporate and Organizational Communication	M
Dentistry	P
Developmental Biology	M,D
East European and Russian Studies	M,O
Ecology	D,O
Economics	M,D
Electrical Engineering	M,D,O*
Engineering and Applied Sciences—General	M,D,O*
Engineering Management	M,D,O
English	M,D
Entrepreneurship	M
Environmental and Occupational Health	M,D
Environmental Design	M
Environmental Engineering	M,D,O
Environmental Management and Policy	M*
Environmental Sciences	M
Epidemiology	M,D
Evolutionary Biology	D,O
Experimental Psychology	M,D
Family Nurse Practitioner Studies	M,O
Film, Television, and Video Production	M
Finance and Banking	M,D
Financial Engineering	M,D,O
French	M,D
Genetics	M,D
Geochemistry	M,D
Geodetic Sciences	M,D
Geophysics	M,D
Geosciences	M,D
German	M,D
Gerontological Nursing	M,O
Health Services Management and Hospital Administration	M
Historic Preservation	M,O
History	M,D
Human Resources Management	M
Industrial/Management Engineering	M,D,O*
Information Studies	M
Inorganic Chemistry	M,D
Interdisciplinary Studies	M
International Affairs	M*
International Business	M
Italian	M,D
Jewish Studies	M,D
Journalism	M,D*
Kinesiology and Movement Studies	M,D
Landscape Architecture	M
Latin American Studies	M,O
Law	P,M,D
Liberal Studies	M
Management of Technology	M
Marketing	M,D
Materials Engineering	M,D,O
Materials Sciences	M,D,O
Maternal and Child Health	M
Maternal and Child/Neonatal Nursing	M,O
Mathematics	M,D*
Mechanical Engineering	M,D,O
Mechanics	M,D,O
Medical Informatics	M,D,O
Medical Physics	M,D,O
Medical/Surgical Nursing	M,O
Medieval and Renaissance Studies	M
Metallurgical Engineering and Metallurgy	M,D,O
Meteorology	M*
Microbiology	M,D
Mineral/Mining Engineering	M,D,O
Molecular Biology	M,D
Music	M,D
Near and Middle Eastern Languages	M,D
Near and Middle Eastern Studies	M,D,O
Neurobiology	D
Nonprofit Management	M
Nurse Anesthesia	M,O
Nurse Midwifery	M
Nursing—General	M,D,O*
Nutrition	M,D*
Occupational Therapy	M,D
Oceanography	M,D
Oncology Nursing	M,O
Operations Research	M,D,O
Oral and Dental Sciences	M,D,O
Organic Chemistry	M,D
Pathobiology	M,D
Pathology	M,D
Pediatric Nursing	M,O
Pharmacology	M,D
Philosophy	M,D
Photography	M
Physical Therapy	D
Physics	M,D
Physiology	M,D
Planetary and Space Sciences	M,D
Political Science	M,D
Psychiatric Nursing	M,O
Psychology—General	M,D
Public Administration	M
Public Health—General	M,D
Public Policy	M
Real Estate	M
Religion	M,D
Romance Languages	M,D
Russian	M,D
Science Education	M,D,O
Slavic Languages	M,D
Social Psychology	M,D
Social Sciences	M
Social Work	M,D

*M—master's degree; P—first professional degree; D—doctorate; O—other advanced degree; *—Close-Up and/or Announcement or Display in one of the other books in this series*

Sociology	M,D
Spanish	M,D
Sports Management	M
Statistics	M,D
Sustainable Development	M,D
Theater	M,D*
Toxicology	M,D
Urban and Regional Planning	M,D
Western European Studies	M,O
Women's Health Nursing	O
Writing	M

COLUMBUS STATE UNIVERSITY

Art Education	M
Business Administration and Management—General	M
Computer Science	M
Counseling Psychology	M,O
Counselor Education	M,O
Criminal Justice and Criminology	M
Early Childhood Education	M,O
Education—General	M,O
Educational Leadership and Administration	M,O
English Education	M,O
Environmental Sciences	M
Health Services Management and Hospital Administration	M
Mathematics Education	M,O
Middle School Education	M,O
Music Education	M
Physical Education	M,O
Public Administration	M
Science Education	M,O
Secondary Education	M,O
Social Sciences Education	M,O
Special Education	M,O

CONCORDIA LUTHERAN SEMINARY

Theology	P,O

CONCORDIA SEMINARY

Theology	P,M,D,O

CONCORDIA THEOLOGICAL SEMINARY

Theology	P,M,D

CONCORDIA UNIVERSITY (CA)

Business Administration and Management—General	M
Curriculum and Instruction	M
Education—General	M
Educational Leadership and Administration	M
International Affairs	M
Physical Education	M
Sports Management	M
Theology	M

CONCORDIA UNIVERSITY (CANADA)

Accounting	M,D,O
Adult Education	M,O
Aerospace/Aeronautical Engineering	M
Anthropology	M
Applied Arts and Design—General	O
Art Education	M,D
Art History	M,D
Art Therapy	M
Art/Fine Arts	M
Aviation Management	M,D,O
Biological and Biomedical Sciences—General	M,D,O
Biotechnology	M,D,O
Business Administration and Management—General	M,D,O
Chemistry	M,D
Child and Family Studies	M
Civil Engineering	M,D,O
Clinical Psychology	M,D,O
Communication—General	M,D,O
Computer and Information Systems Security	M,O
Computer Art and Design	O
Computer Engineering	M,D,O
Computer Science	M,D,O
Construction Engineering	M,D,O
Economic Development	O
Economics	M,D,O
Education—General	M,D,O
Educational Media/Instructional Technology	M,D,O
Electrical Engineering	M,D
Engineering and Applied Sciences—General	M,D,O
English as a Second Language	M,O
English	M
Environmental Engineering	M,D,O
Environmental Management and Policy	M,O
Exercise and Sports Science	M
Film, Television, and Video Production	M
Film, Television, and Video Theory and Criticism	M
French	M,O
Genomic Sciences	M,D,O
Geography	M,D,O
Health Services Management and Hospital Administration	M,D,O
History	M,D
Humanities	D
Industrial/Management Engineering	M,D,O
Internet and Interactive Multimedia	M,O
Investment Management	M,D,O
Jewish Studies	M
Journalism	O
Linguistics	M,O
Mathematics Education	M,D
Mathematics	M,D
Mechanical Engineering	M,D,O
Media Studies	M,D,O
Music	O
Organizational Management	M
Philosophy	M
Physics	M,D
Political Science	M,D
Psychology—General	M,D
Public Administration	M,D
Public Affairs	O
Public Policy	M,D
Religion	M,D
Rural Planning and Studies	M,D,O
Sociology	M
Software Engineering	M,D,O
Sports Management	M,D,O
Systems Engineering	M,O
Telecommunications Management	M,O
Theology	M
Translation and Interpretation	M,O
Transportation Management	M,D,O
Urban and Regional Planning	O
Urban Studies	M,O
Writing	M

CONCORDIA UNIVERSITY (MI)

Educational Leadership and Administration	M
Organizational Management	M

CONCORDIA UNIVERSITY (OR)

Business Administration and Management—General	M
Curriculum and Instruction	M
Education—General	M
Educational Leadership and Administration	M
Elementary Education	M
Secondary Education	M

CONCORDIA UNIVERSITY CHICAGO

Business Administration and Management—General	M
Counseling Psychology	M
Counselor Education	M,O
Curriculum and Instruction	M
Early Childhood Education	M,D
Education—General	M
Educational Leadership and Administration	M,D,O
Elementary Education	M
Exercise and Sports Science	M
Gerontology	M
Human Services	M
Liberal Studies	M
Music	M
Psychology—General	M
Reading Education	M
Religion	M
Religious Education	M
Secondary Education	M

CONCORDIA UNIVERSITY, NEBRASKA

Early Childhood Education	M
Education—General	M
Educational Leadership and Administration	M
Elementary Education	M
Pastoral Ministry and Counseling	M
Reading Education	M
Religious Education	M
Secondary Education	M

CONCORDIA UNIVERSITY, ST. PAUL

Business Administration and Management—General	M
Child and Family Studies	M,O
Criminal Justice and Criminology	M
Curriculum and Instruction	M,O
Early Childhood Education	M,O
Education—General	M,O
Educational Leadership and Administration	M,O
Human Resources Management	M
Organizational Management	M
Pastoral Ministry and Counseling	M,O
Religious Education	M,O
Special Education	M,O
Sports Management	M,O
Theology	M,O

CONCORDIA UNIVERSITY TEXAS

Education—General	M

CONCORDIA UNIVERSITY WISCONSIN

Art Education	M
Business Administration and Management—General	M
Child and Family Studies	M
Corporate and Organizational Communication	M
Counseling Psychology	M
Counselor Education	M
Curriculum and Instruction	M
Early Childhood Education	M
Education—General	M
Educational Leadership and Administration	M
Environmental Education	M
Family Nurse Practitioner Studies	M
Finance and Banking	M
Gerontological Nursing	M
Health Services Management and Hospital Administration	M
Human Resources Management	M
Human Services	M,D
International Business	M
Management Information Systems	M
Marketing	M
Music	M
Nursing Education	M
Nursing—General	M
Occupational Therapy	M
Physical Therapy	M,D
Psychology—General	M
Public Administration	M
Reading Education	M
Rehabilitation Sciences	M
Special Education	M
Student Affairs	M

CONCORD LAW SCHOOL

Law	P

CONNECTICUT COLLEGE

Botany	M
Psychology—General	M

CONSERVATORIO DE MUSICA

Music Education	M
Music	O

CONVERSE COLLEGE

Art Education	M,O
Curriculum and Instruction	O
Early Childhood Education	M,O
Education of the Gifted	M
Education—General	M,O
Educational Leadership and Administration	M,O
Elementary Education	M
English Education	M
English	M
History	M
Liberal Studies	M
Marriage and Family Therapy	O
Mathematics Education	M
Music Education	M
Music	M
Political Science	M
Science Education	M
Secondary Education	M
Social Sciences Education	M
Special Education	M

CONWAY SCHOOL OF LANDSCAPE DESIGN

Landscape Architecture	M

COOPER UNION FOR THE ADVANCEMENT OF SCIENCE AND ART

Architecture	M
Chemical Engineering	M
Civil Engineering	M
Electrical Engineering	M
Engineering and Applied Sciences—General	M
Mechanical Engineering	M

COPPIN STATE UNIVERSITY

Addictions/Substance Abuse Counseling	M
Adult Education	M
Criminal Justice and Criminology	M
Curriculum and Instruction	M
Education—General	M
Family Nurse Practitioner Studies	M,O
Human Services	M
Nursing—General	M,O
Reading Education	M
Rehabilitation Counseling	M
Special Education	M

CORCORAN COLLEGE OF ART AND DESIGN

Art Education	M
Decorative Arts	M
Interior Design	M

CORNELL UNIVERSITY

Accounting	D
Adult Education	M,D
Aerospace/Aeronautical Engineering	M,D
African Studies	M,D
African-American Studies	M,D
Agricultural Economics and Agribusiness	M,D
Agricultural Education	M,D
Agricultural Engineering	M,D
Agronomy and Soil Sciences	M,D
American Studies	M,D
Analytical Chemistry	D
Anatomy	M,D
Animal Behavior	D
Animal Sciences	M,D
Anthropology	D
Applied Economics	D
Applied Mathematics	M,D*
Applied Physics	M,D
Applied Statistics	M,D
Archaeology	M,D
Architectural History	M,D
Architecture	M,D
Art History	D
Art/Fine Arts	M
Artificial Intelligence/Robotics	M,D
Asian Languages	M,D
Asian Studies	M,D
Astronomy	D
Astrophysics	D
Atmospheric Sciences	M,D
Biochemical Engineering	M,D
Biochemistry	D
Bioengineering	M,D
Biological and Biomedical Sciences—General	M,D
Biomedical Engineering	M,D
Biometry	M,D
Biophysics	D
Biopsychology	D
Building Science	M,D
Business Administration and Management—General	M,D
Cell Biology	M,D
Chemical Engineering	M,D
Chemical Physics	D
Chemistry	D*
Child and Family Studies	D
Chinese	M,D
Civil Engineering	M,D
Classics	D
Clothing and Textiles	M,D
Cognitive Sciences	D
Communication—General	M,D
Comparative Literature	D
Computational Biology	D
Computational Sciences	M,D
Computer Art and Design	M,D
Computer Engineering	M,D
Computer Science	M,D
Conflict Resolution and Mediation/Peace Studies	M,D
Consumer Economics	M,D
Cultural Studies	M,D
Curriculum and Instruction	M,D
Demography and Population Studies	M,D
Developmental Biology	M,D
Developmental Psychology	D
East European and Russian Studies	M,D
Ecology	M,D
Economic Development	M,D
Economics	M,D
Education—General	M,D
Electrical Engineering	M,D
Engineering and Applied Sciences—General	M,D
Engineering Management	M,D
Engineering Physics	M,D
English	M,D
Entomology	M,D
Environmental Design	M
Environmental Engineering	M,D
Environmental Management and Policy	M,D
Environmental Sciences	M,D
Epidemiology	M,D
Ergonomics and Human Factors	M
Ethnic Studies	M,D
Evolutionary Biology	D
Experimental Psychology	D
Facilities Management	M
Family and Consumer Sciences-General	M,D
Finance and Banking	D
Fish, Game, and Wildlife Management	M,D
Food Science and Technology	M,D
Foreign Languages Education	M,D
Forestry	M,D
French	D
Gender Studies	M,D
Genetics	D
Geochemistry	M,D
Geology	M,D
Geophysics	M,D
Geosciences	M,D
Geotechnical Engineering	M,D
German	M,D
Health Services Management and Hospital Administration	M,D
Historic Preservation	M,D
History of Science and Technology	M,D
History	M,D
Horticulture	M,D
Hospitality Management	M,D
Human Development	D
Human Resources Management	M,D
Human-Computer Interaction	D
Hydrology	M,D
Immunology	M,D
Industrial and Labor Relations	M,D*
Industrial/Management Engineering	M,D
Infectious Diseases	M,D
Information Science	D
Information Studies	D
Inorganic Chemistry	D
Interior Design	M
International Affairs	D
International Development	M
Italian	D
Japanese	M,D
Jewish Studies	M,D
Landscape Architecture	M
Latin American Studies	M,D
Law	P,M,D
Limnology	D
Linguistics	M,D
Manufacturing Engineering	M,D
Marine Geology	M,D
Marine Sciences	M,D
Marketing	D
Materials Engineering	M,D
Materials Sciences	M,D
Mathematics Education	M,D
Mathematics	D
Mechanical Engineering	M,D
Mechanics	M,D
Medieval and Renaissance Studies	M,D
Microbiology	D
Mineralogy	M,D
Molecular Biology	D
Molecular Medicine	M,D
Music	M,D
Natural Resources	M,D
Near and Middle Eastern Studies	M,D
Neurobiology	D*
Nuclear Engineering	M,D
Nutrition	M,D
Oceanography	D
Operations Research	M,D*
Organic Chemistry	D
Organizational Behavior	M,D
Paleontology	M,D
Pharmacology	M,D*
Philosophy	D
Photography	M
Physical Chemistry	D
Physics	M,D
Physiology	M,D
Planetary and Space Sciences	D
Plant Biology	M,D
Plant Molecular Biology	M,D
Plant Pathology	M,D
Plant Physiology	M,D
Plant Sciences	M,D
Political Science	D
Polymer Science and Engineering	M,D
Psychology—General	D
Public Affairs	M*
Public Policy	M,D
Real Estate	M
Religion	D
Reproductive Biology	M,D
Romance Languages	M,D
Rural Planning and Studies	M
Rural Sociology	M,D
Scandinavian Languages	M,D
Science Education	M,D
Slavic Languages	M,D
Social Psychology	M,D
Social Work	M,D
Sociology	M,D
Spanish	D
Statistics	M,D
Structural Biology	M,D
Structural Engineering	M,D
Systems Engineering	M
Textile Design	M,D
Textile Sciences and Engineering	M,D
Theater	D
Theoretical Chemistry	D
Theoretical Physics	M,D
Toxicology	M,D
Transportation and Highway Engineering	M,D
Urban and Regional Planning	M,D
Urban Design	M,D
Veterinary Medicine	P
Water Resources Engineering	M,D
Western European Studies	M,D
Women's Studies	M,D
Writing	M,D
Zoology	M,D

CORNELL UNIVERSITY, JOAN AND SANFORD I. WEILL MEDICAL COLLEGE AND GRADUATE SCHOOL OF MEDICAL SCIENCES

Biochemistry	M,D
Biological and Biomedical Sciences—General	M,D
Biophysics	M,D
Cell Biology	M,D
Epidemiology	M
Health Services Research	M
Immunology	M,D
Molecular Biology	M,D
Neuroscience	M,D
Pharmacology	M,D
Physiology	M,D
Structural Biology	M,D
Systems Biology	M,D

CORNERSTONE UNIVERSITY

Business Administration and Management—General	M,O
Education—General	M,O
English as a Second Language	M,O

COVENANT COLLEGE

Education—General	M

COVENANT THEOLOGICAL SEMINARY

Theology	P,M,D,O

CRANBROOK ACADEMY OF ART

Applied Arts and Design—General	M
Architecture	M
Art/Fine Arts	M*
Graphic Design	M
Photography	M
Textile Design	M

CREIGHTON UNIVERSITY

Allied Health—General	P,M,D
Allopathic Medicine	P
Anatomy	M
Atmospheric Sciences	M
Biological and Biomedical Sciences—General	M,D
Business Administration and Management—General	M
Conflict Resolution and Mediation/Peace Studies	M,O
Counselor Education	M
Dentistry	P
Education—General	M
Educational Leadership and Administration	M
Elementary Education	M
English	M
Immunology	M,D
International Affairs	M
Law	P,M,O
Liberal Studies	M
Management Information Systems	M
Medical Microbiology	M,D*
Nursing—General	M,D
Occupational Therapy	D
Pharmaceutical Sciences	M,D
Pharmacology	M,D
Pharmacy	P

*M—master's degree; P—first professional degree; D—doctorate; O—other advanced degree; *—Close-Up and/or Announcement or Display in one of the other books in this series*

Physical Therapy D
Physics M
Secondary Education M
Social Psychology M
Special Education M
Student Affairs M
Theology M
Writing M

THE CRISWELL COLLEGE

Jewish Studies P,M
Pastoral Ministry and Counseling P,M
Theology P,M

CROWN COLLEGE

Theology M

CUMBERLAND UNIVERSITY

Business Administration and Management—General M
Education—General M
Human Resources Management M
Organizational Management M
Public Administration M

CUNY GRADUATE SCHOOL OF JOURNALISM

Journalism M*

CURRY COLLEGE

Business Administration and Management—General M,O
Criminal Justice and Criminology M
Education—General M,O
Educational Leadership and Administration M,O
Educational Measurement and Evaluation M,O
Elementary Education M,O
Finance and Banking M,O
Foundations and Philosophy of Education M,O
Reading Education M,O
Special Education M,O

THE CURTIS INSTITUTE OF MUSIC

Music M

DAEMEN COLLEGE

Adult Nursing M,O
Business Administration and Management—General M
Early Childhood Education M
Education—General M
International Business M
Medical/Surgical Nursing M,O
Middle School Education M
Nursing and Healthcare Administration M,O
Nursing Education M,O
Nursing—General M,O
Physical Therapy D,O
Physician Assistant Studies M
Special Education M

DAKOTA STATE UNIVERSITY

Education—General M
Educational Media/Instructional Technology M
Information Science M,D*

DAKOTA WESLEYAN UNIVERSITY

Curriculum and Instruction M
Education—General M
Educational Leadership and Administration M
Secondary Education M

DALHOUSIE UNIVERSITY

Agricultural Engineering M,D
Agricultural Sciences—General M
Allopathic Medicine P,M,D
Anatomy M,D
Anthropology M,D
Applied Mathematics M,D
Architecture M
Biochemistry M,D
Bioengineering M,D
Bioinformatics M,D
Biological and Biomedical Sciences—General M,D
Biomedical Engineering M,D
Biophysics M,D
Business Administration and Management—General M,O
Chemical Engineering M,D
Chemistry M,D
Civil Engineering M,D
Classics M,D
Clinical Psychology M,D
Communication Disorders M,D
Community Health M
Computer Engineering M,D
Computer Science M,D
Economics M,D
Electrical Engineering M,D
Electronic Commerce M,D
Engineering and Applied Sciences—General M,D
English M,D
Environmental Engineering M,D
Environmental Management and Policy M
Epidemiology M
Finance and Banking M
Food Science and Technology M,D
French M,D
Geosciences M,D
German M
Health Education M
Health Services Management and Hospital Administration M,D
History M,D
Human-Computer Interaction M
Immunology M,D
Industrial/Management Engineering M,D
Information Studies M
Interdisciplinary Studies D
International Development M
Kinesiology and Movement Studies M
Law M,D
Leisure Studies M
Library Science M
Management Information Systems M
Marine Affairs M
Materials Engineering M,D
Mathematics M,D
Mechanical Engineering M,D
Medical Informatics M,D
Microbiology M,D
Mineral/Mining Engineering M,D
Music M
Natural Resources M
Neurobiology M,D
Neuroscience M,D
Nursing—General M,D
Occupational Therapy M
Oceanography M,D
Oral and Dental Sciences
Pathology M,D
Pharmacology M,D
Philosophy M,D
Physical Therapy M
Physics M,D
Physiology M,D
Political Science M,D
Psychology—General M,D
Public Administration M,O
Rural Planning and Studies M
Social Work M
Sociology M,D
Statistics M,D
Urban and Regional Planning M

DALLAS BAPTIST UNIVERSITY

Accounting M
Business Administration and Management—General M
Conflict Resolution and Mediation/Peace Studies M
Corporate and Organizational Communication M
Counseling Psychology M
Counselor Education M
Criminal Justice and Criminology M
Curriculum and Instruction M
Education—General M
Educational Leadership and Administration M
Electronic Commerce M
Elementary Education M
Engineering Management M
English as a Second Language M
Entrepreneurship M
Experimental Psychology M
Finance and Banking M
Health Services Management and Hospital Administration M
Higher Education M
Human Resources Management M
Interdisciplinary Studies M
International Business M
Kinesiology and Movement Studies M
Liberal Studies M
Management Information Systems M
Management of Technology M
Marketing M
Missions and Missiology M
Nonprofit Management M
Pastoral Ministry and Counseling M
Project Management M
Reading Education M
Religious Education M
Secondary Education M

DALLAS THEOLOGICAL SEMINARY

Media Studies M,D,O
Missions and Missiology M,D,O
Pastoral Ministry and Counseling M,D,O
Religious Education M,D,O
Theology M,D,O

DANIEL WEBSTER COLLEGE

Aviation Management M
Business Administration and Management—General M

DANIEL WEBSTER COLLEGE–PORTSMOUTH CAMPUS

Business Administration and Management—General M

DARKEI NOAM RABBINICAL COLLEGE

Theology P

DARTMOUTH COLLEGE

Allopathic Medicine P
Astronomy M,D
Biochemical Engineering M,D
Biochemistry D
Biological and Biomedical Sciences—General D*
Biotechnology M,D
Business Administration and Management—General M
Cancer Biology/Oncology D
Cardiovascular Sciences D
Cell Biology D
Chemistry D
Cognitive Sciences D
Comparative Literature M
Computer Engineering M,D
Computer Science M,D
Ecology D
Electrical Engineering M,D
Engineering and Applied Sciences—General M,D*
Engineering Management M
Engineering Physics M,D
Evolutionary Biology D
Genetics D*
Geosciences M,D
Health Services Management and Hospital Administration M,D
Health Services Research M,D*
Immunology D*
Liberal Studies M*
Manufacturing Engineering M,D
Materials Engineering M,D
Materials Sciences M,D
Mathematics D
Mechanical Engineering M,D
Microbiology D*
Molecular Biology D*
Molecular Medicine D*
Molecular Pathogenesis D
Molecular Pharmacology D
Music M
Neuroscience D*
Pharmaceutical Sciences D
Pharmacology D
Physics M,D
Physiology D
Psychology—General D
Public Health—General M
Systems Biology D
Toxicology D

DAVENPORT UNIVERSITY

Accounting M
Business Administration and Management—General M
Computer and Information Systems Security M
Finance and Banking M
Health Services Management and Hospital Administration M
Human Resources Management M
Management Strategy and Policy M
Marketing M
Public Health—General M

DAVENPORT UNIVERSITY

Accounting M
Business Administration and Management—General M
Computer and Information Systems Security M
Finance and Banking M

Health Services Management and Hospital Administration	M
Human Resources Management	M
Management Strategy and Policy	M
Public Health—General	M

DAVENPORT UNIVERSITY

Accounting	M
Business Administration and Management—General	M
Computer and Information Systems Security	M
Finance and Banking	M
Health Services Management and Hospital Administration	M
Human Resources Management	M
Public Health—General	M

DEFIANCE COLLEGE

Adult Education	M
Business Administration and Management—General	M
Criminal Justice and Criminology	M
Education—General	M
Health Services Management and Hospital Administration	M
Management Strategy and Policy	M
Physical Education	M
Secondary Education	M
Special Education	M

DELAWARE STATE UNIVERSITY

Adult Education	M
Applied Mathematics	M,D
Art Education	M
Biological and Biomedical Sciences—General	M
Business Administration and Management—General	M
Chemistry	M
Curriculum and Instruction	M
Education—General	M,D
Educational Leadership and Administration	M,D
Exercise and Sports Science	M
Foreign Languages Education	M
Historic Preservation	M
Mathematics Education	M
Mathematics	M
Natural Resources	M
Neuroscience	M,D
Nursing—General	M
Optical Sciences	M,D
Physics	M,D
Plant Sciences	M
Reading Education	M
Science Education	M,D
Social Work	M
Special Education	M
Theoretical Physics	D

DELAWARE VALLEY COLLEGE

Agricultural Economics and Agribusiness	M
Business Administration and Management—General	M
Educational Leadership and Administration	M

DELL'ARTE SCHOOL OF PHYSICAL THEATRE

Theater	M

DELTA STATE UNIVERSITY

Accounting	M
Aviation Management	M
Biological and Biomedical Sciences—General	M
Business Administration and Management—General	M
Counselor Education	M,D
Criminal Justice and Criminology	M
Education—General	M,D,O
Educational Leadership and Administration	M,D,O
Elementary Education	M,D,O
English Education	M
Family Nurse Practitioner Studies	M
Health Services Management and Hospital Administration	M
Higher Education	D
Marketing	M
Mathematics Education	M
Nursing Education	M
Nursing—General	M
Physical Education	M
Recreation and Park Management	M
Science Education	M
Secondary Education	M,O
Social Sciences Education	M
Special Education	M
Urban and Regional Planning	M

DENVER SEMINARY

Marriage and Family Therapy	P,M,D,O
Pastoral Ministry and Counseling	P,M,D,O
Religion	P,M,D,O
Theology	P,M,D,O

DEPAUL UNIVERSITY

Accounting	M
Adult Education	M
Advertising and Public Relations	M
Applied Mathematics	M,O
Applied Physics	M
Applied Statistics	M,O
Biochemistry	M
Biological and Biomedical Sciences—General	M
Business Administration and Management—General	M
Chemistry	M
Clinical Psychology	M,D
Communication—General	M
Computer and Information Systems Security	M,D
Computer Art and Design	M,D
Computer Science	M,D
Corporate and Organizational Communication	M
Counselor Education	M,D
Curriculum and Instruction	D
Economics	M
Education—General	M,D
Educational Leadership and Administration	D
Electronic Commerce	M,D
Elementary Education	M,D
English	M
Entrepreneurship	M
Experimental Psychology	M,D
Finance and Banking	M,O
Health Law	P,M,O
Health Services Management and Hospital Administration	M,O
History	M
Human Development	M,D
Human Resources Management	M
Human Services	M,D
Human-Computer Interaction	M,D
Industrial and Manufacturing Management	M
Industrial and Organizational Psychology	M,D
Information Science	M,D
Interdisciplinary Studies	M
International Business	M
Internet and Interactive Multimedia	M,D
Journalism	M
Law	P,M
Management Information Systems	M,D
Management of Technology	M,D
Management Strategy and Policy	M
Marketing	M
Mathematical and Computational Finance	M,D
Mathematics Education	M,O
Mathematics	M,O
Media Studies	M
Multilingual and Multicultural Education	M,D
Music Education	M,O
Music	M,O
Nonprofit Management	M,O
Nurse Anesthesia	M
Nursing—General	M
Philosophy	M,D
Physical Education	M,D
Physics	M
Polymer Science and Engineering	M
Project Management	M,D
Psychology—General	M,D
Public Administration	M,O
Public Affairs	M,O
Public Policy	M,O
Publishing	M
Reading Education	M,D
Real Estate	M
Secondary Education	M,D
Social Psychology	M,D
Sociology	M
Software Engineering	M,D
Special Education	M,D
Taxation	M
Telecommunications	M,D
Theater	M
Urban and Regional Planning	M,O
Urban Education	M,D
Writing	M

DESALES UNIVERSITY

Accounting	M
Adult Nursing	M
Business Administration and Management—General	M
Computer Education	M
Criminal Justice and Criminology	M
Education—General	M
Elementary Education	M
English as a Second Language	M
Family Nurse Practitioner Studies	M
Finance and Banking	M
Health Services Management and Hospital Administration	M
Information Science	M
Management Information Systems	M
Marketing	M
Mathematics Education	M
Nurse Midwifery	M
Nursing Education	M
Nursing—General	M
Physician Assistant Studies	M
Project Management	M
Special Education	M

DES MOINES UNIVERSITY

Health Services Management and Hospital Administration	M
Osteopathic Medicine	P
Physical Therapy	D
Physician Assistant Studies	M
Podiatric Medicine	P
Public Health—General	M

DEVRY UNIVERSITY (AZ)

Business Administration and Management—General	M,O

DEVRY UNIVERSITY (CA)

Business Administration and Management—General	M,O

DEVRY UNIVERSITY (CO)

Business Administration and Management—General	M,O

DEVRY UNIVERSITY (FL)

Business Administration and Management—General	M,O

DEVRY UNIVERSITY (GA)

Business Administration and Management—General	M,O

DEVRY UNIVERSITY (IL)

Business Administration and Management—General	M,O

DEVRY UNIVERSITY (IL)

Accounting	M
Business Administration and Management—General	M*
Communication—General	M
Finance and Banking	M
Human Resources Management	M
Management Information Systems	M
Project Management	M
Public Administration	M

DEVRY UNIVERSITY (IN)

Business Administration and Management—General	M,O

DEVRY UNIVERSITY (MD)

Business Administration and Management—General	M,O

*M—master's degree; P—first professional degree; D—doctorate; O—other advanced degree; *—Close-Up and/or Announcement or Display in one of the other books in this series*

DEVRY UNIVERSITY (MO)
- Business Administration and Management—General — M,O

DEVRY UNIVERSITY (NC)
- Business Administration and Management—General — M,O

DEVRY UNIVERSITY (NV)
- Business Administration and Management—General — M,O

DEVRY UNIVERSITY (OH)
- Business Administration and Management—General — M,O

DEVRY UNIVERSITY (OR)
- Business Administration and Management—General — M,O

DEVRY UNIVERSITY (PA)
- Business Administration and Management—General — M,O

DEVRY UNIVERSITY (TX)
- Business Administration and Management—General — M,O

DEVRY UNIVERSITY (UT)
- Business Administration and Management—General — M

DEVRY UNIVERSITY (VA)
- Business Administration and Management—General — M,O

DEVRY UNIVERSITY (WA)
- Business Administration and Management—General — M,O

DEVRY UNIVERSITY (WI)
- Business Administration and Management—General — M,O

DIGIPEN INSTITUTE OF TECHNOLOGY
- Computer Science — M

DIGITAL MEDIA ARTS COLLEGE
- Computer Art and Design — M
- Graphic Design — M
- Media Studies — M

DOANE COLLEGE
- Business Administration and Management—General — M
- Counselor Education — M
- Curriculum and Instruction — M
- Education—General — M
- Educational Leadership and Administration — M

DOMINICAN COLLEGE
- Allied Health—General — M,D
- Business Administration and Management—General — M
- Education—General — M
- Elementary Education — M
- Family Nurse Practitioner Studies — M
- Nursing—General — M
- Occupational Therapy — M
- Physical Therapy — M,D
- Special Education — M

DOMINICAN HOUSE OF STUDIES, PONTIFICAL FACULTY OF THE IMMACULATE CONCEPTION
- Theology — P,M,O

DOMINICAN SCHOOL OF PHILOSOPHY AND THEOLOGY
- Philosophy — M
- Theology — P,O

DOMINICAN UNIVERSITY
- Accounting — M
- Business Administration and Management—General — M
- Curriculum and Instruction — M
- Early Childhood Education — M
- Education—General — M
- Educational Leadership and Administration — M
- Elementary Education — M
- English as a Second Language — M
- Information Studies — M,O
- Library Science — M,O
- Management Information Systems — M
- Organizational Management — M
- Reading Education — M
- Social Work — M
- Special Education — M

DOMINICAN UNIVERSITY OF CALIFORNIA
- Biological and Biomedical Sciences—General — M
- Business Administration and Management—General — M
- Counseling Psychology — M
- Education—General — M,O
- Gerontology — M
- Humanities — M
- International Business — M
- Management Strategy and Policy — M
- Marriage and Family Therapy — M
- Nursing Education — M
- Nursing—General — M
- Occupational Therapy — M
- Public Health—General — M
- Special Education — O
- Sustainability Management — M
- Sustainable Development — M

DONGGUK ROYAL UNIVERSITY
- Acupuncture and Oriental Medicine — M

DORDT COLLEGE
- Education—General — M

DOWLING COLLEGE
- Aviation Management — M,O
- Business Administration and Management—General — M,O
- Education—General — M,D,O
- Educational Leadership and Administration — M,D,O
- Educational Media/Instructional Technology — M,D,O
- Finance and Banking — M,O
- Human Development — M,D,O
- Liberal Studies — M
- Mathematics — M
- Quality Management — M,O
- Reading Education — M,D,O
- Secondary Education — M,D,O
- Special Education — M,D,O

DRAKE UNIVERSITY
- Adult Education — M
- American Studies — M
- Art/Fine Arts — M
- Business Administration and Management—General — M
- Business Education — M
- Communication—General — M
- Counselor Education — M
- Education—General — M,D,O
- Educational Leadership and Administration — M,D,O
- Elementary Education — M
- English Education — M
- History — M
- Journalism — M
- Law — P*
- Mathematics Education — M
- Pharmaceutical Sciences — P
- Pharmacy — P
- Public Administration — M
- Rehabilitation Counseling — M
- Rehabilitation Sciences — M,D,O
- Science Education — M
- Secondary Education — M
- Social Sciences Education — M
- Sociology — M
- Special Education — M
- Speech and Interpersonal Communication — M
- Theater — M

DREW UNIVERSITY
- Bioethics — M,D,O
- English — M,D
- Ethics — M,D
- History — M,D
- Holocaust Studies — M,D,O
- Humanities — M,D,O
- Interdisciplinary Studies — M,D,O
- Near and Middle Eastern Studies — M,D
- Religion — M,D
- Theology — P,M,D,O
- Women's Studies — M

DREXEL UNIVERSITY
- Accounting — M,D,O
- Allied Health—General — M,D,O
- Allopathic Medicine — P
- Applied Arts and Design—General — M
- Architectural Engineering — M,D
- Art Therapy — M,O
- Arts Administration — M
- Biochemical Engineering — M
- Biochemistry — M,D
- Biological and Biomedical Sciences—General — M,D,O*
- Biomedical Engineering — M,D
- Biopsychology — M,D
- Biostatistics — M,D,O
- Business Administration and Management—General — M,D,O
- Cell Biology — M,D
- Chemical Engineering — M,D
- Chemistry — M,D
- Civil Engineering — M,D
- Clinical Psychology — D
- Communication—General — M
- Computer Art and Design — M
- Computer Engineering — M
- Computer Science — M,D
- Corporate and Organizational Communication — M
- Curriculum and Instruction — M
- Economics — M,D,O
- Education—General — M,D,O*
- Educational Leadership and Administration — M,D
- Educational Media/Instructional Technology — M,D
- Electrical Engineering — M*
- Emergency Management — M
- Emergency Medical Services — M
- Engineering and Applied Sciences—General — M,D,O
- Engineering Management — M,O
- English as a Second Language — M,D,O
- Environmental Engineering — M,D
- Environmental Management and Policy — M
- Environmental Sciences — M,D
- Epidemiology — M,D,O
- Film, Television, and Video Production — M
- Finance and Banking — M,D,O
- Forensic Psychology — D
- Genetics — M,D
- Geotechnical Engineering — M,D
- Health Psychology — D
- Higher Education — M
- History of Science and Technology — M
- Hydraulics — M,D
- Hydrology — M,D
- Immunology — M,D
- Information Science — M,D
- Information Studies — M*
- Interior Design — M
- International and Comparative Education — M
- Journalism — M
- Library Science — M,D,O
- Management Strategy and Policy — M,D,O
- Marketing — M,D,O
- Marriage and Family Therapy — M,D
- Mass Communication — M
- Materials Engineering — M,D
- Mathematics — M,D
- Mechanical Engineering — M,D
- Mechanics — M,D
- Media Studies — M
- Medical Informatics — M,D,O
- Microbiology — M,D
- Molecular Biology — M,D
- Neuroscience — M,D
- Nurse Anesthesia — M
- Nursing—General — M
- Nutrition — M
- Organizational Behavior — M,D,O
- Pathobiology — M,D
- Pharmacology — M,D
- Physical Therapy — M,D,O
- Physician Assistant Studies — M
- Physics — M,D
- Psychology—General — M,D
- Public Health—General — M,D,O
- Publishing — M
- Quantitative Analysis — M,D,O
- Software Engineering — M,D,O
- Structural Engineering — M,D
- Technical Communication — M
- Technical Writing — M
- Telecommunications — M
- Textile Design — M
- Therapies—Dance, Drama, and Music — M,O
- Veterinary Sciences — M

DRURY UNIVERSITY
- Art/Fine Arts — M
- Business Administration and Management—General — M
- Communication—General — M
- Criminal Justice and Criminology — M
- Education of the Gifted — M
- Education—General — M

Educational Media/Instructional Technology	M
Elementary Education	M
Human Services	M
Mathematics Education	M
Middle School Education	M
Reading Education	M
Secondary Education	M
Special Education	M

DUKE UNIVERSITY

Acute Care/Critical Care Nursing	M,D,O
Adult Nursing	M,D,O
Allopathic Medicine	P
Anatomy	D
Anthropology	D
Art History	D
Art/Fine Arts	D
Asian Studies	M,O
Biochemistry	D,O
Bioinformatics	D
Biological and Biomedical Sciences—General	D,O
Biological Anthropology	D
Biomedical Engineering	M,D
Biopsychology	D
Business Administration and Management—General	M,D
Cancer Biology/Oncology	D
Cell Biology	D,O
Chemistry	D
Civil Engineering	M,D*
Classics	D
Clinical Laboratory Sciences/Medical Technology	M
Clinical Psychology	D
Clinical Research	M
Cognitive Sciences	D
Comparative Literature	D
Computer Engineering	M,D
Computer Science	M,D
Developmental Biology	D,O
Developmental Psychology	D
Ecology	M,D,O
Economics	M,D
Education—General	M
Electrical Engineering	M,D*
Engineering and Applied Sciences—General	M,D
Engineering Management	M*
English	D
Environmental and Occupational Health	M,D,O
Environmental Engineering	M,D
Environmental Management and Policy	M,D
Environmental Sciences	M,D*
Experimental Psychology	D
Family Nurse Practitioner Studies	M,D,O
Forestry	M
French	D
Genetics	D
Geology	M,D
German	D
Gerontological Nursing	M,D,O
Health Psychology	D
Health Services Management and Hospital Administration	O
History of Medicine	
History	M,D
HIV/AIDS Nursing	M,D,O
Human Development	D
Humanities	M
Immunology	D
International Development	M,O
International Health	M
Latin American Studies	M,D,O
Law	P,M,D
Liberal Studies	M
Marine Affairs	M
Marine Sciences	M*
Materials Sciences	M,D
Maternal and Child/Neonatal Nursing	M,D,O
Mathematics	D
Mechanical Engineering	M,D
Medieval and Renaissance Studies	O
Microbiology	D
Molecular Biology	D,O
Molecular Biophysics	O
Molecular Genetics	D
Music	M,D
Natural Resources	M,D*
Neurobiology	D
Neuroscience	D,O
Nurse Anesthesia	M,D,O
Nursing and Healthcare Administration	M,D,O
Nursing Education	M,D,O
Nursing Informatics	M,D,O
Nursing—General	D
Oncology Nursing	M,D,O
Paleontology	D
Pathology	M,D*
Pediatric Nursing	M,D,O
Pharmacology	D
Philosophy	M,D
Physical Therapy	D
Physician Assistant Studies	M
Physics	M,D
Political Science	M,D
Psychology—General	D
Public Policy	M,D,O
Religion	M,D
Slavic Languages	M
Sociology	M,D
Spanish	D
Statistics	D
Structural Biology	O
Theology	P,M,D
Toxicology	D,O
Water Resources	M
Women's Studies	O

DUQUESNE UNIVERSITY

Accounting	M
Acute Care/Critical Care Nursing	O
Allied Health—General	M,D
Biochemistry	M,D
Bioethics	M,D,O
Biological and Biomedical Sciences—General	M,D
Biotechnology	M
Business Administration and Management—General	M*
Chemistry	M,D*
Clinical Psychology	D
Communication Disorders	M,D
Communication—General	M,D
Community Health	M
Conflict Resolution and Mediation/Peace Studies	M,O
Counselor Education	M,D
Curriculum and Instruction	M,D,O
Early Childhood Education	M
Education—General	M,D,O
Educational Leadership and Administration	M,D,O
Educational Media/Instructional Technology	M,D
Elementary Education	M
English as a Second Language	M,D
English Education	M
English	M,D
Environmental Management and Policy	M,O
Environmental Sciences	M,O
Ethics	M
Family Nurse Practitioner Studies	M,O
Foreign Languages Education	M
Forensic Nursing	M,O
Forensic Sciences	M
Foundations and Philosophy of Education	M
Health Services Management and Hospital Administration	M,D
History	M
Internet and Interactive Multimedia	M,O
Law	P,M
Liberal Studies	M
Management Information Systems	M
Management Strategy and Policy	M
Mathematics Education	M
Mathematics	M
Medicinal and Pharmaceutical Chemistry	M,D
Museum Studies	M
Music Education	M,O
Music	M,O
Nursing Education	M
Nursing—General	M,D,O
Occupational Therapy	M,D
Organizational Management	M
Pharmaceutical Administration	M
Pharmaceutical Sciences	M,D*
Pharmacology	M,D
Pharmacy	P
Philosophy	M,D
Physical Therapy	M,D
Physician Assistant Studies	M,D
Psychology—General	D
Public Administration	M,O
Public Policy	M,O
Reading Education	M
Rhetoric	M,D
School Psychology	M,D,O
Science Education	M
Secondary Education	M
Social Sciences Education	M
Special Education	M
Sports Management	M
Sustainability Management	M
Theology	M,D

D'YOUVILLE COLLEGE

Business Administration and Management—General	M
Chiropractic	P
Community Health Nursing	M,O
Education—General	M,O
Educational Leadership and Administration	D
Elementary Education	M,O
Family Nurse Practitioner Studies	M,O
Health Education	D
Health Services Management and Hospital Administration	M,D,O
International Business	M
Nursing and Healthcare Administration	M,O
Nursing Education	M,O
Nursing—General	M,O*
Nutrition	M
Occupational Therapy	M
Physical Therapy	M,D,O
Physician Assistant Studies	M
Secondary Education	M,O
Special Education	M,O

EARLHAM COLLEGE

Education—General	M

EARLHAM SCHOOL OF RELIGION

Religion	P,M
Theology	P,M

EAST CAROLINA UNIVERSITY

Accounting	M
Addictions/Substance Abuse Counseling	M
Adult Education	M,O
Allied Health—General	M,D
Allopathic Medicine	P
American Studies	M
Anatomy	D
Anthropology	M
Applied Mathematics	M
Art/Fine Arts	M
Biochemistry	D
Biological and Biomedical Sciences—General	M,D
Biophysics	M,D
Biotechnology	M
Business Administration and Management—General	M,D,O
Cell Biology	D
Chemistry	M
Child and Family Studies	M
Child Development	M
Clinical Psychology	M
Communication Disorders	M,D
Computer Science	M,D,O
Counselor Education	M,O
Criminal Justice and Criminology	M
Curriculum and Instruction	M
Economics	M
Education—General	M,D,O
Educational Leadership and Administration	M,D,O
Educational Media/Instructional Technology	M,O
Elementary Education	M
English Education	M
English	M
Environmental and Occupational Health	M
Exercise and Sports Science	M,D
Geography	M
Geology	M
Health Communication	M
Health Education	M
Health Psychology	D
History	M
Immunology	D
Industrial/Management Engineering	M,D,O
Information Science	M
International Affairs	M
Leisure Studies	M
Library Science	M,O
Logistics	M,D,O
Management Information Systems	M,D,O
Management of Technology	M,D,O
Manufacturing Engineering	M,D,O
Marine Affairs	D
Marriage and Family Therapy	M
Mathematics Education	M
Mathematics	M
Medical Physics	M,D
Microbiology	D
Middle School Education	M
Molecular Biology	M,D
Music Education	M
Music	M
Natural Resources	D
Nursing—General	M,D
Nutrition	M
Occupational Therapy	M
Pathology	D
Pharmacology	D
Physical Therapy	M,D
Physician Assistant Studies	M
Physics	M,D
Physiology	D
Political Science	M
Psychology—General	M
Public Administration	M
Public Health—General	M

*M—master's degree; P—first professional degree; D—doctorate; O—other advanced degree; *—Close-Up and/or Announcement or Display in one of the other books in this series*

Reading Education	M
Recreation and Park Management	M
Rehabilitation Counseling	M
Rehabilitation Sciences	M
School Psychology	
Science Education	M
Social Sciences Education	M
Social Work	M
Sociology	M
Special Education	M
Therapies—Dance, Drama, and Music	M
Vocational and Technical Education	M
Western European Studies	M

EAST CENTRAL UNIVERSITY

Counselor Education	M
Criminal Justice and Criminology	M
Education—General	M
Human Resources Management	M
Psychology—General	M
Rehabilitation Counseling	M

EASTERN CONNECTICUT STATE UNIVERSITY

Early Childhood Education	M
Education—General	M
Educational Media/Instructional Technology	M
Elementary Education	M
Organizational Management	M
Reading Education	M
Science Education	M
Secondary Education	M

EASTERN ILLINOIS UNIVERSITY

Accounting	M,O
Art Education	M
Art/Fine Arts	M
Biological and Biomedical Sciences—General	M
Business Administration and Management—General	M,O
Chemistry	M
Clinical Psychology	M,O
Communication Disorders	M
Computer and Information Systems Security	M,O
Computer Science	M,O
Consumer Economics	M
Counselor Education	M
Early Childhood Education	M
Economics	M
Education—General	M,O
Educational Leadership and Administration	M,O
Elementary Education	M
Engineering and Applied Sciences—General	M,O
English	M
Family and Consumer Sciences-General	M
Gerontology	M
History	M
Mathematics Education	M
Mathematics	M
Middle School Education	M
Music	M
Nutrition	M
Physical Education	M
Political Science	M
Psychology—General	M,O
Public History	M
School Psychology	M,O
Special Education	M
Speech and Interpersonal Communication	M
Student Affairs	M
Systems Science	M,O

EASTERN KENTUCKY UNIVERSITY

Agricultural Education	M
Allied Health—General	M
Art Education	M
Biological and Biomedical Sciences—General	M
Business Administration and Management—General	M
Business Education	M
Chemistry	M
Clinical Psychology	M,O
Communication Disorders	M
Community Health	M
Counselor Education	M
Criminal Justice and Criminology	M
Curriculum and Instruction	M
Ecology	M
Education—General	M
Educational Leadership and Administration	M
Elementary Education	M
English Education	M
English	M
Environmental and Occupational Health	M
Family Nurse Practitioner Studies	M
Geology	M,D
Health Education	M
Health Promotion	M
Health Services Management and Hospital Administration	M
Higher Education	M
History	M
Home Economics Education	M
Industrial and Organizational Psychology	M,O
Industrial/Management Engineering	M
Library Science	M
Manufacturing Engineering	M
Mathematics Education	M
Mathematics	M
Music Education	M
Music	M
Nursing—General	M
Nutrition	M
Occupational Therapy	M
Physical Education	M
Political Science	M
Psychology—General	M,O
Public Administration	M
Recreation and Park Management	M
School Psychology	M,O
Science Education	M
Secondary Education	M
Social Sciences Education	M
Special Education	M
Sports Management	M
Urban and Regional Planning	M
Vocational and Technical Education	M
Writing	M

EASTERN MENNONITE UNIVERSITY

Business Administration and Management—General	M
Conflict Resolution and Mediation/Peace Studies	M,O
Education—General	M
Pastoral Ministry and Counseling	P,M,O
Religion	P,M,O
Theology	P,M,O

EASTERN MICHIGAN UNIVERSITY

Accounting	M
Addictions/Substance Abuse Counseling	M,O
Adult Nursing	M,O
African-American Studies	O
American Studies	M,O
Applied Economics	M
Applied Statistics	M
Art Education	M
Art/Fine Arts	M
Artificial Intelligence/Robotics	M,O
Arts Administration	M
Athletic Training and Sports Medicine	M,O
Bioinformatics	M,O
Biological and Biomedical Sciences—General	M
Business Administration and Management—General	M,O
Cell Biology	M
Chemistry	M
Child and Family Studies	M,O
Clinical Psychology	M,D
Clinical Research	M,O
Clothing and Textiles	M
Communication Disorders	M
Communication—General	M
Computer and Information Systems Security	M,O
Computer Science	M,O
Construction Management	M
Counselor Education	M,O
Criminal Justice and Criminology	M,O
Cultural Studies	M
Curriculum and Instruction	M
Developmental Education	M,O
Early Childhood Education	M
Ecology	M
Economic Development	M
Economics	M
Education—General	M,D,O
Educational Leadership and Administration	M,D,O
Educational Measurement and Evaluation	M,O
Educational Media/Instructional Technology	M,O
Educational Psychology	M,O
Electronic Commerce	M,O
Elementary Education	M
Engineering and Applied Sciences—General	M
Engineering Management	M
English as a Second Language	M,O
English Education	M,O
English	M,O
Entrepreneurship	M,O
Exercise and Sports Science	M
Finance and Banking	M,O
Foundations and Philosophy of Education	M
French	M,O
Gender Studies	M
Geographic Information Systems	M,O
Geography	M,O
Geosciences	M
German	M,O
Gerontology	M,O
Health Education	M
Health Promotion	M,O
Health Services Management and Hospital Administration	M,O
Hispanic Studies	M,O
Historic Preservation	M,O
History	M,O
Hospitality Management	M,O
Human Resources Management	M,O
Human Services	M,O
Interior Design	M
International Business	M,O
International Economics	M
Japanese	M,O
Kinesiology and Movement Studies	M
Legal and Justice Studies	O
Linguistics	M
Management Information Systems	M,O
Management of Technology	M,D
Marketing	M
Mathematics Education	M
Mathematics	M
Middle School Education	M
Molecular Biology	M
Multilingual and Multicultural Education	M,D,O
Music Education	M
Music	M
Nonprofit Management	M,O
Nursing and Healthcare Administration	M,O
Nursing Education	M,O
Nutrition	M
Occupational Therapy	M
Organizational Management	M
Physical Education	M
Physics	M
Physiology	M
Political Science	M
Polymer Science and Engineering	M
Psychology—General	M,D
Public Administration	M,O
Public Policy	M,O
Quality Management	M,O
Reading Education	M
Science Education	M
Secondary Education	M
Social Psychology	M,O
Social Sciences	M,O
Social Work	M,O
Sociology	M
Spanish	M,O
Special Education	M,O
Sports Management	M
Supply Chain Management	M,O
Technical Communication	M,O
Technology and Public Policy	M
Theater	M
Travel and Tourism	M,O
Urban and Regional Planning	M,O
Vocational and Technical Education	M
Water Resources	M,O
Women's Studies	M
Writing	M,O

EASTERN NAZARENE COLLEGE

Counseling Psychology	M
Early Childhood Education	M,O
Education—General	M,O
Educational Leadership and Administration	M,O
Elementary Education	M,O
English as a Second Language	M,O
Marriage and Family Therapy	M
Middle School Education	M,O
Reading Education	M,O
Secondary Education	M,O
Special Education	M,O

EASTERN NEW MEXICO UNIVERSITY

Anthropology	M
Biological and Biomedical Sciences—General	M

Business Administration and Management—General M
Chemistry M
Communication Disorders M
Communication—General M
Counselor Education M
Education—General M
English M
Human Services M
Mathematics M
Physical Education M
Special Education M

EASTERN OREGON UNIVERSITY

Education—General M
Elementary Education M
Secondary Education M

EASTERN UNIVERSITY

Business Administration and Management—General M
Counseling Psychology M,O
Counselor Education M,O
Economic Development M
Education—General M,O
Health Education M
Health Services Management and Hospital Administration M
International Development M
Marriage and Family Therapy D
Missions and Missiology D
Multilingual and Multicultural Education M
Nonprofit Management M
Organizational Management M,D
Pastoral Ministry and Counseling D
School Nursing M,O
School Psychology M,O
Social Psychology M,O
Theology P,M,D
Urban and Regional Planning M
Urban Studies M

EASTERN VIRGINIA MEDICAL SCHOOL

Allopathic Medicine P
Art Therapy M
Biological and Biomedical Sciences—General M,D
Clinical Psychology D
Medical/Surgical Nursing O
Physician Assistant Studies M
Public Health—General M
Reproductive Biology M
Vision Sciences O

EASTERN WASHINGTON UNIVERSITY

Adult Education M
Biological and Biomedical Sciences—General M
Business Administration and Management—General M
Clinical Psychology M
Communication Disorders M
Communication—General M
Computer Education M
Computer Science M
Counseling Psychology M
Counselor Education M
Curriculum and Instruction M
Dental Hygiene M
Early Childhood Education M
Education—General M
Educational Leadership and Administration M
Educational Media/Instructional Technology M
Elementary Education M
English as a Second Language M
English M
Exercise and Sports Science M
Experimental Psychology M
Foreign Languages Education M
Foundations and Philosophy of Education M
History M
Interdisciplinary Studies M
Mathematics Education M
Mathematics M
Music Education M
Music M
Nursing Education M
Nursing—General M
Occupational Therapy M
Physical Education M
Physical Therapy D
Psychology—General M
Public Administration M
Reading Education M
Rhetoric M
School Psychology M
Social Work M
Special Education M
Sport Psychology M
Sports Management M
Technical Communication M
Urban and Regional Planning M
Writing M

EAST STROUDSBURG UNIVERSITY OF PENNSYLVANIA

Biological and Biomedical Sciences—General M
Communication Disorders M
Community Health M
Computer Science M
Education—General M
Educational Media/Instructional Technology M
Elementary Education M
Exercise and Sports Science M
Health Education M
History M
Hospitality Management M
Physical Education M
Political Science M
Public Health—General M
Reading Education M
Rehabilitation Sciences M
Science Education M
Secondary Education M
Social Sciences Education M
Special Education M
Sports Management M
Travel and Tourism M

EAST TENNESSEE STATE UNIVERSITY

Accounting M
Allied Health—General M,D,O
Allopathic Medicine P
Anatomy M,D
Art Education M
Art History M
Art/Fine Arts M
Biochemistry M,D
Biological and Biomedical Sciences—General M,D
Biophysics M,D
Business Administration and Management—General M,O
Chemistry M
Clinical Psychology M
Communication Disorders M,D
Communication—General M
Community Health M,O
Computer Art and Design M
Computer Science M
Counselor Education M
Criminal Justice and Criminology M
Curriculum and Instruction M
Early Childhood Education M
Economic Development M
Economics M
Education—General M,D,O
Educational Leadership and Administration M,D,O
Educational Media/Instructional Technology M
Elementary Education M
English M
Environmental and Occupational Health M
Epidemiology M,O
Exercise and Sports Science M
Finance and Banking M
Gerontology M,O
Health Services Management and Hospital Administration M,D,O
History M
Human Development M
Information Science M
Liberal Studies M
Manufacturing Engineering M
Marriage and Family Therapy M
Mathematics M
Microbiology M,D
Nursing—General M,D,O
Nutrition M
Pharmacology M,D
Physical Education M
Physical Therapy D
Physiology M,D
Psychology—General M
Public Health—General M,O
Reading Education M
Secondary Education M
Social Work M
Sociology M
Software Engineering M
Special Education M,D
Sports Management M
Urban and Regional Planning M
Urban Studies M
Vocational and Technical Education M

EAST WEST COLLEGE OF NATURAL MEDICINE

Acupuncture and Oriental Medicine M

ÉCOLE POLYTECHNIQUE DE MONTRÉAL

Aerospace/Aeronautical Engineering M,D,O
Applied Mathematics M,D,O
Biomedical Engineering M,D,O
Chemical Engineering M,D,O
Civil Engineering M,D,O
Computer Engineering M,D,O
Computer Science M,D,O
Electrical Engineering M,D,O
Engineering and Applied Sciences—General M,D,O
Engineering Physics M,D,O
Environmental Engineering M,D,O
Geotechnical Engineering M,D,O
Hydraulics M,D,O
Industrial/Management Engineering M,D,O
Management of Technology M,D,O
Mechanical Engineering M,D,O
Mechanics M,D,O
Nuclear Engineering M,D,O
Operations Research M,D,O
Optical Sciences M,D,O
Structural Engineering M,D,O
Transportation and Highway Engineering M,D,O

ECUMENICAL THEOLOGICAL SEMINARY

Pastoral Ministry and Counseling D
Theology P

EDEN THEOLOGICAL SEMINARY

Theology P,M,D

EDGEWOOD COLLEGE

Accounting M
Business Administration and Management—General M
Education—General M,D,O
Educational Leadership and Administration M,D,O
Marriage and Family Therapy M
Nursing—General M
Religion M
Special Education M,D,O

EDINBORO UNIVERSITY OF PENNSYLVANIA

Art/Fine Arts M
Biological and Biomedical Sciences—General M
Clinical Psychology M
Communication Disorders M
Communication—General M
Counselor Education M,O
Developmental Education M,O
Early Childhood Education M,O
Education—General M,O
Educational Leadership and Administration M,O
Educational Psychology M,O
Elementary Education M,O
Family Nurse Practitioner Studies M
Media Studies M
Nursing—General M
Psychology—General M
Reading Education M,O
Rehabilitation Counseling M,O
School Psychology M,O
Social Sciences M
Social Work M
Special Education M,O

EDWARD VIA VIRGINIA COLLEGE OF OSTEOPATHIC MEDICINE

Osteopathic Medicine P

ELIZABETH CITY STATE UNIVERSITY

Biological and Biomedical Sciences—General M
Education—General M
Educational Leadership and Administration M
Elementary Education M
Mathematics M

ELMHURST COLLEGE

Accounting M
Business Administration and Management—General M
Computer Science M
Educational Leadership and Administration M
English M
Industrial and Organizational Psychology M
Nursing—General M
Special Education M
Supply Chain Management M

*M—master's degree; P—first professional degree; D—doctorate; O—other advanced degree; *—Close-Up and/or Announcement or Display in one of the other books in this series*

ELMS COLLEGE

Communication Disorders	O
Early Childhood Education	M,O
Education—General	M,O
Elementary Education	M,O
English as a Second Language	M,O
English Education	M,O
Foreign Languages Education	M,O
Nursing—General	M
Reading Education	M,O
Religion	M
Science Education	M,O
Secondary Education	M,O
Special Education	M,O

ELON UNIVERSITY

Business Administration and Management—General	M
Education of the Gifted	M
Education—General	M
Elementary Education	M
Internet and Interactive Multimedia	M
Law	P
Physical Therapy	D
Special Education	M

EMBRY-RIDDLE AERONAUTICAL UNIVERSITY (AZ)

Safety Engineering	M

EMBRY-RIDDLE AERONAUTICAL UNIVERSITY (FL)

Aerospace/Aeronautical Engineering	M
Aviation Management	M
Business Administration and Management—General	M
Engineering Physics	M
Ergonomics and Human Factors	M
Mechanical Engineering	M
Planetary and Space Sciences	M
Software Engineering	M
Systems Engineering	M

EMBRY-RIDDLE AERONAUTICAL UNIVERSITY WORLDWIDE

Aerospace/Aeronautical Engineering	M
Aviation Management	M,O
Education—General	M,O
Management of Technology	M,O
Project Management	M

EMERSON COLLEGE

Advertising and Public Relations	M
Broadcast Journalism	M
Communication Disorders	M
Communication—General	M
Corporate and Organizational Communication	M
Health Communication	M
International Business	M
Journalism	M
Marketing	M
Media Studies	M
Publishing	M
Theater	M
Writing	M

EMILY CARR INSTITUTE OF ART + DESIGN

Applied Arts and Design—General	M
Art/Fine Arts	M
Computer Art and Design	M

EMMANUEL COLLEGE

Business Administration and Management—General	M,O
Education—General	M,O
Educational Leadership and Administration	M,O
Elementary Education	M,O
Human Resources Management	M,O
Secondary Education	M,O

EMMANUEL SCHOOL OF RELIGION

Missions and Missiology	P,M,D
Pastoral Ministry and Counseling	P,M,D
Religion	P,M,D
Religious Education	P,M,D
Theology	P,M,D

EMORY & HENRY COLLEGE

American Studies	M
Education—General	M
History	M
Reading Education	M

EMORY UNIVERSITY

Accounting	M,D
Adult Nursing	M
Allied Health—General	M,D
Allopathic Medicine	P
Anesthesiologist Assistant Studies	M
Animal Behavior	D
Anthropology	D
Art History	D
Biochemistry	D*
Biological and Biomedical Sciences—General	D*
Biomedical Engineering	D
Biophysics	D
Biostatistics	M,D
Business Administration and Management—General	M,D
Cell Biology	D
Chemistry	D
Clinical Laboratory Sciences/Medical Technology	M,D
Clinical Psychology	D
Clinical Research	M
Cognitive Sciences	D
Comparative Literature	D,O
Computer Science	M,D*
Condensed Matter Physics	D
Demography and Population Studies	M
Developmental Biology	D
Developmental Psychology	D
Ecology	D*
Economics	D
Education—General	M,D,O
English	D,O
Environmental and Occupational Health	M
Epidemiology	M,D
Ethics	P,M,D
Evolutionary Biology	D
Family Nurse Practitioner Studies	M
Film, Television, and Video Theory and Criticism	M,D,O
Finance and Banking	M,D
French	D,O
Genetics	D*
Gerontological Nursing	M
Gerontology	M
Health Education	M
Health Informatics	M,D
Health Physics/Radiological Health	D
Health Promotion	M
Health Services Management and Hospital Administration	M,D
Health Services Research	M,D
History	D
Immunology	D*
Interdisciplinary Studies	D
International Health	M
Jewish Studies	M
Law	P,M,O
Management Information Systems	M,D
Marketing	M,D
Mathematics	M,D*
Medical/Surgical Nursing	M
Microbiology	D*
Middle School Education	M,D,O
Molecular Biology	D
Molecular Genetics	D
Molecular Pathogenesis	D
Music	M
Near and Middle Eastern Studies	D,O
Neuroscience	D*
Nurse Anesthesia	M,D
Nurse Midwifery	M
Nursing and Healthcare Administration	M
Nursing—General	M,D*
Nutrition	M,D*
Oncology Nursing	M
Organizational Management	M,D
Pediatric Nursing	M
Pharmacology	D*
Philosophy	D,O
Physical Therapy	D
Physician Assistant Studies	M
Physics	D
Political Science	D
Portuguese	D,O
Psychology—General	D
Public Health—General	M,D,O
Religion	D,O
Secondary Education	M,D,O
Sociology	M,D*
Spanish	D,O
Theology	P,M,D
Vision Sciences	M
Women's Health Nursing	M
Women's Studies	D,O

EMPEROR'S COLLEGE OF TRADITIONAL ORIENTAL MEDICINE

Acupuncture and Oriental Medicine	M,D

EMPORIA STATE UNIVERSITY

Art Therapy	M
Biological and Biomedical Sciences—General	M
Botany	M
Business Administration and Management—General	M
Business Education	M
Cell Biology	M
Clinical Psychology	M
Counseling Psychology	M
Counselor Education	M
Curriculum and Instruction	M
Early Childhood Education	M
Education of the Gifted	M
Education—General	M,O
Educational Leadership and Administration	M
Educational Media/Instructional Technology	M
Elementary Education	M
English as a Second Language	M
English	M
Environmental Biology	M
Geosciences	M,O
History	M
Industrial and Organizational Psychology	M
Information Studies	M,D,O
Library Science	M,D,O
Mathematics	M
Microbiology	M
Music Education	M
Music	M
Physical Education	M
Psychology—General	M
Reading Education	M
Rehabilitation Counseling	M
School Psychology	M,O
Secondary Education	M
Social Sciences Education	M
Special Education	M
Zoology	M

ENDICOTT COLLEGE

Art Education	M
Business Administration and Management—General	M
Distance Education Development	M
Early Childhood Education	M
Elementary Education	M
Management Information Systems	M
Organizational Management	M
Reading Education	M
Special Education	M
Sports Management	M

EPISCOPAL DIVINITY SCHOOL

Theology	P,M,D,O

ERIKSON INSTITUTE

Child Development	M
Developmental Psychology	M,O
Early Childhood Education	M,D
English as a Second Language	M,O
Human Development	M,O

ERSKINE THEOLOGICAL SEMINARY

Theology	P,M,D

EVANGELICAL SEMINARY OF PUERTO RICO

Theology	P,M,D

EVANGEL UNIVERSITY

Clinical Psychology	M
Counseling Psychology	M
Counselor Education	M
Education—General	M
Educational Leadership and Administration	M
Organizational Management	M
Psychology—General	M
Reading Education	M
School Psychology	M
Secondary Education	M

EVEREST UNIVERSITY, BOCA RATON

Business Administration and Management—General	M
Criminal Justice and Criminology	M

EVEREST UNIVERSITY, CLEARWATER

Accounting	M
Business Administration and Management—General	M

Human Resources Management M
International Business M

EVEREST UNIVERSITY, JACKSONVILLE

Business Administration and Management—General M

EVEREST UNIVERSITY, LAKELAND

Business Administration and Management—General M
Criminal Justice and Criminology M

EVEREST UNIVERSITY, MELBOURNE

Criminal Justice and Criminology M

EVEREST UNIVERSITY, ORLANDO

Business Administration and Management—General M
Criminal Justice and Criminology M

EVEREST UNIVERSITY, ORLANDO

Business Administration and Management—General M

EVEREST UNIVERSITY, PAMPANO BEACH

Business Administration and Management—General M

EVEREST UNIVERSITY, TAMPA

Accounting M
Business Administration and Management—General M
Human Resources Management M
International Business M

EVERGLADES UNIVERSITY

Aviation M
Business Administration and Management—General M
Information Science M

THE EVERGREEN STATE COLLEGE

Education—General M
English as a Second Language M
Environmental Management and Policy M
Mathematics Education M
Public Administration M

EXCELSIOR COLLEGE

Business Administration and Management—General M
Liberal Studies M
Medical Informatics O
Nursing and Healthcare Administration O
Nursing—General M

FACULTAD DE DERECHO EUGENIO MARÍA DE HOSTOS

Law P

FAIRFIELD UNIVERSITY

Accounting M,O
American Studies M
Business Administration and Management—General M,O*
Communication—General M
Computer Engineering M
Counselor Education M,O
Education—General M,O
Educational Media/Instructional Technology M,O
Electrical Engineering M
Elementary Education M,O
Engineering and Applied Sciences—General M
English as a Second Language M,O
Family Nurse Practitioner Studies M,O
Finance and Banking M,O
Foundations and Philosophy of Education M,O
Health Services Management and Hospital Administration M,O
Human Resources Management M,O
Human Services M,O
Industrial and Organizational Psychology M,O
International Business M,O
Management Information Systems M,O
Management of Technology M
Marketing M,O
Marriage and Family Therapy M
Mathematics M
Mechanical Engineering M
Multilingual and Multicultural Education M,O
Nurse Anesthesia M,O
Nursing and Healthcare Administration M,O
Nursing—General M,O
Psychiatric Nursing M,O
Psychology—General M,O
School Psychology M,O
Secondary Education M,O
Software Engineering M
Special Education M,O
Taxation M,O
Writing M

FAIRLEIGH DICKINSON UNIVERSITY, COLLEGE AT FLORHAM

Accounting M
Biological and Biomedical Sciences—General M
Business Administration and Management—General M,O*
Chemical Engineering M,O
Chemistry M
Corporate and Organizational Communication M
Counseling Psychology M
Education—General M,O
Educational Leadership and Administration M
Educational Media/Instructional Technology M,O
Entrepreneurship M,O
Finance and Banking M,O
Health Services Management and Hospital Administration M
Hospitality Management M*
Human Resources Management M
Industrial and Organizational Psychology M
International Business M,O
Management of Technology M,O
Marketing M,O
Organizational Behavior M,O
Organizational Management M,O
Pharmacology M,O
Psychology—General M,O
Public Administration M
Reading Education M,O
Taxation M,O
Writing M

FAIRLEIGH DICKINSON UNIVERSITY, METROPOLITAN CAMPUS

Accounting M,O
Art/Fine Arts M
Biological and Biomedical Sciences—General M
Business Administration and Management—General M,O*
Chemistry M
Clinical Laboratory Sciences/Medical Technology M
Clinical Psychology M,D*
Communication—General M
Comparative Literature M
Computer Engineering M
Computer Science M*
Curriculum and Instruction M
Education—General M,O*
Educational Leadership and Administration M
Educational Media/Instructional Technology M,O
Electrical Engineering M*
Electronic Commerce M
Engineering and Applied Sciences—General M
English M
Entrepreneurship M,O
Experimental Psychology M,O
Finance and Banking M,O
Forensic Psychology M
Foundations and Philosophy of Education M
Health Services Management and Hospital Administration M
History M
Homeland Security M
Hospitality Management M*
Human Resources Management M,O
International Affairs M
International Business M
Management Information Systems M,O
Marketing M,O
Mathematics M
Media Studies M
Multilingual and Multicultural Education M
Nonprofit Management M,O
Nursing—General M,D,O
Pharmaceutical Administration M,O
Political Science M
Psychology—General M,D,O
Public Administration M,O
Reading Education M,O
School Psychology M,D
Science Education M
Special Education M
Sports Management M
Systems Science M
Taxation M

FAIRMONT STATE UNIVERSITY

Business Administration and Management—General M
Criminal Justice and Criminology M

Distance Education Development M
Education—General M
Educational Leadership and Administration M
Human Services M
Nursing and Healthcare Administration M
Nursing Education M
Nursing—General M
Reading Education M
Special Education M

FAITH BAPTIST BIBLE COLLEGE AND THEOLOGICAL SEMINARY

Pastoral Ministry and Counseling P,M
Religion P,M
Theology P,M

FAITH EVANGELICAL LUTHERAN SEMINARY

Theology P,M,D

FASHION INSTITUTE OF TECHNOLOGY

Applied Arts and Design—General M*
Art History M
Arts Administration M
Business Administration and Management—General M
Clothing and Textiles M
Illustration M
Marketing M
Museum Studies M

FAULKNER UNIVERSITY

Law P

FAYETTEVILLE STATE UNIVERSITY

Biological and Biomedical Sciences—General M
Business Administration and Management—General M
Criminal Justice and Criminology M
Educational Leadership and Administration M,D
Elementary Education M
English M
History M
Mathematics M
Middle School Education M
Political Science M
Psychology—General M
Reading Education M
Secondary Education M
Social Sciences Education M
Social Work M
Sociology M

FELICIAN COLLEGE

Adult Nursing M,O
Business Administration and Management—General M
Counseling Psychology M*
Education—General M*
Educational Leadership and Administration M
Elementary Education M
Entrepreneurship M
Family Nurse Practitioner Studies M,O*
Health Education M,O
Nursing Education M,O
Nursing—General M,O
Religious Education M,O
Special Education M

*M—master's degree; P—first professional degree; D—doctorate; O—other advanced degree; *—Close-Up and/or Announcement or Display in one of the other books in this series*

FERRIS STATE UNIVERSITY

Allied Health—General	M
Applied Arts and Design—General	M
Art/Fine Arts	M
Business Administration and Management—General	M
Computer Science	M
Criminal Justice and Criminology	M
Curriculum and Instruction	M
Database Systems	M
Developmental Education	M
Education—General	M
Educational Leadership and Administration	M
Educational Media/Instructional Technology	M
Electronic Commerce	M
Elementary Education	M
Human Services	M
Management Information Systems	M
Nursing and Healthcare Administration	M
Nursing Education	M
Nursing Informatics	M
Nursing—General	M
Optometry	P
Pharmacy	P
Quality Management	M
Reading Education	M
Special Education	M

FIELDING GRADUATE UNIVERSITY

Clinical Psychology	M,D,O
Educational Leadership and Administration	M,D,O*
Educational Media/Instructional Technology	M,D,O
Human Development	M,D,O
Organizational Management	M,D,O*
Psychology—General	M,D,O*

FISK UNIVERSITY

Biological and Biomedical Sciences—General	M
Chemistry	M
Clinical Psychology	M
Physics	M
Psychology—General	M

FITCHBURG STATE COLLEGE

Accounting	M
Art Education	M,O
Biological and Biomedical Sciences—General	M
Business Administration and Management—General	M
Communication—General	M,O
Computer Science	M
Counseling Psychology	M,O
Counselor Education	M,O
Criminal Justice and Criminology	M
Curriculum and Instruction	M
Early Childhood Education	M
Educational Leadership and Administration	M,O
Educational Media/Instructional Technology	M,O
Elementary Education	M
English Education	M,O
English	M,O
Forensic Nursing	M,O
Higher Education	M,O
History	M,O
Human Resources Management	M,O
Interdisciplinary Studies	O
Marriage and Family Therapy	M,O
Middle School Education	M
Science Education	M
Secondary Education	M
Social Sciences Education	M,O
Special Education	M
Technical Writing	M,O
Vocational and Technical Education	M

FIVE BRANCHES UNIVERSITY: GRADUATE SCHOOL OF TRADITIONAL CHINESE MEDICINE

Acupuncture and Oriental Medicine	M

FIVE TOWNS COLLEGE

Early Childhood Education	M
Music Education	M,D
Music	M,D

FLORIDA AGRICULTURAL AND MECHANICAL UNIVERSITY

Accounting	M
Adult Education	M,D
African-American Studies	M
Agricultural Economics and Agribusiness	M
Agricultural Sciences—General	M
Allied Health—General	M
Animal Sciences	M
Architecture	M
Biological and Biomedical Sciences—General	M
Biomedical Engineering	M,D
Business Administration and Management—General	M
Business Education	M
Chemical Engineering	M,D
Chemistry	M
Civil Engineering	M,D
Counselor Education	M,D
Criminal Justice and Criminology	M
Early Childhood Education	M
Economics	M
Education—General	M,D
Educational Leadership and Administration	M,D
Electrical Engineering	M,D
Elementary Education	M
Engineering and Applied Sciences—General	M,D
English Education	M
Entomology	M
Environmental Engineering	M,D
Environmental Sciences	M,D
Finance and Banking	M
Food Science and Technology	M
Health Education	M
History	M
Industrial/Management Engineering	M,D
International Affairs	M
Journalism	M
Landscape Architecture	M
Law	P
Management Information Systems	M
Marketing	M
Mathematics Education	M
Mechanical Engineering	M,D
Medicinal and Pharmaceutical Chemistry	M,D
Nursing and Healthcare Administration	M
Nursing—General	M
Pharmaceutical Administration	M,D
Pharmaceutical Sciences	M,D
Pharmacology	M,D
Pharmacy	P,D
Physical Education	M
Physical Therapy	M
Physics	M,D
Plant Sciences	M
Political Science	M
Psychology—General	M
Public Administration	M
Public Health—General	M
Recreation and Park Management	M
School Psychology	M
Science Education	M
Secondary Education	M
Social Psychology	M
Social Sciences Education	M
Social Sciences	M
Social Work	M
Sociology	M
Software Engineering	M
Toxicology	M,D
Vocational and Technical Education	M

FLORIDA ATLANTIC UNIVERSITY

Accounting	M,D
Adult Education	M,D,O
Anthropology	M
Applied Arts and Design—General	M
Applied Mathematics	M,D
Art Education	M
Art/Fine Arts	M
Biological and Biomedical Sciences—General	M,D
Business Administration and Management—General	M,D,O
Chemistry	M,D
Civil Engineering	M
Communication Disorders	M
Communication—General	M,O
Comparative and Interdisciplinary Arts	D
Comparative Literature	M
Computer Art and Design	M
Computer Engineering	M,D
Computer Science	M,D
Counseling Psychology	M,D,O
Counselor Education	M,D,O
Criminal Justice and Criminology	M
Curriculum and Instruction	M,D,O
Early Childhood Education	M,D,O
Economic Development	M,O
Economics	M
Education—General	M,D,O
Educational Leadership and Administration	M,D,O
Electrical Engineering	M,D
Elementary Education	M
Engineering and Applied Sciences—General	M,D
English as a Second Language	M,D,O
English Education	M
English	M
Entrepreneurship	M,D
Environmental Design	M,O
Environmental Education	M,O
Environmental Management and Policy	M,O
Environmental Sciences	M
Exercise and Sports Science	M
Film, Television, and Video Production	M,O
Film, Television, and Video Theory and Criticism	M,O
Finance and Banking	M,D
Foundations and Philosophy of Education	M
French	M
Geography	M
Geology	M
Graphic Design	M
Health Promotion	M
Higher Education	M,D,O
History	M,O
International Business	M,D
Journalism	M,O
Liberal Studies	M
Linguistics	M
Management Information Systems	M
Marriage and Family Therapy	M,D,O
Mathematics	M,D
Mechanical Engineering	M,D
Multilingual and Multicultural Education	M,D,O
Music	M
Neuroscience	D
Nonprofit Management	M
Nursing—General	M,D,O
Ocean Engineering	M,D
Physics	M,D
Political Science	M
Psychology—General	M,D
Public Administration	M,D
Reading Education	M
Rehabilitation Counseling	M,D,O
Social Work	M
Sociology	M
Spanish	M
Special Education	M,D
Statistics	M,D
Sustainable Development	M,O
Taxation	M
Theater	M
Travel and Tourism	M,O
Urban and Regional Planning	M,O
Women's Studies	M,O
Writing	M

FLORIDA COASTAL SCHOOL OF LAW

Law	P

FLORIDA COLLEGE OF INTEGRATIVE MEDICINE

Acupuncture and Oriental Medicine	M

FLORIDA GULF COAST UNIVERSITY

Accounting	M
Allied Health—General	M,D
Business Administration and Management—General	M
Computer Science	M
Counselor Education	M
Criminal Justice and Criminology	M
Curriculum and Instruction	M
Early Childhood Education	M
Education—General	M
Educational Leadership and Administration	M
Educational Media/Instructional Technology	M
Elementary Education	M
English Education	M
English	M
Environmental Management and Policy	M
Environmental Sciences	M
Forensic Sciences	M
History	M
Information Science	M
Interdisciplinary Studies	M
Nursing—General	M
Occupational Therapy	M
Physical Therapy	M,D
Public Administration	M
Reading Education	M
Social Work	M
Special Education	M
Taxation	M

FLORIDA HOSPITAL COLLEGE OF HEALTH SCIENCES

Nurse Anesthesia	M

FLORIDA INSTITUTE OF TECHNOLOGY

Accounting M
Aerospace/Aeronautical Engineering M,D*
Applied Mathematics M,D
Biological and Biomedical Sciences—General M,D
Biotechnology M,D
Business Administration and Management—General M
Cell Biology M,D*
Chemical Engineering M,D
Chemistry M,D
Civil Engineering M,D*
Clinical Psychology M,D
Communication—General M
Computer Education M,D,O
Computer Engineering M,D
Computer Science M,D*
Ecology M
Electrical Engineering M,D*
Electronic Commerce M
Elementary Education M,D,O
Engineering and Applied Sciences—General M,D
Engineering Management M*
Environmental Education M,D,O
Environmental Management and Policy M,D
Environmental Sciences M,D*
Ergonomics and Human Factors M
Finance and Banking M
Health Services Management and Hospital Administration M
Human Resources Management M
Industrial and Manufacturing Management M
Industrial and Organizational Psychology M,D
Information Science M
Logistics M
Management Information Systems M
Marine Affairs M,D
Marine Biology M*
Marine Sciences M,D
Marketing M
Mathematics Education M,D,O
Mechanical Engineering M,D*
Meteorology M,D
Molecular Biology M,D
Ocean Engineering M,D*
Oceanography M,D*
Operations Research M,D
Physics M,D
Planetary and Space Sciences M,D
Psychology—General M,D*
Public Administration M
Quality Management M
Science Education M,D,O
Software Engineering M,D
Systems Engineering M
Systems Science M
Transportation Management M

FLORIDA INTERNATIONAL UNIVERSITY

Accounting M
Adult Education M,D
African Studies M
Architecture M
Art Education M,D
Art/Fine Arts M
Asian Studies M
Athletic Training and Sports Medicine M
Biological and Biomedical Sciences—General M,D
Biomedical Engineering M,D*
Biostatistics M,D
Business Administration and Management—General M,D
Chemistry M,D
Civil Engineering M,D*
Communication Disorders M
Computer Engineering M
Computer Science M,D*
Conflict Resolution and Mediation/Peace Studies O
Construction Management M*
Counseling Psychology M
Counselor Education M
Criminal Justice and Criminology M
Curriculum and Instruction M,D,O
Early Childhood Education M,D
Economics M,D
Education—General M,D,O
Educational Leadership and Administration M,D,O
Educational Media/Instructional Technology M,D,O
Electrical Engineering M,D*
Elementary Education M,D
Engineering and Applied Sciences—General M,D*
English as a Second Language M,D,O
English Education M,D
English M
Environmental and Occupational Health M,D
Environmental Engineering M
Environmental Management and Policy M
Environmental Sciences M
Epidemiology M,D
Exercise and Sports Science M
Finance and Banking M
Foreign Languages Education M,D,O
Forensic Sciences M
Geosciences M,D
Health Promotion M,D
Health Services Management and Hospital Administration M,D
Higher Education D
History M,D
Hospitality Management M
Human Resources Development M,D
Human Resources Management M
Information Science M,D
Interior Design M
International Affairs M,D
International and Comparative Education M,D
International Business M
Landscape Architecture M
Latin American Studies M
Law P
Leisure Studies M
Liberal Studies M
Linguistics M
Management Information Systems M
Mass Communication M
Materials Engineering M,D
Mathematics Education M,D
Mathematics M
Mechanical Engineering M,D*
Music Education M
Music M
Nursing—General M,D*
Nutrition M,D
Occupational Therapy M
Physical Education M,D,O
Physical Therapy D
Physics M,D
Political Science M,D
Psychology—General M,D
Public Administration M,D
Public Health—General M,D
Reading Education M,D
Real Estate M
Recreation and Park Management M
Rehabilitation Counseling M
Religion M
School Psychology M,O
Science Education M,D
Social Sciences Education M,D
Social Work M,D
Sociology M,D
Spanish M,D
Special Education M,D,O
Sports Management M
Statistics M
Taxation M
Telecommunications M
Urban Education M
Writing M

FLORIDA SOUTHERN COLLEGE

Accounting M
Business Administration and Management—General M
Education—General M
International Business M
Nursing—General M

FLORIDA STATE UNIVERSITY

Accounting M,D
American Studies M,O
Analytical Chemistry M,D
Anthropology M,D
Applied Mathematics M,D
Applied Statistics M,D
Archaeology M,D
Art Education M,D,O
Art History M,D,O
Art/Fine Arts M
Arts Administration M,D
Asian Studies M
Biochemistry M,D
Biological and Biomedical Sciences—General P,M,D*
Biomedical Engineering M,D
Biostatistics M,D
Business Administration and Management—General M,D
Cell Biology M,D
Chemical Engineering M,D
Chemistry M,D
Child and Family Studies M,D
Civil Engineering M,D
Classics M,D
Clinical Psychology D
Cognitive Sciences D
Communication Disorders M,D
Communication—General M,D
Computational Biology D
Computer and Information Systems Security M,D
Computer Science M,D
Corporate and Organizational Communication M,D
Counseling Psychology M,D,O
Counselor Education M,D,O
Criminal Justice and Criminology M,D
Dance M
Demography and Population Studies M,O
Developmental Psychology D
Distance Education Development M,D,O
Early Childhood Education M,D,O
East European and Russian Studies M
Ecology M,D
Economics M,D
Education—General M,D,O
Educational Leadership and Administration M,D,O
Educational Measurement and Evaluation M,D,O
Educational Media/Instructional Technology M,D,O
Educational Policy M,D,O
Educational Psychology M,D,O
Electrical Engineering M,D
Elementary Education M,D,O
Engineering and Applied Sciences—General M,D
English Education M,D,O
English M,D
Environmental Engineering M,D
Evolutionary Biology M,D
Exercise and Sports Science M,D
Family and Consumer Sciences-General M,D
Family Nurse Practitioner Studies M,O
Film, Television, and Video Production M
Finance and Banking M,D
Food Science and Technology M,D
Foundations and Philosophy of Education M,D,O
French M,D
Genetics M,D
Geographic Information Systems M,D
Geography M,D
Geology M,D
Geophysics D
German M
Health Education M,D
Higher Education M,D,O
History M,D
Human Resources Development M,D,O
Humanities M,D,O
Industrial/Management Engineering M,D
Information Studies M,D,O
Inorganic Chemistry M,D
Insurance M,D
Interior Design M
International Affairs M
International and Comparative Education M,D,O
Italian M
Law P,M
Library Science M,D,O
Management Information Systems M,D
Manufacturing Engineering M,D
Marketing M,D
Marriage and Family Therapy M,D
Mass Communication M,D
Materials Sciences M
Mathematical and Computational Finance M,D
Mathematics Education M,D,O
Mathematics M,D
Mechanical Engineering M,D
Media Studies M,D
Meteorology M,D
Molecular Biology M,D
Molecular Biophysics D
Museum Studies M,D,O
Music Education M,D
Music M,D
Neuroscience D
Nursing Education M,O
Nursing—General M,O
Nutrition M,D
Oceanography M,D
Organic Chemistry M,D
Philosophy M,D
Physical Chemistry M,D
Physical Education M,D,O
Physics M,D*
Political Science M,D
Polymer Science and Engineering M
Psychology—General M,D
Public Administration M,D,O
Public Health—General M
Public History M,D

*M—master's degree; P—first professional degree; D—doctorate; O—other advanced degree; *—Close-Up and/or Announcement or Display in one of the other books in this series*

Public Policy	M,D,O
Reading Education	M,D,O
Recreation and Park Management	M,D,O
Rehabilitation Counseling	M,D,O
Religion	M,D
Rhetoric	M,D
School Psychology	M,O
Science Education	M,D,O
Slavic Languages	M
Social Psychology	D
Social Sciences Education	M,D,O
Social Work	M,D
Sociology	M,D
Software Engineering	M,D
Spanish	M,D
Special Education	M,D,O
Speech and Interpersonal Communication	M,D
Sport Psychology	M,D,O
Sports Management	M,D,O
Statistics	M,D,O
Structural Biology	D
Taxation	M,D
Theater	M,D
Therapies—Dance, Drama, and Music	M,D
Urban and Regional Planning	M,D
Writing	M,D

FONTBONNE UNIVERSITY

Accounting	M
Art/Fine Arts	M
Business Administration and Management—General	M
Communication Disorders	M
Computer Education	M
Education—General	M
Family and Consumer Sciences-General	M
Special Education	M
Taxation	M
Theater	M

FORDHAM UNIVERSITY

Accounting	M
Adult Education	M,D,O
Biological and Biomedical Sciences—General	M,D*
Business Administration and Management—General	M
Classics	M,D
Clinical Psychology	D
Communication—General	M
Computer Science	M
Corporate and Organizational Communication	M
Counseling Psychology	M,D,O
Counselor Education	M,D,O
Curriculum and Instruction	M,D,O
Developmental Psychology	D
Early Childhood Education	M,D,O
Economic Development	M,O
Economics	M,D,O
Education—General	M,D,O
Educational Leadership and Administration	M,D,O
Educational Psychology	M,D,O
Elementary Education	M,D,O
English as a Second Language	M,D,O
English	M,D
Ethics	M,O
Finance and Banking	M
History	M,D
Human Resources Management	M,D,O
International Affairs	M,O
International Development	M,O*
International Economics	M,O
Latin American Studies	M,O
Law	P,M
Liberal Studies	M
Management Information Systems	M
Marketing	M
Mass Communication	M
Media Studies	M
Medieval and Renaissance Studies	M,O
Multilingual and Multicultural Education	M,D,O
Pastoral Ministry and Counseling	M,D,O
Philosophy	M,D
Political Science	M
Psychology—General	D
Reading Education	M,D,O
Religion	M,D,O
Religious Education	M,D,O
School Psychology	M,D,O
Secondary Education	M,D,O
Social Work	M,D*
Sociology	M
Special Education	M,D,O
Taxation	M
Theology	M,D
Urban Studies	M

FORT HAYS STATE UNIVERSITY

Art/Fine Arts	M
Biological and Biomedical Sciences—General	M
Business Administration and Management—General	M
Communication Disorders	M
Communication—General	M
Counselor Education	M
Education—General	M,O
Educational Leadership and Administration	M,O
Educational Media/Instructional Technology	M
English	M
Geography	M
Geology	M
Geosciences	M
Health Education	M
History	M
Liberal Studies	M
Nursing—General	M
Physical Education	M
Psychology—General	M,O
School Psychology	O
Special Education	M

FORT VALLEY STATE UNIVERSITY

Animal Sciences	M
Counseling Psychology	M
Counselor Education	M,O
Environmental and Occupational Health	M
Public Health—General	M
Rehabilitation Counseling	M

FRAMINGHAM STATE COLLEGE

Art/Fine Arts	M
Business Administration and Management—General	M
Curriculum and Instruction	M
Early Childhood Education	M
Educational Leadership and Administration	M
Educational Media/Instructional Technology	M
Elementary Education	M
English as a Second Language	M
English Education	M
Food Science and Technology	M
Foreign Languages Education	M
Health Education	M
Health Services Management and Hospital Administration	M
Human Resources Management	M
Mathematics Education	M
Nursing and Healthcare Administration	M
Nursing Education	M
Nursing—General	M
Nutrition	M
Psychology—General	M
Public Administration	M
Reading Education	M
Social Sciences Education	M
Spanish	M
Special Education	M

FRANCISCAN SCHOOL OF THEOLOGY

Theology	P,M

FRANCISCAN UNIVERSITY OF STEUBENVILLE

Business Administration and Management—General	M
Counseling Psychology	M
Curriculum and Instruction	M
Education—General	M
Educational Leadership and Administration	M
Nursing—General	M
Philosophy	M
Theology	M

FRANCIS MARION UNIVERSITY

Business Administration and Management—General	M
Clinical Psychology	M
Early Childhood Education	M
Education—General	M
Elementary Education	M
Health Services Management and Hospital Administration	M
Psychology—General	M
School Psychology	M
Secondary Education	M
Social Psychology	M
Special Education	M

FRANKLIN PIERCE LAW CENTER

Law	P,M,O

FRANKLIN PIERCE UNIVERSITY

Business Administration and Management—General	M,D,O
Education—General	M,D,O
Health Services Management and Hospital Administration	M,D,O
Human Resources Management	M,D,O
Interdisciplinary Studies	M,D,O
Management Information Systems	M,D,O
Management Strategy and Policy	M,D,O
Nursing—General	M,D,O
Physical Therapy	M,D,O
Sports Management	M,D,O
Telecommunications	M,D,O

FRANKLIN UNIVERSITY

Business Administration and Management—General	M
Computer Science	M
Corporate and Organizational Communication	M
Marketing	M

FRANK LLOYD WRIGHT SCHOOL OF ARCHITECTURE

Architecture	M

FREDERICK S. PARDEE RAND GRADUATE SCHOOL

Public Policy	D

FREED-HARDEMAN UNIVERSITY

Accounting	M
Business Administration and Management—General	M
Counselor Education	M,O
Curriculum and Instruction	M,O
Education—General	M,O
Educational Leadership and Administration	M,O
Ethics	M
Management Strategy and Policy	M
Pastoral Ministry and Counseling	M
Special Education	M,O
Theology	P,M

FRESNO PACIFIC UNIVERSITY

Business Administration and Management—General	M
Conflict Resolution and Mediation/Peace Studies	M
Counselor Education	M
Curriculum and Instruction	M
Education of the Multiply Handicapped	M
Education—General	M
Educational Leadership and Administration	M
Educational Media/Instructional Technology	M
Elementary Education	M
English as a Second Language	M
Interdisciplinary Studies	M
Kinesiology and Movement Studies	M
Mathematics Education	M
Middle School Education	M
Multilingual and Multicultural Education	M
Reading Education	M
School Psychology	M
Science Education	M
Secondary Education	M
Special Education	M
Student Affairs	M

FRIENDS UNIVERSITY

Business Administration and Management—General	M
Education—General	M
Elementary Education	M
Health Services Management and Hospital Administration	M
Human Resources Development	M
Industrial and Manufacturing Management	M
Law	M
Management Information Systems	M
Marriage and Family Therapy	M
Secondary Education	M
Theology	M

FRONTIER SCHOOL OF MIDWIFERY AND FAMILY NURSING

Family Nurse Practitioner Studies	M,O
Nurse Midwifery	M,O

Nursing—General	M,O
Women's Health Nursing	M,O

FROSTBURG STATE UNIVERSITY

Biological and Biomedical Sciences—General	M
Business Administration and Management—General	M
Computer Science	M
Conservation Biology	M
Counseling Psychology	M
Counselor Education	M
Curriculum and Instruction	M
Ecology	M
Education—General	M
Educational Leadership and Administration	M
Educational Media/Instructional Technology	M
Elementary Education	M
Fish, Game, and Wildlife Management	M
Interdisciplinary Studies	M
Psychology—General	M
Reading Education	M
Recreation and Park Management	M
Secondary Education	M
Special Education	M

FULLER THEOLOGICAL SEMINARY

Clinical Psychology	D
Marriage and Family Therapy	M,O
Missions and Missiology	P,M,D
Music	P,M,D
Pastoral Ministry and Counseling	P,M,D
Psychology—General	M,D,O
Theology	P,M,D

FULL SAIL UNIVERSITY

Business Administration and Management—General	M
Educational Media/Instructional Technology	M
Entertainment Management	M*
Internet and Interactive Multimedia	M*
Marketing	M*
Media Studies	M*

FURMAN UNIVERSITY

Chemistry	M
Curriculum and Instruction	M
Early Childhood Education	M
Education—General	M
Educational Leadership and Administration	M
English as a Second Language	M
Reading Education	M
Special Education	M

GALLAUDET UNIVERSITY

Clinical Psychology	D
Communication Disorders	M,D,O
Counseling Psychology	M
Counselor Education	M
Developmental Psychology	M,O
Early Childhood Education	M,D,O
Education of the Multiply Handicapped	M,D,O
Educational Leadership and Administration	M,D,O
Educational Measurement and Evaluation	M,O
Elementary Education	M,D,O
International and Comparative Education	M,O
Leisure Studies	M
Linguistics	M,D
Psychology—General	M,D,O
School Psychology	M,O
Secondary Education	M,D,O
Social Work	M
Special Education	M,D,O

GANNON UNIVERSITY

Accounting	O
Business Administration and Management—General	M,O
Computer Science	M
Counseling Psychology	D
Counselor Education	M,O
Curriculum and Instruction	M
Early Childhood Education	M
Education—General	M,D,O
Educational Leadership and Administration	M,D,O
Educational Media/Instructional Technology	M,O
Electrical Engineering	M
Engineering Management	M
English as a Second Language	O
English	M
Environmental and Occupational Health	O
Environmental Education	M
Environmental Engineering	M
Environmental Sciences	M,O
Family Nurse Practitioner Studies	M,O
Finance and Banking	O
Gerontology	O
Human Resources Management	O
Information Science	M
Investment Management	O
Marketing	O
Mechanical Engineering	M
Medical/Surgical Nursing	M,O
Nurse Anesthesia	M,O
Nursing and Healthcare Administration	M,O
Nursing—General	M,O
Occupational Therapy	M
Organizational Management	D
Pastoral Ministry and Counseling	M,O
Physical Therapy	D
Physician Assistant Studies	M
Public Administration	M,O
Reading Education	M,O
Science Education	M
Software Engineering	M

GARDNER-WEBB UNIVERSITY

Business Administration and Management—General	M
Counseling Psychology	M
Curriculum and Instruction	D
Education—General	M,D
Educational Leadership and Administration	M,D
Elementary Education	M
English Education	M
English	M
Exercise and Sports Science	M
Middle School Education	M
Missions and Missiology	P,D
Nursing—General	M,O
Pastoral Ministry and Counseling	P,D
Physical Education	M
Psychology—General	M
Religious Education	P,D
School Psychology	M
Theology	P,D

GARRETT-EVANGELICAL THEOLOGICAL SEMINARY

Music	P,M,D
Pastoral Ministry and Counseling	P,M,D
Religious Education	P,M,D
Theology	P,M,D

GENERAL THEOLOGICAL SEMINARY

Pastoral Ministry and Counseling	P,M,D,O
Religion	P,M,D,O
Theology	P,M,D,O

GENEVA COLLEGE

Business Administration and Management—General	M
Counseling Psychology	M
Counselor Education	M
Education—General	M
Educational Leadership and Administration	M
Higher Education	M
Marriage and Family Therapy	M
Organizational Management	M
Psychology—General	M
Special Education	M

GEORGE FOX UNIVERSITY

Business Administration and Management—General	M,D
Clinical Psychology	M,D*
Counseling Psychology	M,O
Counselor Education	M,O
Curriculum and Instruction	M,D,O
Education—General	M,D,O
Educational Leadership and Administration	M,D,O
Educational Media/Instructional Technology	M,D,O
English as a Second Language	M,D,O
Foundations and Philosophy of Education	M,D,O
Higher Education	M,D,O
Marriage and Family Therapy	M,O
Missions and Missiology	P,M,D,O
Multilingual and Multicultural Education	M,D,O
Pastoral Ministry and Counseling	P,M,D,O
Psychology—General	M,D
Reading Education	M,D,O
Religion	P,M,D,O
School Psychology	M,O
Secondary Education	M,D,O
Theology	P,M,D,O

GEORGE MASON UNIVERSITY

Accounting	M
Anthropology	M,D
Applied Physics	M
Art Education	M
Art History	M
Arts Administration	M
Atmospheric Sciences	D
Bioinformatics	M,D,O
Biological and Biomedical Sciences—General	M,D,O
Biopsychology	M,D
Biostatistics	M,D,O
Business Administration and Management—General	M
Cell Biology	M,D,O
Chemistry	M
Civil Engineering	M
Clinical Psychology	M,D
Communication—General	M,D
Community College Education	M,D,O
Community Health	M,O
Computational Biology	M,D,O
Computational Sciences	M,D,O
Computer and Information Systems Security	M,D,O
Computer Engineering	M,D,O
Computer Science	M,D
Conflict Resolution and Mediation/Peace Studies	M,D
Counselor Education	M
Criminal Justice and Criminology	M,D
Cultural Studies	D*
Dance	M
Database Systems	M,D,O
Developmental Psychology	M,D
Early Childhood Education	M,O
Education of the Gifted	M,O
Education—General	M,D,O
Educational Leadership and Administration	M,O
Educational Measurement and Evaluation	M
Educational Media/Instructional Technology	M,O
Educational Psychology	M
Electrical Engineering	M,D,O
Electronic Commerce	M,D,O
Engineering and Applied Sciences—General	M,D,O
Engineering Physics	M
English as a Second Language	M,O
Environmental Sciences	M,D
Epidemiology	M,D,O
Evolutionary Biology	M,D,O
Exercise and Sports Science	M
Family Nurse Practitioner Studies	M,D,O
Film, Television, and Video Production	M
Folklore	M
Foreign Languages Education	M
Forensic Sciences	M,D,O
Gender Studies	M
Geodetic Sciences	M,D,O
Geographic Information Systems	M,D,O
Geography	M
Graphic Design	M
Health Promotion	M
Higher Education	M,D,O
History	M,D,O
Homeland Security	M,D
Human Resources Management	M
Industrial and Organizational Psychology	M,D
Information Science	M,D,O
International Affairs	M
International Health	M,O
Law	P,M
Library Science	M,O
Linguistics	M,O
Logistics	M
Management Information Systems	M,D,O
Management of Technology	M,D
Mathematics Education	M,O
Mathematics	M,D
Microbiology	M,D,O
Molecular Biology	M,D,O
Music Education	M,O
Music	M,O
Nanotechnology	M,D,O
Neuroscience	M,D,O
Nursing and Healthcare Administration	M,D,O
Nursing Education	M,D,O

*M—master's degree; P—first professional degree; D—doctorate; O—other advanced degree; *—Close-Up and/or Announcement or Display in one of the other books in this series*

Nursing—General	M,D,O
Nutrition	M,O
Operations Research	M
Organizational Management	M
Philosophy	M
Physical Education	M,O
Physics	M
Political Science	M,D
Public Affairs	M,D
Public Policy	M,D*
Reading Education	M,O
Religion	M
School Psychology	M
Science Education	M,O
Secondary Education	M,O
Social Sciences	M,D,O
Social Work	M
Software Engineering	M,D,O
Special Education	M,O
Statistics	M,D,O
Systems Engineering	M
Telecommunications	M,D,O
Transportation Management	M
Women's Studies	M
Writing	M

GEORGETOWN COLLEGE

Education—General	M

GEORGETOWN UNIVERSITY

Acute Care/Critical Care Nursing	M
Advertising and Public Relations	M,D
Allopathic Medicine	P
American Studies	M,D
Analytical Chemistry	D
Biochemistry	M,D
Bioinformatics	M
Biological and Biomedical Sciences—General	M,D
Biophysics	M,D
Biostatistics	M
Business Administration and Management—General	M
Cell Biology	D
Chemistry	D
Communication—General	M
Comparative Literature	M,D
Computer Science	M
Conflict Resolution and Mediation/Peace Studies	M
East European and Russian Studies	M
Economic Development	D
Economics	D
English as a Second Language	M,D,O
English	M
Epidemiology	M
Ethics	M,D
Family Nurse Practitioner Studies	M
Finance and Banking	D
German	M,D
Health Law	P,M,D
Health Physics/Radiological Health	M
Health Promotion	M,D
History	M,D
Human Resources Management	M,D
Humanities	M,D
Immunology	M,D
Industrial and Labor Relations	D
Industrial and Manufacturing Management	D
Infectious Diseases	M,D
Inorganic Chemistry	D
Interdisciplinary Studies	M,D
International Affairs	P,M,D
International Business	P,M,D
International Health	P,M,D
Internet and Interactive Multimedia	M
Journalism	M,D
Latin American Studies	M,D
Law	P,M,D
Legal and Justice Studies	P,M,D
Liberal Studies	M,D
Linguistics	M,D,O
Materials Sciences	D
Mathematics	M
Media Studies	M,D
Medieval and Renaissance Studies	M,D
Microbiology	M,D
Molecular Biology	M,D
Multilingual and Multicultural Education	M,D,O
Near and Middle Eastern Languages	M,D
Near and Middle Eastern Studies	M,D,O
Neuroscience	D
Nurse Anesthesia	M
Nurse Midwifery	M
Nursing Education	M
Nursing—General	M
Organic Chemistry	D
Pathology	M,D
Pharmacology	M,D
Philosophy	M,D
Physical Chemistry	D
Physiology	M,D
Political Science	M,D
Psychology—General	D
Public Health—General	M,D
Public Policy	M,D
Radiation Biology	M
Real Estate	M,D
Religion	M,D
Spanish	M,D
Sports Management	M,D
Statistics	M
Taxation	P,M,D
Theology	D
Theoretical Chemistry	D
Western European Studies	M

THE GEORGE WASHINGTON UNIVERSITY

Accounting	M,D
Adult Nursing	M,D,O
Aerospace/Aeronautical Engineering	M,D,O
Allopathic Medicine	P
American Studies	M,D
Analytical Chemistry	M,D
Anthropology	M,D
Applied Mathematics	M,D
Art History	M
Art Therapy	M
Art/Fine Arts	M
Asian Studies	M
Biochemistry	M,D*
Bioinformatics	M
Biological and Biomedical Sciences—General	M,D*
Biostatistics	M,D
Biotechnology	M
Business Administration and Management—General	M,D,O
Chemistry	M,D
Civil Engineering	M,D,O
Clinical Psychology	D
Cognitive Sciences	D
Communication Disorders	M
Communication—General	M
Community Health	M
Computer Engineering	M,D
Computer Science	M,D
Counselor Education	M,D,O
Criminal Justice and Criminology	M
Curriculum and Instruction	M,D,O
Early Childhood Education	M
East European and Russian Studies	M
Economics	M,D
Education—General	M,D,O
Educational Leadership and Administration	M,D,O
Educational Media/Instructional Technology	M
Educational Policy	M,D
Electrical Engineering	M,D
Elementary Education	M
Emergency Management	M,D,O
Engineering and Applied Sciences—General	M,D,O*
Engineering Management	M,D,O
English	M,D
Environmental and Occupational Health	M,D
Environmental Engineering	M,D,O
Environmental Management and Policy	M,D
Epidemiology	M,D
Exercise and Sports Science	M
Family Nurse Practitioner Studies	M,D,O
Finance and Banking	M,D
Folklore	M,D
Forensic Sciences	M
Genetics	D
Genomic Sciences	M
Geography	M
Health Communication	M
Health Promotion	M
Health Psychology	D
Health Services Management and Hospital Administration	M,D,O
Health Services Research	M,D,O
Higher Education	M,D,O
Historic Preservation	M
History	M,D
Hospitality Management	M,O
Human Development	M
Human Resources Development	M,D,O
Human Resources Management	M,D
Immunology	D*
Industrial and Organizational Psychology	M,D
Infectious Diseases	M
Inorganic Chemistry	M,D
Interior Design	M
International Affairs	M
International and Comparative Education	M
International Business	M,D
International Development	M
International Health	M,D
International Trade Policy	M
Investment Management	M,D
Latin American Studies	M
Law	P,M,D
Legal and Justice Studies	M,O
Management Information Systems	M,D
Management of Technology	M,D
Management Strategy and Policy	M,D
Marketing	M,D
Mass Communication	M
Materials Sciences	M,D
Maternal and Child Health	M
Mathematics	M,D
Mechanical Engineering	M,D,O
Microbiology	M,D,O
Military and Defense Studies	M
Molecular Biology	M,D
Molecular Genetics	D
Molecular Medicine	D*
Museum Education	M
Museum Studies	M,O
Near and Middle Eastern Studies	M
Nonprofit Management	M
Nursing and Healthcare Administration	M,D,O
Nursing—General	M,D,O
Organic Chemistry	M,D
Organizational Management	M,D
Philosophy	M,D
Photography	M
Physical Chemistry	M,D
Physical Therapy	D
Physician Assistant Studies	M
Physics	M,D
Political Science	M,D
Project Management	M,D
Psychology—General	D
Public Administration	M,D
Public Affairs	M
Public Health—General	M,D,O
Public Policy	M,D
Publishing	M
Real Estate	M
Rehabilitation Counseling	M
Religion	M
Secondary Education	M
Social Psychology	M,D
Sociology	M
Special Education	M,D,O
Sports Management	M,O
Statistics	M,D,O
Systems Engineering	M,D,O
Technology and Public Policy	M
Telecommunications	M,D
Theater	M
Toxicology	M
Travel and Tourism	M,O
Western European Studies	M
Women's Studies	M,D,O

GEORGIA CAMPUS–PHILADELPHIA COLLEGE OF OSTEOPATHIC MEDICINE

Biological and Biomedical Sciences—General	M,O
Osteopathic Medicine	P

GEORGIA COLLEGE & STATE UNIVERSITY

Accounting	M
Adult Nursing	M
Biological and Biomedical Sciences—General	M
Business Administration and Management—General	M
Criminal Justice and Criminology	M
Curriculum and Instruction	M,O
Early Childhood Education	M,O
Education—General	M,O
Educational Leadership and Administration	M,O
Educational Media/Instructional Technology	M,O
English	M
Family Nurse Practitioner Studies	M
Health Education	M
Health Promotion	M
History	M
Logistics	M
Management Information Systems	M
Middle School Education	M,O
Music Education	M
Nursing and Healthcare Administration	M
Nursing—General	M
Physical Education	M
Public Administration	M
Public History	M
Recreation and Park Management	M
Secondary Education	M,O
Special Education	M
Therapies—Dance, Drama, and Music	M
Writing	M

GEORGIA INSTITUTE OF TECHNOLOGY

Accounting	M,D,O
Aerospace/Aeronautical Engineering	M,D
Applied Mathematics	M,D
Architecture	M,D
Atmospheric Sciences	M,D
Biochemistry	M,D
Bioengineering	M,D
Bioinformatics	M,D
Biological and Biomedical Sciences—General	M,D
Biomedical Engineering	D
Building Science	M,D
Business Administration and Management—General*	M,D,O
Chemical Engineering	M,D
Chemistry	M,D
Civil Engineering	M,D
Computer and Information Systems Security	M,D
Computer Art and Design	M,D
Computer Engineering	M,D
Computer Science	M,D
Economic Development	M,D
Economics	M
Electrical Engineering	M,D
Electronic Commerce	M,O
Engineering and Applied Sciences—General	M,D
Entrepreneurship	M,O
Environmental Engineering	M,D
Environmental Management and Policy	M,D
Environmental Sciences	M,D
Ergonomics and Human Factors	M,D
Experimental Psychology	M,D
Finance and Banking	M,D,O
Geochemistry	M,D
Geographic Information Systems	M,D
Geophysics	M,D
Geosciences	M,D*
Health Physics/Radiological Health	M,D
Health Services Management and Hospital Administration	M
History of Science and Technology	M,D
Human-Computer Interaction	M
Hydrology	M,D
Industrial and Organizational Psychology	M,D
Industrial/Management Engineering	M,D
International Affairs	M,D
International Business	M,O
Internet and Interactive Multimedia	M,D
Management Information Systems	M,D,O
Management of Technology	M,O
Management Strategy and Policy	M,D,O
Marketing	M,D,O
Materials Engineering	M,D
Mathematical and Computational Finance	M,D
Mathematics	M,D
Mechanical Engineering	M,D
Mechanics	M,D
Medical Physics	M,D
Natural Resources	M,D
Nuclear Engineering	M,D
Ocean Engineering	M,D
Operations Research	M,D
Organizational Behavior	M,D,O
Physics	M,D
Physiology	M
Polymer Science and Engineering	M,D
Psychology—General	M,D
Public Policy	M,D
Statistics	M,D
Systems Engineering	M,D
Textile Sciences and Engineering	M,D
Urban and Regional Planning	M,D
Urban Design	M,D

GEORGIAN COURT UNIVERSITY

Accounting	M,O
Biological and Biomedical Sciences—General	M,O
Business Administration and Management—General	M,O
Counseling Psychology	M,O
Education—General	M
Educational Leadership and Administration	M,O
Educational Psychology	M,O
Mathematics	M,O
Pastoral Ministry and Counseling	M,O
Religious Education	M,O
Theology	M,O

GEORGIA SOUTHERN UNIVERSITY

Accounting	M
Allied Health—General	M,D,O
Applied Economics	M
Art Education	M
Art/Fine Arts	M
Biological and Biomedical Sciences—General	M
Biostatistics	M,D
Business Administration and Management—General	M
Business Education	M
Community Health Nursing	M,D,O
Community Health	M,D
Counselor Education	M,O
Curriculum and Instruction	D
Early Childhood Education	M
Education—General	M,D,O
Educational Leadership and Administration	M,D,O
Educational Media/Instructional Technology	M
Electrical Engineering	M
Elementary Education	M
English Education	M
English	M
Environmental and Occupational Health	M,D
Epidemiology	M,D
Family Nurse Practitioner Studies	M,O
Foreign Languages Education	M
Health Education	M,D
Health Services Management and Hospital Administration	M,D
Higher Education	M
History	M
Kinesiology and Movement Studies	M
Mathematics Education	M
Mathematics	M
Mechanical Engineering	M
Middle School Education	M
Music	M
Nursing—General	M,D,O
Physical Education	M
Psychology—General	M,D
Public Administration	M
Public Health—General	M,D
Reading Education	M
Recreation and Park Management	M
School Psychology	M,O
Science Education	M
Secondary Education	M
Social Sciences Education	M
Sociology	M
Spanish	M
Special Education	M
Sports Management	M
Vocational and Technical Education	M
Women's Health Nursing	M,D,O

GEORGIA SOUTHWESTERN STATE UNIVERSITY

Business Administration and Management—General	M
Computer Science	M
Early Childhood Education	M,O
Education—General	M,O
Health Education	M,O
Information Science	M
Middle School Education	M,O
Physical Education	M,O
Reading Education	M,O
Secondary Education	M,O
Special Education	M,O

GEORGIA STATE UNIVERSITY

Accounting	M,D,O
Actuarial Science	M
Adult Nursing	M,D,O
Allied Health—General	M,D,O
Anthropology	M
Art Education	M,D,O
Art History	M
Art/Fine Arts	M
Astronomy	D
Athletic Training and Sports Medicine	M
Biochemistry	M,D
Biological and Biomedical Sciences—General	M,D
Business Administration and Management—General	M,D
Cell Biology	M,D
Chemistry	M,D
Communication Disorders	M
Communication—General	M,D
Computer Science	M,D
Counseling Psychology	M,D,O
Counselor Education	M,D,O
Criminal Justice and Criminology	M,D,O
Early Childhood Education	M,D,O
Economic Development	M,D,O
Economics	M,D
Education of the Multiply Handicapped	M
Education—General	M,D,O
Educational Leadership and Administration	M,D,O
Educational Measurement and Evaluation	M,D
Educational Media/Instructional Technology	M,D,O
Educational Policy	M,D,O
Educational Psychology	M,D
Emergency Management	M,D,O
English as a Second Language	M,D,O
English Education	M,D,O
English	M,D
Entrepreneurship	M,D
Environmental Biology	M,D
Exercise and Sports Science	M
Family Nurse Practitioner Studies	M,D,O
Film, Television, and Video Production	M,D
Finance and Banking	M,D,O
Foundations and Philosophy of Education	M,D
French	M,O
Geographic Information Systems	O
Geography	M
Geology	M
Geosciences	M,O
German	M,O
Gerontology	M
Health Education	M
Health Promotion	M,D,O
Health Services Management and Hospital Administration	M
Historic Preservation	M,O
History	M,D
Human Resources Management	M,D
Human Services	M
Hydrogeology	M,O
Information Science	M
Insurance	M,D,O
International Business	M
Kinesiology and Movement Studies	D
Latin American Studies	M,D,O
Law	P
Linguistics	M,D
Management Information Systems	M,D
Management Strategy and Policy	M,D
Marketing	M,D
Mass Communication	M,D
Mathematics Education	M,D,O
Mathematics	M,D
Microbiology	M,D
Middle School Education	M,O
Molecular Biology	M,D
Molecular Genetics	M,D
Music Education	M,D,O
Music	M
Neurobiology	M,D
Nonprofit Management	M,D,O
Nursing—General	M,D,O
Nutrition	M
Operations Research	M,D
Organizational Management	M,D
Pediatric Nursing	M,D,O
Philosophy	M
Photography	M,D
Physical Education	M
Physical Therapy	D
Physics	M,D
Physiology	M,D
Political Science	M,D
Psychiatric Nursing	M,D,O
Psychology—General	M,D
Public Administration	M,D,O
Public Health—General	M,D,O
Public Policy	M,D,O
Quantitative Analysis	M,D
Reading Education	M,D,O
Real Estate	M,D,O
Rehabilitation Counseling	M
Religion	M
Rhetoric	M,D
School Psychology	M,D,O
Science Education	M,D,O
Secondary Education	M,D,O
Social Sciences Education	M,D,O
Social Work	M
Sociology	M,D
Spanish	M,O
Special Education	M,D
Speech and Interpersonal Communication	M,D
Sports Management	M
Statistics	M,D
Taxation	M
Translation and Interpretation	O
Urban and Regional Planning	M,D,O
Women's Health Nursing	M,D,O
Women's Studies	M,O
Writing	M,D

GERSTNER SLOAN-KETTERING GRADUATE SCHOOL OF BIOMEDICAL SCIENCES

Biological and Biomedical Sciences—General	D
Cancer Biology/Oncology	D*

*M—master's degree; P—first professional degree; D—doctorate; O—other advanced degree; *—Close-Up and/or Announcement or Display in one of the other books in this series*

GLOBAL UNIVERSITY

Missions and Missiology	P,M
Religious Education	P,M
Theology	P,M

GODDARD COLLEGE

Business Administration and Management—General	M
Comparative and Interdisciplinary Arts	M
Counseling Psychology	M
Education—General	M
Environmental Management and Policy	M
Health Promotion	M
Industrial and Organizational Psychology	M
Interdisciplinary Studies	M
Sustainability Management	M
Writing	M

GOLDEN GATE BAPTIST THEOLOGICAL SEMINARY

Early Childhood Education	P,M,D,O
Educational Leadership and Administration	P,M,D,O
Pastoral Ministry and Counseling	P,M,D,O
Theology	P,M,D,O

GOLDEN GATE UNIVERSITY

Accounting	M,D,O
Advertising and Public Relations	M,D,O
Business Administration and Management—General	M,D,O
Environmental Law	P,M,D
Finance and Banking	M,D,O
Human Resources Management	M,D,O
International Business	M,D,O
Law	P,M,D
Legal and Justice Studies	P,M,D
Management Information Systems	M,D,O
Management of Technology	M,D,O
Marketing	M,D,O
Psychology—General	M,D,O
Taxation	P,M,D,O

GOLDEY-BEACOM COLLEGE

Business Administration and Management—General	M
Finance and Banking	M
Human Resources Management	M
Management Information Systems	M
Marketing	M

GOLDFARB SCHOOL OF NURSING AT BARNES-JEWISH COLLEGE

Adult Nursing	M
Health Services Management and Hospital Administration	M
Maternal and Child/Neonatal Nursing	M
Nurse Anesthesia	M
Nursing Education	M
Nursing—General	M
Oncology Nursing	M

GONZAGA UNIVERSITY

Accounting	M
Business Administration and Management—General	M
Communication—General	M
Counseling Psychology	M
Education—General	M
Educational Leadership and Administration	M,D
English as a Second Language	M
Law	P
Nurse Anesthesia	M
Nursing—General	M
Organizational Management	M
Pastoral Ministry and Counseling	M
Philosophy	M
Reading Education	M
Religion	M
Special Education	M
Sports Management	M

GOODING INSTITUTE OF NURSE ANESTHESIA

Nurse Anesthesia	M

GORDON COLLEGE

Education—General	M
Music Education	M

GORDON-CONWELL THEOLOGICAL SEMINARY

Archaeology	P,M,D
Missions and Missiology	P,M,D
Pastoral Ministry and Counseling	P,M,D
Religion	P,M,D
Theology	P,M,D

GOUCHER COLLEGE

Arts Administration	M
Biological and Biomedical Sciences—General	O
Education—General	M
Historic Preservation	M
Writing	M

GOVERNORS STATE UNIVERSITY

Accounting	M
Addictions/Substance Abuse Counseling	M
Analytical Chemistry	M
Art/Fine Arts	M
Business Administration and Management—General	M
Communication Disorders	M
Communication—General	M
Computer Science	M
Counseling Psychology	M
Early Childhood Education	M
Education—General	M
Educational Leadership and Administration	M
Educational Media/Instructional Technology	M
English	M
Environmental Biology	M
Health Services Management and Hospital Administration	M
Legal and Justice Studies	M
Management Information Systems	M
Media Studies	M
Nursing—General	M
Occupational Therapy	M
Physical Therapy	M,D
Political Science	M
Psychology—General	M
Public Administration	M
Reading Education	M
Social Work	M
Special Education	M

GRACE COLLEGE

Counseling Psychology	M

GRACELAND UNIVERSITY (IA)

Education—General	M
Educational Leadership and Administration	M
Educational Media/Instructional Technology	M
Family Nurse Practitioner Studies	M,O
Nursing and Healthcare Administration	M,O
Nursing Education	M,O
Nursing—General	M,O
Pastoral Ministry and Counseling	M
Religion	M
Special Education	M

GRACE THEOLOGICAL SEMINARY

Cultural Studies	P,M,D,O
Missions and Missiology	P,M,D,O
Pastoral Ministry and Counseling	P,M,D,O
Theology	P,M,D,O

GRACE UNIVERSITY

Counseling Psychology	M
Pastoral Ministry and Counseling	M
Theology	M

GRADUATE INSTITUTE OF APPLIED LINGUISTICS

Linguistics	M,O
Multilingual and Multicultural Education	M,O

GRADUATE SCHOOL AND UNIVERSITY CENTER OF THE CITY UNIVERSITY OF NEW YORK

Accounting	D
Anthropology	D
Archaeology	D
Architectural History	D
Art History	D
Biochemistry	D
Biological and Biomedical Sciences—General	D
Biomedical Engineering	D
Biopsychology	D
Business Administration and Management—General	D
Chemical Engineering	D
Chemistry	D
Civil Engineering	D
Classics	M,D
Clinical Psychology	D
Cognitive Sciences	D
Communication Disorders	D
Comparative Literature	M,D
Computer Science	D
Criminal Justice and Criminology	D
Developmental Psychology	D
Economics	D
Educational Psychology	D
Electrical Engineering	D
Engineering and Applied Sciences—General	D*
English	D
Environmental Sciences	D
Experimental Psychology	D
Finance and Banking	D
French	D
Geosciences	D
German	M,D
History	D
Industrial and Organizational Psychology	D
Interdisciplinary Studies	M,D
Italian	M,D
Liberal Studies	M
Linguistics	M,D
Management Information Systems	D
Mathematics	D
Mechanical Engineering	D
Medieval and Renaissance Studies	M,D
Music	D
Neuroscience	D
Nursing—General	D
Organizational Behavior	D
Philosophy	M,D
Physical Therapy	D
Physics	D
Political Science	M,D
Psychology—General	D
Public Health—General	D
Public Policy	M,D
Social Psychology	D
Social Work	D
Sociology	D
Spanish	D
Theater	D
Urban Education	D
Urban Studies	M,D
Women's Studies	M,D

GRADUATE THEOLOGICAL UNION

Art History	M,D,O
Cultural Studies	M,D,O
Ethics	M,D,O
Jewish Studies	M,D,O
Religion	M,D,O
Social Sciences	M,D,O
Theology	M,D,O

GRAMBLING STATE UNIVERSITY

Counselor Education	M,D
Criminal Justice and Criminology	M
Curriculum and Instruction	M,D
Developmental Education	M,D
Education—General	M,D
Educational Leadership and Administration	M,D
Educational Media/Instructional Technology	M,D
English	M,D
Family Nurse Practitioner Studies	M,O
Health Services Management and Hospital Administration	M
Higher Education	M,D
Human Resources Management	M
Mass Communication	M
Mathematics Education	M,D
Nursing Education	M,O
Nursing—General	M,O
Political Science	M
Public Administration	M
Reading Education	M
Science Education	M,D,O
Social Sciences Education	M
Social Work	M
Sports Management	M
Student Affairs	M,D

GRAND CANYON UNIVERSITY

Accounting	M
Addictions/Substance Abuse Counseling	M
Adult Nursing	M

Business Administration and Management—General	M
Counselor Education	M
Curriculum and Instruction	M,D
Education—General	M,D*
Educational Leadership and Administration	M,D
Elementary Education	M,D
Family Nurse Practitioner Studies	M
Finance and Banking	M
Health Services Management and Hospital Administration	M
Management Information Systems	M
Marketing	M
Nursing and Healthcare Administration	M
Nursing Education	M
Nursing—General	M
Organizational Management	M,D
Secondary Education	M,D
Special Education	M,D

GRAND RAPIDS THEOLOGICAL SEMINARY OF CORNERSTONE UNIVERSITY

Missions and Missiology	P,M
Pastoral Ministry and Counseling	P,M
Religion	P,M
Religious Education	P,M
Theology	P,M

GRAND VALLEY STATE UNIVERSITY

Accounting	M
Adult Education	M,O
Allied Health—General	M,D
Bioinformatics	M
Biological and Biomedical Sciences—General	M
Biostatistics	M
Business Administration and Management—General	M
Cell Biology	M
Communication—General	M
Computer Engineering	M
Computer Science	M
Criminal Justice and Criminology	M
Early Childhood Education	M,O
Education—General	M,O
Educational Leadership and Administration	M,O
Educational Media/Instructional Technology	M,O
Electrical Engineering	M
Elementary Education	M,O
Engineering and Applied Sciences—General	M
English as a Second Language	M,O
English Education	M
English	M
Health Services Management and Hospital Administration	M,D
Higher Education	M,O
Information Science	M
Management Information Systems	M
Manufacturing Engineering	M
Mechanical Engineering	M
Medical Informatics	M
Middle School Education	M,O
Molecular Biology	M
Nursing and Healthcare Administration	M,D
Nursing Education	M,D
Nursing—General	M,D
Occupational Therapy	M
Physical Therapy	D
Physician Assistant Studies	M
Public Administration	M
Reading Education	M
School Psychology	M
Secondary Education	M,O
Social Work	M
Software Engineering	M
Special Education	M
Taxation	M

GRAND VIEW UNIVERSITY

Business Administration and Management—General	M
Education—General	M
Nursing—General	M
Organizational Management	M

GRANTHAM UNIVERSITY

Business Administration and Management—General	M
Management Information Systems	M
Management of Technology	M
Project Management	M

GRATZ COLLEGE

Education—General	M
Holocaust Studies	M,O
Jewish Studies	M,O
Music	M,O
Religious Education	M,D,O
Social Work	M,O

GREEN MOUNTAIN COLLEGE

Business Administration and Management—General	M
Environmental Management and Policy	M

GREENSBORO COLLEGE

Education—General	M
Elementary Education	M
English as a Second Language	M
Special Education	M

GREENVILLE COLLEGE

Education—General	M
Elementary Education	M
Pastoral Ministry and Counseling	M
Secondary Education	M

GWYNEDD-MERCY COLLEGE

Adult Nursing	M
Business Administration and Management—General	M
Counselor Education	M
Education—General	M
Educational Leadership and Administration	M
Family Nurse Practitioner Studies	M
Gerontological Nursing	M
Nursing—General	M
Oncology Nursing	M
Pediatric Nursing	M
Reading Education	M
Special Education	M

HAMLINE UNIVERSITY

Business Administration and Management—General	M,D
Education—General	M,D
Law	P,M
Liberal Studies	M,O
Nonprofit Management	M,D
Public Administration	M,D

HAMPTON UNIVERSITY

Adult Nursing	M
Applied Mathematics	M
Atmospheric Sciences	M,D
Biological and Biomedical Sciences—General	M
Business Administration and Management—General	M
Chemistry	M
Communication Disorders	M
Community Health Nursing	M
Computational Sciences	M
Computer Science	M
Counselor Education	M
Early Childhood Education	M
Education—General	M
Elementary Education	M
Environmental Biology	M
Gerontological Nursing	M
Medical Physics	M,D
Middle School Education	M
Music Education	M
Nursing—General	M
Pastoral Ministry and Counseling	M
Pediatric Nursing	M
Physical Therapy	D
Physics	M,D
Psychiatric Nursing	M
Secondary Education	M
Special Education	M
Statistics	M
Student Affairs	M
Women's Health Nursing	M

HARDING UNIVERSITY

Accounting	M
Art Education	M,O
Business Administration and Management—General	M
Communication Disorders	M
Counseling Psychology	M
Counselor Education	M,O
Early Childhood Education	M,O
Education—General	M,O
Educational Leadership and Administration	M,O
Elementary Education	M,O
English as a Second Language	M,O
English Education	M,O
Foreign Languages Education	M,O
Health Education	M,O
Health Services Management and Hospital Administration	M
Home Economics Education	M,O
International Business	M
Management Information Systems	M
Marriage and Family Therapy	M
Mathematics Education	M,O
Organizational Management	M
Pastoral Ministry and Counseling	M
Pharmacy	P
Physician Assistant Studies	M
Reading Education	M,O
Science Education	M,O
Secondary Education	M,O
Social Sciences Education	M,O
Special Education	M,O

HARDING UNIVERSITY GRADUATE SCHOOL OF RELIGION

Pastoral Ministry and Counseling	P,M,D
Religion	P,M,D
Theology	P,M,D

HARDIN-SIMMONS UNIVERSITY

Business Administration and Management—General	M
Counselor Education	M
Education of the Gifted	M
Education—General	M
English	M
Environmental Management and Policy	M
Family Nurse Practitioner Studies	M
History	M
Kinesiology and Movement Studies	M
Marriage and Family Therapy	M
Maternal and Child/Neonatal Nursing	M
Mathematics	M,D
Music Education	M
Music	M
Nursing—General	M
Pastoral Ministry and Counseling	M
Physical Therapy	D
Psychology—General	M
Reading Education	M
Recreation and Park Management	M
Religion	M
Science Education	M,D
Theology	P,M

HARRISBURG UNIVERSITY OF SCIENCE AND TECHNOLOGY

Educational Media/Instructional Technology	M
Project Management	M

HARTFORD SEMINARY

Pastoral Ministry and Counseling	M,D,O
Religion	M,D,O
Theology	M,D,O

HARVARD UNIVERSITY

Accounting	D
African Studies	D
African-American Studies	D
Allopathic Medicine	P,D
American Studies	D
Anthropology	M,D
Applied Mathematics	M,D
Applied Physics	M,D
Applied Science and Technology	M,O
Archaeology	M,D
Architectural History	D
Architecture	M,D
Art Education	M
Art History	D
Asian Languages	M,D
Asian Studies	M,D
Astronomy	D
Astrophysics	D
Biochemistry	D
Biological and Biomedical Sciences—General	M,D,O*
Biomedical Engineering	M,D
Biophysics	D*
Biopsychology	D
Biostatistics	M,D
Biotechnology	M,O

*M—master's degree; P—first professional degree; D—doctorate; O—other advanced degree; *—Close-Up and/or Announcement or Display in one of the other books in this series*

Business Administration and Management—General M,D,O
Cell Biology D
Celtic Languages D
Chemical Physics D
Chemistry D*
Chinese D
Classics D
Cognitive Sciences M,D
Communication Disorders D
Communication—General M,O
Comparative Literature D
Computer Science M,D
Curriculum and Instruction M
Demography and Population Studies M,D
Dentistry P,M,D,O
Developmental Psychology D
East European and Russian Studies M
Economics D
Education—General M,D
Educational Leadership and Administration M,D
Educational Measurement and Evaluation D
Educational Media/Instructional Technology M,O
Educational Policy M
Educational Psychology M
Engineering and Applied Sciences—General M,D
English M,D,O
Environmental and Occupational Health M,D*
Environmental Management and Policy M,O
Environmental Sciences M
Epidemiology M,D
Evolutionary Biology D
Experimental Psychology D
Forestry M
Foundations and Philosophy of Education M,O
French M,D
Genetics D
Genomic Sciences D
Geosciences M,D
German D
Health Promotion M,D
Health Services Management and Hospital Administration M,D
Higher Education D
History of Science and Technology M,D
History D
Human Development M,D
Immunology D
Industrial and Manufacturing Management D
Infectious Diseases D
Information Science M,D,O
Inorganic Chemistry D
International Affairs P,D
International and Comparative Education M
International Development M
International Health M,D
Italian M,D
Japanese D
Jewish Studies M,D
Journalism M,O
Landscape Architecture M,D
Law P,M,D
Legal and Justice Studies P
Liberal Studies M,O
Linguistics D
Management of Technology D
Management Strategy and Policy D
Marketing D
Mathematics Education M,O
Mathematics D
Medical Informatics M
Medical Physics D
Medieval and Renaissance Studies D
Microbiology D
Molecular Biology D
Molecular Genetics D
Molecular Pharmacology D
Multilingual and Multicultural Education D
Museum Studies M,O
Music M,D
Near and Middle Eastern Languages M,D
Near and Middle Eastern Studies M,D
Neurobiology D
Neuroscience D
Nutrition D
Oral and Dental Sciences M,D,O
Organic Chemistry D
Organizational Behavior D
Pathology D
Philosophy M,D
Physical Chemistry D
Physics D
Physiology M,D
Planetary and Space Sciences M,D
Political Science M,D
Portuguese M,D
Psychology—General D
Public Administration M
Public Health—General M,D*
Public Policy M,D
Reading Education M
Religion D
Russian D
Scandinavian Languages D
Science Education M
Slavic Languages D
Social Psychology D
Sociology D
Spanish M,D
Statistics M,D
Structural Biology D
Systems Biology D
Technical Communication M
Theology P,M,D
Theoretical Physics D
Urban and Regional Planning M,D
Urban Design M
Urban Education D

HASTINGS COLLEGE

Education—General M

HAWAI'I PACIFIC UNIVERSITY

Accounting M
Business Administration and Management—General M*
Communication—General M*
Community Health Nursing M
Economics M
Electronic Commerce M
English as a Second Language M*
Family Nurse Practitioner Studies M
Finance and Banking M
Human Resources Management M
International Business M
Management Information Systems M*
Marine Sciences M
Marketing M
Military and Defense Studies M*
Nursing—General M*
Organizational Management M
Secondary Education M
Social Work M
Software Engineering M
Sustainable Development M*
Telecommunications Management M
Travel and Tourism M

HAZELDEN GRADUATE SCHOOL OF ADDICTION STUDIES

Addictions/Substance Abuse Counseling M,O

HEBREW COLLEGE

Early Childhood Education M,O
Education—General M,O
Jewish Studies M,O
Middle School Education M,O
Music Education M,O
Music M,O
Religious Education M,O
Special Education M,O
Theology M

HEBREW THEOLOGICAL COLLEGE

Theology O

HEBREW UNION COLLEGE–JEWISH INSTITUTE OF RELIGION (CA)

Education—General M,D,O
Jewish Studies M,D
Religious Education M,D,O
Social Work M,O
Theology P

HEBREW UNION COLLEGE–JEWISH INSTITUTE OF RELIGION (NY)

Education—General M
Jewish Studies M
Music M
Near and Middle Eastern Languages D
Religious Education M
Theology P,D

HEBREW UNION COLLEGE–JEWISH INSTITUTE OF RELIGION (OH)

Jewish Studies P,M,D
Near and Middle Eastern Studies M,D
Religion M,D
Theology P

HEC MONTREAL

Accounting M,O
Applied Economics M
Arts Administration O
Business Administration and Management—General M,D,O
Corporate and Organizational Communication O
Electronic Commerce M,O
Finance and Banking M,O
Financial Engineering M
Human Resources Management M
Industrial and Manufacturing Management M
International Business M
Logistics M
Management Information Systems M
Management Strategy and Policy M
Marketing M
Supply Chain Management O
Sustainable Development O
Taxation M,O

HEIDELBERG UNIVERSITY

Business Administration and Management—General M
Counseling Psychology M
Education—General M

HENDERSON STATE UNIVERSITY

Business Administration and Management—General M
Counselor Education M
Curriculum and Instruction M
Early Childhood Education M
Education—General M,O
Educational Leadership and Administration M,O
Liberal Studies M
Middle School Education M
Physical Education M
Reading Education M
Social Psychology M
Special Education M
Sports Management M

HENDRIX COLLEGE

Accounting M

HERITAGE BAPTIST COLLEGE AND HERITAGE THEOLOGICAL SEMINARY

Pastoral Ministry and Counseling P,M,D,O
Theology P,M,D,O

HERITAGE CHRISTIAN UNIVERSITY

Classics M
Pastoral Ministry and Counseling M
Religion M

HERITAGE UNIVERSITY

Biological and Biomedical Sciences—General M
Counselor Education M
Education—General M
Educational Leadership and Administration M
English as a Second Language M
English M
Multilingual and Multicultural Education M
Reading Education M
Science Education M
Special Education M

HIGH POINT UNIVERSITY

Business Administration and Management—General M
Educational Leadership and Administration M
Elementary Education M
Exercise and Sports Science M
History M
Nonprofit Management M
Special Education M

HILLSDALE FREE WILL BAPTIST COLLEGE

Pastoral Ministry and Counseling M

HODGES UNIVERSITY

Business Administration and Management—General M
Criminal Justice and Criminology M
Education—General M

Interdisciplinary Studies	M
Law	M
Management Information Systems	M
Management of Technology	M
Psychology—General	M
Public Administration	M

HOFSTRA UNIVERSITY

Accounting	M
Applied Mathematics	M
Applied Social Research	M
Art Education	M
Art Therapy	M
Art/Fine Arts	M
Biological and Biomedical Sciences—General	M*
Business Administration and Management—General	M
Business Education	M
Clinical Psychology	M,D
Communication Disorders	M,D
Communication—General	M
Community Health	M
Comparative Literature	M
Computer Science	M
Counseling Psychology	M,O
Counselor Education	M,O
Early Childhood Education	M,O
Education of the Gifted	M,O
Education—General	M,D,O
Educational Leadership and Administration	M,D,O
Educational Media/Instructional Technology	M,O
Elementary Education	M,O
English as a Second Language	M,O
English Education	M
English	M
Entertainment Management	M
Film, Television, and Video Production	M
Finance and Banking	M
Foreign Languages Education	M
Foundations and Philosophy of Education	M,O
French	M
German	M
Gerontology	M,O
Health Education	M
Health Services Management and Hospital Administration	M
Human Development	M,D,O
Human Resources Management	M
Humanities	M
Industrial and Organizational Psychology	M,D
Interdisciplinary Studies	M
International Business	M
Journalism	M
Law	P,M
Legal and Justice Studies	P,M
Linguistics	M,D,O
Management Information Systems	M
Marketing Research	M
Marketing	M
Marriage and Family Therapy	M
Mathematics Education	M
Mathematics	M
Middle School Education	O
Multilingual and Multicultural Education	M,O
Music Education	M
Music	M
Physical Education	M,D,O
Psychology—General	M,D,O
Quality Management	M
Reading Education	M,D,O
Real Estate	M
Rehabilitation Counseling	M,O
Rhetoric	M
Russian	M
School Psychology	M,D,O
Science Education	M
Secondary Education	M,O
Social Psychology	M,D,O
Social Sciences Education	M,O
Sociology	M
Spanish	M
Special Education	M,D,O
Speech and Interpersonal Communication	M
Sports Management	M
Taxation	M
Writing	M

HOLLINS UNIVERSITY

Art/Fine Arts	M,O
Dance	M
Education—General	M
English	M
Film, Television, and Video Production	M
Film, Television, and Video Theory and Criticism	M
Humanities	M,O
Interdisciplinary Studies	M,O
Legal and Justice Studies	M,O
Liberal Studies	M,O
Music	M,O
Social Sciences	M,O
Theater	M
Writing	M

HOLMES INSTITUTE

Pastoral Ministry and Counseling	M

HOLY APOSTLES COLLEGE AND SEMINARY

Theology	P,M,O

HOLY CROSS GREEK ORTHODOX SCHOOL OF THEOLOGY

Theology	P,M

HOLY FAMILY UNIVERSITY

Business Administration and Management—General	M
Community Health Nursing	M
Counseling Psychology	M
Criminal Justice and Criminology	M
Education—General	M
Educational Leadership and Administration	M
Elementary Education	M
Finance and Banking	M
Health Services Management and Hospital Administration	M
Human Resources Management	M
Management Information Systems	M
Nursing and Healthcare Administration	M
Nursing Education	M
Nursing—General	M
Reading Education	M
Secondary Education	M
Special Education	M

HOLY NAMES UNIVERSITY

Business Administration and Management—General	M
Community Health Nursing	M,O
Counseling Psychology	M,O
Education—General	M,O
Educational Psychology	M,O
Energy Management and Policy	M
English as a Second Language	M,O
Family Nurse Practitioner Studies	M,O
Finance and Banking	M
Forensic Psychology	M,O
Marketing	M
Music Education	M,O
Music	M,O
Nursing and Healthcare Administration	M,O
Nursing Education	M,O
Nursing—General	M,O
Pastoral Ministry and Counseling	M,O
Religion	M,O
Special Education	M,O
Sports Management	M
Urban Education	M,O

HOOD COLLEGE

Accounting	M
Art/Fine Arts	M,O
Biological and Biomedical Sciences—General	M,O
Biotechnology	M,O
Business Administration and Management—General	M
Computer Science	M
Curriculum and Instruction	M
Early Childhood Education	M
Education—General	M
Educational Leadership and Administration	M
Elementary Education	M
Environmental Biology	M
Finance and Banking	M
Human Development	M,O
Human Resources Management	M
Humanities	M
Immunology	M,O
Information Science	M
Management Information Systems	M
Marketing	M
Mathematics Education	M,O
Microbiology	M,O
Middle School Education	M,O
Molecular Biology	M,O
Psychology—General	M,O
Public Administration	M
Reading Education	M
Science Education	M
Secondary Education	M,O
Special Education	M
Systems Science	M
Thanatology	M,O

HOOD THEOLOGICAL SEMINARY

Theology	P,M,D

HOPE INTERNATIONAL UNIVERSITY

Business Administration and Management—General	M
Education—General	M
Educational Leadership and Administration	M
International Business	M
International Development	M
Marriage and Family Therapy	M
Missions and Missiology	M
Music	M
Nonprofit Management	M
Religion	M

HOUGHTON COLLEGE

Music	M

HOUSTON BAPTIST UNIVERSITY

Accounting	M
Business Administration and Management—General	M
Counseling Psychology	M
Counselor Education	M
Curriculum and Instruction	M
Education—General	M
Educational Leadership and Administration	M
Educational Measurement and Evaluation	M
English as a Second Language	M
Health Services Management and Hospital Administration	M
Human Resources Management	M
Liberal Studies	M
Pastoral Ministry and Counseling	M
Psychology—General	M
Reading Education	M
Theology	M

HOUSTON GRADUATE SCHOOL OF THEOLOGY

Pastoral Ministry and Counseling	P,M,D
Theology	P,M,D

HOWARD UNIVERSITY

Accounting	M
African Studies	M,D
Allopathic Medicine	P,D
Analytical Chemistry	M,D
Anatomy	M,D
Applied Arts and Design—General	M
Applied Mathematics	M,D
Art History	M
Art/Fine Arts	M
Atmospheric Sciences	M,D
Biochemistry	M,D
Biological and Biomedical Sciences—General	M,D
Biophysics	D
Biopsychology	M,D
Biotechnology	M,D
Business Administration and Management—General	M
Chemical Engineering	M
Chemistry	M,D
Civil Engineering	M
Clinical Psychology	M,D
Communication Disorders	M,D
Communication—General	M,D
Computer Science	M
Corporate and Organizational Communication	M,D
Counseling Psychology	M,D,O
Counselor Education	M,O
Dentistry	P,O
Developmental Psychology	M,D
Early Childhood Education	M,O
Economics	M,D
Education—General	M,D,O
Educational Leadership and Administration	M,D,O
Educational Psychology	M,D,O
Electrical Engineering	M,D
Elementary Education	M
Engineering and Applied Sciences—General	M,D
English	M,D
Environmental Sciences	M,D
Exercise and Sports Science	M
Experimental Psychology	M,D
Family Nurse Practitioner Studies	M,O
Film, Television, and Video Production	M

*M—master's degree; P—first professional degree; D—doctorate; O—other advanced degree; *—Close-Up and/or Announcement or Display in one of the other books in this series*

Finance and Banking M
French M
Health Education M
History M,D
Human Development M
Human Resources Management M
Inorganic Chemistry M,D
International Business M
Law P,M
Leisure Studies M
Management Information Systems M
Marketing M
Mass Communication M,D
Mathematics M,D
Mechanical Engineering M,D
Media Studies M,D
Microbiology D
Molecular Biology M,D
Multilingual and Multicultural Education M,D
Music Education M
Music M
Nursing—General M,O
Nutrition M,D
Oral and Dental Sciences P,O
Organic Chemistry M,D
Pharmacology M,D
Pharmacy P
Philosophy M
Photography M
Physical Chemistry M,D
Physical Education M
Physics M,D
Physiology D
Political Science M,D
Psychology—General M,D
Public Administration M
Public Health—General M
Reading Education M,O
School Psychology M,D,O
Secondary Education M,O
Social Psychology M,D
Social Work M,D
Sociology M,D
Spanish M
Special Education M,O
Sports Management M
Supply Chain Management M
Theology P,M,D

HULT INTERNATIONAL BUSINESS SCHOOL (UNITED STATES)

Advertising and Public Relations M
Business Administration and Management—General M
Conflict Resolution and Mediation/Peace Studies M
Entrepreneurship M
Finance and Banking M
International Affairs M
International Business M
Marketing M
National Security M
Political Science M

HUMBOLDT STATE UNIVERSITY

Athletic Training and Sports Medicine M
Biological and Biomedical Sciences—General M
Business Administration and Management—General M
Counseling Psychology M
Education—General M
English Education M
English M
Environmental Management and Policy M
Environmental Sciences M
Exercise and Sports Science M
Film, Television, and Video Production M
Fish, Game, and Wildlife Management M
Forestry M
Geology M
Hazardous Materials Management M
Kinesiology and Movement Studies M
Natural Resources M
Physical Education M
Physical Therapy M
Psychology—General M
School Psychology M
Social Sciences M
Social Work M
Sociology M
Theater M
Water Resources M

HUMPHREYS COLLEGE

Law P

HUNTER COLLEGE OF THE CITY UNIVERSITY OF NEW YORK

Accounting M
Adult Nursing M
Anthropology M
Applied Mathematics M
Applied Social Research M
Art History M
Art/Fine Arts M
Biochemistry M,D
Biological and Biomedical Sciences—General M,D
Biopsychology M
Biostatistics M
Chemistry M,D
Classics M
Cognitive Sciences M
Communication Disorders M
Community Health Nursing M
Community Health M
Counselor Education M
Early Childhood Education M,O
Economics M
Education of the Multiply Handicapped M
Education—General M,O
Educational Leadership and Administration O
Elementary Education M
English as a Second Language M
English Education M
English M
Environmental and Occupational Health M
Environmental Sciences M,O
Epidemiology M
Foreign Languages Education M
French M
Geographic Information Systems M,O
Geography M,O
Geosciences M,O
Gerontological Nursing M
Health Services Management and Hospital Administration M
History M
Italian M
Mathematics Education M
Mathematics M
Media Studies M
Multilingual and Multicultural Education M
Music Education M
Music M
Nursing—General M,O
Nutrition M
Physics M,D
Psychiatric Nursing M,O
Psychology—General M
Public Health—General M
Reading Education M,O
Rehabilitation Counseling M
Romance Languages M
Science Education M,O
Secondary Education M
Social Psychology M
Social Sciences Education M
Social Work M,D
Sociology M
Spanish M
Special Education M
Theater M
Urban and Regional Planning M
Urban Studies M
Writing M

HUNTINGTON COLLEGE OF HEALTH SCIENCES

Nutrition M

HUNTINGTON UNIVERSITY

Education—General M
Pastoral Ministry and Counseling M

HUSSON UNIVERSITY

Business Administration and Management—General M
Community Health Nursing M,O
Counseling Psychology M
Counselor Education M
Criminal Justice and Criminology M
Family Nurse Practitioner Studies M,O
Health Services Management and Hospital Administration M
Nonprofit Management M
Nursing—General M,O
Occupational Therapy M
Physical Therapy D
Psychiatric Nursing M,O

ICR GRADUATE SCHOOL

Astrophysics M
Biological and Biomedical Sciences—General M
Geology M
Geophysics M
Science Education M

IDAHO STATE UNIVERSITY

Allied Health—General M,D,O
Anthropology M
Applied Physics M,D
Art/Fine Arts M
Biological and Biomedical Sciences—General M,D
Business Administration and Management—General M,O
Chemistry M
Civil Engineering M
Clinical Psychology D
Communication Disorders M,D,O
Community Health O
Counseling Psychology M,D,O
Counselor Education M,D,O
Curriculum and Instruction M,O
Dental Hygiene M
Dentistry O
Education—General M,D,O
Educational Leadership and Administration M,D,O
Educational Media/Instructional Technology M,D,O
Elementary Education M,O
Engineering and Applied Sciences—General M,D,O
English M,D,O
Environmental Engineering M
Environmental Sciences M
Geographic Information Systems M,O
Geology M,O
Geophysics M,O
Geosciences M,O
Hazardous Materials Management M
Health Education M
Health Physics/Radiological Health M,D
History M
Hydrology M,O
Interdisciplinary Studies M
Management Information Systems M,O
Management of Technology M
Marriage and Family Therapy M,D,O
Mathematics Education M,D
Mathematics M,D
Mechanical Engineering M
Medical Microbiology M,D
Medicinal and Pharmaceutical Chemistry M,D
Microbiology M,D
Nuclear Engineering M,D,O
Nursing—General M,O
Nutrition M,O
Occupational Therapy M
Operations Research M
Oral and Dental Sciences O
Pharmaceutical Administration P,M,D
Pharmaceutical Sciences M,D
Pharmacology M,D
Pharmacy P,M,D
Physical Education M
Physical Therapy D
Physician Assistant Studies M
Physics M,D
Political Science M,D
Psychology—General M,D
Public Administration M
Public Health—General M,O
Reading Education M,O
Rhetoric M
School Psychology M,D,O
Secondary Education M,O
Sociology M
Special Education M,D,O
Speech and Interpersonal Communication M
Theater M
Vocational and Technical Education M

ILIFF SCHOOL OF THEOLOGY

Pastoral Ministry and Counseling P,M,D
Religion P,M,D
Theology P,M,D

ILLINOIS COLLEGE OF OPTOMETRY

Optometry P

ILLINOIS INSTITUTE OF TECHNOLOGY

Aerospace/Aeronautical Engineering M,D
Agricultural Engineering M,D
Analytical Chemistry M,D
Applied Arts and Design—General M,D*
Applied Mathematics M,D
Architectural Engineering M,D
Architecture M,D
Bioengineering M,D
Biological and Biomedical Sciences—General M,D

Biomedical Engineering D
Business Administration and Management—General M,D
Chemical Engineering M,D
Chemistry M,D
Civil Engineering M,D
Clinical Psychology M,D
Communication—General M,D
Computer Engineering M,D
Computer Science M,D
Construction Engineering M,D
Corporate and Organizational Communication M
Electrical Engineering M,D
Engineering and Applied Sciences—General M,D
Environmental and Occupational Health M
Environmental Engineering M,D
Environmental Management and Policy M
Finance and Banking P,M
Food Science and Technology M
Geotechnical Engineering M,D
Health Physics/Radiological Health M,D
Human Resources Development M,D
Industrial and Manufacturing Management M
Industrial and Organizational Psychology M,D
Landscape Architecture M,D
Law P,M
Management Information Systems M,D
Manufacturing Engineering M,D
Marketing M
Materials Engineering M,D
Materials Sciences M,D
Mathematical and Computational Finance M
Mathematics Education M,D
Mechanical Engineering M,D
Medical Imaging M,D
Molecular Biology M,D
Molecular Biophysics M,D
Nonprofit Management M
Physics M,D
Psychology—General M,D
Public Administration M
Rehabilitation Counseling M,D
Science Education M,D
Software Engineering M,D
Structural Engineering M,D
Sustainability Management M
Taxation P,M
Technical Writing M,D
Telecommunications M,D
Transportation and Highway Engineering M,D

ILLINOIS STATE UNIVERSITY

Accounting M
Agricultural Economics and Agribusiness M
Agricultural Sciences—General M
Animal Behavior M,D
Archaeology M
Art History M
Art/Fine Arts M
Bacteriology M,D
Biochemistry M,D
Biological and Biomedical Sciences—General M,D
Biophysics M,D
Biotechnology M
Botany M,D
Business Administration and Management—General M
Cell Biology M,D
Chemistry M
Clinical Psychology M,D,O
Communication Disorders M
Communication—General M
Conservation Biology M
Counseling Psychology M,D,O
Criminal Justice and Criminology M
Curriculum and Instruction M,D
Developmental Biology M,D
Developmental Psychology M,D,O
Ecology M,D
Economics M
Education—General M,D
Educational Leadership and Administration M,D
Educational Policy M,D
Educational Psychology M,D,O
English M,D
Entomology M,D
Evolutionary Biology M,D
Experimental Psychology M,D,O
Family and Consumer Sciences-General M
Family Nurse Practitioner Studies M,D,O
French M
Genetics M,D
German M
Graphic Design M
Health Education M
Higher Education M,D
History M
Hydrogeology M
Hydrology M
Immunology M,D
Industrial and Organizational Psychology M,D,O
Industrial/Management Engineering M
Management Information Systems M
Management of Technology M
Mathematics Education D
Mathematics M
Microbiology M,D
Molecular Biology M,D
Molecular Genetics M,D
Music M
Neurobiology M,D
Neuroscience M,D
Nursing—General M,D,O
Parasitology M,D
Photography M
Physical Education M
Physiology M,D
Plant Biology M,D
Plant Molecular Biology M,D
Plant Sciences M,D
Political Science M
Psychology—General M,D,O
Reading Education M
School Psychology D,O
Social Work M
Sociology M
Spanish M
Special Education M,D
Structural Biology M,D
Student Affairs M
Textile Design M
Theater M
Writing M
Zoology M,D

IMCA–INTERNATIONAL MANAGEMENT CENTRES ASSOCIATION

Business Administration and Management—General M

IMMACULATA UNIVERSITY

Clinical Psychology M,D,O
Counseling Psychology M,D,O
Counselor Education M,D,O
Educational Leadership and Administration M,D,O
Elementary Education M,D,O
Multilingual and Multicultural Education M
Nursing—General M
Nutrition M
Organizational Management M
Psychology—General M,D,O
School Psychology M,D,O
Secondary Education M,D,O
Special Education M,D,O
Therapies—Dance, Drama, and Music M

INDEPENDENCE UNIVERSITY

Business Administration and Management—General M
Community Health Nursing M
Community Health M
Gerontological Nursing M
Health Promotion M
Health Services Management and Hospital Administration M
Nursing and Healthcare Administration M
Nursing—General M
Public Health—General M

INDIANA STATE UNIVERSITY

Art/Fine Arts M
Athletic Training and Sports Medicine M
Biological and Biomedical Sciences—General M,D
Business Administration and Management—General M
Clinical Psychology M,D
Communication—General M
Community Health M
Comparative Literature M
Computer Engineering M
Computer Science M
Consumer Economics M
Counseling Psychology M,D,O
Counselor Education M,D,O
Criminal Justice and Criminology M
Curriculum and Instruction M,D
Early Childhood Education M
Ecology M,D
Education—General M,D,O
Educational Leadership and Administration M,D,O
Educational Media/Instructional Technology M,D
Elementary Education M
Engineering and Applied Sciences—General M
English as a Second Language M,O
English Education M
English M
Environmental and Occupational Health M
Exercise and Sports Science M
Family and Consumer Sciences-General M
Geography M,D
Graphic Design M
Health Education M
Health Promotion M
Higher Education M,D,O
History M
Home Economics Education M
Human Resources Development M
Industrial/Management Engineering M
Linguistics M,O
Management of Technology D
Mathematics Education M
Mathematics M
Media Studies M
Microbiology M,D
Multilingual and Multicultural Education M,O
Music M
Nursing—General M
Nutrition M
Photography M
Physical Education M
Physiology M,D
Political Science M
Psychology—General M,D
Public Administration M
School Psychology M,D,O
Science Education M,D
Sports Management M
Student Affairs M,D,O
Vocational and Technical Education M
Writing M

INDIANA TECH

Accounting M
Business Administration and Management—General M
Health Services Management and Hospital Administration M
Human Resources Development M
Human Resources Management M
Marketing M
Organizational Management M
Science Education M

INDIANA UNIVERSITY BLOOMINGTON

African Studies M
African-American Studies M
Analytical Chemistry M,D
Anthropology M,D
Applied Mathematics M,D
Art Education M,D,O
Art History M,D
Art/Fine Arts M,D
Asian Languages M,D
Asian Studies M,D
Astronomy M,D
Astrophysics M,D
Athletic Training and Sports Medicine M,D
Biochemistry M,D
Bioinformatics M,D
Biological and Biomedical Sciences—General M,D*
Biotechnology M,D
Business Administration and Management—General M,D
Cell Biology M,D
Chemistry M,D
Child and Family Studies M,D
Chinese M,D
Classics M,D
Cognitive Sciences M,D
Communication Disorders M,D
Communication—General M,D*
Comparative Literature M,D
Computer Art and Design M,D
Computer Science M,D
Counseling Psychology M,D,O
Counselor Education M,D,O
Criminal Justice and Criminology M,D
Curriculum and Instruction M,D,O
Developmental Psychology M,D
East European and Russian Studies M,O
Ecology M,D
Economics M,D

*M—master's degree; P—first professional degree; D—doctorate; O—other advanced degree; *—Close-Up and/or Announcement or Display in one of the other books in this series*

Education—General	M,D,O*
Educational Leadership and Administration	M,D,O
Educational Measurement and Evaluation	M,D,O
Educational Media/ Instructional Technology	M,D,O
Educational Policy	M,D,O
Educational Psychology	M,D,O
Elementary Education	M,D,O
English as a Second Language	M,D
English	M,D
Environmental Sciences	M,D*
Ergonomics and Human Factors	M,D
Evolutionary Biology	M,D
Exercise and Sports Science	M,D
Film, Television, and Video Theory and Criticism	M,D
Folklore	M,D
Foreign Languages Education	M,D
Foundations and Philosophy of Education	M,D,O
French	M,D
Gender Studies	D
Genetics	M,D
Geochemistry	M,D
Geography	M,D
Geology	M,D
Geophysics	M,D
Geosciences	M,D
German	M,D
Health Education	M,D
Health Informatics	M,D
Health Promotion	M,D
Higher Education	M,D,O
History of Science and Technology	M,D
History	M,D
Human Development	M,D
Human-Computer Interaction	M,D
Hydrogeology	M,D
Information Science	M,D,O
Information Studies	M,D,O
Inorganic Chemistry	M,D
International and Comparative Education	M,D,O
Italian	M,D
Japanese	M,D
Journalism	M,D
Kinesiology and Movement Studies	M,D
Latin American Studies	M
Law	P,M,D,O
Leisure Studies	M,D,O
Library Science	M,D,O*
Linguistics	M,D
Mass Communication	M,D
Mathematics Education	M,D,O
Mathematics	M,D
Media Studies	M,D
Medieval and Renaissance Studies	M,D
Microbiology	M,D
Mineralogy	M,D
Molecular Biology	M,D
Multilingual and Multicultural Education	M,D
Music	M,D,O
Near and Middle Eastern Languages	M,D
Neuroscience	D
Nonprofit Management	M,D,O
Nutrition	M,D
Optometry	P,M,D
Philosophy	M,D
Physical Chemistry	M,D
Physical Education	M,D
Physics	M,D
Plant Biology	M,D
Political Science	M,D
Portuguese	M,D
Psychology—General	M,D
Public Administration	M,D,O
Public Affairs	M,D,O*
Public Health—General	M,D
Public Policy	M,D,O
Reading Education	M,D,O
Recreation and Park Management	M,D,O
Religion	M,D
Rhetoric	M,D
Safety Engineering	M,D
School Psychology	M,D,O
Science Education	M,D,O
Secondary Education	M,D,O
Slavic Languages	M,D
Social Psychology	M,D
Social Sciences Education	M,D,O
Social Sciences	P,M,D,O
Sociology	M,D
Spanish	M,D
Special Education	M,D,O
Speech and Interpersonal Communication	M,D
Sports Management	M,D,O
Statistics	M,D
Telecommunications	M
Theater	M,D
Travel and Tourism	M,D,O
Western European Studies	M
Writing	M,D
Zoology	M,D

INDIANA UNIVERSITY EAST

Education—General	M
Social Work	M

INDIANA UNIVERSITY KOKOMO

Business Administration and Management—General	M
Education—General	M
Elementary Education	M
Liberal Studies	M
Public Administration	M,O

INDIANA UNIVERSITY NORTHWEST

Accounting	M,O
Business Administration and Management—General	M,O
Criminal Justice and Criminology	M,O
Education—General	M
Elementary Education	M
Environmental Sciences	M,O
Health Services Management and Hospital Administration	M,O
Human Services	M,O
Nonprofit Management	M,O
Public Administration	M,O
Public Affairs	M,O
Secondary Education	M
Social Work	M

INDIANA UNIVERSITY OF PENNSYLVANIA

Adult Education	M,D
Applied Mathematics	M
Art/Fine Arts	M
Biological and Biomedical Sciences—General	M
Business Administration and Management—General	M
Chemistry	M
Clinical Psychology	D
Communication Disorders	M
Communication—General	M,D
Counselor Education	M
Criminal Justice and Criminology	M,D
Curriculum and Instruction	M,D
Education—General	M,D,O
Educational Leadership and Administration	M,D,O
Educational Media/ Instructional Technology	M,D
Educational Psychology	M,O
Elementary Education	M
Emergency Management	M
English as a Second Language	M,D
English Education	M,D
English	M,D
Environmental and Occupational Health	M
Exercise and Sports Science	M
Facilities Management	M
Geography	M
Health Education	M
Higher Education	M
History	M
Human Resources Development	M
Industrial and Labor Relations	M
Linguistics	M,D
Mathematics Education	M
Mathematics	M
Media Studies	M,D
Music Education	M
Music	M
Nursing—General	M
Nutrition	M
Physical Education	M
Physics	M
Political Science	M
Psychology—General	M,D
Public Affairs	M
Reading Education	M
Rhetoric	M,D
School Psychology	D,O
Sociology	M
Special Education	M
Sports Management	M
Writing	M,D

INDIANA UNIVERSITY–PURDUE UNIVERSITY FORT WAYNE

Adult Nursing	M,O
Applied Mathematics	M,O
Applied Statistics	M,O
Biological and Biomedical Sciences—General	M
Business Administration and Management—General	M
Communication Disorders	M
Communication—General	M
Computer Engineering	M
Computer Science	M
Counselor Education	M
Education—General	M,O
Educational Leadership and Administration	M
Electrical Engineering	M
Elementary Education	M,O
Engineering and Applied Sciences—General	M
English as a Second Language	M,O
English Education	M,O
English	M,O
Industrial/Management Engineering	M
Information Science	M
Liberal Studies	M
Mathematics	M,O
Mechanical Engineering	M
Nursing and Healthcare Administration	M,O
Nursing Education	M,O
Nursing—General	M,O
Operations Research	M,O
Organizational Management	M
Public Affairs	M,O
Secondary Education	M,O
Sociology	M
Special Education	M
Systems Engineering	M
Women's Health Nursing	M,O

INDIANA UNIVERSITY–PURDUE UNIVERSITY INDIANAPOLIS

Accounting	M
Acute Care/Critical Care Nursing	M,D
Addictions/Substance Abuse Counseling	M,D
Adult Education	M
Adult Nursing	M,D
Allopathic Medicine	P,M,D
Anatomy	M,D
Applied Arts and Design—General	M
Applied Mathematics	M,D
Applied Statistics	M
Art Education	M
Art/Fine Arts	M
Artificial Intelligence/ Robotics	M,D
Biochemistry	D
Bioethics	M,O
Biological and Biomedical Sciences—General	M,D
Biomedical Engineering	M,D,O
Biopsychology	M,D
Business Administration and Management—General	M
Cell Biology	M,D
Chemistry	M,D
Child and Family Studies	M
Clinical Psychology	M,D
Community Health Nursing	M,D
Computer Education	M,O
Computer Engineering	M,D
Computer Science	M,D
Counselor Education	M,O
Criminal Justice and Criminology	M
Curriculum and Instruction	M,O
Dentistry	P,M,D,O
Early Childhood Education	M,O
Economics	M
Education—General	M,O
Educational Leadership and Administration	M,O
Electrical Engineering	M,D
English as a Second Language	M,O
English Education	M
English	M
Environmental Management and Policy	M
Epidemiology	M
Family Nurse Practitioner Studies	M,D
Foreign Languages Education	M,O
Gender Studies	M
Geographic Information Systems	M,O
Geology	M
Health Education	M,D
Health Services Management and Hospital Administration	M
Higher Education	M,O
History	M
Immunology	M,D
Industrial and Organizational Psychology	M
Information Science	M,D
Internet and Interactive Multimedia	M
Law	P,M,D
Liberal Studies	M,D,O
Library Science	M
Maternal and Child/ Neonatal Nursing	M,D
Mathematics Education	M
Mathematics	M,D
Mechanical Engineering	M,D,O
Microbiology	M,D*

Molecular Biology	D
Molecular Genetics	M,D
Museum Studies	M,O
Music	M
Nonprofit Management	M,D
Nursing—General	M,D
Nutrition	M,D
Occupational Therapy	M,D
Pathology	M,D
Pediatric Nursing	M,D
Pharmacology	M,D
Philanthropic Studies	M,D
Philosophy	M,O
Physical Education	M
Physical Therapy	M,D
Physics	M,D
Political Science	M,O
Psychiatric Nursing	M,D
Psychology—General	M,D
Public Administration	M
Public Affairs	M*
Public Health—General	M
Public History	M
Public Policy	M
Reading Education	M,O
Rehabilitation Counseling	M,D
Rehabilitation Sciences	M,D
Social Work	M,D,O
Sociology	M
Special Education	M,O
Student Affairs	M,O
Toxicology	M,D
Women's Health Nursing	M,D

INDIANA UNIVERSITY SOUTH BEND

Accounting	M
Applied Mathematics	M
Art Education	M
Business Administration and Management—General	M
Computer Science	M
Counselor Education	M
Education—General	M
Elementary Education	M
English	M
Health Services Management and Hospital Administration	M,O
Liberal Studies	M
Management Information Systems	M
Music	M
Nonprofit Management	M,O
Psychology—General	M
Public Administration	M,O
Public Affairs	M,O
Secondary Education	M
Social Work	M
Special Education	M

INDIANA UNIVERSITY SOUTHEAST

Business Administration and Management—General	M
Counselor Education	M
Education—General	M
Elementary Education	M
Finance and Banking	M
Liberal Studies	M
Secondary Education	M

INDIANA WESLEYAN UNIVERSITY

Accounting	M
Addictions/Substance Abuse Counseling	M
Business Administration and Management—General	M
Community Health Nursing	M,O
Counseling Psychology	M
Counselor Education	M
Curriculum and Instruction	M
Education—General	M
Human Resources Management	M
Marriage and Family Therapy	M
Nursing and Healthcare Administration	M,O
Nursing Education	M,O
Nursing—General	M,O
Organizational Management	D
Pastoral Ministry and Counseling	M
Social Psychology	M
Theology	P,M

INSTITUTE FOR CHRISTIAN STUDIES

Education—General	M,D
Philosophy	M,D
Political Science	M,D
Theology	M,D

INSTITUTE FOR CLINICAL SOCIAL WORK

Social Work	D

INSTITUTE OF CLINICAL ACUPUNCTURE AND ORIENTAL MEDICINE

Acupuncture and Oriental Medicine	M

INSTITUTE OF PUBLIC ADMINISTRATION

Health Services Management and Hospital Administration	M,O
Public Administration	M,O

INSTITUTE OF TRANSPERSONAL PSYCHOLOGY

Clinical Psychology	M,D
Counseling Psychology	M,D
Psychology—General	M,D,O
Transpersonal and Humanistic Psychology	M,D,O
Women's Studies	M,D

THE INSTITUTE OF WORLD POLITICS

Military and Defense Studies	M,O
National Security	M,O
Political Science	M,O*
Public Affairs	M,O
Public Policy	M,O

INSTITUT FRANCO-EUROPÉEN DE CHIROPRATIQUE

Chiropractic	P

INSTITUTO CENTROAMERICANO DE ADMINISTRACIÓN DE EMPRESAS

Agricultural Economics and Agribusiness	M
Business Administration and Management—General	M
Economics	M
Finance and Banking	M
Sustainable Development	M

INSTITUTO TECNOLOGICO DE SANTO DOMINGO

Allopathic Medicine	P,M
Business Administration and Management—General	M
Education—General	M
Engineering and Applied Sciences—General	M
Environmental Engineering	M
Environmental Sciences	M
Finance and Banking	M
Human Resources Management	M
Industrial/Management Engineering	M
Linguistics	M
Psychology—General	M
Social Sciences Education	M
Structural Engineering	M
Telecommunications	M

INSTITUTO TECNOLÓGICO Y DE ESTUDIOS SUPERIORES DE MONTERREY, CAMPUS CENTRAL DE VERACRUZ

Business Administration and Management—General	M
Computer Science	M
Education—General	M
Educational Leadership and Administration	M
Educational Media/Instructional Technology	M
Electronic Commerce	M
Finance and Banking	M
Humanities	M
International Business	M
Management Information Systems	M
Management of Technology	M
Marketing	M

INSTITUTO TECNOLÓGICO Y DE ESTUDIOS SUPERIORES DE MONTERREY, CAMPUS CHIHUAHUA

Computer Engineering	M,O
Electrical Engineering	M,O
Engineering Management	M,O
Industrial/Management Engineering	M,O
International Business	M,O
Mechanical Engineering	M,O
Systems Engineering	M,O

INSTITUTO TECNOLÓGICO Y DE ESTUDIOS SUPERIORES DE MONTERREY, CAMPUS CIUDAD DE MÉXICO

Business Administration and Management—General	M,D
Computer Science	M,D
Economics	M,D
Education—General	M,D
Educational Media/Instructional Technology	M,D
Environmental Engineering	M,D
Environmental Sciences	M,D
Finance and Banking	M,D
Humanities	M,D
Industrial/Management Engineering	M,D
International Business	M,D
Law	P
Management Information Systems	M,D
Quality Management	M,D
Telecommunications Management	M

INSTITUTO TECNOLÓGICO Y DE ESTUDIOS SUPERIORES DE MONTERREY, CAMPUS CIUDAD JUÁREZ

Business Administration and Management—General	M
Education—General	M
Educational Leadership and Administration	M
Educational Media/Instructional Technology	M,D
Electronic Commerce	M
Humanities	M
Management Information Systems	M
Public Administration	M
Quality Management	M

INSTITUTO TECNOLÓGICO Y DE ESTUDIOS SUPERIORES DE MONTERREY, CAMPUS CIUDAD OBREGÓN

Business Administration and Management—General	M
Communication—General	M
Developmental Education	M
Education—General	M
Engineering and Applied Sciences—General	M
Finance and Banking	M
International Affairs	M
Management Information Systems	M
Marketing	M
Mathematics Education	M
Telecommunications Management	M

INSTITUTO TECNOLÓGICO Y DE ESTUDIOS SUPERIORES DE MONTERREY, CAMPUS CUERNAVACA

Business Administration and Management—General	M
Computer Science	M,D
Finance and Banking	M
Human Resources Management	M
Information Science	M,D
International Business	M
Management of Technology	M,D
Marketing	M

INSTITUTO TECNOLÓGICO Y DE ESTUDIOS SUPERIORES DE MONTERREY, CAMPUS ESTADO DE MÉXICO

Architecture	M,D
Business Administration and Management—General	M,D
Computer Science	M,D
Education—General	M,D
Educational Leadership and Administration	M,D
Educational Media/Instructional Technology	M,D
Electronic Commerce	M,D
Environmental Management and Policy	M,D
Finance and Banking	M,D
Humanities	M,D
Industrial and Manufacturing Management	M,D
Information Science	M,D
Management Information Systems	M,D
Marketing	M,D
Materials Engineering	M,D
Materials Sciences	M,D
Quality Management	M,D

*M—master's degree; P—first professional degree; D—doctorate; O—other advanced degree; *—Close-Up and/or Announcement or Display in one of the other books in this series*

Telecommunications Management M,D

INSTITUTO TECNOLÓGICO Y DE ESTUDIOS SUPERIORES DE MONTERREY, CAMPUS GUADALAJARA

Business Administration and Management—General M
Finance and Banking M

INSTITUTO TECNOLÓGICO Y DE ESTUDIOS SUPERIORES DE MONTERREY, CAMPUS IRAPUATO

Architecture M,D
Business Administration and Management—General M,D
Computer Science M,D
Education—General M,D
Educational Leadership and Administration M,D
Educational Media/Instructional Technology M,D
Electronic Commerce M,D
Environmental Management and Policy M,D
Finance and Banking M,D
Humanities M,D
Industrial and Manufacturing Management M,D
Information Science M,D
International Business M,D
Library Science M,D
Management Information Systems M,D
Management of Technology M,D
Marketing Research M,D
Quality Management M,D
Telecommunications Management M,D

INSTITUTO TECNOLÓGICO Y DE ESTUDIOS SUPERIORES DE MONTERREY, CAMPUS LAGUNA

Business Administration and Management—General M
Industrial/Management Engineering M
Management Information Systems M

INSTITUTO TECNOLÓGICO Y DE ESTUDIOS SUPERIORES DE MONTERREY, CAMPUS LEÓN

Business Administration and Management—General M

INSTITUTO TECNOLÓGICO Y DE ESTUDIOS SUPERIORES DE MONTERREY, CAMPUS MONTERREY

Agricultural Engineering M,D
Agricultural Sciences—General M,D
Applied Statistics M,D
Artificial Intelligence/Robotics M,D
Biotechnology M,D
Business Administration and Management—General M,D
Chemical Engineering M,D
Chemistry M,D
Civil Engineering M,D
Communication—General M,D
Computer Science M,D
Electrical Engineering M,D
Engineering and Applied Sciences—General M,D
Environmental Engineering M,D
Finance and Banking M
Industrial/Management Engineering M,D
Information Science M,D
International Business M
Manufacturing Engineering M,D
Marketing M
Mechanical Engineering M,D
Organic Chemistry M,D
Science Education M,D
Systems Engineering M,D

INSTITUTO TECNOLÓGICO Y DE ESTUDIOS SUPERIORES DE MONTERREY, CAMPUS QUERÉTARO

Business Administration and Management—General M

INSTITUTO TECNOLÓGICO Y DE ESTUDIOS SUPERIORES DE MONTERREY, CAMPUS SONORA NORTE

Business Administration and Management—General M
Education—General M
Information Science M

INSTITUTO TECNOLÓGICO Y DE ESTUDIOS SUPERIORES DE MONTERREY, CAMPUS TOLUCA

Business Administration and Management—General M

INTER AMERICAN UNIVERSITY OF PUERTO RICO, AGUADILLA CAMPUS

Business Administration and Management—General M
Counseling Psychology M
Criminal Justice and Criminology M
Educational Leadership and Administration M
Elementary Education M
Marketing M

INTER AMERICAN UNIVERSITY OF PUERTO RICO, ARECIBO CAMPUS

Acute Care/Critical Care Nursing M
Adult Nursing M
Community Health Nursing M
Counselor Education M
Curriculum and Instruction M
Education—General M
Educational Leadership and Administration M
Elementary Education M
English as a Second Language M
Foreign Languages Education M
Mathematics Education M
Medical/Surgical Nursing M
Nurse Anesthesia M
Nursing—General M
Science Education M
Social Sciences Education M

INTER AMERICAN UNIVERSITY OF PUERTO RICO, BARRANQUITAS CAMPUS

Accounting M
Business Administration and Management—General M
Curriculum and Instruction M
Education—General M
Educational Leadership and Administration M
Elementary Education M
Finance and Banking M
Library Science M

INTER AMERICAN UNIVERSITY OF PUERTO RICO, BAYAMÓN CAMPUS

Electronic Commerce M
Human Resources Management M

INTER AMERICAN UNIVERSITY OF PUERTO RICO, GUAYAMA CAMPUS

Early Childhood Education M
Elementary Education M

INTER AMERICAN UNIVERSITY OF PUERTO RICO, METROPOLITAN CAMPUS

Accounting M
Athletic Training and Sports Medicine M
Business Administration and Management—General M
Clinical Laboratory Sciences/Medical Technology M
Computer Science M
Criminal Justice and Criminology M
Curriculum and Instruction D
Education—General D
Educational Leadership and Administration D
Educational Media/Instructional Technology M
Elementary Education M
English as a Second Language M
English M
Environmental Management and Policy M
Exercise and Sports Science M
Finance and Banking M
Health Education M
Higher Education M
History M
Human Resources Development M
Human Resources Management M
Industrial and Labor Relations M,D
Industrial and Manufacturing Management M
Industrial and Organizational Psychology M,D
International Business M
Management Information Systems M
Marketing M
Mathematics Education M
Microbiology M
Molecular Biology M
Music Education M
Pastoral Ministry and Counseling D
Physical Education M
Psychology—General M,D
Religious Education D
School Psychology M,D
Science Education M
Social Work M
Spanish M
Special Education M
Theology D
Vocational and Technical Education M

INTER AMERICAN UNIVERSITY OF PUERTO RICO, PONCE CAMPUS

Accounting M
Criminal Justice and Criminology M
Elementary Education M
English as a Second Language M
Finance and Banking M
Human Resources Management M
Marketing M
Mathematics Education M
Science Education M
Social Sciences Education M
Spanish M

INTER AMERICAN UNIVERSITY OF PUERTO RICO, SAN GERMÁN CAMPUS

Accounting M,D
Applied Mathematics M
Art/Fine Arts M
Business Administration and Management—General M,D
Business Education M
Counseling Psychology M,D
Counselor Education M,D
Curriculum and Instruction D
Educational Leadership and Administration M,D
Elementary Education M
English as a Second Language M
Entrepreneurship D
Environmental Biology M
Environmental Sciences M
Finance and Banking M,D
Human Resources Development M,D
Human Resources Management M,D
Industrial and Labor Relations M,D
International Business M,D
Kinesiology and Movement Studies M
Library Science M
Management Information Systems M,D
Marketing M,D
Music Education M
Photography M
Physical Education M
Psychology—General M,D
School Psychology M,D
Science Education M
Special Education M
Water Resources M

INTER AMERICAN UNIVERSITY OF PUERTO RICO SCHOOL OF LAW

Law P

INTER AMERICAN UNIVERSITY OF PUERTO RICO SCHOOL OF OPTOMETRY

Optometry P

INTERDENOMINATIONAL THEOLOGICAL CENTER

Theology P,M,D

INTERNATIONAL BAPTIST COLLEGE

Pastoral Ministry and Counseling M,D
Theology M

INTERNATIONAL COLLEGE OF THE CAYMAN ISLANDS

Business Administration and Management—General M
Business Education M
Human Resources Management M

INTERNATIONAL TECHNOLOGICAL UNIVERSITY

Business Administration and Management—General M
Computer Art and Design M
Computer Engineering M
Computer Science M
Electrical Engineering M,D
Engineering Management M
Industrial and Manufacturing Management M
Software Engineering M,D

INTERNATIONAL UNIVERSITY IN GENEVA

Business Administration and Management—General M
Communication—General M
Finance and Banking M
International Business M
Investment Management M
Marketing M
Media Studies M

THE INTERNATIONAL UNIVERSITY OF MONACO

Business Administration and Management—General M
Entrepreneurship M
Finance and Banking M
Financial Engineering M
International Business M
Marketing M

IONA COLLEGE

Advertising and Public Relations M
Business Administration and Management—General M,O*
Computer Science M
Counseling Psychology M
Criminal Justice and Criminology M
Education—General M
Educational Leadership and Administration M
Educational Media/Instructional Technology M,O
English Education M
English M
Experimental Psychology M
Finance and Banking M,O
Foreign Languages Education M
Health Services Management and Hospital Administration M,O
History M
Human Resources Management M,O
Industrial and Organizational Psychology M
International Business M,O
Italian M
Journalism M
Management of Technology M,O
Marketing M,O
Marriage and Family Therapy M,O
Mass Communication M
Mathematics Education M
Pastoral Ministry and Counseling M,O
Psychology—General M
Reading Education M
School Psychology M
Science Education M
Social Sciences Education M
Spanish M
Telecommunications M,O

IOWA STATE UNIVERSITY OF SCIENCE AND TECHNOLOGY

Accounting M
Aerospace/Aeronautical Engineering M,D
Agricultural Economics and Agribusiness M,D
Agricultural Education M,D
Agricultural Engineering M,D
Agricultural Sciences—General M,D
Agronomy and Soil Sciences M,D
Animal Sciences M,D
Anthropology M
Applied Arts and Design—General M
Applied Mathematics M,D
Applied Physics M,D
Architecture M
Astronomy M,D
Astrophysics M,D
Biochemistry M,D*
Bioengineering M,D
Bioinformatics D
Biological and Biomedical Sciences—General M,D
Biophysics M,D
Biostatistics D
Biosystems Engineering M,D
Business Administration and Management—General M
Cell Biology M,D
Chemical Engineering M,D
Chemistry M,D
Child and Family Studies M,D
Civil Engineering M,D
Clothing and Textiles M,D
Cognitive Sciences D
Computational Biology D
Computer Engineering M,D
Computer Science M,D*
Condensed Matter Physics M,D
Construction Engineering M,D
Consumer Economics M,D
Corporate and Organizational Communication M,D
Counseling Psychology D
Counselor Education M,D
Curriculum and Instruction M,D
Developmental Biology M,D
Ecology M,D
Economics M,D
Educational Leadership and Administration M,D
Educational Measurement and Evaluation M,D
Educational Media/Instructional Technology M,D
Electrical Engineering M,D
Elementary Education M,D
Engineering and Applied Sciences—General M,D
English M,D
Entomology M,D
Environmental Engineering M,D
Environmental Sciences M,D
Evolutionary Biology M,D
Family and Consumer Sciences-General M
Fish, Game, and Wildlife Management M,D
Food Science and Technology M,D
Forestry M,D
Foundations and Philosophy of Education M,D
Genetics M,D
Geology M,D
Geosciences M,D
Geotechnical Engineering M,D
Graphic Design M
Higher Education M,D
History of Science and Technology M,D
History M,D
Home Economics Education M,D
Horticulture M,D
Hospitality Management M,D
Human Development M,D
Human Resources Development M,D
Human-Computer Interaction M,D
Immunology M,D
Industrial/Management Engineering M,D
Information Science M
Interdisciplinary Studies M
Interior Design M
Journalism M
Kinesiology and Movement Studies M,D
Landscape Architecture M
Management Information Systems M
Mass Communication M
Materials Engineering M,D
Materials Sciences M,D
Mathematics Education M,D
Mathematics M,D
Mechanical Engineering M,D
Mechanics M,D
Meteorology M,D
Microbiology M,D
Molecular Biology M,D
Natural Resources M,D
Neuroscience M,D
Nutrition M,D
Operations Research M,D
Pathology M,D
Physics M,D
Plant Biology M,D
Plant Pathology M,D
Political Science M
Psychology—General D
Public Administration M
Rhetoric M,D
Rural Planning and Studies M,D
Rural Sociology M,D
Social Psychology D
Sociology M,D
Special Education M,D
Statistics M,D
Structural Biology D
Structural Engineering M,D
Sustainable Development M,D
Systems Engineering M
Toxicology M,D
Transportation and Highway Engineering M,D
Transportation Management M
Urban and Regional Planning M
Veterinary Medicine P,M
Veterinary Sciences M,D
Vocational and Technical Education M,D

ITHACA COLLEGE

Accounting M
Allied Health—General M,D
Business Administration and Management—General M
Communication Disorders M
Communication—General M
Elementary Education M
English Education M
Exercise and Sports Science M
Foreign Languages Education M
Health Education M
Mathematics Education M
Music Education M
Music M
Occupational Therapy M
Physical Education M
Physical Therapy M,D
Science Education M
Secondary Education M
Social Sciences Education M
Sports Management M

ITT TECHNICAL INSTITUTE (IN)

Business Administration and Management—General M

JACKSON STATE UNIVERSITY

Accounting M
Biological and Biomedical Sciences—General M,D
Business Administration and Management—General M,D
Chemistry M,D
Clinical Psychology D
Communication Disorders M
Computer Science M
Counselor Education M,O
Criminal Justice and Criminology M
Early Childhood Education M,D,O
Education—General M,D,O
Educational Leadership and Administration M,D,O
Educational Media/Instructional Technology M,D,O
Elementary Education M,D,O
English Education M
English M
Environmental Sciences M,D
Health Education M
History M
Mass Communication M
Materials Sciences M
Mathematics Education M
Mathematics M
Music Education M
Physical Education M
Political Science M
Psychology—General D
Public Administration M,D
Public Affairs M
Public Policy M,D
Rehabilitation Counseling M,O
Science Education M,D
Secondary Education M,D,O
Social Work M,D
Sociology M
Special Education M,O
Urban and Regional Planning M
Vocational and Technical Education M

JACKSONVILLE STATE UNIVERSITY

Biological and Biomedical Sciences—General M
Business Administration and Management—General M
Computer Science M
Counselor Education M

*M—master's degree; P—first professional degree; D—doctorate; O—other advanced degree; *—Close-Up and/or Announcement or Display in one of the other books in this series*

Criminal Justice and Criminology	M
Early Childhood Education	M
Education—General	M,O
Educational Leadership and Administration	M,O
Educational Media/ Instructional Technology	M
Elementary Education	M
Emergency Management	M
English	M
Health Education	M
History	M
Liberal Studies	M
Mathematics	M
Music	M
Nursing—General	M
Physical Education	M
Political Science	M
Psychology—General	M
Reading Education	M
Secondary Education	M
Software Engineering	M
Special Education	M

JACKSONVILLE UNIVERSITY

Business Administration and Management—General	M
Computer Education	M
Early Childhood Education	M,O
Education—General	M,O
Educational Media/ Instructional Technology	M
Elementary Education	M
Mathematics Education	M
Music Education	M
Nursing—General	M
Oral and Dental Sciences	O
Reading Education	M

JAMES MADISON UNIVERSITY

Accounting	M
Applied Science and Technology	M
Art Education	M
Art History	M
Art/Fine Arts	M
Biological and Biomedical Sciences—General	M
Business Administration and Management—General	M
Clinical Psychology	D
Communication Disorders	M,D
Computer Science	M
Counseling Psychology	M,O
Early Childhood Education	M
Educational Leadership and Administration	M
Elementary Education	M
English	M
Health Education	M
History	M
Kinesiology and Movement Studies	M
Mathematics	M
Middle School Education	M
Music Education	M,D
Music	D
Nursing—General	M
Occupational Therapy	M
Photography	M
Physician Assistant Studies	M
Political Science	M
Psychology—General	M,D,O
Public Administration	M
Reading Education	M
School Psychology	M,D,O
Secondary Education	M
Special Education	M
Statistics	M
Technical Writing	M
Textile Design	M
Vocational and Technical Education	M

JEFFERSON COLLEGE OF HEALTH SCIENCES

Nursing and Healthcare Administration	M
Nursing Education	M
Nursing—General	M
Occupational Therapy	M
Physician Assistant Studies	M

JESUIT SCHOOL OF THEOLOGY AT BERKELEY

Theology	P,M,D,O

THE JEWISH THEOLOGICAL SEMINARY

Jewish Studies	M,D
Music	M
Religion	M,D*
Religious Education	M,D*
Theology	M,D,O*

JEWISH UNIVERSITY OF AMERICA

Jewish Studies	P,D
Pastoral Ministry and Counseling	M,D
Religious Education	M,D

JOHN BROWN UNIVERSITY

Business Administration and Management—General	M
Counselor Education	M
Higher Education	M
International Business	M
Marriage and Family Therapy	M
Pastoral Ministry and Counseling	M

JOHN CARROLL UNIVERSITY

Accounting	M
Biological and Biomedical Sciences—General	M
Business Administration and Management—General	M
Corporate and Organizational Communication	M
Counseling Psychology	M,O
Counselor Education	M,O
Early Childhood Education	M
Education—General	M
Educational Leadership and Administration	M
Educational Psychology	M
English	M
History	M
Humanities	M
Mathematics	M
Middle School Education	M
Nonprofit Management	M
Religion	M
Science Education	M
Secondary Education	M

JOHN F. KENNEDY UNIVERSITY

Art/Fine Arts	M
Business Administration and Management—General	M,O
Comparative and Interdisciplinary Arts	M
Counseling Psychology	M
Education—General	M
Health Education	M
Health Psychology	M
Human Resources Development	M,O
Industrial and Organizational Psychology	M,O
Interdisciplinary Studies	M
Law	P
Museum Studies	M,O
Organizational Management	M,O
Psychology—General	M,D,O
Sport Psychology	M
Transpersonal and Humanistic Psychology	M

JOHN JAY COLLEGE OF CRIMINAL JUSTICE OF THE CITY UNIVERSITY OF NEW YORK

Criminal Justice and Criminology	M,D
Forensic Psychology	M,D
Forensic Sciences	M,D
Legal and Justice Studies	M,D
Organizational Behavior	M,D
Public Administration	M
Public Policy	M,D

JOHN MARSHALL LAW SCHOOL

International Business	P,M
Law	P,M
Legal and Justice Studies	P,M
Management Information Systems	P,M
Real Estate	P,M
Taxation	P,M

THE JOHNS HOPKINS UNIVERSITY

Acute Care/Critical Care Nursing	M,O
Addictions/Substance Abuse Counseling	M,D
Adult Education	M,O
Adult Nursing	M,O
Allopathic Medicine	P
Anatomy	D
Anthropology	D
Applied Economics	M
Applied Mathematics	M,D,O
Applied Physics	M,O
Art History	M,D
Asian Studies	M,D,O
Astronomy	D
Biochemistry	M,D
Bioengineering	M,D
Bioethics	M,D
Bioinformatics	M,D,O
Biological and Biomedical Sciences—General	M,D
Biomedical Engineering	M,D,O
Biophysics	D
Biostatistics	M,D
Biotechnology	M
Business Administration and Management—General	M,O
Cell Biology	D
Chemical Engineering	M,D
Chemistry	D
Civil Engineering	M,D
Classics	D
Clinical Psychology	M,D
Clinical Research	M,D
Cognitive Sciences	D
Communication—General	M
Community Health Nursing	M
Community Health	M,D
Comparative Literature	D
Computer and Information Systems Security	M,O*
Computer Engineering	M,D,O
Computer Science	M,D,O*
Counselor Education	M,O
Criminal Justice and Criminology	M
Curriculum and Instruction	M,O
Demography and Population Studies	M,D
Developmental Biology	D
Early Childhood Education	M,D,O
Economics	D
Education of the Gifted	M,D,O
Education—General	M,D,O
Educational Leadership and Administration	M,D,O
Educational Media/ Instructional Technology	M,D,O
Educational Psychology	M,O
Electrical Engineering	M,D,O*
Elementary Education	M,O
Emergency Management	M,O
Engineering and Applied Sciences—General	M,D,O
English as a Second Language	M,O
English Education	M,O
English	D
Environmental and Occupational Health	M,D
Environmental Engineering	M,D,O
Environmental Management and Policy	M,O
Environmental Sciences	M
Epidemiology	M,D
Evolutionary Biology	D
Family Nurse Practitioner Studies	M,O
Finance and Banking	M,O
Foreign Languages Education	M,O
French	D
Genetic Counseling	M,D
Genetics	M,D
Geography	M,D
Geosciences	M,D
German	D
Health Communication	M,D
Health Education	M,D
Health Informatics	M
Health Services Management and Hospital Administration	M,D,O
Health Services Research	M,D
History of Science and Technology	M,D
History	D
Homeland Security	M,O
Human Genetics	D
Human Resources Development	M,O
Immunology	M,D*
Infectious Diseases	M,D
Information Science	M
International Affairs	M,D,O
International Development	M,D,O
International Economics	M,D,O
International Health	M,D
Investment Management	M,O
Italian	D
Liberal Studies	M,O
Management Information Systems	M,O
Management of Technology	M,O
Marketing	M
Materials Engineering	M,D
Materials Sciences	M,D
Mathematical and Computational Finance	M,D
Mathematics Education	M,O
Mathematics	D
Mechanical Engineering	M,D
Mechanics	M
Medical Illustration	M
Microbiology	M,D
Military and Defense Studies	M
Molecular Biology	M,D
Molecular Biophysics	M,D
Molecular Medicine	D
Museum Studies	M
Music	M,D,O
Nanotechnology	M
Near and Middle Eastern Studies	D
Neuroscience	D
Nursing and Healthcare Administration	M
Nursing—General	M,D,O

Nutrition M,D
Operations Research M,D
Pathobiology D
Pathology D
Pediatric Nursing M,O
Pharmaceutical Sciences M
Pharmacology D*
Philosophy M,D
Physics D*
Physiology M,D
Political Science M,D,O
Psychology—General D
Public Health—General M,D
Public Policy M*
Reading Education M,D,O
Real Estate M
Romance Languages D
School Psychology M,O
Science Education M,O
Secondary Education M,O
Social Sciences Education M,O
Social Sciences M,D
Sociology D
Spanish D
Special Education M,D,O
Statistics M,D
Systems Engineering M,O
Technical Writing M
Telecommunications M,O
Toxicology M,D
Urban Education M,O
Women's Health Nursing M,O
Writing M

JOHNSON & WALES UNIVERSITY

Accounting M
Education—General M
Educational Leadership and Administration D
Finance and Banking M,O
Hospitality Management M,O
Human Resources Development O
International Business M
Marketing M
Organizational Management M

JOHNSON BIBLE COLLEGE

Education—General M
Educational Media/ Instructional Technology M
Marriage and Family Therapy M
Theology M

JOHNSON STATE COLLEGE

Art/Fine Arts M
Counselor Education M
Curriculum and Instruction M
Education of the Gifted M
Education—General M,O
Educational Psychology M
Reading Education M
Science Education M
Secondary Education M,O
Special Education M

JOINT MILITARY INTELLIGENCE COLLEGE

Military and Defense Studies M

JONES INTERNATIONAL UNIVERSITY

Accounting M
Adult Education M
Business Administration and Management—General M
Computer and Information Systems Security M
Conflict Resolution and Mediation/Peace Studies M
Corporate and Organizational Communication M
Curriculum and Instruction M
Distance Education Development M
Education—General M
Educational Leadership and Administration M
Educational Media/ Instructional Technology M
Elementary Education M
Entrepreneurship M
Finance and Banking M
Health Services Management and Hospital Administration M
Higher Education M
Management of Technology M
Organizational Management M
Project Management M
Secondary Education M

THE JUDGE ADVOCATE GENERAL'S SCHOOL, U.S. ARMY

Law M
Military and Defense Studies M

JUDSON UNIVERSITY

Architecture M
Education—General M
Organizational Management M
Reading Education M

THE JUILLIARD SCHOOL

Music M,D,O

KANSAS CITY UNIVERSITY OF MEDICINE AND BIOSCIENCES

Bioethics M
Biological and Biomedical Sciences—General M
Osteopathic Medicine P

KANSAS STATE UNIVERSITY

Accounting M
Adult Education M,D
Agricultural Economics and Agribusiness M,D
Agricultural Engineering M,D
Agricultural Sciences—General M,D
Agronomy and Soil Sciences M,D
Analytical Chemistry M,D
Anatomy M,D
Animal Sciences M,D
Architectural Engineering M
Architecture M
Art/Fine Arts M
Biochemistry M,D
Bioengineering M,D
Biological and Biomedical Sciences—General M,D
Business Administration and Management—General M
Chemical Engineering M,D
Chemistry M,D
Child and Family Studies M,D
Civil Engineering M,D
Clothing and Textiles M,D
Communication—General M
Computer Engineering M,D
Computer Science M,D*
Counselor Education M,D
Curriculum and Instruction M,D
Economics M,D
Education—General M,D
Educational Leadership and Administration M,D
Electrical Engineering M,D
Engineering and Applied Sciences—General M,D*
Engineering Management M,D
English M
Entomology M,D
Family and Consumer Sciences-General M,D
Food Science and Technology M,D
French M
Genetics M,D
Geography M,D
Geology M
German M
History M,D
Horticulture M,D
Hospitality Management M,D
Human Development D
Human Services M
Industrial/Management Engineering M,D
Information Science M,D
Inorganic Chemistry M,D
International Affairs M
Kinesiology and Movement Studies M
Landscape Architecture M
Manufacturing Engineering M,D
Marriage and Family Therapy D
Mass Communication M
Mathematics M,D
Mechanical Engineering M,D
Microbiology D
Music Education M
Music M
National Security M,D
Nuclear Engineering M,D
Nutrition M,D
Operations Research M,D
Organic Chemistry M,D
Pathobiology M,D
Physical Chemistry M,D
Physiology M,D
Plant Pathology M,D
Political Science M
Psychology—General M,D
Public Administration M
Public Health—General M
Range Science M,D
Rhetoric M
Sociology M,D
Software Engineering M,D
Spanish M
Special Education M,D
Speech and Interpersonal Communication M
Statistics M,D
Student Affairs M,D
Theater M
Urban and Regional Planning M
Veterinary Medicine P
Veterinary Sciences M

KANSAS WESLEYAN UNIVERSITY

Business Administration and Management—General M
Sports Management M

KAPLAN UNIVERSITY–DAVENPORT CAMPUS

Business Administration and Management—General M
Computer and Information Systems Security M
Criminal Justice and Criminology M
Education—General M
Educational Leadership and Administration M
Educational Media/ Instructional Technology M
Entrepreneurship M
Finance and Banking M
Health Services Management and Hospital Administration M,O
Higher Education M
Human Resources Management M
International Business M
Law M
Legal and Justice Studies M,O
Logistics M
Management Information Systems M
Marketing M
Mathematics Education M
Nursing and Healthcare Administration M
Nursing Education M
Nursing—General M
Organizational Management M
Political Science M,O
Project Management M
Reading Education M
Science Education M
Secondary Education M
Special Education M
Student Affairs M
Supply Chain Management M

KEAN UNIVERSITY

Accounting M
Addictions/Substance Abuse Counseling M
Adult Education M
Art Education M
Art/Fine Arts M
Biotechnology M
Business Administration and Management—General M
Clinical Psychology D
Communication Disorders M
Communication—General M
Community Health Nursing M
Community Health
Computational Sciences M
Computer Education M
Counseling Psychology M
Counselor Education M
Criminal Justice and Criminology M
Curriculum and Instruction M
Early Childhood Education M
Education—General M
Educational Leadership and Administration M,D
Educational Psychology M
English as a Second Language M
Environmental Management and Policy M
Exercise and Sports Science M
Foreign Languages Education M
Graphic Design M
Health Services Management and Hospital Administration M
Holocaust Studies M
Industrial and Organizational Psychology M
International Business M
Liberal Studies M
Management Information Systems M
Marriage and Family Therapy O
Mathematics Education M
Mathematics M

*M—master's degree; P—first professional degree; D—doctorate; O—other advanced degree; *—Close-Up and/or Announcement or Display in one of the other books in this series*

Multilingual and Multicultural Education	M
Nonprofit Management	M
Nursing and Healthcare Administration	M
Nursing—General	M
Occupational Therapy	M
Political Science	M
Psychology—General	M
Public Administration	M
Reading Education	M
School Nursing	M
School Psychology	D,O
Science Education	M
Social Work	M
Sociology	M
Spanish	M
Special Education	M
Statistics	M
Urban Education	D

KECK GRADUATE INSTITUTE OF APPLIED LIFE SCIENCES

Biological and Biomedical Sciences—General	M,D,O
Computational Biology	M,D,O

KEENE STATE COLLEGE

Curriculum and Instruction	M,O
Education—General	M,O
Educational Leadership and Administration	M,O
Special Education	M,O

KEHILATH YAKOV RABBINICAL SEMINARY

Theology	

KEISER UNIVERSITY

Business Administration and Management—General	M
Criminal Justice and Criminology	M
Education—General	M
Educational Leadership and Administration	M
International Business	M
Marketing	M

KELLER GRADUATE SCHOOL OF MANAGEMENT

Business Administration and Management—General	M,O

KELLER GRADUATE SCHOOL OF MANAGEMENT

Business Administration and Management—General	M

KENNESAW STATE UNIVERSITY

Accounting	M
Applied Statistics	M
Business Administration and Management—General	M
Computer Science	M
Conflict Resolution and Mediation/Peace Studies	M
Early Childhood Education	M
Education—General	M,D,O
Educational Leadership and Administration	M,D,O
Educational Media/Instructional Technology	M
Elementary Education	M
English as a Second Language	M
English Education	M
Exercise and Sports Science	M
Health Services Management and Hospital Administration	M
Information Science	M
Mathematics Education	M
Middle School Education	M
Nursing—General	M
Public Administration	M
Secondary Education	M
Social Work	M
Special Education	M
Writing	M

KENRICK-GLENNON SEMINARY

Theology	P,M

KENT STATE UNIVERSITY

Accounting	M,D
Adult Nursing	M,D
Analytical Chemistry	M,D
Anthropology	M
Applied Mathematics	M,D
Architecture	M,O
Art Education	M
Art History	M
Art/Fine Arts	M
Athletic Training and Sports Medicine	M
Biochemistry	M,D
Biological and Biomedical Sciences—General	M,D*
Biological Anthropology	D
Business Administration and Management—General	M
Cell Biology	M,D
Chemical Physics	M,D
Chemistry	M,D*
Classics	M,D
Clinical Psychology	M,D
Communication Disorders	M,D
Communication—General	M,D
Comparative Literature	M,D
Computer Science	M,D
Counseling Psychology	M
Counselor Education	M,D,O
Criminal Justice and Criminology	M
Curriculum and Instruction	M,D,O
Early Childhood Education	M
Ecology	M,D
Economics	M
Education of the Gifted	M
Education—General	M,D,O
Educational Leadership and Administration	M,D,O
Educational Measurement and Evaluation	M,D
Educational Media/Instructional Technology	M
Educational Psychology	M,D
Elementary Education	M,D,O
Engineering and Applied Sciences—General	M
English as a Second Language	M,D
English Education	M,D
English	M,D
Exercise and Sports Science	M,D
Experimental Psychology	M,D
Family and Consumer Sciences-General	M
Family Nurse Practitioner Studies	M,D
Finance and Banking	D
Financial Engineering	M
Foreign Languages Education	M,D
Foundations and Philosophy of Education	M,D
French	M,D
Geography	M,D
Geology	M,D
German	M,D
Gerontological Nursing	M,D
Gerontology	M
Graphic Design	M
Health Education	M,D
Higher Education	M
Historic Preservation	M,O
History	M,D
Human Development	M,D
Human Services	M,D,O
Illustration	M
Information Science	M
Inorganic Chemistry	M,D
Japanese	M,D
Journalism	M
Leisure Studies	M
Liberal Studies	M
Library Science	M
Management Information Systems	D
Marketing	D
Mass Communication	M
Mathematics	M,D
Middle School Education	M
Molecular Biology	M,D
Music Education	M,D
Music	M,D
Neuroscience	M,D
Nursing and Healthcare Administration	M,D
Nursing—General	M,D
Nutrition	M
Organic Chemistry	M,D
Pediatric Nursing	M,D
Pharmacology	M,D
Philosophy	M
Physical Chemistry	M,D
Physical Education	M,D
Physics	M,D
Physiology	M,D
Political Science	M,D
Psychiatric Nursing	M,D
Psychology—General	M,D
Public Administration	M
Public Health—General	M
Public Policy	M,D
Reading Education	M
Recreation and Park Management	M
Rehabilitation Counseling	M,O
Rhetoric	M,D
Russian	M,D
School Psychology	M,D,O
Secondary Education	M
Sociology	M,D
Spanish	M,D
Special Education	M,D,O
Sports Management	M
Student Affairs	M
Textile Design	M
Theater	M
Translation and Interpretation	M,D
Urban Design	M,O
Vocational and Technical Education	M,O
Women's Health Nursing	M,D
Writing	M,D

KENT STATE UNIVERSITY, STARK CAMPUS

Business Administration and Management—General	M

KENTUCKY CHRISTIAN UNIVERSITY

Religion	M
Theology	M

KENTUCKY STATE UNIVERSITY

Accounting	M
Aquaculture	M
Business Administration and Management—General	M
Computer and Information Systems Security	M
Computer Science	M
Finance and Banking	M
Human Resources Development	M
Information Science	M
International Affairs	M
Management Information Systems	M
Marketing	M
Nonprofit Management	M
Public Administration	M
Special Education	M

KETTERING UNIVERSITY

Automotive Engineering	M
Business Administration and Management—General	M
Computer Engineering	M
Electrical Engineering	M
Engineering Design	M
Engineering Management	M
Industrial and Manufacturing Management	M
Information Science	M
Manufacturing Engineering	M
Mechanical Engineering	M

KEUKA COLLEGE

Business Administration and Management—General	M
Criminal Justice and Criminology	M
Early Childhood Education	M
Occupational Therapy	M

KING COLLEGE

Business Administration and Management—General	M

KING'S COLLEGE

Business Administration and Management—General	M
Health Services Management and Hospital Administration	M
Physician Assistant Studies	M
Reading Education	M

KNOWLEDGE SYSTEMS INSTITUTE

Computer Science	M
Information Science	M

KNOX COLLEGE

Theology	P,M,D

KNOX THEOLOGICAL SEMINARY

Missions and Missiology	M
Pastoral Ministry and Counseling	D
Religion	M
Theology	P,M,O

KOL YAAKOV TORAH CENTER

Theology	O

KUTZTOWN UNIVERSITY OF PENNSYLVANIA

Art Education	M,O
Business Administration and Management—General	M
Computer Science	M
Counseling Psychology	M
Counselor Education	M
Curriculum and Instruction	M,O

Early Childhood Education	M,O
Education—General	M,O
Educational Leadership and Administration	M
Educational Media/ Instructional Technology	M,O
Elementary Education	M,O
English Education	M,O
English	M
Library Science	M,O
Marriage and Family Therapy	M
Mathematics Education	M,O
Media Studies	M
Music Education	O
Public Administration	M
Reading Education	M
School Nursing	M,O
Science Education	M,O
Secondary Education	M,O
Social Sciences Education	M,O
Social Work	M
Special Education	M,O

LAGRANGE COLLEGE

Curriculum and Instruction	M
Education—General	M
Middle School Education	M
Organizational Management	M
Secondary Education	M

LAGUNA COLLEGE OF ART & DESIGN

Art/Fine Arts	M

LAKE ERIE COLLEGE

Business Administration and Management—General	M
Curriculum and Instruction	M
Education—General	M
Educational Leadership and Administration	M
Health Services Management and Hospital Administration	M
Reading Education	M

LAKE ERIE COLLEGE OF OSTEOPATHIC MEDICINE

Biological and Biomedical Sciences—General	P,M,O
Health Education	P,M,O
Osteopathic Medicine	P,M,O
Pharmacy	P,M,O

LAKE FOREST COLLEGE

Liberal Studies	M

LAKE FOREST GRADUATE SCHOOL OF MANAGEMENT

Business Administration and Management—General	M

LAKEHEAD UNIVERSITY

Biological and Biomedical Sciences—General	M
Chemistry	M
Clinical Psychology	M,D
Computer Engineering	M
Computer Science	M
Economics	M
Education—General	M,D
Electrical Engineering	M
Engineering and Applied Sciences—General	M
English	M
Environmental Engineering	M
Exercise and Sports Science	M
Experimental Psychology	M,D
Forestry	M,D
Geology	M
Gerontology	M,D
Health Services Research	M
History	M
Kinesiology and Movement Studies	M
Mathematics	M
Physics	M
Psychology—General	M,D
Social Work	M
Sociology	M
Women's Studies	M,D

LAKELAND COLLEGE

Accounting	M
Business Administration and Management—General	M
Counselor Education	M
Education—General	M
Finance and Banking	M
Health Services Management and Hospital Administration	M
Project Management	M
Theology	M

LAMAR UNIVERSITY

Accounting	M
Applied Arts and Design—General	M
Art History	M
Art/Fine Arts	M
Biological and Biomedical Sciences—General	M
Business Administration and Management—General	M
Chemical Engineering	M,D
Chemistry	M
Civil Engineering	M,D
Clinical Psychology	M
Communication Disorders	M,D
Computer Science	M
Counselor Education	M,D,O
Criminal Justice and Criminology	M
Education—General	M,D,O
Educational Leadership and Administration	M,D,O
Educational Media/ Instructional Technology	M,D,O
Electrical Engineering	M,D
Engineering and Applied Sciences—General	M,D
Engineering Management	M,D
English	M
Entrepreneurship	M
Environmental Engineering	M,D
Environmental Management and Policy	M,D
Family and Consumer Sciences-General	M,O
Finance and Banking	M
Health Services Management and Hospital Administration	M
History	M
Industrial and Organizational Psychology	M
Industrial/Management Engineering	M,D
Information Science	M
Kinesiology and Movement Studies	M
Management Strategy and Policy	M
Mathematics	M
Mechanical Engineering	M,D
Music Education	M
Music	M
Nursing and Healthcare Administration	M
Nursing Education	M
Nursing—General	M
Photography	M
Political Science	M
Psychology—General	M
Public Administration	M
Social Psychology	M
Special Education	M,D
Theater	M

LANCASTER BIBLE COLLEGE

Counselor Education	M
Pastoral Ministry and Counseling	M
Special Education	M
Theology	M

LANCASTER THEOLOGICAL SEMINARY

Theology	P,M,D,O

LANDER UNIVERSITY

Curriculum and Instruction	M
Education—General	M
Elementary Education	M

LANGSTON UNIVERSITY

Education—General	M
Elementary Education	M
English as a Second Language	M
Multilingual and Multicultural Education	M
Physical Therapy	D
Rehabilitation Counseling	M
Urban Education	M

LA ROCHE COLLEGE

Human Resources Management	M,O
Nurse Anesthesia	M
Nursing and Healthcare Administration	M
Nursing Education	M
Nursing—General	M

LA SALLE UNIVERSITY

Business Administration and Management—General	M,O
Clinical Psychology	M,D
Communication Disorders	M
Computer Science	M
Corporate and Organizational Communication	M
Counseling Psychology	M,D
East European and Russian Studies	M
Education—General	M
Educational Media/ Instructional Technology	M
Hispanic Studies	M
History	M
Latin American Studies	M
Management of Technology	M
Marriage and Family Therapy	D
Nursing—General	M,O
Pastoral Ministry and Counseling	M
Psychology—General	D
Rehabilitation Counseling	D
Religion	M
Theology	M

LASELL COLLEGE

Advertising and Public Relations	M,O
Business Administration and Management—General	M,O
Communication—General	M,O
Corporate and Organizational Communication	M,O
Human Resources Management	M,O
Marketing	M,O
Nonprofit Management	M,O
Project Management	M,O

LA SIERRA UNIVERSITY

Accounting	M,O
Advertising and Public Relations	M
Business Administration and Management—General	M,O
Communication—General	M
Counselor Education	M,O
Curriculum and Instruction	M,D,O
Education—General	M,D,O
Educational Leadership and Administration	M,D,O
Educational Psychology	M,O
English	M
Finance and Banking	M,O
Human Resources Management	M,O
Marketing	M,O
Pastoral Ministry and Counseling	P,M
Religion	P,M
Religious Education	P,M
School Psychology	M,O
Writing	M

LAURA AND ALVIN SIEGAL COLLEGE OF JUDAIC STUDIES

Holocaust Studies	M
Humanities	M
Jewish Studies	M
Religious Education	M

LAURENTIAN UNIVERSITY

Analytical Chemistry	M
Applied Physics	M
Applied Social Research	M
Biochemistry	M
Biological and Biomedical Sciences—General	M,D
Business Administration and Management—General	M
Chemistry	M
Ecology	M,D
Engineering and Applied Sciences—General	M,D
Environmental Sciences	M
Experimental Psychology	M
Geology	M,D
History	M
Human Development	M
Humanities	M
Mineral/Mining Engineering	M,D
Natural Resources	M,D
Nursing—General	M
Organic Chemistry	M
Physical Chemistry	M
Psychology—General	M
Public Health—General	D
Science Education	O
Social Work	M
Sociology	M
Technical Writing	O
Theoretical Chemistry	M

LAWRENCE TECHNOLOGICAL UNIVERSITY

Architecture	M
Automotive Engineering	M,D
Business Administration and Management—General	M,D
Civil Engineering	M,D
Computer Engineering	M,D
Computer Science	M
Construction Engineering	M,D
Educational Media/ Instructional Technology	M
Electrical Engineering	M,D

*M—master's degree; P—first professional degree; D—doctorate; O—other advanced degree; *—Close-Up and/or Announcement or Display in one of the other books in this series*

Engineering and Applied Sciences—General	M,D
Engineering Management	M,D
Industrial and Manufacturing Management	M,D
Interior Design	M
Management Information Systems	M,D
Management of Technology	M,D
Manufacturing Engineering	M,D
Mechanical Engineering	M,D
Science Education	M
Technical Communication	M

LEADERSHIP INSTITUTE OF SEATTLE

Counseling Psychology	M
Organizational Behavior	M
Organizational Management	M
Psychology—General	M

LEBANESE AMERICAN UNIVERSITY

Business Administration and Management—General	M
Computer Science	M
International Affairs	M
Pharmacy	P

LEBANON VALLEY COLLEGE

Business Administration and Management—General	M
Music Education	M
Physical Therapy	D
Science Education	M

LEE UNIVERSITY

Counseling Psychology	M
Counselor Education	M
Education—General	M,O
Educational Leadership and Administration	M,O
Elementary Education	M,O
Music Education	M
Music	M
Religion	M
Secondary Education	M,O
Special Education	M,O
Theology	M

LEHIGH UNIVERSITY

Accounting	M
American Studies	M
Applied Mathematics	M,D
Biochemistry	M,D
Bioengineering	M,D
Biological and Biomedical Sciences—General	M,D
Business Administration and Management—General	M,D,O
Chemical Engineering	M,D
Chemistry	M,D
Civil Engineering	M,D
Computational Sciences	M,D
Computer Engineering	M,D
Computer Science	M,D
Counseling Psychology	M,D,O
Counselor Education	M,D,O
Economics	M,D
Education—General	M,D,O
Educational Leadership and Administration	M,D,O
Educational Media/Instructional Technology	M,D,O
Electrical Engineering	M,D
Elementary Education	M,D,O
Engineering and Applied Sciences—General	M,D
English as a Second Language	M,O
English	M,D
Environmental Engineering	M,D
Environmental Management and Policy	M
Environmental Sciences	M,D
Finance and Banking	M
Geology	M,D
Geosciences	M,D
History	M,D
Human Development	M,D
Human Services	M,D,O
Industrial/Management Engineering	M,D
Information Science	M
International and Comparative Education	M,O
Manufacturing Engineering	M
Materials Engineering	M,D
Materials Sciences	M,D
Mathematics	M,D
Mechanical Engineering	M,D
Mechanics	M,D
Molecular Biology	M,D
Neuroscience	M,D
Photonics	M,D
Physics	M,D
Political Science	M
Polymer Science and Engineering	M,D
Project Management	M,D,O
Psychology—General	M,D
Quantitative Analysis	M
School Psychology	M,D,O
Secondary Education	M,D,O
Sociology	M
Special Education	M,D,O
Statistics	M,D
Structural Engineering	M,D
Supply Chain Management	M,D,O
Systems Engineering	M,D

LEHMAN COLLEGE OF THE CITY UNIVERSITY OF NEW YORK

Accounting	M
Adult Nursing	M
Art/Fine Arts	M
Biological and Biomedical Sciences—General	M
Business Education	M
Communication Disorders	M
Computer Science	M
Counselor Education	M
Early Childhood Education	M
Education—General	M
Elementary Education	M
English as a Second Language	M
English Education	M
English	M
Gerontological Nursing	M
Health Education	M
Health Promotion	M
History	M
Maternal and Child/Neonatal Nursing	M
Mathematics Education	M
Mathematics	M
Multilingual and Multicultural Education	M
Music Education	M
Nursing—General	M
Nutrition	M
Pediatric Nursing	M
Plant Sciences	D
Reading Education	M
Recreation and Park Management	M
Science Education	M
Social Sciences Education	M
Spanish	M
Special Education	M

LE MOYNE COLLEGE

Business Administration and Management—General	M
Early Childhood Education	M,O
Education—General	M,O
Educational Leadership and Administration	M,O
Elementary Education	M,O
Middle School Education	M,O
Nursing and Healthcare Administration	M,O
Nursing Education	M,O
Nursing—General	M,O
Physician Assistant Studies	M
Secondary Education	M,O
Special Education	M,O

LENOIR-RHYNE UNIVERSITY

Accounting	M
Athletic Training and Sports Medicine	M
Business Administration and Management—General	M
Counselor Education	M
Early Childhood Education	M
Education—General	M
Entrepreneurship	M
Occupational Therapy	M
School Psychology	M
Social Psychology	M

LESLEY UNIVERSITY

Art Education	M,D,O
Art Therapy	M,D,O*
Art/Fine Arts	M*
Clinical Psychology	M,D,O
Computer Education	M,D,O
Counseling Psychology	M*
Curriculum and Instruction	M,D,O
Early Childhood Education	M,D,O
Ecology	M,D,O
Education—General	M,D,O*
Elementary Education	M,D,O
Environmental Education	M,D,O
Health Psychology	M
Interdisciplinary Studies	M
International Affairs	M,O
Middle School Education	M,D,O
Psychology—General	M,D,O
Reading Education	M,D,O
School Psychology	M
Science Education	M,D,O
Social Psychology	M,D,O
Special Education	M,D,O
Sustainable Development	M
Therapies—Dance, Drama, and Music	M,D,O
Urban and Regional Planning	M
Women's Studies	M
Writing	M*

LETOURNEAU UNIVERSITY

Business Administration and Management—General	M

LEWIS & CLARK COLLEGE

Addictions/Substance Abuse Counseling	M
Communication Disorders	M
Counseling Psychology	M,O
Cultural Studies	M,O
Early Childhood Education	M
Education—General	M
Educational Leadership and Administration	M,D
Elementary Education	M
Environmental Law	P,M
Law	P,M
Marriage and Family Therapy	M
Middle School Education	M
Psychology—General	M,O
School Psychology	M,O
Secondary Education	M
Social Psychology	M
Special Education	M

LEWIS UNIVERSITY

Accounting	M
Adult Nursing	M
Aviation	M
Business Administration and Management—General	M
Computer and Information Systems Security	M
Counseling Psychology	M
Counselor Education	M
Criminal Justice and Criminology	M
Curriculum and Instruction	M
Education—General	M,D,O
Educational Leadership and Administration	M,D,O
Educational Media/Instructional Technology	M
Electronic Commerce	M
Elementary Education	M
English as a Second Language	M
Environmental and Occupational Health	M
Finance and Banking	M
Health Services Management and Hospital Administration	M
Human Resources Management	M
International Business	M
Management Information Systems	M
Management of Technology	M
Marketing	M
Mathematics Education	M
Nursing and Healthcare Administration	M
Nursing Education	M
Nursing—General	M
Organizational Management	M
Project Management	M
Public Administration	M
Reading Education	M
Science Education	M
Secondary Education	M
Social Sciences Education	M
Special Education	M
Student Affairs	M

LEXINGTON THEOLOGICAL SEMINARY

Theology	P,M,D

LIBERTY UNIVERSITY

Business Administration and Management—General	M
Communication—General	M
Counseling Psychology	M,D
Counselor Education	M,D,O
Curriculum and Instruction	M,D,O
Early Childhood Education	M,D,O
Education of the Gifted	M,D,O
Education—General	M,D,O
Educational Leadership and Administration	M,D,O
Elementary Education	M,D,O
Law	P
Nursing—General	M,D
Pastoral Ministry and Counseling	M,D
Reading Education	M,D,O
Religion	P,M,D
Secondary Education	M,D,O

Special Education	M,D,O
Theology	P,M,D

LIFE CHIROPRACTIC COLLEGE WEST

Chiropractic	P*

LIFE UNIVERSITY

Chiropractic	P
Exercise and Sports Science	M

LIM COLLEGE

Business Administration and Management—General	M
Entrepreneurship	M
Textile Design	M

LINCOLN CHRISTIAN SEMINARY

Pastoral Ministry and Counseling	P,M,D
Theology	P,M,D

LINCOLN MEMORIAL UNIVERSITY

Business Administration and Management—General	M
Counselor Education	M,O
Curriculum and Instruction	M,O
Education—General	M,O
Educational Leadership and Administration	M,O
English Education	M,O
Family Nurse Practitioner Studies	M
Nurse Anesthesia	M
Nursing—General	M
Osteopathic Medicine	P

LINCOLN UNIVERSITY (CA)

Business Administration and Management—General	M
Finance and Banking	M
Human Resources Management	M
International Business	M
Investment Management	M
Management Information Systems	M

LINCOLN UNIVERSITY (MO)

Accounting	M
Business Administration and Management—General	M
Counselor Education	M,O
Criminal Justice and Criminology	M
Education—General	M,O
Educational Leadership and Administration	M,O
Elementary Education	M,O
Entrepreneurship	M
History	M
Political Science	M
Public Administration	M
Public Policy	M
Secondary Education	M,O
Social Sciences	M
Sociology	M
Special Education	M,O

LINCOLN UNIVERSITY (PA)

Business Administration and Management—General	M
Early Childhood Education	M
Elementary Education	M
Finance and Banking	M
Human Resources Management	M
Human Services	M
Reading Education	M

LINDENWOOD UNIVERSITY

Accounting	M
American Studies	M
Art/Fine Arts	M
Business Administration and Management—General	M,O
Communication—General	M,O
Counseling Psychology	M,D,O
Criminal Justice and Criminology	M,O
Education—General	M,D,O
Educational Leadership and Administration	M,D,O
Educational Media/Instructional Technology	M,D,O
Entrepreneurship	M
Finance and Banking	M
Gerontology	M,O
Health Services Management and Hospital Administration	M,O
Human Resources Management	M,O
International Business	M
Management Information Systems	M,O
Marketing	M,O
Public Administration	M
School Psychology	M,D,O
Sports Management	M
Theater	M
Writing	M,O

LINDSEY WILSON COLLEGE

Counseling Psychology	M
Human Development	M

LIPSCOMB UNIVERSITY

Accounting	M
Business Administration and Management—General	M
Conflict Resolution and Mediation/Peace Studies	M,O
Counseling Psychology	M,O
Curriculum and Instruction	M
Education—General	M
Educational Leadership and Administration	M
English as a Second Language	M
Finance and Banking	M
Health Services Management and Hospital Administration	M
Nonprofit Management	M
Pharmacy	P
Psychology—General	M,O
Religion	P,M
Special Education	M
Sustainability Management	M
Theology	P,M

LOCK HAVEN UNIVERSITY OF PENNSYLVANIA

Education—General	M
Elementary Education	M
Liberal Studies	M
Physician Assistant Studies	M

LOGAN UNIVERSITY–COLLEGE OF CHIROPRACTIC

Chiropractic	P,M

LOGOS EVANGELICAL SEMINARY

Theology	P,M,D

LOMA LINDA UNIVERSITY

Adult Nursing	M
Allied Health—General	M,D
Allopathic Medicine	P,M,D
Anatomy	M,D
Biochemistry	M,D
Bioethics	M,O
Biological and Biomedical Sciences—General	M,D
Biostatistics	M,D,O
Child and Family Studies	M,D,O
Communication Disorders	M
Counselor Education	M,D,O
Dentistry	P,M,O
Environmental and Occupational Health	M
Epidemiology	M,D,O
Geosciences	M,D
Gerontological Nursing	M
Health Education	M,D
Health Promotion	M,D
Health Services Management and Hospital Administration	M
International Health	M
Microbiology	M,D
Nursing and Healthcare Administration	M
Nursing—General	M
Nutrition	M,D
Occupational Therapy	M,D
Oral and Dental Sciences	M,O
Pastoral Ministry and Counseling	M,O
Pathology	M,D
Pediatric Nursing	M
Pharmacology	M,D
Pharmacy	P
Physical Therapy	M,D
Physician Assistant Studies	M
Physiology	M,D
Psychology—General	D
Public Health—General	M,D,O
Religion	M
Social Work	M,D

LONG ISLAND UNIVERSITY AT RIVERHEAD

Counselor Education	M,O
Early Childhood Education	M
Education—General	M,O
Elementary Education	M
Homeland Security	M,O
Reading Education	M
Special Education	M

LONG ISLAND UNIVERSITY, BRENTWOOD CAMPUS

Counseling Psychology	M
Counselor Education	M
Criminal Justice and Criminology	M
Early Childhood Education	M
Education—General	M
Reading Education	M
Special Education	M

LONG ISLAND UNIVERSITY, BROOKLYN CAMPUS

Accounting	M
Adult Nursing	M,O
Athletic Training and Sports Medicine	M
Biological and Biomedical Sciences—General	M
Business Administration and Management—General	M
Chemistry	M
Clinical Psychology	D
Communication Disorders	M
Community Health	M
Comparative Literature	M
Computer Art and Design	M
Computer Science	M
Counselor Education	M,O
Economics	M
Education—General	M,O
Educational Leadership and Administration	M
Educational Media/Instructional Technology	M
Elementary Education	M
English as a Second Language	M
English Education	M
English	M
Exercise and Sports Science	M
Health Education	M
Health Services Management and Hospital Administration	M
History	M,O
Human Resources Management	M
International Affairs	M,O
Mathematics Education	M
Multilingual and Multicultural Education	M
Nursing and Healthcare Administration	M
Nursing—General	M,O
Pharmaceutical Administration	M
Pharmaceutical Sciences	M,D
Pharmacology	M,D
Physical Education	M
Physical Therapy	D
Political Science	M
Psychology—General	M,D
Public Administration	M
Reading Education	M
School Psychology	M
Social Sciences	M,O
Special Education	M
Taxation	M
Toxicology	M,D
Urban Studies	M
Writing	M

LONG ISLAND UNIVERSITY, C.W. POST CAMPUS

Accounting	M,O
Allied Health—General	M,O
Applied Mathematics	M
Art Education	M
Art Therapy	M
Art/Fine Arts	M
Biological and Biomedical Sciences—General	M
Business Administration and Management—General	M,O
Cardiovascular Sciences	M
Clinical Laboratory Sciences/Medical Technology	M
Clinical Psychology	D
Communication Disorders	M
Computer Art and Design	M
Computer Education	M
Computer Science	M
Counselor Education	M
Criminal Justice and Criminology	M
Early Childhood Education	M
Education—General	M,O
Educational Leadership and Administration	M,O
Educational Media/Instructional Technology	M
Elementary Education	M
Engineering Management	M
English as a Second Language	M
English Education	M
English	M
Environmental Management and Policy	M
Family Nurse Practitioner Studies	M,O
Finance and Banking	M,O
Foreign Languages Education	M

*M—master's degree; P—first professional degree; D—doctorate; O—other advanced degree; *—Close-Up and/or Announcement or Display in one of the other books in this series*

Geosciences	M
Gerontology	M,O
Health Services Management and Hospital Administration	M,O
History	M
Immunology	M
Information Science	M
Information Studies	M,D,O
Interdisciplinary Studies	M
International Affairs	M
International Business	M,O
Internet and Interactive Multimedia	M
Library Science	M,D,O
Management Information Systems	M,O
Marketing	M,O
Mathematics Education	M
Mathematics	M
Medicinal and Pharmaceutical Chemistry	M
Microbiology	M
Middle School Education	M
Multilingual and Multicultural Education	M
Music Education	M
Music	M
Nonprofit Management	M,O
Nursing—General	M,O
Nutrition	M,O
Perfusion	M
Political Science	M
Psychology—General	M,D
Public Administration	M,O
Reading Education	M
Science Education	M
Secondary Education	M
Social Sciences	M
Social Work	M
Spanish	M
Special Education	M
Taxation	M,O
Theater	M

LONG ISLAND UNIVERSITY, ROCKLAND GRADUATE CAMPUS

Business Administration and Management—General	M,O
Counseling Psychology	M
Counselor Education	M
Early Childhood Education	M
Educational Leadership and Administration	M,O
Elementary Education	M
Gerontology	M,O
Health Services Management and Hospital Administration	M,O
Pharmaceutical Sciences	M
Public Administration	M,O
Reading Education	M
Secondary Education	M
Special Education	M

LONG ISLAND UNIVERSITY, WESTCHESTER GRADUATE CAMPUS

Business Administration and Management—General	M
Counseling Psychology	M
Counselor Education	M
Early Childhood Education	M,O
Education—General	M,O
Educational Psychology	M
Elementary Education	M,O
English as a Second Language	M,O
Information Studies	M
Library Science	M
Multilingual and Multicultural Education	M,O
Reading Education	M,O
School Psychology	M
Secondary Education	M,O
Special Education	M,O

LONGWOOD UNIVERSITY

Business Administration and Management—General	M
Communication Disorders	M
Counselor Education	M
Criminal Justice and Criminology	M
Education—General	M
Educational Leadership and Administration	M
Educational Media/Instructional Technology	M
Elementary Education	M
English Education	M
English	M
Reading Education	M
Secondary Education	M
Special Education	M
Writing	M

LONGY SCHOOL OF MUSIC

Music	M,O

LORAS COLLEGE

Educational Leadership and Administration	M
Pastoral Ministry and Counseling	M
Psychology—General	M
Special Education	M
Theology	M

LOUISIANA STATE UNIVERSITY AND AGRICULTURAL AND MECHANICAL COLLEGE

Accounting	M,D
Agricultural Economics and Agribusiness	M,D
Agricultural Education	M,D
Agricultural Engineering	M,D
Agricultural Sciences—General	M,D
Agronomy and Soil Sciences	M,D
Animal Sciences	M,D
Anthropology	M,D
Applied Arts and Design—General	M
Applied Science and Technology	M
Applied Statistics	M
Architecture	M
Art History	M
Art/Fine Arts	M
Astronomy	M,D
Astrophysics	M,D
Biochemistry	M,D
Bioengineering	M,D
Biological and Biomedical Sciences—General	M,D
Biopsychology	M,D
Business Administration and Management—General	M,D
Business Education	M,D
Chemical Engineering	M,D
Chemistry	M,D
Civil Engineering	M,D
Clinical Psychology	M,D
Cognitive Sciences	M,D
Communication Disorders	M,D
Communication—General	M,D
Comparative Literature	M,D
Computer Engineering	M,D
Computer Science	M,D
Counselor Education	M,D,O
Developmental Psychology	M,D
Economics	M,D
Education—General	M,D,O
Educational Leadership and Administration	M,D,O
Educational Measurement and Evaluation	M,D,O
Educational Media/Instructional Technology	M,D,O
Electrical Engineering	M,D
Elementary Education	M,D,O
Engineering and Applied Sciences—General	M,D
English	M,D
Entomology	M,D
Environmental Engineering	M,D
Environmental Management and Policy	M
Environmental Sciences	M,D
Family and Consumer Sciences-General	M,D
Finance and Banking	M,D
Fish, Game, and Wildlife Management	M,D
Food Science and Technology	M,D
Forestry	M,D
French	M,D
Geography	M,D
Geology	M,D
Geophysics	M,D
Geotechnical Engineering	M,D
Graphic Design	M
Higher Education	M,D,O
Hispanic Studies	M
History	M,D
Home Economics Education	M,D
Horticulture	M,D
Human Resources Development	M,D
Industrial and Organizational Psychology	M,D
Industrial/Management Engineering	M,D
Information Studies	M,O
International and Comparative Education	M,D
Kinesiology and Movement Studies	M,D
Landscape Architecture	M
Law	M
Liberal Studies	M
Library Science	M,O
Linguistics	M,D
Management Information Systems	M,D
Marine Affairs	M,D
Marketing	D
Mass Communication	M,D
Mathematics	M,D
Mechanical Engineering	M,D
Mechanics	M,D
Media Studies	M,D
Medical Physics	M,D
Music Education	M,D
Music	M,D
Natural Resources	M,D
Oceanography	M,D
Petroleum Engineering	M,D
Philosophy	M
Photography	M
Physics	M,D
Plant Pathology	M,D
Political Science	M,D
Psychology—General	M,D
Public Administration	M,D
School Psychology	M,D
Secondary Education	M,D,O
Social Work	M,D
Sociology	M,D
Statistics	M
Structural Engineering	M,D
Systems Science	M,D
Theater	M,D
Toxicology	M
Transportation and Highway Engineering	M,D
Veterinary Medicine	P
Veterinary Sciences	M,D
Vocational and Technical Education	M,D
Water Resources Engineering	M,D
Writing	M,D

LOUISIANA STATE UNIVERSITY HEALTH SCIENCES CENTER

Adult Nursing	M,D
Allied Health—General	M
Allopathic Medicine	P,M
Anatomy	M,D
Biological and Biomedical Sciences—General	M,D
Biostatistics	M,D
Cell Biology	M,D
Communication Disorders	M,D
Community Health Nursing	M,D
Dentistry	P
Developmental Biology	M,D
Human Genetics	M,D
Immunology	M,D
Microbiology	M,D
Neurobiology	M,D
Neuroscience	M,D*
Nurse Anesthesia	M,D
Nursing—General	M,D
Occupational Therapy	M
Parasitology	M,D
Pathology	M,D
Pharmacology	M,D
Physical Therapy	D
Physiology	M,D
Rehabilitation Counseling	M

LOUISIANA STATE UNIVERSITY HEALTH SCIENCES CENTER AT SHREVEPORT

Allopathic Medicine	P
Anatomy	M,D
Biochemistry	M,D
Biological and Biomedical Sciences—General	M,D*
Cell Biology	M,D
Immunology	M,D
Microbiology	M,D
Molecular Biology	M,D
Pharmacology	D
Physiology	M,D

LOUISIANA STATE UNIVERSITY IN SHREVEPORT

Business Administration and Management—General	M
Computer Science	M
Counseling Psychology	M
Curriculum and Instruction	M
Education—General	M
Educational Leadership and Administration	M
Health Services Management and Hospital Administration	M
Human Services	M
Liberal Studies	M
School Psychology	O
Systems Science	M

LOUISIANA TECH UNIVERSITY

Accounting	M,D
Applied Arts and Design—General	M
Art/Fine Arts	M
Biological and Biomedical Sciences—General	M
Biomedical Engineering	M,D
Business Administration and Management—General	M,D
Business Education	M,D
Chemical Engineering	M,D
Chemistry	M
Civil Engineering	M,D
Communication Disorders	M

Computational Sciences	M,D
Computer Science	M
Counseling Psychology	M,D
Counselor Education	M,D
Curriculum and Instruction	M,D
Economics	M,D
Education—General	M,D
Educational Leadership and Administration	M,D
Electrical Engineering	M,D
Engineering and Applied Sciences—General	M,D
English Education	M,D
English	M
Exercise and Sports Science	M
Family and Consumer Sciences-General	M
Finance and Banking	M,D
Foreign Languages Education	M,D
Graphic Design	M
Health Education	M,D
History	M
Industrial and Organizational Psychology	M,D
Industrial/Management Engineering	M
Interior Design	M
Marketing	M,D
Mathematics Education	M,D
Mathematics	M
Mechanical Engineering	M,D
Nutrition	M
Photography	M
Physical Education	M,D
Physics	M,D
Psychology—General	M,D
Science Education	M,D
Secondary Education	M,D
Social Sciences Education	M,D
Special Education	M,D
Speech and Interpersonal Communication	M
Statistics	M

LOUISVILLE PRESBYTERIAN THEOLOGICAL SEMINARY

Religion	P,M,D
Theology	P,M,D

LOURDES COLLEGE

Education—General	M
Educational Media/Instructional Technology	M
Organizational Management	M

LOYOLA MARYMOUNT UNIVERSITY

Bioethics	M
Business Administration and Management—General	M
Civil Engineering	M
Computer Science	M
Counselor Education	M
Early Childhood Education	M
Education—General	M,D
Educational Leadership and Administration	M,D
Electrical Engineering	M
Elementary Education	M
Engineering Management	M
English as a Second Language	M
English	M
Environmental Engineering	M
Environmental Sciences	M
Film, Television, and Video Production	M
Law	P,M
Marriage and Family Therapy	M
Mathematics Education	M
Mechanical Engineering	M
Multilingual and Multicultural Education	M
Pastoral Ministry and Counseling	M
Philosophy	M
Reading Education	M
Religious Education	M
School Psychology	M
Secondary Education	M
Special Education	M
Systems Engineering	M
Taxation	P,M
Theology	M
Urban Education	M
Writing	M

LOYOLA UNIVERSITY CHICAGO

Accounting	M
Acute Care/Critical Care Nursing	M,O
Adult Nursing	M,O
Allopathic Medicine	P
Anatomy	M,D
Applied Statistics	M
Biochemistry	M,D*
Biological and Biomedical Sciences—General	M
Business Administration and Management—General	M
Cardiovascular Sciences	M,O
Cell Biology	M,D*
Chemistry	M,D
Clinical Psychology	M,D
Cognitive Sciences	M
Computer Science	M
Corporate and Organizational Communication	M
Counseling Psychology	D
Counselor Education	M,O
Criminal Justice and Criminology	M
Curriculum and Instruction	M,D
Developmental Psychology	M,D
Education—General	M,D,O
Educational Leadership and Administration	M,D,O
Educational Measurement and Evaluation	M,D
Educational Media/Instructional Technology	M
Educational Policy	M,D
Educational Psychology	M
Elementary Education	M
English	M,D
Environmental and Occupational Health	M,O
Family Nurse Practitioner Studies	M,O
Finance and Banking	M
Health Law	P,M,D
Health Services Management and Hospital Administration	M,O
Higher Education	M,D
History	M,D
Human Resources Management	M
Immunology	M,D
Industrial and Labor Relations	M
Infectious Diseases	M,O
Information Science	M
Law	P,M,D
Management Information Systems	M
Marketing	M
Mathematics	M
Microbiology	M,D
Molecular Biology	D
Molecular Physiology	M,D*
Neurobiology	M,D
Neuroscience	M,D
Nursing and Healthcare Administration	M,O
Nursing Informatics	M,O
Nursing—General	M,D
Oncology Nursing	M,O
Pastoral Ministry and Counseling	M,O
Pharmacology	M,D
Philosophy	M,D
Political Science	M,D
Psychology—General	M,D
Public History	M,D
Public Policy	M,D
Reading Education	M
Religion	P,M,O
Religious Education	M
School Psychology	M,D,O
Science Education	M
Secondary Education	M
Social Psychology	M,D
Sociology	M,D
Software Engineering	M
Spanish	M
Special Education	M
Statistics	M
Theology	P,M,D,O
Women's Health Nursing	M

LOYOLA UNIVERSITY MARYLAND

Accounting	M
Business Administration and Management—General	M*
Clinical Psychology	M,D,O
Communication Disorders	M,O*
Computer Science	M
Counseling Psychology	M,O
Counselor Education	M,O
Curriculum and Instruction	M,O
Early Childhood Education	M,O
Education—General	M,O*
Educational Leadership and Administration	M,O
Educational Media/Instructional Technology	M
Finance and Banking	M
International Business	M
Liberal Studies	M
Management Information Systems	M
Marketing	M
Pastoral Ministry and Counseling	M,D,O
Psychology—General	M,D,O*
Reading Education	M,O
Software Engineering	M
Special Education	M,O

LOYOLA UNIVERSITY NEW ORLEANS

Adult Nursing	M
Business Administration and Management—General	M
Counselor Education	M
Criminal Justice and Criminology	M
Family Nurse Practitioner Studies	M
Health Services Management and Hospital Administration	M
Law	P,M
Music	M
Nursing—General	M
Theology	M,O
Therapies—Dance, Drama, and Music	M

LUBBOCK CHRISTIAN UNIVERSITY

Theology	M

LUTHERAN SCHOOL OF THEOLOGY AT CHICAGO

Pastoral Ministry and Counseling	P,M,D
Theology	P,M,D

LUTHERAN THEOLOGICAL SEMINARY

Ethics	P,M,D
Pastoral Ministry and Counseling	P,M,D
Religion	P,M,D
Theology	P,M,D

LUTHERAN THEOLOGICAL SEMINARY AT GETTYSBURG

Pastoral Ministry and Counseling	P,M,D
Religion	P,M,D
Theology	P,M,D

THE LUTHERAN THEOLOGICAL SEMINARY AT PHILADELPHIA

Pastoral Ministry and Counseling	P,M,D,O
Religion	P,M,D,O
Theology	P,M,D,O

LUTHERAN THEOLOGICAL SOUTHERN SEMINARY

Theology	P,M,D

LUTHER RICE UNIVERSITY

Missions and Missiology	P,M,D
Pastoral Ministry and Counseling	P,M,D
Religious Education	P,M,D
Theology	P,M,D

LUTHER SEMINARY

Theology	P,M,D

LYNCHBURG COLLEGE

Business Administration and Management—General	M
Counselor Education	M
Curriculum and Instruction	M
Education—General	M
Educational Leadership and Administration	M
English Education	M
English	M
History	M
Music	M
Reading Education	M
Science Education	M
Social Psychology	M
Special Education	M

LYNDON STATE COLLEGE

Counselor Education	M
Curriculum and Instruction	M
Education—General	M
Reading Education	M
Science Education	M
Special Education	M

LYNN UNIVERSITY

Aviation Management	M,D
Business Administration and Management—General	M,D
Criminal Justice and Criminology	M,O
Education of the Gifted	M,D
Educational Leadership and Administration	M,D
Emergency Management	M,O
Hospitality Management	M,D
International and Comparative Education	M,D
International Business	M,D
Investment Management	M,D
Marketing	M,D
Mass Communication	M,D
Media Studies	M,D
Music	M,O
Psychology—General	M,O

*M—master's degree; P—first professional degree; D—doctorate; O—other advanced degree; *—Close-Up and/or Announcement or Display in one of the other books in this series*

Special Education	M,D
Sports Management	M,D

MACHZIKEI HADATH RABBINICAL COLLEGE

Theology	O

MADONNA UNIVERSITY

Adult Nursing	M
Business Administration and Management—General	M
Clinical Psychology	M
Criminal Justice and Criminology	M
Education—General	M
Educational Leadership and Administration	M
English as a Second Language	M
Health Services Management and Hospital Administration	M
Hospice Nursing	M
International Business	M
Liberal Studies	M
Nursing and Healthcare Administration	M
Nursing—General	M
Pastoral Ministry and Counseling	M
Psychology—General	M
Quality Management	M
Reading Education	M
Special Education	M
Theology	M

MAHARISHI UNIVERSITY OF MANAGEMENT

Accounting	M,D
Asian Studies	M,D
Business Administration and Management—General	M,D
Computer Science	M
Education—General	M
Elementary Education	M
Secondary Education	M
Sustainability Management	M,D

MAINE COLLEGE OF ART

Art/Fine Arts	M

MAINE MARITIME ACADEMY

International Business	M,O
Logistics	M,O
Supply Chain Management	M,O
Transportation Management	M,O

MALONE UNIVERSITY

Business Administration and Management—General	M
Counselor Education	M
Curriculum and Instruction	M
Education—General	M
Educational Media/Instructional Technology	M
Family Nurse Practitioner Studies	M
Nursing—General	M
Pastoral Ministry and Counseling	M
Reading Education	M
Special Education	M
Theology	M

MANHATTAN COLLEGE

Chemical Engineering	M
Civil Engineering	M
Computer Engineering	M
Counselor Education	M,O
Early Childhood Education	M
Education—General	M,O
Educational Leadership and Administration	M,O
Electrical Engineering	M
Engineering and Applied Sciences—General	M
Environmental Engineering	M
Mechanical Engineering	M
Special Education	M

MANHATTAN SCHOOL OF MUSIC

Music	M,D,O

MANHATTANVILLE COLLEGE

Art Education	M
Early Childhood Education	M
Education—General	M*
Educational Leadership and Administration	M
Elementary Education	M
English as a Second Language	M
English Education	M
Exercise and Sports Science	M
Finance and Banking	M
Foreign Languages Education	M
Human Resources Development	M
International Business	M
Liberal Studies	M
Management Strategy and Policy	M
Marketing	M
Mathematics Education	M
Middle School Education	M
Music Education	M
Organizational Management	M
Reading Education	M
Science Education	M
Secondary Education	M
Social Sciences Education	M
Special Education	M
Sports Management	M
Writing	M

MANSFIELD UNIVERSITY OF PENNSYLVANIA

Art Education	M
Education—General	M
Elementary Education	M
Information Studies	M
Library Science	M
Music	M
Nursing—General	M
Secondary Education	M

MAPLE SPRINGS BAPTIST BIBLE COLLEGE AND SEMINARY

Pastoral Ministry and Counseling	P,M,D,O
Religious Education	P,M,D,O
Theology	P,M,D,O

MARANATHA BAPTIST BIBLE COLLEGE

Cultural Studies	M
Pastoral Ministry and Counseling	M
Theology	M

MARIAN UNIVERSITY (IN)

Education—General	M

MARIAN UNIVERSITY (WI)

Adult Nursing	M
Business Administration and Management—General	M
Education—General	M,D
Educational Leadership and Administration	M,D
Nursing Education	M
Nursing—General	M
Organizational Management	M
Quality Management	M

MARIETTA COLLEGE

Corporate and Organizational Communication	M
Education—General	M
Physician Assistant Studies	M
Psychology—General	M

MARIST COLLEGE

Business Administration and Management—General	M,O
Computer Science	M,O
Corporate and Organizational Communication	M
Counseling Psychology	M,O
Education—General	M,O
Educational Psychology	M,O
Industrial and Manufacturing Management	M,O
Management Information Systems	M,O
Management of Technology	M,O
Psychology—General	M,O
Public Administration	M
School Psychology	M,O
Software Engineering	M,O

MARLBORO COLLEGE

Business Administration and Management—General	M
Computer Education	M
Education—General	M
Health Services Management and Hospital Administration	M
Information Science	M
Internet and Interactive Multimedia	M
Sustainability Management	M

MARQUETTE UNIVERSITY

Accounting	M
Adult Nursing	M,D,O
Advertising and Public Relations	M
Analytical Chemistry	M,D
Bioinformatics	M,D
Biological and Biomedical Sciences—General	M,D
Biomedical Engineering	M,D
Business Administration and Management—General	M
Cell Biology	M,D
Chemical Physics	M,D
Chemistry	M,D
Civil Engineering	M,D
Clinical Psychology	M,D
Communication Disorders	M
Communication—General	M
Computational Sciences	M,D
Computer Engineering	M,D
Computer Science	M,D
Construction Management	M,D
Dentistry	P
Developmental Biology	M,D
Ecology	M,D
Economics	M
Education—General	M,D,O
Electrical Engineering	M,D
Engineering and Applied Sciences—General	M,D
Engineering Management	M,D
English	M,D
Entrepreneurship	O
Environmental Engineering	M,D
Ethics	M,D
Evolutionary Biology	M,D
Foreign Languages Education	M
Genetics	M,D
Geotechnical Engineering	M,D
Gerontological Nursing	M,D,O
Health Communication	M
History	M,D
Human Resources Development	M
Human Resources Management	M
Inorganic Chemistry	M,D
Interdisciplinary Studies	M,D
International Affairs	M
Journalism	M
Law	P
Management of Technology	M,D
Manufacturing Engineering	M,D
Mass Communication	M
Maternal and Child/Neonatal Nursing	M,D,O
Mathematics Education	M,D
Mathematics	M,D
Mechanical Engineering	M,D
Media Studies	M
Medieval and Renaissance Studies	M,D
Microbiology	M,D
Molecular Biology	M,D
Neurobiology	M,D
Nurse Midwifery	M,D,O
Nursing—General	M,D,O
Oral and Dental Sciences	M
Organic Chemistry	M,D
Pediatric Nursing	M,D,O
Philosophy	M,D
Physical Chemistry	M,D
Physical Therapy	D
Physician Assistant Studies	M
Physiology	M,D
Political Science	M
Psychology—General	M,D
Public Administration	M
Spanish	M
Speech and Interpersonal Communication	M
Structural Engineering	M,D
Theology	M,D
Transportation and Highway Engineering	M,D
Water Resources Engineering	M,D

MARSHALL UNIVERSITY

Adult Education	M
Allopathic Medicine	P
Art/Fine Arts	M
Biological and Biomedical Sciences—General	M,D
Business Administration and Management—General	M,D,O
Chemistry	M
Classics	M
Clinical Psychology	M,D
Communication Disorders	M
Communication—General	M
Counselor Education	M,O
Criminal Justice and Criminology	M
Early Childhood Education	M
Education—General	M,D,O
Educational Leadership and Administration	M,D,O

Elementary Education	M
Engineering and Applied Sciences—General	M
Engineering Management	M
English	M
Environmental Engineering	M
Environmental Sciences	M
Exercise and Sports Science	M
Family and Consumer Sciences-General	M
Geography	M
Health Education	M
Health Services Management and Hospital Administration	M,D
History	M
Human Resources Management	M
Humanities	M
Industrial and Organizational Psychology	M,D
Information Science	M
Journalism	M
Management of Technology	M
Mass Communication	M
Mathematics	M
Music	M
Nursing—General	M
Nutrition	M
Physics	M
Political Science	M
Psychology—General	M,D
Reading Education	M,O
School Psychology	O
Secondary Education	M
Sociology	M
Spanish	M
Special Education	M
Sports Management	M
Vocational and Technical Education	M

MARS HILL GRADUATE SCHOOL

Counseling Psychology	M
Religion	M
Theology	M

MARTIN UNIVERSITY

Pastoral Ministry and Counseling	M
Psychology—General	M
Social Psychology	M

MARY BALDWIN COLLEGE

Education—General	M
Elementary Education	M
English	M
Middle School Education	M
Theater	M

MARYGROVE COLLEGE

Education—General	M
Educational Leadership and Administration	M
Elementary Education	M
English	M
Human Resources Management	M
Legal and Justice Studies	M
Reading Education	M
Secondary Education	M
Translation and Interpretation	O
Urban Education	M

MARYLAND INSTITUTE COLLEGE OF ART

Art Education	M
Art/Fine Arts	M,O
Graphic Design	M
Photography	M

MARYLHURST UNIVERSITY

Art Therapy	M,O
Business Administration and Management—General	M
Counseling Psychology	M,O
Education—General	M
Finance and Banking	M
Health Services Management and Hospital Administration	M
Interdisciplinary Studies	M
Marketing	M
Nonprofit Management	M
Organizational Behavior	M
Real Estate	M
Theology	P,M

MARYMOUNT UNIVERSITY

Allied Health—General	M,D,O
Business Administration and Management—General	M,O
Computer and Information Systems Security	M,O
Counseling Psychology	M,O
Counselor Education	M
Education—General	M
Educational Leadership and Administration	M,O
Elementary Education	M
English as a Second Language	M
English	M
Family Nurse Practitioner Studies	M,O
Forensic Psychology	M
Health Promotion	M
Health Services Management and Hospital Administration	M,O
Human Resources Management	M,O
Humanities	M
Interior Design	M
Legal and Justice Studies	M,O
Management Information Systems	M,O
Medical Informatics	M,O
Nursing Education	M,O
Nursing—General	M,O
Organizational Management	M,O
Pastoral Ministry and Counseling	M,O
Physical Therapy	D
Project Management	M,O
Secondary Education	M
Social Psychology	
Special Education	M

MARYVILLE UNIVERSITY OF SAINT LOUIS

Accounting	M,O
Actuarial Science	M
Addictions/Substance Abuse Counseling	M
Adult Nursing	M
Allied Health—General	M,D
Art Education	M,D
Business Administration and Management—General	M,O
Business Education	M,O
Early Childhood Education	M,D
Education of the Gifted	M,D
Education—General	M,D
Educational Leadership and Administration	M,D
Educational Psychology	M,D
Electronic Commerce	M,O
Elementary Education	M,D
English Education	M,D
Environmental Education	M,D
Family Nurse Practitioner Studies	M
Marketing	M,O

Marriage and Family Therapy	M
Middle School Education	M,D
Nursing Education	M
Nursing—General	M
Occupational Therapy	M
Physical Therapy	D
Reading Education	M,D
Rehabilitation Counseling	M
Secondary Education	M,D
Therapies—Dance, Drama, and Music	M

MARYWOOD UNIVERSITY

Addictions/Substance Abuse Counseling	M
Architecture	M
Art Education	M
Art Therapy	M,O
Art/Fine Arts	M
Biotechnology	M
Business Administration and Management—General	M
Clinical Psychology	M,D
Communication Disorders	M
Communication—General	M,O
Corporate and Organizational Communication	M,O
Counseling Psychology	M
Counselor Education	M,O
Criminal Justice and Criminology	M
Early Childhood Education	M
Education—General	M
Educational Leadership and Administration	M,D
Electronic Commerce	M,O
Elementary Education	M
Exercise and Sports Science	M
Film, Television, and Video Production	M,O
Finance and Banking	M
Gerontology	M,O
Graphic Design	M
Health Communication	M,O
Health Education	D
Health Services Management and Hospital Administration	M
Higher Education	M,D
Human Development	D
Illustration	M
Information Science	M
Interdisciplinary Studies	M,O
Interior Design	M
Investment Management	M
Library Science	M,O
Management Information Systems	M
Media Studies	M,O
Music Education	M
Nursing and Healthcare Administration	M
Nutrition	M,O
Photography	M
Physician Assistant Studies	M
Psychology—General	M
Public Administration	M
Reading Education	M
School Psychology	M,O
Secondary Education	M
Social Work	M,D
Special Education	M
Textile Design	M
Therapies—Dance, Drama, and Music	M,O

MASSACHUSETTS COLLEGE OF ART AND DESIGN

Applied Arts and Design—General	M
Architecture	M
Art Education	M
Art/Fine Arts	M
Education—General	M
Film, Television, and Video Production	M
Photography	M
Textile Design	M
Theater	M

MASSACHUSETTS COLLEGE OF LIBERAL ARTS

Curriculum and Instruction	M
Education—General	M
Educational Leadership and Administration	M
Reading Education	M
Special Education	M

MASSACHUSETTS COLLEGE OF PHARMACY AND HEALTH SCIENCES

Chemistry	M,D
Health Services Management and Hospital Administration	M
Organic Chemistry	M
Pharmaceutical Sciences	M,D*
Pharmacology	M,D
Pharmacy	P
Physician Assistant Studies	M

MASSACHUSETTS INSTITUTE OF TECHNOLOGY

Aerospace/Aeronautical Engineering	M,D,O
Archaeology	M,D,O
Architectural History	M,D
Architecture	M,D
Art History	M,D
Atmospheric Sciences	M,D
Biochemistry	D
Bioengineering	M,D*
Biological and Biomedical Sciences—General	P,M,D
Biomedical Engineering	M,D
Business Administration and Management—General	M,D
Cell Biology	D
Chemical Engineering	M,D
Chemistry	D
Civil Engineering	M,D,O
Cognitive Sciences	D
Communication Disorders	D
Computational Biology	D
Computational Sciences	M
Computer Science	M,D,O
Construction Engineering	M,D,O
Developmental Biology	D
Economics	M,D
Electrical Engineering	M,D,O
Electronic Materials	M,D,O
Engineering and Applied Sciences—General	M,D,O
Engineering Management	M,D
Environmental Biology	M,D,O
Environmental Engineering	M,D,O
Environmental Sciences	M,D,O
Genetics	D
Geochemistry	M,D
Geology	M,D
Geophysics	M,D
Geosciences	M,D
Geotechnical Engineering	M,D,O
History of Science and Technology	D
Humanities	M
Hydrology	M,D,O
Immunology	D
Information Science	M,D,O
Inorganic Chemistry	D
Linguistics	D
Logistics	M,D
Manufacturing Engineering	M,D,O
Marine Geology	M,D
Materials Engineering	M,D,O
Materials Sciences	M,D,O

*M—master's degree; P—first professional degree; D—doctorate; O—other advanced degree; *—Close-Up and/or Announcement or Display in one of the other books in this series*

Mathematics	D
Mechanical Engineering	M,D,O
Media Studies	M,D
Medical Informatics	M
Medical Physics	D
Metallurgical Engineering and Metallurgy	M,D,O
Microbiology	D
Molecular Biology	D
Molecular Pathogenesis	M,D
Molecular Pharmacology	M,D
Molecular Toxicology	M,D
Neurobiology	D
Neuroscience	D
Nuclear Engineering	M,D,O
Ocean Engineering	M,D,O
Oceanography	M,D,O
Operations Research	M,D
Organic Chemistry	M,D,O
Philosophy	D
Physical Chemistry	D
Physics	M,D
Planetary and Space Sciences	M,D
Political Science	M,D
Polymer Science and Engineering	M,D,O
Real Estate	M
Social Sciences	D
Structural Biology	D
Structural Engineering	M,D,O
Systems Biology	D
Systems Engineering	M,D
Technical Writing	M
Technology and Public Policy	M,D
Toxicology	M,D
Transportation and Highway Engineering	M,D,O
Urban and Regional Planning	M,D
Urban Studies	M,D
Writing	M

MASSACHUSETTS MARITIME ACADEMY

Emergency Management	M
Facilities Management	M

MASSACHUSETTS SCHOOL OF LAW AT ANDOVER

Law	P

MASSACHUSETTS SCHOOL OF PROFESSIONAL PSYCHOLOGY

Clinical Psychology	M,D,O
Counseling Psychology	M,D,O
Forensic Psychology	M,D,O
Industrial and Organizational Psychology	M,D,O
Psychology—General	M,D,O
School Psychology	M,D,O

THE MASTER'S COLLEGE AND SEMINARY

Pastoral Ministry and Counseling	P,M,D
Theology	P,M,D

MAYO GRADUATE SCHOOL

Biochemistry	D
Biological and Biomedical Sciences—General	D
Biomedical Engineering	D
Cancer Biology/Oncology	D
Cell Biology	D
Genetics	D
Immunology	D
Molecular Biology	D
Molecular Pharmacology	D*
Neuroscience	D
Structural Biology	D
Virology	D

MAYO MEDICAL SCHOOL

Allopathic Medicine	P

MAYO SCHOOL OF HEALTH SCIENCES

Nurse Anesthesia	M
Physical Therapy	D

McCORMICK THEOLOGICAL SEMINARY

Pastoral Ministry and Counseling	P,M,D,O
Theology	P,M,D,O

McDANIEL COLLEGE

Counselor Education	M
Curriculum and Instruction	M
Educational Leadership and Administration	M
Educational Media/Instructional Technology	M
Elementary Education	M
Human Resources Development	M
Human Services	M
Liberal Studies	M
Library Science	M
Physical Education	M
Reading Education	M
Secondary Education	M
Special Education	M

McGILL UNIVERSITY

Accounting	M,D,O
Aerospace/Aeronautical Engineering	M,D
Agricultural Economics and Agribusiness	M
Agricultural Engineering	M,D
Agricultural Sciences—General	M,D,O
Agronomy and Soil Sciences	M,D
Allopathic Medicine	M,D
Anatomy	M,D
Animal Sciences	M,D
Anthropology	M,D
Applied Mathematics	M,D
Architecture	M,D,O
Art History	M,D
Asian Studies	M,D
Atmospheric Sciences	M,D
Biochemistry	M,D
Bioengineering	M,D
Bioethics	M,D,O
Bioinformatics	M,D
Biological and Biomedical Sciences—General	M,D*
Biomedical Engineering	M,D
Biostatistics	M,D,O
Biotechnology	M,D,O
Business Administration and Management—General	M,D,O
Cell Biology	M,D
Chemical Engineering	M,D
Chemistry	M,D
Civil Engineering	M,D
Clinical Psychology	M,D
Communication Disorders	M,D
Communication—General	M,D
Community Health	M,D,O
Computational Sciences	M,D
Computer Engineering	M,D
Computer Science	M,D
Counseling Psychology	M,D,O
Curriculum and Instruction	M,D,O
Dentistry	P,M,D,O
Developmental Psychology	M,D,O
Economics	M,D
Education—General	M,D,O
Educational Leadership and Administration	M,D,O
Educational Psychology	M,D,O
Electrical Engineering	M,D
Engineering and Applied Sciences—General	M,D,O
English	M,D
Entomology	M,D
Entrepreneurship	M,D,O
Environmental and Occupational Health	M,D,O
Environmental Engineering	M,D
Environmental Management and Policy	M,D
Epidemiology	M,D,O
Experimental Psychology	M,D
Family Nurse Practitioner Studies	M,D,O
Finance and Banking	M,D,O
Fish, Game, and Wildlife Management	M,D
Food Science and Technology	M,D
Foreign Languages Education	M,D,O
Forensic Sciences	M,D,O
Forestry	M,D
Foundations and Philosophy of Education	M,D,O
French	M,D
Genetic Counseling	M,D
Geography	M,D
Geosciences	M,D
Geotechnical Engineering	M,D
German	M,D
Health Services Management and Hospital Administration	M,D,O
Hispanic Studies	M,D
History of Medicine	M,D
History	M,D
Human Genetics	M,D
Hydraulics	M,D
Immunology	M,D
Industrial and Manufacturing Management	M,D,O
Information Studies	M,D,O
International Business	M,D,O
International Development	M,D,O
Italian	M,D
Jewish Studies	M
Kinesiology and Movement Studies	M,D,O
Law	P,M,D,O
Library Science	M,D,O
Linguistics	M,D
Management Information Systems	M,D,O
Management Strategy and Policy	M,D,O
Marketing	M,D,O
Materials Engineering	M,D,O
Mathematics	M,D
Mechanical Engineering	M,D
Mechanics	M,D
Medical Physics	M,D
Meteorology	M,D
Microbiology	M,D
Mineral/Mining Engineering	M,D,O
Music Education	M,D
Music	M,D
Natural Resources	M,D
Near and Middle Eastern Studies	M,D,O
Neuroscience	M,D
Nursing—General	M,D,O
Nutrition	M,D,O
Oceanography	M,D
Oral and Dental Sciences	M,D,O
Parasitology	M,D,O
Pathology	M,D
Pharmacology	M,D
Philosophy	M,D
Physical Education	M,D,O
Physics	M,D
Physiology	M,D
Planetary and Space Sciences	M,D
Plant Sciences	M,D,O
Political Science	M,D
Psychology—General	M,D
Rehabilitation Sciences	M,D,O
Religion	M,D
Russian	M,D
School Psychology	M,D,O
Social Work	M,D,O
Sociology	M,D,O
Statistics	M,D,O
Structural Engineering	M,D
Theology	M,D
Transportation Management	M,D
Urban and Regional Planning	M,D
Water Resources Engineering	M,D

McKENDREE UNIVERSITY

Business Administration and Management—General	M
Counseling Psychology	M
Education—General	M
Educational Leadership and Administration	M
Human Resources Management	M
International Business	M
Music Education	M
Nursing and Healthcare Administration	M
Nursing Education	M
Nursing—General	M
Special Education	M

McMASTER UNIVERSITY

Analytical Chemistry	M,D
Anthropology	M,D
Applied Statistics	M
Astrophysics	D
Biochemistry	M,D
Biological and Biomedical Sciences—General	M,D
Business Administration and Management—General	M,D
Cancer Biology/Oncology	M,D
Cardiovascular Sciences	M,D
Cell Biology	M,D
Chemical Engineering	M,D
Chemical Physics	M,D
Chemistry	M,D
Civil Engineering	M,D
Classics	M,D
Computer Science	M,D
Cultural Studies	M,D
Economics	M,D
Electrical Engineering	M,D
Engineering and Applied Sciences—General	M,D
Engineering Physics	M,D
English	M,D
French	M
Genetics	M,D
Geochemistry	M,D
Geography	M,D
Geology	M,D
Geosciences	M,D
Health Physics/Radiological Health	M,D
Health Services Research	M,D
History	M,D
Human Resources Management	M,D
Immunology	M,D
Industrial and Labor Relations	M
Inorganic Chemistry	M,D
International Affairs	M,D
Kinesiology and Movement Studies	M,D
Management Information Systems	D
Materials Engineering	M,D
Materials Sciences	M,D

Mathematics	M,D
Mechanical Engineering	M,D
Medical Physics	M,D
Molecular Biology	M,D
Neuroscience	M,D
Nuclear Engineering	M,D
Nursing—General	M,D
Nutrition	M,D
Occupational Therapy	M
Organic Chemistry	M,D
Pastoral Ministry and Counseling	P,M,D,O
Pharmacology	M,D
Philosophy	M,D
Physical Chemistry	M,D
Physical Therapy	M
Physics	D
Physiology	M,D
Political Science	M,D
Psychology—General	M,D
Public Administration	M,D
Public Affairs	M,D
Public Policy	M,D
Rehabilitation Sciences	M,D
Religion	M,D
Social Work	M,D
Sociology	M,D
Software Engineering	M,D
Statistics	M
Theology	P,M,D,O
Virology	M,D

McNEESE STATE UNIVERSITY

Accounting	M
Addictions/Substance Abuse Counseling	M
Agricultural Sciences—General	M
Biological and Biomedical Sciences—General	M
Business Administration and Management—General	M
Chemical Engineering	M
Chemistry	M
Civil Engineering	M
Computer Science	M
Counseling Psychology	M
Counselor Education	M
Curriculum and Instruction	M
Early Childhood Education	M
Education—General	M
Educational Leadership and Administration	M,O
Educational Media/Instructional Technology	M,O
Electrical Engineering	M
Elementary Education	M
Engineering and Applied Sciences—General	M
Engineering Management	M
English	M
Environmental Sciences	M
Exercise and Sports Science	M
Experimental Psychology	M
Family Nurse Practitioner Studies	M
Health Promotion	M
Mathematics	M
Mechanical Engineering	M
Music Education	M
Nursing and Healthcare Administration	M
Nursing Education	M
Nursing—General	M
Nutrition	M
Psychology—General	M
School Psychology	M
Science Education	M
Secondary Education	M
Special Education	M
Statistics	M
Writing	M

MEADVILLE LOMBARD THEOLOGICAL SCHOOL

Pastoral Ministry and Counseling	P,M,D
Theology	P,M,D

MEDAILLE COLLEGE

Business Administration and Management—General	M
Counseling Psychology	M
Curriculum and Instruction	M
Education—General	M
Elementary Education	M
Organizational Management	M
Psychology—General	M
Reading Education	M
Special Education	M

MEDICAL COLLEGE OF GEORGIA

Acute Care/Critical Care Nursing	M
Adult Nursing	M
Allied Health—General	M
Allopathic Medicine	P
Anatomy	D
Biochemistry	D
Biological and Biomedical Sciences—General	M,D,O
Biostatistics	M,D
Cardiovascular Sciences	D
Cell Biology	D
Clinical Research	M,O
Dentistry	P
Family Nurse Practitioner Studies	M
Genomic Sciences	D
Health Informatics	M
Medical Illustration	M
Molecular Biology	D
Molecular Medicine	D
Neuroscience	D
Nurse Anesthesia	M
Nursing and Healthcare Administration	M
Nursing—General	D
Oral and Dental Sciences	M,D
Pediatric Nursing	M
Pharmacology	D
Physiology	D

MEDICAL COLLEGE OF WISCONSIN

Allopathic Medicine	P
Biochemistry	D
Bioethics	M
Bioinformatics	M
Biological and Biomedical Sciences—General	M,D,O
Biophysics	D*
Biostatistics	D*
Cell Biology	D
Clinical Laboratory Sciences/Medical Technology	M
Community Health	M,D,O
Developmental Biology	D
Environmental and Occupational Health	M
Epidemiology	M
Medical Informatics	M
Microbiology	M,D
Molecular Genetics	M,D
Neuroscience	D
Pathology	M,D
Pharmacology	D
Physiology	M,D
Public Health—General	M,D,O
Toxicology	D

MEDICAL UNIVERSITY OF SOUTH CAROLINA

Adult Nursing	M
Allied Health—General	M,D
Allopathic Medicine	P
Biochemistry	M,D
Bioinformatics	M,D
Biological and Biomedical Sciences—General	M,D
Biostatistics	M,D
Cancer Biology/Oncology	M,D
Cardiovascular Sciences	M,D
Cell Biology	M,D
Clinical Research	M,D
Dentistry	P
Developmental Biology	M,D
Epidemiology	M,D
Family Nurse Practitioner Studies	M,D
Genetics	M,D
Health Services Management and Hospital Administration	M,D
Health Services Research	M
Immunology	M,D
Marine Sciences	M,D
Maternal and Child/Neonatal Nursing	M
Microbiology	M,D
Molecular Biology	M,D
Molecular Pharmacology	M,D
Neuroscience	M,D
Nurse Anesthesia	M
Nursing and Healthcare Administration	M
Nursing Education	M
Nursing—General	D
Occupational Therapy	M
Pathobiology	M,D
Pathology	M,D
Pharmaceutical Sciences	D
Pharmacy	P
Physical Therapy	D
Physician Assistant Studies	M
Rehabilitation Sciences	D
Structural Biology	M,D

MEHARRY MEDICAL COLLEGE

Allopathic Medicine	P
Biological and Biomedical Sciences—General	D
Cancer Biology/Oncology	D
Community Health	M
Dentistry	P
Environmental and Occupational Health	M
Health Services Management and Hospital Administration	M
Immunology	D
Microbiology	D
Neuroscience	D
Pharmacology	D

MEMORIAL UNIVERSITY OF NEWFOUNDLAND

Adult Education	M,D,O
Anthropology	M,D
Aquaculture	M
Archaeology	M,D
Biochemistry	M,D
Biological and Biomedical Sciences—General	M,D,O
Biopsychology	M,D
Business Administration and Management—General	M
Cancer Biology/Oncology	M,D
Cardiovascular Sciences	M,D
Chemistry	M,D
Civil Engineering	M,D
Classics	M
Clinical Research	M
Community Health	M,D,O
Computational Sciences	M
Computer Engineering	M,D
Computer Science	M,D
Condensed Matter Physics	M,D
Curriculum and Instruction	M,D,O
Economics	M
Education—General	M,D,O
Educational Leadership and Administration	M,D,O
Educational Media/Instructional Technology	M,D,O
Educational Psychology	M,D,O
Electrical Engineering	M,D
Engineering and Applied Sciences—General	M,D
English	M,D
Environmental Engineering	M
Environmental Sciences	M
Epidemiology	M,D,O
Exercise and Sports Science	M
Experimental Psychology	M,D
Fish, Game, and Wildlife Management	M,O
Folklore	M,D
Food Science and Technology	M,D
French	M
Gender Studies	M,D
Geography	M,D
Geology	M,D
Geophysics	M,D
Geosciences	M,D
German	M
History	M,D
Human Genetics	M,D
Humanities	M
Immunology	M,D
Industrial and Labor Relations	M
Kinesiology and Movement Studies	M
Linguistics	M,D
Marine Affairs	M,D,O
Marine Biology	M,D
Marine Sciences	M,O
Mathematics	M,D
Mechanical Engineering	M,D
Music	M,D
Neuroscience	M,D
Nursing—General	M,O
Ocean Engineering	M,D
Oceanography	M,D
Pharmaceutical Sciences	M,D
Philosophy	M
Physical Education	M
Physics	M,D
Political Science	M
Psychology—General	M,D
Religion	M
Social Psychology	M,D
Social Work	M
Sociology	M,D
Sport Psychology	M
Statistics	M,D
Women's Studies	M

MEMPHIS COLLEGE OF ART

Applied Arts and Design—General	M
Art Education	M
Art/Fine Arts	M*
Computer Art and Design	M
Photography	M

MEMPHIS THEOLOGICAL SEMINARY

Theology	P,M,D

MENNONITE BRETHREN BIBLICAL SEMINARY

Marriage and Family Therapy	M,O
Missions and Missiology	M

*M—master's degree; P—first professional degree; D—doctorate; O—other advanced degree; *—Close-Up and/or Announcement or Display in one of the other books in this series*

Pastoral Ministry and Counseling	M
Theology	P,M

MERCER UNIVERSITY

Accounting	M
Allopathic Medicine	P,M
Biomedical Engineering	M
Business Administration and Management—General	M
Computer Engineering	M
Curriculum and Instruction	M,D,O
Early Childhood Education	M,D,O
Education—General	M,D,O
Educational Leadership and Administration	M,D,O
Electrical Engineering	M
Engineering and Applied Sciences—General	M
Engineering Management	M
Environmental Engineering	M
Environmental Sciences	M
Law	P
Management of Technology	M
Mechanical Engineering	M
Middle School Education	M,D,O
Music	M
Nursing—General	M,D,O
Pharmaceutical Sciences	P,M,D
Pharmacy	P,M,D
Reading Education	M,D,O
Secondary Education	M,D,O
Software Engineering	M
Theology	P,M,D

MERCY COLLEGE

Accounting	M
Addictions/Substance Abuse Counseling	M,O
Allied Health—General	M,D,O
Business Administration and Management—General	M
Communication Disorders	M
Computer and Information Systems Security	M
Counseling Psychology	M,O
Counselor Education	M,O
Early Childhood Education	M
Education—General	M,O
Educational Leadership and Administration	M,O
Electronic Commerce	M
Elementary Education	M
English as a Second Language	M
English	M
Health Services Management and Hospital Administration	M
Human Resources Management	M,O
Marriage and Family Therapy	M
Middle School Education	M
Multilingual and Multicultural Education	M,O
Nursing and Healthcare Administration	M
Nursing Education	M
Nursing—General	M
Occupational Therapy	M
Organizational Management	M
Physical Therapy	M,D
Physician Assistant Studies	M
Psychology—General	M
Reading Education	M
School Psychology	M
Secondary Education	M
Special Education	M,O
Urban Education	M

MERCYHURST COLLEGE

Biological Anthropology	M
Criminal Justice and Criminology	M,O
Educational Leadership and Administration	M,O
Forensic Sciences	M
Multilingual and Multicultural Education	M,O
Organizational Management	M,O
Special Education	M,O

MEREDITH COLLEGE

Business Administration and Management—General	M
Education—General	M
Music	M
Nutrition	M

MERITUS UNIVERSITY

Business Administration and Management—General	M

MERRIMACK COLLEGE

Education—General	M

MESA STATE COLLEGE

Business Administration and Management—General	M
Education—General	M

MESIVTA OF EASTERN PARKWAY–YESHIVA ZICHRON MEILECH

Theology

MESIVTA TIFERETH JERUSALEM OF AMERICA

Theology

MESIVTA TORAH VODAATH RABBINICAL SEMINARY

Theology

METHODIST THEOLOGICAL SCHOOL IN OHIO

Theology	P,M,D

METHODIST UNIVERSITY

Business Administration and Management—General	M
Criminal Justice and Criminology	M
Physician Assistant Studies	M

METROPOLITAN COLLEGE OF NEW YORK

Business Administration and Management—General	M
Corporate and Organizational Communication	M
Elementary Education	M
Media Studies	M
Public Administration	M

METROPOLITAN STATE UNIVERSITY

Business Administration and Management—General	M,O
Computer Science	M
Information Studies	M,O
Liberal Studies	M
Management Information Systems	M,O
Nonprofit Management	M,O
Nursing—General	M,D
Project Management	M,O
Psychology—General	M
Public Administration	M,O
Technical Writing	M

MGH INSTITUTE OF HEALTH PROFESSIONS

Allied Health—General	M,D,O*
Communication Disorders	M,O
Gerontological Nursing	M,D,O
Medical Imaging	O
Nursing Education	M,D,O
Nursing—General	M,D,O
Pediatric Nursing	M,D,O
Physical Therapy	M,D,O
Psychiatric Nursing	M,D,O
Reading Education	M,O
Women's Health Nursing	M,D,O

MIAMI INTERNATIONAL UNIVERSITY OF ART & DESIGN

Art/Fine Arts	M
Computer Art and Design	M
Film, Television, and Video Production	M
Graphic Design	M*
Interior Design	M

MIAMI UNIVERSITY

Accounting	M
Analytical Chemistry	M,D
Architecture	M
Art Education	M
Art/Fine Arts	M
Biochemistry	M,D
Botany	M,D*
Business Administration and Management—General	M
Chemistry	M,D
Child and Family Studies	M
Clinical Psychology	D
Communication Disorders	M
Communication—General	M
Curriculum and Instruction	M
Early Childhood Education	M
Economics	M
Education—General	M,D,O
Educational Leadership and Administration	M,D
Educational Psychology	M,O
Elementary Education	M
Engineering and Applied Sciences—General	M,O
English Education	M,D
English	M,D
Environmental Sciences	M
Exercise and Sports Science	M
Experimental Psychology	D
Finance and Banking	M
French	M
Geography	M
Geology	M,D
Gerontology	M
History	M,D
Inorganic Chemistry	M,D
Management Information Systems	M
Marketing	M
Mass Communication	M
Mathematics Education	M
Mathematics	M
Microbiology	M,D
Music Education	M
Music	M
Operations Research	M
Organic Chemistry	M,D
Paper and Pulp Engineering	M
Philosophy	M
Physical Chemistry	M,D
Physics	M
Plant Biology	M,D
Plant Sciences	M,D
Political Science	M,D
Psychology—General	D
Reading Education	M
Religion	M
Rhetoric	M,D
School Psychology	M,O
Secondary Education	M
Social Psychology	D
Social Sciences Education	M
Software Engineering	M,O
Spanish	M
Special Education	M
Speech and Interpersonal Communication	M
Statistics	M
Student Affairs	M
Systems Science	M
Technical Writing	M
Theater	M
Writing	M,D
Zoology	M,D*

MICHIGAN SCHOOL OF PROFESSIONAL PSYCHOLOGY

Clinical Psychology	M,D
Educational Psychology	M,D
Psychology—General	M,D
Transpersonal and Humanistic Psychology	M,D

MICHIGAN STATE UNIVERSITY

Accounting	M,D
Adult Education	M,D,O
Advertising and Public Relations	M,D
African Studies	M,D
African-American Studies	M,D
Agricultural Economics and Agribusiness	M,D
Agricultural Sciences—General	M,D
Agronomy and Soil Sciences	M,D
Allopathic Medicine	P
American Studies	M,D
Animal Sciences	M,D
Anthropology	M,D
Applied Mathematics	M,D
Applied Statistics	M,D
Art/Fine Arts	M
Astronomy	M,D
Astrophysics	M,D
Biochemistry	M,D*
Bioethics	M
Biological and Biomedical Sciences—General	M,D
Biosystems Engineering	M,D
Business Administration and Management—General	M,D
Cell Biology	M,D
Chemical Engineering	M,D
Chemical Physics	M,D
Chemistry	M,D
Child and Family Studies	M,D
Child Development	M,D
Civil Engineering	M,D
Clinical Laboratory Sciences/Medical Technology	M
Communication Disorders	M,D
Communication—General	M,D
Computer Science	M,D
Construction Management	M,D
Counselor Education	M,D,O
Criminal Justice and Criminology	M,D*
Curriculum and Instruction	M,D,O
Ecology	D
Economics	M,D
Education—General	M,D,O
Educational Leadership and Administration	M,D,O

Educational Measurement and Evaluation	M,D,O
Educational Media/ Instructional Technology	M,D,O
Educational Policy	D
Educational Psychology	M,D,O
Electrical Engineering	M,D
Engineering and Applied Sciences—General	M,D
English as a Second Language	M,D
English	M,D
Entomology	M,D
Environmental Design	M,D
Environmental Engineering	M,D
Environmental Sciences	M,D
Epidemiology	M,D
Evolutionary Biology	D
Finance and Banking	M,D
Fish, Game, and Wildlife Management	M,D
Food Science and Technology	M,D
Foreign Languages Education	D
Forensic Sciences	M,D
Forestry	M,D
French	M,D
Genetics	M,D
Geography	M,D
Geosciences	M,D
German	M,D
Health Communication	M
Higher Education	M,D,O
Hispanic Studies	M,D
History	M,D
Horticulture	M,D
Hospitality Management	M*
Human Resources Management	M,D
Humanities	M
Industrial and Labor Relations	M,D
Interior Design	M,D
International Affairs	M
Journalism	M
Kinesiology and Movement Studies	M,D
Latin American Studies	D
Linguistics	M,D
Management Information Systems	M,D
Manufacturing Engineering	M,D
Marketing	M,D
Marriage and Family Therapy	M,D
Materials Engineering	M,D
Materials Sciences	M,D
Mathematics Education	M,D
Mathematics	M,D
Mechanical Engineering	M,D
Mechanics	M,D
Media Studies	M,D
Microbiology	M,D
Molecular Biology	M,D
Molecular Genetics	M,D
Music Education	M,D
Music	M,D
Natural Resources	M,D
Neuroscience	M,D
Nursing—General	M,D
Nutrition	M,D
Osteopathic Medicine	P
Pathobiology	M,D
Pathology	M,D
Pharmacology	M,D
Philosophy	M,D
Physics	M,D
Physiology	M,D
Plant Biology	M,D
Plant Pathology	M,D
Plant Sciences	M,D
Political Science	M,D
Portuguese	M,D
Psychology—General	M,D
Public Health—General	M
Quantitative Analysis	D
Reading Education	M
Recreation and Park Management	M,D
Rehabilitation Counseling	M,D,O
Rhetoric	M,D
Romance Languages	M,D
School Psychology	M,D,O
Science Education	M
Social Sciences Education	M,D
Social Sciences	M
Social Work	M,D
Sociology	M,D
Spanish	M,D
Special Education	M,D,O
Statistics	M,D
Structural Biology	D
Supply Chain Management	M,D
Systems Biology	D
Telecommunications	M
Theater	M
Therapies—Dance, Drama, and Music	M,D
Toxicology	M,D
Urban and Regional Planning	M,D
Veterinary Medicine	P
Veterinary Sciences	M,D
Writing	M,D
Zoology	M,D

MICHIGAN STATE UNIVERSITY COLLEGE OF LAW

Law	P,M
Legal and Justice Studies	P,M

MICHIGAN TECHNOLOGICAL UNIVERSITY

Archaeology	M,D
Atmospheric Sciences	D
Biological and Biomedical Sciences—General	M,D
Biomedical Engineering	D
Business Administration and Management—General	M
Chemical Engineering	M,D
Chemistry	M,D
Civil Engineering	M,D
Computational Sciences	D
Computer Engineering	D
Computer Science	M,D
Ecology	M
Electrical Engineering	M,D
Engineering and Applied Sciences—General	M,D
Engineering Physics	D
Environmental Engineering	M,D
Environmental Management and Policy	M
Forestry	M,D
Geological Engineering	M,D
Geology	M,D
Geophysics	M
Historic Preservation	D
Materials Engineering	M,D
Mathematics	M,D
Mechanical Engineering	M,D
Mechanics	M
Metallurgical Engineering and Metallurgy	M,D
Mineral Economics	M
Mineral/Mining Engineering	M,D
Physics	M,D
Plant Molecular Biology	M,D
Rhetoric	M,D
Science Education	M
Sustainability Management	O
Sustainable Development	O
Technical Communication	M,D

MICHIGAN THEOLOGICAL SEMINARY

Counseling Psychology	P,M,O
Religion	P,M,O
Religious Education	P,M,O
Theology	P,M,O

MID-AMERICA BAPTIST THEOLOGICAL SEMINARY

Theology	P,M,D

MID-AMERICA BAPTIST THEOLOGICAL SEMINARY NORTHEAST BRANCH

Theology	P

MIDAMERICA NAZARENE UNIVERSITY

Business Administration and Management—General	M
Counseling Psychology	M,O
Education—General	M
Educational Media/ Instructional Technology	M
English as a Second Language	M
Finance and Banking	M
International Business	M
Nonprofit Management	M
Organizational Management	M
Special Education	M

MID-AMERICA REFORMED SEMINARY

Theology	P,M

MIDDLEBURY COLLEGE

Chinese	M
English	M
French	M,D
German	M,D
Italian	M,D
Russian	M,D
Spanish	M,D

MIDDLE TENNESSEE SCHOOL OF ANESTHESIA

Nurse Anesthesia	M

MIDDLE TENNESSEE STATE UNIVERSITY

Accounting	M
Aerospace/Aeronautical Engineering	M
Aviation Management	M
Biological and Biomedical Sciences—General	M
Biostatistics	M
Biotechnology	M
Business Administration and Management—General	M
Business Education	M
Chemistry	M,D
Child and Family Studies	M
Child Development	M
Clinical Psychology	M,O
Computer Science	M
Counseling Psychology	M,O
Counselor Education	M,O
Criminal Justice and Criminology	M
Curriculum and Instruction	M,O
Early Childhood Education	M,O
Economics	M,D
Education—General	M,D,O
Educational Leadership and Administration	M,O
Educational Media/ Instructional Technology	M,O
Elementary Education	M,O
English as a Second Language	M,O
English	M,D
Exercise and Sports Science	M,D
Family Nurse Practitioner Studies	M,O
Food Science and Technology	M
Foreign Languages Education	M
Geosciences	O
Gerontology	O
Health Education	M
Health Services Management and Hospital Administration	O
History	M
Industrial and Organizational Psychology	M,O
Management Information Systems	M
Management Strategy and Policy	M
Marketing	M
Mass Communication	M
Mathematics Education	M
Mathematics	M
Medical Informatics	M
Middle School Education	M,O
Music	M
Nursing—General	M,O
Nutrition	M
Physical Education	M
Psychology—General	M
Public History	M,D
Reading Education	M,D
Recreation and Park Management	M
School Psychology	M,O
Science Education	M
Secondary Education	M,O
Social Sciences	M
Social Work	M
Sociology	M
Special Education	M,O
Vocational and Technical Education	M

MIDWEST COLLEGE OF ORIENTAL MEDICINE

Acupuncture and Oriental Medicine	M,O

MIDWESTERN BAPTIST THEOLOGICAL SEMINARY

Archaeology	P,M,D,O
Linguistics	P,M,D,O
Missions and Missiology	P,M,D,O
Music	P,M,D,O
Pastoral Ministry and Counseling	P,M,D,O
Religion	P,M,D,O
Religious Education	P,M,D,O
Theology	P,M,D,O

MIDWESTERN STATE UNIVERSITY

Biological and Biomedical Sciences—General	M
Business Administration and Management—General	M
Computer Science	M
Counselor Education	M
Criminal Justice and Criminology	M
Curriculum and Instruction	M
Education—General	M
Educational Leadership and Administration	M
Educational Media/ Instructional Technology	M
English	M
Family Nurse Practitioner Studies	M
Health Physics/ Radiological Health	M
Health Services Management and Hospital Administration	M

*M—master's degree; P—first professional degree; D—doctorate; O—other advanced degree; *—Close-Up and/or Announcement or Display in one of the other books in this series*

History M
Human Resources Development M
Kinesiology and Movement Studies M
Nursing Education M
Nursing—General M
Political Science M
Psychology—General M
Public Administration M
Reading Education M
Special Education M

MIDWESTERN UNIVERSITY, DOWNERS GROVE CAMPUS

Allied Health—General M,D
Biological and Biomedical Sciences—General M*
Clinical Psychology M,D*
Occupational Therapy M*
Osteopathic Medicine P*
Pharmacy P*
Physical Therapy D*
Physician Assistant Studies M*

MIDWESTERN UNIVERSITY, GLENDALE CAMPUS

Allied Health—General P,M,D,O
Bioethics M,O
Biological and Biomedical Sciences—General M
Cardiovascular Sciences M
Clinical Psychology D
Dentistry P
Health Education M
Nurse Anesthesia M
Occupational Therapy M
Osteopathic Medicine P*
Pharmacy P
Physician Assistant Studies M
Podiatric Medicine P

MIDWEST UNIVERSITY

English as a Second Language P,M,D
Theology P,M,D

MILLERSVILLE UNIVERSITY OF PENNSYLVANIA

Art Education M
Biological and Biomedical Sciences—General M
Clinical Psychology M
Early Childhood Education M
Education of the Gifted M
Education—General M
Elementary Education M
Emergency Management M
English as a Second Language M
English Education M
English M
Foundations and Philosophy of Education M
French M
German M
History M
Mathematics Education M
Nursing—General M
Psychology—General M
Reading Education M
School Psychology M
Social Work M
Spanish M
Special Education M
Sports Management M
Vocational and Technical Education M

MILLIGAN COLLEGE

Business Administration and Management—General M
Education—General M
Occupational Therapy M

MILLIKIN UNIVERSITY

Business Administration and Management—General M
Nursing and Healthcare Administration M
Nursing Education M
Nursing—General M

MILLSAPS COLLEGE

Accounting M
Business Administration and Management—General M

MILLS COLLEGE

Art Education M,D
Art/Fine Arts M
Biological and Biomedical Sciences—General O
Business Administration and Management—General M
Computer Science M,O
Curriculum and Instruction M,D
Dance M
Early Childhood Education M,D
Education—General M,D
Educational Leadership and Administration M,D
Elementary Education M,D
English Education M,D
English M
Foreign Languages Education M,D
Health Education M,D
Illustration M
Interdisciplinary Studies M,O
Mathematics Education M,D
Music M
Photography M
Public Policy M
Science Education M,D
Secondary Education M,D
Social Sciences Education M,D
Writing M

MILWAUKEE SCHOOL OF ENGINEERING

Business Administration and Management—General M
Cardiovascular Sciences M
Clinical Laboratory Sciences/Medical Technology M
Engineering and Applied Sciences—General M*
Engineering Management M
Environmental Engineering M
Industrial and Manufacturing Management M
International Business M
Marketing M
Medical Informatics M
Nursing—General M
Perfusion M
Structural Engineering M

MINNEAPOLIS COLLEGE OF ART AND DESIGN

Applied Arts and Design—General M
Art/Fine Arts M,O
Computer Art and Design O
Film, Television, and Video Production M
Graphic Design M
Illustration M
Photography M
Sustainable Development O

MINNESOTA STATE UNIVERSITY MANKATO

Accounting M
Allied Health—General M,D,O
Anthropology M
Art Education M
Art/Fine Arts M
Astronomy M
Automotive Engineering M
Biological and Biomedical Sciences—General M
Business Administration and Management—General M
Clinical Psychology M,D
Communication Disorders M
Community Health M
Computer Science M,O
Counselor Education M,D,O
Curriculum and Instruction M,O
Database Systems M,O
Early Childhood Education M
Education of the Gifted M,O
Education—General M,D,O
Educational Leadership and Administration M,O
Educational Media/Instructional Technology M,O
Electrical Engineering M
Elementary Education M
English as a Second Language M,O
English Education M,O
English M,O
Environmental Sciences M
Ethnic Studies M
Family Nurse Practitioner Studies M,D
Finance and Banking M
French M
Geography M
Gerontology M,O
Health Education M
Higher Education M,D,O
History M
Human Services M
Industrial and Organizational Psychology M,D
Interdisciplinary Studies M
International Business M
Management Information Systems M,O
Manufacturing Engineering M
Marketing M
Marriage and Family Therapy M,D,O
Mathematics Education M
Mathematics M
Multilingual and Multicultural Education M
Music M
Nursing and Healthcare Administration M,D
Nursing Education M,D
Nursing—General M,D
Physical Education M,O
Physics M
Psychology—General M,D
Public Administration M
Rehabilitation Counseling M
School Psychology M,D
Science Education M
Secondary Education M,O
Social Psychology M,D,O
Social Sciences Education M
Sociology M
Spanish M
Special Education M,O
Speech and Interpersonal Communication M
Statistics M
Student Affairs M,D,O
Technical Communication M,O
Theater M
Urban and Regional Planning M,O
Urban Studies M,O
Women's Studies M,O
Writing M,O

MINNESOTA STATE UNIVERSITY MOORHEAD

Communication Disorders M
Counselor Education M
Curriculum and Instruction M
Education—General M,O
Educational Leadership and Administration M,O
Human Services M,O
Liberal Studies M
Nursing Education M
Nursing—General M,O
Public Administration M
Reading Education M
School Psychology M,O
Special Education M
Writing M

MINOT STATE UNIVERSITY

Business Administration and Management—General M
Communication Disorders M
Criminal Justice and Criminology M
Early Childhood Education M
Education of the Multiply Handicapped M
Elementary Education M
Management Information Systems M
Mathematics Education M
Music Education M
School Psychology O
Science Education M
Special Education M

MIRRER YESHIVA

Theology

MISERICORDIA UNIVERSITY

Allied Health—General M,D
Business Administration and Management—General M
Communication Disorders M
Curriculum and Instruction M
Education—General M
Nursing—General M
Occupational Therapy M,D
Organizational Management M
Physical Therapy M,D

MISSISSIPPI COLLEGE

Accounting M,O
Advertising and Public Relations M
Art Education M,D,O
Art/Fine Arts M
Biochemistry M
Biological and Biomedical Sciences—General M
Business Administration and Management—General M,O
Business Education M,D,O
Chemistry M
Communication—General M
Computer Education M,D,O
Computer Science M
Corporate and Organizational Communication M
Counseling Psychology M,O
Counselor Education M,O
Criminal Justice and Criminology M,O
Curriculum and Instruction M,D,O

Education—General	M,D,O
Educational Leadership and Administration	M,D,O
Elementary Education	M,D,O
English as a Second Language	M
English Education	M,D,O
English	M
Finance and Banking	M,O
Health Services Management and Hospital Administration	M
Higher Education	M,D,O
History	M,O
Kinesiology and Movement Studies	M
Law	P,O
Legal and Justice Studies	M,O
Liberal Studies	M
Marriage and Family Therapy	M,O
Mathematics Education	M,D,O
Mathematics	M
Music Education	M
Music	M
Political Science	M,O
Science Education	M,D,O
Secondary Education	M,D,O
Social Sciences Education	M,D,O
Social Sciences	M,O
Special Education	M,D,O

MISSISSIPPI STATE UNIVERSITY

Accounting	M,D
Aerospace/Aeronautical Engineering	M,D
Agricultural Economics and Agribusiness	M
Agricultural Education	M,D,O
Agricultural Sciences—General	M,D,O
Agronomy and Soil Sciences	M,D
American Studies	M,D
Animal Sciences	M,D
Anthropology	M
Applied Economics	M,D
Applied Physics	M,D
Architecture	M
Biochemistry	M,D
Bioengineering	M,D
Biological and Biomedical Sciences—General	M,D
Biomedical Engineering	M,D
Business Administration and Management—General	M,D
Chemical Engineering	M,D
Chemistry	M,D
Civil Engineering	M,D
Clinical Psychology	M,D
Cognitive Sciences	M,D
Community College Education	M,D,O
Computer Art and Design	M
Computer Engineering	M,D
Computer Science	M,D
Counselor Education	M,D,O
Curriculum and Instruction	M,D,O
Economics	M,D
Education—General	M,D,O
Educational Leadership and Administration	M,D,O
Educational Media/Instructional Technology	M,D,O
Educational Psychology	M,D,O
Electrical Engineering	M,D
Elementary Education	M,D,O
Engineering and Applied Sciences—General	M,D
English	M
Entomology	M,D
Exercise and Sports Science	M
Experimental Psychology	M,D
Finance and Banking	M,D
Fish, Game, and Wildlife Management	M,D
Food Science and Technology	M,D
Foreign Languages Education	M
Forestry	M,D
French	M
Genetics	M,D
Geosciences	M
German	M
Health Promotion	M,D
History	M,D
Horticulture	M,D
Human Resources Development	M,D,O
Industrial/Management Engineering	M,D
Kinesiology and Movement Studies	M
Landscape Architecture	M
Management Information Systems	M,D
Marketing	D
Mathematics	M,D
Mechanical Engineering	M,D
Molecular Biology	M,D
Nutrition	M,D
Physical Education	M
Physics	M,D
Plant Pathology	M,D
Plant Sciences	M,D
Political Science	M,D
Project Management	M,D
Psychology—General	M,D
Public Administration	M,D
Public Policy	M,D
School Psychology	M,D,O
Secondary Education	M,D,O
Sociology	M,D
Spanish	M
Special Education	M,D,O
Sports Management	M
Statistics	M,D
Student Affairs	M,D,O
Systems Engineering	M,D
Taxation	M
Veterinary Medicine	P
Veterinary Sciences	M,D
Vocational and Technical Education	M,D,O
Western European Studies	M,D

MISSISSIPPI UNIVERSITY FOR WOMEN

Communication Disorders	M,O
Curriculum and Instruction	M
Education of the Gifted	M
Education—General	M
Health Education	M
Nursing—General	M,O

MISSISSIPPI VALLEY STATE UNIVERSITY

Bioinformatics	M
Criminal Justice and Criminology	M
Education—General	M
Elementary Education	M
Environmental and Occupational Health	M

MISSOURI BAPTIST UNIVERSITY

Business Administration and Management—General	M,O
Counselor Education	M,O
Education—General	M,O
Educational Leadership and Administration	M,O
Pastoral Ministry and Counseling	M,O

MISSOURI SOUTHERN STATE UNIVERSITY

Business Administration and Management—General	M
Criminal Justice and Criminology	M
Dental Hygiene	M
Early Childhood Education	M
Education—General	M
Educational Media/Instructional Technology	M
Nursing—General	M

MISSOURI STATE UNIVERSITY

Accounting	M
Agricultural Education	M
Agricultural Sciences—General	M
Applied Science and Technology	M
Art Education	M
Art/Fine Arts	M
Biological and Biomedical Sciences—General	M
Business Administration and Management—General	M*
Cell Biology	M
Chemistry	M
Child and Family Studies	M
Clinical Psychology	M
Communication Disorders	M,D
Communication—General	M
Computer Science	M
Construction Management	M
Counselor Education	M
Criminal Justice and Criminology	M
Curriculum and Instruction	M
Early Childhood Education	M
Educational Leadership and Administration	M,O
Educational Media/Instructional Technology	M
Elementary Education	M,O
English	M
Environmental Management and Policy	M
Experimental Psychology	M
Family and Consumer Sciences-General	M
Family Nurse Practitioner Studies	M
Foreign Languages Education	M
French	M
Geography	M
Geology	M
Geosciences	M
German	M
Health Promotion	M
Health Services Management and Hospital Administration	M
History	M
Industrial and Organizational Psychology	M
Interior Design	M
International Affairs	M*
Management Information Systems	M
Materials Sciences	M
Mathematics	M
Military and Defense Studies	M
Molecular Biology	M
Music Education	M
Music	M
Natural Resources	M
Nurse Anesthesia	M
Nursing Education	M
Nursing—General	M
Physical Education	M
Physical Therapy	D
Physician Assistant Studies	M
Plant Sciences	M
Political Science	M
Project Management	M
Psychology—General	M
Public Administration	M
Public Health—General	M
Reading Education	M
Religion	M
Science Education	M
Secondary Education	M,O
Social Psychology	M
Social Sciences Education	M
Social Work	M
Spanish	M
Special Education	M,D
Sports Management	M
Student Affairs	M
Textile Design	M
Theater	M
Urban and Regional Planning	M

MISSOURI UNIVERSITY OF SCIENCE AND TECHNOLOGY

Aerospace/Aeronautical Engineering	M,D
Applied Mathematics	M,D
Biological and Biomedical Sciences—General	M
Ceramic Sciences and Engineering	M,D
Chemical Engineering	M,D
Chemistry	M,D
Civil Engineering	M,D
Computer Engineering	M,D
Computer Science	M,D
Construction Engineering	M,D
Electrical Engineering	M,D
Engineering and Applied Sciences—General	M,D
Engineering Management	M,D
Environmental Biology	M
Environmental Engineering	M,D
Geochemistry	M,D
Geological Engineering	M,D
Geology	M,D
Geophysics	M,D
Geotechnical Engineering	M,D
Hydraulics	M,D
Hydrology	M,D
Information Science	M
Manufacturing Engineering	M,D
Mathematics Education	M,D
Mathematics	M,D
Mechanical Engineering	M,D
Mechanics	M,D
Metallurgical Engineering and Metallurgy	M,D
Mineral/Mining Engineering	M,D
Nuclear Engineering	M,D
Petroleum Engineering	M,D
Physics	M,D
Statistics	M,D
Systems Engineering	M,D
Water Resources	M,D

MOLLOY COLLEGE

Adult Nursing	M,O
Family Nurse Practitioner Studies	M,O
Nursing and Healthcare Administration	M,O
Nursing Education	M,O
Nursing Informatics	M,O
Nursing—General	M,O
Pediatric Nursing	M,O
Psychiatric Nursing	M,O

MONMOUTH UNIVERSITY

Accounting	M,O
Addictions/Substance Abuse Counseling	M,O

*M—master's degree; P—first professional degree; D—doctorate; O—other advanced degree; *—Close-Up and/or Announcement or Display in one of the other books in this series*

Advertising and Public Relations	M,O
Business Administration and Management—General	M,O
Communication—General	M,O
Computer Science	M
Corporate and Organizational Communication	M,O
Counseling Psychology	M,O
Criminal Justice and Criminology	M,O
Education—General	M,O
Educational Leadership and Administration	M,O
Elementary Education	M,O
English	M
Health Services Management and Hospital Administration	M,O
History	M
Liberal Studies	M
Media Studies	M,O
Nursing—General	M,O
Psychology—General	M,O
Public Policy	M
Reading Education	M,O
School Nursing	M,O
Social Work	M
Software Engineering	M,O
Special Education	M,O

MONROE COLLEGE

Business Administration and Management—General	M

MONTANA STATE UNIVERSITY

Accounting	M
Adult Education	M,D,O
Agricultural Education	M
Agricultural Sciences—General	M,D
American Indian/Native American Studies	M
Animal Sciences	M,D
Architecture	M
Art/Fine Arts	M
Biochemistry	M,D
Biological and Biomedical Sciences—General	M,D
Chemical Engineering	M,D
Chemistry	M,D
Civil Engineering	M,D
Computer Engineering	M,D
Computer Science	M,D
Construction Engineering	M,D
Consumer Economics	M
Counselor Education	M
Curriculum and Instruction	M,D,O
Ecology	M,D
Education—General	M,D,O
Educational Leadership and Administration	M,D,O
Electrical Engineering	M,D
Engineering and Applied Sciences—General	M,D
English	M
Environmental Engineering	M,D
Environmental Sciences	M,D
Exercise and Sports Science	M
Family Nurse Practitioner Studies	M,O
Film, Television, and Video Production	M
Fish, Game, and Wildlife Management	M,D
Geosciences	M,D
Health Promotion	M
Higher Education	M,D,O
History	M,D
Home Economics Education	M
Human Development	M
Industrial/Management Engineering	M,D
Mathematics Education	M,D
Mathematics	M,D
Mechanical Engineering	M,D
Mechanics	M,D
Microbiology	M,D
Molecular Biology	M,D
Natural Resources	M
Neuroscience	M,D
Nursing Education	M,O
Nursing—General	M,O
Nutrition	M
Physics	M,D
Plant Pathology	M,D
Plant Sciences	M,D
Psychology—General	M
Public Administration	M
Range Science	M,D
School Psychology	M,D,O
Statistics	M,D
Veterinary Sciences	M,D
Zoology	M,D

MONTANA STATE UNIVERSITY–BILLINGS

Advertising and Public Relations	M
Athletic Training and Sports Medicine	M
Communication—General	M
Counselor Education	M
Curriculum and Instruction	M
Early Childhood Education	M
Education—General	M,O
Educational Media/Instructional Technology	M
Health Services Management and Hospital Administration	M
Human Services	M
Interdisciplinary Studies	M
Physical Education	M
Psychology—General	M
Public Administration	M
Reading Education	M
Rehabilitation Counseling	M
Secondary Education	M
Special Education	M
Sports Management	M

MONTANA STATE UNIVERSITY–NORTHERN

Counselor Education	M
Education—General	M

MONTANA TECH OF THE UNIVERSITY OF MONTANA

Electrical Engineering	M
Engineering and Applied Sciences—General	M
Environmental Engineering	M
Geochemistry	M
Geological Engineering	M
Geology	M
Geosciences	M
Hydrogeology	M
Industrial Hygiene	M
Industrial/Management Engineering	M
Interdisciplinary Studies	M
Metallurgical Engineering and Metallurgy	M
Mineral/Mining Engineering	M
Petroleum Engineering	M
Project Management	M
Technical Communication	M

MONTCLAIR STATE UNIVERSITY

Accounting	M,O
Addictions/Substance Abuse Counseling	M,D,O
Advertising and Public Relations	M
Applied Mathematics	M,D,O
Applied Statistics	M,O
Art Education	M,O
Art History	M,O
Art/Fine Arts	M,O
Arts Administration	M
Biochemistry	M
Biological and Biomedical Sciences—General	M,O
Business Administration and Management—General	M,O*
Chemistry	M
Clinical Psychology	M,O
Communication Disorders	M,D*
Communication—General	M
Computer Science	M,D,O
Conflict Resolution and Mediation/Peace Studies	M,O
Corporate and Organizational Communication	M
Counseling Psychology	M,D,O
Counselor Education	M,D,O
Curriculum and Instruction	M,D,O
Early Childhood Education	M,O
Economics	M
Education of the Multiply Handicapped	M,O
Education—General	M,D,O*
Educational Leadership and Administration	M,D,O
Educational Media/Instructional Technology	M,O
Educational Psychology	M,O
Elementary Education	M,O
English as a Second Language	M,O
English Education	M,O
English	M,O
Environmental and Occupational Health	M,D,O
Environmental Management and Policy	M,D*
Environmental Sciences	M,D,O
Exercise and Sports Science	M,O
Finance and Banking	M,O
Food Science and Technology	M,O
Foundations and Philosophy of Education	M,D,O
French	M,O
Geographic Information Systems	M,D,O
Geosciences	M,D,O
Health Education	M,O
History	M,O
Home Economics Education	M,O
Industrial and Organizational Psychology	M,O
Information Science	M,O
International Business	M,O
Italian	M,O
Legal and Justice Studies	M,O
Linguistics	M,O
Management Information Systems	M,O
Marketing	M,O
Marriage and Family Therapy	M,O
Mathematics Education	M,D,O*
Mathematics	M,D,O
Middle School Education	M,D,O
Molecular Biology	M,O
Music Education	M,O
Music	M,O
Nutrition	M,O
Philosophy	M,D,O
Physical Education	M,O
Psychology—General	M,O
Reading Education	M,O
School Psychology	M,O
Science Education	M,D,O
Social Psychology	M,D,O
Social Sciences Education	M,O
Social Sciences	M,O
Sociology	M
Spanish	M,O
Special Education	M,O
Speech and Interpersonal Communication	M
Sports Management	M,O
Statistics	M,D,O
Theater	M
Therapies—Dance, Drama, and Music	M,O
Translation and Interpretation	M,O
Water Resources	M,D,O

MONTEREY INSTITUTE OF INTERNATIONAL STUDIES

Business Administration and Management—General	M
English as a Second Language	M*
Environmental Management and Policy	M
Foreign Languages Education	M
International Affairs	M*
International Business	M*
International Trade Policy	M
Public Administration	M
Translation and Interpretation	M*

MONTREAT COLLEGE

Business Administration and Management—General	M
Education—General	M
Elementary Education	M

MOODY BIBLE INSTITUTE

Pastoral Ministry and Counseling	P,M,O
Theology	P,M,O
Urban Studies	P,M,O

MORAVIAN COLLEGE

Allied Health—General	M
Business Administration and Management—General	M
Human Resources Development	M
Human Resources Management	M
Management of Technology	M
Nursing and Healthcare Administration	M
Nursing Education	M
Supply Chain Management	M

MORAVIAN THEOLOGICAL SEMINARY

Theology	P,M

MOREHEAD STATE UNIVERSITY

Adult Education	M,O
Art Education	M
Art/Fine Arts	M
Biological and Biomedical Sciences—General	M
Business Administration and Management—General	M
Clinical Psychology	M
Communication—General	M
Counseling Psychology	M
Counselor Education	M,O
Criminal Justice and Criminology	M
Curriculum and Instruction	M,O
Education—General	M,O
Educational Leadership and Administration	M,O
Elementary Education	M,O
English	M

Environmental Management and Policy	M
Exercise and Sports Science	M
Experimental Psychology	M
Gerontology	M
Health Education	M
Higher Education	M,O
Industrial/Management Engineering	M
International and Comparative Education	M,O
Management Information Systems	M
Middle School Education	M,O
Music Education	M
Music	M
Physical Education	M
Psychology—General	M
Public Administration	M
Reading Education	M,O
Secondary Education	M,O
Sociology	M
Special Education	M,O
Sports Management	M

MOREHOUSE SCHOOL OF MEDICINE

Allopathic Medicine	P
Biological and Biomedical Sciences—General	M,D*
Clinical Research	M
Public Health—General	M

MORGAN STATE UNIVERSITY

African-American Studies	M,D
Architecture	M
Bioinformatics	M
Biological and Biomedical Sciences—General	M,D
Business Administration and Management—General	D
Chemistry	M
Civil Engineering	M,D
Community College Education	D
Economics	M
Education—General	M,D
Educational Leadership and Administration	M,D
Electrical Engineering	M,D
Elementary Education	M
Engineering and Applied Sciences—General	M,D
English	M,D
Environmental Biology	D
Higher Education	D
History	M,D
Industrial/Management Engineering	M,D
International Affairs	M
Landscape Architecture	M
Mathematics Education	M,D
Mathematics	M
Middle School Education	M
Music	M
Nursing—General	M,D
Psychology—General	M,D
Public Health—General	M,D
Science Education	M,D
Secondary Education	M
Social Work	M,D
Sociology	M
Telecommunications Management	M
Transportation and Highway Engineering	M
Transportation Management	M
Urban and Regional Planning	M
Urban Education	M,D

MORNINGSIDE COLLEGE

Education—General	M
Special Education	M

MORRISON UNIVERSITY

Business Administration and Management—General	M

MOUNTAIN STATE UNIVERSITY

Allied Health—General	M
Criminal Justice and Criminology	M
Family Nurse Practitioner Studies	M,O
Interdisciplinary Studies	M*
Management Strategy and Policy	M
Nurse Anesthesia	M,O
Nursing and Healthcare Administration	M,O
Nursing Education	M,O
Nursing—General	M,O*
Physician Assistant Studies	M*

MOUNT ALLISON UNIVERSITY

Biological and Biomedical Sciences—General	M
Chemistry	M

MOUNT ALOYSIUS COLLEGE

Criminal Justice and Criminology	M
Health Services Management and Hospital Administration	M
Psychology—General	M

MOUNT ANGEL SEMINARY

Theology	P,M

MOUNT CARMEL COLLEGE OF NURSING

Adult Nursing	M
Nursing and Healthcare Administration	M
Nursing Education	M
Nursing—General	M*

MOUNT HOLYOKE COLLEGE

Psychology—General	M

MOUNT MARTY COLLEGE

Business Administration and Management—General	M
Nurse Anesthesia	M
Pastoral Ministry and Counseling	M

MOUNT MARY COLLEGE

Art Therapy	M
Business Administration and Management—General	M
Counselor Education	M
Education—General	M
English	M
Health Education	M
Nutrition	M
Occupational Therapy	M

MOUNT SAINT MARY COLLEGE

Adult Nursing	M
Business Administration and Management—General	M
Early Childhood Education	M
Education—General	M
Elementary Education	M
Finance and Banking	M
Middle School Education	M
Nursing and Healthcare Administration	M
Nursing Education	M
Nursing—General	M
Reading Education	M
Secondary Education	M
Special Education	M

MOUNT ST. MARY'S COLLEGE

Business Administration and Management—General	M
Counseling Psychology	M
Education—General	M
Educational Leadership and Administration	M
Elementary Education	M
Humanities	M
Nursing—General	M
Physical Therapy	D
Religion	M
Secondary Education	M
Special Education	M

MOUNT ST. MARY'S UNIVERSITY

Business Administration and Management—General	M
Education—General	M
Theology	P,M

MOUNT SAINT VINCENT UNIVERSITY

Adult Education	M
Child and Family Studies	M
Curriculum and Instruction	M
Education—General	M
Educational Psychology	M
Elementary Education	M
English as a Second Language	M
Foundations and Philosophy of Education	M
Gerontology	M
Middle School Education	M
Nutrition	M
Reading Education	M
School Psychology	M
Special Education	M
Women's Studies	M

MOUNT SINAI SCHOOL OF MEDICINE OF NEW YORK UNIVERSITY

Allopathic Medicine	P
Bioethics	M
Biological and Biomedical Sciences—General	M,D
Clinical Research	M,D
Community Health	M,D
Genetic Counseling	M,D
Neuroscience	M,D

MOUNT VERNON NAZARENE UNIVERSITY

Business Administration and Management—General	M
Education—General	M
Theology	M

MULTNOMAH UNIVERSITY

Counselor Education	M
Education—General	M

MURRAY STATE UNIVERSITY

Accounting	M
Agricultural Education	M
Agricultural Sciences—General	M
Biological and Biomedical Sciences—General	M,D
Business Administration and Management—General	M
Chemistry	M
Clinical Psychology	M
Communication Disorders	M
Corporate and Organizational Communication	M
Counselor Education	M,O
Early Childhood Education	M
Economics	M
Education—General	M,D,O
Educational Leadership and Administration	M,O
Elementary Education	M,O
English as a Second Language	M
English	M
Environmental and Occupational Health	M
Environmental Sciences	M
Exercise and Sports Science	M
Family Nurse Practitioner Studies	M
Geosciences	M
History	M
Human Services	M
Hydrology	M
Industrial Hygiene	M
Leisure Studies	M
Management of Technology	M
Mass Communication	M
Mathematics	M
Middle School Education	M,O
Music Education	M
Music	M
Nurse Anesthesia	M
Nursing—General	M
Physical Education	M,O
Psychology—General	M
Public Affairs	M
Reading Education	M,O
Safety Engineering	M
Secondary Education	M,O
Special Education	M
Statistics	M
Telecommunications Management	M
Vocational and Technical Education	M
Writing	M

MUSKINGUM UNIVERSITY

Education—General	M

NAROPA UNIVERSITY

Art Therapy	M
Asian Languages	M
Clinical Psychology	M
Counseling Psychology	M
Counselor Education	M
Education—General	M
Environmental Management and Policy	M
Psychoanalysis and Psychotherapy	M
Recreation and Park Management	M
Religion	M
Social Psychology	M
Theater	M
Theology	P
Therapies—Dance, Drama, and Music	M
Transpersonal and Humanistic Psychology	M*
Writing	M

NASHOTAH HOUSE

Theology	P,M,O

*M—master's degree; P—first professional degree; D—doctorate; O—other advanced degree; *—Close-Up and/or Announcement or Display in one of the other books in this series*

NATIONAL AMERICAN UNIVERSITY
Business Administration and Management—General M

NATIONAL COLLEGE OF MIDWIFERY
Nurse Midwifery M,D

NATIONAL COLLEGE OF NATURAL MEDICINE
Acupuncture and Oriental Medicine M
Naturopathic Medicine D

NATIONAL DEFENSE UNIVERSITY
Conflict Resolution and Mediation/Peace Studies M
Homeland Security M
Military and Defense Studies M
National Security M

THE NATIONAL GRADUATE SCHOOL OF QUALITY MANAGEMENT
Business Administration and Management—General M
Electronic Commerce M
Quality Management M

NATIONAL-LOUIS UNIVERSITY
Addictions/Substance Abuse Counseling M,O
Adult Education M,D,O
Business Administration and Management—General M
Counselor Education M,O
Curriculum and Instruction M,D,O
Developmental Education M,O
Early Childhood Education M,O
Education—General M,D,O
Educational Leadership and Administration M,D,O
Educational Media/Instructional Technology M,O
Educational Psychology M,D,O
Elementary Education M,O
English Education M,O
Gerontology M,O
Health Psychology M,O
Human Development M,D,O
Human Resources Development M
Human Resources Management M
Human Services M,O
Industrial and Organizational Psychology M,O
Mathematics Education M,O
Psychology—General M,O
Reading Education M,D,O
School Psychology M,D,O
Science Education M,O
Secondary Education M
Social Psychology M,O
Special Education M,O
Writing M

NATIONAL THEATRE CONSERVATORY
Theater M,O

NATIONAL UNIVERSITY
Accounting M
Art/Fine Arts M
Business Administration and Management—General M
Communication Disorders M
Communication—General M
Computer Art and Design M
Computer Science M
Conflict Resolution and Mediation/Peace Studies M
Corporate and Organizational Communication M
Counseling Psychology M
Counselor Education M
Criminal Justice and Criminology M
Database Systems M
Economics M
Education—General M
Educational Leadership and Administration M
Educational Media/Instructional Technology M
Electronic Commerce M
Engineering and Applied Sciences—General M
Engineering Management M
English M
Environmental Engineering M
Finance and Banking M
Forensic Sciences M
Health Services Management and Hospital Administration M
History M
Homeland Security M
Human Resources Management M
Human Services M
Humanities M
Information Science M
International Business M
Internet and Interactive Multimedia M
Management Information Systems M
Management of Technology M
Marketing M
Media Studies M
Multilingual and Multicultural Education M
Organizational Management M
Psychology—General M
Public Administration M
Safety Engineering M
School Psychology M
Software Engineering M
Special Education M
Systems Engineering M
Telecommunications M
Writing M

NATIONAL UNIVERSITY OF HEALTH SCIENCES
Acupuncture and Oriental Medicine P,M,D
Chiropractic P,M,D*
Naturopathic Medicine P,M,D

NATIONAL UNIVERSITY OF SINGAPORE
Public Administration M,D
Public Affairs M,D
Public Policy M,D

NAVAL POSTGRADUATE SCHOOL
Aerospace/Aeronautical Engineering M
Applied Mathematics M,D
Applied Physics M,D
Applied Science and Technology M
Business Administration and Management—General M
Computer Engineering M,D,O
Computer Science M,D
Electrical Engineering M,D,O
Human Resources Development M
Human-Computer Interaction M,D
Information Science M,O
International Affairs M
Management Information Systems M,O
Mathematics M,D
Mechanical Engineering M,D,O
Meteorology M,D
Military and Defense Studies M,D
National Security M
Oceanography M,D
Operations Research M,D
Physics M,D
Political Science M
Software Engineering M,D
Systems Engineering M,D,O

NAVAL WAR COLLEGE
National Security M

NAZARENE THEOLOGICAL SEMINARY
Missions and Missiology P,M,D
Religious Education P,M,D
Theology P,M,D

NAZARETH COLLEGE OF ROCHESTER
Art Education M
Art Therapy M
Business Administration and Management—General M
Business Education M
Communication Disorders M
Early Childhood Education M
Education—General M
Educational Media/Instructional Technology M
Elementary Education M
English as a Second Language M
Gerontological Nursing M
Human Resources Management M
Liberal Studies M
Middle School Education M
Music Education M
Nursing—General M
Physical Therapy M,D
Reading Education M
Social Work M
Therapies—Dance, Drama, and Music M

NEBRASKA METHODIST COLLEGE
Health Promotion M
Health Services Management and Hospital Administration M
Nursing—General M

NEBRASKA WESLEYAN UNIVERSITY
Forensic Sciences M
History M
Nursing—General M

NER ISRAEL RABBINICAL COLLEGE
Theology M,D,O

NER ISRAEL YESHIVA COLLEGE OF TORONTO
Theology

NEUMANN UNIVERSITY
Education—General M,D
Management Strategy and Policy M
Nursing—General M
Pastoral Ministry and Counseling M,O
Physical Therapy D
Sports Management M

NEW BRUNSWICK THEOLOGICAL SEMINARY
Pastoral Ministry and Counseling D
Theology P,M,D

NEW ENGLAND COLLEGE
Business Administration and Management—General M
Counseling Psychology M
Education—General M
Educational Leadership and Administration M
Health Services Management and Hospital Administration M
Human Services M
Nonprofit Management M
Organizational Management M
Public Policy M
Special Education M
Writing M

THE NEW ENGLAND COLLEGE OF OPTOMETRY
Optometry P,M
Vision Sciences P,M

NEW ENGLAND CONSERVATORY OF MUSIC
Music M,D,O

NEW ENGLAND SCHOOL OF ACUPUNCTURE
Acupuncture and Oriental Medicine M

NEW ENGLAND SCHOOL OF LAW
Law P,M

NEW JERSEY CITY UNIVERSITY
Accounting M
Allied Health—General M
Art Education M
Art/Fine Arts M
Business Administration and Management—General M
Community Health M
Counseling Psychology M
Criminal Justice and Criminology M
Early Childhood Education M
Educational Leadership and Administration M
Educational Media/Instructional Technology M
Educational Psychology M,O
Elementary Education M
English as a Second Language M
Finance and Banking M
Health Education M

Health Services Management and Hospital Administration	M
Mathematics Education	M
Multilingual and Multicultural Education	M
Music Education	M
Music	M
Psychology—General	M,O
Reading Education	M
School Psychology	M,O
Secondary Education	M
Special Education	M
Urban Education	M
Urban Studies	M

NEW JERSEY INSTITUTE OF TECHNOLOGY

Applied Mathematics	M
Applied Physics	M,D
Applied Statistics	M
Architecture	M
Bioinformatics	M,D
Biological and Biomedical Sciences—General	M,D
Biomedical Engineering	M,D
Biostatistics	M
Business Administration and Management—General	M
Chemical Engineering	M,D
Chemistry	M,D
Civil Engineering	M,D
Computational Biology	M
Computer Engineering	M,D
Computer Science	M,D
Electrical Engineering	M,D
Emergency Management	M,D
Energy and Power Engineering	M
Engineering and Applied Sciences—General	M,D,O
Engineering Management	M
Environmental Engineering	M,D
Environmental Management and Policy	M
Environmental Sciences	M,D
History	M
Industrial/Management Engineering	M,D
Information Science	M,D
Internet Engineering	M
Management Information Systems	M,D
Management of Technology	M
Manufacturing Engineering	M
Materials Engineering	M,D
Materials Sciences	M,D
Mathematics	D
Mechanical Engineering	M,D,O
Pharmaceutical Engineering	M
Safety Engineering	M
Software Engineering	M,D
Technical Communication	M
Transportation and Highway Engineering	M,D
Transportation Management	M,D
Urban Studies	D

NEW LIFE THEOLOGICAL SEMINARY

Religion	M

NEWMAN THEOLOGICAL COLLEGE

Educational Leadership and Administration	M,O
Religious Education	M,O
Theology	P,M

NEWMAN UNIVERSITY

Business Administration and Management—General	M
Curriculum and Instruction	M
Education—General	M
Educational Leadership and Administration	M
English as a Second Language	M
International Business	M
Management Information Systems	M
Nurse Anesthesia	M
Organizational Management	M
Social Work	M

NEW MEXICO HIGHLANDS UNIVERSITY

American Studies	M
Anthropology	M
Business Administration and Management—General	M
Chemistry	M
Clinical Psychology	M
Computer Science	M
Counselor Education	M
Curriculum and Instruction	M
Education—General	M
Educational Leadership and Administration	M
English	M
Exercise and Sports Science	M
Fish, Game, and Wildlife Management	M
Health Education	M
Human Resources Management	M
International Business	M
Internet and Interactive Multimedia	M
Management Information Systems	M
Media Studies	M
Nonprofit Management	M
Psychology—General	M
Public Affairs	M
Rhetoric	M
School Psychology	M
Social Work	M
Sociology	M
Special Education	M
Sports Management	M
Writing	M

NEW MEXICO INSTITUTE OF MINING AND TECHNOLOGY

Applied Mathematics	M,D
Astrophysics	M,D
Atmospheric Sciences	M,D
Biochemistry	M,D
Biological and Biomedical Sciences—General	M
Chemistry	M,D
Computer Science	M,D
Electrical Engineering	M
Engineering Management	M
Environmental Engineering	M
Environmental Sciences	M,D
Geochemistry	M,D
Geology	M,D
Geophysics	M,D
Geosciences	M,D
Hazardous Materials Management	M
Hydrology	M,D
Materials Engineering	M,D
Mathematical Physics	M,D
Mathematics	M,D
Mechanics	M
Mineral/Mining Engineering	M
Operations Research	M,D
Petroleum Engineering	M,D
Physics	M,D
Science Education	M
Water Resources Engineering	M

NEW MEXICO STATE UNIVERSITY

Accounting	M
Adult Nursing	M
Agricultural Economics and Agribusiness	M,D
Agricultural Education	M
Agricultural Sciences—General	M
Animal Sciences	M,D
Anthropology	M
Applied Arts and Design—General	M
Art History	M
Art/Fine Arts	M
Astronomy	M,D
Biochemistry	M,D
Biological and Biomedical Sciences—General	M,D
Business Administration and Management—General	M,D
Chemical Engineering	M,D
Chemistry	M,D
Civil Engineering	M,D
Communication Disorders	M,D
Communication—General	M
Community Health Nursing	M
Community Health	M
Computer Engineering	M,D
Computer Science	M,D
Corporate and Organizational Communication	M,D
Counseling Psychology	M,D,O
Counselor Education	M,D,O
Criminal Justice and Criminology	M
Curriculum and Instruction	M,D,O
Economic Development	M,D
Economics	M,D
Education—General	M,D,O
Educational Leadership and Administration	M,D
Electrical Engineering	M,D
Engineering and Applied Sciences—General	M,D
English	M,D
Entomology	M
Environmental Engineering	M,D
Environmental Sciences	M,D
Family and Consumer Sciences-General	M
Fish, Game, and Wildlife Management	M
Geography	M
Geology	M
Health Education	M
History	M
Horticulture	M,D
Industrial/Management Engineering	M,D
Interdisciplinary Studies	M,D
Marketing	D
Mathematics	M,D
Mechanical Engineering	M,D
Medical/Surgical Nursing	M
Molecular Biology	M,D
Music Education	M
Music	M
Nursing and Healthcare Administration	M
Nursing—General	M
Photography	M
Physics	M,D
Plant Pathology	M
Plant Sciences	M,D
Political Science	M
Psychiatric Nursing	M
Psychology—General	M,D
Public Health—General	M
Range Science	M,D
Rhetoric	M,D
School Psychology	M,D,O
Social Work	M
Sociology	M
Spanish	M
Special Education	M,D
Statistics	M,D
Writing	M,D

NEW ORLEANS BAPTIST THEOLOGICAL SEMINARY

Music	M,D
Pastoral Ministry and Counseling	P,M,D
Religious Education	P,M,D
Theology	P,M,D

THE NEW SCHOOL: A UNIVERSITY

Anthropology	M,D
Applied Arts and Design—General	M
Applied Social Research	M,D
Architecture	M*
Art/Fine Arts	M*
Clinical Psychology	M,D
Communication—General	M*
Computer Art and Design	M*
Decorative Arts	M*
Economics	M,D
English as a Second Language	M*
Finance and Banking	M
Health Services Management and Hospital Administration	M,O
History	M,D
Human Resources Development	M,O
Interior Design	M*
International Affairs	M*
International Business	M
International Development	M
Liberal Studies	M
Lighting Design	M*
Mass Communication	M
Media Studies	M
Music	M,O
Nonprofit Management	M*
Organizational Management	M*
Philosophy	M,D
Photography	M*
Political Science	M,D
Psychology—General	M,D
Public Policy	D*
Social Sciences	M,D*
Sociology	M,D
Theater	M*
Urban Studies	M*
Writing	M*

NEWSCHOOL OF ARCHITECTURE & DESIGN

Architecture	M

NEW YORK ACADEMY OF ART

Art/Fine Arts	M

NEW YORK CHIROPRACTIC COLLEGE

Acupuncture and Oriental Medicine	M
Anatomy	M
Chiropractic	P*
Health Physics/Radiological Health	M
Nutrition	M

*M—master's degree; P—first professional degree; D—doctorate; O—other advanced degree; *—Close-Up and/or Announcement or Display in one of the other books in this series*

NEW YORK COLLEGE OF HEALTH PROFESSIONS

Acupuncture and Oriental Medicine	M

NEW YORK COLLEGE OF PODIATRIC MEDICINE

Podiatric Medicine	P

NEW YORK COLLEGE OF TRADITIONAL CHINESE MEDICINE

Acupuncture and Oriental Medicine	M

NEW YORK FILM ACADEMY

Film, Television, and Video Production	M

NEW YORK INSTITUTE OF TECHNOLOGY

Accounting	M,O
Architecture	M
Business Administration and Management—General	M,O
Communication—General	M
Computer Engineering	M
Computer Science	M
Counseling Psychology	M
Counselor Education	M
Distance Education Development	M,O
Education—General	M,O
Educational Leadership and Administration	O
Educational Media/Instructional Technology	M,O
Electrical Engineering	M
Elementary Education	M,O
Energy and Power Engineering	M,O
Energy Management and Policy	M,O
Engineering and Applied Sciences—General	M,O
Environmental Engineering	M
Environmental Management and Policy	M,O
Finance and Banking	M,O
Human Development	M
Human Resources Management	M,O
Industrial and Labor Relations	M,O
International Business	M,O
Management Information Systems	M,O
Marketing	M,O
Nutrition	M
Occupational Therapy	M
Osteopathic Medicine	P
Physical Therapy	M
Physician Assistant Studies	M
Urban Design	M

NEW YORK LAW SCHOOL

Law	P,M
Taxation	P,M

NEW YORK MEDICAL COLLEGE

Allopathic Medicine	P
Anatomy	M,D
Biochemistry	M,D
Biological and Biomedical Sciences—General	M,D*
Biostatistics	M,D
Cell Biology	M,D*
Communication Disorders	M*
Disability Studies	M
Environmental and Occupational Health	M
Epidemiology	M,D*
Health Promotion	M,D
Health Services Management and Hospital Administration	M,D*
Immunology	M,D
International Health	M
Microbiology	M,D
Molecular Biology	M,D
Neuroscience	M,D
Pathology	M,D
Pharmacology	M,D
Physical Therapy	D*
Physiology	M,D
Public Health—General	M,D*

NEW YORK SCHOOL OF INTERIOR DESIGN

Interior Design	M*

NEW YORK STUDIO SCHOOL OF DRAWING, PAINTING AND SCULPTURE

Art/Fine Arts	M,O

NEW YORK THEOLOGICAL SEMINARY

Theology	P,M,D

NEW YORK UNIVERSITY

Accounting	M,D
Acute Care/Critical Care Nursing	M,O
Adult Nursing	M,O
Advertising and Public Relations	M
African Studies	M,D,O
Agricultural Engineering	M,D
Allopathic Medicine	P
American Studies	M,D
Anthropology	M,D
Applied Arts and Design—General	M
Applied Economics	M,D,O
Archaeology	M,D
Art Education	M,D
Art History	M,D
Art Therapy	M
Art/Fine Arts	M,D
Arts Administration	M
Asian Studies	M,D
Bioethics	M
Biological and Biomedical Sciences—General	M,D*
Business Administration and Management—General	P,M,D,O
Business Education	M,O
Cancer Biology/Oncology	P,M,D
Cell Biology	P,M,D
Chemistry	M,D
Classics	M,D,O
Clinical Research	P,M,D
Cognitive Sciences	M,D,O
Communication Disorders	M,D
Communication—General	M,D
Comparative Literature	M,D
Computational Biology	D
Computer Art and Design	M
Computer Science	M,D*
Construction Management	M,O
Corporate and Organizational Communication	M
Counseling Psychology	M,D,O
Counselor Education	M,D,O
Cultural Studies	M,D,O
Dance	M,D
Database Systems	M,O
Dentistry	P
Developmental Biology	M,D
Developmental Psychology	M,D
Early Childhood Education	M,D,O
Economics	M,D,O
Education—General	M,D,O
Educational Leadership and Administration	M,D,O
Educational Media/Instructional Technology	M,D,O
Educational Policy	M,D
Educational Psychology	M,D
Elementary Education	M,D,O
English as a Second Language	M,D,O
English Education	M,D,O
English	M,D
Environmental and Occupational Health	M,D
Environmental Education	M
Environmental Management and Policy	M
Epidemiology	M,D
Ergonomics and Human Factors	M,D
Film, Television, and Video Production	M
Film, Television, and Video Theory and Criticism	M,D
Finance and Banking	M,D,O
Food Science and Technology	M,D
Foreign Languages Education	M,D,O
Foundations and Philosophy of Education	M,D
French	M,D,O
Genetics	M,D
German	M,D
Gerontological Nursing	M,O
Graphic Design	M
Health Education	M,D
Health Promotion	M,D,O
Health Services Management and Hospital Administration	M,O
Higher Education	M,D
Hispanic Studies	M,D
Historic Preservation	
History	M,D,O
Hospitality Management	M,D,O
Human Development	M,D,O
Human Resources Development	M,O
Human Resources Management	M,D,O
Humanities	M,O
Immunology	P,M,D
Industrial and Organizational Psychology	M,D,O
Interdisciplinary Studies	M*
International Affairs	M,D,O
International and Comparative Education	M,D,O
International Business	M,D
International Health	M,D
Internet and Interactive Multimedia	M
Italian	M,D
Jewish Studies	M,D,O
Journalism	M,D,O
Kinesiology and Movement Studies	M,D,O
Latin American Studies	M,D,O
Law	P,M,D,O
Legal and Justice Studies	M,D
Linguistics	M,D
Management Information Systems	M,D,O
Management Strategy and Policy	M,D,O
Marketing	M,D,O
Mathematical and Computational Finance	M,D
Mathematics Education	M
Mathematics	M,D*
Media Studies	M,D
Microbiology	P,M,D*
Molecular Biology	P,M,D
Molecular Genetics	M,D
Molecular Pharmacology	D
Molecular Toxicology	M,D
Multilingual and Multicultural Education	M,D,O
Museum Studies	M,D,O
Music Education	M,D,O
Music	M,D,O
National Security	M
Near and Middle Eastern Studies	M,D,O
Neurobiology	M,D
Neuroscience	P,M,D*
Nonprofit Management	M,D,O
Nurse Midwifery	M,O
Nursing Education	M,O
Nursing Informatics	M,O
Nursing—General	M,O
Nutrition	M,D
Occupational Therapy	M,D
Oral and Dental Sciences	M,D,O
Organizational Behavior	M,D
Organizational Management	M,D
Parasitology	P,M,D
Pathobiology	P,M,D
Pediatric Nursing	M,O
Pharmacology	P,M,D
Philosophy	M,D
Physical Therapy	M,D,O
Physics	M,D
Physiology	P,M,D
Plant Biology	M,D
Political Science	M,D
Portuguese	M,D
Psychiatric Nursing	M,O
Psychoanalysis and Psychotherapy	M,D,O
Psychology—General	M,D,O
Public Administration	M,D,O*
Public History	M,D,O
Publishing	M
Quantitative Analysis	M,D,O
Reading Education	M
Real Estate	M,O
Religion	M,O
Romance Languages	M,D
Russian	M
Science Education	M
Slavic Languages	M
Social Psychology	M,D,O
Social Sciences Education	M,D,O
Social Sciences	M,O
Social Work	M,D*
Sociology	M,D
Spanish	M,D
Special Education	M
Speech and Interpersonal Communication	M,D
Sports Management	M,O
Statistics	M,D
Structural Biology	P,M,D
Student Affairs	M,D
Taxation	P,M,D,O
Theater	M,D,O
Therapies—Dance, Drama, and Music	M
Toxicology	M,D
Translation and Interpretation	M,D
Travel and Tourism	M,O
Urban and Regional Planning	M,O
Western European Studies	M
Writing	M,D

NIAGARA UNIVERSITY

Business Administration and Management—General	M
Counselor Education	M,O
Criminal Justice and Criminology	M
Early Childhood Education	M,O
Education—General	M,O
Educational Leadership and Administration	M,O
Elementary Education	M,O
Foundations and Philosophy of Education	M
Interdisciplinary Studies	M
Middle School Education	M,O
Reading Education	M
School Psychology	M,O

Secondary Education	M,O
Special Education	M,O

NICHOLLS STATE UNIVERSITY

Business Administration and Management—General	M
Computer Science	M
Counseling Psychology	M,O
Counselor Education	M
Curriculum and Instruction	M
Education—General	M
Educational Leadership and Administration	M
Environmental Biology	M
Marine Biology	M
Mathematics Education	M
Mathematics	M
School Psychology	M,O

NICHOLS COLLEGE

Business Administration and Management—General	M
Criminal Justice and Criminology	M
Sports Management	M

THE NIGERIAN BAPTIST THEOLOGICAL SEMINARY

Music	P,M,D,O
Pastoral Ministry and Counseling	P,M,D,O
Religious Education	P,M,D,O
Theology	P,M,D,O

NIPISSING UNIVERSITY

Education—General	M,O

NORFOLK STATE UNIVERSITY

Art/Fine Arts	M
Clinical Psychology	M
Communication—General	M
Computer Engineering	M
Computer Science	M
Criminal Justice and Criminology	M
Early Childhood Education	M
Education of the Multiply Handicapped	M
Education—General	M
Educational Leadership and Administration	M
Electrical Engineering	M
Materials Sciences	M
Media Studies	M
Music Education	M
Music	M
Optical Sciences	M
Psychology—General	M,D
Secondary Education	M
Social Psychology	M
Social Work	M,D
Sociology	M
Special Education	M
Urban Education	M
Urban Studies	M

NORTH CAROLINA AGRICULTURAL AND TECHNICAL STATE UNIVERSITY

Adult Education	M,D
African-American Studies	M
Agricultural Economics and Agribusiness	M
Agricultural Education	M
Agricultural Sciences—General	M
Agronomy and Soil Sciences	M
Animal Sciences	M
Applied Economics	M
Art Education	M
Biological and Biomedical Sciences—General	M
Business Administration and Management—General	M,D
Chemical Engineering	M,D
Chemistry	M
Civil Engineering	M
Computer Engineering	M,D
Computer Science	M
Construction Management	M
Counselor Education	M,D
Education—General	M
Educational Leadership and Administration	M,D
Educational Media/Instructional Technology	M
Electrical Engineering	M,D
Elementary Education	M
Energy and Power Engineering	M,D
Engineering and Applied Sciences—General	M,D
English Education	M
English	M
Environmental and Occupational Health	M
Environmental Sciences	M
Health Education	M
Human Resources Development	M,D
Industrial/Management Engineering	M,D
Management of Technology	M,D
Mathematics Education	M
Mechanical Engineering	M,D
Nutrition	M
Optical Sciences	M,D
Organizational Management	M,D
Physical Education	M
Plant Sciences	M
Reading Education	M
Rehabilitation Counseling	M,D
Science Education	M
Social Sciences Education	M
Social Work	M
Systems Engineering	M,D
Vocational and Technical Education	M,D

NORTH CAROLINA CENTRAL UNIVERSITY

Applied Mathematics	M
Biological and Biomedical Sciences—General	M
Business Administration and Management—General	M
Chemistry	M
Communication Disorders	M
Counselor Education	M
Criminal Justice and Criminology	M
Curriculum and Instruction	M
Education—General	M
Educational Leadership and Administration	M
Educational Media/Instructional Technology	M
Elementary Education	M
English	M
Family and Consumer Sciences-General	M
Geosciences	M
History	M
Information Studies	M
Law	P
Library Science	M
Mathematics Education	M
Mathematics	M
Middle School Education	M
Music	M
Physical Education	M
Physics	M
Psychology—General	M
Public Administration	M
Recreation and Park Management	M
Social Psychology	M
Sociology	M
Special Education	M
Sports Management	M

NORTH CAROLINA STATE UNIVERSITY

Accounting	M
Adult Education	M,D
Aerospace/Aeronautical Engineering	M,D
Agricultural Economics and Agribusiness	M
Agricultural Education	M,O
Agricultural Engineering	M,D,O
Agricultural Sciences—General	M,D,O
Agronomy and Soil Sciences	M,D
Animal Sciences	M,D
Anthropology	M
Applied Arts and Design—General	M,D
Applied Mathematics	M,D
Architecture	M
Atmospheric Sciences	M,D
Biochemistry	D
Bioengineering	M,D,O
Bioinformatics	M,D*
Biological and Biomedical Sciences—General	M,D,O
Biomathematics	M,D
Biomedical Engineering	M,D
Biotechnology	M
Botany	M,D
Business Administration and Management—General	M
Business Education	M
Cell Biology	M,D
Chemical Engineering	M,D
Chemistry	M,D
Civil Engineering	M,D
Clothing and Textiles	D
Communication—General	M
Community College Education	M,D
Computer Art and Design	D
Computer Engineering	M,D
Computer Science	M,D
Counselor Education	M,D
Curriculum and Instruction	M,D
Developmental Education	M,D,O
Developmental Psychology	D
Economics	M,D
Education—General	M,D,O
Educational Leadership and Administration	M,D
Educational Measurement and Evaluation	D
Educational Media/Instructional Technology	M,D
Electrical Engineering	M,D
Elementary Education	M
Engineering and Applied Sciences—General	M,D*
English Education	M
English	M
Entomology	M,D
Entrepreneurship	M
Epidemiology	M,D
Ergonomics and Human Factors	D
Experimental Psychology	D
Financial Engineering	M
Fish, Game, and Wildlife Management	M,D
Food Science and Technology	M,D
Forestry	M,D
French	M
Genetics	M,D
Genomic Sciences	M,D*
Geographic Information Systems	M,D
Geosciences	M,D
Graphic Design	M
Higher Education	M,D
History	M
Horticulture	M,D,O
Human Resources Development	M
Immunology	M,D
Industrial and Organizational Psychology	D
Industrial Design	M
Industrial/Management Engineering	M,D
Infectious Diseases	M,D
International Affairs	M
Landscape Architecture	M
Liberal Studies	M
Management of Technology	D
Manufacturing Engineering	M
Marine Sciences	M,D
Materials Engineering	M,D
Materials Sciences	M,D
Mathematical and Computational Finance	M
Mathematics Education	M,D
Mathematics	M,D
Mechanical Engineering	M,D*
Meteorology	M,D
Microbiology	M,D
Middle School Education	M
Molecular Toxicology	M,D
Natural Resources	M,D
Nonprofit Management	M,D,O
Nuclear Engineering	M,D
Nutrition	M,D
Oceanography	M,D
Operations Research	M,D
Paper and Pulp Engineering	M,D
Pathology	M,D
Pharmacology	M,D
Physics	M,D
Physiology	M,D
Plant Biology	M,D
Plant Pathology	M,D
Polymer Science and Engineering	D
Psychology—General	D
Public Administration	M,D
Public History	M
Recreation and Park Management	M,D
Rhetoric	D
School Psychology	D
Science Education	M,D
Secondary Education	M
Social Psychology	M
Social Sciences Education	M
Social Work	M
Sociology	M,D
Spanish	M
Special Education	M
Sports Management	M,D
Statistics	M,D
Supply Chain Management	M
Technical Communication	M
Textile Sciences and Engineering	M,D
Toxicology	M,D
Travel and Tourism	M,D
Veterinary Medicine	P,M
Veterinary Sciences	M,D
Writing	M
Zoology	M,D

NORTH CENTRAL COLLEGE

Business Administration and Management—General	M
Computer Science	M
Curriculum and Instruction	M
Education—General	M

*M—master's degree; P—first professional degree; D—doctorate; O—other advanced degree; *—Close-Up and/or Announcement or Display in one of the other books in this series*

Educational Leadership and Administration	M
Liberal Studies	M
Management Information Systems	M
Nonprofit Management	M

NORTHCENTRAL UNIVERSITY

Business Administration and Management—General	M,D,O
Education—General	M,D,O
Psychology—General	M,D,O

NORTH DAKOTA STATE UNIVERSITY

Adult Education	M,D,O
Agricultural Economics and Agribusiness	M
Agricultural Education	M
Agricultural Engineering	M,D
Agricultural Sciences—General	M,D
Agronomy and Soil Sciences	M,D
Animal Sciences	M,D
Applied Mathematics	M,D
Applied Statistics	M,D,O
Biochemistry	M,D
Bioinformatics	M,D
Biological and Biomedical Sciences—General	M,D
Biosystems Engineering	M,D
Botany	M,D
Business Administration and Management—General	M
Cell Biology	M,D
Chemistry	M,D
Child and Family Studies	M,D
Child Development	M,D
Civil Engineering	M,D
Clinical Psychology	M,D
Cognitive Sciences	M,D
Communication—General	M,D
Computer Engineering	M,D
Computer Science	M,D,O
Conservation Biology	M,D
Construction Management	M
Consumer Economics	M,D
Counselor Education	M,D
Criminal Justice and Criminology	M,D
Ecology	M,D
Education—General	M,D,O
Educational Leadership and Administration	M,O
Electrical Engineering	M,D
Emergency Management	M,D
Engineering and Applied Sciences—General	M,D
English	M
Entomology	M,D
Environmental Engineering	M,D
Environmental Sciences	M,D
Exercise and Sports Science	M
Family and Consumer Sciences-General	M
Food Science and Technology	M,D
Genomic Sciences	M,D
Gerontology	M,D
Health Psychology	M,D
History	M,D
Human Development	D
Industrial/Management Engineering	M,D
Logistics	M,D
Manufacturing Engineering	M,D
Marriage and Family Therapy	M,D
Mass Communication	M,D
Materials Sciences	D
Mathematics Education	M,D,O
Mathematics	M,D
Mechanical Engineering	M,D
Mechanics	M,D
Microbiology	M,D
Molecular Biology	M,D
Molecular Pathogenesis	M,D
Music Education	M,D,O
Music	M,D
Nanotechnology	D
Natural Resources	M,D
Nursing—General	M,D
Nutrition	M
Operations Research	M,D,O
Pathology	M,D
Pharmaceutical Sciences	M,D
Physical Education	M
Physics	M,D
Plant Pathology	M,D
Plant Sciences	M,D
Polymer Science and Engineering	M,D
Psychology—General	M,D
Range Science	M,D
Science Education	M,D,O
Social Psychology	M,D
Social Sciences Education	M,D,O
Social Sciences	M,D
Sociology	M,D
Software Engineering	M,D,O
Speech and Interpersonal Communication	M,D
Sports Management	M
Statistics	M,D,O
Transportation Management	M,D
Veterinary Sciences	M,D
Vocational and Technical Education	M,D,O
Zoology	M,D

NORTHEASTERN ILLINOIS UNIVERSITY

Accounting	M
Biological and Biomedical Sciences—General	M
Business Administration and Management—General	M
Chemistry	M
Computer Science	M
Counselor Education	M
Education of the Gifted	M
Education—General	M
Educational Leadership and Administration	M
English Education	M
English	M
Environmental Management and Policy	M
Finance and Banking	M
Geography	M
Geosciences	M
Gerontology	M
History	M
Human Resources Development	M
Linguistics	M
Marketing	M
Mathematics Education	M
Mathematics	M
Multilingual and Multicultural Education	M
Music	M
Political Science	M
Reading Education	M
Special Education	M
Speech and Interpersonal Communication	M
Urban Education	M
Writing	M

NORTHEASTERN OHIO UNIVERSITIES COLLEGE OF MEDICINE AND PHARMACY

Allopathic Medicine	P
Pharmacy	P

NORTHEASTERN SEMINARY AT ROBERTS WESLEYAN COLLEGE

Theology	P,M,D

NORTHEASTERN STATE UNIVERSITY

Accounting	M
American Studies	M
Business Administration and Management—General	M
Communication Disorders	M
Communication—General	M
Counseling Psychology	M
Counselor Education	M
Criminal Justice and Criminology	M
Early Childhood Education	M
Education—General	M
Educational Leadership and Administration	M
Educational Media/Instructional Technology	M
English	M
Finance and Banking	M
Foundations and Philosophy of Education	M
Health Education	M
Higher Education	M
Industrial and Manufacturing Management	M
Mathematics Education	M
Optometry	P
Psychology—General	M
Reading Education	M
Science Education	M

NORTHEASTERN UNIVERSITY

Accounting	M,O
Acute Care/Critical Care Nursing	M,O
Allied Health—General	P,M,D,O
Analytical Chemistry	M,D
Applied Economics	M,D
Applied Mathematics	M,D
Architecture	M
Biochemistry	M,D
Bioinformatics	M
Biological and Biomedical Sciences—General	M,D
Biotechnology	M,D
Business Administration and Management—General	M,O
Chemical Engineering	M,D
Chemistry	M,D
Civil Engineering	M,D
Communication Disorders	M,D
Computer Engineering	M,D
Computer Science	M,D
Counseling Psychology	M,D,O
Counselor Education	M,D
Criminal Justice and Criminology	M,D
Economics	M,D
Educational Psychology	M,D
Electrical Engineering	M,D
Engineering and Applied Sciences—General	M,D,O
Engineering Management	M,D
English	M,D,O
Entrepreneurship	M
Environmental Engineering	M,D
Exercise and Sports Science	M
Experimental Psychology	M,D
Finance and Banking	M
Health Informatics	M,D
Health Services Management and Hospital Administration	M,O
History	M,D
Industrial/Management Engineering	M,D
Information Science	M,D,O
Inorganic Chemistry	M,D
International Affairs	M,D,O
Journalism	M
Law	P
Legal and Justice Studies	M,D
Management Information Systems	M,D
Manufacturing Engineering	M,D
Marine Biology	M,D
Maternal and Child/Neonatal Nursing	M,O
Mathematics	M,D
Mechanical Engineering	M,D
Nurse Anesthesia	M,O
Nursing and Healthcare Administration	M
Nursing—General	M,O
Operations Research	M,D
Organic Chemistry	M,D
Pharmaceutical Sciences	P,M,D
Pharmacology	M,D
Physical Chemistry	M,D
Physician Assistant Studies	M
Physics	M,D*
Political Science	M,D,O
Psychiatric Nursing	M,O
Psychology—General	M,D,O
Public Administration	M,O
Public Affairs	M,D,O
Public History	M,D
Public Policy	M,D
Rehabilitation Counseling	M
School Psychology	M,D,O
Sociology	M,D
Special Education	M,D,O
Speech and Interpersonal Communication	D
Student Affairs	M
Systems Engineering	M
Taxation	M,O
Telecommunications Management	M,D
Toxicology	M
Urban Studies	M,O

NORTHERN ARIZONA UNIVERSITY

Allied Health—General	M,D
Anthropology	M
Applied Physics	M
Archaeology	M
Biochemistry	M
Biological and Biomedical Sciences—General	M,D
Business Administration and Management—General	M
Chemistry	M
Civil Engineering	M
Clinical Psychology	M
Communication Disorders	M
Communication—General	M
Community College Education	M,D
Computer Science	M
Counseling Psychology	D
Counselor Education	M
Criminal Justice and Criminology	M,O
Curriculum and Instruction	D
Early Childhood Education	M
Education—General	M,D,O
Educational Leadership and Administration	M,D
Educational Media/Instructional Technology	M,O
Educational Psychology	D
Electrical Engineering	M
Elementary Education	M
Engineering and Applied Sciences—General	M,D
English as a Second Language	M,D,O

English Education	M
English	M
Environmental Engineering	M
Environmental Management and Policy	M
Environmental Sciences	M
Family Nurse Practitioner Studies	M
Foreign Languages Education	M
Forestry	M,D
Foundations and Philosophy of Education	M,D
Geographic Information Systems	M,O
Geography	M,O
Geology	M
Geosciences	M
Health Psychology	M
Higher Education	M,D
History	M,D
Liberal Studies	M
Linguistics	M,D,O
Mathematics Education	M
Mathematics	M
Mechanical Engineering	M
Multilingual and Multicultural Education	M
Music Education	M
Music	M
Nursing Education	M
Nursing—General	M
Physical Therapy	D
Physics	M
Political Science	M,D,O
Psychology—General	M
Public Administration	M,D,O
Public Health—General	M
School Psychology	M,D
Science Education	M
Secondary Education	M
Social Psychology	M
Sociology	M
Special Education	M
Statistics	M
Student Affairs	M
Sustainable Development	M
Technical Writing	M
Vocational and Technical Education	M
Writing	M

NORTHERN BAPTIST THEOLOGICAL SEMINARY

Missions and Missiology	P,M,D
Pastoral Ministry and Counseling	P,M,D
Theology	P,M,D

NORTHERN ILLINOIS UNIVERSITY

Accounting	M
Adult Education	M,D
Anthropology	M
Art/Fine Arts	M
Biological and Biomedical Sciences—General	M,D
Business Administration and Management—General	M
Chemistry	M,D
Child and Family Studies	M
Communication Disorders	M,D
Communication—General	M
Computer Science	M
Counselor Education	M,D
Curriculum and Instruction	M,D
Dance	M
Early Childhood Education	M,D
Economics	M,D
Education—General	M,D,O
Educational Leadership and Administration	M,D,O
Educational Media/Instructional Technology	M,D
Educational Psychology	M,D,O
Electrical Engineering	M
Elementary Education	M,D
Engineering and Applied Sciences—General	M
English	M,D
Foundations and Philosophy of Education	M,D,O
French	M
Geography	M
Geology	M,D
Higher Education	M,D
History	M,D
Industrial and Manufacturing Management	M
Industrial/Management Engineering	M
Law	P
Management Information Systems	M
Mathematics	M,D
Mechanical Engineering	M
Music	M,O
Nursing—General	M
Nutrition	M
Philosophy	M
Physical Education	M
Physical Therapy	M
Physics	M,D
Political Science	M,D
Psychology—General	M,D
Public Administration	M
Public Health—General	M
Reading Education	M,D
Romance Languages	M
Secondary Education	M,D
Sociology	M
Spanish	M
Special Education	M,D
Sports Management	M
Statistics	M
Taxation	M
Theater	M

NORTHERN KENTUCKY UNIVERSITY

Accounting	M,O
Business Administration and Management—General	M,O
Communication—General	M
Computer and Information Systems Security	M,O
Computer Science	M,O
Counselor Education	M,O
Education—General	M,D,O
Educational Leadership and Administration	M,D,O
English	M,O
Entrepreneurship	M,O
Family Nurse Practitioner Studies	M,O
Finance and Banking	M,O
Health Informatics	M,O
Health Psychology	M,O
Industrial and Organizational Psychology	M,O
Information Science	M,O
International Business	M,O
Law	P
Liberal Studies	M,O
Marketing	M,O
Nonprofit Management	M,O
Nursing—General	M,O
Organizational Management	M
Project Management	M,O
Public Administration	M,O
Social Psychology	M,O
Software Engineering	M,O
Special Education	M,O
Student Affairs	M,O
Taxation	M,O

NORTHERN MICHIGAN UNIVERSITY

Biological and Biomedical Sciences—General	M
Counselor Education	M
Criminal Justice and Criminology	M
Education—General	M,O
Educational Leadership and Administration	M,O
Elementary Education	M
English	M
Exercise and Sports Science	M
Nursing—General	M
Psychology—General	M
Public Administration	M
Reading Education	M,O
Science Education	M
Secondary Education	M
Special Education	M
Writing	M

NORTHERN STATE UNIVERSITY

Counselor Education	M
Education—General	M
Educational Leadership and Administration	M
Educational Media/Instructional Technology	M
Elementary Education	M
English Education	M
Health Education	M
Physical Education	M
Reading Education	M
Secondary Education	M
Special Education	M

NORTH GEORGIA COLLEGE & STATE UNIVERSITY

Art Education	M,O
Early Childhood Education	M,O
Education—General	M,O
Educational Leadership and Administration	M,O
English Education	M,O
Family Nurse Practitioner Studies	M
Mathematics Education	M,O
Middle School Education	M,O
Nursing Education	M
Physical Education	M,O
Physical Therapy	D
Public Administration	M
Science Education	M,O
Secondary Education	M,O
Social Psychology	M
Social Sciences Education	M,O
Special Education	M,O

NORTH GREENVILLE UNIVERSITY

Business Administration and Management—General	M
Pastoral Ministry and Counseling	M

NORTH PARK THEOLOGICAL SEMINARY

Pastoral Ministry and Counseling	M,O
Theology	P,M,D

NORTH PARK UNIVERSITY

Adult Nursing	M
Business Administration and Management—General	M
Education—General	M
Nursing and Healthcare Administration	M
Nursing—General	M

NORTH SHORE–LIJ GRADUATE SCHOOL OF MOLECULAR MEDICINE

Molecular Medicine	D

NORTHWEST BAPTIST SEMINARY

Theology	P,M,D,O

NORTHWEST CHRISTIAN UNIVERSITY

Business Administration and Management—General	M
Counselor Education	M
Education—General	M

NORTHWESTERN HEALTH SCIENCES UNIVERSITY

Acupuncture and Oriental Medicine	M
Chiropractic	P
Rehabilitation Sciences	O

NORTHWESTERN OKLAHOMA STATE UNIVERSITY

Counseling Psychology	M
Counselor Education	M
Education—General	M
Elementary Education	M
Reading Education	M
Secondary Education	M

NORTHWESTERN POLYTECHNIC UNIVERSITY

Business Administration and Management—General	M
Computer Engineering	M
Computer Science	M
Electrical Engineering	M
Engineering and Applied Sciences—General	M

NORTHWESTERN STATE UNIVERSITY OF LOUISIANA

Adult Education	M
Archaeology	M
Art/Fine Arts	M
Business Education	M
Clinical Psychology	M
Counselor Education	M,O
Curriculum and Instruction	M
Early Childhood Education	M
Education—General	M,O
Educational Leadership and Administration	M,O
Educational Media/Instructional Technology	M,O
Elementary Education	M,O
English Education	M
English	M
Health Education	M
Historic Preservation	M
Home Economics Education	M
Mathematics Education	M
Middle School Education	M
Music	M
Nursing—General	M
Psychology—General	M
Reading Education	M,O
Science Education	M
Secondary Education	M,O
Social Sciences Education	M
Special Education	M,O
Student Affairs	M,O

NORTHWESTERN UNIVERSITY

Accounting	D
Advertising and Public Relations	M
African Studies	O
Allopathic Medicine	
Anthropology	D
Applied Mathematics	M,D
Art History	D
Art/Fine Arts	M*

*M—master's degree; P—first professional degree; D—doctorate; O—other advanced degree; *—Close-Up and/or Announcement or Display in one of the other books in this series*

Astronomy	M,D
Astrophysics	M,D
Biochemistry	D
Bioinformatics	M
Biological and Biomedical Sciences—General	D*
Biomedical Engineering	M,D
Biophysics	D
Biopsychology	D
Biotechnology	D
Broadcast Journalism	M
Business Administration and Management—General	M
Cancer Biology/Oncology	D
Cell Biology	D
Chemical Engineering	M,D
Chemistry	D
Civil Engineering	M,D
Clinical Psychology	D
Clinical Research	M,O
Cognitive Sciences	D
Communication Disorders	M,D*
Communication—General	M,D
Comparative Literature	M,D,O
Computational Biology	M
Computational Sciences	M
Computer Engineering	M,D,O
Computer Science	M,D,O
Corporate and Organizational Communication	M
Counseling Psychology	M
Developmental Biology	D
Economics	M,D
Education—General	M,D*
Educational Media/Instructional Technology	M,D
Electrical Engineering	M,D,O
Electronic Commerce	M
Electronic Materials	M,D,O
Elementary Education	M
Engineering and Applied Sciences—General	M,D,O
Engineering Design	M
Engineering Management	M
English	M,D*
Environmental Engineering	M,D
Evolutionary Biology	D
Film, Television, and Video Production	M,D
Finance and Banking	D
French	D,O
Gender Studies	O
Genetic Counseling	M
Genetics	D
Geology	M,D
Geosciences	M,D
Geotechnical Engineering	M,D
German	D
Higher Education	M
History	D
Human Development	D
Immunology	D
Industrial/Management Engineering	M,D
Information Science	M
International Affairs	P,M,O
Italian	D,O
Journalism	M
Kinesiology and Movement Studies	D
Law	P,M,O
Liberal Studies	M
Linguistics	M,D
Management Information Systems	M
Management Strategy and Policy	D
Manufacturing Engineering	M
Marketing	M,D
Marriage and Family Therapy	M
Materials Engineering	M,D,O
Materials Sciences	M,D,O
Mathematics	D
Mechanical Engineering	M,D
Mechanics	M,D
Media Studies	M,D
Microbiology	D
Molecular Biology	D
Music Education	M,D
Music	M,D,O
Neurobiology	M,D
Neuroscience	D
Operations Research	M,D
Organizational Behavior	M,D
Organizational Management	M,D
Pharmacology	D
Philosophy	D
Physical Therapy	D
Physics	M,D
Physiology	M
Political Science	M,D
Project Management	M
Psychology—General	D*
Public Health—General	M
Public Policy	D*
Publishing	M
Rehabilitation Sciences	D
Reproductive Biology	D
Secondary Education	M
Slavic Languages	D
Social Psychology	D
Social Sciences	M,O
Sociology	D
Special Education	M,D
Speech and Interpersonal Communication	M,D
Statistics	M,D
Structural Biology	D
Structural Engineering	M,D
Taxation	P,M
Theater	M,D
Toxicology	D
Transportation and Highway Engineering	M,D
Writing	M

NORTHWEST MISSOURI STATE UNIVERSITY

Accounting	M
Agricultural Economics and Agribusiness	M
Agricultural Education	M
Agricultural Sciences—General	M
Biological and Biomedical Sciences—General	M
Business Administration and Management—General	M
Computer Science	M,O
Counselor Education	M
Early Childhood Education	M
Education—General	M,O
Educational Leadership and Administration	M,O
Educational Media/Instructional Technology	M
Elementary Education	M,O
English as a Second Language	M,O
English Education	M
English	M
Geographic Information Systems	M,O
Geography	M,O
Health Education	M
Health Services Management and Hospital Administration	M
Higher Education	M,O
History	M
Management Information Systems	M
Mathematics Education	M
Middle School Education	M
Music Education	M
Physical Education	M
Psychology—General	M
Quality Management	M,O
Reading Education	M
Recreation and Park Management	M
Science Education	M
Secondary Education	M,O
Social Sciences Education	M
Special Education	M

NORTHWEST NAZARENE UNIVERSITY

Business Administration and Management—General	M
Counselor Education	M
Curriculum and Instruction	M
Education—General	M
Educational Leadership and Administration	M
Marriage and Family Therapy	M
Missions and Missiology	P,M
Pastoral Ministry and Counseling	P,M
Reading Education	M
Religion	P,M
School Psychology	M
Social Psychology	M
Social Work	M
Special Education	M

NORTHWEST UNIVERSITY

Business Administration and Management—General	M
Counseling Psychology	M
Education—General	M
Psychology—General	M

NORTHWOOD UNIVERSITY

Business Administration and Management—General	M

NORWICH UNIVERSITY

Business Administration and Management—General	M
Civil Engineering	M
Conflict Resolution and Mediation/Peace Studies	M
Criminal Justice and Criminology	M
International Affairs	M
International Business	M
Management Information Systems	M
Military and Defense Studies	M
Nursing and Healthcare Administration	M
Organizational Management	M
Public Administration	M

NOTRE DAME COLLEGE (OH)

Accounting	M,O
Business Administration and Management—General	M,O
Education—General	M,O
Finance and Banking	M,O
Management Information Systems	M,O
Pastoral Ministry and Counseling	M,O
Reading Education	M,O
Special Education	M,O

NOTRE DAME DE NAMUR UNIVERSITY

Art Therapy	M
Biological and Biomedical Sciences—General	O
Business Administration and Management—General	M
Clinical Psychology	M
Education—General	M,O
Educational Leadership and Administration	M,O
English as a Second Language	M,O
English	M,O
Finance and Banking	M
Gerontology	M,O
Human Resources Management	M
Management of Technology	M
Marketing	M
Marriage and Family Therapy	M
Music Education	M
Music	M
Project Management	M
Psychology—General	M,O
Public Administration	M
Public Affairs	M
Reading Education	M,O
Special Education	M,O

NOTRE DAME SEMINARY

Theology	P,M

NOVA SCOTIA AGRICULTURAL COLLEGE

Agricultural Sciences—General	M
Agronomy and Soil Sciences	M
Animal Sciences	M
Aquaculture	M
Botany	M
Ecology	M
Environmental Biology	M
Environmental Management and Policy	M
Environmental Sciences	M
Food Science and Technology	M
Horticulture	M
Physiology	M
Plant Pathology	M
Plant Physiology	M
Water Resources	M

NOVA SOUTHEASTERN UNIVERSITY

Accounting	M,D
Adult Education	D
Allied Health—General	M,D
Art Education	M,O
Biological and Biomedical Sciences—General	M
Business Administration and Management—General	M,D*
Child and Family Studies	M,D
Clinical Psychology	D,O
Communication Disorders	M,D
Computer and Information Systems Security	M,D
Computer Education	M,D,O
Computer Science	M,D*
Conflict Resolution and Mediation/Peace Studies	M,D
Counseling Psychology	M
Counselor Education	M
Criminal Justice and Criminology	M*
Curriculum and Instruction	M,O
Dentistry	P,M
Distance Education Development	M,D
Early Childhood Education	M,O
Education of the Gifted	M,O
Education—General	M,D,O
Educational Leadership and Administration	M,D,O
Educational Media/Instructional Technology	M,D,O
Elementary Education	M,O
English as a Second Language	M,O
English Education	M,O
Entrepreneurship	M
Environmental Education	M,O

Environmental Sciences	M
Finance and Banking	M,D
Health Education	M,D
Health Law	M
Higher Education	D
Human Resources Management	M,D
Human Services	M,D
Humanities	M,O
Industrial and Manufacturing Management	D
Information Science	M,D
Interdisciplinary Studies	M,O
International Business	M,D
Law	P,M,O
Legal and Justice Studies	M,O
Management Information Systems	M,D
Marine Affairs	M
Marine Biology	M,D
Marine Sciences	M
Marriage and Family Therapy	M,D,O
Mathematics Education	M,O
Multilingual and Multicultural Education	M,O
Nursing—General	M,D
Occupational Therapy	M,D
Oceanography	M,D*
Optometry	P,M
Organizational Management	D
Osteopathic Medicine	P,M
Pharmacology	M
Pharmacy	P
Physical Therapy	D
Physician Assistant Studies	M
Psychology—General	M,D,O
Public Administration	M
Public Health—General	M
Reading Education	M,O
Real Estate	M
School Psychology	O
Science Education	M,O
Secondary Education	M,O
Social Sciences Education	M,O
Social Sciences	M,O
Spanish	M,O
Special Education	M,D,O
Sports Management	M,O
Student Affairs	M,O
Taxation	M
Urban Education	M,O
Vision Sciences	P,M
Vocational and Technical Education	D

NSCAD UNIVERSITY

Applied Arts and Design—General	M
Art/Fine Arts	M

NYACK COLLEGE

Accounting	M
Business Administration and Management—General	M
Education—General	M
Elementary Education	M
Organizational Management	M
Social Sciences	M
Special Education	M

OAKLAND CITY UNIVERSITY

Business Administration and Management—General	M
Education—General	M,D
Educational Leadership and Administration	M,D
Theology	P,D

OAKLAND UNIVERSITY

Accounting	M,O
Adult Nursing	M
Allied Health—General	M,D,O
Applied Mathematics	M,D
Applied Statistics	M
Biological and Biomedical Sciences—General	M,D
Business Administration and Management—General	M,O
Chemistry	M,D
Computer Engineering	M
Computer Science	M
Counseling Psychology	M,D,O
Early Childhood Education	M,D,O
Economics	O
Education—General	M,D,O
Educational Leadership and Administration	M,D,O
Educational Media/Instructional Technology	O
Electrical Engineering	M
Engineering and Applied Sciences—General	M,D
Engineering Management	M
English as a Second Language	M,O
English	M
Entrepreneurship	M,O
Environmental and Occupational Health	M
Environmental Sciences	M,D
Exercise and Sports Science	M,O
Family Nurse Practitioner Studies	M,O
Finance and Banking	M,O
Foundations and Philosophy of Education	M
Gerontological Nursing	M,O
Health Promotion	O
Higher Education	M,D,O
History	M
Human Resources Development	M
Human Resources Management	M,O
Industrial and Manufacturing Management	M,O
International Business	M,O
Liberal Studies	M
Linguistics	M,O
Management Information Systems	M,O
Marketing	M,O
Maternal and Child Health	M,D,O
Mathematics Education	M,D,O
Mathematics	M
Mechanical Engineering	M,D
Medical Physics	M,D
Music Education	M,D
Music	M,D
Nurse Anesthesia	M,O
Nursing Education	M,O
Nursing—General	M,D,O
Physical Therapy	M,D,O
Physics	M,D
Public Administration	M
Reading Education	M,D,O
Secondary Education	M
Software Engineering	M
Special Education	M,O
Statistics	O
Systems Engineering	M,D
Systems Science	M

OAKWOOD UNIVERSITY

Pastoral Ministry and Counseling	M

OBERLIN COLLEGE

Early Childhood Education	M
Education—General	M
Middle School Education	M
Music	M,O

OBLATE SCHOOL OF THEOLOGY

Pastoral Ministry and Counseling	P,M,D,O
Religion	P,M,D,O
Theology	P,M,D,O

OCCIDENTAL COLLEGE

Biological and Biomedical Sciences—General	M
Education—General	M
Elementary Education	M
English Education	M
Foreign Languages Education	M
Liberal Studies	M
Mathematics Education	M
Science Education	M
Secondary Education	M
Social Sciences Education	M

OGI SCHOOL OF SCIENCE & ENGINEERING AT OREGON HEALTH & SCIENCE UNIVERSITY

Biochemistry	M,D
Biomedical Engineering	M,D
Business Administration and Management—General	M,O
Computer Engineering	M,D
Computer Science	M,D
Electrical Engineering	M,D
Environmental and Occupational Health	M,D
Environmental Engineering	M,D
Environmental Sciences	M,D
Health Services Management and Hospital Administration	M,O
Management of Technology	M,O
Molecular Biology	M,D
Ocean Engineering	M,D

OGLALA LAKOTA COLLEGE

Business Administration and Management—General	M
Educational Leadership and Administration	M

OGLETHORPE UNIVERSITY

Early Childhood Education	M
Education—General	M

OHIO COLLEGE OF PODIATRIC MEDICINE

Podiatric Medicine	P

OHIO DOMINICAN UNIVERSITY

Business Administration and Management—General	M
Education—General	M
English as a Second Language	M
Liberal Studies	M
Theology	M

OHIO NORTHERN UNIVERSITY

Law	P,M
Pharmacy	P

THE OHIO STATE UNIVERSITY

Accounting	M
Aerospace/Aeronautical Engineering	M,D
African Studies	M
African-American Studies	M
Agricultural Economics and Agribusiness	M,D
Agricultural Education	M,D
Agricultural Engineering	M,D
Agricultural Sciences—General	M,D
Agronomy and Soil Sciences	M,D
Allied Health—General	M
Allopathic Medicine	P
Anatomy	M,D
Animal Sciences	M,D
Anthropology	M,D
Architecture	M
Art Education	M,D
Art History	M,D
Art/Fine Arts	M
Arts Administration	M
Asian Languages	M,D
Astronomy	M,D
Atmospheric Sciences	M,D
Biochemistry	M
Bioengineering	M,D
Biological and Biomedical Sciences—General	M,D
Biomedical Engineering	M,D
Biophysics	M,D
Biostatistics	D
Business Administration and Management—General	M,D
Cardiovascular Sciences	M
Cell Biology	M,D
Chemical Engineering	M,D
Chemical Physics	M,D
Chemistry	M,D
Child and Family Studies	M,D
Chinese	M,D
Civil Engineering	M,D
Classics	M,D
Clinical Psychology	M,D
Clothing and Textiles	M,D
Cognitive Sciences	M,D
Communication Disorders	M,D
Communication—General	M,D
Computer Engineering	M,D
Computer Science	M,D
Consumer Economics	M,D
Dance	D
Dentistry	P,M
Developmental Biology	M,D
Developmental Psychology	M,D
East European and Russian Studies	M
Ecology	M,D
Economics	M,D
Education—General	M,D
Educational Leadership and Administration	M,D
Educational Policy	M,D
Electrical Engineering	M,D
Engineering and Applied Sciences—General	M,D
Engineering Physics	M,D
English	M,D
Entomology	M,D
Environmental Sciences	M,D
Evolutionary Biology	M,D
Family and Consumer Sciences-General	M
Film, Television, and Video Theory and Criticism	M
Finance and Banking	M,D
Food Science and Technology	M,D
French	M,D
Genetics	M,D
Geodetic Sciences	M,D
Geography	M,D
Geology	M,D
German	M,D
Health Services Management and Hospital Administration	M,D
Higher Education	M
History	M,D

*M—master's degree; P—first professional degree; D—doctorate; O—other advanced degree; *—Close-Up and/or Announcement or Display in one of the other books in this series*

Home Economics Education	M
Horticulture	M,D
Hospitality Management	M,D
Human Development	M,D
Human Resources Management	M,D
Immunology	M,D
Industrial and Labor Relations	M,D
Industrial Design	M
Industrial/Management Engineering	M,D
Information Science	M,D
Interdisciplinary Studies	M,D
Interior Design	M
Italian	M,D
Japanese	M,D
Journalism	M
Landscape Architecture	M
Law	P,M
Linguistics	M,D
Logistics	M
Management Information Systems	M,D
Materials Engineering	M,D
Materials Sciences	M,D*
Mathematics	M,D
Mechanical Engineering	M,D
Mechanics	M,D
Medicinal and Pharmaceutical Chemistry	M,D
Metallurgical Engineering and Metallurgy	M,D
Microbiology	M,D
Molecular Biology	M,D
Molecular Genetics	M,D
Music	M,D
Natural Resources	M,D
Near and Middle Eastern Languages	M,D
Neuroscience	M,D
Nuclear Engineering	M,D
Nursing—General	M,D
Nutrition	M,D
Occupational Therapy	M
Optical Sciences	M,D
Optometry	P
Oral and Dental Sciences	D
Pathobiology	M,D
Pathology	M
Pharmaceutical Administration	M,D
Pharmaceutical Sciences	M,D
Pharmacology	M,D
Pharmacy	P
Philosophy	M,D
Photography	M
Physical Education	M,D
Physical Therapy	M
Physics	M,D
Physiology	M,D
Plant Biology	M,D
Plant Pathology	M,D
Political Science	M,D
Portuguese	M,D
Psychology—General	M,D
Public Affairs	M,D
Public Health—General	M,D
Rural Sociology	M,D
Slavic Languages	M,D
Social Psychology	M,D
Social Work	M,D
Sociology	M,D
Spanish	M,D
Statistics	M,D
Student Affairs	M
Surveying Science and Engineering	M,D
Systems Engineering	M,D
Theater	M,D
Toxicology	M,D
Urban and Regional Planning	M,D
Veterinary Medicine	P
Veterinary Sciences	M,D
Virology	M,D
Vocational and Technical Education	D
Women's Studies	M,D

THE OHIO STATE UNIVERSITY AT LIMA

Early Childhood Education	M
Education—General	M
Middle School Education	M
Social Work	M

THE OHIO STATE UNIVERSITY AT MARION

Early Childhood Education	M,D
Education—General	M,D
Middle School Education	M,D
Nursing—General	M,D
Social Work	M,D

THE OHIO STATE UNIVERSITY–MANSFIELD CAMPUS

Early Childhood Education	M
Middle School Education	M
Social Work	M

THE OHIO STATE UNIVERSITY–NEWARK CAMPUS

Early Childhood Education	M
Education—General	M
Middle School Education	M
Social Work	M

OHIO UNIVERSITY

African Studies	M
Applied Economics	M
Art History	M
Art/Fine Arts	M
Asian Studies	M
Astronomy	M,D
Athletic Training and Sports Medicine	M
Biochemistry	M,D
Biological and Biomedical Sciences—General	M,D
Biomedical Engineering	M
Business Administration and Management—General	M
Cell Biology	M,D
Chemical Engineering	M,D
Child and Family Studies	M
Child Development	M
Civil Engineering	M,D
Clinical Psychology	D
Communication Disorders	M,D
Communication—General	M,D
Comparative and Interdisciplinary Arts	D
Computer Education	M,D
Computer Science	M,D
Construction Engineering	M,D
Counselor Education	M,D
Curriculum and Instruction	M,D
Early Childhood Education	M
Ecology	M,D
Economics	M
Education—General	M,D
Educational Leadership and Administration	M,D
Educational Measurement and Evaluation	M,D
Educational Media/ Instructional Technology	M,D
Electrical Engineering	M,D
Engineering and Applied Sciences—General	M,D
English as a Second Language	M
English	M,D
Environmental Biology	M,D
Environmental Engineering	M,D
Environmental Management and Policy	M
Evolutionary Biology	M,D
Exercise and Sports Science	M,D
Experimental Psychology	D
Family and Consumer Sciences-General	M
Film, Television, and Video Production	M
Film, Television, and Video Theory and Criticism	M
Finance and Banking	M
French	M
Geochemistry	M
Geography	M
Geology	M
Geophysics	M
Geotechnical Engineering	M,D
Graphic Design	M
Health Services Management and Hospital Administration	M
Higher Education	M,D
History	M,D
Hydrogeology	M
Industrial and Organizational Psychology	D
Industrial/Management Engineering	M,D
International Affairs	M
International Development	M
Journalism	M,D
Latin American Studies	M
Linguistics	M
Manufacturing Engineering	M,D
Mathematics Education	M,D
Mathematics	M,D
Mechanical Engineering	M,D
Media Studies	M,D
Microbiology	M,D
Middle School Education	M,D
Molecular Biology	M,D*
Multilingual and Multicultural Education	M,D
Music Education	M,O
Music	M,O
Neuroscience	M,D
Nutrition	M
Osteopathic Medicine	P
Philosophy	M
Photography	M
Physical Education	M
Physical Therapy	D
Physics	M,D*
Physiology	M,D
Plant Biology	M,D
Political Science	M
Psychology—General	D
Public Administration	M
Reading Education	M,D
Recreation and Park Management	M
Rehabilitation Counseling	M,D
Science Education	M
Secondary Education	M,D
Social Sciences Education	M,D
Social Sciences	M
Social Work	M
Sociology	M
Spanish	M
Special Education	M,D
Speech and Interpersonal Communication	D
Sports Management	M
Structural Engineering	M,D
Student Affairs	M,D
Systems Engineering	M
Telecommunications	M
Theater	M
Therapies—Dance, Drama, and Music	M,O
Transportation and Highway Engineering	M,D
Water Resources Engineering	M,D

OHR HAMEIR THEOLOGICAL SEMINARY

Theology	

OKLAHOMA CHRISTIAN UNIVERSITY

Pastoral Ministry and Counseling	P,M
Theology	P,M

OKLAHOMA CITY UNIVERSITY

Accounting	M
Art/Fine Arts	M
Business Administration and Management—General	M
Comparative Literature	M
Computer Science	M
Corporate and Organizational Communication	M
Criminal Justice and Criminology	M
Dance	M
Early Childhood Education	M
Education—General	M
Educational Psychology	M
Elementary Education	M
English as a Second Language	M
Finance and Banking	M
Health Services Management and Hospital Administration	M
International Business	M
Law	P
Liberal Studies	M
Management Information Systems	M
Marketing	M
Mass Communication	M
Music	M
Nursing—General	M
Philosophy	M
Religion	M
Theater	M
Writing	M

OKLAHOMA STATE UNIVERSITY

Accounting	M,D
Agricultural Economics and Agribusiness	M,D
Agricultural Education	M,D
Agricultural Engineering	M,D
Agricultural Sciences—General	M,D
Agronomy and Soil Sciences	M,D
Animal Sciences	M,D
Applied Arts and Design—General	M,D
Applied Mathematics	M,D
Applied Science and Technology	M,D
Biochemistry	M,D*
Bioengineering	M,D
Biotechnology	M,D
Botany	M,D
Business Administration and Management—General	M,D*
Chemical Engineering	M,D
Chemistry	M,D
Child and Family Studies	M,D
Civil Engineering	M,D
Clinical Psychology	M,D
Clothing and Textiles	M,D
Communication Disorders	M
Computer Engineering	M,D
Computer Science	M,D
Consumer Economics	M,D
Curriculum and Instruction	M,D
Economics	M,D
Education—General	M,D,O
Educational Leadership and Administration	M,D
Educational Psychology	M,D,O
Electrical Engineering	M,D
Emergency Management	M,D
Engineering and Applied Sciences—General	M,D*
English	M,D

Entomology M,D
Environmental Engineering M,D
Environmental Sciences M,D
Family and Consumer Sciences-General M,D
Finance and Banking M,D
Fire Protection Engineering M,D
Food Science and Technology M,D
Forestry M,D
Geography M,D
Geology M,D
Health Education M,D,O
Higher Education M,D
History M,D
Horticulture M,D
Hospitality Management M,D
Human Development M,D
Industrial/Management Engineering M,D
Information Science M,D
Landscape Architecture M,D
Management Information Systems M,D
Marketing M,D
Mass Communication M
Mathematics Education M,D
Mathematics M,D*
Mechanical Engineering M,D
Microbiology M,D
Molecular Biology M,D
Molecular Genetics M,D
Music Education M
Music M
Natural Resources M,D
Nutrition M,D
Philosophy M
Photonics M,D
Physics M,D
Plant Pathology M,D
Plant Sciences M,D
Political Science M,D
Psychology—General M,D
Quantitative Analysis M,D
Sociology M,D
Statistics M,D
Telecommunications Management M,D
Theater M
Veterinary Medicine P
Veterinary Sciences M,D
Writing M,D
Zoology M,D

OKLAHOMA STATE UNIVERSITY CENTER FOR HEALTH SCIENCES

Biological and Biomedical Sciences—General M,D
Forensic Psychology M,O
Forensic Sciences M,O
Molecular Biology M,O
Osteopathic Medicine P
Toxicology M,O

OLD DOMINION UNIVERSITY

Accounting M
Aerospace/Aeronautical Engineering M,D
Allied Health—General M,D
Analytical Chemistry M,D
Applied Economics M
Athletic Training and Sports Medicine M
Automotive Engineering M
Biochemistry M,D
Biological and Biomedical Sciences—General M,D
Business Administration and Management—General M,D
Business Education M,D
Chemistry M,D
Civil Engineering M,D
Clinical Psychology D
Communication Disorders M
Community College Education M,D
Community Health M
Computer Engineering M,D
Computer Science M,D
Conflict Resolution and Mediation/Peace Studies M,D
Counselor Education M,D,O
Criminal Justice and Criminology D
Curriculum and Instruction M,D
Dental Hygiene M
Early Childhood Education M,D
Ecology D
Economics M
Education—General M,D,O
Educational Leadership and Administration M,D,O
Educational Media/Instructional Technology M,D
Electrical Engineering M,D
Elementary Education M
Engineering and Applied Sciences—General M,D
Engineering Management M,D
English M,D
Environmental and Occupational Health M
Environmental Engineering M,D
Ergonomics and Human Factors D
Exercise and Sports Science M
Experimental Psychology D
Family Nurse Practitioner Studies M
Finance and Banking M,D
Health Promotion M
Health Services Management and Hospital Administration M
Health Services Research D
Higher Education M,D,O
History M
Human-Computer Interaction M,D
Humanities M
Industrial and Organizational Psychology D
Information Science D
International Affairs M,D
International Business M
Kinesiology and Movement Studies D
Library Science M
Linguistics M
Management Information Systems M
Management of Technology M
Manufacturing Engineering M,D
Marine Affairs M
Marketing D
Mathematics M,D
Mechanical Engineering M,D
Middle School Education M
Music Education M
Nurse Anesthesia M
Nurse Midwifery M
Nursing Education M
Nursing—General M,D
Oceanography M,D
Organic Chemistry M,D
Physical Chemistry M,D
Physical Education M
Physical Therapy D
Physics M,D
Psychology—General M,D
Public Administration M,D
Public Health—General M
Reading Education M,D
Recreation and Park Management M
Science Education M
Secondary Education M
Sociology M
Special Education M,D
Sports Management M
Systems Engineering M,D
Travel and Tourism M
Urban Studies D
Vocational and Technical Education M,D
Women's Health Nursing M
Women's Studies M,D
Writing M

OLIVET COLLEGE

Education—General M

OLIVET NAZARENE UNIVERSITY

Business Administration and Management—General M
Curriculum and Instruction M
Education—General M
Educational Leadership and Administration M
Elementary Education M
Library Science M
Organizational Management M
Reading Education M
Religion M
Secondary Education M
Theology M

ORAL ROBERTS UNIVERSITY

Accounting M
Business Administration and Management—General M
Curriculum and Instruction M,D
Education—General M,D
Educational Leadership and Administration M,D
English as a Second Language M,D
Entrepreneurship M
Finance and Banking M
Higher Education M,D
International Business M
Marketing M
Marriage and Family Therapy P,M,D
Missions and Missiology P,M,D
Near and Middle Eastern Languages P,M,D
Nonprofit Management M
Organizational Behavior M
Pastoral Ministry and Counseling P,M,D
Religious Education P,M,D
Theology P,M,D

OREGON COLLEGE OF ORIENTAL MEDICINE

Acupuncture and Oriental Medicine M,D

OREGON HEALTH & SCIENCE UNIVERSITY

Allopathic Medicine P
Biochemistry M,D
Bioinformatics M,D,O
Biological and Biomedical Sciences—General M,D,O
Biomedical Engineering M,D
Biopsychology M,D
Biostatistics M
Cell Biology D
Community Health Nursing M,O
Computer Engineering M,D
Computer Science M,D
Dentistry P,O
Developmental Biology D
Electrical Engineering M,D
Environmental Engineering M,D
Environmental Sciences M,D
Epidemiology M
Family Nurse Practitioner Studies M,O
Genetics D
Gerontological Nursing O
Gerontology M,O
Immunology D
Management of Technology M
Medical Informatics M,D,O
Microbiology D
Molecular Biology M,D
Neuroscience M,D*
Nurse Anesthesia M
Nurse Midwifery M,O
Nursing Education M,O
Nursing—General M,D,O
Nutrition M
Oral and Dental Sciences P,M,O
Pharmacology D
Physiology D
Psychiatric Nursing M,O

OREGON STATE UNIVERSITY

Adult Education M
Agricultural Economics and Agribusiness M,D
Agricultural Education M
Agricultural Sciences—General M,D
Agronomy and Soil Sciences M,D
Analytical Chemistry M,D
Animal Sciences M,D
Anthropology M
Applied Physics M,D
Atmospheric Sciences M,D
Biochemistry M,D
Bioengineering M,D
Biophysics M,D
Botany M,D
Business Administration and Management—General M,O
Cell Biology M,D
Chemical Engineering M,D
Chemistry M,D
Child and Family Studies M,D
Civil Engineering M,D
Clothing and Textiles M,D
Computer Engineering M,D
Computer Science M,D
Construction Engineering M,D
Counselor Education M,D
Economics M,D
Education—General M,D
Educational Leadership and Administration M
Electrical Engineering M,D*
Elementary Education M
Engineering and Applied Sciences—General M,D*
English M
Environmental and Occupational Health M
Environmental Engineering M,D
Environmental Sciences M,D
Ethics M
Exercise and Sports Science M,D
Family and Consumer Sciences-General M
Fish, Game, and Wildlife Management M,D
Food Science and Technology M,D
Foreign Languages Education M
Forestry M,D
Genetics M,D
Geography M,D
Geology M,D
Geophysics M,D

*M—master's degree; P—first professional degree; D—doctorate; O—other advanced degree; *—Close-Up and/or Announcement or Display in one of the other books in this series*

Geosciences	M,D
Geotechnical Engineering	M,D
Gerontology	M
Health Physics/ Radiological Health	M,D
Health Promotion	M,D
Health Services Management and Hospital Administration	M,D
Hispanic Studies	M
History of Science and Technology	M,D
History	M,D
Horticulture	M,D
Human Development	M,D
Industrial/Management Engineering	M,D
Inorganic Chemistry	M,D
Interdisciplinary Studies	M
Kinesiology and Movement Studies	M
Manufacturing Engineering	M,D
Marine Affairs	M
Marine Sciences	M
Materials Sciences	M,D
Mathematics Education	M,D
Mathematics	M,D
Mechanical Engineering	M,D
Microbiology	M,D
Molecular Biology	M,D
Molecular Toxicology	M,D
Music Education	M
Nanotechnology	M,D
Nuclear Engineering	M,D
Nutrition	M,D
Ocean Engineering	M,D
Oceanography	M,D
Operations Research	M,D
Organic Chemistry	M,D
Paper and Pulp Engineering	M,D
Pharmaceutical Sciences	P,M,D
Pharmacy	P,M,D
Philosophy	M
Physical Chemistry	M,D
Physical Education	M
Physics	M,D*
Plant Pathology	M,D
Plant Physiology	M,D
Public Health—General	M,D
Range Science	M,D
Reading Education	M
Science Education	M,D
Statistics	M,D
Structural Engineering	M,D
Student Affairs	M
Systems Engineering	M,D
Toxicology	M,D
Transportation and Highway Engineering	M,D
Veterinary Medicine	P
Veterinary Sciences	D
Water Resources Engineering	M,D
Zoology	M,D

OREGON STATE UNIVERSITY–CASCADES

Education—General	M
School Psychology	M
Social Psychology	M

OTIS COLLEGE OF ART AND DESIGN

Art/Fine Arts	M
Graphic Design	M
Photography	M
Writing	M

OTTAWA UNIVERSITY

Art Therapy	M
Business Administration and Management—General	M
Counseling Psychology	M
Counselor Education	M
Curriculum and Instruction	M
Early Childhood Education	M
Education—General	M
Educational Leadership and Administration	M
Educational Media/ Instructional Technology	M
Elementary Education	M
Finance and Banking	M
Human Resources Development	M
Human Resources Management	M
Marketing	M
Marriage and Family Therapy	M
Pastoral Ministry and Counseling	M
School Psychology	M
Special Education	M

OTTERBEIN COLLEGE

Adult Nursing	M,O
Business Administration and Management—General	M
Education—General	M
Family Nurse Practitioner Studies	M,O
Nursing and Healthcare Administration	M,O
Nursing—General	M,O

OUR LADY OF HOLY CROSS COLLEGE

Counselor Education	M
Curriculum and Instruction	M
Education—General	M
Educational Leadership and Administration	M
Marriage and Family Therapy	M

OUR LADY OF THE LAKE UNIVERSITY OF SAN ANTONIO

Accounting	M
Business Administration and Management—General	M
Communication Disorders	M
Communication—General	M
Computer and Information Systems Security	M
Counseling Psychology	M,D
Counselor Education	M
Curriculum and Instruction	M
Early Childhood Education	M
Education—General	M,D
Educational Leadership and Administration	M
Educational Media/ Instructional Technology	M
Elementary Education	M
English as a Second Language	M
English Education	M
English	M
Finance and Banking	M
Health Services Management and Hospital Administration	M
Human Development	M
Management Information Systems	M
Marriage and Family Therapy	M,D
Mathematics Education	M
Middle School Education	M
Multilingual and Multicultural Education	M
Nonprofit Management	M
Organizational Management	M,D
Psychology—General	M,D
Reading Education	M
School Psychology	M,D
Science Education	M
Secondary Education	M
Social Work	M
Special Education	M
Vocational and Technical Education	M
Writing	M

OXFORD GRADUATE SCHOOL

Child and Family Studies	M,D
Organizational Management	M,D
Religion	M,D

PACE UNIVERSITY

Accounting	M
Addictions/Substance Abuse Counseling	M
Business Administration and Management—General	M,D,O
Computer Science	M,D,O
Counseling Psychology	M
Curriculum and Instruction	M,O
Economics	M
Education—General	M,O
Educational Leadership and Administration	M,O
Environmental Law	P,M,D
Environmental Sciences	M
Family Nurse Practitioner Studies	M,D,O
Finance and Banking	M
Forensic Sciences	M
Health Services Management and Hospital Administration	M
Information Science	M,D,O
International Business	M
Investment Management	M
Law	P,M,D*
Legal and Justice Studies	P,M,D
Management Information Systems	M
Management Strategy and Policy	M
Marketing Research	M
Marketing	M
Nonprofit Management	M
Nursing Education	M,D,O
Nursing—General	M,D,O
Physician Assistant Studies	M
Psychology—General	M
Public Administration	M
Publishing	M
Taxation	M
Telecommunications	M,D,O
Theater	M

PACIFICA GRADUATE INSTITUTE

Clinical Psychology	M,D
Counseling Psychology	M,D
Psychology—General	M,D

PACIFIC COLLEGE OF ORIENTAL MEDICINE

Acupuncture and Oriental Medicine	M,D

PACIFIC COLLEGE OF ORIENTAL MEDICINE-CHICAGO

Acupuncture and Oriental Medicine	M

PACIFIC COLLEGE OF ORIENTAL MEDICINE-NEW YORK

Acupuncture and Oriental Medicine	M

PACIFIC LUTHERAN THEOLOGICAL SEMINARY

Theology	P,M,D,O

PACIFIC LUTHERAN UNIVERSITY

Business Administration and Management—General	M
Curriculum and Instruction	M
Education—General	M
Educational Leadership and Administration	M
Family Nurse Practitioner Studies	M
Management of Technology	M
Marriage and Family Therapy	M
Nursing and Healthcare Administration	M
Nursing—General	M
Writing	M

PACIFIC OAKS COLLEGE

Human Development	M
Marriage and Family Therapy	M

PACIFIC SCHOOL OF RELIGION

Religion	P,M,D,O
Theology	P,M,D,O

PACIFIC STATES UNIVERSITY

Accounting	M,D
Business Administration and Management—General	M,D
Computer Science	M
Finance and Banking	M,D
International Business	M,D
Management Information Systems	M,D
Management of Technology	M,D
Real Estate	M,D

PACIFIC UNION COLLEGE

Education—General	M

PACIFIC UNIVERSITY

Early Childhood Education	M
Education—General	M
Elementary Education	M
Middle School Education	M
Occupational Therapy	M
Pharmacy	P
Physical Therapy	D
Physician Assistant Studies	M
Psychology—General	M,D
Secondary Education	M
Special Education	M

PALM BEACH ATLANTIC UNIVERSITY

Addictions/Substance Abuse Counseling	M
Business Administration and Management—General	M
Counseling Psychology	M
Counselor Education	M
Education—General	M
Marriage and Family Therapy	M
Organizational Management	M
Pharmacy	P

PALMER COLLEGE OF CHIROPRACTIC

Anatomy	M
Chiropractic	P
Clinical Research	M

PALO ALTO UNIVERSITY

Biopsychology	D

Clinical Psychology	D*
Psychology—General	M,D*

PARKER COLLEGE OF CHIROPRACTIC

Chiropractic	P

PARK UNIVERSITY

Business Administration and Management—General	M
Education—General	M
Educational Leadership and Administration	M
Emergency Management	M
Entrepreneurship	M
Health Services Management and Hospital Administration	M
International Business	M
Law	M
Management Information Systems	M
Middle School Education	M
Multilingual and Multicultural Education	M
Nonprofit Management	M
Public Administration	M
Public Affairs	M
Secondary Education	M
Special Education	M

PAYNE THEOLOGICAL SEMINARY

Theology	P

PENN STATE DICKINSON SCHOOL OF LAW

Law	P,M

PENN STATE ERIE, THE BEHREND COLLEGE

Business Administration and Management—General	M
Project Management	M

PENN STATE GREAT VALLEY

Agricultural Engineering	M
Business Administration and Management—General	M
Curriculum and Instruction	M
Education—General	M
Educational Leadership and Administration	M
Educational Media/Instructional Technology	M
Engineering Management	M
Entrepreneurship	M
Health Services Management and Hospital Administration	M
Information Science	M
Management Information Systems	M
Science Education	M
Software Engineering	M
Special Education	M

PENN STATE HARRISBURG

American Studies	M,D
Business Administration and Management—General	M
Business Education	M,D
Clinical Psychology	M,D
Computer Science	M
Criminal Justice and Criminology	M,D
Curriculum and Instruction	M,D
Education—General	M,D
Electrical Engineering	M
Engineering and Applied Sciences—General	M
Engineering Management	M
Environmental Engineering	M
Environmental Sciences	M
Health Education	M,D
Health Services Management and Hospital Administration	M,D
Humanities	M,D
Management Information Systems	M
Psychology—General	M,D
Public Administration	M,D
Reading Education	M,D
Social Psychology	M,D

PENN STATE HERSHEY MEDICAL CENTER

Allopathic Medicine	P,M,D
Anatomy	M,D
Biochemistry	M,D
Bioengineering	M,D
Biological and Biomedical Sciences—General	M,D
Cell Biology	M,D
Genetics	M,D
Health Services Research	M
Immunology	M,D
Microbiology	M,D
Molecular Biology	M,D
Molecular Medicine	M,D
Molecular Toxicology	M,D
Neuroscience	M,D
Pharmacology	M,D
Physiology	M,D
Public Health—General	M
Veterinary Sciences	M
Virology	M,D

PENN STATE UNIVERSITY PARK

Acoustics	M,D
Adult Education	M,D
Aerospace/Aeronautical Engineering	M,D
Agricultural Economics and Agribusiness	M,D
Agricultural Education	M,D
Agricultural Engineering	M,D
Agricultural Sciences—General	M,D
Agronomy and Soil Sciences	M,D
Animal Sciences	M,D
Anthropology	M,D
Applied Mathematics	M,D
Applied Statistics	M,D
Architectural Engineering	M,D
Architecture	M
Art Education	M,D
Art History	M,D
Art/Fine Arts	M,D
Astronomy	M,D
Astrophysics	M,D
Biochemistry	M,D*
Bioengineering	M,D
Biological and Biomedical Sciences—General	M,D
Biomedical Engineering	M,D
Biopsychology	M,D
Biotechnology	M,D*
Business Administration and Management—General	M,D
Cell Biology	M,D
Chemical Engineering	M,D
Chemistry	M,D
Child and Family Studies	M,D
Civil Engineering	M,D
Clinical Psychology	M,D
Cognitive Sciences	M,D
Communication Disorders	M,D
Communication—General	M,D
Comparative Literature	M,D
Computer Engineering	M,D
Computer Science	M,D*
Counseling Psychology	M,D
Counselor Education	M,D
Criminal Justice and Criminology	M,D
Curriculum and Instruction	M,D
Demography and Population Studies	M,D
Developmental Biology	M,D
Developmental Psychology	M,D
Early Childhood Education	M,D
Ecology	M,D
Economics	M,D
Education—General	M,D
Educational Leadership and Administration	M,D
Educational Media/Instructional Technology	M,D
Educational Psychology	M,D
Electrical Engineering	M,D
Elementary Education	M,D
Engineering and Applied Sciences—General	M,D
English Education	M,D
English	M,D
Entomology	M,D
Environmental Engineering	M,D
Environmental Management and Policy	M
Environmental Sciences	M
Evolutionary Biology	M,D
Fish, Game, and Wildlife Management	M,D
Food Science and Technology	M,D
Forestry	M,D
Foundations and Philosophy of Education	M,D
French	M,D
Genetics	M,D
Geochemistry	M,D
Geosciences	M,D
German	M,D
Health Services Management and Hospital Administration	M,D
Higher Education	M,D
History	M,D
Horticulture	M,D
Hospitality Management	M,D
Human Development	M,D
Human Resources Development	M
Immunology	M,D
Industrial and Labor Relations	M
Industrial and Manufacturing Management	M
Industrial and Organizational Psychology	M,D
Industrial/Management Engineering	M,D
Kinesiology and Movement Studies	M,D
Landscape Architecture	M
Leisure Studies	M,D
Manufacturing Engineering	M,D
Materials Engineering	M,D
Materials Sciences	M,D
Mathematics Education	M,D
Mathematics	M,D
Mechanical Engineering	M,D
Mechanics	M,D
Meteorology	M,D
Microbiology	M,D
Molecular Biology	M,D
Molecular Medicine	M,D
Multilingual and Multicultural Education	M,D
Music Education	M,D
Music	M,D
Natural Resources	M,D
Neuroscience	M,D
Nuclear Engineering	M,D
Nursing—General	M,D
Nutrition	M,D
Operations Research	M,D
Pathobiology	D
Philosophy	M,D
Photography	M,D
Physics	M,D*
Physiology	M,D
Plant Pathology	M,D
Plant Physiology	M,D
Political Science	M,D
Psychology—General	M,D
Quality Management	M
Reading Education	M,D
Recreation and Park Management	M,D
Rural Sociology	M,D
Russian	M,D
School Psychology	M,D
Science Education	M,D
Social Psychology	M,D
Social Sciences Education	M,D
Sociology	M,D
Spanish	M,D
Special Education	M,D
Statistics	M,D
Structural Engineering	M,D
Student Affairs	M,D
Supply Chain Management	M,D
Theater	M
Transportation and Highway Engineering	M,D
Veterinary Sciences	D
Vocational and Technical Education	M,D
Water Resources Engineering	M,D
Writing	M,D

PENNSYLVANIA ACADEMY OF THE FINE ARTS

Art/Fine Arts	M,O

PEPPERDINE UNIVERSITY

Business Administration and Management—General	M
Clinical Psychology	M,D
Education—General	M,D
Educational Leadership and Administration	M,D
Educational Media/Instructional Technology	M,D
Finance and Banking	M
International Business	M
Marriage and Family Therapy	M,D
Organizational Management	M
Psychology—General	M,D

PEPPERDINE UNIVERSITY

American Studies	M
Business Administration and Management—General	M
Clinical Psychology	M
Communication—General	M
Conflict Resolution and Mediation/Peace Studies	M
Economics	M
History	M
Humanities	M
International Affairs	M
International Business	M
Law	P
Political Science	M
Psychology—General	M
Public Administration	M
Public Policy	M
Religion	P,M

PERU STATE COLLEGE

Curriculum and Instruction	M
Economics	M
Education—General	M

*M—master's degree; P—first professional degree; D—doctorate; O—other advanced degree; *—Close-Up and/or Announcement or Display in one of the other books in this series*

Entrepreneurship	M
Organizational Management	M

PFEIFFER UNIVERSITY

Business Administration and Management—General	M
Education—General	M
Elementary Education	M
Health Services Management and Hospital Administration	M
Organizational Management	M
Religious Education	M

PHILADELPHIA BIBLICAL UNIVERSITY

Curriculum and Instruction	M
Education—General	M
Educational Leadership and Administration	M
Organizational Management	M
Pastoral Ministry and Counseling	M
Theology	P,M

PHILADELPHIA COLLEGE OF OSTEOPATHIC MEDICINE

Biological and Biomedical Sciences—General	M,O
Clinical Psychology	M,D,O
Counseling Psychology	M,D,O
Forensic Sciences	M
Health Psychology	M,D,O
Industrial and Organizational Psychology	M,D,O
Osteopathic Medicine	P
Physician Assistant Studies	M*
Psychology—General	M,D,O*
School Psychology	M,D,O

PHILADELPHIA UNIVERSITY

Architecture	M
Business Administration and Management—General	M
Clothing and Textiles	M
Computer Art and Design	M
Construction Management	M
Emergency Management	M
Finance and Banking	M
Health Services Management and Hospital Administration	M
International Business	M
Marketing	M
Nurse Midwifery	M,O
Occupational Therapy	M*
Physician Assistant Studies	M
Sustainable Development	M
Taxation	M
Textile Design	M
Textile Sciences and Engineering	M,D

PHILLIPS GRADUATE INSTITUTE

Clinical Psychology	D
Counselor Education	M
Marriage and Family Therapy	M,D
Organizational Behavior	M,D

PHILLIPS THEOLOGICAL SEMINARY

Business Administration and Management—General	P,M,D
Ethics	P,M,D
Higher Education	P,M,D
Missions and Missiology	P,M,D
Music	P,M,D
Pastoral Ministry and Counseling	D
Religious Education	P,M,D
Social Work	P,M,D
Theology	P,M,D

PIEDMONT BAPTIST COLLEGE AND GRADUATE SCHOOL

Theology	M,D

PIEDMONT COLLEGE

Business Administration and Management—General	M
Curriculum and Instruction	M,O
Early Childhood Education	M,O
Education—General	M,O
Secondary Education	M,O

PIKEVILLE COLLEGE

Osteopathic Medicine	P

PITTSBURGH THEOLOGICAL SEMINARY

Theology	P,M,D

PITTSBURG STATE UNIVERSITY

Accounting	M
Applied Physics	M
Art Education	M
Art/Fine Arts	M
Biological and Biomedical Sciences—General	M
Business Administration and Management—General	M
Chemistry	M
Communication—General	M
Community College Education	O
Counselor Education	M
Early Childhood Education	M
Education—General	M,O
Educational Leadership and Administration	M
Educational Media/Instructional Technology	M
Elementary Education	M
Engineering and Applied Sciences—General	M
English	M
Graphic Design	M,O
Higher Education	M,O
History	M
Human Resources Development	M
Mathematics	M
Music Education	M
Music	M
Nursing—General	M
Physical Education	M
Physics	M
Psychology—General	M
Reading Education	M
School Psychology	O
Secondary Education	M
Social Psychology	M
Special Education	M
Theater	M
Vocational and Technical Education	M,O

PLYMOUTH STATE UNIVERSITY

Athletic Training and Sports Medicine	M
Business Administration and Management—General	M
Counselor Education	M
Education—General	O
Educational Leadership and Administration	M
Elementary Education	M
English Education	M
Environmental Management and Policy	M
Health Education	M
Mathematics Education	M
Meteorology	M
Middle School Education	M
Reading Education	M
Science Education	M
Secondary Education	M
Special Education	M,O

POINT LOMA NAZARENE UNIVERSITY

Biological and Biomedical Sciences—General	M
Business Administration and Management—General	M
Education—General	M,O
Nursing—General	M
Religion	M

POINT PARK UNIVERSITY

Business Administration and Management—General	M
Communication—General	M*
Criminal Justice and Criminology	M
Curriculum and Instruction	M
Education—General	M
Educational Leadership and Administration	M
Engineering Management	M
Journalism	M
Mass Communication	M
Music	M
Organizational Management	M
Theater	M

POLYTECHNIC INSTITUTE OF NYU

Bioinformatics	M
Biomedical Engineering	M,D
Biotechnology	M
Business Administration and Management—General	M,D
Chemical Engineering	M,D
Chemistry	M,D
Civil Engineering	M,D
Communication—General	O
Computer and Information Systems Security	O
Computer Engineering	M,O
Computer Science	M,D
Construction Management	M
Criminal Justice and Criminology	M,D,O
Electrical Engineering	M,D
Engineering Physics	M
Entrepreneurship	M
Environmental Engineering	M
Environmental Sciences	M
Film, Television, and Video Production	O
Finance and Banking	M,O
Financial Engineering	M,O
History of Science and Technology	M
Humanities	M,O
Industrial/Management Engineering	M
Internet and Interactive Multimedia	M,O
Journalism	M
Management of Technology	M,D
Manufacturing Engineering	M
Materials Sciences	M
Mathematical and Computational Finance	M,O
Mathematics	M,D
Mechanical Engineering	M,D
Organizational Behavior	M
Physics	M,D
Polymer Science and Engineering	M
Psychology—General	M
Software Engineering	O
Systems Engineering	M
Technical Communication	O
Technical Writing	M
Telecommunications Management	M
Telecommunications	M
Transportation and Highway Engineering	M,D
Transportation Management	M

POLYTECHNIC INSTITUTE OF NYU, LONG ISLAND GRADUATE CENTER

Aerospace/Aeronautical Engineering	M,D
Biological and Biomedical Sciences—General	M,D,O
Biomedical Engineering	M,D,O
Biotechnology	M,D,O
Business Administration and Management—General	M,O
Chemical Engineering	M,D
Chemistry	M,D
Civil Engineering	M,D
Computer Engineering	M
Computer Science	M,D
Electrical Engineering	M,D
Engineering Design	M
Engineering Physics	M
Entrepreneurship	M,D,O
Environmental Engineering	M
Financial Engineering	M,O
Industrial/Management Engineering	M,D
Manufacturing Engineering	M,D
Materials Sciences	M,D
Mechanical Engineering	M,D
Software Engineering	M
Systems Engineering	M
Telecommunications	M
Transportation and Highway Engineering	M

POLYTECHNIC INSTITUTE OF NYU, WESTCHESTER GRADUATE CENTER

Business Administration and Management—General	M
Chemical Engineering	M
Chemistry	M
Computer Engineering	M
Computer Science	M,D
Electrical Engineering	M,D
Finance and Banking	M,O
Financial Engineering	M,O
Information Science	M
Management Information Systems	M,O
Management of Technology	M
Materials Sciences	D
Mathematical and Computational Finance	M,O
Telecommunications	M

POLYTECHNIC UNIVERSITY OF PUERTO RICO

Business Administration and Management—General	M
Civil Engineering	M
Electrical Engineering	M
Engineering Management	M
Environmental Management and Policy	M
Industrial and Manufacturing Management	M

International Business M
Management of Technology M
Manufacturing Engineering M

POLYTECHNIC UNIVERSITY OF THE AMERICAS–MIAMI CAMPUS

Business Administration and Management—General M
Engineering Management M

POLYTECHNIC UNIVERSITY OF THE AMERICAS–ORLANDO CAMPUS

Business Administration and Management—General M
Civil Engineering M
Computer Engineering M
Electrical Engineering M
Engineering Management M

PONCE SCHOOL OF MEDICINE

Allopathic Medicine P
Biological and Biomedical Sciences—General D
Clinical Psychology D
Public Health—General M

PONTIFICAL CATHOLIC UNIVERSITY OF PUERTO RICO

Accounting M
Biological and Biomedical Sciences—General M
Business Administration and Management—General M,D
Business Education M,D
Chemistry M
Clinical Laboratory Sciences/Medical Technology O
Clinical Psychology M,D
Counselor Education M
Criminal Justice and Criminology M
Curriculum and Instruction M,D
Education—General M,D
Educational Leadership and Administration D
Educational Psychology M
English as a Second Language M
Environmental Sciences M
Finance and Banking M
Hispanic Studies M,O
History M
Human Resources Management M
Human Services M,D
Industrial and Organizational Psychology M,D
International Business M
Law P
Management Information Systems M
Marketing M
Medical/Surgical Nursing M
Nursing—General M
Psychiatric Nursing M
Psychology—General M,D
Public Administration M
Rehabilitation Counseling M
Religious Education M
Social Work M
Spanish M,O
Theology P

PONTIFICAL COLLEGE JOSEPHINUM

Theology P,M

PONTIFICIA UNIVERSIDAD CATOLICA MADRE Y MAESTRA

Allopathic Medicine P
Architecture M
Business Administration and Management—General M
Construction Engineering M
Criminal Justice and Criminology M
Energy and Power Engineering M
Environmental Engineering M
Environmental Management and Policy M
Finance and Banking M
Human Resources Management M
Industrial and Labor Relations M
Interior Design M
International Business M
Law M
Logistics M
Marketing M

PORTLAND STATE UNIVERSITY

Adult Education M,D
Anthropology M,D,O
Applied Economics M,D
Applied Social Research M,D
Art/Fine Arts M
Artificial Intelligence/Robotics M,D,O
Biological and Biomedical Sciences—General M,D
Business Administration and Management—General M,D,O
Chemistry M,D
Civil Engineering M,D,O
Communication Disorders M
Computer Engineering M,D
Computer Science M,D
Conflict Resolution and Mediation/Peace Studies M
Counselor Education M,D
Criminal Justice and Criminology M,D
Curriculum and Instruction M,D
Early Childhood Education M,D
Economics M,D,O
Education—General M,D
Educational Leadership and Administration M,D
Educational Media/Instructional Technology M,D
Educational Policy M,D
Electrical Engineering M,D
Elementary Education M,D
Engineering and Applied Sciences—General M,D,O
Engineering Management M,D,O
English as a Second Language M
English M
Environmental Engineering M,D
Environmental Management and Policy M,D
Environmental Sciences M,D
Finance and Banking M
Foreign Languages Education M
French M
Geography M,D
Geology M,D
German M
Gerontology O
Health Education M,O
Health Promotion M,O
Health Services Management and Hospital Administration M
Higher Education M,D
History M
Human Resources Management M
Industrial and Manufacturing Management M,D
International Business M
Japanese M
Management of Technology M,D
Manufacturing Engineering M
Mathematics Education M,D
Mathematics M,D,O
Mechanical Engineering M,D,O
Music Education M
Music M
Physics M,D
Political Science M,D
Psychology—General M,D,O
Public Administration M,D
Public Health—General M,O
Reading Education M,D
Science Education M,D
Secondary Education M,D
Social Sciences Education M
Social Work M,D
Sociology M,D,O
Software Engineering M,D
Spanish M
Special Education M,D
Speech and Interpersonal Communication M,O
Statistics M,D
Systems Engineering M,O
Systems Science M,D,O
Theater M
Urban and Regional Planning M
Urban Studies M,D

PRAIRIE VIEW A&M UNIVERSITY

Accounting M
Agricultural Economics and Agribusiness M
Agricultural Sciences—General M
Agronomy and Soil Sciences M
Animal Sciences M
Architecture M
Biological and Biomedical Sciences—General M
Business Administration and Management—General M
Chemistry M
Clinical Psychology M,D
Computer Science M,D
Counselor Education M,D
Curriculum and Instruction M
Education—General M,D
Educational Leadership and Administration M,D
Electrical Engineering M,D
Engineering and Applied Sciences—General M,D
English M
Family and Consumer Sciences-General M
Family Nurse Practitioner Studies M
Forensic Psychology M,D
Health Education M
Legal and Justice Studies M,D
Management Information Systems M,D
Mathematics M
Nursing and Healthcare Administration M
Nursing Education M
Nursing—General M
Physical Education M
Sociology M
Special Education M
Urban Design M

PRATT INSTITUTE

Applied Arts and Design—General M,O
Architecture M*
Art Education M,O
Art History M
Art Therapy M
Art/Fine Arts M*
Arts Administration M
Educational Media/Instructional Technology M,O
Facilities Management M
Graphic Design M
Historic Preservation M
Industrial Design M
Information Studies M,O*
Interior Design M
Internet and Interactive Multimedia M
Library Science M,O
Photography M
Special Education M
Therapies—Dance, Drama, and Music M
Urban and Regional Planning M
Urban Design M

PRESCOTT COLLEGE

Art Therapy M
Counseling Psychology M
Counselor Education M,D
Early Childhood Education M,D
Education—General M,D
Educational Leadership and Administration M,D
Elementary Education M,D
English as a Second Language M,D
Environmental Education M,D
Environmental Management and Policy M
Health Psychology M
Humanities M
Leisure Studies M
Multilingual and Multicultural Education M,D
Psychoanalysis and Psychotherapy M
Secondary Education M,D
Special Education M,D

PRINCETON THEOLOGICAL SEMINARY

Religion P,M,D
Theology P,M,D

PRINCETON UNIVERSITY

Aerospace/Aeronautical Engineering M,D
Anthropology D
Applied Mathematics D
Applied Physics M,D
Archaeology D
Architecture M,D
Asian Studies D
Astronomy D
Astrophysics D
Atmospheric Sciences D
Chemical Engineering M,D
Chemistry M,D*
Civil Engineering M,D
Classics D
Comparative Literature D
Computational Biology D
Computational Sciences D
Computer Science M,D*
Demography and Population Studies D,O
Ecology D
Economics D,O
Electrical Engineering M,D*
Electronic Materials D
English D

*M—master's degree; P—first professional degree; D—doctorate; O—other advanced degree; *—Close-Up and/or Announcement or Display in one of the other books in this series*

Environmental Engineering M,D
Environmental Management and Policy M,D
Evolutionary Biology D
Finance and Banking M
Financial Engineering M,D
French D
Geosciences D
German D
History of Science and Technology D
History D
International Affairs M,D
Marine Biology D
Materials Sciences D
Mathematics D
Mechanical Engineering M,D
Molecular Biology D
Music D
Near and Middle Eastern Studies M,D
Neuroscience D
Ocean Engineering D
Oceanography D
Operations Research M,D
Philosophy D
Photonics D
Physics D
Plasma Physics D
Political Science D
Portuguese D
Psychology—General D
Public Affairs M,D,O
Public Policy M,D
Religion D
Russian D
Slavic Languages D
Sociology D,O
Spanish D
Structural Engineering M,D
Water Resources Engineering M,D

THE PROTESTANT EPISCOPAL THEOLOGICAL SEMINARY IN VIRGINIA

Theology P,M,D

PROVIDENCE COLLEGE

Accounting M
American Studies M
Business Administration and Management—General M*
Counselor Education M
Economics M
Education—General M
Educational Leadership and Administration M
Elementary Education M
Entrepreneurship M
Finance and Banking M
History M
International Business M
Marketing M
Mathematics Education M
Nonprofit Management M
Quantitative Analysis M
Reading Education M
Religion M
Secondary Education M
Special Education M
Theology M

PROVIDENCE COLLEGE AND THEOLOGICAL SEMINARY

Counseling Psychology P,M,D,O
English as a Second Language P,M,D,O
Missions and Missiology P,M,D,O
Pastoral Ministry and Counseling P,M,D,O
Religious Education P,M,D,O
Student Affairs P,M,D,O
Theology P,M,D,O

PURCHASE COLLEGE, STATE UNIVERSITY OF NEW YORK

Art History M
Art/Fine Arts M
Dance M
Music M
Theater M

PURDUE UNIVERSITY

Aerospace/Aeronautical Engineering M,D
Agricultural Economics and Agribusiness M,D
Agricultural Education M,D,O
Agricultural Engineering M,D
Agricultural Sciences—General M,D
Agronomy and Soil Sciences M,D
American Studies M,D
Analytical Chemistry M,D
Anatomy M,D
Animal Sciences M,D
Anthropology M,D
Applied Arts and Design—General M
Aquaculture M,D
Art Education M,D,O
Art/Fine Arts M
Atmospheric Sciences M,D
Biochemistry M,D
Biological and Biomedical Sciences—General M,D
Biomedical Engineering M,D
Biophysics M,D
Botany M,D
Business Administration and Management—General M,D
Cell Biology M,D
Chemical Engineering M,D
Chemistry M,D
Child and Family Studies M,D
Child Development M,D
Civil Engineering M,D
Clothing and Textiles M,D
Communication Disorders M,D
Communication—General M,D
Comparative Literature M,D
Computer and Information Systems Security M
Computer Engineering M,D
Computer Science M,D
Consumer Economics M,D
Counselor Education M,D,O
Curriculum and Instruction M,D,O
Developmental Biology M,D
Ecology M,D
Economics D
Education of the Gifted M,D,O
Education—General M,D,O
Educational Leadership and Administration M,D,O
Educational Media/Instructional Technology M,D,O
Educational Psychology M,D,O
Electrical Engineering M,D
Elementary Education M,D,O
Engineering and Applied Sciences—General M,D,O
English Education M,D,O
English M,D
Entomology M,D
Environmental Management and Policy M,D
Epidemiology M,D
Evolutionary Biology M,D
Exercise and Sports Science M,D
Family and Consumer Sciences-General M,D
Finance and Banking M
Fish, Game, and Wildlife Management M,D
Food Science and Technology M,D
Foreign Languages Education M,D,O
Forestry M,D
Foundations and Philosophy of Education M,D,O
French M,D
Genetics M,D
Geosciences M,D
German M,D
Health Promotion M,D
Higher Education M,D,O
History M,D
Home Economics Education M,D,O
Horticulture M,D
Hospitality Management M,D
Human Development M,D
Human Resources Management M,D
Immunology M,D
Industrial and Manufacturing Management M
Industrial/Management Engineering M,D
Inorganic Chemistry M,D
International Business M
Linguistics M,D
Marriage and Family Therapy M,D
Materials Engineering M,D
Mathematics Education M,D,O
Mathematics M,D
Mechanical Engineering M,D,O
Medicinal and Pharmaceutical Chemistry M,D
Microbiology M,D
Molecular Biology M,D
Molecular Pharmacology M,D
Natural Resources M,D
Neurobiology M,D
Nuclear Engineering M,D
Nutrition M,D
Organic Chemistry M,D
Organizational Behavior D
Pathobiology M,D
Pathology M,D
Pharmaceutical Administration M,D,O
Pharmaceutical Sciences M,D
Pharmacology M,D
Pharmacy P
Philosophy M,D
Physical Chemistry M,D
Physical Education M,D
Physics M,D
Physiology M,D
Plant Pathology M,D
Plant Physiology M,D
Political Science M,D
Psychology—General D
Public Health—General M,D
Reading Education M,D,O
Science Education M,D,O
Social Sciences Education M,D,O
Sociology M,D
Spanish M,D
Special Education M,D,O
Sport Psychology M,D
Statistics M,D,O
Theater M
Toxicology M,D
Travel and Tourism M,D
Veterinary Medicine P
Veterinary Sciences M,D
Virology M,D
Vocational and Technical Education M,D,O
Writing M,D

PURDUE UNIVERSITY CALUMET

Accounting M
Biological and Biomedical Sciences—General M
Biotechnology M
Business Administration and Management—General M
Communication—General M
Computer Engineering M
Counseling Psychology M
Counselor Education M
Education—General M
Educational Leadership and Administration M
Educational Media/Instructional Technology M
Electrical Engineering M
Engineering and Applied Sciences—General M
English M
History M
Human Services M
Marriage and Family Therapy M
Mathematics Education M
Mathematics M
Mechanical Engineering M
Nursing—General M
School Psychology M
Science Education M
Special Education M

PURDUE UNIVERSITY NORTH CENTRAL

Education—General M
Elementary Education M

QUEENS COLLEGE OF THE CITY UNIVERSITY OF NEW YORK

Accounting M
Art Education M,O
Art History M
Art/Fine Arts M
Biochemistry M
Biological and Biomedical Sciences—General M
Chemistry M
Clinical Psychology M
Communication Disorders M
Computer Science M
Counselor Education M
Early Childhood Education M,O
Education—General M,O
Educational Leadership and Administration O
Elementary Education M,O
English as a Second Language M
English Education M,O
English M
Environmental Sciences M
Exercise and Sports Science M
Family and Consumer Sciences-General M
Foreign Languages Education M,O
French M
Geology M
History M
Home Economics Education M
Information Studies M,O
Italian M
Liberal Studies M
Library Science M,O
Linguistics M
Mathematics Education M,O
Mathematics M
Multilingual and Multicultural Education M,O
Music Education M,O
Music M
Physics M,D
Psychology—General M
Reading Education M
Romance Languages M
School Psychology M,O
Science Education M,O
Secondary Education M,O
Social Sciences Education M,O
Social Sciences M
Sociology M
Spanish M
Special Education M

Urban Studies	M
Writing	M

QUEEN'S UNIVERSITY AT KINGSTON

Allopathic Medicine	P
Anatomy	M,D
Biochemistry	M,D
Biological and Biomedical Sciences—General	M,D
Business Administration and Management—General	M
Canadian Studies	M,D
Cancer Biology/Oncology	M,D
Cardiovascular Sciences	M,D
Cell Biology	M,D
Chemical Engineering	M,D
Chemistry	M,D
Civil Engineering	M,D
Classics	M
Clinical Psychology	M,D
Cognitive Sciences	M,D
Communication—General	M,D
Computer Engineering	M,D
Computer Science	M,D
Developmental Psychology	M,D
Education—General	M,D
Electrical Engineering	M,D
Engineering and Applied Sciences—General	M,D
English	M,D
Entrepreneurship	M
Epidemiology	M,D
Exercise and Sports Science	M,D
Family Nurse Practitioner Studies	M,D,O
Finance and Banking	M
French	M,D
Gender Studies	M,D
Geography	M,D
Geology	M,D
German	M,D
Health Services Management and Hospital Administration	M,D
Hispanic Studies	M
Immunology	M,D
Industrial and Labor Relations	M
Information Studies	M,D
International Affairs	M,D
Law	P,M
Legal and Justice Studies	M,D
Marketing	M
Mathematics	M,D
Mechanical Engineering	M,D
Microbiology	M,D
Mineral/Mining Engineering	M,D
Molecular Biology	M,D
Molecular Medicine	M,D
Neurobiology	M,D
Neuroscience	M,D
Nursing—General	M,D,O
Occupational Therapy	M,D
Pathology	M,D
Pediatric Nursing	M,D,O
Pharmaceutical Sciences	M,D
Pharmacology	M,D
Philosophy	M,D
Physical Therapy	M,D
Physics	M,D
Physiology	M,D
Political Science	M,D
Project Management	M
Psychology—General	M,D
Public Health—General	M,D
Public Policy	M
Rehabilitation Sciences	M,D
Religion	M
Reproductive Biology	M,D
Social Psychology	M,D
Sociology	M,D
Spanish	M
Sport Psychology	M,D
Statistics	M,D
Theology	P,M,O
Toxicology	M,D
Urban and Regional Planning	M
Women's Health Nursing	M,D,O
Women's Studies	M,D

QUEENS UNIVERSITY OF CHARLOTTE

Business Administration and Management—General	M
Corporate and Organizational Communication	M
Education—General	M
Educational Leadership and Administration	M
Elementary Education	M
Nursing and Healthcare Administration	M
Nursing—General	M
Reading Education	M
Writing	M

QUINCY UNIVERSITY

Business Administration and Management—General	M
Counselor Education	M
Education—General	M
Theology	M

QUINNIPIAC UNIVERSITY

Accounting	M
Adult Nursing	M,O
Advertising and Public Relations	M
Allied Health—General	M,D,O*
Biological and Biomedical Sciences—General	M
Business Administration and Management—General	M*
Cardiovascular Sciences	M
Cell Biology	M
Clinical Laboratory Sciences/Medical Technology	M
Communication—General	M*
Education—General	M*
Elementary Education	M
English Education	M
Family Nurse Practitioner Studies	M,O
Finance and Banking	M
Foreign Languages Education	M
Health Law	P,M
Health Physics/Radiological Health	M
Health Services Management and Hospital Administration	M
International Business	M
Internet and Interactive Multimedia	M
Investment Management	M
Journalism	M
Law	P,M
Management Information Systems	M
Marketing	M
Mathematics Education	M
Microbiology	M
Middle School Education	M
Molecular Biology	M
Nursing—General	M,O
Occupational Therapy	M
Pathology	M
Perfusion	M
Physical Therapy	M,D
Physician Assistant Studies	M
Science Education	M
Secondary Education	M
Social Sciences Education	M

RABBI ISAAC ELCHANAN THEOLOGICAL SEMINARY

Theology	O

RABBINICAL ACADEMY MESIVTA RABBI CHAIM BERLIN

Theology	O

RABBINICAL COLLEGE BETH SHRAGA

Theology	

RABBINICAL COLLEGE BOBOVER YESHIVA B'NEI ZION

Theology	

RABBINICAL COLLEGE CH'SAN SOFER

Theology	

RABBINICAL COLLEGE OF LONG ISLAND

Theology	

RABBINICAL SEMINARY M'KOR CHAIM

Theology	

RABBINICAL SEMINARY OF AMERICA

Theology	

RADFORD UNIVERSITY

Adult Nursing	M
Art/Fine Arts	M
Business Administration and Management—General	M
Clinical Psychology	M,D,O
Communication Disorders	M
Corporate and Organizational Communication	M
Counseling Psychology	M,D,O
Counselor Education	M
Criminal Justice and Criminology	M
Education—General	M
Educational Leadership and Administration	M
English	M
Experimental Psychology	M,D,O
Family Nurse Practitioner Studies	M
Industrial and Organizational Psychology	M,D,O
Music Education	M
Music	M
Nursing—General	M
Psychology—General	M,D,O
Reading Education	M
School Psychology	M,D,O
Social Work	M
Special Education	M
Student Affairs	M
Therapies—Dance, Drama, and Music	M

RAMAPO COLLEGE OF NEW JERSEY

Educational Media/Instructional Technology	M
Liberal Studies	M
Nursing Education	M
Nursing—General	M

RECONSTRUCTIONIST RABBINICAL COLLEGE

Theology	P,M,D,O

REED COLLEGE

Liberal Studies	M

REFORMED PRESBYTERIAN THEOLOGICAL SEMINARY

Theology	P,M,D

REFORMED THEOLOGICAL SEMINARY–CHARLOTTE CAMPUS

Pastoral Ministry and Counseling	P,M,D
Religion	P,M,D
Theology	P,M,D

REFORMED THEOLOGICAL SEMINARY–JACKSON CAMPUS

Marriage and Family Therapy	P,M,D,O
Missions and Missiology	P,M,D,O
Pastoral Ministry and Counseling	P,M,D,O
Religious Education	P,M,D,O
Theology	P,M,D,O

REFORMED THEOLOGICAL SEMINARY–ORLANDO CAMPUS

Pastoral Ministry and Counseling	P,M,D
Theology	P,M,D

REFORMED THEOLOGICAL SEMINARY–WASHINGTON D.C.

Religion	P,M
Theology	P,M

REGENT COLLEGE

Theology	P,M,O

REGENT UNIVERSITY

Business Administration and Management—General	M,D,O
Clinical Psychology	M,D,O
Communication—General	M,D
Computer Art and Design	M,D
Counseling Psychology	M,D,O
Counselor Education	M,D,O
Economics	M
Education—General	M,D,O
Educational Leadership and Administration	M,D,O
Elementary Education	M,D,O
English as a Second Language	M,D,O
Entrepreneurship	M,D,O
Film, Television, and Video Production	M,D
Health Services Management and Hospital Administration	M
Homeland Security	M
International Economics	M
Journalism	M,D
Law	P,M
Legal and Justice Studies	P,M
Management Strategy and Policy	M,D,O
Mathematics Education	M,D,O
Missions and Missiology	P,M,D
Near and Middle Eastern Studies	M
Organizational Management	M,D,O
Pastoral Ministry and Counseling	P,M,D
Political Science	M
Public Administration	M
Public Policy	M
Religious Education	M,D,O
Social Psychology	M,D,O
Special Education	M,D,O
Student Affairs	M,D,O

*M—master's degree; P—first professional degree; D—doctorate; O—other advanced degree; *—Close-Up and/or Announcement or Display in one of the other books in this series*

Theater	M,D
Theology	P,M,D

REGIS COLLEGE (CANADA)

Pastoral Ministry and Counseling	P,M,D,O
Theology	P,M,D,O

REGIS COLLEGE (MA)

Biotechnology	M
Business Administration and Management—General	M
Corporate and Organizational Communication	M
Education—General	M
Family Nurse Practitioner Studies	M,O
Nonprofit Management	M,O
Nursing Education	M,O
Nursing—General	M,O
Organizational Management	M
Public Administration	M,O
Public Policy	M,O
Quality Management	M

REGIS UNIVERSITY

Accounting	M,O
Adult Education	M,O
Allied Health—General	P,M,D,O
Art/Fine Arts	M,O
Arts Administration	M,O
Business Administration and Management—General	M,O
Communication—General	M,O
Computer and Information Systems Security	M,O
Computer Science	M,O
Conflict Resolution and Mediation/Peace Studies	M,O
Counseling Psychology	M,O
Criminal Justice and Criminology	M,O
Curriculum and Instruction	M,O
Database Systems	M,O
Early Childhood Education	M,O
Education—General	M,O
Educational Leadership and Administration	M,O
Educational Media/Instructional Technology	M,O
Electronic Commerce	M,O
Elementary Education	M,O
English as a Second Language	M,O
Family Nurse Practitioner Studies	P,M,D,O
Finance and Banking	M,O
Foundations and Philosophy of Education	M,O
Health Education	P,M,D,O
Health Services Management and Hospital Administration	P,M,D,O
Human Resources Management	M,O
Industrial and Manufacturing Management	M,O
Information Science	M,O
Interdisciplinary Studies	M,O
International Business	M,O
Legal and Justice Studies	M,O
Management Information Systems	M,O
Management of Technology	M,O
Marketing	M,O
Marriage and Family Therapy	M,O
Maternal and Child/Neonatal Nursing	P,M,D,O
Music	M,O
Nonprofit Management	M,O
Nursing and Healthcare Administration	P,M,D,O
Nursing—General	P,M,D,O
Organizational Management	M,O
Pharmacy	P,M,D,O
Physical Therapy	P,M,D,O
Physician Assistant Studies	P,M,D,O
Project Management	M,O
Psychology—General	M,O
Reading Education	M,O
Science Education	M,O
Secondary Education	M,O
Social Psychology	M,O
Social Sciences	M,O
Software Engineering	M,O
Special Education	M,O
Systems Engineering	M,O
Technical Writing	M,O

REINHARDT COLLEGE

Business Administration and Management—General	M
Early Childhood Education	M
Education—General	M
Music Education	M
Music	M

RENSSELAER AT HARTFORD

Business Administration and Management—General	M
Computer Engineering	M
Computer Science	M
Electrical Engineering	M
Engineering and Applied Sciences—General	M
Information Science	M
Mechanical Engineering	M
Systems Science	M

RENSSELAER POLYTECHNIC INSTITUTE

Aerospace/Aeronautical Engineering	M,D
Analytical Chemistry	M,D
Applied Mathematics	M
Applied Physics	M,D
Applied Science and Technology	M
Architecture	M,D
Art/Fine Arts	M,D
Astrophysics	M,D
Biochemistry	M,D
Bioengineering	M,D
Biological and Biomedical Sciences—General	M,D
Biomedical Engineering	M,D
Biophysics	M,D
Business Administration and Management—General	M,D
Cell Biology	M,D
Ceramic Sciences and Engineering	M,D
Chemical Engineering	M,D
Chemistry	M,D
Civil Engineering	M,D
Cognitive Sciences	D
Communication—General	M,D
Computer Art and Design	M,D
Computer Engineering	M,D
Computer Science	M,D
Developmental Biology	M,D
Economics	M
Electrical Engineering	M,D
Energy and Power Engineering	M,D
Engineering and Applied Sciences—General	M,D
Engineering Management	M,D
Engineering Physics	M,D
Entrepreneurship	M,D
Environmental Engineering	M,D
Environmental Management and Policy	M,D
Environmental Sciences	M,D
Financial Engineering	M,D
Geochemistry	M,D
Geology	M,D
Geophysics	M,D
Geosciences	M,D
Geotechnical Engineering	M,D
History of Science and Technology	M,D
Human-Computer Interaction	M
Hydrogeology	M,D
Industrial/Management Engineering	M,D
Information Science	M
Inorganic Chemistry	M,D
Interdisciplinary Studies	M,D
Lighting Design	M
Materials Engineering	M,D
Materials Sciences	M,D
Mathematics	M,D
Mechanical Engineering	M,D
Metallurgical Engineering and Metallurgy	M,D
Microbiology	M,D
Molecular Biology	M,D
Nuclear Engineering	M,D
Organic Chemistry	M,D
Physical Chemistry	M,D
Physics	M,D
Polymer Science and Engineering	M,D
Rhetoric	M,D
Science Education	M
Speech and Interpersonal Communication	M,D
Structural Engineering	M,D
Systems Engineering	M,D
Technical Communication	M
Technology and Public Policy	M,D
Transportation and Highway Engineering	M,D

RESEARCH COLLEGE OF NURSING

Family Nurse Practitioner Studies	M
Nursing Education	M
Nursing—General	M

RHODE ISLAND COLLEGE

Accounting	M,O
Art Education	M
Art/Fine Arts	M
Arts Administration	M
Biological and Biomedical Sciences—General	M
Counselor Education	M,O
Early Childhood Education	M
Education—General	D
Educational Leadership and Administration	M,O
Elementary Education	M
English as a Second Language	M
English Education	M
English	M
Finance and Banking	M,O
Foreign Languages Education	M
Health Education	M,O
History	M
Mathematics Education	M
Mathematics	M
Music Education	M
Nursing—General	M
Physical Education	M,O
Psychology—General	M
Public Administration	M
Reading Education	M
Secondary Education	M
Social Sciences Education	M
Social Work	M
Special Education	M,O
Theater	M
Vocational and Technical Education	M
Writing	M

RHODE ISLAND SCHOOL OF DESIGN

Applied Arts and Design—General	M
Architecture	M
Art Education	M
Art/Fine Arts	M
Computer Art and Design	M
Graphic Design	M
Industrial Design	M
Interior Design	M
Landscape Architecture	M
Photography	M
Textile Design	M

RHODES COLLEGE

Accounting	M

RICE UNIVERSITY

Anthropology	M,D
Applied Mathematics	M,D
Applied Physics	M,D
Architecture	M,D
Astronomy	M,D
Biochemistry	M,D
Bioengineering	M,D
Biomedical Engineering	M,D
Biostatistics	M,D
Business Administration and Management—General	M
Cell Biology	M,D
Chemical Engineering	M,D
Chemistry	M,D
Civil Engineering	M,D
Cognitive Sciences	M,D
Computational Sciences	M,D
Computer Engineering	M,D
Computer Science	M,D
Ecology	M,D
Economics	M,D
Education—General	M
Electrical Engineering	M,D
Engineering and Applied Sciences—General	M,D
English	M,D
Environmental Engineering	M,D
Environmental Management and Policy	M
Environmental Sciences	M,D
Evolutionary Biology	M,D
French	M,D
Geophysics	M
Geosciences	M,D
History	M,D
Industrial and Organizational Psychology	M,D
Inorganic Chemistry	M,D
Linguistics	M,D
Materials Sciences	M,D
Mathematical and Computational Finance	M,D
Mathematics	M,D
Mechanical Engineering	M,D
Music	M,D
Organic Chemistry	M,D
Philosophy	M,D
Physical Chemistry	M,D
Physics	M,D
Political Science	M,D
Psychology—General	M,D
Religion	D
Spanish	M
Statistics	M,D
Urban Design	M,D

THE RICHARD STOCKTON COLLEGE OF NEW JERSEY

Business Administration and Management—General	M
Criminal Justice and Criminology	M
Education—General	M
Educational Media/Instructional Technology	M
Holocaust Studies	M
Legal and Justice Studies	O
Nursing—General	M
Occupational Therapy	M
Physical Therapy	D

RICHMOND, THE AMERICAN INTERNATIONAL UNIVERSITY IN LONDON

Art History	M

RICHMONT GRADUATE UNIVERSITY

Counseling Psychology	M
Marriage and Family Therapy	M
Psychology—General	M

RIDER UNIVERSITY

Accounting	M
Business Administration and Management—General	M*
Business Education	O
Counselor Education	M,O
Curriculum and Instruction	M,O
Education—General	M,O*
Educational Leadership and Administration	M,O
Elementary Education	O
English as a Second Language	O
English Education	O
Foreign Languages Education	O
French	O
German	O
Mathematics Education	O
Organizational Management	M
Reading Education	M,O
School Psychology	O
Science Education	O
Social Sciences Education	O
Spanish	O
Special Education	M,O

RIVIER COLLEGE

Business Administration and Management—General	M
Computer Science	M
Counseling Psychology	M,D,O
Counselor Education	M,D,O
Curriculum and Instruction	M,D,O
Early Childhood Education	M,D,O
Education—General	M,D,O
Educational Leadership and Administration	M,D,O
Elementary Education	M,D,O
English	M
Family Nurse Practitioner Studies	M
Foreign Languages Education	M
Management Information Systems	M
Mathematics	M
Nursing Education	M
Nursing—General	M
Organizational Management	M
Reading Education	M,D,O
Social Sciences Education	M
Special Education	M,D,O
Writing	M

ROBERT MORRIS COLLEGE

Accounting	M
Business Administration and Management—General	M
Finance and Banking	M
Human Resources Management	M
Management Information Systems	M

ROBERT MORRIS UNIVERSITY

Business Administration and Management—General	M
Business Education	M,D,O
Computer and Information Systems Security	M,D
Education—General	M,D,O
Educational Leadership and Administration	M,D,O
Engineering and Applied Sciences—General	M
Engineering Management	M
Human Resources Management	M
Information Science	M,D
Internet and Interactive Multimedia	M,D
Management Information Systems	M,D
Nonprofit Management	M
Nursing—General	M,D
Organizational Management	M,D
Project Management	M,D
Taxation	M

ROBERTS WESLEYAN COLLEGE

Business Administration and Management—General	M,O
Child and Family Studies	M
Counselor Education	M
Early Childhood Education	M,O
Education—General	M,O
Health Services Management and Hospital Administration	M
Human Services	M
Management Strategy and Policy	M,O
Marketing	M,O
Middle School Education	M,O
Nonprofit Management	M,O
Nursing and Healthcare Administration	M
Nursing Education	M
Nursing—General	M
Pastoral Ministry and Counseling	M
Reading Education	M,O
School Psychology	M,O
Secondary Education	M,O
Social Work	M
Special Education	M,O
Urban Education	M,O

ROCHESTER INSTITUTE OF TECHNOLOGY

Accounting	M
Applied Mathematics	M
Applied Statistics	M,O
Art Education	M
Art/Fine Arts	M
Astrophysics	M,D
Bioinformatics	M
Biological and Biomedical Sciences—General	M
Business Administration and Management—General	M
Chemistry	M
Clinical Laboratory Sciences/Medical Technology	M
Communication—General	M
Computer and Information Systems Security	M,O
Computer Art and Design	M
Computer Engineering	M
Computer Science	M,D,O
Database Systems	M,O
Electrical Engineering	M
Engineering and Applied Sciences—General	M,D,O
Engineering Design	M
Engineering Management	M
Environmental Management and Policy	M
Environmental Sciences	M
Film, Television, and Video Production	M
Finance and Banking	M
Gerontology	M,O
Graphic Design	M
Health Services Management and Hospital Administration	M,O
Hospitality Management	M
Human Resources Development	M
Human-Computer Interaction	M
Industrial and Manufacturing Management	M
Industrial Design	M
Industrial/Management Engineering	M
Information Science	M,D
Interdisciplinary Studies	M
International Business	M
Internet and Interactive Multimedia	M,O
Management Information Systems	M
Manufacturing Engineering	M
Materials Engineering	M
Materials Sciences	M
Mechanical Engineering	M
Media Studies	M
Medical Illustration	M
Optical Sciences	M,D
Photography	M
Psychology—General	M
Public Policy	M
School Psychology	M,O
Secondary Education	M
Software Engineering	M
Special Education	M
Statistics	M,O
Sustainability Management	D
Sustainable Development	D
Systems Engineering	M,D
Technical Communication	O
Technology and Public Policy	M
Telecommunications	M
Travel and Tourism	M

THE ROCKEFELLER UNIVERSITY

Biological and Biomedical Sciences—General	D*

ROCKFORD COLLEGE

Business Administration and Management—General	M
Education—General	M
Elementary Education	M
Reading Education	M
Secondary Education	M
Special Education	M

ROCKHURST UNIVERSITY

Business Administration and Management—General	M
Communication Disorders	M
Education—General	M
Occupational Therapy	M
Physical Therapy	D

ROGER WILLIAMS UNIVERSITY

Architecture	M
Construction Management	M
Criminal Justice and Criminology	M*
Education—General	M
Elementary Education	M
Forensic Psychology	M*
Law	P
Public Administration	M*
Reading Education	M

ROLLINS COLLEGE

Business Administration and Management—General	M
Counselor Education	M
Education—General	M
Elementary Education	M
English Education	M
Human Resources Development	M
Human Resources Management	M
Liberal Studies	M
Mathematics Education	M
Music Education	M
Secondary Education	M

ROOSEVELT UNIVERSITY

Accounting	M
Actuarial Science	M
Anthropology	M
Applied Economics	M
Biotechnology	M
Business Administration and Management—General	M
Chemistry	M
Clinical Psychology	M,D
Communication—General	M
Computer Science	M
Corporate and Organizational Communication	M
Counselor Education	M
Early Childhood Education	M
Economics	M
Education—General	M,D
Educational Leadership and Administration	M
Elementary Education	M
English	M
Gender Studies	M,O
History	M
Hospitality Management	M
Human Resources Development	M
Human Resources Management	M
Industrial and Organizational Psychology	M
International Business	M
Journalism	M
Management Information Systems	M
Mathematics	M
Music Education	M,O
Music	M,O
Organizational Management	M,D
Political Science	M
Psychology—General	D
Public Administration	M
Reading Education	M
Real Estate	M,O
Secondary Education	M
Sociology	M
Spanish	M
Special Education	M
Telecommunications	M
Theater	M
Women's Studies	M,O
Writing	M

*M—master's degree; P—first professional degree; D—doctorate; O—other advanced degree; *—Close-Up and/or Announcement or Display in one of the other books in this series*

ROSALIND FRANKLIN UNIVERSITY OF MEDICINE AND SCIENCE

Allied Health—General	M,D,O
Allopathic Medicine	P
Biological and Biomedical Sciences—General	M,D*
Clinical Laboratory Sciences/Medical Technology	M
Health Education	M
Health Services Management and Hospital Administration	M,O
Immunology	M,D
Interdisciplinary Studies	D
Medical Physics	M
Microbiology	M,D
Molecular Pharmacology	M,D
Neuroscience	D
Nurse Anesthesia	M
Nutrition	M
Pathology	M
Physical Therapy	M,D
Physician Assistant Studies	M
Podiatric Medicine	P
Psychology—General	M,D
Women's Health Nursing	M,D,O

ROSE-HULMAN INSTITUTE OF TECHNOLOGY

Biomedical Engineering	M
Chemical Engineering	M
Civil Engineering	M
Electrical Engineering	M
Engineering and Applied Sciences—General	M*
Engineering Management	M
Environmental Engineering	M
Mechanical Engineering	M
Optical Sciences	M

ROSEMONT COLLEGE

Business Administration and Management—General	M
Counseling Psychology	M
Counselor Education	M
Curriculum and Instruction	M
Elementary Education	M
English	M
Human Services	M
Publishing	M
Writing	M

ROWAN UNIVERSITY

Advertising and Public Relations	M
Business Administration and Management—General	M
Counseling Psychology	M
Counselor Education	M
Criminal Justice and Criminology	M
Curriculum and Instruction	M
Education—General	M,D,O
Educational Leadership and Administration	M,D
Elementary Education	M
Engineering and Applied Sciences—General	M
Engineering Management	M
Higher Education	M
Library Science	M
Mathematics	M
Music	M
Psychology—General	M
Reading Education	M
School Psychology	M,O
Secondary Education	M
Special Education	M
Theater	M
Writing	M

ROYAL MILITARY COLLEGE OF CANADA

Business Administration and Management—General	M
Chemical Engineering	M,D
Chemistry	M,D
Civil Engineering	M,D
Computer Engineering	M,D
Computer Science	M
Electrical Engineering	M,D
Engineering and Applied Sciences—General	M,D
Environmental Engineering	M,D
Environmental Sciences	M,D
Materials Sciences	M,D
Mathematics	M
Mechanical Engineering	M,D
Military and Defense Studies	M,D
Nuclear Engineering	M,D
Physics	M
Software Engineering	M,D

ROYAL ROADS UNIVERSITY

Advertising and Public Relations	O
Business Administration and Management—General	M,O
Conflict Resolution and Mediation/Peace Studies	M,O
Emergency Management	M,O
Environmental Education	M,O
Environmental Management and Policy	M,O
Health Services Management and Hospital Administration	O
Hospitality Management	M,O
Human Resources Management	M,O
Project Management	O
Travel and Tourism	M,O

RUSH UNIVERSITY

Acute Care/Critical Care Nursing	M,D,O
Adult Nursing	M,D,O
Allopathic Medicine	P
Anatomy	M,D
Biochemistry	D
Bioethics	M,O
Cell Biology	M,D
Clinical Laboratory Sciences/Medical Technology	M
Communication Disorders	M,D
Community Health Nursing	M,D,O
Family Nurse Practitioner Studies	M,D,O
Gerontological Nursing	M,D,O
Health Services Management and Hospital Administration	M,D
Immunology	M,D
Maternal and Child/Neonatal Nursing	M,D,O
Medical Physics	M,D
Medical/Surgical Nursing	M,D,O
Microbiology	M,D
Neuroscience	M,D
Nurse Anesthesia	M,D,O
Nursing—General	M,D,O
Nutrition	M
Occupational Therapy	M
Pediatric Nursing	M,D,O
Pharmaceutical Sciences	M,D
Pharmacology	M,D
Physiology	D
Psychiatric Nursing	M,D,O
Virology	M,D

RUTGERS, THE STATE UNIVERSITY OF NEW JERSEY, CAMDEN

Biological and Biomedical Sciences—General	M
Business Administration and Management—General	M
Chemistry	M
Child Development	M,D
Computer Science	M
Criminal Justice and Criminology	M
Educational Leadership and Administration	M
Educational Policy	M
English	M
History	M
International Affairs	M
International Development	M
Law	P
Liberal Studies	M
Mathematics	M
Physical Therapy	D
Psychology—General	M
Public Administration	M
Public History	M
Public Policy	M
Writing	M

RUTGERS, THE STATE UNIVERSITY OF NEW JERSEY, NEWARK

Accounting	M,D,O
Adult Nursing	M
American Studies	M,D
Analytical Chemistry	M,D
Applied Physics	M,D
Biochemistry	M,D
Biological and Biomedical Sciences—General	M,D
Biopsychology	D
Business Administration and Management—General	M,D,O
Chemistry	M,D
Cognitive Sciences	D*
Community Health Nursing	M
Computational Biology	M
Criminal Justice and Criminology	D
Economics	M
English	M
Environmental Sciences	M,D
Family Nurse Practitioner Studies	M
Finance and Banking	M,D,O
Geology	M
Gerontological Nursing	M
Health Services Management and Hospital Administration	M,D
History	M
Human Resources Management	M,D
Inorganic Chemistry	M,D
International Affairs	M,D
International Business	M,D
Law	P
Liberal Studies	M
Management Information Systems	M,D
Management Strategy and Policy	M
Marketing	M,D
Maternal and Child/Neonatal Nursing	M
Mathematics	D
Music	M
Neuroscience	D
Nursing—General	M
Organic Chemistry	M,D
Organizational Management	D
Physical Chemistry	M,D
Political Science	M
Psychiatric Nursing	M
Psychology—General	D
Public Administration	M,D
Public Policy	M,D
Social Psychology	D
Supply Chain Management	D
Taxation	M
Urban Studies	M,D
Writing	M

RUTGERS, THE STATE UNIVERSITY OF NEW JERSEY, NEW BRUNSWICK

Aerospace/Aeronautical Engineering	M,D
African Studies	D
African-American Studies	D
Agricultural Economics and Agribusiness	M
Animal Sciences	M,D
Anthropology	M,D
Applied Arts and Design—General	M
Applied Mathematics	M,D
Applied Statistics	M,D
Art History	M,D,O
Art/Fine Arts	M
Asian Studies	D
Astronomy	M,D
Atmospheric Sciences	M,D
Biochemical Engineering	M,D
Biochemistry	M,D
Biological and Biomedical Sciences—General	D
Biomedical Engineering	M,D
Biopsychology	D
Biostatistics	M,D
Cell Biology	M,D
Chemical Engineering	M,D
Chemistry	M,D*
Civil Engineering	M,D
Classics	M,D
Clinical Psychology	M,D
Cognitive Sciences	D
Communication—General	D
Comparative Literature	M,D
Computational Biology	D
Computer Engineering	M,D
Computer Science	M,D*
Condensed Matter Physics	M,D
Counseling Psychology	M
Developmental Biology	M,D
Developmental Education	M
Early Childhood Education	M,D
Ecology	M,D
Economics	M,D
Education—General	M,D
Educational Leadership and Administration	M,D
Educational Measurement and Evaluation	M
Educational Policy	D
Educational Psychology	M,D
Electrical Engineering	M,D*
Elementary Education	M,D
English as a Second Language	M,D
English Education	M
English	D
Entomology	M,D
Environmental Biology	M,D
Environmental Engineering	M,D
Environmental Sciences	M,D
Evolutionary Biology	M,D
Food Science and Technology	M,D
Foreign Languages Education	M,D
Foundations and Philosophy of Education	M,D
French	M,D
Gender Studies	M,D
Genetics	M,D
Geography	M,D
Geology	M,D
German	M,D

Hazardous Materials Management	M,D
Health Psychology	D
Historic Preservation	M,D,O
History of Medicine	D
History of Science and Technology	D
History	D
Horticulture	M,D
Human Resources Management	M,D*
Immunology	M,D
Industrial and Labor Relations	M,D*
Industrial and Organizational Psychology	M,D
Industrial/Management Engineering	M,D
Information Studies	M,D
Inorganic Chemistry	M,D
Interdisciplinary Studies	D
International Affairs	D
Italian	M,D
Legal and Justice Studies	D
Library Science	M,D
Linguistics	D
Marine Biology	M,D
Materials Engineering	M,D
Materials Sciences	M,D
Mathematics Education	M,D
Mathematics	M,D
Mechanical Engineering	M,D
Mechanics	M,D
Medical Microbiology	M,D
Medicinal and Pharmaceutical Chemistry	M,D
Medieval and Renaissance Studies	D
Microbiology	M,D
Molecular Biology	M,D
Molecular Biophysics	D
Molecular Genetics	M,D
Molecular Pharmacology	D
Multilingual and Multicultural Education	M,D
Music Education	M,D,O
Music	M,D,O
Neuroscience	D
Nutrition	M,D
Oceanography	M,D
Operations Research	D
Organic Chemistry	M,D
Pharmaceutical Sciences	M,D
Pharmacy	P,M,D
Philosophy	D
Physical Chemistry	M,D
Physics	M,D
Plant Biology	M,D
Plant Molecular Biology	M,D
Plant Pathology	M,D
Political Science	D
Psychology—General	M,D
Public Health—General	M,D
Public Policy	M,D
Quality Management	M,D
Reading Education	M,D
School Psychology	M,D
Science Education	M,D
Social Psychology	D
Social Sciences Education	M,D
Social Work	M,D
Sociology	M,D
Spanish	M,D
Special Education	M,D
Statistics	M,D
Systems Biology	D
Systems Engineering	M,D
Theater	M
Theoretical Physics	M,D
Toxicology	M,D
Translation and Interpretation	M,D
Urban and Regional Planning	M,D
Virology	M,D
Water Resources	M,D
Women's Studies	M,D
Writing	M

RYERSON UNIVERSITY

Arts Administration	M

SACRED HEART MAJOR SEMINARY

Pastoral Ministry and Counseling	P,M
Theology	P,M

SACRED HEART SCHOOL OF THEOLOGY

Theology	P,M

SACRED HEART UNIVERSITY

Business Administration and Management—General	M
Chemistry	M
Computer and Information Systems Security	M,O
Computer Science	M,O
Criminal Justice and Criminology	M
Database Systems	M,O
Education—General	M,O
Educational Leadership and Administration	M,O
Educational Media/Instructional Technology	M,O
Elementary Education	M,O
Exercise and Sports Science	M,D
Family Nurse Practitioner Studies	M
Gerontology	M
Information Science	M,O
Internet and Interactive Multimedia	M,O
Management Information Systems	M,O
Nursing and Healthcare Administration	M
Nursing—General	M
Nutrition	M,D
Occupational Therapy	M
Physical Therapy	M,D
Reading Education	M,O
Religion	M
Secondary Education	M,O

SAGE GRADUATE SCHOOL

Adult Nursing	M,O
Art Education	M
Business Administration and Management—General	M
Child and Family Studies	M
Community Health Nursing	M
Community Health	M
Counselor Education	M,O
Criminal Justice and Criminology	M,O
Education—General	M,D,O
Educational Leadership and Administration	D
Elementary Education	M
English Education	M
Family Nurse Practitioner Studies	M,O
Finance and Banking	M
Forensic Psychology	M,O
Gerontological Nursing	M,D,O
Gerontology	M,O
Health Education	M
Health Services Management and Hospital Administration	M,D,O
Human Resources Management	M
Management Strategy and Policy	M
Marketing	M
Mathematics Education	M
Nursing and Healthcare Administration	M,D,O
Nursing Education	D
Nursing—General	M,D,O
Nutrition	M,O
Occupational Therapy	M
Organizational Management	M
Physical Therapy	D
Psychiatric Nursing	M,O
Psychology—General	M,O
Public Administration	M
Reading Education	M
Social Psychology	M
Social Sciences Education	M
Sociology	M,O
Special Education	M

SAGINAW VALLEY STATE UNIVERSITY

Business Administration and Management—General	M
Communication—General	M
Distance Education Development	M
Early Childhood Education	M
Education—General	M,O
Educational Leadership and Administration	M,O
Educational Media/Instructional Technology	M
Elementary Education	M
Family Nurse Practitioner Studies	M
Health Services Management and Hospital Administration	M
Media Studies	M
Middle School Education	M
Nursing and Healthcare Administration	M
Nursing—General	M
Occupational Therapy	M
Physical Education	M
Public Administration	M
Reading Education	M
Science Education	M
Secondary Education	M
Special Education	M

ST. AMBROSE UNIVERSITY

Accounting	M
Business Administration and Management—General	M,D
Criminal Justice and Criminology	M
Education—General	M
Educational Leadership and Administration	M
Health Services Management and Hospital Administration	M,D
Human Resources Management	M,D
Management of Technology	M
Nursing—General	M
Occupational Therapy	M
Organizational Management	M
Pastoral Ministry and Counseling	M
Physical Therapy	D
Social Work	M
Special Education	M

ST. ANDREW'S COLLEGE IN WINNIPEG

Theology	P

ST. AUGUSTINE'S SEMINARY OF TORONTO

Pastoral Ministry and Counseling	P,M,O
Religious Education	P,M,O
Theology	P,M,O

SAINT BERNARD'S SCHOOL OF THEOLOGY AND MINISTRY

Pastoral Ministry and Counseling	P,M,O
Theology	P,M,O

ST. BONAVENTURE UNIVERSITY

Accounting	M
Business Administration and Management—General	M
Counseling Psychology	M,O
Counselor Education	M,O
Curriculum and Instruction	M,O
Education—General	M,O
Educational Leadership and Administration	M,O
English	M
Finance and Banking	M
International Business	M
Marketing	M
Reading Education	M
Theology	M,O

ST. CATHERINE UNIVERSITY

Education—General	M
Information Studies	M
Library Science	M
Nursing—General	M,D
Occupational Therapy	M
Organizational Management	M
Physical Therapy	D
Public Health—General	M
Social Work	M
Theology	M

ST. CHARLES BORROMEO SEMINARY, OVERBROOK

Religion	M
Theology	P,M

ST. CLOUD STATE UNIVERSITY

Applied Economics	M
Applied Statistics	M
Archaeology	M
Biological and Biomedical Sciences—General	M
Biomedical Engineering	M
Business Administration and Management—General	M
Child and Family Studies	M
Communication Disorders	M
Computer Science	M
Counselor Education	M
Criminal Justice and Criminology	M
Curriculum and Instruction	M
Economics	M
Education—General	M,D,O
Educational Leadership and Administration	M,D
Educational Media/Instructional Technology	M
Electrical Engineering	M
Engineering and Applied Sciences—General	M
Engineering Management	M
English as a Second Language	M
English	M
Environmental Management and Policy	M
Exercise and Sports Science	M
Finance and Banking	M
Geography	M
Gerontology	M
Higher Education	M,D
Historic Preservation	M
History	M

*M—master's degree; P—first professional degree; D—doctorate; O—other advanced degree; *—Close-Up and/or Announcement or Display in one of the other books in this series*

Industrial and Organizational Psychology M
Marketing M
Marriage and Family Therapy M
Mass Communication M
Mathematics M
Mechanical Engineering M
Music Education M
Music M
Nonprofit Management M
Physical Education M
Psychology—General M
Rehabilitation Counseling M
Social Psychology M
Social Work M
Special Education M
Sports Management M
Student Affairs M
Technology and Public Policy M

ST. EDWARD'S UNIVERSITY

Accounting M,O
Business Administration and Management—General M,O
Computer Art and Design M
Conflict Resolution and Mediation/Peace Studies M,O
Counseling Psychology M,O
Education—General M,O
Educational Leadership and Administration M,O
Educational Media/ Instructional Technology M,O
Entrepreneurship M,O
Ethics M
Finance and Banking M,O
Human Resources Management M,O
Human Services M,O
Humanities M,O
International Business M,O
Liberal Studies M,O
Management Information Systems M,O
Marketing M,O
Organizational Management M
Project Management M
Public Administration M,O
Social Sciences M,O
Sports Management M,O
Student Affairs M

SAINT FRANCIS MEDICAL CENTER COLLEGE OF NURSING

Medical/Surgical Nursing M,O
Nursing Education M,O
Nursing—General M,O

SAINT FRANCIS SEMINARY

Pastoral Ministry and Counseling P,M
Theology P,M

SAINT FRANCIS UNIVERSITY

Biological and Biomedical Sciences—General M
Business Administration and Management—General M
Education—General M
Educational Leadership and Administration M
Health Education M
Human Resources Management M
Occupational Therapy M
Physical Therapy D
Physician Assistant Studies M
Reading Education M

ST. FRANCIS XAVIER UNIVERSITY

Adult Education M
Biological and Biomedical Sciences—General M
Chemistry M
Computer Science M
Cultural Studies M
Curriculum and Instruction M
Education—General M
Educational Leadership and Administration M
Geology M
Geosciences M
Physics M

ST. JOHN FISHER COLLEGE

Business Administration and Management—General M
Counseling Psychology M
Education—General M,D,O
Educational Leadership and Administration M,D
Elementary Education M
English Education M
Family Nurse Practitioner Studies M,O
Foreign Languages Education M
Human Resources Development M
International Affairs M
Mathematics Education M
Middle School Education M
Nursing Education M,O
Nursing—General M,D,O
Pharmacy P
Reading Education M
Science Education M
Social Sciences Education M
Special Education M,O

ST. JOHN'S COLLEGE (MD)

Liberal Studies M

ST. JOHN'S COLLEGE (NM)

Asian Languages M
Asian Studies M
Liberal Studies M

ST. JOHN'S SEMINARY (CA)

Pastoral Ministry and Counseling P,M
Theology P,M

SAINT JOHN'S SEMINARY (MA)

Religion P,M
Theology P,M

SAINT JOHN'S UNIVERSITY (MN)

Music P,M
Pastoral Ministry and Counseling P,M
Theology P,M

ST. JOHN'S UNIVERSITY (NY)

Accounting M,O
Actuarial Science M
African Studies M,O
Applied Mathematics M
Asian Studies M,O
Biological and Biomedical Sciences—General M,D
Biotechnology M
Business Administration and Management—General M,O
Chemistry M
Clinical Psychology D
Communication—General M,D,O
Computer Science M
Counselor Education M,O
Criminal Justice and Criminology M
Early Childhood Education M
Education—General M,D,O
Educational Leadership and Administration M,D,O
Elementary Education M
English as a Second Language M
English M,D
Experimental Psychology M
Finance and Banking M,O
History M,D
Information Studies M,O
Insurance M
International Business M,O
Law P
Legal and Justice Studies M
Liberal Studies M
Library Science M,O
Management Information Systems M,O
Marketing M,O
Mathematics M
Multilingual and Multicultural Education M,O
Pastoral Ministry and Counseling P,M,O
Pharmaceutical Administration M
Pharmaceutical Sciences M,D
Pharmacy P
Philosophy M
Political Science M,O
Psychology—General M,D
Quantitative Analysis M,O
Reading Education M,D
Rehabilitation Counseling M,D,O
School Psychology M,D
Secondary Education M
Sociology M
Spanish M,O
Special Education M
Sports Management M
Statistics M
Taxation M,O
Theater M,D,O
Theology P,M,O
Toxicology M

SAINT JOSEPH COLLEGE

Biochemistry M
Biological and Biomedical Sciences—General M
Business Administration and Management—General M
Chemistry M
Child and Family Studies M
Counseling Psychology M
Counselor Education M
Education—General M
Family Nurse Practitioner Studies M,O
Gerontology M,O
Human Development M,O
Marriage and Family Therapy M
Nursing—General M,O
Nutrition M
Social Psychology M
Special Education M

SAINT JOSEPH'S COLLEGE

Music M,O

ST. JOSEPH'S COLLEGE, LONG ISLAND CAMPUS

Accounting M
Business Administration and Management—General M,O
Early Childhood Education M
Health Services Management and Hospital Administration M,O
Human Resources Management M,O
Nursing—General M
Organizational Management M,O
Reading Education M
Special Education M

ST. JOSEPH'S COLLEGE, NEW YORK

Accounting M
Business Administration and Management—General M
Early Childhood Education M
Education—General M
Nursing—General M
Reading Education M
Special Education M

SAINT JOSEPH'S COLLEGE OF MAINE

Business Administration and Management—General M
Education—General M
Health Services Management and Hospital Administration M
Nursing and Healthcare Administration M,O
Nursing Education M,O
Nursing—General M,O
Quality Management M

ST. JOSEPH'S SEMINARY

Theology P,M

SAINT JOSEPH'S UNIVERSITY

Accounting M
Adult Education M,O
Biological and Biomedical Sciences—General M
Business Administration and Management—General M,O
Computer Science M,O
Criminal Justice and Criminology M,O
Education—General M,D
Educational Leadership and Administration M,D
Educational Media/ Instructional Technology M,D
Elementary Education M,D
Environmental and Occupational Health M,O
Finance and Banking M
Gerontology M,O
Health Education M,O
Health Informatics M,O
Health Services Management and Hospital Administration M,O
Homeland Security M,O
Human Resources Management M
Human Services M,O
Industrial and Organizational Psychology M,O
International Business M
Law M,O
Management Strategy and Policy M
Marketing M,O
Mathematics M,O
Nurse Anesthesia M,O
Organizational Management M,D,O
Psychology—General M,O
Reading Education M,D
School Nursing M,O
Secondary Education M,D
Special Education M,D
Writing M

ST. LAWRENCE UNIVERSITY

Counselor Education M,O

Education—General	M,O
Educational Leadership and Administration	M,O
Human Development	M,O

SAINT LEO UNIVERSITY

Accounting	M
Business Administration and Management—General	M
Computer and Information Systems Security	M
Criminal Justice and Criminology	M
Curriculum and Instruction	M
Education of the Gifted	M
Education—General	M
Educational Leadership and Administration	M
Educational Media/Instructional Technology	M
Health Services Management and Hospital Administration	M
Human Resources Management	M
Pastoral Ministry and Counseling	M
Reading Education	M
Sports Management	M

ST. LOUIS COLLEGE OF PHARMACY

Pharmacy	P

SAINT LOUIS UNIVERSITY

Accounting	M
Allied Health—General	M,D,O
Allopathic Medicine	P
American Studies	M,D
Anatomy	M,D
Athletic Training and Sports Medicine	M,D
Biochemistry	D
Bioethics	D,O
Biological and Biomedical Sciences—General	M,D
Biomedical Engineering	M,D
Business Administration and Management—General	M
Chemistry	M,D
Clinical Psychology	M,D
Communication Disorders	M
Communication—General	M
Community Health	M
Counselor Education	M,D,O
Curriculum and Instruction	M,D
Dentistry	M
Education—General	M,D
Educational Leadership and Administration	M,D,O
English	M,D
Experimental Psychology	M,D
Finance and Banking	M
Foundations and Philosophy of Education	M,D
French	M
Geographic Information Systems	M,D,O
Geophysics	M,D
Geosciences	M,D
Health Services Management and Hospital Administration	M,D
Higher Education	M,D,O
History	M,D
Human Development	M,D,O
Immunology	D
Industrial and Organizational Psychology	M,D
International Business	M,D
Law	P,M
Marriage and Family Therapy	M,D,O
Mathematics	M,D
Meteorology	M,D
Microbiology	D
Molecular Biology	D
Nursing—General	M,D,O
Nutrition	M
Occupational Therapy	M
Oral and Dental Sciences	M
Organizational Management	M,D,O
Pathology	D
Pharmacology	D
Philosophy	M,D
Physical Therapy	M,D
Physician Assistant Studies	M
Physiology	D
Political Science	M
Psychology—General	M,D
Public Administration	M,D,O
Public Health—General	M,D
Public Policy	M,D,O
Social Work	M
Spanish	M
Special Education	M,D
Student Affairs	M,D,O
Theology	M,D
Urban Studies	M,D,O

SAINT LOUIS UNIVERSITY–MADRID CAMPUS

English	M
Spanish	M*

SAINT MARTIN'S UNIVERSITY

Business Administration and Management—General	M
Civil Engineering	M
Counseling Psychology	M
Counselor Education	M
Education—General	M
Educational Leadership and Administration	M
Engineering Management	M
English as a Second Language	M
Reading Education	M
Social Psychology	M
Special Education	M
Vocational and Technical Education	M

SAINT MARY-OF-THE-WOODS COLLEGE

Art Therapy	M,O
Environmental Management and Policy	M
Management Strategy and Policy	M
Pastoral Ministry and Counseling	M,O
Theology	M,O
Therapies—Dance, Drama, and Music	M

SAINT MARY'S COLLEGE OF CALIFORNIA

Business Administration and Management—General	M
Counselor Education	M
Curriculum and Instruction	M
Early Childhood Education	M
Education—General	M,D
Educational Leadership and Administration	M,D
Kinesiology and Movement Studies	M
Liberal Studies	M
Marriage and Family Therapy	M
Reading Education	M
Special Education	M
Writing	M

SAINT MARY SEMINARY AND GRADUATE SCHOOL OF THEOLOGY

Theology	P,M,D

ST. MARY'S SEMINARY AND UNIVERSITY

Theology	P,M,D,O*

SAINT MARY'S UNIVERSITY (CANADA)

Astronomy	M,D
Business Administration and Management—General	M,D
Canadian Studies	M
Criminal Justice and Criminology	M
Finance and Banking	M,D
History	M
Industrial and Organizational Psychology	M,D
International Development	M
Philosophy	M
Psychology—General	M,D
Women's Studies	M

ST. MARY'S UNIVERSITY (UNITED STATES)

Accounting	M
Addictions/Substance Abuse Counseling	M,D,O
Business Administration and Management—General	M
Clinical Psychology	M
Communication—General	M
Computer Engineering	M
Computer Science	M
Counseling Psychology	M
Counselor Education	D
Education—General	M,O
Educational Leadership and Administration	M,O
Electrical Engineering	M
Engineering and Applied Sciences—General	M
Engineering Management	M
English	M
Finance and Banking	M
Human Services	M,D,O
Industrial and Organizational Psychology	M
Industrial/Management Engineering	M
Information Science	M
International Affairs	M
International Business	M
Law	P
Marriage and Family Therapy	M,D
Operations Research	M
Pastoral Ministry and Counseling	M
Political Science	M
Psychology—General	M
Public Administration	M
Reading Education	M
Social Psychology	M
Software Engineering	M
Taxation	M
Theology	M

SAINT MARY'S UNIVERSITY OF MINNESOTA

Arts Administration	M
Business Administration and Management—General	M
Counseling Psychology	M,D
Curriculum and Instruction	M,O
Education of the Gifted	M,O
Education—General	M,O
Educational Leadership and Administration	M,D,O
Elementary Education	M,O
Environmental and Occupational Health	M
Geographic Information Systems	M,O
Health Services Management and Hospital Administration	M
Human Development	M
Human Resources Management	M
International Business	M
Marriage and Family Therapy	M,O
Nurse Anesthesia	M
Organizational Management	M
Pastoral Ministry and Counseling	M,O
Philanthropic Studies	M
Project Management	M,O
Reading Education	M,O
Secondary Education	M,O
Special Education	M,O
Telecommunications	M

SAINT MEINRAD SCHOOL OF THEOLOGY

Theology	P,M

SAINT MICHAEL'S COLLEGE

Art Education	M,O
Business Administration and Management—General	M,O
Clinical Psychology	M
Curriculum and Instruction	M,O
Education—General	M,O
Educational Leadership and Administration	M,O
Educational Media/Instructional Technology	M,O
English as a Second Language	M,O
Reading Education	M,O
Special Education	M,O
Theology	M,O

ST. NORBERT COLLEGE

Education—General	M
Liberal Studies	M
Theology	M

ST. PATRICK'S SEMINARY & UNIVERSITY

Theology	P,M

SAINT PAUL SCHOOL OF THEOLOGY

Theology	P,M,D

SAINT PAUL UNIVERSITY

Conflict Resolution and Mediation/Peace Studies	M
Counseling Psychology	M
Marriage and Family Therapy	M
Missions and Missiology	M
Pastoral Ministry and Counseling	M,D,O
Theology	M,D,O

ST. PETERSBURG THEOLOGICAL SEMINARY

Jewish Studies	P,M,D
Pastoral Ministry and Counseling	P,M,D
Religious Education	P,M,D
Theology	P,M,D

*M—master's degree; P—first professional degree; D—doctorate; O—other advanced degree; *—Close-Up and/or Announcement or Display in one of the other books in this series*

SAINT PETER'S COLLEGE

Accounting	M
Adult Nursing	M
Business Administration and Management—General	M
Curriculum and Instruction	M,O
Education—General	M,O
Educational Leadership and Administration	M,O
Elementary Education	M,O
Finance and Banking	M
International Business	M
Management Information Systems	M
Marketing	M
Nursing and Healthcare Administration	M
Nursing—General	M
Reading Education	M
Special Education	M

ST. PETER'S SEMINARY

Theology	P,M

SAINTS CYRIL AND METHODIUS SEMINARY

Pastoral Ministry and Counseling	P,M
Religious Education	P,M
Theology	P,M

ST. STEPHEN'S COLLEGE

Pastoral Ministry and Counseling	M,D
Theology	M,D

ST. THOMAS AQUINAS COLLEGE

Business Administration and Management—General	M*
Education—General	M,O*
Educational Leadership and Administration	M,O
Elementary Education	M,O
Finance and Banking	M
Marketing	M
Middle School Education	M,O
Reading Education	M,O
Secondary Education	M,O
Special Education	M,O

ST. THOMAS UNIVERSITY

Accounting	M,O
Arts Administration	M
Business Administration and Management—General	M,O
Communication—General	M,D,O
Counseling Psychology	M
Counselor Education	M,O
Criminal Justice and Criminology	M,O
Education of the Gifted	M,D,O
Education—General	M,D,O
Educational Leadership and Administration	M,D,O
Educational Media/Instructional Technology	M,D,O
Elementary Education	M,D,O
English as a Second Language	M,D,O
Film, Television, and Video Production	M
Geosciences	M,D,O
Health Services Management and Hospital Administration	M,O
Hispanic Studies	M,O
Human Resources Management	M,O
International Business	M,O
Law	P,M
Marriage and Family Therapy	M,O
Pastoral Ministry and Counseling	M,D,O
Planetary and Space Sciences	M,D,O
Public Administration	M,O
Reading Education	M,D,O
Special Education	M,D,O
Sports Management	M,O
Taxation	P,M
Theology	M,D,O

ST. TIKHON'S ORTHODOX THEOLOGICAL SEMINARY

Theology	P

SAINT VINCENT COLLEGE

Curriculum and Instruction	M
Education—General	M
Educational Leadership and Administration	M
Educational Media/Instructional Technology	M
Environmental Education	M
Nurse Anesthesia	M
Nursing and Healthcare Administration	M
Special Education	M

SAINT VINCENT DE PAUL REGIONAL SEMINARY

Theology	P,M

SAINT VINCENT SEMINARY

Theology	P,M

ST. VLADIMIR'S ORTHODOX THEOLOGICAL SEMINARY

Music	P,M,D
Religious Education	P,M,D
Theology	P,M,D

SAINT XAVIER UNIVERSITY

Adult Nursing	M,O
Business Administration and Management—General	M,O
Communication Disorders	M
Community Health Nursing	M,O
Computer Science	M
Counseling Psychology	M,O
Counselor Education	M
Curriculum and Instruction	M,O
Early Childhood Education	M,O
Education—General	M,O
Educational Leadership and Administration	M,O
Electronic Commerce	M,O
Elementary Education	M,O
English	M,O
Family Nurse Practitioner Studies	M,O
Finance and Banking	M,O
Health Services Management and Hospital Administration	M,O
Information Science	M
Marketing	M,O
Mathematics	M
Nonprofit Management	M,O
Nursing and Healthcare Administration	M,O
Nursing—General	M,O
Psychiatric Nursing	M,O
Psychology—General	M,O
Public Health—General	M,O
Reading Education	M,O
Secondary Education	M,O
Special Education	M,O
Travel and Tourism	M,O
Writing	M,O

SALEM COLLEGE

Early Childhood Education	M
Education—General	M
Elementary Education	M
English as a Second Language	M
Middle School Education	M
Reading Education	M
Secondary Education	M
Special Education	M

SALEM INTERNATIONAL UNIVERSITY

Business Administration and Management—General	M
Computer and Information Systems Security	M
Curriculum and Instruction	M
Education—General	M
Educational Leadership and Administration	M
International Business	M

SALEM STATE COLLEGE

Art Education	M
Business Administration and Management—General	M
Counseling Psychology	M
Counselor Education	M
Criminal Justice and Criminology	M
Early Childhood Education	M
Education—General	M
Educational Leadership and Administration	M
Educational Media/Instructional Technology	M
Elementary Education	M
English as a Second Language	M
English Education	M
English	M
Geography	M
Higher Education	M
History	M
Mathematics Education	M
Mathematics	M
Middle School Education	M
Multilingual and Multicultural Education	M
Nursing—General	M
Occupational Therapy	M
Physical Education	M
Psychology—General	M
Reading Education	M,O
Science Education	M
Secondary Education	M
Social Work	M
Spanish	M
Special Education	M

SALISBURY UNIVERSITY

Accounting	M
Business Administration and Management—General	M
Education—General	M
Educational Leadership and Administration	M
English as a Second Language	M
English	M
Geographic Information Systems	M
History	M
Mathematics Education	M
Nursing—General	M
Physiology	M
Public Administration	M
Reading Education	M
Social Work	M
Writing	M

SALUS UNIVERSITY

Communication Disorders	M,D,O
Optometry	P
Rehabilitation Sciences	M,D,O
Special Education	M,D,O
Vision Sciences	M,D,O

SALVE REGINA UNIVERSITY

Art Therapy	M,O
Business Administration and Management—General	M,O
Counseling Psychology	M,O
Criminal Justice and Criminology	M
Health Services Management and Hospital Administration	M,O
Homeland Security	M,O
Human Resources Development	M,O
Human Resources Management	M,O
Humanities	M,D,O
International Affairs	M,O
Legal and Justice Studies	M
Rehabilitation Counseling	M,O

SAMFORD UNIVERSITY

Business Administration and Management—General	M
Early Childhood Education	M,D,O
Education of the Gifted	M,D,O
Education—General	M,D,O
Educational Leadership and Administration	M,D,O
Elementary Education	M,D,O
Environmental Management and Policy	M
Family Nurse Practitioner Studies	M,D
Law	P,M
Music Education	M
Music	M
Nurse Anesthesia	M,D
Nursing and Healthcare Administration	M,D
Nursing Education	M,D
Nursing—General	M,D
Pharmacy	P
Secondary Education	M,D,O
Theology	P,M,D

SAM HOUSTON STATE UNIVERSITY

Accounting	M
Agricultural Sciences—General	M
Biological and Biomedical Sciences—General	M
Business Administration and Management—General	M
Chemistry	M
Clinical Psychology	M,D
Computational Sciences	M
Computer Science	M
Counselor Education	M,D
Criminal Justice and Criminology	M,D
Curriculum and Instruction	M
Dance	M
Education—General	M,D
Educational Leadership and Administration	M,D
Educational Media/Instructional Technology	M
English	M
Family and Consumer Sciences-General	M
Finance and Banking	M
Forensic Sciences	M,D
History	M
Humanities	M,D
Industrial/Management Engineering	M
Information Science	M
Kinesiology and Movement Studies	M
Library Science	M
Mathematics	M

Music Education	M
Music	M
Nutrition	M
Political Science	M
Psychology—General	M,D
Public Administration	M
Reading Education	M,D
Sociology	M
Special Education	M,D
Statistics	M

SAMRA UNIVERSITY OF ORIENTAL MEDICINE

Acupuncture and Oriental Medicine	M,D

SAMUEL MERRITT UNIVERSITY

Family Nurse Practitioner Studies	M,O
Nurse Anesthesia	M,O
Nursing and Healthcare Administration	M,O
Nursing—General	M,O
Occupational Therapy	M
Physical Therapy	D
Physician Assistant Studies	M

SAN DIEGO STATE UNIVERSITY

Accounting	M
Advertising and Public Relations	M
Aerospace/Aeronautical Engineering	M,D
Anthropology	M
Applied Arts and Design—General	M
Applied Mathematics	M
Art History	M
Art/Fine Arts	M
Asian Studies	M
Astronomy	M
Biological and Biomedical Sciences—General	M,D*
Biometry	M
Biostatistics	M,D
Business Administration and Management—General	M
Cell Biology	M,D
Chemistry	M,D
Child and Family Studies	M
Child Development	M
Civil Engineering	M
Clinical Psychology	M,D
Communication Disorders	M,D
Communication—General	M
Computational Sciences	M,D
Computer Science	M
Counselor Education	M
Criminal Justice and Criminology	M
Curriculum and Instruction	M
Ecology	M,D
Economics	M
Education—General	M,D
Educational Leadership and Administration	M
Educational Media/Instructional Technology	M,D
Electrical Engineering	M
Elementary Education	M
Emergency Management	M,D
Emergency Medical Services	M,D
Engineering and Applied Sciences—General	M,D
Engineering Design	M,D
English as a Second Language	M,O
English	M
Entrepreneurship	M
Environmental and Occupational Health	M,D
Environmental Design	M
Epidemiology	M,D
Exercise and Sports Science	M
Film, Television, and Video Production	M
Finance and Banking	M
Geography	M,D
Geology	M
Gerontology	M
Graphic Design	M
Health Physics/Radiological Health	M
Health Promotion	M,D
Health Psychology	M,D
Health Services Management and Hospital Administration	M,D
Higher Education	M
History	M
Human Resources Management	M
Industrial and Manufacturing Management	M
Industrial and Organizational Psychology	M,D
Interdisciplinary Studies	M
Interior Design	M
International Business	M
International Health	M,D
Internet and Interactive Multimedia	M
Kinesiology and Movement Studies	M
Latin American Studies	M
Liberal Studies	M
Linguistics	M,O
Management Information Systems	M
Marketing	M
Mathematics Education	M,D
Mathematics	M,D
Mechanical Engineering	M,D
Mechanics	M,D
Media Studies	M
Microbiology	M
Molecular Biology	M,D*
Multilingual and Multicultural Education	M,D
Music Education	M
Music	M
Nursing—General	M
Nutrition	M
Pharmaceutical Administration	M
Philosophy	M
Physical Education	M
Physics	M
Political Science	M
Psychology—General	M,D
Public Administration	M
Public Health—General	M,D
Reading Education	M
Rehabilitation Counseling	M
Rhetoric	M
Romance Languages	M
School Psychology	M
Science Education	M,D
Secondary Education	M
Social Work	M
Sociology	M
Spanish	M
Special Education	M
Sports Management	M
Statistics	M
Telecommunications Management	M
Theater	M
Toxicology	M,D
Urban and Regional Planning	M
Western European Studies	M
Women's Studies	M
Writing	M

SAN FRANCISCO ART INSTITUTE

Applied Arts and Design—General	M,O
Art History	M
Art/Fine Arts	M,O*
Film, Television, and Video Production	M,O
Museum Studies	M
Photography	M,O
Urban Studies	M

SAN FRANCISCO CONSERVATORY OF MUSIC

Music	M

SAN FRANCISCO STATE UNIVERSITY

Adult Education	M,O
Anthropology	M
Art History	M
Art/Fine Arts	M
Asian-American Studies	M
Biochemistry	M
Biological and Biomedical Sciences—General	M
Business Administration and Management—General	M
Cell Biology	M
Chemistry	M
Chinese	M
Classics	M
Clinical Laboratory Sciences/Medical Technology	M
Communication Disorders	M
Comparative Literature	M
Computer Science	M
Conservation Biology	M
Counseling Psychology	M
Cultural Studies	M
Early Childhood Education	M
Ecology	M
Economics	M
Education—General	M,D,O
Educational Leadership and Administration	M,O
Educational Media/Instructional Technology	M,O
Elementary Education	M
Engineering and Applied Sciences—General	M
English as a Second Language	M
English Education	M,O
English	M,O
Environmental Management and Policy	M
Ethnic Studies	M
Family and Consumer Sciences-General	M
Family Nurse Practitioner Studies	M
Film, Television, and Video Production	M
Film, Television, and Video Theory and Criticism	M
French	M
Geography	M
Geosciences	M
German	M
Gerontology	M
Health Education	M
History	M
Humanities	M
Industrial Design	M
International Affairs	M
Italian	M
Japanese	M
Kinesiology and Movement Studies	M
Legal and Justice Studies	M,O
Leisure Studies	M
Linguistics	M
Marine Biology	M
Marine Sciences	M
Marriage and Family Therapy	M
Mathematics Education	M
Mathematics	M
Media Studies	M
Microbiology	M
Molecular Biology	M
Museum Studies	M
Music Education	M
Music	M
Natural Resources	M
Nonprofit Management	M
Nursing and Healthcare Administration	M
Nursing Education	M
Nursing—General	M
Philosophy	M,O
Physical Therapy	M,D
Physics	M
Physiology	M
Political Science	M
Psychology—General	M
Public Administration	M
Public Health—General	M
Public Policy	M
Reading Education	M,O
Recreation and Park Management	M
Rehabilitation Counseling	M
Secondary Education	M
Social Work	M
Software Engineering	M
Spanish	M
Special Education	M,D,O
Speech and Interpersonal Communication	M
Theater	M
Women's Studies	M
Writing	M

SAN FRANCISCO THEOLOGICAL SEMINARY

Theology	P,M,D

SAN JOAQUIN COLLEGE OF LAW

Law	P

SAN JOSE STATE UNIVERSITY

Accounting	M
Aerospace/Aeronautical Engineering	M
Anthropology	M
Applied Arts and Design—General	M
Applied Economics	M
Applied Mathematics	M
Art Education	M
Art History	M
Art/Fine Arts	M
Biological and Biomedical Sciences—General	M
Business Administration and Management—General	M
Chemical Engineering	M
Chemistry	M
Child and Family Studies	M
Civil Engineering	M
Clinical Psychology	M
Communication Disorders	M
Communication—General	M
Comparative Literature	M,O
Computer Art and Design	M
Computer Engineering	M
Computer Science	M
Counselor Education	M
Criminal Justice and Criminology	M
Ecology	M
Economics	M
Education—General	M,O
Educational Leadership and Administration	M,O
Educational Media/Instructional Technology	M,O
Electrical Engineering	M
Elementary Education	M,O
Engineering and Applied Sciences—General	M
English as a Second Language	M,O

*M—master's degree; P—first professional degree; D—doctorate; O—other advanced degree; *—Close-Up and/or Announcement or Display in one of the other books in this series*

English Education M,O
English M,O
Environmental Management and Policy M
Ergonomics and Human Factors M
Experimental Psychology M
Film, Television, and Video Production M
French M
Geographic Information Systems M,O
Geography M,O
Geology M
Gerontological Nursing M,O
Gerontology M,O
Health Education M,O
Higher Education M,O
Hispanic Studies M
History M
Industrial and Manufacturing Management M
Industrial and Organizational Psychology M
Industrial/Management Engineering M
Information Studies M,D
Interdisciplinary Studies M
Kinesiology and Movement Studies M
Library Science M,D
Linguistics M,O
Management Information Systems M
Marine Sciences M
Mass Communication M
Materials Engineering M
Mathematics Education M
Mathematics M
Mechanical Engineering M
Meteorology M
Microbiology M
Molecular Biology M
Music M
Nursing and Healthcare Administration M,O
Nursing Education M,O
Nursing—General M,O
Nutrition M
Occupational Therapy M
Philosophy M,O
Photography M
Physics M
Physiology M
Psychology—General M
Public Administration M
Public Health—General M,O
Quality Management M
Recreation and Park Management M
Secondary Education M,O
Social Work M,O
Sociology M
Software Engineering M
Spanish M
Special Education M,O
Speech and Interpersonal Communication M
Statistics M
Student Affairs M
Systems Engineering M
Taxation M
Theater M
Transportation Management M
Urban and Regional Planning M,O
Writing M,O

SAN JUAN BAUTISTA SCHOOL OF MEDICINE

Allopathic Medicine P

SANTA CLARA UNIVERSITY

Applied Mathematics M
Business Administration and Management—General M
Civil Engineering M
Computer Engineering M,D,O
Computer Science M,D,O
Counseling Psychology M
Counselor Education M
Education—General M,O
Educational Leadership and Administration M
Electrical Engineering M,D,O
Engineering and Applied Sciences—General M,D,O
Engineering Design M,D,O
Engineering Management M
Law P,M,O
Management Information Systems M
Materials Engineering M,D,O
Mechanical Engineering M,D,O
Music M
Pastoral Ministry and Counseling M
Religion M
Software Engineering M,D,O
Special Education M,O
Telecommunications Management M,D,O

SARAH LAWRENCE COLLEGE

Child Development M
Dance M*
Education—General M
Genetic Counseling M
History M
Human Genetics M
Interdisciplinary Studies M
Public Health—General M*
Theater M
Women's Studies M*
Writing M

SAVANNAH COLLEGE OF ART AND DESIGN

Advertising and Public Relations M
Applied Arts and Design—General M
Architectural History M
Architecture M
Art History M
Art/Fine Arts M*
Arts Administration M
Computer Art and Design M
Education—General M
Film, Television, and Video Production M
Film, Television, and Video Theory and Criticism M
Graphic Design M
Historic Preservation M
Illustration M
Industrial Design M
Interior Design M
Internet and Interactive Multimedia M
Media Studies M
Music M
Photography M
Textile Design M
Theater M
Urban Design M
Writing M

SAVANNAH STATE UNIVERSITY

Business Administration and Management—General M
Marine Sciences M
Public Administration M
Social Work M
Urban Studies M

SAYBROOK GRADUATE SCHOOL AND RESEARCH CENTER

Clinical Psychology M,D
Health Psychology M,D
Marriage and Family Therapy M,D
Organizational Behavior M,D
Organizational Management M,D
Psychology—General M,D
Transpersonal and Humanistic Psychology M,D

SCHILLER INTERNATIONAL UNIVERSITY (GERMANY)

Business Administration and Management—General M
International Business M
Management Information Systems M

SCHILLER INTERNATIONAL UNIVERSITY

Business Administration and Management—General M
International Affairs M
International Business M

SCHILLER INTERNATIONAL UNIVERSITY (SPAIN)

Business Administration and Management—General M
International Business M

SCHILLER INTERNATIONAL UNIVERSITY

Business Administration and Management—General M
International Business M

SCHILLER INTERNATIONAL UNIVERSITY (UNITED KINGDOM)

Corporate and Organizational Communication M
Hospitality Management M
International Affairs M
International Business M
Management Information Systems M
Travel and Tourism M

SCHILLER INTERNATIONAL UNIVERSITY (UNITED STATES)

Business Administration and Management—General M
Finance and Banking M
Hospitality Management M
International Business M
Management Information Systems M
Travel and Tourism M

SCHOOL OF ADVANCED AIR AND SPACE STUDIES

Military and Defense Studies M

THE SCHOOL OF PROFESSIONAL PSYCHOLOGY AT FOREST INSTITUTE

Clinical Psychology M,D,O
Counseling Psychology M,D,O
Marriage and Family Therapy M,D,O
Psychology—General M,D,O

SCHOOL OF THE ART INSTITUTE OF CHICAGO

Applied Arts and Design—General M
Architecture M
Art Education M
Art History M,O
Art Therapy M
Art/Fine Arts M*
Arts Administration M
Arts Journalism M
Film, Television, and Video Production M
Graphic Design M
Historic Preservation M
Interior Design M
Journalism M
Materials Sciences M
Music M
Photography M
Textile Design M,O
Writing M,O

SCHOOL OF THE MUSEUM OF FINE ARTS, BOSTON

Art/Fine Arts M

SCHOOL OF VISUAL ARTS

Applied Arts and Design—General M
Art Education M
Art Therapy M
Art/Fine Arts M
Computer Art and Design M
Film, Television, and Video Production M
Illustration M
Internet and Interactive Multimedia M
Photography M

SCHREINER UNIVERSITY

Education—General M

SEABURY-WESTERN THEOLOGICAL SEMINARY

Music P,M,D,O
Theology P,M,D,O

SEATTLE INSTITUTE OF ORIENTAL MEDICINE

Acupuncture and Oriental Medicine M

SEATTLE PACIFIC UNIVERSITY

Adult Nursing M,O
Business Administration and Management—General M
Clinical Psychology D
Counselor Education M,D,O
Curriculum and Instruction M
Educational Leadership and Administration M,D,O
English as a Second Language M
Family Nurse Practitioner Studies M,O
Gerontological Nursing M,O
Industrial and Organizational Psychology M,D
Management Information Systems M
Marriage and Family Therapy M,O
Nursing and Healthcare Administration M
Nursing Education M

Nursing Informatics	M
Nursing—General	M
Reading Education	M
Secondary Education	M,O
Writing	M

SEATTLE UNIVERSITY

Accounting	M
Adult Education	M,O
Business Administration and Management—General	M,O
Community Health Nursing	M
Counselor Education	M,O
Criminal Justice and Criminology	M
Curriculum and Instruction	M,O
Education—General	M,D,O
Educational Leadership and Administration	M,D,O
Engineering and Applied Sciences—General	M
English as a Second Language	M,O
Finance and Banking	M,O
Law	P,O
Nonprofit Management	M
Nursing and Healthcare Administration	M
Nursing—General	M
Organizational Management	M,O
Pastoral Ministry and Counseling	M
Psychiatric Nursing	M
Psychology—General	M
Public Administration	M
Reading Education	M,O
School Psychology	M,O
Software Engineering	M
Special Education	M,O
Sports Management	M
Theology	P,M,O
Transpersonal and Humanistic Psychology	M

SEMINARY OF THE IMMACULATE CONCEPTION

Pastoral Ministry and Counseling	P,M,D,O
Theology	P,M,D,O

SEMINARY OF THE SOUTHWEST

Pastoral Ministry and Counseling	P,M,O
Religion	P,M,O
Theology	P,M,O

SETON HALL UNIVERSITY

Accounting	M
Acute Care/Critical Care Nursing	M
Adult Nursing	M
Advertising and Public Relations	M
Allied Health—General	M,D
Analytical Chemistry	M,D
Art/Fine Arts	M
Asian Languages	M
Asian Studies	M*
Athletic Training and Sports Medicine	M
Biochemistry	M,D
Biological and Biomedical Sciences—General	M,D
Business Administration and Management—General	M,O
Chemistry	M,D*
Chinese	M
Communication Disorders	M
Communication—General	M
Corporate and Organizational Communication	M*
Counseling Psychology	M,D
Education—General	M,D,O
Educational Leadership and Administration	D,O
Educational Media/Instructional Technology	M
English	M*
Experimental Psychology	M*
Finance and Banking	M
Gerontological Nursing	M
Health Services Management and Hospital Administration	M,O*
Higher Education	D
History	M*
Holocaust Studies	M
Inorganic Chemistry	M,D
International Affairs	M*
International Business	M,O
Jewish Studies	M
Law	P,M
Management Information Systems	M
Marketing	M
Marriage and Family Therapy	M,D,O
Microbiology	M,D
Molecular Biology	M,D*
Multilingual and Multicultural Education	O
Museum Education	M
Museum Studies	M*
Neuroscience	M,D
Nonprofit Management	M,O
Nursing and Healthcare Administration	M
Nursing Education	M
Nursing—General	M,D
Occupational Therapy	M
Organic Chemistry	M,D
Pastoral Ministry and Counseling	P,M
Pediatric Nursing	M
Pharmaceutical Administration	M
Physical Chemistry	M,D
Physical Therapy	D
Physician Assistant Studies	M
Psychology—General	M,D,O
Public Administration	M,O
Public Policy	M,O*
Religion	M*
School Nursing	M
School Psychology	O
Speech and Interpersonal Communication	M
Sports Management	M
Student Affairs	M
Taxation	M
Theology	P,M
Women's Health Nursing	M
Writing	M

SETON HILL UNIVERSITY

Art Therapy	M,O
Business Administration and Management—General	M
Education—General	M
Elementary Education	M,O
Holocaust Studies	O
Marriage and Family Therapy	M
Physician Assistant Studies	M
Special Education	M,O
Writing	M

SEWANEE: THE UNIVERSITY OF THE SOUTH

English	M
Theology	P,M,D
Writing	M

SHASTA BIBLE COLLEGE

Educational Leadership and Administration	M
Pastoral Ministry and Counseling	M
Religious Education	M

SHAW UNIVERSITY

Curriculum and Instruction	M
Theology	P,M

SHENANDOAH UNIVERSITY

Allied Health—General	M,D,O
Arts Administration	M,D,O
Athletic Training and Sports Medicine	M
Business Administration and Management—General	M,O
Dance	M,D,O
Education—General	M,D,O
Educational Leadership and Administration	M,D,O
Elementary Education	M,D,O
English as a Second Language	M,D,O
Family Nurse Practitioner Studies	M,O
Health Services Management and Hospital Administration	M,O
Management Information Systems	M,O
Middle School Education	M,D,O
Music Education	M,D,O
Music	M,D,O
Nurse Midwifery	M,O
Nursing—General	M,O
Occupational Therapy	M
Pharmacy	P
Physical Therapy	D
Physician Assistant Studies	M
Psychiatric Nursing	M,O
Public Administration	M,D,O
Secondary Education	M,D,O
Therapies—Dance, Drama, and Music	M,D,O

SHEPHERD UNIVERSITY

Curriculum and Instruction	M

SHERMAN COLLEGE OF STRAIGHT CHIROPRACTIC

Chiropractic	P

SHIPPENSBURG UNIVERSITY OF PENNSYLVANIA

Addictions/Substance Abuse Counseling	M,O
Biological and Biomedical Sciences—General	M
Business Administration and Management—General	M,O
Communication—General	M
Computer Science	M
Counseling Psychology	M,O
Counselor Education	M,O
Criminal Justice and Criminology	M
Curriculum and Instruction	M
Early Childhood Education	M
Education—General	M,O
Educational Leadership and Administration	M
Elementary Education	M
English Education	M
Environmental Management and Policy	M
Foreign Languages Education	M
Geography	M
Gerontology	M,O
Higher Education	M
History	M,O
Marriage and Family Therapy	M,O
Mathematics Education	M
Middle School Education	M
Organizational Management	M
Psychology—General	M
Public Administration	M
Public History	M,O
Reading Education	M
Science Education	M
Social Psychology	M,O
Social Work	M,O
Sociology	M
Special Education	M
Student Affairs	M,O

SHORTER COLLEGE

Business Administration and Management—General	M

SH'OR YOSHUV RABBINICAL COLLEGE

Theology	

SIENA HEIGHTS UNIVERSITY

Early Childhood Education	M
Education—General	M
Educational Leadership and Administration	M
Elementary Education	M
Mathematics Education	M
Middle School Education	M
Reading Education	M
Secondary Education	M

SIERRA NEVADA COLLEGE

Education—General	M
Elementary Education	M
Secondary Education	M

SILVER LAKE COLLEGE

Business Administration and Management—General	M
Education—General	M
Educational Leadership and Administration	M
Music Education	M
Organizational Behavior	M
Special Education	M

SIMMONS COLLEGE

Business Administration and Management—General	M,O
Corporate and Organizational Communication	M
Counselor Education	M,D,O
Cultural Studies	M
Education—General	M,D,O
Educational Leadership and Administration	M,O
Educational Media/Instructional Technology	M,D,O
Elementary Education	M,O
English as a Second Language	M,O
English	M
Entrepreneurship	M,O
Gender Studies	M
Health Education	M,D,O
Health Promotion	M,O
Health Services Management and Hospital Administration	M,O
Information Studies	M,D,O
Library Science	M,D,O
Middle School Education	M,O
Nursing—General	M,D,O
Nutrition	M,O
Physical Therapy	D

*M—master's degree; P—first professional degree; D—doctorate; O—other advanced degree; *—Close-Up and/or Announcement or Display in one of the other books in this series*

Public History
Secondary Education M,O
Social Work M,D
Spanish M
Special Education M,D,O
Urban Education M,O

SIMON FRASER UNIVERSITY

Actuarial Science M,D
Anthropology M,D
Applied Mathematics M,D
Archaeology M,D
Art Education M,D
Biochemistry M,D
Biological and Biomedical Sciences—General M,D
Biophysics M,D
Biotechnology M,D
Business Administration and Management—General M,D
Chemical Physics M,D
Chemistry M,D
Communication—General M,D
Community Health M
Comparative and Interdisciplinary Arts M
Computational Sciences M,D
Computer Science M,D
Counselor Education M
Criminal Justice and Criminology M,D
Curriculum and Instruction M,D
Economics M,D
Education—General M,D
Educational Leadership and Administration M,D
Educational Media/ Instructional Technology M,D
Educational Psychology M,D
Engineering and Applied Sciences—General M,D
English as a Second Language M
English M,D
Entomology M,D
Environmental Management and Policy M,D
Finance and Banking M,D
Foundations and Philosophy of Education M,D
French M
Geography M,D
Geosciences M,D
Gerontology M,D
History M,D
Information Science M,D
International Business M,D
Internet and Interactive Multimedia M,D
Kinesiology and Movement Studies M,D
Latin American Studies M
Liberal Studies M
Linguistics M,D
Management of Technology M,D
Mathematics Education M,D
Mathematics M,D
Molecular Biology M,D
Philosophy M,D
Physics M,D
Political Science M,D
Psychology—General M,D
Public Health—General M
Public Policy M
Publishing M
Sociology M,D
Statistics M,D
Toxicology M,D
Urban Studies M,O
Women's Studies M,D

SIMPSON UNIVERSITY

Cultural Studies P,M
Education—General M
Educational Leadership and Administration M
Missions and Missiology P,M
Pastoral Ministry and Counseling P,M
Religion P,M

SINTE GLESKA UNIVERSITY

Education—General M
Elementary Education M

SIOUX FALLS SEMINARY

Marriage and Family Therapy M
Pastoral Ministry and Counseling P,M
Religion M
Theology M,D,O

SIT GRADUATE INSTITUTE

Business Administration and Management—General M
Conflict Resolution and Mediation/Peace Studies M
Education—General M
English as a Second Language M
Entrepreneurship M
Foreign Languages Education M
International Affairs M
International and Comparative Education M
International Business M
Near and Middle Eastern Studies M
Organizational Management M
Sustainable Development M

SKIDMORE COLLEGE

Liberal Studies M

SLIPPERY ROCK UNIVERSITY OF PENNSYLVANIA

Counselor Education M
Education—General M
Educational Leadership and Administration M
Elementary Education M
English M
Environmental Education M
Environmental Management and Policy M
History M
Mathematics Education M
Physical Education M
Physical Therapy D
Reading Education M
Science Education M
Secondary Education M
Special Education M
Sports Management M
Student Affairs M
Sustainable Development M
Writing M

SMITH COLLEGE

Biological and Biomedical Sciences—General M
Chemistry M
Dance M
Education—General M
Elementary Education M
English Education M
Exercise and Sports Science M
Foreign Languages Education M
French M
History M
Mathematics Education M
Mathematics O
Middle School Education M
Science Education M
Secondary Education M
Social Sciences Education M
Social Work M,D
Special Education M
Theater M

SOJOURNER-DOUGLASS COLLEGE

Human Services M
Public Administration M
Reading Education M
Urban Education M

SONOMA STATE UNIVERSITY

Anthropology M
Biological and Biomedical Sciences—General M
Business Administration and Management—General M
Counseling Psychology M
Counselor Education M
Curriculum and Instruction M
Education—General M
Educational Leadership and Administration M
Elementary Education M
English M
Environmental Biology M
Family Nurse Practitioner Studies M
History M
Interdisciplinary Studies M
Kinesiology and Movement Studies M
Marriage and Family Therapy M
Political Science M
Public Administration M
Public History M
Special Education M
Writing M

SOUTH BAYLO UNIVERSITY

Acupuncture and Oriental Medicine M

SOUTH CAROLINA STATE UNIVERSITY

Agricultural Economics and Agribusiness M
Allied Health—General M
Business Education M
Child and Family Studies M
Civil Engineering M
Communication Disorders M
Counselor Education M
Early Childhood Education M
Education—General M
Educational Leadership and Administration D,O
Elementary Education M
English Education M
Entrepreneurship M
Family and Consumer Sciences-General M
Home Economics Education M
Human Services M
Mathematics Education M
Mechanical Engineering M
Nutrition M
Rehabilitation Counseling M
Science Education M
Secondary Education M
Social Sciences Education M
Special Education M
Transportation and Highway Engineering M
Vocational and Technical Education M

SOUTH DAKOTA SCHOOL OF MINES AND TECHNOLOGY

Atmospheric Sciences M,D
Bioengineering M,D
Biomedical Engineering M,D
Chemical Engineering M
Chemistry M
Civil Engineering M
Computer Science M
Electrical Engineering M
Engineering and Applied Sciences—General M,D
Environmental Sciences D
Geological Engineering M,D
Geology M,D
Management of Technology M
Materials Engineering M,D*
Materials Sciences M,D
Mechanical Engineering M
Metallurgical Engineering and Metallurgy M
Nanotechnology D
Paleontology M
Physics M

SOUTH DAKOTA STATE UNIVERSITY

Agricultural Engineering M,D
Agricultural Sciences—General M,D
Agronomy and Soil Sciences M,D
Animal Sciences M,D
Biological and Biomedical Sciences—General M,D
Biosystems Engineering M,D
Chemistry M,D
Civil Engineering M
Clothing and Textiles M
Communication—General M
Computational Sciences M,D
Counselor Education M
Curriculum and Instruction M
Economics M
Education—General M
Educational Leadership and Administration M
Electrical Engineering M,D
Engineering and Applied Sciences—General M,D
English M
Family and Consumer Sciences-General M
Fish, Game, and Wildlife Management M,D
Food Science and Technology M
Geography M
Geosciences M,D
Health Education M
Hospitality Management M
Human Development M
Human Resources Development M
Industrial/Management Engineering M
Interior Design M
Journalism M
Mathematics M,D
Mechanical Engineering M
Microbiology M,D
Nursing—General M,D
Nutrition M
Pharmaceutical Sciences M,D
Pharmacy P
Physical Education M
Physics M
Plant Sciences M,D
Recreation and Park Management M
Rural Sociology M,D
Statistics M,D
Veterinary Sciences M,D

SOUTHEASTERN BAPTIST THEOLOGICAL SEMINARY

Ethics P,M,D
Missions and Missiology P,M,D
Music P,M,D
Philosophy P,M,D

Psychology—General	P,M,D
Religious Education	P,M,D
Theology	P,M,D
Women's Studies	P,M,D

SOUTHEASTERN LOUISIANA UNIVERSITY

Applied Science and Technology	M
Biological and Biomedical Sciences—General	M
Business Administration and Management—General	M
Communication Disorders	M
Communication—General	M
Counselor Education	M
Curriculum and Instruction	M
Education—General	M,D
Educational Leadership and Administration	M,D
Educational Media/Instructional Technology	M,D
Elementary Education	M
English	M
Health Education	M
History	M
Kinesiology and Movement Studies	M
Music	M
Nursing—General	M
Psychology—General	M
Sociology	M
Special Education	M

SOUTHEASTERN OKLAHOMA STATE UNIVERSITY

Aviation Management	M
Aviation	M
Business Administration and Management—General	M
Counselor Education	M
Education—General	M
Educational Leadership and Administration	M
Elementary Education	M
Industrial and Manufacturing Management	M
Mathematics Education	M
Reading Education	M
Social Psychology	M

SOUTHEASTERN UNIVERSITY

Accounting	M
Business Administration and Management—General	M
Computer Science	M
Finance and Banking	M
Health Services Management and Hospital Administration	M
International Business	M
Management Information Systems	M
Marketing	M
Public Administration	M

SOUTHEAST MISSOURI STATE UNIVERSITY

Accounting	M
Biological and Biomedical Sciences—General	M
Business Administration and Management—General	M
Chemistry	M
Communication Disorders	M
Counseling Psychology	M,O
Counselor Education	M,O
Criminal Justice and Criminology	M
Educational Leadership and Administration	M,O
Elementary Education	M
English as a Second Language	M
English	M
Entrepreneurship	M
Environmental Management and Policy	M
Exercise and Sports Science	M
Finance and Banking	M
Forensic Sciences	M
Foundations and Philosophy of Education	M
Health Services Management and Hospital Administration	M
Higher Education	M,O
History	M
Industrial and Manufacturing Management	M
International Business	M
Leisure Studies	M
Management of Technology	M
Mathematics	M
Middle School Education	M
Music Education	M
Nursing—General	M
Nutrition	M
Public Administration	M
School Psychology	M,O
Science Education	M
Secondary Education	M
Special Education	M
Sports Management	M

SOUTHERN ADVENTIST UNIVERSITY

Accounting	M
Adult Nursing	M
Business Administration and Management—General	M
Counseling Psychology	M
Counselor Education	M
Curriculum and Instruction	M
Education—General	M
Educational Leadership and Administration	M
Family Nurse Practitioner Studies	M
Finance and Banking	M
Health Services Management and Hospital Administration	M
Human Resources Management	M
Marketing	M
Missions and Missiology	M
Nursing and Healthcare Administration	M
Nursing—General	M
Psychology—General	M
Reading Education	M
Religion	M
Religious Education	M
Theology	M

SOUTHERN ARKANSAS UNIVERSITY–MAGNOLIA

Agricultural Sciences—General	M
Business Administration and Management—General	M
Computer Science	M
Counseling Psychology	M
Counselor Education	M
Education—General	M
Educational Leadership and Administration	M
Elementary Education	M
Kinesiology and Movement Studies	M
Library Science	M
Public Administration	M
Secondary Education	M

SOUTHERN BAPTIST THEOLOGICAL SEMINARY

Missions and Missiology	P,M,D
Music	P,M,D
Pastoral Ministry and Counseling	P,M,D
Philosophy	P,M,D
Religion	P,M,D
Religious Education	P,M,D
Theology	P,M,D

SOUTHERN CALIFORNIA COLLEGE OF OPTOMETRY

Optometry	P

SOUTHERN CALIFORNIA INSTITUTE OF ARCHITECTURE

Architecture	M

SOUTHERN CALIFORNIA SEMINARY

Counseling Psychology	P,M,D
Psychology—General	P,M,D
Religion	P,M,D
Theology	P,M,D

SOUTHERN CALIFORNIA UNIVERSITY OF HEALTH SCIENCES

Acupuncture and Oriental Medicine	M
Chiropractic	P

SOUTHERN COLLEGE OF OPTOMETRY

Optometry	P

SOUTHERN CONNECTICUT STATE UNIVERSITY

Art Education	M
Biological and Biomedical Sciences—General	M
Business Administration and Management—General	M
Chemistry	M
Communication Disorders	M
Computer Science	M
Counselor Education	M,O
Education—General	M,D,O
Educational Leadership and Administration	M,D,O
Educational Measurement and Evaluation	M
Elementary Education	M,O
English as a Second Language	M
English	M
Environmental Education	M,O
Exercise and Sports Science	M
Foundations and Philosophy of Education	O
Health Education	M
History	M
Information Studies	M,O
Leisure Studies	M
Library Science	M,O
Marriage and Family Therapy	M
Mathematics	M
Multilingual and Multicultural Education	M
Nursing and Healthcare Administration	M
Nursing Education	M
Nursing—General	M
Physical Education	M
Political Science	M
Psychology—General	M
Public Health—General	M
Reading Education	M,O
Recreation and Park Management	M
School Psychology	M,O
Science Education	M,O
Social Work	M
Sociology	M
Special Education	M,O
Sport Psychology	M
Urban Studies	M
Women's Studies	M

SOUTHERN EVANGELICAL SEMINARY

Jewish Studies	M,D,O
Missions and Missiology	P,M,O
Near and Middle Eastern Studies	M,D,O
Pastoral Ministry and Counseling	P,M,O
Philosophy	M,D,O
Religion	P,M,D,O
Religious Education	P,M,O
Theology	P,M,D,O

SOUTHERN ILLINOIS UNIVERSITY CARBONDALE

Accounting	M,D
Agricultural Economics and Agribusiness	M
Agricultural Sciences—General	M*
Agronomy and Soil Sciences	M
Animal Sciences	M
Anthropology	M,D*
Applied Arts and Design—General	M*
Applied Physics	M,D*
Architecture	M
Art/Fine Arts	M
Biochemistry	M,D
Biological and Biomedical Sciences—General	M,D
Biomedical Engineering	M*
Business Administration and Management—General	M,D*
Chemistry	M,D*
Civil Engineering	M*
Clinical Psychology	M,D
Communication Disorders	M
Communication—General	M,D*
Community Health	M
Computer Engineering	M,D
Computer Science	M,D*
Counseling Psychology	M,D
Counselor Education	M,D
Criminal Justice and Criminology	M
Cultural Studies	M
Curriculum and Instruction	M,D*
Economics	M,D*
Education—General	M,D
Educational Leadership and Administration	M,D*
Educational Measurement and Evaluation	M,D
Educational Psychology	M,D*
Electrical Engineering	M,D*
Energy and Power Engineering	D
Engineering and Applied Sciences—General	M,D*
English as a Second Language	M
English	M,D*
Environmental Sciences	D*
Experimental Psychology	M,D
Forestry	M
Geography	M,D
Geology	M,D
Health Education	M,D*
Health Law	M
Health Services Management and Hospital Administration	M
Higher Education	M
History	M,D*
Horticulture	M
Human Development	M,D

M—master's degree; P—first professional degree; D—doctorate; O—other advanced degree; *—Close-Up and/or Announcement or Display in one of the other books in this series

Journalism	D
Law	P,M
Legal and Justice Studies	M
Linguistics	M
Manufacturing Engineering	M*
Mass Communication	M
Mathematics	M,D*
Mechanical Engineering	M*
Mechanics	M,D*
Media Studies	M
Microbiology	M,D
Mineral/Mining Engineering	M*
Molecular Biology	M,D*
Music Education	M
Music	M
Nutrition	M
Pharmacology	M,D*
Philosophy	M,D*
Physical Education	M
Physician Assistant Studies	M
Physics	M,D
Physiology	M,D*
Plant Biology	M,D*
Plant Sciences	M
Political Science	M,D*
Psychology—General	M,D*
Public Administration	M
Recreation and Park Management	M
Rehabilitation Counseling	M,D*
Rhetoric	M,D
Social Work	M
Sociology	M,D*
Special Education	M
Speech and Interpersonal Communication	M,D*
Statistics	M,D
Theater	M,D*
Vocational and Technical Education	M,D*
Writing	M*
Zoology	M,D*

SOUTHERN ILLINOIS UNIVERSITY EDWARDSVILLE

Accounting	M
Art Education	M
Art Therapy	M
Art/Fine Arts	M
Biological and Biomedical Sciences—General	M
Biotechnology	M
Business Administration and Management—General	M
Chemistry	M
Civil Engineering	M
Clinical Psychology	M
Communication Disorders	M
Computer Science	M
Corporate and Organizational Communication	O
Curriculum and Instruction	M
Dentistry	P
Economics	M
Education—General	M,O
Educational Leadership and Administration	M,O
Educational Media/Instructional Technology	M,O
Electrical Engineering	M
Engineering and Applied Sciences—General	M
English as a Second Language	M,O
English Education	M,O
English	M,O
Environmental Management and Policy	M
Environmental Sciences	M
Family Nurse Practitioner Studies	M,O
Finance and Banking	M
Foreign Languages Education	M
Foundations and Philosophy of Education	M
Geography	M
Health Education	M,O
History	M
Industrial and Organizational Psychology	M
Industrial/Management Engineering	M
Kinesiology and Movement Studies	M,O
Management Information Systems	M
Marketing Research	M
Mass Communication	M
Mathematics Education	M
Mathematics	M
Mechanical Engineering	M
Media Studies	O
Museum Studies	O
Music Education	M,O
Music	M
Nurse Anesthesia	M,O
Nursing and Healthcare Administration	M,O
Nursing Education	M,O
Nursing—General	M,O
Pharmacy	P
Physics	M
Project Management	M
Psychology—General	M
Public Administration	M
Reading Education	M,O
School Psychology	O
Science Education	M
Secondary Education	M
Social Sciences Education	M
Social Work	M
Sociology	M
Special Education	M,O
Speech and Interpersonal Communication	M
Writing	M

SOUTHERN METHODIST UNIVERSITY

Accounting	M
Anthropology	M,D
Applied Economics	M,D
Applied Mathematics	M,D
Applied Science and Technology	M,D
Art History	M
Art/Fine Arts	M
Arts Administration	M
Biological and Biomedical Sciences—General	M,D*
Business Administration and Management—General	M
Chemistry	M,D
Civil Engineering	M,D
Clinical Psychology	D
Communication—General	M
Computational Sciences	M,D
Computer Engineering	M,D
Computer Science	M,D
Conflict Resolution and Mediation/Peace Studies	M,O
Counselor Education	M,O
Dance	M
Economics	M,D
Education of the Gifted	M,D,O
Education—General	M,D,O
Electrical Engineering	M,D
Engineering and Applied Sciences—General	M,D
Engineering Management	M,D
English	M,D
Entrepreneurship	M
Environmental Engineering	M,D
Environmental Sciences	M,D
Facilities Management	M,D
Film, Television, and Video Production	M
Finance and Banking	M
Geology	M,D
Geophysics	M,D
Hazardous Materials Management	M,D
History	M,D
Information Science	M,D
Law	P,M,D
Management Information Systems	M
Management Strategy and Policy	M
Manufacturing Engineering	M,D
Marketing	M
Mathematics	M,D
Mechanical Engineering	M,D
Medieval and Renaissance Studies	M
Multilingual and Multicultural Education	M,D,O
Music Education	M,O
Music	M,O
Operations Research	M,D
Photography	M
Physics	M,D
Psychology—General	D
Religion	M,D
Software Engineering	M,D
Statistics	M,D
Systems Engineering	M,D
Systems Science	M,D
Taxation	P,M,D
Telecommunications	M,D
Theater	M
Theology	P,M,D

SOUTHERN NAZARENE UNIVERSITY

Business Administration and Management—General	M
Counseling Psychology	M
Curriculum and Instruction	M
Education—General	M
Educational Leadership and Administration	M
Marriage and Family Therapy	M
Nursing and Healthcare Administration	M
Nursing Education	M
Nursing—General	M
Psychology—General	M
Religion	M
Theology	M

SOUTHERN NEW ENGLAND SCHOOL OF LAW

Law	P

SOUTHERN NEW HAMPSHIRE UNIVERSITY

Accounting	M,D,O
Addictions/Substance Abuse Counseling	M,O
Business Administration and Management—General	M,D,O*
Business Education	M,O
Child Development	M,O
Clinical Psychology	M,O
Community Health	M,O
Computer Education	M,O
Curriculum and Instruction	M,O
Economic Development	M,D
Education—General	M,O
Educational Leadership and Administration	M,O
Elementary Education	M,O
English as a Second Language	M,O
Finance and Banking	M,D,O
Hospitality Management	M,D,O
Human Resources Development	M,O
Human Resources Management	M,D,O
International Business	M,D,O
Management Information Systems	M,D,O
Marketing	M,D,O
Nonprofit Management	M,D,O
Organizational Management	M,D,O
Project Management	M,D,O
Psychology—General	M,O
Public Policy	M,D
Secondary Education	M,O
Special Education	M,O
Sports Management	M,D,O
Taxation	M,D,O
Vocational and Technical Education	M,O
Writing	M,O

SOUTHERN OREGON UNIVERSITY

Business Administration and Management—General	M
Computer Science	M
Counselor Education	M
Early Childhood Education	M
Education—General	M
Educational Leadership and Administration	M
Elementary Education	M
Environmental Education	M
Human Services	M
Mathematics	M
Music	M
Psychology—General	M
Reading Education	M
Secondary Education	M
Social Sciences	M
Special Education	M

SOUTHERN POLYTECHNIC STATE UNIVERSITY

Accounting	M,O
Business Administration and Management—General	M,O
Communication—General	M,O
Computer and Information Systems Security	M,O
Computer Engineering	M
Computer Science	M,O
Construction Management	M
Corporate and Organizational Communication	M,O
Educational Media/Instructional Technology	M,O
Electrical Engineering	M
Engineering and Applied Sciences—General	M,O
Graphic Design	M,O
Industrial/Management Engineering	M,O
Information Science	M,O
Internet and Interactive Multimedia	M,O
Quality Management	M,O
Software Engineering	M,O
Systems Engineering	M,O
Technical Communication	M,O

SOUTHERN UNIVERSITY AND AGRICULTURAL AND MECHANICAL COLLEGE

Agricultural Sciences—General	M
Analytical Chemistry	M
Biochemistry	M
Biological and Biomedical Sciences—General	M
Business Administration and Management—General	M
Chemistry	M
Computer Science	M
Counselor Education	M

Criminal Justice and Criminology	M
Education—General	M,D
Educational Leadership and Administration	M
Educational Media/ Instructional Technology	M
Elementary Education	M
Engineering and Applied Sciences—General	M
Environmental Sciences	M
Family Nurse Practitioner Studies	M,D,O
Forestry	M
Gerontological Nursing	M,D,O
History	M
Inorganic Chemistry	M
Law	P
Mass Communication	M
Mathematics Education	D
Mathematics	M
Nursing and Healthcare Administration	M,D,O
Nursing Education	M,D,O
Nursing—General	M,D,O
Organic Chemistry	M
Physical Chemistry	M
Physics	M
Political Science	M
Psychology—General	M
Public Administration	M
Public Policy	D
Recreation and Park Management	M
Rehabilitation Counseling	M
Science Education	D
Secondary Education	M
Social Sciences	M
Special Education	M,D

SOUTHERN UNIVERSITY AT NEW ORLEANS

Social Work	M

SOUTHERN UTAH UNIVERSITY

Accounting	M
Arts Administration	M
Business Administration and Management—General	M
Communication—General	M
Education—General	M
Exercise and Sports Science	M
Forensic Sciences	M
Public Administration	M

SOUTHERN WESLEYAN UNIVERSITY

Business Administration and Management—General	M
Education—General	M
Pastoral Ministry and Counseling	M

SOUTH TEXAS COLLEGE OF LAW

Law	P

SOUTH UNIVERSITY (AL)

Business Administration and Management—General	M
Counseling Psychology	M*
Health Services Management and Hospital Administration	M

SOUTH UNIVERSITY (FL)

Business Administration and Management—General	M
Counseling Psychology	M*
Health Services Management and Hospital Administration	M

SOUTH UNIVERSITY (GA)

Anesthesiologist Assistant Studies	M
Business Administration and Management—General	M
Counseling Psychology	M*
Pharmacy	P*
Physician Assistant Studies	M*

SOUTH UNIVERSITY (SC)

Business Administration and Management—General	M
Counseling Psychology	M*
Health Services Management and Hospital Administration	M

SOUTHWEST ACUPUNCTURE COLLEGE

Acupuncture and Oriental Medicine	M

SOUTHWEST BAPTIST UNIVERSITY

Business Administration and Management—General	M
Education—General	M,O
Educational Leadership and Administration	M,O
Health Services Management and Hospital Administration	M
Physical Therapy	D

SOUTHWEST COLLEGE OF NATUROPATHIC MEDICINE AND HEALTH SCIENCES

Naturopathic Medicine	D*

SOUTHWESTERN ADVENTIST UNIVERSITY

Accounting	M
Business Administration and Management—General	M
Curriculum and Instruction	M
Education—General	M
Educational Leadership and Administration	M
Finance and Banking	M
Reading Education	M

SOUTHWESTERN ASSEMBLIES OF GOD UNIVERSITY

Counseling Psychology	M
Curriculum and Instruction	M
Education—General	M
Educational Leadership and Administration	M
History	M
Missions and Missiology	P,M
Pastoral Ministry and Counseling	P,M
Religion	P,M
Religious Education	M
Secondary Education	M
Theology	P,M

SOUTHWESTERN BAPTIST THEOLOGICAL SEMINARY

Music	M,D,O
Religious Education	M,D,O
Theology	P,M,D,O

SOUTHWESTERN CHRISTIAN UNIVERSITY

Missions and Missiology	M
Pastoral Ministry and Counseling	M

SOUTHWESTERN COLLEGE (KS)

Business Administration and Management—General	M
Criminal Justice and Criminology	M
Curriculum and Instruction	M
Education—General	M
Organizational Management	M
Pastoral Ministry and Counseling	M
Special Education	M

SOUTHWESTERN COLLEGE (NM)

Art Therapy	M
Counseling Psychology	M,O*
Health Psychology	O
Psychology—General	O
Social Psychology	O
Thanatology	M,O

SOUTHWESTERN LAW SCHOOL

Law	P,M

SOUTHWESTERN OKLAHOMA STATE UNIVERSITY

Allied Health—General	M
Art Education	M
Business Administration and Management—General	M
Counselor Education	M
Early Childhood Education	M
Education—General	M
Educational Leadership and Administration	M
Educational Measurement and Evaluation	M
Elementary Education	M
English Education	M
Kinesiology and Movement Studies	M
Mathematics Education	M
Microbiology	M
Music Education	M
Music	M
Pharmacy	P
Recreation and Park Management	M
School Psychology	M
Science Education	M
Secondary Education	M
Social Sciences Education	M
Special Education	M

SOUTHWEST MINNESOTA STATE UNIVERSITY

Business Administration and Management—General	M
Education—General	M
Special Education	M

SPALDING UNIVERSITY

Adult Nursing	M
Business Administration and Management—General	M
Clinical Psychology	M,D
Communication—General	M
Corporate and Organizational Communication	M
Counselor Education	M
Education—General	M,D
Educational Leadership and Administration	M,D
Elementary Education	M
Family Nurse Practitioner Studies	M
Middle School Education	M
Nursing and Healthcare Administration	M
Nursing—General	M
Occupational Therapy	M
Pediatric Nursing	M
Psychology—General	M,D
Secondary Education	M
Social Work	M
Special Education	M
Writing	M

SPERTUS INSTITUTE OF JEWISH STUDIES

Jewish Studies	M,D
Nonprofit Management	M
Religious Education	M

SPRING ARBOR UNIVERSITY

Business Administration and Management—General	M
Child and Family Studies	M
Communication—General	M
Counseling Psychology	M
Education—General	M
Nursing—General	M
Organizational Management	M
Pastoral Ministry and Counseling	M
Special Education	M
Theology	M

SPRINGFIELD COLLEGE

Addictions/Substance Abuse Counseling	M
Art Therapy	M,O
Athletic Training and Sports Medicine	M,D
Counseling Psychology	M,O
Counselor Education	M,O
Early Childhood Education	M
Education—General	M
Educational Leadership and Administration	M
Elementary Education	M
Exercise and Sports Science	M,D
Health Education	M,D,O
Health Promotion	M,D
Health Services Management and Hospital Administration	M
Human Services	M
Industrial and Organizational Psychology	M,O
Marriage and Family Therapy	M,O
Occupational Therapy	M,O
Organizational Management	M
Physical Education	M,D,O
Physical Therapy	D
Physician Assistant Studies	M
Recreation and Park Management	M
Rehabilitation Counseling	M
Secondary Education	M
Social Psychology	M
Social Work	M
Special Education	M
Sport Psychology	M,D,O
Sports Management	M,D,O
Student Affairs	M,O

SPRING HILL COLLEGE

Business Administration and Management—General	M

*M—master's degree; P—first professional degree; D—doctorate; O—other advanced degree; *—Close-Up and/or Announcement or Display in one of the other books in this series*

Early Childhood Education	M
Education—General	M
Elementary Education	M
Liberal Studies	M
Nursing—General	M
Secondary Education	M
Theology	M

STANFORD UNIVERSITY

Aerospace/Aeronautical Engineering	M,D,O
Allopathic Medicine	P
Anthropology	M,D
Applied Physics	M,D
Art Education	M,D
Art/Fine Arts	M,D
Asian Studies	M
Biochemistry	D
Bioengineering	M,D
Biological and Biomedical Sciences—General	M,D
Biomedical Engineering	M
Biophysics	D
Business Administration and Management—General	M,D
Cancer Biology/Oncology	D
Chemical Engineering	M,D,O
Chemistry	D
Child and Family Studies	D
Chinese	M,D
Civil Engineering	M,D,O
Classics	M,D
Communication—General	M,D
Comparative Literature	D
Computational Sciences	M,D
Computer Education	M,D
Computer Science	M,D
Counseling Psychology	D
Curriculum and Instruction	M,D
Developmental Biology	D
Developmental Psychology	D
East European and Russian Studies	M
Economics	D
Education—General	M,D
Educational Leadership and Administration	M,D
Educational Measurement and Evaluation	M,D
Educational Psychology	D
Electrical Engineering	M,D,O
Engineering and Applied Sciences—General	M,D,O
Engineering Design	M
Engineering Management	M,D
English Education	M,D
English	M,D
Environmental Engineering	M,D,O
Environmental Management and Policy	M
Environmental Sciences	M,D,O
Epidemiology	M,D
Foreign Languages Education	M
Foundations and Philosophy of Education	M,D
French	M,D
Genetics	D
Geophysics	M,D
Geosciences	M,D,O
German	M,D
Health Services Research	M
Higher Education	M,D
History	M,D
Humanities	M
Immunology	D
Industrial/Management Engineering	M,D
Interdisciplinary Studies	M,D
International Affairs	M
International and Comparative Education	M,D
Italian	M,D
Japanese	M,D
Journalism	M,D
Law	P,M,D
Linguistics	M,D
Materials Engineering	M,D,O
Materials Sciences	M,D,O
Mathematical and Computational Finance	M,D
Mathematics Education	M,D
Mathematics	M,D
Mechanical Engineering	M,D,O*
Medical Informatics	M,D
Microbiology	D
Molecular Pharmacology	D
Music	M,D
Neuroscience	D
Petroleum Engineering	M,D,O
Philosophy	M,D
Physics	D
Physiology	D
Political Science	M,D
Psychology—General	D
Religion	M,D
Russian	M,D
Science Education	M,D
Slavic Languages	M,D
Social Sciences Education	M,D
Sociology	D
Spanish	M,D
Statistics	M,D
Structural Biology	D
Theater	D

STARR KING SCHOOL FOR THE MINISTRY

Theology	P

STATE UNIVERSITY OF NEW YORK AT BINGHAMTON

Accounting	M,D
Analytical Chemistry	M,D
Anthropology	M,D
Applied Physics	M
Art History	M,D*
Biological and Biomedical Sciences—General	M,D
Biopsychology	M,D
Business Administration and Management—General	M,D
Chemistry	M,D
Clinical Psychology	M,D
Cognitive Sciences	M,D
Comparative Literature	M,D
Computer Science	M,D
Cultural Studies	M,D
Early Childhood Education	M
Economics	M,D
Education—General	M,D
Electrical Engineering	M,D
Engineering and Applied Sciences—General	M,D*
English Education	M
English	M,D
Finance and Banking	M,D
Foreign Languages Education	M
Foundations and Philosophy of Education	D
French	M
Geography	M
Geology	M,D
Health Services Management and Hospital Administration	M,D
History	M,D
Industrial/Management Engineering	M,D
Inorganic Chemistry	M,D
Italian	M
Legal and Justice Studies	M,D
Materials Engineering	M,D
Materials Sciences	M,D
Mathematics Education	M
Mathematics	M,D
Mechanical Engineering	M,D
Music	M
Nursing—General	M,D,O
Organic Chemistry	M,D
Philosophy	M,D
Physical Chemistry	M,D
Physics	M
Political Science	M,D
Psychology—General	M,D
Public Administration	M
Public Policy	M,D
Reading Education	M
Science Education	M
Secondary Education	M
Social Sciences Education	M
Social Work	M
Sociology	M,D
Spanish	M,O
Special Education	M
Statistics	M,D
Systems Science	M,D
Theater	M
Translation and Interpretation	M,O

STATE UNIVERSITY OF NEW YORK AT FREDONIA

Accounting	M
Biological and Biomedical Sciences—General	M
Business Administration and Management—General	M
Chemistry	M
Communication Disorders	M
Education—General	M,O
Educational Leadership and Administration	O
Elementary Education	M
English as a Second Language	M
English	M
Interdisciplinary Studies	M
Mathematics	M
Music Education	M
Music	M
Reading Education	M
Science Education	M
Secondary Education	M

STATE UNIVERSITY OF NEW YORK AT NEW PALTZ

Accounting	M
Art Education	M
Art/Fine Arts	M
Biological and Biomedical Sciences—General	M
Business Administration and Management—General	M
Communication Disorders	M
Computer Engineering	M
Computer Science	M
Counseling Psychology	M
Counselor Education	M
Early Childhood Education	M
Education—General	M,O
Educational Leadership and Administration	M,O
Electrical Engineering	M
Elementary Education	M
English as a Second Language	M
English Education	M
English	M
Interdisciplinary Studies	M
Multilingual and Multicultural Education	M
Music	M
Psychology—General	M
Reading Education	M
Science Education	M
Secondary Education	M
Social Sciences Education	M
Special Education	M
Therapies—Dance, Drama, and Music	M

STATE UNIVERSITY OF NEW YORK AT OSWEGO

Agricultural Education	M
Art Education	M
Art/Fine Arts	M
Business Administration and Management—General	M
Business Education	M
Chemistry	M
Child and Family Studies	M
Consumer Economics	M
Counseling Psychology	M,O
Education—General	M,O
Educational Leadership and Administration	O
Elementary Education	M
English	M
History	M
Human Services	M
Human-Computer Interaction	M
Reading Education	M
School Psychology	M,O
Secondary Education	M
Special Education	M
Vocational and Technical Education	M

STATE UNIVERSITY OF NEW YORK AT PLATTSBURGH

Communication Disorders	M
Counselor Education	M,O
Curriculum and Instruction	M
Educational Leadership and Administration	O
Elementary Education	M
English Education	M
Foreign Languages Education	M
Liberal Studies	M
Mathematics Education	M
Psychology—General	M,O
Reading Education	M
School Psychology	M,O
Science Education	M
Secondary Education	M
Social Sciences Education	M
Special Education	M

STATE UNIVERSITY OF NEW YORK COLLEGE AT CORTLAND

American Studies	O
Early Childhood Education	M
Education—General	M,O
Educational Leadership and Administration	O
English as a Second Language	M
English Education	M
English	M
Exercise and Sports Science	M
Foreign Languages Education	M
Health Education	M
History	M
Mathematics Education	M
Mathematics	M
Physical Education	M
Reading Education	M
Recreation and Park Management	M
Science Education	M
Secondary Education	M
Social Sciences Education	M
Special Education	M
Sports Management	M

STATE UNIVERSITY OF NEW YORK COLLEGE AT GENESEO

Accounting	M
Business Administration and Management—General	M
Communication Disorders	M
Early Childhood Education	M
Education—General	M
Elementary Education	M
Multilingual and Multicultural Education	M

Reading Education	M
Secondary Education	M

STATE UNIVERSITY OF NEW YORK COLLEGE AT OLD WESTBURY

Accounting	M
Taxation	M

STATE UNIVERSITY OF NEW YORK COLLEGE AT ONEONTA

Biological and Biomedical Sciences—General	M
Counselor Education	M,O
Education—General	M,O
Educational Psychology	M,O
Elementary Education	M
Family and Consumer Sciences-General	M
Geosciences	M
Home Economics Education	M
Middle School Education	M
Museum Studies	M
Nutrition	M
Reading Education	M
Secondary Education	M

STATE UNIVERSITY OF NEW YORK COLLEGE AT POTSDAM

Communication—General	M
Computer Education	M
Curriculum and Instruction	M
Early Childhood Education	M
Educational Media/Instructional Technology	M
Elementary Education	M
English	M
Management Information Systems	M
Mathematics Education	M
Mathematics	M
Middle School Education	M
Music Education	M
Music	M
Organizational Management	M
Reading Education	M
Science Education	M
Secondary Education	M
Social Sciences Education	M
Special Education	M

STATE UNIVERSITY OF NEW YORK COLLEGE OF ENVIRONMENTAL SCIENCE AND FORESTRY

Biochemistry	M,D
Chemistry	M,D
Communication—General	M,D
Conservation Biology	M,D
Construction Management	M,D
Ecology	M,D
Entomology	M,D
Environmental Biology	M,D
Environmental Engineering	M,D
Environmental Management and Policy	M,D
Environmental Sciences	M,D
Fish, Game, and Wildlife Management	M,D
Forestry	M,D
Hydrology	M,D
Landscape Architecture	M
Natural Resources	M,D
Organic Chemistry	M,D
Paper and Pulp Engineering	M,D
Plant Pathology	M,D
Plant Sciences	M,D
Recreation and Park Management	M,D
Urban and Regional Planning	M,D
Urban Design	M
Water Resources	M,D

STATE UNIVERSITY OF NEW YORK COLLEGE OF OPTOMETRY

Optometry	P
Vision Sciences	M,D

STATE UNIVERSITY OF NEW YORK DOWNSTATE MEDICAL CENTER

Allopathic Medicine	P,M
Biological and Biomedical Sciences—General	M,D*
Biomedical Engineering	M,D
Cell Biology	D
Community Health	M
Family Nurse Practitioner Studies	M,O
Medical/Surgical Nursing	M,O
Molecular Biology	D
Neuroscience	D
Nurse Anesthesia	M
Nurse Midwifery	M,O
Nursing—General	M,O
Public Health—General	M*

STATE UNIVERSITY OF NEW YORK EMPIRE STATE COLLEGE

Business Administration and Management—General	M
Education—General	M
Industrial and Labor Relations	M
Liberal Studies	M
Public Policy	M

STATE UNIVERSITY OF NEW YORK INSTITUTE OF TECHNOLOGY

Accounting	M
Adult Nursing	M,O
Business Administration and Management—General	M
Computer Science	M
Engineering and Applied Sciences—General	M
Family Nurse Practitioner Studies	M,O
Gerontological Nursing	M,O
Health Services Management and Hospital Administration	M
Information Science	M
Management of Technology	M
Nursing and Healthcare Administration	M,O
Nursing Education	M,O
Nursing—General	M,O
Sociology	M
Telecommunications	M

STATE UNIVERSITY OF NEW YORK MARITIME COLLEGE

Transportation Management	M

STATE UNIVERSITY OF NEW YORK UPSTATE MEDICAL UNIVERSITY

Allopathic Medicine	P
Anatomy	M,D
Biochemistry	M,D
Biological and Biomedical Sciences—General	M,D
Cancer Biology/Oncology	
Cardiovascular Sciences	
Cell Biology	M,D
Clinical Laboratory Sciences/Medical Technology	M
Family Nurse Practitioner Studies	M,O
Immunology	M,D
Infectious Diseases	
Microbiology	M,D
Molecular Biology	M,D
Neuroscience	D
Nursing—General	M,O
Pharmacology	D
Physical Therapy	D
Physiology	M,D

STEPHEN F. AUSTIN STATE UNIVERSITY

Accounting	M
Agricultural Education	M
Applied Arts and Design—General	M
Art/Fine Arts	M
Athletic Training and Sports Medicine	M
Biological and Biomedical Sciences—General	M
Biotechnology	M
Business Administration and Management—General	M
Chemistry	M
Communication Disorders	M
Communication—General	M
Computer Science	M
Counselor Education	M
Early Childhood Education	M
Education—General	M,D
Educational Leadership and Administration	M,D
Elementary Education	M
English	M
Environmental Sciences	M
Family and Consumer Sciences-General	M
Forestry	M,D
Geology	M
History	M
Interdisciplinary Studies	M
Kinesiology and Movement Studies	M
Marketing	M
Mass Communication	M
Mathematics Education	M
Mathematics	M
Music	M
Physics	M
Psychology—General	M
Public Administration	M
School Psychology	M
Secondary Education	M,D
Social Work	M
Special Education	M
Statistics	M

STEPHENS COLLEGE

Business Administration and Management—General	M
Counseling Psychology	M
Counselor Education	M
Curriculum and Instruction	M
Marriage and Family Therapy	M

STETSON UNIVERSITY

Accounting	M
Business Administration and Management—General	M
Counselor Education	M
Education—General	M
Educational Leadership and Administration	M
English	M
Law	P,M
Marriage and Family Therapy	M
Reading Education	M

STEVENS INSTITUTE OF TECHNOLOGY

Aerospace/Aeronautical Engineering	M,O
Analytical Chemistry	M,D,O
Applied Mathematics	M
Applied Statistics	O
Biochemistry	M,D,O
Bioinformatics	M,D,O
Biomedical Engineering	M,O
Business Administration and Management—General	M
Chemical Engineering	M,D,O
Chemistry	M,D,O
Civil Engineering	M,D,O
Communication—General	M,D,O
Computer and Information Systems Security	M,D,O
Computer Art and Design	M,D,O
Computer Engineering	M,D,O
Computer Science	M,D,O
Construction Engineering	M,O
Construction Management	M,O
Corporate and Organizational Communication	O
Database Systems	M,D,O
Electrical Engineering	M,D,O
Electronic Commerce	M,O
Engineering and Applied Sciences—General	M,D,O
Engineering Design	M
Engineering Management	M,D
Engineering Physics	M,D,O
Entrepreneurship	M,O
Environmental Engineering	M,D,O
Finance and Banking	M
Financial Engineering	M
Health Informatics	M
Human Resources Management	M
Hydrology	M,D,O
Industrial and Manufacturing Management	M
Information Science	M,O
International Business	M
Internet and Interactive Multimedia	M,D,O
Logistics	M,D,O
Management Information Systems	M,D,O
Management of Technology	M,D,O
Management Strategy and Policy	M
Manufacturing Engineering	M
Marine Affairs	M
Materials Engineering	M,D
Mathematics	M,D
Mechanical Engineering	M,D,O
Ocean Engineering	M,D
Organic Chemistry	M,D,O
Pharmaceutical Sciences	M,O
Photonics	M,D,O
Physical Chemistry	M,D,O
Physics	M,D,O
Polymer Science and Engineering	M,D,O
Project Management	M,O
Quality Management	M,O
Software Engineering	M,D,O
Statistics	M,O
Structural Engineering	M,D,O
Systems Engineering	M,D,O
Systems Science	M,D
Telecommunications Management	M,D,O
Telecommunications	M,D,O
Water Resources Engineering	M,D,O

*M—master's degree; P—first professional degree; D—doctorate; O—other advanced degree; *—Close-Up and/or Announcement or Display in one of the other books in this series*

STEVENSON UNIVERSITY

Forensic Sciences	M
Information Science	M
Management of Technology	M

STONY BROOK UNIVERSITY, STATE UNIVERSITY OF NEW YORK

Addictions/Substance Abuse Counseling	M
Adult Nursing	M,O
African Studies	M
Allopathic Medicine	P
Anatomy	D
Anthropology	M,D
Applied Mathematics	M,D
Art History	M,D
Art/Fine Arts	M
Astronomy	D
Atmospheric Sciences	M,D
Biochemistry	D
Biological and Biomedical Sciences—General	D
Biomedical Engineering	M,D,O
Biophysics	D
Biopsychology	D
Business Administration and Management—General	M,O
Cell Biology	M,D
Chemistry	M,D
Clinical Psychology	D
Community Health	M,D
Comparative Literature	M,D
Computer Education	M
Computer Engineering	M,D,O
Computer Science	M,D,O
Cultural Studies	M,D
Dentistry	P,O
Developmental Biology	M,D
Ecology	M,D
Economics	M,D
Educational Leadership and Administration	M,O
Educational Media/Instructional Technology	M,O
Electrical Engineering	M,D
Engineering and Applied Sciences—General	M,D,O
English as a Second Language	M
English Education	M,D,O
English	M,D,O
Environmental and Occupational Health	M,O
Environmental Management and Policy	M,O
Evolutionary Biology	M,D
Experimental Psychology	D
Family Nurse Practitioner Studies	M,O
Finance and Banking	M,O
Foreign Languages Education	M,O
French	M
Genetics	D
Geosciences	M,D
Hazardous Materials Management	M,O
Health Psychology	D
Health Services Management and Hospital Administration	M,D,O
Hispanic Studies	M,D
History	M,D
Human Resources Management	M,O
Immunology	M,D
Italian	M
Liberal Studies	M,O
Linguistics	M,D
Management Information Systems	M,D,O
Management of Technology	M
Marine Sciences	M,D
Marketing	M,O
Materials Engineering	M,D
Materials Sciences	M,D
Maternal and Child/Neonatal Nursing	M,O
Mathematics Education	M,O
Mathematics	M,D
Mechanical Engineering	M,D
Medical Physics	M,D
Microbiology	D
Molecular Biology	M,D
Molecular Genetics	D
Molecular Physiology	D
Music	M,D
Neuroscience	D
Nurse Midwifery	M,O
Nursing—General	M,D,O
Occupational Therapy	M,D,O
Oral and Dental Sciences	P,M,D,O
Pathology	M,D
Pediatric Nursing	M,O
Pharmacology	D
Philosophy	M,D
Physical Education	M,O
Physical Therapy	M,D,O
Physician Assistant Studies	M,D,O
Physics	M,D
Physiology	D
Political Science	M,D
Psychiatric Nursing	M,O
Psychology—General	D
Public Health—General	M
Public Policy	M,D
Romance Languages	M
Science Education	M,D,O
Social Psychology	D
Social Sciences Education	M,O
Social Sciences	M,O
Social Work	M,D
Sociology	M,D
Software Engineering	M,D,O
Statistics	M,D
Structural Biology	D
Systems Engineering	M,D,O
Technology and Public Policy	M,D,O
Theater	M
Women's Health Nursing	M,O
Writing	M

STRATFORD UNIVERSITY

Accounting	M
Business Administration and Management—General	M
Management Information Systems	M
Software Engineering	M

STRAYER UNIVERSITY

Accounting	M
Business Administration and Management—General	M
Computer and Information Systems Security	M
Education—General	M
Educational Media/Instructional Technology	M
Finance and Banking	M
Health Services Management and Hospital Administration	M
Hospitality Management	M
Human Resources Management	M
Information Science	M
Management Information Systems	M
Marketing	M
Public Administration	M
Software Engineering	M
Supply Chain Management	M
Systems Science	M
Taxation	M
Telecommunications Management	M
Travel and Tourism	M

SUFFOLK UNIVERSITY

Accounting	M,O
Adult Education	M,O
Advertising and Public Relations	M
Applied Arts and Design—General	M
Business Administration and Management—General	M,O
Clinical Psychology	D
Communication—General	M
Computer Science	M
Corporate and Organizational Communication	M
Counseling Psychology	M,O
Counselor Education	M,O
Criminal Justice and Criminology	M
Economics	M,D*
Education—General	M,O
Educational Leadership and Administration	M,O
Entrepreneurship	M,O
Ethics	M
Finance and Banking	M,O
Foundations and Philosophy of Education	M,O
Graphic Design	M
Health Education	M
Health Law	P,M
Health Services Management and Hospital Administration	M,O
Human Resources Development	M,O
Interior Design	M
International Business	M,D,O
Law	P,M
Management Strategy and Policy	M,O
Marketing	M,O
Middle School Education	M,O
Nonprofit Management	M,O
Organizational Behavior	M,O
Organizational Management	M,O
Political Science	M,O
Psychology—General	D
Public Administration	M,O
Public Policy	M
Secondary Education	M,O
Taxation	M,O
Women's Studies	M

SULLIVAN UNIVERSITY

Business Administration and Management—General	P,M
Conflict Resolution and Mediation/Peace Studies	P,M
Management Information Systems	P,M
Management of Technology	P,M

SUL ROSS STATE UNIVERSITY

Animal Sciences	M
Applied Arts and Design—General	M
Art Education	M
Art History	M
Art/Fine Arts	M
Biological and Biomedical Sciences—General	M
Business Administration and Management—General	M
Counselor Education	M
Criminal Justice and Criminology	M
Education—General	M
Educational Leadership and Administration	M
Educational Measurement and Evaluation	M
Elementary Education	M
English	M
Fish, Game, and Wildlife Management	M
Geology	M*
History	M
Multilingual and Multicultural Education	M
Physical Education	M
Political Science	M
Psychology—General	M
Public Administration	M
Range Science	M
Reading Education	M
Secondary Education	M
Textile Design	M

SWEDISH INSTITUTE, COLLEGE OF HEALTH SCIENCES

Accounting	M
Acupuncture and Oriental Medicine	M

SWEET BRIAR COLLEGE

Education—General	M

SYRACUSE UNIVERSITY

Accounting	M,D
Adult Education	M,D
Advertising and Public Relations	M
Aerospace/Aeronautical Engineering	M,D
African Studies	M
African-American Studies	M
Anthropology	M,D
Applied Arts and Design—General	M
Applied Statistics	M
Architecture	M
Art Education	M,O
Art History	M
Art/Fine Arts	M
Arts Journalism	M
Biochemistry	D
Bioengineering	M,D
Biological and Biomedical Sciences—General	M,D*
Biophysics	D
Broadcast Journalism	M
Business Administration and Management—General	M,D*
Chemical Engineering	M
Chemistry	M,D
Child and Family Studies	M,D
Civil Engineering	M,D
Clinical Psychology	D
Communication Disorders	M,D
Communication—General	M,D*
Computer and Information Systems Security	O
Computer Art and Design	M
Computer Engineering	M,D
Conflict Resolution and Mediation/Peace Studies	
Counselor Education	M,D
Curriculum and Instruction	M,D,O
Disability Studies	O
Early Childhood Education	M
Economics	M,D
Education of the Multiply Handicapped	M
Education—General	M,D,O
Educational Leadership and Administration	M,D,O
Educational Measurement and Evaluation	M,D,O
Educational Media/Instructional Technology	M,O
Electrical Engineering	M,D
Engineering and Applied Sciences—General	M,D,O*
Engineering Management	M

English as a Second Language	M
English Education	M,D
English	M,D
Entrepreneurship	M
Environmental Engineering	M
Exercise and Sports Science	M
Experimental Psychology	D
Film, Television, and Video Production	M
Film, Television, and Video Theory and Criticism	M
Finance and Banking	M,D
Forensic Sciences	M
Foundations and Philosophy of Education	M,D
French	M
Geography	M,D
Geology	M,D
Health Services Management and Hospital Administration	O
Higher Education	M,D
History	M,D
Human Resources Development	D
Illustration	M
Industrial and Manufacturing Management	D
Information Science	D
Information Studies	M*
International Affairs	M
Journalism	M
Law	P
Library Science	M,O
Linguistics	M
Management Information Systems	M,D,O
Management Strategy and Policy	D
Marketing	M,D
Marriage and Family Therapy	M,D
Mass Communication	M,D
Mathematics Education	M,D
Mathematics	M,D
Mechanical Engineering	M,D
Media Studies	M
Museum Studies	M
Music Education	M
Music	M
Nutrition	M
Organizational Behavior	D
Philosophy	M,D
Photography	M
Physics	M,D
Political Science	M,D
Public Administration	M,D,O
Quantitative Analysis	D
Reading Education	M,D
Rehabilitation Counseling	M
Religion	M,D
Rhetoric	M,D
School Psychology	M,D,O
Science Education	M,D
Social Psychology	M,D
Social Sciences Education	M
Social Sciences	M,D
Social Work	M
Sociology	M,D
Spanish	M
Special Education	M,D
Structural Biology	D
Student Affairs	M
Supply Chain Management	M,D
Telecommunications Management	M,O
Telecommunications	M
Textile Design	M
Writing	M,D

TABOR COLLEGE

Accounting	M
Business Administration and Management—General	M

TAI SOPHIA INSTITUTE

Acupuncture and Oriental Medicine	M,O

TALMUDIC COLLEGE OF FLORIDA

Theology	M,D

TARLETON STATE UNIVERSITY

Accounting	M
Agricultural Education	M
Agricultural Sciences—General	M
Biological and Biomedical Sciences—General	M
Business Administration and Management—General	M
Counseling Psychology	M,O
Counselor Education	M,O
Criminal Justice and Criminology	M
Curriculum and Instruction	M
Economics	M
Education—General	M,D,O
Educational Leadership and Administration	M,D,O
English	M
Environmental Sciences	M
Finance and Banking	M
History	M
Human Resources Management	M
Liberal Studies	M
Management Information Systems	M
Mathematics	M
Music Education	M
Physical Education	M
Political Science	M
School Psychology	M,O
Secondary Education	M,O
Special Education	M,O

TAYLOR COLLEGE AND SEMINARY

Cultural Studies	P,M,O
Missions and Missiology	P,M,O
Theology	P,M,O

TAYLOR UNIVERSITY

Business Administration and Management—General	M
Environmental Sciences	M
Higher Education	M
International Business	M
Management Strategy and Policy	M
Religion	M

TEACHERS COLLEGE, COLUMBIA UNIVERSITY

Adult Education	M,D
Anthropology	M,D
Art Education	M,D
Arts Administration	M
Clinical Psychology	D
Communication Disorders	M,D
Communication—General	M,D
Computer Education	M
Counseling Psychology	M,D
Curriculum and Instruction	M,D
Developmental Psychology	M,D
Early Childhood Education	M,D
Economics	M,D
Education of the Gifted	M,D
Education of the Multiply Handicapped	M
Education—General	M,D,O
Educational Leadership and Administration	M,D
Educational Measurement and Evaluation	M,D
Educational Media/Instructional Technology	M,D
Educational Psychology	M,D
Elementary Education	M
English as a Second Language	M,D
English Education	M,D
Foreign Languages Education	M,D
Foundations and Philosophy of Education	M,D
Health Education	M,D
Higher Education	M,D
History	M,D
Industrial and Organizational Psychology	M,D
Interdisciplinary Studies	M,D
International and Comparative Education	M,D
Kinesiology and Movement Studies	M,D
Linguistics	M,D
Mathematics Education	M,D
Multilingual and Multicultural Education	M
Music Education	M,D
Neuroscience	M,D
Nursing and Healthcare Administration	M,D
Nursing Education	M,D
Nutrition	M,D
Physical Education	M,D
Political Science	M,D
Reading Education	M
Religious Education	M,D
School Psychology	M,D
Science Education	M,D
Social Psychology	M,D
Social Sciences Education	M,D
Sociology	M,D
Special Education	M,D,O
Student Affairs	M,D

TÉLÉ-UNIVERSITÉ

Computer Science	M,D
Distance Education Development	M,D
Finance and Banking	M,D

TELSHE YESHIVA–CHICAGO

Jewish Studies	O

TEMPLE BAPTIST SEMINARY

Archaeology	P,M,D
Religion	P,M,D
Religious Education	P,M,D
Theology	P,M,D

TEMPLE UNIVERSITY

Accounting	M,D
Actuarial Science	M
African-American Studies	M,D
Allied Health—General	M,D
Allopathic Medicine	P
Anatomy	M,D
Anthropology	D
Applied Mathematics	M,D
Art Education	M
Art History	M,D*
Art/Fine Arts	M
Arts Administration	M,D
Biochemistry	M,D
Biological and Biomedical Sciences—General	M,D*
Business Administration and Management—General	M,D
Cell Biology	M,D
Chemistry	M,D
Civil Engineering	M
Clinical Psychology	D
Cognitive Sciences	D
Communication Disorders	M
Communication—General	M,D
Community Health	M
Computational Sciences	M,D
Computer Engineering	M
Computer Science	M,D
Corporate and Organizational Communication	M,D
Counseling Psychology	M,D
Criminal Justice and Criminology	M,D
Dance	M,D
Dentistry	P
Developmental Psychology	D
Early Childhood Education	M,D
Education—General	M,D
Educational Leadership and Administration	M,D
Educational Psychology	M,D
Electrical Engineering	M
Elementary Education	M,D
Engineering and Applied Sciences—General	M,D*
English as a Second Language	M,D
English Education	M,D
English	M,D
Entrepreneurship	D
Environmental and Occupational Health	M
Epidemiology	M
Film, Television, and Video Production	M
Finance and Banking	M,D
Financial Engineering	M
Foreign Languages Education	M,D
Genetics	D
Geography	M
Geology	M
Graphic Design	M
Health Education	M
Health Services Management and Hospital Administration	M
History	M,D
Hospitality Management	M,D
Human Resources Management	M,D
Immunology	M,D
Industrial and Organizational Psychology	M
Information Science	M,D
Insurance	D
International Business	M,D
Journalism	M
Kinesiology and Movement Studies	M,D
Law	P,M,D
Legal and Justice Studies	P,M,D
Leisure Studies	M
Liberal Studies	M
Linguistics	M
Management Information Systems	M,D
Management Strategy and Policy	D
Marketing	M,D
Mass Communication	D
Mathematics Education	M,D
Mathematics	M,D
Mechanical Engineering	M
Media Studies	M,D
Medicinal and Pharmaceutical Chemistry	M,D
Microbiology	M,D
Molecular Biology	D
Music Education	M,D
Music	M,D
Neuroscience	M,D
Nursing—General	M
Occupational Therapy	M

*M—master's degree; P—first professional degree; D—doctorate; O—other advanced degree; *—Close-Up and/or Announcement or Display in one of the other books in this series*

Oral and Dental Sciences	M,O
Pathology	D
Pharmaceutical Administration	M
Pharmaceutical Sciences	M,D
Pharmacology	M,D
Pharmacy	P
Philosophy	M,D
Photography	M
Physical Education	M,D
Physical Therapy	D
Physics	M,D*
Physiology	D
Podiatric Medicine	P
Political Science	M,D
Psychology—General	D
Public Health—General	M,D
Reading Education	M,D
Recreation and Park Management	M
Religion	M,D
School Psychology	M,D
Science Education	M,D
Social Psychology	D
Social Work	M
Sociology	M,D
Spanish	M,D
Special Education	M,D
Sports Management	M,D
Statistics	M,D
Taxation	P,M,D
Textile Design	M
Theater	M
Therapies—Dance, Drama, and Music	M,D
Travel and Tourism	M*
Urban and Regional Planning	M
Urban Education	M,D
Urban Studies	M
Vocational and Technical Education	M,D
Writing	M

TENNESSEE STATE UNIVERSITY

Agricultural Sciences—General	M
Allied Health—General	M,D
Biological and Biomedical Sciences—General	M,D
Business Administration and Management—General	M
Chemistry	M
Communication Disorders	M
Counseling Psychology	M,D
Counselor Education	M,D
Criminal Justice and Criminology	M
Curriculum and Instruction	M,D
Education—General	M,D,O
Educational Leadership and Administration	M,D,O
Elementary Education	M,D
Engineering and Applied Sciences—General	M,D
English	M
Exercise and Sports Science	M
Family and Consumer Sciences-General	M
Family Nurse Practitioner Studies	M
Mathematics	M
Music Education	M
Nursing Informatics	M
Nursing—General	M
Physical Education	M
Physical Therapy	M,D
Psychology—General	M,D
Public Administration	M,D
School Psychology	M,D
Special Education	M,D

TENNESSEE TECHNOLOGICAL UNIVERSITY

Biological and Biomedical Sciences—General	M
Business Administration and Management—General	M*
Chemical Engineering	M,D
Chemistry	M
Civil Engineering	M,D
Computer Science	M
Curriculum and Instruction	M,O
Early Childhood Education	M,O
Education of the Gifted	D
Education—General	M,D,O
Educational Leadership and Administration	M,O
Educational Psychology	M,O
Electrical Engineering	M,D
Elementary Education	M,O
Engineering and Applied Sciences—General	M,D
English	M
Environmental Biology	M
Environmental Sciences	D
Fish, Game, and Wildlife Management	M
Health Education	M
Kinesiology and Movement Studies	M
Library Science	M,O
Management Strategy and Policy	M
Mathematics	M
Mechanical Engineering	M,D
Nursing—General	M
Physical Education	M
Reading Education	M,O
Secondary Education	M,O
Special Education	M,O
Student Affairs	M,O

TENNESSEE TEMPLE UNIVERSITY

Curriculum and Instruction	M
Education—General	M
Educational Leadership and Administration	M

TEXAS A&M HEALTH SCIENCE CENTER

Biological and Biomedical Sciences—General	M,D
Cell Biology	D
Dental Hygiene	M
Dentistry	P
Environmental and Occupational Health	M
Epidemiology	M
Health Education	M
Health Services Management and Hospital Administration	M
Immunology	D
Materials Sciences	M
Microbiology	D
Molecular Biology	D
Molecular Medicine	D
Molecular Pathogenesis	D
Neuroscience	D
Oral and Dental Sciences	P,M,D,O
Public Health—General	M
Systems Biology	D
Translational Biology	D
Virology	D

TEXAS A&M INTERNATIONAL UNIVERSITY

Accounting	M
Biological and Biomedical Sciences—General	M
Business Administration and Management—General	M
Counseling Psychology	M
Counselor Education	M
Criminal Justice and Criminology	M
Curriculum and Instruction	M,D
Early Childhood Education	M,D
Education—General	M,D
Educational Leadership and Administration	M
English	M,D
Finance and Banking	M
Foreign Languages Education	M,D
Hispanic Studies	M,D
History	M
International Business	M
Management Information Systems	M
Mathematics	M
Multilingual and Multicultural Education	M,D
Nursing—General	M
Physics	M
Political Science	M
Psychology—General	M
Public Administration	M
Reading Education	M,D
Social Sciences	M
Sociology	M
Spanish	M,D
Special Education	M

TEXAS A&M UNIVERSITY

Accounting	M,D
Aerospace/Aeronautical Engineering	M,D
Agricultural Economics and Agribusiness	M,D
Agricultural Education	M,D
Agricultural Engineering	M,D
Agricultural Sciences—General	M,D
Agronomy and Soil Sciences	M,D
Anatomy	M,D
Animal Sciences	M,D
Anthropology	M,D
Applied Physics	M,D
Architecture	M,D
Biochemistry	M,D
Bioengineering	M,D
Biological and Biomedical Sciences—General	M,D
Biomedical Engineering	M,D
Biophysics	M,D
Biopsychology	M,D
Botany	M,D
Business Administration and Management—General	M,D
Cell Biology	M,D
Chemical Engineering	M,D
Chemistry	M,D*
Civil Engineering	M,D
Clinical Psychology	M,D
Cognitive Sciences	M,D
Communication—General	M,D
Computer Engineering	M,D
Computer Science	M,D
Construction Engineering	M,D
Construction Management	M,D
Counseling Psychology	M,D
Counselor Education	M,D
Curriculum and Instruction	M,D
Developmental Psychology	M,D
Economics	M,D
Education of the Gifted	M,D
Education—General	M,D
Educational Leadership and Administration	M,D
Educational Measurement and Evaluation	M,D
Educational Media/Instructional Technology	M,D
Educational Psychology	M,D
Electrical Engineering	M,D
Engineering and Applied Sciences—General	M,D
English Education	M,D
English	M,D
Entomology	M,D
Environmental Engineering	M,D
Epidemiology	M,D
Finance and Banking	M,D
Fish, Game, and Wildlife Management	M,D
Food Science and Technology	M,D
Forestry	M,D
Foundations and Philosophy of Education	M,D
Genetics	M,D
Geography	M,D
Geology	M,D
Geophysics	M,D
Geotechnical Engineering	M,D
Health Education	M,D
Health Physics/Radiological Health	M,D
History	M,D
Homeland Security	M,O
Horticulture	M,D
Human Development	M,D
Human Resources Development	M,D
Human Resources Management	M,D
Industrial and Manufacturing Management	M,D
Industrial and Organizational Psychology	M,D
Industrial/Management Engineering	M,D
International Affairs	M,O
International Development	M,O
Kinesiology and Movement Studies	M,D
Landscape Architecture	M,D
Management Information Systems	M,D
Manufacturing Engineering	M
Marketing	M,D
Materials Engineering	M,D
Mathematics Education	M,D
Mathematics	M,D
Mechanical Engineering	M,D
Meteorology	M,D
Microbiology	M,D
Multilingual and Multicultural Education	M,D
National Security	M,O
Natural Resources	M,D
Neuroscience	M,D
Nonprofit Management	M,O
Nuclear Engineering	M,D
Ocean Engineering	M,D
Oceanography	M,D
Parasitology	M,D
Pathobiology	M,D
Pathology	M,D
Petroleum Engineering	M,D
Philosophy	M,D
Physical Education	M,D
Physics	M,D
Physiology	M,D
Plant Biology	M,D
Plant Pathology	M,D
Plant Sciences	M,D
Political Science	M,D
Psychology—General	M,D
Public Administration	M,O
Public Affairs	M,O
Public Health—General	M,D
Public Policy	M,O
Reading Education	M,D
Real Estate	M
Recreation and Park Management	M,D
School Psychology	M,D
Science Education	M,D
Social Psychology	M,D
Sociology	M,D*
Spanish	M,D
Special Education	M,D
Statistics	M,D
Structural Engineering	M,D
Toxicology	M,D
Transportation and Highway Engineering	M,D
Urban and Regional Planning	M,D

Urban Education	M,D
Veterinary Medicine	P,M
Veterinary Sciences	M
Water Resources Engineering	M,D
Zoology	M,D

TEXAS A&M UNIVERSITY AT GALVESTON

Marine Biology	M,D
Marine Sciences	M

TEXAS A&M UNIVERSITY–COMMERCE

Agricultural Education	M
Agricultural Sciences—General	M
Art History	M
Art/Fine Arts	M
Biological and Biomedical Sciences—General	M
Business Administration and Management—General	M
Chemistry	M
Cognitive Sciences	M,D
Computer Science	M
Counseling Psychology	M,D
Counselor Education	M,D
Curriculum and Instruction	M,D
Early Childhood Education	M,D
Economics	M
Education—General	M,D
Educational Leadership and Administration	M,D
Educational Media/Instructional Technology	M,D
Elementary Education	M,D
English as a Second Language	M,D
English Education	M,D
English	M,D
Exercise and Sports Science	M,D
Geosciences	M
Health Education	M,D
Health Promotion	M,D
Higher Education	M,D
History	M
Industrial/Management Engineering	M
Kinesiology and Movement Studies	M,D
Management of Technology	M
Mathematics	M
Multilingual and Multicultural Education	M,D
Music Education	M
Music	M
Physical Education	M,D
Physics	M
Psychology—General	M,D
Reading Education	M,D
Secondary Education	M,D
Social Sciences Education	M
Social Sciences	M
Social Work	M
Sociology	M
Spanish	M,D
Special Education	M,D
Speech and Interpersonal Communication	M
Theater	M

TEXAS A&M UNIVERSITY–CORPUS CHRISTI

Accounting	M
Applied Mathematics	M
Aquaculture	M
Art/Fine Arts	M
Biological and Biomedical Sciences—General	M
Business Administration and Management—General	M
Computer Science	M
Counselor Education	M,D
Curriculum and Instruction	M,D
Early Childhood Education	M,D
Education—General	M,D
Educational Leadership and Administration	M,D
Educational Media/Instructional Technology	M,D
Elementary Education	M
English	M
Environmental Sciences	M
Family Nurse Practitioner Studies	M
Health Services Management and Hospital Administration	M
History	M
International Business	M
Kinesiology and Movement Studies	M,D
Marine Sciences	D
Mathematics Education	M
Mathematics	M
Nursing and Healthcare Administration	M
Nursing—General	M
Psychology—General	M
Public Administration	M
Reading Education	M,D
Secondary Education	M
Special Education	M

TEXAS A&M UNIVERSITY–KINGSVILLE

Adult Education	M
Agricultural Economics and Agribusiness	M
Agricultural Education	M
Agricultural Sciences—General	M,D
Agronomy and Soil Sciences	M,D
Animal Sciences	M
Art/Fine Arts	M
Biological and Biomedical Sciences—General	M
Business Administration and Management—General	M
Chemical Engineering	M
Chemistry	M
Civil Engineering	M
Communication Disorders	M
Computer Science	M
Counselor Education	M
Early Childhood Education	M
Education—General	M,D
Educational Leadership and Administration	M,D
Electrical Engineering	M
Elementary Education	M
Engineering and Applied Sciences—General	M,D
English as a Second Language	M
English	M
Environmental Engineering	M,D
Family and Consumer Sciences-General	M
Fish, Game, and Wildlife Management	M,D
Foreign Languages Education	M
Geology	M
Gerontology	M
Health Education	M
Higher Education	D
History	M
Industrial/Management Engineering	M
Kinesiology and Movement Studies	M
Mathematics	M
Mechanical Engineering	M
Multilingual and Multicultural Education	M,D
Music Education	M
Petroleum Engineering	M
Plant Sciences	M,D
Political Science	M
Psychology—General	M
Range Science	M
Reading Education	M
Secondary Education	M
Sociology	M
Spanish	M
Special Education	M

TEXAS A&M UNIVERSITY–TEXARKANA

Accounting	M
Adult Education	M
Business Administration and Management—General	M
Counseling Psychology	M
Curriculum and Instruction	M
Education—General	M
Educational Leadership and Administration	M
Educational Media/Instructional Technology	M
English	M
History	M
Interdisciplinary Studies	M
Psychology—General	M
Special Education	M

TEXAS CHIROPRACTIC COLLEGE

Chiropractic	P

TEXAS CHRISTIAN UNIVERSITY

Accounting	M
Adult Nursing	M,D
Advertising and Public Relations	M
Allied Health—General	M,D
Art History	M
Art/Fine Arts	M
Astrophysics	M,D
Biological and Biomedical Sciences—General	M
Business Administration and Management—General	M,D
Chemistry	M,D
Communication Disorders	M
Counselor Education	M,O
Curriculum and Instruction	M
Ecology	M
Education—General	M,D,O
Educational Leadership and Administration	M
Educational Psychology	M,O
Elementary Education	M,O
English	M,D
Environmental Sciences	M
Geology	M
Geosciences	M
History	M,D
International Business	M
Journalism	M
Kinesiology and Movement Studies	M
Liberal Studies	M
Mathematics	M
Middle School Education	M
Music Education	M,O
Music	M,O
Nurse Anesthesia	M
Nursing—General	M,D
Physics	M,D
Psychology—General	M,D
Science Education	M,D
Secondary Education	M
Special Education	M
Speech and Interpersonal Communication	M

TEXAS COLLEGE OF TRADITIONAL CHINESE MEDICINE

Acupuncture and Oriental Medicine	M

TEXAS SOUTHERN UNIVERSITY

Art/Fine Arts	M
Biological and Biomedical Sciences—General	M
Business Administration and Management—General	M
Chemistry	M
Communication—General	M
Computer Science	M
Counselor Education	M,D
Criminal Justice and Criminology	M,D
Curriculum and Instruction	M,D
Education—General	M,D
Educational Leadership and Administration	M,D
English	M
Family and Consumer Sciences-General	M
Health Education	M
Higher Education	M,D
History	M
Human Services	M
Industrial/Management Engineering	M
Law	P
Management Information Systems	M
Mathematics	M
Multilingual and Multicultural Education	M,D
Music	M
Pharmacy	P,M,D
Physical Education	M
Psychology—General	M
Public Administration	M
Secondary Education	M,D
Sociology	M
Toxicology	M,D
Transportation and Highway Engineering	M
Transportation Management	M
Urban and Regional Planning	M,D

TEXAS STATE UNIVERSITY–SAN MARCOS

Accounting	M
Agricultural Education	M
Allied Health—General	M,D
Anthropology	M
Applied Mathematics	M
Athletic Training and Sports Medicine	M
Biochemistry	M
Biological and Biomedical Sciences—General	M
Business Administration and Management—General	M
Chemistry	M
Child and Family Studies	M
Communication Disorders	M
Communication—General	M
Computer Art and Design	M
Computer Science	M*
Conservation Biology	M
Counselor Education	M
Criminal Justice and Criminology	M
Developmental Education	M,D
Early Childhood Education	M
Education—General	M,D
Educational Leadership and Administration	M
Elementary Education	M
English	M
Environmental Management and Policy	M
Fish, Game, and Wildlife Management	M
Geographic Information Systems	M,D
Geography	M,D
Graphic Design	M
Health Education	M

*M—master's degree; P—first professional degree; D—doctorate; O—other advanced degree; *—Close-Up and/or Announcement or Display in one of the other books in this series*

Health Psychology	M
Health Services Management and Hospital Administration	M
Health Services Research	M
History	M
Industrial/Management Engineering	M
Interdisciplinary Studies	M
International Affairs	M
Legal and Justice Studies	M
Leisure Studies	M
Management Information Systems	M
Management of Technology	M
Marine Biology	M,D
Mass Communication	M
Mathematics Education	M,D
Mathematics	M,D
Multilingual and Multicultural Education	M
Music Education	M
Music	M
Nutrition	M
Physical Education	M
Physical Therapy	D
Physics	M
Political Science	M
Psychology—General	M
Public Administration	M
Reading Education	M
Recreation and Park Management	M
Rhetoric	M
School Psychology	M
Science Education	M
Secondary Education	M
Social Sciences Education	D
Social Work	M
Sociology	M
Software Engineering	M
Spanish	M
Special Education	M
Technical Communication	M
Theater	M
Vocational and Technical Education	M
Writing	M

TEXAS TECH UNIVERSITY

Accounting	M,D
Agricultural Economics and Agribusiness	M,D
Agricultural Education	M,D
Agricultural Sciences—General	M,D
Agronomy and Soil Sciences	M,D
Animal Sciences	M,D
Anthropology	M
Applied Economics	M,D
Applied Physics	M,D
Architecture	M
Art Education	M,D
Art/Fine Arts	M,D
Atmospheric Sciences	M,D
Bioinformatics	M,D
Biological and Biomedical Sciences—General	M,D
Biotechnology	M
Business Administration and Management—General	M,D
Chemical Engineering	M,D
Chemistry	M,D
Child and Family Studies	M,D
Civil Engineering	M,D
Classics	M
Clinical Psychology	M,D
Communication—General	M
Computer Science	M,D
Consumer Economics	M,D
Counseling Psychology	M,D
Counselor Education	M,D
Curriculum and Instruction	M,D
Dance	M,D
Economics	M,D
Education—General	M,D
Educational Leadership and Administration	M,D
Educational Media/ Instructional Technology	M,D
Educational Psychology	M,D
Electrical Engineering	M,D
Elementary Education	M,D
Engineering and Applied Sciences—General	M,D
Engineering Management	M,D
English Education	M,D
English	M,D
Entomology	M,D
Entrepreneurship	M
Environmental Design	M,D
Environmental Engineering	M,D
Environmental Management and Policy	D
Environmental Sciences	M,D
Exercise and Sports Science	M
Experimental Psychology	M,D
Family and Consumer Sciences-General	M,D
Finance and Banking	M,D
Fish, Game, and Wildlife Management	M,D
Food Science and Technology	M,D
French	M
Genomic Sciences	M
Geosciences	M,D
German	M
Gerontology	M,D
Health Services Management and Hospital Administration	M
Higher Education	M,D
Historic Preservation	M
History	M,D
Home Economics Education	M,D
Horticulture	M,D
Hospitality Management	M,D
Human Development	M,D
Humanities	M,D
Industrial and Manufacturing Management	M,D
Industrial/Management Engineering	M,D
Interdisciplinary Studies	M
Interior Design	M,D
International Business	M
Landscape Architecture	M
Law	P
Linguistics	M
Management Information Systems	M,D
Manufacturing Engineering	M,D
Marketing	M,D
Marriage and Family Therapy	M,D
Mass Communication	M,D
Mathematics	M,D
Mechanical Engineering	M,D
Microbiology	M,D
Multilingual and Multicultural Education	M,D
Museum Studies	M
Music Education	M,D
Music	M,D
Natural Resources	M,D
Nutrition	M,D
Petroleum Engineering	M,D
Philosophy	M
Physics	M,D
Plant Sciences	M,D
Political Science	M,D
Psychology—General	M,D
Public Administration	M,D
Quantitative Analysis	M,D
Range Science	M,D
Reading Education	M,D
Rhetoric	M,D
Romance Languages	M,D
Secondary Education	M,D
Sociology	M
Software Engineering	M,D
Spanish	M,D
Special Education	M,D
Statistics	M
Systems Engineering	M,D
Taxation	M,D
Technical Writing	M,D
Theater	M,D
Toxicology	M,D
Zoology	M,D

TEXAS TECH UNIVERSITY HEALTH SCIENCES CENTER

Acute Care/Critical Care Nursing	M,D,O
Allied Health—General	M,D
Allopathic Medicine	P
Athletic Training and Sports Medicine	M
Biochemistry	M,D
Biological and Biomedical Sciences—General	M,D
Biotechnology	M
Cell Biology	M,D
Communication Disorders	M,D
Family Nurse Practitioner Studies	M,D,O
Gerontological Nursing	M,D,O
Health Services Management and Hospital Administration	M
Medical Microbiology	M,D
Molecular Biophysics	M,D
Molecular Genetics	M,D
Molecular Pathology	M
Molecular Physiology	M,D
Neuroscience	M,D
Nursing and Healthcare Administration	M,D,O
Nursing Education	M,D,O
Nursing—General	M,D,O
Occupational Therapy	M
Pediatric Nursing	M,D,O
Pharmaceutical Sciences	M,D
Pharmacology	M,D
Physical Therapy	M,D
Physician Assistant Studies	M
Rehabilitation Counseling	M
Rehabilitation Sciences	D

TEXAS WESLEYAN UNIVERSITY

Business Administration and Management—General	M
Counseling Psychology	M
Counselor Education	M
Education—General	M
Health Services Management and Hospital Administration	M
Law	P
Nurse Anesthesia	M,D

TEXAS WOMAN'S UNIVERSITY

Acute Care/Critical Care Nursing	M,D
Adult Nursing	M,D
Allied Health—General	M,D
Art/Fine Arts	M
Biological and Biomedical Sciences—General	M,D
Business Administration and Management—General	M
Chemistry	M
Child and Family Studies	M,D
Child Development	M,D
Communication Disorders	M
Community Health	M,D
Counseling Psychology	M,D,O
Counselor Education	M,D
Curriculum and Instruction	M,D
Dance	M,D
Early Childhood Education	M,D
Education—General	M,D
Educational Leadership and Administration	M,D
Elementary Education	M,D
English	M,D
Exercise and Sports Science	M
Family Nurse Practitioner Studies	M,D
Food Science and Technology	M,D
Health Education	M,D
Health Services Management and Hospital Administration	M,D
History	M
Kinesiology and Movement Studies	M,D
Library Science	M,D
Marriage and Family Therapy	M,D
Mathematics Education	M
Mathematics	M
Molecular Biology	M,D
Music	M
Nursing Education	M,D
Nursing—General	M,D
Nutrition	M,D
Occupational Therapy	M,D
Pediatric Nursing	M,D
Physical Therapy	M,D
Political Science	M
Psychology—General	M,D,O
Reading Education	M,D
Rhetoric	M,D
School Psychology	M,D,O
Science Education	M,D
Sociology	M,D
Special Education	M,D
Theater	M
Women's Health Nursing	M,D
Women's Studies	M

THOMAS COLLEGE

Business Administration and Management—General	M
Business Education	M
Computer Education	M
Human Resources Management	M

THOMAS EDISON STATE COLLEGE

Applied Science and Technology	O
Business Administration and Management—General	M
Distance Education Development	O
Educational Leadership and Administration	M
Educational Media/ Instructional Technology	O
Epidemiology	O
Homeland Security	M,O
Human Resources Management	M,O
Liberal Studies	M
Nursing Education	O
Nursing—General	M
Organizational Management	O
Public Administration	O

THOMAS JEFFERSON SCHOOL OF LAW

Law	P

THOMAS JEFFERSON UNIVERSITY

Allopathic Medicine	P
Biochemistry	D*
Biological and Biomedical Sciences—General	M,D,O*
Biomedical Engineering	D
Biophysics	D
Biotechnology	D
Cell Biology	M,D

Clinical Laboratory Sciences/Medical Technology M
Clinical Research O
Developmental Biology M,D
Genetics D*
Health Services Research O
Immunology D*
Marriage and Family Therapy M
Microbiology M,D
Molecular Biology D
Molecular Pharmacology D
Molecular Physiology D
Neuroscience D
Nursing—General M
Occupational Therapy M
Pharmacology M*
Pharmacy P
Physical Therapy M,D
Public Health—General M
Structural Biology D

THOMAS M. COOLEY LAW SCHOOL

Law P,M
Taxation P,M

THOMAS MORE COLLEGE

Business Administration and Management—General M
Education—General M

THOMAS UNIVERSITY

Business Administration and Management—General M
Education—General M
Human Services M
Nursing—General M
Rehabilitation Counseling M
Social Psychology M

THUNDERBIRD SCHOOL OF GLOBAL MANAGEMENT

Business Administration and Management—General M
International Business M

TIFFIN UNIVERSITY

Business Administration and Management—General M
Criminal Justice and Criminology M
Forensic Psychology M
Homeland Security M
Humanities M
Sports Management M

TORONTO SCHOOL OF THEOLOGY

Theology P,M,D

TOURO COLLEGE

Acupuncture and Oriental Medicine M,D
Communication Disorders M,D
Jewish Studies M
Law P,M
Occupational Therapy M
Physical Therapy M,D

TOURO UNIVERSITY

Education—General P,M
Osteopathic Medicine P,M
Pharmacy P,M

Physician Assistant Studies P,M
Public Health—General P,M

TOWSON UNIVERSITY

Accounting M
Advertising and Public Relations O
Allied Health—General M
Applied Mathematics M
Art Education M,O
Art/Fine Arts M
Biological and Biomedical Sciences—General M
Business Administration and Management—General M
Child and Family Studies O
Clinical Psychology M
Communication Disorders M,D
Communication—General M,O
Computer and Information Systems Security D,O
Computer Science M
Corporate and Organizational Communication M
Counseling Psychology O
Database Systems D,O
Early Childhood Education M,O
Education—General M
Educational Media/Instructional Technology M,D
Elementary Education M
Environmental and Occupational Health D
Environmental Management and Policy M
Environmental Sciences M,O
Forensic Sciences M
Geography M
Gerontology M,O
Health Services Management and Hospital Administration O
Homeland Security M,O
Human Resources Development M
Humanities M
Information Science M,D,O
Internet and Interactive Multimedia D,O
Kinesiology and Movement Studies M
Liberal Studies M
Management Information Systems D,O
Management Strategy and Policy O
Mathematics Education M
Music Education M,O
Music M
Nursing Education M,O
Nursing—General M,O
Occupational Therapy M
Organizational Behavior O
Physician Assistant Studies M
Reading Education M,O
School Psychology O
Science Education M
Secondary Education M
Social Sciences M
Software Engineering D,O
Special Education M
Theater M
Women's Studies M,O
Writing M

TRADITIONAL CHINESE MEDICAL COLLEGE OF HAWAII

Acupuncture and Oriental Medicine M

TRENT UNIVERSITY

American Indian/Native American Studies M,D
Anthropology M
Biological and Biomedical Sciences—General M,D
Canadian Studies M,D
Chemistry M
Computer Science M
Cultural Studies D
Environmental Management and Policy M,D
Geography M,D
Materials Sciences M
Physics M

TREVECCA NAZARENE UNIVERSITY

Business Administration and Management—General M
Counseling Psychology M
Counselor Education M,D
Curriculum and Instruction M
Education—General M,D
Educational Leadership and Administration M,D
Elementary Education M
English as a Second Language M
Information Science M
Library Science M
Marriage and Family Therapy M
Organizational Management M
Physician Assistant Studies M
Psychology—General M,D
Reading Education M
Religion M
Secondary Education M
Theology M
Vocational and Technical Education M

TRINE UNIVERSITY

Civil Engineering M
Criminal Justice and Criminology M
Engineering and Applied Sciences—General M
Mechanical Engineering M

TRINITY BAPTIST COLLEGE

Education—General M
Educational Leadership and Administration M
Pastoral Ministry and Counseling M
Religious Education M
Special Education M

TRINITY COLLEGE

American Studies M
Economics M
English M
Public Policy M

TRINITY EPISCOPAL SCHOOL FOR MINISTRY

Missions and Missiology P,M,D,O
Pastoral Ministry and Counseling P,M,D,O
Religion P,M,D,O
Theology P,M,D,O

TRINITY INTERNATIONAL UNIVERSITY

Archaeology P,M,D,O
Bioethics M
Business Administration and Management—General P,M,D,O
Communication—General M
Counseling Psychology P,M,D,O
Education—General M
Educational Leadership and Administration M
Law P
Missions and Missiology P,M,D,O
Pastoral Ministry and Counseling P,M,D,O
Religious Education P,M,D,O
Theology P,M,D,O

TRINITY INTERNATIONAL UNIVERSITY, SOUTH FLORIDA CAMPUS

Counseling Psychology M
Religion M,O

TRINITY LUTHERAN SEMINARY

Music P,M
Theology P,M

TRINITY UNIVERSITY

Accounting M
Business Administration and Management—General M
Education—General M
Educational Leadership and Administration M
Health Services Management and Hospital Administration M
School Psychology M

TRINITY (WASHINGTON) UNIVERSITY

Business Administration and Management—General M
Communication—General M
Counselor Education M
Curriculum and Instruction M
Early Childhood Education M
Education—General M
Educational Leadership and Administration M
Elementary Education M
English as a Second Language M
English Education M
Human Resources Management M
National Security M
Nonprofit Management M
Organizational Management M
Public Health—General M
Reading Education M
Secondary Education M
Social Sciences Education M
Special Education M

TRINITY WESTERN UNIVERSITY

Business Administration and Management—General M
Counseling Psychology M
Educational Leadership and Administration M,O
English as a Second Language M
English M
Health Services Management and Hospital Administration M,O
History M
Humanities M
Interdisciplinary Studies M

*M—master's degree; P—first professional degree; D—doctorate; O—other advanced degree; *—Close-Up and/or Announcement or Display in one of the other books in this series*

International Business	M
Linguistics	M
Nonprofit Management	M,O
Organizational Management	M,O
Pastoral Ministry and Counseling	P,M,D
Philosophy	M
Theology	P,M,D

TRI STATE COLLEGE OF ACUPUNCTURE

Acupuncture and Oriental Medicine	M,O

TROPICAL AGRICULTURE RESEARCH AND HIGHER EDUCATION CENTER

Agricultural Economics and Agribusiness	M,D
Agricultural Sciences—General	M,D
Conservation Biology	M,D
Environmental Management and Policy	M,D
Forestry	M,D
Water Resources	M,D

TROY UNIVERSITY

Adult Education	M
Art/Fine Arts	M
Business Administration and Management—General	M
Clinical Psychology	M
Communication—General	M
Computer Science	M
Counselor Education	M,O
Criminal Justice and Criminology	M
Early Childhood Education	M,O
Education—General	M,O
Educational Leadership and Administration	M,O
Elementary Education	M,O
Environmental Management and Policy	M
Health Services Management and Hospital Administration	M
Human Resources Management	M
International Affairs	M
Management Information Systems	M
National Security	M
Nonprofit Management	M
Nursing—General	M
Public Administration	M
Rehabilitation Counseling	M,O
School Psychology	M
Secondary Education	M,O
Sports Management	M

TRUMAN STATE UNIVERSITY

Accounting	M
Biological and Biomedical Sciences—General	M
Communication Disorders	M
Education—General	M
English	M
Music	M

TUFTS UNIVERSITY

Allopathic Medicine	P
Analytical Chemistry	M,D
Archaeology	M
Art History	M
Art/Fine Arts	M
Biochemistry	D
Bioengineering	M,D,O
Biological and Biomedical Sciences—General	M,D*
Biomedical Engineering	M,D
Biostatistics	M,D
Biotechnology	O
Cell Biology	D
Chemical Engineering	M,D
Chemistry	M,D
Child and Family Studies	M,D,O
Child Development	M,D,O*
Civil Engineering	M,D
Classics	M
Clinical Research	M,D
Computer Science	M,D,O
Conflict Resolution and Mediation/Peace Studies	M,D
Dance	M,D
Dentistry	P
Developmental Biology	D
Early Childhood Education	M,D,O
Economics	M
Education—General	M,D,O
Electrical Engineering	M,D,O
Engineering and Applied Sciences—General	M,D*
Engineering Management	M
English	M,D
Environmental and Occupational Health	M,D
Environmental Engineering	M,D
Environmental Management and Policy	M,D,O
Environmental Sciences	M,D
Epidemiology	M,D,O
Ergonomics and Human Factors	M,D
Family and Consumer Sciences-General	M,D,O
French	M
Genetics	D
Geotechnical Engineering	M,D
German	M
Hazardous Materials Management	M,D
Health Communication	M
History	M,D
Human-Computer Interaction	O
Immunology	D
Inorganic Chemistry	M,D
International Affairs	M,D*
International and Comparative Education	M,D
International Business	M,D
International Development	M,D
International Health	M,D
Management Strategy and Policy	O
Manufacturing Engineering	O
Mathematics	M,D
Mechanical Engineering	M,D
Microbiology	D
Middle School Education	M,D
Molecular Biology	D
Molecular Physiology	D
Museum Studies	O
Music	M
Neuroscience	D
Nonprofit Management	O
Nutrition	M,D
Occupational Therapy	M,D,O
Oral and Dental Sciences	M,O
Organic Chemistry	M,D
Pharmacology	D
Philosophy	M
Physical Chemistry	M,D
Physics	M,D
Physiology	D
Psychology—General	M,D
Public Administration	O
Public Health—General	M
Public Policy	M*
School Psychology	M,O
Secondary Education	M,D
Structural Engineering	M,D
Theater	M,D
Urban and Regional Planning	M
Urban Studies	M
Veterinary Medicine	P
Veterinary Sciences	M,D
Water Resources Engineering	M,D

TUI UNIVERSITY

Adult Education	M
Business Administration and Management—General	M,D
Clinical Research	M,D,O
Computer and Information Systems Security	M,D
Conflict Resolution and Mediation/Peace Studies	M,D
Criminal Justice and Criminology	M,D
Early Childhood Education	M
Education—General	M,D
Educational Leadership and Administration	M,D
Educational Media/Instructional Technology	M,D
Emergency Management	M,D,O
Environmental and Occupational Health	M,D,O
Finance and Banking	M,D
Health Education	M,D,O
Health Informatics	M,D,O
Health Services Management and Hospital Administration	M,D,O
Higher Education	M,D
Human Resources Management	M,D
International Business	M,D
International Health	M,D,O
Legal and Justice Studies	M,D,O
Logistics	M,D
Management Information Systems	M,D,O
Marketing	M,D
Nursing and Healthcare Administration	M,D,O
Project Management	M,D
Public Administration	M,D
Public Health—General	M,D,O
Quality Management	M,D,O
Reading Education	M

TULANE UNIVERSITY

Allopathic Medicine	P
Anthropology	M,D
Applied Mathematics	M,D
Architecture	M
Art History	M
Art/Fine Arts	M
Biochemistry	M,D
Biological and Biomedical Sciences—General	M,D
Biomedical Engineering	M,D
Biostatistics	M,D
Business Administration and Management—General	M,D
Cell Biology	M,D
Chemical Engineering	D
Chemistry	M,D
Classics	M
Dance	M
Ecology	M,D
Economics	M,D
English	M,D
Environmental and Occupational Health	M,D
Environmental Sciences	M,D
Epidemiology	M,D
Evolutionary Biology	M,D
French	M,D
Geology	M,D
Geosciences	M,D
Health Communication	M
Health Education	M
Health Services Management and Hospital Administration	M,D
History	M,D
Human Genetics	M,D
Immunology	M,D
Infectious Diseases	M,D,O
Interdisciplinary Studies	D
International Development	M,D
International Health	M,D
Latin American Studies	M,D
Law	P,M,D
Liberal Studies	M
Maternal and Child Health	M,D
Mathematics	M,D
Microbiology	M,D
Molecular Biology	M,D
Music	M
Neuroscience	M,D
Nutrition	M
Parasitology	M,D,O
Pharmacology	M,D
Philosophy	M,D
Physics	D
Physiology	M,D
Political Science	M,D
Portuguese	M,D
Psychology—General	M,D
Public Health—General	M,D,O
Social Work	M
Sociology	M,D
Spanish	M,D
Statistics	M,D
Structural Biology	M,D
Theater	M

TUSCULUM COLLEGE

Adult Education	M
Education—General	M
Organizational Management	M

TUSKEGEE UNIVERSITY

Agricultural Economics and Agribusiness	M
Agricultural Sciences—General	M
Agronomy and Soil Sciences	M
Animal Sciences	M
Biological and Biomedical Sciences—General	M,D
Chemistry	M
Electrical Engineering	M
Engineering and Applied Sciences—General	M,D
Environmental Sciences	M
Food Science and Technology	M
Materials Engineering	D
Mechanical Engineering	M
Nutrition	M
Plant Sciences	M
Veterinary Medicine	P,M
Veterinary Sciences	P,M

TYNDALE UNIVERSITY COLLEGE & SEMINARY

Missions and Missiology	P,M,O
Pastoral Ministry and Counseling	P,M,O
Theology	P,M,O

UNIFICATION THEOLOGICAL SEMINARY

Theology	P,M,D

UNIFORMED SERVICES UNIVERSITY OF THE HEALTH SCIENCES

Allopathic Medicine	P
Biological and Biomedical Sciences—General	M,D*
Cell Biology	D
Clinical Psychology	D
Environmental and Occupational Health	M,D
Family Nurse Practitioner Studies	M
History of Medicine	M
History of Science and Technology	M,D
Immunology	D
Infectious Diseases	D*
International Health	M,D
Medical/Surgical Nursing	M

Microbiology D
Molecular Biology D*
Neuroscience D*
Nurse Anesthesia M
Nursing—General M
Psychology—General D
Public Health—General M,D
Zoology M,D

UNION COLLEGE (KY)

Clinical Psychology M
Counseling Psychology M
Education—General M
Educational Leadership and Administration M
Elementary Education M
Health Education M
Middle School Education M
Music Education M
Physical Education M
Psychology—General M
Reading Education M
School Psychology M
Secondary Education M
Special Education M

UNION COLLEGE (NE)

Physician Assistant Studies M

UNION GRADUATE COLLEGE

Bioethics M
Business Administration and Management—General M,O
Computer Science M
Education—General M
Electrical Engineering M
Engineering and Applied Sciences—General M
Engineering Management M
English Education M
Finance and Banking M,O
Foreign Languages Education M
Health Services Management and Hospital Administration M,O
Human Resources Management M,O
Mathematics Education M
Mechanical Engineering M
Science Education M
Social Sciences Education M

UNION INSTITUTE & UNIVERSITY

Clinical Psychology D
Counseling Psychology M
Cultural Studies M
Education—General M,D,O
Educational Leadership and Administration D
Health Promotion M
Higher Education D
History M
Interdisciplinary Studies M,D
Psychology—General M
Writing M

UNION THEOLOGICAL SEMINARY AND PRESBYTERIAN SCHOOL OF CHRISTIAN EDUCATION

Religious Education M
Theology P,M,D

UNION THEOLOGICAL SEMINARY IN THE CITY OF NEW YORK

Theology P,M,D

UNION UNIVERSITY

Business Administration and Management—General M
Cultural Studies M
Education—General M,D,O
Educational Leadership and Administration M,D,O
Family Nurse Practitioner Studies M,D,O
Higher Education M,D,O
Nurse Anesthesia M,D,O
Nursing and Healthcare Administration M,D,O
Nursing Education M,D,O
Nursing—General M,D,O
Pastoral Ministry and Counseling M,D
Religion M,D

UNITED STATES ARMY COMMAND AND GENERAL STAFF COLLEGE

Military and Defense Studies M

UNITED STATES INTERNATIONAL UNIVERSITY

Business Administration and Management—General M
Counseling Psychology M
Finance and Banking M
International Affairs M
Management Information Systems M
Management Strategy and Policy M
Marketing M

UNITED STATES SPORTS ACADEMY

Athletic Training and Sports Medicine M
Exercise and Sports Science M
Physical Education M
Sports Management M,D

UNITED TALMUDICAL SEMINARY

Theology

UNITED THEOLOGICAL SEMINARY

Theology P,M,D

UNITED THEOLOGICAL SEMINARY OF THE TWIN CITIES

Art/Fine Arts P,M,D,O
Asian Studies P,M,D,O
Conflict Resolution and Mediation/Peace Studies P,M,D,O
Ethnic Studies P,M,D,O
Pastoral Ministry and Counseling P,M,D,O
Religion P,M,D,O
Theology P,M,D,O
Women's Studies P,M,D,O

UNIVERSIDAD ADVENTISTA DE LAS ANTILLAS

Biological and Biomedical Sciences—General M
Curriculum and Instruction M
Education—General M
Educational Leadership and Administration M
English as a Second Language M
History M
Secondary Education M
Spanish M

UNIVERSIDAD AUTONOMA DE GUADALAJARA

Advertising and Public Relations M,D
Allopathic Medicine P
Architecture M,D
Business Administration and Management—General M,D
Computer Science M,D
Corporate and Organizational Communication M,D
Education—General M,D
Energy and Power Engineering M,D
Environmental and Occupational Health M,D
Environmental Management and Policy M,D
International Business M,D
Internet and Interactive Multimedia M,D
Law M,D
Manufacturing Engineering M,D
Marketing Research M,D
Mathematics Education M,D
Philosophy M,D
Spanish M,D
Systems Science M,D
Translation and Interpretation M,D

UNIVERSIDAD CENTRAL DEL CARIBE

Addictions/Substance Abuse Counseling M
Allopathic Medicine P,M
Anatomy M
Biological and Biomedical Sciences—General M
Cell Biology M
Immunology M
Microbiology M
Pharmacology M
Physiology M

UNIVERSIDAD CENTRAL DEL ESTE

Allopathic Medicine P
Business Administration and Management—General M,D
Educational Policy M,D
Environmental Engineering M,D
Finance and Banking M,D
Higher Education M,D
Human Resources Development M,D
Law P
Public Health—General M,D
Public Policy M,D

UNIVERSIDAD DE CIENCIAS MEDICAS

Allopathic Medicine P,M,O
Anatomy P,M,O
Biological and Biomedical Sciences—General P,M,O
Environmental and Occupational Health P,M,O
Health Services Management and Hospital Administration P,M,O
Pharmacy P,M,O

UNIVERSIDAD DE IBEROAMERICA

Acute Care/Critical Care Nursing P,M
Allopathic Medicine P,M
Clinical Psychology P,M
Educational Psychology P,M
Forensic Psychology P,M
Health Services Management and Hospital Administration P,M

UNIVERSIDAD DE LAS AMERICAS, A.C.

Business Administration and Management—General M
Education—General M
Finance and Banking M
International Affairs M
Marketing Research M
Marriage and Family Therapy M
Organizational Behavior M
Psychology—General M
Quality Management M

UNIVERSIDAD DE LAS AMÉRICAS–PUEBLA

American Studies M
Anthropology M
Archaeology M
Biotechnology M
Business Administration and Management—General M
Chemical Engineering M
Clinical Laboratory Sciences/Medical Technology M
Computer Art and Design M
Computer Science M,D
Construction Management M
Economics M
Education—General M
Electrical Engineering M
Engineering and Applied Sciences—General M,D
English M
Finance and Banking M
Food Science and Technology M
Industrial and Manufacturing Management M
Industrial/Management Engineering M
Linguistics M
Manufacturing Engineering M
Psychology—General M

UNIVERSIDAD DEL ESTE

Accounting M
Adult Education M
Agricultural Economics and Agribusiness M
Business Administration and Management—General M
Computer and Information Systems Security M
Criminal Justice and Criminology M
Elementary Education M
English as a Second Language M
Foreign Languages Education M
Human Resources Management M
Management Information Systems M
Management Strategy and Policy M
Multilingual and Multicultural Education M
Public Policy M
Social Work M
Special Education M

*M—master's degree; P—first professional degree; D—doctorate; O—other advanced degree; *—Close-Up and/or Announcement or Display in one of the other books in this series*

UNIVERSIDAD DEL TURABO

Accounting	M
Adult Nursing	M
Art/Fine Arts	M
Arts Administration	M
Athletic Training and Sports Medicine	M
Business Administration and Management—General	M,D
Communication Disorders	M
Counseling Psychology	M
Counselor Education	M
Criminal Justice and Criminology	M
Curriculum and Instruction	M,D
Early Childhood Education	M
Education—General	M,D
Educational Leadership and Administration	M,D
English as a Second Language	M
Environmental Management and Policy	M
Environmental Sciences	M,D
Family Nurse Practitioner Studies	M,O
Forensic Sciences	M
Health Promotion	M
Human Resources Management	M
Human Services	M
Information Studies	M
Library Science	M
Logistics	M
Management Information Systems	M,D
Marketing	M
Multilingual and Multicultural Education	M
Nursing—General	M
Physical Education	M
Project Management	M
Quality Management	M
School Psychology	M
Special Education	M
Taxation	M
Telecommunications	M

UNIVERSIDAD IBEROAMERICANA

Advertising and Public Relations	P,M
Allopathic Medicine	P
Dentistry	P,M
Educational Leadership and Administration	P,M
Higher Education	P,M
Human Resources Development	P,M
Law	P,M
Marketing	P,M
Special Education	P,M

UNIVERSIDAD METROPOLITANA

Accounting	M,O
Business Administration and Management—General	M,O
Curriculum and Instruction	M
Early Childhood Education	M
Education—General	M
Educational Leadership and Administration	M
Environmental Education	M
Environmental Management and Policy	M
Finance and Banking	M
Human Resources Management	M
International Business	M
Leisure Studies	M
Marketing	M
Natural Resources	M
Physical Education	M
Recreation and Park Management	M
Special Education	M

UNIVERSIDAD NACIONAL PEDRO HENRIQUEZ URENA

Accounting	P,M,D
Allopathic Medicine	P
Animal Sciences	P,M,D
Architecture	P,M,D
Business Administration and Management—General	P,M,D
Construction Engineering	P,M,D
Dentistry	P
Economics	P,M,D
Education—General	P,M,D
Environmental Engineering	P,M,D
Health Services Management and Hospital Administration	P,M,D
Historic Preservation	P,M,D
Horticulture	P,M,D
Humanities	P,M,D
International Affairs	P,M,D
Natural Resources	P,M,D
Project Management	P,M,D
Public Administration	P,M,D
Social Sciences	P,M,D
Veterinary Medicine	P,M,D

UNIVERSITÉ DE MONCTON

Astronomy	M
Biochemistry	M
Biological and Biomedical Sciences—General	M
Business Administration and Management—General	M
Chemistry	M
Civil Engineering	M
Computer Science	M,O
Counselor Education	M
Economics	M
Education—General	M
Educational Leadership and Administration	M
Educational Psychology	M
Electrical Engineering	M
Engineering and Applied Sciences—General	M
Food Science and Technology	M
French	M,D
History	M
Industrial/Management Engineering	M
Law	P,M,O
Mathematics	M
Mechanical Engineering	M
Nutrition	M
Physics	M
Public Administration	M
Social Work	M

UNIVERSITÉ DE MONTRÉAL

Acute Care/Critical Care Nursing	O
Allopathic Medicine	P,O
Anthropology	M,D
Art History	M,D
Biochemistry	M,D,O
Bioethics	M,O
Biological and Biomedical Sciences—General	M,D
Biomedical Engineering	M,D,O
Biophysics	M,D,O
Cancer Biology/Oncology	O
Cell Biology	M,D
Chemistry	M,D
Clinical Laboratory Sciences/Medical Technology	O
Communication Disorders	M
Communication—General	M,D,O
Community Health	M,D,O
Comparative Literature	M,D
Computer Science	M,D
Criminal Justice and Criminology	M,D
Curriculum and Instruction	M,D,O
Demography and Population Studies	M,D
Dental Hygiene	O
Developmental Psychology	M,D,O
Economics	M,D
Education—General	M,D,O
Educational Leadership and Administration	M,D,O
Educational Psychology	M,D,O
Emergency Management	O
English	M,D
Environmental and Occupational Health	M,O
Environmental Design	M,D,O
Environmental Management and Policy	O
Ergonomics and Human Factors	O
Film, Television, and Video Theory and Criticism	M,D
French	M,D
Genetics	O
Geography	M,D,O
German	M
Gerontology	O
Health Physics/Radiological Health	O
Health Services Management and Hospital Administration	M,O
Hispanic Studies	M,D
History	M,D
Human Services	D
Immunology	M,D
Industrial and Labor Relations	M,D,O
Infectious Diseases	O
Information Studies	M,D
Kinesiology and Movement Studies	M,D,O
Law	P,M,D,O
Library Science	M,D
Linguistics	M,D,O
Maternal and Child/Neonatal Nursing	O
Mathematics	M,D
Microbiology	M,D,O
Molecular Biology	M,D
Museum Studies	M
Music	M,D,O
Neuroscience	M,D
Nurse Anesthesia	O
Nursing—General	M,D,O
Nutrition	M,D,O
Optometry	P,O
Oral and Dental Sciences	M,O
Pathology	M,D
Pharmaceutical Sciences	M,D,O
Pharmacology	M,D
Philosophy	M,D
Physical Education	M,D,O
Physical Therapy	O
Physics	M,D
Physiology	M,D,O
Political Science	M,D
Psychology—General	M,D
Public Health—General	M,D,O
Rehabilitation Counseling	O
Social Work	O
Sociology	M,D
Spanish	M
Statistics	M,D
Theology	M,D,O
Toxicology	O
Translation and Interpretation	M,D,O
Veterinary Medicine	P
Veterinary Sciences	M,D,O
Virology	D
Vision Sciences	M,O

UNIVERSITÉ DE SHERBROOKE

Accounting	M
Allopathic Medicine	P
Biochemistry	M,D
Biological and Biomedical Sciences—General	M,D,O
Biophysics	M,D
Biotechnology	P,M,D,O
Business Administration and Management—General	P,M,D,O
Canadian Studies	M,D
Cell Biology	M,D
Chemical Engineering	M,D
Chemistry	M,D,O
Civil Engineering	M,D
Clinical Laboratory Sciences/Medical Technology	M,D
Comparative Literature	M,D
Conflict Resolution and Mediation/Peace Studies	P,M,D,O
Economics	M
Education—General	M,O
Educational Leadership and Administration	M
Electrical Engineering	M,D
Elementary Education	M,O
Engineering and Applied Sciences—General	M,D,O
Engineering Management	M,O
Environmental Engineering	M
Environmental Sciences	M,O
Ethics	M,D,O
Finance and Banking	M
French	M,D
Geography	M,D
Gerontology	M
Health Law	P,M,D,O
Higher Education	M,O
History	M
Immunology	M,D
Information Science	M,D
International Business	M
Kinesiology and Movement Studies	M,O
Law	P,M,D,O
Linguistics	M,D
Management Information Systems	M,O
Marketing	M
Mathematics	M,D
Mechanical Engineering	M,D
Microbiology	M,D
Organizational Behavior	M
Pharmacology	M,D
Philosophy	M,D,O
Physical Education	M,O
Physics	M,D
Physiology	M,D
Psychology—General	M
Radiation Biology	M,D
Religion	M,D,O
Social Work	M
Special Education	M,O
Theater	M,D
Theology	M,D,O

UNIVERSITÉ DU QUÉBEC À CHICOUTIMI

Art/Fine Arts	M
Business Administration and Management—General	M
Canadian Studies	M
Comparative Literature	M
Education—General	M,D
Engineering and Applied Sciences—General	M,D
Environmental Management and Policy	M
Ethics	O
French	O
Genetics	M
Geosciences	M
Linguistics	M
Mineralogy	D
Project Management	M
Theology	M,D

UNIVERSITÉ DU QUÉBEC À MONTRÉAL

Accounting	M,O

Actuarial Science	O
Art History	M,D
Art/Fine Arts	M
Atmospheric Sciences	M,D,O
Biological and Biomedical Sciences—General	M,D
Business Administration and Management—General	M,D,O
Chemistry	M,D
Communication—General	M,D
Comparative Literature	M,D
Dance	M
Economics	M,D
Education—General	M,D,O
Environmental and Occupational Health	O
Environmental Education	M,D,O
Environmental Sciences	M,D,O
Ergonomics and Human Factors	O
Finance and Banking	O
Geographic Information Systems	O
Geography	M
Geology	M,D,O
Geosciences	M,D,O
History	M,D
Kinesiology and Movement Studies	M
Law	O
Linguistics	M,D
Management Information Systems	M
Mathematics	M,D
Meteorology	M,D,O
Mineralogy	M,D,O
Museum Studies	M
Natural Resources	M,D,O
Philosophy	M,D
Political Science	M,D
Project Management	M,O
Psychology—General	D
Public Administration	M
Religion	M,D
Social Work	M
Sociology	M,D
Urban Studies	M,D

UNIVERSITÉ DU QUÉBEC À RIMOUSKI

Business Administration and Management—General	M,O
Comparative Literature	M,D
Education—General	M,D,O
Engineering and Applied Sciences—General	M
Ethics	M,O
Fish, Game, and Wildlife Management	M,D,O
Marine Affairs	M,O
Nursing—General	M,O
Oceanography	M,D
Project Management	M,O
Social Psychology	M
Urban and Regional Planning	M,D,O

UNIVERSITÉ DU QUÉBEC À TROIS-RIVIÈRES

Accounting	M
Biophysics	M,D
Business Administration and Management—General	M,D
Chemistry	M
Chiropractic	P
Communication—General	M,O
Comparative Literature	M
Computer Science	M
Education—General	M,D
Educational Leadership and Administration	O
Educational Psychology	M,D
Electrical Engineering	M,D
Environmental Sciences	M,D
Finance and Banking	O
Industrial and Labor Relations	O
Industrial/Management Engineering	M,O
Leisure Studies	M,O
Mathematics	M
Nursing—General	M,O
Philosophy	M,D
Physical Education	M
Physics	M,D
Psychology—General	D,O
Travel and Tourism	M,O

UNIVERSITÉ DU QUÉBEC, ÉCOLE DE TECHNOLOGIE SUPÉRIEURE

Engineering and Applied Sciences—General	M,D,O

UNIVERSITÉ DU QUÉBEC, ÉCOLE NATIONALE D'ADMINISTRATION PUBLIQUE

International Business	M,O
Public Administration	D,O
Urban Studies	M

UNIVERSITÉ DU QUÉBEC EN ABITIBI-TÉMISCAMINGUE

Biological and Biomedical Sciences—General	M,D
Business Administration and Management—General	M
Education—General	M,D,O
Engineering and Applied Sciences—General	M,O
Environmental Sciences	M,D
Forestry	M,D
Mineral/Mining Engineering	M,O
Natural Resources	M,D
Project Management	M,O
Social Work	M

UNIVERSITÉ DU QUÉBEC EN OUTAOUAIS

Accounting	M,O
Adult Education	O
Computer Science	M,D
Education—General	M,D,O
Educational Psychology	M
Finance and Banking	M,O
Industrial and Labor Relations	M,D,O
Nursing—General	M,O
Project Management	M,O
Social Work	M
Software Engineering	O
Urban and Regional Planning	M

UNIVERSITÉ DU QUÉBEC, INSTITUT NATIONAL DE LA RECHERCHE SCIENTIFIQUE

Biological and Biomedical Sciences—General	M,D
Demography and Population Studies	M,D
Energy Management and Policy	M,D
Environmental Management and Policy	M,D
Geosciences	M,D
Hydrology	M,D
Immunology	M,D
Materials Sciences	M,D
Medical Microbiology	M,D
Microbiology	M,D
Telecommunications	M,D
Urban Studies	M,D
Virology	M,D

UNIVERSITÉ LAVAL

Accounting	M,O
Advertising and Public Relations	O
Aerospace/Aeronautical Engineering	M
Agricultural Economics and Agribusiness	M
Agricultural Engineering	M
Agricultural Sciences—General	M,D
Agronomy and Soil Sciences	M,D
Allopathic Medicine	P,O
Anatomy	M,D,O
Anesthesiologist Assistant Studies	O
Animal Sciences	M,D
Anthropology	M,D
Archaeology	M,D
Architecture	M
Art History	M,D
Art/Fine Arts	M
Biochemistry	M,D,O
Biological and Biomedical Sciences—General	M,D,O
Business Administration and Management—General	M,D,O
Cancer Biology/Oncology	O
Cardiovascular Sciences	O
Cell Biology	M,D
Chemical Engineering	M,D
Chemistry	M,D
Civil Engineering	M,D,O
Clinical Psychology	D
Communication Disorders	M
Community Health	M,D,O
Comparative Literature	M,D
Computer Science	M,D
Consumer Economics	O
Counselor Education	M,D
Curriculum and Instruction	M,D
Dentistry	P
Economics	M,D
Education—General	M,D,O
Educational Leadership and Administration	M,D,O
Educational Measurement and Evaluation	M,D,O
Educational Media/Instructional Technology	M,D
Educational Psychology	M,D
Electrical Engineering	M,D
Electronic Commerce	M,O
Emergency Medical Services	O
Engineering and Applied Sciences—General	M,D,O
English	M,D
Entrepreneurship	M,O
Environmental and Occupational Health	O
Environmental Engineering	M,D
Environmental Management and Policy	M,D,O
Environmental Sciences	M,D
Epidemiology	M,D
Ethics	O
Ethnic Studies	M,D
Facilities Management	M,O
Film, Television, and Video Theory and Criticism	M,D
Finance and Banking	M,O
Food Science and Technology	M,D
Forestry	M,D
Geodetic Sciences	M,D
Geographic Information Systems	M,O
Geography	M,D
Geology	M,D
Geosciences	M,D
Gerontology	O
Graphic Design	M
Health Physics/Radiological Health	O
History	M,D
Immunology	M,D
Industrial and Labor Relations	M,D
Industrial/Management Engineering	O
Infectious Diseases	O
International Affairs	M,D
International Business	M,O
Journalism	O
Kinesiology and Movement Studies	M,D
Law	M,D,O
Legal and Justice Studies	O
Linguistics	M,D
Management Information Systems	M,O
Marketing	M,O
Mass Communication	M,D
Mathematics	M,D
Mechanical Engineering	M,D
Metallurgical Engineering and Metallurgy	M,D
Microbiology	M,D
Mineral/Mining Engineering	M,D
Molecular Biology	M,D
Museum Studies	O
Music Education	M,D
Music	M,D
Neurobiology	M,D
Nursing—General	M,D,O
Nutrition	M,D
Oceanography	D
Oral and Dental Sciences	M,O
Organizational Management	M,O
Pathology	O
Pharmaceutical Sciences	M,D,O
Philosophy	M,D
Physics	M,D
Physiology	M,D
Plant Biology	M,D
Political Science	M,D
Psychology—General	D
Religion	M,D
Rural Planning and Studies	O
Social Psychology	D
Social Work	M,D
Sociology	M,D
Software Engineering	O
Spanish	M,D
Statistics	M
Theater	M,D
Theology	M,D
Translation and Interpretation	M,O
Urban and Regional Planning	M,D
Women's Studies	O

UNIVERSITY AT ALBANY, STATE UNIVERSITY OF NEW YORK

Accounting	M
African Studies	M
African-American Studies	M
Anthropology	M,D
Art/Fine Arts	M
Atmospheric Sciences	M,D
Biochemistry	M,D
Biological and Biomedical Sciences—General	M,D*
Biopsychology	M,D,O
Biostatistics	M,D
Business Administration and Management—General	M
Cell Biology	M,D
Chemistry	M,D
Clinical Psychology	M,D,O
Communication—General	M,D
Computer Science	M,D
Conservation Biology	M
Counseling Psychology	M,D,O
Counselor Education	M,D,O
Criminal Justice and Criminology	M,D
Curriculum and Instruction	M,D,O
Demography and Population Studies	M,D,O

*M—master's degree; P—first professional degree; D—doctorate; O—other advanced degree; *—Close-Up and/or Announcement or Display in one of the other books in this series*

Developmental Biology	M,D
Ecology	M,D
Economics	M,D,O
Education—General	M,D,O
Educational Leadership and Administration	M,D,O
Educational Measurement and Evaluation	M,D,O
Educational Media/ Instructional Technology	M,D,O
Educational Psychology	M,D,O
English	M,D
Environmental and Occupational Health	M,D
Environmental Management and Policy	M
Environmental Sciences	M
Epidemiology	M,D
Evolutionary Biology	M,D
Experimental Psychology	M,D,O
Finance and Banking	M
Forensic Sciences	M,D
French	M,D
Genetics	M,D
Geographic Information Systems	M,O
Geography	M,O
Geology	M,D
Geosciences	M,D
Health Services Management and Hospital Administration	M
History	M,D,O
Human Resources Management	M
Immunology	M,D
Industrial and Organizational Psychology	M,D,O
Information Science	M,D,O
Information Studies	M,O
Italian	M
Latin American Studies	M,O
Liberal Studies	M
Management of Technology	M
Marketing	M
Mathematics Education	M,D
Mathematics	M,D
Molecular Biology	M,D
Molecular Pathogenesis	M,D
Nanotechnology	M,D
Neurobiology	M,D
Neuroscience	M,D
Philosophy	M,D
Physics	M,D
Political Science	M,D
Psychology—General	M,D,O
Public Administration	M,D,O
Public Health—General	M,D
Public History	M,D,O
Public Policy	M,D,O
Reading Education	M,D,O
Rehabilitation Counseling	M
Russian	M,O
School Psychology	M,D,O
Science Education	M,D
Social Psychology	M,D,O
Social Work	M,D
Sociology	M,D,O
Spanish	M,D
Special Education	M
Statistics	M,D,O
Structural Biology	M,D
Taxation	M
Theater	M
Toxicology	M,D*
Translation and Interpretation	M,O
Urban and Regional Planning	M
Urban Studies	M,D,O
Women's Studies	M,D

UNIVERSITY AT BUFFALO, THE STATE UNIVERSITY OF NEW YORK

Accounting	M,D,O
Acute Care/Critical Care Nursing	M,D,O
Adult Nursing	M,D,O
Aerospace/Aeronautical Engineering	M,D
Allied Health—General	M,D,O
Allopathic Medicine	P
American Studies	M,D
Anatomy	M,D
Anthropology	M,D
Architecture	M
Art History	M,O
Art/Fine Arts	M,O
Biochemistry	M,D
Bioengineering	M,D
Biological and Biomedical Sciences—General	M,D*
Biophysics	M,D
Biostatistics	M,D
Biotechnology	M
Business Administration and Management—General	M,D,O
Cancer Biology/Oncology	D
Cell Biology	D
Chemical Engineering	M,D
Chemistry	M,D
Civil Engineering	M,D
Classics	M,D
Clinical Laboratory Sciences/Medical Technology	M
Clinical Psychology	M,D
Cognitive Sciences	M,D
Communication Disorders	M,D
Communication—General	M,D
Community Health	M,D
Comparative Literature	M,D
Computer Science	M,D
Counseling Psychology	M,D,O
Counselor Education	M,D,O
Dentistry	P,M,D,O
Early Childhood Education	M,D,O
Ecology	M,D,O
Economics	M,D,O
Education—General	M,D,O
Educational Leadership and Administration	M,D,O
Educational Psychology	M,D,O
Electrical Engineering	M,D
Electronic Commerce	M,D,O
Elementary Education	M,D,O
Engineering and Applied Sciences—General	M,D*
English as a Second Language	M,D,O
English Education	M,D,O
English	M,D
Environmental Engineering	M,D
Epidemiology	M,D
Evolutionary Biology	M,D,O
Exercise and Sports Science	M,D
Family Nurse Practitioner Studies	M,D,O
Finance and Banking	M,D,O
Foreign Languages Education	M,D,O
French	M,D
Geographic Information Systems	M,D,O
Geography	M,D,O
Geology	M,D
Gerontological Nursing	M,D,O
Higher Education	M,D,O
History	M,D
Human Resources Management	M,D,O
Immunology	M,D*
Industrial/Management Engineering	M,D
Information Studies	M,O
Japanese	M,D,O
Law	P,M
Library Science	M,O
Linguistics	M,D
Logistics	M,D,O
Management Information Systems	M,D,O
Materials Sciences	M
Maternal and Child/ Neonatal Nursing	M,D,O
Mathematics Education	M,D,O
Mathematics	M,D
Mechanical Engineering	M,D
Media Studies	M,O
Medicinal and Pharmaceutical Chemistry	M,D
Microbiology	M,D
Middle School Education	M,D,O
Molecular Biology	D
Molecular Pharmacology	D
Multilingual and Multicultural Education	M,D,O
Museum Studies	M,O
Music Education	M,D,O
Music	M,D
Neuroscience	M,D
Nurse Anesthesia	M,D,O
Nursing—General	M,D,O
Nutrition	M,D
Occupational Therapy	M
Oral and Dental Sciences	M,D,O
Pathology	M,D
Pediatric Nursing	M,D,O
Pharmaceutical Sciences	M,D
Pharmacology	M,D
Pharmacy	P
Philosophy	M,D
Physical Therapy	D
Physics	M,D
Physiology	M,D
Political Science	M,D
Psychiatric Nursing	M,D,O
Psychology—General	M,D
Public Health—General	M,D
Reading Education	M,D,O
Rehabilitation Counseling	M,D,O
Rehabilitation Sciences	M,D,O
Romance Languages	M,D
School Psychology	M,D,O
Science Education	M,D,O
Social Psychology	M,D
Social Sciences Education	M,D,O
Social Work	M,D
Sociology	M,D
Spanish	M,D
Special Education	M,D,O
Structural Biology	M,D
Structural Engineering	M,D
Toxicology	M,D
Transportation Management	M,D,O
Urban and Regional Planning	M
Urban Design	M
Women's Health Nursing	M,D,O

UNIVERSITY OF ADVANCING TECHNOLOGY

Computer and Information Systems Security	M
Computer Science	M
Internet and Interactive Multimedia	M
Management of Technology	M

THE UNIVERSITY OF AKRON

Accounting	M
Applied Mathematics	M,D
Arts Administration	M
Biological and Biomedical Sciences—General	M,D
Biomedical Engineering	M,D
Business Administration and Management—General	M
Chemical Engineering	M,D
Chemistry	M,D
Child and Family Studies	M
Child Development	M
Civil Engineering	M,D
Clothing and Textiles	M
Cognitive Sciences	M,D
Communication Disorders	M,D
Communication—General	M
Computer Engineering	M,D
Computer Science	M
Counseling Psychology	M,D
Counselor Education	M,D
Economics	M
Education—General	M,D
Educational Leadership and Administration	M,D
Electrical Engineering	M,D
Electronic Commerce	M
Elementary Education	M,D
Engineering and Applied Sciences—General	M,D
Engineering Management	M
English	M
Entrepreneurship	M
Exercise and Sports Science	M
Family and Consumer Sciences-General	M
Finance and Banking	M
Geographic Information Systems	M
Geography	M
Geology	M
Geophysics	M
Geosciences	M
Health Services Management and Hospital Administration	M
Higher Education	M
History	M,D
Human Resources Management	M
Industrial and Organizational Psychology	M,D
International Business	M
Law	P
Management Information Systems	M
Management of Technology	M
Marketing	M
Marriage and Family Therapy	M
Mathematics	M
Mechanical Engineering	M,D
Music Education	M
Music	M
Nursing—General	M,D
Nutrition	M
Physical Education	M
Physics	M
Political Science	M
Polymer Science and Engineering	M,D
Psychology—General	M,D
Public Administration	M
Public Health—General	M,D
School Psychology	M
Secondary Education	M,D
Social Work	M
Sociology	M,D
Spanish	M
Special Education	M
Statistics	M
Supply Chain Management	M
Taxation	M
Theater	M
Urban and Regional Planning	M
Urban Studies	M,D
Vocational and Technical Education	M
Writing	M

THE UNIVERSITY OF ALABAMA

Accounting	M,D
Advertising and Public Relations	M
Aerospace/Aeronautical Engineering	M,D
American Studies	M
Anthropology	M,D

Applied Mathematics	M,D
Applied Statistics	M,D
Art History	M
Art/Fine Arts	M
Biological and Biomedical Sciences—General	M,D
Business Administration and Management—General	M,D
Chemical Engineering	M,D
Chemistry	M,D
Child and Family Studies	M
Civil Engineering	M,D
Clinical Psychology	D
Clothing and Textiles	M
Communication Disorders	M
Communication—General	M,D
Community Health	M
Computer Engineering	M,D
Computer Science	M,D
Construction Engineering	M,D
Consumer Economics	M
Counselor Education	M,D,O
Criminal Justice and Criminology	M
Economics	M,D
Education of the Gifted	M,D,O
Educational Leadership and Administration	M,D,O
Electrical Engineering	M,D
Elementary Education	M,D,O
Engineering and Applied Sciences—General	M,D
English as a Second Language	M,D
English	M,D
Environmental Engineering	M,D
Ergonomics and Human Factors	M
Exercise and Sports Science	M,D
Experimental Psychology	D
Family and Consumer Sciences-General	M,D
Film, Television, and Video Production	M
Finance and Banking	M,D
French	M,D
Geography	M
Geology	M,D
German	M,D
Health Education	M,D
Health Promotion	M,D
Higher Education	M,D
History	M,D
Hospitality Management	M
Human Development	M
Industrial/Management Engineering	M
Information Studies	M,D
Interior Design	M
Journalism	M
Kinesiology and Movement Studies	M,D
Law	P,M
Library Science	M,D
Marketing	M,D
Mass Communication	D
Materials Engineering	M,D
Materials Sciences	D
Mathematics	M,D
Mechanical Engineering	M,D
Mechanics	M,D
Media Studies	M
Metallurgical Engineering and Metallurgy	M,D
Music Education	M,D,O
Music	M,D
Nursing—General	M,D
Nutrition	M
Photography	M
Physical Education	M,D
Physics	M,D
Political Science	M,D
Psychology—General	D
Public Administration	M,D
Quality Management	M
Rhetoric	M,D
Romance Languages	M,D
Secondary Education	M,D,O
Social Work	M,D
Spanish	M,D
Special Education	M,D,O
Speech and Interpersonal Communication	M
Sports Management	M,D
Taxation	M,D
Theater	M
Women's Studies	M
Writing	M,D

THE UNIVERSITY OF ALABAMA AT BIRMINGHAM

Accounting	M
Allied Health—General	M,D,O
Allopathic Medicine	P,M,D
Anthropology	M
Applied Mathematics	M,D
Art Education	M
Art History	M
Biochemistry	M,D
Biological and Biomedical Sciences—General	M,D*
Biomedical Engineering	M,D
Biophysics	D
Biostatistics	M,D
Business Administration and Management—General	M,D
Cell Biology	D
Chemistry	M,D
Civil Engineering	M,D
Communication—General	M
Computer Engineering	D
Computer Science	M,D
Counselor Education	M
Criminal Justice and Criminology	M
Dentistry	P
Early Childhood Education	M,D
Education—General	M,D,O
Educational Leadership and Administration	M,D,O
Electrical Engineering	M
Elementary Education	M
Engineering and Applied Sciences—General	M,D
English	M
Environmental and Occupational Health	D
Environmental Engineering	D
Epidemiology	D
Forensic Sciences	M
Genetics	D
Health Education	M,D
Health Informatics	M
Health Promotion	D
Health Services Management and Hospital Administration	M,D
History	M
Information Science	M,D
Management Information Systems	M
Materials Engineering	M,D
Materials Sciences	D
Mathematics	M,D
Mechanical Engineering	M,D
Microbiology	D
Molecular Biology	D
Molecular Genetics	D
Molecular Physiology	M,D
Neurobiology	D*
Neuroscience	D
Nurse Anesthesia	M
Nursing—General	M,D
Nutrition	M,D,O
Occupational Therapy	M
Optometry	P
Oral and Dental Sciences	M
Pathology	D
Pharmacology	D
Physical Education	M
Physical Therapy	D
Physician Assistant Studies	M
Physics	M,D
Physiology	D
Psychology—General	M,D
Public Administration	M
Public Health—General	M,D
Rehabilitation Sciences	O
Secondary Education	M
Sociology	M,D
Special Education	M
Toxicology	M,D
Vision Sciences	M,D

THE UNIVERSITY OF ALABAMA IN HUNTSVILLE

Accounting	M,O
Acute Care/Critical Care Nursing	M,D,O
Aerospace/Aeronautical Engineering	M,D
Applied Mathematics	M,D
Atmospheric Sciences	M,D
Biological and Biomedical Sciences—General	M
Biotechnology	D
Business Administration and Management—General	M,O
Chemical Engineering	M
Chemistry	M
Civil Engineering	M,D
Computer Engineering	M,D
Computer Science	M,D,O
Criminal Justice and Criminology	O
Electrical Engineering	M,D
Engineering and Applied Sciences—General	M,D
Engineering Management	M,D
English as a Second Language	M,O
English	M,O
Environmental Engineering	M,D
Environmental Sciences	M,D
Family Nurse Practitioner Studies	M,D,O
Finance and Banking	M,O
Geotechnical Engineering	M,D
Health Services Management and Hospital Administration	M,D,O
History	M
Human Resources Management	M,O
Industrial/Management Engineering	M,D
Interdisciplinary Studies	M,D,O
Logistics	M,O
Management Information Systems	M,O
Marketing	M,O
Materials Sciences	M,D
Mathematics	M,D
Mechanical Engineering	M,D
Nursing Education	M,D,O
Nursing—General	M,D,O
Operations Research	M
Optical Sciences	M,D
Photonics	M,D
Physics	M,D
Project Management	M,O
Psychology—General	M
Public Affairs	M
Science Education	M,D
Social Sciences Education	M
Software Engineering	M,D,O
Structural Engineering	M,D
Supply Chain Management	M,O
Systems Engineering	M,D
Taxation	M,O
Technical Writing	M,O
Transportation and Highway Engineering	M,D
Vision Sciences	M,D
Water Resources Engineering	M,D

UNIVERSITY OF ALASKA ANCHORAGE

Adult Education	M
Anthropology	M
Biological and Biomedical Sciences—General	M
Business Administration and Management—General	M
Civil Engineering	M,O
Clinical Psychology	M,D
Counselor Education	M
Early Childhood Education	M,O
Education—General	M,O
Educational Leadership and Administration	M,O
Engineering and Applied Sciences—General	M,O
Engineering Management	M
English	M
Environmental Engineering	M
Environmental Sciences	M
Family Nurse Practitioner Studies	M,O
Geological Engineering	M
Interdisciplinary Studies	M
Logistics	M,O
Nursing Education	M,O
Nursing—General	M,O
Ocean Engineering	M,O
Project Management	M
Psychiatric Nursing	M,O
Psychology—General	M,D
Public Administration	M
Public Health—General	M
Social Psychology	M,D
Social Work	M,O
Special Education	M,O
Writing	M

UNIVERSITY OF ALASKA FAIRBANKS

Anthropology	M,D
Art/Fine Arts	M
Astrophysics	M,D
Atmospheric Sciences	M,D
Biochemistry	M,D
Biological and Biomedical Sciences—General	M,D
Botany	M,D
Business Administration and Management—General	M
Chemistry	M,D
Civil Engineering	M,D
Clinical Psychology	D
Communication—General	M
Computational Sciences	M,D
Computer Art and Design	M
Computer Engineering	M,D
Computer Science	M
Corporate and Organizational Communication	M
Counselor Education	M
Criminal Justice and Criminology	M
Cultural Studies	M
Curriculum and Instruction	M,D,O
Economics	M
Education—General	M,D,O
Electrical Engineering	M,D
Elementary Education	M,D,O
Engineering and Applied Sciences—General	M,D
Engineering Management	M,D
English Education	M,D,O
English	M
Environmental Engineering	M,D
Environmental Management and Policy	M,D
Environmental Sciences	M,D

*M—master's degree; P—first professional degree; D—doctorate; O—other advanced degree; *—Close-Up and/or Announcement or Display in one of the other books in this series*

Finance and Banking	M
Fish, Game, and Wildlife Management	M,D
Geological Engineering	M,D
Geology	M,D
Geophysics	M,D
History	M
Interdisciplinary Studies	M,D
Limnology	M,D
Linguistics	M
Marine Biology	M,D
Marine Sciences	M,D
Mathematics	M,D
Mechanical Engineering	M,D
Mineral/Mining Engineering	M
Multilingual and Multicultural Education	M,D,O
Music Education	M
Music	M
Natural Resources	M
Northern Studies	M
Nutrition	M,D
Oceanography	M,D
Petroleum Engineering	M,D
Photography	M
Physics	M,D
Psychology—General	D
Reading Education	M,D,O
Rural Planning and Studies	M
Secondary Education	M,D,O
Social Psychology	M,D
Software Engineering	M
Statistics	M,D
Water Resources	M,D
Writing	M
Zoology	M,D

UNIVERSITY OF ALASKA SOUTHEAST

Business Administration and Management—General	M
Early Childhood Education	M
Education—General	M
Educational Media/Instructional Technology	M
Elementary Education	M
Public Administration	M
Secondary Education	M

UNIVERSITY OF ALBERTA

Accounting	D
Adult Education	M,D,O
Agricultural Economics and Agribusiness	M,D
Agricultural Sciences—General	M,D
Agronomy and Soil Sciences	M,D
Anthropology	M,D
Applied Arts and Design—General	M
Applied Mathematics	M,D,O
Archaeology	M,D
Art History	M
Art/Fine Arts	M
Asian Studies	M
Astrophysics	M,D
Biochemistry	M,D
Biological and Biomedical Sciences—General	P,M,D
Biomedical Engineering	M,D
Biostatistics	M,D,O
Biotechnology	M,D
Business Administration and Management—General	M,D*
Cancer Biology/Oncology	M,D
Cell Biology	M,D
Chemical Engineering	M,D
Chemistry	M,D
Chinese	M
Civil Engineering	M,D
Classics	M,D
Clinical Laboratory Sciences/Medical Technology	M,D
Clothing and Textiles	M,D
Communication Disorders	M,D
Communication—General	M
Community Health	M,D
Computer Engineering	M,D
Computer Science	M,D
Condensed Matter Physics	M,D
Conservation Biology	M,D
Construction Engineering	M,D
Counseling Psychology	M,D
Counselor Education	M,D
Criminal Justice and Criminology	M,D
Demography and Population Studies	M,D
Dental Hygiene	O
Dentistry	P
East European and Russian Studies	M,D
Ecology	M,D
Economics	M,D
Educational Leadership and Administration	M,D,O
Educational Media/Instructional Technology	M,D
Educational Policy	M,D,O
Educational Psychology	M,D
Electrical Engineering	M,D
Elementary Education	M,D
Energy and Power Engineering	M,D
Engineering Management	M,D
English as a Second Language	M,D
English	M,D
Environmental and Occupational Health	M,D
Environmental Biology	M,D
Environmental Engineering	M,D
Environmental Management and Policy	M,D
Environmental Sciences	M,D
Epidemiology	M,D
Evolutionary Biology	M,D
Exercise and Sports Science	M,D
Family and Consumer Sciences-General	M,D
Finance and Banking	M,D
Folklore	M,D
Forestry	M,D
French	M,D
Genetics	M,D
Geophysics	M,D
Geosciences	M,D
Geotechnical Engineering	M,D
German	M,D
Health Physics/Radiological Health	M,D
Health Promotion	M,O
Health Services Management and Hospital Administration	M,D
Health Services Research	M,D
Hispanic Studies	M,D
History	M,D
Immunology	M,D
Industrial and Labor Relations	D
Information Studies	M
International Business	M
International Health	M,D
Italian	M,D
Japanese	M
Law	P,M
Library Science	M
Linguistics	M,D
Marketing	D
Materials Engineering	M,D
Maternal and Child/Neonatal Nursing	P
Mathematical and Computational Finance	M,D,O
Mathematical Physics	M,D,O
Mathematics	M,D,O
Mechanical Engineering	M,D
Medical Microbiology	M,D
Medical Physics	M,D
Microbiology	M,D
Mineral/Mining Engineering	M,D
Molecular Biology	M,D
Multilingual and Multicultural Education	M
Music	M,D
Nanotechnology	M,D
Natural Resources	M,D
Neuroscience	M,D
Nursing—General	M,D
Occupational Therapy	M,D
Oral and Dental Sciences	M,D
Organizational Management	D
Pathology	M,D
Petroleum Engineering	M,D
Pharmaceutical Sciences	M,D
Pharmacology	M,D
Pharmacy	M,D
Philosophy	M,D
Physical Education	M,D
Physical Therapy	M,D
Physics	M,D
Physiology	M,D
Plant Biology	M,D
Political Science	M,D
Psychology—General	M,D
Public Health—General	M,D
Recreation and Park Management	M,D
Rehabilitation Sciences	D
Rural Sociology	M,D
School Psychology	M,D
Secondary Education	M,D
Slavic Languages	M,D
Sociology	M,D
Special Education	M,D
Sports Management	M
Statistics	M,D,O
Structural Engineering	M,D
Systems Engineering	M,D
Telecommunications	M,D
Theater	M
Vision Sciences	M,D
Water Resources Engineering	M,D

THE UNIVERSITY OF ARIZONA

Accounting	M
Aerospace/Aeronautical Engineering	M,D
Agricultural Economics and Agribusiness	M
Agricultural Education	M
Agricultural Engineering	M,D
Agricultural Sciences—General	M,D
Agronomy and Soil Sciences	M,D
Allopathic Medicine	P
American Indian/Native American Studies	M,D
Anatomy	D
Animal Sciences	M,D
Anthropology	M,D
Applied Mathematics	M,D*
Applied Physics	M
Architecture	M
Art Education	M
Art History	M,D
Art/Fine Arts	M
Asian Studies	M,D
Astronomy	M,D
Atmospheric Sciences	M,D
Biochemistry	M,D
Biological and Biomedical Sciences—General	M,D
Biomedical Engineering	M,D
Biostatistics	M,D
Biosystems Engineering	M,D
Business Administration and Management—General	M,D
Cancer Biology/Oncology	D
Cell Biology	M,D
Chemical Engineering	M,D
Chemistry	M,D
Child and Family Studies	M,D
Civil Engineering	M,D
Classics	M
Communication Disorders	M,D
Communication—General	M,D
Computer Engineering	M,D
Computer Science	M,D
Consumer Economics	M,D
Ecology	M,D
Economics	M,D
Education of the Gifted	M,D,O
Education—General	M,D,O
Educational Leadership and Administration	M,D,O
Educational Psychology	M,D,O
Electrical Engineering	M,D*
Elementary Education	M,D
Engineering and Applied Sciences—General	M,D,O
English as a Second Language	D
English Education	D
English	M,D
Entomology	M,D
Environmental Engineering	M,D
Environmental Sciences	M,D
Epidemiology	M,D
Evolutionary Biology	M,D
Family and Consumer Sciences-General	M,D
Family Nurse Practitioner Studies	M,D,O
Finance and Banking	M,D
Fish, Game, and Wildlife Management	M,D
Forestry	M,D
French	M
Genetics	M,D
Geography	M,D
Geological Engineering	M,D,O
Geosciences	M,D
German	M
Higher Education	M,D
History	M,D
Human Development	M,D
Hydrology	M,D
Immunology	M,D*
Industrial/Management Engineering	M,D
Information Studies	M,D
Interdisciplinary Studies	M,D
Landscape Architecture	M
Latin American Studies	M
Law	P,M
Library Science	M,D
Linguistics	M,D
Management Information Systems	M
Management Strategy and Policy	D
Marketing	M,D
Materials Engineering	M,D
Materials Sciences	M,D
Mathematics	M,D
Mechanical Engineering	M,D
Mechanics	M,D
Media Studies	M
Medical Informatics	M,D,O
Microbiology	M,D
Mineral/Mining Engineering	M,O
Molecular Biology	M,D
Multilingual and Multicultural Education	M,D,O
Music Education	M,D
Music	M,D
Near and Middle Eastern Studies	M,D
Neuroscience	D
Nursing—General	M,D,O
Nutrition	M,D
Optical Sciences	M,D
Pathobiology	M,D
Perfusion	M,D
Pharmaceutical Sciences	M,D

Pharmacology	M,D
Pharmacy	P
Philosophy	M,D
Physics	M,D
Physiology	M,D
Planetary and Space Sciences	M,D*
Plant Pathology	M,D
Plant Sciences	M,D
Political Science	M,D
Psychology—General	M,D
Public Administration	M,D
Public Health—General	M,D
Public Policy	M,D
Range Science	M,D
Reading Education	M,D,O
Rehabilitation Counseling	M,D
Reliability Engineering	M
Rhetoric	D
Russian	M
School Psychology	M,D,O
Secondary Education	M,D
Sociology	D
Spanish	M,D
Special Education	M,D,O
Statistics	M,D
Systems Engineering	M,D
Theater	M
Urban and Regional Planning	M
Water Resources	M,D
Women's Studies	M,D
Writing	M

UNIVERSITY OF ARKANSAS

Accounting	M
Agricultural Economics and Agribusiness	M
Agricultural Education	M
Agricultural Engineering	M,D
Agricultural Sciences—General	M,D
Agronomy and Soil Sciences	M,D
Animal Sciences	M,D
Anthropology	M,D
Applied Physics	M
Art/Fine Arts	M
Bioengineering	M
Biological and Biomedical Sciences—General	M,D
Biomedical Engineering	M
Business Administration and Management—General	M,D
Cell Biology	M,D
Chemical Engineering	M,D
Chemistry	M,D
Civil Engineering	M,D
Communication Disorders	M
Communication—General	M
Comparative Literature	M,D
Computer Engineering	M,D
Computer Science	M,D
Counselor Education	M,D,O
Curriculum and Instruction	D
Early Childhood Education	M
Economics	M,D
Education—General	M,D,O
Educational Leadership and Administration	M,D,O
Educational Measurement and Evaluation	M,D
Educational Media/Instructional Technology	M
Educational Policy	D
Electrical Engineering	M,D
Electronic Materials	M,D
Elementary Education	M,O
Engineering and Applied Sciences—General	M,D
English	M,D
Entomology	M,D
Environmental Engineering	M
Family and Consumer Sciences-General	M
Food Science and Technology	M,D
French	M
Geography	M
Geology	M
German	M
Health Education	M,D
Higher Education	M,D,O
History	M,D
Horticulture	M
Industrial and Manufacturing Management	M
Industrial/Management Engineering	M,D
Interdisciplinary Studies	M,D
Journalism	M
Kinesiology and Movement Studies	M,D
Law	P,M
Management Information Systems	M
Mathematics Education	M
Mathematics	M,D
Mechanical Engineering	M,D
Middle School Education	M,D,O
Molecular Biology	M,D
Music	M
Nursing—General	M
Operations Research	M
Philosophy	M,D
Photonics	M,D
Physical Education	M
Physics	M,D
Planetary and Space Sciences	M,D
Plant Pathology	M
Plant Sciences	D
Political Science	M
Psychology—General	M,D
Public Administration	M
Public Policy	D
Recreation and Park Management	M,D
Rehabilitation Counseling	M,D
Secondary Education	M,O
Social Work	M
Sociology	M
Spanish	M
Special Education	M
Statistics	M
Telecommunications	M
Theater	M
Translation and Interpretation	M
Transportation and Highway Engineering	M
Vocational and Technical Education	M,D
Writing	M

UNIVERSITY OF ARKANSAS AT LITTLE ROCK

Accounting	M,O
Adult Education	M
Allied Health—General	M
Applied Mathematics	M,O
Applied Science and Technology	M,D
Applied Statistics	M,O
Art Education	M
Art History	M
Art/Fine Arts	M
Bioinformatics	M,D
Biological and Biomedical Sciences—General	M
Business Administration and Management—General	M,O
Chemistry	M
Computer Science	M
Conflict Resolution and Mediation/Peace Studies	O
Construction Management	M,O
Counselor Education	M
Criminal Justice and Criminology	M
Early Childhood Education	M
Education of the Gifted	M
Education—General	M,D,O
Educational Leadership and Administration	M,D,O
Educational Media/Instructional Technology	M
Foreign Languages Education	M
Geosciences	O
Gerontology	O
Higher Education	D
Information Science	M
Journalism	M
Law	P
Liberal Studies	M
Management Information Systems	M,O
Management of Technology	M,O
Marriage and Family Therapy	O
Mass Communication	M
Mathematics	M,O
Middle School Education	M
Nonprofit Management	O
Psychology—General	M
Public Administration	M
Public Affairs	M,O
Public History	M
Reading Education	M,O
Rehabilitation Counseling	M,O
Rhetoric	M
Secondary Education	M
Social Work	M
Special Education	M,O
Speech and Interpersonal Communication	M
Systems Engineering	O
Taxation	M,O
Technical Writing	M
Writing	M

UNIVERSITY OF ARKANSAS AT MONTICELLO

Education—General	M
Educational Leadership and Administration	M
Forestry	M
Natural Resources	M

UNIVERSITY OF ARKANSAS AT PINE BLUFF

Addictions/Substance Abuse Counseling	M
Aquaculture	M
Education—General	M
Elementary Education	M
Fish, Game, and Wildlife Management	M
Physical Education	M
Science Education	M
Secondary Education	M
Social Sciences Education	M

UNIVERSITY OF ARKANSAS FOR MEDICAL SCIENCES

Anatomy	M,D
Biochemistry	M,D
Biological and Biomedical Sciences—General	M,D
Biophysics	M,D
Communication Disorders	M,D
Environmental and Occupational Health	M
Genetic Counseling	M
Health Services Research	D
Immunology	M,D
Microbiology	M,D
Molecular Biology	M,D
Neurobiology	M,D
Nursing—General	D
Nutrition	M
Pathology	M
Pharmaceutical Administration	M
Pharmaceutical Sciences	M
Pharmacology	M,D
Pharmacy	P,M
Physiology	M,D
Toxicology	M,D

UNIVERSITY OF BALTIMORE

Accounting	M,O
Applied Arts and Design—General	M
Business Administration and Management—General	M,O
Computer Art and Design	M,D
Conflict Resolution and Mediation/Peace Studies	M
Counseling Psychology	M
Criminal Justice and Criminology	M
Ethics	M
Finance and Banking	M
Graphic Design	M,D
Health Services Management and Hospital Administration	M
Human Services	M
Human-Computer Interaction	M,D
Industrial and Organizational Psychology	M
Information Science	M,D
Law	M
Legal and Justice Studies	M
Management Information Systems	M,O
Marketing	M
Psychology—General	M
Public Administration	M,D
Publishing	M
Taxation	P,M
Writing	M

UNIVERSITY OF BRIDGEPORT

Acupuncture and Oriental Medicine	M
Business Administration and Management—General	M
Chiropractic	P
Computer Education	M,O
Computer Engineering	M,D
Computer Science	M,D
Conflict Resolution and Mediation/Peace Studies	M
Dental Hygiene	M
Early Childhood Education	M,O
Education—General	M,D,O
Educational Leadership and Administration	D,O
Electrical Engineering	M
Elementary Education	M,O
Engineering and Applied Sciences—General	M,D
Human Resources Development	M
Human Services	M
International Affairs	M
International and Comparative Education	M,O
Management of Technology	M
Mechanical Engineering	M
Naturopathic Medicine	D
Nutrition	M
Reading Education	M,O
Secondary Education	M,O
Student Affairs	M

THE UNIVERSITY OF BRITISH COLUMBIA

Accounting	D
Adult Education	M,D
Agricultural Economics and Agribusiness	M
Agricultural Sciences—General	M,D
Agronomy and Soil Sciences	M,D

*M—master's degree; P—first professional degree; D—doctorate; O—other advanced degree; *—Close-Up and/or Announcement or Display in one of the other books in this series*

Allopathic Medicine	P,M
Anatomy	M,D
Animal Sciences	M,D
Anthropology	M,D
Applied Mathematics	M,D
Archaeology	M,D
Architecture	M
Art Education	M,D
Art History	M,D,O
Art/Fine Arts	M,D,O
Asian Studies	M,D
Astronomy	M,D
Atmospheric Sciences	M,D
Biochemistry	M,D
Biopsychology	M,D
Botany	M,D
Business Administration and Management—General	M,D
Business Education	M,D
Cell Biology	M,D
Chemical Engineering	M,D
Chemistry	M,D
Civil Engineering	M,D
Classics	M,D
Clinical Psychology	M,D
Cognitive Sciences	M,D
Communication Disorders	M,D
Computer Engineering	M,D
Computer Science	M,D
Counseling Psychology	M,D,O
Curriculum and Instruction	M,D
Dentistry	P
Developmental Psychology	M,D
Early Childhood Education	M,D
East European and Russian Studies	M,D
Economics	M,D
Education—General	M,D,O
Educational Leadership and Administration	M,D
Educational Measurement and Evaluation	M,D,O
Educational Policy	M,D
Electrical Engineering	M,D
Engineering and Applied Sciences—General	M,D
Engineering Physics	M
English as a Second Language	M,D
English	M,D
Environmental and Occupational Health	M,D
Epidemiology	M,D
Film, Television, and Video Production	M,O
Film, Television, and Video Theory and Criticism	M,O
Finance and Banking	D
Food Science and Technology	M,D
Forestry	M,D
Foundations and Philosophy of Education	M,D
French	M,D
Genetic Counseling	M
Genetics	M,D
Geography	M,D
Geological Engineering	M,D
Geology	M,D
Geophysics	M,D
German	M,D
Health Psychology	M,D
Health Services Management and Hospital Administration	M,D
Higher Education	M,D
Hispanic Studies	M,D
History	M,D
Home Economics Education	M,D
Human Development	M,D,O
Immunology	M,D
Information Studies	M,D
International Affairs	M
International Business	D
Journalism	M
Kinesiology and Movement Studies	M,D
Landscape Architecture	M
Law	M,D
Library Science	M,D
Linguistics	M,D
Management Information Systems	D
Management Strategy and Policy	D
Marine Sciences	M,D
Marketing	D
Materials Engineering	M,D
Materials Sciences	M,D
Mathematics Education	M,D
Mathematics	M,D
Mechanical Engineering	M,D
Metallurgical Engineering and Metallurgy	M,D
Microbiology	M,D
Mineral/Mining Engineering	M,D
Molecular Biology	M,D
Museum Studies	M,D,O
Music Education	M,D
Music	M,D
Natural Resources	M,D
Neuroscience	M,D
Nurse Anesthesia	M,D
Nursing—General	M,D
Nutrition	M,D
Occupational Therapy	M
Oceanography	M,D
Operations Research	M
Oral and Dental Sciences	M,D,O
Organizational Behavior	D
Pathology	M,D
Pharmaceutical Sciences	P,M,D
Pharmacology	M,D
Pharmacy	P,M,D
Philosophy	M,D
Physical Education	M,D
Physics	M,D
Physiology	M,D
Plant Sciences	M,D
Political Science	M,D
Psychology—General	M,D
Public Health—General	M,D
Public History	M,D
Quantitative Analysis	M,D
Reading Education	M,D
Rehabilitation Sciences	M,D
Religion	M,D
Reproductive Biology	M,D
School Psychology	M,D,O
Science Education	M,D
Social Psychology	M,D
Social Sciences Education	M,D
Social Work	M,D
Sociology	M,D
Software Engineering	M
Special Education	M,D,O
Statistics	M,D
Theater	M,D
Transportation Management	D
Urban and Regional Planning	M,D
Vocational and Technical Education	M,D
Western European Studies	M
Writing	M,O
Zoology	M,D

UNIVERSITY OF CALGARY

Allopathic Medicine	P
Analytical Chemistry	M,D
Anthropology	M,D
Archaeology	M,D
Architecture	M,D
Art/Fine Arts	M
Astronomy	M,D
Biochemistry	M,D
Biological and Biomedical Sciences—General	M,D
Biomedical Engineering	M,D
Biotechnology	M
Business Administration and Management—General	M,D
Cancer Biology/Oncology	M,D
Cardiovascular Sciences	M,D
Chemical Engineering	M,D
Chemistry	M,D
Civil Engineering	M,D
Classics	M,D
Clinical Psychology	M,D
Communication—General	M,D
Community Health	M,D,O
Computer Engineering	M,D
Computer Science	M,D
Counseling Psychology	M,D
Curriculum and Instruction	M,D,O
Economics	M,D
Education of the Gifted	M,D,O
Educational Leadership and Administration	M,D,O
Educational Measurement and Evaluation	M,D,O
Educational Media/Instructional Technology	M,D,O
Educational Psychology	M,D
Electrical Engineering	M,D
Engineering and Applied Sciences—General	M,D
English as a Second Language	M,D,O
English	M,D
Environmental Design	M,D
Environmental Law	M,O
Environmental Management and Policy	M,D,O
Epidemiology	M,D
Exercise and Sports Science	M,D
Foreign Languages Education	M,D,O
Foundations and Philosophy of Education	M,D,O
Geography	M,D
Geology	M,D
Geophysics	M,D
Geotechnical Engineering	M,D
German	M
Health Education	M,D
Higher Education	M,D,O
History	M,D
Human Development	M,D
Immunology	M,D
Infectious Diseases	M,D
Inorganic Chemistry	M,D
Kinesiology and Movement Studies	M,D
Law	P,M,O
Legal and Justice Studies	M,O
Linguistics	M,D
Management Strategy and Policy	M,D
Manufacturing Engineering	M,D
Mathematics	M,D
Mechanical Engineering	M,D
Microbiology	M,D
Military and Defense Studies	M,D
Molecular Biology	M,D
Music	M,D
Neuroscience	M,D
Nursing—General	M,D,O
Organic Chemistry	M,D
Petroleum Engineering	M,D
Philosophy	M,D
Physical Chemistry	M,D
Physics	M,D
Political Science	M,D
Psychology—General	M,D
Religion	M,D
School Psychology	M,D
Social Work	M,D,O
Sociology	M,D
Software Engineering	M,D
Special Education	M,D
Statistics	M,D
Theater	M
Theoretical Chemistry	M,D
Vocational and Technical Education	M,D,O

UNIVERSITY OF CALIFORNIA, BERKELEY

Accounting	D
African-American Studies	D
Agricultural Economics and Agribusiness	D
Allopathic Medicine	
Anthropology	D
Applied Arts and Design—General	M
Applied Mathematics	D
Applied Science and Technology	D
Archaeology	M,D
Architectural History	M,D
Architecture	M,D
Art History	D
Art/Fine Arts	M
Asian Languages	M,D
Asian Studies	M,D
Astrophysics	D
Biochemistry	D
Bioengineering	D
Biological and Biomedical Sciences—General	D
Biophysics	D
Biostatistics	M,D
Building Science	M,D
Business Administration and Management—General	M,D
Cell Biology	D
Chemical Engineering	M,D
Chemistry	D
Chinese	D
Civil Engineering	M,D
Classics	M,D
Comparative Literature	D
Computer Science	M,D
Demography and Population Studies	M,D
Developmental Education	
Economics	D
Education—General	M,D
Educational Leadership and Administration	M,D
Educational Measurement and Evaluation	M,D
Electrical Engineering	M,D
Energy Management and Policy	M,D
Engineering and Applied Sciences—General	M,D
Engineering Management	M,D
English	D
Environmental and Occupational Health	M,D
Environmental Design	M
Environmental Engineering	M,D
Environmental Management and Policy	M,D
Environmental Sciences	M,D
Epidemiology	M,D
Ethnic Studies	D
Finance and Banking	D
Financial Engineering	M
Folklore	M
Forestry	M,D
Foundations and Philosophy of Education	M,D
French	D
Geography	D
Geology	M,D
Geophysics	M,D
Geotechnical Engineering	M,D
German	D
Health Education	M
Health Services Management and Hospital Administration	M,D
Hispanic Studies	D
History of Science and Technology	D
History	M,D
Human Development	M,D
Immunology	D
Industrial and Labor Relations	D

Industrial/Management Engineering	M,D
Infectious Diseases	M,D
Information Studies	M,D
International Affairs	M
Italian	D
Japanese	D
Jewish Studies	D
Journalism	M
Landscape Architecture	M
Latin American Studies	M
Law	P,M,D
Legal and Justice Studies	D
Linguistics	D
Marketing	D
Materials Engineering	M,D
Materials Sciences	M,D
Maternal and Child Health	M
Mathematics Education	M,D
Mathematics	M,D
Mechanical Engineering	M,D
Mechanics	M,D
Microbiology	D
Molecular Biology	D
Molecular Toxicology	D
Multilingual and Multicultural Education	M,D
Music	D
Natural Resources	M,D
Near and Middle Eastern Studies	M,D
Neuroscience	D*
Nuclear Engineering	M,D
Nutrition	M,D
Operations Research	M,D
Optometry	P,O
Organizational Behavior	D
Philosophy	D
Physical Education	M,D
Physics	D
Physiology	M,D
Plant Biology	D
Political Science	D
Psychology—General	D
Public Health—General	M,D
Public Policy	M,D
Range Science	M
Reading Education	M,D
Real Estate	D
Religion	D
Rhetoric	D
Romance Languages	D
Russian	D
Scandinavian Languages	D
School Psychology	
Science Education	M,D
Slavic Languages	D
Social Work	M,D
Sociology	M,D
Spanish	D
Special Education	D
Statistics	M,D
Structural Engineering	M,D
Theater	D
Transportation and Highway Engineering	M,D
Urban and Regional Planning	M,D
Urban Design	M,D
Vision Sciences	M,D
Water Resources Engineering	M,D

UNIVERSITY OF CALIFORNIA, DAVIS

Aerospace/Aeronautical Engineering	M,D,O
Agricultural Economics and Agribusiness	M,D
Agricultural Sciences—General	M
Agronomy and Soil Sciences	M,D
Allopathic Medicine	P
American Indian/Native American Studies	M,D
Animal Behavior	D
Animal Sciences	M,D
Anthropology	M,D
Applied Mathematics	M,D
Applied Science and Technology	M,D
Art History	M*
Art/Fine Arts	M
Atmospheric Sciences	M,D
Biochemistry	M,D
Bioengineering	M,D
Biomedical Engineering	M,D
Biophysics	M,D
Biostatistics	M,D
Business Administration and Management—General	M
Cell Biology	M,D
Chemical Engineering	M,D
Chemistry	M,D
Child Development	M
Civil Engineering	M,D,O
Clinical Research	M
Clothing and Textiles	M
Communication—General	M
Comparative Literature	D
Computer Engineering	M,D
Computer Science	M,D
Cultural Studies	M,D
Curriculum and Instruction	M,D
Developmental Biology	M,D
Ecology	M,D
Economics	M,D
Education—General	M,D
Educational Psychology	M,D
Electrical Engineering	M,D
Engineering and Applied Sciences—General	M,D,O
English	M,D
Entomology	M,D
Environmental Engineering	M,D,O
Environmental Sciences	M,D
Epidemiology	M,D
Evolutionary Biology	D
Exercise and Sports Science	M
Food Science and Technology	M,D
Forensic Sciences	M
French	D
Genetics	M,D
Geography	M,D
Geology	M,D
German	M,D
History	M,D
Horticulture	M
Human Development	D
Hydrology	M,D
Immunology	M,D
Law	P,M
Linguistics	M,D
Materials Engineering	M,D
Materials Sciences	M,D
Maternal and Child Health	M
Mathematics	M,D
Mechanical Engineering	M,D,O
Medical Informatics	M
Microbiology	M,D*
Molecular Biology	M,D
Music	M,D
Neuroscience	D*
Nutrition	M,D
Pathology	M,D
Pharmacology	M,D
Philosophy	M,D
Physics	M,D
Physiology	M,D
Plant Biology	M,D
Plant Pathology	M,D
Political Science	M,D
Psychology—General	D
Sociology	M,D
Spanish	M,D
Statistics	M,D
Textile Design	M
Theater	M,D
Toxicology	M,D
Transportation and Highway Engineering	M,D
Transportation Management	M,D
Urban and Regional Planning	M
Veterinary Medicine	P
Veterinary Sciences	M,O
Viticulture and Enology	M,D
Writing	M,D
Zoology	M

UNIVERSITY OF CALIFORNIA, HASTINGS COLLEGE OF THE LAW

Law	P,M

UNIVERSITY OF CALIFORNIA, IRVINE

Aerospace/Aeronautical Engineering	M,D
Allopathic Medicine	P
Anatomy	M,D
Anthropology	M,D
Art History	M,D
Art/Fine Arts	M
Artificial Intelligence/Robotics	M
Asian Languages	M,D
Biochemical Engineering	M,D
Biochemistry	M,D
Biological and Biomedical Sciences—General	M,D
Biomedical Engineering	M,D
Biophysics	D
Biotechnology	M
Business Administration and Management—General	M,D
Cell Biology	M,D
Chemical Engineering	M,D
Chemistry	M,D
Chinese	M,D
Civil Engineering	M,D
Classics	M,D
Comparative Literature	M,D
Computer Science	M,D
Criminal Justice and Criminology	M,D
Dance	M
Demography and Population Studies	M
Developmental Biology	M,D
Ecology	M,D
Economics	M,D
Education—General	M,D
Educational Leadership and Administration	M,D
Electrical Engineering	M,D
Elementary Education	M,D
Engineering and Applied Sciences—General	M,D
English	M,D
Environmental Engineering	M,D
Epidemiology	M,D
Evolutionary Biology	M,D
Foreign Languages Education	M,D
French	M,D
Genetic Counseling	M
Genetics	D
Geosciences	M,D
German	M,D
History	M,D
Information Science	M,D
Japanese	M,D
Materials Engineering	M,D
Materials Sciences	M,D
Mathematics	M,D
Mechanical Engineering	M,D
Microbiology	M,D
Molecular Biology	M,D
Molecular Genetics	M,D
Music	M
Neurobiology	M,D
Pharmacology	M,D*
Philosophy	M,D
Physics	M,D
Physiology	D
Political Science	D
Psychology—General	D
Secondary Education	M,D
Social Sciences	M,D
Sociology	M,D
Spanish	M,D
Theater	M,D
Toxicology	M,D
Transportation and Highway Engineering	M,D
Urban and Regional Planning	M,D
Urban Studies	M,D
Writing	M

UNIVERSITY OF CALIFORNIA, LOS ANGELES

Aerospace/Aeronautical Engineering	M,D
African Studies	M
African-American Studies	M
Allopathic Medicine	P
American Indian/Native American Studies	M
Anatomy	D
Anthropology	M,D
Applied Arts and Design—General	M
Applied Social Research	M,D
Archaeology	M,D
Architecture	M,D
Art History	M,D
Art/Fine Arts	M
Asian Languages	M,D
Asian Studies	M,D
Asian-American Studies	M
Astronomy	M,D
Astrophysics	M,D
Atmospheric Sciences	M,D
Biochemistry	M,D
Biological and Biomedical Sciences—General	M,D
Biomathematics	M,D
Biomedical Engineering	M,D
Biometry	M,D*
Biostatistics	M,D
Business Administration and Management—General	M,D*
Cell Biology	D*
Chemical Engineering	M,D
Chemistry	M,D
Civil Engineering	M,D
Classics	M,D
Clinical Research	M
Community Health	M,D
Comparative Literature	M,D
Computer Science	M,D
Dance	M,D
Dentistry	P,O
Developmental Biology	D
Ecology	M,D
Economics	M,D
Education—General	M,D
Educational Leadership and Administration	D
Electrical Engineering	M,D
Engineering and Applied Sciences—General	M,D
English as a Second Language	M,D,O
English	M,D
Environmental and Occupational Health	M,D
Environmental Engineering	M,D
Environmental Sciences	M,D
Epidemiology	M,D
Evolutionary Biology	M,D
Film, Television, and Video Production	M,D,O
French	M,D
Geochemistry	M,D
Geography	M,D
Geology	M,D
Geophysics	M,D
Geosciences	M,D
German	M,D
Health Services Management and Hospital Administration	M,D

*M—master's degree; P—first professional degree; D—doctorate; O—other advanced degree; *—Close-Up and/or Announcement or Display in one of the other books in this series*

Hispanic Studies	D
History	M,D
Human Genetics	M,D
Immunology	M,D
Information Studies	M,D,O
Italian	M,D
Latin American Studies	M
Law	P,M,D
Library Science	M,D,O
Linguistics	M,D
Manufacturing Engineering	M
Materials Engineering	M,D
Materials Sciences	M,D
Mathematics	M,D
Mechanical Engineering	M,D
Medical Physics	M,D
Microbiology	M,D
Molecular Biology	M,D
Molecular Genetics	M,D
Molecular Toxicology	D
Music	M,D
Near and Middle Eastern Languages	M,D
Near and Middle Eastern Studies	M,D
Neurobiology	D
Neuroscience	D
Nursing—General	M,D
Oral and Dental Sciences	M,D
Pathology	M,D
Pharmacology	D
Philosophy	M,D
Physics	M,D*
Physiology	M,D
Planetary and Space Sciences	M,D
Political Science	M,D
Portuguese	M
Psychology—General	M,D
Public Health—General	M,D
Public Policy	M
Scandinavian Languages	M
Science Education	M,D
Slavic Languages	M,D
Social Work	M,D
Sociology	M,D
Spanish	M
Special Education	D
Statistics	M,D
Theater	M,D
Toxicology	D
Urban and Regional Planning	M,D
Urban Design	M,D
Women's Studies	M,D

UNIVERSITY OF CALIFORNIA, RIVERSIDE

Agronomy and Soil Sciences	M,D
Anthropology	M,D
Applied Statistics	M,D
Art History	M
Art/Fine Arts	M
Artificial Intelligence/Robotics	M,D
Asian Studies	M
Biochemistry	M,D
Bioengineering	M,D*
Bioinformatics	D
Biological and Biomedical Sciences—General	M,D
Botany	M,D
Business Administration and Management—General	M
Cell Biology	M,D
Chemical Engineering	M,D
Chemistry	M,D
Classics	D
Comparative Literature	M,D
Computer Engineering	M,D
Computer Science	M,D
Curriculum and Instruction	M,D
Dance	M,D
Developmental Biology	M,D
Economics	M,D*
Education—General	M,D
Educational Leadership and Administration	M,D
Educational Policy	M,D
Educational Psychology	M,D
Electrical Engineering	M,D*
English	M,D
Entomology	M,D
Environmental Engineering	M,D
Ethnic Studies	D
Evolutionary Biology	M,D
Genetics	D
Genomic Sciences	D
Geology	M,D*
Higher Education	M,D
Hispanic Studies	M,D
Historic Preservation	M,D
History	M,D
Mathematics	M,D
Mechanical Engineering	M,D
Microbiology	M,D
Molecular Biology	M,D
Molecular Genetics	D
Museum Studies	M,D
Music	M,D
Neuroscience	D
Philosophy	M,D
Physics	M,D
Plant Biology	M,D
Plant Pathology	M,D
Plant Sciences	M,D
Political Science	M,D
Psychology—General	M,D
Reading Education	M,D
School Psychology	M,D
Sociology	M,D
Spanish	M,D
Special Education	M,D
Statistics	M,D
Toxicology	M,D
Water Resources	M,D
Writing	M

UNIVERSITY OF CALIFORNIA, SAN DIEGO

Aerospace/Aeronautical Engineering	M,D
Allopathic Medicine	P
Anthropology	D
Applied Mathematics	M,D
Applied Physics	M,D
Art/Fine Arts	M,D
Artificial Intelligence/Robotics	M,D
Biochemistry	M,D
Bioengineering	M,D*
Bioinformatics	D*
Biological and Biomedical Sciences—General	M,D*
Biophysics	M,D
Business Administration and Management—General	M
Cancer Biology/Oncology	D
Cardiovascular Sciences	D
Cell Biology	D
Chemical Engineering	M,D
Chemistry	M,D*
Clinical Psychology	D
Clinical Research	M
Cognitive Sciences	D
Communication Disorders	D
Communication—General	M,D
Comparative Literature	M,D
Computer Engineering	M,D
Computer Science	M,D*
Developmental Biology	D
Ecology	D
Economics	M,D
Education—General	M,D
Electrical Engineering	M,D
Engineering Physics	M,D
English	M
Epidemiology	D
Ethnic Studies	M,D
Evolutionary Biology	D
French	M
Genetics	D
Geosciences	M,D
German	M
Health Law	M
Health Services Management and Hospital Administration	M
History of Science and Technology	M,D
History	M,D
Immunology	D
International Affairs	M,D*
Jewish Studies	M,D
Latin American Studies	M
Law	M
Legal and Justice Studies	M
Linguistics	D
Marine Biology	M,D
Marine Sciences	M
Materials Sciences	M,D
Mathematics Education	D
Mathematics	M,D
Mechanical Engineering	M,D*
Mechanics	M,D
Microbiology	D
Molecular Biology	D
Molecular Pathology	D
Music	M,D
Neurobiology	D
Neuroscience	D*
Ocean Engineering	M,D
Oceanography	M,D
Pacific Area/Pacific Rim Studies	M,D
Pharmacology	D
Pharmacy	P
Philosophy	D
Photonics	M,D
Physics	M,D
Physiology	D
Plant Biology	D
Plant Molecular Biology	D
Political Science	M,D
Psychology—General	D
Public Health—General	D
Science Education	D
Sociology	D
Spanish	M
Statistics	M,D
Structural Biology	D
Structural Engineering	M,D
Systems Biology	D
Telecommunications	M,D
Theater	M,D
Virology	D

UNIVERSITY OF CALIFORNIA, SAN FRANCISCO

Allopathic Medicine	P
Anatomy	D
Anthropology	D
Biochemistry	D
Bioengineering	D
Biological and Biomedical Sciences—General	D
Biophysics	D
Cell Biology	D
Chemistry	D
Dentistry	P
Developmental Biology	D
Genetics	D
Genomic Sciences	D
History of Science and Technology	M,D
Immunology	D
Medical Informatics	D
Medicinal and Pharmaceutical Chemistry	D
Microbiology	D
Molecular Biology	D
Neuroscience	D
Nursing—General	M,D
Oral and Dental Sciences	M,D
Pathology	D
Pharmaceutical Sciences	D
Pharmacology	D
Pharmacy	P
Physical Therapy	M,D
Physiology	D
Sociology	D

UNIVERSITY OF CALIFORNIA, SANTA BARBARA

Agricultural Economics and Agribusiness	M,D
Anthropology	M,D
Applied Mathematics	M,D
Applied Statistics	M,D
Archaeology	M,D
Art History	D
Art/Fine Arts	M,D
Asian Languages	M,D
Asian Studies	M,D
Biochemistry	M,D
Cell Biology	M,D
Chemical Engineering	M,D
Chemistry	M,D
Child and Family Studies	M,D
Classics	M,D
Clinical Psychology	M,D
Cognitive Sciences	M,D
Communication—General	D
Comparative Literature	D
Computational Sciences	M,D
Computer Engineering	M,D
Computer Science	M,D
Counseling Psychology	M,D
Developmental Biology	M,D
Developmental Psychology	M,D
Ecology	M,D
Economics	M,D
Education—General	M,D
Educational Leadership and Administration	M,D
Educational Measurement and Evaluation	M,D
Electrical Engineering	M,D
Engineering and Applied Sciences—General	M,D
English	D
Environmental Management and Policy	M,D
Environmental Sciences	M,D
Evolutionary Biology	M,D
Film, Television, and Video Production	D
French	M,D
Geography	M,D
Geology	M,D
Geophysics	M,D
Geosciences	M,D
German	M,D
Hispanic Studies	M,D
History	D
Human Development	D
International Affairs	M,D
International and Comparative Education	M,D
Latin American Studies	M,D
Linguistics	M,D
Marine Biology	M,D
Marine Sciences	M,D
Materials Engineering	M,D
Materials Sciences	M,D
Mathematical and Computational Finance	M,D
Mathematics	M,D
Mechanical Engineering	M,D
Media Studies	M,D
Medieval and Renaissance Studies	M,D
Molecular Biology	M,D
Music	M,D
Philosophy	D
Physics	D
Political Science	M,D
Portuguese	M,D
Psychology—General	M,D
Quantitative Analysis	M,D
Religion	M,D
School Psychology	M,D
Sociology	D
Spanish	M,D
Special Education	M,D

Speech and Interpersonal Communication	D
Statistics	M,D
Theater	M,D
Transportation Management	M,D
Women's Studies	M,D

UNIVERSITY OF CALIFORNIA, SANTA CRUZ

Anthropology	D
Applied Economics	M
Applied Mathematics	M,D
Archaeology	D
Art/Fine Arts	M
Astronomy	D
Astrophysics	D
Biochemistry	M,D
Bioinformatics	M,D*
Cell Biology	M,D
Chemistry	M,D
Communication—General	O
Comparative Literature	M,D
Computer Art and Design	M
Computer Engineering	M,D*
Computer Science	M,D*
Developmental Biology	M,D
Ecology	M,D
Economics	D
Education—General	M,D
Educational Policy	M,D
Electrical Engineering	M,D*
Engineering and Applied Sciences—General	M,D
English	M,D
Environmental Biology	M,D
Environmental Management and Policy	D
Evolutionary Biology	M,D
Finance and Banking	M
Geosciences	M,D
History	M,D
Humanities	D
Illustration	O
International Affairs	D
Linguistics	M,D
Marine Sciences	M,D
Mathematics Education	M,D
Mathematics	M,D
Molecular Biology	M,D
Music	M,D
Philosophy	M,D
Physics	M,D
Planetary and Space Sciences	M,D
Political Science	D
Psychology—General	D
Reading Education	M,D
Science Education	M,D
Social Sciences Education	M
Social Sciences	D
Sociology	D
Statistics	M,D*
Technical Writing	O
Telecommunications	M,D
Theater	O
Toxicology	M,D
Writing	M

UNIVERSITY OF CENTRAL ARKANSAS

Accounting	M
Applied Mathematics	M
Biological and Biomedical Sciences—General	M
Business Administration and Management—General	M
Communication Disorders	M,D
Computer Art and Design	M
Computer Science	M
Counseling Psychology	M
Counselor Education	M
Early Childhood Education	M
Economic Development	M
Economics	M
Education—General	M,O
Educational Leadership and Administration	M,O
Educational Media/Instructional Technology	M
English	M
Family and Consumer Sciences-General	M
Family Nurse Practitioner Studies	M
Film, Television, and Video Production	M
Foreign Languages Education	M
Geographic Information Systems	M,O
Geography	M,O
Health Education	M
History	M
Kinesiology and Movement Studies	M
Library Science	M
Mathematics Education	M
Mathematics	M
Medical Physics	M
Music Education	M
Music	M
Nursing—General	M
Occupational Therapy	M
Physical Therapy	D
Psychology—General	M,D
Reading Education	M
School Psychology	M,D
Social Psychology	M
Special Education	M
Student Affairs	M

UNIVERSITY OF CENTRAL FLORIDA

Accounting	M
Actuarial Science	M,O
Addictions/Substance Abuse Counseling	M,O
Adult Nursing	M,D,O
Aerospace/Aeronautical Engineering	M
Anthropology	M
Applied Mathematics	M,D,O
Art Education	M
Art/Fine Arts	M
Biological and Biomedical Sciences—General	M,D,O
Biotechnology	M
Business Administration and Management—General	M,D,O*
Chemistry	M,D,O
Child and Family Studies	M,O
Civil Engineering	M,D,O
Clinical Psychology	M,D
Communication Disorders	M,D,O
Communication—General	M
Community College Education	M,D,O
Computational Sciences	M,D
Computer Art and Design	M,D
Computer Engineering	M,D
Computer Science	M,D
Conservation Biology	M,D,O
Construction Engineering	M,D,O
Corporate and Organizational Communication	M
Counselor Education	M,D,O
Criminal Justice and Criminology	M,O
Curriculum and Instruction	M,D,O
Early Childhood Education	M
Economics	M,D
Education of the Gifted	M,D,O
Education—General	M,D,O
Educational Leadership and Administration	M,D,O
Educational Media/Instructional Technology	M,D,O
Electrical Engineering	M,D,O
Elementary Education	M,D
Emergency Management	M,O
Engineering and Applied Sciences—General	M,D,O
Engineering Design	M,D,O
Engineering Management	M,D,O
English as a Second Language	M,O
English Education	M
English	M
Entrepreneurship	M,O
Environmental Engineering	M,D
Ergonomics and Human Factors	M,D,O
Exercise and Sports Science	M
Experimental Psychology	M,D
Family Nurse Practitioner Studies	M,D,O
Film, Television, and Video Production	M
Finance and Banking	D
Forensic Sciences	M,D,O
Gerontology	M,O
Health Services Management and Hospital Administration	M,O
Higher Education	M,D,O
History	M
Homeland Security	M,O
Hospitality Management	M
Human Resources Management	M,O
Industrial and Organizational Psychology	M,D
Industrial/Management Engineering	M,D,O
Interdisciplinary Studies	M
International Affairs	M
International and Comparative Education	M,D,O
Internet and Interactive Multimedia	M
Latin American Studies	M,D,O
Management Information Systems	M
Manufacturing Engineering	M,D,O
Marketing	D
Marriage and Family Therapy	M,O
Mass Communication	M
Materials Engineering	M,D
Materials Sciences	M,D
Mathematics Education	M,D,O
Mathematics	M,D,O
Mechanical Engineering	M,D,O
Microbiology	M
Middle School Education	M
Molecular Biology	M
Music	M
Nonprofit Management	M,O
Nursing and Healthcare Administration	M,D,O
Nursing Education	M,D,O
Nursing—General	M,D,O
Operations Research	M,D,O
Optical Sciences	M,D
Pediatric Nursing	M,D,O
Photonics	M,D
Physical Education	M
Physical Therapy	D
Physics	M,D
Political Science	M
Psychology—General	M,D
Public Administration	M,O
Public Affairs	D
Public History	M
Reading Education	M,O
School Psychology	O
Science Education	M,D,O
Social Sciences Education	M,D
Social Work	M,O
Sociology	M,D,O
Spanish	M
Special Education	M,D
Speech and Interpersonal Communication	M
Sports Management	M,O
Statistics	M,O
Structural Engineering	M,D,O
Student Affairs	M,D,O
Systems Engineering	M,D,O
Taxation	M
Technical Writing	M,D,O
Theater	M
Transportation and Highway Engineering	M,D,O
Travel and Tourism	M
Urban and Regional Planning	M,O
Urban Education	M,D,O
Vocational and Technical Education	M
Writing	M

UNIVERSITY OF CENTRAL MISSOURI

Accounting	M
Applied Mathematics	M
Aviation	M
Biological and Biomedical Sciences—General	M
Business Administration and Management—General	M
Communication Disorders	M
Communication—General	M
Counselor Education	M,O
Criminal Justice and Criminology	M,O
Curriculum and Instruction	M,O
Education—General	M,D,O
Educational Leadership and Administration	M,O
Educational Media/Instructional Technology	M,O
Elementary Education	M,O
English as a Second Language	M
English	M
Environmental and Occupational Health	M,O
Exercise and Sports Science	M
Fire Protection Engineering	M,O
Gerontology	M
History	M
Human Services	M,O
Industrial and Manufacturing Management	M
Industrial Hygiene	M,O
Industrial/Management Engineering	M
Information Studies	M,O
Library Science	M,O
Management Information Systems	M
Mass Communication	M
Mathematics	M
Music	M
Nursing—General	M
Physical Education	M
Psychology—General	M
Reading Education	M,O
Secondary Education	M,O
Sociology	M
Special Education	M,O
Speech and Interpersonal Communication	M
Student Affairs	M
Theater	M
Transportation Management	M,O
Vocational and Technical Education	M,O

UNIVERSITY OF CENTRAL OKLAHOMA

Addictions/Substance Abuse Counseling	M
Adult Education	M
American Studies	M
Applied Arts and Design—General	M
Applied Mathematics	M
Biological and Biomedical Sciences—General	M

*M—master's degree; P—first professional degree; D—doctorate; O—other advanced degree; *—Close-Up and/or Announcement or Display in one of the other books in this series*

Business Administration and Management—General M
Chemistry M
Communication Disorders M
Computer Education M
Computer Science M
Counseling Psychology M
Counselor Education M
Criminal Justice and Criminology M
Early Childhood Education M
Education—General M
Educational Leadership and Administration M
Educational Media/Instructional Technology M
Elementary Education M
Engineering and Applied Sciences—General M
English as a Second Language M
English M
Family and Consumer Sciences-General M
Gerontology M
Health Education M
Higher Education M
History M
Home Economics Education M
Human Development M
Interior Design M
International Affairs M
Mathematics Education M
Mathematics M
Museum Studies M
Music Education M
Music M
Nutrition M
Physics M
Political Science M
Psychology—General M
Reading Education M
Secondary Education M
Special Education M
Statistics M
Urban Studies M
Writing M

UNIVERSITY OF CHARLESTON

Accounting
Business Administration and Management—General M
Legal and Justice Studies
Pharmacy P

UNIVERSITY OF CHICAGO

Allopathic Medicine P
Anatomy D
Anthropology M,D
Applied Mathematics M,D
Archaeology M,D
Art History M,D
Art/Fine Arts M
Asian Languages M,D
Asian Studies M,D
Astronomy M,D
Astrophysics M,D
Atmospheric Sciences M,D
Biochemistry D
Biological and Biomedical Sciences—General D
Biophysics D
Business Administration and Management—General M,D
Cancer Biology/Oncology D
Cell Biology D
Chemistry D
Classics M,D
Comparative Literature M,D
Computer Science M
Developmental Biology D
Ecology D
Economics D
English M,D
Environmental Management and Policy M,D
Environmental Sciences M,D
Evolutionary Biology D
Film, Television, and Video Theory and Criticism M,D
French M,D
Genetics D*
Genomic Sciences D
Geophysics M,D
Geosciences M,D
German M,D
Health Promotion M,D
History D
Human Development D
Human Genetics D
Humanities M
Immunology D
Interdisciplinary Studies D
International Affairs M
International Business M
Italian M,D
Latin American Studies M
Law P,M,D
Linguistics M,D
Mathematical and Computational Finance M
Mathematics M,D
Media Studies M,D
Medical Physics D
Microbiology D
Molecular Biology D
Molecular Physiology D
Music M,D
Near and Middle Eastern Languages M,D
Near and Middle Eastern Studies M,D
Neurobiology D
Neuroscience D
Nutrition D
Paleontology M,D
Pathology D
Pharmacology D
Philosophy M,D
Physics M,D
Physiology D
Planetary and Space Sciences M,D
Political Science D
Psychology—General D
Public Policy M,D
Religion P,M,D
Romance Languages M,D
Science Education D
Slavic Languages M,D
Social Sciences M,D
Social Work M,D
Sociology D
Spanish M,D
Statistics M,D
Systems Biology D
Theology P,M,D
Vision Sciences D
Zoology D

UNIVERSITY OF CINCINNATI

Accounting M,D
Acute Care/Critical Care Nursing M,D
Adult Education M,D,O
Adult Nursing M,D
Aerospace/Aeronautical Engineering M,D
Allopathic Medicine P,M
Analytical Chemistry M,D
Anthropology M
Applied Arts and Design—General M
Applied Mathematics M,D
Architecture M
Art Education M
Art History M
Art/Fine Arts M
Arts Administration M,D
Biochemistry M,D
Bioinformatics D
Biological and Biomedical Sciences—General M,D
Biomedical Engineering D
Biophysics D
Biostatistics M,D
Business Administration and Management—General M,D
Cancer Biology/Oncology D
Cell Biology D
Ceramic Sciences and Engineering M,D
Chemical Engineering M,D
Chemistry M,D
Civil Engineering M,D
Classics M,D
Clinical Psychology D
Communication Disorders M,D,O
Communication—General M
Community Health Nursing M,D
Computer Engineering M,D
Computer Science M,D
Counselor Education M,D,O
Criminal Justice and Criminology M,D
Curriculum and Instruction M,D
Developmental Biology D
Early Childhood Education M
Economics M
Education—General M,D,O
Educational Leadership and Administration M,D,O
Electrical Engineering M,D
Elementary Education M
Engineering and Applied Sciences—General M,D
English as a Second Language M,D,O
English M,D
Environmental and Occupational Health M,D
Environmental Engineering M,D
Environmental Sciences M,D
Epidemiology M,D
Ergonomics and Human Factors M,D
Experimental Psychology D
Finance and Banking D
Foundations and Philosophy of Education M,D
French M,D
Genetic Counseling M
Genomic Sciences M,D
Geography M,D
Geology M,D
German M,D
Graphic Design M
Health Education M,D
Health Physics/Radiological Health M
History M,D
Immunology M,D
Industrial and Labor Relations M
Industrial and Manufacturing Management D
Industrial Design M
Industrial Hygiene M,D
Industrial/Management Engineering M,D
Inorganic Chemistry M,D
Interdisciplinary Studies D
Interior Design M
Law P
Management Information Systems M,D
Marketing M,D
Materials Engineering M,D
Materials Sciences M,D
Maternal and Child/Neonatal Nursing M,D
Mathematics Education M,D
Mathematics M,D
Mechanical Engineering M,D
Mechanics M,D
Medical Imaging D
Medical Physics M
Metallurgical Engineering and Metallurgy M,D
Microbiology M,D
Molecular Biology M,D
Molecular Genetics M,D
Molecular Medicine D
Molecular Toxicology M,D
Music Education M
Music M,D,O
Neuroscience D
Nuclear Engineering M,D
Nurse Anesthesia M,D
Nurse Midwifery M,D
Nursing and Healthcare Administration M,D
Nursing—General M,D
Nutrition M
Occupational Health Nursing M,D
Organic Chemistry M,D
Organizational Management M
Pathobiology D
Pathology D
Pediatric Nursing M,D
Pharmaceutical Sciences M,D
Pharmacology D
Pharmacy P
Philosophy M,D
Physical Chemistry M,D
Physics M,D
Physiology D
Political Science M,D
Polymer Science and Engineering M,D
Psychiatric Nursing M,D
Psychology—General D
Quantitative Analysis M,D
Reading Education M,D
Rehabilitation Sciences D
Romance Languages M,D
School Psychology D,O
Science Education M,D,O
Secondary Education M
Social Sciences Education M,D,O
Social Work M
Sociology M,D
Spanish M,D
Special Education M,D
Statistics M,D
Textile Design M
Theater M,D
Urban and Regional Planning M
Women's Health Nursing M,D
Women's Studies M,O

UNIVERSITY OF COLORADO AT BOULDER

Accounting M,D
Aerospace/Aeronautical Engineering M,D
Animal Behavior M,D
Anthropology M,D
Applied Mathematics M,D
Architectural Engineering M,D
Art History M
Art/Fine Arts M
Asian Studies M,D
Astrophysics M,D
Atmospheric Sciences M,D
Biochemistry M,D
Business Administration and Management—General M*
Cell Biology M,D
Chemical Engineering M,D
Chemical Physics M,D
Chemistry M,D
Chinese M,D
Civil Engineering M,D
Classics M,D
Communication Disorders M,D
Communication—General M,D
Comparative Literature M,D
Computer Engineering M,D
Computer Science M,D
Construction Engineering M,D

Curriculum and Instruction	M,D
Dance	M,D
Developmental Biology	M,D
Ecology	M,D
Economics	M,D
Education—General	M,D
Educational Measurement and Evaluation	D
Educational Psychology	M,D
Electrical Engineering	M,D
Engineering and Applied Sciences—General	M,D*
Engineering Management	M
English	M,D
Entrepreneurship	M,D
Environmental Engineering	M,D
Environmental Management and Policy	M,D
Evolutionary Biology	M,D
Finance and Banking	M,D
French	M,D
Genetics	M,D
Geography	M,D
Geology	M,D
Geophysics	M,D
Geotechnical Engineering	M,D
German	M
History	M,D
International Affairs	M,D
Japanese	M,D
Journalism	M,D
Kinesiology and Movement Studies	M,D
Law	P
Linguistics	M,D
Management Information Systems	M,D
Marine Biology	M,D
Marketing	M,D
Mass Communication	M,D
Mathematical Physics	M,D
Mathematics	M,D
Mechanical Engineering	M,D
Media Studies	D
Medical Physics	M,D
Medieval and Renaissance Studies	M,D
Microbiology	M,D
Molecular Biology	M,D
Multilingual and Multicultural Education	M,D
Museum Studies	M
Music Education	M,D
Music	M,D
Neurobiology	M,D
Oceanography	M,D
Operations Research	M
Optical Sciences	M,D
Organizational Management	M,D
Philosophy	M,D
Photography	M
Physics	M,D
Physiology	M,D
Plasma Physics	M,D
Political Science	M,D
Psychology—General	M,D
Public Policy	M,D
Religion	M
Sociology	D
Spanish	M,D
Structural Engineering	M,D
Telecommunications Management	M
Telecommunications	M
Theater	M,D
Water Resources Engineering	M,D
Writing	M,D

UNIVERSITY OF COLORADO AT COLORADO SPRINGS

Accounting	M
Adult Nursing	M,D
Aerospace/Aeronautical Engineering	M
Applied Mathematics	M
Biological and Biomedical Sciences—General	M
Business Administration and Management—General	M
Chemistry	M
Communication—General	M
Community Health Nursing	M,D
Computer Science	M,D
Counselor Education	M,D
Criminal Justice and Criminology	M
Curriculum and Instruction	M,D
Education—General	M,D
Educational Leadership and Administration	M,D
Electrical Engineering	M,D
Engineering and Applied Sciences—General	M,D
Engineering Management	M
Environmental Sciences	M
Family Nurse Practitioner Studies	M,D
Finance and Banking	M
Forensic Nursing	M,D
Geography	M
Gerontological Nursing	M,D
Health Services Management and Hospital Administration	M
History	M
Human Services	M,D
Information Science	M
International Business	M
Management Information Systems	M
Management of Technology	M
Manufacturing Engineering	M
Marketing	M
Maternal and Child/Neonatal Nursing	M,D
Mathematics	M
Mechanical Engineering	M
Nursing and Healthcare Administration	M,D
Nursing—General	M,D
Physics	M
Psychology—General	M,D
Public Administration	M
Public Affairs	M
Sociology	M
Software Engineering	M
Special Education	M,D
Women's Health Nursing	M,D

UNIVERSITY OF COLORADO DENVER

Accounting	M
Allopathic Medicine	P
Anthropology	M
Applied Mathematics	M,D
Applied Science and Technology	M
Architecture	M
Biochemistry	D
Bioinformatics	D
Biological and Biomedical Sciences—General	M,D
Biophysics	M,D
Biostatistics	M,D
Business Administration and Management—General	M
Cancer Biology/Oncology	D
Cell Biology	D
Chemistry	M
Civil Engineering	M,D
Clinical Laboratory Sciences/Medical Technology	M,D
Clinical Psychology	D
Communication—General	M
Computer Engineering	M,D
Computer Science	M,D
Counseling Psychology	M
Counselor Education	M
Criminal Justice and Criminology	M
Curriculum and Instruction	M
Dentistry	P
Developmental Biology	D
Economics	M
Education—General	M,D,O
Educational Leadership and Administration	M,D,O
Educational Media/Instructional Technology	M
Electrical Engineering	M
English as a Second Language	M,O
English Education	M,O
English	M,O
Environmental Sciences	M
Epidemiology	D
Finance and Banking	M
Genetic Counseling	M
Genetics	M,D
Geographic Information Systems	M,D
Health Education	D
Health Psychology	D
Health Services Management and Hospital Administration	M
Health Services Research	D
History	M
Humanities	M
Immunology	D*
Information Science	D
International Business	M
Landscape Architecture	M
Linguistics	M,O
Management Information Systems	M,D
Marketing	M
Mathematics	M
Mechanical Engineering	M
Microbiology	D
Molecular Biology	D
Molecular Genetics	D
Music	M
Neuroscience	D
Nursing—General	D
Pathology	D
Pediatric Nursing	M
Pharmaceutical Sciences	P
Pharmacology	D
Pharmacy	P,D
Physical Therapy	D
Physiology	D
Political Science	M
Psychology—General	D
Public Administration	M
Public Affairs	D
Public Health—General	M,D
Reproductive Biology	D
Social Sciences	M
Sociology	M
Spanish	M
Technical Communication	M
Toxicology	D
Urban and Regional Planning	M,D
Urban Design	M

UNIVERSITY OF CONNECTICUT

Accounting	M,D
Actuarial Science	M,D
Adult Education	M,D
African Studies	M
Agricultural Economics and Agribusiness	M,D
Agricultural Education	M,D,O
Agricultural Sciences—General	M,D
Agronomy and Soil Sciences	M,D
Allied Health—General	M
Animal Sciences	M,D
Anthropology	M,D
Applied Mathematics	M
Art History	M
Art/Fine Arts	M
Biochemistry	M,D
Biological and Biomedical Sciences—General	M,D
Biomedical Engineering	M,D
Biophysics	M,D
Biopsychology	M,D,O
Biotechnology	M
Botany	M,D
Business Administration and Management—General	M,D*
Cell Biology	M,D
Chemical Engineering	M,D
Chemistry	M,D
Child and Family Studies	M,D,O
Civil Engineering	M,D
Clinical Psychology	M,D,O
Clinical Research	M
Cognitive Sciences	M,D,O
Communication Disorders	M,D
Communication—General	M,D
Comparative Literature	M,D
Computer Science	M,D
Corporate and Organizational Communication	M,D
Counseling Psychology	M,D,O
Counselor Education	M,D,O
Developmental Biology	M,D
Developmental Psychology	M,D,O
Ecology	M,D,O
Economics	M,D
Education of the Gifted	M,D,O
Education—General	M,D,O
Educational Leadership and Administration	D,O
Educational Measurement and Evaluation	M,D,O
Educational Media/Instructional Technology	M,D,O
Educational Psychology	M,D,O
Electrical Engineering	M,D
Elementary Education	M,D,O
Engineering and Applied Sciences—General	M,D
English Education	M,D,O
English	M,D
Entomology	M,D
Environmental and Occupational Health	M
Environmental Engineering	M,D
Exercise and Sports Science	M,D
Experimental Psychology	M,D,O
Finance and Banking	M,D,O
Foreign Languages Education	M,D,O
Foundations and Philosophy of Education	D
French	M,D
Genetics	M,D
Genomic Sciences	M
Geographic Information Systems	M,D,O
Geography	M,D,O
Geology	M,D
German	M,D
Health Psychology	M,D,O
Health Services Management and Hospital Administration	M,D
Higher Education	M
History	M,D
Homeland Security	M
Human Development	M,D,O
Human Resources Development	M
Human Resources Management	M
Industrial and Organizational Psychology	M,D,O
International Affairs	M
Italian	M,D
Jewish Studies	M
Latin American Studies	M
Law	P

*M—master's degree; P—first professional degree; D—doctorate; O—other advanced degree; *—Close-Up and/or Announcement or Display in one of the other books in this series*

Leisure Studies	M,D
Linguistics	M,D
Marine Sciences	M,D
Marketing	M,D
Materials Engineering	M,D
Materials Sciences	M,D
Mathematical and Computational Finance	M
Mathematics Education	M,D,O
Mathematics	M,D
Mechanical Engineering	M,D
Medicinal and Pharmaceutical Chemistry	M,D
Medieval and Renaissance Studies	M,D
Metallurgical Engineering and Metallurgy	M,D
Microbiology	M,D
Molecular Biology	M
Multilingual and Multicultural Education	M,D,O
Music Education	M,D,O
Music	M,D,O
Natural Resources	M,D
Neurobiology	M,D
Neuroscience	M,D,O
Nonprofit Management	M,O
Nursing—General	M,D,O
Nutrition	
Oceanography	M,D
Oral and Dental Sciences	M
Pathobiology	M,D
Pharmaceutical Sciences	M,D
Pharmacology	M,D
Pharmacy	P
Philosophy	M,D
Physical Therapy	D
Physics	M,D
Physiology	M,D*
Plant Biology	M,D
Plant Molecular Biology	M,D
Plant Sciences	M,D
Political Science	M,D
Polymer Science and Engineering	M,D*
Psychology—General	M,D,O
Public Administration	M,O
Public Health—General	M
Quantitative Analysis	M,O
Reading Education	M,D,O
School Psychology	M,D,O
Science Education	M,D,O
Secondary Education	M,D,O
Social Psychology	M,D,O
Social Sciences Education	M,D,O
Sociology	M,D
Software Engineering	M,D
Spanish	M,D
Special Education	M,D,O
Statistics	M,D
Structural Biology	M,D
Sustainable Development	M
Theater	M
Toxicology	M,D
Western European Studies	M
Zoology	M,D

UNIVERSITY OF CONNECTICUT HEALTH CENTER

Allopathic Medicine	P
Biochemistry	D
Biological and Biomedical Sciences—General	D*
Cell Biology	D*
Clinical Research	M
Dentistry	P,O
Developmental Biology	D
Genetics	D*
Immunology	D*
Molecular Biology	D*
Molecular Pharmacology	D
Neuroscience	D*
Oral and Dental Sciences	M,D*
Public Health—General	M

UNIVERSITY OF DALLAS

Accounting	M
American Studies	M
Art/Fine Arts	M
Business Administration and Management—General	M
Comparative Literature	D
English	M
Entertainment Management	M
Entrepreneurship	M
Finance and Banking	M
Health Services Management and Hospital Administration	M
Human Resources Management	M
Humanities	M
International Business	M
Logistics	M
Management Information Systems	M
Management of Technology	M
Management Strategy and Policy	M
Marketing	M
Nonprofit Management	M
Organizational Management	M
Pastoral Ministry and Counseling	M
Philosophy	M,D
Political Science	M,D
Project Management	M
Psychology—General	M
Sports Management	M
Supply Chain Management	M
Theology	M

UNIVERSITY OF DAYTON

Accounting	M
Aerospace/Aeronautical Engineering	M,D
Agricultural Engineering	M
Applied Mathematics	M
Art Education	M
Biological and Biomedical Sciences—General	M,D
Business Administration and Management—General	M
Chemical Engineering	M
Chemistry	M
Civil Engineering	M
Clinical Psychology	M
Communication—General	M
Computer Engineering	M,D
Computer Science	M
Counselor Education	M,O
Early Childhood Education	M
Education—General	M,D,O
Educational Leadership and Administration	M,D,O
Educational Media/Instructional Technology	M
Electrical Engineering	M,D
Electronic Commerce	M
Engineering and Applied Sciences—General	M,D
Engineering Management	M
English	M
Entrepreneurship	M
Environmental Engineering	M
Environmental Management and Policy	M,D
Exercise and Sports Science	M,D
Finance and Banking	M
Human Development	M,O
Industrial and Manufacturing Management	M
International Business	M
Law	P,M
Management Information Systems	M
Management Strategy and Policy	M
Marketing	M
Materials Engineering	M,D
Mathematical and Computational Finance	M
Mechanical Engineering	M,D
Mechanics	M
Middle School Education	M
Music Education	M
Optical Sciences	M,D
Pastoral Ministry and Counseling	M,D
Physical Education	M,D
Physical Therapy	M,D
Psychology—General	M
Public Administration	M
Reading Education	M
School Psychology	M,O
Secondary Education	M
Social Psychology	M,O
Special Education	M
Structural Engineering	M
Student Affairs	M,O
Theology	M,D
Transportation and Highway Engineering	M
Water Resources Engineering	M

UNIVERSITY OF DELAWARE

Accounting	M
Adult Nursing	M,O
Agricultural Economics and Agribusiness	M
Agricultural Education	M
Agricultural Sciences—General	M,D
Agronomy and Soil Sciences	M,D
American Studies	M
Animal Sciences	M,D
Applied Arts and Design—General	M
Applied Mathematics	M,D
Art History	M,D
Art/Fine Arts	M
Astronomy	M,D
Atmospheric Sciences	M,D
Biochemistry	M,D
Biological and Biomedical Sciences—General	M,D
Biotechnology	M,D
Business Administration and Management—General	M,D*
Business Education	M,D
Cancer Biology/Oncology	M,D
Cell Biology	M,D
Chemical Engineering	M,D
Chemistry	M,D
Child and Family Studies	M,D
Civil Engineering	M,D
Clinical Psychology	D
Cognitive Sciences	D
Communication—General	M
Computer Engineering	M,D
Computer Science	M,D*
Criminal Justice and Criminology	M,D
Curriculum and Instruction	M,D,O
Developmental Biology	M,D
Ecology	M,D
Economics	M,D
Education—General	M,D,O
Educational Leadership and Administration	M,D,O
Electrical Engineering	M,D
Energy Management and Policy	M,D
Engineering and Applied Sciences—General	M,D
English as a Second Language	M,D,O
English	M,D
Entomology	M,D
Entrepreneurship	M,D
Environmental Engineering	M,D
Environmental Management and Policy	M,D
Evolutionary Biology	M,D
Exercise and Sports Science	M
Family Nurse Practitioner Studies	M,O
Finance and Banking	M
Fish, Game, and Wildlife Management	M,D
Food Science and Technology	M,D
Foreign Languages Education	M
French	M
Genetics	M,D
Geography	M,D
Geotechnical Engineering	M,D
German	M
Gerontological Nursing	M,O
Health Promotion	M
Higher Education	M,D,O
Historic Preservation	M,D
History of Science and Technology	M,D
History	M,D
HIV/AIDS Nursing	M,O
Horticulture	M
Hospitality Management	M
Human Development	M,D
Information Science	M,D
International Affairs	M,D
Kinesiology and Movement Studies	M,D
Liberal Studies	M
Linguistics	M,D
Management Information Systems	M*
Management of Technology	M
Marine Affairs	M,D
Marine Geology	M,D
Marine Sciences	M,D
Materials Engineering	M,D
Materials Sciences	M,D
Maternal and Child/Neonatal Nursing	M,O
Mathematics	M,D*
Mechanical Engineering	M,D
Microbiology	M,D
Molecular Biology	M,D
Multilingual and Multicultural Education	M,D,O
Music Education	M
Music	M
Neuroscience	D
Nonprofit Management	M,D
Nursing and Healthcare Administration	M,O
Nursing—General	M,O
Nutrition	M
Ocean Engineering	M,D
Oceanography	M,D
Oncology Nursing	M,O
Operations Research	M,D
Pediatric Nursing	M,O
Physical Therapy	D
Physics	M,D
Physiology	M,D
Plant Sciences	M,D
Political Science	M,D
Psychiatric Nursing	M,O
Psychology—General	D
Public Administration	M*
Public Policy	M,D
School Psychology	M,D,O
Social Psychology	D
Sociology	M,D
Spanish	M
Statistics	M
Structural Engineering	M,D
Theater	M

Transportation and Highway Engineering M,D
Urban Studies M,D
Water Resources Engineering M,D
Women's Health Nursing M,O

UNIVERSITY OF DENVER

Accounting M
Adult Education M,D,O
Advertising and Public Relations M
Anthropology M
Applied Mathematics M,D
Applied Physics M,D
Art History M
Art/Fine Arts M
Astronomy M,D
Bioengineering M,D
Biological and Biomedical Sciences—General M,D
Business Administration and Management—General M,O
Chemistry M,D
Child and Family Studies M,D,O
Clinical Psychology M,D
Communication—General M,D,O*
Computer Art and Design M
Computer Engineering M
Computer Science M,D,O
Conflict Resolution and Mediation/Peace Studies M
Construction Management M
Counseling Psychology M,D,O
Criminal Justice and Criminology M,O
Curriculum and Instruction M,D,O
Economics M
Education—General M,D,O
Educational Leadership and Administration M,D,O
Educational Measurement and Evaluation M,D,O
Educational Psychology M,D,O
Electrical Engineering M
Electronic Commerce M
English M,D
Environmental Management and Policy M,O
Film, Television, and Video Production M
Finance and Banking M
Geographic Information Systems M,O
Geography M,D
Higher Education M,D,O
Human Resources Management M,O
Information Studies M,O
International Affairs M,D
International Business M
Law P,M
Legal and Justice Studies M,O
Liberal Studies M,O
Library Science M,D,O
Management Information Systems M
Management of Technology M,O
Management Strategy and Policy M,O
Marketing M
Mass Communication M
Materials Engineering M,D
Mathematics M,D
Mechanical Engineering M,D
Media Studies M
Museum Studies M
Music Education M,O
Music M,O
Organizational Management M,O
Physics M,D
Project Management M,O
Psychology—General M,D
Public Policy M
Real Estate M
Religion M,D
School Psychology M,D,O
Social Work M,D,O
Speech and Interpersonal Communication M,D
Statistics M
Taxation M
Telecommunications Management M,O
Telecommunications M,O
Theology D
Translation and Interpretation M,O
Transportation Management M

UNIVERSITY OF DETROIT MERCY

Addictions/Substance Abuse Counseling M,O
Allied Health—General M,O
Architectural Engineering M
Biochemistry M
Business Administration and Management—General M,O
Chemistry M
Civil Engineering M,D
Clinical Psychology M,D
Computer Education M
Computer Engineering M,D
Computer Science M
Counselor Education M
Criminal Justice and Criminology M
Curriculum and Instruction M
Dentistry P
Education—General M
Educational Leadership and Administration M
Electrical Engineering M,D
Engineering and Applied Sciences—General M,D
Engineering Management M
Environmental Engineering M,D
Family Nurse Practitioner Studies M,O
Health Services Management and Hospital Administration M
Industrial and Organizational Psychology M
Information Science M
Law P
Liberal Studies M
Management Information Systems M
Mathematics Education M
Mechanical Engineering M,D
Military and Defense Studies M
Nurse Anesthesia M
Oral and Dental Sciences M,O
Physician Assistant Studies M
Psychology—General M,D,O
Religion M
School Psychology O
Software Engineering M
Special Education M

UNIVERSITY OF DUBUQUE

Business Administration and Management—General M
Communication—General M
Theology P,M,D

UNIVERSITY OF EVANSVILLE

Business Administration and Management—General M
Computer Science M
Education—General M,D
Electrical Engineering M
Engineering and Applied Sciences—General M
Health Services Management and Hospital Administration M
Nursing—General M
Physical Therapy M
Public Administration M

THE UNIVERSITY OF FINDLAY

Athletic Training and Sports Medicine M
Business Administration and Management—General M
Early Childhood Education M
Education—General M
Educational Leadership and Administration M
Educational Media/Instructional Technology M
Elementary Education M
English as a Second Language M
Environmental Management and Policy M
Finance and Banking M
Human Resources Management M
International Business M
Liberal Studies M
Marketing M
Multilingual and Multicultural Education M
Occupational Therapy M
Pharmacy P
Physical Therapy M
Public Administration M
Special Education M

UNIVERSITY OF FLORIDA

Accounting M,D
Advertising and Public Relations M
Aerospace/Aeronautical Engineering M,D,O
African Studies O
Agricultural Economics and Agribusiness M,D
Agricultural Education M,D
Agricultural Engineering M,D,O
Agricultural Sciences—General M,D
Agronomy and Soil Sciences M,D
Allied Health—General M,D
Allopathic Medicine P
Animal Sciences M,D
Anthropology M,D
Aquaculture M,D
Architecture M,D
Art Education M,D
Art History M,D
Art/Fine Arts M,D
Arts Administration M
Astronomy M,D
Athletic Training and Sports Medicine M,D
Biochemistry M,D*
Bioengineering M,D,O
Biological and Biomedical Sciences—General D
Biomedical Engineering M,D,O
Biostatistics M
Botany M,D
Building Science M,D
Business Administration and Management—General M,D,O
Cell Biology M,D*
Chemical Engineering M,D
Chemistry M,D
Civil Engineering M,D,O
Classics M,D
Clinical Psychology D
Clinical Research M
Cognitive Sciences M,D
Communication Disorders M,D
Communication—General M,D
Computer Art and Design M,D
Computer Engineering M,D,O
Computer Science M,D
Construction Engineering M,D
Counseling Psychology M,D
Counselor Education M,D,O
Criminal Justice and Criminology M,D
Curriculum and Instruction M,D,O
Dentistry P,O
Developmental Psychology M,D
Early Childhood Education M,D,O
Ecology M,D
Economics M,D
Education—General M,D,O
Educational Leadership and Administration M,D,O
Educational Measurement and Evaluation M,D,O
Educational Psychology M,D,O
Electrical Engineering M,D,O
Electronic Commerce M
Elementary Education M,D,O
Engineering and Applied Sciences—General M,D,O*
English as a Second Language M,D,O
English Education M,D,O
English M,D
Entomology M,D
Entrepreneurship M,D,O
Environmental and Occupational Health M
Environmental Engineering M,D,O
Environmental Law P,M,D
Epidemiology M
Exercise and Sports Science M,D
Family and Consumer Sciences-General M
Finance and Banking M,D,O
Fish, Game, and Wildlife Management M,D
Food Science and Technology M,D
Forensic Sciences M,O
Forestry M,D
Foundations and Philosophy of Education M,D,O
French M,D
Gender Studies M,O
Genetics D*
Genomic Sciences D
Geography M,D
Geology M,D
Geosciences M,D
German M,D
Graphic Design M,D
Health Communication M,D,O
Health Education M,D,O
Health Psychology D
Health Services Management and Hospital Administration M,D
Health Services Research M,D
Higher Education M,D,O
History M,D
Horticulture M,D
Human Resources Management M
Immunology D*
Industrial/Management Engineering M,D,O
Information Science M,D
Insurance M,D,O
Interior Design M,D
International Affairs M
International Business P,M,D
International Development M,D,O
Internet and Interactive Multimedia M,D
Journalism M
Kinesiology and Movement Studies M,D
Landscape Architecture M,D
Latin American Studies M,O
Law P,M,D
Limnology M,D

*M—master's degree; P—first professional degree; D—doctorate; O—other advanced degree; *—Close-Up and/or Announcement or Display in one of the other books in this series*

Linguistics	M,D,O
Management Information Systems	M,D
Management Strategy and Policy	M
Marine Sciences	M,D
Marketing	M,D
Marriage and Family Therapy	M,D,O
Mass Communication	M,D
Materials Engineering	M,D,O
Materials Sciences	M,D,O
Mathematics Education	M,D,O
Mathematics	M,D
Mechanical Engineering	M,D,O
Media Studies	M
Medical Imaging	M,D
Medicinal and Pharmaceutical Chemistry	P,M,D
Microbiology	M,D
Molecular Biology	M,D
Molecular Genetics	M,D
Multilingual and Multicultural Education	M,D,O
Museum Studies	M,D
Music Education	M,D
Music	M,D
Natural Resources	M,D
Neuroscience	M,D*
Nuclear Engineering	M,D,O
Nursing—General	M,D
Nutrition	M,D
Occupational Therapy	M
Ocean Engineering	M,D,O
Oral and Dental Sciences	M,D,O
Pathology	D
Pharmaceutical Administration	M,D
Pharmaceutical Sciences	D
Pharmacology	M,D
Pharmacy	P
Philosophy	M,D
Photography	M,D
Physical Education	M,D
Physical Therapy	D
Physician Assistant Studies	M
Physics	M,D
Physiology	M,D*
Plant Biology	M,D
Plant Molecular Biology	M,D
Plant Pathology	M,D
Plant Sciences	D
Political Science	M,D,O
Psychology—General	M,D
Public Affairs	M,D,O
Public Health—General	M
Quantitative Analysis	M
Reading Education	M,D,O
Real Estate	M,D,O
Recreation and Park Management	M,D
Rehabilitation Counseling	M
Rehabilitation Sciences	D
Religion	M,D
School Psychology	M,D,O
Science Education	M,D,O
Social Psychology	M,D
Social Sciences Education	M,D,O
Social Sciences	M
Sociology	M,D
Spanish	M,D
Special Education	M,D,O
Sport Psychology	M,D
Sports Management	M,D
Statistics	M,D
Student Affairs	M,D,O
Supply Chain Management	M,D
Systems Engineering	M,D,O
Taxation	P,M,D
Theater	M
Toxicology	M,D,O
Urban and Regional Planning	M,D
Veterinary Medicine	P
Veterinary Sciences	M,D,O
Water Resources	M,D
Women's Studies	M,O
Writing	M,D
Zoology	M,D

UNIVERSITY OF GEORGIA

Accounting	M
Adult Education	M,D,O
Agricultural Economics and Agribusiness	M,D
Agricultural Education	M
Agricultural Engineering	M,D
Agricultural Sciences—General	M,D
Agronomy and Soil Sciences	M,D
Analytical Chemistry	M,D
Anatomy	M
Animal Sciences	M,D
Anthropology	M,D
Applied Economics	M,D
Applied Mathematics	M,D
Archaeology	M,D
Art Education	M,D,O
Art History	M
Art/Fine Arts	M
Artificial Intelligence/Robotics	M
Astronomy	M,D
Biochemistry	M,D
Bioengineering	M,D
Biological and Biomedical Sciences—General	D
Business Administration and Management—General	M,D
Cell Biology	M,D
Chemistry	M,D
Child and Family Studies	M,D,O
Classics	M
Clothing and Textiles	M,D
Communication Disorders	M,D,O
Communication—General	M,D
Comparative Literature	M,D
Computer Science	M,D
Consumer Economics	M,D
Counselor Education	M,D,O
Early Childhood Education	M,D,O
Ecology	M,D
Economics	M,D
Education—General	M,D,O
Educational Leadership and Administration	M,D,O
Educational Media/Instructional Technology	M,D,O
Educational Policy	M,D,O
Educational Psychology	M,D,O
Elementary Education	M,D,O
English Education	M,D,O
English	M,D
Entomology	M,D
Environmental and Occupational Health	M,D
Environmental Design	M
Family and Consumer Sciences-General	M,D
Food Science and Technology	M,D
Foreign Languages Education	M,D,O
Forestry	M,D
Foundations and Philosophy of Education	M,D,O
French	M
Genetics	M,D
Geography	M,D
Geology	M,D
German	M
Gerontology	O
Health Education	M,D
Health Promotion	M,D
Higher Education	D
Historic Preservation	M
History	M,D
Horticulture	M,D
Human Resources Management	M,D,O
Infectious Diseases	M,D
Inorganic Chemistry	M,D
Interior Design	M,D
Internet and Interactive Multimedia	M
Internet Engineering	M
Journalism	M,D
Kinesiology and Movement Studies	M,D
Landscape Architecture	M
Law	P,M
Leisure Studies	M,D,O
Linguistics	M,D
Marine Sciences	M,D
Marketing Research	M
Mass Communication	M,D
Mathematics Education	M,D,O
Mathematics	M,D
Microbiology	M,D*
Middle School Education	M,D,O
Molecular Biology	M,D
Music Education	M,D,O
Music	M,D
Natural Resources	M,D
Neuroscience	D
Nonprofit Management	M,O
Nutrition	M,D
Oceanography	M,D
Organic Chemistry	M,D
Pathology	M,D
Pharmaceutical Sciences	M,D,O
Pharmacology	M,D
Pharmacy	P
Philosophy	M,D
Physical Chemistry	M,D
Physical Education	M,D
Physics	M,D
Physiology	M,D
Plant Biology	M,D
Plant Pathology	M,D
Political Science	M,D
Psychology—General	M,D
Public Administration	M,D
Public Policy	M,D
Reading Education	M,D,O
Religion	M
Romance Languages	M,D
Science Education	M,D,O
Social Sciences Education	M,D,O
Social Work	M,D,O
Sociology	M,D
Spanish	M
Special Education	M,D,O
Speech and Interpersonal Communication	M,D
Statistics	M,D
Student Affairs	M,D,O
Sustainable Development	M,D
Theater	M,D
Toxicology	M,D
Veterinary Medicine	P
Veterinary Sciences	M,D
Vocational and Technical Education	M,D,O
Women's Studies	O
Writing	M,D

UNIVERSITY OF GREAT FALLS

Counseling Psychology	M
Criminal Justice and Criminology	M
Education—General	M
Human Services	M
Secondary Education	M

UNIVERSITY OF GUAM

Art/Fine Arts	M
Biological and Biomedical Sciences—General	M
Business Administration and Management—General	M
Counselor Education	M
Education—General	M
Educational Leadership and Administration	M
English as a Second Language	M
English	M
Environmental Sciences	M
Graphic Design	M
Marine Biology	M
Pacific Area/Pacific Rim Studies	M
Public Administration	M
Reading Education	M
Secondary Education	M
Social Work	M
Special Education	M

UNIVERSITY OF GUELPH

Acute Care/Critical Care Nursing	M,D,O
Agricultural Economics and Agribusiness	M,D
Agricultural Sciences—General	M,D,O
Agronomy and Soil Sciences	M,D
Anatomy	M,D
Anesthesiologist Assistant Studies	M,D,O
Animal Sciences	M,D
Anthropology	M,D
Applied Mathematics	M,D
Applied Statistics	M,D
Aquaculture	M
Art/Fine Arts	M
Atmospheric Sciences	M,D
Biochemistry	M,D
Bioengineering	M,D
Biological and Biomedical Sciences—General	M,D
Biophysics	M,D
Biotechnology	M,D
Botany	M,D
Business Administration and Management—General	M,D
Cardiovascular Sciences	M,D,O
Cell Biology	M,D
Chemistry	M,D
Child and Family Studies	M,D
Clinical Psychology	M,D
Cognitive Sciences	M,D
Comparative Literature	D
Computer Science	M,D
Consumer Economics	M
Criminal Justice and Criminology	M,D
Demography and Population Studies	M,D
Ecology	M,D
Economics	M,D
Emergency Medical Services	M,D,O
Engineering and Applied Sciences—General	M,D
English	M
Entomology	M,D
Environmental Biology	M,D
Environmental Engineering	M,D
Environmental Management and Policy	M,D
Environmental Sciences	M,D
Epidemiology	M,D
Evolutionary Biology	M,D
Food Science and Technology	M,D
French	M
Geography	M,D
History	M,D
Horticulture	M,D
Hospitality Management	M
Human Development	M,D
Immunology	M,D,O
Industrial and Organizational Psychology	M,D
Infectious Diseases	M,D,O
International Development	M,D
Landscape Architecture	M
Marriage and Family Therapy	M,D
Mathematics	M,D
Medical Imaging	M,D,O
Medieval and Renaissance Studies	D
Microbiology	M,D

Molecular Biology	M,D
Molecular Genetics	M,D
Natural Resources	M,D
Neuroscience	M,D,O
Nutrition	M,D
Organizational Management	M
Pathology	M,D,O
Pharmacology	M,D
Philosophy	M,D
Physics	M,D
Physiology	M,D
Plant Pathology	M,D
Political Science	M
Psychology—General	M,D
Public Administration	M
Public Policy	M
Rural Planning and Studies	M,D
Social Psychology	M,D
Sociology	M,D
Statistics	M,D
Theater	M
Toxicology	M,D
Veterinary Medicine	M,D,O
Veterinary Sciences	M,D,O
Vision Sciences	M,D,O
Water Resources Engineering	M,D
Western European Studies	M
Zoology	M,D

UNIVERSITY OF HARTFORD

Accounting	M,O
Architecture	M
Art/Fine Arts	M
Biological and Biomedical Sciences—General	M
Business Administration and Management—General	M
Clinical Psychology	M,D
Communication—General	M
Community Health Nursing	M
Counselor Education	M,O
Early Childhood Education	M
Education—General	M,D,O
Educational Leadership and Administration	D,O
Educational Media/Instructional Technology	M
Elementary Education	M
Engineering and Applied Sciences—General	M
Experimental Psychology	M
Music Education	M,D,O
Music	M,D,O
Neuroscience	M*
Nursing Education	M
Nursing—General	M
Organizational Behavior	M
Physical Therapy	M,D
Psychology—General	M,D
School Psychology	M
Taxation	M,O

UNIVERSITY OF HAWAII AT MANOA

Accounting	M,D
Adult Nursing	M,D,O
Agricultural Sciences—General	M,D
Allopathic Medicine	P
American Studies	M,D,O
Animal Sciences	M
Anthropology	M,D
Architecture	D
Art History	M
Art/Fine Arts	M
Asian Languages	M,D
Asian Studies	O
Astronomy	M,D
Bioengineering	M
Biological and Biomedical Sciences—General	M,D
Botany	M,D
Business Administration and Management—General	M
Chemistry	M,D
Chinese	M,D,O
Civil Engineering	M,D
Clinical Psychology	M,D,O
Communication Disorders	M
Communication—General	M,O
Community Health Nursing	M,D,O
Computer Science	M,D,O
Conflict Resolution and Mediation/Peace Studies	O
Conservation Biology	M,D
Curriculum and Instruction	M,D
Dance	M,D
Demography and Population Studies	O
Disability Studies	O
Early Childhood Education	M
Ecology	M,D
Economics	M,D
Education—General	M,D,O
Educational Leadership and Administration	M,D
Educational Media/Instructional Technology	M,D
Educational Policy	D
Educational Psychology	M,D
Electrical Engineering	M,D
Emergency Management	O
Engineering and Applied Sciences—General	M,D,O
English as a Second Language	M,D,O
English	M,D
Entomology	M,D
Entrepreneurship	M
Environmental Engineering	M,D
Environmental Management and Policy	M,D,O
Epidemiology	M,D,O
Evolutionary Biology	M,D
Family Nurse Practitioner Studies	M,D,O
Finance and Banking	M,D
Financial Engineering	M
Food Science and Technology	M
Foreign Languages Education	M,D,O
Foundations and Philosophy of Education	M,D
French	M
Genetics	M,D
Geochemistry	M,D
Geography	M,D,O
Geological Engineering	M,D
Geology	M,D
Geophysics	M,D
Historic Preservation	O
History	M,D
Horticulture	M,D
Human Resources Management	M
Hydrogeology	M,D
Information Science	M,D
Information Studies	M,O
International Business	M,D
Japanese	M,D,O
Kinesiology and Movement Studies	M,D
Law	P,M,O
Library Science	M,O*
Linguistics	M,D
Management Information Systems	M,D,O
Marine Biology	M,D
Marine Geology	M,D
Marine Sciences	O
Marketing	M,D
Mathematics	M,D
Mechanical Engineering	M,D
Medical Microbiology	M,D
Meteorology	M,D
Microbiology	M,D
Molecular Biology	M,D
Museum Studies	O
Music	M,D
Natural Resources	M,D
Nursing and Healthcare Administration	M,D,O
Nursing—General	M,D,O
Nutrition	M,D
Ocean Engineering	M,D
Oceanography	M,D
Organizational Behavior	M
Organizational Management	M,D
Pacific Area/Pacific Rim Studies	M,O
Philosophy	M,D
Physics	M,D
Physiology	M,D
Planetary and Space Sciences	M,D
Plant Pathology	M,D
Plant Sciences	M,D
Political Science	M,D
Psychology—General	M,D,O
Public Administration	M,O
Public Health—General	M,D,O
Public Policy	O
Real Estate	M
Religion	M
Social Psychology	M,D,O
Social Work	M,D
Sociology	M,D
Spanish	M
Special Education	M,D
Speech and Interpersonal Communication	M
Taxation	M
Telecommunications	O
Theater	M,D
Travel and Tourism	M
Urban and Regional Planning	M,D,O
Women's Studies	O
Zoology	M,D

UNIVERSITY OF HOUSTON

Accounting	M,D
Advertising and Public Relations	M
Aerospace/Aeronautical Engineering	M,D
Anthropology	M
Architecture	M
Art Education	M,D
Art/Fine Arts	M
Biochemistry	M,D
Biological and Biomedical Sciences—General	M,D
Biomedical Engineering	M,D
Business Administration and Management—General	M,D
Chemical Engineering	M,D
Chemistry	M,D
Civil Engineering	M,D
Clinical Psychology	M,D
Communication Disorders	M
Communication—General	M
Computer Engineering	M,D
Computer Science	M,D*
Construction Management	M
Counseling Psychology	M,D
Curriculum and Instruction	M,D
Early Childhood Education	M,D
Economics	M,D
Education of the Gifted	M,D
Education—General	M,D
Educational Leadership and Administration	M,D
Educational Psychology	M,D
Electrical Engineering	M,D
Elementary Education	M,D
Engineering and Applied Sciences—General	M,D
English as a Second Language	M,D
English	M,D
Entrepreneurship	D
Environmental Engineering	M,D
Exercise and Sports Science	M,D
Family and Consumer Sciences-General	M
Finance and Banking	M
Foundations and Philosophy of Education	M,D
French	M,D
Geology	M,D
Geophysics	M,D
Health Education	M,D
Higher Education	M,D
History	M,D
Hospitality Management	M
Human Development	M
Industrial and Organizational Psychology	M,D
Industrial/Management Engineering	M,D
Information Science	M,D
Interior Design	M
Kinesiology and Movement Studies	M,D
Law	P,M
Linguistics	M,D
Logistics	M
Marketing	D
Mass Communication	M
Materials Engineering	M,D
Mathematics Education	M,D
Mathematics	M,D
Mechanical Engineering	M,D
Multilingual and Multicultural Education	M,D
Music Education	M,D
Music	M,D
Optometry	P
Petroleum Engineering	M,D
Pharmaceutical Administration	P,M,D
Pharmaceutical Sciences	P,M,D
Pharmacology	P,M,D
Pharmacy	P,M,D
Philosophy	M
Photography	M
Physical Education	M,D
Physics	M,D
Political Science	M,D
Psychology—General	M,D
Public History	M,D
Reading Education	M,D
Science Education	M,D
Secondary Education	M,D
Social Psychology	M,D
Social Sciences Education	M,D
Social Work	M,D
Sociology	M
Spanish	M,D
Special Education	M,D
Speech and Interpersonal Communication	M
Systems Engineering	M,D
Telecommunications	M
Theater	M
Vision Sciences	M,D
Writing	M,D

UNIVERSITY OF HOUSTON–CLEAR LAKE

Accounting	M
Biological and Biomedical Sciences—General	M
Biotechnology	M
Business Administration and Management—General	M
Chemistry	M
Clinical Psychology	M
Computer Engineering	M
Computer Science	M
Counselor Education	M
Criminal Justice and Criminology	M
Cultural Studies	M
Curriculum and Instruction	M
Early Childhood Education	M
Education—General	M,D

*M—master's degree; P—first professional degree; D—doctorate; O—other advanced degree; *—Close-Up and/or Announcement or Display in one of the other books in this series*

Educational Leadership and Administration	M,D
Educational Media/Instructional Technology	M
English	M
Environmental Management and Policy	M
Environmental Sciences	M
Exercise and Sports Science	M
Finance and Banking	M
Foundations and Philosophy of Education	M
Health Services Management and Hospital Administration	M
History	M
Human Resources Management	M
Humanities	M
Information Science	M
Library Science	M
Management Information Systems	M
Marriage and Family Therapy	M
Mathematics	M
Multilingual and Multicultural Education	M
Physics	M
Psychology—General	M
Reading Education	M
School Psychology	M
Sociology	M
Software Engineering	M
Statistics	M
Systems Engineering	M

UNIVERSITY OF HOUSTON–DOWNTOWN

Criminal Justice and Criminology	M
Curriculum and Instruction	M
Elementary Education	M
English	M
Multilingual and Multicultural Education	M
Secondary Education	M
Technical Communication	M
Urban Education	M
Writing	M

UNIVERSITY OF HOUSTON–VICTORIA

Accounting	M
Business Administration and Management—General	M
Computer Science	M
Counseling Psychology	M
Counselor Education	M
Curriculum and Instruction	M
Economic Development	M
Education—General	M
Educational Leadership and Administration	M
Entrepreneurship	M
Finance and Banking	M
Interdisciplinary Studies	M
International Business	M
Marketing	M
Nursing—General	M
Psychology—General	M
School Psychology	M
Special Education	M

UNIVERSITY OF IDAHO

Accounting	M
Adult Education	M,D,O
Agricultural Economics and Agribusiness	M
Agricultural Education	M
Agricultural Engineering	M,D
Agronomy and Soil Sciences	M,D
Animal Sciences	M,D
Anthropology	M
Applied Arts and Design—General	M
Applied Economics	M
Architecture	M
Art Education	M
Art/Fine Arts	M
Biochemistry	M,D
Bioengineering	M,D
Bioinformatics	M,D
Biological and Biomedical Sciences—General	M,D
Business Administration and Management—General	M
Chemical Engineering	M,D
Chemistry	M,D
Civil Engineering	M,D
Computational Biology	M,D
Computer Engineering	M
Computer Science	M,D
Consumer Economics	M
Counselor Education	M,D,O
Curriculum and Instruction	M,D,O
Education—General	M,D,O
Educational Leadership and Administration	M,D,O
Electrical Engineering	M,D
Engineering and Applied Sciences—General	M,D
Engineering Management	M
English as a Second Language	M
English	M
Entomology	M,D
Environmental Engineering	M
Environmental Sciences	M,D
Fish, Game, and Wildlife Management	M
Food Science and Technology	M,D
Forestry	M
Geography	M,D
Geological Engineering	M
Geology	M,D
History	M,D
Hydrology	M
Interdisciplinary Studies	M
Landscape Architecture	M
Law	P
Materials Engineering	M,D
Materials Sciences	M,D
Mathematics	M,D
Mechanical Engineering	M,D
Metallurgical Engineering and Metallurgy	M,D
Microbiology	M,D
Mineral/Mining Engineering	M,D
Molecular Biology	M,D
Music	M
Natural Resources	M,D
Neuroscience	M,D
Nuclear Engineering	M,D
Physical Education	M,D
Physics	M,D
Plant Sciences	M,D
Political Science	M,D
Psychology—General	M
Public Administration	M
Public Affairs	M,D
Range Science	M
Recreation and Park Management	M
School Psychology	O
Science Education	M,D
Social Sciences	M
Special Education	M,O
Statistics	M
Systems Engineering	M
Theater	M
Urban and Regional Planning	M
Veterinary Sciences	M,D
Vocational and Technical Education	M,D,O
Water Resources	M,D
Writing	M

UNIVERSITY OF ILLINOIS AT CHICAGO

Accounting	M
Acute Care/Critical Care Nursing	M
Adult Nursing	M
Allied Health—General	M,D
Allopathic Medicine	P
Anatomy	D
Anthropology	M,D
Applied Mathematics	M,D
Architecture	M
Art History	M,D
Art/Fine Arts	M
Biochemistry	D
Bioengineering	M,D
Biological and Biomedical Sciences—General	M,D
Biophysics	M,D
Biostatistics	M,D
Biotechnology	D
Business Administration and Management—General	M,D
Cell Biology	D
Chemical Engineering	M,D
Chemistry	M,D
Civil Engineering	M,D
Communication—General	M,D
Community Health Nursing	M
Community Health	M,D
Computer Engineering	M,D
Computer Science	M,D
Criminal Justice and Criminology	M,D
Curriculum and Instruction	M,D
Dentistry	P
Disability Studies	M,D
Economics	M,D
Education—General	M,D
Educational Leadership and Administration	M,D
Educational Policy	M,D
Educational Psychology	D
Electrical Engineering	M,D*
Elementary Education	M,D
Engineering and Applied Sciences—General	M,D
English as a Second Language	M
English Education	M,D
English	M,D
Environmental and Occupational Health	M,D
Epidemiology	M,D
Family Nurse Practitioner Studies	M
Forensic Sciences	M
French	M
Genetics	D
Geography	M
Geology	M,D
Geosciences	M,D
German	M,D
Gerontological Nursing	M
Graphic Design	M
Health Education	M
Health Informatics	M
Health Services Management and Hospital Administration	M,D
Health Services Research	M,D
Hispanic Studies	M,D
History	M,D
Human Development	M,D
Immunology	D
Industrial Design	M
Industrial/Management Engineering	M,D
Kinesiology and Movement Studies	M,D
Linguistics	M
Management Information Systems	M,D
Materials Engineering	M,D
Maternal and Child/Neonatal Nursing	M
Mathematical and Computational Finance	M,D
Mathematics Education	M
Mathematics	M,D
Mechanical Engineering	M,D
Medical Illustration	M
Microbiology	D
Molecular Biology	D
Molecular Genetics	D
Multilingual and Multicultural Education	M,D
Neurobiology	D*
Neuroscience	D
Nurse Midwifery	M
Nursing and Healthcare Administration	M
Nursing—General	M,D
Nutrition	M,D
Occupational Health Nursing	M
Occupational Therapy	M,D
Operations Research	D
Oral and Dental Sciences	M,D
Pediatric Nursing	M
Pharmaceutical Administration	M,D
Pharmaceutical Sciences	M,D
Pharmacology	D*
Pharmacy	P,D
Philosophy	M,D
Photography	M
Physical Therapy	M,D
Physics	M,D
Physiology	M,D
Political Science	M,D
Psychiatric Nursing	M
Psychology—General	D
Public Administration	M,D
Public Health—General	M,D
Quantitative Analysis	M,D
Reading Education	M,D
Real Estate	M
School Nursing	M
Secondary Education	M,D
Social Work	M,D
Sociology	M,D
Spanish	M,D
Special Education	M,D
Statistics	M,D
Urban and Regional Planning	M,D
Urban Education	M,D
Women's Health Nursing	M
Writing	M,D

UNIVERSITY OF ILLINOIS AT SPRINGFIELD

Accounting	M
Addictions/Substance Abuse Counseling	M
Biological and Biomedical Sciences—General	M
Business Administration and Management—General	M
Child and Family Studies	M
Communication—General	M
Computer Science	M
Education—General	M
Educational Leadership and Administration	M
English	M
Environmental Management and Policy	M
Environmental Sciences	M
Gerontology	M
History	M
Human Development	M
Human Services	M
Interdisciplinary Studies	M
Journalism	M
Legal and Justice Studies	M
Management Information Systems	M
Political Science	M
Public Administration	M,D
Public Health—General	M
Public History	M
Social Sciences	M

UNIVERSITY OF ILLINOIS AT URBANA–CHAMPAIGN

Accounting	M,D
Actuarial Science	M,D
Advertising and Public Relations	M
Aerospace/Aeronautical Engineering	M,D
African Studies	M
Agricultural Economics and Agribusiness	M,D
Agricultural Education	M,D
Agricultural Engineering	M,D
Agricultural Sciences—General	M,D
Agronomy and Soil Sciences	M,D
Allopathic Medicine	
Animal Sciences	M,D
Anthropology	M,D
Applied Arts and Design—General	M,D
Applied Mathematics	M,D
Applied Statistics	M,D
Architecture	M,D
Art Education	M,D
Art History	M,D
Art/Fine Arts	M
Asian Languages	M,D
Asian Studies	M,D
Astronomy	M,D
Atmospheric Sciences	M,D
Aviation	M
Biochemistry	M,D
Bioengineering	M,D
Bioinformatics	M,D,O
Biological and Biomedical Sciences—General	M,D
Biophysics	M,D
Business Administration and Management—General	M,D
Cell Biology	D
Chemical Engineering	M,D
Chemical Physics	M,D
Chemistry	M,D
Civil Engineering	M,D
Classics	M,D
Communication Disorders	M,D
Communication—General	M,D
Community Health	M,D
Comparative Literature	M,D
Computational Biology	M,D
Computer Engineering	M,D
Computer Science	M,D
Conservation Biology	M,D
Consumer Economics	M,D
Counselor Education	M,D,O
Curriculum and Instruction	M,D,O
Dance	M
Developmental Biology	D
East European and Russian Studies	M
Ecology	M,D
Economics	M,D*
Education of the Multiply Handicapped	M,D,O
Education—General	M,D,O
Educational Leadership and Administration	M,D,O
Educational Policy	M,D,O
Educational Psychology	M,D,O
Electrical Engineering	M,D
Engineering and Applied Sciences—General	M,D
English as a Second Language	M,D
English	M,D
Entomology	M,D
Environmental Engineering	M,D
Environmental Sciences	M,D
Ergonomics and Human Factors	M
Evolutionary Biology	M,D
Finance and Banking	M,D
Food Science and Technology	M,D
Foreign Languages Education	M,D
French	M,D
Geography	M,D
Geology	M,D
Geosciences	M,D
German	M,D
Graphic Design	M
Health Informatics	M,D,O
Higher Education	M,D,O
History	M,D
Human Development	M,D
Human Resources Development	M,D,O
Human Resources Management	M,D
Human-Computer Interaction	M,D,O
Industrial and Labor Relations	M,D
Industrial Design	M
Industrial/Management Engineering	M,D
Information Science	M,D,O
Information Studies	M,D,O
Italian	M,D
Journalism	M
Kinesiology and Movement Studies	M,D
Landscape Architecture	M,D
Latin American Studies	M
Law	P,M,D
Leisure Studies	M,D
Library Science	M,D,O
Linguistics	M,D
Management of Technology	M,D
Materials Engineering	M,D
Materials Sciences	M,D
Mathematics Education	M,D
Mathematics	M,D
Mechanical Engineering	M,D*
Mechanics	M,D
Media Studies	D
Medical Informatics	M,D,O
Microbiology	M,D*
Molecular Physiology	M,D
Music Education	M,D,O
Music	M,D,O
Natural Resources	M,D
Neuroscience	D
Nuclear Engineering	M,D*
Nutrition	M,D
Pathobiology	M,D
Philosophy	M,D
Photography	M
Physics	M,D
Physiology	M,D
Plant Biology	M,D
Political Science	M,D
Portuguese	M,D
Psychology—General	M,D
Public Health—General	M,D
Rehabilitation Sciences	M,D
Science Education	M,D
Slavic Languages	M,D
Social Work	M,D
Sociology	M,D
Spanish	M,D
Special Education	M,D,O
Statistics	M,D
Systems Engineering	M,D
Taxation	M,D
Theater	M,D
Urban and Regional Planning	M,D
Veterinary Medicine	P
Veterinary Sciences	M,D
Vocational and Technical Education	M,D,O
Writing	M,D
Zoology	M,D

UNIVERSITY OF INDIANAPOLIS

Art Education	M
Art/Fine Arts	M
Biological and Biomedical Sciences—General	M
Business Administration and Management—General	M,O
Clinical Psychology	M,D
Counseling Psychology	M,D
Curriculum and Instruction	M
Education—General	M
Educational Leadership and Administration	M
Elementary Education	M
English Education	M
English	M
Foreign Languages Education	M
Gerontology	M,O
History	M
International Affairs	M
Mathematics Education	M
Nurse Midwifery	M
Nursing and Healthcare Administration	M
Nursing Education	M
Nursing—General	M
Occupational Therapy	M,D
Physical Education	M
Physical Therapy	M,D
Psychology—General	M,D
Science Education	M
Secondary Education	M
Social Sciences Education	M
Sociology	M

THE UNIVERSITY OF IOWA

Accounting	M,D
Actuarial Science	M,D
African-American Studies	M
Allopathic Medicine	P
American Studies	M,D
Anatomy	D
Anthropology	M,D
Applied Mathematics	D
Art Education	M,D
Art History	M,D
Art/Fine Arts	M
Asian Studies	M
Astronomy	M
Bacteriology	M,D
Biochemical Engineering	M,D
Biochemistry	M,D
Biological and Biomedical Sciences—General	M,D*
Biomedical Engineering	M,D
Biophysics	D
Biostatistics	M,D
Business Administration and Management—General	M,D
Cell Biology	M,D
Chemical Engineering	M,D
Chemistry	M,D
Civil Engineering	M,D
Classics	M,D
Clinical Research	M,D
Communication Disorders	M,D
Communication—General	M,D
Community Health	M,D
Comparative Literature	M,D
Computational Biology	M,D,O
Computational Sciences	D
Computer Engineering	M,D
Computer Science	M,D
Counseling Psychology	M,D,O
Counselor Education	M,D
Curriculum and Instruction	M,D
Dance	M
Dentistry	P,M,D,O
Developmental Education	M,D
Early Childhood Education	M,D
Economics	D
Education—General	M,D,O
Educational Leadership and Administration	M,D,O
Educational Measurement and Evaluation	M,D,O
Educational Policy	M,D,O
Educational Psychology	M,D,O
Electrical Engineering	M,D
Elementary Education	M,D
Engineering and Applied Sciences—General	M,D*
English Education	M,D
English	M,D
Entrepreneurship	M
Environmental and Occupational Health	M,D,O
Environmental Engineering	M,D
Epidemiology	M,D
Ergonomics and Human Factors	M,D
Evolutionary Biology	M,D
Exercise and Sports Science	M,D
Film, Television, and Video Production	M
Film, Television, and Video Theory and Criticism	M,D
Finance and Banking	M,D
Foreign Languages Education	M,D
Foundations and Philosophy of Education	M,D,O
French	M,D
Genetics	M,D
Geography	M,D
Geosciences	M,D
German	M,D
Health Informatics	M,D,O
Health Services Management and Hospital Administration	M,D,O
Higher Education	M,D,O
History	M,D
Immunology	M,D
Industrial and Manufacturing Management	M
Industrial/Management Engineering	M,D
Information Science	M,D,O
Information Studies	M
Investment Management	M
Journalism	M
Law	P,M
Leisure Studies	M
Library Science	M
Linguistics	M,D
Management Information Systems	M
Management Strategy and Policy	M
Manufacturing Engineering	M,D
Marketing	M,D
Mass Communication	M,D
Mathematics Education	M,D
Mathematics	M,D
Mechanical Engineering	M,D
Media Studies	M,D
Microbiology	M,D
Molecular Biology	D
Music Education	M,D
Music	M,D
Neurobiology	M,D
Neuroscience	D
Nonprofit Management	M
Nursing—General	M,D
Operations Research	M,D
Oral and Dental Sciences	M,D,O
Pathology	M
Pharmacology	M,D
Pharmacy	M,D
Philosophy	M,D
Physical Education	M,D
Physical Therapy	D
Physician Assistant Studies	M
Physics	M,D
Physiology	D
Plant Biology	M,D
Political Science	M,D
Psychology—General	M,D,O
Public Health—General	M,D,O
Radiation Biology	M,D
Recreation and Park Management	M
Rehabilitation Counseling	M,D

*M—master's degree; P—first professional degree; D—doctorate; O—other advanced degree; *—Close-Up and/or Announcement or Display in one of the other books in this series*

Rehabilitation Sciences	D
Religion	M,D
Rhetoric	M,D
School Psychology	M,D,O
Science Education	M,D
Secondary Education	M,D
Social Sciences Education	M,D
Social Work	M,D
Sociology	M,D
Spanish	M,D
Special Education	M,D
Sport Psychology	M,D
Sports Management	M
Statistics	M,D,O
Student Affairs	M,D
Theater	M
Toxicology	M,D
Translation and Interpretation	M
Translational Biology	M,D
Urban and Regional Planning	M
Virology	M,D
Women's Studies	D
Writing	M,D

THE UNIVERSITY OF KANSAS

Accounting	M
Aerospace/Aeronautical Engineering	M,D
African Studies	M,O
African-American Studies	M,O
Allied Health—General	M,D,O
Allopathic Medicine	P,M,D
American Indian/Native American Studies	M
American Studies	M,D
Anatomy	M,D
Anthropology	M,D
Applied Arts and Design—General	M
Architectural Engineering	M
Architecture	M,D,O
Art Education	M
Art History	M,D
Art/Fine Arts	M
Asian Languages	M
Asian Studies	M
Astronomy	M,D
Biochemistry	M,D
Bioengineering	M,D
Biological and Biomedical Sciences—General	M,D*
Biophysics	M,D
Biotechnology	M
Botany	M,D
Business Administration and Management—General	M,D
Cell Biology	M,D
Chemical Engineering	M,D
Chemistry	M,D
Civil Engineering	M,D
Classics	M
Clinical Psychology	M,D
Cognitive Sciences	M,D
Communication Disorders	M,D
Communication—General	M,D
Community Health Nursing	M,D,O
Computational Sciences	M,D
Computer Art and Design	M
Computer Engineering	M
Computer Science	M,D
Construction Management	M
Counseling Psychology	M,D
Curriculum and Instruction	M,D
Developmental Biology	M,D
Developmental Psychology	M,D
East European and Russian Studies	M
Ecology	M,D
Economics	M,D
Education—General	M,D,O
Educational Leadership and Administration	M,D
Educational Measurement and Evaluation	M,D
Educational Policy	D
Educational Psychology	M,D
Electrical Engineering	M,D
Engineering and Applied Sciences—General	M,D
Engineering Management	M
English	M,D
Entomology	M,D
Environmental Engineering	M,D
Environmental Sciences	M,D
Evolutionary Biology	M,D
Facilities Management	M,D,O
Family Nurse Practitioner Studies	M,D,O
Film, Television, and Video Theory and Criticism	M,D
Foundations and Philosophy of Education	D
French	M,D
Geography	M,D
Geology	M,D
German	M,D
Gerontology	M,D,O
Health Education	M,D,O
Health Services Management and Hospital Administration	M
Higher Education	M,D
History	M,D
Immunology	D
Interdisciplinary Studies	M,D
International Affairs	M
Journalism	M
Latin American Studies	M,O
Law	P
Linguistics	M,D
Management Information Systems	M
Mathematics	M,D
Mechanical Engineering	M,D
Medical Informatics	M,D,O
Medicinal and Pharmaceutical Chemistry	M,D
Microbiology	M,D
Molecular Biology	M,D
Molecular Genetics	D
Museum Studies	M,O
Music Education	M,D
Music	M,D
Near and Middle Eastern Studies	M
Neuroscience	M,D
Nurse Anesthesia	M
Nurse Midwifery	M,D,O
Nursing—General	M,D,O
Nutrition	M,O
Occupational Therapy	M,D
Organizational Management	M,D,O
Pathology	M,D
Petroleum Engineering	M,D
Pharmaceutical Sciences	M
Pharmacology	M,D
Philosophy	M,D
Physical Education	M,D
Physical Therapy	D
Physics	M,D*
Physiology	M,D
Political Science	M,D
Psychiatric Nursing	M,D,O
Psychology—General	M,D
Public Administration	M,D
Public Health—General	M
Rehabilitation Sciences	M,D
Religion	M
School Psychology	D,O
Slavic Languages	M,D
Social Sciences	M,D
Sociology	M,D
Spanish	M,D
Special Education	M,D
Theater	M,D
Therapies—Dance, Drama, and Music	M
Toxicology	M,D
Urban and Regional Planning	M
Water Resources	M
Writing	M,D

UNIVERSITY OF KENTUCKY

Accounting	M
Agricultural Economics and Agribusiness	M,D
Agricultural Engineering	M,D
Agricultural Sciences—General	M,D
Agronomy and Soil Sciences	M,D
Allied Health—General	M,D
Allopathic Medicine	P
Anatomy	D
Animal Sciences	M,D
Anthropology	M,D
Applied Arts and Design—General	M
Applied Mathematics	M,D
Architecture	M
Art Education	M
Art History	M
Art/Fine Arts	M
Astronomy	M,D
Biochemistry	D
Biological and Biomedical Sciences—General	M,D
Biomedical Engineering	M,D
Business Administration and Management—General	M,D
Chemical Engineering	M,D
Chemistry	M,D
Child and Family Studies	M,D
Civil Engineering	M,D
Classics	M
Clinical Laboratory Sciences/Medical Technology	M,D
Clinical Psychology	M,D
Clothing and Textiles	M
Communication Disorders	M
Communication—General	M,D
Computer Science	M,D
Counseling Psychology	M,D,O
Curriculum and Instruction	M,D
Dentistry	P,M
Early Childhood Education	M,D
Economics	M,D
Education—General	M,D,O
Educational Leadership and Administration	M,D,O
Educational Measurement and Evaluation	M,D
Educational Media/Instructional Technology	M,D
Educational Policy	M,D
Educational Psychology	M,D,O
Electrical Engineering	M,D
Engineering and Applied Sciences—General	M,D
English	M,D
Entomology	M,D
Exercise and Sports Science	M,D
Experimental Psychology	M,D
Foreign Languages Education	M
Forestry	M
French	M
Geography	M,D
Geology	M,D
German	M
Gerontology	D
Health Physics/Radiological Health	M
Health Promotion	M,D
Health Services Management and Hospital Administration	M
Higher Education	M,D
Hispanic Studies	M,D
Historic Preservation	M
History	M,D
Hospitality Management	M
Interior Design	M
International Affairs	M
International Business	M
Kinesiology and Movement Studies	M,D
Law	P
Library Science	M
Manufacturing Engineering	M
Materials Sciences	M,D
Mathematics	M,D
Mechanical Engineering	M,D
Medical Physics	M
Microbiology	D
Middle School Education	M,D
Mineral/Mining Engineering	M,D
Music Education	M,D
Music	M,D
Neurobiology	D
Nursing—General	M,D
Nutrition	M,D
Oral and Dental Sciences	M
Pharmaceutical Sciences	M,D
Pharmacology	D
Pharmacy	P
Philosophy	M,D
Physical Therapy	M
Physician Assistant Studies	M
Physics	M,D
Physiology	M,D
Plant Pathology	M,D
Plant Physiology	D
Plant Sciences	M
Political Science	M,D
Psychology—General	M,D
Public Administration	M,D
Public Health—General	M
Rehabilitation Counseling	M,D
Rehabilitation Sciences	D
School Psychology	M,D,O
Social Work	M,D
Sociology	M,D
Special Education	M,D
Statistics	M,D
Theater	M
Toxicology	M,D
Veterinary Sciences	M,D
Vocational and Technical Education	M

UNIVERSITY OF LA VERNE

Accounting	M
Business Administration and Management—General	M,O
Child and Family Studies	M
Child Development	M
Clinical Psychology	D
Counseling Psychology	M
Counselor Education	M,O
Education—General	M,O
Educational Leadership and Administration	M,D,O
Finance and Banking	M
Gerontology	M,O
Health Informatics	M
Health Services Management and Hospital Administration	M,O
Health Services Research	M
International Business	M
Law	P
Management Information Systems	M
Marketing	M
Marriage and Family Therapy	M
Multilingual and Multicultural Education	O
Nonprofit Management	M,O
Organizational Management	M,D,O
Psychology—General	M,D
Public Administration	M,D,O
Reading Education	M,O
Social Psychology	D

Special Education	M
Supply Chain Management	M

UNIVERSITY OF LETHBRIDGE

Accounting	M,D
Addictions/Substance Abuse Counseling	M,D
Agricultural Sciences—General	M,D
American Indian/Native American Studies	M,D
Anthropology	M,D
Archaeology	M,D
Art/Fine Arts	M,D
Biochemistry	M,D
Biological and Biomedical Sciences—General	M,D
Business Administration and Management—General	M,D
Canadian Studies	M,D
Chemistry	M,D
Computational Sciences	M,D
Computer Science	M,D
Counseling Psychology	M,D
Economics	M,D
Education—General	M,D
Educational Leadership and Administration	M,D
English	M,D
Environmental Sciences	M,D
Exercise and Sports Science	M,D
Finance and Banking	M,D
French	M,D
Geographic Information Systems	M,D
Geography	M,D
German	M,D
History	M,D
Human Resources Management	M,D
International Business	M,D
Kinesiology and Movement Studies	M,D
Management Information Systems	M,D
Management Strategy and Policy	M,D
Mathematics	M,D
Media Studies	M,D
Molecular Biology	M,D
Music	M,D
Neuroscience	M,D
Nursing—General	M,D
Philosophy	M,D
Physics	M,D
Political Science	M,D
Psychology—General	M,D
Religion	M,D
Social Sciences	M,D
Sociology	M,D
Spanish	M,D
Theater	M,D
Urban Studies	M,D
Women's Studies	M,D

UNIVERSITY OF LOUISIANA AT LAFAYETTE

American Studies	D
Architectural Engineering	M
Biological and Biomedical Sciences—General	M,D
Business Administration and Management—General	M
Chemical Engineering	M
Civil Engineering	M
Cognitive Sciences	D
Communication Disorders	M,D
Communication—General	M
Computer Engineering	M,D
Computer Science	M,D*
Counselor Education	M
Curriculum and Instruction	M
Education of the Gifted	M
Education—General	M,D
Educational Leadership and Administration	M,D
Engineering Management	M
English	M,D
Environmental Biology	M,D
Evolutionary Biology	M,D
Family and Consumer Sciences-General	M
Folklore	M,D
French	M,D
Geology	M
Health Services Management and Hospital Administration	M
History	M
Mass Communication	M
Mathematics	M,D
Mechanical Engineering	M
Music Education	M
Music	M
Nursing—General	M
Petroleum Engineering	M
Physics	M
Psychology—General	M
Rehabilitation Counseling	M
Rhetoric	M,D
Telecommunications	M
Writing	M,D

UNIVERSITY OF LOUISIANA AT MONROE

Addictions/Substance Abuse Counseling	M
Biological and Biomedical Sciences—General	M
Business Administration and Management—General	M
Communication Disorders	M
Communication—General	M
Counselor Education	M
Criminal Justice and Criminology	M
Curriculum and Instruction	M,D
Education of the Gifted	M,D
Education—General	M,D,O
Educational Leadership and Administration	M,D
Educational Measurement and Evaluation	M,D
Elementary Education	M,D
English	M
Exercise and Sports Science	M
Experimental Psychology	M
Gerontology	M,O
History	M
Marriage and Family Therapy	M,D
Middle School Education	M
Music	M
Pharmaceutical Sciences	M
Pharmacy	P,D
Psychology—General	M,O
Reading Education	M,D
School Psychology	M,O
Secondary Education	M

UNIVERSITY OF LOUISVILLE

Accounting	M
Addictions/Substance Abuse Counseling	M,D,O
Adult Nursing	M,D
African Studies	M
African-American Studies	M
Allopathic Medicine	P
Analytical Chemistry	M,D
Anatomy	M,D
Applied Mathematics	M,D
Art Education	M
Art History	M,D
Art/Fine Arts	M
Biochemistry	M,D
Biological and Biomedical Sciences—General	M
Biophysics	M,D
Biostatistics	M,D
Business Administration and Management—General	M
Chemical Engineering	M,D
Chemical Physics	M,D
Chemistry	M,D
Civil Engineering	M,D
Clinical Psychology	M,D
Clinical Research	M,O
Communication Disorders	M,D
Computer Engineering	M,D
Computer Science	M,D
Counselor Education	M,D
Criminal Justice and Criminology	M
Curriculum and Instruction	D
Dentistry	P
Early Childhood Education	M
Education—General	M,D,O
Educational Leadership and Administration	M,D,O
Educational Media/Instructional Technology	M
Educational Psychology	M,D
Electrical Engineering	M,D
Elementary Education	M
Engineering and Applied Sciences—General	M,D
Engineering Management	M
English	M,D
Entrepreneurship	M,D
Environmental and Occupational Health	M,D
Environmental Biology	D
Environmental Engineering	M,D
Epidemiology	M,D
Exercise and Sports Science	M
Experimental Psychology	D
Family Nurse Practitioner Studies	M,D
French	M
Gerontology	M,D,O
Health Education	M,D
Health Promotion	M,D
Health Services Management and Hospital Administration	M,D
Higher Education	M
History	M
Human Resources Development	M
Human Resources Management	M
Humanities	M,D
Immunology	M,D
Industrial/Management Engineering	M,D
Inorganic Chemistry	M,D
Interdisciplinary Studies	M
Law	P
Marriage and Family Therapy	M,D,O
Maternal and Child/Neonatal Nursing	M,D
Mathematics	M,D
Mechanical Engineering	M
Microbiology	M,D
Middle School Education	M
Molecular Biology	M,D
Museum Studies	M,D
Music Education	M
Music	M,D
Neurobiology	M,D
Nonprofit Management	M
Nursing—General	M,D
Oral and Dental Sciences	M
Organic Chemistry	M,D
Pharmacology	M,D
Philosophy	M
Physical Chemistry	M,D
Physical Education	M
Physics	M,D
Physiology	M,D
Political Science	M
Psychiatric Nursing	M,D
Psychology—General	M,D
Public Administration	M
Public Affairs	D
Public Health—General	M,D
Public Policy	M
Reading Education	M
Rhetoric	M,D
Secondary Education	M
Social Work	M,D,O
Sociology	M
Spanish	M
Special Education	M
Sports Management	M
Theater	M
Toxicology	M,D
Urban and Regional Planning	M
Urban Studies	D
Women's Studies	M,O
Writing	M

UNIVERSITY OF MAINE

Accounting	M
Agricultural Economics and Agribusiness	M
Agricultural Sciences—General	M,D
Agronomy and Soil Sciences	M,D
Animal Sciences	M
Biochemistry	M,D
Bioengineering	M
Biological and Biomedical Sciences—General	D
Botany	M
Business Administration and Management—General	M
Chemical Engineering	M,D
Chemistry	M,D
Civil Engineering	M,D
Clinical Psychology	M,D
Communication Disorders	M
Communication—General	M
Computer Engineering	M,D
Computer Science	M,D
Counselor Education	M,D,O
Curriculum and Instruction	M
Developmental Psychology	M,D
Ecology	M,D
Economics	M
Education—General	M,D,O*
Educational Leadership and Administration	M,D,O
Educational Media/Instructional Technology	M
Electrical Engineering	M,D
Elementary Education	M,O
Engineering and Applied Sciences—General	M,D
Engineering Physics	M
English	M
Entomology	M
Environmental Engineering	M,D
Environmental Sciences	M,D
Experimental Psychology	M,D
Fish, Game, and Wildlife Management	M,D
Food Science and Technology	M,D
Foreign Languages Education	M
Forestry	M,D
French	M
Geology	M,D
Geosciences	M,D
Geotechnical Engineering	M,D
Higher Education	M,D,O
History	M,D
Horticulture	M
Human Development	M
Interdisciplinary Studies	D
Kinesiology and Movement Studies	M
Liberal Studies	M
Management Information Systems	M
Marine Affairs	M
Marine Biology	M,D

*M—master's degree; P—first professional degree; D—doctorate; O—other advanced degree; *—Close-Up and/or Announcement or Display in one of the other books in this series*

Marine Sciences	M,D
Mathematics	M
Mechanical Engineering	M,D
Microbiology	M,D
Molecular Biology	M,D
Music	M
Natural Resources	M,D
Nursing—General	M,O
Nutrition	M,D
Oceanography	M,D
Physical Education	M
Physics	M,D
Plant Biology	M,D
Plant Pathology	M
Plant Sciences	M,D
Psychology—General	M,D
Public Administration	M,D*
Reading Education	M,D,O
Science Education	M,O
Secondary Education	M,O
Social Psychology	M,D
Social Sciences Education	M,O
Social Work	M
Special Education	M,O
Structural Engineering	M,D
Sustainability Management	M
Zoology	M,D

UNIVERSITY OF MAINE AT FARMINGTON

Education—General	M
Educational Leadership and Administration	M
Educational Media/Instructional Technology	M
Reading Education	M

UNIVERSITY OF MANAGEMENT AND TECHNOLOGY

Business Administration and Management—General	M,D,O
Computer Science	M,O
Criminal Justice and Criminology	M
Information Science	M,O
Management Information Systems	M,O
Project Management	M,D,O
Public Administration	M,O
Software Engineering	M,O

UNIVERSITY OF MANITOBA

Adult Education	M
Agricultural Economics and Agribusiness	M,D
Agricultural Sciences—General	M,D
Agronomy and Soil Sciences	M,D
American Indian/Native American Studies	M
Anatomy	M,D
Animal Sciences	M,D
Anthropology	M,D
Architecture	M
Biochemistry	M,D
Biological and Biomedical Sciences—General	M,D,O
Biosystems Engineering	M,D
Botany	M,D
Business Administration and Management—General	M,D
Canadian Studies	M
Cancer Biology/Oncology	M
Chemistry	M,D
Child and Family Studies	M
Civil Engineering	M,D
Classics	M
Clinical Psychology	M,D
Clothing and Textiles	M
Community Health	M,D,O
Computational Sciences	M
Computer Engineering	M,D
Computer Science	M,D
Counselor Education	M
Curriculum and Instruction	M
Dentistry	P
Disability Studies	M
Ecology	M,D
Economics	M,D
Education—General	M,D
Educational Leadership and Administration	M
Educational Psychology	M
Electrical Engineering	M,D
Engineering and Applied Sciences—General	M,D
English as a Second Language	M
English Education	M
English	M,D
Entomology	M,D
Environmental Sciences	M,D
Family and Consumer Sciences-General	M
Food Science and Technology	M,D
Foundations and Philosophy of Education	M
French	M,D
Geography	M,D
Geology	M,D
Geophysics	M,D
German	M
Higher Education	M
History	M,D
Horticulture	M,D
Human Genetics	M,D
Immunology	M,D
Industrial/Management Engineering	M,D
Interdisciplinary Studies	M,D
Interior Design	M
Kinesiology and Movement Studies	M
Landscape Architecture	M
Law	M
Linguistics	M,D
Manufacturing Engineering	M,D
Mathematics	M,D
Mechanical Engineering	M,D
Medical Microbiology	M,D
Microbiology	M,D
Museum Studies	M,D
Music	M
Natural Resources	M,D
Northern Studies	M
Nursing—General	M
Nutrition	M,D
Occupational Therapy	M,D
Oral and Dental Sciences	M,D
Pathology	M
Pharmaceutical Sciences	M,D
Pharmacology	M,D
Philosophy	M
Physical Education	M
Physical Therapy	M,D
Physics	M,D
Physiology	M,D
Plant Physiology	M,D
Plant Sciences	M,D
Political Science	M
Psychology—General	M,D
Public Administration	M
Recreation and Park Management	M
Rehabilitation Sciences	M,D
Religion	M,D
School Psychology	M,D
Slavic Languages	M
Social Work	M,D
Sociology	M,D
Special Education	M
Statistics	M,D
Urban and Regional Planning	M
Zoology	M,D

UNIVERSITY OF MARY

Addictions/Substance Abuse Counseling	M
Business Administration and Management—General	M
Curriculum and Instruction	M
Early Childhood Education	M
Education—General	M
Educational Leadership and Administration	M
Family Nurse Practitioner Studies	M
Health Services Management and Hospital Administration	M
Higher Education	M
Human Resources Management	M
Management Strategy and Policy	M
Nursing and Healthcare Administration	M
Nursing Education	M
Nursing—General	M
Occupational Therapy	M
Physical Therapy	D
Project Management	M
Reading Education	M
School Psychology	M
Social Psychology	M
Special Education	M

UNIVERSITY OF MARY HARDIN-BAYLOR

Accounting	M
Business Administration and Management—General	M
Counseling Psychology	M
Counselor Education	M
Education—General	M,D
Educational Leadership and Administration	M,D
Educational Psychology	M,D
Exercise and Sports Science	M,D
Management Information Systems	M
Marriage and Family Therapy	M
Nursing—General	M
Psychology—General	M
Reading Education	M,D
School Psychology	M
Social Psychology	M

UNIVERSITY OF MARYLAND, BALTIMORE

Allopathic Medicine	P
Biochemistry	M,D
Biological and Biomedical Sciences—General	M,D
Biostatistics	M,D
Cancer Biology/Oncology	M,D
Cell Biology	M,D
Clinical Laboratory Sciences/Medical Technology	M
Clinical Research	M,D
Community Health Nursing	M
Dental Hygiene	M
Dentistry	P,M,O
Environmental Sciences	M,D
Epidemiology	M,D
Gerontological Nursing	M
Gerontology	M,D
Health Services Research	M,D
Human Genetics	M,D
Immunology	D
Law	P
Marine Sciences	M,D*
Maternal and Child/Neonatal Nursing	M
Medical/Surgical Nursing	M
Microbiology	D
Molecular Biology	M,D
Molecular Medicine	M,D
Neurobiology	D
Neuroscience	D
Nurse Midwifery	M
Nursing and Healthcare Administration	M
Nursing Education	M
Nursing—General	M,D
Oral and Dental Sciences	P,M,D,O
Pathology	M
Pediatric Nursing	M
Pharmaceutical Administration	M,D
Pharmaceutical Sciences	D
Pharmacology	M,D
Pharmacy	P,M,D
Physical Therapy	D
Psychiatric Nursing	M
Rehabilitation Sciences	D
Social Work	M,D
Toxicology	M,D

UNIVERSITY OF MARYLAND, BALTIMORE COUNTY

Applied Mathematics	M,D
Applied Physics	M,D
Art/Fine Arts	M
Astrophysics	M,D
Atmospheric Sciences	M,D
Biochemical Engineering	M,D,O
Biochemistry	M,D
Biological and Biomedical Sciences—General	M,D
Biostatistics	M,D
Biotechnology	O
Cell Biology	D
Chemical Engineering	M,D,O
Chemistry	M,D
Civil Engineering	M,D
Cognitive Sciences	D
Communication—General	M
Computer Engineering	M,D
Computer Science	M,D
Curriculum and Instruction	M,O
Developmental Psychology	D
Distance Education Development	M,O
Early Childhood Education	M
Economics	M
Education—General	M,O
Educational Media/Instructional Technology	M,O
Electrical Engineering	M,D
Elementary Education	M
Engineering and Applied Sciences—General	M,D,O
Engineering Management	M,O
English as a Second Language	M,O
Environmental Engineering	M,D
Environmental Management and Policy	M,D
Environmental Sciences	M,D
Epidemiology	M,O
Geographic Information Systems	M,O
Geography	M,D
Gerontology	D
Health Education	M,O
Health Services Management and Hospital Administration	M,O
History	M
Human Services	M,D
Information Science	M,D
Linguistics	M
Marine Sciences	M,D*
Mathematics Education	M,O
Molecular Biology	M,D
Multilingual and Multicultural Education	M,D
Music	O
Neuroscience	D
Nonprofit Management	M,O
Optical Sciences	M,D
Physics	M,D
Psychology—General	M,D
Public Policy	M,D

Science Education	M,O
Secondary Education	M
Social Sciences	D
Sociology	M,O
Statistics	M,D
Systems Engineering	M,O
Women's Studies	O

UNIVERSITY OF MARYLAND, COLLEGE PARK

Advertising and Public Relations	M,D
Aerospace/Aeronautical Engineering	M,D,O
Agricultural Economics and Agribusiness	M,D
Agricultural Sciences—General	P,M,D
Agronomy and Soil Sciences	M,D
American Studies	M,D
Analytical Chemistry	M,D
Animal Sciences	M,D
Anthropology	M
Applied Mathematics	M,D
Architecture	M
Art History	M,D
Art Therapy	M,D,O
Art/Fine Arts	M
Astronomy	M,D
Biochemistry	M,D
Bioengineering	M,D
Biological and Biomedical Sciences—General	M,D
Biostatistics	M,D
Broadcast Journalism	M,D
Business Administration and Management—General	M,D
Cell Biology	M,D
Chemical Engineering	M,D,O
Chemical Physics	M,D
Chemistry	M,D
Child and Family Studies	M,D
Civil Engineering	M,D,O
Classics	M
Clinical Psychology	M,D
Cognitive Sciences	D
Communication Disorders	M,D
Communication—General	M,D
Comparative Literature	M,D
Computer Engineering	M,D
Computer Science	M,D
Conservation Biology	M
Counseling Psychology	M,D,O
Counselor Education	M,D,O
Criminal Justice and Criminology	M,D
Curriculum and Instruction	M,D,O
Dance	M
Developmental Psychology	M,D
Early Childhood Education	M,D
Ecology	M,D
Economics	M,D
Education—General	M,D,O*
Educational Leadership and Administration	M,D,O
Educational Measurement and Evaluation	M,D
Educational Media/Instructional Technology	M,D,O
Educational Policy	M,D
Educational Psychology	M,D
Electrical Engineering	M,D,O
Engineering and Applied Sciences—General	M
English as a Second Language	M,D,O
English	M,D
Entomology	M,D
Environmental and Occupational Health	M,D
Environmental Engineering	M,D
Environmental Sciences	M,D
Epidemiology	M,D
Evolutionary Biology	M,D
Experimental Psychology	M,D
Family and Consumer Sciences-General	M,D
Fire Protection Engineering	M,O
Food Science and Technology	M,D
Foreign Languages Education	M,D
Foundations and Philosophy of Education	M,D,O
French	M,D
Geography	M,D
Geology	M,D
German	M,D
Health Education	M,D
Health Services Management and Hospital Administration	M,D
Higher Education	M,D
Historic Preservation	M,O
History	M,D
Horticulture	D
Human Development	M,D
Industrial and Organizational Psychology	M,D
Information Studies	M,D
Inorganic Chemistry	M,D
International and Comparative Education	M,D
Japanese	M,D
Jewish Studies	M
Journalism	M,D
Kinesiology and Movement Studies	M,D
Law	
Library Science	
Linguistics	M,D
Manufacturing Engineering	M,D
Marine Sciences	M,D*
Marriage and Family Therapy	M,D
Materials Engineering	M,D,O
Materials Sciences	M,D,O
Maternal and Child Health	M,D
Mathematics	M,D
Mechanical Engineering	M,D,O
Mechanics	M,D
Media Studies	M,D
Meteorology	M,D
Molecular Biology	D
Molecular Genetics	M,D
Music Education	M,D
Music	M,D
Natural Resources	M,D
Near and Middle Eastern Languages	M,O
Neuroscience	M,D
Nuclear Engineering	M,D
Nutrition	M,D
Oceanography	M,D
Organic Chemistry	M,D
Philosophy	M,D
Physical Chemistry	M,D
Physics	M,D
Plant Biology	M,D
Political Science	D
Portuguese	M,D
Psychology—General	M,D
Public Administration	M
Public Health—General	M,D
Public Policy	M,D
Reading Education	M,D,O
Real Estate	M
Rehabilitation Counseling	M,D,O
Reliability Engineering	M,D,O
School Psychology	M,D,O
Secondary Education	M,D,O
Social Psychology	M,D
Social Work	
Sociology	M,D
Spanish	M,D
Special Education	M,D,O
Speech and Interpersonal Communication	M,D
Statistics	M,D
Student Affairs	M,D,O
Survey Methodology	M,D
Sustainable Development	M
Systems Engineering	M,O
Telecommunications	M
Theater	M,D
Urban and Regional Planning	M,D
Veterinary Medicine	P
Veterinary Sciences	M,D
Women's Studies	M,D
Writing	M,D

UNIVERSITY OF MARYLAND EASTERN SHORE

Agricultural Sciences—General	M,D
Computer Science	M
Counselor Education	M
Criminal Justice and Criminology	M
Education—General	M
Educational Leadership and Administration	D
Environmental Sciences	M,D
Food Science and Technology	M,D
Marine Sciences	M,D*
Organizational Management	D
Physical Therapy	D
Rehabilitation Counseling	M
Rehabilitation Sciences	M
Special Education	M
Toxicology	M,D
Vocational and Technical Education	M

UNIVERSITY OF MARYLAND UNIVERSITY COLLEGE

Accounting	M,O
Biotechnology	M,O
Business Administration and Management—General	M,D,O
Distance Education Development	M,O
Education—General	M
Environmental Management and Policy	M,O
Finance and Banking	M,O
Health Informatics	M,O
Health Services Management and Hospital Administration	M,O
Information Science	M,O
International Business	M,O
Management Information Systems	M,O
Management of Technology	M,O

UNIVERSITY OF MARY WASHINGTON

Business Administration and Management—General	M
Education—General	M
Management Information Systems	M

UNIVERSITY OF MASSACHUSETTS AMHERST

Accounting	M
African-American Studies	M,D
Agricultural Economics and Agribusiness	M,D
Agronomy and Soil Sciences	M,D
Animal Sciences	M,D
Anthropology	M,D
Applied Mathematics	M
Architecture	M
Art History	M
Art/Fine Arts	M
Astronomy	M,D
Biochemistry	M,D
Biological and Biomedical Sciences—General	M,D
Biotechnology	M,D
Business Administration and Management—General	M,D
Cell Biology	D
Chemical Engineering	M,D
Chemistry	M,D
Child and Family Studies	M,D,O
Chinese	M
Civil Engineering	M,D
Classics	M
Clinical Psychology	M,D
Cognitive Sciences	M,D
Communication Disorders	M,D
Communication—General	M,D
Comparative Literature	M,D
Computer Engineering	M,D
Computer Science	M,D
Conflict Resolution and Mediation/Peace Studies	M,D
Counselor Education	M,D,O
Developmental Biology	D
Developmental Psychology	M,D
Early Childhood Education	M,D,O
Economics	M,D
Education—General	M,D,O
Educational Leadership and Administration	M,D,O
Educational Measurement and Evaluation	M,D,O
Educational Media/Instructional Technology	M,D,O
Educational Policy	M,D,O
Electrical Engineering	M,D
Elementary Education	M,D,O
Engineering and Applied Sciences—General	M,D
Engineering Management	
English as a Second Language	M,D,O
English	M,D
Entomology	M,D
Environmental Biology	M,D
Environmental Engineering	M
Evolutionary Biology	M,D
Fish, Game, and Wildlife Management	M,D
Food Science and Technology	M,D
Foreign Languages Education	M
Forestry	M,D
French	M
Geography	M
Geosciences	M,D
German	M,D
Higher Education	M,D,O
History of Science and Technology	M,D
History	M,D
Hospitality Management	M
Industrial and Labor Relations	M
Industrial/Management Engineering	M,D
Interior Design	M
International and Comparative Education	M,D,O
Italian	M
Japanese	M
Kinesiology and Movement Studies	M,D
Landscape Architecture	M
Linguistics	M,D
Marine Sciences	M
Mathematics	M,D
Mechanical Engineering	M,D
Microbiology	M,D*
Molecular Biophysics	D
Multilingual and Multicultural Education	M,D,O
Music	M,D
Neuroscience	M,D
Nursing—General	M,D
Nutrition	M,D
Operations Research	M,D
Philosophy	M,D
Physics	M,D

*M—master's degree; P—first professional degree; D—doctorate; O—other advanced degree; *—Close-Up and/or Announcement or Display in one of the other books in this series*

Plant Biology	M,D
Plant Molecular Biology	M,D
Plant Physiology	M,D
Plant Sciences	M,D
Political Science	M,D
Polymer Science and Engineering	M,D
Portuguese	M,D
Psychology—General	M,D
Public Administration	M
Public Health—General	M,D
Public History	M,D
Public Policy	M
Reading Education	M,D,O
Scandinavian Languages	M,D
School Psychology	D
Secondary Education	M,D,O
Social Psychology	M,D
Sociology	M,D
Spanish	M,D
Special Education	M,D,O
Sports Management	M,D
Statistics	M,D
Theater	M
Travel and Tourism	M
Urban and Regional Planning	M,D
Writing	M,D

UNIVERSITY OF MASSACHUSETTS BOSTON

American Studies	M
Applied Physics	M
Archaeology	M
Biological and Biomedical Sciences—General	M
Biotechnology	M
Business Administration and Management—General	M
Cell Biology	D
Chemistry	M
Clinical Psychology	D
Computer Science	M,D
Conflict Resolution and Mediation/Peace Studies	M,O
Counseling Psychology	M,O
Counselor Education	M,O
Curriculum and Instruction	M
Education—General	M,D,O
Educational Leadership and Administration	M,D,O
Elementary Education	M,D,O
English as a Second Language	M
English	M
Environmental Biology	D
Environmental Sciences	D
Foreign Languages Education	M
Forensic Psychology	M,O
Gerontology	M,D,O
Health Services Management and Hospital Administration	M,D,O
Higher Education	M,D,O
History	M
Human Services	M
Linguistics	M
Marine Sciences	D
Marriage and Family Therapy	M,O
Molecular Biology	D
Multilingual and Multicultural Education	M
Nursing—General	M,D
Political Science	M,D,O
Public Affairs	M
Public History	M
Public Policy	D
Rehabilitation Counseling	M,O
School Psychology	M,O
Secondary Education	M,D,O
Sociology	M
Special Education	M
Urban Education	M,D,O
Women's Studies	M,D,O

UNIVERSITY OF MASSACHUSETTS DARTMOUTH

Accounting	M,O
Acoustics	M,D,O
Adult Nursing	M,D,O
Applied Arts and Design—General	M
Art Education	M
Art/Fine Arts	M,O
Biological and Biomedical Sciences—General	M
Biomedical Engineering	D
Biotechnology	D
Business Administration and Management—General	M,O
Chemistry	M,D
Civil Engineering	M
Clinical Psychology	M,O
Community Health Nursing	M,D,O
Computer Art and Design	M
Computer Engineering	M,D,O
Computer Science	M,O
Education—General	M,O
Electrical Engineering	M,D,O
Electronic Commerce	M,O
Elementary Education	M,O
Engineering and Applied Sciences—General	M,D,O
Environmental Engineering	M
Environmental Management and Policy	M,O
Finance and Banking	M,O
Graphic Design	M
Illustration	M
Latin American Studies	M,D
Marine Biology	M
Marine Sciences	M,D
Marketing	M,O
Mechanical Engineering	M
Middle School Education	M,O
Nursing—General	M,D,O
Organizational Management	M,O
Photography	M
Physics	M
Portuguese	M,D
Psychology—General	M,O
Public Policy	M,O
Secondary Education	M,O
Software Engineering	M,O
Supply Chain Management	M,O
Telecommunications	M,D,O
Textile Design	M,O
Textile Sciences and Engineering	M
Writing	M,O

UNIVERSITY OF MASSACHUSETTS LOWELL

Allied Health—General	M,D,O
Analytical Chemistry	M,D
Applied Mathematics	M,D
Applied Physics	M,D
Atmospheric Sciences	M,D
Biochemistry	M,D
Biological and Biomedical Sciences—General	M,D
Biotechnology	M,D
Business Administration and Management—General	M,O
Chemical Engineering	M,D
Chemistry	M,D
Civil Engineering	M,D,O
Clinical Laboratory Sciences/Medical Technology	M,O
Computational Sciences	M,D
Computer Engineering	M
Computer Science	M,D
Criminal Justice and Criminology	M
Curriculum and Instruction	M,D,O
Economic Development	M,O
Economics	M,O
Education—General	M,D,O
Educational Leadership and Administration	M,D,O
Electrical Engineering	M,D
Energy and Power Engineering	M,D
Engineering and Applied Sciences—General	M,D,O
Entrepreneurship	M,O
Environmental Engineering	M,D,O
Environmental Management and Policy	M,D,O
Environmental Sciences	M,D,O
Epidemiology	M,D,O
Ergonomics and Human Factors	M,D,O
Family Nurse Practitioner Studies	M
Gerontological Nursing	M,O
Health Informatics	M,O
Health Physics/Radiological Health	M
Health Promotion	D
Health Services Management and Hospital Administration	M,O
Industrial Hygiene	M,D,O
Industrial/Management Engineering	M,D,O
Inorganic Chemistry	M,D
Materials Engineering	M,D,O
Mathematics Education	M,D,O
Mathematics	M,D
Mechanical Engineering	M,D
Mechanics	M,D
Medical/Surgical Nursing	M,D,O
Music Education	M
Music	M
Nuclear Engineering	M,D
Nursing and Healthcare Administration	D
Nursing Education	M,D,O
Nursing—General	M,D,O
Nutrition	M,O
Optical Sciences	M,D
Organic Chemistry	M,D
Pathology	M,O
Physical Therapy	D
Physics	M,D
Polymer Science and Engineering	M,D,O
Psychiatric Nursing	M,O
Psychology—General	M
Public Health—General	M,O
Reading Education	M,D,O
Science Education	M,D,O
Social Psychology	M
Sociology	M,O
Sustainable Development	M,D,O

UNIVERSITY OF MASSACHUSETTS WORCESTER

Acute Care/Critical Care Nursing	M,D,O
Adult Nursing	M,D,O
Allopathic Medicine	P
Biochemistry	D
Biological and Biomedical Sciences—General	D
Biomedical Engineering	D
Cancer Biology/Oncology	D
Cell Biology	D
Clinical Research	M,D
Epidemiology	D
Family Nurse Practitioner Studies	M,D,O
Gerontological Nursing	M,D,O
Health Services Research	D
Immunology	D
Medical Physics	D
Microbiology	D
Molecular Genetics	D
Molecular Pharmacology	D
Molecular Physiology	D
Neuroscience	D
Nursing Education	M,D,O
Nursing—General	M,D,O
Physiology	D
Virology	D

UNIVERSITY OF MEDICINE AND DENTISTRY OF NEW JERSEY

Adult Nursing	M,D,O
Allied Health—General	M,D,O
Allopathic Medicine	P
Biochemistry	M,D
Bioinformatics	M,D
Biological and Biomedical Sciences—General	M,D,O
Biomedical Engineering	M,D,O
Biostatistics	M,D,O
Cardiovascular Sciences	M,D
Cell Biology	M,D
Clinical Laboratory Sciences/Medical Technology	M,D
Counseling Psychology	M,D,O
Dentistry	P,M,O
Environmental Sciences	D
Epidemiology	M,D,O
Family Nurse Practitioner Studies	M,D,O
Health Education	M,D
Health Physics/Radiological Health	M
Health Services Management and Hospital Administration	M
Immunology	M,D
Interdisciplinary Studies	M,D
Kinesiology and Movement Studies	M,D
Medical Imaging	M
Medical Informatics	M,D,O
Microbiology	M,D*
Molecular Biology	M,D
Molecular Genetics	M,D
Molecular Medicine	D
Molecular Pathology	D
Molecular Pharmacology	M,D
Neuroscience	M,D
Nurse Anesthesia	M,D,O
Nurse Midwifery	M,O
Nursing Informatics	M
Nursing—General	M,O
Nutrition	M,D,O
Occupational Health Nursing	M,D,O
Oral and Dental Sciences	P,M,O
Osteopathic Medicine	P
Pathology	D
Pharmacology	D
Physical Therapy	M,D
Physician Assistant Studies	M
Physiology	M,D
Public Health—General	M,D,O
Rehabilitation Counseling	M,D
Transcultural Nursing	D
Women's Health Nursing	M,D,O

UNIVERSITY OF MEMPHIS

Accounting	M,D
Adult Education	M,D
Anthropology	M
Applied Mathematics	M,D
Applied Statistics	M,D
Archaeology	M,O
Architecture	M
Art History	M,O
Art/Fine Arts	M,O
Biological and Biomedical Sciences—General	M,D
Biomedical Engineering	M,D
Business Administration and Management—General	M,D
Chemistry	M,D
Civil Engineering	M,D
Clinical Psychology	M,D
Communication Disorders	M,D
Communication—General	M,D

Computer Engineering	M,D
Computer Science	M,D
Counseling Psychology	M,D
Counselor Education	M,D
Criminal Justice and Criminology	M
Curriculum and Instruction	M,D
Early Childhood Education	M,D
Economics	M,D
Education—General	M,D,O
Educational Leadership and Administration	M,D
Educational Measurement and Evaluation	M,D
Educational Media/ Instructional Technology	M,D
Educational Psychology	M,D
Electrical Engineering	M,D
Elementary Education	M,D
Energy and Power Engineering	M,D
Engineering and Applied Sciences—General	M,D
English	M,D,O
Environmental Engineering	M,D
Exercise and Sports Science	M
Experimental Psychology	M,D
Family and Consumer Sciences-General	M
Film, Television, and Video Production	M,D
Finance and Banking	M,D
French	M
Geology	M,D,O
Graphic Design	M,O
Health Promotion	M
Health Services Management and Hospital Administration	M
Higher Education	M,D
History	M,D
Industrial/Management Engineering	M,D
Interior Design	M,O
International Business	M,D
Journalism	M
Law	P
Leisure Studies	M
Liberal Studies	M
Management Information Systems	M,D
Manufacturing Engineering	M
Marketing	M,D
Mathematics	M,D
Mechanical Engineering	M,D
Middle School Education	M,D
Music Education	M,D
Music	M,D
Nonprofit Management	M
Nursing—General	M,O
Nutrition	M
Philosophy	M,D
Photography	M,O
Physical Education	M
Physics	M
Political Science	M
Psychology—General	M,D
Public Administration	M
Public Health—General	M
Public Policy	M
Reading Education	M,D
Real Estate	M,D
Rehabilitation Counseling	M,D
School Psychology	M,D
Secondary Education	M,D
Sociology	M
Spanish	M
Special Education	M,D
Statistics	M,D
Structural Engineering	M,D
Student Affairs	M,D
Supply Chain Management	M,D
Taxation	M
Theater	M
Transportation and Highway Engineering	M,D
Urban and Regional Planning	M
Water Resources Engineering	M,D
Writing	M,D,O

UNIVERSITY OF MIAMI

Accounting	M
Acute Care/Critical Care Nursing	M,D
Adult Nursing	M,D
Advertising and Public Relations	M,D
Aerospace/Aeronautical Engineering	M,D
Allopathic Medicine	P
Architectural Engineering	M,D
Architecture	M*
Art History	M
Art/Fine Arts	M
Athletic Training and Sports Medicine	M
Biochemistry	D
Biological and Biomedical Sciences—General	M,D*
Biomedical Engineering	M,D
Biophysics	D
Broadcast Journalism	M,D
Business Administration and Management—General	M
Cancer Biology/Oncology	D
Cell Biology	D
Chemistry	M,D
Civil Engineering	M,D
Clinical Psychology	M,D
Communication—General	M,D
Computer Engineering	M,D
Computer Science	M,D
Counseling Psychology	D
Counselor Education	M,O
Developmental Biology	D
Developmental Psychology	M,D
Early Childhood Education	M,O
Economic Development	M,D
Economics	M,D
Education—General	M,D,O*
Educational Leadership and Administration	M,D,O
Educational Measurement and Evaluation	M,D
Electrical Engineering	M,D
Elementary Education	M
Engineering and Applied Sciences—General	M,D
English as a Second Language	M
English	M,D
Environmental and Occupational Health	M
Environmental Management and Policy	M,D
Epidemiology	D
Ergonomics and Human Factors	M
Evolutionary Biology	M,D
Exercise and Sports Science	M,D
Family Nurse Practitioner Studies	M,D
Film, Television, and Video Production	M,D
Film, Television, and Video Theory and Criticism	M,D
Finance and Banking	M
Fish, Game, and Wildlife Management	M,D
French	D
Genetics	M,D
Geography	M
Geophysics	M,D
Graphic Design	M
Higher Education	M,D,O
History	M,D
Immunology	D
Industrial/Management Engineering	M,D
Inorganic Chemistry	M,D
International Affairs	M,D
International Business	M
International Economics	M,D
Internet and Interactive Multimedia	M
Journalism	M,D
Latin American Studies	M
Law	P,M
Liberal Studies	M
Management Information Systems	M
Management of Technology	M,D
Marine Affairs	M
Marine Biology	M,D
Marine Geology	M,D
Marine Sciences	M,D
Marketing	M
Marriage and Family Therapy	M,O
Mathematics Education	D
Mathematics	M,D
Mechanical Engineering	M,D
Meteorology	M,D
Microbiology	D
Molecular Biology	D
Multilingual and Multicultural Education	D
Music Education	M,D,O
Music	M,D,O
Neuroscience	M,D*
Nurse Anesthesia	M,D
Nurse Midwifery	M,D
Nursing—General	M,D
Oceanography	M,D
Organic Chemistry	M,D
Pharmacology	D
Philosophy	M,D
Photography	M
Physical Chemistry	M,D
Physical Therapy	D
Physics	M,D*
Physiology	D
Political Science	M
Psychology—General	M,D
Public Health—General	M
Reading Education	M,D,O
Romance Languages	D
Science Education	D
Sociology	M,D
Spanish	M,D
Special Education	M,D,O
Sports Management	M
Student Affairs	M,D,O
Taxation	M
Therapies—Dance, Drama, and Music	M,D,O
Urban Design	M
Writing	M,D

UNIVERSITY OF MICHIGAN

Acute Care/Critical Care Nursing	M
Adult Nursing	M,O
Aerospace/Aeronautical Engineering	M,D
Allopathic Medicine	P
American Studies	M,D
Analytical Chemistry	D
Anthropology	D
Applied Arts and Design—General	M
Applied Economics	M
Applied Physics	D
Applied Statistics	M,D
Archaeology	D
Architecture	M,D
Art History	D
Art/Fine Arts	M
Asian Languages	M,D
Asian Studies	M,D,O
Astronomy	D
Astrophysics	D
Atmospheric Sciences	M,D
Automotive Engineering	M
Biochemistry	D
Bioinformatics	M,D
Biological and Biomedical Sciences—General	D
Biomedical Engineering	M,D
Biophysics	D
Biopsychology	D
Biostatistics	M,D
Business Administration and Management—General	D
Cell Biology	M,D
Chemical Engineering	M,D,O
Chemistry	D
Civil Engineering	M,D,O
Classics	M,D,O
Clinical Psychology	D
Clinical Research	M
Communication—General	D
Community Health Nursing	M,O
Comparative Literature	D
Computer Education	M,D
Computer Engineering	M,D
Computer Science	M,D
Conservation Biology	M,D
Construction Engineering	M,D,O
Curriculum and Instruction	M,D
Dance	M
Dental Hygiene	M
Dentistry	P
Developmental Biology	M,D
Developmental Psychology	D
Early Childhood Education	M,D
East European and Russian Studies	M,O
Ecology	M,D
Economics	M,D
Education—General	M,D
Educational Leadership and Administration	M,D
Educational Measurement and Evaluation	M,D
Educational Media/ Instructional Technology	M,D
Electrical Engineering	M,D
Engineering and Applied Sciences—General	M,D,O
English as a Second Language	M,D
English Education	M,D
English	M,D,O
Environmental and Occupational Health	M,D
Environmental Engineering	M,D,O
Environmental Management and Policy	M,D
Environmental Sciences	M,D
Epidemiology	M,D
Evolutionary Biology	M,D
Experimental Psychology	D
Family Nurse Practitioner Studies	M,O
Film, Television, and Video Theory and Criticism	D,O
Financial Engineering	M
Foreign Languages Education	M,D
Forestry	M,D,O
Foundations and Philosophy of Education	M,D
French	D
Geochemistry	M,D
Geology	M,D
German	M,D
Gerontological Nursing	M
Health Physics/ Radiological Health	M,D,O
Health Promotion	M,D
Health Services Management and Hospital Administration	M,D
Higher Education	M,D
History	D,O
Human Genetics	M,D

*M—master's degree; P—first professional degree; D—doctorate; O—other advanced degree; *—Close-Up and/or Announcement or Display in one of the other books in this series*

Human-Computer Interaction	M,D
Immunology	D
Industrial Hygiene	M,D
Industrial/Management Engineering	M,D
Information Science	M,D
Information Studies	M,D
Inorganic Chemistry	D
International Health	M,D
Jewish Studies	M,D,O
Kinesiology and Movement Studies	M,D
Landscape Architecture	M,D
Law	P,M,D
Library Science	M,D
Linguistics	D
Manufacturing Engineering	M,D
Marine Geology	M,D
Marine Sciences	M,D
Mass Communication	D
Materials Engineering	M,D
Materials Sciences	M,D*
Mathematics Education	M,D
Mathematics	M,D
Mechanical Engineering	M,D
Media Studies	M
Medical/Surgical Nursing	M
Medicinal and Pharmaceutical Chemistry	D
Medieval and Renaissance Studies	O
Microbiology	D
Molecular Biology	M,D
Molecular Pathology	D
Multilingual and Multicultural Education	M,D
Music Education	M,D,O
Music	M,D,O
Natural Resources	M,D
Near and Middle Eastern Languages	M,D
Near and Middle Eastern Studies	M,D
Neuroscience	D
Nuclear Engineering	M,D,O
Nurse Midwifery	M,O
Nursing and Healthcare Administration	M
Nursing—General	M,D,O
Nutrition	M,D
Occupational Health Nursing	M,O
Ocean Engineering	M,D,O
Oceanography	M,D
Operations Research	M,D
Oral and Dental Sciences	M,D
Organic Chemistry	D
Pathology	D
Pediatric Nursing	M,O
Pharmaceutical Administration	D
Pharmaceutical Engineering	M
Pharmaceutical Sciences	D
Pharmacology	D
Pharmacy	P
Philosophy	M,D
Physical Chemistry	D
Physics	M,D
Physiology	D
Planetary and Space Sciences	M,D
Political Science	M,D
Psychiatric Nursing	M
Psychology—General	D,O
Public Health—General	M,D
Public Policy	M,D
Reading Education	M,D
Real Estate	M,O
Religion	M,D
Romance Languages	D
Russian	M,D
Science Education	M,D
Slavic Languages	M,D
Social Psychology	D
Social Sciences Education	M,D
Social Sciences	D
Social Work	M,D*
Sociology	D,O
Spanish	D
Sports Management	M,D
Statistics	M,D
Structural Engineering	M,D,O
Supply Chain Management	M,D
Survey Methodology	M,D,O
Sustainable Development	M,D
Systems Engineering	M,D
Taxation	P,M,D
Theater	M,D
Toxicology	M,D
Urban and Regional Planning	M,D,O
Urban Design	M
Women's Studies	D,O
Writing	M

UNIVERSITY OF MICHIGAN–DEARBORN

Accounting	M
Applied Mathematics	M
Automotive Engineering	M,D
Business Administration and Management—General	M
Clinical Psychology	M
Computational Sciences	M
Computer Engineering	M
Computer Science	M
Education—General	M
Educational Measurement and Evaluation	M,O
Electrical Engineering	M
Engineering and Applied Sciences—General	M,D*
Engineering Management	M,D
Environmental Sciences	M
Finance and Banking	M
Health Psychology	M
Industrial/Management Engineering	M,D
Information Science	M,D
Liberal Studies	M
Manufacturing Engineering	M,D
Mechanical Engineering	M
Nonprofit Management	M,O
Public Administration	M,O
Public Policy	M
Science Education	M
Software Engineering	M
Special Education	M
Systems Engineering	M,D
Systems Science	M,D

UNIVERSITY OF MICHIGAN–FLINT

American Studies	M
Biological and Biomedical Sciences—General	M
Business Administration and Management—General	M
Computer Science	M*
Early Childhood Education	M
Education—General	M
Educational Media/Instructional Technology	M
Elementary Education	M
English	M
Health Education	M
Information Science	M
Nurse Anesthesia	M
Nursing—General	D
Physical Therapy	D
Public Administration	M
Reading Education	M
Social Sciences	M
Special Education	M

UNIVERSITY OF MINNESOTA, DULUTH

Allopathic Medicine	P
Anthropology	M
Applied Mathematics	M
Art/Fine Arts	M
Biochemistry	M,D
Biological and Biomedical Sciences—General	M,D
Biophysics	M,D
Business Administration and Management—General	M
Chemistry	M
Communication Disorders	M
Computational Sciences	M
Computer Engineering	M
Computer Science	M
Criminal Justice and Criminology	M
Education—General	D
Electrical Engineering	M
Engineering Management	M
English	M
Geology	M,D
Graphic Design	M
Immunology	M,D
Liberal Studies	M
Medical Microbiology	M,D
Molecular Biology	M,D
Music Education	M
Music	M
Pharmacology	M,D
Physics	M
Physiology	M,D
Safety Engineering	M
Social Work	M
Sociology	M
Toxicology	M,D

UNIVERSITY OF MINNESOTA, TWIN CITIES CAMPUS

Accounting	M,D
Adult Education	M,D,O
Adult Nursing	M
Aerospace/Aeronautical Engineering	M,D
Agricultural Education	M,D
Agricultural Sciences—General	M,D
Agronomy and Soil Sciences	M,D
Allopathic Medicine	P
American Studies	D
Animal Behavior	M,D
Animal Sciences	M,D
Anthropology	M,D
Applied Arts and Design—General	M,D,O
Applied Economics	M,D
Archaeology	M,D
Architecture	M
Art Education	M,D,O
Art History	M,D
Art/Fine Arts	M
Asian Languages	D
Asian Studies	D
Astronomy	M,D
Astrophysics	M,D
Biochemistry	D
Biological and Biomedical Sciences—General	M,D
Biomedical Engineering	M,D
Biophysics	M,D
Biopsychology	D
Biostatistics	M,D
Biosystems Engineering	M,D
Biotechnology	M
Business Administration and Management—General	M,D*
Business Education	M,D
Cancer Biology/Oncology	D
Cell Biology	M,D
Chemical Engineering	M,D
Chemistry	M,D
Child and Family Studies	M,D
Child Development	M,D
Civil Engineering	M,D
Classics	M,D
Clinical Psychology	D
Clinical Research	M
Clothing and Textiles	M,D,O
Cognitive Sciences	D
Communication Disorders	M,D
Communication—General	M,D,O
Community Health Nursing	M
Community Health	M
Comparative Literature	D
Computational Sciences	M,D
Computer and Information Systems Security	M
Computer Engineering	M,D
Computer Science	M,D
Conservation Biology	M,D
Counseling Psychology	D
Counselor Education	M,D,O
Cultural Studies	D
Curriculum and Instruction	M,D,O
Dance	M,D
Dentistry	P
Developmental Biology	M,D
Early Childhood Education	M,D,O
Ecology	M,D
Economic Development	M
Economics	D
Education of the Gifted	M,D,O
Education—General	M,D,O
Educational Leadership and Administration	M,D,O
Educational Measurement and Evaluation	M,D
Educational Media/Instructional Technology	M,D,O
Educational Policy	M,D,O
Educational Psychology	M,D,O
Electrical Engineering	M,D
Elementary Education	M,D,O
Engineering and Applied Sciences—General	M,D
English as a Second Language	M
English Education	M
English	M,D
Entomology	M,D
Entrepreneurship	M
Environmental and Occupational Health	M,D,O
Environmental Education	M,D,O
Environmental Management and Policy	M
Epidemiology	M,D
Evolutionary Biology	M,D
Exercise and Sports Science	M,D,O
Family Nurse Practitioner Studies	M
Finance and Banking	M,D
Food Science and Technology	M,D
Foreign Languages Education	M
Foundations and Philosophy of Education	M,D,O
French	M,D
Genetic Counseling	M,D
Genetics	M,D
Geographic Information Systems	M
Geography	M,D
Geological Engineering	M,D
Geology	M,D
Geophysics	M,D
German	M,D
Gerontological Nursing	M
Health Informatics	M,D*
Health Services Management and Hospital Administration	M,D
Health Services Research	M,D
Higher Education	M,D
History of Medicine	M,D
History of Science and Technology	M,D
History	M,D
Human Resources Development	M,D,O
Human Resources Management	M,D*
Immunology	D
Industrial and Labor Relations	M,D

Industrial and Manufacturing Management	M,D
Industrial and Organizational Psychology	D
Industrial Hygiene	M,D
Industrial/Management Engineering	M,D
Infectious Diseases	M,D
Information Science	M,D
Interdisciplinary Studies	D
Interior Design	M,D,O
International and Comparative Education	M,D
International Business	M
International Health	M,D
Kinesiology and Movement Studies	M,D
Landscape Architecture	M
Law	P,M
Leisure Studies	M,D
Linguistics	M,D
Logistics	M,D
Management Information Systems	M,D
Management of Technology	M
Management Strategy and Policy	M,D
Marketing	M,D
Marriage and Family Therapy	M,D
Mass Communication	M,D
Materials Engineering	M,D
Materials Sciences	M,D
Maternal and Child Health	M
Mathematics Education	M
Mathematics	M,D
Mechanical Engineering	M,D
Mechanics	M,D
Medical Physics	M,D*
Medicinal and Pharmaceutical Chemistry	M,D
Medieval and Renaissance Studies	M,D
Microbiology	D
Molecular Biology	M,D
Multilingual and Multicultural Education	M
Music	M,D
Natural Resources	M,D
Neurobiology	M,D
Neuroscience	M,D
Nurse Anesthesia	M
Nurse Midwifery	M
Nursing and Healthcare Administration	M
Nursing—General	M,D
Nutrition	M,D
Occupational Health Nursing	M,D
Oral and Dental Sciences	M,D,O
Pediatric Nursing	M
Pharmaceutical Administration	M,D
Pharmaceutical Sciences	M,D
Pharmacology	M,D
Pharmacy	P,M,D
Philosophy	M,D
Physical Education	M,D,O
Physical Therapy	D
Physics	M,D
Physiology	D
Plant Biology	M,D
Plant Pathology	M,D
Plant Sciences	M,D
Political Science	D
Portuguese	M,D
Psychiatric Nursing	M
Psychology—General	D
Public Affairs	M
Public Health—General	M,D,O
Public Policy	M
Reading Education	M,D,O
Recreation and Park Management	M,D
Religion	M,D
Scandinavian Languages	M,D
School Psychology	M,D,O
Science Education	M
Social Psychology	D
Social Sciences Education	M
Social Work	M,D
Sociology	M,D
Spanish	M,D
Special Education	M,D,O
Sports Management	M,D,O
Statistics	M,D
Structural Biology	D
Student Affairs	M,D,O
Supply Chain Management	M
Systems Engineering	M
Taxation	M
Technology and Public Policy	M
Textile Design	M,D,O
Theater	M,D
Toxicology	M,D
Urban and Regional Planning	M
Veterinary Medicine	P
Veterinary Sciences	M,D
Virology	D
Vocational and Technical Education	M,D,O
Water Resources	M,D
Women's Health Nursing	M
Women's Studies	D

UNIVERSITY OF MISSISSIPPI

Accounting	M,D
American Studies	M
Anthropology	M
Applied Science and Technology	M,D
Art Education	M
Art History	M
Art/Fine Arts	M
Biological and Biomedical Sciences—General	M,D
Business Administration and Management—General	M,D
Chemistry	M,D
Classics	M
Clinical Psychology	M,D
Communication Disorders	M
Computational Sciences	M,D
Counselor Education	M,D,O
Curriculum and Instruction	M,D,O
Economics	M,D
Education—General	M,D,O
Educational Leadership and Administration	M,D,O
Engineering and Applied Sciences—General	M,D
English	M,D
Exercise and Sports Science	M,D
Experimental Psychology	M,D
Family and Consumer Sciences-General	M
French	M
German	M
Higher Education	M,D,O
History	M,D
Journalism	M
Law	P
Legal and Justice Studies	M
Leisure Studies	M,D
Management Information Systems	M,D
Mathematics	M,D
Medicinal and Pharmaceutical Chemistry	M,D
Music	M,D
Pharmaceutical Administration	M,D
Pharmaceutical Sciences	M,D
Pharmacology	M,D
Pharmacy	P
Philosophy	M
Physics	M,D
Political Science	M,D
Psychology—General	M,D
Recreation and Park Management	M,D
Sociology	M
Spanish	M
Student Affairs	M,D,O
Taxation	M,D

UNIVERSITY OF MISSISSIPPI MEDICAL CENTER

Allied Health—General	M
Allopathic Medicine	P
Anatomy	M,D
Biochemistry	M,D*
Biological and Biomedical Sciences—General	M,D
Biophysics	M,D
Clinical Laboratory Sciences/Medical Technology	M,D
Dentistry	P,M,D
Maternal and Child Health	M
Microbiology	M,D
Nursing—General	M,D
Occupational Therapy	M
Oral and Dental Sciences	M,D
Pathology	M,D
Pharmacology	M,D
Physical Therapy	M
Physiology	M,D
Toxicology	M,D

UNIVERSITY OF MISSOURI–COLUMBIA

Accounting	M,D
Adult Education	M,D,O
Aerospace/Aeronautical Engineering	M,D
Agricultural Economics and Agribusiness	M,D
Agricultural Education	M,D,O
Agricultural Engineering	M,D
Agricultural Sciences—General	M,D
Agronomy and Soil Sciences	M,D
Allopathic Medicine	P
Analytical Chemistry	M,D
Anatomy	M
Animal Sciences	M,D
Anthropology	M,D
Applied Mathematics	M
Archaeology	M,D
Architecture	M
Art Education	M,D,O
Art History	M,D
Art/Fine Arts	M
Astronomy	M,D
Atmospheric Sciences	M,D
Biochemistry	M,D
Bioengineering	M,D
Bioinformatics	D
Biological and Biomedical Sciences—General	M,D*
Business Administration and Management—General	M,D
Business Education	M,D,O
Cell Biology	M,D
Chemical Engineering	M,D
Chemistry	M,D
Child and Family Studies	M,D
Civil Engineering	M,D
Classics	M,D
Clothing and Textiles	M
Communication Disorders	M
Communication—General	M,D
Comparative Literature	M,D
Computer Art and Design	M
Computer Science	M,D
Conflict Resolution and Mediation/Peace Studies	M
Consumer Economics	M
Counseling Psychology	M,D,O
Curriculum and Instruction	M,D,O
Early Childhood Education	M,D,O
Ecology	M,D
Economics	M,D
Education of the Gifted	M,D
Education—General	M,D,O
Educational Leadership and Administration	M,D,O
Educational Media/Instructional Technology	M,D,O
Educational Psychology	M,D,O
Electrical Engineering	M,D
Elementary Education	M,D,O
Engineering and Applied Sciences—General	M,D
English Education	M,D,O
English	M,D
Entomology	M,D
Environmental Design	M
Environmental Engineering	M,D
Evolutionary Biology	M,D
Exercise and Sports Science	M,D
Family and Consumer Sciences-General	M,D
Fish, Game, and Wildlife Management	M,D
Food Science and Technology	M,D
Foreign Languages Education	M,D,O
Forestry	M,D
French	M,D
Genetics	M,D
Geography	M
Geology	M,D
Geotechnical Engineering	M,D
German	M
Health Education	M,D,O
Health Informatics	M
Health Physics/Radiological Health	M,D
Health Services Management and Hospital Administration	M
Higher Education	M,D,O
History	M,D
Horticulture	M,D
Hospitality Management	M,D
Human Development	M,D
Immunology	M,D
Industrial/Management Engineering	M,D
Information Studies	M,D,O
Inorganic Chemistry	M,D
Journalism	M,D
Law	P,M
Library Science	M,D,O
Manufacturing Engineering	M,D
Mathematics Education	M,D,O
Mathematics	M,D
Mechanical Engineering	M,D
Medical Physics	M,D
Microbiology	M,D
Music Education	M,D,O
Music	M
Natural Resources	M
Neurobiology	M,D
Neuroscience	M,D
Nuclear Engineering	M,D
Nursing—General	M,D
Nutrition	M,D
Occupational Therapy	M
Organic Chemistry	M,D
Pathobiology	M,D
Pathology	M
Pharmacology	M,D
Philosophy	M,D
Physical Chemistry	M,D
Physical Therapy	M
Physics	M,D
Physiology	M,D
Plant Biology	M,D
Plant Pathology	M,D
Plant Sciences	M,D
Political Science	M,D
Psychology—General	M,D
Public Affairs	M
Public Health—General	M
Reading Education	M,D,O
Recreation and Park Management	M

*M—master's degree; P—first professional degree; D—doctorate; O—other advanced degree; *—Close-Up and/or Announcement or Display in one of the other books in this series*

Religion	M
Romance Languages	M,D
Rural Sociology	M,D
School Psychology	M,D,O
Science Education	M,D,O
Social Sciences Education	M,D,O
Social Work	M
Sociology	M,D
Spanish	M,D
Special Education	M,D
Statistics	M,D
Structural Engineering	M,D
Theater	M,D
Transportation and Highway Engineering	M,D
Veterinary Medicine	P
Veterinary Sciences	M,D
Vocational and Technical Education	M,D,O
Water Resources Engineering	M,D

UNIVERSITY OF MISSOURI–KANSAS CITY

Accounting	M,D
Adult Nursing	M,D
Allopathic Medicine	P
Analytical Chemistry	M,D
Art History	M,D
Art/Fine Arts	M,D
Biochemistry	D
Bioinformatics	M,D
Biological and Biomedical Sciences—General	M,D
Biophysics	D
Business Administration and Management—General	M,D
Cell Biology	D*
Chemistry	M,D
Civil Engineering	M,D
Clinical Psychology	M,D
Computer Engineering	M,D
Computer Science	M,D
Counseling Psychology	M,D,O
Criminal Justice and Criminology	M
Curriculum and Instruction	M,D,O
Dental Hygiene	P,M,D,O
Dentistry	P,M,D,O
Economics	M,D
Education—General	M,D,O
Educational Leadership and Administration	M,D,O
Electrical Engineering	M,D
Engineering and Applied Sciences—General	M,D
English	M,D
Entrepreneurship	M,D
Family Nurse Practitioner Studies	M,D
Geology	M,D
Geosciences	M,D
History	M,D
Inorganic Chemistry	M,D
Interdisciplinary Studies	D
Law	P,M
Maternal and Child/Neonatal Nursing	M,D
Mathematics	M,D
Mechanical Engineering	M,D
Molecular Biology	D*
Music Education	M,D
Music	M,D
Nursing and Healthcare Administration	M,D
Nursing Education	M,D
Nursing—General	M,D
Oral and Dental Sciences	P,M,D,O
Organic Chemistry	M,D
Pediatric Nursing	M,D
Pharmaceutical Sciences	P,M,D
Pharmacy	P,M,D
Physical Chemistry	M,D
Physics	M,D
Political Science	M,D
Polymer Science and Engineering	M,D
Psychology—General	M,D
Public Administration	M,D
Public Affairs	M,D
Reading Education	M,D,O
Romance Languages	M
Social Psychology	M,D
Social Work	M
Sociology	M,D
Software Engineering	M,D
Special Education	M,D,O
Statistics	M,D
Taxation	P,M
Telecommunications	M,D
Theater	M
Women's Health Nursing	M,D

UNIVERSITY OF MISSOURI–ST. LOUIS

Accounting	M,O
Adult Education	M,D,O
Animal Behavior	M,D,O
Applied Mathematics	M,D
Applied Physics	M,D
Astrophysics	M,D
Biochemistry	M,D,O
Biological and Biomedical Sciences—General	M,D,O
Biotechnology	M,D,O
Botany	M,D,O
Business Administration and Management—General	M,O
Cell Biology	M,D,O
Chemistry	M,D
Clinical Psychology	M,D,O
Communication—General	M
Computer Science	M,D
Conflict Resolution and Mediation/Peace Studies	M
Conservation Biology	M,D,O
Counselor Education	M,D
Criminal Justice and Criminology	M,D
Curriculum and Instruction	M,O
Developmental Biology	M,D,O
Early Childhood Education	M,O
Ecology	M,D,O
Economics	M,O
Education—General	M,D,O
Educational Leadership and Administration	M,D,O
Educational Measurement and Evaluation	M,D,O
Educational Psychology	D,O
Elementary Education	M,O
English as a Second Language	M,O
English	M,O
Environmental Management and Policy	M,D,O
Evolutionary Biology	M,D,O
Family Nurse Practitioner Studies	M,D,O
Finance and Banking	M,O
Genetics	M,D,O
Gerontology	M,O
Health Services Management and Hospital Administration	M,O
Higher Education	M,D,O
Human Resources Development	M,O
Human Resources Management	M,O
Industrial and Manufacturing Management	M,O
Industrial and Organizational Psychology	M,D,O
Inorganic Chemistry	M,D
Linguistics	M,O
Logistics	M,D,O
Management Information Systems	M,D
Marketing	M,O
Mathematics	M,D
Middle School Education	M,O
Molecular Biology	M,D,O
Museum Studies	M,O
Music Education	M
Neuroscience	M,D,O
Nonprofit Management	M,O
Nursing—General	M,D,O
Optometry	P
Organic Chemistry	M,D
Philosophy	M
Physical Chemistry	M,D
Physics	M,D
Physiology	M,D,O
Political Science	M,D
Psychology—General	M,D,O
Public Administration	M,D,O
Public Policy	M,D,O
Quantitative Analysis	M,O
Reading Education	M,O
School Psychology	D,O
Secondary Education	M,O
Social Psychology	M,D,O
Social Work	M,O
Sociology	M
Special Education	M,O
Supply Chain Management	M,D,O
Vision Sciences	M,D
Writing	M,O

UNIVERSITY OF MOBILE

Business Administration and Management—General	M
Education—General	M
Marriage and Family Therapy	M
Nursing—General	M
Religion	M
Theology	M

THE UNIVERSITY OF MONTANA

Accounting	M
Analytical Chemistry	M,D
Animal Behavior	M,D,O
Anthropology	M,D
Art/Fine Arts	M
Biochemistry	M,D
Biological and Biomedical Sciences—General	M,D
Business Administration and Management—General	M
Chemistry	M,D
Clinical Psychology	M,D,O
Communication—General	M
Computer Science	M
Counseling Psychology	M,D,O
Counselor Education	M,D,O
Criminal Justice and Criminology	M
Curriculum and Instruction	M,D
Developmental Psychology	M,D,O
Ecology	M,D
Economics	M
Education—General	M,D,O
Educational Leadership and Administration	M,D,O
English Education	M
English	M
Environmental Management and Policy	M
Environmental Sciences	M
Exercise and Sports Science	M
Experimental Psychology	M,D,O
Fish, Game, and Wildlife Management	M,D
Forestry	M,D
French	M
Geographic Information Systems	M
Geography	M
Geology	M,D
Geosciences	M,D
German	M
Health Education	M
Health Promotion	M
History	M,D
Infectious Diseases	D
Inorganic Chemistry	M,D
Interdisciplinary Studies	M,D
Jewish Studies	M
Journalism	M
Law	P
Linguistics	M,D
Mathematics Education	M,D
Mathematics	M,D
Microbiology	M,D
Music Education	M
Music	M
Natural Resources	M,D
Neuroscience	M,D
Organic Chemistry	M,D
Pharmaceutical Sciences	M,D
Pharmacy	P,M,D
Philosophy	M
Physical Chemistry	M,D
Physical Education	M
Physical Therapy	D
Political Science	M
Psychology—General	M,D,O
Public Administration	M
Public Health—General	M,O
Recreation and Park Management	M,D
Rural Planning and Studies	M
Rural Sociology	M
School Psychology	M,D,O
Social Work	M
Sociology	M
Spanish	M
Theater	M
Toxicology	M,D
Writing	M
Zoology	M,D

UNIVERSITY OF MONTEVALLO

Communication Disorders	M
Counselor Education	M
Education—General	M,O
Educational Leadership and Administration	M,O
Elementary Education	M
English	M
Marriage and Family Therapy	M
Secondary Education	M
Social Psychology	M

UNIVERSITY OF NEBRASKA AT KEARNEY

Art Education	M
Biological and Biomedical Sciences—General	M
Business Administration and Management—General	M
Communication Disorders	M
Counselor Education	M,O
Curriculum and Instruction	M
Education—General	M,O
Educational Leadership and Administration	M,O
Educational Media/Instructional Technology	M
English	M
Exercise and Sports Science	M
Foreign Languages Education	M
History	M
Music Education	M
Physical Education	M
Reading Education	M
School Psychology	M,O
Science Education	M
Special Education	M
Writing	M

UNIVERSITY OF NEBRASKA AT OMAHA

Accounting	M
Biological and Biomedical Sciences—General	M
Biopsychology	M,D,O

Business Administration and Management—General	M
Communication Disorders	M
Communication—General	M
Computer Science	M
Counselor Education	M
Criminal Justice and Criminology	M,D
Developmental Psychology	M,D,O
Economics	M
Education—General	M,D,O
Educational Leadership and Administration	M,D,O
Educational Media/Instructional Technology	M,O
Educational Psychology	M,D,O
Elementary Education	M
English as a Second Language	M,O
English	M,O
Foreign Languages Education	M
Geography	M,O
Gerontology	M,O
Health Education	M
History	M
Industrial and Organizational Psychology	M,D,O
Information Science	M,D,O
Management Information Systems	M,D,O
Mathematics	M
Music	M
Physical Education	M
Political Science	M
Psychology—General	M,D,O
Public Administration	M,D,O
Public Health—General	M
Reading Education	M
Recreation and Park Management	M
School Psychology	M,D,O
Secondary Education	M
Social Work	M
Special Education	M
Technical Communication	M,O
Theater	M
Urban Education	M,O
Writing	M,O

UNIVERSITY OF NEBRASKA–LINCOLN

Accounting	M,D
Actuarial Science	M
Adult Education	M,D,O
Advertising and Public Relations	M,D
Agricultural Education	M
Agricultural Engineering	M,D
Agricultural Sciences—General	M,D
Agronomy and Soil Sciences	M,D
Analytical Chemistry	M,D
Animal Sciences	M,D
Anthropology	M
Archaeology	M,D
Architectural Engineering	M,D
Architecture	M,D
Art History	M
Art/Fine Arts	M
Astronomy	M,D
Biochemistry	M,D
Bioengineering	M,D
Bioinformatics	M,D
Biological and Biomedical Sciences—General	M,D
Biopsychology	M,D
Business Administration and Management—General	M,D
Chemical Engineering	M,D
Chemistry	M,D
Child Development	M,D
Civil Engineering	M,D
Classics	M
Clinical Psychology	M,D
Cognitive Sciences	M,D,O
Communication Disorders	M,D
Communication—General	M,D
Comparative Literature	M,D
Computer Engineering	M,D
Computer Science	M,D
Corporate and Organizational Communication	M,D
Counseling Psychology	M,D,O
Curriculum and Instruction	M,D,O
Developmental Psychology	M,D,O
Distance Education Development	M
Early Childhood Education	M,D
Economics	M,D
Educational Leadership and Administration	M,D,O
Educational Measurement and Evaluation	M,D,O
Educational Psychology	M,D,O
Electrical Engineering	M,D
Engineering and Applied Sciences—General	M,D
Engineering Management	M,D
English	M,D
Entomology	M,D
Environmental Engineering	M,D
Exercise and Sports Science	M,D
Family and Consumer Sciences-General	M,D
Finance and Banking	M,D
Food Science and Technology	M,D
French	M,D
Geography	M,D
Geosciences	M,D
German	M,D
Gerontology	M,D
Health Education	M
Health Promotion	M,D
History	M,D
Home Economics Education	M,D
Horticulture	M,D
Human Development	M,D,O
Industrial/Management Engineering	M,D
Information Science	M,D
Inorganic Chemistry	M,D
Interior Design	M,D
Journalism	M
Law	P,M
Legal and Justice Studies	M
Management Information Systems	M
Manufacturing Engineering	M,D
Marketing	M,D
Marriage and Family Therapy	M,D
Mass Communication	M
Materials Engineering	M,D
Materials Sciences	M,D
Mathematics	M,D
Mechanical Engineering	M,D*
Mechanics	M,D
Metallurgical Engineering and Metallurgy	M,D
Music Education	M,D
Music	M,D
Natural Resources	M,D
Nutrition	M,D
Organic Chemistry	M,D
Philosophy	M,D
Physical Chemistry	M,D
Physics	M,D
Psychology—General	M,D
Public Policy	M,D,O
Rhetoric	M,D
School Psychology	M,D,O
Social Psychology	M,D
Sociology	M,D
Spanish	M,D
Special Education	M,D,O
Speech and Interpersonal Communication	M,D
Statistics	M,D
Survey Methodology	M,D
Theater	M
Toxicology	M,D
Urban and Regional Planning	M,D
Veterinary Sciences	M,D
Vocational and Technical Education	M,D,O
Writing	M,D

UNIVERSITY OF NEBRASKA MEDICAL CENTER

Allied Health—General	M,D,O
Allopathic Medicine	P,O
Anatomy	M,D
Biochemistry	M,D
Biological and Biomedical Sciences—General	M,D*
Cancer Biology/Oncology	D
Cell Biology	M,D
Clinical Laboratory Sciences/Medical Technology	M,O
Dentistry	P,M,D,O
Genetics	M,D
Microbiology	M,D
Molecular Biology	M,D
Neuroscience	M,D
Nursing—General	M,D
Nutrition	O
Pathology	M,D
Perfusion	M
Pharmaceutical Sciences	M,D
Pharmacology	M,D
Pharmacy	P
Physical Therapy	D
Physician Assistant Studies	M
Physiology	M,D
Public Health—General	M
Toxicology	M,D

UNIVERSITY OF NEVADA, LAS VEGAS

Accounting	M
Addictions/Substance Abuse Counseling	M,O
Aerospace/Aeronautical Engineering	M,D
Allied Health—General	M,D
Anthropology	M,D
Architecture	M
Art/Fine Arts	M
Astronomy	M,D
Biochemistry	M,D
Biological and Biomedical Sciences—General	M,D
Biomedical Engineering	M,D
Business Administration and Management—General	M
Chemistry	M,D
Civil Engineering	M,D
Communication—General	M
Community Health	M,O
Computer Engineering	M,D
Computer Science	M,D
Construction Management	M
Counselor Education	M,O
Criminal Justice and Criminology	M
Curriculum and Instruction	M,D
Early Childhood Education	M,D,O
Economics	M
Education—General	M,D,O
Educational Leadership and Administration	M,D
Educational Media/Instructional Technology	M,D,O
Educational Psychology	M,D,O
Electrical Engineering	M,D
Emergency Management	M,D,O
Engineering and Applied Sciences—General	M,D
English	M,D
Environmental and Occupational Health	M
Environmental Sciences	M,D
Ethics	M
Exercise and Sports Science	M
Family Nurse Practitioner Studies	M,D,O
Film, Television, and Video Production	M
Forensic Sciences	M,O
Geosciences	M,D
Health Physics/Radiological Health	M
Health Promotion	M
Health Services Management and Hospital Administration	M
Hispanic Studies	M,O
History	M,D
Hospitality Management	M,D,O
Information Science	M,D
Journalism	M
Kinesiology and Movement Studies	M
Law	P
Leisure Studies	M
Management Information Systems	M
Marriage and Family Therapy	M,O
Materials Engineering	M,D
Mathematics	M,D
Mechanical Engineering	M,D
Media Studies	M
Music	M,D
Nonprofit Management	M,D,O
Nuclear Engineering	M,D
Nursing Education	M,D,O
Nursing—General	M,D,O
Physical Education	M,D
Physical Therapy	D
Physics	M,D
Political Science	M,D
Psychology—General	D
Public Administration	M,D,O
Public Affairs	M,D,O
Public Policy	M
Rehabilitation Counseling	M,O
Social Work	M,O
Sociology	M,D
Spanish	M,O
Special Education	M,D,O
Sports Management	M,D
Theater	M
Translation and Interpretation	M,O
Transportation and Highway Engineering	M,D
Water Resources	M
Women's Studies	O
Writing	M,D

UNIVERSITY OF NEVADA, RENO

Accounting	M
Agricultural Economics and Agribusiness	M,D
Agricultural Sciences—General	M,D
Animal Sciences	M
Anthropology	M,D
Applied Economics	M,D
Art/Fine Arts	M
Atmospheric Sciences	M,D
Biochemistry	M,D*
Biological and Biomedical Sciences—General	M
Biomedical Engineering	M,D
Biotechnology	M
Business Administration and Management—General	M
Cell Biology	M,D
Chemical Engineering	M,D
Chemical Physics	D
Chemistry	M,D
Child and Family Studies	M

*M—master's degree; P—first professional degree; D—doctorate; O—other advanced degree; *—Close-Up and/or Announcement or Display in one of the other books in this series*

Civil Engineering	M,D
Clinical Psychology	M,D
Cognitive Sciences	M,D
Communication Disorders	M,D
Computer Engineering	M,D
Computer Science	M,D
Conservation Biology	D
Counselor Education	M,D,O
Criminal Justice and Criminology	M
Curriculum and Instruction	D
Ecology	D
Economics	M
Education—General	M,D,O
Educational Leadership and Administration	M,D,O
Educational Psychology	M,D,O
Electrical Engineering	M,D
Elementary Education	M
Engineering and Applied Sciences—General	M,D
English as a Second Language	M
English	M,D
Environmental and Occupational Health	M,D
Environmental Management and Policy	M
Environmental Sciences	M,D
Evolutionary Biology	D
Finance and Banking	M
Foreign Languages Education	M
French	M
Geochemistry	M,D
Geography	M,D
Geological Engineering	M,D
Geology	M,D
Geophysics	M,D
German	M
History	M,D
Human Development	M
Hydrogeology	M,D
Hydrology	M,D
Journalism	M
Legal and Justice Studies	M,D
Management Information Systems	M
Mathematics Education	M
Mathematics	M
Mechanical Engineering	M,D
Mineral/Mining Engineering	M
Molecular Biology	M,D
Molecular Pharmacology	D
Music	M
Nursing—General	M
Nutrition	M
Philosophy	M
Physics	M,D
Physiology	D
Political Science	M,D
Psychology—General	M,D
Public Administration	M
Public Health—General	M,D
Reading Education	M,D
Secondary Education	M
Social Psychology	D
Social Work	M
Sociology	M
Spanish	M
Special Education	M,D
Speech and Interpersonal Communication	M
Western European Studies	D

UNIVERSITY OF NEW BRUNSWICK FREDERICTON

Anthropology	M
Applied Economics	M
Biological and Biomedical Sciences—General	M,D
Business Administration and Management—General	M
Chemical Engineering	M,D
Chemistry	M,D
Civil Engineering	M,D
Classics	M
Computer Engineering	M,D
Computer Science	M,D
Conflict Resolution and Mediation/Peace Studies	M
Construction Engineering	M,D
Economics	M
Education—General	M,D
Electrical Engineering	M,D
Engineering and Applied Sciences—General	M,D,O
English	M,D
Environmental Engineering	M,D
Environmental Management and Policy	M,D
Exercise and Sports Science	M
Forestry	M,D
Geodetic Sciences	M,D,O
Geology	M,D
Geotechnical Engineering	M,D
Health Services Research	M
History	M,D
Hydrology	M,D
Interdisciplinary Studies	M,D
Law	P
Marketing	M,D
Materials Sciences	M,D
Mathematics	M,D
Mechanical Engineering	M,D
Mechanics	M,D
Nursing Education	M
Nursing—General	M
Philosophy	M
Physical Education	M
Physics	M,D
Political Science	M
Psychology—General	M,D
Public Administration	M
Public Policy	M
Recreation and Park Management	M
Sociology	M,D
Sports Management	M
Statistics	M,D
Structural Engineering	M,D
Surveying Science and Engineering	M,D,O
Sustainable Development	M
Transportation and Highway Engineering	M,D
Water Resources	M,D

UNIVERSITY OF NEW BRUNSWICK SAINT JOHN

Biological and Biomedical Sciences—General	M,D
Business Administration and Management—General	M
Clinical Psychology	M,D
Electronic Commerce	M
Experimental Psychology	M,D
International Business	M
Natural Resources	M
Psychology—General	M,D

UNIVERSITY OF NEW ENGLAND

Addictions/Substance Abuse Counseling	M,O
Biological and Biomedical Sciences—General	M
Education—General	M
Educational Leadership and Administration	O
Educational Measurement and Evaluation	M
Gerontology	M,O
Marine Sciences	M
Nurse Anesthesia	M
Occupational Therapy	M
Osteopathic Medicine	P
Physical Therapy	D
Physician Assistant Studies	M
Public Health—General	M,O
Reading Education	M
Social Work	M,O

UNIVERSITY OF NEW HAMPSHIRE

Accounting	M
Agronomy and Soil Sciences	M
Animal Sciences	M,D
Applied Mathematics	M,D,O
Art/Fine Arts	M
Biochemistry	M,D
Biological and Biomedical Sciences—General	M,D
Business Administration and Management—General	M,O
Chemical Engineering	M,D
Chemistry	M,D
Child and Family Studies	M
Civil Engineering	M,D
Communication Disorders	M,O
Comparative Literature	M,D
Computer Science	M,D
Counselor Education	M,O
Early Childhood Education	M
Economics	M,D*
Education—General	M,D,O
Educational Leadership and Administration	M,O
Electrical Engineering	M,D
Elementary Education	M
English Education	M,D
English	M,D
Environmental Education	M
Environmental Management and Policy	M
Fish, Game, and Wildlife Management	M
Forestry	M
Genetics	M,D
Geochemistry	M
Geology	M
Geosciences	M
Higher Education	M
History	M,D
Hydrology	M
Kinesiology and Movement Studies	M
Legal and Justice Studies	M
Liberal Studies	M
Linguistics	M,D
Logistics	M,D
Management of Technology	M,O
Marriage and Family Therapy	M
Materials Sciences	M,D
Mathematics Education	M,D,O
Mathematics	M,D,O
Mechanical Engineering	M,D
Microbiology	M,D
Museum Studies	M,D
Music Education	M
Music	M
Natural Resources	M,D
Nursing—General	M,O
Nutrition	M,D
Occupational Therapy	M,O
Ocean Engineering	M,D,O
Oceanography	M,D,O
Physics	M,D
Plant Biology	M,D
Political Science	M
Psychology—General	D
Public Administration	M,O
Public Health—General	M,O
Reading Education	M
Recreation and Park Management	M
Science Education	M,D
Secondary Education	M
Social Work	M,O
Sociology	M,D
Spanish	M
Special Education	M,O
Statistics	M,D,O
Water Resources	M
Writing	M,D
Zoology	M,D

UNIVERSITY OF NEW HAVEN

Accounting	M
Advertising and Public Relations	M
Business Administration and Management—General	M
Cell Biology	M*
Computer Science	M
Criminal Justice and Criminology	M
Education—General	M
Electrical Engineering	M
Engineering and Applied Sciences—General	M,O
Engineering Design	M,O
Engineering Management	M
Environmental and Occupational Health	M
Environmental Engineering	M,O
Environmental Sciences	M
Finance and Banking	M
Fire Protection Engineering	M
Forensic Sciences	M
Health Services Management and Hospital Administration	M
Human Resources Management	M
Industrial and Labor Relations	M
Industrial and Organizational Psychology	M,O*
Industrial Hygiene	M
Industrial/Management Engineering	M,O
Information Science	M
International Business	M
Logistics	M,O
Management Information Systems	M
Management of Technology	M
Management Strategy and Policy	M
Marketing	M
Mechanical Engineering	M
Molecular Biology	M
National Security	M*
Nutrition	M
Public Administration	M
Social Psychology	M,O
Software Engineering	M
Sports Management	M
Taxation	M

UNIVERSITY OF NEW MEXICO

Allopathic Medicine	P
American Studies	M,D
Anthropology	M,D
Architecture	M
Art Education	M
Art History	M,D
Art/Fine Arts	M
Biochemistry	M,D
Biological and Biomedical Sciences—General	M,D
Biophysics	M,D
Business Administration and Management—General	M
Cell Biology	M,D
Chemical Engineering	M,D
Chemistry	M,D
Child and Family Studies	M,D
Civil Engineering	M,D
Clinical Laboratory Sciences/Medical Technology	M
Clinical Psychology	M,D
Communication Disorders	M

Communication—General	M,D
Comparative Literature	M,D
Computational Sciences	O
Computer Engineering	M,D
Computer Science	M,D
Construction Management	M
Counselor Education	M,D
Dance	M
Dental Hygiene	M
Economics	M,D
Education—General	M,O
Educational Leadership and Administration	M,D,O
Educational Media/Instructional Technology	M,D,O
Educational Psychology	M,D
Electrical Engineering	M,D*
Elementary Education	M,O
Engineering and Applied Sciences—General	M,D
English	M,D
Exercise and Sports Science	D
Foundations and Philosophy of Education	M,D
French	M,D
Genetics	M,D
Geography	M
Geosciences	M,D
German	M,D
Health Education	M
Historic Preservation	O
History	M,D
Human Resources Management	M
International Business	M
Landscape Architecture	M
Latin American Studies	M,D
Law	P
Linguistics	M,D
Management Information Systems	M
Management of Technology	M
Management Strategy and Policy	M
Manufacturing Engineering	M
Mathematics	M,D
Mechanical Engineering	M,D
Microbiology	M,D
Molecular Biology	M,D
Multilingual and Multicultural Education	D,O
Music	M
Nanotechnology	M,D
Neuroscience	M,D
Nuclear Engineering	M,D
Nursing—General	M,D
Nutrition	M
Occupational Therapy	M
Optical Sciences	M,D
Organizational Management	M
Pathology	M,D
Pharmaceutical Sciences	M,D
Pharmacy	P
Philosophy	M,D
Physical Education	M,D,O
Physical Therapy	M
Physics	M,D
Physiology	M,D
Planetary and Space Sciences	M,D
Political Science	M,D
Portuguese	M,D
Psychology—General	M,D
Public Administration	M
Public Health—General	M
Secondary Education	M,O
Sociology	M,D
Spanish	M,D
Special Education	M,D,O
Statistics	M,D
Taxation	M
Theater	M
Toxicology	M,D
Urban and Regional Planning	M
Urban Design	O
Water Resources	M
Women's Studies	O
Writing	M,D

UNIVERSITY OF NEW ORLEANS

Accounting	M
Art/Fine Arts	M
Arts Administration	M
Biological and Biomedical Sciences—General	M,D
Business Administration and Management—General	M
Chemistry	M,D
Computer Science	M
Counselor Education	M,D,O
Curriculum and Instruction	M,D,O
Economics	D
Education—General	M,D,O
Educational Leadership and Administration	M,D,O
Engineering and Applied Sciences—General	M,D,O
Engineering Management	M,O
English Education	M
English	M
Environmental Sciences	M
Film, Television, and Video Production	M
Finance and Banking	M,D
Geography	M
Geosciences	M
Health Services Management and Hospital Administration	M
History	M
Hospitality Management	M
Mathematics	M
Mechanical Engineering	M
Music	M
Physics	M,D
Political Science	M,D
Psychology—General	M,D
Public Administration	M
Romance Languages	M
Social Sciences Education	M
Sociology	M
Special Education	M,D,O
Taxation	M
Theater	M
Travel and Tourism	M
Urban and Regional Planning	M
Urban Studies	M,D

UNIVERSITY OF NORTH ALABAMA

Business Administration and Management—General	M
Counselor Education	M
Criminal Justice and Criminology	M
Education—General	M,O
Educational Leadership and Administration	O
Elementary Education	M,O
English	M
History	M
Nursing—General	M
Secondary Education	M
Special Education	M

THE UNIVERSITY OF NORTH CAROLINA AT ASHEVILLE

Liberal Studies	M

THE UNIVERSITY OF NORTH CAROLINA AT CHAPEL HILL

Accounting	M,D
Adult Nursing	M,D,O
Allied Health—General	M,D
Allopathic Medicine	P
Anthropology	M,D
Archaeology	M,D
Art History	M,D
Art/Fine Arts	M
Astronomy	M,D
Astrophysics	M,D
Athletic Training and Sports Medicine	M
Atmospheric Sciences	M,D
Biochemistry	M,D
Biological and Biomedical Sciences—General	M,D*
Biomedical Engineering	M,D
Biophysics	M,D
Biostatistics	M,D
Botany	M,D
Business Administration and Management—General	M,D
Cell Biology	D
Chemistry	M,D
Classics	M,D
Clinical Psychology	D
Cognitive Sciences	D
Communication Disorders	M,D
Communication—General	M,D
Community Health Nursing	M
Comparative Literature	M,D
Computer Science	M,D*
Counselor Education	M
Curriculum and Instruction	M,D
Dental Hygiene	M,D
Dentistry	P
Developmental Biology	M,D
Developmental Psychology	D
Early Childhood Education	M,D
East European and Russian Studies	M
Ecology	M,D
Economics	M,D
Education—General	M,D
Educational Leadership and Administration	M,D
Educational Measurement and Evaluation	M,D
Educational Psychology	M,D
English Education	M
English	M,D
Environmental and Occupational Health	M,D
Environmental Engineering	M,D
Environmental Management and Policy	M,D
Environmental Sciences	M,D
Epidemiology	M,D
Evolutionary Biology	M,D
Exercise and Sports Science	M
Experimental Psychology	D
Family Nurse Practitioner Studies	M,D,O
Finance and Banking	D
Folklore	M
Foreign Languages Education	M
French	M,D
Genetics	M,D
Geography	M,D
Geology	M,D
German	M,D
Health Education	M,D
Health Promotion	M
Health Services Management and Hospital Administration	M,D
History	M,D
Immunology	M,D
Industrial Hygiene	M,D
Information Studies	M,D,O
Italian	M,D
Kinesiology and Movement Studies	M,D
Latin American Studies	M,D,O
Law	P
Leisure Studies	M
Library Science	M,D,O
Linguistics	M,D
Management Information Systems	D
Management Strategy and Policy	D
Marine Sciences	M,D
Marketing	D
Mass Communication	M,D
Materials Sciences	M,D
Maternal and Child Health	M,D
Mathematics Education	M
Mathematics	M,D
Microbiology	M,D
Molecular Biology	M,D
Molecular Physiology	D
Music Education	M
Music	M,D
Neurobiology	D
Nursing and Healthcare Administration	M,D,O
Nursing—General	M,D,O
Nutrition	M,D
Occupational Health Nursing	M
Occupational Therapy	M,D
Operations Research	M,D
Oral and Dental Sciences	M,D
Organizational Behavior	D
Pathology	D
Pediatric Nursing	M,D,O
Pharmaceutical Sciences	M,D
Pharmacology	D
Philosophy	M,D
Physical Education	M
Physical Therapy	M,D
Physics	M,D
Political Science	M,D
Portuguese	M,D
Psychiatric Nursing	M,D,O
Psychology—General	D
Public Administration	M
Public Health—General	M,D
Public Policy	D
Reading Education	M,D
Recreation and Park Management	M
Rehabilitation Counseling	M,D
Religion	M,D
Romance Languages	M,D
Russian	M,D
School Psychology	M,D
Science Education	M
Secondary Education	M
Slavic Languages	M,D
Social Psychology	D
Social Sciences Education	M
Social Work	M,D
Sociology	M,D
Spanish	M,D
Sports Management	M
Statistics	M,D
Theater	M
Toxicology	M,D
Urban and Regional Planning	M,D
Women's Health Nursing	M,D,O

THE UNIVERSITY OF NORTH CAROLINA AT CHARLOTTE

Accounting	M
Adult Education	D
Adult Nursing	M
Applied Mathematics	M,D
Applied Physics	M,D
Architecture	M
Art Education	M
Biological and Biomedical Sciences—General	M,D
Business Administration and Management—General	M,D
Chemistry	M
Child Development	M,D
Civil Engineering	M,D
Clinical Psychology	M
Communication—General	M
Computer Engineering	M,D
Computer Science	M
Counselor Education	M,D
Criminal Justice and Criminology	M
Curriculum and Instruction	M,D,O
Dance	M

*M—master's degree; P—first professional degree; D—doctorate; O—other advanced degree; *—Close-Up and/or Announcement or Display in one of the other books in this series*

Economics	M
Education of the Gifted	M,D
Education—General	M
Educational Leadership and Administration	M,D,O
Educational Media/Instructional Technology	M,D,O
Electrical Engineering	M,D
Elementary Education	M
Engineering and Applied Sciences—General	M,D*
Engineering Management	M
English as a Second Language	M
English Education	M
English	M
Environmental Engineering	D
Exercise and Sports Science	M
Foreign Languages Education	M
Geography	M,D
Geosciences	M
Gerontology	M
Health Psychology	D
Health Services Management and Hospital Administration	M
Health Services Research	D
History	M
Industrial and Organizational Psychology	M,D
Information Science	M,D
Kinesiology and Movement Studies	M
Latin American Studies	M
Liberal Studies	M
Marketing	M
Mathematical and Computational Finance	M
Mathematics Education	M
Mathematics	M,D*
Mechanical Engineering	M,D
Middle School Education	M
Music Education	M
Nurse Anesthesia	M
Nursing—General	M
Optical Sciences	M,D
Psychology—General	M,D
Public Administration	M
Public Health—General	M
Public Policy	D
Reading Education	M
Religion	M
Secondary Education	M
Social Psychology	M
Social Work	M
Sociology	M
Spanish	M
Special Education	M,D
Sports Management	M
Systems Engineering	D
Systems Science	M,D
Theater	M

THE UNIVERSITY OF NORTH CAROLINA AT GREENSBORO

Accounting	M,O
Adult Education	M,D,O
Adult Nursing	M,D,O
Applied Economics	M
Architecture	M,O
Art/Fine Arts	M
Biochemistry	M
Biological and Biomedical Sciences—General	M
Business Administration and Management—General	M,O
Chemistry	M
Child and Family Studies	M,D
Classics	M
Clinical Psychology	M,D
Cognitive Sciences	M,D
Communication Disorders	M,D
Communication—General	M
Community Health	M,D
Computer Science	M
Conflict Resolution and Mediation/Peace Studies	M,O
Counseling Psychology	M,D,O
Counselor Education	M,D,O
Criminal Justice and Criminology	M
Curriculum and Instruction	M,D,O
Dance	M
Developmental Psychology	M,D
Early Childhood Education	M,D,O
Economic Development	M,D,O
Economics	D
Education—General	M,D,O
Educational Leadership and Administration	M,D,O
Educational Measurement and Evaluation	D
Educational Media/Instructional Technology	M,D,O
Elementary Education	D
English as a Second Language	M,D,O
English Education	M,D
English	M,D
Exercise and Sports Science	M,D
Family and Consumer Sciences-General	M,D,O
Film, Television, and Video Production	M
Finance and Banking	M,O
Foreign Languages Education	M,D,O
French	M
Gender Studies	M,O
Genetic Counseling	M
Geographic Information Systems	M,D,O
Geography	M,D,O
Gerontological Nursing	M,D,O
Gerontology	M,O
Higher Education	D
Hispanic Studies	M,O
Historic Preservation	M,O
History	M,D,O
Human Development	M,D
Information Studies	M
Interior Design	M,O
Liberal Studies	M
Library Science	M
Management Information Systems	M,D,O
Marketing	M,D
Marriage and Family Therapy	M,D,O
Mathematics Education	M,D,O
Mathematics	M,D
Media Studies	M
Middle School Education	M,D,O
Multilingual and Multicultural Education	M,D,O
Museum Studies	M,D,O
Music Education	M,D
Music	M,D
Nonprofit Management	M,O
Nurse Anesthesia	M,D,O
Nursing and Healthcare Administration	M,D,O
Nursing Education	M,D,O
Nursing—General	M,D,O
Nutrition	M,D
Political Science	M,O
Psychology—General	M,D
Public Affairs	M,O
Reading Education	M,D,O
Recreation and Park Management	M
Rhetoric	M,D
School Psychology	M,D,O
Science Education	M,D,O
Social Psychology	M,D
Social Sciences Education	M,D,O
Social Work	M
Sociology	M
Spanish	M,O
Special Education	M,D,O
Supply Chain Management	M,D,O
Taxation	M,O
Technical Writing	M,D,O
Textile Design	M,D
Theater	M
Women's Studies	M,D,O
Writing	M

THE UNIVERSITY OF NORTH CAROLINA AT PEMBROKE

Art Education	M
Business Administration and Management—General	M
Counselor Education	M
Education—General	M
Educational Leadership and Administration	M
Elementary Education	M
English Education	M
Mathematics Education	M
Middle School Education	M
Music Education	M
Physical Education	M
Public Administration	M
Reading Education	M
Science Education	M
Social Sciences Education	M

UNIVERSITY OF NORTH CAROLINA SCHOOL OF THE ARTS

Film, Television, and Video Production	M
Music	M
Theater	M

THE UNIVERSITY OF NORTH CAROLINA WILMINGTON

Accounting	M
Biological and Biomedical Sciences—General	M,D
Business Administration and Management—General	M
Chemistry	M
Computer Science	M
Criminal Justice and Criminology	M
Curriculum and Instruction	M
Education—General	M,D
Educational Leadership and Administration	M,D
Educational Media/Instructional Technology	M
Elementary Education	M
English	M
Environmental Education	M
Environmental Management and Policy	M
Family Nurse Practitioner Studies	M
Geology	M
Geosciences	M
Gerontology	M
Hispanic Studies	M,O
History	M
Liberal Studies	M
Marine Biology	M,D
Marine Sciences	M,D
Mathematics	M
Middle School Education	M
Nursing Education	M
Nursing—General	M
Psychology—General	M
Public Administration	M
Reading Education	M
Social Work	M
Sociology	M
Systems Science	M
Writing	M

UNIVERSITY OF NORTH DAKOTA

Accounting	M
Allopathic Medicine	P
Anatomy	M,D
Applied Economics	M
Art/Fine Arts	M
Atmospheric Sciences	M,D
Aviation	M
Biochemistry	M,D
Biological and Biomedical Sciences—General	M,D
Botany	M,D
Business Administration and Management—General	M
Chemical Engineering	M
Chemistry	M,D
Civil Engineering	M
Clinical Laboratory Sciences/Medical Technology	M
Clinical Psychology	M,D
Communication Disorders	M,D
Communication—General	M,D
Computer Science	M
Counseling Psychology	M
Criminal Justice and Criminology	D
Early Childhood Education	M
Ecology	M,D
Education—General	M,D,O
Educational Leadership and Administration	M,D,O
Educational Measurement and Evaluation	D
Educational Media/Instructional Technology	M
Electrical Engineering	M
Elementary Education	M,D
Engineering and Applied Sciences—General	D
English	M,D
Entomology	M,D
Environmental Biology	M,D
Environmental Engineering	M
Experimental Psychology	M,D
Fish, Game, and Wildlife Management	M,D
Forensic Psychology	M,D
Genetics	M,D
Geography	M
Geological Engineering	M
Geology	M,D
Geosciences	M,D
History	M,D
Immunology	M,D
Kinesiology and Movement Studies	M
Law	P
Linguistics	M
Mathematics	M
Mechanical Engineering	M
Microbiology	M,D
Mineral/Mining Engineering	M
Music Education	M,D
Music	M,D
Nursing—General	M,D
Occupational Therapy	M
Pharmacology	M,D
Physical Therapy	M,D
Physician Assistant Studies	M
Physics	M,D
Physiology	M,D
Planetary and Space Sciences	M
Psychology—General	M,D
Public Administration	M
Reading Education	M
Secondary Education	D
Social Work	M
Sociology	M
Special Education	M,D
Structural Engineering	M
Theater	M
Zoology	M,D

UNIVERSITY OF NORTHERN BRITISH COLUMBIA

Community Health	M,D,O
Computer Science	M,D,O
Disability Studies	M,D,O
Education—General	M,D,O
Environmental Management and Policy	M,D,O
Gender Studies	M,D,O
History	M,D,O
Interdisciplinary Studies	M,D,O
International Affairs	M,D,O
Mathematics	M,D,O
Natural Resources	M,D,O
Political Science	M,D,O
Psychology—General	M,D,O
Social Work	M,D,O

UNIVERSITY OF NORTHERN COLORADO

Applied Statistics	M,D
Art/Fine Arts	M
Biological and Biomedical Sciences—General	M
Chemistry	M,D
Communication Disorders	M,D
Communication—General	M
Counseling Psychology	D
Counselor Education	M,D
Early Childhood Education	M,D
Education—General	M,D,O
Educational Leadership and Administration	M,D,O
Educational Measurement and Evaluation	M,D
Educational Media/Instructional Technology	M,D
Educational Psychology	M,D
English	M
Exercise and Sports Science	M,D
Family Nurse Practitioner Studies	M,D
Foreign Languages Education	M
Geosciences	M
Gerontology	M
Health Education	M
Higher Education	D
History	M
Library Science	M
Mathematics Education	M,D
Mathematics	M,D
Music Education	M,D
Music	M,D
Nursing Education	M,D
Nursing—General	M,D
Physical Education	M,D
Psychology—General	M,D
Public Health—General	M
Reading Education	M
Rehabilitation Counseling	M,D
School Psychology	D,O
Science Education	M,D
Sociology	M
Spanish	M
Special Education	M,D
Sports Management	M,D
Student Affairs	D

UNIVERSITY OF NORTHERN IOWA

Accounting	M
Art Education	M
Art/Fine Arts	M
Biological and Biomedical Sciences—General	M
Business Administration and Management—General	M
Chemistry	M
Communication Disorders	M
Communication—General	M
Community Health	M,D
Computer Science	M
Counselor Education	M,D
Criminal Justice and Criminology	M
Curriculum and Instruction	M,D
Early Childhood Education	M
Education—General	M,D,O
Educational Leadership and Administration	M,D
Educational Media/Instructional Technology	M
Educational Psychology	M,O
Elementary Education	M
English as a Second Language	M
English	M
Environmental Sciences	M
French	M
Gender Studies	M
Geography	M
German	M
Health Education	M,D
Higher Education	M
History	M
Leisure Studies	M,D
Mathematics Education	M
Mathematics	M
Middle School Education	M
Music Education	M
Music	M
Nonprofit Management	M
Physical Education	M
Physics	M
Political Science	M
Psychology—General	M
Public Policy	M
Reading Education	M
Rehabilitation Sciences	M,D
School Psychology	M,O
Science Education	M
Social Sciences	M
Social Work	M
Sociology	M
Spanish	M
Special Education	M,D
Sports Management	M,D
Student Affairs	M
Vocational and Technical Education	M,D
Women's Studies	M

UNIVERSITY OF NORTH FLORIDA

Accounting	M
Allied Health—General	M,O
Biological and Biomedical Sciences—General	M
Business Administration and Management—General	M
Communication Disorders	M
Community Health	M,O
Computer Science	M
Counseling Psychology	M
Counselor Education	M
Criminal Justice and Criminology	M
Education—General	M,D
Educational Leadership and Administration	M,D
Elementary Education	M
English	M
Ethics	M,O
Gerontology	M,O
Health Services Management and Hospital Administration	M,O
Health Services Research	M,O
History	M
Information Science	M
Mathematics	M
Nursing—General	M,O
Nutrition	M,O
Philosophy	M,O
Physical Therapy	M
Psychology—General	M
Public Administration	M
Public Health—General	M,O
Rehabilitation Counseling	M,O
Secondary Education	M
Sociology	M
Special Education	M
Statistics	M
Writing	M

UNIVERSITY OF NORTH TEXAS

Accounting	M,D
Anthropology	M
Applied Arts and Design—General	M
Applied Economics	M
Art Education	M,D,O
Art History	M,D,O
Art/Fine Arts	M
Biochemistry	M,D
Biological and Biomedical Sciences—General	M,D
Business Administration and Management—General	M,D
Chemistry	M,D
Child and Family Studies	M,O
Clinical Psychology	M,D
Clothing and Textiles	M
Communication Disorders	M,D
Communication—General	M
Community Health	M,D
Computer Education	M,D
Computer Engineering	M,D
Computer Science	M,D
Counseling Psychology	M,D,O
Counselor Education	M,D,O
Criminal Justice and Criminology	M
Curriculum and Instruction	M,D
Early Childhood Education	M,D,O
Economics	M
Education—General	M,D,O
Educational Leadership and Administration	M,D
Educational Measurement and Evaluation	D
Educational Media/Instructional Technology	D
Educational Psychology	M
Electrical Engineering	M
Engineering and Applied Sciences—General	M
English	M,D
Environmental Sciences	M,D
Experimental Psychology	M,D
Film, Television, and Video Production	M
Finance and Banking	M,D
French	M
Geography	M
Gerontology	M,D,O
Health Psychology	M,D
Higher Education	M,D,O
History	M,D
Hospitality Management	M
Human Development	M,O
Industrial and Labor Relations	M
Information Studies	M,D
Interdisciplinary Studies	M
International and Comparative Education	M,D
Journalism	M,O
Kinesiology and Movement Studies	M
Leisure Studies	M,O
Library Science	M,D
Management Information Systems	M,D
Marketing	D
Marriage and Family Therapy	M,D,O
Materials Sciences	M,D
Mathematics	M,D
Molecular Biology	M,D
Museum Studies	M,D,O
Music Education	M,D
Music	M,D
Philosophy	M,D
Physics	M,D
Political Science	M,D
Psychology—General	M,D
Public Administration	M,D
Quantitative Analysis	M,D
Reading Education	M,D
Real Estate	M,D
Recreation and Park Management	M,O
Rehabilitation Counseling	M
Rehabilitation Sciences	M
Religion	M,D
School Psychology	M
Secondary Education	M,O
Social Psychology	M,D,O
Sociology	M,D
Spanish	M
Special Education	M,D,O
Taxation	M,D
Vocational and Technical Education	M,D
Writing	M,D

UNIVERSITY OF NORTH TEXAS HEALTH SCIENCE CENTER AT FORT WORTH

Anatomy	M,D
Biochemistry	M,D
Biological and Biomedical Sciences—General	M,D
Biostatistics	M,D
Biotechnology	M,D
Community Health	M,D
Environmental and Occupational Health	M,D
Epidemiology	M,D
Forensic Sciences	M,D
Genetics	M,D
Health Services Management and Hospital Administration	M,D
Immunology	M,D
Microbiology	M,D
Molecular Biology	M,D
Osteopathic Medicine	P,M
Pharmacology	M,D
Physician Assistant Studies	M
Physiology	M,D
Public Health—General	M,D
Science Education	M,D

UNIVERSITY OF NOTRE DAME

Accounting	M
Aerospace/Aeronautical Engineering	M,D
Applied Arts and Design—General	M
Applied Mathematics	M,D
Architecture	M
Art History	M
Art/Fine Arts	M
Biochemistry	M,D
Bioengineering	M,D
Biological and Biomedical Sciences—General	M,D
Business Administration and Management—General	M
Cell Biology	M,D
Chemical Engineering	M,D
Chemistry	M,D
Civil Engineering	M,D
Cognitive Sciences	D
Comparative Literature	D
Computer Engineering	M,D
Computer Science	M,D
Conflict Resolution and Mediation/Peace Studies	M,D
Counseling Psychology	D
Developmental Psychology	D
Ecology	M,D
Economics	M,D
Education—General	M
Electrical Engineering	M,D*
Engineering and Applied Sciences—General	M,D
English	M,D
Environmental Engineering	M,D
Evolutionary Biology	M,D
French	M

*M—master's degree; P—first professional degree; D—doctorate; O—other advanced degree; *—Close-Up and/or Announcement or Display in one of the other books in this series*

Genetics	M,D
Geosciences	M,D
Graphic Design	M
History of Science and Technology	M,D
History	M,D
Industrial Design	M
Inorganic Chemistry	M,D
Italian	M
Latin American Studies	M
Law	P,M,D
Mathematics	M,D
Mechanical Engineering	M,D
Medieval and Renaissance Studies	M,D
Molecular Biology	M,D
Nonprofit Management	M
Organic Chemistry	M,D
Parasitology	M,D
Philosophy	D
Photography	M
Physical Chemistry	M,D
Physics	M,D
Physiology	M,D
Political Science	D
Psychology—General	D
Religion	M
Romance Languages	M
Sociology	D
Spanish	M
Theology	P,M,D
Writing	M

UNIVERSITY OF OKLAHOMA

Accounting	M
Adult Education	M,D
Advertising and Public Relations	M
Aerospace/Aeronautical Engineering	M,D
American Indian/Native American Studies	M
Anthropology	M,D
Applied Arts and Design—General	M
Architecture	M
Art History	M
Art/Fine Arts	M
Astrophysics	M,D
Biochemistry	M,D
Bioengineering	M,D
Botany	M,D
Business Administration and Management—General	M,D*
Chemical Engineering	M,D
Chemistry	M,D
Civil Engineering	M,D
Communication—General	M,D
Computer Engineering	M,D
Computer Science	M,D
Counseling Psychology	D
Counselor Education	M
Curriculum and Instruction	M,D,O
Dance	M
Early Childhood Education	M,D,O
Ecology	D
Economics	M,D
Education—General	M,D,O
Educational Leadership and Administration	M,D
Educational Psychology	M,D
Electrical Engineering	M,D
Elementary Education	M,D,O
Engineering and Applied Sciences—General	M,D
Engineering Physics	M,D
English Education	M,D,O
English	M,D
Environmental and Occupational Health	M,D
Environmental Engineering	M,D
Environmental Sciences	M,D
Evolutionary Biology	D
Exercise and Sports Science	M,D
Film, Television, and Video Production	M
Foundations and Philosophy of Education	M,D
French	M,D
Geography	M,D
Geological Engineering	M,D
Geology	M,D
Geophysics	M
Geotechnical Engineering	M,D
German	M
Hazardous Materials Management	M,D
Health Services Management and Hospital Administration	M
Higher Education	M,D
History of Science and Technology	M,D
History	M,D
Human Services	M
Industrial/Management Engineering	M,D
Information Studies	M,O
Interdisciplinary Studies	M,D
International Affairs	M
International Business	M
Journalism	M
Landscape Architecture	M
Law	P
Liberal Studies	M
Library Science	M,O
Management Information Systems	M
Management Strategy and Policy	M
Mass Communication	M
Mathematics Education	M,D,O
Mathematics	M,D*
Mechanical Engineering	M,D
Meteorology	M,D
Microbiology	M,D
Multilingual and Multicultural Education	M,D,O
Museum Studies	M
Music Education	M,D
Music	M,D
Natural Resources	M,D
Neurobiology	D
Organizational Behavior	M
Petroleum Engineering	M,D
Philosophy	M,D
Photography	M
Physics	M,D
Political Science	M,D
Psychology—General	M,D
Public Administration	M
Reading Education	M,D,O
School Psychology	M,D
Science Education	M,D,O
Secondary Education	M,D,O
Social Psychology	M
Social Sciences Education	M,D,O
Social Work	M
Sociology	M,D
Spanish	M,D
Special Education	M,D
Structural Engineering	M,D
Telecommunications	M
Theater	M
Urban and Regional Planning	M
Water Resources	M,D
Writing	M
Zoology	M,D*

UNIVERSITY OF OKLAHOMA HEALTH SCIENCES CENTER

Allied Health—General	M,D,O
Allopathic Medicine	P
Biochemistry	M,D
Biological and Biomedical Sciences—General	M,D
Biopsychology	M,D
Biostatistics	M,D
Cell Biology	M,D
Communication Disorders	M,D,O
Dentistry	P,O
Environmental and Occupational Health	M,D
Epidemiology	M,D
Genetic Counseling	M
Health Education	D
Health Physics/Radiological Health	M,D
Health Promotion	M,D
Health Services Management and Hospital Administration	M,D
Immunology	M,D
Medical Physics	M,D
Microbiology	M,D
Molecular Biology	M,D
Neuroscience	M,D
Nursing—General	M
Nutrition	M
Occupational Therapy	M
Oral and Dental Sciences	M
Pathology	D
Pharmaceutical Sciences	M,D
Pharmacy	P
Physical Therapy	M
Physiology	M,D
Public Health—General	M,D
Radiation Biology	M,D
Rehabilitation Sciences	M
Special Education	M,D,O

UNIVERSITY OF OREGON

Accounting	M,D
Anthropology	M,D
Architecture	M
Art History	M,D
Art/Fine Arts	M
Arts Administration	M*
Asian Languages	M,D
Asian Studies	M
Biochemistry	M,D
Biological and Biomedical Sciences—General	M,D
Biopsychology	M,D
Business Administration and Management—General	M,D
Chemistry	M,D
Chinese	M,D
Classics	M
Clinical Psychology	D
Cognitive Sciences	M,D
Communication—General	M,D
Comparative Literature	M,D
Computer Science	M,D*
Dance	M
Developmental Psychology	M,D
Ecology	M,D
Economics	M,D
Education—General	M,D
English	M,D
Environmental Management and Policy	M,D
Evolutionary Biology	M,D
Finance and Banking	D
Folklore	M
French	M
Genetics	M,D
Geography	M,D
Geology	M,D
German	M,D
Historic Preservation	M
History	M,D
Information Science	M,D
Interdisciplinary Studies	M
Interior Design	M
International Affairs	M
Italian	M
Japanese	M,D
Journalism	M,D
Landscape Architecture	M
Law	P,M
Linguistics	M,D
Management Information Systems	M
Marine Biology	M,D
Marketing	D
Mathematics	M,D
Molecular Biology	M,D
Music Education	M,D
Music	M,D
Neuroscience	M,D
Philosophy	M,D
Physics	M,D
Physiology	M,D
Political Science	M,D
Psychology—General	M,D
Public Policy	M
Quantitative Analysis	M
Romance Languages	M,D
Russian	M
Social Psychology	M,D
Sociology	M,D
Spanish	M
Theater	M,D
Urban and Regional Planning	M
Writing	M

UNIVERSITY OF OTTAWA

Aerospace/Aeronautical Engineering	M,D
Allopathic Medicine	P,M,D
Anthropology	M
Biochemistry	M,D
Biological and Biomedical Sciences—General	M,D
Biomedical Engineering	M
Business Administration and Management—General	M*
Canadian Studies	D
Cell Biology	M,D
Chemical Engineering	M,D
Chemistry	M,D
Civil Engineering	M,D
Classics	M,D
Communication Disorders	M
Communication—General	M
Community Health	M,D,O
Computer Engineering	M,D
Computer Science	M,D
Criminal Justice and Criminology	M,D
Economics	M,D
Education—General	M,D,O
Electrical Engineering	M,D
Electronic Commerce	M,D,O
Engineering and Applied Sciences—General	M,D,O
Engineering Management	M,O
English	M,D
Epidemiology	M
Finance and Banking	D,O
French	M,D
Geography	M,D
Geosciences	M,D
Health Services Management and Hospital Administration	M
Health Services Research	D,O
History	M,D
Immunology	M,D
Information Science	M,O
Interdisciplinary Studies	D,O
International Development	M
Kinesiology and Movement Studies	M
Law	M,D
Linguistics	M,D
Mathematics	M,D
Mechanical Engineering	M,D
Microbiology	M,D
Molecular Biology	M,D
Music Education	M,O
Music	M,O
Nursing—General	M,D,O
Philosophy	M,D
Physics	M,D
Political Science	M,D
Project Management	M,O
Psychology—General	D
Public Administration	D,O
Public Health—General	D
Rehabilitation Sciences	M
Religion	M,D
Social Work	M
Sociology	M
Spanish	M,D
Statistics	M,D
Systems Science	M,D,O

Theater	M
Translation and Interpretation	M,D
Women's Studies	M

UNIVERSITY OF PENNSYLVANIA

Accounting	M,D
Acute Care/Critical Care Nursing	M
Adult Nursing	M
Allopathic Medicine	P
Anthropology	M,D
Applied Economics	D
Applied Mathematics	D
Archaeology	M,D
Architecture	M,D,O*
Art History	M,D
Art/Fine Arts	M
Asian Studies	M,D
Astrophysics	M,D
Biochemistry	D
Bioengineering	M,D
Biological and Biomedical Sciences—General	M,D
Biostatistics	M,D
Biotechnology	M*
Business Administration and Management—General	M,D
Cancer Biology/Oncology	D
Cell Biology	D
Chemical Engineering	M,D
Chemistry	M,D
Classics	M,D
Communication—General	D
Comparative Literature	M,D
Computational Biology	D
Computational Sciences	D
Computer Art and Design	M
Computer Science	M,D
Counseling Psychology	M,D
Criminal Justice and Criminology	M,D
Demography and Population Studies	M,D
Dentistry	P
Developmental Biology	D
Economics	M,D
Education—General	M,D*
Educational Leadership and Administration	M,D
Educational Measurement and Evaluation	M,D
Educational Media/Instructional Technology	M
Educational Psychology	M,D
Electrical Engineering	M,D
Elementary Education	M
Engineering and Applied Sciences—General	M,D,O*
English as a Second Language	M,D
English	M,D
Environmental Management and Policy	M
Environmental Sciences	M,D
Epidemiology	M,D
Ethics	M,D
Family Nurse Practitioner Studies	M,O
Finance and Banking	M,D
French	M,D
Genetics	D
Genomic Sciences	D
Geosciences	M,D
German	M,D
Health Services Management and Hospital Administration	M,D
Historic Preservation	M,O
History of Science and Technology	M,D
History	M,D
Human Development	M,D
Immunology	D
Information Science	M,D
Insurance	M,D
International Affairs	M
International and Comparative Education	M,D
International Business	M
Italian	M,D
Landscape Architecture	M,O
Law	P,M,D
Legal and Justice Studies	M,D
Liberal Studies	M
Linguistics	M,D
Management Information Systems	M,D
Management of Technology	M
Marketing	M,D
Materials Engineering	M,D
Materials Sciences	M,D
Maternal and Child/Neonatal Nursing	M,O
Mathematics	M,D
Mechanical Engineering	M,D
Mechanics	M,D
Medical Physics	M,D
Microbiology	D
Molecular Biology	D
Molecular Biophysics	D
Multilingual and Multicultural Education	M,D
Music	M,D
Near and Middle Eastern Studies	M,D
Neuroscience	D
Nurse Anesthesia	M
Nurse Midwifery	M
Nursing and Healthcare Administration	M,D
Nursing—General	M,D,O
Occupational Health Nursing	M
Oncology Nursing	M
Organizational Behavior	M
Organizational Management	M
Parasitology	D
Pediatric Nursing	M
Pharmacology	D
Philosophy	M,D
Physics	M,D
Physiology	D
Political Science	M,D
Psychiatric Nursing	M
Psychology—General	D
Public Administration	M*
Public Policy	M,D
Reading Education	M,D
Real Estate	M,D
Religion	D
Romance Languages	M,D
Secondary Education	M
Social Work	M,D*
Sociology	M,D
Spanish	M,D
Statistics	M,D
Systems Engineering	M,D
Telecommunications Management	M
Telecommunications	M
Urban and Regional Planning	M,D,O
Urban Design	D
Veterinary Medicine	P
Virology	D
Women's Health Nursing	M
Writing	M,D

UNIVERSITY OF PHOENIX

Accounting	M
Adult Education	M
Business Administration and Management—General	M,D
Community Health	M
Computer Education	M
Criminal Justice and Criminology	M
Curriculum and Instruction	M
Early Childhood Education	M
Education—General	M,D
Educational Leadership and Administration	M
Educational Media/Instructional Technology	M
Electronic Commerce	M
Elementary Education	M
English as a Second Language	M
English Education	M
Family Nurse Practitioner Studies	M
Gerontology	M
Health Informatics	M
Health Services Management and Hospital Administration	M,D
Human Resources Management	M
Management Information Systems	M
Management of Technology	M
Marketing	M
Marriage and Family Therapy	M
Mathematics Education	M
Nursing Education	M
Nursing—General	M
Organizational Management	D
Psychology—General	M
Public Administration	M
Secondary Education	M
Social Psychology	M
Special Education	M

UNIVERSITY OF PHOENIX–ATLANTA CAMPUS

Accounting	M
Business Administration and Management—General	M
Criminal Justice and Criminology	M
Health Services Management and Hospital Administration	M
Human Resources Management	M
International Business	M
Management Information Systems	M
Management of Technology	M
Marketing	M
Nursing Education	M
Nursing—General	M
Public Administration	M

UNIVERSITY OF PHOENIX–AUGUSTA CAMPUS

Accounting	M
Business Administration and Management—General	M
Criminal Justice and Criminology	M
Health Services Management and Hospital Administration	M
Human Resources Management	M
International Business	M
Management Information Systems	M
Management of Technology	M
Marketing	M
Nursing Education	M
Nursing—General	M
Public Administration	M

UNIVERSITY OF PHOENIX–AUSTIN CAMPUS

Accounting	M
Business Administration and Management—General	M
Criminal Justice and Criminology	M
Curriculum and Instruction	M
Education—General	M
Electronic Commerce	M
Health Services Management and Hospital Administration	M
Human Resources Management	M
International Business	M
Management Information Systems	M
Management of Technology	M
Marketing	M
Psychology—General	M
Public Administration	M

UNIVERSITY OF PHOENIX–BAY AREA CAMPUS

Accounting	M
Adult Education	M
Business Administration and Management—General	M
Criminal Justice and Criminology	M
Curriculum and Instruction	M
Education—General	M
Electronic Commerce	M
Elementary Education	M
Family Nurse Practitioner Studies	M
Health Services Management and Hospital Administration	M
Human Resources Management	M
International Business	M
Management Information Systems	M
Management of Technology	M
Marketing	M
Marriage and Family Therapy	M
Nursing Education	M
Nursing—General	M
Public Administration	M
Secondary Education	M

UNIVERSITY OF PHOENIX–BIRMINGHAM CAMPUS

Accounting	M
Business Administration and Management—General	M
Community Health	M
Criminal Justice and Criminology	M
Gerontology	M
Health Informatics	M
Health Services Management and Hospital Administration	M
Human Resources Management	M
International Business	M
Management Information Systems	M
Management of Technology	M
Marketing	M
Nursing Education	M
Nursing—General	M
Psychology—General	M
Public Administration	M

*M—master's degree; P—first professional degree; D—doctorate; O—other advanced degree; *—Close-Up and/or Announcement or Display in one of the other books in this series*

UNIVERSITY OF PHOENIX–BOSTON CAMPUS

Business Administration and Management—General M
International Business M
Management Information Systems M
Management of Technology M

UNIVERSITY OF PHOENIX–CENTRAL FLORIDA CAMPUS

Accounting M
Business Administration and Management—General M
Computer Education M
Curriculum and Instruction M
Early Childhood Education M
Education—General M
Educational Leadership and Administration M
Elementary Education M
Health Services Management and Hospital Administration M
Human Resources Management M
International Business M
Management Information Systems M
Management of Technology M
Marketing M
Mathematics Education M
Nursing Education M
Nursing—General M
Public Administration M
Secondary Education M

UNIVERSITY OF PHOENIX–CENTRAL MASSACHUSETTS CAMPUS

Business Administration and Management—General M
Education—General M
Management of Technology M

UNIVERSITY OF PHOENIX–CENTRAL VALLEY CAMPUS

Accounting M
Business Administration and Management—General M
Community Health M
Computer Education M
Curriculum and Instruction M
Education—General M
Elementary Education M
Gerontology M
Health Services Management and Hospital Administration M
Human Resources Management M
International Business M
Management Information Systems M
Management of Technology M
Marketing M
Marriage and Family Therapy M
Nursing—General M
Public Administration M
Secondary Education M

UNIVERSITY OF PHOENIX–CHARLOTTE CAMPUS

Accounting M
Allied Health—General M
Business Administration and Management—General M
International Business M
Management Information Systems M
Management of Technology M
Nursing—General M

UNIVERSITY OF PHOENIX–CHATTANOOGA CAMPUS

Accounting M
Business Administration and Management—General M
Community Health M
Criminal Justice and Criminology M
Curriculum and Instruction M
Education—General M
Educational Leadership and Administration M
Elementary Education M
Gerontology M
Health Services Management and Hospital Administration M
Human Resources Management M
International Business M
Management Information Systems M
Management of Technology M
Marketing M
Psychology—General M
Public Administration M
Secondary Education M

UNIVERSITY OF PHOENIX–CHEYENNE CAMPUS

Business Administration and Management—General M
Criminal Justice and Criminology M
Health Services Management and Hospital Administration M
Human Resources Management M
International Business M
Management Information Systems M
Management of Technology M
Marketing M
Nursing Education M
Nursing—General M
Psychology—General M
Public Administration M

UNIVERSITY OF PHOENIX–CHICAGO CAMPUS

Business Administration and Management—General M
Electronic Commerce M
Human Resources Management M
International Business M
Management Information Systems M
Management of Technology M

UNIVERSITY OF PHOENIX–CINCINNATI CAMPUS

Accounting M
Business Administration and Management—General M
Criminal Justice and Criminology M
Electronic Commerce M
Health Services Management and Hospital Administration M
Human Resources Management M
Information Science M
International Business M
Management Information Systems M
Management of Technology M
Marketing M
Nursing—General M
Psychology—General M
Public Administration M

UNIVERSITY OF PHOENIX–CLEVELAND CAMPUS

Accounting M
Business Administration and Management—General M
Criminal Justice and Criminology M
Health Services Management and Hospital Administration M
Human Resources Management M
International Business M
Management Information Systems M
Management of Technology M
Marketing M
Nursing—General M
Psychology—General M
Public Administration M

UNIVERSITY OF PHOENIX–COLUMBIA CAMPUS

Business Administration and Management—General M
Management of Technology M

UNIVERSITY OF PHOENIX–COLUMBUS GEORGIA CAMPUS

Accounting M
Business Administration and Management—General M
Criminal Justice and Criminology M
Electronic Commerce M
Health Services Management and Hospital Administration M
Human Resources Management M
International Business M
Management Information Systems M
Management of Technology M
Marketing M
Nursing—General M
Public Administration M

UNIVERSITY OF PHOENIX–COLUMBUS OHIO CAMPUS

Accounting M
Business Administration and Management—General M
Criminal Justice and Criminology M
Health Services Management and Hospital Administration M
Human Resources Management M
International Business M
Management Information Systems M
Management of Technology M
Marketing M
Nursing—General M
Psychology—General M
Public Administration M

UNIVERSITY OF PHOENIX–DALLAS CAMPUS

Accounting M
Business Administration and Management—General M
Criminal Justice and Criminology M
Curriculum and Instruction M
Education—General M
Electronic Commerce M
Health Services Management and Hospital Administration M
Human Resources Management M
International Business M
Management Information Systems M
Management of Technology M
Marketing M
Psychology—General M
Public Administration M

UNIVERSITY OF PHOENIX–DENVER CAMPUS

Accounting M
Business Administration and Management—General M
Criminal Justice and Criminology M
Curriculum and Instruction M
Education—General M
Educational Leadership and Administration M
Electronic Commerce M
Elementary Education M
Health Services Management and Hospital Administration M
Human Resources Management M
International Business M
Management Information Systems M
Management of Technology M
Marketing M
Marriage and Family Therapy M
Nursing—General M
Psychology—General M
Public Administration M
School Psychology M
Secondary Education M
Social Psychology M

UNIVERSITY OF PHOENIX–DES MOINES CAMPUS

Accounting M
Business Administration and Management—General M
Criminal Justice and Criminology M
Health Services Management and Hospital Administration M
Human Resources Management M
International Business M
Management Information Systems M
Management of Technology M
Marketing M
Public Administration M

UNIVERSITY OF PHOENIX–EASTERN WASHINGTON CAMPUS

Accounting M
Business Administration and Management—General M
Health Services Management and Hospital Administration M
Human Resources Management M
Management Information Systems M
Management of Technology M
Marketing M
Public Administration M

UNIVERSITY OF PHOENIX–FAIRFIELD COUNTY

Business Administration and Management—General M

UNIVERSITY OF PHOENIX–HARRISBURG CAMPUS

Accounting M
Business Administration and Management—General M
Criminal Justice and Criminology M
Health Services Management and Hospital Administration M
Human Resources Management M
International Business M
Management Information Systems M
Management of Technology M
Marketing M
Nursing Education M
Nursing—General M
Psychology—General M
Public Administration M

UNIVERSITY OF PHOENIX–HAWAII CAMPUS

Accounting M
Business Administration and Management—General M
Community Health M
Criminal Justice and Criminology M
Curriculum and Instruction M
Education—General M
Educational Leadership and Administration M
Elementary Education M
Family Nurse Practitioner Studies M
Gerontology M
Health Services Management and Hospital Administration M
Human Resources Management M
International Business M
Management Information Systems M
Management of Technology M
Marketing M
Marriage and Family Therapy M
Nursing Education M
Nursing—General M
Psychology—General M
Public Administration M
Secondary Education M
Social Psychology M
Special Education M

UNIVERSITY OF PHOENIX–HOUSTON CAMPUS

Accounting M
Business Administration and Management—General M
Criminal Justice and Criminology M
Curriculum and Instruction M
Education—General M
Electronic Commerce M
Health Services Management and Hospital Administration M
Human Resources Management M
International Business M
Management Information Systems M
Management of Technology M
Marketing M
Psychology—General M
Public Administration M

UNIVERSITY OF PHOENIX–IDAHO CAMPUS

Accounting M
Business Administration and Management—General M
Criminal Justice and Criminology M
Curriculum and Instruction M
Education—General M
Educational Leadership and Administration M
Elementary Education M
Health Services Management and Hospital Administration M
Human Resources Management M
International Business M
Management Information Systems M
Management of Technology M
Marketing M
Nursing Education M
Nursing—General M
Psychology—General M
Public Administration M
Secondary Education M

UNIVERSITY OF PHOENIX–INDIANAPOLIS CAMPUS

Accounting M
Business Administration and Management—General M
Criminal Justice and Criminology M
Education—General M
Elementary Education M
Health Services Management and Hospital Administration M
Human Resources Management M
International Business M
Management Information Systems M
Management of Technology M
Marketing M
Nursing Education M
Nursing—General M
Psychology—General M
Public Administration M
Secondary Education M

UNIVERSITY OF PHOENIX–JERSEY CITY CAMPUS

Accounting M
Business Administration and Management—General M
Criminal Justice and Criminology M
Health Services Management and Hospital Administration M
Human Resources Management M
International Business M
Management Information Systems M
Management of Technology M
Marketing M
Psychology—General M
Public Administration M

UNIVERSITY OF PHOENIX–KANSAS CITY CAMPUS

Accounting M
Business Administration and Management—General M
Criminal Justice and Criminology M
Education—General M
Educational Leadership and Administration M
Health Services Management and Hospital Administration M
Human Resources Management M
International Business M
Management of Technology M
Marketing M
Nursing—General M
Public Administration M
Social Psychology M

UNIVERSITY OF PHOENIX–LAS VEGAS CAMPUS

Accounting M
Allied Health—General M
Business Administration and Management—General M
Counseling Psychology M
Criminal Justice and Criminology M
Curriculum and Instruction M
Education—General M
Educational Leadership and Administration M
Elementary Education M
Health Services Management and Hospital Administration M
Human Resources Management M
International Business M
Management Information Systems M
Management of Technology M
Marketing M
Marriage and Family Therapy M
Nursing Education M
Nursing—General M
Psychology—General M
Public Administration M
School Psychology M

UNIVERSITY OF PHOENIX–LITTLE ROCK CAMPUS

Business Administration and Management—General M

UNIVERSITY OF PHOENIX–LOUISIANA CAMPUS

Accounting M
Business Administration and Management—General M
Criminal Justice and Criminology M
Curriculum and Instruction M
Early Childhood Education M
Education—General M
Health Services Management and Hospital Administration M
Human Resources Management M
International Business M
Management Information Systems M
Management of Technology M
Marketing M
Nursing—General M
Psychology—General M
Public Administration M

UNIVERSITY OF PHOENIX–LOUISVILLE CAMPUS

Business Administration and Management—General M
Electronic Commerce M
Health Services Management and Hospital Administration M
Management of Technology M

UNIVERSITY OF PHOENIX–MADISON CAMPUS

Accounting M
Business Administration and Management—General M
Electronic Commerce M
Health Services Management and Hospital Administration M
Human Resources Management M
International Business M
Internet and Interactive Multimedia M
Management Information Systems M
Management of Technology M
Marketing M
Public Administration M

UNIVERSITY OF PHOENIX–MARYLAND CAMPUS

Accounting M
Business Administration and Management—General M
Criminal Justice and Criminology M
Electronic Commerce M
Health Services Management and Hospital Administration M
Human Resources Management M
Human Services M
International Business M
Management Information Systems M
Management of Technology M
Marketing M
Nursing Education M
Nursing—General M
Psychology—General M
Public Administration M

UNIVERSITY OF PHOENIX–MEMPHIS CAMPUS

Accounting M

*M—master's degree; P—first professional degree; D—doctorate; O—other advanced degree; *—Close-Up and/or Announcement or Display in one of the other books in this series*

Business Administration and Management—General	M
Criminal Justice and Criminology	M
Curriculum and Instruction	M
Education—General	M
Educational Leadership and Administration	M
Electronic Commerce	M
Elementary Education	M
Health Services Management and Hospital Administration	M
Human Resources Management	M
International Business	M
Management Information Systems	M
Management of Technology	M
Marketing	M
Public Administration	M
Secondary Education	M

UNIVERSITY OF PHOENIX–METRO DETROIT CAMPUS

Accounting	M
Adult Education	M
Business Administration and Management—General	M
Criminal Justice and Criminology	M
Curriculum and Instruction	M
Education—General	M
Educational Leadership and Administration	M
Elementary Education	M
Health Services Management and Hospital Administration	M
Human Resources Management	M
International Business	M
Management Information Systems	M
Management of Technology	M
Marketing	M
Nursing Education	M
Nursing—General	M
Special Education	M

UNIVERSITY OF PHOENIX–MINNEAPOLIS/ST. LOUIS PARK CAMPUS

Accounting	M
Business Administration and Management—General	M
Family Nurse Practitioner Studies	M
Health Services Management and Hospital Administration	M
Human Resources Management	M
International Business	M
Management of Technology	M
Marketing	M
Nursing Education	M
Nursing—General	M
Public Administration	M
Social Psychology	M

UNIVERSITY OF PHOENIX–NASHVILLE CAMPUS

Business Administration and Management—General	M
Curriculum and Instruction	M
Education—General	M
Educational Leadership and Administration	M
Elementary Education	M
Health Services Management and Hospital Administration	M
Human Resources Management	M
Management Information Systems	M
Management of Technology	M
Secondary Education	M

UNIVERSITY OF PHOENIX–NEW MEXICO CAMPUS

Accounting	M
Business Administration and Management—General	M
Counselor Education	M
Criminal Justice and Criminology	M
Curriculum and Instruction	M
Education—General	M
Educational Leadership and Administration	M
Electronic Commerce	M
Elementary Education	M
Health Services Management and Hospital Administration	M
Human Resources Management	M
International Business	M
Management Information Systems	M
Management of Technology	M
Marketing	M
Marriage and Family Therapy	M
Nursing Education	M
Nursing—General	M
Psychology—General	M
Secondary Education	M

UNIVERSITY OF PHOENIX–NORTHERN NEVADA CAMPUS

Accounting	M
Business Administration and Management—General	M
Criminal Justice and Criminology	M
Curriculum and Instruction	M
Education—General	M
Educational Leadership and Administration	M
Elementary Education	M
Health Services Management and Hospital Administration	M
Human Resources Management	M
International Business	M
Management Information Systems	M
Management of Technology	M
Marketing	M
Marriage and Family Therapy	M
Nursing Education	M
Nursing—General	M
Psychology—General	M
Public Administration	M
School Psychology	M
Secondary Education	M

UNIVERSITY OF PHOENIX–NORTHERN VIRGINIA CAMPUS

Accounting	M
Business Administration and Management—General	M
Criminal Justice and Criminology	M
Education—General	M
Educational Leadership and Administration	M
Electronic Commerce	M
Health Services Management and Hospital Administration	M
Human Resources Management	M
International Business	M
Management Information Systems	M
Management of Technology	M
Marketing	M
Nursing—General	M
Public Administration	M

UNIVERSITY OF PHOENIX–NORTH FLORIDA CAMPUS

Accounting	M
Business Administration and Management—General	M
Computer Education	M
Curriculum and Instruction	M
Early Childhood Education	M
Education—General	M
Educational Leadership and Administration	M
Elementary Education	M
Health Services Management and Hospital Administration	M
Human Resources Management	M
International Business	M
Management Information Systems	M
Marketing	M
Mathematics Education	M
Nursing Education	M
Nursing—General	M
Public Administration	M
Secondary Education	M

UNIVERSITY OF PHOENIX–NORTHWEST ARKANSAS CAMPUS

Accounting	M
Business Administration and Management—General	M
Criminal Justice and Criminology	M
Health Services Management and Hospital Administration	M
Human Resources Management	M
International Business	M
Management Information Systems	M
Management of Technology	M
Marketing	M
Nursing Education	M
Nursing—General	M
Public Administration	M

UNIVERSITY OF PHOENIX–OKLAHOMA CITY CAMPUS

Accounting	M
Business Administration and Management—General	M
Criminal Justice and Criminology	M
Electronic Commerce	M
Health Services Management and Hospital Administration	M
Human Resources Management	M
International Business	M
Management Information Systems	M
Management of Technology	M
Marketing	M
Nursing—General	M
Psychology—General	M

UNIVERSITY OF PHOENIX–OMAHA CAMPUS

Accounting	M
Adult Education	M
Business Administration and Management—General	M
Computer Education	M
Criminal Justice and Criminology	M
Curriculum and Instruction	M
Education—General	M
Educational Leadership and Administration	M
Elementary Education	M
English as a Second Language	M
English Education	M
Health Services Management and Hospital Administration	M
Human Resources Management	M
International Business	M
Management Information Systems	M
Management of Technology	M
Marketing	M
Mathematics Education	M
Public Administration	M
Secondary Education	M
Special Education	M

UNIVERSITY OF PHOENIX–OREGON CAMPUS

Accounting	M
Business Administration and Management—General	M
Criminal Justice and Criminology	M
Curriculum and Instruction	M
Early Childhood Education	M
Education—General	M
Elementary Education	M
Health Services Management and Hospital Administration	M
Human Resources Management	M
International Business	M
Management Information Systems	M
Management of Technology	M
Marketing	M
Middle School Education	M
Psychology—General	M
Public Administration	M
Secondary Education	M

UNIVERSITY OF PHOENIX–PHILADELPHIA CAMPUS

Accounting	M
Business Administration and Management—General	M
Criminal Justice and Criminology	M
Health Services Management and Hospital Administration	M
Human Resources Management	M
International Business	M
Management Information Systems	M
Management of Technology	M
Marketing	M

Nursing Education	M
Nursing—General	M
Psychology—General	M
Public Administration	M

UNIVERSITY OF PHOENIX–PHOENIX CAMPUS

Accounting	M
Adult Education	M
Business Administration and Management—General	M
Computer Education	M
Curriculum and Instruction	M
Early Childhood Education	M
Education—General	M
Educational Leadership and Administration	M
Elementary Education	M
English as a Second Language	M
English Education	M
Family Nurse Practitioner Studies	M,O
Gerontology	M,O
Health Education	M,O
Health Informatics	M,O
Health Services Management and Hospital Administration	M,O
Human Resources Management	M
Information Science	M
International Business	M
Management of Technology	M
Marketing	M
Marriage and Family Therapy	M,O
Mathematics Education	M
Nursing Education	M,O
Nursing—General	M,O
Psychology—General	M,O
Secondary Education	M
Social Psychology	M,O
Special Education	M

UNIVERSITY OF PHOENIX–PITTSBURGH CAMPUS

Accounting	M
Business Administration and Management—General	M
Criminal Justice and Criminology	M
Electronic Commerce	M
Health Services Management and Hospital Administration	M
Human Resources Management	M
International Business	M
Management Information Systems	M
Management of Technology	M
Marketing	M
Nursing Education	M
Psychology—General	M
Public Administration	M

UNIVERSITY OF PHOENIX–PUERTO RICO CAMPUS

Accounting	M
Business Administration and Management—General	M
Counseling Psychology	M
Early Childhood Education	M
Education—General	M
Educational Leadership and Administration	M
Health Services Management and Hospital Administration	M
Human Resources Management	M
International Business	M
Management of Technology	M
Marketing	M
Marriage and Family Therapy	M
School Psychology	M

UNIVERSITY OF PHOENIX–RALEIGH CAMPUS

Accounting	M
Business Administration and Management—General	M
Electronic Commerce	M
Health Services Management and Hospital Administration	M
Human Resources Management	M
International Business	M
Management Information Systems	M
Management of Technology	M
Marketing	M

UNIVERSITY OF PHOENIX–RENTON LEARNING CENTER

Accounting	M
Business Administration and Management—General	M
Criminal Justice and Criminology	M
Health Services Management and Hospital Administration	M
Human Resources Management	M
International Business	M
Management Information Systems	M
Management of Technology	M
Marketing	M
Nursing Education	M
Nursing—General	M
Public Administration	M

UNIVERSITY OF PHOENIX–RICHMOND CAMPUS

Accounting	M
Business Administration and Management—General	M
Criminal Justice and Criminology	M
Curriculum and Instruction	M
Educational Leadership and Administration	M
Health Services Management and Hospital Administration	M
Human Resources Management	M
Human Services	M
International Business	M
Management Information Systems	M
Management of Technology	M
Marketing	M
Nursing Education	M
Nursing—General	M
Psychology—General	M
Public Administration	M

UNIVERSITY OF PHOENIX–SACRAMENTO VALLEY CAMPUS

Accounting	M
Adult Education	M,O
Business Administration and Management—General	M
Counseling Psychology	M
Criminal Justice and Criminology	M
Curriculum and Instruction	M,O
Education—General	M,O
Elementary Education	M,O
Family Nurse Practitioner Studies	M
Health Services Management and Hospital Administration	M
Human Resources Management	M
International Business	M
Management Information Systems	M
Management of Technology	M
Marketing	M
Marriage and Family Therapy	M
Nursing Education	M
Nursing—General	M
Psychology—General	M
Public Administration	M
Secondary Education	M,O

UNIVERSITY OF PHOENIX–ST. LOUIS CAMPUS

Accounting	M
Business Administration and Management—General	M
Criminal Justice and Criminology	M
Health Services Management and Hospital Administration	M
Human Resources Management	M
International Business	M
Management Information Systems	M
Marketing	M
Nursing—General	M
Public Administration	M

UNIVERSITY OF PHOENIX–SAN ANTONIO CAMPUS

Accounting	M
Business Administration and Management—General	M
Criminal Justice and Criminology	M
Curriculum and Instruction	M
Electronic Commerce	M
Health Services Management and Hospital Administration	M
Human Resources Management	M
International Business	M
Management Information Systems	M
Management of Technology	M
Marketing	M
Psychology—General	M
Public Administration	M

UNIVERSITY OF PHOENIX–SAN DIEGO CAMPUS

Accounting	M
Business Administration and Management—General	M
Computer Education	M
Criminal Justice and Criminology	M
Curriculum and Instruction	M
Education—General	M
Elementary Education	M
English as a Second Language	M
Health Services Management and Hospital Administration	M
Human Resources Management	M
International Business	M
Management Information Systems	M
Management of Technology	M
Marketing	M
Marriage and Family Therapy	M
Nursing Education	M
Nursing—General	M
Public Administration	M
Secondary Education	M

UNIVERSITY OF PHOENIX–SAVANNAH CAMPUS

Accounting	M
Business Administration and Management—General	M
Criminal Justice and Criminology	M
Health Services Management and Hospital Administration	M
Human Resources Management	M
International Business	M
Management Information Systems	M
Management of Technology	M
Marketing	M
Nursing Education	M
Nursing—General	M
Public Administration	M

UNIVERSITY OF PHOENIX–SOUTHERN ARIZONA CAMPUS

Accounting	M
Adult Education	M,O
Business Administration and Management—General	M
Counselor Education	M,O
Criminal Justice and Criminology	M,O
Curriculum and Instruction	M,O
Education—General	M,O
Educational Leadership and Administration	M,O
Educational Psychology	M,O
Elementary Education	M,O
Family Nurse Practitioner Studies	M,O
Health Services Management and Hospital Administration	M,O
Human Resources Management	M
International Business	M
Management Information Systems	M
Management of Technology	M
Marketing	M
Marriage and Family Therapy	M,O
Psychology—General	M,O
Secondary Education	M,O
Special Education	M,O

UNIVERSITY OF PHOENIX–SOUTHERN CALIFORNIA CAMPUS

Accounting	M
Adult Education	M
Business Administration and Management—General	M

*M—master's degree; P—first professional degree; D—doctorate; O—other advanced degree; *—Close-Up and/or Announcement or Display in one of the other books in this series*

Criminal Justice and Criminology M,O
Curriculum and Instruction M
Education—General M
Elementary Education M
Family Nurse Practitioner Studies M,O
Health Services Management and Hospital Administration M,O
Human Resources Management M
International Business M
Management Information Systems M
Management of Technology M
Marketing M
Marriage and Family Therapy M,O
Nursing Education M,O
Nursing—General M,O
Psychology—General M,O
Public Administration M
Secondary Education M

UNIVERSITY OF PHOENIX–SOUTHERN COLORADO CAMPUS

Accounting M
Business Administration and Management—General M
Criminal Justice and Criminology M
Curriculum and Instruction M,O
Education—General M,O
Educational Leadership and Administration M,O
Elementary Education M,O
Gerontology M
Health Education M
Health Services Management and Hospital Administration M
Human Resources Management M
International Business M
Management Information Systems M
Management of Technology M
Marketing M
Marriage and Family Therapy M
Nursing—General M
Psychology—General M
Public Administration M
School Psychology M,O
Secondary Education M,O
Social Psychology M

UNIVERSITY OF PHOENIX–SOUTH FLORIDA CAMPUS

Accounting M
Business Administration and Management—General M
Computer Education M
Curriculum and Instruction M
Early Childhood Education M
Education—General M
Educational Leadership and Administration M
Elementary Education M
Health Services Management and Hospital Administration M
Human Resources Management M
International Business M
Management Information Systems M
Marketing M
Mathematics Education M
Nursing Education M
Nursing—General M
Public Administration M
Secondary Education M

UNIVERSITY OF PHOENIX–SPRINGFIELD CAMPUS

Accounting M
Business Administration and Management—General M
Computer Education M
Criminal Justice and Criminology M
Curriculum and Instruction M
Education—General M
Educational Leadership and Administration M
English as a Second Language M
English Education M
Health Services Management and Hospital Administration M
Human Resources Management M
International Business M
Management Information Systems M
Management of Technology M
Marketing M
Mathematics Education M
Nursing—General M
Public Administration M

UNIVERSITY OF PHOENIX–TULSA CAMPUS

Accounting M
Business Administration and Management—General M
Criminal Justice and Criminology M
Health Services Management and Hospital Administration M
Human Resources Management M
International Business M
Management Information Systems M
Management of Technology M
Marketing M
Nursing—General M
Psychology—General M

UNIVERSITY OF PHOENIX–UTAH CAMPUS

Accounting M
Business Administration and Management—General M
Counseling Psychology M
Curriculum and Instruction M
Education—General M
Educational Leadership and Administration M
Elementary Education M
Health Services Management and Hospital Administration M
Human Resources Management M
International Business M
Management Information Systems M
Management of Technology M
Marketing M
Nursing Education M
Nursing—General M
School Psychology M
Secondary Education M
Special Education M

UNIVERSITY OF PHOENIX–VANCOUVER CAMPUS

Accounting M
Business Administration and Management—General M
Computer Education M
Curriculum and Instruction M
Education—General M
Educational Leadership and Administration M
Health Services Management and Hospital Administration M
Human Resources Management M
International Business M
Management Information Systems M
Management of Technology M
Marketing M
Nursing—General M

UNIVERSITY OF PHOENIX–WEST FLORIDA CAMPUS

Accounting M
Business Administration and Management—General M
Computer Education M
Curriculum and Instruction M
Early Childhood Education M
Education—General M
Educational Leadership and Administration M
Educational Media/Instructional Technology M
Elementary Education M
Health Services Management and Hospital Administration M
Human Resources Management M
International Business M
Management Information Systems M
Management of Technology M
Marketing M
Mathematics Education M
Nursing Education M
Nursing—General M
Public Administration M
Secondary Education M

UNIVERSITY OF PHOENIX–WEST MICHIGAN CAMPUS

Accounting M
Business Administration and Management—General M
Curriculum and Instruction M
Education—General M
Educational Leadership and Administration M
Electronic Commerce M
Health Services Management and Hospital Administration M
Human Resources Management M
International Business M
Management Information Systems M
Management of Technology M
Nursing—General M

UNIVERSITY OF PHOENIX–WICHITA CAMPUS

Business Administration and Management—General M

UNIVERSITY OF PHOENIX–WISCONSIN CAMPUS

Accounting M
Business Administration and Management—General M
Health Services Management and Hospital Administration M
Human Resources Management M
International Business M
Management Information Systems M
Management of Technology M
Marketing M
Public Administration M

UNIVERSITY OF PITTSBURGH

Accounting M,D
Acute Care/Critical Care Nursing M,D
Adult Nursing M,D
African Studies O
Allopathic Medicine P
Anthropology M,D
Applied Mathematics M,D
Applied Statistics M,D
Architectural History M,D
Art History M,D
Artificial Intelligence/Robotics D
Asian Studies M,O
Athletic Training and Sports Medicine M
Biochemistry M,D
Bioengineering M,D
Bioethics M
Bioinformatics M,D,O
Biological and Biomedical Sciences—General D
Biostatistics M,D
Business Administration and Management—General M,D
Cell Biology M,D
Chemical Engineering M,D
Chemistry M,D*
Civil Engineering M,D
Classics M,D
Clinical Laboratory Sciences/Medical Technology M,D,O
Clinical Research M,D,O
Cognitive Sciences D
Communication Disorders M,D
Communication—General M,D
Community Health M,D,O
Computational Biology D
Computer Science M,D
Conflict Resolution and Mediation/Peace Studies M
Criminal Justice and Criminology M,D
Cultural Studies M,D
Dentistry P,M,O
Developmental Biology D*
Developmental Psychology M,D
Disability Studies O
Early Childhood Education M
East European and Russian Studies O
Ecology D*
Economics M,D
Education—General M,D
Educational Leadership and Administration M,D
Educational Measurement and Evaluation M,D
Electrical Engineering M,D
Elementary Education M
Emergency Management M,D,O
Engineering and Applied Sciences—General M,D

English as a Second Language	O
English Education	M,D
English	M,D*
Environmental and Occupational Health	M
Environmental Engineering	M,D
Environmental Law	M,O
Environmental Management and Policy	M,O
Epidemiology	M,D
Evolutionary Biology	D
Exercise and Sports Science	M,D
Family Nurse Practitioner Studies	M,D
Finance and Banking	M,D
Foreign Languages Education	M,D
Foundations and Philosophy of Education	M,D
French	M,D
Genetic Counseling	M
Geographic Information Systems	M,D
Geology	M,D
German	M,D
Gerontology	M,D,O
Health Education	M,D,O
Health Informatics	M
Health Law	M,O
Health Promotion	M,D,O
Health Services Management and Hospital Administration	M,D,O
Higher Education	M,D
Hispanic Studies	M,D
History of Science and Technology	M,D
History	M,D
Human Genetics	M,D,O
Human Resources Management	M,D
Immunology	M,D
Industrial/Management Engineering	M,D
Infectious Diseases	M,D,O
Information Science	M,D,O*
Information Studies	M,D,O
Interdisciplinary Studies	D
International Affairs	M,D,O
International and Comparative Education	M,D
International Business	M
International Development	M,O
Italian	M
Latin American Studies	O
Law	P,M,O
Legal and Justice Studies	M,O
Library Science	M,D,O
Linguistics	M,D
Management Information Systems	M
Management Strategy and Policy	M
Marketing	M,D
Materials Sciences	M,D
Mathematical and Computational Finance	M,D
Mathematics Education	M,D
Mathematics	M,D
Mechanical Engineering	M,D
Microbiology	M,D,O*
Military and Defense Studies	M
Molecular Biology	D*
Molecular Biophysics	D
Molecular Genetics	M,D
Molecular Pathology	M,D
Molecular Pharmacology	D
Molecular Physiology	M,D
Music	M,D
National Security	M
Neurobiology	D
Neuroscience	D
Nonprofit Management	M
Nurse Anesthesia	M
Nursing and Healthcare Administration	M
Nursing Education	M
Nursing—General	M
Nutrition	M
Occupational Therapy	M
Oral and Dental Sciences	M,O
Organizational Behavior	M,D
Pathology	M,D
Pediatric Nursing	M,D
Petroleum Engineering	M,D
Pharmaceutical Sciences	M,D
Pharmacy	P
Philosophy	M,D
Physical Therapy	M,D
Physics	M,D*
Planetary and Space Sciences	M,D
Political Science	M,D
Psychiatric Nursing	M,D
Psychology—General	M,D
Public Administration	M,D,O*
Public Health—General	M,D,O*
Public Policy	M,D,O
Quantitative Analysis	D
Reading Education	M,D
Rehabilitation Counseling	M
Rehabilitation Sciences	M,D,O
Religion	M,D
Science Education	M,D
Secondary Education	M,D
Slavic Languages	M,D
Social Sciences Education	M,D
Social Work	M,D,O
Sociology	M,D
Spanish	M,D
Special Education	M,D
Statistics	M,D
Structural Biology	D
Telecommunications	M,D,O
Theater	M,D
Urban and Regional Planning	M,O
Virology	M,D
Western European Studies	O
Women's Studies	O
Writing	M,D

UNIVERSITY OF PORTLAND

Business Administration and Management—General	M
Communication—General	M
Corporate and Organizational Communication	M
Education—General	M
Engineering and Applied Sciences—General	M
Music	M
Nursing—General	M,D
Pastoral Ministry and Counseling	M
Theater	M

UNIVERSITY OF PRINCE EDWARD ISLAND

Anatomy	M,D
Bacteriology	M,D
Biological and Biomedical Sciences—General	M
Chemistry	M
Education—General	M
Educational Leadership and Administration	M
Epidemiology	M,D
Geography	M
Immunology	M,D
Parasitology	M,D
Pathology	M,D
Pharmacology	M,D
Physiology	M,D
Toxicology	M,D
Veterinary Medicine	P
Veterinary Sciences	M,D
Virology	M,D

UNIVERSITY OF PUERTO RICO, MAYAGÜEZ CAMPUS

Agricultural Economics and Agribusiness	M
Agricultural Education	M
Agricultural Sciences—General	M
Agronomy and Soil Sciences	M
Animal Sciences	M
Applied Mathematics	M
Biological and Biomedical Sciences—General	M
Business Administration and Management—General	M
Chemical Engineering	M,D
Chemistry	M,D
Civil Engineering	M,D
Computational Sciences	M
Computer Engineering	M
Electrical Engineering	M
Engineering and Applied Sciences—General	M,D
English Education	M
English	M
Finance and Banking	M
Food Science and Technology	M
Geology	M
Hispanic Studies	M
Horticulture	M
Human Resources Management	M
Industrial and Manufacturing Management	M
Industrial/Management Engineering	M
Information Science	D
Marine Sciences	M,D
Mathematics	M
Mechanical Engineering	M
Physics	M
Statistics	M

UNIVERSITY OF PUERTO RICO, MEDICAL SCIENCES CAMPUS

Acute Care/Critical Care Nursing	M
Allied Health—General	M,D,O
Allopathic Medicine	P
Anatomy	M,D
Biochemistry	M,D
Biological and Biomedical Sciences—General	M,D
Biostatistics	M
Clinical Laboratory Sciences/Medical Technology	M,O
Clinical Research	M,O
Communication Disorders	M,D
Community Health Nursing	M
Demography and Population Studies	M
Dentistry	P
Environmental and Occupational Health	M,D
Epidemiology	M
Family Nurse Practitioner Studies	M
Gerontology	M,O
Health Education	M
Health Informatics	M
Health Services Management and Hospital Administration	M
Health Services Research	M
Industrial Hygiene	M
Maternal and Child Health	M
Microbiology	M,D
Nurse Anesthesia	M
Nurse Midwifery	M,O
Nursing—General	M
Nutrition	M,D,O
Occupational Therapy	M
Oral and Dental Sciences	M,O
Pharmaceutical Sciences	P,M
Pharmacology	M,D
Pharmacy	P,M
Physical Therapy	M
Physiology	M,D
Psychiatric Nursing	M
Public Health—General	M
Special Education	O
Toxicology	M,D

UNIVERSITY OF PUERTO RICO, RÍO PIEDRAS

Accounting	M,D
Architecture	M
Biological and Biomedical Sciences—General	M,D
Business Administration and Management—General	M,D
Chemistry	M,D
Clinical Psychology	M,D
Comparative Literature	M
Counselor Education	M,D
Curriculum and Instruction	M,D
Early Childhood Education	M
Economics	M
Education—General	M,D
Educational Leadership and Administration	M,D
Educational Measurement and Evaluation	M
English as a Second Language	M
English Education	M,D
English	M,D
Exercise and Sports Science	M
Family and Consumer Sciences-General	M
Finance and Banking	M,D
Foreign Languages Education	M,D
Hispanic Studies	M,D
History	M,D
Human Resources Management	M,D
Industrial and Manufacturing Management	M,D
Industrial and Organizational Psychology	M,D
Information Studies	M,O
International Business	M,D
Law	P,M
Library Science	M,O
Linguistics	M
Marketing	M,D
Mass Communication	M
Mathematics Education	M,D
Mathematics	M,D
Nutrition	M
Philosophy	M
Physical Chemistry	M,D
Physics	M,D
Psychology—General	M,D
Public Administration	M
Quantitative Analysis	M,D
Rehabilitation Counseling	M
Science Education	M,D
Secondary Education	M,D
Social Sciences Education	M,D
Social Work	M,D
Sociology	M
Special Education	M
Translation and Interpretation	M,O
Urban and Regional Planning	M

UNIVERSITY OF PUGET SOUND

Counseling Psychology	M
Counselor Education	M
Education—General	M

*M—master's degree; P—first professional degree; D—doctorate; O—other advanced degree; *—Close-Up and/or Announcement or Display in one of the other books in this series*

Elementary Education	M
Occupational Therapy	M
Pastoral Ministry and Counseling	M
Physical Therapy	D
Secondary Education	M

UNIVERSITY OF REDLANDS

Business Administration and Management—General	M
Communication Disorders	M
Education—General	M,D,O
Geographic Information Systems	M
Management Information Systems	M
Music	M

UNIVERSITY OF REGINA

Adult Education	M
American Indian/Native American Studies	M
Analytical Chemistry	M,D
Anthropology	M
Art/Fine Arts	M
Biochemistry	M,D
Biological and Biomedical Sciences—General	M,D
Business Administration and Management—General	M,O
Canadian Studies	M,D
Chemistry	M,D
Clinical Psychology	M,D
Computer Engineering	M,D
Computer Science	M,D
Criminal Justice and Criminology	M
Curriculum and Instruction	M
Economics	M,D,O
Education—General	M,D
Educational Leadership and Administration	M
Educational Psychology	M
Engineering and Applied Sciences—General	M,D
English	M,D
Environmental Engineering	M,D
Experimental Psychology	M,D
French	M
Geography	M,D
Geology	M,D
Gerontology	M
History	M,D
Human Resources Development	M
Human Resources Management	M,O
Industrial/Management Engineering	M,D
Inorganic Chemistry	M,D
International Business	M,O
Kinesiology and Movement Studies	M,D
Linguistics	M
Manufacturing Engineering	M
Mathematics	M,D
Music	M,D
Organic Chemistry	M,D
Petroleum Engineering	M,D
Philosophy	M
Physical Chemistry	M,D
Physics	M,D
Political Science	M
Psychology—General	M,D
Public Administration	M,D,O
Public Policy	M,D,O
Religion	M,D
Social Sciences	M,D
Social Work	M,D
Sociology	M,D
Statistics	M,D
Systems Engineering	M,D
Women's Studies	M

UNIVERSITY OF RHODE ISLAND

Accounting	M
Adult Education	M
Animal Sciences	M,D
Applied Mathematics	M,D,O
Aquaculture	M,D
Biochemistry	M,D
Biological and Biomedical Sciences—General	M,D
Biomedical Engineering	M,D
Biotechnology	M
Business Administration and Management—General	M,D
Cell Biology	M,D
Chemical Engineering	M,D
Chemistry	M,D
Child and Family Studies	M
Civil Engineering	M,D
Clinical Laboratory Sciences/Medical Technology	M
Clinical Psychology	M,D
Clothing and Textiles	M
Communication Disorders	M,D
Communication—General	M
Computer Engineering	M,D
Computer Science	M,D,O
Counseling Psychology	M
Economics	M,D
Education—General	M,D
Electrical Engineering	M,D
Elementary Education	M
Engineering and Applied Sciences—General	M,D
English	M,D
Entomology	M,D
Environmental Engineering	M
Environmental Management and Policy	M,D
Environmental Sciences	M,D
Exercise and Sports Science	M,D
Family Nurse Practitioner Studies	M,D
Finance and Banking	D
Fish, Game, and Wildlife Management	M,D
Food Science and Technology	M,D
Forensic Sciences	M,D,O
Geosciences	M,D
Geotechnical Engineering	M,D
Gerontological Nursing	M,D
Gerontology	M,D
Health Education	M,D
History	M
Human Resources Management	M
Industrial and Labor Relations	M
Industrial and Manufacturing Management	M,D
Industrial/Management Engineering	D
Information Studies	M
International Affairs	M,O
International Business	M,D
Library Science	M
Management Information Systems	D
Manufacturing Engineering	D
Marine Affairs	M,D
Marine Sciences	M,D
Marketing	D
Mathematics	M,D
Mechanical Engineering	M,D
Mechanics	M,D
Medicinal and Pharmaceutical Chemistry	M,D
Microbiology	M,D
Molecular Biology	M,D
Molecular Genetics	M,D
Music Education	M,D
Music	M
Natural Resources	M,D
Nursing and Healthcare Administration	M,D
Nursing Education	M,D
Nursing—General	M,D
Nutrition	M,D
Ocean Engineering	M,D
Oceanography	M,D
Pharmaceutical Sciences	M,D
Pharmacology	M,D
Pharmacy	M,D
Physical Education	M,D
Physical Therapy	D
Physics	M,D
Plant Sciences	M,D
Political Science	M,O
Psychiatric Nursing	M,D
Psychology—General	D
Public Administration	M,O
Public Policy	M,O
Reading Education	M
Recreation and Park Management	M,D
School Psychology	M,D
Secondary Education	M
Spanish	M
Sport Psychology	M,D
Sports Management	M,D
Statistics	M,D,O
Structural Engineering	M,D
Student Affairs	M
Systems Engineering	M,D
Toxicology	M,D
Transportation and Highway Engineering	M

UNIVERSITY OF RICHMOND

Business Administration and Management—General	M
Law	P

UNIVERSITY OF RIO GRANDE

Art Education	M
Education—General	M
Mathematics Education	M
Reading Education	M
Special Education	M

UNIVERSITY OF ROCHESTER

Acute Care/Critical Care Nursing	M,D,O
Adult Nursing	M,D,O
Allopathic Medicine	P
Anatomy	M,D
Art History	M,D
Art/Fine Arts	M,D*
Astronomy	M,D
Biochemistry	M,D
Biological and Biomedical Sciences—General	M,D
Biomedical Engineering	M,D
Biophysics	M,D
Biostatistics	M,D
Business Administration and Management—General	M,D
Chemical Engineering	M,D*
Chemistry	M,D
Clinical Psychology	M,D
Cognitive Sciences	M,D
Computational Biology	M,D
Computer Engineering	M,D
Computer Science	M,D*
Developmental Psychology	M,D
Economics	M,D
Education—General	M,D
Electrical Engineering	M,D
Emergency Management	M,D,O
Engineering and Applied Sciences—General	M,D*
English	M,D
Epidemiology	M,D
Family Nurse Practitioner Studies	M,D,O
Genetics	M,D
Geology	M,D
Geosciences	M,D*
Health Education	M,D,O
Health Promotion	M,D,O
Health Services Research	M,D,O
History	M,D
Immunology	M,D
Marriage and Family Therapy	M
Materials Sciences	M,D
Maternal and Child/Neonatal Nursing	M,D,O
Mathematics	M,D
Mechanical Engineering	M,D
Microbiology	M,D
Music Education	M,D
Music	M,D
Neurobiology	M,D
Neuroscience	M,D
Nursing and Healthcare Administration	M,D,O
Nursing—General	M,D,O
Optical Sciences	M,D
Oral and Dental Sciences	M
Pathology	M,D
Pediatric Nursing	M,D,O
Pharmacology	M,D
Philosophy	M,D
Physics	M,D*
Physiology	M,D
Political Science	M,D
Psychiatric Nursing	M,D,O
Psychology—General	M,D
Public Health—General	M
Social Psychology	M,D
Statistics	M,D
Toxicology	M,D

UNIVERSITY OF ST. AUGUSTINE FOR HEALTH SCIENCES

Occupational Therapy	M,D
Physical Therapy	M,D,O

UNIVERSITY OF ST. FRANCIS (IL)

Adult Nursing	M,D
Allied Health—General	M,D
Business Administration and Management—General	M
Curriculum and Instruction	M
Education—General	M
Educational Leadership and Administration	M
Elementary Education	M
English Education	M
Family Nurse Practitioner Studies	M,D
Health Services Management and Hospital Administration	M
Mathematics Education	M
Nursing—General	M,D
Physician Assistant Studies	M,D
Reading Education	M
Science Education	M
Secondary Education	M
Social Sciences Education	M
Social Work	M
Special Education	M

UNIVERSITY OF SAINT FRANCIS (IN)

Allied Health—General	M
Art/Fine Arts	M
Business Administration and Management—General	M
Counseling Psychology	M
Counselor Education	M
Education—General	M
Nursing—General	M
Pastoral Ministry and Counseling	M

Physician Assistant Studies	M
Psychology—General	M
Special Education	M

UNIVERSITY OF SAINT MARY

Business Administration and Management—General	M
Curriculum and Instruction	M
Education—General	M
Psychology—General	M
Special Education	M

UNIVERSITY OF SAINT MARY OF THE LAKE–MUNDELEIN SEMINARY

Theology	P,M,D,O

UNIVERSITY OF ST. MICHAEL'S COLLEGE

Jewish Studies	P,M,D,O
Pastoral Ministry and Counseling	P,M,D,O
Religious Education	P,M,D,O
Theology	P,M,D,O

UNIVERSITY OF ST. THOMAS (MN)

Accounting	M
Art History	M
Business Administration and Management—General	M*
Computer and Information Systems Security	M,O
Corporate and Organizational Communication	M
Counseling Psychology	M,D,O
Curriculum and Instruction	M,D,O
Education of the Gifted	M,D,O
Education—General	M,O
Educational Leadership and Administration	M,D,O
Educational Media/Instructional Technology	M,D,O
Educational Policy	M,D,O
Elementary Education	M,O
Engineering and Applied Sciences—General	M,O
Engineering Management	M,O
English	M*
Health Services Management and Hospital Administration	M
Human Development	M,D,O
Human Resources Management	M,D,O
Industrial and Manufacturing Management	M,O
Law	P
Management Information Systems	M,O
Management of Technology	M,O
Manufacturing Engineering	M,O
Marriage and Family Therapy	M,D,O
Multilingual and Multicultural Education	M,O
Music Education	M
Organizational Management	M,D,O
Pastoral Ministry and Counseling	M
Psychology—General	M,D,O
Reading Education	M,D,O
Real Estate	M
Religion	M
Religious Education	M
Secondary Education	M,O
Social Work	M
Software Engineering	M,O*
Special Education	M,O
Student Affairs	M,D,O
Systems Engineering	M,O
Theology	P,M

UNIVERSITY OF ST. THOMAS (TX)

Business Administration and Management—General	M
Education—General	M
Liberal Studies	M
Philosophy	M,D
Theology	P,M

UNIVERSITY OF SAN DIEGO

Accounting	M,O
Adult Nursing	M,D
Business Administration and Management—General	M,O
Conflict Resolution and Mediation/Peace Studies	M
Counseling Psychology	M
Counselor Education	M
Curriculum and Instruction	M
Education—General	M,D,O
Educational Leadership and Administration	M,D,O
Family Nurse Practitioner Studies	M,D
Foreign Languages Education	M
Higher Education	M,D,O
History	M
International Affairs	M
Law	P,M,O
Legal and Justice Studies	P,M,O
Marine Affairs	M
Marine Sciences	M
Marriage and Family Therapy	M
Mathematics Education	M
Nonprofit Management	M,D,O
Nursing and Healthcare Administration	M,D
Nursing—General	M,D
Pediatric Nursing	M,D
Reading Education	M
Science Education	M
Special Education	M
Supply Chain Management	M,O
Taxation	P,M,O
Theater	M

UNIVERSITY OF SAN FRANCISCO

Asian Studies	M
Biological and Biomedical Sciences—General	M
Business Administration and Management—General	M
Chemistry	M
Computer Science	M
Counseling Psychology	M,D
Counselor Education	M,D
Curriculum and Instruction	M,D
Economics	M
Education—General	M,D
Educational Leadership and Administration	M,D
Educational Media/Instructional Technology	M,D
Electronic Commerce	M
English as a Second Language	M,D
Entrepreneurship	M
Family Nurse Practitioner Studies	D
Finance and Banking	M
Health Services Management and Hospital Administration	M
International Affairs	M
International and Comparative Education	M,D
International Business	M
International Development	M
Internet and Interactive Multimedia	M
Internet Engineering	M
Investment Management	M
Law	P,M
Management Information Systems	M
Marketing	M
Marriage and Family Therapy	M,D
Multilingual and Multicultural Education	M,D
Natural Resources	M
Nonprofit Management	M
Nursing and Healthcare Administration	D
Nursing—General	M,D
Organizational Management	M
Pacific Area/Pacific Rim Studies	M
Project Management	M
Public Administration	M
Reading Education	M,D
Religious Education	M,D
Sports Management	M
Telecommunications Management	M
Theology	M
Writing	M

UNIVERSITY OF SASKATCHEWAN

Accounting	M
Agricultural Economics and Agribusiness	M,D
Agricultural Engineering	M,D
Agricultural Sciences—General	M,D
Agronomy and Soil Sciences	M,D
Allopathic Medicine	P
Anatomy	M,D
Animal Sciences	M,D
Anthropology	M
Archaeology	M,D
Art/Fine Arts	M
Biochemistry	M,D
Biological and Biomedical Sciences—General	M,D,O
Biomedical Engineering	M,D
Biotechnology	M
Business Administration and Management—General	M
Canadian Studies	M,D
Cell Biology	M,D
Chemical Engineering	M,D
Chemistry	M,D
Civil Engineering	M,D
Community Health	M,D
Computer Science	M,D
Curriculum and Instruction	M,D,O
Dentistry	P
East European and Russian Studies	M
Economics	M
Education—General	M,D,O
Educational Leadership and Administration	M,D,O
Educational Psychology	M,D,O
Electrical Engineering	M,D
Engineering and Applied Sciences—General	M,D,O
Engineering Physics	M,D
English	M,D
Environmental Engineering	M,D,O
Epidemiology	M,D
Finance and Banking	M
Food Science and Technology	M,D
Foundations and Philosophy of Education	M,D,O
French	M
Gender Studies	M,D
Geography	M,D
Geology	M,D,O
German	M
Health Services Management and Hospital Administration	M
History	M,D
Immunology	M,D
Industrial and Labor Relations	M
International Business	M
Kinesiology and Movement Studies	M,D,O
Law	P,M
Marketing	M
Mathematics	M,D
Mechanical Engineering	M,D
Microbiology	M,D
Music	M
Nursing—General	M
Organizational Behavior	M
Pathology	M,D
Pharmaceutical Sciences	M,D
Pharmacology	M,D
Philosophy	M
Physics	M,D
Physiology	M,D
Plant Sciences	M,D
Political Science	M
Psychology—General	M,D
Religion	M
Reproductive Biology	M,D
Sociology	M,D
Special Education	M,D,O
Statistics	M,D
Theater	M
Toxicology	M,D,O
Veterinary Medicine	P,M,D
Veterinary Sciences	M,D
Women's Studies	M,D

THE UNIVERSITY OF SCRANTON

Accounting	M
Adult Nursing	M,O
Biochemistry	M
Business Administration and Management—General	M
Chemistry	M
Counseling Psychology	M,O
Counselor Education	M
Curriculum and Instruction	M
Early Childhood Education	M
Education—General	M
Educational Leadership and Administration	M
Elementary Education	M
English as a Second Language	M
Family Nurse Practitioner Studies	M,O
Finance and Banking	M
Health Services Management and Hospital Administration	M
History	M
Human Resources Development	M
Human Resources Management	M
International Business	M
Management Information Systems	M
Marketing	M
Nurse Anesthesia	M,O
Nursing—General	M,O
Occupational Therapy	M
Organizational Management	M
Physical Therapy	M,D
Reading Education	M
Rehabilitation Counseling	M
Secondary Education	M
Social Psychology	M
Software Engineering	M

*M—master's degree; P—first professional degree; D—doctorate; O—other advanced degree; *—Close-Up and/or Announcement or Display in one of the other books in this series*

Special Education	M
Theology	M

UNIVERSITY OF SIOUX FALLS

Business Administration and Management—General	M
Education—General	M,O
Educational Leadership and Administration	M,O
Educational Media/ Instructional Technology	M,O
Reading Education	M,O

UNIVERSITY OF SOUTH AFRICA

Accounting	M,D
Acute Care/Critical Care Nursing	M,D
Adult Education	M,D
Agricultural Sciences—General	M,D
Anthropology	M,D
Archaeology	M,D
Art History	M,D
Business Administration and Management—General	M,D
Chemical Engineering	M
Classics	M,D
Clinical Psychology	M,D
Communication—General	M,D
Counseling Psychology	M,D
Counselor Education	M,D
Criminal Justice and Criminology	M,D
Curriculum and Instruction	M,D
Economics	M,D
Education—General	M,D
Educational Leadership and Administration	M,D
Educational Media/ Instructional Technology	M,D
Educational Psychology	M,D
Engineering and Applied Sciences—General	M
English as a Second Language	M,D
English	M,D
Environmental Education	M,D
Environmental Management and Policy	M,D
Environmental Sciences	M,D
Ethics	M,D
Family and Consumer Sciences-General	M,D
Foundations and Philosophy of Education	M,D
French	M,D
Geography	M,D
German	M,D
Health Education	M,D
Health Services Management and Hospital Administration	M,D
History	M,D
Horticulture	M,D
Human Development	M,D
Human Resources Development	M,D
Industrial and Organizational Psychology	M,D
Information Science	M,D
International and Comparative Education	M,D
Italian	M,D
Law	M,D
Linguistics	M,D
Logistics	M,D
Management Information Systems	M
Marketing	M,D
Maternal and Child/ Neonatal Nursing	M,D
Mathematics Education	M,D
Medical/Surgical Nursing	M,D
Missions and Missiology	M,D
Music	M,D
Natural Resources	M,D
Near and Middle Eastern Languages	M,D
Near and Middle Eastern Studies	M,D
Nurse Midwifery	M,D
Pastoral Ministry and Counseling	M,D
Philosophy	M,D
Political Science	M,D
Portuguese	M,D
Psychology—General	M,D
Public Administration	M,D
Public Health—General	M,D
Quantitative Analysis	M,D
Real Estate	M,D
Religion	M,D
Romance Languages	M,D
Russian	M,D
Science Education	M,D
Social Work	M,D
Sociology	M,D
Spanish	M,D
Statistics	M,D
Technology and Public Policy	M,D
Telecommunications Management	M,D
Theology	M,D
Travel and Tourism	M,D
Vocational and Technical Education	M,D

UNIVERSITY OF SOUTH ALABAMA

Accounting	M
Adult Nursing	M,D
Allied Health—General	M,D
Allopathic Medicine	P
Biochemistry	D
Biological and Biomedical Sciences—General	M,D*
Business Administration and Management—General	M
Cell Biology	D
Chemical Engineering	M
Civil Engineering	M
Communication Disorders	M,D
Communication—General	M
Community Health Nursing	M,D
Computer Science	M
Counselor Education	M,D
Early Childhood Education	M,O
Education—General	M,D,O
Educational Leadership and Administration	M,O
Educational Media/ Instructional Technology	M,D
Electrical Engineering	M
Elementary Education	M,O
Engineering and Applied Sciences—General	M
English	M
Environmental and Occupational Health	M
Exercise and Sports Science	M
Gerontology	O
Health Education	M
History	M
Immunology	D
Information Science	M
Leisure Studies	M
Management Information Systems	M
Marine Sciences	M,D
Maternal and Child/ Neonatal Nursing	M,D
Mathematics	M
Mechanical Engineering	M
Microbiology	D
Molecular Biology	D
Neuroscience	D
Nursing—General	M,D
Occupational Therapy	M
Pharmacology	D
Physical Education	M
Physical Therapy	D
Physician Assistant Studies	M
Physiology	D
Psychology—General	M
Public Administration	M
Reading Education	M,O
Recreation and Park Management	M
Rehabilitation Counseling	M,D
School Psychology	M,D
Science Education	M,O
Secondary Education	M,O
Sociology	M
Special Education	M,O
Toxicology	M

UNIVERSITY OF SOUTH CAROLINA

Accounting	M
Acute Care/Critical Care Nursing	M,O
Adult Nursing	M
Allopathic Medicine	P
Anthropology	M,D
Applied Statistics	M,D,O
Art Education	M,D
Art History	M
Art/Fine Arts	M
Astronomy	M,D
Biochemistry	M,D
Biological and Biomedical Sciences—General	M,D,O
Biostatistics	M,D
Business Administration and Management—General	M,D
Business Education	M,D
Cell Biology	M,D
Chemical Engineering	M,D
Chemistry	M,D
Civil Engineering	M,D
Clinical Psychology	M,D
Communication Disorders	M,D
Community Health Nursing	M
Comparative Literature	M,D
Computer Engineering	M,D
Computer Science	M,D
Consumer Economics	M
Counselor Education	D,O
Criminal Justice and Criminology	M,D
Curriculum and Instruction	D
Developmental Biology	M,D
Early Childhood Education	M,D
Ecology	M,D
Economics	M,D
Education—General	M,D,O
Educational Leadership and Administration	M,D,O
Educational Measurement and Evaluation	M,D
Educational Media/ Instructional Technology	M
Educational Psychology	M,D
Electrical Engineering	M,D
Elementary Education	M,D
Engineering and Applied Sciences—General	M,D
English as a Second Language	M,D,O
English Education	M,D
English	M,D
Entertainment Management	M
Environmental and Occupational Health	M,D
Environmental Management and Policy	M
Epidemiology	M,D
Evolutionary Biology	M,D
Exercise and Sports Science	M,D
Experimental Psychology	M,D
Family Nurse Practitioner Studies	M
Foreign Languages Education	M,D
Foundations and Philosophy of Education	D
French	M,D
Genetic Counseling	M
Geography	M,D
Geology	M,D
Geosciences	M,D
German	M,D
Gerontology	O
Hazardous Materials Management	M,D
Health Education	M,D,O
Health Promotion	M,D,O
Health Services Management and Hospital Administration	M,D
Higher Education	M
Historic Preservation	M,O
History	M,D,O
Hospitality Management	M
Human Resources Management	M
Industrial Hygiene	M,D
Information Studies	M,D,O
International Affairs	M,D
International Business	M
Journalism	M,D
Law	P
Library Science	M,D,O
Linguistics	M,D,O
Marine Sciences	M,D
Mathematics Education	M,D
Mathematics	M,D
Mechanical Engineering	M,D
Media Studies	M
Medical/Surgical Nursing	M
Molecular Biology	M,D
Museum Studies	M,O
Music Education	M,D,O
Music	M,D,O
Nuclear Engineering	M,D
Nurse Anesthesia	M
Nursing and Healthcare Administration	M
Nursing—General	M,O
Pediatric Nursing	M
Pharmaceutical Sciences	M,D
Pharmacy	P
Philosophy	M,D
Physical Education	M,D
Physics	M,D
Political Science	M,D
Psychiatric Nursing	M,O
Psychology—General	M,D
Public Administration	M
Public Health—General	M
Public History	M,O
Reading Education	M,D
Rehabilitation Counseling	M,O
Rehabilitation Sciences	M,O
Religion	M
School Psychology	D
Science Education	M,D
Secondary Education	M,D
Social Psychology	M,D
Social Sciences Education	M,D
Social Work	M,D
Sociology	M,D
Software Engineering	M,D
Spanish	M,D
Special Education	M,D
Speech and Interpersonal Communication	M,D
Sports Management	M
Statistics	M,D,O
Student Affairs	M
Theater	M,D
Travel and Tourism	M
Women's Health Nursing	M
Women's Studies	O
Writing	M,D

UNIVERSITY OF SOUTH CAROLINA AIKEN

Clinical Psychology	M
Education—General	M
Educational Media/ Instructional Technology	M
Elementary Education	M

UNIVERSITY OF SOUTH CAROLINA UPSTATE

Early Childhood Education	M
Education—General	M
Elementary Education	M
Special Education	M

THE UNIVERSITY OF SOUTH DAKOTA

Accounting	M
Allied Health—General	M,D
Allopathic Medicine	P
Art/Fine Arts	M
Biological and Biomedical Sciences—General	M,D
Business Administration and Management—General	M
Cardiovascular Sciences	M,D
Cell Biology	M,D
Chemistry	M,D
Clinical Psychology	M,D
Communication Disorders	M,D
Communication—General	M
Computational Sciences	M,D
Computer Science	M,D
Counselor Education	M,D,O
Curriculum and Instruction	M,D,O
Education—General	M,D,O
Educational Leadership and Administration	M,D,O
Educational Media/Instructional Technology	M,O
Educational Psychology	M,D,O
Elementary Education	M
English	M,D
Health Education	M
History	M
Immunology	M,D
Interdisciplinary Studies	M
Law	P
Mathematics	M
Microbiology	M,D
Molecular Biology	M,D
Music	M
Neuroscience	M,D
Occupational Therapy	M
Pharmacology	M,D
Physical Education	M
Physical Therapy	D
Physician Assistant Studies	M
Physiology	M,D
Political Science	M,D
Psychology—General	M,D
Public Administration	M,D
Secondary Education	M
Special Education	M
Statistics	M,D
Theater	M

UNIVERSITY OF SOUTHERN CALIFORNIA

Accounting	M
Advertising and Public Relations	M
Aerospace/Aeronautical Engineering	M,D,O
Allopathic Medicine	P
American Studies	D
Applied Mathematics	M,D
Architecture	M,D
Art History	M,D,O
Art/Fine Arts	M,D,O
Artificial Intelligence/Robotics	M,D
Arts Administration	M
Asian Languages	M,D
Asian Studies	M,D
Biochemistry	M,D
Bioinformatics	M,D
Biological and Biomedical Sciences—General	M,D
Biomedical Engineering	M,D
Biometry	M
Biophysics	M,D
Biostatistics	M,D*
Broadcast Journalism	M
Business Administration and Management—General	M,D
Cell Biology	M,D
Chemical Engineering	M,D,O
Chemical Physics	D
Chemistry	M,D
Child and Family Studies	M,D
Civil Engineering	M,D,O
Classics	M,D
Clinical Psychology	M,D
Clinical Research	M,D,O
Cognitive Sciences	M,D
Communication—General	M,D*
Comparative Literature	M,D
Computational Biology	M,D
Computer and Information Systems Security	M,D
Computer Art and Design	M
Computer Engineering	M,D,O
Computer Science	M,D*
Construction Management	M,D,O
Corporate and Organizational Communication	M,D
Counselor Education	M
Dentistry	P
Developmental Psychology	M,D
Economic Development	M,D
Economics	M,D
Educational Leadership and Administration	D
Educational Media/Instructional Technology	M
Educational Policy	D
Educational Psychology	M,D
Electrical Engineering	M,D,O
Engineering and Applied Sciences—General	M,D,O*
Engineering Management	M,D,O
English as a Second Language	M
English	M,D
Environmental Engineering	M,D,O
Epidemiology	M,D
Evolutionary Biology	M,D
Film, Television, and Video Production	M,O
Film, Television, and Video Theory and Criticism	M,D
Food Science and Technology	M,D,O
Genetics	M,D
Geographic Information Systems	M,O
Geography	M,O
Geosciences	M,D
Gerontology	M,D,O
Health Communication	M
Health Promotion	M
Health Services Management and Hospital Administration	M
Health Services Research	D
Higher Education	D
History	D
Immunology	M,D
Industrial/Management Engineering	M,D,O
International Affairs	M,D
International Health	M
Internet and Interactive Multimedia	M,D,O
Journalism	M
Kinesiology and Movement Studies	M,D
Linguistics	M,D
Manufacturing Engineering	M,D,O
Marine Biology	M,D
Marine Sciences	M,D
Marriage and Family Therapy	M
Mass Communication	M,D
Materials Engineering	M,D,O
Materials Sciences	M,D,O
Mathematics	M,D
Mechanical Engineering	M,D,O
Mechanics	M,D,O
Media Studies	M,D
Medical Imaging	M,D
Microbiology	M,D
Molecular Biology	M,D
Molecular Pharmacology	M,D
Multilingual and Multicultural Education	D
Music Education	M,D
Music	M,D
Neurobiology	M,D
Neuroscience	M,D
Occupational Therapy	M,D
Operations Research	M,D,O
Oral and Dental Sciences	M,D,O
Organizational Management	M
Pathobiology	M,D*
Pathology	M,D
Petroleum Engineering	M,D,O
Pharmaceutical Sciences	M,D*
Pharmacy	P
Philosophy	M,D
Physical Therapy	D
Physician Assistant Studies	M
Physics	M,D
Physiology	M,D
Political Science	M,D
Psychology—General	M,D
Public Administration	M
Public Health—General	M*
Public Policy	M
Quantitative Analysis	M,D
Real Estate	M
Safety Engineering	M,D,O
Slavic Languages	M,D
Social Psychology	M,D
Sociology	D
Software Engineering	M,D
Speech and Interpersonal Communication	M,D
Statistics	M,D
Student Affairs	M
Supply Chain Management	M,D,O
Sustainable Development	M,D,O
Systems Biology	D
Systems Engineering	M,D,O
Taxation	M
Telecommunications	M,D,O
Theater	M*
Toxicology	M,D
Transportation and Highway Engineering	M,D,O
Urban and Regional Planning	D
Urban Education	D
Writing	M,D

UNIVERSITY OF SOUTHERN INDIANA

Accounting	M
Business Administration and Management—General	M
Education—General	M
Elementary Education	M
Engineering and Applied Sciences—General	M
Health Services Management and Hospital Administration	M
Industrial and Manufacturing Management	M
Liberal Studies	M
Nursing—General	M,D
Occupational Therapy	M
Public Administration	M
Secondary Education	M
Social Work	M

UNIVERSITY OF SOUTHERN MAINE

Accounting	M
Adult Education	M,O
Adult Nursing	M,O
American Studies	M
Biological and Biomedical Sciences—General	M
Business Administration and Management—General	M
Computer Science	M
Counselor Education	M,O
Education—General	M,D,O
Educational Leadership and Administration	M,O
Educational Psychology	M,O
English as a Second Language	M,O
Family Nurse Practitioner Studies	M,O
Health Services Management and Hospital Administration	M,O
Immunology	M
Law	P
Manufacturing Engineering	M
Medical/Surgical Nursing	M,O
Middle School Education	M,O
Molecular Biology	M
Music	M
Nonprofit Management	M,O
Nursing—General	M,O
Occupational Therapy	M
Psychiatric Nursing	M,O
Public Policy	M,D,O
Reading Education	M,O
School Psychology	M,D
Social Work	M
Special Education	M
Sports Management	M,O
Statistics	M
Urban and Regional Planning	M,O
Writing	M

UNIVERSITY OF SOUTHERN MISSISSIPPI

Accounting	M
Adult Education	M,D,O
Adult Nursing	M,D
Advertising and Public Relations	M,D
Analytical Chemistry	M,D
Anthropology	M
Art Education	M
Biochemistry	M,D
Biological and Biomedical Sciences—General	M,D
Biostatistics	M
Business Administration and Management—General	M
Chemistry	M,D
Child and Family Studies	M
Clinical Laboratory Sciences/Medical Technology	M
Clinical Psychology	M,D
Communication Disorders	M,D
Community Health Nursing	M,D
Computational Sciences	M,D
Computer Science	M,D
Construction Engineering	M
Construction Management	M
Counseling Psychology	M,D
Criminal Justice and Criminology	M,D
Curriculum and Instruction	M,D,O
Early Childhood Education	M,D,O
Economic Development	M,D
Economics	M,D
Education of the Gifted	M,D,O
Education—General	M,D,O
Educational Leadership and Administration	M,D,O
Elementary Education	M,D,O
Engineering and Applied Sciences—General	M,D
English	M,D

*M—master's degree; P—first professional degree; D—doctorate; O—other advanced degree; *—Close-Up and/or Announcement or Display in one of the other books in this series*

Environmental and Occupational Health	M
Environmental Biology	M,D
Epidemiology	M
Exercise and Sports Science	M,D
Experimental Psychology	M,D
Family Nurse Practitioner Studies	M,D
Food Science and Technology	M,D
Foreign Languages Education	M
Geography	M,D
Geology	M,D
Health Education	M
Health Services Management and Hospital Administration	M
Higher Education	M,D,O
History	M,D
Hydrology	M,D
Inorganic Chemistry	M,D
International Affairs	M,D
International Development	M,D
Leisure Studies	M,D
Library Science	M,O
Management Information Systems	M
Marine Biology	M,D
Marine Sciences	M,D
Marriage and Family Therapy	M
Mass Communication	M,D
Maternal and Child/ Neonatal Nursing	M,D
Mathematics Education	M,D
Mathematics	M,D
Microbiology	M,D
Molecular Biology	M,D
Music Education	M,D
Music	M,D
Nursing and Healthcare Administration	M,D
Nursing—General	M,D
Nutrition	M,D
Organic Chemistry	M,D
Philosophy	M
Physical Chemistry	M,D
Physical Education	M,D
Physics	M,D
Political Science	M,D
Polymer Science and Engineering	M,D
Psychiatric Nursing	M,D
Psychology—General	M,D
Public Health—General	M
Reading Education	M,D,O
Recreation and Park Management	M,D
School Psychology	M,D
Science Education	M,D
Secondary Education	M,D,O
Social Sciences Education	M,D,O
Social Work	M
Special Education	M,D,O
Speech and Interpersonal Communication	M,D
Sports Management	M,D
Theater	M
Vocational and Technical Education	M

UNIVERSITY OF SOUTHERN NEVADA

Business Administration and Management—General	M
Pharmacy	P

UNIVERSITY OF SOUTH FLORIDA

Accounting	M
Adult Education	M,D,O
African Studies	M
American Studies	M
Analytical Chemistry	M,D
Anatomy	M,D
Anthropology	M,D
Applied Physics	M,D
Architecture	M
Art History	M
Art/Fine Arts	M
Biochemistry	M,D
Bioinformatics	M,D
Biological and Biomedical Sciences—General	M,D
Biomedical Engineering	M,D
Biophysics	M,D
Biostatistics	M,D
Business Administration and Management—General	M,D
Cancer Biology/Oncology	D*
Cell Biology	M,D
Chemical Engineering	M,D
Chemistry	M,D
Civil Engineering	M,D
Classics	M
Clinical Psychology	M,D
Clinical Research	M,D
Cognitive Sciences	M,D
Communication Disorders	M,D
Communication—General	M,D
Community College Education	M,D,O
Community Health	M,D
Computational Sciences	M,D
Computer Engineering	M,D
Computer Science	M,D
Conservation Biology	M,D
Counselor Education	M,D,O
Criminal Justice and Criminology	M,D
Early Childhood Education	M,D,O
Economics	M,D
Education of the Gifted	M,D,O
Education—General	M,D,O*
Educational Leadership and Administration	M,D,O
Educational Measurement and Evaluation	M,D,O
Educational Media/ Instructional Technology	M,D,O
Electrical Engineering	M,D
Elementary Education	M,D,O
Engineering and Applied Sciences—General	M,D
Engineering Management	M,D
English as a Second Language	M
English Education	M,D,O
English	M,D
Entrepreneurship	M,O
Environmental and Occupational Health	M,D
Environmental Engineering	M,D
Environmental Management and Policy	M
Environmental Sciences	M,D
Epidemiology	M,D
Finance and Banking	M
Foreign Languages Education	M,D,O
French	M
Geography	M,D
Geology	M,D
Gerontology	M,D
Health Services Management and Hospital Administration	M,D
Higher Education	M,D,O
History	M,D
Immunology	M,D
Industrial and Organizational Psychology	M,D
Industrial/Management Engineering	M,D
Infectious Diseases	M,D
Information Studies	M
Inorganic Chemistry	M,D
International Affairs	M,D
International Health	M,D
Latin American Studies	M,D,O
Liberal Studies	M
Library Science	M
Linguistics	M
Management Information Systems	M
Marine Biology	M,D
Marine Sciences	M,D
Mass Communication	M
Materials Sciences	M
Mathematics Education	M,D,O
Mathematics	M,D,O
Mechanical Engineering	M,D
Medical Microbiology	M,D
Middle School Education	M,D,O
Molecular Biology	M,D
Molecular Medicine	M,D
Molecular Pharmacology	M,D
Music Education	M,D
Music	M,D
Neuroscience	M,D
Nursing—General	M,D
Oceanography	M,D
Organic Chemistry	M,D
Pathology	M,D
Pharmacology	M,D
Philosophy	M,D
Physical Chemistry	M,D
Physical Education	M
Physical Therapy	M,D
Physics	M,D
Physiology	M,D
Political Science	M
Polymer Science and Engineering	M,D
Psychology—General	M,D
Public Administration	M
Public Health—General	M,D
Reading Education	M,D
Rehabilitation Counseling	M
Religion	M
School Psychology	M,D,O
Science Education	M,D,O
Secondary Education	M,D,O
Social Sciences Education	M,D,O
Social Work	M,D
Sociology	M,D
Spanish	M
Special Education	M,D,O
Statistics	M,D,O
Student Affairs	M,D,O
Vocational and Technical Education	M,D,O
Women's Studies	M

THE UNIVERSITY OF TAMPA

Accounting	M
Adult Nursing	M
Business Administration and Management—General	M
Curriculum and Instruction	M
Economics	M
Education—General	M
Entrepreneurship	M
Family Nurse Practitioner Studies	M
Finance and Banking	M
International Business	M
Management Information Systems	M
Marketing	M
Mathematics Education	M
Nonprofit Management	M
Nursing—General	M
Science Education	M
Social Sciences Education	M

THE UNIVERSITY OF TENNESSEE

Accounting	M,D
Adult Education	M,D
Advertising and Public Relations	M,D
Aerospace/Aeronautical Engineering	M,D
Agricultural Education	M
Agricultural Engineering	M
Agricultural Sciences—General	M,D
Analytical Chemistry	M,D
Anatomy	M,D
Animal Behavior	M,D
Animal Sciences	M,D
Anthropology	M,D
Applied Mathematics	M,D
Archaeology	M,D
Architecture	M
Art Education	M,D,O
Art/Fine Arts	M
Artificial Intelligence/ Robotics	M,D
Athletic Training and Sports Medicine	M,D
Aviation	M
Biochemistry	M,D
Bioethics	M,D
Biological and Biomedical Sciences—General	M,D
Biomedical Engineering	M,D
Biosystems Engineering	M,D
Business Administration and Management—General	M,D
Chemical Engineering	M,D
Chemical Physics	M,D
Chemistry	M,D
Child and Family Studies	M,D
Civil Engineering	M,D
Clinical Psychology	M,D
Clothing and Textiles	M,D
Communication Disorders	M,D,O
Communication—General	M,D
Community Health	M,D
Computer Engineering	M,D
Computer Science	M,D
Consumer Economics	M,D
Counseling Psychology	M,D
Counselor Education	M,D,O
Criminal Justice and Criminology	M,D
Curriculum and Instruction	M,D,O
Early Childhood Education	M,D,O
Ecology	M,D
Economics	M,D
Education—General	M,D,O
Educational Leadership and Administration	M,D,O
Educational Measurement and Evaluation	M,D,O
Educational Media/ Instructional Technology	M,D,O
Educational Psychology	M,D,O
Electrical Engineering	M,D
Elementary Education	M,D,O
Engineering and Applied Sciences—General	M,D
Engineering Management	M,D
English as a Second Language	M,D,O
English Education	M,D,O
English	M,D
Entomology	M,D
Environmental Engineering	M
Environmental Management and Policy	M,D
Ergonomics and Human Factors	M,D
Evolutionary Biology	M,D
Exercise and Sports Science	M,D,O
Experimental Psychology	M,D
Family and Consumer Sciences-General	D
Finance and Banking	M,D
Fish, Game, and Wildlife Management	M
Food Science and Technology	M,D
Foreign Languages Education	M,D,O
Forestry	M
Foundations and Philosophy of Education	M,D,O
French	M,D
Genetics	M,D
Genomic Sciences	M,D
Geography	M,D

Geology	M,D
German	M,D
Gerontology	M
Graphic Design	M
Health Education	M
Health Promotion	M
Health Services Management and Hospital Administration	M
History	M,D
Hospitality Management	M
Human Resources Development	M
Industrial and Manufacturing Management	M,D
Industrial and Organizational Psychology	D
Industrial/Management Engineering	M,D
Information Science	M,D
Inorganic Chemistry	M,D
Italian	D
Journalism	M,D
Kinesiology and Movement Studies	M,D
Landscape Architecture	M
Law	P
Leisure Studies	M,D
Linguistics	D
Logistics	M,D
Manufacturing Engineering	M,D
Marketing	M,D
Materials Engineering	M,D
Materials Sciences	M,D
Mathematics Education	M,D,O
Mathematics	M,D
Mechanical Engineering	M,D
Mechanics	M,D
Media Studies	M,D
Microbiology	M,D
Multilingual and Multicultural Education	M,D,O
Music Education	M
Music	M
Nuclear Engineering	M,D
Nursing—General	M,D
Nutrition	M
Organic Chemistry	M,D
Philosophy	M,D
Photography	M
Physical Chemistry	M,D
Physics	M,D
Physiology	M,D
Plant Pathology	M,D
Plant Physiology	M,D
Plant Sciences	M
Political Science	M,D
Polymer Science and Engineering	M,D
Portuguese	D
Psychology—General	M,D
Public Administration	M
Public Health—General	M
Reading Education	M,D,O
Recreation and Park Management	M,D
Rehabilitation Counseling	M,D
Religion	M,D
Russian	D
School Psychology	M,D,O
Science Education	M,D,O
Secondary Education	M,D,O
Social Sciences Education	M,D,O
Social Work	M,D
Sociology	M,D
Spanish	M,D
Special Education	M,D,O
Speech and Interpersonal Communication	M,D
Sports Management	M,D
Statistics	M,D
Student Affairs	M
Theater	M
Theoretical Chemistry	M,D
Transportation Management	M,D
Travel and Tourism	M
Veterinary Medicine	P

THE UNIVERSITY OF TENNESSEE AT CHATTANOOGA

Accounting	M
Adult Nursing	M,O
Business Administration and Management—General	M
Chemical Engineering	M
Civil Engineering	M
Computational Sciences	M,D
Computer Science	M,O
Counselor Education	M,O
Criminal Justice and Criminology	M
Education—General	M,D,O
Educational Leadership and Administration	M,D,O
Educational Media/ Instructional Technology	O
Electrical Engineering	M
Elementary Education	M,O
Engineering and Applied Sciences—General	M,D,O
Engineering Management	M,O
English	M
Environmental Sciences	M
Experimental Psychology	M
Family Nurse Practitioner Studies	M,O
Industrial and Organizational Psychology	M
Industrial/Management Engineering	M
Mechanical Engineering	M
Music	M
Nurse Anesthesia	M,O
Nursing and Healthcare Administration	M,O
Nursing Education	M,O
Nursing—General	M,O
Physical Education	M
Physical Therapy	D
Psychology—General	M
Public Administration	M,O
School Psychology	O
Secondary Education	M,O
Special Education	M,O

THE UNIVERSITY OF TENNESSEE AT MARTIN

Agricultural Sciences—General	M
Business Administration and Management—General	M
Child and Family Studies	M
Child Development	M
Counselor Education	M
Education—General	M
Educational Leadership and Administration	M
Elementary Education	M
Family and Consumer Sciences-General	M
Food Science and Technology	M
Nutrition	M
Secondary Education	M
Social Psychology	M

THE UNIVERSITY OF TENNESSEE HEALTH SCIENCE CENTER

Allied Health—General	M,D
Allopathic Medicine	P,M,D
Anatomy	D
Biological and Biomedical Sciences—General	M,D*
Biomedical Engineering	M,D
Dentistry	P,M,O
Neurobiology	D
Nursing—General	M,D
Oral and Dental Sciences	P,M,O
Pharmaceutical Sciences	M,D
Pharmacy	P,M,D
Physical Therapy	M,D

THE UNIVERSITY OF TENNESSEE–OAK RIDGE NATIONAL LABORATORY GRADUATE SCHOOL OF GENOME SCIENCE AND TECHNOLOGY

Biological and Biomedical Sciences—General	M,D
Genomic Sciences	M,D

THE UNIVERSITY OF TENNESSEE SPACE INSTITUTE

Aerospace/Aeronautical Engineering	M,D
Applied Mathematics	M
Aviation	M
Computer Science	M,D
Electrical Engineering	M,D
Engineering and Applied Sciences—General	M,D*
Engineering Management	M,D
Materials Engineering	M
Materials Sciences	M
Mechanical Engineering	M,D
Mechanics	M,D
Physics	M,D

THE UNIVERSITY OF TEXAS AT ARLINGTON

Accounting	M,D
Aerospace/Aeronautical Engineering	M,D
Anthropology	M
Architecture	M
Art/Fine Arts	M
Bioengineering	M,D
Biological and Biomedical Sciences—General	M,D
Business Administration and Management—General	M,D*
Chemistry	M,D
Civil Engineering	M,D
Communication—General	M
Computer Engineering	M,D
Computer Science	M,D
Criminal Justice and Criminology	M
Curriculum and Instruction	M,D
Economics	M
Education—General	M,D
Educational Leadership and Administration	M,D
Electrical Engineering	M,D
Engineering and Applied Sciences—General	M,D
English as a Second Language	M
English	M,D
Environmental Sciences	M,D
Exercise and Sports Science	M,D
Experimental Psychology	M,D
Family Nurse Practitioner Studies	M,D
Finance and Banking	M,D
French	M
Geology	M,D
Health Psychology	M,D
Health Services Management and Hospital Administration	M
History	M,D
Human Resources Management	M
Humanities	M
Industrial and Organizational Psychology	M,D
Industrial/Management Engineering	M
Interdisciplinary Studies	M
Landscape Architecture	M
Linguistics	M,D
Logistics	M
Management Information Systems	M,D
Marketing Research	M
Marketing	M,D
Materials Engineering	M,D
Materials Sciences	M,D
Mathematics	M,D
Mechanical Engineering	M,D
Music Education	M
Music	M
Nursing and Healthcare Administration	M,D
Nursing Education	M,D
Nursing—General	M,D
Physical Education	M,D
Physics	M,D
Political Science	M
Psychology—General	M,D
Public Administration	M
Public Affairs	D
Quantitative Analysis	M,D
Real Estate	M,D
Social Work	M,D
Sociology	M
Software Engineering	M,D
Spanish	M
Systems Engineering	M
Taxation	M
Urban and Regional Planning	M

THE UNIVERSITY OF TEXAS AT AUSTIN

Accounting	M,D
Actuarial Science	M,D
Advertising and Public Relations	M,D
Aerospace/Aeronautical Engineering	M,D
African Studies	M,D
American Studies	M,D
Analytical Chemistry	M,D
Animal Behavior	M,D
Anthropology	M,D
Applied Arts and Design—General	M
Applied Mathematics	M,D
Applied Physics	M,D
Archaeology	M,D
Architectural Engineering	M
Architectural History	M,D
Architecture	M,D
Art Education	M
Art History	M,D
Art/Fine Arts	M
Asian Languages	M,D
Asian Studies	M,D
Astronomy	M,D
Biochemistry	M,D
Biological and Biomedical Sciences—General	M,D
Biomedical Engineering	M,D
Biopsychology	D
Business Administration and Management—General	M,D
Cell Biology	D
Chemical Engineering	M,D
Chemistry	M,D
Child and Family Studies	M,D
Child Development	M,D
Civil Engineering	M,D
Classics	M,D
Cognitive Sciences	M,D
Communication Disorders	M,D
Communication—General	M,D
Comparative Literature	M,D
Computational Sciences	M,D
Computer Engineering	M,D
Computer Science	M,D
Counseling Psychology	M,D
Counselor Education	M,D
Curriculum and Instruction	M,D
Dance	M,D

*M—master's degree; P—first professional degree; D—doctorate; O—other advanced degree; *—Close-Up and/or Announcement or Display in one of the other books in this series*

East European and Russian Studies	M
Ecology	M,D
Economics	M,D
Education—General	M,D
Educational Leadership and Administration	M,D
Educational Psychology	M,D
Electrical Engineering	M,D
Engineering and Applied Sciences—General	M,D
English	M,D
Entrepreneurship	M
Environmental Engineering	M,D
Evolutionary Biology	M,D
Family and Consumer Sciences-General	M,D
Film, Television, and Video Production	M,D
Finance and Banking	D
Folklore	M,D
Foreign Languages Education	M,D
French	M,D
Geography	M,D
Geology	M,D
Geosciences	M,D
Geotechnical Engineering	M,D
German	M,D
Health Education	M,D
Hispanic Studies	M
Historic Preservation	M,D
History	M,D
Human Development	M,D
Industrial and Manufacturing Management	D
Industrial/Management Engineering	M,D
Information Studies	M,D
Inorganic Chemistry	M,D
Italian	M,D
Journalism	M,D
Kinesiology and Movement Studies	M,D
Landscape Architecture	M,D
Latin American Studies	M,D
Law	P,M
Linguistics	M,D
Management Information Systems	D
Marine Sciences	M,D
Marketing	D
Materials Engineering	M,D
Materials Sciences	M,D
Mathematics Education	M,D
Mathematics	M,D
Mechanical Engineering	M,D
Mechanics	M,D
Media Studies	M,D
Microbiology	D
Mineral Economics	M
Mineral/Mining Engineering	M
Molecular Biology	D
Music	M,D
Natural Resources	M
Near and Middle Eastern Languages	M,D
Near and Middle Eastern Studies	M,D
Neurobiology	D
Neuroscience	D
Nursing—General	M,D
Nutrition	M,D
Operations Research	M,D
Organic Chemistry	M,D
Petroleum Engineering	M,D
Pharmaceutical Sciences	M,D
Pharmacy	P
Philosophy	D
Physical Chemistry	M,D
Physics	M,D
Plant Biology	M,D
Political Science	D
Portuguese	M,D
Psychology—General	D
Public Affairs	M,D
Public History	M,D
Public Policy	M,D
Romance Languages	M,D
School Psychology	M,D
Science Education	M,D
Slavic Languages	M,D
Social Work	M,D
Sociology	M,D
Spanish	M,D
Special Education	M,D
Sport Psychology	M,D
Statistics	M
Supply Chain Management	D
Technology and Public Policy	M
Textile Sciences and Engineering	M
Theater	M,D
Urban and Regional Planning	M,D
Urban Design	M,D
Water Resources Engineering	M,D
Writing	M,D

THE UNIVERSITY OF TEXAS AT BROWNSVILLE

Biological and Biomedical Sciences—General	M
Business Administration and Management—General	M
Community Health Nursing	M
Counselor Education	M
Curriculum and Instruction	M
Early Childhood Education	M
Education—General	M
Educational Leadership and Administration	M
Educational Media/Instructional Technology	M
English as a Second Language	M
English	M
History	M
Interdisciplinary Studies	M
Mathematics	M
Multilingual and Multicultural Education	M
Physics	M
Political Science	M
Psychology—General	M
Public Administration	M
Public Policy	M
Reading Education	M
Spanish	M
Special Education	M

THE UNIVERSITY OF TEXAS AT DALLAS

Accounting	M,D
Applied Mathematics	M,D
Biological and Biomedical Sciences—General	M,D
Biotechnology	M,D
Business Administration and Management—General	M,D*
Cell Biology	M,D
Chemistry	M,D
Child and Family Studies	M,D
Cognitive Sciences	M,D
Communication Disorders	M,D
Communication—General	M,D
Comparative Literature	M,D
Computer and Information Systems Security	M
Computer Engineering	M,D
Computer Science	M,D
Criminal Justice and Criminology	M,D
Economics	M,D*
Electrical Engineering	M,D
Electronic Commerce	M
Engineering and Applied Sciences—General	M,D
Entrepreneurship	M
Finance and Banking	M,D
Geochemistry	M,D
Geographic Information Systems	M,D
Geophysics	M,D
Geosciences	M,D
Health Services Management and Hospital Administration	M
Humanities	M,D
Hydrogeology	M,D
Interdisciplinary Studies	M
International Business	M,D
Management Information Systems	M,D
Management Strategy and Policy	M
Marketing	D
Materials Engineering	M,D
Materials Sciences	M,D
Mathematics Education	M
Mathematics	M,D*
Mechanical Engineering	M
Molecular Biology	M,D
Neuroscience	M,D
Nursing and Healthcare Administration	M
Paleontology	M,D
Physics	M,D
Political Science	M,D
Project Management	M
Psychology—General	M,D
Public Affairs	M,D
Public Policy	M,D
Science Education	M
Sociology	M
Software Engineering	M,D
Statistics	M,D
Supply Chain Management	M
Taxation	M
Telecommunications	M,D

THE UNIVERSITY OF TEXAS AT EL PASO

Accounting	M
Allied Health—General	D
Applied Mathematics	M
Art Education	M
Art/Fine Arts	M
Bioinformatics	M
Biological and Biomedical Sciences—General	M,D
Business Administration and Management—General	M
Chemistry	M,D
Civil Engineering	M,D
Clinical Psychology	M,D
Communication Disorders	M
Communication—General	M
Computer Engineering	M,D
Computer Science	M,D
Counselor Education	M
Curriculum and Instruction	M,D
Economics	M
Education—General	M,D
Educational Leadership and Administration	M,D
Educational Measurement and Evaluation	M
Educational Psychology	M
Electrical Engineering	M,D
Engineering and Applied Sciences—General	M,D
English Education	M,D
English	M,D
Environmental Engineering	M,D
Environmental Sciences	D
Experimental Psychology	M,D
Family Nurse Practitioner Studies	M,O
Geology	M,D
Geophysics	M,D
Health Education	M
Health Promotion	M
Health Services Management and Hospital Administration	M,O
History	M,D
Industrial/Management Engineering	M
Information Science	M,D
Interdisciplinary Studies	M
Kinesiology and Movement Studies	M
Linguistics	M
Manufacturing Engineering	M
Materials Engineering	D
Materials Sciences	D
Mathematics	M
Mechanical Engineering	M
Metallurgical Engineering and Metallurgy	M
Military and Defense Studies	M
Music Education	M
Music	M
National Security	M
Nursing and Healthcare Administration	M,O
Nursing Education	M,O
Nursing—General	M,O
Occupational Therapy	M
Physical Therapy	M
Physics	M
Political Science	M
Psychology—General	M,D
Public Administration	M
Public Health—General	M
Public Policy	M
Reading Education	M,D
Rhetoric	M,D
Sociology	M
Spanish	M
Special Education	M
Statistics	M
Women's Health Nursing	M,O
Writing	M,D

THE UNIVERSITY OF TEXAS AT SAN ANTONIO

Accounting	M,D
Adult Education	M,D,O
Anthropology	M,D
Applied Mathematics	M
Applied Statistics	M,D
Architecture	M,O
Art History	M
Art/Fine Arts	M
Biological and Biomedical Sciences—General	M,D*
Biomedical Engineering	M,D
Biotechnology	M,D
Business Administration and Management—General	M,D
Cell Biology	M,D
Chemistry	M,D
Civil Engineering	M,D
Communication—General	M
Computer Engineering	M,D
Computer Science	M,D
Counselor Education	M,D,O
Criminal Justice and Criminology	M
Cultural Studies	M,D
Curriculum and Instruction	M
Demography and Population Studies	D
Early Childhood Education	M
Economics	M
Education—General	M,D,O
Educational Leadership and Administration	M,D
Educational Media/Instructional Technology	M
Electrical Engineering	M,D
Engineering and Applied Sciences—General	M,D
English as a Second Language	M,D
English	M,D,O
Environmental Engineering	M,D
Environmental Sciences	M,D
Finance and Banking	M,D

Geology	M
Health Education	M
Health Promotion	M
Higher Education	M,D,O
Historic Preservation	M,O
History	M
Information Science	M,D
Interdisciplinary Studies	M
International Business	M,D
Kinesiology and Movement Studies	M
Management Information Systems	M,D
Marketing	M,D
Mathematics	M
Mechanical Engineering	M
Molecular Biology	M,D
Multilingual and Multicultural Education	M,D
Music	M,O
Neurobiology	M,D
Organizational Management	M,D
Physics	M,D
Political Science	M
Psychology—General	M
Public Administration	M
Reading Education	M
Social Work	M
Sociology	M
Spanish	M,O
Special Education	M
Statistics	M,D
Taxation	M,D
Translation and Interpretation	M,O
Urban and Regional Planning	M,O
Writing	M,D,O

THE UNIVERSITY OF TEXAS AT TYLER

Art History	M
Art/Fine Arts	M
Biological and Biomedical Sciences—General	M
Business Administration and Management—General	M
Civil Engineering	M
Clinical Psychology	M
Communication—General	M
Computer Science	M
Counseling Psychology	M
Criminal Justice and Criminology	M
Early Childhood Education	M
Educational Leadership and Administration	M
Electrical Engineering	M
English	M
Family Nurse Practitioner Studies	M,D
Health Education	M
Health Services Management and Hospital Administration	M
History	M
Human Resources Development	M,D
Industrial and Manufacturing Management	M,D
Interdisciplinary Studies	M
Kinesiology and Movement Studies	M
Marriage and Family Therapy	M
Mathematics	M
Mechanical Engineering	M
Nursing and Healthcare Administration	M,D
Nursing Education	M,D
Nursing—General	M,D
Political Science	M
Psychology—General	M
Public Administration	M
Reading Education	M
School Psychology	M
Social Sciences	M
Sociology	M
Special Education	M
Vocational and Technical Education	M,D

THE UNIVERSITY OF TEXAS HEALTH SCIENCE CENTER AT HOUSTON

Allopathic Medicine	P
Biochemistry	M,D
Biological and Biomedical Sciences—General	M,D
Biomathematics	M,D
Biostatistics	M,D
Cancer Biology/Oncology	M,D
Cell Biology	M,D
Dentistry	P,M
Developmental Biology	M,D
Genetic Counseling	M
Genetics	M,D
Health Informatics	M,D,O
Human Genetics	M,D
Immunology	M,D
Medical Physics	M,D
Microbiology	M,D
Molecular Biology	M,D
Molecular Genetics	M,D
Molecular Pathology	M,D
Neuroscience	M,D
Nursing—General	M,D
Public Health—General	M,D,O
Virology	M,D

THE UNIVERSITY OF TEXAS HEALTH SCIENCE CENTER AT SAN ANTONIO

Allopathic Medicine	P,M
Biochemistry	M,D
Biological and Biomedical Sciences—General	M,D
Cell Biology	M,D
Clinical Laboratory Sciences/Medical Technology	M
Communication Disorders	M
Dental Hygiene	M
Dentistry	P,M,O
Immunology	D
Medical Physics	M,D
Microbiology	D
Molecular Medicine	M,D
Nursing—General	M,D
Occupational Therapy	M
Oral and Dental Sciences	M,O
Pharmacology	D
Physical Therapy	M
Physician Assistant Studies	M
Physiology	M,D
Structural Biology	M,D

THE UNIVERSITY OF TEXAS MEDICAL BRANCH

Allied Health—General	M,D
Allopathic Medicine	P
Bacteriology	D
Biochemistry	D
Bioinformatics	D
Biological and Biomedical Sciences—General	M,D
Biophysics	D
Cell Biology	D
Clinical Laboratory Sciences/Medical Technology	M,D
Community Health	M,D
Computational Biology	D
Genetics	D
Humanities	M,D
Immunology	M,D
Infectious Diseases	D*
Microbiology	M,D
Molecular Biophysics	M,D
Neuroscience	D
Nursing—General	M,D
Occupational Therapy	M
Pathology	D
Pharmacology	M,D
Physical Therapy	M,D
Physician Assistant Studies	M
Physiology	M,D
Public Health—General	M
Structural Biology	D
Toxicology	M,D
Virology	D

THE UNIVERSITY OF TEXAS OF THE PERMIAN BASIN

Accounting	M
Biological and Biomedical Sciences—General	M
Business Administration and Management—General	M
Clinical Psychology	M
Computer Science	M
Counselor Education	M
Criminal Justice and Criminology	M
Early Childhood Education	M
Education—General	M
Educational Leadership and Administration	M
English as a Second Language	M
English	M
Experimental Psychology	M
Foundations and Philosophy of Education	M
Geology	M
History	M
Kinesiology and Movement Studies	M
Political Science	M
Psychology—General	M
Reading Education	M
Spanish	M
Special Education	M

THE UNIVERSITY OF TEXAS–PAN AMERICAN

Accounting	M
Adult Nursing	M
Art/Fine Arts	M
Biological and Biomedical Sciences—General	M
Business Administration and Management—General	M,D
Chemistry	M
Clinical Psychology	M
Communication Disorders	M
Communication—General	M
Computer Science	M
Counselor Education	M
Criminal Justice and Criminology	M
Early Childhood Education	M
Economics	D
Education of the Gifted	M
Education—General	M,D
Educational Leadership and Administration	M,D.
Educational Measurement and Evaluation	M
Educational Psychology	M
Electrical Engineering	M
Elementary Education	M
English as a Second Language	M
English	M
Experimental Psychology	M
Family Nurse Practitioner Studies	M
Finance and Banking	D
History	M
Interdisciplinary Studies	M
International Business	D
Kinesiology and Movement Studies	M
Management Information Systems	D
Manufacturing Engineering	M
Marketing	D
Mathematics Education	M
Mathematics	M
Mechanical Engineering	M
Multilingual and Multicultural Education	M
Music Education	M
Music	M
Nursing—General	M
Occupational Therapy	M
Pediatric Nursing	M
Psychology—General	M
Public Administration	M
Reading Education	M
Rehabilitation Counseling	M
School Psychology	M
Secondary Education	M
Social Work	M
Sociology	M
Spanish	M
Special Education	M
Theater	M

THE UNIVERSITY OF TEXAS SOUTHWESTERN MEDICAL CENTER AT DALLAS

Allopathic Medicine	P
Biochemistry	D
Biological and Biomedical Sciences—General	M,D*
Biomedical Engineering	M,D
Cell Biology	D
Clinical Psychology	D
Developmental Biology	D
Genetics	D
Immunology	D
Medical Illustration	M
Microbiology	D
Molecular Biophysics	D
Neuroscience	D
Physical Therapy	D
Physician Assistant Studies	M
Radiation Biology	M,D
Rehabilitation Counseling	M

THE UNIVERSITY OF THE ARTS

Art Education	M
Art/Fine Arts	M*
Industrial Design	M
Museum Education	M
Museum Studies	M
Music Education	M
Music	M

UNIVERSITY OF THE CUMBERLANDS

Early Childhood Education	M
Education—General	M,O
Educational Leadership and Administration	M
Elementary Education	M
Middle School Education	M
Reading Education	M
Secondary Education	M
Special Education	M

UNIVERSITY OF THE DISTRICT OF COLUMBIA

Business Administration and Management—General	M
Clinical Psychology	M
Communication Disorders	M
Counseling Psychology	M
Counselor Education	M
Early Childhood Education	M
Education—General	M
English	M
Law	P

*M—master's degree; P—first professional degree; D—doctorate; O—other advanced degree; *—Close-Up and/or Announcement or Display in one of the other books in this series*

Mathematics Education M
Public Administration M
Special Education M

UNIVERSITY OF THE FRASER VALLEY

Criminal Justice and Criminology M

UNIVERSITY OF THE INCARNATE WORD

Accounting M
Adult Education M,D,O
Biological and Biomedical Sciences—General M
Business Administration and Management—General M,O
Communication—General M,O
Early Childhood Education M,D
Education—General M,D
Educational Leadership and Administration M,D
Educational Media/Instructional Technology M,D,O
Elementary Education M
Entrepreneurship M,D
Health Promotion M
Health Services Management and Hospital Administration M,O
Higher Education M,D
Interdisciplinary Studies M
International Business M,O
Kinesiology and Movement Studies M,D
Mathematics Education M,D
Mathematics M
Multilingual and Multicultural Education M,D
Nursing—General M
Nutrition M,O
Optometry P
Organizational Management M,D,O
Pharmacy P
Physical Education M,O
Project Management M,O
Reading Education M,D
Religion M
Science Education M
Secondary Education M
Special Education M,D
Sports Management M,O
Statistics M

UNIVERSITY OF THE PACIFIC

Biological and Biomedical Sciences—General M
Business Administration and Management—General M
Communication Disorders M
Communication—General M
Criminal Justice and Criminology P,M,D
Curriculum and Instruction M,D
Dentistry P,M,O
Education—General M,D,O
Educational Leadership and Administration M,D
Educational Psychology M,D,O
Exercise and Sports Science M
International Affairs P,M,D
Law P,M,D
Legal and Justice Studies P,M,D
Music Education M
Music M
Oral and Dental Sciences M,O
Pharmaceutical Sciences M,D
Pharmacy P
Physical Therapy M,D
Psychology—General M
Public Policy P,M,D
School Psychology M,D,O
Special Education M,D
Taxation P,M,D
Therapies—Dance, Drama, and Music M
Water Resources P,M,D

UNIVERSITY OF THE SACRED HEART

Accounting M
Advertising and Public Relations M
Business Administration and Management—General M
Communication—General M
Conflict Resolution and Mediation/Peace Studies M
Cultural Studies M
Early Childhood Education M
Education—General M
Educational Media/Instructional Technology M
Environmental and Occupational Health M
Film, Television, and Video Production M
Human Resources Management M
Legal and Justice Studies M
Management Information Systems M
Marketing M
Nonprofit Management M
Occupational Health Nursing M
Taxation M
Writing M

UNIVERSITY OF THE SCIENCES IN PHILADELPHIA

Biochemistry M,D
Bioinformatics M
Biotechnology M,D
Cell Biology M,D
Chemistry M,D
Health Psychology M
Health Services Management and Hospital Administration M,D
Medicinal and Pharmaceutical Chemistry M,D
Pharmaceutical Administration M
Pharmaceutical Sciences M,D*
Pharmacology M,D
Public Health—General M,D
Technical Writing M,O
Toxicology M,D

UNIVERSITY OF THE SOUTHWEST

Business Administration and Management—General M
Counselor Education M
Curriculum and Instruction M
Early Childhood Education M
Education—General M
Educational Leadership and Administration M
Educational Measurement and Evaluation M
Special Education M

UNIVERSITY OF THE VIRGIN ISLANDS

Business Administration and Management—General M
Education—General M
Environmental Sciences M
Marine Sciences M
Mathematics Education M
Public Administration M

UNIVERSITY OF THE WEST

Business Administration and Management—General M
Finance and Banking M
International Business M
Management Information Systems M
Nonprofit Management M
Religion M,D

THE UNIVERSITY OF TOLEDO

Accounting M
Adult Nursing M,O
Analytical Chemistry M,D
Applied Mathematics M,D
Art Education M
Biochemistry M,D
Bioengineering M,D
Bioinformatics M,O
Biological and Biomedical Sciences—General M,D,O
Biomedical Engineering D
Biopsychology M,D
Biostatistics M,O
Business Administration and Management—General M,D
Business Education M
Cancer Biology/Oncology M,D
Cardiovascular Sciences M,D
Chemical Engineering M,D
Chemistry M,D
Civil Engineering M,D
Clinical Psychology M,D
Cognitive Sciences M,D
Communication Disorders M
Communication—General O
Computer Science M,D
Counselor Education M,D,O
Criminal Justice and Criminology M,O
Curriculum and Instruction M,D,O
Early Childhood Education M,O
Ecology M,D
Economics M
Education of the Gifted D,O
Education—General M,D,O
Educational Leadership and Administration M,D,O
Educational Measurement and Evaluation M,D
Educational Media/Instructional Technology M,D,O
Educational Psychology M,D
Electrical Engineering M,D
Elementary Education D,O
Engineering and Applied Sciences—General M
English as a Second Language M,O
English Education M
English M,O
Environmental and Occupational Health M,O
Environmental Sciences M,D
Epidemiology M,O
Exercise and Sports Science M,D
Experimental Psychology M,D
Family Nurse Practitioner Studies M,O
Finance and Banking M
Foreign Languages Education M
Foundations and Philosophy of Education M,D
French M
Genomic Sciences M,O
Geographic Information Systems M,O
Geography M,O
Geology M,D
Geosciences M,D
German M
Gerontology O
Health Education M,D
Health Physics/Radiological Health M
Health Services Management and Hospital Administration M,O
Higher Education M,D
History M,D
Homeland Security M,O
Human Resources Management M
Immunology M,D
Industrial and Manufacturing Management M,D
Industrial/Management Engineering M,D
Inorganic Chemistry M,D
International Business M
International Health M,O
Law P
Leisure Studies M
Liberal Studies M
Management Information Systems M
Marketing M
Mathematics Education M
Mathematics M,D
Mechanical Engineering M,D
Medical Physics M
Medicinal and Pharmaceutical Chemistry M,D
Middle School Education M
Molecular Biology M
Music Education M
Music M
Neuroscience M,D
Nursing Education M,O
Nursing—General M,O
Occupational Therapy D
Oral and Dental Sciences M
Organic Chemistry M,D
Pathology O
Pediatric Nursing M,O
Pharmaceutical Administration M
Pharmaceutical Sciences M
Pharmacology M
Philosophy M
Physical Chemistry M,D
Physical Education M
Physical Therapy M,D
Physician Assistant Studies M
Physics M,D
Political Science M
Psychology—General M,D
Public Administration M,O
Public Health—General M,O
School Psychology M,D,O
Science Education M
Secondary Education M,D,O
Social Psychology M,D,O
Social Sciences Education M
Social Work M
Sociology M
Spanish M
Special Education M,D,O
Statistics M,D
Urban and Regional Planning M,O
Vocational and Technical Education M,O
Writing M,O

UNIVERSITY OF TORONTO

Accounting M,D
Aerospace/Aeronautical Engineering M,D
Allopathic Medicine P,M,D
Anthropology M,D
Architecture M
Art History M,D
Art/Fine Arts M,D
Asian Studies M,D
Astronomy M,D
Astrophysics M,D

Biochemistry	M,D
Bioethics	M,D
Biological and Biomedical Sciences—General	M,D
Biomedical Engineering	M,D
Biophysics	M,D
Business Administration and Management—General	M,D
Cell Biology	M,D
Chemical Engineering	M,D
Chemistry	M,D
Civil Engineering	M,D
Classics	M,D
Communication Disorders	M,D
Comparative Literature	M,D
Computer Engineering	M,D
Computer Science	M,D
Criminal Justice and Criminology	M,D
Dentistry	P
East European and Russian Studies	M
Ecology	M,D
Economics	M,D
Education—General	M,D
Electrical Engineering	M,D
Engineering and Applied Sciences—General	M,D
English	M,D
Evolutionary Biology	M,D
Forestry	M,D
French	M,D
Genetic Counseling	M,D
Genetics	M,D
Geography	M,D
Geology	M,D
German	M,D
History of Science and Technology	M,D
History	M,D
Human Resources Management	M,D
Immunology	M,D
Industrial and Labor Relations	M,D
Industrial/Management Engineering	M,D
Information Studies	M,D,O
Italian	M,D
Law	P,M,D
Library Science	M,D,O
Linguistics	M,D
Materials Engineering	M,D
Materials Sciences	M,D
Mathematics	M,D
Mechanical Engineering	M,D
Medieval and Renaissance Studies	M,D
Museum Studies	M,D
Music Education	M,D
Music	M,D
Near and Middle Eastern Studies	M,D
Nursing—General	M,D
Nutrition	M,D
Oral and Dental Sciences	M,D
Pathobiology	M,D
Pharmaceutical Sciences	M,D
Pharmacology	M,D
Philosophy	M,D
Physical Education	M,D
Physics	M,D
Physiology	M,D
Political Science	M,D
Portuguese	M,D
Psychology—General	M,D
Public Health—General	M,D
Rehabilitation Sciences	M,D
Religion	M,D
Slavic Languages	M,D
Social Work	M,D
Sociology	M,D
Spanish	M,D
Statistics	M,D
Systems Biology	M,D
Theater	M,D
Toxicology	M,D
Urban and Regional Planning	M,D
Urban Design	M,D

UNIVERSITY OF TRINITY COLLEGE

Music	P,M,D,O
Pastoral Ministry and Counseling	P,M,D,O
Theology	P,M,D,O

UNIVERSITY OF TULSA

Accounting	M
Anthropology	M
Art/Fine Arts	M
Biochemistry	M
Biological and Biomedical Sciences—General	M,D
Business Administration and Management—General	M
Chemical Engineering	M,D
Chemistry	M,D
Clinical Psychology	M,D
Communication Disorders	M
Computer Science	M,D
Education—General	M
Electrical Engineering	M
Energy Management and Policy	M
Engineering and Applied Sciences—General	M,D
Engineering Physics	M
English	M,D
Environmental Law	P,M,O
Finance and Banking	M*
Financial Engineering	M
Geosciences	M,D
Health Law	P,M,O
History	M
Industrial and Organizational Psychology	M,D
International Business	M
Investment Management	M
Law	P,M,O
Management Information Systems	M
Mathematics Education	M
Mathematics	M
Mechanical Engineering	M,D
Petroleum Engineering	M,D
Physics	M
Psychology—General	M,D
Science Education	M
Taxation	M

UNIVERSITY OF UTAH

Accounting	M,D
Allopathic Medicine	P
American Studies	M,D
Anatomy	D
Anthropology	M,D
Architecture	M
Art Education	M
Art History	M
Art/Fine Arts	M
Asian Studies	M
Atmospheric Sciences	M,D
Biochemistry	M,D
Bioengineering	M,D*
Bioinformatics	M,D,O
Biological and Biomedical Sciences—General	M,D,O*
Biostatistics	M,D
Biotechnology	M
Business Administration and Management—General	M,D
Cancer Biology/Oncology	M,D
Chemical Engineering	M,D
Chemical Physics	M,D
Chemistry	M,D
Child and Family Studies	M
Civil Engineering	M,D
Clinical Laboratory Sciences/Medical Technology	M
Clinical Psychology	D
Communication Disorders	M,D
Communication—General	M,D
Comparative Literature	M,D
Computational Sciences	M
Computer Science	M,D
Consumer Economics	M
Counseling Psychology	M,D
Counselor Education	M,D
Dance	M
Early Childhood Education	M,D
Economics	M,D
Education—General	M,D
Educational Leadership and Administration	M,D
Educational Psychology	M,D
Electrical Engineering	M,D,O
Elementary Education	M,D
Engineering and Applied Sciences—General	M,D,O
English	M,D
Environmental Engineering	M,D
Environmental Sciences	M
Exercise and Sports Science	M,D
Film, Television, and Video Production	M
Finance and Banking	M,D
Foreign Languages Education	M,D
Foundations and Philosophy of Education	M,D
French	M,D
Geography	M,D
Geological Engineering	M,D
Geology	M,D
Geophysics	M,D
German	M,D
Gerontological Nursing	M,O
Gerontology	M,O
Graphic Design	M
Health Education	M,D
Health Promotion	M,D
History	M,D
Human Development	M
Human Genetics	M,D
Humanities	M
International Affairs	M
Law	P,M
Leisure Studies	M,D
Linguistics	M,D
Materials Engineering	M,D
Materials Sciences	M,D
Mathematics	M,D*
Mechanical Engineering	M,D
Medical Physics	D
Medicinal and Pharmaceutical Chemistry	M,D
Metallurgical Engineering and Metallurgy	M,D
Mineral/Mining Engineering	M,D
Molecular Biology	D
Music	M,D
Near and Middle Eastern Languages	M,D
Near and Middle Eastern Studies	M,D
Neurobiology	D
Neuroscience	D*
Nuclear Engineering	M,D
Nursing—General	M,D
Nutrition	M
Occupational Therapy	M
Pathology	M,D
Pharmaceutical Sciences	M
Pharmacology	D
Pharmacy	P
Philosophy	M,D
Photography	M
Physical Therapy	D,O
Physician Assistant Studies	M
Physics	M,D
Physiology	D
Political Science	M,D
Psychology—General	D
Public Administration	M
Public Health—General	M,D
Public Policy	M
Recreation and Park Management	M,D
Rhetoric	M,D
School Psychology	M,D
Science Education	M,D
Secondary Education	M,D
Social Work	M,D
Sociology	M,D
Spanish	M,D
Special Education	M,D
Statistics	M,D
Toxicology	D
Urban and Regional Planning	M,D
Writing	M,D

UNIVERSITY OF VERMONT

Accounting	M
Agricultural Economics and Agribusiness	M
Agricultural Sciences—General	M,D
Agronomy and Soil Sciences	M,D
Allied Health—General	M,D
Allopathic Medicine	P
Animal Sciences	M,D
Applied Economics	M
Biochemistry	M,D
Biological and Biomedical Sciences—General	M,D
Biomedical Engineering	M
Biophysics	M,D
Biostatistics	M
Business Administration and Management—General	M
Cell Biology	M,D
Chemistry	M,D
Civil Engineering	M,D
Classics	M
Clinical Laboratory Sciences/Medical Technology	M,D
Clinical Psychology	D
Communication—General	M
Computer Science	M,D
Counseling Psychology	M
Counselor Education	M
Curriculum and Instruction	M
Education—General	M,D
Educational Leadership and Administration	M,D
Electrical Engineering	M,D
Engineering and Applied Sciences—General	M,D
English	M
Environmental Engineering	M,D
Food Science and Technology	D
Foreign Languages Education	M
Forestry	M,D
French	M
Geology	M
German	M
Historic Preservation	M
History	M
Horticulture	M,D
Materials Sciences	M,D
Mathematics Education	M,D
Mathematics	M,D
Mechanical Engineering	M,D
Microbiology	M,D
Molecular Biology	M,D
Molecular Genetics	M,D*
Molecular Physiology	M,D
Natural Resources	M,D
Neuroscience	D
Nursing—General	M
Nutrition	M,D

*M—master's degree; P—first professional degree; D—doctorate; O—other advanced degree; *—Close-Up and/or Announcement or Display in one of the other books in this series*

Pathology	M
Pharmacology	M,D
Physical Therapy	D
Physics	M
Plant Biology	M,D
Plant Sciences	M,D
Psychology—General	D
Public Administration	M
Reading Education	M
Science Education	M,D
Social Work	M
Special Education	M
Statistics	M

UNIVERSITY OF VICTORIA

Anthropology	M
Art Education	M,D
Art History	M,D
Art/Fine Arts	M
Asian Studies	M
Astronomy	M,D
Astrophysics	M,D
Biochemistry	M,D
Biological and Biomedical Sciences—General	M,D
Business Administration and Management—General	M
Chemistry	M,D
Child and Family Studies	M,D
Classics	M,D
Clinical Psychology	M,D
Computer Art and Design	M
Computer Engineering	M,D
Computer Science	M,D
Condensed Matter Physics	M,D
Conflict Resolution and Mediation/Peace Studies	M,D
Counseling Psychology	M,D
Counselor Education	M,D
Curriculum and Instruction	M,D
Developmental Psychology	M,D
Early Childhood Education	M,D
Economics	M,D
Education—General	M,D
Educational Leadership and Administration	M,D
Educational Measurement and Evaluation	M,D
Educational Psychology	M,D
Electrical Engineering	M,D
Engineering and Applied Sciences—General	M,D
English Education	M,D
English	M,D
Environmental Education	M,D
Experimental Psychology	M,D
Family Nurse Practitioner Studies	M,D
Film, Television, and Video Production	M
Foreign Languages Education	M
Foundations and Philosophy of Education	M,D
French	M
Geography	M,D
Geophysics	M,D
Geosciences	M,D
German	M
Health Informatics	M
Hispanic Studies	M
History	M,D
Human Development	M,D
Italian	M
Kinesiology and Movement Studies	M
Law	P,M,D
Leisure Studies	M
Linguistics	M,D
Mathematics Education	M,D
Mathematics	M,D
Mechanical Engineering	M,D
Medical Physics	M,D
Microbiology	M,D
Music Education	M,D
Music	M,D
Nursing and Healthcare Administration	M,D
Nursing Education	M,D
Nursing—General	M,D
Oceanography	M,D
Pacific Area/Pacific Rim Studies	M
Philosophy	M
Photography	M
Physical Education	M
Physics	M,D
Political Science	M,D
Psychology—General	M,D
Public Administration	M,D
Reading Education	M,D
Science Education	M,D
Social Psychology	M,D
Social Sciences Education	M,D
Social Work	M
Sociology	M,D
Special Education	M,D
Statistics	M,D
Theater	M
Theoretical Physics	M,D
Vocational and Technical Education	M,D
Writing	M

UNIVERSITY OF VIRGINIA

Accounting	M
Acute Care/Critical Care Nursing	M,D
Aerospace/Aeronautical Engineering	M,D
Allopathic Medicine	P,M,D
Anthropology	M,D
Archaeology	M,D
Architectural History	M,D
Architecture	M
Art History	M,D
Asian Studies	M
Astronomy	M,D
Biochemistry	D
Bioethics	M
Biological and Biomedical Sciences—General	M,D
Biomedical Engineering	M,D
Biophysics	M,D
Business Administration and Management—General	M,D
Cell Biology	D
Chemical Engineering	M,D
Chemistry	M,D
Civil Engineering	M,D
Classics	M,D
Clinical Psychology	M,D,O
Clinical Research	M
Communication Disorders	M
Community Health	M,D
Computer Engineering	M,D
Computer Science	M,D
Counselor Education	M,D,O
Curriculum and Instruction	M,D,O
Early Childhood Education	M,D
Economics	M,D
Education of the Gifted	M,D,O
Education—General	M,D,O
Educational Leadership and Administration	M,D,O
Educational Measurement and Evaluation	M,D,O
Educational Media/Instructional Technology	M,D,O
Educational Psychology	M,D,O
Electrical Engineering	M,D
Elementary Education	M,D,O
Engineering and Applied Sciences—General	M,D
Engineering Physics	M,D
English Education	M,D
English	M,D,O
Environmental Sciences	M,D
Finance and Banking	M
Foreign Languages Education	M,D,O
Foundations and Philosophy of Education	M,D
French	M,D
German	M,D
Health Education	M,D
Health Informatics	M
Health Services Management and Hospital Administration	M
Health Services Research	M
Higher Education	M,D,O
History	M,D
Immunology	D
Interdisciplinary Studies	M,D
International Affairs	M,D
Italian	M
Kinesiology and Movement Studies	M,D
Landscape Architecture	M
Law	P,M,D,O
Linguistics	M
Management Information Systems	M
Marketing	M
Materials Sciences	M,D
Mathematics Education	M,D,O
Mathematics	M,D
Mechanical Engineering	M,D
Microbiology	D
Molecular Genetics	D
Molecular Physiology	M,D
Music	M,D
Neuroscience	D
Nursing and Healthcare Administration	M,D
Nursing—General	M,D
Pathology	D
Pharmacology	D
Philosophy	M,D
Physical Education	M,D
Physics	M,D
Physiology	D
Political Science	M,D
Psychiatric Nursing	M,D
Psychology—General	M,D
Public Health—General	M,D
Public Policy	M
Reading Education	M,D,O
Religion	M,D
Romance Languages	M,D
School Psychology	M,D,O
Science Education	M,D,O
Slavic Languages	M,D
Social Sciences Education	M,D,O
Sociology	M,D
Spanish	M,D
Special Education	M,D,O
Statistics	M,D
Student Affairs	M,D,O
Systems Engineering	M,D
Theater	M
Urban and Regional Planning	M,O
Writing	M

UNIVERSITY OF WASHINGTON

Accounting	M,D
Aerospace/Aeronautical Engineering	M,D
Allopathic Medicine	P
Animal Behavior	D
Anthropology	M,D
Applied Arts and Design—General	M
Applied Mathematics	M,D
Applied Physics	M,D
Architecture	M,D,O
Art History	M,D
Art/Fine Arts	M
Asian Languages	M,D
Asian Studies	M,D
Astronomy	M,D
Atmospheric Sciences	M,D
Bacteriology	D
Biochemistry	D
Bioengineering	M,D
Bioethics	M
Bioinformatics	M,D
Biological and Biomedical Sciences—General	M,D
Biophysics	D
Biostatistics	M,D
Biotechnology	D
Business Administration and Management—General	M,D*
Business Education	M,D
Cell Biology	D*
Chemical Engineering	M,D*
Chemistry	M,D
Chinese	M,D
Civil Engineering	M,D
Classics	M,D
Clinical Laboratory Sciences/Medical Technology	M
Clinical Psychology	D
Clinical Research	M,D
Cognitive Sciences	D
Communication Disorders	M,D
Communication—General	M,D
Community Health	M,D
Comparative Literature	M,D
Computational Sciences	M,D
Computer Science	M,D
Construction Engineering	M,D
Construction Management	M
Curriculum and Instruction	M,D
Dance	M
Demography and Population Studies	M,D
Dentistry	P
Developmental Psychology	D
East European and Russian Studies	M
Ecology	M,D
Economics	M,D
Education—General	M,D,O
Educational Leadership and Administration	M,D
Educational Measurement and Evaluation	M,D
Educational Media/Instructional Technology	M,D
Educational Policy	M,D
Educational Psychology	M,D
Electrical Engineering	M,D*
Energy Management and Policy	M,D
English as a Second Language	M,D
English Education	M,D
English	M,D
Environmental and Occupational Health	M,D
Environmental Engineering	M,D
Environmental Management and Policy	M,D
Epidemiology	M,D
Finance and Banking	M,D
Fish, Game, and Wildlife Management	M,D
Forestry	M,D
Foundations and Philosophy of Education	M,D
French	M,D
Genetics	M,D
Genomic Sciences	D
Geography	M,D
Geology	M,D
Geophysics	M,D
Geotechnical Engineering	M,D
German	M,D
Health Informatics	M,D
Health Services Management and Hospital Administration	M
Health Services Research	M,D
Higher Education	M,D
Hispanic Studies	M
Historic Preservation	O
History	M,D
Horticulture	M,D
Human Development	M,D
Hydrology	M,D
Immunology	M,D
Industrial Design	M
Industrial/Management Engineering	M,D

Information Science	M,D
International Affairs	M
International Business	M,D,O
International Health	M,D
Italian	M,D
Japanese	M,D
Landscape Architecture	M
Law	P,M,D
Legal and Justice Studies	P,M,D
Library Science	M,D
Lighting Design	M,D,O
Linguistics	M,D
Logistics	O
Management of Technology	M,D
Marine Affairs	M,O
Marine Geology	M,D
Materials Engineering	M,D
Materials Sciences	M,D
Maternal and Child Health	M,D
Mathematics Education	M,D
Mathematics	M,D
Mechanical Engineering	M,D
Medical Informatics	M,D
Medicinal and Pharmaceutical Chemistry	D
Microbiology	D
Molecular Biology	D
Molecular Medicine	D
Multilingual and Multicultural Education	M,D
Museum Studies	M
Music Education	M,D
Music	M,D
Nanotechnology	M,D
Natural Resources	M,D
Near and Middle Eastern Studies	M,D
Neurobiology	D
Nursing—General	M,D,O
Nutrition	M,D
Occupational Therapy	M,D
Oceanography	M,D
Oral and Dental Sciences	P,M,O
Parasitology	D
Pathobiology	D
Pathology	D
Pharmaceutical Sciences	M,D
Pharmacology	D
Pharmacy	P,M,D
Philosophy	M,D
Photography	M
Physical Education	M,D
Physical Therapy	M,D
Physics	M,D
Physiology	D
Political Science	M,D
Portuguese	M
Psychology—General	D
Public Administration	M,D
Public Affairs	M,D
Public Policy	M,D
Reading Education	M,D
Rehabilitation Sciences	M,D
Religion	M,D
Romance Languages	M,D
Russian	M,D
Scandinavian Languages	M,D
School Psychology	M,D
Science Education	M,D
Slavic Languages	M,D
Social Psychology	D
Social Sciences Education	M,D
Social Sciences	M,D
Social Work	M,D
Sociology	M,D
Spanish	M
Special Education	M,D
Statistics	M,D
Structural Biology	D
Structural Engineering	M,D
Sustainable Development	P,M,D
Taxation	P,M,D
Technical Communication	M,D
Theater	M,D
Toxicology	M,D
Transportation and Highway Engineering	M,D
Transportation Management	O
Urban and Regional Planning	M,D
Urban Design	M,D,O
Veterinary Sciences	M
Water Resources Engineering	M,D
Women's Studies	D
Writing	M,D

UNIVERSITY OF WASHINGTON, BOTHELL

Business Administration and Management—General	M
Education—General	M
Nursing—General	M
Public Policy	M

UNIVERSITY OF WASHINGTON, TACOMA

Accounting	M
Computer Engineering	M
Education—General	M
Educational Leadership and Administration	M
Finance and Banking	M
Interdisciplinary Studies	M
Nursing—General	M
Science Education	M
Secondary Education	M
Social Work	M
Software Engineering	M
Special Education	M

UNIVERSITY OF WATERLOO

Accounting	M,D
Actuarial Science	M,D
Anthropology	M
Applied Mathematics	M,D
Architecture	M
Art/Fine Arts	M
Biochemistry	M,D
Biological and Biomedical Sciences—General	M,D
Biostatistics	M,D
Business Administration and Management—General	M
Chemical Engineering	M,D
Chemistry	M,D
Civil Engineering	M,D
Computer Engineering	M,D
Computer Science	M,D
Economic Development	M
Economics	M,D
Electrical Engineering	M,D
Engineering and Applied Sciences—General	M,D
Engineering Management	M,D
English	M,D
Entrepreneurship	M
Environmental Engineering	M,D
Environmental Management and Policy	M,D
Finance and Banking	M,D
French	M,D
Geography	M,D
Geosciences	M,D
German	M,D
Health Education	M,D
History	M,D
Information Science	M,D
International Affairs	M,D
Kinesiology and Movement Studies	M,D
Leisure Studies	M,D
Management of Technology	M,D
Mathematics	M,D
Mechanical Engineering	M,D
Near and Middle Eastern Studies	M
Operations Research	M,D
Optometry	M,D
Philosophy	M,D
Physics	M,D
Political Science	M,D
Psychology—General	M,D
Public Affairs	M
Public Health—General	M
Recreation and Park Management	M,D
Religion	D
Russian	M,D
Sociology	M,D
Software Engineering	M,D
Statistics	M,D
Systems Engineering	M,D
Taxation	M,D
Technical Writing	M,D
Travel and Tourism	M
Urban and Regional Planning	M,D
Vision Sciences	M,D

THE UNIVERSITY OF WEST ALABAMA

Adult Education	M
Athletic Training and Sports Medicine	M
Counselor Education	M
Early Childhood Education	M
Education—General	M
Educational Leadership and Administration	M
Educational Media/Instructional Technology	M
Elementary Education	M
English Education	M
Foundations and Philosophy of Education	M
Mathematics Education	M
Physical Education	M
Science Education	M
Secondary Education	M
Social Sciences Education	M
Special Education	M

THE UNIVERSITY OF WESTERN ONTARIO

Allopathic Medicine	P,M
Anatomy	M,D
Anthropology	M,D
Applied Mathematics	M,D
Astronomy	M,D
Biochemical Engineering	M,D
Biochemistry	M,D
Biophysics	M,D
Biostatistics	M,D
Business Administration and Management—General	M,D
Cell Biology	M,D
Chemical Engineering	M,D
Chemistry	M,D
Civil Engineering	M,D
Classics	M
Communication Disorders	M
Comparative Literature	M,D
Computer Engineering	M,D
Computer Science	M,D
Counseling Psychology	M
Curriculum and Instruction	M
Dentistry	P
Economics	M,D
Education—General	M
Educational Policy	M
Educational Psychology	M
Electrical Engineering	M,D
Engineering and Applied Sciences—General	M,D
English	M,D
Entrepreneurship	M,D
Environmental Engineering	M,D
Environmental Sciences	M,D
Epidemiology	M,D
Finance and Banking	M,D
French	M,D
Geography	M,D
Geology	M,D
Geophysics	M,D
Geosciences	M,D
Health Services Management and Hospital Administration	M,D
History	M,D
Immunology	M,D
Information Studies	M,D
Interdisciplinary Studies	M,D
International Business	M,D
Journalism	M
Kinesiology and Movement Studies	M,D
Law	P,M,O
Library Science	M,D
Management Strategy and Policy	M,D
Marketing	M,D
Materials Engineering	M,D
Mathematics	M,D
Mechanical Engineering	M,D
Media Studies	M,D
Microbiology	M,D
Molecular Biology	M,D
Music	M,D
Neuroscience	M,D
Nursing—General	M,D
Occupational Therapy	M
Oral and Dental Sciences	M
Pathology	M,D
Philosophy	M,D
Physical Therapy	M,O
Physics	M,D
Physiology	M,D
Plant Biology	M,D
Plant Sciences	M,D
Political Science	M,D
Psychology—General	M,D
Sociology	M,D
Spanish	M,D
Special Education	M
Statistics	M,D
Sustainable Development	M,D
Zoology	M,D

UNIVERSITY OF WEST FLORIDA

Accounting	M
Anthropology	M
Archaeology	M
Biochemistry	M
Biological and Biomedical Sciences—General	M
Biotechnology	M
Business Administration and Management—General	M
Communication—General	M
Computer Science	M
Counseling Psychology	M
Counselor Education	M
Criminal Justice and Criminology	M
Curriculum and Instruction	D,O
Early Childhood Education	M
Educational Leadership and Administration	M,O
Educational Media/Instructional Technology	M
Elementary Education	M
English as a Second Language	M
English	M
Environmental Biology	M
Environmental Sciences	M
Exercise and Sports Science	M
Health Education	M
Historic Preservation	M
History	M
Humanities	M
Industrial and Organizational Psychology	M
Leisure Studies	M
Marine Affairs	M
Mathematics	M
Middle School Education	M

*M—master's degree; P—first professional degree; D—doctorate; O—other advanced degree; *—Close-Up and/or Announcement or Display in one of the other books in this series*

Nursing and Healthcare Administration	M
Pharmaceutical Administration	M
Physical Education	M
Political Science	M
Psychology—General	M
Public Administration	M
Public Health—General	M
Public History	M
Reading Education	M
Science Education	M
Secondary Education	M
Social Work	M
Software Engineering	M
Special Education	M
Student Affairs	M
Vocational and Technical Education	M
Writing	M

UNIVERSITY OF WEST GEORGIA

Accounting	M
Applied Mathematics	M
Art Education	M
Biological and Biomedical Sciences—General	M
Business Administration and Management—General	M
Business Education	M,O
Communication Disorders	M,O
Computer Science	M,O
Counselor Education	M,O
Criminal Justice and Criminology	M
Early Childhood Education	M,O
Education—General	M,D,O
Educational Leadership and Administration	M,O
Educational Measurement and Evaluation	D
Educational Media/Instructional Technology	M,O
English Education	M,O
English	M
Foreign Languages Education	M,O
Geographic Information Systems	O
History	M
Mathematics Education	M,O
Mathematics	M
Middle School Education	M,O
Museum Studies	O
Music Education	M
Music	M
Nursing—General	M
Physical Education	M
Psychology—General	M,D
Public Administration	M,O
Reading Education	M
Rural Planning and Studies	M
Science Education	M,O
Secondary Education	M,O
Social Sciences Education	M,O
Sociology	M
Software Engineering	M,O
Special Education	M,O

UNIVERSITY OF WINDSOR

Art/Fine Arts	M
Biochemistry	M,D
Biological and Biomedical Sciences—General	M,D
Biopsychology	M,D
Business Administration and Management—General	M
Chemistry	M,D
Civil Engineering	M,D
Clinical Psychology	M,D
Communication—General	M
Computer Science	M,D
Criminal Justice and Criminology	M,D
Economics	M
Education—General	M,D
Electrical Engineering	M,D
Engineering and Applied Sciences—General	M,D
English	M
Environmental Engineering	M,D
Environmental Sciences	M,D
Geosciences	M,D
History	M
Industrial/Management Engineering	M,D
Kinesiology and Movement Studies	M
Legal and Justice Studies	M
Manufacturing Engineering	M,D
Materials Engineering	M,D
Mathematics	M,D
Mechanical Engineering	M,D
Nursing—General	M
Philosophy	M
Physics	M,D
Political Science	M
Psychology—General	M,D
Social Psychology	M,D
Social Work	M
Sociology	M,D
Statistics	M,D
Writing	M

THE UNIVERSITY OF WINNIPEG

History	M
Marriage and Family Therapy	P,M,O
Public Administration	M
Religion	M
Theology	P,M,O

UNIVERSITY OF WISCONSIN–EAU CLAIRE

Business Administration and Management—General	M
Communication Disorders	M
Education—General	M
Elementary Education	M
English Education	M
English	M
History	M
Mathematics Education	M
Nursing—General	M
Psychology—General	M,O
Reading Education	M
School Psychology	M,O
Secondary Education	M
Social Sciences Education	M
Special Education	M

UNIVERSITY OF WISCONSIN–GREEN BAY

Business Administration and Management—General	M
Education—General	M
Environmental Management and Policy	M
Environmental Sciences	M
Social Work	M

UNIVERSITY OF WISCONSIN–LA CROSSE

Athletic Training and Sports Medicine	M
Biological and Biomedical Sciences—General	M
Business Administration and Management—General	M
Cell Biology	M
Community Health	M
Education—General	M
Elementary Education	M
Exercise and Sports Science	M
Health Education	M
Marine Sciences	M
Medical Microbiology	M
Microbiology	M
Molecular Biology	M
Nurse Anesthesia	M
Occupational Therapy	M
Physical Education	M
Physical Therapy	M,D
Physician Assistant Studies	M
Physiology	M
Psychology—General	M,O
Public Health—General	M
Reading Education	M
Recreation and Park Management	M
Rehabilitation Sciences	M
School Psychology	M,O
Secondary Education	M
Software Engineering	M
Special Education	M
Sports Management	M
Student Affairs	M

UNIVERSITY OF WISCONSIN–MADISON

Accounting	D
Actuarial Science	M
African Studies	M,D
African-American Studies	M
Agricultural Economics and Agribusiness	M,D
Agricultural Engineering	M,D
Agricultural Sciences—General	M,D
Agronomy and Soil Sciences	M,D
Allopathic Medicine	P
American Studies	M,D
Animal Sciences	M,D
Anthropology	D
Applied Arts and Design—General	M,D
Applied Economics	M,D
Archaeology	D
Art Education	M,D
Art History	M,D
Art/Fine Arts	M
Arts Administration	M
Asian Languages	M,D
Asian Studies	M,D
Astronomy	D
Atmospheric Sciences	M,D
Bacteriology	M
Biochemistry	M,D
Bioengineering	M,D
Biological and Biomedical Sciences—General	M,D
Biomedical Engineering	M,D
Biometry	M
Biophysics	D
Biopsychology	D
Botany	M,D
Business Administration and Management—General	M
Cancer Biology/Oncology	D
Cell Biology	D
Chemical Engineering	M,D
Chemistry	M,D
Child and Family Studies	M,D
Chinese	M,D
Civil Engineering	M,D
Classics	M,D
Clinical Psychology	D
Clinical Research	M
Cognitive Sciences	D
Communication Disorders	M,D
Communication—General	M,D
Comparative Literature	M,D
Computer and Information Systems Security	M
Computer Science	M,D
Conservation Biology	M
Consumer Economics	M,D
Counseling Psychology	D
Counselor Education	M
Curriculum and Instruction	M,D
Developmental Psychology	D
Ecology	M
Economics	D
Education—General	M,D,O
Educational Leadership and Administration	M,D,O
Educational Policy	M,D,O
Educational Psychology	M,D
Electrical Engineering	M,D
Energy and Power Engineering	M,D
Engineering and Applied Sciences—General	M,D,O
Engineering Management	M
Engineering Physics	M,D
English	M,D
Entomology	M,D
Entrepreneurship	M
Environmental Biology	M,D
Environmental Engineering	M,D
Environmental Sciences	M,D
Epidemiology	M,D
Family and Consumer Sciences-General	M,D
Film, Television, and Video Theory and Criticism	M,D
Finance and Banking	M,D
Fish, Game, and Wildlife Management	M,D
Folklore	M,D
Food Science and Technology	M,D
Foreign Languages Education	M,D
Forestry	M,D
French	M,D,O
Genetic Counseling	M
Genetics	M,D*
Geographic Information Systems	M,D,O
Geography	M,D,O
Geological Engineering	M,D
Geology	M,D
Geophysics	M,D
German	M,D
Health Services Research	M,D
History of Science and Technology	M,D
History	M,D
Horticulture	M,D
Human Development	M,D
Human Resources Management	M,D
Industrial/Management Engineering	M,D
Information Studies	M,D
Insurance	M,D
Investment Management	D
Italian	M,D
Japanese	M,D
Jewish Studies	M,D
Journalism	M,D
Kinesiology and Movement Studies	M,D
Landscape Architecture	M
Latin American Studies	M,D
Law	P,M,D
Legal and Justice Studies	M,D
Library Science	M,D
Limnology	M,D
Linguistics	M,D
Management Information Systems	D
Management of Technology	M
Management Strategy and Policy	M
Manufacturing Engineering	M
Marine Sciences	M,D
Marketing Research	M
Marketing	D
Mass Communication	M,D
Materials Engineering	M,D
Materials Sciences	M,D
Mathematics Education	M,D
Mathematics	D
Mechanical Engineering	M,D
Mechanics	M,D
Media Studies	M,D

Medical Microbiology	D
Medical Physics	M,D
Microbiology	D
Molecular Biology	D
Music Education	M,D
Music	M,D
Natural Resources	M,D
Near and Middle Eastern Languages	M,D
Near and Middle Eastern Studies	M,D
Neurobiology	D
Neuroscience	D
Nuclear Engineering	M,D
Nursing—General	D
Nutrition	M,D
Occupational Therapy	M,D
Oceanography	M,D
Pathology	D*
Pharmaceutical Administration	M,D
Pharmaceutical Sciences	M,D
Pharmacology	D
Pharmacy	P
Philosophy	M,D
Physics	M,D
Physiology	M,D
Plant Pathology	M,D
Plant Sciences	M,D
Political Science	D
Polymer Science and Engineering	M,D
Portuguese	M,D
Psychology—General	D
Public Affairs	M
Real Estate	M,D
Rehabilitation Counseling	M,D
Rehabilitation Sciences	M
Rhetoric	M,D
Rural Sociology	M,D
Scandinavian Languages	M,D
Science Education	M,D
Slavic Languages	M,D
Social Psychology	D
Social Sciences	D
Social Work	M,D
Sociology	M,D
Spanish	M,D
Special Education	M,D
Speech and Interpersonal Communication	M,D
Statistics	M,D
Supply Chain Management	M
Sustainable Development	M
Systems Engineering	M,D
Theater	M,D
Toxicology	M,D
Urban and Regional Planning	M,D
Veterinary Medicine	P
Veterinary Sciences	M,D
Water Resources	M
Women's Studies	M,D
Writing	M,D
Zoology	M,D

UNIVERSITY OF WISCONSIN–MILWAUKEE

Adult Education	D
African Studies	D
Allied Health—General	M,D,O
Anthropology	M,D,O
Architecture	M,D,O
Art Education	M
Art History	M,O
Art/Fine Arts	M
Biochemistry	M,D
Biological and Biomedical Sciences—General	M,D
Business Administration and Management—General	M,D,O
Chemistry	M,D
Civil Engineering	M,D,O
Classics	M,O
Clinical Laboratory Sciences/Medical Technology	M
Clinical Psychology	M,D
Communication Disorders	M,O
Communication—General	M,D,O
Comparative Literature	M,D,O
Computer Engineering	M,D,O
Computer Science	M,D
Conflict Resolution and Mediation/Peace Studies	M,O
Counseling Psychology	M,D
Counselor Education	M,D
Criminal Justice and Criminology	M
Curriculum and Instruction	M,D
Dance	M
Developmental Psychology	M,D
Early Childhood Education	M
Economics	M,D
Education—General	M,D,O
Educational Leadership and Administration	M,D,O
Educational Measurement and Evaluation	M,D
Educational Media/Instructional Technology	D
Educational Psychology	M,D
Electrical Engineering	M,D,O
Elementary Education	M
Engineering and Applied Sciences—General	M,D,O
Engineering Management	M,D,O
English	M,D,O
Ergonomics and Human Factors	M,O
Family Nurse Practitioner Studies	M,D,O
Film, Television, and Video Production	M
Foundations and Philosophy of Education	M,D
French	M,O
Geochemistry	M,D
Geographic Information Systems	M,O
Geography	M,D
Geology	M,D
German	M,O
Gerontology	M,D,O
Health Education	M,D,O
Health Informatics	M,O
Historic Preservation	M,D,O
History	M,D
Human Resources Development	M,O
Industrial and Labor Relations	M,O
Industrial/Management Engineering	M,D,O
Information Studies	M,D,O
Interdisciplinary Studies	D
International Business	M,O
Italian	M,O
Jewish Studies	M,O
Kinesiology and Movement Studies	M
Liberal Studies	M
Library Science	M,D,O
Linguistics	M,D,O
Manufacturing Engineering	M,D,O
Marriage and Family Therapy	M,D,O
Materials Engineering	M,D,O
Mathematics	M,D
Mechanical Engineering	M,D,O
Mechanics	M,D,O
Media Studies	M,O
Medical Informatics	D
Middle School Education	M
Multilingual and Multicultural Education	D
Museum Studies	M,D,O
Music Education	M,O
Music	M,O
Nonprofit Management	M,D,O
Nursing—General	M,D,O
Occupational Therapy	M,O
Philosophy	M
Physical Therapy	D
Physics	M,D
Political Science	M,D
Psychology—General	M,D
Public Administration	M
Public Health—General	M,D,O
Reading Education	M
Recreation and Park Management	M,O
Rhetoric	M,D,O
School Psychology	D,O
Secondary Education	M
Slavic Languages	M,O
Social Psychology	M,D
Social Work	M,D,O
Sociology	M
Spanish	M,O
Special Education	M,D,O
Theater	M
Translation and Interpretation	M,O
Urban and Regional Planning	M,O
Urban Education	M,D
Urban Studies	M,D
Writing	M,D,O

UNIVERSITY OF WISCONSIN–OSHKOSH

Adult Nursing	M
Biological and Biomedical Sciences—General	M
Botany	M
Business Administration and Management—General	M
Counselor Education	M
Curriculum and Instruction	M
Early Childhood Education	M
Education—General	M
Educational Leadership and Administration	M
English	M
Experimental Psychology	M
Family Nurse Practitioner Studies	M
Health Services Management and Hospital Administration	M
Industrial and Organizational Psychology	M
International Business	M
Mathematics Education	M
Microbiology	M
Nursing—General	M
Psychology—General	M
Public Administration	M
Reading Education	M
Social Work	M
Special Education	M
Zoology	M

UNIVERSITY OF WISCONSIN–PARKSIDE

Business Administration and Management—General	M
Computer Science	M
Information Science	M
Molecular Biology	M

UNIVERSITY OF WISCONSIN–PLATTEVILLE

Adult Education	M
Computer Science	M
Counselor Education	M
Criminal Justice and Criminology	M
Education—General	M
Elementary Education	M
Engineering and Applied Sciences—General	M
Middle School Education	M
Project Management	M
Secondary Education	M
Vocational and Technical Education	M

UNIVERSITY OF WISCONSIN–RIVER FALLS

Agricultural Education	M
Agricultural Sciences—General	M
Art/Fine Arts	M
Business Administration and Management—General	M
Communication Disorders	M
Counselor Education	M,O
Education—General	M
Elementary Education	M
English as a Second Language	M
Mathematics Education	M
Reading Education	M
School Psychology	M,O
Science Education	M
Social Sciences Education	M

UNIVERSITY OF WISCONSIN–STEVENS POINT

Advertising and Public Relations	M
Business Administration and Management—General	M
Communication Disorders	M,D
Communication—General	M
Corporate and Organizational Communication	M
Counselor Education	M
Education—General	M
Educational Leadership and Administration	M
Elementary Education	M
English	M
Family and Consumer Sciences-General	M
Health Promotion	M
History	M
Human Development	M
Mass Communication	M
Music Education	M
Natural Resources	M
Nutrition	M
Reading Education	M
Science Education	M
Special Education	M
Speech and Interpersonal Communication	M

UNIVERSITY OF WISCONSIN–STOUT

Child and Family Studies	M
Counseling Psychology	M
Education—General	M,O
Food Science and Technology	M
Human Development	M
Human Resources Development	M
Industrial Hygiene	M
Industrial/Management Engineering	M
Information Science	M
Management of Technology	M
Manufacturing Engineering	M
Marriage and Family Therapy	M
Nutrition	M
Psychology—General	M
Rehabilitation Counseling	M
School Psychology	M,O
Telecommunications Management	M
Vocational and Technical Education	M,O

*M—master's degree; P—first professional degree; D—doctorate; O—other advanced degree; *—Close-Up and/or Announcement or Display in one of the other books in this series*

UNIVERSITY OF WISCONSIN–SUPERIOR

Art Education M
Art History M
Art Therapy M
Art/Fine Arts M
Arts Administration M
Communication—General M
Counselor Education M
Curriculum and Instruction M
Education—General M
Educational Leadership and Administration M,O
Mass Communication M
Reading Education M
Social Psychology M
Special Education M
Speech and Interpersonal Communication M
Theater M

UNIVERSITY OF WISCONSIN–WHITEWATER

Accounting M
Business Administration and Management—General M*
Business Education M
Communication Disorders M
Communication—General M
Corporate and Organizational Communication M
Counselor Education M
Curriculum and Instruction M
Education—General M
Educational Leadership and Administration M
Environmental and Occupational Health M
Finance and Banking M
Higher Education M
Human Resources Management M
International Business M
Management of Technology M
Marketing M
Mass Communication M
Psychology—General M,O
Reading Education M
School Psychology M,O
Secondary Education M
Social Psychology M
Special Education M
Supply Chain Management M

UNIVERSITY OF WYOMING

Accounting M
Adult Education M,D,O
Agricultural Economics and Agribusiness M
Agricultural Sciences—General M,D
Agronomy and Soil Sciences M,D
American Studies M
Animal Sciences M,D
Anthropology M,D
Applied Economics M
Atmospheric Sciences M,D
Biotechnology D
Botany M,D
Business Administration and Management—General M
Cell Biology D
Chemical Engineering M,D
Chemistry M,D
Child Development M
Civil Engineering M,D
Communication Disorders M
Communication—General M
Community Health M,D
Computational Biology D
Computer Science M,D
Consumer Economics M
Counselor Education M,D
Curriculum and Instruction M,D
Distance Education Development M,D,O
Ecology M,D
Economics M,D
Educational Leadership and Administration M,D,O
Educational Media/Instructional Technology M,D,O
Electrical Engineering M,D
Engineering and Applied Sciences—General M,D
English M
Entomology M,D
Environmental Engineering M
Finance and Banking M
Food Science and Technology M
French M
Genetics D
Geography M
Geology M,D
Geophysics M,D
German M
Health Education M
History M
International Affairs M
Law P
Mathematics Education M,D
Mathematics M,D
Mechanical Engineering M,D
Microbiology D
Molecular Biology M,D
Music Education M
Music M
Natural Resources M,D
Nursing—General M
Nutrition M
Pathobiology M
Petroleum Engineering M,D
Pharmacy P
Philosophy M
Physical Education M
Physiology M,D
Political Science M
Psychology—General M,D
Public Administration M
Range Science M,D
Reproductive Biology M,D
Rural Planning and Studies M
Science Education M
Social Work M
Sociology M
Spanish M
Special Education M,D,O
Statistics M,D
Student Affairs M,D
Water Resources M,D
Writing M
Zoology M,D

UPPER IOWA UNIVERSITY

Accounting M
Business Administration and Management—General M
Criminal Justice and Criminology M
Finance and Banking M
Homeland Security M
Human Resources Management M
Human Services M
International Business M
Organizational Management M
Public Administration M
Quality Management M

URBANA UNIVERSITY

Business Administration and Management—General M
Education—General M

URSULINE COLLEGE

Art Education M
Art Therapy M
Business Administration and Management—General M
Early Childhood Education M
Education—General M
Educational Leadership and Administration M
Historic Preservation M
Liberal Studies M
Mathematics Education M
Medical/Surgical Nursing M
Middle School Education M
Nursing and Healthcare Administration M
Nursing Education M
Nursing—General M
Reading Education M
Science Education M
Social Sciences Education M
Special Education M
Theology M

UTAH STATE UNIVERSITY

Accounting M
Aerospace/Aeronautical Engineering M,D
Agricultural Education M
Agricultural Engineering M,D
Agricultural Sciences—General M,D
Agronomy and Soil Sciences M,D
American Studies M
Animal Sciences M,D
Applied Economics M
Applied Mathematics M,D
Art/Fine Arts M
Biochemistry M,D
Biological and Biomedical Sciences—General M,D
Business Administration and Management—General M
Business Education M,D
Chemistry M,D
Child and Family Studies M,D
Civil Engineering M,D,O
Clinical Psychology M,D
Communication Disorders M,D,O
Communication—General M
Computer Science M,D
Consumer Economics M
Counseling Psychology M,D
Counselor Education M,D
Curriculum and Instruction D
Disability Studies M,D,O
Ecology M,D
Economics M,D
Education—General M,D,O
Educational Measurement and Evaluation M,D
Educational Media/Instructional Technology M,D,O
Electrical Engineering M,D
Elementary Education M
Engineering and Applied Sciences—General M,D,O
English M
Environmental Engineering M,D,O
Environmental Management and Policy M,D
Family and Consumer Sciences-General M,D
Fish, Game, and Wildlife Management M,D
Folklore M
Food Science and Technology M,D
Forestry M,D
Geography M,D
Geology M
Health Education M
History M
Home Economics Education M
Human Development M,D
Human Resources Management M
Interior Design M
Landscape Architecture M
Management Information Systems M,D
Marriage and Family Therapy M,D
Mathematics M,D
Mechanical Engineering M,D
Meteorology M,D
Microbiology M,D
Molecular Biology M,D
Multilingual and Multicultural Education M
Natural Resources M
Nutrition M,D
Physical Education M
Physics M,D
Plant Sciences M,D
Political Science M
Psychology—General M,D
Range Science M,D
Recreation and Park Management M,D
Rehabilitation Counseling M
School Psychology M,D
Secondary Education M
Sociology M,D
Special Education M,D,O
Statistics M,D
Theater M
Toxicology M,D
Urban and Regional Planning M,D
Veterinary Sciences M,D
Vocational and Technical Education M
Water Resources Engineering M,D
Water Resources M,D
Writing M

UTAH VALLEY UNIVERSITY

Education—General M
Nursing—General M

UTICA COLLEGE

Accounting M
Criminal Justice and Criminology M
Education—General M,O
Health Services Management and Hospital Administration M
Liberal Studies M
Occupational Therapy M
Physical Therapy D

VALDOSTA STATE UNIVERSITY

Business Administration and Management—General M
Clinical Psychology M,O
Counseling Psychology M,O
Counselor Education M,O
Criminal Justice and Criminology M
Early Childhood Education M,O
Educational Leadership and Administration M,D,O
English M
History M
Industrial and Organizational Psychology M,O
Information Studies M

Library Science	M
Marriage and Family Therapy	M
Middle School Education	M,O
Psychology—General	M,O
Reading Education	M,O
School Psychology	M,O
Secondary Education	M,O
Social Work	M
Sociology	M
Special Education	M,O

VALPARAISO UNIVERSITY

Asian Studies	M
Business Administration and Management—General	M,O
Clinical Psychology	M,O
Counseling Psychology	M,O
Education—General	M
Engineering Management	M,O
English as a Second Language	M,O
English	M,O
Ethics	M,O
Gerontology	M,O
History	M,O
International Business	M
Law	P,M
Liberal Studies	M,O
Management Information Systems	M
Nursing Education	M,O
Nursing—General	M,O
Psychology—General	M,O
School Psychology	
Sports Management	M
Theology	M,O

VANCOUVER ISLAND UNIVERSITY

Business Administration and Management—General	M

VANCOUVER SCHOOL OF THEOLOGY

Theology	P,M,O

VANDERBILT UNIVERSITY

Acute Care/Critical Care Nursing	M,D
Adult Nursing	M,D
Allopathic Medicine	M,D
Analytical Chemistry	M,D
Anthropology	M,D
Astronomy	M,D
Biochemistry	M,D
Bioinformatics	M,D
Biological and Biomedical Sciences—General	M,D*
Biomedical Engineering	M,D
Biophysics	M,D
Business Administration and Management—General	M,D
Cancer Biology/Oncology	M,D
Cell Biology	M,D
Chemical Engineering	M,D
Chemistry	M,D
Child and Family Studies	M
Civil Engineering	M,D
Classics	M
Clinical Research	M
Communication Disorders	M,D
Computer Science	M,D
Counselor Education	M
Economic Development	M,D
Economics	P,M,D
Education—General	M,D*
Educational Leadership and Administration	M,D
Educational Measurement and Evaluation	M,D
Educational Policy	M,D
Electrical Engineering	M,D
Elementary Education	M
Engineering and Applied Sciences—General	M,D
English Education	M
English	M,D
Environmental Engineering	M,D
Environmental Management and Policy	M,D
Environmental Sciences	M
Family Nurse Practitioner Studies	M,D
Finance and Banking	M,D
Foreign Languages Education	M,D
Forensic Nursing	M,D
French	M,D
German	M,D
Gerontological Nursing	M,D
Higher Education	M,D
History	M,D
Human Development	M
Human Genetics	D
Human Resources Development	M,D
Immunology	M,D
Inorganic Chemistry	M,D
International and Comparative Education	M,D
Latin American Studies	M
Law	P,M,D
Liberal Studies	M
Marketing	D
Materials Sciences	M,D
Maternal and Child/Neonatal Nursing	M,D
Mathematics	M,D
Mechanical Engineering	M,D
Medical Physics	M
Medical/Surgical Nursing	M,D
Microbiology	M,D
Molecular Biology	M,D
Molecular Physiology	M,D
Multilingual and Multicultural Education	M,D
Neuroscience	D
Nurse Midwifery	M,D
Nursing and Healthcare Administration	M,D
Nursing Informatics	M,D
Nursing—General	M,D
Nutrition	M,D
Organic Chemistry	M,D
Organizational Management	M,D
Pathology	D
Pediatric Nursing	M,D
Pharmacology	D
Philosophy	M,D
Physical Chemistry	M,D
Physics	M,D
Political Science	M,D
Portuguese	M,D
Psychiatric Nursing	M,D
Psychology—General	M,D
Public Health—General	M
Public Policy	M,D
Reading Education	M
Religion	M,D
Science Education	M,D
Secondary Education	M
Sociology	M,D
Spanish	M,D
Special Education	M,D
Theology	P,M
Theoretical Chemistry	M,D
Urban and Regional Planning	M
Urban Education	M
Women's Health Nursing	M,D
Writing	M

VANDERCOOK COLLEGE OF MUSIC

Music Education	M

VANGUARD UNIVERSITY OF SOUTHERN CALIFORNIA

Business Administration and Management—General	M
Clinical Psychology	M
Education—General	M
Religion	M
Theology	M

VASSAR COLLEGE

Biological and Biomedical Sciences—General	M
Chemistry	M

VAUGHN COLLEGE OF AERONAUTICS AND TECHNOLOGY

Aviation Management	M

VERMONT LAW SCHOOL

Environmental Law	M
Environmental Management and Policy	M
Law	P
Legal and Justice Studies	M

VICTORIA UNIVERSITY

Theology	P,M,D,O

VILLANOVA UNIVERSITY

Accounting	M
Adult Nursing	M,D,O
Applied Statistics	M
Artificial Intelligence/Robotics	M,O
Biological and Biomedical Sciences—General	M*
Business Administration and Management—General	M
Chemical Engineering	M
Chemistry	M*
Civil Engineering	M
Communication—General	M
Computer Engineering	M,O
Computer Science	M,O*
Counselor Education	M*
Criminal Justice and Criminology	M
Education—General	M*
Educational Leadership and Administration	M
Electrical Engineering	M,O
Elementary Education	M
Engineering and Applied Sciences—General	M,D,O
English	M*
Environmental Engineering	M
Finance and Banking	M
Gerontological Nursing	M,D,O
Health Services Management and Hospital Administration	M,D,O
Higher Education	M
Hispanic Studies	M
History	M*
Human Resources Development	M
Humanities	M
International Business	M
Law	P
Liberal Studies	M
Management Information Systems	M
Manufacturing Engineering	M,O
Marketing	M
Mathematics	M
Mechanical Engineering	M,O
Nurse Anesthesia	M,D,O
Nursing and Healthcare Administration	M,D,O
Nursing Education	M,D,O
Nursing—General	M,D,O
Pediatric Nursing	M,D,O
Philosophy	D
Political Science	M*
Psychology—General	M*
Public Administration	M
Secondary Education	M
Software Engineering	M
Taxation	M
Theater	M
Theology	M
Transportation and Highway Engineering	M
Water Resources Engineering	M

VIRGINIA COLLEGE AT BIRMINGHAM

Business Administration and Management—General	M
Criminal Justice and Criminology	M

VIRGINIA COMMONWEALTH UNIVERSITY

Accounting	M,D
Adult Education	M
Adult Nursing	M,D,O
Advertising and Public Relations	M
Allied Health—General	D
Allopathic Medicine	P
Analytical Chemistry	M,D
Anatomy	D,O
Applied Arts and Design—General	M
Applied Mathematics	M,O
Applied Physics	M
Applied Social Research	M,O
Architectural History	M,D
Art Education	M
Art History	M,D
Art/Fine Arts	M,D
Athletic Training and Sports Medicine	M
Biochemistry	M,D,O
Bioengineering	M,D
Bioinformatics	M
Biological and Biomedical Sciences—General	M,D,O
Biomedical Engineering	M,D
Biostatistics	M,D
Business Administration and Management—General	M,O
Chemical Engineering	M,D
Chemical Physics	M,D
Chemistry	M,D
Clinical Laboratory Sciences/Medical Technology	M,D
Clinical Psychology	D
Communication—General	D
Community Health	D
Computer Science	M,D,O
Counseling Psychology	M,D,O
Counselor Education	M
Criminal Justice and Criminology	M,O
Curriculum and Instruction	M,O
Dentistry	P,M
Early Childhood Education	M,O
Economics	M
Education—General	M,D,O
Educational Leadership and Administration	D
Educational Measurement and Evaluation	D
Educational Policy	D
Educational Psychology	D
Electrical Engineering	M,D
Emergency Management	M,O
Engineering and Applied Sciences—General	M,D,O
English	M
Environmental and Occupational Health	M
Environmental Management and Policy	M

*M—master's degree; P—first professional degree; D—doctorate; O—other advanced degree; *—Close-Up and/or Announcement or Display in one of the other books in this series*

Environmental Sciences	M
Epidemiology	D
Exercise and Sports Science	M
Family Nurse Practitioner Studies	M,O
Finance and Banking	M
Forensic Sciences	M
Gender Studies	O
Genetics	M,D
Geographic Information Systems	O
Gerontology	M,D,O
Health Physics/ Radiological Health	D
Health Services Management and Hospital Administration	M,D
Health Services Research	D
Historic Preservation	O
History	M,D
Homeland Security	M,O
Human Genetics	M,D,O
Human Resources Development	M
Humanities	M,D,O
Immunology	M,D
Inorganic Chemistry	M,D
Insurance	M
Interdisciplinary Studies	M
Interior Design	M
Internet and Interactive Multimedia	M
Journalism	M
Management Information Systems	M,D
Marketing	O
Mass Communication	M
Mathematics	M,O
Mechanical Engineering	M,D
Media Studies	D
Medical Physics	M,D
Microbiology	M,D,O
Middle School Education	M,O
Molecular Biology	M,D
Museum Studies	M,D
Music Education	M
Music	M
Neurobiology	D
Neuroscience	M,D
Nonprofit Management	O
Nuclear Engineering	M
Nurse Anesthesia	M,D
Nursing and Healthcare Administration	M,D,O
Nursing—General	M,D,O
Occupational Therapy	M,D
Operations Research	M,O
Organic Chemistry	M,D
Pathology	M,D
Pediatric Nursing	M,D,O
Pharmaceutical Sciences	P,M,D
Pharmacology	M,D,O
Pharmacy	P
Photography	M
Physical Chemistry	M,D
Physical Education	M,D
Physical Therapy	M,D
Physics	M
Physiology	M,D,O
Political Science	M,D,O
Psychiatric Nursing	M,D,O
Psychology—General	D
Public Administration	M,O
Public Affairs	M,D,O
Public Policy	D
Quantitative Analysis	M
Reading Education	M
Real Estate	M,O
Recreation and Park Management	M
Rehabilitation Counseling	M,O
Rehabilitation Sciences	D
Rhetoric	M
Secondary Education	M,O
Social Sciences Education	M,O
Social Work	M,D
Sociology	M
Special Education	M,D
Statistics	M,O
Systems Biology	D
Taxation	M
Theater	M
Toxicology	M,D
Urban and Regional Planning	M,O
Urban Education	D
Women's Health Nursing	M,D,O
Writing	M

VIRGINIA INTERNATIONAL UNIVERSITY

Business Administration and Management—General	M
Computer Science	M
Management Information Systems	M

VIRGINIA POLYTECHNIC INSTITUTE AND STATE UNIVERSITY

Accounting	M,D
Acute Care/Critical Care Nursing	M,D
Adult Education	M,D
Aerospace/Aeronautical Engineering	M,D
Agricultural Economics and Agribusiness	M,D
Agricultural Education	M,D
Agricultural Engineering	M,D
Agricultural Sciences—General	M,D
Agronomy and Soil Sciences	M,D
Animal Sciences	M,D
Applied Arts and Design—General	M,D
Applied Economics	M,D
Applied Mathematics	M,D
Applied Physics	M,D
Architecture	M,D
Arts Administration	M
Biochemistry	M,D
Bioengineering	M,D
Bioinformatics	D
Biological and Biomedical Sciences—General	M,D
Biomedical Engineering	M,D
Botany	M,D
Business Administration and Management—General	M,D
Chemical Engineering	M,D
Chemistry	M,D
Child and Family Studies	M,D
Child Development	M,D
Civil Engineering	M,D*
Clinical Psychology	M,D
Clothing and Textiles	M,D
Communication—General	M
Computational Biology	D
Computer Engineering	M,D
Computer Science	M,D
Construction Engineering	M
Consumer Economics	M,D
Counselor Education	M,D,O
Curriculum and Instruction	M,D,O
Developmental Biology	M,D
Developmental Psychology	M,D
Ecology	M,D
Economic Development	M,D
Economics	M,D
Educational Leadership and Administration	D,O
Educational Measurement and Evaluation	D
Educational Media/ Instructional Technology	M,D,O
Educational Psychology	M,D,O
Electrical Engineering	M,D
Engineering and Applied Sciences—General	M,D
Engineering Management	M,D
English Education	M,D,O
English	M,D
Entomology	M,D
Environmental Design	D
Environmental Engineering	M,D
Environmental Management and Policy	M,D
Environmental Sciences	M,D
Evolutionary Biology	M,D
Finance and Banking	M,D
Fish, Game, and Wildlife Management	M,D
Food Science and Technology	M,D
Foreign Languages Education	M
Forestry	M,D
Genetics	M,D
Geography	M,D
Geology	M,D
Geophysics	M,D
Geosciences	M,D
Gerontology	M,D
Health Education	M,D,O
Health Promotion	M,D,O
Higher Education	M,D,O
History of Science and Technology	M,D
History	M
Horticulture	M,D
Hospitality Management	M,D
Human Development	M,D
Human Resources Development	M,D
Industrial and Organizational Psychology	M,D
Industrial/Management Engineering	M,D
Information Science	M
Interdisciplinary Studies	M,D,O
Interior Design	M,D
International Affairs	M,D
International Development	M,D
International Economics	M,D
Landscape Architecture	M,D
Logistics	M,D
Management Information Systems	M,D
Marketing	M,D
Marriage and Family Therapy	M,D
Materials Engineering	M,D
Materials Sciences	M,D
Mathematical Physics	M,D
Mathematics Education	M,D,O
Mathematics	M,D
Mechanical Engineering	M,D
Mechanics	M,D
Microbiology	M,D
Mineral/Mining Engineering	M,D
Natural Resources	M
Nutrition	M,D
Ocean Engineering	M,D
Operations Research	M,D
Philosophy	M
Physical Education	M,D,O
Physics	M,D
Plant Pathology	M,D
Plant Physiology	M,D
Political Science	M
Psychology—General	M,D
Public Administration	M,D,O
Public Affairs	M,D
Public Policy	M,D,O
Recreation and Park Management	M,D
Rural Planning and Studies	M,D
Sociology	M,D
Special Education	D,O
Statistics	M,D
Systems Engineering	M
Theater	M
Travel and Tourism	M,D
Urban and Regional Planning	M,D
Urban Studies	M,D
Veterinary Medicine	P
Veterinary Sciences	M,D
Vocational and Technical Education	M,D,O
Zoology	M,D

VIRGINIA STATE UNIVERSITY

Agricultural Sciences—General	M
Biological and Biomedical Sciences—General	M
Clinical Psychology	M,D
Community Health	M,D
Computer Science	M
Economics	M
Education—General	M,O
Educational Leadership and Administration	M
English	M
Health Education	M,D
Health Psychology	M,D
History	M
Interdisciplinary Studies	M
Mathematics Education	M
Mathematics	M
Physics	M
Plant Sciences	M
Psychology—General	M,D
Vocational and Technical Education	M,O

VIRGINIA UNION UNIVERSITY

Theology	P,D

VIRGINIA UNIVERSITY OF LYNCHBURG

Religion	P

VITERBO UNIVERSITY

Business Administration and Management—General	M
Education—General	M
Nursing—General	M

WAGNER COLLEGE

Accounting	M
Biological and Biomedical Sciences—General	M
Business Administration and Management—General	M
Early Childhood Education	M
Education—General	M,O
Educational Leadership and Administration	O
Elementary Education	M
Family Nurse Practitioner Studies	O
Finance and Banking	M
Health Services Management and Hospital Administration	M
International Business	M
Marketing	M
Microbiology	M
Middle School Education	M
Nursing—General	M
Physician Assistant Studies	M
Reading Education	M
Secondary Education	M

WAKE FOREST UNIVERSITY

Accounting	M
Allopathic Medicine	P
Analytical Chemistry	M,D
Anatomy	D
Biochemistry	D
Biological and Biomedical Sciences—General	M,D
Biomedical Engineering	M,D
Business Administration and Management—General	M
Cancer Biology/Oncology	D

Chemistry	M,D
Communication—General	M
Computer Science	M
Counselor Education	M
Education—General	M
English	M
Entrepreneurship	M
Exercise and Sports Science	M
Finance and Banking	M
Genomic Sciences	D
Health Services Management and Hospital Administration	M
Health Services Research	M
Human Genetics	D
Immunology	D
Industrial and Manufacturing Management	M
Inorganic Chemistry	M,D
Law	P,M,D
Liberal Studies	M
Marketing	M
Mathematics	M
Microbiology	D
Molecular Biology	D
Molecular Genetics	D
Molecular Medicine	M,D
Neurobiology	D
Neuroscience	D
Organic Chemistry	M,D
Pathobiology	M,D
Pharmacology	D
Physical Chemistry	M,D
Physics	M,D*
Physiology	D
Psychology—General	M
Religion	M
Secondary Education	M
Speech and Interpersonal Communication	M
Taxation	M

WALDEN UNIVERSITY

Accounting	M,D
Adult Education	M,D,O
Business Administration and Management—General	M,D
Child and Family Studies	M,D
Clinical Psychology	M,D,O
Clinical Research	M,D
Community College Education	M,D,O
Community Health	M,D
Conflict Resolution and Mediation/Peace Studies	M,D,O
Counseling Psychology	M,D,O
Criminal Justice and Criminology	M,D,O
Curriculum and Instruction	M,D,O
Developmental Psychology	M,D,O
Early Childhood Education	M,D,O
Education—General	M,D,O
Educational Leadership and Administration	M,D,O
Educational Media/Instructional Technology	M,D,O
Elementary Education	M,D,O
Engineering and Applied Sciences—General	M,O
Engineering Management	M,D,O
Entrepreneurship	M,D
Epidemiology	M,D
Finance and Banking	M,D
Forensic Psychology	M,D,O
Health Promotion	M,D
Health Psychology	M,D,O
Health Services Management and Hospital Administration	M,D,O
Higher Education	M,D,O
Homeland Security	M,D,O
Human Resources Management	M,D
Human Services	M,D
Industrial and Organizational Psychology	M,D,O
International Affairs	M,D,O
International Business	M,D
Law	M,D,O
Management Information Systems	M,D
Management of Technology	M,D,O
Marketing	M,D
Mathematics Education	M,D,O
Middle School Education	M,D,O
Nonprofit Management	M,D,O
Nursing and Healthcare Administration	M,O
Nursing Education	M,O
Nursing Informatics	M,O
Nursing—General	M,O
Organizational Management	M,D,O
Project Management	M,D,O
Psychology—General	M,D,O
Public Administration	M,D,O
Public Health—General	M,D
Public Policy	M,D,O
Quantitative Analysis	M,D
Reading Education	M,D,O
School Psychology	M,D,O
Science Education	M,D,O
Social Psychology	M,D,O
Social Work	M,D
Software Engineering	M,O
Special Education	M,D,O
Supply Chain Management	M,D
Sustainability Management	M,D
Sustainable Development	M,D,O
Systems Engineering	M,O

WALLA WALLA UNIVERSITY

Biological and Biomedical Sciences—General	M
Counseling Psychology	M
Curriculum and Instruction	M
Education—General	M
Educational Leadership and Administration	M
Reading Education	M
Social Work	M
Special Education	M

WALSH COLLEGE OF ACCOUNTANCY AND BUSINESS ADMINISTRATION

Accounting	M
Business Administration and Management—General	M
Economics	M
Finance and Banking	M
Management Information Systems	M
Taxation	M

WALSH UNIVERSITY

Business Administration and Management—General	M
Counseling Psychology	M
Counselor Education	M
Education—General	M
Physical Therapy	D
Theology	M

WARNER PACIFIC COLLEGE

Business Administration and Management—General	M
Education—General	M
Ethics	M
Organizational Management	M
Pastoral Ministry and Counseling	M
Religion	M
Theology	M

WARNER UNIVERSITY

Business Administration and Management—General	M
Education—General	M

WARREN WILSON COLLEGE

Writing	M

WARTBURG THEOLOGICAL SEMINARY

Theology	P,M

WASHBURN UNIVERSITY

Business Administration and Management—General	M
Clinical Psychology	M
Criminal Justice and Criminology	M
Curriculum and Instruction	M
Education—General	M
Educational Leadership and Administration	M
Law	P
Liberal Studies	M
Psychology—General	M
Reading Education	M
Social Work	M
Special Education	M

WASHINGTON AND LEE UNIVERSITY

Law	P,M

WASHINGTON COLLEGE

English	M
History	M
Psychology—General	M

WASHINGTON STATE UNIVERSITY

Accounting	M,D
Agricultural Economics and Agribusiness	M,D,O
Agricultural Engineering	M,D
Agricultural Sciences—General	M
Agronomy and Soil Sciences	M,D
American Studies	M,D
Animal Sciences	M,D
Anthropology	M,D
Applied Economics	M,D,O
Applied Mathematics	M,D
Applied Statistics	M
Archaeology	M,D
Architecture	M
Art/Fine Arts	M
Asian Studies	M,D
Biochemistry	M,D
Bioengineering	M,D
Biological and Biomedical Sciences—General	M
Biophysics	M,D
Botany	M,D
Business Administration and Management—General	M,D
Cell Biology	M,D
Chemical Engineering	M,D
Chemistry	M,D
Civil Engineering	M,D
Clinical Psychology	M,D
Clothing and Textiles	M,D
Communication—General	M,D
Computer Art and Design	M
Computer Engineering	M,D
Computer Science	M,D
Corporate and Organizational Communication	M,D
Counseling Psychology	M,D,O
Criminal Justice and Criminology	M,D
Cultural Studies	M,D
Curriculum and Instruction	M,D
Demography and Population Studies	M,D
Economics	M,D,O
Education—General	M,D,O
Educational Leadership and Administration	M,D
Educational Psychology	M,D,O
Electrical Engineering	M,D
Elementary Education	M,D
Engineering and Applied Sciences—General	M,D
English Education	M,D
English	M,D
Entomology	M,D
Environmental Engineering	M
Environmental Sciences	M,D*
Ethnic Studies	M,D
Exercise and Sports Science	M,D
Experimental Psychology	M,D
Finance and Banking	M,D
Food Science and Technology	M,D
Foreign Languages Education	M
Genetics	M,D
Geology	M,D
Geosciences	M,D
Health Communication	M,D
Health Services Management and Hospital Administration	M
Higher Education	M,D,O
History	M,D
Horticulture	M,D
Human Development	M
Industrial and Manufacturing Management	M,D
Insurance	D
Interdisciplinary Studies	D
Interior Design	M,D
International Affairs	M,D
International Business	M,D,O
Landscape Architecture	M,D
Management Information Systems	M,D
Marketing	M,D
Materials Engineering	M
Materials Sciences	M,D
Mathematics Education	M,D
Mathematics	M,D*
Mechanical Engineering	M,D
Media Studies	M,D
Microbiology	M,D
Molecular Biology	M,D
Multilingual and Multicultural Education	M,D
Music Education	M
Music	M
Natural Resources	M,D
Neuroscience	M,D
Nutrition	M,D
Pharmacology	M,D
Pharmacy	P
Philosophy	M
Photography	M
Physics	M,D
Plant Molecular Biology	M,D
Plant Pathology	M,D
Political Science	M,D
Psychology—General	M,D
Public History	M,D
Public Policy	M,D
Reading Education	M,D
Real Estate	D
School Psychology	M,D,O
Secondary Education	M,D
Social Psychology	M,D
Sociology	M,D
Spanish	M
Sports Management	M,D,O
Statistics	M

*M—master's degree; P—first professional degree; D—doctorate; O—other advanced degree; *—Close-Up and/or Announcement or Display in one of the other books in this series*

Student Affairs	M,D,O
Taxation	M
Toxicology	M,D
Veterinary Medicine	P,M,D
Veterinary Sciences	M,D
Western European Studies	M,D
Women's Studies	M,D
Zoology	M,D

WASHINGTON STATE UNIVERSITY SPOKANE

Architecture	M,D
Communication Disorders	M
Criminal Justice and Criminology	M,D
Education—General	M,O
Educational Leadership and Administration	M,O
Engineering Management	M
Exercise and Sports Science	M,O
Health Services Management and Hospital Administration	M
Interior Design	M,D
Landscape Architecture	M,D
Nursing—General	M
Pharmacy	P
Physiology	M,O

WASHINGTON STATE UNIVERSITY TRI-CITIES

Atmospheric Sciences	M,D
Biological and Biomedical Sciences—General	M
Business Administration and Management—General	M
Chemistry	M
Computer Engineering	M,D
Computer Science	M,D
Counselor Education	M,D
Education—General	M,D
Educational Leadership and Administration	M,D
Electrical Engineering	M,D
Engineering and Applied Sciences—General	M,D
Environmental and Occupational Health	M,D
Environmental Sciences	M,D
Geosciences	M,D
Mechanical Engineering	M,D
Nursing—General	M
Reading Education	M,D
Secondary Education	M,D
Toxicology	M,D
Water Resources	M,D

WASHINGTON STATE UNIVERSITY VANCOUVER

Business Administration and Management—General	M
Computer Science	M
Education—General	M,D
Engineering and Applied Sciences—General	M
Environmental Sciences	M
History	M
Mechanical Engineering	M
Nursing—General	M
Public Affairs	M

WASHINGTON THEOLOGICAL UNION

Theology	P,M,D

WASHINGTON UNIVERSITY IN ST. LOUIS

Accounting	M
Aerospace/Aeronautical Engineering	M,D
Allied Health—General	M,D,O
Allopathic Medicine	P
Anthropology	D
Archaeology	M,D
Architecture	M*
Art History	M,D
Art/Fine Arts	M
Asian Languages	M,D
Asian Studies	M*
Biochemistry	D
Biological and Biomedical Sciences—General	D
Biomedical Engineering	M,D
Business Administration and Management—General	M,D
Cell Biology	D
Chemical Engineering	M,D
Chemistry	D
Chinese	M,D
Classics	M
Clinical Psychology	D
Clinical Research	M
Communication Disorders	M,D
Comparative Literature	M,D
Computational Biology	D
Computer Engineering	M,D
Computer Science	M,D*
Developmental Biology	D
Ecology	D
Economics	D
Education—General	M,D
Educational Measurement and Evaluation	D
Electrical Engineering	M,D
Elementary Education	M
Engineering and Applied Sciences—General	M,D
English	M,D
Environmental Biology	D
Environmental Engineering	M,D
Evolutionary Biology	D
Experimental Psychology	D
Finance and Banking	M
French	M,D
Genetics	M,D,O
Geosciences	M,D
German	M,D
History	M,D
Immunology	D
Japanese	M,D
Kinesiology and Movement Studies	D
Law	P,M,D
Mathematics	M,D
Mechanical Engineering	M,D
Microbiology	D
Molecular Biology	D
Molecular Biophysics	D
Molecular Genetics	D
Molecular Pathogenesis	D
Music	M,D
Neuroscience	D
Occupational Therapy	M,D
Philosophy	M,D
Physical Therapy	D,O
Physics	D
Planetary and Space Sciences	M,D
Plant Biology	D
Political Science	M,D
Psychology—General	D
Public Health—General	M,D
Public Policy	M
Romance Languages	M,D
Secondary Education	M
Social Psychology	D
Social Work	M,D*
Spanish	M,D
Special Education	M,D
Speech and Interpersonal Communication	M,D
Statistics	M,D
Structural Engineering	M,D
Systems Science	M,D
Urban Design	M
Writing	M

WAYLAND BAPTIST UNIVERSITY

Business Administration and Management—General	M
Counseling Psychology	M
Criminal Justice and Criminology	M
Education—General	M
Health Services Management and Hospital Administration	M
Homeland Security	M
Human Resources Management	M
Interdisciplinary Studies	M
International Business	M
Management Information Systems	M
Organizational Management	M
Pastoral Ministry and Counseling	M
Public Administration	M
Religion	M

WAYNESBURG UNIVERSITY

Business Administration and Management—General	M,D
Counseling Psychology	M,D
Education—General	M,D
Educational Media/Instructional Technology	M,D
Nursing—General	M,D
Special Education	M,D

WAYNE STATE COLLEGE

Business Administration and Management—General	M
Business Education	M
Communication—General	M
Counselor Education	M
Curriculum and Instruction	M
Early Childhood Education	M
Education—General	M,O
Educational Leadership and Administration	M,O
Elementary Education	M
English as a Second Language	M
English Education	M
Exercise and Sports Science	M
Home Economics Education	M
Mathematics Education	M
Music Education	M
Organizational Management	M
Physical Education	M
Science Education	M
Social Sciences Education	M
Special Education	M
Sports Management	M
Vocational and Technical Education	M

WAYNE STATE UNIVERSITY

Accounting	M,D
Acute Care/Critical Care Nursing	M
Addictions/Substance Abuse Counseling	O
Adult Education	M,D,O
Adult Nursing	M
Advertising and Public Relations	M,D
Allopathic Medicine	P
Anatomy	M,D
Anthropology	M,D
Applied Arts and Design—General	M
Applied Mathematics	M,D
Art Education	M,D,O
Art History	M
Art/Fine Arts	M
Biochemistry	M,D
Biological and Biomedical Sciences—General	M,D
Biomedical Engineering	M,D
Biopsychology	M
Business Administration and Management—General	M,D*
Business Education	M,D,O
Cancer Biology/Oncology	M,D*
Chemical Engineering	M,D
Chemistry	M,D
Child and Family Studies	O
Civil Engineering	M,D
Classics	M
Clinical Laboratory Sciences/Medical Technology	M,O
Clinical Psychology	M,D,O
Cognitive Sciences	M,D
Communication Disorders	M,D
Communication—General	M,D
Community Health Nursing	M
Community Health	M,O
Comparative Literature	M
Computer Engineering	M,D
Computer Science	M,D,O
Conflict Resolution and Mediation/Peace Studies	M,O
Corporate and Organizational Communication	M,D
Counselor Education	M,D,O
Criminal Justice and Criminology	M
Curriculum and Instruction	M,D,O
Developmental Psychology	M,D
Early Childhood Education	M,D,O
Economic Development	O
Economics	M,D,O
Education—General	M,D,O
Educational Leadership and Administration	M,D,O
Educational Measurement and Evaluation	M,D,O
Educational Media/Instructional Technology	M,D,O
Educational Policy	M,D,O
Educational Psychology	M,D,O
Electrical Engineering	M,D
Elementary Education	M,D,O
Engineering and Applied Sciences—General	M,D,O
Engineering Management	M
English Education	M,D,O
English	M,D
Environmental and Occupational Health	M,O
Food Science and Technology	M,D
Foreign Languages Education	M,D,O
Foundations and Philosophy of Education	M,D,O
French	M
Genetics	M,D*
Geography	M
Geology	M
German	M,D
Gerontology	O
Hazardous Materials Management	M,O
Health Education	M,D,O
Health Physics/Radiological Health	M,D
Higher Education	M,D,O
History	M,D
Human Development	M
Human Services	O
Immunology	M,D
Industrial and Labor Relations	M

Industrial and Organizational Psychology	M,D
Industrial/Management Engineering	M,D
Information Studies	M,O
Italian	M
Kinesiology and Movement Studies	M
Law	P,M,D
Library Science	M,O
Linguistics	M
Manufacturing Engineering	M
Materials Engineering	M,D,O
Materials Sciences	M,D,O
Maternal and Child/Neonatal Nursing	M,O
Mathematics Education	M,D,O
Mathematics	M,D
Mechanical Engineering	M,D
Media Studies	M,D
Medical Physics	M,D
Medicinal and Pharmaceutical Chemistry	P,M,D
Metallurgical Engineering and Metallurgy	M,D,O
Microbiology	M,D
Molecular Biology	M,D*
Multilingual and Multicultural Education	M,D,O
Music Education	M,O
Music	M,O
Near and Middle Eastern Studies	M
Neurobiology	D
Nurse Anesthesia	M,O
Nursing Education	M,O
Nursing—General	D
Nutrition	M,D
Occupational Therapy	M
Pathology	M,D
Pediatric Nursing	M,O
Pharmaceutical Administration	P,M,D,O
Pharmaceutical Sciences	P,M,D,O
Pharmacology	P,M,D
Pharmacy	P,M,D,O
Philosophy	M,D
Physical Education	M
Physical Therapy	M
Physician Assistant Studies	M
Physics	M,D
Physiology	M,D
Political Science	M,D
Polymer Science and Engineering	M,D,O
Psychiatric Nursing	M,O
Psychology—General	M,D
Public Administration	M
Public Health—General	M,O
Reading Education	M,D,O
Recreation and Park Management	M
Rehabilitation Counseling	M,D,O
Rehabilitation Sciences	M,O
Russian	M,D
School Psychology	M,D,O
Science Education	M,D,O
Secondary Education	M,D,O
Social Sciences Education	M,D,O
Social Work	M,D,O
Sociology	M,D
Spanish	M
Special Education	M,D,O
Speech and Interpersonal Communication	M,D
Sports Management	M
Statistics	M,D
Taxation	M,D
Theater	M,D
Toxicology	M,D
Urban and Regional Planning	M
Vocational and Technical Education	M,D,O
Writing	M,D

WEBBER INTERNATIONAL UNIVERSITY

Accounting	M
Business Administration and Management—General	M*
Criminal Justice and Criminology	M
Sports Management	M

WEBER STATE UNIVERSITY

Accounting	M
Athletic Training and Sports Medicine	M
Business Administration and Management—General	M
Curriculum and Instruction	M
Education—General	M
English	M
Health Services Management and Hospital Administration	M
Legal and Justice Studies	M

WEBSTER UNIVERSITY

Advertising and Public Relations	M
Aerospace/Aeronautical Engineering	M,D
Art/Fine Arts	M
Arts Administration	M
Business Administration and Management—General	M,D
Communication—General	M
Computer Science	M,O
Corporate and Organizational Communication	M
Counseling Psychology	M
Criminal Justice and Criminology	M,D
Early Childhood Education	M
Education—General	M,O
Educational Leadership and Administration	M,O
Educational Media/Instructional Technology	M,O
Engineering Management	M
English as a Second Language	M
Environmental Management and Policy	M,D
Finance and Banking	M
Gerontology	M
Health Services Management and Hospital Administration	M,D
Human Resources Development	M,D
Human Resources Management	M,D
International Affairs	M
International Business	M
Legal and Justice Studies	M
Management Information Systems	M,D,O
Marketing	M,D
Mathematics Education	M,O
Media Studies	M
Music Education	M
Music	M
Nurse Anesthesia	M
Nursing—General	M
Organizational Management	M
Public Administration	M,D
Quality Management	M,D
Social Sciences Education	M,O
Special Education	M,O
Telecommunications Management	M,D

WESLEYAN COLLEGE

Business Administration and Management—General	M
Early Childhood Education	M
Education—General	M
Mathematics Education	M
Middle School Education	M
Science Education	M

WESLEYAN UNIVERSITY

Astronomy	M
Biochemistry	M,D
Biological and Biomedical Sciences—General	D
Cell Biology	D
Chemical Physics	M,D
Chemistry	M,D*
Developmental Biology	D
Environmental Sciences	M
Evolutionary Biology	D
Genetics	D
Geosciences	M
Inorganic Chemistry	M,D
Liberal Studies	M,O
Mathematics	M,D*
Molecular Biology	D
Music	M,D
Neurobiology	D
Organic Chemistry	M,D
Physics	M,D
Physiology	D
Psychology—General	M
Theoretical Chemistry	M,D

WESLEY BIBLICAL SEMINARY

Marriage and Family Therapy	P,M
Missions and Missiology	P,M
Pastoral Ministry and Counseling	P,M
Religious Education	P,M
Theology	P,M

WESLEY COLLEGE

Business Administration and Management—General	M
Education—General	M
Environmental Management and Policy	M
Nursing—General	M

WESLEY THEOLOGICAL SEMINARY

Theology	P,M,D

WEST CHESTER UNIVERSITY OF PENNSYLVANIA

Anthropology	M,O
Applied Statistics	M,O
Astronomy	M,O
Biological and Biomedical Sciences—General	M,O
Business Administration and Management—General	M,O
Chemistry	M
Classics	M,O
Clinical Psychology	M,O
Communication Disorders	M,O
Communication—General	M
Computer and Information Systems Security	M,O
Computer Science	M,O
Counselor Education	M,O
Criminal Justice and Criminology	M
Early Childhood Education	M,O
Economics	M
Education—General	M,O
Educational Measurement and Evaluation	M,O
Educational Media/Instructional Technology	M,O
Elementary Education	M,O
Emergency Management	M,O
English as a Second Language	M,O
English	M,O
Entrepreneurship	M,O
Ethics	M,O
Exercise and Sports Science	M,O
Foreign Languages Education	M,O
French	M,O
Geographic Information Systems	M,O
Geography	M,O
Geology	M,O
German	M,O
Gerontology	M,O
Health Education	M,O
Health Psychology	M,O
Health Services Management and Hospital Administration	M,O
History	M,O
Holocaust Studies	M,O
Human Resources Management	M,O
Industrial and Organizational Psychology	M,O
Kinesiology and Movement Studies	M,O
Management Information Systems	M,O
Management of Technology	M
Marketing	M
Mathematics	M,O
Music Education	M,O
Music	M,O
Nonprofit Management	M,O
Nursing Education	M,O
Nursing—General	M,O
Philosophy	M,O
Physical Education	M,O
Planetary and Space Sciences	M,O
Political Science	M,O
Psychology—General	M,O
Public Administration	M,O
Public Affairs	M,O
Public Health—General	M,O
Reading Education	M,O
School Nursing	M,O
Science Education	M,O
Secondary Education	M,O
Social Sciences Education	M,O
Social Work	M
Sociology	M,O
Spanish	M,O
Special Education	M,O
Sports Management	M,O
Urban and Regional Planning	M,O
Women's Studies	M,O

WESTERN CAROLINA UNIVERSITY

Accounting	M
Applied Arts and Design—General	M
Art/Fine Arts	M
Biological and Biomedical Sciences—General	M
Business Administration and Management—General	M
Chemistry	M
Communication Disorders	M
Community College Education	M
Computer Science	M
Construction Management	M
Counselor Education	M
Education—General	M,D,O
Educational Leadership and Administration	M,D,O
English as a Second Language	M
English Education	M

*M—master's degree; P—first professional degree; D—doctorate; O—other advanced degree; *—Close-Up and/or Announcement or Display in one of the other books in this series*

English	M
Entrepreneurship	M
Health Services Management and Hospital Administration	M
Higher Education	M
History	M
Human Resources Development	M
Industrial/Management Engineering	M
Mathematics Education	M
Mathematics	M
Music	M
Nursing—General	M
Physical Education	M
Physical Therapy	M
Project Management	M
Psychology—General	M
Public Affairs	M
School Psychology	M
Science Education	M
Social Psychology	M
Social Work	M
Sports Management	M

WESTERN CONNECTICUT STATE UNIVERSITY

Accounting	M
Adult Nursing	M
Art/Fine Arts	M
Biological and Biomedical Sciences—General	M
Business Administration and Management—General	M
Counselor Education	M
Criminal Justice and Criminology	M
Curriculum and Instruction	M
Education—General	M,D
Educational Leadership and Administration	D
Educational Media/Instructional Technology	M
English as a Second Language	M
English Education	M
English	M
Environmental Sciences	M
Geosciences	M
Health Services Management and Hospital Administration	M
History	M
Illustration	M
Mathematics Education	M
Mathematics	M
Music Education	M
Nursing—General	M
Planetary and Space Sciences	M
Reading Education	M
Social Psychology	M
Special Education	M
Writing	M

WESTERN GOVERNORS UNIVERSITY

Business Administration and Management—General	M
Computer and Information Systems Security	M
Education—General	M,O
Educational Leadership and Administration	M,O
Educational Measurement and Evaluation	M,O
Educational Media/Instructional Technology	M,O
English Education	M,O
Higher Education	M,O
Management Information Systems	M
Management Strategy and Policy	M
Mathematics Education	M,O
Science Education	M,O

WESTERN ILLINOIS UNIVERSITY

Accounting	M
Applied Mathematics	M,O
Biological and Biomedical Sciences—General	M,O
Business Administration and Management—General	M
Chemistry	M
Clinical Psychology	M,O
Communication Disorders	M
Communication—General	M
Computer Science	M
Counselor Education	M
Criminal Justice and Criminology	M,O
Distance Education Development	M,O
Economics	M,O
Education—General	M,D,O
Educational Leadership and Administration	M,D,O
Educational Media/Instructional Technology	M,O
Elementary Education	M
English	M,O
Foundations and Philosophy of Education	M
Geographic Information Systems	M,O
Geography	M,O
Graphic Design	M,O
Health Education	M,O
Health Services Management and Hospital Administration	M,O
History	M
Internet and Interactive Multimedia	M,O
Kinesiology and Movement Studies	M
Liberal Studies	M
Manufacturing Engineering	M
Marine Biology	M,O
Mathematics	M,O
Museum Studies	M
Music	M
Nonprofit Management	M,O
Physics	M
Political Science	M,O
Psychology—General	M,O
Public Administration	M,O
Reading Education	M,O
Recreation and Park Management	M
School Psychology	M,O
Social Psychology	M,O
Sociology	M
Special Education	M
Sports Management	M
Student Affairs	M
Sustainable Development	M,O
Technology and Public Policy	M
Theater	M
Travel and Tourism	M
Zoology	M,O

WESTERN INTERNATIONAL UNIVERSITY

Business Administration and Management—General	M
Finance and Banking	M
International Business	M
Management Information Systems	M
Management Strategy and Policy	M
Marketing	M
Organizational Management	M
Public Administration	M
Systems Engineering	M

WESTERN KENTUCKY UNIVERSITY

Agricultural Sciences—General	M
Anthropology	M
Art Education	M
Biological and Biomedical Sciences—General	M
Business Administration and Management—General	M
Business Education	M,O
Chemistry	M
Communication Disorders	M
Communication—General	M
Comparative Literature	M
Computer Science	M
Counselor Education	M,O
Early Childhood Education	M
Educational Leadership and Administration	M,O
Educational Media/Instructional Technology	M
Educational Psychology	M,O
Elementary Education	M,O
English as a Second Language	M
English Education	M
English	M
Geography	M
Geology	M
Health Services Management and Hospital Administration	M
History	M
Interdisciplinary Studies	M
Mathematics	M
Middle School Education	M,O
Music Education	M
Nursing—General	M
Physical Education	M
Political Science	M
Psychology—General	M,O
Public Health—General	M
Reading Education	M
Recreation and Park Management	M
School Psychology	M,O
Science Education	M
Secondary Education	M,O
Social Work	M
Sociology	M
Special Education	M
Student Affairs	M,O
Writing	M

WESTERN MICHIGAN UNIVERSITY

Accounting	M
Anthropology	M
Applied Arts and Design—General	M
Applied Economics	M,D
Applied Mathematics	M
Applied Statistics	M
Art Education	M
Athletic Training and Sports Medicine	M
Biological and Biomedical Sciences—General	M,D
Biotechnology	M,D
Business Administration and Management—General	M
Chemical Engineering	M,D
Chemistry	M,D
Civil Engineering	M
Clinical Psychology	M,D
Communication Disorders	M,D
Communication—General	M
Computational Sciences	M
Computer Engineering	M,D
Computer Science	M,D
Construction Engineering	M
Construction Management	M
Corporate and Organizational Communication	M
Counseling Psychology	M,D
Counselor Education	M,D
Economics	M,D
Education—General	M,D,O
Educational Leadership and Administration	M,D,O
Educational Measurement and Evaluation	M,D,O
Educational Media/Instructional Technology	M,D,O
Electrical Engineering	M,D
Engineering and Applied Sciences—General	M,D
Engineering Management	M
English Education	M,D
English	M,D
Exercise and Sports Science	M
Experimental Psychology	M,D
Family and Consumer Sciences-General	M
Finance and Banking	M
Geography	M
Geosciences	M,D
Graphic Design	M
Health Services Management and Hospital Administration	M,D,O
History	M,D
Human Resources Development	M,D,O
Industrial and Organizational Psychology	M,D
Industrial/Management Engineering	M
Manufacturing Engineering	M
Marriage and Family Therapy	M,D
Mathematics Education	M,D
Mathematics	M,D
Mechanical Engineering	M,D
Medieval and Renaissance Studies	M
Microbiology	M,D
Music Education	M
Music	M
Nanotechnology	M,D
Nonprofit Management	M,D,O
Occupational Therapy	M
Paper and Pulp Engineering	M,D
Philosophy	M
Physical Education	M
Physician Assistant Studies	M
Physics	M,D
Physiology	M
Political Science	M,D
Psychology—General	M,D
Public Administration	M,D,O
Public Affairs	M,D,O
Rehabilitation Counseling	M
Religion	M
Science Education	D*
Social Work	M
Sociology	M,D
Spanish	M,D
Sports Management	M
Statistics	M,D
Structural Engineering	M
Therapies—Dance, Drama, and Music	M
Transportation and Highway Engineering	M
Vocational and Technical Education	M
Writing	M,D

WESTERN NEW ENGLAND COLLEGE

Accounting	M
Business Administration and Management—General	M

Electrical Engineering	M
Elementary Education	M
Engineering and Applied Sciences—General	M
English Education	M
Industrial/Management Engineering	M
Law	P,M
Manufacturing Engineering	M
Mathematics Education	M
Mechanical Engineering	M
Psychology—General	D
Sports Management	M

WESTERN NEW MEXICO UNIVERSITY

Business Administration and Management—General	M
Counselor Education	M
Education—General	M
Educational Leadership and Administration	M
Elementary Education	M
English as a Second Language	M
Interdisciplinary Studies	M
Multilingual and Multicultural Education	M
Reading Education	M
School Psychology	M
Secondary Education	M
Special Education	M

WESTERN OREGON UNIVERSITY

Criminal Justice and Criminology	M
Early Childhood Education	M
Education—General	M
Educational Media/Instructional Technology	M
Health Education	M
Mathematics Education	M
Multilingual and Multicultural Education	M
Music	M
Rehabilitation Counseling	M
Science Education	M
Secondary Education	M
Social Sciences Education	M
Special Education	M

WESTERN SEMINARY

Human Resources Development	M,O
Missions and Missiology	M,O
Pastoral Ministry and Counseling	P,M,D,O
Religion	M,O
Religious Education	D
Special Education	M,O
Theology	M,O
Women's Studies	M,O

WESTERN SEMINARY–SACRAMENTO CAMPUS

Marriage and Family Therapy	P,M
Pastoral Ministry and Counseling	P,M
Theology	P,M

WESTERN SEMINARY–SAN JOSE CAMPUS

Marriage and Family Therapy	P,M
Pastoral Ministry and Counseling	P,M
Theology	P,M

WESTERN STATES CHIROPRACTIC COLLEGE

Chiropractic	P

WESTERN STATE UNIVERSITY COLLEGE OF LAW

Law	P

WESTERN THEOLOGICAL SEMINARY

Theology	P,M,D

WESTERN UNIVERSITY OF HEALTH SCIENCES

Allied Health—General	M,D
Dentistry	P
Family Nurse Practitioner Studies	M
Health Education	M
Nursing—General	M
Optometry	P
Osteopathic Medicine	P
Pharmaceutical Sciences	M
Pharmacy	P
Physical Therapy	D
Physician Assistant Studies	M
Veterinary Medicine	P

WESTERN WASHINGTON UNIVERSITY

Adult Education	M
Anthropology	M
Biological and Biomedical Sciences—General	M
Business Administration and Management—General	M
Chemistry	M
Communication Disorders	M
Computer Science	M
Counseling Psychology	M
Counselor Education	M
Education of the Gifted	M
Education—General	M
Educational Leadership and Administration	M
Elementary Education	M
English	M
Environmental Education	M
Environmental Sciences	M
Exercise and Sports Science	M
Experimental Psychology	M
Geography	M
Geology	M
Higher Education	M
History	M
Marine Sciences	M
Mathematics	M
Music	M
Physical Education	M
Political Science	M
Psychology—General	M
Rehabilitation Counseling	M
Science Education	M
Secondary Education	M

WESTFIELD STATE COLLEGE

Counseling Psychology	M
Counselor Education	M
Criminal Justice and Criminology	M
Early Childhood Education	M
Education—General	M,O
Educational Leadership and Administration	M,O
Educational Media/Instructional Technology	M
Elementary Education	M
English	M
History	M
Physical Education	M
Psychology—General	M
Reading Education	M
Secondary Education	M
Special Education	M
Vocational and Technical Education	M,O

WEST LIBERTY STATE UNIVERSITY

Education—General	M

WESTMINSTER CHOIR COLLEGE OF RIDER UNIVERSITY

Music Education	M*
Music	M

WESTMINSTER COLLEGE (PA)

Counselor Education	M,O
Education—General	M,O
Educational Leadership and Administration	M,O
Reading Education	M,O

WESTMINSTER COLLEGE (UT)

Business Administration and Management—General	M,O
Communication—General	M
Counseling Psychology	M
Education—General	M
Family Nurse Practitioner Studies	M
Management of Technology	M,O
Nurse Anesthesia	M
Nursing Education	M
Nursing—General	M
Public Health—General	M
Writing	M

WESTMINSTER SEMINARY CALIFORNIA

Religion	P,M
Theology	P,M

WESTMINSTER THEOLOGICAL SEMINARY

Missions and Missiology	P,M,D,O
Pastoral Ministry and Counseling	P,M,D,O
Religion	P,M,D,O
Theology	P,M,D,O

WEST TEXAS A&M UNIVERSITY

Accounting	M
Agricultural Economics and Agribusiness	M
Agricultural Sciences—General	M,D
Animal Sciences	M
Art/Fine Arts	M
Biological and Biomedical Sciences—General	M
Business Administration and Management—General	M
Chemistry	M
Communication Disorders	M
Communication—General	M
Counselor Education	M
Criminal Justice and Criminology	M
Curriculum and Instruction	M
Economics	M
Education—General	M
Educational Leadership and Administration	M
Educational Measurement and Evaluation	M
Educational Media/Instructional Technology	M
Engineering and Applied Sciences—General	M
English	M
Environmental Sciences	M
Exercise and Sports Science	M
Finance and Banking	M
History	M
Interdisciplinary Studies	M
Mathematics	M
Music	M
Nursing—General	M
Plant Sciences	M
Political Science	M
Psychology—General	M
Reading Education	M
Special Education	M

WEST VIRGINIA SCHOOL OF OSTEOPATHIC MEDICINE

Osteopathic Medicine	P

WEST VIRGINIA STATE UNIVERSITY

Biotechnology	M
Media Studies	M

WEST VIRGINIA UNIVERSITY

Accounting	M
Aerospace/Aeronautical Engineering	M,D
African Studies	M,D
African-American Studies	M,D
Agricultural Economics and Agribusiness	M
Agricultural Education	M,D
Agricultural Sciences—General	M,D
Agronomy and Soil Sciences	D
Allopathic Medicine	P
American Studies	M,D
Analytical Chemistry	M,D
Animal Sciences	M,D
Applied Mathematics	M,D
Applied Physics	M,D
Applied Social Research	M
Art Education	M
Art History	M
Art/Fine Arts	M
Asian Studies	M,D
Athletic Training and Sports Medicine	M,D
Biochemistry	M,D
Biological and Biomedical Sciences—General	M,D
Business Administration and Management—General	M
Cancer Biology/Oncology	M,D
Cell Biology	M,D
Chemical Engineering	M,D
Chemical Physics	M,D
Chemistry	M,D
Child and Family Studies	M
Civil Engineering	M,D
Clinical Psychology	M,D
Communication Disorders	M,D
Communication—General	M,D
Community Health	M
Computer Engineering	D
Computer Science	M,D
Condensed Matter Physics	M,D
Corporate and Organizational Communication	M,D
Counseling Psychology	D
Counselor Education	M
Curriculum and Instruction	M,D
Dentistry	P
Developmental Biology	M,D
Developmental Psychology	M,D
Early Childhood Education	M,D
Economic Development	M,D
Economics	M,D
Education of the Gifted	M,D
Education of the Multiply Handicapped	M,D
Education—General	M,D
Educational Leadership and Administration	M,D
Educational Media/Instructional Technology	M,D

*M—master's degree; P—first professional degree; D—doctorate; O—other advanced degree; *—Close-Up and/or Announcement or Display in one of the other books in this series*

Educational Psychology	M
Electrical Engineering	M,D
Elementary Education	M
Engineering and Applied Sciences—General	M,D
English as a Second Language	M
English	M,D
Entomology	M,D
Environmental and Occupational Health	D
Environmental Biology	M,D
Environmental Education	M,D
Environmental Engineering	M,D
Environmental Management and Policy	M,D
Evolutionary Biology	M,D
Exercise and Sports Science	M,D
Fish, Game, and Wildlife Management	M
Food Science and Technology	M,D
Forensic Sciences	M,D
Forestry	M,D
French	M
Genetics	M,D
Genomic Sciences	M,D
Geographic Information Systems	M,D
Geography	M,D
Geology	M,D
Geophysics	M,D
Graphic Design	M
Health Education	M,D
Health Promotion	M,D
Higher Education	M,D
History of Science and Technology	M,D
History	M,D
Horticulture	M,D
Human Development	M,D
Human Genetics	M,D
Human Services	M
Hydrogeology	M,D
Immunology	M,D
Industrial and Labor Relations	M
Industrial Hygiene	M
Industrial/Management Engineering	M,D
Inorganic Chemistry	M,D
International Affairs	M,D
International Economics	M,D
Journalism	M
Latin American Studies	M,D
Law	P
Legal and Justice Studies	M
Liberal Studies	M
Linguistics	M
Marketing	M
Mathematics Education	M,D
Mathematics	M,D
Mechanical Engineering	M,D
Medicinal and Pharmaceutical Chemistry	M,D
Microbiology	M,D
Mineral/Mining Engineering	M,D
Molecular Biology	M,D
Music Education	M,D
Music	M,D
Natural Resources	M,D
Neurobiology	M,D
Neuroscience	D
Nursing—General	M,D,O
Nutrition	M
Occupational Therapy	M
Oral and Dental Sciences	M
Organic Chemistry	M,D
Paleontology	M,D
Petroleum Engineering	M,D
Pharmaceutical Administration	M,D
Pharmaceutical Sciences	M,D
Pharmacology	M,D
Pharmacy	P,M,D
Physical Chemistry	M,D
Physical Education	M,D
Physical Therapy	D
Physics	M,D
Physiology	M,D
Plant Pathology	M,D
Plant Sciences	D
Plasma Physics	M,D
Political Science	M,D
Psychology—General	M,D
Public Administration	M
Public Health—General	M
Public Policy	M,D
Reading Education	M
Recreation and Park Management	M
Rehabilitation Counseling	M
Reproductive Biology	M,D
Safety Engineering	M
Secondary Education	M,D
Social Work	M
Sociology	M
Software Engineering	M
Spanish	M
Special Education	M,D
Sport Psychology	M,D
Sports Management	M,D
Statistics	M,D
Sustainable Development	D
Teratology	M,D
Theater	M
Theoretical Chemistry	M,D
Theoretical Physics	M,D
Toxicology	M,D
Urban and Regional Planning	M,D
Writing	M

WEST VIRGINIA UNIVERSITY INSTITUTE OF TECHNOLOGY

Engineering and Applied Sciences—General	M
Systems Engineering	M

WEST VIRGINIA WESLEYAN COLLEGE

Business Administration and Management—General	M

WHEATON COLLEGE

American Studies	M
Archaeology	M
Clinical Psychology	M,D
Cultural Studies	M,O
Education—General	M
Elementary Education	M
English as a Second Language	M,O
Missions and Missiology	M,O
Pastoral Ministry and Counseling	M,D
Psychology—General	M,D
Religion	M
Religious Education	M
Secondary Education	M
Theology	M,D

WHEELING JESUIT UNIVERSITY

Accounting	M
Business Administration and Management—General	M
Nursing—General	M
Organizational Management	M
Physical Therapy	D

WHEELOCK COLLEGE

Child and Family Studies	M
Early Childhood Education	M
Education—General	M
Educational Leadership and Administration	M
Elementary Education	M
Human Development	M
Reading Education	M
Social Work	M
Special Education	M

WHITTIER COLLEGE

Child Development	M
Education—General	M
Educational Leadership and Administration	M
Elementary Education	M
Law	P,M
Legal and Justice Studies	P,M
Secondary Education	M

WHITWORTH UNIVERSITY

Business Administration and Management—General	M
Counselor Education	M
Education of the Gifted	M
Education—General	M
Educational Leadership and Administration	M
Elementary Education	M
International Business	M
Secondary Education	M
Special Education	M

WICHITA STATE UNIVERSITY

Accounting	M
Aerospace/Aeronautical Engineering	M,D
Allied Health—General	M
Anthropology	M
Applied Mathematics	M,D
Art Education	M
Art/Fine Arts	M
Biological and Biomedical Sciences—General	M*
Business Administration and Management—General	M
Chemistry	M,D
Clinical Psychology	M,D
Communication Disorders	M,D
Communication—General	M
Computer Science	M
Counselor Education	M,D,O
Criminal Justice and Criminology	M
Curriculum and Instruction	M
Economics	M
Education—General	M,D,O
Educational Leadership and Administration	M,D,O
Educational Psychology	M,D,O
Electrical Engineering	M,D
Engineering and Applied Sciences—General	M,D
English	M
Environmental Sciences	M
Exercise and Sports Science	M
Family Nurse Practitioner Studies	M
Geology	M
Gerontology	M
History	M
Human Services	M
Industrial/Management Engineering	M,D
Liberal Studies	M
Manufacturing Engineering	M,D
Mathematics	M,D
Mechanical Engineering	M,D
Music Education	M
Music	M
Nurse Midwifery	M
Nursing and Healthcare Administration	M
Nursing—General	M
Physical Education	M
Physical Therapy	M
Physics	M
Political Science	M
Psychology—General	M,D
Public Administration	M
Public Health—General	M
School Psychology	M,D,O
Social Psychology	M,D
Social Work	M
Sociology	M
Spanish	M
Special Education	M
Sports Management	M
Statistics	M,D
Writing	M

WIDENER UNIVERSITY

Accounting	M
Adult Education	M,D
Business Administration and Management—General	M
Chemical Engineering	M
Civil Engineering	M
Clinical Psychology	D*
Computer Engineering	M
Counselor Education	M,D
Criminal Justice and Criminology	M
Early Childhood Education	M,D
Education—General	M,D*
Educational Leadership and Administration	M,D
Educational Media/Instructional Technology	M,D
Educational Psychology	M,D
Elementary Education	M,D
Engineering and Applied Sciences—General	M*
Engineering Management	M
English Education	M,D
Foundations and Philosophy of Education	M,D
Health Education	M,D
Health Law	P,M,D
Health Services Management and Hospital Administration	M
Human Resources Management	M
Law	P,M,D
Liberal Studies	M
Mathematics Education	M,D
Mechanical Engineering	M
Middle School Education	M,D
Nursing—General	M,D,O
Physical Therapy	M,D
Psychology—General	
Public Administration	M
Reading Education	M,D
Science Education	M,D
Social Sciences Education	M,D
Social Work	M,D*
Software Engineering	M
Special Education	M,D
Taxation	M
Telecommunications	M

WILFRID LAURIER UNIVERSITY

Archaeology	M
Biological and Biomedical Sciences—General	M
Business Administration and Management—General	M,D
Chemistry	M
Classics	M
Cognitive Sciences	M,D
Communication—General	M
Cultural Studies	M
Developmental Psychology	M,D
Economics	M
English	M,D
Ethics	P,M,D,O
Film, Television, and Video Theory and Criticism	M,D
Foundations and Philosophy of Education	M
Geography	M,D

History M,D
International Affairs M,D
Kinesiology and Movement Studies M
Mathematics M
Pastoral Ministry and Counseling P,M,D,O
Philosophy M
Physical Education M
Political Science M
Psychology—General M,D
Public Policy M
Religion M,D
Social Psychology M,D
Social Work M,D
Sociology M
Theology P,M,D,O
Therapies—Dance, Drama, and Music M

WILKES UNIVERSITY

Accounting M
Business Administration and Management—General M
Computer Education M,D
Education—General M,D
Educational Leadership and Administration M,D
Educational Measurement and Evaluation M,D
Educational Media/Instructional Technology M,D
Electrical Engineering M
Elementary Education M,D
Engineering and Applied Sciences—General M
English Education M,D
Entrepreneurship M
Finance and Banking M
Higher Education M,D
Human Resources Management M
International Business M
Marketing M
Mathematics Education M,D
Mathematics M
Nursing—General M
Pharmacy P
Science Education M,D
Secondary Education M,D
Social Sciences Education M,D
Special Education M,D
Writing M

WILLAMETTE UNIVERSITY

Business Administration and Management—General M
Education—General M
Law P,M

WILLIAM CAREY UNIVERSITY

Art Education M,O
Business Administration and Management—General M
Counseling Psychology M
Education of the Gifted M,O
Education—General M,O
Elementary Education M,O
English Education M,O
Nursing—General M
Psychology—General M
Secondary Education M,O
Social Sciences Education M,O
Special Education M,O

WILLIAM HOWARD TAFT UNIVERSITY

Education—General M
Law P,M
Legal and Justice Studies P,M
Taxation P,M

WILLIAM MITCHELL COLLEGE OF LAW

Law P

WILLIAM PATERSON UNIVERSITY OF NEW JERSEY

Art/Fine Arts M
Biological and Biomedical Sciences—General M*
Biotechnology M
Business Administration and Management—General M
Clinical Psychology M
Communication Disorders M
Communication—General M
Counseling Psychology M
Counselor Education M
Ecology M
Education—General M
Educational Leadership and Administration M
Elementary Education M
English M
History M
Limnology M
Media Studies M
Molecular Biology M
Music M
Nursing—General M
Physiology M
Public Policy M
Reading Education M
Sociology M
Special Education M

WILLIAMS COLLEGE

Art History M

WILLIAM WOODS UNIVERSITY

Agricultural Economics and Agribusiness M,O
Curriculum and Instruction M,O
Educational Leadership and Administration M,O
Elementary Education M,O
Health Services Management and Hospital Administration M,O
Human Resources Development M,O
Physical Education M,O
Secondary Education M,O
Special Education M,O

WILMINGTON COLLEGE

Education—General M
Reading Education M
Special Education M

WILMINGTON UNIVERSITY

Adult Nursing M
Business Administration and Management—General M
Computer and Information Systems Security M
Counselor Education M
Criminal Justice and Criminology M
Education of the Gifted M
Education—General M
Educational Leadership and Administration M,D
Educational Media/Instructional Technology M
Elementary Education M
Family Nurse Practitioner Studies M
Finance and Banking M
Gerontology M
Health Services Management and Hospital Administration M
Homeland Security M
Human Resources Management M
Human Services M
Internet and Interactive Multimedia M
Internet Engineering M
Logistics M
Management Information Systems M
Nursing—General M
Organizational Management M
Public Administration M
Reading Education M
Secondary Education M
Social Psychology M
Special Education M
Transportation Management M
Vocational and Technical Education M
Women's Health Nursing M

WINEBRENNER THEOLOGICAL SEMINARY

Theology P,M,D

WINGATE UNIVERSITY

Business Administration and Management—General M
Education—General M
Educational Leadership and Administration M
Elementary Education M
Pharmacy P
Physical Education M
Sports Management M

WINONA STATE UNIVERSITY

Adult Nursing M,D,O
Counselor Education M
Education—General M
Educational Leadership and Administration M,O
English M
Family Nurse Practitioner Studies M,D,O
Nursing and Healthcare Administration M,D,O
Nursing Education M,D,O
Nursing—General M,D,O
Recreation and Park Management M,O
Special Education M
Sports Management M,O

WINSTON-SALEM STATE UNIVERSITY

Business Administration and Management—General M
Computer Science M
Elementary Education M
Management Information Systems M
Nursing—General M
Occupational Therapy M
Physical Therapy M
Rehabilitation Counseling M

WINTHROP UNIVERSITY

Art Education M
Art/Fine Arts M
Arts Administration M
Biological and Biomedical Sciences—General M
Business Administration and Management—General M
Counselor Education M
Education—General M
Educational Leadership and Administration M
English M
History M
Liberal Studies M
Middle School Education M
Music Education M
Music M
Nutrition M
Physical Education M
Project Management M,O
Psychology—General M,O
Reading Education M
Secondary Education M
Social Work M
Software Engineering M,O
Spanish M
Special Education M

WISCONSIN SCHOOL OF PROFESSIONAL PSYCHOLOGY

Clinical Psychology M,D
Psychology—General M,D

WITTENBERG UNIVERSITY

Education—General M

WOODBURY UNIVERSITY

Architecture M
Business Administration and Management—General M
Organizational Management M
Real Estate M

WOODS HOLE OCEANOGRAPHIC INSTITUTION

Civil Engineering M,D,O
Electrical Engineering M,D,O
Geochemistry M,D,O
Geophysics M,D,O
Marine Biology M,D,O
Marine Geology M,D,O
Mechanical Engineering M,D,O
Ocean Engineering M,D,O
Oceanography M,D,O

WORCESTER POLYTECHNIC INSTITUTE

Applied Mathematics M,D,O
Applied Statistics M,D,O
Artificial Intelligence/Robotics M,D,O
Biochemistry M,D
Biological and Biomedical Sciences—General M,D*
Biomedical Engineering M,D,O*
Biotechnology M,D
Business Administration and Management—General M,O
Chemical Engineering M,D*
Chemistry M,D*
Civil Engineering M,D,O*
Computer and Information Systems Security M,O
Computer Engineering M,D,O
Computer Science M,D,O*
Construction Management M,D,O
Electrical Engineering M,D,O*
Energy and Power Engineering M,D
Engineering and Applied Sciences—General M,D,O*
Engineering Design M,O
Environmental Engineering M,D,O
Fire Protection Engineering M,D,O*
Interdisciplinary Studies M,D,O
Management Information Systems M,D,O
Manufacturing Engineering M,D,O*
Marketing M,O
Materials Engineering M,D,O
Materials Sciences M,D,O*

*M—master's degree; P—first professional degree; D—doctorate; O—other advanced degree; *—Close-Up and/or Announcement or Display in one of the other books in this series*

Mathematics	M,D,O*
Mechanical Engineering	M,D,O*
Mechanics	M,D,O
Organizational Management	M,O
Physics	M,D*
Social Sciences	M,D,O
Structural Engineering	M,D,O
Systems Engineering	M,D,O
Systems Science	M,D,O

WORCESTER STATE COLLEGE

Accounting	M
Biotechnology	M
Business Administration and Management—General	M
Communication Disorders	M
Community Health Nursing	M
Early Childhood Education	M
Education—General	M,O
Educational Leadership and Administration	M,O
Elementary Education	M
English Education	M
Foreign Languages Education	M
Health Education	M
Health Services Management and Hospital Administration	M
History	M
Middle School Education	M
Nonprofit Management	M
Occupational Therapy	M
Organizational Management	M
Reading Education	M,O
School Psychology	M,O
Secondary Education	M
Social Sciences Education	M
Spanish	M
Special Education	M

WORLD MEDICINE INSTITUTE: COLLEGE OF ACUPUNCTURE AND HERBAL MEDICINE

Acupuncture and Oriental Medicine	M

WRIGHT INSTITUTE

Clinical Psychology	D
Counseling Psychology	M
Psychology—General	D

WRIGHT STATE UNIVERSITY

Accounting	M
Acute Care/Critical Care Nursing	M
Adult Education	O
Adult Nursing	M
Allopathic Medicine	P
Anatomy	M
Applied Economics	M
Applied Mathematics	M
Applied Statistics	M
Biochemistry	M
Biological and Biomedical Sciences—General	M,D
Biomedical Engineering	M
Biophysics	M
Business Administration and Management—General	M
Business Education	M
Chemistry	M
Clinical Psychology	D
Community Health Nursing	M
Computer Education	M
Computer Engineering	M,D
Computer Science	M,D
Counselor Education	M
Criminal Justice and Criminology	M
Curriculum and Instruction	M,O
Early Childhood Education	M
Economics	M
Education of the Gifted	M
Education—General	M,O
Educational Leadership and Administration	M,O
Electrical Engineering	M
Elementary Education	M
Engineering and Applied Sciences—General	M,D
English as a Second Language	M
English	M
Environmental Sciences	M,D
Ergonomics and Human Factors	M,D
Family Nurse Practitioner Studies	M
Finance and Banking	M
Geology	M
Geophysics	M
Health Education	M
Health Promotion	M
Health Services Management and Hospital Administration	M
Higher Education	M,O
History	M
Humanities	M
Immunology	M
Industrial and Organizational Psychology	M,D
Interdisciplinary Studies	M
International and Comparative Education	M
International Business	M
Library Science	M
Logistics	M
Management Information Systems	M
Marketing	M
Materials Engineering	M
Materials Sciences	M
Mathematics Education	M
Mathematics	M
Mechanical Engineering	M
Medical Physics	M
Microbiology	M
Middle School Education	M
Molecular Biology	M
Music Education	M
Music	M
Nursing and Healthcare Administration	M
Nursing—General	M
Pediatric Nursing	M
Pharmacology	M
Physical Education	M
Physics	M
Physiology	M
Project Management	M
Psychology—General	M,D
Public Administration	M
Public Health—General	M
Recreation and Park Management	M
Rehabilitation Counseling	M
Rhetoric	M
School Nursing	M
Science Education	M
Secondary Education	M
Special Education	M
Supply Chain Management	M
Toxicology	M
Urban Studies	M
Vocational and Technical Education	M
Writing	M

WYCLIFFE COLLEGE

Religion	P,M,D,O
Theology	P,M,D,O

XAVIER UNIVERSITY

Business Administration and Management—General	M
Clinical Psychology	M,D
Counselor Education	M
Criminal Justice and Criminology	M
Early Childhood Education	M
Education—General	M
Educational Leadership and Administration	M
Electronic Commerce	M
Elementary Education	M
English	M
Experimental Psychology	M,D
Finance and Banking	M
Health Law	M
Health Services Management and Hospital Administration	M*
Human Resources Development	M
Industrial and Organizational Psychology	M,D
International Business	M
Management Information Systems	M
Marketing	M
Multilingual and Multicultural Education	M
Nursing and Healthcare Administration	M
Nursing—General	M
Occupational Therapy	M
Psychology—General	M,D
Reading Education	M
Secondary Education	M
Special Education	M
Sports Management	M
Theology	M

XAVIER UNIVERSITY OF LOUISIANA

Counselor Education	M
Curriculum and Instruction	M
Education—General	M
Educational Leadership and Administration	M
Pastoral Ministry and Counseling	M
Pharmacy	P
Theology	M

YALE UNIVERSITY

Accounting	D
African Studies	M
African-American Studies	D
Allopathic Medicine	P
American Studies	D
Anthropology	M,D
Applied Arts and Design—General	M
Applied Mathematics	M,D
Applied Physics	M,D
Archaeology	M,D
Architecture	M
Art History	D
Art/Fine Arts	M
Asian Languages	D
Asian Studies	M
Astronomy	M,D
Astrophysics	M,D
Atmospheric Sciences	D
Biochemistry	D
Bioinformatics	D
Biological and Biomedical Sciences—General	D*
Biomedical Engineering	M,D
Biophysics	D
Biostatistics	M,D
Business Administration and Management—General	M,D*
Cancer Biology/Oncology	D
Cell Biology	D
Chemical Engineering	M,D
Chemistry	D
Classics	M,D
Clinical Psychology	D
Cognitive Sciences	D
Comparative Literature	D
Computational Biology	D
Computer Science	M,D*
Developmental Biology	D
Developmental Psychology	D
East European and Russian Studies	M,D
Ecology	D
Economic Development	M
Economics	M,D
Electrical Engineering	M,D
Engineering and Applied Sciences—General	M,D*
Engineering Physics	M,D
English	M,D
Environmental and Occupational Health	M,D
Environmental Design	M
Environmental Engineering	M,D
Environmental Management and Policy	M,D
Environmental Sciences	M,D
Epidemiology	M,D
Evolutionary Biology	D
Film, Television, and Video Theory and Criticism	D
Finance and Banking	D
Forestry	M,D
French	M,D
Genetics	D
Genomic Sciences	D
Geochemistry	D
Geology	D
Geophysics	D
Geosciences	D
German	D
Graphic Design	M
Health Services Management and Hospital Administration	M,D
History of Medicine	M,D
History of Science and Technology	M,D
History	M,D
Immunology	D
Infectious Diseases	D
Inorganic Chemistry	D
International Affairs	M,O
International Economics	M
International Health	M
Italian	D
Latin American Studies	D
Law	P,M,D
Linguistics	D
Marketing	D
Mathematics	M,D
Mechanical Engineering	M,D
Medieval and Renaissance Studies	M,D
Meteorology	D
Microbiology	D
Molecular Biology	D
Molecular Biophysics	D
Molecular Medicine	D
Molecular Pathology	D
Molecular Physiology	D
Music	M,D,O
Near and Middle Eastern Languages	M,D
Near and Middle Eastern Studies	M,D
Neurobiology	D
Neuroscience	D
Nursing—General	M,D,O
Oceanography	D
Organic Chemistry	D
Paleontology	D
Parasitology	D
Pathobiology	D

Pathology	M,D
Pharmacology	D
Philosophy	D
Photography	M
Physical Chemistry	D
Physician Assistant Studies	M,O
Physics	D
Physiology	D
Planetary and Space Sciences	M,D
Plant Biology	D
Political Science	D
Portuguese	D
Psychology—General	D
Public Health—General	M,D
Religion	D
Russian	D
Slavic Languages	D
Social Psychology	D
Social Sciences	M,D
Sociology	D
Spanish	D
Statistics	M,D
Structural Biology	D
Theater	M,D,O
Theology	P,M
Theoretical Chemistry	D
Virology	D

YESHIVA BETH MOSHE

Theology	O

YESHIVA KARLIN STOLIN RABBINICAL INSTITUTE

Theology	O

YESHIVA OF NITRA RABBINICAL COLLEGE

Theology	

YESHIVA SHAAR HATORAH TALMUDIC RESEARCH INSTITUTE

Theology	

YESHIVATH ZICHRON MOSHE

Theology	O

YESHIVA TORAS CHAIM TALMUDICAL SEMINARY

Theology	

YESHIVA UNIVERSITY

Accounting	M
Clinical Psychology	D
Counseling Psychology	M
Educational Leadership and Administration	M,D,O
Health Psychology	D
Jewish Studies	M,D
Law	P,M
Psychology—General	M,D
Religious Education	M,D,O
School Psychology	D
Social Work	M,D

YORK COLLEGE OF PENNSYLVANIA

Business Administration and Management—General	M
Education—General	M
Nursing—General	M

YORK UNIVERSITY

Accounting	M,D
Anthropology	M,D
Applied Arts and Design—General	M
Applied Mathematics	M,D
Art History	M,D
Art/Fine Arts	M,D
Astronomy	M,D
Biological and Biomedical Sciences—General	M,D
Business Administration and Management—General	M,D
Chemistry	M,D
Communication—General	M,D
Computer Science	M,D
Dance	M
Disability Studies	M,D
Economics	M,D
Education—General	M,D
Emergency Management	M
English	M,D
Environmental Management and Policy	M,D
Film, Television, and Video Production	M,D
Finance and Banking	M,D
French	M
Geography	M,D
Geosciences	M,D
History	M,D
Human Resources Management	M,D
Humanities	M,D
Industrial and Labor Relations	M,D
Industrial and Manufacturing Management	M,D
Interdisciplinary Studies	M
International Affairs	M
International Business	M,D
Kinesiology and Movement Studies	M,D
Law	P,M,D
Linguistics	M,D
Management Information Systems	M,D
Management Strategy and Policy	M,D
Marketing	M,D
Mathematics	M,D
Music	M,D
Nursing—General	M
Organizational Behavior	M,D
Philosophy	M,D
Physics	M,D
Planetary and Space Sciences	M,D
Political Science	M,D
Psychology—General	M,D
Public Administration	M,D
Public Affairs	M
Public Policy	M
Social Sciences	M
Social Work	M,D
Sociology	M,D
Statistics	M,D
Theater	M,D
Translation and Interpretation	M
Women's Studies	M,D

YO SAN UNIVERSITY OF TRADITIONAL CHINESE MEDICINE

Acupuncture and Oriental Medicine	M

YOUNGSTOWN STATE UNIVERSITY

Accounting	M
Analytical Chemistry	M
Anatomy	M
Applied Mathematics	M
Biochemistry	M
Biological and Biomedical Sciences—General	M
Business Administration and Management—General	M,O
Chemistry	M
Civil Engineering	M
Computer Engineering	M
Computer Science	M
Counseling Psychology	M
Counselor Education	M
Criminal Justice and Criminology	M
Curriculum and Instruction	M
Early Childhood Education	M
Economics	M
Education of the Gifted	M
Education—General	M,D
Educational Leadership and Administration	M,D
Educational Media/Instructional Technology	M
Electrical Engineering	M
Engineering and Applied Sciences—General	M
English	M
Environmental Biology	M
Environmental Engineering	M
Environmental Management and Policy	M,O
Finance and Banking	M
Foundations and Philosophy of Education	M,D
Health Services Management and Hospital Administration	M
History	M
Human Services	M
Industrial/Management Engineering	M
Information Science	M
Inorganic Chemistry	M
Marketing	M
Mathematics Education	M
Mathematics	M
Mechanical Engineering	M
Microbiology	M
Middle School Education	M
Molecular Biology	M
Music Education	M
Music	M
Nursing—General	M
Organic Chemistry	M
Physical Chemistry	M
Physical Therapy	D
Physiology	M
Psychology—General	M
Reading Education	M
School Psychology	M
Science Education	M
Secondary Education	M
Special Education	M
Statistics	M

*M—master's degree; P—first professional degree; D—doctorate; O—other advanced degree; *—Close-Up and/or Announcement or Display in one of the other books in this series*

PROFILES OF INSTITUTIONS OFFERING GRADUATE AND PROFESSIONAL WORK

ABILENE CHRISTIAN UNIVERSITY, Abilene, TX 79699-9100

General Information Independent-religious, coed, comprehensive institution. CGS member. *Enrollment:* 4,669 graduate, professional, and undergraduate students; 347 full-time matriculated graduate/professional students (200 women), 333 part-time matriculated graduate/professional students (176 women). *Enrollment by degree level:* 644 master's, 20 doctoral, 15 other advanced degrees. *Graduate faculty:* 13 full-time (2 women), 69 part-time/adjunct (23 women). *Tuition:* Full-time $10,728; part-time $596 per hour. *Required fees:* $1090; $53.50 per hour. $10 per term. Tuition and fees vary according to campus/location. *Graduate housing:* On-campus housing not available. *Student services:* Campus employment opportunities, campus safety program, career counseling, exercise/wellness program, grant writing training, international student services, low-cost health insurance, multicultural affairs office, services for students with disabilities, teacher training, writing training. *Library facilities:* Brown Library. *Online resources:* library catalog, web page, access to other libraries' catalogs. *Collection:* 511,000 titles, 1,385 serial subscriptions, 65,246 audiovisual materials. *Research affiliation:* Fermilab (peanut toxins), Los Alamos National Laboratory (particle physics).

Computer facilities: Computer purchase and lease plans are available. 724 computers available on campus for general student use. A campuswide network can be accessed from student residence rooms and from off campus. Online class registration is available. *Web address:* http://www.acu.edu/.

General Application Contact: William Horn, Graduate Admissions Counselor, 325-674-2656, Fax: 325-674-6717, E-mail: gradinfo@acu.edu.

GRADUATE UNITS

Graduate School Students: 347 full-time (200 women), 333 part-time (176 women); includes 70 minority (35 African Americans, 2 American Indian/Alaska Native, 1 Asian American or Pacific Islander, 32 Hispanic Americans), 35 international. Average age 32. 527 applicants, 80% accepted, 288 enrolled. *Faculty:* 13 full-time (2 women), 69 part-time/adjunct (23 women). Expenses: Contact institution. *Financial support:* In 2008–09, 551 students received support, including 36 research assistantships with partial tuition reimbursements available (averaging $5,800 per year), 12 teaching assistantships with partial tuition reimbursements available (averaging $5,800 per year); career-related internships or fieldwork, Federal Work-Study, institutionally sponsored loans, scholarships/grants, and tuition waivers (partial) also available. Support available to part-time students. Financial award application deadline: 4/1; financial award applicants required to submit FAFSA. In 2008, 197 master's, 6 doctorates, 23 other advanced degrees awarded. *Degree program information:* Part-time and evening/weekend programs available. Postbaccalaureate distance learning degree programs offered (no on-campus study). Offers liberal arts (MLA). *Application deadline:* For fall admission, 4/1 priority date for domestic students; for spring admission, 11/1 priority date for domestic students. Applications are processed on a rolling basis. *Application fee:* $40 ($45 for international students). *Application Contact:* William Horn, Graduate Admissions Counselor, 325-674-2656, Fax: 325-674-3717, E-mail: gradinfo@acu.edu. *Graduate Dean,* Dr. Carol G. Williams, 325-674-2223, Fax: 325-674-6717, E-mail: gradinfo@acu.edu.

College of Arts and Sciences Students: 105 full-time (70 women), 86 part-time (61 women); includes 19 minority (11 African Americans, 8 Hispanic Americans), 14 international. 177 applicants, 80% accepted, 94 enrolled. *Faculty:* 2 full-time (0 women), 31 part-time/adjunct (9 women). Expenses: Contact institution. *Financial support:* In 2008–09, 160 students received support, including 21 research assistantships (averaging $5,800 per year), 12 teaching assistantships (averaging $5,800 per year); career-related internships or fieldwork, Federal Work-Study, and tuition waivers (partial) also available. Support available to part-time students. Financial award application deadline: 4/1; financial award applicants required to submit FAFSA. In 2008, 58 master's, 22 other advanced degrees awarded. *Degree program information:* Part-time programs available. Postbaccalaureate distance learning degree programs offered (no on-campus study). Offers arts and sciences (MA, MS, Certificate); clinical psychology (MS); communication (MA); composition/rhetoric (MA); conflict resolution (Certificate); conflict resolution and reconciliation (MA); counseling psychology (MS); gerontology (MS, Certificate); literature (MA); organizational and human resource development (MS); psychology (MS); school psychology (MS); writing (MA). *Application deadline:* For fall admission, 4/1 priority date for domestic students; for spring admission, 11/1 for domestic students. Applications are processed on a rolling basis. *Application fee:* $40 ($45 for international students). Electronic applications accepted. *Application Contact:* William Horn, Graduate Admissions Counselor, 325-674-2656, Fax: 325-674-6717, E-mail: gradinfo@acu.edu. *Interim Dean,* Dr. Greg Straughn, 325-674-2209, Fax: 325-674-6800, E-mail: gregory.straughn@acu.edu.

College of Biblical Studies Students: 102 full-time (31 women), 80 part-time (13 women); includes 11 minority (4 African Americans, 1 American Indian/Alaska Native, 1 Asian American or Pacific Islander, 5 Hispanic Americans), 9 international. 87 applicants, 75% accepted, 46 enrolled. *Faculty:* 11 full-time (2 women), 11 part-time/adjunct (2 women). Expenses: Contact institution. *Financial support:* In 2008–09, 102 students received support; teaching assistantships, career-related internships or fieldwork and Federal Work-Study available. Support available to part-time students. Financial award application deadline: 4/1; financial award applicants required to submit FAFSA. In 2008, 50 master's, 6 doctorates awarded. *Degree program information:* Part-time and evening/weekend programs available. Offers biblical studies (M Div, MA, MACM, MMFT, D Min); Christian ministry (MACM); divinity (M Div); history and theology (MA); marriage and family therapy (MMFT); ministry (D Min); missions (MA); New Testament (MA); Old Testament (MA). *Application deadline:* For fall admission, 4/1 priority date for domestic students; for spring admission, 11/1 for domestic students. Applications are processed on a rolling basis. *Application fee:* $40 ($45 for international students). *Application Contact:* William Horn, Graduate Admissions Counselor, 325-674-2656, Fax: 325-674-6717, E-mail: gradinfo@acu.edu. *Dean,* Dr. Jack Reese, 325-674-3700.

College of Business Administration Students: 37 full-time (13 women), 3 part-time (1 woman); includes 6 minority (1 African American, 1 American Indian/Alaska Native, 4 Hispanic Americans), 6 international. 36 applicants, 86% accepted, 26 enrolled. *Faculty:* 7 part-time/adjunct (0 women). Expenses: Contact institution. *Financial support:* In 2008–09, 38 students received support; teaching assistantships, Federal Work-Study available. Support available to part-time students. Financial award application deadline: 4/1; financial award applicants required to submit FAFSA. In 2008, 28 master's awarded. *Degree program information:* Part-time programs available. Offers business administration (M Acc). *Application deadline:* For fall admission, 4/1 priority date for domestic students; for spring admission, 11/1 for domestic students. Applications are processed on a rolling basis. *Application fee:* $40 ($45 for international students). Electronic applications accepted. *Application Contact:* William Horn, Graduate Admissions Counselor, 325-674-2656, Fax: 325-674-6717, E-mail: gradinfo@acu.edu. *Department Chair,* Bill Fowler, 325-674-2080, Fax: 325-674-2564, E-mail: bill.fowler@coba.acu.edu.

College of Education and Human Services Students: 101 full-time (84 women), 150 part-time (91 women); includes 31 minority (19 African Americans, 12 Hispanic Americans), 6 international. 217 applicants, 81% accepted, 119 enrolled. *Faculty:* 20 part-time/adjunct (12 women). Expenses: Contact institution. *Financial support:* In 2008–09, 216 students received support. Application deadline: 4/1. In 2008, 26 master's awarded. Offers communication sciences and disorders (MS); curriculum and instruction (M Ed); education and human services (M Ed, MS, MSSW); higher education (M Ed); leadership of learning (M Ed); social work (MSSW); special education (M Ed). *Application deadline:* For fall admission, 4/1 priority date for domestic students; for spring admission, 11/1 for domestic students. Applications are processed on a rolling basis. *Application fee:* $40 ($45 for international students). Electronic applications accepted. *Application Contact:* William Horn, Graduate Admissions Counselor, 325-674-2656, Fax: 325-674-6717, E-mail: gradinfo@acu.edu. *Dean,* Dr. Malesa Breeding, 325-674-2700.

School of Nursing Students: 9 part-time (8 women); includes 3 minority (all Hispanic Americans). 5 applicants, 40% accepted, 0 enrolled. Expenses: Contact institution. *Financial support:* In 2008–09, 6 students received support. Application deadline: 4/1. In 2008, 4 master's, 1 other advanced degree awarded. *Degree program information:* Part-time programs available. Offers education and administration (MSN); family nurse practitioner (MSN). *Application deadline:* For fall admission, 4/1 priority date for domestic students; for spring admission, 11/1 for domestic students. Applications are processed on a rolling basis. *Application fee:* $40 ($45 for international students). Electronic applications accepted. *Application Contact:* William Horn, Graduate Admissions Counselor, 325-674-2656, Fax: 325-674-6717, E-mail: gradinfo@acu.edu. *Dean,* Dr. Amy Toone, 325-671-2399, Fax: 325-671-2386, E-mail: atoone@phssn.edu.

ACADEMY FOR FIVE ELEMENT ACUPUNCTURE, Hallandale, FL 33009

General Information Independent, coed, graduate-only institution.

GRADUATE UNITS

Graduate Program

ACADEMY OF ART UNIVERSITY, San Francisco, CA 94105-3410

General Information Proprietary, coed, comprehensive institution. *Enrollment:* 13,335 graduate, professional, and undergraduate students; 1,236 full-time matriculated graduate/professional students (760 women), 2,209 part-time matriculated graduate/professional students (1,242 women). *Enrollment by degree level:* 3,445 master's. *Graduate faculty:* 112 full-time (44 women), 334 part-time/adjunct (124 women). *Tuition:* Full-time $18,400; part-time $770 per unit. Tuition and fees vary according to program. *Graduate housing:* Room and/or apartments guaranteed to single students; on-campus housing not available to married students. Typical cost: $13,400 (including board). Housing application deadline: 9/7. *Student services:* Campus employment opportunities, campus safety program, career counseling, international student services, low-cost health insurance, services for students with disabilities, teacher training, writing training. *Library facilities:* Academy of Art University Library. *Online resources:* library catalog, web page, access to other libraries' catalogs. *Collection:* 36,000 titles, 476 serial subscriptions, 3,500 audiovisual materials.

Computer facilities: 800 computers available on campus for general student use. A campuswide network can be accessed from off campus. Online class registration is available. *Web address:* http://www.academyart.edu/.

General Application Contact: Cindy Cai, Director of Graduate Domestic Admissions, 800-544-ARTS, Fax: 415-263-4130, E-mail: info@academyart.edu.

GRADUATE UNITS

Graduate Program Students: 1,236 full-time (760 women), 2,209 part-time (1,242 women); includes 615 minority (188 African Americans, 15 American Indian/Alaska Native, 253 Asian Americans or Pacific Islanders, 159 Hispanic Americans), 1,278 international. Average age 30. 1,121 applicants. *Faculty:* 112 full-time (44 women), 334 part-time/adjunct (124 women). Expenses: Contact institution. *Financial support:* Career-related internships or fieldwork and Federal Work-Study available. Support available to part-time students. Financial award application deadline: 8/10; financial award applicants required to submit FAFSA. In 2008, 312 master's awarded. *Degree program information:* Part-time and evening/weekend programs available. Postbaccalaureate distance learning degree programs offered (no on-campus study). *Application deadline:* For fall admission, 9/7 for domestic and international students; for spring admission, 2/2 for domestic and international students. Applications are processed on a rolling basis. *Application fee:* $100 ($500 for international students). Electronic applications accepted. *Application Contact:* 800-544-ARTS, Fax: 415-263-4130, E-mail: info@academyart.edu. *Executive Vice President,* Melissa Marshall, 800-544-ARTS, E-mail: info@academyart.edu.

School of Advertising Students: 161 full-time (88 women), 58 part-time (39 women); includes 16 African Americans, 15 Asian Americans or Pacific Islanders, 11 Hispanic Americans, 83 international. Average age 28. 73 applicants. *Faculty:* 4 full-time (2 women), 22 part-time/adjunct (3 women). Expenses: Contact institution. *Financial support:* Fellowships, career-related internships or fieldwork and Federal Work-Study available. Support available to part-time students. Financial award application deadline: 8/10; financial award applicants required to submit FAFSA. In 2008, 29 master's awarded. *Degree program information:* Part-time programs available. Postbaccalaureate distance learning degree programs offered (no on-campus study). Offers advertising (MFA). *Application deadline:* For fall admission, 9/7 for domestic and international students; for spring admission, 2/2 for domestic and international students. Applications are processed on a rolling basis. *Application fee:* $100 ($500 for international students). Electronic applications accepted. *Application Contact:* 800-544-ARTS, Fax: 415-263-4130, E-mail: info@academyart.edu. *Director,* Melinda Mettler, 800-544-ARTS, E-mail: mmettler@academyart.edu.

School of Animation and Visual Effects Students: 497 full-time (172 women), 200 part-time (73 women); includes 123 minority (31 African Americans, 3 American Indian/Alaska Native, 52 Asian Americans or Pacific Islanders, 37 Hispanic Americans), 362 international. Average age 28. 182 applicants. *Faculty:* 18 full-time (3 women), 45 part-time/adjunct (12 women). Expenses: Contact institution. *Financial support:* Career-related internships or fieldwork and Federal Work-Study available. Support available to part-time students. Financial award application deadline: 8/10; financial award applicants required to submit FAFSA. In 2008, 75 master's awarded. *Degree program information:* Part-time programs available. Postbaccalaureate distance learning degree programs offered (no on-campus study). Offers 2D animation (MFA); 3D animation (MFA); 3D modeling (MFA); games (MFA); visual effects (MFA). *Application deadline:* For fall admission, 9/7 for domestic and international students; for spring admission, 2/2 for domestic and international students. Applications are processed on a rolling basis. *Application fee:* $100 ($500 for international students). Electronic applications accepted. *Application Contact:* Information Contact, 800-544-ARTS, Fax: 415-263-4130, E-mail: info@academyart.edu. *Director of Animation 3D,* Tom Bertine, 800-544-ARTS, Fax: 415-263-4130, E-mail: info@academyart.edu.

School of Architecture Students: 64 full-time (35 women), 10 part-time (5 women); includes 2 African Americans, 5 Asian Americans or Pacific Islanders, 2 Hispanic Americans, 40 international. Average age 29. 51 applicants. *Faculty:* 2 full-time (1 woman), 14 part-time/adjunct (5 women). Expenses: Contact institution. *Financial support:* Career-related internships or fieldwork and Federal Work-Study available. Support available to part-time students. Financial award application deadline: 8/10; financial award applicants required to submit FAFSA. In 2008, 8 master's awarded. *Degree program information:* Part-time programs available. Offers architecture (M Arch). *Application deadline:* For fall admission, 9/7 for domestic and international students; for spring admission, 2/2 for domestic and international students. Applications are processed on a rolling basis. *Application fee:* $100 ($500 for international students). Electronic applications accepted. *Application Contact:* Prospective Students Services, 800-544-ARTS, Fax: 415-263-4131, E-mail: info@academyart.edu. *Director,* Alberto Bertoli, 800-544-ARTS, E-mail: info@academyart.edu.

School of Fashion Students: 353 full-time (313 women), 130 part-time (119 women); includes 95 minority (36 African Americans, 2 American Indian/Alaska Native, 39 Asian Americans or Pacific Islanders, 18 Hispanic Americans), 225 international. Average age 28. 179 applicants. *Faculty:* 16 full-time (12 women), 32 part-time/adjunct (22 women). Expenses: Contact institution. *Financial support:* Career-related internships or fieldwork and Federal Work-Study available. Support available to part-time students. Financial award application deadline: 8/10; financial award applicants required to submit FAFSA. In 2008, 48 master's awarded. *Degree program information:* Part-time programs available. Postbaccalaureate distance learning degree programs offered (no on-campus study). Offers fashion design (MFA); fashion merchandising (MFA); fashion textiles (MFA); knitwear (MFA). *Application deadline:* For fall admission, 9/7 for domestic and international students; for spring admission, 2/2 for domestic and international students. Applications are processed on a rolling basis. *Application fee:* $100 ($500 for international students). Electronic applications accepted. *Application Contact:* Prospective Student Services, 800-544-ARTS, Fax: 415-263-4130, E-mail: info@academyart.edu. *Director,* Simon Ungless, 800-544-ARTS, Fax: 415-296-2089, E-mail: info@academyart.edu.

School of Fine Art Students: 135 full-time (86 women), 167 part-time (123 women); includes 52 minority (13 African Americans, 1 American Indian/Alaska Native, 23 Asian Americans or Pacific Islanders, 15 Hispanic Americans), 43 international. Average age 38. 88 applicants. *Faculty:* 14 full-time (9 women), 32 part-time/adjunct (12 women). Expenses: Contact institution. *Financial support:* Career-related internships or fieldwork and Federal Work-Study available. Support available to part-time students. Financial award application deadline: 8/10; financial award applicants required to submit FAFSA. In 2008, 36 master's awarded.

Degree program information: Part-time programs available. Postbaccalaureate distance learning degree programs offered (no on-campus study). Offers figurative painting (MFA); non-figurative painting (MFA); printmaking (MFA); sculpture (MFA). *Application deadline:* For fall admission, 9/7 for domestic and international students; for spring admission, 2/2 for domestic and international students. Applications are processed on a rolling basis. *Application fee:* $100 ($500 for international students). Electronic applications accepted. *Application Contact:* Prospective Student Services, 800-544-ARTS, Fax: 415-263-4130, E-mail: info@academyart.edu. *Director*, William Maughan, 800-544-ARTS, Fax: 415-263-4124, E-mail: info@academyart.edu.

School of Graphic Design Students: 168 full-time (115 women), 134 part-time (94 women); includes 51 minority (15 African Americans, 1 American Indian/Alaska Native, 23 Asian Americans or Pacific Islanders, 12 Hispanic Americans), 107 international. Average age 29. 109 applicants. *Faculty:* 6 full-time (1 woman), 22 part-time/adjunct (10 women). Expenses: Contact institution. *Financial support:* Career-related internships or fieldwork and Federal Work-Study available. Support available to part-time students. Financial award application deadline: 8/10; financial award applicants required to submit FAFSA. In 2008, 18 master's awarded. *Degree program information:* Part-time programs available. Postbaccalaureate distance learning degree programs offered (no on-campus study). Offers graphic design (MFA). *Application deadline:* For fall admission, 9/7 for domestic and international students; for spring admission, 2/2 for domestic and international students. Applications are processed on a rolling basis. *Application fee:* $100 ($500 for international students). Electronic applications accepted. *Application Contact:* Prospective Student Services, 800-544-ARTS, Fax: 415-263-4130, E-mail: info@academyart.edu. *Director*, Phil Hamlett, 800-544-ARTS, Fax: 415-263-4124.

School of Illustration Students: 117 full-time (63 women), 84 part-time (49 women); includes 29 minority (8 African Americans, 1 American Indian/Alaska Native, 12 Asian Americans or Pacific Islanders, 8 Hispanic Americans), 44 international. Average age 31. 61 applicants. *Faculty:* 8 full-time (1 woman), 16 part-time/adjunct (5 women). Expenses: Contact institution. *Financial support:* Career-related internships or fieldwork and Federal Work-Study available. Support available to part-time students. Financial award application deadline: 8/10; financial award applicants required to submit FAFSA. In 2008, 11 master's awarded. *Degree program information:* Part-time programs available. Postbaccalaureate distance learning degree programs offered (no on-campus study). Offers illustration (MFA). *Application deadline:* For fall admission, 9/7 for domestic and international students; for spring admission, 2/2 for domestic and international students. Applications are processed on a rolling basis. *Application fee:* $100 ($500 for international students). Electronic applications accepted. *Application Contact:* Prospective Student Services, 800-544-ARTS, Fax: 415-263-4130, E-mail: info@academyart.edu. *Director*, William Maughan, 800-544-ARTS, Fax: 415-263-4124, E-mail: info@academyart.edu.

School of Industrial Design Students: 103 full-time (36 women), 15 part-time (5 women); includes 2 African Americans, 10 Asian Americans or Pacific Islanders, 1 Hispanic American, 84 international. Average age 28. 62 applicants. *Faculty:* 4 full-time (0 women), 12 part-time/adjunct (1 woman). Expenses: Contact institution. *Financial support:* Career-related internships or fieldwork and Federal Work-Study available. Support available to part-time students. Financial award application deadline: 8/10; financial award applicants required to submit FAFSA. In 2008, 7 master's awarded. *Degree program information:* Part-time programs available. Postbaccalaureate distance learning degree programs offered (no on-campus study). Offers industrial design (MFA). *Application deadline:* For fall admission, 9/7 for domestic and international students; for spring admission, 2/2 for domestic and international students. Applications are processed on a rolling basis. *Application fee:* $100 ($500 for international students). Electronic applications accepted. *Application Contact:* 800-544-ARTS, Fax: 415-263-4130, E-mail: info@academyart.edu. *Director*, Mark Bolick, 800-544-ARTS, Fax: 415-263-4130, E-mail: info@academyart.edu.

School of Interior Architecture and Design Students: 100 full-time (77 women), 76 part-time (62 women); includes 23 minority (9 African Americans, 8 Asian Americans or Pacific Islanders, 6 Hispanic Americans), 63 international. Average age 31. 75 applicants. *Faculty:* 4 full-time (3 women), 24 part-time/adjunct (7 women). Expenses: Contact institution. *Financial support:* Career-related internships or fieldwork and Federal Work-Study available. Support available to part-time students. Financial award application deadline: 8/10; financial award applicants required to submit FAFSA. In 2008, 13 master's awarded. *Degree program information:* Part-time programs available. Postbaccalaureate distance learning degree programs offered (no on-campus study). Offers interior architecture and design (MFA). *Application deadline:* For fall admission, 9/7 for domestic and international students; for spring admission, 2/2 for domestic and international students. Applications are processed on a rolling basis. *Application fee:* $100 ($500 for international students). Electronic applications accepted. *Application Contact:* 800-544-ARTS, Fax: 415-263-4130, E-mail: info@academyart.edu. *Director*, Marlene Farrell, 800-544-ARTS, Fax: 415-263-4130, E-mail: info@academyart.edu.

School of Motion Pictures and Television Students: 185 full-time (71 women), 79 part-time (34 women); includes 62 minority (24 African Americans, 5 American Indian/Alaska Native, 15 Asian Americans or Pacific Islanders, 18 Hispanic Americans), 75 international. Average age 30. 73 applicants. *Faculty:* 6 full-time (2 women), 36 part-time/adjunct (12 women). Expenses: Contact institution. *Financial support:* Career-related internships or fieldwork and Federal Work-Study available. Support available to part-time students. Financial award application deadline: 8/10; financial award applicants required to submit FAFSA. In 2008, 12 master's awarded. *Degree program information:* Part-time programs available. Postbaccalaureate distance learning degree programs offered (no on-campus study). Offers motion pictures and television (MFA). *Application deadline:* For fall admission, 9/7 for domestic and international students; for spring admission, 2/2 for domestic and international students. Applications are processed on a rolling basis. *Application fee:* $100 ($500 for international students). Electronic applications accepted. *Application Contact:* 800-544-ARTS, Fax: 415-263-4130, E-mail: info@academyart.edu. *Director*, Diane Baker, 800-544-ARTS, E-mail: info@academyart.edu.

School of Multimedia Communications Students: 1 (woman) full-time, 6 part-time (4 women); includes 2 minority (1 Asian American or Pacific Islander, 1 Hispanic American). Average age 30. 7 applicants. *Faculty:* 2 full-time (1 woman). Expenses: Contact institution. *Financial support:* Career-related internships or fieldwork and Federal Work-Study available. Support available to part-time students. Financial award applicants required to submit FAFSA. *Degree program information:* Part-time and evening/weekend programs available. Offers multimedia communications (MA). *Application deadline:* For fall admission, 9/7 for domestic and international students; for spring admission, 2/2 for domestic and international students. Applications are processed on a rolling basis. *Application fee:* $100 ($500 for international students). Electronic applications accepted. *Application Contact:* Jan Yanehiro, 800-544-ARTS, E-mail: info@academyart.edu. Jan Yanehiro, 800-544-ARTS, E-mail: info@academyart.edu.

School of Photography Students: 143 full-time (80 women), 147 part-time (76 women); includes 47 minority (13 African Americans, 2 American Indian/Alaska Native, 19 Asian Americans or Pacific Islanders, 13 Hispanic Americans), 39 international. Average age 34. 72 applicants. *Faculty:* 9 full-time (4 women), 30 part-time/adjunct (7 women). Expenses: Contact institution. *Financial support:* Career-related internships or fieldwork and Federal Work-Study available. Support available to part-time students. Financial award application deadline: 8/10; financial award applicants required to submit FAFSA. In 2008, 25 master's awarded. *Degree program information:* Part-time programs available. Postbaccalaureate distance learning degree programs offered (no on-campus study). Offers photography (MFA). *Application deadline:* For fall admission, 9/7 for domestic and international students; for spring admission, 2/2 for domestic and international students. Applications are processed on a rolling basis. *Application fee:* $100 ($500 for international students). Electronic applications accepted. *Application Contact:* 800-544-ARTS, Fax: 415-263-4130, E-mail: info@academyart.edu. *Director*, William Musgrove, 800-544-ARTS, E-mail: info@academyart.edu.

School of Web Design and New Media Students: 181 full-time (104 women), 129 part-time (76 women); includes 66 minority (18 African Americans, 31 Asian Americans or Pacific Islanders, 17 Hispanic Americans), 112 international. Average age 31. 81 applicants. *Faculty:* 3 full-time (2 women), 11 part-time/adjunct (4 women). Expenses: Contact institution. *Financial support:* Career-related internships or fieldwork and Federal Work-Study available. Support available to part-time students. Financial award application deadline: 8/10; financial award applicants required to submit FAFSA. In 2008, 30 master's awarded. *Degree program information:* Part-time and evening/weekend programs available. Offers Web design and new media (MFA). *Application deadline:* For fall admission, 9/7 for domestic and international students; for spring admission, 2/2 for domestic students, 9/2 for international students. Applications are processed on a rolling basis. *Application fee:* $100 for international students). Electronic applications accepted. *Application Contact:* 800-544-ARTS, Fax: 415-263-4130, E-mail: info@academyart.edu. *Director*, Lourdes Livingston, 800-544-ARTS, E-mail: info@academyart.edu.

ACADEMY OF CHINESE CULTURE AND HEALTH SCIENCES, Oakland, CA 94612

General Information Private, coed, graduate-only institution. *Graduate housing:* On-campus housing not available.

GRADUATE UNITS

Program in Traditional Chinese Medicine *Degree program information:* Part-time and evening/weekend programs available. Offers traditional Chinese medicine (MS).

ACADEMY OF ORIENTAL MEDICINE AT AUSTIN, Austin, TX 78757

General Information Proprietary, coed, graduate-only institution.

GRADUATE UNITS

Program in Acupuncture and Oriental Medicine Offers acupuncture and oriental medicine (MAOM). Electronic applications accepted.

ACADIA UNIVERSITY, Wolfville, NS B4P 2R6, Canada

General Information Province-supported, coed, comprehensive institution. *Enrollment:* 3,376 graduate, professional, and undergraduate students; 130 full-time matriculated graduate/professional students (70 women), 373 part-time matriculated graduate/professional students (268 women). *Enrollment by degree level:* 503 master's. *Graduate faculty:* 155 full-time (51 women), 29 part-time/adjunct (8 women). *Graduate tuition:* Tuition and fees charges are reported in Canadian dollars. *Tuition, area resident:* Full-time $3873.50 Canadian dollars; part-time $844 Canadian dollars per course. Tuition, province resident: full-time $4634.50 Canadian dollars; part-time $844 Canadian dollars per course. Tuition, Canadian resident: full-time $9103 Canadian dollars; part-time $1687 Canadian dollars per course. *Required fees:* $503.22 Canadian dollars; $5 Canadian dollars per course. *Graduate housing:* Room and/or apartments available on a first-come, first-served basis to single students; on-campus housing not available to married students. Typical cost: $4176 Canadian dollars per year ($7561 Canadian dollars including board). Housing application deadline: 5/31. *Student services:* Campus employment opportunities, campus safety program, career counseling, exercise/wellness program, free psychological counseling, international student services, low-cost health insurance, services for students with disabilities, writing training. *Library facilities:* Vaughan Memorial Library. *Online resources:* library catalog, web page, access to other libraries' catalogs. *Collection:* 1.3 million titles, 26,644 serial subscriptions, 11,204 audiovisual materials. *Research affiliation:* Atlantic Research Laboratory.

Computer facilities: Computer purchase and lease plans are available. 10 computers available on campus for general student use. A campuswide network can be accessed from student residence rooms and from off campus. Online class registration is available. *Web address:* http://www.acadiau.ca/.

General Application Contact: Theresa Starratt, Graduate Studies Officer, 902-585-1914, Fax: 902-585-1096, E-mail: gradadmissions@acadiau.ca.

GRADUATE UNITS

Divinity College Students: 33 full-time (11 women), 28 part-time (4 women). Average age 43. *Faculty:* 12 full-time (2 women), 12 part-time/adjunct (1 woman). Expenses: Contact institution. *Financial support:* In 2008–09, 8 teaching assistantships (averaging $1,000 per year) were awarded; career-related internships or fieldwork, institutionally sponsored loans, and scholarships/grants also available. Support available to part-time students. Financial award application deadline: 8/12. In 2008, 32 master's, 6 doctorates awarded. *Degree program information:* Part-time programs available. Offers divinity (M Div); theology (MA, D Min). *Application deadline:* For fall admission, 6/30 priority date for domestic students, 4/1 priority date for international students; for spring admission, 4/30 priority date for domestic students. Applications are processed on a rolling basis. *Application fee:* $25. *Application Contact:* Shawna Peverill, Manager of Student Services, 902-585-2215, Fax: 902-585-2233, E-mail: shawna.peverill@acadiau.ca. *President*, Dr. Harry M. Gardner, 902-585-2212, Fax: 902-585-2233, E-mail: harry.gardner@acadiau.ca.

Faculty of Arts Students: 10 full-time (5 women), 7 part-time (5 women). Average age 25. 38 applicants, 50% accepted, 10 enrolled. *Faculty:* 28 full-time (11 women), 1 part-time/adjunct (0 women). Expenses: Contact institution. *Financial support:* Research assistantships, teaching assistantships, scholarships/grants and unspecified assistantships available. Financial award application deadline: 2/1. In 2008, 7 master's awarded. Offers arts (MA); English (MA); political science (MA); sociology (MA). *Application deadline:* For fall admission, 2/1 for domestic and international students. Applications are processed on a rolling basis. *Application fee:* $50. *Application Contact:* Dr. Robert J. Perrins, Dean, 902-585-1485, Fax: 902-585-1070, E-mail: robert.perrins@acadiau.ca. *Dean*, Dr. Robert J. Perrins, 902-585-1485, Fax: 902-585-1070, E-mail: robert.perrins@acadiau.ca.

Faculty of Professional Studies Students: 34 full-time (26 women), 314 part-time (247 women). 191 applicants, 66% accepted, 76 enrolled. *Faculty:* 20 full-time (10 women). Expenses: Contact institution. *Financial support:* Research assistantships, teaching assistantships available. Financial award application deadline: 2/1. In 2008, 103 master's awarded. *Degree program information:* Part-time and evening/weekend programs available. *Application deadline:* Applications are processed on a rolling basis. *Application fee:* $50. *Application Contact:* Rosie Hare, Administrative Assistant, 902-585-1597, Fax: 902-585-1086, E-mail: rosie.hare@acadiau.ca. *Dean*, Dr. Heather Hemming, 902-585-1597, Fax: 902-585-1086, E-mail: heather.hemming@acadiau.ca.

School of Education Students: 33 full-time (25 women), 313 part-time (247 women). 185 applicants, 68% accepted, 75 enrolled. *Faculty:* 20 full-time (10 women). Expenses: Contact institution. *Financial support:* In 2008–09, 7 teaching assistantships (averaging $4,500 per year) were awarded; research assistantships, unspecified assistantships also available. Financial award application deadline: 2/1. In 2008, 103 master's awarded. *Degree program information:* Part-time and evening/weekend programs available. Offers counseling (M Ed); cultural and media studies (M Ed); curriculum studies (M Ed); inclusive education (M Ed); leadership (M Ed); learning and technology (M Ed); science, math and technology (M Ed). *Application fee:* $50. Electronic applications accepted. *Application Contact:* Sheila Langille, Secretary, 902-585-1229, Fax: 902-585-1071, E-mail: sheila.langille@acadiau.ca. *Director*, Ann Vibert.

School of Recreation Management and Kinesiology Students: 1 (woman) full-time, 1 part-time (0 women). 6 applicants, 17% accepted, 1 enrolled. Expenses: Contact institution. *Financial support:* In 2008–09, 1 teaching assistantship (averaging $9,000 per year) was awarded; unspecified assistantships also available. Offers recreation management and kinesiology (MR). *Application deadline:* For fall admission, 2/1 for domestic students. Applications are processed on a rolling basis. *Application fee:* $50. *Application Contact:* Krista Robertson, Secretary, 902-585-1457, Fax: 902-585-1702, E-mail: krista.robertson@acadiau.ca. *Director*, Dr. Gary Ness, 902-585-1566, Fax: 902-585-1702, E-mail: gary.ness@acadiau.ca.

Faculty of Pure and Applied Science Students: 53 full-time (28 women), 24 part-time (12 women). 122 applicants, 46% accepted, 32 enrolled. *Faculty:* 95 full-time (28 women), 16 part-time/adjunct (7 women). Expenses: Contact institution. *Financial support:* Fellowships, research assistantships, teaching assistantships, career-related internships or fieldwork, scholarships/grants, and unspecified assistantships available. Financial award application

Acadia University (continued)

deadline: 2/1. In 2008, 28 master's awarded. Offers applied geomatics (M Sc); applied mathematics and statistics (M Sc); biology (M Sc); chemistry (M Sc); clinical psychology (M Sc); earth and environmental science (M Sc); pure and applied science (M Sc). *Application deadline:* For fall admission, 2/1 for domestic students. *Application fee:* $50. *Application Contact:* Dr. Robert P. Raeside, Dean, 902-585-1472, Fax: 902-585-1637, E-mail: robraeside@acadiau.ca. *Dean,* Dr. Robert P. Raeside, 902-585-1472, Fax: 902-585-1637, E-mail: robraeside@acadiau.ca.

Jodrey School of Computer Science Students: 10 full-time (0 women), 6 part-time (2 women), all international. Average age 28. 29 applicants, 62% accepted, 8 enrolled. *Faculty:* 10 full-time (0 women), 1 part-time/adjunct (0 women). Expenses: Contact institution. *Financial support:* In 2008–09, 7 teaching assistantships were awarded; career-related internships or fieldwork, scholarships/grants, and unspecified assistantships also available. Financial award application deadline: 2/1. In 2008, 6 master's awarded. Offers computer science (M Sc). *Application deadline:* For fall admission, 2/1 for domestic students. Applications are processed on a rolling basis. *Application fee:* $50. *Application Contact:* Dr. Tomasz Muldner, Graduate Chair, 902-585-1578, E-mail: tomasz.muldner@acadiau.ca. *Director,* Dr. Daniel L. Silver, 902-585-1331, Fax: 902-585-1067, E-mail: cs@acadiau.ca.

ACUPUNCTURE & INTEGRATIVE MEDICINE COLLEGE, BERKELEY, Berkeley, CA 94704

General Information Independent, coed, graduate-only institution. *Graduate housing:* On-campus housing not available.

GRADUATE UNITS

Program in Oriental Medicine *Degree program information:* Part-time and evening/weekend programs available. Offers Oriental medicine (MS).

ACUPUNCTURE AND MASSAGE COLLEGE, Miami, FL 33176

General Information Proprietary, coed, graduate-only institution.

GRADUATE UNITS

Program in Oriental Medicine Offers Oriental medicine (MOM).

ADAMS STATE COLLEGE, Alamosa, CO 81102

General Information State-supported, coed, comprehensive institution. *Graduate housing:* Rooms and/or apartments available to single and married students. Housing application deadline: 5/15. *Research affiliation:* Sandia National Laboratories (science education).

GRADUATE UNITS

The Graduate School *Degree program information:* Part-time programs available. Post-baccalaureate distance learning degree programs offered. Offers art (MA); counseling (MA); education (MA); history (MA); human performance and physical education (MA); special education (MA).

ADELPHI UNIVERSITY, Garden City, NY 11530-0701

General Information Independent, coed, university. *Enrollment:* 8,177 graduate, professional, and undergraduate students; 947 full-time matriculated graduate/professional students (780 women), 2,050 part-time matriculated graduate/professional students (1,638 women). *Enrollment by degree level:* 2,780 master's, 217 doctoral. *Graduate faculty:* 295 full-time (155 women), 639 part-time/adjunct (450 women). *Tuition:* Full-time $25,700; part-time $775 per credit hour. *Required fees:* $500. Tuition and fees vary according to course load, degree level, campus/location, program and student level. *Graduate housing:* Room and/or apartments available on a first-come, first-served basis to single students; on-campus housing not available to married students. Typical cost: $10,000 (including board). Room and board charges vary according to board plan. *Student services:* Campus employment opportunities, campus safety program, career counseling, child daycare facilities, exercise/wellness program, free psychological counseling, international student services, low-cost health insurance, multicultural affairs office, services for students with disabilities, teacher training, writing training. *Library facilities:* Swirbul Library plus 1 other. *Online resources:* library catalog, web page, access to other libraries' catalogs. *Collection:* 588,987 titles, 32,138 serial subscriptions, 24,850 audiovisual materials. *Research affiliation:* Teagle Foundation, World Anti-doping Agency, The National Science Foundation, The Research Corporation, The Horace Hagedorn Foundation, Albert Einstein College of Medicine.

Computer facilities: 772 computers available on campus for general student use. A campuswide network can be accessed from student residence rooms and from off campus. Online class registration, payment, drop/add classes, check application status are available. *Web address:* http://www.adelphi.edu/.

General Application Contact: Christine Murphy, Director of Admissions, 516-877-3050, Fax: 516-877-3039, E-mail: graduateadmissions@adelphi.edu.

GRADUATE UNITS

Derner Institute of Advanced Psychological Studies Students: 187 full-time (151 women), 128 part-time (101 women); includes 43 minority (21 African Americans, 10 Asian Americans or Pacific Islanders, 12 Hispanic Americans), 17 international. Average age 29. 590 applicants, 44% accepted, 95 enrolled. *Faculty:* 23 full-time (11 women), 78 part-time/adjunct (51 women). Expenses: Contact institution. *Financial support:* In 2008–09, 77 research assistantships with full and partial tuition reimbursements (averaging $5,527 per year) were awarded; teaching assistantships, career-related internships or fieldwork, Federal Work-Study, institutionally sponsored loans, and unspecified assistantships also available. Financial award application deadline: 2/15; financial award applicants required to submit FAFSA. In 2008, 81 master's, 21 doctorates awarded. *Degree program information:* Part-time programs available. Offers clinical psychology (PhD); general psychology (MA); mental health counseling (MA); school psychology (MA). *Application deadline:* For fall admission, 4/1 priority date for domestic students, 5/1 priority date for international students; for spring admission, 11/1 priority date for international students. *Application fee:* $50. Electronic applications accepted. *Application Contact:* Christine Murphy, Director of Admissions, 516-877-3050, Fax: 516-877-3039, E-mail: graduateadmissions@adelphi.edu. *Dean,* Dr. Jeau Lau Chin, 516-877-4800, E-mail: Chin@adelphi.edu.

Graduate School of Arts and Sciences Students: 19 full-time (11 women), 64 part-time (51 women); includes 14 minority (1 African American, 6 Asian Americans or Pacific Islanders, 7 Hispanic Americans), 9 international. Average age 30. 140 applicants, 53% accepted, 26 enrolled. *Faculty:* 109 full-time (42 women), 149 part-time/adjunct (78 women). Expenses: Contact institution. *Financial support:* In 2008–09, 29 research assistantships with full and partial tuition reimbursements (averaging $8,760 per year) were awarded; fellowships, teaching assistantships, career-related internships or fieldwork, Federal Work-Study, institutionally sponsored loans, tuition waivers (full and partial), and unspecified assistantships also available. Support available to part-time students. Financial award application deadline: 2/15; financial award applicants required to submit FAFSA. In 2008, 32 master's awarded. *Degree program information:* Part-time programs available. Offers art and art history (MA); arts and sciences (MA, MFA, MS); biology (MS); creative writing (MFA); environmental studies (MS); physics (MS). *Application deadline:* For fall admission, 5/1 priority date for international students; for spring admission, 11/1 priority date for international students. Applications are processed on a rolling basis. *Application fee:* $50. Electronic applications accepted. *Application Contact:* Christine Murphy, Director of Admissions, 516-877-3050, Fax: 516-877-3039, E-mail: graduateadmissions@adelphi.edu. *Dean,* Dr. Steven Rubin, 516-877-4124, Fax: 516-877-4191, E-mail: sjr@adelphi.edu.

School of Business Students: 90 full-time (45 women), 177 part-time (89 women); includes 65 minority (38 African Americans, 1 American Indian/Alaska Native, 13 Asian Americans or Pacific Islanders, 13 Hispanic Americans), 63 international. Average age 31. 308 applicants, 42% accepted, 97 enrolled. *Faculty:* 36 full-time (8 women), 38 part-time/adjunct (15 women). Expenses: Contact institution. *Financial support:* In 2008–09, 33 teaching assistantships with partial tuition reimbursements (averaging $5,929 per year) were awarded; research assistantships, career-related internships or fieldwork, Federal Work-Study, institutionally sponsored loans, scholarships/grants, and unspecified assistantships also available. Financial award application deadline: 3/1; financial award applicants required to submit FAFSA. In 2008, 108 master's, 2 other advanced degrees awarded. *Degree program information:* Part-time and evening/weekend programs available. Offers accounting (MBA); business (MBA, Certificate); finance (MBA); human resources management (Certificate); management information systems (MBA); management/human resource management (MBA); marketing/e-commerce (MBA). *Application deadline:* For fall admission, 4/1 for international students; for spring admission, 11/1 for international students. Applications are processed on a rolling basis. *Application fee:* $50. Electronic applications accepted. *Application Contact:* Christine Murphy, Director of Admissions, 516-877-3050, Fax: 516-877-3039, E-mail: graduateadmissions@adelphi.edu. *Associate Dean,* Dr. Rakesh Gupta, 516-877-4629.

School of Education Students: 426 full-time (380 women), 828 part-time (636 women); includes 216 minority (87 African Americans, 33 Asian Americans or Pacific Islanders, 96 Hispanic Americans), 13 international. Average age 30. 1,177 applicants, 52% accepted, 401 enrolled. *Faculty:* 67 full-time (45 women), 150 part-time/adjunct (119 women). Expenses: Contact institution. *Financial support:* In 2008–09, 116 teaching assistantships (averaging $4,898 per year) were awarded; career-related internships or fieldwork, Federal Work-Study, institutionally sponsored loans, tuition waivers (full), and unspecified assistantships also available. Support available to part-time students. Financial award application deadline: 2/15; financial award applicants required to submit FAFSA. In 2008, 566 master's, 1 doctorate, 18 other advanced degrees awarded. *Degree program information:* Part-time and evening/weekend programs available. Offers adolescent education (MA); aging (Certificate); art education (MA); audiology (MS, DA); birth through grade 2 (Certificate); birth-grade 12 (MS); birth-grade 6 (MS); childhood special education (Certificate); childhood special education studies (MS); community health education (MA, Certificate); early childhood education (Certificate); education (MA, MS, DA, Certificate); educational leadership and technology (MA, Certificate); elementary teachers pre K-6 (MA); grades 1-6 (MA, MS); grades 5-12 (MS); in-service (MA, MS); inclusive setting, grades 1-6 preservice or in-service track (MS); physical/educational human performance science (MA); pre-certification (MA); preservice (MS); school health education (MA); special education (MS, Certificate); speech-language pathology (MS, DA); teaching English to speakers of other languages (MA, Certificate). *Application deadline:* For fall admission, 4/1 for international students; for spring admission, 11/1 for international students. Applications are processed on a rolling basis. *Application fee:* $50. Electronic applications accepted. *Application Contact:* Christine Murphy, Director of Admissions, 516-877-3050, Fax: 516-877-3039, E-mail: graduateadmissions@adelphi.edu. *Dean,* Dr. Ronald Feingold, 516-877-4100, E-mail: feingold@adelphi.edu.

School of Nursing Students: 1 (woman) full-time, 161 part-time (152 women); includes 74 minority (50 African Americans, 16 Asian Americans or Pacific Islanders, 8 Hispanic Americans). Average age 44. 48 applicants, 44% accepted, 14 enrolled. *Faculty:* 34 full-time (30 women), 120 part-time/adjunct (116 women). Expenses: Contact institution. *Financial support:* In 2008–09, 15 teaching assistantships (averaging $4,512 per year) were awarded; career-related internships or fieldwork, unspecified assistantships, and graduate achievement awards also available. Support available to part-time students. Financial award application deadline: 2/15; financial award applicants required to submit FAFSA. In 2008, 36 master's, 2 other advanced degrees awarded. *Degree program information:* Part-time and evening/weekend programs available. Offers nursing (MS, PhD, Certificate). *Application deadline:* For fall admission, 3/15 for domestic students, 4/1 for international students; for spring admission, 11/1 for international students. *Application fee:* $50. Electronic applications accepted. *Application Contact:* Christine Murphy, Director of Admissions, 516-877-3050, Fax: 516-877-3039, E-mail: graduateadmissions@adelphi.edu. *Dean,* Dr. Patrick Coonan, 516-877-4511, E-mail: coonan@adelphi.edu.

School of Social Work Students: 221 full-time (190 women), 679 part-time (605 women); includes 370 minority (258 African Americans, 1 American Indian/Alaska Native, 13 Asian Americans or Pacific Islanders, 98 Hispanic Americans), 3 international. Average age 36. 551 applicants, 77% accepted, 291 enrolled. *Faculty:* 28 full-time (20 women), 79 part-time/adjunct (51 women). Expenses: Contact institution. *Financial support:* In 2008–09, 23 teaching assistantships (averaging $3,888 per year) were awarded; career-related internships or fieldwork, Federal Work-Study, institutionally sponsored loans, scholarships/grants, traineeships, tuition waivers (full and partial), and unspecified assistantships also available. Financial award application deadline: 2/15; financial award applicants required to submit FAFSA. In 2008, 288 master's, 2 doctorates awarded. *Degree program information:* Part-time and evening/weekend programs available. Offers social welfare (DSW); social work (MSW, PhD). *Application deadline:* For fall admission, 4/1 for international students; for spring admission, 12/1 for domestic students, 11/1 for international students. *Application fee:* $50. Electronic applications accepted. *Application Contact:* Christine Murphy, Director of Admissions, 516-877-3050, Fax: 516-877-3039, E-mail: graduateadmissions@adelphi.edu. *Dean,* Dr. Andrew Safyer, 516-877-4300, E-mail: asafyer@adelphi.edu.

University College Offers emergency management (Certificate).

ADLER GRADUATE SCHOOL, Richfield, MN 55423

General Information Independent, coed, graduate-only institution. *Graduate housing:* On-campus housing not available.

GRADUATE UNITS

Program in Adlerian Studies *Degree program information:* Part-time and evening/weekend programs available. Offers art therapy specialization (MA); clinical counseling track (MA); coaching and consulting in organizations (Certificate); management consulting and organizational leadership (MA); marriage and family track (MA); non-clinical Adlerian studies track (MA); personal and professional life coaching (Certificate); school counseling (MA).

ADLER SCHOOL OF PROFESSIONAL PSYCHOLOGY, Chicago, IL 60601-7203

General Information Independent, coed, graduate-only institution. *Enrollment by degree level:* 294 master's, 348 doctoral. *Graduate faculty:* 17 full-time (9 women), 47 part-time/adjunct (20 women). *Tuition:* Part-time $850 per credit. Tuition and fees vary according to degree level, campus/location and program. *Graduate housing:* On-campus housing not available. *Student services:* Campus employment opportunities, campus safety program, career counseling, international student services, low-cost health insurance, services for students with disabilities, writing training. *Library facilities:* Sol and Elaine Mosak Library. *Online resources:* library catalog. *Collection:* 12,000 titles, 170 serial subscriptions, 1,500 audiovisual materials. *Research affiliation:* Adler Institute on Social Exclusion, Adler Institute on Public Safety and Social Justice.

Computer facilities: 40 computers available on campus for general student use. A campuswide network can be accessed from off campus. Online class registration is available. *Web address:* http://www.adler.edu/.

General Application Contact: Craig A. Hines, Director of Admissions, 312-201-5900 Ext. 226, Fax: 312-201-5917, E-mail: admissions@adler.edu.

GRADUATE UNITS

Programs in Psychology Students: 514 full-time (404 women), 128 part-time (100 women); includes 147 minority (69 African Americans, 2 American Indian/Alaska Native, 30 Asian Americans or Pacific Islanders, 46 Hispanic Americans), 53 international. Average age 27. 855 applicants, 46% accepted, 195 enrolled. *Faculty:* 36 full-time (17 women), 45 part-time/adjunct (18 women). Expenses: Contact institution. *Financial support:* Career-related internships or fieldwork, Federal Work-Study, scholarships/grants, and tuition waivers (full and partial) available. Support available to part-time students. Financial award application deadline: 5/15; financial award applicants required to submit FAFSA. In 2008, 110 master's, 136 doctorates awarded. *Degree program information:* Part-time and evening/weekend programs available. Postbaccalaureate distance learning degree programs offered (minimal on-campus study). Offers art therapy (Certificate); clinical hypnosis (Certificate); clinical psychology (Psy D); counseling psychology (MACP); counseling psychology/art therapy (MACAT); gerontology (MAGP); marriage and family counseling (MAMFC); marriage and family therapy (Certificate); organizational psychology (MAO); substance abuse counseling (MASAC,

Certificate). *Application deadline:* For fall admission, 2/15 priority date for domestic students, 12/1 priority date for international students. Applications are processed on a rolling basis. *Application fee:* $50. Electronic applications accepted. *Application Contact:* Craig A Hines, Director of Admissions, 312-201-5900 Ext. 226, Fax: 312-201-5917, E-mail: chines@adler.edu. *Vice President of Academic Affairs,* Dr. Frank Gruba-McAllister, 312-201-5900, Fax: 312-207-5917.

AGNES SCOTT COLLEGE, Decatur, GA 30030-3797

General Information Independent-religious, Undergraduate: women only; graduate: coed, comprehensive institution. *Graduate housing:* On-campus housing not available.

GRADUATE UNITS

Secondary English Program *Degree program information:* Evening/weekend programs available. Offers secondary English (MAT).

Secondary Mathematics and Science Program Offers secondary biology (MAT); secondary chemistry (MAT); secondary math (MAT); secondary physics (MAT).

AIR FORCE INSTITUTE OF TECHNOLOGY, Dayton, OH 45433-7765

General Information Federally supported, coed, primarily men, graduate-only institution. CGS member. *Graduate housing:* On-campus housing not available. *Research affiliation:* U.S. Air Force Office of Scientific Research, U.S. Air Force Research Laboratory, Dayton Area Graduate Studies Institute (aerospace), Department of Energy, National Security Agency.

GRADUATE UNITS

Graduate School of Engineering and Management *Degree program information:* Part-time programs available. Offers aeronautical engineering (MS, PhD); applied mathematics (MS, PhD); applied physics (MS, PhD); astronautical engineering (MS, PhD); computer engineering (MS, PhD); computer systems/science (MS); cost analysis (MS); electrical engineering (MS, PhD); electro-optics (MS, PhD); engineering and management (MS, PhD); environmental and engineering management (MS); environmental engineering science (MS); information resource/systems management (MS); logistics management (MS); materials science (MS, PhD); nuclear engineering (MS, PhD); operations research (MS, PhD); space operations (MS); space physics (MS); systems engineering (MS, PhD).

ALABAMA AGRICULTURAL AND MECHANICAL UNIVERSITY, Huntsville, AL 35811

General Information State-supported, coed, university. CGS member. *Enrollment:* 5,124 graduate, professional, and undergraduate students; 312 full-time matriculated graduate/professional students (216 women), 515 part-time matriculated graduate/professional students (352 women). *Enrollment by degree level:* 706 master's, 71 doctoral, 30 other advanced degrees. *Graduate faculty:* 309 full-time (121 women), 69 part-time/adjunct (42 women). Full-time tuition and fees vary according to program. *Graduate housing:* Rooms and/or apartments available on a first-come, first-served basis to single students and available to married students. Typical cost: $2756 per year ($4770 including board) for single students; $2756 per year ($4770 including board) for married students. Housing application deadline: 5/1. *Student services:* Campus employment opportunities, campus safety program, career counseling, child daycare facilities, international student services, low-cost health insurance, services for students with disabilities. *Library facilities:* J. F. Drake Learning Resources Center. *Online resources:* library catalog, access to other libraries' catalogs. *Collection:* 507,500 titles, 2,500 serial subscriptions. *Research affiliation:* NASA (utilization of space resources), Boeing Defense and Space Group (plant science), Lawrence Livermore National Laboratory (chemistry, physics), Alabama Supercomputer Network, Nichols Research Corporation (computer science), Hughes Aircraft Corporation (physics).

Computer facilities: 1,000 computers available on campus for general student use. A campuswide network can be accessed from student residence rooms and from off campus. *Web address:* http://www.aamu.edu/.

General Application Contact: Dr. Frank Archer, Dean, School of Graduate Studies, 256-372-5266, Fax: 256-372-5269, E-mail: caula.beyl@aamu.edu.

GRADUATE UNITS

School of Graduate Studies Students: 312 full-time (216 women), 515 part-time (352 women); includes 559 minority (547 African Americans, 2 American Indian/Alaska Native, 6 Asian Americans or Pacific Islanders, 4 Hispanic Americans), 106 international. Average age 33. *Faculty:* 309 full-time (121 women), 69 part-time/adjunct (42 women). Expenses: Contact institution. *Financial support:* In 2008–09, fellowships with tuition reimbursements (averaging $18,000 per year), research assistantships with tuition reimbursements (averaging $13,500 per year), teaching assistantships with tuition reimbursements (averaging $9,000 per year) were awarded; career-related internships or fieldwork, Federal Work-Study, and institutionally sponsored loans also available. Support available to part-time students. Financial award application deadline: 4/1; financial award applicants required to submit FAFSA. In 2008, 289 master's, 11 doctorates awarded. *Application deadline:* For fall admission, 5/1 priority date for domestic students. Applications are processed on a rolling basis. *Application fee:* $25. Electronic applications accepted. *Application Contact:* Dr. Caula Beyl, Dean, School of Graduate Studies, 256-372-5266, Fax: 256-372-5269, E-mail: caula.beyl@aamu.edu. *Dean, School of Graduate Studies,* Dr. Michael Orok, 256-372-5266, Fax: 256-372-5269.

School of Agricultural and Environmental Sciences Students: 49 full-time (28 women), 120 part-time (67 women); includes 113 minority (109 African Americans, 4 Asian Americans or Pacific Islanders), 44 international. Expenses: Contact institution. *Financial support:* Fellowships, research assistantships, teaching assistantships, career-related internships or fieldwork and Federal Work-Study available. Support available to part-time students. Financial award application deadline: 4/1. In 2008, 32 master's, 8 doctorates awarded. *Degree program information:* Part-time and evening/weekend programs available. Offers agribusiness (MS); agricultural and environmental sciences (MS, MURP, PhD); animal sciences (MS); environmental science (MS); family and consumer sciences (MS); food science (MS, PhD); plant and soil science (PhD); urban and regional planning (MURP). *Application deadline:* For fall admission, 5/1 for domestic students. Applications are processed on a rolling basis. *Application fee:* $25. Electronic applications accepted. *Application Contact:* Dr. Caula Beyl, Dean, School of Graduate Studies, 256-372-5266, Fax: 256-372-5269, E-mail: caula.beyl@aamu.edu. *Dean,* Dr. Robert Taylor, 256-372-5783, Fax: 256-372-5906.

School of Arts and Sciences Students: 90 full-time (74 women), 50 part-time (33 women); includes 99 minority (97 African Americans, 1 Asian American or Pacific Islander, 1 Hispanic American), 17 international. *Faculty:* 38. Expenses: Contact institution. *Financial support:* In 2008–09, 2 fellowships with tuition reimbursements (averaging $15,000 per year), 15 research assistantships with tuition reimbursements (averaging $9,000 per year), 6 teaching assistantships with tuition reimbursements (averaging $9,000 per year) were awarded; career-related internships or fieldwork and Federal Work-Study also available. Financial award application deadline: 4/1. In 2008, 50 master's, 5 doctorates awarded. *Degree program information:* Part-time and evening/weekend programs available. Offers arts and sciences (MS, MSW, PhD); biology (MS); physics (MS, PhD); social work (MSW). *Application deadline:* For fall admission, 5/1 priority date for domestic students. Applications are processed on a rolling basis. *Application fee:* $25. Electronic applications accepted. *Application Contact:* Dr. Caula Beyl, Dean, School of Graduate Studies, 256-372-5266, Fax: 256-372-5269, E-mail: caula.beyl@aamu.edu. *Dean,* Dr. Matthew Edwards, 256-372-5300.

School of Business Students: 20 full-time (7 women), 25 part-time (16 women); includes 38 minority (all African Americans), 7 international. Average age 26. *Faculty:* 24 full-time (2 women). Expenses: Contact institution. *Financial support:* Research assistantships, teaching assistantships, career-related internships or fieldwork, Federal Work-Study, and institutionally sponsored loans available. Financial award application deadline: 4/1. In 2008, 18 master's awarded. *Degree program information:* Part-time and evening/weekend programs available. Offers business (MBA); management and marketing (MBA). *Application deadline:* For fall admission, 5/1 for domestic students. Applications are processed on a rolling basis. *Application fee:* $25. Electronic applications accepted. *Application Contact:* Dr. Caula Beyl, Dean, School of Graduate Studies, 256-372-5266, Fax: 256-372-5269, E-mail: caula.beyl@aamu.edu. *Dean,* Dr. Barbara A. P. Jones, 256-372-5485, Fax: 256-372-5081.

School of Education Students: 129 full-time (97 women), 273 part-time (209 women); includes 274 minority (268 African Americans, 2 American Indian/Alaska Native, 1 Asian American or Pacific Islander, 3 Hispanic Americans), 15 international. *Faculty:* 36 full-time (18 women), 4 part-time/adjunct (1 woman). Expenses: Contact institution. *Financial support:* Fellowships, research assistantships, career-related internships or fieldwork, Federal Work-Study, institutionally sponsored loans, and traineeships available. Support available to part-time students. Financial award application deadline: 4/1. In 2008, 130 master's, 2 other advanced degrees awarded. *Degree program information:* Part-time and evening/weekend programs available. Offers communicative disorders (M Ed, MS); early childhood education (MS Ed, Ed S); education (M Ed, Ed S); elementary education (MS Ed, Ed S); higher administration (MS); music (MS); music education (M Ed); physical education (M Ed, MS); psychology and counseling (MS, Ed S); special education (M Ed, MS). *Application deadline:* For fall admission, 5/1 for domestic students. Applications are processed on a rolling basis. *Application fee:* $25. Electronic applications accepted. *Application Contact:* Dr. Caula Beyl, Dean, School of Graduate Studies, 256-372-5266, Fax: 256-372-5269, E-mail: caula.beyl@aamu.edu. *Dean,* Dr. Larry Powers, 256-372-5500.

School of Engineering and Technology Students: 23 full-time (9 women), 24 part-time (9 women); includes 22 minority (all African Americans), 22 international. *Faculty:* 4 full-time (1 woman). Expenses: Contact institution. *Financial support:* Research assistantships with tuition reimbursements, career-related internships or fieldwork available. Financial award application deadline: 4/1. In 2008, 26 master's awarded. *Degree program information:* Part-time and evening/weekend programs available. Offers computer science (MS); engineering and technology (M Ed, MS); industrial technology (M Ed, MS). *Application deadline:* For fall admission, 5/1 for domestic students. Applications are processed on a rolling basis. *Application fee:* $25. Electronic applications accepted. *Application Contact:* Dr. Caula Beyl, Dean, School of Graduate Studies, 256-372-5266, Fax: 256-372-5269, E-mail: caula.beyl@aamu.edu. *Dean,* Dr. Trent Montgomery, 256-372-5560.

ALABAMA STATE UNIVERSITY, Montgomery, AL 36101-0271

General Information State-supported, coed, comprehensive institution. *Graduate housing:* Rooms and/or apartments available on a first-come, first-served basis to single and married students. Housing application deadline: 7/15.

GRADUATE UNITS

School of Graduate Studies *Degree program information:* Part-time and evening/weekend programs available. Offers instrumental music (M Ed); vocal/choral music (M Ed).

College of Arts and Sciences *Degree program information:* Part-time programs available. Offers arts and sciences (M Ed, MS, Ed S); biological sciences (MS); mathematics (M Ed, MS, Ed S).

College of Business Administration *Degree program information:* Part-time programs available. Offers accountancy (M Acc); business administration (M Acc).

College of Education *Degree program information:* Part-time programs available. Offers biology education (M Ed, Ed S); early childhood education (M Ed, Ed S); education (M Ed, MS, Ed D, Ed S); educational administration (M Ed, Ed D, Ed S); educational leadership, policy and law (Ed D); elementary education (M Ed, Ed S); English/language arts (M Ed); general counseling (MS, Ed S); guidance and counseling (M Ed, MS, Ed S); health education (M Ed); history education (M Ed, Ed S); library education media (M Ed, Ed S); mathematics education (M Ed); physical education (M Ed); school counseling (M Ed, Ed S); secondary education (M Ed, Ed S); social studies (Ed S); special education (M Ed).

College of Health Sciences Offers health sciences (DPT); physical therapy (DPT).

ALASKA PACIFIC UNIVERSITY, Anchorage, AK 99508-4672

General Information Independent, coed, comprehensive institution. *Graduate housing:* Room and/or apartments available on a first-come, first-served basis to single students; on-campus housing not available to married students. Housing application deadline: 8/15.

GRADUATE UNITS

Graduate Programs *Degree program information:* Part-time and evening/weekend programs available. Offers business administration (MBA); counseling psychology (MSCP); environmental science (MSES, MSOEE); health services administration (MBA); information and communication technology (MBAICT); investment (CGS); outdoor and environmental education (MSOEE); self-designed study (MA); teaching (MAT); teaching (K-8) (MAT). Electronic applications accepted.

ALBANY COLLEGE OF PHARMACY AND HEALTH SCIENCES, Albany, NY 12208-3425

General Information Independent, coed, comprehensive institution. *Enrollment:* 1,525 graduate, professional, and undergraduate students; 424 full-time matriculated graduate/professional students (241 women), 2 part-time matriculated graduate/professional students. *Enrollment by degree level:* 426 first professional. *Graduate faculty:* 53 full-time (28 women), 4 part-time/adjunct (all women). *Tuition:* Full-time $22,050; part-time $735 per credit hour. *Required fees:* $1150. *Graduate housing:* Room and/or apartments available on a first-come, first-served basis to single students; on-campus housing not available to married students. Typical cost: $6900 per year ($8700 including board). Housing application deadline: 6/1. *Student services:* Campus employment opportunities, career counseling, free psychological counseling, international student services, low-cost health insurance, writing training. *Library facilities:* George and Leona Lewis Library. *Online resources:* library catalog, web page, access to other libraries' catalogs. *Collection:* 16,124 titles, 3,576 serial subscriptions.

Computer facilities: 30 computers available on campus for general student use. A campuswide network can be accessed from student residence rooms and from off campus. Online class registration is available. *Web address:* http://www.acphs.edu/.

General Application Contact: Director of Admissions, 518-694-7221, Fax: 518-694-7322, E-mail: admissions@acphs.edu.

GRADUATE UNITS

Program in Pharmacy Students: 424 full-time (241 women), 2 part-time (0 women); includes 71 minority (13 African Americans, 54 Asian Americans or Pacific Islanders, 4 Hispanic Americans), 37 international. Average age 26. 2,324 applicants, 7% accepted, 98 enrolled. *Faculty:* 53 full-time (28 women), 4 part-time/adjunct (all women). Expenses: Contact institution. *Financial support:* In 2008–09, 1 fellowship with tuition reimbursement (averaging $40,000 per year) was awarded; Federal Work-Study and scholarships/grants also available. Support available to part-time students. Financial award application deadline: 3/1; financial award applicants required to submit FAFSA. In 2008, 193 first professional degrees awarded. Offers pharmaceutical sciences (MS); pharmacy (Pharm D); pharmacy administration (MS). *Application deadline:* For fall admission, 3/1 for domestic and international students. Applications are processed on a rolling basis. *Application fee:* $75. Electronic applications accepted. *Application Contact:* Director of Admissions, 518-694-7221, Fax: 518-694-7322, E-mail: admissions@acphs.edu. *Dean,* Dr. Mehdi Boroujerdi, 518-694-7212, Fax: 518-694-7063.

ALBANY LAW SCHOOL, Albany, NY 12208-3494

General Information Independent, coed, graduate-only institution. *Enrollment by degree level:* 695 first professional, 13 master's, 26 other advanced degrees. *Graduate faculty:* 45 full-time (27 women), 51 part-time/adjunct (12 women). *Tuition:* Full-time $38,900; part-time $1345 per credit hour. *Graduate housing:* On-campus housing not available. *Student services:* Campus employment opportunities, campus safety program, career counseling, free psychological counseling, low-cost health insurance, services for students with disabilities, writing training. *Library facilities:* Schaffer Law Library. *Online resources:* library catalog, web page. *Collection:* 288,328 titles, 2,408 serial subscriptions, 458 audiovisual materials.

Computer facilities: 54 computers available on campus for general student use. A campuswide network can be accessed from off campus. Online class registration is available. *Web address:* http://www.albanylaw.edu/.

Albany Law School (continued)

General Application Contact: Gail S. Benson, Director of Admissions, 518-445-2326, Fax: 518-445-2369, E-mail: gbens@albanylaw.edu.

GRADUATE UNITS

Professional Program Students: 707 full-time (318 women), 27 part-time (14 women); includes 101 minority (19 African Americans, 4 American Indian/Alaska Native, 53 Asian Americans or Pacific Islanders, 25 Hispanic Americans), 17 international. Average age 26. 2,332 applicants, 43% accepted, 255 enrolled. *Faculty:* 45 full-time (27 women), 51 part-time/adjunct (12 women). Expenses: Contact institution. *Financial support:* In 2008–09, 609 students received support, including 50 research assistantships (averaging $2,000 per year); career-related internships or fieldwork, Federal Work-Study, institutionally sponsored loans, scholarships/grants, health care benefits, and tuition waivers (full and partial) also available. Support available to part-time students. Financial award applicants required to submit FAFSA. In 2008, 221 JDs, 4 master's awarded. *Degree program information:* Part-time programs available. Offers law (JD, LL M, MSLS). *Application deadline:* For fall admission, 3/15 priority date for domestic students. Applications are processed on a rolling basis. *Application fee:* $60. *Application Contact:* Gail S. Benson, Director of Admissions, 518-445-2326, Fax: 518-445-2369, E-mail: gbens@albanylaw.edu. *President and Dean,* Thomas F. Guernsey, 518-445-2321, Fax: 518-472-5865.

ALBANY MEDICAL COLLEGE, Albany, NY 12208-3479

General Information Independent, coed, graduate-only institution. *Graduate housing:* On-campus housing not available. *Research affiliation:* X-Ray Optical Systems (diagnostic equipment), Albany Molecular Research, Inc. (biomedical research), Regenerative Research Foundation (biomedical research), Wadsworth Center for Laboratories and Research (biomedical research), ORDWAY Research Institute (biomedical research), General Electric Corporation (imaging).

GRADUATE UNITS

Alden March Bioethics Institute *Degree program information:* Part-time programs available. Postbaccalaureate distance learning degree programs offered (no on-campus study). Offers bioethics (MS); clinical ethics (Certificate). Electronic applications accepted.

Center for Nurse Anesthesiology Postbaccalaureate distance learning degree programs offered (minimal on-campus study). Offers nurse anesthesiology (MS).

Center for Physician Assistant Studies Offers physician assistant studies (MS).

Graduate Programs in the Biological Sciences *Degree program information:* Part-time programs available. Offers biological sciences (MS, PhD).

Center for Cardiovascular Sciences *Degree program information:* Part-time programs available. Offers cardiovascular sciences (MS, PhD).

Center for Cell Biology and Cancer Research *Degree program information:* Part-time programs available. Offers cell biology and cancer research (MS, PhD).

Center for Immunology and Microbial Disease *Degree program information:* Part-time programs available. Offers immunology and microbial disease (MS, PhD).

Center for Neuropharmacology and Neuroscience Offers neuropharmacology and neuroscience (MS, PhD).

Professional Program Offers medicine (MD). Electronic applications accepted.

ALBANY STATE UNIVERSITY, Albany, GA 31705-2717

General Information State-supported, coed, primarily women, comprehensive institution. CGS member. *Enrollment:* 4,176 graduate, professional, and undergraduate students; 91 full-time matriculated graduate/professional students (66 women), 305 part-time matriculated graduate/professional students (217 women). *Enrollment by degree level:* 261 master's, 43 other advanced degrees. *Graduate faculty:* 79 full-time (29 women), 15 part-time/adjunct (12 women). Tuition, state resident: full-time $4296; part-time $154 per semester hour. Tuition, nonresident: full-time $15,338; part-time $614 per semester hour. *Required fees:* $306 per semester. Tuition and fees vary according to course load. *Graduate housing:* Room and/or apartments available on a first-come, first-served basis to single students; on-campus housing not available to married students. Typical cost: $3466 per year ($5796 including board). Room and board charges vary according to board plan and housing facility selected. Housing application deadline: 6/30. *Student services:* Campus employment opportunities, campus safety program, career counseling, exercise/wellness program, free psychological counseling, grant writing training, international student services, low-cost health insurance, services for students with disabilities. *Library facilities:* James Pendergrast Memorial Library.

Computer facilities: 1,000 computers available on campus for general student use. A campuswide network can be accessed from student residence rooms and from off campus. Online class registration is available. *Web address:* http://www.asurams.edu/.

General Application Contact: Diane P. Frink, Graduate Admissions Counselor, 229-430-5118, Fax: 229-430-6398, E-mail: diane.frink@asurams.edu.

GRADUATE UNITS

College of Arts and Humanities Students: 10 full-time (8 women), 42 part-time (29 women); includes 50 minority (49 African Americans, 1 Asian American or Pacific Islander). Average age 35. *Faculty:* 16 full-time (5 women). Expenses: Contact institution. *Financial support:* Tuition waivers available. Financial award application deadline: 4/1; financial award applicants required to submit FAFSA. In 2008, 16 master's awarded. *Degree program information:* Part-time programs available. Offers arts and humanities (MPA, MS); community and economic development (MPA); criminal justice (MPA); fiscal management (MPA); general management (MPA); health administration and policy (MPA); human resources management (MPA); public policy (MPA); water resource management and policy (MPA). *Application deadline:* For fall admission, 4/15 for domestic and international students; for spring admission, 11/15 for domestic and international students. Applications are processed on a rolling basis. *Application fee:* $20. Electronic applications accepted. *Application Contact:* Diane P. Frink, Graduate Admissions Counselor, 229-430-5118, Fax: 229-430-6398, E-mail: diane.frink@asurams.edu. *Dean,* Dr. Leroy Bynum, 229-430-4832, Fax: 229-430-4765, E-mail: leroy.bynum@asurams.edu.

College of Business Students: 4 full-time (3 women), 18 part-time (14 women); includes 17 minority (15 African Americans, 2 Asian Americans or Pacific Islanders). Average age 43. *Faculty:* 10 full-time (1 woman), 3 part-time/adjunct (2 women). Expenses: Contact institution. *Financial support:* Application deadline: 4/1. In 2008, 15 master's awarded. *Degree program information:* Part-time and evening/weekend programs available. Postbaccalaureate distance learning degree programs offered (no on-campus study). Offers business (MBA). *Application deadline:* For fall admission, 4/15 for domestic and international students; for spring admission, 11/15 for domestic and international students. Applications are processed on a rolling basis. *Application fee:* $20. Electronic applications accepted. *Application Contact:* Diane P. Frink, Graduate Admissions Counselor, 229-430-5118, Fax: 229-430-6398, E-mail: dfrink@asurams.edu. *Interim Dean,* Dr. Michael Rogers, 229-430-4780, Fax: 229-430-5119, E-mail: michael.rogers@asurams.edu.

College of Education Students: 81 full-time (66 women), 165 part-time (131 women); includes 174 minority (172 African Americans, 2 Asian Americans or Pacific Islanders). Average age 35. *Faculty:* 24 full-time (11 women), 7 part-time/adjunct (all women). Expenses: Contact institution. *Financial support:* Fellowships, research assistantships, teaching assistantships, career-related internships or fieldwork, Federal Work-Study, and scholarships/grants available. Support available to part-time students. Financial award application deadline: 4/1; financial award applicants required to submit CSS PROFILE or FAFSA. In 2008, 54 master's, 43 Certificates awarded. *Degree program information:* Part-time programs available. Offers biology (M Ed); chemistry (M Ed); early childhood education (M Ed); education (M Ed, Certificate, Ed S); educational leadership (M Ed, Certificate, Ed S); English education (M Ed); health and physical education (M Ed); middle grades education (M Ed); music education (M Ed); school counseling (M Ed); special education (M Ed). *Application deadline:* For fall admission, 4/15 for domestic and international students; for spring admission, 11/15 for domestic and international students. Applications are processed on a rolling basis. *Application fee:* $20. Electronic applications accepted. *Application Contact:* Diane P. Frink, Graduate Admissions Counselor, 229-430-5118, Fax: 229-430-6398, E-mail: diane.frink@asurams.edu. *Dean,* Dr. Wilburn Campbell, 229-430-4715, Fax: 229-430-4993, E-mail: wilburn.campbell@asurams.edu.

College of Sciences and Health Professions Students: 31 full-time (21 women), 70 part-time (52 women); includes 73 minority (70 African Americans, 3 Asian Americans or Pacific Islanders). Average age 37. *Faculty:* 29 full-time (12 women), 5 part-time/adjunct (3 women). Expenses: Contact institution. *Financial support:* In 2008–09, 16 students received support. Scholarships/grants and traineeships available. Financial award applicants required to submit CSS PROFILE or FAFSA. In 2008, 37 master's awarded. *Degree program information:* Part-time programs available. Offers criminal justice (MS); criminal justice and forensic science (MS); mathematics education (M Ed); nursing (MSN); science education (M Ed). *Application deadline:* For fall admission, 4/15 for domestic and international students; for spring admission, 11/15 for domestic and international students. Applications are processed on a rolling basis. *Application fee:* $20. Electronic applications accepted. *Application Contact:* Linda Grimsley, Chairperson, 229-430-4724, Fax: 229-430-3937, E-mail: linda.grimsley@asurams.edu. *Dean,* Dr. Joyce Johnson, 229-430-4724, Fax: 229-430-3937, E-mail: joyce.johnson@asurams.edu.

ALBERT EINSTEIN COLLEGE OF MEDICINE, Bronx, NY 10461

General Information Independent, coed, graduate-only institution.

GRADUATE UNITS

Medical Scientist Training Program

Professional Program in Medicine Offers medicine (MD).

Sue Golding Graduate Division of Medical Sciences Offers anatomy (PhD); biochemistry (PhD); cell and developmental biology (PhD); medical sciences (PhD); microbiology and immunology (PhD); neuroscience (PhD); pathology (PhD); physiology and biophysics (PhD).

Division of Biological Sciences Offers cell biology (PhD); computational genetics (PhD); developmental and molecular biology (PhD); genetics (PhD); molecular genetics (PhD); molecular pharmacology (PhD); translational genetics (PhD).

ALBERTUS MAGNUS COLLEGE, New Haven, CT 06511-1189

General Information Independent-religious, coed, comprehensive institution. *Graduate housing:* Room and/or apartments available to single students; on-campus housing not available to married students. Housing application deadline: 8/31.

GRADUATE UNITS

Liberal Studies Program *Degree program information:* Part-time and evening/weekend programs available. Offers liberal studies (MALS).

Program in Art Therapy *Degree program information:* Part-time and evening/weekend programs available. Offers art therapy (MAAT).

Program in Leadership Offers leadership (MA).

Program in Management *Degree program information:* Evening/weekend programs available. Offers business administration (MBA); management (MSM). Program also offered in East Hartford, CT.

ALBRIGHT COLLEGE, Reading, PA 19612-5234

General Information Independent-religious, coed, comprehensive institution. *Graduate housing:* On-campus housing not available.

GRADUATE UNITS

Department of Education—Graduate Division *Degree program information:* Part-time and evening/weekend programs available. Offers early childhood education (MS); elementary education (MS); English as a second language (MA); general education (MA); special education (MS). Electronic applications accepted.

ALCORN STATE UNIVERSITY, Alcorn State, MS 39096-7500

General Information State-supported, coed, comprehensive institution. CGS member. *Graduate housing:* Room and/or apartments available on a first-come, first-served basis to single students; on-campus housing not available to married students.

GRADUATE UNITS

School of Graduate Studies *Degree program information:* Part-time programs available. Offers workforce education leadership (MS). Electronic applications accepted.

School of Agriculture and Applied Science Offers agricultural economics (MS Ag); agronomy (MS Ag); animal science (MS Ag).

School of Arts and Sciences Offers arts and sciences (MS); biology (MS); computer and information sciences (MS).

School of Business Offers business (MBA).

School of Nursing Offers rural nursing (MSN).

School of Psychology and Education Offers agricultural education (MS Ed); elementary education (MS Ed, Ed S); guidance and counseling (MS Ed); industrial education (MS Ed); secondary education (MS Ed); special education (MS Ed).

ALDERSON-BROADDUS COLLEGE, Philippi, WV 26416

General Information Independent-religious, coed, comprehensive institution. *Graduate housing:* Rooms and/or apartments available on a first-come, first-served basis to single and married students. Housing application deadline: 8/21.

GRADUATE UNITS

Program in Physician Assistant Studies Offers physician assistant studies (MPAS). Electronic applications accepted.

ALFRED UNIVERSITY, Alfred, NY 14802-1205

General Information Independent, coed, university. CGS member. *Graduate housing:* Room and/or apartments available on a first-come, first-served basis to single students; on-campus housing not available to married students. Housing application deadline: 7/1. *Research affiliation:* Laboratory for Electronic Ceramics, Polymer-Assisted Ceramics Manufacturing Center, New York State Center for Advanced Ceramic Technology, National Science Foundation Industry-University Center for Glass Research, Whitewares Research Center Industry University Center (whitewares processing, traditional ceramics), National Science Foundation Industry-University Center for Biosurfaces (bioceramics).

GRADUATE UNITS

Graduate School *Degree program information:* Part-time programs available. Offers school counseling (MS Ed, CAS); school psychology (MA, Psy D, CAS). Electronic applications accepted.

College of Business *Degree program information:* Part-time programs available. Offers business administration (MBA). Electronic applications accepted.

Division of Education *Degree program information:* Part-time programs available. Offers literacy teacher (MS Ed); numeracy (MS). Electronic applications accepted.

New York State College of Ceramics Offers biomedical materials engineering science (MS); ceramic art (MFA); ceramic engineering (MS); ceramics (MFA, MS, PhD); electrical engineering (MS); electronic integrated arts (MFA); glass art (MFA); glass science (MS, PhD); materials science and engineering (MS, PhD); mechanical engineering (MS); sculpture (MFA). Electronic applications accepted.

ALLEN COLLEGE, Waterloo, IA 50703

General Information Independent, coed, primarily women, comprehensive institution. *Enrollment:* 416 graduate, professional, and undergraduate students; 17 full-time matriculated graduate/professional students (16 women), 80 part-time matriculated graduate/professional students (75 women). *Enrollment by degree level:* 97 master's. *Graduate faculty:* 1 (woman) full-time, 9 part-time/adjunct (all women). *Tuition:* Full-time $12,135; part-time $620 per credit hour. *Required fees:* $727; $62 per credit hour. One-time fee: $415. Tuition and fees vary according to course load, program and student level. *Graduate housing:* Room and/or apartments available on a first-come, first-served basis to single students; on-campus housing not available to married students. Typical cost: $6178 (including board). *Student services:* Career counseling, child daycare facilities, exercise/wellness program, free psychological counseling, low-cost health insurance, multicultural affairs office. *Library facilities:* Barrett Library. *Online resources:* library catalog, web page, access to other libraries' catalogs. *Collection:* 3,200 titles, 199 serial subscriptions, 350 audiovisual materials.

Computer facilities: 26 computers available on campus for general student use. A campuswide network can be accessed from student residence rooms and from off campus. *Web address:* http://www.allencollege.edu/.

General Application Contact: Dina Dowden, Education Secretary, 319-226-2000, Fax: 319-226-2051, E-mail: allcucollegeadmissions@ihs.org.

GRADUATE UNITS

Program in Nursing Students: 17 full-time (16 women), 80 part-time (75 women); includes 1 minority (Asian American or Pacific Islander). Average age 38. 83 applicants, 70% accepted, 52 enrolled. *Faculty:* 1 (woman) full-time, 9 part-time/adjunct (all women). Expenses: Contact institution. *Financial support:* In 2008–09, 95 students received support; teaching assistantships, institutionally sponsored loans, scholarships/grants, and traineeships available. Support available to part-time students. Financial award application deadline: 8/15; financial award applicants required to submit FAFSA. In 2008, 10 master's awarded. *Degree program information:* Part-time programs available. Offers acute care nurse practitioner (MSN); adult psychiatric mental health nurse practitioner (MSN); family nurse practitioner (MSN); health education (MSN); leadership in health care delivery (MSN). *Application deadline:* For fall admission, 7/15 priority date for domestic students; for spring admission, 12/1 priority date for domestic students. Applications are processed on a rolling basis. *Application fee:* $50. Electronic applications accepted. *Application Contact:* Michelle Koehn, Admissions Counselor, 319-226-2002, Fax: 319-226-2051, E-mail: Koehnml@ihs.org. *Chair,* Nancy Kramer, 319-226-2040, Fax: 319-226-2070, E-mail: kramerna@ihs.org.

ALLIANCE THEOLOGICAL SEMINARY, Nyack, NY 10960

General Information Independent-religious, coed, graduate-only institution. *Graduate housing:* Rooms and/or apartments available on a first-come, first-served basis to single and married students. Housing application deadline: 9/1.

GRADUATE UNITS

Graduate and Professional Programs *Degree program information:* Part-time programs available. Offers Christian ministry (MPS); counseling (MA); intercultural studies (MA); missions (MPS); New Testament (MA); Old Testament (MA); theology (M Div); urban ministry (MPS).

ALLIANT INTERNATIONAL UNIVERSITY–FRESNO, Fresno, CA 93727

General Information Independent, coed, graduate-only institution. *Graduate housing:* On-campus housing not available.

GRADUATE UNITS

California School of Professional Psychology Offers clinical psychology (PhD, Psy D); professional psychology (PhD, Psy D).

Center for Forensic Studies Offers forensic psychology (PhD, Psy D). Electronic applications accepted.

Graduate School of Education *Degree program information:* Part-time and evening/weekend programs available. Postbaccalaureate distance learning degree programs offered (no on-campus study). Offers education (MA, Ed D, Certificate, Credential); educational leadership and management (Ed D); teaching (MA); teaching English to speakers of other languages (MA, Ed D, Certificate). Electronic applications accepted.

Marshall Goldsmith School of Management *Degree program information:* Part-time and evening/weekend programs available. Offers management (MA, Psy D).

Organizational Psychology Division *Degree program information:* Part-time and evening/weekend programs available. Offers organizational behavior (MA); organizational development (Psy D). Electronic applications accepted.

ALLIANT INTERNATIONAL UNIVERSITY–IRVINE, Irvine, CA 92612

General Information Independent, coed, graduate-only institution.

GRADUATE UNITS

California School of Professional Psychology *Degree program information:* Part-time programs available. Offers marital and family therapy (MA, Psy D); professional psychology (MA, Psy D). Electronic applications accepted.

Center for Forensic Studies Offers forensic studies (Psy D).

Graduate School of Education *Degree program information:* Part-time and evening/weekend programs available. Postbaccalaureate distance learning degree programs offered. Offers auditory oral education (Certificate); CLAD (Certificate); education (MA, Ed D, Psy D, Certificate, Credential); educational administration (MA, Credential); educational leadership and management (K-12) (Ed D); educational psychology (Psy D); higher education (Ed D); preliminary administrative services (Credential); preliminary multiple subject (Credential); preliminary multiple subject with BCLAD (Credential); preliminary single subject (Credential); professional clear multiple subject (Credential); professional clear single subject (Credential); pupil personnel services (Credential); school psychology (MA); teaching (MA, Credential); teaching English to speakers of other languages (MA, Ed D); technology and learning (MA). Electronic applications accepted.

ALLIANT INTERNATIONAL UNIVERSITY–LOS ANGELES, Alhambra, CA 91803-1360

General Information Independent, coed, graduate-only institution. *Graduate housing:* Room and/or apartments available to single students; on-campus housing not available to married students.

GRADUATE UNITS

California School of Professional Psychology Offers biofeedback (MA); chemical dependency (MA); clinical psychology (PhD, Psy D); gerontology (MA); Latin American family therapy (MA); professional psychology (MA, PhD, Psy D). Electronic applications accepted.

Center for Forensic Studies Offers forensic psychology (Psy D).

Graduate School of Education *Degree program information:* Part-time and evening/weekend programs available. Postbaccalaureate distance learning degree programs offered (no on-campus study). Offers education (MA, Ed D, Psy D, Credential); educational administration (MA); educational leadership and management (K-12) (Ed D); educational psychology (Psy D); higher education (Ed D); preliminary administrative services (Credential); pupil personnel services (Credential); school psychology (MA); teaching (MA). Electronic applications accepted.

Marshall Goldsmith School of Management Offers management (MA, DBA, PhD).

Business Division Offers business (DBA).

Organizational Psychology Division *Degree program information:* Part-time programs available. Offers industrial/organizational psychology (MA, PhD). Electronic applications accepted.

ALLIANT INTERNATIONAL UNIVERSITY–MÉXICO CITY, CP06700 Mexico City, Mexico

General Information Independent, coed, comprehensive institution. *Graduate housing:* On-campus housing not available.

GRADUATE UNITS

California School of Professional Psychology Offers professional psychology (MA).

Graduate School of Education *Degree program information:* Part-time and evening/weekend programs available. Postbaccalaureate distance learning degree programs offered (no on-campus study). Offers teaching (MA).

International Studies Division Offers international relations (MA).

Marshall Goldsmith School of Management *Degree program information:* Part-time and evening/weekend programs available. Offers international business administration (MIBA); international relations (MA). Electronic applications accepted.

Programs in Arts and Science *Degree program information:* Part-time programs available. Offers counseling psychology (MA); international relations (MA). Electronic applications accepted.

ALLIANT INTERNATIONAL UNIVERSITY–SACRAMENTO, Sacramento, CA 95825

General Information Independent, coed, graduate-only institution.

GRADUATE UNITS

California School of Professional Psychology Offers clinical psychology (Psy D); marital and family therapy (MA); professional psychology (MA, Psy D). Electronic applications accepted.

Graduate School of Education Offers education (MA); teaching (MA).

Marshall Goldsmith School of Management Offers management (Psy D); organizational development (Psy D).

ALLIANT INTERNATIONAL UNIVERSITY–SAN DIEGO, San Diego, CA 92131-1799

General Information Independent, coed, graduate-only institution. *Graduate housing:* Rooms and/or apartments available on a first-come, first-served basis to single and married students.

GRADUATE UNITS

California School of Professional Psychology *Degree program information:* Part-time programs available. Offers clinical psychology (PhD, Psy D); marital and family therapy (MA, Psy D); professional psychology (MA, PhD, Psy D).

Graduate School of Education *Degree program information:* Part-time and evening/weekend programs available. Postbaccalaureate distance learning degree programs offered (no on-campus study). Offers education (MA, Ed D, Psy D, Certificate, Credential); educational administration (MA); educational leadership and management (K-12) (Ed D); educational psychology (Psy D); higher education (Ed D, Certificate); preliminary administrative services (Credential); preliminary single subject (Credential); professional clear multiple subject (Credential); professional clear single subject (Credential); pupil personnel services (Credential); school psychology (MA); student personnel services (Certificate); teacher education (MA); teaching English to speakers of other languages (MA, Ed D, Certificate). Electronic applications accepted.

Marshall Goldsmith School of Management *Degree program information:* Part-time and evening/weekend programs available. Offers management (MA, MBA, MIBA, MS, DBA, PhD).

Business and Management Division *Degree program information:* Part-time and evening/weekend programs available. Offers business administration (MBA); information and technology management (DBA); international business (MIBA, DBA); strategic business (DBA); sustainable management (MBA). Electronic applications accepted.

International Studies Division *Degree program information:* Part-time programs available. Offers international relations (MA).

Organizational Psychology Division *Degree program information:* Part-time and evening/weekend programs available. Offers clinical/industrial organizational psychology (PhD); consulting psychology (PhD); industrial/organizational psychology (MA, MS, PhD); organizational behavior (MA). Electronic applications accepted.

ALLIANT INTERNATIONAL UNIVERSITY–SAN FRANCISCO, San Francisco, CA 94133-1221

General Information Independent, coed, graduate-only institution. *Graduate housing:* On-campus housing not available.

GRADUATE UNITS

California School of Professional Psychology Offers clinical psychology (PhD, Psy D, Certificate); professional psychology (Post-Doctoral MS, PhD, Psy D, Certificate); psychopharmacology (Post-Doctoral MS). Electronic applications accepted.

Graduate School of Education *Degree program information:* Part-time and evening/weekend programs available. Postbaccalaureate distance learning degree programs offered (no on-campus study). Offers auditory oral education (Certificate); CLAD (Certificate); community college administration (Ed D); education (MA, Ed D, Psy D, Certificate, Credential); educational administration (MA); educational leadership and management (K-12) (Ed D); educational psychology (Psy D); higher education (Ed D); preliminary administrative services (Credential); preliminary multiple subject (Credential); preliminary multiple subject with BCLAD (Credential); preliminary single subject (Credential); professional clear multiple subject (Credential); professional clear single subject (Credential); pupil personnel services (Credential); school psychology (MA); teaching (MA); university administration (Ed D). Electronic applications accepted.

Marshall Goldsmith School of Management *Degree program information:* Part-time and evening/weekend programs available. Offers management (MA, MBA, PhD). Electronic applications accepted.

Organizational Psychology Division *Degree program information:* Part-time and evening/weekend programs available. Offers organization development (MA); organizational psychology (MA, PhD). Electronic applications accepted.

Presidio School of Management Offers sustainable management (MBA).

ALVERNIA UNIVERSITY, Reading, PA 19607-1799

General Information Independent-religious, coed, comprehensive institution. *Graduate housing:* On-campus housing not available.

GRADUATE UNITS

Graduate Studies *Degree program information:* Part-time and evening/weekend programs available. Offers business (MBA); community counseling (MA); leadership (PhD); liberal studies (MALS); occupational therapy (MSOT); urban education (M Ed). Electronic applications accepted.

ALVERNO COLLEGE, Milwaukee, WI 53234-3922

General Information Independent-religious, Undergraduate: women only; graduate: coed, comprehensive institution. *Graduate housing:* On-campus housing not available.

GRADUATE UNITS

School of Business *Degree program information:* Evening/weekend programs available. Offers business (MBA). Electronic applications accepted.

School of Education *Degree program information:* Part-time and evening/weekend programs available. Offers adaptive education (MA); administrative leadership (MA); adult education and organizational development (MA); adult educational and instructional design (MA); adult

Alverno College (continued)

educational and instructional technology (MA); instructional leadership (MA); instructional technology for K-12 settings (MA); professional development (MA); reading education (MA); reading education with adaptive education (MA); science education (MA); teaching in alternative schools (MA). Electronic applications accepted.

School of Nursing *Degree program information:* Part-time and evening/weekend programs available. Offers nursing (MSN). Electronic applications accepted.

AMBERTON UNIVERSITY, Garland, TX 75041-5595

General Information Independent-religious, coed, upper-level institution. *Graduate housing:* On-campus housing not available.

GRADUATE UNITS

Graduate School *Degree program information:* Part-time and evening/weekend programs available. Offers counseling (MA); general business (MBA); human relations and business (MA, MS); management (MBA); professional development (MA).

AMBROSE UNIVERSITY COLLEGE, Calgary, AB T2P 3T5, Canada

General Information Independent-religious, coed, comprehensive institution. *Enrollment by degree level:* 39 first professional, 78 master's, 18 other advanced degrees. *Graduate faculty:* 7 full-time (0 women), 24 part-time/adjunct (2 women). *Graduate housing:* Room and/or apartments available to single students; on-campus housing not available to married students. Housing application deadline: 8/20. *Student services:* Campus employment opportunities, career counseling, international student services. *Library facilities:* Archibald Foundation Library. *Online resources:* library catalog, access to other libraries' catalogs. *Collection:* 65,000 titles, 546 serial subscriptions.

Computer facilities: A campuswide network can be accessed. *Web address:* http://www.ambrose.edu/.

General Application Contact: Lisa Kelly, Enrollment Coordinator, 403-410-2000 Ext. 2900, Fax: 403-571-2556, E-mail: enrolment@ambrose.edu.

GRADUATE UNITS

Ambrose Seminary *Degree program information:* Part-time programs available. Offers biblical/theological studies (MA); Chinese ministries (Certificate); Christian studies (Diploma); church education (M Div); intercultural ministries (M Div, MA, Certificate, Diploma); leadership and ministry (MA, Certificate, Diploma); pastoral ministries (M Div). Electronic applications accepted.

AMERICAN BAPTIST SEMINARY OF THE WEST, Berkeley, CA 94704-3029

General Information Independent-religious, coed, graduate-only institution. *Enrollment by degree level:* 68 first professional, 2 master's, 1 other advanced degree. *Graduate faculty:* 4 full-time (all women), 5 part-time/adjunct (0 women). *Tuition:* Full-time $12,750; part-time $500 per credit. *Required fees:* $240 per semester. One-time fee: $250. Tuition and fees vary according to degree level. *Graduate housing:* Rooms and/or apartments available on a first-come, first-served basis to single and married students. Housing application deadline: 6/1. *Student services:* Campus employment opportunities, international student services, low-cost health insurance, services for students with disabilities, writing training. *Library facilities:* Graduate Theological Union Library.

Computer facilities: 3 computers available on campus for general student use. Online class registration is available. *Web address:* http://www.absw.edu/.

General Application Contact: Rev. Marie Onwubuariri, Graduate Studies, 510-841-1905, Fax: 510-841-2446, E-mail: recruitment@absw.edu.

GRADUATE UNITS

Graduate and Professional Programs Students: 50 full-time (29 women), 21 part-time (11 women); includes 50 minority (44 African Americans, 6 Asian Americans or Pacific Islanders), 13 international. *Faculty:* 4 full-time (all women), 5 part-time/adjunct (0 women). Expenses: Contact institution. *Financial support:* Career-related internships or fieldwork, institutionally sponsored loans, scholarships/grants, tuition waivers (partial), and tuition discount available. Support available to part-time students. Financial award application deadline: 4/15; financial award applicants required to submit FAFSA. *Degree program information:* Part-time and evening/weekend programs available. Offers community leadership (MA); theology (M Div, MA). *Application deadline:* For fall admission, 4/15 priority date for domestic students, 4/15 for international students. Applications are processed on a rolling basis. *Application fee:* $25. Electronic applications accepted. *Application Contact:* Rev. Michelle M. Holmes, Vice President, 510-841-1905 Ext. 225, Fax: 510-841-2446, E-mail: mmholmes@absw.edu. *President for the Interim,* Dr. Paul M. Martin, 510-841-1905 Ext. 224, Fax: 510-841-2446, E-mail: pmartin@absw.edu.

THE AMERICAN COLLEGE, Bryn Mawr, PA 19010-2105

General Information Independent, coed, graduate-only institution. *Graduate housing:* On-campus housing not available.

GRADUATE UNITS

Richard D. Irwin Graduate School *Degree program information:* Part-time and evening/weekend programs available. Postbaccalaureate distance learning degree programs offered (minimal on-campus study). Offers financial services (MSFS); leadership (MSM). Electronic applications accepted.

AMERICAN COLLEGE OF ACUPUNCTURE AND ORIENTAL MEDICINE, Houston, TX 77063

General Information Proprietary, coed, graduate-only institution. *Research affiliation:* Baylor College of Medicine (acupuncture for osteoarthritis of the knee), Memorial Herman Healthcare System, Tianjing Hospital, China (traditional Chinese medicine), Montrose Clinic (HIV/AIDS research and treatment), Rice University Wellness Center (student and staff care).

GRADUATE UNITS

Graduate Studies *Degree program information:* Part-time programs available.

AMERICAN COLLEGE OF THESSALONIKI, GR-555-10 Pylea, Thessaloniki, Greece

General Information Independent, coed, comprehensive institution. *Enrollment:* 447 graduate, professional, and undergraduate students; 6 full-time matriculated graduate/professional students (3 women), 44 part-time matriculated graduate/professional students (30 women). *Enrollment by degree level:* 50 master's. *Graduate faculty:* 6 full-time (1 woman), 10 part-time/adjunct (2 women). *Student services:* Career counseling, free psychological counseling, international student services, writing training. *Library facilities:* Bissell Library plus 1 other. *Online resources:* library catalog, web page, access to other libraries' catalogs. *Collection:* 24,544 titles, 16,500 serial subscriptions, 960 audiovisual materials.

Computer facilities: 180 computers available on campus for general student use. A campuswide network can be accessed from off campus. *Web address:* http://www.act.edu/.

General Application Contact: Elli Konstantinou, Director of Student Recruitment, 30-310-398238, E-mail: elli@act.edu.

GRADUATE UNITS

Department of Business Administration Students: 6 full-time (3 women), 44 part-time (30 women), 17 international. 30 applicants, 97% accepted, 24 enrolled. *Faculty:* 6 full-time (1 woman), 10 part-time/adjunct (2 women). Expenses: Contact institution. *Degree program information:* Part-time and evening/weekend programs available. Offers banking and finance (MBA); entrepreneurship (MBA, Certificate); finance (Certificate); management (MBA, Certificate); marketing (MBA, Certificate). *Application deadline:* For fall admission, 9/30 priority date for domestic students; for spring admission, 1/31 priority date for domestic students. Applications are processed on a rolling basis. *Application fee:* $70. Electronic applications accepted. *Application Contact:* Elli Konstantinou, Director of Student Recruitment, 30-310-398238, E-mail: elli@act.edu. *Chair, Business Division,* Dr. Nikolaos Kourkoumelis, 30-310-398386, E-mail: nikolaos@act.edu.

AMERICAN COLLEGE OF TRADITIONAL CHINESE MEDICINE, San Francisco, CA 94107

General Information Independent, coed, graduate-only institution. *Graduate housing:* On-campus housing not available.

GRADUATE UNITS

Graduate Program *Degree program information:* Part-time programs available. Offers acupuncture and Oriental medicine (DAOM); shiatsu massage (Certificate); traditional Chinese medicine (MSTCM); tui na massage (Certificate).

AMERICAN CONSERVATORY THEATER, San Francisco, CA 94108-5800

General Information Independent, coed, graduate-only institution. *Graduate housing:* On-campus housing not available.

GRADUATE UNITS

Program in Acting Offers acting (MFA, Certificate). Certificate open only to applicants with undergraduate degree from a non-accredited institution.

AMERICAN FILM INSTITUTE CONSERVATORY, Los Angeles, CA 90027-1657

General Information Independent, coed, graduate-only institution. *Enrollment by degree level:* 357 master's. *Graduate faculty:* 45 full-time (6 women), 64 part-time/adjunct (18 women). *Tuition:* Full-time $34,150. *Required fees:* $2300. *Student services:* Campus employment opportunities, campus safety program, career counseling, free psychological counseling, international student services, services for students with disabilities, writing training. *Library facilities:* Louis B. Mayer Library. *Collection:* 14,000 titles, 100 serial subscriptions, 6,000 audiovisual materials.

Computer facilities: 30 computers available on campus for general student use. A campuswide network can be accessed from off campus. *Web address:* http://www.afi.com/.

General Application Contact: Angela Wheaton, Admissions Counselor, 323-856-7842, Fax: 323-856-7720, E-mail: awheaton@afi.com.

GRADUATE UNITS

Graduate Program Students: 357 full-time (117 women); includes 65 minority (19 African Americans, 1 American Indian/Alaska Native, 21 Asian Americans or Pacific Islanders, 24 Hispanic Americans), 105 international. Average age 26. 651 applicants, 31% accepted, 140 enrolled. *Faculty:* 45 full-time (6 women), 64 part-time/adjunct (18 women). Expenses: Contact institution. *Financial support:* In 2008–09, 95 students received support, including 18 teaching assistantships with partial tuition reimbursements available (averaging $3,000 per year); career-related internships or fieldwork, scholarships/grants, and unspecified assistantships also available. Financial award application deadline: 4/15; financial award applicants required to submit FAFSA. In 2008, 120 master's awarded. Offers cinematography (MFA); directing (MFA); editing (MFA); producing (MFA); production design (MFA); screenwriting (MFA). *Application deadline:* For fall admission, 12/1 for domestic and international students. *Application fee:* $75. *Application Contact:* Angela Wheaton, Admissions Counselor, 323-856-7842, Fax: 323-856-7720, E-mail: awheaton@afi.com. *Dean,* Robert Mandel, 323-856-7600, Fax: 323-467-4578.

AMERICAN GRADUATE SCHOOL OF INTERNATIONAL RELATIONS AND DIPLOMACY, F-75006 Paris, France

General Information Independent, coed, graduate-only institution.

GRADUATE UNITS

Program in International Relations and Diplomacy Offers international relations and diplomacy (MA, PhD).

AMERICAN GRADUATE UNIVERSITY, Covina, CA 91724

General Information Proprietary, coed, graduate-only institution.

GRADUATE UNITS

Program in Acquisition Management *Degree program information:* Part-time programs available. Postbaccalaureate distance learning degree programs offered (no on-campus study). Offers acquisition management (MAM, Certificate). Electronic applications accepted.

Program in Business Administration *Degree program information:* Part-time programs available. Postbaccalaureate distance learning degree programs offered (no on-campus study). Offers business administration (MBA). Electronic applications accepted.

Program in Contract Management *Degree program information:* Part-time programs available. Postbaccalaureate distance learning degree programs offered (no on-campus study). Offers contract management (MCM, Certificate). Electronic applications accepted.

Program in Project Management *Degree program information:* Part-time programs available. Postbaccalaureate distance learning degree programs offered (no on-campus study). Offers project management (MPM, Certificate). Electronic applications accepted.

AMERICAN INTERCONTINENTAL UNIVERSITY, Houston, TX 77042

General Information Proprietary, coed, comprehensive institution.

GRADUATE UNITS

School of Business Offers management (MBA).

AMERICAN INTERCONTINENTAL UNIVERSITY BUCKHEAD CAMPUS, Atlanta, GA 30326-1016

General Information Proprietary, coed, comprehensive institution. *Graduate housing:* Room and/or apartments available on a first-come, first-served basis to single students; on-campus housing not available to married students.

GRADUATE UNITS

Program in Business Administration *Degree program information:* Evening/weekend programs available. Postbaccalaureate distance learning degree programs offered. Offers accounting and finance (MBA); management (MBA); marketing (MBA). Electronic applications accepted.

AMERICAN INTERCONTINENTAL UNIVERSITY DUNWOODY CAMPUS, Atlanta, GA 30328

General Information Proprietary, coed, comprehensive institution. *Graduate housing:* On-campus housing not available.

GRADUATE UNITS

Program in Global Technology Management *Degree program information:* Part-time and evening/weekend programs available. Postbaccalaureate distance learning degree programs offered. Offers global technology management (MBA). Electronic applications accepted.

Program in Information Technology *Degree program information:* Part-time and evening/weekend programs available. Offers information technology (MIT). Electronic applications accepted.

AMERICAN INTERCONTINENTAL UNIVERSITY–LONDON, London W1U 4RY, United Kingdom

General Information Proprietary, coed, comprehensive institution. *Graduate housing:* Room and/or apartments available on a first-come, first-served basis to single students. Housing application deadline: 9/18.

GRADUATE UNITS

Program in Business Administration Offers international business (MBA). Electronic applications accepted.

Program in Information Technology Offers information technology (MIT). Electronic applications accepted.

AMERICAN INTERCONTINENTAL UNIVERSITY ONLINE, Hoffman Estates, IL 60192

General Information Proprietary, coed, comprehensive institution.

GRADUATE UNITS

Program in Business Administration *Degree program information:* Evening/weekend programs available. Postbaccalaureate distance learning degree programs offered (no on-campus study). Offers accounting and finance (MBA); finance (MBA); healthcare management (MBA); human resource management (MBA); international business (MBA); management (MBA); marketing (MBA); operations management (MBA); organizational psychology and development (MBA); project management (MBA). Electronic applications accepted.

Program in Education *Degree program information:* Evening/weekend programs available. Postbaccalaureate distance learning degree programs offered (no on-campus study). Offers curriculum and instruction (M Ed); educational assessment and evaluation (M Ed); instructional technology (M Ed); leadership of educational organizations (M Ed). Electronic applications accepted.

Program in Information Technology *Degree program information:* Evening/weekend programs available. Postbaccalaureate distance learning degree programs offered (no on-campus study). Offers Internet security (MIT); IT project management (MIT). Electronic applications accepted.

AMERICAN INTERCONTINENTAL UNIVERSITY SOUTH FLORIDA, Weston, FL 33326

General Information Proprietary, coed, comprehensive institution.

GRADUATE UNITS

Program in Information Technology *Degree program information:* Part-time and evening/weekend programs available. Offers Internet security (MIT); wireless computer forensics (MIT). Electronic applications accepted.

Program in Instructional Technology *Degree program information:* Part-time and evening/weekend programs available. Offers instructional technology (M Ed). Electronic applications accepted.

Program in International Business *Degree program information:* Part-time and evening/weekend programs available. Postbaccalaureate distance learning degree programs offered. Offers accounting and finance (MBA); human resource management (MBA); management (MBA); marketing (MBA). Electronic applications accepted.

AMERICAN INTERNATIONAL COLLEGE, Springfield, MA 01109-3189

General Information Independent, coed, comprehensive institution. *Graduate housing:* Room and/or apartments available on a first-come, first-served basis to single students; on-campus housing not available to married students. Housing application deadline: 6/1.

GRADUATE UNITS

Center for Human Resource Development *Degree program information:* Evening/weekend programs available. Offers human resource development (MA). Electronic applications accepted.

AMERICAN JEWISH UNIVERSITY, Bel Air, CA 90077-1599

General Information Independent-religious, coed, comprehensive institution. *Graduate housing:* Rooms and/or apartments available on a first-come, first-served basis to single and married students. Housing application deadline: 6/1.

GRADUATE UNITS

Graduate School *Degree program information:* Part-time and evening/weekend programs available.

David Lieber School of Graduate Studies *Degree program information:* Part-time and evening/weekend programs available. Offers general nonprofit administration (MBA); Jewish communal studies (MAJCS); Jewish nonprofit administration (MBA).

Fingerhut School of Education Offers education (MA Ed); education for working professionals (MA Ed).

Ziegler School of Rabbinic Studies Offers rabbinic studies (MARS).

AMERICAN PUBLIC UNIVERSITY SYSTEM, Charles Town, WV 25414

General Information Proprietary, coed, comprehensive institution. *Graduate housing:* On-campus housing not available.

GRADUATE UNITS

AMU/APU Graduate Programs *Degree program information:* Part-time and evening/weekend programs available. Postbaccalaureate distance learning degree programs offered (no on-campus study). Offers air warfare (MA Military Studies); American Revolution (MA Military Studies); business administration (MBA); Civil War (MA Military Studies); criminal justice (MA); defense management (MA Military Studies); emergency and disaster management (MA); environmental policy and management (MS); fire science management (MA); global engagement (MA); history (MA); homeland security (MA); humanities (MA); intelligence (MA Military Studies, MA Strategic Intelligence); international peace and conflict resolution (MA); international relations and conflict resolution (MA); joint warfare (MA Military Studies); land warfare international perspective (MA Military Studies); management (MA); military history (MA); military leadership (MA Military Studies); national security studies (MA); naval warfare international (MA Military Studies); naval warfare US (MA Military Studies); political science (MA); public administration (MA); public health (MA); security management (MA); space studies (MS); special ops/LIC (MA Military Studies); sports management (MA); transportation and logistics management (MA); transportation management (MA); unconventional warfare (MA Military Studies); World War II (MA Military Studies). Programs offered via distance learning only. Electronic applications accepted.

AMERICAN SENTINEL UNIVERSITY, Englewood, CO 80112

General Information Private, coed, upper-level institution.

GRADUATE UNITS

Graduate Programs *Degree program information:* Part-time and evening/weekend programs available. Postbaccalaureate distance learning degree programs offered (no on-campus study). Electronic applications accepted.

AMERICAN UNIVERSITY, Washington, DC 20016-8001

General Information Independent-religious, coed, university. CGS member. *Enrollment:* 11,684 graduate, professional, and undergraduate students; 2,849 full-time matriculated graduate/professional students (1,700 women), 2,353 part-time matriculated graduate/professional students (1,461 women). *Enrollment by degree level:* 1,460 first professional, 3,015 master's, 455 doctoral, 272 other advanced degrees. *Graduate faculty:* 591 full-time (274 women), 500 part-time/adjunct (224 women). *Tuition:* Full-time $21,204; part-time $1178 per credit hour. *Required fees:* $380. Part-time tuition and fees vary according to course load and program. *Graduate housing:* On-campus housing not available. *Student services:* Campus employment opportunities, campus safety program, career counseling, child daycare facilities, exercise/wellness program, free psychological counseling, grant writing training, international student services, low-cost health insurance, multicultural affairs office, services for students with disabilities, teacher training. *Library facilities:* American University Bender Library plus 1 other. *Online resources:* library catalog, web page, access to other libraries' catalogs. *Collection:* 1.1 million titles, 34,838 serial subscriptions, 50,966 audiovisual materials.

Computer facilities: 700 computers available on campus for general student use. A campuswide network can be accessed from student residence rooms and from off campus. Online class registration, printers, scanners, online course support are available. *Web address:* http://www.american.edu/.

General Application Contact: 202-885-1000.

GRADUATE UNITS

College of Arts and Sciences Students: 498 full-time (359 women), 867 part-time (617 women); includes 258 minority (133 African Americans, 16 American Indian/Alaska Native, 45 Asian Americans or Pacific Islanders, 64 Hispanic Americans), 124 international. Average age 28. 1,624 applicants, 57% accepted, 456 enrolled. *Faculty:* 257 full-time (127 women), 190 part-time/adjunct (117 women). Expenses: Contact institution. *Financial support:* Fellowships, research assistantships with full and partial tuition reimbursements, teaching assistantships with full and partial tuition reimbursements, career-related internships or fieldwork, Federal Work-Study, institutionally sponsored loans, scholarships/grants, traineeships, tuition waivers (full and partial), and unspecified assistantships available. Support available to part-time students. Financial award applicants required to submit FAFSA. In 2008, 405 master's, 45 doctorates, 31 other advanced degrees awarded. *Degree program information:* Part-time and evening/weekend programs available. Offers anthropology (PhD); applied microeconomics (Certificate); applied science (MS); applied statistics (Certificate); art history (MA); arts and sciences (M Ed, MA, MAT, MFA, MS, PhD, Certificate); arts management (MA, Certificate); behavior, cognition, and neuroscience (PhD); biology (MA, MS); chemistry (MS); clinical psychology (PhD); computer science (MS, Certificate); creative writing (MFA); economics (MA, PhD); environmental science (MS); ethics, peace, and global affairs (MA); experimental/biological psychology (MA); French (Certificate); general psychology (MA); history (MA, PhD); interdisciplinary studies (MA); international economic relations (Certificate); literature (MA); marine science (MS); mathematics (MA); painting, sculpture and printmaking (MFA); personality/social psychology (MA); philosophy (MA); psychology (MA, PhD); public anthropology (MA, Certificate); Russian (Certificate); social research (Certificate); sociology (MA); Spanish: Latin American studies (MA, Certificate); statistics (MS, Certificate); teaching English to speakers of other languages (MA, Certificate); toxicology (MS); translation (Certificate). *Application deadline:* For fall admission, 2/1 for domestic students; for spring admission, 10/1 for domestic students. *Application fee:* $80. Electronic applications accepted. *Application Contact:* Kathleen Clowery, Director, Graduate Admissions, 202-885-3621, Fax: 202-885-1505. *Dean,* Dr. Peter Starr, 202-885-2446, Fax: 202-885-2429.

School of Education, Teaching, and Health Students: 64 full-time (57 women), 409 part-time (316 women); includes 102 minority (59 African Americans, 13 American Indian/Alaska Native, 12 Asian Americans or Pacific Islanders, 18 Hispanic Americans), 5 international. Average age 26. 308 applicants, 87% accepted, 205 enrolled. *Faculty:* 16 full-time (10 women), 52 part-time/adjunct (33 women). Expenses: Contact institution. *Financial support:* Fellowships, research assistantships with full and partial tuition reimbursements, teaching assistantships with full and partial tuition reimbursements, career-related internships or fieldwork, Federal Work-Study, and institutionally sponsored loans available. Support available to part-time students. Financial award application deadline: 2/1; financial award applicants required to submit FAFSA. In 2008, 195 master's, 6 other advanced degrees awarded. *Degree program information:* Part-time and evening/weekend programs available. Offers curriculum and instruction (M Ed, Certificate); early childhood education (MAT, Certificate); elementary education (MAT); English for speakers of other languages (MAT, Certificate); health promotion management (MS); international training and development (MAT); international training and education (MA); nutrition education (Certificate); secondary teaching (MAT, Certificate); special education (MA); special education: learning disabilities (MA). *Application deadline:* For fall admission, 2/1 priority date for domestic students; for spring admission, 10/1 priority date for domestic students. Applications are processed on a rolling basis. *Application fee:* $80. *Application Contact:* Kathleen Clowery, Director, Graduate Admissions, 202-885-3621, Fax: 202-885-1505. *Dean,* Dr. Sarah Irvine-Belson, 202-885-3714, Fax: 202-885-1187, E-mail: educate@american.edu.

Kogod School of Business Students: 170 full-time (71 women), 262 part-time (126 women); includes 111 minority (51 African Americans, 39 Asian Americans or Pacific Islanders, 21 Hispanic Americans), 70 international. Average age 29. 556 applicants, 60% accepted, 133 enrolled. *Faculty:* 57 full-time (20 women), 35 part-time/adjunct (8 women). Expenses: Contact institution. *Financial support:* In 2008–09, 28 students received support; fellowships, research assistantships with partial tuition reimbursements available, career-related internships or fieldwork, Federal Work-Study, institutionally sponsored loans, and tuition waivers (partial) available. Support available to part-time students. Financial award application deadline: 2/1; financial award applicants required to submit FAFSA. In 2008, 156 master's awarded. *Degree program information:* Part-time and evening/weekend programs available. Postbaccalaureate distance learning degree programs offered. Offers accounting (MS, Certificate); business (MBA, MS, Certificate); consulting (MBA); corporate finance: commercial banking (MBA); corporate finance: corporate financial management (MBA); corporate finance: investment banking (MBA); entrepreneurship (MBA); finance (MS, Certificate); global emerging markets (MBA); information systems (MS, Certificate); international business (Certificate); international trade and global supply chain management (MBA); leadership (MBA); marketing management (MBA); marketing research (MBA); real estate (MS); taxation (MS, Certificate). *Application deadline:* For fall admission, 2/1 priority date for domestic students. Applications are processed on a rolling basis. *Application fee:* $100. *Application Contact:* Shannon Demko, Associate Director of Graduate Admissions, 202-885-1994, Fax: 202-885-1108, E-mail: demko@american.edu. *Dean,* Dr. Richard Durand, 202-885-1900, Fax: 202-885-1955.

School of Communication Students: 126 full-time (75 women), 199 part-time (126 women); includes 76 minority (49 African Americans, 14 Asian Americans or Pacific Islanders, 13 Hispanic Americans), 29 international. Average age 27. 506 applicants, 66% accepted, 177 enrolled. *Faculty:* 42 full-time (18 women), 15 part-time/adjunct. Expenses: Contact institution. *Financial support:* In 2008–09, 64 students received support, including 6 fellowships with partial tuition reimbursements available (averaging $23,000 per year), 15 research assistantships with partial tuition reimbursements available (averaging $18,000 per year), 15 teaching assistantships with partial tuition reimbursements available (averaging $18,000 per year); career-related internships or fieldwork, Federal Work-Study, institutionally sponsored loans, scholarships/grants, and tuition waivers (partial) also available. Financial award application deadline: 2/1; financial award applicants required to submit FAFSA. In 2008, 159 master's awarded. *Degree program information:* Part-time and evening/weekend programs available. Offers broadcast journalism (MA); communication (MA, MFA); film and electronic media (MFA); film and video (MA); interactive journalism (MA); international media (MA); news media studies (MA); print journalism (MA); producing film and video (MA); producing for film and video (MA); public communication (MA). *Application deadline:* For fall admission, 2/1 priority date for domestic students, 4/1 priority date for international students; for spring admission, 11/15 for domestic students. Applications are processed on a rolling basis. *Application fee:* $50. Electronic applications accepted. *Application Contact:* Sharmeen Ahsan-Bracciale, Graduate Admissions Office, 202-885-2040, Fax: 202-885-2019, E-mail: sharmeen@american.edu. *Dean,* Dean Larry Kirkman, 202-885-2058, Fax: 202-885-2099, E-mail: larry@american.edu.

School of International Service Students: 519 full-time (317 women), 335 part-time (205 women); includes 157 minority (54 African Americans, 2 American Indian/Alaska Native, 45 Asian Americans or Pacific Islanders, 56 Hispanic Americans), 116 international. Average age 27. 1,901 applicants, 58% accepted, 277 enrolled. *Faculty:* 70 full-time (28 women), 51 part-time/adjunct (20 women). Expenses: Contact institution. *Financial support:* Career-

American University (continued)

related internships or fieldwork, Federal Work-Study, and institutionally sponsored loans available. Financial award application deadline: 1/15. In 2008, 358 master's, 5 doctorates, 9 other advanced degrees awarded. *Degree program information:* Part-time and evening/weekend programs available. Offers comparative and regional studies (Certificate); cross-cultural communication (Certificate); development management (MS); ethics, peace, and global affairs (MA); European studies (Certificate); global environmental policy (MA, Certificate); international affairs (MA); international communication (MA, Certificate); international development (MA, Certificate); international development management (Certificate); international economic policy (Certificate); international economic relations (Certificate); international media (MA); international peace and conflict resolution (MA, Certificate); international relations (PhD); international service (MIS); peace building (Certificate); the Americas (Certificate); United States foreign policy (Certificate). *Application deadline:* For fall admission, 1/15 priority date for domestic students; for spring admission, 10/1 priority date for domestic students. Applications are processed on a rolling basis. *Application fee:* $50. *Application Contact:* Yasmin Quianzon, Director of Graduate Admissions and Financial Aid, 202-885-2496, Fax: 202-885-1109. *Dean*, Dr. Louis W. Goodman, 202-885-1600, Fax: 202-885-2494.

School of Public Affairs Students: 245 full-time (156 women), 302 part-time (192 women); includes 117 minority (70 African Americans, 5 American Indian/Alaska Native, 30 Asian Americans or Pacific Islanders, 12 Hispanic Americans), 33 international. Average age 30. 817 applicants, 71% accepted, 193 enrolled. *Faculty:* 61 full-time (30 women), 47 part-time/adjunct (14 women). Expenses: Contact institution. *Financial support:* Fellowships, research assistantships, teaching assistantships, career-related internships or fieldwork, Federal Work-Study, institutionally sponsored loans, and tuition waivers (full and partial) available. Financial award application deadline: 2/1. In 2008, 203 master's, 7 doctorates, 5 other advanced degrees awarded. *Degree program information:* Part-time and evening/weekend programs available. Offers advanced organization development (Certificate); fundamentals of organization development (Certificate); justice, law and society (MS, PhD); key executive leadership (MPA); leadership for organizational change (Certificate); non-profit management (Certificate); organization development (MSOD); organizational change (Certificate); political science (MA, PhD); public administration (MPA, PhD); public affairs (MA, MPA, MPP, MS, MSOD, PhD, Certificate); public financial management (Certificate); public management (Certificate); public policy (MPP); public policy analysis (Certificate); women, policy and political leadership (Certificate). *Application deadline:* For fall admission, 2/1 for domestic students; for spring admission, 11/1 for domestic students. *Application fee:* $55. *Application Contact:* Brenda Manley, Admissions and Financial Aid Manager, 202-885-6202, Fax: 202-885-2355, E-mail: bmanley@american.edu. *Dean*, Dr. William Leo Grande, 202-885-6234.

Washington College of Law Students: 1,266 full-time (709 women), 389 part-time (193 women); includes 511 minority (145 African Americans, 19 American Indian/Alaska Native, 158 Asian Americans or Pacific Islanders, 189 Hispanic Americans), 167 international. Average age 26. 8,840 applicants, 24% accepted, 553 enrolled. *Faculty:* 82 full-time (39 women), 125 part-time/adjunct (39 women). Expenses: Contact institution. *Financial support:* In 2008–09, 379 students received support; fellowships with full tuition reimbursements available, career-related internships or fieldwork, Federal Work-Study, institutionally sponsored loans, and tuition waivers (full and partial) available. Support available to part-time students. Financial award application deadline: 2/15; financial award applicants required to submit FAFSA. In 2008, 475 first professional degrees, 135 master's, 1 doctorate awarded. *Degree program information:* Part-time and evening/weekend programs available. Offers human rights and the law (Certificate); international legal studies (LL M, Certificate); judicial sciences (SJD); law (JD, LL M, SJD, Certificate); law and government (LL M). *Application deadline:* Applications are processed on a rolling basis. *Application fee:* $70. *Application Contact:* Akira Shiroma, Assistant Dean of Admissions, 202-274-4101, Fax: 202-274-4107, E-mail: shiroma@wcl.american.edu. *Dean*, Dr. Claudio Grossman, 202-274-4000, Fax: 202-274-4107, E-mail: wcladmit@american.edu.

THE AMERICAN UNIVERSITY IN CAIRO, 11511 Cairo, Egypt

General Information Independent, coed, comprehensive institution. *Graduate housing:* Room and/or apartments available to single students; on-campus housing not available to married students.

GRADUATE UNITS

Center for Migration and Refugee Studies Offers forced migration and refugee studies (Diploma); migration and refugee studies (MA).

Graduate Studies and Research *Degree program information:* Part-time programs available. Electronic applications accepted.

School of Business, Economics and Communication *Degree program information:* Part-time programs available. Offers business, economics and communication (MA, MBA, MPA, Diploma); economics (MA); journalism and mass communication (MA); management (MBA, MPA, Diploma); television and digital journalism (MA). Electronic applications accepted.

School of Humanities and Social Sciences *Degree program information:* Part-time programs available. Offers Arab language and literature (MA); English and comparative literature (MA); gender and development (MA, Diploma); gender and justice (MA, Diploma); gender and women's studies in the Middle East and North Africa (MA, Diploma); humanities and social sciences (MA, Diploma); Islamic art and architecture (MA); Islamic studies (Diploma); Middle East studies (MA, Diploma); Middle Eastern history (MA); political science (MA); public policy and administration (MA, Diploma); sociology and anthropology (MA); teaching Arabic as a foreign language (MA); teaching English as a foreign language (MA, Diploma). Electronic applications accepted.

School of Sciences and Engineering Offers biotechnology (MS); computer science and engineering (MS); construction engineering (M Eng, MS); sciences and engineering (M Eng, MS, Diploma). Electronic applications accepted.

THE AMERICAN UNIVERSITY IN DUBAI, Dubai, United Arab Emirates

General Information Proprietary, coed, comprehensive institution. *Enrollment:* 90 full-time matriculated graduate/professional students (42 women), 29 part-time matriculated graduate/professional students (14 women). *Enrollment by degree level:* 119 master's. *Graduate faculty:* 10 full-time (1 woman). *Graduate housing:* Room and/or apartments available on a first-come, first-served basis to single students; on-campus housing not available to married students. Housing application deadline: 7/31. *Student services:* Campus employment opportunities, campus safety program, career counseling, free psychological counseling, international student services, multicultural affairs office, services for students with disabilities, writing training. *Library facilities:* University Library. *Online resources:* library catalog, web page, access to other libraries' catalogs. *Collection:* 26,047 titles, 200 serial subscriptions, 216 audiovisual materials.

Computer facilities: Computer purchase and lease plans are available. 270 computers available on campus for general student use. A campuswide network can be accessed from student residence rooms and from off campus. *Web address:* http://www.aud.edu.

General Application Contact: Carol Maalouf, Director of Admissions, 971-4-399-9000, Fax: 971-4-399-8899, E-mail: admissions@aud.edu.

GRADUATE UNITS

Master in Business Administration Program Students: 90 full-time (42 women), 29 part-time (14 women). *Faculty:* 10 full-time (1 woman). Expenses: Contact institution. *Financial support:* Scholarships/grants available. In 2008, 39 master's awarded. *Degree program information:* Part-time and evening/weekend programs available. Offers general (MBA); healthcare management (MBA); international finance (MBA); international marketing (MBA); management of construction enterprises (MBA). *Application deadline:* Applications are processed on a rolling basis. *Application fee:* $54. Electronic applications accepted. *Application Contact:* Carol Maalouf, Director of Admissions, 971-4-399-9000, Fax: 971-4-399-8899, E-mail: admissions@aud.edu. *Director of Admissions*, Carol Maalouf, 971-4-399-9000, Fax: 971-4-399-8899, E-mail: admissions@aud.edu.

AMERICAN UNIVERSITY OF ARMENIA, Yerevan 3750198, Armenia

General Information Independent, coed, graduate-only institution.

GRADUATE UNITS

Graduate Programs

THE AMERICAN UNIVERSITY OF ATHENS, GR-115 25 Athens, Greece

General Information Independent, coed, comprehensive institution. *Graduate housing:* Room and/or apartments guaranteed to single students; on-campus housing not available to married students. *Research affiliation:* Dimokritos (engineering and physics), Pasteur Institute (biomedical sciences).

GRADUATE UNITS

The School of Graduate Studies Offers biomedical sciences (MS); business (MBA); business communication (MA); computer sciences (MS); engineering and applied sciences (MS); politics and policy making (MA); systems engineering (MS); telecommunications (MS).

AMERICAN UNIVERSITY OF BEIRUT, Beirut 1107 2020, Lebanon

General Information Independent, coed, university. *Graduate housing:* Room and/or apartments available on a first-come, first-served basis to single students; on-campus housing not available to married students. Housing application deadline: 8/10. *Research affiliation:* University of California, Davis (engineering), Lebanese American University (student exchange), University of Paris—7 Denis Diderot (medicine), University of Poitiers (medicine), University of Cornell (agriculture), The University of Palermo (Italy).

GRADUATE UNITS

Graduate Programs *Degree program information:* Part-time and evening/weekend programs available.

Faculty of Agricultural and Food Sciences *Degree program information:* Part-time programs available. Offers agricultural economics (MS); animal sciences (MS); ecosystem management (MSES); food technology (MS); irrigation (MS); mechanization (MS); nutrition (MS); plant protection (MS); plant science (MS); poultry science (MS); soils (MS).

Faculty of Arts and Sciences *Degree program information:* Part-time programs available. Offers anthropology (MA); Arabic language and literature (MA); archaeology (MA); biology (MS); chemistry (MS); computer science (MS); economics (MA); education (MA); English language (MA); English literature (MA); environmental policy planning (MSES); financial economics (MAFE); geology (MS); history (MA); mathematics (MA, MS); Middle Eastern studies (MA); philosophy (MA); physics (MS); political studies (MA); psychology (MA); public administration (MA); sociology (MA); statistics (MA, MS).

Faculty of Engineering and Architecture *Degree program information:* Part-time programs available. Offers civil engineering (ME, PhD); electrical and computer engineering (ME, PhD); engineering management (MEM); environmental and water resources (ME); environmental and water resources engineering (PhD); environmental technology (MSES); mechanical engineering (ME, PhD); urban design (MUD); urban planning and policy (MUP). Electronic applications accepted.

Faculty of Health Sciences *Degree program information:* Part-time programs available. Offers environmental sciences (MSES); epidemiology (MS); epidemiology and biostatistics (MPH); health behavior and education (MPH); population health (MS); public health (MPH). Electronic applications accepted.

Faculty of Medicine *Degree program information:* Part-time programs available. Offers biochemistry (MS); human morphology (MS); medicine (MD); microbiology and immunology (MS); neuroscience (MS); pharmacology and therapeutics (MS); physiology (MS).

Olayan School of Business *Degree program information:* Part-time and evening/weekend programs available. Offers business administration (MBA); executive business administration (EMBA).

School of Nursing *Degree program information:* Part-time programs available. Offers nursing (MSN).

THE AMERICAN UNIVERSITY OF PARIS, F-75007 Paris, France

General Information Independent, coed, comprehensive institution.

GRADUATE UNITS

Graduate Programs

AMERICAN UNIVERSITY OF PUERTO RICO, Bayamón, PR 00960-2037

General Information Independent, coed, comprehensive institution.

GRADUATE UNITS

Program in Criminal Justice Offers criminal justice (MA).

Program in Education Offers art history (M Ed); elementary education (4-6) (M Ed); elementary education (k-3) (M Ed); general science education (M Ed); physical education (k-12) (M Ed); special education at secondary level (transition) (M Ed).

AMERICAN UNIVERSITY OF SHARJAH, Sharjah, United Arab Emirates

General Information Independent, coed, comprehensive institution. *Enrollment by degree level:* 254 master's. *Graduate faculty:* 35 full-time (7 women). *Graduate tuition:* Tuition and fees charges are reported in United Arab Emirates dirhams. *Tuition:* Full-time 58,500 United Arab Emirates dirhams; part-time 3250 United Arab Emirates dirhams per credit hour. One-time fee: 300 United Arab Emirates dirhams. *Graduate housing:* Room and/or apartments available on a first-come, first-served basis to single students; on-campus housing not available to married students. *Student services:* Campus employment opportunities, campus safety program, career counseling, exercise/wellness program, free psychological counseling, international student services, low-cost health insurance. *Research affiliation:* Cambridge University, UK (Water Resources & Environmental Engineering), Mohammed Bin Rashid Foundation (Education), TESOL Arabian (TESOL Education). *Web address:* http://www.aus.edu/.

General Application Contact: Ghadi Sami, Undergraduate and Graduate Admissions Manager, E-mail: gsami@aus.edu.

GRADUATE UNITS

Graduate Programs Students: 66 full-time (36 women), 188 part-time (83 women). Average age 28. 302 applicants, 65% accepted, 131 enrolled. *Faculty:* 35 full-time (7 women). Expenses: Contact institution. In 2008, 74 master's awarded. *Degree program information:* Part-time and evening/weekend programs available. Offers business (EMBA, MBA); chemical engineering (MS Ch E); civil engineering (MSCE); computer engineering (MS); electrical engineering (MSEE); mechanical engineering (MSME); mechatronics engineering (MS); public administration (MPA); teaching English to speakers of other languages (MA); translation and interpreting (MA); urban planning (MUP). *Application deadline:* For fall admission, 7/30 priority date for domestic students, 7/15 priority date for international students; for spring admission, 12/31 priority date for domestic students, 12/16 for international students. Applications are processed on a rolling basis. *Application fee:* $300. Electronic applications accepted. *Application Contact:* Ghada S Sami, Admissions Manager, 971-65151006 Ext. 1006, Fax: 971-65151020, E-mail: graduateadmission@aus.edu. *Admissions Manager*, Ghada S Sami, 971-65151006 Ext. 1006, Fax: 971-65151020, E-mail: graduateadmission@aus.edu.

AMRIDGE UNIVERSITY, Montgomery, AL 36117

General Information Independent-religious, coed, university. *Enrollment:* 720 graduate, professional, and undergraduate students; 131 full-time matriculated graduate/professional students (61 women), 218 part-time matriculated graduate/professional students (119 women). *Enrollment by degree level:* 58 first professional, 222 master's, 69 doctoral. *Graduate faculty:* 44 full-time (9 women), 18 part-time/adjunct (7 women). *Tuition:* Full-time $9630; part-time $535 per semester hour. *Required fees:* $600 per term. Tuition and fees vary according to course load and degree level. *Graduate housing:* On-campus housing not available. *Student services:* Campus employment opportunities, campus safety program, career counseling, services for students with disabilities. *Library facilities:* Southern Christian University Library. *Online resources:* library catalog, web page, access to other libraries' catalogs. *Collection:* 80,000 titles, 1,200 serial subscriptions, 800 audiovisual materials.

Computer facilities: 5 computers available on campus for general student use. A campuswide network can be accessed from off campus. Online class registration, access to over 20 million monographs and journals online are available. *Web address:* http://www.amridgeuniversity.edu/.

General Application Contact: Ora Davis, Admissions Officer, 334-387-3877 Ext. 7524, Fax: 334-387-3878, E-mail: oradavis@amridgeuniversity.edu.

GRADUATE UNITS

Graduate and Professional Programs Students: 131 full-time (61 women), 218 part-time (119 women); includes 174 minority (164 African Americans, 1 American Indian/Alaska Native, 1 Asian American or Pacific Islander, 8 Hispanic Americans). Average age 35. *Faculty:* 44 full-time (9 women), 18 part-time/adjunct (7 women). Expenses: Contact institution. *Financial support:* Federal Work-Study and scholarships/grants available. Support available to part-time students. Financial award applicants required to submit FAFSA. *Degree program information:* Part-time and evening/weekend programs available. Postbaccalaureate distance learning degree programs offered (no on-campus study). Offers behavioral leadership and management (MA); biblical studies (MA, PhD); family therapy (D Min); leadership and management (MS); marriage and family therapy (M Div, MA, PhD); ministerial leadership (M Div, MS); pastoral counseling (M Div, MS); practical theology (MA); professional counseling (M Div, MA); theology (M Div, D Min). *Application deadline:* For fall admission, 9/1 priority date for domestic students; for spring admission, 1/1 priority date for domestic students. Applications are processed on a rolling basis. *Application fee:* $75. Electronic applications accepted. *Application Contact:* Ora Davis, Admissions Officer, 334-387-3877 Ext. 7524, Fax: 334-387-3878, E-mail: oradavis@amridgeuniversity.edu. *Director of Enrollment Management,* Rick Johnson, 800-351-4040 Ext. 7513, Fax: 334-387-3878, E-mail: rickjohnson@amridgeuniversity.edu.

ANDERSON UNIVERSITY, Anderson, IN 46012-3495

General Information Independent-religious, coed, comprehensive institution. *Graduate housing:* Room and/or apartments available to single students; on-campus housing not available to married students. Housing application deadline: 6/1.

GRADUATE UNITS

Falls School of Business Offers accountancy (MA); business administration (MBA, DBA).

School of Education Offers education (M Ed).

School of Theology *Degree program information:* Part-time programs available. Offers missions (MA); theology (M Div, MTS, D Min).

ANDERSON UNIVERSITY, Anderson, SC 29621-4035

General Information Independent-religious, coed, comprehensive institution.

GRADUATE UNITS

College of Business Offers business (MBA).

College of Education Offers education (M Ed).

Command College Postbaccalaureate distance learning degree programs offered. Offers criminal justice (MA).

School of Christian Ministry Postbaccalaureate distance learning degree programs offered. Offers Christian ministry (M Min).

ANDOVER NEWTON THEOLOGICAL SCHOOL, Newton Centre, MA 02459-2243

General Information Independent-religious, coed, graduate-only institution. *Graduate housing:* Rooms and/or apartments available on a first-come, first-served basis to single and married students. Housing application deadline: 7/1.

GRADUATE UNITS

Graduate and Professional Programs *Degree program information:* Part-time programs available. Offers divinity (M Div); general (MA); psychology and religion (MA); religious education (MA); research (MA); sacred theology (STM); theology (D Min); theology and the arts (MA). Electronic applications accepted.

ANDREW JACKSON UNIVERSITY, Birmingham, AL 35244

General Information Private, coed, comprehensive institution. *Graduate housing:* On-campus housing not available.

GRADUATE UNITS

Brian Tracy College of Business and Entrepreneurship *Degree program information:* Part-time and evening/weekend programs available. Postbaccalaureate distance learning degree programs offered (no on-campus study). Offers entrepreneurship (MBA); finance (MBA); health services management (MBA); hospitality and tourism management (MBA); human resource management (MBA); international business (MBA); management (MBA); marketing (MBA). Electronic applications accepted.

Jeffrey D. Rubenstein College of Criminal Justice *Degree program information:* Part-time and evening/weekend programs available. Postbaccalaureate distance learning degree programs offered (no on-campus study). Offers criminal justice (MPA, MS); public administration (MPA). Electronic applications accepted.

ANDREWS UNIVERSITY, Berrien Springs, MI 49104

General Information Independent-religious, coed, university. CGS member. *Enrollment:* 3,419 graduate, professional, and undergraduate students; 578 full-time matriculated graduate/professional students (185 women), 775 part-time matriculated graduate/professional students (211 women). *Enrollment by degree level:* 363 first professional, 476 master's, 486 doctoral, 28 other advanced degrees. *Graduate faculty:* 162 full-time (49 women), 20 part-time/adjunct (13 women). *Tuition:* Full-time $18,360; part-time $765 per credit hour. *Required fees:* $476; $765 per credit hour. $238 per semester. Tuition and fees vary according to degree level. *Graduate housing:* Rooms and/or apartments available on a first-come, first-served basis to single and married students. Typical cost: $5916 per year ($9500 including board) for single students. *Student services:* Campus employment opportunities, campus safety program, career counseling, child daycare facilities, free psychological counseling, international student services, low-cost health insurance. *Library facilities:* James White Library plus 2 others. *Online resources:* library catalog, web page, access to other libraries' catalogs. *Collection:* 615,937 titles, 39,000 serial subscriptions, 55,998 audiovisual materials. *Research affiliation:* RAND Corporation (drug abuse), Argonne National Laboratory (physics), Deutches Electronen Synchroton (physics).

Computer facilities: Computer purchase and lease plans are available. 130 computers available on campus for general student use. A campuswide network can be accessed from student residence rooms and from off campus. Online class registration, degree audit are available. *Web address:* http://www.andrews.edu/.

General Application Contact: Carolyn Hurst, Supervisor of Graduate Admission, 800-253-2874, Fax: 269-471-3228, E-mail: graduate@andrews.edu.

GRADUATE UNITS

School of Graduate Studies Students: 578 full-time (185 women), 775 part-time (211 women); includes 505 minority (275 African Americans, 6 American Indian/Alaska Native, 58 Asian Americans or Pacific Islanders, 166 Hispanic Americans), 337 international. Average age 38. 589 applicants, 61% accepted, 304 enrolled. *Faculty:* 162 full-time (49 women), 20 part-time/adjunct (13 women). Expenses: Contact institution. *Financial support:* Fellowships, research assistantships, teaching assistantships, career-related internships or fieldwork, Federal Work-Study, institutionally sponsored loans, scholarships/grants, tuition waivers (partial), and unspecified assistantships available. Support available to part-time students. Financial award applicants required to submit FAFSA. In 2008, 103 first professional degrees, 177 master's, 44 doctorates, 8 other advanced degrees awarded. *Degree program information:* Part-time and evening/weekend programs available. Postbaccalaureate distance learning degree programs offered (minimal on-campus study). *Application deadline:* Applications are processed on a rolling basis. *Application fee:* $40. *Application Contact:* Carolyn Hurst, Supervisor of Graduate Admission, 800-253-2874, Fax: 269-471-6321, E-mail: graduate@andrews.edu. *Interim Dean,* Dr. Emilio Garcia-Marenko, 269-471-3405.

College of Arts and Sciences Students: 94 full-time (67 women), 35 part-time (30 women); includes 45 minority (30 African Americans, 4 Asian Americans or Pacific Islanders, 11 Hispanic Americans), 43 international. Average age 30. 125 applicants, 66% accepted, 51 enrolled. *Faculty:* 80 full-time (33 women), 14 part-time/adjunct (10 women). Expenses: Contact institution. *Financial support:* Fellowships, research assistantships, teaching assistantships, career-related internships or fieldwork, Federal Work-Study, and institutionally sponsored loans available. Financial award applicants required to submit FAFSA. In 2008, 59 master's awarded. *Degree program information:* Part-time and evening/weekend programs available. Offers arts and sciences (M Mus, MA, MAT, MS, MSA, MSMT, MSW, Dr Sc PT, TDPT); biology (MAT, MS); clinical and laboratory sciences (MSMT); communication (MA); community services management (MSA); English (MA, MAT); history (MA, MAT); international development (MSA); international language studies (MAT); mathematics and physical science (MS); music (M Mus, MA); nursing (MS); nutrition (MS); physical therapy (DPT, Dr Sc PT, TDPT); social work (MSW). *Application deadline:* Applications are processed on a rolling basis. *Application fee:* $40. *Application Contact:* Carolyn Hurst, Supervisor of Graduate Admission, 800-253-2874, Fax: 269-471-6321, E-mail: graduate@andrews.edu. *Dean,* Dr. Keith Mattingly.

College of Technology Students: 7 full-time (0 women), 4 part-time (0 women), 10 international. Average age 31. 4 applicants, 75% accepted, 2 enrolled. *Faculty:* 6 full-time (1 woman). Expenses: Contact institution. In 2008, 2 master's awarded. Offers software engineering (MS); technology (MS). *Application deadline:* Applications are processed on a rolling basis. *Application fee:* $40. *Application Contact:* Carolyn Hurst, Supervisor of Graduate Admission, 800-253-2874, Fax: 269-471-6321, E-mail: graduate@andrews.edu. *Head,* Dr. Verlyn Benson, 269-471-3413.

Division of Architecture Students: 25 full-time (6 women), 1 (woman) part-time; includes 10 minority (3 African Americans, 1 Asian American or Pacific Islander, 6 Hispanic Americans), 3 international. Average age 24. 34 applicants, 68% accepted, 18 enrolled. *Faculty:* 8 full-time (2 women), 1 part-time/adjunct (0 women). Expenses: Contact institution. In 2008, 29 master's awarded. Offers architecture (M Arch). *Application fee:* $40. *Application Contact:* Carolyn Hurst, Supervisor of Graduate Admission, 800-253-2874, Fax: 269-471-6321, E-mail: graduate@andrews.edu. *Director,* Carey Carscallen, 269-471-6003.

School of Business Students: 4 full-time (3 women), 20 part-time (9 women); includes 9 minority (3 African Americans, 2 Asian Americans or Pacific Islanders, 4 Hispanic Americans), 5 international. Average age 31. *Faculty:* 14 full-time (4 women). Expenses: Contact institution. *Financial support:* Fellowships, research assistantships, teaching assistantships, Federal Work-Study available. In 2008, 16 master's awarded. *Degree program information:* Part-time programs available. Offers accounting, economics and finance (MBA, MSA); business (MBA, MSA); management and marketing (MBA, MSA). *Application deadline:* For fall admission, 8/15 for domestic students. Applications are processed on a rolling basis. *Application fee:* $40. *Application Contact:* Carolyn Hurst, Supervisor of Graduate Admission, 800-253-2874, Fax: 269-471-6321, E-mail: graduate@andrews.edu. *Dean,* Dr. Allen Stembridge, 269-471-3632.

School of Education Students: 71 full-time (46 women), 221 part-time (125 women); includes 105 minority (66 African Americans, 3 American Indian/Alaska Native, 8 Asian Americans or Pacific Islanders, 28 Hispanic Americans), 37 international. Average age 42. *Faculty:* 22 full-time (8 women), 1 (woman) part-time/adjunct. Expenses: Contact institution. *Financial support:* Fellowships, research assistantships, teaching assistantships, career-related internships or fieldwork, Federal Work-Study, institutionally sponsored loans, and tuition waivers (partial) available. Support available to part-time students. In 2008, 45 master's, 21 doctorates, 5 other advanced degrees awarded. *Degree program information:* Part-time programs available. Offers community counseling (MA); counseling psychology (PhD); curriculum and instruction (MA, Ed D, PhD, Ed S); education (MA, MAT, MS, Ed D, PhD, Ed S); educational administration and leadership (MA, Ed D, PhD, Ed S); educational and developmental psychology (MA, Ed D, PhD); educational psychology (Ed D, PhD); elementary education (MAT); leadership (MA, Ed D, PhD); reading (MA); school counseling (MA); school psychology (Ed S); secondary education (MAT); special education (MS); special education/learning disabilities (MS); teacher education (MAT). *Application deadline:* Applications are processed on a rolling basis. *Application fee:* $40. *Application Contact:* Carolyn Hurst, Supervisor of Graduate Admission, 800-253-2874, Fax: 269-471-6321, E-mail: graduate@andrews.edu. *Dean,* Dr. James R. Jeffery, 269-471-3464.

Seventh-day Adventist Theological Seminary Students: 377 full-time (63 women), 494 part-time (46 women); includes 336 minority (173 African Americans, 3 American Indian/Alaska Native, 43 Asian Americans or Pacific Islanders, 117 Hispanic Americans), 239 international. Average age 41. *Faculty:* 35 full-time (3 women), 1 (woman) part-time/adjunct. Expenses: Contact institution. *Financial support:* Fellowships, research assistantships, teaching assistantships, career-related internships or fieldwork, Federal Work-Study, and institutionally sponsored loans available. In 2008, 103 first professional degrees, 26 master's, 23 doctorates, 3 other advanced degrees awarded. Offers ministry (M Div, D Min); pastoral ministry (MA); religious education (MA, Ed D, PhD, Ed S); theology (M Th, Th D); youth ministry (MA). *Application deadline:* Applications are processed on a rolling basis. *Application fee:* $40. *Application Contact:* Carolyn Hurst, Director, 800-253-2874, Fax: 269-471-6321. *Dean,* Dr. Denis Fortin, 269-471-3537.

ANGELO STATE UNIVERSITY, San Angelo, TX 76909

General Information State-supported, coed, comprehensive institution. CGS member. *Enrollment:* 6,155 graduate, professional, and undergraduate students; 202 full-time matriculated graduate/professional students (129 women), 291 part-time matriculated graduate/professional students (197 women). *Enrollment by degree level:* 493 master's. *Graduate faculty:* 70 full-time (27 women), 2 part-time/adjunct (0 women). *Graduate housing:* Room and/or apartments available on a first-come, first-served basis to single students; on-campus housing not available to married students. Housing application deadline: 7/15. *Student services:* Campus employment opportunities, campus safety program, career counseling, free psychological counseling, international student services, low-cost health insurance, multicultural affairs office. *Library facilities:* Porter Henderson Library plus 1 other. *Online resources:* library catalog, web page. *Collection:* 590,221 titles, 33,585 serial subscriptions, 18,054 audiovisual materials.

Computer facilities: Computer purchase and lease plans are available. 715 computers available on campus for general student use. A campuswide network can be accessed from student residence rooms and from off campus. Online class registration, Online courses. Other online services: pay tuition, purchase books, purchase parking permits, university calendar, library card catalog and library resources. Discounted hardware and software programs for personally owned computers. are available. *Web address:* http://www.angelo.edu/.

General Application Contact: Thersa Fortin, Graduate Admissions Assistant, 325-942-2169, Fax: 325-942-2194, E-mail: theresa.fortin@angelo.edu.

GRADUATE UNITS

College of Graduate Studies Students: 202 full-time (129 women), 291 part-time (197 women); includes 77 minority (11 African Americans, 3 American Indian/Alaska Native, 8 Asian Americans or Pacific Islanders, 55 Hispanic Americans), 7 international. Average age 32. 211 applicants, 78% accepted, 128 enrolled. *Faculty:* 70 full-time (27 women), 2 part-

Angelo State University (continued)

time/adjunct (0 women). Expenses: Contact institution. *Financial support:* In 2008–09, 274 students received support, including 9 research assistantships (averaging $9,887 per year), 16 teaching assistantships (averaging $10,251 per year); career-related internships or fieldwork, Federal Work-Study, scholarships/grants, and unspecified assistantships also available. Support available to part-time students. Financial award application deadline: 3/1. In 2008, 143 master's awarded. *Degree program information:* Part-time and evening/weekend programs available. Postbaccalaureate distance learning degree programs offered (minimal on-campus study). Offers interdisciplinary studies (MA, MS). *Application deadline:* For fall admission, 7/15 priority date for domestic students, 6/10 for international students; for spring admission, 12/1 priority date for domestic students, 11/1 for international students. Applications are processed on a rolling basis. *Application fee:* $40 ($50 for international students). Electronic applications accepted. *Application Contact:* Theresa Fortin, Graduate Admissions Assistant, 325-942-2169, Fax: 325-942-2194, E-mail: theresa.fortin@angelo.edu. *Dean of the College of Graduate Studies,* Dr. Brian J. May, 325-942-2169, Fax: 325-942-2194, E-mail: brian.may@angelo.edu.

College of Business and Professional Studies Students: 28 full-time (13 women), 23 part-time (13 women); includes 11 minority (2 African Americans, 2 American Indian/Alaska Native, 1 Asian American or Pacific Islander, 6 Hispanic Americans), 4 international. Average age 25. 15 applicants, 100% accepted, 14 enrolled. *Faculty:* 10 full-time (1 woman). Expenses: Contact institution. *Financial support:* In 2008–09, 36 students received support. Career-related internships or fieldwork, Federal Work-Study, and scholarships/grants available. Support available to part-time students. Financial award application deadline: 3/1; financial award applicants required to submit FAFSA. In 2008, 26 master's awarded. *Degree program information:* Part-time and evening/weekend programs available. Offers accounting (MBA); business (MBA, MPAC); business administration (MBA); professional accountancy (MPAC). *Application deadline:* For fall admission, 7/15 priority date for domestic students, 6/10 for international students; for spring admission, 12/1 priority date for domestic students, 11/1 for international students. Applications are processed on a rolling basis. *Application fee:* $40 ($50 for international students). Electronic applications accepted. *Application Contact:* Theresa Fortin, Graduate Admissions Assistant, 325-942-2169, Fax: 325-942-2194, E-mail: theresa.fortin@angelo.edu. *Dean,* Dr. Corbett Gaulden, 325-942-2337, E-mail: corbett.gaulden@angelo.edu.

College of Education Students: 45 full-time (34 women), 173 part-time (117 women); includes 23 minority (2 African Americans, 1 Asian American or Pacific Islander, 20 Hispanic Americans). Average age 30. 49 applicants, 88% accepted, 31 enrolled. *Faculty:* 10 full-time (7 women). Expenses: Contact institution. *Financial support:* In 2008–09, 73 students received support. Career-related internships or fieldwork, Federal Work-Study, scholarships/grants, and unspecified assistantships available. Support available to part-time students. Financial award application deadline: 3/1; financial award applicants required to submit FAFSA. In 2008, 46 master's awarded. *Degree program information:* Part-time and evening/weekend programs available. Offers curriculum and instruction (MA); education (M Ed, MA, MS); educational diagnostics (M Ed); guidance and counseling (M Ed); kinesiology (MS); reading specialist (M Ed); school administration (M Ed); student development and leadership in higher education (M Ed). *Application deadline:* For fall admission, 7/15 priority date for domestic students, 6/10 for international students; for spring admission, 12/1 priority date for domestic students, 11/1 for international students. Applications are processed on a rolling basis. *Application fee:* $40 ($50 for international students). Electronic applications accepted. *Application Contact:* Theresa Fortin, Graduate Admissions Assistant, 325-942-2169, Fax: 325-942-2194, E-mail: theresa.fortin@angelo.edu. *Dean of the College of Education,* Dr. John J. Miazga, 325-942-2212, E-mail: john.miazga@angelo.edu.

College of Liberal and Fine Arts Students: 45 full-time (27 women), 32 part-time (20 women); includes 17 minority (1 African American, 1 American Indian/Alaska Native, 15 Hispanic Americans), 2 international. Average age 27. 38 applicants, 95% accepted, 28 enrolled. *Faculty:* 21 full-time (4 women). Expenses: Contact institution. *Financial support:* In 2008–09, 68 students received support, including 10 teaching assistantships (averaging $10,251 per year); career-related internships or fieldwork, Federal Work-Study, scholarships/grants, and unspecified assistantships also available. Support available to part-time students. Financial award application deadline: 3/1; financial award applicants required to submit FAFSA. In 2008, 35 master's awarded. *Degree program information:* Part-time and evening/weekend programs available. Offers communication systems management (MA); English (MA); history (MA); liberal and fine arts (MA, MPA, MS); psychology (MS); public administration (MPA). *Application deadline:* For fall admission, 7/15 priority date for domestic students, 6/10 for international students; for spring admission, 12/1 priority date for domestic students, 11/1 for international students. Applications are processed on a rolling basis. *Application fee:* $40 ($50 for international students). Electronic applications accepted. *Application Contact:* Theresa Fortin, Graduate Admissions Assistant, 325-942-2169, Fax: 325-942-2194, E-mail: theresa.fortin@angelo.edu. *Dean,* Dr. Kevin Lambert, 325-942-2115, E-mail: kevin.lambert@angelo.edu.

College of Nursing and Allied Health Students: 64 full-time (46 women), 50 part-time (47 women); includes 23 minority (6 African Americans, 6 Asian Americans or Pacific Islanders, 11 Hispanic Americans), 1 international. Average age 32. Expenses: Contact institution. In 2008, 31 master's awarded. Offers adult nurse practitioner (MSN); nurse educator (MSN); nursing and allied health (MSN, DPT); physical therapy (DPT). *Application deadline:* For fall admission, 7/15 priority date for domestic students, 6/10 for international students; for spring admission, 12/1 priority date for domestic students, 11/1 for international students. *Application Contact:* Theresa Fortin, Graduate Admissions Assistant, 325-942-2169, Fax: 325-942-2194, E-mail: theresa.fortin@angelo.edu. *Dean,* Dr. Leslie M. Mayrand, 325-942-2060 Ext. 247, E-mail: leslie.mayrand@angelo.edu.

College of Sciences Students: 22 full-time (11 women), 15 part-time (2 women); includes 3 minority (all Hispanic Americans). Average age 24. 19 applicants, 95% accepted, 16 enrolled. *Faculty:* 26 full-time (13 women), 1 part-time/adjunct (0 women). Expenses: Contact institution. *Financial support:* In 2008–09, 96 students received support, including 9 research assistantships (averaging $9,887 per year), 2 teaching assistantships (averaging $10,251 per year); career-related internships or fieldwork, Federal Work-Study, scholarships/grants, and unspecified assistantships also available. Support available to part-time students. Financial award application deadline: 8/1; financial award applicants required to submit FAFSA. In 2008, 9 master's awarded. *Degree program information:* Part-time and evening/weekend programs available. Offers animal science (MS); biology (MS); sciences (MS). *Application deadline:* For fall admission, 7/15 priority date for domestic students, 6/10 for international students; for spring admission, 12/1 priority date for domestic students, 11/1 for international students. Applications are processed on a rolling basis. *Application fee:* $40 ($50 for international students). Electronic applications accepted. *Application Contact:* Theresa Fortin, Graduate Admissions Assistant, 325-942-2169, Fax: 325-942-2194, E-mail: theresa.fortin@angelo.edu. *Dean,* Dr. Grady Blount, 325-942-2024 Ext. 242, E-mail: grady.blount@angelo.edu.

See Close-Up on page 849.

ANNA MARIA COLLEGE, Paxton, MA 01612

General Information Independent-religious, coed, comprehensive institution. *Enrollment:* 1,333 graduate, professional, and undergraduate students; 53 full-time matriculated graduate/professional students (29 women), 267 part-time matriculated graduate/professional students (172 women). *Enrollment by degree level:* 305 master's, 15 other advanced degrees. *Graduate faculty:* 18 full-time (8 women), 42 part-time/adjunct (16 women). *Tuition:* Part-time $1400 per course. *Graduate housing:* On-campus housing not available. *Student services:* Career counseling, free psychological counseling, grant writing training, services for students with disabilities, teacher training. *Library facilities:* Mondor-Eagen Library. *Online resources:* library catalog, access to other libraries' catalogs. *Collection:* 85,117 titles, 176 serial subscriptions.

Computer facilities: 63 computers available on campus for general student use. A campuswide network can be accessed from student residence rooms. Student account information available. *Web address:* http://www.annamaria.edu/.

General Application Contact: Dennis Braun, Director, Graduate Studies and Continuing Education, 508-849-3293, Fax: 508-819-3362, E-mail: dbraun@annamaria.edu.

GRADUATE UNITS

Graduate Division Students: 53 full-time (29 women), 267 part-time (172 women); includes 17 minority (9 African Americans, 1 American Indian/Alaska Native, 3 Asian Americans or Pacific Islanders, 4 Hispanic Americans), 3 international. Average age 34. *Faculty:* 18 full-time (8 women), 42 part-time/adjunct (16 women). Expenses: Contact institution. *Financial support:* Applicants required to submit FAFSA. In 2008, 101 master's, 17 other advanced degrees awarded. *Degree program information:* Part-time and evening/weekend programs available. Offers art and visual art (MA); business administration (MBA, AC); counseling psychology (MA); criminal justice (MS); early childhood education (M Ed); education (CAGS); elementary education (M Ed); emergency management (MS, Graduate Certificate); English language arts (M Ed); fire science (MA); justice administration (MS); occupational and environmental health and safety (MS); pastoral ministry (MA); public administration (MPA); security management (MA); teacher of visual art (M Ed); visual arts (M Ed). *Application deadline:* For fall admission, 3/1 priority date for domestic and international students; for spring admission, 11/1 priority date for domestic and international students. Applications are processed on a rolling basis. *Application fee:* $40. Electronic applications accepted. *Application Contact:* Dennis Braun, Director, Graduate Studies and Continuing Education, 508-849-3293, Fax: 508-819-3362, E-mail: dbraun@annamaria.edu. *President,* Dr. Jack P. Calareso, 508-849-3333, Fax: 508-849-3343.

ANTIOCH UNIVERSITY LOS ANGELES, Culver City, CA 90230

General Information Independent, coed, upper-level institution. *Graduate housing:* On-campus housing not available.

GRADUATE UNITS

Graduate Programs *Degree program information:* Part-time and evening/weekend programs available. Postbaccalaureate distance learning degree programs offered. Offers clinical psychology (MA); creative writing (MFA); education (MA); human resource development (MA); leadership (MA); organizational development (MA); pedagogy of creative writing (Certificate); psychology (MA).

See Close-Up on page 851.

ANTIOCH UNIVERSITY MCGREGOR, Yellow Springs, OH 45387-1609

General Information Independent, coed, upper-level institution. *Enrollment:* 630 graduate, professional, and undergraduate students; 318 full-time matriculated graduate/professional students (213 women), 152 part-time matriculated graduate/professional students (108 women). *Enrollment by degree level:* 470 master's. *Graduate faculty:* 14 full-time (7 women), 59 part-time/adjunct (34 women). *Tuition:* Full-time $20,016; part-time $417 per credit hour. *Required fees:* $150 per quarter. *Graduate housing:* On-campus housing not available. *Student services:* International student services, teacher training. *Library facilities:* Olive Kettering Library plus 1 other. *Online resources:* library catalog, web page, access to other libraries' catalogs. *Collection:* 355,000 titles, 12,200 serial subscriptions, 6,400 audiovisual materials.

Computer facilities: 32 computers available on campus for general student use. A campuswide network can be accessed. Online class registration is available. *Web address:* http://www.mcgregor.edu/.

General Application Contact: Seth Gordon, Assistant Director of Admissions, 937-769-1800 Ext. 1825, Fax: 937-769-1804, E-mail: sgordon@antioch.edu.

GRADUATE UNITS

Graduate Programs Students: 318 full-time (213 women), 152 part-time (108 women); includes 96 minority (88 African Americans, 2 American Indian/Alaska Native, 3 Asian Americans or Pacific Islanders, 3 Hispanic Americans). Average age 38. 208 applicants, 85% accepted, 149 enrolled. *Faculty:* 14 full-time (7 women), 59 part-time/adjunct (34 women). Expenses: Contact institution. *Financial support:* Federal Work-Study and scholarships/grants available. Financial award applicants required to submit FAFSA. In 2008, 167 master's awarded. *Degree program information:* Part-time and evening/weekend programs available. Postbaccalaureate distance learning degree programs offered (minimal on-campus study). Offers community college management (MA); conflict analysis and management (MA); liberal and professional studies (MA); management (MA). *Application deadline:* For fall admission, 8/1 for domestic students; for winter admission, 12/1 for domestic students; for spring admission, 3/10 for domestic students. Applications are processed on a rolling basis. *Application fee:* $50. Electronic applications accepted. *Application Contact:* Seth Gordon, Assistant Director of Admissions, 937-769-1800 Ext. 1825, Fax: 937-769-1804, E-mail: sgordon@antioch.edu. *Dean of Students,* Darlene Robertson, 937-769-1800 Ext. 1820, Fax: 937-769-1804, E-mail: drobertson@antioch.edu.

School of Education Students: 238 full-time (169 women), 79 part-time (56 women); includes 100 minority (95 African Americans, 1 American Indian/Alaska Native, 2 Asian Americans or Pacific Islanders, 2 Hispanic Americans). Average age 31. 146 applicants, 88% accepted, 109 enrolled. *Faculty:* 9 full-time (5 women), 34 part-time/adjunct (20 women). Expenses: Contact institution. *Financial support:* Federal Work-Study available. Financial award applicants required to submit FAFSA. In 2008, 112 master's awarded. *Degree program information:* Evening/weekend programs available. Offers education (M Ed). *Application deadline:* For fall admission, 9/7 for domestic students; for winter admission, 12/10 for domestic students; for spring admission, 3/8 for domestic students. Applications are processed on a rolling basis. *Application fee:* $50. Electronic applications accepted. *Application Contact:* Oscar Robinson, Director of Admissions, 937-769-1823, Fax: 937-769-1804, E-mail: orobinson@antioch.edu. *Director,* Dr. Zak Shariff, 937-769-1880, Fax: 937-769-1805, E-mail: zsharif@antioch.edu.

ANTIOCH UNIVERSITY NEW ENGLAND, Keene, NH 03431-3552

General Information Independent, coed, graduate-only institution. *Graduate housing:* On-campus housing not available. *Research affiliation:* Harris Center for Conservation Education (environmental studies), Cheshire Medical Center Cardiac Rehabilitation Program (clinical psychology), Northeast Foundation for Children (education), Pine Hill Waldorf School (education).

GRADUATE UNITS

Graduate School *Degree program information:* Evening/weekend programs available. Offers administration and supervision (M Ed); autism spectrum disorders (Certificate); clinical mental health counseling (MA); clinical psychology (Psy D); conservation biology (MS); dance/movement therapy and counseling (M Ed, MA); early childhood education (M Ed); elementary education (M Ed); environmental advocacy and organizing (MS); environmental education (MS); environmental studies (MS, PhD); experienced educators (M Ed); individualized study (MS); integrated learning (M Ed); marriage and family therapy (MA, PhD); organizational and environmental sustainability (MBA); organizational development (Certificate); organizational leadership and management (MS); resource management and conservation (MS); science teacher certification (MS); Waldorf teacher training (M Ed). Electronic applications accepted.

ANTIOCH UNIVERSITY SANTA BARBARA, Santa Barbara, CA 93101-1581

General Information Independent, coed, upper-level institution. *Enrollment:* 369 graduate, professional, and undergraduate students; 211 full-time matriculated graduate/professional students (162 women), 53 part-time matriculated graduate/professional students (45 women). *Enrollment by degree level:* 209 master's, 55 doctoral. *Graduate faculty:* 13 full-time (9 women), 42 part-time/adjunct (21 women). *Tuition:* Full-time $17,025; part-time $570 per unit. *Required fees:* $26. Tuition and fees vary according to course load, degree level and program. *Graduate housing:* On-campus housing not available. *Student services:* Campus employment opportunities, international student services, services for students with disabilities, writing training. *Library facilities:* AUSB Library.

Computer facilities: 14 computers available on campus for general student use. A campuswide network can be accessed from off campus. Online class registration is available. *Web address:* http://www.antiochsb.edu/.

General Application Contact: Steve Weir, Director of Marketing and Enrollment Management, 805-962-8179 Ext. 152, Fax: 805-962-4786, E-mail: sweir@antioch.edu.

GRADUATE UNITS

Program in Clinical Psychology Students: 50 full-time (37 women), 5 part-time (3 women); includes 17 minority (3 African Americans, 2 Asian Americans or Pacific Islanders, 12 Hispanic Americans), 1 international. *Faculty:* 6 full-time (4 women), 7 part-time/adjunct (3 women). Expenses: Contact institution. Offers clinical psychology (Psy D). *Application deadline:* Applications are processed on a rolling basis. *Application fee:* $60. Electronic applications accepted. *Application Contact:* Steve Weir, Director of Marketing and Enrollment Management, 805-962-8179 Ext. 152, Fax: 805-962-4786, E-mail: sweir@antioch.edu. *Director,* Michele Harway, PhD, 805-962-8179 Ext. 320, Fax: 805-962-4786, E-mail: mharway@antioch.edu.

Program in Education/Teacher Credentialing Students: 20 full-time (17 women), 13 part-time (all women); includes 8 minority (2 Asian Americans or Pacific Islanders, 6 Hispanic Americans), 1 international. *Faculty:* 2 full-time (both women), 7 part-time/adjunct (4 women). Expenses: Contact institution. In 2008, 7 master's awarded. *Degree program information:* Part-time programs available. Offers education/teacher credentialing (MA). *Application deadline:* Applications are processed on a rolling basis. *Application fee:* $60. Electronic applications accepted. *Application Contact:* Steve Weir, Director of Marketing and Enrollment Management, 805-962-8179 Ext. 152, Fax: 805-962-4786, E-mail: admissions@antioch.edu. *Chair,* Michele Britton Bass, EdD, 805-962-8179 Ext. 114, Fax: 805-962-4786, E-mail: britbass@antioch.edu.

Program in Organizational Management Students: 38 full-time (19 women), 12 part-time (8 women); includes 7 minority (2 African Americans, 5 Hispanic Americans), 32 international. *Faculty:* 2 full-time (1 woman), 6 part-time/adjunct (1 woman). Expenses: Contact institution. In 2008, 20 master's awarded. *Degree program information:* Part-time and evening/weekend programs available. Postbaccalaureate distance learning degree programs offered (minimal on-campus study). Offers organizational management (MA). *Application deadline:* Applications are processed on a rolling basis. *Application fee:* $60. Electronic applications accepted. *Application Contact:* Steve Weir, Director of Marketing and Enrollment Management, 805-962-8179 Ext. 152, Fax: 805-962-4786, E-mail: sweir@antioch.edu. *Chair,* Esther Lopez-Mulnix, PhD, 805-962-8179 Ext. 335, Fax: 805-962-4786, E-mail: emulnix@antioch.edu.

Program in Psychology Students: 103 full-time (89 women), 23 part-time (21 women); includes 36 minority (3 African Americans, 1 American Indian/Alaska Native, 5 Asian Americans or Pacific Islanders, 27 Hispanic Americans), 4 international. *Faculty:* 1 (woman) full-time, 22 part-time/adjunct (12 women). Expenses: Contact institution. In 2008, 69 master's awarded. *Degree program information:* Part-time and evening/weekend programs available. Offers psychology (MA). *Application deadline:* Applications are processed on a rolling basis. *Application fee:* $60. Electronic applications accepted. *Application Contact:* Steve Weir, Director of Marketing and Enrollment Management, 805-962-8179 Ext. 152, Fax: 805-962-4786, E-mail: sweir@antioch.edu. *Chair,* Catherine Radecki-Bush, PhD, 805-962-8179 Ext. 229, Fax: 805-962-4786, E-mail: cradecki-bush@antioch.edu.

ANTIOCH UNIVERSITY SEATTLE, Seattle, WA 98121-1814

General Information Independent, coed, upper-level institution. *Graduate housing:* On-campus housing not available.

GRADUATE UNITS

Graduate Programs *Degree program information:* Part-time and evening/weekend programs available. Offers education (MA); psychology (MA, Psy D). Electronic applications accepted.

Center for Creative Change *Degree program information:* Evening/weekend programs available. Offers environment and community (MA); management (MS); organizational psychology (MA); strategic communications (MA); whole system design (MA). Electronic applications accepted.

APEX SCHOOL OF THEOLOGY, Durham, NC 27713

General Information Independent-religious, coed, comprehensive institution. *Graduate housing:* On-campus housing not available.

GRADUATE UNITS

Graduate Programs

APPALACHIAN SCHOOL OF LAW, Grundy, VA 24614

General Information Independent, coed, graduate-only institution. *Enrollment by degree level:* 350 first professional. *Graduate faculty:* 22 full-time (8 women), 2 part-time/adjunct (0 women). *Tuition:* Full-time $25,000; part-time $990 per credit hour. *Required fees:* $325. *Graduate housing:* On-campus housing not available. *Student services:* Campus employment opportunities, career counseling, services for students with disabilities, writing training. *Library facilities:* ASL Library. *Online resources:* library catalog, web page, access to other libraries' catalogs. *Collection:* 111,217 titles, 4,110 serial subscriptions, 381 audiovisual materials.

Computer facilities: 29 computers available on campus for general student use. A campuswide network can be accessed. Online class registration, printing access are available. *Web address:* http://www.asl.edu/.

General Application Contact: Nancy M. Pruitt, Director of Student Services and Registrar, 276-935-4349 Ext. 1229, Fax: 276-935-8261, E-mail: npruitt@asl.edu.

GRADUATE UNITS

Professional Program in Law Students: 350 full-time (126 women); includes 34 minority (16 African Americans, 2 American Indian/Alaska Native, 6 Asian Americans or Pacific Islanders, 10 Hispanic Americans), 2 international. Average age 27. 1,688 applicants, 45% accepted, 115 enrolled. *Faculty:* 22 full-time (8 women), 2 part-time/adjunct (0 women). Expenses: Contact institution. *Financial support:* In 2008–09, 91 students received support; research assistantships, career-related internships or fieldwork, Federal Work-Study, institutionally sponsored loans, scholarships/grants, and tuition waivers (full and partial) available. Financial award application deadline: 7/1; financial award applicants required to submit FAFSA. In 2008, 10,491 JDs awarded. *Degree program information:* Part-time programs available. Offers law (JD). *Application deadline:* For fall admission, 6/1 for domestic students. Applications are processed on a rolling basis. *Application fee:* $60. Electronic applications accepted. *Application Contact:* Nancy M. Pruitt, Director of Student Services and Registrar, 276-935-4349 Ext. 1229, Fax: 276-935-8261, E-mail: npruitt@asl.edu. *Dean,* Clinton W. Shinn, 276-935-4349, Fax: 276-935-8261, E-mail: wshinn@asl.edu.

APPALACHIAN STATE UNIVERSITY, Boone, NC 28608

General Information State-supported, coed, comprehensive institution. CGS member. *Enrollment:* 16,610 graduate, professional, and undergraduate students; 773 full-time matriculated graduate/professional students (462 women), 923 part-time matriculated graduate/professional students (659 women). *Enrollment by degree level:* 1,529 master's, 70 doctoral, 97 other advanced degrees. *Graduate faculty:* 471 full-time (180 women), 90 part-time/adjunct (51 women). Tuition, state resident: full-time $2600; part-time $700 per course. Tuition, nonresident: full-time $5000; part-time $3300 per course. *Required fees:* $2150; $330 per course. Tuition and fees vary according to campus/location. *Graduate housing:* Rooms and/or apartments available on a first-come, first-served basis to single and married students. Typical cost: $4000 per year for single students; $4000 per year for married students. Housing application deadline: 2/28. *Student services:* Campus employment opportunities, campus safety program, career counseling, child daycare facilities, exercise/wellness program, free psychological counseling, grant writing training, international student services, low-cost health insurance, multicultural affairs office, services for students with disabilities, teacher training, writing training. *Library facilities:* Carol Grotnes Belk Library plus 1 other. *Online resources:* library catalog, web page, access to other libraries' catalogs. *Collection:* 1.4 million titles, 7,383 serial subscriptions, 40,686 audiovisual materials.

Computer facilities: 2,500 computers available on campus for general student use. A campuswide network can be accessed from student residence rooms and from off campus. Online class registration is available. *Web address:* http://www.appstate.edu/.

General Application Contact: Sandy Krause, Director of Admissions and Recruiting, 828-262-2130, Fax: 828-262-2709, E-mail: krausesl@appstate.edu.

GRADUATE UNITS

Cratis D. Williams Graduate School Students: 773 full-time (462 women), 923 part-time (659 women); includes 114 minority (79 African Americans, 4 American Indian/Alaska Native, 15 Asian Americans or Pacific Islanders, 16 Hispanic Americans), 26 international. 1,287 applicants, 70% accepted, 595 enrolled. *Faculty:* 471 full-time (180 women), 90 part-time/adjunct (51 women). Expenses: Contact institution. *Financial support:* In 2008–09, 30 fellowships (averaging $3,500 per year) were awarded; research assistantships, teaching assistantships, career-related internships or fieldwork, Federal Work-Study, institutionally sponsored loans, scholarships/grants, and unspecified assistantships also available. Financial award application deadline: 4/1; financial award applicants required to submit FAFSA. In 2008, 509 master's, 14 doctorates, 36 other advanced degrees awarded. *Degree program information:* Part-time and evening/weekend programs available. Postbaccalaureate distance learning degree programs offered (no on-campus study). Offers accounting (MS); business administration (MBA); cell and molecular (MS); child development (MA); clinical health psychology (MA); community counseling (MA); computer science (MS); criminal justice (MS); curriculum specialist (MA); educational administration (Ed S); educational leadership (Ed D); educational media (MA); elementary education (MA); engineering physics (MS); English (MA); English education (MA); exercise science (MS); family and consumer science (MA); family and consumer science education (MA); general (MS); general experimental psychology (MA); geography (MA); gerontology (MA); higher education (MA, Ed S); history (MA); history education (MA); industrial and organizational psychology (MA); industrial technology (MA); library science (MLS); marriage and family therapy (MA); mathematics (MA); mathematics education (MA); middle grades education (MA); political science (MA); public administration (MPA); public history (MA); reading education (MA); romance languages (MA); school administration (MSA); school counseling (MA); social work (MSW); special education (MA); speech-language pathology (MA); student development (MA); technology education (MA). *Application deadline:* For fall admission, 7/1 for domestic students, 2/1 for international students; for spring admission, 11/1 for domestic students, 7/1 for international students. Applications are processed on a rolling basis. *Application fee:* $50. Electronic applications accepted. *Application Contact:* Sandy Krause, Director of Admissions and Recruiting, 828-262-2130, Fax: 828-262-2709, E-mail: krausesl@appstate.edu. *Dean of Research and Graduate Studies,* Dr. Edelma D. Huntley, 828-262-2130, E-mail: huntleyed@appstate.edu.

Center for Appalachian Studies Students: 19 full-time (11 women), 5 part-time (3 women). 20 applicants, 90% accepted, 10 enrolled. *Faculty:* 14 full-time (5 women). Expenses: Contact institution. *Financial support:* In 2008–09, 8 research assistantships (averaging $7,000 per year) were awarded; fellowships, teaching assistantships, career-related internships or fieldwork, Federal Work-Study, scholarships/grants, and unspecified assistantships also available. Financial award application deadline: 4/1; financial award applicants required to submit FAFSA. In 2008, 6 master's awarded. *Degree program information:* Part-time programs available. Offers culture (MA); music (MA); sustainable development (MA). *Application deadline:* For fall admission, 7/1 for domestic students, 2/1 for international students; for spring admission, 11/1 for domestic students, 7/1 for international students. Applications are processed on a rolling basis. *Application fee:* $50. Electronic applications accepted. *Application Contact:* Dr. Bruce Stewart, Graduate Program Director, 828-262-4858, E-mail: stewartbe1@appstate.edu. *Director,* Dr. Pat Beaver, 828-262-2550, E-mail: beaverpd@appstate.edu.

School of Music Students: 25 full-time (13 women), 7 part-time (4 women); includes 2 minority (both African Americans), 1 international. 28 applicants, 86% accepted, 13 enrolled. *Faculty:* 29 full-time (11 women), 2 part-time/adjunct (both women). Expenses: Contact institution. *Financial support:* In 2008–09, 16 research assistantships (averaging $7,000 per year) were awarded; fellowships, teaching assistantships, career-related internships or fieldwork, Federal Work-Study, scholarships/grants, tuition waivers (partial), and unspecified assistantships also available. Financial award application deadline: 4/1; financial award applicants required to submit FAFSA. In 2008, 9 master's awarded. *Degree program information:* Part-time programs available. Offers music education (MM); music performance (MM); music therapy (MMT). *Application deadline:* For fall admission, 7/1 for domestic students, 2/1 for international students; for spring admission, 11/1 for domestic students, 7/1 for international students. Applications are processed on a rolling basis. *Application fee:* $50. Electronic applications accepted. *Application Contact:* Dr. Nancy Schneeloch-Bingham, Graduate Program Director, 828-262-6463, E-mail: schneelochna@appstate.edu. *Dean,* Dr. William Harbinson, 828-262-6446, E-mail: harbinsonwg@appstate.edu.

AQUINAS COLLEGE, Grand Rapids, MI 49506-1799

General Information Independent-religious, coed, comprehensive institution. *Enrollment:* 2,159 graduate, professional, and undergraduate students; 32 full-time matriculated graduate/professional students (21 women), 255 part-time matriculated graduate/professional students (198 women). *Enrollment by degree level:* 287 master's. *Graduate faculty:* 38 full-time (24 women), 24 part-time/adjunct (13 women). *Tuition:* Full-time $9000; part-time $500 per credit hour. *Graduate housing:* On-campus housing not available. *Student services:* Campus employment opportunities, campus safety program, career counseling, child daycare facilities, exercise/wellness program, free psychological counseling, multicultural affairs office, services for students with disabilities, teacher training. *Library facilities:* Grace Hauenstein Library. *Online resources:* library catalog, web page, access to other libraries' catalogs. *Collection:* 99,293 titles, 526 serial subscriptions.

Computer facilities: Computer purchase and lease plans are available. 153 computers available on campus for general student use. A campuswide network can be accessed from student residence rooms and from off campus. *Web address:* http://www.aquinas.edu/.

General Application Contact: Lynn Atkins-Rykert, Executive Assistant, School of Management, 616-632-2924, Fax: 616-732-4489, E-mail: atkinlyn@aquinas.edu.

GRADUATE UNITS

School of Education Students: 24 full-time (16 women), 195 part-time (166 women); includes 19 minority (4 African Americans, 1 American Indian/Alaska Native, 2 Asian Americans or Pacific Islanders, 12 Hispanic Americans). Average age 35. 48 applicants, 96% accepted, 39 enrolled. *Faculty:* 27 full-time (19 women), 18 part-time/adjunct (12 women). Expenses: Contact institution. *Financial support:* In 2008–09, 141 students received support. Scholarships/grants available. Support available to part-time students. Financial award application deadline: 3/15; financial award applicants required to submit FAFSA. In 2008, 101 master's awarded. *Degree program information:* Part-time and evening/weekend programs available. Offers education (MAT, ME, MS). *Application deadline:* Applications are processed on a rolling basis. *Application fee:* $0. *Application Contact:* Michele Polega, Coordinator of Graduate Education Programs, 616-632-2440, E-mail: pciegmic@aquinas.edu. *Dean,* Nanette Clatterbuck, 616-632-2973, Fax: 616-732-4465, E-mail: clattnan@aquinas.edu.

School of Management Students: 8 full-time (5 women), 60 part-time (32 women); includes 7 minority (3 African Americans, 1 American Indian/Alaska Native, 1 Asian American or Pacific Islander, 2 Hispanic Americans). Average age 36. 23 applicants, 74% accepted, 13 enrolled. *Faculty:* 11 full-time (5 women), 6 part-time/adjunct (5 women). Expenses: Contact institution. *Financial support:* In 2008–09, 26 students received support. Scholarships/grants available. Support available to part-time students. Financial award application deadline: 3/15; financial award applicants required to submit FAFSA. In 2008, 25 master's awarded. *Degree program information:* Part-time and evening/weekend programs available. Offers management (M Mgt). *Application deadline:* Applications are processed on a rolling basis. *Application Contact:* Lynn Atkins-Rykert, Executive Assistant, School of Management, 616-632-2924, Fax: 616-732-4489, E-mail: atkinlyn@aquinas.edu. *Dean,* Cynthia VanGelderen, 616-632-2922, Fax: 616-732-4489, E-mail: vangecyn@aquinas.edu.

AQUINAS INSTITUTE OF THEOLOGY, St. Louis, MO 63108

General Information Independent-religious, coed, graduate-only institution. *Enrollment by degree level:* 178 master's, 57 doctoral, 32 other advanced degrees. *Graduate faculty:* 17

Aquinas Institute of Theology (continued)

full-time (10 women), 4 part-time/adjunct (2 women). *Tuition:* Full-time $14,784; part-time $616 per credit hour. *Required fees:* $195 per semester. Tuition and fees vary according to course load. *Graduate housing:* On-campus housing not available. *Student services:* Campus employment opportunities, career counseling, exercise/wellness program, free psychological counseling, international student services, low-cost health insurance, services for students with disabilities, writing training. *Library facilities:* Pius XII Memorial Library plus 3 others. *Online resources:* library catalog, web page, access to other libraries' catalogs. *Collection:* 1.4 million titles, 11,847 serial subscriptions, 4,079 audiovisual materials.

Computer facilities: A campuswide network can be accessed from student residence rooms and from off campus. *Web address:* http://www.ai.edu/.

General Application Contact: David Werthmann, Director of Admissions, 314-256-8806, Fax: 314-256-8888, E-mail: admissions@ai.edu.

GRADUATE UNITS

Graduate and Professional Programs Students: 74 full-time (25 women), 193 part-time (127 women); includes 37 minority (16 African Americans, 1 American Indian/Alaska Native, 10 Asian Americans or Pacific Islanders, 10 Hispanic Americans), 12 international. Average age 41. 76 applicants, 87% accepted, 56 enrolled. *Faculty:* 17 full-time (10 women), 4 part-time/adjunct (2 women). Expenses: Contact institution. *Financial support:* Career-related internships or fieldwork, scholarships/grants, health care benefits, and tuition waivers (partial) available. Support available to part-time students. Financial award application deadline: 3/15; financial award applicants required to submit CSS PROFILE or FAFSA. In 2008, 42 master's, 8 doctorates awarded. *Degree program information:* Part-time and evening/weekend programs available. Postbaccalaureate distance learning degree programs offered (minimal on-campus study). Offers biblical studies (Certificate); health care mission (MAHCM); ministry (M Div); pastoral care (Certificate); pastoral ministry (MAPM); pastoral studies (MAPS); preaching (D Min); spiritual direction (Certificate); theology (M Div, MA); Thomistic studies (Certificate). *Application deadline:* For fall admission, 3/15 priority date for domestic and international students; for spring admission, 11/15 priority date for domestic and international students. Applications are processed on a rolling basis. *Application fee:* $50. *Application Contact:* David Werthmann, Director of Admissions, 314-256-8806, Fax: 314-256-8888, E-mail: admissions@ai.edu. *Academic Dean,* Fr. Gregory Heille, 314-256-8800, Fax: 314-256-8888, E-mail: heille@ai.edu.

ARCADIA UNIVERSITY, Glenside, PA 19038-3295

General Information Independent-religious, coed, comprehensive institution. CGS member. *Enrollment:* 3,894 graduate, professional, and undergraduate students; 487 full-time matriculated graduate/professional students (373 women), 1,163 part-time matriculated graduate/professional students (884 women). *Enrollment by degree level:* 995 master's, 196 doctoral, 459 other advanced degrees. *Graduate faculty:* 71 full-time, 135 part-time/adjunct. Tuition and fees vary according to degree level and program. *Graduate housing:* On-campus housing not available. *Student services:* Campus safety program, career counseling, international student services, low-cost health insurance, multicultural affairs office, writing training.

Computer facilities: 120 computers available on campus for general student use. A campuswide network can be accessed from student residence rooms and from off campus. Online class registration is available. *Web address:* http://www.arcadia.edu/.

General Application Contact: Information Contact, 215-572-2910, Fax: 215-572-4049, E-mail: admiss@arcadia.edu.

GRADUATE UNITS

Graduate Studies Students: 487 full-time (373 women), 1,163 part-time (884 women); includes 161 minority (131 African Americans, 20 Asian Americans or Pacific Islanders, 10 Hispanic Americans), 12 international. Average age 31. *Faculty:* 71 full-time, 135 part-time/adjunct. Expenses: Contact institution. *Financial support:* Research assistantships, teaching assistantships, career-related internships or fieldwork, scholarships/grants, tuition waivers (partial), and unspecified assistantships available. Support available to part-time students. In 2008, 443 master's, 45 doctorates awarded. *Degree program information:* Part-time and evening/weekend programs available. Postbaccalaureate distance learning degree programs offered (minimal on-campus study). Offers allied health (MSHE, MSPH); art education (M Ed, MA Ed); biology education (MA Ed); business administration (MBA); chemistry education (MA Ed); child development (CAS); community counseling (MACP); computer education (M Ed, CAS); computer education 7–12 (MA Ed); early childhood education (M Ed, CAS); educational leadership (M Ed, CAS); educational psychology (CAS); elementary education (M Ed, CAS); English (MAE); English education (MA Ed); environmental education (MA Ed, CAS); fine arts, theater, and music (MAH); forensic science (MSFS); genetic counseling (MSGC); history education (MA Ed); history, philosophy, and religion (MAH); international peace and conflict management (MAIPCR); international relations and diplomacy (MA); language arts (M Ed, CAS); literature and language (MAH); mathematics education (M Ed, MA Ed, CAS); medical science and community health (MM Sc, MSHE, MSPH); music education (MA Ed); physical therapy (DPT); psychology (MA Ed); pupil personnel services (CAS); reading (M Ed, CAS); school counseling (MACP); school library science (M Ed); science education (M Ed, CAS); secondary education (M Ed, CAS); special education (M Ed, Ed D, CAS); theater arts (MA Ed); written communication (MA Ed). *Application fee:* $50. Electronic applications accepted. *Application Contact:* 215-572-2910, Fax: 215-572-4049, E-mail: admiss@arcadia.edu. *Dean of Graduate Studies,* John Hoffman, 215-572-2925, Fax: 215-572-2081, E-mail: hoffman@arcadia.edu.

See Close-Up on page 853.

ARGOSY UNIVERSITY, ATLANTA, Atlanta, GA 30328

General Information Proprietary, coed, university. CGS member.

GRADUATE UNITS

College of Business Offers accounting (DBA); customized professional concentration (MBA, DBA); finance (MBA); healthcare administration (MBA); information systems (DBA); information systems management (MBA); international business (MBA, DBA); management (MBA, MSM, DBA); marketing (MBA, DBA).

College of Education Offers educational leadership (MAEd, Ed D, Ed S); instructional leadership (MAEd, Ed D, Ed S).

College of Psychology and Behavioral Sciences Offers clinical psychology (MA, Psy D, Postdoctoral Respecialization Certificate); community counseling (MA); counselor education and supervision (Ed D); marriage and family therapy (Certificate).

ARGOSY UNIVERSITY, CHICAGO, Chicago, IL 60654

General Information Proprietary, coed, university. CGS member.

GRADUATE UNITS

College of Business Postbaccalaureate distance learning degree programs offered (minimal on-campus study). Offers accounting (DBA); customized professional concentration (MBA, DBA); finance (MBA); healthcare administration (MBA); information systems (DBA); information systems management (MBA); international business (MBA, DBA); management (MBA, MSM, DBA); marketing (MBA, DBA).

College of Education Postbaccalaureate distance learning degree programs offered (minimal on-campus study). Offers community college executive leadership (Ed D); educational leadership (MA Ed, Ed D, Ed S); instructional leadership (MA Ed, Ed D, Ed S).

College of Psychology and Behavioral Sciences Postbaccalaureate distance learning degree programs offered (minimal on-campus study). Offers child and adolescent psychology (Psy D); client-centered and experiential psychotherapies (Psy D); clinical psychology (MA, Psy D); community counseling (MA); counseling psychology (Ed D); counselor education and supervision (Ed D); diversity and multicultural psychology (Psy D); family psychology (Psy D); forensic psychology (Psy D); health psychology (Psy D); organizational leadership (Ed D); psychoanalytic psychology (Psy D); psychology and spirituality (Psy D).

ARGOSY UNIVERSITY, DALLAS, Dallas, TX 75231

General Information Proprietary, coed, university. CGS member.

GRADUATE UNITS

College of Business Offers accounting (AGC); corporate compliance (MBA, Graduate Certificate); customized professional concentration (MBA); finance (MBA, Graduate Certificate); fraud examination (MBA, Graduate Certificate); global business sustainability (AGC); healthcare administration (Graduate Certificate); healthcare management (MBA); information systems (MBA, AGC); information systems management (Graduate Certificate); international business (MBA, AGC, Graduate Certificate); management (MBA, AGC, Graduate Certificate); marketing (MBA, Graduate Certificate); public administration (MBA, Graduate Certificate); sustainable management (MBA, Graduate Certificate).

College of Education Offers educational leadership (MA Ed); instructional leadership (MA Ed).

College of Psychology and Behavioral Sciences Offers clinical psychology (MA, Psy D); community counseling (MA); psychology and behavioral sciences (MA, Psy D).

ARGOSY UNIVERSITY, DENVER, Denver, CO 80203

General Information Proprietary, coed, university.

GRADUATE UNITS

College of Business Offers accounting (DBA); customized professional concentration (MBA, DBA); finance (MBA); healthcare administration (MBA); information systems (DBA); information systems management (MBA); international business (MBA, DBA); management (MBA, MSM, DBA); marketing (MBA, DBA).

College of Education Offers community college executive leadership (Ed D); educational leadership (MA Ed, Ed D); instructional leadership (MA Ed, Ed D).

College of Psychology and Behavioral Sciences Offers clinical psychology (MA, Psy D); community counseling (MA); counseling psychology (Ed D); counselor education and supervision (Ed D); forensic psychology (MA); marriage and family therapy (MA); organizational leadership (Ed D).

ARGOSY UNIVERSITY, HAWAI'I, Honolulu, HI 96813

General Information Proprietary, coed, university. CGS member.

GRADUATE UNITS

College of Business Offers accounting (DBA); customized professional concentration (MBA, DBA); finance (MBA, Certificate); healthcare administration (MBA); information systems (DBA); information systems management (MBA, Certificate); international business (MBA, DBA, Certificate); management (MBA, DBA); marketing (MBA, DBA, Certificate).

College of Education Offers adult education and training (MAEd); educational leadership (MAEd, Ed D); instructional leadership (MAEd, Ed D).

College of Health Sciences Offers healthcare administration (Certificate).

College of Psychology and Behavioral Sciences Offers clinical psychology (MA, Psy D, Postdoctoral Respecialization Certificate); counseling psychology (Ed D); marriage and family therapy (MA); organizational leadership (Ed D); psychology and behavioral sciences (MA, MS, Ed D, Psy D, Certificate, Postdoctoral Respecialization Certificate); psychopharmacology (MS, Certificate); school psychology (MA); substance abuse counseling (Certificate).

ARGOSY UNIVERSITY, INLAND EMPIRE, San Bernardino, CA 92408

General Information Proprietary, coed, university.

GRADUATE UNITS

College of Business Offers accounting (DBA); customized professional concentration (MBA, DBA); finance (MBA); healthcare administration (MBA); information systems (DBA); information systems management (MBA); international business (MBA, DBA); management (MBA, DBA); marketing (MBA, DBA).

College of Education Offers community college executive leadership (Ed D); educational leadership (MA Ed, Ed D); instructional leadership (MA Ed, Ed D).

College of Psychology and Behavioral Sciences Offers clinical psychology/marriage and family therapy (MA); counseling psychology (MA, Ed D); counseling psychology/marriage and family therapy (MA); forensic psychology (MA).

ARGOSY UNIVERSITY, LOS ANGELES, Santa Monica, CA 90405

General Information Proprietary, coed, university.

GRADUATE UNITS

College of Business Offers accounting (DBA); customized professional concentration (MBA, DBA); finance (MBA); healthcare administration (MBA); information systems (DBA); information systems management (MBA); international business (MBA, DBA); management (MBA, MSM, DBA); marketing (MBA, DBA).

College of Education Offers community college executive leadership (Ed D); educational leadership (MA Ed, Ed D); instructional leadership (MA Ed, Ed D).

College of Psychology and Behavioral Sciences Offers clinical psychology/marriage and family therapy (MA); counseling psychology (Ed D); counseling psychology/marriage and family therapy (MA); organizational leadership (Ed D).

ARGOSY UNIVERSITY, NASHVILLE, Nashville, TN 37214

General Information Proprietary, coed, university. CGS member.

GRADUATE UNITS

College of Business Offers accounting (DBA); customized professional concentration (MBA, DBA); finance (MBA); healthcare administration (MBA); information systems (MBA, DBA); international business (MBA, DBA); management (MBA, MSM, DBA); marketing (MBA, DBA).

College of Education Offers education (MA Ed, Ed D, Ed S); educational leadership (MA Ed, Ed S); higher education administration (Ed D); instructional leadership (MA Ed, Ed S); K-12 education (Ed D).

College of Psychology and Behavioral Sciences Offers counselor education and supervision (Ed D); mental health counseling (MA).

Program in Counselor Education and Supervision Offers counselor education and supervision (Ed D).

ARGOSY UNIVERSITY, ORANGE COUNTY, Santa Ana, CA 92704

General Information Proprietary, coed, university. CGS member.

GRADUATE UNITS

College of Business Offers accounting (DBA, Adv C); customized professional concentration (MBA, DBA); finance (MBA, Certificate); healthcare administration (MBA); information systems (DBA, Adv C); information systems management (MBA); international business (MBA, DBA, Adv C, Certificate); management (MBA, MSM, DBA, Adv C); marketing (MBA, DBA, Adv C, Certificate); public administration (MBA, Certificate).

College of Education Offers community college executive leadership (Ed D); educational leadership (MA Ed, Ed D); instructional leadership (MA Ed, Ed D).

College of Psychology and Behavioral Sciences *Degree program information:* Part-time and evening/weekend programs available. Offers child and adolescent psychology (Psy D); counseling psychology (Ed D); forensic psychology (MA); marriage and family therapy (MA); organizational leadership (Ed D); psychology and behavioral sciences (MA, Ed D, Psy D, Postdoctoral Respecialization Certificate); sport-exercise psychology (MA). Electronic applications accepted.

ARGOSY UNIVERSITY, PHOENIX, Phoenix, AZ 85021

General Information Proprietary, coed, university. CGS member.

GRADUATE UNITS

College of Business Offers accounting (DBA); customized professional concentration (MBA, DBA); finance (MBA); healthcare administration (MBA); information systems (DBA); information systems management (MBA); international business (MBA, DBA); management (MBA, DBA); marketing (MBA, DBA).

College of Education Offers community college executive leadership (Ed D); educational leadership (MA Ed, Ed D, Ed S); instructional leadership (MA Ed, Ed D, Ed S).

College of Psychology and Behavioral Sciences Offers clinical psychology (MA); forensic psychology (MA); mental health counseling (MA); psychology and behavioral sciences (MA, Psy D); school psychology (MA, Psy D); sport–exercise psychology (MA); sports-exercise psychology (Psy D).

ARGOSY UNIVERSITY, SALT LAKE CITY, Draper, UT 84020

General Information Proprietary, coed, university.

GRADUATE UNITS

College of Business Offers accounting (DBA); customized professional concentration (MBA, DBA); finance (MBA); fraud examination (MBA); global business sustainability (DBA); healthcare administration (MBA); information systems (DBA); information systems management (MBA); international business (MBA, DBA); management (MBA, DBA); marketing (MBA, DBA); public administration (MBA); sustainable management (MBA).

College of Education Offers educational leadership (MA Ed, Ed D).

College of Psychology and Behavioral Sciences Offers counseling psychology (Ed D); marriage and family therapy (MA).

ARGOSY UNIVERSITY, SAN DIEGO, San Diego, CA 92108

General Information Proprietary, coed, university.

GRADUATE UNITS

College of Business Offers accounting (DBA); customized professional concentration (MBA, DBA); finance (MBA); information systems (DBA); information systems management (MBA); international business (MBA, DBA); management (MBA, MSM, DBA); marketing (MBA, DBA).

College of Education Offers community college executive leadership (Ed D); educational leadership (MA Ed, Ed D); instructional leadership (MA Ed, Ed D).

College of Psychology and Behavioral Sciences Offers clinical psychology/marriage and family therapy (MA); counseling psychology (MA, Ed D); counseling psychology/marriage and family therapy (MA).

ARGOSY UNIVERSITY, SAN FRANCISCO BAY AREA, Alameda, CA 94501

General Information Proprietary, coed, university. CGS member.

GRADUATE UNITS

College of Business Offers accounting (DBA); corporate compliance (MBA); customized professional concentration (MBA, DBA); finance (MBA); healthcare administration (MBA); information systems (DBA); information systems management (MBA); international business (MBA, DBA); management (MBA, MSM, DBA); marketing (MBA, DBA).

College of Education Offers community college executive leadership (Ed D); educational leadership (MA Ed, Ed D); instructional leadership (MA Ed, Ed D).

College of Psychology and Behavioral Sciences Offers clinical psychology (MA, Psy D); counseling psychology (MA, Ed D); forensic psychology (MA); organizational leadership (Ed D).

ARGOSY UNIVERSITY, SARASOTA, Sarasota, FL 34235

General Information Proprietary, coed, university. CGS member.

GRADUATE UNITS

College of Business Offers accounting (DBA, Adv C); customized professional concentration (MBA, DBA); finance (MBA, Certificate); healthcare administration (MBA); information systems (DBA, Adv C, Certificate); information systems management (MBA); international business (MBA, DBA, Adv C, Certificate); management (MBA, MSM, DBA, Adv C); marketing (MBA, DBA, Adv C, Certificate).

College of Education Offers community college executive leadership (Ed D); educational leadership (MA Ed, Ed D, Ed S); instructional leadership (MA Ed, Ed D, Ed S).

College of Health Sciences Offers healthcare administration (Certificate).

College of Psychology and Behavioral Sciences Offers community counseling (MA); counseling psychology (Ed D); counselor education and supervision (Ed D); forensic psychology (MA); marriage and family therapy (MA); mental health counseling (MA); organizational leadership (Ed D); pastoral community counseling (Ed D); school counseling (MA, Ed S); school psychology (MA).

ARGOSY UNIVERSITY, SCHAUMBURG, Schaumburg, IL 60173-5403

General Information Proprietary, coed, university. CGS member.

GRADUATE UNITS

College of Business Offers accounting (DBA, Adv C); customized professional concentration (MBA, DBA); finance (MBA, Certificate); healthcare administration (MBA); information systems (DBA, Adv C, Certificate); information systems management (MBA); international business (MBA, DBA, Adv C, Certificate); management (MBA, MSM, DBA, Adv C, Certificate); marketing (DBA, Adv C, Certificate).

College of Education Offers community college executive leadership (Ed D); educational leadership (MA Ed, Ed D, Ed S); instructional leadership (MA Ed, Ed D, Ed S).

College of Health Sciences Offers healthcare administration (Certificate).

College of Psychology and Behavioral Sciences Offers clinical health psychology (Post-Graduate Certificate); clinical psychology (MA, Psy D); community counseling (MA); counseling psychology (Ed D); counselor education and supervision (Ed D); forensic psychology (Post-Graduate Certificate); organizational leadership (Ed D).

ARGOSY UNIVERSITY, SEATTLE, Seattle, WA 98121

General Information Proprietary, coed, university. CGS member.

GRADUATE UNITS

College of Business Offers accounting (DBA); customized professional concentration (MBA, DBA); finance (MBA); healthcare administration (MBA); information systems (DBA); information systems management (MBA); international business (MBA, DBA); management (MBA, MSM, DBA); marketing (MBA, DBA).

College of Education Offers community college executive leadership (Ed D); educational leadership (MA Ed, Ed D); instructional leadership (MA Ed, Ed D).

College of Psychology and Behavioral Sciences Offers clinical psychology (MA, Psy D, Postdoctoral Respecialization Certificate); counseling psychology (MA, Ed D); psychology and behavioral sciences (MA, Ed D, Psy D, Postdoctoral Respecialization Certificate).

ARGOSY UNIVERSITY, TAMPA, Tampa, FL 33614

General Information Proprietary, coed, university. CGS member.

GRADUATE UNITS

College of Business Offers accounting (DBA); customized professional concentration (MBA, DBA); finance (MBA); healthcare administration (MBA); information systems (DBA); information systems management (MBA); international business (MBA, DBA); management (MBA, MSM, DBA); marketing (MBA, DBA); public administration (MBA).

College of Education Offers community college executive leadership (Ed D); educational leadership (MA Ed, Ed D, Ed S); instructional leadership (MA Ed, Ed D, Ed S).

College of Health Sciences Offers healthcare administration (Certificate).

College of Psychology and Behavioral Sciences Offers clinical psychology (MA, Psy D); counselor education and supervision (Ed D); marriage and family therapy (MA); mental health counseling (MA); organizational leadership (Ed D); school counseling (MA).

ARGOSY UNIVERSITY, TWIN CITIES, Eagan, MN 55121

General Information Proprietary, coed, university.

GRADUATE UNITS

College of Business Offers accounting (DBA); customized professional concentration (MBA, DBA); finance (MBA); healthcare administration (MBA); information systems (DBA); information systems management (MBA); international business (MBA, DBA); management (MBA, MSM, DBA); marketing (MBA, DBA).

College of Education Offers educational leadership (MA Ed, Ed D, Ed S); instructional leadership (MA Ed, Ed D, Ed S).

College of Health Sciences Offers health services management (MS).

College of Psychology and Behavioral Sciences Offers clinical psychology (MA, Psy D); forensic counseling (Post-Graduate Certificate); forensic psychology (MA); marriage and family therapy (MA, DMFT); organizational leadership (Ed D).

ARGOSY UNIVERSITY, WASHINGTON DC, Arlington, VA 22209

General Information Proprietary, coed, university. CGS member.

GRADUATE UNITS

College of Business Offers accounting (DBA); customized professional concentration (MBA, DBA); finance (MBA); healthcare administration (MBA); information systems (DBA); information systems management (MBA); international business (MBA, DBA, Certificate); management (MBA, MSM, DBA); marketing (MBA, DBA, Certificate).

College of Education Offers community college executive leadership (Ed D); educational leadership (MA Ed, Ed D, Ed S); instructional leadership (MA Ed, Ed D, Ed S).

College of Psychology and Behavioral Sciences Offers clinical psychology (MA, Psy D); community counseling (MA); counseling psychology (Ed D); counselor education and supervision (Ed D); forensic psychology (MA); organizational leadership (Ed D).

ARIZONA SCHOOL OF ACUPUNCTURE AND ORIENTAL MEDICINE, Tucson, AZ 85712

General Information Proprietary, coed, graduate-only institution.

GRADUATE UNITS

Graduate Programs

ARIZONA STATE UNIVERSITY, Tempe, AZ 85287

General Information State-supported, coed, university. CGS member. *Graduate housing:* Room and/or apartments available to single students; on-campus housing not available to married students. *Research affiliation:* Semiconductor Industries, Aerospace Industries, Arizona State University Research Park Facilities and Partnerships with Industry, Architecture Research Centers Consortium, Southwest Center for Environmental Research and Policy, Industrial University Cooperative Center for Health Management Research.

GRADUATE UNITS

Graduate College *Degree program information:* Part-time programs available. Offers statistics (MS).

College of Design Offers architecture (M Arch); arts/media/engineering (MSD); building design (MS); design (PhD); healthcare and healing environments (MSD); history, theory, and criticism (PhD); industrial design (MSD); interaction design (MSD); interior design (MSD); landscape architecture (MLA); new product innovation (MSD); planning (MUEP); transportation systems (Certificate); urban design (MUD); visual communication design (MSD).

College of Liberal Arts and Sciences Offers American media and popular culture (MAS); anthropology (PhD); applied mathematics for the life and social sciences (PhD); astrophysics (MS, PhD); audiology (Au D); behavioral neuroscience (PhD); biological design (PhD); biology (MNS, MS, PhD); biology and society (PhD); chemistry and biochemistry (MS, PhD); Chinese (MA); clinical psychology (PhD); cognition, action and perception (PhD); communication (MA, PhD); communication disorders (MS); computational biosciences (PSM, PhD); creative writing (MFA); developmental psychology (PhD); East/Southeast Asian history (MA, PhD); English (MA, PhD); environmental social science (PhD); European history (MA, PhD); family and human development (MS, PhD); film analysis (MLS); French (MA); gender studies (PhD); geographic education (MAS); geographic information systems (MAS); geography (MA, PhD); geological sciences (MS, PhD); German (MA); human and social dimensions of science and technology (PhD); humanities (MA, MAS, MFA, MLS, MTESOL, PhD); infant-family practice (MAS); Japanese (MA); justice studies (MS, PhD); kinesiology (PhD); Latin American studies (MA, PhD); liberal arts and sciences (MA, MAS, MFA, MLS, MNS, MS, MTESOL, PSM, Au D, PhD); marriage and family therapy (MAS); mathematics (MA, MNS, PhD); microbiology (MNS, MS, PhD); molecular and cellular biology (MS, PhD); museum studies in anthropology (MA); nanoscience (PSM); natural sciences (MA, MNS, MS, PSM, Au D, PhD); neuroscience (PhD); North American history (MA, PhD); philosophy (MA, PhD); physics (MNS, MS, PhD); plant biology (MNS, MS, PhD); political science (MA, PhD); public history (MA); quantitative psychology (PhD); religious studies (MA, PhD); screenwriting (MAS); social psychology (PhD); social science and health (PhD); social sciences (MA, MAS, MS, PhD); sociology (MA, PhD); Spanish (MA, PhD); speech and hearing science (PhD); teaching English to speakers of other languages (MTESOL).

Herberger College of the Arts Offers art (MA, MFA, PhD); arts (MA, MFA, MM, DMA, PhD); composition (MM); creative writing (playwriting) (MFA); dance (MFA); music (MA, DMA); music education (MM); music therapy (MM); performance (MM); theatre (MA, MFA, PhD).

Ira A. Fulton School of Engineering *Degree program information:* Part-time programs available. Offers aerospace engineering (MS, MSE, PhD); bioengineering (MS, PhD); biomedical informatics (MS, PhD); chemical engineering (MS, MSE, PhD); civil and environmental engineering (MS, MSE, PhD); computer science (MCS, MS, PhD); construction (MS); electrical engineering (MS, MSE, PhD); embedded systems (M Eng); engineering (M Eng, MCS, MS, MSE, PhD); enterprise systems innovation and management (MSE); industrial engineering (MS, MSE, PhD); materials science and engineering (MS, MSE, PhD); mechanical engineering (MS, MSE, PhD); modeling and simulation (M Eng); quality and reliability engineering (M Eng); semiconductor processing and packaging (MSE); software engineering (MSE); systems engineering (M Eng).

Mary Lou Fulton College of Education *Degree program information:* Part-time programs available. Offers counseling (M Ed, MC); counseling psychology (PhD); curriculum and instruction (M Ed, MA, Ed D, PhD); education (M Ed, MA, MC, Ed D, PhD); educational administration and supervision (M Ed, Ed D); educational leadership and policy studies (M Ed, MA, Ed D, PhD); educational psychology (M Ed, MA, PhD); educational technology (M Ed, PhD); higher and post-secondary education (M Ed); psychology in education (M Ed, MA, MC, PhD); social and philosophical foundations of education (MA); special education (M Ed, MA).

School of Sustainability Offers sustainability (MA, MS, PhD).

Arizona State University (continued)

W.P. Carey School of Business *Degree program information:* Part-time programs available. Offers accountancy (M Acc, M Tax, PhD); agribusiness (PhD); business (M Acc, M Tax, MBA, MHSM, MS, PhD); business administration (MBA); economics (MS, PhD); finance (MBA, PhD); health management and policy (MHSM); health sector management (MBA); information management (MS); information systems (PhD); management (MBA, PhD); marketing (MBA, PhD); supply chain management (MBA, PhD).

Sandra Day O'Connor College of Law Students: 560 full-time (250 women), 19 part-time (14 women); includes 128 minority (18 African Americans, 33 American Indian/Alaska Native, 21 Asian Americans or Pacific Islanders, 56 Hispanic Americans), 8 international. Average age 27. 2,736 applicants, 28% accepted, 181 enrolled. *Faculty:* 61 full-time (21 women), 36 part-time/adjunct (8 women). Expenses: Contact institution. *Financial support:* In 2008–09, 475 students received support; research assistantships, teaching assistantships, career-related internships or fieldwork, Federal Work-Study, institutionally sponsored loans, scholarships/grants, tuition waivers (full and partial), and unspecified assistantships available. Financial award application deadline: 3/5; financial award applicants required to submit FAFSA. In 2008, 240 JDs awarded. Offers biotechnology and genomics (LL M); law (JD); legal studies (MLS); tribal policy, law and government (LL M). *Application deadline:* For fall admission, 11/1 for domestic and international students; for spring admission, 2/1 priority date for domestic and international students. Applications are processed on a rolling basis. *Application fee:* $50. Electronic applications accepted. *Application Contact:* Chitra Damania, Director of Admissions, 480-965-1474, Fax: 480-727-7930, E-mail: law.admissions@asu.edu. *Dean and Foundation Professor of Law,* Dean Paul Schiff Berman, 480-965-6188, Fax: 480-965-6521, E-mail: paul.berman@asu.edu.

ARIZONA STATE UNIVERSITY AT THE DOWNTOWN PHOENIX CAMPUS, Phoenix, AZ 85004

General Information State-supported, coed, comprehensive institution.

GRADUATE UNITS

College of Nursing and Healthcare Innovation Postbaccalaureate distance learning degree programs offered. Offers child and adolescent mental health intervention specialist (Graduate Certificate); community and public health practice (Graduate Certificate); community health (MS); evidence-based practice in nursing (Graduate Certificate); healthcare innovation (MHI); nurse education in academic and practice settings (Graduate Certificate); nurse educator (MS); nursing (MS); nursing and healthcare innovation (PhD); nursing practice (DNP).

College of Public Programs Offers community resources and development (PhD); nonprofit studies (MNpS); public affairs (MPA, MPP, PhD); recreation and tourism studies (MS); social work (MSW, PhD).

Walter Cronkite School of Journalism and Mass Communication Offers journalism and mass communication (MMC). Electronic applications accepted.

ARIZONA STATE UNIVERSITY AT THE POLYTECHNIC CAMPUS, Mesa, AZ 85212

General Information State-supported, coed, comprehensive institution. *Graduate housing:* Rooms and/or apartments available on a first-come, first-served basis to single and married students. Housing application deadline: 3/31.

GRADUATE UNITS

College of Technology and Innovation *Degree program information:* Part-time and evening/weekend programs available. Offers aeronautical management technology (MS); electronic systems (MS); mechanical and manufacturing engineering technology (MS); technology and innovation (MCST, MS); technology management (MS). Electronic applications accepted.

Division of Computing Studies *Degree program information:* Part-time programs available. Offers computing studies (MCST); technology (MS).

Morrison School of Management and Agribusiness *Degree program information:* Part-time and evening/weekend programs available. Offers agribusiness (MS). Electronic applications accepted.

School of Applied Arts and Sciences Offers applied arts and sciences (MS, PhD); applied biological sciences (MS); applied psychology (MS); exercise and wellness (MS); human nutrition (MS); physical activity, nutrition and wellness (PhD). Electronic applications accepted.

The School of Educational Innovation and Teacher Preparation Offers administration/supervision (M Ed); curriculum and instruction (M Ed); physical education (MPE, PhD). Electronic applications accepted.

ARIZONA STATE UNIVERSITY AT THE WEST CAMPUS, Phoenix, AZ 85069-7100

General Information State-supported, coed, comprehensive institution. *Graduate housing:* Room and/or apartments available on a first-come, first-served basis to single students; on-campus housing not available to married students.

GRADUATE UNITS

College of Human Services *Degree program information:* Part-time and evening/weekend programs available. Offers communication (MA); human services (MA, MS, MSW, PhD, Certificate); social work (MSW). Electronic applications accepted.

School of Aging and Lifespan Development *Degree program information:* Part-time and evening/weekend programs available. Offers aging and lifespan development (MS); gerontology (Certificate). Electronic applications accepted.

School of Criminology and Criminal Justice *Degree program information:* Part-time and evening/weekend programs available. Offers criminal justice (MA); criminology and criminal justice (MS, PhD). Electronic applications accepted.

College of Teacher Education and Leadership *Degree program information:* Part-time and evening/weekend programs available. Offers educational administration and supervision (M Ed); elementary education (M Ed, Certificate); leadership/innovation (administration) (Ed D); leadership/innovation (teaching) (Ed D); secondary education (M Ed, Certificate); special education (M Ed). Electronic applications accepted.

New College of Interdisciplinary Arts and Sciences *Degree program information:* Part-time and evening/weekend programs available. Offers interdisciplinary studies (MA); social justice and human rights (MA). Electronic applications accepted.

School of Global Management and Leadership *Degree program information:* Part-time and evening/weekend programs available. Offers accountancy (Certificate); accounting and applied leadership (MAAL); applied leadership and management (MALM); customer-centric innovation and marketing research (MS); financial analysis and portfolio management (MS). Electronic applications accepted.

ARKANSAS STATE UNIVERSITY, Jonesboro, State University, AR 72467

General Information State-supported, coed, university. CGS member. *Enrollment:* 11,490 graduate, professional, and undergraduate students; 567 full-time matriculated graduate/professional students (318 women), 1,159 part-time matriculated graduate/professional students (809 women). *Enrollment by degree level:* 1,394 master's, 142 doctoral, 190 other advanced degrees. *Graduate faculty:* 225 full-time (87 women), 60 part-time/adjunct (33 women). *International tuition:* $7938 full-time. Tuition, state resident: full-time $3744; part-time $208 per credit hour. Tuition, nonresident: full-time $9540; part-time $530 per credit hour. *Required fees:* $896; $47 per credit hour. $25 per term. One-time fee: $50. Tuition and fees vary according to course load and program. *Graduate housing:* Rooms and/or apartments available on a first-come, first-served basis to single and married students. Typical cost: $4876 per year for single students; $4876 per year for married students. Room charges vary according to board plan and housing facility selected. Housing application deadline: 8/21. *Student services:* Campus employment opportunities, campus safety program, career counseling, child daycare facilities, exercise/wellness program, free psychological counseling, international student services, multicultural affairs office, services for students with disabilities. *Library facilities:* Dean B. Ellis Library. *Online resources:* library catalog, web page. *Collection:* 620,610 titles, 2,764 serial subscriptions, 22,892 audiovisual materials. *Research affiliation:* Radiance Technologies, Alaka'i Consulting and Engineering.

Computer facilities: Computer purchase and lease plans are available. 510 computers available on campus for general student use. A campuswide network can be accessed from student residence rooms and from off campus. Online class registration is available. *Web address:* http://www.astate.edu/.

General Application Contact: Dr. Andrew Sustich, Dean of the Graduate School, 870-972-3029, Fax: 870-972-3857, E-mail: sustich@astate.edu.

GRADUATE UNITS

Graduate School Students: 567 full-time (318 women), 1,159 part-time (809 women); includes 263 minority (235 African Americans, 5 American Indian/Alaska Native, 12 Asian Americans or Pacific Islanders, 11 Hispanic Americans), 169 international. Average age 33. 1,365 applicants, 82% accepted, 580 enrolled. *Faculty:* 223 full-time (85 women), 60 part-time/adjunct (33 women). Expenses: Contact institution. *Financial support:* In 2008–09, 358 students received support; fellowships, research assistantships, teaching assistantships, career-related internships or fieldwork, scholarships/grants, and unspecified assistantships available. Financial award application deadline: 7/1; financial award applicants required to submit FAFSA. In 2008, 427 master's, 9 doctorates, 31 other advanced degrees awarded. *Degree program information:* Part-time programs available. *Application deadline:* Applications are processed on a rolling basis. *Application fee:* $50. Electronic applications accepted. *Application Contact:* Dr. Andrew Sustich, Dean of the Graduate School, 870-972-3029, Fax: 870-972-3857, E-mail: sustich@astate.edu. *Dean of the Graduate School,* Dr. Andrew Sustich, 870-972-3029, Fax: 870-972-3857, E-mail: sustich@astate.edu.

College of Agriculture and Technology Students: 8 full-time (3 women), 28 part-time (15 women); includes 5 minority (all African Americans), 3 international. Average age 31. 22 applicants, 95% accepted, 15 enrolled. *Faculty:* 8 full-time (0 women), 3 part-time/adjunct (1 woman). Expenses: Contact institution. *Financial support:* In 2008–09, 9 students received support; teaching assistantships, career-related internships or fieldwork, scholarships/grants, and unspecified assistantships available. Financial award application deadline: 7/1; financial award applicants required to submit FAFSA. In 2008, 13 master's awarded. *Degree program information:* Part-time programs available. Offers agricultural education (MSA, SCCT); agriculture (MSA); molecular biosciences (PhD); vocational-technical administration (MS, SCCT). *Application deadline:* For fall admission, 7/15 for domestic students, 7/1 for international students; for spring admission, 12/1 for domestic students, 11/13 for international students. Applications are processed on a rolling basis. *Application fee:* $30 ($40 for international students). Electronic applications accepted. *Application Contact:* Dr. Andrew Sustich, Dean of the Graduate School, 870-972-3029, Fax: 870-972-3857, E-mail: sustich@astate.edu. *Dean,* Dr. Gregory Phillips, 870-972-2085, Fax: 870-972-3885, E-mail: gphillips@astate.edu.

College of Business Students: 74 full-time (33 women), 131 part-time (56 women); includes 20 minority (16 African Americans, 2 Asian Americans or Pacific Islanders, 2 Hispanic Americans), 44 international. Average age 29. 160 applicants, 79% accepted, 75 enrolled. *Faculty:* 31 full-time (7 women), 2 part-time/adjunct (1 woman). Expenses: Contact institution. *Financial support:* In 2008–09, 35 students received support; teaching assistantships, career-related internships or fieldwork, scholarships/grants, and unspecified assistantships available. Financial award application deadline: 7/1; financial award applicants required to submit FAFSA. In 2008, 75 master's awarded. *Degree program information:* Part-time programs available. Offers accountancy (M Acc); business (EMBA, M Acc, MBA, MS, MSE, SCCT); business administration (EMBA, MBA); business administration education (SCCT); business education (SCCT); business technology education (MSE); information systems and e-commerce (MS). *Application deadline:* For fall admission, 7/15 for domestic students, 7/1 for international students; for spring admission, 12/1 for domestic students, 11/13 for international students. Applications are processed on a rolling basis. *Application fee:* $30 ($40 for international students). Electronic applications accepted. *Application Contact:* Dr. Andrew Sustich, Dean of the Graduate School, 870-972-3029, Fax: 870-972-3857, E-mail: sustich@astate.edu. *Dean,* Dr. Len Frey, 870-972-3035, Fax: 870-972-3744, E-mail: lfrey@astate.edu.

College of Communications Students: 20 full-time (14 women), 19 part-time (7 women); includes 15 minority (all African Americans), 9 international. Average age 28. 34 applicants, 94% accepted, 20 enrolled. *Faculty:* 13 full-time (5 women), 1 part-time/adjunct (0 women). Expenses: Contact institution. *Financial support:* In 2008–09, 15 students received support. Career-related internships or fieldwork, scholarships/grants, and unspecified assistantships available. Financial award application deadline: 7/1; financial award applicants required to submit FAFSA. In 2008, 10 master's awarded. *Degree program information:* Part-time programs available. Offers communication studies and theatre arts (MA); communication studies and theatre arts education (SCCT); communications (MA, MSMC, SCCT); journalism (MSMC); radio-television (MSMC). *Application deadline:* For fall admission, 7/15 for domestic students, 7/1 for international students; for spring admission, 12/1 for domestic students, 11/13 for international students. Applications are processed on a rolling basis. *Application fee:* $30 ($40 for international students). Electronic applications accepted. *Application Contact:* Dr. Andrew Sustich, Dean of the Graduate School, 870-972-3029, Fax: 870-972-3857, E-mail: sustich@astate.edu. *Dean,* Dr. Russell Shain, 870-972-2468, Fax: 870-972-3856, E-mail: rshain@astate.edu.

College of Education Students: 122 full-time (103 women), 584 part-time (407 women); includes 129 minority (116 African Americans, 1 American Indian/Alaska Native, 5 Asian Americans or Pacific Islanders, 7 Hispanic Americans), 5 international. Average age 35. 504 applicants, 78% accepted, 237 enrolled. *Faculty:* 37 full-time (17 women), 29 part-time/adjunct (16 women). Expenses: Contact institution. *Financial support:* In 2008–09, 62 students received support; teaching assistantships, career-related internships or fieldwork, scholarships/grants, and unspecified assistantships available. Financial award application deadline: 7/1; financial award applicants required to submit FAFSA. In 2008, 122 master's, 5 doctorates, 28 other advanced degrees awarded. *Degree program information:* Part-time programs available. Offers college student personnel services (MS); community college administration education (SCCT); counselor education (Ed S); curriculum and instruction (MSE); early childhood education (MSE); early childhood services (MS); education (MRC, MS, MSE, Ed D, Certificate, Ed S, SCCT); education theory and practice (MSE); educational leadership (MSE, Ed D, Ed S); exercise science (MS); middle level education (MSE); physical education (MS, MSE, SCCT); reading (MSE, SCCT); rehabilitation counseling (MRC); school counseling (MSE); special education (MSE); student affairs (Certificate). *Application deadline:* Applications are processed on a rolling basis. *Application fee:* $50. Electronic applications accepted. *Application Contact:* Dr. Andrew Sustich, Dean of the Graduate School, 870-972-3029, Fax: 870-972-3857, E-mail: sustich@astate.edu. *Interim Dean,* Dr. Don Maness, 870-972-3057, Fax: 870-972-3828, E-mail: dmaness@astate.edu.

College of Engineering Students: 1 full-time (0 women), 11 part-time (2 women); includes 1 minority (African American), 2 international. Average age 31. 15 applicants, 87% accepted, 9 enrolled. *Faculty:* 3 part-time/adjunct (0 women). Expenses: Contact institution. *Financial support:* Career-related internships or fieldwork, scholarships/grants, and unspecified assistantships available. *Degree program information:* Part-time programs available. Offers engineering (MEM). *Application deadline:* For fall admission, 6/1 for domestic and international students; for spring admission, 10/15 for domestic and international students. Applications are processed on a rolling basis. *Application fee:* $30 ($40 for international students). Electronic applications accepted. *Application Contact:* Dr. Andrew Sustich, Dean of the Graduate School, 870-972-3029, Fax: 870-972-3857, E-mail: sustich@astate.edu. *Associate Dean,* Dr. Ricky Clifft, 870-972-2088, Fax: 870-972-3948, E-mail: rclifft@astate.edu.

College of Fine Arts Students: 7 full-time (3 women); 13 part-time (5 women); includes 2 minority (1 African American, 1 American Indian/Alaska Native), 1 international. Average age 33. 17 applicants, 76% accepted, 7 enrolled. *Faculty:* 26 full-time (8 women), 2 part-time/adjunct (both women). Expenses: Contact institution. *Financial support:* In 2008–09, 10 students received support; teaching assistantships, career-related internships or fieldwork, scholarships/grants, and unspecified assistantships available. Financial award application deadline: 7/1; financial award applicants required to submit FAFSA. In 2008, 10 master's, 2 other advanced degrees awarded. *Degree program information:* Part-time programs available. Offers art (MA); communication studies and theatre arts (MA); communication studies and theatre arts education (SCCT); fine arts (MA, MM, MME, SCCT); music education (MME, SCCT); performance (MM). *Application deadline:* Applications are processed on a rolling basis. *Application fee:* $30 ($40 for international students). Electronic applications accepted. *Application Contact:* Dr. Andrew Sustich, Dean of the Graduate School, 870-972-3029, Fax: 870-972-3857, E-mail: sustich@astate.edu. *Dean*, Dr. Daniel Reeves, 870-972-3053, Fax: 870-972-3932, E-mail: dreeves@astate.edu.

College of Humanities and Social Sciences Students: 58 full-time (34 women), 118 part-time (69 women); includes 38 minority (all African Americans), 10 international. Average age 35. 99 applicants, 76% accepted, 38 enrolled. *Faculty:* 46 full-time (20 women), 5 part-time/adjunct (4 women). Expenses: Contact institution. *Financial support:* In 2008–09, 52 students received support; fellowships, teaching assistantships, career-related internships or fieldwork, scholarships/grants, and unspecified assistantships available. Financial award application deadline: 7/1; financial award applicants required to submit FAFSA. In 2008, 49 master's, 1 other advanced degree awarded. *Degree program information:* Part-time programs available. Offers criminal justice (MA, Certificate); English (MA); English education (MSE, SCCT); heritage studies (MA, PhD); history (MA); history education (SCCT); humanities and social sciences (MA, MPA, MSE, PhD, Certificate, SCCT); political science (MA); political science education (SCCT); public administration (MPA); social science education (MSE); sociology (MA); sociology education (SCCT). *Application deadline:* Applications are processed on a rolling basis. *Application fee:* $50. Electronic applications accepted. *Application Contact:* Dr. Andrew Sustich, Dean of the Graduate School, 870-972-3029, Fax: 870-972-3857, E-mail: sustich@astate.edu. *Dean*, Dr. Gloria Gibson, 870-972-3973, Fax: 870-972-3976, E-mail: ggibson@astate.edu.

College of Nursing and Health Professions Students: 175 full-time (96 women), 145 part-time (122 women); includes 38 minority (33 African Americans, 1 American Indian/Alaska Native, 3 Asian Americans or Pacific Islanders, 1 Hispanic American), 19 international. Average age 31. 193 applicants, 81% accepted, 87 enrolled. *Faculty:* 19 full-time (13 women), 8 part-time/adjunct (6 women). Expenses: Contact institution. *Financial support:* In 2008–09, 67 students received support. Career-related internships or fieldwork, scholarships/grants, and unspecified assistantships available. Financial award application deadline: 7/1; financial award applicants required to submit FAFSA. In 2008, 119 master's awarded. *Degree program information:* Part-time programs available. Offers aging studies (Certificate); communication disorders (MCD); health sciences (MS); nurse anesthesia (MSN); nursing (MSN); nursing and health professions (MCD, MPT, MS, MSN, MSW, DPT, Certificate); physical therapy (MPT, DPT); social work (MSW). *Application deadline:* Applications are processed on a rolling basis. *Application fee:* $30 ($40 for international students). Electronic applications accepted. *Application Contact:* Dr. Andrew Sustich, Dean of the Graduate School, 870-972-3029, Fax: 870-972-3857, E-mail: sustich@astate.edu. *Dean*, Dr. Susan Hanrahan, 870-972-3112, Fax: 870-972-2040, E-mail: hanrahan@astate.edu.

College of Sciences and Mathematics Students: 100 full-time (31 women), 38 part-time (12 women); includes 8 minority (4 African Americans, 2 American Indian/Alaska Native, 1 Asian American or Pacific Islander, 1 Hispanic American), 76 international. Average age 26. 287 applicants, 80% accepted, 61 enrolled. *Faculty:* 38 full-time (12 women), 7 part-time/adjunct (3 women). Expenses: Contact institution. *Financial support:* In 2008–09, 73 students received support; fellowships, teaching assistantships, career-related internships or fieldwork, scholarships/grants, and unspecified assistantships available. Financial award application deadline: 7/1; financial award applicants required to submit FAFSA. In 2008, 29 master's, 4 doctorates awarded. *Degree program information:* Part-time programs available. Offers biological sciences (MA); biology (MS); biology education (MSE, SCCT); chemistry (MS); chemistry education (MSE, SCCT); computer science (MS); environmental sciences (MS, PhD); mathematics (MS); mathematics education (MSE); sciences and mathematics (MA, MS, MSE, PhD, SCCT). *Application deadline:* Applications are processed on a rolling basis. *Application fee:* $50. Electronic applications accepted. *Application Contact:* Dr. Andrew Sustich, Dean of the Graduate School, 870-972-3029, Fax: 870-972-3857, E-mail: sustich@astate.edu. *Interim Dean*, Dr. Andrew Sustich, 870-972-3079, Fax: 870-972-3827, E-mail: sustich@astate.edu.

ARKANSAS TECH UNIVERSITY, Russellville, AR 72801

General Information State-supported, coed, comprehensive institution. *Enrollment:* 7,492 graduate, professional, and undergraduate students; 124 full-time matriculated graduate/professional students (69 women), 408 part-time matriculated graduate/professional students (277 women). *Enrollment by degree level:* 515 master's, 17 other advanced degrees. *Graduate faculty:* 62 full-time (30 women), 6 part-time/adjunct (5 women). Tuition, state resident: full-time $1575; part-time $175 per credit hour. Tuition, nonresident: full-time $3150; part-time $350 per credit hour. Tuition and fees vary according to course load. *Graduate housing:* Room and/or apartments available on a first-come, first-served basis to single students; on-campus housing not available to married students. Typical cost: $2824 per year ($4888 including board). Room and board charges vary according to board plan, campus/location and housing facility selected. Housing application deadline: 8/1. *Student services:* Campus employment opportunities, campus safety program, career counseling, exercise/wellness program, free psychological counseling, international student services, low-cost health insurance, multicultural affairs office, services for students with disabilities, teacher training. *Library facilities:* Ross Pendergraft Library and Technology Center. *Online resources:* library catalog, web page. *Collection:* 278,540 titles, 1,069 serial subscriptions, 6,975 audiovisual materials.

Computer facilities: Computer purchase and lease plans are available. 700 computers available on campus for general student use. A campuswide network can be accessed from student residence rooms and from off campus. Online class registration is available. *Web address:* http://www.atu.edu/.

General Application Contact: Dr. Eldon G. Clary, Dean of Graduate School, 479-968-0398, Fax: 479-964-0542, E-mail: graduate.school@atu.edu.

GRADUATE UNITS

Graduate School Students: 124 full-time (69 women), 408 part-time (277 women); includes 38 minority (17 African Americans, 6 American Indian/Alaska Native, 6 Asian Americans or Pacific Islanders, 9 Hispanic Americans), 75 international. Average age 33. *Faculty:* 62 full-time (30 women), 6 part-time/adjunct (5 women). Expenses: Contact institution. *Financial support:* In 2008–09, teaching assistantships with full tuition reimbursements (averaging $4,000 per year); research assistantships, career-related internships or fieldwork, Federal Work-Study, scholarships/grants, health care benefits, and unspecified assistantships also available. Support available to part-time students. Financial award application deadline: 4/15; financial award applicants required to submit FAFSA. In 2008, 233 master's, 4 other advanced degrees awarded. *Degree program information:* Part-time and evening/weekend programs available. Postbaccalaureate distance learning degree programs offered (no on-campus study). *Application deadline:* For fall admission, 3/1 priority date for domestic students, 5/1 priority date for international students; for winter admission, 10/1 priority date for international students; for spring admission, 10/1 priority date for domestic and international students. Applications are processed on a rolling basis. *Application fee:* $0 ($30 for international students). Electronic applications accepted. *Application Contact:* Dr. Eldon G. Clary, Dean of Graduate School, 479-968-0398, Fax: 479-964-0542, E-mail: graduate.school@atu.edu. *Dean of Graduate School*, Dr. Eldon G. Clary, 479-968-0398, Fax: 479-964-0542, E-mail: graduate.school@atu.edu.

School of Community Education Students: 14 full-time (2 women), 37 part-time (15 women); includes 4 minority (1 African American, 1 American Indian/Alaska Native, 1 Asian American or Pacific Islander, 1 Hispanic American), 2 international. Average age 31. Expenses: Contact institution. *Financial support:* In 2008–09, teaching assistantships with full tuition reimbursements (averaging $4,000 per year); career-related internships or fieldwork, Federal Work-Study, scholarships/grants, health care benefits, and unspecified assistantships also available. Support available to part-time students. Financial award application deadline: 4/15; financial award applicants required to submit FAFSA. In 2008, 4 master's awarded. *Degree program information:* Part-time programs available. Offers emergency management and homeland security (MS). *Application deadline:* For fall admission, 3/1 priority date for domestic students, 5/1 priority date for international students; for winter admission, 10/1 priority date for international students; for spring admission, 10/1 priority date for domestic and international students. Applications are processed on a rolling basis. *Application fee:* $0 ($30 for international students). Electronic applications accepted. *Application Contact:* Dr. Eldon G. Clary, Dean of Graduate School, 479-968-0398, Fax: 479-964-0542, E-mail: graduate.school@atu.edu. *Dean*, Dr. Mary Ann Rollans, 479-968-0234 Ext. 479, E-mail: maryann.rollans@atu.edu.

School of Education Students: 33 full-time (26 women), 229 part-time (175 women); includes 19 minority (10 African Americans, 3 American Indian/Alaska Native, 1 Asian American or Pacific Islander, 5 Hispanic Americans), 12 international. Average age 34. Expenses: Contact institution. *Financial support:* In 2008–09, teaching assistantships with full tuition reimbursements (averaging $4,000 per year); career-related internships or fieldwork, Federal Work-Study, scholarships/grants, health care benefits, and unspecified assistantships also available. Support available to part-time students. Financial award application deadline: 4/15; financial award applicants required to submit FAFSA. In 2008, 123 master's, 4 other advanced degrees awarded. *Degree program information:* Part-time and evening/weekend programs available. Postbaccalaureate distance learning degree programs offered (no on-campus study). Offers college student personnel (MSE); educational leadership (M Ed, Ed S); English education (M Ed); gifted education (MSE); instructional improvement (M Ed); secondary education (M Ed); teaching, learning and leadership (M Ed). *Application deadline:* For fall admission, 3/1 priority date for domestic students, 5/1 priority date for international students; for winter admission, 10/1 priority date for international students; for spring admission, 10/1 priority date for domestic and international students. Applications are processed on a rolling basis. *Application fee:* $0 ($30 for international students). Electronic applications accepted. *Application Contact:* Dr. Eldon G. Clary, Dean of Graduate School, 479-968-0398, Fax: 479-964-0542, E-mail: graduate.school@atu.edu. *Dean*, Dr. C. Glenn Sheets, 479-968-0350, Fax: 479-968-0350, E-mail: glenn.sheets@atu.edu.

School of Liberal and Fine Arts Students: 40 full-time (31 women), 81 part-time (60 women); includes 10 minority (3 African Americans, 2 American Indian/Alaska Native, 2 Asian Americans or Pacific Islanders, 3 Hispanic Americans), 19 international. Average age 33. Expenses: Contact institution. *Financial support:* In 2008–09, teaching assistantships with full tuition reimbursements (averaging $4,000 per year); career-related internships or fieldwork, Federal Work-Study, scholarships/grants, health care benefits, and unspecified assistantships also available. Support available to part-time students. Financial award application deadline: 4/15; financial award applicants required to submit FAFSA. In 2008, 70 master's awarded. *Degree program information:* Part-time programs available. Offers communication (MLA); English (M Ed, MA); fine arts (MLA); history (MA); multi-media journalism (MA); social science (MLA); social studies (M Ed); Spanish (MA, MLA); teaching English as a second language (MA, MLA). *Application deadline:* For fall admission, 3/1 priority date for domestic students, 5/1 priority date for international students; for winter admission, 10/1 priority date for international students; for spring admission, 10/1 priority date for domestic and international students. Applications are processed on a rolling basis. *Application fee:* $0 ($30 for international students). Electronic applications accepted. *Application Contact:* Dr. Eldon G. Clary, Dean of Graduate School, 479-968-0398, Fax: 479-964-0542, E-mail: graduate.school@atu.edu. *Dean*, Dr. Georgena Duncan, 479-968-0266, Fax: 479-968-0275, E-mail: georgena.duncan@atu.edu.

School of Physical and Life Sciences Students: 6 full-time (4 women), 7 part-time (2 women). Average age 29. Expenses: Contact institution. *Financial support:* In 2008–09, teaching assistantships with full tuition reimbursements (averaging $4,000 per year); career-related internships or fieldwork, Federal Work-Study, scholarships/grants, health care benefits, and unspecified assistantships also available. Support available to part-time students. Financial award application deadline: 4/15; financial award applicants required to submit FAFSA. In 2008, 3 master's awarded. Offers fisheries and wildlife biology (MS); nursing (MSN). *Application deadline:* For fall admission, 3/1 priority date for domestic students, 5/1 priority date for international students; for winter admission, 10/1 priority date for international students; for spring admission, 10/1 priority date for domestic and international students. Applications are processed on a rolling basis. *Application fee:* $0 ($30 for international students). Electronic applications accepted. *Application Contact:* Dr. Eldon G. Clary, Dean of Graduate School, 479-968-0398, Fax: 479-964-0542, E-mail: graduate.school@atu.edu. *Dean*, Dr. Richard Cohoon, 479-964-0816, E-mail: richard.cohoon@atu.edu.

School of Systems Science Students: 31 full-time (6 women), 34 part-time (9 women); includes 5 minority (3 African Americans, 2 Asian Americans or Pacific Islanders), 42 international. Average age 26. Expenses: Contact institution. *Financial support:* In 2008–09, teaching assistantships with full tuition reimbursements (averaging $4,000 per year); career-related internships or fieldwork, Federal Work-Study, scholarships/grants, health care benefits, and unspecified assistantships also available. Support available to part-time students. Financial award application deadline: 4/15; financial award applicants required to submit FAFSA. In 2008, 33 master's awarded. *Degree program information:* Part-time programs available. Offers engineering (M Engr); information technology (MS); mathematics (M Ed). *Application deadline:* For fall admission, 3/1 priority date for domestic students, 5/1 priority date for international students; for winter admission, 10/1 priority date for international students; for spring admission, 10/1 priority date for domestic and international students. Applications are processed on a rolling basis. *Application fee:* $0 ($30 for international students). Electronic applications accepted. *Application Contact:* Dr. Eldon G. Clary, Dean of Graduate School, 479-968-0398, Fax: 479-964-0542, E-mail: graduate.school@atu.edu. *Dean*, Dr. William Hoefler, 479-968-0353 Ext. 501, E-mail: whoeflerjr@atu.edu.

ARMSTRONG ATLANTIC STATE UNIVERSITY, Savannah, GA 31419-1997

General Information State-supported, coed, primarily women, comprehensive institution. *Graduate housing:* Room and/or apartments available on a first-come, first-served basis to single students; on-campus housing not available to married students.

GRADUATE UNITS

School of Graduate Studies *Degree program information:* Part-time and evening/weekend programs available. Postbaccalaureate distance learning degree programs offered (minimal on-campus study). Offers adult education (M Ed); computer science (MS); criminal justice (MS); curriculum and instruction (M Ed); early childhood education (M Ed); education (M Ed); elementary education (M Ed); health services administration (MHSA); history (MA); liberal and professional studies (MALPS); middle grades education (M Ed); nursing (MSN); physical therapy (DPT); public health (MPH); secondary education (M Ed); special education (M Ed); sports health sciences (MSSM). Electronic applications accepted.

ART ACADEMY OF CINCINNATI, Cincinnati, OH 45202

General Information Independent, coed, comprehensive institution. *Enrollment:* 165 graduate, professional, and undergraduate students; 2 part-time matriculated graduate/professional students (1 woman). *Enrollment by degree level:* 2 master's. *Graduate faculty:* 1 full-time (0 women), 1 (woman) part-time/adjunct. *Tuition:* Full-time $9625; part-time $875 per credit hour. *Required fees:* $380; $190 per semester. *Graduate housing:* Rooms and/or apartments available on a first-come, first-served basis to single and married students. Typical cost: $900 per year for single students; $900 per year for married students. Housing application deadline: 5/1. *Student services:* Free psychological counseling.

Computer facilities: 40 computers available on campus for general student use. A campuswide network can be accessed. *Web address:* http://www.artacademy.edu/.

General Application Contact: Joe Fisher, Assistant Director of Admissions, 513-562-8754, Fax: 513-562-8778, E-mail: jfisher@artacademy.edu.

GRADUATE UNITS

Program in Art Education Students: 2 part-time (1 woman); includes 1 minority (African American). Average age 35. *Faculty:* 1 full-time (0 women), 1 (woman) part-time/adjunct. Expenses: Contact institution. *Financial support:* Scholarships/grants available. Support avail-

Art Academy of Cincinnati (continued)
able to part-time students. Financial award application deadline: 5/1; financial award applicants required to submit FAFSA. In 2008, 3 degrees awarded. *Degree program information:* Part-time programs available. Offers art education (MAAE). Offered during summer only. *Application deadline:* Applications are processed on a rolling basis. *Application fee:* $0. Electronic applications accepted. *Application Contact:* Joe Fisher, Assistant Director of Admissions, 513-562-8754, Fax: 513-562-8778, E-mail: jfisher@artacademy.edu. *Chair,* Keith Benjamin, 513-562-6262, Fax: 513-562-8778, E-mail: kbenjamin@artacademy.edu.

ART CENTER COLLEGE OF DESIGN, Pasadena, CA 91103-1999

General Information Independent, coed, comprehensive institution. *Graduate housing:* On-campus housing not available.

GRADUATE UNITS

Graduate Division Offers broadcast cinema (MFA); environmental design (MS); fine arts (MFA); media design (MFA); product design (MS).

THE ART INSTITUTE OF BOSTON AT LESLEY UNIVERSITY, Boston, MA 02215-2598

General Information Independent, coed, comprehensive institution.

GRADUATE UNITS

Program in Visual Arts Offers visual arts (MFA).

THE ART INSTITUTE OF CALIFORNIA–SAN FRANCISCO, San Francisco, CA 94102-4908

General Information Proprietary, coed, comprehensive institution.

GRADUATE UNITS

Master of Fine Arts Program Offers computer animation (MFA).

ASBURY COLLEGE, Wilmore, KY 40390-1198

General Information Independent-religious, coed, comprehensive institution. *Graduate housing:* On-campus housing not available.

GRADUATE UNITS

Graduate Programs *Degree program information:* Part-time programs available.

ASBURY THEOLOGICAL SEMINARY, Wilmore, KY 40390-1199

General Information Independent-religious, coed, primarily men, graduate-only institution. *Enrollment by degree level:* 845 first professional, 441 master's, 259 doctoral, 15 other advanced degrees. *Graduate faculty:* 67 full-time (15 women), 74 part-time/adjunct (14 women). *Tuition:* Full-time $12,474; part-time $462 per credit hour. *Required fees:* $50; $30 per year. Tuition and fees vary according to course level, course load, degree level, campus/location and program. *Graduate housing:* Rooms and/or apartments available on a first-come, first-served basis to single and married students. *Student services:* Campus employment opportunities, campus safety program, exercise/wellness program, free psychological counseling, international student services, low-cost health insurance, multicultural affairs office, services for students with disabilities, writing training. *Library facilities:* B. L. Fisher Library plus 1 other. *Online resources:* library catalog, web page. *Collection:* 339,893 titles, 1,125 serial subscriptions, 40,597 audiovisual materials.

Computer facilities: 55 computers available on campus for general student use. A campuswide network can be accessed from student residence rooms and from off campus. Online class registration, course management system are available. *Web address:* http://www.asburyseminary.edu/.

General Application Contact: Janelle Vernon, Admissions Director, 859-858-2211, Fax: 859-858-2287, E-mail: admissions.office@asburyseminary.edu.

GRADUATE UNITS

Graduate and Professional Programs Students: 708 full-time (219 women), 852 part-time (263 women); includes 110 minority (59 African Americans, 10 American Indian/Alaska Native, 12 Asian Americans or Pacific Islanders, 29 Hispanic Americans), 156 international. Average age 25. 765 applicants, 75% accepted, 364 enrolled. *Faculty:* 67 full-time (15 women), 74 part-time/adjunct (14 women). Expenses: Contact institution. *Financial support:* In 2008–09, 1,317 students received support. Career-related internships or fieldwork, Federal Work-Study, institutionally sponsored loans, and scholarships/grants available. Support available to part-time students. Financial award applicants required to submit FAFSA. In 2008, 95 master's, 15 doctorates, 38 other advanced degrees awarded. *Degree program information:* Part-time programs available. Postbaccalaureate distance learning degree programs offered (minimal on-campus study). Offers theology (MA, MAC, MACE, MACL, MAPC, MAXM, MAYM, Th M, D Miss, PhD, Certificate). *Application deadline:* Applications are processed on a rolling basis. *Application fee:* $50. Electronic applications accepted. *Application Contact:* Janelle Vernon, Admissions Director, 859-858-2211, Fax: 859-858-2287, E-mail: admissions.office@asburyseminary.edu. *Provost,* Dr. Leslie A. Andrews, 859-858-2206, Fax: 859-858-2025, E-mail: leslie.andrews@asburyseminary.edu.

ASHLAND THEOLOGICAL SEMINARY, Ashland, OH 44805

General Information Independent-religious, coed, graduate-only institution. *Graduate housing:* Rooms and/or apartments available on a first-come, first-served basis to single and married students. Housing application deadline: 6/30.

GRADUATE UNITS

Graduate Programs *Degree program information:* Part-time programs available. Offers biblical and theological studies (MA, MAR); Christian ministry (MAPT); Christian studies (Diploma); clinical pastoral counseling (MACPC); historical studies (MA); ministry (D Min); pastoral counseling (MAPC); pastoral ministry (M Div); theological studies (MA). Electronic applications accepted.

ASHLAND UNIVERSITY, Ashland, OH 44805-3702

General Information Independent-religious, coed, comprehensive institution. CGS member. *Enrollment:* 6,475 graduate, professional, and undergraduate students; 784 full-time matriculated graduate/professional students (476 women), 1,277 part-time matriculated graduate/professional students (835 women). *Enrollment by degree level:* 2,006 master's, 55 doctoral. *Graduate faculty:* 72 full-time (34 women), 181 part-time/adjunct (90 women). *Tuition:* Part-time $419 per credit hour. Tuition and fees vary according to degree level and program. *Graduate housing:* On-campus housing not available. *Student services:* Campus employment opportunities, campus safety program, career counseling, exercise/wellness program, free psychological counseling, international student services, low-cost health insurance, multicultural affairs office, services for students with disabilities, teacher training, writing training. *Library facilities:* Ashland Library plus 2 others. *Online resources:* library catalog, web page. *Collection:* 205,200 titles, 1,625 serial subscriptions, 3,550 audiovisual materials. *Research affiliation:* Teacher Quality Project (TQP) (education).

Computer facilities: Computer purchase and lease plans are available. 760 computers available on campus for general student use. A campuswide network can be accessed from student residence rooms and from off campus. Online class registration is available. *Web address:* http://www.exploreashland.com/.

General Application Contact: Dr. W. Gregory Gerrick, Dean, Graduate School, 419-289-5750, Fax: 419-289-5949, E-mail: ggerrick@ashland.edu.

GRADUATE UNITS

College of Arts and Sciences Students: 67 full-time (38 women), 74 part-time (34 women); includes 9 minority (3 African Americans, 1 Asian American or Pacific Islander, 5 Hispanic Americans). Average age 37. *Faculty:* 3 full-time (0 women), 23 part-time/adjunct (5 women). Expenses: Contact institution. *Financial support:* Application deadline: 4/15. In 2008, 1 master's awarded. *Degree program information:* Part-time programs available. Offers American history and government (MAHG); arts and sciences (MAHG, MFA); creative writing (MFA). *Application deadline:* Applications are processed on a rolling basis. *Application fee:* $30. Electronic applications accepted. *Application Contact:* Dr. W. Gregory Gerrick, Dean, Graduate School, 419-289-5750, Fax: 419-289-5949, E-mail: ggerrick@ashland.edu. *Dean,* Dr. Dawn Weber, 419-289-5107.

Dauch College of Business and Economics Students: 271 full-time (114 women), 334 part-time (157 women); includes 99 minority (80 African Americans, 4 American Indian/Alaska Native, 8 Asian Americans or Pacific Islanders, 7 Hispanic Americans), 50 international. Average age 34. *Faculty:* 15 full-time (4 women), 15 part-time/adjunct (5 women). Expenses: Contact institution. *Financial support:* In 2008–09, 158 students received support. Tuition waivers (partial) and unspecified assistantships available. Financial award application deadline: 4/15; financial award applicants required to submit FAFSA. In 2008, 213 master's awarded. *Degree program information:* Part-time and evening/weekend programs available. Offers business and economics (MBA). *Application deadline:* For fall admission, 8/1 priority date for domestic students; for spring admission, 12/1 priority date for domestic students. Applications are processed on a rolling basis. *Application fee:* $30. Electronic applications accepted. *Application Contact:* Stephen W. Krispinsky, Executive Director of MBA Program, 419-289-5236, Fax: 419-289-5910, E-mail: skrispin@ashland.edu. *Chair,* Dr. Beverly Heimann, 419-289-5216, E-mail: bheimann@ashland.edu.

Dwight Schar College of Education Students: 446 full-time (324 women), 869 part-time (644 women); includes 91 minority (64 African Americans, 1 American Indian/Alaska Native, 6 Asian Americans or Pacific Islanders, 20 Hispanic Americans), 19 international. Average age 33. *Faculty:* 70 full-time (37 women), 199 part-time/adjunct (103 women). Expenses: Contact institution. *Financial support:* In 2008–09, 475 students received support; teaching assistantships with partial tuition reimbursements available, scholarships/grants available. Financial award application deadline: 4/15. In 2008, 640 master's, 8 doctorates awarded. *Degree program information:* Part-time and evening/weekend programs available. Offers adapted physical education (M Ed); administration (M Ed); applied exercise science (M Ed); business manager (M Ed); classroom instruction (M Ed); curriculum specialist (M Ed); education (M Ed, Ed D); educational leadership studies (Ed D); intervention specialist-mild/moderate (M Ed); intervention specialist-moderate/intensive (M Ed); literacy (M Ed); principalship (M Ed); pupil services (M Ed); school treasurer (M Ed); sport education (M Ed); sport management (M Ed); superintendency (M Ed); talent development (M Ed). *Application deadline:* For fall admission, 8/27 for domestic students; for spring admission, 1/14 for domestic students. Applications are processed on a rolling basis. *Application fee:* $30. *Application Contact:* Dr. Linda Billman, Director and Chair, Graduate Studies in Education and Associate Dean, 419-289-5369, Fax: 419-289-5331, E-mail: lbillman@ashland.edu. *Dean,* Dr. James P. Van Keuren, 419-289-5377, E-mail: jvankeu1@ashland.edu.

ASPEN UNIVERSITY, Denver, CO 80246

General Information Independent, coed, upper-level institution. *Graduate housing:* On-campus housing not available.

GRADUATE UNITS

Program in Business Administration *Degree program information:* Part-time and evening/weekend programs available. Postbaccalaureate distance learning degree programs offered (no on-campus study). Offers business administration (MBA); finance (MBA); information management (MBA); project management (MBA, Certificate). Electronic applications accepted.

Program in Information Technology *Degree program information:* Part-time and evening/weekend programs available. Postbaccalaureate distance learning degree programs offered (no on-campus study). Offers information technology (MS, Certificate). Electronic applications accepted.

Programs in Information Management *Degree program information:* Part-time and evening/weekend programs available. Postbaccalaureate distance learning degree programs offered (no on-campus study). Offers information management (MS); information systems (Certificate). Electronic applications accepted.

ASSEMBLIES OF GOD THEOLOGICAL SEMINARY, Springfield, MO 65802

General Information Independent-religious, coed, graduate-only institution. *Enrollment by degree level:* 144 first professional, 196 master's, 106 doctoral. *Graduate faculty:* 16 full-time (3 women), 21 part-time/adjunct (4 women). *Graduate housing:* On-campus housing not available. *Student services:* Career counseling, free psychological counseling, international student services, services for students with disabilities. *Library facilities:* Cordas C. Burnett Library. *Online resources:* library catalog, web page, access to other libraries' catalogs. *Collection:* 95,879 titles, 350 serial subscriptions, 5,321 audiovisual materials.

Computer facilities: 23 computers available on campus for general student use. A campuswide network can be accessed. *Web address:* http://www.agts.edu/.

General Application Contact: Natalia Guerreiro, 417-268-1000, Fax: 417-268-1001.

GRADUATE UNITS

Graduate and Professional Programs Students: 220 full-time (69 women), 226 part-time (49 women); includes 49 minority (11 African Americans, 5 American Indian/Alaska Native, 11 Asian Americans or Pacific Islanders, 22 Hispanic Americans), 7 international. Average age 36. *Faculty:* 16 full-time (3 women), 21 part-time/adjunct (4 women). Expenses: Contact institution. *Financial support:* Career-related internships or fieldwork, Federal Work-Study, and scholarships/grants available. Support available to part-time students. Financial award application deadline: 7/15; financial award applicants required to submit FAFSA. *Degree program information:* Part-time and evening/weekend programs available. Postbaccalaureate distance learning degree programs offered (minimal on-campus study). Offers biblical preaching (D Min); Christian ministries (MA); divinity (M Div); intercultural studies (D Miss, PhD); missional leadership (D Min); relief and development (D Miss); self-design study (D Min); women in leadership (D Min). *Application deadline:* For fall admission, 7/1 priority date for domestic students, 6/1 priority date for international students; for spring admission, 12/1 priority date for domestic students, 11/1 priority date for international students. Applications are processed on a rolling basis. *Application fee:* $35. Electronic applications accepted. *Application Contact:* Stephen Lim, Academic Dean, 417-268-1000, Fax: 417-268-1001, E-mail: slim@agts.edu. *Academic Dean,* Stephen Lim, 417-268-1000, Fax: 417-268-1001, E-mail: slim@agts.edu.

ASSOCIATED MENNONITE BIBLICAL SEMINARY, Elkhart, IN 46517-1999

General Information Independent-religious, coed, graduate-only institution. *Graduate housing:* Rooms and/or apartments available on a first-come, first-served basis to single and married students. Housing application deadline: 5/1.

GRADUATE UNITS

Graduate and Professional Programs *Degree program information:* Part-time programs available. Offers Christian formation (MA); divinity (M Div); mission and evangelism (MA); peace studies (MA); theological studies (MA, Certificate). Electronic applications accepted.

ASSUMPTION COLLEGE, Worcester, MA 01609-1296

General Information Independent-religious, coed, comprehensive institution. CGS member. *Enrollment:* 2,626 graduate, professional, and undergraduate students; 126 full-time matriculated graduate/professional students (105 women), 278 part-time matriculated graduate/professional students (179 women). *Enrollment by degree level:* 404 master's. *Graduate faculty:* 18 full-time (5 women), 44 part-time/adjunct (18 women). *Tuition:* Part-time $468 per credit hour. *Required fees:* $20 per semester. One-time fee: $100. *Graduate housing:* On-campus housing not available. *Student services:* Campus employment opportunities, campus safety program, career counseling, exercise/wellness program, international student services, low-cost health insurance, multicultural affairs office, services for students with disabilities. *Library facilities:* Emmanuel d'Alzon Library. *Online resources:* library catalog, web page, access to other libraries' catalogs. *Collection:* 139,170 titles, 1,273 serial subscriptions, 3,313 audiovisual materials.

Computer facilities: Computer purchase and lease plans are available. 300 computers available on campus for general student use. A campuswide network can be accessed from student residence rooms and from off campus. Online class registration is available. *Web address:* http://www.assumption.edu/.

General Application Contact: Adrian O. Dumas, Director of Graduate Enrollment Management and Services, 508-767-7365, Fax: 508-767-7030, E-mail: adumas@assumption.edu.

GRADUATE UNITS

Graduate School Students: 126 full-time (105 women), 278 part-time (179 women); includes 25 minority (12 African Americans, 1 American Indian/Alaska Native, 4 Asian Americans or Pacific Islanders, 8 Hispanic Americans), 6 international. Average age 25. 302 applicants, 91% accepted. *Faculty:* 18 full-time (5 women), 44 part-time/adjunct (18 women). Expenses: Contact institution. *Financial support:* In 2008–09, 244 students received support, including 64 fellowships with partial tuition reimbursements available (averaging $5,966 per year), 2 teaching assistantships with partial tuition reimbursements available (averaging $9,933 per year); scholarships/grants, traineeships, and unspecified assistantships also available. Financial award application deadline: 7/1; financial award applicants required to submit FAFSA. In 2008, 150 master's, 4 other advanced degrees awarded. *Degree program information:* Part-time and evening/weekend programs available. Postbaccalaureate distance learning degree programs offered (minimal on-campus study). Offers accounting (MBA); business administration (CAGS); child and family interventions (MA); cognitive and behavioral therapies (MA); finance/economics (MBA); general business (MBA); general psychology (MA); human resources (MBA); international business (MBA); management (MBA); marketing (MBA); nonprofit leadership (MBA); rehabilitation counseling (MA, CAGS); school counseling (MA, CAGS); special education (MA). *Application deadline:* For fall admission, 6/1 priority date for domestic students, 5/1 priority date for international students; for spring admission, 11/1 priority date for domestic students, 9/1 priority date for international students. Applications are processed on a rolling basis. *Application fee:* $30. Electronic applications accepted. *Application Contact:* Adrian O. Dumas, Director of Graduate Enrollment Management and Services, 508-767-7365, Fax: 508-767-7030, E-mail: adumas@assumption.edu. *Dean,* Dr. Mary Lou Anderson, 508-767-7276, Fax: 508-767-7053, E-mail: mlanders@assumption.edu.

ATHABASCA UNIVERSITY, Athabasca, AB T9S 3A3, Canada

General Information Province-supported, coed, comprehensive institution. *Enrollment:* 34,171 graduate, professional, and undergraduate students; 3,143 part-time matriculated graduate/professional students (2,063 women). *Enrollment by degree level:* 3,143 master's. *Graduate faculty:* 44 full-time (21 women), 25 part-time/adjunct (17 women). *Graduate tuition:* Tuition and fees charges are reported in Canadian dollars. *International tuition:* $15,455 Canadian dollars full-time. Tuition, province resident: full-time $13,255 Canadian dollars; part-time $1205 Canadian dollars per course. Tuition, Canadian resident: full-time $13,255 Canadian dollars; part-time $1205 Canadian dollars per course. One-time fee: $280 Canadian dollars. *Student services:* Services for students with disabilities. *Library facilities:* Athabasca University Library. *Online resources:* library catalog, web page, access to other libraries' catalogs. *Collection:* 178,808 titles, 32,619 serial subscriptions, 17,628 audiovisual materials. *Research affiliation:* SAP (software), IBM (software).

Computer facilities: Computer purchase and lease plans are available. 28 computers available on campus for general student use. A campuswide network can be accessed from off campus. Online class registration is available. *Web address:* http://www.athabascau.ca/.

General Application Contact: Information Contact, 800-788-9041, Fax: 780-675-6437, E-mail: inquire@athabascau.ca.

GRADUATE UNITS

Centre for Distance Education Students: 301 part-time (202 women). Average age 40. 88 applicants, 93% accepted. *Faculty:* 11 full-time (4 women), 5 part-time/adjunct (4 women). Expenses: Contact institution. In 2008, 130 master's awarded. *Degree program information:* Part-time programs available. Postbaccalaureate distance learning degree programs offered (no on-campus study). Offers distance education (MDE); distance education technology (Advanced Diploma). *Application deadline:* For fall admission, 3/1 for domestic and international students. *Application fee:* $65. Electronic applications accepted. *Application Contact:* Glenda Hawryluk, Administrative Assistant, 780-675-6179, Fax: 780-675-6170, E-mail: glendah@athabascau.ca. *Program Director,* Dr. Bob Spencer, 780-675-6238, Fax: 780-675-6170, E-mail: bobs@athabascau.ca.

Centre for Innovative Management Students: 949 part-time (315 women). Average age 38. 264 applicants, 82% accepted, 184 enrolled. *Faculty:* 7 full-time (5 women), 2 part-time/adjunct (0 women). Expenses: Contact institution. *Financial support:* In 2008–09, 34 students received support. Scholarships/grants available. In 2008, 215 master's awarded. *Degree program information:* Part-time and evening/weekend programs available. Postbaccalaureate distance learning degree programs offered (no on-campus study). Offers business administration (MBA); information technology management (MBA); management (GDM); project management (MBA, GDM). *Application deadline:* For fall admission, 6/15 for domestic and international students; for winter admission, 10/15 for domestic and international students; for spring admission, 2/15 for domestic and international students. Applications are processed on a rolling basis. *Application fee:* $165. Electronic applications accepted. *Application Contact:* Shannon LaRose, Customer Service Representative, 800-561-4650, Fax: 800-561-4660, E-mail: shannonl@athabascau.ca. *Executive Director,* Dr. Alexander Kondra, 780-675-6807, Fax: 780-675-6338, E-mail: alexk@athabascau.ca.

Centre for Integrated Studies Students: 651 part-time (467 women). Average age 36. 150 applicants, 87% accepted, 112 enrolled. *Faculty:* 8 full-time (3 women), 16 part-time/adjunct (13 women). Expenses: Contact institution. In 2008, 39 master's awarded. *Degree program information:* Part-time and evening/weekend programs available. Postbaccalaureate distance learning degree programs offered (no on-campus study). Offers adult education (MA); community studies (MA); cultural studies (MA); educational studies (MA); global change (MA); work, organization, and leadership (MA). *Application deadline:* For fall admission, 3/1 for domestic and international students; for winter admission, 10/1 for domestic and international students. *Application fee:* $65. Electronic applications accepted. *Application Contact:* Derek Stovin, Program Administrator, 780-675-6236, Fax: 780-675-6921, E-mail: dereks@athabascau.ca. *Program Director,* Dr. Michael Gismondi, 780-675-6218, Fax: 780-675-6921, E-mail: mikeg@athabascau.ca.

Centre for Nursing and Health Studies Students: 1,193 part-time (1,097 women). Average age 37. 460 applicants, 81% accepted, 335 enrolled. *Faculty:* 9 full-time (7 women). Expenses: Contact institution. In 2008, 133 master's awarded. *Degree program information:* Part-time programs available. Postbaccalaureate distance learning degree programs offered. Offers advanced nursing practice (MN, Advanced Diploma); generalist (MN); health studies-leadership (MHS). *Application deadline:* For fall admission, 3/1 for domestic and international students. *Application fee:* $60. Electronic applications accepted. *Application Contact:* Lisa Bodnarchuk, Administrative Assistant, 780-675-6381, Fax: 780-675-6468, E-mail: lisab@athabascau.ca. *Director,* Dr. Donna Romyn, 780-675-6794, Fax: 780-675-6468, E-mail: dromyn@athabascau.ca.

Graduate Centre for Applied Psychology *Faculty:* 3 full-time (2 women), 2 part-time/adjunct (0 women). Expenses: Contact institution. Offers art therapy (MC); career counseling (MC); counseling (Advanced Certificate); counseling psychology (MC); school counseling (MC). *Application Contact:* Information Contact, 800-788-9041, Fax: 780-675-6437, E-mail: inquire@athabascau.ca. *Program Director,* Dr. Sandra Collins, 888-611-7121, E-mail: sandrac@athabascau.ca.

School of Computing and Information Systems Students: 206 part-time (37 women). Average age 35. 93 applicants, 96% accepted. *Faculty:* 6 full-time (0 women). Expenses: Contact institution. In 2008, 24 master's awarded. *Degree program information:* Part-time programs available. Postbaccalaureate distance learning degree programs offered (no on-campus study). Offers information systems (M Sc). *Application deadline:* For fall admission, 3/1 for domestic students; for winter admission, 10/1 for domestic students. *Application fee:* $250. Electronic applications accepted. *Application Contact:* Claire Gemmell-Mathieu, Administrative Professional Officer, 780-675-6777, Fax: 780-675-6148, E-mail: claire@athabascau.ca. *Director,* Dr. Kinshuk Kinshuk, 780-675-6812, E-mail: kinshuk@athabascau.ca.

THE ATHENAEUM OF OHIO, Cincinnati, OH 45230-5900

General Information Independent-religious, coed, graduate-only institution. *Graduate housing:* Room and/or apartments guaranteed to single students; on-campus housing not available to married students.

GRADUATE UNITS

Graduate Programs *Degree program information:* Part-time and evening/weekend programs available. Offers biblical studies (MABS); divinity (M Div); lay ministry (Certificate); pastoral counseling (MAPC); pastoral ministry (MA); theology (MA Th).

ATLANTA'S JOHN MARSHALL LAW SCHOOL, Atlanta, GA 30309

General Information Private, coed, graduate-only institution.

GRADUATE UNITS

Graduate Program *Degree program information:* Part-time programs available. Offers law (JD). Electronic applications accepted.

ATLANTIC COLLEGE, Guaynabo, PR 00970

General Information Independent, comprehensive institution.

GRADUATE UNITS

Program in Graphic Arts *Degree program information:* Part-time programs available. Offers digital graphic design (MA, MGD).

ATLANTIC INSTITUTE OF ORIENTAL MEDICINE, Fort Lauderdale, FL 33301

General Information Independent, coed, graduate-only institution. *Enrollment by degree level:* 101 master's. *Graduate faculty:* 6 full-time (0 women), 15 part-time/adjunct (5 women). *Tuition:* Full-time $13,000. *Required fees:* $1300. One-time fee: $250 full-time. *Student services:* Campus employment opportunities, campus safety program, career counseling, exercise/wellness program, international student services. *Collection:* 2,302 titles.

Computer facilities: 3 computers available on campus for general student use. *Web address:* http://www.atom.edu/.

General Application Contact: Milagros Ferreira, Registrar, 954-763-9840 Ext. 207, Fax: 954-763-9844, E-mail: registrar@atom.edu.

GRADUATE UNITS

Graduate Program Students: 101 full-time (67 women); includes 23 minority (3 African Americans, 7 Asian Americans or Pacific Islanders, 13 Hispanic Americans), 7 international. *Faculty:* 6 full-time (0 women), 15 part-time/adjunct (5 women). Expenses: Contact institution. *Degree program information:* Evening/weekend programs available. Offers Oriental medicine (MS). *Application deadline:* For fall admission, 7/1 for domestic students, 5/1 for international students; for spring admission, 11/30 for domestic students, 2/28 for international students. Applications are processed on a rolling basis. *Application fee:* $20 ($100 for international students). *Application Contact:* Milagros Ferreira, Registrar, 954-763-9840 Ext. 207, Fax: 954-763-9844, E-mail: registrar@atom.edu. *President,* Dr. Johanna C. Yen, 954-763-9840 Ext. 202, Fax: 954-763-9844, E-mail: president@atom.edu.

ATLANTIC SCHOOL OF THEOLOGY, Halifax, NS B3H 3B5, Canada

General Information Independent, coed, graduate-only institution. *Graduate housing:* Rooms and/or apartments available on a first-come, first-served basis to single and married students. Housing application deadline: 6/1.

GRADUATE UNITS

Graduate and Professional Programs *Degree program information:* Part-time programs available. Postbaccalaureate distance learning degree programs offered (minimal on-campus study). Offers theology (M Div, MTS, Graduate Certificate).

ATLANTIC UNION COLLEGE, South Lancaster, MA 01561-1000

General Information Independent-religious, coed, comprehensive institution. *Graduate housing:* Room and/or apartments available to single students; on-campus housing not available to married students.

GRADUATE UNITS

Graduate Education Program *Degree program information:* Part-time programs available. Postbaccalaureate distance learning degree programs offered (minimal on-campus study). Offers education (M Ed). Offered during summer only.

ATLANTIC UNIVERSITY, Virginia Beach, VA 23451-2061

General Information Independent, coed, primarily women, graduate-only institution. *Enrollment by degree level:* 164 master's. *Graduate faculty:* 16 part-time/adjunct (5 women). *Tuition:* Full-time $3000; part-time $750 per course. *Graduate housing:* On-campus housing not available. *Web address:* http://www.atlanticuniv.edu/.

General Application Contact: Candis Collins, Director of Admissions, 757-631-8101 Ext. 7176, Fax: 757-631-8096, E-mail: candis.collins@atlanticuniv.edu.

GRADUATE UNITS

Program in Transformative Theories and Practices Students: 164 part-time (121 women); includes 6 minority (3 African Americans, 3 Hispanic Americans), 13 international. Average age 45. 102 applicants, 46% accepted, 45 enrolled. *Faculty:* 16 part-time/adjunct (5 women). Expenses: Contact institution. In 2008, 15 master's awarded. *Degree program information:* Part-time and evening/weekend programs available. Postbaccalaureate distance learning degree programs offered (no on-campus study). Offers transformative theories and practices (MA). *Application deadline:* Applications are processed on a rolling basis. *Application fee:* $50. Electronic applications accepted. *Application Contact:* R. Gregory Deming, Director of Admissions, 757-631-8101, Fax: 757-631-8096, E-mail: admissions@atlanticuniv.edu. *Chief Executive Officer,* Kevin J. Todeschi, 757-631-8101, Fax: 757-631-8096, E-mail: info@atlanticuniv.edu.

Program in Visionary Art and Consciousness *Faculty:* 2 part-time/adjunct (1 woman). Expenses: Contact institution. *Degree program information:* Part-time and evening/weekend programs available. Postbaccalaureate distance learning degree programs offered (no on-campus study). Offers visionary art and consciousness (MFA). *Application deadline:* For fall admission, 3/31 for domestic and international students. *Application fee:* $50. *Application Contact:* R. Gregory Deming, Director of Admissions, 757-631-8101, Fax: 757-631-8096, E-mail: admissions@atlanticuniv.edu. *Chief Executive Officer,* Kevin J. Todeschi, 757-631-8101, Fax: 757-631-8096, E-mail: info@atlanticuniv.edu.

A.T. STILL UNIVERSITY OF HEALTH SCIENCES, Kirksville, MO 63501

General Information Independent, coed, graduate-only institution. *Enrollment by degree level:* 1,137 first professional, 903 master's, 1,302 doctoral, 121 other advanced degrees. *Graduate faculty:* 185 full-time (76 women), 630 part-time/adjunct (288 women). Full-time tuition and fees vary according to degree level and program. *Graduate housing:* Rooms and/or apartments available on a first-come, first-served basis to single and married students. Typical cost: $4680 (including board) for single students; $5160 (including board) for married students. Room and board charges vary according to housing facility selected. Housing application deadline: 4/1. *Student services:* Campus employment opportunities, career counsel-

A.T. Still University of Health Sciences (continued)

ing, exercise/wellness program, free psychological counseling, services for students with disabilities. *Library facilities:* A. T. Still Memorial Library. *Online resources:* library catalog, web page, access to other libraries' catalogs. *Collection:* 69,225 titles, 5,140 serial subscriptions, 3,752 audiovisual materials. *Research affiliation:* The Pennsylvania State University College of Medicine (osteopathic clinical research), University of Arizona—College of Medicine—Phoenix (osteopathic/biomedical clinical research), Unitec New Zealand (osteopathic manual medicine), European School of Osteopathy (osteopathic manual medicine), Nordic Academy of Osteopathy (osteopathic clinical research), Ridgway Integrative Medicine (osteopathic clinical research).

Computer facilities: 45 computers available on campus for general student use. A campuswide network can be accessed from student residence rooms and from off campus. *Web address:* http://www.atsu.edu/.

General Application Contact: Donna Sparks, Associate Director for Admissions, 660-626-2237, Fax: 660-626-2969, E-mail: admissions@atsu.edu.

GRADUATE UNITS

Arizona School of Dentistry and Oral Health Students: 244 full-time (126 women); includes 63 minority (3 African Americans, 14 American Indian/Alaska Native, 31 Asian Americans or Pacific Islanders, 15 Hispanic Americans). Average age 25. 3,199 applicants, 3% accepted, 68 enrolled. *Faculty:* 47 full-time (25 women), 132 part-time/adjunct (52 women). Expenses: Contact institution. *Financial support:* In 2008–09, 223 students received support; fellowships, research assistantships, teaching assistantships, Federal Work-Study and scholarships/grants available. Financial award application deadline: 5/1; financial award applicants required to submit FAFSA. In 2008, 54 first professional degrees awarded. Offers dental medicine (DMD); orthodontics (Certificate). *Application deadline:* For fall admission, 12/1 for domestic students. Applications are processed on a rolling basis. *Application fee:* $60. Electronic applications accepted. *Application Contact:* Donna Sparks, Associate Director for Admissions, 660-626-2237, Fax: 660-626-2969, E-mail: admissions@atsu.edu. *Dean,* Dr. Jack Dillenberg, 480-219-6000, Fax: 480-219-6110, E-mail: jdillenberg@atsu.edu.

Arizona School of Health Sciences Students: 485 full-time (347 women), 1,287 part-time (925 women); includes 301 minority (60 African Americans, 12 American Indian/Alaska Native, 167 Asian Americans or Pacific Islanders, 62 Hispanic Americans), 6 international. Average age 33. 1,861 applicants, 35% accepted, 512 enrolled. *Faculty:* 49 full-time (27 women), 216 part-time/adjunct (123 women). Expenses: Contact institution. *Financial support:* In 2008–09, 473 students received support; fellowships, research assistantships, teaching assistantships, Federal Work-Study and scholarships/grants available. Financial award application deadline: 5/1; financial award applicants required to submit FAFSA. In 2008, 156 master's, 482 doctorates awarded. Postbaccalaureate distance learning degree programs offered (no on-campus study). Offers advanced occupational therapy (MS); advanced physician assistant (MS); athletic training (MS); audiology (Au D); health sciences (DHSc); human movement (MS); occupational therapy (MS); physical therapy (MS, DPT); physician assistant (MS); transitional physical therapy (DPT). *Application deadline:* For fall admission, 2/1 priority date for domestic and international students. Applications are processed on a rolling basis. *Application fee:* $60. *Application Contact:* Donna Sparks, Associate Director for Admissions, 660-626-2237, Fax: 660-626-2969, E-mail: admissions@atsu.edu. *Dean,* Dr. Randy Danielsen, 480-219-6000, Fax: 480-219-6110, E-mail: rdanielsen@atsu.edu.

Kirksville College of Osteopathic Medicine Students: 710 full-time (279 women), 9 part-time (4 women); includes 107 minority (9 African Americans, 5 American Indian/Alaska Native, 76 Asian Americans or Pacific Islanders, 17 Hispanic Americans), 17 international. Average age 27. 3,209 applicants, 11% accepted, 184 enrolled. *Faculty:* 59 full-time (16 women), 17 part-time/adjunct (3 women). Expenses: Contact institution. *Financial support:* In 2008–09, 632 students received support, including 12 fellowships with full tuition reimbursements available (averaging $12,000 per year); research assistantships, teaching assistantships, career-related internships or fieldwork, Federal Work-Study, institutionally sponsored loans, and scholarships/grants also available. Financial award application deadline: 5/1; financial award applicants required to submit FAFSA. In 2008, 170 first professional degrees, 14 master's awarded. Offers biomedical sciences (MS); osteopathic medicine (DO). *Application deadline:* For fall admission, 2/1 for domestic and international students. Applications are processed on a rolling basis. *Application fee:* $60. Electronic applications accepted. *Application Contact:* Donna Sparks, Associate Director for Admissions, 660-626-2237, Fax: 660-626-2969, E-mail: admissions@atsu.edu. *Dean,* Dr. Philip C. Slocum, 660-626-2354, Fax: 660-626-2080, E-mail: pslocum@atsu.edu.

School of Health Management Students: 47 full-time (33 women), 477 part-time (310 women); includes 179 minority (106 African Americans, 8 American Indian/Alaska Native, 38 Asian Americans or Pacific Islanders, 27 Hispanic Americans). Average age 32. *Faculty:* 1 (woman) full-time, 52 part-time/adjunct (24 women). Expenses: Contact institution. *Financial support:* In 2008–09, 277 students received support; fellowships, research assistantships, teaching assistantships available. Financial award application deadline: 5/1; financial award applicants required to submit FAFSA. In 2008, 110 master's, 4 doctorates awarded. *Degree program information:* Part-time and evening/weekend programs available. Postbaccalaureate distance learning degree programs offered (no on-campus study). Offers geriatric healthcare (MGH); health administration (MHA); health education (MH Ed, DH Ed); public health (MPH). *Application deadline:* For fall admission, 8/7 for domestic students, 7/27 for international students; for winter admission, 11/30 for domestic students, 10/26 for international students; for spring admission, 2/20 for domestic students, 2/15 for international students. Applications are processed on a rolling basis. *Application fee:* $60. Electronic applications accepted. *Application Contact:* Sarah Bartlett, Director of Recruitment, 660-626-2820, Fax: 660-626-2826, E-mail: sbartlett@atsu.edu. *Interim Dean,* Dr. Kimberly O'Reilly, 660-626-2820, Fax: 660-626-2826, E-mail: koreilley@atsu.edu.

School of Osteopathic Medicine in Arizona Students: 204 full-time (95 women); includes 73 minority (4 African Americans, 11 American Indian/Alaska Native, 39 Asian Americans or Pacific Islanders, 19 Hispanic Americans). Average age 26. 2,809 applicants, 8% accepted, 102 enrolled. *Faculty:* 30 full-time (8 women), 260 part-time/adjunct (114 women). Expenses: Contact institution. *Financial support:* In 2008–09, 206 students received support. Federal Work-Study and scholarships/grants available. Financial award application deadline: 5/1. Offers osteopathic medicine (DO). *Application deadline:* For fall admission, 3/1 for domestic students. Applications are processed on a rolling basis. *Application fee:* $60. Electronic applications accepted. *Application Contact:* Donna Sparks, Associate Director for Admissions, 660-626-2237, Fax: 660-626-2969, E-mail: admissions@atsu.edu. *Dean,* Dr. Douglas Wood, 480-219-6000, Fax: 480-219-6110, E-mail: dwood@atsu.edu.

AUBURN UNIVERSITY, Auburn University, AL 36849

General Information State-supported, coed, university. CGS member. *Enrollment:* 24,530 graduate, professional, and undergraduate students; 2,499 full-time matriculated graduate/professional students (1,321 women), 1,941 part-time matriculated graduate/professional students (897 women). *Enrollment by degree level:* 959 first professional, 2,111 master's, 1,327 doctoral, 43 other advanced degrees. *Graduate faculty:* 1,224 full-time (392 women), 139 part-time/adjunct (58 women). *International tuition:* $17,846 full-time. Tuition, state resident: full-time $5880; part-time $243 per credit hour. Tuition, nonresident: full-time $17,640; part-time $729 per credit hour. Tuition and fees vary according to program and reciprocity agreements. *Graduate housing:* Rooms and/or apartments available on a first-come, first-served basis to single students and available to married students. Housing application deadline: 7/1. *Student services:* Campus employment opportunities, campus safety program, career counseling, exercise/wellness program, free psychological counseling, international student services, low-cost health insurance, multicultural affairs office, services for students with disabilities, teacher training. *Library facilities:* R. B. Draughon Library plus 2 others. *Online resources:* library catalog, web page, access to other libraries' catalogs. *Collection:* 3 million titles, 29,355 serial subscriptions, 14,760 audiovisual materials. *Research affiliation:* Consortium for Vehicle Electronics (Mechanical & Automotive, Electrical Engineering), Tay-Sachs Gene Therapy Consortium (Veterinary Medicine, Clinical sciences), Higher Education Consortium for Special Education (Special & Rehabilitative Education), National Center of Excellence for Airliner Cabin Environmental Research (Aerospace, Polymer & Fibers Engineering), National Textile Center Consortium (Polymer & Fibers Engineering), National Asphalt Pavement Association (Asphalt technology, Civil Engineering).

Computer facilities: Computer purchase and lease plans are available. 1,722 computers available on campus for general student use. A campuswide network can be accessed from student residence rooms and from off campus. Online class registration, pay Bursar online, course materials available online are available. *Web address:* http://www.auburn.edu/.

General Application Contact: Dr. George Flowers, PhD, Dean of the Graduate School, 334-844-2125, E-mail: flowegt@auburn.edu.

GRADUATE UNITS

College of Veterinary Medicine Students: 387 full-time (269 women), 71 part-time (44 women); includes 25 minority (8 African Americans, 2 American Indian/Alaska Native, 6 Asian Americans or Pacific Islanders, 9 Hispanic Americans), 19 international. Average age 27. 917 applicants, 12% accepted, 102 enrolled. *Faculty:* 100 full-time (39 women), 6 part-time/adjunct (1 woman). Expenses: Contact institution. *Financial support:* Fellowships, research assistantships, teaching assistantships, Federal Work-Study available. Support available to part-time students. Financial award application deadline: 3/15. In 2008, 91 first professional degrees, 8 master's, 4 doctorates awarded. *Degree program information:* Part-time programs available. Offers veterinary medicine (DVM, MS, PhD). *Application deadline:* For fall admission, 7/7 for domestic students. Applications are processed on a rolling basis. *Application fee:* $25 ($50 for international students). *Application Contact:* Dr. Joe Pittman, Interim Dean of the Graduate School, 334-844-4700. *Dean,* Dr. Timothy R. Boosinger, 334-844-4546.

Graduate Programs in Veterinary Medicine Students: 11 full-time (4 women), 55 part-time (32 women); includes 5 minority (1 African American, 1 American Indian/Alaska Native, 3 Asian Americans or Pacific Islanders), 19 international. Average age 32. 35 applicants, 31% accepted, 11 enrolled. *Faculty:* 100 full-time (39 women), 6 part-time/adjunct (1 woman). Expenses: Contact institution. *Financial support:* Research assistantships, teaching assistantships, Federal Work-Study available. Support available to part-time students. Financial award application deadline: 3/15. In 2008, 7 master's, 8 doctorates awarded. *Degree program information:* Part-time programs available. Offers biomedical sciences (MS, PhD). *Application deadline:* For fall admission, 7/7 for domestic students; for spring admission, 11/24 for domestic students. Applications are processed on a rolling basis. *Application fee:* $25 ($50 for international students). Electronic applications accepted. *Application Contact:* Dr. George Flowers, Dean of the Graduate School, 334-844-2125. *Dean,* Dr. Timothy R. Boosinger, 334-844-4546.

Graduate School Students: 2,499 full-time (1,321 women), 1,941 part-time (897 women); includes 559 minority (369 African Americans, 19 American Indian/Alaska Native, 93 Asian Americans or Pacific Islanders, 78 Hispanic Americans), 804 international. Average age 30. 3,640 applicants, 48% accepted, 869 enrolled. *Faculty:* 1,190 full-time (381 women), 133 part-time/adjunct (54 women). Expenses: Contact institution. *Financial support:* Fellowships, research assistantships, teaching assistantships, career-related internships or fieldwork and Federal Work-Study available. Support available to part-time students. In 2008, 867 master's, 164 doctorates, 25 other advanced degrees awarded. *Degree program information:* Part-time and evening/weekend programs available. Offers cell and molecular biology (PhD); integrated textile and apparel sciences (PhD); rural sociology (MS); sociology (MA, MS); sociology, anthropology, criminology, and social work (MA, MS). *Application deadline:* For fall admission, 7/7 for domestic students; for spring admission, 11/24 for domestic students. *Application fee:* $25 ($50 for international students). *Application Contact:* Dr. George Flowers, Dean of the Graduate School, 334-844-2125. *Dean,* Dr. George Flowers, 334-844-2125.

College of Agriculture Students: 129 full-time (48 women), 134 part-time (60 women); includes 20 minority (10 African Americans, 2 American Indian/Alaska Native, 5 Asian Americans or Pacific Islanders, 3 Hispanic Americans), 103 international. Average age 30. 123 applicants, 46% accepted, 40 enrolled. *Faculty:* 156 full-time (28 women), 11 part-time/adjunct (0 women). Expenses: Contact institution. *Financial support:* Fellowships, research assistantships, teaching assistantships, Federal Work-Study available. Support available to part-time students. Financial award application deadline: 3/15. In 2008, 50 master's, 19 doctorates awarded. *Degree program information:* Part-time programs available. Offers agricultural economics (M Ag, MS); agriculture (M Ag, M Aq, MS, PhD); agronomy and soils (M Ag, MS, PhD); animal sciences (M Ag, MS, PhD); applied economics (PhD); entomology (M Ag, MS, PhD); fisheries and allied aquacultures (M Aq, MS, PhD); horticulture (M Ag, MS, PhD); plant pathology (M Ag, MS, PhD); poultry science (M Ag, MS, PhD). *Application deadline:* For fall admission, 7/7 for domestic students; for spring admission, 11/24 for domestic students. Applications are processed on a rolling basis. *Application fee:* $25 ($50 for international students). Electronic applications accepted. *Application Contact:* Dr. George Flowers, Dean of the Graduate School, 334-844-2125. *Dean,* Dr. Richard Guthrie, 334-844-2345.

College of Architecture, Design, and Construction Students: 98 full-time (33 women), 14 part-time (5 women); includes 9 minority (5 African Americans, 2 Asian Americans or Pacific Islanders, 2 Hispanic Americans), 10 international. Average age 27. 76 applicants, 54% accepted, 21 enrolled. *Faculty:* 62 full-time (10 women), 4 part-time/adjunct (1 woman). Expenses: Contact institution. *Financial support:* Fellowships, Federal Work-Study available. Support available to part-time students. Financial award application deadline: 3/15. In 2008, 60 master's awarded. *Degree program information:* Part-time programs available. Offers architecture, design, and construction (MBS, MCP, MDB, MID, MLA); building science (MBS); community planning (MCP); construction management (MBS); design-build (MDB); industrial design (MID); landscape architecture (MLA). *Application deadline:* For fall admission, 7/7 for domestic students; for spring admission, 11/24 for domestic students. Applications are processed on a rolling basis. *Application fee:* $25 ($50 for international students). Electronic applications accepted. *Application Contact:* Dr. George Flowers, Dean of the Graduate School, 334-844-2125. *Dean,* Prof. Dan D. Bennett, 334-844-4524.

College of Business Students: 167 full-time (53 women), 416 part-time (120 women); includes 72 minority (30 African Americans, 3 American Indian/Alaska Native, 19 Asian Americans or Pacific Islanders, 20 Hispanic Americans), 45 international. Average age 33. 543 applicants, 57% accepted, 208 enrolled. *Faculty:* 76 full-time (16 women), 13 part-time/adjunct (5 women). Expenses: Contact institution. *Financial support:* Fellowships, research assistantships, teaching assistantships, career-related internships or fieldwork and Federal Work-Study available. Support available to part-time students. Financial award application deadline: 3/15. In 2008, 200 master's, 10 doctorates awarded. *Degree program information:* Part-time programs available. Offers accountancy (M Acc); business (M Acc, MBA, MMIS, MS, PhD); business administration (MBA); economics (MS); finance (MS); human resource management (PhD); management (MS, PhD); management information systems (MMIS, PhD). *Application deadline:* For fall admission, 7/7 for domestic students; for spring admission, 11/24 for domestic students. Applications are processed on a rolling basis. *Application fee:* $25 ($50 for international students). Electronic applications accepted. *Application Contact:* Dr. George Flowers, Dean of the Graduate School, 334-844-2125. *Dean,* Dr. Paul M Bobrowski, 334-844-4832.

College of Education Students: 303 full-time (213 women), 451 part-time (304 women); includes 190 minority (169 African Americans, 3 American Indian/Alaska Native, 5 Asian Americans or Pacific Islanders, 13 Hispanic Americans), 14 international. Average age 34. 455 applicants, 39% accepted, 147 enrolled. *Faculty:* 95 full-time (57 women), 18 part-time/adjunct (10 women). Expenses: Contact institution. *Financial support:* Fellowships, research assistantships, teaching assistantships, career-related internships or fieldwork and Federal Work-Study available. Support available to part-time students. Financial award application deadline: 3/15. In 2008, 205 master's, 50 doctorates, 9 other advanced degrees awarded. *Degree program information:* Part-time programs available. Offers adult education (M Ed, MS, Ed D); business education (M Ed, MS, PhD); collaborative teacher special education (M Ed, MS); community agency counseling (M Ed, MS, Ed D, PhD, Ed S); counseling psychology (PhD); counselor education (Ed D, PhD); curriculum and instruction (M Ed, MS, Ed D, Ed S); curriculum supervision (M Ed, MS, Ed D, Ed S); early childhood education (M Ed, MS, PhD, Ed S); early childhood special education (M Ed, MS); education (M Ed, MS, Ed D, PhD, Ed S); educational psychology (PhD); elementary education (M Ed, MS, PhD, Ed S); exercise science (M Ed, MS, PhD); foreign languages (M Ed, MS); health promotion (M Ed, MS); higher education administration (M Ed, MS, Ed D, Ed S); kinesiology (PhD); media instructional design (MS); media specialist (M Ed); music education (M Ed,

MS, PhD, Ed S); physical education/teacher education (M Ed, MS, Ed D, Ed S); postsecondary education (PhD); reading education (PhD, Ed S); rehabilitation counseling (M Ed, MS, PhD); school administration (M Ed, MS, Ed D, Ed S); school counseling (M Ed, MS, Ed D, PhD, Ed S); school psychometry (M Ed, MS, Ed D, PhD, Ed S); secondary education (M Ed, MS, PhD, Ed S). *Application fee:* $25 ($50 for international students). Electronic applications accepted. *Application Contact:* Dr. George Flowers, Dean of the Graduate School, 334-844-2125. *Dean,* Dr. Frances Kochan, 334-844-4446.

College of Human Sciences Students: 38 full-time (28 women), 54 part-time (46 women); includes 23 minority (14 African Americans, 6 Asian Americans or Pacific Islanders, 3 Hispanic Americans), 19 international. Average age 30. 98 applicants, 37% accepted, 17 enrolled. *Faculty:* 50 full-time (34 women), 1 (woman) part-time/adjunct. Expenses: Contact institution. *Financial support:* Fellowships, research assistantships, teaching assistantships, career-related internships or fieldwork and Federal Work-Study available. Support available to part-time students. Financial award application deadline: 3/15. In 2008, 22 master's, 7 doctorates awarded. *Degree program information:* Part-time programs available. Offers apparel and textiles (MS); human development and family studies (MS, PhD); human sciences (MS, PhD); nutrition and food science (MS, PhD). *Application deadline:* For fall admission, 7/7 for domestic students; for spring admission, 11/24 for domestic students. Applications are processed on a rolling basis. *Application fee:* $25 ($50 for international students). Electronic applications accepted. *Application Contact:* Dr. George Flowers, Dean of the Graduate School, 334-844-2125. *Dean,* Dr. June Henton, 334-844-3790, E-mail: jhenton@humsci.auburn.edu.

College of Liberal Arts Students: 211 full-time (152 women), 230 part-time (131 women); includes 47 minority (33 African Americans, 4 Asian Americans or Pacific Islanders, 10 Hispanic Americans), 11 international. Average age 31. 556 applicants, 36% accepted, 122 enrolled. *Faculty:* 267 full-time (120 women), 53 part-time/adjunct (27 women). Expenses: Contact institution. *Financial support:* Fellowships, research assistantships, teaching assistantships, career-related internships or fieldwork and Federal Work-Study available. Support available to part-time students. Financial award application deadline: 3/15. In 2008, 107 master's, 25 doctorates awarded. *Degree program information:* Part-time programs available. Offers applied behavior analysis in developmental disabilities (MS); audiology (MCD, MS, Au D); clinical psychology (PhD); communication (MA); English (MA, MTPC, PhD); experimental psychology (PhD); history (MA, PhD); industrial/organizational psychology (PhD); liberal arts (MA, MCD, MHS, MPA, MS, MTPC, Au D, PhD); mass communications (MA); public administration (MPA, PhD); Spanish (MA, MHS); speech pathology (MCD, MS). *Application deadline:* For fall admission, 7/7 for domestic students; for spring admission, 11/24 for domestic students. Applications are processed on a rolling basis. *Application fee:* $25 ($50 for international students). Electronic applications accepted. *Application Contact:* Dr. George Flowers, Dean of the Graduate School, 334-844-2125. *Dean,* Dr. Anne-Katrin Gramberg, 334-844-2185.

College of Sciences and Mathematics Students: 175 full-time (66 women), 169 part-time (80 women); includes 29 minority (16 African Americans, 1 American Indian/Alaska Native, 6 Asian Americans or Pacific Islanders, 6 Hispanic Americans), 142 international. Average age 29. 333 applicants, 50% accepted, 82 enrolled. *Faculty:* 155 full-time (24 women), 15 part-time/adjunct (5 women). Expenses: Contact institution. *Financial support:* Fellowships, research assistantships, teaching assistantships, career-related internships or fieldwork and Federal Work-Study available. Support available to part-time students. In 2008, 49 master's, 22 doctorates awarded. *Degree program information:* Part-time programs available. Offers analytical chemistry (MS, PhD); applied mathematics (MAM, MS); biochemistry (MS, PhD); botany (MS, PhD); geography (MS); geology (MS); inorganic chemistry (MS, PhD); mathematics (MS, PhD); microbiology (MS, PhD); organic chemistry (MS, PhD); physical chemistry (MS, PhD); physics (MS, PhD); probability and statistics (M Prob S); sciences and mathematics (M Prob S, MAM, MS, PhD); statistics (MS); zoology (MS, PhD). *Application deadline:* For fall admission, 7/7 for domestic students; for spring admission, 11/24 for domestic students. Applications are processed on a rolling basis. *Application fee:* $25 ($50 for international students). *Application Contact:* Dr. George Flowers, Dean of the Graduate School, 334-844-2125. *Dean,* Dr. Stewart W. Schneller, 334-844-5737.

Ginn College of Engineering Students: 398 full-time (90 women), 322 part-time (67 women); includes 62 minority (39 African Americans, 2 American Indian/Alaska Native, 11 Asian Americans or Pacific Islanders, 10 Hispanic Americans), 376 international. Average age 29. 1,221 applicants, 56% accepted, 188 enrolled. *Faculty:* 141 full-time (9 women), 9 part-time/adjunct (1 woman). Expenses: Contact institution. *Financial support:* Fellowships, research assistantships, teaching assistantships, Federal Work-Study available. Support available to part-time students. Financial award application deadline: 3/15. In 2008, 130 master's, 47 doctorates awarded. *Degree program information:* Part-time programs available. Offers aerospace engineering (MAE, MS, PhD); chemical engineering (M Ch E, MS, PhD); computer science and software engineering (MS, MSWE, PhD); construction engineering and management (MCE, MS, PhD); electrical and computer engineering (MEE, MS, PhD); engineering (M Ch E, M Mtl E, MAE, MCE, MEE, MISE, MME, MS, MSWE, PhD); environmental engineering (MCE, MS, PhD); geotechnical/materials engineering (MCE, MS, PhD); hydraulics/hydrology (MCE, MS, PhD); industrial and systems engineering (MISE, MS, PhD); materials engineering (M Mtl E, MS, PhD); mechanical engineering (MME, MS, PhD); structural engineering (MCE, MS, PhD); transportation engineering (MCE, MS, PhD). *Application deadline:* For fall admission, 7/7 for domestic students; for spring admission, 11/24 for domestic students. Applications are processed on a rolling basis. *Application fee:* $25 ($50 for international students). Electronic applications accepted. *Application Contact:* Dr. George Flowers, Dean of the Graduate School, 334-844-2125. *Dean,* Dr. Larry Benefield, 334-844-2308.

School of Forestry and Wildlife Sciences Students: 30 full-time (12 women), 30 part-time (12 women); includes 2 minority (1 African American, 1 Hispanic American), 18 international. Average age 30. 27 applicants, 56% accepted, 14 enrolled. *Faculty:* 28 full-time (5 women). Expenses: Contact institution. *Financial support:* Fellowships, research assistantships, teaching assistantships, Federal Work-Study available. Support available to part-time students. Financial award application deadline: 3/15. In 2008, 8 master's, 5 doctorates awarded. *Degree program information:* Part-time programs available. Offers forest economics (PhD); forestry (MS, PhD); natural resource conservation (MNR); wildlife sciences (MS, PhD). *Application deadline:* For fall admission, 7/7 for domestic students; for spring admission, 11/24 for domestic students. Applications are processed on a rolling basis. *Application fee:* $25 ($50 for international students). Electronic applications accepted. *Application Contact:* Dr. George Flowers, Dean of the Graduate School, 334-844-2125. *Dean,* Dr. Richard W. Brinker, 334-844-1007, Fax: 334-844-1084, E-mail: brinker@forestry.auburn.edu.

Harrison School of Pharmacy Students: 535 full-time (340 women), 33 part-time (14 women); includes 78 minority (40 African Americans, 6 American Indian/Alaska Native, 30 Asian Americans or Pacific Islanders, 2 Hispanic Americans), 19 international. Average age 27. *Faculty:* 48 full-time (27 women), 1 (woman) part-time/adjunct. Expenses: Contact institution. *Financial support:* Fellowships, research assistantships, teaching assistantships, Federal Work-Study available. Support available to part-time students. In 2008, 126 first professional degrees, 2 doctorates awarded. *Degree program information:* Part-time programs available. Offers pharmacal sciences (MS, PhD); pharmaceutical sciences (PhD); pharmacy (Pharm D, MS, PhD); pharmacy care systems (MS, PhD). *Application deadline:* For fall admission, 7/7 for domestic students; for spring admission, 11/24 for domestic students. Applications are processed on a rolling basis. *Application fee:* $25. Electronic applications accepted. *Application Contact:* Dr. George Flowers, Dean of the Graduate School, 334-844-2125. *Dean,* Dr. R. Lee Evans, 334-844-8348.

AUBURN UNIVERSITY MONTGOMERY, Montgomery, AL 36124-4023

General Information State-supported, coed, comprehensive institution. *Enrollment:* 5,284 graduate, professional, and undergraduate students; 272 full-time matriculated graduate/professional students (179 women), 555 part-time matriculated graduate/professional students (381 women). *Graduate faculty:* 84 full-time (27 women), 12 part-time/adjunct (4 women). Tuition, state resident: full-time $5088; part-time $212 per credit. Tuition, nonresident: full-time $15,264; part-time $636 per credit. *Required fees:* $234. *Graduate housing:* Rooms and/or apartments available to single students and available on a first-come, first-served basis to married students. *Student services:* Campus employment opportunities, campus safety program, career counseling, exercise/wellness program, free psychological counseling, international student services, low-cost health insurance, multicultural affairs office, services for students with disabilities. *Library facilities:* Auburn University Montgomery Library. *Online resources:* library catalog, web page, access to other libraries' catalogs. *Collection:* 331,513 titles, 2,280 serial subscriptions.

Computer facilities: 500 computers available on campus for general student use. A campuswide network can be accessed from student residence rooms and from off campus. Online class registration is available. *Web address:* http://www.aum.edu/.

General Application Contact: Ronnie McKinney, Associate Director of Enrollment Services, 334-244-3598, Fax: 334-244-3795, E-mail: rmckinne@aum.edu.

GRADUATE UNITS

School of Business Students: 85 full-time (34 women), 112 part-time (54 women); includes 39 minority (31 African Americans, 5 Asian Americans or Pacific Islanders, 3 Hispanic Americans), 10 international. Average age 29. *Faculty:* 22 full-time (6 women), 3 part-time/adjunct (1 woman). Expenses: Contact institution. *Financial support:* Research assistantships, career-related internships or fieldwork and scholarships/grants available. Support available to part-time students. Financial award application deadline: 3/1; financial award applicants required to submit FAFSA. In 2008, 76 master's awarded. *Degree program information:* Part-time and evening/weekend programs available. Offers business (MBA). *Application deadline:* Applications are processed on a rolling basis. *Application fee:* $25. Electronic applications accepted. *Application Contact:* Dr. Jane Goodson, Dean, 334-244-3478, Fax: 334-244-3792, E-mail: jgoodson@aum.edu. *Dean,* Dr. Jane Goodson, 334-244-3478, Fax: 334-244-3792, E-mail: jgoodson@aum.edu.

School of Education Students: 132 full-time (115 women), 219 part-time (175 women); includes 151 minority (147 African Americans, 3 Asian Americans or Pacific Islanders, 1 Hispanic American), 2 international. Average age 33. *Faculty:* 24 full-time (18 women), 5 part-time/adjunct (4 women). Expenses: Contact institution. *Financial support:* In 2008–09, 2 teaching assistantships were awarded; career-related internships or fieldwork and scholarships/grants also available. Support available to part-time students. Financial award application deadline: 3/1; financial award applicants required to submit FAFSA. In 2008, 110 master's awarded. *Degree program information:* Part-time and evening/weekend programs available. Offers counseling (M Ed, Ed S); early childhood education (M Ed, Ed S); education (M Ed, Ed S); education administration (M Ed, Ed S); elementary education (M Ed, Ed S); physical education (M Ed); reading education (M Ed, Ed S); secondary education (M Ed, Ed S); special education (M Ed, Ed S). *Application deadline:* Applications are processed on a rolling basis. *Application fee:* $25. Electronic applications accepted. *Application Contact:* Dr. Sam Flynt, Associate Graduate Coordinator, 334-244-3270, Fax: 334-244-3835, E-mail: sflynt@mail.aum.edu. *Dean,* Dr. Jennifer A. Brown, 334-244-3413, Fax: 334-244-3835, E-mail: jbrown@mail.aum.edu.

School of Liberal Arts Students: 4 full-time (2 women), 29 part-time (19 women); includes 8 minority (5 African Americans, 1 American Indian/Alaska Native, 2 Asian Americans or Pacific Islanders). Average age 38. *Faculty:* 30 full-time (10 women). Expenses: Contact institution. *Financial support:* In 2008–09, 2 teaching assistantships were awarded; career-related internships or fieldwork and scholarships/grants also available. Support available to part-time students. Financial award application deadline: 3/1; financial award applicants required to submit FAFSA. In 2008, 6 master's awarded. *Degree program information:* Part-time and evening/weekend programs available. Offers liberal arts (MLA). *Application deadline:* Applications are processed on a rolling basis. *Application fee:* $25. Electronic applications accepted. *Application Contact:* Dr. Eric Sterling, Professor, 334-244-3760, Fax: 334-244-3740, E-mail: esterlin@aum.edu. *Interim Dean,* Dr. Steven Daniell, 334-244-3382, Fax: 334-244-3740.

School of Sciences Students: 51 full-time (28 women), 155 part-time (99 women); includes 89 minority (86 African Americans, 1 American Indian/Alaska Native, 2 Asian Americans or Pacific Islanders), 5 international. Average age 32. *Faculty:* 21 full-time (4 women), 10 part-time/adjunct (2 women). Expenses: Contact institution. *Financial support:* In 2008–09, 8 teaching assistantships were awarded; career-related internships or fieldwork and scholarships/grants also available. Support available to part-time students. Financial award application deadline: 3/1; financial award applicants required to submit FAFSA. In 2008, 70 master's awarded. *Degree program information:* Part-time and evening/weekend programs available. Offers justice and public safety (MSJPS); psychology (MSPG); public administration and political science (MPA, MPS, PhD); sciences (MPA, MPS, MSJPS, MSPG, PhD). *Application deadline:* Applications are processed on a rolling basis. *Application fee:* $25. Electronic applications accepted. *Application Contact:* Dr. Bridgette Harper, Graduate Coordinator, 334-244-3551, Fax: 334-244-3826, E-mail: bharper4@aum.edu. *Dean,* Dr. Bayo Lawal, 334-224-3678, Fax: 334-244-3826, E-mail: blawal@mail.aum.edu.

AUGSBURG COLLEGE, Minneapolis, MN 55454-1351

General Information Independent-religious, coed, comprehensive institution. *Enrollment:* 3,891 graduate, professional, and undergraduate students; 535 full-time matriculated graduate/professional students (329 women), 272 part-time matriculated graduate/professional students (204 women). *Enrollment by degree level:* 807 master's. *Graduate faculty:* 30 full-time (19 women), 18 part-time/adjunct (8 women). *Graduate housing:* On-campus housing not available. *Student services:* Career counseling, free psychological counseling, international student services. *Library facilities:* James G. Lindell Library. *Online resources:* library catalog, web page, access to other libraries' catalogs. *Collection:* 146,166 titles, 754 serial subscriptions.

Computer facilities: 260 computers available on campus for general student use. A campuswide network can be accessed from student residence rooms and from off campus. Online class registration is available. *Web address:* http://www.augsburg.edu/.

General Application Contact: Nathan Gorr, Director, Weekend College and Graduate Admissions, 612-330-1101 Ext. 1390, E-mail: gorr@augsburg.edu.

GRADUATE UNITS

Program in Business Administration Students: 234 full-time (109 women), 18 part-time (10 women); includes 21 minority (8 African Americans, 2 American Indian/Alaska Native, 9 Asian Americans or Pacific Islanders, 2 Hispanic Americans), 3 international. Average age 34. 715 applicants, 13% accepted, 85 enrolled. *Faculty:* 2 full-time (1 woman), 5 part-time/adjunct (2 women). Expenses: Contact institution. In 2008, 161 master's awarded. *Degree program information:* Evening/weekend programs available. Offers business administration (MBA). *Application deadline:* For fall admission, 8/15 priority date for domestic students; for winter admission, 12/15 priority date for domestic students; for spring admission, 3/25 priority date for domestic students. Applications are processed on a rolling basis. *Application fee:* $35. Electronic applications accepted. *Application Contact:* Mike Bilden, Graduate Recruiter, 612-330-1434, E-mail: bilden@augsburg.edu. *Director,* Steven Zitnick, 612-330-1774.

Program in Education Students: 107 full-time (70 women), 79 part-time (56 women); includes 18 minority (8 African Americans, 3 American Indian/Alaska Native, 7 Asian Americans or Pacific Islanders). Average age 34. 405 applicants, 17% accepted, 43 enrolled. *Faculty:* 4 full-time (3 women), 3 part-time/adjunct (all women). Expenses: Contact institution. In 2008, 11 master's awarded. *Degree program information:* Part-time and evening/weekend programs available. Offers education (MAE). *Application deadline:* For fall admission, 8/15 for domestic and international students; for winter admission, 12/15 for domestic and international students; for spring admission, 3/26 for domestic and international students. Applications are processed on a rolling basis. *Application fee:* $35. Electronic applications accepted. *Application Contact:* Karen Howell, Program Coordinator, 612-330-1354, E-mail: howell@augsburg.edu. *Professor,* Vicki Olson, 612-330-1131, E-mail: olsonv@augsburg.edu.

Program in Leadership Students: 22 full-time (19 women), 77 part-time (55 women); includes 10 minority (6 African Americans, 1 American Indian/Alaska Native, 1 Asian American or Pacific Islander, 2 Hispanic Americans). Average age 38. 213 applicants, 17% accepted, 31 enrolled. *Faculty:* 7 full-time (2 women), 2 part-time/adjunct (1 woman). Expenses: Contact institution. *Financial support:* In 2008–09, 9 students received support. Available to part-time students. Application deadline: 8/1. In 2008, 18 master's awarded. *Degree program information:*

Augsburg College (continued)

Part-time and evening/weekend programs available. Offers leadership (MA). *Application deadline:* For fall admission, 8/9 priority date for domestic students; for winter admission, 12/15 for domestic students; for spring admission, 3/7 for domestic students. Applications are processed on a rolling basis. *Application fee:* $35. *Application Contact:* Patricia Park, Program Coordinator, 612-330-1150, E-mail: parkp@augsburg.edu. *Director,* Dr. Norma Noonan, 612-330-1198, Fax: 612-330-1355, E-mail: noonan@augsburg.edu.

Program in Physicians Assistant Studies Students: 81 full-time (69 women); includes 4 minority (3 Asian Americans or Pacific Islanders, 1 Hispanic American). Average age 27. 130 applicants, 22% accepted, 28 enrolled. *Faculty:* 7 full-time (6 women), 1 part-time/adjunct (0 women). Expenses: Contact institution. *Financial support:* In 2008–09, 26 students received support. Application deadline: 8/1. In 2008, 31 master's awarded. Offers physicians assistant studies (MS). *Application deadline:* For spring admission, 10/1 for domestic students. *Application fee:* $20. *Application Contact:* Carrie Benton, Information Contact, 612-330-1039, Fax: 612-330-1757, E-mail: paprog@augsburg.edu. *Director,* Dawn B. Ludwig, 612-330-1331, Fax: 612-330-1757, E-mail: ludwig@augsburg.edu.

Program in Social Work Students: 73 full-time (65 women), 23 part-time (18 women); includes 20 minority (9 African Americans, 2 American Indian/Alaska Native, 7 Asian Americans or Pacific Islanders, 2 Hispanic Americans). Average age 33. 359 applicants, 20% accepted, 36 enrolled. *Faculty:* 8 full-time (5 women), 5 part-time/adjunct (2 women). Expenses: Contact institution. *Financial support:* In 2008–09, 38 students received support. Career-related internships or fieldwork, institutionally sponsored loans, and tuition waivers (partial) available. Support available to part-time students. Financial award application deadline: 4/15. In 2008, 44 master's awarded. *Degree program information:* Part-time and evening/weekend programs available. Offers social work (MSW). *Application deadline:* For fall admission, 1/15 for domestic students; for spring admission, 10/1 for domestic students. *Application fee:* $35. *Application Contact:* Holley Locher, Program Coordinator, 612-330-1763, Fax: 612-330-1493, E-mail: locherh@augsburg.edu. *Director,* Dr. Lois A. Bosch, 612-330-1633, Fax: 612-330-1493, E-mail: bosch@augsburg.edu.

Program in Transcultural Community Health Nursing Students: 15 full-time (14 women), 63 part-time (61 women); includes 3 minority (1 African American, 2 Asian Americans or Pacific Islanders), 1 international. Average age 45. 120 applicants, 18% accepted, 20 enrolled. *Faculty:* 2 full-time (both women). Expenses: Contact institution. *Financial support:* In 2008–09, 5 students received support. Application deadline: 8/1. In 2008, 1 master's awarded. Offers transcultural community health nursing (MA). *Application deadline:* For fall admission, 8/1 for domestic students; for winter admission, 12/4 for domestic students; for spring admission, 3/9 for domestic students. *Application fee:* $35. *Application Contact:* Sharon Wade, Coordinator, 612-330-1209, E-mail: wades@augsburg.edu. *Director,* Dr. Cheryl J. Leuning, 612-330-1214, E-mail: leuning@augsburg.edu.

AUGUSTANA COLLEGE, Sioux Falls, SD 57197

General Information Independent-religious, coed, comprehensive institution. *Graduate housing:* Room and/or apartments available on a first-come, first-served basis to single students.

GRADUATE UNITS

Department of Education *Degree program information:* Part-time and evening/weekend programs available. Offers education (MA); elementary (MA); secondary (MA).

Program in Advanced Nursing Practice in Emerging Health Systems *Degree program information:* Part-time programs available. Postbaccalaureate distance learning degree programs offered (minimal on-campus study). Offers community health nursing (MA).

AUGUSTA STATE UNIVERSITY, Augusta, GA 30904-2200

General Information State-supported, coed, comprehensive institution. *Enrollment:* 6,689 graduate, professional, and undergraduate students; 428 full-time matriculated graduate/professional students (338 women), 482 part-time matriculated graduate/professional students (356 women). *Enrollment by degree level:* 839 master's, 71 other advanced degrees. *Graduate faculty:* 50 full-time (24 women), 34 part-time/adjunct (25 women). Tuition, state resident: full-time $2520; part-time $140 per credit hour. Tuition, nonresident: full-time $10,080; part-time $560 per credit hour. *Required fees:* $546; $273 per semester. *Graduate housing:* Room and/or apartments available on a first-come, first-served basis to single students; on-campus housing not available to married students. Typical cost: $5100 per year. *Student services:* Campus employment opportunities, career counseling, child daycare facilities, low-cost health insurance, services for students with disabilities, teacher training. *Library facilities:* Reese Library plus 1 other. *Online resources:* library catalog, web page, access to other libraries' catalogs. *Collection:* 488,586 titles, 49,502 serial subscriptions, 5,744 audiovisual materials. *Research affiliation:* Veterans Administration Hospital (psychology).

Computer facilities: 325 computers available on campus for general student use. A campuswide network can be accessed from off campus. Online class registration is available. *Web address:* http://www.aug.edu/.

General Application Contact: Katherine Sweeney, Director of Admissions/Registrar, 706-737-1405, Fax: 706-667-4355, E-mail: ksweeney@aug.edu.

GRADUATE UNITS

Graduate Studies Students: 428 full-time (338 women), 482 part-time (356 women); includes 299 minority (254 African Americans, 2 American Indian/Alaska Native, 20 Asian Americans or Pacific Islanders, 23 Hispanic Americans). Average age 34. 342 applicants, 76% accepted, 221 enrolled. *Faculty:* 50 full-time (24 women), 34 part-time/adjunct (25 women). Expenses: Contact institution. *Financial support:* Research assistantships with partial tuition reimbursements, career-related internships or fieldwork, Federal Work-Study, institutionally sponsored loans, and unspecified assistantships available. Support available to part-time students. Financial award application deadline: 4/15; financial award applicants required to submit FAFSA. In 2008, 230 master's, 57 other advanced degrees awarded. *Degree program information:* Part-time and evening/weekend programs available. *Application deadline:* Applications are processed on a rolling basis. *Application fee:* $20. *Application Contact:* Dr. Samuel Sullivan, Vice President for Academic Affairs, 706-737-1422, Fax: 706-737-1585, E-mail: ssullivan@aug.edu. *Vice President for Academic Affairs,* Dr. Samuel Sullivan, 706-737-1422, Fax: 706-737-1585, E-mail: ssullivan@aug.edu.

College of Arts and Sciences Students: 36 full-time (28 women), 32 part-time (25 women); includes 21 minority (14 African Americans, 2 Asian Americans or Pacific Islanders, 5 Hispanic Americans). Average age 30. 62 applicants, 56% accepted, 29 enrolled. *Faculty:* 11 full-time (6 women), 3 part-time/adjunct (1 woman). Expenses: Contact institution. *Financial support:* Research assistantships with partial tuition reimbursements, career-related internships or fieldwork, Federal Work-Study, and institutionally sponsored loans available. Financial award application deadline: 4/15; financial award applicants required to submit FAFSA. In 2008, 23 master's awarded. *Degree program information:* Part-time and evening/weekend programs available. Offers arts and sciences (MPA, MS); political science (MPA); psychology (MS). *Application deadline:* Applications are processed on a rolling basis. *Application fee:* $20. *Application Contact:* Dr. Robert R. Parham, Dean, 706-737-1738, Fax: 706-737-1773, E-mail: rparham@aug.edu. *Dean,* Dr. Robert R. Parham, 706-737-1738, Fax: 706-737-1773, E-mail: rparham@aug.edu.

College of Education Students: 356 full-time (294 women), 389 part-time (307 women); includes 259 minority (233 African Americans, 2 American Indian/Alaska Native, 9 Asian Americans or Pacific Islanders, 15 Hispanic Americans). Average age 36. 239 applicants, 82% accepted, 168 enrolled. *Faculty:* 31 full-time (16 women), 28 part-time/adjunct (23 women). Expenses: Contact institution. *Financial support:* Career-related internships or fieldwork, Federal Work-Study, institutionally sponsored loans, and unspecified assistantships available. Support available to part-time students. Financial award application deadline: 4/15; financial award applicants required to submit FAFSA. In 2008, 72 master's, 97 other advanced degrees awarded. *Degree program information:* Part-time and evening/weekend programs available. Offers counseling/guidance (M Ed); curriculum/instruction (M Ed); education (M Ed, MAT, Ed S); educational leadership (M Ed, Ed S); health and physical education (M Ed); special education (M Ed, Ed S); teaching/learning (MAT, Ed S). *Application deadline:* For fall admission, 7/16 priority date for domestic students. Applications are processed on a rolling basis. *Application fee:* $20. *Application Contact:* Andrea M. Scott, Secretary to the Dean, 706-737-1499, Fax: 706-667-4706, E-mail: ascott1@aug.edu. *Dean,* Dr. Richard Harrison, 706-737-1499, Fax: 706-667-4706, E-mail: vharriso@aug.edu.

Hull College of Business Students: 36 full-time (16 women), 61 part-time (24 women); includes 19 minority (7 African Americans, 9 Asian Americans or Pacific Islanders, 3 Hispanic Americans). Average age 30. 41 applicants, 66% accepted, 24 enrolled. *Faculty:* 8 full-time (2 women), 3 part-time/adjunct (1 woman). Expenses: Contact institution. *Financial support:* Research assistantships with partial tuition reimbursements, Federal Work-Study and institutionally sponsored loans available. Support available to part-time students. Financial award application deadline: 4/15; financial award applicants required to submit FAFSA. In 2008, 35 master's awarded. *Degree program information:* Part-time and evening/weekend programs available. Offers business (MBA). *Application deadline:* For fall admission, 7/15 priority date for domestic students, 7/1 for international students; for spring admission, 12/1 priority date for domestic students, 11/15 for international students. Applications are processed on a rolling basis. *Application fee:* $20. *Application Contact:* Dr. Todd A Schultz, Acting Associate Dean, 706-737-1562, Fax: 706-667-4064, E-mail: tschultz@aug.edu. *Dean,* Dr. Marc D Miller, 706-737-1418, Fax: 706-667-4064, E-mail: mmiller@aug.edu.

AURORA UNIVERSITY, Aurora, IL 60506-4892

General Information Independent, coed, comprehensive institution. *Enrollment:* 4,291 graduate, professional, and undergraduate students; 433 full-time matriculated graduate/professional students (322 women), 1,485 part-time matriculated graduate/professional students (1,082 women). *Enrollment by degree level:* 1,768 master's, 141 doctoral, 9 other advanced degrees. *Graduate faculty:* 39 full-time (19 women), 168 part-time/adjunct (89 women). *Tuition:* Full-time $19,512; part-time $542 per semester hour. Tuition and fees vary according to degree level, campus/location and program. *Graduate housing:* On-campus housing not available. *Student services:* Campus employment opportunities, campus safety program, career counseling, exercise/wellness program, free psychological counseling, international student services, low-cost health insurance, multicultural affairs office, services for students with disabilities, teacher training, writing training. *Library facilities:* Charles B. Phillips Library. *Online resources:* library catalog, web page, access to other libraries' catalogs. *Collection:* 99,000 titles, 210 serial subscriptions, 7,621 audiovisual materials.

Computer facilities: 90 computers available on campus for general student use. A campuswide network can be accessed from student residence rooms and from off campus. Learning Management System available. *Web address:* http://www.aurora.edu/.

General Application Contact: Dr. Donna DeSpain, Dean of Adult and Graduate Studies, 800-742-5281, Fax: 630-844-5535, E-mail: auadmission@aurora.edu.

GRADUATE UNITS

College of Arts and Sciences Students: 109 part-time (73 women); includes 14 minority (3 Asian Americans or Pacific Islanders, 11 Hispanic Americans). Average age 36. 11 applicants, 100% accepted, 11 enrolled. *Faculty:* 1 (woman) part-time/adjunct. Expenses: Contact institution. *Financial support:* Fellowships, research assistantships, teaching assistantships, Federal Work-Study, scholarships/grants, and unspecified assistantships available. Support available to part-time students. Financial award application deadline: 4/15; financial award applicants required to submit FAFSA. *Degree program information:* Part-time and evening/weekend programs available. Offers mathematics (MS). *Application deadline:* For fall admission, 7/15 priority date for domestic students, 3/1 for international students; for spring admission, 12/15 for domestic students, 7/1 for international students. Applications are processed on a rolling basis. *Application fee:* $25. Electronic applications accepted. *Application Contact:* Donna DeSpain, Dean of Adult and Graduate Studies, 800-742-5281, Fax: 630-844-5535, E-mail: auadmission@aurora.edu. *Dean,* Dr. Lora Delacey, 630-844-5510, E-mail: ldelacey@aurora.edu.

College of Education Students: 138 full-time (92 women), 1,167 part-time (865 women); includes 150 minority (41 African Americans, 4 American Indian/Alaska Native, 9 Asian Americans or Pacific Islanders, 96 Hispanic Americans). Average age 35. 451 applicants, 99% accepted, 421 enrolled. *Faculty:* 20 full-time (10 women), 99 part-time/adjunct (55 women). Expenses: Contact institution. *Financial support:* In 2008–09, 355 students received support; fellowships, research assistantships, teaching assistantships, Federal Work-Study and scholarships/grants available. Support available to part-time students. Financial award application deadline: 4/15; financial award applicants required to submit FAFSA. In 2008, 439 master's, 9 doctorates awarded. *Degree program information:* Part-time and evening/weekend programs available. Offers curriculum and instruction (Ed D); education (MAT); education and administration (Ed D); educational leadership (MEL); reading instruction (MA). *Application deadline:* For fall admission, 8/23 priority date for domestic students. Applications are processed on a rolling basis. *Application fee:* $25. Electronic applications accepted. *Application Contact:* Donna DeSpain, Dean of Adult and Graduate Studies, 800-742-5281, Fax: 630-844-5535, E-mail: auadmission@aurora.edu. *Dean,* Dr. Donald C. Wold, 630-844-1542, Fax: 630-844-5530, E-mail: dwold@aurora.edu.

College of Professional Studies Students: 277 full-time (220 women), 199 part-time (137 women); includes 98 minority (48 African Americans, 10 Asian Americans or Pacific Islanders, 40 Hispanic Americans), 1 international. Average age 31. 274 applicants, 98% accepted, 166 enrolled. *Faculty:* 16 full-time (8 women), 24 part-time/adjunct (15 women). Expenses: Contact institution. *Financial support:* In 2008–09, 267 students received support; fellowships, research assistantships, teaching assistantships available. Financial award application deadline: 4/15; financial award applicants required to submit FAFSA. In 2008, 170 master's awarded. *Degree program information:* Part-time and evening/weekend programs available. *Application deadline:* For fall admission, 8/25 priority date for domestic students. Applications are processed on a rolling basis. *Application fee:* $25. Electronic applications accepted. *Application Contact:* Donna DeSpain, Dean of Adult and Graduate Studies, 800-742-5281, Fax: 630-844-5535, E-mail: auadmission@aurora.edu. *Dean,* Dr. Michael Carroll, 630-844-4888.

Dunham School of Business Students: 65 full-time (37 women), 106 part-time (55 women); includes 36 minority (15 African Americans, 7 Asian Americans or Pacific Islanders, 14 Hispanic Americans), 1 international. Average age 33. 46 applicants, 100% accepted, 33 enrolled. *Faculty:* 6 full-time (0 women), 12 part-time/adjunct (4 women). Expenses: Contact institution. *Financial support:* In 2008–09, 43 students received support; fellowships, research assistantships, teaching assistantships, Federal Work-Study and scholarships/grants available. Support available to part-time students. Financial award application deadline: 4/15; financial award applicants required to submit FAFSA. In 2008, 48 master's awarded. *Degree program information:* Part-time and evening/weekend programs available. Offers business (MBA). *Application deadline:* For fall admission, 8/25 priority date for domestic students. Applications are processed on a rolling basis. *Application fee:* $25. Electronic applications accepted. *Application Contact:* Donna DeSpain, Dean of Adult and Graduate Studies, 800-742-5281, Fax: 630-844-5535, E-mail: auadmission@aurora.edu. *Director,* Dr. Shawn Green, 630-844-5527, Fax: 630-844-7830, E-mail: sgreen@aurora.edu.

School of Social Work Students: 212 full-time (183 women), 93 part-time (82 women); includes 62 minority (33 African Americans, 3 Asian Americans or Pacific Islanders, 26 Hispanic Americans). Average age 31. 228 applicants, 97% accepted, 133 enrolled. *Faculty:* 10 full-time (8 women), 12 part-time/adjunct (11 women). Expenses: Contact institution. *Financial support:* In 2008–09, 224 students received support; fellowships, research assistantships, teaching assistantships, Federal Work-Study and scholarships/grants available. Support available to part-time students. Financial award application deadline: 4/15; financial award applicants required to submit FAFSA. In 2008, 122 master's awarded. *Degree program information:* Part-time and evening/weekend programs available. Offers social work (MSW). *Application deadline:* For fall admission, 8/25 priority date for domestic students. Applications are processed on a rolling basis. *Application fee:* $25. Electronic applications accepted. *Application Contact:* Melissa Yovich-Whattam, Graduate Recruiter, 630-844-5292, E-mail: auadmission@aurora.edu. *Dean,* Dr. Fred Mckenzie, 630-844-5420, E-mail: mckenzie@aurora.edu.

George Williams College of Aurora University Students: 18 full-time (10 women), 10 part-time (7 women); includes 2 minority (1 African American, 1 Hispanic American). Average

age 28. Expenses: Contact institution. *Application Contact:* Donna DeSpain, Dean of Adult and Graduate Studies, 800-742-5281, Fax: 630-844-5535, E-mail: auadmission@aurora.edu. *Dean,* Dr. Rita Yerkes, 262-245-8572, E-mail: ryerkes@aurora.edu.

School of Experiential Leadership 30 applicants, 100% accepted, 22 enrolled. *Faculty:* 2 full-time (1 woman), 2 part-time/adjunct (1 woman). Expenses: Contact institution. *Financial support:* In 2008–09, 27 students received support, including 6 fellowships (averaging $5,609 per year); research assistantships, teaching assistantships, Federal Work-Study, scholarships/grants, and unspecified assistantships also available. Support available to part-time students. Financial award application deadline: 4/15. In 2008, 30 master's awarded. *Degree program information:* Part-time and evening/weekend programs available. Offers administration of leisure services (MS); outdoor pursuits recreation administration (MS). *Application deadline:* For fall admission, 8/25 priority date for domestic students. Applications are processed on a rolling basis. *Application fee:* $25. Electronic applications accepted. *Application Contact:* Dr. Rita Yerkes, Dean, 262-245-8572, E-mail: ryerkes@aurora.edu.

AUSTIN COLLEGE, Sherman, TX 75090-4400

General Information Independent-religious, coed, comprehensive institution. *Enrollment:* 1,298 graduate, professional, and undergraduate students; 34 full-time matriculated graduate/professional students (29 women), 1 (woman) part-time matriculated graduate/professional student. *Enrollment by degree level:* 35 master's. *Graduate faculty:* 5 full-time (3 women), 1 (woman) part-time/adjunct. *Graduate housing:* Room and/or apartments available on a first-come, first-served basis to single students; on-campus housing not available to married students. Housing application deadline: 5/1. *Student services:* Campus employment opportunities, campus safety program, career counseling, free psychological counseling, teacher training. *Library facilities:* Abell Library. *Online resources:* library catalog, web page, access to other libraries' catalogs. *Collection:* 240,944 titles, 2,181 serial subscriptions.

Computer facilities: 160 computers available on campus for general student use. A campuswide network can be accessed from student residence rooms and from off campus. Online class registration is available. *Web address:* http://www.austincollege.edu/.

General Application Contact: Dr. Barbara Sylvester, Director of Teaching Program, 903-813-2327, Fax: 903-813-2326, E-mail: bsylvester@austincollege.edu.

GRADUATE UNITS

Program in Education Students: 34 full-time (29 women), 1 (woman) part-time; includes 3 minority (1 Asian American or Pacific Islander, 2 Hispanic Americans). Average age 23. *Faculty:* 5 full-time (3 women), 1 (woman) part-time/adjunct. Expenses: Contact institution. *Financial support:* Career-related internships or fieldwork, Federal Work-Study, scholarships/grants, and unspecified assistantships available. Support available to part-time students. Financial award application deadline: 4/1; financial award applicants required to submit FAFSA. In 2008, 17 master's awarded. *Degree program information:* Part-time programs available. Offers art education (MA); elementary education (MA); middle school education (MA); music education (MA); physical education and coaching (MA); secondary education (MA); theatre education (MA). *Application deadline:* For fall admission, 5/1 priority date for domestic students; for spring admission, 1/15 priority date for domestic students. Applications are processed on a rolling basis. *Application fee:* $35. Electronic applications accepted. *Application Contact:* Dr. Barbara Sylvester, Director of Teaching Program, 903-813-2327, Fax: 903-813-2326, E-mail: bsylvester@austincollege.edu. *Director of Teaching Program,* Dr. Barbara Sylvester, 903-813-2327, Fax: 903-813-2326, E-mail: bsylvester@austincollege.edu.

AUSTIN GRADUATE SCHOOL OF THEOLOGY, Austin, TX 78705-5610

General Information Independent-religious, coed, upper-level institution. *Graduate housing:* On-campus housing not available.

GRADUATE UNITS

Program in Theological Studies *Degree program information:* Part-time programs available. Offers theological studies (MATS).

AUSTIN PEAY STATE UNIVERSITY, Clarksville, TN 37044

General Information State-supported, coed, comprehensive institution. CGS member. *Enrollment:* 9,401 graduate, professional, and undergraduate students; 234 full-time matriculated graduate/professional students (172 women), 584 part-time matriculated graduate/professional students (431 women). *Enrollment by degree level:* 805 master's, 13 other advanced degrees. *Graduate faculty:* 97 full-time (46 women), 14 part-time/adjunct (10 women). Tuition, state resident: full-time $5772; part-time $305 per credit hour. Tuition, nonresident: full-time $16,664; part-time $778 per credit hour. *Required fees:* $1224. *Graduate housing:* Rooms and/or apartments available on a first-come, first-served basis to single and married students. Typical cost: $3640 per year ($5870 including board) for single students; $5600 per year ($7830 including board) for married students. Room and board charges vary according to board plan and housing facility selected. *Student services:* Campus employment opportunities, campus safety program, career counseling, child daycare facilities, exercise/wellness program, free psychological counseling, international student services, low-cost health insurance, multicultural affairs office, services for students with disabilities, teacher training, writing training. *Library facilities:* Felix G. Woodward Library. *Online resources:* library catalog, web page, access to other libraries' catalogs. *Collection:* 552,681 titles, 18,675 serial subscriptions, 6,432 audiovisual materials.

Computer facilities: Computer purchase and lease plans are available. 760 computers available on campus for general student use. A campuswide network can be accessed from student residence rooms and from off campus. Online class registration is available. *Web address:* http://www.apsu.edu/.

General Application Contact: Dr. Charles Pinder, Dean, College of Graduate Studies, 931-221-7414, Fax: 931-221-7641, E-mail: pinderc@apsu.edu.

GRADUATE UNITS

College of Graduate Studies Students: 234 full-time (172 women), 584 part-time (431 women); includes 161 minority (117 African Americans, 2 American Indian/Alaska Native, 18 Asian Americans or Pacific Islanders, 24 Hispanic Americans), 4 international. Average age 33. 387 applicants, 96% accepted, 281 enrolled. *Faculty:* 97 full-time (46 women), 14 part-time/adjunct (10 women). Expenses: Contact institution. *Financial support:* In 2008–09, 105 students received support, including 105 research assistantships with full tuition reimbursements available (averaging $6,996 per year); career-related internships or fieldwork, Federal Work-Study, institutionally sponsored loans, scholarships/grants, and unspecified assistantships also available. Support available to part-time students. Financial award application deadline: 3/1; financial award applicants required to submit FAFSA. In 2008, 214 master's, 8 other advanced degrees awarded. *Degree program information:* Part-time and evening/weekend programs available. Postbaccalaureate distance learning degree programs offered. *Application deadline:* For fall admission, 7/27 priority date for domestic students; for spring admission, 12/17 priority date for domestic students. Applications are processed on a rolling basis. *Application fee:* $25. Electronic applications accepted. *Application Contact:* Dr. Charles Pinder, Dean, College of Graduate Studies, 931-221-7414, Fax: 931-221-7641, E-mail: pinderc@apsu.edu. *Dean, College of Graduate Studies,* Dr. Charles Pinder, 931-221-7414, Fax: 931-221-7641, E-mail: pinderc@apsu.edu.

College of Arts and Letters Students: 54 full-time (31 women), 123 part-time (68 women); includes 31 minority (25 African Americans, 4 Asian Americans or Pacific Islanders, 2 Hispanic Americans), 1 international. Average age 33. 99 applicants, 98% accepted, 69 enrolled. *Faculty:* 39 full-time (15 women), 7 part-time/adjunct (4 women). Expenses: Contact institution. *Financial support:* In 2008–09, 29 research assistantships with full tuition reimbursements (averaging $6,996 per year) were awarded; career-related internships or fieldwork, Federal Work-Study, institutionally sponsored loans, scholarships/grants, and unspecified assistantships also available. Support available to part-time students. Financial award application deadline: 3/1; financial award applicants required to submit FAFSA. In 2008, 40 master's awarded. *Degree program information:* Part-time programs available. Postbaccalaureate distance learning degree programs offered. Offers arts and letters (M Mu, MA); communication arts (MA); English (MA); military history (MA); music education (M Mu); music performance (M Mu). *Application deadline:* For fall admission, 7/27 priority date for domestic students; for spring admission, 12/17 priority date for domestic students. Applications are processed on a rolling basis. *Application fee:* $25. Electronic applications accepted. *Application Contact:* Dr. Charles Pinder, Dean, College of Graduate Studies, 931-221-7414, Fax: 931-221-7641, E-mail: pinderc@apsu.edu. *Interim Dean,* Dixie Webb, 931-221-6445, Fax: 931-221-1024.

College of Professional Programs and Social Sciences Students: 173 full-time (136 women), 425 part-time (333 women); includes 118 minority (83 African Americans, 2 American Indian/Alaska Native, 13 Asian Americans or Pacific Islanders, 20 Hispanic Americans), 3 international. Average age 34. 289 applicants, 95% accepted, 200 enrolled. *Faculty:* 43 full-time (25 women), 7 part-time/adjunct (6 women). Expenses: Contact institution. *Financial support:* In 2008–09, 35 research assistantships with full tuition reimbursements (averaging $6,996 per year) were awarded; career-related internships or fieldwork, Federal Work-Study, institutionally sponsored loans, scholarships/grants, and unspecified assistantships also available. Support available to part-time students. Financial award application deadline: 3/1; financial award applicants required to submit FAFSA. In 2008, 173 master's, 10 other advanced degrees awarded. *Degree program information:* Part-time and evening/weekend programs available. Postbaccalaureate distance learning degree programs offered. Offers administration and supervision (Ed S); advanced practice (MSN); counseling (MS); counseling and guidance (Ed S); curriculum and instruction (MA Ed); educational leadership studies (MA Ed); elementary education (Ed S); family nurse practitioner (MSN); K-6 education (MAT); management (MS); nursing administration (MSN); nursing education (MSN); nursing informatics (MSN); psychology (MA); public and community health (MS); reading (MA Ed); secondary education (MAT, Ed S); social sciences (MA, MA Ed, MAT, MS, MSN, Ed S); special education (MAT). *Application deadline:* For fall admission, 7/27 priority date for domestic students; for spring admission, 12/17 priority date for domestic students. Applications are processed on a rolling basis. *Application fee:* $25. Electronic applications accepted. *Application Contact:* Dr. Charles Pinder, Dean, College of Graduate Studies, 931-221-7414, Fax: 931-221-7641, E-mail: pinderc@apsu.edu. *Dean,* Dr. David Denton, 931-221-7423, E-mail: dentond@apsu.edu.

College of Science and Mathematics Students: 3 full-time (2 women), 15 part-time (12 women); includes 4 minority (1 African American, 1 Asian American or Pacific Islander, 2 Hispanic Americans). Average age 28. 14 applicants, 100% accepted, 4 enrolled. *Faculty:* 13 full-time (4 women). Expenses: Contact institution. *Financial support:* In 2008–09, 12 research assistantships with full tuition reimbursements (averaging $6,996 per year) were awarded; career-related internships or fieldwork, Federal Work-Study, institutionally sponsored loans, scholarships/grants, and unspecified assistantships also available. Support available to part-time students. Financial award application deadline: 3/1; financial award applicants required to submit FAFSA. In 2008, 9 master's awarded. *Degree program information:* Part-time programs available. Offers clinical laboratory science (MS); radiologic science (MS); science and mathematics (MS). *Application deadline:* For fall admission, 7/27 priority date for domestic students; for spring admission, 12/17 priority date for domestic students. Applications are processed on a rolling basis. *Application fee:* $25. Electronic applications accepted. *Application Contact:* Dr. Charles Pinder, Dean, College of Graduate Studies, 931-221-7414, Fax: 931-221-7641, E-mail: pinderc@apsu.edu. *Interim Dean,* Dr. Jaime Taylor, 931-221-7971, E-mail: taylorj@apsu.edu.

AUSTIN PRESBYTERIAN THEOLOGICAL SEMINARY, Austin, TX 78705-5797

General Information Independent-religious, coed, graduate-only institution. *Enrollment by degree level:* 175 master's, 80 doctoral. *Graduate faculty:* 20 full-time (6 women), 3 part-time/adjunct (0 women). *Tuition:* Full-time $8640; part-time $180 per credit. *Required fees:* $135. *Graduate housing:* Rooms and/or apartments available on a first-come, first-served basis to single and married students. Housing application deadline: 5/31. *Student services:* Campus employment opportunities, campus safety program, career counseling, free psychological counseling, international student services, writing training. *Library facilities:* David and Jane Stitt Library. *Online resources:* library catalog, web page, access to other libraries' catalogs. *Collection:* 155,500 titles, 504 serial subscriptions, 5,921 audiovisual materials.

Computer facilities: 20 computers available on campus for general student use. A campuswide network can be accessed from off campus. Biblical Theological Research available. *Web address:* http://www.austinseminary.edu/.

General Application Contact: Jack Barden, Director of Admissions, 512-404-4827, Fax: 512-479-0738, E-mail: jbarden@austinseminary.edu.

GRADUATE UNITS

Graduate and Professional Programs *Degree program information:* Part-time programs available. Offers divinity (M Div); ministry (D Min); theological studies (MA).

AUSTRALASIAN COLLEGE OF HEALTH SCIENCES, Portland, OR 97239-3719

General Information Independent, coed. *Graduate housing:* On-campus housing not available.

GRADUATE UNITS

Graduate Programs Postbaccalaureate distance learning degree programs offered. Offers complementary alternative medicine (MS).

AVE MARIA SCHOOL OF LAW, Ann Arbor, MI 48105-2550

General Information Independent-religious, coed, graduate-only institution. *Graduate housing:* On-campus housing not available.

GRADUATE UNITS

School of Law Offers law (JD). Electronic applications accepted.

AVE MARIA UNIVERSITY, Ave Maria, FL 34142

General Information Independent-religious, coed, comprehensive institution. *Graduate housing:* Room and/or apartments available on a first-come, first-served basis to single students; on-campus housing not available to married students. Housing application deadline: 7/15.

GRADUATE UNITS

Graduate Programs

Institute for Pastoral Theology *Degree program information:* Part-time and evening/weekend programs available. Offers pastoral theology (MTS).

AVERETT UNIVERSITY, Danville, VA 24541-3692

General Information Independent-religious, coed, comprehensive institution. *Graduate housing:* On-campus housing not available.

GRADUATE UNITS

Graduate Studies in Education *Degree program information:* Part-time and evening/weekend programs available. Offers art education (M Ed); biology (M Ed); biology education (M Ed); chemistry (M Ed); chemistry education (M Ed); curriculum and instruction (M Ed); elementary education (M Ed); English (M Ed); English education (M Ed); health and physical education (M Ed); history and social studies education (M Ed); math (M Ed); mathematics education (M Ed); physical science (M Ed); reading specialization (M Ed); special education (learning disabilities specialization PK-12) (M Ed). Program also offered at Richmond, VA regional campus location.

Program in Business Administration *Degree program information:* Part-time programs available. Offers business administration (MBA).

AVILA UNIVERSITY, Kansas City, MO 64145-1698

General Information Independent-religious, coed, comprehensive institution. *Enrollment:* 1,939 graduate, professional, and undergraduate students; 513 full-time matriculated graduate/professional students (344 women), 213 part-time matriculated graduate/professional students (146 women). *Enrollment by degree level:* 726 master's. *Graduate faculty:* 25 full-time (14 women), 57 part-time/adjunct (29 women). *Tuition:* Full-time $7776; part-time $432 per credit hour. *Required fees:* $414; $24 per credit hour. Tuition and fees vary according to program. *Graduate housing:* Room and/or apartments available on a first-come, first-served basis to single students; on-campus housing not available to married students. Typical cost: $2900 per year ($5900 including board). Room and board charges vary according to board plan and housing facility selected. *Student services:* Campus employment opportunities, campus safety program, career counseling, child daycare facilities, exercise/wellness program, free psychological counseling, international student services, low-cost health insurance, multicultural affairs office, services for students with disabilities, teacher training, writing training. *Library facilities:* Hooley Bundshu Library. *Online resources:* library catalog, web page, access to other libraries' catalogs. *Collection:* 80,845 titles, 22,464 serial subscriptions.

Computer facilities: 180 computers available on campus for general student use. A campuswide network can be accessed from student residence rooms and from off campus. Online class registration is available. *Web address:* http://www.avila.edu/.

General Application Contact: Office of Admissions, 816-501-2400.

GRADUATE UNITS

Department of Psychology Students: 116 full-time (93 women), 29 part-time (25 women); includes 31 minority (27 African Americans, 2 Asian Americans or Pacific Islanders, 2 Hispanic Americans), 6 international. Average age 32. 72 applicants, 72% accepted, 41 enrolled. *Faculty:* 7 full-time (5 women), 12 part-time/adjunct (9 women). Expenses: Contact institution. *Financial support:* In 2008–09, 108 students received support. Career-related internships or fieldwork and scholarships/grants available. Support available to part-time students. Financial award applicants required to submit FAFSA. In 2008, 31 master's awarded. *Degree program information:* Part-time and evening/weekend programs available. Offers counseling psychology (MS); general psychology (MS). *Application deadline:* Applications are processed on a rolling basis. *Application fee:* $0. *Application Contact:* Ann Grubbs, Administrative Assistant, 816-501-3698, E-mail: gradpsych@avila.edu. *Director of Graduate Psychology,* Dr. Regina Staves, 816-501-3665, Fax: 816-501-2455, E-mail: gradpsych@avila.edu.

Program in Organizational Development Students: 54 full-time (39 women), 26 part-time (16 women); includes 20 minority (16 African Americans, 2 Asian Americans or Pacific Islanders, 2 Hispanic Americans), 4 international. Average age 36. *Faculty:* 2 full-time (1 woman), 10 part-time/adjunct (7 women). Expenses: Contact institution. *Financial support:* In 2008–09, 50 students received support. Unspecified assistantships available. Support available to part-time students. Financial award applicants required to submit FAFSA. In 2008, 19 master's awarded. *Degree program information:* Part-time and evening/weekend programs available. Offers organizational development (MS); project management (Graduate Certificate). *Application deadline:* Applications are processed on a rolling basis. *Application fee:* $0. Electronic applications accepted. *Application Contact:* School of Professional Studies, 816-501-3737, Fax: 816-941-4650, E-mail: advantage@avila.edu. *Assistant Dean,* Dr. Lacey Smith, 816-501-3737, Fax: 816-941-4650, E-mail: advantage@avila.edu.

School of Business Students: 163 full-time (69 women), 112 part-time (70 women); includes 60 minority (35 African Americans, 2 American Indian/Alaska Native, 14 Asian Americans or Pacific Islanders, 9 Hispanic Americans), 84 international. Average age 32. 65 applicants, 83% accepted, 54 enrolled. *Faculty:* 9 full-time (3 women), 24 part-time/adjunct (5 women). Expenses: Contact institution. *Financial support:* In 2008–09, 86 students received support. Career-related internships or fieldwork available. Support available to part-time students. Financial award applicants required to submit FAFSA. In 2008, 83 master's awarded. *Degree program information:* Part-time and evening/weekend programs available. Offers accounting (MBA); finance (MBA); general management (MBA); health care administration (MBA); international business (MBA); management information systems (MBA); marketing (MBA). *Application deadline:* For fall admission, 7/30 priority date for domestic students, 7/30 for international students; for winter admission, 11/30 priority date for domestic students, 11/30 for international students; for spring admission, 2/28 priority date for domestic students, 2/28 for international students. Applications are processed on a rolling basis. *Application fee:* $0. Electronic applications accepted. *Application Contact:* JoAnna Giffin, MBA Admissions Director, 816-501-3601, Fax: 816-501-2463, E-mail: joanna.giffin@avila.edu. *Dean, School of Business,* Dr. Richard Woodall, 816-501-3720ri, Fax: 816-501-2463, E-mail: richard.woodall@avila.edu.

School of Education Students: 179 full-time (143 women), 44 part-time (34 women); includes 22 minority (17 African Americans, 2 American Indian/Alaska Native, 1 Asian American or Pacific Islander, 2 Hispanic Americans), 1 international. Average age 35. 156 applicants, 93% accepted, 129 enrolled. *Faculty:* 7 full-time (5 women), 11 part-time/adjunct (8 women). Expenses: Contact institution. *Financial support:* In 2008–09, 57 students received support, including 1 research assistantship; career-related internships or fieldwork also available. Support available to part-time students. Financial award applicants required to submit FAFSA. In 2008, 48 master's awarded. *Degree program information:* Part-time and evening/weekend programs available. Offers education (MA); English for speakers of other languages (Advanced Certificate); special reading (Advanced Certificate). *Application deadline:* Applications are processed on a rolling basis. *Application fee:* $0. Electronic applications accepted. *Application Contact:* Deana Angotti, Director of Graduate Education, 816-501-2446, Fax: 816-501-2915, E-mail: deana.augotti@avila.edu. *Director of Graduate Education,* Deana Angotti, 816-501-2446, Fax: 816-501-2915, E-mail: deana.augotti@avila.edu.

AZUSA PACIFIC UNIVERSITY, Azusa, CA 91702-7000

General Information Independent-religious, coed, university. CGS member. *Enrollment:* 8,548 graduate, professional, and undergraduate students; 585 full-time matriculated graduate/professional students (382 women), 3,105 part-time matriculated graduate/professional students (2,139 women). *Enrollment by degree level:* 180 first professional, 3,117 master's, 393 doctoral. *Graduate faculty:* 115 full-time (64 women), 9 part-time/adjunct (1 woman). *Tuition:* Full-time $9180; part-time $510 per unit. *Required fees:* $700; $700 per year. Tuition and fees vary according to degree level and program. *Graduate housing:* On-campus housing not available. *Student services:* Campus employment opportunities, campus safety program, career counseling, exercise/wellness program, free psychological counseling, international student services, low-cost health insurance, multicultural affairs office, services for students with disabilities, teacher training. *Library facilities:* Marshburn Memorial Library plus 2 others. *Online resources:* library catalog, web page. *Collection:* 185,708 titles, 14,031 serial subscriptions, 17,706 audiovisual materials.

Computer facilities: Computer purchase and lease plans are available. 300 computers available on campus for general student use. A campuswide network can be accessed from off campus. Online class registration is available. *Web address:* http://www.apu.edu/.

General Application Contact: Linda Witte, Graduate Admissions Office, 626-969-3434.

GRADUATE UNITS

College of Liberal Arts and Sciences *Degree program information:* Part-time and evening/weekend programs available. Postbaccalaureate distance learning degree programs offered. Offers fine arts in visual art (MFA); liberal arts and sciences (MA, MFA); teaching English to speakers of other languages (MA).

Haggard School of Theology *Degree program information:* Part-time and evening/weekend programs available. Offers Christian education (MAR); Christian non-profit leadership (MA); divinity (M Div); ministry (D Min); ministry management (MAMM); pastoral studies (MAPS); religion: Biblical studies (MAR); religion: theology and ethics (MAR); theology (M Div, MA, MAMM, MAPS, MAR, MAWL, D Min); worship leadership (MAWL).

School of Behavioral and Applied Sciences Offers behavioral and applied sciences (M Ed, MA, MLOS, DPT, Ed D, Psy D); clinical psychology (MA, Psy D); college student affairs (M Ed); entry-level (DPT); higher education leadership (Ed D); leadership and organizational studies (MLOS); organizational leadership (MA); transitional (DPT).

School of Business and Management *Degree program information:* Part-time and evening/weekend programs available. Offers business administration (MBA); human and organizational development (MA); international business (MBA); strategic management (MBA).

School of Education *Degree program information:* Part-time and evening/weekend programs available. Offers curriculum and instruction in a multicultural setting (MA); education (M Ed, MA, Ed D); educational counseling (MA); educational leadership (Ed D); educational psychology (MA); educational technology (M Ed); language development (MA); physical education (M Ed); pupil personnel services (MA); school administration (MA); school librarianship (MA); special education (MA); teaching (MA).

School of Music *Degree program information:* Part-time and evening/weekend programs available. Offers education (M Mus); performance (M Mus).

School of Nursing *Degree program information:* Part-time and evening/weekend programs available. Offers nursing (MSN); nursing education (PhD).

BABEL UNIVERSITY SCHOOL OF TRANSLATION, Honolulu, HI 96815-1302

General Information Proprietary, coed, primarily women, graduate-only institution. *Graduate housing:* On-campus housing not available.

GRADUATE UNITS

Program in Translation *Degree program information:* Part-time and evening/weekend programs available. Postbaccalaureate distance learning degree programs offered (no on-campus study). Offers translation (MS).

BABSON COLLEGE, Wellesley, Babson Park, MA 02457-0310

General Information Independent, coed, comprehensive institution. *Enrollment:* 3,439 graduate, professional, and undergraduate students; 417 full-time matriculated graduate/professional students (141 women), 1,171 part-time matriculated graduate/professional students (305 women). *Enrollment by degree level:* 1,567 master's, 21 other advanced degrees. *Graduate faculty:* 130 full-time (35 women), 41 part-time/adjunct (10 women). Tuition and fees vary according to course load. *Graduate housing:* Rooms and/or apartments available on a first-come, first-served basis to single and married students. Typical cost: $10,440 per year ($14,704 including board) for single students; $13,572 per year ($22,100 including board) for married students. Room and board charges vary according to board plan, campus/location and housing facility selected. Housing application deadline: 5/1. *Student services:* Campus employment opportunities, campus safety program, career counseling, exercise/wellness program, free psychological counseling, international student services, low-cost health insurance, services for students with disabilities, writing training. *Library facilities:* Horn Library plus 1 other. *Online resources:* library catalog, web page, access to other libraries' catalogs. *Collection:* 131,436 titles, 626 serial subscriptions.

Computer facilities: 290 computers available on campus for general student use. A campuswide network can be accessed from student residence rooms and from off campus. Online class registration, network drives and folders are available. *Web address:* http://www.babson.edu/.

General Application Contact: Martha Snelling, Admissions Services Team, 781-239-4317, Fax: 781-239-4194, E-mail: mbaadmission@babson.edu.

GRADUATE UNITS

F. W. Olin Graduate School of Business Students: 417 full-time (141 women), 1,171 part-time (305 women); includes 222 minority (31 African Americans, 3 American Indian/Alaska Native, 150 Asian Americans or Pacific Islanders, 38 Hispanic Americans), 310 international. Average age 33. 999 applicants, 67% accepted, 415 enrolled. *Faculty:* 130 full-time (35 women), 41 part-time/adjunct (10 women). Expenses: Contact institution. *Financial support:* In 2008–09, 245 students received support, including 56 fellowships (averaging $26,811 per year); career-related internships or fieldwork, Federal Work-Study, institutionally sponsored loans, scholarships/grants, and unspecified assistantships also available. Financial award application deadline: 4/15; financial award applicants required to submit FAFSA. In 2008, 770 master's awarded. *Degree program information:* Part-time and evening/weekend programs available. Postbaccalaureate distance learning degree programs offered (minimal on-campus study). Offers accounting (MSA); business administration (MBA); global entrepreneurship (MS); technological entrepreneurship (MS). *Application deadline:* For fall admission, 4/15 priority date for domestic students, 1/15 priority date for international students. *Application fee:* $100. Electronic applications accepted. *Application Contact:* Martha Snelling, Admission Services Team, 781-239-4317, Fax: 781-239-4194, E-mail: mbaadmission@babson.edu. *Dean,* Dr. Raghu Tadepalli, E-mail: rtadepalli@babson.edu.

BAKER COLLEGE CENTER FOR GRADUATE STUDIES, Flint, MI 48507-9843

General Information Independent, coed, graduate-only institution. CGS member. *Graduate housing:* On-campus housing not available.

GRADUATE UNITS

Graduate Programs *Degree program information:* Part-time and evening/weekend programs available. Postbaccalaureate distance learning degree programs offered. Offers accounting (MBA); finance (MBA); general business (MBA); health care management (MBA); human resources management (MBA); information management (MBA); leadership studies (MBA); management information systems (MSIS); marketing (MBA); occupational therapy (MOT). Electronic applications accepted.

BAKER UNIVERSITY, Baldwin City, KS 66006-0065

General Information Independent-religious, coed. *Enrollment:* 409 full-time matriculated graduate/professional students (227 women), 1,554 part-time matriculated graduate/professional students (1,056 women). *Enrollment by degree level:* 1,899 master's, 64 doctoral. *Graduate faculty:* 14 full-time (10 women), 353 part-time/adjunct (178 women). *Tuition:* Full-time $9265; part-time $300 per credit hour. One-time fee: $2535 full-time. Tuition and fees vary according to course load, degree level and program. *Graduate housing:* On-campus housing not available. *Student services:* Campus safety program, international student services, services for students with disabilities. *Library facilities:* Collins Library. *Online resources:* library catalog, web page, access to other libraries' catalogs. *Collection:* 107,255 titles, 676 serial subscriptions, 5,471 audiovisual materials.

Computer facilities: 222 computers available on campus for general student use. A campuswide network can be accessed from student residence rooms. Online class registration is available. *Web address:* http://www.bakeru.edu/.

General Application Contact: Kelly Belk, Director of Marketing, 913-491-4432, Fax: 913-491-0470, E-mail: kbelk@bakeru.edu.

GRADUATE UNITS

School of Education Students: 103 full-time (78 women), 967 part-time (754 women); includes 47 minority (25 African Americans, 5 American Indian/Alaska Native, 3 Asian Americans or Pacific Islanders, 14 Hispanic Americans). Average age 35. *Faculty:* 10 full-time (8 women), 73 part-time/adjunct (47 women). Expenses: Contact institution. *Financial support:* Applicants required to submit FAFSA. In 2008, 468 master's, 14 doctorates awarded. *Degree program information:* Part-time and evening/weekend programs available. Offers education (MA Ed, MASL, MSSE, MST, Ed D). Master's-level programs also offered in Wichita, KS. *Application deadline:* Applications are processed on a rolling basis. *Application fee:* $20. *Application Contact:* Judy Favor, Director of Graduate Program, 913-491-4432, Fax: 913-491-0470, E-mail: jfavor@bakeru.edu. *Vice President and Dean, School of Education,* Dr. Peggy Harris, 785-594-8492, Fax: 785-594-8363, E-mail: peggy.harris@bakeru.edu.

School of Professional and Graduate Studies Students: 306 full-time (149 women), 587 part-time (302 women); includes 154 minority (87 African Americans, 15 American Indian/Alaska Native, 27 Asian Americans or Pacific Islanders, 25 Hispanic Americans), 1 international. Average age 33. *Faculty:* 4 full-time (2 women), 280 part-time/adjunct (131 women). Expenses: Contact institution. *Financial support:* Applicants required to submit FAFSA. In 2008, 370 master's awarded. *Degree program information:* Part-time and evening/weekend programs available. Postbaccalaureate distance learning degree programs offered (minimal on-campus study). Offers business (MBA, MSM); conflict management and dispute resolution (MA); liberal arts (MLA). *Application deadline:* Applications are processed on a rolling basis. *Application fee:* $45. *Application Contact:* Kelly Belk, Director of Marketing, 913-491-4432, Fax: 913-491-0470, E-mail: kbelk@bakeru.edu. *Vice President and Dean,* Dr. Marvin L. Hunt, 913-491-4432, Fax: 913-491-0470, E-mail: marvin.hunt@bakeru.edu.

BAKKE GRADUATE UNIVERSITY, Seattle, WA 98104

General Information Independent-religious, coed, primarily men, graduate-only institution. *Enrollment by degree level:* 87 master's, 197 doctoral. *Graduate faculty:* 5 full-time (2 women), 12 part-time/adjunct (0 women). *Tuition:* Part-time $1700 per course. Tuition and fees vary according to course level. *Graduate housing:* On-campus housing not available. *Student services:* Career counseling, writing training. *Library facilities:* Bakke Graduate University Library. *Online resources:* web page. *Collection:* 5,000 titles, 69 serial subscriptions, 125 audiovisual materials.

Computer facilities: 4 computers available on campus for general student use. A campuswide network can be accessed. Online class registration is available. *Web address:* http://www.bgu.edu/.

General Application Contact: Lauren Geiser, Assistant Registrar, 206-246-9100 Ext. 122, Fax: 206-246-8828, E-mail: laureng@bgu.edu.

GRADUATE UNITS

Programs in Pastoral Ministry and Business Students: 56 full-time (12 women), 149 part-time (31 women); includes 87 minority (50 African Americans, 1 American Indian/Alaska Native, 28 Asian Americans or Pacific Islanders, 8 Hispanic Americans). Average age 36. *Faculty:* 6 full-time (2 women), 29 part-time/adjunct (2 women). Expenses: Contact institution. *Financial support:* In 2008–09, 46 students received support. Scholarships/grants and tuition waivers (partial) available. Financial award applicants required to submit CSS PROFILE. In 2008, 8 master's, 19 doctorates awarded. *Degree program information:* Part-time programs available. Postbaccalaureate distance learning degree programs offered (minimal on-campus study). Offers business (MBA); global urban ministry (MA); social and civic entrepreneurship (MA); transformational leadership for the global city (D Min). *Application deadline:* For fall admission, 7/1 priority date for domestic students; for winter admission, 12/1 for domestic students; for spring admission, 3/15 for domestic students. Applications are processed on a rolling basis. *Application fee:* $75 ($25 for international students). Electronic applications accepted. *Application Contact:* Lauren Geiser, Assistant Registrar, 206-246-9100 Ext. 122, Fax: 206-264-8828, E-mail: laureng@bgu.edu. *Academic Dean,* Dr. Grace Barnes, 206-264-9100 Ext. 119, Fax: 206-264-8828, E-mail: graceb@bgu.edu.

BALDWIN-WALLACE COLLEGE, Berea, OH 44017-2088

General Information Independent-religious, coed, comprehensive institution. *Enrollment:* 4,382 graduate, professional, and undergraduate students; 351 full-time matriculated graduate/professional students (204 women), 350 part-time matriculated graduate/professional students (218 women). *Enrollment by degree level:* 701 master's. *Graduate faculty:* 30 full-time (10 women), 25 part-time/adjunct (5 women). *Tuition:* Full-time $12,330; part-time $690 per credit hour. *Graduate housing:* Room and/or apartments available to single students; on-campus housing not available to married students. *Student services:* Campus employment opportunities, campus safety program, career counseling, exercise/wellness program, free psychological counseling, international student services, low-cost health insurance, multicultural affairs office, services for students with disabilities, teacher training, writing training. *Library facilities:* Ritter Library plus 2 others. *Online resources:* library catalog, web page, access to other libraries' catalogs. *Collection:* 200,000 titles, 22,000 serial subscriptions. *Research affiliation:* Cleveland State University (Partnering in a STEM grant to encourage high school students to enter science and science teaching as a career.), Ohio Board of Regents (Funding for the CSI Summer Academy for high school students to encourage careers in science and science teaching.), Parma City Schools (Cooperating in a STEM curriculum program funded by the Ohio Board of Regents.).

Computer facilities: 465 computers available on campus for general student use. A campuswide network can be accessed from student residence rooms. Online class registration is available. *Web address:* http://www.bw.edu/.

General Application Contact: Winifred W. Gerhardt, Director of Admission for the Evening and Weekend College, 440-826-2222, Fax: 440-826-3830, E-mail: admission@bw.edu.

GRADUATE UNITS

Graduate Programs Students: 351 full-time (204 women), 350 part-time (218 women); includes 64 minority (39 African Americans, 2 American Indian/Alaska Native, 13 Asian Americans or Pacific Islanders, 10 Hispanic Americans), 21 international. Average age 34. 278 applicants, 74% accepted, 124 enrolled. *Faculty:* 30 full-time (10 women), 25 part-time/adjunct (5 women). Expenses: Contact institution. *Financial support:* In 2008–09, 254 students received support. Career-related internships or fieldwork available. Support available to part-time students. Financial award application deadline: 5/1; financial award applicants required to submit FAFSA. In 2008, 259 master's awarded. *Degree program information:* Part-time and evening/weekend programs available. *Application deadline:* Applications are processed on a rolling basis. *Application fee:* $25. Electronic applications accepted. *Application Contact:* Winifred W. Gerhardt, Director of Admission for the Evening and Weekend College, 440-826-2222, Fax: 440-826-3830, E-mail: admission@bw.edu. *Vice President for Academic Affairs and Dean of the College,* Mary Lou Higgerson, 440-826-2251, Fax: 440-826-2329, E-mail: mlhiggers@bw.edu.

Division of Business Students: 267 full-time (132 women), 205 part-time (99 women); includes 48 minority (25 African Americans, 2 American Indian/Alaska Native, 12 Asian Americans or Pacific Islanders, 9 Hispanic Americans), 21 international. Average age 34. 156 applicants, 74% accepted, 83 enrolled. *Faculty:* 22 full-time (7 women), 19 part-time/adjunct (2 women). Expenses: Contact institution. *Financial support:* In 2008–09, 170 students received support. Career-related internships or fieldwork available. Support available to part-time students. Financial award application deadline: 5/1; financial award applicants required to submit FAFSA. In 2008, 175 master's awarded. *Degree program information:* Part-time and evening/weekend programs available. Offers accounting (MBA); business administration-systems management (MBA); entrepreneurship (MBA); executive management (MBA); health care management (MBA); human resources (MBA); international management (MBA). *Application deadline:* For fall admission, 7/25 priority date for domestic students, 4/30 priority date for international students; for spring admission, 12/15 priority date for domestic students, 9/30 priority date for international students. Applications are processed on a rolling basis. *Application fee:* $25. Electronic applications accepted. *Application Contact:* Peggy Shepard, Graduate Business Coordinator, 440-826-2196, Fax: 440-826-3868, E-mail: pshepard@bw.edu. *Chairperson, Business Administration,* Wayne Cunningham, 440-826-2394, Fax: 440-826-3868, E-mail: wcunning@bw.edu.

Division of Education Students: 84 full-time (72 women), 145 part-time (119 women); includes 16 minority (14 African Americans, 1 Asian American or Pacific Islander, 1 Hispanic American). Average age 33. 122 applicants, 75% accepted, 41 enrolled. *Faculty:* 8 full-time (3 women), 6 part-time/adjunct (3 women). Expenses: Contact institution. *Financial support:* In 2008–09, 84 students received support. Career-related internships or fieldwork available. Support available to part-time students. Financial award application deadline: 5/1; financial award applicants required to submit FAFSA. In 2008, 84 master's awarded. *Degree program information:* Part-time and evening/weekend programs available. Offers educational technology (MA Ed); leadership in higher education (MA Ed); mild/moderate educational needs (MA Ed); reading (MA Ed); school leadership (MA Ed); teaching and learning (M Ed, MA Ed). *Application deadline:* For fall admission, 8/15 priority date for domestic students; for spring admission, 12/15 priority date for domestic students. Applications are processed on a rolling basis. *Application fee:* $25. Electronic applications accepted. *Application Contact:* Winifred W. Gerhardt, Director of Admission for the Evening and Weekend College, 440-826-2222, Fax: 440-826-3830, E-mail: admission@bw.edu. *Chair,* Karen Kaye, 440-826-2168, Fax: 440-826-3779, E-mail: kkaye@bw.edu.

BALL STATE UNIVERSITY, Muncie, IN 47306-1099

General Information State-supported, coed, university. CGS member. *Enrollment:* 20,243 graduate, professional, and undergraduate students; 1,014 full-time matriculated graduate/professional students (570 women), 2,175 part-time matriculated graduate/professional students (1,430 women). *Enrollment by degree level:* 2,789 master's, 318 doctoral, 82 other advanced degrees. *Graduate faculty:* 712. *Graduate housing:* Rooms and/or apartments available on a first-come, first-served basis to single and married students. Typical cost: $8300 (including board) for single students; $6300 (including board) for married students. Room and board charges vary according to board plan and housing facility selected. Housing application deadline: 3/1. *Student services:* Campus employment opportunities, campus safety program, career counseling, child daycare facilities, exercise/wellness program, free psychological counseling, international student services, low-cost health insurance, multicultural affairs office, services for students with disabilities, teacher training. *Library facilities:* Bracken Library plus 2 others. *Online resources:* library catalog, web page, access to other libraries' catalogs. *Collection:* 1.1 million titles, 3,243 serial subscriptions, 456,126 audiovisual materials.

Computer facilities: 1,500 computers available on campus for general student use. A campuswide network can be accessed from student residence rooms and from off campus. *Web address:* http://www.bsu.edu/.

General Application Contact: Dr. Robert J. Morris, Associate Provost for Research and Dean of the Graduate School, 765-285-1300, Fax: 765-285-1994, E-mail: rmorris@bsu.edu.

GRADUATE UNITS

Graduate School Students: 1,014 full-time (570 women), 2,175 part-time (1,430 women); includes 192 minority (115 African Americans, 10 American Indian/Alaska Native, 26 Asian Americans or Pacific Islanders, 41 Hispanic Americans), 226 international. 2,540 applicants, 55% accepted, 848 enrolled. *Faculty:* 705. Expenses: Contact institution. *Financial support:* In 2008–09, 2 fellowships with full tuition reimbursements (averaging $15,500 per year), 46 research assistantships with full and partial tuition reimbursements (averaging $9,746 per year), 638 teaching assistantships with full and partial tuition reimbursements (averaging $9,162 per year) were awarded; career-related internships or fieldwork, Federal Work-Study, tuition waivers (partial), and unspecified assistantships also available. Support available to part-time students. Financial award application deadline: 3/1. In 2008, 938 master's, 50 doctorates, 58 other advanced degrees awarded. *Degree program information:* Part-time and evening/weekend programs available. Postbaccalaureate distance learning degree programs offered (no on-campus study). *Application deadline:* For fall admission, 3/1 priority date for domestic students, 1/1 priority date for international students; for spring admission, 12/1 priority date for domestic students, 7/1 priority date for international students. Applications are processed on a rolling basis. *Application fee:* $35 ($40 for international students). Electronic applications accepted. *Application Contact:* Dr. Jacquelyn S. Nelson, Associate Dean, 765-285-1297, Fax: 765-285-1328, E-mail: jnelson@bsu.edu. *Associate Provost for Research and Dean of the Graduate School,* Dr. Robert J. Morris, 765-285-1300, Fax: 765-285-1994, E-mail: rmorris@bsu.edu.

College of Applied Science and Technology Students: 117 full-time (81 women), 829 part-time (596 women); includes 53 minority (31 African Americans, 3 American Indian/Alaska Native, 6 Asian Americans or Pacific Islanders, 13 Hispanic Americans), 15 international. Average age 29. 357 applicants, 43% accepted, 117 enrolled. *Faculty:* 80. Expenses: Contact institution. *Financial support:* In 2008–09, 3 research assistantships with full tuition reimbursements (averaging $10,000 per year), 76 teaching assistantships with full tuition reimbursements (averaging $9,769 per year) were awarded; career-related internships or fieldwork and tuition waivers (full) also available. Financial award application deadline: 3/1. In 2008, 174 master's, 4 doctorates, 6 other advanced degrees awarded. *Degree program information:* Part-time and evening/weekend programs available. Postbaccalaureate distance learning degree programs offered (no on-campus study). Offers applied gerontology (MA); applied science and technology (MA, MAE, MS, PhD, Graduate Certificate); family and consumer sciences (MA, MS); human bioenergetics (PhD); industry and technology (MA, MAE); nursing (MS); physical education (MA, MAE, MS, PhD); wellness management (MA, MS). *Application deadline:* For fall admission, 1/1 for international students; for spring admission, 7/1 for international students. Applications are processed on a rolling basis. *Application fee:* $25 ($35 for international students). Electronic applications accepted. *Application Contact:* Dr. Robert Morris, Associate Provost for Research and Dean of the Graduate School, 765-285-5723, Fax: 765-285-1328, E-mail: rmorris@bsu.edu. *Dean,* Dr. Mitchell Whaley, 765-285-5816, E-mail: mwhaley@bsu.edu.

College of Architecture and Planning Students: 141 full-time (53 women), 27 part-time (12 women); includes 7 minority (2 African Americans, 2 Asian Americans or Pacific Islanders, 3 Hispanic Americans), 14 international. Average age 27. 173 applicants, 73% accepted, 81 enrolled. *Faculty:* 47. Expenses: Contact institution. *Financial support:* In 2008–09, 6 research assistantships with full tuition reimbursements (averaging $9,500 per year), 19 teaching assistantships with full tuition reimbursements (averaging $6,656 per year) were awarded; fellowships with full tuition reimbursements, career-related internships or fieldwork also available. Support available to part-time students. Financial award application deadline: 3/1. In 2008, 44 master's awarded. *Degree program information:* Part-time programs available. Offers architecture (M Arch); architecture and planning (M Arch, MLA, MS, MUD, MURP); historic preservation (M Arch, MS); landscape architecture (MLA); urban design (MUD); urban planning (MURP). *Application deadline:* For fall admission, 1/1 priority date for international students. Applications are processed on a rolling basis. *Application fee:* $25 ($35 for international students). Electronic applications accepted. *Application Contact:* Dr. Robert Morris, Associate Provost for Research and Dean of the Graduate School, E-mail: rmorris@bsu.edu. *Dean,* Dr. Guillermo Vasquez de Velasco, 765-285-5861, Fax: 765-285-3726.

College of Communication, Information, and Media Students: 106 full-time (46 women), 58 part-time (30 women); includes 13 minority (7 African Americans, 2 American Indian/Alaska Native, 1 Asian American or Pacific Islander, 3 Hispanic Americans), 36 international. Average age 25. 150 applicants, 65% accepted, 74 enrolled. *Faculty:* 31. Expenses: Contact institution. *Financial support:* In 2008–09, 6 research assistantships with full tuition reimbursements (averaging $9,878 per year), 65 teaching assistantships with full tuition reimbursements (averaging $7,091 per year) were awarded; career-related internships or fieldwork also available. Financial award application deadline: 3/1. In 2008, 92 master's awarded. *Degree program information:* Part-time programs available. Postbaccalaureate distance learning degree programs offered (no on-campus study). Offers communication, information, and media (MA, MS); digital storytelling (MA); information and communication sciences (MS); journalism (MA); public relations (MA); speech, public address, forensics, and rhetoric (MA). *Application deadline:* For fall admission, 1/1 priority date for international students; for spring admission, 7/1 priority date for international students. Applications are processed on a rolling basis. *Application fee:* $25 ($35 for international students). Electronic applications accepted. *Application Contact:* Dr. Robert Morris, Associate Provost for Research and Dean of the Graduate School, 765-285-4723, Fax: 765-285-1328, E-mail: rmorris@bsu.edu. *Dean,* Roger Lavery, 765-285-6000, Fax: 765-285-6002.

College of Fine Arts Students: 45 full-time (22 women), 56 part-time (32 women); includes 5 minority (2 African Americans, 2 Asian Americans or Pacific Islanders, 1 Hispanic American), 24 international. Average age 26. 65 applicants, 69% accepted, 29 enrolled. *Faculty:* 69. Expenses: Contact institution. *Financial support:* In 2008–09, 66 teaching assistantships with full tuition reimbursements (averaging $6,424 per year) were awarded; fellowships with full tuition reimbursements, research assistantships also available. Support available to part-time students. Financial award application deadline: 3/1. In 2008, 21 master's, 5 doctorates, 2 other advanced degrees awarded. *Degree program information:* Part-time programs available. Offers art (MA); art education (MA, MAE); fine arts (MA, MAE, MM, DA, Graduate Certificate); music education (MA, MM, DA). *Application deadline:* For fall admission, 1/1 priority date for international students; for spring admission, 6/1 priority date for international students. Applications are processed on a rolling basis. *Application fee:* $25 ($35 for international students). Electronic applications accepted. *Application Contact:* Dr. Robert Morris, Associate Provost for Research and Dean of the Graduate School, E-mail: rmorris@bsu.edu. *Dean,* Dr. Robert Kvam, 765-285-5495, Fax: 765-285-3790, E-mail: rkvam@bsu.edu.

Ball State University (continued)

College of Sciences and Humanities Students: 322 full-time (195 women), 227 part-time (123 women); includes 36 minority (14 African Americans, 2 American Indian/Alaska Native, 9 Asian Americans or Pacific Islanders, 11 Hispanic Americans), 80 international. Average age 26. 717 applicants, 58% accepted, 201 enrolled. *Faculty:* 301. Expenses: Contact institution. *Financial support:* In 2008–09, 16 research assistantships with full tuition reimbursements (averaging $10,369 per year), 192 teaching assistantships with full tuition reimbursements (averaging $11,405 per year) were awarded; career-related internships or fieldwork and Federal Work-Study also available. Support available to part-time students. Financial award application deadline: 3/1. In 2008, 190 master's, 10 doctorates, 18 other advanced degrees awarded. *Degree program information:* Part-time programs available. Postbaccalaureate distance learning degree programs offered (minimal on-campus study). Offers actuarial science (MA); anthropology (MA); applied linguistics (PhD); biology (MA, MAE, MS); biology education (Ed D); chemistry (MA, MS); clinical psychology (MA); cognitive and social processes (MA); computer science (MA, MS); earth sciences (MA); English (MA, PhD); geology (MA, MS); health education (MA, MAE); history (MA); linguistics (MA, PhD); linguistics and teaching English to speakers of other languages (MA); mathematical statistics (MA); mathematics (MA, MAE, MS); mathematics education (MAE); natural resources (MA, MS); physics (MA, MS); physiology (MA, MS); political science (MA); public administration (MPA); sciences and humanities (MA, MAE, MPA, MS, Au D, Ed D, PhD, Graduate Certificate); social sciences (MA); sociology (MA); speech pathology and audiology (MA, Au D); teaching English to speakers of other languages (MA). *Application deadline:* For fall admission, 1/1 priority date for international students; for spring admission, 7/1 priority date for international students. Applications are processed on a rolling basis. *Application fee:* $25 ($35 for international students). Electronic applications accepted. *Application Contact:* Dr. Robert Morris, Associate Provost for Research and Dean of the Graduate School, E-mail: rmorris@bsu.edu. *Dean,* Dr. Michael Maggioto, 765-285-1042, Fax: 765-285-8980.

Miller College of Business *Degree program information:* Part-time and evening/weekend programs available. Offers accounting (MS); business (MAE, MBA, MS); business administration (MBA); business education (MAE).

Teachers College Students: 210 full-time (143 women), 808 part-time (571 women); includes 67 minority (52 African Americans, 2 American Indian/Alaska Native, 5 Asian Americans or Pacific Islanders, 8 Hispanic Americans), 38 international. Average age 28. 896 applicants, 49% accepted, 268 enrolled. *Faculty:* 98. Expenses: Contact institution. *Financial support:* In 2008–09, 2 fellowships with full tuition reimbursements (averaging $15,500 per year), 10 research assistantships with full tuition reimbursements (averaging $9,573 per year), 102 teaching assistantships with full tuition reimbursements (averaging $9,070 per year) were awarded; career-related internships or fieldwork and Federal Work-Study also available. Support available to part-time students. Financial award application deadline: 3/1. In 2008, 334 master's, 32 doctorates, 22 other advanced degrees awarded. *Degree program information:* Part-time and evening/weekend programs available. Postbaccalaureate distance learning degree programs offered (no on-campus study). Offers adult and community education (MA); adult education (MA, Ed D); adult, community, and higher education (Ed D); counseling psychology (MA, PhD); curriculum (MAE, Ed S); curriculum and instruction (MAE, Ed S); education (MA, MAE, Ed D, PhD, Ed S, Graduate Certificate); educational administration (MAE, Ed D); educational psychology (MA, PhD, Ed S); educational studies (MAE, PhD); elementary education (MAE, Ed D, PhD); executive development (MA); school psychology (MA, PhD, Ed S); school superintendency (Ed S); secondary education (MA); social psychology (MA); special education (MA, MAE, Ed D, Ed S); student affairs administration in higher education (MA). *Application deadline:* For fall admission, 1/1 priority date for international students. *Application fee:* $25 ($35 for international students). *Application Contact:* Dr. Robert Morris, Associate Provost for Research and Dean of the Graduate School, E-mail: rmorris@bsu.edu. *Dean,* Dr. John E. Jacobson, 765-285-5251, Fax: 765-285-5455, E-mail: jejacobson@bsu.edu.

BALTIMORE HEBREW UNIVERSITY, Baltimore, MD 21215-3996

General Information Independent, coed, comprehensive institution. *Graduate housing:* On-campus housing not available. *Research affiliation:* American Schools of Oriental Research (archaeology).

GRADUATE UNITS

Peggy Meyerhoff Pearlstone School of Graduate Studies *Degree program information:* Part-time programs available. Offers Jewish communal service (MAJCS); Jewish education (MAJE); Jewish studies (MAJS, PhD).

BANGOR THEOLOGICAL SEMINARY, Bangor, ME 04401-4699

General Information Independent-religious, coed, graduate-only institution. *Graduate housing:* On-campus housing not available.

GRADUATE UNITS

Professional Program *Degree program information:* Part-time programs available. Offers theology (M Div, MA, MTS, D Min). M Div not offered at Portland, ME campus.

BANK STREET COLLEGE OF EDUCATION, New York, NY 10025

General Information Independent, coed, graduate-only institution. *Enrollment by degree level:* 940 master's. *Graduate faculty:* 73 full-time (63 women), 58 part-time/adjunct (47 women). *Tuition:* Part-time $1060 per credit. One-time fee: $600 part-time. *Student services:* Campus employment opportunities, campus safety program, career counseling, child daycare facilities, international student services, teacher training, writing training. *Library facilities:* Bank Street College Library. *Online resources:* library catalog, web page, access to other libraries' catalogs. *Collection:* 124,353 titles, 18,880 serial subscriptions, 2,073 audiovisual materials. *Research affiliation:* Center for Teaching Quality (education), Educational Development Corporation (education).

Computer facilities: 42 computers available on campus for general student use. A campuswide network can be accessed from off campus. Online class registration is available. *Web address:* http://www.bankstreet.edu/.

General Application Contact: Ann Morgan, Director of Graduate Admissions, 212-875-4403, Fax: 212-873-4678, E-mail: gradcourses@bankstreet.edu.

GRADUATE UNITS

Graduate School Students: 309 full-time (276 women), 631 part-time (562 women); includes 256 minority (96 African Americans, 43 Asian Americans or Pacific Islanders, 117 Hispanic Americans), 12 international. Average age 30. 580 applicants, 83% accepted, 361 enrolled. *Faculty:* 73 full-time (63 women), 58 part-time/adjunct (47 women). Expenses: Contact institution. *Financial support:* In 2008–09, 690 students received support. Career-related internships or fieldwork, Federal Work-Study, scholarships/grants, and unspecified assistantships available. Support available to part-time students. Financial award application deadline: 4/15; financial award applicants required to submit FAFSA. In 2008, 337 master's awarded. Offers advanced literacy specialization (Ed M); bilingual childhood special education (Ed M, MS Ed); bilingual early childhood education (MS Ed); bilingual early childhood special and general education (MS Ed); bilingual early childhood special education (Ed M, MS Ed); bilingual education (Ed M, MS Ed); bilingual elementary/childhood general education (MS Ed); bilingual elementary/childhood special and general education (MS Ed); bilingual middle school general education (MS Ed); bilingual middle school special and general education (Ed M, MS Ed); bilingual middle school special education (MS Ed); child life (MS); early childhood and elementary/childhood education (MS Ed); early childhood education (MS Ed); early childhood leadership (MS Ed); early childhood special and general education (MS Ed); early childhood special education (Ed M, MS Ed); education (Ed M, MS, MS Ed); educational leadership (MS Ed); elementary/childhood education (MS Ed); elementary/childhood special and general education (MS Ed); elementary/childhood special education (MS Ed); elementary/childhood special education certification (Ed M); infant and family development (MS Ed); infant and family development and early intervention/early childhood special and general education (MS Ed); infant and family development and early intervention/early childhood special education (Ed M); infant and parent development (Ed M, MS Ed); leadership for educational change (Ed M, MS Ed); leadership in mathematics education (MS Ed); leadership in museum education (MS Ed); leadership in the arts: creative writing (MS Ed); leadership in the arts: visual arts (MS Ed); middle school education (MS Ed); middle school special and general education (MS Ed); middle school special education (Ed M, MS Ed); museum education (MS Ed); museum education: elementary education certification (MS Ed); museum education: middle school certification (MS Ed); museum studies (MS Ed); reading and literacy (Ed M, MS Ed); special education (Ed M, MS Ed); teaching literacy (MS Ed). *Application deadline:* For fall admission, 3/1 priority date for domestic and international students; for spring admission, 11/1 priority date for domestic and international students. Applications are processed on a rolling basis. *Application fee:* $50. *Application Contact:* Ann Morgan, Director of Graduate Admissions, 212-875-4403, Fax: 212-875-4678, E-mail: amorgan@bankstreet.edu. *Dean,* Dr. Jon Snyder, 212-875-4466, Fax: 212-875-4753, E-mail: jsnyder@bankstreet.edu.

BAPTIST BIBLE COLLEGE, Springfield, MO 65803-3498

General Information Independent-religious, coed, comprehensive institution. *Graduate housing:* Rooms and/or apartments available on a first-come, first-served basis to single students and available to married students.

GRADUATE UNITS

Graduate School of Theology *Degree program information:* Part-time programs available. Offers biblical counseling (MA); biblical studies (MA); church ministry (MA); intercultural studies (MA); theology (M Div). Electronic applications accepted.

BAPTIST BIBLE COLLEGE OF PENNSYLVANIA, Clarks Summit, PA 18411-1297

General Information Independent-religious, coed, comprehensive institution. *Graduate housing:* Rooms and/or apartments guaranteed to single and married students.

GRADUATE UNITS

Baptist Bible Seminary *Degree program information:* Part-time and evening/weekend programs available. Postbaccalaureate distance learning degree programs offered (minimal on-campus study). Offers biblical studies (PhD); church planting (M Div); global missions (M Div); military chaplaincy (M Div); ministry (M Min, D Min); pastor of church education (M Div); pastor of outreach (M Div); pastoral counseling (M Div); pastoral leadership (M Div); theology (M Div, Th M); youth pastor (M Div). Electronic applications accepted.

Graduate School *Degree program information:* Part-time and evening/weekend programs available. Postbaccalaureate distance learning degree programs offered (no on-campus study). Offers biblical ministries (MS); Christian school education (MS); counseling (MS).

BAPTIST MISSIONARY ASSOCIATION THEOLOGICAL SEMINARY, Jacksonville, TX 75766-5407

General Information Independent-religious, coed, primarily men, comprehensive institution. *Graduate housing:* Rooms and/or apartments available on a first-come, first-served basis to single and married students. Housing application deadline: 6/1.

GRADUATE UNITS

Graduate and Professional Programs *Degree program information:* Part-time programs available. Offers theology (M Div, MAR). Electronic applications accepted.

BAPTIST THEOLOGICAL SEMINARY AT RICHMOND, Richmond, VA 23227

General Information Independent-religious, coed, graduate-only institution. *Enrollment by degree level:* 112 first professional, 22 doctoral. *Graduate faculty:* 14 full-time (6 women), 8 part-time/adjunct (1 woman). *Graduate housing:* Rooms and/or apartments available on a first-come, first-served basis to single and married students. Housing application deadline: 6/1. *Student services:* Campus employment opportunities, campus safety program, free psychological counseling, international student services, services for students with disabilities, writing training. *Online resources:* library catalog, web page, access to other libraries' catalogs. *Collection:* 309,610 titles, 1,358 serial subscriptions, 34,252 audiovisual materials.

Computer facilities: 20 computers available on campus for general student use. *Web address:* http://www.btsr.edu/.

General Application Contact: Tiffany Kellogg Pittman, Director of Admissions, 804-204-1208, Fax: 804-355-8182, E-mail: admissions@btsr.edu.

GRADUATE UNITS

Graduate and Professional Programs Students: 117 full-time (64 women), 17 part-time (7 women); includes 10 minority (6 African Americans, 1 Asian American or Pacific Islander, 3 Hispanic Americans), 1 international. Average age 46. *Faculty:* 14 full-time (6 women), 8 part-time/adjunct (1 woman). Expenses: Contact institution. *Financial support:* In 2008–09, 98 students received support, including 16 teaching assistantships (averaging $1,300 per year); scholarships/grants and tuition waivers (partial) also available. Financial award application deadline: 2/1. In 2008, 37 first professional degrees, 6 doctorates awarded. *Degree program information:* Part-time programs available. Postbaccalaureate distance learning degree programs offered (minimal on-campus study). Offers biblical interpretation (M Div); Christian education (M Div); theology (D Min); youth and student ministries (M Div). *Application deadline:* For fall admission, 8/1 priority date for domestic students, 5/1 priority date for international students; for winter admission, 12/1 priority date for domestic students, 9/1 priority date for international students; for spring admission, 1/1 priority date for domestic students, 10/1 priority date for international students. Applications are processed on a rolling basis. *Application fee:* $35. *Application Contact:* Tiffany Kellogg Pittman, Director of Admissions, 804-204-1208, Fax: 804-355-8182, E-mail: admissions@btsr.edu. *President,* Dr. Ronald W. Crawford, 804-204-1201, Fax: 804-355-8182.

BARD COLLEGE, Annandale-on-Hudson, NY 12504

General Information Independent, coed, comprehensive institution. *Graduate housing:* Room and/or apartments available on a first-come, first-served basis to single students; on-campus housing not available to married students.

GRADUATE UNITS

Bard Center for Environmental Policy Offers environmental policy (MS, Professional Certificate). Electronic applications accepted.

Center for Curatorial Studies Offers curatorial studies (MA). Electronic applications accepted.

Conservatory of Music Offers music (MFA, MM); vocal arts (MM).

The Conductors Institute Offers conducting (MFA).

International Center of Photography Offers advanced photographic studies (MFA).

Master of Arts in Teaching Program Offers teaching (MAT). Electronic applications accepted.

Milton Avery Graduate School of the Arts Offers arts (MFA). Electronic applications accepted.

Program in History of the Decorative Arts, Design and Culture *Degree program information:* Part-time programs available. Offers history of the decorative arts, design and culture (MA, PhD).

BARD GRADUATE CENTER FOR STUDIES IN THE DECORATIVE ARTS, DESIGN, AND CULTURE, New York, NY 10024-3602

General Information Independent, coed, primarily women, graduate-only institution. *Graduate housing:* Rooms and/or apartments available on a first-come, first-served basis to single and married students. Housing application deadline: 5/1. *Research affiliation:* American Museum of Natural History, Brooklyn Museum of Art, Metropolitan Museum of Art, New York Historical Society.

GRADUATE UNITS

Program in History of the Decorative Arts, Design and Culture *Degree program information:* Part-time programs available. Offers history of the decorative arts, design and culture (MA, PhD). Bard Graduate Center for Studies in the Decorative Arts is a unit of Bard College.

BARRY UNIVERSITY, Miami Shores, FL 33161-6695

General Information Independent-religious, coed, university. *Graduate housing:* On-campus housing not available. *Research affiliation:* Baxter Corporation (immunology, diagnostics), Coulter Corporation (immunology, cytology), Cordis Corporation (cardiac product development), Diamedix (immunological diagnostics), Noven Pharmaceutical, Sano Pharmaceuticals.

GRADUATE UNITS

Andreas School of Business *Degree program information:* Part-time and evening/weekend programs available. Offers accounting (MSA); business (MBA, MSA, MSM, Certificate); business administration (MBA); finance (Certificate); health services administration (Certificate); international business (Certificate); management (MSM); management information systems (Certificate); marketing (Certificate). Electronic applications accepted.

College of Health Sciences *Degree program information:* Part-time and evening/weekend programs available. Offers anesthesiology (MS); biology (MS); biomedical sciences (MS); health care leadership (Certificate); health care planning and informatics (Certificate); health sciences (MS, Certificate); health services administration (MS); histotechnology (Certificate); long term care management (Certificate); medical group practice management (Certificate); occupational therapy (MS); quality improvement and outcomes management (Certificate). Electronic applications accepted.

School of Adult and Continuing Education *Degree program information:* Part-time and evening/weekend programs available. Offers administrative studies (MA); adult and continuing education (MA, MPA, MS); information technology (MS); public administration (MPA). Electronic applications accepted.

School of Arts and Sciences *Degree program information:* Part-time and evening/weekend programs available. Offers arts and sciences (MA, MFA, MS, D Min, Certificate, SSP); broadcasting (Certificate); clinical psychology (MS); communication (MA); liberal studies (MA); ministry (D Min); organizational communication (MS); pastoral ministry for Hispanics (MA); pastoral theology (MA); photography (MA, MFA); practical theology (MA); school psychology (MS, SSP). Electronic applications accepted.

School of Education *Degree program information:* Part-time and evening/weekend programs available. Postbaccalaureate distance learning degree programs offered. Offers accomplished teacher (Ed S); advanced teaching and learning with technology (Certificate); counseling (MS, PhD, Ed S); culture, language and literacy (TESOL) (PhD); curriculum evaluation and research (PhD); distance education (Certificate); early childhood (Ed S); early childhood education (PhD); education (MS, Ed D, PhD, Certificate, Ed S); education for teachers of students with hearing impairments (MS); educational computing and technology (MS, Ed S); educational leadership (MS, Ed D, Certificate, Ed S); educational technology (PhD); elementary (Ed S); elementary education (MS, PhD); elementary education/ESOL (MS); ESOL (Ed S); exceptional student education (MS, Ed S); gifted (Ed S); higher education administration (MS); higher education technology integration (Certificate); human resource development (PhD); human resource development and administration (MS); human resources: not for profit and religious organizations (Certificate); K-12 technology integration (Certificate); leadership (PhD); marital, couple and family counseling/therapy (MS, Ed S); mental health counseling (MS, Ed S); Montessori (Ed S); Montessori education (MS, Ed S); PKP/elementary (Ed S); pre-k/primary (MS); pre-k/primary/ESOL (MS); reading (Ed S); reading, language and cognition (PhD); rehabilitation counseling (MS, Ed S); school counseling (MS, Ed S); technology and TESOL (MS, Ed S); TESOL (MS); TESOL international (MS). Electronic applications accepted.

School of Graduate Medical Sciences Offers anatomy (MS); medical sciences (DPM, MCMS, MPH, MS); physician assistant (MCMS); podiatric medicine and surgery (DPM); public health (MPH). Electronic applications accepted.

School of Human Performance and Leisure Sciences *Degree program information:* Part-time and evening/weekend programs available. Offers athletic training (MS); biomechanics (MS); exercise science (MS); general movement science (MS); human performance and leisure sciences (MS); sport and exercise psychology (MS); sport management (MS). Electronic applications accepted.

School of Law Offers law (JD).

School of Nursing *Degree program information:* Part-time and evening/weekend programs available. Offers acute care nurse practitioner (MSN); family nurse practitioner (MSN); nurse practitioner (Certificate); nursing (MSN, PhD, Certificate); nursing administration (MSN, PhD, Certificate); nursing education (MSN, Certificate). Electronic applications accepted.

School of Social Work *Degree program information:* Part-time and evening/weekend programs available. Offers social work (MSW, PhD). Electronic applications accepted.

See Close-Up on page 855.

BASTYR UNIVERSITY, Kenmore, WA 98028-4966

General Information Independent, coed, upper-level institution. *Enrollment:* 969 graduate, professional, and undergraduate students; 653 full-time matriculated graduate/professional students (525 women), 115 part-time matriculated graduate/professional students (96 women). *Enrollment by degree level:* 451 first professional, 291 master's, 9 doctoral, 8 other advanced degrees. *Graduate faculty:* 30 full-time (16 women), 94 part-time/adjunct (58 women). *Tuition:* Full-time $21,915; part-time $450 per credit. Full-time tuition and fees vary according to degree level, program and student level. Part-time tuition and fees vary according to course load. *Graduate housing:* Room and/or apartments available on a first-come, first-served basis to single students; on-campus housing not available to married students. Typical cost: $4100 per year. *Student services:* Campus employment opportunities, campus safety program, career counseling, child daycare facilities, free psychological counseling, international student services, low-cost health insurance, writing training. *Library facilities:* Bastyr University Library. *Online resources:* library catalog, web page. *Collection:* 20,000 titles, 239 serial subscriptions. *Research affiliation:* Cleavage Creek Winery (oncology), Benaroya Research Institute at Virginia Mason (health), University of Washington (health), Fred Hutchinson Cancer Research Center (oncology).

Computer facilities: 53 computers available on campus for general student use. A campuswide network can be accessed from student residence rooms and from off campus. *Web address:* http://www.bastyr.edu/.

General Application Contact: Information Contact, 425-602-3330, Fax: 425-602-2090, E-mail: admissions@bastyr.edu.

GRADUATE UNITS

Graduate and Professional Programs *Degree program information:* Part-time programs available.

School of Acupuncture and Oriental Medicine Students: 84 full-time (57 women), 55 part-time (39 women); includes 21 minority (1 African American, 1 American Indian/Alaska Native, 19 Asian Americans or Pacific Islanders), 12 international. Average age 34. Expenses: Contact institution. *Financial support:* Career-related internships or fieldwork, Federal Work-Study, and scholarships/grants available. Support available to part-time students. Financial award application deadline: 3/15; financial award applicants required to submit FAFSA. In 2008, 41 master's, 3 doctorates, 1 other advanced degree awarded. Offers acupuncture (MS); acupuncture and Oriental medicine (MS, DAOM); Chinese herbal medicine (Certificate). *Application deadline:* For fall admission, 3/15 priority date for domestic and international students. Applications are processed on a rolling basis. *Application fee:* $75. *Application Contact:* Admissions Office, 425-602-3330, Fax: 425-602-3090, E-mail: admissions@bastyr.edu. *Dean,* Terry Courtney, 425-823-1300, Fax: 425-823-6222.

School of Naturopathic Medicine Students: 440 full-time (352 women), 11 part-time (10 women); includes 66 minority (15 African Americans, 3 American Indian/Alaska Native, 34 Asian Americans or Pacific Islanders, 14 Hispanic Americans), 36 international. Average age 30. 275 applicants, 62% accepted, 100 enrolled. Expenses: Contact institution. *Financial support:* Career-related internships or fieldwork, Federal Work-Study, and scholarships/grants available. Support available to part-time students. Financial award application deadline: 4/15; financial award applicants required to submit FAFSA. In 2008, 99 doctorates awarded. Offers midwifery (Certificate); naturopathic medicine (ND). *Application deadline:* For fall admission, 2/1 priority date for domestic and international students. Applications are processed on a rolling basis. *Application fee:* $75. *Application Contact:* Admissions Office, 425-602-3330, Fax: 425-602-3090, E-mail: admissions@bastyr.edu. *Dean,* Dr. Gannady Raskin, 425-823-1300, Fax: 425-823-6222.

School of Nutrition and Exercise Science Students: 88 full-time (80 women), 17 part-time (all women); includes 6 minority (1 African American, 4 Asian Americans or Pacific Islanders, 1 Hispanic American), 7 international. Average age 34. Expenses: Contact institution. *Financial support:* Career-related internships or fieldwork, Federal Work-Study, and scholarships/grants available. Support available to part-time students. Financial award application deadline: 4/15; financial award applicants required to submit FAFSA. In 2008, 75 master's awarded. *Degree program information:* Part-time programs available. Offers nutrition (MS); nutrition and clinical health psychology (MS). *Application deadline:* For fall admission, 3/15 priority date for domestic and international students. Applications are processed on a rolling basis. *Application fee:* $75. *Application Contact:* Admissions Office, 425-602-3330, Fax: 425-602-3090, E-mail: admissions@bastyr.edu. *Dean,* Dr. Mark Kestin, 425-823-1300, Fax: 425-823-6222.

BAYAMÓN CENTRAL UNIVERSITY, Bayamón, PR 00960-1725

General Information Independent-religious, coed, comprehensive institution. *Graduate housing:* On-campus housing not available.

GRADUATE UNITS

Graduate Programs *Degree program information:* Part-time and evening/weekend programs available. Offers accounting (MBA); administration and supervision (MA Ed); commercial education (MA Ed); education of the autistic (MA Ed); elementary education (K–3) (MA Ed); elementary education (K–6) (MA Ed); elementary physical education (MA Ed); finance (MBA); general business (MBA); guidance and counseling (MA Ed); management (MBA); management of security and protection (MBA); marketing (MBA); pre-elementary teacher (MA Ed); psychology (MA); rehabilitation counseling (MA Ed); special education (MA Ed).

BAYLOR COLLEGE OF MEDICINE, Houston, TX 77030-3498

General Information Independent, coed, graduate-only institution. CGS member. *Enrollment by degree level:* 664 first professional, 139 master's, 582 doctoral. *Graduate faculty:* 1,971 full-time, 348 part-time/adjunct. *Graduate housing:* On-campus housing not available. *Student services:* Campus employment opportunities, campus safety program, career counseling, exercise/wellness program, free psychological counseling, grant writing training, international student services, low-cost health insurance, services for students with disabilities. *Library facilities:* Houston Academy of Medicine–Texas Medical Center Library. *Online resources:* library catalog, web page, access to other libraries' catalogs. *Collection:* 270,649 titles, 4,447 serial subscriptions, 786 audiovisual materials. *Research affiliation:* Veterans Affairs Medical Center (biomedical research), Texas Children's Hospital (pediatric biomedical research), The Methodist Hospital (biomedical research), National Space Biomedical Research Institute, Harris County Hospital District (biomedical research), Children's Nutrition Research Center (pediatric nutrition).

Computer facilities: 60 computers available on campus for general student use. A campuswide network can be accessed from off campus. *Web address:* http://www.bcm.edu/.

General Application Contact: Dr. Florence F. Eddins-Folensbee, MD, Associate Dean of the Medical School, 713-798-4842, Fax: 713-798-5563, E-mail: florence@bcm.edu.

GRADUATE UNITS

Graduate School of Biomedical Sciences Students: 582 full-time (316 women); includes 130 minority (23 African Americans, 3 American Indian/Alaska Native, 54 Asian Americans or Pacific Islanders, 50 Hispanic Americans), 211 international. Average age 26. 1,130 applicants, 20% accepted, 103 enrolled. *Faculty:* 410 full-time (101 women). Expenses: Contact institution. *Financial support:* In 2008–09, 16 fellowships (averaging $26,000 per year), 421 research assistantships (averaging $26,000 per year) were awarded; teaching assistantships, career-related internships or fieldwork, Federal Work-Study, institutionally sponsored loans, health care benefits, tuition waivers (full and partial), and stipends also available. Financial award applicants required to submit FAFSA. In 2008, 10 master's, 67 doctorates awarded. Offers biochemistry (PhD); biochemistry and molecular biology (PhD); biomedical sciences (MS, PhD); cardiovascular sciences (PhD); cell and molecular biology (PhD); clinical scientist training (MS, PhD); developmental biology (PhD); genetics (PhD); human genetics (PhD); immunology (PhD); microbiology (PhD); molecular and cellular biology (PhD); molecular and human genetics (PhD); molecular physiology and biophysics (PhD); molecular virology and microbiology (PhD); neuroscience (PhD); pharmacology (PhD); structural and computational biology and molecular biophysics (PhD); translational biology and molecular medicine (PhD); virology (PhD). *Application deadline:* For fall admission, 1/1 priority date for domestic students. Applications are processed on a rolling basis. *Application fee:* $30. Electronic applications accepted. *Application Contact:* Meliss Houghton, Administrator for GSBS Admissions, 713-798-4031, Fax: 713-798-6325, E-mail: melissah@bcm.edu. *Dean of Graduate Sciences,* Dr. William R. Brinkley, 713-798-5263, Fax: 713-798-6325, E-mail: brinkley@bcm.tmc.edu.

Medical School Students: 664 full-time (327 women); includes 368 minority (43 African Americans, 16 American Indian/Alaska Native, 229 Asian Americans or Pacific Islanders, 80 Hispanic Americans), 3 international. Average age 24. 4,879 applicants, 6% accepted, 176 enrolled. Expenses: Contact institution. *Financial support:* In 2008–09, 542 students received support. Career-related internships or fieldwork, Federal Work-Study, institutionally sponsored loans, scholarships/grants, traineeships, and tuition waivers (full and partial) available. Financial award application deadline: 5/11; financial award applicants required to submit FAFSA. In 2008, 162 MDs awarded. Offers medicine (MD). *Application deadline:* For fall admission, 11/1 for domestic students. Applications are processed on a rolling basis. *Application fee:* $80. Electronic applications accepted. *Application Contact:* Dr. Florence F. Eddins-Folensbee, Senior Associate Dean of the Medical School, 713-798-4842, Fax: 713-798-5563, E-mail: florence@bcm.edu. *Senior Vice President and Dean of Medical Education,* Dr. Stephen B. Greenberg, 713-798-8878, Fax: 713-798-3096, E-mail: stepheng@bcm.edu.

Program in Cell and Molecular Biology of Aging Expenses: Contact institution. Offers cell and molecular biology of aging (PhD). *Application Contact:* Dr. Lloyd H. Michael, Senior Associate Dean of the Medical School, 713-798-4842, Fax: 713-798-5563, E-mail: lmichael@bcm.edu.

School of Allied Health Sciences Students: 139 full-time (114 women); includes 35 minority (5 African Americans, 2 American Indian/Alaska Native, 22 Asian Americans or Pacific Islanders, 6 Hispanic Americans). 816 applicants, 7% accepted, 50 enrolled. *Faculty:* 15 full-time (7 women), 4 part-time/adjunct (2 women). Expenses: Contact institution. *Financial support:* In 2008–09, 120 students received support. Career-related internships or fieldwork, Federal Work-Study, institutionally sponsored loans, and scholarships/grants available. Financial award application deadline: 5/1; financial award applicants required to submit FAFSA. In 2008, 38 master's awarded. Offers allied health sciences (MS); nurse anesthesia (MS); physician assistant (MS). *Application deadline:* For fall admission, 11/1 for domestic students. Applications are processed on a rolling basis. *Application fee:* $75. Electronic applications accepted. *Application Contact:* Dr. J. David Holcomb, Senior Vice President and Dean, 713-798-4613, Fax: 713-798-7694, E-mail: jholcomb@bcm.edu. *Senior Vice President and Dean,* Dr. J. David Holcomb, 713-798-4613, Fax: 713-798-7694, E-mail: jholcomb@bcm.edu.

BAYLOR UNIVERSITY, Waco, TX 76798

General Information Independent-religious, coed, university. CGS member. *Enrollment:* 14,541 graduate, professional, and undergraduate students; 2,059 full-time matriculated graduate/professional students (931 women), 348 part-time matriculated graduate/professional students (181 women). *Enrollment by degree level:* 778 first professional, 988 master's, 620 doctoral, 21 other advanced degrees. *Graduate faculty:* 350. *Graduate housing:* Rooms and/or apartments available to single and married students. *Student services:* Campus

Baylor University (continued)

employment opportunities, campus safety program, career counseling, exercise/wellness program, free psychological counseling, international student services, low-cost health insurance, multicultural affairs office, services for students with disabilities. *Library facilities:* Moody Memorial Library plus 8 others. *Online resources:* library catalog, web page, access to other libraries' catalogs. *Collection:* 2.3 million titles, 8,429 serial subscriptions. *Research affiliation:* Sandia National Laboratory (physics), National Center for Supercomputing Applications (physics), Zyvex Corporation (physics), OXiGENE, Inc. (pharmaceuticals), Brookhaven National Laboratory (physics), Fermi National Accelerator Laboratory (physics).

Computer facilities: 1,668 computers available on campus for general student use. A campuswide network can be accessed from student residence rooms and from off campus. Online class registration is available. *Web address:* http://www.baylor.edu/.

General Application Contact: Suzanne Keener, Administrative Assistant, 254-710-3588, Fax: 254-710-3870.

GRADUATE UNITS

George W. Truett Seminary Students: 313 full-time (101 women), 93 part-time (23 women); includes 93 minority (52 African Americans, 2 American Indian/Alaska Native, 7 Asian Americans or Pacific Islanders, 32 Hispanic Americans), 26 international. Average age 29. 144 applicants, 94% accepted, 102 enrolled. *Faculty:* 17 full-time (3 women), 7 part-time/adjunct (1 woman). Expenses: Contact institution. *Financial support:* In 2008–09, 207 students received support, including 1 research assistantship, 12 teaching assistantships; career-related internships or fieldwork, institutionally sponsored loans, scholarships/grants, tuition waivers (partial), and unspecified assistantships also available. Support available to part-time students. Financial award application deadline: 8/1; financial award applicants required to submit FAFSA. In 2008, 70 first professional degrees, 6 master's, 1 doctorate awarded. Offers theology (M Div, MTS, D Min). *Application deadline:* For fall admission, 5/1 priority date for domestic students, 5/1 for international students; for spring admission, 11/1 priority date for domestic students, 11/1 for international students. Applications are processed on a rolling basis. *Application fee:* $35. *Application Contact:* Dr. Grear Howard, Director of Student Services, 254-710-3755, Fax: 254-710-7233, E-mail: grear_howard@baylor.edu. *Dean,* Dr. David E. Garland, 254-710-3755, Fax: 254-710-3753.

Graduate School Students: 1,330 full-time (649 women), 249 part-time (155 women); includes 236 minority (65 African Americans, 13 American Indian/Alaska Native, 63 Asian Americans or Pacific Islanders, 95 Hispanic Americans), 168 international. 1,435 applicants, 46% accepted, 465 enrolled. *Faculty:* 350. Expenses: Contact institution. *Financial support:* Fellowships, research assistantships with full and partial tuition reimbursements, teaching assistantships with full and partial tuition reimbursements, career-related internships or fieldwork, Federal Work-Study, institutionally sponsored loans, scholarships/grants, tuition waivers (full and partial), and unspecified assistantships available. Support available to part-time students. In 2008, 529 master's, 142 doctorates, 4 other advanced degrees awarded. *Degree program information:* Part-time and evening/weekend programs available. Postbaccalaureate distance learning degree programs offered (minimal on-campus study). Offers clinical orthopedics (D Sc); emergency medicine (D Sc PA); health care administration (MHA); health sciences (MHA, MPT, MS, D Sc, D Sc PA, DPT); nutrition (MS); physical therapy (MPT, DPT). *Application deadline:* Applications are processed on a rolling basis. *Application fee:* $25. *Application Contact:* Lori McNamara, Graduate Admissions Coordinator, 254-710-3584, Fax: 254-710-3870, E-mail: lori_mcnamara@baylor.edu. *Dean,* Dr. Larry Lyon, 254-710-3588, Fax: 254-710-3870, E-mail: larry_lyon@baylor.edu.

College of Arts and Sciences Students: 533 full-time (263 women), 87 part-time (52 women); includes 58 minority (7 African Americans, 6 American Indian/Alaska Native, 18 Asian Americans or Pacific Islanders, 27 Hispanic Americans), 89 international. Expenses: Contact institution. *Financial support:* Fellowships, research assistantships with partial tuition reimbursements, teaching assistantships, career-related internships or fieldwork, Federal Work-Study, institutionally sponsored loans, scholarships/grants, tuition waivers (full and partial), unspecified assistantships, and laboratory assistantships, practicum stipends available. Support available to part-time students. In 2008, 123 master's, 42 doctorates awarded. *Degree program information:* Part-time and evening/weekend programs available. Offers air science and environment (IMES); American studies (MA); applied sociology (PhD); arts and sciences (IMES, MA, MES, MFA, MIJ, MPPA, MS, MSCP, MSCSD, MSW, PhD, Psy D); biology (MA, MS, PhD); chemistry (MS, PhD); church-state studies (MA, PhD); clinical psychology (MSCP, Psy D); communication sciences and disorders (MA, MSCSD); communication studies (MA); directing (MFA); earth science (MA); English (MA, PhD); environmental biology (MS); environmental studies (MES, MS); geology (MS, PhD); history (MA); international journalism (MIJ); international studies (MA); journalism (MA); limnology (MS); mathematics (MS, PhD); museum studies (MA); neuroscience (MA, PhD); philosophy (MA, PhD); physics (MA, MS, PhD); political science (MA, PhD); public policy and administration (MPPA); religion (MA, PhD); sociology (MA); Spanish (MA); statistics (MA, PhD). *Application deadline:* Applications are processed on a rolling basis. *Application fee:* $25. Electronic applications accepted. *Application Contact:* Suzanne Keener, Administrative Assistant, 254-710-3588, Fax: 254-710-3870.

Hankamer School of Business Students: 269 full-time (97 women), 14 part-time (7 women); includes 59 minority (23 African Americans, 1 American Indian/Alaska Native, 17 Asian Americans or Pacific Islanders, 18 Hispanic Americans), 36 international. Expenses: Contact institution. *Financial support:* Research assistantships, teaching assistantships, career-related internships or fieldwork, Federal Work-Study, and institutionally sponsored loans available. In 2008, 179 master's awarded. *Degree program information:* Part-time programs available. Offers accounting and business law (M Acc, MT); business (M Acc, MA, MBA, MBAIM, MIM, MS, MS Eco, MSIS, MT); business administration (MBA); economics (MS Eco); information systems (MSIS); information systems management (MBA); international economics (MA, MS); international management (MBA, MBAIM, MIM). *Application deadline:* For fall admission, 8/1 for domestic students; for spring admission, 12/1 for domestic students. Applications are processed on a rolling basis. *Application fee:* $25. *Application Contact:* Laurie Wilson, Director, Graduate Business Degree Programs, 254-710-4163, Fax: 254-710-1066, E-mail: laurie_wilson@baylor.edu. *Director of Graduate Programs,* Dr. Gary Carini, 254-710-3718, Fax: 254-710-1092, E-mail: gary_carini@baylor.edu.

Institute of Biomedical Studies Students: 29 full-time (14 women), 3 part-time (all women); includes 4 minority (3 Asian Americans or Pacific Islanders, 1 Hispanic American), 13 international. Expenses: Contact institution. *Financial support:* Research assistantships, teaching assistantships available. In 2008, 1 master's, 4 doctorates awarded. Offers biomedical studies (MS, PhD). *Application deadline:* Applications are processed on a rolling basis. *Application fee:* $25. *Application Contact:* Rhonda Bellert, Administrative Assistant, 254-710-2514, Fax: 254-710-3870, E-mail: rhonda_bellert@baylor.edu. *Graduate Program Director,* Dr. Chris Kearney, 254-710-2131, Fax: 254-710-3878, E-mail: chris_kearney@baylor.edu.

Louise Herrington School of Nursing Students: 21 full-time (20 women), 31 part-time (all women); includes 12 minority (2 African Americans, 1 American Indian/Alaska Native, 5 Asian Americans or Pacific Islanders, 4 Hispanic Americans). Expenses: Contact institution. In 2008, 12 master's awarded. Offers family nurse practitioner (MSN); neonatal nurse practitioner (MSN); nursing administration and management (MSN). *Application deadline:* For fall admission, 8/1 for domestic students; for spring admission, 12/1 for domestic students. Applications are processed on a rolling basis. *Application fee:* $25. *Application Contact:* Beverly Kurfees, Administrative Assistant, 214-8204111, Fax: 254-710-3870, E-mail: beverly_kurfees@baylor.edu. *Graduate Program Director,* Dr. Mary Brucker, 214-820-4111, Fax: 214-818-8692, E-mail: mary_brucker@baylor.edu.

School of Education Students: 170 full-time (108 women), 63 part-time (41 women); includes 38 minority (15 African Americans, 5 American Indian/Alaska Native, 18 Hispanic Americans), 11 international. Expenses: Contact institution. *Financial support:* Research assistantships, teaching assistantships, career-related internships, career-related internships or fieldwork, Federal Work-Study, institutionally sponsored loans, scholarships/grants, and tuition waivers (partial) available. In 2008, 68 master's, 17 doctorates, 4 other advanced degrees awarded. *Degree program information:* Part-time programs available. Postbaccalaureate distance learning degree programs offered (minimal on-campus study). Offers curriculum and instruction (MA, MS Ed, Ed D, Ed S); education (MA, MS Ed, Ed D, PhD, Ed S); educational administration (MS Ed, Ed S); educational psychology (MA, MS Ed, PhD, Ed S); exercise, nutrition and preventive health (PhD); health, human performance and recreation (MS Ed). *Application deadline:* Applications are processed on a rolling basis. *Application fee:* $25. Electronic applications accepted. *Application Contact:* Julie Baker, Administrative Assistant, 254-710-3050, Fax: 254-710-3870, E-mail: julie_baker@baylor.edu. *Interim Dean,* 254-710-3111, Fax: 254-710-3987.

School of Engineering and Computer Science Students: 37 full-time (6 women), 7 part-time (2 women); includes 11 minority (2 African Americans, 1 American Indian/Alaska Native, 3 Asian Americans or Pacific Islanders, 5 Hispanic Americans), 13 international. Expenses: Contact institution. *Financial support:* Teaching assistantships available. Financial award application deadline: 3/15. In 2008, 12 master's awarded. *Degree program information:* Part-time programs available. Offers biomedical engineering (MSBE); computer science (MS); electrical and computer engineering (MSECE); engineering (ME, MSBE, MSECE, MSME); mechanical engineering (MSME). *Application deadline:* For fall admission, 8/1 for domestic students; for spring admission, 12/1 for domestic students. Applications are processed on a rolling basis. *Application fee:* $25. *Application Contact:* Suzanne Keener, Administrative Assistant, 254-710-3588, Fax: 254-710-3870. *Graduate Program Director,* Dr. Greg Speegle, 254-710-3876, Fax: 254-710-3839, E-mail: greg_speegle@baylor.edu.

School of Music Students: 13 full-time (7 women), 37 part-time (15 women); includes 3 minority (1 American Indian/Alaska Native, 2 Hispanic Americans), 4 international. Expenses: Contact institution. *Financial support:* In 2008–09, 43 teaching assistantships with full tuition reimbursements (averaging $5,990 per year) were awarded; Federal Work-Study and institutionally sponsored loans also available. In 2008, 26 master's awarded. Offers church music (MM); collaborative piano (MM); composition (MM); conducting (MM); music history and literature (MM); music theory (MM); performance (MM); piano pedagogy and performance (MM). *Application deadline:* For fall admission, 8/1 for domestic students; for spring admission, 12/1 for domestic students. Applications are processed on a rolling basis. *Application fee:* $25. *Application Contact:* Melinda Coates, Administrative Assistant, 254-710-2360, Fax: 254-710-3870, E-mail: melinda_coats@baylor.edu. *Graduate Program Director,* Dr. David Music, 254-710-2360, Fax: 254-710-1191, E-mail: david_music@baylor.edu.

School of Law Students: 418 full-time (184 women); includes 62 minority (5 African Americans, 2 American Indian/Alaska Native, 31 Asian Americans or Pacific Islanders, 24 Hispanic Americans). Average age 24. 2,082 applicants, 21% accepted, 94 enrolled. *Faculty:* 24 full-time (4 women), 36 part-time/adjunct (2 women). Expenses: Contact institution. *Financial support:* In 2008–09, 353 students received support. Career-related internships or fieldwork, Federal Work-Study, institutionally sponsored loans, and scholarships/grants available. Financial award applicants required to submit FAFSA. In 2008, 156 JDs awarded. Offers law (JD). *Application deadline:* For fall admission, 3/1 for domestic students; for spring admission, 11/1 for domestic students. Applications are processed on a rolling basis. *Application fee:* $40. Electronic applications accepted. *Application Contact:* Becky Beck, Assistant Dean of Admission, 254-710-1911, Fax: 254-710-2316, E-mail: Becky_Beck@baylor.edu. *Dean,* Dr. Bradley J. B. Toben, 254-710-1911, Fax: 254-710-2316.

School of Social Work Students: 77 full-time (70 women), 7 part-time (4 women); includes 20 minority (8 African Americans, 1 American Indian/Alaska Native, 3 Asian Americans or Pacific Islanders, 8 Hispanic Americans), 2 international. Average age 27. 127 applicants, 86% accepted, 64 enrolled. *Faculty:* 11 full-time (5 women), 13 part-time/adjunct (7 women). Expenses: Contact institution. *Financial support:* In 2008–09, 75 students received support, including 12 research assistantships with tuition reimbursements available (averaging $6,800 per year); career-related internships or fieldwork, Federal Work-Study, institutionally sponsored loans, scholarships/grants, traineeships, tuition waivers (partial), and unspecified assistantships also available. Support available to part-time students. Financial award application deadline: 6/1. In 2008, 63 master's awarded. *Degree program information:* Part-time programs available. Offers social work (MSW). *Application deadline:* For fall admission, 6/1 for domestic and international students. Applications are processed on a rolling basis. *Application fee:* $45. Electronic applications accepted. *Application Contact:* Tracey Kelley, Director of Recruitment/Career Services, 254-710-4479, Fax: 254-710-6455, E-mail: Tracey_Kelley@baylor.edu. *Associate Dean for Graduate Studies,* Dr. Dennis Myers, 254-710-6404, E-mail: dennis_myers@baylor.edu.

BAY PATH COLLEGE, Longmeadow, MA 01106-2292

General Information Independent, Undergraduate: women only; graduate: coed, comprehensive institution. *Graduate housing:* Room and/or apartments available on a first-come, first-served basis to single students; on-campus housing not available to married students. Housing application deadline: 7/2.

GRADUATE UNITS

Program in Communications and Information Management *Degree program information:* Part-time and evening/weekend programs available. Offers information management (MS); information systems (MS). Electronic applications accepted.

Program in Entrepreneurial Thinking and Innovative Practices *Degree program information:* Part-time and evening/weekend programs available. Offers entrepreneurial thinking and innovative practices (MBA). Electronic applications accepted.

Program in Occupational Therapy *Degree program information:* Part-time and evening/weekend programs available. Offers occupational therapy (MOT, MS). Electronic applications accepted.

BEACON UNIVERSITY, Columbus, GA 31909

General Information Independent-religious, coed, graduate-only institution. *Graduate housing:* On-campus housing not available.

GRADUATE UNITS

Graduate Programs *Degree program information:* Part-time and evening/weekend programs available. Postbaccalaureate distance learning degree programs offered (minimal on-campus study). Offers cell church development (MAPM); counseling ministry (MAPM); military chaplaincy (MAPM); organizational leadership (MAPM); pastoral ministry (MAPM); theology (M Div, MABS).

BELHAVEN COLLEGE, Jackson, MS 39202-1789

General Information Independent-religious, coed, comprehensive institution. *Enrollment:* 2,619 graduate, professional, and undergraduate students; 409 full-time matriculated graduate/professional students (304 women), 44 part-time matriculated graduate/professional students (34 women). *Enrollment by degree level:* 453 master's. *Graduate faculty:* 18 full-time (7 women), 18 part-time/adjunct (8 women). *Graduate housing:* On-campus housing not available. *Student services:* Career counseling, free psychological counseling. *Library facilities:* Hood Library. *Online resources:* library catalog, web page. *Collection:* 10,647 titles, 448 serial subscriptions, 2,243 audiovisual materials.

Computer facilities: 36 computers available on campus for general student use. A campuswide network can be accessed from student residence rooms and from off campus. Online class registration is available. *Web address:* http://www.belhaven.edu/.

General Application Contact: Dr. Audrey Kelleher, Vice President for Adult and Graduate Marketing and Development, 407-804-1424, Fax: 407-620-5210, E-mail: akelleher@belhaven.edu.

GRADUATE UNITS

School of Business Students: 231 full-time (155 women), 6 part-time (1 woman); includes 157 minority (135 African Americans, 21 American Indian/Alaska Native, 1 Hispanic American). Average age 34. 222 applicants, 70% accepted, 111 enrolled. *Faculty:* 13 full-time (3 women), 12 part-time/adjunct (3 women). Expenses: Contact institution. *Financial support:* In 2008–09, 2 students received support, including 2 research assistantships. Financial award applicants required to submit FAFSA. In 2008, 105 master's awarded. *Degree program information:* Evening/weekend programs available. Offers business administration (MBA); business management (MSM); public administration (MPA). MBA program also offered in Houston, TX; Memphis,

TN; and Orlando, FL. *Application deadline:* Applications are processed on a rolling basis. *Application fee:* $25. Electronic applications accepted. *Application Contact:* Dr. Audrey Kelleher, Vice President for Adult and Graduate Marketing and Development, 407-804-1424, Fax: 407-620-5210, E-mail: akelleher@belhaven.edu. *Dean, School of Business*, Dr. Ralph Mason, 601-968-8949, Fax: 601-968-8951, E-mail: cmason@belhaven.edu.

School of Education Students: 185 full-time (154 women), 39 part-time (34 women); includes 97 African Americans, 2 American Indian/Alaska Native, 3 Hispanic Americans. Average age 34. 392 applicants, 70% accepted, 140 enrolled. *Faculty:* 6 full-time (all women), 4 part-time/adjunct (all women). Expenses: Contact institution. *Financial support:* Federal Work-Study, scholarships/grants, tuition waivers (full), and unspecified assistantships available. Support available to part-time students. Financial award applicants required to submit FAFSA. In 2008, 46 master's awarded. *Degree program information:* Part-time and evening/weekend programs available. Offers elementary education (M Ed, MAT); secondary education (M Ed, MAT). *Application deadline:* Applications are processed on a rolling basis. *Application fee:* $25. Electronic applications accepted. *Application Contact:* Jenny Mixon, Director of Graduate and Online Admission, 601-968-8947, Fax: 601-968-5953, E-mail: gradadmission@belhaven.edu. *Dean*, Dr. Sandra L. Rasberry, EdD, 601-968-8703, Fax: 601-974-6461, E-mail: srasberry@belhaven.edu.

BELLARMINE UNIVERSITY, Louisville, KY 40205-0671

General Information Independent-religious, coed, comprehensive institution. *Enrollment:* 3,040 graduate, professional, and undergraduate students; 309 full-time matriculated graduate/professional students (198 women), 387 part-time matriculated graduate/professional students (266 women). *Enrollment by degree level:* 587 master's, 109 doctoral. *Graduate faculty:* 54 full-time (29 women), 50 part-time/adjunct (32 women). *Graduate housing:* Room and/or apartments available on a first-come, first-served basis to single students; on-campus housing not available to married students. Housing application deadline: 5/1. *Student services:* Campus employment opportunities, campus safety program, career counseling, exercise/wellness program, free psychological counseling, grant writing training, international student services, multicultural affairs office, services for students with disabilities, teacher training, writing training. *Library facilities:* W.L. Lyons Brown Library. *Online resources:* library catalog, web page. *Collection:* 126,164 titles, 514 serial subscriptions, 5,337 audiovisual materials.

Computer facilities: 350 computers available on campus for general student use. A campuswide network can be accessed from student residence rooms and from off campus. Online class registration is available. *Web address:* http://www.bellarmine.edu/.

General Application Contact: Dr. Sara Yount, Dean of Graduate Admission, 502-452-8401, Fax: 502-452-8002, E-mail: syount@bellarmine.edu.

GRADUATE UNITS

Annsley Frazier Thornton School of Education Students: 84 full-time (66 women), 171 part-time (136 women); includes 17 minority (12 African Americans, 1 American Indian/Alaska Native, 3 Asian Americans or Pacific Islanders, 1 Hispanic American). Average age 34. *Faculty:* 13 full-time (11 women), 17 part-time/adjunct (12 women). Expenses: Contact institution. *Financial support:* Scholarships/grants available. Financial award applicants required to submit FAFSA. In 2008, 151 master's awarded. *Degree program information:* Part-time and evening/weekend programs available. Offers early elementary education (MA, MAT); instructional leadership and school administration/school principal (MA); learning and behavior disorders (MA); middle school education (MA, MAT); reading and writing endorsement (MA); secondary school education (MAT); Waldorf inspired curriculum (MA). *Application deadline:* Applications are processed on a rolling basis. *Application fee:* $25. *Application Contact:* Theresa Klapheke, Administrative Director of Graduate Programs, 502-452-8037, Fax: 502-452-8189, E-mail: tklapheke@bellarmine.edu. *Dean*, Dr. Cindy Gnadinger, 502-452-8191, Fax: 502-452-8189, E-mail: cgnadinger@bellarmine.edu.

Bellarmine College of Arts and Sciences Students: 7 part-time (6 women); includes 1 minority (African American). Average age 46. *Faculty:* 4 full-time (1 woman). Expenses: Contact institution. In 2008, 8 master's awarded. Offers spirituality (MA). *Application deadline:* For spring admission, 3/15 for domestic students. *Application fee:* $25. *Application Contact:* Pat Allen, Office Receptionist, 502-452-8188, E-mail: pallen@bellarmine.edu. *Program Director*, Dr. Gregory Hillis, 502-473-3800, E-mail: ghillis@bellarmine.edu.

Center for Interdisciplinary Technology and Entrepreneurship Students: 8 full-time (2 women), 14 part-time (3 women); includes 3 minority (2 African Americans, 1 Asian American or Pacific Islander). Average age 35. *Faculty:* 2 full-time (0 women), 6 part-time/adjunct (2 women). Expenses: Contact institution. In 2008, 11 master's awarded. *Degree program information:* Part-time and evening/weekend programs available. Offers technology and entrepreneurship (MAIT). *Application fee:* $25. *Application Contact:* Dr. Richard Jones, Program Director, 502-452-8346, E-mail: rcjones@bellarmine.edu. *Dean of Continuing and Professional Studies*, Dr. Michael D. Mattei, 502-452-8441, E-mail: mmattei@bellarmine.edu.

Donna and Allan Lansing School of Nursing and Health Sciences Students: 116 full-time (93 women), 55 part-time (54 women); includes 3 minority (1 African American, 2 Asian Americans or Pacific Islanders). Average age 30. 350 applicants, 48 enrolled. *Faculty:* 16 full-time (11 women), 7 part-time/adjunct (6 women). Expenses: Contact institution. *Financial support:* Career-related internships or fieldwork and scholarships/grants available. In 2008, 10 master's, 36 doctorates awarded. *Degree program information:* Part-time and evening/weekend programs available. Offers family nurse practitioner (MSN); nursing administration (MSN); nursing education (MSN); nursing practice (DNP); physical therapy (DPT). *Application fee:* $25. Electronic applications accepted. *Application Contact:* Julie Armstrong-Binnix, Health Science Recruiter, 800-274-4723 Ext. 8364, E-mail: julieab@bellarmine.edu. *Dean*, Dr. Susan H. Davis, 800-274-4723 Ext. 8217, E-mail: sdavis@bellarmine.edu.

School of Communication Students: 1 full-time (0 women), 29 part-time (20 women); includes 1 minority (African American), 1 international. Average age 37. *Faculty:* 6 full-time (3 women), 1 (woman) part-time/adjunct. Expenses: Contact institution. *Degree program information:* Part-time and evening/weekend programs available. Offers communication (MA, MS). *Application deadline:* Applications are processed on a rolling basis. *Application fee:* $30. *Application Contact:* Dr. Ruth Wagoner, Director of Graduate Studies, 502-452-8417, E-mail: rwagoner@bellarmine.edu. *Director of Graduate Studies*, Dr. Ruth Wagoner, 502-452-8417, E-mail: rwagoner@bellarmine.edu.

W. Fielding Rubel School of Business Students: 109 full-time (47 women), 121 part-time (52 women); includes 13 minority (11 African Americans, 1 Asian American or Pacific Islander, 1 Hispanic American), 1 international. Average age 30. 93 applicants, 90% accepted, 77 enrolled. *Faculty:* 14 full-time (2 women), 4 part-time/adjunct (1 woman). Expenses: Contact institution. *Financial support:* Career-related internships or fieldwork, scholarships/grants, and unspecified assistantships available. Support available to part-time students. Financial award application deadline: 7/1. In 2008, 90 master's awarded. *Degree program information:* Part-time and evening/weekend programs available. Offers business (EMBA, MBA). *Application deadline:* Applications are processed on a rolling basis. *Application fee:* $25. Electronic applications accepted. *Application Contact:* Laura Richardson, Director, 800-274-4723 Ext. 8258, Fax: 502-452-8012, E-mail: lrichardson@bellarmine.edu. *Dean*, Dr. Daniel L. Bauer, 800-274-4723 Ext. 8026, Fax: 502-452-8013, E-mail: dbauer@bellarmine.edu.

BELLEVUE UNIVERSITY, Bellevue, NE 68005-3098

General Information Independent, coed, comprehensive institution. *Graduate housing:* Room and/or apartments available on a first-come, first-served basis to single students; on-campus housing not available to married students.

GRADUATE UNITS

Graduate School *Degree program information:* Part-time and evening/weekend programs available. Postbaccalaureate distance learning degree programs offered (no on-campus study). Offers acquisition and contract management (MS); business administration (MBA); clinical counseling (MS); computer information systems (MS); healthcare administration (MA, MHA, MS); human capital management (MS, PhD); human services (MA, MS); instructional design and development (MS); leadership (MA); management (MA); management information systems (MS); organizational performance (MS); public administration (MPA); public health (MPH); security management (MS).

BELMONT UNIVERSITY, Nashville, TN 37212-3757

General Information Independent-religious, coed, comprehensive institution. *Enrollment:* 4,991 graduate, professional, and undergraduate students; 406 full-time matriculated graduate/professional students (323 women), 395 part-time matriculated graduate/professional students (221 women). *Enrollment by degree level:* 75 first professional, 554 master's, 172 doctoral. *Graduate faculty:* 113 full-time (58 women), 43 part-time/adjunct (24 women). *Tuition:* Full-time $14,270; part-time $810 per credit hour. *Required fees:* $530; $280 per year. Tuition and fees vary according to degree level and program. *Graduate housing:* On-campus housing not available. *Student services:* Campus employment opportunities, campus safety program, career counseling, exercise/wellness program, free psychological counseling, international student services, low-cost health insurance, multicultural affairs office. *Library facilities:* Lila D. Bunch Library. *Online resources:* library catalog, web page, access to other libraries' catalogs. *Collection:* 220,637 titles, 1,072 serial subscriptions, 31,109 audiovisual materials.

Computer facilities: Computer purchase and lease plans are available. 400 computers available on campus for general student use. A campuswide network can be accessed from student residence rooms and from off campus. Online class registration, individual student information via BANNER Web are available. *Web address:* http://www.belmont.edu/.

General Application Contact: Dr. Kathryn Baugher, Dean of Enrollment Services, 615-460-6785, Fax: 615-460-5434, E-mail: baugherk@mail.belmont.edu.

GRADUATE UNITS

College of Arts and Sciences Students: 107 full-time (69 women), 127 part-time (96 women); includes 49 minority (40 African Americans, 3 Asian Americans or Pacific Islanders, 6 Hispanic Americans), 2 international. Average age 29. 82 applicants, 54% accepted, 42 enrolled. *Faculty:* 25 full-time (19 women), 8 part-time/adjunct (4 women). Expenses: Contact institution. *Financial support:* In 2008–09, 50 students received support; fellowships with partial tuition reimbursements available, teaching assistantships with partial tuition reimbursements available, Federal Work-Study, institutionally sponsored loans, scholarships/grants, tuition waivers (partial), and unspecified assistantships available. Financial award application deadline: 4/15; financial award applicants required to submit FAFSA. In 2008, 91 master's awarded. *Degree program information:* Part-time and evening/weekend programs available. Offers arts and sciences (M Ed, MA, MAT, MSA); literature (MA); writing (MA). *Application deadline:* For fall admission, 8/1 for domestic students; for spring admission, 12/1 for domestic students. Applications are processed on a rolling basis. *Application fee:* $50. Electronic applications accepted. *Application Contact:* Dr. Bryce Sullivan, Dean, 615-460-6437, Fax: 615-385-5084, E-mail: bryce.sullivan@belmont.edu. *Dean*, Dr. Bryce Sullivan, 615-460-6437, Fax: 615-385-5084, E-mail: bryce.sullivan@belmont.edu.

School of Education Students: 71 full-time (41 women), 120 part-time (90 women); includes 37 African Americans, 3 Asian Americans or Pacific Islanders, 6 Hispanic Americans, 2 international. Average age 27. 67 applicants, 48% accepted, 30 enrolled. *Faculty:* 9 full-time (7 women), 8 part-time/adjunct (4 women). Expenses: Contact institution. *Financial support:* In 2008–09, 30 students received support; fellowships with partial tuition reimbursements available, teaching assistantships with partial tuition reimbursements available, institutionally sponsored loans, tuition waivers (partial), and unspecified assistantships available. Financial award application deadline: 4/15; financial award applicants required to submit FAFSA. In 2008, 94 master's awarded. *Degree program information:* Part-time and evening/weekend programs available. Offers education (M Ed); elementary education (MAT); English (MAT); history (MAT); mathematics (MAT); middle grade education (MAT); science (MAT); secondary education (MAT); special education (MAT); sports administration (MSA). *Application deadline:* For fall admission, 8/1 priority date for domestic students, 6/1 for international students; for spring admission, 12/1 priority date for domestic students, 10/1 for international students. Applications are processed on a rolling basis. *Application fee:* $50. *Application Contact:* Andrea McClain, Admission/Licensure Officer, 615-460-5483, Fax: 615-460-5556, E-mail: Andrea.Mcclain@belmont.edu. *Associate Dean*, Dr. Trevor F. Hutchins, 615-460-6232, Fax: 615-460-5556, E-mail: Trevor.Hutchins@belmont.edu.

College of Health Sciences Students: 324 full-time (266 women), 17 part-time (all women); includes 31 minority (18 African Americans, 12 Asian Americans or Pacific Islanders, 1 Hispanic American), 1 international. Average age 27. 834 applicants, 34% accepted, 184 enrolled. *Faculty:* 20 full-time (15 women), 19 part-time/adjunct (15 women). Expenses: Contact institution. *Financial support:* In 2008–09, 123 students received support, including teaching assistantships with full tuition reimbursements available (averaging $7,020 per year); career-related internships or fieldwork, scholarships/grants, and traineeships also available. Financial award application deadline: 3/1; financial award applicants required to submit FAFSA. In 2008, 38 master's, 44 doctorates awarded. *Degree program information:* Part-time programs available. Postbaccalaureate distance learning degree programs offered (minimal on-campus study). Offers health sciences (Pharm D, MSN, MSOT, DPT, OTD). *Application deadline:* Applications are processed on a rolling basis. *Application fee:* $50. Electronic applications accepted. *Application Contact:* Dr. Kathryn Baugher, Dean of Enrollment Services, 615-460-6785, Fax: 615-460-5434, E-mail: baugherk@mail.belmont.edu. *Dean*, Dr. Jack Williams, 615-460-6916, Fax: 615-460-6750, E-mail: williamsj@mail.belmont.edu.

School of Nursing Students: 13 full-time (all women), 17 part-time (all women); includes 3 minority (2 African Americans, 1 Asian American or Pacific Islander). Average age 33. 20 applicants, 85% accepted, 15 enrolled. *Faculty:* 1 (woman) full-time, 3 part-time/adjunct (all women). Expenses: Contact institution. *Financial support:* In 2008–09, 21 students received support. Scholarships/grants and traineeships available. Financial award application deadline: 3/1; financial award applicants required to submit FAFSA. In 2008, 7 master's awarded. *Degree program information:* Part-time programs available. Offers nursing (MSN). *Application deadline:* For fall admission, 8/1 for domestic students; for spring admission, 10/15 priority date for domestic students. Applications are processed on a rolling basis. *Application fee:* $50. Electronic applications accepted. *Application Contact:* Admissions Coordinator. *Director, Graduate Program*, Dr. Leslie J. Higgins, 615-460-6027, Fax: 615-460-6125, E-mail: leslie.higgins@belmont.edu.

School of Occupational Therapy Students: 139 full-time (123 women); includes 8 minority (all African Americans), 1 international. Average age 29. 183 applicants, 42% accepted, 62 enrolled. *Faculty:* 10 full-time (9 women), 7 part-time/adjunct (5 women). Expenses: Contact institution. *Financial support:* Fellowships, research assistantships, teaching assistantships available. Financial award applicants required to submit FAFSA. In 2008, 29 master's, 16 doctorates awarded. *Degree program information:* Evening/weekend programs available. Offers occupational therapy (MSOT, OTD). *Application deadline:* For fall admission, 3/1 priority date for domestic students. *Application fee:* $50. Electronic applications accepted. *Application Contact:* Kayla Lyftogt, Admissions Assistant, 615-460-6798, Fax: 615-460-6475, E-mail: msot@mail.belmont.edu. *Associate Dean*, Dr. Ruth Ford, 615-460-6700, Fax: 615-460-6475, E-mail: fordr@mail.belmont.edu.

School of Pharmacy Average age 24. 354 applicants, 32% accepted, 75 enrolled. *Faculty:* 13 full-time (8 women). Expenses: Contact institution. *Financial support:* In 2008–09, 8 students received support. Applicants required to submit FAFSA. Offers pharmacy (Pharm D). *Application deadline:* For fall admission, 8/31 priority date for domestic students; for spring admission, 3/1 for domestic students. Applications are processed on a rolling basis. *Application fee:* $50. Electronic applications accepted. *Application Contact:* Dr. Elinor Chumney, Dean of Enrollment Services, 615-460-6747, Fax: 615-460-6741, E-mail: chumneye@mail.belmont.edu. *Dean*, Dr. Phil Johnston, 615-460-6746, Fax: 615-460-6741, E-mail: johnstonp@mail.belmont.edu.

School of Physical Therapy Students: 97 full-time (82 women); includes 2 minority (1 Asian American or Pacific Islander, 1 Hispanic American). Average age 24. 227 applicants, 34% accepted, 32 enrolled. *Faculty:* 9 full-time (5 women), 9 part-time/adjunct (7 women). Expenses: Contact institution. *Financial support:* In 2008–09, 74 students received support. Scholarships/grants available. Financial award applicants required to submit FAFSA. In 2008, 32 doctorates awarded. Offers physical therapy (DPT). *Application deadline:* For fall admission, 8/31 priority date for domestic and international students. Applications are processed on a rolling basis. *Application fee:* $50. Electronic applications accepted. *Application Contact:* Lucy Baltimore, Program Assistant, 615-460-6726, Fax: 615-460-6729, E-mail: baltimorel@mail.belmont.edu. *Associate Dean*, Dr. John S. Halle, 615-460-6727, Fax: 615-460-6729, E-mail: hallej@mail.belmont.edu.

Belmont University (continued)

College of Visual and Performing Arts Students: 13 full-time (10 women), 33 part-time (17 women); includes 5 minority (2 African Americans, 3 Hispanic Americans), 1 international. Average age 28. 19 applicants, 89% accepted, 13 enrolled. *Faculty:* 26 full-time (8 women), 12 part-time/adjunct (3 women). Expenses: Contact institution. *Financial support:* In 2008–09, 15 fellowships (averaging $2,000 per year), 5 teaching assistantships (averaging $2,000 per year) were awarded; career-related internships or fieldwork, scholarships/grants, and unspecified assistantships also available. Financial award application deadline: 3/1; financial award applicants required to submit FAFSA. In 2008, 15 master's awarded. *Degree program information:* Part-time programs available. Offers visual and performing arts (MM). *Application deadline:* For fall admission, 5/1 priority date for domestic students, 5/11 for international students; for spring admission, 11/1 priority date for domestic students, 11/1 for international students. Applications are processed on a rolling basis. *Application fee:* $50. Electronic applications accepted. *Application Contact:* Russ Cornwall, Graduate Secretary, 615-460-8117, Fax: 615-386-0239, E-mail: cornwallr@mail.belmont.edu. *Dean,* Dr. Cynthia R. Curtis, 615-460-8118.

School of Music Students: 13 full-time (10 women), 33 part-time (17 women); includes 5 minority (2 African Americans, 3 Hispanic Americans), 1 international. Average age 28. 19 applicants, 89% accepted, 13 enrolled. *Faculty:* 26 full-time (8 women), 12 part-time/adjunct (3 women). Expenses: Contact institution. *Financial support:* In 2008–09, 15 fellowships (averaging $2,000 per year), 5 teaching assistantships (averaging $2,000 per year) were awarded; career-related internships or fieldwork, scholarships/grants, and unspecified assistantships also available. Financial award application deadline: 3/1; financial award applicants required to submit FAFSA. In 2008, 17 master's awarded. *Degree program information:* Part-time programs available. Offers church music (MM); composition (MM); music education (MM); pedagogy (MM); performance (MM). *Application deadline:* For fall admission, 5/1 priority date for domestic students, 5/1 for international students; for spring admission, 11/1 priority date for domestic students, 11/1 for international students. Applications are processed on a rolling basis. *Application fee:* $50. Electronic applications accepted. *Application Contact:* Russ Cornwall, Graduate Secretary, 615-460-8117, Fax: 615-386-0239, E-mail: cornwallr@mail.belmont.edu. *Director,* Dr. Robert Gregg, 615-460-8111, Fax: 615-386-0239, E-mail: greggr@mail.belmont.edu.

Jack C. Massey Graduate School of Business Students: 15 full-time (5 women), 175 part-time (71 women); includes 28 minority (13 African Americans, 2 American Indian/Alaska Native, 7 Asian Americans or Pacific Islanders, 6 Hispanic Americans), 6 international. Average age 29. 80 applicants, 74% accepted, 37 enrolled. *Faculty:* 30 full-time (9 women), 4 part-time/adjunct (2 women). Expenses: Contact institution. *Financial support:* In 2008–09, 22 students received support. Scholarships/grants, tuition waivers (full), and unspecified assistantships available. Financial award application deadline: 7/1; financial award applicants required to submit FAFSA. In 2008, 93 master's awarded. *Degree program information:* Part-time and evening/weekend programs available. Offers business (M Acc, MBA). *Application deadline:* For fall admission, 7/1 for domestic and international students; for spring admission, 11/1 for domestic and international students. Applications are processed on a rolling basis. *Application fee:* $50. Electronic applications accepted. *Application Contact:* Tonya Hollin, Admissions Assistant, 615-460-6480, Fax: 615-460-6353, E-mail: masseyadmissions@.belmont.edu. *Dean,* Dr. Patrick Raines, 615-460-6480, Fax: 615-460-6455, E-mail: rainesp@mail.belmont.edu.

BEMIDJI STATE UNIVERSITY, Bemidji, MN 56601-2699

General Information State-supported, coed, comprehensive institution. *Graduate housing:* Room and/or apartments available on a first-come, first-served basis to single students; on-campus housing not available to married students. Housing application deadline: 4/25.

GRADUATE UNITS

School of Graduate Studies *Degree program information:* Part-time programs available. Postbaccalaureate distance learning degree programs offered (no on-campus study). Electronic applications accepted.

College of Arts and Letters *Degree program information:* Part-time programs available. Offers arts and letters (MA, MS); English (MA, MS). Electronic applications accepted.

College of Professional Studies *Degree program information:* Part-time programs available. Postbaccalaureate distance learning degree programs offered (minimal on-campus study). Offers education (M Ed, MS); professional studies (M Ed, M Sp Ed, MS); special education (M Sp Ed, MS); sport studies (MS); technical education (MS); technology/career technical education (MS). Electronic applications accepted.

College of Social and Natural Sciences *Degree program information:* Part-time programs available. Offers biology (MS); environmental studies (MS); mathematics (MS); psychology (MS); science (MS); social and natural sciences (MS). Electronic applications accepted.

BENEDICTINE COLLEGE, Atchison, KS 66002-1499

General Information Independent-religious, coed, comprehensive institution. *Enrollment:* 2,033 graduate, professional, and undergraduate students; 32 full-time matriculated graduate/professional students (9 women), 23 part-time matriculated graduate/professional students (17 women). *Enrollment by degree level:* 55 master's. *Graduate faculty:* 5 full-time (1 woman), 13 part-time/adjunct (6 women). *Tuition:* Full-time $21,000; part-time $530 per credit hour. *Graduate housing:* On-campus housing not available. *Student services:* Campus employment opportunities, career counseling, exercise/wellness program, free psychological counseling, international student services, services for students with disabilities, teacher training. *Library facilities:* Benedictine College Library plus 1 other. *Online resources:* library catalog, web page, access to other libraries' catalogs. *Collection:* 207,316 titles, 32,834 serial subscriptions, 1,032 audiovisual materials.

Computer facilities: 80 computers available on campus for general student use. A campuswide network can be accessed from student residence rooms and from off campus. Online class registration is available. *Web address:* http://www.benedictine.edu/.

General Application Contact: Donna Bonnel, Administrative of Graduation Programs, 913-367-5340 Ext. 2524, Fax: 913-367-5462, E-mail: emba@benedictine.edu.

GRADUATE UNITS

Executive Master of Business Administration Program Students: 14 full-time (5 women), 1 part-time (0 women); includes 2 African Americans. Average age 38. 10 applicants, 100% accepted, 10 enrolled. *Faculty:* 3 full-time (0 women), 8 part-time/adjunct (1 woman). Expenses: Contact institution. *Financial support:* In 2008–09, 5 students received support. Scholarships/grants available. Support available to part-time students. Financial award application deadline: 4/15; financial award applicants required to submit FAFSA. In 2008, 20 master's awarded. *Degree program information:* Part-time and evening/weekend programs available. Offers business administration (EMBA). *Application deadline:* For fall admission, 7/15 priority date for domestic students, 7/1 for international students; for spring admission, 4/15 priority date for domestic students, 4/1 for international students. Applications are processed on a rolling basis. *Application fee:* $100. Electronic applications accepted. *Application Contact:* Donna Bonnel, Administrative of Graduation Programs, 913-367-5340 Ext. 7589, Fax: 913-360-7301, E-mail: dbonnel@benedictine.edu. *Executive Director, School of Business,* Dr. Antonio J Soave, 913-367-5340 Ext. 7302, Fax: 913-360-7301, E-mail: emba@benedictine.edu.

Master of Arts Program in School Leadership Students: 21 full-time (14 women); includes 2 minority (1 American Indian/Alaska Native, 1 Hispanic American). Average age 32. *Faculty:* 4 full-time (2 women), 6 part-time/adjunct (1 woman). Expenses: Contact institution. *Financial support:* Scholarships/grants available. Support available to part-time students. Financial award applicants required to submit FAFSA. In 2008, 17 master's awarded. *Degree program information:* Part-time and evening/weekend programs available. Offers school leadership (MA). *Application deadline:* For fall admission, 8/15 priority date for domestic students; for spring admission, 5/15 priority date for domestic students. Applications are processed on a rolling basis. *Application fee:* $25 ($0 for international students). *Application Contact:* Donna Bonnel, Administrative Assistant of Graduate Program, 913-367-5340 Ext. 2524, Fax: 913-367-5462, E-mail: emba@benedictine.edu. *Director,* Dr. Cheryl Reding, 913-367-7384 Ext. 7384, E-mail: creding@benedictine.edu.

Traditional Business Administration Program Students: 24 full-time (7 women), 16 part-time (11 women); includes 1 minority (Hispanic American), 7 international. Average age 22. 22 applicants, 100% accepted, 20 enrolled. *Faculty:* 6 full-time (2 women), 8 part-time/adjunct (0 women). Expenses: Contact institution. *Financial support:* In 2008–09, 16 students received support. Scholarships/grants and unspecified assistantships available. Support available to part-time students. Financial award application deadline: 3/15; financial award applicants required to submit FAFSA. In 2008, 17 master's awarded. *Degree program information:* Part-time and evening/weekend programs available. Offers business administration (MBA). *Application deadline:* For fall admission, 8/1 priority date for domestic students, 7/1 priority date for international students; for winter admission, 1/7 priority date for domestic students, 12/1 priority date for international students; for spring admission, 5/1 priority date for domestic students, 4/1 priority date for international students. Applications are processed on a rolling basis. *Application fee:* $25. *Application Contact:* Donna Bonnel, Administrative Specialist, 913-360-7589, Fax: 913-360-7301, E-mail: dbonnel@benedictine.edu. *Director,* Dr. Antonio J Soave, 913-367-5340 Ext. 7302, Fax: 913-360-7301, E-mail: emba@benedictine.edu.

BENEDICTINE UNIVERSITY, Lisle, IL 60532-0900

General Information Independent-religious, coed, comprehensive institution. *Graduate housing:* Rooms and/or apartments available on a first-come, first-served basis to single and married students.

GRADUATE UNITS

Graduate Programs *Degree program information:* Part-time and evening/weekend programs available. Postbaccalaureate distance learning degree programs offered (no on-campus study). Offers accountancy (MSA); accounting (MBA); administration of health care institutions (MPH); clinical exercise physiology (MS); clinical psychology (MS); curriculum and instruction and collaborative teaching (M Ed); dietetics (MPH); disaster management (MPH); elementary education (MA Ed); entrepreneurship and managing innovation (MBA); financial management (MBA); health administration (MBA); health education (MPH); health information systems (MPH); higher education and organizational change (Ed D); human resource management (MBA); information systems security (MBA); international business (MBA); leadership and administration (M Ed); management and organizational behavior (MS); management consulting (MBA); management information systems (MBA); marketing management (MBA); nutrition and wellness (MS); operations management and logistics (MBA); organizational development (PhD); organizational leadership (MBA); reading and literacy (M Ed); science content and process (MSSCP); secondary education (MA Ed); special education (MA Ed). Electronic applications accepted.

BENNINGTON COLLEGE, Bennington, VT 05201

General Information Independent, coed, comprehensive institution. *Enrollment:* 759 graduate, professional, and undergraduate students; 119 full-time matriculated graduate/professional students (87 women), 22 part-time matriculated graduate/professional students (10 women). *Enrollment by degree level:* 134 master's, 7 other advanced degrees. *Graduate faculty:* 40 full-time (16 women), 33 part-time/adjunct (16 women). *Tuition:* Full-time $20,640; part-time $2890 per course. One-time fee: $75. Tuition and fees vary according to program. *Graduate housing:* Room and/or apartments available on a first-come, first-served basis to single students; on-campus housing not available to married students. Typical cost: $3100 per year ($8060 including board). *Student services:* Campus employment opportunities, campus safety program, career counseling, child daycare facilities, exercise/wellness program, free psychological counseling, international student services, low-cost health insurance, teacher training, writing training. *Library facilities:* Crossett Library plus 1 other. *Online resources:* library catalog, web page, access to other libraries' catalogs. *Collection:* 121,500 titles, 26,801 serial subscriptions, 5,681 audiovisual materials.

Computer facilities: 100 computers available on campus for general student use. A campuswide network can be accessed from student residence rooms and from off campus. *Web address:* http://www.bennington.edu/.

General Application Contact: Ken Himmelman, Dean of Admissions and Financial Aid, 802-440-4312, Fax: 802-440-4320, E-mail: admissions@bennington.edu.

GRADUATE UNITS

Graduate Programs Students: 119 full-time (87 women), 22 part-time (10 women); includes 10 minority (4 African Americans, 6 Hispanic Americans), 4 international. Average age 38. 216 applicants, 37% accepted, 38 enrolled. *Faculty:* 40 full-time (16 women), 33 part-time/adjunct (16 women). Expenses: Contact institution. *Financial support:* In 2008–09, 16 students received support, including 3 fellowships (averaging $10,320 per year), 3 teaching assistantships; scholarships/grants and unspecified assistantships also available. Financial award application deadline: 4/1; financial award applicants required to submit FAFSA. In 2008, 58 master's, 5 other advanced degrees awarded. *Degree program information:* Part-time programs available. Postbaccalaureate distance learning degree programs offered (minimal on-campus study). Offers allied and health sciences (Certificate); art education (MAT); creative writing (MFA); dance (MFA); early childhood (MAT); education (MATSL); elementary education (MAT); English education (MAT); foreign language education (MAT, MATSL); French (MATSL); mathematics education (MAT); music (MFA); music education (MAT); science education (MAT); secondary education (MAT); social science education (MAT); Spanish (MATSL). *Application deadline:* Applications are processed on a rolling basis. *Application fee:* $60. *Application Contact:* Ken Himmelman, Dean of Admissions and Financial Aid, 802-440-4312, Fax: 802-440-4320, E-mail: admissions@bennington.edu. *Associate Dean for Academic Services,* Duncan Dobbelmann, 802-440-4400, Fax: 802-440-4876, E-mail: duncand@bennington.edu.

BENTLEY UNIVERSITY, Waltham, MA 02452-4705

General Information Independent, coed, comprehensive institution. *Enrollment:* 5,664 graduate, professional, and undergraduate students; 381 full-time matriculated graduate/professional students (168 women), 1,024 part-time matriculated graduate/professional students (442 women). *Enrollment by degree level:* 1,358 master's, 28 doctoral, 18 other advanced degrees. *Graduate faculty:* 285 full-time (110 women), 199 part-time/adjunct (78 women). *Tuition:* Full-time $25,200; part-time $3150 per course. *Required fees:* $404; $105 per year. Tuition and fees vary according to course load. *Graduate housing:* Room and/or apartments available on a first-come, first-served basis to single students; on-campus housing not available to married students. Typical cost: $8760 per year ($13,310 including board). Room and board charges vary according to board plan and housing facility selected. *Student services:* Campus employment opportunities, campus safety program, career counseling, exercise/wellness program, free psychological counseling, international student services, low-cost health insurance, multicultural affairs office, services for students with disabilities. *Library facilities:* Bentley Library. *Online resources:* library catalog, web page, access to other libraries' catalogs. *Collection:* 177,000 titles, 30,700 serial subscriptions, 9,500 audiovisual materials.

Computer facilities: Computer purchase and lease plans are available. 4,789 computers available on campus for general student use. A campuswide network can be accessed from student residence rooms and from off campus. Online class registration, grade checking, online admission, Blackboard, resume review, student employment, interlibrary loan, free software downloads for popular Microsoft titles and many academic applications are available. *Web address:* http://www.bentley.edu.

General Application Contact: Sharon Hill, Assistant Dean/Director of Graduate Admissions, 781-891-2108, Fax: 781-891-2464, E-mail: Bentleygraduateadmissions@bentley.edu.

GRADUATE UNITS

McCallum Graduate School of Business Students: 381 full-time (168 women), 1,024 part-time (442 women); includes 146 minority (23 African Americans, 3 American Indian/Alaska Native, 93 Asian Americans or Pacific Islanders, 27 Hispanic Americans), 251 international. Average age 29. 1,444 applicants, 60% accepted, 496 enrolled. *Faculty:* 285 full-time (110 women), 199 part-time/adjunct (78 women). Expenses: Contact institution. *Financial support:* In 2008–09, 46 research assistantships (averaging $17,873 per year) were awarded; scholarships/grants and unspecified assistantships also available. Financial award application deadline: 6/1; financial award applicants required to submit CSS PROFILE or FAFSA. In 2008, 530 master's awarded. *Degree program information:* Part-time and evening/

weekend programs available. Postbaccalaureate distance learning degree programs offered. Offers accountancy (PhD); accounting (GBC); accounting information systems (GBC); business (GSS); business administration (MBA); business ethics (GBC); data analysis (GBC); finance (MSF); financial planning (GBC); fraud and forensic accounting (GBC); human factors in information design (MSHFID); information technology (MSIT); marketing analytics (MSMA); taxation (MST). *Application deadline:* For fall admission, 12/1 priority date for domestic and international students; for spring admission, 10/1 priority date for domestic and international students. *Application fee:* $50. Electronic applications accepted. *Application Contact:* Sharon Hill, Director of Graduate Admissions, 781-891-2108, Fax: 781-891-2464, E-mail: Bentleygraduateadmissions@bentley.edu. *Vice President for Academic Affairs/Dean of Business,* Dr. Michael J. Page.

BERNARD M. BARUCH COLLEGE OF THE CITY UNIVERSITY OF NEW YORK, New York, NY 10010-5585

General Information State and locally supported, coed, comprehensive institution. *Graduate housing:* On-campus housing not available.

GRADUATE UNITS

School of Public Affairs Students: 185 full-time (132 women), 627 part-time (446 women); includes 353 minority (177 African Americans, 1 American Indian/Alaska Native, 56 Asian Americans or Pacific Islanders, 119 Hispanic Americans). Average age 34. 537 applicants, 77% accepted, 315 enrolled. *Faculty:* 46 full-time (0 women), 31 part-time/adjunct (0 women). Expenses: Contact institution. *Financial support:* In 2008–09, 39 students received support, including 15 fellowships (averaging $2,250 per year), 23 research assistantships (averaging $12,000 per year); teaching assistantships, career-related internships or fieldwork, Federal Work-Study, scholarships/grants, tuition waivers (partial), and unspecified assistantships also available. Support available to part-time students. Financial award application deadline: 5/15; financial award applicants required to submit FAFSA. In 2008, 241 master's awarded. *Degree program information:* Part-time and evening/weekend programs available. Offers educational leadership (MS Ed); higher education administration (MS Ed); nonprofit administration (MPA); public affairs (MPA, MS Ed, AC); public management (MPA). *Application deadline:* For fall admission, 4/1 priority date for domestic and international students; for spring admission, 11/15 priority date for domestic and international students. Applications are processed on a rolling basis. *Application fee:* $125. Electronic applications accepted. *Application Contact:* Michael J. Lovaglio, Director of Student Affairs and Graduate Admissions, 646-660-6750, Fax: 646-660-6751, E-mail: Michael.Lovaglio@baruch.cuny.edu. *Dean,* David Birdsell, 646-660-6700, Fax: 646-660-6721, E-mail: David.Birdsell@baruch.cuny.edu.

Weissman School of Arts and Sciences Offers arts and sciences (MA, MS); corporate communication (MA); financial engineering (MS); industrial organizational psychology (MS).

Zicklin School of Business *Degree program information:* Part-time and evening/weekend programs available. Offers accounting (MBA, MS, PhD); business (MBA, MS, PhD, Certificate); business administration (MBA); computer information systems (MBA, MS, PhD); decision sciences (MBA, MS); economics (MBA); entrepreneurship (MBA); finance (MBA, MS, PhD); general business (MBA); general management and policy (MBA); health care administration (MBA); human resources management (MBA); industrial and labor relations (MS); industrial and organizational psychology (MBA, MS, PhD, Certificate); international executive education (MBA); management planning systems (PhD); management science (MBA); marketing (MBA, MS, PhD); organization and policy studies (PhD); organizational behavior (MBA); statistics (MBA, MS); taxation (MBA, MS). Electronic applications accepted.

BERRY COLLEGE, Mount Berry, GA 30149-0159

General Information Independent-religious, coed, comprehensive institution. *Enrollment:* 1,795 graduate, professional, and undergraduate students; 21 full-time matriculated graduate/professional students (8 women), 88 part-time matriculated graduate/professional students (56 women). *Enrollment by degree level:* 101 master's, 8 other advanced degrees. *Graduate faculty:* 17 part-time/adjunct (10 women). *Tuition:* Full-time $7578; part-time $421 per credit hour. *Required fees:* $150. Tuition and fees vary according to program. *Graduate housing:* On-campus housing not available. *Student services:* Campus employment opportunities, campus safety program, career counseling, child daycare facilities, exercise/wellness program, free psychological counseling, grant writing training, international student services, low-cost health insurance, multicultural affairs office. *Library facilities:* Memorial Library plus 1 other. *Online resources:* library catalog, web page, access to other libraries' catalogs. *Collection:* 281,522 titles, 2,088 serial subscriptions, 4,768 audiovisual materials. *Research affiliation:* Georgia Forestry Commission (biology), National Geographic Society (conservation), Georgia State University (psychology), Auburn University (marketing), University of Georgia (animal science), Gulf Coast Research Laboratory (marine science).

Computer facilities: 140 computers available on campus for general student use. A campuswide network can be accessed from student residence rooms and from off campus. Online class registration is available. *Web address:* http://www.berry.edu/.

General Application Contact: Brett Kennedy, Director of Admissions, 706-236-2215, Fax: 706-290-2178, E-mail: admissions@berry.edu.

GRADUATE UNITS

Graduate Programs Students: 21 full-time (8 women), 88 part-time (56 women); includes 6 minority (3 African Americans, 3 Hispanic Americans), 7 international. Average age 33. *Faculty:* 17 part-time/adjunct (10 women). Expenses: Contact institution. *Financial support:* In 2008–09, 65 students received support, including 9 research assistantships with full tuition reimbursements available (averaging $4,275 per year); scholarships/grants, tuition waivers (partial), and unspecified assistantships also available. Support available to part-time students. Financial award application deadline: 4/1; financial award applicants required to submit FAFSA. In 2008, 27 master's, 1 other advanced degree awarded. *Degree program information:* Part-time and evening/weekend programs available. Offers curriculum and instruction (Ed S); early childhood education (M Ed); educational leadership (Ed S); middle-grades education and reading (M Ed); secondary education (M Ed). *Application deadline:* For fall admission, 7/24 for domestic students, 5/1 for international students; for spring admission, 12/13 for domestic students, 2/1 for international students. Applications are processed on a rolling basis. *Application fee:* $25 ($30 for international students). *Application Contact:* Brett Kennedy, Director of Admissions, 706-236-2215, Fax: 706-290-2178, E-mail: admissions@berry.edu. *Provost,* Dr. Katherine Whatley, 706-236-2216, Fax: 706-290-2179, E-mail: kwhatley@berry.edu.

Campbell School of Business Students: 8 full-time (1 woman), 17 part-time (3 women), 6 international. Average age 29. *Faculty:* 4 part-time/adjunct (3 women). Expenses: Contact institution. *Financial support:* In 2008–09, 14 students received support, including 3 research assistantships with full tuition reimbursements available (averaging $4,836 per year); scholarships/grants, tuition waivers (partial), and unspecified assistantships also available. Support available to part-time students. Financial award application deadline: 4/1; financial award applicants required to submit FAFSA. In 2008, 9 master's awarded. *Degree program information:* Part-time and evening/weekend programs available. Offers business (MBA). *Application deadline:* For fall admission, 7/24 for domestic students; for spring admission, 12/13 for domestic students. Applications are processed on a rolling basis. *Application fee:* $25 ($30 for international students). *Application Contact:* Brett Kennedy, Director of Admissions, 706-236-2215, Fax: 706-290-2178, E-mail: admissions@berry.edu. *Dean,* Dr. John Grout, 706-236-2233, Fax: 706-802-6728, E-mail: jgrout@berry.edu.

BETHANY THEOLOGICAL SEMINARY, Richmond, IN 47374-4019

General Information Independent-religious, coed, graduate-only institution. *Graduate housing:* On-campus housing not available.

GRADUATE UNITS

Graduate and Professional Programs *Degree program information:* Part-time programs available. Postbaccalaureate distance learning degree programs offered (minimal on-campus study). Offers biblical studies (MA Th); ministry studies (M Div); peace studies (M Div, MA Th); theological studies (MA Th, CATS); youth ministry (M Div).

BETHANY UNIVERSITY, Scotts Valley, CA 95066-2820

General Information Independent-religious, coed, comprehensive institution. *Graduate housing:* Rooms and/or apartments available to single students and available on a first-come, first-served basis to married students. Housing application deadline: 7/31.

GRADUATE UNITS

Program in Clinical Psychology *Degree program information:* Part-time and evening/weekend programs available. Offers clinical psychology (MS).

Program in Teacher Education *Degree program information:* Part-time and evening/weekend programs available. Offers education (MA); educational leadership (MA).

BETH BENJAMIN ACADEMY OF CONNECTICUT, Stamford, CT 06901-1202

General Information Independent-religious, men only, comprehensive institution. *Graduate housing:* Rooms and/or apartments available to single and married students.

GRADUATE UNITS

Graduate and Professional Programs

BETHEL COLLEGE, Mishawaka, IN 46545-5591

General Information Independent-religious, coed, comprehensive institution. *Enrollment:* 2,075 graduate, professional, and undergraduate students; 52 full-time matriculated graduate/professional students (30 women), 167 part-time matriculated graduate/professional students (92 women). *Enrollment by degree level:* 219 master's. *Graduate faculty:* 1 full-time (0 women), 30 part-time/adjunct (15 women). *Tuition:* Full-time $6120; part-time $340 per credit hour. Tuition and fees vary according to program. *Graduate housing:* On-campus housing not available. *Student services:* Campus employment opportunities, campus safety program, career counseling, international student services, services for students with disabilities, writing training. *Library facilities:* Otis and Elizabeth Bowen Library. *Online resources:* library catalog, web page, access to other libraries' catalogs. *Collection:* 118,393 titles, 1,496 serial subscriptions, 2,962 audiovisual materials.

Computer facilities: 110 computers available on campus for general student use. A campuswide network can be accessed. Online class registration is available. *Web address:* http://www.bethelcollege.edu.

General Application Contact: Dr. Bradley D. Smith, Dean, 574-257-3363, Fax: 574-257-7616.

GRADUATE UNITS

Division of Graduate Studies Students: 52 full-time (30 women), 167 part-time (92 women); includes 28 minority (23 African Americans, 1 Asian American or Pacific Islander, 4 Hispanic Americans), 2 international. Average age 37. 165 applicants, 90% accepted, 129 enrolled. *Faculty:* 1 full-time (0 women), 30 part-time/adjunct (15 women). Expenses: Contact institution. *Financial support:* Career-related internships or fieldwork and unspecified assistantships available. Financial award applicants required to submit FAFSA. In 2008, 46 master's awarded. *Degree program information:* Part-time and evening/weekend programs available. Offers business administration (MBA); Christian ministries (M Min); education (M Ed, MAT); nursing (MSN); theological studies (MATS). *Application deadline:* For fall admission, 5/1 for international students; for spring admission, 10/1 for international students. Applications are processed on a rolling basis. *Application fee:* $25. Electronic applications accepted. *Application Contact:* Dr. Bradley D. Smith, Dean, 574-257-3363, Fax: 574-257-3357, E-mail: smithb@bethelcollege.edu. *Dean,* Dr. Bradley D. Smith, 574-257-3363, Fax: 574-257-3357, E-mail: smithb@bethelcollege.edu.

BETHEL COLLEGE, McKenzie, TN 38201

General Information Independent-religious, coed, comprehensive institution. *Graduate housing:* Room and/or apartments available on a first-come, first-served basis to single students; on-campus housing not available to married students. Housing application deadline: 7/31.

GRADUATE UNITS

Program in Education *Degree program information:* Part-time and evening/weekend programs available. Offers administration and supervision (MA Ed); biology education K8-12 (MAT); elementary education (MAT); English education K8-12 (MAT); history education K8-12 (MAT); physical education K8-12 (MAT); special education K8-12 (MAT).

BETHEL SEMINARY, St. Paul, MN 55112-6998

General Information Independent-religious, coed, graduate-only institution. *Enrollment by degree level:* 421 first professional, 505 master's, 97 doctoral, 81 other advanced degrees. *Graduate faculty:* 26 full-time (2 women), 93 part-time/adjunct (29 women). *Graduate housing:* Rooms and/or apartments available on a first-come, first-served basis to single and married students. *Student services:* Campus employment opportunities, campus safety program, career counseling, child daycare facilities, free psychological counseling, international student services, multicultural affairs office, writing training. *Library facilities:* Carl H. Lundquist Library plus 1 other. *Online resources:* library catalog, web page, access to other libraries' catalogs. *Collection:* 237,121 titles, 596 serial subscriptions, 8,762 audiovisual materials.

Computer facilities: 19 computers available on campus for general student use. A campuswide network can be accessed from student residence rooms and from off campus. Online class registration is available. *Web address:* http://www.bethel.edu/seminary/btshome.htm.

General Application Contact: Joseph V. Dworak, Director of Admissions, 651-638-6288, Fax: 651-638-6002, E-mail: j-dworak@bethel.edu.

GRADUATE UNITS

Graduate and Professional Programs Students: 397 full-time (124 women), 707 part-time (299 women); includes 218 minority (123 African Americans, 1 American Indian/Alaska Native, 67 Asian Americans or Pacific Islanders, 27 Hispanic Americans), 14 international. Average age 36. 470 applicants, 90% accepted, 270 enrolled. *Faculty:* 26 full-time (2 women), 93 part-time/adjunct (29 women). Expenses: Contact institution. *Financial support:* In 2008–09, 688 students received support, including 20 teaching assistantships; career-related internships or fieldwork, Federal Work-Study, scholarships/grants, and tuition waivers (full) also available. Financial award application deadline: 7/15; financial award applicants required to submit FAFSA. In 2008, 63 first professional degrees, 101 master's, 10 doctorates awarded. *Degree program information:* Part-time and evening/weekend programs available. Postbaccalaureate distance learning degree programs offered (minimal on-campus study). Offers applied ministry (MA); biblical studies (MATS, Certificate); children's and family ministry (MACFM); Christian education (MACE); Christian thought (M Div, MACT); church leadership (D Min); community ministry leadership (MA, Certificate); congregation and family care (D Min); global and contextual studies (MA, MATS); historical studies (MATS); lay ministry (Certificate); marriage and family studies (M Div); marriage and family therapy (MAMFT, Certificate); pastoral ministries (M Div); spiritual formation (Certificate); theological studies (MATS, Certificate); transformational leadership (MATL); youth ministries (MACE). *Application deadline:* For fall admission, 8/1 priority date for domestic students, 3/1 for international students; for winter admission, 12/1 priority date for domestic students; for spring admission, 3/1 priority date for domestic students. Applications are processed on a rolling basis. *Application fee:* $20. Electronic applications accepted. *Application Contact:* Joseph V. Dworak, Director of Admissions, 651-638-6288, Fax: 651-638-6002, E-mail: j-dworak@bethel.edu. *Executive Vice President and Provost,* Dr. Leland Eliason, 651-638-6182.

BETHEL UNIVERSITY, St. Paul, MN 55112-6999

General Information Independent-religious, coed, comprehensive institution. *Graduate housing:* On-campus housing not available.

GRADUATE UNITS

Graduate School *Degree program information:* Part-time and evening/weekend programs available. Postbaccalaureate distance learning degree programs offered (minimal on-campus

Bethel University (continued)

study). Offers business administration (MBA); child and adolescent mental health (Certificate); Christian health ministry (MA); communication (MA); counseling psychology (MA); education K-12 (MA); educational administration (Ed D); gerontology (MA); healthcare leadership (MA); literacy (Certificate); literacy education (MA); nursing education (MA, Certificate); organizational leadership (MA); post-secondary teaching (Certificate); secondary education (MA); special education (M Ed). Electronic applications accepted.

BETHESDA CHRISTIAN UNIVERSITY, Anaheim, CA 92801

General Information Independent-religious, coed, comprehensive institution.

GRADUATE UNITS

Graduate and Professional Programs Offers biblical studies (MA); music (MA); theology (M Div).

BETH HAMEDRASH SHAAREI YOSHER INSTITUTE, Brooklyn, NY 11204

General Information Independent-religious, men only, comprehensive institution.

GRADUATE UNITS

Graduate Programs

BETH HATALMUD RABBINICAL COLLEGE, Brooklyn, NY 11214

General Information Independent-religious, men only, comprehensive institution.

GRADUATE UNITS

Graduate Programs

BETH MEDRASH GOVOHA, Lakewood, NJ 08701-2797

General Information Independent-religious, men only, upper-level institution.

GRADUATE UNITS

Graduate Programs

BETHUNE-COOKMAN UNIVERSITY, Daytona Beach, FL 32114-3099

General Information Independent-religious, coed, comprehensive institution.

GRADUATE UNITS

School of Graduate and Professional Studies Postbaccalaureate distance learning degree programs offered (minimal on-campus study). Offers transformative leadership (MS). Electronic applications accepted.

BEULAH HEIGHTS UNIVERSITY, Atlanta, GA 30316

General Information Independent-religious, coed, comprehensive institution.

GRADUATE UNITS

Graduate School Offers biblical studies (MA); leadership studies (MA). Electronic applications accepted.

BEXLEY HALL EPISCOPAL SEMINARY, Columbus, OH 43209-2325

General Information Independent-religious, coed, graduate-only institution.

GRADUATE UNITS

Graduate Programs Offers ministry (M Div, MA).

BIBLICAL THEOLOGICAL SEMINARY, Hatfield, PA 19440-2499

General Information Independent-religious, coed, graduate-only institution. *Graduate housing:* Rooms and/or apartments available to single students and available on a first-come, first-served basis to married students. *Research affiliation:* Christian Counseling and Education Foundation (psychology).

GRADUATE UNITS

Graduate and Professional Programs *Degree program information:* Part-time programs available. Postbaccalaureate distance learning degree programs offered. Offers advanced missional leadership (D Min); advanced pastoral studies (Certificate); biblical counseling (Certificate); biblical studies (MA, Certificate); counseling (MA); ministry (MA); missional theology (MA); theology (M Div); youth ministry (Certificate).

BIOLA UNIVERSITY, La Mirada, CA 90639-0001

General Information Independent-religious, coed, university. *Graduate housing:* Rooms and/or apartments available on a first-come, first-served basis to single and married students.

GRADUATE UNITS

Crowell School of Business *Degree program information:* Part-time and evening/weekend programs available. Offers business (MBA).

Rosemead School of Psychology Offers psychology (MA, PhD, Psy D).

School of Arts and Sciences *Degree program information:* Part-time and evening/weekend programs available. Offers arts and sciences (MA Ed).

School of Intercultural Studies *Degree program information:* Part-time and evening/weekend programs available. Offers applied linguistics (MA); intercultural education (PhD); intercultural studies (MAICS); missiology (D Miss); missions (MA); teaching English to speakers of other languages (MA, Certificate). Electronic applications accepted.

School of Professional Studies *Degree program information:* Part-time and evening/weekend programs available. Offers Christian apologetics (MA); organizational leadership (MA).

Talbot School of Theology *Degree program information:* Part-time and evening/weekend programs available. Offers Bible exposition (MA); biblical and theological studies (MA); Christian education (MACE); Christian ministry and leadership (MA); divinity (M Div); education (PhD); ministry (MA Min); New Testament (MA); Old Testament (MA); philosophy of religion and ethics (MA); spiritual formation (MA); spiritual formation and soul care (MA); theology (MA, Th M, D Min).

BIRMINGHAM-SOUTHERN COLLEGE, Birmingham, AL 35254

General Information Independent-religious, coed, comprehensive institution. *Enrollment:* 1,458 graduate, professional, and undergraduate students; 52 full-time matriculated graduate/professional students (26 women). *Enrollment by degree level:* 52 master's. *Graduate faculty:* 16 full-time (6 women), 1 part-time/adjunct. *Tuition:* Full-time $9875. *Required fees:* $145. One-time fee: $270 full-time. *Graduate housing:* On-campus housing not available. *Student services:* Campus employment opportunities, campus safety program, career counseling, exercise/wellness program, free psychological counseling, international student services, low-cost health insurance, multicultural affairs office, services for students with disabilities, writing training. *Library facilities:* Charles Andrew Rush Learning Center/N. E. Miles Library. *Online resources:* library catalog, web page. *Collection:* 215,565 titles, 540 serial subscriptions, 21,720 audiovisual materials.

Computer facilities: Computer purchase and lease plans are available. 156 computers available on campus for general student use. A campuswide network can be accessed from student residence rooms and from off campus. Online class registration is available. *Web address:* http://www.bsc.edu/.

General Application Contact: Brenda D Durham, Director of MPPM Admission, 205-226-4803, Fax: 205-226-4843, E-mail: graduate@bsc.edu.

GRADUATE UNITS

Program in Music Offers music (MM).

Program in Public and Private Management *Degree program information:* Part-time and evening/weekend programs available. Offers public and private management (MPPM).

BISHOP'S UNIVERSITY, Sherbrooke, QC J1M 0C8, Canada

General Information Province-supported, coed, comprehensive institution. *Graduate housing:* Room and/or apartments available on a first-come, first-served basis to single students; on-campus housing not available to married students. Housing application deadline: 7/1.

GRADUATE UNITS

School of Education *Degree program information:* Part-time programs available. Postbaccalaureate distance learning degree programs offered (minimal on-campus study). Offers advanced studies in education (Diploma); education (M Ed, MA); teaching English as a second language (Certificate).

BLACK HILLS STATE UNIVERSITY, Spearfish, SD 57799

General Information State-supported, coed, comprehensive institution. *Graduate housing:* Rooms and/or apartments available on a first-come, first-served basis to single and married students. Housing application deadline: 3/1.

GRADUATE UNITS

College of Business and Technology *Degree program information:* Part-time programs available. Offers business services management (MS).

College of Education *Degree program information:* Part-time programs available. Offers curriculum and instruction (MS).

BLESSED JOHN XXIII NATIONAL SEMINARY, Weston, MA 02493-2618

General Information Independent-religious, men only, graduate-only institution. *Enrollment by degree level:* 60 first professional. *Graduate faculty:* 9 full-time (0 women), 19 part-time/adjunct (3 women). *Tuition:* Full-time $21,500. *Graduate housing:* Room and/or apartments available to single students; on-campus housing not available to married students. Housing application deadline: 8/1. *Student services:* Campus safety program, career counseling, exercise/wellness program. *Collection:* 48,482 titles, 262 serial subscriptions.

Computer facilities: 6 computers available on campus for general student use. A campuswide network can be accessed from student residence rooms and from off campus. *Web address:* http://www.blessedjohnxxiii.edu/.

General Application Contact: Rev. Peter J. Uglietto, President and Rector, 781-899-5500, Fax: 781-891-9057, E-mail: rev.uglietto@blessedjohnxxiii.edu.

GRADUATE UNITS

School of Theology Students: 60 full-time (0 women); includes 12 minority (3 African Americans, 1 American Indian/Alaska Native, 4 Asian Americans or Pacific Islanders, 4 Hispanic Americans). Average age 45. *Faculty:* 9 full-time (0 women), 19 part-time/adjunct (3 women). Expenses: Contact institution. *Financial support:* Career-related internships or fieldwork available. In 2008, 15 M Divs awarded. Offers theology (M Div). *Application deadline:* For fall admission, 7/15 priority date for domestic students. Applications are processed on a rolling basis. *Application fee:* $0. *Application Contact:* Rev. Peter J. Uglietto, President and Rector, 781-899-5500, Fax: 781-891-9057, E-mail: rev.uglietto@blessedjohnxxiii.edu. *President and Rector,* Rev. Peter J. Uglietto, 781-899-5500, Fax: 781-891-9057, E-mail: rev.uglietto@blessedjohnxxiii.edu.

BLESSING-RIEMAN COLLEGE OF NURSING, Quincy, IL 62305-7005

General Information Independent, coed, primarily women, comprehensive institution. *Enrollment:* 219 graduate, professional, and undergraduate students; 8 part-time matriculated graduate/professional students (7 women). *Enrollment by degree level:* 8 master's. *Graduate faculty:* 8 full-time (all women). *Tuition:* Part-time $300 per credit hour. One-time fee: $175 part-time. *Graduate housing:* Rooms and/or apartments available on a first-come, first-served basis to single and married students. Typical cost: $28,040 per year for single students; $47,070 per year for married students. *Student services:* Child daycare facilities, free psychological counseling, services for students with disabilities, teacher training, writing training. *Library facilities:* Blessing Health Professions Library plus 1 other. *Online resources:* library catalog, web page, access to other libraries' catalogs. *Collection:* 3,767 titles, 125 serial subscriptions.

Computer facilities: 28 computers available on campus for general student use. A campuswide network can be accessed. *Web address:* http://www.brcn.edu/.

General Application Contact: Heather Mutter, Admissions Counselor, 217-228-5520 Ext. 6964, Fax: 217-223-4661, E-mail: hmutter@brcn.edu.

GRADUATE UNITS

Program in Nursing Students: 8 part-time (7 women). *Faculty:* 8 full-time (all women). Expenses: Contact institution. *Degree program information:* Part-time programs available. Offers nursing (MSN).

BLOOMSBURG UNIVERSITY OF PENNSYLVANIA, Bloomsburg, PA 17815-1301

General Information State-supported, coed, comprehensive institution. CGS member. *Graduate housing:* Room and/or apartments available to single students; on-campus housing not available to married students. *Research affiliation:* American Chemical Society/Petroleum Research Fund (chemistry), Consortium of Big Ten Universities Research and Training Reactors (physics), Melanoma Research Fund (biology), Merck Corp (biology), Marine Science Consortium (biology).

GRADUATE UNITS

School of Graduate Studies *Degree program information:* Part-time and evening/weekend programs available. Electronic applications accepted.

College of Business Offers business (M Ed, MBA); business administration (MBA); business education (M Ed). Electronic applications accepted.

College of Liberal Arts *Degree program information:* Part-time programs available. Offers clinical athletic training (MS); exercise science (MS); liberal arts (MS). Electronic applications accepted.

College of Professional Studies Offers adult and family nurse practitioner (MSN); adult health and illness (MSN); audiology (Au D); community health (MSN); curriculum and instruction (M Ed); early childhood education (MS); education (M Ed, MS); education of the deaf/hard of hearing (MS); elementary education (M Ed); exceptionality programs (MS); guidance counseling and student affairs (M Ed); health sciences (MS, MSN, Au D); nursing (MSN); nursing administration (MSN); reading (M Ed); special education (MS); speech pathology (MS). Electronic applications accepted.

College of Science and Technology Offers biology (MS); biology education (M Ed); instructional technology (MS); radiologist assistant (MS); science and technology (M Ed, MS).

BLUFFTON UNIVERSITY, Bluffton, OH 45817

General Information Independent-religious, coed, comprehensive institution.

GRADUATE UNITS

Program in Education Students: 8 full-time (5 women), 24 part-time (21 women); includes 1 African American, 1 Hispanic American. 32 applicants, 69% accepted, 20 enrolled. *Faculty:* 3 full-time (1 woman), 2 part-time/adjunct (both women). Expenses: Contact institution. *Financial support:* In 2008–09, 2 students received support. Health care benefits available. Support available to part-time students. Financial award application deadline: 9/15; financial award applicants required to submit FAFSA. In 2008, 18 master's awarded. *Degree program information:* Part-time programs available. Offers education (MA Ed). *Application deadline:* For fall admission, 8/15 priority date for domestic students, 6/15 priority date for international students; for spring admission, 12/15 priority date for domestic students, 9/15 priority date for international students. Applications are processed on a rolling basis. *Application fee:* $20. Electronic applications accepted. *Application Contact:* Nancey Schortgen, Program Representative, 419-358-3202, Fax: 419-358-3399, E-mail: schortgenn@bluffton.edu. *Director of Teacher Education*, Dr. George Metz, 419-358-3560, Fax: 419-358-3399, E-mail: metzg@bluffton.edu.

Programs in Business *Degree program information:* Evening/weekend programs available. Offers business administration (MBA); organizational management (MA). Electronic applications accepted.

BOB JONES UNIVERSITY, Greenville, SC 29614

General Information Independent-religious, coed, university.

GRADUATE UNITS

Graduate Programs

BOISE STATE UNIVERSITY, Boise, ID 83725-0399

General Information State-supported, coed, university. CGS member. *Enrollment:* 19,667 graduate, professional, and undergraduate students; 634 full-time matriculated graduate/professional students (367 women), 1,062 part-time matriculated graduate/professional students (583 women). *Enrollment by degree level:* 1,638 master's, 58 doctoral. *Graduate faculty:* 658. Tuition, state resident: full-time $3763; part-time $204 per credit. Tuition, nonresident: full-time $11,467; part-time $204 per credit. *Required fees:* $1741; $81 per credit. *Graduate housing:* Rooms and/or apartments available on a first-come, first-served basis to single and married students. Typical cost: $3775 per year ($6255 including board) for single students; $3000 per year ($5480 including board) for married students. Room and board charges vary according to board plan, campus/location and housing facility selected. Housing application deadline: 6/1. *Student services:* Campus employment opportunities, campus safety program, career counseling, child daycare facilities, exercise/wellness program, free psychological counseling, grant writing training, international student services, low-cost health insurance, multicultural affairs office, services for students with disabilities, writing training. *Library facilities:* Albertsons Library. *Online resources:* library catalog, web page. *Collection:* 838,932 titles, 5,575 serial subscriptions, 58,047 audiovisual materials. *Research affiliation:* Federal Aviation Administration (airliner cabin environment research), Lee Pesky Learning Center (elementary mathematics education), Prewitt & Associates, Inc. (C-130 drop zones), Bechtel BWXT Idaho, LLC (energy policy analysis), Arsonne National Laboratory (energy policy analysis), American Chemical Society (petroleum research).

Computer facilities: 900 computers available on campus for general student use. A campuswide network can be accessed from student residence rooms and from off campus. Online class registration is available. *Web address:* http://www.boisestate.edu/.

General Application Contact: Dr. John R. Pelton, Dean, 208-426-3647, Fax: 208-426-2789, E-mail: jpelton@boisestate.edu.

GRADUATE UNITS

Graduate College Students: 634 full-time (367 women), 1,062 part-time (583 women); includes 149 minority (27 African Americans, 8 American Indian/Alaska Native, 43 Asian Americans or Pacific Islanders, 71 Hispanic Americans), 95 international. Average age 37. 644 applicants, 81% accepted, 372 enrolled. *Faculty:* 415 full-time (132 women), 242 part-time/adjunct (94 women). Expenses: Contact institution. *Financial support:* In 2008–09, 11 fellowships (averaging $11,333 per year), 81 research assistantships with full and partial tuition reimbursements (averaging $10,498 per year), 84 teaching assistantships with full and partial tuition reimbursements (averaging $8,522 per year) were awarded; career-related internships or fieldwork, Federal Work-Study, institutionally sponsored loans, scholarships/grants, tuition waivers (full and partial), and unspecified assistantships also available. Support available to part-time students. Financial award application deadline: 3/1; financial award applicants required to submit FAFSA. In 2008, 482 master's, 1 doctorate awarded. *Degree program information:* Part-time programs available. Postbaccalaureate distance learning degree programs offered (no on-campus study). *Application deadline:* For fall admission, 3/1 priority date for domestic students; for spring admission, 10/1 priority date for domestic students. Applications are processed on a rolling basis. *Application fee:* $55. Electronic applications accepted. *Application Contact:* Linda Platt, Office Services Supervisor, Graduate Admission and Degree Services, 208-426-1074, Fax: 208-426-2789, E-mail: lplatt@boisestate.edu. *Dean*, Dr. John R. Pelton, 208-426-3647, Fax: 208-426-2789, E-mail: jpelton@boisestate.edu.

College of Arts and Sciences *Degree program information:* Part-time programs available. Offers art education (MA); arts and sciences (MA, MFA, MM, MS, PhD); biology (MA, MS); creative writing (MFA); earth science (MS); English (MA, MFA); geology (MS, PhD); geophysics (MS, PhD); interdisciplinary studies (MA, MS); music (MM); music education (MM); pedagogy (MM); performance (MM); raptor biology (MS); technical communication (MA); visual arts (MFA). Electronic applications accepted.

College of Business and Economics *Degree program information:* Part-time programs available. Offers accountancy (MSA); business administration (MBA); business and economics (MBA, MSA); information technology management (MBA); taxation (MSA). Electronic applications accepted.

College of Education *Degree program information:* Part-time programs available. Offers athletic administration (MPE); counseling (MA); counselor education (MA); curriculum and instruction (Ed D); curriculum instruction (MA); early childhood education (M Ed, MA); education (M Ed, MA, MET, MPE, MS, MS Ed, Ed D); educational leadership (M Ed); educational technology (MET, MS, MS Ed); exercise and sports studies (MS); physical education (MPE); reading (MA); special education (M Ed, MA). Electronic applications accepted.

College of Engineering *Degree program information:* Part-time programs available. Postbaccalaureate distance learning degree programs offered (no on-campus study). Offers civil engineering (M Engr, MS); computer engineering (M Engr, MS); computer science (MS); electrical and computer engineering (PhD); electrical engineering (M Engr, MS); engineering (M Engr, MS, PhD); instructional and performance technology (MS); materials science and engineering (M Engr, MS); mechanical engineering (M Engr, MS). Electronic applications accepted.

College of Health Science *Degree program information:* Part-time programs available. Offers health science (MHS). Electronic applications accepted.

College of Social Sciences and Public Affairs *Degree program information:* Part-time programs available. Offers communication (MA); criminal justice administration (MA); environmental and natural resources policy and administration (MPA); general public administration (MPA); history (MA); social sciences and public affairs (MA, MPA, MSW); social work (MSW); state and local government policy and administration (MPA). Electronic applications accepted.

BORICUA COLLEGE, New York, NY 10032-1560

General Information Independent, coed, comprehensive institution.

GRADUATE UNITS

Program in Human Services (Brooklyn Campus) *Degree program information:* Evening/weekend programs available. Offers human services (MS).

Program in Human Services (Manhattan Campus) *Degree program information:* Evening/weekend programs available. Offers human services (MS).

Program in Latin American and Caribbean Studies (Brooklyn Campus) *Degree program information:* Evening/weekend programs available. Offers Latin American and Caribbean studies (MA).

Program in Latin American and Caribbean Studies (Manhattan Campus) *Degree program information:* Evening/weekend programs available. Offers Latin American and Caribbean studies (MA).

BOSTON ARCHITECTURAL COLLEGE, Boston, MA 02115-2795

General Information Independent, coed, comprehensive institution.

GRADUATE UNITS

Graduate Programs Offers architecture (M Arch); interior design (MID). Electronic applications accepted.

BOSTON COLLEGE, Chestnut Hill, MA 02467-3800

General Information Independent-religious, coed, university. CGS member. *Enrollment:* 13,903 graduate, professional, and undergraduate students; 2,540 full-time matriculated graduate/professional students (1,457 women), 2,303 part-time matriculated graduate/professional students (1,268 women). *Graduate faculty:* 679. *Tuition:* Part-time $1148 per credit. *Graduate housing:* Rooms and/or apartments available on a first-come, first-served basis to single and married students. *Student services:* Campus employment opportunities, campus safety program, career counseling, child daycare facilities, exercise/wellness program, free psychological counseling, grant writing training, international student services, low-cost health insurance, multicultural affairs office, services for students with disabilities, teacher training, writing training. *Library facilities:* Thomas P. O'Neill Library plus 7 others. *Online resources:* library catalog, web page. *Collection:* 2.7 million titles, 31,664 serial subscriptions, 171,099 audiovisual materials.

Computer facilities: Computer purchase and lease plans are available. 1,000 computers available on campus for general student use. A campuswide network can be accessed from student residence rooms and from off campus. Online class registration is available. *Web address:* http://www.bc.edu/.

General Application Contact: Robert V. Howe, Associate Dean, 617-552-3265, Fax: 617-552-3700, E-mail: hower@bc.edu.

GRADUATE UNITS

The Carroll School of Management Students: 376 full-time (140 women), 549 part-time (168 women); includes 95 minority (10 African Americans, 1 American Indian/Alaska Native, 73 Asian Americans or Pacific Islanders, 11 Hispanic Americans), 132 international. Average age 28. 2,099 applicants, 30% accepted, 360 enrolled. *Faculty:* 89 full-time (31 women), 121 part-time/adjunct. Expenses: Contact institution. *Financial support:* In 2008–09, 241 fellowships with full tuition reimbursements, 149 research assistantships with full and partial tuition reimbursements were awarded; teaching assistantships, career-related internships or fieldwork, Federal Work-Study, institutionally sponsored loans, scholarships/grants, tuition waivers (full and partial), and unspecified assistantships also available. Support available to part-time students. Financial award application deadline: 3/1; financial award applicants required to submit FAFSA. In 2008, 372 master's, 6 doctorates awarded. *Degree program information:* Part-time and evening/weekend programs available. Offers accounting (MSA); business administration (MBA); finance (MSF, PhD); management (MBA, MSA, MSF, PhD); organization studies (PhD). *Application fee:* $100. Electronic applications accepted. *Application Contact:* Shelley A. Burt, Director of Graduate Enrollment, 617-552-3920, Fax: 617-552-8078, E-mail: bcmba@bc.edu. *Associate Dean for Graduate Programs*, Dr. Jeffrey L. Ringuest, 617-552-9100, Fax: 617-552-0514, E-mail: jeffrey.ringuest@bc.edu.

Graduate School of Arts and Sciences Students: 303 full-time (143 women), 656 part-time (295 women); includes 92 minority (18 African Americans, 2 American Indian/Alaska Native, 41 Asian Americans or Pacific Islanders, 31 Hispanic Americans), 219 international. 2,600 applicants, 15% accepted, 175 enrolled. *Faculty:* 428 full-time (132 women). Expenses: Contact institution. *Financial support:* Fellowships with full and partial tuition reimbursements, research assistantships with full and partial tuition reimbursements, teaching assistantships with full and partial tuition reimbursements, career-related internships or fieldwork, Federal Work-Study, scholarships/grants, and tuition waivers (full and partial) available. Support available to part-time students. Financial award application deadline: 3/1; financial award applicants required to submit FAFSA. In 2008, 113 master's, 38 doctorates awarded. *Degree program information:* Part-time programs available. Offers arts and sciences (M Div, MA, MS, MST, MTS, Th M, PhD, STD, STL); biochemistry (PhD); biology (PhD); classics (MA); economics (PhD); English (MA, PhD); European national studies (MA); French (MA, PhD); geology and geophysics (MS); Greek (MA); history (MA, PhD); inorganic chemistry (PhD); Italian (MA); Latin (MA); linguistics (MA); mathematics (MA); medieval language (PhD); medieval studies (MA); organic chemistry (PhD); philosophy (MA, PhD); physical chemistry (PhD); physics (MS, PhD); political science (MA, PhD); psychology (MA, PhD); Russian and Slavic languages and literature (MA); science education (MST); Slavic studies (MA); sociology (MA, PhD); Spanish (MA, PhD); theology (PhD). *Application deadline:* For fall admission, 1/2 priority date for domestic and international students. *Application fee:* $70. Electronic applications accepted. *Application Contact:* Robert V. Howe, Associate Dean, 617-552-3265, Fax: 617-552-3700, E-mail: hower@bc.edu. *Dean*, Dr. David Quigley, 617-552-2393, E-mail: david.quigley@bc.edu.

School of Theology and Ministry *Degree program information:* Part-time programs available. Offers church leadership (MA); divinity (M Div); pastoral ministry (MA); religious education (MA, PhD); sacred theology (STD, STL); social justice/social ministry (MA); spiritual direction (MA); theological studies (MTS); theology (Th M, PhD); youth ministry (MA). Electronic applications accepted.

Graduate School of Social Work Students: 420 full-time (362 women), 77 part-time (72 women); includes 89 minority (36 African Americans, 1 American Indian/Alaska Native, 26 Asian Americans or Pacific Islanders, 26 Hispanic Americans), 19 international. 728 applicants, 67% accepted, 184 enrolled. *Faculty:* 17 full-time (9 women), 37 part-time/adjunct (23 women). Expenses: Contact institution. *Financial support:* In 2008–09, 378 students received support, including 15 fellowships with full tuition reimbursements available (averaging $18,000 per year), 2 research assistantships with full tuition reimbursements available (averaging $6,000 per year); teaching assistantships, career-related internships or fieldwork, Federal Work-Study, institutionally sponsored loans, scholarships/grants, traineeships, tuition waivers (partial), and unspecified assistantships also available. Support available to part-time students. Financial award applicants required to submit FAFSA. In 2008, 213 master's, 6 doctorates awarded. *Degree program information:* Part-time programs available. Offers social work (MSW, PhD). *Application deadline:* For fall admission, 3/1 for domestic students. Applications are processed on a rolling basis. *Application fee:* $40. *Application Contact:* Dr. William Howard, Director of Admission, 617-552-4024, Fax: 617-552-1690, E-mail: william.howard@bc.edu. *Dean*, Dr. Alberto Godenzi, 617-552-0866, Fax: 617-552-2374, E-mail: godenzi@bc.edu.

Law School Students: 799 full-time (369 women); includes 168 minority (34 African Americans, 4 American Indian/Alaska Native, 83 Asian Americans or Pacific Islanders, 47 Hispanic Americans), 17 international. Average age 24. 6,552 applicants, 20% accepted, 299 enrolled. *Faculty:* 53 full-time (19 women), 40 part-time/adjunct (17 women). Expenses: Contact institution. *Financial support:* In 2008–09, 426 students received support. Career-related internships or fieldwork, Federal Work-Study, institutionally sponsored loans, scholarships/grants, and tuition waivers (partial) available. Financial award application deadline: 3/15; financial award applicants required to submit FAFSA. In 2008, 271 JDs awarded. Offers law (JD). *Application deadline:* For fall admission, 3/1 for domestic and international students. Applications are processed on a rolling basis. *Application fee:* $75. Electronic applications accepted. *Application Contact:* Rita C. Jones, Assistant Dean for Admissions and Financial Aid, 617-552-4351, Fax: 617-552-2917, E-mail: rita.jones@bc.edu. *Dean*, John H. Garvey, 617-552-4340, Fax: 617-552-2851.

Lynch Graduate School of Education *Degree program information:* Part-time and evening/weekend programs available. Offers biology (MST); chemistry (MST); counseling psychology (MA, PhD); curriculum and instruction (M Ed, PhD, CAES); developmental and educational psychology (MA, PhD); early childhood education/teacher option (M Ed); early childhood/specialist option (MA); education (M Ed, MA, MAT, MST, Ed D, PhD, CAES); educational administration (M Ed, CAES); educational research, measurement, and evaluation (M Ed, PhD); elementary education (M Ed); English (MAT); French (MAT); geology (MST); higher education (MA, PhD); history (MAT); Latin and classical humanities (MAT); mathematics (MST); physics (MST); professional school administrator (Ed D); reading specialist (M Ed, CAES); religious education (M Ed, CAES); secondary education (M Ed, MAT, MST); second-

Boston College (continued)

ary teaching (M Ed); Spanish (MAT); special needs: moderate disabilities (M Ed, CAES); special needs: severe disabilities (M Ed). Electronic applications accepted.

William F. Connell School of Nursing Students: 185 full-time (173 women), 77 part-time (75 women); includes 23 minority (7 African Americans, 1 American Indian/Alaska Native, 13 Asian Americans or Pacific Islanders, 2 Hispanic Americans), 7 international. Average age 34. 327 applicants, 54% accepted, 96 enrolled. *Faculty:* 46 full-time (44 women), 26 part-time/adjunct (25 women). Expenses: Contact institution. *Financial support:* In 2008–09, 102 students received support, including 11 fellowships with partial tuition reimbursements available (averaging $12,092 per year), 10 research assistantships (averaging $19,500 per year), 5 teaching assistantships (averaging $13,346 per year); Federal Work-Study, institutionally sponsored loans, scholarships/grants, traineeships, health care benefits, and tuition waivers (partial) also available. Support available to part-time students. Financial award application deadline: 3/1; financial award applicants required to submit FAFSA. In 2008, 57 master's, 7 doctorates awarded. *Degree program information:* Part-time programs available. Offers adult health nursing (MS); community health nursing (MS); family health (MS); forensic nursing (MS); gerontology (MS); maternal/child health nursing (MS); nurse anesthesia (MS); nursing (PhD); palliative care (MS); psychiatric-mental health nursing (MS). *Application deadline:* For fall admission, 11/1 for domestic and international students; for winter admission, 12/31 for domestic and international students; for spring admission, 9/15 for domestic and international students. Applications are processed on a rolling basis. *Application fee:* $40. Electronic applications accepted. *Application Contact:* Zanifer John-Bayard, Graduate Programs Assistant, 617-552-4928, Fax: 617-552-0745, E-mail: csongrad@bc.edu. *Dean,* Dr. Susan Gennaro, 617-552-4251, Fax: 617-552-0931, E-mail: susan.gennaro@bc.edu.

THE BOSTON CONSERVATORY, Boston, MA 02215

General Information Independent, coed, comprehensive institution. *Graduate housing:* Room and/or apartments available on a first-come, first-served basis to single students; on-campus housing not available to married students. Housing application deadline: 12/1.

GRADUATE UNITS

Graduate Division *Degree program information:* Part-time programs available. Offers choral conducting (MM); composition (MM); music (MM, ADP, Certificate); music education (MM); music performance (MM, ADP, Certificate); opera (MM, ADP, Certificate); theater (MM). Electronic applications accepted.

BOSTON GRADUATE SCHOOL OF PSYCHOANALYSIS, Brookline, MA 02446-4602

General Information Independent, coed, graduate-only institution. *Research affiliation:* Boston Institute for Psychotherapy (psychotherapy).

GRADUATE UNITS

Master's, Certificate, and Doctoral Programs *Degree program information:* Part-time programs available. Offers psychoanalysis (MA, Psya D, Certificate). Electronic applications accepted.

Master's Program—New York *Degree program information:* Part-time programs available. Offers psychoanalysis (MA).

Program in Psychoanalytic Counseling Offers psychoanalytic counseling (MA). Electronic applications accepted.

Programs in Psychoanalysis and Culture *Degree program information:* Evening/weekend programs available. Offers psychoanalysis and culture (MA, Psya D). Electronic applications accepted.

BOSTON UNIVERSITY, Boston, MA 02215

General Information Independent, coed, university. CGS member. *Enrollment:* 8,709 full-time matriculated graduate/professional students (4,700 women), 4,390 part-time matriculated graduate/professional students (2,300 women). *Enrollment by degree level:* 2,230 first professional, 8,361 master's, 2,339 doctoral, 169 other advanced degrees. *Tuition:* Full-time $36,540; part-time $1142 per credit. *Required fees:* $224 per semester. Tuition and fees vary according to course level, course load and program. *Graduate housing:* On-campus housing not available. *Student services:* Campus employment opportunities, campus safety program, career counseling, child daycare facilities, exercise/wellness program, free psychological counseling, international student services, low-cost health insurance, services for students with disabilities, writing training. *Library facilities:* Mugar Memorial Library plus 18 others. *Online resources:* library catalog, web page, access to other libraries' catalogs. *Collection:* 2.4 million titles, 33,983 serial subscriptions. *Research affiliation:* NASA–Ames Research Center, Society for the Preservation of New England Antiquities, Massachusetts Historical Society, Woods Hole Oceanographic Institution–Marine Biological Laboratory.

Computer facilities: Computer purchase and lease plans are available. 750 computers available on campus for general student use. A campuswide network can be accessed from student residence rooms and from off campus. Online class registration, research and educational networks are available. *Web address:* http://www.bu.edu/.

GRADUATE UNITS

College of Communication Students: 286 full-time (184 women), 25 part-time (15 women); includes 31 minority (9 African Americans, 2 American Indian/Alaska Native, 14 Asian Americans or Pacific Islanders, 6 Hispanic Americans), 65 international. Average age 26. 875 applicants, 48% accepted. *Faculty:* 57 full-time, 81 part-time/adjunct. Expenses: Contact institution. *Financial support:* In 2008–09, 290 students received support, including 18 teaching assistantships with partial tuition reimbursements available; career-related internships or fieldwork, Federal Work-Study, institutionally sponsored loans, scholarships/grants, and unspecified assistantships also available. Support available to part-time students. Financial award application deadline: 2/1; financial award applicants required to submit FAFSA. In 2008, 146 master's awarded. *Degree program information:* Part-time programs available. Offers advertising (MS); broadcast journalism (MS); business and economics journalism (MS); communication (MFA, MS); communication research (MS); communication studies (MS); film production (MFA); film studies (MFA); media ventures (MS); photojournalism (MS); print journalism (MS); public relations (MS); science journalism (MS); screenwriting (MFA); television production (MS). *Application deadline:* For fall admission, 2/1 for domestic and international students. *Application fee:* $70. Electronic applications accepted. *Application Contact:* Kate Iserman, Administrator of Graduate Services, 617-353-3481, Fax: 617-358-0399, E-mail: comgrad@bu.edu. *Dean,* Thomas Fiedler, 617-353-3450, Fax: 617-358-0399, E-mail: com@bu.edu.

College of Engineering Students: 452 full-time (111 women), 49 part-time (9 women); includes 50 minority (7 African Americans, 33 Asian Americans or Pacific Islanders, 10 Hispanic Americans), 208 international. Average age 25. 1,541 applicants, 25% accepted, 139 enrolled. *Faculty:* 119 full-time (14 women), 2 part-time/adjunct (0 women). Expenses: Contact institution. *Financial support:* In 2008–09, 390 students received support, including 41 fellowships with full tuition reimbursements available (averaging $26,250 per year), 225 research assistantships with full tuition reimbursements available (averaging $17,500 per year), 58 teaching assistantships with full tuition reimbursements available (averaging $17,500 per year); career-related internships or fieldwork, Federal Work-Study, institutionally sponsored loans, scholarships/grants, traineeships, health care benefits, and tuition waivers (full and partial) also available. Financial award application deadline: 1/15; financial award applicants required to submit FAFSA. In 2008, 100 master's, 45 doctorates awarded. *Degree program information:* Part-time programs available. Postbaccalaureate distance learning degree programs offered (no on-campus study). Offers biomedical engineering (M Eng, MS, PhD); computer engineering (MS, PhD); electrical engineering (MS, PhD); engineering (M Eng, MS, PhD); general engineering (MS); mechanical engineering (MS, PhD); photonics (MS). *Application deadline:* For fall admission, 4/1 for domestic and international students; for spring admission, 10/1 for domestic and international students. Applications are processed on a rolling basis. *Application fee:* $70. Electronic applications accepted. *Application Contact:* Cheryl Kelley, Director of Graduate Programs, 617-353-9760, Fax: 617-353-0259, E-mail: enggrad@bu.edu. *Dean,* Dr. Kenneth R. Lutchen, 617-353-2800, Fax: 617-358-3468, E-mail: klutch@bu.edu.

Division of Materials Science and Engineering Students: 18 full-time (2 women), 11 international. Average age 26. 23 applicants, 78% accepted, 12 enrolled. Expenses: Contact institution. *Financial support:* In 2008–09, 18 students received support, including 3 fellowships with full tuition reimbursements available (averaging $27,300 per year), 12 research assistantships with full tuition reimbursements available (averaging $18,200 per year), 3 teaching assistantships with full tuition reimbursements available (averaging $18,200 per year); career-related internships or fieldwork, Federal Work-Study, institutionally sponsored loans, scholarships/grants, traineeships, and health care benefits also available. Financial award application deadline: 1/15; financial award applicants required to submit FAFSA. *Degree program information:* Part-time programs available. Offers materials science and engineering (MS, PhD). *Application deadline:* For fall admission, 4/1 for domestic and international students; for spring admission, 10/1 for domestic and international students. Applications are processed on a rolling basis. *Application fee:* $70. Electronic applications accepted. *Application Contact:* Cheryl Kelley, Director of Graduate Programs, 617-353-9760, Fax: 617-353-0259, E-mail: enggrad@bu.edu. *Division Head,* Dr. Uday Pal, 617-353-7708, Fax: 617-353-5548, E-mail: upal@bu.edu.

Division of Systems Engineering Students: 28 full-time (5 women), 1 part-time (0 women); includes 1 minority (Asian American or Pacific Islander), 21 international. Average age 27. 2 applicants, 50% accepted, 1 enrolled. Expenses: Contact institution. *Financial support:* In 2008–09, 26 students received support, including 5 fellowships with full tuition reimbursements available (averaging $27,300 per year), 17 research assistantships with full tuition reimbursements available (averaging $18,200 per year), 3 teaching assistantships with full tuition reimbursements available (averaging $18,200 per year); career-related internships or fieldwork, Federal Work-Study, institutionally sponsored loans, scholarships/grants, traineeships, and health care benefits also available. Financial award application deadline: 1/15; financial award applicants required to submit FAFSA. In 2008, 4 doctorates awarded. *Degree program information:* Part-time programs available. Offers systems engineering (M Eng, MS, PhD). *Application deadline:* For fall admission, 4/1 for domestic and international students; for spring admission, 10/1 for domestic and international students. Applications are processed on a rolling basis. *Application fee:* $70. Electronic applications accepted. *Application Contact:* Cheryl Kelley, Director of Graduate Programs, 617-353-9760, Fax: 617-353-0259, E-mail: enggrad@bu.edu. *Division Head,* Dr. Christos Cassandras, 617-353-7154, Fax: 617-353-5548, E-mail: cgc@bu.edu.

College of Fine Arts Students: 879 full-time (515 women), 212 part-time (116 women); includes 118 minority (51 African Americans, 8 American Indian/Alaska Native, 24 Asian Americans or Pacific Islanders, 35 Hispanic Americans), 152 international. Average age 24. 1,335 applicants, 38% accepted. *Faculty:* 70 full-time, 38 part-time/adjunct. Expenses: Contact institution. *Financial support:* Fellowships, teaching assistantships, Federal Work-Study and scholarships/grants available. Support available to part-time students. Financial award application deadline: 2/1. In 2008, 129 master's, 11 doctorates, 13 other advanced degrees awarded. *Degree program information:* Part-time programs available. Offers art education (MA); collaborative piano (MM, DMA); composition (MM, DMA); conducting (MM, Artist Diploma, Performance Diploma); costume design (MFA); costume production (MFA); directing (MFA); fine arts (MFA, MM, DMA, Artist Diploma, Certificate, Performance Diploma); graphic design (MFA); historical performance (MM, DMA, Artist Diploma, Performance Diploma); lighting design (MFA); music education (MM, DMA); music theory (MM); musicology (MM); opera performance (Certificate); painting (MFA); performance (MM, DMA, Artist Diploma, Performance Diploma); scene design (MFA); sculpture (MFA); studio teaching (MA); technical production (MFA, Certificate); theatre crafts (Certificate); theatre education (MFA). *Application deadline:* For fall admission, 1/15 priority date for domestic and international students. *Application fee:* $70. Electronic applications accepted. *Application Contact:* Mark Krone, Manager, Graduate Admissions, 617-353-3350, E-mail: arts@bu.edu. *Interim Dean,* Walt Meissner, 617-353-3350.

College of Health and Rehabilitation Sciences—Sargent College Students: 340 full-time (303 women), 111 part-time (87 women); includes 46 minority (4 African Americans, 1 American Indian/Alaska Native, 27 Asian Americans or Pacific Islanders, 14 Hispanic Americans), 20 international. Average age 27. 763 applicants, 42% accepted, 110 enrolled. *Faculty:* 54 full-time (42 women), 44 part-time/adjunct (28 women). Expenses: Contact institution. *Financial support:* In 2008–09, 300 students received support, including 119 fellowships with full and partial tuition reimbursements available (averaging $15,000 per year), 9 research assistantships with partial tuition reimbursements available (averaging $18,000 per year), 15 teaching assistantships with partial tuition reimbursements available (averaging $6,000 per year); career-related internships or fieldwork, Federal Work-Study, institutionally sponsored loans, scholarships/grants, and health care benefits also available. Support available to part-time students. Financial award application deadline: 4/15; financial award applicants required to submit FAFSA. In 2008, 140 master's, 141 doctorates awarded. Postbaccalaureate distance learning degree programs offered (minimal on-campus study). Offers applied anatomy and physiology (MS, PhD); audiology (PhD); health and rehabilitation sciences (MS, MSOT, D Sc, DPT, OTD, PhD, CAGS); nutrition (MS); occupational therapy (MS, MSOT, OTD); physical therapy (DPT); rehabilitation sciences (D Sc); speech-language pathology (MS, PhD, CAGS). *Application deadline:* For fall admission, 2/1 priority date for domestic students. Applications are processed on a rolling basis. *Application fee:* $70. Electronic applications accepted. *Application Contact:* Sharon Sankey, Director, Student Services, 617-353-2713, Fax: 617-353-7500, E-mail: ssankey@bu.edu. *Dean,* Dr. Gloria S. Waters, 617-353-2704, Fax: 617-353-7500, E-mail: gwaters@bu.edu.

Goldman School of Dental Medicine Students: 796 full-time (386 women); includes 184 minority (11 African Americans, 3 American Indian/Alaska Native, 141 Asian Americans or Pacific Islanders, 29 Hispanic Americans), 279 international. Average age 28. Expenses: Contact institution. *Financial support:* In 2008–09, 480 students received support. Career-related internships or fieldwork and institutionally sponsored loans available. Financial award application deadline: 4/15; financial award applicants required to submit CSS PROFILE or FAFSA. In 2008, 169 first professional degrees, 21 master's, 13 doctorates, 58 other advanced degrees awarded. Offers advanced general dentistry (CAGS); dental medicine (DMD, MS, MSD, D Sc, D Sc D, PhD, CAGS); dental public health (MS, MSD, D Sc D, CAGS); dentistry (DMD); endodontics (MSD, D Sc D, CAGS); implantology (CAGS); operative dentistry (MSD, D Sc D, CAGS); oral and maxillofacial surgery (MSD, D Sc D, CAGS); oral biology (MSD, D Sc, D Sc D, PhD); orthodontics (MSD, D Sc D, CAGS); pediatric dentistry (MSD, D Sc D, CAGS); periodontology (MSD, D Sc D, CAGS); prosthodontics (MSD, D Sc D, CAGS). *Application deadline:* For fall admission, 3/1 for domestic students. Applications are processed on a rolling basis. *Application fee:* $60. *Application Contact:* 617-638-4787, Fax: 617-638-4798. *Interim Dean,* Dr. Jeffrey W. Hutter, 617-638-4780.

Graduate School of Arts and Sciences Students: 1,678 full-time (814 women), 237 part-time (137 women); includes 150 minority (40 African Americans, 6 American Indian/Alaska Native, 66 Asian Americans or Pacific Islanders, 38 Hispanic Americans), 610 international. Average age 30. 6,836 applicants, 25% accepted, 612 enrolled. Expenses: Contact institution. *Financial support:* In 2008–09, 1,200 students received support, including 102 fellowships with full tuition reimbursements available, 499 research assistantships with full tuition reimbursements available, 408 teaching assistantships with full tuition reimbursements available; career-related internships or fieldwork, Federal Work-Study, scholarships/grants, traineeships, and unspecified assistantships also available. Support available to part-time students. Financial award application deadline: 1/15; financial award applicants required to submit FAFSA. In 2008, 385 master's, 198 doctorates awarded. Offers African American studies (MA); African studies (Certificate); American and New England studies (PhD); anthropology (PhD); applied anthropology (MA); applied linguistics (MA, PhD); archaeological heritage management (MA); archaeology (MA, PhD); art history (MA, PhD); arts and sciences (MA, MAEP, MAPE, MFA, MS, PhD, Certificate); astronomy (MA, PhD); bioinformatics (MS, PhD); biology (MA, PhD); biostatistics (MA, PhD); cellular biophysics (PhD); chemistry (MA, PhD); classical studies (MA, PhD); cognitive and neural systems (MA, PhD); composition (MA); computer science (MA, PhD); creative writing (MA); earth sciences (MA, PhD); economic policy (MAEP); economics (MA, PhD); energy and environmental analysis (MA); English (MA, PhD); environmental remote sensing and GIs (MA); French language and literature (MA, PhD); geoarchaeology (MA); geography (MA); geography and environment (PhD); Hispanic language and literatures (MA, PhD); history (MA, PhD); international relations (MA); international relations and environmental policy (MA); international relations and environmental policy management (MA); international relations and international communication (MA); mathematical finance (MA); mathematics (MA, PhD); molecular biology, cell biology, and biochemistry (MA, PhD); museum studies (Certificate); music education (MA); music history/theory (PhD); musicology (MA, PhD); neuroscience (MA, PhD); philosophy (MA, PhD); physics (MA, PhD); political economy (MAPE); political science (MA, PhD); preservation studies (MA); psychology (MA, PhD); religious and theological studies (MA, PhD); sociology (MA, PhD); sociology and social work (PhD). *Application deadline:* For fall admission, 1/15 priority date for domestic and international students; for spring admission, 10/15 priority date for domestic and international students. *Application fee:* $70. Electronic applications accepted. *Application Contact:* Patricia A. Schiavoni, Admissions Officer, 617-353-2696, Fax: 617-358-5492, E-mail: grs@bu.edu. *Associate Dean,* J. Scott Whittaker, 617-353-2690, Fax: 617-358-0540.

Editorial Institute Students: 14 full-time (6 women), 1 international. Average age 35. 11 applicants, 64% accepted, 7 enrolled. Expenses: Contact institution. *Financial support:* In 2008–09, 12 students received support, including 3 teaching assistantships with full tuition reimbursements available (averaging $17,500 per year); Federal Work-Study, scholarships/grants, and unspecified assistantships also available. Support available to part-time students. Financial award application deadline: 1/15; financial award applicants required to submit FAFSA. Offers editorial studies (MA, PhD). *Application deadline:* For fall admission, 3/30 for domestic and international students. *Application fee:* $70. *Application Contact:* Alex Effgen, Administrative Assistant, 617-353-6631, Fax: 617-353-6917, E-mail: editinst@bu.edu. *Co-Director,* Archie Burnett, 617-353-6631, E-mail: burnetta@bu.edu.

Metropolitan College Students: 217 full-time (103 women), 2,046 part-time (892 women); includes 195 minority (52 African Americans, 6 American Indian/Alaska Native, 87 Asian Americans or Pacific Islanders, 50 Hispanic Americans), 375 international. Average age 34. *Faculty:* 33 full-time (6 women), 219 part-time/adjunct (63 women). Expenses: Contact institution. *Financial support:* In 2008–09, 948 students received support; fellowships, research assistantships, teaching assistantships, career-related internships or fieldwork, Federal Work-Study, institutionally sponsored loans, scholarships/grants, tuition waivers (full and partial), and unspecified assistantships available. Support available to part-time students. In 2008, 883 master's awarded. *Degree program information:* Part-time and evening/weekend programs available. Offers actuarial science (MS); advertising (MS); arts administration (MS, Graduate Certificate); banking and financial management (MSM); business continuity in emergency management (MSM); city planning (MCP); computer information systems (MS); computer science (MS); criminal justice (MCJ); economics development and tourism management (MSAS); electronic commerce, systems, and technology (MSAS); financial economics (MSAS); fundraising management (Graduate Certificate); gastronomy (MLA); health communication (MS); human resource management (MSM); innovation and technology (MSAS); insurance management (MSM); interdisciplinary studies (MLA); international market management (MSM); multinational commerce (MSAS); project management (MSM); telecommunications (MS); urban affairs (MUA). *Application deadline:* Applications are processed on a rolling basis. *Application fee:* $70. Electronic applications accepted. *Application Contact:* Dr. Jay Halfond, Dean, 617-353-6776, Fax: 617-353-6066, E-mail: jhalfond@bu.edu. *Dean,* Dr. Jay Halfond, 617-353-6776, Fax: 617-353-6066, E-mail: jhalfond@bu.edu.

School of Education *Degree program information:* Part-time programs available. Offers administration, training, and policy studies (Ed D); bilingual education (Ed M, CAGS); counseling (Ed M, CAGS); counseling psychology (Ed D); curriculum and teaching (Ed M, MAT, Ed D, CAGS); developmental studies (Ed M, Ed D, CAGS); early childhood education (Ed M, Ed D, CAGS); education (Ed M, MAT, Ed D, CAGS); education of the deaf (Ed M, CAGS); educational administration (Ed M); educational media and technology (Ed M, Ed D, CAGS); elementary education (Ed M); English and language arts education (Ed M, CAGS); health education (Ed M, CAGS); human resource education (Ed M, CAGS); international educational development (Ed M); Latin and classical studies (MAT); literacy and language (Ed D); mathematics education (Ed M, MAT, Ed D, CAGS); modern foreign language education (Ed M, MAT); physical education and coaching (Ed M, Ed D, CAGS); policy, planning, and administration (Ed M, CAGS); reading education (Ed M, Ed D, CAGS); science education (Ed M, MAT, Ed D, CAGS); social studies education (Ed M, MAT, Ed D, CAGS); special education (Ed M, Ed D, CAGS); teaching of English to speakers of other languages (Ed M, CAGS). Electronic applications accepted.

School of Law Students: 1,004 full-time (495 women), 107 part-time (59 women); includes 188 minority (37 African Americans, 3 American Indian/Alaska Native, 94 Asian Americans or Pacific Islanders, 54 Hispanic Americans), 161 international. Average age 27. 5,907 applicants, 29% accepted, 284 enrolled. *Faculty:* 58 full-time (19 women), 95 part-time/adjunct (31 women). Expenses: Contact institution. *Financial support:* In 2008–09, 493 students received support. Career-related internships or fieldwork, Federal Work-Study, institutionally sponsored loans, and scholarships/grants available. Financial award application deadline: 3/1; financial award applicants required to submit FAFSA. In 2008, 278 JDs, 197 master's awarded. Offers American law (LL M); banking (LL M); intellectual property law (LL M); law (JD); taxation (LL M). *Application deadline:* For fall admission, 3/1 for domestic and international students. Applications are processed on a rolling basis. *Application fee:* $75. Electronic applications accepted. *Application Contact:* Alissa Leonard, Director of Admissions and Financial Aid, 617-353-3100, Fax: 617-353-0578, E-mail: bulawadm@bu.edu. *Dean,* Maureen A. O'Rourke, 617-353-3112, Fax: 617-353-7400, E-mail: lawdean@bu.edu.

School of Management Students: 423 full-time (183 women), 671 part-time (267 women); includes 158 minority (19 African Americans, 2 American Indian/Alaska Native, 109 Asian Americans or Pacific Islanders, 28 Hispanic Americans), 222 international. Average age 32. 1,989 applicants, 35% accepted, 377 enrolled. *Faculty:* 74 full-time (17 women), 37 part-time/adjunct (7 women). Expenses: Contact institution. *Financial support:* Career-related internships or fieldwork, Federal Work-Study, institutionally sponsored loans, and tuition waivers (partial) available. Support available to part-time students. Financial award applicants required to submit FAFSA. In 2008, 347 master's, 7 doctorates awarded. *Degree program information:* Part-time and evening/weekend programs available. Offers accounting (DBA); advanced accounting (Certificate); business administration (Exec MBA, MBA, DBA, Certificate); entrepreneurship (MBA); finance (MBA); health sector management (MBA); information systems (DBA); international management (MBA); investment management (MSIM); management (Exec MBA, MA, MBA, MS, MSIM, DBA, PhD, Certificate); management policy (DBA); marketing (MBA, DBA); mathematical finance (MA, MS, PhD); operations management (DBA); organizational behavior (DBA); public and nonprofit management (MBA); strategy and business analysis (MBA). *Application deadline:* For fall admission, 1/5 for domestic students; for spring admission, 11/1 for domestic students. Applications are processed on a rolling basis. *Application fee:* $125. Electronic applications accepted. *Application Contact:* Hayden Estrada, Assistant Dean, Admissions, 617-353-2670, Fax: 617-353-7368, E-mail: mba@bu.edu. *Dean,* Louis Lataif, 617-353-2668, Fax: 617-353-5581, E-mail: lelataif@bu.edu.

School of Medicine Students: 1,429 full-time (797 women), 129 part-time (83 women); includes 341 minority (76 African Americans, 1 American Indian/Alaska Native, 203 Asian Americans or Pacific Islanders, 61 Hispanic Americans), 153 international. Average age 27. Expenses: Contact institution. *Financial support:* Fellowships, research assistantships, teaching assistantships, career-related internships or fieldwork, Federal Work-Study, and institutionally sponsored loans available. Support available to part-time students. In 2008, 149 first professional degrees, 248 master's, 38 doctorates awarded. *Degree program information:* Part-time and evening/weekend programs available. Offers medicine (MD, MA, MS, PhD). *Application Contact:* Dr. Robert Witzburg, Associate Dean for Admissions, 617-638-4630. *Dean,* Dr. Karen H. Antman, 617-638-5300.

Division of Graduate Medical Sciences Students: 505 full-time (246 women), 32 part-time (18 women); includes 106 minority (15 African Americans, 71 Asian Americans or Pacific Islanders, 20 Hispanic Americans), 59 international. Average age 26. *Faculty:* 80 full-time (20 women), 134 part-time/adjunct (19 women). Expenses: Contact institution. *Financial support:* In 2008–09, 38 fellowships with tuition reimbursements, 121 research assistantships with tuition reimbursements, 6 teaching assistantships with tuition reimbursements were awarded; Federal Work-Study, scholarships/grants, and traineeships also available. *Degree program information:* Part-time programs available. Offers biochemistry (MA, PhD); cell and molecular biology (PhD); immunology (PhD); medical sciences (MA, MS, PhD); microbiology (MA, PhD); molecular medicine (PhD); pharmacology and experimental therapeutics (MA, PhD). *Application deadline:* For spring admission, 10/15 priority date for domestic students. Electronic applications accepted. *Application Contact:* Michelle Hall, Assistant Director of Admissions, 617-638-5121, Fax: 617-638-5740, E-mail: natashah@bu.edu. *Associate Dean,* Dr. Carl Franzblau, 617-638-5120, Fax: 617-638-4842, E-mail: medsci@bu.edu.

School of Public Health Students: 764 (610 women); includes 142 minority (38 African Americans, 1 American Indian/Alaska Native, 74 Asian Americans or Pacific Islanders, 29 Hispanic Americans), 63 international. Average age 29. 1,829 applicants, 70% accepted, 272 enrolled. *Faculty:* 153 full-time, 271 part-time/adjunct. Expenses: Contact institution. *Financial support:* Fellowships, career-related internships or fieldwork, Federal Work-Study, institutionally sponsored loans, scholarships/grants, and traineeships available. Support available to part-time students. Financial award application deadline: 3/1; financial award applicants required to submit FAFSA. In 2008, 300 master's, 12 doctorates awarded. *Degree program information:* Part-time and evening/weekend programs available. Offers biostatistics (MA, MPH, PhD); environmental health (MPH, PhD); epidemiology (M Sc, MPH, PhD); health behavior, health promotion, and disease prevention (MPH); health law, bioethics and human rights (MPH); health policy and management (MPH); health services research (M Sc, PhD); international health (MPH, Dr PH, Certificate); maternal and child health (MPH, Dr PH); public health (M Sc, MA, MPH, Dr PH, PhD, Certificate); social behavioral sciences (Dr PH). *Application deadline:* For fall admission, 2/1 priority date for domestic and international students; for spring admission, 10/15 priority date for domestic and international students. Applications are processed on a rolling basis. *Application fee:* $95. Electronic applications accepted. *Application Contact:* LePhan Quan, Associate Director of Admissions, 617-638-4640, Fax: 617-638-5299, E-mail: asksph@bu.edu. *Dean,* Dr. Robert F. Meenan, 617-638-4640, Fax: 617-638-5299.

School of Social Work Students: 149 full-time (140 women), 190 part-time (163 women); includes 45 minority (19 African Americans, 1 American Indian/Alaska Native, 9 Asian Americans or Pacific Islanders, 16 Hispanic Americans), 5 international. Average age 31. *Faculty:* 22 full-time (16 women), 29 part-time/adjunct (23 women). Expenses: Contact institution. *Financial support:* In 2008–09, 1 research assistantship with full tuition reimbursement (averaging $8,000 per year) was awarded; career-related internships or fieldwork, Federal Work-Study, institutionally sponsored loans, and scholarships/grants also available. Support available to part-time students. Financial award application deadline: 3/1; financial award applicants required to submit FAFSA. In 2008, 147 master's awarded. *Degree program information:* Part-time programs available. Offers clinical practice with groups (MSW); clinical practice with individuals and families (MSW); macro social work practice (MSW); social work and sociology (PhD). *Application deadline:* For fall admission, 3/1 for domestic and international students. Applications are processed on a rolling basis. *Application fee:* $70. Electronic applications accepted. *Application Contact:* Edward M. Greene, Director of Admissions, 617-353-3765, Fax: 617-353-5612, E-mail: busswad@bu.edu. *Interim Dean,* Gail Steketee, 617-353-3760, Fax: 617-353-5612.

School of Theology Students: 249 full-time (111 women), 25 part-time (13 women); includes 37 minority (19 African Americans, 1 American Indian/Alaska Native, 7 Asian Americans or Pacific Islanders, 10 Hispanic Americans), 89 international. Average age 36. 229 applicants, 70% accepted. *Faculty:* 24 full-time (10 women), 18 part-time/adjunct (5 women). Expenses: Contact institution. *Financial support:* Fellowships, research assistantships, teaching assistantships, Federal Work-Study, institutionally sponsored loans, and scholarships/grants available. Support available to part-time students. Financial award application deadline: 7/15; financial award applicants required to submit FAFSA. In 2008, 36 first professional degrees, 55 master's, 9 doctorates awarded. *Degree program information:* Part-time programs available. Offers theology (M Div, MSM, MTS, STM, D Min, Th D). *Application deadline:* For fall admission, 1/15 priority date for domestic students; for spring admission, 10/1 priority date for domestic students. Applications are processed on a rolling basis. *Application fee:* $70. Electronic applications accepted. *Application Contact:* Rev. Earl R. Beane, Director of Admissions, 617-353-3036, Fax: 617-358-0140, E-mail: sthadmis@bu.edu. *Interim Dean,* Dr. Ray Hart, 617-353-3050, Fax: 617-353-3061.

See Close-Up on page 857.

BOWIE STATE UNIVERSITY, Bowie, MD 20715-9465

General Information State-supported, coed, comprehensive institution. CGS member. *Graduate housing:* Room and/or apartments available on a first-come, first-served basis to single students; on-campus housing not available to married students. Housing application deadline: 8/1.

GRADUATE UNITS

Graduate Programs *Degree program information:* Part-time and evening/weekend programs available. Offers administration of nursing services (MS); applied and computational mathematics (MS); business administration (MBA); computer science (MS, App Sc D); counseling psychology (MA); educational leadership (Ed D); elementary and secondary school administration (M Ed); elementary education (M Ed); English (MA); family nurse practitioner (MS); guidance and counseling (M Ed); human resource development (MA); information systems analyst (Certificate); management information systems (MS); mental halth counseling (MA); nursing education (MS); organizational communication (MA, Certificate); public administration (MPA); reading education (M Ed); school administration and supervision (M Ed); secondary education (M Ed); special education (M Ed); teaching (MAT). Electronic applications accepted.

BOWLING GREEN STATE UNIVERSITY, Bowling Green, OH 43403

General Information State-supported, coed, university. CGS member. *Graduate housing:* On-campus housing not available. *Research affiliation:* Spectra Group, Inc. (photoscience).

GRADUATE UNITS

Graduate College *Degree program information:* Part-time and evening/weekend programs available. Electronic applications accepted.

College of Arts and Sciences *Degree program information:* Part-time programs available. Offers 2-D studio art (MA, MFA); 3-D studio art (MA, MFA); American culture studies (MA, PhD); applied philosophy (PhD); applied statistics (MS); art education (MA); art history (MA); arts and sciences (MA, MAT, MFA, MPA, MS, PhD); biological sciences (MAT, MS, PhD); chemistry (MAT, MS); clinical psychology (MA, PhD); communication studies (MA, PhD); computer art (MA); computer science (MS); creative writing (MFA); demography and population studies (MA); design (MFA); developmental psychology (MA, PhD); digital arts (MFA); English (MA, PhD); experimental psychology (MA, PhD); fiction (MFA); French (MA, MAT); French education (MAT); geology (MS); geophysics (MS); German (MA, MAT); graphics (MFA); history (MA, MAT, PhD); industrial/organizational psychology (MA, PhD); institutional theory and history (PhD); literature (MA); mathematics (MA, MAT, PhD); philosophy (MA); photochemical sciences (PhD); physics (MAT, MS); poetry (MFA); popular culture (MA); public administration (MPA); public history (MA); quantitative psychology (MA, PhD); rhetoric and writing (PhD); scientific and technical communication (MA); social psychology (MA); sociology (PhD); Spanish (MA, MAT); Spanish education (MAT); statistics (PhD); theatre and film (MA, PhD). Electronic applications accepted.

College of Business Administration *Degree program information:* Part-time and evening/weekend programs available. Offers accountancy (M Acc); applied statistics (MS); business (MBA); business administration (M Acc, MA, MBA, MOD, MS); economics (MA); organization development (MOD). Electronic applications accepted.

College of Education and Human Development *Degree program information:* Part-time and evening/weekend programs available. Offers assistive technology (M Ed); business education (M Ed); classroom technology (M Ed); college student personnel (MA); counseling (M Ed, MA); cross-cultural and international education (MA); curriculum (M Ed); curriculum and teaching (M Ed); developmental kinesiology (M Ed); early childhood intervention

Bowling Green State University (continued)

(M Ed); education and human development (M Ed, MA, MFCS, MRC, Ed D, PhD, Ed S, Sp Ed); education and intervention services (M Ed, MA, MRC, Ed S, Sp Ed); educational administration and supervision (M Ed, Ed S); food and nutrition (MFCS); gifted education (M Ed); hearing impaired intervention (M Ed); higher education administration (PhD); human development and family studies (MFCS); leadership and policy studies (M Ed, MA, Ed D, PhD, Ed S); leadership studies (Ed D); master teaching (M Ed); mental health counseling (MA); mild/moderate intervention (M Ed); moderate/intensive intervention (M Ed); reading (M Ed, Ed S); recreation and leisure (M Ed); rehabilitation counseling (MRC); school counseling (M Ed); school psychology (M Ed, Sp Ed); special education (M Ed); sport administration (M Ed). Electronic applications accepted.

College of Health and Human Services *Degree program information:* Part-time and evening/weekend programs available. Offers communication disorders (PhD); criminal justice (MSCJ); health and human services (MPH, MS, MSCJ, PhD); public health (MPH); speech-language pathology (MS). Electronic applications accepted.

College of Musical Arts *Degree program information:* Part-time programs available. Offers composition (MM); contemporary music (DMA); ethnomusicology (MM); music education (MM); music history (MM); music theory (MM); performance (MM). Electronic applications accepted.

College of Technology *Degree program information:* Part-time programs available. Offers career and technology education (M Ed); construction management (MIT); manufacturing technology (MIT); technology (M Ed, MIT). Electronic applications accepted.

Interdisciplinary Studies *Degree program information:* Part-time programs available. Offers interdisciplinary studies (M Ed, MA, MS, PhD). Electronic applications accepted.

See Close-Up on page 859.

BRADLEY UNIVERSITY, Peoria, IL 61625-0002

General Information Independent, coed, comprehensive institution. CGS member. *Graduate housing:* Room and/or apartments available to single students; on-campus housing not available to married students. *Research affiliation:* Northern Research Laboratory, Peoria School of Medicine, Caterpillar, Inc., Ford Motor Credit/Visteon, Illinois Manufacturing Extension Center.

GRADUATE UNITS

Graduate School *Degree program information:* Part-time and evening/weekend programs available.

College of Education and Health Sciences *Degree program information:* Part-time and evening/weekend programs available. Offers curriculum and instruction (MA, Certificate); education and health sciences (MA, MSN, DPT, Certificate); human development counseling (MA); leadership in educational administration (MA); leadership in human service administration (MA); nurse administered anesthesia (MSN); nursing administration (MSN); physical therapy (DPT).

College of Engineering and Technology *Degree program information:* Part-time and evening/weekend programs available. Offers civil engineering and construction (MSCE); electrical engineering (MSEE); engineering and technology (MSCE, MSEE, MSIE, MSME, MSMFE); industrial engineering (MSIE); manufacturing engineering (MSIE); mechanical engineering (MSME).

College of Liberal Arts and Sciences *Degree program information:* Part-time and evening/weekend programs available. Offers biology (MS); chemistry (MS); computer information systems (MS); computer science (MS); English (MA); liberal arts and sciences (MA, MLS, MS); liberal studies (MLS).

Foster College of Business Administration *Degree program information:* Part-time and evening/weekend programs available. Offers accounting (MSA); business administration (MBA, MSA).

Slane College of Communications and Fine Arts *Degree program information:* Part-time and evening/weekend programs available. Offers ceramics (MA, MFA); communications and fine arts (MA, MFA); drawing/illustration (MA, MFA); interdisciplinary art (MA, MFA); painting (MA, MFA); photography (MA, MFA); printmaking (MA, MFA); sculpture (MA, MFA); visual communication and design (MA, MFA).

BRANDEIS UNIVERSITY, Waltham, MA 02454-9110

General Information Independent, coed, university. *Enrollment:* 5,327 graduate, professional, and undergraduate students; 1,535 full-time matriculated graduate/professional students (851 women), 347 part-time matriculated graduate/professional students (118 women). *Enrollment by degree level:* 1,147 master's, 693 doctoral, 42 other advanced degrees. *Graduate faculty:* 360 full-time (138 women), 176 part-time/adjunct (86 women). *Tuition:* Full-time $36,122; part-time $4515 per course. *Required fees:* $294; $294 per year. Full-time tuition and fees vary according to course load, program and student level. *Graduate housing:* Room and/or apartments available on a first-come, first-served basis to single students; on-campus housing not available to married students. Typical cost: $6950 per year. Housing application deadline: 6/1. *Student services:* Campus employment opportunities, campus safety program, career counseling, child daycare facilities, exercise/wellness program, free psychological counseling, grant writing training, international student services, low-cost health insurance, multicultural affairs office, services for students with disabilities, teacher training, writing training. *Library facilities:* Goldfarb Library plus 2 others. *Online resources:* library catalog, web page, access to other libraries' catalogs. *Collection:* 1.2 million titles, 35,125 serial subscriptions, 40,773 audiovisual materials.

Computer facilities: Computer purchase and lease plans are available. 104 computers available on campus for general student use. A campuswide network can be accessed from student residence rooms and from off campus. Online class registration, educational software are available. *Web address:* http://www.brandeis.edu/.

General Application Contact: 781-736-3410, Fax: 781-736-2000.

GRADUATE UNITS

Graduate School of Arts and Sciences Students: 774 full-time (404 women), 27 part-time (17 women); includes 58 minority (19 African Americans, 1 American Indian/Alaska Native, 15 Asian Americans or Pacific Islanders, 23 Hispanic Americans), 199 international. Average age 30. 1,856 applicants, 40% accepted, 314 enrolled. *Faculty:* 317 full-time (119 women), 91 part-time/adjunct (58 women). Expenses: Contact institution. *Financial support:* Fellowships with full and partial tuition reimbursements, research assistantships with full and partial tuition reimbursements, teaching assistantships with full and partial tuition reimbursements, career-related internships or fieldwork, institutionally sponsored loans, scholarships/grants, health care benefits, tuition waivers (full and partial), and unspecified assistantships available. Support available to part-time students. Financial award applicants required to submit FAFSA. In 2008, 172 master's, 65 doctorates, 14 other advanced degrees awarded. *Degree program information:* Part-time programs available. Offers acting (MFA); ancient Greek and Roman studies (MA, Graduate Certificate); anthropology (MA, PhD); anthropology and women's and gender studies (MA); arts and sciences (MA, MAT, MFA, MS, PhD, Certificate, Graduate Certificate, Postbaccalaureate Certificate); biochemistry (MS, PhD); biophysics and structural biology (MS, PhD); brain, body and behavior (PhD); coexistence and conflict (MA); cognitive neuroscience (PhD); composition and theory (MA, MFA, PhD); computational linguistics (MA); cultural production (MA); design (MFA); English and American literature (MA, PhD); English and women's and gender studies (MA); English and women's studies (MA); general psychology (MA); genetic counseling (MS); genetics (PhD); global studies (MA); history (MA, PhD); inorganic chemistry (MS, PhD); Jewish day school (MAT); Jewish professional leadershipmathematics (MA, PhD, Postbaccalaureate Certificate); microbiology (PhD); molecular and cell biology (MS, PhD); molecular biology (PhD); music and women's and gender studies (MA); music and women's studies (MA); musicology (MA, MFA, PhD); Near Eastern and Judaic studies (MA, PhD); Near Eastern and Judaic studies and sociology (PhD); Near Eastern and Judaic studies and women's and gender studies (MA); Near Eastern and Judaic studies and women's studies (MA); neurobiology (PhD); neuroscience (MS, PhD); organic chemistry (MS, PhD); philosophy (MA); physical chemistry (MS, PhD); physics (MS, PhD); politics (MA, PhD); premedical studies (Certificate); public education elementary (MAT); public policy and gender studies (MA); secondary education (English, history, biology, Bible) (MAT); social policy and sociology (PhD); social/developmental psychology (PhD); sociology (MA, PhD); sociology and women';s and gender studies (MA); sociology and women's and gender studies (MA); studio art (Certificate); sustainable international development and women';s/gender studies (MA); teaching of Hebrew (MAT). *Application deadline:* For fall admission, 1/15 priority date for domestic and international students; for spring admission, 11/1 for domestic and international students. Applications are processed on a rolling basis. *Application fee:* $75. Electronic applications accepted. *Application Contact:* David F. Cotter, Assistant Dean, Graduate School of Arts and Sciences, 781-736-3410, Fax: 781-736-3412, E-mail: gradschool@brandeis.edu. *Dean,* Dr. Gregory L. Freeze, 781-736-3410, Fax: 781-736-3412, E-mail: gradschool@brandeis.edu.

Michtom School of Computer Science Students: 42 full-time (11 women), 2 part-time (0 women); includes 3 minority (1 African American, 2 Asian Americans or Pacific Islanders), 18 international. Average age 26. 68 applicants, 76% accepted, 20 enrolled. *Faculty:* 10 full-time (1 woman), 1 part-time/adjunct (0 women). Expenses: Contact institution. *Financial support:* In 2008–09, 23 students received support, including 10 fellowships with full tuition reimbursements available (averaging $17,500 per year), 12 research assistantships with full tuition reimbursements available (averaging $17,500 per year), 1 teaching assistantship with partial tuition reimbursement available (averaging $3,200 per year); scholarships/grants, health care benefits, and tuition waivers (full and partial) also available. Support available to part-time students. Financial award application deadline: 4/15; financial award applicants required to submit FAFSA. In 2008, 11 master's, 4 doctorates, 1 other advanced degree awarded. *Degree program information:* Part-time programs available. Offers computer science (MA, PhD); computer science and IT entrepreneurship (MA). *Application deadline:* For fall admission, 1/15 for domestic students. *Application fee:* $75. Electronic applications accepted. *Application Contact:* Myrna Fox, Department Administrator, 781-736-2701, E-mail: maf@cs.brandeis.edu. *Graduate Chair,* Dr. Richard Alterman, 781-736-2700, Fax: 781-736-2741, E-mail: ralterma@brandeis.edu.

The Heller School for Social Policy and Management Expenses: Contact institution. *Financial support:* Fellowships with full and partial tuition reimbursements, research assistantships, teaching assistantships, institutionally sponsored loans, scholarships/grants, traineeships, health care benefits, tuition waivers (full and partial), and unspecified assistantships available. Financial award application deadline: 2/15; financial award applicants required to submit CSS PROFILE or FAFSA. *Degree program information:* Part-time programs available. Offers aging (MPP); aging services management (MBA); assets and inequalities (PhD); behavioral health (MPP); child, youth, and family management (MBA); children, youth and families (MPP, PhD); general social policy (MPP); health (MPP); health and behavioral health (PhD); health care management (MBA); international development (MA); international health policy and management (MS); poverty alleviation and development (MPP); social impact management (MBA); social policy and management (MBA); sustainable development (MA, MBA). *Application deadline:* For fall admission, 12/15 for domestic students; for winter admission, 2/15 for domestic students; for spring admission, 6/1 for domestic students. Applications are processed on a rolling basis. *Application fee:* $50. Electronic applications accepted. *Application Contact:* Lisa Hamlin Sherry, Assistant Director for Admissions and Financial Aid, 781-736-3835, Fax: 781-736-3881, E-mail: sherry@brandeis.edu. *Dean,* Stuart Altman, 781-736-3803, E-mail: altman@brandeis.edu.

International Business School *Degree program information:* Part-time and evening/weekend programs available. Offers finance (MSF); international business (MBAi); international economics and finance (MA, PhD); international finance/international economics (MBAi). Electronic applications accepted.

Rabb School of Continuing Studies, Division of Graduate Professional Studies Students: 3 full-time (0 women), 226 part-time (58 women); includes 35 minority (9 African Americans, 22 Asian Americans or Pacific Islanders, 4 Hispanic Americans). Average age 35. 76 applicants, 100% accepted, 76 enrolled. *Faculty:* 2 full-time (both women), 34 part-time/adjunct (7 women). Expenses: Contact institution. In 2008, 94 master's, 14 other advanced degrees awarded. *Degree program information:* Part-time and evening/weekend programs available. Postbaccalaureate distance learning degree programs offered (no on-campus study). Offers bioinformatics (MS, Graduate Certificate); information assurance (MS, Graduate Certificate); information technology management (MS, Graduate Certificate); management of projects and programs (MS, Graduate Certificate); software engineering (MSE, Graduate Certificate); virtual team management and communication (MS, Graduate Certificate). *Application deadline:* For fall admission, 6/15 priority date for domestic students; for winter admission, 10/15 priority date for domestic students; for spring admission, 2/15 priority date for domestic students. Applications are processed on a rolling basis. *Application fee:* $50. Electronic applications accepted. *Application Contact:* Frances Stearns, Associate Director of Admissions and Student Services, 781-736-8785, Fax: 781-736-3420, E-mail: fstearns@brandeis.edu. *Executive Director,* Sybil P. Smith, 781-736-3443, Fax: 781-736-3420, E-mail: sysmith@brandeis.edu.

BRANDON UNIVERSITY, Brandon, MB R7A 6A9, Canada

General Information Province-supported, coed, comprehensive institution. *Graduate housing:* Room and/or apartments available on a first-come, first-served basis to single students; on-campus housing not available to married students.

GRADUATE UNITS

Department of Rural Development Offers rural development (MRD, Diploma). Electronic applications accepted.

Faculty of Education Offers curriculum and instruction (M Ed, Diploma); educational administration (M Ed, Diploma); guidance and counseling (M Ed, Diploma); special education (M Ed, Diploma).

School of Music *Degree program information:* Part-time programs available. Offers composition (M Mus); music education (M Mus); performance and literature (M Mus). Electronic applications accepted.

BRENAU UNIVERSITY, Gainesville, GA 30501

General Information Independent, women only, comprehensive institution. *Enrollment:* 893 graduate, professional, and undergraduate students; 316 full-time matriculated graduate/professional students (271 women), 384 part-time matriculated graduate/professional students (300 women). *Enrollment by degree level:* 664 master's, 36 other advanced degrees. *Graduate faculty:* 54 full-time (35 women), 69 part-time/adjunct (34 women). Tuition and fees vary according to course load, campus/location and program. *Student services:* Campus employment opportunities, career counseling, exercise/wellness program, international student services, teacher training. *Library facilities:* Trustee Library. *Online resources:* library catalog, web page. *Collection:* 86,878 titles, 15,541 serial subscriptions, 2,954 audiovisual materials.

Computer facilities: 200 computers available on campus for general student use. A campuswide network can be accessed from student residence rooms. Online class registration is available. *Web address:* http://www.brenau.edu/.

General Application Contact: Michelle Leavell, Graduate Admissions Specialist, 770-538-4390, Fax: 770-538-4701, E-mail: mleavell@brenau.edu.

GRADUATE UNITS

Graduate Programs Students: 316 full-time (271 women), 384 part-time (300 women); includes 135 minority (106 African Americans, 2 American Indian/Alaska Native, 11 Asian Americans or Pacific Islanders, 16 Hispanic Americans), 18 international. Average age 34. 472 applicants, 56% accepted, 210 enrolled. *Faculty:* 54 full-time (35 women), 69 part-time/adjunct (34 women). Expenses: Contact institution. *Financial support:* In 2008–09, 35 students received support. Scholarships/grants, traineeships, and Athletic Grant-in-Aid available. Support available to part-time students. Financial award application deadline: 7/15; financial award applicants required to submit FAFSA. In 2008, 284 master's awarded. *Degree program information:* Part-time and evening/weekend programs available. Postbaccalaureate distance learning degree programs offered (no on-campus study). *Application deadline:* Applications are processed on a rolling basis. *Application fee:* $35. *Application Contact:* Michelle Leavell,

Graduate Admissions Specialist, 770-538-4390, Fax: 770-538-4701, E-mail: mleavell@brenau.edu. *Vice President for Academic Services/Dean of Faculty*, Dr. James Southerland, 770-534-6119.

School of Business and Mass Communication Students: 87 full-time (54 women), 178 part-time (115 women); includes 63 minority (53 African Americans, 5 Asian Americans or Pacific Islanders, 5 Hispanic Americans), 13 international. Average age 34. 148 applicants, 67% accepted, 76 enrolled. *Faculty:* 12 full-time (4 women), 29 part-time/adjunct (5 women). Expenses: Contact institution. *Financial support:* In 2008–09, 1 student received support. Athletic Grant-in-Aid available. Financial award application deadline: 7/15; financial award applicants required to submit FAFSA. In 2008, 101 master's awarded. *Degree program information:* Part-time and evening/weekend programs available. Postbaccalaureate distance learning degree programs offered (no on-campus study). Offers accounting (MBA); advanced management studies (MBA); business administration (MBA); healthcare management (MBA); organizational leadership (MS); project management (MBA). *Application deadline:* Applications are processed on a rolling basis. *Application fee:* $35. Electronic applications accepted. *Application Contact:* Michelle Leavell, Graduate Admissions Specialist, 770-538-4390, Fax: 770-538-4701, E-mail: mleavell@brenau.edu. *Dean*, Dr. William S. Lightfoot, 770-538-5330, Fax: 770-537-4701, E-mail: wlightfoot@brenau.edu.

School of Education Students: 154 full-time (144 women), 147 part-time (131 women); includes 36 minority (25 African Americans, 3 Asian Americans or Pacific Islanders, 8 Hispanic Americans), 3 international. Average age 35. 226 applicants, 44% accepted, 74 enrolled. *Faculty:* 15 full-time (10 women), 31 part-time/adjunct (21 women). Expenses: Contact institution. *Financial support:* In 2008–09, 2 students received support. Scholarships/grants available. Support available to part-time students. Financial award application deadline: 7/15; financial award applicants required to submit FAFSA. In 2008, 143 master's awarded. *Degree program information:* Part-time and evening/weekend programs available. Postbaccalaureate distance learning degree programs offered (no on-campus study). Offers early childhood (Ed S); early childhood education (M Ed, MAT); middle grades (Ed S); middle grades education (M Ed, MAT); secondary education (MAT); special education (M Ed, MAT). *Application deadline:* Applications are processed on a rolling basis. *Application fee:* $35. Electronic applications accepted. *Application Contact:* Michelle Leavell, Graduate Admissions Specialist, 770-538-4390, Fax: 770-538-4701, E-mail: mleavell@brenau.edu. *Dean*, Dr. Lora Bailey, 770-534-6220, Fax: 770-534-6221, E-mail: lbailey@brenau.edu.

School of Fine Arts and Humanities Students: 6 full-time (all women). Average age 29. 77 applicants, 65% accepted, 20 enrolled. *Faculty:* 5 full-time (4 women), 1 (woman) part-time/adjunct. Expenses: Contact institution. *Degree program information:* Part-time programs available. Offers interior design (MID). *Application deadline:* Applications are processed on a rolling basis. *Application fee:* $35. Electronic applications accepted. *Application Contact:* Michelle Leavell, Admissions Coordinator, 770-538-4390, Fax: 770-538-4701, E-mail: mleavell@brenau.edu. *Dean*, Dr. Andrea Birch, E-mail: abirch@brenau.edu.

School of Health and Science Students: 69 full-time (67 women), 59 part-time (54 women); includes 36 minority (28 African Americans, 2 American Indian/Alaska Native, 3 Asian Americans or Pacific Islanders, 3 Hispanic Americans), 2 international. Average age 33. 75 applicants, 55% accepted, 28 enrolled. *Faculty:* 22 full-time (17 women), 8 part-time/adjunct (7 women). Expenses: Contact institution. *Financial support:* In 2008–09, 32 students received support. Scholarships/grants and traineeships available. Support available to part-time students. Financial award application deadline: 7/15; financial award applicants required to submit FAFSA. In 2008, 40 master's awarded. *Degree program information:* Part-time and evening/weekend programs available. Offers family nurse practitioner (MSN); nurse educator (MSN); nursing management (MSN); occupational therapy (MS); psychology (MS). *Application deadline:* Applications are processed on a rolling basis. *Application fee:* $35. Electronic applications accepted. *Application Contact:* Michelle Leavell, Admissions Coordinator, 770-538-4390, Fax: 770-538-4701, E-mail: mleavell@brenau.edu. *Dean*, Dr. Gale Starich, 777-718-5305, Fax: 770-297-5929, E-mail: gstarich@brenau.edu.

BRESCIA UNIVERSITY, Owensboro, KY 42301-3023

General Information Independent-religious, coed, comprehensive institution. *Graduate housing:* Room and/or apartments available to single students.

GRADUATE UNITS

Program in Curriculum and Instruction *Degree program information:* Part-time and evening/weekend programs available. Offers curriculum and instruction (MSCI). Electronic applications accepted.

Program in Management *Degree program information:* Part-time and evening/weekend programs available. Offers management (MSM).

BRIAR CLIFF UNIVERSITY, Sioux City, IA 51104-0100

General Information Independent-religious, coed, comprehensive institution. *Graduate housing:* Room and/or apartments available on a first-come, first-served basis to single students; on-campus housing not available to married students. Housing application deadline: 6/1.

GRADUATE UNITS

Program in Education Postbaccalaureate distance learning degree programs offered (minimal on-campus study). Offers education (MA). Program offered during the summer only. Electronic applications accepted.

Program in Human Resource Management *Degree program information:* Part-time and evening/weekend programs available. Offers human resource management (MA).

Program in Nursing *Degree program information:* Part-time and evening/weekend programs available. Offers nursing (MSN).

BRIDGEWATER STATE COLLEGE, Bridgewater, MA 02325-0001

General Information State-supported, coed, comprehensive institution. CGS member. *Graduate housing:* On-campus housing not available.

GRADUATE UNITS

School of Graduate Studies *Degree program information:* Part-time and evening/weekend programs available.

School of Arts and Sciences *Degree program information:* Part-time and evening/weekend programs available. Offers art (MAT); arts and sciences (MA, MAT, MPA, MS, MSW); biological sciences (MAT); computer science (MS); criminal justice (MS); English (MA, MAT); history (MAT); mathematics (MAT); physical sciences (MAT); physics (MAT); psychology (MA); public administration (MPA); social work (MSW).

School of Business *Degree program information:* Part-time and evening/weekend programs available. Offers accounting and finance (MSM); business (MSM); management (MSM).

School of Education and Allied Science *Degree program information:* Part-time and evening/weekend programs available. Offers counseling (M Ed, CAGS); early childhood education (M Ed); education and allied science (M Ed, MAT, MS, CAGS); educational leadership (M Ed, CAGS); elementary education (M Ed); health promotion (M Ed); instructional technology (M Ed); physical education (MS); reading (M Ed, CAGS); secondary education (MAT); special education (M Ed).

BRIERCREST SEMINARY, Caronport, SK S0H 0S0, Canada

General Information Independent-religious, coed, graduate-only institution. *Graduate housing:* Rooms and/or apartments guaranteed to single students and available on a first-come, first-served basis to married students.

GRADUATE UNITS

Graduate Programs *Degree program information:* Part-time programs available. Offers Biblical studies (M Div); leadership (MA); leadership and management (M Div); marriage and family counseling (MA); missions (MA); New Testament (MATS); Old Testament (MATS); organizational leadership (MA); pastoral counseling (M Div, MA); pastoral ministry (M Div); theological studies (M Div); theology (MATS); worship (M Div, MA); youth and family ministry (M Div, MA).

BRIGHAM YOUNG UNIVERSITY, Provo, UT 84602-1001

General Information Independent-religious, coed, university. CGS member. *Enrollment:* 34,244 graduate, professional, and undergraduate students; 1,927 full-time matriculated graduate/professional students (683 women), 1,228 part-time matriculated graduate/professional students (474 women). *Enrollment by degree level:* 446 first professional, 2,154 master's, 478 doctoral, 77 other advanced degrees. *Graduate faculty:* 1,048 full-time (177 women), 2 part-time/adjunct (1 woman). *Tuition:* Full-time $5160; part-time $287 per credit hour. Tuition and fees vary according to program and student's religious affiliation. *Graduate housing:* Rooms and/or apartments available on a first-come, first-served basis to single and married students. Typical cost: $3000 per year ($6000 including board) for single students; $4500 per year ($7500 including board) for married students. Room and board charges vary according to board plan. Housing application deadline: 7/1. *Student services:* Campus employment opportunities, campus safety program, career counseling, exercise/wellness program, free psychological counseling, international student services, low-cost health insurance, multicultural affairs office, services for students with disabilities, teacher training, writing training. *Library facilities:* Main library plus 2 others. *Online resources:* library catalog, web page, access to other libraries' catalogs. *Collection:* 3.5 million titles, 27,161 serial subscriptions.

Computer facilities: Computer purchase and lease plans are available. 2,000 computers available on campus for general student use. A campuswide network can be accessed from student residence rooms and from off campus. Online class registration is available. *Web address:* http://www.byu.edu/.

General Application Contact: Graduate Studies, 801-422-4091, Fax: 801-422-0270, E-mail: gradstudies@byu.edu.

GRADUATE UNITS

Graduate Studies Students: 1,927 full-time (683 women), 1,228 part-time (474 women); includes 226 minority (19 African Americans, 27 American Indian/Alaska Native, 101 Asian Americans or Pacific Islanders, 79 Hispanic Americans), 357 international. Average age 30. 2,828 applicants, 50% accepted, 1061 enrolled. *Faculty:* 1,048 full-time (177 women), 2 part-time/adjunct (1 woman). Expenses: Contact institution. *Financial support:* Fellowships, research assistantships, teaching assistantships, career-related internships or fieldwork, institutionally sponsored loans, and tuition waivers (full and partial) available. Support available to part-time students. Financial award applicants required to submit FAFSA. In 2008, 152 first professional degrees, 1,220 master's, 76 doctorates, 36 other advanced degrees awarded. *Degree program information:* Part-time and evening/weekend programs available. *Application deadline:* For fall admission, 1/10 priority date for domestic students; for winter admission, 2/1 priority date for domestic students; for spring admission, 2/1 priority date for domestic students. Applications are processed on a rolling basis. *Application fee:* $50. Electronic applications accepted. *Application Contact:* Kevin Green, Adviser, 801-422-7308, Fax: 801-422-0270, E-mail: gradstudies@byu.edu. *Dean*, Bonnie Brinton, 801-422-4465, Fax: 801-422-0270, E-mail: gradstudies@byu.edu.

College of Family, Home, and Social Sciences Students: 260 full-time (129 women), 14 part-time (6 women); includes 40 minority (3 African Americans, 5 American Indian/Alaska Native, 19 Asian Americans or Pacific Islanders, 13 Hispanic Americans), 11 international. Average age 28. 277 applicants, 42% accepted, 101 enrolled. *Faculty:* 79 full-time (20 women), 17 part-time/adjunct (7 women). Expenses: Contact institution. *Financial support:* In 2008–09, 148 students received support, including 5 fellowships with tuition reimbursements available (averaging $5,160 per year), 79 research assistantships with partial tuition reimbursements available (averaging $7,084 per year), 41 teaching assistantships with partial tuition reimbursements available (averaging $5,615 per year); career-related internships or fieldwork, institutionally sponsored loans, tuition waivers (full and partial), and administrative aides, paid field practica also available. Support available to part-time students. Financial award application deadline: 2/1; financial award applicants required to submit FAFSA. In 2008, 69 master's, 15 doctorates awarded. Offers anthropology (MA); clinical psychology (PhD); family, home, and social sciences (MA, MPP, MS, MSW, PhD); general psychology (MS); geography (MS); marriage and family therapy (MS, PhD); marriage, family and human development (MS, PhD); psychology (PhD); public policy (MPP); social work (MSW); sociology (MS). *Application deadline:* For fall admission, 1/5 for domestic and international students. *Application fee:* $50. Electronic applications accepted. *Application Contact:* Adviser, 801-422-4541, Fax: 801-378-5238, E-mail: gradstudies@byu.edu. *Dean*, Dr. David B. Magleby, 801-422-2083, Fax: 801-422-2084, E-mail: david_magleby@byu.edu.

College of Fine Arts and Communications Students: 110 full-time (69 women), 48 part-time (23 women); includes 15 minority (1 African American, 1 American Indian/Alaska Native, 10 Asian Americans or Pacific Islanders, 3 Hispanic Americans). Average age 29. 99 applicants, 54% accepted, 42 enrolled. *Faculty:* 99 full-time (23 women), 4 part-time/adjunct (2 women). Expenses: Contact institution. *Financial support:* In 2008–09, 129 students received support, including 28 research assistantships with full and partial tuition reimbursements available (averaging $3,903 per year), 61 teaching assistantships with full and partial tuition reimbursements available (averaging $4,319 per year); career-related internships or fieldwork, institutionally sponsored loans, scholarships/grants, tuition waivers (partial), unspecified assistantships, and administrative aides, supplementary awards also available. Support available to part-time students. Financial award applicants required to submit FAFSA. In 2008, 57 master's awarded. Offers art education (MA); art history (MA); composition (MM); conducting (MM); fine arts and communications (MA, MFA, MM); mass communications (MA); music education (MA, MM); musicology (MA); performance (MM); studio art (MFA); theatre and media arts (MA). *Application fee:* $50. Electronic applications accepted. *Application Contact:* Adviser, 801-422-4541, Fax: 801-378-5238, E-mail: gradstudies@byu.edu. *Dean*, Dr. Stephen M. Jones, 801-422-8271, Fax: 801-422-0253, E-mail: amber_louw@byu.edu.

College of Health and Human Performance Students: 53 full-time (35 women), 55 part-time (25 women); includes 8 minority (2 American Indian/Alaska Native, 5 Asian Americans or Pacific Islanders, 1 Hispanic American), 1 international. Average age 28. 78 applicants, 45% accepted, 29 enrolled. *Faculty:* 44 full-time (7 women), 1 (woman) part-time/adjunct. Expenses: Contact institution. *Financial support:* In 2008–09, 74 students received support, including 46 research assistantships with full and partial tuition reimbursements available (averaging $3,438 per year), 32 teaching assistantships with full and partial tuition reimbursements available (averaging $10,106 per year); fellowships, career-related internships or fieldwork, institutionally sponsored loans, scholarships/grants, tuition waivers (full and partial), unspecified assistantships, and administrative aides also available. Support available to part-time students. Financial award application deadline: 3/1. In 2008, 27 master's, 2 doctorates awarded. Offers athletic training (MS); exercise physiology (MS, PhD); health and human performance (MPH, MS, PhD); health promotion (MS, PhD); health science (MPH); physical medicine and rehabilitation (PhD); youth and family recreation (MS). *Application deadline:* For fall admission, 2/1 for domestic students. *Application fee:* $50. Electronic applications accepted. *Application Contact:* Sandra L. Alger, Graduate Secretary, 801-422-4271, Fax: 801-422-0557, E-mail: sandy_alger@byu.edu. *Dean*, Sara Lee Gibb, 801-422-2645, Fax: 801-422-0557, E-mail: sara_lee_gibb@byu.edu.

College of Humanities Students: 223 full-time (151 women), 43 part-time (24 women); includes 27 minority (1 African American, 15 Asian Americans or Pacific Islanders, 11 Hispanic Americans), 18 international. Average age 27. 177 applicants, 68% accepted, 101 enrolled. *Faculty:* 171 full-time (36 women), 2 part-time/adjunct (both women). Expenses: Contact institution. *Financial support:* In 2008–09, 217 students received support, including 20 fellowships with partial tuition reimbursements available (averaging $4,169 per year), 33 research assistantships with partial tuition reimbursements available (averaging $3,408 per year), 149 teaching assistantships with partial tuition reimbursements available (averaging $4,415 per year); career-related internships or fieldwork, institutionally sponsored loans, tuition waivers (full and partial), and student instructorships also available. Support available to part-time students. In 2008, 77 master's, 24 other advanced degrees awarded. *Degree program information:* Part-time programs available. Offers comparative literature

Brigham Young University (continued)

(MA); comparative studies (MA); English (MA); French studies (MA); general linguistics (MA); German studies (MA); humanities (MA, Certificate); language acquisition and teaching (MA); Portuguese linguistics (MA); Portuguese literature (MA); Spanish linguistics (MA); Spanish teaching (MA); Spanish/Latin American Literature (MA); Spanish/Peninsular literature (MA); teaching English as a second language (MA, Certificate). *Application fee:* $50. Electronic applications accepted. *Application Contact:* Adviser, 801-422-4541, Fax: 801-378-5238, E-mail: gradstudies@byu.edu. *Dean,* Dr. John R. Rosenberg, 801-422-2779, Fax: 801-422-0308, E-mail: john_rosenberg@byu.edu.

College of Life Sciences Students: 100 full-time (45 women), 24 part-time (7 women); includes 19 minority (1 African American, 1 American Indian/Alaska Native, 5 Asian Americans or Pacific Islanders, 12 Hispanic Americans), 7 international. Average age 28. 71 applicants, 61% accepted, 32 enrolled. *Faculty:* 92 full-time (11 women), 13 part-time/adjunct (3 women). Expenses: Contact institution. *Financial support:* In 2008–09, 114 students received support, including 1 fellowship with partial tuition reimbursement available (averaging $7,100 per year), 78 research assistantships with full and partial tuition reimbursements available (averaging $13,543 per year), 112 teaching assistantships with full and partial tuition reimbursements available (averaging $13,423 per year); career-related internships or fieldwork, institutionally sponsored loans, scholarships/grants, tuition waivers (full and partial), and tuition awards also available. Support available to part-time students. Financial award application deadline: 4/15. In 2008, 40 master's, 2 doctorates awarded. *Degree program information:* Part-time programs available. Offers biological science education (MS); biology (MS, PhD); environmental science (MS); food science (MS); genetics and biotechnology (MS); life sciences (MS, PhD); microbiology (MS, PhD); molecular biology (MS, PhD); neuroscience (MS, PhD); nutrition (MS); physiology and developmental biology (MS, PhD); wildlife and wildlands conservation (MS, PhD). *Application deadline:* For fall admission, 1/31 for domestic and international students. *Application fee:* $50. Electronic applications accepted. *Application Contact:* Sue Pratley, Application Contact, 801-422-3963, Fax: 801-422-0050, E-mail: sue_pratley@byu.edu. *Dean,* Dr. Rodney J. Brown, 801-422-3963, Fax: 801-422-0050.

College of Nursing Students: 28 full-time (24 women); includes 4 minority (1 African American, 3 Asian Americans or Pacific Islanders). Average age 31. 23 applicants, 65% accepted, 15 enrolled. *Faculty:* 26 full-time (24 women). Expenses: Contact institution. *Financial support:* In 2008–09, 28 students received support, including 2 research assistantships with full and partial tuition reimbursements available (averaging $10,000 per year), 3 teaching assistantships with full and partial tuition reimbursements available (averaging $10,000 per year); institutionally sponsored loans, scholarships/grants, tuition waivers (full), and unspecified assistantships also available. Support available to part-time students. Financial award application deadline: 2/1; financial award applicants required to submit FAFSA. In 2008, 13 master's awarded. Offers family nurse practitioner (MS). *Application deadline:* For spring admission, 12/1 for domestic students. Applications are processed on a rolling basis. *Application fee:* $50. Electronic applications accepted. *Application Contact:* Denise Gibbons Davis, Graduate Secretary, 801-422-4142, Fax: 801-422-0538, E-mail: denise_gibbons@byu.edu. *Dean,* Dr. Beth Vaughan Cole, 801-422-8296, Fax: 801-422-0536, E-mail: bethcole@byu.edu.

College of Physical and Mathematical Sciences Students: 312 full-time (86 women), 10 part-time (5 women); includes 29 minority (26 Asian Americans or Pacific Islanders, 3 Hispanic Americans), 71 international. Average age 27. 178 applicants, 66% accepted, 77 enrolled. *Faculty:* 162 full-time (12 women), 6 part-time/adjunct (0 women). Expenses: Contact institution. *Financial support:* In 2008–09, 276 students received support, including 14 fellowships with full tuition reimbursements available (averaging $20,500 per year), 127 research assistantships with full and partial tuition reimbursements available (averaging $14,658 per year), 135 teaching assistantships with full and partial tuition reimbursements available (averaging $13,779 per year); career-related internships or fieldwork, institutionally sponsored loans, scholarships/grants, health care benefits, tuition waivers (full and partial), and unspecified assistantships also available. Support available to part-time students. In 2008, 70 master's, 9 doctorates awarded. *Degree program information:* Part-time programs available. Offers applied statistics (MS); biochemistry (MS, PhD); chemistry (MS, PhD); computer science (MS, PhD); geological sciences (MS); mathematics (MS, PhD); mathematics education (MA); physical and mathematical sciences (MA, MS, PhD); physics (MS, PhD); physics and astronomy (PhD). *Application deadline:* Applications are processed on a rolling basis. *Application fee:* $50. Electronic applications accepted. *Application Contact:* Lynn Patten, Executive Secretary, 801-422-4022, Fax: 801-422-0550, E-mail: lynn_patten@byu.edu. *Chair,* Dr. Scott D. Sommerfeldt, 801-422-2205, Fax: 801-422-0553, E-mail: scott_sommerfeldt@byu.edu.

College of Religious Education Students: 8 full-time (1 woman). Average age 32. *Faculty:* 69 full-time (4 women). Expenses: Contact institution. *Financial support:* In 2008–09, 17 students received support. Scholarships/grants available. In 2008, 2 master's awarded. Offers religious education (MA). *Application deadline:* For fall admission, 12/1 for international students; for winter admission, 12/1 for domestic students. *Application fee:* $50. *Application Contact:* Dr. Clyde J. Williams, Professor of Ancient Scripture, 801-422-2124, Fax: 801-422-0616. *Dean,* Dr. Terry B. Ball, 801-422-2736, Fax: 801-422-0616, E-mail: terry_ball@byu.edu.

David O. McKay School of Education Students: 183 full-time (135 women), 115 part-time (71 women); includes 20 minority (1 African American, 2 American Indian/Alaska Native, 11 Asian Americans or Pacific Islanders, 6 Hispanic Americans), 18 international. Average age 30. 256 applicants, 63% accepted, 125 enrolled. *Faculty:* 65 full-time (28 women), 27 part-time/adjunct (10 women). Expenses: Contact institution. *Financial support:* In 2008–09, 146 students received support, including 63 research assistantships (averaging $10,506 per year), 36 teaching assistantships (averaging $7,220 per year); fellowships, career-related internships or fieldwork, institutionally sponsored loans, scholarships/grants, tuition waivers (partial), and unspecified assistantships also available. Support available to part-time students. Financial award applicants required to submit FAFSA. In 2008, 59 master's, 21 doctorates, 12 other advanced degrees awarded. *Degree program information:* Part-time programs available. Offers counseling psychology (PhD); education (M Ed, MA, MS, PhD, Ed S); educational leadership and foundations (M Ed, PhD); instructional psychology and technology (MS, PhD); literacy education (MA); school psychology (Ed S); special education (MS); speech-language pathology (MS); teacher education (MA). *Application deadline:* For fall admission, 2/1 for domestic and international students; for winter admission, 2/1 for domestic and international students; for spring admission, 2/15 for domestic and international students. *Application fee:* $50. Electronic applications accepted. *Application Contact:* Jay Oliver, Director, Education Advisement Center, 801-422-1202, Fax: 801-422-0195, E-mail: jay_oliver@byu.edu. *Dean,* Dr. K. Richard Young, 801-422-3695, Fax: 801-422-0200, E-mail: richard_young@byu.edu.

Ira A. Fulton College of Engineering and Technology Students: 286 full-time (31 women), 75 part-time (6 women); includes 23 minority (1 American Indian/Alaska Native, 19 Asian Americans or Pacific Islanders, 3 Hispanic Americans), 38 international. Average age 26. 134 applicants, 75% accepted, 74 enrolled. *Faculty:* 107 full-time (2 women), 18 part-time/adjunct (2 women). Expenses: Contact institution. *Financial support:* In 2008–09, 9 fellowships with partial tuition reimbursements (averaging $11,400 per year), 191 research assistantships with partial tuition reimbursements (averaging $12,382 per year), 109 teaching assistantships with partial tuition reimbursements (averaging $7,916 per year) were awarded; career-related internships or fieldwork, institutionally sponsored loans, and scholarships/grants also available. Support available to part-time students. Financial award application deadline: 3/15; financial award applicants required to submit FAFSA. In 2008, 96 master's, 8 doctorates awarded. Offers chemical engineering (MS, PhD); civil engineering (MS, PhD); construction management (MS); electrical and computer engineering (MS, PhD); engineering and technology (MS, PhD); information technology (MS); manufacturing systems (MS); mechanical engineering (MS, PhD); technology and engineering education (MS). *Application deadline:* For fall admission, 1/15 for domestic and international students; for winter admission, 9/15 for domestic students, 2/15 for international students. Applications are processed on a rolling basis. *Application fee:* $0. Electronic applications accepted. *Application Contact:* Adviser, 801-422-4541, Fax: 801-378-5238, E-mail: gradstudies@byu.edu. *Dean,* Dr. Alan R. Parkinson, 801-422-4327, Fax: 801-422-0218, E-mail: college@et.byu.edu.

J. Reuben Clark Law School Students: 458 full-time (156 women); includes 77 minority (9 African Americans, 6 American Indian/Alaska Native, 35 Asian Americans or Pacific Islanders, 27 Hispanic Americans), 1 international. Average age 25. 790 applicants, 31% accepted, 146 enrolled. *Faculty:* 34 full-time (8 women), 34 part-time/adjunct (8 women). Expenses: Contact institution. *Financial support:* In 2008–09, 252 students received support, including 151 fellowships (averaging $5,000 per year); research assistantships, teaching assistantships, career-related internships or fieldwork, institutionally sponsored loans, scholarships/grants, and health care benefits also available. Financial award application deadline: 6/1; financial award applicants required to submit FAFSA. In 2008, 157 JDs, 8 master's awarded. Offers law (JD, LL M). *Application deadline:* For fall admission, 3/1 priority date for domestic students. Applications are processed on a rolling basis. *Application fee:* $50. Electronic applications accepted. *Application Contact:* GaeLynn Kuchar, Admissions Director, 801-422-4277, Fax: 801-422-0389, E-mail: kucharg@lawgate.byu.edu. *Dean,* James D. Gordon, 801-422-6383, Fax: 801-422-0389, E-mail: jim.gordon@byu.edu.

Marriott School of Management Students: 646 full-time (133 women), 253 part-time (50 women); includes 57 minority (6 African Americans, 8 American Indian/Alaska Native, 23 Asian Americans or Pacific Islanders, 20 Hispanic Americans), 71 international. Average age 30. 1,092 applicants, 62% accepted, 531 enrolled. *Faculty:* 123 full-time (11 women), 73 part-time/adjunct (23 women). Expenses: Contact institution. *Financial support:* In 2008–09, 559 students received support. Career-related internships or fieldwork, institutionally sponsored loans, scholarships/grants, and tuition waivers (full and partial) available. Financial award application deadline: 4/15; financial award applicants required to submit FAFSA. In 2008, 507 master's awarded. Offers accountancy (M Acc); business administration (MBA); information systems (MISM); management (EMPA, M Acc, MBA, MISM, MPA); public administration (EMPA, MPA). *Application fee:* $50. Electronic applications accepted. *Application Contact:* Adviser, 801-422-4541, Fax: 801-378-5238, E-mail: gradstudies@byu.edu. *Dean,* Dr. Gary C. Cornia, 801-422-4121, Fax: 801-422-4501.

BRITISH AMERICAN COLLEGE LONDON, London NW1 4NS, United Kingdom

General Information Coed, comprehensive institution.

GRADUATE UNITS

Webster Graduate School *Degree program information:* Part-time programs available. Offers business (MBA); finance (MS); human resources (MA); information technology management (MA); international business (MA); international non-governmental organizations (MA); international relations (MA); management and leadership (MA); marketing (MA).

BROCK UNIVERSITY, St. Catharines, ON L2S 3A1, Canada

General Information Province-supported, coed, university. *Graduate housing:* Room and/or apartments available on a first-come, first-served basis to single students; on-campus housing not available to married students. Housing application deadline: 5/28. *Research affiliation:* Registered Nurses Association of Ontario (nursing best practices), Canadian Honey Council (agriculture/therapeutic product development), Fly Fishing Canada/Trout Unlimited Canada (fisheries management), Henry Ford Health Centre (cance epidemiology).

GRADUATE UNITS

Faculty of Graduate Studies *Degree program information:* Part-time and evening/weekend programs available. Electronic applications accepted.

Faculty of Applied Health Sciences Offers applied health sciences (M Sc, MA). Electronic applications accepted.

Faculty of Business *Degree program information:* Part-time programs available. Offers accountancy (M Acc); business administration (MBA); management (M Sc). Electronic applications accepted.

Faculty of Education *Degree program information:* Part-time and evening/weekend programs available. Offers education (M Ed, PhD). Electronic applications accepted.

Faculty of Humanities *Degree program information:* Part-time programs available. Offers applied linguistics (MA); classics (MA); English (MA); history (MA); philosophy (MA); studies in comparative literatures and arts (MA). Electronic applications accepted.

Faculty of Mathematics and Science *Degree program information:* Part-time programs available. Offers biological sciences (M Sc, PhD); biology (M Sc, PhD); biotechnology (M Sc, PhD); chemistry (M Sc, PhD); computer science (M Sc); earth sciences (M Sc); mathematics and statistics (M Sc); physics (M Sc). Electronic applications accepted.

Faculty of Social Sciences *Degree program information:* Part-time programs available. Offers applied disability studies (MA, MADS, Diploma); behavioral neuroscience (MA, PhD); business economics (MBE); Canadian politics (MA); child and youth studies (MA); geography (MA); international and comparative politics (MA); life span development (MA, PhD); political philosophy (MA); political science (MA); popular culture (MA); psychology (MA, PhD); public administration (MA); social justice and equity studies (MA); social personality (MA, PhD). Electronic applications accepted.

BROOKLYN COLLEGE OF THE CITY UNIVERSITY OF NEW YORK, Brooklyn, NY 11210-2889

General Information State and locally supported, coed, comprehensive institution. *Enrollment:* 518 full-time matriculated graduate/professional students (375 women), 2,722 part-time matriculated graduate/professional students (1,832 women). *Enrollment by degree level:* 3,179 master's, 61 other advanced degrees. Tuition, state resident: full-time $7360; part-time $310 per credit hour. Tuition, nonresident: full-time $13,800; part-time $575 per credit hour. *Graduate housing:* On-campus housing not available. *Student services:* Campus employment opportunities, career counseling, child daycare facilities, exercise/wellness program, free psychological counseling, international student services, low-cost health insurance, multicultural affairs office, services for students with disabilities, writing training. *Library facilities:* Brooklyn College Library plus 1 other. *Online resources:* library catalog, web page, access to other libraries' catalogs. *Collection:* 1.3 million titles, 13,500 serial subscriptions, 21,731 audiovisual materials. *Research affiliation:* Ajinomoto Co. Inc (Amino Acids), Crohn's & Colitis Foundation of America (Crohn's, ulcerative colitis, and other inflammatory bowel diseases), Teagle Foundation (Higher Education), The After School Corporation (Psychology), American Heart Assoication (Public Health, Heart and Stroke), American Psychological Foundation (Psychology).

Computer facilities: 800 computers available on campus for general student use. A campuswide network can be accessed from off campus. Online class registration is available. *Web address:* http://www.brooklyn.cuny.edu/.

General Application Contact: Office of Admissions, 718-951-5001, Fax: 718-951-4506, E-mail: adminqry@brooklyn.cuny.edu.

GRADUATE UNITS

Division of Graduate Studies Students: 518 full-time (375 women), 2,722 part-time (1,832 women); includes 1,308 minority (822 African Americans, 6 American Indian/Alaska Native, 182 Asian Americans or Pacific Islanders, 298 Hispanic Americans), 250 international. Average age 34. 3,166 applicants, 62% accepted, 1290 enrolled. Expenses: Contact institution. *Financial support:* Career-related internships or fieldwork, Federal Work-Study, institutionally sponsored loans, and scholarships/grants available. Support available to part-time students. Financial award application deadline: 5/1; financial award applicants required to submit FAFSA. In 2008, 1,008 master's, 129 other advanced degrees awarded. *Degree program information:* Part-time and evening/weekend programs available. Offers accounting (MS); acting (MFA); applied physics (MA); art history (MA, PhD); audiology (Au D); biology (MA, PhD); chemistry (MA, PhD); community health (MA, MPH, MS); community health education (MA); computer science (MA, PhD); computer science and health science (MS); creative writing (MFA); criticism and history (MA); design and technical production (MFA); digital art (MFA); directing (MFA); dramaturgy (MFA); drawing and painting (MFA); economics (MA); English (MA, PhD); exercise science and rehabilitation (MS); experimental psychology (MA);

fiction (MFA); French (MA); geology (MA, PhD); grief counseling (CAS); health care management (MPH); health care policy and administration (MPH); history (MA, PhD); industrial and organizational psychology (MA); information systems (MS); international affairs (MA); Judaic studies (MA); liberal studies (MA); mathematics (MA, PhD); mental health counseling (MA); modern languages and literature (PhD); nutrition (MS); parallel and distributed computing (Advanced Certificate); performance and interactive media arts (MFA, CAS); performing arts management (MFA); photography (MFA); physical education (MS); physics (MA, PhD); playwriting (MFA); poetry (MFA); political science (MA, PhD); political science, urban policy and administration (MA); printmaking (MFA); psychology (PhD); public health (MPH); sculpture (MFA); sociology (MA, PhD); Spanish (MA); speech (MA); speech and hearing sciences (PhD); speech pathology (MS); television and radio (MS); television production (MFA); thanatology (MA); theater (PhD). The division offers courses at Brooklyn College that are creditable toward the CUNY doctoral program. *Application deadline:* For fall admission, 3/1 priority date for domestic students, 2/1 priority date for international students; for spring admission, 11/1 priority date for domestic students, 10/1 priority date for international students. Applications are processed on a rolling basis. *Application fee:* $125. Electronic applications accepted. *Application Contact:* Hernan Sierra, Graduate Admissions Coordinator, 718-951-4536, Fax: 718-951-4506, E-mail: grads@brooklyn.cuny.edu. *Dean,* Dr. Louise Hainline, 718-951-5252, Fax: 718-951-4727, E-mail: louiseh@brooklyn.cuny.edu.

Conservatory of Music Students: 64 full-time (36 women); includes 9 minority (4 African Americans, 1 Asian American or Pacific Islander, 4 Hispanic Americans), 19 international. Average age 29. 69 applicants, 74% accepted, 30 enrolled. Expenses: Contact institution. *Financial support:* Career-related internships or fieldwork, Federal Work-Study, institutionally sponsored loans, and scholarships/grants available. Support available to part-time students. Financial award application deadline: 5/1; financial award applicants required to submit FAFSA. In 2008, 22 master's awarded. *Degree program information:* Part-time programs available. Offers composition (MM); music (DMA, PhD); music education (MA); musicology (MA); performance (MM); performance practice (MA). The department offers courses at Brooklyn College that are creditable toward the CUNY doctoral degree (with permission of the executive officer of the doctoral program). *Application deadline:* For fall admission, 3/1 priority date for domestic students, 2/1 priority date for international students; for spring admission, 11/1 priority date for domestic students, 10/1 priority date for international students. Applications are processed on a rolling basis. *Application fee:* $125. Electronic applications accepted. *Application Contact:* Hernan Sierra, Graduate Admissions Coordinator, 718-951-4536, Fax: 718-951-4506, E-mail: grads@brooklyn.cuny.edu. *Chairperson,* Dr. Bruce MacIntyre, 718-951-5286, E-mail: brucem@brooklyn.cuny.edu.

School of Education Students: 229 full-time (173 women), 1,451 part-time (1,068 women); includes 748 minority (477 African Americans, 4 American Indian/Alaska Native, 84 Asian Americans or Pacific Islanders, 183 Hispanic Americans), 31 international. Average age 32. 1,256 applicants, 78% accepted, 709 enrolled. Expenses: Contact institution. *Financial support:* Fellowships, career-related internships or fieldwork, Federal Work-Study, institutionally sponsored loans, scholarships/grants, and tuition waivers (full and partial) available. Support available to part-time students. Financial award application deadline: 5/1; financial award applicants required to submit FAFSA. In 2008, 557 master's, 127 other advanced degrees awarded. *Degree program information:* Part-time and evening/weekend programs available. Offers adolescence science education (MAT); art teacher (MA); bilingual education (MS Ed); biology (MA); biology teacher (MA); birth-grade 2 (MS Ed); chemistry (MA); chemistry teacher (MA); earth science (MA); education (MA, MAT, MS Ed, CAS); educational leadership (MS Ed); English teacher (MA); French teacher (MA); general science (MA); guidance and counseling (CAS); health and nutrition sciences: health teacher (MS Ed); liberal arts (MS Ed); mathematics (MS Ed); mathematics teacher (MA); middle childhood education (math) (MS Ed); music education (CAS); music teacher (MA); physical education teacher (MS Ed); physics (MA); physics teacher (MA); school psychologist (MS Ed, CAS); school psychologist-bilingual (CAS); science/environmental education (MS Ed); social studies teacher (MA); Spanish teacher (MA); teacher of students with disabilities (MS Ed). *Application deadline:* For fall admission, 3/1 priority date for domestic students, 2/1 priority date for international students; for spring admission, 11/1 priority date for domestic students, 10/1 priority date for international students. Applications are processed on a rolling basis. *Application fee:* $125. Electronic applications accepted. *Application Contact:* Hernan Sierra, Graduate Admissions Coordinator, 718-951-4536, Fax: 718-951-4506, E-mail: grads@brooklyn.cuny.edu. *Dean,* Dr. Deborah Shanley, 718-951-5214, Fax: 718-951-4816, E-mail: dshanley@brooklyn.cuny.edu.

See Close-Up on page 861.

BROOKLYN LAW SCHOOL, Brooklyn, NY 11201-3798

General Information Independent, coed, graduate-only institution. *Enrollment by degree level:* 1,490 first professional. *Graduate faculty:* 63 full-time (29 women), 77 part-time/adjunct (20 women). *Graduate housing:* Rooms and/or apartments available to single students and guaranteed to married students. Housing application deadline: 5/1. *Student services:* Campus employment opportunities, campus safety program, career counseling, free psychological counseling, international student services, low-cost health insurance, services for students with disabilities, writing training. *Library facilities:* Brooklyn Law School Library plus 2 others. *Online resources:* library catalog, web page, access to other libraries' catalogs. *Collection:* 265,438 titles, 2,109 serial subscriptions.

Computer facilities: 138 computers available on campus for general student use. A campuswide network can be accessed from student residence rooms and from off campus. Online class registration is available. *Web address:* http://www.brooklaw.edu/.

General Application Contact: Henry W. Haverstick, Dean of Admissions and Financial Aid, 718-780-7906, Fax: 718-780-0395, E-mail: admitq@brooklaw.edu.

GRADUATE UNITS

Professional Program Students: 1,211 full-time (588 women), 279 part-time (136 women); includes 404 minority (90 African Americans, 2 American Indian/Alaska Native, 222 Asian Americans or Pacific Islanders, 90 Hispanic Americans), 9 international. Average age 26. 4,860 applicants, 31% accepted, 493 enrolled. *Faculty:* 63 full-time (29 women), 77 part-time/adjunct (20 women). Expenses: Contact institution. *Financial support:* In 2008–09, 1,328 students received support, including 48 fellowships with partial tuition reimbursements available (averaging $5,000 per year), 91 research assistantships with partial tuition reimbursements available (averaging $5,000 per year); career-related internships or fieldwork, Federal Work-Study, scholarships/grants, and tuition waivers (partial) also available. Support available to part-time students. Financial award application deadline: 4/28; financial award applicants required to submit FAFSA. In 2008, 470 JDs awarded. *Degree program information:* Part-time and evening/weekend programs available. Offers law (JD). *Application deadline:* For fall admission, 2/1 priority date for domestic and international students. Applications are processed on a rolling basis. Electronic applications accepted. *Application Contact:* Henry W. Haverstick, Dean of Admissions and Financial Aid, 718-780-7906, Fax: 718-780-0395, E-mail: admitq@brooklaw.edu. *Dean,* Joan G. Wexler, 718-780-7900, Fax: 718-780-0393.

BROOKS INSTITUTE, Santa Barbara, CA 93101

General Information Proprietary, coed, comprehensive institution. *Graduate housing:* On-campus housing not available.

GRADUATE UNITS

Graduate Program in Professional Photography *Degree program information:* Evening/weekend programs available. Offers professional photography (MFA). Electronic applications accepted.

BROWN UNIVERSITY, Providence, RI 02912

General Information Independent, coed, university. CGS member. *Graduate housing:* Room and/or apartments available to single students; on-campus housing not available to married students. *Research affiliation:* Woods Hole Oceanographic Institution–Marine Biological Laboratory, Rhode Island Reactor, International Center for Numismatic Studies, Meeting Street School.

GRADUATE UNITS

Graduate School *Degree program information:* Part-time programs available. Offers acting and directing (MFA); American civilization (MA, PhD); ancient Judaism (PhD); anthropology (AM, PhD); behavioral neuroscience (PhD); biochemistry (PhD); chemistry (AM, Sc M, PhD); classics (MA, PhD); cognitive processes (PhD); cognitive science (Sc M, PhD); comparative literature (PhD); computer science (Sc M, PhD); early Christianity (PhD); economics (PhD); Egyptology (AM, PhD); electronic music and multimedia (PhD); elementary education 1-6 (MAT); ethnomusicology (PhD); French studies (PhD); geological sciences (MA, Sc M, PhD); German (PhD); Hispanic studies (MA, PhD); history (MA, PhD); history of art and architecture (MA, PhD); Italian studies (PhD); linguistics (AM, PhD); literatures and cultures in English (MA, PhD); mathematics (M Sc, MA, PhD); museum studies (AM); neuroscience (PhD); nonfiction writing (MFA); philosophy (MA, PhD); physics (Sc M, PhD); political science (PhD); public humanities (MA); religion and critical thought (PhD); religion in the ancient Mediterranean (PhD); religion, culture, and comparison (PhD); Russian language and literature (AM); secondary biology (MAT); secondary English (MAT); secondary history/social studies (MAT); sensation and perception (PhD); Slavic languages (AM); Slavic studies (PhD); social/developmental (PhD); sociology (AM, MA, PhD); theatre and performance studies (PhD); theatre arts (AM).

A. Alfred Taubman Center for Public Policy and American Institutions Offers public policy and American institutions (MPA, MPP).

Center for Environmental Studies Students: 16 full-time (10 women), 1 international. Average age 24. 26 applicants, 46% accepted, 8 enrolled. *Faculty:* 7 full-time (2 women), 11 part-time/adjunct (3 women). Expenses: Contact institution. *Financial support:* In 2008–09, 16 students received support, including 2 teaching assistantships with full tuition reimbursements available (averaging $14,000 per year); career-related internships or fieldwork, Federal Work-Study, health care benefits, and tuition waivers (partial) also available. Financial award application deadline: 1/2; financial award applicants required to submit FAFSA. In 2008, 7 master's awarded. *Degree program information:* Part-time programs available. Offers environmental studies (AM). *Application deadline:* For fall admission, 1/2 priority date for domestic and international students. Applications are processed on a rolling basis. *Application fee:* $70. Electronic applications accepted. *Application Contact:* Patricia Caton, Administrative Manager, 401-863 Ext. 3449, Fax: 401-863-3503, E-mail: Patricia-Ann_Caton@Brown.EDU. *Interim Director,* Phil Brown, PhD, 401-863-3449, Fax: 401-863-3503, E-mail: Phil_Brown@Brown.EDU.

Center for Portuguese and Brazilian Studies Offers Brazilian studies (AM); Portuguese and Brazilian studies (AM, PhD); Portuguese Bilingual Education and Cross-Cultural Studies (AM).

Division of Applied Mathematics Offers applied mathematics (Sc M, PhD).

Division of Biology and Medicine *Degree program information:* Part-time programs available. Offers artificial organs, biomaterials, and cell technology (MA, Sc M, PhD); biochemistry (M Med Sc, Sc M, PhD); biology (MA, PhD); biology and medicine (M Med Sc, MA, MPH, MS, Sc M, PhD); biomedical engineering (MS, PhD); biostatistics (MS, PhD); cancer biology (PhD); cell biology (M Med Sc, Sc M, PhD); developmental biology (M Med Sc, Sc M, PhD); ecology and evolutionary biology (PhD); epidemiology (MS, PhD); health services research (MS, PhD); immunology (M Med Sc, Sc M, PhD); immunology and infection (PhD); medical science (PhD); molecular microbiology (M Med Sc, Sc M, PhD); molecular pharmacology and physiology (MA, Sc M, PhD); neuroscience (PhD); pathobiology (Sc M); public health (MPH); statistical science (MS, PhD); toxicology and environmental pathology (PhD). Electronic applications accepted.

Division of Engineering Offers biomedical engineering (Sc M, PhD); electrical sciences and computer engineering (Sc M, PhD); fluid, thermal and chemical processes (Sc M, PhD); materials science and engineering (Sc M, PhD); mechanics of solids (Sc M, PhD).

Joukowsky Institute for Archaeology and the Ancient World Offers archaeology and the ancient world (PhD).

National Institutes of Health Sponsored Programs Offers neuroscience (PhD).

Program in Medicine Offers medicine (MD).

BRYANT UNIVERSITY, Smithfield, RI 02917-1284

General Information Independent, coed, comprehensive institution. *Enrollment:* 3,800 graduate, professional, and undergraduate students; 38 full-time matriculated graduate/professional students (18 women), 266 part-time matriculated graduate/professional students (83 women). *Enrollment by degree level:* 304 master's. *Graduate faculty:* 38 full-time (9 women), 2 part-time/adjunct (0 women). *Tuition:* Part-time $26,928 per degree program. One-time fee: $750 part-time. *Graduate housing:* On-campus housing not available. *Student services:* Campus employment opportunities, campus safety program, career counseling, exercise/wellness program, free psychological counseling, international student services, low-cost health insurance, multicultural affairs office, services for students with disabilities, writing training. *Library facilities:* Douglas and Judith Krupp Library. *Online resources:* library catalog, web page, access to other libraries' catalogs. *Collection:* 143,393 titles, 26,451 serial subscriptions, 1,208 audiovisual materials.

Computer facilities: Computer purchase and lease plans are available. 467 computers available on campus for general student use. A campuswide network can be accessed from student residence rooms and from off campus. Online class registration, e-mail, online library, wireless network, student Web hosts are available. *Web address:* http://www.bryant.edu/.

General Application Contact: Kristopher T. Sullivan, Assistant Dean of the Graduate School, 401-232-6230, Fax: 401-232-6494, E-mail: gradprog@bryant.edu.

GRADUATE UNITS

Graduate School of Business Students: 38 full-time (18 women), 266 part-time (83 women); includes 13 minority (3 African Americans, 8 Asian Americans or Pacific Islanders, 2 Hispanic Americans), 10 international. Average age 31. 162 applicants, 66% accepted, 75 enrolled. *Faculty:* 20 full-time (6 women), 2 part-time/adjunct (0 women). Expenses: Contact institution. *Financial support:* In 2008–09, 12 research assistantships with partial tuition reimbursements were awarded; unspecified assistantships also available. Support available to part-time students. Financial award applicants required to submit FAFSA. In 2008, 166 master's awarded. *Degree program information:* Part-time and evening/weekend programs available. Offers business administration (MBA); general business (MBA); professional accountancy (MPAC); taxation (MST). *Application deadline:* For fall admission, 7/15 for domestic and international students; for spring admission, 11/15 for domestic and international students. Applications are processed on a rolling basis. *Application fee:* $80. Electronic applications accepted. *Application Contact:* Kristopher T Sullivan, Assistant Dean of the Graduate School, 401-232-6230, Fax: 401-232-6494, E-mail: gradprog@bryant.edu. *Dean of the College of Business,* Dr. Jack W. Trifts, 401-232-6308, Fax: 401-232-6573, E-mail: jtrifts@bryant.edu.

BRYN ATHYN COLLEGE OF THE NEW CHURCH, Bryn Athyn, PA 19009-0717

General Information Independent-religious, coed, comprehensive institution. *Graduate housing:* Room and/or apartments available on a first-come, first-served basis to single students; on-campus housing not available to married students. Housing application deadline: 1/31.

GRADUATE UNITS

Academy of the New Church Theological School *Degree program information:* Part-time programs available. Postbaccalaureate distance learning degree programs offered (minimal on-campus study). Offers divinity (M Div); religious studies (MA).

BRYN MAWR COLLEGE, Bryn Mawr, PA 19010-2899

General Information Independent, Undergraduate: women only; graduate: coed, university. CGS member. *Graduate housing:* Room and/or apartments available on a first-come, first-served basis to single students.

Bryn Mawr College (continued)

GRADUATE UNITS

Graduate School of Arts and Sciences *Degree program information:* Part-time programs available. Offers arts and sciences (MA, PhD); chemistry (MA, PhD); classical and Near Eastern archaeology (MA, PhD); clinical developmental psychology (PhD); French (MA, PhD); Greek, Latin, and Classical studies (MA, PhD); history of art (MA, PhD); mathematics (MA, PhD); physics (MA, PhD); Russian (MA, PhD).

Graduate School of Social Work and Social Research Students: 130 full-time (113 women), 95 part-time (86 women); includes 45 minority (39 African Americans, 3 Asian Americans or Pacific Islanders, 3 Hispanic Americans), 2 international. Average age 35. 175 applicants, 91% accepted, 81 enrolled. *Faculty:* 14 full-time (8 women), 27 part-time/adjunct (23 women). Expenses: Contact institution. *Financial support:* In 2008–09, 199 students received support, including 29 fellowships with full and partial tuition reimbursements available (averaging $2,517 per year), 6 teaching assistantships with full and partial tuition reimbursements available (averaging $9,076 per year); research assistantships with full and partial tuition reimbursements available, career-related internships or fieldwork, Federal Work-Study, institutionally sponsored loans, scholarships/grants, tuition waivers (full and partial), and PhD dissertation award also available. Support available to part-time students. Financial award application deadline: 3/1; financial award applicants required to submit FAFSA. In 2008, 108 master's, 3 doctorates awarded. *Degree program information:* Part-time and evening/weekend programs available. Offers social work and social research (MLSP, MSS, PhD). *Application deadline:* For fall admission, 3/31 priority date for domestic and international students. Applications are processed on a rolling basis. *Application fee:* $50. Electronic applications accepted. *Application Contact:* Nancy J. Kirby, Assistant Dean and Director of Admissions, 610-520-2601, Fax: 610-520-2655, E-mail: swadmiss@brynmawr.edu. *Director,* Dr. Marcia L. Martin, 610-520-2603, Fax: 610-520-2613, E-mail: mmartin@brynmawr.edu.

See Close-Up on page 863.

BUCKNELL UNIVERSITY, Lewisburg, PA 17837

General Information Independent, coed, comprehensive institution. *Graduate housing:* On-campus housing not available.

GRADUATE UNITS

Graduate Studies *Degree program information:* Part-time programs available.

College of Arts and Sciences *Degree program information:* Part-time programs available. Offers animal behavior (MA, MS); arts and sciences (MA, MS, MS Ed); biology (MA, MS); chemistry (MA, MS); classroom teaching (MS Ed); educational research (MS Ed); elementary and secondary counseling (MA, MS Ed); elementary and secondary principalship (MA, MS Ed); English (MA); mathematics (MA, MS); psychology (MA, MS); reading (MA, MS Ed); school psychology (MS Ed); supervision of curriculum and instruction (MA, MS Ed).

College of Engineering *Degree program information:* Part-time programs available. Offers chemical engineering (MS, MS Ch E); civil and environmental engineering (MS, MSCE, MSEV); electrical engineering (MS, MSEE); engineering (MS, MS Ch E, MSCE, MSEE, MSEV, MSME); mechanical engineering (MS, MSME).

BUENA VISTA UNIVERSITY, Storm Lake, IA 50588

General Information Independent-religious, coed, comprehensive institution. *Enrollment:* 1,070 graduate, professional, and undergraduate students; 50 full-time matriculated graduate/professional students (40 women). *Enrollment by degree level:* 50 master's. *Graduate faculty:* 3 full-time (2 women), 3 part-time/adjunct (all women). *Graduate housing:* Room and/or apartments available on a first-come, first-served basis to single students; on-campus housing not available to married students. Housing application deadline: 5/1. *Student services:* Campus employment opportunities, campus safety program, career counseling, exercise/wellness program, free psychological counseling, multicultural affairs office, services for students with disabilities, writing training. *Library facilities:* BVU Library. *Online resources:* library catalog, web page. *Collection:* 144,000 titles, 632 serial subscriptions, 5,648 audiovisual materials.

Computer facilities: 400 computers available on campus for general student use. A campuswide network can be accessed from student residence rooms and from off campus. Online class registration is available. *Web address:* http://www.bvu.edu/.

General Application Contact: Rita Mckenzie, Director of Graduate Studies, 712-749-2156, Fax: 712-749-1408, E-mail: mckenzie@bvu.edu.

GRADUATE UNITS

School of Education Students: 50 full-time (40 women). Average age 36. 38 applicants, 58% accepted, 20 enrolled. *Faculty:* 3 full-time (2 women), 3 part-time/adjunct (all women). Expenses: Contact institution. *Financial support:* In 2008–09, teaching assistantships with full tuition reimbursements (averaging $6,000 per year); career-related internships or fieldwork also available. Financial award application deadline: 5/15; financial award applicants required to submit FAFSA. In 2008, 24 master's awarded. *Degree program information:* Part-time and evening/weekend programs available. Postbaccalaureate distance learning degree programs offered (minimal on-campus study). Offers curriculum and instruction (M Ed); school guidance and counseling (MS Ed). Program offered in summer only. *Application deadline:* For spring admission, 4/15 for domestic students. *Application fee:* $0. Electronic applications accepted. *Application Contact:* Rita Mckenzie, Director of Graduate Studies, 712-749-2156, Fax: 712-749-1408, E-mail: mckenzie@bvu.edu. *Dean,* Dr. susan Kalsow, 712-749-2163, Fax: 712-749-1408, E-mail: kalsow@bvu.edu.

BUFFALO STATE COLLEGE, STATE UNIVERSITY OF NEW YORK, Buffalo, NY 14222-1095

General Information State-supported, coed, comprehensive institution. CGS member. *Enrollment:* 11,224 graduate, professional, and undergraduate students; 614 full-time matriculated graduate/professional students (428 women), 1,249 part-time matriculated graduate/professional students (858 women). *Enrollment by degree level:* 1,863 master's. *Graduate faculty:* 274 full-time (92 women), 57 part-time/adjunct (20 women). *International tuition:* $6625 full-time. *Tuition, area resident:* Full-time $3940; part-time $328 per credit. Tuition, state resident: full-time $3940; part-time $328 per credit. Tuition, nonresident: full-time $6625; part-time $552 per credit. *Required fees:* $575; $23.95 per credit. *Graduate housing:* Room and/or apartments available on a first-come, first-served basis to single students; on-campus housing not available to married students. Housing application deadline: 8/15. *Student services:* Campus employment opportunities, campus safety program, career counseling, child daycare facilities, exercise/wellness program, free psychological counseling, grant writing training, international student services, low-cost health insurance, multicultural affairs office, services for students with disabilities, teacher training, writing training. *Library facilities:* E. H. Butler Library. *Online resources:* library catalog, web page, access to other libraries' catalogs. *Collection:* 618,429 titles, 2,847 serial subscriptions. *Research affiliation:* Hauptman Woodward Institute, Ecology and Environment Corporation, Phillip Morris Foundation, Friends of Buffalo River, Research Institute on Addictions at the University of Buffalo, Roswell Park Memorial Institute.

Computer facilities: 1,700 computers available on campus for general student use. A campuswide network can be accessed from student residence rooms and from off campus. Online class registration is available. *Web address:* http://www.buffalostate.edu/.

General Application Contact: The Graduate School, 716-878-5601, Fax: 716-878-5630, E-mail: gradoffc@buffalostate.edu.

GRADUATE UNITS

The Graduate School Students: 614 full-time (428 women), 1,249 part-time (858 women); includes 236 minority (136 African Americans, 10 American Indian/Alaska Native, 28 Asian Americans or Pacific Islanders, 62 Hispanic Americans), 42 international. Average age 32. 803 applicants, 71% accepted, 481 enrolled. *Faculty:* 274 full-time (92 women), 57 part-time/adjunct (20 women). Expenses: Contact institution. *Financial support:* In 2008–09, 26 fellowships with full tuition reimbursements (averaging $7,000 per year), 55 research assistantships with full tuition reimbursements (averaging $5,000 per year) were awarded; Federal Work-Study, scholarships/grants, health care benefits, and unspecified assistantships also available. Support available to part-time students. Financial award application deadline: 2/1; financial award applicants required to submit FAFSA. In 2008, 768 master's, 19 other advanced degrees awarded. *Degree program information:* Part-time and evening/weekend programs available. Postbaccalaureate distance learning degree programs offered (no on-campus study). Offers multidisciplinary studies (MA, MS). *Application deadline:* For fall admission, 5/1 priority date for domestic and international students; for spring admission, 10/1 priority date for domestic and international students. Applications are processed on a rolling basis. *Application fee:* $50. *Application Contact:* Graduate Admissions Counselor, 716-878-5601, E-mail: gradoffc@buffalostate.edu. *Associate Provost/Dean,* Dr. Kevin Railey, 716-878-5601, Fax: 716-878-5630, E-mail: raileykj@buffalostate.edu.

Faculty of Applied Science and Education *Degree program information:* Part-time and evening/weekend programs available. Postbaccalaureate distance learning degree programs offered (no on-campus study). Offers adult education (MS, Certificate); applied science and education (MPS, MS, MS Ed, CAS, Certificate); business and marketing education (MS Ed); career and technical education (MS Ed); childhood education (grades 1-6) (MS Ed); creative studies (MS); criminal justice (MS); early childhood and childhood curriculum and instruction (MS Ed); early childhood education (birth-grade 2) (MS Ed); educational computing (MS Ed); educational leadership and facilitation (CAS); elementary education (MS Ed); human resources development (Certificate); industrial technology (MS); literacy specialist (MPS, MS Ed); literacy specialist (birth-grade 6) (MS Ed); literacy specialist (grades 5-12) (MPS); special education (MS Ed); special education: adolescents (MS Ed); special education: childhood (MS Ed); special education: early childhood (MS Ed); speech language pathology (MS Ed); student personnel administration (MS); teaching bilingual exceptional individuals (MS Ed); technology education (MS Ed).

Faculty of Arts and Humanities *Degree program information:* Part-time and evening/weekend programs available. Offers art conservation (CAS); art education (MS Ed); arts and humanities (MA, MS Ed, CAS); conservation of historic works and art works (MA); English (MA); secondary education (MS Ed).

Faculty of Natural and Social Sciences *Degree program information:* Part-time and evening/weekend programs available. Offers applied economics (MA); biology (MA); chemistry (MA); history (MA); mathematics education (MS Ed); natural and social sciences (MA, MS Ed); secondary education (MS Ed); secondary education physics (MS Ed).

BUTLER UNIVERSITY, Indianapolis, IN 46208-3485

General Information Independent, coed, comprehensive institution. *Enrollment:* 4,438 graduate, professional, and undergraduate students; 372 full-time matriculated graduate/professional students (248 women), 356 part-time matriculated graduate/professional students (174 women). *Enrollment by degree level:* 245 first professional, 483 master's. *Graduate faculty:* 66 full-time (26 women), 36 part-time/adjunct (20 women). *Graduate housing:* Room and/or apartments available on a first-come, first-served basis to single students; on-campus housing not available to married students. Housing application deadline: 8/1. *Student services:* Campus employment opportunities, campus safety program, career counseling, child daycare facilities, free psychological counseling, international student services, low-cost health insurance, multicultural affairs office. *Library facilities:* Irwin Library System plus 1 other. *Online resources:* library catalog, web page, access to other libraries' catalogs. *Collection:* 361,690 titles, 25,965 serial subscriptions, 16,359 audiovisual materials.

Computer facilities: 450 computers available on campus for general student use. A campuswide network can be accessed from student residence rooms and from off campus. Online class registration is available. *Web address:* http://www.butler.edu/.

General Application Contact: Pamela Bender, Student Services Specialist, 317-940-8100, Fax: 317-940-8250, E-mail: pbender@butler.edu.

GRADUATE UNITS

College of Business Administration Students: 39 full-time (15 women), 179 part-time (49 women); includes 8 minority (6 African Americans, 1 Asian American or Pacific Islander, 1 Hispanic American), 20 international. Average age 30. 220 applicants, 29% accepted, 34 enrolled. *Faculty:* 15 full-time (4 women), 8 part-time/adjunct (0 women). Expenses: Contact institution. *Financial support:* Career-related internships or fieldwork and institutionally sponsored loans available. Support available to part-time students. Financial award application deadline: 7/15; financial award applicants required to submit FAFSA. In 2008, 58 master's awarded. *Degree program information:* Part-time and evening/weekend programs available. Offers business administration (MBA, MP Acc). *Application deadline:* For fall admission, 8/15 priority date for domestic students. Applications are processed on a rolling basis. *Application fee:* $35. Electronic applications accepted. *Application Contact:* Stephanie Judge, Director of Marketing, 317-940-9886, Fax: 317-940-9455, E-mail: sjudge@butler.edu. *Dean,* Dr. Chuck Williams, 317-940-8491, Fax: 317-940-9455, E-mail: crwillia@butler.edu.

College of Education Students: 19 full-time (11 women), 136 part-time (104 women); includes 16 minority (8 African Americans, 1 American Indian/Alaska Native, 3 Asian Americans or Pacific Islanders, 4 Hispanic Americans), 10 international. Average age 31. 77 applicants, 53% accepted, 26 enrolled. *Faculty:* 11 full-time (7 women), 14 part-time/adjunct (12 women). Expenses: Contact institution. *Financial support:* Institutionally sponsored loans available. Support available to part-time students. Financial award application deadline: 7/15; financial award applicants required to submit FAFSA. In 2008, 78 master's awarded. *Degree program information:* Part-time and evening/weekend programs available. Offers administration (MS); elementary education (MS); reading (MS); school counseling (MS); secondary education (MS); special education (MS). *Application deadline:* For fall admission, 8/15 priority date for domestic students. Applications are processed on a rolling basis. *Application fee:* $35. Electronic applications accepted. *Application Contact:* Karen Farrell, Department Secretary, 317-940-9220, E-mail: kfarrell@butler.edu. *Dean,* Dr. Ena Shelley, 317-940-9752, Fax: 317-940-6481.

College of Liberal Arts and Sciences Students: 4 full-time (3 women), 22 part-time (14 women), 3 international. Average age 37. 36 applicants, 58% accepted, 15 enrolled. *Faculty:* 3 full-time (2 women). Expenses: Contact institution. *Financial support:* Career-related internships or fieldwork, institutionally sponsored loans, and tuition waivers (full and partial) available. Support available to part-time students. Financial award applicants required to submit FAFSA. In 2008, 8 master's awarded. *Degree program information:* Part-time and evening/weekend programs available. Offers English (MA); history (MA); liberal arts and sciences (MA). *Application deadline:* For fall admission, 8/15 priority date for domestic students. Applications are processed on a rolling basis. *Application fee:* $35. Electronic applications accepted. *Application Contact:* Pamela Bender, Student Services Specialist, 317-940-8100, Fax: 317-940-8250, E-mail: pbender@butler.edu. *Interim Dean,* Dr. Judi Morrel, 317-940-9723, E-mail: jmorrel@butler.edu.

College of Pharmacy Students: 287 full-time (209 women), 7 part-time (4 women); includes 10 minority (1 African American, 7 Asian Americans or Pacific Islanders, 2 Hispanic Americans), 9 international. Average age 24. 118 applicants, 2% accepted, 1 enrolled. *Faculty:* 23 full-time (10 women), 3 part-time/adjunct (all women). Expenses: Contact institution. *Financial support:* Applicants required to submit FAFSA. In 2008, 156 first professional degrees, 29 master's awarded. *Degree program information:* Part-time and evening/weekend programs available. Offers pharmaceutical science (Pharm D, MS); physician assistance studies (MS). *Application deadline:* For fall admission, 8/1 priority date for domestic students; for spring admission, 12/15 for domestic students. Applications are processed on a rolling basis. *Application fee:* $35. Electronic applications accepted. *Application Contact:* Dr. Bruce Clayton, Professor, 317-940-9830, E-mail: bclayton@butler.edu. *Dean,* Dr. Mary Andritz, 317-940-9451, Fax: 317-940-6172, E-mail: mandritz@butler.edu.

Jordan College of Fine Arts Students: 23 full-time (10 women), 12 part-time (3 women); includes 1 minority (Hispanic American), 5 international. Average age 28. 38 applicants, 74% accepted, 9 enrolled. *Faculty:* 14 full-time (3 women), 11 part-time/adjunct (5 women). Expenses: Contact institution. *Financial support:* In 2008–09, 15 teaching assistantships with full tuition reimbursements (averaging $2,500 per year) were awarded; fellowships, career-related internships or fieldwork, institutionally sponsored loans, and scholarships/grants also available. Support available to part-time students. Financial award application deadline: 7/15;

financial award applicants required to submit FAFSA. In 2008, 14 master's awarded. *Degree program information:* Part-time and evening/weekend programs available. Offers composition (MM); conducting (MM); fine arts (MM); music (MM); music education (MM); music history (MM); organ (MM); performance (MM). *Application deadline:* For fall admission, 8/15 priority date for domestic students. Applications are processed on a rolling basis. *Application fee:* $35. Electronic applications accepted. *Application Contact:* Kathy Lang, Admission Representative, 317-940-9646, Fax: 317-940-9658, E-mail: klang@butler.edu. *Dean,* Dr. Peter Alexander, 317-940-9231, Fax: 317-940-9658, E-mail: palexand@butler.edu.

CABRINI COLLEGE, Radnor, PA 19087-3698

General Information Independent-religious, coed, comprehensive institution. CGS member. *Enrollment:* 3,580 graduate, professional, and undergraduate students; 123 full-time matriculated graduate/professional students (93 women), 1,621 part-time matriculated graduate/professional students (1,252 women). *Enrollment by degree level:* 1,744 master's. *Graduate faculty:* 6 full-time (3 women), 106 part-time/adjunct (61 women). *Tuition:* Part-time $540 per credit hour. *Required fees:* $45 per semester. Tuition and fees vary according to campus/location. *Graduate housing:* On-campus housing not available. *Student services:* Campus safety program, career counseling, exercise/wellness program, free psychological counseling, international student services, low-cost health insurance, multicultural affairs office, services for students with disabilities, teacher training. *Library facilities:* Holy Spirit Library. *Online resources:* library catalog, web page. *Collection:* 108,713 titles, 23,553 serial subscriptions, 3,030 audiovisual materials.

Computer facilities: 460 computers available on campus for general student use. A campuswide network can be accessed from student residence rooms. Online class registration, account balances and other services are available. *Web address:* http://www.cabrini.edu/.

General Application Contact: Bruce D. Bryde, Director of Enrollment and Recruiting, 610-902-8291, Fax: 610-902-8522, E-mail: bruce.d.bryde@cabrini.edu.

GRADUATE UNITS

Graduate and Professional Studies Students: 123 full-time (93 women), 1,621 part-time (1,252 women); includes 206 minority (150 African Americans, 1 American Indian/Alaska Native, 24 Asian Americans or Pacific Islanders, 31 Hispanic Americans), 1 international. Average age 32. 559 applicants, 67% accepted, 358 enrolled. *Faculty:* 6 full-time (3 women), 106 part-time/adjunct (61 women). Expenses: Contact institution. *Financial support:* Career-related internships or fieldwork and unspecified assistantships available. Support available to part-time students. Financial award applicants required to submit FAFSA. In 2008, 182 master's awarded. *Degree program information:* Part-time and evening/weekend programs available. Offers biotechnology (Certificate); education (M Ed); instructional systems technology (MS); organization leadership (MS). *Application deadline:* For fall admission, 7/29 priority date for domestic students; for spring admission, 12/9 for domestic students. Applications are processed on a rolling basis. *Application fee:* $50. Electronic applications accepted. *Application Contact:* Bruce D. Bryde, Director of Enrollment and Recruiting, 610-902-8291, Fax: 610-902-8522, E-mail: bruce.d.bryde@cabrini.edu. *Interim Dean for Graduate and Professional Studies,* Dr. Dennis R. Dougherty, 610-902-8501, Fax: 610-902-8522, E-mail: dennis.dougherty@cabrini.edu.

CALDWELL COLLEGE, Caldwell, NJ 07006-6195

General Information Independent-religious, coed, comprehensive institution. CGS member. *Graduate housing:* On-campus housing not available.

GRADUATE UNITS

Graduate Studies *Degree program information:* Part-time and evening/weekend programs available. Postbaccalaureate distance learning degree programs offered (minimal on-campus study). Offers accounting (MBA); applied behavior analysis (MA); art therapy (MA); business administration (MBA); counseling psychology (MA); curriculum and instruction (MA); educational administration (MA); pastoral ministry (MA); school counseling (MA); special education (MA). Electronic applications accepted.

See Close-Up on page 865.

CALIFORNIA BAPTIST UNIVERSITY, Riverside, CA 92504-3206

General Information Independent-religious, coed, comprehensive institution. *Enrollment:* 4,013 graduate, professional, and undergraduate students; 279 full-time matriculated graduate/professional students (191 women), 638 part-time matriculated graduate/professional students (477 women). *Enrollment by degree level:* 917 master's. *Graduate faculty:* 47 full-time (23 women), 23 part-time/adjunct (11 women). *Tuition:* Full-time $8172; part-time $454 per credit hour. *Required fees:* $510. *Graduate housing:* On-campus housing not available. *Student services:* Campus employment opportunities, campus safety program, career counseling, exercise/wellness program, free psychological counseling, international student services, low-cost health insurance, services for students with disabilities, teacher training. *Library facilities:* Annie Gabriel Library. *Online resources:* library catalog, web page, access to other libraries' catalogs. *Collection:* 180,946 titles, 11,166 serial subscriptions, 3,633 audiovisual materials.

Computer facilities: Computer purchase and lease plans are available. 279 computers available on campus for general student use. A campuswide network can be accessed from student residence rooms and from off campus. Online class registration is available. *Web address:* http://www.calbaptist.edu/.

General Application Contact: Gail Ronveaux, Dean of Graduate Enrollment, 951-343-5045, Fax: 951-343-5095, E-mail: graduateadmissions@calbaptist.edu.

GRADUATE UNITS

Program in Athletic Training Students: 20 full-time (11 women); includes 9 minority (3 African Americans, 2 Asian Americans or Pacific Islanders, 4 Hispanic Americans), 2 international. 20 applicants, 60% accepted, 10 enrolled. *Faculty:* 1 (woman) full-time. Expenses: Contact institution. *Financial support:* Federal Work-Study and scholarships/grants available. Financial award applicants required to submit FAFSA. *Degree program information:* Part-time programs available. Offers athletic training (MS). *Application deadline:* For fall admission, 8/1 priority date for domestic students, 7/1 for international students; for spring admission, 12/1 priority date for domestic students, 10/15 for international students. Applications are processed on a rolling basis. *Application fee:* $45. Electronic applications accepted. *Application Contact:* Gail Ronveaux, Dean of Graduate Enrollment, 951-343-5045, Fax: 951-343-5095, E-mail: graduateadmissions@calbaptist.edu. *Director,* Dr. Nicole MacDonald, 951-343-4379.

Program in Business Administration Students: 44 full-time (22 women), 58 part-time (20 women); includes 30 minority (11 African Americans, 2 American Indian/Alaska Native, 4 Asian Americans or Pacific Islanders, 13 Hispanic Americans), 17 international. 116 applicants, 55% accepted, 52 enrolled. *Faculty:* 5 full-time (2 women), 4 part-time/adjunct (1 woman). Expenses: Contact institution. *Financial support:* In 2008–09, 30 students received support. Federal Work-Study and scholarships/grants available. Support available to part-time students. Financial award applicants required to submit FAFSA. In 2008, 23 master's awarded. *Degree program information:* Part-time and evening/weekend programs available. Offers management (MBA). *Application deadline:* For fall admission, 8/1 priority date for domestic students, 7/1 priority date for international students; for spring admission, 12/1 priority date for domestic students, 10/15 priority date for international students. Applications are processed on a rolling basis. *Application fee:* $45. Electronic applications accepted. *Application Contact:* Gail Ronveaux, Dean of Graduate Enrollment, 951-343-5045, Fax: 951-343-5095, E-mail: graduateadmissions@calbaptist.edu. *Dean, School of Business,* Dr. Andrew Herrity, 951-343-4427, Fax: 951-343-4361, E-mail: aherrity@calbaptist.edu.

Program in Counseling Ministry Students: 2 full-time (both women), 6 part-time (5 women); includes 4 minority (1 African American, 3 Hispanic Americans). 6 applicants, 50% accepted, 3 enrolled. *Faculty:* 2 full-time (0 women). Expenses: Contact institution. *Financial support:* Federal Work-Study and scholarships/grants available. Support available to part-time students. Financial award applicants required to submit FAFSA. In 2008, 4 master's awarded. *Degree program information:* Part-time programs available. Offers counseling ministry (MA). *Application deadline:* For fall admission, 8/1 priority date for domestic students, 7/1 priority date for international students; for spring admission, 12/1 priority date for domestic students, 10/15 priority date for international students. Applications are processed on a rolling basis. *Application fee:* $45. Electronic applications accepted. *Application Contact:* Gail Ronveaux, Dean of Graduate Enrollment, 951-343-5045, Fax: 951-343-5095, E-mail: graduateadmissions@calbaptist.edu. *Director,* Dr. Nathan Lewis, 951-343-4348, Fax: 951-343-4569, E-mail: nlewis@calbaptist.edu.

Program in Counseling Psychology Students: 79 full-time (61 women), 54 part-time (42 women); includes 58 minority (14 African Americans, 1 American Indian/Alaska Native, 9 Asian Americans or Pacific Islanders, 34 Hispanic Americans), 3 international. 116 applicants, 54% accepted, 48 enrolled. *Faculty:* 4 full-time (2 women), 4 part-time/adjunct (2 women). Expenses: Contact institution. *Financial support:* Career-related internships or fieldwork, Federal Work-Study, and scholarships/grants available. Support available to part-time students. Financial award applicants required to submit FAFSA. In 2008, 45 master's awarded. *Degree program information:* Part-time programs available. Offers professional counseling (MS); professional ministry (MS). *Application deadline:* For fall admission, 9/1 for domestic students, 7/1 priority date for international students; for spring admission, 1/3 for domestic students, 10/15 priority date for international students. Applications are processed on a rolling basis. *Application fee:* $45. Electronic applications accepted. *Application Contact:* Gail Ronveaux, Dean of Graduate Enrollment, 951-343-5045, Fax: 951-343-5095, E-mail: graduateadmissions@calbaptist.edu. *Director and Associate Dean, School of Business,* Dr. Gary Collins, 951-343-4304, Fax: 951-343-4569, E-mail: gcollins@calbaptist.edu.

Program in Education Students: 61 full-time (49 women), 454 part-time (367 women); includes 197 minority (39 African Americans, 9 American Indian/Alaska Native, 16 Asian Americans or Pacific Islanders, 133 Hispanic Americans), 4 international. 259 applicants, 68% accepted, 156 enrolled. *Faculty:* 16 full-time (9 women), 10 part-time/adjunct (5 women). Expenses: Contact institution. *Financial support:* Career-related internships or fieldwork, Federal Work-Study, and scholarships/grants available. Support available to part-time students. Financial award applicants required to submit FAFSA. In 2008, 98 master's awarded. *Degree program information:* Part-time programs available. Offers cross-cultural language and academic development (MA); educational leadership (MS); educational leadership and faith-based instruction (MS); educational technology (MS); instructional computer applications (MS); reading (MS); school counseling (MS); school psychology (MS); special education (MS); special education in mild/moderate disabilities (MS); special education in moderate/severe disabilities (MS); teaching (MS); teaching and learning (MS Ed). *Application deadline:* For fall admission, 8/1 priority date for domestic students, 7/1 priority date for international students; for spring admission, 12/1 priority date for domestic students, 10/15 priority date for international students. Applications are processed on a rolling basis. *Application fee:* $45. Electronic applications accepted. *Application Contact:* Gail Ronveaux, Dean of Graduate Enrollment, 951-343-5045, Fax: 951-343-5095, E-mail: graduateadmissions@calbaptist.edu. *Dean, School of Education,* Dr. Mary Crist, 951-343-4313, Fax: 951-343-4516, E-mail: mcrist@calbaptist.edu.

Program in English Students: 4 full-time (all women), 27 part-time (20 women); includes 5 minority (1 African American, 1 Asian American or Pacific Islander, 3 Hispanic Americans), 5 international. 17 applicants, 59% accepted, 10 enrolled. *Faculty:* 5 full-time (4 women), 2 part-time/adjunct (1 woman). Expenses: Contact institution. *Financial support:* Federal Work-Study available. Support available to part-time students. Financial award applicants required to submit FAFSA. In 2008, 10 master's awarded. *Degree program information:* Part-time programs available. Offers English pedagogy (MA); literature (MA); teaching English as a second language (TESOL) (MA). *Application deadline:* For fall admission, 8/1 priority date for domestic students, 7/1 priority date for international students; for spring admission, 12/1 priority date for domestic students, 10/15 priority date for international students. Applications are processed on a rolling basis. *Application fee:* $45. Electronic applications accepted. *Application Contact:* Gail Ronveaux, Dean of Graduate Enrollment, 951-343-5045, Fax: 951-343-5095, E-mail: graduateadmissions@calbaptist.edu. *Director,* Dr. Jennifer Newton, 951-343-4276, Fax: 951-343-4661, E-mail: jnewton@calbaptist.edu.

Program in Forensic Psychology Students: 15 full-time (12 women), 4 part-time (3 women); includes 9 minority (2 African Americans, 1 American Indian/Alaska Native, 2 Asian Americans or Pacific Islanders, 4 Hispanic Americans). 19 applicants, 63% accepted, 11 enrolled. *Faculty:* 2 full-time (both women), 1 part-time/adjunct (0 women). Expenses: Contact institution. *Financial support:* Federal Work-Study and scholarships/grants available. Support available to part-time students. Financial award applicants required to submit FAFSA. *Degree program information:* Part-time programs available. Offers forensic psychology (MA). *Application deadline:* For fall admission, 8/1 priority date for domestic students, 7/1 for international students; for spring admission, 12/1 priority date for domestic students, 10/15 for international students. Applications are processed on a rolling basis. *Application fee:* $45. Electronic applications accepted. *Application Contact:* Gail Ronveaux, Dean of Graduate Enrollment, 951-343-5045, Fax: 951-343-5095, E-mail: graduateadmissions@calbaptist.edu. *Director,* Dr. Anne-Marie Larsen, 951-343-4761.

Program in Kinesiology Students: 11 full-time (4 women), 8 part-time (4 women); includes 9 minority (1 African American, 1 Asian American or Pacific Islander, 7 Hispanic Americans). 15 applicants, 87% accepted, 8 enrolled. *Faculty:* 2 full-time (0 women). Expenses: Contact institution. *Financial support:* Federal Work-Study and scholarships/grants available. Support available to part-time students. Financial award applicants required to submit FAFSA. In 2008, 24 master's awarded. *Degree program information:* Part-time programs available. Offers physical education pedagogy (MS); sport management (MS). *Application deadline:* For fall admission, 8/1 priority date for domestic students, 7/1 priority date for international students; for spring admission, 12/1 priority date for domestic students, 10/15 priority date for international students. Applications are processed on a rolling basis. *Application fee:* $45. Electronic applications accepted. *Application Contact:* Gail Ronveaux, Dean of Graduate Enrollment, 951-343-5045, Fax: 951-343-5095, E-mail: graduateadmissions@calbaptist.edu. *Chair, Department of Kinesiology,* Dr. Sean Sullivan, 951-343-4528, E-mail: ssullivan@calbaptist.edu.

Program in Music Students: 16 full-time (9 women), 1 part-time (0 women); includes 5 minority (2 African Americans, 1 Asian American or Pacific Islander, 2 Hispanic Americans), 5 international. 15 applicants, 73% accepted, 9 enrolled. *Faculty:* 5 full-time (1 woman). Expenses: Contact institution. *Financial support:* Federal Work-Study and scholarships/grants available. Support available to part-time students. Financial award applicants required to submit FAFSA. In 2008, 3 master's awarded. *Degree program information:* Part-time programs available. Offers conducting (MM); music education (MM); performance (MM). *Application deadline:* For fall admission, 8/1 priority date for domestic students, 7/1 for international students; for spring admission, 12/1 priority date for domestic students, 10/15 for international students. Applications are processed on a rolling basis. *Application fee:* $45. Electronic applications accepted. *Application Contact:* Gail Ronveaux, Dean of Graduate Enrollment, 951-343-5045, Fax: 951-343-5095, E-mail: graduateadmissions@calbaptist.edu. *Dean, School of Music,* Dr. Gary Bonner, 951-343-4251, Fax: 951-343-4570, E-mail: gbonner@calbaptist.edu.

Program in Nursing Students: 9 full-time (8 women); includes 3 minority (1 African American, 1 Asian American or Pacific Islander, 1 Hispanic American), 1 international. *Faculty:* 2 full-time (1 woman), 2 part-time/adjunct (both women). Expenses: Contact institution. Offers nursing (MS). *Application deadline:* For fall admission, 8/1 priority date for domestic students; for spring admission, 12/1 priority date for domestic students. Applications are processed on a rolling basis. Electronic applications accepted. *Application Contact:* Gail Ronveaux, Dean of Graduate Enrollment, 951-343-5045, Fax: 951-343-5095, E-mail: graduateadmissions@calbaptist.edu. *Dean, School of Nursing,* Dr. Constance Milton, 951-343-4700, E-mail: cmilton@calbaptist.edu.

Program in Public Administration Students: 19 full-time (10 women), 21 part-time (11 women); includes 13 minority (7 African Americans, 6 Hispanic Americans), 3 international. 29 applicants, 62% accepted, 14 enrolled. *Faculty:* 3 full-time (1 woman). Expenses: Contact institution. *Financial support:* Federal Work-Study and scholarships/grants available. Support available to part-time students. Financial award applicants required to submit FAFSA. In 2008, 4 master's awarded. *Degree program information:* Part-time programs available. Offers public administration (MPA). *Application deadline:* For fall admission, 8/1 priority date for domestic students, 7/1 priority date for international students; for spring admission, 12/1

California Baptist University (continued)
priority date for domestic students, 10/15 priority date for international students. Applications are processed on a rolling basis. *Application fee:* $45. Electronic applications accepted. *Application Contact:* Gail Ronveaux, Dean of Graduate Enrollment, 951-343-5045, Fax: 951-343-5095, E-mail: graduateadmissions@calbaptist.edu. *Director,* Dr. Patricia Kircher, 951-343-4306, Fax: 951-343-4661, E-mail: pkircher@calbaptist.edu.

CALIFORNIA COAST UNIVERSITY, Santa Ana, CA 92701

General Information Proprietary, coed, comprehensive institution.

GRADUATE UNITS

Program in Psychology *Degree program information:* Part-time programs available. Postbaccalaureate distance learning degree programs offered (no on-campus study). Offers psychology (MS).

Programs in Business Administration *Degree program information:* Part-time programs available. Postbaccalaureate distance learning degree programs offered (no on-campus study). Offers human resources (MBA); management (MS).

Programs in Education *Degree program information:* Part-time programs available. Postbaccalaureate distance learning degree programs offered (no on-campus study). Offers administration (M Ed); curriculum and instruction (M Ed).

CALIFORNIA COLLEGE OF THE ARTS, San Francisco, CA 94107

General Information Independent, coed, comprehensive institution. *Graduate housing:* Room and/or apartments available on a first-come, first-served basis to single students; on-campus housing not available to married students. Housing application deadline: 4/1.

GRADUATE UNITS

Graduate Programs Offers architecture (M Arch); ceramics (MFA); curatorial practice (MA); design (MFA); design strategy (MBA); film/video/performance (MFA); glass (MFA); jewelry/metal arts (MFA); painting/drawing (MFA); photography (MFA); printmaking (MFA); sculpture (MFA); textiles (MFA); visual and critical studies (MA); wood/furniture (MFA); writing (MFA).

CALIFORNIA INSTITUTE OF INTEGRAL STUDIES, San Francisco, CA 94103

General Information Independent, coed, upper-level institution. CGS member. *Enrollment:* 867 full-time matriculated graduate/professional students (626 women), 215 part-time matriculated graduate/professional students (146 women). *Enrollment by degree level:* 580 master's, 502 doctoral, 1,082 other advanced degrees. *Graduate faculty:* 57 full-time, 91 part-time/adjunct. *Tuition:* Part-time $815 per contact hour. *Required fees:* $135 per semester. Tuition and fees vary according to degree level. *Graduate housing:* On-campus housing not available. *Student services:* Campus employment opportunities, career counseling, grant writing training, international student services, low-cost health insurance, multicultural affairs office, services for students with disabilities, writing training. *Library facilities:* The Laurance S. Rockefeller. *Collection:* 4,000 titles. *Research affiliation:* Bay Area Reference Service.

Computer facilities: A campuswide network can be accessed from off campus. *Web address:* http://www.ciis.edu/.

General Application Contact: Cori Watkins, Admissions Inquiries Coordinator, 415-575-6151, Fax: 415-575-1268, E-mail: cwatkins@ciis.edu.

GRADUATE UNITS

School of Consciousness and Transformation Students: 334 full-time (218 women), 126 part-time (77 women); includes 102 minority (39 African Americans, 4 American Indian/Alaska Native, 35 Asian Americans or Pacific Islanders, 24 Hispanic Americans), 1 international. Average age 37. 223 applicants, 78% accepted, 110 enrolled. *Faculty:* 29 full-time, 32 part-time/adjunct. Expenses: Contact institution. *Financial support:* In 2008–09, 271 students received support; research assistantships, teaching assistantships, career-related internships or fieldwork, Federal Work-Study, institutionally sponsored loans, scholarships/grants, and tuition waivers (partial) available. Support available to part-time students. Financial award application deadline: 3/15; financial award applicants required to submit FAFSA. In 2008, 93 master's, 30 doctorates awarded. *Degree program information:* Part-time and evening/weekend programs available. Postbaccalaureate distance learning degree programs offered (minimal on-campus study). Offers cultural anthropology and social transformation (MA); East-West psychology (MA, PhD); integrative health studies (MA); philosophy and religion (MA, PhD), social and cultural anthropology (PhD); transformative leadership (MA); transformative studies (PhD). *Application deadline:* For fall admission, 2/1 priority date for domestic and international students; for spring admission, 10/15 priority date for domestic and international students. Applications are processed on a rolling basis. *Application fee:* $65. Electronic applications accepted. *Application Contact:* Allyson Werner, Senior Admissions Counselor, 415-575-6155, Fax: 415-575-1268.

School of Professional Psychology Students: 553 full-time (408 women), 88 part-time (69 women); includes 132 minority (25 African Americans, 3 American Indian/Alaska Native, 57 Asian Americans or Pacific Islanders, 47 Hispanic Americans). Average age 37. 506 applicants, 61% accepted, 181 enrolled. *Faculty:* 28 full-time, 59 part-time/adjunct. Expenses: Contact institution. *Financial support:* In 2008–09, 496 students received support; research assistantships with tuition reimbursements available, teaching assistantships with tuition reimbursements available, career-related internships or fieldwork, Federal Work-Study, institutionally sponsored loans, scholarships/grants, and tuition waivers (partial) available. Support available to part-time students. Financial award application deadline: 3/15; financial award applicants required to submit FAFSA. In 2008, 109 master's, 20 doctorates awarded. *Degree program information:* Part-time programs available. Offers clinical psychology (Psy D); community mental health (MA); drama therapy (MA); expressive arts therapy (MA); integral counseling psychology (MA); integral counseling, psychology-weekend (MA); somatic psychology (MA). *Application deadline:* For fall admission, 2/1 priority date for domestic and international students; for spring admission, 10/15 priority date for domestic and international students. Applications are processed on a rolling basis. *Application fee:* $65. Electronic applications accepted. *Application Contact:* David Townes, Senior Admissions Counselor, 415-575-6152, Fax: 415-575-1268, E-mail: dtownes@ciis.edu.

CALIFORNIA INSTITUTE OF TECHNOLOGY, Pasadena, CA 91125-0001

General Information Independent, coed, university. CGS member. *Graduate housing:* Rooms and/or apartments available on a first-come, first-served basis to single students and available to married students. Housing application deadline: 5/1. *Research affiliation:* Scripps Institute of Oceanography, Stanford Linear Accelerator Center (high-energy physics), European Center for Nuclear Research (high-energy physics), National Science Foundation Center for Research in Parallel Computing, Cosmic Gravitational Waves Observatory (laser interferometer gravitational waves).

GRADUATE UNITS

Division of Biology Offers biochemistry and molecular biophysics (MS, PhD); cell biology and biophysics (PhD); developmental biology (PhD); genetics (PhD); immunology (PhD); molecular biology (PhD); neurobiology (PhD). Electronic applications accepted.

Division of Chemistry and Chemical Engineering Students: 323 full-time (122 women). Average age 27. 656 applicants, 23% accepted, 48 enrolled. *Faculty:* 57 full-time (13 women). Expenses: Contact institution. *Financial support:* Fellowships, research assistantships, teaching assistantships, Federal Work-Study, institutionally sponsored loans, scholarships/grants, traineeships, health care benefits, and unspecified assistantships available. Financial award application deadline: 1/1. In 2008, 11 master's, 47 doctorates awarded. *Degree program information:* Part-time and evening/weekend programs available. Postbaccalaureate distance learning degree programs offered (minimal on-campus study). Offers biochemistry and molecular biophysics (MS, PhD); chemical engineering (MS, PhD); chemistry (MS, PhD). *Application deadline:* For fall admission, 1/1 for domestic and international students. *Application fee:* $80. Electronic applications accepted. *Application Contact:* Natalie Gilmore, Graduate Office, 626-395-3812, Fax: 626-577-9246, E-mail: ngilmore@its.caltech.edu. *Chair,* Prof. Jacqueline K. Barton, 626-395-3646, Fax: 626-568-8824, E-mail: jkbarton@caltech.edu.

Division of Engineering and Applied Science Offers aeronautics (MS, PhD, Engr); applied and computational mathematics (MS, PhD); applied mechanics (MS, PhD); applied physics (MS, PhD); bioengineering (MS, PhD); civil engineering (MS, PhD, Engr); computation and neural systems (MS, PhD); computer science (MS, PhD); control and dynamical systems (MS, PhD); electrical engineering (MS, PhD, Engr); environmental science and engineering (MS, PhD); materials science (MS, PhD); mechanical engineering (MS, PhD, Engr). Electronic applications accepted.

Division of Geological and Planetary Sciences Students: 72 full-time (37 women); includes 23 minority (1 African American, 19 Asian Americans or Pacific Islanders, 3 Hispanic Americans). Average age 26. 127 applicants, 24% accepted, 16 enrolled. *Faculty:* 37 full-time (5 women). Expenses: Contact institution. *Financial support:* In 2008–09, 72 students received support, including 23 fellowships with full tuition reimbursements available (averaging $26,050 per year), 49 research assistantships with full tuition reimbursements available (averaging $26,050 per year); teaching assistantships with full tuition reimbursements available, institutionally sponsored loans, scholarships/grants, health care benefits, and unspecified assistantships also available. Financial award applicants required to submit FAFSA. In 2008, 13 master's, 9 doctorates awarded. Offers geobiology (PhD); geochemistry (MS, PhD); geology (MS, PhD); geophysics (MS, PhD); planetary science (MS, PhD). *Application deadline:* For fall admission, 1/1 for domestic and international students. *Application fee:* $80. Electronic applications accepted. *Application Contact:* Dr. Robert W. Clayton, Academic Officer, 626-395-6909, Fax: 626-795-6028, E-mail: dianb@gps.caltech.edu. *Chairman,* Dr. Kenneth A. Farley, 626-395-6111, Fax: 626-795-6028, E-mail: dianb@gps.caltech.edu.

Division of Physics, Mathematics and Astronomy Offers astronomy (PhD); mathematics (PhD); physics (PhD).

Division of the Humanities and Social Sciences Students: 35 full-time (9 women); includes 3 minority (2 Asian Americans or Pacific Islanders, 1 Hispanic American), 18 international. Average age 27. 173 applicants, 15% accepted, 6 enrolled. *Faculty:* 31 full-time (3 women). Expenses: Contact institution. *Financial support:* In 2008–09, 35 students received support, including 11 fellowships with tuition reimbursements available (averaging $25,500 per year), 13 research assistantships with tuition reimbursements available (averaging $25,500 per year), 11 teaching assistantships with tuition reimbursements available (averaging $25,500 per year); Federal Work-Study, institutionally sponsored loans, and scholarships/grants also available. In 2008, 7 master's, 4 doctorates awarded. Offers humanities and social sciences (MS, PhD); social science (MS, PhD). *Application deadline:* For fall admission, 12/15 for domestic and international students. *Application fee:* $80. Electronic applications accepted. *Application Contact:* Laurel Auchampaugh, Graduate Secretary, 626-395-4206, Fax: 626-405-9841, E-mail: gradsec@hss.caltech.edu. Dr. Jonathan Katz.

CALIFORNIA INSTITUTE OF THE ARTS, Valencia, CA 91355-2340

General Information Independent, coed, comprehensive institution. *Graduate housing:* Room and/or apartments available on a first-come, first-served basis to single students; on-campus housing not available to married students. Housing application deadline: 7/1.

GRADUATE UNITS

School of Art Offers art (MFA, Adv C); graphic design (MFA, Adv C); photography (MFA, Adv C). Electronic applications accepted.

School of Critical Studies Offers writing (MFA, Adv C).

School of Dance Offers dance (MFA, Adv C).

School of Film/Video Offers experimental animation (MFA); film directing (MFA, Adv C); film/video (Adv C). Electronic applications accepted.

School of Music *Degree program information:* Part-time programs available. Offers African music (MFA, Adv C); composition (MFA, Adv C); composition/new media (MFA, Adv C); Indonesian music (MFA, Adv C); jazz (MFA, Adv C); North Indian music (MFA, Adv C); performance (MFA, Adv C); performer/composer (MFA, Adv C); voice (MFA, Adv C); world music performance (MFA). Electronic applications accepted.

School of Theatre Offers acting (MFA, Adv C); design and technology (Adv C); directing (MFA); performing arts design and technology (MFA); theater management (MFA, Adv C); writing for performance (MFA). Electronic applications accepted.

CALIFORNIA INTERCONTINENTAL UNIVERSITY, Diamond Bar, CA 91765

General Information Proprietary, coed, comprehensive institution.

GRADUATE UNITS

Hollywood College of the Entertainment Industry Offers Hollywood and entertainment management (MBA).

School of Business Offers banking and finance (MBA); entrepreneurship and business management (DBA); global business leadership (DBA); international management and marketing (MBA); organizational management and human resource management (MBA).

School of Healthcare Offers healthcare management and leadership (MBA, DBA).

School of Information Technology Offers information systems and enterprise resource management (DBA); information systems and knowledge management (MBA); project and quality management (MBA).

CALIFORNIA INTERNATIONAL BUSINESS UNIVERSITY, San Diego, CA 92101

General Information Independent, coed, graduate-only institution.

GRADUATE UNITS

Graduate Programs Offers business (MBA, MSIM, DBA).

CALIFORNIA LUTHERAN UNIVERSITY, Thousand Oaks, CA 91360-2787

General Information Independent-religious, coed, comprehensive institution. CGS member. *Enrollment:* 3,499 graduate, professional, and undergraduate students; 839 full-time matriculated graduate/professional students (579 women), 458 part-time matriculated graduate/professional students (233 women). *Enrollment by degree level:* 1,163 master's, 93 doctoral, 41 other advanced degrees. *Graduate faculty:* 34 full-time (18 women), 80 part-time/adjunct (42 women). *Graduate housing:* Rooms and/or apartments available on a first-come, first-served basis to single and married students. *Student services:* Campus employment opportunities, career counseling, free psychological counseling, international student services, low-cost health insurance, multicultural affairs office, services for students with disabilities, writing training. *Library facilities:* Pearson Library. *Online resources:* library catalog, web page. *Collection:* 132,744 titles, 1,497 serial subscriptions.

Computer facilities: 300 computers available on campus for general student use. A campuswide network can be accessed from student residence rooms and from off campus. Online class registration is available. *Web address:* http://www.callutheran.edu/.

General Application Contact: Information Contact, 805-493-3127, Fax: 805-493-3542, E-mail: clugrad@clunet.edu.

GRADUATE UNITS

Graduate Studies Students: 839 full-time (260 women), 458 part-time (225 women); includes 363 minority (44 African Americans, 4 American Indian/Alaska Native, 97 Asian Americans or Pacific Islanders, 218 Hispanic Americans), 131 international. Average age 33. 674 applicants, 76% accepted. *Faculty:* 34 full-time (18 women), 80 part-time/adjunct (42 women). Expenses: Contact institution. *Financial support:* In 2008–09, 584 students received support. Available to part-time students. Applicants required to submit FAFSA. In 2008, 390 master's, 16 doctorates awarded. *Degree program information:* Part-time and evening/weekend programs available. Offers clinical psychology (MS); marital and family therapy (MS); public policy and administration (MPPA). *Application deadline:* Applications are processed on a rolling basis. *Application fee:* $50. *Application Contact:* 805-493-3127, Fax: 805-493-3542, E-mail: clugrad@clunet.edu. *Provost/Vice President for Academic Affairs*, Dr. Leanne Neilson, 805-493-3145, E-mail: neilson@clunet.edu.

School of Business Students: 259 full-time (115 women), 273 part-time (109 women); includes 148 minority (22 African Americans, 1 American Indian/Alaska Native, 67 Asian Americans or Pacific Islanders, 58 Hispanic Americans), 103 international. Average age 33. 238 applicants, 68% accepted. *Faculty:* 12 full-time (3 women), 27 part-time/adjunct (6 women). Expenses: Contact institution. *Financial support:* In 2008–09, 134 students received support. In 2008, 213 master's awarded. *Degree program information:* Evening/weekend programs available. Postbaccalaureate distance learning degree programs offered. Offers business (IMBA); entrepreneurship (MBA, Certificate); finance (MBA, Certificate); financial planning (MBA, Certificate); information systems and technology (MS); information technology management (MBA, Certificate); international business (MBA, Certificate); management and organization behavior (MBA); management and organizational behavior (Certificate); marketing (MBA, Certificate). *Application deadline:* Applications are processed on a rolling basis. *Application fee:* $50. *Application Contact:* 805-493-3127, Fax: 805-493-3542, E-mail: clugrad@clunet.edu. *Director*, Dr. Ronald Hagler, 805-493-3371.

School of Education Students: 417 full-time (338 women), 117 part-time (95 women); includes 159 minority (15 African Americans, 2 American Indian/Alaska Native, 19 Asian Americans or Pacific Islanders, 123 Hispanic Americans), 12 international. Average age 34. 194 applicants, 81% accepted. *Faculty:* 22 full-time (15 women), 36 part-time/adjunct (24 women). Expenses: Contact institution. *Financial support:* In 2008–09, 323 students received support. In 2008, 105 master's, 16 doctorates awarded. *Degree program information:* Part-time and evening/weekend programs available. Offers counseling and guidance (MS); curriculum and instruction (MA); educational leadership (MA, Ed D); educational leadership (k-12) (Ed D); higher education leadership (Ed D); reading education (MA); special education (MS); teaching (M Ed). *Application deadline:* For fall admission, 6/28 priority date for domestic students; for spring admission, 11/2 priority date for domestic students. Applications are processed on a rolling basis. *Application fee:* $50. *Application Contact:* 805-493-3127, Fax: 805-493-3542, E-mail: clugrad@clunet.edu. *Dean*, Dr. Carol Bartell, 805-493-3421.

CALIFORNIA NATIONAL UNIVERSITY FOR ADVANCED STUDIES, Northridge, CA 91325-3576

General Information Proprietary, coed, comprehensive institution.

GRADUATE UNITS

College of Business Administration *Degree program information:* Part-time programs available. Postbaccalaureate distance learning degree programs offered (no on-campus study). Offers business administration (MBA, MHRM). Electronic applications accepted.

College of Engineering *Degree program information:* Part-time programs available. Postbaccalaureate distance learning degree programs offered (no on-campus study). Offers engineering (MS Eng). Electronic applications accepted.

College of Quality and Engineering Management *Degree program information:* Part-time programs available. Offers quality and engineering management (MEM).

CALIFORNIA POLYTECHNIC STATE UNIVERSITY, SAN LUIS OBISPO, San Luis Obispo, CA 93407

General Information State-supported, coed, comprehensive institution. CGS member. *Enrollment:* 19,471 graduate, professional, and undergraduate students; 537 full-time matriculated graduate/professional students (230 women), 251 part-time matriculated graduate/professional students (101 women). *Enrollment by degree level:* 788 master's. *Graduate faculty:* 168 full-time (40 women), 30 part-time/adjunct (12 women). Tuition, nonresident: full-time $10,170; part-time $226 per unit. *Required fees:* $5751; $1265 per quarter. *Student services:* Campus employment opportunities, campus safety program, career counseling, child daycare facilities, exercise/wellness program, free psychological counseling, grant writing training, international student services, low-cost health insurance, multicultural affairs office, services for students with disabilities, teacher training, writing training. *Library facilities:* Kennedy Library plus 1 other. *Online resources:* library catalog, web page, access to other libraries' catalogs. *Collection:* 763,651 titles, 5,529 serial subscriptions.

Computer facilities: A campuswide network can be accessed from student residence rooms and from off campus. Online class registration is available. *Web address:* http://www.calpoly.edu/.

General Application Contact: Dr. James Maraviglia, Assistant Vice President for Admissions, Recruitment and Financial Aid, 805-756-2311, Fax: 805-756-5400, E-mail: admissions@calpoly.edu.

GRADUATE UNITS

College of Agriculture, Food and Environmental Sciences Students: 76 full-time (41 women), 42 part-time (21 women); includes 24 minority (2 African Americans, 2 American Indian/Alaska Native, 5 Asian Americans or Pacific Islanders, 15 Hispanic Americans), 3 international. Average age 28. 100 applicants, 62% accepted, 45 enrolled. *Faculty:* 38 full-time (7 women), 4 part-time/adjunct (0 women). Expenses: Contact institution. *Financial support:* Fellowships, research assistantships, teaching assistantships, career-related internships or fieldwork, Federal Work-Study, institutionally sponsored loans, and scholarships/grants available. Support available to part-time students. Financial award application deadline: 3/2; financial award applicants required to submit FAFSA. In 2008, 28 master's awarded. *Degree program information:* Part-time programs available. Offers agribusiness (MS); agriculture (MS); agriculture, food and environmental sciences (MS); forestry sciences (MS). *Application deadline:* For fall admission, 7/1 for domestic students, 11/30 for international students; for winter admission, 11/1 for domestic students, 6/30 for international students; for spring admission, 2/1 for domestic students. Applications are processed on a rolling basis. *Application fee:* $55. Electronic applications accepted. *Application Contact:* Dr. Mark Shelton, Associate Dean/Graduate Coordinator, 805-756-2161, Fax: 805-756-6577, E-mail: mshelton@calpoly.edu. *Dean*, Dr. David J. Wehner, 805-756-2161, Fax: 805-756-6577, E-mail: dwehner@calpoly.edu.

College of Architecture and Environmental Design Students: 54 full-time (24 women), 10 part-time (6 women); includes 14 minority (8 Asian Americans or Pacific Islanders, 6 Hispanic Americans), 1 international. Average age 27. 87 applicants, 62% accepted, 31 enrolled. *Faculty:* 12 full-time (2 women), 5 part-time/adjunct (2 women). Expenses: Contact institution. *Financial support:* Research assistantships, teaching assistantships, career-related internships or fieldwork, Federal Work-Study, and institutionally sponsored loans available. Support available to part-time students. Financial award application deadline: 3/2; financial award applicants required to submit FAFSA. In 2008, 13 master's awarded. *Degree program information:* Part-time programs available. Offers architecture (MS); architecture and environmental design (MCRP, MS); city and regional planning (MCRP). *Application deadline:* For fall admission, 7/1 for domestic students, 11/30 for international students; for winter admission, 11/1 for domestic students, 6/30 for international students. Applications are processed on a rolling basis. *Application fee:* $55. Electronic applications accepted. *Application Contact:* Dr. James Maraviglia, Assistant Vice President for Admissions, Recruitment and Financial Aid, 805-756-2311, Fax: 805-756-5400, E-mail: admissions@calpoly.edu. *Dean*, R. Thomas Jones, 805-756-1414, Fax: 805-756-2765, E-mail: rtjones@calpoly.edu.

College of Education Students: 68 full-time (56 women), 8 part-time (all women); includes 19 minority (5 Asian Americans or Pacific Islanders, 14 Hispanic Americans). Average age 31. 117 applicants, 55% accepted, 49 enrolled. *Faculty:* 7 full-time (4 women), 6 part-time/adjunct (5 women). Expenses: Contact institution. *Financial support:* Research assistantships, career-related internships or fieldwork, Federal Work-Study, and institutionally sponsored loans available. Support available to part-time students. Financial award application deadline: 3/2; financial award applicants required to submit FAFSA. In 2008, 66 master's awarded. *Degree program information:* Part-time and evening/weekend programs available. Offers education (MA). *Application deadline:* For fall admission, 2/1 priority date for domestic students, 11/30 for international students. *Application fee:* $55. *Application Contact:* Dr. James Maraviglia, Assistant Vice President for Admissions, Recruitment and Financial Aid, 805-756-2311, Fax: 805-756-5400, E-mail: admissions@calpoly.edu. *Dean*, Dr. Bonnie Konopak, 805-756-2126, Fax: 805-756-5682, E-mail: bkonopak@calpoly.edu.

College of Engineering Students: 209 full-time (27 women), 77 part-time (13 women); includes 83 minority (4 African Americans, 1 American Indian/Alaska Native, 53 Asian Americans or Pacific Islanders, 25 Hispanic Americans), 11 international. Average age 26. 221 applicants, 74% accepted, 119 enrolled. *Faculty:* 66 full-time (14 women), 7 part-time/adjunct (1 woman). Expenses: Contact institution. *Financial support:* Fellowships, research assistantships, teaching assistantships, career-related internships or fieldwork, Federal Work-Study, institutionally sponsored loans, and unspecified assistantships available. Support available to part-time students. Financial award application deadline: 3/2; financial award applicants required to submit FAFSA. In 2008, 149 master's awarded. *Degree program information:* Part-time programs available. Offers aerospace engineering (MS); civil and environmental engineering (MS); computer science (MS); electrical engineering (MS); engineering (MS); general engineering (MS); industrial engineering (MS); mechanical engineering (MS). *Application deadline:* For fall admission, 7/1 for domestic students, 11/30 for international students; for winter admission, 11/1 for domestic students, 6/30 for international students; for spring admission, 2/1 for domestic students. Applications are processed on a rolling basis. *Application fee:* $55. Electronic applications accepted. *Application Contact:* Dr. Mohammad Noori, Dean, 805-756-2131, Fax: 805-756-6503, E-mail: mnoori@calpoly.edu. *Dean*, Dr. Mohammad Noori, 805-756-2131, Fax: 805-756-6503, E-mail: mnoori@calpoly.edu.

College of Liberal Arts Students: 49 full-time (40 women), 78 part-time (39 women); includes 16 minority (2 African Americans, 2 Asian Americans or Pacific Islanders, 12 Hispanic Americans). Average age 29. 161 applicants, 52% accepted, 49 enrolled. *Faculty:* 12 full-time (8 women), 3 part-time/adjunct (2 women). Expenses: Contact institution. *Financial support:* Teaching assistantships, career-related internships or fieldwork, Federal Work-Study, institutionally sponsored loans, scholarships/grants, and tutorships, writing laboratory assistantships available. Support available to part-time students. Financial award application deadline: 3/2; financial award applicants required to submit FAFSA. In 2008, 53 master's awarded. *Degree program information:* Part-time programs available. Offers English (MA); history (MA); liberal arts (MA, MPP, MS); political science (MPP); psychology (MS). *Application deadline:* For fall admission, 5/1 for domestic students, 11/30 for international students; for winter admission, 11/1 for domestic students, 6/30 for international students; for spring admission, 2/1 for domestic students. *Application fee:* $55. *Application Contact:* Dr. Linda Halisky, Dean, 805-756-2706, Fax: 805-756-5748, E-mail: lhalisky@calpoly.edu. *Dean*, Dr. Linda Halisky, 805-756-2706, Fax: 805-756-5748, E-mail: lhalisky@calpoly.edu.

College of Science and Mathematics Students: 37 full-time (23 women), 22 part-time (7 women); includes 11 minority (1 American Indian/Alaska Native, 8 Asian Americans or Pacific Islanders, 2 Hispanic Americans), 1 international. Average age 26. 79 applicants, 61% accepted, 27 enrolled. *Faculty:* 22 full-time (5 women), 4 part-time/adjunct (2 women). Expenses: Contact institution. *Financial support:* Research assistantships, teaching assistantships, career-related internships or fieldwork and Federal Work-Study available. Support available to part-time students. Financial award application deadline: 3/2; financial award applicants required to submit FAFSA. In 2008, 23 master's awarded. *Degree program information:* Part-time programs available. Offers biological sciences (MS); kinesiology (MS); mathematics (MS); polymers and coating science (MS); science and mathematics (MS). *Application deadline:* For fall admission, 7/1 for domestic students, 11/30 for international students; for winter admission, 11/1 for domestic students, 6/30 for international students; for spring admission, 2/1 for domestic students. *Application fee:* $55. Electronic applications accepted. *Application Contact:* Dr. James Maraviglia, Assistant Vice President for Admissions, Recruitment and Financial Aid, 805-756-2311, Fax: 805-756-5400, E-mail: admissions@calpoly.edu. *Dean*, Dr. Philip S. Bailey, 805-756-2226, Fax: 805-756-1670, E-mail: pbailey@calpoly.edu.

Orfalea College of Business Students: 44 full-time (19 women), 14 part-time (7 women); includes 10 minority (1 American Indian/Alaska Native, 1 Asian American or Pacific Islander, 8 Hispanic Americans), 2 international. Average age 27. 110 applicants, 45% accepted, 41 enrolled. *Faculty:* 11 full-time (2 women), 1 part-time/adjunct (0 women). Expenses: Contact institution. *Financial support:* Career-related internships or fieldwork, Federal Work-Study, institutionally sponsored loans, scholarships/grants, and unspecified assistantships available. Support available to part-time students. Financial award application deadline: 3/2; financial award applicants required to submit FAFSA. In 2008, 103 master's awarded. Offers business (MBA); industrial and technical studies (MS); taxation (MSA). *Application deadline:* For fall admission, 7/1 for domestic students, 11/30 for international students. Applications are processed on a rolling basis. *Application fee:* $55. Electronic applications accepted. *Application Contact:* Dr. Chris Carr, Associate Dean, 805-756-2637, Fax: 805-756-0110, E-mail: ccarr@calpoly.edu. *Dean*, Dr. David P. Christy, 805-756-2705, Fax: 805-756-5452, E-mail: dchristy@calpoly.edu.

CALIFORNIA SCHOOL OF PODIATRIC MEDICINE AT SAMUEL MERRITT COLLEGE, Oakland, CA 94609

General Information Independent, coed, graduate-only institution. *Graduate housing:* Room and/or apartments available on a first-come, first-served basis to single students; on-campus housing not available to married students. *Research affiliation:* University of Southern California–Los Angeles County Medical Center, University of California, San Francisco Health Sciences Center, University of Texas Health Science Center–San Antonio.

GRADUATE UNITS

Graduate and Professional Programs Offers podiatric medicine (DPM).

CALIFORNIA STATE POLYTECHNIC UNIVERSITY, POMONA, Pomona, CA 91768-2557

General Information State-supported, coed, comprehensive institution. CGS member. *Enrollment:* 21,190 graduate, professional, and undergraduate students; 426 full-time matriculated graduate/professional students (243 women), 996 part-time matriculated graduate/professional students (511 women). *Enrollment by degree level:* 1,422 master's. *Graduate faculty:* 559 full-time (238 women), 456 part-time/adjunct (171 women). Tuition, nonresident: full-time $7232; part-time $226 per credit. *Required fees:* $4272. One-time fee: $2694 part-time. Tuition and fees vary according to course load. *Graduate housing:* Room and/or apartments available on a first-come, first-served basis to single students; on-campus housing not available to married students. Typical cost: $5580 per year ($9120 including board). Room and board charges vary according to board plan and housing facility selected. Housing application deadline: 5/1. *Student services:* Campus employment opportunities, campus safety program, career counseling, child daycare facilities, free psychological counseling, international student services, low-cost health insurance, multicultural affairs office, services for students with disabilities. *Library facilities:* University Library. *Online resources:* library catalog, web page, access to other libraries' catalogs. *Collection:* 757,460 titles, 8,445 serial subscriptions, 11,280 audiovisual materials.

Computer facilities: Computer purchase and lease plans are available. 1,850 computers available on campus for general student use. A campuswide network can be accessed from student residence rooms and from off campus. Online class registration is available. *Web address:* http://www.csupomona.edu/.

General Application Contact: Scott J. Duncan, Director, Admissions, 909-869-3258, Fax: 909-869-4529, E-mail: sjduncan@csupomona.edu.

GRADUATE UNITS

Academic Affairs Students: 426 full-time (243 women), 996 part-time (511 women); includes 634 minority (58 African Americans, 4 American Indian/Alaska Native, 311 Asian Americans or Pacific Islanders, 261 Hispanic Americans), 141 international. Average age 31. 1,234 applicants, 46% accepted, 312 enrolled. *Faculty:* 559 full-time (238 women), 456 part-time/adjunct (171 women). Expenses: Contact institution. *Financial support:* In 2008–09, 4 fellow-

California State Polytechnic University, Pomona (continued)

ships, 5 research assistantships, 3 teaching assistantships were awarded; career-related internships or fieldwork, Federal Work-Study, institutionally sponsored loans, and unspecified assistantships also available. Support available to part-time students. Financial award application deadline: 3/2; financial award applicants required to submit FAFSA. In 2008, 348 master's awarded. *Degree program information:* Part-time programs available. *Application deadline:* Applications are processed on a rolling basis. *Application fee:* $55. Electronic applications accepted. *Application Contact:* Scott J. Duncan, Director, Admissions, 909-869-3258, Fax: 909-869-4529, E-mail: sjduncan@csupomona.edu. *Provost/Vice President for Academic Affairs,* Dr. Marten L. denBoer, 909-869-3443, E-mail: mdenboer@csupomona.edu.

College of Agriculture Students: 20 full-time (17 women), 44 part-time (36 women); includes 25 minority (2 African Americans, 14 Asian Americans or Pacific Islanders, 9 Hispanic Americans), 3 international. Average age 29. 61 applicants, 59% accepted, 28 enrolled. *Faculty:* 38 full-time (11 women), 17 part-time/adjunct (11 women). Expenses: Contact institution. *Financial support:* Career-related internships or fieldwork, Federal Work-Study, and institutionally sponsored loans available. Support available to part-time students. Financial award application deadline: 3/2; financial award applicants required to submit FAFSA. In 2008, 12 master's awarded. *Degree program information:* Part-time programs available. Offers agriculture (MS). *Application deadline:* For fall admission, 5/1 priority date for domestic students; for winter admission, 10/15 priority date for domestic students; for spring admission, 1/2 priority date for domestic students. Applications are processed on a rolling basis. *Application fee:* $55. Electronic applications accepted. *Application Contact:* Scott J. Duncan, Director, Admissions, 909-869-3258, Fax: 909-869-4529, E-mail: sjduncan@csupomona.edu. *Interim Dean,* Dr. Lester C. Young, 909-869-2203, E-mail: lcyoung@csupomona.edu.

College of Business Administration Students: 33 full-time (19 women), 120 part-time (49 women); includes 66 minority (8 African Americans, 43 Asian Americans or Pacific Islanders, 15 Hispanic Americans), 36 international. Average age 31. 195 applicants, 41% accepted, 41 enrolled. *Faculty:* 82 full-time (50 women), 36 part-time/adjunct (11 women). Expenses: Contact institution. *Financial support:* In 2008–09, 5 research assistantships, 3 teaching assistantships were awarded; career-related internships or fieldwork, Federal Work-Study, and institutionally sponsored loans also available. Support available to part-time students. Financial award application deadline: 3/2; financial award applicants required to submit FAFSA. In 2008, 58 master's awarded. *Degree program information:* Part-time programs available. Postbaccalaureate distance learning degree programs offered (minimal on-campus study). Offers business administration (MBA, MSBA, PMBA). *Application deadline:* For fall admission, 5/1 priority date for domestic students; for winter admission, 10/15 priority date for domestic students; for spring admission, 1/2 priority date for domestic students. Applications are processed on a rolling basis. *Application fee:* $55. Electronic applications accepted. *Application Contact:* Dr. Tarique Hossain, Faculty Associate, Graduate Program, 909-869-2363, E-mail: gba@csupomona.edu. *Interim Dean,* Dr. Lynn H. Turner, 909-869-2347, E-mail: lhturner@csupomona.edu.

College of Education and Integrative Studies Students: 52 full-time (34 women), 277 part-time (190 women); includes 168 minority (23 African Americans, 1 American Indian/Alaska Native, 52 Asian Americans or Pacific Islanders, 92 Hispanic Americans), 2 international. Average age 36. 49 applicants, 78% accepted, 22 enrolled. *Faculty:* 41 full-time (28 women), 44 part-time/adjunct (26 women). Expenses: Contact institution. *Financial support:* Career-related internships or fieldwork, Federal Work-Study, and institutionally sponsored loans available. Support available to part-time students. Financial award application deadline: 3/2; financial award applicants required to submit FAFSA. In 2008, 100 master's awarded. *Degree program information:* Part-time programs available. Offers education and integrative studies (MA). *Application deadline:* For fall admission, 5/1 priority date for domestic students; for winter admission, 10/15 priority date for domestic students; for spring admission, 1/20 priority date for domestic students. Applications are processed on a rolling basis. *Application fee:* $55. Electronic applications accepted. *Application Contact:* Dr. Gary Kinsey, Associate Dean, 909-869-2316, Fax: 909-869-4963, E-mail: gwkinsey@csupomona.edu. *Dean,* Dr. Peggy Kelly, 909-869-2307, E-mail: pkelly@csupomona.edu.

College of Engineering Students: 25 full-time (3 women), 179 part-time (36 women); includes 99 minority (1 African American, 69 Asian Americans or Pacific Islanders, 29 Hispanic Americans), 33 international. Average age 28. 188 applicants, 54% accepted, 46 enrolled. *Faculty:* 92 full-time (17 women), 77 part-time/adjunct (5 women). Expenses: Contact institution. *Financial support:* In 2008–09, 1 fellowship, 6 research assistantships, 5 teaching assistantships were awarded; career-related internships or fieldwork, Federal Work-Study, institutionally sponsored loans, and unspecified assistantships also available. Support available to part-time students. Financial award application deadline: 3/2; financial award applicants required to submit FAFSA. In 2008, 32 master's awarded. *Degree program information:* Part-time programs available. Offers civil engineering (MS); electrical engineering (MSEE); engineering (MSE); engineering management (MS); mechanical engineering (MS). *Application deadline:* For fall admission, 5/1 priority date for domestic students; for winter admission, 10/15 priority date for domestic students; for spring admission, 1/2 priority date for domestic students. Applications are processed on a rolling basis. *Application fee:* $55. Electronic applications accepted. *Application Contact:* Dr. Edward Hohmann, Dean, 909-869-2472, Fax: 909-869-4370, E-mail: echohmann@csupomona.edu. *Dean,* Dr. Edward Hohmann, 909-869-2472, Fax: 909-869-4370, E-mail: echohmann@csupomona.edu.

College of Environmental Design Students: 161 full-time (84 women), 69 part-time (37 women); includes 68 minority (5 African Americans, 1 American Indian/Alaska Native, 41 Asian Americans or Pacific Islanders, 21 Hispanic Americans), 12 international. Average age 30. 332 applicants, 31% accepted, 52 enrolled. *Faculty:* 44 full-time (21 women), 44 part-time/adjunct (17 women). Expenses: Contact institution. *Financial support:* Career-related internships or fieldwork, Federal Work-Study, and institutionally sponsored loans available. Support available to part-time students. Financial award application deadline: 3/2; financial award applicants required to submit FAFSA. In 2008, 35 master's awarded. *Degree program information:* Part-time programs available. Offers architecture (M Arch); environmental design (M Arch, M Land Arch, MS, MURP); landscape architecture (M Land Arch); regenerative studies (MS); urban and regional planning (MURP). *Application deadline:* For fall admission, 5/1 priority date for domestic students; for winter admission, 10/15 priority date for domestic students; for spring admission, 1/20 priority date for domestic students. Applications are processed on a rolling basis. *Application fee:* $55. Electronic applications accepted. *Application Contact:* Scott J. Duncan, Director, Admissions, 909-869-3258, Fax: 909-869-4529, E-mail: sjduncan@csupomona.edu. *Interim Dean,* Dr. Kyle D. Brown, 909-869-5178, E-mail: kdbrown@csupomona.edu.

College of Letters, Arts, and Social Sciences Students: 76 full-time (54 women), 174 part-time (98 women); includes 118 minority (17 African Americans, 1 American Indian/Alaska Native, 35 Asian Americans or Pacific Islanders, 65 Hispanic Americans), 24 international. Average age 31. 231 applicants, 48% accepted, 65 enrolled. *Faculty:* 118 full-time (63 women), 159 part-time/adjunct (74 women). Expenses: Contact institution. *Financial support:* In 2008–09, 2 fellowships were awarded; Federal Work-Study and institutionally sponsored loans also available. Support available to part-time students. Financial award application deadline: 3/2; financial award applicants required to submit FAFSA. In 2008, 66 master's awarded. *Degree program information:* Part-time programs available. Offers economics (MS); English (MA); history (MA); kinesiology (MS); letters, arts, and social sciences (MA, MPA, MS); psychology (MS); public administration (MPA). *Application deadline:* Applications are processed on a rolling basis. *Application fee:* $55. Electronic applications accepted. *Application Contact:* Scott J. Duncan, Director, Admissions, 909-869-3258, Fax: 909-869-4529, E-mail: sjduncan@csupomona.edu. *Dean,* Dr. Carol P. Richardson, 909-869-3943, E-mail: cprichardson@csupomona.edu.

College of Science Students: 59 full-time (32 women), 133 part-time (65 women); includes 90 minority (2 African Americans, 1 American Indian/Alaska Native, 57 Asian Americans or Pacific Islanders, 30 Hispanic Americans), 31 international. Average age 28. 178 applicants, 52% accepted, 58 enrolled. *Faculty:* 127 full-time (42 women), 74 part-time/adjunct (24 women). Expenses: Contact institution. *Financial support:* Career-related internships or fieldwork, Federal Work-Study, and institutionally sponsored loans available. Support available to part-time students. Financial award application deadline: 3/2; financial award applicants required to submit FAFSA. In 2008, 45 master's awarded. *Degree program information:* Part-time programs available. Offers applied mathematics (MS); biological sciences (MS); chemistry (MS); computer science (MS); pure mathematics (MS); science (MS). *Application deadline:* For fall admission, 5/1 priority date for domestic students; for winter admission, 10/15 priority date for domestic students; for spring admission, 1/20 priority date for domestic students. Applications are processed on a rolling basis. *Application fee:* $55. Electronic applications accepted. *Application Contact:* Scott J. Duncan, Director, Admissions, 909-869-3258, Fax: 909-869-4529, E-mail: sjduncan@csupomona.edu. *Dean,* Dr. Donald O. Straney, 909-869-3600, E-mail: dostraney@csupomona.edu.

CALIFORNIA STATE UNIVERSITY, BAKERSFIELD, Bakersfield, CA 93311-1022

General Information State-supported, coed, comprehensive institution. *Graduate housing:* Room and/or apartments available on a first-come, first-served basis to single students; on-campus housing not available to married students. Housing application deadline: 8/1.

GRADUATE UNITS

Division of Graduate Studies *Degree program information:* Part-time and evening/weekend programs available. Postbaccalaureate distance learning degree programs offered (no on-campus study). Offers administration (MS); interdisciplinary studies (MA).

School of Business and Public Administration Offers business administration (MBA); business and public administration (MBA, MPA, MSA); health care management (MSA); public administration (MPA).

School of Education Offers bilingual/multicultural education (MA Ed); curriculum and instruction (MA Ed); early childhood education (MA); education (MA, MA Ed, MS, Certificate); educational administration (MA); educational technology (MA Ed); reading/literacy (MA Ed, Certificate); school counseling (MS); special education (MA); student affairs (MS).

School of Humanities and Social Sciences *Degree program information:* Part-time and evening/weekend programs available. Offers anthropology (MA); counseling psychology (MS); English (MA); history (MA); humanities and social sciences (MA, MS, MSW); psychology (MA); social work (MSW); sociology (MA); Spanish (MA).

School of Natural Sciences and Mathematics Offers biology (MS); geology (MS); hydrogeology (MS); natural sciences and mathematics (MA, MS); nursing (MS); petroleum geology (MS); teaching mathematics (MA).

CALIFORNIA STATE UNIVERSITY CHANNEL ISLANDS, Camarillo, CA 93012

General Information State-supported, coed, comprehensive institution. *Enrollment:* 3,599 graduate, professional, and undergraduate students; 400 matriculated graduate/professional students. *Enrollment by degree level:* 400 master's. *Graduate housing:* Room and/or apartments available on a first-come, first-served basis to single students; on-campus housing not available to married students. Housing application deadline: 6/1. *Student services:* Campus employment opportunities, campus safety program, career counseling, exercise/wellness program, international student services, low-cost health insurance, multicultural affairs office, services for students with disabilities, teacher training, writing training. *Library facilities:* John Spoor Broome Library at Channel Islands. *Online resources:* library catalog, web page. *Web address:* http://www.csuci.edu/.

General Application Contact: Christian Cash, Application Contact, 805-437-2748, Fax: 805-437-8859, E-mail: exed@csuci.edu.

GRADUATE UNITS

Extended Education Students: 500. Expenses: Contact institution. *Financial support:* Teaching assistantships, career-related internships or fieldwork, Federal Work-Study, scholarships/grants, and tuition waivers (full and partial) available. *Degree program information:* Part-time and evening/weekend programs available. Offers biotechnology and bioinformatics (MS); business administration (MBA); computer science (MS); educational leadership (MAEd); mathematics (MS). *Application deadline:* For fall admission, 6/1 for domestic and international students. Applications are processed on a rolling basis. *Application Contact:* Christian Cash, Application Contact, 805-437-2748, Fax: 805-437-8859, E-mail: exed@csuci.edu. *Dean of Extended Education,* Dr. Gary A. Berg, 805-437-8580, Fax: 805-437-8859, E-mail: gary.berg@csuci.edu.

CALIFORNIA STATE UNIVERSITY, CHICO, Chico, CA 95929-0722

General Information State-supported, coed, comprehensive institution. CGS member. *Graduate housing:* Room and/or apartments available on a first-come, first-served basis to single students; on-campus housing not available to married students. Housing application deadline: 3/22. *Research affiliation:* Hewlett-Packard Company (computer science).

GRADUATE UNITS

Graduate School *Degree program information:* Part-time programs available. Postbaccalaureate distance learning degree programs offered (no on-campus study). Offers interdisciplinary studies (MA, MS); science teaching (MS); simulation science (MS); teaching international languages (MA). Electronic applications accepted.

College of Behavioral and Social Sciences *Degree program information:* Part-time programs available. Offers applied psychology (MA); behavioral and social sciences (MA, MPA, MS, MSW); geography (MA); health administration (MPA); local government management (MPA); marriage and family therapy (MS); museum studies (MA); political science (MA); psychological science (MA); psychology (MA); public administration (MPA); rural and town planning (MA); social science (MA); social science education (MA); social work (MSW). Electronic applications accepted.

College of Business *Degree program information:* Part-time programs available. Offers business (MBA); business administration (MBA). Electronic applications accepted.

College of Communication and Education *Degree program information:* Part-time programs available. Offers communication and education (MA); communication science and disorders (MA); communication studies (MA); curriculum and instruction (MA); education (MA); kinesiology (MA); linguistically and culturally diverse learners (MA); reading/language arts (MA); recreation administration (MA); special education (MA). Electronic applications accepted.

College of Engineering, Computer Science, and Technology *Degree program information:* Part-time programs available. Postbaccalaureate distance learning degree programs offered. Offers computer engineering (MS); computer science (MS); electronics engineering (MS); engineering, computer science, and technology (MS). Electronic applications accepted.

College of Humanities and Fine Arts Offers art history (MA); English (MA); fine arts (MFA); history (MA); humanities and fine arts (MA, MFA); music (MA). Electronic applications accepted.

College of Natural Sciences *Degree program information:* Part-time programs available. Offers biological sciences (MS); botany (MS); environmental science (MS); geosciences (MS); hydrology/hydrogeology (MS); math education (MS); natural sciences (MS); nursing (MS); nutrition education (MS); nutritional sciences (MS). Electronic applications accepted.

CALIFORNIA STATE UNIVERSITY, DOMINGUEZ HILLS, Carson, CA 90747-0001

General Information State-supported, coed, comprehensive institution. CGS member. *Enrollment:* 12,851 graduate, professional, and undergraduate students; 1,496 full-time matriculated graduate/professional students (1,134 women), 1,865 part-time matriculated graduate/professional students (1,421 women). *Enrollment by degree level:* 2,541 master's, 820 other advanced degrees. *Graduate faculty:* 112 full-time (70 women), 143 part-time/adjunct (107 women). Tuition, nonresident: part-time $339 per unit. *Required fees:* $1300 per semester. *Graduate housing:* Rooms and/or apartments available on a first-come, first-served basis to single and married students. Typical cost: $4500 per year ($9970 including board) for single students; $4500 per year ($9970 including board) for married students. Housing application deadline: 4/15. *Student services:* Campus employment opportunities, campus safety program, career counseling, child daycare facilities, free psychological counseling, international student services, low-cost health insurance, services for students with disabilities. *Library facilities:* Leo F. Cain Educational Resource Center. *Online resources:* library catalog, web page, access to other libraries' catalogs. *Collection:* 438,746 titles, 70,691 serial subscriptions. *Research affiliation:* Los Angeles Biomedical Research Institute at Harbor UCLA Medical Center (biomedical science), Drew Medical School.

Computer facilities: 256 computers available on campus for general student use. A campuswide network can be accessed from student residence rooms. Online class registration is available. *Web address:* http://www.csudh.edu/.

General Application Contact: Dr. Gayle Ball-Parker, Director of Admissions, 310-243-3645, E-mail: gball@csudh.edu.

GRADUATE UNITS

College of Arts and Humanities Students: 60 full-time (37 women), 259 part-time (157 women); includes 149 minority (67 African Americans, 18 Asian Americans or Pacific Islanders, 64 Hispanic Americans), 12 international. Average age 39. 230 applicants, 77% accepted, 84 enrolled. *Faculty:* 31 full-time (16 women), 5 part-time/adjunct (3 women). Expenses: Contact institution. *Financial support:* Institutionally sponsored loans available. Support available to part-time students. In 2008, 76 master's awarded. *Degree program information:* Part-time and evening/weekend programs available. Offers arts and humanities (MA, MS, Certificate); English (MA); humanities (MA); negotiation, conflict resolution and peacebuilding (MA); rhetoric and composition (Certificate); teaching English as a second language (Certificate). *Application deadline:* For fall admission, 6/1 for domestic students. *Application fee:* $55. *Application Contact:* Dr. Gayle Ball-Parker, Director of Admissions, 310-243-3645, E-mail: gball@csudh.edu. *Dean,* Dr. George Arasimowicz, 310-243-3389, E-mail: garasimowicz@csudh.edu.

College of Business Administration and Public Policy Students: 115 full-time (66 women), 290 part-time (159 women); includes 207 minority (105 African Americans, 3 American Indian/Alaska Native, 52 Asian Americans or Pacific Islanders, 47 Hispanic Americans), 36 international. Average age 35. 376 applicants, 44% accepted, 57 enrolled. *Faculty:* 15 full-time (8 women), 16 part-time/adjunct (7 women). Expenses: Contact institution. In 2008, 165 master's awarded. *Degree program information:* Part-time and evening/weekend programs available. Postbaccalaureate distance learning degree programs offered (no on-campus study). Offers business administration (MBA); business administration and public policy (MBA, MPA); public administration (MPA). *Application deadline:* For fall admission, 4/1 for domestic and international students; for spring admission, 11/1 for domestic students, 10/1 for international students. *Application fee:* $55. *Application Contact:* Eileen Hall, Graduate Advisor, 310-243-3465, E-mail: ehall@csudh.edu. *Dean,* Dr. James Strong, 310-243-3548, E-mail: jstrong@csudh.edu.

College of Extended and International Education Students: 14 full-time (6 women), 763 part-time (358 women); includes 160 minority (33 African Americans, 9 American Indian/Alaska Native, 58 Asian Americans or Pacific Islanders, 60 Hispanic Americans), 47 international. Average age 43. 173 applicants, 76% accepted, 97 enrolled. *Faculty:* 8 full-time (4 women), 52 part-time/adjunct (17 women). Expenses: Contact institution. In 2008, 131 master's awarded. *Degree program information:* Part-time and evening/weekend programs available. Postbaccalaureate distance learning degree programs offered. Offers extended and international education (MA, MS); humanities (MA); quality assurance (MS). *Application fee:* $55. Electronic applications accepted. *Application Contact:* Dr. Gayle Ball-Parker, Director of Admissions, 310-243-3645, E-mail: gball@csudh.edu. *Dean,* Dr. Margaret Gordon, 310-243-3737, Fax: 310-516-4423, E-mail: mgordon@csudh.edu.

College of Natural and Behavioral Sciences Students: 52 full-time (44 women), 109 part-time (71 women); includes 110 minority (55 African Americans, 12 Asian Americans or Pacific Islanders, 43 Hispanic Americans), 3 international. Average age 35. 107 applicants, 73% accepted, 44 enrolled. *Faculty:* 38 full-time (16 women), 11 part-time/adjunct (5 women). Expenses: Contact institution. In 2008, 45 master's awarded. Offers biology (MS); clinical psychology (MA); computer science (MSCS); natural and behavioral sciences (MA, MS, MSCS, Certificate); social research (Certificate); sociology (MA); teaching of mathematics (MA). *Application Contact:* Dr. Gayle Ball-Parker, Director of Admissions, 310-243-3645, E-mail: gball@csudh.edu. *Interim Dean,* Dr. Laura Robles, 310-243-2547, E-mail: lrobles@csudh.edu.

College of Professional Studies Students: 1,317 full-time (1,012 women), 1,426 part-time (1,126 women); includes 1,667 minority (584 African Americans, 10 American Indian/Alaska Native, 322 Asian Americans or Pacific Islanders, 751 Hispanic Americans), 7 international. Average age 37. 1,331 applicants, 78% accepted, 661 enrolled. *Faculty:* 85 full-time (61 women), 121 part-time/adjunct (91 women). Expenses: Contact institution. In 2008, 488 master's awarded. *Application fee:* $55. Electronic applications accepted. *Application Contact:* Dr. Gayle Ball-Parker, Director of Admissions, 310-243-3645, E-mail: gball@csudh.edu. *Dean,* Dr. Mitchell T. Maki, 301-243-2046, Fax: 310-217-6800, E-mail: mmaki@csudh.edu.

School of Education Students: 952 full-time (715 women), 907 part-time (661 women); includes 1,184 minority (407 African Americans, 9 American Indian/Alaska Native, 156 Asian Americans or Pacific Islanders, 612 Hispanic Americans), 4 international. Average age 36. 827 applicants, 78% accepted, 401 enrolled. *Faculty:* 54 full-time (36 women), 74 part-time/adjunct (54 women). Expenses: Contact institution. In 2008, 281 master's awarded. *Degree program information:* Part-time and evening/weekend programs available. Offers counseling (MA); curriculum and instruction (MA); early childhood (MA); education (MA, Certificate); educational administration (MA); individualized education (MA); mild/moderate (MA); moderate/severe (MA); multicultural education (MA); special education (MA); technology-based education (MA, Certificate). *Application deadline:* For fall admission, 6/1 priority date for domestic students; for spring admission, 10/1 priority date for domestic students. Applications are processed on a rolling basis. *Application fee:* $55. *Application Contact:* Dr. Sharon E. Russell, Acting Director, 310-243-3510, Fax: 310-243-3518, E-mail: srussell@csudh.edu. *Acting Director,* Dr. Sharon Russell, 310-243-3510, Fax: 310-243-3518, E-mail: srussell@csudhe.du.

School of Health and Human Services Students: 365 full-time (297 women), 519 part-time (465 women); includes 483 minority (177 African Americans, 1 American Indian/Alaska Native, 166 Asian Americans or Pacific Islanders, 139 Hispanic Americans), 3 international. Average age 38. 504 applicants, 77% accepted, 260 enrolled. *Faculty:* 31 full-time (25 women), 47 part-time/adjunct (37 women). Expenses: Contact institution. In 2008, 207 master's awarded. Offers health and human services (MA, MS, MSN, MSW); health sciences (MS); marital and family therapy (MS); nursing (MSN); occupational therapy (MS); physical education administration (MA); social work (MSW). *Application deadline:* For fall admission, 6/1 for domestic students. *Application fee:* $55. *Application Contact:* Dr. Gayle Ball-Parker, Director of Admissions, 310-243-3645, E-mail: gball@csudh.edu. *Dean,* Dr. Mitchell T. Maki, 310-243-2046, Fax: 310-217-6800, E-mail: mmaki@csudh.edu.

CALIFORNIA STATE UNIVERSITY, EAST BAY, Hayward, CA 94542-3000

General Information State-supported, coed, comprehensive institution. CGS member. *Enrollment:* 14,167 graduate, professional, and undergraduate students; 1,722 full-time matriculated graduate/professional students (1,171 women), 1,792 part-time matriculated graduate/professional students (1,166 women). *Enrollment by degree level:* 3,514 master's. *Graduate faculty:* 365. *Graduate housing:* Room and/or apartments available on a first-come, first-served basis to single students; on-campus housing not available to married students. Housing application deadline: 4/30. *Student services:* Campus employment opportunities, campus safety program, career counseling, child daycare facilities, free psychological counseling, international student services, low-cost health insurance, services for students with disabilities. *Research affiliation:* Sandia National Laboratories (technology marketing assessment), Stanford University (complex learning), Lawrence Livermore National Laboratory (technology transfer), NASA–Ames Research Center, Academy of Economy, Moscow (business management training), Pacific Telesis (urban education).

Computer facilities: 700 computers available on campus for general student use. A campuswide network can be accessed from student residence rooms and from off campus. Online class registration is available. *Web address:* http://www.csueastbay.edu/.

General Application Contact: Rita Nakasone, Graduate Prospect Specialist, 510-885-3286, Fax: 510-885-3543, E-mail: rita.nakasone@csueastbay.edu.

GRADUATE UNITS

Academic Programs and Graduate Studies Students: 1,041 full-time (730 women), 1,402 part-time (870 women); includes 926 minority (223 African Americans, 6 American Indian/Alaska Native, 493 Asian Americans or Pacific Islanders, 204 Hispanic Americans), 334 international. Average age 34. 2,191 applicants, 57% accepted. Expenses: Contact institution. *Financial support:* Fellowships, teaching assistantships, career-related internships or fieldwork, Federal Work-Study, institutionally sponsored loans, and scholarships/grants available. Support available to part-time students. Financial award application deadline: 3/2; financial award applicants required to submit FAFSA. In 2008, 1,072 master's awarded. *Degree program information:* Part-time and evening/weekend programs available. Offers interdisciplinary studies (MA, MS, Certificate); multimedia (MA). *Application deadline:* For fall admission, 7/31 for domestic students, 4/30 for international students; for winter admission, 9/31 for domestic students, 9/30 for international students; for spring admission, 12/31 for domestic students, 11/30 for international students. Applications are processed on a rolling basis. *Application fee:* $55. Electronic applications accepted. *Application Contact:* Rita Nakasone, Administrative Support Coordinator, 510-885-3286, Fax: 510-885-3543, E-mail: rita.nakasone@csueastbay.edu. *Associate Vice President,* Dr. Carl Bellone, 510-885-3716, Fax: 510-885-4777, E-mail: carl.bellone@csueastbay.edu.

College of Business and Economics Students: 219 full-time (117 women), 356 part-time (161 women); includes 228 minority (22 African Americans, 177 Asian Americans or Pacific Islanders, 29 Hispanic Americans), 166 international. Average age 32. 503 applicants, 47% accepted, 114 enrolled. *Faculty:* 37 full-time (7 women), 8 part-time/adjunct (3 women). Expenses: Contact institution. *Financial support:* Career-related internships or fieldwork, Federal Work-Study, and institutionally sponsored loans available. Support available to part-time students. Financial award application deadline: 3/2. In 2008, 426 master's awarded. *Degree program information:* Part-time and evening/weekend programs available. Offers accounting (MBA); business administration (MS); business and economics (MA, MBA, MS); business economics (MBA); e-business (MBA); economics (MA, MBA); economics for teachers (MBA); entrepreneurship (MBA); finance (MBA); human resources management (MBA); information technology management (MBA); international business (MBA); management sciences (MBA); marketing management (MBA); new ventures/small business management (MBA); operations and materials management (MBA); strategic management (MBA); supply chain management (MBA); taxation (MS); telecommunications (MS). *Application deadline:* For fall admission, 6/31 for domestic students, 4/30 for international students; for winter admission, 10/31 for domestic students, 9/30 for international students; for spring admission, 12/31 for domestic students, 11/30 for international students. Applications are processed on a rolling basis. *Application fee:* $55. Electronic applications accepted. *Application Contact:* Rita Nakasone, Administrative Support Coordinator, 510-885-3286, Fax: 510-885-3543, E-mail: rita.nakasone@csueastbay.edu. *Dean,* Dr. Terri Swartz, 510-885-3291, Fax: 510-885-4884, E-mail: terri.swartz@csueastbay.edu.

College of Education and Allied Studies Students: 296 full-time (232 women), 303 part-time (229 women); includes 190 minority (52 African Americans, 4 American Indian/Alaska Native, 64 Asian Americans or Pacific Islanders, 70 Hispanic Americans), 5 international. Average age 36. 516 applicants, 68% accepted, 223 enrolled. Expenses: Contact institution. *Financial support:* Career-related internships or fieldwork, Federal Work-Study, and institutionally sponsored loans available. Support available to part-time students. Financial award application deadline: 3/2. In 2008, 259 master's awarded. *Degree program information:* Part-time and evening/weekend programs available. Offers counseling (MS); education (MS); education and allied studies (MS); educational leadership (MS); physical education (MS); special education (MS); specializing in urban teaching leadership (MS). *Application deadline:* For fall admission, 7/31 for domestic students, 4/30 for international students; for winter admission, 10/31 for domestic students, 9/30 for international students; for spring admission, 12/31 for domestic students, 11/30 for international students. *Application fee:* $55. Electronic applications accepted. *Application Contact:* Rita Nakasone, Administrative Support Coordinator, 510-885-3286, Fax: 510-885-3543, E-mail: rita.nakasone@csueastbay.edu. *Dean,* Dr. Deidre Badejo, 510-885-3161, Fax: 510-885-3164, E-mail: deidre.badejo@csueastbay.edu.

College of Letters, Arts, and Social Sciences Students: 368 full-time (287 women), 454 part-time (333 women); includes 348 minority (137 African Americans, 1 American Indian/Alaska Native, 122 Asian Americans or Pacific Islanders, 88 Hispanic Americans), 38 international. Average age 34. 600 applicants, 59% accepted, 249 enrolled. Expenses: Contact institution. *Financial support:* Fellowships, research assistantships, teaching assistantships, career-related internships or fieldwork, Federal Work-Study, institutionally sponsored loans, and scholarships/grants available. Support available to part-time students. Financial award application deadline: 3/2. In 2008, 283 master's awarded. *Degree program information:* Part-time and evening/weekend programs available. Offers anthropology (MA); communication (MA); English (MA); geography (MA); health care administration (MS); history (MA); letters, arts, and social sciences (MA, MPA, MS, MSW); music (MA); public administration (MPA); social work (MSW); sociology (MA); speech pathology and audiology (MS). *Application deadline:* For fall admission, 7/31 for domestic students, 4/30 for international students; for winter admission, 10/31 for domestic students, 9/30 for international students; for spring admission, 12/31 for domestic students, 11/30 for international students. Applications are processed on a rolling basis. *Application fee:* $55. Electronic applications accepted. *Application Contact:* Rita Nakasone, Administrative Support Coordinator, 510-885-4476, Fax: 510-885-3543, E-mail: rita.nakasone@csueastbay.edu. *Dean,* Dr. Deidre Badejo, 510-885-3161, Fax: 510-885-3164, E-mail: deidre.badejo@csueastbay.edu.

College of Science Students: 139 full-time (84 women), 274 part-time (140 women); includes 148 minority (9 African Americans, 1 American Indian/Alaska Native, 126 Asian Americans or Pacific Islanders, 12 Hispanic Americans), 123 international. Average age 32. 322 applicants, 57% accepted, 112 enrolled. Expenses: Contact institution. *Financial support:* Career-related internships or fieldwork, Federal Work-Study, and institutionally sponsored loans available. Support available to part-time students. Financial award application deadline: 3/2. In 2008, 74 master's awarded. *Degree program information:* Part-time and evening/weekend programs available. Offers actuarial statistics (MS); biochemistry (MS); biological sciences (MS); biostatistics (MS); chemistry (MS); computational statistics (MS); computer science (MS); engineering management (MS); geology (MS); marine sciences (MS); mathematical statistics (MS); mathematics (MS); multimedia (MA); science (MA, MS); statistics (MS); telecommunication (MS); theoretical and applied statistics (MS). *Application deadline:* For fall admission, 7/31 for domestic students, 4/30 for international students; for winter admission, 10/31 for domestic students, 9/30 for international students; for spring admission, 12/31 for domestic students, 11/30 for international students. *Application fee:* $55. Electronic applications accepted. *Application Contact:* Rita Nakasone, Administrative Support Coordinator, 510-885-3286, Fax: 510-885-3543, E-mail: rita.nakasone@csueastbay.edu. *Dean,* Dr. Michael Leung, 510-885-3441, Fax: 510-885-2035, E-mail: michael.leung@csueastbay.edu.

CALIFORNIA STATE UNIVERSITY, FRESNO, Fresno, CA 93740-8027

General Information State-supported, coed, comprehensive institution. CGS member. *Graduate housing:* Room and/or apartments available on a first-come, first-served basis to single students; on-campus housing not available to married students. Housing application deadline: 4/1. *Research affiliation:* Coleman Foundation (administration), Starburst Foundation (engineering), Garabedian Foundation (agribusiness), California Endowment (arts and humanities).

GRADUATE UNITS

Division of Graduate Studies *Degree program information:* Part-time and evening/weekend programs available. Electronic applications accepted.

California State University, Fresno (continued)

College of Agricultural Sciences and Technology *Degree program information:* Part-time and evening/weekend programs available. Offers agricultural sciences and technology (MS); animal science (MS); family and consumer sciences (MS); food science and nutritional sciences (MS); industrial technology (MS); plant science (MS); viticulture and enology (MS). Electronic applications accepted.

College of Arts and Humanities *Degree program information:* Part-time and evening/weekend programs available. Offers art (MA); arts and humanities (MA, MFA); communication (MA); composition theory (MA); creative writing (MFA); linguistics (MA); literature (MA); mass communication and journalism (MA); music (MA); music education (MA); performance (MA); Spanish (MA). Electronic applications accepted.

College of Engineering and Computer Science *Degree program information:* Part-time and evening/weekend programs available. Offers civil engineering (MS); electrical engineering (MS); engineering and computer science (MS); mechanical engineering (MS). Electronic applications accepted.

College of Health and Human Services *Degree program information:* Part-time and evening/weekend programs available. Offers communicative disorders (MA); exercise science (MA); health and human services (MA, MPH, MPT, MS, MSW, DPT); health policy and management (MPH); health promotion (MPH); nursing (MS); physical therapy (MPT, DPT); social work education (MSW); sport psychology (MA). Electronic applications accepted.

College of Science and Mathematics *Degree program information:* Part-time and evening/weekend programs available. Offers biology (MA); biotechnology (MBT); chemistry (MS); computer science (MS); geology (MS); marine sciences (MS); mathematics (MA); physics (MS); psychology (MA, MS); science and mathematics (MA, MBT, MS); teaching (MA). Electronic applications accepted.

College of Social Sciences *Degree program information:* Part-time and evening/weekend programs available. Offers criminology (MS); history-teaching option (MA); history-traditional track (MA); international relations (MA); public administration (MPA); social sciences (MA, MPA, MS). Electronic applications accepted.

Craig School of Business *Degree program information:* Part-time programs available. Offers accountancy (MS); business (MBA, MS); business administration (MBA). Electronic applications accepted.

School of Education and Human Development *Degree program information:* Part-time and evening/weekend programs available. Offers counseling and student services (MS); education (MA); education and human development (MA, MS, Ed D); educational leadership (Ed D); marriage and family therapy (MS); rehabilitation counseling (MS); special education (MA). Electronic applications accepted.

CALIFORNIA STATE UNIVERSITY, FULLERTON, Fullerton, CA 92834-9480

General Information State-supported, coed, comprehensive institution. CGS member. *Enrollment:* 36,996 graduate, professional, and undergraduate students; 1,671 full-time matriculated graduate/professional students (1,072 women), 2,805 part-time matriculated graduate/professional students (1,712 women). *Enrollment by degree level:* 4,418 master's, 58 doctoral. Tuition and fees vary according to degree level. *Graduate housing:* On-campus housing not available. *Student services:* Campus employment opportunities, campus safety program, career counseling, child daycare facilities, exercise/wellness program, free psychological counseling, international student services, low-cost health insurance, multicultural affairs office, services for students with disabilities, teacher training, writing training. *Library facilities:* Pollack Library. *Online resources:* library catalog, web page, access to other libraries' catalogs. *Collection:* 1.3 million titles, 10,902 serial subscriptions, 7,417 audiovisual materials.

Computer facilities: 2,000 computers available on campus for general student use. A campuswide network can be accessed from student residence rooms and from off campus. Online class registration is available. *Web address:* http://www.fullerton.edu/.

General Application Contact: Admissions/Applications, 657-278-2371, E-mail: admissions@fullerton.edu.

GRADUATE UNITS

Graduate Studies Students: 1,671 full-time (1,072 women), 2,805 part-time (1,712 women); includes 1,677 minority (114 African Americans, 11 American Indian/Alaska Native, 850 Asian Americans or Pacific Islanders, 702 Hispanic Americans), 588 international. Average age 31. 4,832 applicants, 49% accepted, 1508 enrolled. Expenses: Contact institution. *Financial support:* Research assistantships, teaching assistantships, career-related internships or fieldwork, Federal Work-Study, institutionally sponsored loans, and scholarships/grants available. Support available to part-time students. Financial award application deadline: 3/1. In 2008, 1,328 master's awarded. *Degree program information:* Part-time and evening/weekend programs available. *Application deadline:* Applications are processed on a rolling basis. *Application fee:* $55. Electronic applications accepted. *Application Contact:* Admissions/Applications, 714-278-2300, E-mail: admissions@fullerton.edu. *Associate Vice President, Graduate Programs and Research,* Dr. Dorota Huizinga, 657-278-3602.

College of Communications Students: 97 full-time (85 women), 82 part-time (69 women); includes 58 minority (7 African Americans, 15 Asian Americans or Pacific Islanders, 36 Hispanic Americans), 14 international. Average age 30. 343 applicants, 22% accepted, 50 enrolled. Expenses: Contact institution. *Financial support:* Teaching assistantships, career-related internships or fieldwork, Federal Work-Study, institutionally sponsored loans, and scholarships/grants available. Support available to part-time students. Financial award application deadline: 3/1. In 2008, 70 master's awarded. *Degree program information:* Part-time programs available. Offers communications (MA); communications—advertising (MA); communications—entertainment and tourism (MA); communications—journalism (MA); communications—public relations (MA); communicative disorders (MA); speech communication (MA). *Application fee:* $55. *Application Contact:* Admissions/Applications, 657-278-2300. *Dean,* Dr. Rick Pullen, 657-278-3355.

College of Education Students: 112 full-time (94 women), 760 part-time (609 women); includes 323 minority (15 African Americans, 1 American Indian/Alaska Native, 100 Asian Americans or Pacific Islanders, 207 Hispanic Americans), 10 international. Average age 35. 497 applicants, 64% accepted, 279 enrolled. Expenses: Contact institution. *Financial support:* Teaching assistantships available. In 2008, 348 master's awarded. Offers bilingual/bicultural education (MS); education (MS, Ed D); educational leadership (MS, Ed D); elementary curriculum and instruction (MS); instructional design and technology (MS); middle school mathematics (MS); reading (MS); secondary education (MS); special education (MS); teacher induction (MS). *Application fee:* $55. *Application Contact:* Admissions/Applications, 657-278-2300. *Dean,* Dr. Claire Cavallaro, 657-278-4021.

College of Engineering and Computer Science Students: 221 full-time (48 women), 407 part-time (91 women); includes 215 minority (16 African Americans, 1 American Indian/Alaska Native, 167 Asian Americans or Pacific Islanders, 31 Hispanic Americans), 248 international. Average age 30. 924 applicants, 61% accepted, 204 enrolled. Expenses: Contact institution. *Financial support:* Teaching assistantships, career-related internships or fieldwork, Federal Work-Study, institutionally sponsored loans, and scholarships/grants available. Support available to part-time students. Financial award application deadline: 3/1. In 2008, 158 master's awarded. *Degree program information:* Part-time programs available. Offers civil engineering and engineering mechanics (MS); computer science (MS); electrical engineering (MS); engineering and computer science (MS); mechanical engineering (MS); software engineering (MS); systems engineering (MS). *Application fee:* $55. *Application Contact:* Dr. Susamma Barua, Associate Dean, 657-278-3362. *Dean,* Dr. Raman Unnikrishnan, 657-278-3362.

College of Health and Human Development Students: 474 full-time (380 women), 330 part-time (277 women); includes 370 minority (38 African Americans, 5 American Indian/Alaska Native, 174 Asian Americans or Pacific Islanders, 153 Hispanic Americans), 21 international. Average age 32. 1,054 applicants, 41% accepted, 352 enrolled. Expenses: Contact institution. *Financial support:* Teaching assistantships, career-related internships or fieldwork, Federal Work-Study, institutionally sponsored loans, and scholarships/grants available. Support available to part-time students. Financial award application deadline: 3/1. In 2008, 165 master's awarded. *Degree program information:* Part-time programs available. Offers counseling (MS); health and human development (MPH, MS, MSW); kinesiology (MS); nursing (MS); public health (MPH); social work (MSW). *Application fee:* $55. *Application Contact:* Admissions/Applications, 657-278-2300. *Dean,* Dr. Roberta Rikli, 657-278-3311.

College of Humanities and Social Sciences Students: 343 full-time (239 women), 578 part-time (360 women); includes 335 minority (16 African Americans, 2 American Indian/Alaska Native, 127 Asian Americans or Pacific Islanders, 190 Hispanic Americans), 64 international. Average age 31. 756 applicants, 54% accepted, 262 enrolled. Expenses: Contact institution. *Financial support:* Teaching assistantships, career-related internships or fieldwork, Federal Work-Study, institutionally sponsored loans, and scholarships/grants available. Support available to part-time students. Financial award application deadline: 3/1. In 2008, 261 master's awarded. *Degree program information:* Part-time programs available. Offers American studies (MA); analysis of specific language structures (MA); anthropological linguistics (MA); anthropology (MA); applied linguistics (MA); clinical/community psychology (MS); communication and semantics (MA); comparative literature (MA); disorders of communication (MA); English (MA); environmental sciences (MS); experimental phonetics (MA); French (MA); geography (MA); German (MA); gerontology (MS); history (MA); humanities and social sciences (MA, MPA, MS); political science (MA); psychology (MA); public administration (MPA); sociology (MA); Spanish (MA); teaching English to speakers of other languages (MS). *Application fee:* $55. *Application Contact:* Admissions/Applications, 657-278-2300. *Dean,* Dr. Thomas Klammer, 657-278-3256.

College of Natural Science and Mathematics Students: 53 full-time (31 women), 158 part-time (87 women); includes 85 minority (1 African American, 1 American Indian/Alaska Native, 56 Asian Americans or Pacific Islanders, 27 Hispanic Americans), 20 international. Average age 29. 229 applicants, 52% accepted, 76 enrolled. Expenses: Contact institution. *Financial support:* Research assistantships, teaching assistantships, career-related internships or fieldwork, Federal Work-Study, institutionally sponsored loans, and scholarships/grants available. Support available to part-time students. Financial award application deadline: 3/1. In 2008, 69 master's awarded. *Degree program information:* Part-time programs available. Offers applied mathematics (MA); biological science (MS); chemistry (MS); geochemistry (MS); geological sciences (MS); mathematics (MA); mathematics for secondary school teachers (MA); natural science and mathematics (MA, MAT, MS); physics (MA); teaching science (MAT). *Application fee:* $55. *Application Contact:* Admissions/Applications, 657-278-2300. *Dean,* Dr. Steven Murray, 657-278-2638.

College of the Arts Students: 96 full-time (57 women), 91 part-time (49 women); includes 52 minority (6 African Americans, 1 American Indian/Alaska Native, 29 Asian Americans or Pacific Islanders, 16 Hispanic Americans), 21 international. Average age 31. 180 applicants, 38% accepted, 56 enrolled. Expenses: Contact institution. *Financial support:* Teaching assistantships, career-related internships or fieldwork, Federal Work-Study, institutionally sponsored loans, and scholarships/grants available. Support available to part-time students. Financial award application deadline: 3/1. In 2008, 47 master's awarded. *Degree program information:* Part-time programs available. Offers acting (MFA); acting and directing (MA); art (MA, MFA); art history (MA); arts (MA, MFA, MM); dance (MA); design (MA); directing (MFA); dramatic literature/criticism (MA); music education (MA); music history and literature (MA); oral interpretation (MA); performance (MM); piano pedagogy (MA); playwriting (MA); technical theater (MA); technical theater and design (MFA); television (MA); theatre for children (MA); theatre history (MA); theory-composition (MM). *Application fee:* $55. *Application Contact:* Admissions/Applications, 657-278-2300. *Dean,* Jerry Samuelson, 657-278-3256.

Mihaylo College of Business and Economics Students: 275 full-time (138 women), 399 part-time (170 women); includes 239 minority (15 African Americans, 182 Asian Americans or Pacific Islanders, 42 Hispanic Americans), 189 international. Average age 29. 849 applicants, 45% accepted, 229 enrolled. Expenses: Contact institution. *Financial support:* Teaching assistantships, Federal Work-Study, institutionally sponsored loans, and scholarships/grants available. Support available to part-time students. Financial award application deadline: 3/1. In 2008, 210 master's awarded. *Degree program information:* Part-time and evening/weekend programs available. Offers accounting (MBA, MS); business and economics (MA, MBA, MS); business economics (MBA); e-commerce (MBA); economics (MA); entrepreneurship (MBA); finance (MBA); information systems (MS); information systems (decision sciences) (MS); information systems (e-commerce) (MS); information technology (MS); international business (MBA); management (MBA); management science (MBA); marketing (MBA); taxation (MS). *Application deadline:* Applications are processed on a rolling basis. *Application fee:* $55. Electronic applications accepted. *Application Contact:* Robert Miyake, Assistant Dean, 657-278-2211. *Dean,* Dr. Anil Puri, 657-773-2592.

CALIFORNIA STATE UNIVERSITY, LONG BEACH, Long Beach, CA 90840

General Information State-supported, coed, comprehensive institution. CGS member. *Enrollment:* 37,891 graduate, professional, and undergraduate students; 2,052 full-time matriculated graduate/professional students (1,316 women), 2,762 part-time matriculated graduate/professional students (1,709 women). *Enrollment by degree level:* 4,742 master's, 72 doctoral. *Graduate faculty:* 427 full-time (184 women), 170 part-time/adjunct (78 women). Tuition, nonresident: full-time $11,160; part-time $372 per unit. *Required fees:* $4100; $1261 per semester. *Graduate housing:* Room and/or apartments available on a first-come, first-served basis to single students; on-campus housing not available to married students. Housing application deadline: 4/1. *Student services:* Campus employment opportunities, campus safety program, career counseling, child daycare facilities, exercise/wellness program, free psychological counseling, grant writing training, international student services, low-cost health insurance, multicultural affairs office, services for students with disabilities, teacher training, writing training. *Library facilities:* University Library. *Online resources:* library catalog, web page, access to other libraries' catalogs. *Collection:* 1.2 million titles, 39,682 serial subscriptions, 37,378 audiovisual materials. *Research affiliation:* Boeing Company (aerospace engineering and manufacturing).

Computer facilities: 2,000 computers available on campus for general student use. A campuswide network can be accessed from off campus. *Web address:* http://www.csulb.edu/.

General Application Contact: Rachel Brophy, Student Programs Coordinator, 562-985-4546, Fax: 562-985-7786, E-mail: rpbrophy@csulb.edu.

GRADUATE UNITS

Graduate Studies Students: 2,701 full-time (1,738 women), 3,626 part-time (2,318 women); includes 3,128 minority (382 African Americans, 35 American Indian/Alaska Native, 1,311 Asian Americans or Pacific Islanders, 1,400 Hispanic Americans). Average age 33. *Faculty:* 975 full-time, 1,429 part-time/adjunct. Expenses: Contact institution. *Financial support:* Fellowships, research assistantships, teaching assistantships, career-related internships or fieldwork, Federal Work-Study, institutionally sponsored loans, scholarships/grants, traineeships, tuition waivers (partial), and unspecified assistantships available. Financial award application deadline: 3/2; financial award applicants required to submit FAFSA. *Degree program information:* Part-time and evening/weekend programs available. Postbaccalaureate distance learning degree programs offered (no on-campus study). Offers interdisciplinary studies (MA, MS). *Application deadline:* For fall admission, 7/1 for domestic and international students; for spring admission, 12/1 for domestic and international students. Applications are processed on a rolling basis. *Application fee:* $55. Electronic applications accepted. *Application Contact:* Rachel Brophy, Student Programs Coordinator, 562-985-4546, Fax: 562-985-7786, E-mail: rpbrophy@csulb.edu. *Director,* Dr. Cecile Lindsay, 562-985-8225, Fax: 562-985-1680, E-mail: clindsay@csulb.edu.

College of Business Administration Students: 93 full-time (34 women), 199 part-time (88 women); includes 92 minority (3 African Americans, 1 American Indian/Alaska Native, 54 Asian Americans or Pacific Islanders, 34 Hispanic Americans), 45 international. Average age 32. 464 applicants, 44% accepted, 66 enrolled. *Faculty:* 20 full-time (3 women), 1 part-time/adjunct (0 women). Expenses: Contact institution. *Financial support:* Career-related internships or fieldwork and scholarships/grants available. Financial award application deadline: 3/2; financial award applicants required to submit FAFSA. *Degree program information:* Part-time and evening/weekend programs available. Offers accelerated (MBA);

evening (MBA); fully employed (MBA); theatre management (MBA). *Application deadline:* For fall admission, 3/30 for domestic students. Applications are processed on a rolling basis. *Application fee:* $55. Electronic applications accepted. *Application Contact:* Dr. H Michael Chung, Director, Graduate Programs and Executive Education, 562-985-5565, Fax: 562-985-5742, E-mail: hmchung@csulb.edu. *Dean*, Dr. Michael E. Solt, 562-985-5307, Fax: 562-985-5742, E-mail: msolt@csulb.edu.

College of Education Students: 254 full-time (195 women), 594 part-time (485 women); includes 456 minority (77 African Americans, 4 American Indian/Alaska Native, 127 Asian Americans or Pacific Islanders, 248 Hispanic Americans), 18 international. Average age 33. 918 applicants, 38% accepted, 283 enrolled. *Faculty:* 37 full-time (26 women), 39 part-time/adjunct (24 women). Expenses: Contact institution. *Financial support:* Federal Work-Study, institutionally sponsored loans, and scholarships/grants available. Financial award application deadline: 3/2. *Degree program information:* Part-time and evening/weekend programs available. Offers counseling (MS); education (MA, Ed D); marriage and family therapy (MS); school counseling (MS); special education (MS). *Application deadline:* For fall admission, 3/1 for domestic students. Applications are processed on a rolling basis. *Application fee:* $55. Electronic applications accepted. *Application Contact:* Nancy L. McGlothin, Coordinator for Graduate Studies and Research, 562-985-8476, Fax: 562-985-4951, E-mail: nmcgloth@csulb.edu. *Dean*, Dr. Marquita Grenot-Scheyer, 562-985-4513, Fax: 562-985-4951, E-mail: mgrenot@csulb.edu.

College of Engineering Students: 279 full-time (51 women), 348 part-time (63 women); includes 201 minority (22 African Americans, 1 American Indian/Alaska Native, 139 Asian Americans or Pacific Islanders, 39 Hispanic Americans), 276 international. Average age 32. 820 applicants, 67% accepted, 189 enrolled. *Faculty:* 28 full-time (5 women), 9 part-time/adjunct (0 women). Expenses: Contact institution. *Financial support:* Research assistantships, teaching assistantships, career-related internships or fieldwork, Federal Work-Study, institutionally sponsored loans, scholarships/grants, and unspecified assistantships available. Financial award application deadline: 3/2. *Degree program information:* Part-time and evening/weekend programs available. Offers aerospace engineering (MSAE); civil engineering (MSCE); computer engineering and computer science (MS); electrical engineering (MSEE); engineering (MS, MSAE, MSCE, MSE, MSEE, MSME, PhD); engineering and industrial applied mathematics (PhD); interdisciplinary engineering (MSE); management engineering (MSE); mechanical engineering (MSME). *Application deadline:* For fall admission, 4/20 for domestic students. *Application fee:* $55. Electronic applications accepted. *Application Contact:* Dr. Sandra Cynar, Associate Dean for Instruction, 562-985-1512, Fax: 562-985-7561, E-mail: cynar@csulb.edu. *Dean*, Dr. Forouzan Golshani, 562-985-5123, Fax: 562-985-7561, E-mail: golshani@csulb.edu.

College of Health and Human Services Students: 871 full-time (703 women), 918 part-time (681 women); includes 1,040 minority (175 African Americans, 13 American Indian/Alaska Native, 352 Asian Americans or Pacific Islanders, 500 Hispanic Americans), 63 international. Average age 33. 2,195 applicants, 50% accepted, 690 enrolled. *Faculty:* 57 full-time (34 women), 38 part-time/adjunct (18 women). Expenses: Contact institution. *Financial support:* Fellowships, research assistantships, teaching assistantships, career-related internships or fieldwork, Federal Work-Study, institutionally sponsored loans, and scholarships/grants available. Financial award application deadline: 3/2; financial award applicants required to submit FAFSA. *Degree program information:* Part-time and evening/weekend programs available. Postbaccalaureate distance learning degree programs offered (no on-campus study). Offers adapted physical education (MA); adult clinical nurse specialist (MS); children, youth and families (MSW); coaching and student athlete development (MA); communicative disorders (MA); concurrent degree in nursing/health care administration (MS); criminal justice (MS); emergency services administration (MS); exercise physiology and nutrition (MS); exercise science (MS); family and consumer sciences (MA); food science (MS); gerontology (MS); health and human services (MA, MPA, MPH, MPT, MS, MSN, MSW, Certificate); health care administration (MS, Certificate); health science (MS); hospitality foodservice and hotel management (MS); individualized studies (MA); kinesiology (MA); nursing (MSN); nutritional science (MS); nutritional sciences/dietetics and food administration (MS); occupational studies (MA); older adults and families (MSW); pedagogical studies (MA); physical therapy (MPT); public policy and administration (MPA); recreation administration (MS); sport and exercise psychology (MS); sport management (MA); sports medicine and injury studies (MS). *Application deadline:* For fall admission, 7/1 for domestic students; for spring admission, 12/1 for domestic students. Applications are processed on a rolling basis. *Application fee:* $55. Electronic applications accepted. *Application Contact:* Dr. Michael Lacourse, Chair, 562-985-4066, Fax: 562-985-7581, E-mail: mlacourse@csulb.edu. *Dean*, Dr. Ronald Vogel, 562-985-4691, Fax: 562-985-7581, E-mail: rvogel@csulb.edu.

College of Liberal Arts Students: 295 full-time (195 women), 394 part-time (234 women); includes 231 minority (28 African Americans, 4 American Indian/Alaska Native, 76 Asian Americans or Pacific Islanders, 123 Hispanic Americans), 75 international. Average age 33. 770 applicants, 44% accepted, 214 enrolled. *Faculty:* 137 full-time (63 women), 29 part-time/adjunct (14 women). Expenses: Contact institution. *Financial support:* Research assistantships, teaching assistantships, career-related internships or fieldwork, Federal Work-Study, institutionally sponsored loans, and scholarships/grants available. Financial award application deadline: 3/2. *Degree program information:* Part-time and evening/weekend programs available. Offers Africa and the Middle East (MA); ancient/Medieval Europe (MA); anthropology (MA); applied anthropology (MA); Asia (MA); Asian American studies (Certificate); Asian studies (MA); communication studies (MA); creative writing (MFA); economics (MA); English (MA); French (MA); general linguistics (MA); geography (MA); German (MA); human factors (MS); language and culture (MA); Latin America (MA); liberal arts (MA, MFA, MS, Certificate); modern Europe (MA); philosophy (MA); political science (MA); psychology (MA); religious studies (MA); Spanish (MA); special concentration (MA); teaching English as a second language (MA); United States (MA); world (MA). *Application deadline:* For fall admission, 7/1 for domestic and international students; for spring admission, 12/1 for international students. Applications are processed on a rolling basis. *Application fee:* $55. Electronic applications accepted. *Application Contact:* Dr. Mark Wiley, Associate Dean, 562-985-5381, Fax: 562-985-2463, E-mail: mwiley@csulb.edu. *Dean*, Dr. Gerry Riposa, 562-985-5381, Fax: 562-985-2463, E-mail: griposa@csulb.edu.

College of Natural Sciences and Mathematics Students: 105 full-time (44 women), 222 part-time (102 women); includes 130 minority (10 African Americans, 2 American Indian/Alaska Native, 75 Asian Americans or Pacific Islanders, 43 Hispanic Americans), 39 international. Average age 31. 297 applicants, 58% accepted, 94 enrolled. *Faculty:* 79 full-time (24 women), 11 part-time/adjunct (7 women). Expenses: Contact institution. *Financial support:* Research assistantships, teaching assistantships, Federal Work-Study, institutionally sponsored loans, scholarships/grants, traineeships, and unspecified assistantships available. Financial award application deadline: 3/2. *Degree program information:* Part-time programs available. Offers applied physics (MS); biochemistry (MS); biology (MS); chemistry (MS); general physics (MS); geology (MS); geophysics (MS); mathematics (MS); microbiology (MS); natural sciences and mathematics (MS). *Application deadline:* For fall admission, 7/1 for domestic students. Applications are processed on a rolling basis. *Application fee:* $55. Electronic applications accepted. *Application Contact:* Dr. Henry Fung, Associate Dean for Curriculum and Instruction, 562-985-7898, Fax: 562-985-2315, E-mail: hcfung@csulb.edu. *Dean*, Dr. Laura Kingsford, 562-985-4707, Fax: 562-985-2315, E-mail: lking@csulb.edu.

College of the Arts Students: 153 full-time (93 women), 83 part-time (53 women); includes 43 minority (2 African Americans, 20 Asian Americans or Pacific Islanders, 21 Hispanic Americans), 17 international. Average age 36. 353 applicants, 41% accepted, 86 enrolled. *Faculty:* 69 full-time (29 women), 44 part-time/adjunct (15 women). Expenses: Contact institution. *Financial support:* Research assistantships, teaching assistantships, Federal Work-Study, institutionally sponsored loans, scholarships/grants, and traineeships available. Financial award application deadline: 3/2. *Degree program information:* Part-time programs available. Offers acting (MFA); art education (MA); art history (MFA); arts (MA, MFA, MM); composition (MM); conducting-choral (MM); conducting-instrumental (MM); dance (MA, MFA); dramatic writing (MFA); instrument/vocal performance (MM); jazz studies (MM); music (MA); opera performance (MM); studio art (MA); technical theatre/design (MFA); theatre management (MFA). *Application deadline:* For fall admission, 1/31 for domestic students. Applications are processed on a rolling basis. *Application fee:* $55. Electronic applications accepted. *Application Contact:* Dr. Jay Kvapil, Associate Dean, 562-985-7885, Fax: 562-985-7883, E-mail: kvapil@csulb.edu. *Dean*, Dr. Donald Para, 562-985-4364, Fax: 562-985-7883, E-mail: para@csulb.edu.

CALIFORNIA STATE UNIVERSITY, LOS ANGELES, Los Angeles, CA 90032-8530

General Information State-supported, coed, comprehensive institution. CGS member. *Enrollment:* 20,743 graduate, professional, and undergraduate students; 2,135 full-time matriculated graduate/professional students (1,436 women), 2,741 part-time matriculated graduate/professional students (1,700 women). *Enrollment by degree level:* 4,863 master's, 13 doctoral. *Graduate faculty:* 263 full-time (119 women), 101 part-time/adjunct (49 women). Tuition, nonresident: part-time $226 per credit. *Required fees:* $4019. *Graduate housing:* Room and/or apartments available to single students; on-campus housing not available to married students. Typical cost: $5424 per year ($9105 including board). Room and board charges vary according to housing facility selected. Housing application deadline: 10/24. *Student services:* Campus employment opportunities, career counseling, child daycare facilities, free psychological counseling, international student services, multicultural affairs office, services for students with disabilities, writing training. *Library facilities:* John F. Kennedy Memorial Library plus 1 other. *Online resources:* library catalog, web page. *Collection:* 1.2 million titles, 24,031 serial subscriptions, 11,605 audiovisual materials.

Computer facilities: 1,500 computers available on campus for general student use. A campuswide network can be accessed from student residence rooms and from off campus. Online class registration is available. *Web address:* http://www.calstatela.edu/.

General Application Contact: Dr. Jose L. Galvan, Dean of Graduate Studies, 323-343-3820, Fax: 323-343-5653, E-mail: jgalvan@cslanet.calstatela.edu.

GRADUATE UNITS

Graduate Studies Students: 2,135 full-time (1,436 women), 2,741 part-time (1,700 women); includes 2,665 minority (303 African Americans, 20 American Indian/Alaska Native, 773 Asian Americans or Pacific Islanders, 1,569 Hispanic Americans), 705 international. Average age 32. 2,431 applicants, 97% accepted, 1136 enrolled. *Faculty:* 263 full-time (119 women), 101 part-time/adjunct (49 women). Expenses: Contact institution. *Financial support:* Fellowships, teaching assistantships, career-related internships or fieldwork and Federal Work-Study available. Support available to part-time students. Financial award application deadline: 3/1. In 2008, 1,032 master's awarded. *Degree program information:* Part-time and evening/weekend programs available. *Application deadline:* For fall admission, 6/15 for domestic students, 5/1 for international students; for winter admission, 11/1 for domestic students, 9/1 for international students; for spring admission, 2/1 for domestic students, 10/1 for international students. Applications are processed on a rolling basis. *Application fee:* $55. Electronic applications accepted. *Application Contact:* Dr. Jose L. Galvan, Dean of Graduate Studies, 323-343-3820, Fax: 323-343-5653, E-mail: jgalvan@cslanet.calstatela.edu. *Dean of Graduate Studies*, Dr. Jose L. Galvan, 323-343-3820, Fax: 323-343-5653, E-mail: jgalvan@cslanet.calstatela.edu.

Charter College of Education Students: 853 full-time (625 women), 950 part-time (693 women); includes 1,137 minority (109 African Americans, 7 American Indian/Alaska Native, 247 Asian Americans or Pacific Islanders, 774 Hispanic Americans), 87 international. Average age 34. 463 applicants, 99% accepted, 286 enrolled. *Faculty:* 76 full-time (45 women). Expenses: Contact institution. *Financial support:* Career-related internships or fieldwork and Federal Work-Study available. Support available to part-time students. Financial award application deadline: 3/1. In 2008, 418 master's awarded. *Degree program information:* Part-time and evening/weekend programs available. Offers applied and advanced studies in education (MA); counseling (MS); education (MA, MS, PhD); elementary teaching (MA); reading (MA); secondary teaching (MA); special education (MA, PhD). *Application deadline:* For fall admission, 6/15 for domestic students, 5/1 for international students; for winter admission, 11/1 for domestic students, 9/1 for international students; for spring admission, 2/1 for domestic students, 10/1 for international students. Applications are processed on a rolling basis. *Application fee:* $55. Electronic applications accepted. *Application Contact:* Dr. Jose L. Galvan, Dean of Graduate Studies, 323-343-3820, Fax: 323-343-5653, E-mail: jgalvan@cslanet.calstatela.edu. *Dean*, Dr. Mary Falvey, 323-343-4300, Fax: 323-343-4318, E-mail: mfalvey@calstatela.edu.

College of Arts and Letters Students: 192 full-time (100 women), 283 part-time (181 women); includes 211 minority (33 African Americans, 6 American Indian/Alaska Native, 47 Asian Americans or Pacific Islanders, 125 Hispanic Americans), 46 international. Average age 34. 236 applicants, 97% accepted, 114 enrolled. *Faculty:* 62 full-time (22 women), 12 part-time/adjunct (7 women). Expenses: Contact institution. *Financial support:* Career-related internships or fieldwork and Federal Work-Study available. Support available to part-time students. Financial award application deadline: 3/1. In 2008, 89 master's awarded. *Degree program information:* Part-time and evening/weekend programs available. Offers art (MA); arts and letters (MA, MFA, MM); English (MA); fine arts (MFA); French (MA); music composition (MM); music education (MA); musicology (MA); performance (MM); philosophy (MA); Spanish (MA); speech communication (MA); television, film and theatre (MFA); theater arts (MA). *Application deadline:* For fall admission, 6/5 for domestic students, 5/1 for international students; for winter admission, 11/1 for domestic students, 9/1 for international students; for spring admission, 2/1 for domestic students, 10/1 for international students. Applications are processed on a rolling basis. *Application fee:* $55. Electronic applications accepted. *Application Contact:* Dr. Jose L. Galvan, Dean of Graduate Studies, 323-343-3820, Fax: 323-343-5653, E-mail: jgalvan@cslanet.calstatela.edu. *Dean*, Dr. Terry Allison, 323-343-4001, Fax: 323-343-6440, E-mail: talliso@calstatela.edu.

College of Business and Economics Students: 110 full-time (59 women), 239 part-time (140 women); includes 116 minority (20 African Americans, 67 Asian Americans or Pacific Islanders, 29 Hispanic Americans), 146 international. Average age 30. 193 applicants, 89% accepted, 85 enrolled. *Faculty:* 16 full-time (3 women), 11 part-time/adjunct (2 women). Expenses: Contact institution. *Financial support:* Fellowships, career-related internships or fieldwork and Federal Work-Study available. Support available to part-time students. Financial award application deadline: 3/1. In 2008, 104 master's awarded. *Degree program information:* Part-time and evening/weekend programs available. Offers accountancy (MS); accounting (MBA); analytical quantitative economics (MA); business and economics (MA, MBA, MS); business economics (MA, MBA, MS); business information systems (MBA); economics (MA); finance and banking (MBA, MS); health care management (MS); international business (MBA, MS); management (MBA, MS); management information systems (MS); marketing management (MBA, MS); office management (MBA). *Application deadline:* For fall admission, 6/15 for domestic students, 5/1 for international students; for winter admission, 11/1 for domestic students, 9/1 for international students; for spring admission, 11/30 for domestic students, 10/1 for international students. Applications are processed on a rolling basis. *Application fee:* $55. Electronic applications accepted. *Application Contact:* Dr. Jose L. Galvan, Dean of Graduate Studies, 323-343-3820, Fax: 323-343-5653, E-mail: jgalvan@cslanet.calstatela.edu. *Acting Dean*, Dr. Philip Romero, 323-343-2800, Fax: 323-343-2813, E-mail: promero@calstatela.edu.

College of Engineering, Computer Science, and Technology Students: 192 full-time (48 women), 330 part-time (52 women); includes 155 minority (19 African Americans, 1 American Indian/Alaska Native, 84 Asian Americans or Pacific Islanders, 51 Hispanic Americans), 302 international. Average age 28. 439 applicants, 96% accepted, 165 enrolled. *Faculty:* 17 full-time (3 women), 7 part-time/adjunct (2 women). Expenses: Contact institution. *Financial support:* Federal Work-Study available. Support available to part-time students. Financial award application deadline: 3/1. In 2008, 80 master's awarded. *Degree program information:* Part-time and evening/weekend programs available. Offers civil engineering (MS); computer science (MS); electrical engineering (MS); engineering, computer science, and technology (MA, MS); industrial and technical studies (MA); mechanical engineering (MS). *Application deadline:* For fall admission, 6/15 for domestic students, 5/1 for international students; for winter admission, 10/1 for domestic students, 9/1 for international students; for spring admission, 2/1 for domestic students, 10/1 for international students. Applications are processed on a rolling basis. *Application fee:* $55. Electronic applications accepted. *Applica-*

California State University, Los Angeles (continued)

tion Contact: Dr. Jose L. Galvan, Dean of Graduate Studies, 323-343-3820, Fax: 323-343-5653, E-mail: jgalvan@cslanet.calstatela.edu. *Dean*, Dr. Keith Moo-Young, 323-343-4500, Fax: 323-343-4555, E-mail: kmooyou@exchange.calstatela.edu.

College of Health and Human Services Students: 439 full-time (381 women), 328 part-time (272 women); includes 486 minority (53 African Americans, 2 American Indian/Alaska Native, 180 Asian Americans or Pacific Islanders, 251 Hispanic Americans), 32 international. Average age 32. 530 applicants, 98% accepted, 200 enrolled. *Faculty:* 30 full-time (20 women), 45 part-time/adjunct (32 women). Expenses: Contact institution. *Financial support:* Career-related internships or fieldwork and Federal Work-Study available. Support available to part-time students. Financial award application deadline: 3/1. In 2008, 203 master's awarded. *Degree program information:* Part-time and evening/weekend programs available. Offers child development (MA); criminal justice (MS); criminalistics (MS); health and human services (MA, MS, MSW); health science (MA); nursing (MS); nutritional science (MS); physical education and kinesiology (MA, MS); social work (MSW); speech and hearing (MA); speech-language pathology (MA). *Application deadline:* For fall admission, 6/15 for domestic students, 5/1 for international students; for winter admission, 11/1 for domestic students, 9/1 for international students; for spring admission, 2/1 for domestic students, 10/1 for international students. Applications are processed on a rolling basis. *Application fee:* $55. Electronic applications accepted. *Application Contact:* Dr. Jose L. Galvan, Dean of Graduate Studies, 323-343-3820, Fax: 323-343-5653, E-mail: jgalvan@cslanet.calstatela.edu. *Dean*, Dr. Beatrice Yorker, 323-343-4600, Fax: 323-343-5598, E-mail: byorker@calstatela.edu.

College of Natural and Social Sciences Students: 310 full-time (197 women), 532 part-time (303 women); includes 481 minority (55 African Americans, 4 American Indian/Alaska Native, 120 Asian Americans or Pacific Islanders, 302 Hispanic Americans), 89 international. Average age 30. 495 applicants, 97% accepted, 252 enrolled. *Faculty:* 61 full-time (26 women), 25 part-time/adjunct (6 women). Expenses: Contact institution. *Financial support:* Teaching assistantships, career-related internships or fieldwork and Federal Work-Study available. Support available to part-time students. Financial award application deadline: 3/1. In 2008, 138 master's awarded. *Degree program information:* Part-time and evening/weekend programs available. Offers analytical chemistry (MS); anthropology (MA); biochemistry (MS); biology (MS); chemistry (MS); geography (MA); geological sciences (MS); history (MA); inorganic chemistry (MS); Latin American studies (MA); mathematics (MS); Mexican-American studies (MA); natural and social sciences (MA, MS); organic chemistry (MS); physical chemistry (MS); physics (MS); political science (MA); psychology (MA, MS); public administration (MS); sociology (MA). *Application deadline:* For fall admission, 6/15 for domestic students, 5/1 for international students; for winter admission, 11/1 for domestic students, 9/1 for international students; for spring admission, 2/1 for domestic students, 10/1 for international students. Applications are processed on a rolling basis. *Application fee:* $55. *Application Contact:* Dr. Jose L. Galvan, Dean of Graduate Studies, 323-343-3820, Fax: 323-343-5653, E-mail: jgalvan@cslanet.calstatela.edu. *Dean*, Dr. James Henderson, 323-343-2000, Fax: 323-343-2011, E-mail: jhender3@calstatela.edu.

CALIFORNIA STATE UNIVERSITY, MONTEREY BAY, Seaside, CA 93955-8001

General Information State-supported, coed, comprehensive institution. *Enrollment:* 4,340 graduate, professional, and undergraduate students; 106 full-time matriculated graduate/professional students (66 women), 136 part-time matriculated graduate/professional students (101 women). *Enrollment by degree level:* 242 master's. *Graduate faculty:* 14 full-time (8 women), 8 part-time/adjunct (4 women). Tuition, nonresident: full-time $10,700; part-time $4068 per year. *Required fees:* $4243; $2178 per year. $244 per term. *Graduate housing:* Rooms and/or apartments available on a first-come, first-served basis to single and married students. Typical cost: $6750 per year ($9360 including board) for single students; $6750 per year ($9360 including board) for married students. Room and board charges vary according to board plan and housing facility selected. *Student services:* Campus employment opportunities, campus safety program, career counseling, child daycare facilities, exercise/wellness program, free psychological counseling, international student services, low-cost health insurance, services for students with disabilities, teacher training, writing training. *Library facilities:* The Tanimura & Antle Family Memorial library. *Online resources:* library catalog, web page, access to other libraries' catalogs. *Collection:* 90,500 titles, 13,295 serial subscriptions, 2,541 audiovisual materials.

Computer facilities: Computer purchase and lease plans are available. 800 computers available on campus for general student use. A campuswide network can be accessed from student residence rooms and from off campus. Online class registration is available. *Web address:* http://www.csumb.edu/.

General Application Contact: Victor Torres, Admissions Evaluator, 831-582-3628, Fax: 831-582-3783, E-mail: victor_torres@csumb.edu.

GRADUATE UNITS

College of Professional Studies Students: 33 full-time (25 women), 72 part-time (57 women); includes 31 minority (4 African Americans, 5 Asian Americans or Pacific Islanders, 22 Hispanic Americans), 4 international. Average age 39. 96 applicants, 65% accepted, 36 enrolled. *Faculty:* 8 full-time (6 women), 4 part-time/adjunct (2 women). Expenses: Contact institution. *Financial support:* In 2008–09, 43 students received support. Scholarships/grants available. Support available to part-time students. Financial award application deadline: 3/2; financial award applicants required to submit FAFSA. In 2008, 17 master's awarded. *Degree program information:* Part-time and evening/weekend programs available. Postbaccalaureate distance learning degree programs offered. Offers professional studies (EMBA, MA, MPP); public policy (MPP). *Application deadline:* For fall admission, 2/2 for domestic students. *Application fee:* $55. Electronic applications accepted. *Application Contact:* Victor Torres, Evaluator, 831-582-3628, Fax: 831-582-3783, E-mail: victor_torres@csumb.edu. *Dean*, Dr. Brian Simmons, 831-582-3898, Fax: 831-582-4568, E-mail: brian_simmons@csumb.edu.

Institute for Advanced Studies in Education Students: 5 full-time (all women), 58 part-time (47 women); includes 22 minority (3 African Americans, 5 Asian Americans or Pacific Islanders, 14 Hispanic Americans), 4 international. Average age 41. 36 applicants, 64% accepted, 14 enrolled. *Faculty:* 5 full-time (4 women), 1 part-time/adjunct (0 women). Expenses: Contact institution. *Financial support:* In 2008–09, 20 students received support. Scholarships/grants available. Support available to part-time students. Financial award application deadline: 3/2; financial award applicants required to submit FAFSA. In 2008, 11 master's awarded. *Degree program information:* Part-time and evening/weekend programs available. Offers education (MA). *Application deadline:* For fall admission, 7/15 for domestic students, 4/1 for international students. Applications are processed on a rolling basis. *Application fee:* $55. Electronic applications accepted. *Application Contact:* Jazmine Contreras, Administrative Support Coordinator, 831-582-3639, Fax: 831-582-3585, E-mail: jazmine_contreras@csumb.edu. *Department Chair*, Irene Nares-Guzicki, 831-582-5081, Fax: 831-582-3585, E-mail: irene_nares-guzicki@csumb.edu.

School of Business Students: 5 part-time (3 women). Average age 36. 24 applicants, 50% accepted, 5 enrolled. *Faculty:* 1 (woman) full-time. Expenses: Contact institution. *Financial support:* In 2008–09, 4 students received support. Application deadline: 3/2. *Degree program information:* Part-time and evening/weekend programs available. Postbaccalaureate distance learning degree programs offered (no on-campus study). Offers business (EMBA). *Application deadline:* Applications are processed on a rolling basis. *Application fee:* $55. Electronic applications accepted. *Application Contact:* Dr. Murray Millson, Director, 831-582-4517, Fax: 831-582-4251, E-mail: murray_milson@csumb.edu. *Director*, Dr. Murray Millson, 831-582-4517, Fax: 831-582-4251, E-mail: murray_milson@csumb.edu.

College of Science, Media Arts and Technology Students: 73 full-time (41 women), 64 part-time (44 women); includes 25 minority (1 African American, 15 Asian Americans or Pacific Islanders, 9 Hispanic Americans), 4 international. Average age 32. 120 applicants, 57% accepted, 56 enrolled. *Faculty:* 6 full-time (2 women), 4 part-time/adjunct (2 women). Expenses: Contact institution. *Financial support:* In 2008–09, 61 students received support; research assistantships, teaching assistantships, career-related internships or fieldwork available. Financial award application deadline: 3/2; financial award applicants required to submit FAFSA. In 2008, 22 master's awarded. *Degree program information:* Part-time programs available. Offers coastal and watershed science and policy (MS); marine science (MS); science, media arts and technology (MA, MS, MSMIT). *Application deadline:* For fall admission, 2/15 for domestic students. *Application fee:* $55. Electronic applications accepted. *Application Contact:* Victor Torres, Admission Evaluator, 831-582-3628, Fax: 831-582-3783, E-mail: victor_torres@csumb.edu. *Dean*, Dr. Marsha Moroh, 831-582-4107, Fax: 831-582-3311, E-mail: marsha_moroh@csumb.edu.

School of Information Technology and Communication Design Students: 50 full-time (30 women), 16 part-time (12 women); includes 19 minority (1 African American, 12 Asian Americans or Pacific Islanders, 6 Hispanic Americans), 3 international. Average age 40. 55 applicants, 71% accepted, 31 enrolled. *Faculty:* 2 full-time (1 woman), 4 part-time/adjunct (2 women). Expenses: Contact institution. *Financial support:* In 2008–09, 18 students received support. Application deadline: 3/2. In 2008, 15 master's awarded. Offers interdisciplinary studies (MA); management and information technology (MA). *Application deadline:* For fall admission, 12/15 for domestic students; for spring admission, 3/1 for domestic students. *Application fee:* $55. Electronic applications accepted. *Application Contact:* Chris Khan, Program Coordinator, 831-582-4791, Fax: 831-582-4484, E-mail: chris_khan@csumb.edu. *Director*, Dr. Eric Y. Tao, 831-582-4222, Fax: 831-582-4484, E-mail: eric_tao@csumb.edu.

CALIFORNIA STATE UNIVERSITY, NORTHRIDGE, Northridge, CA 91330

General Information State-supported, coed, comprehensive institution. CGS member. *Enrollment:* 36,208 graduate, professional, and undergraduate students; 1,980 full-time matriculated graduate/professional students (1,256 women), 2,295 part-time matriculated graduate/professional students (1,470 women). *Enrollment by degree level:* 4,275 master's. *Graduate faculty:* 726 full-time (312 women), 1,107 part-time/adjunct (507 women). *Graduate housing:* Room and/or apartments available to single students; on-campus housing not available to married students. *Student services:* Campus employment opportunities, campus safety program, career counseling, child daycare facilities, free psychological counseling, international student services, low-cost health insurance, multicultural affairs office, services for students with disabilities, teacher training. *Library facilities:* Oviatt Library. *Online resources:* library catalog, web page. *Collection:* 1.4 million titles, 1,584 serial subscriptions, 14,130 audiovisual materials. *Research affiliation:* California Institute of Technology (science), Haagen Company (archaeology), Northridge Hospital (biology), Warner Center Institute (child care), Jet Propulsion Laboratory (engineering), Hughes Aircraft Corporation (engineering).

Computer facilities: A campuswide network can be accessed from student residence rooms and from off campus. Online class registration is available. *Web address:* http://www.csun.edu/.

General Application Contact: Dr. Mack Johnson, Associate Vice President, 818-677-2138.

GRADUATE UNITS

Graduate Studies Students: 1,980 full-time (1,256 women), 2,295 part-time (1,470 women); includes 1,503 minority (215 African Americans, 16 American Indian/Alaska Native, 403 Asian Americans or Pacific Islanders, 869 Hispanic Americans), 527 international. Average age 32. 6,886 applicants, 55% accepted, 1967 enrolled. *Faculty:* 726 full-time (312 women), 1,107 part-time/adjunct (507 women). Expenses: Contact institution. *Financial support:* Fellowships, research assistantships, teaching assistantships, career-related internships or fieldwork, Federal Work-Study, institutionally sponsored loans, scholarships/grants, tuition waivers (partial), and unspecified assistantships available. Support available to part-time students. Financial award applicants required to submit FAFSA. In 2008, 1,543 master's awarded. *Degree program information:* Part-time and evening/weekend programs available. Offers interdisciplinary studies (MA, MS). *Application deadline:* For fall admission, 3/31 for domestic students; for spring admission, 10/31 for domestic students. Applications are processed on a rolling basis. *Application fee:* $55. *Application Contact:* 818-677-3755. *Associate Vice President*, Dr. Mack Johnson, 818-677-2138.

College of Arts, Media, and Communication Students: 108 full-time (65 women), 154 part-time (108 women); includes 61 minority (11 African Americans, 1 American Indian/Alaska Native, 16 Asian Americans or Pacific Islanders, 33 Hispanic Americans), 20 international. Average age 33. 376 applicants, 44% accepted, 103 enrolled. *Faculty:* 87 full-time (39 women), 177 part-time/adjunct (64 women). Expenses: Contact institution. *Financial support:* Teaching assistantships, career-related internships or fieldwork, Federal Work-Study, and unspecified assistantships available. Support available to part-time students. Financial award application deadline: 3/1. In 2008, 69 master's awarded. *Degree program information:* Part-time and evening/weekend programs available. Offers art education (MA); art history (MA); arts, media, and communication (MA, MFA, MM); communication studies (MA); composition (MM); conducting (MM); mass communication (MA); music education (MA); performance (MM); screenwriting (MA); studio art (MA, MFA); theatre (MA); visual communications (MA, MFA). *Application deadline:* For fall admission, 11/30 for domestic students. *Application fee:* $55. *Application Contact:* Robert Bucker, Dean, 818-677-2246, E-mail: robert.bucker@csun.edu. *Dean*, Robert Bucker, 818-677-2246, E-mail: robert.bucker@csun.edu.

College of Business and Economics Students: 40 full-time (19 women), 162 part-time (75 women); includes 53 minority (5 African Americans, 34 Asian Americans or Pacific Islanders, 14 Hispanic Americans), 27 international. Average age 33. 508 applicants, 23% accepted, 40 enrolled. *Faculty:* 88 full-time (21 women), 51 part-time/adjunct (8 women). Expenses: Contact institution. *Financial support:* Teaching assistantships, Federal Work-Study available. Support available to part-time students. Financial award application deadline: 3/1. In 2008, 73 master's awarded. *Degree program information:* Part-time programs available. Offers business and economics (MBA). *Application deadline:* For fall admission, 11/30 for domestic students. *Application fee:* $55. *Application Contact:* Dr. Deborah Cours, Director of Graduate Programs, 818-677-2466, E-mail: deborah.cours@csun.edu. *Dean*, Dr. William Jennings, 818-677-2455.

College of Education Students: 637 full-time (510 women), 819 part-time (625 women); includes 673 minority (108 African Americans, 8 American Indian/Alaska Native, 110 Asian Americans or Pacific Islanders, 447 Hispanic Americans), 31 international. Average age 35. 943 applicants, 55% accepted, 416 enrolled. *Faculty:* 81 full-time (50 women), 189 part-time/adjunct (101 women). Expenses: Contact institution. *Financial support:* Fellowships, career-related internships or fieldwork, Federal Work-Study, institutionally sponsored loans, scholarships/grants, and tuition waivers (partial) available. Support available to part-time students. Financial award application deadline: 3/1. In 2008, 690 master's awarded. *Degree program information:* Part-time and evening/weekend programs available. Offers counseling (MS); curriculum and instruction (MA); early childhood special education (MA); education (MA, MA Ed, MS, Ed D); education of the deaf and hard of hearing (MA); educational administration (MA); educational leadership (Ed D); educational psychology (MA Ed); educational technology (MA); educational therapy (MA); English education (MA); language and literacy (MA); mathematics education (MA); mild/moderate disabilities (MA); moderate/severe disabilities (MA); multilingual/multicultural education (MA); secondary science education (MA); teaching and learning (MA). *Application deadline:* For fall admission, 11/30 for domestic students. *Application fee:* $55. *Application Contact:* Dr. Michael E. Spagna, Dean, 818-677-2590. *Dean*, Dr. Michael E. Spagna, 818-677-2590.

College of Engineering and Computer Science Students: 334 full-time (51 women), 285 part-time (58 women); includes 132 minority (10 African Americans, 1 American Indian/Alaska Native, 73 Asian Americans or Pacific Islanders, 48 Hispanic Americans), 327 international. Average age 28. 1,231 applicants, 55% accepted, 220 enrolled. *Faculty:* 52 full-time (8 women), 85 part-time/adjunct (13 women). Expenses: Contact institution. *Financial support:* Teaching assistantships, career-related internships or fieldwork and Federal Work-Study available. Support available to part-time students. Financial award application deadline: 3/1. In 2008, 159 master's awarded. *Degree program information:* Part-time and evening/weekend programs available. Offers computer science (MS); electrical engineering (MS); engineering (MS); engineering and computer science (MS); engineering automation (MS); engineering management (MS); manufacturing systems engineering (MS); materials engineering (MS); mechanical engineering (MS); software engineering (MS). *Application* *deadline:* For fall admission, 11/30 for domestic students. *Application fee:* $55. *Application Contact:* Dr. S.K. Ramesh, Dean, 818-677-4501. *Dean*, Dr. S.K. Ramesh, 818-677-4501.

College of Health and Human Development Students: 405 full-time (313 women), 289 part-time (226 women); includes 218 minority (36 African Americans, 2 American Indian/Alaska Native, 91 Asian Americans or Pacific Islanders, 89 Hispanic Americans), 56 international. Average age 30. 1,148 applicants, 50% accepted, 285 enrolled. *Faculty:* 81 full-time (48 women), 172 part-time/adjunct (99 women). Expenses: Contact institution. *Financial support:* Teaching assistantships, career-related internships or fieldwork, Federal Work-Study, and institutionally sponsored loans available. Support available to part-time students. Financial award application deadline: 3/1. In 2008, 178 master's awarded. *Degree program information:* Part-time and evening/weekend programs available. Offers audiology (MS); environmental and occupational health (MS); family and consumer sciences (MS); health administration (MS); health and human development (MPH, MPT, MS); hospitality and tourism (MS); industrial hygiene (MS); kinesiology (MS); physical therapy (MPT); public health (MPH); recreational sport management/campus recreation (MS); speech language pathology (MS). *Application deadline:* For fall admission, 11/30 for domestic students. *Application fee:* $55. *Application Contact:* Dr. Sylvia A. Alva, Dean, 818-677-3001. *Dean*, Dr. Sylvia A. Alva, 818-677-3001.

College of Humanities Students: 80 full-time (52 women), 198 part-time (143 women); includes 108 minority (4 African Americans, 1 American Indian/Alaska Native, 20 Asian Americans or Pacific Islanders, 83 Hispanic Americans), 9 international. Average age 34. 200 applicants, 66% accepted, 83 enrolled. *Faculty:* 104 full-time (54 women), 187 part-time/adjunct (112 women). Expenses: Contact institution. *Financial support:* Teaching assistantships, Federal Work-Study available. Support available to part-time students. Financial award application deadline: 3/1. In 2008, 59 master's awarded. *Degree program information:* Part-time and evening/weekend programs available. Offers Chicana and Chicano studies (MA); creative writing (MA); humanities (MA); linguistics (MA); literature (MA); rhetoric and composition theory (MA); Spanish (MA). *Application deadline:* For fall admission, 11/30 for domestic students. *Application fee:* $55. *Application Contact:* Dr. Elizabeth Say, Dean, 818-677-3301. *Dean*, Dr. Elizabeth Say, 818-677-3301.

College of Science and Mathematics Students: 106 full-time (60 women), 154 part-time (84 women); includes 9 African Americans, 24 Asian Americans or Pacific Islanders, 44 Hispanic Americans, 40 international. Average age 29. 338 applicants, 57% accepted, 101 enrolled. *Faculty:* 103 full-time (33 women), 91 part-time/adjunct (41 women). Expenses: Contact institution. *Financial support:* Research assistantships, teaching assistantships, Federal Work-Study, institutionally sponsored loans, tuition waivers (partial), and unspecified assistantships available. Support available to part-time students. Financial award applicants required to submit FAFSA. In 2008, 42 master's awarded. *Degree program information:* Part-time and evening/weekend programs available. Offers applied mathematics (MS); biochemistry (MS); biology (MS); chemistry (MS); geology (MS); mathematics (MS); mathematics for educational careers (MS); physics (MS); science and mathematics (MS). *Application fee:* $55. *Application Contact:* Dr. Jerry Stinner, Dean, 818-677-2004. *Dean*, Dr. Jerry Stinner, 818-677-2004.

College of Social and Behavioral Sciences Students: 262 full-time (181 women), 211 part-time (137 women); includes 165 minority (21 African Americans, 3 American Indian/Alaska Native, 33 Asian Americans or Pacific Islanders, 108 Hispanic Americans), 15 international. Average age 31. 988 applicants, 60% accepted, 187 enrolled. *Faculty:* 129 full-time (59 women), 142 part-time/adjunct (64 women). Expenses: Contact institution. *Financial support:* Teaching assistantships, career-related internships or fieldwork, Federal Work-Study, and institutionally sponsored loans available. Support available to part-time students. Financial award application deadline: 3/1. In 2008, 257 master's awarded. *Degree program information:* Part-time and evening/weekend programs available. Offers clinical psychology (MA); general anthropology (MA); general-experimental psychology (MA); geography (MA); history (MA); human factors and applied experimental psychology (MA); political science (MA); public archaeology (MA); social and behavioral sciences (MA, MSW); social work (MSW); sociology (MA). *Application deadline:* For fall admission, 11/30 for domestic students. *Application fee:* $55. *Application Contact:* Dr. Stella Z. Theodoulou, Dean, 818-677-3317. *Dean*, Dr. Stella Z. Theodoulou, 818-677-3317.

The Tseng College of Extended Learning Expenses: Contact institution. Offers knowledge management (MKM); public administration (MPA); taxation (MS). *Application Contact:* Joyce Feucht-Haviar, Dean, 866-873-6439. *Dean*, Joyce Feucht-Haviar, 866-873-6439.

CALIFORNIA STATE UNIVERSITY, SACRAMENTO, Sacramento, CA 95819-6048

General Information State-supported, coed, comprehensive institution. CGS member. *Graduate housing:* Room and/or apartments available on a first-come, first-served basis to single students; on-campus housing not available to married students.

GRADUATE UNITS

Graduate Studies *Degree program information:* Part-time and evening/weekend programs available. Electronic applications accepted.

College of Arts and Letters *Degree program information:* Part-time and evening/weekend programs available. Offers arts and letters (MA, MM); communication studies (MA); creative writing (MA); foreign languages (MA); music (MM); public history (MA); studio art (MA); teaching English to speakers of other languages (MA); theatre and dance (MA). Electronic applications accepted.

College of Business Administration *Degree program information:* Part-time and evening/weekend programs available. Offers accountancy (MS); business administration (MBA); human resources (MBA); management information science (MS); urban land development (MBA). Electronic applications accepted.

College of Education *Degree program information:* Part-time programs available. Offers bilingual/multicultural education (MA); career counseling (MS); curriculum and instruction (MA); early childhood education (MA); education (MA, MS); educational leadership (MA); generic counseling (MS); guidance (MA); reading education (MA); school counseling (MS); school psychology (MS); special education (MA); vocational rehabilitation (MS). Electronic applications accepted.

College of Engineering and Computer Science *Degree program information:* Part-time and evening/weekend programs available. Offers civil engineering (MS); computer systems (MS); electrical engineering (MS); engineering and computer science (MS); mechanical engineering (MS); software engineering (MS). Electronic applications accepted.

College of Health and Human Services *Degree program information:* Part-time programs available. Offers audiology (MS); criminal justice (MS); family and children's services (MSW); health and human services (MS, MSW); health care (MSW); mental health (MSW); nursing (MS); physical education (MS); recreation administration (MS); social justice and corrections (MSW); speech pathology (MS). Electronic applications accepted.

College of Natural Sciences and Mathematics *Degree program information:* Part-time programs available. Offers biological sciences (MA, MS); chemistry (MS); immunohematology (MS); marine science (MS); mathematics and statistics (MA); natural sciences and mathematics (MA, MS). Electronic applications accepted.

College of Social Sciences and Interdisciplinary Studies *Degree program information:* Part-time programs available. Offers anthropology (MA); counseling psychology (MA); French (MA); German (MA); government (MA); international affairs (MA); public policy and administration (MPPA); social sciences and interdisciplinary studies (MA, MPPA); sociology (MA); Spanish (MA); theater arts (MA). Electronic applications accepted.

CALIFORNIA STATE UNIVERSITY, SAN BERNARDINO, San Bernardino, CA 92407-2397

General Information State-supported, coed, comprehensive institution. CGS member. *Enrollment:* 17,646 graduate, professional, and undergraduate students; 1,615 full-time matriculated graduate/professional students (1,088 women), 761 part-time matriculated graduate/professional students (470 women). *Enrollment by degree level:* 2,352 master's, 24 doctoral. *Graduate faculty:* 238 full-time (101 women), 121 part-time/adjunct (51 women). Tuition and fees vary according to degree level and student level. *Graduate housing:* Room and/or apartments available on a first-come, first-served basis to single students; on-campus housing not available to married students. Typical cost: $4594 (including board). Housing application deadline: 8/1. *Student services:* Campus employment opportunities, campus safety program, career counseling, child daycare facilities, exercise/wellness program, free psychological counseling, international student services, low-cost health insurance, multicultural affairs office, services for students with disabilities, teacher training. *Library facilities:* Pfau Library. *Online resources:* library catalog. *Collection:* 731,259 titles, 2,028 serial subscriptions.

Computer facilities: Computer purchase and lease plans are available. 1,300 computers available on campus for general student use. A campuswide network can be accessed from student residence rooms and from off campus. Online class registration is available. *Web address:* http://www.csusb.edu/.

General Application Contact: Olivia Rosas, Director of Admissions, 909-537-5188, Fax: 909-537-7034, E-mail: orosas@csusb.edu.

GRADUATE UNITS

Graduate Studies Students: 1,615 full-time (1,088 women), 761 part-time (470 women); includes 1,035 minority (260 African Americans, 16 American Indian/Alaska Native, 145 Asian Americans or Pacific Islanders, 614 Hispanic Americans), 196 international. Average age 31. 3,022 applicants, 54% accepted, 1048 enrolled. *Faculty:* 238 full-time (101 women), 121 part-time/adjunct (51 women). Expenses: Contact institution. *Financial support:* Fellowships, research assistantships, teaching assistantships, career-related internships or fieldwork, Federal Work-Study, institutionally sponsored loans, scholarships/grants, and unspecified assistantships available. Support available to part-time students. Financial award applicants required to submit FAFSA. In 2008, 754 master's awarded. *Degree program information:* Part-time and evening/weekend programs available. Offers interdisciplinary studies (MA). *Application deadline:* Applications are processed on a rolling basis. *Application fee:* $55. Electronic applications accepted. *Application Contact:* Olivia Rosas, Director of Admissions, 909-537-7577, Fax: 909-537-7034, E-mail: orosas@csusb.edu.

College of Arts and Letters Students: 100 full-time (75 women), 123 part-time (85 women); includes 90 minority (25 African Americans, 2 American Indian/Alaska Native, 9 Asian Americans or Pacific Islanders, 54 Hispanic Americans), 15 international. Average age 33. 179 applicants, 46% accepted, 65 enrolled. *Faculty:* 50 full-time (29 women), 7 part-time/adjunct (3 women). Expenses: Contact institution. *Financial support:* Research assistantships, teaching assistantships, career-related internships or fieldwork, Federal Work-Study, institutionally sponsored loans, and writing center tutorships available. Support available to part-time students. Financial award application deadline: 3/1. In 2008, 56 master's awarded. *Degree program information:* Part-time and evening/weekend programs available. Offers art (MA); arts and letters (MA, MFA); communication studies (MA); creative writing (MFA); English composition (MA); integrated marketing communication (MA); Spanish (MA); theatre arts (MA); theatre education (MA); theatre for youth (MA). *Application deadline:* For fall admission, 8/31 priority date for domestic students. *Application fee:* $55. *Application Contact:* Olivia Rosas, Director of Admissions, 909-537-7577, Fax: 909-537-7034, E-mail: orosas@csusb.edu. *Dean*, Dr. Eri F. Yasuhara, 909-537-5800, Fax: 909-537-5926, E-mail: eyasuha@csusb.edu.

College of Business and Public Administration Students: 442 full-time (240 women), 123 part-time (64 women); includes 203 minority (53 African Americans, 4 American Indian/Alaska Native, 40 Asian Americans or Pacific Islanders, 106 Hispanic Americans), 142 international. Average age 32. 610 applicants, 42% accepted, 201 enrolled. *Faculty:* 32 full-time (3 women), 19 part-time/adjunct (5 women). Expenses: Contact institution. *Financial support:* Career-related internships or fieldwork, Federal Work-Study, and institutionally sponsored loans available. Support available to part-time students. Financial award application deadline: 3/1. In 2008, 150 master's awarded. *Degree program information:* Part-time and evening/weekend programs available. Offers business administration (MBA); business and public administration (MBA, MPA); for executives (MBA); public administration (MPA). *Application deadline:* For fall admission, 8/31 priority date for domestic students. Applications are processed on a rolling basis. *Application fee:* $55. *Application Contact:* Olivia Rosas, Director of Admissions, 909-537-7577, Fax: 909-537-7034, E-mail: orosas@csusb.edu. *Dean*, Dr. Karen Dill-Bowerman, 909-537-3390, Fax: 909-537-7026, E-mail: karenb@csusb.edu.

College of Education Students: 636 full-time (483 women), 359 part-time (244 women); includes 490 minority (117 African Americans, 8 American Indian/Alaska Native, 46 Asian Americans or Pacific Islanders, 319 Hispanic Americans), 10 international. Average age 41. 546 applicants, 66% accepted, 192 enrolled. *Faculty:* 45 full-time (25 women), 70 part-time/adjunct (35 women). Expenses: Contact institution. *Financial support:* Career-related internships or fieldwork and Federal Work-Study available. Support available to part-time students. In 2008, 379 master's awarded. *Degree program information:* Part-time and evening/weekend programs available. Offers bilingual/cross-cultural education (MA); correctional and alternative education (MA); counseling and guidance (MS); curriculum and instruction (MA); educational administration (MA); educational leadership and curriculum (Ed D); educational psychology and counseling (MA, MS); elementary education (MA); English as a second language (MA); environmental education (MA); history and English for secondary teachers (MA); instructional technology (MA); reading (MA); rehabilitation counseling (MA); secondary education (MA); special education (MA); special education and rehabilitation counseling (MA); teaching of science (MA); vocational and career education (MA). *Application deadline:* For fall admission, 8/31 priority date for domestic students. *Application fee:* $55. *Application Contact:* Olivia Rosas, Director of Admissions, 909-537-7577, Fax: 909-537-7034, E-mail: orosas@csusb.edu. *Dean*, Dr. Patricia Arlin, 909-537-5600, Fax: 909-537-7011, E-mail: parlin@csusb.edu.

College of Natural Sciences Students: 105 full-time (56 women), 104 part-time (56 women); includes 87 minority (27 African Americans, 1 American Indian/Alaska Native, 21 Asian Americans or Pacific Islanders, 38 Hispanic Americans), 31 international. Average age 34. 241 applicants, 46% accepted, 82 enrolled. *Faculty:* 51 full-time (18 women), 3 part-time/adjunct (2 women). Expenses: Contact institution. *Financial support:* Fellowships, research assistantships, teaching assistantships, career-related internships or fieldwork and Federal Work-Study available. In 2008, 51 master's awarded. *Degree program information:* Part-time programs available. Offers biology (MS); computer science (MS); health science (MS); health services administration (MS); kinesiology (MA Ed); mathematics (MA); natural sciences (MA, MA Ed, MAT, MPH, MS); nursing (MS); public health (MPH); teaching mathematics (MAT). *Application fee:* $55. *Application Contact:* Olivia Rosas, Director of Admissions, 909-537-7577, Fax: 909-537-7034, E-mail: orosas@csusb.edu. *Dean*, Dr. B. Robert Carlson, 909-537-5300, Fax: 909-537-7005, E-mail: carlson@csusb.edu.

College of Social and Behavioral Sciences Students: 339 full-time (247 women), 92 part-time (46 women); includes 182 minority (44 African Americans, 1 American Indian/Alaska Native, 29 Asian Americans or Pacific Islanders, 108 Hispanic Americans), 10 international. Average age 31. 478 applicants, 40% accepted, 153 enrolled. *Faculty:* 62 full-time (27 women), 22 part-time/adjunct (6 women). Expenses: Contact institution. *Financial support:* Fellowships, research assistantships, teaching assistantships, career-related internships or fieldwork, Federal Work-Study, institutionally sponsored loans, and unspecified assistantships available. Support available to part-time students. In 2008, 118 master's awarded. *Degree program information:* Part-time and evening/weekend programs available. Offers child development (MA); clinical psychology (MS); clinical/counseling psychology (MS); criminal justice (MA); environmental sciences (MS); general/experimental psychology (MA); industrial/organizational psychology (MS); national security studies (MA); organizational psychology (MS); psychology (MA); psychology-life span (MA); social and behavioral sciences (MA, MS, MSW); social sciences (MA); social work (MSW). *Application Contact:* Olivia Rosas, Director of Admissions, 909-537-7577, Fax: 909-537-7034, E-mail: orosas@csusb.edu. *Dean*, Jamal Nassar, 909-537-7500, Fax: 909-537-7107, E-mail: jnassar@csusb.edu.

CALIFORNIA STATE UNIVERSITY, SAN MARCOS, San Marcos, CA 92096-0001

General Information State-supported, coed, comprehensive institution. CGS member. *Graduate housing:* Room and/or apartments available on a first-come, first-served basis to single students; on-campus housing not available to married students. Housing application deadline: 10/1.

GRADUATE UNITS

College of Arts and Sciences *Degree program information:* Part-time and evening/weekend programs available. Offers arts and sciences (MA, MS); biological sciences (MS); computer science (MS); literature and writing studies (MA); mathematics (MS); psychology (MA); sociological practice (MA); Spanish (MA). Electronic applications accepted.

College of Business Administration *Degree program information:* Evening/weekend programs available. Offers business management (MBA); government management (MBA).

College of Education *Degree program information:* Part-time and evening/weekend programs available. Offers education (MA).

CALIFORNIA STATE UNIVERSITY, STANISLAUS, Turlock, CA 95382

General Information State-supported, coed, comprehensive institution. CGS member. *Graduate housing:* Room and/or apartments available on a first-come, first-served basis to single students; on-campus housing not available to married students. Housing application deadline: 8/1. *Research affiliation:* EDAW, Inc. (environmental sustainable development), Mathematical Association of America (mathematics), Kaiser permanente (healthcare), California Campus Compact-Carnegie Fellowship Program (teaching development for faculty), Valley Mountain Regional Center (development disability), Friends of Turlock Library (public library).

GRADUATE UNITS

College of Business Administration *Degree program information:* Part-time and evening/weekend programs available. Offers business administration (EMBA, MBA, MSBA); finance and international finance (MSBA).

College of Education *Degree program information:* Part-time and evening/weekend programs available. Offers community college leadership (Ed D); curriculum and instruction (MA); education (MA); educational leadership (Ed D); educational technology (MA); middle/junior high studies (Graduate Certificate); P-12 leadership (Ed D); physical education (MA); school administration (MA); school counseling (MA); special education (MA).

College of Human and Health Sciences Offers behavior analysis (MS); child development (Graduate Certificate); counseling (MS); human and health sciences (MA, MS, MSW, Graduate Certificate); psychology (MA, MS); social work (MSW).

College of Humanities and Social Sciences Offers criminal justice (MA); English (MA); gerontology (Certificate); history (MA); humanities and social sciences (MA, MPA, Certificate); international relations (MA); literature (MA); public administration (MPA); rhetoric and teaching of writing (MA); secondary school teachers (MA); TESOL (MA, Certificate).

College of Natural Sciences Offers ecology and sustainability (MS); genetic counseling (MS); marine sciences (MS); natural sciences (MS).

College of the Arts *Degree program information:* Part-time and evening/weekend programs available. Offers arts (Certificate); printmaking (Certificate). Electronic applications accepted.

Programs in Interdisciplinary Studies *Degree program information:* Part-time and evening/weekend programs available. Offers interdisciplinary studies (MA, MS). Electronic applications accepted.

CALIFORNIA UNIVERSITY OF PENNSYLVANIA, California, PA 15419-1394

General Information State-supported, coed, comprehensive institution. CGS member. *Graduate housing:* Room and/or apartments available on a first-come, first-served basis to single students; on-campus housing not available to married students. *Research affiliation:* The Center for Rural Pennsylvania (agriculture), The Technology Collaborative (robotics), International Technical Education Association (curricular development), NCAA (tobacco use), Gettysburg Travel Council (travel and tourism), NASA (space grant consortium).

GRADUATE UNITS

School of Graduate Studies and Research *Degree program information:* Part-time and evening/weekend programs available. Postbaccalaureate distance learning degree programs offered (no on-campus study). Offers legal studies (MS). Electronic applications accepted.

College of Liberal Arts *Degree program information:* Part-time and evening/weekend programs available. Offers liberal arts (MA); social science—criminal justice (MA). Electronic applications accepted.

School of Education *Degree program information:* Part-time and evening/weekend programs available. Postbaccalaureate distance learning degree programs offered (minimal on-campus study). Offers athletic training (MS); communication disorders (MS); education (M Ed, MAT, MS, MSW); exercise science and health promotion (MS); fitness and wellness (MS); guidance and counseling (M Ed, MS); mentally and/or physically handicapped education (M Ed); performance enhancement and injury prevention (MS); reading specialist (M Ed); rehabilitation sciences (MS); school administration (M Ed); school psychology (MS); secondary education (MAT); social work (MSW); sport management (MS), sport psychology (MS), technology education (M Ed). Electronic applications accepted.

School of Science and Technology *Degree program information:* Part-time and evening/weekend programs available. Postbaccalaureate distance learning degree programs offered. Offers business administration (MSBA); multimedia technology (MS); science and technology (MS, MSBA). Electronic applications accepted.

CALIFORNIA WESTERN SCHOOL OF LAW, San Diego, CA 92101-3090

General Information Independent, coed, graduate-only institution. *Graduate housing:* On-campus housing not available.

GRADUATE UNITS

Graduate and Professional Programs *Degree program information:* Part-time programs available. Offers law (JD, LL M). Electronic applications accepted.

CALUMET COLLEGE OF SAINT JOSEPH, Whiting, IN 46394-2195

General Information Independent-religious, coed, comprehensive institution.

GRADUATE UNITS

Program in Leadership in Teaching Offers leadership in teaching (MS Ed).

Program in Public Safety Administration Offers public safety administration (MS).

Program in Quality Assurance Offers quality assurance (MS).

CALVARY BIBLE COLLEGE AND THEOLOGICAL SEMINARY, Kansas City, MO 64147-1341

General Information Independent-religious, coed, comprehensive institution. *Enrollment:* 300 graduate, professional, and undergraduate students; 21 full-time matriculated graduate/professional students (7 women), 37 part-time matriculated graduate/professional students (16 women). *Enrollment by degree level:* 6 first professional, 52 master's. *Graduate faculty:* 3 full-time (0 women), 2 part-time/adjunct (0 women). *Graduate housing:* Rooms and/or apartments available on a first-come, first-served basis to single and married students. *Student services:* Campus employment opportunities, services for students with disabilities, writing training. *Library facilities:* Hilda Kroeker Library. *Online resources:* library catalog, web page. *Collection:* 61,188 titles, 12,965 serial subscriptions, 492 audiovisual materials.

Computer facilities: 23 computers available on campus for general student use. A campuswide network can be accessed from student residence rooms. Online class registration is available. *Web address:* http://www.calvary.edu/.

General Application Contact: Bob Crank, Director of Admissions, 800-326-3960 Ext. 1326, Fax: 816-331-4474.

GRADUATE UNITS

Calvary Theological Seminary Students: 21 full-time (7 women), 37 part-time (16 women); includes 5 African Americans, 4 Asian Americans or Pacific Islanders, 3 Hispanic Americans, 2 international. Average age 38. *Faculty:* 3 full-time (0 women), 2 part-time/adjunct (0 women). Expenses: Contact institution. *Financial support:* In 2008–09, 13 students received support. Scholarships/grants available. Financial award application deadline: 11/5. In 2008, 13 master's awarded. *Degree program information:* Part-time and evening/weekend programs available. Offers Bible and theology (MS); Biblical counseling (MA); Biblical studies (MA); Christian ministry (MA); Christian studies (MS); Christian theology (MA); New Testament (MA); Old Testament (MA); pastoral studies (M Div). *Application deadline:* For fall admission, 7/15 priority date for domestic and international students; for spring admission, 12/1 priority date for domestic and international students. *Application fee:* $25. *Application Contact:* Bob Crank, Director of Admissions, 800-326-3960 Ext. 1326, Fax: 816-331-4474. *Academic Dean,* Dr. Thomas Baurain, 816-322-0110 Ext. 1502, Fax: 816-331-4474.

CALVIN COLLEGE, Grand Rapids, MI 49546-4388

General Information Independent-religious, coed, comprehensive institution. *Enrollment:* 4,171 graduate, professional, and undergraduate students; 6 full-time matriculated graduate/professional students (5 women), 130 part-time matriculated graduate/professional students (87 women). *Enrollment by degree level:* 136 master's. *Graduate faculty:* 3 full-time (2 women), 4 part-time/adjunct (1 woman). *Tuition:* Part-time $420 per credit hour. *Graduate housing:* Room and/or apartments available on a first-come, first-served basis to single students; on-campus housing not available to married students. Typical cost: $3780 per year ($7970 including board). Housing application deadline: 5/1. *Student services:* Campus employment opportunities, campus safety program, career counseling, exercise/wellness program, free psychological counseling, international student services, low-cost health insurance, multicultural affairs office, services for students with disabilities, writing training. *Library facilities:* Hekman Library plus 1 other. *Online resources:* library catalog, web page. *Collection:* 1 million titles, 15,697 serial subscriptions, 25,557 audiovisual materials.

Computer facilities: Computer purchase and lease plans are available. 800 computers available on campus for general student use. A campuswide network can be accessed from student residence rooms and from off campus. Online class registration is available. *Web address:* http://www.calvin.edu/.

General Application Contact: Cindi Hoekstra, Graduate Program Coordinator, 616-516-6158, Fax: 616-526-6505, E-mail: choekstr@calvin.edu.

GRADUATE UNITS

Graduate Programs in Education Students: 6 full-time (5 women), 130 part-time (87 women); includes 9 minority (3 African Americans, 5 Asian Americans or Pacific Islanders, 1 Hispanic American). Average age 29. *Faculty:* 3 full-time (2 women), 4 part-time/adjunct (1 woman). Expenses: Contact institution. *Financial support:* Federal Work-Study, scholarships/grants, and tuition waivers (full and partial) available. Support available to part-time students. Financial award application deadline: 4/3. *Degree program information:* Part-time programs available. Offers curriculum and instruction (M Ed); educational leadership (M Ed); learning disabilities (M Ed); literacy (M Ed). *Application deadline:* For fall admission, 8/1 priority date for domestic students, 5/1 priority date for international students; for spring admission, 1/1 priority date for domestic students, 11/1 priority date for international students. Applications are processed on a rolling basis. *Application fee:* $0. Electronic applications accepted. *Application Contact:* Debra Abbott, Administrative Assistant, 616-526-6105, Fax: 616-526-6505, E-mail: dka2@calvin.edu. *Graduate Program Director,* Dr. Debra Buursma, 616-526-6231, Fax: 616-526-6505, E-mail: dbuursma@calvin.edu.

CALVIN THEOLOGICAL SEMINARY, Grand Rapids, MI 49546-4387

General Information Independent-religious, coed, graduate-only institution. *Graduate housing:* Rooms and/or apartments available on a first-come, first-served basis to single and married students. Housing application deadline: 4/1.

GRADUATE UNITS

Graduate and Professional Programs *Degree program information:* Part-time programs available. Offers divinity (M Div); educational ministry (MA); historical theology (PhD); missions: church growth (MA); philosophical and moral theology (PhD); systematic theology (PhD); theological studies (MTS); theology (Th M). Electronic applications accepted.

CAMBRIDGE COLLEGE, Cambridge, MA 02138-5304

General Information Independent, coed, comprehensive institution. *Enrollment:* 6,098 graduate, professional, and undergraduate students; 2,108 full-time matriculated graduate/professional students (1,620 women), 1,743 part-time matriculated graduate/professional students (1,328 women). *Enrollment by degree level:* 3,228 master's, 60 doctoral, 563 other advanced degrees. *Graduate faculty:* 10 full-time (8 women), 814 part-time/adjunct (478 women). *Tuition:* Full-time $6960; part-time $435 per credit. One-time fee: $140 full-time. Tuition and fees vary according to degree level, campus/location and program. *Graduate housing:* On-campus housing not available. *Student services:* Career counseling, free psychological counseling, international student services, services for students with disabilities, writing training. *Library facilities:* Cambridge College Online Library. *Online resources:* web page. *Collection:* 30,000 titles, 21 serial subscriptions.

Computer facilities: A campuswide network can be accessed. Online class registration is available. *Web address:* http://www.cambridgecollege.edu/.

General Application Contact: Farah Favanbakhsh, Assistant Vice President of Undergraduate Admissions, 617-868-1000 Ext. 1124, Fax: 617-349-3561, E-mail: admit@cambridgecollege.edu.

GRADUATE UNITS

School of Education Students: 1,036 full-time (830 women), 1,191 part-time (928 women); includes 1,163 minority (802 African Americans, 6 American Indian/Alaska Native, 36 Asian Americans or Pacific Islanders, 319 Hispanic Americans), 17 international. Average age 37. 866 applicants, 77% accepted, 524 enrolled. *Faculty:* 9 full-time (3 women), 461 part-time/adjunct (263 women). Expenses: Contact institution. *Financial support:* In 2008–09, 1,722 students received support. Career-related internships or fieldwork, Federal Work-Study, and scholarships/grants available. Financial award applicants required to submit FAFSA. In 2008, 927 master's, 11 doctorates, 223 CAGSs awarded. *Degree program information:* Part-time and evening/weekend programs available. Postbaccalaureate distance learning degree programs offered (minimal on-campus study). Offers art education (M Ed); autism spectrum disorders (M Ed); behavioral management (M Ed); early childhood teacher (M Ed); education specialist: curriculum and instruction (CAGS); educational leadership (Ed D); elementary teacher (M Ed); English as a second language (M Ed); general science (M Ed); health/family and consumer sciences (M Ed); history (M Ed); humane education (M Ed); individualized (M Ed); information technology literacy (M Ed); instructional technology (M Ed); interdisciplinary studies (M Ed); library teacher (M Ed); literacy education (M Ed); mathematics (M Ed); mathematics education (M Ed); middle school mathematics and science (M Ed); school administration (M Ed, CAGS); school guidance counselor (M Ed); school nurse education (M Ed); science (M Ed); science education (M Ed); special education administrator (CAGS); special education/moderate disabilities (M Ed); teaching skills and methodologies (M Ed); workforce education (M Ed). *Application deadline:* For fall admission, 9/8 priority date for domestic students; for winter admission, 1/8 for domestic students; for spring admission, 5/21 priority date for domestic students. Applications are processed on a rolling basis. *Application* *fee:* $30. Electronic applications accepted. *Application Contact:* Robin Laskey, Associate Director of Admissions, 800-877-4723 Ext. 1141, E-mail: robin.laskey@cambridgecollege.edu. *Acting Dean*, Dr. Jo-Ann Testaverde, EdD, 617-873-0187, Fax: 617-873-0222, E-mail: joann.testaverde@cambridgecollege.edu.

School of Management Students: 422 full-time (255 women), 226 part-time (144 women); includes 258 minority (160 African Americans, 1 American Indian/Alaska Native, 40 Asian Americans or Pacific Islanders, 57 Hispanic Americans), 70 international. Average age 39. 229 applicants, 77% accepted, 134 enrolled. *Faculty:* 4 full-time (3 women), 170 part-time/adjunct (130 women). Expenses: Contact institution. *Financial support:* In 2008–09, 324 students received support. Federal Work-Study and scholarships/grants available. Financial award applicants required to submit FAFSA. In 2008, 253 master's awarded. *Degree program information:* Part-time and evening/weekend programs available. Offers business negotiation and conflict resolution (M Mgt); general business (M Mgt); health care informatics (M Mgt); healthcare management (M Mgt); leadership in human organizational dynamics (M Mgt); non-profit and public organization management (M Mgt); small business development (M Mgt); technology management (M Mgt). *Application deadline:* Applications are processed on a rolling basis. *Application fee:* $30. *Application Contact:* Jessie Haigh, Admissions Counselor, 617-873-0285, Fax: 617-873-0673, E-mail: jessie.haigh@cambridgecollege.edu. *Acting Dean*, Dr. Mary Ann Joseph, PhD, 617-873-0127, Fax: 617-873-0673, E-mail: maryann.joseph@cambridgecollege.edu.

School of Psychology and Counseling Students: 476 full-time (384 women), 313 part-time (245 women); includes 396 minority (300 African Americans, 2 American Indian/Alaska Native, 13 Asian Americans or Pacific Islanders, 81 Hispanic Americans), 13 international. Average age 37. 307 applicants, 81% accepted, 192 enrolled. *Faculty:* 5 full-time (2 women), 183 part-time/adjunct (85 women). Expenses: Contact institution. *Financial support:* In 2008–09, 857 students received support. Career-related internships or fieldwork, Federal Work-Study, and scholarships/grants available. Financial award applicants required to submit FAFSA. In 2008, 226 master's, 9 CAGSs awarded. *Degree program information:* Part-time and evening/weekend programs available. Offers addiction counseling (M Ed); counseling psychology (M Ed); counseling psychology: forensic counseling (M Ed); marriage and family therapy (M Ed); mental health and addiction counseling (M Ed); mental health counseling (M Ed); mental health counseling for school guidance counselors (Certificate); mental health, addiction and school adjustment counseling (M Ed); psychological studies (M Ed); school adjustment counseling (M Ed); school guidance counseling (M Ed). *Application deadline:* Applications are processed on a rolling basis. *Application fee:* $30. Electronic applications accepted. *Application Contact:* Kathryn Lenehan, Admission Counselor, 800-877-0280, E-mail: kathryn.lenehan@cambridgecollege.edu. *Dean*, Dr. Niti Seth, EdD, 617-873-0208, Fax: 617-349-3545, E-mail: nseth@cambridgecollege.edu.

CAMERON UNIVERSITY, Lawton, OK 73505-6377

General Information State-supported, coed, comprehensive institution. *Graduate housing:* Room and/or apartments available on a first-come, first-served basis to single students; on-campus housing not available to married students. *Research affiliation:* Telos-Ok (simulations), Army Research Institute (human factors), Advanced Systems Technology, Inc. (informational systems), Dynamics Research Corporation (multimedia systems), Eagle Systems, Inc. (multimedia systems), Halliburton (energy systems).

GRADUATE UNITS

Office of Graduate Studies *Degree program information:* Part-time and evening/weekend programs available. Postbaccalaureate distance learning degree programs offered (no on-campus study). Offers behavioral sciences (MS); business administration (MBA); education (M Ed); educational leadership (MS); entrepreneurial studies (MS); teaching (MAT). Electronic applications accepted.

CAMPBELLSVILLE UNIVERSITY, Campbellsville, KY 42718-2799

General Information Independent-religious, coed, comprehensive institution. *Enrollment:* 2,830 graduate, professional, and undergraduate students; 301 full-time matriculated graduate/professional students (192 women), 97 part-time matriculated graduate/professional students (61 women). *Enrollment by degree level:* 301 master's. *Graduate faculty:* 50 full-time (19 women), 46 part-time/adjunct (21 women). *Tuition:* Full-time $6570; part-time $365 per credit hour. *Required fees:* $60 per term. *Graduate housing:* Rooms and/or apartments available on a first-come, first-served basis to single and married students. Typical cost: $6410 (including board) for single students. Housing application deadline: 6/30. *Student services:* Campus safety program, career counseling, exercise/wellness program, international student services, teacher training, writing training. *Library facilities:* Montgomery Library plus 2 others. *Online resources:* library catalog, web page. *Collection:* 172,000 titles, 12,777 serial subscriptions.

Computer facilities: 148 computers available on campus for general student use. *Web address:* http://www.campbellsville.edu/.

General Application Contact: Monica Bamwine, Assistant Director of Admissions, 270-789-5221, Fax: 270-789-5071, E-mail: mkbamwine@campbellsville.edu.

GRADUATE UNITS

Carver School of Social Work *Degree program information:* Evening/weekend programs available. Electronic applications accepted.

College of Arts and Sciences *Degree program information:* Part-time programs available. Offers social science (MA). Electronic applications accepted.

School of Business and Economics *Degree program information:* Part-time and evening/weekend programs available. Offers business administration (MBA). Electronic applications accepted.

School of Education *Degree program information:* Part-time and evening/weekend programs available. Postbaccalaureate distance learning degree programs offered (minimal on-campus study). Offers curriculum and instruction (MAE); special education (MASE). Electronic applications accepted.

School of Music *Degree program information:* Part-time programs available. Offers church music (MM); music (MA); music education (MM). Electronic applications accepted.

School of Theology *Degree program information:* Part-time programs available. Offers theology (M Th). Electronic applications accepted.

CAMPBELL UNIVERSITY, Buies Creek, NC 27506

General Information Independent-religious, coed, university. *Graduate housing:* Rooms and/or apartments available on a first-come, first-served basis to single and married students. Housing application deadline: 6/2.

GRADUATE UNITS

Graduate and Professional Programs *Degree program information:* Part-time and evening/weekend programs available.

Divinity School Offers Christian education (MA); divinity (M Div); ministry (D Min).

Lundy-Fetterman School of Business *Degree program information:* Part-time and evening/weekend programs available. Offers business (MBA, MTIM).

Norman Adrian Wiggins School of Law Offers law (JD). Electronic applications accepted.

School of Education *Degree program information:* Part-time and evening/weekend programs available. Offers administration (MSA); community counseling (MA); elementary education (M Ed); English education (M Ed); interdisciplinary studies (M Ed); mathematics education (M Ed); middle grades education (M Ed); physical education (M Ed); school counseling (M Ed); secondary education (M Ed); social science education (M Ed).

School of Pharmacy *Degree program information:* Part-time and evening/weekend programs available. Offers clinical research (MS); pharmaceutical science (MS); pharmacy (Pharm D). Electronic applications accepted.

CANADIAN COLLEGE OF NATUROPATHIC MEDICINE, Toronto, ON M2K 1E2, Canada

General Information Independent, coed, primarily women, graduate-only institution. *Enrollment by degree level:* 529 other advanced degrees. *Graduate faculty:* 32 full-time, 85 part-time/adjunct. *Graduate tuition:* Tuition charges are reported in Canadian dollars. *Tuition:* Full-time $18,355 Canadian dollars. Part-time tuition and fees vary according to course load. *Graduate housing:* Room and/or apartments available on a first-come, first-served basis to single students; on-campus housing not available to married students. Typical cost: $3840 Canadian dollars per year. Housing application deadline: 6/1. *Student services:* Campus employment opportunities, campus safety program, career counseling, exercise/wellness program, free psychological counseling, international student services, low-cost health insurance, services for students with disabilities. *Library facilities:* Learning Resource Centre. *Online resources:* library catalog. *Collection:* 11 titles, 100 serial subscriptions, 1,500 audiovisual materials. *Research affiliation:* Sick Children's Hospital, Sherbourne Health Center, Mayo Clinic, Toronto General Hospital, Sunnybrook and Women's College Hospital.

Computer facilities: 40 computers available on campus for general student use. A campuswide network can be accessed. *Web address:* http://www.ccnm.edu/.

General Application Contact: Student Services and Admissions Office, 416-498-1225 Ext. 245, Fax: 416-498-3197, E-mail: info@ccnm.edu.

GRADUATE UNITS

Doctor of Naturopathic Medicine Program Average age 25. 163 applicants, 87% accepted, 80 enrolled. *Faculty:* 32 full-time, 85 part-time/adjunct. Expenses: Contact institution. *Financial support:* In 2008–09, 280 students received support, including 3 research assistantships, 2 teaching assistantships; career-related internships or fieldwork, scholarships/grants, and health care benefits also available. Support available to part-time students. Financial award application deadline: 7/31. Offers naturopathic medicine (ND). *Application deadline:* For fall admission, 1/31 priority date for domestic and international students; for winter admission, 5/30 priority date for domestic and international students. Applications are processed on a rolling basis. *Application fee:* $150. *Application Contact:* Student Services, 416-498-1225 Ext. 245, Fax: 416-498-3197, E-mail: info@ccnm.edu. *President/CEO*, Bob Bernhardt, 416-498-1255, Fax: 416-498-3197, E-mail: bbernhardt@ccnm.edu.

CANADIAN MEMORIAL CHIROPRACTIC COLLEGE, Toronto, ON M2H 3J1, Canada

General Information Independent, coed, graduate-only institution. *Graduate housing:* On-campus housing not available. *Research affiliation:* University of Waterloo, University of Calgary, University of Toronto.

GRADUATE UNITS

Certificate Programs Offers chiropractic clinical sciences (Certificate); chiropractic radiology (Certificate); chiropractic sports sciences (Certificate); clinical acupuncture (Certificate).

Professional Program Offers chiropractic (DC).

CANADIAN SOUTHERN BAPTIST SEMINARY, Cochrane, AB T4C 2G1, Canada

General Information Independent-religious, coed, graduate-only institution. *Enrollment by degree level:* 44 master's. *Graduate faculty:* 8 full-time (0 women), 3 part-time/adjunct (1 woman). *Graduate tuition:* Tuition charges are reported in Canadian dollars. *Tuition:* Full-time $4800 Canadian dollars. Tuition and fees vary according to course load and campus/location. *Graduate housing:* Rooms and/or apartments available on a first-come, first-served basis to single and married students. Typical cost: $655 Canadian dollars per year for single students; $7860 Canadian dollars per year for married students. Room charges vary according to housing facility selected. Housing application deadline: 6/30. *Student services:* Campus employment opportunities, free psychological counseling. *Library facilities:* Keith C. Willis Library. *Online resources:* library catalog, access to other libraries' catalogs. *Collection:* 34,892 titles, 11,413 serial subscriptions, 2,743 audiovisual materials.

Computer facilities: 12 computers available on campus for general student use. A campuswide network can be accessed from off campus. *Web address:* http://www.csbs.edu/.

General Application Contact: Alain Laundriault, Recruitment Director, 403-932-6622 Ext. 251, Fax: 403-932-7049, E-mail: alain.laundriault@csbs.ca.

GRADUATE UNITS

Graduate Programs Students: 22 full-time (4 women), 22 part-time (5 women); includes 9 minority (1 African American, 5 Asian Americans or Pacific Islanders, 3 Hispanic Americans), 12 international. Average age 30. *Faculty:* 8 full-time (0 women), 3 part-time/adjunct (1 woman). Expenses: Contact institution. *Degree program information:* Part-time programs available. Offers ministry (M Div); religious education (MRE). *Application deadline:* For fall admission, 7/1 priority date for domestic and international students; for winter admission, 11/15 priority date for domestic and international students. Applications are processed on a rolling basis. *Application fee:* $50. *Application Contact:* Kathleen McNaughton, Registrar, 403-932-6622 Ext. 221, E-mail: registrar@csbs.ca.

CANISIUS COLLEGE, Buffalo, NY 14208-1098

General Information Independent-religious, coed, comprehensive institution. *Enrollment:* 4,916 graduate, professional, and undergraduate students; 838 full-time matriculated graduate/professional students (563 women), 732 part-time matriculated graduate/professional students (410 women). *Enrollment by degree level:* 1,570 master's. *Graduate faculty:* 99 full-time (40 women), 128 part-time/adjunct (65 women). *Tuition:* Full-time $33,750; part-time $680 per credit hour. *Required fees:* $18.50 per credit hour. *Graduate housing:* Room and/or apartments available on a first-come, first-served basis to single students; on-campus housing not available to married students. Typical cost: $5990 per year ($10,150 including board). Housing application deadline: 5/1. *Student services:* Campus employment opportunities, campus safety program, career counseling, exercise/wellness program, free psychological counseling, international student services, multicultural affairs office, services for students with disabilities, teacher training. *Library facilities:* Andrew L. Bouwhuis Library plus 1 other. *Online resources:* library catalog, web page, access to other libraries' catalogs. *Collection:* 379,498 titles, 24,000 serial subscriptions, 9,596 audiovisual materials.

Computer facilities: Computer purchase and lease plans are available. 500 computers available on campus for general student use. A campuswide network can be accessed from student residence rooms and from off campus. Online class registration, online accounts are available. *Web address:* http://www.canisius.edu/.

General Application Contact: Graduate Education Office, 716-888-2545, Fax: 716-888-3290, E-mail: graded@canisius.edu.

GRADUATE UNITS

Graduate Division Students: 838 full-time (563 women), 727 part-time (406 women); includes 114 minority (70 African Americans, 5 American Indian/Alaska Native, 18 Asian Americans or Pacific Islanders, 21 Hispanic Americans), 319 international. Average age 29. *Faculty:* 84 full-time (29 women), 107 part-time/adjunct (59 women). Expenses: Contact institution. *Financial support:* Research assistantships, teaching assistantships, career-related internships or fieldwork, Federal Work-Study, institutionally sponsored loans, tuition waivers (partial), and unspecified assistantships available. Support available to part-time students. Financial award applicants required to submit FAFSA. In 2008, 840 master's awarded. *Degree program information:* Part-time and evening/weekend programs available. *Application deadline:* Applications are processed on a rolling basis. *Application fee:* $25. Electronic applications accepted. *Application Contact:* Ann Marie Muscovic, Director of Admissions, 716-888-2200, Fax: 716-888-3230, E-mail: admissions@canisius.edu. *Vice President for Academic Affairs*, Dr. Scott A. Chadwick, 716-888-2120, Fax: 716-888-2120, E-mail: chadwics@canisius.edu.

College of Arts and Sciences Students: 5 full-time (2 women), 38 part-time (30 women); includes 8 minority (4 African Americans, 1 Asian American or Pacific Islander, 3 Hispanic Americans), 1 international. Average age 32. *Faculty:* 10 full-time (4 women). Expenses: Contact institution. *Financial support:* Research assistantships with tuition reimbursements

Canisius College (continued)

available. Financial award applicants required to submit FAFSA. In 2008, 15 master's awarded. *Degree program information:* Part-time and evening/weekend programs available. Offers arts and sciences (MS); communication and leadership (MS). *Application deadline:* For fall admission, 7/15 priority date for domestic students; for spring admission, 4/15 priority date for domestic students. Applications are processed on a rolling basis. *Application fee:* $25. Electronic applications accepted. *Application Contact:* Dr. Rosanne L. Hartman, Director, Communication and Leadership, 716-888-2589, Fax: 716-888-3118, E-mail: hartmanr@canisius.edu. *Dean,* Dr. Paula McNutt, 716-888-2130, E-mail: mcnutt@canisius.edu.

Richard J. Wehle School of Business Students: 94 full-time (47 women), 203 part-time (85 women); includes 24 minority (8 African Americans, 11 Asian Americans or Pacific Islanders, 5 Hispanic Americans), 18 international. Average age 29. *Faculty:* 41 full-time (8 women), 3 part-time/adjunct (0 women). Expenses: Contact institution. *Financial support:* In 2008–09, 10 research assistantships (averaging $7,812 per year) were awarded; career-related internships or fieldwork, institutionally sponsored loans, scholarships/grants, and unspecified assistantships also available. Support available to part-time students. Financial award application deadline: 6/15; financial award applicants required to submit FAFSA. In 2008, 137 master's awarded. *Degree program information:* Part-time and evening/weekend programs available. Offers accounting (MBA); business (MBA, MBAPA); business administration (MBA); professional accounting (MBAPA). *Application deadline:* For fall admission, 7/1 priority date for domestic students; for spring admission, 11/1 priority date for domestic students. Applications are processed on a rolling basis. *Application fee:* $25. Electronic applications accepted. *Application Contact:* Laura McEwen, Director, Graduate Business Programs, 716-888-2142, Fax: 716-888-2145, E-mail: mcewenl@canisius.edu. *Dean,* Dr. Antone Alber, 716-888-2160, Fax: 716-888-2145, E-mail: gradubus@canisius.edu.

School of Education and Human Services Students: 739 full-time (514 women), 486 part-time (291 women); includes 82 minority (58 African Americans, 5 American Indian/Alaska Native, 6 Asian Americans or Pacific Islanders, 13 Hispanic Americans), 300 international. Average age 27. *Faculty:* 33 full-time (17 women), 104 part-time/adjunct (59 women). Expenses: Contact institution. *Financial support:* Career-related internships or fieldwork, institutionally sponsored loans, scholarships/grants, health care benefits, tuition waivers (partial), and unspecified assistantships available. Financial award applicants required to submit FAFSA. In 2008, 688 master's awarded. *Degree program information:* Part-time and evening/weekend programs available. Offers adolescence education (grades 7-12) (MS); childhood education (grades 1-6) (MS); college student personnel administration (MS); community mental health counseling (MS); deaf education (MS); differentiated instruction (MS Ed); education and human services (MS, MS Ed); educational administration and supervision (MS); general counseling (MS); general education (MS Ed); health and human performance (MS); initial teacher certification (elementary education) (MS); initial teacher certification (secondary education) (MS); literacy (MS Ed); physical education (MS); physical education (Pre-K to Grade 12) (MS); school counseling (MS); special education (MS); sport administration (MS). *Application deadline:* Applications are processed on a rolling basis. *Application fee:* $25. Electronic applications accepted. *Application Contact:* James D. Bagwell, Director of Graduate Recruitment and Admissions, 716-888-2544, Fax: 716-888-3290, E-mail: bagwellj@canisius.edu. *Dean,* Dr. Margaret C. McCarthy, 716-888-2548, Fax: 716-888-3290.

CAPE BRETON UNIVERSITY, Sydney, NS B1P 6L2, Canada

General Information Province-supported, coed, comprehensive institution. *Enrollment:* 3,491 graduate, professional, and undergraduate students; 98 full-time matriculated graduate/professional students (46 women), 182 part-time matriculated graduate/professional students (107 women). *Graduate faculty:* 13 full-time (5 women), 26 part-time/adjunct (10 women). *Graduate housing:* Room and/or apartments available on a first-come, first-served basis to single students; on-campus housing not available to married students. Housing application deadline: 3/31. *Student services:* Campus employment opportunities, campus safety program, career counseling, child daycare facilities, exercise/wellness program, free psychological counseling, international student services, low-cost health insurance, multicultural affairs office, services for students with disabilities, teacher training, writing training. *Research affiliation:* Hyperspectral Data International Ltd. (marine remote sensing), Sable Offshore Energy, Inc. (petroleum resources), Fortress Louisbourg National Historic Park (museum/heritage projects), Dynagen Industrial Mine Technology (mining industry equipment), Atlantic Geomatics (computer networking and software development), Advanced Glazing, Limited (transparent insulation).

Computer facilities: 206 computers available on campus for general student use. A campuswide network can be accessed from off campus. Online class registration is available. *Web address:* http://www.capebretonu.ca/.

General Application Contact: Brendan MacDonald, Admissions Coordinator, 902-563-1117, Fax: 902-563-1371, E-mail: brendan_macdonald@cbu.ca.

GRADUATE UNITS

School of Education, Health, and Wellness Students: 171 part-time (103 women). Average age 30. *Faculty:* 15 part-time/adjunct (5 women). Expenses: Contact institution. In 2008, 22 Certificates awarded. *Degree program information:* Part-time and evening/weekend programs available. Postbaccalaureate distance learning degree programs offered (no on-campus study). Offers educational counseling (Diploma); educational studies-arts education (Certificate); educational technology (Diploma). *Application deadline:* For fall admission, 8/1 priority date for domestic students. Applications are processed on a rolling basis. *Application fee:* $50. Electronic applications accepted. *Application Contact:* Terry MacDonald, Coordinator, Teacher/Distance Education, 902-563-1647, Fax: 902-563-1449, E-mail: terry_macdonald@capebretonu.ca. *Dean,* Dr. Jane Lewis, 902-563-1305, Fax: 902-563-1861.

Shannon School of Business Students: 98 full-time (46 women), 11 part-time (4 women). Average age 38. 60 applicants, 92% accepted. *Faculty:* 13 full-time (5 women), 11 part-time/adjunct (5 women). Expenses: Contact institution. *Financial support:* In 2008–09, 6 students received support. Scholarships/grants and tuition waivers (full and partial) available. Financial award application deadline: 5/31. In 2008, 6 master's awarded. Offers community economic development (MBA). *Application deadline:* For spring admission, 5/31 for domestic students. Applications are processed on a rolling basis. *Application fee:* $80. *Application Contact:* Anne Michelle Chiasson, Program Coordinator, 902-563-1664, Fax: 902-563-1366, E-mail: anne_chiasson@cbu.ca. *Dean, School of Business,* Ed Grimm, 902-563-1221, Fax: 902-563-1453, E-mail: ed_grimm@cbu.ca.

CAPELLA UNIVERSITY, Minneapolis, MN 55402

General Information Proprietary, coed, upper-level institution. CGS member. *Enrollment:* 1,344 full-time matriculated graduate/professional students (980 women), 19,666 part-time matriculated graduate/professional students (14,246 women). *Enrollment by degree level:* 11,554 master's, 9,216 doctoral, 240 other advanced degrees. *Library facilities:* Capella University Library. *Online resources:* library catalog, web page.

Computer facilities: Online class registration is available. *Web address:* http://www.capella.edu/.

General Application Contact: Enrollment Services Office, 888-CAPELLA, Fax: 612-977-5060, E-mail: info@capella.edu.

GRADUATE UNITS

Harold Abel School of Psychology Students: 686 full-time (517 women), 3,006 part-time (2,299 women); includes 1,141 minority (848 African Americans, 35 American Indian/Alaska Native, 58 Asian Americans or Pacific Islanders, 200 Hispanic Americans), 50 international. Average age 39. Expenses: Contact institution. *Financial support:* Institutionally sponsored loans and scholarships/grants available. Support available to part-time students. Financial award application deadline: 6/15; financial award applicants required to submit FAFSA. In 2008, 228 master's, 103 doctorates, 5 other advanced degrees awarded. *Degree program information:* Part-time and evening/weekend programs available. Postbaccalaureate distance learning degree programs offered (minimal on-campus study). Offers child and adolescent development (MS); clinical psychology (MS, Psy D); counseling psychology (MS); educational psychology (MS, PhD); evaluation, research, and measurement (MS); general psychology (MS, PhD); industrial/organizational psychology (MS, PhD); leadership coaching psychology (MS); organizational leader development (MS); school psychology (MS); sport psychology (MS). *Application deadline:* Applications are processed on a rolling basis. *Application fee:* $75 ($175 for international students). Electronic applications accepted. *Application Contact:* Enrollment Services, 888-CAPELLA Ext. 1, Fax: 612-977-5060, E-mail: info@capella.edu. *Dean,* Dr. Deborah Bushway, 888-CAPELLA Ext. 4463, Fax: 612-977-5060, E-mail: deborah.bushway@capella.edu.

School of Business and Technology *Degree program information:* Part-time and evening/weekend programs available. Postbaccalaureate distance learning degree programs offered (minimal on-campus study). Offers accounting (MBA); business (Certificate); finance (MBA); general business (MBA); health care management (MBA); information technology (MS, Certificate); information technology management (MBA); marketing (MBA); organization and management (MBA, MS, PhD); project management (MBA). Electronic applications accepted.

School of Public Service Leadership Offers criminal justice (MS, PhD); emergency management (MS, PhD); general human services (MS, PhD); general public administration (MPA, DPA); gerontology (MS); health care administration (MS, PhD); health management and policy (MSPH); management of nonprofit agencies (MS, PhD); nurse educator (MS); public safety leadership (MS, PhD); social and community services (MS, PhD); social behavioral sciences (MSPH).

CAPITAL BIBLE SEMINARY, Lanham, MD 20706-3599

General Information Independent-religious, coed, graduate-only institution. *Graduate housing:* Rooms and/or apartments available on a first-come, first-served basis to single and married students. Housing application deadline: 7/15.

GRADUATE UNITS

Graduate and Professional Programs *Degree program information:* Part-time and evening/weekend programs available. Offers biblical studies (MA, Certificate); Christian counseling (MA); Christian counseling and discipleship (Certificate); ministry leadership (MA); theology (M Div, Th M).

CAPITAL UNIVERSITY, Columbus, OH 43209-2394

General Information Independent-religious, coed, comprehensive institution. *Graduate housing:* On-campus housing not available.

GRADUATE UNITS

Conservatory of Music *Degree program information:* Part-time programs available. Offers music education (MM). Program offered only in summer. Electronic applications accepted.

Law School *Degree program information:* Part-time and evening/weekend programs available. Offers business (LL M); business and taxation (LL M); law (JD, LL M, MT); taxation (LL M, MT). Electronic applications accepted.

School of Management *Degree program information:* Part-time and evening/weekend programs available. Offers management (MBA). Electronic applications accepted.

School of Nursing *Degree program information:* Part-time and evening/weekend programs available. Offers administration (MSN); legal studies (MSN); theological studies (MSN).

CAPITOL COLLEGE, Laurel, MD 20708-9759

General Information Independent, coed, comprehensive institution. *Graduate housing:* On-campus housing not available.

GRADUATE UNITS

Graduate Programs *Degree program information:* Part-time and evening/weekend programs available. Postbaccalaureate distance learning degree programs offered (no on-campus study). Offers business administration (MBA); computer science (MS); electrical engineering (MS); information and telecommunications systems management (MS); information architecture (MS); network security (MS). Electronic applications accepted.

CARDINAL STRITCH UNIVERSITY, Milwaukee, WI 53217-3985

General Information Independent-religious, coed, comprehensive institution. *Graduate housing:* Room and/or apartments available on a first-come, first-served basis to single students; on-campus housing not available to married students.

GRADUATE UNITS

College of Arts and Sciences *Degree program information:* Part-time and evening/weekend programs available. Offers arts and sciences (MA, MM, MS); clinical psychology (MA); history (MA); lay ministries (MA); ministry (MA); piano (MM); religious studies (MA); sport management (MS); visual studies (MA).

College of Business and Management *Degree program information:* Part-time and evening/weekend programs available. Offers business and management (MBA, MSM). Programs also offered in Madison, WI and Minneapolis-St. Paul, MN.

College of Education *Degree program information:* Part-time and evening/weekend programs available. Offers education (MA, MAT, ME, MS, Ed D, PhD); educational leadership (MS); instructional technology (ME, MS); leadership for the advancement of learning and service (Ed D, PhD); literacy/English as a second language (MA); reading/language arts (MA); reading/learning disability (MA); special education (MA); teaching (MAT); urban education (MA).

College of Nursing *Degree program information:* Part-time and evening/weekend programs available. Offers nursing (MSN). Electronic applications accepted.

CAREY THEOLOGICAL COLLEGE, Vancouver, BC V6T 1J6, Canada

General Information Independent-religious, coed, graduate-only institution. *Enrollment by degree level:* 79 master's, 44 doctoral. *Graduate faculty:* 8 full-time (2 women), 17 part-time/adjunct (3 women). *Graduate tuition:* Tuition and fees charges are reported in Canadian dollars. *Tuition:* Full-time $7500 Canadian dollars; part-time $250 Canadian dollars per credit. One-time fee: $350 Canadian dollars. *Graduate housing:* Rooms and/or apartments available on a first-come, first-served basis to single and married students. Housing application deadline: 5/31. *Student services:* Services for students with disabilities. *Library facilities:* John Allison Library plus 3 others. *Online resources:* library catalog, web page, access to other libraries' catalogs. *Collection:* 112 titles, 13,923 serial subscriptions, 9,540 audiovisual materials.

Computer facilities: Online class registration is available. *Web address:* http://www.careycentre.com/.

General Application Contact: Myrna Sears, Registrar, 604-224-4308, Fax: 604-224-5014, E-mail: msears@careytheologicalcollege.ca.

GRADUATE UNITS

Graduate Programs Students: 1 full-time (0 women), 103 part-time (23 women); includes 38 minority (1 African American, 31 Asian Americans or Pacific Islanders, 6 Hispanic Americans). Average age 45. 27 applicants, 78% accepted, 21 enrolled. *Faculty:* 8 full-time (2 women), 17 part-time/adjunct (3 women). Expenses: Contact institution. *Financial support:* In 2008–09, 4 students received support. Scholarships/grants available. In 2008, 8 master's, 5 doctorates awarded. *Degree program information:* Part-time programs available. Offers theology (MPM, D Min). *Application deadline:* Applications are processed on a rolling basis. *Application fee:* $60. Electronic applications accepted. *Application Contact:* Rev. Myrna Sears, Registrar, 604-224-4308, Fax: 604-224-5014, E-mail: msears@careytheologicalcollege.ca. *Academic Vice President,* Dr. Barbara Mutch, 604-224-4308, Fax: 604-224-5014, E-mail: barmutch@careytheologicalcollege.ca.

CARIBBEAN UNIVERSITY, Bayamón, PR 00960-0493

General Information Independent, coed, comprehensive institution.

CARLETON UNIVERSITY, Ottawa, ON K1S 5B6, Canada

General Information Province-supported, coed, university. *Graduate housing:* Room and/or apartments guaranteed to single students; on-campus housing not available to married students. Housing application deadline: 5/31.

GRADUATE UNITS

Faculty of Graduate Studies *Degree program information:* Part-time and evening/weekend programs available. Electronic applications accepted.

Faculty of Arts and Social Sciences *Degree program information:* Part-time and evening/weekend programs available. Offers anthropology (MA); applied language studies (MA); art history: art and its institutions (MA); arts and social sciences (M Sc, MA, PhD); Canadian studies (MA, PhD); cognitive science (PhD); cultural mediations (PhD); English (MA, PhD); film studies (MA); French (MA); geography (M Sc, MA, PhD); history (MA, PhD); music and culture (MA); neuroscience (M Sc); philosophy (MA); psychology (MA, PhD); sociology (MA, PhD).

Faculty of Business Offers business (MBA, PhD); business administration (MBA); management (PhD).

Faculty of Engineering and Design Offers aerospace engineering (M Eng, MA Sc, PhD); biomedical engineering (MA Sc); civil and environmental engineering (M Eng, MA Sc, PhD); design studies (M Arch); electrical engineering (M Eng, M Sc, MA Sc, PhD); engineering and design (M Arch, M Des, M Eng, M Sc, MA Sc, PhD); industrial design (M Des); information and systems science (M Sc); materials engineering (M Eng, MA Sc); mechanical engineering (M Eng, MA Sc, PhD); technology innovation management (M Eng, MA Sc).

Faculty of Public Affairs and Management *Degree program information:* Part-time programs available. Offers communication (MA, PhD); conflict resolution (Certificate); economics (MA, PhD); European and European Union studies (MA); European integration studies (Diploma); international affairs (MA, PhD); journalism (MJ); legal studies (MA); political economy (MA, PhD); political science (MA, PhD); public administration (MA, DPA); public affairs and management (MA, MJ, MSW, DPA, PhD, Certificate, Diploma); public policy (PhD); Russian, Eurasian and transition studies (MA); social work (MSW).

Faculty of Science *Degree program information:* Part-time and evening/weekend programs available. Offers biology (M Sc, PhD); chemistry (M Sc, PhD); computer science (MCS, PhD); earth science (M Sc, PhD); information and system science (M Sc); information and systems science (M Sc); mathematics (M Sc, PhD); physics (M Sc, PhD); science (M Sc, MCS, PhD).

CARLOS ALBIZU UNIVERSITY, San Juan, PR 00901

General Information Independent, coed, primarily women, university. *Enrollment:* 888 graduate, professional, and undergraduate students; 566 full-time matriculated graduate/professional students (470 women), 149 part-time matriculated graduate/professional students (122 women). *Enrollment by degree level:* 215 master's, 500 doctoral. *Graduate faculty:* 22 full-time (11 women), 52 part-time/adjunct (38 women). *Tuition:* Full-time $6912; part-time $288 per credit. *Required fees:* $512 per semester. Tuition and fees vary according to degree level. *Graduate housing:* On-campus housing not available. *Student services:* Career counseling, free psychological counseling, services for students with disabilities, teacher training. *Library facilities:* Carlos Albizu. *Online resources:* library catalog.

Computer facilities: 55 computers available on campus for general student use. A campuswide network can be accessed. *Web address:* http://www.albizu.edu/.

General Application Contact: Carlos Rodriguez, Director of Students Affairs, 787-725-6500 Ext. 21, Fax: 787-721-7187, E-mail: crodriguez@prip.ccas.edu.

GRADUATE UNITS

Graduate Programs Students: 566 full-time (470 women), 149 part-time (122 women); all minorities (all Hispanic Americans). Average age 28. 238 applicants, 79% accepted, 170 enrolled. *Faculty:* 22 full-time (11 women), 52 part-time/adjunct (38 women). Expenses: Contact institution. *Financial support:* In 2008–09, 564 students received support, including 272 fellowships (averaging $1,786 per year); career-related internships or fieldwork, Federal Work-Study, institutionally sponsored loans, scholarships/grants, traineeships, and tuition waivers (partial) also available. Support available to part-time students. Financial award application deadline: 4/21; financial award applicants required to submit FAFSA. In 2008, 100 master's, 84 doctorates awarded. *Degree program information:* Part-time and evening/weekend programs available. Offers clinical psychology (MS, PhD, Psy D); general psychology (PhD); industrial/organizational psychology (MS, PhD); speech and language pathology (MS). *Application deadline:* For fall admission, 2/15 for domestic students, 7/19 for international students; for winter admission, 11/15 for international students; for spring admission, 11/15 for domestic students, 4/21 for international students. *Application fee:* $75. *Application Contact:* Carlos Rodriguez, Director of Admission's Office, 787-725-6500 Ext. 1521, Fax: 787-721-7187, E-mail: jveray@albizu.edu. *Chancellor,* Dr. Jose J Cabiya, 787-725-6500 Ext. 1435, Fax: 787-721-7187, E-mail: jcabiya@sju.albizu.edu.

CARLOS ALBIZU UNIVERSITY, MIAMI CAMPUS, Miami, FL 33172-2209

General Information Independent, coed, primarily women, comprehensive institution. *Enrollment:* 1,139 graduate, professional, and undergraduate students; 498 full-time matriculated graduate/professional students (409 women), 199 part-time matriculated graduate/professional students (153 women). *Enrollment by degree level:* 382 master's, 315 doctoral. *Graduate faculty:* 19 full-time (12 women), 70 part-time/adjunct (35 women). *Tuition:* Full-time $9090; part-time $505 per credit. *Required fees:* $298 per term. Tuition and fees vary according to course load, degree level and program. *Graduate housing:* On-campus housing not available. *Student services:* Campus employment opportunities, campus safety program, career counseling, exercise/wellness program, international student services, services for students with disabilities, writing training. *Library facilities:* Albizu Library. *Online resources:* library catalog. *Collection:* 32,315 titles, 383 serial subscriptions, 1,554 audiovisual materials.

Computer facilities: 105 computers available on campus for general student use. A campuswide network can be accessed. *Web address:* http://www.mia.albizu.edu/.

General Application Contact: Barbara De la Cruz, Admission Officer, 305-593-1223 Ext. 218, Fax: 305-593-1854, E-mail: bdelacruz@albizu.edu.

GRADUATE UNITS

Graduate Programs Students: 498 full-time (409 women), 199 part-time (153 women); includes 515 minority (56 African Americans, 1 American Indian/Alaska Native, 7 Asian Americans or Pacific Islanders, 451 Hispanic Americans). Average age 33. 179 applicants, 67% accepted, 113 enrolled. *Faculty:* 19 full-time (12 women), 70 part-time/adjunct (35 women). Expenses: Contact institution. *Financial support:* In 2008–09, 111 students received support. Federal Work-Study, scholarships/grants, and tuition discounts available. Financial award application deadline: 6/1; financial award applicants required to submit FAFSA. In 2008, 185 master's, 21 doctorates awarded. *Degree program information:* Part-time and evening/weekend programs available. Offers clinical psychology (Psy D); entrepreneurship (MBA); exceptional student education (MS); industrial/organizational psychology (MS); marriage and family therapy (MS); mental health counseling (MS); nonprofit management (MBA); organizational management (MBA); psychology (MS); school counseling (MS); teaching English as a second language (MS). *Application deadline:* For fall admission, 8/1 priority date for domestic students; for spring admission, 11/30 priority date for domestic students. Applications are processed on a rolling basis. *Application fee:* $50. Electronic applications accepted. *Application Contact:* Barbara De la Cruz, Admission Officer, 305-593-1223 Ext. 218, Fax: 305-593-1854, E-mail: bdelacruz@albizu.edu. *Chancellor,* Dr. Carmen S. Roca, PhD, 305-593-1223 Ext. 120, Fax: 305-629-8052, E-mail: croca@albizu.edu.

CARLOW UNIVERSITY, Pittsburgh, PA 15213-3165

General Information Independent-religious, coed, primarily women, comprehensive institution. *Enrollment:* 2,128 graduate, professional, and undergraduate students; 175 full-time matriculated graduate/professional students (163 women), 438 part-time matriculated graduate/professional students (398 women). *Enrollment by degree level:* 582 master's, 21 doctoral, 10 other advanced degrees. *Graduate faculty:* 25 full-time (20 women), 56 part-time/adjunct (37 women). *Tuition:* Part-time $700 per credit. *Graduate housing:* Room and/or apartments available on a first-come, first-served basis to single students; on-campus housing not available to married students. Typical cost: $8146 (including board). Room and board charges vary according to board plan. *Student services:* Campus employment opportunities, campus safety program, career counseling, exercise/wellness program, free psychological counseling, international student services, low-cost health insurance, multicultural affairs office, services for students with disabilities. *Library facilities:* Grace Library. *Online resources:* library catalog, web page, access to other libraries' catalogs. *Collection:* 131,831 titles, 363 serial subscriptions, 5,005 audiovisual materials.

Computer facilities: 151 computers available on campus for general student use. A campuswide network can be accessed from student residence rooms and from off campus. Online class registration is available. *Web address:* http://www.carlow.edu/.

General Application Contact: Jo Danhires, Administrative Assistant, Admissions, 412-578-6059, Fax: 412-578-6321, E-mail: gradstudies@carlow.edu.

GRADUATE UNITS

Humanities Division Students: 30 part-time (27 women); includes 3 minority (all African Americans). Average age 41. *Faculty:* 8 part-time/adjunct (4 women). Expenses: Contact institution. *Financial support:* Career-related internships or fieldwork, Federal Work-Study, and scholarships/grants available. Support available to part-time students. Financial award application deadline: 4/1; financial award applicants required to submit FAFSA. In 2008, 8 master's awarded. *Degree program information:* Part-time and evening/weekend programs available. Offers creative writing (MFA). *Application deadline:* For fall admission, 6/15 priority date for domestic and international students; for spring admission, 11/15 priority date for domestic and international students. Applications are processed on a rolling basis. *Application fee:* $20. *Application Contact:* Jo Danhires, Administrative Assistant, Admissions, 412-578-6059, Fax: 412-578-6321, E-mail: gradstudies@carlow.edu. *Director of MFA Program,* Ellie Wymard, PhD, 412-578-6597, Fax: 412-578-8706, E-mail: wymardex@carlow.edu.

School for Social Change Students: 98 full-time (92 women), 85 part-time (79 women); includes 38 minority (36 African Americans, 2 Asian Americans or Pacific Islanders). Average age 31. 146 applicants, 47% accepted, 63 enrolled. *Faculty:* 5 full-time (3 women), 10 part-time/adjunct (5 women). Expenses: Contact institution. *Financial support:* Federal Work-Study available. Financial award application deadline: 4/1; financial award applicants required to submit FAFSA. In 2008, 64 master's awarded. *Degree program information:* Part-time and evening/weekend programs available. Offers professional counseling (MS); professional counseling: school counseling (MS); professional leadership: management for nonprofit organizations (MS); professional leadership: organizational influence and policy (MS); professional leadership: training and development (MS). *Application deadline:* For fall admission, 6/15 priority date for domestic and international students; for spring admission, 11/15 priority date for domestic and international students. Applications are processed on a rolling basis. *Application fee:* $20. Electronic applications accepted. *Application Contact:* Jo Danhires, Administrative Assistant, Admissions, 412-578-6059, Fax: 412-578-6321, E-mail: gradstudies@carlow.edu. *Chair, Department of Psychology and Counseling,* Robert A Reed, PsyD, 412-575-6349, E-mail: reedra@carlow.edu.

School of Education Students: 30 full-time (27 women), 136 part-time (123 women); includes 22 minority (21 African Americans, 1 Hispanic American), 1 international. Average age 34. 105 applicants, 45% accepted, 33 enrolled. *Faculty:* 8 full-time (7 women), 15 part-time/adjunct (10 women). Expenses: Contact institution. *Financial support:* Application deadline: 4/1. In 2008, 41 master's awarded. *Degree program information:* Part-time and evening/weekend programs available. Offers art education (M Ed); early childhood education (M Ed); early childhood supervision (M Ed); education (M Ed); educational leadership (M Ed); educational praxis (MA); elementary education (M Ed); instructional technology specialist (M Ed); secondary education (M Ed); special education (M Ed). *Application deadline:* For fall admission, 6/15 priority date for domestic and international students; for spring admission, 11/15 priority date for domestic and international students. Applications are processed on a rolling basis. *Application fee:* $20. Electronic applications accepted. *Application Contact:* Jo Danhires, Administrative Assistant, Admissions, 412-578-6059, Fax: 412-578-6321, E-mail: gradstudies@carlow.edu. *Associate Dean and Director,* Dr. Roberta Schomburg, 412-578-6312, Fax: 412-578-8816, E-mail: schomburgrl@carlow.edu.

School of Management Students: 4 full-time (3 women), 88 part-time (73 women); includes 14 minority (12 African Americans, 1 Asian American or Pacific Islander, 1 Hispanic American), 4 international. Average age 37. 91 applicants, 51% accepted, 45 enrolled. *Faculty:* 4 full-time (2 women), 9 part-time/adjunct (5 women). Expenses: Contact institution. *Financial support:* Federal Work-Study and scholarships/grants available. Support available to part-time students. Financial award application deadline: 4/1; financial award applicants required to submit FAFSA. In 2008, 2 master's awarded. *Degree program information:* Part-time and evening/weekend programs available. Postbaccalaureate distance learning degree programs offered (minimal on-campus study). Offers business administration (MBA). *Application deadline:* For fall admission, 6/15 priority date for domestic and international students; for spring admission, 11/15 priority date for domestic and international students. Applications are processed on a rolling basis. *Application fee:* $20. Electronic applications accepted. *Application Contact:* Jo Danhires, Administrative Assistant, Admissions, 412-578-6088, Fax: 412-578-6321, E-mail: gradstudies@carlow.edu. *Director, MBA Program,* Dr. Enrique Mu, 412-578-8729, Fax: 412-587-6367, E-mail: muex@carlow.edu.

School of Nursing Students: 43 full-time (41 women), 48 part-time (46 women); includes 7 minority (3 African Americans, 3 Asian Americans or Pacific Islanders, 1 Hispanic American), 2 international. Average age 39. 38 applicants, 74% accepted, 21 enrolled. *Faculty:* 5 full-time (all women), 11 part-time/adjunct (10 women). Expenses: Contact institution. *Financial support:* Application deadline: 4/1. In 2008, 38 master's awarded. *Degree program information:* Part-time and evening/weekend programs available. Postbaccalaureate distance learning degree programs offered (minimal on-campus study). Offers family nurse practitioner (MSN); home health advanced practice nursing (MSN); nursing (DNP); nursing case management/leadership (MSN); nursing leadership (MSN). *Application deadline:* For fall admission, 6/15 priority date for domestic and international students; for spring admission, 11/15 priority date for domestic and international students. Applications are processed on a rolling basis. *Application fee:* $20. Electronic applications accepted. *Application Contact:* Jo Danhires, Administrative Assistant, Admissions, 412-578-6059, Fax: 412-578-6321, E-mail: gradstudies@carlow.edu. *Associate Dean and Director,* Clare M Hopkins, PhD, RN, 412-578-6108, Fax: 412-578-6114, E-mail: hopkinscm@carlow.edu.

CARNEGIE MELLON UNIVERSITY, Pittsburgh, PA 15213-3891

General Information Independent, coed, university. CGS member. *Graduate housing:* On-campus housing not available. *Research affiliation:* National Census Data Research Center (public policy), Robotics Engineering Consortium (computer science and engineering), Software Engineering Institute (computer science and engineering), Carnegie Bosch Institute for Applied Studies in International Management (business and management), Pittsburgh Supercomputer Center.

GRADUATE UNITS

Carnegie Institute of Technology *Degree program information:* Part-time and evening/weekend programs available. Offers advanced infrastructure systems (MS, PhD); bioengineering (MS, PhD); biomedical engineering (MS, PhD); chemical engineering (M Ch E, MS, PhD); civil and environmental engineering (MS, PhD); civil and environmental engineering/engineering and public policy (PhD); civil engineering (MS, PhD); colloids, polymers and surfaces (MS); computational science and engineering (MS, PhD); electrical and computer engineering (MS, PhD); engineering and public policy (PhD); environmental engineering (MS, PhD); environmental management and science (MS, PhD); materials science and engineering (MS, PhD); mechanical engineering (MS, PhD); product development (MPD); technology (M Ch E, MPD, MS, PhD).

Information Networking Institute Students: 177 full-time (51 women), 1 part-time (0 women). Average age 24. *Faculty:* 66 full-time. Expenses: Contact institution. *Financial support:* In

Carnegie Mellon University (continued)

2008–09, 170 students received support; fellowships with full and partial tuition reimbursements available, research assistantships with partial tuition reimbursements available, teaching assistantships with partial tuition reimbursements available, career-related internships or fieldwork, scholarships/grants, tuition waivers (partial), and unspecified assistantships available. Financial award application deadline: 2/1. Offers information networking (MS); information security technology and management (MS); information technology—information security (MS); information technology—mobility (MS); information technology—software management (MS). *Application deadline:* For fall admission, 2/1 for domestic and international students. *Application fee:* $65. *Application Contact:* Kari Gazdich, Director of Admissions, 412-268-9598, Fax: 412-268-7196, E-mail: kgaz@cmu.edu. *Director,* Dr. Dena Haritos Tsamitis, 412-268-7195, Fax: 412-268-7196, E-mail: denat@ece.cmu.edu.

Center for the Neural Basis of Cognition Offers neural basis of cognition (PhD).

College of Fine Arts *Degree program information:* Part-time programs available. Offers fine arts (M Des, M Sc, MAM, MET, MFA, MM, MPD, MSA, PhD). Electronic applications accepted.

School of Architecture Offers architectural engineering construction management (M Sc); architecture (MSA); architecture, engineering, and construction management (PhD); building performance and diagnostics (M Sc, PhD); computational design (M Sc, PhD); sustainable design (M Sc); urban design (M Sc).

School of Art Offers art (MFA).

School of Design Offers communication planning and information design (M Des); design (PhD); design theory (PhD); interaction design (M Des, PhD); new product development (PhD); product development (MPD); typography and information design (PhD).

School of Drama Offers design (MFA); directing (MFA); dramatic writing (MFA); production technology and management (MFA).

School of Music *Degree program information:* Part-time programs available. Offers composition (MM); conducting (MM); instrumental performance (MM); music education (MM); vocal performance (MM).

College of Humanities and Social Sciences *Degree program information:* Part-time programs available. Offers African and African-American diaspora (PhD); behavioral decision research (PhD); behavioral decision research and psychology (PhD); cognitive neuroscience (PhD); cognitive psychology (PhD); communication planning and design (M Des); culture and power (PhD); developmental psychology (PhD); editing and publishing (MAPW); gender and the family (PhD); history (MA, MS); history and policy (MA); humanities and social sciences (M Des, MA, MAPW, MS, PhD); labor and politics (PhD); literary and cultural studies (MA, PhD); logic and computation (MS); logic, computation and methodology (PhD); machine learning and statistics (PhD); mathematical finance (PhD); philosophy (MA); policy and non-profit communication (MAPW); professional writing (MAPW); public and media relations / corporate communications (MAPW); rhetoric (MA, PhD); science or healthcare communication (MAPW); science, technology, medicine and environment (PhD); second language acquisition (PhD); social and decision science (PhD); social/personality/health psychology (PhD); statistics (MS, PhD); statistics and public policy (PhD); strategy, entrepreneurship, and technological change (PhD); technical writing (MAPW); writing for new media (MAPW); writing for print media (MAPW). Electronic applications accepted.

Center for Innovation in Learning Offers instructional science (PhD).

H. John Heinz III College *Degree program information:* Part-time and evening/weekend programs available. Offers arts management (MAM); entertainment industry management (MEIM); public policy and management (MAM, MEIM, MIS, MISM, MMM, MPM, MS, MSED, MSHCPM, MSISPM, MSIT, PhD). Electronic applications accepted.

School of Information Systems and Management Offers information security policy and management (MSISPM); information systems and management (MISM, MSISPM, MSIT); information systems management (MISM); information technology (MSIT).

School of Public Policy and Management Offers biotechnology and management (MS); health care policy and management (MSHCPM); medical management (MMM); public management (MPM); public policy and management (MMM, MPM, MS, MSHCPM, PhD).

Joint CMU-Pitt PhD Program in Computational Biology Offers computational biology (PhD).

Mellon College of Science *Degree program information:* Part-time programs available. Offers algorithms, combinatorics, and optimization (PhD); applied mathematics (PhD); applied physics (PhD); biochemistry (PhD); biophysics (PhD); biotechnology and management (MS); cell biology (PhD); chemistry (PhD); colloids, polymers and surfaces (MS); computational biology (MS); computational finance (MS); developmental biology (PhD); genetics (PhD); mathematical finance (PhD), mathematical sciences (MS, DA, PhD); molecular biology (PhD); molecular biophysics and structural biology (PhD); neuroscience (PhD); physics (MS, PhD); pure and applied logic (PhD); science (MS, DA, PhD). Electronic applications accepted.

School of Computer Science Offers algorithms, combinatorics, and optimization (PhD); computer science (MS, PhD); entertainment technology (MET); human-computer interaction (MHCI, PhD); machine learning (PhD); pure and applied logic (PhD); software engineering (MSE, PhD).

Language Technologies Institute Offers language technologies (MLT, PhD).

Robotics Institute Offers robotics (MS, PhD).

Tepper School of Business *Degree program information:* Part-time programs available. Offers accounting (PhD); algorithms, combinatorics, and optimization (MS, PhD); business management and software engineering (MBMSE); civil engineering and industrial management (MS); computational finance (MSCF); economics (PhD); electronic commerce (MS); environmental engineering and management (MEEM); finance (PhD); financial economics (PhD); industrial administration (MBA); information systems (PhD); management of manufacturing and automation (PhD); marketing (PhD); mathematical finance (PhD); operations research (PhD); organizational behavior and theory (PhD); political economy (PhD); production and operations management (PhD); public policy and management (MS, MSED); software engineering and business management (MS).

CARROLL UNIVERSITY, Waukesha, WI 53186-5593

General Information Independent-religious, coed, comprehensive institution. *Enrollment:* 3,316 graduate, professional, and undergraduate students; 176 full-time matriculated graduate/professional students (145 women), 81 part-time matriculated graduate/professional students (40 women). *Enrollment by degree level:* 196 master's, 61 doctoral. *Graduate faculty:* 24 full-time (11 women), 26 part-time/adjunct (21 women). *Tuition:* Full-time $21,560; part-time $345 per credit. *Required fees:* $400. *Graduate housing:* Room and/or apartments available on a first-come, first-served basis to single students; on-campus housing not available to married students. Typical cost: $4500 per year. *Student services:* Campus employment opportunities, campus safety program, career counseling, exercise/wellness program, free psychological counseling, international student services, multicultural affairs office, services for students with disabilities. *Library facilities:* Todd Wehr Memorial Library. *Online resources:* library catalog, web page, access to other libraries' catalogs. *Collection:* 150,000 titles, 18,000 serial subscriptions, 1,025 audiovisual materials.

Computer facilities: Computer purchase and lease plans are available. 250 computers available on campus for general student use. A campuswide network can be accessed from student residence rooms and from off campus. Online class registration is available. *Web address:* http://www.cc.edu/.

General Application Contact: Tami Bartunek, Graduate Admission Counselor, 262-524-7643, E-mail: tbartune@carrollu.edu.

GRADUATE UNITS

Graduate Program in Education Students: 113 full-time (96 women), 56 part-time (36 women); includes 9 minority (4 African Americans, 1 American Indian/Alaska Native, 2 Asian Americans or Pacific Islanders, 2 Hispanic Americans), 1 international. Average age 34. 141 applicants, 54% accepted, 67 enrolled. *Faculty:* 7 full-time (4 women), 13 part-time/adjunct (11 women). Expenses: Contact institution. *Financial support:* Available to part-time students. Application deadline: 3/15. In 2008, 42 master's awarded. *Degree program information:* Part-time and evening/weekend programs available. Offers education (M Ed); learning and teaching (M Ed). *Application deadline:* For fall admission, 8/15 priority date for domestic students. Applications are processed on a rolling basis. *Application fee:* $0. Electronic applications accepted. *Application Contact:* Tami Bartunek, Graduate Admission Counselor, 262-524-7643, E-mail: tbartune@carrollu.edu. *Chair,* Dr. Bruce Strom, 262-524-7130, Fax: 262-524-7139, E-mail: bstrom@cc.edu.

Program in Physical Therapy Students: 61 full-time (49 women). Average age 24. 71 applicants, 79% accepted, 37 enrolled. *Faculty:* 4 full-time (2 women), 3 part-time/adjunct (2 women). Expenses: Contact institution. *Financial support:* Available to part-time students. Application deadline: 3/15. In 2008, 15 doctorates awarded. Offers physical therapy (MPT, DPT). *Application deadline:* For fall admission, 7/14 for domestic students. Applications are processed on a rolling basis. *Application fee:* $25. *Application Contact:* Tami Bartunek, Graduate Admission Counselor, 262-524-7643, E-mail: tbartune@carrollu.edu. *Dean, Natural and Health Sciences,* Dr. Jane F. Hopp, 262-524-7294, E-mail: jhopp@carrollu.edu.

Program in Software Engineering Students: 2 full-time (0 women), 25 part-time (4 women); includes 3 minority (1 African American, 1 Asian American or Pacific Islander, 1 Hispanic American), 5 international. Average age 34. 15 applicants, 53% accepted, 2 enrolled. *Faculty:* 4 full-time (0 women). Expenses: Contact institution. *Financial support:* In 2008–09, 2 students received support. Institutionally sponsored loans available. Support available to part-time students. In 2008, 1 master's awarded. *Degree program information:* Part-time and evening/weekend programs available. Offers software engineering (MSE). *Application deadline:* For fall admission, 9/15 priority date for domestic students. Applications are processed on a rolling basis. *Application fee:* $0. Electronic applications accepted. *Application Contact:* Tami Bartunek, Graduate Admission Counselor, 262-524-7643, E-mail: tbartune@carrollu.edu. *Associate Professor of Computer Science and Program Director,* Dr. Chenglie Hu, 262-524-7170, E-mail: gli@cc.edu.

CARSON-NEWMAN COLLEGE, Jefferson City, TN 37760

General Information Independent-religious, coed, comprehensive institution. *Enrollment:* 2,032 graduate, professional, and undergraduate students; 113 full-time matriculated graduate/professional students (86 women), 96 part-time matriculated graduate/professional students (63 women). *Enrollment by degree level:* 209 master's. *Graduate faculty:* 14 full-time (8 women), 5 part-time/adjunct (2 women). *Tuition:* Full-time $5310. *Required fees:* $200. *Graduate housing:* Rooms and/or apartments available to single and married students. Housing application deadline: 7/15. *Student services:* Campus employment opportunities, career counseling, free psychological counseling, international student services, low-cost health insurance. *Library facilities:* Stephens-Burnett Library plus 1 other. *Online resources:* library catalog, web page. *Collection:* 218,371 titles, 3,966 serial subscriptions.

Computer facilities: 200 computers available on campus for general student use. A campuswide network can be accessed from student residence rooms and from off campus. *Web address:* http://www.cn.edu/.

General Application Contact: Graduate Admissions and Services Adviser, 865-473-3468, Fax: 865-472-3475.

GRADUATE UNITS

Department of Nursing Offers family nurse practitioner (MSN).

Graduate Program in Education *Degree program information:* Part-time and evening/weekend programs available. Offers curriculum and instruction (M Ed); elementary education (MAT); school counseling (M Ed); secondary education (MAT); teaching English as a second language (MATESL).

CARTHAGE COLLEGE, Kenosha, WI 53140

General Information Independent-religious, coed, comprehensive institution. *Graduate housing:* On-campus housing not available.

GRADUATE UNITS

Division of Teacher Education *Degree program information:* Part-time and evening/weekend programs available. Offers classroom guidance and counseling (M Ed); creative arts (M Ed); gifted and talented children (M Ed); language arts (M Ed); modern language (M Ed); natural sciences (M Ed); reading (M Ed, Certificate); social sciences (M Ed); teacher leadership (M Ed).

CASE WESTERN RESERVE UNIVERSITY, Cleveland, OH 44106

General Information Independent, coed, university. CGS member. *Enrollment:* 9,814 graduate, professional, and undergraduate students; 4,223 full-time matriculated graduate/professional students (2,014 women), 1,113 part-time matriculated graduate/professional students (705 women). *Enrollment by degree level:* 1,671 first professional, 1,923 master's, 1,698 doctoral, 44 other advanced degrees. *Graduate faculty:* 2,646 full-time (905 women). *Tuition:* Full-time $31,000; part-time $1292 per credit hour. *Required fees:* $22. *Graduate housing:* On-campus housing not available. *Student services:* Campus employment opportunities, campus safety program, career counseling, exercise/wellness program, free psychological counseling, grant writing training, international student services, low-cost health insurance, multicultural affairs office, services for students with disabilities, teacher training, writing training. *Library facilities:* University Library plus 6 others. *Online resources:* library catalog, web page, access to other libraries' catalogs. *Collection:* 2.5 million titles, 54,252 serial subscriptions, 53,892 audiovisual materials. *Research affiliation:* Cleveland Clinic Foundation (biomedical science), Universities Space Research Association (space exploration), Rockwell Automation (sensors), Dow Chemical Company (polymers), Cleveland Hearing and Speech Center (speech-language pathology and audiology), University Hospitals of Cleveland (biomedical science).

Computer facilities: Computer purchase and lease plans are available. 415 computers available on campus for general student use. A campuswide network can be accessed from student residence rooms and from off campus. Online class registration, software library, online reference databases, electronic books and journals are available. *Web address:* http://www.case.edu/.

General Application Contact: Susan M. Benedict, Admissions Coordinator, 216-368-4400, Fax: 216-368-4250, E-mail: susan.benedict@case.edu.

GRADUATE UNITS

Frances Payne Bolton School of Nursing *Degree program information:* Part-time programs available. Postbaccalaureate distance learning degree programs offered (minimal on-campus study). Offers acute care cardiovascular nursing (MSN); acute care nurse practitioner (MSN, DNP); acute care/flight nurse (MSN); adult nurse practitioner (MSN, DNP); community health nursing (MSN); family nurse practitioner (MSN, DNP); gerontological nurse practitioner (MSN, DNP); graduate entry/pre-licensure option (DNP); medical-surgical nursing (MSN, DNP); midwifery/family nursing (DNP); neonatal nurse practitioner (MSN, DNP); nurse anesthesia (MSN); nurse midwifery (MSN); nurse practitioner (MSN); nursing (MSN, DNP, PhD); nursing informatics (MSN); pediatric nurse practitioner (MSN, DNP); post-licensure option (DNP); psychiatric-mental health nurse practitioner (MSN, DNP); women's health nurse practitioner (MSN, DNP).

Mandel School of Applied Social Sciences *Degree program information:* Evening/weekend programs available. Offers social administration (MSSA); social welfare (PhD). Electronic applications accepted.

School of Dental Medicine Offers advanced general dentistry (Certificate); dental medicine (DMD, MSD, Certificate); dentistry (DMD, MSD, Certificate); endodontics (MSD, Certificate); oral surgery (Certificate); orthodontics (MSD, Certificate); pedodontics (MSD, Certificate); periodontics (MSD, Certificate). Electronic applications accepted.

School of Graduate Studies Students: 1,626 full-time (761 women), 313 part-time (156 women); includes 217 minority (62 African Americans, 8 American Indian/Alaska Native, 118 Asian Americans or Pacific Islanders, 29 Hispanic Americans), 622 international. Average age 29. 3,762 applicants, 29% accepted, 495 enrolled. *Faculty:* 2,620 full-time (897 women). Expenses: Contact institution. *Financial support:* Fellowships with tuition reimbursements, research assistantships with tuition reimbursements, teaching assistantships with tuition reimbursements, career-related internships or fieldwork, Federal Work-Study, institutionally sponsored loans, scholarships/grants, traineeships, health care benefits, tuition waivers (full and partial), and unspecified assistantships available. Support available to part-time students. In 2008, 343 master's, 205 doctorates awarded. *Degree program information:* Part-time and evening/weekend programs available. Offers acting (MFA); anthropology (MA, PhD); applied mathematics (MS, PhD); art education (MA); art history (MA, PhD); art history and museum studies (MA, PhD); astronomy (MS, PhD); biology (MS, PhD); chemistry (MS, PhD); clinical psychology (PhD); cognitive linguistics (MA); contemporary dance (MFA); dance (MA); early music (MA, D Mus A); English (MA, PhD); experimental psychology (PhD); French (MA); geological sciences (MS, PhD); history (MA, PhD); mathematics (MS, PhD); music education (MA, PhD); music history (MA); musicology (PhD); physics (MS, PhD); political science (MA, PhD); sociology (MA, PhD); speech-language pathology (MA, PhD); statistics (MS, PhD); theater (MFA); world literature (MA). *Application deadline:* For fall admission, 3/1 for domestic students; for spring admission, 11/1 for domestic students. *Application fee:* $50. Electronic applications accepted. *Application Contact:* Susan M. Benedict, Admissions Coordinator, 216-368-4400, Fax: 216-368-4250, E-mail: susan.benedict@case.edu. *Dean,* Dr. Charles E. Rozek, 216-368-4400, Fax: 216-368-4250, E-mail: charles.rozek@case.edu.

The Case School of Engineering Students: 511 full-time (108 women), 87 part-time (16 women); includes 52 minority (13 African Americans, 3 American Indian/Alaska Native, 32 Asian Americans or Pacific Islanders, 4 Hispanic Americans), 278 international. 1,329 applicants, 33% accepted, 143 enrolled. *Faculty:* 109 full-time (13 women). Expenses: Contact institution. *Financial support:* In 2008–09, 102 fellowships with full and partial tuition reimbursements, 293 research assistantships with full and partial tuition reimbursements, 39 teaching assistantships were awarded; career-related internships or fieldwork, Federal Work-Study, and institutionally sponsored loans also available. Support available to part-time students. Financial award applicants required to submit FAFSA. In 2008, 132 master's, 56 doctorates awarded. *Degree program information:* Part-time and evening/weekend programs available. Postbaccalaureate distance learning degree programs offered (minimal on-campus study). Offers aerospace engineering (MS, PhD); biomedical engineering (MS, PhD); ceramics and materials science (MS); chemical engineering (MS, PhD); civil engineering (MS, PhD); computer engineering (MS, PhD); computing and information science (MS, PhD); electrical engineering (MS, PhD); engineering (ME, MEM, MS, PhD); engineering mechanics (MS); fluid and thermal engineering sciences (MS, PhD); integration of management and engineering (MEM); macromolecular science (MS, PhD); materials science and engineering (MS, PhD); mechanical engineering (MS, PhD); systems and control engineering (MS, PhD). *Application deadline:* Applications are processed on a rolling basis. *Application fee:* $50. Electronic applications accepted. *Application Contact:* Dr. Patrick Crago, Associate Dean and Professor of Biomedical Engineering, 216-368-4436, Fax: 216-368-6939, E-mail: cseinfo@case.edu. *Dean,* Norman C. Tien, 216-368-4436, Fax: 216-368-6939, E-mail: csedean@case.edu.

Cleveland Clinic Lerner Research Institute–Molecular Medicine PhD Program Students: 17 full-time (10 women); includes 4 minority (1 African American, 3 Asian Americans or Pacific Islanders), 7 international. Average age 26. 48 applicants, 35% accepted, 9 enrolled. *Faculty:* 122 full-time (34 women). Expenses: Contact institution. *Financial support:* Fellowships with full tuition reimbursements, health care benefits and stipends available. Offers molecular medicine (PhD). *Application deadline:* For fall admission, 1/15 for domestic and international students. *Application fee:* $50. Electronic applications accepted. *Application Contact:* Dr. Marcia Takacs Jarrett, Director of Research Education, 216-445-6690, E-mail: molmedphd@ccf.org. *Director,* Dr. Martha Cathcart, 216-444-5222, E-mail: molmedphd@ccf.org.

School of Law Students: 624 full-time (279 women), 34 part-time (16 women); includes 86 minority (26 African Americans, 2 American Indian/Alaska Native, 51 Asian Americans or Pacific Islanders, 7 Hispanic Americans), 18 international. Average age 24. 2,212 applicants, 37% accepted, 204 enrolled. *Faculty:* 62 full-time (24 women), 78 part-time/adjunct (24 women). Expenses: Contact institution. *Financial support:* In 2008–09, 546 students received support. Career-related internships or fieldwork, Federal Work-Study, and scholarships/grants available. Support available to part-time students. Financial award application deadline: 5/1; financial award applicants required to submit FAFSA. In 2008, 214 JDs, 45 master's awarded. *Degree program information:* Part-time programs available. Offers law (JD); U.S. legal studies (LL M). *Application deadline:* For fall admission, 4/1 priority date for domestic and international students. Applications are processed on a rolling basis. *Application fee:* $40. Electronic applications accepted. *Application Contact:* Elaine Greaves, Assistant Dean for Admissions, 216-368-3600, Fax: 216-368-1042, E-mail: lawadmissions@case.edu. *Interim Dean,* Robert H. Rawson, 216-368-3283.

School of Medicine *Degree program information:* Part-time programs available. Offers clinical research (MS); medicine (MD, MA, MPH, MS, PhD).

Graduate Programs in Medicine *Degree program information:* Part-time programs available. Offers anesthesiology (MS); applied anatomy (MS); biochemical research (MS); biochemistry (MS, PhD); bioethics (MA); biological anthropology (MS); biomedical sciences (PhD); biostatistics (MS, PhD); cancer biology (PhD); cell and molecular physiology (MS); cell biology (MS, PhD); cell physiology (PhD); cellular biology (MS, PhD); dietetics (MS); epidemiology (MS, PhD); genetic and molecular epidemiology (MS, PhD); genetic counseling (MS); health services research (MS, PhD); human, molecular, and developmental genetics and genomics (PhD); immunology (MS, PhD); medicine (MA, MPH, MS, PhD); microbiology (PhD); molecular biology (PhD); molecular medicine (PhD); molecular virology (PhD); molecular/cellular biophysics (PhD); neurobiology (PhD); neuroscience (PhD); nutrition (MS, PhD); pathology (MS, PhD); pharmacology (PhD); physiology and biophysics (PhD); public health (MPH); public health nutrition (MS); RNA biology (PhD); systems physiology (PhD). Electronic applications accepted.

Weatherhead School of Management Students: 518 full-time (246 women), 336 part-time (143 women); includes 108 minority (59 African Americans, 34 Asian Americans or Pacific Islanders, 15 Hispanic Americans), 218 international. Average age 28. *Faculty:* 71 full-time (13 women), 36 part-time/adjunct (10 women). Expenses: Contact institution. *Financial support:* Fellowships with full and partial tuition reimbursements, career-related internships or fieldwork, Federal Work-Study, institutionally sponsored loans, scholarships/grants, tuition waivers (full and partial), and unspecified assistantships available. Financial award application deadline: 5/1; financial award applicants required to submit FAFSA. *Degree program information:* Part-time and evening/weekend programs available. Offers accountancy (M Acc, PhD); banking and finance (MBA); business administration (EMBA, MBA); economics (MBA); information systems (MBA); labor and human resource policy (MBA); management (MS, MSM, EDM); management for liberal arts graduates (MSM); management policy (MBA); marketing (MBA); operations research (MSM, PhD); organizational behavior and analysis (MBA, MPOD, MS); positive organization development and change (MS); supply chain (MSM). *Application deadline:* Applications are processed on a rolling basis. *Application fee:* $75. Electronic applications accepted. *Application Contact:* N. Mohan Reddy, Head, 216-368-2038, E-mail: mohan.reddy@case.edu. *Head,* N. Mohan Reddy, 216-368-2038, E-mail: mohan.reddy@case.edu.

Mandel Center for Nonprofit Organizations Average age 31. Expenses: Contact institution. *Financial support:* In 2008–09, 39 students received support, including 1 fellowship with full and partial tuition reimbursement available; career-related internships or fieldwork, Federal Work-Study, and scholarships/grants also available. Financial award application deadline: 5/1; financial award applicants required to submit FAFSA. *Degree program information:* Part-time and evening/weekend programs available. Offers nonprofit organizations (MNO, CNM). *Application deadline:* For fall admission, 6/1 priority date for domestic students; for spring admission, 11/15 priority date for domestic students. Applications are processed on a rolling basis. *Application fee:* $25. *Application Contact:* Wendy Jelinek, Director, 216-368-8566, Fax: 216-368-8592, E-mail: wendy.jelinek@case.edu. *Director,* Wendy Jelinek, 216-368-8566, Fax: 216-368-8592, E-mail: wendy.jelinek@case.edu.

CASTLETON STATE COLLEGE, Castleton, VT 05735

General Information State-supported, coed, comprehensive institution. *Graduate housing:* Room and/or apartments available on a first-come, first-served basis to single students; on-campus housing not available to married students. Housing application deadline: 5/19.

GRADUATE UNITS

Division of Graduate Studies *Degree program information:* Part-time and evening/weekend programs available. Offers curriculum and instruction (MA Ed); educational leadership (MA Ed, CAGS); forensic psychology (MA); language arts and reading (MA Ed, CAGS); special education (MA Ed, CAGS).

CATAWBA COLLEGE, Salisbury, NC 28144-2488

General Information Independent-religious, coed, comprehensive institution. *Enrollment:* 1,261 graduate, professional, and undergraduate students; 36 part-time matriculated graduate/professional students (all women). *Enrollment by degree level:* 36 master's. *Graduate faculty:* 4 full-time (3 women), 3 part-time/adjunct (2 women). *Tuition:* Part-time $140 per credit hour. *Graduate housing:* On-campus housing not available. *Student services:* Campus safety program, career counseling, teacher training. *Library facilities:* Corriher-Linn-Black Memorial Library plus 1 other. *Online resources:* library catalog.

Computer facilities: 97 computers available on campus for general student use. A campuswide network can be accessed from student residence rooms and from off campus. *Web address:* http://www.catawba.edu/.

General Application Contact: Dr. Lou W. Kasias, Director, Graduate Program, 704-637-4462, Fax: 704-637-4732, E-mail: lakasias@catawba.edu.

GRADUATE UNITS

Program in Education Students: 36 part-time (all women). *Faculty:* 4 full-time (3 women), 3 part-time/adjunct (2 women). Expenses: Contact institution. *Financial support:* Scholarships/grants available. *Degree program information:* Part-time and evening/weekend programs available. Offers elementary education (M Ed). *Application deadline:* For fall admission, 8/1 priority date for domestic students; for winter admission, 12/1 priority date for domestic students; for spring admission, 5/1 priority date for domestic students. Applications are processed on a rolling basis. *Application fee:* $0. *Application Contact:* Dr. Lou W. Kasias, Director, Graduate Program, 704-637-4462, Fax: 704-637-4732, E-mail: lakasias@catawba.edu. *Chair, Department of Teacher Education,* Dr. James K. Stringfield, 704-637-4337, Fax: 704-637-4732, E-mail: jstringf@catawba.edu.

THE CATHOLIC DISTANCE UNIVERSITY, Hamilton, VA 20158

General Information Independent-religious, coed, graduate-only institution. *Graduate housing:* On-campus housing not available.

GRADUATE UNITS

Graduate Programs *Degree program information:* Part-time and evening/weekend programs available. Postbaccalaureate distance learning degree programs offered (no on-campus study). Offers religious studies (MRS); theology (MA).

CATHOLIC THEOLOGICAL UNION AT CHICAGO, Chicago, IL 60615-5698

General Information Independent-religious, coed, graduate-only institution. *Graduate housing:* Rooms and/or apartments available on a first-come, first-served basis to single and married students. Housing application deadline: 7/1.

GRADUATE UNITS

Graduate and Professional Programs *Degree program information:* Part-time and evening/weekend programs available. Offers biblical spirituality (Certificate); cross-cultural ministries (D Min); cross-cultural missions (Certificate); divinity (M Div); liturgical studies (Certificate); liturgy (D Min); pastoral studies (MAPS, Certificate); spiritual formation (Certificate); spirituality (D Min); theology (MA).

THE CATHOLIC UNIVERSITY OF AMERICA, Washington, DC 20064

General Information Independent-religious, coed, university. CGS member. *Enrollment:* 6,705 graduate, professional, and undergraduate students; 1,348 full-time matriculated graduate/professional students (647 women), 1,766 part-time matriculated graduate/professional students (931 women). *Enrollment by degree level:* 984 first professional, 1,235 master's, 895 doctoral. *Graduate faculty:* 352 full-time (128 women), 342 part-time/adjunct (155 women). *Tuition:* Full-time $30,520; part-time $1195 per credit hour. *Required fees:* $50; $25 per semester. One-time fee: $425. *Graduate housing:* Room and/or apartments available on a first-come, first-served basis to single students; on-campus housing not available to married students. Typical cost: $13,946 (including board). Housing application deadline: 5/15. *Student services:* Campus employment opportunities, campus safety program, career counseling, exercise/wellness program, free psychological counseling, international student services, low-cost health insurance, services for students with disabilities, teacher training, writing training. *Library facilities:* Mullen Library plus 7 others. *Online resources:* library catalog, web page, access to other libraries' catalogs. *Collection:* 1.6 million titles, 10,428 serial subscriptions, 41,679 audiovisual materials. *Research affiliation:* EnergySolutions (Waste vitrification), Alion, Inc. (Support of military programs), CareFirst (Nurse education), Henry Jackson Foundation (Medical research), Lily Foundation (Religion and young Americans), Various Catholic dioceses (Secondary school development).

Computer facilities: Computer purchase and lease plans are available. 450 computers available on campus for general student use. A campuswide network can be accessed from student residence rooms and from off campus. Online class registration, internet 2, video streaming, online voting, pedagogical software are available. *Web address:* http://www.cua.edu/.

General Application Contact: Christine Mica, Dean, University Admissions, 202-319-5305, Fax: 202-319-6533, E-mail: cua-admissions@cua.edu.

GRADUATE UNITS

The Benjamin T. Rome School of Music Students: 52 full-time (33 women), 83 part-time (59 women); includes 19 minority (4 African Americans, 8 Asian Americans or Pacific Islanders, 7 Hispanic Americans), 29 international. Average age 33. 97 applicants, 68% accepted, 30 enrolled. *Faculty:* 17 full-time (4 women), 22 part-time/adjunct (9 women). Expenses: Contact institution. *Financial support:* Fellowships, research assistantships, teaching assistantships, Federal Work-Study, scholarships/grants, tuition waivers (full and partial), and unspecified assistantships available. Financial award application deadline: 2/1; financial award applicants required to submit FAFSA. In 2008, 19 master's, 10 doctorates awarded. *Degree program information:* Part-time programs available. Offers chamber music (MM); composition (DMA); compostition (MM); music (Certificate); musicology (MA, PhD); orchestral instruments (DMA); piano pedagogy (MM, DMA); piano performance (MM); rchestral conducting (MM); sacred music (MMSM, DMA); vocal pedagogy (MM); vocal performance (MM). *Application deadline:* For fall admission, 8/1 priority date for domestic students, 7/1 for international students; for spring admission, 12/1 priority date for domestic students, 11/15 for international students. Applications are processed on a rolling basis. *Application fee:* $55. Electronic applications accepted. *Application Contact:* Christine Mica, Dean, University Admissions, 202-319-5305, Fax: 202-319-6533, E-mail: cua-admissions@cua.edu. *Dean,* Murry Sidlin, 202-319-5414, Fax: 202-319-6280, E-mail: cua-music@cua.edu.

Columbus School of Law *Degree program information:* Part-time and evening/weekend programs available. Offers law (JD). Electronic applications accepted.

Metropolitan College Students: 15 full-time (11 women), 50 part-time (37 women); includes 26 minority (21 African Americans, 4 Asian Americans or Pacific Islanders, 1 Hispanic American), 8 international. Average age 32. 79 applicants, 56% accepted, 34 enrolled. *Faculty:* 37 part-time/adjunct (17 women). Expenses: Contact institution. *Degree program information:* Part-time and evening/weekend programs available. Offers human resource management (MA); management (MS). *Application deadline:* For fall admission, 8/1 priority date for domestic students, 7/1 for international students; for spring admission, 11/15 for international students. *Application Contact:* Christine Mica, Dean, University Admissions, 202-319-5305, Fax: 202-319-6533, E-mail: cua-admissions@cua.edu. *Dean,* Dr. Sara Thompson, 202-319-5256, Fax: 202-319-6032, E-mail: thompsons@cua.edu.

The Catholic University of America (continued)

National Catholic School of Social Service Students: 71 full-time (61 women), 179 part-time (153 women); includes 51 minority (30 African Americans, 7 Asian Americans or Pacific Islanders, 14 Hispanic Americans), 7 international. Average age 35. 194 applicants, 73% accepted, 85 enrolled. *Faculty:* 16 full-time (14 women), 24 part-time/adjunct (22 women). Expenses: Contact institution. *Financial support:* Fellowships, research assistantships, teaching assistantships, Federal Work-Study, scholarships/grants, tuition waivers (full and partial), and unspecified assistantships available. Financial award application deadline: 2/1; financial award applicants required to submit FAFSA. In 2008, 66 master's, 2 doctorates awarded. *Degree program information:* Part-time programs available. Offers clinical (MSW); combined (clinical and macro) (MSW); contract research and theory in clinical social work (PhD); macro (MSW); research and theory in macro social work (PhD). *Application deadline:* For fall admission, 6/1 priority date for domestic students, 7/1 for international students; for spring admission, 11/30 priority date for domestic students, 11/15 for international students. Applications are processed on a rolling basis. *Application fee:* $55. Electronic applications accepted. *Application Contact:* Christine Mica, Dean, University Admissions, 202-319-5305, Fax: 202-319-6533, E-mail: cua-admissions@cua.edu. *Dean,* Dr. James R. Zabora, 202-319-5454, Fax: 202-319-5093, E-mail: zabora@cua.edu.

School of Architecture and Planning Students: 105 full-time (43 women), 23 part-time (10 women); includes 31 minority (10 African Americans, 9 Asian Americans or Pacific Islanders, 12 Hispanic Americans), 7 international. Average age 27. 135 applicants, 77% accepted, 46 enrolled. *Faculty:* 22 full-time (5 women), 35 part-time/adjunct (9 women). Expenses: Contact institution. *Financial support:* Fellowships, research assistantships, teaching assistantships, Federal Work-Study, scholarships/grants, tuition waivers (full and partial), and unspecified assistantships available. Financial award application deadline: 2/1; financial award applicants required to submit FAFSA. In 2008, 33 master's awarded. *Degree program information:* Part-time programs available. Offers cultural studies/sacred space (M Arch); design technologies (M Arch); digital media (M Arch); urban design (M Arch). *Application deadline:* For fall admission, 1/15 priority date for domestic students; for spring admission, 10/15 priority date for domestic students. Applications are processed on a rolling basis. *Application fee:* $55. Electronic applications accepted. *Application Contact:* Christine Mica, Dean, University Admissions, 202-319-5305, Fax: 202-319-6533, E-mail: cua-admissions@cua.edu. *Dean,* Randall Ott, 202-319-5784, Fax: 202-319-2023, E-mail: ott@cua.edu.

School of Arts and Sciences Students: 150 full-time (83 women), 388 part-time (210 women); includes 75 minority (28 African Americans, 2 American Indian/Alaska Native, 22 Asian Americans or Pacific Islanders, 23 Hispanic Americans), 46 international. Average age 32. 656 applicants, 45% accepted, 126 enrolled. *Faculty:* 144 full-time (53 women), 88 part-time/adjunct (43 women). Expenses: Contact institution. *Financial support:* Fellowships, research assistantships, teaching assistantships, Federal Work-Study, scholarships/grants, tuition waivers (full and partial), and unspecified assistantships available. Financial award application deadline: 2/1; financial award applicants required to submit FAFSA. In 2008, 112 master's, 35 doctorates awarded. *Degree program information:* Part-time programs available. Offers acting, directing, and playwriting (MFA); American government (MA, PhD); Ancient Near East (Biblical Hebrew/Aramaic) (MA); ancient Near East (Biblical Hebrew/Aramaic) (PhD); anthropology (MA); applied experimental psychology (PhD); Arabic (PhD); arts and sciences (MA, MFA, MS, PhD, Certificate); Catholic educational leadership (PhD); cell and microbial biology (MS, PhD); chemistry (MS); Christian Near East (Biblical Hebrew/Aramaic) (MA); clinical laboratory science (MS, PhD); clinical psychology (PhD); comparative literature (MA); Congressional and presidential studies (MA); Coptic (MA, PhD); early Christian studies (MA, PhD); education (Certificate); educational psychology (PhD); English language and literature (MA, PhD); general psychology (MA); Greek and Latin (MA, PhD); human factors (MA); international affairs (MA); international political economics (MA); Irish studies (MA); Latin (MA); learning and instruction (MA); medieval and Byzantine studies (MA, PhD, Certificate); Medieval Europe (MA, PhD); modern Europe (PhD); physics (MS, PhD); political theory (MA, PhD); religon and society in the Late Medieval and early modern world (MA); rhetoric (MA, PhD); secondary education (MA); sociology (MA); Spanish (MA, PhD); special education (MA); Syriac (MA); theatre education (MA); theatre history and criticism (MA); United States (MA); world politics (MA, PhD). *Application deadline:* For fall admission, 8/1 priority date for domestic students, 7/1 for international students; for spring admission, 12/1 priority date for domestic students, 11/15 for international students. Applications are processed on a rolling basis. *Application fee:* $55. Electronic applications accepted. *Application Contact:* Christine Mica, Dean, University Admissions, 202-319-5305, Fax: 202-319-6533, E-mail: cua-admissions@cua.edu. *Dean,* Dr. Lawrence R. Poos, 202-319-5115, Fax: 202-319-6076, E-mail: poos@cua.edu.

School of Canon Law Students: 30 full-time (3 women), 60 part-time (10 women); includes 5 minority (2 African Americans, 2 Asian Americans or Pacific Islanders, 1 Hispanic American), 20 international. Average age 41. 43 applicants, 79% accepted, 28 enrolled. *Faculty:* 6 full-time (0 women), 1 part-time/adjunct (0 women). Expenses: Contact institution. *Financial support:* Fellowships, research assistantships, teaching assistantships, Federal Work-Study, scholarships/grants, tuition waivers (full and partial), and unspecified assistantships available. Financial award application deadline: 2/1; financial award applicants required to submit FAFSA. *Degree program information:* Part-time programs available. Offers canon law (JCD, JCL). *Application deadline:* For fall admission, 8/1 priority date for domestic students, 7/1 for international students; for spring admission, 12/1 priority date for domestic students, 11/15 for international students. Applications are processed on a rolling basis. *Application fee:* $55. Electronic applications accepted. *Application Contact:* Christine Mica, Dean, University Admissions, 202-319-5305, Fax: 202-319-6533, E-mail: cua-admissions@cua.edu. *Interim Dean,* Sr. Rose McDermott, 202-319-5492, Fax: 202-319-4187, E-mail: cua-canonlaw@cua.edu.

School of Engineering Students: 56 full-time (16 women), 92 part-time (21 women); includes 25 minority (11 African Americans, 7 Asian Americans or Pacific Islanders, 7 Hispanic Americans), 40 international. Average age 31. 166 applicants, 59% accepted, 55 enrolled. *Faculty:* 25 full-time (3 women), 18 part-time/adjunct (0 women). Expenses: Contact institution. *Financial support:* Fellowships, research assistantships, teaching assistantships, Federal Work-Study, scholarships/grants, tuition waivers (full and partial), and unspecified assistantships available. Financial award application deadline: 2/1; financial award applicants required to submit FAFSA. In 2008, 43 master's, 6 doctorates awarded. *Degree program information:* Part-time programs available. Offers active control and smart materials/systems (MME, MSE, PhD); antennas and electromagnetic propagation (MEE, MSCS, D Engr); bioimaging (MEE, MSCS, PhD); bioinformatics and intelligent information systems (MEE, D Engr, PhD); bioinstrumentation (MBE, MSE, D Engr); biomechanics (MBE, D Engr, PhD); biosignal processing and medical imaging (MBE, MSE, PhD); combustion (MME, MSE, D Engr); computational fluid dynamics (MME, MSE, D Engr); controls (MME, MSE, D Engr, PhD); distributed and real-time systems (MEE, MSCS, D Engr, PhD); dynamics (MME, MSE, PhD); electronic packaging (MME, MSE, PhD); engineering (MBE, MCE, MEE, MME, MSCS, MSE, D Engr, PhD, Certificate); engineering management (MSE, Certificate); environmental engineering (MCE, MSE, D Engr, PhD, Certificate); environmental engineering and management (MCE, MSE, PhD, Certificate); environmental engineering and management (D Engr); fluid and solid mechanics (MCE, MSE, PhD, Certificate); geotechnical engineering (MCE, MSE, PhD, Certificate); high speed communications and networking (MSCS, D Engr, PhD); home care technologies (MBE, MSE, D Engr); human thermal comfort (MME, MSE, D Engr, PhD); HVAC and refrigeration (MME, MSE, D Engr, PhD); information security (MEE, MSCS, PhD); management of construction (MCE, MSE, D Engr, PhD); MEMS (MSE, D Engr, PhD); micro-optics (MEE, MSCS, D Engr, PhD); nano-mechanics (MME, D Engr, PhD); rehabilitation engineering (MBE, MSE, D Engr); signal and image processing (MEE, MSCS, D Engr); structural engineering (MSE, D Engr, PhD); systems engineering (MSE, D Engr, PhD, Certificate); telemedicine (MBE, MSE, D Engr); thermal/fluid sciences (MME, MSE, D Engr, PhD); vibrations (MSE, D Engr, PhD). *Application deadline:* For fall admission, 8/1 priority date for domestic students, 7/1 for international students; for spring admission, 12/1 priority date for domestic students, 11/15 for international students. Applications are processed on a rolling basis. *Application fee:* $55. Electronic applications accepted. *Application Contact:* Christine Mica, Dean, University Admissions, 202-319-5305, Fax: 202-319-6533, E-mail: cua-admissions@cua.edu. *Dean,* Dr. Charles C. Nguyen, 202-319-5160, Fax: 202-319-4499, E-mail: nguyen@cua.edu.

School of Library and Information Science Students: 24 full-time (20 women), 187 part-time (150 women); includes 36 minority (19 African Americans, 11 Asian Americans or Pacific Islanders, 6 Hispanic Americans), 5 international. Average age 36. 136 applicants, 86% accepted, 62 enrolled. *Faculty:* 6 full-time (4 women), 17 part-time/adjunct (10 women). Expenses: Contact institution. *Financial support:* Fellowships, research assistantships, teaching assistantships, Federal Work-Study, scholarships/grants, tuition waivers (full and partial), and unspecified assistantships available. Financial award application deadline: 2/1; financial award applicants required to submit FAFSA. In 2008, 103 master's awarded. *Degree program information:* Part-time programs available. Offers library and information science (MSLS). *Application deadline:* For fall admission, 8/1 priority date for domestic students, 7/1 for international students; for spring admission, 11/1 priority date for domestic students, 11/15 for international students. Applications are processed on a rolling basis. *Application fee:* $55. Electronic applications accepted. *Application Contact:* Christine Mica, Dean, University Admissions, 202-319-5305, Fax: 202-319-6533, E-mail: cua-admissions@cua.edu. *Dean,* Dr. Kimberly B. Kelley, 202-319-5085, Fax: 202-319-5574, E-mail: kelleyk@cua.edu.

School of Nursing Students: 43 full-time (40 women), 59 part-time (56 women); includes 41 minority (29 African Americans, 8 Asian Americans or Pacific Islanders, 4 Hispanic Americans), 6 international. Average age 41. 84 applicants, 48% accepted, 24 enrolled. *Faculty:* 15 full-time (all women), 29 part-time/adjunct (27 women). Expenses: Contact institution. *Financial support:* Fellowships, research assistantships, teaching assistantships, Federal Work-Study, scholarships/grants, tuition waivers (full and partial), and unspecified assistantships available. Financial award application deadline: 2/1; financial award applicants required to submit FAFSA. In 2008, 16 master's, 6 doctorates awarded. *Degree program information:* Part-time programs available. Offers adult health specialist with functional role as nurse educator (MSN); adult nurse practitioner (MSN); community/public health nurse specialist educator (MSN); family nurse practitioner (MSN); geriatric nurse practioner (MSN); immigrant, refugee, and global health clinical nurse specialist (MSN); nursing (DNP, PhD, Certificate); pediatric nurse practitioner (MSN); promoting healthy families in vulnerable communities (MSN); psychiatric-mental health nursing (MSN). *Application deadline:* For fall admission, 8/1 priority date for domestic students, 7/1 for international students; for spring admission, 12/1 priority date for domestic students, 11/15 for international students. Applications are processed on a rolling basis. *Application fee:* $55. Electronic applications accepted. *Application Contact:* Christine Mica, Dean, University Admissions, 202-319-5305, Fax: 202-319-6533, E-mail: cua-admissions@cua.edu. *Dean,* Dr. Nalini N. Jairath, 202-319-5403, Fax: 202-319-6485, E-mail: cua-deanschoolofnursing@cua.edu.

School of Philosophy Students: 45 full-time (4 women), 83 part-time (21 women); includes 5 minority (1 African American, 3 Asian Americans or Pacific Islanders, 1 Hispanic American), 19 international. Average age 32. 102 applicants, 64% accepted, 34 enrolled. *Faculty:* 15 full-time (3 women), 6 part-time/adjunct (2 women). Expenses: Contact institution. *Financial support:* Fellowships, research assistantships, teaching assistantships, Federal Work-Study, scholarships/grants, tuition waivers (full and partial), and unspecified assistantships available. Financial award application deadline: 2/1; financial award applicants required to submit FAFSA. In 2008, 12 master's, 3 doctorates awarded. *Degree program information:* Part-time programs available. Offers philosophy (MA, PhD, Ph L). *Application deadline:* For fall admission, 8/1 priority date for domestic students, 7/1 for international students; for spring admission, 12/1 priority date for domestic students, 11/15 for international students. Applications are processed on a rolling basis. *Application fee:* $55. Electronic applications accepted. *Application Contact:* Christine Mica, Dean, University Admissions, 202-319-5305, Fax: 202-319-6533, E-mail: cua-admissions@cua.edu. *Dean,* Rev. Kurt J. Pritzl, OP, 202-319-5259, Fax: 202-319-4731, E-mail: pritzl@cua.edu.

School of Theology and Religious Studies Students: 172 full-time (19 women), 213 part-time (56 women); includes 37 minority (11 African Americans, 1 American Indian/Alaska Native, 14 Asian Americans or Pacific Islanders, 11 Hispanic Americans), 69 international. Average age 37. 248 applicants, 77% accepted, 87 enrolled. *Faculty:* 39 full-time (5 women), 8 part-time/adjunct (1 woman). Expenses: Contact institution. *Financial support:* Fellowships, research assistantships, teaching assistantships, Federal Work-Study, scholarships/grants, tuition waivers (full and partial), and unspecified assistantships available. Financial award application deadline: 2/1; financial award applicants required to submit FAFSA. In 2008, 5 first professional degrees, 19 master's, 21 doctorates awarded. *Degree program information:* Part-time programs available. Offers Biblical studies (STB, MA, PhD, STL); Catholic educational leadership (MA); church history (PhD); Hispanic pastoral leadership (Certificate); Hispanic/Latino ministry (M Div); historical theology (STB, STD); history of religions (Hinduism/Islam) (MA, PhD); liturgical studies/sacramental theology (MA, PhD, STD, STL); moral theology/ethics (STB, MA, PhD, STD, STL); pastoral studies (M Div, Certificate); religion and culture (PhD); religious education/catechetics (MA, MRE, PhD); spirituality (STB, PhD, STD, STL); systematic and historical theology (MA, PhD, STD, STL). *Application deadline:* For fall admission, 8/1 priority date for domestic students, 7/1 for international students; for spring admission, 12/1 priority date for domestic students, 11/15 for international students. Applications are processed on a rolling basis. *Application fee:* $55. Electronic applications accepted. *Application Contact:* Christine Mica, Dean, University Admissions, 202-319-5305, Fax: 202-319-6533, E-mail: cua-admissions@cua.edu. *Dean,* Msgr. Kevin W. Irwin, 202-319-5683, Fax: 202-319-4967, E-mail: irwin@cua.edu.

CEDAR CREST COLLEGE, Allentown, PA 18104-6196

General Information Independent-religious, women only, comprehensive institution.

GRADUATE UNITS

Department of Education *Degree program information:* Part-time and evening/weekend programs available. Offers education (M Ed).

Program in Forensic Science Offers forensic science (MS). Electronic applications accepted.

CEDARS-SINAI MEDICAL CENTER, Los Angeles, CA 90048

General Information Independent, coed, graduate-only institution. *Enrollment by degree level:* 9 doctoral. *Graduate faculty:* 60 full-time (15 women). *Graduate housing:* On-campus housing not available.

General Application Contact: Emma Yates Casler, Program Coordinator, 310-423 8294, E-mail: yatese@cshs.org.

GRADUATE UNITS

Graduate Program in Biomedical Sciences and Translational Medicine Students: 9 full-time (7 women); includes 3 minority (2 Asian Americans or Pacific Islanders, 1 Hispanic American). Average age 29. 20 applicants, 45% accepted, 9 enrolled. *Faculty:* 60 full-time (15 women). Expenses: Contact institution. *Financial support:* Health care benefits and annual stipends ($36,000) available. Offers biomedical sciences and translational medicine (PhD). *Application deadline:* For fall admission, 1/15 for domestic students. Applications are processed on a rolling basis. *Application fee:* $30. *Application Contact:* Emma Yates Casler, Program Coordinator, 310-423 8294, E-mail: yatese@cshs.org. *Program Coordinator,* Emma Yates Casler, 310-423-8294, E-mail: yatese@cshs.org.

CEDARVILLE UNIVERSITY, Cedarville, OH 45314-0601

General Information Independent-religious, coed, comprehensive institution. *Enrollment:* 3,077 graduate, professional, and undergraduate students; 81 part-time matriculated graduate/professional students (58 women). *Enrollment by degree level:* 81 master's. *Graduate faculty:* 12 part-time/adjunct (2 women). *Tuition:* Part-time $320 per credit hour. *Graduate housing:* Room and/or apartments available on a first-come, first-served basis to single students; on-campus housing not available to married students. Housing application deadline: 5/1. *Student services:* Campus safety program, career counseling, exercise/wellness program, free psychological counseling. *Library facilities:* Centennial Library. *Online resources:* library catalog, web page. *Collection:* 181,053 titles, 21,050 serial subscriptions, 16,464 audiovisual materials.

Computer facilities: 2,600 computers available on campus for general student use. A campuswide network can be accessed from student residence rooms and from off campus. Online class registration, over 150 software packages are available. *Web address:* http://www.cedarville.edu/.

General Application Contact: Scott Van Loo, Admissions Director, 937-766-7700, Fax: 937-766-7575, E-mail: smithr@cedarville.edu.

GRADUATE UNITS

Graduate Programs Students: 81 part-time (58 women); includes 1 minority (African American), 1 international. Average age 33. 100 applicants, 81% accepted, 81 enrolled. *Faculty:* 12 part-time/adjunct (2 women). Expenses: Contact institution. *Financial support:* Scholarships/grants available. Support available to part-time students. Financial award applicants required to submit FAFSA. In 2008, 3 master's awarded. *Degree program information:* Part-time and evening/weekend programs available. Offers education (M Ed). *Application deadline:* Applications are processed on a rolling basis. *Application fee:* $30. Electronic applications accepted. *Application Contact:* Roscoe Smith, Admissions Director, 937-766-7700, Fax: 937-766-7575, E-mail: smithr@cedarville.edu. *Director of Graduate Recruitment,* Bruce Traeger, 888-CEDARVILLE, Fax: 937-66-7575, E-mail: traegerb@cedarville.edu.

CENTENARY COLLEGE, Hackettstown, NJ 07840-2100

General Information Independent-religious, coed, comprehensive institution. *Graduate housing:* Room and/or apartments available on a first-come, first-served basis to single students; on-campus housing not available to married students. Housing application deadline: 6/1.

GRADUATE UNITS

Program in Business Administration *Degree program information:* Part-time and evening/weekend programs available. Postbaccalaureate distance learning degree programs offered (minimal on-campus study). Offers business administration (MBA).

Program in Counseling Psychology *Degree program information:* Part-time and evening/weekend programs available. Postbaccalaureate distance learning degree programs offered (minimal on-campus study). Offers counseling (MA); counseling psychology (MA).

Program in Education *Degree program information:* Part-time and evening/weekend programs available. Postbaccalaureate distance learning degree programs offered (minimal on-campus study). Offers instructional leadership (MA); special education (MA).

Program in Professional Accounting *Degree program information:* Part-time and evening/weekend programs available. Postbaccalaureate distance learning degree programs offered (minimal on-campus study). Offers professional accounting (MS).

CENTENARY COLLEGE OF LOUISIANA, Shreveport, LA 71104

General Information Independent-religious, coed, comprehensive institution. *Graduate housing:* Rooms and/or apartments available on a first-come, first-served basis to single students and available to married students.

GRADUATE UNITS

Graduate Programs *Degree program information:* Part-time and evening/weekend programs available. Offers administration (M Ed); elementary education (MAT); secondary education (MAT); supervision of instruction (M Ed).

Frost School of Business *Degree program information:* Part-time and evening/weekend programs available. Offers business (MBA).

CENTRAL BAPTIST THEOLOGICAL SEMINARY, Shawnee, KS 66226

General Information Independent-religious, coed, graduate-only institution. *Graduate housing:* On-campus housing not available.

GRADUATE UNITS

Graduate and Professional Programs *Degree program information:* Part-time programs available. Offers missional church studies (MA); theological studies (MA); theology (M Div, Diploma). Electronic applications accepted.

CENTRAL BAPTIST THEOLOGICAL SEMINARY OF VIRGINIA BEACH, Virginia Beach, VA 23464

General Information Independent-religious, coed, graduate-only institution.

GRADUATE UNITS

Graduate Programs Offers biblical studies (M Div, MBS, Th M). Electronic applications accepted.

CENTRAL CONNECTICUT STATE UNIVERSITY, New Britain, CT 06050-4010

General Information State-supported, coed, comprehensive institution. CGS member. *Enrollment:* 12,233 graduate, professional, and undergraduate students; 497 full-time matriculated graduate/professional students (339 women), 1,535 part-time matriculated graduate/professional students (1,035 women). *Enrollment by degree level:* 1,576 master's, 44 doctoral, 412 other advanced degrees. *Graduate faculty:* 343 full-time (140 women), 410 part-time/adjunct (182 women). *Tuition, area resident:* Full-time $4377; part-time $420 per credit. Tuition, state resident: full-time $6566; part-time $420 per credit. Tuition, nonresident: full-time $12,195; part-time $420 per credit. *Required fees:* $3462. One-time fee: $62 part-time. *Graduate housing:* Room and/or apartments available on a first-come, first-served basis to single students; on-campus housing not available to married students. Typical cost: $5020 per year ($8618 including board). Room and board charges vary according to board plan. Housing application deadline: 4/1. *Student services:* Campus employment opportunities, campus safety program, career counseling, child daycare facilities, exercise/wellness program, free psychological counseling, international student services, low-cost health insurance, multicultural affairs office, services for students with disabilities, teacher training, writing training. *Library facilities:* Elihu Burritt Library. *Online resources:* library catalog, web page, access to other libraries' catalogs. *Collection:* 717,553 titles, 31,195 serial subscriptions, 8,851 audiovisual materials.

Computer facilities: 1,000 computers available on campus for general student use. A campuswide network can be accessed from student residence rooms and from off campus. Online class registration is available. *Web address:* http://www.ccsu.edu/.

General Application Contact: Patricia Gardner, Graduate Admissions, 860-832-2350, Fax: 860-832-2362, E-mail: graduateadmissions@mail.ccsu.edu.

GRADUATE UNITS

School of Graduate Studies Students: 497 full-time (339 women), 1,535 part-time (1,035 women); includes 251 minority (91 African Americans, 4 American Indian/Alaska Native, 51 Asian Americans or Pacific Islanders, 105 Hispanic Americans), 41 international. Average age 33. 1,173 applicants, 64% accepted, 490 enrolled. *Faculty:* 343 full-time (140 women), 410 part-time/adjunct (182 women). Expenses: Contact institution. *Financial support:* In 2008–09, 165 students received support, including 72 research assistantships (averaging $4,800 per year); career-related internships or fieldwork, Federal Work-Study, scholarships/grants, and unspecified assistantships also available. Support available to part-time students. Financial award application deadline: 3/1; financial award applicants required to submit FAFSA. In 2008, 552 master's, 1 doctorate, 100 other advanced degrees awarded. *Degree program information:* Part-time and evening/weekend programs available. *Application deadline:* For fall admission, 7/1 for domestic students; for spring admission, 12/1 for domestic students. Applications are processed on a rolling basis. *Application fee:* $50. Electronic applications accepted. *Application Contact:* Patricia Gardner, Graduate Admissions, 860-832-2350, Fax: 860-832-2362, E-mail: graduateadmissions@mail.ccsu.edu. *Graduate Admissions,* Patricia Gardner, 860-832-2350, Fax: 860-832-2362, E-mail: graduateadmissions@mail.ccsu.edu.

School of Arts and Sciences Students: 263 full-time (161 women), 475 part-time (290 women); includes 117 minority (32 African Americans, 1 American Indian/Alaska Native, 34 Asian Americans or Pacific Islanders, 50 Hispanic Americans), 28 international. Average age 33. 420 applicants, 61% accepted, 161 enrolled. *Faculty:* 222 full-time (95 women), 290 part-time/adjunct (123 women). Expenses: Contact institution. *Financial support:* In 2008–09, 76 students received support, including 32 research assistantships; career-related internships or fieldwork, Federal Work-Study, scholarships/grants, and unspecified assistantships also available. Support available to part-time students. Financial award application deadline: 3/1; financial award applicants required to submit FAFSA. In 2008, 171 master's, 23 other advanced degrees awarded. *Degree program information:* Part-time and evening/weekend programs available. Offers anesthesia (MS); art education (MS, Certificate); arts and sciences (MA, MS, Certificate); biological sciences (MA, MS); biology (Certificate); community psychology (MA); computer information technology (MS); criminal justice (MS); data mining (MS, Certificate); English (MA, Certificate); French (MA); general health (MS); general psychology (MA); geography (MS); graphic information design (MA); health psychology (MA); history (MA, Certificate); international studies (MS); Italian (Certificate); mathematics (MA, MS, Certificate); modern language (MA, Certificate); music education (MS, Certificate); natural sciences (MS); organizational communication (MS); physics and earth science (MS, Certificate); public history (MA); public relations/promotions (Certificate); social studies (Certificate); Spanish (MA, MS, Certificate); Spanish language and Hispanic culture (MA); teaching English to speakers of other languages (MS, Certificate). *Application deadline:* For fall admission, 7/1 for domestic students; for spring admission, 12/1 for domestic students. Applications are processed on a rolling basis. *Application fee:* $50. Electronic applications accepted. *Application Contact:* Dr. Susan Pease, Dean, 860-832-2600, E-mail: pease@ccsu.edu. *Dean,* Dr. Susan Pease, 860-832-2600, E-mail: pease@ccsu.edu.

School of Business Students: 2 full-time (both women), 2 part-time (both women). Average age 36. 3 applicants, 100% accepted, 1 enrolled. *Faculty:* 11 full-time (2 women), 11 part-time/adjunct (2 women). Expenses: Contact institution. *Financial support:* Career-related internships or fieldwork, Federal Work-Study, scholarships/grants, and unspecified assistantships available. Support available to part-time students. Financial award application deadline: 3/1; financial award applicants required to submit FAFSA. In 2008, 31 master's, 1 other advanced degree awarded. *Degree program information:* Part-time and evening/weekend programs available. Offers business (MS, Certificate); business education (MS, Certificate). *Application deadline:* For fall admission, 7/1 for domestic students; for spring admission, 12/1 for domestic students. Applications are processed on a rolling basis. *Application fee:* $50. Electronic applications accepted. *Application Contact:* Dr. Siamack Shojai, Dean, 860-832-3205. *Dean,* Dr. Siamack Shojai, 860-832-3205.

School of Education and Professional Studies Students: 200 full-time (165 women), 939 part-time (725 women); includes 111 minority (55 African Americans, 3 American Indian/Alaska Native, 6 Asian Americans or Pacific Islanders, 47 Hispanic Americans), 9 international. Average age 33. 648 applicants, 64% accepted, 274 enrolled. *Faculty:* 65 full-time (33 women), 82 part-time/adjunct (51 women). Expenses: Contact institution. *Financial support:* In 2008–09, 75 students received support, including 35 research assistantships; career-related internships or fieldwork, Federal Work-Study, scholarships/grants, and unspecified assistantships also available. Support available to part-time students. Financial award application deadline: 3/1; financial award applicants required to submit FAFSA. In 2008, 317 master's, 1 doctorate, 74 other advanced degrees awarded. *Degree program information:* Part-time and evening/weekend programs available. Offers early childhood education (MS); education and professional studies (MS, Ed D, Certificate, Sixth Year Certificate); educational foundations policy/secondary education (MS); educational leadership (MS, Ed D, Sixth Year Certificate); educational technology and media (MS); elementary education (MS, Certificate); marriage and family therapy (MS); physical education (MS, Certificate); professional counseling (MS, Certificate); reading and language arts (MS, Sixth Year Certificate); school counseling (MS); special education (Certificate); special education for special educators (MS); special education for teachers certified in areas other than education (MS); student development in higher education (MS). *Application deadline:* For fall admission, 7/1 for domestic students; for spring admission, 12/1 for domestic students. Applications are processed on a rolling basis. *Application fee:* $50. Electronic applications accepted. *Application Contact:* Dr. Mitchell Sakofs, Dean, 860-832-2100, E-mail: sakofsm@ccsu.edu. *Dean,* Dr. Mitchell Sakofs, 860-832-2100, E-mail: sakofsm@ccsu.edu.

School of Technology Students: 32 full-time (11 women), 119 part-time (18 women); includes 23 minority (4 African Americans, 11 Asian Americans or Pacific Islanders, 8 Hispanic Americans), 4 international. Average age 34. 102 applicants, 76% accepted, 54 enrolled. *Faculty:* 45 full-time (10 women), 27 part-time/adjunct (6 women). Expenses: Contact institution. *Financial support:* In 2008–09, 14 students received support, including 5 research assistantships; career-related internships or fieldwork, Federal Work-Study, scholarships/grants, and unspecified assistantships also available. Support available to part-time students. Financial award application deadline: 3/1; financial award applicants required to submit FAFSA. In 2008, 33 master's, 2 other advanced degrees awarded. *Degree program information:* Part-time and evening/weekend programs available. Offers biomolecular sciences (MA); engineering (MS); technology (MA, MS, Certificate); technology education (MS, Certificate); technology management (MS). *Application deadline:* For fall admission, 7/1 for domestic students; for spring admission, 12/1 for domestic students. Applications are processed on a rolling basis. *Application fee:* $50. Electronic applications accepted. *Application Contact:* Dr. Zdzislaw Kremens, Dean, 860-832-1800. *Dean,* Dr. Zdzislaw Kremens, 860-832-1800.

CENTRAL EUROPEAN UNIVERSITY, H-1051 Budapest, Hungary

General Information Independent, coed, graduate-only institution. *Graduate housing:* Room and/or apartments guaranteed to single students; on-campus housing not available to married students. *Research affiliation:* Institute of Human Sciences Vienna (social sciences), Open Society Institute, NY.

GRADUATE UNITS

CEU Business School *Degree program information:* Part-time and evening/weekend programs available. Offers finance (MBA); general management (MBA); information technology (M Sc); information technology management (MBA); management (EMBA); marketing (MBA); real estate management (MBA). Electronic applications accepted.

Graduate Studies Offers comparative constitutional law (LL M); economic and legal studies (LL M, MA); environmental sciences and policy (MS, PhD); history (MA, PhD); human rights (LL M, MA); international business law (LL M); legal studies (SJD). Electronic applications accepted.

School of Social Sciences and Humanities Offers economics (MA, PhD); gender studies (MA, PhD); international relations and European studies (MA, PhD); mathematics and its applications (MS, PhD); medieval studies (MA, PhD); nationalism studies (MA, PhD); philosophy (MA, PhD); political science (MA, PhD); public policy (MA, PhD); sociology and social anthropology (MA, PhD). Electronic applications accepted.

CENTRAL METHODIST UNIVERSITY, Fayette, MO 65248-1198

General Information Independent-religious, coed, comprehensive institution. *Graduate housing:* Rooms and/or apartments available on a first-come, first-served basis to single and married students. Housing application deadline: 5/1.

GRADUATE UNITS

College of Graduate and Extended Studies *Degree program information:* Part-time and evening/weekend programs available. Postbaccalaureate distance learning degree programs offered (no on-campus study). Electronic applications accepted.

CENTRAL MICHIGAN UNIVERSITY, Mount Pleasant, MI 48859

General Information State-supported, coed, university. CGS member. *Enrollment:* 27,225 graduate, professional, and undergraduate students; 869 full-time matriculated graduate/professional students, 923 part-time matriculated graduate/professional students. *Enrollment by degree level:* 1,387 master's, 405 doctoral. *Graduate faculty:* 349 full-time (134 women), 52 part-time/adjunct (26 women). Tuition, state resident: full-time $3717; part-time $413 per credit. Tuition, nonresident: full-time $6894; part-time $766 per credit. *Graduate housing:* Rooms and/or apartments available on a first-come, first-served basis to single and married students. *Student services:* Campus employment opportunities, campus safety program,

Central Michigan University (continued)

career counseling, exercise/wellness program, free psychological counseling, grant writing training, international student services, low-cost health insurance, multicultural affairs office, services for students with disabilities, teacher training, writing training. *Library facilities:* Charles V. Park Library plus 1 other. *Online resources:* library catalog, web page. *Collection:* 1.1 million titles, 7,711 serial subscriptions. *Research affiliation:* SAP (information technology), IBM (information technology), Dendritic Nanotechnologies Inc (chemistry/physics), Dow Corning Corporation (silicon-based technology), Dow Chemical Company (chemicals and plastics), SAS (business analysis).

Computer facilities: Computer purchase and lease plans are available. 3,000 computers available on campus for general student use. A campuswide network can be accessed from student residence rooms and from off campus. Online class registration, Blackboard are available. *Web address:* http://www.cmich.edu/.

General Application Contact: Judith L. Prince, Director of Graduate Student Services, 989-774-1059, Fax: 989-774-1587, E-mail: judith.l.prince@cmich.edu.

GRADUATE UNITS

Central Michigan University Off-Campus Programs Students: 7,826 part-time (5,267 women); includes 2,159 minority (1,868 African Americans, 47 American Indian/Alaska Native, 108 Asian Americans or Pacific Islanders, 136 Hispanic Americans), 187 international. Average age 37. *Faculty:* 1,362 part-time/adjunct. Expenses: Contact institution. *Financial support:* In 2008–09, 2,925 students received support. Scholarships/grants and tuition waivers (partial) available. Support available to part-time students. Financial award applicants required to submit FAFSA. In 2008, 1,531 master's, 29 doctorates, 124 other advanced degrees awarded. *Degree program information:* Part-time and evening/weekend programs available. Postbaccalaureate distance learning degree programs offered (no on-campus study). Offers acquisitions administration (MSA, Certificate); adult education (MA); community college (MA); education (MA); educational administration (Ed S); educational administration and community leadership (Ed D); general administration (MSA, Certificate); guidance and development (MA); health administration (DHA); health services administration (MSA, Certificate); human resources administration (MSA, Certificate); humanities (MA); information resource management (MSA, Certificate); instructional (MA); international administration (MSA, Certificate); leadership (MSA, Certificate); professional counseling (MA); public administration (MSA, Certificate); public management (MPA); SAP (MBA); school counseling (MA); school principalship (MA); sport administration (MA); state and local government (MPA); value-driven organization (MBA); vehicle design and manufacturing administration (MSA, Certificate). *Application deadline:* Applications are processed on a rolling basis. *Application fee:* $50. Electronic applications accepted. *Application Contact:* Off-Campus Programs Call Center, 877-268-4636, Fax: 989-774-2461, E-mail: cmuoffcampus@cmich.edu. *Vice President and Executive Director,* Dr. Merodie Hancock, 989-774-3865, Fax: 989-774-3542.

College of Graduate Studies Students: 869 full-time (518 women), 923 part-time (532 women); includes 129 minority (53 African Americans, 26 American Indian/Alaska Native, 24 Asian Americans or Pacific Islanders, 26 Hispanic Americans), 259 international. Average age 29. 2,472 applicants, 34% accepted. *Faculty:* 349 full-time (134 women), 52 part-time/adjunct (26 women). Expenses: Contact institution. *Financial support:* Fellowships with full and partial tuition reimbursements, research assistantships with full and partial tuition reimbursements, teaching assistantships with full and partial tuition reimbursements, career-related internships or fieldwork, Federal Work-Study, unspecified assistantships, and out-of-state merit awards available. *Degree program information:* Part-time and evening/weekend programs available. Postbaccalaureate distance learning degree programs offered (no on-campus study). Offers acquisitions administration (MSA, Graduate Certificate); general administration (MSA, Graduate Certificate); health services administration (MSA, Graduate Certificate); human resource administration (Graduate Certificate); human resources administration (MSA); information resource management (MSA, Graduate Certificate); international administration (MSA, Graduate Certificate); leadership (MSA); organizational communication (MSA, Graduate Certificate); public administration (MSA, Graduate Certificate); recreation and park administration (MSA); sport administration (MSA). *Application deadline:* Applications are processed on a rolling basis. *Application fee:* $35 ($45 for international students). Electronic applications accepted. *Application Contact:* Judith L. Prince, Director of Graduate Student Services, 989-774-1059, Fax: 989-774-1857, E-mail: judith.l.prince@cmich.edu. *Interim Dean, College of Graduate Studies,* Dr. Roger Coles, 989-774-6099, Fax: 989-774-3439, E-mail: grad@cmich.edu.

College of Business Administration Students: 120 full-time (35 women), 78 part-time (28 women); includes 13 minority (6 African Americans, 1 American Indian/Alaska Native, 3 Asian Americans or Pacific Islanders, 3 Hispanic Americans), 91 international. Average age 27. *Faculty:* 35 full-time (5 women), 3 part-time/adjunct (2 women). Expenses: Contact institution. *Financial support:* Fellowships with tuition reimbursements, research assistantships with tuition reimbursements, teaching assistantships with tuition reimbursements, career-related internships or fieldwork, Federal Work-Study, unspecified assistantships, and out-of-state merit awards available. *Degree program information:* Part-time and evening/weekend programs available. Offers accounting (MBA); business computing (Graduate Certificate); business economics (MBA); business information systems (MS, Graduate Certificate); economics (MA); finance (MBA); finance and law (MBA); human resource management (MBA); information systems (MS); international business (MBA); management (MBA); management information systems (MBA); management information systems/SAP (MBA); marketing (MBA); marketing and hospitality services administration (MBA). *Application deadline:* Applications are processed on a rolling basis. *Application fee:* $35 ($45 for international students). Electronic applications accepted. *Application Contact:* Dr. Monica Holmes, Associate Dean, 989-774-3337, Fax: 989-774-1329, E-mail: holme1mc@cmich.edu. *Dean,* Dr. Michael Fields, 989-774-3337, Fax: 989-774-1320, E-mail: field1dm@cmich.edu.

College of Communication and Fine Arts Students: 38 full-time (18 women), 58 part-time (33 women); includes 9 minority (3 African Americans, 1 American Indian/Alaska Native, 3 Asian Americans or Pacific Islanders, 2 Hispanic Americans), 2 international. Average age 28. *Faculty:* 64 full-time (24 women), 4 part-time/adjunct (1 woman). Expenses: Contact institution. *Financial support:* Fellowships with tuition reimbursements, research assistantships with tuition reimbursements, teaching assistantships with tuition reimbursements, career-related internships or fieldwork, Federal Work-Study, unspecified assistantships, and out-of-state merit awards available. *Degree program information:* Part-time programs available. Offers communication and fine arts (MA, MM); conducting (MM); electronic media management (MA); electronic media studies (MA); film theory and criticism (MA); interpersonal and public communication (MA); media production (MA); music composition (MM); music education (MM); music performance (MM); piano pedagogy (MM). *Application fee:* $35 ($45 for international students). Electronic applications accepted. *Application Contact:* Judith L. Prince, Director of Graduate Student Services, 989-774-1059, Fax: 989-774-1857, E-mail: judith.l.prince@cmich.edu. *Dean,* Dr. Salma Ghanem, 989-774-1885, Fax: 989-774-1890, E-mail: ghane1si@cmich.edu.

College of Education and Human Services Students: 74 full-time (52 women), 257 part-time (189 women); includes 18 minority (5 African Americans, 7 American Indian/Alaska Native, 1 Asian American or Pacific Islander, 5 Hispanic Americans), 8 international. Average age 32. *Faculty:* 61 full-time (40 women), 18 part-time/adjunct (12 women). Expenses: Contact institution. *Financial support:* Fellowships with tuition reimbursements, research assistantships with tuition reimbursements, teaching assistantships with tuition reimbursements, career-related internships or fieldwork, Federal Work-Study, unspecified assistantships, and out-of-state merit awards available. *Degree program information:* Part-time and evening/weekend programs available. Offers apparel product development and merchandising technology (MS); autism (Graduate Certificate); counseling (MA); education and human services (MA, MS, Ed D, Ed S, Graduate Certificate); educational leadership (MA, Ed D); educational technology (MA); elementary education (MA); general educational administration (Ed S); human development and family studies (MA); middle level education (MA); nutrition and dietetics (MS); reading and literacy K-12 (MA); recreation and park administration (MA); school principalship (MA); secondary education (MA); special education (MA); therapeutic recreation (MA). *Application deadline:* Applications are processed on a rolling basis. *Application fee:* $35 ($45 for international students). Electronic applications accepted. *Application Contact:* Judith L. Prince, Director of Graduate Student Services, 989-774-1059, Fax: 989-774-1857, E-mail: judith.l.prince@cmich.edu. *Interim Dean,* Dr. Kathy Koch, 989-774-6995, Fax: 989-774-1999, E-mail: koch1ke@cmich.edu.

College of Humanities and Social and Behavioral Sciences Students: 161 full-time (82 women), 177 part-time (93 women); includes 20 minority (9 African Americans, 6 American Indian/Alaska Native, 1 Asian American or Pacific Islander, 4 Hispanic Americans), 31 international. Average age 29. *Faculty:* 86 full-time (32 women), 4 part-time/adjunct (2 women). Expenses: Contact institution. *Financial support:* Fellowships with tuition reimbursements, research assistantships with tuition reimbursements, teaching assistantships with tuition reimbursements, career-related internships or fieldwork, Federal Work-Study, unspecified assistantships, and out-of-state merit awards available. *Degree program information:* Part-time and evening/weekend programs available. Offers applied experimental psychology (PhD); clinical psychology (MA, PhD); English composition and communication (MA); English language and literature (MA); European history (Graduate Certificate); experimental psychology (MS, PhD); history (MA, PhD); humanities (MA); humanities and social and behavioral sciences (MA, MPA, MS, PhD, Graduate Certificate, S Psy S); industrial and organizational psychology (MA, PhD); modern history (Graduate Certificate); neuroscience (MS, PhD); political science (MA); professional development in public administration (Graduate Certificate); psychological services (S Psy S); public administration (MPA, Graduate Certificate); public management (MPA); school psychology (PhD, S Psy S); Spanish (MA); state and local government (MPA); teaching English to speakers of other languages (TESOL) (MA); United States history (Graduate Certificate). *Application deadline:* Applications are processed on a rolling basis. *Application fee:* $35 ($45 for international students). Electronic applications accepted. *Application Contact:* Judith L. Prince, Director of Graduate Student Services, 989-774-1059, Fax: 989-774-1857, E-mail: judith.l.prince@cmich.edu. *Dean,* Dr. Gary Shapiro, 989-774-3341, Fax: 989-774-7106, E-mail: gary.shapiro@cmich.edu.

College of Science and Technology Students: 50 full-time (20 women), 131 part-time (49 women); includes 9 minority (3 African Americans, 2 American Indian/Alaska Native, 3 Asian Americans or Pacific Islanders, 1 Hispanic American), 75 international. Average age 29. *Faculty:* 68 full-time (15 women), 8 part-time/adjunct (2 women). Expenses: Contact institution. *Financial support:* Fellowships with tuition reimbursements, research assistantships with tuition reimbursements, teaching assistantships with tuition reimbursements, career-related internships or fieldwork, Federal Work-Study, unspecified assistantships, and out-of-state merit awards available. *Degree program information:* Part-time and evening/weekend programs available. Offers biology (MS); chemistry (MS); computer science (MS); conservation biology (MS); industrial management and technology (MA); mathematics (MA, PhD); physics (MS); science and technology (MA, MS, PhD, Graduate Certificate); science of advanced materials (PhD); teaching chemistry (MA). *Application deadline:* Applications are processed on a rolling basis. *Application fee:* $35 ($45 for international students). Electronic applications accepted. *Application Contact:* Judith L. Prince, Director of Graduate Student Services, 989-774-1059, Fax: 989-774-1857, E-mail: judith.l.prince@cmich.edu. *Dean,* Dr. Ian R. Davison, 989-774-1870, Fax: 989-774-1874, E-mail: davis1ir@cmich.edu.

The Herbert H. and Grace A. Dow College of Health Professions Students: 321 full-time (257 women), 37 part-time (20 women); includes 19 minority (5 African Americans, 3 American Indian/Alaska Native, 8 Asian Americans or Pacific Islanders, 3 Hispanic Americans), 14 international. Average age 26. *Faculty:* 45 full-time (18 women), 11 part-time/adjunct (7 women). Expenses: Contact institution. *Financial support:* Fellowships with tuition reimbursements, research assistantships with tuition reimbursements, teaching assistantships with tuition reimbursements, career-related internships or fieldwork, Federal Work-Study, unspecified assistantships, and out-of-state merit awards available. Offers audiology (Au D); health professions (MA, MS, Au D, DHA, DPT); health sciences (DHA); physical education (MA); physical therapy (DPT); physician assistant (MS); speech-language pathology (MA); sport education (MA). *Application fee:* $35 ($45 for international students). Electronic applications accepted. *Application Contact:* Clint Fitzpatrick, Director of Admissions and Enrollment Management, 989-774-1730, Fax: 989-774-2223, E-mail: fitzp1tc@cmich.edu. *Dean,* Dr. Chris Ingersoll, 989-774-1850, Fax: 989-774-1853, E-mail: inger1c@cmich.edu.

CENTRAL STATE UNIVERSITY, Wilberforce, OH 45384

General Information State-supported, coed, comprehensive institution. *Graduate housing:* Room and/or apartments available on a first-come, first-served basis to single students; on-campus housing not available to married students. Housing application deadline: 6/15.

GRADUATE UNITS

Program in Education *Degree program information:* Part-time and evening/weekend programs available. Offers education (M Ed).

CENTRAL WASHINGTON UNIVERSITY, Ellensburg, WA 98926

General Information State-supported, coed, comprehensive institution. CGS member. *Graduate housing:* Rooms and/or apartments available on a first-come, first-served basis to single and married students. *Research affiliation:* East-West Center (Pacific area studies), Associated Western Universities (science and engineering), JPL.

GRADUATE UNITS

Graduate Studies, Research and Continuing Education *Degree program information:* Part-time and evening/weekend programs available. Offers individual studies (M Ed, MA, MS). Electronic applications accepted.

College of Arts and Humanities *Degree program information:* Part-time programs available. Offers art (MA, MFA); arts and humanities (MA, MFA, MM); English (MA); history (MA); music (MM); teaching English as a second language (MA); theatre production (MA). Electronic applications accepted.

College of Business *Degree program information:* Part-time programs available. Offers accounting (MPA); business (MPA). Electronic applications accepted.

College of Education and Professional Studies *Degree program information:* Part-time programs available. Offers education and professional studies (M Ed, MS); engineering technology (MS); family and consumer sciences education (MS); family studies (MS); health, physical education and nutrition (MS); master teacher (M Ed); nutrition (MS); reading education (M Ed); special education (M Ed). Electronic applications accepted.

College of the Sciences *Degree program information:* Part-time and evening/weekend programs available. Offers biological sciences (MS); chemistry (MS); experimental psychology (MS); geological sciences (MS); mathematics (MAT); mental health counseling (MS); resource management (MS); school counseling (M Ed); school psychology (M Ed); sciences (M Ed, MAT, MS). Electronic applications accepted.

Announcement: CWU's mission is to enable graduate students to competently confront the complexities of modern global society and to prepare them for successful careers as well as for independent, lifelong learning. CWU provides high-quality graduate programs in selected fields, taught by faculty members dedicated to excellence in teaching and research. Classes are small, and the opportunity to work closely with professors is a hallmark of CWU, as is hands-on research activity. The University is located in an attractive and safe community on the eastern slopes of the Cascade Mountains, 2 hours from Seattle by car.

See Close-Up on page 867.

CENTRAL YESHIVA TOMCHEI TMIMIM-LUBAVITCH, Brooklyn, NY 11230

General Information Independent-religious, men only, comprehensive institution.

GRADUATE UNITS

Graduate Programs

CENTRO DE ESTUDIOS AVANZADOS DE PUERTO RICO Y EL CARIBE, Old San Juan, PR 00902-3970

General Information Independent, coed, graduate-only institution. *Graduate housing:* On-campus housing not available. *Research affiliation:* Museo de las Americas, Museo Hombre Dominicano (Santo Domingo), Archivo General, Museo Universidad del Turabo.

GRADUATE UNITS

Graduate Program in Puerto Rican and Caribbean Studies *Degree program information:* Part-time and evening/weekend programs available. Offers Puerto Rican and Caribbean history (MA, PhD); Puerto Rican and Caribbean literature (MA, PhD); Puerto Rican studies (MA).

CHADRON STATE COLLEGE, Chadron, NE 69337

General Information State-supported, coed, comprehensive institution. *Graduate housing:* Rooms and/or apartments available on a first-come, first-served basis to single and married students. Housing application deadline: 6/1.

GRADUATE UNITS

School of Professional and Graduate Studies *Degree program information:* Part-time and evening/weekend programs available. Postbaccalaureate distance learning degree programs offered (minimal on-campus study). Offers business (MA Ed); business and economics (MBA); community counseling (MA Ed); educational administration (MS Ed, Sp Ed); elementary education (MS Ed); history (MA Ed); language and literature (MA Ed); secondary administration (MS Ed); secondary education (MS Ed). Electronic applications accepted.

CHAMINADE UNIVERSITY OF HONOLULU, Honolulu, HI 96816-1578

General Information Independent-religious, coed, comprehensive institution. *Graduate housing:* On-campus housing not available.

GRADUATE UNITS

Graduate Services *Degree program information:* Part-time and evening/weekend programs available. Offers business administration (MBA); counseling psychology (MSCP); criminal justice administration (MSCJA); forensic science (MSFS); homeland security (Certificate); pastoral leadership (MAPL); pastoral theology (MPT); social science via peace education (M Ed). Electronic applications accepted.

CHAMPLAIN COLLEGE, Burlington, VT 05402-0670

General Information Independent, coed, comprehensive institution. CGS member.

GRADUATE UNITS

Program in Managing Innovation and Information Technology *Degree program information:* Part-time programs available. Postbaccalaureate distance learning degree programs offered (no on-campus study). Offers management of technology (MS). Electronic applications accepted.

CHANCELLOR UNIVERSITY, Cleveland, OH 44114-4624

General Information Independent, coed, comprehensive institution. *Graduate housing:* On-campus housing not available.

GRADUATE UNITS

Charles R. McDonald School of Business *Degree program information:* Part-time and evening/weekend programs available. Postbaccalaureate distance learning degree programs offered (no on-campus study). Offers business (MBA, MMG).

CHAPMAN UNIVERSITY, Orange, CA 92866

General Information Independent-religious, coed, comprehensive institution. *Enrollment:* 6,128 graduate, professional, and undergraduate students; 1,256 full-time matriculated graduate/professional students (675 women), 569 part-time matriculated graduate/professional students (363 women). *Enrollment by degree level:* 544 first professional, 1,022 master's, 172 doctoral, 87 other advanced degrees. *Graduate faculty:* 198 full-time (71 women), 148 part-time/adjunct (54 women). *Tuition:* Full-time $11,970; part-time $665 per credit. *Required fees:* $456; $456 per year. Tuition and fees vary according to course load, degree level and program. *Graduate housing:* Rooms and/or apartments available on a first-come, first-served basis to single and married students. Typical cost: $11,355 (including board) for single students. Room and board charges vary according to board plan and housing facility selected. Housing application deadline: 6/1. *Student services:* Campus employment opportunities, campus safety program, career counseling, exercise/wellness program, free psychological counseling, grant writing training, international student services, low-cost health insurance, services for students with disabilities, teacher training, writing training. *Library facilities:* Leatherby Libraries plus 1 other. *Online resources:* library catalog, web page, access to other libraries' catalogs. *Collection:* 238,260 titles, 35,884 serial subscriptions, 13,127 audiovisual materials. *Research affiliation:* National Science Foundation (NSF) (science/engineering), US Department of Education (DOE) (education), US Geological Survey (USGS) (earth sciences), National Endowment for the Arts (NEA) (art), US Department of Agriculture (USDA) (agriculture/food/nutrition).

Computer facilities: Computer purchase and lease plans are available. 453 computers available on campus for general student use. A campuswide network can be accessed from student residence rooms and from off campus. Online class registration is available. *Web address:* http://www.chapman.edu/.

General Application Contact: Saundra Hoover, Director of Graduate Admissions, 714-997-6786, Fax: 714-997-6713, E-mail: shoover@chapman.edu.

GRADUATE UNITS

Graduate Studies Students: 1,256 full-time (675 women), 569 part-time (363 women); includes 430 minority (29 African Americans, 8 American Indian/Alaska Native, 207 Asian Americans or Pacific Islanders, 186 Hispanic Americans), 99 international. Average age 28. 3,691 applicants, 37% accepted, 646 enrolled. *Faculty:* 198 full-time (71 women), 148 part-time/adjunct (54 women). Expenses: Contact institution. *Financial support:* Fellowships, Federal Work-Study and scholarships/grants available. Financial award application deadline: 6/30; financial award applicants required to submit FAFSA. In 2008, 182 first professional degrees, 380 master's, 39 doctorates awarded. *Degree program information:* Part-time and evening/weekend programs available. *Application deadline:* Applications are processed on a rolling basis. *Application fee:* $55. Electronic applications accepted. *Application Contact:* Saundra Hoover, Director of Graduate Admissions, 714-997-6786, Fax: 714-997-6713, E-mail: shoover@chapman.edu. *Associate Provost,* Dr. Raymond Sfeir, 714-997-6733, Fax: 714-628-7358, E-mail: sfeir@chapman.edu.

College of Educational Studies Students: 223 full-time (193 women), 239 part-time (188 women); includes 151 minority (7 African Americans, 1 American Indian/Alaska Native, 41 Asian Americans or Pacific Islanders, 102 Hispanic Americans), 2 international. Average age 30. 219 applicants, 72% accepted, 126 enrolled. *Faculty:* 20 full-time (13 women), 24 part-time/adjunct (17 women). Expenses: Contact institution. *Financial support:* Fellowships, Federal Work-Study and scholarships/grants available. Financial award application deadline: 6/30; financial award applicants required to submit FAFSA. In 2008, 140 master's awarded. *Degree program information:* Part-time and evening/weekend programs available. Offers administrative services (Tier I) (Credential); communication sciences and disorders (MS); curriculum and instruction (MA); education: cultural and curricular studies (PhD); education: disability studies (PhD); education: school psychology (PhD); educational leadership and administration (MA); educational psychology (MA, Ed S); multiple subjects (Credential); multiple subjects with bilingual emphasis (Credential); professional clear (Ryan 5th year) (Credential); pupil personnel services school counseling (Credential); pupil personnel services school psychology (Credential); reading Certificate (Credential); reading education (MA); school counseling (MA); school psychology (Ed S); single subject (Credential); special education (MA); special education level I mild/moderate (Credential); special education level I moderate/severe (Credential); special education level II mild/moderate (Credential); special education level II moderate/severe (Credential); teaching: elementary education (MA); teaching: secondary education (MA). Credentials are conferred by the State of California upon verification by Chapman of completion of all requirements. *Application deadline:* Applications are processed on a rolling basis. *Application fee:* $50. Electronic applications accepted. *Application Contact:* Brianna Keitel, Admissions Coordinator, 714-997-6714, E-mail: keitel@chapman.edu. *Dean,* Dr. Don Cardinal, 714-997-6781, E-mail: cardinal@chapman.edu.

Dodge College of Film and Media Arts Students: 210 full-time (74 women), 10 part-time (2 women); includes 32 minority (7 African Americans, 2 American Indian/Alaska Native, 8 Asian Americans or Pacific Islanders, 15 Hispanic Americans), 38 international. Average age 27. 319 applicants, 50% accepted, 94 enrolled. *Faculty:* 35 full-time (5 women), 48 part-time/adjunct (14 women). Expenses: Contact institution. *Financial support:* Fellowships, Federal Work-Study and scholarships/grants available. Financial award application deadline: 6/30; financial award applicants required to submit FAFSA. In 2008, 93 master's awarded. *Degree program information:* Part-time and evening/weekend programs available. Offers film and media arts (MA, MFA); film and television producing (MFA); film production (MFA); film studies (MA); production design (MFA); screenwriting (MFA). *Application deadline:* For fall admission, 2/1 priority date for domestic students. *Application fee:* $55. Electronic applications accepted. *Application Contact:* Alexandra Rose, Chair, Graduate Conservatory, 714-744-7941, E-mail: arose@chapman.edu. *Dean,* Robert Bassett, 714-997-6765, E-mail: bassett@chapman.edu.

The George L. Argyros School of Business and Economics Students: 136 full-time (42 women), 97 part-time (28 women); includes 56 minority (1 African American, 33 Asian Americans or Pacific Islanders, 22 Hispanic Americans), 29 international. Average age 29. 173 applicants, 83% accepted, 92 enrolled. *Faculty:* 50 full-time (11 women), 16 part-time/adjunct (6 women). Expenses: Contact institution. *Financial support:* Fellowships, Federal Work-Study and scholarships/grants available. Financial award application deadline: 6/30; financial award applicants required to submit FAFSA. In 2008, 78 master's awarded. *Degree program information:* Part-time and evening/weekend programs available. Offers business and economics (Exec MBA, MBA). *Application deadline:* For fall admission, 2/1 priority date for domestic students; for spring admission, 10/15 priority date for domestic students. *Application fee:* $50. Electronic applications accepted. *Application Contact:* Debra Gonda, Associate Dean, 714-997-6894, E-mail: gonda@chapman.edu. *Dean,* Dr. Arthur Kraft, 714-997-6684.

Schmid College of Science Students: 143 full-time (109 women), 89 part-time (66 women); includes 61 minority (7 African Americans, 3 American Indian/Alaska Native, 40 Asian Americans or Pacific Islanders, 11 Hispanic Americans), 24 international. Average age 27. 402 applicants, 45% accepted, 84 enrolled. *Faculty:* 25 full-time (14 women), 6 part-time/adjunct (3 women). Expenses: Contact institution. *Financial support:* Fellowships, Federal Work-Study and scholarships/grants available. Financial award application deadline: 6/30; financial award applicants required to submit FAFSA. In 2008, 28 master's, 39 doctorates awarded. *Degree program information:* Part-time programs available. Offers food science (MS); health communication (MS); marriage and family therapy (MA); physical therapy (DPT); science (MA, MS, DPT). *Application fee:* $50. *Application Contact:* Saundra Hoover, Director of Graduate Admissions, 714-997-6786, Fax: 714-997-6713, E-mail: shoover@chapman.edu. *Interim Dean,* Dr. Janeen Hill, 714-628-7223, E-mail: jhill@chapman.edu.

School of Law Students: 514 full-time (238 women), 97 part-time (51 women); includes 123 minority (6 African Americans, 1 American Indian/Alaska Native, 82 Asian Americans or Pacific Islanders, 34 Hispanic Americans), 8 international. Average age 27. 2,521 applicants, 27% accepted, 225 enrolled. *Faculty:* 50 full-time (20 women), 32 part-time/adjunct (4 women). Expenses: Contact institution. *Financial support:* Fellowships, Federal Work-Study and scholarships/grants available. Financial award application deadline: 6/30; financial award applicants required to submit FAFSA. In 2008, 182 JDs, 13 master's awarded. *Degree program information:* Part-time and evening/weekend programs available. Offers advocacy and dispute resolution (JD); entertainment law (JD); environmental, land use, and real estate (JD); international law (JD); law (LL M); prosecutorial science (LL M); tax law (JD); taxation (LL M). *Application deadline:* For fall admission, 4/1 priority date for domestic students. Applications are processed on a rolling basis. *Application fee:* $65. Electronic applications accepted. *Application Contact:* Marissa Vargas, Admissions Recruiter/Financial Aid Counselor, 877-CHAPLAW, E-mail: mvargas@chapman.edu. *Dean,* Dr. John Eastman, 714-628-2500.

Wilkinson College of Humanities and Social Sciences Students: 40 full-time (21 women), 37 part-time (28 women); includes 7 minority (1 African American, 1 American Indian/Alaska Native, 3 Asian Americans or Pacific Islanders, 2 Hispanic Americans). Average age 30. 57 applicants, 67% accepted, 25 enrolled. *Faculty:* 18 full-time (8 women), 22 part-time/adjunct (10 women). Expenses: Contact institution. *Financial support:* Fellowships, Federal Work-Study and scholarships/grants available. Financial award application deadline: 3/2; financial award applicants required to submit FAFSA. In 2008, 28 master's awarded. *Degree program information:* Part-time and evening/weekend programs available. Offers creative writing (MFA); English (MA); humanities and social sciences (MA, MFA); international studies (MA). *Application deadline:* For fall admission, 5/1 priority date for domestic students. *Application fee:* $50. *Application Contact:* Saundra Hoover, Director of Graduate Admissions, 714-997-6786, Fax: 714-997-6713, E-mail: shoover@chapman.edu. *Dean,* Dr. Roberta Lessor, 714-997-6947, E-mail: lessor@chapman.edu.

See Close-Up on page 869.

CHARLES R. DREW UNIVERSITY OF MEDICINE AND SCIENCE, Los Angeles, CA 90059

General Information Independent, coed, comprehensive institution. *Graduate housing:* On-campus housing not available.

GRADUATE UNITS

College of Science and Health

Professional Program in Medicine Offers medicine (MD).

CHARLESTON SOUTHERN UNIVERSITY, Charleston, SC 29423-8087

General Information Independent-religious, coed, comprehensive institution. *Enrollment:* 22 full-time matriculated graduate/professional students (10 women), 387 part-time matriculated graduate/professional students (223 women). *Enrollment by degree level:* 409 master's. *Graduate faculty:* 19 full-time (5 women), 6 part-time/adjunct (2 women). *Tuition:* Full-time $8832; part-time $368 per credit hour. *Required fees:* $30. One-time fee: $30. Tuition and fees vary according to course load and program. *Graduate housing:* On-campus housing not available. *Student services:* Campus employment opportunities, campus safety program, career counseling, free psychological counseling, international student services, services for students with disabilities. *Library facilities:* L. Mendel Rivers Library. *Online resources:* library catalog, web page, access to other libraries' catalogs. *Collection:* 192,600 titles, 1,111 serial subscriptions. *Research affiliation:* Santee Lynches Council of Governments (economic forecasting), Waccamaw Regional Planning and Development Council (economic forecasting), Metro Charleston Chamber of Commerce (economic forecasting).

Computer facilities: 250 computers available on campus for general student use. A campuswide network can be accessed from student residence rooms and from off campus. Online class registration, online course work are available. *Web address:* http://www.charlestonsouthern.edu/.

General Application Contact: Alison Harrison, Graduate Enrollment Counselor, 843-863-7534, Fax: 843-863-7070, E-mail: aharrison@csuniv.edu.

GRADUATE UNITS

Department of Criminal Justice Students: 6 full-time (2 women), 20 part-time (13 women); includes 8 minority (7 African Americans, 1 Hispanic American), 1 international. Average age 31. 18 applicants, 72% accepted, 12 enrolled. *Faculty:* 2 full-time (both women), 1 part-time/adjunct. Expenses: Contact institution. *Financial support:* Research assistantships with full

Charleston Southern University (continued)

tuition reimbursements available. Financial award application deadline: 4/15; financial award applicants required to submit FAFSA. *Degree program information:* Part-time and evening/weekend programs available. Offers criminal justice (MSCJ). *Application deadline:* Applications are processed on a rolling basis. *Application fee:* $30. *Application Contact:* Alison Harrison, Graduate Enrollment Counselor, 843-863-7534, Fax: 843-863-7070, E-mail: aharrison@csuniv.edu. *Chair*, Dr. Jacqueline Fish, 843-863-7131, Fax: 843-863-7198, E-mail: jfish@csuniv.edu.

Program in Business Students: 14 full-time (6 women), 297 part-time (155 women); includes 82 minority (73 African Americans, 2 American Indian/Alaska Native, 4 Asian Americans or Pacific Islanders, 3 Hispanic Americans), 16 international. Average age 32. 133 applicants, 88% accepted, 85 enrolled. *Faculty:* 13 full-time (1 woman), 5 part-time/adjunct (1 woman). Expenses: Contact institution. *Financial support:* Research assistantships with full tuition reimbursements available. Financial award application deadline: 4/15; financial award applicants required to submit FAFSA. *Degree program information:* Part-time and evening/weekend programs available. Offers accounting (MBA); finance (MBA); health care administration (MBA); information systems (MBA); organizational development (MBA). *Application deadline:* Applications are processed on a rolling basis. *Application fee:* $30. *Application Contact:* Alison Harrison, Graduate Enrollment Counselor, 843-863-7534, Fax: 843-863-7070, E-mail: aharrison@cusniv.edu. *Director of the MBA Program*, Dr. Scott Pearson, 843-863-7038, Fax: 843-863-7922, E-mail: spearson@csuniv.edu.

School of Education Students: 2 full-time (both women), 70 part-time (55 women); includes 20 minority (18 African Americans, 1 Asian American or Pacific Islander, 1 Hispanic American). Average age 34. 46 applicants, 85% accepted, 24 enrolled. *Faculty:* 5 full-time (3 women), 1 (woman) part-time/adjunct. Expenses: Contact institution. *Financial support:* Research assistantships with full tuition reimbursements, career-related internships or fieldwork and Federal Work-Study available. Financial award application deadline: 4/15; financial award applicants required to submit FAFSA. *Degree program information:* Part-time and evening/weekend programs available. Offers administration and supervision (M Ed); elementary education (M Ed); secondary education (M Ed). *Application deadline:* Applications are processed on a rolling basis. *Application fee:* $30. *Application Contact:* Alison Harrison, Graduate Enrollment Counselor, 843-863-7534, Fax: 843-863-7070, E-mail: aharrison@cwuniv.edu. *Dean*, Dr. Norma Harper, 843-863-7765, Fax: 843-863-7085, E-mail: nharper@csuniv.edu.

CHARLOTTE SCHOOL OF LAW, Charlotte, NC 28204

General Information Independent, coed, graduate-only institution. *Enrollment by degree level:* 310 first professional. *Graduate faculty:* 22 full-time (10 women), 11 part-time/adjunct (6 women). *Tuition:* Full-time $28,620; part-time $11,448 per semester. *Required fees:* $1348; $674 per semester. *Student services:* Campus employment opportunities, campus safety program, career counseling, services for students with disabilities, writing training. *Library facilities:* Charlotte School of Law, Law Library. *Online resources:* library catalog, web page, access to other libraries' catalogs. *Collection:* 45,000 titles, 9,650 serial subscriptions, 100 audiovisual materials.

Computer facilities: 50 computers available on campus for general student use. A campuswide network can be accessed from off campus. Online class registration is available. *Web address:* http://www.charlottelaw.org/.

General Application Contact: Carrie Mansfield, Admissions Recruiter, 704-971-8541, Fax: 704-971-8599, E-mail: admissions@charlottelaw.edu.

GRADUATE UNITS

Professional Program Students: 243 full-time (124 women), 67 part-time (25 women). *Faculty:* 22 full-time (10 women), 11 part-time/adjunct (6 women). Expenses: Contact institution. Offers law (JD). *Application Contact:* Carrie Mansfield, Admissions Recruiter, 704-971-8541, Fax: 704-971-8599, E-mail: admissions@charlottelaw.edu. *Dean*, Dennis Stone, 704-971-8515, E-mail: dstone@charlottelaw.edu.

CHATHAM UNIVERSITY, Pittsburgh, PA 15232-2826

General Information Independent, Undergraduate: women only; graduate: coed, university. CGS member. *Enrollment:* 2,184 graduate, professional, and undergraduate students; 633 full-time matriculated graduate/professional students (506 women), 447 part-time matriculated graduate/professional students (351 women). *Enrollment by degree level:* 832 master's, 248 doctoral. *Graduate faculty:* 88 full-time, 79 part-time/adjunct. *Tuition:* Part-time $686 per credit. Tuition and fees vary according to program. *Graduate housing:* Rooms and/or apartments available on a first-come, first-served basis to single and married students. *Student services:* Campus employment opportunities, campus safety program, career counseling, exercise/wellness program, free psychological counseling, international student services, low-cost health insurance, teacher training, writing training. *Library facilities:* Jennie King Mellon Library. *Online resources:* library catalog, web page, access to other libraries' catalogs. *Collection:* 90,780 titles, 365 serial subscriptions, 1,205 audiovisual materials.

Computer facilities: 250 computers available on campus for general student use. A campuswide network can be accessed from student residence rooms and from off campus. Online class registration is available. *Web address:* http://www.chatham.edu/.

General Application Contact: Michael May, Director of Graduate Admissions, 412-365-1141, Fax: 412-365-1609, E-mail: gradadmissions@chatham.edu.

GRADUATE UNITS

Program in Accounting Students: 8 full-time (3 women), 8 part-time (7 women). Average age 38. 21 applicants, 71% accepted, 9 enrolled. Expenses: Contact institution. *Financial support:* Applicants required to submit FAFSA. *Degree program information:* Part-time and evening/weekend programs available. Offers accounting (M Acc). *Application deadline:* For fall admission, 7/1 for domestic students, 6/1 for international students; for spring admission, 12/1 for domestic students, 11/1 for international students. Applications are processed on a rolling basis. *Application fee:* $45. Electronic applications accepted. *Application Contact:* Michael May, Director of Graduate Admissions, 412-365-1141, Fax: 412-365-1609, E-mail: gradadmissions@chatham.edu.

Program in Biology Students: 11 full-time (7 women), 8 part-time (6 women). Average age 26. 30 applicants, 70% accepted, 9 enrolled. Expenses: Contact institution. *Financial support:* Applicants required to submit FAFSA. In 2008, 8 master's awarded. *Degree program information:* Part-time programs available. Offers environmental biology-non-thesis track (MS); environmental biology-thesis track (MS); human biology-non-thesis track (MS); human biology-thesis track (MS). *Application deadline:* For fall admission, 5/1 priority date for domestic and international students; for spring admission, 11/1 priority date for domestic and international students. Applications are processed on a rolling basis. *Application fee:* $45. Electronic applications accepted. *Application Contact:* Maureen Stokan, Assistant Director of Graduate Admissions, 412-365-2988, Fax: 412-365-1609, E-mail: gradadmissions@chatham.edu. *Director*, Dr. Lisa Lambert, 412-365-1217, E-mail: lambert@chatham.edu.

Program in Business Administration Students: 29 full-time (21 women), 50 part-time (43 women). Average age 32. 79 applicants, 58% accepted, 28 enrolled. Expenses: Contact institution. *Financial support:* Applicants required to submit FAFSA. In 2008, 21 master's awarded. *Degree program information:* Part-time and evening/weekend programs available. Offers business administration (MBA); healthcare professionals (MBA). *Application deadline:* For fall admission, 7/1 for domestic students, 6/1 for international students; for spring admission, 12/1 for domestic students, 11/1 for international students. Applications are processed on a rolling basis. *Application fee:* $45. Electronic applications accepted. *Application Contact:* Michael May, Director of Graduate Admissions, 412-365-1141, Fax: 412-365-1609, E-mail: gradadmissions@chatham.edu.

Program in Counseling Psychology Students: 121 full-time (104 women), 72 part-time (63 women). Average age 30. 117 applicants, 79% accepted, 60 enrolled. Expenses: Contact institution. *Financial support:* Career-related internships or fieldwork available. Financial award applicants required to submit FAFSA. In 2008, 63 master's awarded. *Degree program information:* Part-time and evening/weekend programs available. Offers child, adolescent and family (MSCP); counseling psychology (Psy D); health and holistic (MSCP); infant mental health (MSCP); organization and supervision (MSCP); sport and exercise (MSCP). *Application deadline:* For fall admission, 5/1 priority date for domestic and international students; for spring admission, 10/15 for domestic students, 10/15 priority date for international students. Applications are processed on a rolling basis. *Application fee:* $45. Electronic applications accepted. *Application Contact:* Dory Perry, Associate Director of Graduate Admissions, 412-365-2758, Fax: 412-365-1609, E-mail: gradadmissions@chatham.edu. *Director*, Dr. Mary Beth Mannarino, 412-365-1196, Fax: 412-365-1505, E-mail: mmannarino@chatham.edu.

Program in Education Students: 53 full-time (41 women), 29 part-time (27 women). Average age 30. 45 applicants, 80% accepted, 29 enrolled. Expenses: Contact institution. *Financial support:* Career-related internships or fieldwork available. Financial award applicants required to submit FAFSA. In 2008, 37 master's awarded. Offers early childhood education (MAT); elementary education (MAT); English—secondary (MAT); environmental education (K-12) (MAT); secondary art (MAT); secondary biology education (MAT); secondary chemistry education (MAT); secondary English education (MAT); secondary math education (MAT); secondary physics education (MAT); secondary social studies education (MAT); special education (MAT). *Application deadline:* For fall admission, 5/1 priority date for domestic and international students; for spring admission, 10/15 priority date for domestic and international students. Applications are processed on a rolling basis. *Application fee:* $45. Electronic applications accepted. *Application Contact:* Dory Perry, Associate Director of Graduate Admissions, 412-365-2758, Fax: 412-365-1609, E-mail: gradadmissions@chatham.edu. *Director*, Dr. Tracey Johnson, 412-365-1285, Fax: 412-365-1647, E-mail: tjohnson@chatham.edu.

Program in Film and Digital Technology Students: 9 full-time (6 women), 2 part-time (0 women). Average age 35. 16 applicants, 88% accepted, 10 enrolled. Expenses: Contact institution. *Financial support:* Applicants required to submit FAFSA. *Degree program information:* Part-time and evening/weekend programs available. Offers emerging media (MFA). *Application deadline:* For fall admission, 7/1 priority date for domestic students, 6/1 priority date for international students; for spring admission, 12/1 priority date for domestic students, 11/1 priority date for international students. Applications are processed on a rolling basis. *Application fee:* $45. Electronic applications accepted. *Application Contact:* Dory Perry, Associate Director of Graduate Admissions, 412-365-2758, Fax: 412-365-1609, E-mail: gradadmissions@chatham.edu. *Director*, Dr. Prajna Parasher, 412-365-1182, E-mail: parasher@chatham.edu.

Program in Health Science Students: 6 full-time (5 women), 13 part-time (9 women). Average age 37. 13 applicants, 46% accepted, 5 enrolled. Expenses: Contact institution. *Degree program information:* Part-time and evening/weekend programs available. Postbaccalaureate distance learning degree programs offered (no on-campus study). Offers health science (MHS). *Application deadline:* Applications are processed on a rolling basis. *Application fee:* $0. Electronic applications accepted. *Application Contact:* College for Continuing and Professional Studies, 866-815-2050, Fax: 412-365-1720, E-mail: ccps@chatham.edu. *Dean, College of Continuing Education and Professional Studies*, Dr. Janet Littrell, 412-365-1147, E-mail: jlittrel@chatham.edu.

Program in Interior Architecture Students: 24 full-time (20 women), 9 part-time (8 women). Average age 34. 25 applicants, 80% accepted, 11 enrolled. Expenses: Contact institution. *Financial support:* Applicants required to submit FAFSA. In 2008, 6 master's awarded. *Degree program information:* Part-time and evening/weekend programs available. Postbaccalaureate distance learning degree programs offered (no on-campus study). Offers interior architecture (MIA, MSIA). *Application deadline:* For fall admission, 7/1 priority date for domestic students, 6/1 priority date for international students; for spring admission, 12/1 priority date for domestic students, 11/1 priority date for international students. Applications are processed on a rolling basis. *Application fee:* $45. Electronic applications accepted. *Application Contact:* Michael May, Director of Graduate Admissions, 412-365-1141, Fax: 412-365-1609, E-mail: gradadmissions@chatham.edu. *Director*, Prof. Lori Anthony, 412-365-2977, E-mail: lanthony@chatham.edu.

Program in Landscape Architecture Students: 14 full-time (9 women), 19 part-time (12 women). Average age 35. 26 applicants, 65% accepted, 10 enrolled. Expenses: Contact institution. *Financial support:* Career-related internships or fieldwork available. Financial award applicants required to submit FAFSA. In 2008, 6 master's awarded. *Degree program information:* Part-time and evening/weekend programs available. Offers landscape architecture (ML Arch); landscape studies (MA). *Application deadline:* For fall admission, 7/1 priority date for domestic students, 6/1 priority date for international students; for spring admission, 12/1 priority date for domestic students, 11/1 priority date for international students. Applications are processed on a rolling basis. *Application fee:* $45. Electronic applications accepted. *Application Contact:* Michael May, Director of Graduate Admissions, 412-365-1825, Fax: 412-365-1609, E-mail: gradadmissions@chatham.edu. *Director*, Prof. Lisa Kunst Vavaro, 412-365-1882, E-mail: lvavro@chatham.edu.

Program in Nursing Students: 47 full-time (40 women), 57 part-time (50 women). Average age 45. 48 applicants, 79% accepted, 28 enrolled. Expenses: Contact institution. *Financial support:* Applicants required to submit FAFSA. Offers education/leadership (MSN); nursing (DNP). *Application deadline:* For fall admission, 5/1 priority date for domestic and international students. Applications are processed on a rolling basis. *Application fee:* $45. Electronic applications accepted. *Application Contact:* Dory Perry, Associate Director of Graduate Admissions, 412-365-2758, Fax: 412-365-1609, E-mail: gradadmissions@chatham.edu. *Director*, Dr. Carol Patton, 412-365-2726, E-mail: cpatton@chatham.edu.

Program in Occupational Therapy Students: 47 full-time (40 women), 15 part-time (13 women). Average age 34. 60 applicants, 45% accepted, 24 enrolled. Expenses: Contact institution. *Financial support:* Applicants required to submit FAFSA. Offers occupational therapy (MOT, OTD). *Application deadline:* For fall admission, 5/1 priority date for domestic and international students. Applications are processed on a rolling basis. *Application fee:* $45. Electronic applications accepted. *Application Contact:* Dory Perry, Associate Director of Graduate Admissions, 412-365-2758, Fax: 412-365-1609, E-mail: gradadmissions@chatham.edu. *Director*, Dr. Joyce Salls, 412-365-1177, E-mail: salls@chatham.edu.

Program in Physical Therapy Students: 83 full-time (64 women), 51 part-time (29 women). Average age 30. 169 applicants, 49% accepted, 30 enrolled. Expenses: Contact institution. *Financial support:* Career-related internships or fieldwork available. Financial award applicants required to submit FAFSA. In 2008, 28 doctorates awarded. Offers physical therapy (DPT, TDPT). *Application deadline:* For fall admission, 12/1 priority date for domestic and international students. *Application fee:* $45. *Application Contact:* Maureen Stokan, Assistant Director of Graduate Admissions, 412-365-2988, Fax: 412-365-1609, E-mail: gradadmissions@chatham.edu. *Director*, Dr. Patricia Downey, 412-365-1199, Fax: 412-365-1505, E-mail: downey@chatham.edu.

Program in Physician Assistant Studies Students: 98 full-time (87 women), 1 (woman) part-time. Average age 25. 508 applicants, 18% accepted, 54 enrolled. Expenses: Contact institution. *Financial support:* Career-related internships or fieldwork available. Financial award applicants required to submit FAFSA. In 2008, 43 master's awarded. Offers physician assistant studies (MPAS). *Application deadline:* For fall admission, 10/1 priority date for domestic and international students. *Application fee:* $45. *Application Contact:* Maureen Stokan, Assistant Director of Graduate Admissions, 412-365-2988, Fax: 412-365-1609, E-mail: gradadmissions@chatham.edu. *Director*, Luis Ramos, 412-365-1314, Fax: 412-365-1213, E-mail: lramos@chatham.edu.

Program in Wellness Students: 2 full-time (both women), 10 part-time (9 women). Average age 40. Expenses: Contact institution. *Degree program information:* Part-time and evening/weekend programs available. Postbaccalaureate distance learning degree programs offered (no on-campus study). Offers wellness (MA). *Application deadline:* Applications are processed on a rolling basis. *Application fee:* $0. Electronic applications accepted. *Application Contact:* College for Continuing and Professional Studies, 866-815-2050, Fax: 412-365-1720, E-mail: ccps@chatham.edu. *Dean, College of Continuing Education and Professional Studies*, Dr. Janet Littrell, 412-365-1147, E-mail: jlittrel@chatham.edu.

Program in Writing Students: 57 full-time (47 women), 88 part-time (67 women). Average age 33. 67 applicants, 85% accepted, 57 enrolled. Expenses: Contact institution. *Financial support:* Career-related internships or fieldwork available. Financial award applicants required to submit FAFSA. In 2008, 43 master's awarded. *Degree program information:* Part-time and evening/weekend programs available. Postbaccalaureate distance learning degree programs offered (minimal on-campus study). Offers children's writing (MFA); fiction (MFA); non-fiction (MFA); poetry (MFA); professional writing (MPW); screenwriting (MFA). *Application deadline:* For fall admission, 3/15 priority date for domestic students, 5/1 priority date for international students; for spring admission, 10/15 priority date for domestic students, 10/1 priority date for international students. Applications are processed on a rolling basis. *Application fee:* $45. Electronic applications accepted. *Application Contact:* Dory Perry, Associate Director of Graduate Admissions, 412-365-2758, Fax: 412-365-1609, E-mail: gradadmissions@chatham.edu. *Director,* Dr. Sheryl St. Germain, 412-365-1190, Fax: 412-365-1505, E-mail: sstgermain@chatham.edu.

CHESTNUT HILL COLLEGE, Philadelphia, PA 19118-2693

General Information Independent-religious, coed, comprehensive institution. CGS member. *Enrollment:* 2,085 graduate, professional, and undergraduate students; 210 full-time matriculated graduate/professional students (176 women), 533 part-time matriculated graduate/professional students (440 women). *Enrollment by degree level:* 574 master's, 107 doctoral, 62 other advanced degrees. *Graduate faculty:* 28 full-time (17 women), 84 part-time/adjunct (53 women). *Tuition:* Part-time $510 per credit hour. *Graduate housing:* On-campus housing not available. *Student services:* Campus employment opportunities, career counseling, free psychological counseling, international student services, low-cost health insurance, services for students with disabilities, teacher training, writing training. *Library facilities:* Logue Library. *Online resources:* library catalog, web page, access to other libraries' catalogs. *Collection:* 132,434 titles, 1,296 serial subscriptions, 4,893 audiovisual materials.

Computer facilities: 60 computers available on campus for general student use. A campuswide network can be accessed from student residence rooms. Online class registration is available. *Web address:* http://www.chc.edu/.

General Application Contact: Jayne Mashett, Director of Graduate Admissions, 215-248-7020, Fax: 215-248-7161, E-mail: mashettj@chc.edu.

GRADUATE UNITS

School of Graduate Studies Students: 210 full-time (176 women), 533 part-time (440 women); includes 140 minority (118 African Americans, 11 Asian Americans or Pacific Islanders, 11 Hispanic Americans), 4 international. Average age 31. 176 applicants, 97% accepted. *Faculty:* 29 full-time (17 women), 91 part-time/adjunct (57 women). Expenses: Contact institution. In 2008, 184 master's, 18 doctorates awarded. *Degree program information:* Part-time and evening/weekend programs available. Offers administration of human services (MS); adult and aging services (CAS); clinical and counseling psychology (MA, MS, CAS); clinical psychology (Psy D); early childhood education (M Ed); educational leadership (M Ed); elementary education (M Ed); holistic spirituality (MA); holistic spirituality and healthcare (MA); holistic spirituality and spiritual direction (MA); holistic spirituality/health care (CAS); instructional technology (MS, CAS); leadership development (CAS); secondary education (M Ed); spiritual direction (CAS); spirituality (CAS); supervision of spiritual directors (CAS). *Application deadline:* For fall admission, 7/17 priority date for domestic students, 7/17 for international students; for spring admission, 12/15 priority date for domestic students, 12/15 for international students. Applications are processed on a rolling basis. *Application fee:* $50. *Application Contact:* Amy Boorse, Administrative Assistant, School of Graduate Studies Office, 215-248-7170, Fax: 215-248-7161, E-mail: gradadmissions@chc.edu. *Dean of the School of Graduate Studies,* Dr. Steven Guerriero, 215-248-7120, Fax: 215-248-7161, E-mail: guerrieros@chc.edu.

See Close-Up on page 871.

CHEYNEY UNIVERSITY OF PENNSYLVANIA, Cheyney, PA 19319-0200

General Information State-supported, coed, comprehensive institution. *Enrollment:* 1,488 graduate, professional, and undergraduate students; 48 full-time matriculated graduate/professional students (36 women), 107 part-time matriculated graduate/professional students (78 women). *Enrollment by degree level:* 143 master's, 12 other advanced degrees. *Graduate faculty:* 6 full-time (1 woman), 3 part-time/adjunct (2 women). *Graduate housing:* On-campus housing not available. *Student services:* Career counseling, international student services, low-cost health insurance. *Library facilities:* Leslie Pickney Hill. *Online resources:* library catalog. *Collection:* 293,295 titles.

Computer facilities: Computer purchase and lease plans are available. 250 computers available on campus for general student use. A campuswide network can be accessed from student residence rooms and from off campus. Online class registration, online tutorials, various software packages, online payment/online Praxis study guide are available. *Web address:* http://www.cheyney.edu/.

General Application Contact: Dr. Ivan Banks, Provost, 610-399-2271, Fax: 610-399-2070, E-mail: ibanks@cheyney.edu.

GRADUATE UNITS

School of Education and Professional Studies Students: 48 full-time (36 women), 107 part-time (78 women); includes 125 minority (119 African Americans, 1 Asian American or Pacific Islander, 5 Hispanic Americans). Average age 39. *Faculty:* 6 full-time (1 woman), 3 part-time/adjunct (2 women). Expenses: Contact institution. *Financial support:* Career-related internships or fieldwork, institutionally sponsored loans, tuition waivers (full), and unspecified assistantships available. Financial award application deadline: 5/1. In 2008, 50 master's awarded. *Degree program information:* Part-time and evening/weekend programs available. Offers adult and continuing education (MS); early childhood education (Certificate); education and professional studies (M Ed, MAT, MPA, MS, Certificate); educational administration and supervision (M Ed, Certificate); educational administration of adult and continuing education (M Ed, MS); elementary and secondary principalship (Certificate); elementary education (M Ed, MAT); public administration (MPA); special education (M Ed, MS). *Application deadline:* For fall admission, 8/1 priority date for domestic students; for spring admission, 12/15 for domestic students. Applications are processed on a rolling basis. *Application fee:* $25. Electronic applications accepted. *Application Contact:* Dr. S. Jean Wilson, Chair, 610-399-2086, Fax: 610-399-2307, E-mail: sjwilson@cheyney.edu. *Provost,* Dr. Ivan Banks, 610-399-2271, Fax: 610-399-2070, E-mail: ibanks@cheyney.edu.

THE CHICAGO SCHOOL OF PROFESSIONAL PSYCHOLOGY, Chicago, IL 60610

General Information Independent, coed, primarily women, graduate-only institution. CGS member. *Graduate housing:* On-campus housing not available.

GRADUATE UNITS

Program in Applied Behavior Analysis Offers developmental disabilities (Psy D); instructional design (Psy D); supervision and consulting (Psy D).

Program in Business Psychology Offers business psychology (Psy D).

Program in Clinical Forensic Psychology Offers clinical forensic psychology (Psy D).

Program in Clinical Psychology Offers applied behavior analysis (MA, Certificate); clinical psychology (Psy D); counseling (MA); general psychology (Certificate); Latino mental health (Certificate). Electronic applications accepted.

Program in Forensic Psychology Offers forensic psychology (MA).

Program in Industrial and Organizational Psychology *Degree program information:* Part-time and evening/weekend programs available. Offers industrial and organizational psychology (MA). Electronic applications accepted.

Program in School Psychology *Degree program information:* Part-time programs available. Offers school psychology (Ed S).

THE CHICAGO SCHOOL OF PROFESSIONAL PSYCHOLOGY: DOWNTOWN LOS ANGELES CAMPUS, Los Angeles, CA 90017

General Information Independent, graduate-only institution.

GRADUATE UNITS

Program in Applied Behavior Analysis Offers applied behavior analysis (Psy D).

Program in Clinical Forensic Psychology Offers clinical forensic psychology (Psy D).

Program in Clinical Psychology Offers applied behavior analysis (MA); clinical psychology (Psy D); marital and family therapy (MA).

Program in Industrial and Organizational Psychology Offers industrial and organizational psychology (MA).

THE CHICAGO SCHOOL OF PROFESSIONAL PSYCHOLOGY: GRAYSLAKE CAMPUS, Grayslake, IL 60030

General Information Independent, graduate-only institution.

GRADUATE UNITS

Program in Clinical Psychology Offers counseling (MA).

Program in School Psychology Offers school psychology (Ed S).

THE CHICAGO SCHOOL OF PROFESSIONAL PSYCHOLOGY: IRVINE CAMPUS, Irvine, CA 92612

General Information Independent, graduate-only institution.

GRADUATE UNITS

Program in Clinical Psychology Offers marital and family therapy (MA).

Program in Marital and Family Therapy Offers management practice (Psy D); psychodynamic psychotherapy (Psy D).

Program in Psychology Offers generalist (Psy D); psychodynamic psychotherapy (Psy D).

THE CHICAGO SCHOOL OF PROFESSIONAL PSYCHOLOGY: ONLINE, Chicago, IL 60654

General Information Independent, graduate-only institution.

GRADUATE UNITS

Program in Applied Forensic Psychology Services Offers applied forensic psychology services (MA, Certificate).

Program in Applied Industrial and Organizational Psychology Offers applied industrial and organizational psychology (MA, Certificate).

Program in International Psychology Offers international psychology (PhD).

Program in Organizational Leadership Offers organizational leadership (PhD).

Program in Psychology Offers child and adolescent psychology (MA); generalist (MA); gerontology (MA); international psychology (MA); organizational leadership (MA); sport and exercise psychology (MA).

THE CHICAGO SCHOOL OF PROFESSIONAL PSYCHOLOGY: WESTWOOD CAMPUS, Los Angeles, CA 90024

General Information Independent, graduate-only institution.

GRADUATE UNITS

Program in Clinical Psychology Offers marital and family therapy (MA).

Program in Marital and Family Therapy Offers management practice (Psy D); psychodynamic psychotherapy (Psy D).

Program in Psychology Offers generalist (Psy D); psychodynamic psychotherapy (Psy D).

CHICAGO STATE UNIVERSITY, Chicago, IL 60628

General Information State-supported, coed, comprehensive institution. *Graduate housing:* Room and/or apartments available on a first-come, first-served basis to single students; on-campus housing not available to married students.

GRADUATE UNITS

School of Graduate and Professional Studies *Degree program information:* Part-time and evening/weekend programs available. Electronic applications accepted.

College of Arts and Sciences *Degree program information:* Part-time and evening/weekend programs available. Offers arts and sciences (MA, MFA, MS, MSW); biological sciences (MS); computer science (MS); counseling (MA); creative writing (MFA); criminal justice (MS); English (MA); geography and economic development (MA); history, philosophy, and political science (MA); mathematics (MS); social work (MSW).

College of Education *Degree program information:* Part-time programs available. Offers bilingual education (M Ed); curriculum and instruction (MS Ed); early childhood education (MAT, MS Ed); education (M Ed, MA, MAT, MS Ed, Ed D); educational leadership (MA, Ed D); elementary education (MAT); general administration (MA); higher education administration (MA); instructional foundations (MS Ed); library information and media studies (MS Ed); middle school education (MAT); physical education (MS Ed); reading (MS Ed); secondary education (MAT); special education (M Ed); teaching of reading (MS Ed); technology and education (MS Ed).

CHICAGO THEOLOGICAL SEMINARY, Chicago, IL 60637-1507

General Information Independent-religious, coed, graduate-only institution. *Enrollment by degree level:* 81 first professional, 18 master's, 98 doctoral. *Graduate faculty:* 13 full-time (5 women). *Graduate housing:* On-campus housing not available. *Student services:* Campus employment opportunities, career counseling, international student services, writing training. *Library facilities:* Hammond Library. *Collection:* 110,000 titles, 221 serial subscriptions.

Computer facilities: 8 computers available on campus for general student use. A campuswide network can be accessed from student residence rooms and from off campus. Online class registration is available. *Web address:* http://www.ctschicago.edu/.

General Application Contact: Rev. Lin Sanford Keppert, Director of Admissions, Recruitment and Financial Aid, E-mail: lkeppert@ctschicago.edu.

GRADUATE UNITS

Graduate and Professional Programs Students: 71 full-time (32 women), 139 part-time (76 women); includes 54 minority (45 African Americans, 6 Asian Americans or Pacific Islanders, 3 Hispanic Americans), 33 international. *Faculty:* 13 full-time (5 women). Expenses: Contact institution. *Financial support:* Fellowships, institutionally sponsored loans, scholarships/grants, and tuition waivers (partial) available. Support available to part-time students. Financial award application deadline: 3/1; financial award applicants required to submit FAFSA. *Degree program information:* Part-time programs available. Offers preaching (D Min); religion and health (D Min); religious studies (MA); spirituality and spiritual direction (D Min); theology (M Div); theology, ethics and the human sciences (PhD). *Application deadline:* For fall admission, 2/15 priority date for domestic and international students; for spring admission, 11/1 for domestic and international students. *Application fee:* $50. *Application Contact:* Rev. Lin Sanford Keppert, Director of Admissions, Recruitment and Financial Aid, E-mail: lkeppert@ctschicago.edu. *Acting Dean,* Dr. Theodore W. Jennings, 773-752-5757, Fax: 773-752-1903, E-mail: tjennings@ctschicago.edu.

CHRISTENDOM COLLEGE, Front Royal, VA 22630-5103

General Information Independent-religious, coed, comprehensive institution. *Graduate housing:* On-campus housing not available.

GRADUATE UNITS

Notre Dame Graduate School *Degree program information:* Part-time and evening/weekend programs available. Offers theological studies (MA). Electronic applications accepted.

CHRISTIAN BROTHERS UNIVERSITY, Memphis, TN 38104-5581

General Information Independent-religious, coed, comprehensive institution. *Enrollment:* 1,869 graduate, professional, and undergraduate students; 65 full-time matriculated graduate/professional students (39 women), 382 part-time matriculated graduate/professional students (217 women). *Enrollment by degree level:* 447 master's. *Graduate faculty:* 9 full-time (6 women), 18 part-time/adjunct (7 women). Tuition and fees vary according to program. *Graduate housing:* On-campus housing not available. *Student services:* Campus safety program, career counseling, free psychological counseling, low-cost health insurance. *Library facilities:* Plough Memorial Library and Media Center. *Online resources:* library catalog, web page, access to other libraries' catalogs. *Collection:* 182,060 titles, 384 serial subscriptions, 930 audiovisual materials.

Computer facilities: 310 computers available on campus for general student use. A campuswide network can be accessed from student residence rooms and from off campus. Online class registration, online class listings, course assignments are available. *Web address:* http://www.cbu.edu/.

General Application Contact: Dr. Patrick B. Wilson, Dean, Graduate and Professional Studies Programs, 901-321-3296, E-mail: pwilson4@cbu.edu.

GRADUATE UNITS

Graduate and Professional Studies Students: 65 full-time (39 women), 382 part-time (217 women); includes 170 minority (121 African Americans, 11 Asian Americans or Pacific Islanders, 38 Hispanic Americans), 12 international. Average age 33. *Faculty:* 9 full-time (6 women), 18 part-time/adjunct (7 women). Expenses: Contact institution. *Financial support:* Institutionally sponsored loans available. Support available to part-time students. In 2008, 122 master's awarded. *Degree program information:* Part-time and evening/weekend programs available. *Application deadline:* Applications are processed on a rolling basis. *Application fee:* $25. *Application Contact:* Dr. Patrick B. Wilson, Dean, 901-321-3296, E-mail: pwilson4@cbu.edu. *Dean*, Dr. Patrick B. Wilson, 901-321-3296, E-mail: pwilson4@cbu.edu.

School of Arts Students: 45 full-time (35 women), 171 part-time (126 women); includes 66 minority (61 African Americans, 1 Asian American or Pacific Islander, 4 Hispanic Americans), 2 international. Average age 33. *Faculty:* 6 full-time (5 women), 13 part-time/adjunct (7 women). Expenses: Contact institution. *Financial support:* Institutionally sponsored loans available. Support available to part-time students. In 2008, 72 master's awarded. *Degree program information:* Part-time and evening/weekend programs available. Offers Catholic studies (MACS); curriculum and instruction (M Ed); educational leadership (MSEL); teacher-leadership (M Ed); teaching (MAT). *Application deadline:* Applications are processed on a rolling basis. *Application fee:* $25. *Application Contact:* Dr. Talana L. Vogel, Director, 901-321-4101, Fax: 901-321-3408, E-mail: tvogel@cbu.edu. *Dean*, Dr. Marius Carriere, 901-321-3366, Fax: 901-321-4340, E-mail: mcarrier@cbu.edu.

School of Business Students: 20 full-time (4 women), 138 part-time (74 women); includes 59 minority (54 African Americans, 5 Asian Americans or Pacific Islanders), 9 international. Average age 34. *Faculty:* 2 full-time (1 woman), 4 part-time/adjunct (0 women). Expenses: Contact institution. *Financial support:* Institutionally sponsored loans available. Support available to part-time students. In 2008, 45 master's awarded. *Degree program information:* Part-time and evening/weekend programs available. Offers business (MBA); executive leadership (MAEL); financial planning (Certificate); project management (Certificate). *Application deadline:* Applications are processed on a rolling basis. *Application fee:* $25. *Application Contact:* Dr. Scott Lawyer, Director, Graduate Business Programs, 901-321-3104, Fax: 901-321-3566, E-mail: mlawyer@cbu.edu. *Dean*, Dr. Scott Lawyer, 901-321-3104, Fax: 901-321-3566, E-mail: mlawyer@cbu.edu.

School of Engineering Students: 73 part-time (17 women); includes 14 minority (6 African Americans, 5 Asian Americans or Pacific Islanders, 3 Hispanic Americans), 32 international. Average age 34. *Faculty:* 1 full-time (0 women), 1 part-time/adjunct (0 women). Expenses: Contact institution. *Financial support:* Institutionally sponsored loans available. In 2008, 5 master's awarded. *Degree program information:* Part-time and evening/weekend programs available. Postbaccalaureate distance learning degree programs offered (no on-campus study). Offers engineering (MEM, MSEM). *Application fee:* $25. *Application Contact:* Dr. Neal Jackson, Director, 901-321-3283, Fax: 901-321-3494, E-mail: njackson@cbu.edu. *Dean*, Dr. Eric B Welch, 901-321-3425, Fax: 901-321-3402, E-mail: ewelch@cbu.edu.

CHRISTIAN THEOLOGICAL SEMINARY, Indianapolis, IN 46208-3301

General Information Independent-religious, coed, graduate-only institution. *Graduate housing:* Rooms and/or apartments available on a first-come, first-served basis to single and married students. Housing application deadline: 5/1.

GRADUATE UNITS

Graduate and Professional Programs *Degree program information:* Part-time programs available. Offers marriage and family (MA); pastoral care and counseling (D Min); practical theology (D Min); psychotherapy and faith (MA); sacred theology (STM); specialized ministries (MA); theological studies (MTS); theology (M Div). Electronic applications accepted.

CHRISTIE'S EDUCATION, New York, NY 10036

General Information Proprietary, coed, primarily women, graduate-only institution. *Graduate housing:* On-campus housing not available.

GRADUATE UNITS

Program in Modern Art, Connoisseurship, and the History of the Art Market Offers modern art, connoisseurship, and the history of the art market (MA).

CHRISTOPHER NEWPORT UNIVERSITY, Newport News, VA 23606-2998

General Information State-supported, coed, comprehensive institution. *Graduate housing:* On-campus housing not available. *Research affiliation:* Langley Research Center, Center for Distance Learning (flow visualization), Thomas Jefferson National Acceleration Facility (instrument and nuclear physics), Applied Research Center (biology, engineering, physics), JDH Technologies (computer software), National Science Foundation (science).

GRADUATE UNITS

Graduate Studies *Degree program information:* Part-time and evening/weekend programs available. Offers applied physics and computer science (MS); art (PK-12) (MAT); biology (6-12) (MAT); computer science (6-12) (MAT); elementary (PK-6) (MAT); English (6-12) (MAT); environmental science (MS); French (PK-12) (MAT); history (6-12) (MAT); history and social science (MAT); mathematics (6-12) (MAT); music (PK-12) (MAT); physics (6-12) (MAT); Spanish (PK-12) (MAT); theater (PK-12) (MAT). Electronic applications accepted.

CHRIST THE KING SEMINARY, East Aurora, NY 14052

General Information Independent-religious, coed, graduate-only institution. *Graduate housing:* On-campus housing not available.

GRADUATE UNITS

Graduate and Professional Programs *Degree program information:* Part-time and evening/weekend programs available. Offers divinity (M Div); pastoral ministry (MA); pastoral studies (Certificate); theology (MA).

CHURCH DIVINITY SCHOOL OF THE PACIFIC, Berkeley, CA 94709-1217

General Information Independent-religious, coed, graduate-only institution. *Graduate housing:* Rooms and/or apartments available on a first-come, first-served basis to single and married students. Housing application deadline: 5/1.

GRADUATE UNITS

Graduate and Professional Programs *Degree program information:* Part-time programs available. Offers theology (M Div, MA, MTS, D Min, Certificate). Electronic applications accepted.

CHURCH OF GOD THEOLOGICAL SEMINARY, Cleveland, TN 37320-3330

General Information Independent-religious, coed, graduate-only institution. *Graduate housing:* Rooms and/or apartments available to single and married students.

GRADUATE UNITS

Graduate and Professional Programs *Degree program information:* Part-time programs available. Offers counseling (MA); discipleship and Christian formations (MA); ministry (D Min); theology (M Div).

CINCINNATI CHRISTIAN UNIVERSITY, Cincinnati, OH 45204-3200

General Information Independent-religious, coed, comprehensive institution. *Graduate housing:* On-campus housing not available.

GRADUATE UNITS

Graduate School *Degree program information:* Part-time programs available. Offers biblical studies (MA); church history (MA); counseling (MAC); divinity (M Div); ministry (M Min); practical ministries (MA); theological studies (MA). Electronic applications accepted.

THE CITADEL, THE MILITARY COLLEGE OF SOUTH CAROLINA, Charleston, SC 29409

General Information State-supported, coed, comprehensive institution. *Enrollment:* 3,328 graduate, professional, and undergraduate students; 188 full-time matriculated graduate/professional students (127 women), 594 part-time matriculated graduate/professional students (362 women). *Enrollment by degree level:* 702 master's, 80 other advanced degrees. *Graduate faculty:* 70 full-time (24 women), 19 part-time/adjunct (7 women). Tuition, state resident: full-time $5850; part-time $325 per credit hour. Tuition, nonresident: full-time $9612; part-time $534 per credit hour. *Required fees:* $15 per semester. *Graduate housing:* On-campus housing not available. *Student services:* Campus employment opportunities, career counseling, exercise/wellness program, free psychological counseling, international student services, low-cost health insurance, multicultural affairs office, teacher training, writing training. *Library facilities:* Daniel Library. *Online resources:* library catalog, web page, access to other libraries' catalogs. *Collection:* 232,918 titles, 1,122 serial subscriptions, 4,112 audiovisual materials.

Computer facilities: 350 computers available on campus for general student use. A campuswide network can be accessed from student residence rooms and from off campus. Online class registration is available. *Web address:* http://www.citadel.edu.

GRADUATE UNITS

Citadel Graduate College Students: 188 full-time (127 women), 594 part-time (362 women); includes 108 minority (87 African Americans, 1 American Indian/Alaska Native, 11 Asian Americans or Pacific Islanders, 9 Hispanic Americans), 8 international. Average age 29. *Faculty:* 70 full-time (24 women), 19 part-time/adjunct (7 women). Expenses: Contact institution. *Financial support:* Fellowships, research assistantships, career-related internships or fieldwork, health care benefits, and unspecified assistantships available. Support available to part-time students. Financial award application deadline: 7/1; financial award applicants required to submit FAFSA. In 2008, 214 master's, 7 other advanced degrees awarded. *Degree program information:* Part-time and evening/weekend programs available. Offers biology (MA); computer and information science (MS); English (MA); health, exercise, and sport science (MS); history (MA); mathematics education (MAE); physical education (MAT); psychology (MA); social science (MA). *Application deadline:* For fall admission, 8/1 priority date for domestic students. Applications are processed on a rolling basis. *Application fee:* $30. Electronic applications accepted. *Application Contact:* Brig. Gen. Samuel M. Hines, Provost/Dean of the College, 843-953-5007, Fax: 843-953-7240, E-mail: sam.hines@citadel.edu. *Provost/Dean of the College*, Brig. Gen. Samuel M. Hines, 843-953-5007, Fax: 843-953-7240, E-mail: sam.hines@citadel.edu.

School of Business Administration Students: 55 full-time (21 women), 202 part-time (82 women); includes 29 minority (20 African Americans, 7 Asian Americans or Pacific Islanders, 2 Hispanic Americans), 4 international. Average age 28. *Faculty:* 18 full-time (3 women), 5 part-time/adjunct (1 woman). Expenses: Contact institution. *Financial support:* Fellowships, career-related internships or fieldwork, health care benefits, and unspecified assistantships available. Support available to part-time students. Financial award application deadline: 7/1; financial award applicants required to submit FAFSA. In 2008, 80 master's awarded. *Degree program information:* Part-time and evening/weekend programs available. Offers business administration (MBA); sport management (MBA). *Application deadline:* For fall admission, 7/20 for domestic students; for spring admission, 12/1 for domestic students. *Application fee:* $30. Electronic applications accepted. *Application Contact:* Kathy Jones, Director, MBA Program, 843-953-5257, Fax: 843-953-6764, E-mail: kathy.jones@citadel.edu. *Dean*, Dr. Ronald F. Green, 843-953-5056, Fax: 843-953-6764, E-mail: ron.green@citadel.edu.

School of Education Students: 94 full-time (82 women), 255 part-time (194 women); includes 56 minority (50 African Americans, 3 Asian Americans or Pacific Islanders, 3 Hispanic Americans), 1 international. Average age 30. *Faculty:* 14 full-time (9 women), 9 part-time/adjunct (4 women). Expenses: Contact institution. *Financial support:* Fellowships, career-related internships or fieldwork, health care benefits, and unspecified assistantships available. Support available to part-time students. Financial award application deadline: 7/1; financial award applicants required to submit FAFSA. In 2008, 91 master's, 7 other advanced degrees awarded. *Degree program information:* Part-time and evening/weekend programs available. Offers biology (MAT); education (M Ed, MA, MAT, Ed S); elementary/secondary school administration and supervision (M Ed); elementary/secondary school counseling (M Ed); English language arts (MAT); literacy education (M Ed); mathematics (MAT); school psychology (MA, Ed S); school superintendency (Ed S); social studies (MAT); student affairs and college counseling (M Ed). *Application deadline:* Applications are processed on a rolling basis. *Application fee:* $30. Electronic applications accepted. *Application Contact:* Dr. Tony Johnson, Dean, 843-953-5871, Fax: 843-953-7258, E-mail: tony.johnson@citadel.edu. *Dean*, Dr. Tony Johnson, 843-953-5871, Fax: 843-953-7258, E-mail: tony.johnson@citadel.edu.

CITY COLLEGE OF THE CITY UNIVERSITY OF NEW YORK, New York, NY 10031-9198

General Information State and locally supported, coed, comprehensive institution. *Enrollment:* 14,536 graduate, professional, and undergraduate students; 307 full-time matriculated graduate/professional students (149 women), 3,052 part-time matriculated graduate/professional students (1,861 women). *Enrollment by degree level:* 3,336 master's, 23 doctoral. *Graduate faculty:* 519 full-time (199 women), 610 part-time/adjunct (291 women). Tuition, state resident: full-time $6400; part-time $270 per credit. Tuition, nonresident: full-time $12,000; part-time $500 per credit. *Required fees:* $260.70; $80.35 per semester. One-time fee: $125. Tuition and fees vary according to course level, course load, degree level, program and student level. *Graduate housing:* Room and/or apartments available on a first-come, first-served basis to single students; on-campus housing not available to married students. Typical cost: $9250 per year. Room charges vary according to housing facility selected. *Student services:* Campus employment opportunities, campus safety program, career counseling, child daycare facilities, exercise/wellness program, free psychological counseling, international student services, multicultural affairs office, services for students with disabilities. *Library facilities:* Morris Raphael Cohen Library plus 3 others. *Online resources:* library catalog, web page, access to other libraries' catalogs. *Collection:* 1.4 million titles, 31,000 serial subscriptions, 26,380 audiovisual materials. *Research affiliation:* New York Center for Biological Structures, Lucent Laboratories (engineering), Hospital for Joint Diseases (biomedical engineering), Museum of Natural History.

Computer facilities: 4,000 computers available on campus for general student use. A campuswide network can be accessed from off campus. Online class registration is available. *Web address:* http://www.ccny.cuny.edu/.

General Application Contact: Chad K Austein, Assistant Director of Graduate Admissions, 212-650-6977, Fax: 212-650-6417, E-mail: gradadm@ccny.cuny.edu.

GRADUATE UNITS

Graduate School Students: 307 full-time (149 women), 3,052 part-time (1,861 women); includes 2,513 minority (861 African Americans, 504 Asian Americans or Pacific Islanders, 1,148 Hispanic Americans), 475 international. 1,454 applicants, 63% accepted. Expenses: Contact institution. *Financial support:* Fellowships, research assistantships, teaching assistantships, career-related internships or fieldwork, Federal Work-Study, institutionally sponsored loans, scholarships/grants, health care benefits, tuition waivers (full and partial), and unspecified assistantships available. Support available to part-time students. Financial award applicants required to submit FAFSA. In 2008, 921 master's awarded. *Degree program information:* Part-time and evening/weekend programs available. *Application deadline:* Applications are processed on a rolling basis. *Application fee:* $125. *Application Contact:* 212-650-6977, Fax: 212-650-6417, E-mail: gradadm@ccny.cuny.edu.

College of Liberal Arts and Science 559 applicants, 59% accepted. Expenses: Contact institution. *Financial support:* Fellowships, research assistantships, teaching assistantships, career-related internships or fieldwork, Federal Work-Study, institutionally sponsored loans, scholarships/grants, and tuition waivers (full and partial) available. Support available to part-time students. Financial award applicants required to submit FAFSA. In 2008, 280 master's awarded. *Degree program information:* Part-time and evening/weekend programs available. Offers advertising design (MFA); art history (MA); art history and museum studies (MA); biochemistry (MA, PhD); biology (MA, PhD); ceramic design (MFA); chemistry (MA, PhD); clinical psychology (PhD); creative writing (MA, MFA); earth and environmental science (PhD); earth systems science (MA); economics (MA); English and American literature (MA); experimental cognition (PhD); fine arts (MFA); general psychology (MA); history (MA); humanities and arts (MA, MFA); international relations (MA); language and literacy (MA); liberal arts and science (MA, MFA, MPA, PhD); mathematics (MA); media arts production (MFA); mental health counseling (MA); museum studies (MA); music (MA); painting (MFA); physics (MA, PhD); printmaking (MFA); psychology (MA, PhD); public service management (MPA); science (MA, PhD); sculpture (MFA); sociology (MA); Spanish (MA); wood and metal design (MFA). *Application deadline:* For fall admission, 5/1 for domestic and international students; for spring admission, 11/15 for domestic and international students. Applications are processed on a rolling basis. *Application fee:* $125. Electronic applications accepted. *Application Contact:* 212-650-6977, Fax: 212-650-6417, E-mail: gradadm@ccny.cuny.edu.

Grove School of Engineering *Degree program information:* Part-time programs available. Offers biomedical engineering (ME, PhD); chemical engineering (ME, MS, PhD); civil engineering (ME, MS, PhD); computer sciences (MS, PhD); electrical engineering (ME, MS, PhD); engineering (ME, MS, PhD); mechanical engineering (ME, MS, PhD).

School of Architecture and Environmental Studies *Degree program information:* Part-time programs available. Offers architecture (M Arch, PD); landscape architecture (PD); urban design (MUP).

School of Education *Degree program information:* Part-time and evening/weekend programs available. Offers administration and supervision (MS, AC); adolescent mathematics education (MA, AC); bilingual education (MS); childhood education (MS); education (MA, MS, AC); English education (MA); middle school mathematics education (MS); science education (MA); social studies education (AC); teaching students with disabilities (MA).

See Close-Up on page 873.

CITY OF HOPE NATIONAL MEDICAL CENTER/BECKMAN RESEARCH INSTITUTE, Duarte, CA 91010

General Information Independent, coed, graduate-only institution. *Graduate housing:* Rooms and/or apartments available on a first-come, first-served basis to single and married students. Housing application deadline: 7/14.

GRADUATE UNITS

City of Hope Graduate School of Biological Sciences Offers biological sciences (PhD).

CITY UNIVERSITY OF NEW YORK SCHOOL OF LAW AT QUEENS COLLEGE, Flushing, NY 11367-1358

General Information State and locally supported, coed, graduate-only institution. *Enrollment by degree level:* 387 first professional. *Graduate faculty:* 37 full-time (23 women), 14 part-time/adjunct (9 women). Tuition, state resident: full-time $8900. Tuition, nonresident: full-time $14,800. *Required fees:* $1710. *Graduate housing:* On-campus housing not available. *Student services:* Campus employment opportunities, career counseling, child daycare facilities, free psychological counseling, low-cost health insurance, services for students with disabilities, writing training. *Library facilities:* City University of New York School of Law Library. *Online resources:* library catalog, web page, access to other libraries' catalogs. *Collection:* 111,105 titles.

Computer facilities: 104 computers available on campus for general student use. A campuswide network can be accessed from off campus. Online class registration, free wireless internet access are available. *Web address:* http://www.law.cuny.edu/.

General Application Contact: Yvonne Cherena-Pacheco, Assistant Dean for Enrollment Management and Director of Admissions, 718-340-4210, Fax: 718-340-4435, E-mail: admissions@mail.law.cuny.edu.

GRADUATE UNITS

Professional Program Students: 385 full-time (241 women), 2 part-time (0 women); includes 123 minority (25 African Americans, 63 Asian Americans or Pacific Islanders, 35 Hispanic Americans), 8 international. Average age 26. 2,206 applicants, 26% accepted, 129 enrolled. *Faculty:* 37 full-time (23 women), 14 part-time/adjunct (9 women). Expenses: Contact institution. *Financial support:* In 2008–09, 106 students received support, including 23 fellowships (averaging $8,900 per year), 63 research assistantships (averaging $761 per year), 17 teaching assistantships (averaging $10,993 per year); career-related internships or fieldwork, Federal Work-Study, scholarships/grants, and tuition waivers (partial) also available. Financial award application deadline: 5/1; financial award applicants required to submit FAFSA. In 2008, 132 JDs awarded. Offers law (JD). *Application deadline:* For fall admission, 3/16 priority date for domestic students. Applications are processed on a rolling basis. *Application fee:* $50. Electronic applications accepted. *Application Contact:* Yvonne Cherena-Pacheco, Assistant Dean for Enrollment Management and Director of Admissions, 718-340-4210, Fax: 718-340-4435, E-mail: admissions@mail.law.cuny.edu. *Dean and Professor of Law,* Michelle J. Anderson, 718-340-4201, Fax: 718-340-4482.

CITY UNIVERSITY OF SEATTLE, Bellevue, WA 98005

General Information Independent, coed, comprehensive institution. *Enrollment:* 3,592 graduate, professional, and undergraduate students; 1,194 full-time matriculated graduate/professional students (751 women), 705 part-time matriculated graduate/professional students (359 women). *Enrollment by degree level:* 1,899 master's. *Graduate faculty:* 31 full-time (16 women), 1,142 part-time/adjunct (633 women). *Tuition:* Part-time $586 per credit. One-time fee: $50. Tuition and fees vary according to program. *Graduate housing:* On-campus housing not available. *Student services:* Campus employment opportunities, career counseling, international student services, services for students with disabilities. *Library facilities:* City University Library. *Online resources:* library catalog, web page, access to other libraries' catalogs. *Collection:* 32,329 titles, 1,518 serial subscriptions, 5,184 audiovisual materials.

Computer facilities: 145 computers available on campus for general student use. A campuswide network can be accessed from off campus. Online class registration is available. *Web address:* http://www.cityu.edu/.

General Application Contact: Information Contact, 800-426-5596, Fax: 425-701-5361, E-mail: info@cityu.edu.

GRADUATE UNITS

Graduate Division Students: 1,194 full-time (751 women), 705 part-time (359 women); includes 189 minority (81 African Americans, 21 American Indian/Alaska Native, 49 Asian Americans or Pacific Islanders, 38 Hispanic Americans), 165 international. Average age 36. 1,587 applicants, 100% accepted, 390 enrolled. *Faculty:* 31 full-time (16 women), 1,142 part-time/adjunct (633 women). Expenses: Contact institution. *Financial support:* In 2008–09, 85 students received support. Federal Work-Study and scholarships/grants available. Support available to part-time students. Financial award applicants required to submit FAFSA. In 2008, 1,167 master's awarded. *Degree program information:* Part-time and evening/weekend programs available. Postbaccalaureate distance learning degree programs offered (no on-campus study). *Application deadline:* For fall admission, 9/1 for international students; for winter admission, 12/1 for international students; for spring admission, 3/1 for international students. Applications are processed on a rolling basis. *Application fee:* $50. Electronic applications accepted. *Application Contact:* 800-426-5596, Fax: 425-709-5361, E-mail: info@cityu.edu. *Interim Provost,* Dr. Steven Olswang, 425-637-1010 Ext. 7623, Fax: 425-709-5366, E-mail: solswang@cityu.edu.

Division of Arts and Sciences Students: 340. Average age 36. 200 applicants, 100% accepted, 165 enrolled. *Faculty:* 7 full-time (2 women), 58 part-time/adjunct (37 women). Expenses: Contact institution. *Financial support:* In 2008–09, 29 students received support. Federal Work-Study available. Support available to part-time students. Financial award applicants required to submit FAFSA. In 2008, 98 master's awarded. *Degree program information:* Part-time and evening/weekend programs available. Offers counseling psychology (MA). *Application deadline:* Applications are processed on a rolling basis. *Application fee:* $50. Electronic applications accepted. *Application Contact:* Alysa Borelli, 800-426-5596, Fax: 425-709-5361, E-mail: info@citryu.edu. *Interim Dean,* Judy Hinrichs, 425-637-101 Ext. 5465, Fax: 425-709-5363, E-mail: jhinrichs@cityu.edu.

Gordon Albright School of Education Students: 679; includes 85 minority (21 African Americans, 14 American Indian/Alaska Native, 30 Asian Americans or Pacific Islanders, 20 Hispanic Americans), 1 international. Average age 36. 700 applicants, 100% accepted, 200 enrolled. *Faculty:* 23 full-time (13 women), 345 part-time/adjunct (212 women). Expenses: Contact institution. *Financial support:* In 2008–09, 40 students received support. Federal Work-Study and scholarships/grants available. Support available to part-time students. Financial award applicants required to submit FAFSA. In 2008, 476 master's awarded. *Degree program information:* Part-time and evening/weekend programs available. Postbaccalaureate distance learning degree programs offered (no on-campus study). Offers curriculum and instruction (M Ed); educational leadership (M Ed); educational leadership: administrator certification (Certificate); executive leadership: superintendent certification (Certificate); guidance and counseling (M Ed); leadership (M Ed); leadership and school counseling (M Ed); professional certification for teachers (Certificate); reading and literacy (M Ed); reading and literacy in education (M Ed); teacher certification (elementary K-8) (MIT); teacher certification (special education K-12) (MIT); technology, curriculum, and instruction (M Ed). *Application deadline:* For fall admission, 9/1 for international students; for winter admission, 12/1 for international students; for spring admission, 3/1 for international students. Applications are processed on a rolling basis. *Application fee:* $50. Electronic applications accepted. *Application Contact:* 800-426-5596, Fax: 425-709-5363, E-mail: info@cityu.edu. *Dean,* Judy Hinrichs, 425-637-101 Ext. 5465, Fax: 425-709-5363, E-mail: jhinrichs@cityu.edu.

School of Management Students: 1,030; includes 131 minority (53 African Americans, 4 American Indian/Alaska Native, 63 Asian Americans or Pacific Islanders, 11 Hispanic Americans), 156 international. Average age 36. 771 applicants, 100% accepted, 224 enrolled. *Faculty:* 15 full-time (8 women), 513 part-time/adjunct (148 women). Expenses: Contact institution. *Financial support:* In 2008–09, 12 students received support. Federal Work-Study available. Support available to part-time students. Financial award applicants required to submit FAFSA. In 2008, 731 master's awarded. *Degree program information:* Part-time and evening/weekend programs available. Postbaccalaureate distance learning degree programs offered (no on-campus study). Offers accounting (Certificate); change leadership (MBA, Certificate); financial management (MBA, Certificate); general management (MBA); general management-Europe (MBA); global leadership (Certificate); global marketing (MBA); individualized study (MBA); information security (MS); information systems (MBA); leadership (MA); marketing (MBA, Certificate); project management (MBA, MS, Certificate); sustainable business (Certificate); technology management (MBA, MS, Certificate). *Application deadline:* For fall admission, 9/1 for international students; for winter admission, 12/1 for international students; for spring admission, 3/1 for international students. Applications are processed on a rolling basis. *Application fee:* $50. Electronic applications accepted. *Application Contact:* 800-426-5596, Fax: 425-709-5363, E-mail: info@cityu.edu. *Dean,* Dr. Kurt Kirstein, 425-637-1010 Ext. 5456, Fax: 425-709-5363, E-mail: kdkirstein@cityu.edu.

CLAFLIN UNIVERSITY, Orangeburg, SC 29115

General Information Independent-religious, coed, comprehensive institution. *Enrollment:* 1,773 graduate, professional, and undergraduate students; 61 full-time matriculated graduate/professional students (40 women), 22 part-time matriculated graduate/professional students (12 women). *Enrollment by degree level:* 83 master's. *Tuition:* Full-time $8208; part-time $456 per credit hour. *Required fees:* $456 per credit hour. One-time fee: $150 part-time. *Graduate housing:* Room and/or apartments available on a first-come, first-served basis to single students; on-campus housing not available to married students. Typical cost: $3034 per year ($6806 including board). Housing application deadline: 4/15. *Student services:* Campus employment opportunities, career counseling, services for students with disabilities. *Library facilities:* H. V. Manning Library. *Online resources:* library catalog, web page. *Collection:* 162,027 titles, 495 serial subscriptions, 1,146 audiovisual materials.

Computer facilities: 500 computers available on campus for general student use. A campuswide network can be accessed from student residence rooms and from off campus. Online class registration is available. *Web address:* http://www.claflin.edu/.

General Application Contact: Dr. Jan Bowman, Dean, Center for Professional and Continuing Studies and Graduate Programs, 803-535-5573, Fax: 803-535-5576, E-mail: janbowman@claflin.edu.

GRADUATE UNITS

Graduate Programs Students: 61 full-time (40 women), 22 part-time (12 women); includes 66 African Americans, 15 international. Expenses: Contact institution. *Financial support:* In 2008–09, 6 research assistantships (averaging $15,000 per year), 10 teaching assistantships (averaging $10,000 per year) were awarded. Financial award application deadline: 4/15; financial award applicants required to submit FAFSA. In 2008, 31 master's awarded. *Degree program information:* Part-time programs available. Offers biotechnology (MS); business administration (MBA); educational studies (M Ed). *Application deadline:* For fall admission, 7/15 priority date for domestic students; for spring admission, 11/1 priority date for domestic students. *Application fee:* $40 ($55 for international students). *Application Contact:* Dr. Jan Bowman, Dean, Center for Professional and Continuing Studies and Graduate Programs, 803-535-5573, Fax: 803-535-5576, E-mail: janbowman@claflin.edu. *Dean, Center for Professional and Continuing Studies and Graduate Programs,* Dr. Jan Bowman, 803-535-5573, Fax: 803-535-5576, E-mail: janbowman@claflin.edu.

CLAREMONT GRADUATE UNIVERSITY, Claremont, CA 91711-6160

General Information Independent, coed, graduate-only institution. CGS member. *Enrollment by degree level:* 918 master's, 1,264 doctoral, 25 other advanced degrees. *Graduate faculty:* 117 full-time (46 women), 14 part-time/adjunct (1 woman). *Tuition:* Full-time $33,698; part-time $1465 per unit. *Required fees:* $310; $155 per semester. Tuition and fees vary according to program. *Graduate housing:* Rooms and/or apartments available on a first-come, first-served basis to single and married students. Typical cost: $6500 per year for single students; $6500 per year for married students. Room charges vary according to housing facility selected. *Student services:* Campus employment opportunities, campus safety program, career counseling, free psychological counseling, international student services, low-cost health insurance, multicultural affairs office, teacher training, writing training. *Library facilities:* Honnold Library plus 3 others. *Online resources:* library catalog, web page, access to other libraries' catalogs. *Collection:* 3.4 million titles, 6,000 serial subscriptions, 606

Claremont Graduate University (continued)

audiovisual materials. *Research affiliation:* Claremont School of Theology (religion), Rancho Santa Ana Botanic Garden (botany/native plants).

Computer facilities: 90 computers available on campus for general student use. A campuswide network can be accessed. Online class registration is available. *Web address:* http://www.cgu.edu/.

General Application Contact: Julia Evans, Director of Central Recruitment, 909-607-3689, Fax: 909-607-7285, E-mail: admiss@cgu.edu.

GRADUATE UNITS

Graduate Programs Students: 1,746 full-time (887 women), 461 part-time (267 women); includes 554 minority (135 African Americans, 6 American Indian/Alaska Native, 190 Asian Americans or Pacific Islanders, 223 Hispanic Americans), 335 international. Average age 35. *Faculty:* 117 full-time (46 women), 14 part-time/adjunct (1 woman). Expenses: Contact institution. *Financial support:* Fellowships, research assistantships, teaching assistantships, career-related internships or fieldwork, Federal Work-Study, institutionally sponsored loans, scholarships/grants, tuition waivers (full and partial), and unspecified assistantships available. Support available to part-time students. Financial award application deadline: 2/15; financial award applicants required to submit FAFSA. In 2008, 367 master's, 139 doctorates, 72 other advanced degrees awarded. *Degree program information:* Part-time programs available. Offers arts management (MA); botany (MS, PhD); financial engineering (MSFE); public policy and evaluation (MA). *Application deadline:* For fall admission, 2/1 priority date for domestic and international students; for spring admission, 11/1 priority date for domestic and international students. Applications are processed on a rolling basis. *Application fee:* $60. Electronic applications accepted. *Application Contact:* Yi Feng, Provost and Vice President for Academic Affairs, 909-626-8694, Fax: 909-621-8450, E-mail: yi.feng@cgu.edu. *Provost and Vice President for Academic Affairs,* Yi Feng, 909-626-8694, Fax: 909-621-8450, E-mail: yi.feng@cgu.edu.

Peter F. Drucker and Masatoshi Ito Graduate School of Management Students: 159 full-time (68 women), 108 part-time (47 women); includes 74 minority (14 African Americans, 1 American Indian/Alaska Native, 33 Asian Americans or Pacific Islanders, 26 Hispanic Americans), 58 international. Average age 37. *Faculty:* 14 full-time (3 women). Expenses: Contact institution. *Financial support:* Fellowships, research assistantships, teaching assistantships, Federal Work-Study, institutionally sponsored loans, and scholarships/grants available. Support available to part-time students. Financial award application deadline: 2/15; financial award applicants required to submit FAFSA. In 2008, 86 master's, 4 doctorates, 69 other advanced degrees awarded. *Degree program information:* Part-time programs available. Offers advanced management (MS); executive management (EMBA); leadership (Certificate); management (EMBA, MA, MBA, MS, PhD, Certificate); strategy (Certificate). *Application deadline:* For fall admission, 2/15 priority date for domestic students. Applications are processed on a rolling basis. *Application fee:* $60. Electronic applications accepted. *Application Contact:* Albert Ramos, Admissions Coordinator, 909-621-8067, Fax: 909-621-8551, E-mail: albert.ramos@cgu.edu. *Henry Y. Hwang Dean and Professor of Management,* Ira A. Jackson, 909-607-9209, Fax: 909-621-8543, E-mail: ira.jackson@cgu.edu.

School of Arts and Humanities Students: 358 full-time (200 women), 47 part-time (25 women); includes 89 minority (19 African Americans, 3 American Indian/Alaska Native, 29 Asian Americans or Pacific Islanders, 38 Hispanic Americans), 26 international. Average age 35. *Faculty:* 12 full-time (2 women), 9 part-time/adjunct (1 woman). Expenses: Contact institution. *Financial support:* Fellowships, research assistantships, teaching assistantships, Federal Work-Study, institutionally sponsored loans, and scholarships/grants available. Support available to part-time students. Financial award application deadline: 2/15; financial award applicants required to submit FAFSA. In 2008, 64 master's, 27 doctorates awarded. *Degree program information:* Part-time programs available. Offers Africana history (Certificate); Africana studies (Certificate); American studies (MA, PhD); American studies and U.S. history (MA, PhD); applied women's studies (MA); archival studies (MA); arts and humanities (M Phil, MA, MFA, DCM, DMA, PhD, Certificate); church music (MA, DCM); composition (MA, DMA); critical theory (MA, PhD); cultural studies (MA, PhD); digital media (MA, MFA); drawing (MA, MFA); early modern studies (MA, PhD); English (M Phil, MA, PhD); European studies (MA, PhD); historical performance practices (MA, DMA); installation (MA, MFA); literary theory (PhD); literature (MA, PhD); literature and creative writing (MA); literature and film (MA); media studies (MA, PhD); museum studies (MA); musicology (MA, PhD); new genre (MA, MFA); oral history (MA, PhD); painting (MA, MFA); performance (MA, MFA, DMA); philosophy (MA, PhD); photography (MA, MFA); sculpture (MA, MFA). *Application deadline:* For fall admission, 2/1 priority date for domestic students. Applications are processed on a rolling basis. *Application fee:* $60. Electronic applications accepted. *Application Contact:* Justin Evans, Admissions Coordinator, 909-607-1278, Fax: 909-607-1221, E-mail: humanities@cgu.edu. *Interim Dean,* Marc Redfield, 909-607-3337, Fax: 909-607-1221, E-mail: marc.redfield@cgu.edu.

School of Behavioral and Organizational Sciences Students: 234 full-time (168 women), 29 part-time (22 women); includes 58 minority (18 African Americans, 1 American Indian/Alaska Native, 25 Asian Americans or Pacific Islanders, 14 Hispanic Americans), 18 international. Average age 30. *Faculty:* 17 full-time (7 women), 1 part-time/adjunct (0 women). Expenses: Contact institution. *Financial support:* Fellowships, research assistantships, teaching assistantships, Federal Work-Study, institutionally sponsored loans, scholarships/grants, and tuition waivers (full and partial) available. Support available to part-time students. Financial award application deadline: 2/15; financial award applicants required to submit FAFSA. In 2008, 51 master's, 12 doctorates, 2 other advanced degrees awarded. *Degree program information:* Part-time programs available. Offers advanced study in evaluation (Certificate); behavioral and organizational sciences (MA, MS, PhD, Certificate); cognitive psychology (MA, PhD); developmental psychology (MA, PhD); evaluation and applied research methods (MA, PhD); health behavior research and evaluation (MA, PhD); human resource development and evaluation (MA); human resources design (MS); industrial/organizational psychology (MA, PhD); organizational behavior (MA, PhD); organizational psychology (MA, PhD); social psychology (MA, PhD). *Application deadline:* For fall admission, 1/15 priority date for domestic students. Applications are processed on a rolling basis. *Application fee:* $60. Electronic applications accepted. *Application Contact:* Paul Thomas, Director, External Affairs, 909-607-9016, Fax: 909-621-8905, E-mail: paul.thomas@cgu.edu. *Dean,* Stewart Donaldson, 909-607-9001, E-mail: stewart.donaldson@cgu.edu.

School of Educational Studies Students: 267 full-time (190 women), 202 part-time (146 women); includes 204 minority (55 African Americans, 1 American Indian/Alaska Native, 43 Asian Americans or Pacific Islanders, 105 Hispanic Americans), 7 international. Average age 37. *Faculty:* 19 full-time (13 women), 1 part-time/adjunct (0 women). Expenses: Contact institution. *Financial support:* Fellowships, research assistantships, Federal Work-Study, institutionally sponsored loans, and scholarships/grants available. Support available to part-time students. Financial award application deadline: 2/15; financial award applicants required to submit FAFSA. In 2008, 81 master's, 34 doctorates, 1 other advanced degree awarded. *Degree program information:* Part-time programs available. Offers Africana education (Certificate); education and policy (MA, PhD); higher education/student affairs (MA, PhD); human development (MA, PhD); public school administration (MA, PhD); quantitative evaluation (MA, PhD); special education (MA, PhD); teacher education (MA); teaching and learning (MA, PhD); urban leadership (PhD). *Application deadline:* For fall admission, 2/1 priority date for domestic students. Applications are processed on a rolling basis. *Application fee:* $60. Electronic applications accepted. *Application Contact:* Nicole Kouyoumdjian, Director of External Affairs, 909-607-8493, Fax: 909-621-8734, E-mail: nicole.kouyoumdjian@cgu.edu. *Dean,* Margaret Grogan, 909-621-8075, Fax: 909-621-8734, E-mail: margaret.grogan@cgu.edu.

School of Information Systems and Technology Students: 82 full-time (28 women), 31 part-time (13 women); includes 34 minority (6 African Americans, 20 Asian Americans or Pacific Islanders, 8 Hispanic Americans), 25 international. Average age 37. *Faculty:* 6 full-time (1 woman). Expenses: Contact institution. *Financial support:* Fellowships, research assistantships, teaching assistantships, Federal Work-Study, institutionally sponsored loans, and scholarships/grants available. Support available to part-time students. Financial award application deadline: 2/15; financial award applicants required to submit FAFSA. In 2008, 13 master's, 11 doctorates awarded. *Degree program information:* Part-time programs available. Offers electronic commerce (MS, PhD); health information management (MS); information systems (Certificate); knowledge management (MS, PhD); systems development (MS, PhD); telecommunications and networking (MS, PhD). *Application deadline:* For fall admission, 2/1 priority date for domestic students. Applications are processed on a rolling basis. *Application fee:* $60. Electronic applications accepted. *Application Contact:* Matt Hutter, Director of External Affairs, 909-621-3180, Fax: 909-621-8564, E-mail: matt.hutter@cgu.edu. *Dean,* Terry Ryan, 909-607-9591, Fax: 909-621-8564, E-mail: terry.ryan@cgu.edu.

School of Mathematical Sciences Students: 54 full-time (16 women), 7 part-time (1 woman); includes 14 minority (1 African American, 9 Asian Americans or Pacific Islanders, 4 Hispanic Americans), 16 international. Average age 34. *Faculty:* 5 full-time (0 women), 3 part-time/adjunct (0 women). Expenses: Contact institution. *Financial support:* Fellowships, research assistantships, Federal Work-Study, institutionally sponsored loans, scholarships/grants, and tuition waivers (full and partial) available. Support available to part-time students. Financial award application deadline: 2/15; financial award applicants required to submit FAFSA. In 2008, 5 master's, 3 doctorates awarded. *Degree program information:* Part-time programs available. Offers computational and systems biology (PhD); computational mathematics and numerical analysis (MA, MS); computational science (PhD); engineering and industrial applied mathematics (PhD); mathematics (PhD); operations research and statistics (MA, MS); physical applied mathematics (MA, MS); pure mathematics (MA, MS); scientific computing (MA, MS); systems and control theory (MA, MS). *Application deadline:* For fall admission, 2/1 priority date for domestic students. Applications are processed on a rolling basis. *Application fee:* $60. Electronic applications accepted. *Application Contact:* Susan Townzen, Program Coordinator, 909-621-8080, Fax: 909-607-8261, E-mail: susan.n.townzen@cgu.edu. *Dean,* John Angus, 909-621-8080, Fax: 909-607-8261, E-mail: john.angus@cgu.edu.

School of Politics and Economics Students: 266 full-time (84 women), 25 part-time (7 women); includes 40 minority (7 African Americans, 16 Asian Americans or Pacific Islanders, 17 Hispanic Americans), 96 international. Average age 33. *Faculty:* 17 full-time (5 women), 4 part-time/adjunct (0 women). Expenses: Contact institution. *Financial support:* Fellowships, research assistantships, teaching assistantships, Federal Work-Study, institutionally sponsored loans, and scholarships/grants available. Support available to part-time students. Financial award application deadline: 2/15; financial award applicants required to submit FAFSA. In 2008, 39 master's, 32 doctorates awarded. *Degree program information:* Part-time programs available. Offers American politics (MA, PhD); business and financial economics (MA, PhD); comparative politics (PhD); economic development (Certificate); economics (PhD); industrial organization (PhD); international and development economics (PhD); international economics policy and development (MA); international money and finance (PhD); international political economy (MA); international studies (MA); neuroeconomics (PhD); political economy and public policy (MA); political philosophy (PhD); political science (PhD); politics and economics (MA, PhD, Certificate); politics, economics and business (MA); public choice and public economics (PhD); public policy (MA, PhD); world politics (PhD). *Application deadline:* For fall admission, 2/1 priority date for domestic students. Applications are processed on a rolling basis. *Application fee:* $60. Electronic applications accepted. *Application Contact:* Laura Carillo, Recruiter and Admissions Coordinator, 909-621-8699, Fax: 909-621-7545, E-mail: laura.carillo@cga.edu. *Interim Dean,* Yi Feng, 909-621-8079, Fax: 909-621-7545, E-mail: yi.feng@cgu.edu.

School of Religion Students: 231 full-time (96 women), 4 part-time (2 women); includes 32 minority (13 African Americans, 11 Asian Americans or Pacific Islanders, 8 Hispanic Americans), 29 international. Average age 37. *Faculty:* 7 full-time (2 women), 2 part-time/adjunct (0 women). Expenses: Contact institution. *Financial support:* Fellowships, research assistantships, teaching assistantships, Federal Work-Study, institutionally sponsored loans, and scholarships/grants available. Support available to part-time students. Financial award application deadline: 2/15; financial award applicants required to submit FAFSA. In 2008, 13 master's, 16 doctorates awarded. *Degree program information:* Part-time programs available. Offers Hebrew Bible (MA, PhD); history of Christianity and religions of North America (MA, PhD); New Testament (MA, PhD); philosophy of religion and theology (MA, PhD); theology, ethics and culture (MA, PhD); women's studies in religion (MA, PhD). *Application deadline:* For fall admission, 2/1 priority date for domestic students. Applications are processed on a rolling basis. *Application fee:* $60. Electronic applications accepted. *Application Contact:* Brent Smith, Recruiter, 909-607-2653, Fax: 909-607-9587, E-mail: brent.smith@cgu.edu. *Dean,* Karen Torjesen, 909-607-3214, Fax: 909-621-9587, E-mail: karen.torjesen@cgu.edu.

CLAREMONT SCHOOL OF THEOLOGY, Claremont, CA 91711-3199

General Information Independent-religious, coed, graduate-only institution. *Graduate housing:* Rooms and/or apartments guaranteed to single and married students. Housing application deadline: 6/1. *Research affiliation:* Moore Multicultural Resource and Research Center, Institute for Antiquity and Christianity, Center for Process Studies, National United Methodist Native American Center, Center for Pacific and Asian-American Ministries, Ancient Biblical Manuscript Center.

GRADUATE UNITS

Graduate and Professional Programs *Degree program information:* Part-time programs available. Offers divinity (M Div); ministry (D Min); practical theology (PhD); religion and theology (MA); religious education (MARE). Electronic applications accepted.

CLARION UNIVERSITY OF PENNSYLVANIA, Clarion, PA 16214

General Information State-supported, coed, comprehensive institution. CGS member. *Graduate housing:* Room and/or apartments available on a first-come, first-served basis to single students; on-campus housing not available to married students.

GRADUATE UNITS

Office of Research and Graduate Studies *Degree program information:* Part-time and evening/weekend programs available.

College of Arts and Sciences *Degree program information:* Part-time programs available. Offers arts and sciences (MA, MS); biology (MS); English (MA); mass media arts, journalism, and communication studies (MS). Electronic applications accepted.

College of Business Administration *Degree program information:* Part-time and evening/weekend programs available. Offers business administration (MBA). Electronic applications accepted.

College of Education and Human Services *Degree program information:* Part-time programs available. Offers curriculum and instruction (M Ed); early childhood (M Ed); education (M Ed); education and human services (M Ed, MS, MSLS, CAS); English (M Ed); history (M Ed); library science (MSLS, CAS); literacy (M Ed); reading (M Ed); rehabilitative sciences (MS); science (M Ed); science education (M Ed); special education (MS); speech language pathology (MS); technology (M Ed).

School of Nursing Offers nursing (MSN).

See Close-Up on page 875.

CLARK ATLANTA UNIVERSITY, Atlanta, GA 30314

General Information Independent-religious, coed, university. CGS member. *Enrollment:* 4,068 graduate, professional, and undergraduate students; 309 full-time matriculated graduate/professional students (223 women), 379 part-time matriculated graduate/professional students (244 women). *Enrollment by degree level:* 455 master's, 212 doctoral, 21 other advanced degrees. *Graduate faculty:* 97 full-time (28 women), 29 part-time/adjunct (13 women). *Tuition:* Full-time $12,240; part-time $680 per credit hour. *Required fees:* $710; $355 per semester. *Graduate housing:* Room and/or apartments available to single students; on-campus housing not available to married students. Typical cost: $4984 per year ($8098 including board). Housing application deadline: 6/1. *Student services:* Campus employment opportunities, campus safety program, career counseling, free psychological counseling, international student services, low-cost health insurance. *Library facilities:* Robert W. Woodruff Library. *Online resources:* library catalog, web page, access to other libraries' catalogs. *Collection:* 383,985 titles, 35,440 serial subscriptions, 8,457 audiovisual materials.

Computer facilities: 650 computers available on campus for general student use. A campuswide network can be accessed from student residence rooms. Online class registration is available. *Web address:* http://www.cau.edu/.

General Application Contact: Michelle Clark-Davis, Graduate Program Admissions, 404-880-8709, E-mail: mdowis@cau.edu.

GRADUATE UNITS

School of Arts and Sciences Students: 69 full-time (46 women), 169 part-time (100 women); includes 211 minority (207 African Americans, 3 Asian Americans or Pacific Islanders, 1 Hispanic American), 11 international. Average age 34. 101 applicants, 75% accepted, 39 enrolled. *Faculty:* 59 full-time (10 women), 7 part-time/adjunct (5 women). Expenses: Contact institution. *Financial support:* Fellowships, research assistantships, teaching assistantships, career-related internships or fieldwork, Federal Work-Study, institutionally sponsored loans, scholarships/grants, and unspecified assistantships available. Support available to part-time students. Financial award application deadline: 4/30; financial award applicants required to submit FAFSA. In 2008, 36 master's, 16 doctorates awarded. *Degree program information:* Part-time programs available. Offers African-American studies (MA, DAH); Africana women's studies (MA, DAH); arts and sciences (MA, MPA, MS, DAH, PhD); biology (MS, PhD); chemistry (MS, PhD); computer and information science (MS); criminal justice (MA); English (MA, DAH); history (MA, DAH); mathematical sciences (MS); physics (MS); political science (MA, PhD); public administration (MPA); Romance languages (MA, DAH); sociology (MA). *Application deadline:* For fall admission, 4/1 for domestic and international students; for spring admission, 11/1 for domestic and international students. Applications are processed on a rolling basis. *Application fee:* $40 ($55 for international students). *Application Contact:* Michelle Clark-Davis, Graduate Program Admissions, 404-880-6605, E-mail: cauadmissions@cau.edu. *Dean,* Dr. Shirley Williams-Kirksey, 404-880-6774, E-mail: skirksey@cau.edu.

School of Business Administration Students: 62 full-time (30 women), 25 part-time (16 women); includes 72 minority (all African Americans), 5 international. Average age 27. 100 applicants, 76% accepted, 46 enrolled. *Faculty:* 15 full-time (5 women), 3 part-time/adjunct (1 woman). Expenses: Contact institution. *Financial support:* Fellowships, career-related internships or fieldwork, Federal Work-Study, scholarships/grants, and unspecified assistantships available. Support available to part-time students. Financial award application deadline: 4/30; financial award applicants required to submit FAFSA. In 2008, 43 master's awarded. *Degree program information:* Part-time programs available. Offers accounting (MA); business administration (MA, MBA); economics (MA). *Application deadline:* For fall admission, 4/1 for domestic and international students; for spring admission, 11/1 for domestic and international students. Applications are processed on a rolling basis. *Application fee:* $40 ($55 for international students). Electronic applications accepted. *Application Contact:* Michelle Clark-Davis, Graduate Program Admissions, 404-880-6605, E-mail: cauadmissions@cau.edu. *Interim Dean,* Dr. Edward Davis, 404-880-8454, E-mail: edavis@cau.edu.

School of Education Students: 50 full-time (34 women), 128 part-time (82 women); includes 167 minority (164 African Americans, 2 Asian Americans or Pacific Islanders, 1 Hispanic American), 2 international. Average age 34. 87 applicants, 83% accepted, 40 enrolled. *Faculty:* 15 full-time (7 women), 6 part-time/adjunct (3 women). Expenses: Contact institution. *Financial support:* Fellowships, career-related internships or fieldwork, Federal Work-Study, scholarships/grants, and unspecified assistantships available. Support available to part-time students. Financial award application deadline: 4/30; financial award applicants required to submit FAFSA. In 2008, 30 master's, 14 doctorates, 1 other advanced degree awarded. *Degree program information:* Part-time and evening/weekend programs available. Offers counseling and psychological studies (MA); curriculum (MA, MAT); education (MA, MAT, Ed D, Ed S); educational leadership (MA, Ed D, Ed S). *Application deadline:* For fall admission, 4/1 for domestic and international students; for spring admission, 11/1 for domestic and international students. Applications are processed on a rolling basis. *Application fee:* $40 ($55 for international students). Electronic applications accepted. *Application Contact:* Michelle Clark-Davis, Graduate Program Admissions, 404-880-6605, E-mail: cauadmissions@cau.edu. *Interim Dean,* Dr. Trevor Turner, 404-880-8504, E-mail: tturner@cau.edu.

School of Social Work Students: 128 full-time (113 women), 57 part-time (46 women); includes 164 minority (163 African Americans, 1 Hispanic American), 2 international. Average age 32. 89 applicants, 91% accepted, 63 enrolled. *Faculty:* 10 full-time (7 women), 13 part-time/adjunct (4 women). Expenses: Contact institution. *Financial support:* Fellowships, career-related internships or fieldwork, Federal Work-Study, scholarships/grants, and unspecified assistantships available. Support available to part-time students. Financial award application deadline: 4/30; financial award applicants required to submit FAFSA. In 2008, 65 master's, 6 doctorates awarded. *Degree program information:* Part-time programs available. Offers social work (MSW, PhD). *Application deadline:* For fall admission, 4/1 for domestic and international students; for spring admission, 11/1 for domestic and international students. Applications are processed on a rolling basis. *Application fee:* $40 ($55 for international students). Electronic applications accepted. *Application Contact:* Michelle Clark-Davis, Graduate Program Admissions, 404-880-6605, E-mail: cauadmissions@cau.edu. *Interim Dean,* Dr. Vimala Pillari, 404-880-8006, E-mail: rlyle@cau.edu.

CLARKE COLLEGE, Dubuque, IA 52001-3198

General Information Independent-religious, coed, comprehensive institution. *Enrollment:* 1,156 graduate, professional, and undergraduate students; 99 full-time matriculated graduate/professional students (68 women), 101 part-time matriculated graduate/professional students (83 women). *Enrollment by degree level:* 139 master's, 61 doctoral. *Graduate faculty:* 25 full-time (17 women), 6 part-time/adjunct (all women). *Tuition:* Part-time $602 per credit hour. *Graduate housing:* On-campus housing not available. *Student services:* Campus employment opportunities, career counseling, exercise/wellness program, free psychological counseling, international student services, low-cost health insurance, multicultural affairs office, writing training. *Library facilities:* Nicholas J. Schrupp Library. *Online resources:* library catalog, web page, access to other libraries' catalogs. *Collection:* 120,000 titles, 9,600 serial subscriptions, 1,400 audiovisual materials.

Computer facilities: 237 computers available on campus for general student use. A campuswide network can be accessed from student residence rooms and from off campus. Online class registration is available. *Web address:* http://www.clarke.edu/.

General Application Contact: Carrie Kirk, Graduate Studies Program Coordinator, 563-588-6635, Fax: 563-588-6789, E-mail: graduate@clarke.edu.

GRADUATE UNITS

Department of Nursing and Health *Degree program information:* Part-time programs available. Offers administration of nursing systems (MSN); advanced practice nursing (MSN); education (MSN); family nurse practitioner (MSN, PMC). Electronic applications accepted.

Physical Therapy Program Offers physical therapy (DPT). Freshman-entry master's degree program; entry to the MSPT is determined after junior year of the BS program.

Program in Business Administration *Degree program information:* Part-time and evening/weekend programs available. Offers business administration (MBA). Electronic applications accepted.

Program in Education *Degree program information:* Part-time and evening/weekend programs available. Postbaccalaureate distance learning degree programs offered (minimal on-campus study). Offers early childhood/special education (MA); educational administration: elementary and secondary (MA); educational media: elementary and secondary (MA); multi-categorical resource K–12 (MA); multidisciplinary studies (MA); reading: elementary (MA); technology in education (MA). Electronic applications accepted.

CLARKSON COLLEGE, Omaha, NE 68131-2739

General Information Independent, coed, primarily women, comprehensive institution. *Enrollment:* 820 graduate, professional, and undergraduate students; 9 full-time matriculated graduate/professional students, 160 part-time matriculated graduate/professional students. *Enrollment by degree level:* 164 master's, 5 other advanced degrees. *Graduate faculty:* 1 (woman) full-time, 7 part-time/adjunct (all women). *Tuition:* Part-time $457 per credit hour. *Required fees:* $65 per credit hour. *Graduate housing:* Room and/or apartments available on a first-come, first-served basis to single students; on-campus housing not available to married students. Typical cost: $6100 per year. Room charges vary according to housing facility selected. Housing application deadline: 6/30. *Student services:* Campus employment opportunities, campus safety program, career counseling, child daycare facilities, free psychological counseling. *Library facilities:* Clarkson College Library. *Online resources:* library catalog, web page. *Collection:* 8,807 titles, 262 serial subscriptions, 530 audiovisual materials.

Computer facilities: 40 computers available on campus for general student use. A campuswide network can be accessed from off campus. Online class registration is available. *Web address:* http://www.clarksoncollege.edu/.

General Application Contact: Denise Work, Director of Admissions, 402-552-3100, Fax: 402-552-6057, E-mail: workdenise@clarksoncollege.edu.

GRADUATE UNITS

Graduate Programs *Degree program information:* Part-time and evening/weekend programs available. Postbaccalaureate distance learning degree programs offered (minimal on-campus study). Offers adult nurse practitioner (MSN, Post-Master's Certificate); family nurse practitioner (MSN, Post-Master's Certificate); health care administration (MHCA); nursing education (MSN, Post-Master's Certificate); nursing health care leadership (MSN, Post-Master's Certificate). Electronic applications accepted.

CLARKSON UNIVERSITY, Potsdam, NY 13699

General Information Independent, coed, university. *Enrollment:* 3,045 graduate, professional, and undergraduate students; 400 full-time matriculated graduate/professional students (114 women), 46 part-time matriculated graduate/professional students (16 women). *Enrollment by degree level:* 51 first professional, 244 master's, 151 doctoral. *Graduate faculty:* 139 full-time (29 women), 9 part-time/adjunct (3 women). *Tuition:* Part-time $1011 per credit hour. *Graduate housing:* On-campus housing not available. *Student services:* Campus employment opportunities, campus safety program, career counseling, free psychological counseling, international student services, low-cost health insurance, multicultural affairs office, services for students with disabilities. *Library facilities:* Andrew S. Schuler Educational Resources Center plus 1 other. *Online resources:* library catalog, web page. *Collection:* 309,235 titles, 3,396 serial subscriptions, 2,095 audiovisual materials.

Computer facilities: Computer purchase and lease plans are available. 400 computers available on campus for general student use. A campuswide network can be accessed from student residence rooms and from off campus. Online class registration is available. *Web address:* http://www.clarkson.edu/.

GRADUATE UNITS

Graduate School Students: 400 full-time (114 women), 46 part-time (16 women); includes 13 minority (4 African Americans, 1 American Indian/Alaska Native, 6 Asian Americans or Pacific Islanders, 2 Hispanic Americans), 219 international. Average age 27. 794 applicants, 58% accepted, 155 enrolled. *Faculty:* 139 full-time (29 women), 9 part-time/adjunct (3 women). Expenses: Contact institution. *Financial support:* In 2008–09, 365 students received support, including 8 fellowships (averaging $25,000 per year), 100 research assistantships (averaging $20,150 per year), 68 teaching assistantships (averaging $20,150 per year); institutionally sponsored loans, scholarships/grants, tuition waivers (partial), unspecified assistantships, and merit-based scholarships also available. Financial award applicants required to submit FAFSA. In 2008, 124 master's, 21 doctorates awarded. *Degree program information:* Part-time and evening/weekend programs available. *Application deadline:* For fall admission, 5/15 priority date for domestic students; for spring admission, 10/15 priority date for domestic students. Applications are processed on a rolling basis. *Application fee:* $25 ($35 for international students). Electronic applications accepted.

Coulter School of Engineering Students: 197 full-time (46 women), 4 part-time (all women); includes 5 minority (1 American Indian/Alaska Native, 4 Asian Americans or Pacific Islanders), 137 international. Average age 27. 411 applicants, 61% accepted, 53 enrolled. *Faculty:* 70 full-time (9 women), 4 part-time/adjunct (0 women). Expenses: Contact institution. *Financial support:* In 2008–09, 180 students received support, including 5 fellowships (averaging $25,000 per year), 76 research assistantships (averaging $20,150 per year), 34 teaching assistantships (averaging $20,150 per year); scholarships/grants, tuition waivers (partial), and unspecified assistantships also available. In 2008, 57 master's, 17 doctorates awarded. *Degree program information:* Part-time programs available. Offers chemical engineering (ME, MS, PhD); civil and environmental engineering (PhD); civil engineering (ME, MS); computer engineering (ME, MS); electrical and computer engineering (PhD); electrical engineering (ME, MS); engineering (ME, MS, PhD); environmental science and engineering (MS, PhD); interdisciplinary engineering science (MS, PhD); mechanical engineering (ME, MS, PhD). *Application deadline:* For fall admission, 5/15 priority date for domestic students, 5/15 for international students; for spring admission, 10/15 priority date for domestic students, 10/15 for international students. Applications are processed on a rolling basis. *Application fee:* $25 ($35 for international students). Electronic applications accepted. *Application Contact:* Kelly Sharlow, Assistant to the Dean, 315-268-7929, Fax: 315-268-4494, E-mail: ksharlow@clarkson.edu. *Dean,* Dr. Goodarz Ahmadi, 315-268-6446, Fax: 315-268-4494, E-mail: ahmadi@clarkson.edu.

Division of Health Sciences Students: 51 full-time (38 women); includes 2 minority (both Hispanic Americans), 1 international. Average age 24. 37 applicants, 59% accepted, 19 enrolled. *Faculty:* 8 full-time (5 women), 1 (woman) part-time/adjunct. Expenses: Contact institution. *Financial support:* In 2008–09, 51 students received support. Tuition waivers (partial) available. Financial award applicants required to submit FAFSA. *Degree program information:* Part-time programs available. Offers health sciences (DPT); physical therapy (DPT). *Application deadline:* For fall admission, 3/15 priority date for domestic students. Applications are processed on a rolling basis. *Application fee:* $25 ($35 for international students). Electronic applications accepted. *Application Contact:* Dr. Scott D Minor, Associate Dean, 315-268-3786, Fax: 315-268-1539, E-mail: sminor@clarkson.edu. *Associate Dean,* Dr. Scott D Minor, 315-268-3786, Fax: 315-268-1539, E-mail: sminor@clarkson.edu.

School of Arts and Sciences Students: 95 full-time (16 women), 3 part-time (1 woman); includes 1 minority (Asian American or Pacific Islander), 61 international. Average age 27. 185 applicants, 55% accepted, 22 enrolled. *Faculty:* 41 full-time (9 women), 2 part-time/adjunct (1 woman). Expenses: Contact institution. *Financial support:* In 2008–09, 86 students received support, including 3 fellowships (averaging $25,000 per year), 24 research assistantships (averaging $20,150 per year), 34 teaching assistantships (averaging $20,150 per year); scholarships/grants and tuition waivers (partial) also available. In 2008, 15 master's, 4 doctorates awarded. *Degree program information:* Part-time programs available. Offers analytical chemistry (MS, PhD); arts and sciences (MS, PhD); computer science (MS); information technology (MS); inorganic chemistry (MS, PhD); mathematics (MS, PhD); organic chemistry (MS, PhD); physical chemistry (MS, PhD); physics (MS, PhD). *Application deadline:* For fall admission, 5/15 priority date for domestic students, 5/15 for international students; for spring admission, 10/15 priority date for domestic students, 10/15 for international students. Applications are processed on a rolling basis. *Application fee:* $25 ($35 for international students). Electronic applications accepted. *Application Contact:* Jennifer E Reed, Graduate School Coordinator/School of Arts and Sciences, 315-268-3802, Fax: 315-268-3989, E-mail: jreed@clarkson.edu. *Dean,* Dr. Peter Turner, 315-268-6544, Fax: 315-268-3983, E-mail: pturner@clarkson.edu.

School of Business Students: 57 full-time (14 women), 39 part-time (11 women); includes 5 minority (4 African Americans, 1 Asian American or Pacific Islander), 20 international. Average age 29. 161 applicants, 52% accepted, 61 enrolled. *Faculty:* 20 full-time (5 women), 2 part-time/adjunct (1 woman). Expenses: Contact institution. *Financial support:* In 2008–09, 48 students received support. Institutionally sponsored loans, unspecified assistantships, and merit-based scholarships available. In 2008, 52 master's awarded. *Degree program information:* Part-time and evening/weekend programs available. Offers business (MBA, MS); engineering and global operations management (MS); environmental management (MBA); general business administration (MBA); global supply chain management (MBA); innovation and new venture management (MBA). *Application deadline:* For fall admission, 5/15 priority date for domestic students; for spring admission, 10/15 priority

Clarkson University (continued)

date for domestic students. Applications are processed on a rolling basis. *Application fee:* $25 ($35 for international students). Electronic applications accepted. *Application Contact:* Karen Fuhr, Assistant to the Graduate Director, 315-268-6613, Fax: 315-268-3810, E-mail: fuhrk@clarkson.edu. *Dean*, Dr. Timothy Sugrue, 315-268-2300, Fax: 315-268-3810, E-mail: sugrue@clarkson.edu.

CLARK UNIVERSITY, Worcester, MA 01610-1477

General Information Independent, coed, university. CGS member. *Enrollment:* 3,330 graduate, professional, and undergraduate students; 626 full-time matriculated graduate/professional students (353 women), 295 part-time matriculated graduate/professional students (146 women). *Enrollment by degree level:* 717 master's, 197 doctoral, 7 other advanced degrees. *Graduate faculty:* 189 full-time (80 women), 68 part-time/adjunct (27 women). *Tuition:* Full-time $34,900; part-time $1091 per credit hour. *Required fees:* $30. *Graduate housing:* Rooms and/or apartments available on a first-come, first-served basis to single and married students. Typical cost: $7000 per year ($9750 including board) for single students; $7000 per year ($9750 including board) for married students. *Student services:* Campus employment opportunities, campus safety program, career counseling, exercise/wellness program, free psychological counseling, grant writing training, international student services, low-cost health insurance, multicultural affairs office, services for students with disabilities, teacher training, writing training. *Library facilities:* Robert Hutchings Goddard Library plus 4 others. *Online resources:* library catalog, web page, access to other libraries' catalogs. *Collection:* 289,658 titles, 1,383 serial subscriptions. *Research affiliation:* Massachusetts Biotechnology Research Institute, Worcester Area Computation Center, Worcester Foundation for Experimental Biology.

Computer facilities: 96 computers available on campus for general student use. A campuswide network can be accessed from student residence rooms and from off campus. Online class registration, online course support are available. *Web address:* http://www.clarku.edu/.

General Application Contact: Denise Robertson, Graduate School Coordinator, 508-793-7676, Fax: 508-793-8834, E-mail: gradadmissions@clarku.edu.

GRADUATE UNITS

Graduate School Students: 626 full-time (353 women), 295 part-time (146 women); includes 52 minority (24 African Americans, 1 American Indian/Alaska Native, 15 Asian Americans or Pacific Islanders, 12 Hispanic Americans), 404 international. Average age 30. 1,530 applicants, 61% accepted, 401 enrolled. *Faculty:* 189 full-time (80 women), 68 part-time/adjunct (27 women). Expenses: Contact institution. *Financial support:* In 2008–09, 5 fellowships with full and partial tuition reimbursements (averaging $12,500 per year), 54 research assistantships with full and partial tuition reimbursements (averaging $12,500 per year), 99 teaching assistantships with full and partial tuition reimbursements (averaging $12,500 per year) were awarded; career-related internships or fieldwork, Federal Work-Study, institutionally sponsored loans, scholarships/grants, and tuition waivers (full and partial) also available. Support available to part-time students. In 2008, 333 master's, 34 doctorates, 1 other advanced degree awarded. *Degree program information:* Part-time and evening/weekend programs available. Offers American history (PhD); biology (MA, PhD); chemistry (MA, PhD); clinical psychology (PhD); community development and planning (MA); developmental psychology (PhD); economics (PhD); education (MA Ed); English (MA); environmental science and policy (MA); geographic information science (MA); geographic information science for development and environment (MA); geography (PhD); history (MA, CAGS); holocaust history (PhD); international development and social change (MA); physics (MA, PhD); social-personality psychology (PhD). *Application deadline:* Applications are processed on a rolling basis. *Application fee:* $50. Electronic applications accepted. *Application Contact:* Denise Robertson, Graduate School Coordinator, 508-793-7676, Fax: 508-793-8834, E-mail: gradadmissions@clarku.edu. *Director*, Dr. Nancy Budwig, 508-793-7274.

College of Professional and Continuing Education Students: 57 full-time (35 women), 75 part-time (43 women); includes 9 minority (4 African Americans, 3 Asian Americans or Pacific Islanders, 2 Hispanic Americans), 26 international. Average age 32. 53 applicants, 100% accepted, 53 enrolled. *Faculty:* 21 part-time/adjunct (7 women). Expenses: Contact institution. *Financial support:* Career-related internships or fieldwork available. Support available to part-time students. In 2008, 69 master's, 1 other advanced degree awarded. *Degree program information:* Part-time and evening/weekend programs available. Offers information technology (MIT); liberal studies (MALA); professional and continuing education (MALA, MIT, MPA, MSPC, CAGS, Certificate); professional communication (MSPC); public administration (MPA, Certificate). *Application deadline:* Applications are processed on a rolling basis. *Application fee:* $50. Electronic applications accepted. *Application Contact:* Julia Parent, Director of Marketing, Communications, and Admissions, 508-793-7217, Fax: 508-793-7232, E-mail: jparent@clarku.edu. *Director*, Dr. Thomas Massey, 508-793-7217.

Graduate School of Management Students: 229 full-time (116 women), 145 part-time (58 women); includes 23 minority (11 African Americans, 8 Asian Americans or Pacific Islanders, 4 Hispanic Americans), 221 international. Average age 27. 714 applicants, 73% accepted, 158 enrolled. *Faculty:* 19 full-time (7 women), 11 part-time/adjunct (3 women). Expenses: Contact institution. *Financial support:* In 2008–09, 14 research assistantships with partial tuition reimbursements (averaging $4,800 per year), 14 teaching assistantships with partial tuition reimbursements (averaging $4,800 per year) were awarded; fellowships, career-related internships or fieldwork, Federal Work-Study, institutionally sponsored loans, and tuition waivers (partial) also available. Support available to part-time students. Financial award application deadline: 5/31. In 2008, 137 master's awarded. *Degree program information:* Part-time and evening/weekend programs available. Offers accounting (MBA); finance (MBA); global business (MBA); health care management (MBA); management (MBA, MSF); management of information technology (MBA); marketing (MBA). *Application deadline:* For fall admission, 6/1 priority date for domestic students; for spring admission, 12/1 priority date for domestic students. Applications are processed on a rolling basis. *Application fee:* $50. Electronic applications accepted. *Application Contact:* Lynn Davis, Enrollment and Marketing Director, 508-793-7406, Fax: 508-793-8822, E-mail: clarkmba@clarku.edu. *Dean*, Dr. Edward Ottensmeyer, 508-793-7406, Fax: 508-793-8822.

See Close-Up on page 877.

CLAYTON STATE UNIVERSITY, Morrow, GA 30260-0285

General Information State-supported, coed, comprehensive institution. *Enrollment:* 6,074 graduate, professional, and undergraduate students; 86 full-time matriculated graduate/professional students (47 women), 67 part-time matriculated graduate/professional students (33 women). *Enrollment by degree level:* 153 master's. *Graduate faculty:* 79 full-time (40 women). Tuition, state resident: full-time $2754; part-time $153 per credit hour. Tuition, nonresident: full-time $11,070; part-time $615 per credit hour. *Required fees:* $754; $377 per semester. *Graduate housing:* On-campus housing not available. *Student services:* Campus employment opportunities, career counseling, exercise/wellness program, free psychological counseling, international student services, low-cost health insurance, multicultural affairs office, services for students with disabilities. *Library facilities:* Clayton State University Library. *Online resources:* library catalog, web page, access to other libraries' catalogs. *Collection:* 77,043 titles, 4,250 serial subscriptions.

Computer facilities: 3,500 computers available on campus for general student use. A campuswide network can be accessed from off campus. Online class registration is available. *Web address:* http://www.clayton.edu/.

General Application Contact: Elizabeth Taylor, Assistant to the Dean of Graduate Studies, 678-466-4113, Fax: 678-466-4119, E-mail: elizabethtaylor@clayton.edu.

GRADUATE UNITS

School of Graduate Studies Students: 1 (woman) part-time. Average age 37. *Faculty:* 1 full-time (0 women). Expenses: Contact institution. *Financial support:* In 2008–09, 1 student received support. Application deadline: 7/1. Offers business administration (MBA); English (MAT); health administration (MHA); liberal studies (MALS); mathematics (MAT); nursing (MSN). *Application deadline:* For fall admission, 7/15 for domestic students, 5/1 for international students; for spring admission, 4/15 for domestic students, 2/1 for international students. *Application fee:* $50. Electronic applications accepted. *Application Contact:* Dr. Thomas Eaves, Associate Provost, 678-466-4100, Fax: 678-466-4119, E-mail: graduate@clayton.edu. *Associate Provost*, Dr. Thomas Eaves, 678-466-4100, Fax: 678-466-4119, E-mail: graduate@clayton.edu.

CLEARWATER CHRISTIAN COLLEGE, Clearwater, FL 33759-4595

General Information Independent-religious, coed, comprehensive institution.

GRADUATE UNITS

Program in Educational Leadership Postbaccalaureate distance learning degree programs offered (minimal on-campus study). Offers educational leadership (M Ed).

CLEARY UNIVERSITY, Ann Arbor, MI 48105-2659

General Information Independent, coed, comprehensive institution. *Enrollment:* 855 graduate, professional, and undergraduate students; 1 (woman) full-time matriculated graduate/professional student, 115 part-time matriculated graduate/professional students (67 women). *Enrollment by degree level:* 116 master's. *Graduate faculty:* 1 (woman) full-time, 20 part-time/adjunct (8 women). *Tuition:* Part-time $465 per credit hour. *Graduate housing:* On-campus housing not available. *Student services:* Campus employment opportunities, career counseling, writing training.

Computer facilities: 60 computers available on campus for general student use. A campuswide network can be accessed from off campus. Student portal available. *Web address:* http://www.cleary.edu/.

General Application Contact: Carrie Bonofiglio, Director of Student Recruiting, 800-686-1883, Fax: 517-552-7805, E-mail: cbono@cleary.edu.

GRADUATE UNITS

Online Program in Business Administration Students: 1 (woman) full-time, 115 part-time (67 women); includes 30 minority (21 African Americans, 1 American Indian/Alaska Native, 6 Asian Americans or Pacific Islanders, 2 Hispanic Americans), 7 international. Average age 34. 62 applicants, 77% accepted, 36 enrolled. *Faculty:* 1 (woman) full-time, 20 part-time/adjunct (8 women). Expenses: Contact institution. *Financial support:* In 2008–09, 80 students received support, including 80 fellowships (averaging $12,501 per year); Federal Work-Study and scholarships/grants also available. Support available to part-time students. Financial award application deadline: 8/15; financial award applicants required to submit FAFSA. In 2008, 22 master's awarded. *Degree program information:* Part-time and evening/weekend programs available. Postbaccalaureate distance learning degree programs offered (no on-campus study). Offers accounting (MBA); financial planning (MBA); financial planning (Graduate Certificate); green business strategy (MBA); management (MBA); nonprofit management (MBA); organizational leadership (MBA). *Application deadline:* For fall admission, 8/15 for domestic students, 7/15 for international students; for spring admission, 4/2 for domestic students, 1/2 for international students. Applications are processed on a rolling basis. *Application fee:* $50. Electronic applications accepted. *Application Contact:* Carrie Bonofiglio, Director of Student Recruiting, 800-686-1883, Fax: 517-552-7805, E-mail: cbono@cleary.edu. *Provost and Vice President for Academic Affairs*, Dr. Vincent Linder, 800-686-1883, Fax: 734-332-4646, E-mail: vlinder@cleary.edu.

CLEMSON UNIVERSITY, Clemson, SC 29634

General Information State-supported, coed, university. CGS member. *Enrollment:* 18,317 graduate, professional, and undergraduate students; 2,278 full-time matriculated graduate/professional students (945 women), 885 part-time matriculated graduate/professional students (454 women). *Enrollment by degree level:* 1,933 master's, 1,230 doctoral, 14 other advanced degrees. *Graduate faculty:* 802 full-time (214 women), 235 part-time/adjunct (83 women). Full-time tuition and fees vary according to program. *Graduate housing:* Rooms and/or apartments available on a first-come, first-served basis to single and married students. Typical cost: $2642 per year ($3914 including board) for single students; $2642 per year ($3914 including board) for married students. Room and board charges vary according to board plan, campus/location and housing facility selected. Housing application deadline: 1/30. *Student services:* Campus safety program, career counseling, exercise/wellness program, free psychological counseling, grant writing training, international student services, low-cost health insurance, multicultural affairs office, services for students with disabilities. *Library facilities:* Robert Muldrow Cooper Library plus 1 other. *Online resources:* library catalog, web page. *Collection:* 1.2 million titles, 5,587 serial subscriptions. *Research affiliation:* Savannah National Research Lab (energy), National Textile Center (textile and fiber technology), Greenville Hospital System (biological sciences), South Carolina Universities Research and Education Foundation (energy), Oak Ridge National Laboratory.

Computer facilities: Computer purchase and lease plans are available. 1,250 computers available on campus for general student use. A campuswide network can be accessed from student residence rooms and from off campus. Online class registration is available. *Web address:* http://www.clemson.edu/.

General Application Contact: Information Contact, 864-656-3195, E-mail: gradapp@clemson.edu.

GRADUATE UNITS

Graduate School Students: 2,278 full-time (945 women), 899 part-time (464 women); includes 240 minority (153 African Americans, 13 American Indian/Alaska Native, 39 Asian Americans or Pacific Islanders, 35 Hispanic Americans), 871 international. Average age 29. 4,268 applicants, 49% accepted, 962 enrolled. *Faculty:* 798 full-time (213 women), 223 part-time/adjunct (76 women). Expenses: Contact institution. *Financial support:* In 2008–09, 2,129 students received support, including 145 fellowships (averaging $4,827 per year), 773 research assistantships (averaging $16,143 per year), 1,018 teaching assistantships (averaging $13,063 per year); career-related internships or fieldwork, Federal Work-Study, institutionally sponsored loans, scholarships/grants, traineeships, health care benefits, tuition waivers (full and partial), and unspecified assistantships also available. Support available to part-time students. Financial award applicants required to submit FAFSA. In 2008, 708 master's, 132 doctorates, 3 other advanced degrees awarded. *Degree program information:* Part-time and evening/weekend programs available. Postbaccalaureate distance learning degree programs offered. *Application deadline:* For fall admission, 7/15 for international students; for spring admission, 9/15 for international students. Applications are processed on a rolling basis. *Application fee:* $50. Electronic applications accepted. *Application Contact:* Dr. Tristam Aldridge, Interim Associate Dean, 864-656-2561, Fax: 864-656-5344, E-mail: saldrid@clemson.edu. *Dean*, Dr. J. Bruce Rafert, 864-656-4172, Fax: 864-656-5344, E-mail: jbruce@mail.clemson.edu.

College of Agriculture, Forestry and Life Sciences Students: 384 full-time (187 women), 83 part-time (35 women); includes 24 minority (13 African Americans, 1 American Indian/Alaska Native, 4 Asian Americans or Pacific Islanders, 6 Hispanic Americans), 148 international. Average age 30. 483 applicants, 38% accepted, 128 enrolled. *Faculty:* 180 full-time (40 women), 39 part-time/adjunct (13 women). Expenses: Contact institution. *Financial support:* In 2008–09, 422 students received support, including 56 fellowships (averaging $4,100 per year), 192 research assistantships (averaging $14,200 per year), 150 teaching assistantships (averaging $15,700 per year); career-related internships or fieldwork, Federal Work-Study, institutionally sponsored loans, scholarships/grants, and unspecified assistantships also available. Financial award applicants required to submit FAFSA. In 2008, 44 master's, 35 doctorates awarded. *Degree program information:* Part-time programs available. Offers agricultural education (M Ag Ed); agriculture, forestry and life sciences (M Ag Ed, MFR, MS, PhD); animal and veterinary sciences (MS, PhD); applied economics and statistics (MS); biochemistry and molecular biology (MS, PhD); biological sciences (MS, PhD); biosystems engineering (MS, PhD); entomology (PhD); environmental toxicology (MS, PhD); food technology (PhD); food, nutrition, and culinary science (MS); forest resources (MFR, MS, PhD); genetics (MS, PhD); microbiology (MS, PhD); packaging science (MS); plant and environmental sciences (MS, PhD); wildlife and fisheries biology (MS, PhD). *Application deadline:* For fall admission, 4/15 for international students; for spring admission, 9/15 for international students. Applications are processed on a rolling basis. *Application fee:* $55. Electronic applications accepted. *Application Contact:*

Dr. Joseph Culin, Associate Dean for Research and Graduate Studies, 864-656-2810, E-mail: jculin@clemson.edu. *Dean*, Dr. Alan Sams, 864-656-7592, Fax: 864-656-1286.

College of Architecture, Arts, and Humanities Students: 349 full-time (162 women), 63 part-time (30 women); includes 35 minority (16 African Americans, 2 American Indian/Alaska Native, 9 Asian Americans or Pacific Islanders, 8 Hispanic Americans), 35 international. Average age 29. 515 applicants, 52% accepted, 160 enrolled. *Faculty:* 151 full-time (58 women), 35 part-time/adjunct (16 women). Expenses: Contact institution. *Financial support:* In 2008–09, 53 fellowships (averaging $4,386 per year), 46 research assistantships (averaging $9,337 per year), 212 teaching assistantships (averaging $9,165 per year) were awarded; career-related internships or fieldwork, Federal Work-Study, scholarships/grants, and unspecified assistantships also available. Financial award applicants required to submit FAFSA. In 2008, 112 master's, 1 doctorate awarded. *Degree program information:* Part-time programs available. Offers architecture (M Arch, MS); architecture, arts, and humanities (M Arch, MA, MCRP, MCSM, MFA, MLA, MRED, MS, PhD); city and regional planning (MCRP); construction science and management (MCSM); developmental planning (MCRP); digital production arts (MFA); English (MA); environmental design and planning (PhD); historic preservation (MS); history (MA); landscape architecture (MLA); professional communication (MA); real estate development (MRED); rhetorics, communication and information design (PhD); visual arts (MFA). *Application deadline:* For fall admission, 4/15 for international students; for spring admission, 9/15 for international students. Applications are processed on a rolling basis. *Application fee:* $55. Electronic applications accepted. *Application Contact:* Dr. James B London, Associate Dean for Research and Graduate Studies, 864-656-3927, E-mail: london1@clemson.edu. *Interim Dean*, Dr. Clifton Egan, 864-656-3084, Fax: 964-656-0204.

College of Business and Behavioral Science Students: 221 full-time (99 women), 182 part-time (60 women); includes 26 minority (14 African Americans, 2 American Indian/Alaska Native, 3 Asian Americans or Pacific Islanders, 7 Hispanic Americans), 60 international. Average age 30. 526 applicants, 42% accepted, 160 enrolled. *Faculty:* 130 full-time (31 women), 26 part-time/adjunct (8 women). Expenses: Contact institution. *Financial support:* In 2008–09, 197 students received support, including 10 fellowships (averaging $6,600 per year), 36 research assistantships (averaging $14,137 per year), 115 teaching assistantships (averaging $10,055 per year); career-related internships or fieldwork, Federal Work-Study, institutionally sponsored loans, and unspecified assistantships also available. Support available to part-time students. Financial award applicants required to submit FAFSA. In 2008, 132 master's, 9 doctorates awarded. *Degree program information:* Part-time and evening/weekend programs available. Offers accountancy and legal studies (MP Acc); applied economics (PhD); applied psychology (MS); applied sociology (MS); business administration (MBA); business and behavioral science (MA, MBA, MP Acc, MPA, MRED, MS, PhD); economics (MA); graphic communications (MS); human factors psychology (PhD); industrial/organizational psychology (PhD); management (MS, PhD); marketing (MS); policy studies (PhD); public administration (MPA). *Application deadline:* For fall admission, 4/15 for international students; for spring admission, 9/15 for international students. Applications are processed on a rolling basis. *Application fee:* $50. *Application Contact:* Dr. Caron St. John, Associate Dean for Graduate Programs, 864-656-3177, Fax: 864-656-5344, E-mail: scaron@clemson.edu. *Dean*, Dr. Claude C. Lilly, 864-656-3178.

College of Engineering and Science Students: 1,006 full-time (263 women), 106 part-time (20 women); includes 59 minority (36 African Americans, 4 American Indian/Alaska Native, 14 Asian Americans or Pacific Islanders, 5 Hispanic Americans), 598 international. Average age 28. 2,345 applicants, 49% accepted, 357 enrolled. *Faculty:* 249 full-time (29 women), 103 part-time/adjunct (27 women). Expenses: Contact institution. *Financial support:* In 2008–09, 32 fellowships (averaging $6,265 per year), 417 research assistantships (averaging $17,872 per year), 415 teaching assistantships (averaging $15,374 per year) were awarded; career-related internships or fieldwork, institutionally sponsored loans, and unspecified assistantships also available. Support available to part-time students. Financial award applicants required to submit FAFSA. In 2008, 170 master's, 74 doctorates awarded. *Degree program information:* Part-time programs available. Offers applied and pure mathematics (MS, PhD); automotive engineering (MS, PhD); bioengineering (MS, PhD); chemical engineering (MS, PhD); chemistry (MS, PhD); civil engineering (MS, PhD); computational mathematics (MS, PhD); computer engineering (MS, PhD); computer science (MS, PhD); electrical engineering (M Engr, MS, PhD); engineering and science (M Engr, MS, PhD); environmental engineering and science (M Engr, MS, PhD); environmental health physics (MS); hydrogeology (MS); industrial engineering (MS, PhD); materials science and engineering (MS, PhD); mechanical engineering (MS, PhD); operations research (MS, PhD); physics (MS, PhD); polymer and fiber science (MS, PhD); statistics (MS, PhD). *Application fee:* $55. Electronic applications accepted. *Application Contact:* Dr. R. Larry Dooley, Associate Dean for Research and Graduate Studies, 864-656-3200, Fax: 864-656-4466, E-mail: dooley@eng.clemson.edu. *Dean*, Dr. Esin Gulari, 864-656-3202.

College of Health, Education, and Human Development Students: 300 full-time (217 women), 464 part-time (318 women); includes 95 minority (74 African Americans, 4 American Indian/Alaska Native, 8 Asian Americans or Pacific Islanders, 9 Hispanic Americans), 20 international. Average age 33. 384 applicants, 65% accepted, 157 enrolled. *Faculty:* 88 full-time (55 women), 20 part-time/adjunct (12 women). Expenses: Contact institution. *Financial support:* In 2008–09, 9 fellowships, 54 research assistantships (averaging $11,600 per year), 120 teaching assistantships (averaging $9,850 per year) were awarded; career-related internships or fieldwork, Federal Work-Study, tuition waivers (full and partial), and unspecified assistantships also available. Support available to part-time students. Financial award applicants required to submit FAFSA. In 2008, 250 master's, 13 doctorates, 2 other advanced degrees awarded. *Degree program information:* Part-time and evening/weekend programs available. Postbaccalaureate distance learning degree programs offered. Offers administration and supervision (M Ed, Ed S); community counseling (M Ed); counselor education (M Ed); curriculum and instruction (PhD); educational leadership (M Ed, PhD); elementary education (M Ed); English (M Ed); health, education, and human development (M Ed, MAT, MHRD, MPRTM, MS, PhD, Ed S); human resource development (MHRD); mathematics (M Ed); middle grades education (MAT); natural sciences (M Ed); nursing (MS); parks, recreation, and tourism management (MPRTM, MS, PhD); reading (M Ed); school counseling (M Ed); secondary education (M Ed); special education (M Ed); student affairs (M Ed); youth development (MS). *Application deadline:* Applications are processed on a rolling basis. *Application fee:* $55. Electronic applications accepted. *Application Contact:* Dr. Larry Allen, Dean, 864-656-7640, Fax: 864-656-5488. *Dean*, Dr. Larry Allen, 864-656-7640, Fax: 864-656-5488.

Institute on Family and Neighborhood Life Students: 18 full-time (17 women), 1 (woman) part-time; includes 1 minority (Asian American or Pacific Islander), 10 international. Average age 32. 15 applicants, 13% accepted, 0 enrolled. *Faculty:* 4 full-time (1 woman), 7 part-time/adjunct (6 women). Expenses: Contact institution. *Financial support:* In 2008–09, 17 research assistantships (averaging $21,996 per year) were awarded; fellowships also available. Offers family and neighborhood life (PhD). *Application fee:* $55. *Application Contact:* Information Contact, 861-656-3195, E-mail: gradapp@clemson.edu. *Director*, Dr. Gary B. Melton, 964-656-6271.

CLEVELAND CHIROPRACTIC COLLEGE–KANSAS CITY CAMPUS, Overland Park, KS 66210

General Information Independent, coed, upper-level institution. *Enrollment:* 432 full-time matriculated graduate/professional students (154 women), 42 part-time matriculated graduate/professional students (24 women). *Enrollment by degree level:* 474 first professional. *Graduate faculty:* 38 full-time (6 women), 8 part-time/adjunct (3 women). *Tuition:* Full-time $17,500; part-time $18.06 per contact hour. *Required fees:* $170 per trimester. One-time fee: $150 full-time. *Graduate housing:* On-campus housing not available. *Student services:* Campus employment opportunities, campus safety program, career counseling, child daycare facilities, exercise/wellness program, free psychological counseling, international student services, low-cost health insurance, services for students with disabilities. *Library facilities:* Ruth R. Cleveland Memorial Library. *Online resources:* library catalog, web page. *Collection:* 15,000 titles, 6,100 serial subscriptions, 12,300 audiovisual materials.

Computer facilities: A campuswide network can be accessed. Educational software available. *Web address:* http://www.cleveland.edu/.

General Application Contact: Melissa Denton, Director of Admissions, 913-234-0744, Fax: 913-234-0906, E-mail: kc.admissions@cleveland.edu.

GRADUATE UNITS

Professional Program Students: 432 full-time (154 women), 42 part-time (24 women); includes 47 minority (13 African Americans, 3 American Indian/Alaska Native, 14 Asian Americans or Pacific Islanders, 17 Hispanic Americans), 11 international. Average age 33. 187 applicants, 50% accepted, 58 enrolled. *Faculty:* 38 full-time (6 women), 8 part-time/adjunct (3 women). Expenses: Contact institution. *Financial support:* Federal Work-Study, institutionally sponsored loans, and scholarships/grants available. Financial award application deadline: 3/1; financial award applicants required to submit FAFSA. In 2008, 103 DCs awarded. *Degree program information:* Part-time programs available. Offers chiropractic (DC). *Application deadline:* For fall admission, 7/1 priority date for domestic and international students; for winter admission, 11/1 priority date for domestic and international students; for spring admission, 3/1 priority date for domestic and international students. Applications are processed on a rolling basis. *Application fee:* $50. Electronic applications accepted. *Application Contact:* Melissa Denton, Director of Admissions, 913-234-0744, Fax: 913-234-0906, E-mail: kc.admissions@cleveland.edu. *Academic Dean*, Dr. Paul Barlett, 913-234-0643.

CLEVELAND CHIROPRACTIC COLLEGE–LOS ANGELES CAMPUS, Los Angeles, CA 90004-2196

General Information Independent, coed, upper-level institution. *Enrollment:* 342 graduate, professional, and undergraduate students; 256 full-time matriculated graduate/professional students (107 women), 12 part-time matriculated graduate/professional students (6 women). *Enrollment by degree level:* 268 first professional. *Graduate faculty:* 24 full-time (8 women), 10 part-time/adjunct (3 women). *Tuition:* Part-time $13,365 per year. *Required fees:* $375 per course. $125 per trimester. One-time fee: $265 part-time. *Graduate housing:* On-campus housing not available. *Student services:* Campus employment opportunities, campus safety program, career counseling, free psychological counseling, international student services. *Library facilities:* Carl Cleveland Jr. plus 1 other. *Online resources:* library catalog, web page, access to other libraries' catalogs. *Collection:* 23,937 titles, 152 serial subscriptions, 2,323 audiovisual materials. *Research affiliation:* Unihealth Foundation—Nonprofit philanthropic organization supports health & well-being of community (Chiropractic).

Computer facilities: 30 computers available on campus for general student use. A campuswide network can be accessed. Internet available. *Web address:* http://www.clevelandchiropractic.edu/.

General Application Contact: Dan Justin, Director of Admission, 800-466-CCLA, Fax: 323-906-2094, E-mail: dan.justin@cleveland.edu.

GRADUATE UNITS

Professional Program Students: 256 full-time (107 women), 12 part-time (6 women); includes 85 minority (10 African Americans, 1 American Indian/Alaska Native, 48 Asian Americans or Pacific Islanders, 26 Hispanic Americans), 14 international. Average age 29. 41 applicants, 76% accepted, 31 enrolled. *Faculty:* 24 full-time (8 women), 10 part-time/adjunct (3 women). Expenses: Contact institution. *Financial support:* In 2008–09, 97 students received support; fellowships, research assistantships with partial tuition reimbursements available, Federal Work-Study and scholarships/grants available. Financial award application deadline: 7/1. In 2008, 63 DCs awarded. Offers chiropractic medicine (DC). *Application deadline:* For fall admission, 8/10 priority date for domestic and international students; for spring admission, 12/7 priority date for domestic and international students. Applications are processed on a rolling basis. *Application fee:* $50. Electronic applications accepted. *Application Contact:* Dan Justin, Director of Admission, 800-466-CCLA, Fax: 323-906-2094, E-mail: dan.justin@cleveland.edu. *Vice President for Academic Affairs*, Dr. Ruth Sandefur, 816-501-0100, Fax: 323-660-5387.

THE CLEVELAND INSTITUTE OF ART, Cleveland, OH 44106-1700

General Information Independent, coed.

GRADUATE UNITS

Program in Medical Illustration

CLEVELAND INSTITUTE OF MUSIC, Cleveland, OH 44106-1776

General Information Independent, coed, comprehensive institution. *Graduate housing:* Room and/or apartments available on a first-come, first-served basis to single students; on-campus housing not available to married students. Housing application deadline: 5/30.

GRADUATE UNITS

Graduate Programs Offers performance (MM, DMA, AD, CPS). Electronic applications accepted.

CLEVELAND STATE UNIVERSITY, Cleveland, OH 44115

General Information State-supported, coed, university. CGS member. *Enrollment:* 15,809 graduate, professional, and undergraduate students; 1,833 full-time matriculated graduate/professional students (1,096 women), 1,852 part-time matriculated graduate/professional students (1,157 women). *Enrollment by degree level:* 227 first professional, 3,222 master's, 158 doctoral, 105 other advanced degrees. *Graduate faculty:* 383 full-time (145 women), 151 part-time/adjunct (55 women). *Graduate housing:* Room and/or apartments available on a first-come, first-served basis to single students; on-campus housing not available to married students. Housing application deadline: 7/15. *Student services:* Campus employment opportunities, campus safety program, career counseling, child daycare facilities, exercise/wellness program, free psychological counseling, grant writing training, international student services, low-cost health insurance, services for students with disabilities, teacher training. *Library facilities:* University Library plus 1 other. *Online resources:* library catalog, web page, access to other libraries' catalogs. *Collection:* 847,731 titles, 7,826 serial subscriptions, 143,894 audiovisual materials. *Research affiliation:* Metro Health System, Cleveland Clinic Foundation.

Computer facilities: Computer purchase and lease plans are available. 600 computers available on campus for general student use. A campuswide network can be accessed. Online class registration is available. *Web address:* http://www.csuohio.edu/.

General Application Contact: Deborah L. Brown, Interim Assistant Director, Graduate Admissions, 216-523-7572, Fax: 216-687-9214, E-mail: d.l.brown@csuohio.edu.

GRADUATE UNITS

Cleveland-Marshall College of Law Students: 453 full-time (189 women), 224 part-time (110 women); includes 83 minority (47 African Americans, 2 American Indian/Alaska Native, 22 Asian Americans or Pacific Islanders, 12 Hispanic Americans), 9 international. Average age 28. 1,627 applicants, 39% accepted, 200 enrolled. *Faculty:* 42 full-time (20 women), 37 part-time/adjunct (9 women). Expenses: Contact institution. *Financial support:* In 2008–09, 212 students received support, including 8 teaching assistantships with partial tuition reimbursements available (averaging $1,650 per year); career-related internships or fieldwork, Federal Work-Study, institutionally sponsored loans, scholarships/grants, tuition waivers (full and partial), and unspecified assistantships also available. Support available to part-time students. Financial award application deadline: 5/1; financial award applicants required to submit FAFSA. In 2008, 205 JDs, 2 master's awarded. *Degree program information:* Part-time and evening/weekend programs available. Offers business law (JD); civil litigation and dispute resolution (JD); criminal law (JD); employment labor law (JD); law (JD, LL M). *Application deadline:* For fall admission, 5/1 for domestic and international students. Applications are processed on a rolling basis. *Application fee:* $0. Electronic applications accepted. *Application Contact:* Christopher Lucak, Assistant Dean for Admissions, 216-687-4692, Fax: 216-

Cleveland State University (continued)

687-6881, E-mail: christopher.lucak@law.csuohio.edu. *Dean*, Geoffrey S. Mearns, 216-687-2300, Fax: 216-687-6881, E-mail: geoffrey.mearns@law.csuohio.edu.

College of Graduate Studies Students: 1,833 full-time (1,096 women), 1,852 part-time (1,157 women); includes 1,031 minority (572 African Americans, 9 American Indian/Alaska Native, 374 Asian Americans or Pacific Islanders, 76 Hispanic Americans). Average age 33. 4,010 applicants, 60% accepted. *Faculty:* 383 full-time (145 women), 151 part-time/adjunct (55 women). Expenses: Contact institution. *Financial support:* In 2008–09, 306 research assistantships with full and partial tuition reimbursements (averaging $3,480 per year), 123 teaching assistantships with full and partial tuition reimbursements (averaging $3,480 per year) were awarded; career-related internships or fieldwork, scholarships/grants, tuition waivers (full and partial), and unspecified assistantships also available. In 2008, 1,496 master's, 58 doctorates, 14 other advanced degrees awarded. *Degree program information:* Part-time and evening/weekend programs available. Postbaccalaureate distance learning degree programs offered (minimal on-campus study). *Application deadline:* For fall admission, 7/14 priority date for domestic students, 5/15 priority date for international students; for spring admission, 12/8 priority date for domestic students, 11/1 priority date for international students. Applications are processed on a rolling basis. *Application fee:* $30. Electronic applications accepted. *Application Contact:* Deborah L. Brown, Interim Assistant Director, Graduate Admissions, 216-523-7572, Fax: 216-687-9214, E-mail: d.l.brown@csuohio.edu. *Dean, College of Graduate Studies*, Dr. Vera Vogelsang-Coombs, 216-687-3595, Fax: 216-687-9214, E-mail: dean.graduatestudies@csuohio.edu.

College of Education and Human Services Students: 315 full-time (241 women), 1,255 part-time (988 women); includes 423 minority (372 African Americans, 1 American Indian/Alaska Native, 18 Asian Americans or Pacific Islanders, 32 Hispanic Americans), 36 international. Average age 35. 809 applicants, 61% accepted, 368 enrolled. *Faculty:* 86 full-time (60 women), 106 part-time/adjunct (81 women). Expenses: Contact institution. *Financial support:* In 2008–09, 64 students received support, including 38 research assistantships with full tuition reimbursements available (averaging $6,960 per year), 2 teaching assistantships with full tuition reimbursements available (averaging $7,800 per year); career-related internships or fieldwork, Federal Work-Study, scholarships/grants, tuition waivers (partial), and unspecified assistantships also available. Support available to part-time students. Financial award application deadline: 8/1; financial award applicants required to submit FAFSA. In 2008, 474 master's, 17 doctorates, 20 other advanced degrees awarded. *Degree program information:* Part-time and evening/weekend programs available. Postbaccalaureate distance learning degree programs offered (minimal on-campus study). Offers accelerated degree in adult learning and development (M Ed); adult learning and development (M Ed); art education (M Ed); chemical dependency counseling (Certificate); clinical nursing leader (MSN); community agency counseling (M Ed); community health education (M Ed); counseling (PhD); counseling and pupil personnel administration (Ed S); counseling psychology (PhD); early childhood education (M Ed); early childhood mental health counseling (Certificate); education and human services (M Ed, MPH, MSN, PhD, Certificate, Ed S); educational administration and supervision (M Ed); executive track (MSN); exercise science (M Ed); foreign language education (M Ed); forensic nursing (MSN); human performance (M Ed); leadership and lifelong learning (PhD); learning and development (PhD); mathematics and science education (M Ed); middle childhood education (M Ed); nursing education (MSN); physical education pedagogy (M Ed); policy studies (PhD); population health nursing (MSN); public health (MPH); school administration (PhD, Ed S); school counseling (M Ed); school health education (M Ed); special education (M Ed); sport and exercise psychology (M Ed); sports management (M Ed); teaching English to speakers of other languages (M Ed). *Application deadline:* For fall admission, 7/14 priority date for domestic students, 5/15 for international students; for spring admission, 12/8 priority date for domestic students, 11/1 for international students. Applications are processed on a rolling basis. *Application fee:* $30. Electronic applications accepted. *Application Contact:* Deborah L. Brown, Interim Assistant Director of Graduate Admissions, 216-687-5599, Fax: 216-687-5400, E-mail: d.l.brown@csuohio.edu. *Dean*, Dr. James A. McLoughlin, 216-687-3737, Fax: 216-687-5415, E-mail: j.mcloughlin@csuohio.edu.

College of Liberal Arts and Social Sciences Students: 243 full-time (180 women), 239 part-time (161 women); includes 121 minority (107 African Americans, 4 Asian Americans or Pacific Islanders, 10 Hispanic Americans), 18 international. Average age 34. 439 applicants, 49% accepted, 151 enrolled. *Faculty:* 156 full-time (64 women), 184 part-time/adjunct (79 women). Expenses: Contact institution. *Financial support:* In 2008–09, 99 research assistantships with full and partial tuition reimbursements (averaging $4,172 per year), 67 teaching assistantships with full and partial tuition reimbursements (averaging $4,657 per year) were awarded; fellowships, career-related internships or fieldwork, Federal Work-Study, institutionally sponsored loans, tuition waivers (full and partial), and unspecified assistantships also available. Support available to part-time students. In 2008, 174 master's awarded. *Degree program information:* Part-time and evening/weekend programs available. Offers applied communication theory and methodology (MA); art education (M Ed); art history (MA); bioethics (MA, Certificate); composition (MM); creative writing (MFA); culture, communication and health care (Certificate); economics (MA); English (MA); French (M Ed); history (MA); liberal arts and social sciences (M Ed, MA, MFA, MM, MSW, Certificate); museum studies (MA); music education (MM); performance (MM); philosophy (MA); social work (MSW); sociology (MA); Spanish (M Ed, MA). *Application deadline:* For fall admission, 7/15 priority date for domestic students; for spring admission, 12/2 priority date for domestic students. Applications are processed on a rolling basis. *Application fee:* $30. Electronic applications accepted. *Application Contact:* Deborah Brown, Interim Assistant Director, Graduate Admissions, 216-523-7572, Fax: 216-687-5400, E-mail: d.l.brown@csuohio.edu. *Dean*, Dr. Gregory M. Sadlek, 216-687-3660.

College of Science Students: 382 full-time (266 women), 226 part-time (152 women); includes 70 minority (44 African Americans, 1 American Indian/Alaska Native, 12 Asian Americans or Pacific Islanders, 13 Hispanic Americans), 95 international. Average age 29. 758 applicants, 39% accepted, 173 enrolled. *Faculty:* 107 full-time (35 women), 76 part-time/adjunct (43 women). Expenses: Contact institution. *Financial support:* In 2008–09, 174 students received support, including 47 research assistantships with full tuition reimbursements available (averaging $17,000 per year), 127 teaching assistantships with full and partial tuition reimbursements available (averaging $10,700 per year); unspecified assistantships also available. In 2008, 148 master's, 17 doctorates, 4 other advanced degrees awarded. *Degree program information:* Part-time and evening/weekend programs available. Postbaccalaureate distance learning degree programs offered (no on-campus study). Offers adult development and aging (PhD); analytical chemistry (MS); applied optics (MS); biology (MS); clinical chemistry (MS); clinical psychology (MA); clinical/bioanalytical chemistry (PhD); condensed matter physics (MS); consumer/industrial research (MA); diversity management (MA); environmental chemistry (MS); environmental science (MS); experimental research psychology (MA); health sciences (MS); inorganic chemistry (MS); mathematics (MA, MS); medical physics (MS); museum studies for natural historians (MS); occupational therapy (MOT); online health sciences (MS); optics and materials (MS); optics and medical imaging (MS); organic chemistry (MS); physical chemistry (MS); physical therapy (DPT); physician's assistant (MS); regulatory biology (PhD); school psychology (Psy S); science (MA, MOT, MS, DPT, PhD, Psy S); speech pathology and audiology (MA). *Application deadline:* For fall admission, 7/15 priority date for domestic and international students; for spring admission, 12/8 priority date for domestic and international students. Applications are processed on a rolling basis. *Application fee:* $30. *Application Contact:* Dr. Deborah L. Brown, Interim Assistant Director, Graduate Admissions, 216-523-7572, Fax: 216-687-5400, E-mail: d.l.brown@csuohio.edu. *Dean*, Dr. Bette R. Bonder, 216-687-5580, E-mail: b.bonder@csuohio.edu.

Fenn College of Engineering Students: 129 full-time (31 women), 242 part-time (36 women); includes 19 minority (9 African Americans, 8 Asian Americans or Pacific Islanders, 2 Hispanic Americans), 238 international. Average age 27. 686 applicants, 52% accepted, 80 enrolled. *Faculty:* 54 full-time (5 women), 12 part-time/adjunct (0 women). Expenses: Contact institution. *Financial support:* In 2008–09, 93 students received support, including 1 fellowship with full tuition reimbursement available, 120 research assistantships with full and partial tuition reimbursements available (averaging $8,694 per year), 20 teaching assistantships with full and partial tuition reimbursements available (averaging $8,082 per year); career-related internships or fieldwork, institutionally sponsored loans, scholarships/grants, tuition waivers (full and partial), and unspecified assistantships also available. Support available to part-time students. Financial award application deadline: 3/30. In 2008, 130 master's, 10 doctorates awarded. *Degree program information:* Part-time and evening/weekend programs available. Offers accelerated program civil engineering (MS); accelerated program environmental engineering (MS); applied biomedical engineering (D Eng); chemical engineering (MS, D Eng); civil engineering (MS, D Eng); electrical engineering (MS, D Eng); engineering (MS, D Eng); engineering mechanics (MS); environmental engineering (MS); industrial engineering (MS, D Eng); mechanical engineering (MS, D Eng); software engineering (MS). *Application deadline:* For fall admission, 7/18 for domestic students, 5/15 for international students; for spring admission, 12/5 for domestic students, 11/1 for international students. Applications are processed on a rolling basis. *Application fee:* $30. Electronic applications accepted. *Application Contact:* Dr. Paul P. Lin, Associate Dean, 216-687-2556, Fax: 216-687-9280, E-mail: p.lin@csuohio.edu. *Associate Dean*, Dr. Paul P. Lin, 216-687-2556, Fax: 216-687-9280, E-mail: p.lin@csuohio.edu.

Maxine Goodman Levin College of Urban Affairs Students: 88 full-time (43 women), 199 part-time (115 women); includes 65 minority (54 African Americans, 1 American Indian/Alaska Native, 2 Asian Americans or Pacific Islanders, 8 Hispanic Americans), 39 international. Average age 32. 259 applicants, 46% accepted, 63 enrolled. *Faculty:* 26 full-time (10 women), 11 part-time/adjunct (6 women). Expenses: Contact institution. *Financial support:* In 2008–09, 60 students received support, including 40 research assistantships with full tuition reimbursements available (averaging $8,000 per year), 15 teaching assistantships with full and partial tuition reimbursements available (averaging $7,000 per year); career-related internships or fieldwork, Federal Work-Study, institutionally sponsored loans, scholarships/grants, and unspecified assistantships also available. Support available to part-time students. Financial award application deadline: 3/1; financial award applicants required to submit FAFSA. In 2008, 74 master's, 7 doctorates, 23 other advanced degrees awarded. *Degree program information:* Part-time and evening/weekend programs available. Offers environmental studies (MAES); geographic information systems (Certificate); local and urban management (Certificate); non-profit management (Certificate); nonprofit administration and leadership (MNAL); nonprofit management (Certificate); public administration (MPA); urban affairs (MAES, MNAL, MPA, MS, MUPDD, PhD, Certificate); urban economic development (Certificate); urban planning, design, and development (MUPDD); urban real estate development (Certificate); urban real estate development and finance (Certificate); urban studies (MS); urban studies and public affairs (PhD). *Application deadline:* For fall admission, 7/15 priority date for domestic students, 5/15 for international students; for spring admission, 11/1 for international students. Applications are processed on a rolling basis. *Application fee:* $30. Electronic applications accepted. *Application Contact:* Graduate Program Coordinator, 216-523-7522, Fax: 216-687-5398, E-mail: urbanprograms@csuohio.edu. *Dean*, Dr. Edward W. Hill, 216-687-2135, E-mail: e.hill@csuohio.edu.

Nance College of Business Administration Students: 356 full-time (164 women), 600 part-time (258 women); includes 114 minority (69 African Americans, 1 American Indian/Alaska Native, 34 Asian Americans or Pacific Islanders, 10 Hispanic Americans), 186 international. Average age 30. 859 applicants, 60% accepted, 230 enrolled. *Faculty:* 79 full-time (19 women), 55 part-time/adjunct (13 women). Expenses: Contact institution. *Financial support:* In 2008–09, 110 students received support, including 45 research assistantships with full tuition reimbursements available (averaging $6,960 per year), 1 teaching assistantship with full tuition reimbursement available (averaging $7,800 per year); career-related internships or fieldwork, scholarships/grants, tuition waivers (full), and unspecified assistantships also available. Financial award application deadline: 5/17; financial award applicants required to submit FAFSA. In 2008, 374 master's, 4 doctorates, 2 other advanced degrees awarded. *Degree program information:* Part-time and evening/weekend programs available. Offers business administration (AMBA, EMBA, M Acc, MBA, MCIS, MLRHR, DBA, Graduate Certificate); computer and information science (MCIS); executive business administration (EMBA); finance (DBA); financial accounting/audit (M Acc); global business (Graduate Certificate); health care administration (MBA); information systems (DBA); labor relations and human resources (MLRHR); marketing (MBA, DBA); marketing analytics (Graduate Certificate); off-campus programs (MBA); operations management (DBA); taxation (M Acc). *Application deadline:* For fall admission, 7/15 priority date for domestic students, 5/15 for international students; for spring admission, 12/15 priority date for domestic students, 11/1 for international students. Applications are processed on a rolling basis. *Application fee:* $30. Electronic applications accepted. *Application Contact:* Kenneth Dippong, Director, Student Services, 216-523-7545, Fax: 216-687-9354, E-mail: K.DIPPONG@csuohio.edu. *Dean*, Dr. Robert F. Scherer, 216-687-3786, Fax: 216-687-9354, E-mail: r.scherer@csuohio.edu.

COASTAL CAROLINA UNIVERSITY, Conway, SC 29528-6054

General Information State-supported, coed, comprehensive institution. *Enrollment:* 8,154 graduate, professional, and undergraduate students; 103 full-time matriculated graduate/professional students (59 women), 128 part-time matriculated graduate/professional students (87 women). *Enrollment by degree level:* 231 master's. *Graduate faculty:* 35 full-time (8 women), 9 part-time/adjunct (8 women). Tuition, state resident: full-time $9192; part-time $383 per credit hour. Tuition, nonresident: full-time $11,400; part-time $475 per credit hour. *Required fees:* $80; $40 per term. Tuition and fees vary according to program. *Graduate housing:* On-campus housing not available. *Student services:* Campus safety program, career counseling, free psychological counseling, international student services, multicultural affairs office, services for students with disabilities. *Library facilities:* Kimbel Library. *Online resources:* library catalog, web page, access to other libraries' catalogs. *Collection:* 166,515 titles, 17,452 serial subscriptions, 6,344 audiovisual materials.

Computer facilities: Computer purchase and lease plans are available. 600 computers available on campus for general student use. A campuswide network can be accessed from student residence rooms. Online class registration is available. *Web address:* http://www.coastal.edu/.

General Application Contact: Dr. Richard L. Johnson, Associate Provost for Graduate Studies and Academic Outreach, 843-349-2192, Fax: 843-349-6444, E-mail: rjohnson@coastal.edu.

GRADUATE UNITS

College of Natural and Applied Sciences Students: 10 full-time (6 women), 29 part-time (15 women). Average age 26. 21 applicants, 67% accepted, 10 enrolled. *Faculty:* 15 full-time (1 woman). Expenses: Contact institution. *Financial support:* Fellowships, research assistantships, unspecified assistantships available. Support available to part-time students. Financial award application deadline: 3/1; financial award applicants required to submit FAFSA. In 2008, 13 master's awarded. *Degree program information:* Part-time and evening/weekend programs available. Offers coastal marine and wetland studies (MS). *Application deadline:* For fall admission, 3/1 priority date for domestic and international students; for spring admission, 11/1 priority date for domestic and international students. Applications are processed on a rolling basis. *Application fee:* $45. Electronic applications accepted. *Application Contact:* Dr. Richard L. Johnson, Associate Provost for Graduate Studies and Academic Outreach, 843-349-2192, Fax: 843-349-6444, E-mail: rjohnson@coastal.edu. *Dean*, Dr. Michael H. Roberts, 843-349-2282, Fax: 843-349-2545, E-mail: mroberts@coastal.edu.

Spadoni College of Education Students: 72 full-time (45 women), 67 part-time (55 women); includes 15 minority (10 African Americans, 5 Hispanic Americans), 1 international. Average age 31. 145 applicants, 91% accepted, 91 enrolled. *Faculty:* 10 full-time (4 women), 9 part-time/adjunct (8 women). Expenses: Contact institution. *Financial support:* Fellowships, research assistantships, unspecified assistantships available. Support available to part-time students. Financial award application deadline: 3/1; financial award applicants required to submit FAFSA. In 2008, 50 master's awarded. *Degree program information:* Part-time and evening/weekend programs available. Offers early childhood education (M Ed); education (MAT); elementary education (M Ed); secondary education (M Ed). *Application deadline:* For fall admission, 7/1 priority date for domestic and international students; for spring admission, 11/15 priority date for domestic and international students. Applications are processed on a rolling basis. *Application fee:* $45. Electronic applications accepted. *Application Contact:* Dr.

Richard L. Johnson, Associate Provost for Graduate Studies and Academic Outreach, 843-349-2192, Fax: 843-349-6444, E-mail: rjohnson@coastal.edu. *Dean*, Dr. Diane L. Mark, 843-349-2629, Fax: 843-349-2106, E-mail: dmark@coastal.edu.

Wall College of Business Administration Students: 21 full-time (8 women), 32 part-time (17 women); includes 3 minority (2 African Americans, 1 Asian American or Pacific Islander), 3 international. Average age 28. 29 applicants, 69% accepted, 14 enrolled. *Faculty:* 10 full-time (3 women). Expenses: Contact institution. *Financial support:* Application deadline: 3/1. In 2008, 17 master's awarded. *Degree program information:* Part-time and evening/weekend programs available. Offers accounting (MBA); business (MBA). *Application deadline:* For fall admission, 3/15 priority date for domestic and international students; for spring admission, 10/15 priority date for domestic and international students. Applications are processed on a rolling basis. *Application fee:* $45. Electronic applications accepted. *Application Contact:* Dr. Richard L. Johnson, Associate Provost for Graduate Studies and Academic Outreach, 843-349-2192, Fax: 843-349-6444, E-mail: rjohnson@coastal.edu. *MBA Director*, John O. Lox, 843-349-2469, Fax: 843-349-2455, E-mail: jlox@coastal.edu.

COE COLLEGE, Cedar Rapids, IA 52402-5092

General Information Independent-religious, coed, comprehensive institution. *Enrollment:* 1,326 graduate, professional, and undergraduate students; 31 part-time matriculated graduate/professional students (23 women). *Enrollment by degree level:* 31 master's. *Graduate faculty:* 5 full-time (2 women), 7 part-time/adjunct (3 women). *Tuition:* Part-time $385 per semester hour. *Graduate housing:* On-campus housing not available. *Student services:* Campus safety program, career counseling, international student services, teacher training, writing training.

Computer facilities: A campuswide network can be accessed from student residence rooms and from off campus. Online class registration is available. *Web address:* http://www.coe.edu/.

General Application Contact: Dr. Roger P. Johanson, Professor, 319-399-8510, Fax: 319-399-8721, E-mail: rjohanso@coe.edu.

GRADUATE UNITS

Department of Education Students: 31 part-time (23 women). Average age 30. 10 applicants, 100% accepted. *Faculty:* 5 full-time (2 women), 7 part-time/adjunct (3 women). Expenses: Contact institution. *Financial support:* Institutionally sponsored loans and tuition waivers (partial) available. Support available to part-time students. Financial award applicants required to submit FAFSA. In 2008, 8 master's awarded. *Degree program information:* Part-time programs available. Offers education (MAT). *Application deadline:* For fall admission, 8/1 priority date for domestic students; for spring admission, 3/1 priority date for domestic students. *Application fee:* $25. *Application Contact:* Betsy Kigin, Professor, 319-399-8575, Fax: 319-399-8721, E-mail: bkigin@coe.edu. *Associate Professor*, Dr. Roger P Johanson, 319-399-8510, Fax: 319-399-8721, E-mail: tmcnabb@coe.edu.

COLD SPRING HARBOR LABORATORY, WATSON SCHOOL OF BIOLOGICAL SCIENCES, Cold Spring Harbor, NY 11724

General Information Independent, coed, graduate-only institution. *Graduate housing:* Rooms and/or apartments guaranteed to single students and available to married students.

GRADUATE UNITS

Graduate Program Offers biological sciences (PhD).

COLEMAN COLLEGE, San Diego, CA 92123

General Information Independent, coed, comprehensive institution. *Graduate housing:* On-campus housing not available.

GRADUATE UNITS

Program in Business and Technology Management *Degree program information:* Evening/weekend programs available. Postbaccalaureate distance learning degree programs offered (no on-campus study). Offers business and technology management (MS).

Program in Information Technology *Degree program information:* Evening/weekend programs available. Offers information technology (MSIT).

COLGATE ROCHESTER CROZER DIVINITY SCHOOL, Rochester, NY 14620-2530

General Information Independent-religious, coed, graduate-only institution. *Enrollment by degree level:* 66 first professional, 15 master's, 34 doctoral. *Graduate faculty:* 8 full-time (4 women), 15 part-time/adjunct (7 women). *Tuition:* Full-time $8670; part-time $482 per credit hour. *Required fees:* $155. Tuition and fees vary according to course load and student level. *Graduate housing:* Rooms and/or apartments available on a first-come, first-served basis to single and married students. Typical cost: $6165 per year for single students; $6165 per year for married students. Housing application deadline: 7/1. *Student services:* Campus employment opportunities, low-cost health insurance, services for students with disabilities. *Library facilities:* Ambrose Swasey Library plus 1 other. *Online resources:* library catalog, access to other libraries' catalogs. *Collection:* 18,113 titles, 68 serial subscriptions, 752 audiovisual materials.

Computer facilities: 8 computers available on campus for general student use. A campuswide network can be accessed from student residence rooms and from off campus. Online class registration is available. *Web address:* http://www.crcds.edu/.

General Application Contact: Melissa M. Morral, Vice President for Enrollment Services, 585-340-9500, Fax: 585-340-9644, E-mail: mmorral@crcds.edu.

GRADUATE UNITS

Graduate and Professional Programs Students: 69 full-time, 46 part-time; includes 36 minority (27 African Americans, 2 American Indian/Alaska Native, 4 Asian Americans or Pacific Islanders, 3 Hispanic Americans), 7 international. Average age 43. 46 applicants, 98% accepted, 37 enrolled. *Faculty:* 8 full-time (4 women), 15 part-time/adjunct (7 women). Expenses: Contact institution. *Financial support:* In 2008–09, 49 students received support. Scholarships/grants available. Financial award application deadline: 9/1; financial award applicants required to submit FAFSA. In 2008, 18 first professional degrees, 1 master's, 2 doctorates awarded. *Degree program information:* Part-time programs available. Postbaccalaureate distance learning degree programs offered (minimal on-campus study). Offers theology (M Div, MA, D Min, Certificate). *Application deadline:* For fall admission, 7/1 priority date for domestic students, 3/1 for international students; for spring admission, 12/1 priority date for domestic students. Applications are processed on a rolling basis. *Application fee:* $35. *Application Contact:* Melissa M. Morral, Vice President for Enrollment Services, 585-340-9500, Fax: 585-340-9644, E-mail: mmorral@crcds.edu. *President*, Dr. Eugene C. Bay, 585-271-1320 Ext. 680, Fax: 585-271-8013.

COLGATE UNIVERSITY, Hamilton, NY 13346-1386

General Information Independent, coed, comprehensive institution. *Enrollment:* 2,844 graduate, professional, and undergraduate students; 5 full-time matriculated graduate/professional students (4 women), 2 part-time matriculated graduate/professional students (1 woman). *Enrollment by degree level:* 7 master's. *Graduate faculty:* 5 full-time (4 women), 3 part-time/adjunct (2 women). *Tuition:* Full-time $34,911; part-time $4364 per course. *Required fees:* $135 per semester. Tuition and fees vary according to course load. *Graduate housing:* On-campus housing not available. *Student services:* Campus safety program, career counseling, exercise/wellness program, free psychological counseling, low-cost health insurance, services for students with disabilities, teacher training, writing training. *Library facilities:* Case Library and Geyer Cnter for Information Technology plus 1 other. *Online resources:* library catalog, web page, access to other libraries' catalogs. *Collection:* 1.2 million titles, 29,632 serial subscriptions, 16,184 audiovisual materials.

Computer facilities: Computer purchase and lease plans are available. A campuswide network can be accessed from student residence rooms and from off campus. Online class registration, software applications are available. *Web address:* http://www.colgate.edu/.

General Application Contact: Ginger Babich, Administrative Assistant, Department of Educational Studies, 315-228-7256, Fax: 315-228-7857, E-mail: gbabich@colgate.edu.

GRADUATE UNITS

Master of Arts in Teaching Program Students: 5 full-time (4 women), 2 part-time (1 woman); includes 2 minority (1 African American, 1 Hispanic American). Average age 25. 8 applicants, 63% accepted, 4 enrolled. *Faculty:* 5 full-time (4 women), 3 part-time/adjunct (2 women). Expenses: Contact institution. *Financial support:* In 2008–09, 6 students received support. Scholarships/grants and unspecified assistantships available. Financial award application deadline: 2/15; financial award applicants required to submit FAFSA. In 2008, 3 master's awarded. Offers adolescence education NY state certification (MAT). *Application deadline:* For fall admission, 2/15 for domestic students. *Application fee:* $50. *Application Contact:* Ginger Babich, Administrative Assistant, 315-228-7256, Fax: 315-228-7857, E-mail: gbabich@colgate.edu. *Associate Dean of the Faculty*, Dr. Douglas Johnson, 315-228-7220.

THE COLLEGE AT BROCKPORT, STATE UNIVERSITY OF NEW YORK, Brockport, NY 14420-2997

General Information State-supported, coed, comprehensive institution. CGS member. *Enrollment:* 8,275 graduate, professional, and undergraduate students; 318 full-time matriculated graduate/professional students (201 women), 805 part-time matriculated graduate/professional students (520 women). *Enrollment by degree level:* 927 master's, 196 other advanced degrees. *Graduate housing:* Room and/or apartments available on a first-come, first-served basis to single students; on-campus housing not available to married students. Housing application deadline: 6/1. *Student services:* Campus employment opportunities, campus safety program, career counseling, child daycare facilities, exercise/wellness program, free psychological counseling, grant writing training, international student services, low-cost health insurance, multicultural affairs office, services for students with disabilities, teacher training, writing training. *Library facilities:* Drake Memorial Library.

Computer facilities: 700 computers available on campus for general student use. A campuswide network can be accessed from student residence rooms and from off campus. Online class registration is available. *Web address:* http://www.brockport.edu/.

General Application Contact: Danielle A. Welch, Graduate Admissions Counselor, 585-395-5465, Fax: 585-395-2515.

GRADUATE UNITS

Office of the Vice Provost Offers accounting (MS); forensic accounting (MS); liberal studies (MA).

School of Arts, Humanities and Social Sciences Offers arts, humanities and social sciences (MA, MFA); communication (MA); dance (MA, MFA); English (MA); history (MA); visual studies (MFA).

School of Education and Human Services Offers adolescence biology education (MS Ed); adolescence chemistry education (MS Ed); adolescence earth science education (MS Ed); adolescence education (MS Ed); adolescence English education (MS Ed); adolescence mathematics education (MS Ed); adolescence physics education (MS Ed); adolescence social studies education (MS Ed); alternate adolescence English inclusive education (MS Ed); alternate adolescence inclusive education (MS Ed); alternate adolescence mathematics inclusive education (MS Ed); alternate adolescence science inclusive education (MS Ed); alternate adolescence social studies inclusive education (MS Ed); arts administration (AGC); bilingual education (MS Ed, AGC); childhood curriculum specialist (MS Ed); childhood literacy (MS Ed); college counseling (MS Ed); education and human services (MPA, MS, MS Ed, MSW, AGC, CAS); educational administration (CAS); mental health counseling (MS); nonprofit management (AGC); public administration (MPA); school business administration (CAS); school counseling (MS Ed, CAS); social work (MSW).

School of Health and Human Performance Offers health and human performance (MS, MS Ed); health education (MS Ed); physical education (MS Ed); recreation and leisure (MS).

School of Science and Mathematics Offers biological sciences (MS); computational science (MS); environmental science and biology (MS); mathematics (MA); psychology (MA); science and mathematics (MA, MS).

See Close-Up on page 879.

COLLÈGE DOMINICAIN DE PHILOSOPHIE ET DE THÉOLOGIE, Ottawa, ON K1R 7G3, Canada

General Information Independent-religious, coed, comprehensive institution. *Enrollment:* 227 graduate, professional, and undergraduate students; 55 full-time matriculated graduate/professional students (10 women), 3 part-time matriculated graduate/professional students (1 woman). *Enrollment by degree level:* 39 master's, 19 doctoral. *Graduate faculty:* 11 full-time (1 woman), 7 part-time/adjunct (2 women). *Graduate tuition:* Tuition and fees charges are reported in Canadian dollars. *Tuition:* Full-time $1715 Canadian dollars; part-time $130 Canadian dollars per credit. *Required fees:* $125 Canadian dollars. One-time fee: $105 Canadian dollars part-time. Tuition and fees vary according to degree level and program. *Graduate housing:* Room and/or apartments available on a first-come, first-served basis to single students; on-campus housing not available to married students. Typical cost: $6600 Canadian dollars (including board). *Student services:* Campus safety program. *Library facilities:* Bibliothéque du College Dominicain. *Online resources:* library catalog. *Collection:* 125,000 titles, 500 serial subscriptions.

Computer facilities: 4 computers available on campus for general student use. *Web address:* http://www.collegedominicain.ca/.

General Application Contact: Francis Peddle, Master of Studies, 613-233-3696 Ext. 325, Fax: 613-233-6064, E-mail: francis.peddle@collegedominicain.ca.

GRADUATE UNITS

Graduate Programs Students: 55 full-time (10 women), 3 part-time (1 woman); includes 5 minority (2 African Americans, 3 Asian Americans or Pacific Islanders), 16 international. Average age 42. 13 applicants, 92% accepted, 6 enrolled. *Faculty:* 11 full-time (1 woman), 7 part-time/adjunct (2 women). Expenses: Contact institution. In 2008, 4 master's, 2 doctorates awarded. *Degree program information:* Part-time and evening/weekend programs available. Offers philosophy (MA Ph, PhD); theology (M Th, MA Th, PhD, Th D, L Th). *Application deadline:* For fall admission, 8/1 priority date for domestic students, 3/1 priority date for international students; for winter admission, 11/18 priority date for domestic students, 8/1 priority date for international students; for spring admission, 4/1 priority date for domestic students, 2/1 priority date for international students. Applications are processed on a rolling basis. *Application fee:* $40. *Application Contact:* Francis Peddle, Master of Studies, 613-233-3696 Ext. 325, Fax: 613-233-6064, E-mail: francis.peddle@collegedominicain.ca.

COLLEGE FOR FINANCIAL PLANNING, Greenwood Village, CO 80111

General Information Proprietary, coed, primarily men, graduate-only institution. *Graduate housing:* On-campus housing not available.

GRADUATE UNITS

Program in Financial Planning *Degree program information:* Part-time and evening/weekend programs available. Postbaccalaureate distance learning degree programs offered (no on-campus study). Offers finance (MS); financial analysis (MS); personal financial planning (MS). Electronic applications accepted.

COLLEGE OF CHARLESTON, Charleston, SC 29424-0001

General Information State-supported, coed, comprehensive institution. CGS member. *Enrollment:* 11,367 graduate, professional, and undergraduate students; 281 full-time matriculated graduate/professional students (193 women), 226 part-time matriculated graduate/professional students (161 women). *Enrollment by degree level:* 498 master's, 9 other advanced degrees. *Graduate faculty:* 210 full-time (93 women), 38 part-time/adjunct (20 women). Tuition, state resident: part-time $368 per credit hour. Tuition, nonresident: part-time

College of Charleston (continued)

$893 per credit hour. *Required fees:* $30 per course. One-time fee: $45 part-time. *Graduate housing:* Room and/or apartments available on a first-come, first-served basis to single students; on-campus housing not available to married students. Typical cost: $3202 per year. *Student services:* Campus employment opportunities, campus safety program, career counseling, child daycare facilities, exercise/wellness program, free psychological counseling, international student services, low-cost health insurance, multicultural affairs office, services for students with disabilities, teacher training, writing training. *Library facilities:* Marlene and Nathan Addlestone Library plus 1 other. *Online resources:* library catalog, web page, access to other libraries' catalogs. *Collection:* 762,034 titles, 3,075 serial subscriptions, 8,815 audiovisual materials. *Research affiliation:* Oak Ridge Associated Universities (science), South Carolina Department of Natural Resources, Marine Resources Division (marine biology, Environmental studies), National Institute of Standards and Technology (NIST) (marine biology, Environmental Studies,), NOAA (Marine Biology, Environmental Studies), US. Department of Agriculture (Environmental Studies), South Carolina Aquarium (Marine Biology, Environmental Studies).

Computer facilities: Computer purchase and lease plans are available. 578 computers available on campus for general student use. A campuswide network can be accessed from student residence rooms and from off campus. Online class registration is available. *Web address:* http://www.cofc.edu/.

General Application Contact: Susan Hallatt, Director of Admissions, 843-953-5614, Fax: 843-953-1434, E-mail: hallatts@cofc.edu.

GRADUATE UNITS

Graduate School Students: 281 full-time (193 women), 226 part-time (161 women); includes 36 minority (20 African Americans, 4 American Indian/Alaska Native, 3 Asian Americans or Pacific Islanders, 9 Hispanic Americans), 21 international. Average age 27. 341 applicants, 66% accepted, 170 enrolled. *Faculty:* 210 full-time (93 women), 38 part-time/adjunct (20 women). Expenses: Contact institution. *Financial support:* In 2008–09, 160 students received support, including 5 fellowships (averaging $22,000 per year), 30 research assistantships (averaging $18,000 per year), 32 teaching assistantships (averaging $13,300 per year); career-related internships or fieldwork, Federal Work-Study, institutionally sponsored loans, scholarships/grants, tuition waivers (partial), unspecified assistantships, and 75 graduate assistantships also available. Support available to part-time students. Financial award application deadline: 5/1; financial award applicants required to submit FAFSA. In 2008, 185 master's, 8 other advanced degrees awarded. *Degree program information:* Part-time and evening/weekend programs available. *Application deadline:* For fall admission, 7/1 priority date for domestic students, 4/1 for international students; for spring admission, 4/1 priority date for domestic students, 8/1 for international students. *Application fee:* $45. Electronic applications accepted. *Application Contact:* Susan Hallatt, Director of Admissions, 843-953-5614, Fax: 843-953-1434, E-mail: hallatts@cofc.edu. *Dean of the Graduate School,* Dr. Amy Thompson McCandless, 843-953-5730, Fax: 843-953-1434, E-mail: mccandlessa@cofc.edu.

School of Business and Economics Students: 44 full-time (16 women), 13 part-time (11 women); includes 3 minority (1 African American, 1 Asian American or Pacific Islander, 1 Hispanic American), 3 international. Average age 26. 55 applicants, 76% accepted, 31 enrolled. *Faculty:* 9 full-time (2 women). Expenses: Contact institution. *Financial support:* In 2008–09, 2 research assistantships were awarded; scholarships/grants and unspecified assistantships also available. Support available to part-time students. Financial award applicants required to submit FAFSA. In 2008, 31 master's awarded. Offers accountancy (MS); business and economics (MS). *Application deadline:* Applications are processed on a rolling basis. *Application fee:* $45. Electronic applications accepted. *Application Contact:* Susan Hallatt, Director of Graduate Admissions, 843-953-5614, Fax: 843-953-1434, E-mail: hallatts@cofc.edu. *Dean,* Dr. Alan Shao, 843-953-6651, Fax: 843-953-5697, E-mail: shaoa@cofc.edu.

School of Education, Health, and Human Performance Students: 77 full-time (64 women), 30 part-time (29 women); includes 5 minority (4 African Americans, 1 American Indian/Alaska Native), 5 international. Average age 28. 49 applicants, 76% accepted, 30 enrolled. *Faculty:* 29 full-time (23 women), 10 part-time/adjunct (9 women). Expenses: Contact institution. *Financial support:* In 2008–09, research assistantships (averaging $19,000 per year), teaching assistantships (averaging $13,300 per year) were awarded; career-related internships or fieldwork, Federal Work-Study, scholarships/grants, and unspecified assistantships also available. Support available to part-time students. Financial award application deadline: 4/1; financial award applicants required to submit FAFSA. In 2008, 44 master's awarded. *Degree program information:* Part-time and evening/weekend programs available. Offers early childhood education (MAT); education, health, and human performance (M Ed, MAT, Certificate); elementary education (MAT); English to speakers of other languages (Certificate); languages (M Ed); performing arts education (MAT); science and mathematics for teachers (M Ed); special education (MAT). *Application deadline:* Applications are processed on a rolling basis. *Application fee:* $45. Electronic applications accepted. *Application Contact:* Susan Hallatt, Director of Graduate Admissions, 843-953-5614, Fax: 843-953-1434, E-mail: hallatts@cofc.edu. *Dean,* Dr. Frances Welch, 843-953-5613, Fax: 843-953-5407, E-mail: welchf@cofc.edu.

School of Humanities and Social Sciences Students: 82 full-time (60 women), 68 part-time (49 women); includes 13 minority (7 African Americans, 1 American Indian/Alaska Native, 1 Asian American or Pacific Islander, 4 Hispanic Americans), 2 international. Average age 26. 106 applicants, 60% accepted, 51 enrolled. *Faculty:* 56 full-time (20 women), 7 part-time/adjunct (4 women). Expenses: Contact institution. *Financial support:* In 2008–09, research assistantships (averaging $19,000 per year); fellowships, career-related internships or fieldwork, Federal Work-Study, scholarships/grants, and unspecified assistantships also available. Support available to part-time students. Financial award applicants required to submit FAFSA. In 2008, 42 master's, 4 other advanced degrees awarded. *Degree program information:* Part-time and evening/weekend programs available. Offers communication (MA); English (MA); history (MA); humanities and social sciences (MA, MPA, Certificate); organizational and corporate communication (Certificate); public administration (MPA). *Application fee:* $45. Electronic applications accepted. *Application Contact:* Susan Hallatt, Director of Graduate Admissions, 843-953-5614, Fax: 843-953-1434, E-mail: hallatts@cofc.edu. *Dean,* Dr. Cynthia Lowenthal, 843-953-0760, Fax: 843-953-0758.

School of Languages, Cultures, and World Affairs Students: 9 full-time (8 women), 28 part-time (27 women); includes 10 minority (5 African Americans, 1 American Indian/Alaska Native, 4 Hispanic Americans), 3 international. Average age 34. 32 applicants, 59% accepted, 12 enrolled. *Faculty:* 9 full-time (8 women), 28 part-time/adjunct (27 women). Expenses: Contact institution. *Financial support:* Research assistantships, teaching assistantships, scholarships/grants and unspecified assistantships available. Financial award applicants required to submit FAFSA. In 2008, 10 master's, 3 other advanced degrees awarded. *Degree program information:* Part-time programs available. Offers bilingual legal interpreting (MA, Certificate); healthcare and medical interpreting (Certificate); languages, cultures, and world affairs (MA, Certificate). *Application fee:* $45. Electronic applications accepted. *Application Contact:* Susan Hallatt, Director of Graduate Admissions, 843-953-5614, Fax: 843-953-1434, E-mail: hallatts@cofc.edu. *Dean,* Dr. David Cohen, 843-953-5770, E-mail: cohend@cofc.edu.

School of Sciences and Mathematics Students: 69 full-time (45 women), 86 part-time (44 women); includes 5 minority (3 African Americans, 1 American Indian/Alaska Native, 1 Asian American or Pacific Islander), 8 international. Average age 27. 99 applicants, 65% accepted, 46 enrolled. *Faculty:* 68 full-time (18 women), 19 part-time/adjunct (6 women). Expenses: Contact institution. *Financial support:* In 2008–09, 5 fellowships (averaging $20,000 per year), 20 research assistantships (averaging $19,000 per year), 30 teaching assistantships (averaging $13,300 per year) were awarded; career-related internships or fieldwork, Federal Work-Study, institutionally sponsored loans, scholarships/grants, and unspecified assistantships also available. Support available to part-time students. Financial award application deadline: 6/1; financial award applicants required to submit FAFSA. In 2008, 58 master's awarded. Offers computer and information sciences (MS); environmental studies (MS); marine biology (MS); mathematics (MS); sciences and mathematics (MS, Certificate). *Application deadline:* Applications are processed on a rolling basis. *Application fee:* $45. Electronic applications accepted. *Application Contact:* Susan Hallatt, Director of Graduate Admissions, 843-953-5614, Fax: 843-953-1434, E-mail: hallatts@cofc.edu. *Dean,* Dr. George Pothering, 843-953-5991, E-mail: potheringg@cofc.edu.

School of the Arts Students: 10 full-time (8 women), 1 (woman) part-time. Average age 28. *Faculty:* 11 full-time (5 women), 4 part-time/adjunct (2 women). Expenses: Contact institution. *Financial support:* Scholarships/grants and unspecified assistantships available. Financial award applicants required to submit FAFSA. Offers arts (MPA, MS, Certificate); arts management (MPA, Certificate); historic preservation (MS). *Application fee:* $45. *Application Contact:* Susan Hallatt, Director of Graduate Admissions, 843-953-5614, Fax: 843-953-1434, E-mail: hallatts@cofc.edu. *Dean,* Dr. Valerie B. Morris, 843-953-8222, Fax: 843-953-4988, E-mail: morrisv@cofc.edu.

COLLEGE OF EMMANUEL AND ST. CHAD, Saskatoon, SK S7N 0W6, Canada

General Information Independent-religious, coed, graduate-only institution. *Graduate housing:* Room and/or apartments available on a first-come, first-served basis to single students; on-campus housing not available to married students. Housing application deadline: 6/15.

GRADUATE UNITS

Bachelor of Theology Program *Degree program information:* Part-time programs available. Postbaccalaureate distance learning degree programs offered (minimal on-campus study). Offers theology (B Th).

Graduate Programs *Degree program information:* Part-time programs available. Offers theology (M Div, MTS, STM).

THE COLLEGE OF IDAHO, Caldwell, ID 83605-4494

General Information Independent, coed, comprehensive institution. *Enrollment:* 944 graduate, professional, and undergraduate students; 16 full-time matriculated graduate/professional students (12 women). *Enrollment by degree level:* 16 master's. *Graduate faculty:* 4 full-time (2 women), 2 part-time/adjunct (1 woman). *Graduate housing:* Rooms and/or apartments available on a first-come, first-served basis to single and married students. Typical cost: $3450 per year ($7160 including board) for single students; $4700 per year ($8410 including board) for married students. Room and board charges vary according to board plan and housing facility selected. *Student services:* Campus employment opportunities, campus safety program, career counseling, free psychological counseling, low-cost health insurance, multicultural affairs office, services for students with disabilities. *Library facilities:* Terteling Library. *Online resources:* library catalog, web page. *Collection:* 154,437 titles, 1,758 serial subscriptions, 1,656 audiovisual materials.

Computer facilities: 242 computers available on campus for general student use. A campuswide network can be accessed from student residence rooms and from off campus. Online class registration, online course syllabi, course assignments, course discussion, online yearly catalog, College YouTube are available. *Web address:* http://www.collegeofidaho.edu/.

General Application Contact: Dr. Dennis Cartwright, Director of Education Programs, 208-459-5814, E-mail: dcartwright@collegeofidaho.edu.

GRADUATE UNITS

Program in Teacher Education Students: 16 full-time (12 women); includes 2 minority (1 African American, 1 Asian American or Pacific Islander). Average age 24. *Faculty:* 4 full-time (2 women), 2 part-time/adjunct (1 woman). Expenses: Contact institution. *Financial support:* Applicants required to submit FAFSA. In 2008, 11 master's awarded. Offers teacher education (MAT). *Application deadline:* For fall admission, 3/15 priority date for domestic students. *Application fee:* $0. *Application Contact:* Dr. Dennis Cartwright, Director of Education Programs, 208-459-5814, E-mail: dcartwright@collegeofidaho.edu. *Chair/Director,* Dr. Dennis Cartwright, 208-459-5815, Fax: 208-459-5043, E-mail: dcartwright@collegeofidaho.edu.

COLLEGE OF MOUNT ST. JOSEPH, Cincinnati, OH 45233-1670

General Information Independent-religious, coed, comprehensive institution. CGS member. *Enrollment:* 2,133 graduate, professional, and undergraduate students; 131 full-time matriculated graduate/professional students (103 women), 171 part-time matriculated graduate/professional students (126 women). *Enrollment by degree level:* 236 master's, 66 doctoral. *Graduate faculty:* 40 full-time (23 women), 17 part-time/adjunct (15 women). *Tuition:* Full-time $11,400; part-time $475 per credit hour. *Required fees:* $100 per semester. Tuition and fees vary according to program. *Graduate housing:* Room and/or apartments available on a first-come, first-served basis to single students; on-campus housing not available to married students. Typical cost: $3400 per year ($6900 including board). Housing application deadline: 3/31. *Student services:* Campus employment opportunities, campus safety program, career counseling, child daycare facilities, exercise/wellness program, free psychological counseling, international student services, low-cost health insurance, multicultural affairs office, services for students with disabilities, teacher training, writing training. *Library facilities:* Archbishop Alter Library. *Online resources:* library catalog, web page, access to other libraries' catalogs. *Collection:* 97,141 titles, 9,394 serial subscriptions, 4,047 audiovisual materials.

Computer facilities: Computer purchase and lease plans are available. 270 computers available on campus for general student use. A campuswide network can be accessed from student residence rooms and from off campus. Online class registration, computer-aided instruction are available. *Web address:* http://www.msj.edu/.

General Application Contact: Marilyn Hoskins, Assistant Director of Admissions for Graduate Recruitment, 513-244-4723, Fax: 513-244-4629, E-mail: marilyn_hoskins@mail.msj.edu.

GRADUATE UNITS

Graduate Education Program Students: 48 full-time (38 women), 93 part-time (73 women); includes 17 minority (13 African Americans, 2 American Indian/Alaska Native, 2 Hispanic Americans). Average age 35. 89 applicants, 93% accepted, 58 enrolled. *Faculty:* 15 full-time (11 women), 6 part-time/adjunct (5 women). Expenses: Contact institution. *Financial support:* In 2008–09, 6 students received support. Career-related internships or fieldwork and scholarships/grants available. Support available to part-time students. Financial award application deadline: 6/1; financial award applicants required to submit FAFSA. In 2008, 96 master's awarded. *Degree program information:* Part-time and evening/weekend programs available. Postbaccalaureate distance learning degree programs offered (minimal on-campus study). Offers adolescent young adult education (MA); art (MA); inclusive early childhood education (MA); instructional leadership (MA); middle childhood education (MA); multicultural special education (MA); music (MA); reading (MA). *Application deadline:* Applications are processed on a rolling basis. *Application fee:* $50. Electronic applications accepted. *Application Contact:* Marilyn Hoskins, Assistant Director of Admissions for Graduate Recruitment, 513-244-4723, Fax: 513-244-4629, E-mail: marilyn_hoskins@mail.msj.edu. *Chair,* Dr. Mifrando Obach, 513-244-3263, Fax: 513-244-4867, E-mail: mifrando_obach@mail.msj.edu.

Graduate Program in Religious Studies Students: 24 part-time (18 women); includes 2 minority (both African Americans). Average age 49. 10 applicants, 100% accepted, 2 enrolled. *Faculty:* 4 full-time (2 women). Expenses: Contact institution. *Financial support:* In 2008–09, 18 students received support. Career-related internships or fieldwork and scholarships/grants available. Support available to part-time students. Financial award application deadline: 6/1; financial award applicants required to submit FAFSA. In 2008, 8 master's awarded. *Degree program information:* Part-time and evening/weekend programs available. Offers spiritual and pastoral care (MA). *Application deadline:* Applications are processed on a rolling basis. *Application fee:* $50. Electronic applications accepted. *Application Contact:* Marilyn Hoskins, Assistant Director of Admissions for Graduate Recruitment, 513-244-4723, Fax: 513-244-4629, E-mail: marilyn_hoskins@mail.msj.edu. *Chair,* Dr. John Trokan, 513-244-4272, Fax: 513-244-4222, E-mail: john_trokan@mail.msj.edu.

Master of Nursing Program Students: 21 full-time (19 women); includes 2 minority (1 African American, 1 Asian American or Pacific Islander). Average age 28. 39 applicants, 82% accepted, 22 enrolled. *Faculty:* 6 full-time (3 women), 8 part-time/adjunct (7 women). Expenses: Contact institution. *Financial support:* Career-related internships or fieldwork available. Financial award application deadline: 6/1; financial award applicants required to submit FAFSA. In 2008, 24 master's awarded. Offers nursing (MN). *Application deadline:* Applications are processed on a rolling basis. *Application fee:* $50. Electronic applications accepted. *Application Contact:* Marilyn Hoskins, Assistant Director of Admissions for Graduate Recruitment, 513-244-4723, Fax: 513-244-4629, E-mail: marilyn_hoskins@mail.msj.edu. *Chair, Health Sciences Department,* Dr. Darla Vale, 513-244-4322, Fax: 513-451-2547, E-mail: darla_vale@mail.msj.edu.

Master of Science in Organizational Leadership Program Students: 48 part-time (31 women); includes 9 minority (8 African Americans, 1 American Indian/Alaska Native). Average age 40. 16 applicants, 100% accepted, 7 enrolled. *Faculty:* 6 full-time (1 woman), 1 (woman) part-time/adjunct. Expenses: Contact institution. *Financial support:* In 2008–09, 2 students received support. Application deadline: 6/1. In 2008, 117 master's awarded. *Degree program information:* Part-time and evening/weekend programs available. Offers organizational leadership (MS). *Application deadline:* Applications are processed on a rolling basis. *Application fee:* $50. Electronic applications accepted. *Application Contact:* Marilyn Hoskins, Assistant Director of Admissions for Graduate Recruitment, 513-244-4723, Fax: 513-244-4629, E-mail: marilyn_hoskins@mail.msj.edu. *Interim Chair,* Joseph Ahern, 513-244-4918, Fax: 513-244-4270, E-mail: joseph_ahern@mail.msj.edu.

Physical Therapy Program Students: 62 full-time (46 women), 4 part-time (3 women); includes 3 minority (1 African American, 1 American Indian/Alaska Native, 1 Asian American or Pacific Islander). Average age 24. 71 applicants, 68% accepted, 29 enrolled. *Faculty:* 7 full-time (5 women), 1 (woman) part-time/adjunct. Expenses: Contact institution. *Financial support:* In 2008–09, 5 students received support. Career-related internships or fieldwork, Federal Work-Study, and scholarships/grants available. Support available to part-time students. Financial award application deadline: 6/1; financial award applicants required to submit FAFSA. In 2008, 10 doctorates awarded. Offers physical therapy (MPT, DPT). *Application deadline:* For spring admission, 9/1 priority date for domestic and international students. *Application fee:* $50. Electronic applications accepted. *Application Contact:* Marilyn Hoskins, Assistant Director of Admissions for Graduate Recruitment, 513-244-4723, Fax: 513-244-4629, E-mail: marilyn_hoskins@mail.msj.edu. *Chair, Health Sciences Department,* Dr. Darla Vale, 513-244-4322, Fax: 513-451-2547, E-mail: darla_vale@mail.msj.edu.

See Close-Up on page 881.

COLLEGE OF MOUNT SAINT VINCENT, Riverdale, NY 10471-1093

General Information Independent, coed, comprehensive institution. *Graduate housing:* On-campus housing not available.

GRADUATE UNITS

School of Professional and Continuing Studies Offers adult nurse practitioner (MSN, PMC); family nurse practitioner (MSN, PMC); instructional technology and global perspectives (Certificate); middle level education (Certificate); multicultural studies (Certificate); nurse educator (PMC); nursing administration (MSN); nursing for the adult and aged (MSN); urban and multicultural education (MS Ed).

THE COLLEGE OF NEW JERSEY, Ewing, NJ 08628

General Information State-supported, coed, comprehensive institution. CGS member. *Enrollment:* 6,949 graduate, professional, and undergraduate students; 104 full-time matriculated graduate/professional students (83 women), 601 part-time matriculated graduate/professional students (479 women). *Enrollment by degree level:* 583 master's, 122 other advanced degrees. *Tuition, area resident:* Part-time $557 per credit. Tuition, state resident: part-time $557 per credit. Tuition, nonresident: part-time $845 per credit. *Required fees:* $135 per credit. *Graduate housing:* On-campus housing not available. *Student services:* Campus employment opportunities, career counseling, exercise/wellness program, free psychological counseling, international student services, low-cost health insurance, services for students with disabilities, teacher training. *Library facilities:* New Library. *Online resources:* library catalog, web page. *Collection:* 674,051 titles, 133,506 serial subscriptions, 14,916 audiovisual materials.

Computer facilities: Computer purchase and lease plans are available. 782 computers available on campus for general student use. A campuswide network can be accessed from student residence rooms and from off campus. Online class registration is available. *Web address:* http://www.tcnj.edu/.

General Application Contact: Susan L. Hydro, Assistant Dean, Office of Graduate Studies, 609-771-2300, Fax: 609-637-5105, E-mail: graduate@tcnj.edu.

GRADUATE UNITS

Graduate Division Students: 104 full-time (83 women), 601 part-time (479 women); includes 113 minority (46 African Americans, 1 American Indian/Alaska Native, 30 Asian Americans or Pacific Islanders, 36 Hispanic Americans), 3 international. 498 applicants, 90% accepted. Expenses: Contact institution. *Financial support:* Tuition waivers (partial) and unspecified assistantships available. Financial award application deadline: 5/1; financial award applicants required to submit FAFSA. In 2008, 377 master's, 97 other advanced degrees awarded. *Degree program information:* Part-time and evening/weekend programs available. Offers overseas education (M Ed, Certificate). *Application deadline:* For fall admission, 2/1 priority date for domestic students; for spring admission, 10/1 priority date for domestic students. *Application fee:* $70. Electronic applications accepted. *Application Contact:* Susan L. Hydro, Assistant Dean, Office of Graduate Studies, 609-771-2300, Fax: 609-637-5105, E-mail: graduate@tcnj.edu.

School of Culture and Society Students: 23 part-time (16 women); includes 1 minority (African American). 16 applicants, 100% accepted. Expenses: Contact institution. *Financial support:* Tuition waivers (partial) and unspecified assistantships available. Financial award application deadline: 5/1; financial award applicants required to submit FAFSA. In 2008, 15 master's awarded. *Degree program information:* Part-time programs available. Offers applied Spanish studies (MA); culture and society (MA); English (MA). *Application deadline:* For fall admission, 2/1 priority date for domestic students; for spring admission, 10/1 priority date for domestic students. *Application fee:* $70. Electronic applications accepted. *Application Contact:* Susan L. Hydro, Assistant Dean, Office of Graduate Studies, 609-771-2300, Fax: 609-637-5105, E-mail: graduate@tcnj.edu. *Dean,* Dr. Benjamin Rifkin, 609-771-3434, Fax: 609-637-5173.

School of Education Students: 102 full-time (82 women), 494 part-time (399 women); includes 90 minority (37 African Americans, 21 Asian Americans or Pacific Islanders, 32 Hispanic Americans), 2 international. 438 applicants, 90% accepted. Expenses: Contact institution. *Financial support:* Tuition waivers (partial) and unspecified assistantships available. Financial award application deadline: 5/1; financial award applicants required to submit FAFSA. In 2008, 307 master's, 33 other advanced degrees awarded. *Degree program information:* Part-time and evening/weekend programs available. Offers community counseling: human services (MA); community counseling: substance abuse and addiction (MA, Certificate); developmental reading (M Ed); education (M Ed, MA, MAT, MS, Certificate, Ed S); educational leadership (M Ed, Certificate); educational technology (MS); elementary education (M Ed, MAT); elementary teaching (MAT); English as a second language (M Ed); marriage and family therapy (Ed S); reading certification (Certificate); school counseling (MA); school personnel licensure: preschool-grade 3 (M Ed, MAT); secondary education (MAT); special education (M Ed, MAT); special education with learning disabilities (Certificate); speech pathology (MA); teaching English as a second language (M Ed, Certificate). *Application deadline:* For fall admission, 2/1 priority date for domestic students; for spring admission, 10/1 priority date for domestic students. *Application fee:* $70. Electronic applications accepted. *Application Contact:* Susan L. Hydro, Assistant Dean, Office of Graduate Studies, 609-771-2300, Fax: 609-637-5105, E-mail: graduate@tcnj.edu. *Dean, School of Education,* Dr. William Behre, 609-771-2100.

School of Nursing, Health and Exercise Science Students: 1 (woman) full-time, 46 part-time (39 women); includes 18 minority (8 African Americans, 1 American Indian/Alaska Native, 6 Asian Americans or Pacific Islanders, 3 Hispanic Americans). 28 applicants, 100% accepted. *Faculty:* 3. Expenses: Contact institution. *Financial support:* Tuition waivers (partial) and unspecified assistantships available. Financial award application deadline: 5/1; financial award applicants required to submit FAFSA. In 2008, 24 master's awarded. *Degree program information:* Part-time programs available. Offers health (MAT); health education (M Ed, MAT); nursing (MSN, Certificate); nursing, health and exercise science (M Ed, MAT, MSN, Certificate); physical education (M Ed, MAT). *Application deadline:* For fall admission, 2/1 priority date for domestic students; for spring admission, 10/1 priority date for domestic students. *Application fee:* $70. Electronic applications accepted. *Application Contact:* Susan L. Hydro, Assistant Dean, Office of Graduate Studies, 609-771-2300, Fax: 609-637-5105, E-mail: graduate@tcnj.edu. *Dean,* Dr. Susan Bakewell-Sachs, 609-771-2541, Fax: 609-637-5159.

See Close-Up on page 883.

THE COLLEGE OF NEW ROCHELLE, New Rochelle, NY 10805-2308

General Information Independent, coed, primarily women, comprehensive institution. CGS member. *Graduate housing:* Room and/or apartments available on a first-come, first-served basis to single students; on-campus housing not available to married students. Housing application deadline: 8/1.

GRADUATE UNITS

Graduate School *Degree program information:* Part-time and evening/weekend programs available. Offers acute care nurse practitioner (MS, Certificate); clinical specialist in holistic nursing (MS, Certificate); family nurse practitioner (MS, Certificate); nursing and health care management (MS); nursing education (Certificate).

Division of Art and Communication Studies *Degree program information:* Part-time and evening/weekend programs available. Offers art education (MA); art therapy (MS); art therapy/counseling (MS); communication studies (MS, Certificate); studio art (MS).

Division of Education *Degree program information:* Part-time and evening/weekend programs available. Offers bilingual education (Certificate); creative teaching and learning (MS Ed, Certificate); dual certification: school building leader/school district leader (MS); elementary education/early childhood education (MS Ed); literacy education (MS Ed); school administration and supervision (MS, Advanced Certificate, Advanced Diploma); school building leader (MS, Advanced Certificate); school district leader (MS, Advanced Diploma); special education (MS Ed); teaching English as a second language (MS Ed); teaching English as a second language and multilingual/multicultural education (MS Ed, Certificate).

Division of Human Services *Degree program information:* Part-time and evening/weekend programs available. Offers career development (MS); community-school psychology (MS); gerontology (MS, Certificate); guidance and counseling (MS); mental health counseling (Certificate).

COLLEGE OF NOTRE DAME OF MARYLAND, Baltimore, MD 21210-2476

General Information Independent-religious, Undergraduate: women only; graduate: coed, comprehensive institution. *Graduate housing:* On-campus housing not available.

GRADUATE UNITS

Graduate Studies *Degree program information:* Part-time and evening/weekend programs available. Offers contemporary communication (MA); instructional leadership for changing populations (PhD); leadership in teaching (MA); liberal studies (MA); management (MA); nonprofit management (MA); teaching (MA); teaching English to speakers of other languages (MA). Electronic applications accepted.

COLLEGE OF SAINT ELIZABETH, Morristown, NJ 07960-6989

General Information Independent-religious, Undergraduate: women only; graduate: coed, comprehensive institution. CGS member. *Enrollment:* 2,111 graduate, professional, and undergraduate students; 212 full-time matriculated graduate/professional students (177 women), 633 part-time matriculated graduate/professional students (552 women). *Enrollment by degree level:* 620 master's, 38 doctoral, 187 other advanced degrees. *Graduate faculty:* 27 full-time (14 women), 57 part-time/adjunct (33 women). *Tuition:* Part-time $759 per credit. *Required fees:* $380 per semester. *Graduate housing:* On-campus housing not available. *Student services:* Campus employment opportunities, campus safety program, career counseling, exercise/wellness program, free psychological counseling, international student services, low-cost health insurance, multicultural affairs office, services for students with disabilities, teacher training, writing training. *Library facilities:* Mahoney Library. *Online resources:* library catalog, web page, access to other libraries' catalogs. *Collection:* 109,352 titles, 561 serial subscriptions, 2,418 audiovisual materials. *Research affiliation:* Cornell University and University of Texas Houston (food biotechnology (attitude research)), National Figure Skating Association (sports nutrition), National Institute of Mental Health (mental health service).

Computer facilities: 127 computers available on campus for general student use. A campuswide network can be accessed from student residence rooms and from off campus. *Web address:* http://www.cse.edu/.

General Application Contact: Donna Tatarka, Dean of Admission, 973-290-4705, Fax: 973-290-4710, E-mail: dtatarka@cse.edu.

GRADUATE UNITS

Department of Business Administration and Economics Students: 31 full-time (23 women), 51 part-time (43 women); includes 29 minority (19 African Americans, 2 Asian Americans or Pacific Islanders, 8 Hispanic Americans), 5 international. Average age 37. 49 applicants, 88% accepted, 35 enrolled. *Faculty:* 4 full-time (1 woman), 10 part-time/adjunct (5 women). Expenses: Contact institution. *Financial support:* Career-related internships or fieldwork, tuition waivers (partial), and unspecified assistantships available. Support available to part-time students. Financial award application deadline: 3/15; financial award applicants required to submit FAFSA. In 2008, 64 master's awarded. *Degree program information:* Part-time and evening/weekend programs available. Offers management (MS). *Application deadline:* Applications are processed on a rolling basis. *Application fee:* $35. Electronic applications accepted. *Application Contact:* Donna Tatarka, Dean of Admission, 973-290-4705, Fax: 973-290-4710, E-mail: dtatarka@cse.edu. *Director of the Graduate Program in Management,* Dr. Kathleen Reddick, 973-290-4041, Fax: 973-290-4177, E-mail: kreddick@cse.edu.

Department of Education Students: 135 full-time (110 women), 330 part-time (290 women); includes 55 minority (27 African Americans, 1 American Indian/Alaska Native, 7 Asian Americans or Pacific Islanders, 20 Hispanic Americans). Average age 38. 180 applicants, 83% accepted, 142 enrolled. *Faculty:* 11 full-time (3 women), 30 part-time/adjunct (16 women). Expenses: Contact institution. *Financial support:* Career-related internships or fieldwork, tuition waivers (partial), and unspecified assistantships available. Support available to part-time students. Financial award application deadline: 3/15; financial award applicants required to submit FAFSA. In 2008, 129 master's, 118 other advanced degrees awarded. *Degree program information:* Part-time and evening/weekend programs available. Offers accelerated certification for teachers (Certificate); assistive technology (Certificate); education: human services leadership (MA); educational leadership (MA, Ed D); educational technology (MA). *Application deadline:* For fall admission, 6/30 priority date for domestic students; for spring admission, 11/30 for domestic students. Applications are processed on a rolling basis. *Application fee:* $35. Electronic applications accepted. *Application Contact:* Donna Tatarka, Dean of Admission, 973-290-4705, Fax: 973-290-4710, E-mail: dtatarka@cse.edu. *Director of Graduate Education Programs,* Dr. Alan H. Markowitz, 973-290-4374, Fax: 973-290-4389, E-mail: amarkowitz@cse.edu.

Department of Foods and Nutrition Students: 19 full-time (all women), 25 part-time (23 women); includes 1 minority (Asian American or Pacific Islander), 1 international. Average age 34. 27 applicants, 96% accepted, 21 enrolled. *Faculty:* 1 (woman) full-time, 3 part-time/adjunct (all women). Expenses: Contact institution. *Financial support:* Tuition waivers (partial) and unspecified assistantships available. Support available to part-time students. Financial award application deadline: 3/15; financial award applicants required to submit FAFSA. In 2008, 3 master's, 20 other advanced degrees awarded. *Degree program information:* Part-time and evening/weekend programs available. Offers dietetic internship (Certificate); nutrition (MS). *Application deadline:* Applications are processed on a rolling basis. *Application fee:* $35. Electronic applications accepted. *Application Contact:* Donna Tatarka, Dean of Admis-

College of Saint Elizabeth (continued)

sion, 973-290-4705, Fax: 973-290-4710, E-mail: dtatarka@cse.edu. *Director of the Graduate Program in Nutrition*, Dr. Jean C. Burge, 973-290-4127, Fax: 973-290-4167, E-mail: nutrition@cse.edu.

Department of Health Professions and Related Sciences Students: 3 full-time (2 women), 111 part-time (92 women); includes 23 minority (9 African Americans, 1 American Indian/Alaska Native, 4 Asian Americans or Pacific Islanders, 9 Hispanic Americans), 3 international. Average age 46. 24 applicants, 71% accepted, 15 enrolled. *Faculty:* 2 full-time (both women), 4 part-time/adjunct (all women). Expenses: Contact institution. *Financial support:* Career-related internships or fieldwork, tuition waivers (partial), and unspecified assistantships available. Support available to part-time students. Financial award application deadline: 3/15; financial award applicants required to submit FAFSA. In 2008, 8 master's awarded. *Degree program information:* Part-time and evening/weekend programs available. Offers health care management (MS). *Application deadline:* Applications are processed on a rolling basis. *Application fee:* $35. Electronic applications accepted. *Application Contact:* Donna Tatarka, Dean of Admission, 973-290-4705, Fax: 973-290-4710, E-mail: dtatarka@cse.edu. *Director of the Graduate Program in Health Care Management*, Linda Hunter, 973-290-4040, Fax: 973-290-4167, E-mail: lhunter@cse.edu.

Department of Nursing Students: 12 full-time (all women), 13 part-time (12 women); includes 12 minority (4 African Americans, 5 Asian Americans or Pacific Islanders, 3 Hispanic Americans). Average age 48. *Faculty:* 1 (woman) full-time, 4 part-time/adjunct (all women). Expenses: Contact institution. Offers nursing (MSN). *Application Contact:* Donna Tatarka, Dean of Admission, 973-290-4705, Fax: 973-290-4710, E-mail: dtatarka@cse.edu. *Director of Graduate Program in Nursing*, Dr. Sharon Hellwig, 973-290-1074, E-mail: shellwig@cse.edu.

Department of Psychology Students: 11 full-time (10 women), 84 part-time (77 women); includes 23 minority (10 African Americans, 3 Asian Americans or Pacific Islanders, 10 Hispanic Americans), 2 international. Average age 34. 104 applicants, 58% accepted, 47 enrolled. *Faculty:* 4 full-time (2 women), 10 part-time/adjunct (5 women). Expenses: Contact institution. *Financial support:* Career-related internships or fieldwork, tuition waivers (partial), and unspecified assistantships available. Support available to part-time students. Financial award application deadline: 3/15; financial award applicants required to submit FAFSA. In 2008, 11 master's, 1 other advanced degree awarded. *Degree program information:* Part-time and evening/weekend programs available. Offers counseling psychology (MA); forensic psychology (MA); student affairs in higher education (Certificate). *Application deadline:* For fall admission, 4/14 priority date for domestic students; for spring admission, 11/15 for domestic students. Applications are processed on a rolling basis. *Application fee:* $35. Electronic applications accepted. *Application Contact:* Donna Tatarka, Dean of Admission, 973-290-4705, Fax: 973-290-4710, E-mail: dtatarka@cse.edu. *Director of the Graduate Program in Counseling Psychology*, Dr. Valerie Scott, 973-290-4102, Fax: 973-290-4676, E-mail: vscott@cse.edu.

Department of Theology Students: 15 part-time (11 women), 1 international. Average age 54. 9 applicants, 78% accepted, 3 enrolled. *Faculty:* 2 full-time (1 woman), 4 part-time/adjunct (1 woman). Expenses: Contact institution. *Financial support:* Tuition waivers (partial) and unspecified assistantships available. Support available to part-time students. Financial award applicants required to submit FAFSA. In 2008, 4 master's awarded. *Degree program information:* Part-time and evening/weekend programs available. Offers theology (MA). *Application deadline:* For fall admission, 3/1 priority date for domestic students; for spring admission, 9/1 for domestic students. Applications are processed on a rolling basis. *Application fee:* $35. Electronic applications accepted. *Application Contact:* Donna Tatarka, Dean of Admission, 973-290-4705, Fax: 973-290-4710, E-mail: dtatarka@cse.edu. *Director of the Graduate Program in Theology*, Sr. Kathleen Flanagan, 973-290-4336, Fax: 973-290-4312, E-mail: kflanagan@cse.edu.

COLLEGE OF ST. JOSEPH, Rutland, VT 05701-3899

General Information Independent-religious, coed, comprehensive institution. *Graduate housing:* Room and/or apartments available on a first-come, first-served basis to single students; on-campus housing not available to married students. Housing application deadline: 5/1.

GRADUATE UNITS

Graduate Programs *Degree program information:* Part-time and evening/weekend programs available. Electronic applications accepted.

Division of Business *Degree program information:* Part-time and evening/weekend programs available. Offers business administration (MBA). Electronic applications accepted.

Division of Education *Degree program information:* Part-time and evening/weekend programs available. Offers elementary education (M Ed); English (M Ed); general education (M Ed); reading (M Ed); secondary education (M Ed); social studies (M Ed); special education (M Ed). Electronic applications accepted.

Division of Psychology and Human Services *Degree program information:* Part-time and evening/weekend programs available. Offers alcohol and substance abuse counseling (MS); clinical mental health counseling (MS); clinical psychology (MS); community counseling (MS); school guidance counseling (MS). Electronic applications accepted.

THE COLLEGE OF SAINT ROSE, Albany, NY 12203-1419

General Information Independent, coed, comprehensive institution. CGS member. *Graduate housing:* On-campus housing not available.

GRADUATE UNITS

Graduate Studies *Degree program information:* Part-time and evening/weekend programs available. Electronic applications accepted.

School of Arts and Humanities *Degree program information:* Part-time and evening/weekend programs available. Offers art education (MS Ed, Certificate); arts and humanities (MA, MS Ed, Certificate); English (MA); history/political science (MA); music (MA); music education (MS Ed, Certificate); public communications (MA).

School of Business *Degree program information:* Part-time and evening/weekend programs available. Offers accounting (MS); business (MBA, MS, Certificate); business administration (MBA); not-for-profit management (Certificate). Electronic applications accepted.

School of Education *Degree program information:* Part-time and evening/weekend programs available. Offers applied technology education (MS Ed); bilingual pupil personnel services (Certificate); business and marketing (MS Ed); childhood education (MS Ed); college student personnel (MS Ed); college student services administration (MS Ed); communication disorders (MS Ed); community counseling (MS Ed); counseling (MS Ed); curriculum and instruction (MS Ed); early childhood education (MS Ed); education (MS, MS Ed, Certificate); educational administration and supervision (MS Ed, Certificate); educational leadership and administration (MS Ed); educational leadership and administrationûschool building leader (Certificate); educational leadership and administrationûschool district leader (Certificate); educational psychology (MS Ed); elementary education (K-6) (MS Ed); literacy: birth-grade 6 (MS Ed); literacy: grades 5-12 (MS Ed); reading (Certificate); school administrator and supervisor (Certificate); school counseling (MS Ed); school psychology (MS, Certificate); secondary education (MS Ed, Certificate); special education (MS Ed); teacher education (MS Ed, Certificate). Electronic applications accepted.

School of Mathematics and Sciences *Degree program information:* Part-time and evening/weekend programs available. Offers computer information systems (MS); mathematics and sciences (MS). Electronic applications accepted.

See Close-Up on page 885.

THE COLLEGE OF ST. SCHOLASTICA, Duluth, MN 55811-4199

General Information Independent-religious, coed, comprehensive institution. *Graduate housing:* Room and/or apartments available on a first-come, first-served basis to single students; on-campus housing not available to married students. Housing application deadline: 5/15.

GRADUATE UNITS

Graduate Studies *Degree program information:* Part-time and evening/weekend programs available. Postbaccalaureate distance learning degree programs offered (minimal on-campus study). Offers computer information systems (MA, Certificate); educational media and technology (M Ed); exercise physiology (MA); health information management (MA, Certificate); management (MA, Certificate); nursing (MA, PMC); occupational therapy (MA); physical therapy (DPT); teaching (M Ed, Certificate). Electronic applications accepted.

COLLEGE OF SANTA FE, Santa Fe, NM 87505-7634

General Information Independent, coed. *Graduate housing:* Room and/or apartments available on a first-come, first-served basis to single students; on-campus housing not available to married students.

GRADUATE UNITS

Department of Business Administration *Degree program information:* Part-time and evening/weekend programs available. Offers finance (MBA); human resources (MBA). Program also available at Albuquerque campus.

Department of Education *Degree program information:* Part-time and evening/weekend programs available. Offers at-risk youth (MA); curriculum and instruction (MA); multicultural special education (MA).

COLLEGE OF STATEN ISLAND OF THE CITY UNIVERSITY OF NEW YORK, Staten Island, NY 10314-6600

General Information State and locally supported, coed, comprehensive institution. *Enrollment:* 13,092 graduate, professional, and undergraduate students; 45 full-time matriculated graduate/professional students (38 women), 784 part-time matriculated graduate/professional students (569 women). *Enrollment by degree level:* 782 master's, 37 other advanced degrees. *Graduate faculty:* 50 full-time (23 women), 19 part-time/adjunct (11 women). Tuition, state resident: full-time $6400; part-time $270 per credit. Tuition, nonresident: full-time $12,000; part-time $500 per credit. *Required fees:* $378; $113 per semester. *Graduate housing:* On-campus housing not available. *Student services:* Campus employment opportunities, campus safety program, career counseling, child daycare facilities, exercise/wellness program, free psychological counseling, international student services, low-cost health insurance, multicultural affairs office, services for students with disabilities, teacher training, writing training. *Library facilities:* College of Staten Island Library. *Online resources:* library catalog, web page, access to other libraries' catalogs. *Collection:* 235,000 titles, 28,000 serial subscriptions, 5,000 audiovisual materials. *Research affiliation:* Pall Corporation (service contract), Ciba (service contract), Pall Corporation (membrane for size selective filtration), Dynavax Technologies (biopharmaceutical chemistry), Nulastin (polymer based wound care preparations involving tropelastin).

Computer facilities: 1,254 computers available on campus for general student use. A campuswide network can be accessed from off campus. Online class registration is available. *Web address:* http://www.csi.cuny.edu/.

General Application Contact: Sasha Spence, Assistant Director of Graduate Recruitment and Admissions, 718-982-2699, Fax: 718-982-2500, E-mail: spence@mail.csi.cuny.edu.

GRADUATE UNITS

Graduate Programs Students: 45 full-time (38 women), 784 part-time (569 women); includes 138 minority (46 African Americans, 1 American Indian/Alaska Native, 36 Asian Americans or Pacific Islanders, 55 Hispanic Americans), 44 international. Average age 31. *Faculty:* 50 full-time (23 women), 19 part-time/adjunct (11 women). Expenses: Contact institution. In 2008, 309 master's, 26 other advanced degrees awarded. Offers adolescence education (MS Ed); adult health nursing (MS, 6th Year Certificate); biology (MS); business management (MS); childhood education (MS Ed); cinema and media studies (MA); computer science (MS); cultural competence (6th Year Certificate); English (MA); gerontological nursing (MS, 6th Year Certificate); history (MA); leadership in education (6th Year Certificate); liberal studies (MA); mental health counseling (MA); nursing education (6th Year Certificate); special education (MS Ed). *Application Contact:* Sasha Spence, Assistant Director of Graduate Recruitment and Admissions, 718-982-2699, Fax: 718-982-2500, E-mail: spence@mail.csi.cuny.edu. *Provost and Senior Vice President for Academic Affairs*, Dr. William J. Fritz, 718-982-2440, Fax: 718-982-2442, E-mail: william.fritz@csi.cuny.edu.

Center for Developmental Neuroscience and Developmental Disabilities Students: 1 full-time (0 women), 31 part-time (19 women); includes 7 minority (4 African Americans, 2 Asian Americans or Pacific Islanders, 1 Hispanic American), 3 international. Average age 30. 39 applicants, 72% accepted, 23 enrolled. *Faculty:* 4 full-time (0 women), 1 (woman) part-time/adjunct. Expenses: Contact institution. *Financial support:* In 2008–09, 1 student received support; fellowships with partial tuition reimbursements available, career-related internships or fieldwork, Federal Work-Study, and scholarships/grants available. Support available to part-time students. Financial award application deadline: 4/1; financial award applicants required to submit CSS PROFILE or FAFSA. In 2008, 3 master's awarded. *Degree program information:* Part-time and evening/weekend programs available. Offers neuroscience, mental retardation and developmental disabilities (MS). *Application deadline:* Applications are processed on a rolling basis. *Application fee:* $125. Electronic applications accepted. *Application Contact:* Sasha Spence, Assistant Director of Graduate Recruitment and Admissions, 718-982-2699, Fax: 718-982-2500, E-mail: spence@mail.csi.cuny.edu. *Coordinator*, Dr. Probal Banerjee, 718-982-3950, Fax: 718-982-3953, E-mail: banerjee@mail.csi.cuny.edu.

Center for Environmental Science Students: 31 part-time (7 women); includes 14 minority (5 African Americans, 9 Asian Americans or Pacific Islanders), 1 international. Average age 35. 23 applicants, 100% accepted, 15 enrolled. *Faculty:* 3 full-time (0 women), 1 (woman) part-time/adjunct. Expenses: Contact institution. *Financial support:* In 2008–09, 1 fellowship with partial tuition reimbursement (averaging $10,000 per year), 7 research assistantships (averaging $2,000 per year) were awarded; career-related internships or fieldwork, Federal Work-Study, and scholarships/grants also available. Support available to part-time students. Financial award application deadline: 4/1; financial award applicants required to submit CSS PROFILE or FAFSA. In 2008, 4 master's awarded. *Degree program information:* Part-time and evening/weekend programs available. Offers environmental science (MS). *Application deadline:* Applications are processed on a rolling basis. *Application fee:* $125. Electronic applications accepted. *Application Contact:* Sasha Spence, Assistant Director of Graduate Recruitment and Admissions, 718-982-2699, Fax: 718-982-2500, E-mail: spence@mail.csi.cuny.edu. *Director*, Dr. Alfred Levine, 718-982-2822, Fax: 718-982-3923, E-mail: envirscimasters@mail.csi.cuny.edu.

See Close-Up on page 887.

COLLEGE OF THE ATLANTIC, Bar Harbor, ME 04609-1198

General Information Independent, coed, comprehensive institution. *Graduate housing:* Room and/or apartments available to single students; on-campus housing not available to married students. Housing application deadline: 6/1. *Research affiliation:* Acadia National Park, National Park Service (research management, environmental education), Mount Desert Island Biological Laboratory, Jackson Laboratory (genetics), Society for Human Ecology (ecological decision making in society).

GRADUATE UNITS

Program in Human Ecology Offers human ecology (M Phil).

COLLEGE OF THE HUMANITIES AND SCIENCES, HARRISON MIDDLETON UNIVERSITY, Tempe, AZ 85282

General Information Independent, coed, comprehensive institution.

GRADUATE UNITS

Graduate Program *Degree program information:* Part-time and evening/weekend programs available. Postbaccalaureate distance learning degree programs offered (no on-campus study). Electronic applications accepted.

THE COLLEGE OF WILLIAM AND MARY, Williamsburg, VA 23187-8795

General Information State-supported, coed, university. CGS member. *Enrollment:* 7,892 graduate, professional, and undergraduate students; 1,569 full-time matriculated graduate/professional students (803 women), 389 part-time matriculated graduate/professional students (195 women). *Enrollment by degree level:* 625 first professional, 874 master's, 438 doctoral, 21 other advanced degrees. *Graduate faculty:* 628 full-time (232 women), 173 part-time/adjunct (72 women). Tuition, state resident: full-time $6400; part-time $300 per credit hour. Tuition, nonresident: full-time $19,720; part-time $800 per credit hour. *Required fees:* $3860. *Graduate housing:* Rooms and/or apartments available on a first-come, first-served basis to single and married students. Typical cost: $5126 per year ($8410 including board) for single students. Housing application deadline: 2/13. *Student services:* Campus employment opportunities, campus safety program, career counseling, child daycare facilities, exercise/wellness program, free psychological counseling, grant writing training, international student services, low-cost health insurance, multicultural affairs office, services for students with disabilities, teacher training, writing training. *Library facilities:* Swem Library plus 8 others. *Online resources:* library catalog, web page. *Collection:* 1.8 million titles, 18,000 serial subscriptions, 32,827 audiovisual materials. *Research affiliation:* Incogen, Inc. (computer science, applied science, bioinformatics), Center for Excellence in Aging and Geriatric Health (public policy, kinesiology), Luna Innovations, Inc. (nanotechnology, defense-related technology, applied science), Colonial Williamsburg (archaeology, history), Thomas Jefferson National Accelerator Center (nuclear physics), Virginia Bioinformatics Institute (computer science, applied science, bioinformatics).

Computer facilities: Computer purchase and lease plans are available. 350 computers available on campus for general student use. A campuswide network can be accessed from student residence rooms and from off campus. Online class registration is available. *Web address:* http://www.wm.edu/.

General Application Contact: Dr. Laurie Sanderson, Dean of Graduate Studies and Research, 757-221-2468, E-mail: slsand@wm.edu.

GRADUATE UNITS

Faculty of Arts and Sciences Students: 384 full-time (193 women), 42 part-time (27 women); includes 38 minority (20 African Americans, 5 American Indian/Alaska Native, 7 Asian Americans or Pacific Islanders, 6 Hispanic Americans), 82 international. Average age 28. 705 applicants, 34% accepted, 130 enrolled. *Faculty:* 438 full-time (167 women), 117 part-time/adjunct (46 women). Expenses: Contact institution. *Financial support:* Fellowships, research assistantships, teaching assistantships, career-related internships or fieldwork, Federal Work-Study, institutionally sponsored loans, and unspecified assistantships available. Financial award applicants required to submit FAFSA. In 2008, 102 master's, 20 doctorates awarded. *Degree program information:* Part-time programs available. Offers American studies (MA, PhD); anthropology (MA, PhD); applied science (MS, PhD); arts and sciences (MA, MPP, MS, PhD, Psy D); biology (MS); chemistry (MA, MS); clinical psychology (Psy D); computational operations research (MS); computer science (MS, PhD); general experimental psychology (MA); history (MA, PhD); physics (MS, PhD); public policy (MPP). *Application deadline:* For fall admission, 1/15 for domestic and international students. *Application fee:* $45. *Application Contact:* Wanda Carter, Administrator of Graduate Student Services, 757-221-2467, Fax: 757-221-4874, E-mail: wdcart@wm.edu. *Dean of Graduate Studies and Research,* Dr. Laurie Sanderson, 757-221-2468, E-mail: slsand@wm.edu.

Mason School of Business Students: 289 full-time (94 women), 186 part-time (48 women); includes 41 minority (22 African Americans, 11 Asian Americans or Pacific Islanders, 8 Hispanic Americans), 73 international. Average age 29. 652 applicants, 63% accepted, 283 enrolled. *Faculty:* 49 full-time (11 women), 11 part-time/adjunct (1 woman). Expenses: Contact institution. *Financial support:* In 2008–09, 74 students received support, including 46 fellowships (averaging $14,189 per year), 45 research assistantships with partial tuition reimbursements available (averaging $3,867 per year); career-related internships or fieldwork, scholarships/grants, and unspecified assistantships also available. Financial award application deadline: 3/1; financial award applicants required to submit FAFSA. In 2008, 200 master's awarded. *Degree program information:* Part-time and evening/weekend programs available. Offers accounting (M Acc); business administration (EMBA, MBA). *Application deadline:* Applications are processed on a rolling basis. *Application fee:* $100. Electronic applications accepted. *Application Contact:* Priscilla Case, Director, Full-time MBA Admissions, 757-221-2900, Fax: 757-221-2958, E-mail: priscilla.case@mason.wm.edu. *Dean,* Dr. Lawrence Pulley, 757-221-2891, Fax: 757-221-2937, E-mail: larry.pulley@mason.wm.edu.

School of Education Students: 189 full-time (156 women), 167 part-time (120 women); includes 67 minority (55 African Americans, 2 American Indian/Alaska Native, 5 Asian Americans or Pacific Islanders, 5 Hispanic Americans), 3 international. Average age 33. 392 applicants, 55% accepted, 138 enrolled. *Faculty:* 40 full-time (22 women), 26 part-time/adjunct (23 women). Expenses: Contact institution. *Financial support:* In 2008–09, 193 students received support, including 1 fellowship with full tuition reimbursement available (averaging $20,000 per year), 113 research assistantships with full and partial tuition reimbursements available (averaging $10,000 per year); teaching assistantships, career-related internships or fieldwork, Federal Work-Study, institutionally sponsored loans, scholarships/grants, and unspecified assistantships also available. Financial award application deadline: 1/15; financial award applicants required to submit FAFSA. In 2008, 121 master's, 27 doctorates, 13 other advanced degrees awarded. *Degree program information:* Part-time and evening/weekend programs available. Offers community and addictions counseling (M Ed); community counseling (M Ed); counselor education (PhD); curriculum and educational technology (Ed D, PhD); curriculum leadership (Ed D, PhD); education (M Ed, MA Ed, Ed D, PhD, Ed S); educational leadership (M Ed); educational policy, planning, and leadership (Ed D, PhD); elementary education (MA Ed); family counseling (M Ed); gifted education (MA Ed); gifted education administration (M Ed); reading education (MA Ed); school counseling (M Ed); school psychology (M Ed, Ed S); secondary education (MA Ed); special education (MA Ed). *Application deadline:* For fall admission, 1/15 for domestic and international students; for spring admission, 10/1 for domestic and international students. *Application fee:* $45. Electronic applications accepted. *Application Contact:* Dorothy Smith Osborne, Director of Admissions, 757-221-2317, Fax: 757-221-2293, E-mail: dsosbo@wm.edu. *Dean,* Dr. Virginia McLaughlin, 757-221-2317, E-mail: vamcla@wm.edu.

Virginia Institute of Marine Science Students: 90 full-time (54 women), 9 part-time (2 women); includes 12 minority (6 African Americans, 1 American Indian/Alaska Native, 2 Asian Americans or Pacific Islanders, 3 Hispanic Americans), 15 international. Average age 28. 113 applicants, 28% accepted, 22 enrolled. *Faculty:* 51 full-time (11 women), 1 (woman) part-time/adjunct. Expenses: Contact institution. *Financial support:* In 2008–09, 93 students received support, including 20 fellowships with full tuition reimbursements available (averaging $19,005 per year), 65 research assistantships with full tuition reimbursements available (averaging $19,005 per year), 8 teaching assistantships with full tuition reimbursements available (averaging $6,500 per year); career-related internships or fieldwork, Federal Work-Study, scholarships/grants, health care benefits, and unspecified assistantships also available. Support available to part-time students. Financial award application deadline: 6/15; financial award applicants required to submit FAFSA. In 2008, 13 master's, 11 doctorates awarded. Offers marine science (MS, PhD). *Application deadline:* For fall admission, 1/15 for domestic and international students. *Application fee:* $50. Electronic applications accepted. *Application Contact:* Fonda J. Powell, Admissions Coordinator, 804-684-7106, Fax: 804-684-7881, E-mail: snpres@vims.edu. *Dean/Director,* Dr. John T. Wells, 804-684-7102, Fax: 804-684-7009, E-mail: wells@vims.edu.

William and Mary Law School Students: 626 full-time (306 women); includes 100 minority (77 African Americans, 3 American Indian/Alaska Native, 13 Asian Americans or Pacific Islanders, 7 Hispanic Americans), 4 international. Average age 25. 4,585 applicants, 25% accepted, 220 enrolled. *Faculty:* 44 full-time (18 women), 34 part-time/adjunct (10 women). Expenses: Contact institution. *Financial support:* In 2008–09, 334 students received support, including 189 fellowships with partial tuition reimbursements available (averaging $4,000 per year), 60 research assistantships (averaging $2,250 per year), 17 teaching assistantships (averaging $4,904 per year); career-related internships or fieldwork, scholarships/grants, and unspecified assistantships also available. Financial award application deadline: 2/15; financial award applicants required to submit FAFSA. In 2008, 209 JDs, 14 master's awarded. Offers law (JD, LL M). *Application deadline:* For fall admission, 3/1 priority date for domestic and international students. *Application fee:* $50. Electronic applications accepted. *Application Contact:* Faye F. Shealy, Associate Dean for Admission, 757-221-3785, Fax: 757-221-3261, E-mail: ffshea@wm.edu. *Dean and Hanson Professor of Law,* Davison M Douglas, 757-221-3790, Fax: 757-221-3261, E-mail: dmdoug@wm.edu.

See Close-Up on page 889.

COLLÈGE UNIVERSITAIRE DE SAINT-BONIFACE, Saint-Boniface, MB R2H 0H7, Canada

General Information Independent-religious, comprehensive institution.

GRADUATE UNITS

Department of Education Offers education (M Ed).

Program in Canadian Studies Offers Canadian studies (MA).

COLORADO CHRISTIAN UNIVERSITY, Lakewood, CO 80226

General Information Independent-religious, coed, comprehensive institution. *Graduate housing:* On-campus housing not available.

GRADUATE UNITS

Program in Business Administration *Degree program information:* Part-time and evening/weekend programs available. Postbaccalaureate distance learning degree programs offered (minimal on-campus study). Offers business administration (MBA). Electronic applications accepted.

Program in Counseling *Degree program information:* Part-time and evening/weekend programs available. Offers counseling (MA). Electronic applications accepted.

Program in Curriculum and Instruction *Degree program information:* Part-time and evening/weekend programs available. Offers curriculum and instruction (MA). Electronic applications accepted.

THE COLORADO COLLEGE, Colorado Springs, CO 80903-3294

General Information Independent, coed, comprehensive institution. *Enrollment:* 2,026 graduate, professional, and undergraduate students; 29 full-time matriculated graduate/professional students (22 women). *Enrollment by degree level:* 29 master's. *Graduate faculty:* 3 full-time (2 women), 12 part-time/adjunct (7 women). *Tuition:* Full-time $30,657. *Required fees:* $2086. *Graduate housing:* On-campus housing not available. *Student services:* Campus safety program, career counseling, child daycare facilities, exercise/wellness program, free psychological counseling, grant writing training, international student services, low-cost health insurance, multicultural affairs office, services for students with disabilities, teacher training, writing training. *Library facilities:* Tutt Library plus 1 other. *Online resources:* library catalog, web page, access to other libraries' catalogs. *Collection:* 540,276 titles, 26,233 serial subscriptions, 36,649 audiovisual materials.

Computer facilities: 208 computers available on campus for general student use. A campuswide network can be accessed from student residence rooms and from off campus. Online class registration is available. *Web address:* http://www.coloradocollege.edu/.

General Application Contact: Marsha E. Unruh, Director of Education Career Services, 719-389-6472, Fax: 719-389-6473, E-mail: munruh@coloradocollege.edu.

GRADUATE UNITS

Department of Education Students: 29 full-time (22 women); includes 5 minority (1 American Indian/Alaska Native, 1 Asian American or Pacific Islander, 3 Hispanic Americans). Average age 27. 44 applicants, 86% accepted, 29 enrolled. *Faculty:* 3 full-time (2 women), 12 part-time/adjunct (7 women). Expenses: Contact institution. *Financial support:* In 2008–09, 29 students received support, including 18 teaching assistantships (averaging $16,000 per year); career-related internships or fieldwork, institutionally sponsored loans, health care benefits, and tuition waivers (partial) also available. Financial award application deadline: 2/15; financial award applicants required to submit FAFSA. In 2008, 22 master's awarded. Offers art teaching (K-12) (MAT); elementary education (MAT); elementary school teaching (MAT); English teaching (MAT); foreign language teaching (MAT); mathematics teaching (MAT); music teaching (MAT); science teaching (MAT); secondary education (MAT); social studies teaching (MAT). *Application deadline:* For fall admission, 12/1 for domestic and international students. Applications are processed on a rolling basis. *Application fee:* $50. *Application Contact:* Marsha E. Unruh, Director of Education Career Services, 719-389-6472, Fax: 719-389-6473, E-mail: munruh@coloradocollege.edu. *Chair,* Paul Kuerbis, 719-389-6726, Fax: 719-389-6473, E-mail: pkuerbis@coloradocollege.edu.

Programs for Experienced Teachers *Degree program information:* Part-time programs available. Offers American Southwest studies for all teachers (MAT); arts and humanities for secondary school teachers and administrators (MAT); integrated natural science for all teachers (MAT); liberal arts for elementary school teachers and administrators (MAT). Programs offered during summer only.

COLORADO SCHOOL OF MINES, Golden, CO 80401-1887

General Information State-supported, coed, university. CGS member. *Enrollment:* 4,488 graduate, professional, and undergraduate students; 770 full-time matriculated graduate/professional students (206 women), 166 part-time matriculated graduate/professional students (46 women). *Enrollment by degree level:* 568 master's, 368 doctoral. *Graduate faculty:* 313 full-time (69 women), 94 part-time/adjunct (21 women). Tuition, state resident: full-time $9810; part-time $477 per credit hour. Tuition, nonresident: full-time $23,814; part-time $1158 per credit hour. *Required fees:* $1428.76; $714.38 per semester. *Graduate housing:* Rooms and/or apartments available on a first-come, first-served basis to single and married students. Typical cost: $6894 per year for single students; $8064 per year for married students. *Student services:* Campus employment opportunities, campus safety program, career counseling, exercise/wellness program, free psychological counseling, international student services, low-cost health insurance, services for students with disabilities, teacher training, writing training. *Library facilities:* Arthur Lakes Library. *Online resources:* library catalog, web page, access to other libraries' catalogs. *Collection:* 412,560 titles, 26,399 serial subscriptions, 306 audiovisual materials.

Computer facilities: Computer purchase and lease plans are available. 400 computers available on campus for general student use. A campuswide network can be accessed from student residence rooms and from off campus. Online class registration is available. *Web address:* http://www.mines.edu/.

General Application Contact: Kay Leaman, Graduate Admissions Coordinator, 303-273-3249, Fax: 303-273-3244, E-mail: grad-app@mines.edu.

GRADUATE UNITS

Graduate School Students: 770 full-time (206 women), 166 part-time (46 women); includes 83 minority (16 African Americans, 4 American Indian/Alaska Native, 31 Asian Americans or Pacific Islanders, 32 Hispanic Americans), 250 international. Average age 31. 1,052 applicants, 61% accepted, 318 enrolled. *Faculty:* 313 full-time (69 women), 94 part-time/adjunct (21 women). Expenses: Contact institution. *Financial support:* In 2008–09, 610 students received support, including 113 fellowships with full tuition reimbursements available (averaging $20,000 per year), 306 research assistantships with full tuition reimbursements available (averaging $20,000 per year), 191 teaching assistantships with full tuition reimbursements available (averaging $20,000 per year); career-related internships or fieldwork, Federal Work-Study, institutionally sponsored loans, scholarships/grants, health care benefits, and unspecified assistantships also available. Financial award application deadline: 1/15; financial award applicants required to submit FAFSA. In 2008, 241 master's, 41 doctorates awarded. *Degree program information:* Part-time programs available. Offers applied chemistry (PhD); applied physics (MS, PhD); chemical engineering (MS, PhD); chemistry (MS, PhD); engineer of mines (ME); geochemistry (MS, PhD); geological engineering (ME, MS, PhD); geology (MS, PhD); geophysical engineering (ME, MS, PhD); geophysics (MS, PhD); materials science (MS, PhD); mathematical and computer sciences (MS, PhD); metallurgical and materials

Colorado School of Mines (continued)

engineering (ME, MS, PhD); mineral exploration and mining geosciences (PMS); mining and earth systems engineering (MS); nuclear engineering (MS, PhD); petroleum engineering (ME, MS, PhD); petroleum reservoir systems (PMS). *Application deadline:* For fall admission, 1/15 priority date for domestic and international students; for spring admission, 9/1 priority date for domestic and international students. *Application fee:* $50 ($70 for international students). Electronic applications accepted. *Application Contact:* Kay Leaman, Graduate Admissions Coordinator, 303-273-3249, Fax: 303-273-3244, E-mail: grad-app@mines.edu. *Dean of Graduate Studies*, Dr. Tom M. Boyd, 303-273-3020, Fax: 303-273-3244, E-mail: tboyd@mines.edu.

Division of Economics and Business Students: 67 full-time (15 women), 25 part-time (4 women); includes 8 minority (1 African American, 1 Asian American or Pacific Islander, 6 Hispanic Americans), 30 international. 114 applicants, 80% accepted, 43 enrolled. *Faculty:* 12 full-time (4 women), 7 part-time/adjunct (1 woman). Expenses: Contact institution. *Financial support:* In 2008–09, 35 students received support, including 8 fellowships with full tuition reimbursements available (averaging $20,000 per year), 2 research assistantships with full tuition reimbursements available (averaging $20,000 per year), 25 teaching assistantships with full tuition reimbursements available (averaging $20,000 per year); scholarships/grants, health care benefits, and unspecified assistantships also available. Financial award application deadline: 1/15; financial award applicants required to submit FAFSA. In 2008, 45 master's, 3 doctorates awarded. *Degree program information:* Part-time programs available. Offers engineering and technology management (MS); mineral economics (MS, PhD). *Application deadline:* For fall admission, 1/15 priority date for domestic and international students; for spring admission, 9/1 priority date for domestic and international students. *Application fee:* $50 ($70 for international students). Electronic applications accepted. *Application Contact:* Kathleen A. Feighny, Administrative Faculty, 303-273-3979, Fax: 303-273-3416, E-mail: kfeighny@mines.edu. *Division Head*, Dr. Rod Eggert, 303-273-3981, Fax: 303-273-3416, E-mail: reggert@mines.edu.

Division of Engineering Students: 121 full-time (22 women), 38 part-time (8 women); includes 12 minority (4 African Americans, 4 Asian Americans or Pacific Islanders, 4 Hispanic Americans), 28 international. 130 applicants, 92% accepted, 76 enrolled. *Faculty:* 45 full-time (9 women), 14 part-time/adjunct (2 women). Expenses: Contact institution. *Financial support:* In 2008–09, 76 students received support, including 15 fellowships with full tuition reimbursements available (averaging $20,000 per year), 37 research assistantships with full tuition reimbursements available (averaging $20,000 per year), 24 teaching assistantships with full tuition reimbursements available (averaging $20,000 per year); scholarships/grants, health care benefits, and unspecified assistantships also available. Financial award application deadline: 1/15; financial award applicants required to submit FAFSA. In 2008, 38 master's, 7 doctorates awarded. *Degree program information:* Part-time programs available. Offers engineering systems (ME, MS, PhD). *Application deadline:* For fall admission, 1/15 priority date for domestic and international students; for spring admission, 9/1 priority date for domestic and international students. *Application fee:* $50 ($70 for international students). Electronic applications accepted. *Application Contact:* Kathy Burris, Administrative Assistant, 303-384-2394, Fax: 303-273-3602, E-mail: kburris@mines.edu. *Division Director*, Dr. Terence Parker, 303-273-3657, Fax: 303-273-3602, E-mail: tparker@mines.edu.

Division of Environmental Science and Engineering Students: 59 full-time (25 women), 28 part-time (12 women); includes 17 minority (4 African Americans, 5 Asian Americans or Pacific Islanders, 8 Hispanic Americans), 5 international. 70 applicants, 69% accepted, 21 enrolled. *Faculty:* 26 full-time (7 women), 5 part-time/adjunct (1 woman). Expenses: Contact institution. *Financial support:* In 2008–09, 47 students received support, including 12 fellowships with full tuition reimbursements available (averaging $20,000 per year), 30 research assistantships with full tuition reimbursements available (averaging $20,000 per year), 5 teaching assistantships with full tuition reimbursements available (averaging $20,000 per year); scholarships/grants, health care benefits, and unspecified assistantships also available. Financial award application deadline: 1/15; financial award applicants required to submit FAFSA. In 2008, 30 master's, 5 doctorates awarded. *Degree program information:* Part-time programs available. Offers environmental science and engineering (MS, PhD). *Application deadline:* For fall admission, 1/15 priority date for domestic and international students; for spring admission, 9/1 priority date for domestic and international students. *Application fee:* $50 ($70 for international students). Electronic applications accepted. *Application Contact:* Tim VanHaverbeke, Research Faculty, 303-273-3467, Fax: 303-273-3413, E-mail: tvanhave@mines.edu. *Division Director*, Dr. Robert Siegrist, 303-384-2158, Fax: 303-273-3413, E-mail: siegrist@mines.edu.

Division of Liberal Arts and International Studies Students: 17 full-time (6 women), 7 part-time (0 women); includes 9 minority (2 African Americans, 1 American Indian/Alaska Native, 2 Asian Americans or Pacific Islanders, 4 Hispanic Americans), 3 international. 16 applicants, 88% accepted, 10 enrolled. *Faculty:* 23 full-time (11 women), 24 part-time/adjunct (11 women). Expenses: Contact institution. *Financial support:* In 2008–09, 10 students received support, including fellowships with full tuition reimbursements available (averaging $20,000 per year), 1 research assistantship with full tuition reimbursement available (averaging $20,000 per year), 9 teaching assistantships with full tuition reimbursements available (averaging $20,000 per year); scholarships/grants, health care benefits, and unspecified assistantships also available. Financial award application deadline: 1/15. In 2008, 12 master's awarded. *Degree program information:* Part-time programs available. Offers international political economy (Graduate Certificate); liberal arts and international studies (MIPER); science and technology policy (Graduate Certificate). *Application deadline:* For fall admission, 1/15 priority date for domestic and international students; for spring admission, 9/1 priority date for domestic and international students. *Application fee:* $50 ($70 for international students). Electronic applications accepted. *Application Contact:* Connie Warren, Program Assistant, 303-273-3590, Fax: 303-273-3751, E-mail: cwarren@mines.edu. *Director*, Dr. James Jesudason, 303-273-3425, Fax: 303-273-3751, E-mail: jjesudas@mines.edu.

See Close-Up on page 891.

COLORADO SCHOOL OF TRADITIONAL CHINESE MEDICINE, Denver, CO 80206-2127

General Information Independent, coed, graduate-only institution. *Enrollment by degree level:* 97 master's. *Graduate faculty:* 36 part-time/adjunct (11 women). *Graduate housing:* On-campus housing not available. *Collection:* 7,400 titles, 80 audiovisual materials.

Computer facilities: 3 computers available on campus for general student use. Wireless Internet available. *Web address:* http://www.cstcm.edu/.

General Application Contact: Chris Duxbury-Edwards, Recruiting Director, 303-329-6355 Ext. 21, Fax: 303-388-8165, E-mail: director@cstcm.edu.

GRADUATE UNITS

Graduate Programs Students: 86 full-time (70 women), 11 part-time (9 women); includes 23 minority (2 African Americans, 2 American Indian/Alaska Native, 13 Asian Americans or Pacific Islanders, 6 Hispanic Americans), 3 international. Average age 33. 28 applicants, 100% accepted, 28 enrolled. *Faculty:* 36 part-time/adjunct (11 women). Expenses: Contact institution. *Financial support:* In 2008–09, 86 students received support. Applicants required to submit FAFSA. In 2008, 22 master's awarded. *Degree program information:* Part-time and evening/weekend programs available. Offers traditional Chinese medicine (MS). *Application deadline:* For fall admission, 8/26 for domestic students, 8/15 for international students; for winter admission, 12/24 for domestic students, 12/1 for international students; for spring admission, 4/26 for domestic students, 4/15 for international students. Applications are processed on a rolling basis. *Application fee:* $50 ($100 for international students). *Application Contact:* Lera Atwater, Registrar, 303-329-6355 Ext. 12, Fax: 303-388-8165, E-mail: registrar@cstcm.edu. *Administrative Director*, Vladimir Dibrigida, 303-329-6355 Ext. 11, Fax: 303-388-8165, E-mail: director@cstcm.edu.

COLORADO STATE UNIVERSITY, Fort Collins, CO 80523-0015

General Information State-supported, coed, comprehensive institution. CGS member. *Enrollment:* 27,800 graduate, professional, and undergraduate students; 2,651 full-time matriculated graduate/professional students (1,598 women), 3,362 part-time matriculated graduate/professional students (1,417 women). *Enrollment by degree level:* 527 first professional, 3,976 master's, 1,510 doctoral. *Graduate faculty:* 941 full-time (296 women), 43 part-time/adjunct (8 women). Tuition, state resident: full-time $5620; part-time $312.25 per credit. Tuition, nonresident: full-time $17,253; part-time $958.50 per credit. *Required fees:* $1449.56; $82.35 per credit. *Graduate housing:* Rooms and/or apartments available on a first-come, first-served basis to single and married students. Typical cost: $4114 per year ($8134 including board) for single students; $6318 per year for married students. Room and board charges vary according to board plan, campus/location and housing facility selected. *Student services:* Campus employment opportunities, campus safety program, career counseling, child daycare facilities, exercise/wellness program, free psychological counseling, international student services, low-cost health insurance, multicultural affairs office, services for students with disabilities, teacher training, writing training. *Library facilities:* William E. Morgan Library plus 3 others. *Online resources:* library catalog, web page, access to other libraries' catalogs. *Collection:* 2 million titles, 36,133 serial subscriptions, 1,635 audiovisual materials. *Research affiliation:* Natural Resources Research Center / Agencies of the USDA and Interior (infectious disease), Department of Commerce/NOAA Joint Institutes (meteorological satellite imagery), National Center for Genetic Resources Preservation (genetic resources of crops), National Wildlife Research Center (interactions of wild animals and society), National Centers for Atmospheric Research (Climate, Meteorology), Solix (Biofuels (Algae produced)).

Computer facilities: Computer purchase and lease plans are available. 2,700 computers available on campus for general student use. A campuswide network can be accessed from student residence rooms and from off campus. Online class registration, personalized portal services including transcripts and financials (billing, financial aid) are available. *Web address:* http://www.colostate.edu/.

General Application Contact: Sandra Dailey, Graduate School Administrative Assistant III, 970-491-6817, Fax: 970-491-2194, E-mail: gschool@grad.colostate.edu.

GRADUATE UNITS

College of Veterinary Medicine and Biomedical Sciences Students: 740 full-time (536 women), 137 part-time (83 women); includes 112 minority (8 African Americans, 11 American Indian/Alaska Native, 49 Asian Americans or Pacific Islanders, 44 Hispanic Americans), 37 international. Average age 28. 2,003 applicants, 14% accepted, 253 enrolled. *Faculty:* 146 full-time (50 women), 4 part-time/adjunct (1 woman). Expenses: Contact institution. *Financial support:* In 2008–09, 174 students received support, including 56 fellowships with full tuition reimbursements available (averaging $36,393 per year), 98 research assistantships with full tuition reimbursements available (averaging $18,876 per year), 20 teaching assistantships with partial tuition reimbursements available (averaging $11,623 per year); Federal Work-Study, institutionally sponsored loans, scholarships/grants, tuition waivers (partial), and unspecified assistantships also available. Financial award applicants required to submit FAFSA. In 2008, 136 first professional degrees, 70 master's, 31 doctorates awarded. Offers biomedical sciences (MS, PhD); clinical sciences (MS, PhD); environmental health (MS, PhD); microbiology (MS, PhD); pathology (PhD); radiological health sciences (MS, PhD); veterinary medicine (DVM); veterinary medicine and biomedical sciences (DVM, MS, PhD). *Application deadline:* For fall admission, 3/1 priority date for domestic and international students; for spring admission, 10/1 priority date for domestic and international students. *Application fee:* $50. Electronic applications accepted. *Application Contact:* Dr. Terry Nett, Associate Dean for Research and Graduate Education, 970-491-7053, Fax: 970-491-2250, E-mail: terry.nett@colostate.edu. *Dean*, Dr. Lance Perryman, 970-491-7051, Fax: 970-491-2250, E-mail: lance.perryman@colostate.edu.

Graduate School Students: 1,911 full-time (1,062 women), 3,225 part-time (1,334 women); includes 571 minority (84 African Americans, 78 American Indian/Alaska Native, 175 Asian Americans or Pacific Islanders, 234 Hispanic Americans), 540 international. Average age 33. 5,247 applicants, 40% accepted, 1291 enrolled. *Faculty:* 795 full-time (246 women), 39 part-time/adjunct (7 women). Expenses: Contact institution. *Financial support:* Fellowships, research assistantships, teaching assistantships, career-related internships or fieldwork, Federal Work-Study, institutionally sponsored loans, scholarships/grants, traineeships, tuition waivers (full and partial), and unspecified assistantships available. Support available to part-time students. In 2008, 954 master's, 175 doctorates awarded. *Degree program information:* Part-time programs available. Postbaccalaureate distance learning degree programs offered (no on-campus study). Offers cell and molecular biology (MS, PhD); ecology (MS, PhD); molecular, cellular and integrative neurosciences (PhD). *Application fee:* $50. Electronic applications accepted. *Application Contact:* Sandra Dailey, Graduate School Administrative Assistant III, 970-491-6817, Fax: 970-491-2194, E-mail: gschool@grad.colostate.edu. *Vice Provost for Graduate Studies*, Peter K. Dorhout, 970-491-6817, Fax: 970-491-2194, E-mail: peter.dorhout@colostate.edu.

College of Agricultural Sciences Students: 131 full-time (69 women), 121 part-time (53 women); includes 15 minority (3 African Americans, 7 American Indian/Alaska Native, 1 Asian American or Pacific Islander, 4 Hispanic Americans), 35 international. Average age 31. 217 applicants, 44% accepted, 65 enrolled. *Faculty:* 92 full-time (17 women), 4 part-time/adjunct (0 women). Expenses: Contact institution. *Financial support:* In 2008–09, 113 students received support, including 12 fellowships (averaging $33,390 per year), 84 research assistantships (averaging $15,876 per year), 17 teaching assistantships (averaging $12,877 per year); career-related internships or fieldwork, Federal Work-Study, institutionally sponsored loans, scholarships/grants, traineeships, and unspecified assistantships also available. Support available to part-time students. Financial award application deadline: 3/1; financial award applicants required to submit FAFSA. In 2008, 37 master's, 8 doctorates awarded. *Degree program information:* Part-time programs available. Postbaccalaureate distance learning degree programs offered. Offers agricultural and resource economics (MS, PhD); agricultural sciences (M Agr, MS, PhD); animal sciences (MS, PhD); entomology (MS, PhD); horticulture (MS, PhD); plant pathology and weed science (MS, PhD); soil and crop sciences (MS, PhD). *Application deadline:* For fall admission, 4/1 priority date for domestic and international students; for spring admission, 9/1 priority date for domestic and international students. Applications are processed on a rolling basis. *Application fee:* $50. Electronic applications accepted. *Application Contact:* Pam Schell, Administrative Assistant, 970-491-2410, Fax: 970-491-4895, E-mail: pam.schell@colostate.edu. *Interim Dean*, Dr. Lee Sommers, 970-491-1421, Fax: 970-491-4895, E-mail: lee.sommers@colostate.edu.

College of Applied Human Sciences Students: 529 full-time (418 women), 594 part-time (373 women); includes 156 minority (30 African Americans, 18 American Indian/Alaska Native, 34 Asian Americans or Pacific Islanders, 74 Hispanic Americans), 38 international. Average age 35. 1,013 applicants, 36% accepted, 252 enrolled. *Faculty:* 105 full-time (52 women), 6 part-time/adjunct (3 women). Expenses: Contact institution. *Financial support:* In 2008–09, 99 students received support, including 2 fellowships with full and partial tuition reimbursements available (averaging $16,521 per year), 33 research assistantships with full tuition reimbursements available (averaging $10,977 per year), 64 teaching assistantships with full and partial tuition reimbursements available (averaging $10,779 per year); career-related internships or fieldwork, Federal Work-Study, institutionally sponsored loans, scholarships/grants, traineeships, tuition waivers (full and partial), and unspecified assistantships also available. Support available to part-time students. Financial award applicants required to submit FAFSA. In 2008, 288 master's, 38 doctorates awarded. *Degree program information:* Part-time programs available. Postbaccalaureate distance learning degree programs offered. Offers adult education and training (M Ed); applied human sciences (M Ed, MS, MSW, PhD); community college leadership (PhD); construction management (MS); counseling and career development (M Ed); design and merchandising (MS); education and human resource studies (M Ed, PhD); educational leadership (M Ed, PhD); food science and human nutrition (MS, PhD); health and exercise science (MS); human bioenergetics (PhD); human development and family studies (MS); interdisciplinary studies (PhD); occupational therapy (MS); organizational performance and change (M Ed, PhD); social work (MSW); student affairs in higher education (MS). *Application deadline:* For fall admission, 1/31 priority date for domestic and international students. *Application fee:* $50. Electronic applications accepted. *Application Contact:* Thomas Mazzarisi, Assistant to Dean, 970-491-5236, Fax: 970-491-7859, E-mail: thomas.mazzarisi@colostate.edu. *Dean*, April C. Mason, 977-491-5841, Fax: 970-491-7859, E-mail: april.mason@colostate.edu.

College of Business Students: 144 full-time (75 women), 836 part-time (223 women); includes 151 minority (31 African Americans, 13 American Indian/Alaska Native, 60 Asian Americans or Pacific Islanders, 47 Hispanic Americans), 67 international. Average age 35. 602 applicants, 78% accepted, 391 enrolled. *Faculty:* 56 full-time (13 women). Expenses: Contact institution. *Financial support:* In 2008–09, 3 students received support, including 3 teaching assistantships with full and partial tuition reimbursements available (averaging $6,165 per year); fellowships, research assistantships with full and partial tuition reimbursements available, career-related internships or fieldwork, Federal Work-Study, scholarships/grants, and unspecified assistantships also available. Financial award application deadline: 6/1; financial award applicants required to submit FAFSA. In 2008, 191 master's awarded. *Degree program information:* Part-time and evening/weekend programs available. Postbaccalaureate distance learning degree programs offered. Offers accounting (M Acc); business (M Acc, MBA, MMP, MS, MSBA); business administration (MBA); computer information systems (MSBA); global social and sustainable enterprise (MSBA); management practice (MMP). *Application deadline:* For fall admission, 7/15 for domestic students, 4/1 for international students; for spring admission, 11/15 for domestic students, 10/1 for international students. Applications are processed on a rolling basis. *Application fee:* $50. Electronic applications accepted. *Application Contact:* Rachel Stoll, Admissions Coordinator, 970-491-3704, Fax: 970-491-3481, E-mail: rachel.stoll@colostate.edu. *Associate Dean,* Dr. John Hoxmeier, 970-491-2142, Fax: 970-491-0596, E-mail: john.hoxmeier@colostate.edu.

College of Engineering Students: 226 full-time (53 women), 333 part-time (69 women); includes 43 minority (5 African Americans, 7 American Indian/Alaska Native, 15 Asian Americans or Pacific Islanders, 16 Hispanic Americans), 167 international. Average age 30. 859 applicants, 38% accepted, 123 enrolled. *Faculty:* 93 full-time (8 women), 10 part-time/adjunct (1 woman). Expenses: Contact institution. *Financial support:* In 2008–09, 249 students received support, including 23 fellowships with full tuition reimbursements available (averaging $26,886 per year), 188 research assistantships with full tuition reimbursements available (averaging $18,495 per year), 38 teaching assistantships with full tuition reimbursements available (averaging $9,762 per year); career-related internships or fieldwork, Federal Work-Study, institutionally sponsored loans, scholarships/grants, traineeships, health care benefits, and unspecified assistantships also available. Financial award application deadline: 1/15. In 2008, 104 master's, 36 doctorates awarded. *Degree program information:* Part-time programs available. Offers atmospheric science (MS, PhD); chemical engineering (MS, PhD); civil engineering (ME, MS, PhD); electrical engineering (MEE, MS, PhD); engineering (ME, MEE, MS, PhD); mechanical engineering (ME, MS, PhD). *Application deadline:* For fall admission, 2/1 priority date for domestic and international students; for spring admission, 10/1 priority date for domestic and international students. Applications are processed on a rolling basis. *Application fee:* $50. Electronic applications accepted. *Application Contact:* Dr. Tom Siller, Associate Dean, 970-491-6220, Fax: 970-491-3429, E-mail: thomas.siller@colostate.edu. *Dean,* Dr. Sandra L. Woods, 970-491-3366, Fax: 970-491-5569, E-mail: sandra.woods@colostate.edu.

College of Liberal Arts Students: 387 full-time (231 women), 263 part-time (157 women); includes 49 minority (4 African Americans, 5 American Indian/Alaska Native, 13 Asian Americans or Pacific Islanders, 27 Hispanic Americans), 57 international. Average age 31. 766 applicants, 47% accepted, 195 enrolled. *Faculty:* 216 full-time (91 women), 8 part-time/adjunct (3 women). Expenses: Contact institution. *Financial support:* In 2008–09, 4 research assistantships (averaging $34,763 per year), 224 teaching assistantships with full and partial tuition reimbursements (averaging $11,510 per year) were awarded; fellowships, career-related internships or fieldwork, Federal Work-Study, institutionally sponsored loans, scholarships/grants, traineeships, and unspecified assistantships also available. Support available to part-time students. Financial award application deadline: 3/1; financial award applicants required to submit FAFSA. In 2008, 145 master's, 6 doctorates awarded. *Degree program information:* Part-time programs available. Offers anthropology (MA); art (MFA); communication studies (MA); creative writing (MFA); economics (MA, PhD); English (MA); foreign languages and literatures (MA); history (MA); liberal arts (MA, MFA, MM, MS, PhD); music (MM); philosophy (MA); political science (MA, PhD); public communication and technology (MS, PhD); sociology (MA, PhD); technical communication (MS). *Application deadline:* Applications are processed on a rolling basis. *Application fee:* $50. Electronic applications accepted. *Application Contact:* Dr. John Didier, Associate Dean, 970-491-5421, Fax: 970-491-0528, E-mail: john.didier@colostate.edu. *Dean,* Dr. Ann Gill, 970-491-5421, Fax: 970-491-0528, E-mail: ann.gill@colostate.edu.

College of Natural Sciences Students: 318 full-time (136 women), 372 part-time (116 women); includes 84 minority (8 African Americans, 13 American Indian/Alaska Native, 28 Asian Americans or Pacific Islanders, 35 Hispanic Americans), 129 international. Average age 29. 1,344 applicants, 24% accepted, 169 enrolled. *Faculty:* 166 full-time (47 women), 11 part-time/adjunct (0 women). Expenses: Contact institution. *Financial support:* In 2008–09, 521 students received support, including 66 fellowships (averaging $31,032 per year), 173 research assistantships with full tuition reimbursements available (averaging $15,058 per year), 282 teaching assistantships with full tuition reimbursements available (averaging $14,186 per year); health care benefits also available. Financial award application deadline: 1/15; financial award applicants required to submit FAFSA. In 2008, 116 master's, 56 doctorates awarded. Postbaccalaureate distance learning degree programs offered (no on-campus study). Offers biochemistry (MS, PhD); botany (MS, PhD); chemistry (MS, PhD); computer science (MCS, MS, PhD); mathematics (MAT, MS, PhD); natural sciences (MAT, MCS, MS, PhD); physics (MS, PhD); psychology (MS, PhD); statistics (MS, PhD); zoology (MS, PhD). *Application deadline:* For fall admission, 9/15 priority date for domestic and international students; for spring admission, 1/15 priority date for domestic and international students. Applications are processed on a rolling basis. *Application fee:* $50. Electronic applications accepted. *Application Contact:* Dr. Don Mykles, Associate Dean for Graduate Education, 970-491-6864, Fax: 970-491-6639, E-mail: donald.mykles@colostate.edu. *Interim Dean,* Dr. Jan Nerger, 970-491-6864, Fax: 970-491-6639, E-mail: jan.nerger@colostate.edu.

School of Biomedical Engineering Students: 9 full-time (5 women), 1 part-time (0 women); includes 2 minority (both Asian Americans or Pacific Islanders). Average age 29. 65 applicants, 31% accepted, 6 enrolled. Expenses: Contact institution. *Financial support:* In 2008–09, 8 research assistantships with full tuition reimbursements (averaging $9,836 per year), 3 teaching assistantships with full tuition reimbursements (averaging $7,477 per year) were awarded; fellowships, unspecified assistantships also available. Financial award application deadline: 3/1; financial award applicants required to submit FAFSA. *Degree program information:* Part-time programs available. Offers biomedical engineering (ME, MS, PhD). *Application deadline:* For fall admission, 1/15 priority date for domestic and international students; for spring admission, 9/1 priority date for domestic students, 8/1 priority date for international students. *Application fee:* $50. *Application Contact:* Lori Dwyer, Academic Advisor, 970-491-7157, E-mail: lori.dwyer@colostate.edu. *Director,* Dr. Susan James, 970-491-2842, Fax: 970-491-3827, E-mail: susan.james@colostate.edu.

Warner College of Natural Resources Students: 88 full-time (30 women), 158 part-time (69 women); includes 20 minority (7 American Indian/Alaska Native, 3 Asian Americans or Pacific Islanders, 10 Hispanic Americans), 17 international. Average age 32. 177 applicants, 51% accepted, 57 enrolled. *Faculty:* 58 full-time (15 women). Expenses: Contact institution. *Financial support:* In 2008–09, 118 students received support, including 10 fellowships (averaging $30,563 per year), 79 research assistantships (averaging $14,569 per year), 29 teaching assistantships with tuition reimbursements available (averaging $8,742 per year); career-related internships or fieldwork, Federal Work-Study, institutionally sponsored loans, scholarships/grants, traineeships, and unspecified assistantships also available. Support available to part-time students. Financial award applicants required to submit FAFSA. In 2008, 52 master's, 10 doctorates awarded. *Degree program information:* Part-time programs available. Offers earth sciences (PhD); fish, wildlife and conservation biology (MFWCB); fishery and wildlife biology (MFWB, MS, PhD); forest sciences (MS, PhD); geosciences (MS); human dimensions of natural resources (MS, PhD); natural resources (MFWB, MFWCB, MNRS, MS, PhD); natural resources stewardship (MNRS); rangeland ecosystem science (MS, PhD); watershed science (MS). *Application deadline:* Applications are processed on a rolling basis. *Application fee:* $50. Electronic applications accepted. *Application Contact:* Ethan Billingsley, Coordinator, 970-491-4994, E-mail: ethan.billingsley@colostate.edu. *Dean,* Dr. Joseph T. O'Leary, 970-491-5405, Fax: 970-491-0279, E-mail: joseph.oleary@colostate.edu.

COLORADO STATE UNIVERSITY–PUEBLO, Pueblo, CO 81001-4901

General Information State-supported, coed, comprehensive institution. *Graduate housing:* Room and/or apartments available on a first-come, first-served basis to single students; on-campus housing not available to married students. Housing application deadline: 8/1.

GRADUATE UNITS

College of Education, Engineering and Professional Studies *Degree program information:* Part-time and evening/weekend programs available. Offers art education (M Ed); education, engineering and professional studies (M Ed, MS); foreign language education (M Ed); health and physical education (M Ed); industrial and systems engineering (MS); instructional technology (M Ed); linguistically diverse education (M Ed); music education (M Ed); nursing (MS); special education (M Ed). Electronic applications accepted.

College of Science and Mathematics *Degree program information:* Part-time and evening/weekend programs available. Offers applied natural science (MS).

Malik and Seeme Hasan School of Business *Degree program information:* Part-time and evening/weekend programs available. Offers business (MBA).

COLORADO TECHNICAL UNIVERSITY COLORADO SPRINGS, Colorado Springs, CO 80907-3896

General Information Proprietary, coed, university. *Graduate housing:* On-campus housing not available.

GRADUATE UNITS

Graduate Studies *Degree program information:* Part-time and evening/weekend programs available. Offers accounting (MBA, MSA); business administration (MBA); computer engineering (MSCE); computer science (DCS); computer systems security (MSCS); criminal justice (MSM); database systems (MSCS); electrical engineering (MSEE); finance (MBA); human resources management (MBA); information systems security (MSM); logistics/supply chain management (MBA); management (DM); marketing (MBA); mediation and dispute resolution (MBA); operations management (MBA); project management (MBA); software engineering (MSCS); systems engineering (MS); technology management (MBA).

COLORADO TECHNICAL UNIVERSITY DENVER, Greenwood Village, CO 80111

General Information Proprietary, coed, comprehensive institution. *Graduate housing:* On-campus housing not available.

GRADUATE UNITS

Program in Computer Engineering Offers computer engineering (MS).

Program in Computer Science *Degree program information:* Part-time and evening/weekend programs available. Offers computer systems security (MSCS); database systems (MSCS); software engineering (MSCS).

Program in Electrical Engineering Offers electrical engineering (MS).

Program in Information Science Offers information systems security (MSM).

Program in Systems Engineering Offers systems engineering (MS).

Programs in Business Administration and Management *Degree program information:* Part-time and evening/weekend programs available. Offers accounting (MBA); business administration (MBA); business administration and management (EMBA); finance (MBA); human resource management (MBA); marketing (MBA); mediation and dispute resolution (MBA); operations management (MBA); project management (MBA); technology management (MBA).

COLORADO TECHNICAL UNIVERSITY SIOUX FALLS, Sioux Falls, SD 57108

General Information Proprietary, coed, comprehensive institution. *Graduate housing:* On-campus housing not available.

GRADUATE UNITS

Program in Computing Offers computer systems security (MSCS); software engineering (MSCS).

Program in Criminal Justice Offers criminal justice (MSM).

Programs in Business Administration and Management *Degree program information:* Evening/weekend programs available. Offers business administration (MBA); business management (MSM); health science management (MSM); human resources management (MSM); information technology (MSM); organizational leadership (MSM); project management (MBA); technology management (MBA).

COLUMBIA COLLEGE, Columbia, MO 65216-0002

General Information Independent-religious, coed, comprehensive institution. *Enrollment:* 1,353 graduate, professional, and undergraduate students; 622 full-time matriculated graduate/professional students (386 women). *Enrollment by degree level:* 622 master's. *Graduate faculty:* 14 full-time (6 women), 40 part-time/adjunct (9 women). *Tuition:* Full-time $3420; part-time $285 per semester hour. Full-time tuition and fees vary according to campus/location. *Graduate housing:* On-campus housing not available. *Student services:* Campus safety program, career counseling, exercise/wellness program, free psychological counseling, international student services, low-cost health insurance, services for students with disabilities, teacher training, writing training. *Library facilities:* Stafford Library. *Online resources:* library catalog, web page, access to other libraries' catalogs. *Collection:* 73,862 titles, 239 serial subscriptions, 1,986 audiovisual materials.

Computer facilities: 83 computers available on campus for general student use. A campuswide network can be accessed from student residence rooms and from off campus. Online class registration is available. *Web address:* http://www.ccis.edu/.

General Application Contact: White Samantha, Director of Admissions, 573-875-7352, Fax: 573-875-7506, E-mail: shwhite@ccis.edu.

GRADUATE UNITS

Master of Arts in Teaching Program Students: 104 full-time (89 women); includes 9 minority (6 African Americans, 1 Asian American or Pacific Islander, 2 Hispanic Americans), 1 international. Average age 32. 80 applicants, 70% accepted, 27 enrolled. *Faculty:* 5 full-time (3 women), 10 part-time/adjunct (6 women). Expenses: Contact institution. *Financial support:* In 2008–09, 69 students received support. Career-related internships or fieldwork, Federal Work-Study, and scholarships/grants available. Financial award application deadline: 3/15; financial award applicants required to submit FAFSA. In 2008, 16 master's awarded. *Degree program information:* Evening/weekend programs available. Postbaccalaureate distance learning degree programs offered (no on-campus study). Offers teaching (MAT). *Application deadline:* For fall admission, 8/1 priority date for domestic and international students; for spring admission, 12/15 priority date for domestic and international students. Applications are processed on a rolling basis. *Application fee:* $55. Electronic applications accepted. *Application Contact:* Samantha White, Director of Admissions, 573-875-7352, Fax: 573-875-7506, E-mail: sjwhite@ccis.edu. *MAT Graduate Program Coordinator,* Dr. Kristina Miller, 573-875-7590, Fax: 573-876-4493, E-mail: kmiller@ccis.edu.

Master of Business Administration Program Students: 432 full-time (259 women); includes 106 minority (69 African Americans, 4 American Indian/Alaska Native, 15 Asian Americans or Pacific Islanders, 18 Hispanic Americans), 9 international. Average age 37. 203 applicants, 68% accepted, 80 enrolled. *Faculty:* 3 full-time (2 women), 39 part-time/adjunct (16 women). Expenses: Contact institution. *Financial support:* In 2008–09, 201 students received support.

Columbia College (continued)

Federal Work-Study and scholarships/grants available. Financial award applicants required to submit FAFSA. In 2008, 82 master's awarded. *Degree program information:* Evening/weekend programs available. Postbaccalaureate distance learning degree programs offered (no on-campus study). Offers business administration (MBA). *Application deadline:* For fall admission, 8/1 priority date for domestic and international students; for winter admission, 1/1 priority date for domestic and international students. Applications are processed on a rolling basis. *Application fee:* $55. Electronic applications accepted. *Application Contact:* Samantha White, Director of Admissions, 573-875-7352, Fax: 573-875-7506, E-mail: sjwhite@ccis.edu. *MBA Graduate Program Coordinator,* Dr. Diane Suhler, 573-875-7640, Fax: 573-876-4493, E-mail: drsuhlern@email.ccis.edu.

Master of Science in Criminal Justice Program Students: 86 full-time (38 women); includes 24 minority (17 African Americans, 1 American Indian/Alaska Native, 1 Asian American or Pacific Islander, 5 Hispanic Americans). Average age 35. 46 applicants, 70% accepted, 15 enrolled. *Faculty:* 3 full-time (0 women), 6 part-time/adjunct (3 women). Expenses: Contact institution. *Financial support:* In 2008–09, 53 students received support. Federal Work-Study and scholarships/grants available. Financial award applicants required to submit FAFSA. In 2008, 14 master's awarded. *Degree program information:* Evening/weekend programs available. Postbaccalaureate distance learning degree programs offered (no on-campus study). Offers criminal justice (MSCJ). *Application deadline:* For fall admission, 8/1 priority date for domestic and international students; for spring admission, 12/15 priority date for domestic and international students. Applications are processed on a rolling basis. *Application fee:* $55. Electronic applications accepted. *Application Contact:* Samantha White, Director of Admissions, 573-875-7352, Fax: 573-875-7506, E-mail: sjwhite@ccis.edu. *MSCJ Graduate Program Coordinator,* Dr. Joseph Carrier, 573-875-7275, Fax: 573-876-4493, E-mail: jjcarrier@ccis.edu.

COLUMBIA COLLEGE, Columbia, SC 29203-5998

General Information Independent-religious, Undergraduate: women only; graduate: coed, comprehensive institution. *Enrollment:* 1,444 graduate, professional, and undergraduate students; 144 full-time matriculated graduate/professional students (129 women), 69 part-time matriculated graduate/professional students (57 women). *Enrollment by degree level:* 213 master's. *Graduate faculty:* 5 full-time (3 women), 28 part-time/adjunct (17 women). *Tuition:* Full-time $3015; part-time $335 per semester hour. *Graduate housing:* On-campus housing not available. *Student services:* Campus safety program, career counseling. *Library facilities:* J. Drake Edens Library plus 1 other. *Online resources:* library catalog, web page, access to other libraries' catalogs. *Collection:* 146,135 titles, 28,391 serial subscriptions, 7,804 audiovisual materials.

Computer facilities: Computer purchase and lease plans are available. 150 computers available on campus for general student use. A campuswide network can be accessed from student residence rooms. Online class registration is available. *Web address:* http://www.columbiacollegesc.edu/.

General Application Contact: Carolyn Emeneker, Director of Graduate School and Evening College Admissions, 803-786-3766, Fax: 803-786-3674, E-mail: emeneker@colacoll.edu.

GRADUATE UNITS

Graduate Programs Students: 144 full-time (129 women), 69 part-time (57 women); includes 75 minority (69 African Americans, 2 Asian Americans or Pacific Islanders, 4 Hispanic Americans), 1 international. Average age 33. 111 applicants, 98% accepted, 98 enrolled. *Faculty:* 5 full-time (3 women), 28 part-time/adjunct (17 women). Expenses: Contact institution. *Financial support:* Available to part-time students. Application deadline: 7/1. In 2008, 195 master's awarded. *Degree program information:* Part-time and evening/weekend programs available. Postbaccalaureate distance learning degree programs offered (minimal on-campus study). Offers divergent learning (M Ed); human behavior and conflict management (MA); interpersonal relations/conflict management (Certificate); organizational behavior/conflict management (Certificate). *Application deadline:* For fall admission, 8/22 priority date for domestic students, 8/22 for international students. Applications are processed on a rolling basis. *Application fee:* $50. Electronic applications accepted. *Application Contact:* Carolyn Emeneker, Director of Graduate School and Evening College Admissions, 803-786-3766, Fax: 803-786-3674, E-mail: emeneker@colacoll.edu. *Provost and Vice President for Academic Affairs,* Dr. Laurie B. Hopkins, 803-786-3669, Fax: 803-754-3178, E-mail: lhopkins@colacoll.edu.

COLUMBIA COLLEGE CHICAGO, Chicago, IL 60605-1996

General Information Independent, coed, comprehensive institution. *Enrollment:* 370 full-time matriculated graduate/professional students (249 women), 236 part-time matriculated graduate/professional students (169 women). *Enrollment by degree level:* 604 master's, 2 other advanced degrees. *Graduate faculty:* 128. *Tuition:* Full-time $15,992; part-time $633 per credit hour. *Graduate housing:* Room and/or apartments available on a first-come, first-served basis to single students; on-campus housing not available to married students. Typical cost: $10,000 per year ($12,000 including board). Room and board charges vary according to board plan and housing facility selected. Housing application deadline: 5/1. *Student services:* Campus employment opportunities, campus safety program, career counseling, exercise/wellness program, free psychological counseling, international student services, low-cost health insurance, multicultural affairs office, services for students with disabilities, teacher training. *Library facilities:* Columbia College Library plus 2 others. *Online resources:* library catalog, web page, access to other libraries' catalogs. *Collection:* 258,883 titles, 1,232 serial subscriptions, 21,257 audiovisual materials.

Computer facilities: 730 computers available on campus for general student use. A campuswide network can be accessed. *Web address:* http://www.colum.edu/.

General Application Contact: Royal Dawson, Director of Institutional Research, 312-369-7478, Fax: 312-369-8052, E-mail: rdawson@colum.edu.

GRADUATE UNITS

Graduate School Students: 370 full-time (249 women), 236 part-time (169 women); includes 133 minority (76 African Americans, 4 American Indian/Alaska Native, 13 Asian Americans or Pacific Islanders, 40 Hispanic Americans), 25 international. Average age 29. 876 applicants, 45% accepted, 185 enrolled. *Faculty:* 128. Expenses: Contact institution. *Financial support:* In 2008–09, 202 students received support; fellowships with full and partial tuition reimbursements available, research assistantships, teaching assistantships, career-related internships or fieldwork, Federal Work-Study, scholarships/grants, and tuition waivers (partial) available. Support available to part-time students. Financial award application deadline: 8/13; financial award applicants required to submit FAFSA. In 2008, 318 master's, 3 other advanced degrees awarded. *Degree program information:* Part-time and evening/weekend programs available. Offers architectural studies (MFA); arts, entertainment and media management (MA); creative writing (MFA); dance/movement therapy (MA, Certificate); elementary education (MAT); English (MAT); film and video (MFA); interdisciplinary arts (MA, MAT); interdisciplinary book and paper arts (MFA); interior design (MFA); multicultural education (MA); photography (MA, MFA); poetry (MFA); public affairs journalism (MA); teaching of writing (MA); urban teaching (MA). *Application deadline:* Applications are processed on a rolling basis. *Application fee:* $55. Electronic applications accepted. *Application Contact:* Dr. Keith Cleveland, Office of Provost/Senior Vice President, 312-369-7261, Fax: 312-369-8022, E-mail: kcleveland@colum.edu. *Office of Provost/Senior Vice President,* Dr. Keith Cleveland, 312-369-7261, Fax: 312-369-8022, E-mail: kcleveland@colum.edu.

COLUMBIA INTERNATIONAL UNIVERSITY, Columbia, SC 29230-3122

General Information Independent-religious, coed, university. *Graduate housing:* Room and/or apartments available on a first-come, first-served basis to single students; on-campus housing not available to married students. Housing application deadline: 8/27.

GRADUATE UNITS

Columbia Biblical Seminary and School of Missions *Degree program information:* Part-time and evening/weekend programs available. Offers academic ministries (M Div); bible exposition (M Div, MABE); biblical studies (Certificate); counseling ministries (Certificate); divinity (M Div); educational ministries (M Div, MAEM, Certificate); intercultural studies (M Div, MAIS, Certificate); leadership (D Min); leadership for evangelism/mobilization (MALM); member care (D Min); ministry (Certificate); missions (D Min); pastoral counseling and spiritual formation (M Div, MAPS); preaching (D Min); theology (MA). Electronic applications accepted.

Columbia Graduate School *Degree program information:* Part-time and evening/weekend programs available. Offers Bible teaching (MABT); Christian higher education leadership (Ed D); Christian school educational leadership (Ed D); counseling (MACN); curriculum and instruction (M Ed); early childhood and elementary education (MAT); educational administration (M Ed); teaching English as a foreign language (Certificate); teaching English as a foreign language and intercultural studies (MATF). Electronic applications accepted.

COLUMBIA SOUTHERN UNIVERSITY, Orange Beach, AL 36561

General Information Proprietary, coed, primarily men, comprehensive institution. *Graduate housing:* On-campus housing not available.

GRADUATE UNITS

College of Safety and Emergency Services *Degree program information:* Part-time and evening/weekend programs available. Postbaccalaureate distance learning degree programs offered (no on-campus study). Offers criminal justice (MS); environmental management (MS); occupational safety and health (MS); occupational safety and health/environmental management (MS). Electronic applications accepted.

DBA Program *Degree program information:* Part-time and evening/weekend programs available. Postbaccalaureate distance learning degree programs offered (minimal on-campus study). Offers business administration (DBA). Electronic applications accepted.

MBA Program *Degree program information:* Part-time and evening/weekend programs available. Postbaccalaureate distance learning degree programs offered (no on-campus study). Offers electronic business and technology (MBA); finance (MBA); general (MBA); healthcare management (MBA); hospitality and tourism (MBA); human resources management (MBA); international management (MBA); marketing (MBA); project management (MBA); public administration (MBA); sport management (MBA). Electronic applications accepted.

COLUMBIA THEOLOGICAL SEMINARY, Decatur, GA 30031-0520

General Information Independent-religious, coed, graduate-only institution. *Graduate housing:* Rooms and/or apartments available on a first-come, first-served basis to single students and available to married students. Housing application deadline: 4/30.

GRADUATE UNITS

Graduate and Professional Programs Offers theology (M Div, MATS, Th M, D Min, Th D).

COLUMBIA UNION COLLEGE, Takoma Park, MD 20912-7796

General Information Independent-religious, coed, comprehensive institution.

GRADUATE UNITS

MBA Program *Degree program information:* Part-time programs available. Offers business administration (MBA).

Program in Nursing—Business Leadership Offers nursing—business leadership (MSN).

Program in Religion Offers religion (MAR).

COLUMBIA UNIVERSITY, New York, NY 10027

General Information Independent, coed, university. CGS member. *Enrollment by degree level:* 2,199 first professional, 7,280 master's, 6,043 doctoral, 177 other advanced degrees. *Graduate faculty:* 3,608 full-time (1,394 women), 1,053 part-time/adjunct (412 women). *Tuition:* Full-time $34,364; part-time $1362 per credit. *Required fees:* $1769; $73 per credit. $760 per term. One-time fee: $95. Part-time tuition and fees vary according to course load, degree level, program and student level. *Graduate housing:* Rooms and/or apartments available on a first-come, first-served basis to single and married students. Typical cost: $7416 per year ($9186 including board) for single students; $7500 per year ($10,141 including board) for married students. Room and board charges vary according to board plan and housing facility selected. Housing application deadline: 7/10. *Student services:* Campus employment opportunities, campus safety program, career counseling, exercise/wellness program, free psychological counseling, international student services, low-cost health insurance, multicultural affairs office, services for students with disabilities, writing training. *Library facilities:* Butler plus 25 others. *Online resources:* library catalog. *Collection:* 9.5 million titles, 117,264 serial subscriptions. *Research affiliation:* Long Island Biological Laboratory, Brookhaven National Laboratory, New York Botanical Gardens, American Museum of Natural History, Marine Biological Laboratory, Goddard Space Flight Center.

Computer facilities: Computer purchase and lease plans are available. 400 computers available on campus for general student use. A campuswide network can be accessed from student residence rooms and from off campus. Online class registration is available. *Web address:* http://www.columbia.edu/.

General Application Contact: Information Contact, 212-854-1754.

GRADUATE UNITS

College of Dental Medicine Offers advanced education in general dentistry (Certificate); biomedical informatics (MA, PhD); dental and oral surgery (DDS); dental medicine (DDS, MA, MS, PhD, Certificate); endodontics (Certificate); orthodontics (MS, Certificate); periodontics (MS, Certificate); prosthodontics (MS, Certificate); science education (MA).

College of Physicians and Surgeons *Degree program information:* Part-time programs available. Offers anatomy (M Phil, MA, PhD); anatomy and cell biology (PhD); biochemistry and molecular biophysics (M Phil, PhD); biomedical informatics (M Phil, MA, PhD); biomedical sciences (M Phil, MA, PhD); biophysics (PhD); cellular, molecular and biophysical studies (M Phil, MA, PhD); genetics (M Phil, MA, PhD); medicine (MD, M Phil, MA, MS, DN Sc, DPT, Ed D, PhD, Adv C); movement science (Ed D); neurobiology and behavior (PhD); occupational therapy (professional) (MS); occupational therapy administration or education (post-professional) (MS); pathobiology (M Phil, MA, PhD); pharmacology (M Phil, MA, PhD); pharmacology-toxicology (M Phil, MA, PhD); physical therapy (DPT); physiology and cellular biophysics (M Phil, MA, PhD).

Institute of Human Nutrition *Degree program information:* Part-time and evening/weekend programs available. Offers nutrition (MS, PhD).

Columbia University Mailman School of Public Health Students: 478 full-time (400 women), 554 part-time (397 women); includes 300 minority (80 African Americans, 3 American Indian/Alaska Native, 148 Asian Americans or Pacific Islanders, 69 Hispanic Americans), 133 international. Average age 30. 1,752 applicants, 58% accepted, 365 enrolled. *Faculty:* 312 full-time (155 women), 284 part-time/adjunct (128 women). Expenses: Contact institution. *Financial support:* In 2008–09, 588 students received support; fellowships, research assistantships, teaching assistantships, career-related internships or fieldwork, Federal Work-Study, and traineeships available. Support available to part-time students. Financial award application deadline: 2/1; financial award applicants required to submit FAFSA. In 2008, 363 master's, 29 doctorates awarded. *Degree program information:* Part-time and evening/weekend programs available. Offers biostatistics (MPH, MS, Dr PH, PhD); environmental health sciences (MPH, Dr PH, PhD); epidemiology (MPH, MS, Dr PH, PhD); health policy and management (Exec MPH, MPH); population and family health (MPH); public health (Exec MPH, MPH, MS, Dr PH, PhD); sociomedical sciences (MPH, Dr PH, PhD). PhD offered in cooperation with the Graduate School of Arts and Sciences. *Application deadline:* For fall admission, 1/5 for domestic and international students. *Application fee:* $60. Electronic applications accepted. *Application Contact:* Dr. Joseph Korevec, Director of Admissions and Financial Aid, 212-305-8698, Fax: 212-342-1861, E-mail: ph-admit@columbia.edu. *Dean/Professor,* Dr. Linda P. Fried, 212-305-9300, Fax: 212-305-9342, E-mail: lpfried@columbia.edu.

Fu Foundation School of Engineering and Applied Science Students: 1,140 full-time (270 women), 507 part-time (106 women); includes 140 minority (9 African Americans, 1 American Indian/Alaska Native, 104 Asian Americans or Pacific Islanders, 26 Hispanic Americans), 1,040 international. Average age 28. 4,287 applicants, 34% accepted, 747 enrolled. *Faculty:*

164 full-time (17 women), 114 part-time/adjunct (9 women). Expenses: Contact institution. *Financial support:* In 2008–09, 498 students received support, including 51 fellowships with full and partial tuition reimbursements available (averaging $27,300 per year), 371 research assistantships with full tuition reimbursements available (averaging $27,000 per year), 145 teaching assistantships with full tuition reimbursements available (averaging $24,060 per year); institutionally sponsored loans, scholarships/grants, health care benefits, and unspecified assistantships also available. Support available to part-time students. Financial award application deadline: 12/1; financial award applicants required to submit FAFSA. In 2008, 599 master's, 81 doctorates, 6 other advanced degrees awarded. *Degree program information:* Part-time programs available. Postbaccalaureate distance learning degree programs offered (no on-campus study). Offers applied physics (Eng Sc D); applied physics and applied mathematics (MS, PhD, Engr); biomedical engineering (MS, Eng Sc D, PhD); chemical engineering (MS, Eng Sc D, PhD); civil engineering (MS, Eng Sc D, PhD, Engr); computer engineering (MS); computer science (MS, Eng Sc D, PhD, Engr); construction engineering and management (MS); earth and environmental engineering (MS, Eng Sc D, PhD); electrical engineering (MS, Eng Sc D, PhD, Engr); engineering and applied science (MS, Eng Sc D, PhD, Engr); engineering management systems (MS); engineering mechanics (MS, Eng Sc D, PhD, Engr); financial engineering (MS); industrial engineering (Engr); industrial engineering and operations research (MS, Eng Sc D, PhD); materials science and engineering (MS, Eng Sc D, PhD); mechanical engineering (MS, Eng Sc D, PhD, Engr); medical physics (MS); metallurgical engineering (Engr); mining engineering (Engr); solid state science and engineering (MS, Eng Sc D, PhD). *Application deadline:* For fall admission, 12/1 priority date for domestic and international students; for spring admission, 10/1 priority date for domestic and international students. Applications are processed on a rolling basis. *Application fee:* $70. Electronic applications accepted. *Application Contact:* Jocelyn Morales, Admissions Officer, 212-854-6901, Fax: 212-854-5900, E-mail: jm2388@columbia.edu. *Dean,* Dr. Feniosky Pena-Mora, 212-854-2993, Fax: 212-864-0104, E-mail: seasgradmit@columbia.edu.

Graduate School of Architecture, Planning, and Preservation Offers advanced architectural design (MS); architecture (M Arch, PhD); architecture, planning, and preservation (M Arch, MS, PhD, Certificate); historic preservation (MS, Certificate); real estate development (MS); urban planning (MS, PhD). PhD offered through the Graduate School of Arts and Sciences.

Graduate School of Arts and Sciences *Degree program information:* Part-time and evening/weekend programs available. Offers African-American studies (MA); American studies (MA); arts and sciences (M Phil, MA, DMA, PhD, Certificate); climate and society (MA); conservation biology (MA); East Asian regional studies (MA); East Asian studies (MA); French cultural studies (MA); human rights studies (MA); Islamic culture studies (MA); Jewish studies (MA); medieval studies (MA); modern European studies (MA); quantitative methods in the social sciences (MA); Russian, Eurasian and East European regional studies (MA); South Asian studies (MA); sustainable development (PhD); theatre (M Phil, MA, PhD); Yiddish studies (MA).

Division of Humanities *Degree program information:* Part-time programs available. Offers archaeology (M Phil, MA, PhD); art history and archaeology (M Phil, MA, PhD); classics (M Phil, MA, PhD); comparative literature (M Phil, MA, PhD); East Asian languages and cultures (M Phil, MA, PhD); English literature (M Phil, MA, PhD); French and Romance philology (M Phil, PhD); Germanic languages (M Phil, MA, PhD); Hebrew language and literature (M Phil, MA, PhD); humanities (M Phil, MA, DMA, PhD); Italian (M Phil, MA, PhD); Jewish studies (M Phil, MA, PhD); literature-writing (M Phil, MA, PhD); Middle Eastern languages and cultures (M Phil, MA, PhD); modern art (MA); music (M Phil, MA, DMA, PhD); Oriental studies (M Phil, MA, PhD); philosophy (M Phil, MA, PhD); religion (M Phil, MA, PhD); Romance languages (MA); Russian literature (M Phil, MA, PhD); Slavic languages (M Phil, MA, PhD); South Asian languages and cultures (M Phil, MA, PhD); Spanish and Portuguese (M Phil, MA, PhD).

Division of Natural Sciences *Degree program information:* Part-time programs available. Offers astronomy (M Phil, MA, PhD); atmospheric and planetary science (M Phil, PhD); biological sciences (M Phil, MA, PhD); chemical physics (M Phil, PhD); conservation biology (Certificate); ecology and evolutionary biology (PhD); environmental policy (Certificate); experimental psychology (M Phil, MA, PhD); geochemistry (M Phil, MA, PhD); geodetic sciences (M Phil, MA, PhD); geophysics (M Phil, MA, PhD); inorganic chemistry (M Phil, MA, PhD); mathematics (M Phil, MA, PhD); natural sciences (M Phil, MA, PhD, Certificate); oceanography (M Phil, MA, PhD); organic chemistry (M Phil, MA, PhD); philosophical foundations of physics (MA); physics (M Phil, PhD); psychobiology (M Phil, MA, PhD); social psychology (M Phil, MA, PhD); statistics (M Phil, MA, PhD).

Division of Social Sciences *Degree program information:* Part-time programs available. Offers American history (M Phil, MA, PhD); anthropology (M Phil, MA, PhD); economics (M Phil, MA, PhD); history (M Phil, MA, PhD); political science (M Phil, MA, PhD); social sciences (M Phil, MA, PhD); sociology (M Phil, MA, PhD).

Graduate School of Business Offers accounting (MBA); business (PhD); business administration (EMBA, MBA); decision, risk, and operations (MBA); entrepreneurship (MBA); finance and economics (MBA); global business administration (EMBA); human resource management (MBA); international business (MBA); management/leadership (MBA); marketing (MBA); media (MBA); real estate (MBA); social enterprise (MBA). Electronic applications accepted.

Graduate School of Journalism *Degree program information:* Part-time programs available. Offers journalism (MA, MS, PhD).

School of Continuing Education *Degree program information:* Part-time and evening/weekend programs available. Offers actuarial science (MS); construction administration (MS); fundraising management (MS); information and archive management (MS); landscape design (MS); negotiation and conflict resolution (MS); sports management (MS); strategic communications (MS); technology management (Exec MS). Electronic applications accepted.

School of International and Public Affairs Offers development practice (MPA); environmental science and policy (MPA); international affairs (MIA); international and public affairs (MA, MIA, MPA, Certificate); public policy and administration (MPA). Electronic applications accepted.

The East Central Europe Center Offers East Central European studies (Certificate). Students must be enrolled in a separate graduate degree program at Columbia University. Electronic applications accepted.

The Harriman Institute *Degree program information:* Part-time programs available. Offers Russian, Eurasian, and Eastern European studies (Certificate). Students must be enrolled in a separate graduate degree program at Columbia University. Electronic applications accepted.

Institute for the Study of Europe Offers European studies (Certificate). Students must be enrolled in a separate graduate degree program at Columbia University. Electronic applications accepted.

Institute of African Studies Offers African studies (Certificate). Students must be enrolled in a separate graduate degree program at Columbia University. Electronic applications accepted.

Institute of Latin American Studies Offers Latin American and Caribbean studies (MA); Latin American studies (Certificate). Students must also be enrolled in a separate graduate degree program at Columbia University. Electronic applications accepted.

Middle East Institute Offers Middle East studies (Certificate). Students must also be enrolled in a separate graduate degree program at Columbia University. Electronic applications accepted.

Southern Asian Institute Offers Southern Asian studies (Certificate). Students must be enrolled in a separate graduate degree program at Columbia University. Electronic applications accepted.

Weatherhead East Asian Institute Offers Asian studies (Certificate). Students must be enrolled in a separate graduate degree program at Columbia University. Electronic applications accepted.

School of Law Offers law (JD, LL M, JSD). Electronic applications accepted.

School of Nursing *Degree program information:* Part-time programs available. Offers acute care nurse practitioner (MS, Adv C); adult nurse practitioner (MS, Adv C); family nurse practitioner (MS, Adv C); geriatric nurse practitioner (MS, Adv C); neonatal nurse practitioner (MS, Adv C); nurse anesthesia (MS, Adv C); nurse midwifery (MS); nursing (MS, DN Sc, DNP, Adv C); nursing practice (DNP); nursing science (DN Sc); oncology nursing (MS, Adv C); pediatric nurse practitioner (MS, Adv C); psychiatric mental health nursing (MS, Adv C); women's health nurse practitioner (Adv C). Electronic applications accepted.

School of Social Work Offers social work (MSSW, PhD). PhD offered through the Graduate School of Arts and Sciences. Electronic applications accepted.

School of the Arts Offers arts (MA, MFA); directing (MFA); fiction (MFA); film studies (MA); new genres (MFA); nonfiction (MFA); painting (MFA); photography (MFA); poetry (MFA); printmaking (MFA); producing (MFA); screen writing (MFA); sculpture (MFA). Electronic applications accepted.

Theatre Arts Division Offers acting (MFA); directing (MFA); dramaturgy (MFA); playwriting (MFA); stage management (MFA); theater management (MFA). Electronic applications accepted.

COLUMBUS STATE UNIVERSITY, Columbus, GA 31907-5645

General Information State-supported, coed, comprehensive institution. *Enrollment:* 7,953 graduate, professional, and undergraduate students; 386 full-time matriculated graduate/professional students (245 women), 707 part-time matriculated graduate/professional students (395 women). *Enrollment by degree level:* 953 master's, 140 other advanced degrees. *Graduate faculty:* 59 full-time (28 women), 36 part-time/adjunct (15 women). *Tuition, area resident:* Full-time $3410; part-time $143 per credit hour. Tuition, state resident: full-time $3411; part-time $143 per credit hour. Tuition, nonresident: full-time $13,634; part-time $569 per credit hour. *Required fees:* $1348. *Graduate housing:* Room and/or apartments available on a first-come, first-served basis to single students; on-campus housing not available to married students. Typical cost: $3800 per year ($6300 including board). Room and board charges vary according to board plan, campus/location and housing facility selected. Housing application deadline: 7/1. *Student services:* Campus employment opportunities, campus safety program, career counseling, exercise/wellness program, free psychological counseling, international student services, low-cost health insurance, multicultural affairs office, services for students with disabilities, teacher training. *Library facilities:* Simon Schwob Memorial Library. *Online resources:* library catalog, web page, access to other libraries' catalogs. *Collection:* 382,400 titles, 1,713 serial subscriptions, 10,962 audiovisual materials.

Computer facilities: 311 computers available on campus for general student use. A campuswide network can be accessed from student residence rooms and from off campus. Online class registration is available. *Web address:* http://www.colstate.edu/.

General Application Contact: Katie Thornton, Graduate Admissions Specialist, 706-568-2035, Fax: 706-568-2462, E-mail: thornton_katie@colstate.edu.

GRADUATE UNITS

Graduate Studies Students: 386 full-time (245 women), 707 part-time (395 women); includes 310 minority (273 African Americans, 2 American Indian/Alaska Native, 18 Asian Americans or Pacific Islanders, 17 Hispanic Americans), 14 international. Average age 36. 559 applicants, 59% accepted, 287 enrolled. *Faculty:* 59 full-time (28 women), 36 part-time/adjunct (15 women). Expenses: Contact institution. *Financial support:* In 2008–09, 449 students received support, including 50 research assistantships with partial tuition reimbursements available (averaging $3,000 per year); career-related internships or fieldwork, Federal Work-Study, institutionally sponsored loans, scholarships/grants, tuition waivers (partial), and unspecified assistantships also available. Support available to part-time students. Financial award application deadline: 5/1; financial award applicants required to submit FAFSA. In 2008, 307 master's, 150 other advanced degrees awarded. *Degree program information:* Part-time and evening/weekend programs available. Postbaccalaureate distance learning degree programs offered (minimal on-campus study). *Application deadline:* For fall admission, 5/1 priority date for domestic students, 5/1 for international students; for spring admission, 11/1 for domestic and international students. Applications are processed on a rolling basis. *Application fee:* $25. Electronic applications accepted. *Application Contact:* Katie Thornton, Graduate Admissions Specialist, 706-568-2035, Fax: 706-568-2462, E-mail: thornton_katie@colstate.edu. *Vice President for Academic Affairs,* Dr. Inessa Levi, 706-568-2061, Fax: 706-569-3168, E-mail: levi_inessa@colstate.edu.

College of Arts and Letters Students: 126 full-time (53 women), 230 part-time (79 women); includes 109 minority (102 African Americans, 2 American Indian/Alaska Native, 2 Asian Americans or Pacific Islanders, 3 Hispanic Americans), 1 international. Average age 36. 100 applicants, 67% accepted, 59 enrolled. *Faculty:* 15 full-time (7 women), 16 part-time/adjunct (2 women). Expenses: Contact institution. *Financial support:* In 2008–09, 90 students received support, including 14 research assistantships with partial tuition reimbursements available (averaging $3,000 per year); career-related internships or fieldwork, Federal Work-Study, institutionally sponsored loans, scholarships/grants, tuition waivers (partial), and unspecified assistantships also available. Support available to part-time students. Financial award application deadline: 5/1; financial award applicants required to submit FAFSA. In 2008, 154 master's awarded. *Degree program information:* Part-time and evening/weekend programs available. Postbaccalaureate distance learning degree programs offered (minimal on-campus study). Offers art education (M Ed); arts and letters (M Ed, MM, MPA); justice administration (MPA); music education (MM). *Application deadline:* For fall admission, 5/1 priority date for domestic students, 5/1 for international students; for spring admission, 11/1 for domestic and international students. Applications are processed on a rolling basis. *Application fee:* $25. Electronic applications accepted. *Application Contact:* Katie Thornton, Graduate Admissions Specialist, 706-568-2035, Fax: 706-568-2462, E-mail: thornton_katie@colstate.edu. *Acting Dean,* Dr. James Patrick McHenry, 706-568-2055, Fax: 706-569-3123, E-mail: mchenry_james@colstate.edu.

College of Education Students: 196 full-time (158 women), 321 part-time (255 women); includes 138 minority (121 African Americans, 6 Asian Americans or Pacific Islanders, 11 Hispanic Americans), 3 international. Average age 36. 318 applicants, 54% accepted, 147 enrolled. *Faculty:* 27 full-time (17 women), 17 part-time/adjunct (12 women). Expenses: Contact institution. *Financial support:* In 2008–09, 266 students received support, including 25 research assistantships with partial tuition reimbursements available (averaging $3,000 per year); career-related internships or fieldwork, Federal Work-Study, institutionally sponsored loans, scholarships/grants, tuition waivers (partial), and unspecified assistantships also available. Support available to part-time students. Financial award application deadline: 5/1; financial award applicants required to submit FAFSA. In 2008, 116 master's, 150 other advanced degrees awarded. *Degree program information:* Part-time and evening/weekend programs available. Postbaccalaureate distance learning degree programs offered (minimal on-campus study). Offers accomplished teaching (M Ed); community counseling (MS); early childhood education (M Ed, Ed S); education (M Ed, MS, Ed S); educational leadership (M Ed, Ed S); instructional technology (MS); middle grades education (M Ed, Ed S); physical education (M Ed); school counseling (M Ed); secondary education (M Ed, Ed S); special education (M Ed). *Application deadline:* For fall admission, 5/1 priority date for domestic students, 5/1 for international students; for spring admission, 11/11 for domestic students, 11/1 for international students. Applications are processed on a rolling basis. *Application fee:* $25. Electronic applications accepted. *Application Contact:* Katie Thornton, Graduate Admissions Specialist, 706-568-2035, Fax: 706-568-2462, E-mail: thornton_katie@colstate.edu. *Dean,* Dr. David Rock, 706-568-2212, Fax: 706-569-3134, E-mail: rock_david@colstate.edu.

College of Science Students: 40 full-time (23 women), 111 part-time (39 women); includes 50 minority (44 African Americans, 3 Asian Americans or Pacific Islanders, 3 Hispanic Americans), 8 international. Average age 36. 92 applicants, 71% accepted, 58 enrolled. *Faculty:* 10 full-time (3 women), 2 part-time/adjunct (1 woman). Expenses: Contact institution. *Financial support:* In 2008–09, 59 students received support, including 10 research assistantships with tuition reimbursements available (averaging $3,000 per year); career-related internships or fieldwork, Federal Work-Study, institutionally sponsored loans, scholarships/grants, tuition waivers (partial), and unspecified assistantships also available. Support available to part-time students. Financial award application deadline: 5/1; financial award applicants required to submit FAFSA. In 2008, 18 master's awarded. *Degree program information:* Part-time and evening/weekend programs available. Postbaccalaureate distance

Columbus State University (continued)

learning degree programs offered (no on-campus study). Offers applied computer science (MS); environmental science (MS); health services administration (MPA); science (MPA, MS). *Application deadline:* For fall admission, 5/1 priority date for domestic students, 5/1 for international students; for spring admission, 11/1 for domestic students, 4/1 for international students. Applications are processed on a rolling basis. *Application fee:* $25. Electronic applications accepted. *Application Contact:* Katie Thornton, Graduate Admissions Specialist, 706-568-2035, Fax: 706-568-2462, E-mail: thornton_katie@colstate.edu. *Dean,* Dr. Glenn Stokes, 706-568-2056, E-mail: stokes_glenn@colstate.edu.

D. Abbott Turner College of Business Students: 24 full-time (11 women), 45 part-time (22 women); includes 13 minority (6 African Americans, 7 Asian Americans or Pacific Islanders), 2 international. Average age 36. 46 applicants, 48% accepted, 22 enrolled. *Faculty:* 4 full-time (1 woman). Expenses: Contact institution. *Financial support:* In 2008–09, 28 students received support, including 1 research assistantship (averaging $3,000 per year). Financial award application deadline: 5/1. In 2008, 19 master's awarded. Offers business administration (MBA). *Application deadline:* For fall admission, 5/1 priority date for domestic students, 5/1 for international students; for spring admission, 11/1 for domestic and international students. Applications are processed on a rolling basis. *Application fee:* $25. Electronic applications accepted. *Application Contact:* Katie Thornton, Graduate Admissions Specialist, 706-568-2035, Fax: 706-568-2462, E-mail: thornton_katie@colstate.edu. *Dean,* Dr. Linda U. Hadley, 706-568-2044, Fax: 706-568-2184, E-mail: hadley_linda@colstate.edu.

CONCORDIA LUTHERAN SEMINARY, Edmonton, AB T5B 4E3, Canada

General Information Independent-religious, coed, primarily men, graduate-only institution. *Enrollment by degree level:* 17 first professional, 5 other advanced degrees. *Graduate faculty:* 4 full-time (0 women), 4 part-time/adjunct (0 women). *Graduate tuition:* Tuition and fees charges are reported in Canadian dollars. *Tuition:* Full-time $7200 Canadian dollars; part-time $200 Canadian dollars per credit hour. *Required fees:* $25 Canadian dollars per semester. One-time fee: $455 Canadian dollars full-time. *Graduate housing:* On-campus housing not available. *Student services:* Campus employment opportunities. *Library facilities:* Concordia Lutheran Seminary Library. *Online resources:* library catalog, access to other libraries' catalogs. *Collection:* 27,159 titles, 262 serial subscriptions, 931 audiovisual materials.

Computer facilities: 2 computers available on campus for general student use. *Web address:* http://www.concordiasem.ab.ca/.

General Application Contact: Jeffrey Nachtigall, Director of Admissions, 780-474-1468, Fax: 780-479-5067, E-mail: admissions@concordiasem.ab.ca.

GRADUATE UNITS

Graduate and Professional Programs Students: 17 full-time (0 women), 5 part-time (1 woman); includes 2 minority (both Asian Americans or Pacific Islanders). Average age 31. *Faculty:* 4 full-time (0 women), 4 part-time/adjunct (0 women). Expenses: Contact institution. *Financial support:* Scholarships/grants available. Financial award application deadline: 8/30. *Degree program information:* Part-time programs available. Offers theology (M Div, Graduate Certificate). *Application deadline:* For fall admission, 4/1 priority date for domestic students; for winter admission, 10/30 priority date for domestic students. *Application fee:* $30 ($100 for international students). *Application Contact:* Jeffrey Nachtigall, Director of Admissions, 780-474-1468, Fax: 780-479-5067, E-mail: admissions@concordiasem.ab.ca.

CONCORDIA SEMINARY, St. Louis, MO 63105-3199

General Information Independent-religious, coed, primarily men, graduate-only institution. *Graduate housing:* Rooms and/or apartments guaranteed to single students and available to married students. Housing application deadline: 3/4. *Research affiliation:* Center for Reformation Research, Concordia Historical Institute.

GRADUATE UNITS

Graduate Programs Offers theology (M Div, MA, STM, D Min, PhD, Certificate).

CONCORDIA THEOLOGICAL SEMINARY, Fort Wayne, IN 46825-4996

General Information Independent-religious, coed, primarily men, graduate-only institution. *Graduate housing:* Room and/or apartments available to single students; on-campus housing not available to married students.

GRADUATE UNITS

Graduate and Professional Programs *Degree program information:* Part-time programs available. Offers theology (M Div, MA, STM, D Min, PhD).

CONCORDIA UNIVERSITY, Irvine, CA 92612-3299

General Information Independent-religious, coed, comprehensive institution. *Graduate housing:* On-campus housing not available.

GRADUATE UNITS

School of Arts and Sciences Postbaccalaureate distance learning degree programs offered. Offers coaching and athletic administration (MA).

School of Business and Professional Studies *Degree program information:* Part-time programs available. Offers entrepreneurial business administration (MBA); international studies (MA).

School of Education *Degree program information:* Part-time and evening/weekend programs available. Postbaccalaureate distance learning degree programs offered (minimal on-campus study). Offers curriculum and instruction (MA); education (M Ed); educational administration and administrative services credential (MA).

School of Theology *Degree program information:* Part-time programs available. Offers theology (MA).

CONCORDIA UNIVERSITY, Montréal, QC H3G 1M8, Canada

General Information Province-supported, coed, university. *Graduate housing:* Room and/or apartments available on a first-come, first-served basis to single students; on-campus housing not available to married students. *Research affiliation:* Centre de recherche en plasturgie et composites (CREPEC) (mechanical and industrial engineering), Centre de recherche informatique de Montréal (CRIM) (computer science), Center d'experise et de services en application multimédia (multimedia), Blue Metropolis Literary Series (English), Canadian Journalism Project (journalism), Canadian Rural Revitalization Foundation (sociology).

GRADUATE UNITS

School of Graduate Studies *Degree program information:* Part-time and evening/weekend programs available. Offers individualized research (M Sc, MA, PhD).

Faculty of Arts and Science Offers écriture (Certificate); adult education (Diploma); anglais-français en langue et techniques de localisation (Certificate); applied linguistics (MA); arts and science (M Sc, MA, MTM, PhD, Certificate, Diploma); biology (M Sc, PhD); biotechnology and genomics (Diploma); chemistry (M Sc, PhD); child study (MA); communication (PhD); communication studies (Diploma); community economic development (Diploma); creative writing (MA); economics (MA, PhD, Diploma); educational studies (MA); educational technology (MA, PhD); English (MA); environmental impact assessment (Diploma); exercise science (M Sc); geography, urban and environmental studies (M Sc); history (MA, PhD); history and philosophy of religion (MA); human systems intervention (MA); humanities (PhD); instructional technology (Diploma); journalism (Diploma); Judaic studies (MA); littératures francophones et résonances médiatiques (MA); mathematics (M Sc, MA, PhD); media studies (MA); philosophy (MA); physics (M Sc, PhD); political science (PhD); psychology (clinical) (MA, PhD, Certificate); psychology (general) (MA, PhD); public policy and public administration (MA); religion (PhD); social and cultural anthropology (MA); sociology (MA); teaching English as a second language (Certificate); teaching of mathematics (MTM); theological studies (MA); traductologie (MA); translation (Diploma).

Faculty of Engineering and Computer Science Offers 3D graphics and game development (Certificate); aerospace engineering (M Eng); building engineering (M Eng, MA Sc, PhD, Certificate); civil engineering (M Eng, MA Sc, PhD); composites (M Eng); computer science (M App Comp Sc, M Comp Sc, PhD, Diploma); electrical and computer engineering (M Eng, MA Sc, PhD); engineering and computer science (M App Comp Sc, M Comp Sc, M Eng, MA Sc, PhD, Certificate, Diploma); environmental engineering (Certificate); industrial engineering (M Eng, MA Sc); information systems security (M Eng, MA Sc); mechanical engineering (M Eng, MA Sc, PhD, Certificate); quality systems engineering (M Eng, MA Sc); service engineering and network management (Certificate); software engineering (MA Sc); software systems for industrial engineering (Certificate).

Faculty of Fine Arts *Degree program information:* Part-time programs available. Offers advanced music performance studies (Diploma); art education (MA, PhD); art history (MA, PhD); creative arts therapies (MA); digital technologies in design art practice (Certificate); film studies (MA); fine arts (MA, MFA, PhD, Certificate, Diploma); studio arts (MFA).

John Molson School of Business *Degree program information:* Part-time and evening/weekend programs available. Offers administration (M Sc, Diploma); aviation management (Certificate, Diploma); business administration (MBA, UA Undergraduate Associate, PhD); chartered accountancy (Diploma); community organizational development (Certificate); event management and fundraising (Certificate); executive business administration (EMBA); investment management (Diploma); investment management option (MBA); management accounting (Certificate); management of healthcare organizations (Certificate); sport administration (Diploma).

See Close-Up on page 893.

CONCORDIA UNIVERSITY, Ann Arbor, MI 48105-2797

General Information Independent-religious, coed, comprehensive institution. *Enrollment:* 1,075 graduate, professional, and undergraduate students; 12 full-time matriculated graduate/professional students (10 women), 384 part-time matriculated graduate/professional students (281 women). *Enrollment by degree level:* 396 master's. *Graduate faculty:* 2 full-time (1 woman), 91 part-time/adjunct (46 women). *Tuition:* Full-time $5850; part-time $390 per credit hour. Tuition and fees vary according to course load. *Graduate housing:* On-campus housing not available. *Student services:* Low-cost health insurance. *Online resources:* library catalog.

Computer facilities: 60 computers available on campus for general student use. A campuswide network can be accessed from student residence rooms and from off campus. Online class registration is available. *Web address:* http://www.cuaa.edu/.

General Application Contact: Jean Christensen, Associate Director of Graduate Admission, 734-995-7521, Fax: 734-995-7448, E-mail: graduate.admissions@cuaa.edu.

GRADUATE UNITS

Graduate Programs Students: 12 full-time (10 women), 384 part-time (281 women). 276 applicants, 70% accepted, 167 enrolled. *Faculty:* 2 full-time (1 woman), 91 part-time/adjunct (46 women). Expenses: Contact institution. *Financial support:* Applicants required to submit FAFSA. *Degree program information:* Part-time and evening/weekend programs available. Offers educational leadership (MS); organizational leadership and administration (MS). *Application deadline:* For fall admission, 9/2 priority date for domestic students, 8/15 priority date for international students; for winter admission, 1/2 priority date for domestic students, 12/15 priority date for international students; for spring admission, 5/1 priority date for domestic students, 4/15 priority date for international students. Applications are processed on a rolling basis. *Application fee:* $100. *Application Contact:* Jean Christensen, Associate Director of Graduate Admission, 734-995-7521, Fax: 734-995-7448, E-mail: christj@cuaa.edu.

CONCORDIA UNIVERSITY, Portland, OR 97211-6099

General Information Independent-religious, coed, comprehensive institution. *Graduate housing:* Room and/or apartments available on a first-come, first-served basis to single students; on-campus housing not available to married students. Housing application deadline: 8/1.

GRADUATE UNITS

College of Education *Degree program information:* Part-time programs available. Postbaccalaureate distance learning degree programs offered (no on-campus study). Offers curriculum and instruction (elementary) (M Ed); educational administration (M Ed); elementary education (MAT); secondary education (MAT). Electronic applications accepted.

School of Management *Degree program information:* Evening/weekend programs available. Offers management (MBA).

CONCORDIA UNIVERSITY CHICAGO, River Forest, IL 60305-1499

General Information Independent-religious, coed, comprehensive institution. CGS member. *Graduate housing:* Rooms and/or apartments available on a first-come, first-served basis to single and married students.

GRADUATE UNITS

College of Education Offers Christian education (MA); curriculum and instruction (MA); early childhood education (MAT); elementary education (MAT); reading education (MA); school leadership (MA, Ed D, CAS); secondary education (MAT).

College of Graduate and Innovative Programs Offers business administration (MBA); church music (MCM); community counseling (MA); gerontology (MA); human services (MA); liberal studies (MA); music (MA); psychology (MA); religion (MA); school counseling (MA, CAS).

CONCORDIA UNIVERSITY, NEBRASKA, Seward, NE 68434-1599

General Information Independent-religious, coed, comprehensive institution. *Graduate housing:* Rooms and/or apartments available on a first-come, first-served basis to single and married students.

GRADUATE UNITS

Graduate Programs in Education *Degree program information:* Part-time and evening/weekend programs available. Offers early childhood education (M Ed); education (M Ed, MPE, MS); elementary and secondary education (M Ed); elementary education (M Ed); family life ministry (MS); parish education (MPE); reading education (M Ed); secondary education (M Ed). Electronic applications accepted.

CONCORDIA UNIVERSITY, ST. PAUL, St. Paul, MN 55104-5494

General Information Independent-religious, coed, comprehensive institution. CGS member. *Enrollment:* 2,644 graduate, professional, and undergraduate students; 933 full-time matriculated graduate/professional students (698 women), 20 part-time matriculated graduate/professional students (10 women). *Enrollment by degree level:* 928 master's, 25 other advanced degrees. *Graduate faculty:* 29 full-time (19 women), 76 part-time/adjunct (43 women). *Student services:* Campus employment opportunities, campus safety program, career counseling, child daycare facilities, exercise/wellness program, free psychological counseling, international student services, low-cost health insurance, multicultural affairs office, services for students with disabilities, writing training. *Library facilities:* Library Technology Center. *Online resources:* library catalog, web page, access to other libraries' catalogs. *Collection:* 151,912 titles, 21,950 serial subscriptions, 3,227 audiovisual materials.

Computer facilities: A campuswide network can be accessed from student residence rooms and from off campus. Online class registration is available. *Web address:* http://www.csp.edu/.

General Application Contact: Kimberly Craig, Director of Graduate and Cohort Admission, 651-603-6223, Fax: 651-603-6320, E-mail: craig@csp.edu.

GRADUATE UNITS

College of Business and Organizational Leadership Students: 267 full-time (161 women), 11 part-time (3 women); includes 35 minority (22 African Americans, 10 Asian Americans or Pacific Islanders, 3 Hispanic Americans), 5 international. Average age 33. *Faculty:* 12 full-time (6 women), 26 part-time/adjunct (10 women). Expenses: Contact institution. *Financial support:* Applicants required to submit FAFSA. In 2008, 110 master's awarded. *Degree program information:* Evening/weekend programs available. Postbaccalaureate distance learning degree programs offered (minimal on-campus study). Offers business and organizational leadership (MBA); criminal justice leadership (MA); human resources management (MA); organizational management (MA). *Application deadline:* Applications are processed on a rolling basis. *Application fee:* $50. Electronic applications accepted. *Application Contact:* Kimberly Craig, Director of Graduate and Cohort Admission, 651-603-6223, Fax: 651-603-6320, E-mail: craig@csp.edu. *Dean,* Dr. Bruce Corrie, 651-641-8226, Fax: 651-641-8807, E-mail: corrie@csp.edu.

College of Education Students: 651 full-time (532 women), 5 part-time (4 women); includes 60 minority (36 African Americans, 17 Asian Americans or Pacific Islanders, 7 Hispanic Americans), 1 international. Average age 35. *Faculty:* 16 full-time (13 women), 46 part-time/adjunct (32 women). Expenses: Contact institution. *Financial support:* Applicants required to submit FAFSA. In 2008, 95 master's, 4 other advanced degrees awarded. *Degree program information:* Evening/weekend programs available. Postbaccalaureate distance learning degree programs offered (minimal on-campus study). Offers curriculum and instruction (MA Ed); differentiated instruction (MA Ed); early childhood education (MA Ed); educational leadership (MA Ed); family life education (MA); special education (Certificate); sports management (MA). *Application deadline:* Applications are processed on a rolling basis. *Application fee:* $50. Electronic applications accepted. *Application Contact:* Kimberly Craig, Director of Graduate and Cohort Admission, 651-603-6223, Fax: 651-603-6320, E-mail: craig@csp.edu. *Dean,* Prof. Lonn Maly, 651-641-8278, Fax: 651-641-8807, E-mail: maly@csp.edu.

College of Vocation and Ministry Students: 15 full-time (5 women), 4 part-time (3 women). Average age 32. *Faculty:* 1 full-time (0 women), 4 part-time/adjunct (1 woman). Expenses: Contact institution. *Financial support:* Applicants required to submit FAFSA. In 2008, 2 master's, 10 other advanced degrees awarded. *Degree program information:* Evening/weekend programs available. Postbaccalaureate distance learning degree programs offered (minimal on-campus study). Offers Christian education (Certificate); Christian outreach (MA). *Application deadline:* Applications are processed on a rolling basis. *Application fee:* $50. Electronic applications accepted. *Application Contact:* Kimberly Craig, Director of Graduate and Cohort Admission, 651-603-6223, Fax: 651-603-6320, E-mail: craig@csp.edu. *Dean,* Dr. David Lumpp, 651-641-8217, E-mail: lumpp@csp.edu.

CONCORDIA UNIVERSITY TEXAS, Austin, TX 78726

General Information Independent-religious, coed, comprehensive institution.

GRADUATE UNITS

College of Education *Degree program information:* Part-time and evening/weekend programs available. Offers education (M Ed).

CONCORDIA UNIVERSITY WISCONSIN, Mequon, WI 53097-2402

General Information Independent-religious, coed, comprehensive institution. *Graduate housing:* Room and/or apartments available to single students; on-campus housing not available to married students. Housing application deadline: 8/1.

GRADUATE UNITS

Graduate Programs *Degree program information:* Part-time and evening/weekend programs available. Postbaccalaureate distance learning degree programs offered (minimal on-campus study). Offers art education (MS Ed); curriculum and instruction (MS Ed); early childhood (MS Ed); educational administration (MS Ed); environmental education (MS Ed); family studies (MS Ed); professional counseling (MPC); reading (MS Ed); school counseling (MS Ed); special education (MS Ed). Electronic applications accepted.

School of Arts and Sciences Offers arts and sciences (MCM); church music (MCM).

School of Business and Legal Studies Offers business and legal studies (MBA, MSSPA); finance (MBA); health care administration (MBA); human resource management (MBA); international business (MBA); international business-bilingual English/Chinese (MBA); management (MBA); management information systems (MBA); managerial communications (MBA); marketing (MBA); public administration (MBA); risk management (MBA); student personnel administration (MSSPA).

School of Health and Human Services Offers family nurse practitioner (MSN); geriatric nurse practitioner (MSN); health and human services (MOT, MSN, MSPT, MSRS, DPT); nurse educator (MSN); occupational therapy (MOT); physical therapy (MSPT, DPT); rehabilitation science (MSRS).

CONCORD LAW SCHOOL, Los Angeles, CA 90024

General Information Proprietary, coed, graduate-only institution.

GRADUATE UNITS

Program in Law *Degree program information:* Part-time and evening/weekend programs available. Postbaccalaureate distance learning degree programs offered (no on-campus study). Offers law (EJD, JD). Electronic applications accepted.

CONNECTICUT COLLEGE, New London, CT 06320-4196

General Information Independent, coed, comprehensive institution. *Enrollment:* 1,852 graduate, professional, and undergraduate students; 1 (woman) full-time matriculated graduate/professional student, 6 part-time matriculated graduate/professional students (5 women). *Enrollment by degree level:* 7 master's. *Tuition:* Part-time $1700 per course. *Graduate housing:* On-campus housing not available. *Student services:* Career counseling, low-cost health insurance. *Library facilities:* Charles Shain Library plus 1 other. *Online resources:* library catalog, web page, access to other libraries' catalogs. *Collection:* 496,817 titles, 2,279 serial subscriptions. *Research affiliation:* Hartford Hospital (neuropsychology and clinical psychology).

Computer facilities: Computer purchase and lease plans are available. A campuswide network can be accessed from student residence rooms and from off campus. Online class registration is available. *Web address:* http://www.conncoll.edu/.

General Application Contact: Ann W. Whitlatch, Director of Continuing Education, 860-439-2062, Fax: 860-439-5421, E-mail: awwhi@conncoll.edu.

GRADUATE UNITS

Graduate School Students: 1 (woman) full-time, 6 part-time (5 women), 1 international. Average age 25. 13 applicants, 62% accepted, 4 enrolled. Expenses: Contact institution. *Financial support:* In 2008–09, 5 students received support. 10 course remissions total (2 for each of 5 students) available. Financial award application deadline: 2/1. In 2008, 2 master's awarded. *Degree program information:* Part-time programs available. Offers botany (MA); psychology (MA). *Application deadline:* For fall admission, 2/1 for domestic and international students. *Application fee:* $60. *Application Contact:* Ann W. Whitlatch, Director of Registration, 860-439-2062, Fax: 860-439-5421, E-mail: awwhi@conncoll.edu. *Associate Dean of the Faculty,* Julie H. Rivkin, 860-439-2198.

CONSERVATORIO DE MUSICA, San Juan, PR 00918-2199

General Information Public, coed, comprehensive institution.

GRADUATE UNITS

Program in Musical Performance Offers instrumental performance (Diploma); vocal performance (Diploma).

Program in Music Education Offers music education (MM Ed).

CONVERSE COLLEGE, Spartanburg, SC 29302-0006

General Information Independent, Undergraduate: women only; graduate: coed, comprehensive institution. *Graduate housing:* On-campus housing not available.

GRADUATE UNITS

Carroll McDaniel Petrie School of Music *Degree program information:* Part-time and evening/weekend programs available. Offers instrumental performance (M Mus); music education (M Mus); piano pedagogy (M Mus); vocal performance (M Mus). Electronic applications accepted.

School of Education and Graduate Studies *Degree program information:* Part-time and evening/weekend programs available. Offers administration and supervision (Ed S); art education (M Ed); biology (MAT); chemistry (MAT); curriculum and instruction (Ed S); early childhood education (MAT); education (Ed S); elementary education (M Ed, MAT); English (M Ed, MAT, MLA); gifted education (M Ed); history (MLA); leadership (M Ed); learning disabilities (MAT); liberal arts (MLA); marriage and family therapy (Ed S); mathematics (M Ed, MAT); mental disabilities (MAT); natural sciences (M Ed); political science (MLA); secondary education (M Ed, MAT); social sciences (M Ed, MAT); special education (M Ed, MAT). Electronic applications accepted.

CONWAY SCHOOL OF LANDSCAPE DESIGN, Conway, MA 01341-0179

General Information Independent, coed, graduate-only institution. *Enrollment by degree level:* 19 master's. *Graduate faculty:* 2 full-time (0 women), 4 part-time/adjunct (2 women). *Tuition:* Full-time $25,075. *Required fees:* $3750. *Graduate housing:* On-campus housing not available. *Student services:* Career counseling. *Collection:* 3,250 titles, 35 serial subscriptions.

Computer facilities: 2 computers available on campus for general student use. A campuswide network can be accessed from student residence rooms and from off campus. *Web address:* http://www.csld.edu/.

General Application Contact: Nancy E. Braxton, Director of Admissions, 413-369-4044 Ext. 5, Fax: 413-369-4032, E-mail: braxton@csld.edu.

GRADUATE UNITS

Graduate Program in Landscape Design Offers landscape design/environmental planning (MA).

COOPER UNION FOR THE ADVANCEMENT OF SCIENCE AND ART, New York, NY 10003-7120

General Information Independent, coed, comprehensive institution. *Enrollment:* 969 graduate, professional, and undergraduate students; 40 full-time matriculated graduate/professional students (7 women), 12 part-time matriculated graduate/professional students (1 woman). *Enrollment by degree level:* 52 master's. *Graduate faculty:* 27 full-time (1 woman), 15 part-time/adjunct (2 women). *Tuition:* Full-time $35,000. *Required fees:* $1600. *Graduate housing:* Room and/or apartments available to single students; on-campus housing not available to married students. Typical cost: $9900 per year ($13,900 including board). *Student services:* Campus employment opportunities, campus safety program, career counseling, international student services, low-cost health insurance, writing training. *Library facilities:* Cooper Union Library. *Online resources:* library catalog, web page, access to other libraries' catalogs. *Collection:* 107,348 titles, 2,471 serial subscriptions, 1,684 audiovisual materials. *Research affiliation:* Transpo, Howard Hughes Medical Institute, Lucent, Con Edison, Pfizer, Zimmer.

Computer facilities: Computer purchase and lease plans are available. 400 computers available on campus for general student use. A campuswide network can be accessed from student residence rooms and from off campus. *Web address:* http://www.cooper.edu/.

General Application Contact: Student Contact, 212-353-4120, E-mail: admissions@cooper.edu.

GRADUATE UNITS

Albert Nerken School of Engineering *Faculty:* 27 full-time (1 woman), 15 part-time/adjunct (2 women). Expenses: Contact institution. *Financial support:* Fellowships with tuition reimbursements, career-related internships or fieldwork, Federal Work-Study, scholarships/grants, and tuition waivers (full) available. Support available to part-time students. Financial award application deadline: 6/1; financial award applicants required to submit CSS PROFILE or FAFSA. *Degree program information:* Part-time programs available. Offers chemical engineering (ME); civil engineering (ME); electrical engineering (ME); mechanical engineering (ME). *Application deadline:* For fall admission, 5/1 for domestic and international students. Applications are processed on a rolling basis. *Application fee:* $65. *Application Contact:* Student Contact, 212-353-4120, E-mail: admissions@cooper.edu. *Dean of Engineering,* Eleanor Baum, 212-353-4285, E-mail: baum@cooper.edu.

Irwin S. Chanin School of Architecture Expenses: Contact institution. Offers architecture (M Arch II). *Application deadline:* For fall admission, 2/1 for domestic students. *Application fee:* $65. *Application Contact:* Student Contact, 212-353-4120, E-mail: admissions@cooper.edu. *Dean,* Anthony Vidler.

COPPIN STATE UNIVERSITY, Baltimore, MD 21216-3698

General Information State-supported, coed, comprehensive institution. CGS member. *Graduate housing:* On-campus housing not available.

GRADUATE UNITS

Division of Graduate Studies *Degree program information:* Part-time and evening/weekend programs available. Postbaccalaureate distance learning degree programs offered.

Division of Arts and Sciences *Degree program information:* Part-time and evening/weekend programs available. Offers alcohol and substance abuse counseling (MS); arts and sciences (M Ed, MA, MS); criminal justice (MS); human services administration (MS); rehabilitation counseling (M Ed).

Division of Education *Degree program information:* Part-time and evening/weekend programs available. Postbaccalaureate distance learning degree programs offered. Offers adult and general education (MS); curriculum and instruction (M Ed, MAT, MS); reading education (MS); special education (M Ed); teacher education (MAT); teaching (MAT).

Helene Fuld School of Nursing *Degree program information:* Part-time and evening/weekend programs available. Offers family nurse practitioner (PMC); nursing (MSN).

CORCORAN COLLEGE OF ART AND DESIGN, Washington, DC 20006-4804

General Information Independent, coed, comprehensive institution. *Graduate housing:* Rooms and/or apartments available on a first-come, first-served basis to single and married students. Housing application deadline: 5/15.

GRADUATE UNITS

Graduate Programs *Degree program information:* Part-time programs available.

CORNELL UNIVERSITY, Ithaca, NY 14853-0001

General Information Independent, coed, university. CGS member. *Enrollment:* 20,273 graduate, professional, and undergraduate students; 6,427 full-time matriculated graduate/professional students (2,729 women). *Enrollment by degree level:* 913 first professional, 2,564 master's, 2,950 doctoral. *Graduate faculty:* 1,553 full-time (410 women), 80 part-time/adjunct (18 women). *Tuition:* Full-time $29,500. *Required fees:* $70. Full-time tuition and fees vary according to degree level, program and student level. *Graduate housing:* Rooms and/or apartments available on a first-come, first-served basis to single and married students. Typical cost: $5450 per year ($10,440 including board) for single students; $9790 per year ($14,740 including board) for married students. Room and board charges vary according to board plan, campus/location and housing facility selected. Housing application deadline: 7/1. *Student services:* Campus employment opportunities, campus safety program, career counsel-

Cornell University (continued)

ing, exercise/wellness program, free psychological counseling, grant writing training, international student services, low-cost health insurance, multicultural affairs office, services for students with disabilities, teacher training, writing training. *Library facilities:* Main library plus 18 others. *Online resources:* library catalog, web page. *Collection:* 8.1 million titles, 89,000 serial subscriptions, 161,135 audiovisual materials. *Research affiliation:* Brookhaven National Laboratory, Fermi National Accelerator Laboratory, Boyce Thompson Institute for Plant Research.

Computer facilities: Computer purchase and lease plans are available. 2,650 computers available on campus for general student use. A campuswide network can be accessed from student residence rooms and from off campus. Online class registration is available. *Web address:* http://www.cornell.edu/.

General Application Contact: Graduate School Application Requests, Caldwell Hall, 607-255-5820, Fax: 607-255-1816, E-mail: gradadmissions@cornell.edu.

GRADUATE UNITS

College of Veterinary Medicine Students: 342 full-time (261 women); includes 66 minority (17 African Americans, 1 American Indian/Alaska Native, 16 Asian Americans or Pacific Islanders, 32 Hispanic Americans), 1 international. Average age 26. 918 applicants, 15% accepted, 86 enrolled. *Faculty:* 186 full-time (70 women). Expenses: Contact institution. *Financial support:* In 2008–09, 302 students received support; fellowships, research assistantships, teaching assistantships, Federal Work-Study, institutionally sponsored loans, and scholarships/grants available. Financial award application deadline: 2/1; financial award applicants required to submit CSS PROFILE or FAFSA. Offers veterinary medicine (DVM). *Application deadline:* For fall admission, 10/2 for domestic and international students. *Application fee:* $60. Electronic applications accepted. *Application Contact:* Jennifer A. Mailey, Director of Admissions, 607-253-3700, Fax: 607-253-3709, E-mail: jam333@cornell.edu. *Dean*, Dr. Michael Kotlikoff, 607-253-3771, Fax: 607-253-3701.

Cornell Law School Offers law (JD, LL M, JSD). JD/MLLP offered jointly with Humboldt University, Berlin; JD/DESS offered jointly with Institut d[0092][00c9]tudes Politiques de Paris ('Sciences Po") and Paris I. Electronic applications accepted.

Graduate School Students: 4,757 full-time (1,987 women); includes 643 minority (118 African Americans, 28 American Indian/Alaska Native, 332 Asian Americans or Pacific Islanders, 165 Hispanic Americans), 1,860 international. Average age 29. 13,338 applicants, 23% accepted, 1455 enrolled. *Faculty:* 3,229 full-time (791 women). Expenses: Contact institution. *Financial support:* In 2008–09, 3,013 students received support, including 682 fellowships with full tuition reimbursements available, 1,218 research assistantships with full tuition reimbursements available, 1,113 teaching assistantships with full tuition reimbursements available; career-related internships or fieldwork, institutionally sponsored loans, scholarships/grants, traineeships, tuition waivers (full and partial), and unspecified assistantships also available. Financial award applicants required to submit FAFSA. In 2008, 1,320 master's, 507 doctorates awarded. Offers acarology (MS, PhD); advanced composites and structures (M Eng); advanced materials processing (M Eng, MS, PhD); aerospace engineering (M Eng, MS, PhD); African history (MA, PhD); African studies (MPS); African-American literature (PhD); African-American studies (MPS); agricultural economics (MPS, MS, PhD); agricultural education (MAT); agriculture and life sciences (M Eng, MAT, MFS, MLA, MPS, MS, PhD); agronomy (MS, PhD); algorithms (M Eng, PhD); American art (PhD); American history (MA, PhD); American literature after 1865 (PhD); American literature to 1865 (PhD); American politics (PhD); American studies (PhD); analytical chemistry (PhD); ancient art and archaeology (PhD); ancient history (MA, PhD); ancient Near Eastern studies (MA, PhD); ancient philosophy (PhD); animal breeding (MS, PhD); animal cytology (MS, PhD); animal genetics (MS, PhD); animal nutrition (MPS, MS, PhD); animal science (MPS, MS, PhD); apiculture (MS, PhD); apparel design (MA, MPS); applied economics (PhD); applied entomology (MS, PhD); applied linguistics (MA, PhD); applied logic and automated reasoning (M Eng, PhD); applied mathematics (PhD); applied mathematics and computational methods (M Eng, MS, PhD); applied physics (PhD); applied probability and statistics (PhD); applied research in human-environment relations (MS); applied statistics (MPS); aquatic entomology (MS, PhD); aquatic science (MPS, MS, PhD); Arabic and Islamic studies (MA, PhD); archaeological anthropology (PhD); artificial intelligence (M Eng, PhD); arts and sciences (MA, MFA, MPA, MPS, MS, DMA, PhD); Asian art (PhD); Asian religions (MA, PhD); astronomy (PhD); astrophysics (PhD); atmospheric science (MS, PhD); baroque art (PhD); basic analytical economics (PhD); behavioral biology (PhD); behavioral physiology (MS, PhD); biblical studies (MA, PhD); bio-organic chemistry (PhD); biochemical engineering (M Eng, MS, PhD); biochemistry (PhD); biological anthropology (PhD); biological control (MS, PhD); biological engineering (M Eng, MPS, MS, PhD); biology (7-12) (MAT); biomechanical engineering (M Eng, MS, PhD); biomedical engineering (M Eng, MS, PhD); biometry (MS, PhD); biophysical chemistry (PhD); biophysics (PhD); biopsychology (PhD); cardiovascular and respiratory physiology (MS, PhD); cell biology (PhD); cellular and molecular medicine (MS, PhD); cellular and molecular toxicology (MS, PhD); cellular immunology (MS, PhD); chemical biology (PhD); chemical physics (PhD); chemical reaction engineering (M Eng, MS, PhD); chemistry (7-12) (MAT); Chinese linguistics (MA, PhD); Chinese philology (MA, PhD); classical and statistical thermodynamics (M Eng, MS, PhD); classical archaeology (PhD); classical Chinese literature (MA, PhD); classical Japanese literature (MA, PhD); classical myth (PhD); classical rhetoric (PhD); cognition (PhD); collective bargaining, labor law and labor history (MILR, MPS, MS, PhD); colonial and postcolonial literature (PhD); combustion (M Eng, MS, PhD); communication (MPS, MS, PhD); communication research methods (MS, PhD); community and regional society (MS); community and regional sociology (MPS, PhD); community development process (MPS); community nutrition (MPS, MS, PhD); comparative and functional anatomy (MS, PhD); comparative biomedical sciences (MS, PhD); comparative literature (PhD); comparative politics (PhD); composition (DMA); computational behavioral biology (PhD); computational biology (PhD); computational cell biology (PhD); computational ecology (PhD); computational macromolecular biology (PhD); computational organismal biology (PhD); computer engineering (M Eng, PhD); computer graphics (M Eng, PhD); computer science (M Eng, PhD); computer vision (M Eng, PhD); concurrency and distributed computing (M Eng, PhD); consumer policy (PhD); controlled environment agriculture (MPS, PhD); controlled environment horticulture (MS); creative writing (MFA); cultural studies (PhD); curriculum and instruction (MPS, MS, PhD); cytology (MS, PhD); dairy science (MPS, MS, PhD); decision theory (MS, PhD); development policy (MPS); developmental and reproductive biology (MS, PhD); developmental biology (MS, PhD); developmental psychology (PhD); drama and the theatre (PhD); dramatic literature (PhD); dynamics and space mechanics (MS, PhD); early modern European history (MA, PhD); earth science (7-12) (MAT); East Asian linguistics (MA, PhD); East Asian studies (MA); ecological and environmental plant pathology (MPS, MS, PhD); ecology (MS, PhD); econometrics and economic statistics (PhD); economic and social statistics (MILR, MS, PhD); economic development (MPS); economic development and planning (PhD); economic geology (M Eng, MS, PhD); economic theory (PhD); economy and society (MA, PhD); ecotoxicology and environmental chemistry (MS, PhD); electrical engineering (M Eng, PhD); electrical systems (M Eng, PhD); electrophysics (M Eng, PhD); endocrinology (MS, PhD); energy (M Eng, MPS, MS, PhD); energy and power systems (M Eng, MS, PhD); engineering (M Eng, MPS, MS, PhD); engineering geology (M Eng, MS, PhD); engineering management (M Eng, MS, PhD); engineering physics (M Eng); engineering statistics (MS, PhD); English history (MA, PhD); English linguistics (MA, PhD); English poetry (PhD); English Renaissance to 1660 (PhD); environmental and comparative physiology (MS, PhD); environmental archaeology (MA); environmental engineering (M Eng, MPS, MS, PhD); environmental fluid mechanics and hydrology (M Eng, MS, PhD); environmental geophysics (M Eng, MS, PhD); environmental information science (MS, PhD); environmental management (MPS); environmental systems engineering (M Eng, MS, PhD); epidemiological plant pathology (MPS, MS, PhD); evaluation (PhD); evolutionary biology (PhD); experimental design (MS, PhD); experimental physics (MS, PhD); extension, and adult education (MPS, MS, PhD); facilities planning and management (MS); family and social welfare policy (PhD); fiber science (MS, PhD); field crop science (MS, PhD); fishery science (MPS, MS, PhD); fluid dynamics, rheology and biorheology (M Eng, MS, PhD); fluid mechanics (M Eng, MS, PhD); food chemistry (MPS, MS, PhD); food engineering (MPS, MS, PhD); food microbiology (MPS, MS, PhD); food processing engineering (M Eng, MPS, MS, PhD); food processing waste technology (MPS, MS, PhD); food science (MFS, MPS, MS, PhD); forest science (MPS, MS, PhD); French history (MA, PhD); French linguistics (PhD); French literature (PhD); gastrointestinal and metabolic physiology (MS, PhD); gender and life course (MA, PhD); general geology (M Eng, MS, PhD); general linguistics (MA, PhD); general space sciences (PhD); genetics (PhD); geobiology (M Eng, MS, PhD); geochemistry and isotope geology (M Eng, MS, PhD); geohydrology (M Eng, MS, PhD); geomorphology (M Eng, MS, PhD); geophysics (M Eng, MS, PhD); geotechnical engineering (M Eng, MS, PhD); geotectonics (M Eng, MS, PhD); German area studies (MA, PhD); German history (MA, PhD); German intellectual history (MA, PhD); Germanic linguistics (MA, PhD); Germanic literature (MA, PhD); Greek and Latin language and linguistics (PhD); Greek language and literature (PhD); greenhouse crops (MPS, MS, PhD); health administration (MHA); health management and policy (PhD); heat and mass transfer (M Eng, MS, PhD); heat transfer (M Eng, MS, PhD); Hebrew and Judaic studies (MA, PhD); Hispanic literature (PhD); histology (MS, PhD); historical archaeology (MA); history and philosophy of science and technology (MA, PhD); history of science (MA, PhD); horticultural business management (MPS, MS, PhD); horticultural physiology (MPS, MS, PhD); hospitality management (MMH); hotel administration (MS, PhD); housing and design (MS); human computer interaction (PhD); human development and family studies (PhD); human ecology (MA, MHA, MPS, MS, PhD); human experimental psychology (PhD); human factors and ergonomics (MS); human nutrition (MPS, MS, PhD); human resource studies (MILR, MPS, MS, PhD); human-environment relations (MS); immunochemistry (MS, PhD); immunogenetics (MS, PhD); immunopathology (MS, PhD); Indo-European linguistics (MA, PhD); industrial and labor relations problems (MILR, MPS, MS, PhD); industrial organization and control (PhD); infection and immunity (MS, PhD); infectious diseases (MS, PhD); information organization and retrieval (M Eng, PhD); information systems (PhD); infrared astronomy (PhD); inorganic chemistry (PhD); insect behavior (MS, PhD); insect biochemistry (MS, PhD); insect ecology (MS, PhD); insect genetics (MS, PhD); insect morphology (MS, PhD); insect pathology (MS, PhD); insect physiology (MS, PhD); insect systematics (MS, PhD); insect toxicology and insecticide chemistry (MS, PhD); integrated pest management (MS, PhD); interior design (MA, MPS); international agriculture (M Eng, MPS, MS, PhD); international agriculture and development (MPS); international and comparative labor (MILR, MPS, MS, PhD); international communication (MS, PhD); international economics (PhD); international food science (MPS, MS, PhD); international nutrition (MPS, MS, PhD); international planning (MPS); international population (MPS); international relations (PhD); Italian linguistics (PhD); Italian literature (PhD); Japanese linguistics (MA, PhD); kinetics and catalysis (M Eng, MS, PhD); Korean literature (MA, PhD); labor economics (MILR, MPS, MS, PhD); landscape architecture (MLA); landscape horticulture (MPS, MS, PhD); Latin American archaeology (MA); Latin American history (MA, PhD); Latin language and literature (PhD); lesbian, bisexual, and gay literature studies (PhD); literary criticism and theory (PhD); local government organizations and operations (MPS); local roads (M Eng, MPS, MS, PhD); machine systems (M Eng, MPS, MS, PhD); manufacturing systems engineering (PhD); marine geology (MS, PhD); materials and manufacturing engineering (M Eng, MS, PhD); materials chemistry (PhD); materials engineering (M Eng, PhD); materials science (M Eng, PhD); mathematical programming (PhD); mathematical statistics (MS, PhD); mathematics (PhD); mathematics (7-12) (MAT); mechanical systems and design (M Eng, MS, PhD); mechanics of materials (MS, PhD); medical and veterinary entomology (MS, PhD); medieval and Renaissance Latin literature (PhD); medieval archaeology (MA, PhD); medieval art (PhD); medieval Chinese history (MA, PhD); medieval history (MA, PhD); medieval literature (PhD); medieval music (PhD); medieval philology and linguistics (PhD); medieval philosophy (PhD); Mediterranean and Near Eastern archaeology (MA); membrane and epithelial physiology (MS, PhD); methodology (MA, PhD); methods of social research (MPS, MS, PhD); microbiology (PhD); mineralogy (M Eng, MS, PhD); modern art (PhD); modern Chinese history (MA, PhD); modern Chinese literature (MA, PhD); modern European history (MA, PhD); modern Japanese history (MA, PhD); modern Japanese literature (MA, PhD); molecular and cell biology (PhD); molecular and cellular physiology (MS, PhD); molecular biology (PhD); molecular plant pathology (MPS, MS, PhD); monetary and macroeconomics (PhD); multiphase flows (M Eng, MS, PhD); musicology (PhD); mycology (MPS, MS, PhD); neural and sensory physiology (MS, PhD); neurobiology (PhD); nineteenth century (PhD); nuclear engineering (M Eng, MS, PhD); nuclear science (MS, PhD); nursery crops (MPS, MS, PhD); nutrition of horticultural crops (MPS, MS, PhD); nutritional and food toxicology (MS, PhD); nutritional biochemistry (MPS, MS, PhD); Old and Middle English (PhD); old Norse (MA, PhD); operating systems (M Eng, PhD); operations research and industrial engineering (M Eng); organic chemistry (PhD); organizational behavior (MILR, MPS, MS, PhD); organizations (MA, PhD); organometallic chemistry (PhD); paleobotany (MS, PhD); paleontology (M Eng, MS, PhD); parallel computing (M Eng, PhD); performance practice (DMA); personality and social psychology (PhD); petroleum geology (M Eng, MS, PhD); petrology (M Eng, MS, PhD); pharmacology (MS, PhD); philosophy (PhD); phonetics (MA, PhD); phonological theory (MA, PhD); physical chemistry (PhD); physics (MS, PhD); physics (7-12) (MAT); physiological genomics (MS, PhD); physiology of reproduction (MPS, MS, PhD); planetary geology (M Eng, MS, PhD); planetary studies (PhD); plant breeding (MPS, MS, PhD); plant cell biology (MS, PhD); plant disease epidemiology (MPS, MS, PhD); plant ecology (MS, PhD); plant genetics (MPS, MS, PhD); plant molecular biology (MS, PhD); plant morphology, anatomy and biomechanics (MS, PhD); plant pathology (MPS, MS, PhD); plant physiology (MS, PhD); plant propagation (MPS, MS, PhD); plant protection (MPS); policy analysis (MA, PhD); political methodology (PhD); political sociology/social movements (MA, PhD); political thought (PhD); polymer chemistry (PhD); polymer science (MS, PhD); polymers (M Eng, MS, PhD); pomology (MPS, MS, PhD); population and development (MPS, MS, PhD); population medicine and epidemiology (MS, PhD); Precambrian geology (M Eng, MS, PhD); premodern Islamic history (MA, PhD); premodern Japanese history (MA, PhD); probability (MS, PhD); program development and planning (MPS); programming environments (M Eng, PhD); programming languages and methodology (M Eng, PhD); prose fiction (PhD); public affairs (MPA); public finance (PhD); public garden management (MPS, MS, PhD); public policy (MPA, PhD); Quaternary geology (M Eng, MS, PhD); racial and ethnic relations (MA, PhD); radio astronomy (PhD); radiophysics (PhD); remote sensing (M Eng, MS, PhD); Renaissance art (PhD); Renaissance history (MA, PhD); reproductive physiology (MS, PhD); resource economics (MPS, MS, PhD); resource policy and management (MPS, MS, PhD); Restoration and eighteenth century (PhD); restoration ecology (MPS, MS, PhD); risk assessment, management and public policy (MS, PhD); robotics (M Eng, PhD); rock mechanics (M Eng, MS, PhD); Romance linguistics (MA, PhD); rural and environmental sociology (MPS, MS, PhD); Russian history (MA, PhD); sampling (MS, PhD); science and environmental communication (MS, PhD); science and technology policy (MPS); scientific computing (M Eng, PhD); second language acquisition (MA, PhD); sedimentology (M Eng, MS, PhD); seismology (M Eng, MS, PhD); semantics (MA, PhD); sensory evaluation (MPS, MS, PhD); Slavic linguistics (MA, PhD); social aspects of information (PhD); social networks (MA, PhD); social psychology (MA, PhD); social psychology of communication (MS, PhD); social stratification (MA, PhD); social studies of science and technology (MA, PhD); sociocultural anthropology (PhD); sociolinguistics (MA, PhD); soil and water engineering (M Eng, MPS, MS, PhD); soil science (MS, PhD); solid mechanics (MS, PhD); South Asian linguistics (MA, PhD); South Asian studies (MA); Southeast Asian art (PhD); Southeast Asian history (MA, PhD); Southeast Asian linguistics (MA, PhD); Southeast Asian studies (MA); Spanish linguistics (PhD); state, economy, and society (MPS, MS, PhD); statistical computing (MS, PhD); stochastic processes (MS, PhD); Stone Age archaeology (MA); stratigraphy (M Eng, MS, PhD); structural and functional biology (MS, PhD); structural engineering (M Eng, MS, PhD); structural geology (M Eng, MS, PhD); structural mechanics (M Eng, MS); structures and environment (M Eng, MPS, MS, PhD); surface science (M Eng, MS, PhD); syntactic theory (MA, PhD); systematic botany (MS, PhD); systems engineering (M Eng); taxonomy of ornamental plants (MPS, MS, PhD); textile science (MS, PhD); theatre history (PhD); theatre theory and aesthetics (PhD); theoretical astrophysics (PhD); theoretical chemistry (PhD); theoretical physics (MS, PhD); theory and criticism (PhD); theory of computation (M Eng, PhD); theory of music (MA); transportation engineering (MS, PhD); transportation systems engineering (M Eng); turfgrass science (MPS, MS, PhD); twentieth century (PhD); urban horticulture (MPS, MS, PhD); uses and effects of communication (MS, PhD); vegetable crops (MPS, MS, PhD); water resource systems (M Eng, MS, PhD); weed science (MPS, MS, PhD); wildlife science (MPS, MS, PhD); women's literature (PhD). *Application deadline:* For fall admission, 1/15 for domestic and international students; for spring admission, 11/1 for domestic and international students. *Application fee:* $70. Electronic applications accepted. *Application Contact:* Graduate School Application Requests, 607-255-5816, E-mail: gradadmissions@cornell.edu. *Dean*, Dr. Alison G. Power, 607-255-5417.

Field of Environmental Management Expenses: Contact institution. Offers environmental management (MPS). *Application Contact:* Tad McGalliard, Education Coordinator, 607-255-9996, Fax: 607-255-0238, E-mail: tnm2@cornell.edu.

Graduate Field in the Law School Students: 8 full-time (2 women), 7 international. Average age 31. 25 applicants, 12% accepted, 2 enrolled. *Faculty:* 46 full-time (13 women). Expenses: Contact institution. *Financial support:* Fellowships with full tuition reimbursements, research assistantships with full tuition reimbursements, teaching assistantships with full tuition reimbursements, institutionally sponsored loans, scholarships/grants, health care benefits, tuition waivers (full and partial), and unspecified assistantships available. Financial award applicants required to submit FAFSA. In 2008, 2 doctorates awarded. Offers law (JSD). *Application deadline:* For fall admission, 5/1 for domestic students. *Application fee:* $70. Electronic applications accepted. *Application Contact:* Graduate Field Assistant, 607-255-5141, E-mail: gradlaw@law.mail.cornell.edu. *Director of Graduate Studies*, 607-255-5141.

Graduate Field of Management Students: 38 full-time (14 women); includes 2 minority (both Asian Americans or Pacific Islanders), 21 international. Average age 31. 448 applicants, 5% accepted, 7 enrolled. *Faculty:* 63 full-time (11 women). Expenses: Contact institution. *Financial support:* In 2008–09, 38 students received support, including 2 fellowships with full tuition reimbursements available, 36 research assistantships with full tuition reimbursements available; teaching assistantships with full tuition reimbursements available, institutionally sponsored loans, scholarships/grants, health care benefits, tuition waivers (full and partial), and unspecified assistantships also available. Financial award applicants required to submit FAFSA. In 2008, 6 doctorates awarded. Offers accounting (PhD); behavioral decision theory (PhD); finance (PhD); marketing (PhD); organizational behavior (PhD); production and operations management (PhD). *Application deadline:* For fall admission, 1/3 for domestic students. *Application fee:* $70. Electronic applications accepted. *Application Contact:* Graduate Field Assistant, 607-255-9431, E-mail: js_phd@cornell.edu. *Director of Graduate Studies*, 607-255-3669.

Graduate Fields of Architecture, Art and Planning Students: 284 full-time (130 women); includes 35 minority (8 African Americans, 16 Asian Americans or Pacific Islanders, 11 Hispanic Americans), 97 international. Average age 30. 1,005 applicants, 27% accepted, 130 enrolled. *Faculty:* 109 full-time (30 women). Expenses: Contact institution. *Financial support:* In 2008–09, 60 students received support, including 18 fellowships with full tuition reimbursements available, 9 research assistantships with full tuition reimbursements available, 33 teaching assistantships with full tuition reimbursements available; institutionally sponsored loans, scholarships/grants, health care benefits, tuition waivers (full and partial), and unspecified assistantships also available. Financial award applicants required to submit FAFSA. In 2008, 57 master's, 7 doctorates awarded. Offers architectural design (M Arch); architectural science (MS); architecture, art and planning (M Arch, MA, MFA, MPSRE, MRP, MS, PhD); building technology and environmental science (MS); city and regional planning (MRP, PhD); computer graphics (MS); creative visual arts (MFA); environmental planning and design (MRP, PhD); environmental studies (MA, MS, PhD); historic preservation planning (MA); history of architecture (MA, PhD); history of urban development (MA, PhD); international development planning (MRP, PhD); international spatial problems (MA, MS, PhD); location theory (MA, MS, PhD); multiregional economic analysis (MA, MS, PhD); peace science (MA, MS, PhD); planning methods (MA, MS, PhD); planning theory and systems analysis (MRP, PhD); real estate (MPSRE); regional economics and development planning (MRP, PhD); regional science (MRP, PhD); social and health systems planning (MRP, PhD); theory and criticism of architecture (M Arch); urban and regional economics (MA, MS, PhD); urban and regional theory (MRP, PhD); urban design (M Arch); urban planning history (MRP, PhD). *Application fee:* $70. Electronic applications accepted. *Application Contact:* Graduate School Application Requests, Caldwell Hall, 607-255-5820.

Johnson Graduate School of Management Students: 932 full-time (274 women); includes 187 minority (34 African Americans, 3 American Indian/Alaska Native, 130 Asian Americans or Pacific Islanders, 20 Hispanic Americans), 278 international. Average age 28. 3,255 applicants, 500 enrolled. *Faculty:* 52 full-time (11 women), 4 part-time/adjunct (0 women). Expenses: Contact institution. *Financial support:* Fellowships, research assistantships, career-related internships or fieldwork, Federal Work-Study, institutionally sponsored loans, and tuition waivers (full and partial) available. Financial award application deadline: 2/15; financial award applicants required to submit FAFSA. In 2008, 431 master's awarded. Offers management (MBA). *Application deadline:* For fall admission, 3/15 for domestic students, 1/1 for international students. *Application fee:* $200. Electronic applications accepted. *Application Contact:* 800-847-2082, Fax: 607-255-0065, E-mail: mba@johnson.cornell.edu. *Dean*, Dr. L. Joseph Thomas, 607-255-4854, E-mail: ljt3@cornell.edu.

CORNELL UNIVERSITY, JOAN AND SANFORD I. WEILL MEDICAL COLLEGE AND GRADUATE SCHOOL OF MEDICAL SCIENCES, New York, NY 10065

General Information Independent, coed, graduate-only institution. *Enrollment by degree level:* 410 first professional, 436 doctoral, 67 other advanced degrees. *Graduate faculty:* 1,112 full-time (454 women), 3,359 part-time/adjunct (964 women). *Graduate housing:* Rooms and/or apartments guaranteed to single students and available to married students. Housing application deadline: 4/30. *Student services:* Campus employment opportunities, campus safety program, career counseling, grant writing training, international student services, low-cost health insurance, multicultural affairs office. *Library facilities:* Samuel J. Wood Library. *Research affiliation:* Strong Cancer Prevention Center (cancer prevention), Burke Medical Research Institute (neurology).

Computer facilities: 173 computers available on campus for general student use. A campuswide network can be accessed from student residence rooms and from off campus. *Web address:* http://www.med.cornell.edu/.

General Application Contact: Liliana Montano, Assistant Dean of Admissions, 212-746-1067, Fax: 212-746-8052, E-mail: cumc-admissions@med.cornell.edu.

GRADUATE UNITS

Weill Cornell Graduate School of Medical Sciences Students: 583 full-time (351 women); includes 104 minority (19 African Americans, 56 Asian Americans or Pacific Islanders, 29 Hispanic Americans), 174 international. Average age 24. 570 applicants, 24% accepted, 69 enrolled. *Faculty:* 244 full-time (70 women). Expenses: Contact institution. *Financial support:* In 2008–09, 44 fellowships (averaging $20,772 per year) were awarded; scholarships/grants, health care benefits, and full tuition scholarships and stipends (given to all students) also available. In 2008, 13 master's, 38 doctorates awarded. Offers biochemistry, cell and molecular biology (MS, PhD); chemical biology (PhD); clinical epidemiology and health services research (MS); immunology (MS, PhD); medical sciences (MS, PhD); neuroscience (MS, PhD); pharmacology (MS, PhD); physiology, biophysics and systems biology (MS, PhD). *Application deadline:* For fall admission, 12/1 for domestic students. *Application fee:* $60. Electronic applications accepted. *Application Contact:* Dr. Randi Silver, PhD, Associate Dean, 212-746-6565, Fax: 212-746-8906, E-mail: gsms@med.cornell.edu. *Dean*, Dr. David P. Hajjar, PhD, 212-746-6900, E-mail: dphajjar@med.cornell.edu.

CORNERSTONE UNIVERSITY, Grand Rapids, MI 49525-5897

General Information Independent-religious, coed, comprehensive institution. *Graduate housing:* Rooms and/or apartments available on a first-come, first-served basis to single and married students.

GRADUATE UNITS

Graduate Programs *Degree program information:* Part-time programs available. Postbaccalaureate distance learning degree programs offered. Offers business administration (MBA); education (MA Ed); management (MSM); teaching English to speakers of other languages (MA, Graduate Certificate). Programs also offered at Holland, Kalamazoo, and Troy, MI campuses. Electronic applications accepted.

COVENANT COLLEGE, Lookout Mountain, GA 30750

General Information Independent-religious, coed, comprehensive institution. *Graduate housing:* Room and/or apartments available on a first-come, first-served basis to single students; on-campus housing not available to married students. Housing application deadline: 5/1.

GRADUATE UNITS

Program in Education *Degree program information:* Part-time programs available. Offers education (M Ed).

COVENANT THEOLOGICAL SEMINARY, St. Louis, MO 63141-8697

General Information Independent-religious, coed, graduate-only institution. *Enrollment by degree level:* 379 first professional, 332 master's, 81 doctoral, 20 other advanced degrees. *Graduate faculty:* 23 full-time (0 women), 23 part-time/adjunct (8 women). *Tuition:* Full-time $9720. *Graduate housing:* Rooms and/or apartments available on a first-come, first-served basis to single and married students. *Student services:* Campus employment opportunities, career counseling, free psychological counseling, international student services, services for students with disabilities, writing training. *Library facilities:* J. Oliver Buswell Jr. Library plus 1 other. *Online resources:* library catalog. *Collection:* 65,181 titles, 362 serial subscriptions, 2,454 audiovisual materials.

Computer facilities: 20 computers available on campus for general student use. A campuswide network can be accessed from off campus. Online class registration is available. *Web address:* http://www.covenantseminary.edu/.

General Application Contact: Jeremy Kicklighter, Director of Admissions, 314-434-4044, Fax: 314-434-4819, E-mail: admissions@covenantseminary.edu.

GRADUATE UNITS

Graduate and Professional Programs Students: 375 full-time (67 women), 437 part-time (126 women); includes 97 minority (36 African Americans, 1 American Indian/Alaska Native, 46 Asian Americans or Pacific Islanders, 14 Hispanic Americans), 47 international. Average age 34. 269 applicants, 98% accepted, 198 enrolled. *Faculty:* 23 full-time (0 women), 23 part-time/adjunct (8 women). Expenses: Contact institution. *Financial support:* In 2008–09, 588 students received support. Career-related internships or fieldwork, institutionally sponsored loans, scholarships/grants, and tuition waivers (full and partial) available. Support available to part-time students. Financial award application deadline: 4/15; financial award applicants required to submit FAFSA. In 2008, 62 first professional degrees, 64 master's, 4 doctorates awarded. *Degree program information:* Part-time and evening/weekend programs available. Postbaccalaureate distance learning degree programs offered (minimal on-campus study). Offers theology (M Div, MA, MAC, MAEM, Th M, D Min, Certificate). *Application deadline:* Applications are processed on a rolling basis. *Application fee:* $50. Electronic applications accepted. *Application Contact:* Jeremy Kicklighter, Director of Admissions, 314-434-4044, Fax: 314-434-4819, E-mail: admissions@covenantseminary.edu. *Chief Academic Officer*, Dr. Sean Lucas, 314-434-4044.

CRANBROOK ACADEMY OF ART, Bloomfield Hills, MI 48303-0801

General Information Independent, coed, graduate-only institution. *Graduate housing:* Room and/or apartments available on a first-come, first-served basis to single students; on-campus housing not available to married students. Housing application deadline: 2/1.

GRADUATE UNITS

Graduate School Offers architecture (M Arch); ceramics (MFA); design (MFA); fiber arts (MFA); metalsmithing (MFA); painting (MFA); photography (MFA); printmaking (MFA); sculpture (MFA).

CREIGHTON UNIVERSITY, Omaha, NE 68178-0001

General Information Independent-religious, coed, university. CGS member. *Enrollment:* 7,051 graduate, professional, and undergraduate students; 2,464 full-time matriculated graduate/professional students (1,318 women), 500 part-time matriculated graduate/professional students (256 women). *Enrollment by degree level:* 2,345 first professional, 583 master's, 36 doctoral. *Graduate faculty:* 287. *Tuition:* Full-time $11,250; part-time $625 per credit hour. *Required fees:* $121 per semester. *Graduate housing:* Rooms and/or apartments available on a first-come, first-served basis to single and married students. Typical cost: $7000 per year ($10,000 including board) for single students; $7000 per year ($10,000 including board) for married students. Room and board charges vary according to board plan and housing facility selected. Housing application deadline: 5/1. *Student services:* Campus employment opportunities, campus safety program, career counseling, child daycare facilities, exercise/wellness program, free psychological counseling, international student services, low-cost health insurance, multicultural affairs office, services for students with disabilities, teacher training. *Library facilities:* Reinert Alumni Memorial Library plus 2 others. *Online resources:* library catalog, web page, access to other libraries' catalogs. *Collection:* 925,385 titles, 42,374 serial subscriptions, 21,005 audiovisual materials. *Research affiliation:* Global Weather Central (Atmospheric Science), Omaha Veterans Administration Hospital, Boys Town Institute for Communication Disorders in Children, Children's Memorial Hospital, Creighton University Medical Center.

Computer facilities: Computer purchase and lease plans are available. A campuswide network can be accessed from student residence rooms and from off campus. Online class registration, financial aid information are available. *Web address:* http://www.creighton.edu/.

General Application Contact: Jami E. Monico, Senior Program Coordinator, 402-280-2870, Fax: 402-280-2899, E-mail: jamimonico@creighton.edu.

GRADUATE UNITS

Graduate School Students: 221 full-time (113 women), 398 part-time (184 women); includes 61 minority (21 African Americans, 3 American Indian/Alaska Native, 27 Asian Americans or Pacific Islanders, 10 Hispanic Americans), 57 international. Average age 30. 496 applicants, 59% accepted, 256 enrolled. *Faculty:* 284. Expenses: Contact institution. *Financial support:* In 2008–09, research assistantships with tuition reimbursements (averaging $15,700 per year), teaching assistantships with tuition reimbursements (averaging $15,700 per year) were awarded; career-related internships or fieldwork, institutionally sponsored loans, and tuition waivers (partial) also available. Support available to part-time students. Financial award applicants required to submit FAFSA. In 2008, 206 master's awarded. *Degree program information:* Part-time and evening/weekend programs available. Postbaccalaureate distance learning degree programs offered (minimal on-campus study). *Application deadline:* For fall admission, 3/1 priority date for domestic and international students; for winter admission, 10/1 for domestic students, 7/1 for international students; for spring admission, 4/1 for domestic students, 10/1 for international students. Applications are processed on a rolling basis. *Application fee:* $50. Electronic applications accepted. *Application Contact:* Jami E. Monico, Senior Program Coordinator, 402-280-2870, Fax: 402-280-2899, E-mail: jamimonico@creighton.edu. *Dean*, Dr. Gail M. Jensen, 402-280-2870, Fax: 402-280-2899, E-mail: gjenson@creighton.edu.

College of Arts and Sciences Students: 45 full-time (19 women), 119 part-time (67 women); includes 13 minority (4 African Americans, 2 American Indian/Alaska Native, 5 Asian Americans or Pacific Islanders, 2 Hispanic Americans), 13 international. Average age 31. 67 applicants, 84% accepted, 31 enrolled. Expenses: Contact institution. *Financial support:* In 2008–09, teaching assistantships (averaging $10,438 per year); tuition waivers (partial) also available. Financial award applicants required to submit FAFSA. In 2008, 89 master's awarded. *Degree program information:* Part-time and evening/weekend programs available. Postbaccalaureate distance learning degree programs offered (minimal on-campus study). Offers arts and sciences (M Ed, MA, MLS, MS); atmospheric sciences (MS); Christian spirituality (MA); college student affairs (MS); community counseling (MS); counselor education (MS); creative writing (MA); educational leadership (MS); elementary school guidance (MS); elementary teaching (M Ed); international relations (MA); liberal studies (MLS); literature (MA); ministry (MA); physics (MS); secondary school administration (MS); secondary school guidance (MS); secondary teaching (M Ed); special populations in education (MS); teaching (M Ed); theology (MA). *Application deadline:* For fall admission, 3/1 for domestic and international students; for winter admission, 10/1 for domestic students, 7/1 for international students; for spring admission, 4/1 for domestic students, 10/1 for international students. Applications are processed on a rolling basis. *Application fee:* $50. Electronic applications accepted. *Application Contact:* Jami E. Monico, Senior Program

Creighton University (continued)

Coordinator, 402-280-2870, Fax: 402-280-2899, E-mail: jamimonico@creighton.edu. *Dean*, Dr. Robert J. Lueger, 402-280-2431, E-mail: robertlueger@creighton.edu.

Eugene C. Eppley College of Business Administration Students: 29 full-time (4 women), 173 part-time (42 women); includes 21 minority (4 African Americans, 15 Asian Americans or Pacific Islanders, 2 Hispanic Americans), 18 international. Average age 30. 150 applicants, 76% accepted, 82 enrolled. *Faculty:* 38 full-time (5 women). Expenses: Contact institution. *Financial support:* In 2008–09, 8 research assistantships with full tuition reimbursements (averaging $8,650 per year) were awarded; career-related internships or fieldwork, tuition waivers (partial), and unspecified assistantships also available. Financial award application deadline: 3/1. In 2008, 53 master's awarded. *Degree program information:* Part-time and evening/weekend programs available. Postbaccalaureate distance learning degree programs offered (minimal on-campus study). Offers business administration (MBA); information technology management (MS); securities and portfolio management (MSAPM). *Application deadline:* For fall admission, 7/1 priority date for domestic students, 3/1 for international students; for winter admission, 10/1 priority date for domestic students, 7/1 for international students; for spring admission, 4/1 priority date for domestic students, 10/1 for international students. Applications are processed on a rolling basis. *Application fee:* $50. Electronic applications accepted. *Application Contact:* Gail Hafer, 402-280-2829, Fax: 402-280-2172, E-mail: ghafer@creighton.edu. *Director*, Dr. Robert Moorman, 402-280-2091, E-mail: rmoorman@creighton.edu.

School of Dentistry Offers dentistry (DDS).

School of Law Students: 446 full-time (168 women), 17 part-time (10 women); includes 35 minority (7 African Americans, 16 Asian Americans or Pacific Islanders, 12 Hispanic Americans), 1 international. Average age 24. 1,146 applicants, 56% accepted, 169 enrolled. *Faculty:* 33 full-time (9 women), 35 part-time/adjunct (13 women). Expenses: Contact institution. *Financial support:* In 2008–09, 429 students received support. Career-related internships or fieldwork, institutionally sponsored loans, and scholarships/grants available. Support available to part-time students. Financial award application deadline: 7/1; financial award applicants required to submit FAFSA. In 2008, 146 first professional degrees awarded. *Degree program information:* Part-time programs available. Offers law (JD, MS, Certificate); negotiation and dispute resolution (MS, Certificate). *Application deadline:* For fall admission, 5/1 priority date for domestic and international students. Applications are processed on a rolling basis. *Application fee:* $50. Electronic applications accepted. *Application Contact:* Andrea D. Bashara, Assistant Dean, 402-280-2586, Fax: 402-280-3161, E-mail: bashara@creighton.edu. *Dean and Professor of Law*, Eric A. Chiappinelli, 402-280-2874, Fax: 402-280-3161.

School of Medicine Offers biomedical sciences (MS, PhD); clinical anatomy (MS); medical microbiology and immunology (MS, PhD); medicine (MD, MS, PhD); pharmaceutical sciences (MS); pharmacology (MS, PhD). Electronic applications accepted.

School of Nursing Students: 39 full-time (38 women), 35 part-time (33 women); includes 4 minority (2 African Americans, 2 Hispanic Americans). Average age 33. 49 applicants, 92% accepted, 37 enrolled. *Faculty:* 27 full-time (26 women), 1 (woman) part-time/adjunct. Expenses: Contact institution. *Financial support:* Career-related internships or fieldwork, Federal Work-Study, institutionally sponsored loans, and traineeships available. Financial award applicants required to submit FAFSA. In 2008, 21 master's awarded. *Degree program information:* Part-time programs available. Postbaccalaureate distance learning degree programs offered (minimal on-campus study). Offers nursing (MS, DNP). *Application deadline:* For fall admission, 3/15 priority date for domestic and international students; for spring admission, 10/15 priority date for domestic and international students. Applications are processed on a rolling basis. *Application fee:* $40. Electronic applications accepted. *Application Contact:* Dr. Mary Kunes-Connell, Associate Dean for Academic and Clinical Affairs, 402-280-2024, Fax: 402-280-2045, E-mail: mkc@creighton.edu. *Dean*, Dr. Eleanor V. Howell, 402-280-2004, Fax: 402-280-2045, E-mail: howell@creighton.edu.

School of Pharmacy and Health Professions Students: 956 full-time (660 women); includes 151 minority (23 African Americans, 3 American Indian/Alaska Native, 94 Asian Americans or Pacific Islanders, 31 Hispanic Americans), 1 international. Average age 26. 1,771 applicants, 23% accepted, 264 enrolled. *Faculty:* 98 full-time (59 women), 3 part-time/adjunct (1 woman). Expenses: Contact institution. *Financial support:* In 2008–09, 59 students received support. Scholarships/grants available. Financial award application deadline: 4/1; financial award applicants required to submit CSS PROFILE or FAFSA. In 2008, 234 doctorates awarded. Postbaccalaureate distance learning degree programs offered (minimal on-campus study). Offers occupational therapy (OTD); pharmaceutical sciences (MS); pharmacy (Pharm D); pharmacy and health professions (Pharm D, MS, DPT, OTD); physical therapy (DPT). *Application deadline:* For fall admission, 2/1 for domestic and international students. Applications are processed on a rolling basis. *Application fee:* $60. Electronic applications accepted. *Application Contact:* Kimberly Johnson, Director of Admission, 402-280-2662, Fax: 402-280-5739, E-mail: kimjohnson@creighton.edu. *Dean*, Dr. J. Chris Bradberry, 402-280-2950, Fax: 402-280-5738.

THE CRISWELL COLLEGE, Dallas, TX 75246-1537

General Information Independent-religious, coed, comprehensive institution. *Graduate housing:* On-campus housing not available.

GRADUATE UNITS

Graduate School of the Bible *Degree program information:* Part-time programs available. Offers biblical studies (M Div); Christian leadership (MA); counseling (MA); Jewish studies (MA); ministry (MA); theological and biblical studies (MA). Electronic applications accepted.

CROWN COLLEGE, St. Bonifacius, MN 55375-9001

General Information Independent-religious, coed, comprehensive institution. *Enrollment:* 1,229 graduate, professional, and undergraduate students; 94 full-time matriculated graduate/professional students (32 women), 29 part-time matriculated graduate/professional students (18 women). *Enrollment by degree level:* 123 master's. *Graduate faculty:* 15 part-time/adjunct (4 women). *Tuition:* Part-time $379 per credit. *Required fees:* $100 per term. *Graduate housing:* Room and/or apartments available on a first-come, first-served basis to married students; on-campus housing not available to single students. Housing application deadline: 7/1. *Student services:* Campus employment opportunities, career counseling, free psychological counseling, teacher training. *Library facilities:* Peter Watne Memorial Library. *Online resources:* library catalog, web page, access to other libraries' catalogs. *Collection:* 101,468 titles, 28,000 serial subscriptions, 1,503 audiovisual materials.

Computer facilities: 95 computers available on campus for general student use. A campuswide network can be accessed from student residence rooms and from off campus. Online class registration is available. *Web address:* http://www.crown.edu/.

General Application Contact: Nate Erickson, Enrollment Coordinator, 952-446-4370, Fax: 952-446-4349, E-mail: grad@crown.edu.

GRADUATE UNITS

Graduate Studies Students: 94 full-time (32 women), 29 part-time (18 women); includes 17 minority (9 African Americans, 5 Asian Americans or Pacific Islanders, 3 Hispanic Americans). Average age 37. 75 applicants, 77% accepted, 43 enrolled. *Faculty:* 15 part-time/adjunct (4 women). Expenses: Contact institution. *Financial support:* Scholarships/grants available. In 2008, 41 master's awarded. *Degree program information:* Part-time and evening/weekend programs available. Postbaccalaureate distance learning degree programs offered (no on-campus study). Offers Christian studies (MA); educational leadership (MA); intercultural leadership studies (MA); ministry leadership (MA); organizational leadership (MA). *Application deadline:* For fall admission, 8/1 priority date for domestic students; for winter admission, 1/1 priority date for domestic students; for spring admission, 6/1 priority date for domestic students. Applications are processed on a rolling basis. *Application fee:* $20. *Application Contact:* Nate Erickson, Enrollment Coordinator, 952-446-4370, Fax: 952-446-4349, E-mail: grad@crown.edu. *Director of Adult and Graduate Studies*, Don Bouchard, 952-446-4224, Fax: 952-416-4349, E-mail: grad@crown.edu.

CUMBERLAND UNIVERSITY, Lebanon, TN 37087-3408

General Information Independent, coed, comprehensive institution. *Graduate housing:* Room and/or apartments available on a first-come, first-served basis to single students; on-campus housing not available to married students.

GRADUATE UNITS

Program in Business Administration *Degree program information:* Part-time and evening/weekend programs available. Offers business administration (MBA).

Program in Education *Degree program information:* Part-time and evening/weekend programs available. Postbaccalaureate distance learning degree programs offered (no on-campus study). Offers education (MAE).

Program in Organizational Leadership and Human Relations Management *Degree program information:* Part-time and evening/weekend programs available. Offers organizational leadership and human relations management (MS).

Program in Public Service Administration *Degree program information:* Part-time and evening/weekend programs available. Offers public service administration (MS).

CUNY GRADUATE SCHOOL OF JOURNALISM, New York, NY 10036

General Information City-supported, coed, graduate-only institution.

GRADUATE UNITS

Graduate Program Offers journalism (MA). Electronic applications accepted.

CURRY COLLEGE, Milton, MA 02186-9984

General Information Independent, coed, comprehensive institution. *Graduate housing:* On-campus housing not available. *Research affiliation:* Public School Systems, Literacy Centers/GED Programs.

GRADUATE UNITS

Division of Continuing Education and Graduate Studies *Degree program information:* Part-time and evening/weekend programs available. Offers business administration (MBA); criminal justice (MA); educational administration (M Ed); educational diagnostic assessment (Certificate); educational therapy (Certificate); elementary education (M Ed); finance (Certificate); foundations (non-license) (M Ed); learning disabilities across the lifespan (Certificate); reading (M Ed, Certificate); special education (M Ed).

THE CURTIS INSTITUTE OF MUSIC, Philadelphia, PA 19103-6107

General Information Independent, coed, comprehensive institution. *Graduate housing:* On-campus housing not available.

GRADUATE UNITS

Graduate Studies Offers opera (MM).

DAEMEN COLLEGE, Amherst, NY 14226-3592

General Information Independent, coed, comprehensive institution. *Enrollment:* 2,716 graduate, professional, and undergraduate students; 630 full-time matriculated graduate/professional students (551 women), 318 part-time matriculated graduate/professional students (275 women). *Enrollment by degree level:* 846 master's, 95 doctoral, 7 other advanced degrees. *Graduate faculty:* 28 full-time (16 women), 61 part-time/adjunct (48 women). *Tuition:* Part-time $740 per credit hour. Tuition and fees vary according to course load and program. *Graduate housing:* Room and/or apartments available on a first-come, first-served basis to single students; on-campus housing not available to married students. Typical cost: $9240 (including board). Housing application deadline: 7/15. *Student services:* Campus employment opportunities, campus safety program, career counseling, low-cost health insurance, services for students with disabilities, teacher training. *Library facilities:* Research and Information Commons plus 1 other. *Online resources:* library catalog, web page, access to other libraries' catalogs. *Collection:* 152,081 titles, 24,960 serial subscriptions, 5,763 audiovisual materials.

Computer facilities: 99 computers available on campus for general student use. A campuswide network can be accessed from student residence rooms and from off campus. Online class registration is available. *Web address:* http://www.daemen.edu/.

General Application Contact: Karl Shallowhorn, Associate Director of Graduate Admissions, 716-839-8225, Fax: 716-839-8229, E-mail: kshallow@daemen.edu.

GRADUATE UNITS

Department of Accounting and Business Administration Students: 18 full-time (8 women), 3 part-time (2 women); includes 4 minority (2 African Americans, 1 Asian American or Pacific Islander, 1 Hispanic American), 7 international. Average age 26. 16 applicants, 63% accepted, 6 enrolled. *Faculty:* 4 full-time (2 women), 1 part-time/adjunct (0 women). Expenses: Contact institution. *Financial support:* In 2008–09, 4 students received support. Institutionally sponsored loans and scholarships/grants available. Financial award application deadline: 2/15; financial award applicants required to submit FAFSA. In 2008, 12 master's awarded. *Degree program information:* Part-time and evening/weekend programs available. Offers global business (MS). *Application deadline:* For fall admission, 3/1 priority date for domestic and international students; for spring admission, 10/1 priority date for domestic and international students. Applications are processed on a rolling basis. *Application fee:* $25. Electronic applications accepted. *Application Contact:* Karl Shallowhorn, Associate Director of Graduate Admissions, 716-839-8225, Fax: 716-839-8229, E-mail: kshallow@daemen.edu. *Chair*, Dr. Linda J. Kuechler, 716-839-8398, Fax: 716-839-8261, E-mail: lkuechle@daemen.edu.

Department of Nursing Students: 9 full-time (all women), 101 part-time (91 women); includes 15 minority (11 African Americans, 1 Asian American or Pacific Islander, 3 Hispanic Americans), 1 international. Average age 42. 38 applicants, 89% accepted, 33 enrolled. *Faculty:* 3 full-time (all women), 3 part-time/adjunct (all women). Expenses: Contact institution. *Financial support:* In 2008–09, 1 student received support. Institutionally sponsored loans and scholarships/grants available. Financial award application deadline: 2/15; financial award applicants required to submit FAFSA. In 2008, 23 master's awarded. *Degree program information:* Part-time programs available. Offers adult nurse practitioner (MS, Certificate); nursing education (MS, Post Master's Certificate); nursing executive leadership (MS, Post Master's Certificate); palliative care nursing (MS, Certificate). *Application deadline:* For fall admission, 3/1 priority date for domestic and international students; for spring admission, 10/1 priority date for domestic and international students. Applications are processed on a rolling basis. *Application fee:* $25. Electronic applications accepted. *Application Contact:* Karl Shallowhorn, Associate Director of Graduate Admissions, 716-839-8225, Fax: 716-839-8229, E-mail: kshallow@daemen.edu. *Chair*, Dr. Mary Lou Rusin, 716-839-8387, Fax: 716-839-8403, E-mail: mrusin@daemen.edu.

Department of Physical Therapy Students: 82 full-time (58 women), 21 part-time (14 women); includes 8 minority (2 American Indian/Alaska Native, 4 Asian Americans or Pacific Islanders, 2 Hispanic Americans), 5 international. Average age 27. 68 applicants, 31% accepted, 18 enrolled. *Faculty:* 8 full-time (5 women), 4 part-time/adjunct (1 woman). Expenses: Contact institution. *Financial support:* In 2008–09, 2 students received support; teaching assistantships, institutionally sponsored loans and scholarships/grants available. Financial award application deadline: 2/15; financial award applicants required to submit FAFSA. In 2008, 50 doctorates awarded. *Degree program information:* Part-time programs available. Offers orthopedic manual physical therapy (Advanced Certificate); physical therapy (DPT, TDPT). *Application deadline:* For fall admission, 3/1 priority date for domestic and international students; for spring admission, 10/1 priority date for domestic and international students. Applications are processed on a rolling basis. *Application fee:* $25. Electronic applications accepted. *Application Contact:* Karl Shallowhorn, Associate Director of Graduate Admissions, 716-839-8225, Fax: 716-839-8229, E-mail: kshallow@daemen.edu. *Chair*, Dr. Sharon L. Held, 716-839-8344, Fax: 716-839-8537, E-mail: sheld@daemen.edu.

Education Department Students: 442 full-time (409 women), 171 part-time (147 women); includes 7 minority (1 African American, 1 American Indian/Alaska Native, 2 Asian Americans or Pacific Islanders, 3 Hispanic Americans), 206 international. Average age 25. 283 applicants, 71% accepted, 145 enrolled. *Faculty:* 9 full-time (6 women), 50 part-time/adjunct (43 women). Expenses: Contact institution. *Financial support:* In 2008–09, 16 students received support. Institutionally sponsored loans, scholarships/grants, and some discounted programs available. Financial award application deadline: 2/15; financial award applicants required to submit FAFSA. In 2008, 277 master's awarded. *Degree program information:* Part-time programs available. Offers adolescence education (MS); childhood education (MS); childhood special education (MS). *Application deadline:* For fall admission, 3/1 priority date for domestic and international students; for spring admission, 10/1 priority date for domestic and international students. Applications are processed on a rolling basis. *Application fee:* $25. Electronic applications accepted. *Application Contact:* Karl Shallowhorn, Associate Director of Graduate Admissions, 716-839-8225, Fax: 716-839-8229, E-mail: kshallow@daemen.edu. *Chair,* Dr. Mary H. Fox, 716-839-8530, Fax: 716-839-8516, E-mail: mfox@daemen.edu.

Physician Assistant Department Students: 70 full-time (61 women); includes 6 minority (2 African Americans, 3 Asian Americans or Pacific Islanders, 1 Hispanic American). Average age 25. 339 applicants, 8% accepted, 17 enrolled. *Faculty:* 3 full-time (0 women). Expenses: Contact institution. *Financial support:* Institutionally sponsored loans and scholarships/grants available. Financial award application deadline: 2/15; financial award applicants required to submit FAFSA. In 2008, 38 master's awarded. Offers physician assistant (MS). *Application deadline:* For fall admission, 3/1 priority date for domestic and international students; for spring admission, 10/1 priority date for domestic and international students. Applications are processed on a rolling basis. *Application fee:* $25. Electronic applications accepted. *Application Contact:* Karl Shallowhorn, Associate Director of Graduate Admissions, 716-839-8225, Fax: 716-839-8229, E-mail: kshallow@daemen.edu. *Director,* Gregg L. Shutts, 716-839-8316, Fax: 716-839-8252, E-mail: shutts@daemen.edu.

Program in Executive Leadership and Change Students: 9 full-time (6 women), 22 part-time (21 women); includes 4 minority (3 African Americans, 1 Hispanic American). Average age 43. 15 applicants, 47% accepted, 5 enrolled. *Faculty:* 1 full-time (0 women), 3 part-time/adjunct (1 woman). Expenses: Contact institution. *Financial support:* In 2008–09, 1 student received support. Institutionally sponsored loans and scholarships/grants available. Financial award application deadline: 2/15; financial award applicants required to submit FAFSA. In 2008, 5 master's awarded. *Degree program information:* Part-time and evening/weekend programs available. Offers executive leadership and change (MS). *Application deadline:* For fall admission, 3/1 priority date for domestic and international students; for spring admission, 10/1 priority date for domestic and international students. Applications are processed on a rolling basis. *Application fee:* $25. Electronic applications accepted. *Application Contact:* Karl Shallowhorn, Associate Director of Graduate Admissions, 716-839-8225, Fax: 716-839-8229, E-mail: kshallow@daemen.edu. *Executive Director,* Dr. John S. Frederick, 716-839-8342, Fax: 716-839-8261, E-mail: jfrederi@daemen.edu.

DAKOTA STATE UNIVERSITY, Madison, SD 57042-1799

General Information State-supported, coed, comprehensive institution. CGS member. *Enrollment:* 2,675 graduate, professional, and undergraduate students; 55 full-time matriculated graduate/professional students (10 women), 168 part-time matriculated graduate/professional students (59 women). *Enrollment by degree level:* 187 master's, 36 doctoral. *Graduate faculty:* 48 full-time (14 women), 6 part-time/adjunct (2 women). *Graduate housing:* Room and/or apartments available on a first-come, first-served basis to single students; on-campus housing not available to married students. *Student services:* Campus employment opportunities, campus safety program, career counseling, exercise/wellness program, free psychological counseling, grant writing training, international student services, low-cost health insurance, multicultural affairs office, services for students with disabilities, writing training. *Library facilities:* Karl E. Mundt Library plus 1 other. *Online resources:* library catalog, web page, access to other libraries' catalogs. *Collection:* 95,819 titles, 350 serial subscriptions, 436 audiovisual materials. *Research affiliation:* SBS-Secure Banking Solutions, LLC (information security).

Computer facilities: Computer purchase and lease plans are available. 144 computers available on campus for general student use. A campuswide network can be accessed from student residence rooms and from off campus. Online class registration, wireless computing initiative requires full-time students to have a tablet computer are available. *Web address:* http://www.dsu.edu/.

General Application Contact: Annette Miller, Secretary, Office of Graduate Studies and Research, 605-256-5799, Fax: 605-256-5093, E-mail: annette.miller@dsu.edu.

GRADUATE UNITS

College of Business and Information Systems Students: 54 full-time (10 women), 122 part-time (29 women); includes 11 minority (3 African Americans, 2 American Indian/Alaska Native, 3 Asian Americans or Pacific Islanders, 3 Hispanic Americans), 56 international. Average age 34. 114 applicants, 65% accepted, 56 enrolled. *Faculty:* 20 full-time (2 women), 2 part-time/adjunct (1 woman). Expenses: Contact institution. *Financial support:* In 2008–09, 47 students received support, including 9 fellowships with partial tuition reimbursements available (averaging $31,837 per year), 15 research assistantships with partial tuition reimbursements available (averaging $10,688 per year), 3 teaching assistantships with partial tuition reimbursements available (averaging $31,837 per year); Federal Work-Study, scholarships/grants, unspecified assistantships, and administrative assistantships also available. Support available to part-time students. Financial award applicants required to submit FAFSA. In 2008, 28 master's awarded. *Degree program information:* Part-time and evening/weekend programs available. Postbaccalaureate distance learning degree programs offered (minimal on-campus study). Offers business and information systems (MSIA, MSIS, D Sc IS). *Application deadline:* For fall admission, 8/1 for domestic students, 6/1 for international students; for spring admission, 12/1 for domestic students, 10/1 for international students. Applications are processed on a rolling basis. *Application fee:* $35 ($85 for international students). Electronic applications accepted. *Application Contact:* Annette Miller, Secretary, Office of Graduate Studies and Research, 605-256-5799, Fax: 605-256-5093, E-mail: annette.miller@dsu.edu. *Dean,* Dr. Tom Halverson, 605-256-5165, Fax: 605-256-5060, E-mail: tom.halverson@dsu.edu.

College of Education Students: 1 full-time (0 women), 46 part-time (30 women); includes 1 minority (Hispanic American), 2 international. Average age 35. 17 applicants, 100% accepted, 17 enrolled. *Faculty:* 5 full-time (2 women), 4 part-time/adjunct (1 woman). Expenses: Contact institution. *Financial support:* In 2008–09, 16 students received support, including 3 research assistantships with partial tuition reimbursements available (averaging $10,688 per year); teaching assistantships, Federal Work-Study, scholarships/grants, tuition waivers (partial), unspecified assistantships, and administrative assistantships also available. Support available to part-time students. Financial award applicants required to submit FAFSA. In 2008, 27 master's awarded. *Degree program information:* Part-time programs available. Postbaccalaureate distance learning degree programs offered (minimal on-campus study). Offers instructional technology (MSET). *Application deadline:* For fall admission, 8/1 for domestic students, 6/1 for international students. Applications are processed on a rolling basis. *Application fee:* $35 ($85 for international students). Electronic applications accepted. *Application Contact:* Annette Miller, Secretary, Office of Graduate Studies and Research, 605-256-5799, Fax: 605-256-5093, E-mail: annette.miller@dsu.edu. *Interim Dean,* Dr. Judy Dittman, 605-256-5177, Fax: 605-256-7300, E-mail: judy.dittman@dsu.edu.

DAKOTA WESLEYAN UNIVERSITY, Mitchell, SD 57301-4398

General Information Independent-religious, coed, comprehensive institution. *Enrollment:* 711 graduate, professional, and undergraduate students; 34 part-time matriculated graduate/professional students (18 women). *Enrollment by degree level:* 34 master's. *Graduate faculty:* 1 (woman) full-time, 13 part-time/adjunct (8 women). *Student services:* Campus employment opportunities, campus safety program, career counseling, child daycare facilities, exercise/wellness program, free psychological counseling, international student services, low-cost health insurance, multicultural affairs office, services for students with disabilities, teacher training, writing training. *Library facilities:* George and Eleanor McGovern Library. *Online resources:* library catalog. *Collection:* 92,910 titles, 164 serial subscriptions, 3,944 audiovisual materials.

Computer facilities: 100 computers available on campus for general student use. A campuswide network can be accessed from student residence rooms and from off campus. Online class registration, portal, course management system are available. *Web address:* http://www.dwu.edu/.

General Application Contact: Coordinator of Graduate Admissions, 605-995-2650, Fax: 605-995-2699, E-mail: admissions@dwv.edu.

GRADUATE UNITS

Program in Education Students: 34 part-time (18 women); includes 2 African Americans, 2 American Indian/Alaska Native. Average age 30. 8 applicants, 100% accepted, 8 enrolled. *Faculty:* 5 full-time (4 women), 2 part-time/adjunct (both women). Expenses: Contact institution. In 2008, 14 master's awarded. *Degree program information:* Part-time and evening/weekend programs available. Offers curriculum and instruction (MA Ed); educational policy and administration (MA Ed); pre K-12 principal with certification (MA Ed); secondary with certification (MA Ed). *Application deadline:* For fall admission, 8/1 priority date for domestic and international students; for winter admission, 12/1 priority date for domestic students; for spring admission, 4/1 priority date for domestic students, 12/1 priority date for international students. Applications are processed on a rolling basis. *Application fee:* $50. Electronic applications accepted. *Application Contact:* Coordinator of Graduate Admissions, 800-333-8506, Fax: 605-995-2699, E-mail: admissions@dwv.edu. *Director of Graduate Studies,* Dr. Ruth Haidle, 605-995-2630, Fax: 605-995-2609, E-mail: ruhaidle@dwv.edu.

DALHOUSIE UNIVERSITY, Halifax, NS B3H 4R2, Canada

General Information Province-supported, coed, university. *Enrollment:* 15,367 graduate, professional, and undergraduate students; 1,823 full-time matriculated graduate/professional students (873 women), 876 part-time matriculated graduate/professional students (492 women). *Enrollment by degree level:* 74 first professional, 2,190 master's, 433 doctoral, 2 other advanced degrees. *Graduate faculty:* 1,320. *Graduate housing:* Rooms and/or apartments available on a first-come, first-served basis to single and married students. Housing application deadline: 8/1. *Student services:* Campus employment opportunities, campus safety program, career counseling, child daycare facilities, free psychological counseling, international student services, services for students with disabilities, writing training. *Library facilities:* The Killam Library. *Online resources:* library catalog, web page, access to other libraries' catalogs. *Collection:* 164 serial subscriptions.

Computer facilities: Computer purchase and lease plans are available. 710 computers available on campus for general student use. A campuswide network can be accessed from student residence rooms and from off campus. Online class registration is available. *Web address:* http://www.dal.ca/.

General Application Contact: Heather Nowlan, Admissions and Convocation Officer, 902-494-2485, Fax: 902-494-8797, E-mail: graduate.studies@dal.ca.

GRADUATE UNITS

Faculty of Architecture and Planning Expenses: Contact institution. *Financial support:* Career-related internships or fieldwork and scholarships/grants available. Offers architecture and planning (M Arch, M Eng, M Plan, MEDS, MPS). *Application deadline:* For fall admission, 6/1 priority date for domestic students, 4/1 priority date for international students; for winter admission, 11/15 priority date for domestic students, 8/31 priority date for international students; for spring admission, 2/28 priority date for domestic students, 12/31 priority date for international students. Applications are processed on a rolling basis. *Application fee:* $70. Electronic applications accepted. *Application Contact:* Bev Nightingale, Graduate Secretary, 902-494-3973, Fax: 902-423-6672, E-mail: grad.arch@dal.ca. *Dean,* Christine Macy, 902-494-3973, Fax: 902-423-6672, E-mail: Christine.Macy@dal.ca.

School of Planning Expenses: Contact institution. *Financial support:* Career-related internships or fieldwork and scholarships/grants available. Offers planning (M Eng, M Plan, MPS). *Application deadline:* For fall admission, 6/1 priority date for domestic students, 4/1 for international students; for winter admission, 11/15 for domestic students, 8/31 for international students; for spring admission, 1/28 for domestic students, 12/31 for international students. Applications are processed on a rolling basis. *Application fee:* $70. Electronic applications accepted. *Application Contact:* Frank Palermo, Graduate Coordinator, 902-494-3978, Fax: 902-423-6672, E-mail: frank.palermo@dal.ca. *Director,* Prof. Jill Grant, 902-494-3260, Fax: 902-423-6672, E-mail: plan.office@dal.ca.

Faculty of Arts and Social Science Expenses: Contact institution. *Financial support:* Fellowships, research assistantships, teaching assistantships available. In 2008, 62 master's, 6 doctorates awarded. *Degree program information:* Part-time programs available. Offers arts and social science (MA, PhD); classics (MA, PhD); English (MA, PhD); French (MA, PhD); German (MA); history (MA, PhD); international development studies (MA); musicology (MA); philosophy (MA, PhD); political science (MA, PhD); social anthropology (MA, PhD); sociology (MA, PhD). *Application deadline:* For fall admission, 6/1 for domestic students, 4/1 for international students; for winter admission, 10/31 for domestic students, 8/31 for international students; for spring admission, 2/28 for domestic students, 12/31 for international students. *Application fee:* $70. Electronic applications accepted. *Dean,* Dr. Marian Binkley, 902-494-1440, Fax: 902-494-1957, E-mail: fass@dal.ca.

Faculty of Computer Science Students: 96 full-time (31 women), 52 part-time (22 women). 140 applicants, 70% accepted. *Faculty:* 20 full-time (1 woman), 5 part-time/adjunct (0 women). Expenses: Contact institution. *Financial support:* Fellowships, research assistantships, teaching assistantships, career-related internships or fieldwork, scholarships/grants, and unspecified assistantships available. In 2008, 26 master's, 2 doctorates awarded. Offers computational biology and bioinformatics (M Sc); computer science (PhD); computer science (project-based) (MA Sc); computer science (thesis-based) (MC Sc); electronic commerce (MEC); health informatics (MHI). *Application deadline:* For fall admission, 6/1 priority date for domestic students, 4/1 for international students; for winter admission, 10/31 priority date for domestic students, 8/31 for international students; for spring admission, 2/28 priority date for domestic students, 12/31 for international students. Applications are processed on a rolling basis. *Application fee:* $70. Electronic applications accepted. *Application Contact:* Malcolm Heywood, Graduate Coordinator, 902-494-2951, Fax: 902-494-3149, E-mail: mheywood@cs.dal.ca. *Dean,* Dr. Michael Shepherd, 902-494-2093, Fax: 902-492-1517, E-mail: shepherd@cs.dal.ca.

Faculty of Dentistry Expenses: Contact institution. *Financial support:* Fellowships, research assistantships, teaching assistantships available. Offers dentistryoral and maxillofacial surgery. *Application deadline:* For fall admission, 12/1 for domestic and international students. Applications are processed on a rolling basis. *Application fee:* $70. *Application Contact:* JoAnne Roski, Coordinator of Admissions, 902-494-2274, Fax: 902-494-2527, E-mail: j.roski@dal.ca. *Assistant Dean,* Dr. Mark Filiaggi, 902-494-7102, Fax: 902-494-2527, E-mail: mark.filiaggi@dal.ca.

Faculty of Engineering Expenses: Contact institution. *Financial support:* Career-related internships or fieldwork, scholarships/grants, and health care benefits available. Offers biological engineering (M Eng, MA Sc, PhD); biomedical engineering (MA Sc, PhD); chemical engineering (M Eng, MA Sc, PhD); civil and resource engineering (M Eng, MA Sc, PhD); electrical and computer engineering (M Eng, MA Sc, PhD); engineering (M Eng, M Sc, MA Sc, PhD); engineering mathematics (M Sc, PhD); environmental engineering (M Eng, MA Sc, PhD); food science and technology (M Sc, PhD); industrial engineering (M Eng, MA Sc, PhD); internetworking (M Eng); materials engineering (M Eng, MA Sc, PhD); mechanical engineering (M Eng, MA Sc, PhD); mineral resource engineering (M Eng, MA Sc, PhD). *Application deadline:* For fall admission, 6/1 priority date for domestic students, 4/1 priority date for international students; for winter admission, 10/31 priority date for domestic students, 8/31 priority date for international students; for spring admission, 2/28 priority date for domestic students, 12/31 priority date for international students. Applications are processed on a rolling basis. *Application fee:* $70. *Application Contact:* Heather Hillyard, Admissions Coordinator, Graduate Studies and Research, 902-494-1288, Fax: 902-494-3011, E-mail: gsr@dal.ca. *Dean,* Dr. L. Joshua Leon, PhD, 902-494-6217, Fax: 902-429-3011, E-mail: Joshua.Leon@Dal.Ca.

Dalhousie University (continued)

Faculty of Graduate Studies Students: 1,596 full-time (841 women), 805 part-time (442 women). *Faculty:* 615 full-time, 186 part-time/adjunct. Expenses: Contact institution. *Financial support:* Fellowships, research assistantships, teaching assistantships, career-related internships or fieldwork, institutionally sponsored loans, and tuition waivers (partial) available. In 2008, 494 master's, 64 doctorates awarded. *Degree program information:* Part-time programs available. Postbaccalaureate distance learning degree programs offered. Offers anatomy and neurobiology (M Sc, PhD); interdisciplinary studies (PhD); medicine (M Sc, PhD); neuroscience (M Sc, PhD); pathology (M Sc, PhD); pharmacology (M Sc, PhD). *Application deadline:* For fall admission, 6/1 for domestic students, 4/1 for international students; for winter admission, 10/31 for domestic students, 8/31 for international students; for spring admission, 2/28 for domestic students, 12/31 for international students. *Application fee:* $70. Electronic applications accepted. *Application Contact:* Heather Nowlan, Admissions and Convocation Officer, 902-494-2485, Fax: 902-494-8797, E-mail: admissions.convocation@dal.ca. *Administrative Assistant to the Deans,* Marsha Scott, 902-494-6722, Fax: 902-494-8797, E-mail: graduate.studies@dal.ca.

Dalhousie Law School Students: 17 full-time (5 women), 6 part-time (4 women). 65 applicants, 20% accepted. *Faculty:* 36 full-time, 1 part-time/adjunct. Expenses: Contact institution. *Financial support:* Fellowships available. Financial award application deadline: 1/1. In 2008, 12 master's, 2 doctorates awarded. *Degree program information:* Part-time programs available. Offers law (LL M, JSD). *Application deadline:* For fall admission, 5/1 for domestic students, 4/1 for international students. Applications are processed on a rolling basis. *Application fee:* $70. Electronic applications accepted. *Application Contact:* Sheila Wile, Graduate Secretary, 902-494-1036, Fax: 902-494-1316, E-mail: sheila.wile@dal.ca. *Graduate Coordinator,* Richard Devlin, 902-494-1014, Fax: 902-494-1316, E-mail: law.admissions@dal.ca.

Nova Scotia Agricultural College Students: 35 full-time (24 women), 16 part-time (8 women); includes 1 African American, 3 Asian Americans or Pacific Islanders. 51 applicants, 76% accepted. *Faculty:* 28 full-time (3 women), 8 part-time/adjunct (0 women). Expenses: Contact institution. *Financial support:* In 2008–09, 26 students received support, including research assistantships (averaging $13,500 per year); teaching assistantships, career-related internships or fieldwork also available. In 2008, 16 master's awarded. *Degree program information:* Part-time programs available. Offers agriculture (M Sc). *Application deadline:* For fall admission, 6/1 for domestic students, 4/1 for international students; for winter admission, 10/31 for domestic students, 8/31 for international students; for spring admission, 2/28 for domestic students, 12/31 for international students. Applications are processed on a rolling basis. *Application fee:* $70. Electronic applications accepted. *Application Contact:* Marie Law, Administrative Program Assistant, 902-893-6502, Fax: 902-897-9399, E-mail: mlaw@nsac.ca. *Graduate Coordinator,* Dr. Rajasekaran Lada, 902-893-6502, Fax: 902-897-9399, E-mail: rlada@nsac.ca.

Faculty of Health Professions Students: 190 full-time (166 women), 173 part-time (150 women). *Faculty:* 75 full-time, 11 part-time/adjunct. Expenses: Contact institution. *Financial support:* Fellowships, research assistantships, teaching assistantships, career-related internships or fieldwork and institutionally sponsored loans available. *Degree program information:* Part-time programs available. Postbaccalaureate distance learning degree programs offered. Offers health professions (M Sc, MA, MAHSR, MHA, MN, MPH, MSW, PhD). *Application fee:* $70. *Application Contact:* Dr. William Webster, Dean, 902-494-3327, Fax: 902-494-1966. *Dean,* Dr. William Webster, 902-494-3327, Fax: 902-494-1966.

School of Health Administration Students: 33 full-time (27 women), 22 part-time (18 women); includes 9 minority (1 African American, 8 Asian Americans or Pacific Islanders). Average age 30. 31 applicants, 71% accepted. *Faculty:* 5 full-time (1 woman), 15 part-time/adjunct (8 women). Expenses: Contact institution. *Financial support:* In 2008–09, 13 students received support, including fellowships (averaging $2,000 per year), 5 teaching assistantships (averaging $630 per year). In 2008, 12 master's awarded. *Degree program information:* Part-time programs available. Postbaccalaureate distance learning degree programs offered (minimal on-campus study). Offers health administration (MAHSR, MHA, MPH, PhD). *Application deadline:* For fall admission, 6/1 for domestic and international students. Applications are processed on a rolling basis. *Application fee:* $70. Electronic applications accepted. *Application Contact:* Sandra Drew, Administrative Officer, 902-494-1547, Fax: 902-494-6849, E-mail: sandra.drew@dal.ca. *Graduate Coordinator,* Dr. Joesph Byrne, 902-494-7097, Fax: 902-494-6849, E-mail: healthadmin@dal.ca.

School of Health and Human Performance Students: 34 full-time (24 women), 6 part-time (4 women); includes 3 minority (all Asian Americans or Pacific Islanders). 23 applicants, 52% accepted. *Faculty:* 17 full-time (8 women), 4 part-time/adjunct (0 women). Expenses: Contact institution. *Financial support:* In 2008–09, 20 students received support; fellowships, research assistantships, teaching assistantships, institutionally sponsored loans available. In 2008, 10 master's awarded. *Degree program information:* Part-time programs available. Offers health and human performance (M Sc, MA); health promotion (MA); kinesiology (M Sc); leisure studies (MA). *Application deadline:* For fall admission, 6/1 for domestic and international students. Applications are processed on a rolling basis. *Application fee:* $70. Electronic applications accepted. *Application Contact:* Tracy Powell, Graduate Administrative Secretary, 902-494-1154, Fax: 902-494-5120, E-mail: tracy.powell@dal.ca. *Associate Director, Graduate Studies,* Dr. David Westwood, 902-494-1164, Fax: 902-494-5120, E-mail: david.westwood@dal.ca.

School of Human Communication Disorders Students: 92 full-time (87 women); includes 7 minority (4 Asian Americans or Pacific Islanders, 3 Hispanic Americans). Average age 25. 190 applicants, 17% accepted. *Faculty:* 8 full-time (6 women), 8 part-time/adjunct (4 women). Expenses: Contact institution. *Financial support:* In 2008–09, 16 students received support, including 14 research assistantships (averaging $1,500 per year), 2 teaching assistantships (averaging $500 per year); career-related internships or fieldwork and bursaries also available. In 2008, 27 master's awarded. Offers audiology (M Sc); speech-language pathology (M Sc). *Application deadline:* For fall admission, 1/15 priority date for domestic and international students. Applications are processed on a rolling basis. *Application fee:* $70. Electronic applications accepted. *Application Contact:* Joanne Fenerty, Administrative Assistant, 902-494-5161, Fax: 902-494-5151, E-mail: jfenerty@dal.ca. *Graduate Coordinator,* Dr. Joy Armson, 902-494-7052, Fax: 902-494-5151, E-mail: hcdwww@dal.ca.

School of Nursing Students: 16 full-time (15 women), 73 part-time (all women). Average age 32. 31 applicants, 94% accepted. *Faculty:* 16 full-time (15 women). Expenses: Contact institution. *Financial support:* Fellowships, research assistantships, teaching assistantships available. In 2008, 20 master's awarded. *Degree program information:* Part-time programs available. Postbaccalaureate distance learning degree programs offered (minimal on-campus study). Offers nursing (MN, PhD). *Application deadline:* For fall admission, 2/1 priority date for domestic students, 2/1 for international students. Applications are processed on a rolling basis. *Application fee:* $70. Electronic applications accepted. *Application Contact:* Jackie Gilby, Graduate Programs Secretary, 902-494-2397, Fax: 902-494-3487, E-mail: nursing@dal.ca. *Graduate Coordinator,* Dr. Ruth Martin-Misener, 902-494-2143, Fax: 902-494-3487, E-mail: ruth.martin-misener@dal.ca.

School of Occupational Therapy Students: 2 full-time (1 woman), 4 part-time (all women). Average age 25. 6 applicants, 67% accepted. *Faculty:* 2 full-time (both women), 9 part-time/adjunct (7 women). Expenses: Contact institution. *Financial support:* In 2008–09, 1 student received support, including 1 teaching assistantship; psychiatry practicum award also available. *Degree program information:* Part-time and evening/weekend programs available. Postbaccalaureate distance learning degree programs offered (no on-campus study). Offers occupational therapy (entry to profession) (M Sc); occupational therapy (post-professional) (M Sc). *Application deadline:* Applications are processed on a rolling basis. *Application fee:* $70. Electronic applications accepted. *Application Contact:* Pauline Fitzgerald, Graduate and Alumni Secretary, 902-494-6351, Fax: 902-494-1229, E-mail: p.fitzgerald@dal.ca. *Director,* Dr. Elizabeth Townsend, 902-494-8804, Fax: 902-494-1229, E-mail: occupational.therapy@dal.ca.

School of Physiotherapy Expenses: Contact institution. Offers physiotherapy (entry to profession) (M Sc); physiotherapy (rehabilitation research) (M Sc). *Application deadline:* For fall admission, 1/31 priority date for domestic and international students. *Application fee:* $70. Electronic applications accepted. *Application Contact:* Kelly Underwood, Admissions Assistant, 902-494-1947, Fax: 902-494-1941, E-mail: kelly.underwood@dal.ca. *Head,* Dr. Sandy Rennie, 902-494-2524, Fax: 902-494-1941, E-mail: physiotherapy@dal.ca.

School of Social Work Students: 26 full-time (24 women), 65 part-time (50 women); includes 12 minority (4 African Americans, 8 American Indian/Alaska Native). Average age 37. 50 applicants, 32% accepted. *Faculty:* 12 full-time (8 women), 3 part-time/adjunct (all women). Expenses: Contact institution. *Financial support:* In 2008–09, 13 students received support, including 4 fellowships with tuition reimbursements available, 3 teaching assistantships (averaging $2,520 per year); institutionally sponsored loans, scholarships/grants, and bursaries also available. In 2008, 19 master's awarded. *Degree program information:* Part-time programs available. Postbaccalaureate distance learning degree programs offered (minimal on-campus study). Offers social work (MSW). *Application deadline:* For spring admission, 12/1 priority date for domestic and international students. *Application fee:* $70. Electronic applications accepted. *Application Contact:* Lisa Calda, Admissions Coordinator, 902-494-1361, Fax: 902-494-6709, E-mail: social.work@dal.ca. *Graduate Coordinator,* Catrina Brown, 902-494-7150, Fax: 902-494-6709, E-mail: social.work@dal.ca.

Faculty of Management Students: 262 full-time (149 women), 391 part-time (171 women). *Faculty:* 51 full-time, 22 part-time/adjunct. Expenses: Contact institution. *Financial support:* Fellowships, research assistantships, teaching assistantships, career-related internships or fieldwork and scholarships/grants available. *Degree program information:* Part-time programs available. Offers management (MBA, MEC, MES, MIM, MLIS, MMM, MPA, MREM, GDPA); marine affairs (MMM). *Application deadline:* For fall admission, 6/1 for domestic students, 4/1 for international students; for winter admission, 10/31 for domestic students, 8/31 for international students; for spring admission, 2/28 for domestic students, 12/31 for international students. Applications are processed on a rolling basis. *Application fee:* $70. Electronic applications accepted. *Application Contact:* Dr. David Wheeler, Dean, 902-494-7487, Fax: 902-494-1195, E-mail: managementdean@dal.ca. *Dean,* Dr. David Wheeler, 902-494-7487, Fax: 902-494-1195, E-mail: managementdean@dal.ca.

Centre for Advanced Management Education Students: 19 part-time (4 women). Average age 27. 50 applicants, 42% accepted. *Faculty:* 10 full-time (5 women). Expenses: Contact institution. *Degree program information:* Part-time programs available. Postbaccalaureate distance learning degree programs offered. Offers financial services (MBA); information management (MIM); management (MPA); natural resources (MBA). *Application deadline:* Applications are processed on a rolling basis. *Application fee:* $70. Electronic applications accepted. *Application Contact:* Deborah McColl, Admissions and Registration Coordinator, 902-494-6391, E-mail: mbafs@dal.ca. *Associate Director (Administration),* Michelle Hunter, 902-494-1828, Fax: 902-494-7154, E-mail: mhunter@dal.ca.

School for Resource and Environmental Studies Students: 50 full-time (35 women), 10 part-time (6 women); includes 3 minority (1 African American, 2 Asian Americans or Pacific Islanders), 2 international. Average age 28. 70 applicants, 50% accepted. *Faculty:* 5 full-time, 25 part-time/adjunct. Expenses: Contact institution. *Financial support:* In 2008–09, 17 students received support, including 15 fellowships (averaging $9,000 per year), 5 teaching assistantships; scholarships/grants also available. Financial award application deadline: 2/1. In 2008, 15 master's awarded. *Degree program information:* Part-time programs available. Offers resource and environmental studies (MES, MREM). *Application deadline:* For fall admission, 2/1 for domestic and international students. Applications are processed on a rolling basis. *Application fee:* $70. Electronic applications accepted. *Application Contact:* Susan MacDonald, Administrative Officer, 902-494-1375, Fax: 902-494-3728, E-mail: susan.macdonald@dal.ca. *Graduate Coordinator,* Dr. Peter Duinker, 902-494-7100, Fax: 902-494-3728, E-mail: sres@dal.ca.

School of Business Administration Students: 156 full-time (56 women), 122 part-time (51 women). Average age 26. 504 applicants, 38% accepted. *Faculty:* 34 full-time. Expenses: Contact institution. *Financial support:* In 2008–09, 12 students received support; fellowships, teaching assistantships available. Financial award application deadline: 5/15. *Degree program information:* Part-time programs available. Offers business administration (MBA); financial services (MBA). *Application deadline:* For spring admission, 5/15 priority date for domestic students, 12/31 priority date for international students. Applications are processed on a rolling basis. *Application fee:* $70. Electronic applications accepted. *Application Contact:* Cathy Richard, Admissions and Registration Coordinator, 902-494-6391, Fax: 902-494-1107, E-mail: mbaoffice@mgmtdal.ca. *Graduate Coordinator,* Marianne Hagen, 902-494-1814, Fax: 902-494-1107, E-mail: mba.admissions@dal.ca.

School of Information Management Students: 41 full-time (30 women), 27 part-time (19 women). 59 applicants, 73% accepted. *Faculty:* 5 full-time (3 women), 9 part-time/adjunct (6 women). Expenses: Contact institution. *Financial support:* In 2008–09, 25 students received support, including 15 fellowships (averaging $4,560 per year), 1 research assistantship (averaging $1,300 per year); career-related internships or fieldwork and scholarships/grants also available. Financial award application deadline: 3/1. In 2008, 32 master's awarded. *Degree program information:* Part-time programs available. Offers information management (MIM, MLIS). *Application deadline:* For fall admission, 6/1 for domestic and international students. Applications are processed on a rolling basis. *Application fee:* $70. Electronic applications accepted. *Application Contact:* Joann Watson, MLIS Program Coordinator, 902-494-2471, Fax: 902-494-2451, E-mail: mlsi@dal.ca. *Director,* Dr. Fiona Black, 902-494-3656, Fax: 902-494-2451, E-mail: sim@dal.ca.

School of Public Administration Students: 59 full-time (36 women), 25 part-time (13 women). 58 applicants, 79% accepted. *Faculty:* 9 full-time (1 woman), 6 part-time/adjunct (1 woman). Expenses: Contact institution. *Financial support:* Fellowships, teaching assistantships, career-related internships or fieldwork available. *Degree program information:* Part-time programs available. Offers management (MPA); public administration (MPA, GDPA). *Application deadline:* Applications are processed on a rolling basis. *Application fee:* $70. Electronic applications accepted. *Application Contact:* Jeffrey Roy, Graduate Coordinator, 902-494-2752, Fax: 902-494-7023, E-mail: Roy@dal.ca. *Director,* Fazley Siddiq, 902-494-8802, Fax: 902-494-7023, E-mail: dalmpa@dal.ca.

Faculty of Medicine 688 applicants, 14% accepted. Expenses: Contact institution. Offers biochemistry and molecular biology (M Sc, PhD); community health and epidemiology (M Sc); medicine (MD, M Sc, PhD); microbiology and immunology (M Sc, PhD); physiology and biophysics (M Sc, PhD). *Application deadline:* For fall admission, 11/3 for domestic students. Applications are processed on a rolling basis. *Application fee:* $70. Electronic applications accepted. *Application Contact:* Sharon Graham, Director, Admissions and Student Affairs, 902-494-1874, E-mail: sharon.graham@dal.ca. *Dean,* Dr. Harold W. Cook, 902-494-1846, Fax: 902-494-7119, E-mail: dean.medicine@dal.ca.

Faculty of Science Expenses: Contact institution. *Financial support:* Fellowships, research assistantships, teaching assistantships, career-related internships or fieldwork, scholarships/grants, and health care benefits available. In 2008, 66 master's, 30 doctorates awarded. Offers biology (M Sc, PhD); chemistry (M Sc, PhD); clinical psychology (PhD); earth sciences (M Sc, PhD); economics (MA, MDE, PhD); mathematics (M Sc, PhD); oceanography (M Sc, PhD); physics and atmospheric science (M Sc, PhD); psychology (M Sc, PhD); psychology/neuroscience (M Sc, PhD); science (M Sc, MA, MDE, PhD); statistics (M Sc, PhD). *Application deadline:* For fall admission, 6/1 for domestic students, 4/1 for international students; for winter admission, 11/15 for domestic students, 8/31 for international students; for spring admission, 2/28 for domestic students, 12/31 for international students. *Application fee:* $70. Electronic applications accepted. *Dean,* Dr. Marty Leonard, 902-494-3540, E-mail: dean.science@dal.ca.

DALLAS BAPTIST UNIVERSITY, Dallas, TX 75211-9299

General Information Independent-religious, coed, comprehensive institution. *Enrollment:* 5,297 graduate, professional, and undergraduate students; 538 full-time matriculated graduate/professional students (308 women), 1,184 part-time matriculated graduate/professional students (762 women). *Enrollment by degree level:* 1,589 master's, 133 doctoral. *Graduate faculty:* 68 full-time (30 women), 113 part-time/adjunct (47 women). *Tuition:* Part-time $558 per credit hour. *Graduate housing:* Rooms and/or apartments available on a first-come, first-served basis to single and married students. Typical cost: $2150 per year ($5409 including board) for single students. Housing application deadline: 6/19. *Student services:* Campus employment opportunities, campus safety program, career counseling, free psychological counseling, international student services, low-cost health insurance, services for students with disabilities, writing training. *Library facilities:* Vance Memorial Library. *Online resources:* library catalog, web page, access to other libraries' catalogs. *Collection:* 296,549 titles, 409 serial subscriptions, 7,021 audiovisual materials.

Computer facilities: 190 computers available on campus for general student use. A campuswide network can be accessed from student residence rooms and from off campus. Online class registration is available. *Web address:* http://www.dbu.edu/.

General Application Contact: Kit P. Montgomery, Director of Graduate Programs, 214-333-5242, Fax: 214-333-5579, E-mail: graduate@dbu.edu.

GRADUATE UNITS

College of Adult Education Students: 11 full-time, 118 part-time. *Faculty:* 68 full-time (30 women), 113 part-time/adjunct (47 women). Expenses: Contact institution. *Financial support:* Federal Work-Study, institutionally sponsored loans, scholarships/grants, and tuition waivers (full and partial) available. Support available to part-time students. Financial award applicants required to submit FAFSA. In 2008, 56 master's awarded. *Degree program information:* Part-time and evening/weekend programs available. Offers accounting (MA); adult education (MA, MLA); arts (MLA); Christian ministry (MLA); church leadership (MA); counseling (MA); criminal justice (MA); English (MLA); English as a second language (MA, MLA); finance (MA); fine arts (MLA); higher education (MA); history (MLA); leadership studies (MA); management (MA); management information systems (MA); marketing (MA); missions (MA, MLA); political science (MLA). *Application deadline:* Applications are processed on a rolling basis. *Application fee:* $25. Electronic applications accepted. *Application Contact:* Kit P. Montgomery, Director of Graduate Programs, 214-333-5242, Fax: 214-333-5579, E-mail: graduate@dbu.edu. *Dean,* Dr. Donovan Fredrickson, 214-333-5337, Fax: 214-333-5579, E-mail: graduate@dbu.edu.

College of Business Students: 171 full-time, 459 part-time. 329 applicants, 55% accepted, 168 enrolled. *Faculty:* 68 full-time (30 women), 113 part-time/adjunct (47 women). Expenses: Contact institution. *Financial support:* Federal Work-Study, institutionally sponsored loans, scholarships/grants, and tuition waivers (full and partial) available. Support available to part-time students. Financial award applicants required to submit FAFSA. In 2008, 215 master's awarded. *Degree program information:* Part-time and evening/weekend programs available. Postbaccalaureate distance learning degree programs offered (no on-campus study). Offers accounting (MBA); business (MA, MBA); business communication (MA, MBA); conflict resolution management (MA, MBA); e-business (MBA); entrepreneurship (MBA); finance (MBA); general management (MA); health care management (MA, MBA); human resource management (MA); international business (MBA); leading the non-profit organization (MBA); management (MBA); management information systems (MBA); marketing (MBA); performance management (MA); project management (MBA); technology and engineering management (MBA). *Application deadline:* Applications are processed on a rolling basis. *Application fee:* $25. Electronic applications accepted. *Application Contact:* Kit P. Montgomery, Director of Graduate Programs, 214-333-5242, Fax: 214-333-5579, E-mail: graduate@dbu.edu. *Dean,* Dr. Charlene Conner, 214-333-5244, Fax: 214-333-8857, E-mail: graduate@dbu.edu.

College of Humanities and Social Sciences Students: 7 full-time, 200 part-time. *Faculty:* 68 full-time (30 women), 113 part-time/adjunct (47 women). Expenses: Contact institution. *Financial support:* Federal Work-Study, institutionally sponsored loans, scholarships/grants, and tuition waivers (full and partial) available. Support available to part-time students. Financial award applicants required to submit FAFSA. In 2008, 44 master's awarded. *Degree program information:* Part-time and evening/weekend programs available. Offers counseling (MA); humanities and social sciences (MA). *Application deadline:* Applications are processed on a rolling basis. *Application fee:* $25. Electronic applications accepted. *Application Contact:* Kit P. Montgomery, Director of Graduate Programs, 214-333-5242, Fax: 214-333-5579, E-mail: graduate@dbu.edu. *Dean,* Dr. Michael Williams, 214-333-5242, Fax: 214-333-5579, E-mail: graduate@dbu.edu.

Dorothy M. Bush College of Education Students: 34 full-time, 339 part-time. 169 applicants, 56% accepted, 89 enrolled. *Faculty:* 68 full-time (30 women), 113 part-time/adjunct (47 women). Expenses: Contact institution. *Financial support:* Federal Work-Study, institutionally sponsored loans, scholarships/grants, and tuition waivers (full and partial) available. Support available to part-time students. Financial award applicants required to submit FAFSA. In 2008, 120 master's awarded. *Degree program information:* Part-time and evening/weekend programs available. Offers curriculum and instruction (M Ed); education (M Ed, MAT); educational leadership (M Ed); elementary (MAT); English as a second language (M Ed, MAT); hi-level (MAT); kinesiology (M Ed); master reading teacher (M Ed); reading specialist (M Ed); school counseling (M Ed); secondary (MAT). *Application deadline:* Applications are processed on a rolling basis. *Application fee:* $25. Electronic applications accepted. *Application Contact:* Kit P. Montgomery, Director of Graduate Programs, 214-333-5242, Fax: 214-333-5579, E-mail: graduate@dbu.edu. *Dean,* Dr. Charles Carona, 214-333-5242, Fax: 214-333-5579, E-mail: graduate@dbu.edu.

Gary Cook School of Leadership Students: 49 full-time, 185 part-time. 105 applicants, 63% accepted. *Faculty:* 68 full-time (30 women), 113 part-time/adjunct (47 women). Expenses: Contact institution. *Financial support:* Federal Work-Study, institutionally sponsored loans, scholarships/grants, and tuition waivers (full and partial) available. Support available to part-time students. Financial award applicants required to submit FAFSA. In 2008, 48 master's awarded. *Degree program information:* Part-time and evening/weekend programs available. Offers adult ministry (MA); business communication (MA); business ministry (MA); childhood ministry (MA); Christian education and business administration (MA, MBA); Christian education/missions (MA); Christian education: childhood ministry (MA); Christian education: student ministry (MA); collegiate ministry (MA); communication ministry (MA); counseling ministry (MA); education in higher education (M Ed); education ministry (MA); ESL (MA); general ministry (MA); general studies (MA); global studies (MA); international business (MA); leadership (M Ed, MA, MBA); missions (MA); missions ministry (MA); student ministry (MA); worship leadership (MA); worship ministry (MA); worship/missions (MA). *Application deadline:* Applications are processed on a rolling basis. *Application fee:* $25. Electronic applications accepted. *Application Contact:* Kit P. Montgomery, Director of Graduate Programs, 214-333-5242, Fax: 214-333-5579, E-mail: graduate@dbu.edu. *Dean,* Dr. Rick Gregory, 214-333-5484, Fax: 214-333-5673, E-mail: graduate@dbu.edu.

DALLAS THEOLOGICAL SEMINARY, Dallas, TX 75204-6499

General Information Independent, coed, graduate-only institution. *Graduate housing:* Rooms and/or apartments available on a first-come, first-served basis to single and married students. *Student services:* Campus employment opportunities, campus safety program, career counseling, exercise/wellness program, international student services, low-cost health insurance, multicultural affairs office, services for students with disabilities. *Library facilities:* Turpin Library. *Online resources:* library catalog, access to other libraries' catalogs. *Collection:* 172,376 titles, 1,043 serial subscriptions, 16,843 audiovisual materials.

Computer facilities: 48 computers available on campus for general student use. A campuswide network can be accessed. *Web address:* http://www.dts.edu/.

General Application Contact: Josh Bleeker, Director of Admissions, 214-841-3661, Fax: 214-841-3664, E-mail: admissions@dts.edu.

GRADUATE UNITS

Graduate Programs Expenses: Contact institution. *Financial support:* Career-related internships or fieldwork, institutionally sponsored loans, scholarships/grants, and tuition waivers (full and partial) available. Financial award application deadline: 2/28. *Degree program information:* Part-time and evening/weekend programs available. Offers academic ministries (Th M); Bible translation (Th M); biblical and theological studies (CGS); biblical counseling (MA, Th M); biblical exegesis and linguistics (MA); biblical exposition (PhD); biblical studies (MA); Christian education (MA, D Min); cross-cultural ministries (MA, Th M); educational leadership (Th M); evangelism and discipleship (Th M); interdisciplinary studies (Th M); media and communication (MA); media arts in ministry (Th M); ministry (D Min); New Testament studies (Th M, PhD); Old Testament studies (PhD); parachurch ministries (Th M); pastoral ministries (Th M); sacred theology (STM); theological studies (PhD); women's ministry (Th M). *Application deadline:* For fall admission, 7/1 priority date for domestic students, 1/15 for international students; for winter admission, 11/1 priority date for domestic students; for spring admission, 11/1 priority date for domestic students. Applications are processed on a rolling basis. *Application fee:* $30. Electronic applications accepted. *Application Contact:* Josh Bleeker, Director of Admissions, 214-841-3661, Fax: 214-841-3664, E-mail: admissions@dts.edu. *President,* Dr. Mark L. Bailey, 214-841-3676, Fax: 214-841-3565.

DANIEL WEBSTER COLLEGE, Nashua, NH 03063-1300

General Information Independent, coed, comprehensive institution. *Enrollment:* 1,007 graduate, professional, and undergraduate students; 119 full-time matriculated graduate/professional students (41 women). *Enrollment by degree level:* 119 master's. *Graduate faculty:* 9 full-time, 9 part-time/adjunct. *Student services:* Campus safety program, career counseling, exercise/wellness program, free psychological counseling, services for students with disabilities, writing training. *Library facilities:* Ann Bridge Baddour Library.

Computer facilities: Computer purchase and lease plans are available. 155 computers available on campus for general student use. A campuswide network can be accessed from student residence rooms and from off campus. Online class registration is available. *Web address:* http://www.dwc.edu/.

General Application Contact: Chrissy Harrington, Graduate Admissions Specialist, 866-458-7525, Fax: 603-577-6503, E-mail: mba@dwc.edu.

DANIEL WEBSTER COLLEGE–PORTSMOUTH CAMPUS, Portsmouth, NH 03801

General Information Independent, coed, comprehensive institution. *Enrollment by degree level:* 11 master's. *Graduate faculty:* 2 full-time, 2 part-time/adjunct. *Tuition:* Part-time $510 per credit. *Graduate housing:* On-campus housing not available. *Student services:* Career counseling, services for students with disabilities, writing training. *Web address:* http://www.dwc.edu/gcde/portsmouth/.

General Application Contact: Chrissy Harrington, Graduate Admissions Specialist, 866-458-7528, Fax: 603-577-6503, E-mail: harrington@dwc.edu.

GRADUATE UNITS

MBA Program Students: 11 full-time (6 women). Average age 34. *Faculty:* 2 full-time, 2 part-time/adjunct. Expenses: Contact institution. In 2008, 8 master's awarded. *Degree program information:* Part-time and evening/weekend programs available. Offers applied management (MBA). *Application deadline:* Applications are processed on a rolling basis. *Application fee:* $25. Electronic applications accepted. *Application Contact:* Chrissy Harrington, Graduate Admissions Specialist, 866-458-7525, Fax: 603-577-6503, E-mail: mba@dwc.edu. *Dean, School of Business, Management and Professional Studies,* Neil Pamonter, 603-577-6650, Fax: 603-577-6503, E-mail: parmonter@dwc.edu.

DARKEI NOAM RABBINICAL COLLEGE, Brooklyn, NY 11210

General Information Independent-religious, men only, comprehensive institution.

GRADUATE UNITS

Graduate Programs

DARTMOUTH COLLEGE, Hanover, NH 03755

General Information Independent, coed, university. CGS member. *Enrollment:* 5,848 graduate, professional, and undergraduate students; 1,597 full-time matriculated graduate/professional students (650 women), 104 part-time matriculated graduate/professional students (63 women). *Enrollment by degree level:* 317 first professional, 817 master's, 470 doctoral, 97 other advanced degrees. *Graduate faculty:* 339 full-time (88 women), 83 part-time/adjunct (29 women). *Tuition:* Full-time $36,690. *Required fees:* $50. *Graduate housing:* Rooms and/or apartments available to single and married students. Typical cost: $17,214 (including board) for single students. Housing application deadline: 5/15. *Student services:* Campus safety program, career counseling, free psychological counseling, international student services, low-cost health insurance, services for students with disabilities, teacher training, writing training. *Library facilities:* Baker-Berry Library plus 10 others. *Online resources:* library catalog, web page, access to other libraries' catalogs.

Computer facilities: Computer purchase and lease plans are available. 200 computers available on campus for general student use. A campuswide network can be accessed from student residence rooms and from off campus. Online class registration is available. *Web address:* http://www.dartmouth.edu/.

General Application Contact: Gary Hutchins, Assistant Dean, School of Arts and Sciences, 603-646-2107, Fax: 603-646-3488, E-mail: g.hutchins@dartmouth.edu.

GRADUATE UNITS

Arts and Sciences Graduate Programs Students: 502 full-time (229 women), 80 part-time (50 women); includes 51 minority (9 African Americans, 4 American Indian/Alaska Native, 20 Asian Americans or Pacific Islanders, 18 Hispanic Americans), 165 international. Average age 28. 1,352 applicants, 29% accepted, 165 enrolled. *Faculty:* 339 full-time (88 women), 83 part-time/adjunct (29 women). Expenses: Contact institution. *Financial support:* In 2008–09, 468 students received support, including fellowships with full tuition reimbursements available (averaging $23,364 per year), research assistantships with full tuition reimbursements available (averaging $23,364 per year), teaching assistantships with full tuition reimbursements available (averaging $23,364 per year); career-related internships or fieldwork, institutionally sponsored loans, scholarships/grants, traineeships, tuition waivers (full and partial), and unspecified assistantships also available. Support available to part-time students. Financial award applicants required to submit CSS PROFILE. In 2008, 96 master's, 69 doctorates awarded. Offers arts and sciences (AM, MALS, MS, PhD); biology of integrated systems (PhD); cancer biology and molecular therapeutics (PhD); chemistry (PhD); cognitive neuroscience (PhD); comparative literature (AM); computer science (MS, PhD); earth sciences (MS, PhD); ecology and evolutionary biology (PhD); electro-acoustic music (AM); liberal studies (MALS); mathematics (PhD); molecular pharmacology, toxicology and experimental therapeutics (PhD); neuroscience (PhD); pharmacology and toxicology (PhD); physics and astronomy (MS, PhD); physiology (PhD); psychology (PhD); vascular biology (PhD). *Application deadline:* For fall admission, 1/15 for domestic students. Electronic applications accepted. *Application Contact:* Gary Hutchins, Assistant Dean, School of Arts and Sciences, 603-646-2107, Fax: 603-646-3488, E-mail: g.hutchins@dartmouth.edu. *Dean of Graduate Studies,* Dr. Brian Pogue, 603-646-2106, Fax: 603-646-3488, E-mail: Brian.W.Pogue@Dartmouth.edu.

The Dartmouth Institute Students: 60 full-time (33 women), 40 part-time (23 women); includes 16 minority (1 African American, 1 American Indian/Alaska Native, 13 Asian Americans or Pacific Islanders, 1 Hispanic American), 8 international. Average age 33. 279 applicants, 35% accepted, 69 enrolled. *Faculty:* 32 full-time (17 women), 10 part-time/adjunct (7 women). Expenses: Contact institution. *Financial support:* In 2008–09, 5 students received support. In 2008, 77 master's, 1 doctorate awarded. *Degree program information:* Part-time programs available. Offers evaluative clinical sciences (MS, PhD); public health (MPH). *Application deadline:* For fall admission, 1/15 for domestic students. *Application fee:* $50. *Application Contact:* Gary Hutchins, Assistant Dean, School of Arts and Sciences, 603-646-2107, Fax: 603-646-3488, E-mail: g.hutchins@dartmouth.edu.

Dartmouth Medical School Students: 315 full-time (154 women), 2 part-time (1 woman); includes 76 minority (5 African Americans, 1 American Indian/Alaska Native, 56 Asian Americans or Pacific Islanders, 14 Hispanic Americans), 38 international. Average age 26. 5,419 applicants, 4% accepted, 75 enrolled. *Faculty:* 252 full-time (81 women), 64 part-time/adjunct (33 women). Expenses: Contact institution. In 2008, 62 MDs awarded. Offers medicine (MD). *Application Contact:* Gary Hutchins, Assistant Dean, School of Arts and Sciences, 603-646-2107, Fax: 603-646-3488, E-mail: g.hutchins@dartmouth.edu. *Dean,* Dr. William Green, 603-650-1200.

Graduate Program in Molecular and Cellular Biology Students: 158 full-time (75 women); includes 11 minority (4 African Americans, 2 Asian Americans or Pacific Islanders, 5 Hispanic Americans), 59 international. Average age 27. 275 applicants, 25% accepted, 30 enrolled. *Faculty:* 65 full-time (17 women), 5 part-time/adjunct (1 woman). Expenses: Contact institution. *Financial support:* In 2008–09, 121 students received support, including fellowships with full tuition reimbursements available (averaging $25,250 per year), research assistantships with

Dartmouth College (continued)

full tuition reimbursements available (averaging $25,250 per year), teaching assistantships with full tuition reimbursements available (averaging $25,250 per year); institutionally sponsored loans, scholarships/grants, traineeships, tuition waivers (full), unspecified assistantships, and stipends and full tuition scholarships also available. In 2008, 25 doctorates awarded. Offers biochemistry (PhD); biological sciences (PhD); genetics (PhD); immunology (PhD); microbiology and immunology (PhD); molecular and cellular biology (PhD); molecular pathogenesis (PhD). *Application deadline:* For fall admission, 1/4 for domestic and international students. *Application fee:* $60. *Application Contact:* Janet Cheney, Program Coordinator, 603-650-1612, Fax: 603-650-1006, E-mail: Molecular.and.Cellular.Biology@Dartmouth.edu.

Program in Experimental and Molecular Medicine Students: 23 full-time (16 women); includes 2 minority (1 Asian American or Pacific Islander, 1 Hispanic American), 9 international. Average age 28. 103 applicants, 22% accepted, 9 enrolled. *Faculty:* 71 full-time (13 women). Expenses: Contact institution. *Financial support:* In 2008–09, 22 students received support, including fellowships with full tuition reimbursements available (averaging $25,500 per year), research assistantships with full tuition reimbursements available (averaging $25,500 per year), teaching assistantships with full tuition reimbursements available (averaging $25,500 per year); institutionally sponsored loans, traineeships, and unspecified assistantships also available. Offers biology of integrated systems (PhD); cancer biology and molecular therapeutics (PhD); molecular pharmacology, toxicology and experimental therapeutics (PhD); neuroscience (PhD); systems biology (PhD); vascular biology (PhD). *Application deadline:* For fall admission, 1/15 for domestic students, 10/1 for international students. *Application fee:* $50. Electronic applications accepted. *Application Contact:* Gail L. Paige, Program Coordinator, 603-650-4933, Fax: 603-650-6122, E-mail: molecular.medicine@dartmouth.edu. *Director*, Dr. Murray Korc, 603-650-7936, Fax: 603-650-6122, E-mail: murray.korc@dartmouth.edu.

Thayer School of Engineering Students: 166 full-time (53 women); includes 13 minority (1 American Indian/Alaska Native, 11 Asian Americans or Pacific Islanders, 1 Hispanic American), 73 international. Average age 24. 589 applicants, 32% accepted, 116 enrolled. *Faculty:* 50 full-time (7 women), 13 part-time/adjunct (1 woman). Expenses: Contact institution. *Financial support:* In 2008–09, 13 fellowships with full tuition reimbursements (averaging $22,320 per year), 66 research assistantships with full tuition reimbursements (averaging $22,320 per year), 34 teaching assistantships with partial tuition reimbursements (averaging $7,200 per year) were awarded; career-related internships or fieldwork, institutionally sponsored loans, scholarships/grants, and tuition waivers (full and partial) also available. Financial award application deadline: 2/15; financial award applicants required to submit CSS PROFILE. In 2008, 49 master's, 12 doctorates awarded. Offers biotechnology and biochemical engineering (MS, PhD); computer engineering (MS, PhD); electrical engineering (MS, PhD); engineering (MEM, MS, PhD); engineering management (MEM); engineering physics (MS, PhD); manufacturing systems (MS, PhD); materials sciences and engineering (MS, PhD); mechanical engineering (MS, PhD). *Application deadline:* For fall admission, 1/1 priority date for domestic and international students. Applications are processed on a rolling basis. *Application fee:* $45. Electronic applications accepted. *Application Contact:* Candace S. Potter, Graduate Admissions Administrator, 603-646-3844, Fax: 603-646-1620, E-mail: candace.potter@dartmouth.edu. *Dean*, Dr. Joseph J. Helbie, 603-646-2238, Fax: 603-646-2580, E-mail: joseph.j.helbie@dartmouth.edu.

Tuck School of Business at Dartmouth Offers business (MBA). Electronic applications accepted.

See Close-Up on page 895.

DAVENPORT UNIVERSITY, Dearborn, MI 48126-3799

General Information Independent, coed, comprehensive institution. *Graduate housing:* On-campus housing not available.

GRADUATE UNITS

Sneden Graduate School *Degree program information:* Part-time and evening/weekend programs available. Postbaccalaureate distance learning degree programs offered (no on-campus study). Offers accounting (MBA); business administration (EMBA); finance (MBA); health care management (MBA); human resources management (MBA); information assurance (MS); marketing (MBA); public health (MPH); strategic management (MBA).

DAVENPORT UNIVERSITY, Grand Rapids, MI 49503

General Information Independent, coed, comprehensive institution. *Graduate housing:* Room and/or apartments available on a first-come, first-served basis to single students; on-campus housing not available to married students. *Research affiliation:* Human Synergistic Center for Applied Research, Inc. (leadership, organizational culture, strategy).

GRADUATE UNITS

Sneden Graduate School *Degree program information:* Evening/weekend programs available. Offers accounting (MBA); business administration (EMBA); finance (MBA); health care management (MBA); human resources (MBA); information assurance (MS); public health (MPH); strategic management (MBA). Electronic applications accepted.

DAVENPORT UNIVERSITY, Warren, MI 48092-5209

General Information Independent, coed, comprehensive institution.

GRADUATE UNITS

Sneden Graduate School Offers accounting (MBA); business administration (EMBA); finance (MBA); health care management (MBA); human resources management (MBA); information assurance (MS); public health (MPH); strategic management (MBA).

DEFIANCE COLLEGE, Defiance, OH 43512-1610

General Information Independent-religious, coed, comprehensive institution. *Graduate housing:* On-campus housing not available.

GRADUATE UNITS

Program in Business Administration *Degree program information:* Part-time and evening/weekend programs available. Offers criminal justice (MBA); health care (MBA); leadership (MBA).

Program in Education *Degree program information:* Part-time programs available. Offers adolescent and young adult (MA); mild and moderate intervention specialist (MA); sport science (MA).

DELAWARE STATE UNIVERSITY, Dover, DE 19901-2277

General Information State-supported, coed, university. *Graduate housing:* Room and/or apartments available on a first-come, first-served basis to single students; on-campus housing not available to married students.

GRADUATE UNITS

Graduate Programs *Degree program information:* Part-time and evening/weekend programs available. Offers applied chemistry (MS, PhD); applied mathematics (MS); applied mathematics and theoretical physics (PhD); applied optics (MS); biological sciences (MA, MS); biology education (MS); chemistry (MS, PhD); French (MA); historic preservation (MA); mathematics (MS); mathematics education (MS); molecular and cellular neuroscience (MS); natural resources (MS); neuroscience (PhD); nursing (MS); optics (PhD); physics (MS); physics teaching (MS); plant science (MS); social work (MSW); Spanish (MA); sport administration (MS).

College of Business Administration *Degree program information:* Part-time and evening/weekend programs available. Offers business administration (MBA). Electronic applications accepted.

College of Education *Degree program information:* Part-time and evening/weekend programs available. Offers adult literacy and basic education (MA); art education (MA); curriculum and instruction (MA); education (MA, Ed D); educational leadership (MA, Ed D); science education (MA); special education (MA); teaching (MA). Electronic applications accepted.

DELAWARE VALLEY COLLEGE, Doylestown, PA 18901-2697

General Information Independent, coed, comprehensive institution. *Graduate housing:* On-campus housing not available.

GRADUATE UNITS

Program in Educational Leadership *Degree program information:* Part-time and evening/weekend programs available. Offers educational leadership (MS).

Program in Food and Agribusiness Offers food and agribusiness (MBA).

Program in General Business Offers general business (MBA).

DELL'ARTE SCHOOL OF PHYSICAL THEATRE, Blue Lake, CA 95525

General Information Independent, coed, graduate-only institution. *Graduate housing:* Rooms and/or apartments available on a first-come, first-served basis to single and married students.

GRADUATE UNITS

MFA Program Offers ensemble based physical theatre (MFA). Electronic applications accepted.

DELTA STATE UNIVERSITY, Cleveland, MS 38733-0001

General Information State-supported, coed, comprehensive institution. *Enrollment:* 4,065 graduate, professional, and undergraduate students; 242 full-time matriculated graduate/professional students (174 women), 610 part-time matriculated graduate/professional students (476 women). *Enrollment by degree level:* 708 master's, 55 doctoral, 89 other advanced degrees. *Graduate faculty:* 74 full-time (37 women), 20 part-time/adjunct (9 women). *Tuition, area resident:* Full-time $4450; part-time $247 per credit hour. Tuition, nonresident: full-time $11,182; part-time $621 per credit hour. *Graduate housing:* Rooms and/or apartments available on a first-come, first-served basis to single and married students. Typical cost: $5476 (including board) for single students; $3300 per year for married students. Housing application deadline: 6/1. *Student services:* Campus employment opportunities, campus safety program, career counseling, child daycare facilities, exercise/wellness program, free psychological counseling, grant writing training, international student services, low-cost health insurance, services for students with disabilities, writing training. *Library facilities:* Roberts-LaForge Library. *Online resources:* library catalog, web page. *Collection:* 424,979 titles, 23,184 serial subscriptions.

Computer facilities: Computer purchase and lease plans are available. 350 computers available on campus for general student use. A campuswide network can be accessed from student residence rooms and from off campus. Online class registration is available. *Web address:* http://www.deltastate.edu/.

General Application Contact: Dr. Albert Nylander, Dean of Graduate Studies, 662-846-4875, Fax: 662-846-4313, E-mail: grad-info@deltastate.edu.

GRADUATE UNITS

Graduate Programs Students: 242 full-time (174 women), 610 part-time (476 women); includes 431 minority (420 African Americans, 1 American Indian/Alaska Native, 6 Asian Americans or Pacific Islanders, 4 Hispanic Americans), 17 international. Average age 33. 782 applicants, 59% accepted, 301 enrolled. *Faculty:* 74 full-time (37 women), 20 part-time/adjunct (9 women). Expenses: Contact institution. *Financial support:* In 2008–09, 735 students received support, including 82 research assistantships with full and partial tuition reimbursements available (averaging $7,800 per year); fellowships with full tuition reimbursements available, career-related internships or fieldwork, Federal Work-Study, institutionally sponsored loans, scholarships/grants, tuition waivers (full and partial), and unspecified assistantships also available. Support available to part-time students. Financial award application deadline: 6/1; financial award applicants required to submit FAFSA. In 2008, 191 master's, 5 doctorates, 21 other advanced degrees awarded. *Degree program information:* Part-time and evening/weekend programs available. Postbaccalaureate distance learning degree programs offered (minimal on-campus study). *Application deadline:* For fall admission, 8/1 priority date for domestic students; for spring admission, 12/1 priority date for domestic students. Applications are processed on a rolling basis. *Application fee:* $25. Electronic applications accepted. *Application Contact:* Dr. Albert Nylander, Dean of Graduate Studies, 662-846-4875, Fax: 662-846-4313, E-mail: grad-info@deltastate.edu. *Provost and Vice President for Academic Affairs*, Dr. Ann Lotven, 662-846-4010, Fax: 662-846-4015.

College of Arts and Sciences *Degree program information:* Part-time programs available. Offers arts and sciences (M Ed, MSCD, MSCJ, MSNS); biological science (MSNS); community development (MS); criminal justice (MS); English education (M Ed); history education (M Ed); mathematics education (M Ed); physical science (MSNS); social science secondary education (M Ed).

College of Business *Degree program information:* Part-time and evening/weekend programs available. Postbaccalaureate distance learning degree programs offered (minimal on-campus study). Offers accountancy (MPAC); business (MBA, MCA, MPA); commercial aviation (MCA); management (MBA); marketing (MBA).

College of Education *Degree program information:* Part-time and evening/weekend programs available. Offers administration and supervision (M Ed); administrative and supervision (Ed S); counseling (M Ed); counselor education (Ed D); education (M Ed, MAT, Ed D, Ed S); educational administration and supervision (Ed S); educational leadership (M Ed, Ed D); elementary education (M Ed, MAT, Ed D, Ed S); higher education (Ed D); physical education and recreation (M Ed); secondary education (Ed S); special education (M Ed); teaching (Ed D).

School of Nursing *Degree program information:* Part-time programs available. Offers family nurse practitioner (MSN); nurse administrator (MSN); nurse educator (MSN). Electronic applications accepted.

DENVER SEMINARY, Littleton, CO 80120

General Information Independent-religious, coed, graduate-only institution. *Enrollment by degree level:* 248 first professional, 403 master's, 144 doctoral, 15 other advanced degrees. *Graduate faculty:* 23 full-time (4 women), 94 part-time/adjunct (39 women). *Tuition:* Full-time $12,450; part-time $510 per credit hour. *Graduate housing:* Rooms and/or apartments available on a first-come, first-served basis to single and married students. Housing application deadline: 6/1. *Student services:* Campus employment opportunities, campus safety program, career counseling, free psychological counseling, international student services, low-cost health insurance, services for students with disabilities, writing training. *Library facilities:* Carey S. Thomas Library. *Online resources:* library catalog, access to other libraries' catalogs. *Collection:* 175,000 titles, 500 serial subscriptions.

Computer facilities: 32 computers available on campus for general student use. A campuswide network can be accessed from student residence rooms and from off campus. Online class registration is available. *Web address:* http://www.denverseminary.edu/.

General Application Contact: Adam Kennerly, Director of Admissions, 303-357-5801, Fax: 303-783-3122, E-mail: info@denverseminary.edu.

GRADUATE UNITS

Graduate and Professional Programs *Degree program information:* Part-time and evening/weekend programs available. Postbaccalaureate distance learning degree programs offered. Offers apologetics (Certificate); biblical studies (MA); Christian formation and soul care (MA, Certificate); Christian studies (MA, Certificate); church and parachurch leadership (D Min); counseling licensure (MA); counseling ministry (MA); intercultural ministry (Certificate); leadership (MA, Certificate); marriage and family counseling (D Min); pastoral ministry (D Min); philosophy of religion (MA); spiritual guidance (Certificate); theology (M Div, Certificate); worship (Certificate); youth and family ministry (MA). Electronic applications accepted.

DEPAUL UNIVERSITY, Chicago, IL 60604-2287

General Information Independent-religious, coed, university. *Enrollment:* 24,352 graduate, professional, and undergraduate students; 4,169 full-time matriculated graduate/professional students (2,182 women), 3,184 part-time matriculated graduate/professional students (1,579 women). *Enrollment by degree level:* 1,024 first professional, 7,112 master's, 212 doctoral.

Graduate faculty: 899 full-time (406 women), 943 part-time/adjunct (430 women). *Graduate housing:* On-campus housing not available. *Student services:* Campus employment opportunities, campus safety program, career counseling, exercise/wellness program, free psychological counseling, international student services, low-cost health insurance, multicultural affairs office, services for students with disabilities, writing training. *Library facilities:* John T. Richardson Library plus 2 others. *Online resources:* library catalog, web page, access to other libraries' catalogs. *Collection:* 897,564 titles, 28,514 serial subscriptions, 27,242 audiovisual materials. *Research affiliation:* Civic Federation (public services), Metro Chicago Information Center (public services), International Institute of Higher Studies in the Criminal Sciences (law).

Computer facilities: 1,500 computers available on campus for general student use. A campuswide network can be accessed from student residence rooms and from off campus. Online class registration is available. *Web address:* http://www.depaul.edu/.

General Application Contact: Information Contact, 312-362-6709.

GRADUATE UNITS

Charles H. Kellstadt Graduate School of Business Students: 1,343 full-time (534 women), 839 part-time (320 women); includes 284 minority (59 African Americans, 7 American Indian/Alaska Native, 149 Asian Americans or Pacific Islanders, 69 Hispanic Americans), 219 international. Average age 27. 1,276 applicants, 48% accepted, 408 enrolled. *Faculty:* 148 full-time (68 women). Expenses: Contact institution. *Financial support:* In 2008–09, 12 research assistantships (averaging $25,768 per year) were awarded; career-related internships or fieldwork, Federal Work-Study, institutionally sponsored loans, scholarships/grants, tuition waivers (full and partial), and unspecified assistantships also available. Support available to part-time students. Financial award application deadline: 4/1. In 2008, 657 master's awarded. *Degree program information:* Part-time and evening/weekend programs available. Offers applied economics (MBA); behavioral finance (MBA); brand management (MBA); business (M Acc, MA, MBA, MS, MSA, MSEPA, MSF, MSHR, MSMA, MSRE, MST); computational finance (MS); customer relationship management (MBA); economics (MA); economics and policy analysis (MA); entrepreneurship (MBA); finance (MBA, MSF); financial analysis (MBA); financial management and control (MBA); health sector management (MBA); human resource management (MBA, MSHR); integrated marketing communication (MBA); international business (MBA); international marketing and finance (MBA); leadership/change management (MBA); management planning and strategy (MBA); managerial finance (MBA); marketing analysis (MSMA); marketing and management (MBA); marketing strategy and analysis (MBA); marketing strategy and planning (MBA); new product management (MBA); operations management (MBA); real estate (MS); real estate finance and investment (MBA); sales leadership (MBA); strategy, execution and valuation (MBA). *Application deadline:* For fall admission, 7/1 for domestic students, 6/1 for international students; for winter admission, 10/1 for domestic students, 9/1 for international students; for spring admission, 2/1 for domestic students, 1/1 for international students. Applications are processed on a rolling basis. *Application fee:* $60. Electronic applications accepted. *Application Contact:* Dustin Carnwell, Director of Recruiting and Admission, 312-362-8810, Fax: 312-362-6677, E-mail: kgsb@depaul.edu. *Assistant Dean and Director,* Robert T. Ryan, 312-362-8810, Fax: 312-362-6677, E-mail: rryan1@depaul.edu.

School of Accountancy and Management Information Systems *Faculty:* 30 full-time (9 women), 54 part-time/adjunct (7 women). Expenses: Contact institution. *Financial support:* In 2008–09, 7 research assistantships with full tuition reimbursements (averaging $4,100 per year) were awarded; institutionally sponsored loans also available. Financial award application deadline: 4/2. In 2008, 141 master's awarded. *Degree program information:* Part-time and evening/weekend programs available. Offers accountancy (M Acc, MSA); business information technology (MS); e-business (MBA, MS); financial management and control (MBA); management accounting (MBA); management information systems (MBA); taxation (MST). *Application deadline:* For fall admission, 7/1 for domestic students; for winter admission, 10/1 for domestic students; for spring admission, 2/1 for domestic students. Applications are processed on a rolling basis. *Application fee:* $60. *Application Contact:* Christopher E. Kinsella, Director of Cohort MBA Programs, 312-362-8810, Fax: 312-362-6677, E-mail: kgsb@depaul.edu.

College of Communication Students: 135 full-time (106 women), 43 part-time (35 women); includes 49 minority (25 African Americans, 7 Asian Americans or Pacific Islanders, 17 Hispanic Americans), 8 international. Average age 29. 242 applicants, 47% accepted, 68 enrolled. *Faculty:* 31 full-time (17 women), 15 part-time/adjunct (7 women). Expenses: Contact institution. *Financial support:* In 2008–09, 8 students received support, including 4 research assistantships with partial tuition reimbursements available, 2 teaching assistantships with full tuition reimbursements available (averaging $12,000 per year); fellowships with full tuition reimbursements available, career-related internships or fieldwork, scholarships/grants, and tuition waivers (partial) also available. Support available to part-time students. Financial award applicants required to submit FAFSA. In 2008, 64 master's awarded. *Degree program information:* Part-time and evening/weekend programs available. Offers journalism (MA); media, culture and society (MA); organizational and multicultural communication (MA); public relations and advertising (MA). *Application fee:* $40. Electronic applications accepted. *Application Contact:* Ann Spittle, Director of Graduate Admission, 773-325-8369, Fax: 773-325-2395, E-mail: aspittle@depaul.edu. *Dean,* Dr. Jacqueline Taylor, 773-325-7216, Fax: 773-325-7584, E-mail: jtaylor@depaul.edu.

College of Computing and Digital Media Students: 966 full-time (254 women), 932 part-time (217 women); includes 429 minority (194 African Americans, 3 American Indian/Alaska Native, 149 Asian Americans or Pacific Islanders, 83 Hispanic Americans), 395 international. Average age 31. 930 applicants, 73% accepted, 319 enrolled. *Faculty:* 76 full-time (15 women), 182 part-time/adjunct (43 women). Expenses: Contact institution. *Financial support:* In 2008–09, 69 students received support, including 2 fellowships with full tuition reimbursements available (averaging $18,000 per year), 75 teaching assistantships with full and partial tuition reimbursements available (averaging $5,780 per year); research assistantships, Federal Work-Study, scholarships/grants, tuition waivers (full and partial), and unspecified assistantships also available. Support available to part-time students. Financial award application deadline: 4/30; financial award applicants required to submit FAFSA. In 2008, 444 master's, 4 doctorates awarded. *Degree program information:* Part-time and evening/weekend programs available. Postbaccalaureate distance learning degree programs offered (no on-campus study). Offers business information technology (MS); computational finance (MS); computer game development (MS); computer graphics and motion technology (MS); computer science (MS, PhD); computer, information and network security (MS); digital cinema (MFA, MS); e-commerce technology (MS); human-computer interaction (MS); information systems (MS); information technology (MA); information technology project management (MS); software engineering (MS); telecommunications systems (MS). *Application deadline:* For fall admission, 8/15 priority date for domestic students, 6/1 priority date for international students; for winter admission, 2/15 priority date for domestic students, 9/15 priority date for international students; for spring admission, 3/1 priority date for domestic students, 12/15 priority date for international students. Applications are processed on a rolling basis. *Application fee:* $25. Electronic applications accepted. *Application Contact:* Dr. Liz Friedman, Assistant Dean of Student Services, 312-362-8714, Fax: 312-362-5327, E-mail: efriedm2@cdm.depaul.edu. *Dean,* Dr. David Miller, 312-362-8381, Fax: 312-362-5185.

College of Law Students: 1,030 full-time (524 women), 14 part-time (8 women); includes 237 minority (68 African Americans, 2 American Indian/Alaska Native, 59 Asian Americans or Pacific Islanders, 108 Hispanic Americans), 29 international. Average age 27. 5,141 applicants, 37% accepted, 370 enrolled. *Faculty:* 60 full-time (23 women), 65 part-time/adjunct (27 women). Expenses: Contact institution. *Financial support:* In 2008–09, 534 students received support, including 35 fellowships with partial tuition reimbursements available, 84 research assistantships (averaging $1,400 per year), 24 teaching assistantships with partial tuition reimbursements available; career-related internships or fieldwork, Federal Work-Study, scholarships/grants, and tuition waivers (full and partial) also available. Support available to part-time students. Financial award application deadline: 3/1; financial award applicants required to submit FAFSA. In 2008, 308 JDs awarded. *Degree program information:* Part-time and evening/weekend programs available. Offers health law (LL M); intellectual property law (LL M); international law (LL M); law (JD); tax law (LL M). *Application deadline:* For fall admission, 3/1 for domestic and international students. Applications are processed on a rolling basis. *Application fee:* $60. Electronic applications accepted. *Application Contact:* Michael S Burns, Director of Law Admission and Associate Dean, 312-362-6831, Fax: 312-362-5280, E-mail: lawinfo@depaul.edu. *Dean,* Glen Weissenberger, 312-362-8088, E-mail: gweissen@depaul.edu.

College of Liberal Arts and Sciences Students: 1,142 full-time (613 women), 786 part-time (544 women); includes 414 minority (204 African Americans, 5 American Indian/Alaska Native, 79 Asian Americans or Pacific Islanders, 126 Hispanic Americans), 67 international. Average age 29. 1,779 applicants, 39% accepted, 405 enrolled. *Faculty:* 336 full-time (162 women), 211 part-time/adjunct (102 women). Expenses: Contact institution. *Financial support:* In 2008–09, 80 research assistantships with full and partial tuition reimbursements, 20 teaching assistantships were awarded; career-related internships or fieldwork, Federal Work-Study, institutionally sponsored loans, scholarships/grants, traineeships, tuition waivers (full and partial), and unspecified assistantships also available. Support available to part-time students. Financial award applicants required to submit FAFSA. In 2008, 402 master's, 22 doctorates awarded. *Degree program information:* Part-time and evening/weekend programs available. Postbaccalaureate distance learning degree programs offered (minimal on-campus study). Offers advanced practice nursing (MS); applied mathematics (MS); applied physics (MS); applied statistics (MS, Certificate); biochemistry (MS); biological sciences (MA, MS); chemistry (MS); clinical psychology (MA, PhD); English (MA); experimental psychology (MA, PhD); general psychology (MS); history (MA); industrial/organizational psychology (MA, PhD); interdisciplinary studies (MA, MS); liberal arts and sciences (MA, MS, PhD, Certificate); masters entry into nursing practice (MS); mathematics education (MA); nurse anesthesia (MS); philosophy (MA, PhD); polymer chemistry and coatings technology (MS); sociology (MA); writing and publishing (MA). *Application deadline:* Applications are processed on a rolling basis. *Application fee:* $40. Electronic applications accepted. *Application Contact:* Ann Spittle, Director of Graduate Admission, 773-325-7315, Fax: 773-325-2395, E-mail: graduatelas@depaul.edu. *Dean,* Charles Suchar, 773-325-7305, Fax: 773-325-7304, E-mail: csuchar@depaul.edu.

School for New Learning Students: 41 full-time (29 women), 94 part-time (72 women); includes 66 minority (29 African Americans, 1 American Indian/Alaska Native, 25 Asian Americans or Pacific Islanders, 11 Hispanic Americans), 1 international. Average age 42. 30 applicants, 80% accepted. *Faculty:* 8 full-time (2 women), 9 part-time/adjunct (5 women). Expenses: Contact institution. *Financial support:* In 2008–09, 7 students received support. Scholarships/grants and tuition waivers (partial) available. Financial award applicants required to submit FAFSA. In 2008, 20 master's awarded. *Degree program information:* Part-time and evening/weekend programs available. Offers applied technology (MS); educating adults (MA); integrated professional studies (MA). *Application deadline:* For fall admission, 9/1 priority date for domestic students; for spring admission, 3/1 priority date for domestic students. Applications are processed on a rolling basis. *Application fee:* $25. Electronic applications accepted. *Application Contact:* Sarah Hellstrom, Assistant Director, 312-362-5744, Fax: 312-362-8809, E-mail: shellstr@depaul.edu. *Program Director,* Dr. Russ Rogers, 312-362-8512, Fax: 312-362-8809, E-mail: rrogers@depaul.edu.

School of Education Students: 863 full-time (694 women), 447 part-time (332 women); includes 262 minority (131 African Americans, 2 American Indian/Alaska Native, 53 Asian Americans or Pacific Islanders, 76 Hispanic Americans), 16 international. Average age 30. 635 applicants, 74% accepted, 318 enrolled. *Faculty:* 61 full-time (40 women), 66 part-time/adjunct (41 women). Expenses: Contact institution. *Financial support:* In 2008–09, 14 research assistantships with tuition reimbursements (averaging $5,800 per year) were awarded; career-related internships or fieldwork also available. In 2008, 604 master's, 5 doctorates awarded. *Degree program information:* Part-time and evening/weekend programs available. Offers bilingual and bicultural education (M Ed, MA); curriculum studies (M Ed, MA, Ed D); education (Ed D); educational leadership (M Ed, MA, Ed D); human development and learning (MA); human services and counseling (M Ed, MA); reading and learning disabilities (M Ed, MA); social culture studies in education and development (M Ed, MA); teaching and learning (early childhood, elementary and secondary) (M Ed); teaching and learning (early childhood, elementary, and secondary) (MA). *Application deadline:* Applications are processed on a rolling basis. *Application fee:* $40. Electronic applications accepted. *Application Contact:* Brandon Washington, Data Project Manager, 773-325-1152, Fax: 773-325-2270, E-mail: bwashin3@depaul.edu. *Dean,* Dr. Marie Donovan, 773-325-7581, Fax: 773-325-7713, E-mail: mdonovan@depaul.edu.

School of Music Students: 61 full-time (23 women), 65 part-time (31 women); includes 13 minority (2 African Americans, 6 Asian Americans or Pacific Islanders, 5 Hispanic Americans), 26 international. Average age 24. 175 applicants, 46% accepted. *Faculty:* 11 full-time (2 women), 50 part-time/adjunct (14 women). Expenses: Contact institution. *Financial support:* In 2008–09, 4 fellowships with partial tuition reimbursements were awarded; teaching assistantships, career-related internships or fieldwork, Federal Work-Study, scholarships/grants, and tuition waivers also available. Support available to part-time students. Financial award application deadline: 1/15. In 2008, 40 master's, 5 Certificates awarded. *Degree program information:* Part-time and evening/weekend programs available. Offers applied music (performance) (MM, Certificate); jazz studies (MM); music composition (MM); music education (MM). *Application deadline:* For fall admission, 1/15 priority date for domestic and international students. Applications are processed on a rolling basis. Electronic applications accepted. *Application Contact:* Ross Beacraft, Director of Admissions, 773-325-7444, Fax: 773-325-7429, E-mail: rbeacraf@depaul.edu. *Dean,* Dr. Donald E. Casey, 773-325-7256, E-mail: Dcasey@depaul.edu.

School of Public Service Students: 90 full-time (59 women), 204 part-time (154 women); includes 101 minority (63 African Americans, 10 Asian Americans or Pacific Islanders, 28 Hispanic Americans), 11 international. Average age 26. 162 applicants, 100% accepted, 94 enrolled. *Faculty:* 14 full-time (3 women), 43 part-time/adjunct (24 women). Expenses: Contact institution. *Financial support:* In 2008–09, 60 students received support, including 3 research assistantships with full tuition reimbursements available (averaging $7,000 per year); career-related internships or fieldwork, Federal Work-Study, institutionally sponsored loans, scholarships/grants, tuition waivers (partial), and unspecified assistantships also available. Support available to part-time students. Financial award application deadline: 7/1; financial award applicants required to submit FAFSA. In 2008, 108 master's awarded. *Degree program information:* Part-time and evening/weekend programs available. Postbaccalaureate distance learning degree programs offered (minimal on-campus study). Offers financial administration management (Certificate); health administration (Certificate); health law and policy (MS); international public services (MS); leadership and policy studies (MS); metropolitan planning (Certificate); public administration (MPA); public service management (MS); public services (Certificate). *Application deadline:* Applications are processed on a rolling basis. *Application fee:* $40. Electronic applications accepted. *Application Contact:* Megan B. Balderston, Director of Admissions and Marketing, 312-362-5565, Fax: 312-362-5506, E-mail: pubserv@depaul.edu. *Director,* Dr. J. Patrick Murphy, 312-362-5608, Fax: 312-362-5506, E-mail: jpmurphy@depaul.edu.

The Theatre School Students: 39 full-time (20 women); includes 7 minority (6 African Americans, 1 Hispanic American). Average age 28. 233 applicants, 8% accepted, 14 enrolled. *Faculty:* 18 full-time (9 women), 24 part-time/adjunct (13 women). Expenses: Contact institution. *Financial support:* In 2008–09, 38 students received support, including 38 fellowships (averaging $16,600 per year); career-related internships or fieldwork, Federal Work-Study, institutionally sponsored loans, and scholarships/grants also available. Financial award application deadline: 2/15; financial award applicants required to submit FAFSA. In 2008, 11 master's awarded. Offers acting (MFA); arts leadership (MFA); directing (MFA). *Application deadline:* For fall admission, 1/15 priority date for domestic and international students. *Application fee:* $65. Electronic applications accepted. *Application Contact:* Jason Beck, Director of Admissions, 773-325-7999, Fax: 773-325-7920, E-mail: jbeck1@depaul.edu. *Dean,* John Culbert, 773-325-7954, Fax: 773-325-7920, E-mail: jculbert@depaul.edu.

DESALES UNIVERSITY, Center Valley, PA 18034-9568

General Information Independent-religious, coed, comprehensive institution. *Enrollment:* 3,059 graduate, professional, and undergraduate students; 51 full-time matriculated graduate/professional students (33 women), 722 part-time matriculated graduate/professional students (436 women). *Enrollment by degree level:* 773 master's. *Graduate faculty:* 41. *Tuition:* Full-time $16,720. *Required fees:* $800. Tuition and fees vary according to program. *Graduate*

DeSales University (continued)

housing: On-campus housing not available. *Student services:* International student services, multicultural affairs office, services for students with disabilities. *Library facilities:* Trexler Library. *Online resources:* library catalog, web page, access to other libraries' catalogs. *Collection:* 157,761 titles, 12,600 serial subscriptions, 7,699 audiovisual materials.

Computer facilities: 200 computers available on campus for general student use. A campuswide network can be accessed from student residence rooms and from off campus. Online class registration is available. *Web address:* http://www.desales.edu.

General Application Contact: Caryn Stopper, Director of Graduate Admissions, 610-282-1100 Ext. 1768, Fax: 610-282-0525, E-mail: caryn.stopper@desales.edu.

GRADUATE UNITS

Graduate Division Students: 51 full-time (33 women), 722 part-time (436 women). *Faculty:* 41. Expenses: Contact institution. *Financial support:* Career-related internships or fieldwork available. Support available to part-time students. Financial award applicants required to submit FAFSA. In 2008, 233 master's awarded. Offers accounting (MBA); adult advanced practice nurse specialist (MSN); business administration (MBA); certified nurse midwives (MSN); certified nurse practitioners (MSN); computer information systems (MBA); criminal justice (MACJ); elementary education (M Ed); family nurse practitioner (MSN); finance (MBA); health care systems management (MBA); information systems (MSIS); interdisciplinary (M Ed); management (MBA); marketing (MBA); mathematics (M Ed); nurse educator (MSN); physician assistant studies (MSPAS); project management (MBA); self-design (MBA); special education (M Ed); technology in education (K-12) (M Ed); TESOL/ESL (M Ed). *Application deadline:* Applications are processed on a rolling basis. *Application Contact:* Caryn Stopper, Director of Graduate Admissions, 610-282-1100 Ext. 1768, Fax: 610-282-0525, E-mail: caryn.stopper@desales.edu. *Director of Graduate Admissions*, Caryn Stopper, 610-282-1100 Ext. 1768, Fax: 610-282-0525, E-mail: caryn.stopper@desales.edu.

DES MOINES UNIVERSITY, Des Moines, IA 50312-4104

General Information Independent, coed, graduate-only institution. *Enrollment:* 1,386 full-time matriculated graduate/professional students (762 women), 343 part-time matriculated graduate/professional students (189 women). *Enrollment by degree level:* 1,385 first professional, 344 master's. *Graduate faculty:* 68 full-time (28 women), 22 part-time/adjunct (6 women). *Graduate housing:* On-campus housing not available. *Student services:* Campus employment opportunities, campus safety program, career counseling, exercise/wellness program, free psychological counseling, international student services, low-cost health insurance, multicultural affairs office. *Library facilities:* University Library. *Online resources:* library catalog, web page, access to other libraries' catalogs. *Collection:* 58,039 titles, 581 serial subscriptions, 5,074 audiovisual materials.

Computer facilities: A campuswide network can be accessed from off campus. Online class registration, online classes are available. *Web address:* http://www.dmu.edu/.

General Application Contact: Margie Gehringer, Director of Enrollment Management, 515-271-7498, Fax: 515-271-7190, E-mail: margie.gehringer@dmu.edu.

GRADUATE UNITS

College of Health Sciences Students: 308 full-time (169 women), 318 part-time (175 women); includes 99 minority (25 African Americans, 1 American Indian/Alaska Native, 68 Asian Americans or Pacific Islanders, 5 Hispanic Americans). Average age 24. 1,117 applicants, 40% accepted, 358 enrolled. *Faculty:* 14 full-time (7 women), 5 part-time/adjunct (3 women). Expenses: Contact institution. *Financial support:* Career-related internships or fieldwork, institutionally sponsored loans, scholarships/grants, and university employment available. Support available to part-time students. Financial award application deadline: 4/15; financial award applicants required to submit FAFSA. *Degree program information:* Part-time and evening/weekend programs available. Postbaccalaureate distance learning degree programs offered (minimal on-campus study). Offers health sciences (MHA, MPH, MS, DPT); healthcare administration (MHA); physical therapy (DPT); physician assistant (MS); public health (MPH). *Application deadline:* Applications are processed on a rolling basis. Electronic applications accepted. *Application Contact:* Josh Kvinlaug, Admissions Coordinator, 515-271-7875, Fax: 515-271-7145, E-mail: paadmit@dmu.edu. *Dean*, Jodi Cahalan, PhD, 515-271-1415, E-mail: jodi.cahalan@dmu.edu.

College of Osteopathic Medicine Students: 850 full-time (412 women); includes 93 minority (6 African Americans, 1 American Indian/Alaska Native, 72 Asian Americans or Pacific Islanders, 14 Hispanic Americans). Average age 25. 3,273 applicants, 14% accepted, 221 enrolled. *Faculty:* 40 full-time (16 women), 22 part-time/adjunct (4 women). Expenses: Contact institution. *Financial support:* In 2008–09, 102 students received support, including 0 fellowships with tuition reimbursements available (averaging $6,000 per year); institutionally sponsored loans, scholarships/grants, and university employment also available. Support available to part-time students. Financial award application deadline: 7/15; financial award applicants required to submit FAFSA. In 2008, 198 DOs awarded. Offers osteopathic medicine (DO). *Application deadline:* For fall admission, 2/1 for domestic students, 2/1 priority date for international students. Applications are processed on a rolling basis. *Application fee:* $50. Electronic applications accepted. *Application Contact:* Jamie Rehmann, Director of Admissions, 515-271-1451, Fax: 515-271-7163, E-mail: doadmit@dmu.edu. *Dean*, Dr. Kendall Reed, DO, 515-271-1515, Fax: 515-271-1532, E-mail: kendall.reed@dmu.edu.

College of Podiatric Medicine and Surgery Students: 221 full-time (73 women); includes 22 minority (4 African Americans, 1 American Indian/Alaska Native, 13 Asian Americans or Pacific Islanders, 4 Hispanic Americans). Average age 24. 391 applicants, 23% accepted, 58 enrolled. *Faculty:* 5 full-time (1 woman), 1 part-time/adjunct (0 women). Expenses: Contact institution. *Financial support:* In 2008–09, 82 students received support. Institutionally sponsored loans, scholarships/grants, and university employment available. Support available to part-time students. Financial award application deadline: 7/15; financial award applicants required to submit FAFSA. In 2008, 40 DPMs awarded. Offers podiatric medicine and surgery (DPM). *Application deadline:* For fall admission, 6/1 for domestic and international students. Applications are processed on a rolling basis. *Application fee:* $0. Electronic applications accepted. *Application Contact:* Gina Smith, Admissions Coordinator, 515-271-7497, E-mail: cpmsadmit@dmu.edu. *Dean*, Dr. Robert Yoho, 515-271-1464, Fax: 515-271-1521, E-mail: robert.yoho@dmu.edu.

DEVRY UNIVERSITY, Houston, TX 77041

General Information Proprietary, coed, comprehensive institution.

GRADUATE UNITS

Keller Graduate School of Management Offers management (MAFM, MBA, MISM, MPM, Graduate Certificate).

DEVRY UNIVERSITY, Phoenix, AZ 85021-2995

General Information Proprietary, coed, comprehensive institution.

GRADUATE UNITS

Keller Graduate School of Management Offers management (MAFM, MBA, MHRM, MISM, MNCM, MPA, MPM, Graduate Certificate).

DEVRY UNIVERSITY, Tampa, FL 33607-5901

General Information Proprietary, coed, comprehensive institution.

GRADUATE UNITS

Keller Graduate School of Management Offers management (MAFM, MBA, MHRM, MISM, MNCM, MPA, MPM, Graduate Certificate).

DEVRY UNIVERSITY, Orlando, FL 32839

General Information Proprietary, coed, comprehensive institution.

GRADUATE UNITS

Keller Graduate School of Management Offers management (MAFM, MBA, MHRM, MISM, MNCM, MPA, MPM, Graduate Certificate).

DEVRY UNIVERSITY, Mesa, AZ 85210-2011

General Information Proprietary, coed, comprehensive institution.

GRADUATE UNITS

Keller Graduate School of Management Offers management (MAFM, MBA, MHRM, MISM, MNCM, MPA, MPM, Graduate Certificate).

DEVRY UNIVERSITY, Elk Grove, CA 95758

General Information Proprietary, coed, comprehensive institution.

GRADUATE UNITS

Keller Graduate School of Management Offers management (MAFM, MBA, MHRM, MISM, MNCM, MPA, MPM, Graduate Certificate).

DEVRY UNIVERSITY, Fremont, CA 94555

General Information Proprietary, coed, comprehensive institution.

GRADUATE UNITS

Keller Graduate School of Management Offers management (MAFM, MBA, MHRM, MISM, MNCM, MPA, MPM, Graduate Certificate).

DEVRY UNIVERSITY, Irvine, CA 92612-1682

General Information Proprietary, coed, comprehensive institution.

GRADUATE UNITS

Keller Graduate School of Management Offers management (MAFM, MBA, MHRM, MISM, MNCM, MPA, MPM, Graduate Certificate).

DEVRY UNIVERSITY, Long Beach, CA 90806

General Information Proprietary, coed, comprehensive institution.

GRADUATE UNITS

Keller Graduate School of Management Offers management (MAFM, MBA, MHRM, MISM, MNCM, MPA, MPM, Graduate Certificate).

DEVRY UNIVERSITY, Palmdale, CA 93550

General Information Proprietary, coed, comprehensive institution.

GRADUATE UNITS

Keller Graduate School of Management Offers management (MAFM, MBA, MHRM, MPM, Graduate Certificate).

DEVRY UNIVERSITY, Pomona, CA 91768-2642

General Information Proprietary, coed, comprehensive institution.

GRADUATE UNITS

Keller Graduate School of Management Offers management (MAFM, MBA, MHRM, MISM, MNCM, MPA, MPM, Graduate Certificate).

DEVRY UNIVERSITY, San Diego, CA 92108-1633

General Information Proprietary, coed, comprehensive institution.

GRADUATE UNITS

Keller Graduate School of Management Offers management (MAFM, MBA, MHRM, MISM, MNCM, MPA, MPM, Graduate Certificate).

DEVRY UNIVERSITY, San Francisco, CA 94105-2472

General Information Proprietary, coed, comprehensive institution.

GRADUATE UNITS

Keller Graduate School of Management Offers management (MAFM, MBA, MHRM, MISM, MNCM, MPA, MPM, Graduate Certificate).

DEVRY UNIVERSITY, Kansas City, MO 64105-2112

General Information Proprietary, coed, comprehensive institution.

GRADUATE UNITS

Keller Graduate School of Management Offers management (MAFM, MBA, MHRM, MISM, MNCM, MPA, MPM, Graduate Certificate).

DEVRY UNIVERSITY, Colorado Springs, CO 80910

General Information Proprietary, coed, comprehensive institution.

GRADUATE UNITS

Keller Graduate School of Management Offers management (MAFM, MBA, MHRM, MISM, MNCM, MPA, MPM, Graduate Certificate).

DEVRY UNIVERSITY, Atlanta, GA 30305-1543

General Information Proprietary, coed, comprehensive institution.

GRADUATE UNITS

Keller Graduate School of Management Offers management (MAFM, MBA, MHRM, MISM, MNCM, MPA, MPM, Graduate Certificate).

DEVRY UNIVERSITY, Miami, FL 33131-5351

General Information Proprietary, coed, comprehensive institution.

GRADUATE UNITS

Keller Graduate School of Management Offers management (MAFM, MBA, MHRM, MISM, MNCM, MPA, MPM, Graduate Certificate).

DEVRY UNIVERSITY, Miramar, FL 33027-4150

General Information Proprietary, coed, comprehensive institution.

GRADUATE UNITS

Keller Graduate School of Management Offers management (MAFM, MBA, MHRM, MISM, MNCM, MPA, MPM, Graduate Certificate).

DEVRY UNIVERSITY, Alpharetta, GA 30004

General Information Proprietary, coed, comprehensive institution.

GRADUATE UNITS

Keller Graduate School of Management Offers management (MAFM, MBA, MHRM, MISM, MNCM, MPA, MPM, Graduate Certificate).

DEVRY UNIVERSITY, Decatur, GA 30030-2556

General Information Proprietary, coed, comprehensive institution.

GRADUATE UNITS

Keller Graduate School of Management Offers management (MAFM, MBA, MHRM, MISM, MNCM, MPA, MPM, Graduate Certificate).

DEVRY UNIVERSITY, Duluth, GA 30096-7671

General Information Proprietary, coed, comprehensive institution.

GRADUATE UNITS

Keller Graduate School of Management Offers management (MAFM, MBA, MHRM, MISM, MNCM, MPA, MPM, Graduate Certificate).

DEVRY UNIVERSITY, Elgin, IL 60123-9341

General Information Proprietary, coed, comprehensive institution.

GRADUATE UNITS

Keller Graduate School of Management Offers management (MAFM, MBA, MHRM, MISM, MNCM, MPA, MPM, Graduate Certificate).

DEVRY UNIVERSITY, Gurnee, IL 60031-9126

General Information Proprietary, coed, comprehensive institution.

GRADUATE UNITS

Keller Graduate School of Management Offers management (MAFM, MBA, MHRM, MISM, MNCM, MPA, MPM, Graduate Certificate).

DEVRY UNIVERSITY, Lincolnshire, IL 60069-4460

General Information Proprietary, coed, graduate-only institution.

GRADUATE UNITS

Keller Graduate School of Management Offers management (MAFM, MBA, MHRM, MISM, MNCM, MPA, MPM, Graduate Certificate).

DEVRY UNIVERSITY, Naperville, IL 60563-2361

General Information Proprietary, coed, comprehensive institution.

GRADUATE UNITS

Keller Graduate School of Management Offers management (MAFM, MBA, MHRM, MISM, MNCM, MPA, MPM, Graduate Certificate).

DEVRY UNIVERSITY, Oakbrook Terrace, IL 60181

General Information Proprietary, coed, comprehensive institution. *Graduate housing:* On-campus housing not available.

GRADUATE UNITS

Keller Graduate School of Management Offers accounting and financial management (MAFM); business administration (MBA); human resources management (MHRM); information systems management (MISM); network and communications management (MNCM); project management (MPM); public administration (MPA).

DEVRY UNIVERSITY, Schaumburg, IL 60173-5009

General Information Proprietary, coed, graduate-only institution.

GRADUATE UNITS

Keller Graduate School of Management Offers management (MAFM, MBA, MHRM, MISM, MNCM, MPA, MPM, Graduate Certificate).

DEVRY UNIVERSITY, Tinley Park, IL 60477

General Information Proprietary, coed, comprehensive institution.

GRADUATE UNITS

Keller Graduate School of Management Offers management (MAFM, MBA, MHRM, MISM, MNCM, MPA, MPM, Graduate Certificate).

DEVRY UNIVERSITY, Indianapolis, IN 46240-2158

General Information Proprietary, coed, comprehensive institution.

GRADUATE UNITS

Keller Graduate School of Management Offers management (MAFM, MBA, MHRM, MISM, MNCM, MPA, MPM, Graduate Certificate).

DEVRY UNIVERSITY, Merrillville, IN 46410-5673

General Information Proprietary, coed, comprehensive institution.

GRADUATE UNITS

Keller Graduate School of Management Offers management (MAFM, MBA, MHRM, MISM, MNCM, MPA, MPM, Graduate Certificate).

DEVRY UNIVERSITY, Bethesda, MD 20814-3304

General Information Proprietary, coed, comprehensive institution.

GRADUATE UNITS

Keller Graduate School of Management Offers management (MAFM, MBA, MHRM, MISM, MNCM, MPA, MPM, Graduate Certificate).

DEVRY UNIVERSITY, St. Louis, MO 63146-4020

General Information Proprietary, coed, comprehensive institution.

GRADUATE UNITS

Keller Graduate School of Management Offers management (MAFM, MBA, MHRM, MISM, MNCM, MPA, MPM, Graduate Certificate).

DEVRY UNIVERSITY, Henderson, NV 89074-7120

General Information Proprietary, coed, comprehensive institution.

GRADUATE UNITS

Keller Graduate School of Management Offers management (MAFM, MBA, MHRM, MISM, MNCM, MPA, MPM, Graduate Certificate).

DEVRY UNIVERSITY, Charlotte, NC 28211-3627

General Information Proprietary, coed, comprehensive institution.

GRADUATE UNITS

Keller Graduate School of Management Offers management (MAFM, MBA, MHRM, MISM, MNCM, MPA, MPM, Graduate Certificate).

DEVRY UNIVERSITY, Phoenix, AZ 85054

General Information Proprietary, coed, graduate-only institution.

GRADUATE UNITS

Keller Graduate School of Management Offers management (MAFM, MBA, MHRM, MISM, MNCM, MPA, MPM, Graduate Certificate).

DEVRY UNIVERSITY, Columbus, OH 43209-2705

General Information Proprietary, coed, comprehensive institution.

GRADUATE UNITS

Keller Graduate School of Management Offers management (MAFM, MBA, MHRM, MISM, MNCM, MPA, MPM, Graduate Certificate).

DEVRY UNIVERSITY, Seven Hills, OH 44131

General Information Proprietary, coed, comprehensive institution.

GRADUATE UNITS

Keller Graduate School of Management Offers management (MAFM, MBA, MHRM, MISM, MNCM, MPA, MPM, Graduate Certificate).

DEVRY UNIVERSITY, Portland, OR 97225-6651

General Information Proprietary, coed, comprehensive institution.

GRADUATE UNITS

Keller Graduate School of Management Offers management (MAFM, MBA, MHRM, MISM, MNCM, MPA, MPM, Graduate Certificate).

DEVRY UNIVERSITY, Chesterbrook, PA 19087-5612

General Information Proprietary, coed, comprehensive institution.

GRADUATE UNITS

Keller Graduate School of Management Offers management (MAFM, MBA, MHRM, MISM, MNCM, MPA, MPM, Graduate Certificate).

DEVRY UNIVERSITY, Fort Washington, PA 19034

General Information Proprietary, coed, comprehensive institution.

GRADUATE UNITS

Keller Graduate School of Management Offers management (MAFM, MBA, MHRM, MISM, MNCM, MPA, MPM, Graduate Certificate).

DEVRY UNIVERSITY, Pittsburgh, PA 15222-9123

General Information Proprietary, coed, comprehensive institution.

GRADUATE UNITS

Keller Graduate School of Management Offers management (MAFM, MBA, MHRM, MISM, MNCM, MPA, MPM, Graduate Certificate).

DEVRY UNIVERSITY, Irving, TX 75063-2439

General Information Proprietary, coed, comprehensive institution.

GRADUATE UNITS

Keller Graduate School of Management Offers management (MAFM, MBA, MHRM, MISM, MNCM, MPM, Graduate Certificate).

DEVRY UNIVERSITY, Richardson, TX 75080

General Information Proprietary, coed, comprehensive institution.

GRADUATE UNITS

Keller Graduate School of Management Offers management (MBA, Graduate Certificate).

DEVRY UNIVERSITY, Sandy, UT 84070

General Information Proprietary, coed, comprehensive institution.

GRADUATE UNITS

Keller Graduate School of Management Offers management (MAFM, MBA, MHRM, MISM, MNCM, MPA, MPM).

DEVRY UNIVERSITY, Arlington, VA 22202

General Information Proprietary, coed, comprehensive institution.

GRADUATE UNITS

Keller Graduate School of Management Offers management (MAFM, MBA, MHRM, MISM, MNCM, MPA, MPM, Graduate Certificate).

DEVRY UNIVERSITY, McLean, VA 22102-3832

General Information Proprietary, coed, comprehensive institution.

GRADUATE UNITS

Keller Graduate School of Management Offers management (MAFM, MBA, MHRM, MISM, MNCM, MPA, MPM, Graduate Certificate).

DEVRY UNIVERSITY, Bellevue, WA 98004-5519

General Information Proprietary, coed, comprehensive institution.

GRADUATE UNITS

Keller Graduate School of Management Offers management (MAFM, MBA, MHRM, MISM, MNCM, MPA, MPM, Graduate Certificate).

DEVRY UNIVERSITY, Federal Way, WA 98001

General Information Proprietary, coed, comprehensive institution.

GRADUATE UNITS

Keller Graduate School of Management Offers management (MAFM, MBA, MHRM, MISM, MNCM, MPA, MPM, Graduate Certificate).

DEVRY UNIVERSITY, Milwaukee, WI 53202-4107

General Information Proprietary, coed, comprehensive institution.

GRADUATE UNITS

Keller Graduate School of Management Offers management (MAFM, MBA, MHRM, MISM, MNCM, MPA, MPM, Graduate Certificate).

DEVRY UNIVERSITY, Waukesha, WI 53186-4047

General Information Proprietary, coed, comprehensive institution.

GRADUATE UNITS

Keller Graduate School of Management Offers management (MAFM, MBA, MHRM, MISM, MNCM, MPA, MPM, Graduate Certificate).

DIGIPEN INSTITUTE OF TECHNOLOGY, Redmond, WA 98052

General Information Proprietary, coed, comprehensive institution. *Enrollment:* 867 graduate, professional, and undergraduate students; 22 full-time matriculated graduate/professional students (2 women), 11 part-time matriculated graduate/professional students (1 woman). *Enrollment by degree level:* 33 master's. *Graduate faculty:* 15 full-time, 2 part-time/adjunct. Tuition and fees vary according to course load. *Graduate housing:* On-campus housing not available. *Student services:* Campus employment opportunities, career counseling, free psychological counseling, international student services, services for students with disabilities. *Library facilities:* DigiPen Library plus 2 others. *Online resources:* library catalog, web page. *Collection:* 4,834 titles, 52 serial subscriptions, 631 audiovisual materials.

Computer facilities: Computer purchase and lease plans are available. A campuswide network can be accessed. Online class registration is available. *Web address:* http://www.digipen.edu/.

General Application Contact: Office of Admissions, 866-478-5236, Fax: 425-558-0378, E-mail: admissions@digipen.edu.

GRADUATE UNITS

Master of Science in Computer Science Program Students: 25 full-time, 27 part-time; includes 1 African American, 4 Asian Americans or Pacific Islanders, 4 Hispanic Americans, 5 international. Average age 26. *Faculty:* 15 full-time, 2 part-time/adjunct. Expenses: Contact institution. *Financial support:* In 2008–09, 1 student received support, including 1 fellowship (averaging $11,268 per year); career-related internships or fieldwork and scholarships/grants also available. Financial award application deadline: 5/1. In 2008, 24 master's awarded.

DigiPen Institute of Technology (continued)

Degree program information: Part-time programs available. Offers computer science (MS). *Application deadline:* For fall admission, 2/1 priority date for domestic students; for spring admission, 7/1 for domestic students. Applications are processed on a rolling basis. *Application fee:* $35. Electronic applications accepted. *Application Contact:* Admissions Office, 425-558-0299, Fax: 425-558-0378, E-mail: admissions@digipen.edu. *Dean of Sciences*, Xin Li, 425-895-4425, E-mail: xli@digipen.edu.

DIGITAL MEDIA ARTS COLLEGE, Boca Raton, FL 33431

General Information Proprietary, coed, comprehensive institution.

GRADUATE UNITS

Graduate Programs Offers graphic design (MFA); special FX animation (MFA).

DOANE COLLEGE, Crete, NE 68333-2430

General Information Independent-religious, coed, comprehensive institution. *Graduate housing:* On-campus housing not available.

GRADUATE UNITS

Program in Counseling *Degree program information:* Evening/weekend programs available. Offers counseling (MAC).

Program in Education *Degree program information:* Part-time and evening/weekend programs available. Offers curriculum and instruction (M Ed); educational leadership (M Ed). Electronic applications accepted.

Program in Management *Degree program information:* Part-time and evening/weekend programs available. Offers management (MA).

DOMINICAN COLLEGE, Orangeburg, NY 10962-1210

General Information Independent, coed, comprehensive institution. *Graduate housing:* Room and/or apartments available on a first-come, first-served basis to single students; on-campus housing not available to married students.

GRADUATE UNITS

Division of Allied Health Offers allied health (MS, DPT); occupational therapy (MS); physical therapy (MS, DPT).

Division of Nursing *Degree program information:* Part-time and evening/weekend programs available. Offers family nurse practitioner (MSN); nursing (MSN).

Division of Teacher Education Offers childhood education (MS Ed); teacher education (MS Ed); teacher of students with disabilities (MS Ed); teacher of visually impaired (MS Ed).

MBA Program *Degree program information:* Evening/weekend programs available. Offers business administration (MBA). Electronic applications accepted.

See Close-Up on page 897.

DOMINICAN HOUSE OF STUDIES, PONTIFICAL FACULTY OF THE IMMACULATE CONCEPTION, Washington, DC 20017-1585

General Information Independent-religious, coed, primarily men, graduate-only institution. *Enrollment by degree level:* 53 first professional, 5 master's, 19 other advanced degrees. *Graduate faculty:* 10 full-time (1 woman), 9 part-time/adjunct (2 women). *Tuition:* Full-time $13,680; part-time $570 per credit. *Required fees:* $50 per semester. *Graduate housing:* On-campus housing not available. *Student services:* Career counseling, writing training. *Library facilities:* Dominican Theological Library. *Online resources:* library catalog, web page, access to other libraries' catalogs. *Collection:* 75,000 titles, 397 serial subscriptions, 350 audiovisual materials. *Research affiliation:* Washington Theological Consortium (academics/ecuminism), The Thomist (theological journal).

Computer facilities: 8 computers available on campus for general student use. A campuswide network can be accessed. Online course descriptions and academic calendar available. *Web address:* http://www.dhs.edu/.

General Application Contact: Tobias J Nathe, Registrar, 202-495-3836, Fax: 202-495-3873, E-mail: registrar@dhs.edu.

GRADUATE UNITS

Graduate and Professional Programs in Theology Students: 68 full-time (4 women), 9 part-time (3 women); includes 4 minority (1 Asian American or Pacific Islander, 3 Hispanic Americans), 24 international. Average age 32. 44 applicants, 95% accepted, 34 enrolled. *Faculty:* 10 full-time (1 woman), 9 part-time/adjunct (2 women). Expenses: Contact institution. *Financial support:* In 2008–09, 8 students received support. Career-related internships or fieldwork and Federal Work-Study available. Financial award application deadline: 6/30; financial award applicants required to submit FAFSA. In 2008, 1 first professional degree, 1 master's, 2 other advanced degrees awarded. *Degree program information:* Part-time programs available. Offers moral theology (STL); sacred scripture (STL); systematic theology (STL); theology (STB, MA). *Application deadline:* For fall admission, 7/1 priority date for domestic and international students; for spring admission, 12/1 priority date for domestic and international students. Applications are processed on a rolling basis. *Application fee:* $50. *Application Contact:* Tobias John Nathe, Registrar, 202-495-3836, Fax: 202-495-3873, E-mail: registrar@dhs.edu. *Academic Dean*, Fr. Gabriel O'Donnell, OP, 202-495-3832, Fax: 202-495-3873, E-mail: dean@dhs.edu.

DOMINICAN SCHOOL OF PHILOSOPHY AND THEOLOGY, Berkeley, CA 94708

General Information Independent-religious, coed, graduate-only institution. *Enrollment:* 68 full-time matriculated graduate/professional students (9 women), 32 part-time matriculated graduate/professional students (12 women). *Enrollment by degree level:* 25 first professional, 49 master's, 26 other advanced degrees. *Graduate faculty:* 15 full-time (3 women), 8 part-time/adjunct (1 woman). *Tuition:* Full-time $13,200; part-time $550 per unit. *Required fees:* $550 per unit. *Graduate housing:* Rooms and/or apartments available on a first-come, first-served basis to single and married students. *Student services:* Campus employment opportunities, career counseling, international student services, low-cost health insurance. *Library facilities:* Flora Lamson Hewlett Library. *Online resources:* web page. *Collection:* 450,000 titles, 1,500 serial subscriptions.

Computer facilities: 6 computers available on campus for general student use. Online class registration is available. *Web address:* http://www.dspt.edu/.

General Application Contact: John Knutsen, Director of Admissions, 510-883-2073, Fax: 510-849-1372, E-mail: admissions@dspt.edu.

GRADUATE UNITS

Graduate Programs *Degree program information:* Part-time programs available. Offers philosophy (MA); theology (M Div, Certificate). Electronic applications accepted.

DOMINICAN UNIVERSITY, River Forest, IL 60305-1099

General Information Independent-religious, coed, comprehensive institution. *Enrollment:* 3,413 graduate, professional, and undergraduate students; 334 full-time matriculated graduate/professional students (238 women), 1,050 part-time matriculated graduate/professional students (828 women). *Enrollment by degree level:* 1,379 master's, 5 other advanced degrees. *Graduate faculty:* 53 full-time (28 women), 169 part-time/adjunct (101 women). *Tuition:* Full-time $12,060; part-time $670 per credit hour. *Graduate housing:* Room and/or apartments available on a first-come, first-served basis to single students; on-campus housing not available to married students. Typical cost: $4680 per year ($7930 including board). Housing application deadline: 7/1. *Student services:* Campus employment opportunities, campus safety program, career counseling, child daycare facilities, free psychological counseling, international student services, low-cost health insurance, multicultural affairs office, teacher training, writing training. *Library facilities:* Rebecca Crown Library. *Online resources:* library catalog, web page, access to other libraries' catalogs. *Collection:* 348,474 titles, 30,249 serial subscriptions.

Computer facilities: Computer purchase and lease plans are available. 625 computers available on campus for general student use. A campuswide network can be accessed from student residence rooms and from off campus. Online class registration, online student account information, online financial aid information are available. *Web address:* http://www.dom.edu/.

General Application Contact: Mary Ann Rowan, Vice President of Enrollment Management, 708-524-6544, E-mail: marowan@dom.edu.

GRADUATE UNITS

Edward A. and Lois L. Brennan School of Business Students: 107 full-time (53 women), 164 part-time (97 women); includes 21 minority (5 African Americans, 4 Asian Americans or Pacific Islanders, 12 Hispanic Americans), 38 international. Average age 30. 110 applicants, 85% accepted, 78 enrolled. *Faculty:* 15 full-time (3 women), 26 part-time/adjunct (8 women). Expenses: Contact institution. *Financial support:* Career-related internships or fieldwork, tuition waivers (partial), and unspecified assistantships available. Support available to part-time students. Financial award applicants required to submit FAFSA. In 2008, 174 master's awarded. *Degree program information:* Part-time and evening/weekend programs available. Offers accounting (MSA); business administration (MBA); computer information systems (MSCIS); management information systems (MSMIS); organization management (MSOM). *Application deadline:* Applications are processed on a rolling basis. *Application fee:* $25. Electronic applications accepted. *Application Contact:* Linda Puvogel, Assistant Dean for Graduate Business Programs, 708-524-6507, Fax: 708-524-6939, E-mail: lpuvogel@dom.edu. *Dean*, Dr. Arvid Johnson, 708-524-6465, Fax: 708-524-6939, E-mail: ajohnson@dom.edu.

Graduate School of Library and Information Science Students: 125 full-time (96 women), 383 part-time (311 women); includes 61 minority (18 African Americans, 1 American Indian/Alaska Native, 14 Asian Americans or Pacific Islanders, 28 Hispanic Americans). Average age 35. 160 applicants, 94% accepted, 122 enrolled. *Faculty:* 15 full-time (8 women), 23 part-time/adjunct (16 women). Expenses: Contact institution. *Financial support:* Fellowships, research assistantships, career-related internships or fieldwork, Federal Work-Study, scholarships/grants, and tuition waivers (partial) available. Support available to part-time students. Financial award application deadline: 4/15; financial award applicants required to submit FAFSA. In 2008, 256 master's, 3 other advanced degrees awarded. *Degree program information:* Part-time and evening/weekend programs available. Postbaccalaureate distance learning degree programs offered (minimal on-campus study). Offers library and information science (MLIS); special studies (CSS). *Application deadline:* For fall admission, 6/1 priority date for domestic students; for winter admission, 3/1 priority date for domestic students; for spring admission, 10/1 priority date for domestic students. Applications are processed on a rolling basis. *Application fee:* $25. *Application Contact:* Dr. Susan Roman, Dean, 708-524-6986, Fax: 708-524-6657, E-mail: sroman@dom.edu. *Dean*, Dr. Susan Roman, 708-524-6986, Fax: 708-524-6657, E-mail: sroman@dom.edu.

Graduate School of Social Work Students: 112 full-time (105 women), 88 part-time (82 women); includes 29 minority (22 African Americans, 1 American Indian/Alaska Native, 2 Asian Americans or Pacific Islanders, 4 Hispanic Americans). Average age 32. 122 applicants, 71% accepted, 57 enrolled. *Faculty:* 6 full-time (3 women), 14 part-time/adjunct (5 women). Expenses: Contact institution. *Financial support:* In 2008–09, 45 students received support, including 4 research assistantships (averaging $4,000 per year); scholarships/grants and unspecified assistantships also available. In 2008, 62 master's awarded. *Degree program information:* Part-time programs available. Offers social work (MSW). *Application deadline:* For fall admission, 7/1 for domestic and international students; for spring admission, 11/1 for domestic and international students. Applications are processed on a rolling basis. *Application fee:* $25. Electronic applications accepted. *Application Contact:* Felicia L. Townsend, Assistant Dean of Recruitment, Admissions and Marketing, 708-771-5298, Fax: 708-366-3446, E-mail: ftownsend@dom.edu. *Dean*, Dr. Mark Rodgers, 708-366-3316, E-mail: mrodgers@dom.edu.

School of Education Students: 21 full-time (16 women), 383 part-time (325 women); includes 65 minority (24 African Americans, 3 American Indian/Alaska Native, 6 Asian Americans or Pacific Islanders, 32 Hispanic Americans), 2 international. Average age 33. 140 applicants, 84% accepted, 89 enrolled. *Faculty:* 15 full-time (11 women), 26 part-time/adjunct (18 women). Expenses: Contact institution. *Financial support:* Career-related internships or fieldwork, scholarships/grants, and tuition waivers (partial) available. Support available to part-time students. Financial award application deadline: 8/15; financial award applicants required to submit FAFSA. In 2008, 184 master's awarded. *Degree program information:* Part-time and evening/weekend programs available. Postbaccalaureate distance learning degree programs offered. Offers curriculum and instruction (MA Ed); early childhood education (MS); education (MAT); educational administration (MA); elementary (online) (MS); English as a second language (online) (MS); reading (online) (MS); special education (MS). *Application deadline:* Applications are processed on a rolling basis. *Application fee:* $25. *Application Contact:* Keven Hansen, Coordinator of Recruitment and Admissions, 708-524-6921, Fax: 708-524-6665, E-mail: educate@dom.edu. *Dean*, Dr. Colleen Reardon, 718-524-6643, Fax: 708-524-6665, E-mail: creardon@dom.edu.

School of Leadership and Continuing Studies Students: 8 full-time (7 women), 53 part-time (34 women); includes 19 minority (16 African Americans, 3 Hispanic Americans). Average age 41. *Faculty:* 10 part-time/adjunct (3 women). Expenses: Contact institution. In 2008, 11 master's awarded. *Degree program information:* Part-time and evening/weekend programs available. Offers leadership (MA); organizational leadership (MSOL). *Application deadline:* Applications are processed on a rolling basis. *Application fee:* $25. *Application Contact:* Monica Halloran, Associate Director of Academic Advising, 708-714-9007, Fax: 708-714-9126, E-mail: mhallora@dom.edu. *Executive Director*, Dr. Bryan J. Watkins, 708-714-9001, E-mail: bwatkins@dom.edu.

DOMINICAN UNIVERSITY OF CALIFORNIA, San Rafael, CA 94901-2298

General Information Independent-religious, coed, comprehensive institution. *Enrollment:* 2,071 graduate, professional, and undergraduate students; 347 full-time matriculated graduate/professional students (268 women), 266 part-time matriculated graduate/professional students (198 women). *Enrollment by degree level:* 435 master's, 178 other advanced degrees. *Tuition:* Full-time $14,040; part-time $780 per unit. *Graduate housing:* Room and/or apartments available on a first-come, first-served basis to single students; on-campus housing not available to married students. *Student services:* Career counseling, free psychological counseling, international student services. *Library facilities:* Archbishop Alemany Library. *Online resources:* library catalog, web page, access to other libraries' catalogs. *Collection:* 118,375 titles, 57,534 serial subscriptions, 2,376 audiovisual materials.

Computer facilities: 260 computers available on campus for general student use. A campuswide network can be accessed from student residence rooms and from off campus. Online class registration, Microsoft Office Applications (Word, Excel, PowerPoint) are available. *Web address:* http://www.dominican.edu/.

General Application Contact: Shannon Lovelace, Assistant Director, 415-485-3246, Fax: 415-485-3214.

GRADUATE UNITS

Graduate Programs Students: 347 full-time (268 women), 266 part-time (198 women); includes 90 minority (15 African Americans, 3 American Indian/Alaska Native, 33 Asian Americans or Pacific Islanders, 39 Hispanic Americans), 61 international. Average age 36. Expenses: Contact institution. *Financial support:* Applicants required to submit FAFSA. In 2008, 138 master's, 114 other advanced degrees awarded. *Degree program information:* Part-time and evening/weekend programs available. *Application deadline:* For fall admission, 3/2 priority date for domestic students. Applications are processed on a rolling basis. *Application fee:* $40. Electronic applications accepted. *Application Contact:* Shannon Lovelace, Assistant Director, 415-485-3246, Fax: 415-485-3214. *Provost/Vice President for Academic Affairs*, Dr. Kenneth Porada, 415-485-3290, Fax: 415-485-3205, E-mail: kporada@dominican.edu.

School of Arts and Sciences Students: 123 full-time (111 women), 90 part-time (73 women); includes 42 minority (9 African Americans, 2 American Indian/Alaska Native, 17 Asian Americans or Pacific Islanders, 14 Hispanic Americans), 3 international. Average age 39. 73 applicants, 56% accepted, 41 enrolled. Expenses: Contact institution. *Financial support:* Federal Work-Study and scholarships/grants available. Support available to part-time students. Financial award applicants required to submit FAFSA. In 2008, 57 master's awarded. *Degree program information:* Part-time and evening/weekend programs available. Offers arts and sciences (MA, MFT, MS); biology (MS); counseling psychology (MFT, MS); geriatric and nurse educator (MS); humanities (MA); integrated health practices (clinical nursing specialist) (MS); occupational therapy (MS). *Application deadline:* For fall admission, 3/2 priority date for domestic students. Applications are processed on a rolling basis. *Application fee:* $40. Electronic applications accepted. *Application Contact:* Shannon Lovelace, Assistant Director, 415-485-3246, Fax: 415-485-3214. *Dean,* Dr. Martha Nelson, 415-257-1310, Fax: 415-257-0120, E-mail: nelson@dominican.edu.

School of Business, Education and Leadership Students: 224 full-time (157 women), 186 part-time (125 women); includes 48 minority (6 African Americans, 1 American Indian/Alaska Native, 16 Asian Americans or Pacific Islanders, 25 Hispanic Americans), 58 international. Average age 34. Expenses: Contact institution. *Financial support:* Tuition discounts available. Financial award applicants required to submit FAFSA. *Degree program information:* Part-time and evening/weekend programs available. Offers business, education and leadership (MAM, MBA, MS, Credential); education (MS, Credential); global strategic management (MBA); management (MAM); multiple subject teaching (Credential); single subject teaching (Credential); special education (Credential); strategic leadership (MBA); sustainable development (MBA). Programs also offered in Ukiah, CA. *Application deadline:* Applications are processed on a rolling basis. *Application fee:* $40. Electronic applications accepted. *Application Contact:* Shannon Lovelace, Assistant Director, 415-485-3246, Fax: 415-485-3214. *Dean,* Dr. Ed Kujawa, 415-485-3245, Fax: 415-458-3790, E-mail: kujawa@dominican.edu.

DONGGUK ROYAL UNIVERSITY, Los Angeles, CA 90020

General Information Independent, coed, graduate-only institution. *Enrollment by degree level:* 205 master's. *Graduate faculty:* 50 part-time/adjunct (15 women). *Graduate housing:* On-campus housing not available. *Student services:* Campus employment opportunities, career counseling, exercise/wellness program, international student services, low-cost health insurance, multicultural affairs office. *Collection:* 15,000 titles.

Computer facilities: 10 computers available on campus for general student use. A campuswide network can be accessed from off campus. Online class registration is available. *Web address:* http://www.dru.edu/dru/.

General Application Contact: Ronald Sokolsky, Vice President, 213-487-0110 Ext. 114, Fax: 213-487-0527, E-mail: provost@dru.edu.

GRADUATE UNITS

Program in Oriental Medicine *Degree program information:* Part-time and evening/weekend programs available. Offers Oriental medicine (MS).

DORDT COLLEGE, Sioux Center, IA 51250-1697

General Information Independent-religious, coed, comprehensive institution. *Graduate housing:* Rooms and/or apartments available to single and married students.

GRADUATE UNITS

Program in Education *Degree program information:* Part-time programs available. Postbaccalaureate distance learning degree programs offered (minimal on-campus study). Offers education (M Ed). Electronic applications accepted.

DOWLING COLLEGE, Oakdale, NY 11769-1999

General Information Independent, coed, comprehensive institution. *Graduate housing:* Room and/or apartments available on a first-come, first-served basis to single students; on-campus housing not available to married students. Housing application deadline: 9/1.

GRADUATE UNITS

Graduate Programs in Education *Degree program information:* Part-time and evening/weekend programs available. Postbaccalaureate distance learning degree programs offered. Offers educational administration (Ed D, PD); human development and learning (MS Ed); literacy (MS Ed); literacy/special education (MS Ed); secondary education (MS Ed); special education (MS Ed). Electronic applications accepted.

Programs in Arts and Sciences *Degree program information:* Part-time and evening/weekend programs available. Offers integrated math and science (MS); liberal studies (MA). Electronic applications accepted.

School of Business *Degree program information:* Part-time and evening/weekend programs available. Offers aviation management (MBA, Certificate); banking and finance (MBA, Certificate); general management (MBA); public management (MBA, Certificate); total quality management (MBA, Certificate). Electronic applications accepted.

DRAKE UNIVERSITY, Des Moines, IA 50311-4516

General Information Independent, coed, university. *Enrollment:* 5,668 graduate, professional, and undergraduate students; 1,031 full-time matriculated graduate/professional students (562 women), 1,121 part-time matriculated graduate/professional students (754 women). *Enrollment by degree level:* 915 first professional, 995 master's, 96 doctoral, 146 other advanced degrees. *Graduate faculty:* 32 full-time (14 women), 58 part-time/adjunct (25 women). *Graduate housing:* Room and/or apartments available on a first-come, first-served basis to single students; on-campus housing not available to married students. Typical cost: $3960 per year ($7170 including board). Housing application deadline: 8/1. *Student services:* Campus employment opportunities, campus safety program, career counseling, exercise/wellness program, free psychological counseling, international student services, low-cost health insurance, services for students with disabilities, teacher training, writing training. *Library facilities:* Cowles Library plus 2 others. *Online resources:* library catalog, web page, access to other libraries' catalogs. *Collection:* 525,093 titles, 28,499 serial subscriptions, 2,123 audiovisual materials. *Research affiliation:* NASA Through Iowa State University (arts and sciences), Albertson's Inc. (pharmacy), USDA (agriculture), U.S. Department of Education (education), National Science Foundation (biology, physics), Iowa Department of Education (education).

Computer facilities: 1,000 computers available on campus for general student use. A campuswide network can be accessed from student residence rooms and from off campus. Online class registration is available. *Web address:* http://www.drake.edu/.

General Application Contact: Ann J. Martin, Graduate Coordinator, 515-271-2034, Fax: 515-271-2831, E-mail: ann.martin@drake.edu.

GRADUATE UNITS

College of Business and Public Administration Students: 42 full-time (13 women), 404 part-time (222 women); includes 27 minority (13 African Americans, 1 American Indian/Alaska Native, 8 Asian Americans or Pacific Islanders, 5 Hispanic Americans), 16 international. Average age 30. 259 applicants, 74% accepted, 116 enrolled. *Faculty:* 19 full-time (4 women), 2 part-time/adjunct (0 women). Expenses: Contact institution. *Financial support:* Fellowships with tuition reimbursements, teaching assistantships, career-related internships or fieldwork and institutionally sponsored loans available. Support available to part-time students. Financial award application deadline: 3/1; financial award applicants required to submit FAFSA. In 2008, 188 master's awarded. *Degree program information:* Part-time and evening/weekend programs available. Offers business and public administration (M Acc, MBA, MFM, MPA). *Application deadline:* For fall admission, 8/15 priority date for domestic students; for winter admission, 12/20 priority date for domestic students; for spring admission, 12/1 priority date for domestic students. Applications are processed on a rolling basis. *Application fee:* $25. Electronic applications accepted. *Application Contact:* Danette Kenne, Director of Graduate Programs, 515-271-2188, Fax: 515-271-4518, E-mail: cbpa.gradprograms@drake.edu. *Dean,* Dr. Charles Edwards, 515-271-2871, Fax: 515-271-4518, E-mail: charles.edwards@drake.edu.

College of Pharmacy and Health Sciences Students: 325 full-time (209 women), 2 part-time (1 woman); includes 27 minority (1 African American, 25 Asian Americans or Pacific Islanders, 1 Hispanic American), 6 international. Average age 21. 307 applicants, 46% accepted, 107 enrolled. *Faculty:* 33 full-time (19 women), 9 part-time/adjunct (6 women). Expenses: Contact institution. *Financial support:* In 2008–09, 10 teaching assistantships (averaging $3,200 per year) were awarded; career-related internships or fieldwork, Federal Work-Study, institutionally sponsored loans, and scholarships/grants also available. Support available to part-time students. Financial award application deadline: 3/1; financial award applicants required to submit FAFSA. In 2008, 127 Pharm Ds awarded. Offers pharmaceutical sciences (Pharm D); pharmacy and health sciences (Pharm D); pharmacy practice (Pharm D). *Application deadline:* For fall admission, 2/1 priority date for domestic students. *Application fee:* $135. Electronic applications accepted. *Application Contact:* Dr. Renae J. Chesnut, Associate Dean for Student Affairs, 515-271-3018, Fax: 515-271-4171, E-mail: renae.chesnut@drake.edu. *Dean,* Dr. Raylene Rospond, 515-271-1814, Fax: 515-271-4171, E-mail: raylene.rospond@drake.edu.

Law School Students: 442 full-time (188 women), 10 part-time (8 women); includes 44 minority (26 African Americans, 7 Asian Americans or Pacific Islanders, 11 Hispanic Americans), 9 international. Average age 26. 1,201 applicants, 49% accepted, 154 enrolled. *Faculty:* 28 full-time (10 women), 15 part-time/adjunct (6 women). Expenses: Contact institution. *Financial support:* In 2008–09, 20 research assistantships (averaging $757 per year), 6 teaching assistantships (averaging $2,142 per year) were awarded; career-related internships or fieldwork, Federal Work-Study, institutionally sponsored loans, scholarships/grants, and tuition waivers (full and partial) also available. Support available to part-time students. Financial award application deadline: 3/1; financial award applicants required to submit FAFSA. In 2008, 156 JDs awarded. Offers law (JD). *Application deadline:* For fall admission, 4/1 priority date for domestic and international students. Applications are processed on a rolling basis. *Application fee:* $40. Electronic applications accepted. *Application Contact:* Jason Allen, Director of Admission, 515-271-2040, Fax: 515-271-2530, E-mail: jason.allen@drake.edu. *Dean,* David Walker, 515-271-1805, Fax: 515-271-4118, E-mail: david.walker@drake.edu.

School of Education Students: 87 full-time (65 women), 666 part-time (491 women); includes 25 African Americans, 7 Asian Americans or Pacific Islanders, 23 Hispanic Americans, 9 international. Average age 34. 394 applicants, 53% accepted, 184 enrolled. *Faculty:* 22 full-time (12 women), 48 part-time/adjunct (27 women). Expenses: Contact institution. *Financial support:* In 2008–09, 14 research assistantships were awarded; career-related internships or fieldwork and unspecified assistantships also available. Support available to part-time students. In 2008, 206 master's, 10 doctorates, 24 other advanced degrees awarded. *Degree program information:* Part-time and evening/weekend programs available. Offers adult learning and organizational development (MS); adult learning and performance development (MS); art (MAT); biology (MAT); business (MAT); chemistry (MAT); community agency counseling (MS); education (MAT, MS, MSE, MST, Ed D, Ed S); education leadership (MSE, Ed D, Ed S); effective teaching, learning and leadership (MSE); elementary education (MST); English (MAT); general science (MAT); guidance counseling (MS); history-American (MAT); history-world (MAT); journalism (MAT); mathematics (MAT); mental health counseling (MS); physical science (MAT); physics (MAT); rehabilitation administration (MS); rehabilitation counseling (MS); rehabilitation placement (MS); secondary education (MAT); sociology (MAT); special education (MSE); speech (MAT); speech communication (MAT); teacher education (MST); theatre (MAT). *Application deadline:* For fall admission, 7/1 priority date for domestic students, 6/1 priority date for international students; for spring admission, 11/1 priority date for domestic students, 10/1 priority date for international students. Applications are processed on a rolling basis. *Application fee:* $25. Electronic applications accepted. *Application Contact:* Ann J. Martin, Graduate Coordinator, 515-271-2034, Fax: 515-271-2831, E-mail: ann.martin@drake.edu. *Dean,* Dr. Janet McMahill, 515-271-3829, E-mail: janet.mcmahill@drake.edu.

School of Journalism and Mass Communication Students: 31 part-time (26 women); includes 1 American Indian/Alaska Native. Average age 33. 24 applicants, 67% accepted, 16 enrolled. *Faculty:* 3 full-time (2 women). Expenses: Contact institution. Offers communication leadership (MCL); journalism and mass communication (MCL). *Application Contact:* Ann J. Martin, Graduate Coordinator, 515-271-2034, Fax: 515-271-2831, E-mail: ann.martin@drake.edu. *Dean,* Dr. Charles Edwards, 515-271-2871, Fax: 515-271-4518, E-mail: charles.edwards@drake.edu.

See Close-Up on page 899.

DREW UNIVERSITY, Madison, NJ 07940-1493

General Information Independent-religious, coed, university. CGS member. *Graduate housing:* Rooms and/or apartments available on a first-come, first-served basis to single and married students. Housing application deadline: 7/1. *Research affiliation:* Center for Research Libraries (humanities), Dana Rise Institute (science), Raritan Bay Medical Center (medical humanities), Society for the History of Authorship, Readership and Publishing (book history), Methodist Archives (religion).

GRADUATE UNITS

Caspersen School of Graduate Studies *Degree program information:* Part-time and evening/weekend programs available. Offers anthropology of religion (MA, PhD); Christian social ethics (MA, PhD); English literature (MA, PhD); historical studies (MA, PhD); holocaust and genocide studies (Certificate); interdisciplinary studies (M Litt, D Litt); liturgical studies (MA, PhD); medical humanities (MMH, DMH, CMH); Methodist studies (PhD); modern history and literature (MA, PhD); philosophy of religion (MA, PhD); psychology and religion (MA, PhD); religion in ancient Israel (MA, PhD); sociology of religion (MA, PhD); systematic theology (MA, PhD); the New Testament and early Christianity (MA, PhD); theological ethics (MA, PhD); Wesleyan and Methodist studies (MA, PhD); women's studies (MA).

The Theological School *Degree program information:* Part-time programs available. Postbaccalaureate distance learning degree programs offered (minimal on-campus study). Offers theology (M Div, MTS, STM, D Min, Certificate). Electronic applications accepted.

See Close-Up on page 901.

DREXEL UNIVERSITY, Philadelphia, PA 19104-2875

General Information Independent, coed, university. CGS member. *Graduate housing:* On-campus housing not available.

GRADUATE UNITS

College of Arts and Sciences *Degree program information:* Part-time and evening/weekend programs available. Offers arts and sciences (MA, MS, PhD); biological sciences (MS, PhD); chemistry (MS, PhD); clinical psychology (PhD); communication (MS); environmental policy (MS); environmental science (MS, PhD); forensic psychology (PhD); health psychology (PhD); human nutrition (MS); law-psychology (PhD); mathematics (MS, PhD); neuropsychology (PhD); physics (MS, PhD); psychology (MS); public communication (MS); publication management (MS); science communication (MS); science, technology and society (MS); technical communication (MS). Electronic applications accepted.

College of Engineering *Degree program information:* Part-time and evening/weekend programs available. Offers architectural / building systems engineering (MS, PhD); biochemical engineering (MS); chemical engineering (MS, PhD); civil engineering (MS, PhD); computer engineering (MS); computer science (MS, PhD); electrical and computer engineering (PhD); electrical engineering (MSEE); engineering (MS, MSEE, MSSE, PhD, Certificate); engineering management (MS, Certificate); environmental engineering (MS, PhD); geotechnical, geoenvironmental and geosynthetics (MS, PhD); geotechnical, geoenvironmental and geosynthetics engineering (MS, PhD); hydraulics, hydrology and water resources engineering (MS, PhD); materials engineering (MS, PhD); mechanical engineering (MS, PhD); software engineering (MSSE); structures (MS); telecommunications engineering (MSEE). Electronic applications accepted.

Drexel University (continued)

College of Media Arts and Design *Degree program information:* Part-time and evening/weekend programs available. Offers arts administration (MS); design (MS); digital media (MS); fashion design (MS); interior design (MS); media arts (MS); performing arts (MS); television management (MS). Electronic applications accepted.

College of Medicine *Degree program information:* Part-time programs available. Offers medicine (MD, MLAS, MMS, MS, PhD, Certificate). Electronic applications accepted.

Biomedical Graduate Programs *Degree program information:* Part-time programs available. Offers biochemistry (MS, PhD); biomedical sciences (MLAS, MMS, MS, PhD, Certificate); laboratory animal science (MLAS); medical science (MMS, Certificate); microbiology and immunology (MS, PhD); molecular and cell biology and genetics (MS, PhD); molecular pathobiology (MS, PhD); neuroscience (MS, PhD); pharmacology and physiology (MS, PhD). Electronic applications accepted.

College of Nursing and Health Professions *Degree program information:* Part-time and evening/weekend programs available. Offers art therapy (MA, PMC); couples and family therapy (PhD); dance/movement therapy (MA, PMC); emergency and public safety services (MS); family therapy (MFT); hand and upper quarter rehabilitation (MHS, Certificate, PPDPT); movement science (PhD); music therapy (MA, PMC); nurse anesthesia (MSN); nursing (MSN); nursing and health professions (MA, MFT, MHS, MS, MSN, DPT, PhD, Certificate, PMC, PPDPT); orthopedics (MHS, PhD, PPDPT); pediatrics (MHS, PhD, PPDPT); physical therapy (DPT); physician assistant studies (MHS). Electronic applications accepted.

The iSchool at Drexel, College of Information Science and Technology Students: 231 full-time (158 women), 597 part-time (408 women); includes 121 minority (47 African Americans, 3 American Indian/Alaska Native, 47 Asian Americans or Pacific Islanders, 24 Hispanic Americans), 49 international. Average age 35. 502 applicants, 79% accepted, 253 enrolled. *Faculty:* 38 full-time (19 women), 73 part-time/adjunct (29 women). Expenses: Contact institution. *Financial support:* In 2008–09, 174 students received support, including 36 fellowships with partial tuition reimbursements available, 12 research assistantships with full tuition reimbursements available (averaging $18,292 per year), 6 teaching assistantships with full tuition reimbursements available (averaging $19,500 per year); institutionally sponsored loans, scholarships/grants, health care benefits, tuition waivers (partial), unspecified assistantships, and fellowships also available. Support available to part-time students. Financial award applicants required to submit FAFSA. In 2008, 332 master's, 9 doctorates awarded. *Degree program information:* Part-time and evening/weekend programs available. Postbaccalaureate distance learning degree programs offered (no on-campus study). Offers archival studies (MS); competitive intelligence and knowledge management (MS); digital libraries (MS); healthcare informatics (Certificate); information science and technology (PMC); information studies (PhD); information studies and technology (Advanced Certificate); information systems (MSIS); library and information science (MS); library and information services (MS); school library media (MS); software engineering (MSSE); youth services (MS). *Application deadline:* For fall admission, 9/1 for domestic students, 8/1 for international students; for spring admission, 3/1 for domestic students, 2/1 for international students. Applications are processed on a rolling basis. Electronic applications accepted. *Application Contact:* Matthew Lechtenberg, Graduate Admissions Manager, 215-895-1951, Fax: 215-895-2303, E-mail: ml333@drexel.edu. *Dean and Isaac L. Auerbach Professor of Information Science*, Dr. David E. Fenske, 215-895-2475, Fax: 215-895-6378, E-mail: fenske@drexel.edu.

LeBow College of Business *Degree program information:* Part-time and evening/weekend programs available. Offers accounting (MS); business administration (MBA, PhD, APC); business and administration (MBA, MS, PhD, APC); finance (MS). Electronic applications accepted.

School of Biomedical Engineering, Science and Health Systems Offers biomedical engineering (MS, PhD); biomedical science (MS, PhD); biostatistics (MS); clinical/rehabilitation engineering (MS). Electronic applications accepted.

School of Education *Degree program information:* Part-time and evening/weekend programs available. Postbaccalaureate distance learning degree programs offered. Offers educational administration (MS); educational administration and collaborative learning (MS); educational leadership and learning technology (PhD); global and international education (MS); graduate intern teaching (Certificate); higher education (MS); instructional technology (Spt); post-bachelor's teaching (Certificate); school principal (Certificate); school superintendent (Certificate); science of instruction (MS); teaching English as a second language (Certificate); teaching, learning and curriculum (MS). Electronic applications accepted.

School of Journalism Offers journalism (MA).

School of Public Health Offers biostatistics (MS); epidemiology (PhD); epidemiology and biostatistics (Certificate); public health (MPH, MS, PhD, Certificate). Electronic applications accepted.

DRURY UNIVERSITY, Springfield, MO 65802

General Information Independent, coed, comprehensive institution. *Graduate housing:* Rooms and/or apartments available on a first-come, first-served basis to single and married students. *Research affiliation:* Yale University (child development).

GRADUATE UNITS

Breech School of Business Administration *Degree program information:* Part-time and evening/weekend programs available. Offers business administration (MBA). Electronic applications accepted.

Graduate Programs in Education *Degree program information:* Part-time and evening/weekend programs available. Offers elementary education (M Ed); gifted education (M Ed); human services (M Ed); instructional mathematics K-8 (M Ed); instructional technology (M Ed); middle school teaching (M Ed); secondary education (M Ed); special education (M Ed); special reading (M Ed). Electronic applications accepted.

Program in Communication *Degree program information:* Part-time and evening/weekend programs available. Offers communication (MA). Electronic applications accepted.

Program in Criminology/Criminal Justice *Degree program information:* Part-time and evening/weekend programs available. Offers criminal justice (MS); criminology (MA). Electronic applications accepted.

Program in Studio Art and Theory Offers studio art and theory (MA). Electronic applications accepted.

DUKE UNIVERSITY, Durham, NC 27708-0586

General Information Independent-religious, coed, university. CGS member. *Graduate housing:* Rooms and/or apartments available on a first-come, first-served basis to single students and available to married students. *Research affiliation:* Highlands Biological Station, U.S. Forest Sciences Laboratory, Organization for Tropical Studies.

GRADUATE UNITS

Divinity School Students: 491 full-time (216 women), 36 part-time (20 women); includes 111 minority (69 African Americans, 4 American Indian/Alaska Native, 26 Asian Americans or Pacific Islanders, 12 Hispanic Americans). Average age 29. 619 applicants, 50% accepted, 197 enrolled. *Faculty:* 40 full-time (11 women), 19 part-time/adjunct (6 women). Expenses: Contact institution. *Financial support:* In 2008–09, 472 students received support. Career-related internships or fieldwork, Federal Work-Study, institutionally sponsored loans, scholarships/grants, and field education stipends available. Financial award application deadline: 5/2; financial award applicants required to submit FAFSA. In 2008, 140 first professional degrees, 32 master's awarded. *Degree program information:* Part-time programs available. Offers theology (M Div, MTS, Th M, Th D). *Application deadline:* For fall admission, 4/1 for domestic students, 3/1 for international students. *Application fee:* $50. Electronic applications accepted. *Application Contact:* Rev. Cheryl Brown, Director of Admissions, 919-660-3436, Fax: 919-660-3535, E-mail: admissions@div.duke.edu. *Dean*, Dr. L. Gregory Jones, 919-660-3434, Fax: 919-660-3474, E-mail: gjones@div.duke.edu.

Duke Global Health Institute Offers global health (MS).

The Fuqua School of Business *Degree program information:* Evening/weekend programs available. Postbaccalaureate distance learning degree programs offered. Offers business (EMBA, GEMBA, MBA, MMS, WEMBA, PhD, Certificate); cross continent executive business administration (EMBA); executive business administration (EMBA); global executive business administration (GEMBA); health sector management (Certificate); weekend executive business administration (WEMBA). Electronic applications accepted.

Graduate School *Degree program information:* Part-time and evening/weekend programs available. Offers art, art history and visual studies (PhD); biological and biologically inspired materials (PhD, Certificate); biological chemistry (PhD, Certificate); biological psychology (PhD); biology (PhD); business administration (PhD); cell biology (PhD); cellular and molecular biology (PhD); chemistry (PhD); classical studies (PhD); clinical psychology (PhD); cognitive neuroscience (PhD, Certificate); cognitive psychology (PhD); computational biology and bioinformatics (PhD); computer science (MS, PhD); crystallography of macromolecules (PhD); developmental biology (PhD, Certificate); developmental psychology (PhD); East Asian studies (AM, Certificate); ecology (PhD, Certificate); economics (AM, PhD); English (PhD); enzyme mechanisms (PhD); experimental psychology (PhD); French (PhD); genetics and genomics (PhD); German studies (PhD); gross anatomy and physical anthropology (PhD); health psychology (PhD); history (AM, PhD); human social development (PhD); humanities (AM); immunology (PhD); integrated toxicology and environmental health (PhD, Certificate); Latin American studies (PhD); liberal studies (AM); lipid biochemistry (PhD); literature (PhD); mathematics (PhD); medical physics (MS, PhD); medieval and Renaissance studies (Certificate); membrane structure and function (PhD); molecular cancer biology (PhD); molecular genetics (PhD); molecular genetics and microbiology (PhD); music composition (AM, PhD); musicology (AM, PhD); natural resource economics/policy (AM, PhD); natural resource science/ecology (AM, PhD); natural resource systems science (AM, PhD); neuroanatomy (PhD); neurobiology (PhD); neurochemistry (PhD); nucleic acid structure and function (PhD); pathology (PhD); performance practice (AM, PhD); pharmacology (PhD); philosophy (AM, PhD); physical anthropology (PhD); physics (PhD); political science (AM, PhD); protein structure and function (PhD); religion (MA, PhD); Slavic languages and literatures (AM); social/cultural anthropology (PhD); sociology (AM, PhD); Spanish (PhD); structural biology and biophysics (Certificate); teaching (MAT); women's studies (Certificate). Electronic applications accepted.

Center for Latin American and Caribbean Studies Offers Latin American and Caribbean studies (Certificate).

Division of Earth and Ocean Sciences *Degree program information:* Part-time programs available. Offers earth and ocean sciences (MS, PhD). Electronic applications accepted.

Duke Sanford Institute of Public Policy Offers international development policy (AM, Certificate); public policy (AM, MPP, PhD, Certificate). Electronic applications accepted.

Institute of Statistics and Decision Sciences *Degree program information:* Part-time programs available. Offers statistics and decision sciences (PhD). Electronic applications accepted.

Pratt School of Engineering *Degree program information:* Part-time programs available. Offers biomedical engineering (MS, PhD); civil and environmental engineering (MS, PhD); electrical and computer engineering (MS, PhD); engineering (MEM, MS, PhD); engineering management (MEM); environmental engineering (MS, PhD); materials science (MS, PhD); mechanical engineering (MS, PhD).

Nicholas School of the Environment *Degree program information:* Part-time programs available. Offers coastal environmental management (MEM); DEL-environmental leadership (MEM); energy and environment (MEM); environmental economics and policy (MEM); environmental health and security (MEM); forest resource management (MF); global environmental change (MEM); resource ecology (MEM); water and air resources (MEM). Electronic applications accepted.

School of Law Offers law (JD, LL M, MLS, SJD). LL M and SJD offered only to international students. Electronic applications accepted.

School of Medicine Students: 724 full-time (449 women), 105 part-time (64 women); includes 256 minority (95 African Americans, 5 American Indian/Alaska Native, 128 Asian Americans or Pacific Islanders, 28 Hispanic Americans), 43 international. 6,095 applicants, 8% accepted, 306 enrolled. Expenses: Contact institution. *Financial support:* In 2008–09, 468 students received support. Institutionally sponsored loans and scholarships/grants available. Financial award application deadline: 5/1; financial award applicants required to submit CSS PROFILE or FAFSA. In 2008, 83 master's, 132 doctorates awarded. *Degree program information:* Part-time programs available. Offers clinical leadership program (MHS); clinical research (MHS); medicine (MD, MHS, DPT); pathologists' assistant (MHS); physician assistant (MHS). *Application Contact:* Dr. Brenda E. Armstrong, Director of Admissions, 919-684-2985, Fax: 919-684-8893, E-mail: mcdadm@mc.duke.edu. *Vice Dean, Medical Education*, Dr. Edward G. Buckley, 919-668-3381, Fax: 919-660-7040, E-mail: buckl002@mc.duke.edu.

Physical Therapy Division Students: 169 full-time (139 women); includes 17 minority (6 African Americans, 9 Asian Americans or Pacific Islanders, 2 Hispanic Americans), 2 international. 180 applicants, 59% accepted, 59 enrolled. *Faculty:* 5 full-time (0 women), 2 part-time/adjunct (0 women). Expenses: Contact institution. *Financial support:* In 2008–09, 143 students received support; fellowships, research assistantships, teaching assistantships, Federal Work-Study available. Financial award application deadline: 5/1; financial award applicants required to submit FAFSA. In 2008, 42 doctorates awarded. Offers physical therapy (DPT). *Application deadline:* For fall admission, 12/1 priority date for domestic and international students. Applications are processed on a rolling basis. *Application fee:* $75. Electronic applications accepted. *Application Contact:* Anita Aiken, Admissions Coordinator, 919-668-5206, Fax: 919-688-3024, E-mail: anita.aiken@duke.edu. *Interim Chief and Professor*, Dr. Pam Duncan, 919-681-2060, Fax: 919-668-3024, E-mail: pamela.duncan@duke.edu.

School of Nursing *Degree program information:* Part-time programs available. Postbaccalaureate distance learning degree programs offered (minimal on-campus study). Offers adult acute care (Certificate); adult cardiovascular (Certificate); adult oncology/HIV (Certificate); adult primary care (Certificate); clinical nurse specialist (MSN); clinical research management (MSN, Certificate); family (Certificate); gerontology (Certificate); health and nursing ministries (MSN, Certificate); health systems leadership and outcomes (Certificate); leadership in community based long term care (MSN, Certificate); neonatal (Certificate); neonatal/pediatric in rural health (MSN, Certificate); nurse anesthetist (MSN, Certificate); nurse practitioner (MSN); nursing (MSN, PhD, Certificate); nursing and healthcare leadership (MSN); nursing education (MSN); nursing informatics (MSN, Certificate); pediatric (Certificate); pediatric acute care (Certificate).

DUQUESNE UNIVERSITY, Pittsburgh, PA 15282-0001

General Information Independent-religious, coed, university. CGS member. *Enrollment:* 10,106 graduate, professional, and undergraduate students; 3,402 full-time matriculated graduate/professional students (2,039 women), 1,048 part-time matriculated graduate/professional students (607 women). *Enrollment by degree level:* 1,484 first professional, 2,966 master's. *Tuition:* Part-time $819 per credit. *Required fees:* $78 per credit. Tuition and fees vary according to course load. *Graduate housing:* Rooms and/or apartments available on a first-come, first-served basis to single and married students. Typical cost: $4848 per year ($8888 including board) for single students; $11,400 per year for married students. Room and board charges vary according to housing facility selected. Housing application deadline: 8/22. *Student services:* Campus employment opportunities, campus safety program, career counseling, child daycare facilities, exercise/wellness program, free psychological counseling, international student services, low-cost health insurance, multicultural affairs office, services for students with disabilities, teacher training, writing training. *Library facilities:* Gumberg Library plus 1 other. *Online resources:* library catalog, web page. *Collection:* 700,245 titles, 30,980 serial subscriptions, 84,901 audiovisual materials.

Computer facilities: Computer purchase and lease plans are available. 1,000 computers available on campus for general student use. A campuswide network can be accessed from student residence rooms and from off campus. Online class registration is available. *Web address:* http://www.duq.edu/.

General Application Contact: Dr. Ralph L. Pearson, Provost and Academic Vice President, 412-396-6054, E-mail: rlpearson@duq.edu.

GRADUATE UNITS

Bayer School of Natural and Environmental Sciences Students: 113 full-time (70 women), 35 part-time (14 women); includes 10 minority (4 African Americans, 6 Asian Americans or Pacific Islanders), 21 international. Average age 26. 166 applicants, 54% accepted, 55 enrolled. *Faculty:* 32 full-time (7 women), 17 part-time/adjunct (6 women). Expenses: Contact institution. *Financial support:* In 2008–09, 1 fellowship with full tuition reimbursement (averaging $21,300 per year), 13 research assistantships with full tuition reimbursements (averaging $20,800 per year), 57 teaching assistantships with full tuition reimbursements (averaging $20,800 per year) were awarded; career-related internships or fieldwork, scholarships/grants, tuition waivers (partial), and unspecified assistantships also available. Support available to part-time students. Financial award application deadline: 5/31; financial award applicants required to submit FAFSA. In 2008, 50 master's, 6 doctorates, 5 other advanced degrees awarded. *Degree program information:* Part-time programs available. Offers biological sciences (MS, PhD); biotechnology (MS); chemistry (MS, PhD); environmental management (MEM, Certificate); environmental science (Certificate); environmental science and management (MS); forensic science and law (MS); natural and environmental sciences (MEM, MS, PhD, Certificate). *Application deadline:* For fall admission, 2/15 priority date for domestic students, 2/15 for international students; for spring admission, 10/1 priority date for domestic students, 10/1 for international students. Applications are processed on a rolling basis. *Application fee:* $40. Electronic applications accepted. *Application Contact:* Heather Costello, Graduate Academic Advisor, 412-396-6339, Fax: 412-396-4881, E-mail: gradinfo@duq.edu. *Dean,* Dr. David W. Seybert, 412-396-4877, Fax: 412-396-4881, E-mail: seybert@duq.edu.

Graduate School of Liberal Arts Students: 512 full-time (259 women), 185 part-time (117 women); includes 17 minority (10 African Americans, 1 Asian American or Pacific Islander, 6 Hispanic Americans), 71 international. Average age 30. 392 applicants, 60% accepted, 163 enrolled. *Faculty:* 111 full-time (35 women), 66 part-time/adjunct (33 women). Expenses: Contact institution. *Financial support:* In 2008–09, 32 research assistantships with full tuition reimbursements (averaging $10,000 per year), 71 teaching assistantships with full tuition reimbursements (averaging $13,000 per year) were awarded; fellowships with full tuition reimbursements, career-related internships or fieldwork, Federal Work-Study, institutionally sponsored loans, scholarships/grants, and tuition waivers (full and partial) also available. Support available to part-time students. Financial award application deadline: 5/1. In 2008, 98 master's, 32 doctorates awarded. *Degree program information:* Part-time and evening/weekend programs available. Offers archival, museum, and editing studies (MA); clinical psychology (PhD); communication (MA); computational mathematics (MA, MS); English (MA, PhD); health care ethics (MA, DHCE, PhD, Certificate); history (MA); liberal arts (MA, MS, DHCE, PhD, Certificate); multimedia technology (MS, Certificate); pastoral ministry (MA); philosophy (MA, PhD); religious education (MA); rhetoric (PhD); systematic theology (PhD); theology (MA). *Application deadline:* For fall admission, 8/1 for domestic students, 5/1 for international students; for spring admission, 11/1 for domestic students, 9/1 for international students. Applications are processed on a rolling basis. *Application fee:* $50. Electronic applications accepted. *Application Contact:* Linda L. Rendulic, Assistant to the Dean, 412-396-6400, Fax: 412-396-5265, E-mail: rendulic@duq.edu. *Acting Dean,* Dr. Evan Stoddard, 412-396-6400.

Graduate Center for Social and Public Policy Students: 37 full-time (25 women), 12 part-time (9 women); includes 1 minority (African American), 7 international. Average age 27. 29 applicants, 90% accepted, 18 enrolled. *Faculty:* 15 full-time (3 women), 1 (woman) part-time/adjunct. Expenses: Contact institution. *Financial support:* In 2008–09, 20 students received support, including 12 research assistantships with full and partial tuition reimbursements available (averaging $9,000 per year), 4 teaching assistantships with full and partial tuition reimbursements available (averaging $9,000 per year); career-related internships or fieldwork, institutionally sponsored loans, scholarships/grants, tuition waivers (full and partial), and unspecified assistantships also available. Support available to part-time students. Financial award application deadline: 5/1. In 2008, 9 master's awarded. *Degree program information:* Part-time and evening/weekend programs available. Offers conflict resolution and peace studies (Certificate); social and public policy (MA, Certificate). Programs are a collaboration between the Departments of Political Science and Sociology. *Application deadline:* For fall admission, 4/30 priority date for domestic and international students; for spring admission, 11/1 priority date for domestic and international students. Applications are processed on a rolling basis. *Application fee:* $50. Electronic applications accepted. *Application Contact:* Linda L. Rendulic, Assistant to the Dean, 412-396-6400, Fax: 412-396-5265, E-mail: rendulic@duq.edu. *Director,* Dr. Joseph Yenerall, 412-396-6485, Fax: 412-396-5265, E-mail: socialpolicy@duq.edu.

John F. Donahue Graduate School of Business Students: 115 full-time (50 women), 225 part-time (93 women); includes 14 minority (6 African Americans, 2 American Indian/Alaska Native, 6 Hispanic Americans), 34 international. Average age 31. 244 applicants, 65% accepted, 109 enrolled. *Faculty:* 32 full-time (8 women), 19 part-time/adjunct (3 women). Expenses: Contact institution. *Financial support:* In 2008–09, 37 students received support, including 7 fellowships with partial tuition reimbursements available, 27 research assistantships with partial tuition reimbursements available; career-related internships or fieldwork and unspecified assistantships also available. Support available to part-time students. Financial award application deadline: 7/1; financial award applicants required to submit FAFSA. In 2008, 123 master's awarded. *Degree program information:* Part-time and evening/weekend programs available. Offers accountancy (MS); business administration (MBA); information systems management (MSISM); sustainability (MBA). *Application deadline:* For fall admission, 5/1 priority date for domestic students, 5/1 for international students; for spring admission, 10/1 for domestic and international students. Applications are processed on a rolling basis. *Application fee:* $0. Electronic applications accepted. *Application Contact:* Patricia Moore, Assistant Director, 412-396-6276, Fax: 412-396-1726, E-mail: moorep@duq.edu. *Dean,* Alan R. Miciak, 412-396-5848, Fax: 412-396-5304, E-mail: miciaka@duq.edu.

John G. Rangos, Sr. School of Health Sciences Students: 290 full-time (234 women), 11 part-time (8 women); includes 12 minority (7 African Americans, 4 Asian Americans or Pacific Islanders, 1 Hispanic American), 8 international. Average age 23. 400 applicants, 12% accepted, 20 enrolled. *Faculty:* 35 full-time (23 women), 17 part-time/adjunct (10 women). Expenses: Contact institution. *Financial support:* Federal Work-Study available. In 2008, 76 master's, 28 doctorates awarded. Offers health management systems (MHMS); health sciences (PhD); occupational therapy (MS); physical therapy (DPT); physician assistant (MPA); speech–language pathology (MS). *Application deadline:* For fall admission, 12/1 priority date for domestic students; for winter admission, 5/1 priority date for domestic students. Applications are processed on a rolling basis. *Application fee:* $45. Electronic applications accepted. *Application Contact:* Christopher R. Hilf, Recruiter/Academic Advisor, 412-396-5653, Fax: 412-396-5554, E-mail: hilfc@duq.edu. *Dean,* Dr. Gregory H. Frazer, 412-396-5303, Fax: 412-396-5554, E-mail: frazer@duq.edu.

Mary Pappert School of Music Students: 71 full-time (35 women), 22 part-time (10 women); includes 8 minority (3 African Americans, 5 Asian Americans or Pacific Islanders), 26 international. Average age 23. 96 applicants, 81% accepted, 43 enrolled. *Faculty:* 26 full-time (8 women), 71 part-time/adjunct (18 women). Expenses: Contact institution. *Financial support:* In 2008–09, 45 fellowships with full and partial tuition reimbursements were awarded; career-related internships or fieldwork, Federal Work-Study, institutionally sponsored loans, and tuition waivers (full and partial) also available. Support available to part-time students. Financial award application deadline: 4/1. In 2008, 41 master's, 11 ADs awarded. *Degree program information:* Part-time programs available. Postbaccalaureate distance learning degree programs offered (minimal on-campus study). Offers music composition (MM); music education (MM); music performance (MM, AD); music technology (MM); music theory (MM); sacred music (MM). *Application deadline:* For fall admission, 9/1 priority date for domestic students; for spring admission, 12/1 for domestic students. Applications are processed on a rolling basis. *Application fee:* $50. *Application Contact:* Peggy Eiseman, Administrative Assistant of Admissions, 412-396-5064, Fax: 412-396-5479, E-mail: eiseman@duq.edu. *Dean,* Dr. Edward W. Kocher, 412-396-6082, Fax: 412-396-1524, E-mail: kocher@duq.edu.

Mylan School of Pharmacy Students: 1,166 full-time (728 women), 13 part-time (7 women); includes 47 minority (19 African Americans, 24 Asian Americans or Pacific Islanders, 4 Hispanic Americans), 60 international. *Faculty:* 44 full-time (17 women), 2 part-time/adjunct (0 women). Expenses: Contact institution. In 2008, 147 first professional degrees, 10 master's awarded. Offers pharmacy (Pharm D, MS, PhD). *Application fee:* $50. *Application Contact:* Dr. J. Douglas Bricker, Dean, 412-396-6380. *Dean,* Dr. J. Douglas Bricker, 412-396-6380.

Graduate School of Pharmaceutical Sciences Students: 54 full-time (24 women), 13 part-time (7 women); includes 2 minority (both African Americans), 47 international. 261 applicants, 6% accepted, 11 enrolled. *Faculty:* 20 full-time (4 women). Expenses: Contact institution. *Financial support:* In 2008–09, 53 students received support, including 7 research assistantships with full tuition reimbursements available, 46 teaching assistantships with full tuition reimbursements available; unspecified assistantships also available. In 2008, 10 master's awarded. Offers medicinal chemistry (MS, PhD); pharmaceutical administration (MS); pharmaceutics (MS, PhD); pharmacology (MS, PhD); pharmacy administration (MS). *Application deadline:* For fall admission, 2/1 priority date for domestic and international students; for spring admission, 10/1 priority date for domestic and international students. Applications are processed on a rolling basis. *Application fee:* $50. Electronic applications accepted. *Application Contact:* Information Contact, 412-396-1172, E-mail: gsps-adm@duq.edu. *Associate Dean for Research and Graduate Programs,* Dr. James K. Drennen, 412-396-5520.

School of Education Students: 534 full-time (395 women), 253 part-time (198 women); includes 41 minority (27 African Americans, 1 American Indian/Alaska Native, 8 Asian Americans or Pacific Islanders, 5 Hispanic Americans), 17 international. Average age 34. 451 applicants, 30% accepted, 132 enrolled. *Faculty:* 57 full-time (29 women), 40 part-time/adjunct (23 women). Expenses: Contact institution. *Financial support:* Research assistantships, teaching assistantships with tuition reimbursements, career-related internships or fieldwork, Federal Work-Study, institutionally sponsored loans, and tuition waivers available. Support available to part-time students. In 2008, 239 master's, 39 doctorates, 19 other advanced degrees awarded. *Degree program information:* Part-time and evening/weekend programs available. Offers child psychology (MS Ed); community counseling (MS Ed); counselor education (MS Ed, Ed D); counselor education and supervision (Ed D); early childhood education (MS Ed); education (MS Ed, Ed D, PhD, CAGS, Post-Master's Certificate); educational leaders (Ed D); educational studies (MS Ed); elementary education (MS Ed); elementary education/early childhood (MS Ed); English as a second language (MS Ed); instructional technology (MS Ed, Ed D); marriage and family therapy (MS Ed); reading and language arts (MS Ed); school administration (MS Ed); school administration and supervision (MS Ed, Post-Master's Certificate); school counseling (MS Ed); school psychology (MS Ed, PhD, CAGS); school supervision (MS Ed); secondary education (MS Ed); special education (MS Ed). *Application deadline:* For fall admission, 8/1 for domestic and international students; for spring admission, 12/1 for domestic and international students. Applications are processed on a rolling basis. *Application fee:* $0. Electronic applications accepted. *Application Contact:* Michael Dolinger, Director of Student and Academic Services, 412-396-6647, Fax: 412-396-5585, E-mail: mcelligott@duq.edu. *Dean,* Dr. Olga Welch, 412-396-6102, Fax: 412-396-5585.

School of Law Students: 707 full-time (369 women); includes 49 minority (31 African Americans, 3 American Indian/Alaska Native, 8 Asian Americans or Pacific Islanders, 7 Hispanic Americans), 11 international. Average age 26. *Faculty:* 26 full-time (4 women), 51 part-time/adjunct (11 women). Expenses: Contact institution. *Financial support:* In 2008–09, 267 students received support; research assistantships, teaching assistantships, career-related internships or fieldwork, Federal Work-Study, scholarships/grants, tuition waivers (partial), and grant-in-aid awards available. Support available to part-time students. Financial award application deadline: 5/31. In 2008, 182 JDs awarded. *Degree program information:* Part-time and evening/weekend programs available. Offers law (JD, LL M). *Application deadline:* For fall admission, 4/1 for domestic students. Applications are processed on a rolling basis. *Application fee:* $60. *Application Contact:* Joseph P. Campion, Director, Admissions, 412-396-6296, Fax: 412-396-6659, E-mail: campion@duq.edu. *Interim Dean,* Ken Gormley, 412-396-6300, Fax: 412-396-6659, E-mail: gormley@duq.edu.

School of Leadership and Professional Advancement Students: 535 (263 women); includes 51 minority (43 African Americans, 1 American Indian/Alaska Native, 3 Asian Americans or Pacific Islanders, 4 Hispanic Americans). 231 applicants, 84% accepted, 121 enrolled. *Faculty:* 1 full-time (0 women), 59 part-time/adjunct (30 women). Expenses: Contact institution. *Financial support:* Applicants required to submit FAFSA. In 2008, 134 master's awarded. *Degree program information:* Part-time and evening/weekend programs available. Postbaccalaureate distance learning degree programs offered (no on-campus study). Offers community leadership (MS); leadership and business ethics (MS); leadership and information technology (MS); leadership and liberal studies (MA); sports leadership (MS). *Application deadline:* Applications are processed on a rolling basis. *Application fee:* $0. Electronic applications accepted. *Application Contact:* Marianne Leister, Director of Student Services, 412-396-4933, Fax: 412-396-5072, E-mail: leister@duq.edu. *Dean,* Dr. Dorothy Bassett, PhD, 412-396-5839, Fax: 412-396-4711, E-mail: bassettd@duq.edu.

School of Nursing Students: 100 full-time (96 women), 111 part-time (103 women); includes 25 minority (19 African Americans, 2 Asian Americans or Pacific Islanders, 4 Hispanic Americans), 18 international. 100 applicants, 73% accepted, 61 enrolled. *Faculty:* 54 full-time (49 women), 11 part-time/adjunct (8 women). Expenses: Contact institution. *Financial support:* In 2008–09, 22 students received support, including 11 research assistantships with partial tuition reimbursements available (averaging $2,100 per year), 5 teaching assistantships with partial tuition reimbursements available (averaging $1,500 per year); institutionally sponsored loans, scholarships/grants, traineeships, tuition waivers (partial), and unspecified assistantships also available. Financial award applicants required to submit FAFSA. In 2008, 28 master's, 13 doctorates, 8 other advanced degrees awarded. *Degree program information:* Part-time and evening/weekend programs available. Postbaccalaureate distance learning degree programs offered (minimal on-campus study). Offers acute care nursing (Post-Master's Certificate); family nurse practitioner (MSN, Post-Master's Certificate); forensic nursing (MSN, Post-Master's Certificate); nursing (MSN, DNP, PhD, Post-Master's Certificate); nursing education (MSN); nursing practice (DNP); transcultural/international nursing (Post-Master's Certificate). *Application deadline:* For fall admission, 4/1 for domestic and international students; for spring admission, 11/1 for domestic and international students. *Application fee:* $50. *Application Contact:* Susan Hardner, Nurse Recruiter, 412-396-4945, Fax: 412-396-6346, E-mail: nursing@duq.edu. *Dean/Professor,* Dr. Eileen Zungolo, 412-396-6554, Fax: 412-396-5974, E-mail: zungolo@duq.edu.

D'YOUVILLE COLLEGE, Buffalo, NY 14201-1084

General Information Independent, coed, comprehensive institution. *Enrollment:* 2,943 graduate, professional, and undergraduate students; 1,031 full-time matriculated graduate/professional students (751 women), 521 part-time matriculated graduate/professional students (401 women). *Enrollment by degree level:* 170 first professional, 1,219 master's, 66 doctoral, 97 other advanced degrees. *Graduate faculty:* 79 full-time (47 women), 91 part-time/adjunct (56 women). *Tuition:* Full-time $12,150; part-time $675 per credit hour. *Required fees:* $2 per credit hour. $37 per semester. One-time fee: $115. Tuition and fees vary according to degree level and program. *Graduate housing:* Room and/or apartments available on a first-come, first-served basis to single students; on-campus housing not available to married students. Typical cost: $3800 per year ($4650 including board). Housing application deadline: 8/1. *Student services:* Campus employment opportunities, campus safety program, career counseling, exercise/wellness program, free psychological counseling, grant writing training, international student services, low-cost health insurance, multicultural affairs office, services for students with disabilities, writing training. *Library facilities:* Montante Family Library. *Online resources:* library catalog, web page, access to other libraries' catalogs. *Collection:* 116,237 titles, 725 serial subscriptions, 3,668 audiovisual materials.

Computer facilities: 72 computers available on campus for general student use. A campuswide network can be accessed from student residence rooms and from off campus. Online class registration is available. *Web address:* http://www.dyc.edu/.

General Application Contact: Linda Fisher, Graduate Admissions Director, 716-829-8400, Fax: 716-829-7900, E-mail: graduateadmissions@dyc.edu.

GRADUATE UNITS

Department of Business Students: 57 full-time (31 women), 30 part-time (16 women); includes 23 minority (14 African Americans, 1 Asian American or Pacific Islander, 8 Hispanic Americans), 21 international. Average age 31. 88 applicants, 52% accepted, 18 enrolled.

D'Youville College (continued)

Faculty: 4 full-time (1 woman), 7 part-time/adjunct (2 women). Expenses: Contact institution. *Financial support:* In 2008–09, 1 research assistantship with partial tuition reimbursement (averaging $3,000 per year) was awarded; career-related internships or fieldwork, Federal Work-Study, and scholarships/grants also available. Support available to part-time students. Financial award application deadline: 3/1; financial award applicants required to submit FAFSA. In 2008, 11 master's awarded. *Degree program information:* Part-time and evening/weekend programs available. Offers business administration (MBA); international business (MS). *Application deadline:* For fall admission, 5/1 priority date for international students; for spring admission, 9/1 priority date for international students. Applications are processed on a rolling basis. *Application fee:* $25. Electronic applications accepted. *Application Contact:* Linda Fisher, Graduate Admissions Director, 716-829-8400, Fax: 716-829-7900, E-mail: graduateadmissions@dyc.edu. *Chair,* Dr. Susan Kowalewski, 716-829-7839, Fax: 716-829-7760.

Department of Dietetics Students: 47 full-time (43 women), 7 part-time (6 women); includes 2 minority (1 African American, 1 Hispanic American), 3 international. Average age 24. 64 applicants, 63% accepted, 9 enrolled. *Faculty:* 2 full-time (1 woman), 3 part-time/adjunct (all women). Expenses: Contact institution. In 2008, 13 master's awarded. Offers dietetics (MS). Five-year program that begins at freshman entry. *Application deadline:* For fall admission, 5/1 priority date for international students; for spring admission, 9/1 priority date for international students. Applications are processed on a rolling basis. *Application fee:* $25. Electronic applications accepted. *Application Contact:* Dr. Steven Smith, Director of Admissions, 716-829-7600, Fax: 716-829-7900, E-mail: admiss@dyc.edu. *Chair,* Dr. Charlotte Baumgart, 716-829-7752, Fax: 716-829-8137.

Department of Education Students: 431 full-time (307 women), 224 part-time (178 women); includes 22 minority (9 African Americans, 2 American Indian/Alaska Native, 1 Asian American or Pacific Islander, 10 Hispanic Americans), 517 international. Average age 28. 852 applicants, 52% accepted, 241 enrolled. *Faculty:* 29 full-time (18 women), 29 part-time/adjunct (17 women). Expenses: Contact institution. *Financial support:* In 2008–09, 1 research assistantship with partial tuition reimbursement (averaging $3,000 per year) was awarded; career-related internships or fieldwork, Federal Work-Study, institutionally sponsored loans, scholarships/grants, tuition waivers (full and partial), and unspecified assistantships also available. Support available to part-time students. Financial award application deadline: 3/1; financial award applicants required to submit FAFSA. In 2008, 245 master's, 323 other advanced degrees awarded. *Degree program information:* Part-time and evening/weekend programs available. Offers elementary education (MS Ed, Teaching Certificate); secondary education (MS Ed, Teaching Certificate); special education (MS Ed). *Application deadline:* For fall admission, 5/1 priority date for international students; for spring admission, 9/1 priority date for international students. Applications are processed on a rolling basis. *Application fee:* $25. Electronic applications accepted. *Application Contact:* Linda Fisher, Graduate Admissions Director, 716-829-8400, Fax: 716-829-7900, E-mail: graduateadmissions@dyc.edu. *Chair,* Dr. Kushnood Haq, 716-829-7629, Fax: 716-829-7660.

Department of Health Services Administration Students: 10 full-time (7 women), 46 part-time (32 women); includes 15 minority (11 African Americans, 2 Asian Americans or Pacific Islanders, 2 Hispanic Americans), 17 international. Average age 36. 37 applicants, 51% accepted, 15 enrolled. *Faculty:* 4 full-time (2 women), 4 part-time/adjunct (0 women). Expenses: Contact institution. *Financial support:* In 2008–09, 1 research assistantship with partial tuition reimbursement (averaging $3,000 per year) was awarded; career-related internships or fieldwork, Federal Work-Study, and scholarships/grants also available. Support available to part-time students. Financial award application deadline: 3/1; financial award applicants required to submit FAFSA. In 2008, 8 master's, 1 other advanced degree awarded. *Degree program information:* Part-time and evening/weekend programs available. Offers clinical research associate (Certificate); health services administration (MS, Certificate); long term care administration (Certificate). *Application deadline:* For fall admission, 5/1 priority date for international students; for spring admission, 9/1 priority date for international students. Applications are processed on a rolling basis. *Application fee:* $25. Electronic applications accepted. *Application Contact:* Linda Fisher, Graduate Admissions Director, 716-829-8400, Fax: 716-829-7900, E-mail: graduateadmissions@dyc.edu. *Chair,* Dr. Walter Iwanenko, 716-829-7612, Fax: 716-829-8184.

Department of Holistic Health Studies Students: 77 full-time (35 women); includes 6 minority (2 African Americans, 3 Asian Americans or Pacific Islanders, 1 Hispanic American), 15 international. Average age 25. 107 applicants, 54% accepted, 31 enrolled. *Faculty:* 6 full-time (0 women), 6 part-time/adjunct (5 women). Expenses: Contact institution. In 2008, 4 DCs awarded. Offers chiropractic (DC). *Application fee:* $25. *Application Contact:* Linda Fisher, Graduate Admissions Director, 716-829-8400, Fax: 716-829-7900, E-mail: graduateadmissions@dyc.edu. *Director, Chiropractic Program,* Dr. Peter Hagman, 716-829-7606 Ext. 7793, Fax: 716-829-7893.

Department of Nursing Students: 121 full-time (109 women), 74 part-time (71 women); includes 16 minority (14 African Americans, 2 American Indian/Alaska Native), 95 international. Average age 35. 189 applicants, 62% accepted, 53 enrolled. *Faculty:* 7 full-time (all women), 7 part-time/adjunct (6 women). Expenses: Contact institution. *Financial support:* In 2008–09, 1 research assistantship with partial tuition reimbursement (averaging $3,000 per year) was awarded; Federal Work-Study and scholarships/grants also available. Support available to part-time students. Financial award application deadline: 3/1; financial award applicants required to submit FAFSA. In 2008, 41 master's awarded. *Degree program information:* Part-time and evening/weekend programs available. Offers community health nursing/education (MSN); community health nursing/high risk parents and children (MSN); community health nursing/management (MSN); family nurse practitioner (MS, Post-Master's Certificate); nursing and health-related professions (Certificate); nursing with clinical focus choice (MSN). *Application deadline:* For fall admission, 5/1 priority date for international students; for spring admission, 9/1 priority date for international students. Applications are processed on a rolling basis. *Application fee:* $25. Electronic applications accepted. *Application Contact:* Linda Fisher, Graduate Admissions Director, 716-829-8400, Fax: 716-829-7900, E-mail: graduateadmissions@dyc.edu. *Chair,* Dr. Kathleen Mariano, 716-829-7613, Fax: 716-829-8159.

Department of Physical Therapy Students: 83 full-time (52 women), 14 part-time (8 women); includes 7 minority (4 African Americans, 3 Asian Americans or Pacific Islanders), 43 international. Average age 25. 168 applicants, 53% accepted, 49 enrolled. *Faculty:* 7 full-time (4 women), 4 part-time/adjunct (3 women). Expenses: Contact institution. *Financial support:* In 2008–09, 3 research assistantships with partial tuition reimbursements were awarded; Federal Work-Study and scholarships/grants also available. Financial award application deadline: 3/1; financial award applicants required to submit FAFSA. In 2008, 42 master's, 17 doctorates awarded. *Degree program information:* Part-time programs available. Postbaccalaureate distance learning degree programs offered (minimal on-campus study). Offers advanced orthopedic physical therapy (Certificate); manual physical therapy (Certificate); physical therapy (MPT, MS, DPT). *Application deadline:* For fall admission, 5/1 priority date for international students; for spring admission, 9/1 priority date for international students. Applications are processed on a rolling basis. *Application fee:* $25. Electronic applications accepted. *Application Contact:* Linda Fisher, Graduate Admissions Director, 716-829-8400, Fax: 716-829-7900, E-mail: graduateadmissions@dyc.edu. *Chair,* Dr. Lynn Rivers, 716-829-7708 Ext. 7708, Fax: 716-829-8137, E-mail: riversl@dyc.edu.

Doctoral Programs Students: 1 full-time (0 women), 65 part-time (42 women); includes 5 minority (3 African Americans, 1 Asian American or Pacific Islander, 1 Hispanic American), 16 international. Average age 46. 16 applicants, 69% accepted, 8 enrolled. *Faculty:* 6 full-time (2 women), 23 part-time/adjunct (13 women). Expenses: Contact institution. *Financial support:* In 2008–09, research assistantships with tuition reimbursements (averaging $3,000 per year); scholarships/grants also available. In 2008, 5 doctorates awarded. *Degree program information:* Part-time and evening/weekend programs available. Offers educational leadership (Ed D); health education (Ed D); health policy (Ed D). *Application Contact:* Linda Fisher, Graduate Admissions Director, 716-829-8400, Fax: 716-829-7900, E-mail: graduateadmissions@dyc.edu. *Director of Doctoral Programs,* Dr. Mark Garrison, 716-829-8125, E-mail: garrisonm@dyc.edu.

Occupational Therapy Department Students: 118 full-time (108 women), 9 part-time (6 women); includes 8 minority (3 African Americans, 1 American Indian/Alaska Native, 3 Asian Americans or Pacific Islanders, 1 Hispanic American), 31 international. Average age 23. 159 applicants, 70% accepted, 42 enrolled. *Faculty:* 8 full-time (all women), 2 part-time/adjunct (both women). Expenses: Contact institution. *Financial support:* In 2008–09, 1 research assistantship with partial tuition reimbursement (averaging $3,000 per year) was awarded; scholarships/grants, tuition waivers (partial), and unspecified assistantships also available. In 2008, 23 master's awarded. Offers occupational therapy (MS). *Application deadline:* For fall admission, 5/1 priority date for international students; for spring admission, 9/1 priority date for international students. Applications are processed on a rolling basis. *Application fee:* $25. Electronic applications accepted. *Application Contact:* Linda Fisher, Graduate Admissions Director, 716-829-8400, Fax: 716-829-7900, E-mail: graduateadmissions@dyc.edu. *Chair,* Dr. Amy Nwora, 716-829-7707, Fax: 716-829-8137.

Physician Assistant Department Students: 133 full-time (97 women), 5 part-time (4 women); includes 14 minority (5 African Americans, 1 American Indian/Alaska Native, 3 Asian Americans or Pacific Islanders, 5 Hispanic Americans), 10 international. Average age 27. 190 applicants, 27% accepted, 23 enrolled. *Faculty:* 5 full-time (4 women), 1 part-time/adjunct (0 women). Expenses: Contact institution. In 2008, 19 master's awarded. Offers physician assistant (MS). *Application deadline:* For fall admission, 5/1 priority date for international students; for spring admission, 9/1 priority date for international students. Applications are processed on a rolling basis. *Application fee:* $25. Electronic applications accepted. *Application Contact:* Linda Fisher, Graduate Admissions Director, 716-829-8400, Fax: 716-829-7900, E-mail: graduateadmissions@dyc.edu. *Chair,* Dr. Maureen F. Finney, 716-829-7730, E-mail: finneym@dyc.edu.

See Close-Up on page 903.

EARLHAM COLLEGE, Richmond, IN 47374-4095

General Information Independent-religious, coed, comprehensive institution. *Graduate housing:* On-campus housing not available.

GRADUATE UNITS

Graduate Programs Offers education (M Ed, MAT).

EARLHAM SCHOOL OF RELIGION, Richmond, IN 47374-5360

General Information Independent-religious, coed, graduate-only institution. *Graduate housing:* On-campus housing not available.

GRADUATE UNITS

Graduate Programs *Degree program information:* Part-time programs available. Postbaccalaureate distance learning degree programs offered (minimal on-campus study). Offers religion (MA); theology (M Div, M Min). Electronic applications accepted.

EAST CAROLINA UNIVERSITY, Greenville, NC 27858-4353

General Information State-supported, coed, university. CGS member. *Graduate housing:* Room and/or apartments available on a first-come, first-served basis to single students; on-campus housing not available to married students. Housing application deadline: 5/1.

GRADUATE UNITS

Brody School of Medicine Offers anatomy and cell biology (PhD); biochemistry and molecular biology (PhD); medicine (MD, MPH, PhD); microbiology and immunology (PhD); Pathology (PhD); pharmacology (PhD); physiology (PhD); public health (MPH).

Graduate School *Degree program information:* Part-time and evening/weekend programs available. Postbaccalaureate distance learning degree programs offered (no on-campus study). Offers coastal resources management (PhD).

College of Business *Degree program information:* Part-time and evening/weekend programs available. Offers accounting (MS); business (MBA, MS, MSA); management (MBA).

College of Education *Degree program information:* Part-time and evening/weekend programs available. Postbaccalaureate distance learning degree programs offered (no on-campus study). Offers adult education (MA Ed); behavior/emotional disabilities (MA Ed); counselor education (MS, Ed S); education (MA, MA Ed, MLS, MS, MSA, Ed D, CAS, Ed S); educational administration and supervision (Ed S); educational leadership (Ed D); elementary education (MA Ed); English education (MA Ed); higher education administration (Ed D); information technologies (MS); instruction technology specialist (MA Ed); learning disabilities (MA Ed); library science (MLS, CAS); low incidence disabilities (MA Ed); mathematics (MA Ed), mental retardation (MA Ed), middle grade education (MA Ed); reading education (MA Ed); school administration (MSA); science education (MA, MA Ed); social studies education (MA Ed); supervision (MA Ed); vocation education (MA Ed).

College of Fine Arts and Communication Offers art and design (MA, MA Ed, MFA); fine arts and communication (MA, MA Ed, MFA, MM); health communication (MA); music education (MM); music therapy (MM); performance (MM); theory and composition (MM).

College of Health and Human Performance *Degree program information:* Part-time and evening/weekend programs available. Offers bioenergetics (PhD); environmental health (MS); exercise and sport science (MA, MA Ed); health and human performance (MA, MA Ed, MS, PhD); health education (MA, MA Ed); recreation and leisure services administration (MS); therapeutic recreation administration (MS).

College of Human Ecology *Degree program information:* Part-time programs available. Offers child development and family relations (MS); criminal justice (MS); human ecology (MS, MSW); marriage and family therapy (MS); nutrition (MS); social work (MSW).

College of Nursing *Degree program information:* Part-time programs available. Offers nursing (MSN, PhD).

College of Technology and Computer Science *Degree program information:* Part-time programs available. Offers computer network professional (Certificate); computer science (MS); industrial technology (MS); information assurance (Certificate); occupational safety (MS); technology and computer science (MS, PhD, Certificate); technology management (PhD); Website developer (Certificate).

School of Allied Health Sciences *Degree program information:* Part-time and evening/weekend programs available. Postbaccalaureate distance learning degree programs offered (no on-campus study). Offers allied health sciences (MPT, MS, MSOT, DPT, PhD); communication sciences and disorders (PhD); occupational therapy (MSOT); physical therapy (MPT, DPT); physician assistant studies (MS); rehabilitation counseling (MS); speech, language and auditory pathology (MS); substance abuse and clinical counseling (MS); vocational evaluation (MS).

Thomas Harriot College of Arts and Sciences *Degree program information:* Part-time and evening/weekend programs available. Offers American history (MA); anthropology (MA); applied and biomedical physics (MS); applied mathematics (MA); applied resource economics (MS); arts and sciences (MA, MA Ed, MPA, MS, PhD); biology (MS); chemistry (MS); clinical psychology (MA); English (MA); European history (MA); general psychology (MA); geography (MA); geology (MS); health psychology (PhD); international studies (MA); maritime history (MA); mathematics (MA); medical physics (MS); molecular biology/biotechnology (MS); physics (PhD); public administration (MPA); sociology (MA).

EAST CENTRAL UNIVERSITY, Ada, OK 74820-6899

General Information State-supported, coed, comprehensive institution. CGS member. *Enrollment:* 196 full-time matriculated graduate/professional students (143 women), 584 part-time matriculated graduate/professional students (426 women). *Enrollment by degree level:* 780 master's. *Graduate faculty:* 48. Tuition, state resident: full-time $1175; part-time $130.50 per credit hour. Tuition, nonresident: full-time $3335; part-time $370.50 per credit hour. *Required fees:* $38 per credit hour. *Graduate housing:* Rooms and/or apartments available on a first-come, first-served basis to single and married students. Typical cost: $3400 per year ($4706 including board) for single students; $2000 per year for married students. *Student services:* Campus employment opportunities, career counseling, child daycare facilities, exercise/wellness program, free psychological counseling, grant writing training, international student services, multicultural affairs office, services for students with disabilities, teacher training, writing training. *Library facilities:* Linscheid Library. *Online resources:* library catalog, web page. *Collection:* 182,126 titles, 25,076 serial subscriptions, 906 audiovisual materials.

Computer facilities: 500 computers available on campus for general student use. A campuswide network can be accessed. *Web address:* http://www.ecok.edu/.

General Application Contact: Dr. G. Richard Wetherill, Interim Dean, 580-559-5709 Ext. 709, Fax: 580-332-8691, E-mail: rwethrll@mailclerk.ecok.edu.

GRADUATE UNITS

School of Graduate Studies *Degree program information:* Part-time and evening/weekend programs available. Offers administration (MSHR); counseling (MSHR); criminal justice (MSHR); education (M Ed); psychology (MSPS); rehabilitation counseling (MSHR). Electronic applications accepted.

EASTERN CONNECTICUT STATE UNIVERSITY, Willimantic, CT 06226-2295

General Information State-supported, coed, comprehensive institution. *Enrollment:* 5,427 graduate, professional, and undergraduate students; 66 full-time matriculated graduate/professional students (42 women), 210 part-time matriculated graduate/professional students (160 women). *Enrollment by degree level:* 276 master's. *Graduate faculty:* 11 full-time (6 women), 16 part-time/adjunct (10 women). *Tuition, area resident:* Full-time $4000; part-time $400 per credit. Tuition, nonresident: full-time $12,000. *Required fees:* $50 per term. *Graduate housing:* On-campus housing not available. *Student services:* Campus employment opportunities, campus safety program, career counseling, child daycare facilities, exercise/wellness program, free psychological counseling, grant writing training, international student services, low-cost health insurance, multicultural affairs office, services for students with disabilities, teacher training, writing training. *Library facilities:* J. Eugene Smith Library. *Online resources:* library catalog, web page, access to other libraries' catalogs. *Collection:* 239,218 titles, 1,729 serial subscriptions. *Research affiliation:* Department of Education (early childhood education, mathematics and science education).

Computer facilities: Computer purchase and lease plans are available. 637 computers available on campus for general student use. A campuswide network can be accessed from student residence rooms and from off campus. Online class registration is available. *Web address:* http://www.easternct.edu/.

General Application Contact: Graduate Division, School of Education and Professional Studies, 860-465-5292, E-mail: graduateadmissions@easternct.edu.

GRADUATE UNITS

School of Education and Professional Studies/Graduate Division Students: 66 full-time (42 women), 219 part-time (161 women); includes 22 minority (9 African Americans, 4 Asian Americans or Pacific Islanders, 9 Hispanic Americans), 4 international. Average age 34. 89 applicants, 69% accepted, 31 enrolled. *Faculty:* 11 full-time (6 women), 16 part-time/adjunct (10 women). Expenses: Contact institution. *Financial support:* Teaching assistantships, career-related internships or fieldwork, scholarships/grants, and unspecified assistantships available. Support available to part-time students. Financial award application deadline: 3/15. In 2008, 112 master's awarded. *Degree program information:* Part-time and evening/weekend programs available. Offers early childhood education (MS); education and professional studies (MS); educational technology (MS); elementary education (MS); organizational management (MS); reading and language arts (MS); science education (MS); secondary education (MS). *Application deadline:* For fall admission, 7/6 priority date for domestic and international students; for spring admission, 11/3 priority date for domestic and international students. Applications are processed on a rolling basis. *Application fee:* $50. *Application Contact:* Graduate Division, School of Education and Professional Studies, 860-465-5292, E-mail: graduateadmissions@easternct.edu. *Dean,* Dr. Patricia A. Kleine, 860-465-5293, Fax: 860-465-4538, E-mail: kleinep@easternct.edu.

EASTERN ILLINOIS UNIVERSITY, Charleston, IL 61920-3099

General Information State-supported, coed, comprehensive institution. CGS member. *Graduate housing:* Rooms and/or apartments available to single and married students.

GRADUATE UNITS

Graduate School *Degree program information:* Part-time and evening/weekend programs available. Electronic applications accepted.

College of Arts and Humanities *Degree program information:* Part-time programs available. Offers art (MA); art education (MA); arts and humanities (MA); communication studies (MA); English (MA); historical administration (MA); history (MA); music (MA).

College of Education and Professional Studies *Degree program information:* Part-time and evening/weekend programs available. Offers clinical counseling (MS); college student affairs (MS); education and professional studies (MS, MS Ed, Ed S); educational administration (MS Ed, Ed S); elementary education (MS Ed); physical education (MS); school counseling (MS); special education (MS Ed).

College of Sciences *Degree program information:* Part-time programs available. Offers biological sciences (MS); chemistry (MS); clinical psychology (MA); communication disorders and sciences (MS); economics (MA); mathematics (MA); mathematics and computer science (MA); mathematics education (MA); natural sciences (MS); political science (MA); psychology (MA, SSP); school psychology (SSP).

Lumpkin College of Business and Applied Sciences *Degree program information:* Part-time and evening/weekend programs available. Offers accountancy (Certificate); business and applied sciences (MA, MBA, MS, Certificate); computer technology (Certificate); dietetics (MS); family and consumer sciences (MS); general management (MBA); gerontology (MA); quality systems (Certificate); technology (MS); technology security (Certificate); work performance improvement (Certificate).

EASTERN KENTUCKY UNIVERSITY, Richmond, KY 40475-3102

General Information State-supported, coed, comprehensive institution. CGS member. *Graduate housing:* Rooms and/or apartments guaranteed to single students and available to married students.

GRADUATE UNITS

The Graduate School *Degree program information:* Part-time and evening/weekend programs available. Postbaccalaureate distance learning degree programs offered. Electronic applications accepted.

College of Arts and Sciences *Degree program information:* Part-time and evening/weekend programs available. Offers arts and sciences (MA, MFA, MM, MPA, MS, PhD, Psy S); biological sciences (MS); chemistry (MS); choral conducting (MM); clinical psychology (MS); community development (MPA); community health administration (MPA); creative writing (MFA); ecology (MS); English (MA); general public administration (MPA); geology (MS, PhD); history (MA); industrial/organizational psychology (MS); mathematical sciences (MS); performance (MM); political science (MA); school psychology (Psy S); theory/composition (MM).

College of Business and Technology *Degree program information:* Part-time programs available. Offers business administration (MBA); business and technology (MBA, MS); industrial education (MS); industrial technology (MS); occupational training and development (MS); technical administration (MS); technology education (MS).

College of Education *Degree program information:* Part-time programs available. Postbaccalaureate distance learning degree programs offered (minimal on-campus study). Offers communication disorders (MA Ed); education (MA, MA Ed, MAT); elementary education (MA Ed); human services (MA); instructional leadership (MA Ed); library science (MA Ed); mental health counseling (MA); music education (MA Ed); school counseling (MA Ed); secondary and higher education (MA Ed); secondary education (MA Ed); teaching (MAT).

College of Health Sciences *Degree program information:* Part-time programs available. Offers community health (MPH); community nutrition (MS); environmental health science (MPH); exercise and sport science (MS); exercise and wellness (MS); health sciences (MPH, MS, MSN); occupational therapy (MS); recreation and park administration (MS); rural community health care (MSN); rural health family nurse practitioner (MSN); sports administration (MS).

College of Justice and Safety *Degree program information:* Part-time programs available. Offers correctional and juvenile justice studies (MS); criminal justice (MS); criminal justice education (MS); justice and safety (MS); loss prevention and safety (MS); police studies (MS).

EASTERN MENNONITE UNIVERSITY, Harrisonburg, VA 22802-2462

General Information Independent-religious, coed, comprehensive institution. *Enrollment:* 1,387 graduate, professional, and undergraduate students; 114 full-time matriculated graduate/professional students (68 women), 190 part-time matriculated graduate/professional students (120 women). *Enrollment by degree level:* 78 first professional, 226 master's. *Graduate faculty:* 22 full-time (7 women), 22 part-time/adjunct (6 women). *Tuition:* Part-time $455 per credit hour. Tuition and fees vary according to program. *Graduate housing:* Rooms and/or apartments available on a first-come, first-served basis to single and married students. Typical cost: $7200 per year ($14,400 including board) for single students. Housing application deadline: 4/15. *Student services:* Campus employment opportunities, career counseling, exercise/wellness program, free psychological counseling, international student services, low-cost health insurance, multicultural affairs office, services for students with disabilities, teacher training, writing training. *Library facilities:* Sadie Hartzler Library. *Online resources:* library catalog, web page. *Collection:* 168,135 titles, 965 serial subscriptions, 8,077 audiovisual materials.

Computer facilities: 152 computers available on campus for general student use. A campuswide network can be accessed from student residence rooms and from off campus. Online class registration is available. *Web address:* http://www.emu.edu/.

General Application Contact: Don A. Yoder, Director of Seminary and Graduate Admissions, 540-432-4257, Fax: 540-432-4598, E-mail: yoderda@emu.edu.

GRADUATE UNITS

Eastern Mennonite Seminary Students: 48 full-time (21 women), 30 part-time (10 women); includes 6 minority (5 African Americans, 1 Hispanic American), 12 international. Average age 40. 40 applicants, 100% accepted, 37 enrolled. *Faculty:* 8 full-time (2 women), 8 part-time/adjunct (2 women). Expenses: Contact institution. *Financial support:* Application deadline: 6/30. In 2008, 15 first professional degrees, 9 master's awarded. *Degree program information:* Part-time programs available. Offers church leadership (MA); divinity (M Div); ministry studies (Certificate); online theological studies (Certificate); religion (MA); theological studies (Certificate). *Application deadline:* For fall admission, 6/15 priority date for domestic and international students; for winter admission, 11/15 priority date for domestic and international students; for spring admission, 3/15 priority date for domestic and international students. Applications are processed on a rolling basis. *Application fee:* $25. *Application Contact:* Don A. Yoder, Director of Seminary and Graduate Admissions, 540-432-4257, Fax: 540-432-4598, E-mail: yoderda@emu.edu. *Seminary Dean,* Dr. Ervin R. Stutzman, 540-432-4261, Fax: 540-432-4444, E-mail: stutzerv@emu.edu.

Program in Business Administration Students: 41 part-time (18 women); includes 1 minority (African American), 1 international. Average age 38. 15 applicants, 100% accepted, 12 enrolled. *Faculty:* 6 full-time (0 women), 9 part-time/adjunct (1 woman). Expenses: Contact institution. *Financial support:* Application deadline: 6/30. In 2008, 12 master's awarded. *Degree program information:* Part-time and evening/weekend programs available. Offers business administration (MBA). *Application deadline:* For fall admission, 3/1 priority date for domestic and international students. Applications are processed on a rolling basis. *Application fee:* $25. *Application Contact:* Patricia S. Eckard, Office Coordinator, Business and Economics, 540-432-4150, Fax: 540-432-4071, E-mail: eckardp@emu.edu. *Co-Director, MBA Program,* Dr. Ronald L. Stoltzfus, 540-432-4155, Fax: 540-432 -4071, E-mail: stoltzfr@emu.edu.

Program in Conflict Transformation Students: 40 full-time (28 women), 12 part-time (5 women); includes 1 minority (African American), 7 international. Average age 37. *Faculty:* 7 full-time (2 women), 3 part-time/adjunct (1 woman). Expenses: Contact institution. *Financial support:* In 2008–09, 4 students received support. Scholarships/grants available. Financial award application deadline: 6/30; financial award applicants required to submit FAFSA. *Degree program information:* Part-time programs available. Offers conflict transformation (MA, Graduate Certificate). *Application deadline:* For fall admission, 2/15 priority date for domestic and international students. Applications are processed on a rolling basis. *Application fee:* $25. Electronic applications accepted. *Application Contact:* Janelle Myers-Benner, Administrative Assistant, 540-432-4986, Fax: 540-432-4449, E-mail: bennerj@emu.edu. *Academic Director,* Dr. David Brubaker, 540-432-4423, Fax: 540-432-4449, E-mail: david.brubaker@emu.edu.

Program in Counseling Students: 25 full-time (18 women), 9 part-time (8 women); includes 2 minority (1 African American, 1 Asian American or Pacific Islander), 3 international. Average age 38. 28 applicants, 75% accepted, 17 enrolled. *Faculty:* 3 full-time (2 women), 3 part-time/adjunct (2 women). Expenses: Contact institution. *Financial support:* In 2008–09, 7 students received support. Scholarships/grants available. Financial award application deadline: 6/30; financial award applicants required to submit FAFSA. In 2008, 20 master's awarded. *Degree program information:* Part-time programs available. Offers counseling (MA). *Application deadline:* For fall admission, 3/1 for domestic students. *Application fee:* $25. *Application Contact:* Brenda C. Fairweather, Administrative Assistant, 540-432-4243, Fax: 540-432-4444, E-mail: fairweat@emu.edu. *Professor of Counselor Education,* Dr. P. David Glanzer, 540-432-4244, Fax: 540-432-4444, E-mail: glanzerd@emu.edu.

Program in Education Students: 1 (woman) full-time, 98 part-time (79 women); includes 4 minority (3 African Americans, 1 Hispanic American), 4 international. Average age 34. *Faculty:* 5 full-time (4 women), 11 part-time/adjunct (5 women). Expenses: Contact institution. *Financial support:* Federal Work-Study and scholarships/grants available. Financial award application deadline: 6/30; financial award applicants required to submit FAFSA. *Degree program information:* Part-time programs available. Offers education (MA). *Application deadline:* Applications are processed on a rolling basis. *Application fee:* $25. *Application Contact:* Yvonne Martin, Education Secretary, 540-432-4350, Fax: 540-432-4071, E-mail: yvonne.martin@emu.edu. *Director,* Dr. Donovan D. Steiner, 540-432-4144, Fax: 540-432-4071, E-mail: steinerd@emu.edu.

EASTERN MICHIGAN UNIVERSITY, Ypsilanti, MI 48197

General Information State-supported, coed, comprehensive institution. CGS member. *Enrollment:* 21,926 graduate, professional, and undergraduate students; 1,071 full-time matriculated graduate/professional students (623 women), 3,294 part-time matriculated graduate/professional students (2,116 women). *Enrollment by degree level:* 3,710 master's, 205 doctoral, 450 other advanced degrees. *Graduate faculty:* 705 full-time (329 women). Tuition, state resident: full-time $9636; part-time $401.50 per credit hour. Tuition, nonresident: full-time $18,996; part-time $791.50 per credit hour. *Required fees:* $36.60 per credit hour. $43 per term. One-time fee: $88. Tuition and fees vary according to course level, course load, degree level, program and reciprocity agreements. *Graduate housing:* Rooms and/or apartments available on a first-come, first-served basis to single and married students. Typical cost: $7352 (including board) for single students. Room and board charges vary according to board plan, campus/location and housing facility selected. *Student services:* Campus employment opportunities, campus safety program, career counseling, child daycare facilities, exercise/wellness program, free psychological counseling, grant writing training, international student services, low-cost health insurance, multicultural affairs office, services for students with disabilities, teacher training, writing training. *Library facilities:* Bruce T. Halle Library. *Online resources:* library catalog. *Collection:* 970,268 titles, 2,375 serial subscriptions, 16,314 audiovisual materials. *Research affiliation:* TRACO (coatings research), 3M (coatings research), Toyota (coatings research), Beckers-Fusion (coatings research), Dima-Shield (coatings research), Signal Medical Company (textiles research).

Eastern Michigan University (continued)

Computer facilities: 1,500 computers available on campus for general student use. A campuswide network can be accessed from student residence rooms and from off campus. Online class registration is available. *Web address:* http://www.emich.edu/.

General Application Contact: Graduate Admissions, 734-487-2400, Fax: 734-487-6559, E-mail: graduate.admissions@emich.edu.

GRADUATE UNITS

Graduate School Students: 1,071 full-time (623 women), 3,294 part-time (2,116 women); includes 784 minority (559 African Americans, 31 American Indian/Alaska Native, 124 Asian Americans or Pacific Islanders, 70 Hispanic Americans), 583 international. Average age 33. 3,599 applicants, 68% accepted, 1578 enrolled. *Faculty:* 705 full-time (329 women). Expenses: Contact institution. *Financial support:* In 2008–09, 2,346 students received support; fellowships, research assistantships with full tuition reimbursements available, teaching assistantships with full tuition reimbursements available, career-related internships or fieldwork, Federal Work-Study, institutionally sponsored loans, scholarships/grants, tuition waivers (partial), and unspecified assistantships available. Support available to part-time students. Financial award applicants required to submit FAFSA. In 2008, 1,227 master's, 18 doctorates, 134 other advanced degrees awarded. *Degree program information:* Part-time and evening/weekend programs available. Postbaccalaureate distance learning degree programs offered (minimal on-campus study). *Application deadline:* For fall admission, 2/15 priority date for domestic students, 5/1 priority date for international students; for winter admission, 10/15 priority date for domestic students, 10/1 priority date for international students; for spring admission, 3/15 priority date for domestic students, 3/1 priority date for international students. Applications are processed on a rolling basis. *Application fee:* $35. Electronic applications accepted. *Application Contact:* Graduate Admissions, 734-487-3400, Fax: 734-487-6559, E-mail: graduate.admissions@emich.edu. *Interim Dean,* Dr. Deborah deLaski-Smith, 734-487-0042, Fax: 734-487-0050, E-mail: deb.delaski-smith@emich.edu.

Academic Affairs Division Students: 30 full-time (23 women), 48 part-time (33 women); includes 18 minority (15 African Americans, 1 Asian American or Pacific Islander, 2 Hispanic Americans). Average age 34. Expenses: Contact institution. In 2008, 19 master's awarded. Offers individualized studies (MA, MS); integrated marketing communications (MS).

College of Arts and Sciences Students: 338 full-time (211 women), 750 part-time (472 women); includes 191 minority (124 African Americans, 10 American Indian/Alaska Native, 37 Asian Americans or Pacific Islanders, 20 Hispanic Americans), 156 international. Average age 31. *Faculty:* 398 full-time (161 women). Expenses: Contact institution. *Financial support:* Fellowships, research assistantships with full tuition reimbursements, teaching assistantships with full tuition reimbursements, career-related internships or fieldwork, Federal Work-Study, institutionally sponsored loans, and tuition waivers (partial) available. Support available to part-time students. Financial award applicants required to submit FAFSA. In 2008, 321 master's, 6 doctorates, 16 other advanced degrees awarded. *Degree program information:* Part-time and evening/weekend programs available. Offers African-American studies (Graduate Certificate); applied economics (MA); applied statistics (MA); art (MA); art education (MA); artificial intelligence (Graduate Certificate); arts administration (MA); arts and sciences (MA, MFA, MLS, MM, MPA, MS, PhD, Graduate Certificate); bioinformatics (MS, Graduate Certificate); cell and molecular biology (MS); chemistry (MS); children's literature (MA); clinical behavioral psychology (MS); clinical psychology (MS, PhD); communication (MA); community college biology teaching (MS); computer science (MA, MS); creative writing (MA); criminology and criminal justice (MA); drama/theatre for the young (MA, MFA); earth science education (MS); ecology and organismal biology (MS); economics (MA); English linguistics (MA); English studies for teachers (MA); foreign languages (MA, Graduate Certificate); French (MA); general biology (MS); general science (MS); geographic information systems (MS, Graduate Certificate); geography (MA, MS); geography and geology (MA, MS, Graduate Certificate); German (MA); German for business (Graduate Certificate); GIS educator (Graduate Certificate); GIS professional (Graduate Certificate); GIS-planning (MS); health economics (MA); heritage interpretation and tourism (MS); Hispanic language and cultures (Graduate Certificate); historic preservation (MS, Graduate Certificate); history (MA, Graduate Certificate); international economics and development (MA); interpretation/performance studies (MA); Japanese business practices (Graduate Certificate); language and international trade (MA); language technology (Graduate Certificate); literature (MA, Graduate Certificate); local government management (Graduate Certificate); management of public healthcare services (Graduate Certificate); mathematics (MA); mathematics education (MA); music composition (MM); music education (MM); music pedagogy (MM); music performance (MM); physics (MS); physics education (MS); political science (MPA, Graduate Certificate); psychology (MS); public administration (MPA, Graduate Certificate); public budget management (Graduate Certificate); public land planning (Graduate Certificate); public management (Graduate Certificate); public personnel management (Graduate Certificate); public policy analysis (Graduate Certificate); schools, society and violence (MA); social science (MA, MLS, Graduate Certificate); social science and American culture (MLS); sociology (MA); sociology—family specialty (MA); Spanish (MA); state and local history (Graduate Certificate); studio art (MA, MFA); teaching English to speakers of other languages (MA, Graduate Certificate); teaching of writing (MA, Graduate Certificate); technical communications (MA, Graduate Certificate); theatre arts (MA); theatre arts-arts administration (MA); trade and development (MA); urban and regional planning (MS); water resources (MS, Graduate Certificate); women's and gender studies (MLS); written communication (MA, Graduate Certificate); written communications (MA). *Application deadline:* Applications are processed on a rolling basis. *Application fee:* $35. *Application Contact:* Dr. Thomas Venner, Dean, 734-487-4344, Fax: 734-485-9592, E-mail: tom.venner@emich.edu. *Dean,* Dr. Thomas Venner, 734-487-4344, Fax: 734-485-9592, E-mail: tom.venner@emich.edu.

College of Business Students: 294 full-time (135 women), 482 part-time (267 women); includes 135 minority (83 African Americans, 7 American Indian/Alaska Native, 36 Asian Americans or Pacific Islanders, 9 Hispanic Americans), 230 international. Average age 30. *Faculty:* 64 full-time (19 women). Expenses: Contact institution. *Financial support:* Fellowships, research assistantships with full tuition reimbursements, teaching assistantships with full tuition reimbursements, career-related internships or fieldwork, Federal Work-Study, institutionally sponsored loans, traineeships, tuition waivers (partial), and unspecified assistantships available. Support available to part-time students. Financial award applicants required to submit FAFSA. In 2008, 272 master's, 41 other advanced degrees awarded. *Degree program information:* Part-time and evening/weekend programs available. Postbaccalaureate distance learning degree programs offered (minimal on-campus study). Offers accounting (MS); accounting information systems (MS); business (MBA, MS, MSHROD, MSIS, Graduate Certificate); business administration (MBA); e-business (MBA); enterprise business intelligence (MBA); entrepreneurship (MBA, Graduate Certificate); finance (MBA); human resources (MBA); human resources management and organizational development (MSHROD); information systems (MBA, MSIS); internal auditing (MBA); international business (MBA); nonprofit management (MBA); supply chain management (MBA). *Application deadline:* Applications are processed on a rolling basis. *Application fee:* $35. *Application Contact:* Dawn Gaymer, Assistant Dean, Graduate Business Programs, 734-487-4444, Fax: 734-483-1316, E-mail: cob.grad@emich.edu. *Dean,* Dr. David Mielke, 734-487-4140, Fax: 734-487-7099, E-mail: dmielke@emich.edu.

College of Education Students: 169 full-time (132 women), 1,123 part-time (856 women); includes 221 minority (172 African Americans, 10 American Indian/Alaska Native, 21 Asian Americans or Pacific Islanders, 18 Hispanic Americans), 15 international. Average age 35. *Faculty:* 112 full-time (85 women). Expenses: Contact institution. *Financial support:* Fellowships, research assistantships with full tuition reimbursements, teaching assistantships with full tuition reimbursements, career-related internships or fieldwork, Federal Work-Study, institutionally sponsored loans, scholarships/grants, tuition waivers (partial), and unspecified assistantships available. Support available to part-time students. Financial award applicants required to submit FAFSA. In 2008, 325 master's, 9 doctorates, 20 other advanced degrees awarded. *Degree program information:* Part-time and evening/weekend programs available. Postbaccalaureate distance learning degree programs offered (minimal on-campus study). Offers autism spectrum disorders (MA); cognitive impairment (MA); college counseling (MA); college student personnel (MA); community college leadership (Graduate Certificate); community counseling (MA); counseling (MA, Graduate Certificate, Post Master's Certificate); culture and diversity (MA); curriculum and instruction (MA); early childhood education (MA); education (MA, Ed D, PhD, Graduate Certificate, Post Master's Certificate, SPA); educational assessment (Graduate Certificate); educational leadership (MA, Ed D, SPA); educational media and technology (MA, Graduate Certificate); educational psychology (MA); educational psychology and assessment (MA, Graduate Certificate); educational studies (PhD); elementary education (MA); emotional impairment (MA); hearing impairment (MA); helping interventions in a multicultural society (Graduate Certificate); higher education general administration (MA); higher education student affairs (MA); K-12 administration (MA); K-12 education (MA); leadership (MA, Ed D, Graduate Certificate, SPA); learning disabilities (MA); mentally impaired (MA); middle school education (MA); physical/other health impairment (MA); reading (MA); school counseling (MA); school counselor (MA); school counselor licensure (Post Master's Certificate); secondary school education (MA); social foundations (MA); special education (MA, SPA); special education-administration and supervision (SPA); special education-curriculum development (SPA); speech and language pathology (MA); visual impairment (MA). *Application deadline:* Applications are processed on a rolling basis. *Application fee:* $35. *Application Contact:* Graduate Admissions, 734-487-3400, Fax: 734-487-6559, E-mail: graduate.admissions@emich.edu. *Dean,* Dr. Vernon C. Polite, 734-487-1414, Fax: 734-484-6471, E-mail: vpolite@emich.edu.

College of Health and Human Services Students: 151 full-time (105 women), 445 part-time (357 women); includes 136 minority (104 African Americans, 3 American Indian/Alaska Native, 17 Asian Americans or Pacific Islanders, 12 Hispanic Americans), 39 international. Average age 34. *Faculty:* 86 full-time (61 women). Expenses: Contact institution. *Financial support:* Fellowships, research assistantships with full tuition reimbursements, teaching assistantships with full tuition reimbursements, career-related internships or fieldwork, Federal Work-Study, institutionally sponsored loans, scholarships/grants, tuition waivers (partial), and unspecified assistantships available. Support available to part-time students. Financial award applicants required to submit FAFSA. In 2008, 166 master's, 51 other advanced degrees awarded. *Degree program information:* Part-time and evening/weekend programs available. Postbaccalaureate distance learning degree programs offered (minimal on-campus study). Offers adapted physical education (MS); clinical research administration (MS, Graduate Certificate); community building (Graduate Certificate); exercise physiology (MS); family and children's services (MSW); gerontology (Graduate Certificate); gerontology-dementia (Graduate Certificate); health administration (MHA, MS, Graduate Certificate); health and human services (MHA, MOT, MPA, MS, MSN, MSW, Graduate Certificate); health education (MS); health promotion and human performance (MS, Graduate Certificate); health sciences (MHA, MOT, MS, Graduate Certificate); human nutrition (MS); human nutrition-coordinated program in dietetics (MS); mental health and chemical dependency (MSW); nonprofit management (Graduate Certificate); nursing (MSN); occupational therapy (MOT, MS); orthotics (Graduate Certificate); orthotics/prosthetics (MS); physical education pedagogy (MS); prosthetics (Graduate Certificate); quality improvement in health care systems (Graduate Certificate); services to the aging (MSW); sports management (MS); sports medicine-biomechanics (MS); sports medicine-corporate adult fitness (MS); sports medicine-exercise physiology (MS); teaching in health care systems (MSN, Graduate Certificate). *Application deadline:* Applications are processed on a rolling basis. *Application fee:* $35. *Application Contact:* Dr. Deborah deLaski-Smith, Interim Dean, 734-487-0077, Fax: 734-487-8536, E-mail: ddelaski@emich.edu. *Interim Dean,* Dr. Deborah deLaski-Smith, 734-487-0077, Fax: 734-487-8536, E-mail: ddelaski@emich.edu.

College of Technology Students: 89 full-time (17 women), 446 part-time (131 women); includes 83 minority (61 African Americans, 1 American Indian/Alaska Native, 12 Asian Americans or Pacific Islanders, 9 Hispanic Americans), 143 international. Average age 35. *Faculty:* 60 full-time (17 women). Expenses: Contact institution. *Financial support:* Fellowships, research assistantships with full tuition reimbursements, teaching assistantships with full tuition reimbursements, career-related internships or fieldwork, Federal Work-Study, institutionally sponsored loans, scholarships/grants, tuition waivers (partial), and unspecified assistantships available. Support available to part-time students. Financial award applicants required to submit FAFSA. In 2008, 124 master's, 3 doctorates, 6 other advanced degrees awarded. *Degree program information:* Part-time and evening/weekend programs available. Postbaccalaureate distance learning degree programs offered (minimal on-campus study). Offers apparel, textile merchandising (MS); CAD/CAM (MS); career, technical and workforce education (MS); computer aided technology (MS); construction management (MS); engineering management (MS); engineering technology (MS, Graduate Certificate); hotel and restaurant management (MS, Graduate Certificate); information assurance (MLS, Graduate Certificate); interdisciplinary technology (MLS); interior design (MS); legal administration (Graduate Certificate); polymer technology (MS); quality (MS, Graduate Certificate); quality management (MS); technology (MLS, MS, PhD, Graduate Certificate); technology studies (MLS, MS). *Application deadline:* Applications are processed on a rolling basis. *Application fee:* $35. *Application Contact:* Dr. Morell Boone, Dean, 734-487-0354, Fax: 734-487-0843, E-mail: mboone@emich.edu. *Dean,* Dr. Morell Boone, 734-487-0354, Fax: 734-487-0843, E-mail: mboone@emich.edu.

EASTERN NAZARENE COLLEGE, Quincy, MA 02170-2999

General Information Independent-religious, coed, comprehensive institution. *Graduate housing:* Rooms and/or apartments available to single students and available on a first-come, first-served basis to married students.

GRADUATE UNITS

Adult and Graduate Studies *Degree program information:* Part-time and evening/weekend programs available. Offers marriage and family therapy (MS).

Division of Education *Degree program information:* Part-time and evening/weekend programs available. Offers early childhood education (M Ed, Certificate); elementary education (M Ed, Certificate); English as a second language (M Ed, Certificate); instructional enrichment and development (M Ed, Certificate); middle school education (M Ed, Certificate); moderate special needs education (M Ed, Certificate); principal (Certificate); program development and supervision (M Ed, Certificate); secondary education (M Ed, Certificate); special education administrator (Certificate); supervisor (Certificate); teacher of reading (M Ed, Certificate). M Ed and Certificate also available through weekend program for administration, special needs, and reading only.

EASTERN NEW MEXICO UNIVERSITY, Portales, NM 88130

General Information State-supported, coed, comprehensive institution. CGS member. *Enrollment:* 4,300 graduate, professional, and undergraduate students; 31 full-time matriculated graduate/professional students (21 women), 487 part-time matriculated graduate/professional students (349 women). *Enrollment by degree level:* 518 master's. *Graduate faculty:* 73 full-time (27 women), 2 part-time/adjunct (1 woman). Tuition, state resident: full-time $2748; part-time $114.50 per hour. Tuition, nonresident: full-time $8292; part-time $345.50 per hour. *Required fees:* $978; $40.75 per unit. *Graduate housing:* Rooms and/or apartments available on a first-come, first-served basis to single and married students. Typical cost: $1234 per year ($2611 including board) for single students. Room and board charges vary according to board plan and housing facility selected. *Student services:* Campus employment opportunities, career counseling, child daycare facilities, free psychological counseling, international student services, low-cost health insurance, multicultural affairs office, services for students with disabilities. *Library facilities:* Golden Library. *Online resources:* library catalog, web page, access to other libraries' catalogs. *Collection:* 325,122 titles, 21,537 serial subscriptions, 25,659 audiovisual materials.

Computer facilities: 476 computers available on campus for general student use. A campuswide network can be accessed from student residence rooms and from off campus. Online class registration is available. *Web address:* http://www.enmu.edu/.

General Application Contact: Dr. Linda Weems, Dean, Graduate School, 575-562-2147, Fax: 575-562-2500, E-mail: linda.weems@enmu.edu.

GRADUATE UNITS

Graduate School Students: 31 full-time (21 women), 487 part-time (349 women); includes 135 minority (13 African Americans, 12 American Indian/Alaska Native, 5 Asian Americans or

Pacific Islanders, 105 Hispanic Americans), 18 international. Average age 34. 340 applicants, 57% accepted, 122 enrolled. *Faculty:* 73 full-time (27 women), 2 part-time/adjunct (1 woman). Expenses: Contact institution. *Financial support:* In 2008–09, 3 fellowships, 52 research assistantships with tuition reimbursements (averaging $4,250 per year), 35 teaching assistantships with tuition reimbursements (averaging $4,250 per year) were awarded; career-related internships or fieldwork and unspecified assistantships also available. Support available to part-time students. Financial award applicants required to submit FAFSA. In 2008, 120 master's awarded. *Degree program information:* Part-time and evening/weekend programs available. Postbaccalaureate distance learning degree programs offered (minimal on-campus study). *Application deadline:* For fall admission, 7/20 priority date for domestic students, 6/20 priority date for international students. Applications are processed on a rolling basis. *Application fee:* $10. Electronic applications accepted. *Application Contact:* Dr. Linda Weems, Dean, Graduate School, 575-562-2147, Fax: 575-562-2500, E-mail: linda.weems@enmu.edu. *Dean, Graduate School*, Dr. Linda Weems, 575-562-2147, Fax: 575-562-2500, E-mail: linda.weems@enmu.edu.

College of Business Students: 3 full-time (all women), 50 part-time (31 women); includes 11 minority (2 African Americans, 9 Hispanic Americans), 3 international. Average age 35. 39 applicants, 56% accepted, 18 enrolled. *Faculty:* 6 full-time (1 woman). Expenses: Contact institution. *Financial support:* In 2008–09, 5 research assistantships with tuition reimbursements (averaging $4,250 per year), teaching assistantships (averaging $4,250 per year) were awarded; fellowships, unspecified assistantships also available. Support available to part-time students. Financial award applicants required to submit FAFSA. In 2008, 19 master's awarded. *Degree program information:* Part-time and evening/weekend programs available. Postbaccalaureate distance learning degree programs offered (minimal on-campus study). Offers business (MBA). *Application deadline:* For fall admission, 7/20 priority date for domestic students, 6/20 priority date for international students. Applications are processed on a rolling basis. *Application fee:* $10. Electronic applications accepted. *Application Contact:* Dr. Sue Stockly, Graduate Coordinator, 575-562-2364, E-mail: sue.stockly@enmu.edu. *Graduate Coordinator*, Dr. Sue Stockly, 575-562-2364, E-mail: sue.stockly@enmu.edu.

College of Education and Technology Students: 18 full-time (11 women), 295 part-time (221 women); includes 89 minority (10 African Americans, 7 American Indian/Alaska Native, 2 Asian Americans or Pacific Islanders, 70 Hispanic Americans), 2 international. Average age 36. 154 applicants, 55% accepted, 78 enrolled. *Faculty:* 26 full-time (15 women). Expenses: Contact institution. *Financial support:* In 2008–09, 15 research assistantships with tuition reimbursements (averaging $4,250 per year), 10 teaching assistantships with tuition reimbursements (averaging $4,250 per year) were awarded; career-related internships or fieldwork and unspecified assistantships also available. Support available to part-time students. Financial award applicants required to submit FAFSA. In 2008, 76 master's awarded. *Degree program information:* Part-time and evening/weekend programs available. Postbaccalaureate distance learning degree programs offered (minimal on-campus study). Offers counseling (MA); education (M Ed); education and technology (M Ed, M Sp Ed, MA, MS); physical education (MS); school counseling (M Ed); special education (M Ed, M Sp Ed). *Application deadline:* For fall admission, 7/20 priority date for domestic students, 6/20 priority date for international students. Applications are processed on a rolling basis. *Application fee:* $10. Electronic applications accepted. *Application Contact:* Dr. Jerry Harmon, Dean, 575-562-2443, E-mail: jerry.harmon@enmu.edu. *Dean*, Dr. Jerry Harmon, 575-562-2443, E-mail: jerry.harmon@enmu.edu.

College of Liberal Arts and Sciences Students: 10 full-time (7 women), 142 part-time (97 women); includes 35 minority (1 African American, 5 American Indian/Alaska Native, 3 Asian Americans or Pacific Islanders, 26 Hispanic Americans), 13 international. Average age 31. 113 applicants, 50% accepted, 43 enrolled. *Faculty:* 41 full-time (11 women), 2 part-time/adjunct (1 woman). Expenses: Contact institution. *Financial support:* In 2008–09, 3 fellowships (averaging $5,125 per year), 33 research assistantships with tuition reimbursements (averaging $4,250 per year), 25 teaching assistantships with tuition reimbursements (averaging $4,250 per year) were awarded; career-related internships or fieldwork also available. Support available to part-time students. Financial award applicants required to submit FAFSA. In 2008, 33 master's awarded. *Degree program information:* Part-time and evening/weekend programs available. Postbaccalaureate distance learning degree programs offered. Offers anthropology (MA); biology (MS); chemistry (MS); communicative arts and sciences (MA); English (MA); liberal arts and sciences (MA, MS); mathematical sciences (MA); speech pathology and audiology (MS). *Application deadline:* For fall admission, 7/20 priority date for domestic students, 6/20 priority date for international students. Applications are processed on a rolling basis. *Application fee:* $10. Electronic applications accepted. *Application Contact:* Dr. Linda Weems, Dean, Graduate School, 575-562-2147, Fax: 575-562-2500, E-mail: linda.weems@enmu.edu. *Dean*, Dr. Mary Ayala, 575-562-2421, E-mail: mary.ayala@enmu.edu.

EASTERN OREGON UNIVERSITY, La Grande, OR 97850-2899

General Information State-supported, coed, comprehensive institution. *Graduate housing:* Rooms and/or apartments available to single and married students.

GRADUATE UNITS

School of Education and Business *Degree program information:* Part-time programs available. Postbaccalaureate distance learning degree programs offered (minimal on-campus study). Offers education (MS); education and business (MS, MTE); elementary education (MTE); secondary education (MTE).

EASTERN UNIVERSITY, St. Davids, PA 19087-3696

General Information Independent-religious, coed, comprehensive institution. *Graduate housing:* On-campus housing not available.

GRADUATE UNITS

Department of Counseling Psychology Offers community/clinical counseling (MA); school counseling (MA, Certificate); school psychology (MS, Certificate).

Graduate Education Programs *Degree program information:* Part-time programs available. Offers multicultural education (M Ed); school health services (M Ed); school nurse (Certificate).

Office of Interdisciplinary Programs Offers organizational leadership (PhD).

Palmer Theological Seminary *Degree program information:* Part-time and evening/weekend programs available. Offers marriage and family (D Min); renewal of the church for mission (D Min); theology (M Div, MTS, D Min).

School for Social Change Offers urban studies (MA).

School of Leadership and Development *Degree program information:* Part-time and evening/weekend programs available. Offers economic development (MBA); international development (MA); nonprofit management (MS); organizational leadership (MA).

School of Management Studies Offers health administration (MBA); management (MBA).

EASTERN VIRGINIA MEDICAL SCHOOL, Norfolk, VA 23501-1980

General Information Independent, coed, graduate-only institution. *Graduate faculty:* 320 full-time (121 women), 1,255 part-time/adjunct (312 women). *Graduate housing:* On-campus housing not available. *Student services:* Campus employment opportunities, campus safety program, career counseling, low-cost health insurance. *Library facilities:* Edward E. Brickell Medical Library. *Online resources:* web page. *Collection:* 100,000 titles, 2,200 serial subscriptions.

Computer facilities: 70 computers available on campus for general student use. A campuswide network can be accessed from student residence rooms and from off campus. *Web address:* http://www.evms.edu/.

General Application Contact: Rose Mwayungu, Executive Director of Operations and Compliance, 757-446-7153, Fax: 757-446-6179, E-mail: mwayunra@evms.edu.

GRADUATE UNITS

Doctoral Program in Biomedical Sciences Students: 26. 22 applicants, 27% accepted, 4 enrolled. Expenses: Contact institution. *Financial support:* Research assistantships with full tuition reimbursements available. In 2008, 6 doctorates awarded. Offers biomedical sciences (PhD). *Application deadline:* For fall admission, 2/1 for domestic students. Applications are processed on a rolling basis. *Application fee:* $60. Electronic applications accepted. *Application Contact:* Leah Solomon, Administrative Support Coordinator, 757-446-5944, Fax: 757-446-6179, E-mail: solomoLJ@evms.edu. *Director*, Dr. Earl Godfrey, 757-446-5609, Fax: 757-624-2255, E-mail: godfreEW@evms.edu.

Graduate Art Therapy and Counseling Program Students: 25. 32 applicants, 72% accepted, 13 enrolled. *Faculty:* 3 full-time, 8 part-time/adjunct. Expenses: Contact institution. In 2008, 10 master's awarded. Offers art therapy and counseling (MS). *Application deadline:* For fall admission, 1/15 priority date for domestic and international students. *Application fee:* $60. Electronic applications accepted. *Application Contact:* Kiera Dorsey, Administrative Support Coordinator, 757-446-5895, Fax: 757-446-6179, E-mail: dorseyks@evms.edu. *Director*, Abby Calisch, 757-446-5895, Fax: 757-446-6179, E-mail: artthrpy@evms.edu.

Master of Physician Assistant Program Students: 97. 624 applicants, 9% accepted, 50 enrolled. *Faculty:* 9 full-time (3 women). Expenses: Contact institution. *Financial support:* Applicants required to submit FAFSA. In 2008, 47 master's awarded. Offers physician assistant (MPA). *Application deadline:* For spring admission, 3/1 for domestic students. Applications are processed on a rolling basis. *Application fee:* $60. Electronic applications accepted. *Application Contact:* Rose Mwayungu, Director of Health Professions Enrollment, 757-446-7158, Fax: 757-446-8915, E-mail: mwayunra@evms.edu. *Director*, Dr. Thomas Parish, 757-446-7126, Fax: 757-446-7403, E-mail: parishtg@evms.edu.

Master of Public Health Program Students: 62. 56 applicants, 63% accepted, 21 enrolled. *Faculty:* 5 full-time (3 women), 6 part-time/adjunct (3 women). Expenses: Contact institution. *Financial support:* Applicants required to submit FAFSA. In 2008, 29 master's awarded. *Degree program information:* Evening/weekend programs available. Offers public health (MPH). *Application deadline:* For fall admission, 4/30 for domestic and international students. Applications are processed on a rolling basis. *Application fee:* $60. Electronic applications accepted. *Application Contact:* Paula M. Swartz, Administrative Support Coordinator, 757-446-6120, Fax: 757-446-6121, E-mail: swartzpm@evms.edu. *Director*, Dr. David O. Matson, 757-466-6120, Fax: 757-446-6121, E-mail: matsondo@evms.edu.

Master's Program in Biomedical Sciences (Clinical Embryology and Andrology) Students: 53 full-time. 32 applicants, 75% accepted, 21 enrolled. *Faculty:* 12 full-time, 8 part-time/adjunct. Expenses: Contact institution. In 2008, 11 master's awarded. Postbaccalaureate distance learning degree programs offered (minimal on-campus study). Offers biomedical sciences (MS). *Application deadline:* For winter admission, 1/1 for domestic and international students. Applications are processed on a rolling basis. *Application fee:* $60. Electronic applications accepted. *Application Contact:* Nancy Garcia, Administrator, 757-446-8935, Fax: 757-446-5905, E-mail: garcianw@evms.edu. *Director*, Dr. Jacob Mayer, 757-446-5049, Fax: 757-446-5905.

Master's Program in Biomedical Sciences (Medical Master's) Students: 23. 343 applicants, 12% accepted, 23 enrolled. *Faculty:* 25. Expenses: Contact institution. *Financial support:* Institutionally sponsored loans available. In 2008, 21 master's awarded. Offers biomedical sciences (MS). *Application deadline:* For fall admission, 4/1 for domestic students. Applications are processed on a rolling basis. *Application fee:* $60. Electronic applications accepted. *Application Contact:* Leah Solomon, Administrative Support Coordinator, 757-446-5944, Fax: 757-446-6179, E-mail: solomoLJ@evms.edu. *Director*, Dr. Donald Meyer, 757-446-5615, Fax: 757-446-6179, E-mail: meyerdc@evms.edu.

Master's Program in Biomedical Sciences Research Students: 7. 10 applicants, 70% accepted, 4 enrolled. *Faculty:* 57. Expenses: Contact institution. In 2008, 2 master's awarded. Offers biomedical sciences research (MS). *Application deadline:* For fall admission, 3/1 for domestic students. Applications are processed on a rolling basis. *Application fee:* $60. Electronic applications accepted. *Application Contact:* Leah Solomon, Administrative Support Coordinator, 757-446-5944, Fax: 757-446-6179, E-mail: solomoLJ@evms.edu. *Director*, Dr. Earl Godfrey, 757-446-5609, Fax: 757-624-2255, E-mail: godfreEW@evms.edu.

Ophthalmic Technology Program Students: 7. 13 applicants, 31% accepted, 4 enrolled. *Faculty:* 1 full-time. Expenses: Contact institution. Offers ophthalmic technology (Certificate). *Application deadline:* For fall admission, 4/1 for domestic students. Applications are processed on a rolling basis. *Application fee:* $60. Electronic applications accepted. *Application Contact:* Rose Mwayungu, Executive Director of Operations and Compliance, 757-446-7153, Fax: 757-446-6179, E-mail: mwayunra@evms.edu. *Director*, Lori J. Williams, 757-388-3747, E-mail: optech@evms.edu.

Professional Program in Medicine Students: 437. 4,997 applicants, 115 enrolled. Expenses: Contact institution. In 2008, 108 MDs awarded. Offers medicine (MD). *Application deadline:* For fall admission, 11/15 priority date for domestic students. Applications are processed on a rolling basis. *Application fee:* $95. Electronic applications accepted. *Application Contact:* Susan Castora, Director of Admissions, 757-446-5812, Fax: 757-446-5896, E-mail: castorsl@evms.edu. *Associate Dean for Academic Affairs*, Dr. Michael J. Solhaug, 757-446-5805, Fax: 757-446-5896, E-mail: solhaumj@evms.edu.

Surgical Assistant Program Students: 22. 19 applicants, 79% accepted, 12 enrolled. *Faculty:* 8. Expenses: Contact institution. Offers surgical assistant (Certificate, Graduate Certificate). *Application deadline:* For fall admission, 2/1 for domestic students. Applications are processed on a rolling basis. *Application fee:* $60. Electronic applications accepted. *Application Contact:* Nancy Stromann, Health Professions Supervisor, 757-446-6100, Fax: 757-446-6179, E-mail: stromand@evms.edu. *Program Director*, R. Clinton Crews, 757-446-8961, Fax: 757-446-6179, E-mail: crewsrc@evms.edu.

The Virginia Consortium Program in Clinical Psychology Students: 53. 249 applicants, 6% accepted, 10 enrolled. *Faculty:* 33. Expenses: Contact institution. In 2008, 4 doctorates awarded. Offers clinical psychology (Psy D). *Application deadline:* For fall admission, 1/15 for domestic students. *Application fee:* $40. *Application Contact:* Eileen O'Neill, Administrative Coordinator, 757-368-1820, Fax: 757-446-8401, E-mail: exoneill@odu.edu. *Director*, Dr. Michael L. Stutts, 757-446-8400, Fax: 757-446-8401, E-mail: stuttsml@evms.edu.

EASTERN WASHINGTON UNIVERSITY, Cheney, WA 99004-2431

General Information State-supported, coed, comprehensive institution. CGS member. *Graduate housing:* Rooms and/or apartments available on a first-come, first-served basis to single and married students. Housing application deadline: 5/1.

GRADUATE UNITS

Graduate Studies *Degree program information:* Part-time and evening/weekend programs available. Offers interdisciplinary studies (MA, MS).

College of Arts and Letters *Degree program information:* Part-time programs available. Offers arts and letters (M Ed, MA, MFA); composition (MA); creative writing (MFA); French education (M Ed); instrumental/vocal performance (MA); literature (MA); music education (MA); music history and literature (MA); rhetoric, composition, and technical communication (MA); teaching English as a second language (MA).

College of Business and Public Administration *Degree program information:* Part-time and evening/weekend programs available. Offers business administration (MBA); business and public administration (MBA, MPA, MURP); public administration (MPA); urban and regional planning (MURP).

College of Education and Human Development *Degree program information:* Part-time programs available. Offers adult education (M Ed); applied psychology (MS); curriculum development (M Ed); early childhood education (M Ed); education and human development (M Ed, MS); educational leadership (M Ed); elementary teaching (M Ed); exercise science (MS); foundations of education (M Ed); instructional media and technology (M Ed); literacy (M Ed); mental health counseling (MS); school counseling (MS); school psychology (MS); special education (M Ed); sport and exercise psychology (MS); sports administration/pedagogy (MS).

College of Science, Health and Engineering *Degree program information:* Part-time programs available. Offers biology (MS); communication disorders (MS); computer and technology-supported education (M Ed); computer science (MS); dental hygiene (MS); mathematics (MS); occupational therapy (MOT); physical therapy (DPT); science, health and engineering (M Ed, MA, MOT, MS, DPT); teaching mathematics (MA).

Eastern Washington University (continued)

College of Social and Behavioral Sciences *Degree program information:* Part-time and evening/weekend programs available. Offers clinical psychology (MS); communication studies (MSC); experimental psychology (MS); history (MA); psychology (MS); school psychology (MS); social and behavioral sciences (MA, MS, MSC).

Intercollegiate College of Nursing Offers nursing (MN).

School of Social Work and Human Services *Degree program information:* Part-time programs available. Offers social work and human services (MSW).

EAST STROUDSBURG UNIVERSITY OF PENNSYLVANIA, East Stroudsburg, PA 18301-2999

General Information State-supported, coed, comprehensive institution. CGS member. *Enrollment:* 7,234 graduate, professional, and undergraduate students; 333 full-time matriculated graduate/professional students (207 women), 644 part-time matriculated graduate/professional students (478 women). *Enrollment by degree level:* 977 master's. *Graduate faculty:* 85 full-time (39 women), 20 part-time/adjunct (7 women). Tuition, state resident: full-time $6430; part-time $357 per credit. Tuition, nonresident: full-time $10,288; part-time $572 per credit. *Graduate housing:* Room and/or apartments available on a first-come, first-served basis to single students; on-campus housing not available to married students. Housing application deadline: 5/1. *Student services:* Campus employment opportunities, campus safety program, career counseling, child daycare facilities, exercise/wellness program, free psychological counseling, international student services, low-cost health insurance, multicultural affairs office, services for students with disabilities. *Library facilities:* Kemp Library. *Online resources:* library catalog, web page, access to other libraries' catalogs. *Collection:* 554,964 titles, 25,747 serial subscriptions, 12,419 audiovisual materials.

Computer facilities: 500 computers available on campus for general student use. A campuswide network can be accessed from student residence rooms and from off campus. Online class registration, online classes are available. *Web address:* http://www.esu.edu/.

General Application Contact: Kevin Quintero, Associate Provost for Enrollment Management, 570-422-3890, Fax: 570-422-3711, E-mail: KQuintero@po-box.esu.edu.

GRADUATE UNITS

Graduate School Students: 333 full-time (207 women), 644 part-time (478 women); includes 89 minority (39 African Americans, 3 American Indian/Alaska Native, 9 Asian Americans or Pacific Islanders, 38 Hispanic Americans), 12 international. Average age 33. *Faculty:* 85 full-time (39 women), 20 part-time/adjunct (7 women). Expenses: Contact institution. *Financial support:* In 2008–09, 152 research assistantships with full and partial tuition reimbursements (averaging $1,986 per year) were awarded; career-related internships or fieldwork, Federal Work-Study, and institutionally sponsored loans also available. Financial award application deadline: 3/1; financial award applicants required to submit FAFSA. In 2008, 312 master's awarded. *Degree program information:* Part-time and evening/weekend programs available. *Application deadline:* For fall admission, 7/31 priority date for domestic students, 3/1 priority date for international students; for spring admission, 11/30 for domestic students, 10/1 for international students. Applications are processed on a rolling basis. *Application fee:* $50. *Application Contact:* Kevin Quintero, Graduate Admissions Coordinator, 570-422-3890, Fax: 570-422-3711, E-mail: kquintero@po-box.esu.edu. *Graduate Dean,* Dr. Marilyn Wells, 570-422-3536, Fax: 570-422-3711, E-mail: mwells@po-box.esu.edu.

College of Arts and Sciences Students: 58 full-time (26 women), 97 part-time (55 women); includes 20 minority (9 African Americans, 2 Asian Americans or Pacific Islanders, 9 Hispanic Americans), 5 international. Average age 31. *Faculty:* 29 full-time (8 women). Expenses: Contact institution. *Financial support:* In 2008–09, 32 research assistantships with full and partial tuition reimbursements (averaging $1,986 per year) were awarded; career-related internships or fieldwork, Federal Work-Study, and institutionally sponsored loans also available. Financial award application deadline: 3/1; financial award applicants required to submit FAFSA. In 2008, 43 master's awarded. *Degree program information:* Part-time and evening/weekend programs available. Offers arts and sciences (M Ed, MA, MS); biology (M Ed, MS); computer science (MS); history (M Ed, MA); political science (M Ed, MA). *Application deadline:* For fall admission, 7/31 for domestic students, 5/1 priority date for international students; for spring admission, 11/30 for domestic students, 10/1 for international students. Applications are processed on a rolling basis. *Application fee:* $50. *Application Contact:* Kevin Quintero, Graduate Admissions Coordinator, 570-422-3890, Fax: 570-422-3711, E-mail: kquintero@po-box.esu.edu. *Provost,* Dr. Marilyn Wells, 570-422-3536, Fax: 570-422-3711, E-mail: mwells@po-box.esu.edu.

College of Business and Management Students: 40 full-time (9 women), 18 part-time (3 women); includes 9 minority (8 African Americans, 1 Asian American or Pacific Islander), 3 international. Average age 27. *Faculty:* 6 full-time (2 women). Expenses: Contact institution. *Financial support:* In 2008–09, 23 research assistantships (averaging $1,958 per year) were awarded; career-related internships or fieldwork, Federal Work-Study, and institutionally sponsored loans also available. Financial award application deadline: 3/1; financial award applicants required to submit FAFSA. In 2008, 28 master's awarded. *Degree program information:* Part-time and evening/weekend programs available. Offers business and management (MS); management and leadership (MS); sports management (MS). *Application deadline:* For fall admission, 7/31 for domestic students, 5/1 priority date for international students; for spring admission, 11/30 for domestic students, 10/1 for international students. Applications are processed on a rolling basis. *Application fee:* $50. *Application Contact:* Kevin Quintero, Associate Provost for Enrollment Management, 570-422-3890, Fax: 570-422-2711, E-mail: kquintero@po-box.esu.edu. *Dean,* Dr. Alla Wilson, 570-422-3589, Fax: 570-422-3506, E-mail: awilson@po-box.esu.edu.

College of Education Students: 112 full-time (75 women), 485 part-time (386 women); includes 43 minority (15 African Americans, 2 American Indian/Alaska Native, 4 Asian Americans or Pacific Islanders, 22 Hispanic Americans). Average age 32. *Faculty:* 28 full-time (17 women), 18 part-time/adjunct (6 women). Expenses: Contact institution. *Financial support:* In 2008–09, 26 research assistantships with full and partial tuition reimbursements (averaging $2,069 per year) were awarded; career-related internships or fieldwork, Federal Work-Study, and institutionally sponsored loans also available. Financial award application deadline: 3/1; financial award applicants required to submit FAFSA. In 2008, 173 master's awarded. *Degree program information:* Part-time and evening/weekend programs available. Offers education (M Ed); elementary education (M Ed); instructional technology (M Ed); professional and secondary education (M Ed); reading (M Ed); special education (M Ed). *Application deadline:* For fall admission, 7/31 priority date for domestic students, 5/1 priority date for international students; for spring admission, 11/30 for domestic students, 10/1 for international students. Applications are processed on a rolling basis. *Application fee:* $50. *Application Contact:* Kevin Quintero, Graduate Admissions Coordinator, 570-422-3890, Fax: 570-422-3711, E-mail: kquintero@po-box.esu.edu. *Dean,* Dr. Pamela Kramer, 570-422-3377, Fax: 570-422-3506, E-mail: pkramer@po-box.esu.edu.

College of Health Sciences Students: 123 full-time (97 women), 44 part-time (34 women); includes 17 minority (7 African Americans, 1 American Indian/Alaska Native, 2 Asian Americans or Pacific Islanders, 7 Hispanic Americans), 4 international. Average age 28. *Faculty:* 22 full-time (12 women), 2 part-time/adjunct (1 woman). Expenses: Contact institution. *Financial support:* In 2008–09, 71 research assistantships with full and partial tuition reimbursements (averaging $1,965 per year) were awarded; career-related internships or fieldwork, Federal Work-Study, and institutionally sponsored loans also available. Financial award application deadline: 3/1; financial award applicants required to submit FAFSA. In 2008, 68 master's awarded. *Degree program information:* Part-time and evening/weekend programs available. Offers cardiac rehabilitation and exercise science (MS); community health education (MPH); health and physical education (M Ed); health education (MS); health sciences (M Ed, MPH, MS); speech pathology and audiology (MS). *Application deadline:* For fall admission, 7/31 priority date for domestic students, 5/1 priority date for international students; for spring admission, 11/30 for domestic students, 10/1 for international students. Applications are processed on a rolling basis. *Application fee:* $50. *Application Contact:* Kevin Quintero, Graduate Admissions Coordinator, 570-422-3890, Fax: 570-422-2711, E-mail: kquintero@po-box.esu.edu. *Dean,* Dr. Mark Kilker, 570-422-3425, Fax: 570-422-3347, E-mail: mkilker@po-box.esu.edu.

EAST TENNESSEE STATE UNIVERSITY, Johnson City, TN 37614

General Information State-supported, coed, university. CGS member. *Graduate housing:* Rooms and/or apartments available on a first-come, first-served basis to single and married students. Housing application deadline: 7/1. *Research affiliation:* Oak Ridge National Laboratory (biomedical physical science), Eastman Chemical Corporation (biomedical science), Tennessee Mouse Genome Consortium (biomedical science), Tennessee Biotechnology Association (biotechnology), Siemens (scientific and biomedical manufacturing), Marshall Space Flight Center (general).

GRADUATE UNITS

James H. Quillen College of Medicine *Degree program information:* Part-time programs available. Offers anatomy (MS, PhD); biochemistry (MS, PhD); biophysics (MS, PhD); medicine (MD, MS, PhD); microbiology (MS, PhD); pharmacology (MS, PhD); physiology (MS, PhD).

School of Graduate Studies *Degree program information:* Part-time and evening/weekend programs available.

College of Arts and Sciences *Degree program information:* Part-time and evening/weekend programs available. Offers applied sociology (MA); art education (MA); art history (MA); arts and sciences (MA, MFA, MS, MSW); biology (MS); chemistry (MS); clinical psychology (MA); communication (MA); criminal justice and criminology (MA); English (MA); general psychology (MA); general sociology (MA); history (MA); mathematics (MS); microbiology (MS); social work (MSW); studio art (MA, MFA).

College of Business and Technology *Degree program information:* Part-time and evening/weekend programs available. Offers accountancy (M Acc); business administration (MBA, Certificate); business and technology (M Acc, MBA, MCM, MPM, MS, Certificate); city management (MCM); clinical nutrition (MS); community development (MPM); computer science (MS); digital media (MS); engineering technology (MS); general administration (MPM); health care management (Certificate); industrial arts/technology education (MS); information systems science (MS); municipal service management (MPM); software engineering (MS); urban and regional economic development (MPM); urban and regional planning (MPM).

College of Education *Degree program information:* Part-time and evening/weekend programs available. Offers 7-12 (MAT); administrative endorsement (M Ed, Ed D, Ed S); advanced practitioner (M Ed); classroom leadership (Ed D); classroom technology (M Ed); community agency counseling (M Ed, MA); comprehensive concentration (M Ed); counseling (M Ed, MA); early childhood education (M Ed, MA); early childhood general (M Ed); early childhood special education (M Ed); early childhood teaching (M Ed); education (M Ed, MA, MAT, Ed D, Ed S); educational communication (M Ed); educational leadership (M Ed, Ed D, Ed S); educational media/educational technology (M Ed); elementary and secondary (school counseling) (M Ed, MA); elementary education (M Ed, MAT); exercise physiology (MA); fitness leadership (MA); K-12 (MAT); marriage and family therapy (M Ed, MA); modified concentration (M Ed); physical education (M Ed, MA); post secondary and private sector leadership (Ed D); reading and storytelling (M Ed, MA); reading education (M Ed, MA); school leadership (Ed D); school library media (M Ed); school system leadership (Ed S); secondary education (M Ed, MAT); sports management (MA); sports sciences (MA); teacher leadership (Ed S).

College of Nursing *Degree program information:* Part-time programs available. Offers advanced nursing practice (Post Master's Certificate); health care management (Certificate); nursing (MSN, DSN).

College of Public and Allied Health *Degree program information:* Part-time and evening/weekend programs available. Offers audiology (MS, Au D); communicative disorders (MS); community health (MPH); environmental health (MSEH); epidemiology (Certificate); gerontology (Certificate); health care management (Certificate); physical therapy (DPT); public and allied health (MPH, MS, MSEH, Au D, DPT, Certificate); public health (MPH); public health administration (MPH); special education audiology pre-K-12 (MS); special education speech pathology pre-K-12 (MS); speech pathology (MS).

Division of Cross-Disciplinary Studies Offers liberal studies (MALS).

See Close-Up on page 905.

EAST WEST COLLEGE OF NATURAL MEDICINE, Sarasota, FL 34234

General Information Proprietary, coed, graduate-only institution.

GRADUATE UNITS

Graduate Programs

ÉCOLE POLYTECHNIQUE DE MONTRÉAL, Montréal, QC H3C 3A7, Canada

General Information Province-supported, coed, graduate-only institution. *Enrollment by degree level:* 673 master's, 472 doctoral. *Graduate faculty:* 230. *Graduate housing:* Room and/or apartments available on a first-come, first-served basis to single students; on-campus housing not available to married students. Typical cost: $3200 Canadian dollars per year. Housing application deadline: 2/1. *Student services:* Campus employment opportunities, career counseling, child daycare facilities, free psychological counseling, international student services, low-cost health insurance, multicultural affairs office, services for students with disabilities. *Library facilities:* Biblioth??que de l'??cole Polytechnique. *Online resources:* library catalog, web page, access to other libraries' catalogs. *Collection:* 301,671 titles, 1,683 serial subscriptions. *Research affiliation:* Hydro-Quebec (Energy), Bell Canada (Telecommunications), Bombardier (Aircraft and aviation), IBM (Computer), Pratt and Whitney (Aircraft and aviation), Ubisoft (Video games).

Computer facilities: A campuswide network can be accessed from student residence rooms and from off campus. Online class registration is available. *Web address:* http://www.polymtl.ca/.

General Application Contact: Jenny Deschenes, Counselor for Prospective Students, Communication and Recruitment Services, 514-340-4711 Ext. 4019, E-mail: jenny.deschenes@polymtl.ca.

GRADUATE UNITS

Graduate Programs Students: 1,479 (365 women), 241 international. Average age 24. *Faculty:* 230. Expenses: Contact institution. *Financial support:* Fellowships, research assistantships, teaching assistantships, career-related internships or fieldwork, institutionally sponsored loans, scholarships/grants, and unspecified assistantships available. In 2008, 249 master's, 67 doctorates awarded. *Degree program information:* Part-time and evening/weekend programs available. Offers aerothermics (M Eng, M Sc A, PhD); applied mechanics (M Eng, M Sc A, PhD); automation (M Eng, M Sc A, PhD); chemical engineering (M Eng, M Sc A, PhD, DESS); civil, geological and mining engineering (DESS); computer science (M Eng, M Sc A, PhD); electrical engineering (DESS); electrotechnology (M Eng, M Sc A, PhD); environmental engineering (M Eng, M Sc A, PhD); ergonomy (M Eng, M Sc A, DESS); geotechnical engineering (M Eng, M Sc A, PhD); hydraulics engineering (M Eng, M Sc A, PhD); mathematical method in CA engineering (M Eng, M Sc A, PhD); microelectronics (M Eng, M Sc A, PhD); microwave technology (M Eng, M Sc A, PhD); operational research (M Eng, M Sc A, PhD); optical engineering (M Eng, M Sc A, PhD); production (M Eng, M Sc A); solid-state physics and engineering (M Eng, M Sc A, PhD); structural engineering (M Eng, M Sc A, PhD); technology management (M Eng, M Sc A); tool design (M Eng, M Sc A, PhD); transportation engineering (M Eng, M Sc A, PhD). *Application deadline:* For fall admission, 5/1 priority date for domestic students, 3/15 priority date for international students; for winter admission, 6/1 priority date for domestic and international students; for spring admission, 11/15 priority date for domestic and international students. Applications are processed on a rolling basis. *Application fee:* $70. Electronic applications accepted. *Application Contact:* Jenny Deschenes, Counselor for Prospective Students, Communication and Recruitment Services, 514-340-4711 Ext. 4019, E-mail: jenny.deschenes@polymtl.ca. *Associate Dean of Graduate Studies,* Dr. Jean Dansereau, 514-340-4711 Ext. 4713.

Institute of Biomedical Engineering *Degree program information:* Part-time programs available. Offers biomedical engineering (M Sc A, PhD, DESS).

Institute of Nuclear Engineering Offers nuclear engineering (M Eng, PhD, DESS); nuclear engineering, socio-economics of energy (M Sc A).

ECUMENICAL THEOLOGICAL SEMINARY, Detroit, MI 48201

General Information Independent-religious, coed, graduate-only institution. *Graduate housing:* On-campus housing not available.

GRADUATE UNITS

Professional Program Offers theology (M Div).

Program in Ministry Offers ministry (D Min).

EDEN THEOLOGICAL SEMINARY, St. Louis, MO 63119-3192

General Information Independent-religious, coed, graduate-only institution. *Graduate housing:* Rooms and/or apartments available on a first-come, first-served basis to single and married students. Housing application deadline: 7/30.

GRADUATE UNITS

Graduate and Professional Programs Offers theology (M Div, MAPS, MTS, D Min). Electronic applications accepted.

EDGEWOOD COLLEGE, Madison, WI 53711-1997

General Information Independent-religious, coed, primarily women, comprehensive institution. *Enrollment:* 2,544 graduate, professional, and undergraduate students; 68 full-time matriculated graduate/professional students (45 women), 487 part-time matriculated graduate/professional students (311 women). *Enrollment by degree level:* 422 master's, 133 doctoral. *Graduate faculty:* 189. *Tuition:* Part-time $655 per credit. *Graduate housing:* On-campus housing not available. *Student services:* Campus employment opportunities, career counseling, free psychological counseling, international student services, low-cost health insurance, multi-cultural affairs office, writing training. *Library facilities:* Oscar Rennebohm Library. *Online resources:* library catalog, web page. *Collection:* 107,873 titles, 164 serial subscriptions, 6,197 audiovisual materials.

Computer facilities: Computer purchase and lease plans are available. 146 computers available on campus for general student use. A campuswide network can be accessed from student residence rooms and from off campus. Online class registration is available. *Web address:* http://www.edgewood.edu/.

General Application Contact: Paula O'Malley, Director for Admissions and Recruitment, 608-663-2217, Fax: 608-663-2214, E-mail: pomalley@edgewood.edu.

GRADUATE UNITS

Program in Business Students: 18 full-time (10 women), 141 part-time (69 women); includes 7 minority (1 African American, 1 American Indian/Alaska Native, 4 Asian Americans or Pacific Islanders, 1 Hispanic American), 6 international. Average age 34. Expenses: Contact institution. *Financial support:* Career-related internships or fieldwork available. In 2008, 36 master's awarded. *Degree program information:* Part-time and evening/weekend programs available. Offers accountancy (MS); business (MBA). *Application deadline:* For fall admission, 8/26 for domestic students, 8/1 for international students; for spring admission, 1/10 for domestic students, 10/1 for international students. Applications are processed on a rolling basis. *Application fee:* $25. Electronic applications accepted. *Application Contact:* Paula O'Malley, Director of Graduate and Professional Studies, 608-663-2217, Fax: 608-663-3496, E-mail: gps@edgewood.edu. *Dean,* Dr. Charles Taylor, 608-663-4180, Fax: 608-663-3291, E-mail: ctaylor@edgewood.edu.

Program in Education Students: 33 full-time (22 women), 157 part-time (83 women); includes 25 minority (7 African Americans, 3 American Indian/Alaska Native, 7 Asian Americans or Pacific Islanders, 8 Hispanic Americans), 2 international. Average age 40. Expenses: Contact institution. In 2008, 27 master's, 19 doctorates awarded. *Degree program information:* Part-time and evening/weekend programs available. Offers director of instruction (Certificate); director of special education and pupil services (Certificate); education (MA Ed); educational administration (MA); educational leadership (Ed D); program coordinator (Certificate); school business administration (Certificate); school principalship K-12 (Certificate). *Application deadline:* For fall admission, 8/24 for domestic students, 8/1 for international students; for spring admission, 1/10 for domestic students, 10/1 for international students. Applications are processed on a rolling basis. *Application fee:* $25. Electronic applications accepted. *Application Contact:* Paula O'Malley, Director of Graduate and Professional Studies, 608-663-2217, Fax: 608-663-3496, E-mail: gps@edgewood.edu. *Dean,* Dr. Joseph Schmiedicke, 608-663-2293, Fax: 608-663-3291, E-mail: schmied@edgewood.edu.

Program in Marriage and Family Therapy Students: 13 full-time (10 women), 17 part-time (14 women); includes 3 minority (2 African Americans, 1 Hispanic American). Average age 32. Expenses: Contact institution. In 2008, 15 master's awarded. *Degree program information:* Part-time and evening/weekend programs available. Offers marriage and family therapy (MS). *Application deadline:* For fall admission, 3/1 for domestic students. *Application fee:* $25. Electronic applications accepted. *Application Contact:* Paula O'Malley, Director of Graduate and Professional Studies, 608-663-2217, Fax: 608-663-3496, E-mail: gps@edgewood.edu. *Director,* Dr. Peter Fabian, 608-663-2233, Fax: 608-663-3291, E-mail: fabian@edgewood.edu.

Program in Nursing Students: 34 part-time (31 women). Average age 40. Expenses: Contact institution. In 2008, 9 master's awarded. Offers nursing (MS). *Application deadline:* For fall admission, 8/24 priority date for domestic students, 8/1 for international students; for spring admission, 1/10 priority date for domestic students, 10/1 for international students. Applications are processed on a rolling basis. *Application fee:* $25. Electronic applications accepted. *Application Contact:* Paula O'Malley, Director of Graduate and Professional Studies, 608-663-2217, Fax: 608-663-3496, E-mail: gps@edgewood.edu. *Dean,* Dr. Margaret Noreuil, 608-663-2820, Fax: 608-663-3291, E-mail: mnoreuil@edgewood.edu.

Program in Religious Studies Students: 1 (woman) full-time, 8 part-time (7 women); includes 2 minority (both Hispanic Americans). Average age 47. Expenses: Contact institution. *Financial support:* Career-related internships or fieldwork, institutionally sponsored loans, scholarships/grants, and tuition waivers (partial) available. *Degree program information:* Part-time and evening/weekend programs available. Offers religious studies (MA). *Application deadline:* For fall admission, 8/24 for domestic students, 8/1 for international students; for spring admission, 1/10 for domestic students, 10/1 for international students. Applications are processed on a rolling basis. *Application fee:* $25. Electronic applications accepted. *Application Contact:* Paula O'Malley, Director of Graduate and Professional Studies, 608-663-2217, Fax: 608-663-3496, E-mail: gps@edgewood.edu. *Chairperson,* Dr. John Leonard, 608-663-2823, Fax: 608-663-3291, E-mail: jleonard@edgewood.edu.

EDINBORO UNIVERSITY OF PENNSYLVANIA, Edinboro, PA 16444

General Information State-supported, coed, comprehensive institution. *Enrollment:* 7,671 graduate, professional, and undergraduate students; 455 full-time matriculated graduate/professional students (328 women), 965 part-time matriculated graduate/professional students (749 women). *Enrollment by degree level:* 1,229 master's, 233 other advanced degrees. *Graduate faculty:* 71 full-time (35 women). *International tuition:* $15,171.58 full-time. Tuition, state resident: full-time $6430; part-time $357 per credit. Tuition, nonresident: full-time $8038; part-time $572 per credit. *Required fees:* $2113; $60 per credit. Tuition and fees vary according to course load. *Graduate housing:* Room and/or apartments available on a first-come, first-served basis to single students; on-campus housing not available to married students. Typical cost: $4200 per year ($6450 including board). Room and board charges vary according to board plan. Housing application deadline: 4/3. *Student services:* Campus employment opportunities, campus safety program, career counseling, exercise/wellness program, free psychological counseling, international student services, low-cost health insurance, multicultural affairs office, services for students with disabilities, teacher training. *Library facilities:* Baron-Forness Library plus 1 other. *Online resources:* library catalog, web page, access to other libraries' catalogs. *Collection:* 492,293 titles, 1,315 serial subscriptions, 11,321 audiovisual materials. *Research affiliation:* Mid Continent Research for Education and Learning (Education and Learning), ASM International (Materials Research), Pennsylvania Department of Education (Technical Education), U.S. Department of Education (Education), U.S. Department of Justice (Criminal Justice/Forensics), Pennsylvania Historical and Museum Commission (Pennsylvania History).

Computer facilities: Computer purchase and lease plans are available. 997 computers available on campus for general student use. A campuswide network can be accessed from student residence rooms and from off campus. Online class registration, software are available. *Web address:* http://www.edinboro.edu/.

General Application Contact: Dr. R. Scott Baldwin, Dean of Graduate Studies and Research, 814-732-2856, Fax: 814-732-2611, E-mail: sbaldwin@edinboro.edu.

GRADUATE UNITS

Graduate Studies and Research Students: 455 full-time (328 women), 965 part-time (749 women); includes 63 minority (42 African Americans, 4 American Indian/Alaska Native, 8 Asian Americans or Pacific Islanders, 9 Hispanic Americans), 12 international. Average age 32. 1,051 applicants, 75% accepted, 597 enrolled. *Faculty:* 71 full-time (35 women). Expenses: Contact institution. *Financial support:* In 2008–09, 161 research assistantships with full and partial tuition reimbursements (averaging $3,850 per year) were awarded; career-related internships or fieldwork, Federal Work-Study, institutionally sponsored loans, scholarships/grants, and unspecified assistantships also available. Support available to part-time students. Financial award application deadline: 2/15; financial award applicants required to submit FAFSA. In 2008, 287 master's, 47 other advanced degrees awarded. *Degree program information:* Part-time and evening/weekend programs available. *Application deadline:* Applications are processed on a rolling basis. *Application fee:* $30. Electronic applications accepted. *Application Contact:* Dr. R. Scott Baldwin, Dean of Graduate Studies and Research, 814-732-2856, Fax: 814-732-2611, E-mail: sbaldwin@edinboro.edu. *Dean,* Dr. R. Scott Baldwin, 814-732-2752, Fax: 814-732-2268, E-mail: sbaldwin@edinboro.edu.

School of Education Students: 255 full-time (177 women), 823 part-time (632 women); includes 40 minority (29 African Americans, 3 American Indian/Alaska Native, 2 Asian Americans or Pacific Islanders, 6 Hispanic Americans), 1 international. Average age 31. *Faculty:* 32 full-time (19 women). Expenses: Contact institution. *Financial support:* In 2008–09, 66 research assistantships with full and partial tuition reimbursements (averaging $3,850 per year) were awarded; career-related internships or fieldwork, Federal Work-Study, institutionally sponsored loans, scholarships/grants, and unspecified assistantships also available. Support available to part-time students. Financial award application deadline: 2/15; financial award applicants required to submit FAFSA. In 2008, 251 master's, 25 other advanced degrees awarded. *Degree program information:* Part-time and evening/weekend programs available. Offers behavior management (Certificate); character education (Certificate); counseling (MA); education (M Ed, MA, Certificate); educational leadership (M Ed); educational psychology (M Ed); elementary education (M Ed); letter of eligibility (Certificate); reading (M Ed, Certificate); special education (M Ed). Certificates issued by a state agency. *Application deadline:* Applications are processed on a rolling basis. *Application fee:* $30. Electronic applications accepted. *Application Contact:* Dr. R. Scott Baldwin, Dean, 814-732-2752, Fax: 814-732-2268, E-mail: sbaldwin@edinboro.edu. *Dean,* Dr. Kenneth Adams, 814-732-2752, Fax: 814-732-2268, E-mail: kadams@edinboro.edu.

School of Liberal Arts Students: 194 full-time (146 women), 74 part-time (56 women); includes 21 minority (11 African Americans, 1 American Indian/Alaska Native, 6 Asian Americans or Pacific Islanders, 3 Hispanic Americans), 11 international. Average age 31. *Faculty:* 33 full-time (12 women). Expenses: Contact institution. *Financial support:* In 2008–09, 58 research assistantships with full and partial tuition reimbursements (averaging $3,850 per year) were awarded; career-related internships or fieldwork, Federal Work-Study, institutionally sponsored loans, scholarships/grants, and unspecified assistantships also available. Support available to part-time students. Financial award application deadline: 2/15; financial award applicants required to submit FAFSA. In 2008, 81 master's awarded. *Degree program information:* Part-time and evening/weekend programs available. Offers art (MA); clinical psychology (MA); communications and media studies (MA); fine arts (MFA); liberal arts (MA, MFA, MSW); social sciences (MA); social work (MSW); speech language pathology (MA). *Application deadline:* Applications are processed on a rolling basis. *Application fee:* $30. Electronic applications accepted. *Application Contact:* Dr. R. Scott Baldwin, Dean, 814-732-2752, Fax: 814-732-2268, E-mail: sbaldwin@edinboro.edu. *Dean,* Dr. Terry L. Smith, 814-732-2477, Fax: 814-732-2629, E-mail: tlsmith@edinboro.edu.

School of Science, Management and Technology Students: 6 full-time (5 women), 64 part-time (57 women); includes 2 minority (both African Americans). Average age 36. *Faculty:* 6 full-time (4 women). Expenses: Contact institution. *Financial support:* In 2008–09, 12 research assistantships with full and partial tuition reimbursements (averaging $3,850 per year) were awarded; career-related internships or fieldwork, Federal Work-Study, scholarships/grants, and unspecified assistantships also available. Support available to part-time students. Financial award application deadline: 2/15; financial award applicants required to submit FAFSA. In 2008, 4 master's awarded. *Degree program information:* Part-time and evening/weekend programs available. Offers biology (MS); family nurse practitioner (MSN); science, management and technology (MS, MSN). *Application deadline:* Applications are processed on a rolling basis. *Application fee:* $30. Electronic applications accepted. *Application Contact:* Dr. R. Scott Baldwin, Dean, 814-732-2752, Fax: 814-732-2268, E-mail: sbaldwin@edinboro.edu. *Dean,* Dr. Eric Randall, 814-732-2400, Fax: 814-732-2422, E-mail: erandall@edinboro.edu.

EDWARD VIA VIRGINIA COLLEGE OF OSTEOPATHIC MEDICINE, Blacksburg, VA 24060

General Information Independent, coed, graduate-only institution. *Graduate housing:* On-campus housing not available.

GRADUATE UNITS

Graduate Program

ELIZABETH CITY STATE UNIVERSITY, Elizabeth City, NC 27909-7806

General Information State-supported, coed, comprehensive institution. CGS member. *Graduate housing:* Room and/or apartments available on a first-come, first-served basis to single students; on-campus housing not available to married students. Housing application deadline: 5/31.

GRADUATE UNITS

School of Education and Psychology *Degree program information:* Part-time and evening/weekend programs available. Offers education and psychology (M Ed, MSA); elementary education (M Ed); school administration (MSA). Electronic applications accepted.

School of Mathematics, Science and Technology *Degree program information:* Part-time and evening/weekend programs available. Offers biology (MS); mathematics (MS); mathematics, science and technology (MS). Electronic applications accepted.

ELIZABETHTOWN COLLEGE, Elizabethtown, PA 17022-2298

General Information Independent-religious, coed, comprehensive institution.

GRADUATE UNITS

Department of Occupational Therapy

ELMHURST COLLEGE, Elmhurst, IL 60126-3296

General Information Independent-religious, coed, comprehensive institution. *Enrollment:* 3,316 graduate, professional, and undergraduate students; 1 (woman) full-time matriculated graduate/professional student, 270 part-time matriculated graduate/professional students (156 women). *Enrollment by degree level:* 271 master's. *Graduate faculty:* 17 full-time (11 women), 21 part-time/adjunct (5 women). *Tuition:* Part-time $675 per semester hour. Tuition

Elmhurst College (continued)

and fees vary according to program. *Graduate housing:* On-campus housing not available. *Student services:* Campus employment opportunities, campus safety program, career counseling, child daycare facilities, exercise/wellness program, free psychological counseling, international student services, low-cost health insurance, multicultural affairs office, services for students with disabilities, teacher training, writing training. *Library facilities:* Buehler Library. *Online resources:* library catalog, web page, access to other libraries' catalogs. *Collection:* 225,254 titles, 1,414 serial subscriptions, 48,004 audiovisual materials.

Computer facilities: 620 computers available on campus for general student use. A campuswide network can be accessed from student residence rooms and from off campus. Online class registration is available. *Web address:* http://www.elmhurst.edu/.

General Application Contact: Elizabeth D. Kuebler, Director of Adult and Graduate Admission, 630-617-3069, Fax: 630-617-5501, E-mail: betsyk@elmhurst.edu.

GRADUATE UNITS

Graduate Programs Students: 1 (woman) full-time, 270 part-time (156 women); includes 37 minority (17 African Americans, 13 Asian Americans or Pacific Islanders, 7 Hispanic Americans), 1 international. Average age 30. 252 applicants, 71% accepted, 122 enrolled. *Faculty:* 17 full-time (11 women), 21 part-time/adjunct (5 women). Expenses: Contact institution. *Financial support:* In 2008–09, 52 students received support. Federal Work-Study and scholarships/grants available. Support available to part-time students. Financial award application deadline: 6/1; financial award applicants required to submit FAFSA. In 2008, 128 master's awarded. *Degree program information:* Part-time and evening/weekend programs available. Postbaccalaureate distance learning degree programs offered (minimal on-campus study). Offers business administration (MBA); computer network systems (MS); early childhood special education (M Ed); English studies (MA); industrial/organizational psychology (MA); nursing (MSN); professional accountancy (MPA); supply chain management (MS); teacher leadership (M Ed). *Application deadline:* For fall admission, 5/1 priority date for domestic and international students. Applications are processed on a rolling basis. *Application fee:* $25. Electronic applications accepted. *Application Contact:* Elizabeth D. Kuebler, Director of Adult and Graduate Admission, 630-617-3069, Fax: 630-617-5501, E-mail: betsyk@elmhurst.edu. *Dean of Graduate Studies,* Dr. John E. Bohnert, 630-617-3069, Fax: 630-617-5501, E-mail: gradadm@elmhurst.edu.

ELMS COLLEGE, Chicopee, MA 01013-2839

General Information Independent-religious, coed, primarily women, comprehensive institution. *Enrollment:* 16 full-time matriculated graduate/professional students (15 women), 216 part-time matriculated graduate/professional students (190 women). *Enrollment by degree level:* 209 master's, 23 other advanced degrees. *Graduate faculty:* 17 full-time (13 women), 11 part-time/adjunct (7 women). *Tuition:* Full-time $10,116; part-time $562 per credit. *Required fees:* $40; $20 per semester. *Graduate housing:* On-campus housing not available. *Student services:* Career counseling, low-cost health insurance. *Library facilities:* Alumnae Library. *Online resources:* library catalog. *Collection:* 111,379 titles, 529 serial subscriptions, 2,948 audiovisual materials.

Computer facilities: 70 computers available on campus for general student use. A campuswide network can be accessed from student residence rooms and from off campus. *Web address:* http://www.elms.edu/.

General Application Contact: Joseph P. Wagner, Director of Admission Office, 413-594-2761 Ext. 238, Fax: 413-594-2781, E-mail: wagnerj@elms.edu.

GRADUATE UNITS

Division of Education Students: 17 full-time (14 women), 126 part-time (116 women); includes 7 minority (2 African Americans, 2 Asian Americans or Pacific Islanders, 3 Hispanic Americans). Average age 36. 40 applicants, 73% accepted, 29 enrolled. *Faculty:* 9 full-time (6 women), 4 part-time/adjunct (2 women). Expenses: Contact institution. *Financial support:* In 2008–09, 2 teaching assistantships with partial tuition reimbursements were awarded; tuition waivers (partial) also available. Support available to part-time students. Financial award application deadline: 4/15; financial award applicants required to submit FAFSA. In 2008, 14 master's, 10 other advanced degrees awarded. *Degree program information:* Part-time and evening/weekend programs available. Offers early childhood education (MAT); education (M Ed, CAGS); elementary education (MAT); English as a second language (MAT); reading (MAT); secondary education (MAT); special education (MAT). *Application deadline:* For fall admission, 7/1 priority date for domestic students; for spring admission, 11/1 priority date for domestic students. Applications are processed on a rolling basis. *Application fee:* $30. *Application Contact:* Dana Malone, Associate Director for Graduate Studies and Continuing Education, 413-265-2459, E-mail: Maloned@elms.edu. *Director,* Dr. Mary Janeczek, 413-594-2761, Fax: 413-592-4871, E-mail: janeczeke@elms.edu.

Division of Nursing Students: 27 part-time (26 women); includes 1 African American. 36 applicants, 78% accepted, 27 enrolled. *Faculty:* 6 full-time (all women). Expenses: Contact institution. *Financial support:* Application deadline: 5/1. *Degree program information:* Part-time and evening/weekend programs available. Offers nursing (MSN). *Application deadline:* For fall admission, 7/1 priority date for domestic students; for spring admission, 11/1 priority date for domestic students. Applications are processed on a rolling basis. *Application fee:* $30. *Application Contact:* Joseph P. Wagner, Director of Admission Office, 413-594-2761 Ext. 238, Fax: 413-594-2781, E-mail: wagnerj@elms.edu. *Director,* Dr. Kathleen Scoble, 413-265-2204, E-mail: scoblek@elms.edu.

Program in Communication Sciences and Disorders Students: 21 part-time (all women); includes 1 Hispanic American. Average age 35. 28 applicants, 82% accepted, 21 enrolled. *Faculty:* 1 (woman) full-time, 5 part-time/adjunct (3 women). Expenses: Contact institution. *Financial support:* Application deadline: 4/15. In 2008, 2 degrees awarded. *Degree program information:* Part-time programs available. Offers communication sciences and disorders (CAGS). *Application deadline:* For fall admission, 7/1 priority date for domestic students; for spring admission, 11/1 priority date for domestic students. *Application fee:* $30. *Application Contact:* Joseph P. Wagner, Director of Admission Office, 413-594-2761 Ext. 238, Fax: 413-594-2781, E-mail: wagnerj@elms.edu. *Chair-CSD Department,* Dr. Kathryn James, 413-265-2215, E-mail: jamesk@elms.edu.

Religious Studies Department Students: 12 part-time (6 women). Average age 35. 1 applicant, 100% accepted, 1 enrolled. *Faculty:* 2 full-time (1 woman), 2 part-time/adjunct (0 women). Expenses: Contact institution. *Financial support:* Tuition waivers (partial) available. Financial award application deadline: 4/15; financial award applicants required to submit FAFSA. In 2008, 7 degrees awarded. *Degree program information:* Part-time and evening/weekend programs available. Offers religious studies (MAAT). *Application deadline:* For fall admission, 7/1 priority date for domestic students; for spring admission, 11/1 priority date for domestic students. Applications are processed on a rolling basis. *Application fee:* $30. *Application Contact:* Dr. Martin Pion, Director of MALA/MAAT Programs, 413-265-3581, Fax: 413-594-3951, E-mail: pionm@elms.edu. *Director of MALA/MAAT Programs,* Dr. Martin Pion, 413-265-3581, Fax: 413-594-3951, E-mail: pionm@elms.edu.

ELON UNIVERSITY, Elon, NC 27244-2010

General Information Independent-religious, coed, comprehensive institution. CGS member. *Enrollment:* 5,628 graduate, professional, and undergraduate students; 473 full-time matriculated graduate/professional students (236 women), 163 part-time matriculated graduate/professional students (99 women). *Enrollment by degree level:* 427 first professional, 209 master's. *Graduate faculty:* 71 full-time (33 women), 34 part-time/adjunct (16 women). *Graduate housing:* On-campus housing not available. *Student services:* Campus employment opportunities, campus safety program, career counseling, exercise/wellness program, free psychological counseling, international student services, low-cost health insurance, multicultural affairs office, services for students with disabilities, teacher training, writing training. *Library facilities:* Carol Grotnes Belk. *Online resources:* library catalog, web page, access to other libraries' catalogs. *Collection:* 290,938 titles, 8,805 serial subscriptions, 24,558 audiovisual materials.

Computer facilities: 850 computers available on campus for general student use. A campuswide network can be accessed from student residence rooms and from off campus. Online class registration is available. *Web address:* http://www.elon.edu/.

General Application Contact: Art Fadde, Director of Graduate Admissions, 800-334-8448 Ext. 3, Fax: 336-278-7699, E-mail: afadde@elon.edu.

GRADUATE UNITS

Program in Business Administration Students: 158 part-time (63 women); includes 19 minority (11 African Americans, 1 American Indian/Alaska Native, 6 Asian Americans or Pacific Islanders, 1 Hispanic American), 7 international. Average age 31. 132 applicants, 56% accepted, 58 enrolled. *Faculty:* 23 full-time (7 women), 1 (woman) part-time/adjunct. Expenses: Contact institution. *Financial support:* In 2008–09, 6 students received support. Federal Work-Study and scholarships/grants available. Support available to part-time students. Financial award application deadline: 3/15; financial award applicants required to submit FAFSA. In 2008, 39 master's awarded. *Degree program information:* Part-time and evening/weekend programs available. Offers business administration (MBA). *Application deadline:* For fall admission, 8/1 priority date for domestic students; for spring admission, 2/1 priority date for domestic students. Applications are processed on a rolling basis. *Application fee:* $50. Electronic applications accepted. *Application Contact:* Art Fadde, Director of Graduate Admissions, 800-334-8448 Ext. 3, Fax: 336-278-7699, E-mail: afadde@elon.edu. *Director,* Dr. William Burpit, 336-278-5949, Fax: 336-278-5952, E-mail: wburpitt@elon.edu.

Program in Education Students: 82 part-time (67 women); includes 11 African Americans, 1 Asian American or Pacific Islander, 1 Hispanic American, 3 international. Average age 35. 58 applicants, 81% accepted, 44 enrolled. *Faculty:* 12 full-time (9 women), 4 part-time/adjunct (all women). Expenses: Contact institution. *Financial support:* In 2008–09, 8 students received support. Federal Work-Study and scholarships/grants available. Support available to part-time students. Financial award application deadline: 6/1; financial award applicants required to submit FAFSA. In 2008, 27 master's awarded. *Degree program information:* Part-time programs available. Offers elementary education (M Ed); gifted education (M Ed); special education (M Ed). *Application deadline:* For winter admission, 6/1 priority date for domestic students. Applications are processed on a rolling basis. *Application fee:* $50. Electronic applications accepted. *Application Contact:* Art Fadde, Director of Graduate Admissions, 800-334-8448 Ext. 3, Fax: 336-278-7699, E-mail: afadde@elon.edu. *Director,* Dr. Judith B. Howard, 336-278-5885, Fax: 336-278-5919, E-mail: howardj@elon.edu.

Program in Interactive Media Expenses: Contact institution. Offers interactive media (MA). *Application deadline:* For fall admission, 5/1 priority date for domestic students. Applications are processed on a rolling basis. *Application fee:* $50. Electronic applications accepted. *Application Contact:* Art Fadde, Director of Graduate Admissions, 800-334-8448 Ext. 3, Fax: 336-278-7699, E-mail: afadde@elon.edu. *Director,* Dr. David Alan Copeland, 336-278-5662, Fax: 336-278-5734, E-mail: dcopeland@elon.edu.

Program in Law Students: 311 full-time (137 women); includes 14 African Americans, 1 American Indian/Alaska Native, 8 Asian Americans or Pacific Islanders. Average age 26. 536 applicants, 44% accepted, 106 enrolled. *Faculty:* 23 full-time (8 women), 23 part-time/adjunct (8 women). Expenses: Contact institution. *Financial support:* In 2008–09, 217 students received support. Federal Work-Study and scholarships/grants available. Financial award applicants required to submit FAFSA. Offers law (JD). *Application deadline:* For spring admission, 4/1 priority date for domestic students. Applications are processed on a rolling basis. *Application fee:* $50. Electronic applications accepted. *Application Contact:* Alan Woodlief, Associate Dean of the Elon University School of Law and Director of Law School Admissions, 336-279-9203, E-mail: awoodlief@elon.edu. *Dean,* George Johnson, 336-279-9201, E-mail: gjohnson8@elon.edu.

Program in Physical Therapy Students: 116 full-time (83 women); includes 2 African Americans, 1 Asian American or Pacific Islander, 1 Hispanic American. Average age 23. 249 applicants, 25% accepted, 38 enrolled. *Faculty:* 13 full-time (9 women), 6 part-time/adjunct (3 women). Expenses: Contact institution. *Financial support:* In 2008–09, 6 students received support. Federal Work-Study and scholarships/grants available. Financial award application deadline: 10/1; financial award applicants required to submit FAFSA. Offers physical therapy (DPT). *Application deadline:* For winter admission, 12/1 priority date for domestic students. Applications are processed on a rolling basis. *Application fee:* $50. Electronic applications accepted. *Application Contact:* Art Fadde, Director of Graduate Admissions, 800-334-8448 Ext. 3, Fax: 336-278-7699, E-mail: afadde@elon.edu. *Chair,* Dr. Elizabeth A. Rogers, 336-278-6400, Fax: 336-278-6414, E-mail: rogers@elon.edu.

EMBRY-RIDDLE AERONAUTICAL UNIVERSITY, Prescott, AZ 86301-3720

General Information Independent, coed, comprehensive institution. *Enrollment:* 1,719 graduate, professional, and undergraduate students; 23 full-time matriculated graduate/professional students (10 women), 6 part-time matriculated graduate/professional students. *Enrollment by degree level:* 29 master's. *Graduate faculty:* 5 full-time (1 woman). *Tuition:* Full-time $13,200; part-time $1100 per credit hour. *Graduate housing:* Rooms and/or apartments available on a first-come, first-served basis to single and married students. Typical cost: $4350 per year ($7590 including board) for single students. Housing application deadline: 6/30. *Student services:* Campus employment opportunities, campus safety program, career counseling, free psychological counseling, international student services, low-cost health insurance, services for students with disabilities. *Library facilities:* Christine & Steven F. Udvar-Hazy Library. *Online resources:* library catalog, web page, access to other libraries' catalogs. *Collection:* 40,505 titles, 668 serial subscriptions, 2,350 audiovisual materials. *Research affiliation:* Honeywell Engines & Systems (human factors evaluation of Honeywell enhanced ground proximity), Safeware Corporation (paradrogue aerodynamics phase I: modeling and analysis for mid-air).

Computer facilities: 470 computers available on campus for general student use. A campuswide network can be accessed from student residence rooms and from off campus. Online class registration is available. *Web address:* http://www.embryriddle.edu/.

General Application Contact: Deborah Pfingston, Graduate Admissions Coordinator, 928-777-6993, Fax: 928-777-6958, E-mail: deborah.pfingston@erau.edu.

GRADUATE UNITS

Program in Safety Science Students: 23 full-time (10 women), 6 part-time (0 women); includes 4 minority (2 African Americans, 1 Asian American or Pacific Islander, 1 Hispanic American), 3 international. Average age 27. 17 applicants, 94% accepted, 10 enrolled. *Faculty:* 5 full-time (1 woman). Expenses: Contact institution. *Financial support:* In 2008–09, 36 students received support, including 14 research assistantships with full tuition reimbursements available (averaging $2,194 per year); career-related internships or fieldwork, Federal Work-Study, and unspecified assistantships also available. Support available to part-time students. Financial award application deadline: 4/15; financial award applicants required to submit FAFSA. In 2008, 16 master's awarded. Offers safety science (MSSS). *Application deadline:* For fall admission, 8/1 priority date for domestic students; for spring admission, 12/1 priority date for domestic students. Applications are processed on a rolling basis. *Application fee:* $50. Electronic applications accepted. *Application Contact:* Deborah Pfingston, Graduate Admissions Coordinator, 928-777-6993, Fax: 928-777-6958, E-mail: deborahipfingston@erau.edu. *Chair, Safety Science Department,* Dr. Gary Northam, 928-777-3964, Fax: 928-777-6958.

EMBRY-RIDDLE AERONAUTICAL UNIVERSITY, Daytona Beach, FL 32114-3900

General Information Independent, coed, comprehensive institution. *Enrollment:* 5,062 graduate, professional, and undergraduate students; 282 full-time matriculated graduate/professional students (72 women), 120 part-time matriculated graduate/professional students (30 women). *Enrollment by degree level:* 402 master's. *Graduate faculty:* 51 full-time (6 women), 10 part-time/adjunct (3 women). *Tuition:* Full-time $13,200; part-time $1100 per credit hour. *Graduate housing:* Rooms and/or apartments available on a first-come, first-served basis to single and married students. Typical cost: $5000 per year ($8240 including board) for single students. Housing application deadline: 6/30. *Student services:* Campus employment opportunities, campus safety program, career counseling, free psychological counseling, international student services, low-cost health insurance, services for students with disabilities. *Library facilities:* Jack R. Hunt Memorial Library. *Online resources:* library catalog, web page. *Collection:* 120,550 titles, 811 serial subscriptions, 4,600 audiovisual materials. *Research affiliation:* Chilean Nat'l Directorate of Airports (assessment and operational analysis of airspace and locations for new airports in the central zone of Chile), Boeing (passenger behavior and modeling for enplane/deplane efficiency), Lockheed Martin (transportation and security), Gulfstream Aerospace (design and delivery of courses), JetBlue (enriched quality of instruction), Jet Set (mesospheric dynamics).

Computer facilities: 1,013 computers available on campus for general student use. A campuswide network can be accessed from student residence rooms and from off campus. Online class registration is available. *Web address:* http://www.embryriddle.edu/.

General Application Contact: Keath Deaton, Associate Director, International and Graduate Admissions, 800-388-3728, Fax: 386-226-7070, E-mail: graduate.admissions@erau.edu.

GRADUATE UNITS

Daytona Beach Campus Graduate Program Students: 282 full-time (72 women), 120 part-time (30 women); includes 55 minority (23 African Americans, 3 American Indian/Alaska Native, 13 Asian Americans or Pacific Islanders, 16 Hispanic Americans), 128 international. Average age 27. 362 applicants, 63% accepted, 133 enrolled. *Faculty:* 51 full-time (6 women), 10 part-time/adjunct (3 women). Expenses: Contact institution. *Financial support:* In 2008–09, 262 students received support, including 32 research assistantships with full and partial tuition reimbursements available (averaging $7,470 per year), 43 teaching assistantships with full and partial tuition reimbursements available (averaging $7,470 per year); career-related internships or fieldwork, Federal Work-Study, and unspecified assistantships also available. Support available to part-time students. Financial award application deadline: 4/15; financial award applicants required to submit FAFSA. In 2008, 133 master's awarded. *Degree program information:* Part-time and evening/weekend programs available. Offers aeronautics (MBAA, MSA, MSAE, MSE, MSEP, MSHFS, MSME); aerospace engineering (MSAE); applied aviation sciences (MSA); business administration in aviation (MBAA); engineering physics (space science) (MSEP); human factors engineering (MSHFS); mechanical engineering (MSME); software engineering (MSE); systems engineering (MSHFS). *Application deadline:* For fall admission, 8/1 priority date for domestic students; for spring admission, 12/1 priority date for domestic students. Applications are processed on a rolling basis. *Application fee:* $50. Electronic applications accepted. *Application Contact:* Keith Deaton, Associate Director, International and Graduate Admissions, 800-388-3728, Fax: 386-226-7070, E-mail: graduate.admissions@erau.edu. *Executive Vice President and Chief Academic Officer,* Dr. Richard H Heist, 386-226-6216.

EMBRY-RIDDLE AERONAUTICAL UNIVERSITY WORLDWIDE, Daytona Beach, FL 32114-3900

General Information Independent, coed, comprehensive institution. *Enrollment:* 16,331 graduate, professional, and undergraduate students; 1,703 full-time matriculated graduate/professional students (267 women), 2,349 part-time matriculated graduate/professional students (360 women). *Enrollment by degree level:* 4,052 master's. *Graduate faculty:* 68 full-time (9 women), 316 part-time/adjunct (52 women). *Tuition:* Full-time $4152; part-time $346 per credit hour. *Graduate housing:* On-campus housing not available. *Student services:* Career counseling, international student services. *Library facilities:* Jack R. Hunt Memorial Library. *Online resources:* library catalog, web page. *Collection:* 120,550 titles, 811 serial subscriptions, 4,600 audiovisual materials. *Web address:* http://www.embryriddle.edu/.

General Application Contact: Bill Hampton, Executive Director of Enrollment Management, 386-226-6910, Fax: 386-226-6984, E-mail: ecinfo@erau.edu.

GRADUATE UNITS

Worldwide Headquarters Students: 1,703 full-time (267 women), 2,349 part-time (360 women); includes 723 minority (253 African Americans, 35 American Indian/Alaska Native, 154 Asian Americans or Pacific Islanders, 281 Hispanic Americans), 19 international. Average age 35. 1,363 applicants, 84% accepted, 897 enrolled. *Faculty:* 68 full-time (9 women), 316 part-time/adjunct (52 women). Expenses: Contact institution. *Financial support:* In 2008–09, 202 students received support. Available to part-time students. Applicants required to submit FAFSA. In 2008, 1,029 master's awarded. *Degree program information:* Part-time and evening/weekend programs available. Postbaccalaureate distance learning degree programs offered (minimal on-campus study). Offers aeronautics (MAS); management (MSM, MSM/MBAA); project management (MSPM); space education (MSSE); technical management (MSTM). *Application deadline:* Applications are processed on a rolling basis. *Application fee:* $50. Electronic applications accepted. *Application Contact:* Bill Hampton, Executive Director of Enrollment Management, 386-226-6910, Fax: 386-226-6984, E-mail: ecinfo@erau.edu. *Executive Vice President,* Dr. Martin A. Smith, 386-226-6961, Fax: 386-226-6984, E-mail: martin.smith@erau.edu.

EMERSON COLLEGE, Boston, MA 02116-4624

General Information Independent, coed, comprehensive institution. CGS member. *Enrollment:* 4,536 graduate, professional, and undergraduate students; 731 full-time matriculated graduate/professional students (549 women), 161 part-time matriculated graduate/professional students (112 women). *Enrollment by degree level:* 892 master's. *Graduate faculty:* 162 full-time (70 women), 242 part-time/adjunct (118 women). *Tuition:* Full-time $17,720; part-time $886 per credit. *Required fees:* $60 per year. One-time fee: $170. *Graduate housing:* On-campus housing not available. *Student services:* Campus employment opportunities, campus safety program, career counseling, exercise/wellness program, free psychological counseling, grant writing training, international student services, low-cost health insurance, multicultural affairs office, services for students with disabilities, writing training. *Library facilities:* Iwasaki Library plus 1 other. *Online resources:* library catalog, web page, access to other libraries' catalogs. *Collection:* 179,380 titles, 31,258 serial subscriptions, 11,596 audiovisual materials.

Computer facilities: Computer purchase and lease plans are available. 480 computers available on campus for general student use. A campuswide network can be accessed from student residence rooms and from off campus. Online class registration is available. *Web address:* http://www.emerson.edu/.

General Application Contact: Office of Graduate Admission, 617-824-8610, Fax: 617-824-8614, E-mail: gradapp@emerson.edu.

GRADUATE UNITS

Graduate Studies Students: 731 full-time (549 women), 161 part-time (112 women); includes 96 minority (27 African Americans, 4 American Indian/Alaska Native, 39 Asian Americans or Pacific Islanders, 26 Hispanic Americans), 110 international. Average age 27. 1,588 applicants, 51% accepted, 365 enrolled. *Faculty:* 162 full-time (70 women), 242 part-time/adjunct (118 women). Expenses: Contact institution. *Financial support:* In 2008–09, 183 students received support, including 26 fellowships with partial tuition reimbursements available (averaging $14,900 per year), 115 research assistantships with partial tuition reimbursements available (averaging $10,000 per year); career-related internships or fieldwork, Federal Work-Study, institutionally sponsored loans, scholarships/grants, and unspecified assistantships also available. Support available to part-time students. Financial award application deadline: 3/1; financial award applicants required to submit CSS PROFILE or FAFSA. In 2008, 383 master's awarded. *Degree program information:* Part-time and evening/weekend programs available. *Application deadline:* For fall admission, 3/1 priority date for domestic students, 5/1 for international students; for spring admission, 11/1 for domestic and international students. Applications are processed on a rolling basis. *Application fee:* $60 ($75 for international students). Electronic applications accepted. *Application Contact:* Office of Graduate Admission, 617-824-8610, Fax: 617-824-8614, E-mail: gradapp@emerson.edu. *Director,* Dr. Donna Schroth, 617-824-8612.

School of Communication Students: 368 full-time (311 women), 61 part-time (50 women); includes 46 minority (13 African Americans, 1 American Indian/Alaska Native, 20 Asian Americans or Pacific Islanders, 12 Hispanic Americans), 86 international. Average age 26. 947 applicants, 48% accepted, 196 enrolled. Expenses: Contact institution. *Financial support:* In 2008–09, 94 students received support, including 11 fellowships (averaging $14,000 per year), 55 research assistantships (averaging $9,045 per year); career-related internships or fieldwork, Federal Work-Study, institutionally sponsored loans, scholarships/grants, and unspecified assistantships also available. Support available to part-time students. Financial award applicants required to submit CSS PROFILE or FAFSA. In 2008, 211 master's awarded. Offers communication (MA, MS); communication disorders (MS); communication management (MA); global marketing communication and advertising (MA); health communication (MA); integrated marketing communication (MA); journalism (MA). *Application deadline:* Applications are processed on a rolling basis. *Application fee:* $60 ($75 for international students). Electronic applications accepted. *Application Contact:* Office of Graduate Admission, 617-824-8610, Fax: 617-824-8614, E-mail: gradapp@emerson.edu. *Dean,* Dr. Janis Andersen, 617-824-8573, E-mail: Janis_Andersen@emerson.edu.

School of the Arts Students: 363 full-time (238 women), 100 part-time (62 women); includes 50 minority (14 African Americans, 3 American Indian/Alaska Native, 19 Asian Americans or Pacific Islanders, 14 Hispanic Americans), 24 international. Average age 28. 641 applicants, 54% accepted, 169 enrolled. Expenses: Contact institution. *Financial support:* In 2008–09, 89 students received support, including 15 fellowships (averaging $15,200 per year), 60 research assistantships (averaging $10,000 per year); career-related internships or fieldwork, Federal Work-Study, institutionally sponsored loans, scholarships/grants, and unspecified assistantships also available. Support available to part-time students. Financial award application deadline: 3/1; financial award applicants required to submit FAFSA. In 2008, 172 master's awarded. *Degree program information:* Part-time programs available. Offers arts (MA, MFA); creative writing (MFA); media art (MFA); publishing and writing (MA); theatre education (MA); visual and media arts (MFA). *Application deadline:* Applications are processed on a rolling basis. *Application fee:* $60 ($75 for international students). Electronic applications accepted. *Application Contact:* Office of Graduate Admission, 617-824-8610, Fax: 617-824-8614, E-mail: gradapp@emerson.edu. *Dean,* Grafton Nunes, 617-824-8983, E-mail: Grafton_Nunes@emerson.edu.

EMILY CARR INSTITUTE OF ART + DESIGN, Vancouver, BC V6H 3R9, Canada

General Information Province-supported, coed, comprehensive institution. *Enrollment by degree level:* 27 master's. *Graduate faculty:* 6 full-time (2 women), 2 part-time/adjunct (1 woman). *Graduate tuition:* Tuition and fees charges are reported in Canadian dollars. *Tuition, area resident:* Full-time $11,132 Canadian dollars. *Required fees:* $131.40 Canadian dollars. One-time fee: $144 Canadian dollars full-time. *Graduate housing:* On-campus housing not available. *Student services:* Campus employment opportunities, campus safety program, career counseling, free psychological counseling, grant writing training, international student services, low-cost health insurance, services for students with disabilities, writing training. *Research affiliation:* Children's Hospital, Vancouver BC (Health Care Research), Aldrich Pears + Associates (Experience Design), Kodak Communications Group (Interaction Design), Donat Group (E Learning), Paperny Films (Television and Film Production), Fuel Cell Research Centre, National Research Council (Clean Technology). *Web address:* http://www.eciad.ca/.

General Application Contact: Terry Plummer, Assistant to Dean of Graduate Studies, E-mail: tplum@ecuad.ca.

GRADUATE UNITS

Program in Applied Arts Tuition and fees charges are reported in Canadian dollars. Offers design (MAA); media arts (MAA); visual arts (MAA). Electronic applications accepted.

Program in Digital Media Tuition and fees charges are reported in Canadian dollars. Offers digital media (MDM). Electronic applications accepted.

EMMANUEL COLLEGE, Boston, MA 02115

General Information Independent-religious, coed, comprehensive institution. *Enrollment:* 1,902 graduate, professional, and undergraduate students; 4 full-time matriculated graduate/professional students (all women), 202 part-time matriculated graduate/professional students (149 women). *Enrollment by degree level:* 174 master's, 32 other advanced degrees. *Graduate faculty:* 31 part-time/adjunct (4 women). *Tuition:* Part-time $1950 per course. *Graduate housing:* On-campus housing not available. *Student services:* Campus safety program, career counseling, free psychological counseling, international student services, low-cost health insurance, multicultural affairs office, services for students with disabilities, teacher training, writing training. *Library facilities:* Cardinal Cushing Library. *Online resources:* library catalog, web page, access to other libraries' catalogs. *Collection:* 131,000 titles, 1,063 serial subscriptions, 800 audiovisual materials.

Computer facilities: Computer purchase and lease plans are available. 145 computers available on campus for general student use. A campuswide network can be accessed from student residence rooms and from off campus. Online class registration, software applications are available. *Web address:* http://www.emmanuel.edu/.

General Application Contact: Enrollment Counselor, 617-735-9700, Fax: 617-735-9708, E-mail: gpp@emmanuel.edu.

GRADUATE UNITS

Graduate Programs Students: 4 full-time (all women), 202 part-time (149 women); includes 40 minority (28 African Americans, 4 Asian Americans or Pacific Islanders, 8 Hispanic Americans). Average age 35. 120 applicants, 64% accepted, 75 enrolled. *Faculty:* 31 part-time/adjunct (4 women). Expenses: Contact institution. In 2008, 70 master's, 8 other advanced degrees awarded. *Degree program information:* Part-time and evening/weekend programs available. Offers educational leadership (CAGS); elementary education (MAT); human resource management (MS, Certificate); management (MSM); management and leadership (Certificate); research administration (Certificate); school administration (M Ed); secondary education (MAT). *Application deadline:* For fall admission, 8/15 priority date for domestic students; for spring admission, 12/8 priority date for domestic students. Applications are processed on a rolling basis. *Application fee:* $50. Electronic applications accepted. *Application Contact:* Enrollment Counselor, 617-735-9700, Fax: 617-735-9708, E-mail: gpp@emmanuel.edu. *Dean, Graduate and Professional Programs,* Dr. Judith Marley, 617-735-9700, Fax: 617-735-9708, E-mail: gpp@emmanuel.edu.

EMMANUEL SCHOOL OF RELIGION, Johnson City, TN 37601-9438

General Information Independent-religious, coed, primarily men, graduate-only institution. *Enrollment by degree level:* 90 first professional, 27 master's, 11 doctoral. *Graduate faculty:* 12 full-time (2 women), 2 part-time/adjunct (0 women). *Tuition:* Full-time $7800; part-time $325 per credit. *Required fees:* $122.50 per semester. Tuition and fees vary according to degree level and program. *Graduate housing:* Rooms and/or apartments available on a first-come, first-served basis to single and married students. Typical cost: $1890 per year for single students; $3780 per year for married students. Housing application deadline: 8/1. *Student services:* Campus employment opportunities, career counseling, international student services, low-cost health insurance. *Library facilities:* Emmanuel School of Religion Library. *Online resources:* library catalog, web page. *Collection:* 144,248 titles, 735 serial subscriptions, 4,522 audiovisual materials. *Research affiliation:* American Schools of Oriental Research (Ancient Near East), Disciples of Christ Historical Society (Church History—Stone-Campbell movement).

Computer facilities: 14 computers available on campus for general student use. A campuswide network can be accessed from student residence rooms and from off campus. *Web address:* http://www.esr.edu/.

General Application Contact: Shelley Gasser, Administrative Assistant for Admissions, 423-461-1535, Fax: 423-926-6198, E-mail: gassers@esr.edu.

GRADUATE UNITS

Graduate and Professional Programs Students: 86 full-time (26 women), 42 part-time (10 women); includes 5 minority (4 African Americans, 1 Hispanic American), 14 international. Average age 32. 47 applicants, 98% accepted, 34 enrolled. *Faculty:* 12 full-time (2 women), 2 part-time/adjunct (0 women). Expenses: Contact institution. *Financial support:* In 2008–09,

Emmanuel School of Religion (continued)

90 students received support, including 10 teaching assistantships with partial tuition reimbursements available; career-related internships or fieldwork, institutionally sponsored loans, scholarships/grants, and tuition waivers (partial) also available. Support available to part-time students. Financial award application deadline: 4/1; financial award applicants required to submit FAFSA. In 2008, 16 first professional degrees, 6 master's, 2 doctorates awarded. *Degree program information:* Part-time programs available. Offers Christian care and counseling (M Div); Christian doctrine (M Div); Christian education (M Div); Christian ministries (M Div); church history (M Div, MAR); ministry (D Min); New Testament (M Div, MAR); Old Testament (M Div, MAR); urban ministry (M Div); world mission (M Div). *Application deadline:* For fall admission, 8/1 priority date for domestic students. Applications are processed on a rolling basis. *Application fee:* $25. *Application Contact:* Shelley Gasser, Administrative Assistant for Admissions, 423-461-1535, Fax: 423-926-6198, E-mail: GasserS@esr.edu. *Dean and Professor of New Testament*, Dr. Rollin A Ramsaran, 423-461-1524, Fax: 423-926-6198, E-mail: RamsaranR@esr.edu.

EMORY & HENRY COLLEGE, Emory, VA 24327-0947

General Information Independent-religious, coed, comprehensive institution. *Graduate housing:* Room and/or apartments guaranteed to single students; on-campus housing not available to married students.

GRADUATE UNITS

Graduate Programs *Degree program information:* Part-time and evening/weekend programs available.

EMORY UNIVERSITY, Atlanta, GA 30322-1100

General Information Independent-religious, coed, university. CGS member. *Enrollment:* 10,921 graduate, professional, and undergraduate students; 5,094 full-time matriculated graduate/professional students (2,932 women), 771 part-time matriculated graduate/professional students (386 women). *Enrollment by degree level:* 1,334 first professional, 2,586 master's, 1,695 doctoral, 8 other advanced degrees. *Graduate faculty:* 3,129 full-time (1,172 women), 547 part-time/adjunct (286 women). *Tuition:* Full-time $32,800; part-time $1025 per credit hour. Tuition and fees vary according to course load and program. *Graduate housing:* Rooms and/or apartments available on a first-come, first-served basis to single and married students. Typical cost: $552 per year for single students; $1058 per year for married students. Room charges vary according to campus/location and housing facility selected. *Student services:* Campus employment opportunities, campus safety program, career counseling, child daycare facilities, exercise/wellness program, free psychological counseling, grant writing training, international student services, low-cost health insurance, multicultural affairs office, services for students with disabilities, teacher training, writing training. *Library facilities:* Robert W. Woodruff Library plus 7 others. *Online resources:* library catalog, web page, access to other libraries' catalogs. *Collection:* 3.4 million titles, 54,295 serial subscriptions, 92,260 audiovisual materials. *Research affiliation:* Georgia Research Consortium, Emory and Georgia Technical Biomedical Research Center, Oak Ridge Associated Universities (energy, health and environment), Georgia Mental Health Institute, Centers for Disease Control, Highlands Biological Station.

Computer facilities: Computer purchase and lease plans are available. 600 computers available on campus for general student use. A campuswide network can be accessed from student residence rooms and from off campus. Online class registration is available. *Web address:* http://www.emory.edu/.

General Application Contact: Kharen Fulton, Director of Admissions, 404-727-0184, Fax: 404-727-4990, E-mail: gradkef@emory.edu.

GRADUATE UNITS

Candler School of Theology Students: 444 full-time (223 women), 49 part-time (29 women); includes 119 minority (111 African Americans, 5 Asian Americans or Pacific Islanders, 3 Hispanic Americans), 59 international. Average age 32. 530 applicants, 78% accepted, 181 enrolled. *Faculty:* 53 full-time (15 women), 26 part-time/adjunct (8 women). Expenses: Contact institution. *Financial support:* In 2008–09, 397 students received support, including 345 fellowships (averaging $12,890 per year); career-related internships or fieldwork, Federal Work-Study, institutionally sponsored loans, and scholarships/grants also available. Support available to part-time students. Financial award application deadline: 1/15; financial award applicants required to submit CSS PROFILE or FAFSA. In 2008, 118 first professional degrees, 28 master's awarded. *Degree program information:* Part-time programs available. Offers formation and witness (M Div); leadership in church and community (M Div); religion and race (M Div); religion, health and science (M Div); scripture and interpretation (M Div); society and personality (M Div); theology (MTS, Th M, Th D); theology and ethics (M Div); theology and the arts (M Div); traditions of the church (M Div); women and religion (M Div). *Application deadline:* For fall admission, 7/1 for domestic and international students; for spring admission, 11/1 for domestic and international students. Applications are processed on a rolling basis. *Application fee:* $50. Electronic applications accepted. *Application Contact:* Rev. Shonda R Jones, Assistant Dean of Admissions and Financial Aid, 404-727-6326, Fax: 404-727-2915, E-mail: candleradmissions@emory.edu. *Registrar*, Missy Page, 404-727-6480, Fax: 404-727-4373, E-mail: candlerregistrar@emory.edu.

Goizueta Business School *Degree program information:* Part-time and evening/weekend programs available. Postbaccalaureate distance learning degree programs offered (minimal on-campus study). Offers business (EMBA, MBA, WEMBA, PhD). Electronic applications accepted.

Graduate School of Arts and Sciences Offers anthropology (PhD); art history (PhD); arts and sciences (M Ed, MA, MAT, MM, MPH, MS, MSM, MSPH, PhD, Certificate, DAST); biophysics (PhD); biostatistics (MPH, MSPH, PhD); chemistry (PhD); choral conducting (MM, MSM); clinical psychology (PhD); clinical research (MS); cognition and development (PhD); comparative literature (PhD, Certificate); computer science (MS); condensed matter physics (PhD); economics (PhD); English (PhD); film studies (Certificate); French (PhD, Certificate); French and educational studies (PhD); history (PhD); Jewish studies (MA); mathematics (PhD); Middle Eastern studies (PhD); neuroscience and animal behavior (PhD); non-linear physics (PhD); nursing (PhD); organ performance (MM, MSM); philosophy (PhD); political science (PhD); psychoanalytic studies (PhD); public health informatics (MSPH); radiological physics (PhD); religion (PhD); sociology (MA, PhD); soft condensed matter physics (PhD); solid-state physics (PhD); Spanish (PhD, Certificate); statistical physics (PhD); women studies (Certificate); women's studies (PhD). Electronic applications accepted.

Division of Biological and Biomedical Sciences Students: 429 full-time (282 women); includes 86 minority (39 African Americans, 1 American Indian/Alaska Native, 26 Asian Americans or Pacific Islanders, 20 Hispanic Americans), 66 international. Average age 27. 677 applicants, 18% accepted, 59 enrolled. *Faculty:* 309 full-time (76 women). Expenses: Contact institution. *Financial support:* In 2008–09, 148 students received support, including 147 fellowships (averaging $24,000 per year); institutionally sponsored loans, health care benefits, and tuition waivers (full) also available. In 2008, 63 doctorates awarded. Offers biochemistry, cell and developmental biology (PhD); biological and biomedical sciences (PhD); genetics and molecular biology (PhD); immunology and molecular pathogenesis (PhD); microbiology and molecular genetics (PhD); molecular and systems pharmacology (PhD); neuroscience (PhD); nutrition and health sciences (PhD); population biology, ecology and evolution (PhD). *Application deadline:* For fall admission, 1/3 for domestic and international students. *Application fee:* $50. Electronic applications accepted. *Application Contact:* Kathy Smith, 404-727-2545, Fax: 404-727-3322. *Director*, Dr. Keith Wilkinson, 404-727-2545, Fax: 404-727-3322.

Division of Educational Studies Offers educational studies (MA, PhD, DAST); middle grades teaching (M Ed, MAT); secondary teaching (M Ed, MAT). Electronic applications accepted.

Division of Religion Offers religion (PhD). Electronic applications accepted.

Graduate Institute of Liberal Arts Offers liberal arts (PhD). Electronic applications accepted.

Nell Hodgson Woodruff School of Nursing *Degree program information:* Part-time programs available. Offers adult and elder health advanced practice nursing (MSN); emergency nurse practitioner (MSN); family nurse practitioner (MSN); family nurse-midwife (MSN); leadership in healthcare (MSN); nurse midwifery (MSN); nursing administration (MSN); pediatric advanced nursing practice (MSN); public health nursing (MSN); women's health nurse practitioner (MSN). Electronic applications accepted.

Rollins School of Public Health Students: 358 full-time (277 women); includes 99 minority (42 African Americans, 44 Asian Americans or Pacific Islanders, 13 Hispanic Americans), 15 international. Average age 27. 1,916 applicants, 58% accepted, 358 enrolled. *Faculty:* 208 full-time (88 women), 275 part-time/adjunct (90 women). Expenses: Contact institution. *Financial support:* In 2008–09, 14 fellowships with full and partial tuition reimbursements were awarded; research assistantships, teaching assistantships, career-related internships or fieldwork, Federal Work-Study, institutionally sponsored loans, scholarships/grants, traineeships, health care benefits, and unspecified assistantships also available. Support available to part-time students. Financial award application deadline: 1/5; financial award applicants required to submit FAFSA. In 2008, 302 master's awarded. *Degree program information:* Part-time and evening/weekend programs available. Postbaccalaureate distance learning degree programs offered (minimal on-campus study). Offers applied epidemiology (MPH); behavioral sciences and health education (MPH); biostatistics and bioinformatics (MPH, MSPH); environmental and occupational health (MPH, MSPH); epidemiology (MPH, MSPH, PhD); global demography (MSPH); global environmental health (MPH); health policy (MPH); health policy research (MSPH); health services management (MPH); healthcare outcomes (MPH); prevention science (MPH); public health (MPH, MSPH, PhD, MM Sc/MPH); public health informatics (MSPH); public nutrition (MSPH). *Application deadline:* For fall admission, 1/5 priority date for domestic and international students. *Application fee:* $95. Electronic applications accepted. *Application Contact:* Kara Brown Robinson, Director of Admissions and Recruitment/Assistant Dean for Student Affairs, 404-727-3956, Fax: 404-727-3962, E-mail: admit@sph.emory.edu. *Executive Associate Dean for Academic Affairs*, Dr. Richard Levinson, 404-727-3956, Fax: 404-727-3962, E-mail: admit@sph.emory.edu.

School of Law Students: 697 full-time (332 women); includes 193 minority (71 African Americans, 3 American Indian/Alaska Native, 63 Asian Americans or Pacific Islanders, 56 Hispanic Americans), 28 international. Average age 24. 4,209 applicants, 24% accepted, 224 enrolled. *Faculty:* 54 full-time (29 women), 44 part-time/adjunct (10 women). Expenses: Contact institution. *Financial support:* In 2008–09, 650 students received support, including 15 fellowships with full tuition reimbursements available (averaging $3,000 per year), 47 research assistantships (averaging $9,360 per year); career-related internships or fieldwork, Federal Work-Study, institutionally sponsored loans, scholarships/grants, and tuition waivers (full and partial) also available. Financial award application deadline: 3/1; financial award applicants required to submit FAFSA. In 2008, 245 first professional degrees, 12 Certificates awarded. Offers law (JD, LL M, Certificate). *Application deadline:* For fall admission, 3/1 for domestic and international students. Applications are processed on a rolling basis. *Application fee:* $70. Electronic applications accepted. *Application Contact:* Lynell A. Cadray, Assistant Dean for Admissions, 404-727-6802, Fax: 404-727-2477, E-mail: lawinfo@law.emory.edu. *Dean*, David F. Partlett, 404-712-8815, Fax: 404-727-0866, E-mail: david.partlett@emory.edu.

School of Medicine Offers anesthesiology (MM Sc); anesthesiology/patient monitoring systems (MM Sc); biomedical engineering (PhD); medicine (MD, MM Sc, DPT, PhD); ophthalmic technology (MM Sc); physical therapy (DPT); physician assistant (MM Sc). Electronic applications accepted.

See Close-Up on page 907.

EMPEROR'S COLLEGE OF TRADITIONAL ORIENTAL MEDICINE, Santa Monica, CA 90403

General Information Private, coed, graduate-only institution. *Graduate housing:* On-campus housing not available. *Research affiliation:* Lotus Herbs (herbs), LA Free Clinic (herbs), UCLA Ashe Center (student health).

GRADUATE UNITS

Graduate Programs *Degree program information:* Part-time and evening/weekend programs available. Offers oriental medicine (MTOM, DAOM).

EMPORIA STATE UNIVERSITY, Emporia, KS 66801-5087

General Information State-supported, coed, comprehensive institution. CGS member. *Enrollment:* 6,404 graduate, professional, and undergraduate students; 257 full-time matriculated graduate/professional students (182 women), 1,446 part-time matriculated graduate/professional students (1,000 women). *Enrollment by degree level:* 1,678 master's, 18 doctoral, 7 other advanced degrees. *Graduate faculty:* 260 full-time (120 women), 33 part-time/adjunct (20 women). Tuition, state resident: full-time $3976; part-time $166 per credit hour. Tuition, nonresident: full-time $12,028; part-time $501 per credit hour. *Required fees:* $51 per credit hour. Tuition and fees vary according to campus/location. *Graduate housing:* Rooms and/or apartments available on a first-come, first-served basis to single and married students. Typical cost: $3027 per year ($5858 including board) for single students; $2529 per year for married students. Room and board charges vary according to board plan and housing facility selected. Housing application deadline: 8/25. *Student services:* Campus employment opportunities, campus safety program, career counseling, child daycare facilities, exercise/wellness program, free psychological counseling, grant writing training, international student services, low-cost health insurance, multicultural affairs office, services for students with disabilities, teacher training, writing training. *Library facilities:* William Allen White Library. *Online resources:* library catalog, web page, access to other libraries' catalogs. *Collection:* 2.4 million titles, 37,675 serial subscriptions, 9,256 audiovisual materials.

Computer facilities: 410 computers available on campus for general student use. A campuswide network can be accessed from student residence rooms and from off campus. Online class registration, various software packages are available. *Web address:* http://www.emporia.edu/.

General Application Contact: Mary Sewell, Admissions Coordinator, 800-950-GRAD, Fax: 620-341-5909, E-mail: msewell@emporia.edu.

GRADUATE UNITS

School of Graduate Studies Students: 257 full-time (182 women), 1,446 part-time (1,000 women); includes 99 minority (32 African Americans, 8 American Indian/Alaska Native, 17 Asian Americans or Pacific Islanders, 42 Hispanic Americans), 104 international. Average age 34. 396 applicants, 83% accepted, 321 enrolled. *Faculty:* 260 full-time (120 women), 33 part-time/adjunct (20 women). Expenses: Contact institution. *Financial support:* In 2008–09, 44 research assistantships with full tuition reimbursements (averaging $6,905 per year), 106 teaching assistantships with full tuition reimbursements (averaging $7,128 per year) were awarded; career-related internships or fieldwork, Federal Work-Study, institutionally sponsored loans, scholarships/grants, health care benefits, and unspecified assistantships also available. Financial award application deadline: 3/15; financial award applicants required to submit FAFSA. In 2008, 521 master's, 5 doctorates, 18 other advanced degrees awarded. *Degree program information:* Part-time and evening/weekend programs available. Postbaccalaureate distance learning degree programs offered (no on-campus study). *Application deadline:* Applications are processed on a rolling basis. *Application fee:* $30 ($75 for international students). Electronic applications accepted. *Application Contact:* Mary Sewell, Admissions Coordinator, 800-950-GRAD, Fax: 620-341-5909, E-mail: msewell@emporia.edu. *Dean*, Dr. Gerrit Bleeker, 620-341-5403, Fax: 620-341-5909, E-mail: gbleeker@emporia.edu.

College of Liberal Arts and Sciences Students: 33 full-time (20 women), 110 part-time (54 women); includes 10 minority (1 African American, 1 American Indian/Alaska Native, 4 Asian Americans or Pacific Islanders, 4 Hispanic Americans), 19 international. 33 applicants, 79% accepted, 26 enrolled. *Faculty:* 142 full-time (57 women), 22 part-time/adjunct (15 women). Expenses: Contact institution. *Financial support:* In 2008–09, 7 research assistantships with full tuition reimbursements (averaging $7,059 per year), 45 teaching assistantships with full tuition reimbursements (averaging $7,508 per year) were awarded; career-related internships or fieldwork, Federal Work-Study, institutionally sponsored loans, health care benefits, and unspecified assistantships also available. Financial award application deadline: 3/15; financial award applicants required to submit FAFSA. In 2008, 30 master's,

1 other advanced degree awarded. *Degree program information:* Part-time programs available. Offers American history (MA, MAT); anthropology (MAT); botany (MS); earth science (MS); economics (MAT); English (MA); environmental biology (MS); general biology (MS); geography (MAT); geospatial analysis (Postbaccalaureate Certificate); history (MA); liberal arts and sciences (MA, MAT, MM, MS, Postbaccalaureate Certificate); mathematics (MS); microbial and cellular biology (MS); music education (MM); performance (MM); physical science (MS); political science (MAT); social sciences (MAT); social studies education (MAT); sociology (MAT); teaching English to speakers of other languages (MA); world history (MA, MAT); zoology (MS). *Application deadline:* For fall admission, 8/15 priority date for domestic students. Applications are processed on a rolling basis. *Application fee:* $30 ($75 for international students). Electronic applications accepted. *Application Contact:* Mary Sewell, Admissions Coordinator, 800-950-GRAD, Fax: 620-341-5909, E-mail: msewell@emporia.edu. *Dean,* Dr. Steven Brown, 620-341-5278, Fax: 620-341-5681, E-mail: sbrown10@emporia.edu.

School of Business Students: 69 full-time (39 women), 61 part-time (34 women); includes 5 minority (2 African Americans, 3 Asian Americans or Pacific Islanders), 57 international. 35 applicants, 83% accepted, 29 enrolled. *Faculty:* 28 full-time (6 women), 1 part-time/adjunct (0 women). Expenses: Contact institution. *Financial support:* In 2008–09, 4 research assistantships with full tuition reimbursements (averaging $7,374 per year), 6 teaching assistantships with full tuition reimbursements (averaging $6,695 per year) were awarded; career-related internships or fieldwork, Federal Work-Study, institutionally sponsored loans, health care benefits, and unspecified assistantships also available. Financial award application deadline: 3/15; financial award applicants required to submit FAFSA. In 2008, 52 master's awarded. *Degree program information:* Part-time programs available. Postbaccalaureate distance learning degree programs offered (minimal on-campus study). Offers business (MBA, MSBE); business administration (MBA); business education (MSBE). *Application deadline:* For fall admission, 8/15 priority date for domestic students. Applications are processed on a rolling basis. *Application fee:* $30 ($75 for international students). Electronic applications accepted. *Application Contact:* Dr. Donald Miller, Director, MBA Program, 620-341-5456, Fax: 620-341-6523, E-mail: dmiller1@emporia.edu. *Dean,* Dr. Joseph Wen, 620-341-5274, Fax: 620-341-5892, E-mail: hwen@emporia.edu.

School of Library and Information Management Students: 20 full-time (17 women), 294 part-time (225 women); includes 27 minority (6 African Americans, 1 American Indian/Alaska Native, 6 Asian Americans or Pacific Islanders, 14 Hispanic Americans), 2 international. 73 applicants, 79% accepted, 58 enrolled. *Faculty:* 8 full-time (7 women), 1 part-time/adjunct (0 women). Expenses: Contact institution. *Financial support:* In 2008–09, 6 research assistantships (averaging $8,105 per year), 7 teaching assistantships with full tuition reimbursements (averaging $7,808 per year) were awarded; Federal Work-Study, institutionally sponsored loans, and unspecified assistantships also available. Financial award application deadline: 3/15; financial award applicants required to submit FAFSA. In 2008, 90 master's, 5 doctorates awarded. *Degree program information:* Part-time and evening/weekend programs available. Postbaccalaureate distance learning degree programs offered (minimal on-campus study). Offers archives studies (Certificate); legal information management (Certificate); library and information management (MLS, PhD, Certificate). *Application deadline:* For fall admission, 8/15 priority date for domestic students. *Application fee:* $30 ($75 for international students). *Application Contact:* Candace Boardman, Director, Kansas MLS Program, 620-341-6159, E-mail: cboardma@emporia.edu. *Interim Dean,* Dr. Gwen Alexander, 620-341-5203, Fax: 620-341-5233, E-mail: galexan1@emporia.edu.

The Teachers College Students: 135 full-time (106 women), 981 part-time (687 women); includes 57 minority (23 African Americans, 6 American Indian/Alaska Native, 4 Asian Americans or Pacific Islanders, 24 Hispanic Americans), 26 international. 235 applicants, 84% accepted, 197 enrolled. *Faculty:* 82 full-time (51 women), 9 part-time/adjunct (6 women). Expenses: Contact institution. *Financial support:* In 2008–09, 31 teaching assistantships with full tuition reimbursements (averaging $6,588 per year) were awarded; career-related internships or fieldwork, Federal Work-Study, institutionally sponsored loans, health care benefits, and unspecified assistantships also available. Financial award application deadline: 3/15; financial award applicants required to submit FAFSA. In 2008, 349 master's, 7 other advanced degrees awarded. *Degree program information:* Part-time programs available. Postbaccalaureate distance learning degree programs offered (no on-campus study). Offers art therapy (MS); behavior disorders (MS); clinical psychology (MS); curriculum and instruction (MS); curriculum leadership (MS); early childhood curriculum (MS); early childhood education (MS); early childhood special education (MS); education (MS, Ed S); educational administration (MS); effective practitioner (MS); elementary administration (MS); elementary subject matter (MS); elementary/secondary administration (MS); English as a second language (MS); general psychology (MS); gifted, talented, and creative (MS); industrial/organizational psychology (MS); instructional design and technology (MS); interrelated special education (MS); learning disabilities (MS); master teacher (MS); mental health counseling (MS); mental retardation (MS); national board certification (MS); physical education (MS); psychology (MS); reading (MS); rehabilitation counseling (MS); school counseling (MS); school psychology (MS, Ed S); secondary administration (MS); secondary subject matter (MS); special education (MS). *Application deadline:* Applications are processed on a rolling basis. *Application fee:* $30 ($75 for international students). Electronic applications accepted. *Application Contact:* Mary Sewell, Admissions Coordinator, 800-950-GRAD, Fax: 620-341-5909, E-mail: msewell@emporia.edu. *Dean,* Dr. J. Phillip Bennett, 620-341-5367, Fax: 620-341-5785, E-mail: pbennett@emporia.edu.

See Close-Up on page 909.

ENDICOTT COLLEGE, Beverly, MA 01915-2096

General Information Independent, coed, comprehensive institution. *Enrollment:* 3,947 graduate, professional, and undergraduate students; 104 full-time matriculated graduate/professional students (58 women), 210 part-time matriculated graduate/professional students (143 women). *Enrollment by degree level:* 314 master's. *Graduate faculty:* 19 full-time (6 women), 46 part-time/adjunct (22 women). *Tuition:* Part-time $311 per credit hour. Tuition and fees vary according to program. *Graduate housing:* Room and/or apartments available to single students; on-campus housing not available to married students. Typical cost: $7930 per year ($11,380 including board). Room and board charges vary according to board plan and housing facility selected. *Student services:* Campus employment opportunities, campus safety program, career counseling, international student services, low-cost health insurance, multicultural affairs office, services for students with disabilities, teacher training, writing training. *Library facilities:* Endicott College Library. *Online resources:* library catalog, web page, access to other libraries' catalogs. *Collection:* 120,476 titles, 67,643 serial subscriptions. *Research affiliation:* North Shore Consortium (special needs), Peabody Essex Museum (history).

Computer facilities: Computer purchase and lease plans are available. 167 computers available on campus for general student use. A campuswide network can be accessed from student residence rooms and from off campus. Online class registration is available. *Web address:* http://www.endicott.edu/.

General Application Contact: Dr. Mary Huegel, Dean of Graduate and Professional Studies, 978-232-2084, Fax: 978-232-3000, E-mail: mhuegel@endicott.edu.

GRADUATE UNITS

Van Loan School of Graduate and Professional Studies Students: 104 full-time (58 women), 210 part-time (143 women); includes 7 minority (3 African Americans, 2 Asian Americans or Pacific Islanders, 2 Hispanic Americans), 2 international. Average age 35. *Faculty:* 19 full-time (6 women), 46 part-time/adjunct (22 women). Expenses: Contact institution. *Financial support:* Career-related internships or fieldwork, Federal Work-Study, institutionally sponsored loans, and tuition waivers (partial) available. In 2008, 129 master's awarded. *Degree program information:* Part-time and evening/weekend programs available. Postbaccalaureate distance learning degree programs offered (minimal on-campus study). Offers arts and learning (M Ed); business administration (MBA); computer systems technology (MSIT); initial and professional licensure (M Ed); integrative learning (M Ed); Montessori early childhood education (M Ed); organizational management (M Ed); sport management (M Ed). *Application deadline:* Applications are processed on a rolling basis. *Application fee:* $50. *Application Contact:* Dr. Mary Huegel, Dean of Graduate and Professional Studies, 978-232-2084, Fax: 978-232-3000, E-mail: mhuegel@endicott.edu. *Dean of Graduate and Professional Studies,* Dr. Mary Huegel, 978-232-2084, Fax: 978-232-3000, E-mail: mhuegel@endicott.edu.

EPISCOPAL DIVINITY SCHOOL, Cambridge, MA 02138-3494

General Information Independent-religious, coed, graduate-only institution. *Graduate housing:* Rooms and/or apartments available on a first-come, first-served basis to single and married students. Housing application deadline: 7/31. *Research affiliation:* Boston Theological Institute.

GRADUATE UNITS

Graduate and Professional Programs *Degree program information:* Part-time programs available.

ERIKSON INSTITUTE, Chicago, IL 60654

General Information Independent, coed, primarily women, graduate-only institution.

GRADUATE UNITS

Academic Programs *Degree program information:* Part-time and evening/weekend programs available. Offers administration (Certificate); bilingual/ESL (Certificate); child development (MS); early childhood education (MS); infant mental health (Certificate); infant studies (Certificate).

ERSKINE THEOLOGICAL SEMINARY, Due West, SC 29639-0668

General Information Independent-religious, coed, graduate-only institution. *Graduate housing:* Room and/or apartments available on a first-come, first-served basis to single students; on-campus housing not available to married students. Housing application deadline: 6/1.

GRADUATE UNITS

Graduate and Professional Programs *Degree program information:* Part-time and evening/weekend programs available. Offers theology (M Div, MACE, MACM, MAPM, MATS, MCM, D Min). Electronic applications accepted.

EVANGELICAL SEMINARY OF PUERTO RICO, San Juan, PR 00925-2207

General Information Independent-religious, coed, graduate-only institution. *Graduate housing:* Rooms and/or apartments available on a first-come, first-served basis to single and married students. Housing application deadline: 12/15.

GRADUATE UNITS

Graduate and Professional Programs *Degree program information:* Part-time programs available. Offers theology (M Div, MAR, D Min).

EVANGELICAL THEOLOGICAL SEMINARY, Myerstown, PA 17067-1212

General Information Independent-religious, coed, graduate-only institution. *Graduate housing:* Rooms and/or apartments available on a first-come, first-served basis to single and married students. Housing application deadline: 6/1.

EVANGEL UNIVERSITY, Springfield, MO 65802-2191

General Information Independent-religious, coed, comprehensive institution. *Graduate housing:* Rooms and/or apartments available on a first-come, first-served basis to single and married students. Housing application deadline: 5/1.

GRADUATE UNITS

Department of Education *Degree program information:* Part-time and evening/weekend programs available. Offers educational leadership (M Ed); reading education (M Ed); secondary teaching (M Ed); teaching (MA).

Department of Psychology *Degree program information:* Part-time and evening/weekend programs available. Offers clinical psychology (MS); counseling psychology (MS).

Organizational Leadership Program *Degree program information:* Part-time and evening/weekend programs available. Offers organizational leadership (MOL).

School Counseling Program *Degree program information:* Part-time and evening/weekend programs available. Offers school counseling (MS).

EVEREST UNIVERSITY, Tampa, FL 33614-5899

General Information Proprietary, coed, comprehensive institution. *Graduate housing:* On-campus housing not available.

GRADUATE UNITS

Department of Business Administration *Degree program information:* Part-time and evening/weekend programs available. Offers accounting (MBA); human resources (MBA); international business (MBA).

EVEREST UNIVERSITY, Tampa, FL 33619

General Information Proprietary, coed, comprehensive institution. *Enrollment:* 5,984 graduate, professional, and undergraduate students; 28 full-time matriculated graduate/professional students (20 women), 38 part-time matriculated graduate/professional students (30 women). *Enrollment by degree level:* 66 master's. *Graduate faculty:* 3 part-time/adjunct (all women). *Tuition:* Full-time $16,160; part-time $505 per credit hour. One-time fee: $45 full-time. *Graduate housing:* On-campus housing not available. *Student services:* Campus employment opportunities, career counseling. *Library facilities:* Everest University Library. *Online resources:* library catalog, web page. *Collection:* 5,076 titles, 89 serial subscriptions, 305 audiovisual materials.

Computer facilities: 125 computers available on campus for general student use. A campuswide network can be accessed. *Web address:* http://www.everest.edu/.

General Application Contact: Shandretta Pointer, Director, 813-621-0091 Ext. 106, E-mail: spointer@cci.edu.

GRADUATE UNITS

Program in Business Administration Students: 19 full-time (14 women), 153 part-time (117 women); includes 89 minority (66 African Americans, 4 American Indian/Alaska Native, 2 Asian Americans or Pacific Islanders, 17 Hispanic Americans). Average age 37. *Faculty:* 1 (woman) part-time/adjunct. Expenses: Contact institution. *Financial support:* Federal Work-Study, institutionally sponsored loans, and scholarships/grants available. In 2008, 28 master's awarded. *Degree program information:* Part-time and evening/weekend programs available. Postbaccalaureate distance learning degree programs offered (minimal on-campus study). Offers business administration (MBA). *Application deadline:* Applications are processed on a rolling basis. *Application fee:* $25. *Application Contact:* Shandretta Pointer, Admissions Office, 813-621-0041 Ext. 106, Fax: 813-628-0919, E-mail: spointer@cci.edu. *Chair,* James Jehs, 813-621-0041 Ext. 140, Fax: 813-623-5769, E-mail: JJehs@cci.edu.

Program in Criminal Justice Students: 3 full-time (all women), 127 part-time (103 women); includes 67 minority (59 African Americans, 1 American Indian/Alaska Native, 1 Asian American or Pacific Islander, 6 Hispanic Americans). Average age 37. *Faculty:* 2 part-time/adjunct (both women). Expenses: Contact institution. *Financial support:* Federal Work-Study, institutionally sponsored loans, and scholarships/grants available. In 2008, 11 master's awarded. *Degree program information:* Part-time and evening/weekend programs available. Postbaccalaureate distance learning degree programs offered (minimal on-campus study). Offers criminal justice (MS). *Application deadline:* Applications are processed on a rolling basis. *Application fee:* $25.. *Application Contact:* Shandretta Pointer, Admissions Office, 813-621-0041 Ext. 106, Fax: 813-628-0919, E-mail: spointer@cci.edu. *Chair,* Jim Pingel, 813-621-0041 Ext. 148, Fax: 813-623-5769, E-mail: JPingel@cci.edu.

EVEREST UNIVERSITY, Orlando, FL 32810-5674

General Information Proprietary, coed, comprehensive institution. *Graduate housing:* On-campus housing not available.

GRADUATE UNITS

Division of Business Administration *Degree program information:* Part-time and evening/weekend programs available. Offers business administration (MBA).

EVEREST UNIVERSITY, Orlando, FL 32819

General Information Proprietary, coed, comprehensive institution. *Graduate housing:* On-campus housing not available.

GRADUATE UNITS

Program in Business Administration Offers accounting (MBA); general management (MBA); human resources (MBA); international management (MBA).

EVEREST UNIVERSITY, Clearwater, FL 33759

General Information Proprietary, coed, comprehensive institution.

GRADUATE UNITS

Graduate School of Business Offers business (MBA).

EVEREST UNIVERSITY, Jacksonville, FL 32256

General Information Proprietary, coed, comprehensive institution.

GRADUATE UNITS

Graduate Programs

EVEREST UNIVERSITY, Lakeland, FL 33801

General Information Proprietary, coed, comprehensive institution.

GRADUATE UNITS

Program in Criminal Justice Offers criminal justice (MS).

EVEREST UNIVERSITY, Melbourne, FL 32935-6657

General Information Proprietary, coed, comprehensive institution.

GRADUATE UNITS

Program in Business Administration Offers business administration (MBA).

EVEREST UNIVERSITY, Pompano Beach, FL 33062

General Information Proprietary, coed, comprehensive institution. *Graduate housing:* On-campus housing not available.

GRADUATE UNITS

Program in Criminal Justice Offers criminal justice (MS).

School of Business *Degree program information:* Part-time and evening/weekend programs available. Offers business (MBA).

EVERGLADES UNIVERSITY, Boca Raton, FL 33431

General Information Independent, coed, comprehensive institution.

GRADUATE UNITS

Graduate Programs Offers aviation science (MSA); business administration (MBA); information technology (MIT). Electronic applications accepted.

THE EVERGREEN STATE COLLEGE, Olympia, WA 98505

General Information State-supported, coed, comprehensive institution. *Enrollment:* 4,696 graduate, professional, and undergraduate students; 171 full-time matriculated graduate/professional students (116 women), 140 part-time matriculated graduate/professional students (96 women). *Enrollment by degree level:* 311 master's. *Graduate faculty:* 17 full-time (8 women), 12 part-time/adjunct (5 women). Tuition, state resident: full-time $6567; part-time $219 per credit. Tuition, nonresident: full-time $20,004; part-time $667 per credit. *Required fees:* $7.85 per credit. $50 per quarter. Tuition and fees vary according to course load. *Graduate housing:* Rooms and/or apartments available on a first-come, first-served basis to single and married students. Typical cost: $5454 per year ($8052 including board) for single students; $5454 per year ($8052 including board) for married students. Housing application deadline: 6/1. *Student services:* Campus employment opportunities, campus safety program, career counseling, child daycare facilities, exercise/wellness program, free psychological counseling, grant writing training, international student services, multicultural affairs office, services for students with disabilities, teacher training, writing training. *Library facilities:* Daniel J. Evans Library. *Online resources:* library catalog, web page, access to other libraries' catalogs. *Collection:* 475,610 titles, 12,579 serial subscriptions, 91,552 audiovisual materials. *Research affiliation:* Washington State Institute for Public Policy.

Computer facilities: 375 computers available on campus for general student use. A campuswide network can be accessed from student residence rooms and from off campus. Online class registration, online payment and student accounts history are available. *Web address:* http://www.evergreen.edu/.

GRADUATE UNITS

Graduate Programs Students: 171 full-time (116 women), 140 part-time (96 women); includes 55 minority (12 African Americans, 23 American Indian/Alaska Native, 10 Asian Americans or Pacific Islanders, 10 Hispanic Americans). Average age 34. 252 applicants, 84% accepted, 169 enrolled. *Faculty:* 17 full-time (8 women), 12 part-time/adjunct (5 women). Expenses: Contact institution. *Financial support:* In 2008–09, 33 students received support, including 33 fellowships (averaging $1,928 per year); research assistantships, career-related internships or fieldwork, Federal Work-Study, scholarships/grants, tuition waivers (partial), and unspecified assistantships also available. Support available to part-time students. Financial award application deadline: 3/15; financial award applicants required to submit FAFSA. In 2008, 97 master's awarded. *Degree program information:* Part-time and evening/weekend programs available. Offers English as a second language (M Ed); environmental studies (MES); mathematics (M Ed); public administration (MPA); teaching (MIT). *Application deadline:* For fall admission, 1/4 priority date for domestic and international students. Applications are processed on a rolling basis. *Application fee:* $50. Electronic applications accepted. *Application Contact:* Dr. Don Bantz, Vice President and Provost, 360-867-6400, Fax: 360-867-6745, E-mail: bantzd@evergreen.edu. *Vice President and Provost,* Dr. Don Bantz, 360-867-6400, Fax: 360-867-6745, E-mail: bantzd@evergreen.edu.

EXCELSIOR COLLEGE, Albany, NY 12203-5159

General Information Independent, coed, comprehensive institution.

GRADUATE UNITS

School of Business and Technology *Degree program information:* Part-time and evening/weekend programs available. Postbaccalaureate distance learning degree programs offered (no on-campus study). Offers business and technology (MBA).

School of Health Sciences *Degree program information:* Part-time and evening/weekend programs available. Postbaccalaureate distance learning degree programs offered (no on-campus study). Offers healthcare informatics (Certificate); hospice and palliative care (Certificate); nursing management (Certificate). Electronic applications accepted.

School of Liberal Arts *Degree program information:* Part-time and evening/weekend programs available. Postbaccalaureate distance learning degree programs offered (no on-campus study). Offers liberal studies (MA). Electronic applications accepted.

School of Nursing *Degree program information:* Part-time and evening/weekend programs available. Postbaccalaureate distance learning degree programs offered (no on-campus study). Offers clinical systems management (MS); nursing (MS). Electronic applications accepted.

FACULTAD DE DERECHO EUGENIO MARÍA DE HOSTOS, Mayagüez, PR 00681

General Information Independent, graduate-only institution.

GRADUATE UNITS

School of Law Offers law (JD).

FAIRFIELD UNIVERSITY, Fairfield, CT 06824-5195

General Information Independent-religious, coed, comprehensive institution. *Enrollment:* 5,128 graduate, professional, and undergraduate students; 250 full-time matriculated graduate/professional students (162 women), 794 part-time matriculated graduate/professional students (541 women). *Enrollment by degree level:* 1,024 master's, 20 other advanced degrees. *Graduate faculty:* 141 full-time (75 women), 65 part-time/adjunct (24 women). *Tuition:* Full-time $9450; part-time $525 per credit hour. *Required fees:* $25 per semester. Tuition and fees vary according to course load and program. *Graduate housing:* On-campus housing not available. *Student services:* Campus employment opportunities, campus safety program, career counseling, child daycare facilities, exercise/wellness program, free psychological counseling, international student services, low-cost health insurance, multicultural affairs office, services for students with disabilities, teacher training. *Library facilities:* Dimenna-Nyselius Library. *Online resources:* library catalog, web page. *Collection:* 351,091 titles, 31,424 serial subscriptions, 17,983 audiovisual materials.

Computer facilities: Computer purchase and lease plans are available. 220 computers available on campus for general student use. A campuswide network can be accessed from student residence rooms and from off campus. Online class registration is available. *Web address:* http://www.fairfield.edu/.

General Application Contact: Marianne Gumpper, Director of Graduate and Continuing Studies Admissions, 203-254-4184, Fax: 203-254-4100, E-mail: gradadmis@mail.fairfield.edu.

GRADUATE UNITS

Charles F. Dolan School of Business Students: 60 full-time (22 women), 115 part-time (51 women); includes 4 African Americans, 2 Asian Americans or Pacific Islanders, 2 Hispanic Americans, 21 international. Average age 29. 102 applicants, 45% accepted, 45 enrolled. *Faculty:* 42 full-time (15 women), 8 part-time/adjunct (1 woman). Expenses: Contact institution. *Financial support:* In 2008–09, 48 students received support. Scholarships/grants, unspecified assistantships, and merit based one-time entrance scholarship available. Financial award applicants required to submit FAFSA. In 2008, 79 master's awarded. *Degree program information:* Part-time and evening/weekend programs available. Offers accounting (MBA, MS, CAS); finance (MBA, MS, CAS); general management (MBA); human resource management (MBA, CAS); information systems and operations (MBA); information systems and operations management (CAS); international business (MBA, CAS); marketing (MBA, CAS); taxation (MBA, MS). *Application deadline:* For fall admission, 5/15 for international students; for spring admission, 10/15 for international students. Applications are processed on a rolling basis. *Application fee:* $60. Electronic applications accepted. *Application Contact:* Marianne Gumpper, Director of Graduate and Continuing Studies Admissions, 203-254-4184, Fax: 203-254-4073, E-mail: gradadmis@fairfield.edu. *Dean,* Dr. Norman A. Solomon, 203-254-4000 Ext. 4070, Fax: 203-254-4105, E-mail: nsolomon@fairfield.edu.

College of Arts and Sciences Students: 6 full-time (1 woman), 53 part-time (26 women); includes 1 African American, 2 Hispanic Americans. Average age 41. 23 applicants, 78% accepted, 14 enrolled. *Faculty:* 46 full-time (20 women), 15 part-time/adjunct (7 women). Expenses: Contact institution. *Financial support:* In 2008–09, 19 students received support. Unspecified assistantships available. Financial award applicants required to submit FAFSA. In 2008, 36 master's awarded. *Degree program information:* Part-time and evening/weekend programs available. Offers American studies (MA); communication (MA); creative writing (MFA); mathematics (MS). *Application deadline:* For fall admission, 5/15 for international students; for spring admission, 10/15 for international students. Applications are processed on a rolling basis. *Application fee:* $60. Electronic applications accepted. *Application Contact:* Marianne Gumpper, Director of Graduate and Continuing Studies Admissions, 203-254-4184, Fax: 203-254-4073, E-mail: gradadmis@fairfield.edu. *Dean,* Dr. Robbin Crabtree, 203-254-4000 Ext. 3263, Fax: 203-254-4119, E-mail: rcrabtree@fairfield.edu.

Graduate School of Education and Allied Professions Students: 152 full-time (128 women), 391 part-time (339 women); includes 63 minority (11 African Americans, 1 American Indian/Alaska Native, 8 Asian Americans or Pacific Islanders, 43 Hispanic Americans), 6 international. Average age 33. 261 applicants, 65% accepted, 86 enrolled. *Faculty:* 22 full-time (17 women), 31 part-time/adjunct (16 women). Expenses: Contact institution. *Financial support:* In 2008–09, 189 students received support. Career-related internships or fieldwork and unspecified assistantships available. Financial award applicants required to submit FAFSA. In 2008, 147 master's, 19 other advanced degrees awarded. *Degree program information:* Part-time and evening/weekend programs available. Offers applied psychology (MA); bilingual education (CAS); community counseling (MA, CAS); education and allied professions (MA, CAS); elementary education (MA); marriage and family therapy (MA); media/educational technology (MA); school counseling (MA, CAS); school media specialist (MA); school psychology (MA, CAS); secondary education (MA); special education (MA, CAS); teaching and foundations (MA, CAS); TESOL, foreign language and bilingual/multicultural education (MA, CAS). *Application deadline:* For fall admission, 4/15 for international students; for spring admission, 10/1 for international students. *Application fee:* $60. Electronic applications accepted. *Application Contact:* Marianne Gumpper, Director of Graduate and Continuing Studies Admissions, 203-254-4184, Fax: 203-254-4073, E-mail: gradadmis@fairfield.edu. *Dean,* Dr. Susan D. Franzosa, 203-254-4000 Ext. 4250, Fax: 203-254-4241, E-mail: sfranzosa@fairfield.edu.

School of Engineering Students: 29 full-time (8 women), 109 part-time (13 women); includes 29 minority (5 African Americans, 19 Asian Americans or Pacific Islanders, 5 Hispanic Americans), 32 international. Average age 35. 51 applicants, 69% accepted, 11 enrolled. *Faculty:* 8 full-time (1 woman), 11 part-time/adjunct (0 women). Expenses: Contact institution. *Financial support:* In 2008–09, 25 students received support. Unspecified assistantships available. Financial award applicants required to submit FAFSA. In 2008, 52 master's awarded. *Degree program information:* Part-time and evening/weekend programs available. Offers electrical and computer engineering (MS); management of technology (MS); mechanical engineering (MS); software engineering (MS). *Application deadline:* For fall admission, 5/15 for international students; for spring admission, 10/15 for international students. Applications are processed on a rolling basis. *Application fee:* $60. Electronic applications accepted. *Application Contact:* Marianne Gumpper, Director of Graduate and Continuing Studies Admissions, 203-254-4184, Fax: 203-254-4073, E-mail: gradadmis@fairfield.edu. *Dean,* Dr. Evangelos Hadjimichael, 203-254-4000 Ext. 4147, Fax: 203-254-4013, E-mail: ehadjimichael@fairfield.edu.

School of Nursing Students: 3 full-time (all women), 115 part-time (102 women); includes 24 minority (10 African Americans, 2 American Indian/Alaska Native, 8 Asian Americans or Pacific Islanders, 4 Hispanic Americans). Average age 39. 65 applicants, 68% accepted, 23 enrolled. *Faculty:* 23 full-time (22 women). Expenses: Contact institution. *Financial support:* In 2008–09, 43 students received support. Traineeships, unspecified assistantships, and Traineeships is a federally funded grant program available. Financial award applicants required to submit FAFSA. In 2008, 10 master's awarded. *Degree program information:* Part-time programs available. Offers clinical nurse leader (MSN); family nurse practitioner (MSN, PMC); healthcare management (MSN); nurse anesthesia (MSN); psychiatric nurse practitioner (MSN, PMC). *Application deadline:* For fall admission, 5/15 for international students; for spring admission, 10/15 for international students. Applications are processed on a rolling basis. *Application fee:* $60. Electronic applications accepted. *Application Contact:* Marianne Gumpper, Director of Graduate and Continuing Studies Admissions, 203-254-4184, Fax:

203-254-4073, E-mail: gradadmis@fairfield.edu. *Dean,* Dr. Jeanne M. Novotny, 203-254-4000 Ext. 2701, Fax: 203-254-4126, E-mail: jnovotny@fairfield.edu.

FAIRLEIGH DICKINSON UNIVERSITY, COLLEGE AT FLORHAM, Madison, NJ 07940-1099

General Information Independent, coed, comprehensive institution. *Enrollment:* 3,465 graduate, professional, and undergraduate students; 364 full-time matriculated graduate/professional students (176 women), 632 part-time matriculated graduate/professional students (263 women). *Enrollment by degree level:* 974 master's, 22 other advanced degrees. *Graduate housing:* Room and/or apartments available on a first-come, first-served basis to single students; on-campus housing not available to married students. *Student services:* Campus employment opportunities, career counseling, exercise/wellness program, free psychological counseling, international student services, teacher training, writing training. *Library facilities:* College of Florham Library. *Online resources:* library catalog. *Collection:* 238,383 titles, 1,090 serial subscriptions, 988 audiovisual materials.

Computer facilities: Computer purchase and lease plans are available. 140 computers available on campus for general student use. A campuswide network can be accessed from student residence rooms and from off campus. Online class registration is available. *Web address:* http://www.fdu.edu/.

General Application Contact: Susan Brooman, University Director, Graduate Admissions, 973-443-8905, Fax: 973-443-8088, E-mail: grad@fdu.edu.

GRADUATE UNITS

Anthony J. Petrocelli College of Continuing Studies Students: 7 full-time (4 women), 31 part-time (13 women), 2 international. Average age 34. 12 applicants, 100% accepted, 18 enrolled. Expenses: Contact institution. In 2008, 14 master's awarded. Offers continuing studies (MAS, MPA, MS). *Application deadline:* Applications are processed on a rolling basis. *Application fee:* $40. *Application Contact:* Susan Brooman, University Director, Graduate Admissions, 973-443-8905, Fax: 973-443-8088, E-mail: grad@fdu.edu. *Dean,* Kenneth Vehrkens, 973-443-8500.

International School of Hospitality and Tourism Management Students: 4 full-time (1 woman), 30 part-time (13 women), 1 international. Average age 35. 11 applicants, 100% accepted, 15 enrolled. Expenses: Contact institution. In 2008, 13 master's awarded. Offers hospitality management studies (MS). *Application deadline:* Applications are processed on a rolling basis. *Application fee:* $40. *Application Contact:* Susan Brooman, University Director, Graduate Admissions, 973-443-8905, Fax: 973-443-8088, E-mail: grad@fdu.edu.

Public Administration Institute Students: 2 full-time (both women), 1 part-time (0 women), 1 international. Average age 28. 1 applicant, 100% accepted, 2 enrolled. Expenses: Contact institution. Offers public administration (MPA). *Application fee:* $40. *Application Contact:* Susan Brooman, University Director, Graduate Admissions, 973-443-8905, Fax: 973-443-8088, E-mail: grad@fdu.edu. *Head,* Dr. William Roberts, 973-443-8500.

School of Administrative Science Students: 1 (woman) full-time. Average age 21. Expenses: Contact institution. In 2008, 1 master's awarded. Offers administrative science (MAS). *Application fee:* $40. *Application Contact:* Susan Brooman, University Director, Graduate Admissions, 973-443-8905, Fax: 973-443-8088, E-mail: grad@fdu.edu.

Maxwell Becton College of Arts and Sciences Students: 188 full-time (91 women), 153 part-time (87 women), 103 international. Average age 29. 333 applicants, 61% accepted, 96 enrolled. Expenses: Contact institution. In 2008, 91 master's awarded. Offers arts and sciences (MA, MFA, MS, Certificate); biology (MS); chemistry (MS); corporate and organizational communication (MA); counseling (MA); creative writing (MFA); industrial/organizational psychology (MA); organizational behavior (MA, Certificate); organizational leadership (Certificate). *Application deadline:* Applications are processed on a rolling basis. *Application fee:* $40. *Application Contact:* Susan Brooman, University Director, Graduate Admissions, 973-443-8905, Fax: 973-443-8088, E-mail: grad@fdu.edu. *Dean,* Dr. Geoffrey Weinman, 973-443-8500.

Silberman College of Business Students: 110 full-time (43 women), 398 part-time (135 women), 31 international. Average age 32. 219 applicants, 75% accepted, 137 enrolled. Expenses: Contact institution. In 2008, 130 master's awarded. *Degree program information:* Part-time and evening/weekend programs available. Offers accounting (MS); business (EMBA, MBA, MS, Certificate); business administration (MBA); entrepreneurial studies (MBA, Certificate); evolving technology (Certificate); finance (MBA, Certificate); health care and life sciences (EMBA); international business (MBA, Certificate); international taxation (Certificate); management (EMBA, MBA, Certificate); marketing (MBA, Certificate); pharmaceutical studies (MBA, Certificate); taxation (MS, Certificate). *Application deadline:* Applications are processed on a rolling basis. *Application fee:* $40. *Application Contact:* Susan Brooman, University Director of Graduate Admissions. *Dean,* Dr. William Moore, 973-443-8500.

Center for Human Resource Management Studies Students: 10 full-time (4 women), 10 part-time (6 women), 1 international. Average age 30. 7 applicants, 86% accepted, 4 enrolled. Expenses: Contact institution. In 2008, 9 master's awarded. Offers human resource management (MBA); human resource management studies (MBA). *Application fee:* $40. *Application Contact:* Dr. Gerard Farias, Head, 973-443-8500. *Head,* Dr. Gerard Farias, 973-443-8500.

University College: Arts, Sciences, and Professional Studies Students: 59 full-time (38 women), 50 part-time (28 women). Average age 28. 61 applicants, 92% accepted, 57 enrolled. Expenses: Contact institution. In 2008, 82 master's awarded. Offers arts, sciences, and professional studies (MA, MAT, Certificate). *Application deadline:* Applications are processed on a rolling basis. *Application fee:* $40. *Application Contact:* Susan Brooman, University Director, Graduate Admissions, 973-443-8905, Fax: 973-443-8088, E-mail: grad@fdu.edu. *Dean,* Patti Mills, 973-443-8500.

Peter Sammartino School of Education Students: 59 full-time (38 women), 50 part-time (28 women). Average age 28. 61 applicants, 92% accepted, 57 enrolled. Expenses: Contact institution. In 2008, 82 master's awarded. Offers education for certified teachers (MA, Certificate); educational leadership (MA); instructional technology (Certificate); literacy/reading (Certificate); teaching (MAT). *Application deadline:* Applications are processed on a rolling basis. *Application fee:* $40. *Application Contact:* Susan Brooman, University Director, Graduate Admissions, 973-443-8905, Fax: 973-443-8088, E-mail: grad@fdu.edu.

See Close-Up on page 911.

FAIRLEIGH DICKINSON UNIVERSITY, METROPOLITAN CAMPUS, Teaneck, NJ 07666-1914

General Information Independent, coed, comprehensive institution. *Enrollment:* 8,693 graduate, professional, and undergraduate students; 1,101 full-time matriculated graduate/professional students (561 women), 1,711 part-time matriculated graduate/professional students (1,049 women). *Enrollment by degree level:* 2,392 master's, 179 doctoral, 241 other advanced degrees. *Graduate housing:* Room and/or apartments available on a first-come, first-served basis to single students; on-campus housing not available to married students. *Student services:* Campus employment opportunities, career counseling, exercise/wellness program, free psychological counseling, international student services, teacher training, writing training. *Library facilities:* Weiner Library plus 3 others. *Online resources:* library catalog, web page. *Collection:* 375,348 titles, 1,440 serial subscriptions, 2,682 audiovisual materials.

Computer facilities: Computer purchase and lease plans are available. 160 computers available on campus for general student use. A campuswide network can be accessed from student residence rooms and from off campus. Online class registration is available. *Web address:* http://www.fdu.edu/.

General Application Contact: Susan Brooman, University Director of Graduate Admissions, 201-692-2554, Fax: 201-692-2560, E-mail: globaleducation@fdu.edu.

GRADUATE UNITS

Anthony J. Petrocelli College of Continuing Studies Students: 224 full-time (113 women), 699 part-time (320 women), 166 international. Average age 37. 524 applicants, 86% accepted, 280 enrolled. Expenses: Contact institution. In 2008, 365 master's awarded. Offers continuing studies (MAS, MPA, MS, MSA, MSHS, Certificate); sports administration (MSA). *Application deadline:* Applications are processed on a rolling basis. *Application fee:* $40. *Application Contact:* Susan Brooman, University Director of Graduate Admissions, 201-692-2554, Fax: 201-692-2560, E-mail: globaleducation@fdu.edu. *Dean,* Kenneth T. Vehrkens, 201-692-2000.

International School of Hospitality and Tourism Management Students: 9 full-time (8 women), 14 part-time (9 women), 9 international. Average age 34. 27 applicants, 63% accepted, 10 enrolled. Expenses: Contact institution. In 2008, 20 master's awarded. Offers hospitality (MS); hospitality management (MS). *Application deadline:* Applications are processed on a rolling basis. *Application fee:* $40. *Application Contact:* Susan Brooman, University Director of Graduate Admissions, 201-692-2554, Fax: 201-692-2560, E-mail: globaleducation@fdu.edu. *Director,* Dr. Richard Wisch, 201-692-2000.

Public Administration Institute Students: 138 full-time (62 women), 118 part-time (61 women), 116 international. Average age 32. 230 applicants, 75% accepted, 83 enrolled. Expenses: Contact institution. In 2008, 78 master's awarded. Offers public administration (MPA, Certificate); public non-profit management (Certificate). *Application deadline:* Applications are processed on a rolling basis. *Application fee:* $40. *Application Contact:* Susan Brooman, University Director of Graduate Admissions, 201-692-2554, Fax: 201-692-2560, E-mail: globaleducation@fdu.edu. *Director,* Dr. William Roberts, 201-692-2000.

School of Administrative Science Students: 77 full-time (43 women), 567 part-time (250 women), 41 international. Average age 39. 267 applicants, 98% accepted, 187 enrolled. Expenses: Contact institution. In 2008, 267 master's awarded. Offers administrative science (MAS, MSHS, Certificate); homeland security (MSHS). *Application deadline:* Applications are processed on a rolling basis. *Application fee:* $40. *Application Contact:* Susan Brooman, University Director of Graduate Admissions, 201-692-2554, Fax: 201-692-2560, E-mail: globaleducation@fdu.edu. *Director/Executive Associate Dean,* Ronald Calissi, 201-692-2000.

Silberman College of Business Students: 322 full-time (117 women), 168 part-time (67 women), 211 international. Average age 30. 475 applicants, 54% accepted, 138 enrolled. Expenses: Contact institution. In 2008, 180 master's awarded. Offers accounting (MS, Certificate); business (EMBA, MBA, MS, Certificate); business administration (MBA); chemical studies (Certificate); entrepreneurial studies (MBA, Certificate); executive management (EMBA); finance (MBA, Certificate); international business (MBA); management (MBA, Certificate); management information systems (Certificate); marketing (MBA, Certificate); pharmaceutical studies (MBA, Certificate); taxation (MS). *Application deadline:* Applications are processed on a rolling basis. *Application fee:* $40. *Application Contact:* Susan Brooman, University Director of Graduate Admissions, 201-692-2554, Fax: 201-692-2560, E-mail: globaleducation@fdu.edu. *Dean,* Dr. William Moore, 201-692-2000.

Center for Healthcare Management Studies Students: 42 full-time (13 women), 37 part-time (11 women). Average age 38. 40 applicants, 95% accepted, 22 enrolled. Expenses: Contact institution. In 2008, 32 master's awarded. Offers healthcare and life sciences (EMBA); healthcare management studies (EMBA). *Application deadline:* Applications are processed on a rolling basis. *Application fee:* $40. *Application Contact:* Susan Brooman, University Director of Graduate Admissions, 201-692-2554, Fax: 201-692-2560, E-mail: globaleducation@fdu.edu. *Director,* Dr. Peter Caligiuri, 201-692-2000.

Center for Human Resources Management Studies Students: 8 full-time (7 women), 7 part-time (6 women), 6 international. Average age 28. 19 applicants, 47% accepted, 6 enrolled. Expenses: Contact institution. In 2008, 8 master's awarded. Offers human resource management (MBA, Certificate); human resources management studies (MBA, Certificate). *Application deadline:* Applications are processed on a rolling basis. *Application fee:* $40. *Application Contact:* Susan Brooman, University Director of Graduate Admissions, 201-692-2554, Fax: 201-692-2560, E-mail: globaleducation@fdu.edu.

University College: Arts, Sciences, and Professional Studies Students: 555 full-time (331 women), 844 part-time (662 women), 324 international. Average age 33. 1,581 applicants, 60% accepted, 460 enrolled. Expenses: Contact institution. In 2008, 409 master's, 11 doctorates awarded. Offers arts, sciences, and professional studies (MA, MAT, MS, MSEE, MSN, DNP, PhD, Psy D, Certificate); English and literature (MA); systems science (MS). *Application deadline:* Applications are processed on a rolling basis. *Application fee:* $40. *Application Contact:* Susan Brooman, University Director of Graduate Admissions, 201-692-2554, Fax: 201-692-2560, E-mail: globaleducation@fdu.edu. *Dean,* Patti Mills, 201-692-2000.

Henry P. Becton School of Nursing and Allied Health Students: 41 full-time (35 women), 84 part-time (74 women). Average age 42. 49 applicants, 73% accepted, 21 enrolled. Expenses: Contact institution. In 2008, 15 master's awarded. Offers medical technology (MS); nursing (MSN, Certificate); nursing practice (DNP). *Application deadline:* Applications are processed on a rolling basis. *Application fee:* $40. *Application Contact:* Susan Brooman, University Director of Graduate Admissions, 201-692-2554, Fax: 201-692-2560, E-mail: globaleducation@fdu.edu.

Peter Sammartino School of Education Students: 59 full-time (47 women), 509 part-time (445 women), 16 international. Average age 36. 261 applicants, 90% accepted, 187 enrolled. Expenses: Contact institution. In 2008, 121 master's awarded. *Degree program information:* Part-time programs available. Offers dyslexia specialist (Certificate); education for certified teachers (MA); educational leadership (MA); instructional technology (Certificate); learning disabilities (MA); literacy/reading (Certificate); multilingual education (MA); teacher of the handicapped (Certificate); teaching (MAT). *Application deadline:* Applications are processed on a rolling basis. *Application fee:* $40. *Application Contact:* Susan Brooman, University Director of Graduate Admissions, 201-692-2554, Fax: 201-692-2560, E-mail: globaleducation@fdu.edu. *Director,* Dr. Vicki Cohen, 201-692-2525, Fax: 201-692-2603, E-mail: vicki_cohen@fdu.edu.

School of Art and Media Studies Students: 6 full-time (5 women), 12 part-time (7 women), 5 international. Average age 31. 15 applicants, 67% accepted, 7 enrolled. Expenses: Contact institution. In 2008, 4 master's awarded. Offers art and media studies (MA); media and communications (MA). *Application deadline:* Applications are processed on a rolling basis. *Application fee:* $40. *Application Contact:* Susan Brooman, University Director of Graduate Admissions, 201-692-2554, Fax: 201-692-2560, E-mail: globaleducation@fdu.edu.

School of Computer Sciences and Engineering Students: 172 full-time (56 women), 121 part-time (58 women), 216 international. Average age 27. 793 applicants, 51% accepted, 108 enrolled. Expenses: Contact institution. In 2008, 185 master's awarded. Offers computer engineering (MS); computer science (MS); e-commerce (MS); electrical engineering (MSEE); management information systems (MS); mathematical foundation (MS). *Application deadline:* Applications are processed on a rolling basis. *Application fee:* $40. *Application Contact:* Susan Brooman, University Director of Graduate Admissions, 201-692-2554, Fax: 201-692-2560, E-mail: globaleducation@fdu.edu. *Director,* Dr. Alfredo Tan, 201-692-2000.

School of History, Political and International Studies Students: 8 full-time (5 women), 10 part-time (8 women), 4 international. Average age 29. 25 applicants, 28% accepted, 0 enrolled. Expenses: Contact institution. In 2008, 1 master's awarded. Offers history (MA); international studies (MA); political science (MA). *Application deadline:* Applications are processed on a rolling basis. *Application fee:* $40. *Application Contact:* Susan Brooman, University Director of Graduate Admissions, 201-692-2554, Fax: 201-692-2560, E-mail: globaleducation@fdu.edu.

School of Natural Sciences Students: 68 full-time (36 women), 54 part-time (36 women), 75 international. Average age 26. 245 applicants, 44% accepted, 53 enrolled. Expenses: Contact institution. In 2008, 46 master's awarded. Offers biology (MS); chemistry (MS); science (MA). *Application deadline:* Applications are processed on a rolling basis. *Application fee:* $40. *Application Contact:* Susan Brooman, University Director of Graduate Admissions, 201-692-2554, Fax: 201-692-2560, E-mail: globaleducation@fdu.edu. *Director,* Dr. Irwin Isquith, 201-692-2000.

School of Psychology Students: 198 full-time (145 women), 50 part-time (31 women), 7 international. Average age 32. 174 applicants, 79% accepted, 79 enrolled. Expenses: Contact institution. In 2008, 27 master's, 11 doctorates awarded. Offers clinical psychology (MA, PhD); clinical psychopharmacology (MA); forensic psychology (MA); general-theoretical psychology (MA, Certificate); school psychology (MA, Psy D). *Application deadline:* Applications are processed on a rolling basis. *Application fee:* $40. *Application Contact:* Susan

Fairleigh Dickinson University, Metropolitan Campus (continued)

Brooman, University Director of Graduate Admissions, 201-692-2554, Fax: 201-692-2560, E-mail: globaleducation@fdu.edu.

See Close-Up on page 911.

FAIRMONT STATE UNIVERSITY, Fairmont, WV 26554

General Information State-supported, coed, comprehensive institution. CGS member.

GRADUATE UNITS

Graduate Studies Offers business administration (MBA); criminal justice (MS); education (MAT); human and community service administration (MS); leadership studies (M Ed); nursing administration (MS); nursing education (MS); online learning (M Ed); professional studies (M Ed); reading (M Ed); special education (M Ed).

FAITH BAPTIST BIBLE COLLEGE AND THEOLOGICAL SEMINARY, Ankeny, IA 50021

General Information Independent-religious, coed, comprehensive institution. *Enrollment:* 387 graduate, professional, and undergraduate students; 37 full-time matriculated graduate/professional students (5 women), 23 part-time matriculated graduate/professional students (4 women). *Enrollment by degree level:* 33 first professional, 27 master's. *Graduate faculty:* 4 full-time (0 women), 7 part-time/adjunct (0 women). *Tuition:* Full-time $10,228; part-time $392 per credit hour. *Required fees:* $95 per semester. One-time fee: $50. Tuition and fees vary according to class time and course load. *Graduate housing:* Rooms and/or apartments available on a first-come, first-served basis to single and married students. Typical cost: $2288 per year ($5010 including board) for single students; $2288 per year ($5010 including board) for married students. Housing application deadline: 8/1. *Student services:* Campus employment opportunities, career counseling, free psychological counseling, international student services, low-cost health insurance. *Library facilities:* Patten Hall. *Online resources:* library catalog, web page. *Collection:* 63,840 titles, 395 serial subscriptions, 6,563 audiovisual materials.

Computer facilities: 50 computers available on campus for general student use. A campuswide network can be accessed from student residence rooms and from off campus. Online class registration is available. *Web address:* http://www.faith.edu/.

General Application Contact: Patrick Odle, Vice President of Enrollment, 888-FAITH4U, Fax: 515-964-1638, E-mail: odlep@faith.edu.

GRADUATE UNITS

Graduate Program Students: 28 full-time (3 women), 28 part-time (2 women); includes 1 minority (Hispanic American), 1 international. Average age 29. *Faculty:* 4 full-time (0 women), 7 part-time/adjunct (0 women). Expenses: Contact institution. *Financial support:* Career-related internships or fieldwork and scholarships/grants available. Support available to part-time students. Financial award application deadline: 3/1; financial award applicants required to submit FAFSA. In 2008, 9 first professional degrees, 12 master's awarded. *Degree program information:* Part-time programs available. Offers biblical studies (MA); pastoral studies (M Div); pastoral training (MA); religion (MA); theological studies (MA). *Application deadline:* For fall admission, 8/1 priority date for domestic students, 8/1 for international students; for spring admission, 12/15 for domestic and international students. Applications are processed on a rolling basis. *Application fee:* $25. *Application Contact:* Patrick Odle, Vice President of Enrollment, 888-FAITH4U, Fax: 515-964-1638, E-mail: odlep@faith.edu. *Dean of Seminary,* Dr. Ernest Schmidt, 515-964-0601, Fax: 514-964-1638, E-mail: schmidte@faith.edu.

FAITH EVANGELICAL LUTHERAN SEMINARY, Tacoma, WA 98407

General Information Independent-religious, coed, graduate-only institution.

GRADUATE UNITS

Graduate and Professional Programs *Degree program information:* Part-time and evening/weekend programs available. Postbaccalaureate distance learning degree programs offered (minimal on-campus study). Offers theology (B Th, M Div, MCM, MTS, D Min).

FASHION INSTITUTE OF TECHNOLOGY, New York, NY 10001-5992

General Information State and locally supported, coed, primarily women, comprehensive institution. *Graduate housing:* Room and/or apartments available on a first-come, first-served basis to single students; on-campus housing not available to married students. *Research affiliation:* IDEO (design and management innovation), Grove Dictionary of Art, Oxford University Press (costume history), Exhibition Designers and Producers Association (exhibition design), Society for Environmental Graphic Design (exhibition design), Lolita, SA (global fashion management).

GRADUATE UNITS

School of Graduate Studies *Degree program information:* Part-time and evening/weekend programs available. Offers art market: principles and practices (MA); cosmetics and fragrance marketing and management (MPS); exhibition design (MA); fashion and textile studies: history, theory, and museum practice (MA); global fashion management (MPS); illustration (MA). Electronic applications accepted.

FAULKNER UNIVERSITY, Montgomery, AL 36109-3398

General Information Independent-religious, coed, comprehensive institution. *Enrollment:* 2,873 graduate, professional, and undergraduate students; 263 full-time matriculated graduate/professional students (99 women), 41 part-time matriculated graduate/professional students (18 women). *Enrollment by degree level:* 304 first professional. *Graduate faculty:* 29 full-time (9 women), 6 part-time/adjunct (3 women). *Graduate housing:* On-campus housing not available. *Student services:* Campus employment opportunities, career counseling, services for students with disabilities, writing training. *Library facilities:* Gus Nichols Library plus 2 others. *Online resources:* library catalog. *Collection:* 230,000 titles, 4,708 serial subscriptions, 3,195 audiovisual materials.

Computer facilities: 228 computers available on campus for general student use. A campuswide network can be accessed from student residence rooms and from off campus. Student account access available. *Web address:* http://www.faulkner.edu/.

General Application Contact: Rachel R. Wishum, Admissions Counselor, 334-386-7520, Fax: 334-386-7908, E-mail: rwishum@faulkner.edu.

GRADUATE UNITS

Thomas Goode Jones School of Law Students: 263 full-time (99 women), 41 part-time (18 women); includes 37 minority (19 African Americans, 4 American Indian/Alaska Native, 7 Asian Americans or Pacific Islanders, 7 Hispanic Americans), 2 international. Average age 26. 589 applicants, 55% accepted, 126 enrolled. *Faculty:* 29 full-time (9 women), 6 part-time/adjunct (3 women). Expenses: Contact institution. *Financial support:* In 2008–09, 93 students received support. Career-related internships or fieldwork, scholarships/grants, and tuition waivers (full and partial) available. Financial award application deadline: 7/1; financial award applicants required to submit FAFSA. In 2008, 65 JDs awarded. Offers law (JD). *Application deadline:* For fall admission, 6/15 for domestic and international students. Applications are processed on a rolling basis. *Application fee:* $30. Electronic applications accepted. *Application Contact:* Andrew R. Matthews, Assistant Dean for Student Services, 334-386-7210, Fax: 334-386-7908, E-mail: amatthews@faulkner.edu. *Dean,* Charles I. Nelson, 334-386-7220, Fax: 334-386-7545, E-mail: cnelson@faulkner.edu.

FAYETTEVILLE STATE UNIVERSITY, Fayetteville, NC 28301-4298

General Information State-supported, coed, comprehensive institution. CGS member. *Graduate housing:* On-campus housing not available. *Research affiliation:* Research Triangle Park.

GRADUATE UNITS

Graduate School *Degree program information:* Part-time and evening/weekend programs available. Offers biology (MA Ed, MS); business administration (MBA); criminal justice (MA); educational leadership (Ed D); elementary education (MA Ed); English (MA); history (MA, MA Ed); mathematics (MA Ed, MS); middle grades (MA Ed); political science (MA, MA Ed); psychology (MA); reading (MA Ed); school administration (MSA); social work (MSW); sociology (MA); special education (MA Ed).

FELICIAN COLLEGE, Lodi, NJ 07644-2117

General Information Independent-religious, coed, comprehensive institution. *Graduate housing:* Room and/or apartments available on a first-come, first-served basis to single students; on-campus housing not available to married students.

GRADUATE UNITS

Program in Business *Degree program information:* Part-time and evening/weekend programs available. Offers innovation and entrepreneurship (MBA).

Program in Counseling Psychology Offers counseling psychology (MS).

Program in Education *Degree program information:* Part-time and evening/weekend programs available. Offers elementary education (MA); supervisory (MA); teacher for students with disabilities (MA).

Program in Nursing *Degree program information:* Part-time and evening/weekend programs available. Postbaccalaureate distance learning degree programs offered (no on-campus study). Offers adult nurse practitioner (MSN, PMC); family nurse practitioner (MSN, PMC); nursing education (MSN); school nurse/teacher of health education (Certificate).

Program in Religious Education *Degree program information:* Part-time and evening/weekend programs available. Postbaccalaureate distance learning degree programs offered (no on-campus study). Offers religious education (MA, Certificate, PMC).

FERRIS STATE UNIVERSITY, Big Rapids, MI 49307

General Information State-supported, coed, comprehensive institution. CGS member. *Graduate housing:* Rooms and/or apartments available on a first-come, first-served basis to single and married students. *Research affiliation:* Research Technology Institute (materials science, manufacturing sciences), Vistakon–Johnson & Johnson (optometry), Allergan-Hydron (optometry), Bausch & Lomb (optometry), Ciba Vision Care (optometry).

GRADUATE UNITS

College of Allied Health Sciences Offers allied health sciences (MS).

School of Nursing *Degree program information:* Part-time and evening/weekend programs available. Postbaccalaureate distance learning degree programs offered (minimal on-campus study). Offers nursing (MS); nursing administration (MS); nursing education (MS); nursing informatics (MS). Electronic applications accepted.

College of Business *Degree program information:* Part-time and evening/weekend programs available. Offers application development (MSISM); database administration (MSISM); e-business (MSISM); information systems (MBA); networking (MSISM); quality management (MBA); security (MSISM). Electronic applications accepted.

College of Education and Human Services *Degree program information:* Part-time and evening/weekend programs available. Postbaccalaureate distance learning degree programs offered. Offers education and human services (M Ed, MS, MSCTE).

School of Criminal Justice *Degree program information:* Part-time programs available. Offers criminal justice administration (MS). Electronic applications accepted.

School of Education *Degree program information:* Part-time and evening/weekend programs available. Postbaccalaureate distance learning degree programs offered (no on-campus study). Offers administration (MSCTE); curriculum and instruction (M Ed); education technology (MSCTE); instructor (MSCTE); post-secondary administration (MSCTE); training and development (MSCTE).

College of Pharmacy Offers pharmacy (Pharm D).

Kendall College of Art and Design *Degree program information:* Part-time programs available. Offers art and design (MFA).

Michigan College of Optometry Offers optometry (OD). Electronic applications accepted.

FIELDING GRADUATE UNIVERSITY, Santa Barbara, CA 93105-3538

General Information Independent, coed, graduate-only institution. CGS member. *Enrollment by degree level:* 216 master's, 1,237 doctoral, 221 other advanced degrees. *Graduate faculty:* 89 full-time (44 women), 25 part-time/adjunct (8 women). *Tuition:* Full-time $20,475; part-time $2725 per course. *Graduate housing:* On-campus housing not available. *Student services:* International student services, low-cost health insurance, services for students with disabilities, writing training. *Library facilities:* The Fielding Graduate Univesity Library Services. *Online resources:* web page. *Collection:* 50,832 titles, 27,312 serial subscriptions.

Computer facilities: Online class registration is available. *Web address:* http://www.fielding.edu/.

General Application Contact: Admission Office, 800-340-1099, Fax: 805-687-9793, E-mail: admission@fielding.edu.

GRADUATE UNITS

Graduate Programs Students: 1,407 full-time (1,009 women), 267 part-time (178 women); includes 414 minority (219 African Americans, 25 American Indian/Alaska Native, 70 Asian Americans or Pacific Islanders, 100 Hispanic Americans), 71 international. Average age 45. 512 applicants, 62% accepted, 228 enrolled. *Faculty:* 89 full-time (44 women), 25 part-time/adjunct (8 women). Expenses: Contact institution. *Financial support:* In 2008–09, 1,124 students received support, including 6 research assistantships (averaging $4,765 per year); institutionally sponsored loans, scholarships/grants, health care benefits, and tuition waivers (partial) also available. Support available to part-time students. Financial award application deadline: 5/15; financial award applicants required to submit FAFSA. In 2008, 85 master's, 104 doctorates, 119 other advanced degrees awarded. Postbaccalaureate distance learning degree programs offered (minimal on-campus study). *Application deadline:* For fall admission, 2/15 for domestic and international students; for spring admission, 8/15 for domestic and international students. *Application fee:* $75. Electronic applications accepted. *Application Contact:* Kathy Bellway, Admission Assistant, 800-340-1099, Fax: 805-687-9793, E-mail: admission@fielding.edu. *President,* Dr. Judith Kuipers, 805-898-2903, Fax: 805-687-4590, E-mail: jkuipers@fielding.edu.

School of Educational Leadership and Change Students: 387 full-time (274 women), 10 part-time (8 women); includes 167 minority (115 African Americans, 13 American Indian/Alaska Native, 15 Asian Americans or Pacific Islanders, 24 Hispanic Americans), 3 international. Average age 45. 50 applicants, 94% accepted, 32 enrolled. *Faculty:* 21 full-time (12 women), 13 part-time/adjunct (5 women). Expenses: Contact institution. *Financial support:* In 2008–09, 292 students received support, including 1 research assistantship (averaging $10,000 per year); scholarships/grants, health care benefits, and tuition waivers (partial) also available. Support available to part-time students. Financial award application deadline: 5/15; financial award applicants required to submit FAFSA. In 2008, 51 master's, 28 doctorates, 30 other advanced degrees awarded. Postbaccalaureate distance learning degree programs offered (minimal on-campus study). Offers collaborative educational leadership (MA); educational leadership and change (Ed D); teaching in the virtual classroom (Graduate Certificate). *Application deadline:* For fall admission, 7/31 priority date for domestic students, 7/31 for international students; for spring admission, 11/19 priority date for domestic students, 11/19 for international students. *Application fee:* $75. Electronic applications accepted. *Application Contact:* Violet Hatipoglu, Admission Counselor, 800-340-1099, Fax: 805-687-9793, E-mail: vhatipog@fielding.edu. *Dean,* Dr. Judy Witt, 805-898-2940, E-mail: jwitt@fielding.edu.

School of Human and Organization Development Students: 498 full-time (353 women), 181 part-time (123 women); includes 126 minority (66 African Americans, 6 American

Indian/Alaska Native, 27 Asian Americans or Pacific Islanders, 27 Hispanic Americans), 56 international. Average age 47. 178 applicants, 91% accepted, 120 enrolled. *Faculty:* 28 full-time (13 women), 10 part-time/adjunct (3 women). Expenses: Contact institution. *Financial support:* In 2008–09, 392 students received support, including 2 research assistantships (averaging $5,448 per year); scholarships/grants and health care benefits also available. Support available to part-time students. Financial award application deadline: 5/15; financial award applicants required to submit FAFSA. In 2008, 34 master's, 38 doctorates, 60 other advanced degrees awarded. Postbaccalaureate distance learning degree programs offered (minimal on-campus study). Offers evidence-based coaching (Certificate); human and organizational systems (PhD); human development (PhD); integral studies (Certificate); organization management and development (MA). *Application deadline:* For fall admission, 3/1 for domestic and international students; for spring admission, 9/1 for domestic and international students. *Application fee:* $75. Electronic applications accepted. *Application Contact:* Carmen Kuchera, Admission Counselor, 800-340-1099, Fax: 805-687-9793, E-mail: ckuchera@fielding.edu. *Dean,* Dr. Charles McClintock, 805-898-2930, Fax: 805-687-4590, E-mail: cmcclintock@fielding.edu.

School of Psychology Students: 522 full-time (382 women), 76 part-time (47 women); includes 121 minority (38 African Americans, 6 American Indian/Alaska Native, 28 Asian Americans or Pacific Islanders, 49 Hispanic Americans), 12 international. Average age 44. 284 applicants, 38% accepted, 76 enrolled. *Faculty:* 35 full-time (17 women), 2 part-time/adjunct (0 women). Expenses: Contact institution. *Financial support:* In 2008–09, 440 students received support, including 3 research assistantships (averaging $2,565 per year); scholarships/grants and health care benefits also available. Support available to part-time students. Financial award application deadline: 5/15; financial award applicants required to submit FAFSA. In 2008, 38 doctorates, 29 other advanced degrees awarded. Postbaccalaureate distance learning degree programs offered (minimal on-campus study). Offers clinical psychology (PhD); clinical psychology respecialization (Post-Doctoral Certificate); media psychology (PhD); media psychology and social change (MA); neuropsychology (Post-Doctoral Certificate). *Application deadline:* For fall admission, 2/23 for domestic and international students; for spring admission, 8/25 for domestic and international students. *Application fee:* $75. Electronic applications accepted. *Application Contact:* Kathryn Romero, Admission Counselor, 800-340-1099, Fax: 805-687-9793, E-mail: kromero@fielding.edu. *Dean,* Dr. Raymond Trybus, 805-898-2909, E-mail: rtrybus@fielding.edu.

FISK UNIVERSITY, Nashville, TN 37208-3051

General Information Independent-religious, coed, comprehensive institution. *Graduate housing:* Rooms and/or apartments available on a first-come, first-served basis to single and married students. Housing application deadline: 4/6. *Research affiliation:* Oak Ridge Associated Universities (chemical physics).

GRADUATE UNITS

Graduate Programs *Degree program information:* Part-time programs available. Offers biology (MA); chemistry (MA); clinical psychology (MA); physics (MA); psychology (MA).

FITCHBURG STATE COLLEGE, Fitchburg, MA 01420-2697

General Information State-supported, coed, comprehensive institution. *Enrollment:* 6,761 graduate, professional, and undergraduate students; 248 full-time matriculated graduate/professional students (172 women), 754 part-time matriculated graduate/professional students (531 women). *Enrollment by degree level:* 905 master's, 97 other advanced degrees. Tuition, state resident: full-time $3600; part-time $150 per credit. Tuition, nonresident: full-time $3600; part-time $150 per credit. *Required fees:* $109 per credit. *Graduate housing:* On-campus housing not available. *Student services:* Campus employment opportunities, campus safety program, career counseling, exercise/wellness program, free psychological counseling, international student services, low-cost health insurance, multicultural affairs office, services for students with disabilities, teacher training, writing training. *Library facilities:* Amelia V. Galucci-Cirio Library. *Online resources:* library catalog, web page, access to other libraries' catalogs. *Collection:* 259,321 titles, 2,967 serial subscriptions, 2,211 audiovisual materials.

Computer facilities: Computer purchase and lease plans are available. 150 computers available on campus for general student use. A campuswide network can be accessed from student residence rooms and from off campus. Online class registration is available. *Web address:* http://www.fsc.edu/.

General Application Contact: Director of Admissions, 978-665-3144, Fax: 978-665-4540, E-mail: admissions@fsc.edu.

GRADUATE UNITS

Division of Graduate and Continuing Education Students: 270 full-time (155 women), 687 part-time (504 women); includes 28 minority (9 African Americans, 1 American Indian/Alaska Native, 4 Asian Americans or Pacific Islanders, 14 Hispanic Americans), 117 international. Average age 34. 564 applicants, 90% accepted, 385 enrolled. Expenses: Contact institution. *Financial support:* In 2008–09, research assistantships with partial tuition reimbursements (averaging $5,500 per year); Federal Work-Study, scholarships/grants, and unspecified assistantships also available. Support available to part-time students. Financial award application deadline: 3/1; financial award applicants required to submit FAFSA. In 2008, 475 master's, 55 other advanced degrees awarded. *Degree program information:* Part-time and evening/weekend programs available. Offers accounting (MBA); applied communications (MS, Certificate); arts education (M Ed); biology and teaching biology (MA, MAT); computer science (MS); criminal justice (MS); curriculum and teaching (M Ed); early childhood education (M Ed); educational technology (Certificate); elementary education (M Ed); elementary school guidance counseling (MS); English and teaching English (secondary level) (MA, MAT, Certificate); fine arts director (Certificate); forensic nursing (MS, Certificate); guided studies (M Ed); higher education administration (CAGS); history and teaching history (secondary level) (MA, MAT, Certificate); human resource management (MBA); interdisciplinary studies (CAGS); library media (MS); management (MBA); marriage and family therapy (Certificate); mental health counseling (MS); middle school education (M Ed); non-licensure (M Ed, CAGS); occupational education (M Ed); professional mentoring for teachers (Certificate); reading specialist (M Ed); school principal (M Ed, CAGS); science education (M Ed); secondary education (M Ed); secondary school guidance counseling (MS); supervisor director (M Ed, CAGS); teaching students with moderate disabilities (M Ed); teaching students with severe disabilities (M Ed); technical and professional writing (MS); technology education (M Ed); technology leader (M Ed, CAGS). *Application deadline:* Applications are processed on a rolling basis. *Application fee:* $25 ($50 for international students). *Application Contact:* Director of Admissions, 978-665-3144, Fax: 978-665-4540, E-mail: admissions@fsc.edu. *Dean, Graduate and Continuing Education,* Catherine Canney, 978-665-3182, Fax: 978-665-3658, E-mail: gce@fsc.edu.

FIVE BRANCHES UNIVERSITY: GRADUATE SCHOOL OF TRADITIONAL CHINESE MEDICINE, Santa Cruz, CA 95062

General Information Independent, coed, graduate-only institution. *Graduate housing:* On-campus housing not available.

GRADUATE UNITS

Program in Traditional Chinese Medicine Offers traditional Chinese medicine (MTCM). Electronic applications accepted.

FIVE TOWNS COLLEGE, Dix Hills, NY 11746-6055

General Information Independent, coed, comprehensive institution. *Enrollment:* 1,163 graduate, professional, and undergraduate students; 2 full-time matriculated graduate/professional students (1 woman), 65 part-time matriculated graduate/professional students (22 women). *Enrollment by degree level:* 46 master's, 21 doctoral. *Graduate faculty:* 2 full-time (both women), 12 part-time/adjunct (4 women). *Tuition:* Part-time $495 per credit. *Graduate housing:* On-campus housing not available. *Student services:* Campus employment opportunities, campus safety program, career counseling, international student services, low-cost health insurance, teacher training, writing training. *Library facilities:* Five Towns College Library. *Online resources:* library catalog, access to other libraries' catalogs. *Collection:* 40,000 titles, 565 serial subscriptions.

Computer facilities: 110 computers available on campus for general student use. A campuswide network can be accessed. *Web address:* http://www.fivetowns.edu/.

General Application Contact: Jerry Cohen, Dean of Enrollment, 631-656-2110, Fax: 631-656-2172, E-mail: admissions@ftc.edu.

GRADUATE UNITS

Department of Music *Degree program information:* Part-time programs available. Offers jazz/commercial music (MM); music (DMA); music education (MM).

Program in Childhood Education *Degree program information:* Part-time and evening/weekend programs available. Offers childhood education (MS Ed).

FLORIDA AGRICULTURAL AND MECHANICAL UNIVERSITY, Tallahassee, FL 32307-3200

General Information State-supported, coed, university. CGS member. *Graduate housing:* Rooms and/or apartments available on a first-come, first-served basis to single and married students. Housing application deadline: 6/1. *Research affiliation:* The Boeing Company (aerospace science), Minority Health Professions Foundation (health science), Pfizer, Inc.

GRADUATE UNITS

College of Law Offers law (JD).

Division of Graduate Studies, Research, and Continuing Education *Degree program information:* Part-time and evening/weekend programs available.

College of Arts and Sciences *Degree program information:* Part-time programs available. Offers African American history (MASS); arts and sciences (MASS, MS, MSW, PhD); biology (MS); chemistry (MS); community psychology (MS); criminal justice (MASS); economics (MASS); history (MASS); history and political sciences (MASS, MSW); physics (MS, PhD); political science (MASS); public administration (MASS); public management (MASS); school psychology (MS); social work (MSW); sociology (MASS); software engineering (MS).

College of Education *Degree program information:* Part-time and evening/weekend programs available. Offers administration and supervision (M Ed, MS Ed, PhD); adult education (M Ed, MS Ed); biology (M Ed); business education (MBE); chemistry (MS Ed); early childhood and elementary education (M Ed, MS Ed); education (M Ed, MBE, MS Ed, PhD); educational leadership (PhD); English (MS Ed); guidance and counseling (M Ed, MS Ed); health, physical education, and recreation (M Ed, MS Ed); history (MS Ed); industrial education (M Ed, MS Ed); math (MS Ed); physics (MS Ed).

College of Engineering Science, Technology, and Agriculture Offers agribusiness (MS); animal science (MS); engineering science, technology, and agriculture (MS); engineering technology (MS); entomology (MS); food science (MS); international programs (MS); plant science (MS).

College of Pharmacy and Pharmaceutical Sciences Offers environmental toxicology (PhD); medicinal chemistry (MS, PhD); pharmaceutics (MS, PhD); pharmacology/toxicology (MS, PhD); pharmacy administration (MS); pharmacy and pharmaceutical sciences (Pharm D, MPH, MS, Ex Doc, PhD); public health (MPH).

FAMU-FSU College of Engineering Offers biomedical engineering (MS, PhD); chemical engineering (MS, PhD); civil engineering (MS, PhD); electrical engineering (MS, PhD); engineering (MS, PhD); environmental engineering (MS, PhD); industrial engineering (MS, PhD); mechanical engineering (MS, PhD). College administered jointly by Florida State University.

School of Allied Health Sciences Offers health administration (MS); physical therapy (MPT).

School of Architecture *Degree program information:* Part-time programs available. Offers architectural studies (MS Arch); architecture (professional) (M Arch); landscape architecture (MLA).

School of Business and Industry Offers accounting (MBA); finance (MBA); management information systems (MBA); marketing (MBA).

School of Journalism and Graphic Communication Offers journalism (MS).

School of Nursing Offers nursing (MS).

Environmental Sciences Institute Students: 30 full-time (22 women), 3 part-time (2 women); includes 26 minority (24 African Americans, 1 Asian American or Pacific Islander, 1 Hispanic American), 6 international. Average age 25. 27 applicants, 19% accepted, 2 enrolled. *Faculty:* 10 full-time (2 women), 1 part-time/adjunct (0 women). Expenses: Contact institution. *Financial support:* In 2008–09, 9 fellowships with full and partial tuition reimbursements, 21 research assistantships were awarded; career-related internships or fieldwork, institutionally sponsored loans, scholarships/grants, and unspecified assistantships also available. Financial award application deadline: 6/1; financial award applicants required to submit FAFSA. In 2008, 4 master's, 1 doctorate awarded. Offers environmental sciences (MS, PhD). *Application deadline:* For fall admission, 4/1 priority date for domestic and international students; for spring admission, 11/1 priority date for domestic and international students. *Application fee:* $20. *Application Contact:* Ora S. Mukes, Coordinator, Academic Support Services, 850-561-2641, Fax: 850-412-5504, E-mail: ora.mukes@famu.edu. *Director,* Dr. Henry Neal Williams, 850-599-3550, Fax: 850-599-8183, E-mail: henryneal.williams@famu.edu.

FLORIDA ATLANTIC UNIVERSITY, Boca Raton, FL 33431-0991

General Information State-supported, coed, university. CGS member. *Enrollment:* 26,897 graduate, professional, and undergraduate students; 1,552 full-time matriculated graduate/professional students (896 women), 2,338 part-time matriculated graduate/professional students (1,542 women). *Enrollment by degree level:* 3,890 first professional, 3,194 master's, 696 doctoral. *Graduate faculty:* 1,063 full-time (478 women), 510 part-time/adjunct (265 women). Tuition, state resident: full-time $4867; part-time $270.40 per credit hour. Tuition, nonresident: full-time $16,486; part-time $915.87 per credit hour. *Graduate housing:* Room and/or apartments available on a first-come, first-served basis to single students; on-campus housing not available to married students. Typical cost: $8960 (including board). Room and board charges vary according to board plan and housing facility selected. Housing application deadline: 5/1. *Student services:* Campus employment opportunities, campus safety program, career counseling, exercise/wellness program, free psychological counseling, international student services, low-cost health insurance, multicultural affairs office, services for students with disabilities, teacher training. *Library facilities:* S. E. Wimberly Library plus 2 others. *Online resources:* library catalog, web page, access to other libraries' catalogs. *Collection:* 1.3 million titles, 12,811 serial subscriptions. *Research affiliation:* Smithsonian Marine Station (marine resources characterization), Harbor Branch Oceanographic Institution (harnessing ocean power), Motorola Corporation (engineering), Children's Services Council (urban redevelopment), Shell Oil Co. (engineering), Florida Power & Light (solar energy).

Computer facilities: 1,000 computers available on campus for general student use. A campuswide network can be accessed from student residence rooms and from off campus. Online class registration is available. *Web address:* http://www.fau.edu/.

General Application Contact: Joanna Arlington, Manager, Graduate Admissions, 561-297-2428, Fax: 561-297-2117, E-mail: arlingto@fau.edu.

GRADUATE UNITS

Barry Kaye College of Business Students: 348 full-time (154 women), 776 part-time (382 women); includes 321 minority (93 African Americans, 66 Asian Americans or Pacific Islanders, 162 Hispanic Americans), 75 international. Average age 32. 1,147 applicants, 51% accepted, 199 enrolled. *Faculty:* 109 full-time (36 women), 62 part-time/adjunct (17 women). Expenses: Contact institution. *Financial support:* Fellowships with partial tuition reimbursements, research assistantships with partial tuition reimbursements, teaching assistantships with full tuition reimbursements, career-related internships or fieldwork, Federal Work-Study, institutionally sponsored loans, tuition waivers (full and partial), and unspecified assistantships available. Support available to part-time students. Financial award application deadline: 3/1. In 2008, 281 master's, 12 doctorates awarded. *Degree program information:* Part-time

Florida Atlantic University (continued)

and evening/weekend programs available. Postbaccalaureate distance learning degree programs offered (minimal on-campus study). Offers business (Exec MBA, M Ac, M Tax, MBA, MHA, MS, PhD, Certificate); economics (MS); finance (MS, PhD); global entrepreneurship (MBA); international business (MBA, MS); management (PhD); management information systems (MS); music business administration (MS). *Application deadline:* For fall admission, 7/11 priority date for domestic students, 2/15 priority date for international students; for winter admission, 11/1 priority date for domestic students, 8/15 priority date for international students; for spring admission, 4/1 priority date for domestic students, 1/15 priority date for international students. Applications are processed on a rolling basis. *Application fee:* $30. *Application Contact:* Fredrick G. Taylor, Graduate Adviser, 561-297-3196, Fax: 561-297-1315, E-mail: ftaylor@fau.edu. *Dean*, Dr. Dennis Coates, 561-297-3635, Fax: 561-297-3686, E-mail: coates@fau.edu.

School of Accounting Students: 70 full-time (32 women), 292 part-time (167 women); includes 99 minority (28 African Americans, 14 Asian Americans or Pacific Islanders, 57 Hispanic Americans), 9 international. Average age 32. 384 applicants, 55% accepted, 64 enrolled. *Faculty:* 22 full-time (10 women), 12 part-time/adjunct (1 woman). Expenses: Contact institution. *Financial support:* Fellowships, research assistantships with partial tuition reimbursements, teaching assistantships, career-related internships or fieldwork, Federal Work-Study, institutionally sponsored loans, scholarships/grants, and tuition waivers (partial) available. Support available to part-time students. Financial award application deadline: 3/1. In 2008, 94 master's awarded. *Degree program information:* Part-time and evening/weekend programs available. Postbaccalaureate distance learning degree programs offered (minimal on-campus study). Offers accounting (M Ac, M Tax, PhD); taxation (M Tax). *Application deadline:* For fall admission, 7/1 priority date for domestic students, 2/15 priority date for international students; for spring admission, 11/1 priority date for domestic students, 7/15 priority date for international students. Applications are processed on a rolling basis. *Application fee:* $30. *Application Contact:* Dr. Kim Dunn, Graduate Adviser, 561-297-3643, Fax: 561-297-1315, E-mail: kdunn@fau.edu. *Director*, Dr. Somnath Bhattacharya, 561-297-3638, Fax: 561-297-7023, E-mail: sbhatt@fau.edu.

Charles E. Schmidt College of Science Students: 284 full-time (148 women), 84 part-time (50 women); includes 57 minority (13 African Americans, 3 American Indian/Alaska Native, 18 Asian Americans or Pacific Islanders, 23 Hispanic Americans), 95 international. Average age 31. 330 applicants, 37% accepted, 61 enrolled. *Faculty:* 128 full-time (29 women), 20 part-time/adjunct (5 women). Expenses: Contact institution. *Financial support:* Fellowships with partial tuition reimbursements, research assistantships with partial tuition reimbursements, teaching assistantships with partial tuition reimbursements, career-related internships or fieldwork, Federal Work-Study, institutionally sponsored loans, scholarships/grants, tuition waivers (partial), and unspecified assistantships available. In 2008, 91 master's, 22 doctorates awarded. *Degree program information:* Part-time programs available. Offers applied mathematics and statistics (MS); biological sciences (MS, MST); chemistry (MS, MST, PhD); environmental sciences (MS); geography (MA); geology (MS); mathematical sciences (MS, MST, PhD); physics (MS, PhD); psychology (MA, PhD); science (MA, MS, MST, PhD). *Application deadline:* For fall admission, 6/1 for domestic students, 2/15 for international students; for spring admission, 11/1 for domestic students, 8/15 for international students. Applications are processed on a rolling basis. *Application fee:* $30. Electronic applications accepted. *Application Contact:* Dr. Leslie Terry, Associate Dean of External Affairs and Community Relations, 561-297-0347, Fax: 561-297-3388. *Dean*, Dr. Gary W. Perry, 561-297-3288, Fax: 561-297-3792.

Center for Complex Systems and Brain Sciences Students: 13 full-time (7 women), 3 part-time (0 women); includes 2 minority (1 American Indian/Alaska Native, 1 Hispanic American), 5 international. Average age 34. 8 applicants, 0% accepted. *Faculty:* 3 full-time (1 woman). Expenses: Contact institution. *Financial support:* Fellowships with full tuition reimbursements, research assistantships with partial tuition reimbursements, teaching assistantships with partial tuition reimbursements, Federal Work-Study, traineeships, and unspecified assistantships available. In 2008, 3 doctorates awarded. Offers complex systems and brain sciences (PhD). *Application deadline:* For fall admission, 1/15 priority date for domestic and international students. *Application fee:* $30. *Application Contact:* Rhona Frankel, Associate Director, 561-297-2230, E-mail: frankel@fau.edu. *Director*, Dr. Janet Blanks, 561-297-2229, Fax: 561-297-3634, E-mail: blanks@ccs.fau.edu.

Christine E. Lynn College of Nursing Students: 72 full-time (64 women), 327 part-time (304 women); includes 166 minority (104 African Americans, 2 American Indian/Alaska Native, 19 Asian Americans or Pacific Islanders, 41 Hispanic Americans), 1 international. Average age 40. 365 applicants, 44% accepted, 119 enrolled. *Faculty:* 38 full-time (3 women), 18 part-time/adjunct (17 women). Expenses: Contact institution. *Financial support:* Research assistantships with partial tuition reimbursements, teaching assistantships with partial tuition reimbursements, career-related internships or fieldwork, Federal Work-Study, institutionally sponsored loans, scholarships/grants, and traineeships available. Support available to part-time students. In 2008, 119 master's, 2 doctorates awarded. *Degree program information:* Part-time programs available. Offers nursing (MS, DNP, PhD, Post Master's Certificate). *Application deadline:* For fall admission, 6/1 for domestic students, 2/15 for international students; for spring admission, 10/1 for domestic students, 7/15 for international students. Applications are processed on a rolling basis. *Application fee:* $30. *Application Contact:* Carol Kruse, Graduate Coordinator, 561-297-3261, Fax: 561-297-0088, E-mail: ckruse@fau.edu. *Dean*, Dr. Anne J. Boykin, 561-297-3206, Fax: 561-297-3687, E-mail: boykina@fau.edu.

College of Architecture, Urban and Public Affairs Students: 99 full-time (68 women), 189 part-time (131 women); includes 103 minority (52 African Americans, 3 Asian Americans or Pacific Islanders, 48 Hispanic Americans), 10 international. Average age 34. 351 applicants, 52% accepted, 78 enrolled. *Faculty:* 49 full-time (21 women), 42 part-time/adjunct (18 women). Expenses: Contact institution. *Financial support:* Fellowships with partial tuition reimbursements, research assistantships with partial tuition reimbursements, teaching assistantships with partial tuition reimbursements, career-related internships or fieldwork, Federal Work-Study, and institutionally sponsored loans available. Support available to part-time students. Financial award application deadline: 4/1. In 2008, 107 master's, 5 doctorates awarded. *Degree program information:* Part-time and evening/weekend programs available. Offers architecture, urban and public affairs (MNM, MPA, MS, MSW, MURP, PhD, Certificate). *Application deadline:* For fall admission, 7/1 for domestic students, 2/15 for international students; for spring admission, 11/1 for domestic students, 7/15 for international students. Applications are processed on a rolling basis. *Application fee:* $30. *Application Contact:* Dr. Rosalyn Carter, Dean, 954-762-5660, Fax: 954-762-5673, E-mail: rcarter@fau.edu. *Dean*, Dr. Rosalyn Carter, 954-762-5660, Fax: 954-762-5673, E-mail: rcarter@fau.edu.

School of Criminology and Criminal Justice Students: 5 full-time (1 woman), 15 part-time (8 women); includes 5 minority (2 African Americans, 3 Hispanic Americans), 1 international. Average age 31. 33 applicants, 42% accepted, 11 enrolled. *Faculty:* 13 full-time (4 women), 16 part-time/adjunct (2 women). Expenses: Contact institution. *Financial support:* Research assistantships with partial tuition reimbursements, institutionally sponsored loans, scholarships/grants, and unspecified assistantships available. Financial award application deadline: 4/1. In 2008, 10 master's awarded. *Degree program information:* Part-time and evening/weekend programs available. Postbaccalaureate distance learning degree programs offered. Offers criminology and criminal justice (MS). *Application deadline:* For fall admission, 7/1 priority date for domestic students, 2/15 for international students; for spring admission, 11/1 priority date for domestic students, 7/15 for international students. Applications are processed on a rolling basis. *Application fee:* $30. Electronic applications accepted. *Application Contact:* Dr. Mara Schiff, Graduate Program Coordinator, 954-762-5638, Fax: 954-762-5673, E-mail: mschiff@fau.edu. *Chair*, Dr. Gordon Bazemore, 561-297-3240.

School of Public Administration Students: 18 full-time (9 women), 86 part-time (52 women); includes 41 minority (28 African Americans, 2 Asian Americans or Pacific Islanders, 11 Hispanic Americans), 7 international. Average age 36. 96 applicants, 44% accepted, 24 enrolled. *Faculty:* 10 full-time (3 women), 6 part-time/adjunct (0 women). Expenses: Contact institution. *Financial support:* Fellowships with full tuition reimbursements, research assistantships with partial tuition reimbursements, teaching assistantships with partial tuition reimbursements, career-related internships or fieldwork, Federal Work-Study, institutionally sponsored loans, and tuition waivers (partial) available. Support available to part-time students. Financial award application deadline: 4/1. In 2008, 33 master's, 5 doctorates awarded. *Degree program information:* Part-time and evening/weekend programs available. Offers nonprofit management (MNM); public administration (MNM, MPA, PhD). *Application deadline:* For fall admission, 7/1 priority date for domestic students, 2/15 for international students; for spring admission, 11/1 for domestic students, 7/15 for international students. Applications are processed on a rolling basis. *Application fee:* $30. *Application Contact:* Dr. Hugh T. Miller, Director, 954-762-5650, Fax: 954-762-5693, E-mail: hmiller@fau.edu. *Director*, Dr. Hugh T. Miller, 954-762-5650, Fax: 954-762-5693, E-mail: hmiller@fau.edu.

School of Social Work Students: 55 full-time (46 women), 77 part-time (66 women); includes 42 minority (17 African Americans, 1 Asian American or Pacific Islander, 24 Hispanic Americans), 1 international. Average age 33. 172 applicants, 60% accepted, 35 enrolled. *Faculty:* 18 full-time (8 women), 19 part-time/adjunct (15 women). Expenses: Contact institution. *Financial support:* Fellowships with tuition reimbursements, research assistantships with tuition reimbursements, career-related internships or fieldwork, Federal Work-Study, institutionally sponsored loans, and tuition waivers (partial) available. Financial award application deadline: 4/1. In 2008, 52 master's awarded. *Degree program information:* Part-time and evening/weekend programs available. Offers social work (MSW). *Application deadline:* For fall admission, 5/1 priority date for domestic students, 2/15 for international students. Applications are processed on a rolling basis. *Application fee:* $30. *Application Contact:* Dr. Elwood Hamlin, Coordinator, 501-297-3234, E-mail: ehamlin@fau.edu. *Director*, Dr. Michele Hawkins, 561-297-3234, Fax: 561-297-2866, E-mail: mhawkins@fau.edu.

School of Urban and Regional Planning Students: 21 full-time (12 women), 11 part-time (5 women); includes 15 minority (5 African Americans, 10 Hispanic Americans), 1 international. Average age 33. 47 applicants, 47% accepted, 8 enrolled. *Faculty:* 8 full-time (6 women), 1 (woman) part-time/adjunct. Expenses: Contact institution. *Financial support:* Fellowships with full tuition reimbursements, research assistantships, career-related internships or fieldwork, Federal Work-Study, institutionally sponsored loans, and tuition waivers (partial) available. Financial award application deadline: 4/1. In 2008, 12 master's awarded. *Degree program information:* Part-time and evening/weekend programs available. Offers economic development and tourism (Certificate); environmental planning (Certificate); sustainable community planning (Certificate); urban and regional planning (MURP); visual planning technology (Certificate). *Application deadline:* For fall admission, 7/1 priority date for domestic students, 2/15 for international students; for spring admission, 11/1 priority date for domestic students, 7/15 for international students. Applications are processed on a rolling basis. *Application fee:* $30. *Application Contact:* Dr. Jaap Vos, Chair, 954-762-5653, Fax: 954-762-5673, E-mail: jvos@fau.edu. *Chair*, Dr. Jaap Vos, 954-762-5653, Fax: 954-762-5673, E-mail: jvos@fau.edu.

College of Biomedical Science Students: 43 full-time (21 women), 14 part-time (8 women); includes 19 minority (4 African Americans, 7 Asian Americans or Pacific Islanders, 8 Hispanic Americans), 9 international. Average age 25. 69 applicants, 32% accepted, 17 enrolled. *Faculty:* 14 full-time (5 women), 2 part-time/adjunct (1 woman). Expenses: Contact institution. *Financial support:* Research assistantships available. In 2008, 31 master's awarded. Offers biomedical science (MS); integrative biology (PhD). *Application deadline:* For fall admission, 5/1 for domestic students, 3/15 for international students; for spring admission, 10/1 for domestic and international students. *Application fee:* $30. *Application Contact:* Julie Sivigny, Academic Program Specialist for Graduate Studies, 561-297-2216, E-mail: jsivigny@fau.edu. *Dean*, Dr. Michael L. Friedland, 561-297-4341.

College of Education Students: 326 full-time (254 women), 633 part-time (506 women); includes 264 minority (128 African Americans, 1 American Indian/Alaska Native, 19 Asian Americans or Pacific Islanders, 116 Hispanic Americans), 13 international. Average age 35. 848 applicants, 50% accepted, 269 enrolled. *Faculty:* 97 full-time (62 women), 168 part-time/adjunct (110 women). Expenses: Contact institution. *Financial support:* Fellowships with partial tuition reimbursements, research assistantships with partial tuition reimbursements, teaching assistantships with partial tuition reimbursements, career-related internships or fieldwork, Federal Work-Study, and unspecified assistantships available. In 2008, 282 master's, 25 doctorates awarded. *Degree program information:* Part-time and evening/weekend programs available. Offers adult and community education (M Ed, PhD, Ed S); counselor education (M Ed, PhD, Ed S); curriculum and instruction (M Ed, Ed D, Ed S); early childhood education (M Ed); education (M Ed, MS, Ed D, PhD, Ed S); educational leadership (M Ed, PhD, Ed S); elementary education (M Ed); environmental education (M Ed); exceptional student education (M Ed, Ed D); exercise science and health promotion (MS); higher education (M Ed, PhD); K-12 school leadership (M Ed, PhD, Ed S); marriage and family therapy (Ed S); mental health counseling (M Ed, Ed S); multicultural education (M Ed); reading education (M Ed); rehabilitation counseling (M Ed); school counseling (M Ed, Ed S); social foundations of education (M Ed); speech-language pathology (MS); teaching English to speakers of other languages (TESOL) (M Ed). *Application deadline:* Applications are processed on a rolling basis. *Application fee:* $30. Electronic applications accepted. *Application Contact:* Dr. Eliah Watlington, Associate Dean, 561-296-8520, Fax: 261-297-2991, E-mail: ewatling@fau.edu. *Dean*, Dr. Valerie J. Bristor, 561-297-3564, E-mail: bristor@fau.edu.

College of Engineering and Computer Science Students: 146 full-time (33 women), 106 part-time (26 women); includes 78 minority (16 African Americans, 29 Asian Americans or Pacific Islanders, 33 Hispanic Americans), 90 international. Average age 31. 239 applicants, 49% accepted, 44 enrolled. *Faculty:* 73 full-time (9 women), 2 part-time/adjunct (0 women). Expenses: Contact institution. *Financial support:* In 2008–09, research assistantships with partial tuition reimbursements (averaging $15,000 per year), teaching assistantships with partial tuition reimbursements (averaging $15,000 per year) were awarded; fellowships, career-related internships or fieldwork, Federal Work-Study, and unspecified assistantships also available. Support available to part-time students. Financial award applicants required to submit FAFSA. In 2008, 107 master's, 9 doctorates awarded. *Degree program information:* Part-time and evening/weekend programs available. Postbaccalaureate distance learning degree programs offered (minimal on-campus study). Offers civil engineering (MS); computer engineering (MS, PhD); computer science (MS, PhD); electrical engineering (MS, PhD); engineering and computer science (MS, PhD); mechanical engineering (MS, PhD); ocean engineering (MS, PhD). *Application deadline:* For fall admission, 7/1 for domestic students, 2/15 for international students; for spring admission, 11/1 for domestic students, 7/15 for international students. Applications are processed on a rolling basis. *Application fee:* $30. *Application Contact:* Dr. Karl K. Stevens, Dean, 561-297-3400, Fax: 561-297-2659, E-mail: stevens@fau.edu. *Dean*, Dr. Karl K. Stevens, 561-297-3400, Fax: 561-297-2659, E-mail: stevens@fau.edu.

Dorothy F. Schmidt College of Arts and Letters Students: 234 full-time (154 women), 209 part-time (135 women); includes 93 minority (28 African Americans, 2 American Indian/Alaska Native, 11 Asian Americans or Pacific Islanders, 52 Hispanic Americans), 28 international. Average age 34. 332 applicants, 49% accepted, 71 enrolled. *Faculty:* 199 full-time (99 women), 97 part-time/adjunct (41 women). Expenses: Contact institution. *Financial support:* Fellowships with partial tuition reimbursements, research assistantships, teaching assistantships, career-related internships or fieldwork, Federal Work-Study, institutionally sponsored loans, and tuition waivers (partial) available. Support available to part-time students. In 2008, 97 master's, 8 doctorates awarded. *Degree program information:* Part-time programs available. Offers acting (MFA); anthropology (MA); art education (MAT); arts and letters (MA, MAT, MFA, PhD, Certificate); British and American literature (MA); ceramics (MFA); commercial music (MA); comparative literature (MA); comparative studies (PhD); computer art (MFA); creative nonfiction (MFA); creative writing (MA); design and technology (MFA); environmental studies (Certificate); fiction (MFA); French (MA); graphic design (MFA); history (MA); liberal studies (MA); linguistics (MA); multicultural literatures and literacies (MA); music history/literature (MA); painting (MFA); performance (MA); poetry (MFA); political science (MA, MAT); science fiction and fantasy (MA); sociology (MA); Spanish (MA); teaching English (MAT). *Application deadline:* For fall admission, 6/1 priority date for domestic students. Applications are processed on a rolling basis. *Application fee:* $30. Electronic applications accepted. *Application Contact:* Dr. Emily Stockard, Associate Dean, 561-297-2817, Fax: 561-297-2744, E-mail: stockard@fau.edu. *Dean*, Dr. Manjunath Pendakur, 561-297-3803.

School of Communication and Multimedia Studies Students: 15 full-time (11 women), 10 part-time (5 women); includes 2 minority (1 Asian American or Pacific Islander, 1 Hispanic American), 3 international. Average age 29. 35 applicants, 37% accepted, 7 enrolled.

Faculty: 21 full-time (10 women), 14 part-time/adjunct (3 women). Expenses: Contact institution. *Financial support:* Teaching assistantships with partial tuition reimbursements, Federal Work-Study and institutionally sponsored loans available. Support available to part-time students. Financial award application deadline: 3/1. In 2008, 8 master's awarded. *Degree program information:* Part-time programs available. Offers communication studies (MA); film and video (Certificate); film studies (MA); multimedia journalism studies (MA). *Application deadline:* For fall admission, 7/1 priority date for domestic students, 4/1 for international students; for spring admission, 11/1 for domestic students, 10/1 for international students. Applications are processed on a rolling basis. *Application fee:* $30. Electronic applications accepted. *Application Contact:* Dr. Eric M. Freedman, Graduate Coordinator, 561-297-2534, Fax: 561-297-2615, E-mail: efreedma@fau.edu. *Director,* Dr. Susan S. Reilly, 561-297-1095, Fax: 561-297-2615, E-mail: sreilly@fau.edu.

Women's Studies Center Students: 5 full-time (4 women), 4 part-time (all women); includes 1 minority (Hispanic American). Average age 31. 8 applicants, 25% accepted, 1 enrolled. *Faculty:* 2 full-time (both women), 1 (woman) part-time/adjunct. Expenses: Contact institution. *Financial support:* Fellowships with full and partial tuition reimbursements, teaching assistantships with full and partial tuition reimbursements, career-related internships or fieldwork, Federal Work-Study, institutionally sponsored loans, scholarships/grants, and unspecified assistantships available. Support available to part-time students. In 2008, 3 master's awarded. Offers women's studies (MA, Certificate). *Application deadline:* For fall admission, 7/1 for domestic students, 2/15 for international students; for spring admission, 11/1 for domestic students, 7/15 for international students. Applications are processed on a rolling basis. *Application fee:* $30. *Application Contact:* Dr. Jane Caputi, Professor, 561-297-2056, Fax: 561-297-2127, E-mail: jcaputi@fau.edu. *Director,* Dr. Josephine Beoku-Betts, 561-297-3865, Fax: 561-297-2127.

FLORIDA COASTAL SCHOOL OF LAW, Jacksonville, FL 32256

General Information Proprietary, coed, graduate-only institution. *Enrollment by degree level:* 1,395 first professional. *Graduate faculty:* 77 full-time (45 women), 45 part-time/adjunct (15 women). *Tuition:* Full-time $29,362. *Required fees:* $1454. *Student services:* Campus employment opportunities, campus safety program, career counseling, exercise/wellness program, free psychological counseling, grant writing training, international student services, low-cost health insurance, multicultural affairs office, services for students with disabilities, teacher training, writing training. *Library facilities:* Law Library. *Online resources:* library catalog, web page, access to other libraries' catalogs. *Collection:* 12,710 titles, 2,105 serial subscriptions, 145 audiovisual materials.

Computer facilities: 76 computers available on campus for general student use. A campuswide network can be accessed from off campus. Online class registration is available. *Web address:* http://www.fcsl.edu/.

General Application Contact: Admissions Office, 904-680-7710, Fax: 904-680-7692, E-mail: admissions@fcsl.edu.

GRADUATE UNITS

Professional Program Students: 1,308 full-time (598 women), 162 part-time (82 women); includes 283 minority (94 African Americans, 24 American Indian/Alaska Native, 82 Asian Americans or Pacific Islanders, 83 Hispanic Americans). Average age 26. 4,940 applicants, 48% accepted, 553 enrolled. *Faculty:* 77 full-time (45 women), 45 part-time/adjunct (15 women). Expenses: Contact institution. *Financial support:* Research assistantships, teaching assistantships, scholarships/grants and tuition waivers (full and partial) available. Support available to part-time students. Financial award applicants required to submit FAFSA. *Degree program information:* Part-time programs available. Offers law (JD). *Application deadline:* Applications are processed on a rolling basis. *Application fee:* $50. Electronic applications accepted. *Application Contact:* Admissions Office, 904-680-7710, Fax: 904-680-7692, E-mail: admissions@fcsl.edu. *Dean,* Peter Goplerud, 904-680-7707, E-mail: pgoplerud@fcsl.edu.

FLORIDA COLLEGE OF INTEGRATIVE MEDICINE, Orlando, FL 32809

General Information Proprietary, coed, graduate-only institution. *Graduate housing:* On-campus housing not available.

GRADUATE UNITS

Graduate Program *Degree program information:* Evening/weekend programs available. Offers Oriental medicine (MSOM). Electronic applications accepted.

FLORIDA GULF COAST UNIVERSITY, Fort Myers, FL 33965-6565

General Information State-supported, coed, comprehensive institution. CGS member. *Enrollment:* 10,214 graduate, professional, and undergraduate students; 445 full-time matriculated graduate/professional students (312 women), 1,114 part-time matriculated graduate/professional students (791 women). *Enrollment by degree level:* 1,536 master's, 23 doctoral. *Graduate faculty:* 324 full-time (154 women), 249 part-time/adjunct (113 women). *Graduate housing:* Room and/or apartments available on a first-come, first-served basis to single students; on-campus housing not available to married students. Typical cost: $3138 per year ($7642 including board). Room and board charges vary according to board plan. Housing application deadline: 3/15. *Student services:* Campus employment opportunities, campus safety program, career counseling, child daycare facilities, exercise/wellness program, free psychological counseling, international student services, low-cost health insurance, multicultural affairs office, services for students with disabilities, teacher training. *Library facilities:* Library Services. *Online resources:* library catalog, web page, access to other libraries' catalogs. *Collection:* 387,860 titles, 8,007 serial subscriptions, 10,134 audiovisual materials.

Computer facilities: Computer purchase and lease plans are available. 323 computers available on campus for general student use. A campuswide network can be accessed from student residence rooms and from off campus. Online class registration, online admissions and advising are available. *Web address:* http://www.fgcu.edu/.

General Application Contact: Michael Savarese, Director of Graduate Studies, 239-590-7988, Fax: 239-590-7843, E-mail: graduate@fgcu.edu.

GRADUATE UNITS

College of Arts and Sciences Students: 50 full-time (28 women), 27 part-time (15 women); includes 6 minority (1 Asian American or Pacific Islander, 5 Hispanic Americans). Average age 34. 75 applicants, 60% accepted, 30 enrolled. *Faculty:* 155 full-time (65 women), 123 part-time/adjunct (47 women). Expenses: Contact institution. In 2008, 20 master's awarded. *Degree program information:* Part-time programs available. Offers arts and sciences (MA, MS); English (MA); environmental science (MS); history (MA). *Application deadline:* For fall admission, 2/15 priority date for domestic students; for spring admission, 10/1 for domestic students. Applications are processed on a rolling basis. *Application fee:* $30. Electronic applications accepted. *Application Contact:* Patricia Rice, Executive Secretary, 239-590-7196, Fax: 239-590-7200, E-mail: price@fgcu.edu. *Dean,* Dr. Donna Price Henry, 239-590-7155, Fax: 239-590-7200, E-mail: dhenry@fgcu.edu.

College of Education Students: 231 full-time (188 women), 90 part-time (84 women); includes 51 minority (15 African Americans, 2 American Indian/Alaska Native, 2 Asian Americans or Pacific Islanders, 32 Hispanic Americans). Average age 35. 215 applicants, 76% accepted, 133 enrolled. *Faculty:* 31 full-time (24 women), 39 part-time/adjunct (28 women). Expenses: Contact institution. In 2008, 91 master's awarded. *Degree program information:* Part-time and evening/weekend programs available. Postbaccalaureate distance learning degree programs offered (minimal on-campus study). Offers behavior disorders (MA); counseling (MA); early childhood education (M Ed); education (M Ed, MA); educational leadership (M Ed, MA); educational technology (M Ed, MA); elementary curriculum (M Ed); elementary education (MA); English education (M Ed); mental retardation (MA); reading education (M Ed); specific learning disabilities (MA); varying exceptionalities (MA). *Application deadline:* For fall admission, 7/1 priority date for domestic students; for spring admission, 10/15 for domestic students. Applications are processed on a rolling basis. *Application fee:* $30. Electronic applications accepted. *Application Contact:* Edward Beckett, Adviser/Counselor, 239-590-7759, Fax: 239-590-7801, E-mail: ebeckett@fgcu.edu. *Dean,* Dr. Marci Greene, 239-590-7781, Fax: 239-590-7801, E-mail: mgreene@fgcu.edu.

College of Health Professions Students: 128 full-time (102 women), 61 part-time (45 women); includes 25 minority (10 African Americans, 1 American Indian/Alaska Native, 9 Asian Americans or Pacific Islanders, 5 Hispanic Americans). Average age 33. 188 applicants, 44% accepted, 64 enrolled. *Faculty:* 42 full-time (33 women), 30 part-time/adjunct (20 women). Expenses: Contact institution. *Financial support:* Career-related internships or fieldwork, Federal Work-Study, and institutionally sponsored loans available. In 2008, 36 master's awarded. *Degree program information:* Part-time and evening/weekend programs available. Postbaccalaureate distance learning degree programs offered (minimal on-campus study). Offers health professions (MS, MSN, DPT); health sciences (MS); occupational therapy (MS); physical therapy (MS, DPT). *Application deadline:* Applications are processed on a rolling basis. *Application fee:* $30. Electronic applications accepted. *Application Contact:* Lynn O'Hare, Administrative Assistant, 239-590-7451, Fax: 239-590-7474, E-mail: lohare@fgcu.edu. *Dean,* Dr. Denise Heinemann, 239-590-7511, Fax: 239-590-7474.

School of Nursing Students: 52 full-time (48 women), 7 part-time (all women); includes 7 minority (5 African Americans, 2 Asian Americans or Pacific Islanders). Average age 39. 42 applicants, 36% accepted, 9 enrolled. *Faculty:* 42 full-time (33 women), 30 part-time/adjunct (20 women). Expenses: Contact institution. In 2008, 7 master's awarded. *Degree program information:* Part-time programs available. Offers nursing (MSN). *Application deadline:* For fall admission, 4/15 priority date for domestic students; for spring admission, 6/1 for domestic students. Applications are processed on a rolling basis. *Application fee:* $30. Electronic applications accepted. *Application Contact:* Lynn O'Hare, Administrative Assistant, 239-590-7451, Fax: 239-590-7474, E-mail: lohare@fgcu.edu. *Director,* Dr. Marianne Rodgers, 239-590-7454, Fax: 239-590-7474, E-mail: mrodgers@fgcu.edu.

College of Professional Studies Students: 94 full-time (67 women), 75 part-time (57 women); includes 32 minority (11 African Americans, 3 Asian Americans or Pacific Islanders, 18 Hispanic Americans), 3 international. Average age 31. 132 applicants, 68% accepted, 73 enrolled. *Faculty:* 32 full-time (11 women), 29 part-time/adjunct (12 women). Expenses: Contact institution. *Financial support:* Research assistantships, career-related internships or fieldwork and tuition waivers (full and partial) available. Support available to part-time students. In 2008, 42 master's awarded. *Degree program information:* Part-time and evening/weekend programs available. Offers criminal forensic studies (MS); criminal justice (MPA); criminal justice studies (MS); environmental policy (MPA); general public administration (MPA); management (MPA); professional studies (MPA, MS, MSW); social work (MSW). *Application deadline:* Applications are processed on a rolling basis. *Application fee:* $30. Electronic applications accepted. *Application Contact:* Dr. Kenneth Millar, Dean, 239-590-7724, Fax: 239-590-7846, E-mail: kmillar@fgcu.edu. *Dean,* Dr. Kenneth Millar, 239-590-7724, Fax: 239-590-7846, E-mail: kmillar@fgcu.edu.

Lutgert College of Business Students: 160 full-time (70 women), 70 part-time (39 women); includes 31 minority (6 African Americans, 5 Asian Americans or Pacific Islanders, 20 Hispanic Americans), 6 international. Average age 31. 132 applicants, 77% accepted, 77 enrolled. *Faculty:* 63 full-time (20 women), 19 part-time/adjunct (2 women). Expenses: Contact institution. In 2008, 79 master's awarded. *Degree program information:* Part-time and evening/weekend programs available. Offers accounting and taxation (MS); business (MBA, MS); business administration (MBA); computer and information systems (MS). *Application deadline:* For fall admission, 7/1 priority date for domestic students; for spring admission, 11/1 for domestic students. Applications are processed on a rolling basis. *Application fee:* $30. Electronic applications accepted. *Application Contact:* Carol Burnette, Associate Dean, 239-590-7350, Fax: 239-590-7330, E-mail: burnette@fgcu.edu. *Dean,* Dr. Richard Pegnetter, 239-590-7310, Fax: 239-590-7330, E-mail: epegnett@fgcu.edu.

FLORIDA HOSPITAL COLLEGE OF HEALTH SCIENCES, Orlando, FL 32803

General Information Independent, coed.

GRADUATE UNITS

Program in Nurse Anesthesia Offers nurse anesthesia (MS).

FLORIDA INSTITUTE OF TECHNOLOGY, Melbourne, FL 32901-6975

General Information Independent, coed, university. *Enrollment:* 6,400 graduate, professional, and undergraduate students; 704 full-time matriculated graduate/professional students (325 women), 1,957 part-time matriculated graduate/professional students (778 women). *Enrollment by degree level:* 2,386 master's, 275 doctoral. *Graduate faculty:* 161 full-time (26 women), 150 part-time/adjunct (27 women). *Tuition:* Part-time $980 per credit hour. *Graduate housing:* Room and/or apartments available on a first-come, first-served basis to single students; on-campus housing not available to married students. Typical cost: $6000 per year ($10,250 including board). *Student services:* Campus employment opportunities, career counseling, exercise/wellness program, free psychological counseling, international student services, low-cost health insurance, services for students with disabilities, teacher training, writing training. *Library facilities:* Evans Library. *Online resources:* library catalog, web page, access to other libraries' catalogs. *Collection:* 295,624 titles, 28,597 serial subscriptions, 6,165 audiovisual materials. *Research affiliation:* IBM (software technology, information assurance), Harris—Assurance (Information Security), Boeing Corporation (digital signal processing aeronautics), General Electric-Harris (software testing), Microsoft Corporation (simulation software development), Lockheed Martin Corporation (biological sciences).

Computer facilities: 400 computers available on campus for general student use. A campuswide network can be accessed from student residence rooms and from off campus. Online class registration is available. *Web address:* http://www.fit.edu/.

General Application Contact: Thomas M. Shea, Director of Graduate Admissions, 321-674-7577, Fax: 321-723-9468, E-mail: tshea@fit.edu.

GRADUATE UNITS

Graduate Programs Students: 704 full-time (325 women), 1,957 part-time (778 women); includes 615 minority (349 African Americans, 15 American Indian/Alaska Native, 113 Asian Americans or Pacific Islanders, 138 Hispanic Americans), 344 international. Average age 33. 2,496 applicants, 49% accepted, 848 enrolled. *Faculty:* 161 full-time (26 women), 150 part-time/adjunct (27 women). Expenses: Contact institution. *Financial support:* In 2008–09, 209 students received support, including 5 fellowships with full and partial tuition reimbursements available (averaging $7,240 per year), 81 research assistantships with full and partial tuition reimbursements available (averaging $8,352 per year), 123 teaching assistantships with full and partial tuition reimbursements available (averaging $8,498 per year); career-related internships or fieldwork, institutionally sponsored loans, tuition waivers (partial), unspecified assistantships, and tuition remissions also available. Support available to part-time students. Financial award application deadline: 3/1; financial award applicants required to submit FAFSA. In 2008, 786 master's, 45 doctorates awarded. *Degree program information:* Part-time and evening/weekend programs available. Postbaccalaureate distance learning degree programs offered (no on-campus study). *Application deadline:* Applications are processed on a rolling basis. *Application fee:* $50. Electronic applications accepted. *Application Contact:* Thomas M. Shea, Director of Graduate Admissions, 321-674-7577, Fax: 321-723-9468, E-mail: tshea@fit.edu. *Director,* Vacant.

College of Aeronautics Students: 20 full-time (7 women), 21 part-time (5 women); includes 3 minority (1 African American, 1 Asian American or Pacific Islander, 1 Hispanic American), 20 international. Average age 26. 36 applicants, 58% accepted, 15 enrolled. *Faculty:* 7 full-time (0 women), 1 part-time/adjunct (0 women). Expenses: Contact institution. *Financial support:* Career-related internships or fieldwork, institutionally sponsored loans, tuition waivers (partial), and tuition remissions available. Support available to part-time students. Financial award application deadline: 3/1. *Degree program information:* Part-time and evening/weekend programs available. Offers airport development and management (MSA); applied aviation safety (MSA); aviation human factors (MS). *Application deadline:* Applications are processed on a rolling basis. *Application fee:* $50. Electronic applications accepted. *Application Contact:* Thomas M. Shea, Director of Graduate Admissions, 321-674-7577,

Florida Institute of Technology (continued)

Fax: 321-723-9468, E-mail: tshea@fit.edu. *Dean*, Dr. Winston E. Scott, 321-674-8971, Fax: 321-674-7368, E-mail: wscott@fit.edu.

College of Business Students: 14 full-time (9 women), 29 part-time (12 women); includes 5 minority (2 African Americans, 2 Asian Americans or Pacific Islanders, 1 Hispanic American), 5 international. Average age 30. 91 applicants, 57% accepted, 17 enrolled. *Faculty:* 7 full-time (3 women), 3 part-time/adjunct (0 women). Expenses: Contact institution. *Financial support:* Career-related internships or fieldwork, institutionally sponsored loans, unspecified assistantships, and tuition remissions available. Support available to part-time students. Financial award application deadline: 3/1; financial award applicants required to submit FAFSA. In 2008, 37 master's awarded. *Degree program information:* Part-time and evening/weekend programs available. Offers accounting and finance (MBA); business (EMBA, MBA); healthcare management (MBA); management (MBA); marketing (MBA). *Application deadline:* Applications are processed on a rolling basis. *Application fee:* $50. Electronic applications accepted. *Application Contact:* Thomas M. Shea, Director of Graduate Admissions, 321-674-7577, Fax: 321-723-9468, E-mail: tshea@fit.edu. *Dean*, Dr. Robert E. Niebuhr, 321-674-7327, Fax: 321-674-8896, E-mail: rniebuhr@fit.edu.

College of Engineering Students: 242 full-time (52 women), 341 part-time (66 women); includes 67 minority (22 African Americans, 19 Asian Americans or Pacific Islanders, 26 Hispanic Americans), 185 international. Average age 31. 825 applicants, 58% accepted, 141 enrolled. *Faculty:* 63 full-time (4 women), 14 part-time/adjunct (3 women). Expenses: Contact institution. *Financial support:* In 2008–09, 90 students received support, including 5 fellowships with full and partial tuition reimbursements available (averaging $7,240 per year), 31 research assistantships with full and partial tuition reimbursements available (averaging $7,006 per year), 54 teaching assistantships with full and partial tuition reimbursements available (averaging $6,111 per year); career-related internships or fieldwork, institutionally sponsored loans, unspecified assistantships, and tuition remissions also available. Financial award application deadline: 3/1; financial award applicants required to submit FAFSA. In 2008, 124 master's, 10 doctorates awarded. *Degree program information:* Part-time and evening/weekend programs available. Offers aerospace engineering (MS, PhD); biological oceanography (MS); chemical engineering (MS, PhD); chemical oceanography (MS); civil engineering (MS, PhD); coastal zone management (MS); computer engineering (MS, PhD); computer science (MS, PhD); earth remote sensing (MS); electrical engineering (MS, PhD); engineering (MS, PhD); engineering management (MS); environmental resource management (MS); environmental science (MS, PhD); geological oceanography (MS); mechanical engineering (MS, PhD); meteorology (MS); ocean engineering (MS, PhD); oceanography (MS, PhD); physical oceanography (MS); software engineering (MS); systems engineering (MS). *Application deadline:* Applications are processed on a rolling basis. *Application fee:* $50. Electronic applications accepted. *Application Contact:* Thomas M. Shea, Director of Graduate Admissions, 321-674-7577, Fax: 321-723-9468, E-mail: tshea@fit.edu. *Dean*, Dr. Thomas Waite, 321-674-8020, Fax: 321-674-7270, E-mail: twaite@fit.edu.

College of Psychology and Liberal Arts Students: 179 full-time (144 women), 21 part-time (12 women); includes 33 minority (9 African Americans, 1 American Indian/Alaska Native, 6 Asian Americans or Pacific Islanders, 17 Hispanic Americans), 14 international. Average age 28. 376 applicants, 49% accepted, 72 enrolled. *Faculty:* 24 full-time (9 women), 9 part-time/adjunct (3 women). Expenses: Contact institution. *Financial support:* In 2008–09, 23 students received support, including 19 research assistantships with full and partial tuition reimbursements available (averaging $2,750 per year), 4 teaching assistantships with full and partial tuition reimbursements available (averaging $4,001 per year); career-related internships or fieldwork, institutionally sponsored loans, tuition waivers (partial), unspecified assistantships, and tuition remissions also available. Support available to part-time students. Financial award application deadline: 3/1. In 2008, 76 master's, 20 doctorates awarded. *Degree program information:* Part-time programs available. Offers applied behavior analysis (MS); clinical psychology (Psy D); communication (MS); humanities and communication (MS); industrial/organizational psychology (MS, PhD); psychology (MS, PhD, Psy D). *Application deadline:* Applications are processed on a rolling basis. *Application fee:* $50. Electronic applications accepted. *Application Contact:* Thomas M. Shea, Director of Graduate Admissions, 321-674-7577, Fax: 321-723-9468, E-mail: tshea@fit.edu. *Dean*, Dr. Mary Beth Kenkel, 321-674-8142, Fax: 321-674-7105, E-mail: mkenkel@fit.edu.

College of Science Students: 161 full-time (75 women), 73 part-time (33 women); includes 22 minority (8 African Americans, 4 Asian Americans or Pacific Islanders, 10 Hispanic Americans), 85 international. Average age 31. 385 applicants, 39% accepted, 58 enrolled. *Faculty:* 51 full-time (7 women), 5 part-time/adjunct (2 women). Expenses: Contact institution. *Financial support:* In 2008–09, 96 students received support, including 31 research assistantships with full and partial tuition reimbursements available (averaging $13,133 per year), 65 teaching assistantships with full and partial tuition reimbursements available (averaging $10,758 per year); fellowships with full and partial tuition reimbursements available, career-related internships or fieldwork, institutionally sponsored loans, tuition waivers (partial), unspecified assistantships, and tuition remissions also available. Support available to part-time students. Financial award application deadline: 3/1; financial award applicants required to submit FAFSA. In 2008, 28 master's, 15 doctorates, 1 other advanced degree awarded. *Degree program information:* Part-time and evening/weekend programs available. Offers applied mathematics (MS, PhD); biological sciences (PhD); biotechnology (MS); cell and molecular biology (MS, PhD); chemistry (MS, PhD); computer education (MS); ecology (MS); elementary science education (M Ed); environmental education (MS); informal science education (M Ed); marine biology (MS); mathematics education (MS, Ed D, PhD, Ed S); operations research (MS, PhD); physics (MS, PhD); science (M Ed, MAT, MS, Ed D, PhD, Ed S); science education (MS, Ed D, PhD, Ed S); space sciences (MS, PhD); teaching (MAT). *Application deadline:* Applications are processed on a rolling basis. *Application fee:* $50. Electronic applications accepted. *Application Contact:* Thomas M. Shea, Director of Graduate Admissions, 321-674-7577, Fax: 321-723-9468, E-mail: tshea@fit.edu. *Dean*, Dr. Gordon L. Nelson, 321-674-7260, Fax: 321-674-8864, E-mail: nelson@fit.edu.

University College Students: 84 full-time (38 women), 1,052 part-time (485 women); includes 351 minority (236 African Americans, 13 American Indian/Alaska Native, 50 Asian Americans or Pacific Islanders, 52 Hispanic Americans), 22 international. Average age 36. 484 applicants, 51% accepted, 337 enrolled. *Faculty:* 9 full-time (3 women), 110 part-time/adjunct (18 women). Expenses: Contact institution. *Financial support:* Institutionally sponsored loans available. Financial award application deadline: 3/1; financial award applicants required to submit FAFSA. In 2008, 521 master's awarded. *Degree program information:* Part-time and evening/weekend programs available. Postbaccalaureate distance learning degree programs offered (no on-campus study). Offers acquisition and contract management (MS, PMBA); aerospace engineering (MS); business administration (PMBA); computer information systems (MS); computer science (PMBA); e-business (PMBA); electrical engineering (MS); engineering management (MS); human resource management (PMBA); human resources management (MS); information systems (PMBA); information technology (MS); logistics management (MS); management (MS); materiel acquisition management (MS); mechanical engineering (MS); operations research (MS); project management (MS); public administration (MPA); quality management (MS); software engineering (MS); space systems (MS); space systems management (MS); systems management (MS). *Application deadline:* Applications are processed on a rolling basis. *Application fee:* $50. Electronic applications accepted. *Application Contact:* Carolyn Farrior, Director of Graduate Admissions Online Learning and Off Campus Programs, 321-674-7375, Fax: 321-674-8216, E-mail: cfarrior@fit.edu. *Dean*, Dr. Clifford Bragdon, 321-674-8821, Fax: 321-674-7597, E-mail: cbragdon@fit.edu.

See Close-Up on page 913.

FLORIDA INTERNATIONAL UNIVERSITY, Miami, FL 33199

General Information State-supported, coed, university. CGS member. *Enrollment by degree level:* 533 first professional, 4,982 master's, 1,139 doctoral. *Graduate faculty:* 859 full-time (315 women), 16 part-time/adjunct (4 women). Tuition, state resident: full-time $7167; part-time $298.64 per credit hour. Tuition, nonresident: full-time $19,265; part-time $802.71 per credit hour. *Required fees:* $319 per semester. *Graduate housing:* Rooms and/or apartments available on a first-come, first-served basis to single and married students. Typical cost: $11,120 (including board) for single students; $11,120 (including board) for married students. Room and board charges vary according to housing facility selected. *Student services:* Campus employment opportunities, campus safety program, career counseling, child daycare facilities, exercise/wellness program, free psychological counseling, international student services, low-cost health insurance, multicultural affairs office, services for students with disabilities. *Library facilities:* University Park Library plus 2 others. *Online resources:* library catalog, web page, access to other libraries' catalogs. *Collection:* 2 million titles, 40,813 serial subscriptions, 159,978 audiovisual materials. *Research affiliation:* Montgomery Watson (environmental engineering), Fairchild Tropical Botanic Garden (architecture/biology), Lockheed Martin (engineering), Innovia, LLCa (biomedical engineering), Boeing Company (mechanical engineering/industrial and systems engineering), American Heart Association (biomedical engineering).

Computer facilities: A campuswide network can be accessed from student residence rooms and from off campus. Online class registration, online financial aid and cashier's information are available. *Web address:* http://www.fiu.edu/.

General Application Contact: Nanett Rojas, Assistant Director of Graduate Admissions, 305-348-7442, Fax: 305-348-7441, E-mail: gradadm@fiu.edu.

GRADUATE UNITS

Alvah H. Chapman, Jr. Graduate School of Business Students: 670 full-time (352 women), 477 part-time (215 women); includes 660 minority (85 African Americans, 1 American Indian/Alaska Native, 48 Asian Americans or Pacific Islanders, 526 Hispanic Americans), 307 international. Average age 32. 1,499 applicants, 47% accepted, 507 enrolled. *Faculty:* 81 full-time (25 women). Expenses: Contact institution. *Financial support:* Fellowships, research assistantships, teaching assistantships, Federal Work-Study, institutionally sponsored loans, and scholarships/grants available. Financial award application deadline: 3/1; financial award applicants required to submit FAFSA. In 2008, 672 master's, 8 doctorates awarded. *Degree program information:* Part-time and evening/weekend programs available. Offers business (EMBA, IMBA, M Acc, MBA, MIB, MIS, MSF, MSHRM, MSRE, MST, PhD); business administration (EMBA, IMBA, MBA, PhD); decision sciences and information systems (MIS); finance (MSF); human resources management (MSHRM); international business (MIB); real estate (MSRE). *Application deadline:* For fall admission, 6/1 for domestic students, 4/1 for international students; for spring admission, 10/1 for domestic students, 9/1 for international students. Applications are processed on a rolling basis. *Application fee:* $30. Electronic applications accepted. *Application Contact:* Nanett Rojas, Coordinator of Graduate Admissions, 305-348-7442, Fax: 305-348-7441, E-mail: gradadm@fiu.edu. *Associate Director, Chapman Graduate School Admissions*, Anna M Pietraszek, 305-348-7299, Fax: 305-348-2368, E-mail: anna.pietraszek@fiu.edu.

School of Accounting Students: 70 full-time (42 women), 25 part-time (19 women); includes 81 minority (15 African Americans, 6 Asian Americans or Pacific Islanders, 60 Hispanic Americans), 1 international. Average age 29. 163 applicants, 59% accepted, 71 enrolled. *Faculty:* 20 full-time (6 women). Expenses: Contact institution. *Financial support:* Institutionally sponsored loans and scholarships/grants available. Financial award application deadline: 3/1; financial award applicants required to submit FAFSA. In 2008, 133 master's awarded. *Degree program information:* Part-time and evening/weekend programs available. Offers accounting (M Acc); taxation (MST). *Application deadline:* For fall admission, 6/1 for domestic students, 4/1 for international students; for spring admission, 10/1 for domestic students, 9/1 for international students. Applications are processed on a rolling basis. *Application fee:* $30. Electronic applications accepted. *Application Contact:* Dr. Sharon Lassar, Director, 305-348-3501, Fax: 305-348-2914, E-mail: Sharon.Lassar@fiu.edu. *Director*, Dr. Sharon Lassar, 305-348-3501, Fax: 305-348-2914, E-mail: Sharon.Lassar@fiu.edu.

College of Architecture and the Arts Students: 143 full-time (78 women), 40 part-time (23 women); includes 108 minority (14 African Americans, 3 Asian Americans or Pacific Islanders, 91 Hispanic Americans), 13 international. Average age 31. 237 applicants, 43% accepted, 53 enrolled. *Faculty:* 63 full-time (21 women). Expenses: Contact institution. *Financial support:* Application deadline: 3/1. In 2008, 61 master's awarded. *Degree program information:* Part-time and evening/weekend programs available. Offers architecture and the arts (M Arch, MFA, MID, MLA, MM, MS). *Application deadline:* For fall admission, 4/1 for domestic and international students; for spring admission, 10/1 for domestic students, 9/1 for international students. Applications are processed on a rolling basis. *Application fee:* $30. Electronic applications accepted. *Application Contact:* Nanett Rojas, Assistant Director of Graduate Admissions, 305-348-7442, Fax: 305-348-7441, E-mail: gradadm@fiu.edu. *Acting Dean*, Dr. Brian Schriner, 305-348-3181, Fax: 305-348-6716, E-mail: Brian.Schriner@fiu.edu.

School of Architecture Students: 111 full-time (64 women), 20 part-time (14 women); includes 80 minority (11 African Americans, 2 Asian Americans or Pacific Islanders, 67 Hispanic Americans), 7 international. Average age 30. 177 applicants, 41% accepted, 40 enrolled. *Faculty:* 14 full-time (5 women). Expenses: Contact institution. *Financial support:* Research assistantships, teaching assistantships, institutionally sponsored loans and scholarships/grants available. Financial award application deadline: 3/1; financial award applicants required to submit FAFSA. In 2008, 33 master's awarded. *Degree program information:* Part-time and evening/weekend programs available. Offers architecture (M Arch, MID, MLA); interior design (MID); landscape architecture (MLA). *Application deadline:* For fall admission, 2/1 for domestic and international students. *Application fee:* $30. Electronic applications accepted. *Application Contact:* Nanett Rojas, Assistant Director of Graduate Admissions, 305-348-7441, Fax: 305-348-7442, E-mail: gradadm@fiu.edu. *Interim Dean*, Prof. Brian Schriner, 305-348-6442, Fax: 305-348-2650, E-mail: SCHRINER@fiu.edu.

School of Art and Art History Students: 8 full-time (5 women); includes 3 minority (all Hispanic Americans). Average age 31. 22 applicants, 18% accepted, 4 enrolled. *Faculty:* 13 full-time (6 women). Expenses: Contact institution. *Financial support:* Teaching assistantships, scholarships/grants and traineeships available. Financial award application deadline: 3/1; financial award applicants required to submit FAFSA. In 2008, 9 master's awarded. *Degree program information:* Part-time programs available. Offers visual arts (MFA). *Application deadline:* For fall admission, 2/15 for domestic and international students. *Application fee:* $30. Electronic applications accepted. *Application Contact:* Susie Novoa, Graduate Secretary, 305-348-2897, Fax: 305-348-0513, E-mail: susan.novoa@fiu.edu. *Interim Dean*, Prof. Brian Schriner, 305-348-6442, Fax: 305-348-2650, E-mail: schriner@fiu.edu.

School of Music Students: 24 full-time (9 women), 20 part-time (9 women); includes 25 minority (3 African Americans, 1 Asian American or Pacific Islander, 21 Hispanic Americans), 6 international. Average age 33. 38 applicants, 63% accepted, 9 enrolled. *Faculty:* 21 full-time (5 women). Expenses: Contact institution. *Financial support:* Teaching assistantships, institutionally sponsored loans and scholarships/grants available. Financial award application deadline: 3/1; financial award applicants required to submit FAFSA. In 2008, 19 master's awarded. *Degree program information:* Part-time and evening/weekend programs available. Offers music (MM); music education (MS). *Application deadline:* For fall admission, 6/1 for domestic students, 4/1 for international students; for spring admission, 10/1 for domestic students, 9/1 for international students. Applications are processed on a rolling basis. *Application fee:* $30. *Application Contact:* Nanett Rojas, Assistant Director of Graduate Admissions, 305-348-7442, Fax: 305-348-7441, E-mail: gradadm@fiu.edu. *Director*, Kathleen Wilson, 305-348-2896, Fax: 305-348-4073, E-mail: kathleen.wilson@fiu.edu.

College of Arts and Sciences Students: 688 full-time (403 women), 541 part-time (323 women); includes 635 minority (155 African Americans, 1 American Indian/Alaska Native, 43 Asian Americans or Pacific Islanders, 436 Hispanic Americans), 209 international. Average age 32. 962 applicants, 45% accepted, 264 enrolled. *Faculty:* 359 full-time (121 women), 6 part-time/adjunct (1 woman). Expenses: Contact institution. *Financial support:* Fellowships, research assistantships, teaching assistantships, career-related internships or fieldwork, Federal Work-Study, institutionally sponsored loans, and scholarships/grants available. Financial award application deadline: 3/1; financial award applicants required to submit FAFSA. In 2008, 300 master's, 41 doctorates awarded. *Degree program information:* Part-time and evening/weekend programs available. Offers African-new world studies (MA); arts and sciences (MA, MFA, MPA, MS, PhD); Asian studies (MA); biology (MS, PhD); chemistry (MS, PhD); comparative sociology (MA, PhD); creative writing (MFA); criminal justice (MS); earth sciences (MS, PhD); economics (MA, PhD); English (MA, MFA); environmental studies (MS); forensic science (MS); history (MA, PhD); international relations (MA, PhD); Latin American and

Caribbean studies (MA); liberal studies (MA); linguistics (MA); mathematical sciences (MS); physics (MS, PhD); political science (MS, PhD); psychology (MS, PhD); public administration (MPA, PhD); religious studies (MA); Spanish (MA, PhD); statistics (MS). *Application deadline:* For fall admission, 6/1 for domestic students, 4/1 for international students; for spring admission, 10/1 for domestic students, 9/1 for international students. Applications are processed on a rolling basis. *Application fee:* $30. Electronic applications accepted. *Application Contact:* Nanett Rojas, Assistant Director of Graduate Admissions, 305-348-7442, Fax: 305-348-7441, E-mail: gradadm@fiu.edu. *Dean,* Dr. Kenneth Furton, 305-348-2864, Fax: 305-348-4172, E-mail: furtonk@fiu.edu.

College of Education *Degree program information:* Part-time and evening/weekend programs available. Offers adult education (MS); adult education in human resource development (Ed D); advanced athletic injury training/sports medicine (MS); advanced teacher preparation (MS); art education (MAT, MS, Ed D); conflict resolution and consensus building (Certificate); counselor education (MS); curriculum and instruction (Ed S); curriculum development (MS); curriculum studies (PhD); early childhood education (MS, Ed D); education (MA, MAT, MS, Ed D, PhD, Certificate, Ed S); educational administration and supervision (Ed D); educational leadership (MS, Certificate, Ed S); elementary education (MS, Ed D); English education (MAT, MS, Ed D); exceptional student education (MS, Ed D); exercise and sports science (MS); foreign language education (Certificate); foreign language education—teaching English to speakers of other languages (TESOL) (Certificate); foreign language education- teaching English to speakers of other languages (TESOL) (MS); French education—initial teacher preparation (MAT); higher education (Ed D); higher education administration (MS); human resource development (MS); international and intercultural development education (Ed D); international and intercultural developmental education (MS); language, literacy and culture (PhD); learning technologies (MS, Ed D, PhD); leisure services (MS); mathematics education (MAT, MS, Ed D, PhD); mental health counseling (MS); modern language education/bilingual education (MS, Ed D); parks and recreation management (MS); physical education (MS); reading education (MS, Ed D); rehabilitation counseling (MS); school counseling (MS); school psychology (Ed S); science education (MAT, MS, Ed D, PhD); social studies education (MAT, MS, Ed D); Spanish education—initial teacher preparation (MAT); special education (MS); sports management (MS); strength and conditioning (MS); teaching English (MS); therapeutic recreation (MS); urban education (MS). Electronic applications accepted.

College of Engineering and Computing Students: 458 full-time (111 women), 305 part-time (56 women); includes 303 minority (51 African Americans, 1 American Indian/Alaska Native, 44 Asian Americans or Pacific Islanders, 207 Hispanic Americans), 370 international. Average age 30. 1,240 applicants, 46% accepted, 184 enrolled. *Faculty:* 90 full-time (8 women), 1 part-time/adjunct (0 women). Expenses: Contact institution. *Financial support:* Fellowships, research assistantships, teaching assistantships, career-related internships or fieldwork, Federal Work-Study, institutionally sponsored loans, and scholarships/grants available. Financial award application deadline: 3/1; financial award applicants required to submit FAFSA. In 2008, 268 master's, 43 doctorates awarded. *Degree program information:* Part-time and evening/weekend programs available. Postbaccalaureate distance learning degree programs offered. Offers biomedical engineering (MS, PhD); civil engineering (MS, PhD); computer engineering (MS); construction management (MS); electrical engineering (MS, PhD); engineering and computing (MS, PhD); environmental engineering (MS); materials science and engineering (MS, PhD); mechanical engineering (MS, PhD); telecommunications and networking (MS). *Application deadline:* For fall admission, 6/1 for domestic students, 4/1 for international students; for spring admission, 10/1 for domestic students, 9/1 for international students. Applications are processed on a rolling basis. *Application fee:* $30. Electronic applications accepted. *Application Contact:* Nanett Rojas, Assistant Director of Graduate Admissions, 305-348-7442, Fax: 305-348-7441, E-mail: gradadm@fiu.edu. *Dean,* Dr. Amir Mirmiran, 305-348-2522, Fax: 305-348-1401, E-mail: amir.mirmiran@fiu.edu.

School of Computing and Information Sciences Students: 73 full-time (23 women), 45 part-time (6 women); includes 38 minority (1 African American, 5 Asian Americans or Pacific Islanders, 32 Hispanic Americans), 64 international. Average age 29. 204 applicants, 41% accepted, 21 enrolled. *Faculty:* 25 full-time (2 women), 1 part-time/adjunct (0 women). Expenses: Contact institution. *Financial support:* Fellowships, research assistantships, teaching assistantships, institutionally sponsored loans and scholarships/grants available. Financial award application deadline: 3/1; financial award applicants required to submit FAFSA. In 2008, 28 master's, 8 doctorates awarded. *Degree program information:* Part-time and evening/weekend programs available. Offers computing and information sciences (MS, PhD). *Application deadline:* For fall admission, 6/1 for domestic students, 4/1 for international students; for spring admission, 10/1 for domestic students, 9/1 for international students. Applications are processed on a rolling basis. *Application fee:* $30. Electronic applications accepted. *Application Contact:* Maria Parrilla, Graduate Admissions Assistant, 305-348-1890, Fax: 305-348-6142, E-mail: grad_eng@fiu.edu. *Director,* Dr. Yi Deng, 305-348-2744, Fax: 305-348-3549, E-mail: yi.deng@fiu.edu.

College of Law Students: 520 full-time (242 women), 13 part-time (5 women); includes 46 African Americans, 11 Asian Americans or Pacific Islanders, 237 Hispanic Americans, 4 international. Average age 32. 2,549 applicants, 26% accepted, 217 enrolled. *Faculty:* 28 full-time (14 women). Expenses: Contact institution. *Financial support:* Scholarships/grants and loans available. Financial award application deadline: 3/1; financial award applicants required to submit FAFSA. In 2008, 90 JDs awarded. *Degree program information:* Part-time programs available. Offers law (JD). *Application deadline:* For fall admission, 5/1 for domestic and international students. *Application fee:* $20. Electronic applications accepted. *Application Contact:* Alma Miro, Director of Admissions and Financial Aid, 305-348-8006, Fax: 305-348-2965, E-mail: lawadmit@fiu.edu. *Dean,* Dr. Leonard Strickman, 305-348-1118, Fax: 305-348-1159, E-mail: leonard.strickman@fiu.edu.

College of Nursing and Health Sciences Students: 475 full-time (370 women), 197 part-time (158 women); includes 479 minority (97 African Americans, 42 Asian Americans or Pacific Islanders, 340 Hispanic Americans), 10 international. Average age 34. 755 applicants, 31% accepted, 203 enrolled. *Faculty:* 51 full-time (42 women), 1 (woman) part-time/adjunct. Expenses: Contact institution. *Financial support:* Fellowships, research assistantships, teaching assistantships, career-related internships or fieldwork, Federal Work-Study, institutionally sponsored loans, and scholarships/grants available. Financial award application deadline: 3/1; financial award applicants required to submit FAFSA. In 2008, 211 master's, 1 doctorate awarded. *Degree program information:* Part-time and evening/weekend programs available. Offers nursing (MSN, PhD); nursing and health sciences (MS, MSN, DPT, PhD); occupational therapy (MS); physical therapy (DPT); speech-language pathology (MS). *Application deadline:* For fall admission, 6/1 for domestic students, 4/1 for international students; for spring admission, 10/1 for domestic students, 9/1 for international students. Applications are processed on a rolling basis. *Application fee:* $30. Electronic applications accepted. *Application Contact:* Nanett Rojas, Assistant Director of Graduate Admissions, 305-348-7441, Fax: 305-348-7442, E-mail: gradadm@fiu.edu. *Dean,* Dr. Divina Grossman, 305-348-7703, Fax: 305-348-7764, E-mail: divina.grossman@fiu.edu.

School of Hospitality and Tourism Management Students: 112 full-time (87 women), 58 part-time (28 women); includes 61 minority (19 African Americans, 1 American Indian/Alaska Native, 7 Asian Americans or Pacific Islanders, 34 Hispanic Americans), 75 international. Average age 31. 186 applicants, 54% accepted, 62 enrolled. *Faculty:* 12 full-time (4 women), 1 part-time/adjunct (0 women). Expenses: Contact institution. *Financial support:* Teaching assistantships, scholarships/grants available. Financial award application deadline: 3/1; financial award applicants required to submit FAFSA. In 2008, 60 master's awarded. *Degree program information:* Evening/weekend programs available. Postbaccalaureate distance learning degree programs offered. Offers hospitality and tourism management (MS); hospitality management (MS). *Application deadline:* For fall admission, 6/1 for domestic students, 4/1 for international students; for spring admission, 10/1 for domestic students, 9/1 for international students. Applications are processed on a rolling basis. *Application fee:* $30. Electronic applications accepted. *Application Contact:* Nanett Rojas, Coordinator of Graduate Admissions, 305-348-7442, Fax: 305-348-7441, E-mail: gradadm@fiu.edu. *Dean,* Dr. Joseph West, 305-919-4500, Fax: 305-919-4555, E-mail: jwest@fiu.edu.

School of Journalism and Mass Communication Students: 61 full-time (47 women), 58 part-time (46 women); includes 88 minority (15 African Americans, 7 Asian Americans or Pacific Islanders, 66 Hispanic Americans), 15 international. Average age 29. 110 applicants, 71% accepted, 54 enrolled. *Faculty:* 20 full-time (12 women). Expenses: Contact institution. *Financial support:* Institutionally sponsored loans, scholarships/grants, and unspecified assistantships available. Financial award application deadline: 3/1; financial award applicants required to submit FAFSA. In 2008, 53 master's awarded. *Degree program information:* Part-time and evening/weekend programs available. Offers mass communication (MS). *Application deadline:* For fall admission, 6/1 for domestic students, 4/1 for international students; for spring admission, 10/1 for domestic students, 9/1 for international students. Applications are processed on a rolling basis. *Application fee:* $30. Electronic applications accepted. *Application Contact:* Nanett Rojas, Assistant Director of Graduate Admissions, 305-348-7442, Fax: 305-348-7441, E-mail: gradadm@fiu.edu. *Dean,* Dr. Lillian Kopenhaver, 305-919-5674, Fax: 305-919-5203, E-mail: kopenha@fiu.edu.

Stempel College of Public Health and Social Work Students: 394 full-time (317 women), 262 part-time (210 women); includes 459 minority (197 African Americans, 34 Asian Americans or Pacific Islanders, 228 Hispanic Americans), 77 international. Average age 33. 671 applicants, 61% accepted, 220 enrolled. *Faculty:* 43 full-time (22 women). Expenses: Contact institution. *Financial support:* Fellowships, research assistantships, teaching assistantships, institutionally sponsored loans, scholarships/grants, and unspecified assistantships available. Financial award application deadline: 3/1; financial award applicants required to submit FAFSA. In 2008, 209 master's, 12 doctorates awarded. Offers biostatistics (MPH); community nutrition (MPH, PhD); dietetics and nutrition (MS, PhD); environmental and occupational health (MPH, PhD); epidemiology (MPH, PhD); general public health (MPH); health policy and management (MPH); health promotion and disease prevention (PhD); health promotion and diseases prevention (MPH); public health and social work (MHSA, MPH, MS, MSW, PhD). *Application deadline:* For fall admission, 6/1 for domestic students, 4/1 for international students; for spring admission, 10/1 for domestic students, 9/1 for international students. Applications are processed on a rolling basis. *Application fee:* $30. Electronic applications accepted. *Application Contact:* Nanett Rojas, Assistant Director of Graduate Admissions, 305-348-7442, Fax: 305-348-7441, E-mail: gradadm@fiu.edu. *Interim Dean,* Dr. Fernando Trevino, 305-348-4903, Fax: 305-348-4901, E-mail: phadvise@fiu.edu.

School of Social Work Students: 107 full-time (102 women), 70 part-time (60 women); includes 153 minority (61 African Americans, 4 Asian Americans or Pacific Islanders, 88 Hispanic Americans), 3 international. Average age 34. 129 applicants, 50% accepted, 46 enrolled. *Faculty:* 13 full-time (9 women). Expenses: Contact institution. *Financial support:* Fellowships, research assistantships, teaching assistantships, institutionally sponsored loans and scholarships/grants available. Financial award application deadline: 3/1; financial award applicants required to submit FAFSA. In 2008, 114 master's, 8 doctorates awarded. *Degree program information:* Part-time and evening/weekend programs available. Offers social work (MSW, PhD). *Application deadline:* For fall admission, 6/1 for domestic students, 4/1 for international students; for spring admission, 10/1 for domestic students, 9/1 for international students. Applications are processed on a rolling basis. *Application fee:* $30. Electronic applications accepted. *Application Contact:* Nanett Rojas, Assistant Director of Graduate Admissions, 305-348-7442, Fax: 305-348-7441, E-mail: gradadm@fiu.edu. *Director,* Dr. Paul Stuart, 305-348-5880, Fax: 305-348-5312, E-mail: paul.stuart@fiu.edu.

See Close-Up on page 915.

FLORIDA SOUTHERN COLLEGE, Lakeland, FL 33801-5698

General Information Independent-religious, coed, comprehensive institution. *Enrollment:* 1,874 graduate, professional, and undergraduate students; 5 full-time matriculated graduate/professional students (3 women), 103 part-time matriculated graduate/professional students (77 women). *Enrollment by degree level:* 108 master's. *Graduate faculty:* 12 full-time (5 women), 4 part-time/adjunct (3 women). *Graduate housing:* On-campus housing not available. *Student services:* Campus employment opportunities, campus safety program, career counseling, exercise/wellness program, free psychological counseling, international student services, multicultural affairs office, services for students with disabilities, teacher training. *Library facilities:* Roux Library. *Online resources:* library catalog, web page. *Collection:* 166,595 titles, 31,092 serial subscriptions, 9,936 audiovisual materials.

Computer facilities: Computer purchase and lease plans are available. 382 computers available on campus for general student use. A campuswide network can be accessed from student residence rooms and from off campus. Online class registration, campus portal are available. *Web address:* http://www.flsouthern.edu/.

General Application Contact: Craig Story, Evening Program Director, 863-680-4205, Fax: 863-680-3872, E-mail: cstory@flsouthern.edu.

GRADUATE UNITS

Program in Business Administration *Degree program information:* Part-time and evening/weekend programs available. Offers accounting (MBA); business administration (MBA); international business (MBA).

Program in Nursing *Degree program information:* Part-time and evening/weekend programs available. Offers nursing (MSN).

Programs in Teaching *Degree program information:* Part-time and evening/weekend programs available. Offers teaching (MAT); teaching and learning (M Ed).

FLORIDA STATE UNIVERSITY, Tallahassee, FL 32306

General Information State-supported, coed, university. CGS member. *Enrollment:* 38,682 graduate, professional, and undergraduate students; 5,651 full-time matriculated graduate/professional students (2,943 women), 2,725 part-time matriculated graduate/professional students (1,734 women). *Enrollment by degree level:* 1,172 first professional, 4,518 master's, 2,597 doctoral, 83 other advanced degrees. *Graduate faculty:* 1,179 full-time (415 women), 176 part-time/adjunct (86 women). Tuition, state resident: full-time $5537.52. Tuition, nonresident: full-time $14,432. One-time fee: $20 full-time. *Graduate housing:* Rooms and/or apartments available on a first-come, first-served basis to single students and available to married students. *Student services:* Campus employment opportunities, campus safety program, career counseling, child daycare facilities, exercise/wellness program, free psychological counseling, grant writing training, international student services, low-cost health insurance, multicultural affairs office, services for students with disabilities, teacher training, writing training. *Library facilities:* Robert Manning Strozier Library. *Online resources:* access to other libraries' catalogs. *Research affiliation:* Center for the Study of Southern Culture and Religion, Southeastern Archaeological Studies, Fermi National Accelerator Laboratory, National Center for Atmospheric Research.

Computer facilities: 3,821 computers available on campus for general student use. A campuswide network can be accessed from student residence rooms and from off campus. Online class registration, course home pages, course search, online fee payment are available. *Web address:* http://www.fsu.edu/.

General Application Contact: Melanie Booker, Associate Director for Graduate Admissions, 850-644-3420, Fax: 850-644-0197, E-mail: mbooker@admin.fsu.edu.

GRADUATE UNITS

College of Law Students: 772 full-time (318 women); includes 123 minority (54 African Americans, 4 American Indian/Alaska Native, 19 Asian Americans or Pacific Islanders, 46 Hispanic Americans), 5 international. Average age 24. 3,013 applicants, 33% accepted, 251 enrolled. *Faculty:* 42 full-time (18 women), 27 part-time/adjunct (8 women). Expenses: Contact institution. *Financial support:* In 2008–09, 289 fellowships (averaging $2,000 per year), 58 research assistantships (averaging $3,300 per year), 12 teaching assistantships (averaging $1,034 per year) were awarded; scholarships/grants also available. Financial award application deadline: 4/1; financial award applicants required to submit FAFSA. In 2008, 314 JDs awarded. Offers law (JD, LL M). *Application deadline:* For fall admission, 4/1 priority date for domestic students. Applications are processed on a rolling basis. *Application fee:* $30. Electronic applications accepted. *Application Contact:* Jennifer L. Kessinger, Director of Admissions and Records, 850-644-3787, Fax: 850-644-7284, E-mail: jkessing@law.fsu.edu. *Dean,* Donald J. Weidner, 850-644-3400, Fax: 850-644-5487, E-mail: dweidner@law.fsu.edu.

College of Medicine Students: 357 full-time (213 women), 1 (woman) part-time; includes 123 minority (46 African Americans, 3 American Indian/Alaska Native, 42 Asian Americans or Pacific Islanders, 32 Hispanic Americans). Average age 25. 1,505 applicants, 15% accepted,

Florida State University (continued)

120 enrolled. *Faculty:* 105 full-time (32 women), 568 part-time/adjunct (122 women). Expenses: Contact institution. *Financial support:* In 2008–09, 156 students received support, including 2 fellowships (averaging $5,000 per year), 18 research assistantships with full tuition reimbursements available (averaging $21,500 per year); scholarships/grants also available. Financial award application deadline: 7/1; financial award applicants required to submit FAFSA. In 2008, 48 first professional degrees awarded. Offers biomedical sciences (PhD); medicine (MD). *Application deadline:* For fall admission, 12/1 for domestic students. Applications are processed on a rolling basis. *Application fee:* $30. Electronic applications accepted. *Application Contact:* Admissions Coordinator, 850-644-7904, Fax: 850-645-2846, E-mail: medadmissions@med.fsu.edu. *Dean*, Dr. J. Ocie Harris, 850-644-1855, Fax: 850-645-1420, E-mail: ocie.harris@med.fsu.edu.

The Graduate School Students: 4,470 full-time (2,382 women), 2,709 part-time (1,728 women); includes 1,288 minority (623 African Americans, 46 American Indian/Alaska Native, 206 Asian Americans or Pacific Islanders, 413 Hispanic Americans), 973 international. Average age 31. 7,519 applicants, 46% accepted. *Faculty:* 1,066 full-time (370 women), 111 part-time/adjunct (66 women). Expenses: Contact institution. *Financial support:* Fellowships, research assistantships, teaching assistantships, career-related internships or fieldwork, Federal Work-Study, institutionally sponsored loans, scholarships/grants, traineeships, health care benefits, tuition waivers (partial), and unspecified assistantships available. Support available to part-time students. Financial award applicants required to submit FAFSA. In 2008, 2,079 master's, 337 doctorates, 54 other advanced degrees awarded. *Degree program information:* Part-time and evening/weekend programs available. Offers computational materials science and mechanics (MS); functional materials (MS); nanoscale materials, composite materials, and interfaces (MS); polymers and bio-inspired materials (MS). *Application deadline:* For fall admission, 7/1 for domestic and international students. *Application fee:* $30. Electronic applications accepted. *Application Contact:* Melanie Booker, Associate Director for Graduate Admissions, 850-644-3420, Fax: 850-644-0197, E-mail: mbooker@admin.fsu.edu. *Dean, The Graduate School*, Dr. Nancy Marcus, 850-644-3500, Fax: 850-644-2969, E-mail: nmarcus@fsu.edu.

College of Arts and Sciences Students: 1,505 full-time (650 women), 234 part-time (115 women); includes 239 minority (81 African Americans, 10 American Indian/Alaska Native, 50 Asian Americans or Pacific Islanders, 98 Hispanic Americans), 387 international. Average age 31. *Faculty:* 458 full-time (118 women). Expenses: Contact institution. *Financial support:* Fellowships, research assistantships, teaching assistantships, career-related internships or fieldwork, institutionally sponsored loans, scholarships/grants, traineeships, and unspecified assistantships available. Support available to part-time students. Financial award applicants required to submit FAFSA. In 2008, 267 master's, 142 doctorates awarded. *Degree program information:* Part-time programs available. Offers American and Florida studies (MA, Certificate); analytical chemistry (MS, PhD); anthropology (MA, MS, PhD); applied behavior analysis (MS); applied computational mathematics (MS, PhD); applied statistics (MS); arts and sciences (MA, MFA, MS, PhD, Certificate); biochemistry (MS, PhD); biochemistry, molecular and cell biology (PhD); biomedical mathematics (MS, PhD); biostatistics (MS, PhD); cell and molecular biology and genetics (MS, PhD); classical archaeology (MA); classical civilization (MA); classics (MA, PhD); clinical psychology (PhD); cognitive psychology (PhD); computational structural biology (PhD); computer science (MS, PhD); creative writing (MFA); developmental psychology (PhD); ecology and evolutionary biology (MS, PhD); English (PhD); financial mathematics (MS, PhD); French (MA, PhD); geological sciences (MS, PhD); geophysical fluid dynamics (PhD); German (MA); Greek (MA); Greek and Latin (MA); historical administration (MA); history (MA, PhD); history and philosophy of science (MA); humanities (PhD); information security (MS); inorganic chemistry (MS, PhD); interdisciplinary humanities (PhD); Italian (MA); Italian studies (MA); Latin (MA); literature (MA); mathematical statistics (MS, PhD); meteorology (MS, PhD); molecular biophysics (PhD); neuroscience (PhD); oceanography (MS, PhD); organic chemistry (MS, PhD); philosophy (MA, PhD); physical chemistry (MS, PhD); physics (MS, PhD); pure mathematics (MS, PhD); religion (MA, PhD); rhetoric and composition (MA); Slavic languages and literatures (MA); Slavic languages/Russian (MA); social psychology (PhD); software engineering (MS); Spanish (MA, PhD). *Application fee:* $30. *Application Contact:* Ginger Martin, Senior Academic Coordinator, 850-644-1081, Fax: 850-644-9656, E-mail: vmartin@fsu.edu. *Dean*, Dr. Joseph Travis, 850-644-1081.

College of Business Students: 249 full-time (106 women), 446 part-time (158 women); includes 135 minority (55 African Americans, 7 American Indian/Alaska Native, 31 Asian Americans or Pacific Islanders, 42 Hispanic Americans), 55 international. Average age 30. 696 applicants, 54% accepted, 269 enrolled. *Faculty:* 101 full-time (22 women), 11 part-time/adjunct (2 women). Expenses: Contact institution. *Financial support:* In 2008–09, 102 students received support, including 32 fellowships with full tuition reimbursements available (averaging $6,900 per year), 30 research assistantships with full tuition reimbursements available (averaging $4,500 per year), 40 teaching assistantships with full tuition reimbursements available (averaging $11,500 per year); career-related internships or fieldwork, scholarships/grants, health care benefits, and unspecified assistantships also available. Support available to part-time students. Financial award application deadline: 1/1. In 2008, 268 master's, 17 doctorates awarded. *Degree program information:* Part-time programs available. Postbaccalaureate distance learning degree programs offered (no on-campus study). Offers accounting (M Acc); business administration (MBA, PhD); insurance (MSM); management information systems (MS). *Application deadline:* For fall admission, 5/1 for domestic and international students; for spring admission, 10/1 for domestic students, 9/1 for international students. Applications are processed on a rolling basis. *Application fee:* $30. Electronic applications accepted. *Application Contact:* Lisa Beverly, Director, Graduate Programs Admissions, 850-644-6458, Fax: 850-644-0588, E-mail: lbeverly@cob.fsu.edu. *Dean*, Dr. Caryn Beck-Dudley, 850-644-3090, Fax: 850-644-0915.

College of Communication Students: 193 full-time (155 women), 130 part-time (93 women); includes 79 minority (48 African Americans, 3 Asian Americans or Pacific Islanders, 28 Hispanic Americans), 31 international. Average age 25. 380 applicants, 64% accepted, 112 enrolled. *Faculty:* 42 full-time (21 women), 12 part-time/adjunct (10 women). Expenses: Contact institution. *Financial support:* In 2008–09, 87 students received support, including 2 fellowships with full tuition reimbursements available, 29 research assistantships with full and partial tuition reimbursements available, 56 teaching assistantships with full and partial tuition reimbursements available; career-related internships or fieldwork, Federal Work-Study, institutionally sponsored loans, tuition waivers (partial), and unspecified assistantships also available. Support available to part-time students. Financial award application deadline: 1/1; financial award applicants required to submit FAFSA. In 2008, 120 master's, 14 doctorates awarded. *Degree program information:* Part-time programs available. Offers communication (Adv M, MA, MS, PhD); communication sciences and disorders (Adv M, MS, PhD); corporate and public communication (MA, MS); integrated marketing communication (MA, MS); mass communication (PhD); media and communication studies (MA, MS); speech communication (PhD). *Application deadline:* For fall admission, 7/1 priority date for domestic students, 2/1 for international students; for winter admission, 3/1 priority date for domestic students; for spring admission, 11/1 priority date for domestic students. Applications are processed on a rolling basis. *Application fee:* $30. Electronic applications accepted. *Application Contact:* Dr. Barbara C. Robinson, Assistant Dean for Student Affairs, 850-644-9698, Fax: 850-644-0611, E-mail: dc.gradinfo@comm.fsu.edu. *Interim Dean*, Dr. Gary Heald, 850-644-9698, Fax: 850-644-0611.

College of Criminology and Criminal Justice Students: 81 full-time (40 women), 60 part-time (31 women); includes 23 minority (13 African Americans, 1 American Indian/Alaska Native, 4 Asian Americans or Pacific Islanders, 5 Hispanic Americans). 178 applicants, 51% accepted, 53 enrolled. *Faculty:* 20 full-time (3 women). Expenses: Contact institution. *Financial support:* In 2008–09, fellowships with full tuition reimbursements (averaging $18,000 per year), 21 research assistantships with full tuition reimbursements (averaging $14,500 per year), 3 teaching assistantships with full tuition reimbursements (averaging $14,500 per year) were awarded; institutionally sponsored loans, scholarships/grants, tuition waivers (partial), and unspecified assistantships also available. Financial award application deadline: 2/15; financial award applicants required to submit FAFSA. In 2008, 37 master's, 2 doctorates awarded. *Degree program information:* Part-time and evening/weekend programs available. Postbaccalaureate distance learning degree programs offered (no on-campus study). Offers criminology and criminal justice (MA, MSC, PhD). *Application deadline:* For fall admission, 7/1 for domestic and international students; for spring admission, 11/1 for domestic and international students. Applications are processed on a rolling basis. *Application fee:* $30. Electronic applications accepted. *Application Contact:* Margarita Frankeberger, Graduate Student Coordinator, 850-644-7373, Fax: 850-644-9614, E-mail: mfrankeberger@fsu.edu. *Dean*, Dr. Thomas Blomberg, 850-644-7365, Fax: 850-644-9614.

College of Education Students: 1,247; includes 355 minority (164 African Americans, 3 American Indian/Alaska Native, 125 Asian Americans or Pacific Islanders, 63 Hispanic Americans). 1,114 applicants, 52% accepted, 335 enrolled. *Faculty:* 94 full-time (55 women), 34 part-time/adjunct (16 women). Expenses: Contact institution. *Financial support:* In 2008–09, 17 fellowships, 207 research assistantships, 205 teaching assistantships were awarded; career-related internships or fieldwork and traineeships also available. Financial award applicants required to submit FAFSA. In 2008, 225 master's, 42 doctorates, 17 other advanced degrees awarded. *Degree program information:* Part-time and evening/weekend programs available. Postbaccalaureate distance learning degree programs offered. Offers counseling/school psychology (PhD); early childhood education (MS, Ed D, PhD, Ed S); education (MS, Ed D, PhD, Ed S); educational administration/leadership (MS, Ed D, PhD, Ed S); educational leadership/administration (MS, Ed D, PhD, Ed S); educational policy and planning analysis (PhD, Ed S); educational psychology (MS, PhD, Ed S); elementary education (MS, Ed D, PhD, Ed S); emotional disturbance/learning disabilities (MS); English education (MS, PhD, Ed S); higher education (MS, Ed D, PhD, Ed S); history and philosophy of education (MS, PhD, Ed S); instructional systems (MS, PhD, Ed S); international and intercultural education (PhD); learning and cognition (MS, PhD, Ed S); mathematics education (MS, PhD, Ed S); measurement and statistics (MS, PhD, Ed S); mental health counseling (PhD); mental retardation (MS); open and distance learning (MS); performance improvement and human resources (MS); physical education (MS, Ed D, PhD, Ed S); program evaluation (MS, PhD, Ed S); psychological services (MS, PhD, Ed S); reading education/language arts (MS, Ed D, PhD, Ed S); recreation management (MS); rehabilitation counseling (MS, PhD, Ed S); school psychology (MS, Ed S); science education (MS, PhD, Ed S); social science education (MS, PhD, Ed S); social, history and philosophy of education (MS, PhD, Ed S); sociocultural and international developmental education (MS, PhD, Ed S); special education (MS, PhD, Ed S); sport management (MS, Ed D, PhD); sports psychology (MS, PhD); visual disabilities (MS). *Application deadline:* For fall admission, 6/1 priority date for domestic and international students; for spring admission, 10/1 for domestic and international students. Applications are processed on a rolling basis. *Application fee:* $30. Electronic applications accepted. *Application Contact:* Dr. Pamela S. Carroll, Academic Dean, 850-644-0372, Fax: 850-644-1258, E-mail: pcarroll@fsu.edu. *Dean*, Dr. Marcy P Driscoll, 850-644-6885, Fax: 850-644-2725, E-mail: driscoll@coe.fsu.edu.

College of Human Sciences Students: 151 full-time (112 women), 47 part-time (35 women); includes 53 minority (25 African Americans, 1 American Indian/Alaska Native, 7 Asian Americans or Pacific Islanders, 20 Hispanic Americans), 24 international. 164 applicants, 48% accepted, 44 enrolled. *Faculty:* 42 full-time (30 women). Expenses: Contact institution. *Financial support:* In 2008–09, 108 students received support, including 4 fellowships with partial tuition reimbursements available (averaging $12,825 per year), 22 research assistantships with partial tuition reimbursements available (averaging $9,068 per year), 67 teaching assistantships with partial tuition reimbursements available (averaging $8,000 per year); career-related internships or fieldwork, Federal Work-Study, institutionally sponsored loans, scholarships/grants, and unspecified assistantships also available. Financial award application deadline: 1/15; financial award applicants required to submit FAFSA. In 2008, 53 master's, 13 doctorates awarded. *Degree program information:* Part-time programs available. Offers exercise science (MS, PhD); family and child sciences (MS); family relations (PhD); human sciences (MS, PhD); marriage and family therapy (PhD); nutrition and food sciences (MS, PhD). *Application deadline:* For fall admission, 7/1 for domestic students, 5/1 for international students; for spring admission, 11/1 for domestic students, 12/1 for international students. Applications are processed on a rolling basis. *Application fee:* $30. Electronic applications accepted. *Application Contact:* Tara L. Hartman, Academic Program Specialist, 850-644-7221, Fax: 850-644-0700, E-mail: thartman@fsu.edu. *Dean*, Dr. Billie J. Collier, 850-644-1281, Fax: 850-644-0700, E-mail: bcollier@fsu.edu.

College of Information Students: 47 full-time (31 women), 716 part-time (534 women); includes 149 minority (74 African Americans, 4 American Indian/Alaska Native, 23 Asian Americans or Pacific Islanders, 48 Hispanic Americans), 47 international. Average age 35. 420 applicants, 77% accepted, 228 enrolled. *Faculty:* 29 full-time (14 women), 8 part-time/adjunct (4 women). Expenses: Contact institution. *Financial support:* In 2008–09, 200 students received support, including 13 fellowships with full tuition reimbursements available, 102 research assistantships with full tuition reimbursements available, 94 teaching assistantships with full tuition reimbursements available; career-related internships or fieldwork, Federal Work-Study, scholarships/grants, and unspecified assistantships also available. Financial award application deadline: 3/1; financial award applicants required to submit FAFSA. In 2008, 243 master's, 4 doctorates, 3 other advanced degrees awarded. *Degree program information:* Part-time and evening/weekend programs available. Postbaccalaureate distance learning degree programs offered (no on-campus study). Offers library and information studies (MS, PhD, Specialist). *Application deadline:* For fall admission, 6/1 priority date for domestic students, 6/1 for international students; for spring admission, 11/1 for domestic and international students. Applications are processed on a rolling basis. *Application fee:* $30. Electronic applications accepted. *Application Contact:* Delores Bryant, Graduate Program Assistant, 850-644-5775, Fax: 850-644-9763, E-mail: grad@ci.fsu.edu. *Dean*, Dr. Lawrence Dennis, 850-644-2216, Fax: 850-644-9763, E-mail: ldennis@ci.fsu.edu.

College of Motion Picture, Television, and Recording Arts Students: 57 full-time (14 women); includes 16 minority (7 African Americans, 6 Asian Americans or Pacific Islanders, 3 Hispanic Americans), 9 international. Average age 27. 207 applicants, 14% accepted, 30 enrolled. *Faculty:* 14 full-time (3 women), 4 part-time/adjunct (1 woman). Expenses: Contact institution. *Financial support:* In 2008–09, 23 students received support, including 1 fellowship with partial tuition reimbursement available (averaging $6,300 per year), 23 teaching assistantships with partial tuition reimbursements available (averaging $4,100 per year); Federal Work-Study and unspecified assistantships also available. Financial award application deadline: 1/1; financial award applicants required to submit FAFSA. In 2008, 28 master's awarded. Offers production (MFA); screen and play writing (MFA). *Application deadline:* For fall admission, 12/15 for domestic and international students. *Application fee:* $30. *Application Contact:* Carla Hobson, Assistant to Associate Dean, 850-644-8524, Fax: 850-644-2626, E-mail: chobson@film.fsu.edu. *Dean*, Frank Patterson, 850-644-0453, Fax: 850-644-2626.

College of Music Students: 406 full-time (211 women); includes 98 minority (28 African Americans, 38 Asian Americans or Pacific Islanders, 32 Hispanic Americans). Average age 26. 525 applicants, 38% accepted, 145 enrolled. *Faculty:* 88 full-time, 13 part-time/adjunct. Expenses: Contact institution. *Financial support:* In 2008–09, 225 students received support, including 3 fellowships with full tuition reimbursements available (averaging $15,000 per year), 9 research assistantships with full tuition reimbursements available (averaging $4,000 per year), 173 teaching assistantships with full tuition reimbursements available (averaging $4,000 per year); career-related internships or fieldwork, Federal Work-Study, and tuition waivers (partial) also available. Support available to part-time students. Financial award application deadline: 2/28; financial award applicants required to submit FAFSA. In 2008, 102 master's, 41 doctorates awarded. Offers accompanying (MM); arts administration (MA); choral conducting (MM); composition (MM, DM); ethnomusicology (MM); general music (MA); instrumental accompanying (MM); instrumental conducting (MM); jazz studies (MM); music education (MM Ed, PhD); music theory (MM, PhD); music therapy (MM); musicology (MM, PhD); opera (MM); performance (MM, DM); piano pedagogy (MM); piano technology (MA); vocal accompanying (MM). *Application deadline:* For fall admission, 7/1 for domestic students, 5/2 for international students; for spring admission, 11/3 for domestic students, 9/1 for international students. Applications are processed on a rolling basis. *Application fee:* $30. Electronic applications accepted. *Application Contact:* Dr. Seth Beckman, Assistant Dean for Academic Affairs/Director of Graduate Studies, 850-644-

5848, Fax: 850-644-2033, E-mail: sbeckman@admin.fsu.edu. *Dean*, Don Gibson, 850-644-4361, Fax: 850-644-2033.

College of Nursing Students: 8 full-time (4 women), 84 part-time (79 women); includes 15 minority (8 African Americans, 4 Asian Americans or Pacific Islanders, 3 Hispanic Americans). Average age 35. 42 applicants, 71% accepted, 29 enrolled. *Faculty:* 10 full-time (9 women), 1 part-time/adjunct (0 women). Expenses: Contact institution. *Financial support:* In 2008–09, 67 students received support, including fellowships with partial tuition reimbursements available (averaging $6,300 per year), research assistantships with partial tuition reimbursements available (averaging $3,000 per year), 3 teaching assistantships with partial tuition reimbursements available (averaging $3,000 per year); career-related internships or fieldwork, Federal Work-Study, institutionally sponsored loans, scholarships/grants, traineeships, and tuition waivers (partial) also available. Financial award application deadline: 4/15; financial award applicants required to submit FAFSA. In 2008, 16 master's, 7 other advanced degrees awarded. *Degree program information:* Part-time programs available. Postbaccalaureate distance learning degree programs offered (no on-campus study). Offers family nurse practitioner (MSN, Certificate); nurse educator (MSN, Certificate). *Application deadline:* For fall admission, 7/1 for domestic students; for spring admission, 10/15 for domestic students. Applications are processed on a rolling basis. *Application fee:* $30. Electronic applications accepted. *Application Contact:* Brenda Pereira, Graduate Program Coordinator, 850-644-5638, Fax: 850-645-7249, E-mail: info@nursing.fsu.edu. *Dean*, Dr. Lisa Ann Plowfield, 850-644-5417, Fax: 850-644-7660, E-mail: lplowfield@nursing.fsu.edu.

College of Social Sciences Students: 440 full-time (158 women), 313 part-time (153 women); includes 140 minority (67 African Americans, 4 American Indian/Alaska Native, 16 Asian Americans or Pacific Islanders, 53 Hispanic Americans), 92 international. Average age 26. 774 applicants, 67% accepted, 310 enrolled. *Faculty:* 129 full-time (35 women), 26 part-time/adjunct (9 women). Expenses: Contact institution. *Financial support:* In 2008–09, 239 students received support, including 25 fellowships with full and partial tuition reimbursements available (averaging $16,957 per year), 101 research assistantships with full and partial tuition reimbursements available (averaging $9,909 per year), 91 teaching assistantships with full and partial tuition reimbursements available (averaging $13,150 per year); career-related internships or fieldwork, Federal Work-Study, institutionally sponsored loans, scholarships/grants, health care benefits, tuition waivers (full and partial), and unspecified assistantships also available. Support available to part-time students. Financial award application deadline: 1/15; financial award applicants required to submit FAFSA. In 2008, 205 master's, 29 doctorates awarded. *Degree program information:* Part-time programs available. Offers Asian studies (MA); demography and population health (MS, Certificate); economics (MS, PhD); geographic information science (MS); geography (MA, MS, PhD); international affairs (MA, MS); political science (MA, MS, PhD); public administration and policy (MPA, PhD, Certificate); public health (MPH); Russian and East European studies (MA); social sciences (MA, MPA, MPH, MS, MSP, PhD, Certificate); sociology (MA, MS, PhD); urban and regional planning (MSP, PhD). *Application deadline:* For fall admission, 6/1 priority date for domestic students, 7/1 priority date for international students; for spring admission, 10/15 priority date for domestic students, 9/1 priority date for international students. Applications are processed on a rolling basis. *Application fee:* $30. Electronic applications accepted. *Application Contact:* Melanie Booker, Associate Director for Graduate Admissions, 850-644-3420, Fax: 850-644-0197, E-mail: mbooker@admin.fsu.edu. *Dean*, Dr. David W. Rasmussen, 850-644-5488, Fax: 850-645-4923, E-mail: drasmuss@coss.fsu.edu.

College of Social Work Students: 130 full-time (117 women), 129 part-time (104 women); includes 91 minority (63 African Americans, 5 American Indian/Alaska Native, 7 Asian Americans or Pacific Islanders, 16 Hispanic Americans), 1 international. Average age 31. 384 applicants, 62% accepted, 0 enrolled. *Faculty:* 38 full-time (25 women), 26 part-time/adjunct (20 women). Expenses: Contact institution. *Financial support:* In 2008–09, 25 students received support, including 34 fellowships with partial tuition reimbursements available, 57 research assistantships with partial tuition reimbursements available (averaging $3,500 per year), 2 teaching assistantships with full tuition reimbursements available (averaging $15,000 per year); career-related internships or fieldwork, Federal Work-Study, institutionally sponsored loans, scholarships/grants, traineeships, health care benefits, and unspecified assistantships also available. Support available to part-time students. Financial award application deadline: 3/1; financial award applicants required to submit FAFSA. In 2008, 193 master's, 7 doctorates awarded. *Degree program information:* Part-time and evening/weekend programs available. Postbaccalaureate distance learning degree programs offered (no on-campus study). Offers clinical social work (MSW); social policy and administration (MSW); social work (PhD). *Application deadline:* For fall admission, 5/1 priority date for domestic students; for winter admission, 3/1 priority date for domestic students; for spring admission, 10/1 priority date for domestic students. Applications are processed on a rolling basis. *Application fee:* $30. Electronic applications accepted. *Application Contact:* Vicky Verano, Director of Admissions, 800-378-9550, Fax: 850-644-9750, E-mail: vveranoc@mailer.fsu.edu. *Dean*, Dr. Nicholas Mazza, 850-644-4752, Fax: 850-644-9750.

College of Visual Arts, Theatre and Dance Students: 285 full-time (209 women), 93 part-time (67 women); includes 56 minority (22 African Americans, 21 Asian Americans or Pacific Islanders, 13 Hispanic Americans), 2 international. Average age 26. 270 applicants, 57% accepted, 130 enrolled. *Faculty:* 88 full-time (46 women), 13 part-time/adjunct (12 women). Expenses: Contact institution. *Financial support:* In 2008–09, 5 fellowships with partial tuition reimbursements (averaging $18,000 per year), 90 research assistantships with partial tuition reimbursements (averaging $4,957 per year), 78 teaching assistantships with partial tuition reimbursements (averaging $8,001 per year) were awarded; career-related internships or fieldwork, Federal Work-Study, institutionally sponsored loans, scholarships/grants, and unspecified assistantships also available. Support available to part-time students. Financial award applicants required to submit FAFSA. In 2008, 92 master's, 15 doctorates, 12 other advanced degrees awarded. *Degree program information:* Part-time programs available. Offers American dance studies (MA); art education (MA, MS, Ed D, PhD, Ed S); art history (MA, PhD); dance (MFA); interior design (MA, MFA, MS); museum studies (Certificate); studio and related studies (MA); studio art (MFA); visual arts, theatre and dance (MA, MFA, MS, Ed D, PhD, Certificate, Ed S). *Application deadline:* For fall admission, 7/1 priority date for domestic students; for spring admission, 11/1 priority date for domestic students. Applications are processed on a rolling basis. *Application fee:* $30. Electronic applications accepted. *Application Contact:* Melanie Booker, Associate Director for Graduate Admissions, 850-644-3420, Fax: 850-644-0197, E-mail: mbooker@admin.fsu.edu. *Dean*, Dr. Sally E. McRorie, 850-664-5244, Fax: 850-644-2604, E-mail: smcrorie@mailer.fsu.edu.

FAMU-FSU College of Engineering *Degree program information:* Part-time programs available. Postbaccalaureate distance learning degree programs offered (minimal on-campus study). Offers biomedical engineering (MS, PhD); chemical engineering (MS, PhD); civil and environmental engineering (MS, PhD); electrical engineering (MS, PhD); engineering (MS, PhD); industrial engineering (MS, PhD); mechanical engineering (MS, PhD).

School of Theatre Students: 102 full-time (51 women), 9 part-time (6 women); includes 8 minority (3 African Americans, 1 Asian American or Pacific Islander, 4 Hispanic Americans). Average age 25. 139 applicants, 24% accepted, 27 enrolled. *Faculty:* 20 full-time (10 women). Expenses: Contact institution. *Financial support:* In 2008–09, 1 fellowship with full tuition reimbursement (averaging $18,000 per year), 30 research assistantships with full tuition reimbursements (averaging $8,300 per year), 57 teaching assistantships with full tuition reimbursements (averaging $8,900 per year) were awarded; career-related internships or fieldwork, Federal Work-Study, institutionally sponsored loans, scholarships/grants, health care benefits, and unspecified assistantships also available. Financial award application deadline: 1/1; financial award applicants required to submit FAFSA. In 2008, 28 master's, 1 doctorate awarded. Offers acting (MFA); directing (MFA); lighting, costume, and scenic design (MFA); technical production (MFA); theater management (MFA); theatre (MA, MS, PhD). *Application deadline:* For fall admission, 2/15 priority date for domestic and international students. Applications are processed on a rolling basis. *Application fee:* $30. Electronic applications accepted. *Application Contact:* Barbara Thomas, Program Assistant, 850-644-7234, Fax: 850-644-7246, E-mail: bgthomas@admin.fsu.edu. *Director*, Cameron Jackson, 850-644-7257, Fax: 850-644-7408, E-mail: ccjackson@admin.fsu.edu.

See Close-Up on page 917.

FONTBONNE UNIVERSITY, St. Louis, MO 63105-3098

General Information Independent-religious, coed, primarily women, comprehensive institution. *Enrollment:* 2,967 graduate, professional, and undergraduate students; 474 full-time matriculated graduate/professional students (321 women), 409 part-time matriculated graduate/professional students (323 women). *Enrollment by degree level:* 883 master's. *Graduate faculty:* 46 full-time (30 women), 139 part-time/adjunct (66 women). *Tuition:* Part-time $540 per credit hour. *Required fees:* $270 per year. *Graduate housing:* Room and/or apartments available on a first-come, first-served basis to single students; on-campus housing not available to married students. Typical cost: $7411 (including board). Housing application deadline: 3/8. *Student services:* Career counseling, exercise/wellness program, free psychological counseling, international student services, multicultural affairs office, services for students with disabilities. *Library facilities:* Fontbonne University Library. *Online resources:* library catalog, web page, access to other libraries' catalogs. *Collection:* 88,063 titles, 19,532 serial subscriptions, 3,084 audiovisual materials.

Computer facilities: Computer purchase and lease plans are available. 285 computers available on campus for general student use. A campuswide network can be accessed from student residence rooms and from off campus. Online class registration is available. *Web address:* http://www.fontbonne.edu/.

General Application Contact: Peggy Musen, Vice President of Enrollment Management, 314-889-1400, Fax: 314-889-1451, E-mail: pmusen@fontbonne.edu.

GRADUATE UNITS

Graduate Programs Students: 474 full-time (321 women), 409 part-time (323 women); includes 298 minority (280 African Americans, 3 American Indian/Alaska Native, 9 Asian Americans or Pacific Islanders, 6 Hispanic Americans), 50 international. *Faculty:* 46 full-time (30 women), 139 part-time/adjunct (66 women). Expenses: Contact institution. *Financial support:* Fellowships with full tuition reimbursements, teaching assistantships with partial tuition reimbursements available. Support available to part-time students. Financial award application deadline: 4/1; financial award applicants required to submit FAFSA. In 2008, 344 master's awarded. *Degree program information:* Part-time and evening/weekend programs available. Offers art (MA); computer education (MS); early intervention in deaf education (MA); education (MA); family and consumer sciences (MA); fine arts (MFA); speech-language pathology (MS); theater education (MA). *Application deadline:* For fall admission, 8/1 for international students; for spring admission, 12/1 for international students. Applications are processed on a rolling basis. *Application fee:* $25 ($30 for international students). Electronic applications accepted. *Application Contact:* Peggy Musen, Vice President for Enrollment Management, 314-889-1400, E-mail: pmusen@fontbonne.edu. *Vice President and Dean for Academic and Student Affairs*, Dr. Nancy Blattner, 314-889-1401, Fax: 314-889-1451, E-mail: nblattner@fontbonne.edu.

College of Global Business and Professional Studies Students: 353 full-time (220 women), 99 part-time (55 women); includes 196 minority (183 African Americans, 2 American Indian/Alaska Native, 7 Asian Americans or Pacific Islanders, 4 Hispanic Americans), 46 international. Average age 40. *Faculty:* 5 full-time (2 women), 88 part-time/adjunct (24 women). Expenses: Contact institution. *Financial support:* Available to part-time students. Application deadline: 4/1. In 2008, 196 master's awarded. *Degree program information:* Part-time and evening/weekend programs available. Offers accounting (MS); business administration (MBA); options in business administration (MBA); options in management (MM); taxation (MST). *Application deadline:* For fall admission, 8/1 priority date for domestic students. Applications are processed on a rolling basis. *Application fee:* $25. *Application Contact:* Fontbonne University OPTIONS, 314-863-2220, Fax: 314-9630327, E-mail: OPTIONS@fontbonne.edu. *Dean of the College of Global Business and Professional Studies*, Dean Linda Maurer, 314-889-1423, E-mail: lmaurer@fontbonne.edu.

FORDHAM UNIVERSITY, New York, NY 10458

General Information Independent-religious, coed, university. CGS member. *Enrollment:* 3,417 full-time matriculated graduate/professional students (2,075 women), 2,793 part-time matriculated graduate/professional students (1,698 women). *Enrollment by degree level:* 1,455 first professional, 3,783 master's, 857 doctoral, 115 other advanced degrees. *Graduate faculty:* 502 full-time, 416 part-time/adjunct. *Graduate housing:* Room and/or apartments available on a first-come, first-served basis to single students; on-campus housing not available to married students. Housing application deadline: 4/10. *Student services:* Campus employment opportunities, campus safety program, career counseling, free psychological counseling, international student services, low-cost health insurance, services for students with disabilities, teacher training, writing training. *Library facilities:* Walsh Library plus 3 others. *Online resources:* library catalog, web page, access to other libraries' catalogs. *Collection:* 2.4 million titles, 32,300 serial subscriptions, 32,621 audiovisual materials. *Research affiliation:* Equator Initiative /UNDP, Folger Shakespeare Library, New York Botanical Gardens, New York Ocean Science Library, Wildlife Conservation Society, Memorial Sloan-Kettering Cancer Center.

Computer facilities: Computer purchase and lease plans are available. 1,400 computers available on campus for general student use. A campuswide network can be accessed from student residence rooms and from off campus. Online class registration is available. *Web address:* http://www.fordham.edu/.

General Application Contact: Charlene Dundie, Director of Graduate Admissions, 718-817-4420, Fax: 718-817-3566, E-mail: dundie@fordham.edu.

GRADUATE UNITS

Graduate School of Arts and Sciences Students: 411 full-time (211 women), 314 part-time (151 women); includes 90 minority (33 African Americans, 3 American Indian/Alaska Native, 24 Asian Americans or Pacific Islanders, 30 Hispanic Americans), 104 international. Average age 30. 1,512 applicants, 32% accepted, 165 enrolled. *Faculty:* 249 full-time (81 women), 6 part-time/adjunct. Expenses: Contact institution. *Financial support:* In 2008–09, 28 fellowships with full and partial tuition reimbursements (averaging $22,625 per year), 168 research assistantships with full and partial tuition reimbursements (averaging $18,900 per year), 47 teaching assistantships with full and partial tuition reimbursements (averaging $20,400 per year) were awarded; career-related internships or fieldwork, Federal Work-Study, institutionally sponsored loans, scholarships/grants, health care benefits, tuition waivers (full and partial), and unspecified assistantships also available. Support available to part-time students. Financial award application deadline: 1/4; financial award applicants required to submit FAFSA. In 2008, 212 master's, 44 doctorates, 20 other advanced degrees awarded. *Degree program information:* Part-time and evening/weekend programs available. Offers applied developmental psychology (PhD); arts and sciences (MA, MS, PhD, Certificate); biological sciences (MS, PhD); classical Greek and Latin literature (MA); classics (PhD); clinical psychology (PhD); computer science (MS); economics (MA, PhD); elections and campaign management (MA); English language and literature (MA, PhD); history (MA, PhD); humanities and sciences (MA); international political economy and development (MA, Certificate); Latin American and Latino studies (MA, Certificate); philosophical resources (MA); philosophy (MA, PhD); psychometrics (PhD); public communications (MA); sociology (MA); theology (MA, PhD); urban studies (MA). *Application deadline:* For fall admission, 1/4 priority date for domestic and international students; for spring admission, 10/31 for domestic and international students. *Application fee:* $70. Electronic applications accepted. *Application Contact:* Charlene Dundie, Director of Graduate Admissions, 718-817-4420, Fax: 718-817-3566, E-mail: dundie@fordham.edu. *Dean*, Dr. Nancy A. Busch, 718-817-4400, Fax: 718-817-4474, E-mail: busch@fordham.edu.

Center for Ethics Education Program Students: 1 full-time (0 women). Expenses: Contact institution. *Financial support:* In 2008–09, 1 student received support. Federal Work-Study, institutionally sponsored loans, scholarships/grants, tuition waivers (partial), and unspecified assistantships available. Financial award application deadline: 1/4. *Degree program information:* Part-time programs available. Offers ethics and society (MA); health care ethics (Certificate). *Application deadline:* For fall admission, 1/4 priority date for domestic students; for spring admission, 10/31 for domestic students. *Application fee:* $65. Electronic applications accepted. *Application Contact:* Charlene Dundie, Director of Graduate Admissions, 718-817-4420, Fax: 718-817-3566, E-mail: dundie@fordham.edu. *Director*, Dr. Celia Fisher, 718-817-3793, Fax: 212-759-2009, E-mail: fisher@fordham.edu.

Fordham University (continued)

Center for Medieval Studies Students: 4 full-time (2 women), 9 part-time (6 women). Average age 28. 28 applicants, 79% accepted, 6 enrolled. Expenses: Contact institution. *Financial support:* In 2008–09, 4 students received support, including 4 research assistantships with tuition reimbursements available (averaging $17,915 per year); institutionally sponsored loans, tuition waivers (full and partial), and unspecified assistantships also available. Financial award application deadline: 1/4; financial award applicants required to submit FAFSA. In 2008, 5 master's awarded. *Degree program information:* Part-time and evening/weekend programs available. Offers medieval studies (MA, Certificate). *Application deadline:* For fall admission, 1/4 priority date for domestic students; for spring admission, 11/1 for domestic students. *Application fee:* $70. Electronic applications accepted. *Application Contact:* Charlene Dundie, Director of Graduate Admissions, 718-817-4420, Fax: 718-817-3566, E-mail: dundie@fordham.edu. *Director,* Dr. Maryanne Kowaleski, 718-817-4655, E-mail: kowaleski@fordham.edu.

Graduate School of Business Administration *Degree program information:* Part-time and evening/weekend programs available. Offers accounting (MBA); business administration (EMBA, MBA, MS, MTA); communications and media management (MBA); executive business administration (EMBA); finance (MBA, MS); information systems (MBA, MS); management systems (MBA); marketing (MBA); media management (MS); taxation (MS); taxation and accounting (MTA). Electronic applications accepted.

Graduate School of Education *Degree program information:* Part-time and evening/weekend programs available. Offers education (MAT, MS, MSE, MST, Ed D, PhD, Adv C).

Division of Curriculum and Teaching Offers adult education (MS, MSE); bilingual teacher education (MSE); curriculum and teaching (MSE); early childhood education (MSE); elementary education (MST); language, literacy, and learning (PhD); reading education (MSE, Adv C); secondary education (MAT, MSE); special education (MSE, Adv C); teaching English as a second language (MSE).

Division of Educational Leadership, Administration and Policy Offers administration and supervision (MSE, Adv C); administration and supervision for church leaders (PhD); educational administration and supervision (Ed D, PhD); human resource program administration (MS).

Division of Psychological and Educational Services Offers counseling and personnel services (MSE, Adv C); counseling psychology (PhD); educational psychology (MSE, PhD); school psychology (PhD); urban and urban bilingual school psychology (Adv C).

Graduate School of Religion and Religious Education *Degree program information:* Part-time programs available. Offers pastoral counseling and spiritual care (MA); pastoral ministry/spirituality/pastoral counseling (D Min); religion and religious education (MA); religious education (MS, PhD, PD); spiritual direction (Certificate). Electronic applications accepted.

Graduate School of Social Service *Degree program information:* Part-time and evening/weekend programs available. Offers social work (PhD).

School of Law *Degree program information:* Part-time and evening/weekend programs available. Offers banking, corporate and finance law (LL M); intellectual property and information law (LL M); international business and trade law (LL M); law (JD). Electronic applications accepted.

FORT HAYS STATE UNIVERSITY, Hays, KS 67601-4099

General Information State-supported, coed, comprehensive institution. CGS member. *Enrollment:* 7,403 graduate, professional, and undergraduate students; 359 full-time matriculated graduate/professional students (226 women), 781 part-time matriculated graduate/professional students (540 women). *Enrollment by degree level:* 1,133 master's, 7 other advanced degrees. *Graduate faculty:* 127 full-time (31 women). Tuition, state resident: full-time $3131; part-time $174 per credit hour. Tuition, nonresident: full-time $8317; part-time $462 per credit hour. Full-time tuition and fees vary according to course level, course load and degree level. *Graduate housing:* Rooms and/or apartments available to single and married students. Typical cost: $3335 per year ($6560 including board) for single students; $3335 per year ($6560 including board) for married students. Room and board charges vary according to board plan and housing facility selected. Housing application deadline: 8/1. *Student services:* Campus employment opportunities, career counseling, child daycare facilities, exercise/wellness program, free psychological counseling, grant writing training, international student services, low-cost health insurance, multicultural affairs office, services for students with disabilities. *Library facilities:* Forsyth Library. *Online resources:* library catalog, web page, access to other libraries' catalogs. *Collection:* 624,637 titles, 1,689 serial subscriptions.

Computer facilities: Computer purchase and lease plans are available. 813 computers available on campus for general student use. A campuswide network can be accessed from student residence rooms and from off campus. *Web address:* http://www.fhsu.edu/.

General Application Contact: Dr. Timothy R. Crowley, Dean, 785-628-4236, Fax: 785-628-4479, E-mail: tcrowley@fhsu.edu.

GRADUATE UNITS

Graduate School *Degree program information:* Part-time programs available. Electronic applications accepted.

College of Arts and Sciences *Degree program information:* Part-time programs available. Offers arts and sciences (MA, MFA, MLS, MS, Ed S); communication (MS); English (MA); geography (MS); geology (MS); geosciences (MS); history (MA); liberal studies (MLS); psychology (MS); school psychology (Ed S); studio art (MFA). Electronic applications accepted.

College of Business and Leadership *Degree program information:* Part-time programs available. Offers business and leadership (MBA); management (MBA). Electronic applications accepted.

College of Education and Technology *Degree program information:* Part-time programs available. Offers counseling (MS); education (MSE); education and technology (MS, MSE, Ed S); educational administration (MS, Ed S); instructional technology (MS); special education (MS). Electronic applications accepted.

College of Health and Life Sciences *Degree program information:* Part-time programs available. Offers biology (MS); health and human performance (MS); health and life sciences (MS, MSN); nursing (MSN); speech-language pathology (MS). Electronic applications accepted.

FORT VALLEY STATE UNIVERSITY, Fort Valley, GA 31030-4313

General Information State-supported, coed, comprehensive institution. *Graduate housing:* Room and/or apartments available on a first-come, first-served basis to single students; on-campus housing not available to married students. Housing application deadline: 7/21.

GRADUATE UNITS

College of Graduate Studies and Extended Education *Degree program information:* Part-time programs available. Offers animal science (MS); environmental health (MPH); guidance and counseling (Ed S); mental health counseling (MS); rehabilitation counseling (MS).

FRAMINGHAM STATE COLLEGE, Framingham, MA 01701-9101

General Information State-supported, coed, comprehensive institution. *Graduate housing:* On-campus housing not available.

GRADUATE UNITS

Division of Graduate and Continuing Education *Degree program information:* Part-time and evening/weekend programs available. Offers art (M Ed); business administration (MBA); counseling psychology (MA); curriculum and instructional technology (M Ed); dietetics (MS); early childhood education (M Ed); educational leadership (MA); elementary education (M Ed); English (M Ed); food science and nutrition science (MS); health care administration (MA); history (M Ed); human nutrition: education and media technologies (MS); human resource management (MA); literacy and language (M Ed); mathematics (M Ed); nursing education (MSN); nursing leadership (MSN); public administration (MA); Spanish (M Ed); special education (M Ed); teaching of English as a second language (M Ed).

FRANCISCAN SCHOOL OF THEOLOGY, Berkeley, CA 94709-1294

General Information Independent-religious, coed, graduate-only institution. *Graduate housing:* Rooms and/or apartments available on a first-come, first-served basis to single and married students. Housing application deadline: 5/15.

GRADUATE UNITS

Graduate and Professional Programs *Degree program information:* Part-time programs available. Offers theology (M Div, MA, MAMC, MTS).

FRANCISCAN UNIVERSITY OF STEUBENVILLE, Steubenville, OH 43952-1763

General Information Independent-religious, coed, comprehensive institution. *Graduate housing:* On-campus housing not available.

GRADUATE UNITS

Graduate Programs *Degree program information:* Part-time and evening/weekend programs available. Postbaccalaureate distance learning degree programs offered (minimal on-campus study). Offers administration (MS Ed); business (MBA); counseling (MA); nursing (MSN); philosophy (MA); teaching (MS Ed); theology and Christian ministry (MA).

FRANCIS MARION UNIVERSITY, Florence, SC 29501-0547

General Information State-supported, coed, comprehensive institution. *Enrollment:* 4,019 graduate, professional, and undergraduate students; 46 full-time matriculated graduate/professional students (38 women), 173 part-time matriculated graduate/professional students (143 women). *Enrollment by degree level:* 219 master's. *Graduate faculty:* 114 full-time (35 women), 10 part-time/adjunct (5 women). Tuition, state resident: full-time $7547; part-time $377.35 per credit hour. Tuition, nonresident: full-time $15,094; part-time $754.70 per credit hour. *Required fees:* $22 per credit hour. $30 per semester. *Graduate housing:* Room and/or apartments available on a first-come, first-served basis to single students; on-campus housing not available to married students. Typical cost: $3424 per year ($6024 including board). Housing application deadline: 8/1. *Student services:* Campus employment opportunities, campus safety program, career counseling, child daycare facilities, free psychological counseling, international student services, low-cost health insurance, multicultural affairs office, services for students with disabilities, teacher training. *Library facilities:* James A. Rogers Library plus 1 other. *Online resources:* library catalog, web page, access to other libraries' catalogs. *Collection:* 396,526 titles, 1,498 serial subscriptions, 9,552 audiovisual materials.

Computer facilities: 551 computers available on campus for general student use. A campuswide network can be accessed from student residence rooms and from off campus. Online class registration, Blackboard are available. *Web address:* http://www.fmarion.edu/.

General Application Contact: Rannie Gamble, Administrative Manager, 843-661-1286, Fax: 843-661-4688, E-mail: rgamble@fmarion.edu.

GRADUATE UNITS

Graduate Programs Students: 46 full-time (38 women), 173 part-time (143 women); includes 58 minority (53 African Americans, 2 Asian Americans or Pacific Islanders, 3 Hispanic Americans), 6 international. Average age 38. 379 applicants, 100% accepted, 228 enrolled. *Faculty:* 114 full-time (35 women), 10 part-time/adjunct (5 women). Expenses: Contact institution. *Financial support:* In 2008–09, 6 research assistantships (averaging $5,166 per year), 3 teaching assistantships (averaging $8,000 per year) were awarded; career-related internships or fieldwork and unspecified assistantships also available. Support available to part-time students. Financial award application deadline: 3/1; financial award applicants required to submit FAFSA. In 2008, 75 master's awarded. *Degree program information:* Part-time and evening/weekend programs available. Offers applied clinical psychology (MS); applied community psychology (MS); school psychology (MS). *Application deadline:* For fall admission, 4/15 priority date for domestic students; for spring admission, 10/15 priority date for domestic students. Applications are processed on a rolling basis. *Application fee:* $30. *Application Contact:* Provost's Office, 843-661-1284, Fax: 843-661-4688. *Provost's Office,* 843-661-1284, Fax: 843-661-4688.

School of Business Students: 12 full-time (6 women), 32 part-time (18 women); includes 11 minority (8 African Americans, 2 Asian Americans or Pacific Islanders, 1 Hispanic American), 4 international. Average age 38. 21 applicants, 100% accepted, 7 enrolled. *Faculty:* 15 full-time (1 woman), 1 part-time/adjunct (0 women). Expenses: Contact institution. *Financial support:* In 2008–09, 2 research assistantships (averaging $3,000 per year) were awarded; unspecified assistantships also available. Support available to part-time students. Financial award application deadline: 3/1; financial award applicants required to submit FAFSA. In 2008, 16 master's awarded. *Degree program information:* Part-time and evening/weekend programs available. Offers business (MBA); health management (MBA). *Application deadline:* For fall admission, 4/15 priority date for domestic students; for spring admission, 10/15 priority date for domestic students. Applications are processed on a rolling basis. *Application fee:* $30. *Application Contact:* Dr. M. Barry O'Brien, Dean, 843-661-1419, Fax: 843-661-1432, E-mail: mbobrien@fmarion.edu. *Dean,* Dr. M. Barry O'Brien, 843-661-1419, Fax: 843-661-1432, E-mail: mbobrien@fmarion.edu.

School of Education Students: 19 full-time (17 women), 113 part-time (100 women); includes 42 minority (40 African Americans, 2 Hispanic Americans), 1 international. Average age 38. 319 applicants, 100% accepted, 209 enrolled. *Faculty:* 19 full-time (13 women), 2 part-time/adjunct (1 woman). Expenses: Contact institution. *Financial support:* In 2008–09, 3 research assistantships (averaging $6,000 per year) were awarded; unspecified assistantships also available. Support available to part-time students. Financial award application deadline: 3/1; financial award applicants required to submit FAFSA. In 2008, 44 master's awarded. *Degree program information:* Part-time programs available. Offers early childhood education (M Ed); elementary education (M Ed); learning disabilities (M Ed, MAT); remedial education (M Ed); secondary education (M Ed). *Application deadline:* For fall admission, 4/15 priority date for domestic students; for spring admission, 10/15 priority date for domestic students. Applications are processed on a rolling basis. *Application fee:* $30. *Application Contact:* Dr. James R. Faulkenberry, Dean, 843-661-1460, Fax: 843-661-4647. *Dean,* Dr. James R. Faulkenberry, 843-661-1460, Fax: 843-661-4647.

FRANKLIN PIERCE LAW CENTER, Concord, NH 03301-4197

General Information Independent, coed, graduate-only institution. *Graduate housing:* On-campus housing not available. *Research affiliation:* Patent, Trademark, and Copyright Research Foundation, Institute for Health Law and Ethics, Academy of Applied Science.

GRADUATE UNITS

Professional Program Offers intellectual property (Diploma); intellectual property, commerce and technology (LL M, MIP); law (JD). Diploma awarded as part of Intellectual Property Summer Institute. Electronic applications accepted.

FRANKLIN PIERCE UNIVERSITY, Rindge, NH 03461-0060

General Information Independent, coed, comprehensive institution. *Enrollment:* 2,601 graduate, professional, and undergraduate students; 275 full-time matriculated graduate/professional students (163 women), 223 part-time matriculated graduate/professional students (141 women). *Enrollment by degree level:* 251 master's, 185 doctoral. *Graduate faculty:* 27 full-time (16 women), 18 part-time/adjunct (4 women). Tuition and fees vary according to course load, degree level, campus/location and program. *Graduate housing:* On-campus housing not available. *Student services:* Campus employment opportunities, career counseling, exercise/wellness program, low-cost health insurance, services for students with disabilities. *Library facilities:* Franklin Pierce College Library plus 1 other. *Online resources:* library catalog, web page. *Collection:* 137,458 titles, 19,414 serial subscriptions, 14,635 audiovisual materials.

Computer facilities: Computer purchase and lease plans are available. 109 computers available on campus for general student use. A campuswide network can be accessed from student residence rooms. *Web address:* http://www.franklinpierce.edu/.

General Application Contact: Nichole Johnson, Information Contact, 800-325-1090, Fax: 603-626-4815, E-mail: cgps@franklinpierce.edu.

GRADUATE UNITS

Graduate Studies Students: 275 full-time (163 women), 223 part-time (141 women); includes 6 minority (1 African American, 2 Asian Americans or Pacific Islanders, 3 Hispanic Americans). Average age 38. *Faculty:* 27 full-time (16 women), 18 part-time/adjunct (4 women). Expenses: Contact institution. *Financial support:* Available to part-time students. Applicants required to submit FAFSA. *Degree program information:* Part-time and evening/weekend programs available. Offers emerging network technology (Graduate Certificate); health practice management (MBA, Graduate Certificate); human resource management (MBA); human resources management (Graduate Certificate); information technology management (MS); leadership (MBA, DA); nursing (MS); physical therapy (DPT); sports facilities management (MS); teacher education (M Ed). *Application deadline:* Applications are processed on a rolling basis. *Application fee:* $0. Electronic applications accepted. *Application Contact:* 800-325-1090, Fax: 603-898-0827, E-mail: gpsadmin@franklinpierce.edu. *Assistant Dean*, Dr. Robert G. Goddard, 603-899-4361, Fax: 603-229-4580, E-mail: goddardr@franklinpierce.edu.

FRANKLIN UNIVERSITY, Columbus, OH 43215-5399

General Information Independent, coed, comprehensive institution. *Enrollment:* 7,559 graduate, professional, and undergraduate students; 721 full-time matriculated graduate/professional students (422 women), 133 part-time matriculated graduate/professional students (63 women). *Enrollment by degree level:* 854 master's. *Graduate faculty:* 6 full-time (0 women), 73 part-time/adjunct (22 women). *Tuition:* Full-time $7470; part-time $450 per credit hour. *Graduate housing:* On-campus housing not available. *Student services:* Campus employment opportunities, international student services, services for students with disabilities, writing training. *Library facilities:* Franklin University Library. *Online resources:* library catalog, web page, access to other libraries' catalogs. *Collection:* 27,547 titles, 15,290 serial subscriptions, 246 audiovisual materials.

Computer facilities: A campuswide network can be accessed. Online class registration is available. *Web address:* http://www.franklin.edu/.

General Application Contact: Graduate Services Office, 614-797-4700, Fax: 614-221-7723, E-mail: gradschl@franklin.edu.

GRADUATE UNITS

Computer Science Program Students: 33 full-time (10 women), 20 part-time (4 women); includes 6 minority (1 African American, 5 Asian Americans or Pacific Islanders), 20 international. Average age 34. 17 applicants, 100% accepted, 10 enrolled. *Faculty:* 4 full-time (0 women), 4 part-time/adjunct (0 women). Expenses: Contact institution. *Financial support:* In 2008–09, 10 students received support. Application deadline: 6/15. In 2008, 28 master's awarded. *Degree program information:* Part-time and evening/weekend programs available. Offers computer science (MS). *Application deadline:* For fall admission, 8/1 priority date for domestic students; for winter admission, 12/15 priority date for domestic students; for spring admission, 3/15 priority date for domestic students. Applications are processed on a rolling basis. *Application fee:* $30. Electronic applications accepted. *Application Contact:* 614-797-4700, Fax: 614-221-7723, E-mail: gradschl@franklin.edu. *Program Chair*, Dr. Ron Hartung, 614-947-6139, Fax: 614-224-4025, E-mail: hartung@franklin.edu.

Graduate School of Business Students: 593 full-time (345 women), 100 part-time (51 women); includes 192 minority (158 African Americans, 24 Asian Americans or Pacific Islanders, 10 Hispanic Americans), 38 international. Average age 35. 263 applicants, 89% accepted, 200 enrolled. *Faculty:* 5 full-time (0 women), 92 part-time/adjunct (25 women). Expenses: Contact institution. *Financial support:* In 2008–09, 490 students received support. Institutionally sponsored loans available. Financial award application deadline: 6/15; financial award applicants required to submit FAFSA. In 2008, 378 master's awarded. *Degree program information:* Part-time and evening/weekend programs available. Postbaccalaureate distance learning degree programs offered (minimal on-campus study). Offers business (MBA). *Application deadline:* For fall admission, 8/1 priority date for domestic students; for winter admission, 12/15 priority date for domestic students; for spring admission, 3/15 priority date for domestic students. Applications are processed on a rolling basis. *Application fee:* $30. Electronic applications accepted. *Application Contact:* Graduate Services Office, 614-797-4700, Fax: 614-221-7723, E-mail: gradschl@franklin.edu. *Program Chair*, Dr. Terry Boyd, 614-947-6140, Fax: 614-224-4025.

Marketing and Communications Program Students: 84 full-time (61 women), 9 part-time (7 women); includes 23 minority (18 African Americans, 2 Asian Americans or Pacific Islanders, 3 Hispanic Americans), 4 international. Average age 34. 29 applicants, 93% accepted, 21 enrolled. *Faculty:* 12 part-time/adjunct (2 women). Expenses: Contact institution. *Financial support:* In 2008–09, 84 students received support. Application deadline: 6/30. In 2008, 51 master's awarded. *Degree program information:* Part-time and evening/weekend programs available. Offers marketing and communications (MS). *Application deadline:* For fall admission, 8/15 priority date for domestic students; for winter admission, 12/20 priority date for domestic students; for spring admission, 4/4 priority date for domestic students. Applications are processed on a rolling basis. *Application fee:* $30. Electronic applications accepted. *Application Contact:* Graduate Services Office, 614-797-4700, Fax: 614-224-7723, E-mail: gradschl@franklin.edu. *Program Chair*, Dr. Doug Ross, 614-947-6149.

FRANK LLOYD WRIGHT SCHOOL OF ARCHITECTURE, Scottsdale, AZ 85261-4430

General Information Independent, coed, graduate-only institution. *Graduate housing:* Rooms and/or apartments guaranteed to single students and available on a first-come, first-served basis to married students.

GRADUATE UNITS

Graduate Program Offers architecture (M Arch). Summer session held in Spring Green, WI.

FREDERICK S. PARDEE RAND GRADUATE SCHOOL, Santa Monica, CA 90407-2138

General Information Independent, coed, graduate-only institution. *Graduate housing:* On-campus housing not available. *Research affiliation:* RAND (not for profit research).

GRADUATE UNITS

Program in Policy Analysis Offers policy analysis (PhD). Electronic applications accepted.

FREED-HARDEMAN UNIVERSITY, Henderson, TN 38340-2399

General Information Independent-religious, coed, comprehensive institution. *Enrollment:* 2,061 graduate, professional, and undergraduate students; 85 full-time matriculated graduate/professional students (51 women), 442 part-time matriculated graduate/professional students (274 women). *Enrollment by degree level:* 13 first professional, 448 master's, 66 other advanced degrees. *Graduate faculty:* 32 full-time (7 women), 10 part-time/adjunct (2 women). *Tuition:* Full-time $4284; part-time $357 per credit hour. *Required fees:* $16 per credit hour. *Graduate housing:* Room and/or apartments available on a first-come, first-served basis to single students; on-campus housing not available to married students. Housing application deadline: 8/22. *Student services:* Campus employment opportunities, campus safety program, career counseling, child daycare facilities, exercise/wellness program, free psychological counseling, grant writing training, international student services, services for students with disabilities, teacher training. *Library facilities:* Loden-Daniel Library. *Online resources:* library catalog. *Collection:* 147,821 titles, 33,319 serial subscriptions, 43,759 audiovisual materials.

Computer facilities: Computer purchase and lease plans are available. 250 computers available on campus for general student use. A campuswide network can be accessed from student residence rooms and from off campus. Online class registration is available. *Web address:* http://www.fhu.edu/.

General Application Contact: Dr. Samuel T. Jones, Vice President for Academics, 731-989-6004, Fax: 731-989-6945, E-mail: sjones@fhu.edu.

GRADUATE UNITS

Program in Business Administration Students: 6 full-time (3 women), 34 part-time (14 women); includes 4 minority (all African Americans). Average age 30. 26 applicants, 85% accepted, 20 enrolled. *Faculty:* 4 full-time (2 women), 1 part-time/adjunct (0 women). Expenses: Contact institution. *Financial support:* Career-related internships or fieldwork, Federal Work-Study, institutionally sponsored loans, scholarships/grants, and unspecified assistantships available. Support available to part-time students. Financial award applicants required to submit FAFSA. In 2008, 11 master's awarded. *Degree program information:* Part-time and evening/weekend programs available. Postbaccalaureate distance learning degree programs offered (no on-campus study). Offers accounting (MBA); corporate responsibility (MBA); leadership (MBA). *Application deadline:* For fall admission, 8/17 for domestic students. *Application fee:* $35. *Application Contact:* Dr. Samuel T. Jones, Vice President for Academics, 731-989-6004, Fax: 731-989-6945, E-mail: sjones@fhu.edu. *Director of Graduate Studies, School of Business*, Dr. Tom Deberry, 731-989-6659, E-mail: tdeberry@fhu.edu.

Program in Counseling Students: 26 full-time (18 women), 35 part-time (22 women); includes 21 minority (20 African Americans, 1 Asian American or Pacific Islander). Average age 31. 11 applicants, 100% accepted, 11 enrolled. *Faculty:* 6 full-time (0 women), 1 part-time/adjunct (0 women). Expenses: Contact institution. *Financial support:* Career-related internships or fieldwork, Federal Work-Study, tuition waivers (partial), and unspecified assistantships available. Support available to part-time students. Financial award application deadline: 8/1; financial award applicants required to submit FAFSA. In 2008, 25 master's awarded. *Degree program information:* Part-time and evening/weekend programs available. Offers counseling (MS). *Application deadline:* For fall admission, 8/1 priority date for domestic students; for spring admission, 12/1 for domestic students. Applications are processed on a rolling basis. *Application fee:* $35. *Application Contact:* Dr. Samuel T. Jones, Vice President for Academics, 731-989-6004, Fax: 731-989-6945, E-mail: sjones@fhu.edu. *Graduate Director*, Dr. Mike Cravens, 731-989-6666, Fax: 731-989-6065, E-mail: mcravens@fhu.edu.

Program in Education Students: 41 full-time (30 women), 325 part-time (237 women); includes 226 minority (224 African Americans, 1 American Indian/Alaska Native, 1 Asian American or Pacific Islander). Average age 34. 70 applicants, 74% accepted. *Faculty:* 11 full-time (5 women), 5 part-time/adjunct (2 women). Expenses: Contact institution. *Financial support:* Career-related internships or fieldwork, Federal Work-Study, tuition waivers (partial), and unspecified assistantships available. Support available to part-time students. Financial award application deadline: 8/1; financial award applicants required to submit FAFSA. In 2008, 78 master's, 24 Ed Ss awarded. *Degree program information:* Part-time and evening/weekend programs available. Offers curriculum and instruction (M Ed); school counseling (M Ed); school leadership (Ed S). *Application deadline:* For fall admission, 8/1 for domestic students; for spring admission, 12/1 for domestic students. Applications are processed on a rolling basis. *Application fee:* $35. *Application Contact:* Dr. Samuel T. Jones, Vice President for Academics, 731-989-6004, Fax: 731-989-6945, E-mail: sjones@fhu.edu. *Graduate Director*, Dr. Elizabeth Saunders, 731-989-6082, Fax: 731-989-6065, E-mail: esaunders@fhu.edu.

School of Biblical Studies Students: 12 full-time (0 women), 48 part-time (1 woman); includes 9 minority (1 African American, 1 American Indian/Alaska Native, 5 Asian Americans or Pacific Islanders, 2 Hispanic Americans). Average age 31. 8 applicants, 100% accepted, 8 enrolled. *Faculty:* 10 full-time (0 women), 2 part-time/adjunct (0 women). Expenses: Contact institution. *Financial support:* Career-related internships or fieldwork, Federal Work-Study, tuition waivers (partial), and unspecified assistantships available. Support available to part-time students. Financial award application deadline: 8/1; financial award applicants required to submit FAFSA. In 2008, 20 master's awarded. *Degree program information:* Part-time programs available. Offers biblical studies (M Div, M Min, MA); divinity (M Div); ministry (M Min); New Testament (MA). *Application deadline:* For fall admission, 8/1 priority date for domestic students; for spring admission, 12/1 for domestic students. Applications are processed on a rolling basis. *Application fee:* $35. *Application Contact:* Dr. Samuel T. Jones, Vice President for Academics, 731-989-6004, Fax: 731-989-6945, E-mail: sjones@fhu.edu. *Director of Graduate Studies*, Dr. Mark Blackwelder, 731-989-6769, Fax: 731-989-6400, E-mail: mblackwelder@fhu.edu.

FRESNO PACIFIC UNIVERSITY, Fresno, CA 93702-4709

General Information Independent-religious, coed, comprehensive institution. *Graduate housing:* On-campus housing not available.

GRADUATE UNITS

Graduate Programs *Degree program information:* Part-time and evening/weekend programs available. Offers individualized study (MA); kinesiology (MA); leadership and organizational studies (MA); peacemaking and conflict studies (MA). Electronic applications accepted.

School of Education *Degree program information:* Part-time and evening/weekend programs available. Offers administration (MA Ed); administrative services (MA Ed); bilingual/cross-cultural education (MA Ed); curriculum and teaching (MA Ed); educational technology (MA Ed); elementary and middle school mathematics (MA Ed); foundations, curriculum and teaching (MA Ed); integrated mathematics/science education (MA Ed); language development (MA Ed); language, literacy, and culture (MA Ed); literacy in multilingual contexts (MA Ed); mathematics education (MA Ed); mathematics/science/computer education (MA Ed); mild/moderate (MA Ed); moderate/severe (MA Ed); physical and health impairments (MA Ed); pupil personnel services (MA Ed); reading (MA Ed); reading/English as a second language (MA Ed); reading/language arts (MA Ed); school counseling (MA Ed); school library and information technology (MA Ed); school psychology (MA Ed); secondary school mathematics (MA Ed); special education (MA Ed); teaching English to speakers of other languages (MA). Electronic applications accepted.

FRIENDS UNIVERSITY, Wichita, KS 67213

General Information Independent, coed, comprehensive institution. *Enrollment:* 2,826 graduate, professional, and undergraduate students; 650 full-time matriculated graduate/professional students. *Graduate faculty:* 19 full-time (7 women). *Graduate housing:* Rooms and/or apartments available on a first-come, first-served basis to single and married students. Housing application deadline: 8/1. *Student services:* Campus employment opportunities, campus safety program, career counseling, free psychological counseling, international student services, services for students with disabilities, writing training. *Library facilities:* Edmund Stanley Library plus 3 others. *Online resources:* library catalog. *Collection:* 105,989 titles, 857 serial subscriptions.

Computer facilities: 190 computers available on campus for general student use. A campuswide network can be accessed from student residence rooms and from off campus. *Web address:* http://www.friends.edu/.

General Application Contact: Craig Davis, Director of Graduate Admissions, 800-794-6945 Ext. 5573, Fax: 316-295-5050, E-mail: cdavis@friends.edu.

GRADUATE UNITS

Graduate School *Degree program information:* Evening/weekend programs available. Postbaccalaureate distance learning degree programs offered (minimal on-campus study). Electronic applications accepted.

Division of Business, Technology, and Leadership *Degree program information:* Evening/weekend programs available. Offers business administration (MBA); business law (MBL); business, technology, and leadership (MBA, MBL, MHCL, MMIS, MSM, MSOD, MSOM); health care leadership (MHCL); management (MSM); management information systems (MMIS); operations management (MSOM); organization development (MSOD). Electronic applications accepted.

Division of Science, Arts, and Education *Degree program information:* Evening/weekend programs available. Postbaccalaureate distance learning degree programs offered (minimal on-campus study). Offers Christian ministry (MACM); elementary education (MAT); family therapy (MSFT); science, arts, and education (MACM, MAT, MSFT); secondary education (MAT). Electronic applications accepted.

FRONTIER SCHOOL OF MIDWIFERY AND FAMILY NURSING, Hyden, KY 41749

General Information Independent, coed, primarily women, graduate-only institution.

GRADUATE UNITS

Graduate Programs

FROSTBURG STATE UNIVERSITY, Frostburg, MD 21532-1099

General Information State-supported, coed, comprehensive institution. *Enrollment:* 5,215 graduate, professional, and undergraduate students; 194 full-time matriculated graduate/professional students (125 women), 391 part-time matriculated graduate/professional students (257 women). *Enrollment by degree level:* 585 master's. *Graduate faculty:* 64 full-time (25 women), 20 part-time/adjunct (8 women). Tuition, state resident: full-time $5706; part-time $317 per credit hour. Tuition, nonresident: full-time $6552; part-time $364 per credit hour. *Required fees:* $77 per credit hour. $11 per semester. One-time fee: $30 part-time. *Graduate housing:* Room and/or apartments available to single students; on-campus housing not available to married students. Housing application deadline: 6/1. *Student services:* Career counseling, child daycare facilities, free psychological counseling, international student services. *Library facilities:* Lewis J. Ort Library. *Online resources:* library catalog, web page, access to other libraries' catalogs. *Collection:* 261,712 titles, 2,430 serial subscriptions.

Computer facilities: 577 computers available on campus for general student use. A campuswide network can be accessed from student residence rooms and from off campus. Online class registration is available. *Web address:* http://www.frostburg.edu/.

General Application Contact: Vickie Mazer, Director, Graduate Services, 301-687-7053, Fax: 301-687-4597, E-mail: vmmazer@frostburg.edu.

GRADUATE UNITS

Graduate School Students: 194 full-time (125 women), 391 part-time (257 women); includes 27 minority (17 African Americans, 2 American Indian/Alaska Native, 4 Asian Americans or Pacific Islanders, 4 Hispanic Americans), 8 international. Average age 31. 446 applicants, 74% accepted, 262 enrolled. *Faculty:* 74 full-time (30 women), 24 part-time/adjunct (13 women). Expenses: Contact institution. *Financial support:* In 2008–09, 245 students received support, including 93 research assistantships with full tuition reimbursements available (averaging $5,000 per year); fellowships, career-related internships or fieldwork, Federal Work-Study, and scholarships/grants also available. Financial award application deadline: 4/1; financial award applicants required to submit FAFSA. In 2008, 236 master's awarded. *Degree program information:* Part-time and evening/weekend programs available. *Application deadline:* Applications are processed on a rolling basis. *Application fee:* $30. Electronic applications accepted. *Application Contact:* Vickie Mazer, Director, Graduate Services, 301-687-7053, Fax: 301-687-4597, E-mail: vmmazer@frostburg.edu. *Director, Graduate Services,* Vickie Mazer, 301-687-7053, Fax: 301-687-4597, E-mail: vmmazer@frostburg.edu.

College of Business Students: 38 full-time (17 women), 71 part-time (29 women); includes 7 minority (6 African Americans, 1 Asian American or Pacific Islander), 3 international. Average age 32. 64 applicants, 72% accepted, 36 enrolled. *Faculty:* 16 full-time (8 women). Expenses: Contact institution. *Financial support:* In 2008–09, 8 research assistantships with full tuition reimbursements (averaging $5,000 per year) were awarded; career-related internships or fieldwork and Federal Work-Study also available. Financial award application deadline: 4/1; financial award applicants required to submit FAFSA. In 2008, 37 master's awarded. *Degree program information:* Part-time and evening/weekend programs available. Offers business (MBA); business administration (MBA). *Application deadline:* For fall admission, 7/15 priority date for domestic students. Applications are processed on a rolling basis. *Application fee:* $30. Electronic applications accepted. *Application Contact:* Vickie Mazer, Director, Graduate Services, 301-687-7053, Fax: 301-687-4597, E-mail: vmmazer@frostburg.edu. *Interim Dean,* Dr. Ahmad Tootoonchi, 301-687-4019, E-mail: tootoonchi@frostburg.edu.

College of Education Students: 109 full-time (73 women), 302 part-time (214 women); includes 15 minority (10 African Americans, 1 American Indian/Alaska Native, 1 Asian American or Pacific Islander, 3 Hispanic Americans), 1 international. Average age 31. 250 applicants, 76% accepted, 158 enrolled. *Faculty:* 32 full-time (15 women), 15 part-time/adjunct (10 women). Expenses: Contact institution. *Financial support:* In 2008–09, 29 research assistantships with full tuition reimbursements (averaging $5,000 per year) were awarded; career-related internships or fieldwork and Federal Work-Study also available. Financial award application deadline: 4/1; financial award applicants required to submit FAFSA. In 2008, 178 master's awarded. *Degree program information:* Part-time and evening/weekend programs available. Offers curriculum and instruction (M Ed); education (M Ed, MAT, MS); educational administration and supervision (M Ed); educational technology (M Ed); elementary (M Ed); elementary education (M Ed); elementary teaching (MAT); interdisciplinary education (M Ed); parks and recreational management (MS); reading (M Ed); school counseling (M Ed); secondary (M Ed); secondary education (M Ed); secondary teaching (MAT); special education (M Ed). *Application deadline:* For fall admission, 7/15 priority date for domestic students. Applications are processed on a rolling basis. *Application fee:* $30. Electronic applications accepted. *Application Contact:* Vickie Mazer, Director, Graduate Services, 301-687-7053, Fax: 301-687-4597, E-mail: vmmazer@frostburg.edu. *Dean,* Dr. Kenneth Witmer, 301-687-4759, E-mail: kwitmer@frostburg.edu.

College of Liberal Arts and Sciences Students: 47 full-time (35 women), 18 part-time (14 women); includes 5 minority (1 African American, 1 American Indian/Alaska Native, 2 Asian Americans or Pacific Islanders, 1 Hispanic American), 4 international. Average age 27. 66 applicants, 45% accepted, 22 enrolled. *Faculty:* 28 full-time (9 women), 9 part-time/adjunct (3 women). Expenses: Contact institution. *Financial support:* In 2008–09, 31 research assistantships with full tuition reimbursements (averaging $5,000 per year) were awarded; career-related internships or fieldwork and Federal Work-Study also available. Financial award application deadline: 4/1; financial award applicants required to submit FAFSA. In 2008, 21 master's awarded. *Degree program information:* Part-time and evening/weekend programs available. Offers applied computer science (MS); applied ecology and conservation biology (MS); counseling psychology (MS); fisheries and wildlife management (MS); liberal arts and sciences (MS). *Application deadline:* Applications are processed on a rolling basis. *Application fee:* $30. Electronic applications accepted. *Application Contact:* Vickie Mazer, Director, Graduate Services, 301-687-7053, Fax: 301-687-4597, E-mail: vmmazer@frostburg.edu. *Dean,* Dr. Joseph Hoffman, 301-687-4120, E-mail: jhoffman@frostburg.edu.

FULLER THEOLOGICAL SEMINARY, Pasadena, CA 91182

General Information Independent-religious, coed, graduate-only institution. *Graduate housing:* Rooms and/or apartments available on a first-come, first-served basis to single students and available to married students.

GRADUATE UNITS

Graduate School of Psychology Offers clinical psychology (PhD, Psy D); family studies (MA); marital and family therapy (MS); marriage and family enrichment (Certificate); psychology (MA, MS, PhD, Psy D, Certificate).

Graduate School of Theology *Degree program information:* Part-time and evening/weekend programs available. Offers Christian leadership (MACL); evangelism (MA); family life education (MA); ministry (M Div, D Min); pastoral ministry (MA); recovery ministry (MA); theology (MAT, Th M, PhD); worship music ministry (MA); worship, theology, and the arts (MA); youth, family, and culture (MA). M Div offered jointly with Denver Conservative Baptist Seminary.

School of Intercultural Studies *Degree program information:* Part-time and evening/weekend programs available. Offers cross-cultural studies (MA); global leadership (MA); global ministries (D Min); global ministry (Korean language) (D Min); intercultural studies (MA, Th M, PhD); intercultural studies (Korean language) (MA); missiology (D Miss); missiology (Korean language) (Th M).

FULL SAIL UNIVERSITY, Winter Park, FL 32792-7437

General Information Proprietary, coed, primarily men, comprehensive institution. *Graduate housing:* On-campus housing not available.

GRADUATE UNITS

Online Program in Entertainment Business Postbaccalaureate distance learning degree programs offered. Offers entertainment business (MS).

Online Program in Internet Marketing Postbaccalaureate distance learning degree programs offered. Offers Internet marketing (MS).

Online Program in Media Design Postbaccalaureate distance learning degree programs offered. Offers media design (MFA).

Program in Education Media Design and Technology Postbaccalaureate distance learning degree programs offered (no on-campus study). Offers education media design and technology (MS).

Program in Entertainment Business (On-Campus) Offers entertainment business (MS).

Program in Game Design Offers game design (MS).

FURMAN UNIVERSITY, Greenville, SC 29613

General Information Independent, coed, comprehensive institution. *Enrollment:* 2,977 graduate, professional, and undergraduate students; 22 full-time matriculated graduate/professional students (13 women), 135 part-time matriculated graduate/professional students (119 women). *Enrollment by degree level:* 157 master's. *Graduate faculty:* 23 full-time (11 women), 10 part-time/adjunct (6 women). *Graduate housing:* On-campus housing not available. *Student services:* Campus employment opportunities, campus safety program, career counseling, child daycare facilities, exercise/wellness program, free psychological counseling, international student services, multicultural affairs office, services for students with disabilities, teacher training. *Library facilities:* James Buchanan Duke Library plus 2 others. *Online resources:* library catalog, web page, access to other libraries' catalogs. *Collection:* 453,211 titles, 2,052 serial subscriptions.

Computer facilities: Computer purchase and lease plans are available. 425 computers available on campus for general student use. A campuswide network can be accessed from student residence rooms and from off campus. Online class registration is available. *Web address:* http://www.furman.edu/.

General Application Contact: Dr. Troy M. Terry, Director of Graduate Studies, 864-294-2213, Fax: 864-294-3579, E-mail: troy.terry@furman.edu.

GRADUATE UNITS

Graduate Division Students: 22 full-time (13 women), 135 part-time (119 women); includes 17 minority (11 African Americans, 1 Asian American or Pacific Islander, 5 Hispanic Americans), 1 international. Average age 29. 27 applicants, 100% accepted, 21 enrolled. *Faculty:* 23 full-time (11 women), 10 part-time/adjunct (6 women). Expenses: Contact institution. *Financial support:* In 2008–09, 102 students received support, including 5 fellowships (averaging $4,350 per year); career-related internships or fieldwork, scholarships/grants, and unspecified assistantships also available. Financial award application deadline: 5/15; financial award applicants required to submit FAFSA. In 2008, 71 master's awarded. *Degree program information:* Part-time programs available. Postbaccalaureate distance learning degree programs offered (minimal on-campus study). Offers chemistry (MS); curriculum and instruction (MA); early childhood education (MA); English as a second language (MA); literacy (MA); school leadership (MA); special education (MA). *Application deadline:* For fall admission, 8/1 priority date for domestic and international students; for spring admission, 12/15 priority date for domestic and international students. Applications are processed on a rolling basis. *Application fee:* $50. *Application Contact:* Helen Reynolds, Department Assistant, 864-294-2213, Fax: 864-294-3579, E-mail: helen.reynolds@furman.edu. *Director of Graduate Studies,* Dr. Troy M. Terry, 864-294-2213, Fax: 864-294-3579, E-mail: troy.terry@furman.edu.

GALLAUDET UNIVERSITY, Washington, DC 20002-3625

General Information Independent, coed, university. CGS member. *Graduate housing:* Rooms and/or apartments available on a first-come, first-served basis to single and married students. Housing application deadline: 4/1. *Research affiliation:* George Washington University (minority involvement in science), Georgia State University (vocabulary development in deaf children), Medical College of Virginia (genetics and deafness), University of Maryland College Park (audiology and speech science), University of Wisconsin (telecommunications access for deaf and hard of hearing people), Delmarva Foundation for Medical Care (cultural competence for health service providers).

GRADUATE UNITS

The Graduate School *Degree program information:* Part-time programs available. Offers administration (MS); administration and supervision (PhD); change leadership on deaf education (Ed S); early childhood education (MA, Ed S); education of deaf and hard of hearing students and multihandicapped deaf and hard of hearing students (MA, Ed S); elementary education (MA, Ed S); hearing, speech, and language sciences (MA, MS, Au D); individualized program of study (PhD); international development (MA, Certificate); interpretation (MA); leadership (Certificate); leisure services administration (MS); linguistics (MA, PhD); management (Certificate); mental health counseling (MA); parent/infant specialty (MA, Ed S); school counseling (MA); secondary education (MA, Ed S); special education administration (PhD). Electronic applications accepted.

College of Arts and Sciences Offers arts and sciences (MA, MSW, PhD, Psy S); clinical psychology (PhD); developmental psychology (MA); school psychology (MA, Psy S); social work (MSW). Electronic applications accepted.

GANNON UNIVERSITY, Erie, PA 16541-0001

General Information Independent-religious, coed, comprehensive institution. CGS member. *Enrollment:* 4,197 graduate, professional, and undergraduate students; 524 full-time matriculated graduate/professional students (243 women), 835 part-time matriculated graduate/professional students (525 women). *Enrollment by degree level:* 1,069 master's, 173 doctoral, 117 other advanced degrees. *Graduate faculty:* 86 full-time (35 women), 64 part-time/adjunct (21 women). *Tuition:* Full-time $13,050; part-time $725 per credit. *Required fees:* $502; $16 per credit. Tuition and fees vary according to course load, degree level, campus/location and program. *Graduate housing:* On-campus housing not available. *Student services:* Campus employment opportunities, campus safety program, career counseling, exercise/wellness program, free psychological counseling, grant writing training, international student services, low-cost health insurance, multicultural affairs office, services for students with disabilities, teacher training. *Library facilities:* Nash Library plus 1 other. *Online resources:* library catalog, web page. *Collection:* 259,510 titles, 28,463 serial subscriptions, 3,809 audiovisual materials. *Research affiliation:* Biofuels LLC (biohydrogen product), Precision Rehab Manufacturing, Inc. (PRM) (software maintenance and development), Erie Housing Authority (nursing), General Electric Company (GE) (electrical and mechanical engineering/computer and information science graduate research), Thomas Erie (progressive dies), Immersimap (mechanics; sliding arm).

Computer facilities: 350 computers available on campus for general student use. A campuswide network can be accessed from student residence rooms and from off campus. Online class registration is available. *Web address:* http://www.gannon.edu/.

General Application Contact: Kara Morgan, Assistant Director of Graduate Admissions, 814-871-5831, Fax: 814-871-5827, E-mail: graduate@gannon.edu.

GRADUATE UNITS

School of Graduate Studies Students: 524 full-time (243 women), 835 part-time (525 women); includes 40 minority (24 African Americans, 3 American Indian/Alaska Native, 7 Asian Americans or Pacific Islanders, 6 Hispanic Americans), 262 international. Average age 30. 1,630 applicants, 54% accepted, 357 enrolled. *Faculty:* 86 full-time (35 women), 64 part-time/adjunct (21 women). Expenses: Contact institution. *Financial support:* In 2008–09, 45 fellowships (averaging $3,905 per year), 5 teaching assistantships (averaging $6,300 per year) were awarded; career-related internships or fieldwork, Federal Work-Study, scholarships/

grants, traineeships, tuition waivers (partial), unspecified assistantships, and administrative assistantships also available. Support available to part-time students. Financial award application deadline: 7/1; financial award applicants required to submit FAFSA. In 2008, 449 master's, 30 doctorates, 5 other advanced degrees awarded. *Degree program information:* Part-time and evening/weekend programs available. *Application deadline:* Applications are processed on a rolling basis. *Application fee:* $25. Electronic applications accepted. *Application Contact:* Kara Morgan, Assistant Director of Graduate Admissions, 814-871-5831, Fax: 814-871-5827, E-mail: graduate@gannon.edu. *Dean,* Michael J. O'Neill, 814-871-7339, E-mail: oneill001@gannon.edu.

College of Engineering and Business Students: 246 full-time (42 women), 176 part-time (60 women); includes 12 minority (4 African Americans, 1 American Indian/Alaska Native, 4 Asian Americans or Pacific Islanders, 3 Hispanic Americans), 254 international. Average age 27. 1,072 applicants, 44% accepted, 105 enrolled. *Faculty:* 42 full-time (6 women), 9 part-time/adjunct (0 women). Expenses: Contact institution. *Financial support:* In 2008–09, 13 fellowships (averaging $3,000 per year) were awarded; career-related internships or fieldwork, Federal Work-Study, scholarships/grants, traineeships, unspecified assistantships, and administrative assistantships also available. Financial award application deadline: 7/1; financial award applicants required to submit FAFSA. In 2008, 139 master's, 3 other advanced degrees awarded. *Degree program information:* Part-time and evening/weekend programs available. Postbaccalaureate distance learning degree programs offered (no on-campus study). Offers accounting (Certificate); business (MBA, MPA, Certificate); business administration (MBA); computer and information science (MSCIS); electrical engineering (MSEE); embedded software engineering (MSES); engineering and business (M Ed, MBA, MPA, MS, MSCIS, MSEE, MSEM, MSES, MSME, Certificate); engineering and computer science (M Ed, MS, MSCIS, MSEE, MSEM, MSES, MSME, Certificate); engineering management (MSEM); environmental and occupational science and health (Certificate); environmental science and engineering (MS); finance (Certificate); human resources management (Certificate); investments (Certificate); marketing (Certificate); mechanical engineering (MSME); natural and environmental sciences (M Ed); public administration (MPA, Certificate); risk management (Certificate). *Application deadline:* Applications are processed on a rolling basis. *Application fee:* $25. Electronic applications accepted. *Application Contact:* Kara Morgan, Assistant Director of Graduate Admissions, 814-871-5831, Fax: 814-871-5827, E-mail: graduate@gannon.edu. *Dean,* Dr. Melanie Hatch, 814-871-7582, Fax: 814-871-7616, E-mail: hatch004@gannon.edu.

College of Humanities, Education, and Social Sciences Students: 72 full-time (52 women), 601 part-time (426 women); includes 25 minority (18 African Americans, 2 American Indian/Alaska Native, 2 Asian Americans or Pacific Islanders, 3 Hispanic Americans), 3 international. Average age 32. 320 applicants, 87% accepted, 201 enrolled. *Faculty:* 23 full-time (12 women), 45 part-time/adjunct (18 women). Expenses: Contact institution. *Financial support:* In 2008–09, 13 fellowships (averaging $3,827 per year), 5 teaching assistantships (averaging $6,300 per year) were awarded; career-related internships or fieldwork, Federal Work-Study, scholarships/grants, traineeships, and unspecified assistantships also available. Financial award application deadline: 7/1; financial award applicants required to submit FAFSA. In 2008, 225 master's, 5 doctorates, 1 other advanced degree awarded. *Degree program information:* Part-time and evening/weekend programs available. Postbaccalaureate distance learning degree programs offered. Offers advanced counselor studies (Certificate); community counseling (MS, Certificate); counseling psychology (PhD); curriculum and instruction (M Ed); early intervention (MS); education (M Ed, MS, PhD, Certificate); educational computing technology (M Ed); educational leadership (M Ed); English (MA); English as a second language (Certificate); gerontology (Certificate); humanities (MA, MS, PhD, Certificate); humanities, education, and social sciences (M Ed, MA, MS, PhD, Certificate); instructional technology specialist (Certificate); organizational learning and leadership (PhD); pastoral studies (MA, Certificate); principal certification (Certificate); reading (M Ed, Certificate); school counselor preparation (Certificate); superintendent letter of eligibility certification (Certificate). *Application deadline:* Applications are processed on a rolling basis. *Application fee:* $25. Electronic applications accepted. *Application Contact:* Kara Morgan, Assistant Director of Graduate Admissions, 814-871-5831, Fax: 814-871-5827, E-mail: graduate@gannon.edu. *Dean,* Dr. Timothy Downs, 814-871-7549, Fax: 814-871-7652, E-mail: downs001@gannon.edu.

Morosky College of Health Professions and Sciences Students: 206 full-time (149 women), 58 part-time (39 women); includes 3 minority (2 African Americans, 1 Asian American or Pacific Islander), 5 international. Average age 28. 238 applicants, 55% accepted, 51 enrolled. *Faculty:* 23 full-time (17 women), 10 part-time/adjunct (3 women). Expenses: Contact institution. *Financial support:* In 2008–09, 8 fellowships (averaging $3,392 per year) were awarded; career-related internships or fieldwork, Federal Work-Study, scholarships/grants, traineeships, and unspecified assistantships also available. Financial award application deadline: 7/1; financial award applicants required to submit FAFSA. In 2008, 85 master's, 25 doctorates, 1 other advanced degree awarded. *Degree program information:* Part-time and evening/weekend programs available. Offers anesthesia (MSN); business administration (MSN); family nurse practitioner (Certificate); health professions (MPAS, MS, MSN, DPT, Certificate); health professions and sciences (MPAS, MS, MSN, DPT, Certificate); medical-surgical nursing (MSN); nurse anesthesia (Certificate); nursing rural practitioner (MSN); occupational therapy (MS); physical therapy (DPT); physician assistant (MPAS). *Application fee:* $25. Electronic applications accepted. *Application Contact:* Kara Morgan, Assistant Director of Graduate Admissions, 814-871-5831, Fax: 814-871-5827, E-mail: graduate@gannon.edu. *Dean,* Dr. Carolynn Masters, 814-871-7605, E-mail: masters004@gannon.edu.

GARDNER-WEBB UNIVERSITY, Boiling Springs, NC 28017

General Information Independent-religious, coed, comprehensive institution. *Enrollment:* 3,892 graduate, professional, and undergraduate students; 206 full-time matriculated graduate/professional students (92 women), 1,029 part-time matriculated graduate/professional students (659 women). *Enrollment by degree level:* 182 first professional, 979 master's, 74 doctoral. *Graduate faculty:* 50 full-time (18 women), 18 part-time/adjunct (5 women). *Tuition:* Part-time $290 per credit hour. *Graduate housing:* Room and/or apartments available on a first-come, first-served basis to single students; on-campus housing not available to married students. *Student services:* Campus employment opportunities, campus safety program, career counseling, exercise/wellness program, free psychological counseling, international student services, low-cost health insurance, services for students with disabilities, teacher training. *Library facilities:* Dover Memorial Library plus 1 other. *Online resources:* library catalog, web page. *Collection:* 224,226 titles, 1,607 serial subscriptions, 10,540 audiovisual materials.

Computer facilities: 150 computers available on campus for general student use. A campuswide network can be accessed from student residence rooms and from off campus. Online class registration is available. *Web address:* http://www.gardner-webb.edu/.

General Application Contact: Dr. Jackson Rainer, Dean, Graduate School, 704-406-4724, Fax: 704-406-4329, E-mail: gradschool@gardner-webb.edu.

GRADUATE UNITS

Graduate School Students: 206 full-time (92 women), 1,029 part-time (659 women); includes 296 minority (255 African Americans, 4 American Indian/Alaska Native, 15 Asian Americans or Pacific Islanders, 22 Hispanic Americans), 2 international. Average age 29. 471 applicants, 89% accepted, 329 enrolled. *Faculty:* 50 full-time (18 women), 18 part-time/adjunct (5 women). Expenses: Contact institution. *Financial support:* Fellowships, Federal Work-Study, institutionally sponsored loans, and unspecified assistantships available. Support available to part-time students. In 2008, 313 master's, 19 doctorates awarded. *Degree program information:* Part-time and evening/weekend programs available. Offers English (MA); English education (MA); sport science and pedagogy (MA). *Application deadline:* Applications are processed on a rolling basis. *Application fee:* $25. Electronic applications accepted. *Application Contact:* Dr. Jackson Rainer, Dean, Graduate School, 704-406-4724, Fax: 704-406-4329, E-mail: gradschool@gardner-webb.edu. *Dean,* Dr. Gayle B. Price, 704-406-4723, Fax: 704-406-4329, E-mail: gradschool@gardner-webb.edu.

Graduate School of Business Students: 38 full-time (18 women), 369 part-time (201 women); includes 96 minority (76 African Americans, 2 American Indian/Alaska Native, 11 Asian Americans or Pacific Islanders, 7 Hispanic Americans). Average age 34. 147 applicants, 80% accepted, 117 enrolled. *Faculty:* 10 full-time (0 women), 5 part-time/adjunct (1 woman). Expenses: Contact institution. *Financial support:* In 2008–09, 23 students received support. Unspecified assistantships available. Support available to part-time students. Financial award applicants required to submit FAFSA. In 2008, 138 master's awarded. *Degree program information:* Part-time and evening/weekend programs available. Postbaccalaureate distance learning degree programs offered (no on-campus study). Offers business (IMBA, M Acc, MBA). *Application deadline:* For fall admission, 8/29 for domestic students; for spring admission, 1/13 for domestic students. Applications are processed on a rolling basis. *Application fee:* $25. Electronic applications accepted. *Application Contact:* Kristen J. Setzer, Director of Admissions, 800-457-4622, Fax: 704-434-3895, E-mail: ksetzer@gardner-webb.edu. *Director,* Dr. Anthony Negbenebor, 704-406-4622, Fax: 704-406-3895, E-mail: anegbenebor@gardner-webb.edu.

School of Education Students: 9 full-time (all women), 431 part-time (297 women); includes 134 minority (123 African Americans, 1 American Indian/Alaska Native, 3 Asian Americans or Pacific Islanders, 7 Hispanic Americans). Average age 36. *Faculty:* 7 full-time (3 women), 11 part-time/adjunct (2 women). Expenses: Contact institution. *Financial support:* Unspecified assistantships available. In 2008, 137 master's, 6 doctorates awarded. *Degree program information:* Part-time and evening/weekend programs available. Offers curriculum and instruction (Ed D); educational leadership (Ed D); elementary education (MA); middle grades education (MA); school administration (MA). *Application deadline:* For fall admission, 8/1 priority date for domestic students. Applications are processed on a rolling basis. *Application fee:* $25. Electronic applications accepted. *Application Contact:* Dr. Jackson Rainer, Dean, Graduate School, 704-406-4724, Fax: 704-406-4329, E-mail: gradschool@gardner-webb.edu. *Chair,* Dr. Donna Simmons, 704-406-4406, Fax: 704-406-3921, E-mail: dsimmons@gardner-webb.edu.

School of Nursing Students: 2 full-time (1 woman), 94 part-time (89 women); includes 9 African Americans, 1 American Indian/Alaska Native. Average age 42. *Faculty:* 5 full-time (all women). Expenses: Contact institution. In 2008, 14 master's awarded. Offers nursing (MSN, PMC). *Application Contact:* Dr. Jackson Rainer, Dean, Graduate School, 704-406-4724, Fax: 704-406-4329, E-mail: gradschool@gardner-webb.edu. *Dean,* Dr. Gayle B. Price, 704-406-4723, Fax: 704-406-4329, E-mail: gradschool@gardner-webb.edu.

School of Psychology Students: 12 full-time (9 women), 66 part-time (48 women); includes 12 minority (8 African Americans, 4 Hispanic Americans). Average age 33. *Faculty:* 7 full-time (4 women), 1 part-time/adjunct (0 women). Expenses: Contact institution. *Financial support:* Unspecified assistantships available. In 2008, 26 master's awarded. *Degree program information:* Part-time and evening/weekend programs available. Offers mental health counseling (MA); school counseling (MA). *Application deadline:* For fall admission, 7/1 priority date for domestic students. Applications are processed on a rolling basis. *Application fee:* $25. Electronic applications accepted. *Application Contact:* Dr. Jackson Rainer, Dean, Graduate School, 704-406-4724, Fax: 704-406-4329, E-mail: gradschool@gardner-webb.edu. *Chair,* Dr. David Carscaddon, 704-406-4437, Fax: 704-406-4329, E-mail: dcarscaddon@gardner-webb.edu.

M. Christopher White School of Divinity *Degree program information:* Part-time programs available. Offers Christian education (M Div); ministry (D Min); missiology (M Div); pastoral care and counseling (M Div); pastoral ministry (M Div).

GARRETT-EVANGELICAL THEOLOGICAL SEMINARY, Evanston, IL 60201-3298

General Information Independent-religious, coed, graduate-only institution. *Graduate housing:* Rooms and/or apartments guaranteed to single students and available to married students. Housing application deadline: 4/1.

GRADUATE UNITS

Graduate and Professional Programs *Degree program information:* Part-time programs available. Offers Bible and culture (PhD); Christian education (MA); Christian education and congregational studies (PhD); contemporary theology and culture (PhD); divinity (M Div); ethics, church, and society (MA); liturgical studies (PhD); ministry (D Min); music ministry (MA); pastoral care and counseling (MA); pastoral theology, personality, and culture (PhD); spiritual formation and evangelism (MA); theological studies (MTS). Electronic applications accepted.

GENERAL THEOLOGICAL SEMINARY, New York, NY 10011-4977

General Information Independent-religious, coed, graduate-only institution. *Graduate housing:* Rooms and/or apartments available to single and married students. Housing application deadline: 6/1.

GRADUATE UNITS

Graduate and Professional Programs *Degree program information:* Part-time and evening/weekend programs available. Offers Anglican studies (STM, Th D, Certificate); ascetical theology (Certificate); biblical studies (Certificate); congregational development (Certificate); divinity (M Div); historical and theological studies (Certificate); spiritual direction (MASD, STM, Certificate); theology (MA).

GENEVA COLLEGE, Beaver Falls, PA 15010-3599

General Information Independent-religious, coed, comprehensive institution. *Graduate housing:* On-campus housing not available.

GRADUATE UNITS

Program in Business Administration *Degree program information:* Part-time and evening/weekend programs available. Offers business administration (MBA). Electronic applications accepted.

Program in Counseling *Degree program information:* Part-time and evening/weekend programs available. Offers marriage and family (MA); mental health (MA); school counseling (MA). Electronic applications accepted.

Program in Higher Education *Degree program information:* Part-time and evening/weekend programs available. Postbaccalaureate distance learning degree programs offered (minimal on-campus study). Offers campus ministry (MA); college teaching (MA); educational leadership (MA); student affairs administration (MA). Electronic applications accepted.

Program in Organizational Leadership *Degree program information:* Evening/weekend programs available. Offers organizational leadership (MS). Electronic applications accepted.

Program in Special Education *Degree program information:* Part-time and evening/weekend programs available. Offers special education (M Ed). Electronic applications accepted.

GEORGE FOX UNIVERSITY, Newberg, OR 97132-2697

General Information Independent-religious, coed, university. *Enrollment:* 3,383 graduate, professional, and undergraduate students; 374 full-time matriculated graduate/professional students (241 women), 1,029 part-time matriculated graduate/professional students (553 women). *Enrollment by degree level:* 69 first professional, 889 master's, 283 doctoral, 162 other advanced degrees. *Graduate faculty:* 88 full-time (37 women), 92 part-time/adjunct (52 women). *Graduate housing:* On-campus housing not available. *Student services:* Campus employment opportunities, campus safety program, career counseling, free psychological counseling, international student services, low-cost health insurance, multicultural affairs office, services for students with disabilities, teacher training. *Library facilities:* Murdock Learning Resource Center. *Online resources:* library catalog, web page, access to other libraries' catalogs. *Collection:* 218,240 titles, 6,369 serial subscriptions, 7,266 audiovisual materials.

Computer facilities: Computer purchase and lease plans are available. 140 computers available on campus for general student use. A campuswide network can be accessed from student residence rooms and from off campus. Online class registration is available. *Web address:* http://www.georgefox.edu/.

George Fox University (continued)

General Application Contact: Bonnie Nakashimada, Director for Graduate and SPS Admissions and Regional Sites, 503-554-6149, Fax: 503-554-3110, E-mail: bnakashimada@georgefox.edu.

GRADUATE UNITS

George Fox Evangelical Seminary Students: 51 full-time (6 women), 289 part-time (94 women); includes 27 minority (6 African Americans, 2 American Indian/Alaska Native, 15 Asian Americans or Pacific Islanders, 4 Hispanic Americans), 6 international. Average age 41. 134 applicants, 94% accepted, 97 enrolled. *Faculty:* 7 full-time (2 women), 17 part-time/adjunct (7 women). Expenses: Contact institution. *Financial support:* In 2008–09, 33 students received support. Career-related internships or fieldwork and scholarships/grants available. Financial award application deadline: 5/1; financial award applicants required to submit FAFSA. In 2008, 9 first professional degrees, 18 master's, 20 doctorates, 5 other advanced degrees awarded. *Degree program information:* Part-time and evening/weekend programs available. Postbaccalaureate distance learning degree programs offered (minimal on-campus study). Offers divinity (M Div); ministry (D Min); ministry leadership (MA); spiritual formation (MA); spiritual formation and discipleship (Certificate); theological studies (MA). *Application deadline:* For fall admission, 7/1 for domestic and international students; for spring admission, 11/1 for domestic and international students. Applications are processed on a rolling basis. *Application fee:* $40. Electronic applications accepted. *Application Contact:* Sheila Bartlett, Admissions Counselor, 800-631-0921, Fax: 503-554-6122, E-mail: sbartlett@georgefox.edu. *Vice President and Dean, George Fox Evangelical Seminary*, Dr. Chuck Conniry, 503-554-6152, E-mail: cconniry@georgefox.edu.

Graduate Department of Clinical Psychology Students: 105 full-time (69 women), 4 part-time (all women); includes 11 minority (2 African Americans, 3 American Indian/Alaska Native, 2 Asian Americans or Pacific Islanders, 4 Hispanic Americans). Average age 29. 76 applicants, 45% accepted, 24 enrolled. *Faculty:* 8 full-time (3 women), 8 part-time/adjunct (3 women). Expenses: Contact institution. *Financial support:* In 2008–09, 15 students received support, including 8 research assistantships (averaging $2,000 per year), 6 teaching assistantships (averaging $3,000 per year); scholarships/grants also available. Financial award application deadline: 5/15; financial award applicants required to submit FAFSA. In 2008, 21 master's, 21 doctorates awarded. Offers clinical psychology (MA, Psy D). *Application deadline:* For fall admission, 1/15 priority date for domestic and international students. Applications are processed on a rolling basis. *Application fee:* $40. Electronic applications accepted. *Application Contact:* Adina McConaughey, Admission Counselor, 800-631-0921 Ext. 2263, Fax: 503-554-2263, E-mail: amcconaughey@georgefox.edu. *Professor and Chairperson, Graduate Department of Clinical Psychology*, Dr. Wayne Adams, 800-765-4369 Ext. 2372, E-mail: wadams@georgefox.edu.

School of Education Students: 161 full-time (113 women), 331 part-time (234 women); includes 41 minority (2 African Americans, 5 American Indian/Alaska Native, 9 Asian Americans or Pacific Islanders, 25 Hispanic Americans), 2 international. Average age 36. 156 applicants, 89% accepted, 133 enrolled. *Faculty:* 25 full-time (15 women), 38 part-time/adjunct (29 women). Expenses: Contact institution. *Financial support:* Career-related internships or fieldwork available. Financial award applicants required to submit FAFSA. In 2008, 188 master's, 9 doctorates, 2 other advanced degrees awarded. Postbaccalaureate distance learning degree programs offered (minimal on-campus study). Offers continuing administrator license (Certificate); counseling (MA, Certificate, Ed S); curriculum and instruction (M Ed); educational foundations and leadership (M Ed, Ed D); higher education (M Ed); initial administrator license (Certificate); library media (Certificate); literacy (M Ed); marriage and family therapy (MA, Certificate); mental health trauma (Certificate); reading (M Ed); school counseling (MA, Certificate); school psychology (Certificate, Ed S); secondary education (M Ed); teaching (MAT); teaching plus ESOL (MAT); teaching plus ESOL/bilingual (MAT); teaching plus reading (MAT). *Application deadline:* For fall admission, 6/1 for domestic students; for spring admission, 10/1 for domestic students. Applications are processed on a rolling basis. *Application fee:* $40. Electronic applications accepted. *Application Contact:* Beth Molzahn, Admissions Counselor, Oregon Master of Arts in Teaching Programs, 800-631-0921, Fax: 503-554-3110, E-mail: bmolzahn@georgefox.edu. *Dean, School of Education*, Dr. Linda Samek, 503-554-2871, E-mail: lsamek@georgefox.edu.

School of Management Students: 3 full-time (2 women), 200 part-time (70 women); includes 24 minority (8 African Americans, 1 American Indian/Alaska Native, 7 Asian Americans or Pacific Islanders, 8 Hispanic Americans), 1 international. Average age 37. 55 applicants, 91% accepted, 47 enrolled. *Faculty:* 11 full-time (3 women), 9 part-time/adjunct (3 women). Expenses: Contact institution. *Financial support:* In 2008–09, 2 students received support. Scholarships/grants available. Financial award applicants required to submit FAFSA. In 2008, 87 master's awarded. *Degree program information:* Part-time programs available. Postbaccalaureate distance learning degree programs offered (minimal on-campus study). Offers executive management (D Mgt); management (MBA); management education (D Mgt). MBA offered in part-time and full-time formats; also offered in Portland, OR and Boise, ID. *Application deadline:* For fall admission, 8/1 for domestic and international students; for spring admission, 12/1 for domestic and international students. Applications are processed on a rolling basis. *Application fee:* $40. Electronic applications accepted. *Application Contact:* Robin Halverson, Admissions Counselor, 800-493-4937, Fax: 503-554-6111, E-mail: rhalverson@georgefox.edu. *Professor of Management and Dean, School of Management*, Dr. Ken Armstrong, 800-631-0921, E-mail: karmstrong@georgefox.edu.

GEORGE MASON UNIVERSITY, Fairfax, VA 22030

General Information State-supported, coed, university. CGS member. *Enrollment:* 30,714 graduate, professional, and undergraduate students; 2,378 full-time matriculated graduate/professional students (1,321 women), 7,649 part-time matriculated graduate/professional students (4,339 women). *Enrollment by degree level:* 681 first professional, 7,177 master's, 1,839 doctoral, 330 other advanced degrees. *Graduate faculty:* 1,249 full-time (511 women), 972 part-time/adjunct (461 women). Tuition, state resident: full-time $6894; part-time $287.25 per credit. Tuition, nonresident: full-time $20,286; part-time $853.75 per credit. *Required fees:* $1986; $82.75. *Graduate housing:* On-campus housing not available. *Student services:* Campus employment opportunities, campus safety program, career counseling, child daycare facilities, exercise/wellness program, free psychological counseling, grant writing training, international student services, low-cost health insurance, multicultural affairs office, services for students with disabilities, teacher training, writing training. *Library facilities:* Fenwick Library plus 4 others. *Online resources:* library catalog, web page, access to other libraries' catalogs. *Collection:* 1.6 million titles, 388,085 serial subscriptions, 39,942 audiovisual materials. *Research affiliation:* MicroWave Technology, Inc. (High-tech Communication Technology), Metron Aviation, Inc. (Research and Development in the field of Air Traffic Management), Science Applications International Corporation (Science and Technology), Shared Spectrum Company (High-tech Communication Technology), Lockheed Martin (Science and Technology), INOVA Health System (Health Care and Medical Research).

Computer facilities: Computer purchase and lease plans are available. 1,545 computers available on campus for general student use. A campuswide network can be accessed from student residence rooms and from off campus. Online class registration is available. *Web address:* http://www.gmu.edu/.

General Application Contact: Dan Robb, Director of Graduate Admissions, 703-993-9700, Fax: 703-993-4622, E-mail: masongrad@gmu.edu.

GRADUATE UNITS

College of Education and Human Development Students: 312 full-time (256 women), 2,334 part-time (1,844 women); includes 319 minority (151 African Americans, 3 American Indian/Alaska Native, 80 Asian Americans or Pacific Islanders, 85 Hispanic Americans), 70 international. Average age 34. 1,528 applicants, 74% accepted, 814 enrolled. *Faculty:* 85 full-time (63 women), 160 part-time/adjunct (121 women). Expenses: Contact institution. *Financial support:* Fellowships, research assistantships with tuition reimbursements, teaching assistantships, career-related internships or fieldwork, Federal Work-Study, scholarships/grants, health care benefits, unspecified assistantships, and health care benefits (research or teaching assistantship recipients) available. Support available to part-time students. Financial award application deadline: 3/1; financial award applicants required to submit FAFSA. In 2008, 889 master's, 26 doctorates, 138 other advanced degrees awarded. *Degree program information:* Part-time and evening/weekend programs available. Postbaccalaureate distance learning degree programs offered (minimal on-campus study). Offers counseling and development (M Ed); early childhood education (M Ed); education (PhD); education and human development (M Ed, MA, MS, PhD, Graduate Certificate); education leadership (M Ed); educational psychology (MS); English as a second language (M Ed); exercise, science and health (MS); gifted child education (M Ed); history (M Ed); instructional technology (M Ed); library media (M Ed); literacy and reading (M Ed); mathematics (M Ed); new professional studies (MA); physical education (M Ed); science (M Ed); secondary education (M Ed); special education (M Ed, Graduate Certificate); teacher leadership (M Ed). *Application deadline:* For fall admission, 3/1 priority date for domestic students, 2/1 priority date for international students; for spring admission, 10/1 priority date for domestic students, 9/1 priority date for international students. *Application fee:* $60 ($75 for international students). Electronic applications accepted. *Application Contact:* Information Contact, 703-993-2010. *Dean*, Jeffrey Gorrell, 703-993-2008, E-mail: gseinfo@gmu.edu.

School of Recreation, Health and Tourism Students: 4 full-time (3 women), 16 part-time (12 women); includes 1 minority (Asian American or Pacific Islander), 1 international. Average age 30. 24 applicants, 58% accepted, 8 enrolled. *Faculty:* 26 full-time (10 women), 48 part-time/adjunct (28 women). Expenses: Contact institution. *Financial support:* In 2008–09, 5 students received support. In 2008, 9 master's awarded. Offers exercise, fitness, and health promotion (MS). *Application deadline:* For fall admission, 11/1 priority date for domestic students, 11/1 for international students; for spring admission, 4/1 for domestic and international students. Electronic applications accepted. *Application Contact:* Dr. Pierre Rodgers, Associate Professor/Co-Coordinator of the Graduate Program, 703-993-8317, E-mail: prodgers@gmu.edu. *Director*, David Wiggins, 703-993-2057, E-mail: dwiggin1@gmu.edu.

College of Health and Human Services Students: 185 full-time (158 women), 450 part-time (397 women); includes 167 minority (84 African Americans, 2 American Indian/Alaska Native, 56 Asian Americans or Pacific Islanders, 25 Hispanic Americans), 31 international. Average age 37. 548 applicants, 74% accepted, 262 enrolled. *Faculty:* 72 full-time (54 women), 93 part-time/adjunct (82 women). Expenses: Contact institution. *Financial support:* Fellowships, research assistantships, teaching assistantships, health care benefits, tuition waivers (partial), and health care benefits (research or teaching assistantship recipients) available. Support available to part-time students. Financial award application deadline: 3/1; financial award applicants required to submit FAFSA. In 2008, 132 master's, 13 doctorates, 17 other advanced degrees awarded. Offers epidemiology (Certificate); global health (MS); health administration and policy (MS); health and human services (MPH, MS, MSN, MSW, PhD, Certificate); health science (MS); nutrition (Certificate); public health (MPH); social work (MSW). *Application deadline:* For fall admission, 5/1 for domestic students; for spring admission, 11/1 for domestic students. *Application fee:* $60 ($75 for international students). Electronic applications accepted. *Application Contact:* Sandy Kellerhals, Administrative Office Specialist, 703-993-2120, E-mail: skelleh@gmu.edu. *Dean*, Dr. Shirley S. Travis, 703-993-1918.

School of Nursing Students: 50 full-time (47 women), 275 part-time (257 women); includes 90 minority (47 African Americans, 2 American Indian/Alaska Native, 29 Asian Americans or Pacific Islanders, 12 Hispanic Americans), 11 international. Average age 41. 212 applicants, 73% accepted, 111 enrolled. *Faculty:* 38 full-time (all women), 59 part-time/adjunct (54 women). Expenses: Contact institution. *Financial support:* In 2008–09, 28 students received support; teaching assistantships, institutionally sponsored loans and nurse faculty loan available. In 2008, 72 master's, 13 doctorates, 15 other advanced degrees awarded. Offers epidemiology and biostatistics (MS); nurse educator (MSN); nurse practitioner (MSN); nursing (MSN, PhD); nursing administration (MSN); nursing education (Certificate). *Application deadline:* For fall admission, 4/1 priority date for domestic students. Applications are processed on a rolling basis. Electronic applications accepted. *Application Contact:* Janice Lee-Beverly, Program Support, 703-993-1947, E-mail: jleebev1@gmu.edu. *Dean*, Dr. Shirley S. Travis, 703-993-1918.

College of Humanities and Social Sciences Students: 490 full-time (291 women), 1,336 part-time (805 women); includes 251 minority (92 African Americans, 8 American Indian/Alaska Native, 87 Asian Americans or Pacific Islanders, 64 Hispanic Americans), 112 international. Average age 32. 2,143 applicants, 41% accepted, 512 enrolled. *Faculty:* 393 full-time (181 women), 244 part-time/adjunct (120 women). Expenses: Contact institution. *Financial support:* Fellowships, research assistantships, teaching assistantships, career-related internships or fieldwork, Federal Work-Study, health care benefits, and health care benefits (research or teaching assistantship recipients) available. Support available to part-time students. Financial award application deadline: 3/1; financial award applicants required to submit FAFSA. In 2008, 442 master's, 47 doctorates, 42 other advanced degrees awarded. *Degree program information:* Part-time and evening/weekend programs available. Offers anthropology (MA, MAIS); applied developmental psychology (MA, PhD); art history (MA); biodefense (MS, PhD); biopsychology (MA, PhD); clinical psychology (MA, PhD); communications (MA, PhD); community college teaching (MAIS); creative writing (MFA); cultural studies (PhD); economic systems design (Graduate Certificate); economics (MA, PhD); English (MA); English literature (MA); folklore (MAIS); foreign languages (MA); global interaction (MAIS); higher education (MAIS); history (MA, PhD); human factors engineering psychology (MA, PhD); humanities and social sciences (MA, MAIS, MFA, MPA, MS, DA Ed, PhD, Certificate, Graduate Certificate); individualized studies (MAIS); industrial/organizational psychology (MA, PhD); justice, law, and crime policy (MA, PhD); linguistics (MA); philosophy (MA); political science (MA, PhD); professional writing and editing (MA, Certificate); psychology (MA, PhD); public administration (MPA); religion, cultures, and values (MAIS); school psychology (MA); sociology (MA, PhD); teaching English as a second language (Certificate); teaching writing and literature (MA); video-based production (MAIS); women and gender studies (MAIS); women's studies (MAIS); zoo and aquarium leadership (MAIS). *Application deadline:* Applications are processed on a rolling basis. *Application fee:* $60. Electronic applications accepted. *Application Contact:* Laura Laylord, Graduate Admissions Assistant, 703-993-4783, E-mail: llayland@gmu.edu. *Dean*, Jack Censer, 703-993-8715, Fax: 703-993-8714, E-mail: jcenser@gmu.edu.

Higher Education Program Students: 6 full-time (4 women), 53 part-time (33 women); includes 16 minority (11 African Americans, 2 Asian Americans or Pacific Islanders, 3 Hispanic Americans). Average age 49. 17 applicants, 76% accepted, 8 enrolled. *Faculty:* 2 full-time (both women), 1 part-time/adjunct (0 women). Expenses: Contact institution. *Financial support:* In 2008–09, 2 students received support; fellowships, assistantships available. Financial award application deadline: 3/1; financial award applicants required to submit FAFSA. In 2008, 11 doctorates, 4 Certificates awarded. Offers college teaching (Certificate); community college education (DA Ed). *Application deadline:* For fall admission, 4/15 for domestic students; for spring admission, 11/1 for domestic students. Applications are processed on a rolling basis. *Application fee:* $60 ($75 for international students). Electronic applications accepted. *Application Contact:* Nina Joshi, Administrative Coordinator, 703-993-2310, E-mail: njoshi@gmu.edu. *Director*, John O'Connor, 703-993-2310, E-mail: joconnor@gmu.edu.

College of Science *Degree program information:* Part-time and evening/weekend programs available. Offers applied and engineering physics (MS); biodefense (MS, PhD); bioinformatics and computational biology (MS, PhD, Certificate); biology (MS, PhD); chemistry (MS); chemistry and biochemistry (MS); climate dynamics (PhD); computational and data sciences (MS, PhD, Certificate); computational social science (PhD); computational techniques and applications (Certificate); earth systems and geoinformation sciences (MS, PhD, Certificate); environmental science and policy (MS, PhD); geographic and cartographic sciences (MS); geography (MS); mathematical sciences (MS, PhD); mathematics (MS, PhD); nanotechnology and nanoscience (Certificate); neuroscience (PhD); physical sciences (PhD); physics and astronomy (MS); remote sensing and earth image processing (Certificate). Electronic applications accepted.

College of Visual and Performing Arts Students: 69 full-time (55 women), 122 part-time (92 women); includes 29 minority (19 African Americans, 8 Asian Americans or Pacific Islanders, 2 Hispanic Americans), 10 international. Average age 30. 170 applicants, 43% accepted, 57 enrolled. *Faculty:* 51 full-time (25 women), 54 part-time/adjunct (29 women). Expenses: Contact institution. *Financial support:* Fellowships with partial tuition reimbursements, research assistantships with partial tuition reimbursements, teaching assistantships with partial tuition reimbursements, career-related internships or fieldwork, Federal Work-Study, institutionally sponsored loans, health care benefits, tuition waivers (partial), and health care benefits (research or teaching assistantship recipients) available. Support available to part-time students. Financial award application deadline: 3/1; financial award applicants required to submit FAFSA. In 2008, 45 master's, 2 other advanced degrees awarded. *Degree program information:* Part-time and evening/weekend programs available. Offers art and visual technology (MA, MFA); art education (MAT); artist certificate (Certificate); arts management (MA); composition (MA, MM); conducting (MA, MM); dance (MFA); music (MM); music education (MA, MM, Certificate); pedagogy and performance (MA); performance (MA, MM); visual and performing arts (MA, MAT, MFA, MM, Certificate). *Application deadline:* For fall admission, 5/1 priority date for domestic students; for spring admission, 11/1 for domestic students. *Application fee:* $60 ($75 for international students). Electronic applications accepted. *Application Contact:* Patricia Diefenbach, Graduate Studies Assistant, 703-993-9773, E-mail: pdiefenb@gmu.edu. *Dean,* William Reeder, 703-993-8624, Fax: 703-993-8883.

Institute for Conflict Analysis and Resolution Students: 71 full-time (48 women), 196 part-time (120 women); includes 38 minority (18 African Americans, 1 American Indian/Alaska Native, 7 Asian Americans or Pacific Islanders, 12 Hispanic Americans), 50 international. Average age 35. 364 applicants, 46% accepted, 112 enrolled. *Faculty:* 20 full-time (8 women), 15 part-time/adjunct (7 women). Expenses: Contact institution. *Financial support:* In 2008–09, 29 students received support, including 3 fellowships, 15 research assistantships with partial tuition reimbursements available (averaging $11,500 per year), 1 teaching assistantship (averaging $10,500 per year); career-related internships or fieldwork, Federal Work-Study, scholarships/grants, health care benefits, unspecified assistantships, and health care benefits (research or teaching assistantship recipients) also available. Support available to part-time students. Financial award application deadline: 3/1; financial award applicants required to submit FAFSA. In 2008, 36 master's, 13 doctorates awarded. *Degree program information:* Part-time and evening/weekend programs available. Offers conflict analysis and resolution (MS, PhD). *Application deadline:* For fall admission, 4/1 for domestic students, 1/15 for international students; for spring admission, 11/1 for domestic students. *Application fee:* $60. Electronic applications accepted. *Application Contact:* Erin Oglivie, Graduate Admissions and Student Services Director, 703-993-9683, E-mail: eogilvie@gmu.edu. *Director,* Dr. Sara Cobb, 703-993-4453, Fax: 703-993-1302, E-mail: icarinfo@gmu.edu.

School of Law Students: 458 full-time (187 women), 227 part-time (86 women); includes 114 minority (24 African Americans, 1 American Indian/Alaska Native, 62 Asian Americans or Pacific Islanders, 27 Hispanic Americans), 9 international. Average age 26. 5,236 applicants, 19% accepted, 163 enrolled. *Faculty:* 56 full-time (15 women), 131 part-time/adjunct (30 women). Expenses: Contact institution. *Financial support:* In 2008–09, 3 fellowships with full tuition reimbursements (averaging $27,543 per year) were awarded; career-related internships or fieldwork, scholarships/grants, health care benefits, and tuition waivers (partial) also available. Support available to part-time students. Financial award applicants required to submit FAFSA. In 2008, 223 JDs, 7 master's awarded. *Degree program information:* Part-time and evening/weekend programs available. Offers intellectual property (LL M); law (JD); law and economics (LL M). *Application deadline:* For fall admission, 4/1 for domestic and international students. Applications are processed on a rolling basis. *Application fee:* $35. Electronic applications accepted. *Application Contact:* Alison H. Price, Associate Dean/Director of Admission, 703-993-8010, Fax: 703-993-8088, E-mail: lawadmit@gmu.edu. *Dean,* Dean Daniel D. Polsby, 703-993-8006, Fax: 703-993-8088.

School of Management Students: 97 full-time (40 women), 376 part-time (135 women); includes 59 minority (13 African Americans, 2 American Indian/Alaska Native, 34 Asian Americans or Pacific Islanders, 10 Hispanic Americans), 37 international. Average age 31. 391 applicants, 56% accepted, 136 enrolled. *Faculty:* 81 full-time (27 women), 68 part-time/adjunct (17 women). Expenses: Contact institution. *Financial support:* Fellowships, research assistantships, teaching assistantships, career-related internships or fieldwork, Federal Work-Study, health care benefits, and health care benefits (research or teaching assistantship recipients) available. Support available to part-time students. Financial award application deadline: 3/1; financial award applicants required to submit FAFSA. In 2008, 189 master's awarded. *Degree program information:* Part-time and evening/weekend programs available. Offers accounting (MS); business administration (EMBA, MBA); management (EMBA, MBA, MS); technology management (MS). *Application deadline:* For fall admission, 5/1 priority date for domestic students; for spring admission, 11/1 for domestic students. Applications are processed on a rolling basis. *Application fee:* $60 ($75 for international students). Electronic applications accepted. *Application Contact:* Melanie Stewart, Administrative Coordinator to Dean's Office, 703-993-3638, E-mail: mstewarb@gmu.edu. *Dean,* Richard Klimoski, 703-993-1875, E-mail: rklimosk@gmu.edu.

School of Public Policy Students: 240 full-time (122 women), 682 part-time (347 women); includes 120 minority (41 African Americans, 2 American Indian/Alaska Native, 47 Asian Americans or Pacific Islanders, 30 Hispanic Americans), 91 international. Average age 31. 725 applicants, 70% accepted, 287 enrolled. *Faculty:* 66 full-time (15 women), 31 part-time/adjunct (5 women). Expenses: Contact institution. *Financial support:* In 2008–09, 12 research assistantships with full tuition reimbursements (averaging $16,000 per year) were awarded; career-related internships or fieldwork, Federal Work-Study, scholarships/grants, tuition waivers (partial), and unspecified assistantships also available. Support available to part-time students. Financial award application deadline: 3/1; financial award applicants required to submit FAFSA. In 2008, 289 master's, 12 doctorates awarded. *Degree program information:* Part-time and evening/weekend programs available. Offers international commerce and policy (MA); organization development and knowledge management (MS); peace operations (MNPS); public policy (MA, MNPS, MPP, MS, PhD); transportation policy, operations and logistics (MA). *Application deadline:* Applications are processed on a rolling basis. *Application fee:* $60. Electronic applications accepted. *Application Contact:* Leslie Metzger Levin, Assistant Dean of Graduate Admissions and Marketing, 703-993-8099, Fax: 703-993-4876, E-mail: lmetzger@gmu.edu. *Dean,* Dr. Kingsley Haynes, 703-993-8200, Fax: 703-993-2284, E-mail: khaynes@gmu.edu.

Volgenau School of Information Technology and Engineering Students: 294 full-time (78 women), 1,301 part-time (273 women); includes 293 minority (69 African Americans, 3 American Indian/Alaska Native, 177 Asian Americans or Pacific Islanders, 44 Hispanic Americans), 484 international. Average age 31. 1,683 applicants, 59% accepted, 438 enrolled. *Faculty:* 140 full-time (26 women), 116 part-time/adjunct (18 women). Expenses: Contact institution. *Financial support:* Fellowships, research assistantships, teaching assistantships, career-related internships or fieldwork, Federal Work-Study, institutionally sponsored loans, health care benefits, unspecified assistantships, and health care benefits (research or teaching assistantship recipients) available. Support available to part-time students. Financial award application deadline: 3/1; financial award applicants required to submit FAFSA. In 2008, 425 master's, 29 doctorates, 99 other advanced degrees awarded. *Degree program information:* Part-time and evening/weekend programs available. Offers applied information technology (MS); biostatistics (Certificate); civil and infrastructure engineering (MS); communications and networking (Certificate); computer engineering (MS); computer forensics (MS); Computer Science (MS); computer science (MS, PhD); data mining (Certificate); database management (Certificate); e-commerce (MS, Certificate); electrical and computer engineering (PhD); electrical engineering (MS); epidemiology and biostatistics (MS); federal statistics (Certificate); information and security assurance (MS); information engineering (Certificate); information security and assurance (MS, PhD, Certificate); information systems (MS, PhD); information technology (PhD, Engr); information technology and engineering (MS, PhD, Certificate, Engr); operations research (MS); operations research and management science (MS); signal processing (Certificate); software engineering (MS, PhD); software systems and engineering (MS); software systems engineering (MS); statistical science (MS, PhD); systems engineering (MS); telecommunications (MS); VLSI design/manufacturing (Certificate); web-based software engineering (Certificate). *Application deadline:* For fall admission, 5/1 for domestic students; for spring admission, 11/1 for domestic students. *Application fee:* $75. Electronic applications accepted. *Application Contact:* Nicole Sealey, Graduate Admission and Enrollment Services Director, 703-993-3932, E-mail: nsealey@gmu.edu. *Dean,* Lloyd Griffiths, 703-993-1500, Fax: 703-993-1734, E-mail: lgriffiths@gmu.edu.

GEORGE MEANY CENTER FOR LABOR STUDIES–THE NATIONAL LABOR COLLEGE, Silver Spring, MD 20903

General Information Independent, coed, comprehensive institution.

GRADUATE UNITS

Graduate Studies

GEORGETOWN COLLEGE, Georgetown, KY 40324-1696

General Information Independent-religious, coed, comprehensive institution. *Enrollment:* 1,856 graduate, professional, and undergraduate students; 547 matriculated graduate/professional students (426 women). *Enrollment by degree level:* 547 master's. *Graduate faculty:* 15 full-time (9 women), 14 part-time/adjunct (8 women). *Tuition:* Part-time $270 per credit hour. *Required fees:* $270 per credit hour. *Graduate housing:* On-campus housing not available. *Student services:* Career counseling, international student services, services for students with disabilities, teacher training, writing training. *Library facilities:* Anna Ashcraft Ensor Learning Resource Center. *Online resources:* library catalog, web page, access to other libraries' catalogs. *Collection:* 174,300 titles, 458 serial subscriptions, 8,237 audiovisual materials.

Computer facilities: Computer purchase and lease plans are available. 175 computers available on campus for general student use. A campuswide network can be accessed from student residence rooms and from off campus. Online class registration is available. *Web address:* http://www.georgetowncollege.edu/.

General Application Contact: Dr. Eve Proffitt, Associate Dean of Graduate Education, 502-863-8176, Fax: 502-868-7741, E-mail: eve_proffitt@georgetowncollege.edu.

GRADUATE UNITS

Department of Education *Degree program information:* Part-time programs available. Offers education (MA Ed).

GEORGETOWN UNIVERSITY, Washington, DC 20057

General Information Independent-religious, coed, university. CGS member. *Graduate housing:* On-campus housing not available.

GRADUATE UNITS

Graduate School of Arts and Sciences Offers American government (MA, PhD); analytical chemistry (PhD); Arab studies (MA, Certificate); Arabic area studies (PhD); arts and sciences (IEMBA, MA, MALS, MAT, MBA, MPM, MPP, MPS, MS, DLS, PhD, Certificate); bilingual education (Certificate); biochemistry (PhD); bioethics (MA); biology (MS, PhD); British and American literature (MA); communication, culture, and technology (MA); comparative government (PhD); computational chemistry (PhD); computer science (MS); conflict resolution (MA); democracy and governance (MA); econometrics (PhD); economic development (PhD); economic theory (PhD); German (MA, MS, PhD); history (MA, PhD); industrial organization (PhD); inorganic chemistry (PhD); international law and government (MA); international macro and finance (PhD); international relations (PhD); international trade (PhD); Islamic studies (MA, PhD); labor economics (PhD); language and communication (MA); linguistics (MA, MS, PhD); macroeconomics (PhD); materials chemistry (PhD); mathematics and statistics (MS); organic chemistry (PhD); philosophy (PhD); physical chemistry (PhD); political theory (PhD); psychology (PhD); public economics and political economics (PhD); Russian and East European studies (MA); Spanish (MS, PhD); teaching English as a second language (MAT, Certificate); teaching English as a second language and bilingual education (MAT); theology (PhD); theoretical chemistry (PhD).

BMW Center for German and European Studies Offers German and European studies (MA).

Center for Latin American Studies Offers Latin American studies (MA).

Edmund A. Walsh School of Foreign Service Offers foreign service (MS); security studies (MA).

The Georgetown Public Policy Institute Offers public policy (MPM, MPP).

McDonough School of Business Offers business administration (IEMBA, MBA).

Programs in Biomedical Sciences Offers biochemistry and molecular biology (MS, PhD); biohazardous threat agents and emerging infectious diseases (MS); biomedical sciences (MS, PhD); biostatistics (MS); cell biology (PhD); general microbiology and immunology (MS); global infectious diseases (PhD); health physics (MS); microbiology and immunology research (PhD); neuroscience (PhD); pathology (MS, PhD); pharmacology (MS, PhD); physiology and biophysics (MS, PhD); radiobiology (MS); science policy and advocacy (MS).

School of Continuing Studies Offers American studies (MALS); Catholic studies (MALS); classical civilizations (MALS); ethics and the professions (MALS); human resources management (MPS); humanities (MALS); individualized study (MALS); international affairs (MALS); Islam and Muslim-Christian relations (MALS); journalism (MPS); liberal studies (DLS); literature and society (MALS); medieval and early modern European studies (MALS); public relations (MPS); real estate (MPS); religious studies (MALS); social and public policy (MALS); sports industry management (MPS); the theory and practice of American democracy (MALS); visual culture (MALS).

School of Nursing & Health Studies Offers acute care nurse practitioner (MS); clinical nurse specialist (MS); family nurse practitioner (MS); nurse anesthesia (MS); nurse-midwifery (MS); nursing education (MS).

Law Center *Degree program information:* Part-time and evening/weekend programs available. Offers general (LL M); global health law (LL M); international and comparative law (LL M); international business and economic law (LL M); international legal studies (LL M); law (JD, SJD); securities and financial regulation (LL M); taxation (LL M).

National Institutes of Health Sponsored Programs Offers biomedical sciences (MS, PhD).

School of Medicine Offers medicine (MD).

THE GEORGE WASHINGTON UNIVERSITY, Washington, DC 20052

General Information Independent, coed, university. CGS member. *Enrollment:* 25,116 graduate, professional, and undergraduate students; 5,413 full-time matriculated graduate/professional students (3,036 women), 4,273 part-time matriculated graduate/professional students (2,337 women). *Enrollment by degree level:* 2,400 first professional, 5,558 master's, 1,585 doctoral, 143 other advanced degrees. *Graduate faculty:* 1,705 full-time (707 women), 3,213 part-time/adjunct (1,190 women). *Graduate housing:* On-campus housing not available. *Student services:* Campus employment opportunities, campus safety program, career counseling, exercise/wellness program, free psychological counseling, international student services, low-cost health insurance, multicultural affairs office, services for students with disabilities, teacher training, writing training. *Library facilities:* Gelman Library plus 2 others. *Online resources:* library catalog, web page, access to other libraries' catalogs. *Collection:* 2 million titles, 15,365 serial subscriptions, 171,397 audiovisual materials. *Research affiliation:* Children's Hospital National Medical Center, Goddard Space Flight Center (radar modeling analysis, space systems technologies), Library of Congress, Smithsonian Institution, National Institutes of Health (biostatistics), NASA–Langley Research Center (aeroacoustics, aeronautics, astronautics).

Computer facilities: 550 computers available on campus for general student use. A campuswide network can be accessed from student residence rooms and from off campus. *Web address:* http://www.gwu.edu/.

General Application Contact: Kristin Williams, Assistant Vice President for Graduate and Special Enrollment Management, 202-994-0467, Fax: 202-994-0371, E-mail: ksw@gwu.edu.

GRADUATE UNITS

College of Professional Studies Students: 81 full-time (54 women), 507 part-time (334 women); includes 100 minority (52 African Americans, 5 American Indian/Alaska Native, 19 Asian Americans or Pacific Islanders, 24 Hispanic Americans), 29 international. Average age 33. 759 applicants, 65% accepted, 280 enrolled. *Faculty:* 14 full-time (3 women), 7 part-time/

The George Washington University (continued)

adjunct (5 women). Expenses: Contact institution. In 2008, 135 master's, 77 other advanced degrees awarded. Offers healthcare corporate compliance (Graduate Certificate); law firm management (MPS, Graduate Certificate); molecular biotechnology (MPS); paralegal studies (MPS, Graduate Certificate); publishing (MPS). *Application Contact:* Kristin Williams, Assistant Vice President for Graduate and Special Enrollment Management, 202-994-0467, Fax: 202-994-0371, E-mail: ksw@gwu.edu. *Dean,* Kathleen M Burke, 202-994-9711.

Graduate School of Political Management Students: 34 full-time (16 women), 145 part-time (69 women); includes 24 minority (10 African Americans, 2 American Indian/Alaska Native, 4 Asian Americans or Pacific Islanders, 8 Hispanic Americans), 14 international. Average age 28. 190 applicants, 68% accepted, 77 enrolled. *Faculty:* 6 full-time (0 women). Expenses: Contact institution. *Financial support:* In 2008–09, 18 students received support; fellowships with tuition reimbursements available, scholarships/grants and tuition waivers available. Financial award application deadline: 2/1. In 2008, 51 master's, 8 other advanced degrees awarded. Offers legislative affairs (MA); PAC management (Graduate Certificate); political management (MA). *Application deadline:* For fall admission, 6/15 priority date for domestic students, 4/1 priority date for international students; for spring admission, 11/15 priority date for domestic students, 10/1 priority date for international students. Applications are processed on a rolling basis. *Application fee:* $60. Electronic applications accepted. *Application Contact:* Information Contact, 202-994-6000, Fax: 202-994-6006. *Dean,* Dr. Christopher Arterton, 202-994-5843, Fax: 202-994-5806, E-mail: gspmmail@gwu.edu.

Columbian College of Arts and Sciences Students: 964 full-time (674 women), 1,067 part-time (699 women); includes 311 minority (93 African Americans, 19 American Indian/Alaska Native, 121 Asian Americans or Pacific Islanders, 78 Hispanic Americans), 269 international. Average age 29. 3,950 applicants, 29% accepted, 469 enrolled. *Faculty:* 464 full-time (189 women), 447 part-time/adjunct (229 women). Expenses: Contact institution. *Financial support:* Fellowships with tuition reimbursements, research assistantships, teaching assistantships with tuition reimbursements, career-related internships or fieldwork, Federal Work-Study, scholarships/grants, tuition waivers, and unspecified assistantships available. Support available to part-time students. Financial award application deadline: 2/1. In 2008, 702 master's, 123 doctorates, 26 other advanced degrees awarded. *Degree program information:* Part-time and evening/weekend programs available. Offers American studies (PhD); analytical chemistry (MS, PhD); anthropology (MA); applied mathematics (MA, MS, PhD); applied social psychology (PhD); art history (MA); art therapy (MA); arts and sciences (MA, MFA, MFS, MPA, MPP, MS, PhD, Psy D, Certificate, Graduate Certificate); biological sciences (MS, PhD); biostatistics (MS, PhD); ceramics (MFA); classical acting (MFA); clinical psychology (PhD); cognitive neuroscience (PhD); crime scene investigation (MFS); criminology (MA); design (MFA); drawing/painting (MFA); economics (MA, PhD); English (MA, PhD); epidemiology (MS, PhD); folklife (MA); forensic chemistry (MFS); forensic molecular biology (MFS); forensic toxicology (MFS); geography (MA); high-technology crime investigation (MFS); Hinduism and Islam (MA); historic preservation (MA); history (MA, PhD); hominid paleobiology (MS, PhD); human resources management (MA); industrial/organizational psychology (PhD); inorganic chemistry (MS, PhD); interior design (MFA); international development (MA); material culture (MA); materials science (MS, PhD); museum studies (MA, Certificate); museum training (MA); new media (MFA); organic chemistry (MS, PhD); organizational management (MA); photography (MFA); physical chemistry (MS, PhD); physics (MA, PhD); political science (MA, PhD); professional psychology (Psy D); pure mathematics (MA, MS, PhD); sculpture (MFA); security management (MFS); sociology (MA); speech-language pathology (MA); statistics (MS, PhD); survey design and data analysis (Graduate Certificate); women's studies (MA, Certificate). *Application deadline:* For fall admission, 1/15 priority date for domestic and international students; for spring admission, 10/1 priority date for domestic and international students. Applications are processed on a rolling basis. *Application fee:* $60. Electronic applications accepted. *Application Contact:* 202-994-6210, Fax: 202-994-6213, E-mail: askccas@gwu.edu. *Dean,* Peg Barratt, 202-994-6130, E-mail: barratt@gwu.edu.

Institute for Biomedical Sciences Students: 51 full-time (31 women), 96 part-time (60 women); includes 21 minority (6 African Americans, 1 American Indian/Alaska Native, 11 Asian Americans or Pacific Islanders, 3 Hispanic Americans), 32 international. Average age 30. 260 applicants, 9% accepted, 15 enrolled. Expenses: Contact institution. *Financial support:* In 2008–09, 49 students received support; fellowships with full tuition reimbursements available, Federal Work-Study, institutionally sponsored loans, and tuition waivers available. In 2008, 18 doctorates awarded. *Degree program information:* Part-time and evening/weekend programs available. Offers biochemistry and molecular genetics (PhD); microbiology and immunology (PhD); molecular and cellular oncology (PhD); molecular medicine (PhD); neurosciences (PhD); pharmacology and physiology (PhD). *Application deadline:* For fall admission, 1/2 priority date for domestic and international students. Applications are processed on a rolling basis. *Application fee:* $60. Electronic applications accepted. *Application Contact:* 202-994-2179, Fax: 202-994-0967, E-mail: gwibs@gwu.edu. *Director,* Dr. Linda L. Werling, 202-994-2918, Fax: 202-994-0967.

School of Media and Public Affairs Students: 12 full-time (8 women), 3 part-time (2 women); includes 2 minority (1 Asian American or Pacific Islander, 1 Hispanic American), 1 international. Average age 26. 94 applicants, 27% accepted, 9 enrolled. *Faculty:* 24 full-time (7 women), 13 part-time/adjunct (2 women). Expenses: Contact institution. *Financial support:* In 2008–09, fellowships with tuition reimbursements (averaging $10,000 per year), teaching assistantships with tuition reimbursements (averaging $5,000 per year) were awarded. Financial award application deadline: 1/15. In 2008, 12 master's awarded. Offers media and public affairs (MA). *Application deadline:* For fall admission, 4/1 priority date for domestic students, 1/15 priority date for international students; for spring admission, 10/1 priority date for domestic students, 9/1 priority date for international students. Applications are processed on a rolling basis. *Application fee:* $60. Electronic applications accepted. *Application Contact:* Information Contact, 202-994-6227, Fax: 202-994-5806, E-mail: smpa@gwu.edu. *Director,* Lee W. Huebner, 202-994-6227, E-mail: huebner@gwu.edu.

Trachtenberg School of Public Policy and Public Administration Students: 82 full-time (57 women), 130 part-time (80 women); includes 28 minority (9 African Americans, 1 American Indian/Alaska Native, 10 Asian Americans or Pacific Islanders, 8 Hispanic Americans), 28 international. Average age 31. 225 applicants, 38% accepted, 31 enrolled. *Faculty:* 19 full-time (8 women), 12 part-time/adjunct (3 women). Expenses: Contact institution. *Financial support:* In 2008–09, 87 students received support; fellowships, teaching assistantships, institutionally sponsored loans and tuition waivers available. Financial award application deadline: 1/15. In 2008, 64 master's, 7 doctorates awarded. *Degree program information:* Part-time and evening/weekend programs available. Offers budget and public finance (MPA); environmental and resource policy (MA); federal policy, politics, and management (MPA); international development management (MPA); managing public organizations (MPA); managing state and local governments (MPA); nonprofit management (MPA); philosophy and social policy (MA); policy analysis and evaluation (MPA); public administration (MPA); public policy (MA, MPP); public policy and administration (PhD); public-private policy and management (MPA); women's studies (MA). *Application deadline:* For fall admission, 1/15 priority date for domestic and international students; for spring admission, 10/1 priority date for domestic students, 9/1 priority date for international students. Applications are processed on a rolling basis. *Application fee:* $60. Electronic applications accepted. *Application Contact:* Information Contact, 202-994-8500, Fax: 202-994-8913, E-mail: pubpol@gwu.edu. *Director,* Dr. Joseph J. Cordes, 202-994-5826, Fax: 202-994-8913, E-mail: cordes@gwu.edu.

Elliott School of International Affairs Students: 505 full-time (277 women), 283 part-time (154 women); includes 100 minority (14 African Americans, 2 American Indian/Alaska Native, 54 Asian Americans or Pacific Islanders, 30 Hispanic Americans), 88 international. Average age 27. 1,829 applicants, 60% accepted, 332 enrolled. *Faculty:* 51 full-time (14 women), 78 part-time/adjunct (18 women). Expenses: Contact institution. *Financial support:* In 2008–09, 155 students received support; fellowships with tuition reimbursements available, research assistantships with tuition reimbursements available, teaching assistantships with tuition reimbursements available, career-related internships or fieldwork, Federal Work-Study, institutionally sponsored loans, and tuition waivers (full and partial) available. Financial award application deadline: 1/15; financial award applicants required to submit FAFSA. In 2008, 286 master's awarded. *Degree program information:* Part-time and evening/weekend programs available. Offers Asian studies (MA); European and Eurasian studies (MA); global communication (MA); international affairs (MA, MIPP, MIS); international development studies (MA); international policy and practice (MIPP); international science and technology policy (MA); international studies (MIS); international trade and investment policy (MA); Latin American and hemispheric studies (MA); Middle East studies (MA); security policy studies (MA). *Application deadline:* For fall admission, 2/1 for domestic and international students; for spring admission, 10/1 for domestic and international students. *Application fee:* $60. Electronic applications accepted. *Application Contact:* Jeff V. Miles, Director of Graduate Admissions, 202-994-7050, Fax: 202-994-9537, E-mail: esiagrad@gwu.edu. *Dean,* Michael Brown, 202-994-6241, Fax: 202-994-0335, E-mail: esiadean@gwu.edu.

Graduate School of Education and Human Development Students: 463 full-time (365 women), 1,575 part-time (1,144 women); includes 638 minority (433 African Americans, 18 American Indian/Alaska Native, 110 Asian Americans or Pacific Islanders, 77 Hispanic Americans), 64 international. Average age 37. 1,735 applicants, 71% accepted, 806 enrolled. *Faculty:* 77 full-time (45 women), 61 part-time/adjunct (47 women). Expenses: Contact institution. *Financial support:* In 2008–09, 279 students received support; fellowships with tuition reimbursements available, research assistantships with tuition reimbursements available, teaching assistantships with tuition reimbursements available, career-related internships or fieldwork, Federal Work-Study, and tuition waivers (full and partial) available. Support available to part-time students. Financial award application deadline: 1/15. In 2008, 469 master's, 54 doctorates, 180 other advanced degrees awarded. *Degree program information:* Part-time and evening/weekend programs available. Postbaccalaureate distance learning degree programs offered (no on-campus study). Offers community counseling (MA Ed); counseling (PhD, Ed S); counseling: school, community and rehabilitation (MA Ed); curriculum and instruction (MA Ed, Ed D, Ed S); early childhood special education (MA Ed); education and human development (M Ed, MA Ed, MAT, Ed D, PhD, Certificate, Ed S, Graduate Certificate); education policy (Ed D); education policy studies (MA Ed); educational administration (Ed D); educational administration and policy studies (Ed D); educational leadership and administration (MA Ed, Certificate, Ed S); educational technology leadership (MA Ed); elementary education (M Ed); higher education administration (MA Ed, Ed D, Ed S); human and organizational learning (MA Ed, Ed D, Graduate Certificate); human resource development (MA Ed); international education (MA Ed); leadership development (Graduate Certificate); museum education (MAT); rehabilitation counseling (MA Ed); school counseling (MA Ed); secondary education (M Ed); special education (Ed D, Ed S); special education for children with emotional and behavioral disabilities (MA Ed); transition special education (MA Ed, Certificate). *Application deadline:* For fall admission, 1/15 priority date for domestic students; for spring admission, 10/1 for domestic students. Applications are processed on a rolling basis. *Application fee:* $60. Electronic applications accepted. *Application Contact:* Sarah Lang, Director of Graduate Admissions, 202-994-1447, Fax: 202-994-7207, E-mail: slang@gwu.edu. *Dean,* Dr. Mary Hatwood Futrell, 202-994-6161, Fax: 202-994-7207, E-mail: mfutrell@gwu.edu.

Law School Students: 1,528 full-time (675 women), 473 part-time (176 women); includes 455 minority (137 African Americans, 14 American Indian/Alaska Native, 174 Asian Americans or Pacific Islanders, 130 Hispanic Americans), 52 international. Average age 27. 235 applicants, 100% accepted, 185 enrolled. *Faculty:* 87 full-time (34 women), 208 part-time/adjunct (67 women). Expenses: Contact institution. *Financial support:* Research assistantships, career-related internships or fieldwork, Federal Work-Study, institutionally sponsored loans, scholarships/grants, and tuition waivers (full and partial) available. Support available to part-time students. Financial award application deadline: 3/1; financial award applicants required to submit CSS PROFILE or FAFSA. In 2008, 529 JDs, 177 master's, 3 doctorates awarded. *Degree program information:* Part-time and evening/weekend programs available. Offers law (JD, LL M, SJD). *Application deadline:* For fall admission, 3/1 for domestic students. Applications are processed on a rolling basis. *Application fee:* $65. *Application Contact:* Robert V. Stanek, Assistant Dean of Admissions and Financial Aid, 202-739-0648, Fax: 202-739-0624, E-mail: jd@admit.nlc.gwu.edu. *Dean,* Frederick M. Lawrence, 202-994-6288, Fax: 202-994-5157, E-mail: flawrence@law.gwu.edu.

School of Business Students: 841 full-time (370 women), 1,295 part-time (544 women); includes 492 minority (177 African Americans, 13 American Indian/Alaska Native, 230 Asian Americans or Pacific Islanders, 72 Hispanic Americans), 439 international. Average age 32. 2,610 applicants, 46% accepted, 685 enrolled. *Faculty:* 120 full-time (35 women), 48 part-time/adjunct (15 women). Expenses: Contact institution. *Financial support:* In 2008–09, 194 students received support; fellowships with tuition reimbursements available, teaching assistantships with tuition reimbursements available, career-related internships or fieldwork, Federal Work-Study, institutionally sponsored loans, and tuition waivers (partial) available. Financial award application deadline: 4/1. In 2008, 850 master's, 17 doctorates, 3 other advanced degrees awarded. *Degree program information:* Part-time and evening/weekend programs available. Offers accountancy (M Accy, MBA, PhD); business (M Accy, MBA, MS, MSF, MSIST, MTA, PMBA, PhD, Professional Certificate); event and meeting management (MTA); event management (Professional Certificate); finance (MSF, PhD); finance and investments (MBA); hospitality management (MTA, Professional Certificate); information and decision systems (PhD); information systems (MSIST); information systems development (MSIST); information systems management (MBA); information systems project management (MSIST); international business (MBA, PhD); management (MBA, PhD); management information systems (MSIST); management of science, technology, and innovation (MBA, PhD); marketing (MBA, PhD); project management (MS); real estate and urban development (MBA); sports business management (Professional Certificate); sports management (MTA); strategic management and public policy (MBA, PhD); sustainable destination management (MTA); tourism administration (MTA); tourism and hospitality management (MBA); tourism destination management (Professional Certificate). PMBA program also offered in Alexandria and Ashburn, VA. *Application deadline:* For fall admission, 4/1 priority date for domestic students; for spring admission, 10/1 for domestic students. Applications are processed on a rolling basis. *Application fee:* $60. Electronic applications accepted. *Application Contact:* Kristin Williams, Assistant Vice President for Graduate and Special Enrollment Management, 202-994-0467, Fax: 202-994-0371, E-mail: ksw@gwu.edu. *Dean,* Dr. Susan M. Phillips, 202-994-6380, Fax: 202-994-6382.

School of Engineering and Applied Science Students: 374 full-time (81 women), 1,700 part-time (418 women); includes 525 minority (190 African Americans, 15 American Indian/Alaska Native, 228 Asian Americans or Pacific Islanders, 92 Hispanic Americans), 398 international. Average age 34. 1,231 applicants, 67% accepted, 488 enrolled. *Faculty:* 83 full-time (8 women), 74 part-time/adjunct (6 women). Expenses: Contact institution. *Financial support:* In 2008–09, 216 students received support; fellowships with full and partial tuition reimbursements available, research assistantships with full and partial tuition reimbursements available, teaching assistantships with full and partial tuition reimbursements available, career-related internships or fieldwork, Federal Work-Study, institutionally sponsored loans, and tuition waivers (full and partial) available. Financial award application deadline: 3/1; financial award applicants required to submit FAFSA. In 2008, 440 master's, 51 doctorates, 343 other advanced degrees awarded. *Degree program information:* Part-time and evening/weekend programs available. Offers civil and environmental engineering (MS, D Sc, App Sc, Engr); computer science (MS, D Sc); electrical and computer engineering (MS, D Sc); engineering and applied science (MS, D Sc, App Sc, Engr, Graduate Certificate); engineering management and systems engineering (MS, D Sc, App Sc, Engr, Graduate Certificate); mechanical and aerospace engineering (MS, D Sc, App Sc, Engr, Graduate Certificate); telecommunication and computers (MS). *Application deadline:* For fall admission, 3/1 for domestic students; for spring admission, 10/1 for domestic students. Applications are processed on a rolling basis. *Application fee:* $60. *Application Contact:* Adina Lav, Marketing, Recruiting and Admissions, 202-994-5827, Fax: 202-994-0909, E-mail: engineering@gwu.edu. *Dean,* David S. Dolling, 202-994-6080, E-mail: dolling@gwu.edu.

School of Medicine and Health Sciences Students: 1,013 full-time (631 women), 447 part-time (374 women); includes 308 minority (77 African Americans, 9 American Indian/Alaska Native, 189 Asian Americans or Pacific Islanders, 33 Hispanic Americans), 24 international. Average age 31. 1,669 applicants, 29% accepted, 282 enrolled. *Faculty:* 706 full-time (331 women), 1,794 part-time/adjunct (578 women). Expenses: Contact institution.

Financial support: Career-related internships or fieldwork, Federal Work-Study, and institutionally sponsored loans available. In 2008, 154 first professional degrees, 156 master's, 21 doctorates, 40 other advanced degrees awarded. Offers adult nurse practitioner (MSN, Post Master's Certificate); biochemistry and molecular biology (MS); biochemistry and molecular genetics (PhD); clinical practice management (MSHS); clinical research administration (MSHS); clinical research administration for nurses (MSN); emergency services management (MSHS); end-of-life care (MSHS, MSN); family nurse practitioner (MSN, Post Master's Certificate); genomics and bioinformatics (MS); immunohematology (MSHS); medicine (MD); medicine and health sciences (MD, MS, MSHS, MSN, DNP, DPT, PhD, Post Master's Certificate); nursing (DNP); nursing leadership and management (MSN); physical therapy (DPT); physician assistant (MSHS). *Application deadline:* Applications are processed on a rolling basis. *Application Contact:* Admissions, 202-994-3748, Fax: 202-994-1753, E-mail: medadmit@gwu.edu. *Senior Associate Dean,* Dr. Jean Johnson, 202-994-3725, E-mail: hspjej@gwumc.edu.

School of Public Health and Health Services Students: 393 full-time (317 women), 437 part-time (362 women); includes 300 minority (126 African Americans, 5 American Indian/Alaska Native, 116 Asian Americans or Pacific Islanders, 53 Hispanic Americans), 42 international. Average age 28. 1,561 applicants, 57% accepted, 256 enrolled. *Faculty:* 86 full-time (45 women), 279 part-time/adjunct (123 women). Expenses: Contact institution. *Financial support:* In 2008–09, 71 students received support. Career-related internships or fieldwork, Federal Work-Study, institutionally sponsored loans, scholarships/grants, and tuition waivers (partial) available. Support available to part-time students. Financial award application deadline: 2/15. In 2008, 246 master's, 4 doctorates, 12 other advanced degrees awarded. *Degree program information:* Part-time and evening/weekend programs available. Offers biostatistics (MPH); community-oriented primary care (MPH); environmental and occupational health (Dr PH); environmental health science and policy (MPH); epidemiology (MPH); exercise science (MS); global health (Dr PH); health behavior (Dr PH); health management and leadership (MHSA); health policy (MPH, MS); health promotion (MPH); health services administration (Specialist); maternal and child health (MPH); microbiology and emerging infectious diseases (MSPH); public health (MPH); public health and health services (MHSA, MPH, MS, MSPH, Dr PH, Specialist); public health communication and marketing (MPH); public health management (MPH). *Application deadline:* For fall admission, 2/15 priority date for domestic students, 2/15 for international students. Applications are processed on a rolling basis. *Application Contact:* Jane Smith, Director of Admissions, 202-994-2160, Fax: 202-994-1860, E-mail: sphhsinfo@gwumc.edu. *Associate Dean,* Dr. Josef J. Reum, 202-994-5179, E-mail: josefr@gwu.edu.

GEORGIA CAMPUS–PHILADELPHIA COLLEGE OF OSTEOPATHIC MEDICINE, Suwanee, GA 30024

General Information Independent, coed, graduate-only institution.

GRADUATE UNITS

Program in Biomedical Sciences Offers biomedical sciences (MS, Certificate).

Program in Osteopathic Medicine Offers osteopathic medicine (DO).

GEORGIA COLLEGE & STATE UNIVERSITY, Milledgeville, GA 31061

General Information State-supported, coed, comprehensive institution. *Enrollment:* 6,506 graduate, professional, and undergraduate students; 433 full-time matriculated graduate/professional students (274 women), 583 part-time matriculated graduate/professional students (395 women). *Enrollment by degree level:* 926 master's, 90 other advanced degrees. *Graduate faculty:* 321 full-time (164 women). *Tuition, area resident:* Full-time $3942; part-time $219 per semester hour. Tuition, state resident: full-time $3942; part-time $876 per semester hour. Tuition, nonresident: full-time $15,768; part-time $876 per semester hour. *Required fees:* $930; $465 per semester. One-time fee: $100. Tuition and fees vary according to campus/location. *Graduate housing:* Room and/or apartments available on a first-come, first-served basis to single students; on-campus housing not available to married students. Typical cost: $4308 per year ($7698 including board). Room and board charges vary according to board plan, campus/location and housing facility selected. *Student services:* Campus employment opportunities, campus safety program, career counseling, free psychological counseling, international student services, multicultural affairs office, services for students with disabilities, teacher training. *Library facilities:* Ina Dillard Russell Library. *Online resources:* library catalog, web page, access to other libraries' catalogs. *Collection:* 199,506 titles, 5,625 serial subscriptions, 11,232 audiovisual materials.

Computer facilities: Computer purchase and lease plans are available. 180 computers available on campus for general student use. A campuswide network can be accessed from student residence rooms and from off campus. Online class registration is available. *Web address:* http://www.gcsu.edu/.

General Application Contact: Maryllis Wolfgang, Director, Graduate Admissions, 478-445-6289, Fax: 478-445-1336, E-mail: grad-admit@gcsu.edu.

GRADUATE UNITS

Graduate School Students: 433 full-time (274 women), 583 part-time (395 women); includes 232 minority (196 African Americans, 2 American Indian/Alaska Native, 15 Asian Americans or Pacific Islanders, 19 Hispanic Americans), 32 international. Average age 32. 617 applicants, 85% accepted, 387 enrolled. Expenses: Contact institution. *Financial support:* In 2008–09, 131 research assistantships with tuition reimbursements were awarded; career-related internships or fieldwork and unspecified assistantships also available. Support available to part-time students. Financial award application deadline: 3/1. In 2008, 318 master's, 74 other advanced degrees awarded. *Degree program information:* Part-time and evening/weekend programs available. Postbaccalaureate distance learning degree programs offered (no on-campus study). *Application deadline:* Applications are processed on a rolling basis. *Application fee:* $40. Electronic applications accepted. *Application Contact:* Maryllis Wolfgang, Director of Graduate Programs, 478-445-6289, Fax: 478-445-1336, E-mail: grad-admit@gcsu.edu. *Director of Graduate Programs,* Maryllis Wolfgang, 478-445-6289, Fax: 478-445-1336, E-mail: grad-admit@gcsu.edu.

College of Arts and Sciences Students: 85 full-time (45 women), 188 part-time (107 women); includes 66 minority (48 African Americans, 8 Asian Americans or Pacific Islanders, 10 Hispanic Americans), 9 international. *Faculty:* 175 full-time (77 women). Expenses: Contact institution. *Financial support:* In 2008–09, 67 research assistantships with tuition reimbursements were awarded; career-related internships or fieldwork and unspecified assistantships also available. Support available to part-time students. Financial award application deadline: 3/1; financial award applicants required to submit FAFSA. In 2008, 85 master's awarded. *Degree program information:* Part-time programs available. Offers biology (MS); creative writing (MFA); criminal justice (MS); English (MA); history (advanced studies option) (MA); history (predoctoral option) (MA); liberal arts and sciences (MA, MFA, MM Ed, MPA, MS, MSA); logistics (MSA); logistics management (MSA); music and theatre (MM Ed); public administration (MPA); public history (MA). *Application deadline:* Applications are processed on a rolling basis. *Application fee:* $40. Electronic applications accepted. *Application Contact:* Kenneth Proctor, Dean, 478-445-4441, E-mail: ken.proctor@gcsu.edu. *Dean,* Kenneth Proctor, 478-445-4441, E-mail: ken.proctor@gcsu.edu.

College of Health Sciences Students: 30 full-time (17 women), 71 part-time (65 women); includes 17 minority (15 African Americans, 2 Hispanic Americans), 2 international. Average age 33. 85 applicants, 45% accepted, 31 enrolled. *Faculty:* 38 full-time (29 women). Expenses: Contact institution. *Financial support:* In 2008–09, 23 research assistantships with tuition reimbursements were awarded; career-related internships or fieldwork and unspecified assistantships also available. Support available to part-time students. In 2008, 25 master's awarded. *Degree program information:* Part-time and evening/weekend programs available. Offers adult health (MSN); family nurse practitioner (MSN); health promotion (M Ed); health sciences (M Ed, MMT, MSN); music therapy (MMT); nursing administration (MSN); outdoor education (M Ed). *Application deadline:* For fall admission, 7/1 priority date for domestic students. Applications are processed on a rolling basis. *Application fee:* $25. Electronic applications accepted. *Application Contact:* Dr. Sandra Gangstead, Dean, 478-445-4092. *Dean,* Dr. Sandra Gangstead, 478-445-4092.

The John H. Lounsbury College of Education Students: 264 full-time (193 women), 169 part-time (149 women); includes 117 minority (107 African Americans, 2 American Indian/Alaska Native, 1 Asian American or Pacific Islander, 7 Hispanic Americans), 1 international. Average age 35. 248 applicants, 95% accepted, 170 enrolled. *Faculty:* 42 full-time (29 women). Expenses: Contact institution. *Financial support:* In 2008–09, 14 research assistantships were awarded; career-related internships or fieldwork, Federal Work-Study, and unspecified assistantships also available. Support available to part-time students. Financial award application deadline: 3/1; financial award applicants required to submit FAFSA. In 2008, 151 master's, 57 other advanced degrees awarded. *Degree program information:* Part-time programs available. Offers curriculum and instruction (Ed S); early childhood education (M Ed, Ed S); education (M Ed, MAT, Ed S); educational leadership (M Ed, Ed S); instructional technology (M Ed); middle grades education (M Ed, Ed S); secondary education (M Ed, MAT); special education (M Ed, MAT); special education and educational leadership (M Ed, MAT, Ed S). *Application deadline:* For fall admission, 7/1 priority date for domestic students. Applications are processed on a rolling basis. *Application fee:* $40. Electronic applications accepted. *Application Contact:* Dr. W. Bee Crews, Coordinator of Graduate Programs, 478-445-4056, E-mail: b.crews@gcsu.edu. *Dean,* Dr. Linda Irwin-Devitis, 478-445-4546, E-mail: linda.irwin-devitis@gcsu.edu.

The J. Whitney Bunting School of Business Students: 54 full-time (19 women), 155 part-time (74 women); includes 32 minority (26 African Americans, 6 Asian Americans or Pacific Islanders), 20 international. Average age 30. 180 applicants, 72% accepted, 88 enrolled. *Faculty:* 46 full-time (19 women). Expenses: Contact institution. *Financial support:* In 2008–09, 27 research assistantships with full tuition reimbursements were awarded; career-related internships or fieldwork and unspecified assistantships also available. Support available to part-time students. Financial award application deadline: 3/1. In 2008, 78 master's awarded. *Degree program information:* Part-time and evening/weekend programs available. Postbaccalaureate distance learning degree programs offered (no on-campus study). Offers accountancy (MACCT); business (MBA); information systems (MIS). *Application deadline:* For fall admission, 7/1 priority date for domestic students; for spring admission, 11/15 priority date for domestic students. Applications are processed on a rolling basis. *Application fee:* $40. Electronic applications accepted. *Application Contact:* Lynn Hanson, Director of Graduate Programs in Business, 478-445-5115, E-mail: lynn.hanson@gcsu.edu. *Interim Dean,* Dr. Dale Young, 478-445-5497, E-mail: dale.young@gcsu.edu.

GEORGIA INSTITUTE OF TECHNOLOGY, Atlanta, GA 30332-0001

General Information State-supported, coed, primarily men, university. CGS member. *Graduate housing:* Rooms and/or apartments available on a first-come, first-served basis to single and married students. Housing application deadline: 5/1. *Research affiliation:* Oak Ridge National Laboratory (energy, health, environment), Yerkes Regional Primate Research Center (biomedicine, physiology and behavior), Skidaway Institute of Oceanography (marine geology), Southeastern Universities Research Association (high-energy physics), Emory University Medical School (biomedical engineering), Zoo Atlanta (environmental design, environmental psychology).

GRADUATE UNITS

Graduate Studies and Research *Degree program information:* Part-time and evening/weekend programs available. Postbaccalaureate distance learning degree programs offered. Offers algorithms, combinatorics, and optimization (PhD); statistics (MS Stat). Electronic applications accepted.

College of Architecture Offers architecture (M Arch, MCRP, MS, PhD); building construction (PhD); city and regional planning (PhD); economic development (MCRP); environmental planning and management (MCRP); geographic information systems (MCRP); integrated facility management (MS); integrated project delivery systems (MS); land and community development (MCRP); land use planning (MCRP); residential construction development (MS); transportation (MCRP); urban design (MCRP). Electronic applications accepted.

College of Computing *Degree program information:* Part-time programs available. Offers algorithms, combinatorics, and optimization (PhD); computational science and engineering (MS, PhD); computer science (MS, MSCS, PhD); human computer interaction (MSHCI); human-centered computing (PhD); information security (MS).

College of Engineering *Degree program information:* Part-time programs available. Postbaccalaureate distance learning degree programs offered. Offers aerospace engineering (MS, MSAE, PhD); algorithms, combinatorics, and optimization (PhD); bioengineering (MS Bio E, PhD); bioinformatics (PhD); biomedical engineering (MS Bio E, PhD); chemical engineering (MS Ch E, PhD); civil engineering (MS, MSCE, PhD); electrical and computer engineering (MS, MSEE, PhD); engineering (MS, MS Bio E, MS Ch E, MS Env E, MS Poly, MS Stat, MSAE, MSCE, MSEE, MSESM, MSHS, MSIE, MSME, MSNE, MSOR, PhD); engineering science and mechanics (MS, MSESM, PhD); environmental engineering (MS, MS Env E, PhD); health systems (MSHS); industrial and systems engineering (MS, MS Stat, MSIE, PhD); industrial engineering (MS, MSIE); materials science and engineering (MS, PhD); mechanical engineering (MS, MS Bio E, MSME, PhD); medical physics (MS); nuclear and radiological engineering (MSNE, PhD); nuclear and radiological engineering and medical physics (MS, MSNE, PhD); operations research (MSOR, PhD); paper science and engineering (MS, PhD); polymer, textile and fiber engineering (MS, PhD); polymers (MS Poly); statistics (MS Stat). Electronic applications accepted.

College of Management Offers accounting (MBA, PhD); e-commerce (Certificate); engineering entrepreneurship (MBA); entrepreneurship (Certificate); finance (MBA, PhD); information technology management (MBA, PhD); international business (MBA, Certificate); management (EMBA, MBA, MS, PhD, Certificate); management of technology (Certificate); marketing (MBA, PhD); operations management (MBA, PhD); organizational behavior (MBA, PhD); quantitative and computational finance (MS); strategic management (MBA, PhD). Electronic applications accepted.

College of Sciences *Degree program information:* Part-time programs available. Offers algorithms, combinatorics, and optimization (PhD); applied biology (MS, PhD); applied mathematics (MS); atmospheric chemistry and air pollution (MS, PhD); atmospheric dynamics and climate (MS, PhD); bioinformatics (MS, PhD); biology (MS); chemistry and biochemistry (MS, MS Chem, PhD); geochemistry (MS, PhD); human computer interaction (MSHCI); hydrologic cycle (MS, PhD); mathematics (PhD); ocean sciences (MS, PhD); physics (MS, PhD); prosthetics and orthotics (MS); psychology (MS, MS Psy, PhD); quantitative and computational finance (MS); sciences (MS, MS Chem, MS Phys, MS Psy, MS Stat, MSA Phy, MSHCI, PhD); solid-earth and environmental geophysics (MS, PhD); statistics (MS Stat). Electronic applications accepted.

Ivan Allen College of Policy and International Affairs *Degree program information:* Part-time and evening/weekend programs available. Offers digital media (MS, PhD); economics (MS); history and sociology of technology and science (MS, PhD); human computer interaction (MSHCI); international affairs (MS Int A, PhD); policy and international affairs (MS, MS Int A, MS Pub P, MSHCI, MSIDT, PhD); public policy (MS Pub P, PhD). Electronic applications accepted.

GEORGIAN COURT UNIVERSITY, Lakewood, NJ 08701-2697

General Information Independent-religious, Undergraduate: women only; graduate: coed, comprehensive institution. *Enrollment:* 3,189 graduate, professional, and undergraduate students; 257 full-time matriculated graduate/professional students (222 women), 865 part-time matriculated graduate/professional students (689 women). *Enrollment by degree level:* 866 master's, 256 other advanced degrees. *Graduate faculty:* 55 full-time (31 women), 64 part-time/adjunct (37 women). *Tuition:* Full-time $12,276; part-time $682 per credit. *Required fees:* $400 per year. Tuition and fees vary according to campus/location. *Graduate housing:* On-campus housing not available. *Student services:* Campus employment opportunities, campus safety program, career counseling, exercise/wellness program, free psychological counseling, low-cost health insurance, services for students with disabilities, teacher training.

Georgian Court University (continued)

Library facilities: The Sister Mary Joseph Cunningham Library. *Online resources:* library catalog, web page. *Collection:* 146,129 titles, 673 serial subscriptions.

Computer facilities: 192 computers available on campus for general student use. A campuswide network can be accessed. Online class registration is available. *Web address:* http://www.georgian.edu/.

General Application Contact: Eugene Soltys, Director of Graduate Admissions, 732-987-2770, Fax: 732-987-2084, E-mail: graduateadmissions@georgian.edu.

GRADUATE UNITS

School of Arts and Humanities Students: 23 part-time (18 women); includes 3 minority (1 African American, 1 Asian American or Pacific Islander, 1 Hispanic American). Average age 54. 7 applicants, 100% accepted, 5 enrolled. *Faculty:* 3 full-time (1 woman). Expenses: Contact institution. *Financial support:* Scholarships/grants, health care benefits, and unspecified assistantships available. Financial award application deadline: 4/15; financial award applicants required to submit FAFSA. In 2008, 6 master's awarded. *Degree program information:* Part-time and evening/weekend programs available. Offers Catholic school leadership (Certificate); parish business management (Certificate); pastoral administration (Certificate); pastoral ministry (Certificate); religious education (Certificate); theology (MA, Certificate). *Application deadline:* For fall admission, 8/1 priority date for domestic students, 4/1 for international students; for spring admission, 1/1 priority date for domestic students, 7/1 for international students. Applications are processed on a rolling basis. *Application fee:* $40. Electronic applications accepted. *Application Contact:* Eugene Soltys, Director of Graduate Admissions, 732-987-2770, Fax: 732-987-2084, E-mail: graduateadmissions@georgian.edu. *Dean,* Dr. Linda James, 732-987-2617, Fax: 732-987-2007.

School of Business Students: 31 full-time (25 women), 121 part-time (78 women); includes 33 minority (12 African Americans, 10 Asian Americans or Pacific Islanders, 11 Hispanic Americans), 3 international. Average age 35. 75 applicants, 91% accepted, 46 enrolled. *Faculty:* 9 full-time (4 women), 8 part-time/adjunct (4 women). Expenses: Contact institution. *Financial support:* Scholarships/grants, health care benefits, and unspecified assistantships available. Financial award application deadline: 4/15; financial award applicants required to submit FAFSA. In 2008, 62 master's, 7 other advanced degrees awarded. *Degree program information:* Part-time and evening/weekend programs available. Offers accounting (Certificate); business administration (MBA). *Application deadline:* For fall admission, 8/1 priority date for domestic students, 4/1 for international students; for spring admission, 1/1 priority date for domestic students, 7/1 for international students. Applications are processed on a rolling basis. *Application fee:* $40. Electronic applications accepted. *Application Contact:* Eugene Soltys, Director of Graduate Admissions, 732-987-2770, Fax: 732-987-2084, E-mail: graduateadmissions@georgian.edu. *Dean,* Binetta Dolan, 732-987-2661, Fax: 732-987-2024.

School of Education Students: 174 full-time (149 women), 619 part-time (511 women); includes 65 minority (22 African Americans, 2 American Indian/Alaska Native, 12 Asian Americans or Pacific Islanders, 29 Hispanic Americans), 1 international. Average age 33. 728 applicants, 78% accepted, 278 enrolled. *Faculty:* 27 full-time (16 women), 50 part-time/adjunct (29 women). Expenses: Contact institution. *Financial support:* In 2008–09, 183 students received support. Scholarships/grants, health care benefits, and unspecified assistantships available. Financial award application deadline: 4/15; financial award applicants required to submit FAFSA. In 2008, 91 master's awarded. *Degree program information:* Part-time and evening/weekend programs available. Offers administration and leadership (MA); education (MA). *Application deadline:* For fall admission, 8/1 priority date for domestic students, 4/1 for international students; for spring admission, 1/1 priority date for domestic students, 7/1 for international students. Applications are processed on a rolling basis. *Application fee:* $40. Electronic applications accepted. *Application Contact:* Eugene Soltys, Director of Graduate Admissions, 732-987-2770, Fax: 732-987-2084, E-mail: graduateadmissions@georgian.edu. *Dean,* Dr. Jacqueline Kress, 732-987-2525.

School of Sciences and Mathematics Students: 52 full-time (48 women), 102 part-time (82 women); includes 18 minority (8 African Americans, 3 Asian Americans or Pacific Islanders, 7 Hispanic Americans), 2 international. Average age 34. 119 applicants, 66% accepted, 58 enrolled. *Faculty:* 16 full-time (10 women), 6 part-time/adjunct (4 women). Expenses: Contact institution. *Financial support:* Scholarships/grants, health care benefits, and unspecified assistantships available. Financial award application deadline: 4/15; financial award applicants required to submit FAFSA. In 2008, 27 master's, 2 other advanced degrees awarded. *Degree program information:* Part-time and evening/weekend programs available. Offers biology (MS); counseling psychology (MA); holistic health (Certificate); holistic health studies (MA); mathematics (MA); professional counselor (Certificate); school psychology (Certificate). *Application deadline:* For fall admission, 8/1 priority date for domestic students, 4/1 for international students; for spring admission, 1/1 priority date for domestic students, 7/1 for international students. Applications are processed on a rolling basis. *Application fee:* $40. Electronic applications accepted. *Application Contact:* Eugene Soltys, Director of Graduate Admissions, 732-987-2770, Fax: 732-987-2084, E-mail: graduateadmissions@georgian.edu. *Dean,* Dr. Linda James, 732-987-2617, Fax: 732-987-2007.

GEORGIA SOUTHERN UNIVERSITY, Statesboro, GA 30460

General Information State-supported, coed, university. CGS member. *Enrollment:* 17,764 graduate, professional, and undergraduate students; 732 full-time matriculated graduate/professional students (456 women), 1,416 part-time matriculated graduate/professional students (1,017 women). *Enrollment by degree level:* 1,407 master's, 531 doctoral, 210 other advanced degrees. *Graduate faculty:* 482 full-time (215 women), 19 part-time/adjunct (9 women). Tuition, state resident: full-time $3840; part-time $160 per semester hour. Tuition, nonresident: full-time $15,336; part-time $639 per semester hour. *Required fees:* $1152. *Graduate housing:* Room and/or apartments available on a first-come, first-served basis to single students; on-campus housing not available to married students. Typical cost: $4630 per year ($7300 including board). Housing application deadline: 5/1. *Student services:* Campus employment opportunities, campus safety program, career counseling, exercise/wellness program, free psychological counseling, grant writing training, international student services, low-cost health insurance, multicultural affairs office, services for students with disabilities, teacher training, writing training. *Library facilities:* Henderson Library. *Online resources:* library catalog, web page, access to other libraries' catalogs. *Collection:* 603,315 titles, 2,484 serial subscriptions, 29,154 audiovisual materials. *Research affiliation:* Oak Ridge National Laboratory (physical sciences), Mount Desert Island Biological Laboratory (marine biology), Space Telescope Science Institute (astronomy, physics), St. Catherine's Island Foundation (marine science, life sciences), Skidaway Institute of Oceanography (marine sciences).

Computer facilities: 2,385 computers available on campus for general student use. A campuswide network can be accessed from student residence rooms and from off campus. Online class registration is available. *Web address:* http://www.georgiasouthern.edu/.

General Application Contact: Office of Graduate Admissions, 912-478-5384, Fax: 912-478-0740, E-mail: gradadmissions@georgiasouthern.edu.

GRADUATE UNITS

Jack N. Averitt College of Graduate Studies Students: 732 full-time (456 women), 1,416 part-time (1,017 women); includes 499 minority (445 African Americans, 2 American Indian/Alaska Native, 21 Asian Americans or Pacific Islanders, 31 Hispanic Americans), 74 international. Average age 33. 1,001 applicants, 80% accepted, 482 enrolled. *Faculty:* 482 full-time (215 women), 19 part-time/adjunct (9 women). Expenses: Contact institution. *Financial support:* In 2008–09, 1,350 students received support, including 192 research assistantships with partial tuition reimbursements available (averaging $6,850 per year), teaching assistantships with partial tuition reimbursements available (averaging $6,850 per year); career-related internships or fieldwork, Federal Work-Study, scholarships/grants, traineeships, tuition waivers (partial), unspecified assistantships, and doctoral stipends also available. Support available to part-time students. Financial award application deadline: 4/15; financial award applicants required to submit FAFSA. In 2008, 459 master's, 69 doctorates, 58 other advanced degrees awarded. *Degree program information:* Part-time programs available. Postbaccalaureate distance learning degree programs offered (minimal on-campus study). *Application deadline:* For fall admission, 3/1 priority date for domestic and international students; for spring admission, 10/1 priority date for domestic students, 10/1 for international students. Applications are processed on a rolling basis. *Application fee:* $50. Electronic applications accepted. *Application Contact:* 912-478-5384, Fax: 912-478-0740, E-mail: gradadmissions@georgiasouthern.edu. *Associate Dean of Graduate Studies and Research,* Dr. Dick Diebolt, 912-478-1710, Fax: 912-478-0605, E-mail: diebolt@georgiasouthern.edu.

Allen E. Paulson College of Science and Technology Students: 58 full-time (27 women), 30 part-time (15 women); includes 12 minority (7 African Americans, 1 Asian American or Pacific Islander, 4 Hispanic Americans), 12 international. Average age 28. 55 applicants, 69% accepted, 26 enrolled. *Faculty:* 96 full-time (25 women), 6 part-time/adjunct (0 women). Expenses: Contact institution. *Financial support:* In 2008–09, 60 students received support, including 38 research assistantships with partial tuition reimbursements available (averaging $6,850 per year), teaching assistantships with partial tuition reimbursements available (averaging $6,850 per year); career-related internships or fieldwork, Federal Work-Study, scholarships/grants, tuition waivers (partial), and unspecified assistantships also available. Support available to part-time students. Financial award application deadline: 4/15; financial award applicants required to submit FAFSA. In 2008, 25 master's awarded. *Degree program information:* Part-time programs available. Offers biology (MS); mathematics (MS); mechanical and electrical engineering technology (M Tech); science and technology (M Tech, MS). *Application deadline:* For fall admission, 3/1 priority date for domestic and international students; for spring admission, 10/1 priority date for domestic students, 10/1 for international students. Applications are processed on a rolling basis. *Application fee:* $50. Electronic applications accepted. *Application Contact:* 912-478-5384, Fax: 912-478-0740, E-mail: gradadmissions@georgiasouthern.edu. *Dean,* Dr. Bret Danilowicz, 912-478-5111, Fax: 912-478-0836, E-mail: bdanilowicz@georgiasouthern.edu.

College of Business Administration Students: 125 full-time (48 women), 160 part-time (73 women); includes 52 minority (37 African Americans, 9 Asian Americans or Pacific Islanders, 6 Hispanic Americans), 25 international. Average age 28. 212 applicants, 74% accepted, 99 enrolled. *Faculty:* 68 full-time (20 women), 1 part-time/adjunct (0 women). Expenses: Contact institution. *Financial support:* In 2008–09, 176 students received support, including 23 research assistantships with partial tuition reimbursements available (averaging $6,850 per year), teaching assistantships with partial tuition reimbursements available (averaging $6,850 per year); career-related internships or fieldwork, Federal Work-Study, scholarships/grants, tuition waivers (partial), and unspecified assistantships also available. Support available to part-time students. Financial award application deadline: 4/15; financial award applicants required to submit FAFSA. In 2008, 114 master's awarded. *Degree program information:* Part-time and evening/weekend programs available. Postbaccalaureate distance learning degree programs offered (no on-campus study). Offers accounting (M Acc); applied economics (MS); business administration (M Acc, MBA, MS). *Application deadline:* For fall admission, 3/1 priority date for domestic and international students; for spring admission, 10/1 priority date for domestic students, 10/1 for international students. Applications are processed on a rolling basis. *Application fee:* $50. Electronic applications accepted. *Application Contact:* 912-478-5384, Fax: 912-478-0740, E-mail: gradadmissions@georgiasouthern.edu. *Dean,* Dr. Ron Shiffler, 912-478-5106, Fax: 912-478-0292, E-mail: shiffler@georgiasouthern.edu.

College of Education Students: 266 full-time (218 women), 1,024 part-time (803 women); includes 340 minority (320 African Americans, 2 American Indian/Alaska Native, 5 Asian Americans or Pacific Islanders, 13 Hispanic Americans), 8 international. Average age 36. 409 applicants, 86% accepted, 190 enrolled. *Faculty:* 66 full-time (47 women), 8 part-time/adjunct (6 women). Expenses: Contact institution. *Financial support:* In 2008–09, 696 students received support, including 26 research assistantships with partial tuition reimbursements available (averaging $6,850 per year), teaching assistantships with partial tuition reimbursements available (averaging $6,850 per year); career-related internships or fieldwork, Federal Work-Study, scholarships/grants, tuition waivers (partial), unspecified assistantships, and doctoral stipends also available. Support available to part-time students. Financial award application deadline: 4/15; financial award applicants required to submit FAFSA. In 2008, 188 master's, 69 doctorates, 58 other advanced degrees awarded. *Degree program information:* Part-time and evening/weekend programs available. Postbaccalaureate distance learning degree programs offered (no on-campus study). Offers accomplished teaching (M Ed); art education (MAT); business education (MAT); counselor education (M Ed, Ed S); curriculum studies (Ed D); early childhood education (MAT); education (M Ed, MAT, Ed D, Ed S); educational administration (Ed D); educational leadership (M Ed, Ed S); English education (M Ed, MAT); French education (M Ed); health and physical education (M Ed); higher education (M Ed); instructional technology (M Ed); mathematics education (M Ed, MAT); middle grades education (M Ed, MAT); reading education (M Ed); school psychology (M Ed, Ed S); science education (M Ed, MAT); secondary and p-12 education (M Ed); social science education (M Ed, MAT); Spanish education (MAT); special education (M Ed, MAT); teaching and learning (Ed S); technology education (M Ed). *Application deadline:* For fall admission, 3/1 priority date for domestic and international students; for spring admission, 10/1 priority date for domestic students, 10/1 for international students. Applications are processed on a rolling basis. *Application fee:* $50. Electronic applications accepted. *Application Contact:* 912-478-5384, Fax: 912-478-0740, E-mail: gradadmissions@georgiasouthern.edu. *Dean,* Dr. Lucindia Chance, 912-478-5649, Fax: 912-478-5093, E-mail: lchance@georgiasouthern.edu.

College of Health and Human Sciences Students: 81 full-time (46 women), 118 part-time (81 women); includes 29 minority (26 African Americans, 1 Asian American or Pacific Islander, 2 Hispanic Americans), 1 international. Average age 30. 137 applicants, 75% accepted, 72 enrolled. *Faculty:* 57 full-time (36 women). Expenses: Contact institution. *Financial support:* In 2008–09, 180 students received support, including 57 research assistantships with partial tuition reimbursements available (averaging $6,850 per year), teaching assistantships with tuition reimbursements available (averaging $6,850 per year); career-related internships or fieldwork, Federal Work-Study, scholarships/grants, traineeships, tuition waivers (partial), and unspecified assistantships also available. Support available to part-time students. Financial award application deadline: 4/15; financial award applicants required to submit FAFSA. In 2008, 53 master's awarded. *Degree program information:* Part-time and evening/weekend programs available. Postbaccalaureate distance learning degree programs offered (no on-campus study). Offers clinical nurse specialist (MSN, Certificate); health and human sciences (MS, MSN, DNP, Certificate); health and kinesiology (MS); nurse practitioner (MSN, Certificate); nursing science (DNP); recreation administration (MS); rural community health nurse practitioner (MSN); rural community health nurse specialist (Certificate); rural family nurse practitioner (MSN, Certificate); sport management (MS); women's health nurse practitioner (MSN, Certificate). *Application deadline:* For fall admission, 3/1 priority date for domestic students, 3/1 for international students; for spring admission, 10/1 priority date for domestic students, 10/1 for international students. Applications are processed on a rolling basis. *Application fee:* $50. Electronic applications accepted. *Application Contact:* 912-681-5384, Fax: 912-681-0740, E-mail: gradadmissions@georgiasouthern.edu. *Dean,* Dr. Frederick Whitt, 912-681-5322, Fax: 912-681-5349, E-mail: fwhitt@georgiasouthern.edu.

College of Liberal Arts and Social Sciences Students: 118 full-time (68 women), 62 part-time (31 women); includes 30 minority (24 African Americans, 6 Hispanic Americans), 3 international. Average age 29. 112 applicants, 81% accepted, 54 enrolled. *Faculty:* 147 full-time (67 women), 3 part-time/adjunct (all women). Expenses: Contact institution. *Financial support:* In 2008–09, 151 students received support, including 46 research assistantships with partial tuition reimbursements available (averaging $6,850 per year), teaching assistantships with partial tuition reimbursements available (averaging $6,850 per year); career-related internships or fieldwork, Federal Work-Study, scholarships/grants, tuition waivers (partial), and unspecified assistantships also available. Support available to part-time students. Financial award application deadline: 4/15; financial award applicants required to submit FAFSA. In 2008, 64 master's awarded. *Degree program information:* Part-time programs available. Offers English (MA); fine arts (MFA); history (MA); liberal arts and social sciences (MA, MFA, MM, MPA, MS, Psy D); music (MM); psychology (MS, Psy D); public administration (MPA); sociology and anthropology (MA); Spanish (MA). *Application deadline:* For fall admission, 3/1 priority date for domestic and international students; for spring admission, 10/1 priority date for domestic students, 10/1 for international students.

Applications are processed on a rolling basis. *Application fee:* $50. Electronic applications accepted. *Application Contact:* 912-478-5384, Fax: 912-478-0740, E-mail: gradadmissions@georgiasouthern.edu. *Dean*, Dr. Sue M. Moore, 912-478-0779, Fax: 912-478-5346, E-mail: smoore@georgiasouthern.edu.

Jiann-Ping Hsu College of Public Health Students: 84 full-time (49 women), 22 part-time (14 women); includes 36 minority (31 African Americans, 5 Asian Americans or Pacific Islanders), 25 international. Average age 30. 76 applicants, 83% accepted, 41 enrolled. *Faculty:* 19 full-time (9 women). Expenses: Contact institution. *Financial support:* In 2008–09, 87 students received support, including research assistantships with partial tuition reimbursements available (averaging $6,850 per year), teaching assistantships with partial tuition reimbursements available (averaging $6,850 per year); career-related internships or fieldwork, Federal Work-Study, scholarships/grants, tuition waivers (partial), and unspecified assistantships also available. Support available to part-time students. Financial award application deadline: 4/15; financial award applicants required to submit FAFSA. In 2008, 15 master's awarded. *Degree program information:* Part-time programs available. Offers biostatistics (MPH, Dr PH); community health behavior and education (Dr PH); community health education (MPH); environmental health sciences (MPH); epidemiology (MPH); health services administration (MHSA); health services policy management (MPH); public health (MHSA, MPH, Dr PH); public health leadership (Dr PH). *Application deadline:* For fall admission, 3/1 priority date for domestic and international students; for spring admission, 10/1 priority date for domestic students, 10/1 for international students. Applications are processed on a rolling basis. *Application fee:* $50. Electronic applications accepted. *Application Contact:* 912-478-5384, Fax: 912-478-0740, E-mail: gradadmissions@georgiasouthern.edu. *Dean*, Dr. Charlie Hardy, 912-478-5653, Fax: 912-478-0381, E-mail: chardy@georgiasouthern.edu.

GEORGIA SOUTHWESTERN STATE UNIVERSITY, Americus, GA 31709-4693

General Information State-supported, coed, comprehensive institution. *Graduate housing:* Room and/or apartments available on a first-come, first-served basis to single students; on-campus housing not available to married students. Housing application deadline: 8/1.

GRADUATE UNITS

Graduate Studies *Degree program information:* Part-time programs available. Electronic applications accepted.

School of Business Administration Offers business administration (MBA). Electronic applications accepted.

School of Computer and Information Sciences *Degree program information:* Part-time programs available. Offers computer information systems (MS); computer science (MS). Electronic applications accepted.

School of Education Offers early childhood education (M Ed, Ed S); health and physical education (M Ed); middle grades education (M Ed, Ed S); reading (M Ed); secondary education (M Ed); special education (M Ed). Electronic applications accepted.

GEORGIA STATE UNIVERSITY, Atlanta, GA 30303-3083

General Information State-supported, coed, university. CGS member. *Enrollment:* 28,238 graduate, professional, and undergraduate students; 4,538 full-time matriculated graduate/professional students (2,684 women), 2,854 part-time matriculated graduate/professional students (1,767 women). *Enrollment by degree level:* 656 first professional, 4,595 master's, 1,502 doctoral, 167 other advanced degrees. *Graduate faculty:* 707 full-time (299 women). Tuition, state resident: full-time $5722; part-time $239 per credit hour. Tuition, nonresident: full-time $22,878; part-time $954 per credit hour. *Required fees:* $600 per semester. *Graduate housing:* Rooms and/or apartments available on a first-come, first-served basis to single and married students. Typical cost: $6746 per year for single students; $5800 per year for married students. *Student services:* Campus employment opportunities, campus safety program, career counseling, child daycare facilities, exercise/wellness program, international student services. *Library facilities:* Pullen Library plus 1 other. *Online resources:* library catalog, web page, access to other libraries' catalogs. *Collection:* 2.2 million titles, 7,398 serial subscriptions, 22,542 audiovisual materials. *Research affiliation:* Brookhaven National Laboratory (Physics), Lowell Observatory (Astronomy), Argonne National Laboratory, Advanced Photon Source (crystallography), Cerro Tololo Interamerican Observatory (astronomy), Research Atlanta Inc. (policy studies), Oak Ridge National Laboratory (environmental policy).

Computer facilities: 1,000 computers available on campus for general student use. A campuswide network can be accessed from student residence rooms and from off campus. Online class registration is available. *Web address:* http://www.gsu.edu/.

General Application Contact: Daniel Niccum, Associate Director, 404-413-2049, E-mail: admissions@gsu.edu.

GRADUATE UNITS

Andrew Young School of Policy Studies Students: 212 full-time (121 women), 123 part-time (71 women); includes 152 minority (92 African Americans, 1 American Indian/Alaska Native, 43 Asian Americans or Pacific Islanders, 16 Hispanic Americans), 47 international. Average age 30. 445 applicants, 47% accepted, 113 enrolled. *Faculty:* 60 full-time (21 women), 11 part-time/adjunct (0 women). Expenses: Contact institution. *Financial support:* In 2008–09, 15 fellowships with full tuition reimbursements (averaging $25,000 per year), 113 research assistantships with full tuition reimbursements (averaging $15,000 per year), 7 teaching assistantships with full tuition reimbursements (averaging $15,000 per year) were awarded; career-related internships or fieldwork, Federal Work-Study, institutionally sponsored loans, scholarships/grants, and tuition waivers (partial) also available. Support available to part-time students. Financial award application deadline: 2/15; financial award applicants required to submit FAFSA. In 2008, 94 master's, 17 doctorates, 6 other advanced degrees awarded. *Degree program information:* Part-time and evening/weekend programs available. Offers disaster management (Certificate); economics (MA, PhD); non-profit management (Certificate); planning and economic development (Certificate); policy studies (MA, MPA, MPP, MS, PhD, Certificate); public administration (MPA); public adminsitration (MPA); public policy (MPP, PhD). *Application deadline:* For fall admission, 4/1 for domestic and international students; for spring admission, 10/1 for domestic and international students. Applications are processed on a rolling basis. *Application fee:* $50. Electronic applications accepted. *Application Contact:* Shelly-Ann Williams, Director, Office of Academic Assistance, 404-413-0021, Fax: 404-413-0023, E-mail: swilliams@gsu.edu. *Dean*, Dr. W. Bartley Hildreth, 404-413-0000, Fax: 404-413-0004.

College of Arts and Sciences Students: 1,326 full-time (787 women), 616 part-time (346 women); includes 402 minority (251 African Americans, 4 American Indian/Alaska Native, 77 Asian Americans or Pacific Islanders, 70 Hispanic Americans), 407 international. Average age 32. 2,208 applicants, 33% accepted, 466 enrolled. *Faculty:* 593 full-time (264 women). Expenses: Contact institution. *Financial support:* Fellowships, research assistantships with full tuition reimbursements, teaching assistantships with full tuition reimbursements, career-related internships or fieldwork, Federal Work-Study, institutionally sponsored loans, scholarships/grants, health care benefits, tuition waivers (full and partial), and unspecified assistantships available. Support available to part-time students. Financial award applicants required to submit FAFSA. In 2008, 350 master's, 78 doctorates, 7 other advanced degrees awarded. *Degree program information:* Part-time and evening/weekend programs available. Offers anthropology (MA); applied and environmental microbiology (MS, PhD); applied linguistics (MA, PhD); arts and sciences (M Mu, MA, MA Ed, MFA, MHP, MS, PhD, Certificate, Graduate Certificate); astronomy (PhD); cellular and molecular biology and physiology (MS, PhD); chemistry (MS, PhD); computer science (MS, PhD); creative writing (MA, MFA, PhD); English (MA, PhD); fiction (MFA); fiction/poetry (MA, MFA); film/video/digital imaging (MA); French (MA, Certificate); geographic information systems (Certificate); geography (MA); geology (MA); German (MA, Certificate); heritage preservation (MHP, Certificate); history (MA, PhD); human communication and social influence (MA); hydrogeology (Certificate); Latin American studies (Certificate); literary studies (MA, PhD); mass communication (MA); mathematics (MA, MS); mathematics and statistics (PhD); molecular genetics and biochemistry (MS, PhD); moving image studies (PhD); neurobiology and behavior (MS, PhD); philosophy (MA); physics (MS, PhD); poetry (MFA); political science (MA, PhD); psychology (MA, PhD); public communication (PhD); religious studies (MA); rhetoric and composition (MA, PhD); sociology (MA, PhD); Spanish (MA, Certificate); translation and interpretation (Certificate). *Application deadline:* For fall admission, 8/1 for domestic students; for winter admission, 10/1 for domestic students; for spring admission, 12/1 for domestic students. Applications are processed on a rolling basis. *Application fee:* $50. Electronic applications accepted. *Application Contact:* Amber Amari, Manager, Graduate and Scheduling Services, 404-413-5037, E-mail: aamari@gsu.edu. *Dean*, Dr. Lauren B. Adamson, 404-413-5114, Fax: 404-413-5117, E-mail: ladamson@gsu.edu.

Ernest G. Welch School of Art and Design Offers art and design (MA, MA Ed, MFA); art education (MA Ed); art history (MA); studio art (MFA). Electronic applications accepted.

Gerontology Institute Students: 18 full-time (17 women), 9 part-time (7 women); includes 7 minority (6 African Americans, 1 Asian American or Pacific Islander), 4 international. 11 applicants, 73% accepted, 7 enrolled. *Faculty:* 28 full-time (22 women). Expenses: Contact institution. *Financial support:* In 2008–09, 8 students received support, including 14 research assistantships with full tuition reimbursements available (averaging $9,000 per year); career-related internships or fieldwork, scholarships/grants, and health care benefits also available. Financial award application deadline: 4/15. In 2008, 6 master's awarded. *Degree program information:* Part-time programs available. Offers gerontology (MA). *Application deadline:* For fall admission, 4/15 for domestic and international students; for spring admission, 10/15 for domestic and international students. Applications are processed on a rolling basis. *Application fee:* $50. Electronic applications accepted. *Application Contact:* Mary MacKinnon, Assistant Director for Student Affairs, 404-413-5211, E-mail: mmackinnon@gsu.edu. *Director*, Dr. Frank J. Whittington, 404-413-5213, Fax: 404-413-5219, E-mail: fwhittington@gsu.edu.

School of Music Students: 79 full-time (35 women); includes 21 minority (16 African Americans, 3 Asian Americans or Pacific Islanders, 2 Hispanic Americans), 9 international. 68 applicants, 66% accepted, 40 enrolled. *Faculty:* 23 full-time (3 women). Expenses: Contact institution. *Financial support:* In 2008–09, 40 students received support, including 1 fellowship with full tuition reimbursement available (averaging $5,000 per year), 36 research assistantships with full tuition reimbursements available (averaging $4,000 per year), 3 teaching assistantships with full tuition reimbursements available (averaging $12,000 per year); career-related internships or fieldwork, Federal Work-Study, institutionally sponsored loans, tuition waivers (full), and unspecified assistantships also available. Support available to part-time students. Financial award application deadline: 4/15; financial award applicants required to submit FAFSA. In 2008, 24 master's awarded. *Degree program information:* Part-time and evening/weekend programs available. Offers music (M Mu). *Application deadline:* For fall admission, 3/15 for domestic and international students; for spring admission, 10/15 for domestic and international students. Applications are processed on a rolling basis. *Application fee:* $50. Electronic applications accepted. *Application Contact:* Dr. Steven Andrew Harper, Director of Graduate Studies, 404-413-5943, Fax: 404-413-5910, E-mail: sharper@gsu.edu. *Director*, W. Dwight Coleman, 404-413-5919, Fax: 404-413-5910, E-mail: wcoleman@gsu.edu.

Women's Studies Institute Students: 6 full-time (all women), 9 part-time (8 women); includes 9 minority (all African Americans). 10 applicants, 60% accepted, 5 enrolled. *Faculty:* 5 full-time (all women). Expenses: Contact institution. *Financial support:* In 2008–09, 1 fellowship with tuition reimbursement (averaging $4,000 per year), 1 research assistantship with tuition reimbursement (averaging $8,000 per year), teaching assistantships with tuition reimbursements (averaging $8,000 per year) were awarded; tuition waivers also available. Financial award application deadline: 2/15; financial award applicants required to submit FAFSA. In 2008, 2 master's awarded. *Degree program information:* Part-time programs available. Offers women's studies (MA, Graduate Certificate). *Application deadline:* For fall admission, 2/15 for domestic and international students. *Application fee:* $50. *Application Contact:* Dr. Susan Talburt, Director of Graduate Studies, 404-413-6581, E-mail: stalburt.gsu.edu. *Director*, Dr. Susan Talburt, 404-413-6581, E-mail: stalburt@gsu.edu.

College of Education Students: 1,010 full-time (770 women), 1,013 part-time (816 women); includes 603 minority (533 African Americans, 4 American Indian/Alaska Native, 41 Asian Americans or Pacific Islanders, 25 Hispanic Americans), 41 international. 2,093 applicants, 29% accepted, 479 enrolled. *Faculty:* 117 full-time (73 women), 92 part-time/adjunct (73 women). Expenses: Contact institution. *Financial support:* In 2008–09, 19 fellowships with full tuition reimbursements (averaging $30,000 per year), 343 research assistantships with full and partial tuition reimbursements, 68 teaching assistantships with full and partial tuition reimbursements were awarded; career-related internships or fieldwork, Federal Work-Study, institutionally sponsored loans, scholarships/grants, tuition waivers (partial), and unspecified assistantships also available. Support available to part-time students. In 2008, 480 master's, 57 doctorates, 62 other advanced degrees awarded. *Degree program information:* Part-time and evening/weekend programs available. Postbaccalaureate distance learning degree programs offered (no on-campus study). Offers art education (Ed S); behavior and learning disabilities (M Ed); communication disorders (M Ed); counseling psychology (PhD); counselor education and practice (PhD); early childhood education (M Ed, MAT, PhD, Ed S); education (M Ed, MAT, MLM, MS, PhD, Ed S); education of students with exceptionalities (PhD); educational leadership (M Ed, PhD, Ed S); educational psychology (MS, PhD); educational research (MS, PhD); English education (M Ed, Ed S); exercise science (MS); health and physical education (M Ed); instructional technology (MS, PhD, Ed S); kinesiology (PhD); library media technology (MLM, PhD, Ed S); library science/media (MLM, MS, PhD, Ed S); mathematics education (M Ed, PhD, Ed S); middle childhood education (M Ed, Ed S); multiple and severe disabilities (M Ed, MAT); music education (PhD); professional counseling (MS, PhD, Ed S); reading instruction (M Ed, PhD, Ed S); reading, language and literacy (M Ed); reading, language, and literacy (PhD, Ed S); rehabilitation counseling (MS); research, measurements and statistics (PhD); school counseling (M Ed, Ed S); school psychology (M Ed, PhD, Ed S); science education (M Ed, PhD, Ed S); secondary education (M Ed, PhD, Ed S); social foundations of education (MS, PhD); social studies education (M Ed, PhD, Ed S); sports administration (MS); sports medicine (MS); teaching English as a second language (M Ed). *Application fee:* $50. Electronic applications accepted. *Application Contact:* Nancy Keita, Office of Academic Assistance, 404-413-8000, E-mail: nkeita@gsu.edu. *Dean*, Dr. Randy W. Kamphaus, 404-413-8100, Fax: 404-413-8103.

College of Health and Human Sciences *Degree program information:* Part-time and evening/weekend programs available. Offers criminal justice (MS); health and human sciences (MPH, MS, MSW, DPT, PhD, Certificate). Electronic applications accepted.

Byrdine F. Lewis School of Nursing Students: 79 full-time (77 women), 128 part-time (118 women); includes 66 minority (52 African Americans, 8 Asian Americans or Pacific Islanders, 6 Hispanic Americans), 2 international. Average age 34. 155 applicants, 45% accepted, 63 enrolled. *Faculty:* 35 full-time (all women), 1 (woman) part-time/adjunct. Expenses: Contact institution. *Financial support:* In 2008–09, 18 students received support, including research assistantships with full and partial tuition reimbursements available (averaging $3,108 per year); fellowships with full tuition reimbursements available, teaching assistantships, Federal Work-Study, institutionally sponsored loans, scholarships/grants, traineeships, health care benefits, tuition waivers (partial), and unspecified assistantships also available. Support available to part-time students. Financial award application deadline: 4/1; financial award applicants required to submit FAFSA. In 2008, 49 master's, 3 doctorates awarded. *Degree program information:* Part-time and evening/weekend programs available. Postbaccalaureate distance learning degree programs offered (minimal on-campus study). Offers adult health (MS); adult health nursing (Certificate); child health (MS); family nurse practitioner (MS, Certificate); health promotion, protection and restoration (PhD); perinatal/women's health (MS); psychiatric mental health nursing (Certificate); psychiatric/mental health (MS); women's health nursing (Certificate). *Application deadline:* For fall admission, 3/1 priority date for domestic students; for spring admission, 10/1 priority date for domestic students. Applications are processed on a rolling basis. *Application fee:* $50. Electronic applications accepted. *Application Contact:* Barbara Smith, Admissions Counselor II, 404-413-1007, E-mail: bbsmith@gsu.edu. *Director*, Dr. Barbara C Woodring, 404-413-1201, Fax: 404-413-1203, E-mail: bwoodring@gsu.edu.

Institute of Public Health Students: 49 full-time (40 women), 60 part-time (49 women). Average age 27. 207 applicants, 29% accepted. *Faculty:* 10 full-time (4 women), 14 part-time/adjunct (7 women). Expenses: Contact institution. *Financial support:* In 2008–09,

Georgia State University (continued)

fellowships with full and partial tuition reimbursements (averaging $2,500 per year), research assistantships with full and partial tuition reimbursements (averaging $4,000 per year) were awarded; Federal Work-Study, scholarships/grants, tuition waivers (partial), and unspecified assistantships also available. Support available to part-time students. In 2008, 30 master's, 1 other advanced degree awarded. *Degree program information:* Part-time and evening/weekend programs available. Offers public health (MPH, Certificate). *Application deadline:* For fall admission, 2/15 for domestic and international students; for spring admission, 9/1 for domestic and international students. *Application fee:* $50. Electronic applications accepted. *Application Contact:* Denise Gouveia, Application Contact, 404-413-1000, Fax: 404-413-1001, E-mail: dgouveia@gsu.edu. *Director,* Dr. Michael P Eriksen, 404-413-1130, Fax: 404-413-1140, E-mail: meriksen@gsu.edu.

School of Health Professions Expenses: Contact institution. *Financial support:* Scholarships/grants and unspecified assistantships available. Offers health professions (MS, DPT); nutrition (MS); physical therapy (DPT); respiratory therapy (MS). *Application Contact:* Dr. Lynda Goodfellow, Director, 404-413-1225, Fax: 404-413-1230, E-mail: ltgoodfellow@gsu.edu. *Director,* Dr. Lynda Goodfellow, 404-413-1225, Fax: 404-413-1230, E-mail: ltgoodfellow@gsu.edu.

School of Social Work Students: 54 full-time (47 women), 9 part-time (7 women); includes 25 minority (23 African Americans, 1 Asian American or Pacific Islander, 1 Hispanic American). Average age 26. 84 applicants, 73% accepted, 38 enrolled. *Faculty:* 16 full-time (11 women), 2 part-time/adjunct (both women). Expenses: Contact institution. *Financial support:* In 2008–09, research assistantships with full and partial tuition reimbursements (averaging $3,108 per year); Federal Work-Study, scholarships/grants, tuition waivers (partial), and unspecified assistantships also available. Support available to part-time students. Financial award application deadline: 4/1; financial award applicants required to submit FAFSA. In 2008, 43 master's awarded. *Degree program information:* Part-time programs available. Offers community partnerships (MSW). *Application deadline:* For fall admission, 2/1 priority date for domestic students. Applications are processed on a rolling basis. *Application fee:* $50. Electronic applications accepted. *Application Contact:* Renanda Dear, Director, Student and Community Services, 404-413-1057, Fax: 404-413-1057, E-mail: rwood@gsu.edu. *Director,* Dr. Nancy Kropf, 404-413-1052, E-mail: nkropf@gsu.edu.

College of Law *Degree program information:* Part-time and evening/weekend programs available. Offers law (JD). Electronic applications accepted.

J. Mack Robinson College of Business *Degree program information:* Part-time and evening/weekend programs available. Offers accounting/information systems (MBA); actuarial science (MAS, MBA); business (EMBA, MAS, MBA, MHA, MIB, MPA, MS, MSHA, MSIS, MSRE, MTX, PMBA, PhD, Certificate); business analysis (MBA, MS); computer information systems (MBA, MSIS, PhD); decision sciences (PhD); economics (MBA, MS); enterprise risk management (MBA); entrepreneurship (MBA); finance (MBA, MS, PhD); general business (MBA); general business administration (EMBA, PMBA); human resources management (MBA, MS); information systems consulting (MBA); information systems risk management (MBA); international business and information technology (MBA); international entrepreneurship (MBA); management (MBA, PhD); marketing (MBA, MS, PhD); operations management (MBA, MS); organization change (MS); personal financial planning (MBA, MS, Certificate); personnel employee relations (PhD); real estate (MBA, MSRE, PhD, Certificate); risk management and insurance (MBA, MS, PhD, Certificate); strategic management (PhD). Electronic applications accepted.

Institute of Health Administration Students: 34 full-time (16 women), 33 part-time (17 women); includes 17 minority (11 African Americans, 6 Asian Americans or Pacific Islanders), 6 international. Average age 30. 34 applicants, 44% accepted, 11 enrolled. *Faculty:* 5 full-time (2 women). Expenses: Contact institution. *Financial support:* Career-related internships or fieldwork and tuition waivers (partial) available. Support available to part-time students. Financial award applicants required to submit FAFSA. In 2008, 14 master's awarded. Offers health administration (MBA, MHA, MSHA). *Application deadline:* For fall admission, 5/1 for domestic students, 2/1 for international students; for spring admission, 10/15 for domestic students, 5/1 for international students. Applications are processed on a rolling basis. *Application fee:* $50. Electronic applications accepted. *Application Contact:* Dr. Andrew T. Sumner, Director, 404-413-7634. *Director,* Dr. Andrew T. Sumner, 404-413-7634.

Institute of International Business Students: 52 full-time (27 women), 58 part-time (25 women); includes 17 minority (6 African Americans, 5 Asian Americans or Pacific Islanders, 6 Hispanic Americans), 8 international. Average age 31. 61 applicants, 64% accepted, 8 enrolled. *Faculty:* 12 full-time (2 women). Expenses: Contact institution. *Financial support:* Fellowships, research assistantships, teaching assistantships, career-related internships or fieldwork and tuition waivers (partial) available. Support available to part-time students. Financial award application deadline: 5/1; financial award applicants required to submit FAFSA. In 2008, 50 master's awarded. *Degree program information:* Part-time and evening/weekend programs available. Offers international business (MBA, MIB). *Application deadline:* For fall admission, 5/1 for domestic students, 2/1 for international students; for spring admission, 10/15 for domestic students, 5/1 for international students. Applications are processed on a rolling basis. *Application fee:* $50. Electronic applications accepted. *Application Contact:* Yiandria Boswell, Assistant to Director, 404-413-7275, Fax: 404-413-7276, E-mail: yboswell@gsu.edu. *Director,* Dr. Tamer Cavusgil, 404-413-7284, Fax: 404-413-7276, E-mail: cavusgil@gsu.edu.

School of Accountancy Students: 124 full-time (71 women), 101 part-time (43 women); includes 79 minority (18 African Americans, 53 Asian Americans or Pacific Islanders, 8 Hispanic Americans). Average age 31. 208 applicants, 43% accepted, 71 enrolled. *Faculty:* 13 full-time (4 women), 6 part-time/adjunct (0 women). Expenses: Contact institution. *Financial support:* Fellowships, research assistantships, teaching assistantships, career-related internships or fieldwork and tuition waivers (partial) available. Support available to part-time students. Financial award applicants required to submit FAFSA. In 2008, 72 master's awarded. *Degree program information:* Part-time and evening/weekend programs available. Offers accountancy (MBA, MPA, MTX, PhD, Certificate); taxation (MTX). *Application deadline:* For fall admission, 4/1 for domestic students, 2/1 for international students; for spring admission, 9/15 for domestic students, 4/1 for international students. Applications are processed on a rolling basis. *Application fee:* $50. Electronic applications accepted. *Application Contact:* Karen A Pierre, Graduate Student and Alumni Services, 404-413 Ext. 7146, E-mail: dbakap@langate.gsu.edu. *Interim Director,* Dr. Galen R. Sevcik, 404-413-7231, E-mail: gsevcik@gsu.edu.

GERSTNER SLOAN-KETTERING GRADUATE SCHOOL OF BIOMEDICAL SCIENCES, New York, NY 10021

General Information Independent, coed, graduate-only institution. *Graduate housing:* Rooms and/or apartments available on a first-come, first-served basis to single and married students.

GRADUATE UNITS

Program in Cancer Biology Offers cancer biology (PhD).

GLION INSTITUTE OF HIGHER EDUCATION, CH-1823 Glion-sur-Montreux, Switzerland

General Information Proprietary, coed, comprehensive institution.

GRADUATE UNITS

Graduate Programs

GLOBAL UNIVERSITY, Springfield, MO 65804

General Information Independent-religious, coed, comprehensive institution. *Enrollment:* 200 full-time matriculated graduate/professional students (27 women), 175 part-time matriculated graduate/professional students (48 women). *Enrollment by degree level:* 29 first professional, 346 master's. *Graduate faculty:* 12 full-time (2 women), 90 part-time/adjunct (10 women). *Tuition:* Full-time $3690; part-time $205 per credit hour. *Required fees:* $205 per credit hour. One-time fee: $50 full-time. *Graduate housing:* On-campus housing not available. *Library facilities:* Global University Library. *Online resources:* web page. *Collection:* 180 serial subscriptions. *Web address:* http://www.globaluniversity.edu/.

General Application Contact: Joe Patterson, Graduate Student Enrollment Representative, 417-862-9533 Ext. 2347, Fax: 417-862-0863, E-mail: gradenroll@globaluniversity.edu.

GRADUATE UNITS

Graduate School of Theology Students: 200 full-time (27 women), 175 part-time (48 women); includes 250 minority (150 African Americans, 25 American Indian/Alaska Native, 50 Asian Americans or Pacific Islanders, 25 Hispanic Americans). Average age 49. 148 applicants, 94% accepted, 139 enrolled. *Faculty:* 10 full-time (1 woman), 83 part-time/adjunct (10 women). Expenses: Contact institution. In 2008, 1 first professional degree, 27 master's awarded. *Degree program information:* Part-time and evening/weekend programs available. Post-baccalaureate distance learning degree programs offered (no on-campus study). Offers biblical studies (MA); divinity (M Div); ministerial studies (MA). *Application deadline:* Applications are processed on a rolling basis. *Application fee:* $50. Electronic applications accepted. *Application Contact:* Jody Patterson, Graduate Student Enrollment Representative, 417-862-9533 Ext. 2347, Fax: 417-862-0863, E-mail: gradenroll@globaluniversity.edu. *Dean,* Dr. Carl Chrisner, 417-862-9533 Ext. 2237, Fax: 417-869-5623, E-mail: cchrisner@globaluniversity.edu.

GODDARD COLLEGE, Plainfield, VT 05667-9432

General Information Independent, coed, comprehensive institution. *Enrollment:* 478 full-time matriculated graduate/professional students (335 women), 1 (woman) part-time matriculated graduate/professional student. *Enrollment by degree level:* 479 master's. *Graduate faculty:* 5 full-time (2 women), 84 part-time/adjunct (60 women). *Tuition:* Full-time $14,446. Full-time tuition and fees vary according to campus/location and program. Part-time tuition and fees vary according to course load and program. *Graduate housing:* On-campus housing not available. *Student services:* Services for students with disabilities, writing training. *Library facilities:* Eliot Pratt Center. *Online resources:* library catalog, web page. *Collection:* 70,000 titles, 17 serial subscriptions, 300 audiovisual materials.

Computer facilities: 55 computers available on campus for general student use. A campuswide network can be accessed from student residence rooms and from off campus. Library services available. *Web address:* http://www.goddard.edu/.

General Application Contact: Josh Castle, Associate Dean for Enrollment, 800-906-8312, Fax: 802-454-1029, E-mail: admissions@goddard.edu.

GRADUATE UNITS

Graduate Programs Students: 478 full-time (335 women), 1 (woman) part-time; includes 68 minority (30 African Americans, 11 American Indian/Alaska Native, 13 Asian Americans or Pacific Islanders, 14 Hispanic Americans), 14 international. Average age 39. 185 applicants, 78% accepted. *Faculty:* 5 full-time (2 women), 84 part-time/adjunct (60 women). Expenses: Contact institution. *Financial support:* In 2008–09, 438 students received support. Tuition waivers (full) available. Financial award applicants required to submit FAFSA. In 2008, 165 master's awarded. *Degree program information:* Part-time programs available. Post-baccalaureate distance learning degree programs offered (minimal on-campus study). Offers community education (MA); consciousness studies (MA); creative writing (MFA); environmental studies (MA); health arts and sciences (MA); interdisciplinary arts (MFA); organizational development (MA); psychology and counseling (MA); sexual orientation (MA); socially responsible business and sustainable communities (MA); teacher licensure (MA); transformative language arts (MA). *Application deadline:* Applications are processed on a rolling basis. *Application fee:* $40. Electronic applications accepted. *Application Contact:* Josh Castle, Associate Dean for Enrollment, 800-906-8312, Fax: 802-454-1029, E-mail: admissions@goddard.edu. *Vice President,* Robert Kenny, 802-454-8311 Ext. 228, Fax: 802-454-1451, E-mail: robert.kenny@goddard.edu.

GOLDEN GATE BAPTIST THEOLOGICAL SEMINARY, Mill Valley, CA 94941-3197

General Information Independent-religious, coed, graduate-only institution. *Graduate housing:* Rooms and/or apartments available on a first-come, first-served basis to single and married students. Housing application deadline: 6/15.

GRADUATE UNITS

Graduate and Professional Programs *Degree program information:* Part-time and evening/weekend programs available. Offers divinity (M Div); early childhood education (Certificate); education leadership (MAEL, Diploma); ministry (D Min); theological studies (MTS); theology (Th M); youth ministry (Certificate). Electronic applications accepted.

GOLDEN GATE UNIVERSITY, San Francisco, CA 94105-2968

General Information Independent, coed, university. *Graduate housing:* On-campus housing not available.

GRADUATE UNITS

Ageno School of Business Students: 385 full-time (212 women), 729 part-time (375 women); includes 402 minority (99 African Americans, 1 American Indian/Alaska Native, 229 Asian Americans or Pacific Islanders, 73 Hispanic Americans), 200 international. Average age 34. 675 applicants, 72% accepted, 251 enrolled. Expenses: Contact institution. *Financial support:* Career-related internships or fieldwork, Federal Work-Study, and institutionally sponsored loans available. Support available to part-time students. Financial award applicants required to submit FAFSA. In 2008, 550 master's, 13 doctorates awarded. *Degree program information:* Part-time and evening/weekend programs available. Offers accounting (MBA); business administration (EMBA, MBA, DBA); finance (MBA, MS, Certificate); financial planning (MS, Certificate); human resource management (MBA, MS); human resources management (Certificate); information technology (MBA); information technology management (MS, Certificate); integrated marketing and communications (MS, Certificate); international business (MBA); management (MBA); marketing (MBA, MS, Certificate); operations management (Certificate); psychology (MA, Certificate); public relations (MS, Certificate). *Application deadline:* Applications are processed on a rolling basis. *Application fee:* $55 ($90 for international students). *Application Contact:* Enrollment Services, 415-442-7800, Fax: 415-442-7807, E-mail: info@ggu.edu. *Dean,* Terry Connelly, 415-442-6519, Fax: 415-442-5369.

School of Accounting Students: 69 full-time (42 women), 117 part-time (71 women); includes 67 minority (4 African Americans, 1 American Indian/Alaska Native, 54 Asian Americans or Pacific Islanders, 8 Hispanic Americans), 45 international. Average age 32. 92 applicants, 82% accepted, 38 enrolled. Expenses: Contact institution. In 2008, 61 master's awarded. Offers accounting (M Ac, Graduate Certificate). *Application fee:* $55 ($90 for international students). *Application Contact:* Angela Williams, Enrollment Services, 415-442-7800, Fax: 415-442-7807, E-mail: info@ggu.edu.

School of Law *Degree program information:* Part-time and evening/weekend programs available. Offers environmental law (LL M); intellectual property law (LL M); international legal studies (LL M, SJD); law (JD); taxation (LL M); U.S. legal studies (LL M). Electronic applications accepted.

School of Taxation Students: 55 full-time (32 women), 650 part-time (387 women); includes 227 minority (18 African Americans, 184 Asian Americans or Pacific Islanders, 25 Hispanic Americans), 41 international. Average age 36. 292 applicants, 88% accepted, 144 enrolled. Expenses: Contact institution. *Financial support:* Career-related internships or fieldwork, Federal Work-Study, and institutionally sponsored loans available. Support available to part-time students. Financial award applicants required to submit FAFSA. In 2008, 242 master's awarded. *Degree program information:* Part-time and evening/weekend programs available. Offers taxation (MS, Certificate). *Application deadline:* For fall admission, 7/1 priority date for domestic students. Applications are processed on a rolling basis. *Application fee:* $55 ($90 for international students). *Application Contact:* Enrollment Services, 415-442-7800, Fax: 415-442-7807, E-mail: info@ggu.edu. *Dean,* Mary Canning, 415-442-7885.

GOLDEY-BEACOM COLLEGE, Wilmington, DE 19808-1999

General Information Independent, coed, comprehensive institution. *Graduate housing:* Room and/or apartments available on a first-come, first-served basis to single students; on-campus housing not available to married students.

GRADUATE UNITS

Graduate Program *Degree program information:* Part-time and evening/weekend programs available. Offers business administration (MBA); financial management (MBA); human resource management (MBA); information technology (MBA); management (MM); marketing management (MBA). Electronic applications accepted.

GOLDFARB SCHOOL OF NURSING AT BARNES-JEWISH COLLEGE, St. Louis, MO 63110

General Information Independent, coed, comprehensive institution. *Graduate housing:* Room and/or apartments available on a first-come, first-served basis to single students; on-campus housing not available to married students.

GRADUATE UNITS

Nursing Programs *Degree program information:* Part-time and evening/weekend programs available. Offers adult nurse practitioner (MSN); neonatal nurse practitioner (MSN); nurse administrator (MSN); nurse anesthesia (MSN); nurse educator (MSN); oncology nurse practitioner (MSN).

GONZAGA UNIVERSITY, Spokane, WA 99258

General Information Independent-religious, coed, comprehensive institution. *Graduate housing:* Rooms and/or apartments available on a first-come, first-served basis to single and married students.

GRADUATE UNITS

College of Arts and Sciences *Degree program information:* Part-time programs available. Offers arts and sciences (MA); pastoral ministry (MA); philosophy (MA); religious studies (MA); spirituality (MA).

Program in Teaching English as a Second Language Offers teaching English as a second language (MATESL). Electronic applications accepted.

School of Business Administration *Degree program information:* Part-time and evening/weekend programs available. Offers business administration (M Acc, MBA).

School of Education *Degree program information:* Part-time and evening/weekend programs available. Offers administration and curriculum (MAA); anesthesiology education (M Anesth Ed); counseling psychology (MAC, MAP); education (M Anesth Ed, M Ed, MA Ed Ad, MAA, MAC, MAP, MASPAA, MAT, MES, MIT); educational administration (MA Ed Ad); initial teaching (MIT); literacy (M Ed); special education (MES); sports and athletic administration (MASPAA); teaching at-risk students (MAT).

School of Law *Degree program information:* Part-time programs available. Offers law (JD).

School of Professional Studies Offers communication and leadership studies (MA); leadership studies (PhD); nursing (MSN); organizational leadership (MOL).

GOODING INSTITUTE OF NURSE ANESTHESIA, Panama City, FL 32401

General Information County-supported, coed, graduate-only institution. *Graduate housing:* On-campus housing not available.

GRADUATE UNITS

Program in Nurse Anesthesia Offers nurse anesthesia (MS).

GORDON COLLEGE, Wenham, MA 01984-1899

General Information Independent-religious, coed, comprehensive institution. *Enrollment:* 1,718 graduate, professional, and undergraduate students; 7 full-time matriculated graduate/professional students (5 women), 141 part-time matriculated graduate/professional students (119 women). *Enrollment by degree level:* 148 master's. *Graduate faculty:* 6 full-time (5 women), 11 part-time/adjunct (9 women). *Tuition:* Full-time $7650; part-time $425 per credit. *Required fees:* $50 per term. One-time fee: $50. *Graduate housing:* On-campus housing not available. *Student services:* Campus employment opportunities, campus safety program, career counseling, exercise/wellness program, free psychological counseling, international student services, low-cost health insurance, services for students with disabilities, teacher training. *Library facilities:* Jenks Learning Resource Center. *Online resources:* library catalog, access to other libraries' catalogs. *Collection:* 142,688 titles, 8,555 serial subscriptions.

Computer facilities: 141 computers available on campus for general student use. A campuswide network can be accessed from student residence rooms and from off campus. Online class registration is available. *Web address:* http://www.gordon.edu/.

General Application Contact: Rebecca Lord, Program Administrator, 978-867-4322, Fax: 978-867-4737, E-mail: graduate-education@gordon.edu.

GRADUATE UNITS

Graduate Education Students: 7 full-time (5 women), 141 part-time (119 women). *Faculty:* 6 full-time (5 women), 11 part-time/adjunct (9 women). Expenses: Contact institution. *Degree program information:* Part-time and evening/weekend programs available. Offers education (M Ed, MAT); music education (MME). *Application deadline:* Applications are processed on a rolling basis. *Application fee:* $50. *Application Contact:* E. Jean Bilsbury, Program Coordinator, 978-867-4322, Fax: 978-867-4663, E-mail: jean.bilsbury@gordon.edu. *Dean of Graduate Studies,* Dr. Malcolm L. Patterson, 978-867-4355, Fax: 978-867-4663, E-mail: malcolm.patterson@gordon.edu.

GORDON-CONWELL THEOLOGICAL SEMINARY, South Hamilton, MA 01982-2395

General Information Independent-religious, coed, graduate-only institution. *Graduate housing:* Rooms and/or apartments available to single and married students. Housing application deadline: 4/1.

GRADUATE UNITS

Graduate and Professional Programs *Degree program information:* Part-time and evening/weekend programs available. Offers Biblical languages (MABL); church history (MACH); counseling (MACO); ministry (D Min); missions/evangelism (MAME); New Testament (MANT); Old Testament (MAOT); religion (MAR); theology (M Div, MATH, Th M, Th D).

GOUCHER COLLEGE, Baltimore, MD 21204-2794

General Information Independent, coed, comprehensive institution. CGS member. *Graduate housing:* On-campus housing not available. *Research affiliation:* Sheppard-Pratt Hospital (education).

GRADUATE UNITS

Historic Preservation Program *Degree program information:* Part-time and evening/weekend programs available. Postbaccalaureate distance learning degree programs offered (minimal on-campus study). Offers historic preservation (MA).

Program in Arts Administration *Degree program information:* Part-time programs available. Postbaccalaureate distance learning degree programs offered (minimal on-campus study). Offers arts administration (MA).

Program in Creative Nonfiction *Degree program information:* Part-time and evening/weekend programs available. Postbaccalaureate distance learning degree programs offered (minimal on-campus study). Offers creative nonfiction (MFA).

Program in Post-Baccalaureate Premedical Studies Offers premedical studies (Certificate).

Programs in Education *Degree program information:* Part-time and evening/weekend programs available. Offers education (M Ed, MAT).

GOVERNORS STATE UNIVERSITY, University Park, IL 60466-0975

General Information State-supported, coed, upper-level institution. CGS member. *Graduate housing:* On-campus housing not available.

GRADUATE UNITS

College of Arts and Sciences *Degree program information:* Part-time and evening/weekend programs available. Offers analytical chemistry (MS); art (MA); arts and sciences (MA, MS); communication studies (MA); computer science (MS); English (MA); environmental biology (MS); instructional and training technology (MA); media communication (MA); political and justice studies (MA).

College of Business and Public Administration *Degree program information:* Part-time and evening/weekend programs available. Offers accounting (MS); business administration (MBA); business and public administration (MBA, MPA, MS); management information systems (MS); public administration (MPA).

College of Education *Degree program information:* Part-time and evening/weekend programs available. Offers counseling (MA); early childhood education (MA); education (MA); educational administration and supervision (MA); multi-categorical special education (MA); psychology (MA); reading (MA).

College of Health Professions *Degree program information:* Part-time and evening/weekend programs available. Offers addictions studies (MHS); communication disorders (MHS); health administration (MHA); health professions (MHA, MHS, MOT, MPT, MSN, MSW, DPT); nursing (MSN); occupational therapy (MOT); physical therapy (MPT, DPT); social work (MSW).

GRACE COLLEGE, Winona Lake, IN 46590-1294

General Information Independent-religious, coed, comprehensive institution. *Graduate housing:* On-campus housing not available.

GRADUATE UNITS

Graduate School in Counseling and Interpersonal Relations *Degree program information:* Part-time programs available. Offers counseling (MA); counseling and interpersonal relations (MA); interpersonal relations (MA). Electronic applications accepted.

GRACELAND UNIVERSITY, Lamoni, IA 50140

General Information Independent-religious, coed, comprehensive institution. *Enrollment:* 2,444 graduate, professional, and undergraduate students; 634 full-time matriculated graduate/professional students (513 women), 131 part-time matriculated graduate/professional students (105 women). *Enrollment by degree level:* 765 master's. *Graduate faculty:* 15 full-time (13 women), 56 part-time/adjunct (43 women). *Tuition:* Part-time $360 per semester hour. *Required fees:* $65 per course. One-time fee: $230 part-time. Tuition and fees vary according to program. *Graduate housing:* On-campus housing not available. *Student services:* Campus safety program, career counseling, free psychological counseling, services for students with disabilities, teacher training, writing training. *Library facilities:* Frederick Madison Smith Library. *Online resources:* library catalog, web page, access to other libraries' catalogs. *Collection:* 124,399 titles, 559 serial subscriptions.

Computer facilities: 106 computers available on campus for general student use. A campuswide network can be accessed from student residence rooms and from off campus. Online class registration is available. *Web address:* http://www.graceland.edu/.

General Application Contact: Cathy Porter, Program Consultant, 816-833-0524 Ext. 4816, Fax: 816-833-2990, E-mail: cgporter@graceland.edu.

GRADUATE UNITS

Community of Christ Seminary Students: 13 full-time (5 women), 6 part-time (3 women); includes 1 minority (American Indian/Alaska Native), 1 international. Average age 43. 9 applicants, 78% accepted, 7 enrolled. *Faculty:* 2 full-time (1 woman), 14 part-time/adjunct (6 women). Expenses: Contact institution. *Financial support:* Scholarships/grants available. Financial award application deadline: 12/15; financial award applicants required to submit FAFSA. In 2008, 10 master's awarded. *Degree program information:* Part-time programs available. Postbaccalaureate distance learning degree programs offered (minimal on-campus study). Offers Christian ministry (MACM); religion (MAR). *Application deadline:* For fall admission, 8/15 priority date for domestic students; for winter admission, 10/15 priority date for domestic students; for spring admission, 4/15 priority date for domestic students. Applications are processed on a rolling basis. *Application fee:* $50. *Application Contact:* Judy K. Luffman, Executive Assistant, 816-833-0524 Ext. 4508, Fax: 816-833-2990, E-mail: luffman@graceland.edu. *Dean,* Dr. Don H. Compier, 800-833-0524 Ext. 4900, Fax: 816-833-2990, E-mail: dcompier@graceland.edu.

Gleazer School of Education Students: 503 full-time (399 women); includes 13 minority (6 African Americans, 2 American Indian/Alaska Native, 2 Asian Americans or Pacific Islanders, 3 Hispanic Americans), 5 international. Average age 32. 101 applicants, 95% accepted, 94 enrolled. *Faculty:* 3 full-time (2 women), 20 part-time/adjunct (16 women). Expenses: Contact institution. *Financial support:* In 2008–09, 437 students received support. Institutionally sponsored loans and scholarships/grants available. Financial award application deadline: 12/15; financial award applicants required to submit FAFSA. In 2008, 280 master's awarded. *Degree program information:* Part-time and evening/weekend programs available. Postbaccalaureate distance learning degree programs offered (minimal on-campus study). Offers collaborative learning and teaching (M Ed); differentiated instruction (M Ed); instructional leadership (M Ed); mild/moderate special education (M Ed); quality schools (M Ed); technology integration (M Ed). *Application deadline:* For spring admission, 1/15 priority date for domestic students. *Application fee:* $50. Electronic applications accepted. *Application Contact:* Tom Kotz, Associate Dean, 641-784-5313 Ext. 4520, E-mail: kotz@graceland.edu. *Dean,* Dr. Nancy Halferty, 641-784-5000 Ext. 5251, E-mail: halferty@graceland.edu.

School of Nursing Students: 126 full-time (111 women), 102 part-time (82 women); includes 14 minority (8 African Americans, 1 American Indian/Alaska Native, 4 Asian Americans or Pacific Islanders, 1 Hispanic American). Average age 40. 53 applicants, 85% accepted, 43 enrolled. *Faculty:* 10 full-time (all women), 22 part-time/adjunct (21 women). Expenses: Contact institution. *Financial support:* In 2008–09, 117 students received support. Institutionally sponsored loans and traineeships available. Support available to part-time students. Financial award applicants required to submit FAFSA. In 2008, 100 master's, 7 other advanced degrees awarded. *Degree program information:* Part-time programs available. Postbaccalaureate distance learning degree programs offered (minimal on-campus study). Offers family nurse practitioner (MSN, PMC); health care administration (MSN, PMC); nurse educator (MSN, PMC). *Application deadline:* For fall admission, 6/1 priority date for domestic students; for winter admission, 10/1 priority date for domestic students; for spring admission, 3/1 priority date for domestic students. *Application fee:* $50. Electronic applications accepted. *Application Contact:* Jesse Bolinger, Program Consultant, 816-833-0524 Ext. 4803, Fax: 816-833-2990, E-mail: bolinger@graceland.edu. *Dean,* Dr. Claudia D. Horton, 816-833-0524 Ext. 4214, Fax: 816-833-2990, E-mail: horton@graceland.edu.

GRACE THEOLOGICAL SEMINARY, Winona Lake, IN 46590-9907

General Information Independent-religious, coed, primarily men, graduate-only institution. *Graduate housing:* On-campus housing not available.

GRADUATE UNITS

Graduate and Professional Programs *Degree program information:* Part-time programs available. Postbaccalaureate distance learning degree programs offered (no on-campus study). Offers biblical studies (Certificate); camp administration (MA); counseling (M Div);

Grace Theological Seminary (continued)
exegetical studies (MA); intercultural studies (M Div, MA); local church studies (MA); pastoral studies (M Div); theological studies (MA); theology (D Min, Diploma). Electronic applications accepted.

GRACE UNIVERSITY, Omaha, NE 68108

General Information Independent-religious, coed, comprehensive institution. *Graduate housing:* Rooms and/or apartments available on a first-come, first-served basis to single and married students.

GRADUATE UNITS

College of Graduate Studies *Degree program information:* Part-time and evening/weekend programs available. Offers biblical studies (MA); counseling (MA). Electronic applications accepted.

GRADUATE INSTITUTE OF APPLIED LINGUISTICS, Dallas, TX 75236

General Information Independent, coed, graduate-only institution.

GRADUATE UNITS

Graduate Programs *Degree program information:* Part-time programs available. Offers applied linguistics (MA, Certificate); language development (MA). Electronic applications accepted.

GRADUATE SCHOOL AND UNIVERSITY CENTER OF THE CITY UNIVERSITY OF NEW YORK, New York, NY 10016-4039

General Information State and locally supported, coed, graduate-only institution. CGS member. *Graduate housing:* Rooms and/or apartments available to single and married students. Housing application deadline: 5/1. *Research affiliation:* American Museum of Natural History (anthropology), Roche Institute of Molecular Biology (biological sciences), New York Botanical Gardens (biological sciences).

GRADUATE UNITS

Graduate Studies Students: 4,248 full-time (2,444 women), 327 part-time (194 women); includes 652 minority (207 African Americans, 5 American Indian/Alaska Native, 167 Asian Americans or Pacific Islanders, 273 Hispanic Americans), 986 international. Average age 35. 3,574 applicants, 35% accepted, 650 enrolled. *Faculty:* 1,471 full-time (318 women). Expenses: Contact institution. *Financial support:* In 2008–09, 2,460 fellowships, 156 research assistantships, 224 teaching assistantships were awarded; career-related internships or fieldwork, Federal Work-Study, institutionally sponsored loans, and tuition waivers (full and partial) also available. Financial award application deadline: 2/1; financial award applicants required to submit FAFSA. In 2008, 50 master's, 342 doctorates awarded. Offers accounting (PhD); anthropological linguistics (PhD); archaeology (PhD); architecture (PhD); audiology (Au D); basic applied neurocognition (PhD); behavioral science (PhD); biochemistry (PhD); biology (PhD); biomedical engineering (PhD); biopsychology (PhD); chemical engineering (PhD); chemistry (PhD); civil engineering (PhD); classics (MA, PhD); clinical psychology (PhD); comparative literature (MA, PhD); computer science (PhD); criminal justice (PhD); cultural anthropology (PhD); developmental psychology (PhD); earth and environmental sciences (PhD); economics (PhD); educational psychology (PhD); electrical engineering (PhD); English (PhD); environmental psychology (PhD); experimental psychology (PhD); finance (PhD); French (PhD); Germanic languages and literatures (MA, PhD); graphic arts (PhD); Hispanic and Luso-Brazilian literatures and languages (PhD); history (PhD); industrial psychology (PhD); learning processes (PhD); liberal studies (MA); linguistics (MA, PhD); management planning systems (PhD); mathematics (PhD); mechanical engineering (PhD); music (DMA, PhD); neuropsychology (PhD); nursing science (DNS); painting (PhD); philosophy (MA, PhD); photography (PhD); physical anthropology (PhD); physical therapy (DPT); physics (PhD); political science (MA, PhD); psychology (PhD); public health (DPH); sculpture (PhD); social personality (PhD); social welfare (DSW, PhD); sociology (PhD); speech and hearing sciences (PhD); theatre (PhD); urban education (PhD). *Application fee:* $125. Electronic applications accepted. *Application Contact:* Les Gribben, Director of Admissions, 212-817-7470, Fax: 212-817-1624, E-mail: lgribben@gc.cuny.edu. *Acting Provost and Senior Vice President for Academic Affairs,* Dr. Linda Edwards, 212-817-7200, Fax: 212-817-1612, E-mail: provost@gc.cuny.edu.

Interdisciplinary Studies Offers language in social context (PhD); medieval studies (PhD); public policy (MA, PhD); urban studies (MA, PhD); women's studies (MA, PhD).

GRADUATE THEOLOGICAL UNION, Berkeley, CA 94709-1212

General Information Independent-religious, coed, graduate-only institution. *Enrollment by degree level:* 128 master's, 202 doctoral, 7 other advanced degrees. *Graduate faculty:* 110 full-time (43 women), 43 part-time/adjunct (13 women). *Tuition:* Full-time $24,230; part-time $3000 per course. *Graduate housing:* Rooms and/or apartments available on a first-come, first-served basis to single and married students. Housing application deadline: 6/1. *Student services:* Campus employment opportunities, international student services, low-cost health insurance, services for students with disabilities, teacher training, writing training. *Library facilities:* Flora Lamson Hewlett Library. *Online resources:* library catalog, web page, access to other libraries' catalogs. *Collection:* 475,028 titles, 1,572 serial subscriptions, 10,052 audiovisual materials.

Computer facilities: 60 computers available on campus for general student use. A campuswide network can be accessed from student residence rooms and from off campus. Online class registration is available. *Web address:* http://www.gtu.edu/.

General Application Contact: Dr. Kathleen Kook, Associate Dean for Admissions, 800-826-4488, Fax: 510-649-1730, E-mail: gtuadm@gtu.edu.

GRADUATE UNITS

Graduate Programs Students: 304 full-time (142 women), 33 part-time (15 women); includes 49 minority (15 African Americans, 2 American Indian/Alaska Native, 21 Asian Americans or Pacific Islanders, 11 Hispanic Americans), 74 international. *Faculty:* 110 full-time (43 women), 43 part-time/adjunct (13 women). Expenses: Contact institution. *Financial support:* Fellowships, research assistantships, teaching assistantships, Federal Work-Study, scholarships/grants, and tuition waivers (partial) available. Support available to part-time students. Financial award application deadline: 2/1; financial award applicants required to submit FAFSA. Offers art and religion (MA, PhD, Th D); biblical languages (MA); Biblical studies (PhD, Th D); biblical studies (MA); Buddhist studies (MA); Christian spirituality (MA, PhD, Th D); cultural and historical studies of religions (MA, PhD, Th D); ethics and social theory (PhD, Th D); history (MA, PhD, Th D); homiletics (MA, PhD, Th D); interdisciplinary studies (PhD, Th D); Jewish studies (MA, PhD, Th D, Certificate); liturgical studies (MA, PhD, Th D); Near Eastern religions (PhD, Th D); Orthodox Christian studies (MA); religion and psychology (MA, PhD, Th D); religion and society/ethics and social theory (MA); systematic and philosophical theology (MA, PhD, Th D). *Application deadline:* For fall admission, 12/15 for domestic and international students; for winter admission, 2/15 for domestic and international students; for spring admission, 9/30 for domestic and international students. *Application fee:* $40. Electronic applications accepted. *Application Contact:* Dr. Kathleen Kook, Associate Dean for Admissions, 800-826-4488, Fax: 510-649-1730, E-mail: gtuadm@gtu.edu. *Dean,* Dr. Arthur G. Holder, 510-649-2440, Fax: 510-649-1417, E-mail: aholder@gtu.edu.

GRAMBLING STATE UNIVERSITY, Grambling, LA 71245

General Information State-supported, coed, university. CGS member. *Enrollment:* 5,253 graduate, professional, and undergraduate students; 259 full-time matriculated graduate/professional students (198 women), 171 part-time matriculated graduate/professional students (117 women). *Enrollment by degree level:* 362 master's, 66 doctoral, 2 other advanced degrees. *Graduate faculty:* 52 full-time (28 women), 15 part-time/adjunct (7 women). Tuition, state resident: full-time $3637; part-time $134 per credit hour. Tuition, nonresident: full-time $7651; part-time $134 per credit hour. *Required fees:* $1225; $430 per semester. *Graduate housing:* On-campus housing not available. *Student services:* Campus employment opportunities, campus safety program, career counseling, free psychological counseling, international student services, low-cost health insurance, multicultural affairs office, services for students with disabilities, teacher training, writing training. *Library facilities:* A. C. Lewis Memorial Library. *Online resources:* library catalog, web page, access to other libraries' catalogs. *Collection:* 230,243 titles, 5,434 audiovisual materials. *Research affiliation:* National Science Foundation (science and engineering), NASA (aeronautics research), US Environmental Protection Agency (human health and environment).

Computer facilities: 600 computers available on campus for general student use. A campuswide network can be accessed from student residence rooms and from off campus. Online class registration is available. *Web address:* http://www.gram.edu/.

General Application Contact: Katina Crowe, Special Assistant to Associate Vice President/Dean, 318-274-2158, Fax: 318-274-7373, E-mail: croweks@gram.edu.

GRADUATE UNITS

School of Graduate Studies and Research Students: 259 full-time (198 women), 171 part-time (117 women); includes 346 minority (341 African Americans, 2 American Indian/Alaska Native, 1 Asian American or Pacific Islander, 2 Hispanic Americans), 20 international. Average age 34. 165 applicants, 92% accepted, 118 enrolled. *Faculty:* 52 full-time (28 women), 15 part-time/adjunct (7 women). Expenses: Contact institution. *Financial support:* In 2008–09, 299 students received support, including 39 research assistantships (averaging $5,806 per year), 2 teaching assistantships (averaging $6,139 per year); career-related internships or fieldwork, traineeships, health care benefits, tuition waivers (full), and unspecified assistantships also available. Financial award application deadline: 5/31; financial award applicants required to submit FAFSA. In 2008, 93 master's, 3 doctorates, 1 other advanced degree awarded. *Degree program information:* Part-time and evening/weekend programs available. *Application deadline:* For fall admission, 7/1 for domestic and international students; for spring admission, 12/1 for domestic and international students. Applications are processed on a rolling basis. *Application fee:* $20 ($30 for international students). Electronic applications accepted. *Application Contact:* Katina Crowe, Special Assistant to Associate Vice President/Dean, 318-274-2158, Fax: 318-274-7373, E-mail: croweks@gram.edu. *Associate Vice President/Dean, School of Graduate Studies and Research,* Dr. Janet Guyden, 318-274-7374, Fax: 318-274-7373, E-mail: guydenj@gram.edu.

College of Arts and Sciences Students: 39 full-time (29 women), 38 part-time (25 women); includes 71 minority (all African Americans), 5 international. Average age 31. *Faculty:* 7 full-time (2 women), 5 part-time/adjunct (3 women). Expenses: Contact institution. *Financial support:* In 2008–09, 3 research assistantships (averaging $5,056 per year) were awarded; career-related internships or fieldwork, health care benefits, tuition waivers (full), and unspecified assistantships also available. Financial award application deadline: 5/31; financial award applicants required to submit FAFSA. In 2008, 27 master's awarded. *Degree program information:* Part-time programs available. Offers arts and sciences (MAT, MPA); health service administration (MPA); human resource management (MPA); public management (MPA); social sciences (MAT); state and local government (MPA). *Application deadline:* For fall admission, 7/1 for domestic and international students; for spring admission, 12/1 for domestic and international students. Applications are processed on a rolling basis. *Application fee:* $20 ($30 for international students). Electronic applications accepted. *Application Contact:* Katina Crowe, Special Assistant to Associate Vice President/Dean, 318-274-2158, Fax: 318-274-7373, E-mail: croweks@gram.edu. *Dean,* Dr. Connie Walton, 318-274-6202, Fax: 318-274-6041, E-mail: waltonc@gram.edu.

College of Education Students: 61 full-time (39 women), 98 part-time (66 women); includes 125 minority (122 African Americans, 2 American Indian/Alaska Native, 1 Asian American or Pacific Islander), 6 international. Average age 37. *Faculty:* 24 full-time (14 women), 1 part-time/adjunct (0 women). Expenses: Contact institution. *Financial support:* In 2008–09, 10 research assistantships (averaging $7,303 per year) were awarded; career-related internships or fieldwork, health care benefits, tuition waivers (full), and unspecified assistantships also available. Financial award application deadline: 5/31. In 2008, 16 master's, 3 doctorates awarded. *Degree program information:* Part-time and evening/weekend programs available. Offers curriculum and instruction (Ed D); developmental education (MS, Ed D); education (MS, Ed D); educational leadership (MS, Ed D); sports administration (MS). *Application deadline:* For fall admission, 7/1 for domestic and international students; for spring admission, 12/1 for domestic and international students. Applications are processed on a rolling basis. *Application fee:* $20 ($30 for international students). Electronic applications accepted. *Application Contact:* Laketha Richards, Administrative Assistant III, 318-274-6105, Fax: 318-274-6249, E-mail: richardsl@gram.edu. *Dean,* Dr. Sean Warner, 318-274-3235, Fax: 318-274-2799, E-mail: warners@gram.edu.

College of Professional Studies Students: 159 full-time (130 women), 35 part-time (26 women); includes 150 minority (148 African Americans, 2 Hispanic Americans), 9 international. Average age 33. *Faculty:* 21 full-time (12 women), 9 part-time/adjunct (4 women). Expenses: Contact institution. *Financial support:* In 2008–09, 12 research assistantships (averaging $4,414 per year) were awarded; career-related internships or fieldwork, health care benefits, tuition waivers (full and partial), and unspecified assistantships also available. Financial award application deadline: 5/31; financial award applicants required to submit FAFSA. In 2008, 49 master's awarded. *Degree program information:* Part-time programs available. Offers criminal justice (MS); family nurse practitioner (MSN, PMC); mass communication (MA); nurse educator (MSN); social work (MSW). *Application deadline:* For fall admission, 7/1 for domestic and international students; for spring admission, 12/1 for domestic and international students. Applications are processed on a rolling basis. *Application fee:* $20 ($30 for international students). Electronic applications accepted. *Application Contact:* Katina Crowe, Special Assistant to Associate Vice President/Dean, 318-274-2158, Fax: 318-274-7373, E-mail: croweks@gram.edu. *Interim Dean,* Dr. Rama Tunuguntla, 318-274-3185, Fax: 318-274-2355, E-mail: tunuguntla@gram.edu.

GRAND CANYON UNIVERSITY, Phoenix, AZ 85017-1097

General Information Independent-religious, coed, university. CGS member. *Enrollment:* 1,074 full-time matriculated graduate/professional students (801 women), 11,179 part-time matriculated graduate/professional students (8,308 women). *Enrollment by degree level:* 12,162 master's, 75 doctoral, 16 other advanced degrees. *Graduate faculty:* 69 full-time (34 women), 432 part-time/adjunct (300 women). *Graduate housing:* Rooms and/or apartments available on a first-come, first-served basis to single and married students. *Student services:* Campus employment opportunities, campus safety program, career counseling, exercise/wellness program, international student services, low-cost health insurance, multicultural affairs office, services for students with disabilities, teacher training, writing training. *Library facilities:* Grand Canyon University Library. *Online resources:* library catalog, web page.

Computer facilities: 65 computers available on campus for general student use. A campuswide network can be accessed from student residence rooms and from off campus. Online class registration is available. *Web address:* http://www.gcu.edu/.

General Application Contact: Becky Schildt, Online Enrollment Manager, 800-557-9551, Fax: 888-695-6316, E-mail: bschildt@online.gcu.edu.

GRADUATE UNITS

College of Business Students: 137 full-time (53 women), 1,548 part-time (845 women); includes 84 minority (40 African Americans, 3 American Indian/Alaska Native, 17 Asian Americans or Pacific Islanders, 24 Hispanic Americans), 30 international. Average age 38. *Faculty:* 8 full-time (4 women), 302 part-time/adjunct (141 women). Expenses: Contact institution. *Financial support:* Federal Work-Study available. Support available to part-time students. Financial award applicants required to submit FAFSA. In 2008, 400 master's awarded. *Degree program information:* Part-time and evening/weekend programs available. Postbaccalaureate distance learning degree programs offered (no on-campus study). Offers accounting (MBA); executive fire service leadership (MS); finance (MBA); general management (MBA); health systems management (MBA); leadership (MBA, MS); management of information system (MBA); marketing (MBA); six sigma (MBA). *Application deadline:* For fall admission, 8/21 for domestic students, 7/2 for international students; for spring admission, 12/24 for domestic students, 11/1 for international students. Applications are processed on a rolling basis. *Application fee:* $100. Electronic applications accepted. *Application Contact:*

Matt Tidwell, Enrollment Manager, 602-639-6020, E-mail: mtidwell@gcu.edu. *Dean*, Kim Donaldson, 602-639-6597, E-mail: kdonaldson@gcu.edu.

College of Education Students: 894 full-time (714 women), 8,731 part-time (6,779 women); includes 484 minority (312 African Americans, 15 American Indian/Alaska Native, 33 Asian Americans or Pacific Islanders, 124 Hispanic Americans), 3 international. Average age 38. *Faculty:* 397 part-time/adjunct (305 women). Expenses: Contact institution. *Financial support:* Federal Work-Study available. Support available to part-time students. Financial award applicants required to submit FAFSA. In 2008, 2,928 master's awarded. *Degree program information:* Part-time and evening/weekend programs available. Postbaccalaureate distance learning degree programs offered (no on-campus study). Offers curriculum and instruction (M Ed); education administration (M Ed); elementary education (M Ed); organizational leadership (Ed D); secondary education (M Ed); special education (M Ed); teaching (MA). *Application deadline:* For fall admission, 8/21 for domestic students, 7/2 for international students; for spring admission, 12/24 for domestic students, 11/1 for international students. Applications are processed on a rolling basis. *Application fee:* $100. Electronic applications accepted. *Application Contact:* Becky Schildt, Online Enrollment Manager, 800-557-9551, Fax: 888-695-6316, E-mail: bschildt@online.gcu.edu. *Dean*, Dr. Cindy K. Knott, 602-639-6002, E-mail: cknott@gcu.edu.

College of Nursing and Health Sciences Students: 87 full-time (72 women), 783 part-time (665 women); includes 123 minority (71 African Americans, 6 American Indian/Alaska Native, 13 Asian Americans or Pacific Islanders, 33 Hispanic Americans), 5 international. Average age 44. *Faculty:* 21 full-time (16 women), 224 part-time/adjunct (164 women). Expenses: Contact institution. *Financial support:* Federal Work-Study available. Support available to part-time students. Financial award applicants required to submit FAFSA. In 2008, 151 master's awarded. *Degree program information:* Part-time and evening/weekend programs available. Postbaccalaureate distance learning degree programs offered (no on-campus study). Offers addiction counseling (MS); nursing (MS); professional counseling (MS). *Application deadline:* For fall admission, 8/21 for domestic students, 7/2 for international students; for spring admission, 12/24 for domestic students, 11/1 for international students. *Application fee:* $100. *Application Contact:* Andrea Wolochuk, Information Contact, 602-639-6429, E-mail: awolochuk@gcu.edu. *Vice President*, Dr. Fran Roberts, 602-639-6163, E-mail: froberts@gcu.edu.

GRAND RAPIDS THEOLOGICAL SEMINARY OF CORNERSTONE UNIVERSITY, Grand Rapids, MI 49525-5897

General Information Independent-religious, coed, graduate-only institution. *Graduate housing:* Rooms and/or apartments available on a first-come, first-served basis to single and married students. Housing application deadline: 6/1.

GRADUATE UNITS

Graduate Programs *Degree program information:* Part-time programs available. Postbaccalaureate distance learning degree programs offered (minimal on-campus study). Offers biblical counseling (MA); Biblical counseling (M Div); chaplaincy (M Div); Christian education (M Div, MA); intercultural studies (M Div, MA); New Testament (MA, Th M); Old Testament (MA, Th M); pastoral studies (M Div); systematic theology (MA); theology (Th M). Electronic applications accepted.

GRAND VALLEY STATE UNIVERSITY, Allendale, MI 49401-9403

General Information State-supported, coed, comprehensive institution. CGS member. *Enrollment:* 23,892 graduate, professional, and undergraduate students; 814 full-time matriculated graduate/professional students (538 women), 2,216 part-time matriculated graduate/professional students (1,529 women). *Enrollment by degree level:* 2,895 master's, 122 doctoral, 13 other advanced degrees. *Graduate faculty:* 181 full-time (81 women), 63 part-time/adjunct (31 women). *Graduate housing:* Rooms and/or apartments available on a first-come, first-served basis to single and married students. Housing application deadline: 2/1. *Student services:* Campus employment opportunities, campus safety program, career counseling, child daycare facilities, exercise/wellness program, free psychological counseling, grant writing training, international student services, low-cost health insurance, multicultural affairs office, services for students with disabilities, teacher training, writing training. *Library facilities:* James H. Zumberge Library plus 2 others. *Online resources:* library catalog. *Collection:* 664,000 titles, 8,000 serial subscriptions. *Research affiliation:* Elkins Innovations (life sciences), Progressive AE (water quality).

Computer facilities: 2,600 computers available on campus for general student use. A campuswide network can be accessed from student residence rooms and from off campus. Online class registration, transcript, degree audit, credit card payments are available. *Web address:* http://www.gvsu.edu/.

General Application Contact: Tracey James-Heer, Associate Director for Graduate Recruitment, 616-331-2025, Fax: 616-486-6476, E-mail: james-ht@gvsu.edu.

GRADUATE UNITS

College of Community and Public Service Students: 191 full-time (147 women), 351 part-time (277 women); includes 82 minority (47 African Americans, 8 American Indian/Alaska Native, 8 Asian Americans or Pacific Islanders, 19 Hispanic Americans), 19 international. Average age 31. 233 applicants, 91% accepted, 162 enrolled. *Faculty:* 31 full-time (14 women), 16 part-time/adjunct (13 women). Expenses: Contact institution. *Financial support:* In 2008–09, 20 students received support, including research assistantships with full and partial tuition reimbursements available (averaging $8,000 per year); fellowships, teaching assistantships, career-related internships or fieldwork, Federal Work-Study, institutionally sponsored loans, scholarships/grants, and unspecified assistantships also available. Financial award application deadline: 5/1. In 2008, 240 master's awarded. *Degree program information:* Part-time and evening/weekend programs available. Postbaccalaureate distance learning degree programs offered (no on-campus study). Offers community and public service (MHA, MPA, MS, MSW). *Application deadline:* For fall admission, 5/1 priority date for domestic students; for winter admission, 11/1 priority date for domestic students; for spring admission, 4/10 priority date for domestic students. Applications are processed on a rolling basis. *Application fee:* $30. Electronic applications accepted. *Application Contact:* Tracey James-Heer, Associate Director for Graduate Recruitment, 616-331-2025, Fax: 616-486-6476, E-mail: james-ht@gvsu.edu. *Dean*, George Grant, 616-331-6550.

School of Criminal Justice Students: 11 full-time (9 women), 8 part-time (5 women); includes 2 minority (both American Indian/Alaska Native), 1 international. Average age 27. 11 applicants, 73% accepted, 6 enrolled. *Faculty:* 6 full-time (4 women). Expenses: Contact institution. *Financial support:* In 2008–09, 12 students received support, including 1 research assistantship with full tuition reimbursement available (averaging $8,000 per year); career-related internships or fieldwork, Federal Work-Study, scholarships/grants, and unspecified assistantships also available. Support available to part-time students. Financial award application deadline: 5/1. In 2008, 5 master's awarded. *Degree program information:* Part-time and evening/weekend programs available. Offers criminal justice (MS). *Application deadline:* For fall admission, 7/30 priority date for domestic students; for winter admission, 12/10 priority date for domestic students; for spring admission, 4/10 priority date for domestic students. *Application fee:* $30. *Application Contact:* Dr. Debra Ross, Information Contact, 616-331-7150, Fax: 616-331-7155, E-mail: rossd@gvsu.edu. *Director*, Dr. William Crawley, 616-331-7143, Fax: 616-331-7155, E-mail: crawleyw@gvsu.edu.

School of Public and Nonprofit Administration Students: 58 full-time (34 women), 120 part-time (77 women); includes 33 minority (21 African Americans, 1 American Indian/Alaska Native, 4 Asian Americans or Pacific Islanders, 7 Hispanic Americans), 10 international. Average age 32. 83 applicants, 94% accepted, 58 enrolled. *Faculty:* 11 full-time (4 women), 15 part-time/adjunct (5 women). Expenses: Contact institution. *Financial support:* In 2008–09, 28 students received support, including 13 research assistantships with partial tuition reimbursements available (averaging $8,000 per year); career-related internships or fieldwork, Federal Work-Study, scholarships/grants, and unspecified assistantships also available. Financial award application deadline: 5/1. In 2008, 58 master's awarded. *Degree program information:* Part-time and evening/weekend programs available. Offers health administration (MHA); public and nonprofit administration (MHA, MPA). *Application deadline:* For fall admission, 5/1 priority date for domestic students; for winter admission, 11/1 priority date for domestic students. Applications are processed on a rolling basis. *Application fee:* $30. Electronic applications accepted. *Application Contact:* Tracey James-Heer, Associate Director for Graduate Recruitment, 616-331-2025, Fax: 616-486-6476, E-mail: james-ht@gvsu.edu. *Director*, Dr. Mark Hoffman, 616-331-6575, Fax: 616-331-7120, E-mail: hoffman@gvsu.edu.

School of Social Work Students: 104 full-time (93 women), 194 part-time (172 women); includes 41 minority (24 African Americans, 3 American Indian/Alaska Native, 3 Asian Americans or Pacific Islanders, 11 Hispanic Americans), 8 international. Average age 31. 124 applicants, 92% accepted, 89 enrolled. *Faculty:* 13 full-time (6 women), 13 part-time/adjunct (12 women). Expenses: Contact institution. *Financial support:* In 2008–09, 32 research assistantships with full and partial tuition reimbursements (averaging $6,000 per year) were awarded; career-related internships or fieldwork, Federal Work-Study, institutionally sponsored loans, and unspecified assistantships also available. In 2008, 115 master's awarded. *Degree program information:* Part-time programs available. Offers social work (MSW). *Application deadline:* For fall admission, 5/1 priority date for domestic students; for winter admission, 10/1 priority date for domestic students; for spring admission, 3/15 priority date for domestic students. Applications are processed on a rolling basis. *Application fee:* $30. Electronic applications accepted. *Application Contact:* Prof. Lois Smith Owens, Chair, Admissions, 616-331-6577, E-mail: owensl@gvsu.edu.

College of Education Students: 161 full-time (103 women), 1,309 part-time (991 women); includes 103 minority (53 African Americans, 7 American Indian/Alaska Native, 14 Asian Americans or Pacific Islanders, 29 Hispanic Americans), 2 international. Average age 32. 268 applicants, 96% accepted, 195 enrolled. *Faculty:* 58 full-time (29 women), 24 part-time/adjunct (14 women). Expenses: Contact institution. *Financial support:* In 2008–09, 46 research assistantships with full and partial tuition reimbursements (averaging $8,000 per year) were awarded; career-related internships or fieldwork, Federal Work-Study, scholarships/grants, and unspecified assistantships also available. In 2008, 493 master's, 5 Ed Ss awarded. *Degree program information:* Part-time and evening/weekend programs available. Postbaccalaureate distance learning degree programs offered (minimal on-campus study). Offers adult and higher education (M Ed); college student affairs leadership (M Ed); early childhood developmental delay (M Ed); early childhood education (M Ed); education (M Ed, Ed S); educational differentiation (M Ed); educational leadership (M Ed); educational technology integration (M Ed); elementary education (M Ed); emotional impairment (M Ed); learning disabilities (M Ed); middle level education (M Ed); reading and language arts (M Ed); school counseling (M Ed); school library media services (M Ed); secondary level education (M Ed); special education administration (M Ed); teaching English to speakers of other languages (M Ed). *Application deadline:* Applications are processed on a rolling basis. *Application fee:* $30. Electronic applications accepted. *Application Contact:* Stephen Worst, Admissions Office, 616-331-2025, Fax: 616-331-2000. *Dean*, Dr. Elaine C. Collins, 616-331-6821, Fax: 616-331-6515, E-mail: collinse@gvsu.edu.

College of Health Professions Students: 249 full-time (192 women), 3 part-time (2 women); includes 13 minority (3 African Americans, 6 Asian Americans or Pacific Islanders, 4 Hispanic Americans). Average age 25. 285 applicants, 37% accepted, 98 enrolled. *Faculty:* 21 full-time (12 women), 3 part-time/adjunct (2 women). Expenses: Contact institution. *Financial support:* In 2008–09, 11 research assistantships with full tuition reimbursements (averaging $8,000 per year) were awarded; career-related internships or fieldwork, Federal Work-Study, institutionally sponsored loans, and scholarships/grants also available. Financial award application deadline: 2/15. In 2008, 46 master's, 37 doctorates awarded. Offers health professions (MPAS, MS, DPT); occupational therapy (MS); physical therapy (DPT); physician assistant studies (MPAS). *Application deadline:* For winter admission, 1/15 priority date for domestic and international students. Applications are processed on a rolling basis. Electronic applications accepted. *Application Contact:* Darlene Zwart, Student Services Coordinator, 616-331-3958, E-mail: zwartda@gvsu.edu. *Dean*, Dr. Roy Olson, 616-331-3356, Fax: 616-331-3350.

College of Liberal Arts and Sciences Students: 72 full-time (43 women), 104 part-time (64 women); includes 16 minority (8 African Americans, 1 American Indian/Alaska Native, 3 Asian Americans or Pacific Islanders, 4 Hispanic Americans), 29 international. Average age 30. 144 applicants, 56% accepted, 54 enrolled. *Faculty:* 24 full-time (13 women), 4 part-time/adjunct (0 women). Expenses: Contact institution. *Financial support:* In 2008–09, 22 research assistantships with full and partial tuition reimbursements (averaging $8,000 per year), teaching assistantships with full and partial tuition reimbursements (averaging $8,000 per year) were awarded; fellowships, career-related internships or fieldwork, Federal Work-Study, institutionally sponsored loans, scholarships/grants, and unspecified assistantships also available. In 2008, 54 master's awarded. *Degree program information:* Part-time and evening/weekend programs available. Offers biology (MS); biomedical sciences (MHS); biostatistics (MS); cell and molecular biology (MS); English (MA); liberal arts and sciences (MA, MHS, MS). *Application fee:* $30. Electronic applications accepted. *Application Contact:* Tracey James-Heer, Associate Director for Graduate Recruitment, 616-331-2025, Fax: 616-486-6476, E-mail: james-ht@gvsu.edu. *Dean*, Dr. Frederick Antczak, 616-331-2261.

School of Communications Students: 14 full-time (12 women), 37 part-time (23 women); includes 13 minority (8 African Americans, 2 Asian Americans or Pacific Islanders, 3 Hispanic Americans), 5 international. Average age 31. 17 applicants, 88% accepted, 10 enrolled. *Faculty:* 3 full-time (1 woman), 2 part-time/adjunct (0 women). Expenses: Contact institution. *Financial support:* In 2008–09, 5 research assistantships with tuition reimbursements (averaging $8,000 per year) were awarded; career-related internships or fieldwork, Federal Work-Study, and institutionally sponsored loans also available. Support available to part-time students. Financial award application deadline: 4/15. In 2008, 25 master's awarded. *Degree program information:* Part-time and evening/weekend programs available. Offers communications (MS). *Application deadline:* For fall admission, 8/15 priority date for domestic students; for winter admission, 12/15 priority date for domestic students; for spring admission, 4/15 priority date for domestic students. Applications are processed on a rolling basis. *Application fee:* $30. Electronic applications accepted. *Application Contact:* Dr. William Michael Pritchard, Coordinator, 616-331-3668, Fax: 616-331-2700, E-mail: pritchmi@gvsu.edu. *Director*, Dr. Alex Nesterenko, 616-331-3668, Fax: 616-895-2700, E-mail: nesterea@gvsu.edu.

Kirkhof College of Nursing Students: 6 full-time (5 women), 76 part-time (68 women); includes 3 minority (all African Americans), 1 international. Average age 37. 16 applicants, 94% accepted, 12 enrolled. *Faculty:* 14 full-time (13 women). Expenses: Contact institution. *Financial support:* In 2008–09, 9 research assistantships with full and partial tuition reimbursements (averaging $8,000 per year) were awarded; career-related internships or fieldwork, Federal Work-Study, institutionally sponsored loans, and traineeships also available. Financial award application deadline: 2/15. In 2008, 19 master's awarded. *Degree program information:* Part-time programs available. Offers advanced practice (MSN); case management (MSN); nursing administration (MSN); nursing education (MSN); nursing practice (DNP). *Application deadline:* For fall admission, 3/15 priority date for domestic students. Applications are processed on a rolling basis. *Application fee:* $30. Electronic applications accepted. *Application Contact:* Dr. Jean Martin, Director of Graduate Programs, 616-331-7167, Fax: 616-331-7362, E-mail: martinj@gvsu.edu. *Dean*, Dr. Cynthia McCurren, 616-331-7161, Fax: 616-331-7362.

Padnos College of Engineering and Computing Students: 47 full-time (15 women), 83 part-time (16 women); includes 11 minority (5 African Americans, 6 Asian Americans or Pacific Islanders), 38 international. Average age 30. 149 applicants, 46% accepted, 29 enrolled. *Faculty:* 18 full-time (1 woman), 2 part-time/adjunct (0 women). Expenses: Contact institution. *Financial support:* In 2008–09, 5 research assistantships with full and partial tuition reimbursements (averaging $8,000 per year) were awarded; unspecified assistantships also available. In 2008, 41 master's awarded. *Degree program information:* Part-time programs available. Offers engineering and computing (MS, MSE); medical and bioinformatics (MS). *Application deadline:* For fall admission, 2/1 for domestic students. Applications are processed on a rolling basis. *Application fee:* $30. Electronic applications accepted. *Application Contact:* Tracey James-Heer, Associate Director for Graduate Recruitment, 616-331-2025, Fax: 616-486-6476, E-mail: james-ht@gvsu.edu. *Dean*, Dr. Paul Plotkowski, 616-331-6260, Fax: 616-331-6770, E-mail: plotkowp@gvsu.edu.

School of Computing and Information Systems Students: 37 full-time (13 women), 41 part-time (11 women); includes 7 minority (4 African Americans, 3 Asian Americans or Pacific Islanders), 33 international. Average age 30. 64 applicants, 75% accepted, 19

Grand Valley State University (continued)

enrolled. *Faculty:* 10 full-time (1 woman), 2 part-time/adjunct (0 women). Expenses: Contact institution. *Financial support:* In 2008–09, 4 research assistantships with full and partial tuition reimbursements (averaging $8,000 per year) were awarded. In 2008, 32 master's awarded. *Degree program information:* Part-time and evening/weekend programs available. Offers computer information systems (MS). *Application deadline:* For fall admission, 6/1 for international students; for winter admission, 9/1 for international students. Applications are processed on a rolling basis. *Application fee:* $30. Electronic applications accepted. *Application Contact:* D. Robert Adams, Graduate Program Chair, 616-331-3885, Fax: 616-331-2106, E-mail: adams@cis.gvsu.edu. *Director*, Paul Leidig, 616-331-2038, Fax: 616-331-2106, E-mail: leidigp@gvsu.edu.

School of Engineering Students: 10 full-time (2 women), 42 part-time (5 women); includes 4 minority (1 African American, 3 Asian Americans or Pacific Islanders), 5 international. Average age 29. 85 applicants, 25% accepted, 10 enrolled. *Faculty:* 9 full-time (1 woman). Expenses: Contact institution. *Financial support:* In 2008–09, 14 research assistantships with full tuition reimbursements (averaging $11,000 per year), 3 teaching assistantships with full tuition reimbursements (averaging $8,000 per year) were awarded; career-related internships or fieldwork, Federal Work-Study, institutionally sponsored loans, scholarships/grants, and unspecified assistantships also available. In 2008, 9 master's awarded. *Degree program information:* Part-time and evening/weekend programs available. Offers electrical and computer engineering (MSE); manufacturing operations (MSE); mechanical engineering (MSE); product design and manufacturing engineering (MSE). *Application deadline:* Applications are processed on a rolling basis. *Application fee:* $30. Electronic applications accepted. *Application Contact:* Dr. Pranod Chaphalkar, Graduate Director, 616-331-6843, Fax: 616-331-7215, E-mail: chaphalp@gvsu.edu. *Acting Director*, Dr. Charles Standridge, 616-331-6750, Fax: 616-331-7215, E-mail: standric@gvsu.edu.

Seidman College of Business Students: 88 full-time (33 women), 290 part-time (111 women); includes 17 minority (5 African Americans, 9 Asian Americans or Pacific Islanders, 3 Hispanic Americans), 17 international. Average age 29. 126 applicants, 84% accepted, 81 enrolled. *Faculty:* 22 full-time (6 women), 14 part-time/adjunct (2 women). Expenses: Contact institution. *Financial support:* In 2008–09, 104 students received support, including 27 research assistantships with full and partial tuition reimbursements available (averaging $4,889 per year); fellowships, Federal Work-Study, institutionally sponsored loans, and unspecified assistantships also available. Support available to part-time students. Financial award application deadline: 2/15; financial award applicants required to submit FAFSA. In 2008, 136 master's awarded. *Degree program information:* Part-time and evening/weekend programs available. Offers accounting (MSA); business (MBA, MSA, MST); business administration (MBA); taxation (MST). *Application deadline:* For fall admission, 8/1 priority date for domestic students, 5/1 priority date for international students; for winter admission, 12/1 priority date for domestic students, 11/1 priority date for international students; for spring admission, 4/1 priority date for domestic students, 3/1 priority date for international students. Applications are processed on a rolling basis. *Application fee:* $30. Electronic applications accepted. *Application Contact:* Claudia J. Bajema, Director, Graduate Business Programs, 616-331-7387, Fax: 616-331-7389, E-mail: bajemac@gvsu.edu. *Dean*, Dr. H. James Williams, 616-331-7385, Fax: 616-331-7380, E-mail: williahj@gvsu.edu.

See Close-Up on page 919.

GRAND VIEW UNIVERSITY, Des Moines, IA 50316-1599

General Information Independent-religious, coed, comprehensive institution.

GRADUATE UNITS

Program in Innovative Leadership Offers business (MS); education (MS); nursing (MS). Electronic applications accepted.

GRANTHAM UNIVERSITY, Kansas City, MO 64153

General Information Proprietary, coed, comprehensive institution. *Enrollment:* 6,423 graduate, professional, and undergraduate students; 488 full-time matriculated graduate/professional students. *Enrollment by degree level:* 488 master's. *Graduate faculty:* 8 full-time (3 women), 34 part-time/adjunct (16 women). *Tuition:* Full-time $7950; part-time $265 per credit hour. One-time fee: $30. *Student services:* Career counseling, international student services, services for students with disabilities. *Online resources:* library catalog.

Computer facilities: Online class registration is available. *Web address:* http://www.grantham.edu/.

General Application Contact: DeAnn Wandler, Vice President of Enrollment Management, 800-955-2527, Fax: 816-595-5757, E-mail: admissions@grantham.edu.

GRADUATE UNITS

College of Arts and Sciences Expenses: Contact institution. *Financial support:* Institutionally sponsored loans and scholarships/grants available. In 2008, 48 master's awarded. *Degree program information:* Part-time and evening/weekend programs available. Postbaccalaureate distance learning degree programs offered (no on-campus study). Offers information management technology (MS); information technology (MS); project management (MS). *Application deadline:* Applications are processed on a rolling basis. Electronic applications accepted. *Application Contact:* DeAnn Wandler, Vice President of Enrollment Management, 800-955-2527, Fax: 816-595-5757, E-mail: admissions@grantham.edu. *Dean of the College of Arts and Sciences*, Dr. Duane Geiken, 800-955-2527, Fax: 816-595-5757, E-mail: admissions@grantham.edu.

Mark Skousen School of Business Expenses: Contact institution. *Financial support:* Institutionally sponsored loans and scholarships/grants available. In 2008, 48 master's awarded. *Degree program information:* Part-time and evening/weekend programs available. Postbaccalaureate distance learning degree programs offered (no on-campus study). Offers general business administration (MBA); information management (MBA); project management (MBA). *Application deadline:* Applications are processed on a rolling basis. *Application fee:* $0. Electronic applications accepted. *Application Contact:* DeAnn Wandler, Vice President of Enrollment Management, 800-955-2527, Fax: 816-595-5757, E-mail: admissions@grantham.edu. *Dean of the Mark Skousen School of Business*, Dr. John Theodore, 800-955-2527, Fax: 816-595-5757, E-mail: admissions@grantham.edu.

GRATZ COLLEGE, Melrose Park, PA 19027

General Information Independent-religious, coed, comprehensive institution. *Graduate housing:* On-campus housing not available.

GRADUATE UNITS

Graduate Programs *Degree program information:* Part-time and evening/weekend programs available. Postbaccalaureate distance learning degree programs offered (minimal on-campus study). Offers classical studies (MA); education (MA); Holocaust studies (Certificate); Jewish communal service (MA, Certificate); Jewish education (MA, Ed D, Certificate); Jewish music (MA, Certificate); Jewish studies (MA, Certificate); modern studies (MA).

GREEN MOUNTAIN COLLEGE, Poultney, VT 05764-1199

General Information Independent, coed, comprehensive institution.

GRADUATE UNITS

Program in Business Administration Postbaccalaureate distance learning degree programs offered (no on-campus study). Offers business administration (MBA). Distance learning only. Electronic applications accepted.

Program in Environmental Studies *Degree program information:* Part-time and evening/weekend programs available. Postbaccalaureate distance learning degree programs offered (no on-campus study). Offers environmental studies (MS). Distance learning only. Electronic applications accepted.

GREENSBORO COLLEGE, Greensboro, NC 27401-1875

General Information Independent-religious, coed, comprehensive institution. *Graduate housing:* Rooms and/or apartments guaranteed to single and married students. Housing application deadline: 6/1.

GRADUATE UNITS

Program in Education *Degree program information:* Part-time and evening/weekend programs available. Offers elementary education (M Ed); special education (M Ed). Electronic applications accepted.

Program in Teaching English to Speakers of Other Languages *Degree program information:* Part-time and evening/weekend programs available. Offers teaching English to speakers of other languages (MA). Electronic applications accepted.

GREENVILLE COLLEGE, Greenville, IL 62246-0159

General Information Independent-religious, coed, comprehensive institution. *Graduate housing:* On-campus housing not available.

GRADUATE UNITS

Program in Education Offers education (MAT); elementary education (MAE); secondary education (MAE). Electronic applications accepted.

Program in Leadership and Ministry *Degree program information:* Part-time programs available. Offers leadership and ministry (MA). Electronic applications accepted.

GWYNEDD-MERCY COLLEGE, Gwynedd Valley, PA 19437-0901

General Information Independent-religious, coed, comprehensive institution. *Enrollment:* 2,548 graduate, professional, and undergraduate students; 115 full-time matriculated graduate/professional students (77 women), 415 part-time matriculated graduate/professional students (342 women). *Enrollment by degree level:* 530 master's. *Graduate faculty:* 9 full-time (7 women), 17 part-time/adjunct (11 women). *Tuition:* Part-time $555 per credit hour. *Graduate housing:* On-campus housing not available. *Student services:* Campus employment opportunities, campus safety program, career counseling, free psychological counseling, international student services, low-cost health insurance, services for students with disabilities, teacher training. *Library facilities:* Lourdes Library plus 1 other. *Online resources:* library catalog, web page, access to other libraries' catalogs. *Collection:* 105,070 titles, 667 serial subscriptions, 11,448 audiovisual materials.

Computer facilities: Computer purchase and lease plans are available. 218 computers available on campus for general student use. A campuswide network can be accessed from student residence rooms and from off campus. Online class registration is available. *Web address:* http://www.gmc.edu/.

General Application Contact: Information Contact, 800-342-5462, Fax: 215-641-5556.

GRADUATE UNITS

Center for Lifelong Learning Students: 38 full-time (24 women), 20 part-time (14 women); includes 24 minority (20 African Americans, 4 Hispanic Americans), 2 international. Average age 38. *Faculty:* 7 part-time/adjunct (1 woman). Expenses: Contact institution. Offers lifelong learning (MSM). *Application Contact:* Information Contact, 800-342-5462, Fax: 215-641-5556. *Executive Director*, Joseph Coleman, 215-643-8458.

School of Education Students: 61 full-time (38 women), 369 part-time (302 women); includes 35 minority (25 African Americans, 5 Asian Americans or Pacific Islanders, 5 Hispanic Americans), 2 international. Average age 33. *Faculty:* 8 full-time (5 women), 38 part-time/adjunct (24 women). Expenses: Contact institution. *Financial support:* In 2008–09, 2 research assistantships were awarded; career-related internships or fieldwork, Federal Work-Study, tuition waivers (full and partial), unspecified assistantships, and Federal Stafford Loans, Federal Work Study, Alternative Loans, Graduate Assistantships also available. Financial award applicants required to submit FAFSA. In 2008, 186 master's awarded. *Degree program information:* Part-time and evening/weekend programs available. Offers educational administration (MS); master teacher (MS); reading (MS); school counseling (MS); special education (MS). *Application deadline:* Applications are processed on a rolling basis. *Application fee:* $25. *Application Contact:* Gillian Ricchetti, Graduate Program Coordinator, 215-542-4647, E-mail: ricchetti.g@gmc.edu. *Dean*, Dr. Lorraine Cavaliere, EdD, 215-641-5549, Fax: 215-542-4695, E-mail: cavaliere.l@gmc.edu.

School of Nursing Students: 16 full-time (15 women), 26 part-time (all women); includes 7 minority (5 African Americans, 2 Asian Americans or Pacific Islanders). Average age 42. 23 applicants, 83% accepted, 11 enrolled. *Faculty:* 3 full-time (all women), 2 part-time/adjunct (both women). Expenses: Contact institution. *Financial support:* In 2008–09, 21 students received support. Scholarships/grants, traineeships, and unspecified assistantships available. Financial award application deadline: 8/30. In 2008, 7 master's awarded. Offers clinical nurse specialist (MSN); nurse practitioner (MSN). *Application deadline:* For fall admission, 8/1 priority date for domestic students; for winter admission, 12/1 priority date for domestic students. Applications are processed on a rolling basis. *Application fee:* $25. Electronic applications accepted. *Application Contact:* Dr. Barbara A. Jones, Director, 215-646-7300 Ext. 407, Fax: 215-641-5564, E-mail: jones.b@gmc.edu. *Dean*, Dr. Andrea D. Hollingsworth, 215-646-7300 Ext. 539, Fax: 215-641-5517, E-mail: hollingsworth.a@gmc.edu.

HAMLINE UNIVERSITY, St. Paul, MN 55104-1284

General Information Independent-religious, coed, comprehensive institution. *Enrollment:* 4,876 graduate, professional, and undergraduate students; 1,261 full-time matriculated graduate/professional students (733 women), 1,076 part-time matriculated graduate/professional students (750 women). *Enrollment by degree level:* 715 first professional, 1,518 master's, 75 doctoral, 29 other advanced degrees. *Graduate faculty:* 92 full-time (51 women), 259 part-time/adjunct (167 women). *Tuition:* Full-time $6400; part-time $400 per credit. *Required fees:* $6 per credit. One-time fee: $205. Tuition and fees vary according to degree level and program. *Graduate housing:* Rooms and/or apartments available on a first-come, first-served basis to single and married students. Typical cost: $3976 per year ($7784 including board) for single students; $7326 per year ($11,134 including board) for married students. Room and board charges vary according to board plan and housing facility selected. Housing application deadline: 5/1. *Student services:* Campus employment opportunities, campus safety program, career counseling, free psychological counseling, international student services, low-cost health insurance, multicultural affairs office, services for students with disabilities, teacher training, writing training. *Library facilities:* Bush Library plus 1 other. *Online resources:* library catalog, web page, access to other libraries' catalogs. *Collection:* 239,643 titles, 1,738 serial subscriptions, 5,547 audiovisual materials. *Research affiliation:* Minnesota Women Elected Officials.

Computer facilities: 150 computers available on campus for general student use. A campuswide network can be accessed from student residence rooms and from off campus. Online class registration is available. *Web address:* http://www.hamline.edu/.

General Application Contact: Rae A. Lenway, Director, Graduate Recruitment and Admission, 651-523-2900, Fax: 651-523-3058, E-mail: gradprog@hamline.edu.

GRADUATE UNITS

Graduate School of Liberal Studies Students: 95 full-time (71 women), 127 part-time (97 women); includes 9 minority (7 African Americans, 1 American Indian/Alaska Native, 1 Hispanic American), 3 international. Average age 37. 66 applicants, 74% accepted, 37 enrolled. *Faculty:* 6 full-time (4 women), 13 part-time/adjunct (10 women). Expenses: Contact institution. *Financial support:* Federal Work-Study available. Financial award applicants required to submit FAFSA. In 2008, 49 master's awarded. *Degree program information:* Part-time and evening/weekend programs available. Offers liberal studies (MALS, MFA, CALS). *Application deadline:* For fall admission, 3/1 priority date for domestic students; for spring admission, 9/1 priority date for domestic students. Applications are processed on a rolling basis. *Application fee:* $0. Electronic applications accepted. *Application Contact:* Rae A. Lenway, Director, Graduate Recruitment and Admission, 651-523-2900, Fax: 651-523-3058, E-mail: rlenway@hamline.edu. *Dean*, Mary Francois Rockcastle, 651-523-2047, Fax: 651-523-2490, E-mail: mrockcastle@hamline.edu.

School of Business Students: 401 full-time (207 women), 138 part-time (81 women); includes 75 minority (39 African Americans, 3 American Indian/Alaska Native, 26 Asian Americans or Pacific Islanders, 7 Hispanic Americans), 83 international. Average age 32. 340 applicants, 64% accepted, 159 enrolled. *Faculty:* 18 full-time (10 women), 45 part-time/adjunct (10 women). Expenses: Contact institution. *Financial support:* Federal Work-Study available. Financial award applicants required to submit FAFSA. In 2008, 82 master's, 3 doctorates awarded. *Degree program information:* Part-time and evening/weekend programs available. Offers business (MBA); nonprofit management (MANM); public administration (MPA, DPA). *Application deadline:* For fall admission, 3/30 priority date for domestic students. Applications are processed on a rolling basis. *Application fee:* $0. Electronic applications accepted. *Application Contact:* Rae A. Lenway, Director, Graduate Recruitment and Admission, 651-523-2900, Fax: 651-523-3058, E-mail: rlenway@hamline.edu. *Dean,* Julian Schuster, 651-523-2284, Fax: 651-523-3098, E-mail: jschuster01@hamline.edu.

School of Education Students: 241 full-time (173 women), 612 part-time (476 women); includes 61 minority (24 African Americans, 3 American Indian/Alaska Native, 18 Asian Americans or Pacific Islanders, 16 Hispanic Americans), 20 international. Average age 33. 212 applicants, 80% accepted, 144 enrolled. *Faculty:* 33 full-time (23 women), 152 part-time/adjunct (122 women). Expenses: Contact institution. *Financial support:* Federal Work-Study available. Financial award applicants required to submit FAFSA. In 2008, 220 master's, 3 doctorates awarded. *Degree program information:* Part-time and evening/weekend programs available. Offers education (MA Ed, MAESL, MAT, Ed D). *Application deadline:* For fall admission, 6/15 priority date for domestic students; for spring admission, 10/1 priority date for domestic students. Applications are processed on a rolling basis. *Application fee:* $0. Electronic applications accepted. *Application Contact:* Rae A. Lenway, Director, Graduate Recruitment and Admission, 651-523-2900, Fax: 651-523-3058, E-mail: rlenway@hamline.edu. *Interim Dean,* Barbara Swanson, 651-523-2600, Fax: 651-523-2489, E-mail: bswanson@hamline.edu.

School of Law Students: 509 full-time (276 women), 207 part-time (101 women); includes 94 minority (21 African Americans, 6 American Indian/Alaska Native, 36 Asian Americans or Pacific Islanders, 31 Hispanic Americans), 7 international. Average age 27. 1,450 applicants, 48% accepted, 233 enrolled. *Faculty:* 43 full-time (20 women), 82 part-time/adjunct (32 women). Expenses: Contact institution. *Financial support:* In 2008–09, 620 students received support, including 20 fellowships with full and partial tuition reimbursements available (averaging $3,000 per year); career-related internships or fieldwork, Federal Work-Study, and scholarships/grants also available. Support available to part-time students. Financial award applicants required to submit FAFSA. In 2008, 202 JDs awarded. *Degree program information:* Part-time and evening/weekend programs available. Offers law (JD, LL M). *Application deadline:* For fall admission, 5/1 priority date for domestic and international students. Applications are processed on a rolling basis. *Application fee:* $35. Electronic applications accepted. *Application Contact:* Robin C. Ingli, Director of Admissions, 800-388-3688, Fax: 651-523-3064, E-mail: ringli@hamline.edu. *Dean,* Donald M. Lewis, 651-523-2968, Fax: 651-523-2435, E-mail: dlewis02@hamline.edu.

HAMPTON UNIVERSITY, Hampton, VA 23668

General Information Independent, coed, university. CGS member. *Graduate housing:* Rooms and/or apartments available to single and married students. Housing application deadline: 6/1. *Research affiliation:* NASA–Langley Research Center (physical sciences), Southeastern Universities Research Association (science), Continuous Electron Beam Accelerator Facility (science).

GRADUATE UNITS

Graduate College *Degree program information:* Part-time and evening/weekend programs available. Offers advanced adult nursing (MS); atmospheric physics (MS, PhD); biology (MS); business (MBA); chemistry (MS); college student development (MA); communicative sciences and disorders (MA); community agency counseling (MA); community health nursing (MS); community mental health/psychiatric nursing (MS); computational mathematics (MS); computer science (MS); counseling (MA); early childhood education (MT); elementary education (MA); environmental science (MS); family nursing (MS); gerontological nursing for the nurse practitioner (MS); medical physics (MS, PhD); medical science (MS); middle school education (MT); music education (MT); nonlinear science (MS); nuclear physics (MS, PhD); optical physics (MS, PhD); pastoral counseling (MA); pediatric nursing (MS); physical therapy (DPT); school counseling (MA); secondary education (MT); special education (MA, MT); statistics and probability (MS); teaching (MT); women's health nursing (MS).

HARDING UNIVERSITY, Searcy, AR 72149-0001

General Information Independent-religious, coed, comprehensive institution. *Enrollment:* 6,447 graduate, professional, and undergraduate students; 399 full-time matriculated graduate/professional students (234 women), 553 part-time matriculated graduate/professional students (339 women). *Enrollment by degree level:* 61 first professional, 848 master's, 21 doctoral, 22 other advanced degrees. *Graduate faculty:* 36 full-time (11 women), 106 part-time/adjunct (41 women). *Tuition:* Full-time $9360; part-time $520 per credit hour. *Required fees:* $21 per credit hour. Tuition and fees vary according to course load and program. *Graduate housing:* Rooms and/or apartments available on a first-come, first-served basis to single and married students. Typical cost: $3500 per year for single students; $3500 per year for married students. Room charges vary according to board plan and housing facility selected. *Student services:* Campus employment opportunities, campus safety program, career counseling, exercise/wellness program, free psychological counseling, international student services, services for students with disabilities, writing training. *Library facilities:* Brackett Library plus 1 other. *Online resources:* library catalog, web page, access to other libraries' catalogs. *Collection:* 237,892 titles, 22,180 serial subscriptions, 10,437 audiovisual materials.

Computer facilities: 465 computers available on campus for general student use. A campuswide network can be accessed from student residence rooms and from off campus. Online class registration is available. *Web address:* http://www.harding.edu/.

General Application Contact: Dr. Cheri Yecke, Dean of Graduate Programs, 501-279-4335, Fax: 501-279-5192, E-mail: cyecke@harding.edu.

GRADUATE UNITS

College of Bible and Religion Students: 30 full-time (11 women), 40 part-time (4 women); includes 5 minority (3 African Americans, 1 American Indian/Alaska Native, 1 Hispanic American), 1 international. Average age 33. 33 applicants, 91% accepted, 28 enrolled. *Faculty:* 4 full-time (0 women), 10 part-time/adjunct (2 women). Expenses: Contact institution. *Financial support:* In 2008–09, 51 students received support. Career-related internships or fieldwork, Federal Work-Study, scholarships/grants, and unspecified assistantships available. Financial award applicants required to submit FAFSA. In 2008, 18 master's awarded. *Degree program information:* Part-time programs available. Postbaccalaureate distance learning degree programs offered. Offers Bible and religion (M Min, MS); marriage and family therapy (MS); mental health counseling (MS); ministry (M Min). *Application fee:* $25. *Application Contact:* Dr. Monte Cox, Dean, 501-279-4448, Fax: 501-279-4042, E-mail: mcox@harding.edu. *Dean,* Dr. Monte Cox, 501-279-4448, Fax: 501-279-4042, E-mail: mcox@harding.edu.

College of Business Administration Students: 111 full-time (44 women), 124 part-time (56 women); includes 18 minority (12 African Americans, 1 American Indian/Alaska Native, 2 Asian Americans or Pacific Islanders, 3 Hispanic Americans), 56 international. Average age 29. 82 applicants, 96% accepted, 67 enrolled. *Faculty:* 34 part-time/adjunct (5 women). Expenses: Contact institution. *Financial support:* In 2008–09, 85 students received support. Federal Work-Study, scholarships/grants, and unspecified assistantships available. Financial award application deadline: 7/30; financial award applicants required to submit FAFSA. In 2008, 98 master's awarded. *Degree program information:* Part-time and evening/weekend programs available. Postbaccalaureate distance learning degree programs offered (no on-campus study). Offers accounting (MBA); health care management (MBA); information technology (MBA); international business (MBA); leadership and organizational management (MBA). *Application deadline:* For fall admission, 8/1 priority date for domestic and international students; for spring admission, 12/1 priority date for domestic and international students. *Application fee:* $35. Electronic applications accepted. *Application Contact:* Glen Metheny, Director of Graduate Studies, 501-279-5851, Fax: 501-279-4805, E-mail: mba@harding.edu. *Director of Graduate Studies,* Glen Metheny, 501-279-5851, Fax: 501-279-4805, E-mail: gmetheny@harding.edu.

College of Communication Students: 15 full-time (all women); includes 4 minority (all African Americans). Average age 27. 20 applicants, 100% accepted, 15 enrolled. *Faculty:* 7 part-time/adjunct (5 women). Expenses: Contact institution. *Financial support:* In 2008–09, 1 student received support. Federal Work-Study, scholarships/grants, and unspecified assistantships available. Financial award applicants required to submit FAFSA. Offers speech-language pathology (MS). *Application deadline:* For fall admission, 3/1 for domestic students. *Application fee:* $25. *Application Contact:* Martha Vendetti, Secretary, 501-279-4648, Fax: 501-4325, E-mail: mvendett@harding.edu. *Chair, Department of Communication Sciences and Disorders/Graduate Program Director,* Dr. Rebecca O Weaver, 501-279-4640, Fax: 501-279-4325, E-mail: bweaver@harding.edu.

College of Education Students: 118 full-time (93 women), 388 part-time (279 women); includes 65 minority (57 African Americans, 5 American Indian/Alaska Native, 3 Hispanic Americans), 4 international. Average age 30. 181 applicants, 88% accepted, 150 enrolled. *Faculty:* 13 full-time (4 women), 52 part-time/adjunct (29 women). Expenses: Contact institution. *Financial support:* In 2008–09, 441 students received support. Federal Work-Study, scholarships/grants, and unspecified assistantships available. In 2008, 213 master's, 8 other advanced degrees awarded. *Degree program information:* Part-time programs available. Offers advanced studies in teaching and learning (M Ed); art (MSE); behavioral science (MSE); counseling (MS, Ed S); early childhood special education (M Ed, MSE); education (MSE); educational leadership (M Ed, Ed S); elementary education (M Ed); English (MSE); family and consumer science (MSE); French (MSE); history/social science (MSE); kinesiology (MSE); math (MSE); physical science (MSE); reading (M Ed); secondary education (M Ed); Spanish (MSE); special education licensure (M Ed); teaching (MAT); teaching English as a second language (M Ed). *Application deadline:* For fall admission, 8/1 for domestic and international students; for spring admission, 1/1 for domestic and international students. Applications are processed on a rolling basis. *Application fee:* $35. *Application Contact:* Information Contact, 501-279-4315, E-mail: gradstudiesedu@harding.edu. *Chair,* Pat Bashaw, 501-279-4183, Fax: 501-279-4083, E-mail: pbashaw@harding.edu.

College of Pharmacy Students: 61 full-time (30 women); includes 24 minority (6 African Americans, 2 American Indian/Alaska Native, 16 Asian Americans or Pacific Islanders), 1 international. Average age 26. 358 applicants, 22% accepted, 61 enrolled. *Faculty:* 14 full-time (6 women), 4 part-time/adjunct (0 women). Expenses: Contact institution. *Financial support:* In 2008–09, 6 students received support. Federal Work-Study and scholarships/grants available. Financial award applicants required to submit FAFSA. Offers pharmacy (Pharm D). *Application deadline:* For fall admission, 3/15 priority date for domestic and international students. Applications are processed on a rolling basis. *Application fee:* $50. Electronic applications accepted. *Application Contact:* Carol Kell, Director of Admissions, 501-279-5523, Fax: 501-279-5525, E-mail: ckell@harding.edu. *Dean,* Dr. Julie Ann Hixson-Wallace, 501-279-5205, Fax: 501-279-5525, E-mail: jahixson@harding.edu.

College of Sciences Students: 64 full-time (41 women), 1 part-time (0 women); includes 7 minority (4 American Indian/Alaska Native, 3 Hispanic Americans). Average age 27. 300 applicants, 11% accepted, 32 enrolled. *Faculty:* 5 full-time (1 woman), 2 part-time/adjunct (1 woman). Expenses: Contact institution. *Financial support:* In 2008–09, 1 student received support. Federal Work-Study and scholarships/grants available. Financial award applicants required to submit FAFSA. In 2008, 22 master's awarded. Offers physician assistant studies (MS). *Application deadline:* For fall admission, 11/1 for domestic students. Applications are processed on a rolling basis. *Application fee:* $25. Electronic applications accepted. *Application Contact:* Marcia Murphy, Admissions Director, Physician Assistant Program, 501-279-5642, Fax: 501-279-4188, E-mail: paprogram@haridng.edu. *Director,* Michael Murphy, 501-279-5642, E-mail: mmurphy1@harding.edu.

HARDING UNIVERSITY GRADUATE SCHOOL OF RELIGION, Memphis, TN 38117-5499

General Information Independent-religious, coed, primarily men, graduate-only institution. *Graduate housing:* Rooms and/or apartments available to single and married students.

GRADUATE UNITS

Graduate Programs *Degree program information:* Part-time programs available. Postbaccalaureate distance learning degree programs offered (minimal on-campus study). Offers Christian ministry (MA); counseling (MA); ministry (M Div, D Min); religion (MA). Electronic applications accepted.

HARDIN-SIMMONS UNIVERSITY, Abilene, TX 79698-0001

General Information Independent-religious, coed, comprehensive institution. *Enrollment:* 2,387 graduate, professional, and undergraduate students; 249 full-time matriculated graduate/professional students (134 women), 203 part-time matriculated graduate/professional students (123 women). *Enrollment by degree level:* 89 first professional, 259 master's, 104 doctoral. *Graduate faculty:* 80 full-time (30 women), 19 part-time/adjunct (5 women). *Tuition:* Full-time $10,620; part-time $590 per credit hour. *Required fees:* $590; $110 per semester. Tuition and fees vary according to course load and degree level. *Graduate housing:* Rooms and/or apartments available on a first-come, first-served basis to single and married students. Typical cost: $2492 per year ($5180 including board) for single students; $3780 per year ($5253 including board) for married students. Room and board charges vary according to board plan and housing facility selected. *Student services:* Campus employment opportunities, career counseling, free psychological counseling. *Library facilities:* Richardson Library plus 1 other. *Online resources:* library catalog, web page, access to other libraries' catalogs. *Collection:* 263,075 titles, 33,942 serial subscriptions, 11,715 audiovisual materials.

Computer facilities: 217 computers available on campus for general student use. A campuswide network can be accessed from student residence rooms and from off campus. *Web address:* http://www.hsutx.edu/.

General Application Contact: Dr. Gary Stanlake, Dean of Graduate Studies, 325-670-1298, Fax: 325-670-1564, E-mail: gradoff@hsutx.edu.

GRADUATE UNITS

The Acton MBA in Entrepreneurship Expenses: Contact institution. Offers entrepreneurship (MBA). *Application deadline:* For fall admission, 5/1 for domestic students, 2/25 for international students. *Application fee:* $150. *Application Contact:* Jessica Blanchard, Director of Recruiting, 512-703-1231, E-mail: jblanchard@actonmba.org.

Graduate School Students: 249 full-time (134 women), 203 part-time (123 women); includes 57 minority (13 African Americans, 2 American Indian/Alaska Native, 2 Asian Americans or Pacific Islanders, 40 Hispanic Americans), 1 international. Average age 30. 163 applicants, 77% accepted, 99 enrolled. *Faculty:* 80 full-time (30 women), 19 part-time/adjunct (5 women). Expenses: Contact institution. *Financial support:* In 2008–09, 324 students received support, including 53 fellowships (averaging $1,282 per year); career-related internships or fieldwork, scholarships/grants, unspecified assistantships, and recreation assistantships, coaching assistantships also available. Support available to part-time students. Financial award application deadline: 6/30; financial award applicants required to submit FAFSA. In 2008, 12 first professional degrees, 64 master's awarded. *Degree program information:* Part-time programs available. *Application deadline:* For fall admission, 8/15 priority date for domestic students, 4/1 for international students; for spring admission, 1/5 priority date for domestic students, 9/1 for international students. Applications are processed on a rolling basis. *Application fee:* $50. *Application Contact:* Dr. Gary Stanlake, Dean of Graduate Studies, 325-670-1298, Fax: 325-670-1564, E-mail: gradoff@hsutx.edu. *Dean of Graduate Studies,* Dr. Gary Stanlake, 325-670-1298, Fax: 325-670-1564, E-mail: gradoff@hsutx.edu.

Cynthia Ann Parker College of Liberal Arts Students: 15 full-time (8 women), 20 part-time (14 women); includes 2 African Americans, 5 Hispanic Americans. Average age 28. 21 applicants, 48% accepted, 9 enrolled. *Faculty:* 14 full-time (5 women). Expenses: Contact institution. *Financial support:* In 2008–09, 35 students received support, including 15 fellowships (averaging $1,160 per year); scholarships/grants also available. Support available to part-time students. Financial award application deadline: 6/30; financial award applicants required to submit FAFSA. In 2008, 13 master's awarded. *Degree program*

Hardin-Simmons University (continued)

information: Part-time programs available. Offers English (MA); family psychology (MA); history (MA); liberal arts (MA). *Application deadline:* For fall admission, 8/15 priority date for domestic students, 4/1 for international students; for spring admission, 1/5 priority date for domestic students, 9/1 for international students. Applications are processed on a rolling basis. *Application fee:* $50. *Application Contact:* Dr. Gary Stanlake, Dean of Graduate Studies, 325-670-1298, Fax: 325-670-1564, E-mail: gradoff@hsutx.edu. *Dean,* Dr. Alan R. Stafford, 325-670-1487, E-mail: stafford@hsutx.edu.

Holland School of Sciences and Mathematics Students: 3 full-time (1 woman), 1 part-time (0 women); includes 1 minority (Hispanic American). Average age 26. 58 applicants, 7% accepted, 2 enrolled. *Faculty:* 4 full-time (0 women). Expenses: Contact institution. *Financial support:* In 2008–09, 5 students received support; fellowships, career-related internships or fieldwork and scholarships/grants available. Support available to part-time students. Financial award application deadline: 6/30; financial award applicants required to submit FAFSA. In 2008, 3 master's awarded. *Degree program information:* Part-time programs available. Offers environmental management (MS); physical therapy (DPT); sciences and mathematics (MS, DPT). *Application deadline:* For fall admission, 8/15 priority date for domestic students, 4/1 for international students; for spring admission, 1/5 priority date for domestic students, 9/1 for international students. Applications are processed on a rolling basis. *Application fee:* $50. *Application Contact:* Dr. Gary Stanlake, Dean of Graduate Studies, 325-670-1298, Fax: 325-670-1564, E-mail: gradoff@hsutx.edu. *Dean,* Dr. Christopher McNair, 325-670-1401, Fax: 325-670-1385, E-mail: cmcnair@hsutx.edu.

Irvin School of Education Students: 50 full-time (33 women), 71 part-time (55 women); includes 22 minority (7 African Americans, 15 Hispanic Americans). Average age 30. 57 applicants, 84% accepted, 36 enrolled. *Faculty:* 12 full-time (7 women), 5 part-time/adjunct (3 women). Expenses: Contact institution. *Financial support:* In 2008–09, 114 students received support, including 25 fellowships (averaging $1,198 per year); career-related internships or fieldwork, scholarships/grants, unspecified assistantships, and coaching assistantships also available. Support available to part-time students. Financial award application deadline: 6/30; financial award applicants required to submit FAFSA. In 2008, 31 master's awarded. *Degree program information:* Part-time programs available. Offers counseling and human development (M Ed); education (M Ed); gifted education (M Ed); kinesiology, sport, and recreation (M Ed); reading specialist education (M Ed). *Application deadline:* For fall admission, 8/15 priority date for domestic students, 4/1 for international students; for spring admission, 1/5 priority date for domestic students, 9/1 for international students. Applications are processed on a rolling basis. *Application fee:* $50. *Application Contact:* Dr. Gary Stanlake, Dean of Graduate Studies, 325-670-1298, Fax: 325-670-1564, E-mail: gradoff@hsutx.edu. *Dean,* Dr. Pam Williford, 325-670-1352, Fax: 325-670-5859, E-mail: pwilliford@hsutx.edu.

Kelley College of Business Students: 15 full-time (6 women), 19 part-time (7 women); includes 2 minority (both Hispanic Americans). Average age 31. 17 applicants, 71% accepted, 11 enrolled. *Faculty:* 6 full-time (2 women), 1 part-time/adjunct (0 women). Expenses: Contact institution. *Financial support:* In 2008–09, 31 students received support; fellowships, scholarships/grants available. Support available to part-time students. Financial award application deadline: 6/30; financial award applicants required to submit FAFSA. In 2008, 7 master's awarded. *Degree program information:* Part-time and evening/weekend programs available. Offers business (MBA). *Application deadline:* For fall admission, 8/15 priority date for domestic students, 4/1 for international students; for spring admission, 1/5 priority date for domestic students, 9/1 for international students. Applications are processed on a rolling basis. *Application fee:* $50. *Application Contact:* Dr. Gary Stanlake, Dean of Graduate Studies, 325-670-1298, Fax: 325-670-1564, E-mail: gradoff@hsutx.edu. *Director,* Dr. Nancy Kucinski, 325-670-1503, Fax: 325-670-1523, E-mail: kucinski@hsutx.edu.

Logsdon School of Theology Students: 74 full-time (20 women), 46 part-time (11 women); includes 12 minority (3 African Americans, 2 American Indian/Alaska Native, 7 Hispanic Americans). Average age 31. 35 applicants, 80% accepted, 23 enrolled. *Faculty:* 15 full-time (1 woman), 9 part-time/adjunct (1 woman). Expenses: Contact institution. *Financial support:* In 2008–09, 107 students received support, including 7 fellowships (averaging $1,686 per year); scholarships/grants also available. Support available to part-time students. Financial award application deadline: 6/30; financial award applicants required to submit FAFSA. In 2008, 12 first professional degrees, 6 master's awarded. *Degree program information:* Part-time and evening/weekend programs available. Offers family ministry (MA); religion (MA); theology (M Div). *Application deadline:* For fall admission, 8/15 priority date for domestic students, 4/1 for international students; for spring admission, 1/5 priority date for domestic students, 9/1 for international students. Applications are processed on a rolling basis. *Application fee:* $50. *Application Contact:* Dr. Gary Stanlake, Dean of Graduate Studies, 325-670-1298, Fax: 325-670-1564, E-mail: gradoff@hsutx.edu. *Dean,* Dr. Thomas V. Brisco, 325-670-1266, Fax: 325-670-1406, E-mail: tbrisco@hsutx.edu.

Patty Hanks Shelton School of Nursing Students: 8 full-time (7 women), 14 part-time (all women); includes 4 minority (1 Asian American or Pacific Islander, 3 Hispanic Americans). Average age 36. 19 applicants, 79% accepted, 14 enrolled. *Faculty:* 6 full-time (all women). Expenses: Contact institution. *Financial support:* In 2008–09, 20 students received support. Career-related internships or fieldwork and scholarships/grants available. Support available to part-time students. Financial award application deadline: 6/30; financial award applicants required to submit FAFSA. In 2008, 2 master's awarded. *Degree program information:* Part-time programs available. Offers advanced healthcare delivery (MSN); family nurse practitioner (MSN). *Application deadline:* For fall admission, 8/15 priority date for domestic students, 4/1 for international students; for spring admission, 1/5 priority date for domestic students, 9/1 for international students. Applications are processed on a rolling basis. *Application fee:* $50. *Application Contact:* Dr. Gary Stanlake, Dean of Graduate Studies, 325-670-1298, Fax: 325-670-1564, E-mail: gradoff@hsutx.edu. *Director,* Dr. Amy Toone, 325-671-2361, Fax: 325-671-2386, E-mail: atoone@phssn.edu.

School of Music Students: 8 full-time (3 women), 4 part-time (3 women). Average age 28. 9 applicants, 89% accepted, 4 enrolled. *Faculty:* 14 full-time (4 women), 2 part-time/adjunct (1 woman). Expenses: Contact institution. *Financial support:* In 2008–09, 15 students received support, including 6 fellowships (averaging $1,467 per year); career-related internships or fieldwork and scholarships/grants also available. Support available to part-time students. Financial award application deadline: 6/30; financial award applicants required to submit FAFSA. In 2008, 2 master's awarded. *Degree program information:* Part-time programs available. Offers church music (MM); music education (MM); music performance (MM); theory-composition (MM). *Application deadline:* For fall admission, 8/15 priority date for domestic students, 4/1 for international students; for spring admission, 1/5 priority date for domestic students, 9/1 for international students. Applications are processed on a rolling basis. *Application fee:* $50. *Application Contact:* Dr. Gary Stanlake, Dean of Graduate Studies, 325-670-1298, Fax: 325-670-1564, E-mail: gradoff@hsutx.edu. *Director,* Dr. Leigh Anne Hunsaker, 325-670-1391, Fax: 325-670-5873, E-mail: hunsaker@hsutx.edu.

HARRISBURG UNIVERSITY OF SCIENCE AND TECHNOLOGY, Harrisburg, PA 17101

General Information Independent, coed, comprehensive institution. *Enrollment:* 214 graduate, professional, and undergraduate students; 2 full-time matriculated graduate/professional students, 21 part-time matriculated graduate/professional students (3 women). *Enrollment by degree level:* 23 master's. *Graduate faculty:* 2 full-time (0 women), 2 part-time/adjunct (0 women). *Tuition:* Part-time $500 per credit hour. *Graduate housing:* On-campus housing not available. *Library facilities:* Information Commons. *Online resources:* library catalog, web page. *Collection:* 40,000 titles, 25 serial subscriptions.

Computer facilities: Computer purchase and lease plans are available. 10 computers available on campus for general student use. A campuswide network can be accessed from off campus. *Web address:* http://www.harrisburgu.net/.

General Application Contact: Julie Cullings, Information Contact, 717-901-5163, Fax: 717-901-3163, E-mail: admissions@HarrisburgU.net.

GRADUATE UNITS

Program in Information Technology Project Management Students: 2 full-time (0 women), 21 part-time (3 women). Average age 30. *Faculty:* 2 full-time (0 women), 2 part-time/adjunct (0 women). Expenses: Contact institution. In 2008, 2 master's awarded. *Degree program information:* Part-time and evening/weekend programs available. Offers IT project management (MS). *Application deadline:* For fall admission, 8/1 priority date for domestic students, 7/1 priority date for international students. Applications are processed on a rolling basis. *Application fee:* $0. Electronic applications accepted. *Application Contact:* Julie Cullings, Information Contact, 717-901-5163, Fax: 717-901-3163, E-mail: admissions@HarrisburgU.net.

Program in Learning Technologies Expenses: Contact institution. *Degree program information:* Part-time and evening/weekend programs available. Offers learning technologies (MS). *Application deadline:* Applications are processed on a rolling basis. *Application fee:* $0. *Application Contact:* Julie Cullings, Information Contact, 717-901-5163, Fax: 717-901-3163, E-mail: admissions@harrisburgu.net.

HARTFORD SEMINARY, Hartford, CT 06105-2279

General Information Independent-religious, coed, graduate-only institution. *Graduate housing:* Rooms and/or apartments available on a first-come, first-served basis to single and married students. Housing application deadline: 7/15.

GRADUATE UNITS

Graduate Programs *Degree program information:* Part-time and evening/weekend programs available. Postbaccalaureate distance learning degree programs offered (no on-campus study). Offers black ministry (Certificate); Islamic studies (MA); ministerios Hispanos (Certificate); ministry (D Min); religious studies (MA); women's leadership institute (Certificate).

HARVARD UNIVERSITY, Cambridge, MA 02138

General Information Independent, coed, university. CGS member. *Enrollment:* 19,230 graduate, professional, and undergraduate students; 11,972 full-time matriculated graduate/professional students (5,742 women), 1,192 part-time matriculated graduate/professional students (602 women). *Enrollment by degree level:* 2,763 first professional, 5,754 master's, 4,393 doctoral, 254 other advanced degrees. *Graduate faculty:* 2,517. *Tuition:* Full-time $32,556. *Required fees:* $1426. Full-time tuition and fees vary according to program and student level. *Graduate housing:* Rooms and/or apartments available to single and married students. Housing application deadline: 5/1. *Student services:* Campus employment opportunities, campus safety program, career counseling, child daycare facilities, exercise/wellness program, free psychological counseling, grant writing training, international student services, low-cost health insurance, multicultural affairs office, services for students with disabilities, teacher training, writing training. *Library facilities:* Widener Library plus 80 others. *Online resources:* library catalog, web page, access to other libraries' catalogs. *Collection:* 16 million titles, 110,463 serial subscriptions. *Research affiliation:* Woods Hole Oceanographic Institution (Biology).

Computer facilities: Computer purchase and lease plans are available. 605 computers available on campus for general student use. A campuswide network can be accessed from student residence rooms and from off campus. Online class registration is available. *Web address:* http://www.harvard.edu/.

General Application Contact: Admissions Office, 617-495-1814, E-mail: gsas@fas.harvard.edu.

GRADUATE UNITS

Cyprus International Institute for the Environment and Public Health in Association with Harvard School of Public Health Offers environmental health (MS). Electronic applications accepted.

Extension School *Degree program information:* Part-time and evening/weekend programs available. Offers applied sciences (CAS); biotechnology (ALM); educational technologies (ALM); educational technology (CET); English for graduate and professional studies (DGP); environmental management (ALM, CEM); information technology (ALM); journalism (ALM); liberal arts (ALM); management (ALM, CM); mathematics for teaching (ALM); museum studies (ALM); premedical studies (Diploma); publication and communication (CPC).

Graduate School of Arts and Sciences Offers African and African American studies (PhD); African history (PhD); Akkadian and Sumerian (AM, PhD); American history (PhD); ancient art (PhD); ancient Near Eastern art (PhD); ancient, medieval, early modern, and modern Europe (PhD); anthropology and Middle Eastern studies (PhD); Arabic (AM, PhD); archaeology (PhD); architecture (PhD); Armenian (AM, PhD); arts and sciences (AM, ME, MFS, SM, PhD); astronomy (PhD); astrophysics (PhD); baroque art (PhD); biblical history (AM, PhD); biochemical chemistry (PhD); biological anthropology (PhD); biological sciences in dental medicine (PhD); biology (PhD); biophysics (PhD); biostatistics (PhD); business economics (PhD); Byzantine art (PhD); Byzantine Greek (PhD); chemical biology (PhD); chemical physics (PhD); Chinese (PhD); Chinese studies (AM); classical archaeology (PhD); classical art (PhD); classical philology (PhD); classical philosophy (PhD); comparative literature (PhD); composition (AM, PhD); critical theory (PhD); descriptive linguistics (PhD); diplomatic history (PhD); earth and planetary sciences (AM, PhD); East Asian history (PhD); economic and social history (PhD); economics (PhD); economics and Middle Eastern studies (PhD); eighteenth-century literature (PhD); experimental physics (PhD); fine arts and Middle Eastern studies (PhD); forest science (MFS); French (AM, PhD); German (PhD); health policy (PhD); Hebrew (AM, PhD); historical linguistics (PhD); history and Middle Eastern studies (PhD); history of American civilization (PhD); history of science (AM, PhD); Indian art (PhD); Indian philosophy (AM, PhD); Indo-Muslim culture (AM, PhD); information, technology and management (PhD); Inner Asian and Altaic studies (PhD); inorganic chemistry (PhD); intellectual history (PhD); Iranian (AM, PhD); Irish (PhD); Islamic art (PhD); Italian (AM, PhD); Japanese (PhD); Japanese and Chinese art (PhD); Japanese studies (AM); Jewish history and literature (AM, PhD); Korean (PhD); Korean studies (AM); landscape architecture (PhD); Latin American history (PhD); legal anthropology (AM); literature: nineteenth-century to the present (PhD); mathematics (PhD); medical anthropology (AM); medical engineering/medical physics (PhD); medieval art (PhD); medieval Latin (PhD); medieval literature and language (PhD); modern art (PhD); modern British and American literature (PhD); molecular and cellular biology (PhD); Mongolian (PhD); Mongolian studies (AM); musicology (AM); musicology and ethnomusicology (PhD); Near Eastern history (PhD); neurobiology (PhD); oceanic history (PhD); oral literature (PhD); organic chemistry (PhD); organizational behavior (PhD); Pali (AM, PhD); Persian (AM, PhD); philosophy (PhD); physical chemistry (PhD); Polish (PhD); political economy and government (PhD); political science (PhD); Portuguese (AM, PhD); psychology (PhD); public policy (PhD); regional studies–Middle East (AM); regional studies-Russia, Eastern Europe, and Central Asia (AM); Renaissance and modern architecture (PhD); Renaissance art (PhD); Renaissance literature (PhD); Russian (PhD); Sanskrit (AM, PhD); Scandinavian (PhD); Semitic philology (AM, PhD); Serbo-Croatian (PhD); Slavic philology (PhD); social anthropology (AM, PhD); social change and development (AM); social policy (PhD); social psychology (PhD); sociology (PhD); Spanish (AM, PhD); statistics (AM, PhD); study of religion (PhD); Syro-Palestinian archaeology (AM, PhD); systems biology (PhD); theoretical linguistics (PhD); theoretical physics (PhD); theory (AM, PhD); Tibetan (AM, PhD); Turkish (AM, PhD); Ukrainian (PhD); urban planning (PhD); Urdu (AM, PhD); Vietnamese (PhD); Vietnamese studies (AM); Welsh (PhD). Electronic applications accepted.

Division of Medical Sciences Offers biological chemistry and molecular pharmacology (PhD); cell biology (PhD); genetics (PhD); microbiology and molecular genetics (PhD); pathology (PhD).

School of Engineering and Applied Sciences Students: 369 full-time (97 women), 10 part-time (1 woman); includes 46 minority (6 African Americans, 2 American Indian/Alaska Native, 33 Asian Americans or Pacific Islanders, 5 Hispanic Americans), 177 international. 1,331 applicants, 15% accepted, 94 enrolled. *Faculty:* 56 full-time (6 women), 14 part-time/adjunct (4 women). Expenses: Contact institution. *Financial support:* In 2008–09, 121 fellowships with full tuition reimbursements (averaging $21,240 per year), 238 research assistantships with full and partial tuition reimbursements (averaging $28,320 per year), 55 teaching assistantships with full and partial tuition reimbursements (averaging $5,413 per year) were awarded; Federal Work-Study, institutionally sponsored loans, traineeships, and health care benefits also available. In 2008, 69 master's, 28 doctorates awarded. *Degree program information:* Part-time programs available. Offers applied mathematics (ME, SM, PhD); applied physics (ME, SM, PhD); computer science (ME, SM, PhD); engineering science (ME); engineering sciences (SM, PhD). *Application deadline:* For fall admission, 12/15 priority date for domestic and international students; for winter admission, 1/2 for domestic and international students. *Application fee:* $105. Electronic applications accepted. *Application Contact:* Office of Admissions and Financial Aid, 617-495-5315, E-mail: admissions@seas.harvard.edu. *Dean,* Cherry Murray, 617-495-5829, Fax: 617-495-5264, E-mail: dean@seas.harvard.edu.

Graduate School of Design Offers architecture (M Arch); design (M Arch, M Des S, MAUD, MLA, MLAUD, MUP, Dr DES); design studies (M Des S); landscape architecture (MLA); urban planning (MUP); urban planning and design (MAUD, MLAUD). Electronic applications accepted.

Graduate School of Education Students: 802 full-time (612 women), 97 part-time (71 women); includes 225 minority (76 African Americans, 4 American Indian/Alaska Native, 94 Asian Americans or Pacific Islanders, 51 Hispanic Americans), 123 international. Average age 30. 1,758 applicants, 46% accepted, 577 enrolled. *Faculty:* 61 full-time (29 women), 40 part-time/adjunct (24 women). Expenses: Contact institution. *Financial support:* In 2008–09, 594 students received support, including 149 fellowships with full and partial tuition reimbursements available (averaging $13,934 per year), 73 research assistantships (averaging $9,295 per year), 145 teaching assistantships (averaging $9,237 per year); career-related internships or fieldwork, Federal Work-Study, institutionally sponsored loans, scholarships/grants, health care benefits, tuition waivers (full and partial), and unspecified assistantships also available. Support available to part-time students. Financial award application deadline: 2/1; financial award applicants required to submit FAFSA. In 2008, 567 master's, 40 doctorates awarded. *Degree program information:* Part-time programs available. Offers arts in education (Ed M); culture, communities and education (Ed D); education (Ed M, Ed D); education policy and management (Ed M); education policy, leadership and instructional practice (Ed D); higher education (Ed M, Ed D); human development and education (Ed D); human development and psychology (Ed M); international education policy (Ed M); language and literacy (Ed M); learning and teaching (Ed M); mid-career mathematics and science (teaching certificate) (Ed M); mind brain and education (Ed M); quantitative policy analysis in education (Ed D); risk and prevention (Ed M); school leadership (Ed M); special studies (Ed M); teaching and curriculum (teaching certificate) (Ed M); technology innovation and education (Ed M); urban superintendency (Ed D). *Application deadline:* For fall admission, 1/5 for domestic and international students. *Application fee:* $85. Electronic applications accepted. *Application Contact:* Information Contact, 617-495-3414, Fax: 617-496-3577, E-mail: gseadmissions@harvard.edu. *Dean,* Dr. Kathleen McCartney, 617-495-3401.

Harvard Business School Offers accounting and management (DBA); business (MBA, DBA, PhD); business administration (MBA); business economics (PhD); health policy management (PhD); management (DBA); marketing (DBA); organizational behavior (PhD); science, technology and management (PhD); strategy (DBA); technology and operations management (DBA).

Harvard Divinity School Students: 432 full-time (235 women); includes 78 minority (33 African Americans, 4 American Indian/Alaska Native, 20 Asian Americans or Pacific Islanders, 21 Hispanic Americans), 41 international. Average age 26. 677 applicants, 37% accepted, 161 enrolled. *Faculty:* 36 full-time (15 women), 81 part-time/adjunct (35 women). Expenses: Contact institution. *Financial support:* In 2008–09, 418 students received support, including 398 fellowships with tuition reimbursements available (averaging $21,469 per year); teaching assistantships, career-related internships or fieldwork, Federal Work-Study, and scholarships/grants also available. Support available to part-time students. Financial award application deadline: 2/1; financial award applicants required to submit FAFSA. In 2008, 43 first professional degrees, 119 master's, 11 doctorates awarded. Offers divinity (M Div, MTS, Th M, PhD, Th D). PhD offered by Harvard Graduate School of Arts and Sciences. *Application deadline:* For fall admission, 1/11 for domestic and international students. *Application fee:* $75. Electronic applications accepted. *Application Contact:* Loida Feliz, Director of Admissions, 617-495-5796, Fax: 617-495-0345, E-mail: lfeliz@hds.harvard.edu. *Dean,* William A. Graham, 917-495-4513, Fax: 617-496-8026.

Harvard Medical School Students: 728 full-time (358 women); includes 340 minority (71 African Americans, 9 American Indian/Alaska Native, 203 Asian Americans or Pacific Islanders, 57 Hispanic Americans), 53 international. Average age 27. 5,139 applicants, 4% accepted, 165 enrolled. *Faculty:* 8,074 full-time, 2,810 part-time/adjunct. Expenses: Contact institution. *Financial support:* In 2008–09, 614 students received support; fellowships, research assistantships, teaching assistantships, Federal Work-Study, institutionally sponsored loans, and scholarships/grants available. Financial award application deadline: 4/15; financial award applicants required to submit CSS PROFILE or FAFSA. In 2008, 174 first professional degrees awarded. Offers medicine (MD, M Eng, SM, PhD, Sc D). *Application deadline:* For fall admission, 10/15 for domestic students. *Application fee:* $85. Electronic applications accepted. *Application Contact:* 617-432-1550, Fax: 617-432-3307, E-mail: admissions_office@hms.harvard.edu. *Dean of the Faculty of Medicine,* Dr. Jeffrey S. Flier, 617-432-1501.

Division of Health Sciences and Technology Students: 410 full-time (145 women); includes 164 minority (9 African Americans, 4 American Indian/Alaska Native, 135 Asian Americans or Pacific Islanders, 16 Hispanic Americans), 62 international. Average age 28. 985 applicants, 9% accepted, 71 enrolled. *Faculty:* 68 full-time (6 women), 183 part-time/adjunct (31 women). Expenses: Contact institution. *Financial support:* In 2008–09, 247 students received support, including 119 fellowships with full and partial tuition reimbursements available (averaging $35,574 per year), 142 research assistantships with full and partial tuition reimbursements available (averaging $37,221 per year), 50 teaching assistantships with full and partial tuition reimbursements available (averaging $12,029 per year); career-related internships or fieldwork, scholarships/grants, traineeships, health care benefits, and unspecified assistantships also available. Support available to part-time students. Financial award application deadline: 12/15; financial award applicants required to submit FAFSA. In 2008, 33 first professional degrees, 9 master's, 29 doctorates awarded. Offers biomedical engineering (M Eng); biomedical enterprise (SM); biomedical informatics (SM); health sciences and technology (MD, M Eng, SM, PhD, Sc D); medical engineering (PhD); medical engineering/medical physics (Sc D); medical physics (PhD); medical sciences (MD); speech and hearing bioscience and technology (PhD, Sc D). *Application deadline:* For fall admission, 12/15 for domestic students. *Application fee:* $70.

John F. Kennedy School of Government Students: 587 full-time (239 women); includes 113 minority (27 African Americans, 8 American Indian/Alaska Native, 48 Asian Americans or Pacific Islanders, 30 Hispanic Americans), 252 international. Average age 30. 2,426 applicants, 36% accepted, 587 enrolled. *Faculty:* 70. Expenses: Contact institution. *Financial support:* Fellowships, research assistantships, teaching assistantships, career-related internships or fieldwork, Federal Work-Study, institutionally sponsored loans, scholarships/grants, and unspecified assistantships available. Support available to part-time students. Financial award applicants required to submit CSS PROFILE or FAFSA. Offers government (MPA, MPAID, MPP, MPPUP, PhD); political economy and government (PhD); public administration (MPA); public administration/international development (MPAID); public policy (MPP, PhD); public policy and urban planning (MPPUP). *Application fee:* $80. Electronic applications accepted. *Application Contact:* 617-495-1155, Fax: 617-496-1165, E-mail: hks_admissions@harvard.edu. *Dean,* Dr. David Ellwood, 617-495-1122.

Law School Offers international and comparative law (JD); law (JD, LL M, SJD); law and business (JD); law and government (JD); law and social change (JD); law, science and technology (JD).

School of Dental Medicine Offers advanced general dentistry (Certificate); dental medicine (DMD, M Med Sc, D Med Sc, Certificate); dental public health (Certificate); endodontics (Certificate); general practice residency (Certificate); oral biology (M Med Sc, D Med Sc); oral implantology (Certificate); oral medicine (Certificate); oral pathology (Certificate); oral surgery (Certificate); orthodontics (Certificate); pediatric dentistry (Certificate); periodontics (Certificate); prosthodontics (Certificate).

School of Public Health Students: 814 full-time, 271 part-time; includes 190 minority (54 African Americans, 4 American Indian/Alaska Native, 102 Asian Americans or Pacific Islanders, 30 Hispanic Americans), 350 international. Average age 31. 2,004 applicants, 38% accepted, 533 enrolled. *Faculty:* 345 full-time (132 women), 13 part-time/adjunct (5 women). Expenses: Contact institution. *Financial support:* Fellowships, research assistantships, teaching assistantships, career-related internships or fieldwork, Federal Work-Study, scholarships/grants, traineeships, tuition waivers (partial), and unspecified assistantships available. Support available to part-time students. Financial award application deadline: 2/8; financial award applicants required to submit FAFSA. In 2008, 401 master's, 84 doctorates awarded. *Degree program information:* Part-time programs available. Offers biological sciences in public health (PhD); biostatistics (SM, PhD); cancer epidemiology (SM, DPH); cardiovascular epidemiology (SM, DPH, SD); clinical effectiveness (MPH); clinical epidemiology (SM, DPH, SD); environmental health (MOH, SM, DPH, PhD, SD); environmental/occupational epidemiology (SM, SD); epidemiologic methods (DPH, SD); epidemiology (SM, DPH, SD); epidemiology of aging (SM, DPH, SD); family and community health (MPH); genetics and complex diseases (PhD); global health (MPH); global health and population (SM, DPH, SD); health care management and policy (MPH); health policy (PhD); health policy and management (SM, SD); immunology and infectious diseases (PhD, SD); infectious diseases (SM, DPH, SD); molecular/genetic epidemiology (DPH, SD); neuroepidemiology (DPH, SD); nutrition (DPH, PhD, SD); nutritional epidemiology (DPH, SD); occupational and environmental health (MPH); occupational health (MOH, SM, DPH, SD); oral and dental health epidemiology (SM, SD); pharmacoepidemiology (SM, DPH, SD); physiology (PhD, SD); psychiatric epidemiology (SM, DPH); public health (MOH, MPH, SM, DPH, PhD, SD); public health nutrition (DPH, SD); quantitative methods (MPH); reproductive epidemiology (SM, SD); society, human development and health (SM, DPH, SD). *Application deadline:* For fall admission, 12/15 for domestic and international students. *Application fee:* $0. Electronic applications accepted. *Application Contact:* Vincent W. James, Director of Admissions, 617-432-1031, Fax: 617-432-7080, E-mail: admisofc@hsph.harvard.edu. *Dean of the Faculty,* Dr. Julio Frenk, 617-432-1025, Fax: 617-277-5320, E-mail: deansoff@hsph.harvard.edu.

See Close-Up on page 921.

HASTINGS COLLEGE, Hastings, NE 68901-7696

General Information Independent-religious, coed, comprehensive institution. *Graduate housing:* On-campus housing not available.

GRADUATE UNITS

Department of Teacher Education *Degree program information:* Part-time programs available. Offers teacher education (MAT). Electronic applications accepted.

HAWAI'I PACIFIC UNIVERSITY, Honolulu, HI 96813

General Information Independent, coed, comprehensive institution. *Enrollment:* 8,293 graduate, professional, and undergraduate students; 590 full-time matriculated graduate/professional students (319 women), 590 part-time matriculated graduate/professional students (313 women). *Enrollment by degree level:* 1,155 master's, 25 other advanced degrees. *Graduate faculty:* 83 full-time (32 women), 34 part-time/adjunct (7 women). *Tuition:* Full-time $10,800; part-time $600 per credit. *Graduate housing:* Room and/or apartments available on a first-come, first-served basis to single students; on-campus housing not available to married students. *Student services:* Campus employment opportunities, campus safety program, career counseling, international student services, low-cost health insurance. *Library facilities:* Meader Library plus 2 others. *Online resources:* library catalog, web page, access to other libraries' catalogs. *Collection:* 160,800 titles, 38,050 serial subscriptions, 4,850 audiovisual materials. *Research affiliation:* Oceanic Institute (marine science).

Computer facilities: 590 computers available on campus for general student use. A campuswide network can be accessed from student residence rooms and from off campus. Online class registration is available. *Web address:* http://www.hpu.edu/.

General Application Contact: Danny Lam, Assistant Director of Graduate Admissions, 808-544-1135, Fax: 808-544-0280, E-mail: graduate@hpu.edu.

GRADUATE UNITS

College of Business Administration Students: 227 full-time (117 women), 214 part-time (102 women); includes 140 minority (11 African Americans, 5 American Indian/Alaska Native, 110 Asian Americans or Pacific Islanders, 14 Hispanic Americans), 167 international. Average age 30. 275 applicants, 80% accepted, 149 enrolled. *Faculty:* 19 full-time (6 women), 12 part-time/adjunct (2 women). Expenses: Contact institution. *Financial support:* In 2008–09, 164 students received support; research assistantships, career-related internships or fieldwork, Federal Work-Study, scholarships/grants, and unspecified assistantships available. Support available to part-time students. Financial award application deadline: 3/1; financial award applicants required to submit FAFSA. In 2008, 183 master's awarded. *Degree program information:* Part-time and evening/weekend programs available. Offers accounting/CPA (MBA); e-business (MBA); economics (MBA); finance (MBA); human resource management (MBA); information systems (MBA); international business (MBA); management (MBA); marketing (MBA); organizational change (MBA); travel industry management (MBA). *Application deadline:* For fall admission, 2/15 priority date for domestic students; for spring admission, 10/15 priority date for domestic students. Applications are processed on a rolling basis. *Application fee:* $50. Electronic applications accepted. *Application Contact:* Danny Lam, Assistant Director of Graduate Admissions, 808-544-1135, Fax: 808-544-0280, E-mail: graduate@hpu.edu. *Dean,* Dr. Aytun Ozturk, 808-544-9301, Fax: 808-544-0283, E-mail: uozturk@hpu.edu.

College of Communication Students: 66 full-time (47 women), 51 part-time (33 women); includes 35 minority (7 African Americans, 2 American Indian/Alaska Native, 23 Asian Americans or Pacific Islanders, 3 Hispanic Americans), 40 international. Average age 28. 75 applicants, 81% accepted, 29 enrolled. *Faculty:* 11 full-time (4 women), 3 part-time/adjunct (1 woman). Expenses: Contact institution. *Financial support:* In 2008–09, 65 students received support. Career-related internships or fieldwork, Federal Work-Study, scholarships/grants, and unspecified assistantships available. Support available to part-time students. Financial award application deadline: 3/1; financial award applicants required to submit FAFSA. In 2008, 36 master's awarded. *Degree program information:* Part-time and evening/weekend programs available. Offers communication (MA). *Application deadline:* For fall admission, 2/15 priority date for domestic students; for spring admission, 10/15 priority date for domestic students. Applications are processed on a rolling basis. *Application fee:* $50. Electronic applications accepted. *Application Contact:* Danny Lam, Assistant Director of Graduate Admissions, 808-544-1135, Fax: 808-544-0280, E-mail: graduate@hpu.edu. *Dean,* Dr. Steven Combs, 808-544-0828, Fax: 808-544-0835, E-mail: scombs@hpu.edu.

College of International Studies Students: 28 full-time (19 women), 18 part-time (9 women); includes 21 minority (1 African American, 19 Asian Americans or Pacific Islanders, 1 Hispanic American), 13 international. Average age 35. 41 applicants, 78% accepted, 18 enrolled. *Faculty:* 9 full-time (4 women), 3 part-time/adjunct (1 woman). Expenses: Contact institution. *Financial support:* In 2008–09, 23 students received support. Career-related internships or fieldwork, Federal Work-Study, scholarships/grants, and unspecified assistantships available. Support available to part-time students. Financial award application deadline: 3/1; financial award applicants required to submit FAFSA. In 2008, 14 master's awarded. *Degree program information:* Part-time and evening/weekend programs available. Offers teaching English as a second language (MA). *Application deadline:* For fall admission, 2/15 priority date for domestic students; for spring admission, 10/15 priority date for domestic students. Applications are processed on a rolling basis. *Application fee:* $50. Electronic applications accepted. *Application Contact:* Danny Lam, Assistant Director of Graduate Admissions, 808-544-1135, Fax: 808-544-0280, E-mail: graduate@hpu.edu. *Dean,* Dr. Carlos Juarez, 808-566-2493, Fax: 808-544-0834, E-mail: cjuarez@hpu.edu.

College of Liberal Arts Students: 86 full-time (52 women), 136 part-time (76 women); includes 87 minority (9 African Americans, 4 American Indian/Alaska Native, 69 Asian Americans or Pacific Islanders, 5 Hispanic Americans), 13 international. Average age 32. 152 applicants, 82% accepted, 71 enrolled. *Faculty:* 17 full-time (8 women), 8 part-time/adjunct (1 woman). Expenses: Contact institution. *Financial support:* In 2008–09, 116 students received support. Career-related internships or fieldwork, Federal Work-Study, scholarships/grants, and unspecified assistantships available. Support available to part-time students. Financial award application deadline: 3/1; financial award applicants required to submit FAFSA. In 2008, 49 master's awarded. *Degree program information:* Part-time and evening/weekend programs available. Offers diplomacy and military studies (MA); secondary education (M Ed); social work (MSW). *Application deadline:* For fall admission, 2/15 priority date for domestic students; for spring

Hawai'i Pacific University (continued)

admission, 10/15 priority date for domestic students. Applications are processed on a rolling basis. *Application fee:* $50. Electronic applications accepted. *Application Contact:* Danny Lam, Assistant Director of Graduate Admissions, 808-544-1135, Fax: 808-544-0280, E-mail: graduate@hpu.edu. *Associate Vice President and Dean,* Dr. William Potter, 808-544-0228, Fax: 808-544-1424, E-mail: wpotter@hpu.edu.

College of Natural Sciences Students: 16 full-time (10 women), 5 part-time (4 women); includes 1 minority (Asian American or Pacific Islander), 1 international. Average age 25. 24 applicants, 63% accepted, 13 enrolled. *Faculty:* 9 full-time (3 women), 2 part-time/adjunct. Expenses: Contact institution. *Financial support:* In 2008–09, 21 students received support. Federal Work-Study, scholarships/grants, and unspecified assistantships available. Support available to part-time students. Offers marine science (MS). *Application deadline:* For fall admission, 2/15 priority date for domestic students; for spring admission, 10/15 priority date for domestic students. Applications are processed on a rolling basis. *Application fee:* $50. Electronic applications accepted. *Application Contact:* Danny Lam, Assistant Director of Graduate Admissions, 808-544-1135, Fax: 808-544-0280, E-mail: graduate@hpu.edu. *Vice President, Research/Dean,* Dr. Andrew Brittain, 808-236-3553, Fax: 808-236-5880, E-mail: abrittain@hpu.edu.

College of Professional Studies Students: 144 full-time (52 women), 128 part-time (61 women); includes 94 minority (13 African Americans, 3 American Indian/Alaska Native, 70 Asian Americans or Pacific Islanders, 8 Hispanic Americans), 91 international. Average age 31. 202 applicants, 83% accepted, 74 enrolled. *Faculty:* 13 full-time (2 women), 5 part-time/adjunct (2 women). Expenses: Contact institution. *Financial support:* In 2008–09, 120 students received support. Career-related internships or fieldwork, Federal Work-Study, scholarships/grants, and unspecified assistantships available. Support available to part-time students. Financial award application deadline: 3/1; financial award applicants required to submit FAFSA. In 2008, 85 master's awarded. *Degree program information:* Part-time and evening/weekend programs available. Offers global leadership and sustainable development (MA); human resource management (MA); information systems (MSIS); knowledge management (MSIS); organizational change (MA); software engineering (MSIS); telecommunications security (MSIS). *Application deadline:* For fall admission, 2/15 priority date for domestic students; for spring admission, 10/15 priority date for domestic students. Applications are processed on a rolling basis. *Application fee:* $50. Electronic applications accepted. *Application Contact:* Danny Lam, Assistant Director of Graduate Admissions, 808-544-1135, Fax: 808-544-0280, E-mail: graduate@hpu.edu. *Dean,* Dr. Gordon Jones, 808-544-1181, Fax: 808-544-0247, E-mail: gjones@hpu.edu.

School of Nursing Students: 22 full-time (21 women), 20 part-time (18 women); includes 17 minority (3 African Americans, 13 Asian Americans or Pacific Islanders, 1 Hispanic American), 3 international. Average age 38. 22 applicants, 68% accepted, 14 enrolled. *Faculty:* 5 full-time (all women), 1 part-time/adjunct (0 women). Expenses: Contact institution. *Financial support:* In 2008–09, 17 students received support. Career-related internships or fieldwork, Federal Work-Study, scholarships/grants, and traineeships available. Support available to part-time students. Financial award application deadline: 3/1; financial award applicants required to submit FAFSA. In 2008, 13 master's awarded. *Degree program information:* Part-time and evening/weekend programs available. Offers community clinical nurse specialist (MSN); community clinical nurse specialist educator option (MSN); family nurse practitioner (MSN). *Application deadline:* Applications are processed on a rolling basis. *Application fee:* $50. Electronic applications accepted. *Application Contact:* Danny Lam, Assistant Director of Graduate Admissions, 808-544-1135, Fax: 808-544-0280, E-mail: graduate@hpu.edu. *Associate Dean of Nursing for Administration,* Dr. Patricia Lange-Otsuka, 808-236-5812, Fax: 808-236-5818, E-mail: potsuka@hpu.edu.

See Close-Up on page 923.

HAZELDEN GRADUATE SCHOOL OF ADDICTION STUDIES, Center City, MN 55012

General Information Independent, coed, graduate-only institution. *Graduate housing:* On-campus housing not available.

GRADUATE UNITS

Graduate Programs *Degree program information:* Part-time programs available. Offers addiction counseling (MA, Certificate).

HEBREW COLLEGE, Newton Centre, MA 02459

General Information Independent-religious, coed, comprehensive institution. *Graduate housing:* On-campus housing not available.

GRADUATE UNITS

Cantor Educator Program Offers cantor educator (MJ Ed).

Program in Jewish Studies *Degree program information:* Part-time and evening/weekend programs available. Postbaccalaureate distance learning degree programs offered (minimal on-campus study). Offers Jewish liturgical music (Certificate); Jewish music education (Certificate); Jewish studies (MA).

Rabbinical School

Shoolman Graduate School of Education *Degree program information:* Part-time and evening/weekend programs available. Postbaccalaureate distance learning degree programs offered. Offers early childhood Jewish education (Certificate); Jewish day school education (Certificate); Jewish education (MJ Ed); Jewish family education (Certificate); Jewish special education (Certificate); Jewish youth education, informal education and camping (Certificate).

HEBREW THEOLOGICAL COLLEGE, Skokie, IL 60077-3263

General Information Independent-religious, comprehensive institution.

GRADUATE UNITS

Department of Talmud and Rabbinics Offers Talmud and rabbinics (Rabbi).

HEBREW UNION COLLEGE–JEWISH INSTITUTE OF RELIGION, Los Angeles, CA 90007-3796

General Information Independent-religious, coed, graduate-only institution. *Graduate housing:* On-campus housing not available.

GRADUATE UNITS

Edgar F. Magnin School of Graduate Studies *Degree program information:* Part-time programs available. Offers religion (MAJS, DHL, DHS). Electronic applications accepted.

Rhea Hirsch School of Education Offers day school teaching: California state teaching credential (Certificate); Jewish education (MAJE, PhD). Electronic applications accepted.

School of Jewish Communal Service Offers Jewish communal service (MAJCS, Certificate). Electronic applications accepted.

School of Rabbinical Studies Offers rabbinical studies (MAHL). Electronic applications accepted.

HEBREW UNION COLLEGE–JEWISH INSTITUTE OF RELIGION, New York, NY 10012-1186

General Information Independent-religious, coed, graduate-only institution. *Graduate housing:* On-campus housing not available.

GRADUATE UNITS

Rabbinical School Offers rabbinical studies (MAHL).

School of Education *Degree program information:* Part-time programs available. Offers education (MARE).

School of Graduate Studies *Degree program information:* Part-time programs available. Offers Hebrew letters (DHL); Judaic studies (MAJS); pastoral counseling (D Min).

School of Sacred Music Offers sacred music (MSM).

HEBREW UNION COLLEGE–JEWISH INSTITUTE OF RELIGION, Cincinnati, OH 45220-2488

General Information Independent-religious, coed, graduate-only institution. CGS member. *Graduate housing:* Room and/or apartments available on a first-come, first-served basis to single students. Housing application deadline: 7/31. *Research affiliation:* Union for Reform Judaism (Jewish education, survey and analysis of reform education), Oriental Institute (neo-Babylonian texts).

GRADUATE UNITS

Rabbinic School Offers rabbinic studies (MAHL).

School of Graduate Studies *Degree program information:* Part-time programs available. Offers Bible and the ancient Near East (M Phil, MA, PhD); Hebrew letters (DHL); history of biblical interpretation (M Phil, MA, PhD); Jewish and Christian studies in the Greco-Roman period (M Phil, PhD); Jewish and cognate studies (M Phil); Judaic and cognate studies (MA, PhD); modern Jewish history (M Phil, MA, PhD); philosophy and Jewish religious thought (M Phil, MA, PhD); rabbinics (M Phil, MA, PhD).

HEC MONTREAL, Montréal, QC H3T 2A7, Canada

General Information Province-supported, coed, comprehensive institution. *Enrollment:* 12,464 graduate, professional, and undergraduate students; 1,335 full-time matriculated graduate/professional students (593 women), 1,339 part-time matriculated graduate/professional students (652 women). *Enrollment by degree level:* 1,148 master's, 142 doctoral, 1,384 other advanced degrees. *Graduate faculty:* 267 full-time (78 women), 346 part-time/adjunct (108 women). *Graduate tuition:* Tuition and fees charges are reported in Canadian dollars. *International tuition:* $15,111.72 Canadian dollars full-time. *Tuition, area resident:* Part-time $62.27 Canadian dollars per credit. Tuition, province resident: full-time $2241.72 Canadian dollars; part-time $179.28 Canadian dollars per credit. Tuition, Canadian resident: full-time $6454 Canadian dollars; part-time $419.77 Canadian dollars per credit. *Required fees:* $1218.75 Canadian dollars; $28.25 Canadian dollars per credit. $88 Canadian dollars per term. Tuition and fees vary according to degree level and program. *Graduate housing:* Rooms and/or apartments available on a first-come, first-served basis to single and married students. Typical cost: $3197 Canadian dollars per year for single students; $5400 Canadian dollars per year for married students. *Student services:* Campus employment opportunities, career counseling, child daycare facilities, free psychological counseling, international student services, multicultural affairs office, services for students with disabilities. *Library facilities:* Myriam et J.-Robert Ouimet Library plus 1 other. *Online resources:* library catalog, web page, access to other libraries' catalogs. *Collection:* 369,207 titles, 28,531 serial subscriptions, 2,566 audiovisual materials. *Research affiliation:* CGI (information systems), Center for InterUniversity Research and Analysis on Organizations (economics and finance), Hydro Quebec (finance), Ad Opt (operational research), Centre Francophone de Recherche en Informatisation des Organisations (information systems), Centre de recherche en informatique (CRIM) (information systems).

Computer facilities: Computer purchase and lease plans are available. 250 computers available on campus for general student use. A campuswide network can be accessed from off campus. Online class registration, Corporate calendar and Web site for all the resources available for classes are available. *Web address:* http://www.hec.ca/.

General Application Contact: Manon Vaillant, Registrar, 514-340-6110, Fax: 514-340-5640, E-mail: registraire.info@hec.ca.

GRADUATE UNITS

School of Business Administration Students: 1,335 full-time (593 women), 1,339 part-time (652 women). Average age 29. 1,904 applicants, 57% accepted, 731 enrolled. *Faculty:* 267 full-time (78 women), 346 part-time/adjunct (108 women). Expenses: Contact institution. *Financial support:* Research assistantships, teaching assistantships, scholarships/grants available. In 2008, 453 master's, 22 doctorates, 472 other advanced degrees awarded. *Degree program information:* Part-time and evening/weekend programs available. Offers administration (LL M, M Sc, PhD, Diploma); applied economics (M Sc); applied financial economics (M Sc); business administration (LL M, M Sc, MBA, PhD, Diploma); business administration and management (MBA); business intelligence (M Sc); controllership (M Sc); e-business (Diploma); electronic commerce (M Sc); finance (M Sc); financial engineering (M Sc); human resources management (M Sc); information systems (M Sc); international business (M Sc); international management (M Sc); logistics (M Sc); management (M Sc, Diploma); management and sustainable development (Diploma); management of cultural organizations (Diploma); marketing (M Sc); marketing communication (Diploma); private wealth management (Diploma); production and operations management (M Sc); public accountancy (Diploma); supply chain management (Diploma); taxation (LL M, Diploma). Most courses are given in French. *Application fee:* $76 Canadian dollars. Electronic applications accepted. *Application Contact:* Manon Vaillant, Registrar, 514-340-6110, Fax: 514-340-5640, E-mail: registraire.info@hec.ca. *Director,* Dr. Michel Patry, 514-340-6110, Fax: 514-340-5640.

HEIDELBERG UNIVERSITY, Tiffin, OH 44883-2462

General Information Independent-religious, coed, comprehensive institution. *Graduate housing:* On-campus housing not available.

GRADUATE UNITS

Program in Business *Degree program information:* Part-time and evening/weekend programs available. Offers business (MBA).

Program in Counseling *Degree program information:* Part-time and evening/weekend programs available. Offers counseling (MA).

Program in Education *Degree program information:* Part-time and evening/weekend programs available. Offers education (MA).

HENDERSON STATE UNIVERSITY, Arkadelphia, AR 71999-0001

General Information State-supported, coed, comprehensive institution. CGS member. *Enrollment:* 3,649 graduate, professional, and undergraduate students; 137 full-time matriculated graduate/professional students (80 women), 379 part-time matriculated graduate/professional students (282 women). *Enrollment by degree level:* 511 master's, 5 other advanced degrees. *Graduate faculty:* 70 full-time (25 women), 14 part-time/adjunct (4 women). Tuition, state resident: full-time $2448; part-time $204 per credit hour. Tuition, nonresident: full-time $4896; part-time $408 per credit hour. *Required fees:* $754. Tuition and fees vary according to course load. *Graduate housing:* Room and/or apartments available on a first-come, first-served basis to single students; on-campus housing not available to married students. Typical cost: $5426 (including board). Room and board charges vary according to board plan. *Student services:* Campus employment opportunities, career counseling, free psychological counseling, international student services, services for students with disabilities. *Library facilities:* Huie Library. *Online resources:* library catalog, web page, access to other libraries' catalogs. *Collection:* 264,367 titles, 216,738 serial subscriptions, 20,566 audiovisual materials.

Computer facilities: 125 computers available on campus for general student use. A campuswide network can be accessed from student residence rooms and from off campus. Online class registration is available. *Web address:* http://www.hsu.edu/.

General Application Contact: Dr. Marck L. Beggs, Graduate Dean, 870-230-5126, Fax: 870-230-5479, E-mail: beggsm@hsu.edu.

GRADUATE UNITS

Graduate Studies Students: 139 full-time (79 women), 323 part-time (237 women); includes 63 minority (58 African Americans, 1 American Indian/Alaska Native, 1 Asian American or Pacific Islander, 3 Hispanic Americans), 56 international. Average age 31. 353 applicants, 29% accepted, 66 enrolled. *Faculty:* 49 full-time (25 women), 11 part-time/adjunct (3 women). Expenses: Contact institution. *Financial support:* Teaching assistantships with tuition reimbursements available. In 2008, 160 master's, 7 other advanced degrees awarded. *Degree program* *information:* Part-time programs available. *Application deadline:* For fall admission, 8/1 priority date for domestic students, 6/30 priority date for international students; for spring admission, 1/1 priority date for domestic students, 11/30 priority date for international students. *Application fee:* $25 ($75 for international students). Electronic applications accepted. *Application Contact:* Yvette Bragg, Administrative Assistant I, 870-230-5126, Fax: 870-230-5479, E-mail: braggy@hsu.edu. *Graduate Dean,* Dr. Marck L. Beggs, 870-230-5126, Fax: 870-230-5479, E-mail: beggsm@hsu.edu.

Ellis College of Arts and Sciences Students: 9 full-time (6 women), 28 part-time (21 women); includes 3 minority (2 African Americans, 1 Asian American or Pacific Islander), 2 international. Average age 32. *Faculty:* 9 full-time (8 women). Expenses: Contact institution. *Financial support:* Teaching assistantships with tuition reimbursements available. In 2008, 8 master's awarded. *Degree program information:* Part-time programs available. Offers arts and sciences (MLA). *Application deadline:* For fall admission, 8/1 priority date for domestic students, 6/30 priority date for international students; for spring admission, 1/1 priority date for domestic students, 11/30 priority date for international students. *Application fee:* $25 ($75 for international students). Electronic applications accepted. *Application Contact:* Dr. Marck L. Beggs, Graduate Dean, 870-230-5126, Fax: 870-230-5479, E-mail: beggsm@hsu.edu. *Dean,* Dr. Maralyn Sommer, 870-230-5404, Fax: 870-230-5144, E-mail: sommerm@hsu.edu.

School of Business Administration Students: 65 full-time (26 women), 29 part-time (17 women); includes 9 minority (8 African Americans, 1 Hispanic American), 42 international. Average age 27. 36 applicants, 100% accepted, 36 enrolled. *Faculty:* 14 full-time (5 women), 2 part-time/adjunct (0 women). Expenses: Contact institution. *Financial support:* Teaching assistantships with tuition reimbursements, Federal Work-Study and institutionally sponsored loans available. Support available to part-time students. In 2008, 31 degrees awarded. *Degree program information:* Part-time programs available. Offers business administration (MBA). *Application deadline:* For fall admission, 8/1 priority date for domestic students, 6/30 priority date for international students; for spring admission, 1/1 priority date for domestic students, 11/30 priority date for international students. *Application fee:* $25 ($75 for international students). Electronic applications accepted. *Application Contact:* Dr. Marck L. Beggs, Graduate Dean, 870-230-5126, Fax: 870-230-5479, E-mail: beggsm@hsu.edu. *Interim Dean,* Dr. Margaret Hoskins, 870-230-5310, Fax: 870-230-5286, E-mail: hoskins@hsu.edu.

School of Education Students: 65 full-time (47 women), 266 part-time (199 women); includes 51 minority (48 African Americans, 1 American Indian/Alaska Native, 2 Hispanic Americans), 12 international. Average age 34. 28 applicants, 100% accepted, 28 enrolled. *Faculty:* 26 full-time (12 women), 9 part-time/adjunct (3 women). Expenses: Contact institution. *Financial support:* Teaching assistantships with tuition reimbursements available. In 2008, 121 master's, 7 other advanced degrees awarded. *Degree program information:* Part-time programs available. Offers community counseling (MS); early childhood (P-4) (MSE); education (MAT); educational leadership (Ed S); elementary school counseling (MSE); middle school (MSE); reading (MSE); recreation (MS); school administration (MSE); secondary school counseling (MSE); special education (MSE); sports administration (MS). *Application deadline:* For fall admission, 8/1 priority date for domestic students, 6/30 priority date for international students; for spring admission, 1/1 priority date for domestic students, 11/30 priority date for international students. *Application fee:* $25 ($75 for international students). Electronic applications accepted. *Application Contact:* Dr. Marck L. Beggs, Graduate Dean, 870-230-5126, Fax: 870-230-5479, E-mail: beggsm@hsu.edu. *Dean,* Dr. Judy Harrison, 870-230-5358, Fax: 870-230-5455, E-mail: harrisj@hsu.edu.

HENDRIX COLLEGE, Conway, AR 72032-3080

General Information Independent-religious, coed, comprehensive institution. *Graduate housing:* Room and/or apartments available on a first-come, first-served basis to single students. Housing application deadline: 6/1.

GRADUATE UNITS

Program in Accounting Students: 8 full-time (2 women), 1 international. Average age 22. 8 applicants, 100% accepted. *Faculty:* 6 full-time (2 women), 1 part-time/adjunct (0 women). Expenses: Contact institution. *Financial support:* In 2008–09, 4 students received support. Career-related internships or fieldwork, Federal Work-Study, scholarships/grants, and tuition waivers (partial) available. Financial award application deadline: 2/1; financial award applicants required to submit FAFSA. In 2008, 4 master's awarded. *Degree program information:* Part-time programs available. Offers accounting (MA). *Application deadline:* For fall admission, 2/1 priority date for domestic and international students. Applications are processed on a rolling basis. *Application fee:* $50. *Application Contact:* Prof. Stephen W. Kerr, Professor of Economics and Business, 501-329-6811, Fax: 501-450-1400, E-mail: kerr@hendrix.edu. *Professor of Economics and Business,* Prof. Stephen W. Kerr, 501-329-6811, Fax: 501-450-1400, E-mail: kerr@hendrix.edu.

HERITAGE BAPTIST COLLEGE AND HERITAGE THEOLOGICAL SEMINARY, Cambridge, ON N3C 3T2, Canada

General Information Independent-religious, coed, comprehensive institution.

GRADUATE UNITS

Program in Theological Studies Offers chaplaincy (M Div); counselling (M Div); general (M Div); ministry (D Min); pastoral (M Div); research (M Div); theological studies (MA, Certificate).

HERITAGE CHRISTIAN UNIVERSITY, Florence, AL 35630

General Information Independent-religious, coed, primarily men, comprehensive institution.

GRADUATE UNITS

Graduate Programs Offers counseling (MM); Greek (MA); ministry (MM); New Testament (MA).

HERITAGE UNIVERSITY, Toppenish, WA 98948-9599

General Information Independent, coed, comprehensive institution. *Graduate housing:* On-campus housing not available.

GRADUATE UNITS

Graduate Programs in Education *Degree program information:* Part-time and evening/weekend programs available. Offers bilingual education/ESL (M Ed); biology (M Ed); counseling (M Ed); educational administration (M Ed); English and literature (M Ed); professional studies (M Ed); reading/literacy (M Ed); special education (M Ed); teaching (MIT).

HIGH POINT UNIVERSITY, High Point, NC 27262-3598

General Information Independent-religious, coed, comprehensive institution. CGS member. *Graduate housing:* Rooms and/or apartments available on a first-come, first-served basis to single and married students. Housing application deadline: 5/31.

GRADUATE UNITS

Norcross Graduate School *Degree program information:* Part-time and evening/weekend programs available. Offers business administration (MBA); educational leadership (M Ed); elementary education (M Ed); history (MA); nonprofit management (MA); special education (M Ed); sport studies (MS). Electronic applications accepted.

HILLSDALE FREE WILL BAPTIST COLLEGE, Moore, OK 73160-1208

General Information Independent-religious, coed, comprehensive institution. *Graduate housing:* Room and/or apartments available on a first-come, first-served basis to single students.

GRADUATE UNITS

Department of Bible Studies *Degree program information:* Part-time and evening/weekend programs available. Offers ministry (MA).

HODGES UNIVERSITY, Naples, FL 34119

General Information Independent, coed, comprehensive institution. *Enrollment:* 1,906 graduate, professional, and undergraduate students; 21 full-time matriculated graduate/professional students (13 women), 210 part-time matriculated graduate/professional students (138 women). *Enrollment by degree level:* 231 master's. *Graduate faculty:* 13 full-time (4 women), 3 part-time/adjunct (2 women). *Tuition:* Part-time $600 per credit hour. *Graduate housing:* On-campus housing not available. *Student services:* Career counseling, services for students with disabilities. *Library facilities:* Information Resource Center plus 1 other. *Online resources:* library catalog, web page, access to other libraries' catalogs. *Collection:* 38,008 titles, 230 serial subscriptions.

Computer facilities: 500 computers available on campus for general student use. A campuswide network can be accessed. *Web address:* http://www.hodges.edu/.

General Application Contact: Rita Lampus, Vice President of Student Enrollment Management, 239-513-1122, Fax: 239-598-6253, E-mail: rlampus@hodges.edu.

GRADUATE UNITS

Graduate Programs Students: 21 full-time (13 women), 210 part-time (138 women); includes 68 minority (33 African Americans, 2 Asian Americans or Pacific Islanders, 33 Hispanic Americans). Average age 36. *Faculty:* 13 full-time (4 women), 3 part-time/adjunct (2 women). Expenses: Contact institution. *Financial support:* In 2008–09, 200 students received support. Federal Work-Study and scholarships/grants available. Financial award application deadline: 7/9; financial award applicants required to submit FAFSA. In 2008, 82 master's awarded. *Degree program information:* Part-time and evening/weekend programs available. Postbaccalaureate distance learning degree programs offered (no on-campus study). Offers business administration (MBA); computer information technology (MS); criminal justice (MCJ); education (MPS); information systems management (MIS); interdisciplinary (MPS); law (MPS); management (MSM); professional studies (MPS); psychology (MPS); public administration (MPA). *Application deadline:* Applications are processed on a rolling basis. *Application fee:* $50. Electronic applications accepted. *Application Contact:* Rita Lampus, Vice President of Student Enrollment Management, 239-513-1122, Fax: 239-598-6253, E-mail: rlampus@hodges.edu. *President,* Terry McMahan, 239-513-1122, Fax: 239-598-6253, E-mail: tmcmahan@hodges.edu.

HOFSTRA UNIVERSITY, Hempstead, NY 11549

General Information Independent, coed, university. CGS member. *Enrollment:* 12,333 graduate, professional, and undergraduate students; 2,109 full-time matriculated graduate/professional students (1,276 women), 1,724 part-time matriculated graduate/professional students (1,097 women). *Enrollment by degree level:* 1,143 first professional, 2,319 master's, 288 doctoral, 83 other advanced degrees. *Graduate faculty:* 271 full-time (116 women), 193 part-time/adjunct (83 women). *Tuition:* Full-time $15,300; part-time $850 per credit. *Required fees:* $970; $165 per term. Tuition and fees vary according to program. *Graduate housing:* Room and/or apartments available on a first-come, first-served basis to single students; on-campus housing not available to married students. Typical cost: $12,500 per year. Room charges vary according to housing facility selected. Housing application deadline: 5/1. *Student services:* Campus employment opportunities, campus safety program, career counseling, child daycare facilities, exercise/wellness program, free psychological counseling, grant writing training, international student services, low-cost health insurance, multicultural affairs office, services for students with disabilities, teacher training, writing training. *Library facilities:* Axinn Library plus 1 other. *Online resources:* library catalog, web page, access to other libraries' catalogs. *Collection:* 1.2 million titles, 11,229 serial subscriptions, 15,740 audiovisual materials.

Computer facilities: Computer purchase and lease plans are available. 1,628 computers available on campus for general student use. A campuswide network can be accessed from student residence rooms and from off campus. Online class registration, Gmail/Google Apps for students; Emergency Notification System; Online course management system; Online card services balance update; Online portfolio are available. *Web address:* http://www.hofstra.edu/.

General Application Contact: Carol Drummer, Dean of Graduate Admissions, 516-463-4876, Fax: 516-463-4664, E-mail: gradstudent@hofstra.edu.

GRADUATE UNITS

College of Liberal Arts and Sciences Students: 308 full-time (230 women), 119 part-time (74 women); includes 56 minority (18 African Americans, 20 Asian Americans or Pacific Islanders, 18 Hispanic Americans), 9 international. Average age 27. 761 applicants, 40% accepted, 134 enrolled. *Faculty:* 85 full-time (31 women), 31 part-time/adjunct (13 women). Expenses: Contact institution. *Financial support:* In 2008–09, 251 students received support, including 128 fellowships with full and partial tuition reimbursements available (averaging $6,371 per year), 12 research assistantships with full and partial tuition reimbursements available (averaging $8,834 per year); career-related internships or fieldwork, Federal Work-Study, institutionally sponsored loans, scholarships/grants, tuition waivers (full and partial), and unspecified assistantships also available. Support available to part-time students. Financial award applicants required to submit FAFSA. In 2008, 123 master's, 26 doctorates, 8 other advanced degrees awarded. *Degree program information:* Part-time and evening/weekend programs available. Postbaccalaureate distance learning degree programs offered (no on-campus study). Offers applied linguistics (MA); applied mathematics (MS); applied organizational psychology (PhD); applied social research and policy analysis (MA); audiology (Au D); biology (MA, MS); clinical psychology (MA, PhD); comparative arts and culture (MA); computer science (MA, MS); English and creative writing (MA); English literature (MA); industrial/organizational psychology (MA); liberal arts and sciences (MA, MS, Au D, PhD, Psy D, CAS); mathematics (MA); school-community psychology (MS, Psy D, CAS); Spanish (MA); speech-language pathology (MA). *Application deadline:* Applications are processed on a rolling basis. *Application fee:* $60. Electronic applications accepted. *Application Contact:* Carol Drummer, Dean of Graduate Admissions, 516-463-4876, Fax: 516-463-4664, E-mail: gradstudent@hofstra.edu. *Dean,* Dr. Bernard J. Firestone, 516-463-5411, Fax: 516-463-4861, E-mail: lasbjf@hofstra.edu.

New College 5 applicants, 40% accepted, 0 enrolled. Expenses: Contact institution. *Financial support:* Fellowships with full and partial tuition reimbursements, research assistantships with full and partial tuition reimbursements, Federal Work-Study, institutionally sponsored loans, scholarships/grants, tuition waivers (full and partial), and unspecified assistantships available. Support available to part-time students. Financial award applicants required to submit FAFSA. In 2008, 2 master's awarded. *Degree program information:* Part-time and evening/weekend programs available. Offers interdisciplinary studies (MA). *Application deadline:* Applications are processed on a rolling basis. *Application fee:* $60. Electronic applications accepted. *Application Contact:* Carol Drummer, Dean of Graduate Admissions, 516-463-4876, Fax: 516-463-4664, E-mail: gradstudent@hofstra.edu. *Vice Dean,* Dr. Barry Nass, 516-463-5820, Fax: 516-463-4832, E-mail: barry.n.nass@hofstra.edu.

Frank G. Zarb School of Business Students: 262 full-time (103 women), 407 part-time (160 women); includes 117 minority (40 African Americans, 46 Asian Americans or Pacific Islanders, 31 Hispanic Americans), 95 international. Average age 30. 519 applicants, 78% accepted, 191 enrolled. *Faculty:* 47 full-time (10 women), 15 part-time/adjunct (2 women). Expenses: Contact institution. *Financial support:* In 2008–09, 113 students received support, including 90 fellowships with full and partial tuition reimbursements available (averaging $8,060 per year), 6 research assistantships with full and partial tuition reimbursements available (averaging $13,338 per year); career-related internships or fieldwork, Federal Work-Study, institutionally sponsored loans, scholarships/grants, tuition waivers (full and partial), and unspecified assistantships also available. Support available to part-time students. Financial award applicants required to submit FAFSA. In 2008, 182 master's awarded. *Degree program information:* Part-time and evening/weekend programs available. Offers accounting (MS); business (EMBA, MBA, MS); business administration (MBA); finance (MS); human resource management (MS); information technology (MS); marketing (MS); marketing research (MS); quantitative finance (MS); real estate (MBA); taxation (MS). *Application deadline:* Applications are processed on a rolling basis. *Application fee:* $60. Electronic applications accepted. *Application Contact:* Carol Drummer, Dean of Graduate Admissions, 516-463-4876, Fax: 516-463-4664, E-mail:

Hofstra University (continued)

gradstudent@hofstra.edu. *Dean*, Salvatore F. Sodano, 516-463-5685, Fax: 516-463-5268, E-mail: bizsfs@hofstra.edu.

School of Communication Students: 26 full-time (11 women), 29 part-time (18 women); includes 13 minority (7 African Americans, 3 Asian Americans or Pacific Islanders, 3 Hispanic Americans), 1 international. Average age 28. 56 applicants, 93% accepted, 25 enrolled. *Faculty:* 10 full-time (5 women), 5 part-time/adjunct (2 women). Expenses: Contact institution. *Financial support:* In 2008–09, 28 students received support, including 4 fellowships with full and partial tuition reimbursements available (averaging $3,325 per year), 2 research assistantships with full and partial tuition reimbursements available (averaging $9,480 per year); Federal Work-Study, institutionally sponsored loans, scholarships/grants, tuition waivers (full and partial), and unspecified assistantships also available. Support available to part-time students. Financial award applicants required to submit FAFSA. In 2008, 6 master's awarded. *Degree program information:* Part-time and evening/weekend programs available. Offers communication (MA, MFA); documentary studies and production (MFA); journalism (MA); speech communication and rhetorical studies (MA). *Application deadline:* Applications are processed on a rolling basis. *Application fee:* $60. Electronic applications accepted. *Application Contact:* Carol Drummer, Dean of Graduate Admissions, 516-463-4876, Fax: 516-463-4664, E-mail: gradstudent@hofstra.edu. *Acting Dean*, Dr. Cliff Jernigan, 516-463-5214, Fax: 516-463-4866, E-mail: avfczj@hofstra.edu.

School of Education, Health, and Human Services Students: 657 full-time (503 women), 864 part-time (694 women); includes 263 minority (126 African Americans, 3 American Indian/Alaska Native, 38 Asian Americans or Pacific Islanders, 96 Hispanic Americans), 26 international. Average age 29. 956 applicants, 82% accepted, 487 enrolled. *Faculty:* 70 full-time (48 women), 95 part-time/adjunct (59 women). Expenses: Contact institution. *Financial support:* In 2008–09, 729 students received support, including 150 fellowships with full and partial tuition reimbursements available (averaging $3,459 per year), 26 research assistantships with full and partial tuition reimbursements available (averaging $13,213 per year); career-related internships or fieldwork, Federal Work-Study, institutionally sponsored loans, scholarships/grants, traineeships, health care benefits, tuition waivers (full and partial), unspecified assistantships, and tuition vouchers for cooperating teachers also available. Support available to part-time students. Financial award applicants required to submit FAFSA. In 2008, 584 master's, 11 doctorates, 59 other advanced degrees awarded. *Degree program information:* Part-time and evening/weekend programs available. Postbaccalaureate distance learning degree programs offered (minimal on-campus study). Offers bilingual education (MA); bilingual extension education (CAS); business education (MS Ed); community health (MS); counseling (MA, MS Ed, Advanced Certificate, PD); creative arts therapy (MA); early childhood and childhood education (MS Ed); early childhood education (MA, MS Ed); early childhood special education (MS Ed, Advanced Certificate); education, health, and human services (MA, MHA, MS, MS Ed, Ed D, PhD, Advanced Certificate, CAS, PD); educational and policy leadership (MS Ed, Ed D, CAS); educational leadership (CAS); educational technology (CAS); elementary education (MA, MS Ed); elementary education-math/science/technology (MA); English education (MA, MS Ed); fine arts education (MA, MS Ed); foreign language education (MA, MS Ed); foundations of education (MA, CAS); gerontology (MS, Advanced Certificate); gifted education (Advanced Certificate); health administration (MHA); health education (MS); inclusive early childhood special education (MS Ed); inclusive elementary special education (MS Ed); inclusive secondary special education (MS Ed); learning and teaching (Ed D); literacy studies (MA, MS Ed, Ed D, PhD, CAS, PD); literacy studies and special education (MS Ed); marriage and family therapy (MA); mathematics education (MA, MS Ed); mental health counseling (MA); middle level education (Advanced Certificate); middle school extension (grades 5-6) (Advanced Certificate); middle school extension (grades 7-9) (Advanced Certificate); music education (MA, MS Ed); physical education (MA, MS); rehabilitation administration (PD); rehabilitation counseling (MS Ed, PD); rehabilitation counseling in mental health (MS Ed); school counselor (MS Ed); school counselor-bilingual extension (Advanced Certificate); science education (MA, MS Ed); secondary education (Advanced Certificate); social studies education (MA, MS Ed); special education (MA, MS Ed, Advanced Certificate, PD); special education assessment and diagnosis (Advanced Certificate); teaching students with severe or multiple disabilities (Advanced Certificate); TESL/bilingual education (MA, MS Ed, CAS); TESOL (MS Ed, CAS); wind conducting (MA). *Application deadline:* Applications are processed on a rolling basis. *Application fee:* $60. Electronic applications accepted. *Application Contact:* Carol Drummer, Dean of Graduate Admissions, 516-463-4876, Fax: 516-463-4664, E-mail: gradstudent@hofstra.edu. *Dean*, Dr. David Foulk, 516-463-5740, Fax: 516-463-6461, E-mail: soedff@hofstra.edu.

School of Law Students: 856 full-time (429 women), 305 part-time (151 women); includes 300 minority (112 African Americans, 3 American Indian/Alaska Native, 100 Asian Americans or Pacific Islanders, 85 Hispanic Americans), 24 international. Average age 26. 5,050 applicants, 39% accepted, 415 enrolled. *Faculty:* 58 full-time (22 women), 47 part-time/adjunct (7 women). Expenses: Contact institution. *Financial support:* In 2008–09, 480 students received support, including 430 fellowships with full and partial tuition reimbursements available (averaging $18,183 per year); research assistantships with full and partial tuition reimbursements available, Federal Work-Study, institutionally sponsored loans, scholarships/grants, tuition waivers (full and partial), and unspecified assistantships also available. Support available to part-time students. Financial award applicants required to submit FAFSA. In 2008, 347 JDs, 6 master's awarded. *Degree program information:* Part-time programs available. Offers American legal studies (LL M); family law (LL M); law (JD). *Application deadline:* For fall admission, 4/15 priority date for domestic and international students. Applications are processed on a rolling basis. *Application fee:* $75. Electronic applications accepted. *Application Contact:* John Chalmers, Director of Law School Enrollment Operations, 516-463463-5791, Fax: 516-463-6264, E-mail: lawadmissions@hofstra.edu. *Dean*, Nora V. Demleitner, 516-463-5854, Fax: 516-463-6264, E-mail: lawnao@hofstra.edu.

HOLLINS UNIVERSITY, Roanoke, VA 24020-1603

General Information Independent, Undergraduate: women only; graduate: coed, comprehensive institution. *Enrollment:* 1,058 graduate, professional, and undergraduate students; 202 full-time matriculated graduate/professional students (161 women), 128 part-time matriculated graduate/professional students (94 women). *Enrollment by degree level:* 321 master's, 9 other advanced degrees. *Graduate faculty:* 20 full-time (7 women), 30 part-time/adjunct (18 women). *Tuition:* Full-time $26,720; part-time $590 per credit hour. *Required fees:* $280. *Graduate housing:* Room and/or apartments available on a first-come, first-served basis to single students; on-campus housing not available to married students. Typical cost: $6235 per year. Housing application deadline: 8/1. *Student services:* Campus safety program, career counseling, international student services, low-cost health insurance, multicultural affairs office, services for students with disabilities, teacher training, writing training. *Library facilities:* Wyndham Robertson Library plus 1 other. *Online resources:* library catalog, web page, access to other libraries' catalogs. *Collection:* 236,427 titles, 32,031 serial subscriptions, 7,344 audiovisual materials.

Computer facilities: Computer purchase and lease plans are available. 100 computers available on campus for general student use. A campuswide network can be accessed from student residence rooms and from off campus. Online class registration, applications software are available. *Web address:* http://www.hollins.edu/.

General Application Contact: Cathy S. Koon, Manager of Graduate Services, 540-362-6326, Fax: 540-362-6288, E-mail: ckoon@hollins.edu.

GRADUATE UNITS

Graduate Programs Students: 202 full-time (161 women), 128 part-time (94 women); includes 43 minority (28 African Americans, 3 Asian Americans or Pacific Islanders, 12 Hispanic Americans), 10 international. Average age 34. 410 applicants, 46% accepted, 128 enrolled. *Faculty:* 20 full-time (7 women), 30 part-time/adjunct (18 women). Expenses: Contact institution. *Financial support:* In 2008–09, 236 students received support, including 119 fellowships (averaging $3,510 per year), 8 teaching assistantships; Federal Work-Study and scholarships/grants also available. Support available to part-time students. Financial award application deadline: 7/15; financial award applicants required to submit FAFSA. In 2008, 113 master's awarded. *Degree program information:* Part-time and evening/weekend programs available. Offers children's literature (MA, MFA); creative writing (MFA); dance (MFA); humanities (MALS); interdisciplinary studies (MALS); justice and legal studies (MALS); liberal studies (CAS); playwriting (MFA); screenwriting and film studies (MA, MFA); social science (MALS); teaching (MAT); visual and performing arts (MALS). *Application deadline:* For fall admission, 1/6 priority date for domestic and international students. Applications are processed on a rolling basis. *Application fee:* $40. Electronic applications accepted. *Application Contact:* Cathy S. Koon, Manager of Graduate Services, 540-362-6326, Fax: 540-362-6288, E-mail: ckoon@hollins.edu. *Vice President for Academic Affairs*, Dr. Jeanine S. Stewart, 540-362-6491, Fax: 540-362-6288.

HOLMES INSTITUTE, Burbank, CA 91505

General Information Independent-religious, coed, graduate-only institution. *Enrollment by degree level:* 105 master's. *Graduate faculty:* 50. *Tuition:* Part-time $5966 per year.

Computer facilities: Online class registration is available. *Web address:* http://www.holmesinstitute.org/.

General Application Contact: Maureen Thurston, Administrative Registrar, 720-279-8992, Fax: 303-5260-0913, E-mail: mthurston@religiousscience.org.

GRADUATE UNITS

Graduate Program Average age 40. 16 applicants, 100% accepted, 16 enrolled. *Faculty:* 50 part-time/adjunct (35 women). Expenses: Contact institution. Offers consciousness studies (MS). *Application deadline:* Applications are processed on a rolling basis. *Application fee:* $100.

HOLY APOSTLES COLLEGE AND SEMINARY, Cromwell, CT 06416-2005

General Information Independent-religious, coed, primarily men, comprehensive institution. *Graduate housing:* On-campus housing not available.

GRADUATE UNITS

Department of Theology *Degree program information:* Part-time and evening/weekend programs available. Postbaccalaureate distance learning degree programs offered (no on-campus study). Offers bioethics (MA, Certificate, Post Master's Certificate); church history (MA, Certificate, Post Master's Certificate); dogmatic theology (MA, Certificate, Post Master's Certificate); liturgical music (MA, Certificate, Post Master's Certificate); liturgy (MA, Certificate, Post Master's Certificate); moral theology (MA, Certificate, Post Master's Certificate); philosophical theology (MA, Certificate, Post Master's Certificate); religious education (MA, Certificate, Post Master's Certificate); sacred scripture (MA, Post Master's Certificate); sacred scriptures (Certificate); theology (M Div). Electronic applications accepted.

HOLY CROSS GREEK ORTHODOX SCHOOL OF THEOLOGY, Brookline, MA 02445-7496

General Information Independent-religious, coed, primarily men, graduate-only institution. *Graduate housing:* Rooms and/or apartments available on a first-come, first-served basis to single and married students.

GRADUATE UNITS

Theological Programs *Degree program information:* Part-time programs available. Offers theology (M Div, MTS, Th M).

HOLY FAMILY UNIVERSITY, Philadelphia, PA 19114-2094

General Information Independent-religious, coed, primarily women, comprehensive institution. *Enrollment:* 3,524 graduate, professional, and undergraduate students; 88 full-time matriculated graduate/professional students (67 women), 996 part-time matriculated graduate/professional students (789 women). *Enrollment by degree level:* 1,084 master's. *Graduate faculty:* 18 full-time (11 women), 51 part-time/adjunct (25 women). *Tuition:* Part-time $555 per credit. *Required fees:* $85 per semester. One-time fee: $25 part-time. *Graduate housing:* On-campus housing not available. *Student services:* Campus safety program, career counseling, exercise/wellness program, free psychological counseling, services for students with disabilities. *Library facilities:* Holy Family College Library plus 1 other. *Online resources:* library catalog. *Collection:* 135,740 titles, 752 serial subscriptions, 1,975 audiovisual materials.

Computer facilities: 450 computers available on campus for general student use. A campuswide network can be accessed from student residence rooms. Online class registration is available. *Web address:* http://www.holyfamily.edu/.

General Application Contact: Gidget Marie Montelibano, Graduate Admissions Counselor, 267-341-3358, Fax: 215-637-1478, E-mail: gmontelibano@holyfamily.edu.

GRADUATE UNITS

Division of Extended Learning Students: 107 part-time (61 women); includes 23 minority (12 African Americans, 7 Asian Americans or Pacific Islanders, 4 Hispanic Americans). Average age 35. 30 applicants, 93% accepted, 19 enrolled. *Faculty:* 78 part-time/adjunct (32 women). Expenses: Contact institution. *Financial support:* Applicants required to submit FAFSA. In 2008, 50 master's awarded. *Degree program information:* Part-time and evening/weekend programs available. Offers business administration (MBA); finance (MBA); health care administration (MBA). *Application deadline:* Applications are processed on a rolling basis. *Application fee:* $50. Electronic applications accepted. *Application Contact:* Don Reinmold, Director of Admissions—Division of Extended Learning, 267-341-5001 Ext. 3230, Fax: 215-633-0558, E-mail: dreinmold@holyfamily.edu. *Associate Vice President, Division of Extended Learning*, Honour Moore, 267-341-5008, Fax: 215-633-0558, E-mail: hmoore@holyfamily.edu.

Graduate School Students: 88 full-time (67 women), 996 part-time (789 women); includes 99 minority (50 African Americans, 22 Asian Americans or Pacific Islanders, 27 Hispanic Americans), 2 international. Average age 32. 283 applicants, 72% accepted, 157 enrolled. *Faculty:* 19 full-time (11 women), 50 part-time/adjunct (26 women). Expenses: Contact institution. *Financial support:* Research assistantships with partial tuition reimbursements, Federal Work-Study and unspecified assistantships available. Support available to part-time students. Financial award application deadline: 2/15; financial award applicants required to submit FAFSA. In 2008, 376 master's awarded. *Degree program information:* Part-time and evening/weekend programs available. *Application deadline:* For fall admission, 7/1 priority date for domestic students; for spring admission, 11/1 priority date for domestic students. Applications are processed on a rolling basis. *Application fee:* $25. Electronic applications accepted. *Application Contact:* Gidget Marie Montelibano, Graduate Admissions Counselor, 267-341-3558, Fax: 215-637-1478, E-mail: gmontelibano@holyfamily.edu. *Director of Graduate Admissions*, Margaret Wendling Bacheler, 267-341-3555, Fax: 215-637-1478, E-mail: mbacheler@holyfamily.edu.

School of Arts and Sciences Students: 34 full-time (26 women), 122 part-time (98 women); includes 26 minority (13 African Americans, 3 Asian Americans or Pacific Islanders, 10 Hispanic Americans), 1 international. Average age 30. 72 applicants, 61% accepted, 35 enrolled. *Faculty:* 1 full-time (0 women), 4 part-time/adjunct (2 women). Expenses: Contact institution. *Financial support:* Research assistantships with full and partial tuition reimbursements, Federal Work-Study available. Support available to part-time students. Financial award application deadline: 2/15; financial award applicants required to submit FAFSA. In 2008, 4 master's awarded. *Degree program information:* Part-time and evening/weekend programs available. Offers counseling psychology (MS); criminal justice (MA). *Application deadline:* For fall admission, 7/1 priority date for domestic students; for winter admission, 11/1 for domestic students. Applications are processed on a rolling basis. *Application fee:* $25. *Application Contact:* Gidget Marie Montelibans, Graduate Admissions Counselor, 267-341-3558, Fax: 215-637-1478, E-mail: gmontelibano@holyfamily.edu. *Dean of the School of Arts and Sciences*, Dr. Regina Hobaugh, 267-341-3278, Fax: 215-827-0492, E-mail: hobaugh@holyfamily.edu.

School of Business Students: 5 full-time (3 women), 62 part-time (39 women); includes 8 minority (4 African Americans, 3 Asian Americans or Pacific Islanders, 1 Hispanic American). Average age 32. 17 applicants, 71% accepted, 10 enrolled. *Faculty:* 3 full-time (0 women), 3 part-time/adjunct (0 women). Expenses: Contact institution. *Financial support:* Federal

Work-Study available. Support available to part-time students. Financial award application deadline: 2/15; financial award applicants required to submit FAFSA. In 2008, 25 master's awarded. *Degree program information:* Part-time and evening/weekend programs available. Offers human resources management (MS); information systems management (MS). *Application deadline:* For fall admission, 7/1 priority date for domestic students; for winter admission, 11/1 priority date for domestic students. Applications are processed on a rolling basis. *Application fee:* $25. *Application Contact:* Gidget Marie Montelibano, Graduate Admissions Counselor, 267-341-3558, Fax: 215-637-1478, E-mail: gmontelibano@holyfamily.edu. *Dean of the School of Business,* Dr. Jan Duggar, 267-341-3373, Fax: 215-637-5937, E-mail: jduggar@holyfamily.edi.

School of Education Students: 49 full-time (38 women), 665 part-time (552 women); includes 39 minority (20 African Americans, 8 Asian Americans or Pacific Islanders, 11 Hispanic Americans), 1 international. Average age 32. 177 applicants, 77% accepted, 106 enrolled. *Faculty:* 14 full-time (10 women), 42 part-time/adjunct (23 women). Expenses: Contact institution. *Financial support:* Research assistantships, Federal Work-Study available. Support available to part-time students. Financial award application deadline: 2/15; financial award applicants required to submit FAFSA. In 2008, 287 master's awarded. *Degree program information:* Part-time and evening/weekend programs available. Offers education (M Ed); education leadership (M Ed); elementary education (M Ed); reading specialist (M Ed); secondary education (M Ed); special education (M Ed). *Application deadline:* For fall admission, 7/1 priority date for domestic students; for winter admission, 11/1 priority date for domestic students. Applications are processed on a rolling basis. *Application fee:* $25. *Application Contact:* Gidget Marie Montelibano, Graduate Admissions Counselor, 267-341-3558, Fax: 215-637-1478, E-mail: gmontelibano@holyfamily.edu. *Dean of the School of Education,* Dr. Leonard Soroka, 267-341-3565, Fax: 215-824-2438, E-mail: lsoroka@holyfanily.edu.

School of Nursing Students: 40 part-time (39 women); includes 3 minority (1 African American, 1 Asian American or Pacific Islander, 1 Hispanic American). Average age 41. 17 applicants, 59% accepted, 6 enrolled. *Faculty:* 1 (woman) full-time, 1 (woman) part-time/adjunct. Expenses: Contact institution. *Financial support:* Federal Work-Study available. Support available to part-time students. Financial award application deadline: 2/15; financial award applicants required to submit FAFSA. In 2008, 10 master's awarded. *Degree program information:* Part-time and evening/weekend programs available. Offers community health nursing (MSN); nursing administration (MSN); nursing education (MSN). *Application deadline:* For fall admission, 7/1 priority date for domestic students; for winter admission, 11/1 priority date for domestic students. Applications are processed on a rolling basis. *Application fee:* $25. *Application Contact:* Gidget Matie Montelibano, Graduate Admissions Counselor, 267-341-3558, Fax: 215-637-1478, E-mail: gmontelibano@holyfamily.edu. *Dean of the School of Nursing,* Dr. Christine Rosner, 267-341-3292, Fax: 215-637-6598, E-mail: crosner@holyfamily.edu.

HOLY NAMES UNIVERSITY, Oakland, CA 94619-1699

General Information Independent-religious, coed, primarily women, comprehensive institution. *Enrollment:* 1,105 graduate, professional, and undergraduate students; 91 full-time matriculated graduate/professional students (71 women), 287 part-time matriculated graduate/professional students (236 women). *Enrollment by degree level:* 344 master's, 34 other advanced degrees. *Graduate faculty:* 17 full-time (13 women), 58 part-time/adjunct (37 women). *Tuition:* Full-time $6255; part-time $695 per unit. *Required fees:* $340. Tuition and fees vary according to course load, program, reciprocity agreements and student's religious affiliation. *Graduate housing:* Room and/or apartments available on a first-come, first-served basis to single students; on-campus housing not available to married students. Typical cost: $4640 per year ($8830 including board). Room and board charges vary according to board plan. Housing application deadline: 8/15. *Student services:* Campus employment opportunities, campus safety program, career counseling, free psychological counseling, international student services, low-cost health insurance. *Library facilities:* Cushing Library. *Online resources:* library catalog, web page. *Collection:* 117,760 titles, 8,003 serial subscriptions, 5,093 audiovisual materials.

Computer facilities: 80 computers available on campus for general student use. A campuswide network can be accessed from student residence rooms and from off campus. *Web address:* http://www.hnu.edu/.

General Application Contact: Annie Wenzel, Graduate Admissions Office, 510-436 Ext. 1642, Fax: 510-436-1325, E-mail: admissions@hnu.edu.

GRADUATE UNITS

Graduate Division Students: 91 full-time (71 women), 287 part-time (236 women); includes 154 minority (77 African Americans, 39 Asian Americans or Pacific Islanders, 38 Hispanic Americans), 16 international. Average age 41. 186 applicants, 77% accepted, 73 enrolled. *Faculty:* 17 full-time (13 women), 58 part-time/adjunct (37 women). Expenses: Contact institution. *Financial support:* In 2008–09, 184 students received support. Scholarships/grants available. Support available to part-time students. Financial award application deadline: 3/2; financial award applicants required to submit FAFSA. In 2008, 112 master's, 12 other advanced degrees awarded. *Degree program information:* Part-time and evening/weekend programs available. Offers administration/management (MS, Certificate); clinical faculty (MS, Certificate); community health nursing/case manager (MS); counseling psychology (MA); educational therapy (Certificate); energy and environment management (MBA); family nurse practitioner (MS, Certificate); finance (MBA); forensic psychology (MA, Certificate); Kodaly specialist certificate (Certificate); Kodaly summer certificate (Certificate); level 1 education specialist mild/moderate disabilities (Credential); level 2 education specialist mild/moderate disabilities (Credential); management and leadership (MBA); marketing (MBA); multiple subject teaching credential (Credential); music education with Kodaly emphasis (MM); pastoral counseling (MA, Certificate); pastoral ministries (MA, Certificate); piano pedagogy (MM); piano pedagogy with Suzuki emphasis (MM); single subject teaching credential (Credential); sports management (MBA); teaching English as a second language (TESL) (M Ed); urban education: educational therapy (M Ed); urban education: K-12 education (M Ed); urban education: special education (M Ed); vocal pedagogy (MM). *Application deadline:* For fall admission, 8/1 priority date for domestic students, 8/1 for international students; for spring admission, 12/1 priority date for domestic students, 12/1 for international students. Applications are processed on a rolling basis. *Application fee:* $65. Electronic applications accepted. *Application Contact:* Graduate Admissions Office, 510-436-1321, Fax: 510-436-1325, E-mail: AdultEd@hnu.edu. *Dean of Enrollment Services,* Murad Dibbini, 510-436-1430, Fax: 510-436-1325, E-mail: dibbini@hnu.edu.

Sophia Center in Culture and Spirituality Students: 9 full-time (7 women), 22 part-time (18 women); includes 2 minority (1 African American, 1 Hispanic American), 4 international. Average age 55. 18 applicants, 67% accepted, 8 enrolled. *Faculty:* 2 full-time (0 women), 11 part-time/adjunct (5 women). Expenses: Contact institution. *Financial support:* In 2008–09, 20 students received support. Available to part-time students. Application deadline: 3/2. In 2008, 26 master's, 12 other advanced degrees awarded. Offers culture and spirituality (MA, Certificate). *Application deadline:* For fall admission, 8/1 priority date for domestic students, 8/1 for international students; for spring admission, 12/1 priority date for domestic students, 2/1 for international students. Applications are processed on a rolling basis. *Application fee:* $65. *Application Contact:* 800-430-1321, Fax: 510-436-1325, E-mail: AdultEd@hnu.edu. *Program Director,* Dr. James Conlon, 510-436-1046, E-mail: conlon@hnu.edu.

HOOD COLLEGE, Frederick, MD 21701-8575

General Information Independent, coed, comprehensive institution. CGS member. *Enrollment:* 2,533 graduate, professional, and undergraduate students; 75 full-time matriculated graduate/professional students (56 women), 1,009 part-time matriculated graduate/professional students (713 women). *Enrollment by degree level:* 881 master's, 203 other advanced degrees. *Graduate faculty:* 31 full-time (15 women), 78 part-time/adjunct (39 women). *Tuition:* Full-time $6480. *Required fees:* $100; $50 per semester. *Graduate housing:* On-campus housing not available. *Student services:* Campus employment opportunities, campus safety program, career counseling, international student services, multicultural affairs office, services for students with disabilities, teacher training. *Library facilities:* Beneficial-Hodson Library and Information Technology Center. *Online resources:* library catalog, web page, access to other libraries' catalogs. *Collection:* 208,950 titles, 32,910 serial subscriptions, 5,696 audiovisual materials. *Research affiliation:* NCI (Biomedical Science), USDA (Biomedical Science and Environmental Biology), USAMRID (Biomedical Science).

Computer facilities: Computer purchase and lease plans are available. 283 computers available on campus for general student use. A campuswide network can be accessed from student residence rooms and from off campus. Online class registration is available. *Web address:* http://www.hood.edu/.

General Application Contact: Dr. Allen Flora, Dean of Graduate School, 301-696-3811, Fax: 301-696-3597, E-mail: gofurther@hood.edu.

GRADUATE UNITS

Graduate School Students: 75 full-time (56 women), 1,009 part-time (713 women); includes 88 minority (51 African Americans, 24 Asian Americans or Pacific Islanders, 13 Hispanic Americans), 30 international. Average age 34. 348 applicants, 89% accepted, 223 enrolled. *Faculty:* 31 full-time (15 women), 78 part-time/adjunct (39 women). Expenses: Contact institution. *Financial support:* In 2008–09, 3 research assistantships with full tuition reimbursements (averaging $10,609 per year) were awarded. Financial award applicants required to submit FAFSA. In 2008, 193 master's, 28 other advanced degrees awarded. *Degree program information:* Part-time and evening/weekend programs available. Offers accounting (MBA); administration and management (MBA); biomedical science (MS); ceramic arts (Certificate); ceramics (MFA); computer and information sciences (MS); computer science (MS); curriculum and instruction (MS); educational leadership (MS); environmental biology (MS); finance (MBA); human resource management (MBA); human sciences (MA); humanities (MA); information systems (MBA); management of information technology (MS); marketing (MBA); mathematics education (MS); public management (MBA); reading specialization (MS); regulatory compliance (Certificate); secondary mathematics education (Certificate); thanatology (MA, Certificate). *Application deadline:* For fall admission, 7/15 for domestic and international students; for spring admission, 12/15 for domestic and international students. Applications are processed on a rolling basis. *Application fee:* $35. Electronic applications accepted. *Application Contact:* Dr. Allen P. Flora, Dean of Graduate School, 301-696-3811, Fax: 301-696-3597, E-mail: gofurther@hood.edu. *Dean of the Graduate School,* Dr. Allen P. Flora, 301-696-3811, Fax: 301-696-3597, E-mail: gofurther@hood.edu.

HOOD THEOLOGICAL SEMINARY, Salisbury, NC 28144

General Information Independent-religious, coed, graduate-only institution. *Graduate housing:* Rooms and/or apartments guaranteed to single students and available on a first-come, first-served basis to married students. Housing application deadline: 8/15.

GRADUATE UNITS

Graduate and Professional Programs *Degree program information:* Evening/weekend programs available. Offers theology (M Div, MTS, D Min).

HOPE INTERNATIONAL UNIVERSITY, Fullerton, CA 92831-3138

General Information Independent-religious, coed, comprehensive institution. *Graduate housing:* Room and/or apartments available on a first-come, first-served basis to single students; on-campus housing not available to married students. Housing application deadline: 7/1.

GRADUATE UNITS

School of Graduate Studies *Degree program information:* Part-time and evening/weekend programs available. Postbaccalaureate distance learning degree programs offered (minimal on-campus study). Offers business administration (MBA); Christian leadership (MCM); church music (MA); church music (Korean track) (MCM); church planting (MCM); education (ME); educational administration (MSM); intercultural studies (MCM); international development (MBA, MSM); management (MBA); marriage and family therapy (MA, MFT); nonprofit management (MBA); worship (MCM). Electronic applications accepted.

HOUGHTON COLLEGE, Houghton, NY 14744

General Information Independent-religious, coed, comprehensive institution. *Graduate housing:* On-campus housing not available.

GRADUATE UNITS

Greatbatch School of Music Offers collaborative studies (MMus); composition (MMus); conducting (MMus); music (MA); performance (MMus). Electronic applications accepted.

HOUSTON BAPTIST UNIVERSITY, Houston, TX 77074-3298

General Information Independent-religious, coed, comprehensive institution. *Graduate housing:* Room and/or apartments available on a first-come, first-served basis to single students; on-campus housing not available to married students.

GRADUATE UNITS

College of Arts and Humanities *Degree program information:* Part-time and evening/weekend programs available. Offers arts and humanities (MATS, MLA); liberal arts (MLA); theological studies (MATS).

College of Business and Economics *Degree program information:* Part-time and evening/weekend programs available. Offers accounting (MACCT); business administration (MBA, MSM); business and economics (MACCT, MBA, MSHA, MSHRM, MSM); health administration (MSHA); human resources management (MSHRM).

College of Education and Behavioral Sciences *Degree program information:* Part-time and evening/weekend programs available. Offers bilingual education (M Ed); Christian counseling (MACC); counselor education (M Ed); curriculum and instruction (M Ed); education and behavioral sciences (M Ed, MACC, MAP); educational administration (M Ed); educational diagnostician (M Ed); psychology (MAP); reading education (M Ed).

HOUSTON GRADUATE SCHOOL OF THEOLOGY, Houston, TX 77092

General Information Independent-religious, coed, graduate-only institution. *Graduate housing:* On-campus housing not available.

GRADUATE UNITS

Graduate School *Degree program information:* Part-time and evening/weekend programs available. Offers counseling (MA); pastoral ministry (M Div, D Min); theology (MA).

HOWARD UNIVERSITY, Washington, DC 20059-0002

General Information Independent, coed, university. CGS member. *Graduate housing:* Rooms and/or apartments available on a first-come, first-served basis to single and married students. Housing application deadline: 4/1. *Research affiliation:* National Oceanic and Atmospheric Administration (atmospheric science and nanotechnology), NIMH (National Institute of Mental Health) (genomic study), Akilu Lamma Institute of Pathobiology (HIV/AIDS infection, water resources development, population movement), Labor Research Laboratories and Medical Center in Benin City, Nigeria (infectious diseases), Ewing Marion Kauffman Foundation (science education), The Tokyo Foundation (women's studies/international affairs).

GRADUATE UNITS

College of Dentistry Offers advanced education program general dentistry (Certificate); dentistry (DDS); general dentistry (Certificate); oral and maxillofacial surgery (Certificate); orthodontics (Certificate); pediatric dentistry (Certificate).

College of Engineering, Architecture, and Computer Sciences *Degree program information:* Part-time programs available. Offers engineering, architecture, and computer sciences (M Eng, MCS, MS, PhD). Electronic applications accepted.

School of Engineering and Computer Science *Degree program information:* Part-time programs available. Offers chemical engineering (MS); civil engineering (M Eng); electrical engineering (M Eng, PhD); engineering and computer science (M Eng, MCS, MS, PhD);

Howard University (continued)

mechanical engineering (M Eng, PhD); systems and computer science (MCS). Electronic applications accepted.

College of Medicine Offers biochemistry and molecular biology (PhD); biotechnology (MS); medicine (MD, MPH, MS, PhD); microbiology (PhD); pharmacology (MS, PhD); public health (MPH).

College of Pharmacy, Nursing and Allied Health Sciences *Degree program information:* Part-time programs available. Offers pharmacy, nursing and allied health sciences (Pharm D, MSN, Certificate). Electronic applications accepted.

Division of Nursing *Degree program information:* Part-time programs available. Offers nurse practitioner (Certificate); primary family health nursing (MSN).

School of Pharmacy Postbaccalaureate distance learning degree programs offered (minimal on-campus study). Offers pharmacy (Pharm D). Electronic applications accepted.

Graduate School *Degree program information:* Part-time and evening/weekend programs available. Offers African diaspora (MA, PhD); African history (MA, PhD); African studies (MA, PhD); analytical chemistry (MS, PhD); anatomy (MS, PhD); applied mathematics (MS, PhD); atmospheric (MS, PhD); atmospheric sciences (MS, PhD); biochemistry (MS, PhD); biology (MS, PhD); biophysics (PhD); clinical psychology (PhD); developmental psychology (PhD); economics (MA, PhD); English (MA, PhD); environmental (MS, PhD); exercise physiology (MS); experimental psychology (PhD); French (MA); health education (MS); inorganic chemistry (MS, PhD); Latin America and the Caribbean (MA, PhD); mathematics (MS, PhD); neuropsychology (PhD); nutrition (MS, PhD); organic chemistry (MS, PhD); personality psychology (PhD); philosophy (MA); physical chemistry (MS, PhD); physics (MS, PhD); physiology (PhD); political science (MA, MAPA, PhD); psychology (MS); public administration (MAPA); public history (MA); social psychology (PhD); sociology (MA, PhD); Spanish (MA); sports studies (MS); United States history (MA, PhD); urban recreation (MS). Electronic applications accepted.

Division of Fine Arts *Degree program information:* Part-time programs available. Offers 3D reality (sculpture and ceramics) (MFA); applied music (MM); art history (MA); design (MFA); electronic studio (MFA); fine arts (MFA); history of art and visual culture (MA); instrument (MM Ed); jazz studies (MM); organ (MM Ed); painting (MFA); photography (MFA); piano (MM Ed); voice (MM Ed).

School of Business *Degree program information:* Part-time and evening/weekend programs available. Postbaccalaureate distance learning degree programs offered (no on-campus study). Offers accounting (MBA); business (MBA); entrepreneurship (MBA); finance (MBA); general management (MBA); human resources management (MBA); information systems (MBA); international business (MBA); marketing (MBA); supply chain management (MBA).

School of Communications *Degree program information:* Part-time and evening/weekend programs available. Offers communication sciences (PhD); communications (MA, MFA, MS, PhD); film (MFA); intercultural communication (MA, PhD); organizational communication (MA, PhD); speech pathology (MS). Electronic applications accepted.

Division of Mass Communication and Media Studies *Degree program information:* Part-time and evening/weekend programs available. Offers mass communication (MA, PhD); media studies (MA, PhD). Electronic applications accepted.

School of Divinity *Degree program information:* Part-time and evening/weekend programs available. Offers theology (M Div, MARS, D Min). Electronic applications accepted.

School of Education Students: 132 full-time (96 women), 87 part-time (61 women); includes 178 minority (170 African Americans, 3 Asian Americans or Pacific Islanders, 5 Hispanic Americans), 9 international. Average age 32. 183 applicants, 44% accepted, 28 enrolled. *Faculty:* 28 full-time (17 women), 16 part-time/adjunct (10 women). Expenses: Contact institution. *Financial support:* In 2008–09, 30 students received support, including 7 fellowships with full tuition reimbursements available (averaging $15,000 per year), 16 research assistantships with full tuition reimbursements available (averaging $13,000 per year); career-related internships or fieldwork, Federal Work-Study, institutionally sponsored loans, scholarships/grants, tuition waivers (full and partial), and unspecified assistantships also available. Financial award application deadline: 2/15; financial award applicants required to submit FAFSA. In 2008, 48 master's, 9 doctorates, 2 other advanced degrees awarded. *Degree program information:* Part-time and evening/weekend programs available. Offers counseling and guidance (M Ed, MA, CAGS); counseling psychology (M Ed, MA, PhD, CAGS); early childhood education (M Ed, MA, MAT, CAGS); education (M Ed, MA, MAT, MS, Ed D, PhD, CAGS); educational administration (M Ed, MA, CAGS); educational administration and policy (M Ed, MA, Ed D, CAGS); educational psychology (M Ed, MA, Ed D, PhD, CAGS); elementary education (M Ed); human development (MS); reading (M Ed, MA, MAT, CAGS); school psychology (M Ed, MA, Ed D, PhD, CAGS); secondary education (M Ed, MA, MAT, CAGS); special education (M Ed, MA, CAGS). *Application deadline:* For fall admission, 2/15 priority date for domestic students; for spring admission, 11/1 for domestic students. Applications are processed on a rolling basis. *Application fee:* $45. Electronic applications accepted. *Application Contact:* Dr. Melanie Carter, Associate Dean for Academic Programs and Student Affairs, 202-806-7340, Fax: 202-806-5302, E-mail: melcarter@howard.edu. *Head,* Dr. Leslie T. Fenwick, 202-806-7334, Fax: 202-806-5302, E-mail: lfenwick@howard.edu.

School of Law Offers law (JD, LL M). Electronic applications accepted.

School of Social Work *Degree program information:* Part-time programs available. Offers social work (MSW, PhD).

HULT INTERNATIONAL BUSINESS SCHOOL, Cambridge, MA 02141

General Information Independent, coed, primarily men, graduate-only institution. *Graduate housing:* On-campus housing not available.

GRADUATE UNITS

Program in Business Administration Offers business administration (MBA). Electronic applications accepted.

Program in Business Administration—Hult London Campus *Degree program information:* Part-time programs available. Offers entrepreneurship (MBA); international business (MBA); international finance (MBA); marketing (MBA). Electronic applications accepted.

Program in Finance—Hult London Campus Offers finance (MS). Electronic applications accepted.

Program in International Relations—Hult London Campus *Degree program information:* Part-time programs available. Offers conflict resolution (MA); diplomacy (MA); international public law (MA); international relations (MA); Middle East international security (MA); politics (MA); security studies (MA); terrorism (MA); U.S. foreign policy (MA). Electronic applications accepted.

Program in Marketing—Hult London Campus Offers advertising (MA); marketing (MA); public relations (MA). Electronic applications accepted.

HUMBOLDT STATE UNIVERSITY, Arcata, CA 95521-8299

General Information State-supported, coed, comprehensive institution. CGS member. *Enrollment:* 7,800 graduate, professional, and undergraduate students; 333 full-time matriculated graduate/professional students (218 women), 146 part-time matriculated graduate/professional students (85 women). *Enrollment by degree level:* 479 master's. *Graduate faculty:* 269 full-time (100 women), 252 part-time/adjunct (154 women). Tuition, nonresident: full-time $6102. *Required fees:* $5236. *Graduate housing:* Room and/or apartments available on a first-come, first-served basis to single students; on-campus housing not available to married students. Typical cost: $8972 (including board). Room and board charges vary according to board plan and housing facility selected. Housing application deadline: 2/1. *Student services:* Campus employment opportunities, campus safety program, career counseling, child daycare facilities, free psychological counseling, low-cost health insurance, multicultural affairs office, services for students with disabilities. *Library facilities:* Humbolot State University Library. *Online resources:* library catalog, web page, access to other libraries' catalogs. *Collection:* 1 million titles, 1,737 serial subscriptions, 20,962 audiovisual materials. *Research affiliation:* McIntire-Stennis (forestry), National Sea Grant, U.S. Fish and Wildlife Service–Wildlife Field Station, Redwood Sciences Laboratory of the Pacific Southwest Forest and Range Experiment Station, California Cooperative Fisheries Research Unit.

Computer facilities: Computer purchase and lease plans are available. 1,191 computers available on campus for general student use. A campuswide network can be accessed from student residence rooms and from off campus. Online class registration is available. *Web address:* http://www.humboldt.edu/.

General Application Contact: Cynthia Werner, Research and Graduate Studies, 707-826-3949, E-mail: werner@humboldt.edu.

GRADUATE UNITS

Graduate Studies Students: 333 full-time (218 women), 146 part-time (85 women); includes 76 minority (11 African Americans, 19 American Indian/Alaska Native, 14 Asian Americans or Pacific Islanders, 32 Hispanic Americans), 4 international. Average age 32. 515 applicants, 57% accepted, 181 enrolled. Expenses: Contact institution. *Financial support:* Fellowships, research assistantships, teaching assistantships, career-related internships or fieldwork, Federal Work-Study, and institutionally sponsored loans available. Support available to part-time students. Financial award application deadline: 3/1; financial award applicants required to submit FAFSA. In 2008, 133 master's awarded. *Degree program information:* Part-time and evening/weekend programs available. *Application deadline:* Applications are processed on a rolling basis. *Application fee:* $55. Electronic applications accepted. *Application Contact:* Cynthia Werner, Administrative Support Coordinator, 707-826-3949, Fax: 707-826-3939. *Interim Dean,* Dr. Chris Hopper, 707-826-3949, Fax: 707-826-3939, E-mail: cah3@humboldt.edu.

College of Arts, Humanities, and Social Sciences Students: 75 full-time (55 women), 24 part-time (13 women); includes 13 minority (3 African Americans, 2 American Indian/Alaska Native, 2 Asian Americans or Pacific Islanders, 6 Hispanic Americans). Average age 32. 115 applicants, 57% accepted, 35 enrolled. Expenses: Contact institution. *Financial support:* Fellowships, teaching assistantships, career-related internships or fieldwork, Federal Work-Study, and institutionally sponsored loans available. Support available to part-time students. Financial award application deadline: 3/1; financial award applicants required to submit FAFSA. In 2008, 20 master's awarded. *Degree program information:* Part-time programs available. Offers arts, humanities, and social sciences (MA, MFA); English (MA); environment and community (MA); sociology (MA); theatre arts (MA, MFA). *Application deadline:* Applications are processed on a rolling basis. *Application fee:* $55. Electronic applications accepted. *Application Contact:* Dr. Ken Ayoob, Interim Dean, 707-826-4491, Fax: 707-826-4498. *Interim Dean,* Dr. Ken Ayoob, 707-826-4491, Fax: 707-826-4498.

College of Natural Resources and Sciences Students: 153 full-time (95 women), 68 part-time (33 women); includes 25 minority (2 African Americans, 5 American Indian/Alaska Native, 6 Asian Americans or Pacific Islanders, 12 Hispanic Americans), 3 international. Average age 30. 238 applicants, 46% accepted, 69 enrolled. Expenses: Contact institution. *Financial support:* Fellowships, career-related internships or fieldwork and Federal Work-Study available. Support available to part-time students. Financial award application deadline: 3/1; financial award applicants required to submit FAFSA. In 2008, 39 master's awarded. *Degree program information:* Part-time programs available. Offers biological sciences (MA); environmental systems (MS); natural resources (MS); natural resources and sciences (MA, MS); psychology (MA). *Application deadline:* Applications are processed on a rolling basis. *Application fee:* $55. *Application Contact:* Cynthina Werner, Administrative Support Coordinator, 707-826-3949, Fax: 707-826-3939, E-mail: werner@humboldt.edu. *Dean,* Dr. Jim Howard, 707-826-3256, Fax: 707-826-3562, E-mail: howard@humboldt.edu.

College of Professional Studies Students: 105 full-time (68 women), 54 part-time (39 women); includes 38 minority (6 African Americans, 12 American Indian/Alaska Native, 6 Asian Americans or Pacific Islanders, 14 Hispanic Americans), 1 international. Average age 33. 163 applicants, 73% accepted, 77 enrolled. Expenses: Contact institution. *Financial support:* Fellowships, teaching assistantships, career-related internships or fieldwork, Federal Work-Study, and institutionally sponsored loans available. Support available to part-time students. Financial award application deadline: 3/1; financial award applicants required to submit FAFSA. In 2008, 120 master's awarded. *Degree program information:* Part-time and evening/weekend programs available. Offers athletic training education (MS); business (MBA); education (MA); exercise science/wellness management (MS); pre-physical therapy (MS); social work (MSW); teaching/coaching (MS). *Application deadline:* Applications are processed on a rolling basis. *Application fee:* $55. *Application Contact:* Cynthia Werner, Research and Graduate Studies, 707-826-3949, Fax: 707-826-3939. *Interim Dean,* Dr. Nancy Hurlbut, 707-826-3961, Fax: 707-826-3963, E-mail: nancy.hurlbut@humboldt.edu.

HUMPHREYS COLLEGE, Stockton, CA 95207-3896

General Information Independent, coed, comprehensive institution. *Graduate housing:* Room and/or apartments available on a first-come, first-served basis to single students; on-campus housing not available to married students.

GRADUATE UNITS

Laurence Drivon School of Law *Degree program information:* Part-time and evening/weekend programs available. Offers law (JD). Electronic applications accepted.

HUNTER COLLEGE OF THE CITY UNIVERSITY OF NEW YORK, New York, NY 10021-5085

General Information State and locally supported, coed, comprehensive institution. *Enrollment:* 21,258 graduate, professional, and undergraduate students; 981 full-time matriculated graduate/professional students (808 women), 3,330 part-time matriculated graduate/professional students (2,576 women). *Enrollment by degree level:* 4,147 master's, 164 other advanced degrees. *Graduate faculty:* 315 full-time (166 women), 290 part-time/adjunct (169 women). Tuition, state resident: full-time $6400; part-time $270 per credit. Tuition, nonresident: full-time $15,000; part-time $500 per credit. *Required fees:* $399 per semester. *Graduate housing:* Room and/or apartments available on a first-come, first-served basis to single students; on-campus housing not available to married students. *Student services:* Campus employment opportunities, campus safety program, career counseling, child daycare facilities, exercise/wellness program, free psychological counseling, international student services, services for students with disabilities, teacher training, writing training. *Library facilities:* Hunter College Library. *Online resources:* library catalog, web page, access to other libraries' catalogs. *Collection:* 789,718 titles, 4,282 serial subscriptions. *Research affiliation:* Cornell University Medical Center, New York Hospital, The Mount Sinai Medical Center, Bellevue Hospital Center.

Computer facilities: 750 computers available on campus for general student use. A campuswide network can be accessed. *Web address:* http://www.hunter.cuny.edu/.

General Application Contact: William Zlata, Director for Graduate Admissions, 212-772-4482, Fax: 212-650-3336, E-mail: admissions@hunter.cuny.edu.

GRADUATE UNITS

Graduate School Students: 981 full-time (808 women), 3,330 part-time (2,575 women); includes 791 minority (255 African Americans, 4 American Indian/Alaska Native, 220 Asian Americans or Pacific Islanders, 312 Hispanic Americans). Average age 33. 4,694 applicants, 39% accepted, 1259 enrolled. *Faculty:* 329 full-time (175 women), 269 part-time/adjunct (180 women). Expenses: Contact institution. *Financial support:* Fellowships with full and partial tuition reimbursements, research assistantships with partial tuition reimbursements, teaching assistantships, career-related internships or fieldwork, Federal Work-Study, institutionally sponsored loans, scholarships/grants, traineeships, tuition waivers (full and partial), unspecified assistantships, and lesson stipends available. Support available to part-time students. Financial award applicants required to submit FAFSA. In 2008, 1,566 master's, 82 other advanced degrees awarded. *Degree program information:* Part-time and evening/weekend programs available. *Application deadline:* For fall admission, 4/1 for domestic students; for spring admission, 11/1 for domestic students. *Application fee:* $125. *Application Contact:* Milena Solo, Director for Graduate Admissions, 212-772-4288, Fax: 212-650-3336, E-mail: milena.solo@hunter.cuny.edu. *Director of Admissions,* William Zlata, 212-772-4288, Fax: 212-650-3336, E-mail: bill.zlata@hunter.cuny.edu.

School of Arts and Sciences Students: 126 full-time (70 women), 909 part-time (580 women); includes 154 minority (36 African Americans, 1 American Indian/Alaska Native, 63 Asian Americans or Pacific Islanders, 54 Hispanic Americans). Average age 32. 1,664 applicants, 29% accepted, 270 enrolled. *Faculty:* 179 full-time (78 women), 43 part-time/adjunct (13 women). Expenses: Contact institution. *Financial support:* Fellowships, research assistantships, teaching assistantships, career-related internships or fieldwork, Federal Work-Study, institutionally sponsored loans, scholarships/grants, tuition waivers (full and partial), unspecified assistantships, and lesson stipends available. Support available to part-time students. In 2008, 388 master's awarded. *Degree program information:* Part-time and evening/weekend programs available. Offers accounting (MS); analytical geography (MA); anthropology (MA); applied and evaluative psychology (MA); applied mathematics (MA); applied social research (MS); art history (MA); arts and sciences (MA, MFA, MS, MUP, PhD, Certificate); biochemistry (MA, PhD); biological sciences (MA, PhD); biopsychology and comparative psychology (MA); British and American literature (MA); chemistry (PhD); creative writing (MFA); earth system science (MA); economics (MA); English education (MA); environmental and social issues (MA); fiction (MFA); fine arts (MFA); French (MA); French education (MA); geographic information science (Certificate); geographic information systems (MA); history (MA); integrated media arts (MA, MFA); Italian (MA); Italian education (MA); mathematics for secondary education (MA); music (MA); music education (MA); nonfiction (MFA); physics (MA, PhD); poetry (MFA); pure mathematics (MA); social, cognitive, and developmental psychology (MA); Spanish (MA); Spanish education (MA); studio art (MFA); teaching earth science (MA); teaching Latin (MA); theatre (MA); urban affairs (MS); urban planning (MUP); urban studies/affairs (MS). *Application deadline:* For fall admission, 2/1 for domestic and international students; for spring admission, 11/1 for domestic students, 9/1 for international students. *Application fee:* $125. *Application Contact:* Milena Solo, Director for Graduate Admissions, 212-772-4482, Fax: 212-650-3336, E-mail: milena.solo@hunter.cuny.edu. *Dean,* Dr. Shirley Clay Scott, 212-772-5121, Fax: 212-772-5138, E-mail: shirley.scott@hunter.cuny.edu.

School of Education Students: 253 full-time (221 women), 1,381 part-time (1,115 women); includes 256 minority (77 African Americans, 2 American Indian/Alaska Native, 63 Asian Americans or Pacific Islanders, 114 Hispanic Americans). Average age 31. 1,225 applicants, 56% accepted, 456 enrolled. *Faculty:* 51 full-time (38 women), 130 part-time/adjunct (103 women). Expenses: Contact institution. *Financial support:* Fellowships, career-related internships or fieldwork, Federal Work-Study, institutionally sponsored loans, and tuition waivers (full and partial) available. Support available to part-time students. In 2008, 583 master's, 4 other advanced degrees awarded. Offers bilingual education (MS); biology education (MA); blind or visually impaired (MS Ed); chemistry education (MA); corrective reading (K–12) (MS Ed); deaf or hard of hearing (MS Ed); early childhood education (MS); earth science (MA); education (MA, MS, MS Ed, AC); educational supervision and administration (AC); elementary education (MS); English education (MA); French education (MA); Italian education (MA); literacy education (MS); mathematics education (MA); music education (MA); physics education (MA); rehabilitation counseling (MS Ed); school counseling (MS Ed); school counseling with bilingual extension (MS Ed); school counselor (MS Ed); severe/multiple disabilities (MS Ed); social studies education (MA); Spanish education (MA); special education (MS Ed); teaching English as a second language (MA). *Application deadline:* For fall admission, 4/1 for domestic students, 2/1 for international students; for spring admission, 11/1 for domestic students, 9/1 for international students. Applications are processed on a rolling basis. *Application fee:* $125. *Application Contact:* Milena Solo, Director for Graduate Admissions, 212-772-4482, Fax: 212-650-3336, E-mail: milena.solo@hunter.cuny.edu. *Dean,* Dr. David Steiner, 212-772-4622, E-mail: david.steiner@hunter.cuny.edu.

School of Social Work Students: 499 full-time (411 women), 347 part-time (263 women); includes 187 minority (91 African Americans, 15 Asian Americans or Pacific Islanders, 81 Hispanic Americans). Average age 34. 1,159 applicants, 36% accepted, 369 enrolled. *Faculty:* 38 full-time (21 women), 51 part-time/adjunct (33 women). Expenses: Contact institution. *Financial support:* In 2008–09, 120 fellowships (averaging $1,000 per year) were awarded; career-related internships or fieldwork, Federal Work-Study, and tuition waivers (partial) also available. Support available to part-time students. In 2008, 338 master's awarded. Offers social work (MSW, DSW). *Application deadline:* For fall admission, 1/15 for domestic and international students. Applications are processed on a rolling basis. *Application fee:* $125. *Application Contact:* Raymond Montero, Coordinator of Admissions, 212-452-7005, E-mail: grad.socworkadvisor@hunter.cuny.edu. *Dean/Professor,* Dr. Jacqueline B. Mondros, 212-452-7085, Fax: 212-452-7150, E-mail: jmondros@hunter.cuny.edu.

Schools of the Health Professions Students: 86 full-time (83 women), 382 part-time (306 women); includes 115 minority (42 African Americans, 49 Asian Americans or Pacific Islanders, 24 Hispanic Americans). Average age 33. 646 applicants, 43% accepted, 164 enrolled. *Faculty:* 44 full-time (35 women), 12 part-time/adjunct (11 women). Expenses: Contact institution. *Financial support:* Federal Work-Study and tuition waivers (partial) available. Support available to part-time students. In 2008, 157 master's, 2 other advanced degrees awarded. *Degree program information:* Part-time and evening/weekend programs available. Offers adult nurse practitioner (MS); audiology (MS); community health education (MPH); community health nursing (MS); environmental and occupational health education (MS); epidemiology and biostatistics (MPH); gerontological nurse practitioner (MS); health policy management (MPH); health professions (MPH, MS, DPT, AC); health sciences (MPH, MS, DPT); nursing (MS, AC); nutrition and public health (MPH); psychiatric nursing (MS, AC); speech language pathology (MS); teacher of speech and hearing handicapped (MS). *Application deadline:* For fall admission, 4/1 for domestic students, 2/1 for international students; for spring admission, 11/1 for domestic students, 9/1 for international students. *Application fee:* $125. *Application Contact:* Milena Solo, Director for Graduate Admissions, 212-772-4288, Fax: 212-650-3336, E-mail: milena.solo@hunter.cuny.edu. *Dean,* Lauren N. Sherwen, 212-481-4314.

HUNTINGTON COLLEGE OF HEALTH SCIENCES, Knoxville, TN 37919-7736

General Information Proprietary, coed, comprehensive institution. *Enrollment:* 460 graduate, professional, and undergraduate students; 46 full-time matriculated graduate/professional students (42 women). *Enrollment by degree level:* 46 master's. *Graduate faculty:* 10 full-time (6 women). *Web address:* http://www.hchs.edu/.

General Application Contact: Cheryl Freeman, Director of Student Services, 865-524-8079, E-mail: cfreeman@hchs.edu.

GRADUATE UNITS

Program in Nutrition Students: 46 full-time (42 women), 10 international. Average age 28. *Faculty:* 10 full-time (6 women). Expenses: Contact institution. *Degree program information:* Part-time and evening/weekend programs available. Postbaccalaureate distance learning degree programs offered (no on-campus study). Offers nutrition (MS). *Application fee:* $200. *Application Contact:* Office of Graduate Admissions, 865-524-8079. *Director of Student Services,* Cheryl A. Freeman, 865-524-8079, E-mail: cfreeman@hchs.edu.

HUNTINGTON UNIVERSITY, Huntington, IN 46750-1299

General Information Independent-religious, coed, comprehensive institution. *Enrollment:* 1,211 graduate, professional, and undergraduate students; 9 full-time matriculated graduate/professional students (5 women), 67 part-time matriculated graduate/professional students (14 women). *Enrollment by degree level:* 76 master's. *Graduate faculty:* 4 full-time (0 women), 16 part-time/adjunct (4 women). *Tuition:* Part-time $425 per credit hour. Tuition and fees vary according to program. *Graduate housing:* On-campus housing not available. *Student services:* Campus employment opportunities, career counseling, free psychological counseling, low-cost health insurance, writing training. *Library facilities:* Richlyn Library plus 1 other. *Online resources:* library catalog, web page. *Collection:* 176,744 titles. *Research affiliation:* Link Institute (youth ministry).

Computer facilities: 261 computers available on campus for general student use. A campuswide network can be accessed from student residence rooms and from off campus. Online class registration is available. *Web address:* http://www.huntington.edu/.

General Application Contact: Lori Garde, Program Coordinator, 260-359-4039, Fax: 260-359-4126, E-mail: lgarde@huntington.edu.

GRADUATE UNITS

Graduate School Students: 9 full-time (5 women), 67 part-time (14 women); includes 2 minority (both African Americans), 2 international. Average age 39. 27 applicants, 89% accepted, 24 enrolled. *Faculty:* 4 full-time (0 women), 16 part-time/adjunct (4 women). Expenses: Contact institution. *Financial support:* In 2008–09, 51 students received support. Scholarships/grants available. Support available to part-time students. Financial award application deadline: 8/1; financial award applicants required to submit FAFSA. In 2008, 4 master's awarded. *Degree program information:* Part-time programs available. Postbaccalaureate distance learning degree programs offered (minimal on-campus study). Offers counseling (MA); education (M Ed); ministry leadership (MA); youth ministry leadership (MA). *Application deadline:* For fall admission, 7/1 priority date for domestic and international students; for winter admission, 11/1 priority date for domestic and international students; for spring admission, 2/1 priority date for domestic and international students. Applications are processed on a rolling basis. *Application fee:* $20. Electronic applications accepted. *Application Contact:* Lori Garde, Program Coordinator, 260-359-4039, Fax: 260-359-4126, E-mail: lgarde@huntington.edu. *Associate Dean for Graduate and Adult Studies,* Dr. Steven Holtrop, 260-359-4166, Fax: 260-359-4126, E-mail: sholtrop@huntington.edu.

HUSSON UNIVERSITY, Bangor, ME 04401-2999

General Information Independent, coed, comprehensive institution. *Graduate housing:* Room and/or apartments available on a first-come, first-served basis to single students; on-campus housing not available to married students. Housing application deadline: 6/1.

GRADUATE UNITS

School of Graduate and Professional Studies *Degree program information:* Part-time and evening/weekend programs available. Offers advanced practice psychiatric nursing (MSN, PMC); counseling psychology (MS); criminal justice administration (MS); family and community nurse practitioner (MSN, PMC); health care management (MSB); nonprofit management (MSB); occupational therapy (MSOT); physical therapy (DPT); school counseling (MS).

ICR GRADUATE SCHOOL, Santee, CA 92071

General Information Independent-religious, coed, graduate-only institution. *Graduate housing:* On-campus housing not available.

GRADUATE UNITS

Graduate Programs *Degree program information:* Part-time programs available. Offers astro/geophysics (MS); biology (MS); geology (MS); science education (MS).

IDAHO STATE UNIVERSITY, Pocatello, ID 83209

General Information State-supported, coed, university. CGS member. *Enrollment:* 12,653 graduate, professional, and undergraduate students; 1,101 full-time matriculated graduate/professional students (550 women), 1,005 part-time matriculated graduate/professional students (567 women). *Enrollment by degree level:* 243 first professional, 1,444 master's, 419 doctoral. *Graduate faculty:* 273 full-time (83 women), 7 part-time/adjunct (3 women). Tuition, state resident: full-time $3114; part-time $276 per credit hour. Tuition, nonresident: full-time $12,318; part-time $404 per credit hour. *Required fees:* $2360. Tuition and fees vary according to course load and reciprocity agreements. *Graduate housing:* Rooms and/or apartments available on a first-come, first-served basis to single and married students. Typical cost: $3080 per year ($6030 including board) for single students; $7080 per year ($10,030 including board) for married students. Room and board charges vary according to board plan and housing facility selected. Housing application deadline: 5/1. *Student services:* Campus employment opportunities, campus safety program, career counseling, child daycare facilities, exercise/wellness program, free psychological counseling, grant writing training, international student services, low-cost health insurance, multicultural affairs office, services for students with disabilities, teacher training, writing training. *Library facilities:* Eli M. Oboler Library. *Online resources:* library catalog, web page. *Collection:* 835,638 titles, 4,867 serial subscriptions, 6,626 audiovisual materials. *Research affiliation:* S. M. Stoller Corporation (ecology, waste management), ON Semiconductor (computer sciences, environmental management), Inland Northwest Research Alliance (science), J. R. Simplot Company, Idaho (plant sciences, environmental studies), Bechtel BWXT ID, LLC (environmental management, nuclear sciences), Environmental Science and Research Foundation (waste management, ecology).

Computer facilities: 519 computers available on campus for general student use. A campuswide network can be accessed from student residence rooms and from off campus. Online class registration is available. *Web address:* http://www.isu.edu/.

General Application Contact: Dr. Thomas Jackson, Dean, 208-282-2390, Fax: 208-282-4847, E-mail: tjackson@isu.edu.

GRADUATE UNITS

Office of Graduate Studies Students: 1,101 full-time (550 women), 1,005 part-time (567 women); includes 125 minority (14 African Americans, 14 American Indian/Alaska Native, 43 Asian Americans or Pacific Islanders, 54 Hispanic Americans), 160 international. Average age 35. 1,116 applicants, 33% accepted, 269 enrolled. *Faculty:* 273 full-time (83 women), 7 part-time/adjunct (3 women). Expenses: Contact institution. *Financial support:* In 2008–09, 26 fellowships with full and partial tuition reimbursements (averaging $13,155 per year), 95 research assistantships with full and partial tuition reimbursements (averaging $6,800 per year), 195 teaching assistantships with full and partial tuition reimbursements (averaging $9,401 per year) were awarded; career-related internships or fieldwork, Federal Work-Study, institutionally sponsored loans, scholarships/grants, traineeships, health care benefits, tuition waivers (full and partial), and unspecified assistantships also available. Support available to part-time students. Financial award application deadline: 1/1; financial award applicants required to submit FAFSA. In 2008, 63 first professional degrees, 316 master's, 67 doctorates, 25 other advanced degrees awarded. *Degree program information:* Part-time and evening/weekend programs available. Offers general interdisciplinary (M Ed, MA, MNS); waste management and environmental science (MS). *Application deadline:* For fall admission, 7/1 for domestic students, 6/1 for international students; for spring admission, 12/1 for domestic students, 11/1 for international students. Applications are processed on a rolling basis. *Application fee:* $55. Electronic applications accepted. *Application Contact:* Ellen Combs, Graduate School Technical Records Specialist, 208-282-2150, Fax: 208-282-4847, E-mail: combelle@isu.edu. *Dean,* Dr. Thomas Jackson, 208-282-2390, Fax: 208-282-4847, E-mail: tjackson@isu.edu.

College of Arts and Sciences Students: 255 full-time (109 women), 221 part-time (111 women); includes 26 minority (5 American Indian/Alaska Native, 6 Asian Americans or Pacific Islanders, 15 Hispanic Americans), 58 international. Average age 35. 100 applicants, 57% accepted, 43 enrolled. *Faculty:* 150 full-time (39 women), 4 part-time/adjunct (2 women). Expenses: Contact institution. *Financial support:* In 2008–09, 5 fellowships with full and partial tuition reimbursements (averaging $13,155 per year), 64 research assistantships with full and partial tuition reimbursements (averaging $6,800 per year), 119 teaching assistantships with full and partial tuition reimbursements (averaging $9,401 per year) were awarded; career-related internships or fieldwork, Federal Work-Study, institutionally sponsored loans, scholarships/grants, traineeships, health care benefits, tuition waivers (full and partial), and unspecified assistantships also available. Support available to part-time students. Financial award application deadline: 1/1; financial award applicants required to submit FAFSA. In 2008, 64 master's, 30 doctorates, 2 other advanced degrees awarded. *Degree program information:* Part-time programs available. Offers anthropology (MA, MS); applied physics (PhD); art (MFA); arts and sciences (MA, MFA, MNS, MPA, MS, DA, PhD, Post-Master's Certificate, Postbaccalaureate Certificate); biology (MNS, MS, DA, PhD); chemistry (MNS, MS); clinical laboratory science (MS); clinical psychology (PhD); communication and rhetorical studies (MA); English (MA, DA, PhD, Post-Master's Certificate); geographic information science (MS); geology (MNS, MS); geophysics/hydrology (MS); geotechnology (Postbaccalaureate Certificate); health physics (MS); historical resources management (MA); mathematics (MS, DA); mathematics for secondary teachers (MA); microbiology (MS); physics (MNS); political science (MA, DA); psychology (MS); public

Idaho State University (continued)

administration (MPA); sociology (MA); theatre (MA). *Application deadline:* For fall admission, 7/1 for domestic students, 6/1 for international students; for spring admission, 12/1 for domestic students, 11/1 for international students. Applications are processed on a rolling basis. *Application fee:* $55. Electronic applications accepted. *Application Contact:* Ellen Combs, Graduate School Technical Records Specialist, 208-282-2150, Fax: 208-282-4847, E-mail: combelle@isu.edu. *Interim Dean,* Dr. Scott Hughes, 208-282-3053, Fax: 208-282-4847, E-mail: hughscot@isu.edu.

College of Business Students: 44 full-time (16 women), 79 part-time (21 women); includes 8 minority (1 American Indian/Alaska Native, 4 Asian Americans or Pacific Islanders, 3 Hispanic Americans), 7 international. Average age 32. *Faculty:* 27 full-time (5 women). Expenses: Contact institution. *Financial support:* In 2008–09, 11 teaching assistantships with full and partial tuition reimbursements (averaging $9,401 per year) were awarded; career-related internships or fieldwork, Federal Work-Study, institutionally sponsored loans, scholarships/grants, health care benefits, tuition waivers (full and partial), and unspecified assistantships also available. Support available to part-time students. Financial award application deadline: 1/1; financial award applicants required to submit FAFSA. In 2008, 30 master's, 1 other advanced degree awarded. *Degree program information:* Part-time programs available. Offers business administration (MBA, Postbaccalaureate Certificate); computer information systems (MS, Postbaccalaureate Certificate). *Application deadline:* For fall admission, 7/1 for domestic students, 6/1 for international students; for spring admission, 12/1 for domestic students, 11/1 for international students. Applications are processed on a rolling basis. *Application fee:* $55. Electronic applications accepted. *Application Contact:* Ellen Combs, Graduate School Technical Records Specialist, 208-282-2150, Fax: 208-282-4847, E-mail: combelle@isu.edu. *Dean,* Dr. Ken Smith, 208-282-3585, Fax: 208-282-4367, E-mail: smithken@isu.edu.

College of Education Students: 58 full-time (30 women), 305 part-time (168 women); includes 19 minority (6 African Americans, 3 American Indian/Alaska Native, 2 Asian Americans or Pacific Islanders, 8 Hispanic Americans), 14 international. Average age 39. *Faculty:* 24 full-time (11 women), 1 (woman) part-time/adjunct. Expenses: Contact institution. *Financial support:* In 2008–09, 2 research assistantships with full and partial tuition reimbursements (averaging $6,800 per year), 22 teaching assistantships with full and partial tuition reimbursements (averaging $9,401 per year) were awarded; career-related internships or fieldwork, Federal Work-Study, institutionally sponsored loans, scholarships/grants, health care benefits, tuition waivers (full and partial), and unspecified assistantships also available. Support available to part-time students. Financial award application deadline: 1/1; financial award applicants required to submit FAFSA. In 2008, 67 master's, 4 doctorates, 10 other advanced degrees awarded. *Degree program information:* Part-time programs available. Offers child and family studies (M Ed); curriculum leadership (M Ed); education (M Ed); educational administration (M Ed, 6th Year Certificate, Ed S); educational foundations (5th Year Certificate); educational leadership (Ed D); elementary education (M Ed); human exceptionality (M Ed); instructional design (PhD); instructional technology (M Ed); physical education (MPE); school psychology (Ed S); special education (Ed S). *Application deadline:* For fall admission, 7/1 for domestic students, 6/1 for international students; for spring admission, 12/1 for domestic students, 11/1 for international students. Applications are processed on a rolling basis. *Application fee:* $55. Electronic applications accepted. *Application Contact:* Dr. Peter Denner, Director, Office of Standards and Assessment, 208-282-2783, Fax: 208-282-4697, E-mail: dennpete@isu.edu. *Dean,* Dr. Deborah Hedeen, 208-282-3259, Fax: 208-282-4697, E-mail: hededebo@isu.edu.

College of Engineering Students: 47 full-time (12 women), 39 part-time (5 women); includes 2 minority (both Asian Americans or Pacific Islanders), 38 international. Average age 33. *Faculty:* 17 full-time (1 woman). Expenses: Contact institution. *Financial support:* In 2008–09, 23 research assistantships with full and partial tuition reimbursements (averaging $6,800 per year), 5 teaching assistantships with full and partial tuition reimbursements (averaging $9,401 per year) were awarded; career-related internships or fieldwork, Federal Work-Study, institutionally sponsored loans, scholarships/grants, traineeships, health care benefits, tuition waivers (full and partial), and unspecified assistantships also available. Support available to part-time students. Financial award application deadline: 1/1; financial award applicants required to submit FAFSA. In 2008, 10 master's, 3 doctorates, 1 other advanced degree awarded. *Degree program information:* Part-time programs available. Offers civil engineering (MS); engineering (MS, PhD, Postbaccalaureate Certificate); engineering and applied science (PhD); environmental engineering (MS); measurement and control engineering (MS); mechanical engineering (MS); nuclear science and engineering (MS, PhD, Postbaccalaureate Certificate). *Application deadline:* For fall admission, 7/1 for domestic students, 6/1 for international students; for spring admission, 12/1 for domestic students, 11/1 for international students. Applications are processed on a rolling basis. *Application fee:* $55. Electronic applications accepted. *Application Contact:* Ellen Combs, Graduate School Technical Records Specialist, 208-282-2150, Fax: 208-282-4847, E-mail: combelle@isu.edu. *Dean,* Dr. Richard Jacobsen, 208-282-2902, Fax: 208-282-4538, E-mail: jacorich@isu.edu.

College of Pharmacy Students: 259 full-time (104 women), 13 part-time (7 women); includes 21 minority (2 African Americans, 2 American Indian/Alaska Native, 12 Asian Americans or Pacific Islanders, 5 Hispanic Americans), 23 international. Average age 28. *Faculty:* 17 full-time (4 women). Expenses: Contact institution. *Financial support:* In 2008–09, 5 research assistantships with full and partial tuition reimbursements (averaging $6,800 per year), 7 teaching assistantships with full and partial tuition reimbursements (averaging $9,401 per year) were awarded; career-related internships or fieldwork, Federal Work-Study, institutionally sponsored loans, scholarships/grants, traineeships, health care benefits, tuition waivers (full and partial), and unspecified assistantships also available. Support available to part-time students. Financial award application deadline: 1/1; financial award applicants required to submit FAFSA. In 2008, 63 first professional degrees, 1 master's, 3 doctorates awarded. *Degree program information:* Part-time programs available. Offers biopharmaceutical analysis (PhD); biopharmaceutics (PhD); pharmaceutical chemistry (MS); pharmaceutical science (PhD); pharmaceutics (MS); pharmacognosy (MS); pharmacokinetics (PhD); pharmacology (MS, PhD); pharmacy (Pharm D); pharmacy administration (MS, PhD). *Application deadline:* For fall admission, 7/1 for domestic students, 6/1 for international students; for spring admission, 12/1 for domestic students, 11/1 for international students. Applications are processed on a rolling basis. *Application fee:* $55. Electronic applications accepted. *Application Contact:* Ellen Combs, Graduate School Technical Records Specialist, 208-282-2150, Fax: 208-282-4847, E-mail: combelle@isu.edu. *Dean,* Dr. Joseph Steiner, 208-282-2175, Fax: 208-282-4482, E-mail: jsteiner@pharmacy.isu.edu.

College of Technology Students: 11 full-time (6 women), 57 part-time (34 women); includes 3 minority (1 American Indian/Alaska Native, 2 Hispanic Americans), 2 international. Average age 43. *Faculty:* 2 full-time (1 woman). Expenses: Contact institution. *Financial support:* In 2008–09, 1 teaching assistantship with full and partial tuition reimbursement (averaging $9,401 per year) was awarded; career-related internships or fieldwork, Federal Work-Study, institutionally sponsored loans, scholarships/grants, health care benefits, tuition waivers (full and partial), and unspecified assistantships also available. Support available to part-time students. Financial award application deadline: 1/1; financial award applicants required to submit FAFSA. In 2008, 8 master's awarded. *Degree program information:* Part-time and evening/weekend programs available. Offers human resource training and development (MTD); technology (MTD). *Application deadline:* For fall admission, 7/1 for domestic students, 6/1 for international students; for spring admission, 12/1 for domestic students, 11/1 for international students. Applications are processed on a rolling basis. *Application fee:* $55. Electronic applications accepted. *Application Contact:* Debra K. Ronneburg, Director of Admissions/Student Services, 208-282-2622, Fax: 208-282-5195, E-mail: ctech@isu.edu. *Dean,* Dr. Marilyn Davis, 208-282-2507, Fax: 208-282-4641, E-mail: mdavis@isu.edu.

Kasiska College of Health Professions Students: 419 full-time (270 women), 176 part-time (137 women); includes 41 minority (5 African Americans, 2 American Indian/Alaska Native, 16 Asian Americans or Pacific Islanders, 18 Hispanic Americans), 17 international. Average age 32. *Faculty:* 34 full-time (21 women), 1 part-time/adjunct (0 women). Expenses: Contact institution. *Financial support:* In 2008–09, 1 research assistantship with full and partial tuition reimbursement (averaging $6,800 per year), 23 teaching assistantships with full and partial tuition reimbursements (averaging $9,401 per year) were awarded; career-related internships or fieldwork, Federal Work-Study, institutionally sponsored loans, scholarships/grants, traineeships, health care benefits, tuition waivers (full and partial), and unspecified assistantships also available. Support available to part-time students. Financial award application deadline: 1/1; financial award applicants required to submit FAFSA. In 2008, 135 master's, 27 doctorates, 11 other advanced degrees awarded. *Degree program information:* Part-time programs available. Offers advanced general dentistry (Post-Doctoral Certificate); audiology (MS, Au D); counseling (M Coun, Ed S); counselor education and counseling (PhD); deaf education (MS); dental hygiene (MS); dietetics (Certificate); family medicine (Post-Master's Certificate); health education (MHE); health professions (M Coun, MHE, MOT, MPAS, MPH, MS, Au D, DPT, PhD, Certificate, Ed S, Post-Doctoral Certificate, Post-Master's Certificate, Postbaccalaureate Certificate); Nursing (MS, Post-Master's Certificate); occupational therapy (MOT); physical therapy (DPT); physician assistant studies (MPAS); public health (MPH); speech language pathology (MS). *Application deadline:* For fall admission, 7/1 for domestic students, 6/1 for international students; for spring admission, 12/1 for domestic students, 11/1 for international students. Applications are processed on a rolling basis. *Application fee:* $55. Electronic applications accepted. *Application Contact:* Ellen Combs, Graduate School Technical Records Specialist, 208-282-2150, Fax: 208-282-4847, E-mail: combelle@isu.edu. *Dean,* Dr. Linda Hatzenbuehler, 208-282-3992, Fax: 208-282-4000, E-mail: hatzlind@isu.edu.

ILIFF SCHOOL OF THEOLOGY, Denver, CO 80210-4798

General Information Independent-religious, coed, graduate-only institution. *Graduate housing:* Rooms and/or apartments available on a first-come, first-served basis to single and married students.

GRADUATE UNITS

Graduate and Professional Programs *Degree program information:* Part-time and evening/weekend programs available. Offers biblical studies (MA); church history (MA); religion (MA); religion and social change (MA); specialized ministry (MASM); theology (M Div, MTS, D Min, PhD); theology/ethics (MA). Electronic applications accepted.

ILLINOIS COLLEGE OF OPTOMETRY, Chicago, IL 60616-3878

General Information Independent, coed, graduate-only institution. *Graduate housing:* Rooms and/or apartments guaranteed to single students and available on a first-come, first-served basis to married students. Housing application deadline: 6/1. *Research affiliation:* University of Chicago (vision science), Rush University (cataract development), Ocular Science (contact lenses), University of Illinois at Chicago (neuropharmacology), Vision Service Plan (pediatric optometry), Ciba Vision (contact lenses).

GRADUATE UNITS

Professional Program Offers optometry (OD). Electronic applications accepted.

ILLINOIS INSTITUTE OF TECHNOLOGY, Chicago, IL 60616-3793

General Information Independent, coed, university. CGS member. *Enrollment:* 7,613 graduate, professional, and undergraduate students; 3,151 full-time matriculated graduate/professional students (1,231 women), 1,629 part-time matriculated graduate/professional students (580 women). *Enrollment by degree level:* 958 first professional, 1,006 master's, 586 doctoral, 71 other advanced degrees. *Graduate faculty:* 364 full-time (71 women), 263 part-time/adjunct (57 women). *Graduate housing:* Rooms and/or apartments available on a first-come, first-served basis to single and married students. Housing application deadline: 6/1. *Student services:* Campus employment opportunities, campus safety program, career counseling, free psychological counseling, grant writing training, international student services, low-cost health insurance, multicultural affairs office, services for students with disabilities, teacher training, writing training. *Library facilities:* Paul V. Galvin Library plus 5 others. *Online resources:* library catalog, web page, access to other libraries' catalogs. *Collection:* 1.7 million titles, 33,535 serial subscriptions, 1,071 audiovisual materials.

Computer facilities: 500 computers available on campus for general student use. A campuswide network can be accessed from student residence rooms. Online class registration is available. *Web address:* http://www.iit.edu/.

General Application Contact: Morgan Frederick, Office of Graduate Admissions, 866-472-3448, Fax: 312-567-3138, E-mail: inquiry.grad@iit.edu.

GRADUATE UNITS

Chicago-Kent College of Law *Degree program information:* Part-time and evening/weekend programs available. Offers family law (LL M); financial services (LL M); international intellectual property (LL M); international law (LL M); law (JD); taxation (LL M). Electronic applications accepted.

Graduate College Students: 1,835 full-time (609 women), 1,197 part-time (407 women); includes 295 minority (99 African Americans, 1 American Indian/Alaska Native, 132 Asian Americans or Pacific Islanders, 63 Hispanic Americans), 1,879 international. Average age 28. 6,909 applicants, 51% accepted, 1113 enrolled. *Faculty:* 276 full-time (48 women), 173 part-time/adjunct (35 women). Expenses: Contact institution. *Financial support:* Fellowships with full and partial tuition reimbursements, research assistantships with full and partial tuition reimbursements, teaching assistantships with full and partial tuition reimbursements, career-related internships or fieldwork, Federal Work-Study, institutionally sponsored loans, scholarships/grants, traineeships, health care benefits, tuition waivers (full and partial), and unspecified assistantships available. Support available to part-time students. Financial award applicants required to submit FAFSA. In 2008, 877 master's, 65 doctorates awarded. *Degree program information:* Part-time and evening/weekend programs available. Postbaccalaureate distance learning degree programs offered (no on-campus study). *Application deadline:* Applications are processed on a rolling basis. *Application fee:* $40. Electronic applications accepted. *Application Contact:* Morgan Frederick, Assistant Director of Graduate Communications, 866-472-3448, Fax: 312-567-3138, E-mail: inquiry.grad@iit.edu. *Dean/Vice Provost,* Dr. Ali Cinar, 312-567-3637, Fax: 312-567-7517, E-mail: gradstu@iit.edu.

Armour College of Engineering Students: 700 full-time (146 women), 457 part-time (79 women); includes 77 minority (20 African Americans, 45 Asian Americans or Pacific Islanders, 12 Hispanic Americans), 859 international. Average age 26. 3,231 applicants, 49% accepted, 408 enrolled. *Faculty:* 86 full-time (6 women), 34 part-time/adjunct (4 women). Expenses: Contact institution. *Financial support:* In 2008–09, 15 fellowships with tuition reimbursements, 106 research assistantships with tuition reimbursements, 70 teaching assistantships with tuition reimbursements were awarded; career-related internships or fieldwork, Federal Work-Study, institutionally sponsored loans, scholarships/grants, health care benefits, tuition waivers (full and partial), and unspecified assistantships also available. Support available to part-time students. Financial award applicants required to submit FAFSA. In 2008, 329 master's, 27 doctorates awarded. *Degree program information:* Part-time and evening/weekend programs available. Postbaccalaureate distance learning degree programs offered (no on-campus study). Offers architectural engineering (M Arch E); biological engineering (MBE); biomedical engineering (PhD); biomedical imaging and signals (MBMI); chemical engineering (M Ch E, MS, PhD); civil engineering (MS, PhD); computer engineering (MS, PhD); construction engineering and management (MCEM); electrical and computer engineering (MECE); electrical engineering (MS, PhD); electricity markets (MEM); engineering (M Arch E, M Ch E, M Env E, M Geoenv E, M Trans E, MBE, MBMI, MCEM, MECE, MEM, MFPE, MGE, MGE, MMAE, MME, MMME, MNE, MPE, MPW, MS, MSE, MTSE, MVM, PhD); environmental engineering (M Env E, MS, PhD); food process engineering (MFPE); food processing engineering (MS); gas engineering (MGE); geoenvironmental engineering (M Geoenv E); geotechnical engineering (MGE); manufacturing engineering (MME, MS); materials science and engineering (MMME, MS, PhD); mechanical and aerospace engineering (MMAE, MS, PhD); network engineering (MNE); power engineering (MPE); public works (MPW); structural engineering (MSE); telecommunications and software engineering (MTSE); transportation engineering (M Trans E); VLSI and microelectronics (MVM). *Application deadline:* For fall admission, 5/1 for domestic and international students; for spring admission, 10/15 for domestic and international students. Applications are processed on a rolling basis. *Application fee:* $40. Electronic applications accepted. *Applica-*

tion Contact: Morgan Frederick, Assistant Director of Graduate Communications, 866-472-3448, Fax: 312-567-3138, E-mail: inquiry.grad@iit.edu. *Dean*, Dr. Natacha DePaola, 312-567-3009, Fax: 312-567-7961, E-mail: engineering@iit.edu.

Center for Professional Development Students: 221 full-time (63 women), 85 part-time (23 women); includes 23 minority (5 African Americans, 11 Asian Americans or Pacific Islanders, 7 Hispanic Americans), 242 international. 298 applicants, 58% accepted, 106 enrolled. *Faculty:* 4 full-time (0 women), 23 part-time/adjunct (2 women). Expenses: Contact institution. *Financial support:* In 2008–09, 21 fellowships with tuition reimbursements, 1 research assistantship with tuition reimbursement, 18 teaching assistantships with tuition reimbursements were awarded; career-related internships or fieldwork, Federal Work-Study, institutionally sponsored loans, scholarships/grants, traineeships, health care benefits, tuition waivers (partial), and unspecified assistantships also available. Support available to part-time students. Financial award applicants required to submit FAFSA. In 2008, 96 master's awarded. *Degree program information:* Part-time and evening/weekend programs available. Postbaccalaureate distance learning degree programs offered (no on-campus study). Offers industrial technology and management (MITO); information technology and management (MITM). *Application deadline:* For fall admission, 5/1 for domestic and international students; for spring admission, 1/5 for domestic and international students. Applications are processed on a rolling basis. *Application fee:* $40. Electronic applications accepted. *Application Contact:* Barbara C. Kozi, Administrator, 630-682-6040, Fax: 630-682-6010, E-mail: kozi@iit.edu. *Director*, C. Robert Carlson, 630-682-6002, Fax: 630-682-6010, E-mail: carlson@iit.edu.

College of Architecture Students: 202 full-time (85 women), 27 part-time (11 women); includes 19 minority (2 African Americans, 6 Asian Americans or Pacific Islanders, 11 Hispanic Americans), 96 international. Average age 28. 427 applicants, 78% accepted, 105 enrolled. *Faculty:* 40 full-time (5 women), 55 part-time/adjunct (15 women). Expenses: Contact institution. *Financial support:* In 2008–09, 125 teaching assistantships (averaging $4,000 per year) were awarded; fellowships, career-related internships or fieldwork, Federal Work-Study, institutionally sponsored loans, scholarships/grants, and health care benefits also available. Support available to part-time students. Financial award applicants required to submit FAFSA. In 2008, 54 master's, 2 doctorates awarded. *Degree program information:* Part-time programs available. Offers architecture (M Ar, PhD); integrated building delivery (M IBD); landscape architecture (MLA). *Application deadline:* For fall admission, 1/15 for domestic and international students. Applications are processed on a rolling basis. *Application fee:* $40. Electronic applications accepted. *Application Contact:* Sarah Pariseau, Coordinator for Academic Affairs, 312-567-3231, Fax: 312-567-5820. *John and Jeanne Rowe Chair*, Donna V. Robertson, 312-567-3230, Fax: 312-567-5820, E-mail: robertson@iit.edu.

College of Science and Letters Students: 499 full-time (167 women), 504 part-time (214 women); includes 112 minority (60 African Americans, 1 American Indian/Alaska Native, 31 Asian Americans or Pacific Islanders, 20 Hispanic Americans), 613 international. Average age 29. 2,469 applicants, 49% accepted, 634 enrolled. *Faculty:* 117 full-time (28 women), 45 part-time/adjunct (8 women). Expenses: Contact institution. *Financial support:* In 2008–09, 18 fellowships with tuition reimbursements, 77 research assistantships with tuition reimbursements, 85 teaching assistantships with tuition reimbursements were awarded; career-related internships or fieldwork, Federal Work-Study, institutionally sponsored loans, scholarships/grants, traineeships, health care benefits, tuition waivers (partial), and unspecified assistantships also available. Support available to part-time students. Financial award applicants required to submit FAFSA. In 2008, 305 master's, 22 doctorates awarded. *Degree program information:* Part-time and evening/weekend programs available. Postbaccalaureate distance learning degree programs offered (no on-campus study). Offers analytical chemistry (M Ch); applied mathematics (MS, PhD); biology (MBS, MS, PhD); chemistry (M Ch, M Chem, MS, PhD); collegiate mathematics education (PhD); computer science (MCS, MS, PhD); food safety and technology (MFST, MS); health physics (MHP); information architecture (MS); materials and chemical synthesis (M Ch); mathematical finance (MMF); mathematics education (MME, MS, PhD); molecular biochemistry and biophysics (MS, PhD); nonprofit management (MPA); physics (MHP, MS, PhD); public administration (MPA); public safety and crisis management (MPA); science and letters (M Ch, M Chem, MBS, MCS, MFST, MHP, MME, MMF, MPA, MS, MSE, MST, MTSE, PhD); science education (MS, MSE, PhD); teaching (MST); technical communication (PhD); technical communication and information design (MS); telecommunications and software engineering (MTSE). *Application deadline:* For fall admission, 5/1 for domestic and international students; for spring admission, 1/5 for domestic and international students. Applications are processed on a rolling basis. *Application fee:* $40. Electronic applications accepted. *Application Contact:* Morgan Frederick, Assistant Director of Graduate Communications, 866-472-3448, Fax: 312-567-3138, E-mail: inquiry.grad@iit.edu. *Dean*, Dr. R. Russell Betts, 312-567-3800, Fax: 312-567-3802, E-mail: betts@iit.edu.

Institute of Design Students: 115 full-time (70 women), 30 part-time (11 women); includes 28 minority (2 African Americans, 23 Asian Americans or Pacific Islanders, 3 Hispanic Americans), 45 international. Average age 31. 183 applicants, 64% accepted, 51 enrolled. *Faculty:* 10 full-time (1 woman), 11 part-time/adjunct (1 woman). Expenses: Contact institution. *Financial support:* In 2008–09, fellowships (averaging $5,400 per year), research assistantships (averaging $10,000 per year), teaching assistantships (averaging $10,000 per year) were awarded; career-related internships or fieldwork, Federal Work-Study, institutionally sponsored loans, scholarships/grants, health care benefits, and unspecified assistantships also available. Support available to part-time students. Financial award applicants required to submit FAFSA. In 2008, 56 master's, 1 doctorate awarded. Offers design (M Des, MSDM, PhD). *Application deadline:* For fall admission, 2/15 priority date for domestic students, 2/15 for international students; for spring admission, 10/15 priority date for domestic students, 10/15 for international students. *Application fee:* $75. *Application Contact:* Rachel Williams Smothers, Director of Admissions and Retention, 312-808-4900, Fax: 312-808-4901, E-mail: rachels@iit.edu. *Director of Admissions and Retention*, Rachel Williams Smothers, 312-808-4900, Fax: 312-808-4901, E-mail: rachels@iit.edu.

Institute of Psychology Students: 98 full-time (78 women), 94 part-time (69 women); includes 36 minority (10 African Americans, 16 Asian Americans or Pacific Islanders, 10 Hispanic Americans), 24 international. Average age 29. 301 applicants, 40% accepted, 54 enrolled. *Faculty:* 19 full-time (8 women), 5 part-time/adjunct (all women). Expenses: Contact institution. *Financial support:* In 2008–09, 39 fellowships with partial tuition reimbursements (averaging $2,798 per year), 1 research assistantship with partial tuition reimbursement, 24 teaching assistantships with partial tuition reimbursements (averaging $4,405 per year) were awarded; career-related internships or fieldwork, Federal Work-Study, institutionally sponsored loans, scholarships/grants, traineeships, health care benefits, tuition waivers (partial), and unspecified assistantships also available. Support available to part-time students. Financial award applicants required to submit FAFSA. In 2008, 37 master's, 13 doctorates awarded. *Degree program information:* Evening/weekend programs available. Offers clinical psychology (PhD); industrial/organizational psychology (PhD); personnel/human resource development (MS); psychology (MS); rehabilitation counseling (MS); rehabilitation counselor education (PhD). *Application deadline:* For fall admission, 1/15 for domestic and international students. *Application fee:* $40. Electronic applications accepted. *Application Contact:* Application Contact, 312-567-3500, Fax: 312-567-3493, E-mail: psychology@iit.edu. *Dean*, Dr. M. Ellen Mitchell, 312-567-3362, Fax: 312-567-3493, E-mail: mitchelle@itt.edu.

Stuart School of Business Students: 488 full-time (199 women), 155 part-time (50 women); includes 33 minority (6 African Americans, 22 Asian Americans or Pacific Islanders, 5 Hispanic Americans), 482 international. Average age 27. 1,370 applicants, 63% accepted, 283 enrolled. *Faculty:* 29 full-time (3 women), 16 part-time/adjunct (6 women). Expenses: Contact institution. *Financial support:* Career-related internships or fieldwork, Federal Work-Study, institutionally sponsored loans, scholarships/grants, traineeships, health care benefits, and tuition waivers (partial) available. Support available to part-time students. Financial award applicants required to submit FAFSA. In 2008, 190 master's, 1 doctorate awarded. *Degree program information:* Part-time and evening/weekend programs available. Offers business (MBA, MMF, MS, PhD); environmental management and sustainability (MS); finance (MS); financial management (MBA); innovation and emerging enterprises (MBA); management science (PhD); marketing (MBA); marketing communication (MS); mathematical finance (MMF); sustainable enterprise (MBA). *Application deadline:* For fall admission, 5/1 for domestic and international students; for spring admission, 1/5 for domestic and international students. Applications are processed on a rolling basis. *Application fee:* $75. Electronic applications accepted. *Application Contact:* Dr. Harvey Kahalas, Dean, 312-906-6576, Fax: 312-906-6549, E-mail: kahalas@stuart.iit.edu. *Dean*, Dr. Harvey Kahalas, 312-906-6576, Fax: 312-906-6549, E-mail: kahalas@stuart.iit.edu.

ILLINOIS STATE UNIVERSITY, Normal, IL 61790-2200

General Information State-supported, coed, university. CGS member. *Graduate housing:* Rooms and/or apartments available to single and married students. Housing application deadline: 4/1.

GRADUATE UNITS

Graduate School *Degree program information:* Part-time programs available.

College of Applied Science and Technology *Degree program information:* Part-time programs available. Offers agribusiness (MS); applied science and technology (MA, MS); criminal justice sciences (MA, MS); family and consumer sciences (MA, MS); health education (MS); information technology (MS); physical education (MS); technology (MS).

College of Arts and Sciences *Degree program information:* Part-time programs available. Offers animal behavior (MS); arts and sciences (MA, MS, MSW, PhD, SSP); bacteriology (MS); biochemistry (MS); biological sciences (MS); biology (PhD); biophysics (MS); biotechnology (MS); botany (MS, PhD); cell biology (MS); chemistry (MS); communication (MA, MS); communication sciences and disorders (MA, MS); conservation biology (MS); developmental biology (MS); ecology (MS, PhD); economics (MA, MS); English (MA, MS, PhD); English studies (PhD); entomology (MS); evolutionary biology (MS); French (MA); French and German (MA); French and Spanish (MA); genetics (MS, PhD); German (MA); German and Spanish (MA); historical archaeology (MA, MS); history (MA, MS); hydrogeology (MS); immunology (MS); mathematics (MA, MS, PhD); mathematics education (PhD); microbiology (MS, PhD); molecular biology (MS); molecular genetics (MS); neurobiology (MS); neuroscience (MS); parasitology (MS); physiology (MS, PhD); plant biology (MS); plant molecular biology (MS); plant sciences (MS); politics and government (MA, MS); psychology (MA, MS); school psychology (PhD, SSP); social work (MSW); sociology (MA, MS); Spanish (MA); structural biology (MS); writing (MA, MS); zoology (MS, PhD).

College of Business *Degree program information:* Part-time programs available. Offers accounting (MPA, MS); business (MBA, MPA, MS); business administration (MBA).

College of Education *Degree program information:* Part-time programs available. Offers college student personnel administration (MS); curriculum and instruction (MS, MS Ed, Ed D); education (MS, MS Ed, Ed D, PhD); educational administration (MS, MS Ed, Ed D, PhD); educational policies (Ed D); postsecondary education (Ed D); reading (MS Ed); special education (MS, MS Ed, Ed D); supervision (Ed D).

College of Fine Arts *Degree program information:* Part-time programs available. Offers art history (MA, MS); arts technology (MS); ceramics (MFA, MS); drawing (MFA, MS); fibers (MFA, MS); fine arts (MA, MFA, MM, MM Ed, MS); glass (MFA, MS); graphic design (MFA, MS); metals (MFA, MS); music (MM, MM Ed); painting (MFA, MS); photography (MFA, MS); printmaking (MFA, MS); sculpture (MFA, MS); theatre (MA, MFA, MS).

Mennonite College of Nursing Offers family nurse practitioner (PMC); nursing (MSN, PhD).

IMCA–INTERNATIONAL MANAGEMENT CENTRES ASSOCIATION, Buckingham MK18 1BP, United Kingdom

General Information Independent, graduate-only institution.

GRADUATE UNITS

Programs in Business Administration Postbaccalaureate distance learning degree programs offered (no on-campus study). Offers business administration (M Mgt, M Phil, MBA, MS).

IMMACULATA UNIVERSITY, Immaculata, PA 19345

General Information Independent-religious, coed, primarily women, comprehensive institution. CGS member. *Graduate housing:* On-campus housing not available.

GRADUATE UNITS

College of Graduate Studies *Degree program information:* Part-time and evening/weekend programs available. Offers clinical psychology (Psy D); counseling psychology (MA, Certificate); cultural and linguistic diversity (MA); educational leadership and administration (MA, Ed D); elementary education (Certificate); music therapy (MA); nursing (MSN); nutrition education (MA); nutrition education/approved pre-professional practice program (MA); organization studies (MA); school principal (Certificate); school superintendent (Certificate); secondary education (Certificate); special education (Certificate).

See Close-Up on page 925.

INDEPENDENCE UNIVERSITY, Salt Lake City, UT 84107

General Information Proprietary, coed, comprehensive institution. *Graduate housing:* On-campus housing not available.

GRADUATE UNITS

Program in Business Administration Offers business administration (MBA).

Program in Business Administration in Health Care *Degree program information:* Part-time and evening/weekend programs available. Postbaccalaureate distance learning degree programs offered (no on-campus study). Offers health care administration (MBA).

Program in Health Care Administration *Degree program information:* Part-time and evening/weekend programs available. Postbaccalaureate distance learning degree programs offered (no on-campus study). Offers health care administration (MSHCA).

Program in Health Services *Degree program information:* Part-time and evening/weekend programs available. Postbaccalaureate distance learning degree programs offered (no on-campus study). Offers community health (MSHS); wellness promotion (MSHS).

Program in Nursing Offers community health (MSN); gerontology (MSN); nursing administration (MSN); wellness promotion (MSN).

Program in Public Health *Degree program information:* Part-time and evening/weekend programs available. Postbaccalaureate distance learning degree programs offered (no on-campus study). Offers public health (MPH).

INDIANA STATE UNIVERSITY, Terre Haute, IN 47809-1401

General Information State-supported, coed, university. CGS member. *Graduate housing:* Rooms and/or apartments available on a first-come, first-served basis to single and married students. *Research affiliation:* Boston Museum of Science (remote sensing, biology), Great Lakes–Northern Forest Cooperative Ecosystem Study Unit (biology, life sciences), Indiana Space Grant (remote sensing), Indiana University School of Medicine (cancer and Lupus research), Cranberry Lake Biological Station (psychosocial impacts of cancer).

GRADUATE UNITS

School of Graduate Studies *Degree program information:* Part-time and evening/weekend programs available. Postbaccalaureate distance learning degree programs offered (no on-campus study). Offers technology management (PhD). Electronic applications accepted.

College of Arts and Sciences *Degree program information:* Part-time and evening/weekend programs available. Offers arts and sciences (MA, MFA, MM, MPA, MS, PhD, Psy D, CAS); ceramics (MA, MFA); clinical psychology (Psy D); communication studies (MA, MS); criminology and criminal justice (MA, MS); dietetics (MS); drawing (MA, MFA); ecology (PhD); English teaching (MA); family and consumer sciences education (MS); general psychology (MA, MS); geography (MA); geology (MS); graphic design (MA, MFA); history (MA); inter-area option (MS); life sciences (MS); linguistics/teaching English as a second language (MA); literature (MA); math teaching (MA, MS); mathematics and computer science (MA); mathematics and computer sciences (MS); microbiology (PhD); music performance (MM); painting (MA, MFA); photography (MA, MFA); physical geography (PhD); physiology (PhD); political science (MA, MS); printmaking (MA, MFA); public administration (MPA); radio,

Indiana State University (continued)

television and film (MA, MS); science education (MS); sculpture (MA, MFA); TESL/TEFL (CAS). Electronic applications accepted.

College of Business *Degree program information:* Part-time and evening/weekend programs available. Offers business (MBA). Electronic applications accepted.

College of Education *Degree program information:* Part-time and evening/weekend programs available. Offers counseling psychology (MS, PhD); counselor education (PhD); curriculum and instruction (M Ed, PhD); early childhood education (M Ed); education (M Ed, MS, PhD, Ed S); educational administration (PhD); educational technology (MS); elementary education (M Ed); leadership in higher education (PhD); mental health counseling (MS); school administration (Ed S); school administration and supervision (M Ed); school counseling (M Ed); school psychology (PhD, Ed S); student affairs in higher education (MS). Electronic applications accepted.

College of Nursing, Health and Human Services Offers adult fitness (MA, MS); athletic training (MS); coaching (MA, MS); community health promotion (MA, MS); exercise science (MA, MS); health and safety education (MA, MS); nursing (MS); nursing, health and human services (MA, MS); occupational safety management (MA, MS); recreation and sport management (MA, MS). Electronic applications accepted.

College of Technology Offers career and technical education (MS); electronics and computer technology (MS); human resource development (MS); industrial technology (MS); technology (MS); technology education (MS). Electronic applications accepted.

See Close-Up on page 927.

INDIANA TECH, Fort Wayne, IN 46803-1297

General Information Independent, coed, comprehensive institution. *Enrollment:* 3,512 graduate, professional, and undergraduate students; 198 full-time matriculated graduate/professional students (91 women), 162 part-time matriculated graduate/professional students (83 women). *Enrollment by degree level:* 360 master's. *Graduate faculty:* 16 full-time (5 women), 58 part-time/adjunct (11 women). *Graduate housing:* On-campus housing not available. *Student services:* Career counseling. *Library facilities:* McMillen Library. *Online resources:* library catalog, access to other libraries' catalogs. *Collection:* 20,000 titles, 80 serial subscriptions, 102 audiovisual materials.

Computer facilities: 330 computers available on campus for general student use. A campuswide network can be accessed from student residence rooms and from off campus. Online class registration is available. *Web address:* http://www.indianatech.edu.

General Application Contact: Steve Herendeen, Manager of Campus Development and Support, 260-422-5561 Ext. 2278, Fax: 260-422-1518, E-mail: saherendeen@indianatech.edu.

GRADUATE UNITS

Program in Business Administration Students: 125 full-time (66 women), 124 part-time (64 women); includes 66 minority (49 African Americans, 5 American Indian/Alaska Native, 8 Asian Americans or Pacific Islanders, 4 Hispanic Americans), 4 international. Average age 36. *Faculty:* 16 full-time (5 women), 58 part-time/adjunct (11 women). Expenses: Contact institution. *Financial support:* In 2008–09, 228 students received support. Application deadline: 3/1. In 2008, 89 master's awarded. *Degree program information:* Part-time and evening/weekend programs available. Offers accounting (MBA); health care administration (MBA); human resources (MBA); management (MBA); marketing (MBA). *Application deadline:* Applications are processed on a rolling basis. *Application fee:* $25. Electronic applications accepted. *Application Contact:* Steve Herendeen, Manager of Campus Development and Support, 260-422-5561 Ext. 2121, E-mail: SAHerendeen@indianatech.edu. *Dean of College of Business*, Dr. William Mayfield, 260-422-5561 Ext. 2117, E-mail: WMMayfield@indianatech.edu.

Program in Management Students: 24 full-time (13 women), 19 part-time (11 women); includes 13 minority (12 African Americans, 1 Hispanic American). Average age 41. *Faculty:* 16 full-time (5 women), 58 part-time/adjunct (11 women). Expenses: Contact institution. *Financial support:* In 2008–09, 4 students received support. Application deadline: 3/1. In 2008, 24 master's awarded. *Degree program information:* Part-time and evening/weekend programs available. Offers management (MSM). *Application deadline:* Applications are processed on a rolling basis. *Application fee:* $25. Electronic applications accepted. *Application Contact:* Steve Herendeen, Manager of Campus Development and Support, 260-422-TECH Ext. 2121, E-mail: SAHerendeen@indianatech.edu. *Dean of College of Business*, Dr. William Mayfield, 260-422-5561 Ext. 2117.

Program in Organizational Leadership Offers organizational leadership (MS).

Program in Science Students: 18 full-time (1 woman), 6 part-time (1 woman); includes 3 African Americans, 1 international. Average age 33. *Faculty:* 16 full-time (5 women), 58 part-time/adjunct (11 women). Expenses: Contact institution. *Financial support:* In 2008–09, 12 students received support. Application deadline: 3/1. In 2008, 6 master's awarded. *Degree program information:* Part-time and evening/weekend programs available. Offers science (MSE). *Application deadline:* Applications are processed on a rolling basis. *Application fee:* $25. Electronic applications accepted. *Application Contact:* Steve Herendeen, Manager of Campus Development and Support, 260-422-5561 Ext. 2121, E-mail: SAHerendeen@indianatech.edu. *Dean of Engineering*, Dave Aschliman, 260-422-5561 Ext. 2102, E-mail: DAAschliman@indianatech.edu.

INDIANA UNIVERSITY BLOOMINGTON, Bloomington, IN 47405-7000

General Information State-supported, coed, university. CGS member. *Enrollment:* 40,354 graduate, professional, and undergraduate students; 7,248 full-time matriculated graduate/professional students (3,589 women), 971 part-time matriculated graduate/professional students (577 women). *Enrollment by degree level:* 910 first professional, 3,584 master's, 3,487 doctoral, 224 other advanced degrees. *Graduate faculty:* 1,080 full-time (328 women), 4 part-time/adjunct (2 women). *Tuition, area resident:* Part-time $291.97 per credit hour. Tuition, state resident: part-time $291.97 per credit hour. Tuition, nonresident: part-time $850.33 per credit hour. *Required fees:* $110 per semester. Tuition and fees vary according to course load and program. *Graduate housing:* Rooms and/or apartments available to single and married students. *Student services:* Campus employment opportunities, campus safety program, career counseling, child daycare facilities, exercise/wellness program, free psychological counseling, international student services, low-cost health insurance, multicultural affairs office, services for students with disabilities, writing training. *Library facilities:* Indiana University Library plus 27 others. *Online resources:* library catalog, web page, access to other libraries' catalogs. *Collection:* 6.6 million titles.

Computer facilities: A campuswide network can be accessed from student residence rooms and from off campus. Online class registration, various software packages are available. *Web address:* http://www.iub.edu/.

General Application Contact: Information Contact, 812-855-0661, Fax: 812-855-5102, E-mail: iuadmit@indiana.edu.

GRADUATE UNITS

Jacobs School of Music Students: 788 full-time (414 women), 97 part-time (49 women); includes 89 minority (21 African Americans, 2 American Indian/Alaska Native, 50 Asian Americans or Pacific Islanders, 16 Hispanic Americans), 245 international. Average age 29. 1,312 applicants, 34% accepted, 236 enrolled. *Faculty:* 139 full-time (35 women), 11 part-time/adjunct (3 women). Expenses: Contact institution. *Financial support:* In 2008–09, 225 students received support, including 6 fellowships with full and partial tuition reimbursements available (averaging $17,000 per year), 85 teaching assistantships with full tuition reimbursements available (averaging $6,000 per year); research assistantships with tuition reimbursements available, Federal Work-Study, institutionally sponsored loans, scholarships/grants, tuition waivers (full and partial), and unspecified assistantships also available. Support available to part-time students. Financial award application deadline: 3/1; financial award applicants required to submit FAFSA. In 2008, 170 master's, 46 doctorates, 68 other advanced degrees awarded. Offers church music (DM); music (MA, MM, MM/MLS, MME, MS, DM, DME, PhD, AD, Performance Diploma, Spec); music literature and performance (DM); performance (MM); performance and church music (MM). *Application deadline:* For fall admission, 12/1 for domestic and international students; for spring admission, 9/1 for domestic and international students. Applications are processed on a rolling basis. *Application fee:* $100 ($110 for international students). Electronic applications accepted. *Application Contact:* Music Admissions, 812-855-7998, Fax: 812-856-6086, E-mail: musicadm@indiana.edu. *Dean*, Gwyn Richards, 812-855-2435, E-mail: jln@indiana.edu.

Kelley School of Business Students: 757 full-time (227 women), 41 part-time (15 women); includes 81 minority (24 African Americans, 1 American Indian/Alaska Native, 43 Asian Americans or Pacific Islanders, 13 Hispanic Americans), 314 international. Average age 27. 2,108 applicants, 34% accepted, 387 enrolled. *Faculty:* 71 full-time (10 women). Expenses: Contact institution. *Financial support:* Fellowships with full and partial tuition reimbursements, research assistantships, teaching assistantships, career-related internships or fieldwork, Federal Work-Study, institutionally sponsored loans, tuition waivers (full and partial), and unspecified assistantships available. Support available to part-time students. Financial award application deadline: 3/1; financial award applicants required to submit FAFSA. In 2008, 400 master's, 11 doctorates awarded. Offers business (MBA, MPA, MS, DBA, PhD); business economics and public policy (PhD). PhD offered through University Graduate School. *Application deadline:* For fall admission, 1/15 priority date for domestic students, 12/1 priority date for international students; for winter admission, 3/1 priority date for domestic students; for spring admission, 4/15 for domestic students, 9/1 for international students. *Application fee:* $50 ($60 for international students). Electronic applications accepted. *Application Contact:* Director of Admissions and Financial Aid, 812-855-8006, Fax: 812-855-9039. *Dean*, Daniel Smith, 812-855-8100, Fax: 812-855-8679, E-mail: business@indiana.edu.

Maurer School of Law Students: 695 full-time (291 women), 23 part-time (10 women); includes 111 minority (49 African Americans, 31 Asian Americans or Pacific Islanders, 31 Hispanic Americans), 119 international. Average age 27. 2,384 applicants, 25% accepted, 205 enrolled. *Faculty:* 72 full-time (28 women), 14 part-time/adjunct (4 women). Expenses: Contact institution. *Financial support:* In 2008–09, 581 students received support, including 496 fellowships (averaging $11,669 per year), 76 research assistantships (averaging $1,152 per year), 5 teaching assistantships (averaging $3,060 per year); career-related internships or fieldwork, Federal Work-Study, institutionally sponsored loans, scholarships/grants, health care benefits, and unspecified assistantships also available. Financial award application deadline: 3/1; financial award applicants required to submit FAFSA. In 2008, 216 first professional degrees, 62 master's, 6 doctorates, 1 other advanced degree awarded. Offers comparative law (MCL); juridical science (SJD); law (JD, LL M); law and social sciences (PhD); legal studies (Certificate). PhD offered through University Graduate School. *Application deadline:* For fall admission, 3/1 priority date for domestic and international students. Applications are processed on a rolling basis. *Application fee:* $50 ($60 for international students). Electronic applications accepted. *Application Contact:* Kelly M. Compton, Director of Admissions, 812-855-2704, Fax: 812-855-0555, E-mail: kmcompto@indiana.edu. *Dean*, Lauren K. Robel, 812-855-8885, Fax: 812-855-7057, E-mail: lrobel@indiana.edu.

School of Education Students: 695 full-time (462 women), 256 part-time (178 women); includes 157 minority (67 African Americans, 2 American Indian/Alaska Native, 43 Asian Americans or Pacific Islanders, 45 Hispanic Americans), 197 international. Average age 33. 823 applicants, 55% accepted, 272 enrolled. *Faculty:* 102 full-time (43 women), 112 part-time/adjunct (45 women). Expenses: Contact institution. *Financial support:* Fellowships with full and partial tuition reimbursements, research assistantships with tuition reimbursements, teaching assistantships with tuition reimbursements, Federal Work-Study, scholarships/grants, tuition waivers (full and partial), and unspecified assistantships available. Financial award application deadline: 3/1. In 2008, 251 master's, 93 doctorates, 31 other advanced degrees awarded. *Degree program information:* Part-time programs available. Postbaccalaureate distance learning degree programs offered. Offers art education (MS, Ed D, PhD); counseling (MS, PhD, Ed S); counseling psychology (PhD); counselor education (MS, Ed S); curriculum studies (Ed D, PhD); education (MS, Ed D, PhD, Ed S); education policy studies (PhD); educational leadership (MS, Ed D, PhD, Ed S); educational psychology (MS, PhD); elementary education (MS, Ed D, PhD, Ed S); higher education (MS, Ed D, PhD); history and philosophy of education (MS); history of education (PhD); inquiry methodology (PhD); instructional systems technology (MS, PhD, Ed S); international and comparative education (MS, PhD); learning and developmental sciences (MS, PhD); literacy, culture, and language education (MS, Ed D, PhD, Ed S); mathematics education (MS, Ed D, PhD); philosophy of education (PhD); school psychology (PhD, Ed S); science education (MS, Ed D, PhD); secondary education (MS, Ed D, PhD); social studies education (MS, PhD); special education (MS, Ed D, PhD, Ed S); student affairs administration (MS). *Application deadline:* For fall admission, 1/15 priority date for domestic students, 12/1 priority date for international students; for spring admission, 11/1 priority date for domestic students, 9/1 priority date for international students. Applications are processed on a rolling basis. *Application fee:* $50 ($65 for international students). Electronic applications accepted. *Application Contact:* Elizabeth Tilghman, Admissions Coordinator, 812-856-8552, Fax: 812-856-8505, E-mail: etilghma@indiana.edu. *Dean*, Dr. Gerardo Gonzalez, 812-856-8001, Fax: 812-856-8088, E-mail: gonzalez@indiana.edu.

School of Health, Physical Education and Recreation Students: 264 full-time (134 women), 100 part-time (57 women); includes 77 minority (34 African Americans, 2 American Indian/Alaska Native, 33 Asian Americans or Pacific Islanders, 8 Hispanic Americans), 43 international. Average age 30. 316 applicants, 61% accepted, 112 enrolled. *Faculty:* 67 full-time (29 women), 2 part-time/adjunct (both women). Expenses: Contact institution. *Financial support:* In 2008–09, 182 students received support, including 28 fellowships with full and partial tuition reimbursements available (averaging $2,623 per year), 95 research assistantships with tuition reimbursements available (averaging $8,742 per year), 78 teaching assistantships with tuition reimbursements available (averaging $10,884 per year); career-related internships or fieldwork, Federal Work-Study, institutionally sponsored loans, scholarships/grants, and tuition waivers (full and partial) also available. Support available to part-time students. Financial award application deadline: 3/1. In 2008, 112 master's, 18 doctorates awarded. *Degree program information:* Part-time programs available. Postbaccalaureate distance learning degree programs offered (no on-campus study). Offers adapted physical education (MS); applied sport science (MS); athletic administration/sport management (MS); athletic training (MS); biomechanics (MS); ergonomics (MS); exercise physiology (MS); fitness management (MS); health behavior (PhD); health promotion (MS); health, physical education and recreation (MPH, MS, PhD, Re Dir); human development/family studies (MS); human performance (PhD); leisure behavior (PhD); motor learning/control (MS); nutrition science (MS); outdoor recreation (MS); public health (MPH); recreation (Re Dir); recreation administration (MS); recreational sports administration (MS); safety management (MS); school and college health programs (MS); therapeutic recreation (MS); tourism management (MS). *Application deadline:* For fall admission, 3/1 for domestic students, 1/1 for international students; for spring admission, 11/1 for domestic students, 9/1 for international students. *Application fee:* $50 ($60 for international students). *Application Contact:* Dr. Robert Goodman, Dean, 812-855-1561, Fax: 812-855-4983, E-mail: rmg@indiana.edu. *Dean*, Dr. Robert Goodman, 812-855-1561, Fax: 812-855-4983, E-mail: rmg@indiana.edu.

School of Informatics Students: 317 full-time (78 women), 30 part-time (9 women); includes 14 minority (4 African Americans, 8 Asian Americans or Pacific Islanders, 2 Hispanic Americans), 213 international. Average age 28. 680 applicants, 62% accepted, 176 enrolled. *Faculty:* 63 full-time (12 women). Expenses: Contact institution. *Financial support:* In 2008–09, 2 fellowships with full and partial tuition reimbursements (averaging $20,000 per year), 41 research assistantships (averaging $14,000 per year), 84 teaching assistantships (averaging $13,000 per year) were awarded; Federal Work-Study, institutionally sponsored loans, scholarships/grants, health care benefits, tuition waivers (full and partial), and unspecified assistantships also available. Support available to part-time students. In 2008, 77 master's, 10 doctorates awarded. *Degree program information:* Part-time programs available. Postbaccalaureate distance learning degree programs offered (no on-campus study). Offers bioinformatics (MS); chemical informatics (MS); computer science (MS, PhD); health informatics (MS); human computer interaction (MS); informatics (PhD); laboratory informatics (MS); media arts and science (MS); music informatics (MS); security informatics (MS). PhD offered through University Graduate School. *Application deadline:* For fall admission, 1/15 for domestic students, 12/1 for international students. *Application fee:* $50 ($60 for international students). Electronic applications accepted. *Application Contact:* Rachel Lawmaster, Manager of Graduate Admissions and Graduate Studies, 812-856-3622, Fax: 812-856-3825, E-mail: raclee@indiana.edu. *Associate Dean for Graduate Studies,* Dr. David Leake, 812-855-9756, E-mail: leake@cs.indiana.edu.

School of Journalism Students: 61 full-time (32 women), 15 part-time (8 women); includes 6 minority (2 African Americans, 3 Asian Americans or Pacific Islanders, 1 Hispanic American), 23 international. Average age 30. 132 applicants, 73% accepted, 45 enrolled. *Faculty:* 11 full-time (5 women). Expenses: Contact institution. *Financial support:* Fellowships, research assistantships with full tuition reimbursements, teaching assistantships with partial tuition reimbursements, career-related internships or fieldwork, Federal Work-Study, institutionally sponsored loans, and tuition waivers (full) available. Financial award application deadline: 1/15. In 2008, 20 master's, 5 doctorates awarded. Offers journalism (MA, MAT); mass communication (PhD). *Application deadline:* For fall admission, 1/15 priority date for domestic students; for spring admission, 9/1 priority date for domestic students. Applications are processed on a rolling basis. *Application fee:* $50 ($60 for international students). *Application Contact:* Amy Reynolds, Associate Dean of Graduate Studies, 812-855-8111. *Dean,* Bradley Hamm, 812-855-9247.

School of Library and Information Science Students: 241 full-time (161 women), 109 part-time (74 women); includes 30 minority (10 African Americans, 1 American Indian/Alaska Native, 7 Asian Americans or Pacific Islanders, 12 Hispanic Americans), 45 international. Average age 29. 372 applicants, 92% accepted, 163 enrolled. *Faculty:* 16 full-time (7 women). Expenses: Contact institution. *Financial support:* Fellowships with full and partial tuition reimbursements, research assistantships with full and partial tuition reimbursements, career-related internships or fieldwork, Federal Work-Study, institutionally sponsored loans, scholarships/grants, tuition waivers (partial), and unspecified assistantships available. Support available to part-time students. Financial award application deadline: 1/15. In 2008, 145 master's, 2 other advanced degrees awarded. *Degree program information:* Part-time programs available. Offers library and information science (MIS, MLS, PhD, Sp LIS). *Application deadline:* For fall admission, 5/15 priority date for domestic students, 12/1 priority date for international students; for spring admission, 10/15 priority date for domestic students, 9/1 priority date for international students. Applications are processed on a rolling basis. *Application fee:* $50 ($60 for international students). Electronic applications accepted. *Application Contact:* Rhonda Spencer, Director of Admissions, 812-855-2018, Fax: 812-855-6166, E-mail: slis@indiana.edu. *Dean,* Dr. Blaise Cronin, 812-855-2848, Fax: 812-855-6166, E-mail: bcronin@indiana.edu.

School of Optometry Students: 345 full-time (205 women), 3 part-time (2 women); includes 40 minority (15 African Americans, 2 American Indian/Alaska Native, 21 Asian Americans or Pacific Islanders, 2 Hispanic Americans), 15 international. Average age 26. 475 applicants, 34% accepted, 87 enrolled. *Faculty:* 36 full-time (11 women), 7 part-time/adjunct (5 women). Expenses: Contact institution. *Financial support:* In 2008–09, 48 students received support; fellowships with full tuition reimbursements available, research assistantships with full tuition reimbursements available, Federal Work-Study, institutionally sponsored loans, scholarships/grants, health care benefits, and research assistantships available. Support available to part-time students. Financial award application deadline: 12/1; financial award applicants required to submit FAFSA. In 2008, 82 first professional degrees, 2 master's, 4 doctorates awarded. Offers optometry (OD, MS, PhD). *Application deadline:* For fall admission, 1/15 for domestic students; for winter admission, 2/1 for domestic and international students; for spring admission, 9/1 for domestic students. Applications are processed on a rolling basis. *Application fee:* $50 ($60 for international students). Electronic applications accepted. *Application Contact:* Patricia Reyes, Associate Director of Student Services, 812-855-1292, Fax: 812-855-4389, E-mail: patreyes@indiana.edu. *Interim Dean,* Dr. P. Sarita Soni, 812-855-4440, Fax: 812-855-8664, E-mail: sonip@indiana.edu.

School of Public and Environmental Affairs Students: 425 full-time (227 women), 48 part-time (28 women); includes 42 minority (12 African Americans, 2 American Indian/Alaska Native, 12 Asian Americans or Pacific Islanders, 16 Hispanic Americans), 102 international. Average age 28. 858 applicants, 74% accepted, 291 enrolled. Expenses: Contact institution. *Financial support:* Fellowships with full tuition reimbursements, research assistantships with partial tuition reimbursements, teaching assistantships with partial tuition reimbursements, Federal Work-Study, scholarships/grants, tuition waivers (partial), unspecified assistantships, and service corps program available. Financial award application deadline: 2/1; financial award applicants required to submit FAFSA. In 2008, 275 master's, 18 doctorates, 2 other advanced degrees awarded. *Degree program information:* Part-time programs available. Offers environmental science (MSES, PhD); nonprofit management (Certificate); public affairs (MPA, PhD); public and environmental affairs (MA, MPA, MSES, PhD, Certificate); public management (Certificate); public policy (PhD). *Application deadline:* For fall admission, 2/1 priority date for domestic students, 12/1 priority date for international students; for spring admission, 5/1 for domestic and international students. *Application fee:* $50 ($60 for international students). Electronic applications accepted. *Application Contact:* Jennifer Forney, Director, Graduate Student Services, 812-855-9485, E-mail: jjforney@indiana.edu. *Interim Dean,* Charles Kurt Zorn, 812-855-5058, Fax: 812-855-6234, E-mail: zorn@indiana.edu.

University Graduate School Students: 3,930 full-time (1,999 women), 249 part-time (147 women); includes 463 minority (158 African Americans, 23 American Indian/Alaska Native, 126 Asian Americans or Pacific Islanders, 156 Hispanic Americans), 1,241 international. Average age 30. 6,346 applicants, 30% accepted, 814 enrolled. Expenses: Contact institution. *Financial support:* Fellowships with full and partial tuition reimbursements, research assistantships, teaching assistantships, career-related internships or fieldwork, Federal Work-Study, institutionally sponsored loans, and tuition waivers (full and partial) available. Support available to part-time students. In 2008, 451 master's, 388 doctorates, 1 other advanced degree awarded. *Degree program information:* Part-time programs available. *Application deadline:* For fall admission, 1/15 priority date for domestic students, 12/15 for international students; for spring admission, 9/1 for domestic and international students. *Application fee:* $50 ($60 for international students). Electronic applications accepted. *Application Contact:* Graduate School, 812-855-8853, E-mail: grdschl@indiana.edu. *Dean,* Dr. James Wimbush, 812-855-4848.

College of Arts and Sciences Students: 2,660 full-time (1,358 women), 249 part-time (147 women); includes 329 minority (107 African Americans, 20 American Indian/Alaska Native, 85 Asian Americans or Pacific Islanders, 117 Hispanic Americans), 754 international. Average age 30. 4,794 applicants, 28% accepted, 565 enrolled. *Faculty:* 620 full-time (184 women). Expenses: Contact institution. *Financial support:* Fellowships with full and partial tuition reimbursements, research assistantships, teaching assistantships, career-related internships or fieldwork, Federal Work-Study, institutionally sponsored loans, and tuition waivers (full and partial) available. Support available to part-time students. In 2008, 372 master's, 240 doctorates, 1 other advanced degree awarded. *Degree program information:* Part-time programs available. Offers acting (MFA); African American and African diaspora studies (MA); African languages and linguistics (PhD); African studies (MA); analytical chemistry (PhD); anthropology (MA, PhD); applied mathematics–numerical analysis (MA, PhD); arts and sciences (MA, MAT, MFA, MS, Au D, PhD, Certificate); astronomy (MA, PhD); astrophysics (PhD); audiology (Au D); auditory sciences (PhD); biochemistry (PhD); biogeochemistry (MS, PhD); biological chemistry (PhD); biology and behavior (PhD); biology teaching (MAT); biotechnology (MA); Central Eurasian studies (MA, PhD); chemistry (MAT); Chinese (MA, PhD); classical studies (MA, MAT, PhD); clinical science (PhD); cognitive psychology (PhD); cognitive science (PhD); comparative literature (MA, MAT, PhD); composition, literacy, and culture (PhD); computational linguistics (MA, PhD); creative writing (MA, MFA); criminal justice (MA, PhD); criminology (MA, PhD); cross-cultural perspectives of crime and justice (MA, PhD); design and technology (MFA); developmental psychology (PhD); directing (MFA); East Asian languages and cultures (PhD); East Asian studies (MA); economic geology (MS, PhD); economics (MA, PhD); evolution, ecology, and behavior (MA, PhD); film and media studies (PhD); fine arts (MA, MFA, PhD); folklore (MA, PhD); French (MA, PhD); gender studies (PhD); genetics (PhD); geobiology (MS, PhD); geography (MA, MAT, MS, PhD); geophysics, structural geology and tectonics (MS, PhD); German philology and linguistics (PhD); German studies (MA, PhD); Hispanic linguistics (MA, PhD); Hispanic literature (MA); history (MA, MAT, PhD); history and philosophy of science (MA, PhD); history of art (MA, PhD); hydrogeology (MS, PhD); inorganic chemistry (PhD); Italian (MA, PhD); Japanese (MA, PhD); language (MA); language pedagogy (MA); language sciences (PhD); Latin American and Caribbean studies (MA); law and society (MA, PhD); linguistics (MA, PhD); literature (MA, PhD); Luso-Brazilian literature (MA); Luso-Brazilian studies (PhD); mass communications (PhD); mathematics education (MAT); medieval German studies (PhD); microbiology (MA, PhD); mineralogy (MS, PhD); molecular, cellular, and developmental biology (PhD); Near Eastern languages and cultures (MA, PhD); neuroscience (PhD); performance and ethnography (PhD); philosophy (MA, PhD); physical chemistry (PhD); physics (MAT, MS, PhD); plant sciences (MA, PhD); playwriting (MFA); political science (MA, PhD); probability-statistics (MA, PhD); psychological and brain sciences (MA, PhD); psychology and the law (MA); pure mathematics (MA); religious studies (MA, PhD); rhetoric and public culture (PhD); Russian and East European studies (MA, Certificate); second language studies (MA, PhD); Slavic languages and literatures (MA, MAT, PhD); social psychology (PhD); sociology (MA, PhD); Spanish literatures (PhD); speech and hearing sciences (MA, PhD); speech and voice sciences (PhD); speech-language pathology (MA); stratigraphy and sedimentology (MS, PhD); teaching German (MAT); teaching Spanish (MAT); telecommunications (MA, MS, PhD); TESOL and applied linguistics (MA); theatre and drama (MAT); theatre history (MA, PhD); theory (MA, PhD); West European studies (MA); writing (MA); zoology (MA, PhD). *Application deadline:* For fall admission, 1/15 priority date for domestic students, 12/15 for international students; for spring admission, 9/1 for domestic and international students. *Application fee:* $50 ($60 for international students). Electronic applications accepted. *Application Contact:* Mitchell Byler, Assistant Dean, 812-855-4871, E-mail: mbyler@indiana.edu. *Dean,* Dr. Bennett Bertenthal, 812-855-2392, E-mail: bbertent@indiana.edu.

INDIANA UNIVERSITY EAST, Richmond, IN 47374-1289

General Information State-supported, coed, comprehensive institution.

GRADUATE UNITS

School of Education Offers education (MS Ed).

School of Social Work Offers social work (MSW).

INDIANA UNIVERSITY KOKOMO, Kokomo, IN 46904-9003

General Information State-supported, coed, comprehensive institution. *Graduate housing:* On-campus housing not available.

GRADUATE UNITS

Division of Education *Degree program information:* Part-time and evening/weekend programs available. Offers elementary education (MS Ed).

School of Arts and Sciences Offers liberal studies (MALS).

School of Business *Degree program information:* Part-time and evening/weekend programs available. Offers business administration (MBA).

School of Public and Environmental Affairs Offers public management (MS, Graduate Certificate).

INDIANA UNIVERSITY NORTHWEST, Gary, IN 46408-1197

General Information State-supported, coed, comprehensive institution. *Graduate housing:* On-campus housing not available.

GRADUATE UNITS

Division of Social Work *Degree program information:* Part-time and evening/weekend programs available. Offers social work (MSW).

School of Business and Economics *Degree program information:* Part-time and evening/weekend programs available. Offers accountancy (M Acc); accounting (Certificate); business administration (MBA).

School of Education *Degree program information:* Part-time and evening/weekend programs available. Offers elementary education (MS Ed); secondary education (MS Ed).

School of Public and Environmental Affairs *Degree program information:* Part-time programs available. Offers criminal justice (MPA); environmental affairs (Graduate Certificate); health services administration (MPA); human services administration (MPA); nonprofit management (Graduate Certificate); public management (MPA, Graduate Certificate).

INDIANA UNIVERSITY OF PENNSYLVANIA, Indiana, PA 15705-1087

General Information State-supported, coed, university. CGS member. *Enrollment:* 14,310 graduate, professional, and undergraduate students; 1,046 full-time matriculated graduate/professional students (535 women), 1,336 part-time matriculated graduate/professional students (860 women). *Enrollment by degree level:* 1,650 master's, 732 doctoral. *Graduate faculty:* 284 full-time (122 women), 10 part-time/adjunct (5 women). Tuition, state resident: full-time $6430; part-time $357 per credit. Tuition, nonresident: full-time $10,288; part-time $572 per credit. *Required fees:* $1547.50; $107 per credit. $283 per year. *Graduate housing:* Room and/or apartments available on a first-come, first-served basis to single students; on-campus housing not available to married students. Housing application deadline: 4/15. *Student services:* Campus employment opportunities, campus safety program, career counseling, free psychological counseling, international student services, low-cost health insurance, multicultural affairs office, services for students with disabilities. *Library facilities:* Stapleton Library. *Online resources:* library catalog, web page, access to other libraries' catalogs. *Collection:* 863,626 titles, 16,298 serial subscriptions, 56,540 audiovisual materials.

Computer facilities: Computer purchase and lease plans are available. 3,500 computers available on campus for general student use. A campuswide network can be accessed from student residence rooms and from off campus. Online class registration is available. *Web address:* http://www.iup.edu/.

General Application Contact: Donna Griffith, Assistant Dean, 724-357-2222, Fax: 724-357-4862, E-mail: graduate-admissions@iup.edu.

GRADUATE UNITS

School of Graduate Studies and Research Students: 1,046 full-time (535 women), 1,336 part-time (860 women); includes 135 minority (80 African Americans, 4 American Indian/Alaska Native, 31 Asian Americans or Pacific Islanders, 20 Hispanic Americans), 413 international. Average age 30. 2,684 applicants, 51% accepted, 942 enrolled. *Faculty:* 284 full-time (122 women), 10 part-time/adjunct (5 women). Expenses: Contact institution. *Financial support:* In 2008–09, 24 fellowships with full tuition reimbursements (averaging $1,806 per year), 384 research assistantships with full and partial tuition reimbursements (averaging $4,424 per year), 39 teaching assistantships with partial tuition reimbursements (averaging $14,475 per year) were awarded; career-related internships or fieldwork, Federal Work-Study, scholarships/grants, and tuition waivers (full) also available. Support available to part-time students. Financial award application deadline: 3/15; financial award applicants required to submit FAFSA. In 2008, 698 master's, 101 doctorates, 20 other advanced degrees awarded. *Degree program information:* Part-time and evening/weekend programs available. *Application deadline:* Applications are processed on a rolling basis. *Application fee:* $30. *Application Contact:* Donna Griffith, Assistant Dean, 724-357-2222, Fax: 724-357-4862, E-mail: graduate-admissions@iup.edu. *Dean,* Dr. Timothy Mack, 724-357-2222, Fax: 724-357-4862, E-mail: Timothy.Mack@iup.edu.

College of Education and Educational Technology Students: 261 full-time (203 women), 552 part-time (396 women); includes 45 minority (30 African Americans, 2 American Indian/Alaska Native, 5 Asian Americans or Pacific Islanders, 8 Hispanic Americans), 15 international. Average age 32. 1,059 applicants, 53% accepted, 341 enrolled. *Faculty:* 68 full-time (38 women), 8 part-time/adjunct (4 women). Expenses: Contact institution. *Financial support:* In 2008–09, 7 fellowships (averaging $1,417 per year), 110 research assistantships (averaging $4,773 per year), 10 teaching assistantships with partial tuition reimbursements (averaging $15,682 per year) were awarded; career-related internships or fieldwork and Federal Work-Study also available. Support available to part-time students. Financial award application deadline: 3/15; financial award applicants required to submit FAFSA. In

Indiana University of Pennsylvania (continued)

2008, 248 master's, 41 doctorates, 17 other advanced degrees awarded. *Degree program information:* Part-time and evening/weekend programs available. Offers administration and leadership studies (D Ed); adult education and communication technology (MA); adult education and communications technology (MA); communications media and instructional technology (PhD); communications technology (MA); community counseling (MA); counselor education (M Ed); curriculum and instruction (M Ed, D Ed); education (M Ed, Certificate); education and educational technology (M Ed, MA, MS, D Ed, PhD, Certificate); education of exceptional persons (M Ed); educational psychology (M Ed, Certificate); elementary education (M Ed); literacy (M Ed); principal (Certificate); reading (M Ed); school psychology (D Ed, Certificate); speech-language pathology (MS); student affairs in higher education (MA). *Application deadline:* Applications are processed on a rolling basis. *Application fee:* $30. *Application Contact:* Dr. Edward Nardi, Associate Dean, 724-357-2480, Fax: 724-357-5595, E-mail: ewnardi@iup.edu. *Dean,* Dr. Mary Ann Rafoth, 724-357-2480, Fax: 724-357-5595.

College of Fine Arts Students: 25 full-time (11 women), 18 part-time (10 women); includes 1 minority (Asian American or Pacific Islander), 5 international. Average age 29. 45 applicants, 49% accepted, 16 enrolled. *Faculty:* 21 full-time (9 women). Expenses: Contact institution. *Financial support:* In 2008–09, 16 research assistantships with full and partial tuition reimbursements (averaging $4,590 per year) were awarded; fellowships, career-related internships or fieldwork and Federal Work-Study also available. Support available to part-time students. Financial award application deadline: 3/15; financial award applicants required to submit FAFSA. In 2008, 6 master's awarded. *Degree program information:* Part-time programs available. Offers art (MA, MFA); fine arts (MA, MFA); music (MA); music education (MA); music history and literature (MA); music theory and composition (MA); performance (MA). *Application deadline:* For fall admission, 7/1 priority date for domestic students; for spring admission, 11/1 for domestic students. Applications are processed on a rolling basis. *Application fee:* $30. *Application Contact:* Dr. Douglas Bish, Associate Dean, 724-357-2397, E-mail: dbish@iup.edu. *Dean,* Michael Hood, 724-357-2397, E-mail: mhood@iup.edu.

College of Health and Human Services Students: 172 full-time (74 women), 291 part-time (166 women); includes 31 minority (20 African Americans, 1 American Indian/Alaska Native, 6 Asian Americans or Pacific Islanders, 4 Hispanic Americans), 42 international. Average age 32. 500 applicants, 50% accepted, 211 enrolled. *Faculty:* 42 full-time (23 women), 2 part-time/adjunct (1 woman). Expenses: Contact institution. *Financial support:* In 2008–09, 3 fellowships (averaging $2,000 per year), 63 research assistantships with full and partial tuition reimbursements (averaging $4,241 per year), 5 teaching assistantships (averaging $18,818 per year) were awarded; career-related internships or fieldwork and Federal Work-Study also available. Support available to part-time students. Financial award application deadline: 3/15; financial award applicants required to submit FAFSA. In 2008, 176 master's, 10 doctorates, 3 other advanced degrees awarded. *Degree program information:* Part-time and evening/weekend programs available. Offers aquatics administration and facilities management (MS); criminology (MA, PhD); exercise science (MS); food and nutrition (MS); health and human services (MA, MS, PhD, Certificate); industrial and labor relations (MA); nursing (MS); safety sciences (MS, Certificate); sport management (MS); sport science (MS). *Application deadline:* For fall admission, 7/1 priority date for domestic students; for spring admission, 11/1 for domestic students. Applications are processed on a rolling basis. *Application fee:* $30. *Application Contact:* Dr. Jacqueline Beck, Associate Dean, 724-357-2560, E-mail: jbeck@iup.edu. *Dean,* Dr. Carleen Zoni, 724-357-2555, E-mail: cczoni@iup.edu.

College of Humanities and Social Sciences Students: 192 full-time (100 women), 334 part-time (206 women); includes 34 minority (22 African Americans, 1 American Indian/Alaska Native, 6 Asian Americans or Pacific Islanders, 5 Hispanic Americans), 112 international. Average age 36. 420 applicants, 40% accepted, 112 enrolled. *Faculty:* 70 full-time (32 women). Expenses: Contact institution. *Financial support:* In 2008–09, 9 fellowships (averaging $2,000 per year), 78 research assistantships (averaging $5,347 per year), 22 teaching assistantships (averaging $12,355 per year) were awarded; career-related internships or fieldwork, Federal Work-Study, and tuition waivers (full) also available. Support available to part-time students. Financial award application deadline: 3/15; financial award applicants required to submit FAFSA. In 2008, 70 master's, 35 doctorates awarded. *Degree program information:* Part-time and evening/weekend programs available. Offers administration and leadership studies (PhD); composition and teaching English to speakers of other languages (MA, MAT, PhD); generalist (MA); geography (MA, MS); history (MA); humanities and social sciences (MA, MAT, MS, PhD); literature (MA); literature and criticism (MA, PhD); public affairs (MA); rhetoric and linguistics (PhD); sociology (MA); teaching English (MAT); teaching English to speakers of other languages (MA). *Application deadline:* For fall admission, 7/1 priority date for domestic students; for spring admission, 11/1 for domestic students. Applications are processed on a rolling basis. *Application fee:* $30. *Application Contact:* Dr. Yaw Asamoah, Dean, 724-357-5764. *Dean,* Dr. Yaw Asamoah, 724-357-5764.

College of Natural Sciences and Mathematics Students: 97 full-time (59 women), 49 part-time (34 women); includes 8 minority (3 African Americans, 3 Asian Americans or Pacific Islanders, 2 Hispanic Americans), 14 international. Average age 28. 232 applicants, 28% accepted, 43 enrolled. *Faculty:* 49 full-time (13 women). Expenses: Contact institution. *Financial support:* In 2008–09, 5 fellowships (averaging $2,200 per year), 67 research assistantships with full and partial tuition reimbursements (averaging $4,667 per year), 2 teaching assistantships (averaging $20,909 per year) were awarded; career-related internships or fieldwork and Federal Work-Study also available. Support available to part-time students. Financial award application deadline: 3/15; financial award applicants required to submit FAFSA. In 2008, 38 master's, 15 doctorates awarded. *Degree program information:* Part-time programs available. Offers applied mathematics (MS); biology (MS); chemistry (MA, MS); clinical psychology (Psy D); elementary and middle school mathematics education (M Ed); mathematics education (M Ed); natural sciences and mathematics (M Ed, MA, MS, Psy D); physics (MA, MS); psychology (MA); science for disaster response (MS). *Application deadline:* Applications are processed on a rolling basis. *Application fee:* $30. *Application Contact:* Dr. Jacqueline Gorman, Dean's Associate, 724-357-2609, E-mail: jgorman@iup.edu. *Interim Dean,* Dr. Gerald Buriok, 724-357-2609.

Eberly College of Business and Information Technology Students: 295 full-time (86 women), 60 part-time (34 women); includes 13 minority (5 African Americans, 8 Asian Americans or Pacific Islanders), 222 international. Average age 26. 346 applicants, 67% accepted, 187 enrolled. *Faculty:* 33 full-time (7 women). Expenses: Contact institution. *Financial support:* In 2008–09, fellowships (averaging $250 per year), 50 research assistantships with full and partial tuition reimbursements (averaging $2,069 per year) were awarded; career-related internships or fieldwork and Federal Work-Study also available. Support available to part-time students. Financial award application deadline: 3/15; financial award applicants required to submit FAFSA. In 2008, 160 master's awarded. *Degree program information:* Part-time and evening/weekend programs available. Offers business (M Ed, MBA); business administration (MBA); business/workforce development (M Ed). *Application deadline:* For fall admission, 7/1 priority date for domestic students; for spring admission, 11/1 for domestic students. Applications are processed on a rolling basis. *Application fee:* $30. *Application Contact:* Donna Griffith, Assistant Dean, 724-357-2222, Fax: 724-357-4862, E-mail: graduate-admissions@iup.edu. *Dean,* Dr. Robert Camp, 724-357-4783, E-mail: bobcamp@iup.edu.

See Close-Up on page 929.

INDIANA UNIVERSITY–PURDUE UNIVERSITY FORT WAYNE, Fort Wayne, IN 46805-1499

General Information State-supported, coed, comprehensive institution. CGS member. *Enrollment:* 12,338 graduate, professional, and undergraduate students; 80 full-time matriculated graduate/professional students (45 women), 604 part-time matriculated graduate/professional students (352 women). *Enrollment by degree level:* 648 master's, 36 other advanced degrees. *Graduate faculty:* 196 full-time (73 women), 11 part-time/adjunct (2 women). Tuition, state resident: full-time $4376; part-time $243 per credit. Tuition, nonresident: full-time $10,337; part-time $574 per credit. *Required fees:* $503; $27.95 per credit. Tuition and fees vary according to course load. *Graduate housing:* Room and/or apartments available on a first-come, first-served basis to single students; on-campus housing not available to married students. Typical cost: $5400 per year. *Student services:* Campus employment opportunities, campus safety program, career counseling, child daycare facilities, exercise/wellness program, free psychological counseling, international student services, low-cost health insurance, multicultural affairs office, services for students with disabilities, teacher training, writing training. *Library facilities:* Helmke Library. *Online resources:* library catalog, web page, access to other libraries' catalogs. *Collection:* 455,020 titles, 22,433 serial subscriptions, 3,967 audiovisual materials. *Research affiliation:* Johnson & Johnson (Health & Human Services), Central Indiana Corporate Partnership Foundation (Education), Lincoln Financial Group (Public & Environmental Affairs), Indiana Economic Development Corporation (Public & Environmental Affairs), Tuthill Controls Group (Electrical & Computer Engineering Technology), Earthwatch Institute (Biology).

Computer facilities: Computer purchase and lease plans are available. 472 computers available on campus for general student use. A campuswide network can be accessed from student residence rooms and from off campus. Online class registration, student academic records are available. *Web address:* http://www.ipfw.edu/.

General Application Contact: Susan Humphreys, Graduate Applications Coordinator, 260-481-6145, Fax: 260-481-6880, E-mail: ask@ipfw.edu.

GRADUATE UNITS

College of Arts and Sciences Students: 34 full-time (23 women), 116 part-time (66 women); includes 15 minority (7 African Americans, 1 American Indian/Alaska Native, 2 Asian Americans or Pacific Islanders, 5 Hispanic Americans), 4 international. Average age 34. 76 applicants, 99% accepted, 56 enrolled. *Faculty:* 83 full-time (27 women), 4 part-time/adjunct (2 women). Expenses: Contact institution. *Financial support:* In 2008–09, 6 research assistantships with partial tuition reimbursements (averaging $12,740 per year), 37 teaching assistantships with partial tuition reimbursements (averaging $12,740 per year) were awarded; career-related internships or fieldwork, institutionally sponsored loans, and scholarships/grants also available. Support available to part-time students. Financial award application deadline: 3/1; financial award applicants required to submit FAFSA. In 2008, 35 master's, 2 other advanced degrees awarded. *Degree program information:* Part-time and evening/weekend programs available. Offers applied mathematics (MS); applied statistics (Certificate); arts and sciences (MA, MAT, MLS, MS, Certificate); biology (MS); English (MA, MAT); liberal studies (MLS); mathematics (MS); operations research (MS); professional communication (MA, MS); sociological practice (MA); speech and language pathology (MA); TENL (teaching English as a new language) (Certificate). *Application deadline:* For fall admission, 2/15 for domestic students; for spring admission, 9/1 for domestic students. Applications are processed on a rolling basis. *Application fee:* $30. *Application Contact:* Dr. Carl Drummond, Dean, 260-481-6160, Fax: 260-481-6985, E-mail: drummond@ipfw.edu. *Dean,* Dr. Carl Drummond, 260-481-6160, Fax: 260-481-6985, E-mail: drummond@ipfw.edu.

College of Engineering, Technology, and Computer Science Students: 14 full-time (6 women), 74 part-time (21 women); includes 9 minority (6 African Americans, 3 Asian Americans or Pacific Islanders), 9 international. Average age 33. 43 applicants, 88% accepted, 38 enrolled. *Faculty:* 41 full-time (11 women), 7 part-time/adjunct (0 women). Expenses: Contact institution. *Financial support:* In 2008–09, 1 research assistantship with partial tuition reimbursement (averaging $12,740 per year), 6 teaching assistantships with partial tuition reimbursements (averaging $12,740 per year) were awarded; career-related internships or fieldwork, scholarships/grants, and unspecified assistantships also available. Support available to part-time students. Financial award application deadline: 3/1; financial award applicants required to submit FAFSA. In 2008, 6 master's awarded. *Degree program information:* Part-time programs available. Offers applied computer science (MS); computer engineering (MS); electrical engineering (MS); engineering, technology, and computer science (MS); industrial technology/manufacturing (MS); information technology/advanced computer applications (MS); mechanical engineering (MS); organizational leadership and supervision (MS); systems engineering (MS). *Application deadline:* For fall admission, 7/15 for domestic students, 5/15 for international students; for spring admission, 11/1 for domestic students, 10/15 for international students. Applications are processed on a rolling basis. *Application fee:* $55. *Application Contact:* Dr. Gerard Voland, Dean, 260-481-6839, Fax: 260-481-5734, E-mail: volandg@ipfw.edu. *Dean,* Dr. Gerard Voland, 260-481-6839, Fax: 260-481-5734, E-mail: volandg@ipfw.edu.

College of Health and Human Services Students: 21 part-time (all women); includes 3 minority (all African Americans). Average age 36. 20 applicants, 85% accepted, 16 enrolled. *Faculty:* 9 full-time (all women). Expenses: Contact institution. *Financial support:* In 2008–09, 7 teaching assistantships with partial tuition reimbursements (averaging $12,740 per year) were awarded; scholarships/grants also available. Support available to part-time students. Financial award application deadline: 3/1; financial award applicants required to submit FAFSA. In 2008, 2 master's awarded. *Degree program information:* Part-time programs available. Offers adult nursing practice (MS); health and human services (MS, Certificate); nursing administration (MS, Certificate); nursing education (MS); women's health nursing practice (MS). *Application deadline:* For fall admission, 5/1 priority date for domestic and international students. Applications are processed on a rolling basis. *Application fee:* $55. Electronic applications accepted. *Application Contact:* Dr. Susan Ahrens, Chair, 260-481-6816, Fax: 260-481-5767, E-mail: ahrenss@ipfw.edu. *Dean,* Dr. Linda M. Finke, 260-481-6564, Fax: 260-481-5767, E-mail: finkel@ipfw.edu.

Division of Public and Environmental Affairs Students: 9 full-time (6 women), 35 part-time (23 women); includes 1 minority (African American). Average age 31. 21 applicants, 100% accepted, 17 enrolled. *Faculty:* 10 full-time (3 women). Expenses: Contact institution. *Financial support:* In 2008–09, 1 research assistantship with partial tuition reimbursement (averaging $12,740 per year) was awarded; career-related internships or fieldwork and scholarships/grants also available. Support available to part-time students. Financial award application deadline: 3/1; financial award applicants required to submit FAFSA. In 2008, 15 master's awarded. *Degree program information:* Part-time programs available. Offers public affairs (MPA); public management (MPM, Certificate). *Application deadline:* For fall admission, 8/1 priority date for domestic students; for spring admission, 12/1 for domestic students. Applications are processed on a rolling basis. *Application fee:* $30. *Application Contact:* Dr. Brian L. Fife, Graduate Administrator, 260-481-6961, Fax: 260-481-6346, E-mail: fifeb@ipfw.edu. *Interim Assistant Dean and Graduate Program Director,* Dr. Jane Grant, 260-481-6349, Fax: 260-481-6346, E-mail: grant@ipfw.edu.

School of Business and Management Sciences Students: 22 full-time (9 women), 110 part-time (41 women); includes 11 minority (2 African Americans, 9 Asian Americans or Pacific Islanders), 9 international. Average age 31. 42 applicants, 95% accepted, 36 enrolled. *Faculty:* 29 full-time (10 women). Expenses: Contact institution. *Financial support:* In 2008–09, 7 teaching assistantships with partial tuition reimbursements (averaging $12,740 per year) were awarded; scholarships/grants and unspecified assistantships also available. Support available to part-time students. Financial award application deadline: 3/1; financial award applicants required to submit FAFSA. In 2008, 59 master's awarded. *Degree program information:* Part-time programs available. Offers business administration (MBA). *Application deadline:* For fall admission, 7/15 for domestic students, 5/1 for international students; for spring admission, 11/15 for domestic students, 10/1 for international students. Applications are processed on a rolling basis. *Application fee:* $30. *Application Contact:* Dr. Lyman Lewis, MBA Program Administrator, 260-481-6474, Fax: 260-481-6879, E-mail: lewisl@ipfw.edu. *Dean,* Dr. Otto Chang, 260-481-0219, Fax: 260-481-6879, E-mail: chango@ipfw.edu.

School of Education Students: 1 (woman) full-time, 248 part-time (180 women); includes 21 minority (13 African Americans, 4 Asian Americans or Pacific Islanders, 4 Hispanic Americans), 1 international. Average age 34. 127 applicants, 84% accepted, 101 enrolled. *Faculty:* 24 full-time (13 women). Expenses: Contact institution. *Financial support:* In 2008–09, 1 teaching assistantship with partial tuition reimbursement (averaging $12,740 per year) was awarded; scholarships/grants also available. Support available to part-time students. Financial award application deadline: 3/1; financial award applicants required to submit FAFSA. In 2008, 98 master's awarded. *Degree program information:* Part-time programs available. Offers counselor education (MS Ed); education (MS Ed, Certificate); educational administration (MS Ed);

elementary education (MS Ed, Certificate); secondary education (MS Ed, Certificate); special education (MS Ed). *Application deadline:* For fall admission, 4/1 priority date for domestic and international students. Applications are processed on a rolling basis. *Application fee:* $30. *Application Contact:* Vicky L. Schmidt, Graduate Recorder, 260-481-6450, Fax: 260-481-5408, E-mail: schmidt@ipfw.edu. *Dean,* Dr. Barry Kanpol, 260-481-6456, Fax: 260-481-5408, E-mail: kanpolb@ipfw.edu.

INDIANA UNIVERSITY–PURDUE UNIVERSITY INDIANAPOLIS, Indianapolis, IN 46202-2896

General Information State-supported, coed, university. *Graduate housing:* Rooms and/or apartments available on a first-come, first-served basis to single and married students.

GRADUATE UNITS

Department of Economics Offers economics (MA).

Department of English Offers English (MA); teaching English (MA).

Department of History *Degree program information:* Part-time and evening/weekend programs available. Offers history (MA); public history (MA).

Herron School of Art and Design *Degree program information:* Part-time and evening/weekend programs available. Offers art education (MAE); furniture design (MFA); printmaking (MFA); sculpture (MFA); visual communication (MFA). Electronic applications accepted.

Indiana University School of Medicine Offers anatomy and cell biology (MS, PhD); behavioral health science (MPH); biochemistry and molecular biology (PhD); epidemiology (MPH); genetic counseling (MS); health policy and management (MPH); medical and molecular genetics (MS, PhD); medicine (MD, MPH, MS, DPT, PhD); microbiology and immunology (MS, PhD); pathology and laboratory medicine (MS, PhD); pharmacology (MS, PhD); toxicology (MS, PhD).

School of Health and Rehabilitation Sciences *Degree program information:* Part-time and evening/weekend programs available. Offers health sciences education (MS); nutrition and dietetics (MS); occupational therapy (MS); physical therapy (DPT).

Kelley School of Business *Degree program information:* Part-time and evening/weekend programs available. Postbaccalaureate distance learning degree programs offered (minimal on-campus study). Offers accounting (MSA); business (MBA). Electronic applications accepted.

School of Continuing Studies Offers adult education (MS).

School of Dentistry Offers dentistry (DDS, MS, MSD, PhD, Certificate).

School of Education *Degree program information:* Part-time and evening/weekend programs available. Offers computer education (Certificate); curriculum and instruction (MS); early childhood (MS); educational leadership (MS, Certificate); English as a second language (Certificate); higher education and student affairs (MS); kindergarten (Certificate); language education (MS); reading (Certificate); school counseling (MS); special education (MS, Certificate).

School of Engineering and Technology *Degree program information:* Part-time and evening/weekend programs available. Offers biomedical engineering (MS, MS Bm E, PhD); computer-aided mechanical engineering (Certificate); electrical and computer engineering (MS, MSECE, PhD); engineering (interdisciplinary) (MSE); engineering and technology (MS, MS Bm E, MSE, MSECE, MSME, PhD, Certificate); mechanical engineering (MSME, PhD).

School of Informatics *Degree program information:* Part-time and evening/weekend programs available. Offers informatics (PhD); media arts and science (MS).

School of Law Offers law (JD, LL M, SJD).

School of Liberal Arts Offers American philosophy (Certificate); bioethics (Certificate); family/gender studies (MA); geographic information systems (MS, Certificate); liberal arts (MA, MS, XMA, PhD, Certificate); medical sociology (MA); museum studies (MS, Certificate); philanthropic studies (MA, XMA, PhD); philosophy (MA); political science (MA, Certificate); work/occupations (MA).

Center on Philanthropy *Degree program information:* Part-time and evening/weekend programs available. Postbaccalaureate distance learning degree programs offered (minimal on-campus study). Offers philanthropic studies (MA, PhD).

School of Library and Information Science *Degree program information:* Part-time and evening/weekend programs available. Offers library and information science (MLS).

School of Music *Degree program information:* Part-time and evening/weekend programs available. Postbaccalaureate distance learning degree programs offered. Offers music technology (MS).

School of Nursing *Degree program information:* Part-time programs available. Offers acute care nurse practitioner (MSN); adult health clinical nurse specialist (MSN); adult health nursing (MSN); adult nurse practitioner (MSN); adult psychiatric/mental health nursing (MSN); child psychiatric/mental health nursing (MSN); community health nursing (MSN); family nurse practitioner (MSN); neonatal nurse practitioner (MSN); nursing science (PhD); pediatric clinical nurse specialist (MSN); women's health nurse practitioner (MSN).

School of Physical Education and Tourism Management Offers physical education (MS).

School of Public and Environmental Affairs *Degree program information:* Part-time and evening/weekend programs available. Offers health administration (MHA); public affairs (MPA).

School of Science *Degree program information:* Part-time and evening/weekend programs available. Offers applied mathematics (MS, PhD); applied statistics (MS); biology (MS, PhD); chemistry (MS, PhD); clinical rehabilitation psychology (MS); computer science (MS, PhD); geology (MS); industrial/organizational psychology (MS); math education (MS); mathematics (MS, PhD); physics (MS, PhD); psychobiology of addictions (MS, PhD); science (MS, PhD). Electronic applications accepted.

School of Social Work *Degree program information:* Part-time and evening/weekend programs available. Offers social work (MSW, PhD, Certificate).

INDIANA UNIVERSITY SOUTH BEND, South Bend, IN 46634-7111

General Information State-supported, coed, comprehensive institution. *Graduate housing:* On-campus housing not available.

GRADUATE UNITS

College of Liberal Arts and Sciences *Degree program information:* Part-time and evening/weekend programs available. Offers applied mathematics and computer science (MS); applied psychology (MA); English (MA); liberal studies (MLS).

School of Business and Economics *Degree program information:* Part-time and evening/weekend programs available. Offers accounting (MSA); business administration (MBA); management of information technologies (MS).

School of Education *Degree program information:* Part-time and evening/weekend programs available. Offers counseling and human services (MS Ed); elementary education (MS Ed); secondary education (MS Ed); special education (MS Ed). Electronic applications accepted.

School of Public and Environmental Affairs *Degree program information:* Part-time and evening/weekend programs available. Offers health systems administration and policy (MPA); health systems management (Certificate); nonprofit management (Certificate); public and community services administration and policy (MPA); public management (Certificate); urban affairs (Certificate).

School of Social Work *Degree program information:* Part-time and evening/weekend programs available. Offers social work (MSW).

School of the Arts *Degree program information:* Part-time programs available. Offers music (MM); studio teaching (MM).

INDIANA UNIVERSITY SOUTHEAST, New Albany, IN 47150-6405

General Information State-supported, coed, comprehensive institution. *Graduate housing:* On-campus housing not available.

GRADUATE UNITS

Program in Liberal Studies Offers liberal studies (MLS).

School of Business Offers business administration (MBA); strategic finance (MS).

School of Education *Degree program information:* Part-time and evening/weekend programs available. Offers counselor education (MS Ed); elementary education (MS Ed); secondary education (MS Ed).

INDIANA WESLEYAN UNIVERSITY, Marion, IN 46953-4974

General Information Independent-religious, coed, comprehensive institution. *Enrollment:* 4,623 full-time matriculated graduate/professional students (2,890 women), 393 part-time matriculated graduate/professional students (252 women). *Enrollment by degree level:* 4,897 master's, 119 doctoral. *Graduate faculty:* 66 full-time (28 women), 308 part-time/adjunct (131 women). *Tuition:* Full-time $7020; part-time $390 per credit hour. One-time fee: $290 full-time; $85 part-time. Full-time tuition and fees vary according to course load. *Graduate housing:* On-campus housing not available. *Student services:* Campus employment opportunities, campus safety program, exercise/wellness program, teacher training. *Library facilities:* Lewis A. Jackson Library. *Online resources:* library catalog, web page, access to other libraries' catalogs. *Collection:* 164,272 titles, 85,642 serial subscriptions, 12,648 audiovisual materials.

Computer facilities: 675 computers available on campus for general student use. A campuswide network can be accessed from student residence rooms. *Web address:* http://www.indwes.edu/.

General Application Contact: Dr. Jim Freemyer, Director of Graduate Education, 765-677-2278, Fax: 765-677-2023, E-mail: jfreemyer@indwes.edu.

GRADUATE UNITS

College of Adult and Professional Studies Students: 3,922 full-time (2,371 women), 255 part-time (161 women); includes 922 minority (773 African Americans, 13 American Indian/Alaska Native, 66 Asian Americans or Pacific Islanders, 70 Hispanic Americans). Average age 35. *Faculty:* 21 full-time (6 women), 294 part-time/adjunct (85 women). Expenses: Contact institution. *Financial support:* Available to part-time students. Applicants required to submit FAFSA. In 2008, 1,644 master's awarded. *Degree program information:* Part-time and evening/weekend programs available. Postbaccalaureate distance learning degree programs offered (no on-campus study). Offers accounting (MBA); applied management (MBA); business administration (MBA); curriculum and instruction (M Ed); health care (MBA); human resources (MBA); management (MS). *Application deadline:* Applications are processed on a rolling basis. *Application fee:* $25. Electronic applications accepted. *Application Contact:* Tom Leas, Director of Adult Enrollment Services, 800-895-0036, Fax: 765-677-2404, E-mail: graduate@indwes.edu. *Dean,* Bradford Sample, 765-677-2645, Fax: 765-677-2040, E-mail: bradford.sample@indwes.edu.

College of Graduate Studies Students: 701 full-time (519 women), 138 part-time (91 women); includes 105 minority (86 African Americans, 3 American Indian/Alaska Native, 6 Asian Americans or Pacific Islanders, 10 Hispanic Americans). Average age 34. *Faculty:* 20 full-time (10 women), 33 part-time/adjunct (24 women). Expenses: Contact institution. *Financial support:* In 2008–09, 15 fellowships were awarded; career-related internships or fieldwork, Federal Work-Study, scholarships/grants, and traineeships also available. Support available to part-time students. Financial award applicants required to submit FAFSA. In 2008, 224 master's, 3 doctorates awarded. *Degree program information:* Part-time and evening/weekend programs available. Postbaccalaureate distance learning degree programs offered. Offers addictions counseling (MS); community counseling (MS); divinity (M Div); marriage and family counseling (MS); organizational leadership (Ed D); school counseling (MS). *Application deadline:* Applications are processed on a rolling basis. *Application fee:* $25. Electronic applications accepted. *Application Contact:* Tom Leas, Director of Enrollment Management, 800-895-0036, Fax: 765-677-2404, E-mail: graduate@indwes.edu. *Dean,* Dr. Jim Fuller, 765-677-2090, Fax: 765-677-2380.

School of Nursing Students: 434 full-time (410 women), 31 part-time (30 women); includes 49 minority (38 African Americans, 1 American Indian/Alaska Native, 5 Asian Americans or Pacific Islanders, 5 Hispanic Americans). Average age 42. *Faculty:* 7 full-time (5 women), 21 part-time/adjunct (all women). Expenses: Contact institution. *Financial support:* In 2008–09, 15 fellowships were awarded; career-related internships or fieldwork, scholarships/grants, and traineeships also available. Support available to part-time students. Financial award application deadline: 3/15; financial award applicants required to submit FAFSA. In 2008, 159 master's awarded. *Degree program information:* Part-time programs available. Postbaccalaureate distance learning degree programs offered (minimal on-campus study). Offers community health nursing (MS); nursing (Post Master's Certificate); nursing administration (MS); nursing education (MS); primary care nursing (MS). *Application deadline:* Applications are processed on a rolling basis. *Application Contact:* Tom Leas, Director of Adult Enrollment Services, 800-895-0036, Fax: 765-677-2404, E-mail: graduate@indwes.edu. *Executive Director of Nursing Programs,* Dr. Barbara Ihrke, 765-677-2813, Fax: 765-677-1768, E-mail: barbara.ihrke@indwes.edu.

Wesleyan Seminary Expenses: Contact institution. Offers divinity (M Div); ministerial leadership (MA); ministry (MA); youth ministries (MA). *Application Contact:* Dr. Jim Freemyer, Director of Graduate Education, 765-677-2278, Fax: 765-677-2023, E-mail: jfreemyer@indwes.edu.

INSTITUTE FOR CHRISTIAN STUDIES, Toronto, ON M5T 1R4, Canada

General Information Independent-religious, coed, graduate-only institution. *Graduate housing:* On-campus housing not available.

GRADUATE UNITS

Graduate Programs *Degree program information:* Part-time programs available. Postbaccalaureate distance learning degree programs offered (minimal on-campus study). Offers education (M Phil F, PhD); history of philosophy (M Phil F, PhD); philosophical aesthetics (M Phil F, PhD); philosophy of religion (M Phil F, PhD); political theory (M Phil F, PhD); systematic philosophy (M Phil F, PhD); theology (M Phil F, PhD); worldview studies (MWS).

INSTITUTE FOR CLINICAL SOCIAL WORK, Chicago, IL 60601

General Information Independent, coed, primarily women, graduate-only institution. CGS member. *Graduate housing:* On-campus housing not available.

GRADUATE UNITS

Graduate Programs *Degree program information:* Part-time programs available. Offers clinical social work (PhD).

INSTITUTE OF CLINICAL ACUPUNCTURE AND ORIENTAL MEDICINE, Honolulu, HI 96817

General Information Proprietary, coed, graduate-only institution.

GRADUATE UNITS

Program in Oriental Medicine Offers Oriental medicine (MSOM).

INSTITUTE OF PUBLIC ADMINISTRATION, Dublin 4, Ireland

General Information Proprietary, coed, comprehensive institution.

GRADUATE UNITS

Programs in Public Administration Offers healthcare management (MA); local government management (MA); public management (MA, Diploma).

INSTITUTE OF TRANSPERSONAL PSYCHOLOGY, Palo Alto, CA 94303

General Information Independent, coed, graduate-only institution. *Enrollment by degree level:* 241 master's, 238 doctoral. *Graduate faculty:* 28 full-time (16 women), 96 part-time/adjunct (60 women). *Tuition:* Full-time $24,543; part-time $577 per unit. Tuition and fees vary according to degree level. *Graduate housing:* On-campus housing not available. *Student services:* Campus employment opportunities, international student services. *Library facilities:* Institute of Transpersonal Psychology Library. *Online resources:* library catalog. *Collection:* 13,000 titles, 140 serial subscriptions.

Computer facilities: 10 computers available on campus for general student use. A campuswide network can be accessed. *Web address:* http://www.itp.edu/.

General Application Contact: Elisabeth Borghi, Admissions Office, 650-493-4430, E-mail: info@itp.edu.

GRADUATE UNITS

Global Programs Students: 184 full-time (153 women), 25 part-time (21 women); includes 32 minority (11 African Americans, 2 American Indian/Alaska Native, 5 Asian Americans or Pacific Islanders, 14 Hispanic Americans), 15 international. Average age 43. 142 applicants, 83% accepted, 90 enrolled. *Faculty:* 8 full-time (4 women), 27 part-time/adjunct (20 women). Expenses: Contact institution. *Financial support:* In 2008–09, 68 students received support. Federal Work-Study and scholarships/grants available. Support available to part-time students. Financial award application deadline: 6/30; financial award applicants required to submit FAFSA. In 2008, 19 master's, 8 doctorates awarded. Postbaccalaureate distance learning degree programs offered (minimal on-campus study). Offers psychology (PhD); transpersonal psychology (MTP); transpersonal studies (Certificate). *Application deadline:* Applications are processed on a rolling basis. *Application fee:* $55. *Application Contact:* Dawn Campagnola, Admissions Assistant, 650-493-4430 Ext. 240, Fax: 650-493-6835, E-mail: info@itp.edu. *Academic Vice President,* Dr. Paul Roy, 650-493-4430 Ext. 243, Fax: 650-493-6835, E-mail: proy@itp.edu.

Residential Programs Students: 268 full-time (189 women), 40 part-time (31 women); includes 53 minority (9 African Americans, 3 American Indian/Alaska Native, 21 Asian Americans or Pacific Islanders, 20 Hispanic Americans), 14 international. Average age 38. 168 applicants, 52% accepted, 56 enrolled. *Faculty:* 17 full-time (9 women), 31 part-time/adjunct (18 women). Expenses: Contact institution. *Financial support:* In 2008–09, 178 students received support; teaching assistantships, career-related internships or fieldwork, Federal Work-Study, and scholarships/grants available. Support available to part-time students. Financial award application deadline: 7/1; financial award applicants required to submit FAFSA. In 2008, 47 master's, 16 doctorates awarded. *Degree program information:* Part-time and evening/weekend programs available. Offers clinical psychology (PhD); counseling psychology (MA); transpersonal psychology (MA, PhD); women's spirituality (PhD). *Application deadline:* For fall admission, 2/15 priority date for domestic students. Applications are processed on a rolling basis. *Application fee:* $55. *Application Contact:* 650-493-4430 Ext. 16, Fax: 650-493-6835, E-mail: itpinfo@itp.edu. *Academic Vice President,* Dr. Paul Roy, 650-493-4430 Ext. 243, Fax: 650-493-6835, E-mail: proy@itp.edu.

THE INSTITUTE OF WORLD POLITICS, Washington, DC 20036

General Information Independent, coed, graduate-only institution. *Graduate housing:* On-campus housing not available.

GRADUATE UNITS

Graduate Programs in National Security, Intelligence, and International Affairs *Degree program information:* Part-time and evening/weekend programs available. Offers American foreign policy (Certificate); comparative political culture (Certificate); counterintelligence (Certificate); democracy building (Certificate); intelligence (Certificate); international politics (Certificate); national security affairs (Certificate); public diplomacy and political warfare (Certificate); statecraft and national security affairs (MA); statecraft and world politics (MA); strategic intelligence studies (MA). Electronic applications accepted.

INSTITUT FRANCO-EUROPÉEN DE CHIROPRATIQUE, F-94200 Ivry-sur-Seine, France

General Information Independent, coed, graduate-only institution.

GRADUATE UNITS

Professional Program Offers chiropractic (DC).

INSTITUTO CENTROAMERICANO DE ADMINISTRACIÓN DE EMPRESAS, La Garita, Alajuela, Costa Rica

General Information Independent, coed, graduate-only institution. *Graduate housing:* Rooms and/or apartments guaranteed to single students and available to married students. *Research affiliation:* Tropical Agricultural Research and Higher Education Center (agribusiness), Harvard Institute for International Development (macroeconomics and environment), Earth University (agribusiness), Inter-American Institute for Cooperation on Agriculture (agribusiness), David Rockefeller Center for Latin American Studies (competitiveness), Zamarono (agribusiness).

GRADUATE UNITS

Graduate Programs Offers agribusiness (MIAM); business administration (EMBA); economics and finance (MBA); industry and technology (MBA); sustainable development (MBA). Electronic applications accepted.

INSTITUTO TECNOLÓGICO Y DE ESTUDIOS SUPERIORES DE MONTERREY, CAMPUS CENTRAL DE VERACRUZ, 94500 Córdoba, Veracruz, Mexico

General Information Independent, coed, comprehensive institution.

GRADUATE UNITS

Graduate Programs *Degree program information:* Part-time and evening/weekend programs available. Postbaccalaureate distance learning degree programs offered (minimal on-campus study). Electronic applications accepted.

INSTITUTO TECNOLÓGICO Y DE ESTUDIOS SUPERIORES DE MONTERREY, CAMPUS CHIAPAS, 29000 Tuxtla Gutiérrez, Chiapas, Mexico

General Information Independent, coed, comprehensive institution.

INSTITUTO TECNOLÓGICO Y DE ESTUDIOS SUPERIORES DE MONTERREY, CAMPUS CHIHUAHUA, 31300 Chihuahua, Chihuahua, Mexico

General Information Independent, coed, comprehensive institution.

GRADUATE UNITS

Graduate Programs Offers computer systems engineering (Ingeniero); electrical engineering (Ingeniero); electromechanical engineering (Ingeniero); electronic engineering (Ingeniero); engineering administration (MEA); industrial engineering (MIE, Ingeniero); international trade (MIT); mechanical engineering (Ingeniero).

INSTITUTO TECNOLÓGICO Y DE ESTUDIOS SUPERIORES DE MONTERREY, CAMPUS CIUDAD DE MÉXICO, 14380 Ciudad de Mexico, DF, Mexico

General Information Independent, coed, comprehensive institution. *Graduate housing:* On-campus housing not available. *Research affiliation:* McGill University (management), Concordia University (business and management), Eli Lilly S.A. de C.U. (technological development), Ford Motor Company (industrial organization), German Research Center on Artificial Intelligence (informatics), Brent University (telecommunications).

GRADUATE UNITS

Division of Business *Degree program information:* Part-time and evening/weekend programs available. Postbaccalaureate distance learning degree programs offered (minimal on-campus study). Offers business administration (EMBA, MBA, PhD); economy (MBA); finance (MBA).

Division of Engineering and Architecture *Degree program information:* Part-time and evening/weekend programs available. Postbaccalaureate distance learning degree programs offered (minimal on-campus study). Offers management (MA); telecommunications (MA).

Division of Humanities and Social Sciences *Degree program information:* Part-time and evening/weekend programs available. Offers humanities and social sciences (LL B).

Virtual University Division *Degree program information:* Part-time and evening/weekend programs available. Postbaccalaureate distance learning degree programs offered (minimal on-campus study).

INSTITUTO TECNOLÓGICO Y DE ESTUDIOS SUPERIORES DE MONTERREY, CAMPUS CIUDAD JUÁREZ, 32320 Ciudad Juárez, Chihuahua, Mexico

General Information Independent, coed, comprehensive institution.

GRADUATE UNITS

Program in Administration of Information Technology Offers administration of information technology (MAIT).

Program in Applied Public Management Offers applied public management (MPM).

Program in Business Administration *Degree program information:* Part-time programs available. Postbaccalaureate distance learning degree programs offered. Offers business administration (MBA).

Program in Education Offers education (M Ed).

Program in Educational Administration Offers educational administration (MEA).

Program in Educational Innovation Offers educational innovation (DE).

Program in Educational Technology Offers educational technology (MTE).

Program in Electronic Commerce Offers electronic commerce (MEC).

Program in Humanistic Studies Offers humanistic studies (MEH).

Program in Quality Management Offers quality management (MQM).

INSTITUTO TECNOLÓGICO Y DE ESTUDIOS SUPERIORES DE MONTERREY, CAMPUS CIUDAD OBREGÓN, 85000 Ciudad Obregón, Sonora, Mexico

General Information Independent, coed, comprehensive institution.

GRADUATE UNITS

Program in Administration Offers administration (MA).

Program in Administration of Information Technology Offers administration of information technology (MATI).

Program in Administration of Telecommunications Offers administration of telecommunications (MAT).

Program in Engineering Offers engineering (ME).

Program in Finance Offers finance (MF).

Program in International Relations Offers international relations (MIR).

Program in Marketing Technology Offers marketing technology (MMT).

Programs in Education Offers cognitive development (ME); communications (ME); mathematics (ME).

INSTITUTO TECNOLÓGICO Y DE ESTUDIOS SUPERIORES DE MONTERREY, CAMPUS COLIMA, 28010 Colima, Colima, Mexico

General Information Independent, coed, comprehensive institution.

INSTITUTO TECNOLÓGICO Y DE ESTUDIOS SUPERIORES DE MONTERREY, CAMPUS CUERNAVACA, 62000 Temixco, Morelos, Mexico

General Information Independent, coed, comprehensive institution.

GRADUATE UNITS

Programs in Business Administration Offers finance (MA); human resources management (MA); international business (MA); marketing (MA).

Programs in Information Science Offers administration of information technology (MATI); computer science (MCC, DCC); information technology (MTI).

INSTITUTO TECNOLÓGICO Y DE ESTUDIOS SUPERIORES DE MONTERREY, CAMPUS ESTADO DE MÉXICO, Estado de Mexico 52926, Mexico

General Information Independent, coed, comprehensive institution. *Graduate housing:* On-campus housing not available. *Research affiliation:* Transportadora San Marcos, S.A. de C.V. (quality control), Microsoft (Visual Studio.Net) (computer science), Trinity (new products), Texas Instruments (semiconductors), Sony Electronics (new products), Kaltex (quality control).

GRADUATE UNITS

Professional and Graduate Division *Degree program information:* Part-time programs available. Postbaccalaureate distance learning degree programs offered (minimal on-campus study). Offers administration of information technologies (MITA); architecture (M Arch); business administration (GMBA, MBA); computer sciences (MCS, PhD); education (M Ed); educational institution administration (MAD); educational technology and innovation (PhD); electronic commerce (MEC); environmental systems (MS); finance (MAF); humanistic studies (MHS); information sciences and knowledge management (MISKM); information systems (MS); manufacturing systems (MS); marketing (MEM); quality systems and productivity (MS); science and materials engineering (PhD); telecommunications management (MTM).

INSTITUTO TECNOLÓGICO Y DE ESTUDIOS SUPERIORES DE MONTERREY, CAMPUS GUADALAJARA, 45140 Zapopan, Jalisco, Mexico

General Information Independent, coed, comprehensive institution. *Graduate housing:* Rooms and/or apartments available to single and married students. Housing application deadline: 8/30.

GRADUATE UNITS

Program in Business Administration *Degree program information:* Part-time and evening/weekend programs available. Postbaccalaureate distance learning degree programs offered. Offers business administration (IEMBA, M Ad).

Program in Finance Offers finance (MF).

INSTITUTO TECNOLÓGICO Y DE ESTUDIOS SUPERIORES DE MONTERREY, CAMPUS HIDALGO, 42090 Pachuca, Hidalgo, Mexico

General Information Independent, coed, comprehensive institution.

INSTITUTO TECNOLÓGICO Y DE ESTUDIOS SUPERIORES DE MONTERREY, CAMPUS IRAPUATO, 36660 Irapuato, Guanajuato, Mexico

General Information Independent, coed, comprehensive institution.

GRADUATE UNITS

Graduate Programs Offers administration (MBA); administration of information technology (MAIT); administration of telecommunications (MAT); architecture (M Arch); computer science (MCS); education (M Ed); educational administration (MEA); educational innovation and technology (DEIT); educational technology (MET); electronic commerce (MBA); environmental administration and planning (MEAP); environmental systems (MES); finances (MBA); humanistic studies (MHS); international management for Latin American executives (MIMLAE); library and information science (MLIS); manufacturing quality management (MMQM); marketing research (MBA).

INSTITUTO TECNOLÓGICO Y DE ESTUDIOS SUPERIORES DE MONTERREY, CAMPUS LAGUNA, 27250 Torreón, Coahuila, Mexico

General Information Independent, coed, comprehensive institution. *Graduate housing:* On-campus housing not available.

GRADUATE UNITS

Graduate School *Degree program information:* Part-time programs available. Offers business administration (MBA); industrial engineering (MIE); management information systems (MS).

INSTITUTO TECNOLÓGICO Y DE ESTUDIOS SUPERIORES DE MONTERREY, CAMPUS LEÓN, 37120 León, Guanajuato, Mexico

General Information Independent, coed, comprehensive institution.

GRADUATE UNITS

Program in Business Administration *Degree program information:* Part-time programs available. Offers business administration (MBA).

INSTITUTO TECNOLÓGICO Y DE ESTUDIOS SUPERIORES DE MONTERREY, CAMPUS MAZATLÁN, 82000 Mazatlán, Sinaloa, Mexico

General Information Independent, coed, comprehensive institution.

INSTITUTO TECNOLÓGICO Y DE ESTUDIOS SUPERIORES DE MONTERREY, CAMPUS MONTERREY, 64849 Monterrey, Nuevo León, Mexico

General Information Independent, coed, university. *Graduate housing:* Room and/or apartments available to single students; on-campus housing not available to married students. *Research affiliation:* IBM de México (computer science), Southwest Research Institute (environment), Hylsa (steel), Vitro (glass products), Cydsa (petrochemicals), Cemex (cement).

GRADUATE UNITS

Graduate and Research Division *Degree program information:* Part-time and evening/weekend programs available. Offers agricultural parasitology (PhD); agricultural sciences (MS); applied statistics (M Eng); artificial intelligence (PhD); automation engineering (M Eng); biotechnology (MS); chemical engineering (M Eng); chemistry (MS, PhD); civil engineering (M Eng); communications (MS); computer science (MS); education (MA); electrical engineering (M Eng); electronic engineering (M Eng); environmental engineering (M Eng); farming productivity (MS); food processing engineering (MS); industrial engineering (M Eng, PhD); informatics (PhD); information systems (MS); information technology (MS); manufacturing engineering (M Eng); mechanical engineering (M Eng); phytopathology (MS); systems and quality engineering (M Eng).

Graduate School of Business Administration and Leadership *Degree program information:* Part-time programs available. Offers business administration (MA, MBA); finance (M Sc); international business (M Sc); management (PhD); management and leadership (M Sc, MA, MBA, PhD); marketing (M Sc).

INSTITUTO TECNOLÓGICO Y DE ESTUDIOS SUPERIORES DE MONTERREY, CAMPUS QUERÉTARO, 76130 Querétaro, Querétaro, Mexico

General Information Independent, coed, comprehensive institution. *Graduate housing:* Room and/or apartments guaranteed to single students; on-campus housing not available to married students. Housing application deadline: 6/15. *Research affiliation:* Transmisiones y Equipos Mecanicos (manufacturing designing).

GRADUATE UNITS

School of Business Offers business (MBA).

INSTITUTO TECNOLÓGICO Y DE ESTUDIOS SUPERIORES DE MONTERREY, CAMPUS SALTILLO, 25270 Saltillo, Coahuila, Mexico

General Information Independent, coed, comprehensive institution.

INSTITUTO TECNOLÓGICO Y DE ESTUDIOS SUPERIORES DE MONTERREY, CAMPUS SAN LUIS POTOSÍ, 78140 San Luis Potosí, SLP, Mexico

General Information Independent, coed, comprehensive institution.

INSTITUTO TECNOLÓGICO Y DE ESTUDIOS SUPERIORES DE MONTERREY, CAMPUS SINALOA, 80800 Culiacán, Sinaloa, Mexico

General Information Independent, coed, comprehensive institution.

INSTITUTO TECNOLÓGICO Y DE ESTUDIOS SUPERIORES DE MONTERREY, CAMPUS SONORA NORTE, 83000 Hermosillo, Sonora, Mexico

General Information Independent, coed, comprehensive institution. *Graduate housing:* On-campus housing not available. *Research affiliation:* National Council for Science and Technology (engineering).

GRADUATE UNITS

Program in Business Offers business (MA).

Program in Education Offers education (MA).

Program in Technological Information Management Offers technological information management (MA).

INSTITUTO TECNOLÓGICO Y DE ESTUDIOS SUPERIORES DE MONTERREY, CAMPUS TAMPICO, 89120 Altimira, Tamaulipas, Mexico

General Information Independent, coed, comprehensive institution.

INSTITUTO TECNOLÓGICO Y DE ESTUDIOS SUPERIORES DE MONTERREY, CAMPUS TOLUCA, 50252 Toluca, Estado de Mexico, Mexico

General Information Independent, coed, comprehensive institution.

GRADUATE UNITS

Graduate Programs *Degree program information:* Part-time and evening/weekend programs available.

INSTITUTO TECNOLÓGICO Y DE ESTUDIOS SUPERIORES DE MONTERREY, CAMPUS ZACATECAS, 98000 Zacatecas, Zacatecas, Mexico

General Information Independent, coed, comprehensive institution.

INTER AMERICAN UNIVERSITY OF PUERTO RICO, AGUADILLA CAMPUS, Aguadilla, PR 00605

General Information Independent, coed, comprehensive institution.

GRADUATE UNITS

Graduate School *Degree program information:* Part-time and evening/weekend programs available. Electronic applications accepted.

INTER AMERICAN UNIVERSITY OF PUERTO RICO, ARECIBO CAMPUS, Arecibo, PR 00614-4050

General Information Independent, coed, comprehensive institution.

GRADUATE UNITS

Program in Anesthesia Offers anesthesia (MS).

Program in Nursing Offers community nursing (MS); critical care nursing (MS); primary care nursing (MS); surgical nursing (MS).

Programs in Education Offers administration and educational supervision (MA Ed); counseling and guidance (MA Ed); curriculum and teaching (MA Ed); elementary education (MA Ed).

INTER AMERICAN UNIVERSITY OF PUERTO RICO, BARRANQUITAS CAMPUS, Barranquitas, PR 00794

General Information Independent, coed, comprehensive institution. *Graduate housing:* Rooms and/or apartments available to single and married students.

GRADUATE UNITS

Program in Business Administration Offers accounting (IMBA); finance (IMBA).

Program in Education Offers curriculum and teaching (M Ed); educational administration and supervision (MA); elementary education (M Ed); information and library service technology (M Ed). Electronic applications accepted.

INTER AMERICAN UNIVERSITY OF PUERTO RICO, BAYAMÓN CAMPUS, Bayamón, PR 00957

General Information Independent, coed, comprehensive institution. *Graduate housing:* On-campus housing not available.

GRADUATE UNITS

Graduate School *Degree program information:* Part-time and evening/weekend programs available.

INTER AMERICAN UNIVERSITY OF PUERTO RICO, GUAYAMA CAMPUS, Guayama, PR 00785

General Information Independent, coed, comprehensive institution.

GRADUATE UNITS

Department of Education and Social Sciences *Degree program information:* Part-time programs available. Offers early childhood education (MA); elementary education (MA). Electronic applications accepted.

INTER AMERICAN UNIVERSITY OF PUERTO RICO, METROPOLITAN CAMPUS, San Juan, PR 00919-1293

General Information Independent, coed, comprehensive institution. CGS member. *Graduate housing:* On-campus housing not available. *Research affiliation:* Innovation Technology (electronics).

GRADUATE UNITS

Graduate Programs *Degree program information:* Part-time and evening/weekend programs available. Offers accounting (MBA); administration of clinical laboratories (MS); advanced clinical services (MSW); advanced social work administration (MSW); Christian education (PhD); clinical services (MSW); criminal justice (MA); curriculum and instruction (Ed D); educational administration (Ed D); educational computing (MA); elementary education (MA); English (MA); environmental evaluation and protection (MS); finance (MBA); general business (MBA); higher education (MA); history (MA); human resources (MBA); industrial management (MBA); industrial/organizational psychology (MA, PhD); international business (MIB); labor relations (MA); management information systems (MBA); marketing (MBA); molecular microbiology (MS); music education (MM); occupational education (MA); open information systems (MS); pastoral theology (PhD); psychology (MA, PhD); school psychology (MA, PhD); social work administration (MSW); Spanish (MA); special education (MA); special education administration (Ed D); teaching English as a second language (MA); teaching of math (MA); teaching of physical education (MA); teaching of science (MA); theological studies (PhD); training and sport performance (MA). Electronic applications accepted.

INTER AMERICAN UNIVERSITY OF PUERTO RICO, PONCE CAMPUS, Mercedita, PR 00715-1602

General Information Independent, coed, comprehensive institution.

GRADUATE UNITS

Graduate School

INTER AMERICAN UNIVERSITY OF PUERTO RICO, SAN GERMÁN CAMPUS, San Germán, PR 00683-5008

General Information Independent, coed, university. *Graduate housing:* Room and/or apartments available on a first-come, first-served basis to single students; on-campus housing not available to married students. Housing application deadline: 6/15.

GRADUATE UNITS

Graduate Studies Center *Degree program information:* Part-time and evening/weekend programs available. Offers accounting (MBA); administration and supervision (MA, Ed D); applied mathematics (MA); art (MFA); business education (MA); ceramics (MFA); counseling psychology (MA, PhD); curriculum and instruction (Ed D); drawing (MFA); elementary education (MA); engraving (MFA); environmental biology (MS); environmental chemistry (MS); finance (MBA); financial accounting (M Acc); guidance and counseling (MA, Ed D); human

Inter American University of Puerto Rico, San Germán Campus (continued)

resources (MBA, PhD); industrial relations (MBA); international business (PhD); interregional and international business (PhD); labor relations (PhD); library and information sciences (MLS); management information systems (MBA); managerial accounting (M Acc); marketing (MBA); music education (MA); painting (MFA); photography (MFA); physical education and scientific analysis of human body movement (MA); quality organizational design (MBA); school psychology (MA, PhD); science education (MA); sculpture (MFA); special education (MA); teaching English as a second language (MA); water analysis (MS).

INTER AMERICAN UNIVERSITY OF PUERTO RICO SCHOOL OF LAW, San Juan, PR 00936-8351

General Information Independent, coed, graduate-only institution.

GRADUATE UNITS

Professional Program *Degree program information:* Part-time and evening/weekend programs available. Offers law (JD).

INTER AMERICAN UNIVERSITY OF PUERTO RICO SCHOOL OF OPTOMETRY, Bayam¾n, PR 00957

General Information Independent, coed, graduate-only institution. *Graduate housing:* Room and/or apartments available on a first-come, first-served basis to single students; on-campus housing not available to married students.

GRADUATE UNITS

Professional Program Offers optometry (OD). Electronic applications accepted.

INTERDENOMINATIONAL THEOLOGICAL CENTER, Atlanta, GA 30314-4112

General Information Independent-religious, coed, graduate-only institution. *Enrollment by degree level:* 399 first professional, 27 doctoral. *Graduate faculty:* 20 full-time (6 women), 33 part-time/adjunct (13 women). *Tuition:* Full-time $10,780; part-time $632 per credit. *Required fees:* $604; $632 per credit. *Graduate housing:* Rooms and/or apartments available on a first-come, first-served basis to single and married students. Typical cost: $4052 per year for single students; $4052 per year for married students. Housing application deadline: 8/1. *Student services:* Campus employment opportunities, campus safety program, exercise/wellness program, free psychological counseling, international student services, low-cost health insurance. *Library facilities:* Robert W. Woodruff Library. *Online resources:* library catalog, access to other libraries' catalogs. *Collection:* 353,745 titles, 1,739 serial subscriptions. *Research affiliation:* Atlanta University Center, Inc., Columbia Theological Seminary Library, Candler School of Theology Library, Emory University Library.

Computer facilities: 50 computers available on campus for general student use. A campuswide network can be accessed. Online class registration is available. *Web address:* http://www.itc.edu/.

General Application Contact: Walter Cabassa, Office of Admission and Recruitment, 404-527-7792, E-mail: wcabassa@itc.edu.

GRADUATE UNITS

Graduate and Professional Programs Students: 259 full-time (109 women), 167 part-time (71 women); includes 386 minority (384 African Americans, 2 Hispanic Americans), 17 international. Average age 40. 163 applicants, 83% accepted, 102 enrolled. *Faculty:* 20 full-time (6 women), 33 part-time/adjunct (13 women). Expenses: Contact institution. *Financial support:* In 2008–09, 375 students received support, including 4 research assistantships; career-related internships or fieldwork and Federal Work-Study also available. Support available to part-time students. Financial award application deadline: 6/15; financial award applicants required to submit FAFSA. In 2008, 80 first professional degrees, 4 master's, 5 doctorates awarded. *Degree program information:* Part-time and evening/weekend programs available. Postbaccalaureate distance learning degree programs offered (minimal on-campus study). Offers theology (M Div, MACE, MACM, D Min, Th D). *Application deadline:* For fall admission, 7/1 for domestic and international students; for spring admission, 11/3 for domestic and international students. Applications are processed on a rolling basis. *Application fee:* $50. *Application Contact:* Walter Cabassa, Office of Admission and Recruitment, 404-527-7792, E-mail: wcabassa@itc.edu. *President,* Dr. Michael A. Battle, 404-527-7702, Fax: 404-527-7770, E-mail: mbattle@itc.edu.

INTERNATIONAL BAPTIST COLLEGE, Chandler, AZ 85286

General Information Independent-religious, coed, comprehensive institution. *Graduate housing:* Room and/or apartments available on a first-come, first-served basis to single students; on-campus housing not available to married students.

GRADUATE UNITS

Program in Biblical Studies Offers Biblical studies (MA).

Program in Ministry Offers ministry (M Min, D Min).

INTERNATIONAL COLLEGE OF THE CAYMAN ISLANDS, Newlands, Grand Cayman, Cayman Islands

General Information Independent, coed, comprehensive institution. *Graduate housing:* Room and/or apartments available on a first-come, first-served basis to single students; on-campus housing not available to married students.

GRADUATE UNITS

Graduate Program in Management *Degree program information:* Part-time and evening/weekend programs available. Offers business administration (MBA); management (MS).

INTERNATIONAL TECHNOLOGICAL UNIVERSITY, Santa Clara, CA 95050

General Information Independent, coed, upper-level institution. *Research affiliation:* Linux Works, Inc. (software), @Channel (software), New Trends Technology, Inc. (hardware), Pico Turbo, Inc. (hardware).

GRADUATE UNITS

Program in Business Administration *Degree program information:* Part-time and evening/weekend programs available. Offers business administration (MBA).

Program in Computer Engineering Offers computer engineering (MSCE).

Program in Computer Science Offers computer science (MS).

Program in Digital Arts Offers digital arts (MA).

Program in Electrical Engineering *Degree program information:* Part-time and evening/weekend programs available. Offers electrical engineering (MSEE, PhD).

Program in Engineering Management Offers engineering management (MEM).

Program in Industrial Management Offers industrial management (MIM).

Program in Software Engineering Offers software engineering (MSSE, PhD).

INTERNATIONAL UNIVERSITY IN GENEVA, CH-1215 Geneva 15, Switzerland

General Information Private, coed, comprehensive institution. *Enrollment:* 44 full-time matriculated graduate/professional students (29 women). *Enrollment by degree level:* 44 master's. *Graduate faculty:* 9 full-time (2 women), 23 part-time/adjunct (11 women). *Graduate housing:* Room and/or apartments available on a first-come, first-served basis to single students; on-campus housing not available to married students. Housing application deadline: 7/31. *Student services:* Career counseling, exercise/wellness program, international student services, low-cost health insurance, writing training. *Library facilities:* IUG Library. *Online resources:* web page. *Collection:* 6,000 titles, 2,000 serial subscriptions.

Computer facilities: 30 computers available on campus for general student use. A campuswide network can be accessed from off campus. *Web address:* http://www.iun.ch/.

General Application Contact: Patrice Nuq, Dean for Student Affairs, 41-22710-7110, Fax: 41-22710-7111, E-mail: info@iun.ch.

GRADUATE UNITS

Master of Arts in Media and Communication Program Students: 7 full-time (all women); includes 1 Asian American or Pacific Islander, 1 Hispanic American. Average age 31. 30 applicants, 53% accepted, 7 enrolled. *Faculty:* 9 full-time (2 women), 23 part-time/adjunct (11 women). Expenses: Contact institution. In 2008, 1 master's awarded. Offers luxury management (MA); marketing (MA). *Application deadline:* For fall admission, 7/31 priority date for domestic students, 7/1 priority date for international students; for winter admission, 11/2 priority date for domestic students, 10/9 priority date for international students; for spring admission, 2/12 priority date for domestic students, 1/22 priority date for international students. Applications are processed on a rolling basis. *Application fee:* $150. Electronic applications accepted. *Application Contact:* Uliana Horler, Admissions Officer, 41-22710-7110, Fax: 41-22710-7111, E-mail: master@iun.ch. *Unit Coordinator,* Dr. Leonid Androuchko, 41-22710-7110, Fax: 41-22710-7111, E-mail: info@iun.ch.

Master of Business Administration Program Students: 8 full-time (5 women); includes 2 minority (1 Asian American or Pacific Islander, 1 Hispanic American), 6 international. Average age 31. 61 applicants, 26% accepted, 8 enrolled. *Faculty:* 9 full-time (2 women), 23 part-time/adjunct (11 women). Expenses: Contact institution. *Financial support:* In 2008–09, 5 students received support, including 5 research assistantships with full and partial tuition reimbursements available. Financial award application deadline: 6/28. In 2008, 1 master's awarded. *Degree program information:* Part-time and evening/weekend programs available. Offers finance (MBA); international business (MIB); investment management (MBA); luxury management (MBA); marketing (MBA); wealth management (MBA). *Application deadline:* For fall admission, 7/31 priority date for domestic students, 7/1 priority date for international students; for winter admission, 11/2 priority date for domestic students, 10/9 priority date for international students; for spring admission, 2/12 priority date for domestic students, 1/22 priority date for international students. Applications are processed on a rolling basis. *Application fee:* $150. Electronic applications accepted. *Application Contact:* Uliana Horler, Admissions Officer, 41-22710-7110, Fax: 41-22710-7111, E-mail: master@iun.ch. *Unit Coordinator,* Dr. Leonid Androuchko, 41-22710-7110, Fax: 41-22710-7111, E-mail: info@iun.ch.

THE INTERNATIONAL UNIVERSITY OF MONACO, MC-98000 Principality of Monaco, Monaco

General Information Independent, coed, comprehensive institution. *Graduate housing:* Rooms and/or apartments guaranteed to single and married students. *Research affiliation:* Alpstar (hedge funds).

GRADUATE UNITS

Graduate Programs *Degree program information:* Part-time programs available. Offers entrepreneurship (EMBA, MBA); financial engineering (M Sc); hedge fund and private equity (M Sc); international marketing (EMBA, MBA); international wealth management (M Sc); luxury goods and services (EMBA, M Sc, MBA); wealth and asset management (EMBA, MBA). Electronic applications accepted.

IONA COLLEGE, New Rochelle, NY 10801-1890

General Information Independent-religious, coed, comprehensive institution. *Enrollment:* 4,375 graduate, professional, and undergraduate students; 236 full-time matriculated graduate/professional students (158 women), 672 part-time matriculated graduate/professional students (380 women). *Enrollment by degree level:* 904 master's, 4 other advanced degrees. *Graduate faculty:* 117 full-time (42 women), 64 part-time/adjunct (28 women). *Tuition:* Part-time $755 per credit. *Required fees:* $175 per term. *Graduate housing:* On-campus housing not available. *Student services:* Campus employment opportunities, campus safety program, career counseling, exercise/wellness program, free psychological counseling, international student services, multicultural affairs office, services for students with disabilities. *Library facilities:* Ryan Library plus 2 others. *Online resources:* library catalog, web page, access to other libraries' catalogs. *Collection:* 282,761 titles, 744 serial subscriptions, 3,750 audiovisual materials. *Research affiliation:* IBM (teacher preparation).

Computer facilities: Computer purchase and lease plans are available. 625 computers available on campus for general student use. A campuswide network can be accessed from student residence rooms and from off campus. Online class registration is available. *Web address:* http://www.iona.edu/.

General Application Contact: Kevin Cavanagh, Assistant Vice President for College Admissions, 914-633-2120, Fax: 914-633-2642, E-mail: kcavanagh@iona.edu.

GRADUATE UNITS

Hagan School of Business Students: 79 full-time (41 women), 324 part-time (139 women); includes 55 minority (22 African Americans, 11 Asian Americans or Pacific Islanders, 22 Hispanic Americans), 13 international. Average age 30. 179 applicants, 73% accepted, 113 enrolled. *Faculty:* 23 full-time (6 women), 14 part-time/adjunct (3 women). Expenses: Contact institution. *Financial support:* Fellowships with tuition reimbursements, Federal Work-Study, scholarships/grants, tuition waivers (partial), and unspecified assistantships available. Support available to part-time students. Financial award application deadline: 4/15; financial award applicants required to submit FAFSA. In 2008, 102 master's, 47 other advanced degrees awarded. *Degree program information:* Part-time and evening/weekend programs available. Offers business (MBA, PMC); financial management (MBA, PMC); human resource management (MBA, PMC); information systems (MBA, PMC); international business (PMC); management (MBA, PMC); marketing (MBA). *Application deadline:* For fall admission, 8/15 priority date for domestic students, 8/1 for international students; for winter admission, 11/15 priority date for domestic students, 11/1 for international students; for spring admission, 2/15 priority date for domestic students, 2/1 for international students. Applications are processed on a rolling basis. *Application fee:* $50. Electronic applications accepted. *Application Contact:* Jude Fleurismond, Director of MBA Admissions, 914-633-2289, Fax: 914-637-2708, E-mail: jfleurismond@iona.edu. *Dean,* Dr. Vincent Calluzo, 914-633-2256, E-mail: vcalluzo@iona.edu.

School of Arts and Science Students: 157 full-time (117 women), 348 part-time (241 women); includes 86 minority (37 African Americans, 1 American Indian/Alaska Native, 10 Asian Americans or Pacific Islanders, 38 Hispanic Americans), 7 international. Average age 31. 311 applicants, 61% accepted, 101 enrolled. *Faculty:* 94 full-time (36 women), 50 part-time/adjunct (25 women). Expenses: Contact institution. *Financial support:* Career-related internships or fieldwork, tuition waivers (partial), and unspecified assistantships available. Support available to part-time students. Financial award application deadline: 4/15; financial award applicants required to submit FAFSA. In 2008, 153 master's, 4 other advanced degrees awarded. *Degree program information:* Part-time and evening/weekend programs available. Offers arts and science (MA, MS, MS Ed, MST, Certificate); biology education (MS Ed, MST); computer science (MS); criminal justice (MS); educational leadership (MS Ed); educational technology (MS, Certificate); English (MA); English education (MS Ed, MST); experimental psychology (MA); family counseling (MS, Certificate); health service administration (MS, Certificate); history (MA); industrial-organizational psychology (MA); Italian (MA); journalism (MS); literacy education (MS Ed, MST); mathematics education (MS Ed, MST); mental health counseling (MA); pastoral counseling (MS); psychology (MA); public relations (MA); school psychology (MA); social studies education (MS Ed, MST); Spanish (MA); Spanish education (MS Ed, MST); teaching in childhood education (MS Ed, MST); telecommunications (MS, Certificate). *Application deadline:* For fall admission, 8/1 priority date for domestic students, 5/1 priority date for international students; for winter admission, 12/1 priority date for domestic students, 8/1 priority date for international students; for spring admission, 1/1 priority date for domestic students, 9/1 priority date for international students. Applications are processed on a rolling basis. *Application fee:* $50. Electronic applications accepted. *Application Contact:* Veronica Jarek-Prinz, Director of Graduate Admissions, 914-633-2420, Fax: 914-633-2277,

E-mail: vjarekprinz@iona.edu. *Dean,* Dr. Brian J. Nickerson, 914-633-2112, Fax: 914-633-2023, E-mail: BNickerson@iona.edu.

See Close-Up on page 931.

IOWA STATE UNIVERSITY OF SCIENCE AND TECHNOLOGY, Ames, IA 50011

General Information State-supported, coed, university. CGS member. *Enrollment:* 26,856 graduate, professional, and undergraduate students; 2,524 full-time matriculated graduate/professional students (984 women), 1,628 part-time matriculated graduate/professional students (713 women). *Enrollment by degree level:* 2,036 master's, 2,047 doctoral, 69 other advanced degrees. *Graduate faculty:* 1,388 full-time (380 women), 182 part-time/adjunct (76 women). Tuition, state resident: full-time $6446; part-time $359 per credit. Tuition, nonresident: full-time $17,330; part-time $963 per credit. *Required fees:* $790; $249.25 per semester. Tuition and fees vary according to course load and program. *Graduate housing:* Rooms and/or apartments available on a first-come, first-served basis to single and married students. Typical cost: $3785 per year for single students; $4275 per year for married students. Room charges vary according to board plan, campus/location and housing facility selected. Housing application deadline: 6/15. *Student services:* Campus employment opportunities, campus safety program, career counseling, child daycare facilities, exercise/wellness program, free psychological counseling, international student services, low-cost health insurance, multicultural affairs office, services for students with disabilities, teacher training. *Library facilities:* University Library plus 1 other. *Online resources:* library catalog, web page, access to other libraries' catalogs. *Collection:* 2.5 million titles, 66,195 serial subscriptions. *Research affiliation:* National Veterinary Services Laboratories, National Animal Disease Center, National Soil Tilth Laboratory, North Central Regional Center for Rural Development, U.S. Department of Energy–Ames Laboratory.

Computer facilities: Computer purchase and lease plans are available. 2,400 computers available on campus for general student use. A campuswide network can be accessed from student residence rooms and from off campus. Online class registration, network services are available. *Web address:* http://www.iastate.edu/.

General Application Contact: Information Contact, 515-294-5836, Fax: 515-294-2592, E-mail: grad_admissions@iastate.edu.

GRADUATE UNITS

College of Veterinary Medicine Students: 544 full-time (404 women), 33 part-time (19 women); includes 15 minority (1 African American, 2 American Indian/Alaska Native, 3 Asian Americans or Pacific Islanders, 9 Hispanic Americans), 16 international. 67 applicants, 15% accepted, 9 enrolled. *Faculty:* 122 full-time (22 women), 24 part-time/adjunct (4 women). Expenses: Contact institution. *Financial support:* In 2008–09, 21 research assistantships with full and partial tuition reimbursements (averaging $15,003 per year), 4 teaching assistantships with full and partial tuition reimbursements (averaging $13,500 per year) were awarded; career-related internships or fieldwork, Federal Work-Study, institutionally sponsored loans, scholarships/grants, health care benefits, and unspecified assistantships also available. In 2008, 5 master's, 4 doctorates awarded. *Degree program information:* Part-time programs available. Offers biomedical sciences (MS, PhD); veterinary clinical sciences (MS); veterinary diagnostic and production animal medicine (MS); veterinary medicine (DVM, MS, PhD); veterinary microbiology (MS, PhD); veterinary microbiology and preventive medicine (MS, PhD); veterinary pathology (MS, PhD); veterinary preventative medicine (MS). Electronic applications accepted. *Application Contact:* Information Contact, 515-294-5836, Fax: 515-294-2592, E-mail: grad_admissions@iastate.edu. *Dean,* Dr. John Thomson, 515-294-1250.

Graduate College Students: 2,524 full-time (984 women), 1,628 part-time (713 women); includes 304 minority (133 African Americans, 15 American Indian/Alaska Native, 88 Asian Americans or Pacific Islanders, 68 Hispanic Americans), 1,455 international. 5,597 applicants, 32% accepted, 1169 enrolled. *Faculty:* 1,395 full-time (382 women), 182 part-time/adjunct (74 women). Expenses: Contact institution. *Financial support:* In 2008–09, 1,359 research assistantships with full and partial tuition reimbursements (averaging $17,100 per year), 690 teaching assistantships with full and partial tuition reimbursements (averaging $17,100 per year) were awarded; fellowships, career-related internships or fieldwork, Federal Work-Study, institutionally sponsored loans, scholarships/grants, traineeships, health care benefits, and unspecified assistantships also available. Support available to part-time students. In 2008, 789 master's, 308 doctorates awarded. *Degree program information:* Part-time and evening/weekend programs available. Postbaccalaureate distance learning degree programs offered (minimal on-campus study). Offers bioinformatics and computational biology (PhD); biorenewable resources and technology (MS, PhD); ecology and evolutionary biology (MS, PhD); environmental sciences (MS, PhD); genetics (MS, PhD); human-computer interaction (MS, PhD); immunobiology (MS, PhD); information assurance (MS); interdisciplinary graduate studies (MA, MS); interdisciplinary studies (MA, MBA, MS, PhD); microbiology (MS, PhD); molecular, cellular, and developmental biology (MS, PhD); neuroscience (MS, PhD); nutritional sciences (MS, PhD); plant biology (MS, PhD); sustainable agriculture (MS, PhD); toxicology (MS, PhD); transportation (MS). *Application deadline:* Applications are processed on a rolling basis. *Application fee:* $30 ($70 for international students). Electronic applications accepted. *Application Contact:* Information Contact, 515-294-5836, Fax: 515-294-2592, E-mail: grad_admissions@iastate.edu. *Associate Provost for Academic Progress and Dean of the Graduate College,* Dr. David K. Holger, 515-294-7184, E-mail: grad_admissions@iastate.edu.

College of Agriculture Students: 246 full-time (89 women), 201 part-time (69 women); includes 24 minority (9 African Americans, 3 American Indian/Alaska Native, 7 Asian Americans or Pacific Islanders, 5 Hispanic Americans), 118 international. 378 applicants, 37% accepted, 104 enrolled. *Faculty:* 299 full-time (143 women), 55 part-time/adjunct (38 women). Expenses: Contact institution. *Financial support:* In 2008–09, 224 research assistantships with full and partial tuition reimbursements (averaging $13,860 per year), 35 teaching assistantships with full and partial tuition reimbursements (averaging $15,030 per year) were awarded; fellowships, Federal Work-Study, scholarships/grants, health care benefits, and unspecified assistantships also available. Support available to part-time students. In 2008, 78 master's, 34 doctorates awarded. *Degree program information:* Part-time programs available. Postbaccalaureate distance learning degree programs offered (no on-campus study). Offers agricultural education and studies (MS, PhD); agricultural meteorology (MS, PhD); agriculture (M Ag, MS, PhD); agronomy (MS); animal breeding and genetics (MS, PhD); animal physiology (MS); animal psychology (PhD); animal science (MS, PhD); biochemistry (MS, PhD); biophysics (MS, PhD); crop production and physiology (MS, PhD); entomology (MS, PhD); forestry (MS, PhD); genetics (MS, PhD); horticulture (MS, PhD); industrial agriculture and technology (MS, PhD); meat science (MS, PhD); molecular, cellular, and developmental biology (MS, PhD); plant breeding (MS, PhD); plant pathology (MS, PhD); soil science (MS, PhD); toxicology (MS, PhD); wildlife ecology (MS). *Application deadline:* Applications are processed on a rolling basis. *Application fee:* $30 ($70 for international students). Electronic applications accepted. *Application Contact:* Information Contact, 515-294-5836, Fax: 515-294-2592, E-mail: grad_admissions@iastate.edu. *Dean,* Dr. Wendy Wintersteen, 515-294-2518, Fax: 515-294-6800.

College of Business Students: 84 full-time (45 women), 190 part-time (80 women); includes 18 minority (6 African Americans, 9 Asian Americans or Pacific Islanders, 3 Hispanic Americans), 69 international. 230 applicants, 58% accepted, 97 enrolled. *Faculty:* 62 full-time (13 women), 5 part-time/adjunct (1 woman). Expenses: Contact institution. *Financial support:* In 2008–09, 49 research assistantships with full and partial tuition reimbursements (averaging $13,680 per year), 1 teaching assistantship with full and partial tuition reimbursement (averaging $12,240 per year) were awarded; scholarships/grants, health care benefits, and unspecified assistantships also available. In 2008, 126 master's awarded. Offers accounting (M Acc); business (M Acc, MBA, MS); business administration (MBA, MS); information systems (MS). *Application fee:* $30 ($70 for international students). Electronic applications accepted. *Application Contact:* Dr. Labh S Hira, Dean, 515-294-2422, E-mail: busgrad@iastate.edu. *Dean,* Dr. Labh S Hira, 515-294-2422, E-mail: busgrad@iastate.edu.

College of Design Students: 75 full-time (45 women), 45 part-time (26 women); includes 8 minority (4 African Americans, 1 Asian American or Pacific Islander, 3 Hispanic Americans), 27 international. Average age 32. 139 applicants, 55% accepted, 52 enrolled. *Faculty:* 73 full-time (62 women), 15 part-time/adjunct (13 women). Expenses: Contact institution. *Financial support:* In 2008–09, 36 research assistantships with full and partial tuition reimbursements (averaging $14,130 per year), 33 teaching assistantships with full and partial tuition reimbursements (averaging $14,130 per year) were awarded; career-related internships or fieldwork, Federal Work-Study, institutionally sponsored loans, tuition waivers (partial), and unspecified assistantships also available. Support available to part-time students. Financial award applicants required to submit FAFSA. In 2008, 47 master's awarded. *Degree program information:* Part-time programs available. Offers architectural studies (MSAS); architecture (M Arch); art and design (MA); community and regional planning (MCRP); design (M Arch, MA, MCRP, MFA, MLA, MS, MSAS); graphic design (MFA); integrated visual arts (MFA); interior design (MFA); landscape architecture (MLA); transportation (MS). *Application deadline:* Applications are processed on a rolling basis. *Application fee:* $30 ($70 for international students). Electronic applications accepted. *Application Contact:* Mark Engelbrecht, Dean, 515-294-7427, Fax: 515-294-9755, E-mail: mengelbr@iastate.edu. *Dean,* Mark Engelbrecht, 515-294-7427, Fax: 515-294-9755, E-mail: mengelbr@iastate.edu.

College of Engineering Students: 577 full-time (99 women), 221 part-time (32 women); includes 40 minority (7 African Americans, 3 American Indian/Alaska Native, 20 Asian Americans or Pacific Islanders, 10 Hispanic Americans), 442 international. 2,048 applicants, 16% accepted, 190 enrolled. *Faculty:* 198 full-time (73 women), 23 part-time/adjunct (7 women). Expenses: Contact institution. *Financial support:* In 2008–09, 459 research assistantships with full and partial tuition reimbursements (averaging $13,500 per year), 110 teaching assistantships with full and partial tuition reimbursements (averaging $13,500 per year) were awarded; fellowships, Federal Work-Study, scholarships/grants, health care benefits, and unspecified assistantships also available. Support available to part-time students. In 2008, 144 master's, 69 doctorates awarded. *Degree program information:* Part-time programs available. Offers aerospace engineering (M Eng, MS, PhD); agricultural and biosystems engineering (M Eng, MS, PhD); chemical and biological engineering (M Eng, MS, PhD); civil engineering (MS, PhD); computer engineering (M Eng, MS, PhD); electrical engineering (M Eng, MS, PhD); engineering (M Eng, MS, PhD); engineering mechanics (M Eng, MS, PhD); industrial engineering (M Eng, MS, PhD); materials science and engineering (MS, PhD); mechanical engineering (MS, PhD); mechanical engineering (coursework only) (M Eng); operations research (MS); systems engineering (M Eng). *Application fee:* $30 ($70 for international students). Electronic applications accepted. *Application Contact:* Dr. Jonathan Wickert, Dean, 515-294-9988. *Dean,* Dr. Jonathan Wickert, 515-294-9988.

College of Human Sciences Students: 280 full-time (193 women), 407 part-time (268 women); includes 79 minority (46 African Americans, 4 American Indian/Alaska Native, 10 Asian Americans or Pacific Islanders, 19 Hispanic Americans), 77 international. 337 applicants, 68% accepted, 161 enrolled. *Faculty:* 138 full-time (51 women), 14 part-time/adjunct (3 women). Expenses: Contact institution. *Financial support:* In 2008–09, 199 research assistantships with full and partial tuition reimbursements (averaging $13,392 per year), 56 teaching assistantships with full and partial tuition reimbursements (averaging $13,392 per year) were awarded; fellowships, career-related internships or fieldwork, Federal Work-Study, scholarships/grants, health care benefits, and unspecified assistantships also available. Support available to part-time students. In 2008, 152 master's, 66 doctorates awarded. *Degree program information:* Part-time programs available. Offers counselor education (M Ed, MS); curriculum and instructional technology (M Ed, MS, PhD); educational administration (M Ed, MS); educational leadership (PhD); elementary education (M Ed, MS); family and consumer sciences (MFCS); family and consumer sciences education and studies (M Ed, MS, PhD); food science and technology (MS, PhD); foodservice and lodging management (MFCS, MS, PhD); higher education (M Ed, MS); historical, philosophical, and comparative studies in education (M Ed, MS); human development and family studies (MFCS, MS, PhD); human sciences (M Ed, MFCS, MS, PhD); kinesiology (MS, PhD); nutrition (MS, PhD); organizational learning and human resource development (M Ed, MS); research and evaluation (MS); special education (M Ed, MS); textiles and clothing (MFCS, MS, PhD). *Application fee:* $30 ($70 for international students). Electronic applications accepted. *Application Contact:* Information Contact, 515-294-5836, Fax: 515-294-2592, E-mail: grad_admissions@iastate.edu. *Dean,* Dr. Pamela White, 515-294-7000.

College of Liberal Arts and Sciences Students: 789 full-time (304 women), 272 part-time (128 women); includes 61 minority (27 African Americans, 2 American Indian/Alaska Native, 21 Asian Americans or Pacific Islanders, 11 Hispanic Americans), 480 international. 163,741 applicants, 0% accepted, 248 enrolled. *Faculty:* 503 full-time (18 women), 40 part-time/adjunct (4 women). Expenses: Contact institution. *Financial support:* In 2008–09, 371 research assistantships with full and partial tuition reimbursements (averaging $17,100 per year), 450 teaching assistantships with full and partial tuition reimbursements (averaging $17,100 per year) were awarded; fellowships, Federal Work-Study, institutionally sponsored loans, scholarships/grants, health care benefits, and unspecified assistantships also available. Support available to part-time students. In 2008, 144 master's, 76 doctorates awarded. *Degree program information:* Part-time programs available. Offers agricultural economics (MS, PhD); agricultural history and rural studies (PhD); anthropology (MA); applied mathematics (MS, PhD); applied physics (MS, PhD); astrophysics (MS, PhD); chemistry (MS, PhD); cognitive psychology (PhD); computer science (MS, PhD); condensed matter physics (MS, PhD); counseling psychology (PhD); earth science (MS, PhD); ecology, evolution, and organismal biology (MS, PhD); economics (MS, PhD); English (MA); environmental science (MS, PhD); genetics, developmental and cell biology (MS, PhD); geology (MS, PhD); high energy physics (MS, PhD); history (MA); history of technology and science (MA, PhD); journalism and mass communication (MS); liberal arts and sciences (MA, MPA, MS, MSM, PhD); mathematics (MS, PhD); meteorology (MS, PhD); nuclear physics (MS, PhD); physics (MS, PhD); political science (MA); public administration (MPA); rhetoric and professional communication (PhD); rural sociology (MS, PhD); school mathematics (MSM); social psychology (PhD); sociology (MS, PhD); statistics (MS, PhD). *Application fee:* $30 ($70 for international students). Electronic applications accepted. *Application Contact:* Information Contact, 515-294-5836, Fax: 515-294-2592, E-mail: grad_admissions@iastate.edu. *Dean,* Dr. Michael Whiteford, 515-294-3220, Fax: 515-294-1303.

ITHACA COLLEGE, Ithaca, NY 14850-7020

General Information Independent, coed, comprehensive institution. CGS member. *Enrollment:* 6,448 graduate, professional, and undergraduate students; 372 full-time matriculated graduate/professional students (268 women), 32 part-time matriculated graduate/professional students (21 women). *Enrollment by degree level:* 346 master's, 58 doctoral. *Graduate faculty:* 149 full-time (64 women), 10 part-time/adjunct (8 women). *Tuition:* Full-time $18,090; part-time $603 per hour. *Graduate housing:* On-campus housing not available. *Student services:* Campus employment opportunities, campus safety program, career counseling, exercise/wellness program, free psychological counseling, international student services, low-cost health insurance, multicultural affairs office, services for students with disabilities, writing training. *Library facilities:* Ithaca College Library. *Online resources:* library catalog, web page, access to other libraries' catalogs. *Collection:* 366,970 titles, 28,314 serial subscriptions, 32,270 audiovisual materials. *Research affiliation:* Foundation for HSBC Environmental Education (Environmental Science), National Science Foundation (Physics), National Science Foundation (Computer Science), Department of Health and Human Services, National Institutes of Health (Physical Therapy), National Aeronautics and Space Administration (Astronomy).

Computer facilities: Computer purchase and lease plans are available. 640 computers available on campus for general student use. A campuswide network can be accessed from student residence rooms and from off campus. Online class registration is available. *Web address:* http://www.ithaca.edu/.

General Application Contact: Rob Gearhart, Interim Dean, Graduate and Professional Studies, 607-274-3527, Fax: 607-274-1263, E-mail: gps@ithaca.edu.

GRADUATE UNITS

Division of Graduate and Professional Studies Students: 372 full-time (268 women), 32 part-time (21 women); includes 20 minority (3 African Americans, 1 American Indian/Alaska Native, 6 Asian Americans or Pacific Islanders, 10 Hispanic Americans), 32 international.

Ithaca College (continued)

Average age 24. 553 applicants, 52% accepted, 256 enrolled. *Faculty:* 149 full-time (64 women), 10 part-time/adjunct (8 women). Expenses: Contact institution. *Financial support:* In 2008–09, 346 students received support, including 6 fellowships (averaging $4,661 per year), 139 teaching assistantships (averaging $8,950 per year); career-related internships or fieldwork, Federal Work-Study, scholarships/grants, and unspecified assistantships also available. Support available to part-time students. Financial award applicants required to submit FAFSA. In 2008, 246 master's awarded. *Degree program information:* Part-time programs available. *Application deadline:* Applications are processed on a rolling basis. *Application fee:* $40. Electronic applications accepted. *Application Contact:* Rob Gearhart, Interim Dean, Graduate and Professional Studies, 607-274-3527, Fax: 607-274-1263, E-mail: gps@ithaca.edu. *Interim Dean, Graduate and Professional Studies*, Rob Gearhart, 607-274-3527, Fax: 607-274-1263, E-mail: gps@ithaca.edu.

Roy H. Park School of Communications Students: 22 full-time (16 women), 10 part-time (7 women); includes 1 minority (African American), 8 international. Average age 28. 39 applicants, 74% accepted, 16 enrolled. *Faculty:* 6 full-time (1 woman). Expenses: Contact institution. *Financial support:* In 2008–09, 27 students received support, including 18 teaching assistantships (averaging $7,360 per year); career-related internships or fieldwork, Federal Work-Study, scholarships/grants, and unspecified assistantships also available. Support available to part-time students. Financial award application deadline: 3/1; financial award applicants required to submit FAFSA. In 2008, 20 master's awarded. *Degree program information:* Part-time programs available. Offers communications (MS). *Application deadline:* For fall admission, 7/5 for domestic and international students; for spring admission, 12/1 for domestic and international students. Applications are processed on a rolling basis. *Application fee:* $40. Electronic applications accepted. *Application Contact:* Rob Gearhart, Interim Dean, Graduate and Professional Studies, 607-274-3527, Fax: 607-274-1263, E-mail: gps@ithaca.edu. *Interim Dean, Roy H. Park School of Communications*, Dr. Diane Gayeski, 607-274-1021.

School of Business Students: 27 full-time (10 women), 2 part-time (1 woman); includes 2 minority (1 Asian American or Pacific Islander, 1 Hispanic American), 4 international. Average age 25. 58 applicants, 62% accepted, 25 enrolled. *Faculty:* 20 full-time (5 women). Expenses: Contact institution. *Financial support:* In 2008–09, 22 students received support, including 6 fellowships (averaging $4,661 per year); career-related internships or fieldwork, Federal Work-Study, and scholarships/grants also available. Support available to part-time students. Financial award application deadline: 4/15; financial award applicants required to submit FAFSA. In 2008, 21 master's awarded. *Degree program information:* Part-time programs available. Offers accountancy (MBA); business (MBA); business administration (MBA). *Application deadline:* For fall admission, 8/1 for domestic and international students; for spring admission, 12/1 for domestic and international students. Applications are processed on a rolling basis. *Application fee:* $40. Electronic applications accepted. *Application Contact:* Rob Gearhart, Interim Dean, Graduate and Professional Studies, 607-274-3527, Fax: 607-274-1263, E-mail: gps@ithaca.edu. *Interim Dean, School of Business*, Dr. Mark Cordano, 607-274-3117.

School of Health Sciences and Human Performance Students: 262 full-time (204 women), 18 part-time (12 women); includes 14 minority (1 African American, 1 American Indian/Alaska Native, 4 Asian Americans or Pacific Islanders, 8 Hispanic Americans), 19 international. Average age 23. *Faculty:* 46 full-time (28 women), 4 part-time/adjunct (all women). Expenses: Contact institution. *Financial support:* In 2008–09, 236 students received support, including 65 teaching assistantships (averaging $9,679 per year); career-related internships or fieldwork, Federal Work-Study, scholarships/grants, and unspecified assistantships also available. Support available to part-time students. Financial award applicants required to submit FAFSA. In 2008, 163 master's awarded. *Degree program information:* Part-time programs available. Offers exercise and sport sciences (MS); health education (MS); health sciences and human performance (MS, DPT); occupational therapy (MS); physical education (MS); physical therapy (MS, DPT); speech pathology (MS); sport management (MS); teacher of students with speech and language disabilities (MS). *Application fee:* $40. *Application Contact:* Rob Gearhart, Interim Dean, Graduate and Professional Studies, 607-274-3527, Fax: 607-274-1263, E-mail: gps@ithaca.edu. *Dean, School of Health Sciences and Human Performance*, Dr. Steven Siconolfi, 607-274-3237, Fax: 607-274-1263, E-mail: gps@ithaca.edu.

School of Humanities and Sciences Students: 26 full-time (17 women), 1 (woman) part-time; includes 2 minority (1 African American, 1 Asian American or Pacific Islander). Average age 24. 51 applicants, 55% accepted, 26 enrolled. *Faculty:* 19 full-time (8 women). Expenses: Contact institution. *Financial support:* In 2008–09, 27 students received support, including 24 teaching assistantships (averaging $7,231 per year); career-related internships or fieldwork, Federal Work-Study, scholarships/grants, and unspecified assistantships also available. Support available to part-time students. Financial award applicants required to submit FAFSA. In 2008, 29 master's awarded. *Degree program information:* Part-time programs available. Offers biology 7-12 (MAT); chemistry 7-12 (MAT); childhood education (MS); English 7-12 (MAT); French 7-12 (MAT); humanities and sciences (MAT, MS); math 7-12 (MAT); physics 7-12 (MAT); social studies 7-12 (MAT); Spanish (MAT). *Application deadline:* For fall admission, 5/15 for domestic and international students; for spring admission, 12/1 for domestic and international students. Applications are processed on a rolling basis. *Application fee:* $40. Electronic applications accepted. *Application Contact:* Rob Gearhart, Interim Dean, Graduate and Professional Studies, 607-274-3527, Fax: 607-274-1263, E-mail: gps@ithaca.edu. *Dean, School of Humanities and Sciences*, Dr. Leslie Lewis, 607-274-3533.

School of Music Students: 35 full-time (21 women), 1 part-time (0 women); includes 1 minority (Hispanic American), 1 international. Average age 24. 109 applicants, 28% accepted, 21 enrolled. *Faculty:* 58 full-time (22 women), 6 part-time/adjunct (4 women). Expenses: Contact institution. *Financial support:* In 2008–09, 34 students received support, including 32 teaching assistantships (averaging $9,653 per year); career-related internships or fieldwork, Federal Work-Study, scholarships/grants, and unspecified assistantships also available. Support available to part-time students. Financial award application deadline: 4/1; financial award applicants required to submit FAFSA. In 2008, 33 master's awarded. *Degree program information:* Part-time programs available. Offers composition (MM); conducting (MM); music (MM, MS); music education (MM, MS); performance (MM); Suzuki pedagogy (MM). *Application deadline:* For fall admission, 3/1 for domestic and international students; for spring admission, 12/1 for domestic and international students. Applications are processed on a rolling basis. *Application fee:* $40. Electronic applications accepted. *Application Contact:* Rob Gearhart, Interim Dean, Graduate and Professional Studies, 607-274-3527, Fax: 607-274-1263, E-mail: gps@ithaca.edu. *Dean*, Dr. Gregory Woodward, 607-274-3343.

See Close-Up on page 933.

ITT TECHNICAL INSTITUTE, Indianapolis, IN 46268-1119

General Information Proprietary, coed.

GRADUATE UNITS

Online MBA Program Offers business (MBA).

JACKSON STATE UNIVERSITY, Jackson, MS 39217

General Information State-supported, coed, university. CGS member. *Graduate housing:* Room and/or apartments available on a first-come, first-served basis to single students; on-campus housing not available to married students. Housing application deadline: 7/15. *Research affiliation:* Lawrence A. Berkeley Laboratories (biology, chemistry), U.S. Department of Energy (biology), National Science Foundation (biology, chemistry), U.S. Environmental Protection Agency, Oak Ridge Associated Universities (science), Raytheon Systems Company (computer science).

GRADUATE UNITS

Graduate School *Degree program information:* Part-time and evening/weekend programs available. Postbaccalaureate distance learning degree programs offered (minimal on-campus study).

College of Public Service Offers communicative disorders (MS); public service (MS).

School of Business *Degree program information:* Part-time and evening/weekend programs available. Offers accounting (MPA); business (MBA, MPA, PhD); business administration (MBA).

School of Education *Degree program information:* Part-time and evening/weekend programs available. Offers community and agency counseling (MS); early childhood education (MS Ed, Ed D); education (MS, MS Ed, Ed D, PhD, Ed S); education administration (Ed S); educational administration (MS Ed, PhD); elementary education (MS Ed, Ed S); guidance and counseling (MS, MS Ed, Ed S); health, physical education and recreation (MS Ed); rehabilitative counseling (MS Ed); rehabilitative counseling service (MS Ed); secondary education (MS Ed, Ed S); special education (MS Ed, Ed S).

School of Liberal Arts *Degree program information:* Part-time and evening/weekend programs available. Offers clinical psychology (PhD); criminology and justice service (MA); English (MA); history (MA); liberal arts (MA, MAT, MM Ed, MPPA, MS, PhD); mass communications (MS); music education (MM Ed); political science (MA); public policy and administration (MPPA, PhD); sociology (MA); teaching English (MAT); urban and regional planning (MS).

School of Science and Technology *Degree program information:* Part-time and evening/weekend programs available. Offers biology education (MST); chemistry (MS, PhD); computer science (MS); environmental science (MS, PhD); hazardous materials management (MS); industrial arts education (MS Ed); mathematics (MS); mathematics education (MST); science and technology (MS, MS Ed, MST, PhD); science education (MST).

School of Social Work *Degree program information:* Evening/weekend programs available. Offers social work (MSW, PhD).

JACKSONVILLE STATE UNIVERSITY, Jacksonville, AL 36265-1602

General Information State-supported, coed, comprehensive institution. *Enrollment:* 9,481 graduate, professional, and undergraduate students; 308 full-time matriculated graduate/professional students (210 women), 1,255 part-time matriculated graduate/professional students (767 women). *Enrollment by degree level:* 1,273 master's, 290 other advanced degrees. *Graduate faculty:* 125 full-time (45 women), 5 part-time/adjunct (0 women). Tuition, state resident: full-time $4560; part-time $225 per credit hour. Tuition, nonresident: full-time $9120; part-time $450 per credit hour. *Graduate housing:* Rooms and/or apartments available on a first-come, first-served basis to single and married students. Typical cost: $4215 (including board) for single students; $4215 (including board) for married students. Room and board charges vary according to board plan and housing facility selected. *Student services:* Campus employment opportunities, campus safety program, career counseling, child daycare facilities, exercise/wellness program, free psychological counseling, international student services, multicultural affairs office, services for students with disabilities. *Library facilities:* Houston Cole Library. *Online resources:* library catalog, web page, access to other libraries' catalogs. *Collection:* 685,991 titles, 14,376 serial subscriptions.

Computer facilities: 330 computers available on campus for general student use. A campuswide network can be accessed from student residence rooms and from off campus. *Web address:* http://www.jsu.edu/.

General Application Contact: Dr. William D. Carr, Dean of the College of Graduate Studies and Continuing Education, 256-782-5329, Fax: 256-782-5321, E-mail: graduate@jsu.edu.

GRADUATE UNITS

College of Graduate Studies and Continuing Education Students: 308 full-time (210 women), 1,255 part-time (767 women); includes 357 minority (336 African Americans, 5 American Indian/Alaska Native, 5 Asian Americans or Pacific Islanders, 11 Hispanic Americans), 41 international. Average age 33. 858 applicants, 43% accepted, 312 enrolled. *Faculty:* 125 full-time (45 women), 5 part-time/adjunct (0 women). Expenses: Contact institution. *Financial support:* In 2008–09, 1,171 students received support. Available to part-time students. Application deadline: 4/1. In 2008, 438 master's, 155 other advanced degrees awarded. *Degree program information:* Part-time and evening/weekend programs available. *Application deadline:* Applications are processed on a rolling basis. *Application fee:* $30. *Application Contact:* Dr. Jean Pugliese, Associate Dean, 256-782-8278, Fax: 256-782-5321, E-mail: pugliese@jsu.edu. *Dean*, Dr. William D. Carr, 256-782-5329, Fax: 256-782-5321, E-mail: bcarr@jsu.edu.

College of Arts and Sciences Students: 99 full-time (57 women), 418 part-time (179 women); includes 146 minority (134 African Americans, 1 American Indian/Alaska Native, 2 Asian Americans or Pacific Islanders, 9 Hispanic Americans), 22 international. Average age 33. 292 applicants, 53% accepted, 138 enrolled. *Faculty:* 78 full-time (19 women), 1 part-time/adjunct (0 women). Expenses: Contact institution. *Financial support:* In 2008–09, 330 students received support. Available to part-time students. Application deadline: 4/1. In 2008, 136 master's awarded. *Degree program information:* Part-time and evening/weekend programs available. Offers arts and sciences (MA, MPA, MS); biology (MS); computer systems and software design (MS); criminal justice (MS); emergency management (MS); English (MA); history (MA); liberal studies (MA); mathematics (MS); music (MA); political science (MPA); psychology (MS). *Application deadline:* Applications are processed on a rolling basis. *Application fee:* $30. *Application Contact:* Dr. Jean Pugliese, Associate Dean, 256-782-8278, Fax: 256-782-5321, E-mail: pugliese@jsu.edu. *Dean*, Dr. Earl Wade, 256-782-5649.

College of Commerce and Business Administration Students: 12 full-time (10 women), 57 part-time (32 women); includes 18 minority (16 African Americans, 2 Asian Americans or Pacific Islanders), 5 international. Average age 29. 62 applicants, 24% accepted, 11 enrolled. *Faculty:* 9 full-time (3 women). Expenses: Contact institution. *Financial support:* In 2008–09, 49 students received support. Available to part-time students. Application deadline: 4/1. In 2008, 17 master's awarded. *Degree program information:* Part-time and evening/weekend programs available. Offers commerce and business administration (MBA). *Application deadline:* Applications are processed on a rolling basis. *Application fee:* $30. Electronic applications accepted. *Application Contact:* Dr. Jean Pugliese, Associate Dean, 256-782-8278, Fax: 256-782-5321, E-mail: pugliese@jsu.edu. *Dean*, Dr. William Fielding, 256-782-5508.

College of Education and Professional Studies Students: 193 full-time (141 women), 659 part-time (457 women); includes 177 minority (174 African Americans, 1 Asian American or Pacific Islander, 2 Hispanic Americans), 10 international. Average age 33. 412 applicants, 33% accepted, 118 enrolled. *Faculty:* 36 full-time (21 women), 4 part-time/adjunct (0 women). Expenses: Contact institution. *Financial support:* In 2008–09, 511 students received support. Available to part-time students. Application deadline: 4/1. In 2008, 273 master's, 144 other advanced degrees awarded. *Degree program information:* Part-time and evening/weekend programs available. Offers early childhood education (MS Ed); education (Ed S); education and professional studies (MS, MS Ed, Ed S); educational administration (MS Ed, Ed S); elementary education (MS Ed); guidance and counseling (MS); health and physical education (MS Ed); instructional media (MS Ed); reading specialist (MS Ed); secondary education (MS Ed); special education (MS Ed). *Application deadline:* Applications are processed on a rolling basis. *Application fee:* $30. Electronic applications accepted. *Application Contact:* Dr. Jean Pugliese, Associate Dean, 256-782-8278, Fax: 256-782-5321, E-mail: pugliese@jsu.edu. *Dean*, Dr. John Hammett, 256-782-8212, E-mail: jhammett@jsu.edu.

College of Nursing Students: 1 (woman) full-time, 64 part-time (56 women); includes 10 minority (all African Americans), 1 international. Average age 38. 34 applicants, 47% accepted, 13 enrolled. *Faculty:* 2 full-time (both women). Expenses: Contact institution. *Financial support:* In 2008–09, 36 students received support. Available to part-time students. Application deadline: 4/1. In 2008, 15 master's awarded. *Degree program information:* Part-time and evening/weekend programs available. Offers nursing (MSN). *Application deadline:* Applications are processed on a rolling basis. *Application fee:* $30. Electronic applications accepted. *Application Contact:* Dr. Jean Pugliese, Associate Dean, 256-782-8278, Fax: 256-782-5321, E-mail: pugliese@jsu.edu. *Dean*, Dr. Sarah Latham, 256-782-5431.

JACKSONVILLE UNIVERSITY, Jacksonville, FL 32211-3394

General Information Independent, coed, comprehensive institution. *Graduate housing:* Room and/or apartments available on a first-come, first-served basis to single students; on-campus housing not available to married students. Housing application deadline: 8/1.

GRADUATE UNITS

College of Arts and Sciences *Degree program information:* Part-time and evening/weekend programs available. Offers arts and sciences (MAT, MSN, Certificate).

School of Education *Degree program information:* Part-time and evening/weekend programs available. Offers computer sciences (MAT); early childhood education (Certificate); elementary education (MAT); integrated learning with educational technology (MAT); mathematics education (MAT); music education (MAT); reading education (MAT); second career as a teacher (Certificate); second careers as a teacher (Certificate).

School of Nursing *Degree program information:* Part-time programs available. Offers nursing (MSN).

School of Orthodontics Offers orthodontics (Certificate).

Davis College of Business *Degree program information:* Part-time and evening/weekend programs available. Offers business (Exec MBA, MBA); business administration (Exec MBA, MBA).

JAMES MADISON UNIVERSITY, Harrisonburg, VA 22807

General Information State-supported, coed, comprehensive institution. CGS member. *Enrollment:* 18,454 graduate, professional, and undergraduate students; 887 full-time matriculated graduate/professional students (647 women), 354 part-time matriculated graduate/professional students (181 women). *Enrollment by degree level:* 1,124 master's, 88 doctoral, 29 other advanced degrees. *Graduate faculty:* 243 full-time (116 women), 72 part-time/adjunct (42 women). Tuition, state resident: full-time $7008; part-time $292 per credit hour. Tuition, nonresident: full-time $20,352; part-time $848 per credit hour. *Graduate housing:* Room and/or apartments available on a first-come, first-served basis to single students; on-campus housing not available to married students. Typical cost: $4888 per year. Housing application deadline: 5/1. *Student services:* Campus employment opportunities, campus safety program, career counseling, free psychological counseling, international student services, multicultural affairs office, services for students with disabilities, teacher training. *Library facilities:* Carrier Library plus 2 others. *Online resources:* library catalog, web page. *Collection:* 788,639 titles, 17,078 serial subscriptions, 41,478 audiovisual materials. *Research affiliation:* National Institute of Standards & Technology through George Mason University (network risk assessment), National Science Foundation (Step Ahead STEM Majors), National Oceanic & Atmospheric Administration (applied metrological research), National Science Foundation (quantitative skills in biology), National Science Foundation (development of a detector array for Compton Scattering using polarized beams and targets).

Computer facilities: Computer purchase and lease plans are available. 600 computers available on campus for general student use. A campuswide network can be accessed from student residence rooms and from off campus. Online class registration is available. *Web address:* http://www.jmu.edu/.

General Application Contact: Dr. Reid Linn, Dean, The Graduate School, 540-568-6131, Fax: 540-568-7860, E-mail: grad_programs@jmu.edu.

GRADUATE UNITS

The Graduate School Students: 887 full-time (647 women), 354 part-time (181 women); includes 102 minority (49 African Americans, 4 American Indian/Alaska Native, 35 Asian Americans or Pacific Islanders, 14 Hispanic Americans), 32 international. Average age 27. 1,147 applicants, 45% accepted, 299 enrolled. *Faculty:* 243 full-time (116 women), 72 part-time/adjunct (42 women). Expenses: Contact institution. *Financial support:* In 2008–09, 351 students received support, including 32 teaching assistantships with full tuition reimbursements available (averaging $8,664 per year); career-related internships or fieldwork, Federal Work-Study, and 19 athletic assistantships ($8664), 5 service assistantships ($7,382), 258 graduate assistantships ($7,382), 47 doctoral assistantships ($14,500) also available. Financial award application deadline: 3/1; financial award applicants required to submit FAFSA. In 2008, 601 master's, 13 doctorates, 25 other advanced degrees awarded. *Degree program information:* Part-time and evening/weekend programs available. Postbaccalaureate distance learning degree programs offered (no on-campus study). *Application deadline:* For fall admission, 5/1 priority date for domestic students, 5/1 for international students; for spring admission, 9/1 priority date for domestic students, 9/1 for international students. Applications are processed on a rolling basis. *Application fee:* $55. Electronic applications accepted. *Application Contact:* Lynette M. Bible, Director of Graduate Admissions, 540-568-6395, Fax: 540-568-7860, E-mail: biblelm@jmu.edu. *Dean,* Dr. Reid Linn, 540-568-6131, Fax: 540-568-7860, E-mail: grad_programs@jmu.edu.

College of Arts and Letters Students: 79 full-time (43 women), 52 part-time (31 women); includes 9 minority (4 African Americans, 3 Asian Americans or Pacific Islanders, 2 Hispanic Americans), 1 international. Average age 27. *Faculty:* 37 full-time (13 women), 6 part-time/adjunct (2 women). Expenses: Contact institution. *Financial support:* In 2008–09, 38 students received support, including 10 teaching assistantships with full tuition reimbursements available (averaging $8,664 per year); Federal Work-Study, unspecified assistantships, and 27 assistantships ($7,382), 1 service assistant ($7,382) also available. Financial award application deadline: 3/1; financial award applicants required to submit FAFSA. In 2008, 36 master's awarded. *Degree program information:* Part-time programs available. Offers arts and letters (MA, MPA, MS); English (MA); history (MA); political science (MA, MPA); public administration (MPA); writing, rhetoric, and technical communication (MA, MS). *Application deadline:* For fall admission, 5/1 priority date for domestic students; for spring admission, 9/1 priority date for domestic students. Applications are processed on a rolling basis. *Application fee:* $55. Electronic applications accepted. *Application Contact:* Lynette M. Bible, Director of Graduate Admissions, 540-568-6395, Fax: 540-568-7860, E-mail: biblelm@jmu.edu. *Dean,* Dr. David K. Jeffrey, 540-568-6334.

College of Business Students: 72 full-time (25 women), 63 part-time (19 women); includes 14 minority (2 African Americans, 1 American Indian/Alaska Native, 10 Asian Americans or Pacific Islanders, 1 Hispanic American), 8 international. Average age 27. *Faculty:* 19 full-time (5 women). Expenses: Contact institution. *Financial support:* In 2008–09, 25 students received support. Federal Work-Study and 22 graduate assistantships ($7,382) available. Financial award application deadline: 3/1; financial award applicants required to submit FAFSA. In 2008, 110 master's awarded. *Degree program information:* Part-time and evening/weekend programs available. Postbaccalaureate distance learning degree programs offered (no on-campus study). Offers accounting (MS); business (MBA, MS); business administration (MBA). *Application deadline:* For fall admission, 5/1 priority date for domestic students, 5/1 for international students; for spring admission, 9/1 priority date for domestic students, 9/1 for international students. Applications are processed on a rolling basis. *Application fee:* $55. Electronic applications accepted. *Application Contact:* Lynette M. Bible, Director of Graduate Admissions, 540-568-6395, Fax: 540-568-7860, E-mail: biblelm@jmu.edu. *Dean,* Dr. Robert D. Reid, 540-568-3254.

College of Education Students: 272 full-time (228 women), 47 part-time (33 women); includes 18 minority (9 African Americans, 6 Asian Americans or Pacific Islanders, 3 Hispanic Americans), 1 international. Average age 27. *Faculty:* 37 full-time (30 women), 38 part-time/adjunct (22 women). Expenses: Contact institution. *Financial support:* In 2008–09, 30 students received support. Career-related internships or fieldwork, Federal Work-Study, unspecified assistantships, and 39 assistantships ($7,382) available. Financial award application deadline: 3/1; financial award applicants required to submit FAFSA. In 2008, 231 master's awarded. *Degree program information:* Part-time and evening/weekend programs available. Offers adult education/human resource development (MS Ed); early childhood education (M Ed); education (M Ed, MAT, MS Ed); educational leadership (M Ed); elementary education (M Ed); exceptional education (M Ed); middle education (MAT); reading education (M Ed); secondary education (MAT). *Application deadline:* For fall admission, 5/1 priority date for domestic students; for spring admission, 9/1 priority date for domestic students. Applications are processed on a rolling basis. *Application fee:* $55. Electronic applications accepted. *Application Contact:* Lynette M. Bible, Director of Graduate Admissions, 540-568-6395, Fax: 540-568-7860, E-mail: biblelm@jmu.edu. *Dean,* Dr. Phillip M. Wishon, 540-568-6572.

College of Integrated Science and Technology Students: 417 full-time (327 women), 172 part-time (88 women); includes 56 minority (32 African Americans, 3 American Indian/Alaska Native, 14 Asian Americans or Pacific Islanders, 7 Hispanic Americans), 17 international. Average age 27. *Faculty:* 99 full-time (47 women), 24 part-time/adjunct (15 women). Expenses: Contact institution. *Financial support:* In 2008–09, 203 students received support, including 17 teaching assistantships with full tuition reimbursements available (averaging $8,664 per year); Federal Work-Study, unspecified assistantships, and 147 assistantships, 9 athletic assistants, 4 service assistants ($7,382), 33 doctoral assistants ($14,500) also available. Financial award application deadline: 3/1; financial award applicants required to submit FAFSA. In 2008, 203 master's, 13 doctorates, 25 other advanced degrees awarded. *Degree program information:* Part-time programs available. Postbaccalaureate distance learning degree programs offered (no on-campus study). Offers assessment and measurement (PhD); audiology (Au D, PhD); clinical audiology (PhD); college student personnel administration (M Ed); combined-integrated clinical and school psychology (PhD, Psy D); community counseling psychology (M Ed, MA, Ed S); computer science (MS); health education (MS, MS Ed); integrated science and technology (M Ed, MA, MOT, MPAS, MS, MS Ed, MSN, Au D, PhD, Psy D, Ed S); kinesiology (MS); nursing (MSN); occupational therapy (MOT); physician assistant studies (MPAS); psychological sciences (MA); school counseling (Ed S); school psychology (M Ed, MA, Ed S); speech-language pathology (MS, PhD). *Application deadline:* For fall admission, 2/1 priority date for domestic students; for spring admission, 9/1 priority date for domestic students. Applications are processed on a rolling basis. *Application fee:* $55. Electronic applications accepted. *Application Contact:* Lynette M. Bible, Director of Graduate Admissions, 540-568-6395, Fax: 540-568-7860, E-mail: biblelm@jmu.edu. *Interim Dean,* Dr. Sharon E. Lovell, 540-568-3283.

College of Science and Mathematics Students: 10 full-time (6 women), 13 part-time (7 women); includes 1 minority (Asian American or Pacific Islander), 1 international. Average age 27. *Faculty:* 12 full-time (4 women), 1 (woman) part-time/adjunct. Expenses: Contact institution. *Financial support:* In 2008–09, 10 students received support. Federal Work-Study and 10 graduate assistantships ($7,382) available. Financial award application deadline: 3/1; financial award applicants required to submit FAFSA. In 2008, 8 master's awarded. *Degree program information:* Part-time programs available. Offers biology (MS); mathematics and statistics (M Ed); science and mathematics (M Ed, MS). *Application deadline:* For fall admission, 2/15 priority date for domestic students; for spring admission, 9/1 priority date for domestic students. Applications are processed on a rolling basis. *Application fee:* $55. Electronic applications accepted. *Application Contact:* Lynette M. Bible, Director of Graduate Admissions, 540-568-6395, Fax: 540-568-7860, E-mail: biblelm@jmu.edu. *Dean,* Dr. David F. Brakke, 540-568-3508.

College of Visual and Performing Arts Students: 37 full-time (18 women), 7 part-time (3 women); includes 4 minority (2 African Americans, 1 Asian American or Pacific Islander, 1 Hispanic American), 4 international. Average age 27. *Faculty:* 39 full-time (17 women), 3 part-time/adjunct (2 women). Expenses: Contact institution. *Financial support:* In 2008–09, 25 students received support, including 5 teaching assistantships with full tuition reimbursements available (averaging $8,664 per year); 13 graduate assistantships ($7,382), 14 doctoral assistantships ($14,500) also available. Financial award application deadline: 3/1; financial award applicants required to submit FAFSA. In 2008, 13 master's awarded. *Degree program information:* Part-time programs available. Offers art education (MA); art history (MA); ceramics (MFA); conducting (MM); drawing/painting (MFA); metal/jewelry (MFA); music education (MM); musical arts (DMA); performance (MM); photography (MFA); printmaking (MFA); sculpture (MFA); studio art (MA); theory-composition (MM); visual and performing arts (MA, MFA, MM, DMA); weaving/fibers (MFA). *Application deadline:* For fall admission, 2/15 priority date for domestic students; for spring admission, 10/15 priority date for domestic students. Applications are processed on a rolling basis. *Application fee:* $55. Electronic applications accepted. *Application Contact:* Lynette M. Bible, Director of Graduate Admissions, 540-568-6395, Fax: 540-568-7860, E-mail: biblelm@jmu.edu. *Dean,* Dr. George Sparks, 540-568-6247.

JEFFERSON COLLEGE OF HEALTH SCIENCES, Roanoke, VA 24031-3186

General Information Independent, coed, comprehensive institution. *Enrollment:* 995 graduate, professional, and undergraduate students; 86 full-time matriculated graduate/professional students (78 women), 2 part-time matriculated graduate/professional students (both women). *Enrollment by degree level:* 88 master's. *Graduate faculty:* 13 full-time (6 women), 3 part-time/adjunct (2 women). *Tuition:* Full-time $9000; part-time $545 per credit hour. Tuition and fees vary according to program. *Graduate housing:* Room and/or apartments available on a first-come, first-served basis to single students; on-campus housing not available to married students. Typical cost: $7010 (including board). *Student services:* Campus employment opportunities, campus safety program, career counseling, exercise/wellness program, free psychological counseling, grant writing training, low-cost health insurance, services for students with disabilities, writing training. *Library facilities:* Learning Resource Center. *Online resources:* library catalog, web page. *Collection:* 10,533 titles, 376 serial subscriptions, 1,071 audiovisual materials. *Research affiliation:* Carilion Clinic (hospital and medical services), Virginia Tech/Carilion Medical School (medical school).

Computer facilities: 56 computers available on campus for general student use. A campuswide network can be accessed from student residence rooms and from off campus. Online class registration is available. *Web address:* http://www.jchs.edu/.

General Application Contact: Judith McKeon, Director of Admissions, 540-985-9083, Fax: 540-985-9773, E-mail: jmckeon@jchs.edu.

GRADUATE UNITS

Program in Nursing Students: 33 full-time (32 women); includes 4 minority (2 African Americans, 1 Asian American or Pacific Islander, 1 Hispanic American). Average age 45. 41 applicants, 63% accepted, 20 enrolled. *Faculty:* 6 full-time (5 women). Expenses: Contact institution. *Financial support:* Career-related internships or fieldwork, Federal Work-Study, scholarships/grants, traineeships, health care benefits, and tuition waivers (full) available. Support available to part-time students. Financial award applicants required to submit FAFSA. In 2008, 13 master's awarded. *Degree program information:* Part-time programs available. Offers nursing education (MSN); nursing management (MSN). *Application fee:* $35. *Application Contact:* Judith McKeon, Director of Admissions, 540-985-9083, Fax: 540-985-9773, E-mail: jmckeon@jchs.edu. *Department Chair,* Dr. Carolyn Melby, 888-224-6007, E-mail: csmelby@jchs.edu.

Program in Occupational Therapy Students: 14 full-time (12 women), 1 (woman) part-time, 14 international. Average age 28. 37 applicants, 43% accepted, 15 enrolled. *Faculty:* 3 full-time (2 women), 1 (woman) part-time/adjunct. Expenses: Contact institution. *Financial support:* Career-related internships or fieldwork, Federal Work-Study, scholarships/grants, traineeships, and tuition waivers (full and partial) available. Support available to part-time students. Financial award applicants required to submit FAFSA. *Degree program information:* Part-time programs available. Offers occupational therapy (MS). *Application deadline:* Applications are processed on a rolling basis. *Application fee:* $35. Electronic applications accepted. *Application Contact:* Judith McKeon, Director of Admissions, 540-985-9083, Fax: 540-985-9773, E-mail: jmckeon@jchs.edu. *Program Director,* Dr. David Haynes, 540-985-4020, E-mail: dhaynes@jchs.edu.

Program in Physician Assistant Students: 40 full-time (35 women); includes 1 American Indian/Alaska Native, 1 Asian American or Pacific Islander, 2 Hispanic Americans. Average age 25. 498 applicants, 13% accepted, 40 enrolled. *Faculty:* 3 full-time (2 women), 3 part-time/adjunct (1 woman). Expenses: Contact institution. *Financial support:* Career-related internships or fieldwork, Federal Work-Study, scholarships/grants, traineeships, health care benefits, and tuition waivers (full and partial) available. Support available to part-time students. Financial award applicants required to submit FAFSA. Offers physician assistant (MS). *Application deadline:* Applications are processed on a rolling basis. *Application fee:* $35. Electronic applications accepted. *Application Contact:* Judith McKeon, Director of Admissions, 540-985-9083, Fax: 540-985-9773, E-mail: jmckeon@jchs.edu. *Director,* Dr. Wilton Kennedy, 540-985-8256, E-mail: wkennedy@jchs.edu.

JESUIT SCHOOL OF THEOLOGY AT BERKELEY, Berkeley, CA 94709-1193

General Information Independent-religious, coed, graduate-only institution. *Graduate housing:* Room and/or apartments available to single students; on-campus housing not available to married students.

GRADUATE UNITS

Programs in Theology *Degree program information:* Part-time programs available. Offers theology (M Div, MA, MABL, MTS, Th M, STD, STL).

THE JEWISH THEOLOGICAL SEMINARY, New York, NY 10027-4649

General Information Independent-religious, coed, university. *Enrollment:* 566 graduate, professional, and undergraduate students; 295 full-time matriculated graduate/professional students (147 women), 59 part-time matriculated graduate/professional students (35 women). *Enrollment by degree level:* 169 first professional, 94 master's, 91 doctoral. *Graduate faculty:* 62 full-time (21 women), 69 part-time/adjunct (33 women). *Tuition:* Full-time $21,200; part-time $1000 per credit. *Required fees:* $400 per semester. Tuition and fees vary according to degree level, program and student level. *Graduate housing:* Rooms and/or apartments available on a first-come, first-served basis to single and married students. Typical cost: $9990 per year for single students; $15,120 per year for married students. Room charges vary according to housing facility selected. Housing application deadline: 5/15. *Student services:* Campus employment opportunities, career counseling, free psychological counseling, low-cost health insurance. *Library facilities:* Library of the Jewish Theological Seminary. *Online resources:* library catalog, web page, access to other libraries' catalogs. *Collection:* 380,000 titles, 720 serial subscriptions, 5,250 audiovisual materials.

Computer facilities: 50 computers available on campus for general student use. A campuswide network can be accessed from student residence rooms and from off campus. Online class registration is available. *Web address:* http://www.jtsa.edu/.

General Application Contact: Dr. Stephen Garfinkel, Dean, Graduate School, 212-678-8024, E-mail: stgarfinkel@jtsa.edu.

GRADUATE UNITS

The Graduate School Students: 91 full-time (49 women), 27 part-time (14 women), 15 international. Average age 37. 77 applicants, 68% accepted, 23 enrolled. *Faculty:* 60 full-time (19 women), 73 part-time/adjunct (39 women). Expenses: Contact institution. *Financial support:* Fellowships, career-related internships or fieldwork and tuition waivers (full and partial) available. Support available to part-time students. Financial award application deadline: 3/1; financial award applicants required to submit FAFSA. In 2008, 23 master's, 3 doctorates awarded. *Degree program information:* Part-time programs available. Offers ancient Judaism (MA, DHL, PhD); Bible (MA, DHL, PhD); Jewish education (PhD); Jewish history (MA, DHL, PhD); Jewish literature (MA, DHL, PhD); Jewish philosophy (MA, DHL, PhD); liturgy (MA, DHL, PhD); medieval Jewish studies (MA, DHL, PhD); Midrash (MA, DHL, PhD); modern Jewish studies (MA, DHL, PhD); Talmud and rabbinics (MA, DHL, PhD). *Application deadline:* For fall admission, 1/15 priority date for domestic students. Applications are processed on a rolling basis. *Application fee:* $50. *Application Contact:* Abby Eisenberg, Director of Graduate School Admissions, 212-678-8032, Fax: 212-280-6022, E-mail: abeisenberg@jtsa.edu. *Dean,* Dr. Stephen Garfinkel, 212-678-8024, Fax: 212-678-8947, E-mail: gradschool@jtsa.edu.

H. L. Miller Cantorial School and College of Jewish Music Students: 37 full-time (18 women), 1 (woman) part-time, 5 international. Average age 31. 15 applicants, 53% accepted, 6 enrolled. *Faculty:* 60 full-time (19 women), 73 part-time/adjunct (39 women). Expenses: Contact institution. *Financial support:* Fellowships, career-related internships or fieldwork available. Support available to part-time students. Financial award application deadline: 3/1; financial award applicants required to submit FAFSA. In 2008, 10 master's awarded. Offers Jewish music (MSM). *Application deadline:* For fall admission, 1/1 priority date for domestic students. Applications are processed on a rolling basis. *Application fee:* $50. *Application Contact:* Rita Gordon, Admissions Coordinator, 212-678-8907, E-mail: rigordon@jtsa.edu. *Dean,* Hazzan Henry Rosenblum, 212-678-8036, Fax: 212-678-8947, E-mail: herosenblum@jtsa.edu.

The Rabbinical School Students: 120 full-time (43 women), 11 part-time (4 women); includes 1 minority (Hispanic American), 15 international. Average age 29. 50 applicants, 60% accepted, 24 enrolled. *Faculty:* 60 full-time (19 women), 73 part-time/adjunct (39 women). Expenses: Contact institution. *Financial support:* Fellowships, career-related internships or fieldwork available. Support available to part-time students. Financial award application deadline: 3/1; financial award applicants required to submit FAFSA. In 2008, 13 master's, 31 other advanced degrees awarded. Offers theology (MA, Rabbi). *Application deadline:* For fall admission, 12/31 for domestic students. Applications are processed on a rolling basis. *Application fee:* $65. *Application Contact:* Rabbi Marcus Schwartz, Director of Admission, 212-678-8818, Fax: 212-280-6022, E-mail: moschwartz@jtsa.edu. *Dean,* Rabbi Daniel Nevins, 212-678-8907, E-mail: danevins@jtsa.edu.

William Davidson Graduate School of Jewish Education Students: 80 full-time (7 women), 26 part-time (18 women); includes 1 minority (Hispanic American), 10 international. Average age 35. 38 applicants, 92% accepted, 25 enrolled. *Faculty:* 60 full-time (19 women), 73 part-time/adjunct (39 women). Expenses: Contact institution. *Financial support:* Fellowships, career-related internships or fieldwork available. Financial award application deadline: 3/1. In 2008, 35 master's, 1 doctorate awarded. *Degree program information:* Part-time programs available. Postbaccalaureate distance learning degree programs offered (minimal on-campus study). Offers Jewish education (MA, Ed D). Offered in conjunction with Rabbinical School; H. L. Miller Cantorial School and College of Jewish Music; Teacher's College, Columbia University; and Union Theological Seminary. *Application deadline:* For fall admission, 7/15 priority date for domestic students. Applications are processed on a rolling basis. *Application fee:* $50. *Application Contact:* Abby Eisenberg, Director of Admissions, 212-678-8032, Fax: 212-280-6022, E-mail: abeisenberg@jtsa.edu. *Dean,* Dr. Barry Holtz, 212-678-8030, Fax: 212-749-9085, E-mail: baholtz@jtsa.edu.

JEWISH UNIVERSITY OF AMERICA, Skokie, IL 60077-3248

General Information Independent-religious, men only, graduate-only institution. *Graduate housing:* On-campus housing not available.

GRADUATE UNITS

Graduate School *Degree program information:* Part-time and evening/weekend programs available. Offers Jewish education (MJ Ed, DJ Ed).

Abrams Institute of Pastoral Counseling Offers counseling (MA); pastoral counseling (MPC, DPC).

Graduate Research Division *Degree program information:* Part-time programs available. Offers Bible (MHL, DHL); Hebrew (MHL, DHL); history (MHL, DHL); Jewish studies (MHL, DHL); philosophy (MHL, DHL); rabbinics (MHL, DHL).

JOHN BROWN UNIVERSITY, Siloam Springs, AR 72761-2121

General Information Independent-religious, coed, comprehensive institution. *Enrollment:* 2,017 graduate, professional, and undergraduate students; 107 full-time matriculated graduate/professional students (79 women), 201 part-time matriculated graduate/professional students (95 women). *Enrollment by degree level:* 308 master's. *Graduate faculty:* 11 full-time (2 women), 43 part-time/adjunct (10 women). *Tuition:* Full-time $7740; part-time $430 per credit hour. *Graduate housing:* Rooms and/or apartments available on a first-come, first-served basis to single and married students. *Student services:* Career counseling, exercise/wellness program, free psychological counseling, international student services, services for students with disabilities. *Library facilities:* Arutunoff Learning Resource Center plus 6 others. *Online resources:* library catalog, web page, access to other libraries' catalogs. *Collection:* 102,031 titles, 751 serial subscriptions, 11,097 audiovisual materials.

Computer facilities: 100 computers available on campus for general student use. A campuswide network can be accessed from student residence rooms and from off campus. Online class registration is available. *Web address:* http://www.jbu.edu/.

General Application Contact: Lori Walker, Director of Recruitment, Graduate and Professional Studies, 479-524-7343, Fax: 479-524-9548, E-mail: lwalker@jbu.edu.

GRADUATE UNITS

Graduate Business Division Students: 27 full-time (19 women), 90 part-time (29 women); includes 12 minority (3 African Americans, 4 American Indian/Alaska Native, 1 Asian American or Pacific Islander, 4 Hispanic Americans), 4 international. Average age 32. *Faculty:* 2 full-time (0 women), 7 part-time/adjunct (2 women). Expenses: Contact institution. *Financial support:* In 2008–09, 8 fellowships (averaging $5,500 per year) were awarded; scholarships/grants, tuition waivers (full), and unspecified assistantships also available. Financial award application deadline: 3/1; financial award applicants required to submit FAFSA. In 2008, 42 master's awarded. *Degree program information:* Part-time and evening/weekend programs available. Postbaccalaureate distance learning degree programs offered (minimal on-campus study). Offers business administration (MBA); leadership and ethics (MS). *Application deadline:* For fall admission, 8/11 priority date for domestic students; for spring admission, 1/12 priority date for domestic students. Applications are processed on a rolling basis. *Application fee:* $35 ($100 for international students). Electronic applications accepted. *Application Contact:* Brent Young, Graduate Business Representative, 479-631-0496, E-mail: byoung@jbu.edu. *Program Director,* Dr. Joe Walenciak, 479-524-7170, Fax: 479-524-9548.

Graduate Counseling Division Students: 62 full-time (51 women), 83 part-time (59 women); includes 12 minority (3 African Americans, 6 American Indian/Alaska Native, 1 Asian American or Pacific Islander, 2 Hispanic Americans), 1 international. Average age 32. 47 applicants, 100% accepted, 41 enrolled. *Faculty:* 5 full-time (1 woman), 6 part-time/adjunct (2 women). Expenses: Contact institution. *Financial support:* In 2008–09, 3 research assistantships (averaging $6,210 per year) were awarded; scholarships/grants, tuition waivers (full), and unspecified assistantships also available. Financial award application deadline: 3/1; financial award applicants required to submit FAFSA. In 2008, 9 master's awarded. *Degree program information:* Part-time and evening/weekend programs available. Offers community counseling (MS); marriage and family therapy (MS); school counseling (MS). *Application deadline:* For fall admission, 8/11 priority date for domestic students; for spring admission, 1/12 for domestic students. Applications are processed on a rolling basis. *Application fee:* $35 ($100 for international students). Electronic applications accepted. *Application Contact:* Associate Director of Graduate Recruitment, 479-524-7100. *Program Director,* Dr. John V. Carmack, 479-524-7460, Fax: 479-524-9548, E-mail: jcarmack@jbu.edu.

Graduate Studies Division of Christian Ministry Students: 27 full-time (19 women), 26 part-time (12 women); includes 10 minority (9 African Americans, 1 Hispanic American). Average age 37. *Faculty:* 4 part-time/adjunct (1 woman). Expenses: Contact institution. *Financial support:* Application deadline: 3/1. In 2008, 2 master's awarded. *Degree program information:* Part-time and evening/weekend programs available. Offers leadership and ethics (MA); ministry leadership (MA); pastoral counseling (MA); youth ministry (MA). *Application deadline:* For fall admission, 8/11 priority date for domestic students; for spring admission, 1/12 priority date for domestic students. Applications are processed on a rolling basis. *Application fee:* $35 ($100 for international students). Electronic applications accepted. *Application Contact:* Dr. Dan Lambert, Director, 479-524-7264, Fax: 479-238-8574, E-mail: dlambert@jbu.edu. *Director,* Dr. Dan Lambert, 479-524-7264, Fax: 479-238-8574, E-mail: dlambert@jbu.edu.

JOHN CARROLL UNIVERSITY, University Heights, OH 44118-4581

General Information Independent-religious, coed, comprehensive institution. CGS member. *Graduate housing:* On-campus housing not available.

GRADUATE UNITS

Graduate School *Degree program information:* Part-time and evening/weekend programs available. Offers administration (M Ed, MA); biology (MA, MS); clinical counseling (Certificate); communications management (MA); community counseling (MA); educational and school psychology (M Ed, MA); English (MA); history (MA); humanities (MA); integrated science (MA); mathematics (MA, MS); nonprofit administration (MA); professional teacher education (M Ed, MA); religious studies (MA); school based adolescent-young adult education (M Ed); school based early childhood education (M Ed); school based middle childhood education (M Ed); school based multi-age education (M Ed); school counseling (M Ed, MA). Electronic applications accepted.

John M. and Mary Jo Boler School of Business *Degree program information:* Part-time and evening/weekend programs available. Offers accountancy (MS); business (MBA). Electronic applications accepted.

JOHN F. KENNEDY UNIVERSITY, Pleasant Hill, CA 94523-4817

General Information Independent, coed, primarily women, upper-level institution. *Graduate housing:* On-campus housing not available.

GRADUATE UNITS

Graduate School of Holistic Studies *Degree program information:* Part-time and evening/weekend programs available. Offers consciousness studies (MA); counseling psychology (MA); dream studies (Certificate); holistic health education (MA); holistic studies (MA, MFA, Certificate); integral psychology (MA, Certificate); life coaching (Certificate); somatic psychology (MA); studio arts (MFA); transformative arts (MA); transpersonal psychology (MA).

Graduate School of Professional Psychology *Degree program information:* Part-time and evening/weekend programs available. Offers counseling psychology (MA); organizational psychology (MA, Certificate); professional psychology (MA, Psy D, Certificate); psychology (Psy D); sport psychology (MA).

School of Education and Liberal Arts *Degree program information:* Part-time and evening/weekend programs available. Offers education (MAT); education and liberal arts (MA, MAT, Certificate); museum studies (MA, Certificate).

School of Law *Degree program information:* Part-time and evening/weekend programs available. Offers law (JD).

School of Management *Degree program information:* Part-time and evening/weekend programs available. Offers business administration (MBA); career coaching (Certificate); career development (MA, Certificate); management (MA, MBA, Certificate); organizational leadership (Certificate).

JOHN JAY COLLEGE OF CRIMINAL JUSTICE OF THE CITY UNIVERSITY OF NEW YORK, New York, NY 10019-1093

General Information State and locally supported, coed, comprehensive institution. *Graduate housing:* On-campus housing not available. *Research affiliation:* Criminal Justice Center, Criminal Justice Research and Evaluation Center, Center on Violence and Human Survival, Center for Dispute Resolution, The Fire Science Institute, The Institute For Criminal Justice Ethics.

GRADUATE UNITS

Graduate Studies *Degree program information:* Part-time and evening/weekend programs available. Offers criminal justice (MA, PhD); criminology and deviance (PhD); forensic computing (MS); forensic psychology (PhD); forensic science (PhD); law and philosophy (PhD); organizational behavior (PhD); protection management (MS); public administration (MPA); public policy (PhD).

JOHN MARSHALL LAW SCHOOL, Chicago, IL 60604-3968

General Information Independent, coed, graduate-only institution. *Enrollment by degree level:* 1,354 first professional, 31 master's, 164 other advanced degrees. *Graduate faculty:* 68 full-time (24 women), 97 part-time/adjunct (31 women). *Tuition:* Full-time $33,880; part-time $1210 per credit hour. *Required fees:* $50 per semester. *Graduate housing:* On-campus housing not available. *Student services:* Campus employment opportunities, campus safety program, career counseling, free psychological counseling, international student services, low-cost health insurance, multicultural affairs office, services for students with disabilities, writing training. *Library facilities:* The John Marshall Law School Library. *Online resources:* library catalog, web page, access to other libraries' catalogs. *Collection:* 249,780 titles, 5,364 serial subscriptions, 1,230 audiovisual materials.

Computer facilities: 80 computers available on campus for general student use. A campuswide network can be accessed from off campus. Online class registration is available. *Web address:* http://www.jmls.edu/.

General Application Contact: William B. Powers, Associate Dean of Admission and Student Affairs, 800-537-4280, Fax: 312-427-5136, E-mail: admission@jmls.edu.

GRADUATE UNITS

Graduate and Professional Programs Students: 1,116 full-time (481 women), 433 part-time (206 women); includes 311 minority (108 African Americans, 15 American Indian/Alaska Native, 87 Asian Americans or Pacific Islanders, 101 Hispanic Americans), 63 international. Average age 27. 3,580 applicants, 41% accepted, 344 enrolled. *Faculty:* 68 full-time (24 women), 97 part-time/adjunct (31 women). Expenses: Contact institution. *Financial support:* In 2008–09, 1,350 students received support. Scholarships/grants and tuition waivers (full and partial) available. Support available to part-time students. Financial award application deadline: 6/1; financial award applicants required to submit FAFSA. In 2008, 350 first professional degrees, 4 master's awarded. *Degree program information:* Part-time and evening/weekend programs available. Offers comparative legal studies (LL M); employee benefits (LL M, MS); information technology (LL M, MS); intellectual property (LL M); international business and trade (LL M); law (JD); real estate (LL M, MS); taxation (LL M, MS). *Application deadline:* For fall admission, 3/1 priority date for domestic and international students; for spring admission, 10/15 priority date for domestic and international students. Applications are processed on a rolling basis. *Application fee:* $60. Electronic applications accepted. *Application Contact:* William B. Powers, Associate Dean of Admission and Student Affairs, 800-537-4280, Fax: 312-427-5136, E-mail: admission@jmls.edu. *Dean,* John Corkery, 312-427-2737.

THE JOHNS HOPKINS UNIVERSITY, Baltimore, MD 21218-2699

General Information Independent, coed, university. CGS member. *Enrollment:* 6,174 full-time matriculated graduate/professional students (2,980 women), 7,245 part-time matriculated graduate/professional students (3,440 women). *Enrollment by degree level:* 473 first professional, 9,253 master's, 2,973 doctoral, 720 other advanced degrees. *Graduate faculty:* 3,597 full-time (1,388 women), 442 part-time/adjunct (142 women). *Tuition:* Full-time $37,700; part-time $2035 per course. *Graduate housing:* On-campus housing not available. *Student services:* Campus employment opportunities, campus safety program, career counseling, exercise/wellness program, free psychological counseling, grant writing training, international student services, low-cost health insurance, multicultural affairs office, services for students with disabilities, teacher training, writing training. *Library facilities:* Milton S. Eisenhower Library plus 6 others. *Online resources:* library catalog, web page, access to other libraries' catalogs. *Collection:* 2.9 million titles, 55,000 serial subscriptions. *Research affiliation:* General Electric (medical technology), Carnegie Institution of Washington (biological sciences), SmithKline Beecham (asthma and allergy), Bristol-Myers Squibb (human nutrition), Howard Hughes Medical Institute (biomedical sciences), Space Telescope Science Institute (astronomy).

Computer facilities: Computer purchase and lease plans are available. 140 computers available on campus for general student use. A campuswide network can be accessed from student residence rooms and from off campus. Online class registration is available. *Web address:* http://www.jhu.edu/.

General Application Contact: Graduate Admissions Office, 410-516-8174.

GRADUATE UNITS

Bloomberg School of Public Health Students: 1,280 full-time (916 women), 416 part-time (272 women); includes 407 minority (110 African Americans, 4 American Indian/Alaska Native, 241 Asian Americans or Pacific Islanders, 52 Hispanic Americans), 368 international. Average age 30. 3,165 applicants, 53% accepted, 917 enrolled. *Faculty:* 535 full-time (270 women), 663 part-time/adjunct (270 women). Expenses: Contact institution. *Financial support:* In 2008–09, 1,658 students received support, including 38 fellowships (averaging $34,333 per year), 59 research assistantships (averaging $23,525 per year), 11 teaching assistantships (averaging $3,126 per year); career-related internships or fieldwork, Federal Work-Study, institutionally sponsored loans, scholarships/grants, traineeships, health care benefits, and stipends also available. Support available to part-time students. Financial award application deadline: 3/15; financial award applicants required to submit FAFSA. In 2008, 618 master's, 144 doctorates awarded. *Degree program information:* Part-time and evening/weekend programs available. Postbaccalaureate distance learning degree programs offered (minimal on-campus study). Offers biochemistry and molecular biology (MHS, Sc M, PhD); bioethics and policy (PhD); bioinformatics (MHS); biostatistics (MHS, Sc M, PhD); cancer epidemiology (MHS, Sc M, PhD, Sc D); cardiovascular disease epidemiology (MHS, Sc M, PhD, Sc D); child and adolescent health and development (Dr PH, PhD); children's mental health services (PhD); clinical epidemiology (MHS, Sc M, PhD, Sc D); clinical investigation (MHS, Sc M, PhD); clinical trials (PhD, Sc D); demography (MHS); drug dependence epidemiology (PhD); economic evaluation and policy (PhD); environmental health engineering (PhD); environmental health sciences (MHS, Dr PH); epidemiology (Dr PH); epidemiology (general) (MHS, Sc M, PhD, Sc D); epidemiology of aging (MHS, Sc M, PhD, Sc D); genetic counseling (Sc M); global disease epidemiology and control (MHS, PhD); health and public policy (PhD); health care management and leadership (Dr PH); health education and health communication (MHS); health finance and management (MHA, MHS); health policy (MHS); health services research and policy (PhD); health systems (MHS, PhD); human genetics/genetic epidemiology (MHS, Sc M, PhD, Sc D); human nutrition (MHS, PhD); infectious disease epidemiology (MHS, Sc M, PhD, Sc D); international health (Dr PH); mental health (MHS, Dr PH); molecular microbiology and immunology (MHS, Sc M, PhD); occupational and environmental health (PhD); occupational and environmental hygiene (MHS, MHS); occupational/environmental epidemiology (MHS, Sc M, PhD, Sc D); physiology (PhD); population and health (Dr PH, PhD); population, family and reproductive health (MHS); psychiatric epidemiology (PhD); public health (MHA, MHS, MPH, Sc M, Dr PH, PhD, Sc D); reproductive, perinatal women's health (Dr PH, PhD); social and behavioral interventions (MHS, PhD); social and behavioral sciences (PhD, Sc D); toxicology (PhD). *Application deadline:* Applications are processed on a rolling basis. *Application fee:* $45. Electronic applications accepted. *Application Contact:* Leslie K. Vink, Associate Director of Admissions: Communications, Recruitment and Special Projects, 410-955-3543, Fax: 410-955-0464, E-mail: lvink@jhsph.edu. *Dean,* Dr. Michael J. Klag, 410-955-3540, Fax: 410-955-0121, E-mail: mklag@jhsph.edu.

Carey Business School Students: 214 full-time (95 women), 1,457 part-time (625 women); includes 465 minority (259 African Americans, 3 American Indian/Alaska Native, 154 Asian Americans or Pacific Islanders, 49 Hispanic Americans), 230 international. Average age 33. 1,028 applicants, 47% accepted, 350 enrolled. *Faculty:* 20 full-time (5 women), 167 part-time/adjunct (41 women). Expenses: Contact institution. *Financial support:* In 2008–09, 476 students received support. Federal Work-Study and scholarships/grants available. Support available to part-time students. Financial award application deadline: 6/1; financial award applicants required to submit FAFSA. In 2008, 583 master's, 103 other advanced degrees awarded. *Degree program information:* Part-time and evening/weekend programs available. Postbaccalaureate distance learning degree programs offered (minimal on-campus study). Offers business administration (MBA); business of health (MBA, Certificate); business of medicine (Certificate); business of nursing (Certificate); competitive intelligence (Certificate); finance (MS, Certificate); financial management (Certificate); information and telecommunication systems (Certificate); information security management (Certificate); information technology (MS, Certificate); information technology and telecommunication systems for business (MS); investments (Certificate); leadership and management in the life sciences (MBA, Certificate); leadership development (Certificate); management (MS, Certificate); marketing (MS); medical services management (MBA); organization development and strategic human resources (MS); real estate (MS); senior living and health care real estate (Certificate); skilled facilitator (Certificate). *Application deadline:* For fall admission, 5/1 for international students; for spring admission, 10/15 for international students. Applications are processed on a rolling basis. *Application fee:* $70. Electronic applications accepted. *Application Contact:* Robin Greenberg, Admissions Coordinator, 410-516-4234, Fax: 410-516-0826, E-mail: carey.admissions@jhu.edu. *Dean,* Dr. Yash Gupta, 410-516-2858, Fax: 410-516-0734, E-mail: yash.gupta@jhu.edu.

Engineering Programs for Professionals Students: 75 full-time (18 women), 1,814 part-time (390 women); includes 418 minority (152 African Americans, 5 American Indian/Alaska Native, 199 Asian Americans or Pacific Islanders, 62 Hispanic Americans), 42 international. Average age 31. *Faculty:* 235 part-time/adjunct (30 women). Expenses: Contact institution. In 2008, 617 master's, 34 other advanced degrees awarded. Offers applied and computational mathematics (MS, Post-Master's Certificate); applied biomedical engineering (MS, Post-Master's Certificate); applied physics (MS, Post-Master's Certificate); bioinformatics (MS); chemical and biomolecular engineering (M Ch E); civil engineering (MCE); computer science (MS, Post-Master's Certificate); electrical and computer engineering (MS, Post-Master's Certificate); engineering (M Ch E, M Mat SE, MCE, MEE, MME, MS, MSE, Graduate Certificate, Post-Master's Certificate); environmental engineering (MS, Graduate Certificate, Post-Master's Certificate); environmental engineering and science (MEE, MS, Graduate Certificate, Post-Master's Certificate); environmental planning and management (MS, Post-Master's Certificate); information systems and technology (MS, Post-Master's Certificate); materials science and engineering (M Mat SE, MSE); mechanical engineering (MME); systems engineering (MS, Graduate Certificate, Post-Master's Certificate); technical management (MS, Graduate Certificate, Post-Master's Certificate); telecommunications and networking (MS). *Application deadline:* Applications are processed on a rolling basis. *Application fee:* $75. Electronic applications accepted. *Application Contact:* Toni M. Riley, Director, Student Services, 410-516-2300, Fax: 410-579-8049, E-mail: triley4@jhu.edu. *Associate Dean,* Dr. Allan Bjerkaas, 410-516-2300, Fax: 410-579-8049, E-mail: bjerkaas@jhu.edu.

G. W. C. Whiting School of Engineering Students: 815 full-time (230 women), 42 part-time (10 women); includes 118 minority (20 African Americans, 1 American Indian/Alaska Native, 79 Asian Americans or Pacific Islanders, 18 Hispanic Americans), 419 international. Average age 27. 1,856 applicants, 40% accepted, 244 enrolled. *Faculty:* 177 full-time (33 women), 75 part-time/adjunct (9 women). Expenses: Contact institution. *Financial support:* In 2008–09, 63 fellowships with full tuition reimbursements (averaging $22,494 per year), 472 research assistantships with full tuition reimbursements (averaging $23,536 per year), 48 teaching assistantships with full tuition reimbursements (averaging $21,744 per year) were awarded; Federal Work-Study, institutionally sponsored loans, scholarships/grants, health care benefits, tuition waivers (full and partial), and unspecified assistantships also available. Support available to part-time students. Financial award applicants required to submit FAFSA. In 2008, 186 master's, 81 doctorates awarded. Offers bioengineering innovation and design (MSE); biomaterials (MSEM); biomedical engineering (MSE, PhD); chemical and biomolecular engineering (MSE, PhD); civil engineering (MCE, MSE, PhD); communications science (MSEM); computational medicine (PhD); computer science (MSE, PhD); discrete mathematics (MA, MSE, PhD); electrical and computer engineering (MSE, PhD); engineering (M Ch E, M Mat SE, MA, MCE, MEE, MME, MS, MSE, MSEM, MSSI, PhD, Certificate, Post-Master's Certificate); financial mathematics (MSE); fluid mechanics (MSEM); geography and environmental engineering (MA, MS, MSE, PhD); materials science and engineering (MSEM); mechanical engineering (MSEM); mechanics and materials (MSEM); nano-biotechnology (MSEM); nanomaterials and nanotechnology (MSEM); operations research/optimization/decision science (MA, MSE, PhD); probability and statistics (MSEM); smart product and device design (MSEM); statistics/probability/stochastic processes (MA, MSE, PhD); systems analysis, management and environmental policy (MSEM). *Application fee:* $75. Electronic applications accepted. *Application Contact:* Dennis McIver, Coordinator of Graduate Admissions, 410-516-8174, Fax: 410-516-0780, E-mail: graduateadmissions@jhu.edu. *Interim Dean,* Dr. Nicholas P. Jones, 410-516-8350 Ext. 3, Fax: 410-516-8627.

Information Security Institute Students: 23 full-time (0 women), 15 part-time (4 women); includes 3 minority (all African Americans), 17 international. Average age 25. 90 applicants, 37% accepted, 21 enrolled. *Faculty:* 4 part-time/adjunct (0 women). Expenses: Contact institution. *Financial support:* In 2008–09, 28 students received support, including 3 teaching assistantships with tuition reimbursements available (averaging $3,000 per year); fellowships with full tuition reimbursements available, career-related internships or fieldwork, Federal Work-Study, institutionally sponsored loans, scholarships/grants, traineeships, health care benefits, tuition waivers (partial), and unspecified assistantships also available. In 2008, 19 master's awarded. *Degree program information:* Part-time programs available. Offers information security (MSSI). *Application deadline:* For fall admission, 6/15 priority date for domestic students, 3/15 for international students; for spring admission, 11/15 for domestic students, 11/1 for international students. Applications are processed on a rolling basis. *Application fee:* $25. Electronic applications accepted. *Application Contact:* Deborah K. Higgins, Graduate Coordinator, 410-516-8521, Fax: 410-516-3301, E-mail: dhiggins@jhu.edu. *Director,* Dr. Gerald M. Masson, 410-516-7013, Fax: 410-516-3301, E-mail: masson@jhu.edu.

National Institutes of Health Sponsored Programs Students: 126 full-time (72 women); includes 36 minority (3 African Americans, 1 American Indian/Alaska Native, 21 Asian Americans or Pacific Islanders, 11 Hispanic Americans), 19 international. 282 applicants, 26% accepted, 36 enrolled. *Faculty:* 25 full-time (4 women). Expenses: Contact institution. *Financial support:* In 2008–09, 24 fellowships (averaging $23,000 per year), 93 research assistantships (averaging $23,000 per year), 22 teaching assistantships (averaging $23,000 per year) were awarded; Federal Work-Study, institutionally sponsored loans, scholarships/grants, traineeships, health care benefits, tuition waivers (partial), and unspecified assistantships also available. Financial award application deadline: 4/15; financial award applicants required to submit FAFSA. In 2008, 15 doctorates awarded. Offers biology (PhD); cell, molecular, and developmental biology and biophysics (PhD). *Application deadline:* For fall admission, 12/15 priority date for domestic students. *Application fee:* $60. Electronic applications accepted. *Application Contact:* Joan Miller, Academic Affairs Manager, 410-516-5502, Fax: 410-516-5213, E-mail: joan@jhu.edu. *Chair,* Dr. Allen Shearn, 410-516-4693, Fax: 410-516-5213, E-mail: bio_cals@jhu.edu.

Paul H. Nitze School of Advanced International Studies Students: 630 full-time (265 women), 44 part-time (20 women); includes 94 minority (19 African Americans, 53 Asian Americans or Pacific Islanders, 22 Hispanic Americans), 195 international. Average age 28. 1,404 applicants, 41% accepted, 198 enrolled. *Faculty:* 61 full-time (22 women), 158 part-time/adjunct (61 women). Expenses: Contact institution. *Financial support:* In 2008–09, 445 students received support, including 445 fellowships (averaging $8,300 per year), 28 teaching assistantships (averaging $3,556 per year); career-related internships or fieldwork, Federal Work-Study, and scholarships/grants also available. Financial award application deadline: 2/15; financial award applicants required to submit FAFSA. In 2008, 415 master's, 8 doctorates awarded. Offers international development (MA, Certificate); international public policy (MIPP); international relations (PhD); international studies (Certificate); Japan studies (MA); Korea Studies (MA); South Asia studies (MA); Southeast Asia studies (MA). *Application deadline:* For fall admission, 1/7 for domestic and international students. *Application fee:* $80. Electronic applications accepted. *Application Contact:* SAIS Admissions, 202-663-5700, Fax: 202-663-7788, E-mail: admissions.sais@jhu.edu. *Director of Admissions,* Sidney Jackson, 202-663-5700, Fax: 202-663-7788.

Peabody Conservatory of Music Students: 304 full-time (174 women), 24 part-time (17 women); includes 43 minority (11 African Americans, 1 American Indian/Alaska Native, 20 Asian Americans or Pacific Islanders, 11 Hispanic Americans), 117 international. Average age 25. 740 applicants, 45% accepted, 161 enrolled. *Faculty:* 69 full-time (19 women), 59 part-time/adjunct (18 women). Expenses: Contact institution. *Financial support:* In 2008–09, 280 students received support, including 60 teaching assistantships (averaging $23,005 per year); Federal Work-Study, institutionally sponsored loans, scholarships/grants, and unspecified assistantships also available. Financial award application deadline: 2/1; financial award applicants required to submit FAFSA. In 2008, 122 master's, 5 doctorates, 43 other advanced degrees awarded. Offers music (MA, MM, DMA, AD, GPD). *Application deadline:* For fall admission, 12/1 for domestic students. *Application fee:* $100. *Application Contact:* David Lane, Director of Admissions, 800-368-2521, Fax: 410-659-8102, E-mail: admissions@peabody.jhu.edu. *Director,* Jeffrey Sharkey, 410-659-8100 Ext. 3060, Fax: 410-659-8131.

School of Education Students: 488 full-time (308 women), 1,453 part-time (1,151 women); includes 453 minority (321 African Americans, 11 American Indian/Alaska Native, 69 Asian

The Johns Hopkins University (continued)

Americans or Pacific Islanders, 52 Hispanic Americans), 33 international. Average age 32. 690 applicants, 73% accepted, 398 enrolled. *Faculty:* 54 full-time (33 women), 197 part-time/adjunct (122 women). Expenses: Contact institution. *Financial support:* In 2008–09, 624 students received support, including 10 fellowships; scholarships/grants also available. Support available to part-time students. Financial award application deadline: 6/1; financial award applicants required to submit FAFSA. In 2008, 647 master's, 6 doctorates, 273 other advanced degrees awarded. *Degree program information:* Part-time and evening/weekend programs available. Postbaccalaureate distance learning degree programs offered (minimal on-campus study). Offers adult learning (Certificate); advanced methods for differentiated instruction and inclusive education (Certificate); assistive technology (Certificate); clinical community counseling (Certificate); counseling (MS, CAGS); counseling at-risk youth (Certificate); data-based decision making and organizational improvement (Certificate); early intervention/preschool special education specialist (Certificate); earth/space science (Certificate); education (MAT, MS, Ed D, CAGS, Certificate); education of students with autism and other pervasive developmental disorders (Certificate); education of students with severe disabilities (Certificate); educational leadership for independent schools (Certificate); educational studies (MS); effective teaching of reading (Certificate); elementary education (MAT); English as a second language instruction (Certificate); English for speakers of other languages (MAT); gifted education (Certificate); K-8 mathematics lead-teacher (Certificate); K-8 science lead-teacher (Certificate); leadership for school, family, and community collaboration (Certificate); leadership in technology integration (Certificate); mind, brain, and teaching (Certificate); organizational counseling (Certificate); out-of-school time leadership (Certificate); play therapy (Certificate); reading (MS); school administration and supervision (MS, Certificate); secondary education (MAT); special education (MS, Ed D, CAGS); teacher development and leadership (MS, Ed D, Certificate); teacher leadership (Certificate); technology for educators (MS); urban education (Certificate). *Application deadline:* For fall admission, 5/1 for international students; for spring admission, 10/1 for international students. Applications are processed on a rolling basis. *Application fee:* $80. Electronic applications accepted. *Application Contact:* Jennifer Shaffer, Associate Director of Admissions, 410-516-9797, Fax: 410-516-9799, E-mail: educationinfo@jhu.edu. *Dean,* Dr. Ralph Fessler, 410-516-7820, Fax: 410-516-6697, E-mail: emayotte@jhu.edu.

Division of Public Safety Leadership Students: 162 full-time (46 women), 2 part-time (1 woman); includes 59 minority (50 African Americans, 2 American Indian/Alaska Native, 4 Asian Americans or Pacific Islanders, 3 Hispanic Americans). Average age 37. 58 applicants, 72% accepted, 38 enrolled. *Faculty:* 9 full-time (3 women). Expenses: Contact institution. *Financial support:* Scholarships/grants available. Support available to part-time students. Financial award application deadline: 6/1; financial award applicants required to submit FAFSA. In 2008, 73 master's awarded. *Degree program information:* Part-time and evening/weekend programs available. Offers intelligence analysis (MS); management (MS). *Application deadline:* For fall admission, 5/1 for international students; for spring admission, 10/1 for international students. Applications are processed on a rolling basis. *Application fee:* $0. Electronic applications accepted. *Application Contact:* Jennifer Shaffer, Associate Director of Admissions, 410-516-9797, Fax: 410-516-9799, E-mail: educationinfo@jhu.edu. *Associate Dean,* Dr. Sheldon Greenberg, 410-516-9900, Fax: 410-290-1061, E-mail: psl@jhu.edu.

School of Medicine Students: 1,318 full-time (652 women), 1 (woman) part-time; includes 431 minority (92 African Americans, 7 American Indian/Alaska Native, 280 Asian Americans or Pacific Islanders, 52 Hispanic Americans), 287 international. 5,165 applicants, 10% accepted, 263 enrolled. *Faculty:* 2,592 full-time (963 women), 1,272 part-time/adjunct (412 women). Expenses: Contact institution. *Financial support:* In 2008–09, fellowships with full tuition reimbursements (averaging $23,000 per year); research assistantships, teaching assistantships, career-related internships or fieldwork, Federal Work-Study, institutionally sponsored loans, and tuition waivers (full) also available. In 2008, 101 first professional degrees, 18 master's, 92 doctorates awarded. Offers medicine (MD, MA, MS, PhD). *Application deadline:* Applications are processed on a rolling basis. *Application fee:* $75. Electronic applications accepted. *Application Contact:* Dr. James Weiss, Associate Dean of Admissions, 410-955-3182. *Dean of Medical Faculty and Chief Executive Officer,* Dr. Edward D. Miller, 410-955-3180.

Division of Health Sciences Informatics Students: 3 full-time (1 woman); includes 1 minority (African American). 20 applicants, 15% accepted, 1 enrolled. *Faculty:* 40 part-time/adjunct (10 women). Expenses: Contact institution. *Financial support:* In 2008–09, 1 fellowship with full tuition reimbursement (averaging $42,750 per year) was awarded; career-related internships or fieldwork and health care benefits also available. In 2008, 6 master's awarded. Offers health sciences informatics (MS). *Application deadline:* For spring admission, 2/15 priority date for domestic students. *Application fee:* $75. Electronic applications accepted. *Application Contact:* Kersti Winny, Senior Academic Program Coordinator, 410-502-3768, Fax: 410-614-2064, E-mail: kwinny@jhmi.edu. *Director, Training Program,* Dr. Harold P. Lehmann, 410-502-2569, Fax: 410-614-2064, E-mail: lehmann@jhmi.edu.

Graduate Programs in Medicine Students: 845 full-time (432 women), 1 (woman) part-time; includes 215 minority (58 African Americans, 3 American Indian/Alaska Native, 122 Asian Americans or Pacific Islanders, 32 Hispanic Americans), 275 international. Average age 24. 1,245 applicants, 22% accepted, 145 enrolled. *Faculty:* 246 full-time (79 women), 30 part-time/adjunct (11 women). Expenses: Contact institution. *Financial support:* In 2008–09, fellowships with full tuition reimbursements (averaging $23,000 per year); research assistantships, teaching assistantships with tuition reimbursements, career-related internships or fieldwork, Federal Work-Study, institutionally sponsored loans, and tuition waivers (full) also available. Financial award applicants required to submit FAFSA. In 2008, 18 master's, 92 doctorates awarded. Offers biochemistry, cellular and molecular biology (PhD); biological chemistry (PhD); cellular and molecular medicine (PhD); cellular and molecular physiology (PhD); functional anatomy and evolution (PhD); human genetics (PhD); immunology (PhD); medical and biological illustration (MA); medicine (MA, MS, PhD); molecular biophysics (MS, PhD); neuroscience (PhD); pathobiology (PhD); pharmacology and molecular sciences (PhD); physiology (PhD). *Application deadline:* For fall admission, 1/10 priority date for domestic and international students. Applications are processed on a rolling basis. *Application fee:* $80. Electronic applications accepted. *Application Contact:* Dr. James Weiss, Associate Dean of Admissions, 410-955-3182. *Associate Dean for Graduate Programs,* Dr. Peter Maloney, 410-614-3385.

School of Nursing Students: 114 full-time (106 women), 189 part-time (178 women); includes 67 minority (21 African Americans, 4 American Indian/Alaska Native, 36 Asian Americans or Pacific Islanders, 6 Hispanic Americans), 4 international. Average age 36. 259 applicants, 74% accepted, 160 enrolled. *Faculty:* 27 full-time (26 women), 7 part-time/adjunct (6 women). Expenses: Contact institution. *Financial support:* In 2008–09, 124 students received support, including 6 fellowships with partial tuition reimbursements available (averaging $23,272 per year); research assistantships with full tuition reimbursements available, teaching assistantships with full tuition reimbursements available, career-related internships or fieldwork, Federal Work-Study, scholarships/grants, traineeships, and tuition waivers (partial) also available. Support available to part-time students. Financial award application deadline: 3/1; financial award applicants required to submit FAFSA. In 2008, 69 master's, 5 doctorates awarded. *Degree program information:* Part-time programs available. Offers adult acute/critical care (MSN, Certificate); adult and pediatric primary care (MSN); adult or pediatric primary care (Certificate); business of nursing (Certificate); clinical nurse specialist (MSN); clinical nurse specialist and health systems management (MSN); emergency preparedness/disaster response (Certificate); family primary care (MSN, Certificate); health systems management (MSN); nursing (MSN, DNP, PhD, Certificate); public health nursing (MSN); women's health (Certificate). *Application deadline:* For fall admission, 3/1 priority date for domestic and international students; for winter admission, 7/1 priority date for domestic and international students; for spring admission, 7/1 priority date for domestic and international students. Applications are processed on a rolling basis. *Application fee:* $75. Electronic applications accepted. *Application Contact:* Mary O'Rourke, Director of Admissions/Student Services, 410-955-7548, Fax: 410-614-7086, E-mail: orourke@son.jhmi.edu. *Dean,* Dr. Martha N. Hill, 410-955-7544, Fax: 410-955-4890, E-mail: mnhill@son.jhmi.edu.

Zanvyl Krieger School of Arts and Sciences Students: 953 full-time (432 women), 4 part-time (2 women); includes 82 minority (12 African Americans, 1 American Indian/Alaska Native, 45 Asian Americans or Pacific Islanders, 24 Hispanic Americans), 317 international. Average age 27. 2,744 applicants, 18% accepted, 299 enrolled. *Faculty:* 400 full-time (115 women), 105 part-time/adjunct (37 women). Expenses: Contact institution. *Financial support:* In 2008–09, fellowships with full and partial tuition reimbursements (averaging $18,295 per year), research assistantships with full and partial tuition reimbursements (averaging $19,584 per year), teaching assistantships with full and partial tuition reimbursements (averaging $17,773 per year) were awarded; career-related internships or fieldwork, Federal Work-Study, institutionally sponsored loans, scholarships/grants, health care benefits, tuition waivers (full and partial), and unspecified assistantships also available. Support available to part-time students. Financial award applicants required to submit FAFSA. In 2008, 198 master's, 124 doctorates awarded. Offers anthropology (PhD); applied economics (MA); arts and sciences (MA, MFA, MS, PhD, Certificate); astronomy (PhD); bioinformatics (MS); biology (PhD); bioscience regulatory affairs (MS); biotechnology (MS); chemistry (PhD); chemistry-biology (PhD); classics (PhD); cognitive science (PhD); communication in contemporary society (MA); earth and planetary sciences (MA, PhD); economics (PhD); English and American literature (PhD); environmental sciences and policy (MS); fiction writing (MFA); French (PhD); German (PhD); government (MA, Certificate); history (PhD); history of art (MA, PhD); history of science and technology (MA, PhD); Italian (PhD); liberal arts (MA, Certificate); mathematics (PhD); molecular biophysics (PhD); museum studies (MA); national securities study (Certificate); Near Eastern studies (PhD); philosophy (MA, PhD); physics (PhD); poetry (MFA); political science (MA, PhD); psychological and brain sciences (PhD); romance languages (PhD); science writing (MA); sociology (PhD); Spanish (PhD); writing (MA, MFA). *Application fee:* $75. Electronic applications accepted. *Application Contact:* Dennis McIver, Graduate Admissions Coordinator, 410-516-8174, Fax: 410-516-0780, E-mail: graduateadmissions@jhu.edu. *Dean,* Dr. Adam Falk, 410-516-8212, Fax: 410-516-6017.

Humanities Center Students: 16 full-time (7 women), 1 part-time (0 women); includes 2 minority (both Asian Americans or Pacific Islanders), 4 international. Average age 29. 52 applicants, 6% accepted, 1 enrolled. *Faculty:* 6 full-time (3 women), 3 part-time/adjunct (2 women). Expenses: Contact institution. *Financial support:* In 2008–09, 20 students received support, including 4 fellowships with full tuition reimbursements available (averaging $17,000 per year), 7 teaching assistantships with full tuition reimbursements available (averaging $17,000 per year); Federal Work-Study, institutionally sponsored loans, tuition waivers (full), and unspecified assistantships also available. Financial award application deadline: 3/14; financial award applicants required to submit FAFSA. In 2008, 2 doctorates awarded. *Degree program information:* Part-time programs available. Offers humanities (PhD). *Application deadline:* For fall admission, 12/1 for domestic and international students. *Application fee:* $75. Electronic applications accepted. *Application Contact:* Marva Philip, Administrator, 410-516-7619, Fax: 410-516-4897, E-mail: mphilip@jhu.edu. *Chair,* Prof. Ruth Leys, 410-516-7368, Fax: 410-516-4897, E-mail: leys@jhu.edu.

Institute for Public Policy Students: 57 full-time (38 women); includes 7 minority (2 African Americans, 4 Asian Americans or Pacific Islanders, 1 Hispanic American), 10 international. Average age 26. 149 applicants, 60% accepted, 35 enrolled. *Faculty:* 6 full-time (3 women), 4 part-time/adjunct (2 women). Expenses: Contact institution. *Financial support:* Career-related internships or fieldwork, Federal Work-Study, and unspecified assistantships available. Financial award application deadline: 4/15; financial award applicants required to submit FAFSA. In 2008, 33 master's awarded. Offers public policy (MA). *Application deadline:* For fall admission, 1/15 for domestic and international students. *Application fee:* $75. Electronic applications accepted. *Application Contact:* Dr. Carey Borkoski, Assistant Director, 410-516-4624, Fax: 410-516-8233, E-mail: cborkoski@jhu.edu. *Director,* Dr. Sandra J. Newman, 410-516-7180, Fax: 410-516-8233, E-mail: sjn@jhu.edu.

JOHNSON & WALES UNIVERSITY, Providence, RI 02903-3703

General Information Independent, coed, comprehensive institution. *Graduate housing:* Room and/or apartments available to single students; on-campus housing not available to married students. *Research affiliation:* Consortium of Rhode Island Academic and Research Libraries, Association of Institutional Research.

GRADUATE UNITS

The Alan Shawn Feinstein Graduate School *Degree program information:* Part-time and evening/weekend programs available. Offers accounting (MBA); business education and secondary special education (MAT); educational leadership (Ed D); elementary education and special education (MAT); event leadership (MBA); financial management (MBA); food service education and secondary special education (MAT); international trade (MBA); marketing (MBA); organizational leadership (MBA).

JOHNSON BIBLE COLLEGE, Knoxville, TN 37998-1001

General Information Independent-religious, coed, comprehensive institution. *Enrollment:* 801 graduate, professional, and undergraduate students; 35 full-time matriculated graduate/professional students (26 women), 81 part-time matriculated graduate/professional students (15 women). *Enrollment by degree level:* 116 master's. *Graduate faculty:* 10 full-time (1 woman), 6 part-time/adjunct (1 woman). *Tuition:* Full-time $7010; part-time $290 per credit hour. *Graduate housing:* Rooms and/or apartments available on a first-come, first-served basis to single students and available to married students. Typical cost: $2250 per year ($4890 including board) for single students. Housing application deadline: 8/1. *Student services:* Campus employment opportunities, child daycare facilities, free psychological counseling, low-cost health insurance, services for students with disabilities. *Library facilities:* Glass Memorial Library plus 1 other. *Online resources:* library catalog, web page. *Collection:* 107,954 titles, 390 serial subscriptions, 12,914 audiovisual materials.

Computer facilities: 34 computers available on campus for general student use. A campuswide network can be accessed from student residence rooms and from off campus. Online class registration is available. *Web address:* http://www.jbc.edu/.

General Application Contact: Dr. Tim W. Wingfield, Dean of Enrollment Management, 865-251-2403, Fax: 865-251-2336, E-mail: twingfield@jbc.edu.

GRADUATE UNITS

Department of Marriage and Family Therapy Offers marriage and family therapy/professional counseling (MA).

Program in New Testament *Degree program information:* Part-time and evening/weekend programs available. Postbaccalaureate distance learning degree programs offered (no on-campus study). Offers preaching (MA); research (MA).

Teacher Education Program *Degree program information:* Part-time programs available. Offers Bible and educational technology (MA); holistic education (MA).

JOHNSON STATE COLLEGE, Johnson, VT 05656-9405

General Information State-supported, coed, comprehensive institution. *Enrollment:* 1,898 graduate, professional, and undergraduate students; 73 full-time matriculated graduate/professional students (47 women), 194 part-time matriculated graduate/professional students (159 women). *Enrollment by degree level:* 267 master's. *Graduate faculty:* 11 full-time (6 women), 15 part-time/adjunct (12 women). Tuition, state resident: part-time $390 per credit. Tuition, nonresident: part-time $842 per credit. *Graduate housing:* Rooms and/or apartments available on a first-come, first-served basis to single and married students. Housing application deadline: 5/15. *Student services:* Child daycare facilities, low-cost health insurance, services for students with disabilities, teacher training. *Library facilities:* Library and Learning Center. *Online resources:* library catalog, access to other libraries' catalogs. *Collection:* 100,053 titles, 522 serial subscriptions.

Computer facilities: 131 computers available on campus for general student use. A campuswide network can be accessed from student residence rooms and from off campus. Online class registration is available. *Web address:* http://www.johnsonstatecollege.edu/.

General Application Contact: Catherine H. Higley, Program Coordinator, 800-635-2356 Ext. 1244, Fax: 802-635-1248, E-mail: catherine.higley@jsc.edu.

GRADUATE UNITS

Graduate Program in Education *Faculty:* 5 full-time (3 women), 6 part-time/adjunct (5 women). Expenses: Contact institution. *Financial support:* Career-related internships or fieldwork, Federal Work-Study, institutionally sponsored loans, and unspecified assistantships available. Support available to part-time students. Financial award application deadline: 3/1; financial award applicants required to submit FAFSA. *Degree program information:* Part-time programs available. Offers applied behavior analysis (MA Ed); children's mental health (MA Ed); curriculum and instruction (MA Ed); gifted and talented (MA Ed); literacy (MA Ed); science education (MA Ed); secondary education (MA Ed, CAGS); special education (MA Ed). *Application deadline:* For fall admission, 7/15 priority date for domestic students, 4/15 priority date for international students; for spring admission, 11/1 priority date for domestic students, 8/15 priority date for international students. Applications are processed on a rolling basis. *Application fee:* $35. *Application Contact:* Catherine H. Higley, Program Coordinator, 800-635-2356 Ext. 1244, Fax: 802-635-1248, E-mail: catherine.higley@jsc.edu.

Program in Counseling Students: 28 full-time (21 women), 71 part-time (58 women). *Faculty:* 4 full-time (2 women), 7 part-time/adjunct (6 women). Expenses: Contact institution. *Financial support:* Career-related internships or fieldwork, Federal Work-Study, institutionally sponsored loans, and unspecified assistantships available. Support available to part-time students. Financial award application deadline: 3/1; financial award applicants required to submit FAFSA. *Degree program information:* Part-time programs available. Offers counseling (MA). *Application deadline:* For fall admission, 4/1 priority date for domestic students, 4/15 priority date for international students; for spring admission, 11/1 priority date for domestic students, 8/15 priority date for international students. Applications are processed on a rolling basis. *Application fee:* $35. *Application Contact:* Catherine H. Higley, Program Coordinator, 800-635-2356 Ext. 1244, Fax: 802-635-1248, E-mail: catherine.higley@jsc.edu.

Program in Studio Arts Students: 33 part-time (30 women). *Faculty:* 3 full-time (2 women). Expenses: Contact institution. *Financial support:* Federal Work-Study and unspecified assistantships available. Support available to part-time students. Financial award application deadline: 3/1; financial award applicants required to submit FAFSA. *Degree program information:* Part-time programs available. Postbaccalaureate distance learning degree programs offered (minimal on-campus study). Offers drawing (MFA); mixed media (MFA); painting (MFA); sculpture (MFA). *Application deadline:* For fall admission, 2/15 for domestic and international students. *Application fee:* $35. *Application Contact:* Catherine H. Higley, Program Coordinator, 800-635-2356 Ext. 1244, Fax: 802-635-1248, E-mail: catherine.higley@jsc.edu.

JOINT MILITARY INTELLIGENCE COLLEGE, Washington, DC 20340-5100

General Information Federally supported, coed, graduate-only institution. *Graduate housing:* On-campus housing not available.

GRADUATE UNITS

School of Intelligence Studies *Degree program information:* Part-time and evening/weekend programs available. Offers intelligence studies (MSSI). Open only to federal government employees.

JONES INTERNATIONAL UNIVERSITY, Centennial, CO 80112

General Information Proprietary, coed, university. *Graduate housing:* On-campus housing not available.

GRADUATE UNITS

Graduate School of Education *Degree program information:* Part-time and evening/weekend programs available. Postbaccalaureate distance learning degree programs offered (no on-campus study). Offers adult education (M Ed); corporate training and knowledge management (M Ed); curriculum and instruction (M Ed); e-learning technology and design (M Ed); educational leadership and administration (M Ed); educational leadership and administration: principal and administrator licensure (M Ed); elementary curriculum instruction and assessment (M Ed); higher education leadership and administration (M Ed); K-12 instructional technology (M Ed); K-12 instructional technology: teacher licensure (M Ed); secondary curriculum instruction and assessment (M Ed); technology and design (M Ed). Electronic applications accepted.

School of Business *Degree program information:* Part-time and evening/weekend programs available. Postbaccalaureate distance learning degree programs offered (no on-campus study). Offers accounting (MBA); business communication (MABC); entrepreneurship (MABC, MBA); finance (MBA); global enterprise management (MBA); health care management (MBA); information security management (MBA); information technology management (MBA); leadership and influence (MABC); leading the customer-driven organization (MABC); negotiation and conflict management (MBA); project management (MABC, MBA). Program only offered online. Electronic applications accepted.

THE JUDGE ADVOCATE GENERAL'S SCHOOL, U.S. ARMY, Charlottesville, VA 22903-1781

General Information Federally supported, coed, primarily men, graduate-only institution. *Graduate housing:* On-campus housing not available.

GRADUATE UNITS

Graduate Programs Offers military law (LL M). Only active duty military lawyers attend this school.

JUDSON UNIVERSITY, Elgin, IL 60123-1498

General Information Independent-religious, coed, comprehensive institution.

GRADUATE UNITS

Graduate Programs *Degree program information:* Part-time and evening/weekend programs available. Postbaccalaureate distance learning degree programs offered (no on-campus study).

THE JUILLIARD SCHOOL, New York, NY 10023-6588

General Information Independent, coed, comprehensive institution. *Graduate housing:* Room and/or apartments available on a first-come, first-served basis to single students; on-campus housing not available to married students. Housing application deadline: 5/1.

GRADUATE UNITS

Program in Music Offers music (MM, DMA, Artist Diploma, Diploma). Electronic applications accepted.

KANSAS CITY UNIVERSITY OF MEDICINE AND BIOSCIENCES, Kansas City, MO 64106-1453

General Information Independent, coed, graduate-only institution. *Graduate housing:* On-campus housing not available. *Research affiliation:* Boehringer Ingelheim (HIV), Mylanta-Bertek (hypertension), Covance (hypertension), Novartis (COPD).

GRADUATE UNITS

College of Biosciences Offers bioethics (MA); biomedical sciences (MS).

College of Osteopathic Medicine Offers osteopathic medicine (DO).

KANSAS STATE UNIVERSITY, Manhattan, KS 66506

General Information State-supported, coed, university. CGS member. *Enrollment:* 23,520 graduate, professional, and undergraduate students; 2,321 full-time matriculated graduate/professional students (1,175 women), 1,346 part-time matriculated graduate/professional students (715 women). *Enrollment by degree level:* 439 first professional, 2,179 master's, 1,049 doctoral. *Graduate faculty:* 913 full-time (246 women), 138 part-time/adjunct (28 women). Tuition, state resident: full-time $6466; part-time $269.40 per credit hour. Tuition, nonresident: full-time $14,874; part-time $619.75 per credit hour. *Required fees:* $673; $23.40 per credit hour. Tuition and fees vary according to campus/location. *Graduate housing:* Rooms and/or apartments available on a first-come, first-served basis to single and married students. Housing application deadline: 2/1. *Student services:* Campus employment opportunities, campus safety program, career counseling, child daycare facilities, exercise/wellness program, free psychological counseling, grant writing training, international student services, low-cost health insurance, multicultural affairs office, services for students with disabilities, teacher training. *Library facilities:* Hale Library plus 3 others. *Online resources:* library catalog, web page, access to other libraries' catalogs. *Collection:* 2.4 million titles, 18,718 serial subscriptions. *Research affiliation:* VISTEON, Midwest Research Institute, NASA-Research Center, U.S. Grain Marketing Research Laboratory.

Computer facilities: 326 computers available on campus for general student use. A campuswide network can be accessed from student residence rooms and from off campus. Online class registration is available. *Web address:* http://www.ksu.edu/.

General Application Contact: Dr. Carol W Shanklin, Dean, 785-532-6191, Fax: 785-532-2983, E-mail: shanklin@ksu.edu.

GRADUATE UNITS

College of Veterinary Medicine Students: 468 full-time (326 women), 35 part-time (20 women); includes 27 minority (3 African Americans, 4 American Indian/Alaska Native, 8 Asian Americans or Pacific Islanders, 12 Hispanic Americans), 27 international. 1,227 applicants, 10% accepted, 128 enrolled. *Faculty:* 73 full-time (19 women), 12 part-time/adjunct (6 women). Expenses: Contact institution. *Financial support:* In 2008–09, 47 research assistantships (averaging $19,893 per year) were awarded; teaching assistantships, Federal Work-Study, institutionally sponsored loans, and scholarships/grants also available. Financial award application deadline: 3/1; financial award applicants required to submit FAFSA. In 2008, 112 first professional degrees, 11 master's, 7 doctorates awarded. Offers anatomy and physiology (MS, PhD); biomedical science (MS); clinical sciences (MS); diagnostic medicine/pathobiology (MS, PhD); physiology (PhD); veterinary medicine (DVM, MS, PhD). *Application deadline:* For fall admission, 2/1 priority date for domestic students. Applications are processed on a rolling basis. *Application fee:* $30 ($55 for international students). Electronic applications accepted. *Application Contact:* Gail Eyestone, Administrative Assistant, 785-532-4005, Fax: 785-532-5884, E-mail: geyestone@vet.ksu.edu. *Dean,* Ralph Richardson, 785-532-5660, Fax: 785-532-5884, E-mail: dean@vet.ksu.edu.

Graduate School Students: 1,853 full-time (849 women), 1,311 part-time (695 women); includes 264 minority (107 African Americans, 23 American Indian/Alaska Native, 53 Asian Americans or Pacific Islanders, 81 Hispanic Americans), 779 international. Average age 31. 2,015 applicants, 53% accepted, 730 enrolled. *Faculty:* 840 full-time (227 women), 126 part-time/adjunct (22 women). Expenses: Contact institution. *Financial support:* In 2008–09, 3 research assistantships (averaging $13,827 per year) were awarded; career-related internships or fieldwork, Federal Work-Study, institutionally sponsored loans, scholarships/grants, and tuition waivers (full and partial) also available. Support available to part-time students. Financial award application deadline: 3/1; financial award applicants required to submit FAFSA. In 2008, 816 master's, 152 doctorates awarded. *Degree program information:* Part-time and evening/weekend programs available. Postbaccalaureate distance learning degree programs offered (minimal on-campus study). *Application deadline:* Applications are processed on a rolling basis. *Application fee:* $30 ($55 for international students). Electronic applications accepted. *Application Contact:* Shannon Fox, Administrative Assistant, 785-532-6191, Fax: 785-532-2983, E-mail: grad@ksu.edu. *Dean,* Dr. Carol W Shanklin, 785-532-6191, Fax: 785-532-2983, E-mail: shanklin@ksu.edu.

College of Agriculture Students: 249 full-time (109 women), 166 part-time (75 women); includes 34 minority (15 African Americans, 4 American Indian/Alaska Native, 7 Asian Americans or Pacific Islanders, 8 Hispanic Americans), 134 international. Average age 30. 275 applicants, 41% accepted, 81 enrolled. *Faculty:* 177 full-time (27 women), 35 part-time/adjunct (2 women). Expenses: Contact institution. *Financial support:* In 2008–09, 16 fellowships (averaging $21,719 per year), 236 research assistantships (averaging $16,049 per year), 28 teaching assistantships (averaging $15,643 per year) were awarded; career-related internships or fieldwork, Federal Work-Study, institutionally sponsored loans, scholarships/grants, and tuition waivers (partial) also available. Support available to part-time students. Financial award application deadline: 3/1; financial award applicants required to submit FAFSA. In 2008, 87 master's, 32 doctorates awarded. *Degree program information:* Part-time programs available. Postbaccalaureate distance learning degree programs offered (minimal on-campus study). Offers agricultural economics (MAB, MS, PhD); agriculture (MAB, MS, PhD); animal breeding and genetics (MS, PhD); crop science (MS, PhD); entomology (MS, PhD); food science (MS, PhD); genetics (MS, PhD); grain science and industry (MS, PhD); horticulture (MS, PhD); meat science (MS, PhD); monogastric nutrition (MS, PhD); physiology (MS, PhD); plant pathology (MS, PhD); range management (MS, PhD); ruminant nutrition (MS, PhD); soil science (MS, PhD); weed science (MS, PhD). *Application deadline:* For fall admission, 2/1 for domestic students; for spring admission, 10/1 for domestic students. *Application fee:* $30 ($55 for international students). Electronic applications accepted. *Application Contact:* Fred Cholick, Dean, 785-532-7137, Fax: 785-532-6563, E-mail: fcholick@ksu.edu. *Dean,* Fred Cholick, 785-532-7137, Fax: 785-532-6563, E-mail: fcholick@ksu.edu.

College of Architecture, Planning and Design Students: 246 full-time (119 women), 33 part-time (18 women); includes 15 minority (4 African Americans, 2 American Indian/Alaska Native, 3 Asian Americans or Pacific Islanders, 6 Hispanic Americans), 18 international. Average age 25. 177 applicants, 89% accepted, 151 enrolled. *Faculty:* 48 full-time (13 women), 5 part-time/adjunct (1 woman). Expenses: Contact institution. *Financial support:* In 2008–09, 1 research assistantship (averaging $8,500 per year), 19 teaching assistantships with full tuition reimbursements (averaging $9,032 per year) were awarded; fellowships, career-related internships or fieldwork, Federal Work-Study, institutionally sponsored loans, and scholarships/grants also available. Support available to part-time students. Financial award application deadline: 3/1; financial award applicants required to submit FAFSA. In 2008, 91 master's awarded. *Degree program information:* Part-time and evening/weekend programs available. Postbaccalaureate distance learning degree programs offered (minimal on-campus study). Offers architecture (M Arch); architecture, planning and design (M Arch, MLA, MRCP); landscape architecture and regional and community planning (MLA); regional and community planning (MRCP). *Application deadline:* For fall admission, 2/1 for domestic students, 2/1 priority date for international students; for spring admission, 8/1 for domestic students, 8/1 priority date for international students. Applications are processed on a rolling basis. *Application fee:* $70 ($80 for international students). Electronic applications accepted. *Application Contact:* Dennis Law, Dean, 785-532-5950, Fax: 785-532-6722, E-mail: delaw@ksu.edu. *Dean,* Dennis Law, 785-532-5950, Fax: 785-532-6722, E-mail: delaw@ksu.edu.

College of Arts and Sciences Students: 703 full-time (313 women), 242 part-time (112 women); includes 65 minority (24 African Americans, 3 American Indian/Alaska Native, 17 Asian Americans or Pacific Islanders, 21 Hispanic Americans), 310 international. Average age 30. 888 applicants, 45% accepted, 213 enrolled. *Faculty:* 352 full-time (101 women), 34 part-time/adjunct (4 women). Expenses: Contact institution. *Financial support:* In 2008–09, 165 research assistantships (averaging $15,040 per year), 432 teaching assistantships with full tuition reimbursements (averaging $12,152 per year) were awarded; career-related internships or fieldwork, Federal Work-Study, institutionally sponsored loans, scholarships/grants, and tuition waivers also available. Support available to part-time students. Financial award application deadline: 3/1; financial award applicants required to submit FAFSA. In 2008, 186 master's, 47 doctorates awarded. *Degree program information:* Part-time programs available. Postbaccalaureate distance learning degree programs offered (minimal on-campus study). Offers analytical chemistry (MS); art (MFA); arts and sciences (MA, MFA, MM, MPA, MS, PhD); biochemistry (MS, PhD); biological chemistry (MS); biology (MS, PhD); chemistry (PhD); economics (MA, PhD); English (MA); French (MA); geography (MA, PhD); geology (MS); German (MA); history (MA); inorganic chemistry (MS); international service (MA); kinesiology (MS); mass communications (MS); materials chemistry (MS); mathematics (MS, PhD); microbiology (PhD); music education (MM); music education/band conducting (MM); music history and literature (MM); organic chemistry (MS); performance (MM); performance with pedagogy emphasis (MM); physical chemistry (MS); political science (MA); psychology (MS, PhD); public administration (MPA); rhetoric/communication (MA); security studies (MA, PhD); sociology (MA, PhD); Spanish (MA); statistics (MS, PhD); theatre (MA); theory and composition (MM). *Application deadline:* Applications are processed on a rolling basis. *Application fee:* $30 ($55 for international students). Electronic applica-

Kansas State University (continued)

tions accepted. *Application Contact:* Stephen White, Dean, 785-532-6900, Fax: 785-532-7004, E-mail: sewhite@ksu.edu. *Dean*, Stephen White, 785-532-6900, Fax: 785-532-7004, E-mail: sewhite@ksu.edu.

College of Business Administration Students: 87 full-time (42 women), 15 part-time (7 women); includes 4 minority (2 African Americans, 1 Asian American or Pacific Islander, 1 Hispanic American), 17 international. Average age 26. 131 applicants, 66% accepted, 48 enrolled. *Faculty:* 35 full-time (7 women), 1 part-time/adjunct (0 women). Expenses: Contact institution. *Financial support:* In 2008–09, 7 fellowships (averaging $3,000 per year), 24 research assistantships with partial tuition reimbursements (averaging $9,342 per year), 14 teaching assistantships with partial tuition reimbursements (averaging $10,155 per year) were awarded; Federal Work-Study, institutionally sponsored loans, and scholarships/grants also available. Support available to part-time students. Financial award application deadline: 3/1; financial award applicants required to submit FAFSA. In 2008, 79 master's awarded. *Degree program information:* Part-time programs available. Offers accounting (M Acc); business administration (M Acc, MBA). *Application deadline:* For fall admission, 7/1 for domestic students, 2/1 for international students; for spring admission, 12/1 for domestic students, 8/1 for international students. Applications are processed on a rolling basis. *Application fee:* $50 ($60 for international students). *Application Contact:* Lynn S. Waugh, Information Contact, 785-532-7190, Fax: 785-532-7024, E-mail: lwaugh@ksu.edu. *Dean*, Yar M. Ebadi, 785-532-7227, Fax: 785-532-7024, E-mail: ebadi@ksu.edu.

College of Education Students: 115 full-time (71 women), 450 part-time (303 women); includes 69 minority (31 African Americans, 7 American Indian/Alaska Native, 7 Asian Americans or Pacific Islanders, 24 Hispanic Americans), 18 international. Average age 38. 213 applicants, 76% accepted, 123 enrolled. *Faculty:* 42 full-time (21 women), 13 part-time/adjunct (2 women). Expenses: Contact institution. *Financial support:* In 2008–09, 8 research assistantships (averaging $17,393 per year), 13 teaching assistantships with full tuition reimbursements (averaging $12,922 per year) were awarded; career-related internships or fieldwork, Federal Work-Study, institutionally sponsored loans, and scholarships/grants also available. Support available to part-time students. Financial award application deadline: 3/1; financial award applicants required to submit FAFSA. In 2008, 173 master's, 27 doctorates awarded. *Degree program information:* Part-time and evening/weekend programs available. Postbaccalaureate distance learning degree programs offered. Offers academic advising (MS); adult and continuing education (MS, Ed D); college student development (MS); counselor education and supervision (PhD); curriculum and instruction (MS, Ed D, PhD); education (MS, Ed D, PhD); educational administration (MS, Ed D); school counseling (MS); special education (MS). *Application deadline:* For fall admission, 3/1 priority date for domestic students, 2/1 priority date for international students; for spring admission, 10/1 priority date for domestic students, 8/1 priority date for international students. Applications are processed on a rolling basis. *Application fee:* $30 ($55 for international students). Electronic applications accepted. *Application Contact:* Paul R. Burden, Assistant Dean, 785-532-5595, Fax: 785-532-7304, E-mail: burden@ksu.edu. *Dean*, Michael Holen, 785-532-5525, Fax: 785-532-7304, E-mail: mholen@ksu.edu.

College of Engineering Students: 287 full-time (62 women), 192 part-time (40 women); includes 31 minority (6 African Americans, 3 American Indian/Alaska Native, 13 Asian Americans or Pacific Islanders, 9 Hispanic Americans), 243 international. 654 applicants, 50% accepted, 116 enrolled. *Faculty:* 116 full-time (15 women), 19 part-time/adjunct (4 women). Expenses: Contact institution. *Financial support:* In 2008–09, 187 research assistantships (averaging $16,328 per year), 53 teaching assistantships (averaging $16,575 per year) were awarded; career-related internships or fieldwork, Federal Work-Study, institutionally sponsored loans, and scholarships/grants also available. Support available to part-time students. Financial award application deadline: 3/1; financial award applicants required to submit FAFSA. In 2008, 119 master's, 21 doctorates awarded. *Degree program information:* Part-time programs available. Postbaccalaureate distance learning degree programs offered (minimal on-campus study). Offers architectural engineering (MS); bioengineering (MS, PhD); biological and agricultural engineering (MS); chemical engineering (MS); civil engineering (MS); communications systems (MS, PhD); computer engineering (MS, PhD); computer science (MS, PhD); control systems (MS, PhD); electromagnetics (MS, PhD); engineering (PhD); engineering management (MEM); industrial engineering (MS, PhD); instrumentation (MS, PhD); mechanical engineering (MS); nuclear engineering (MS); operations research (MS); power systems (MS, PhD); signal processing (MS, PhD); software engineering (MSE); solid-state electronics (MS, PhD). *Application deadline:* For fall admission, 2/1 priority date for domestic and international students; for spring admission, 8/1 priority date for domestic and international students. Applications are processed on a rolling basis. *Application fee:* $30 ($55 for international students). Electronic applications accepted. *Application Contact:* Maureen Lockhart, Administrative Assistant to the Dean, 785-532-5441, Fax: 785-532-7810, E-mail: maureen@ksu.edu. *Dean*, John English, 785-532-5590, Fax: 785-532-7810, E-mail: jenglish@ksu.edu.

College of Human Ecology Students: 159 full-time (128 women), 212 part-time (139 women); includes 39 minority (25 African Americans, 4 American Indian/Alaska Native, 5 Asian Americans or Pacific Islanders, 5 Hispanic Americans), 39 international. 257 applicants, 55% accepted, 110 enrolled. *Faculty:* 48 full-time (33 women), 6 part-time/adjunct (5 women). Expenses: Contact institution. *Financial support:* In 2008–09, 61 research assistantships (averaging $13,041 per year), 37 teaching assistantships with full and partial tuition reimbursements (averaging $12,222 per year) were awarded; career-related internships or fieldwork, Federal Work-Study, institutionally sponsored loans, scholarships/grants, and tuition waivers (full) also available. Support available to part-time students. Financial award application deadline: 3/1; financial award applicants required to submit FAFSA. In 2008, 71 master's, 18 doctorates awarded. *Degree program information:* Part-time programs available. Postbaccalaureate distance learning degree programs offered. Offers apparel and textiles (MS, PhD); dietetics and administration (MS); family life education and consultation (PhD); family studies and human services (MS); food science (MS, PhD); food service and hospitality management (MS); food service, hospitality management, and administrative dietetics (PhD); human ecology (MS, PhD); human nutrition (MS, PhD); institutional management (PhD); lifespan and human development (PhD); marriage and family therapy (PhD); public health (MS). *Application deadline:* For fall admission, 2/1 priority date for domestic and international students; for spring admission, 9/1 for domestic students, 9/1 priority date for international students. *Application fee:* $30 ($55 for international students). Electronic applications accepted. *Application Contact:* Patricia Haas, Administrative Specialist, 785-532-5500, Fax: 785-532-5504, E-mail: haas@humec.ksu.edu. *Dean*, Virginia Moxley, 785-532-5500, Fax: 785-532-5504, E-mail: moxley@ksu.edu.

See Close-Up on page 935.

KANSAS WESLEYAN UNIVERSITY, Salina, KS 67401-6196

General Information Independent-religious, coed, comprehensive institution. *Graduate housing:* Rooms and/or apartments available to single and married students.

GRADUATE UNITS

Program in Business Administration *Degree program information:* Part-time and evening/weekend programs available. Offers business administration (MBA); sports management (MBA).

KAPLAN UNIVERSITY–DAVENPORT CAMPUS, Davenport, IA 52807-2095

General Information Proprietary, coed. CGS member.

GRADUATE UNITS

School of Business *Degree program information:* Part-time and evening/weekend programs available. Postbaccalaureate distance learning degree programs offered (no on-campus study). Offers business administration (MBA); change leadership (MS); entrepreneurship (MBA); finance (MBA); health care management (MBA, MS); human resource (MBA); international business (MBA); management (MS); marketing (MBA); project management (MBA, MS); supply chain management and logistics (MBA, MS). Electronic applications accepted.

School of Criminal Justice *Degree program information:* Part-time and evening/weekend programs available. Postbaccalaureate distance learning degree programs offered (no on-campus study). Offers corrections (MSCJ); global issues in criminal justice (MSCJ); law (MSCJ); leadership and executive management (MSCJ); policing (MSCJ). Electronic applications accepted.

School of Higher Education Studies *Degree program information:* Part-time and evening/weekend programs available. Postbaccalaureate distance learning degree programs offered (no on-campus study). Offers college administration and leadership (MS); college teaching and learning (MS); student services (MS).

School of Information Technology *Degree program information:* Part-time and evening/weekend programs available. Postbaccalaureate distance learning degree programs offered (no on-campus study). Offers decision support systems (MS); information security and assurance (MS).

School of Legal Studies *Degree program information:* Part-time and evening/weekend programs available. Postbaccalaureate distance learning degree programs offered (no on-campus study). Offers health care delivery (MS); pathway to paralegal (Postbaccalaureate Certificate); state and local government (MS).

School of Nursing *Degree program information:* Part-time and evening/weekend programs available. Postbaccalaureate distance learning degree programs offered (no on-campus study). Offers nurse administrator (MS); nurse educator (MS).

School of Teacher Education *Degree program information:* Part-time and evening/weekend programs available. Postbaccalaureate distance learning degree programs offered (no on-campus study). Offers education (M Ed); secondary education (M Ed); teaching and learning (MA); teaching literacy and language: grades 6-12 (MA); teaching literacy and language: grades K-6 (MA); teaching mathematics: grades 6-8 (MA); teaching mathematics: grades 9-12 (MA); teaching mathematics: grades K-5 (MA); teaching science: grades 6-12 (MA); teaching science: grades K-6 (MA); teaching students with special needs (MA); teaching with technology (MA).

KEAN UNIVERSITY, Union, NJ 07083

General Information State-supported, coed, comprehensive institution. CGS member. *Enrollment:* 14,203 graduate, professional, and undergraduate students; 582 full-time matriculated graduate/professional students (458 women), 1,697 part-time matriculated graduate/professional students (1,304 women). *Enrollment by degree level:* 2,204 master's, 19 doctoral, 56 other advanced degrees. *Graduate faculty:* 218 full-time (115 women). Tuition, state resident: full-time $10,128; part-time $422 per credit. Tuition, nonresident: full-time $13,728; part-time $572 per credit. *Required fees:* $2570; $107 per credit. Part-time tuition and fees vary according to course load, degree level and program. *Graduate housing:* On-campus housing not available. *Student services:* Campus employment opportunities, campus safety program, career counseling, child daycare facilities, exercise/wellness program, free psychological counseling, grant writing training, international student services, low-cost health insurance, multicultural affairs office, services for students with disabilities, teacher training, writing training. *Library facilities:* Nancy Thompson Library. *Online resources:* library catalog, web page, access to other libraries' catalogs. *Collection:* 327,883 titles, 6,198 serial subscriptions, 7,914 audiovisual materials. *Research affiliation:* Robert Wood Johnson Foundation (the effect of tobacco control policy), Institute of Vertebrate Paleontology and Paleoanthropology, China (paleoanthropology), University of Medicine and Dentistry of New Jersey (biochemistry, molecular biology and neuroscience), Shodor Foundation (intelligent Internet search engines for science research and education), New Jersey Institute of Technology (partitioning to support auditing and extending the UMLS), National Bureau of Economic Research (alcoholic advertising and youth).

Computer facilities: 1,700 computers available on campus for general student use. A campuswide network can be accessed from student residence rooms and from off campus. Online class registration is available. *Web address:* http://www.kean.edu/.

General Application Contact: Steven Koch, Pre-Admissions Coordinator, 908-737-4723, Fax: 908-737-5965, E-mail: grad-adm@kean.edu.

GRADUATE UNITS

College of Business and Public Administration Students: 64 full-time (40 women), 141 part-time (84 women); includes 108 minority (73 African Americans, 1 American Indian/Alaska Native, 8 Asian Americans or Pacific Islanders, 26 Hispanic Americans), 19 international. Average age 32. 116 applicants, 72% accepted, 49 enrolled. *Faculty:* 22 full-time (8 women). Expenses: Contact institution. *Financial support:* In 2008–09, 15 research assistantships with full tuition reimbursements (averaging $3,217 per year) were awarded; unspecified assistantships also available. In 2008, 83 master's awarded. *Degree program information:* Part-time and evening/weekend programs available. Offers accounting (MS); business and public administration (MA, MPA, MS); criminal justice (MA); environmental management (MPA); health services administration (MPA); non-profit management (MPA); public administration (MPA). *Application deadline:* For fall admission, 5/1 for domestic students; for spring admission, 11/1 for domestic students. *Application fee:* $60 ($150 for international students). Electronic applications accepted. *Application Contact:* Steven Koch, Pre-Admissions Coordinator, 908-737-4723, Fax: 908-737-5965, E-mail: grad-adm@kean.edu. *Dean*, Dr. Alfred Ntoko, 908-737-4120, Fax: 908-737-4125, E-mail: antoko@kean.edu.

College of Education Students: 212 full-time (186 women), 879 part-time (761 women); includes 274 minority (123 African Americans, 1 American Indian/Alaska Native, 26 Asian Americans or Pacific Islanders, 124 Hispanic Americans), 7 international. Average age 32. 592 applicants, 73% accepted, 291 enrolled. *Faculty:* 73 full-time (47 women). Expenses: Contact institution. *Financial support:* In 2008–09, 24 research assistantships with full tuition reimbursements (averaging $3,217 per year) were awarded; unspecified assistantships also available. In 2008, 241 master's awarded. *Degree program information:* Part-time programs available. Offers administration in early childhood and family studies (MA); adult literacy (MA); advanced curriculum and teaching (MA); alcohol and drug abuse counseling (MA); basic skills (MA); bilingual/bicultural education (MA); business and industry counseling (MA); classroom instruction (MA); community/agency counseling (MA); earth science (MA); education (MA, MS); education for family living (MA); exercise science (MS); high incidence disabilities (MA); low incidence disabilities (MA); mathematics/science/computer education (MA); reading specialization (MA); school counseling (MA); speech language pathology (MA); teaching (MA); teaching English as a second language (MA); world languages (Spanish) (MA). *Application deadline:* For fall admission, 5/1 for domestic students; for spring admission, 11/1 for domestic students. *Application fee:* $60 ($150 for international students). Electronic applications accepted. *Application Contact:* Steven Koch, Pre-Admissions Coordinator, 908-737-4723, Fax: 908-737-5965, E-mail: grad-adm@kean.edu. *Dean*, Dr. Susan Polirstok, 908-737-3750, Fax: 908-737-3760, E-mail: fpolirst@kean.edu.

College of Humanities and Social Sciences Students: 143 full-time (117 women), 87 part-time (71 women); includes 36 African Americans, 7 Asian Americans or Pacific Islanders, 35 Hispanic Americans, 8 international. Average age 29. 288 applicants, 54% accepted, 85 enrolled. *Faculty:* 54 full-time (31 women). Expenses: Contact institution. *Financial support:* In 2008–09, 29 research assistantships with full tuition reimbursements (averaging $3,217 per year) were awarded; unspecified assistantships also available. In 2008, 88 master's, 19 other advanced degrees awarded. *Degree program information:* Part-time and evening/weekend programs available. Offers advanced standing (MSW); communication studies (MA); educational psychology (MA); human behavior and organizational psychology (MA); humanities and social sciences (MA, MSW, Diploma); marriage and family therapy (Diploma); political science (MA); psychological services (MA); school psychology (Diploma); social work (MSW); sociology and social justice (MA). *Application deadline:* For fall admission, 5/1 for domestic students; for spring admission, 11/1 for domestic students. *Application fee:* $60 ($150 for international students). Electronic applications accepted. *Application Contact:* Steven Koch, Pre-Admissions Coordinator, 908-737-4723, Fax: 908-737-5965, E-mail: grad-adm@kean.edu. *Dean*, Dr. Kenneth Dollarhide, 908-737-0430, Fax: 908-737-3914, E-mail: kdollarh@kean.edu.

College of Natural, Applied and Health Sciences Students: 65 full-time (57 women), 128 part-time (113 women); includes 75 minority (42 African Americans, 20 Asian Americans or

Pacific Islanders, 13 Hispanic Americans), 3 international. Average age 35. 165 applicants, 48% accepted, 59 enrolled. *Faculty:* 25 full-time (16 women). Expenses: Contact institution. *Financial support:* In 2008–09, 8 research assistantships with full tuition reimbursements (averaging $3,217 per year) were awarded; unspecified assistantships also available. In 2008, 61 master's awarded. *Degree program information:* Part-time and evening/weekend programs available. Offers clinical management (MSN); community health (MSN); computer applications (MA); computing, statistics and mathematics (MS); natural, applied and health sciences (MA, MS, MSN); occupational therapy (MS); school nursing (MSN); supervision of math education (MA); teaching of math (MA). *Application deadline:* For fall admission, 5/1 for domestic students; for spring admission, 11/1 for domestic students. *Application fee:* $60 ($150 for international students). Electronic applications accepted. *Application Contact:* Steven Koch, Pre-Admissions Coordinator, 908-737-4723, Fax: 908-737-5965, E-mail: grad-adm@kean.edu. *Dean*, Dr. Jeffrey H. Toney, 908-737-3600, Fax: 908-737-3606, E-mail: jtoney@kean.edu.

Nathan Weiss Graduate College Students: 71 full-time (37 women), 396 part-time (235 women); includes 77 African Americans, 15 Asian Americans or Pacific Islanders, 41 Hispanic Americans, 24 international. Average age 35. 261 applicants, 72% accepted, 142 enrolled. *Faculty:* 16 full-time (4 women). Expenses: Contact institution. *Financial support:* In 2008–09, 22 research assistantships with full tuition reimbursements (averaging $3,217 per year) were awarded; unspecified assistantships also available. In 2008, 137 master's awarded. *Degree program information:* Evening/weekend programs available. Offers biotechnology (MS); executive management (MBA); global management (MBA); Holocaust and genocide studies (MA); school and clinical psychology (Psy D); school business administration (MA); supervisors and principals (MA); urban leadership (Ed D). *Application deadline:* For fall admission, 5/1 for domestic students. *Application fee:* $60 ($150 for international students). Electronic applications accepted. *Application Contact:* Steven Koch, Director of Graduate Admissions, 908-737-4723, Fax: 908-737-5965, E-mail: grad-adm@kean.edu. *Vice President of Research and Graduate Studies and Dean*, Dr. Kristie Reilly, 908-737-5900, Fax: 908-737-5905, E-mail: kreilly@kean.edu.

School of Visual and Performing Arts Students: 27 full-time (21 women), 66 part-time (40 women); includes 21 minority (10 African Americans, 2 Asian Americans or Pacific Islanders, 9 Hispanic Americans), 3 international. Average age 36. 23 applicants, 96% accepted, 19 enrolled. *Faculty:* 28 full-time (9 women). Expenses: Contact institution. *Financial support:* In 2008–09, 12 research assistantships with full tuition reimbursements (averaging $3,217 per year) were awarded; unspecified assistantships also available. In 2008, 47 master's awarded. *Degree program information:* Part-time and evening/weekend programs available. Offers certification (MA); graphic communication technology management (MS); liberal studies (MA); studio/research (MA); supervision (MA); visual and performing arts (MA, MS). *Application deadline:* For fall admission, 5/1 for domestic students; for spring admission, 11/1 for domestic students. *Application fee:* $60 ($150 for international students). Electronic applications accepted. *Application Contact:* Steven Koch, Pre-Admissions Coordinator, 908-737-4723, Fax: 908-737-5965, E-mail: grad-adm@kean.edu. *Dean*, Dr. Holly Logue, 908-737-4376, Fax: 908-737-4377, E-mail: hlogue@kean.edu.

KECK GRADUATE INSTITUTE OF APPLIED LIFE SCIENCES, Claremont, CA 91711

General Information Independent, coed, graduate-only institution. CGS member.

GRADUATE UNITS

Bioscience Program Offers applied life science (PhD); bioscience (MBS); bioscience management (Certificate); computational systems biology (PhD). Electronic applications accepted.

KEENE STATE COLLEGE, Keene, NH 03435

General Information State-supported, coed, comprehensive institution. *Enrollment:* 5,271 graduate, professional, and undergraduate students; 15 full-time matriculated graduate/professional students (12 women), 67 part-time matriculated graduate/professional students (58 women). *Enrollment by degree level:* 82 master's. *Graduate faculty:* 16 full-time (11 women), 5 part-time/adjunct (4 women). Tuition, state resident: full-time $6600; part-time $386 per credit. Tuition, nonresident: full-time $14,450; part-time $416 per credit. *Required fees:* $2178; $86 per credit. *Graduate housing:* Rooms and/or apartments available on a first-come, first-served basis to single and married students. Typical cost: $6202 per year ($8742 including board) for single students; $6570 per year ($9110 including board) for married students. Room and board charges vary according to board plan and housing facility selected. Housing application deadline: 5/1. *Student services:* Campus employment opportunities, campus safety program, career counseling, child daycare facilities, exercise/wellness program, free psychological counseling, international student services, low-cost health insurance, multicultural affairs office, services for students with disabilities, teacher training, writing training. *Library facilities:* Mason Library. *Online resources:* library catalog, web page, access to other libraries' catalogs. *Collection:* 324,561 titles, 969 serial subscriptions, 11,776 audiovisual materials.

Computer facilities: Computer purchase and lease plans are available. 500 computers available on campus for general student use. A campuswide network can be accessed from student residence rooms and from off campus. Online class registration, personal Web pages are available. *Web address:* http://www.keene.edu/.

General Application Contact: Peggy Richmond, Director of Admissions, 603-358-2276, Fax: 603-358-2767, E-mail: admissions@keene.edu.

GRADUATE UNITS

School of Professional and Graduate Studies Students: 20 full-time (16 women), 75 part-time (66 women), 1 international. Average age 34. 64 applicants, 70% accepted, 34 enrolled. *Faculty:* 18 full-time (14 women), 14 part-time/adjunct (7 women). Expenses: Contact institution. *Financial support:* Research assistantships, career-related internships or fieldwork, Federal Work-Study, institutionally sponsored loans, and unspecified assistantships available. Support available to part-time students. Financial award application deadline: 3/1; financial award applicants required to submit FAFSA. In 2008, 62 master's, 19 other advanced degrees awarded. *Degree program information:* Part-time and evening/weekend programs available. Offers curriculum and instruction (M Ed); educational leadership (M Ed); special education (M Ed); teacher certification (Postbaccalaureate Certificate). *Application deadline:* For fall admission, 4/1 for domestic students; for spring admission, 12/1 for domestic students. *Application fee:* $40. *Application Contact:* Peggy Richmond, Director of Admissions, 603-358-2276, Fax: 603-358-2767, E-mail: admissions@keene.edu. *Dean*, Dr. Melinda Treadwell, 603-358-2220.

KEHILATH YAKOV RABBINICAL SEMINARY, Ossining, NY 10562

General Information Independent-religious, men only, comprehensive institution.

GRADUATE UNITS

Graduate Programs

KEISER UNIVERSITY, Fort Lauderdale, FL 33309

General Information Proprietary, coed, comprehensive institution. *Enrollment by degree level:* 145 master's. *Graduate faculty:* 11 full-time (4 women), 15 part-time/adjunct (8 women). *Tuition:* Full-time $21,108; part-time $586 per credit hour. *Required fees:* $1800; $587 per credit hour. One-time fee: $195. *Graduate housing:* Room and/or apartments available to single students. *Student services:* Campus employment opportunities, campus safety program, career counseling, writing training. *Library facilities:* Jim Bishop Memorial Library. *Online resources:* library catalog, web page. *Collection:* 5,000 titles, 30 serial subscriptions.

Computer facilities: A campuswide network can be accessed. *Web address:* http://www.keiseruniversity.edu/.

General Application Contact: Manuel Christiansen, Associate Director of Admissions, 954-318-1620 Ext. 309, E-mail: mchristiansen@keiseruniversity.edu.

GRADUATE UNITS

Program in Business Administration Students: 18 full-time (14 women), 83 part-time (51 women); includes 51 minority (30 African Americans, 2 American Indian/Alaska Native, 2 Asian Americans or Pacific Islanders, 17 Hispanic Americans), 1 international. Average age 42. 30 applicants, 77% accepted, 18 enrolled. *Faculty:* 8 full-time (3 women), 7 part-time/adjunct (2 women). Expenses: Contact institution. *Financial support:* In 2008–09, 95 students received support. Federal Work-Study available. Financial award applicants required to submit FAFSA. In 2008, 21 master's awarded. *Degree program information:* Part-time programs available. Postbaccalaureate distance learning degree programs offered (minimal on-campus study). Offers international business (MBA); leadership for managers (MBA); marketing (MBA). *Application deadline:* Applications are processed on a rolling basis. *Application fee:* $50. Electronic applications accepted. *Application Contact:* Manuel Christiansen, Associate Director of Admissions, 954-318-1620 Ext. 309, E-mail: mchristiansen@keiseruniversity.edu. *Dean*, Dr. Sara Malmstrom, PhD, 954-318-1620.

Program in Criminal Justice Students: 8 full-time (5 women), 14 part-time (9 women); includes 8 minority (5 African Americans, 1 American Indian/Alaska Native, 2 Hispanic Americans). Average age 36. 19 applicants, 89% accepted, 13 enrolled. *Faculty:* 1 (woman) full-time, 5 part-time/adjunct (all women). Expenses: Contact institution. *Financial support:* In 2008–09, 18 students received support. Federal Work-Study available. Financial award applicants required to submit FAFSA. *Degree program information:* Part-time programs available. Postbaccalaureate distance learning degree programs offered (no on-campus study). Offers criminal justice (MA). *Application deadline:* Applications are processed on a rolling basis. *Application fee:* $50. Electronic applications accepted. *Application Contact:* Manuel Christiansen, Associate Director of Admissions, 954-318-1620 Ext. 309, E-mail: mchristiansen@keiseruniversity.edu. *Dean of the Graduate School*, Dr. Sara Malmstrom, PhD, 954-318-1620.

Program in Education Students: 9 full-time (7 women), 13 part-time (11 women); includes 17 minority (14 African Americans, 1 American Indian/Alaska Native, 2 Hispanic Americans). Average age 35. 16 applicants, 88% accepted, 11 enrolled. *Faculty:* 2 full-time (both women), 3 part-time/adjunct (2 women). Expenses: Contact institution. *Financial support:* In 2008–09, 10 students received support. Federal Work-Study available. Financial award applicants required to submit FAFSA. *Degree program information:* Part-time programs available. Postbaccalaureate distance learning degree programs offered (no on-campus study). Offers college administration (MS); leadership (MS); teaching and learning (MS). *Application deadline:* Applications are processed on a rolling basis. *Application fee:* $50. Electronic applications accepted. *Application Contact:* Manuel Christiansen, Associate Director of Admissions, 954-318-1620 Ext. 309, E-mail: mchristiansen@keiseruniversity.edu. *Dean, Graduate School*, Dr. Sara Malmstrom, 954-318-1620.

KELLER GRADUATE SCHOOL OF MANAGEMENT, Long Island City, NY 11101-3051

General Information Proprietary, coed, graduate-only institution.

GRADUATE UNITS

Keller Graduate School of Management Offers management (MAFM, MBA, MISM, Graduate Certificate).

KELLER GRADUATE SCHOOL OF MANAGEMENT, New York, NY 10036-4041

General Information Proprietary, coed, graduate-only institution.

GRADUATE UNITS

Keller Graduate School of Management Offers management (MBA, MISM).

KENNESAW STATE UNIVERSITY, Kennesaw, GA 30144-5591

General Information State-supported, coed, comprehensive institution. CGS member. *Enrollment:* 21,449 graduate, professional, and undergraduate students; 901 full-time matriculated graduate/professional students (561 women), 1,092 part-time matriculated graduate/professional students (614 women). *Enrollment by degree level:* 1,945 master's, 48 doctoral. *Graduate faculty:* 221 full-time (88 women), 34 part-time/adjunct (12 women). Tuition, state resident: full-time $3668; part-time $153 per semester hour. Tuition, nonresident: full-time $14,670; part-time $612 per semester hour. *Required fees:* $474 per semester. *Graduate housing:* Room and/or apartments available on a first-come, first-served basis to single students; on-campus housing not available to married students. *Student services:* Campus employment opportunities, campus safety program, career counseling, exercise/wellness program, free psychological counseling, international student services, low-cost health insurance, multicultural affairs office, services for students with disabilities, teacher training, writing training. *Library facilities:* Horace W. Sturgis Library. *Online resources:* library catalog, web page, access to other libraries' catalogs. *Collection:* 645,788 titles, 889 serial subscriptions, 10,137 audiovisual materials.

Computer facilities: Computer purchase and lease plans are available. 1,087 computers available on campus for general student use. A campuswide network can be accessed from student residence rooms and from off campus. Online class registration is available. *Web address:* http://www.kennesaw.edu/.

General Application Contact: Vilma Marquez, Admissions Counselor, 770-420-4377, Fax: 770-423-6885, E-mail: ksugrad@kennesaw.edu.

GRADUATE UNITS

College of Health and Human Services Students: 150 full-time (125 women), 25 part-time (17 women); includes 49 minority (32 African Americans, 9 Asian Americans or Pacific Islanders, 8 Hispanic Americans), 4 international. Average age 34. 191 applicants, 54% accepted, 86 enrolled. *Faculty:* 7 full-time (6 women), 15 part-time/adjunct (10 women). Expenses: Contact institution. *Financial support:* In 2008–09, 2 research assistantships with full tuition reimbursements (averaging $15,000 per year) were awarded; Federal Work-Study also available. Support available to part-time students. Financial award application deadline: 6/15; financial award applicants required to submit FAFSA. In 2008, 78 master's awarded. *Degree program information:* Part-time and evening/weekend programs available. Offers advanced care management and leadership (MSN); applied exercise and health science (MS); health and human services (MS, MSN, MSW); primary care nurse practitioner (MSN); social work (MSW). *Application deadline:* For fall admission, 5/31 for domestic and international students. *Application fee:* $60. Electronic applications accepted. *Application Contact:* Vilma Marquez, Admissions Counselor, 770-420-4377, Fax: 770-423-6885, E-mail: ksugrad@kennesaw.edu. *Dean*, Dr. Richard Sowell, 770-423-6565, Fax: 770-423-6627, E-mail: rsowell@kennesaw.edu.

College of Humanities and Social Sciences Students: 130 full-time (82 women), 120 part-time (87 women); includes 52 minority (43 African Americans, 3 American Indian/Alaska Native, 4 Asian Americans or Pacific Islanders, 2 Hispanic Americans), 39 international. Average age 34. 165 applicants, 65% accepted, 75 enrolled. *Faculty:* 35 full-time (19 women), 6 part-time/adjunct (2 women). Expenses: Contact institution. *Financial support:* In 2008–09, 2 research assistantships with full tuition reimbursements (averaging $15,000 per year) were awarded; Federal Work-Study and unspecified assistantships also available. Support available to part-time students. Financial award application deadline: 6/15; financial award applicants required to submit FAFSA. In 2008, 78 master's awarded. *Degree program information:* Part-time and evening/weekend programs available. Offers conflict management (MSCM); humanities and social sciences (MAPW, MPA, MSCM); professional writing (MAPW); public administration (MPA). *Application deadline:* For fall admission, 7/1 priority date for domestic and international students; for spring admission, 10/1 priority date for domestic and international students. Applications are processed on a rolling basis. *Application fee:* $60. Electronic applications accepted. *Application Contact:* Vilma Marquez, Admissions Counselor, 770-420-4377, Fax: 770-423-6885, E-mail: ksugrad@kennesaw.edu. *Dean*, Dr. Richard Vengroff, 770-423-6124, E-mail: rvengrof@kennesaw.edu.

College of Science and Mathematics Students: 40 full-time (14 women), 111 part-time (37 women); includes 34 minority (23 African Americans, 7 Asian Americans or Pacific Islanders,

Kennesaw State University (continued)

4 Hispanic Americans), 20 international. Average age 32. 91 applicants, 58% accepted, 38 enrolled. *Faculty:* 22 full-time (3 women), 1 (woman) part-time/adjunct. Expenses: Contact institution. *Financial support:* In 2008–09, 2 research assistantships with full tuition reimbursements (averaging $15,000 per year) were awarded; Federal Work-Study and unspecified assistantships also available. Support available to part-time students. Financial award application deadline: 6/15; financial award applicants required to submit FAFSA. In 2008, 64 master's awarded. *Degree program information:* Part-time programs available. Offers applied computer science (MSaCS); applied statistics (MSAS); information systems (MSIS); science and mathematics (MSAS, MSIS, MSaCS). *Application deadline:* For fall admission, 7/1 for domestic and international students; for spring admission, 10/1 for domestic and international students. Applications are processed on a rolling basis. *Application fee:* $60. Electronic applications accepted. *Application Contact:* Vilma Marquez, Admissions Counselor, 770-420-4377, Fax: 770-423-6885, E-mail: ksugrad@kennesaw.edu. *Dean,* Dr. Laurence I. Peterson, 770-423-6160, Fax: 770-423-6530, E-mail: lpeterso@kennesaw.edu.

Leland and Clarice C. Bagwell College of Education Students: 181 full-time (161 women), 369 part-time (275 women); includes 89 minority (56 African Americans, 9 Asian Americans or Pacific Islanders, 24 Hispanic Americans), 17 international. Average age 32. 131 applicants, 77% accepted, 77 enrolled. *Faculty:* 60 full-time (38 women), 12 part-time/adjunct (4 women). Expenses: Contact institution. *Financial support:* Federal Work-Study available. Support available to part-time students. Financial award application deadline: 6/15; financial award applicants required to submit FAFSA. In 2008, 398 master's awarded. *Degree program information:* Part-time programs available. Offers adolescent education (M Ed); education (M Ed, MAT, Ed D, Ed S); educational leadership (M Ed); educational leadership technology (M Ed); elementary and early childhood education (M Ed); leadership for learning (Ed D, Ed S); secondary English or mathematics (MAT); special education (M Ed); teaching English to speakers of other languages (M Ed, MAT). *Application deadline:* For fall admission, 7/1 for domestic and international students; for spring admission, 10/1 for domestic and international students. *Application fee:* $60. Electronic applications accepted. *Application Contact:* Alisha Bello, Administrative Coordinator, 770-423-6043, Fax: 770-420-4435, E-mail: abello2@kennesaw.edu. *Dean,* Dr. Arlinda Eaton, 770-423-6117, Fax: 770-423-6567.

Michael J. Coles College of Business Students: 400 full-time (179 women), 467 part-time (198 women); includes 211 minority (141 African Americans, 47 Asian Americans or Pacific Islanders, 23 Hispanic Americans), 93 international. Average age 35. 579 applicants, 54% accepted, 243 enrolled. *Faculty:* 62 full-time (21 women), 9 part-time/adjunct (2 women). Expenses: Contact institution. *Financial support:* In 2008–09, 8 research assistantships with tuition reimbursements (averaging $4,000 per year) were awarded; Federal Work-Study also available. Support available to part-time students. Financial award application deadline: 6/15; financial award applicants required to submit FAFSA. In 2008, 348 master's awarded. *Degree program information:* Part-time and evening/weekend programs available. Offers accounting (M Acc); business (M Acc, MBA); business administration (MBA). *Application deadline:* For fall admission, 8/1 for domestic and international students; for spring admission, 12/1 for domestic and international students. Applications are processed on a rolling basis. *Application fee:* $60. Electronic applications accepted. *Application Contact:* Vilma Marquez, Admissions Counselor, 770-420-4377, Fax: 770-423-6885, E-mail: ksugrad@kennesaw.edu. *Dean,* Dr. Timothy Mescon, 770-423-6425, Fax: 770-423-6141, E-mail: tmescon@coles2.kennesaw.edu.

KENRICK-GLENNON SEMINARY, St. Louis, MO 63119-4330

General Information Independent-religious, men only, graduate-only institution. *Graduate housing:* Room and/or apartments available to single students; on-campus housing not available to married students.

GRADUATE UNITS

Graduate and Professional Programs Offers theology (M Div, MA).

KENT STATE UNIVERSITY, Kent, OH 44242-0001

General Information State-supported, coed, university. CGS member. *Graduate housing:* Rooms and/or apartments available on a first-come, first-served basis to single students and available to married students.

GRADUATE UNITS

College of Architecture and Environmental Design *Degree program information:* Part-time programs available. Offers architecture (M Arch); preservation architecture (Certificate); urban design (M Arch, MUD, Certificate). Electronic applications accepted.

College of Arts and Sciences *Degree program information:* Part-time programs available. Offers analytical chemistry (MS, PhD); anthropology (MA); applied geology (PhD); applied mathematics (MA, MS, PhD); arts and sciences (MA, MFA, MLS, MPA, MS, PhD); biochemistry (MS, PhD); chemical physics (MS, PhD); chemistry (MA, MS, PhD); clinical psychology (MA, PhD); comparative literature (MA); computer science (MA, MS, PhD); creative writing (MFA); ecology (MS, PhD); English (PhD); English for teachers (MA); experimental psychology (MA, PhD); French literature (MA); French, Spanish, German and Latin pedagogy (MA); geography (MA, PhD); geology (MS, PhD); German literature (MA); history (MA, PhD); inorganic chemistry (MS, PhD); justice studies (MA); liberal studies (MLS); literature and writing (MA); organic chemistry (MS, PhD); philosophy (MA); physical chemistry (MS, PhD); physics (MA, MS, PhD); physiology (MS, PhD); political science (MA); public administration (MPA); public policy (PhD); pure mathematics (MA, MS, PhD); rhetoric and composition (PhD); sociology (MA, PhD); Spanish literature (MA); teaching English as a second language (MA); translation (MA); translation studies (PhD). Electronic applications accepted.

College of Communication and Information Offers communication and information (MA, MFA, MLIS, MS, PhD); information architecture and knowledge management (MS).

School of Communication Studies Offers communication studies (MA, PhD). Electronic applications accepted.

School of Journalism and Mass Communication *Degree program information:* Part-time programs available. Offers journalism and mass communication (MA). Electronic applications accepted.

School of Library and Information Science Offers library and information science (MLIS).

School of Visual Communication Design *Degree program information:* Part-time programs available. Offers visual communication design (MA, MFA).

College of Nursing *Degree program information:* Part-time programs available. Offers adult nurse practitioner (MSN); family nurse practitioner (MSN); geriatric nurse practitioner (MSN); nursing (PhD); nursing and health care management (MSN); nursing of adults (clinical nurse specialist) (MSN); pediatric nurse practitioner (MSN); psychiatric/mental health nursing (MSN); women's health nursing (MSN). Electronic applications accepted.

College of Technology *Degree program information:* Part-time programs available. Postbaccalaureate distance learning degree programs offered. Offers technology (MT). Electronic applications accepted.

College of the Arts Offers arts (MA, MFA, MM, PhD). Electronic applications accepted.

Hugh A. Glauser School of Music Offers composition (MA); conducting (MM); ethnomusicology (MA); music education (MM, PhD); musicology (MA); musicology-ethnomusicology (PhD); performance (MM); theory (MA); theory and composition (PhD). Electronic applications accepted.

School of Art Offers art education (MA); art history (MA); crafts (MA, MFA); fine art (MA, MFA). Electronic applications accepted.

School of Theatre and Dance *Degree program information:* Part-time programs available. Offers acting (MFA); design and technology (MFA); theatre (MA, MFA). Electronic applications accepted.

Graduate School of Education, Health, and Human Services Students: 842 full-time (663 women), 787 part-time (620 women); includes 141 minority (102 African Americans, 20 Asian Americans or Pacific Islanders, 19 Hispanic Americans), 3 international. 932 applicants, 55% accepted. *Faculty:* 227 full-time (137 women), 175 part-time/adjunct (128 women). Expenses: Contact institution. *Financial support:* In 2008–09, 14 fellowships with full tuition reimbursements (averaging $11,123 per year), 87 research assistantships with full tuition reimbursements (averaging $7,576 per year) were awarded; teaching assistantships with full tuition reimbursements, career-related internships or fieldwork, Federal Work-Study, institutionally sponsored loans, scholarships/grants, health care benefits, and unspecified assistantships also available. Support available to part-time students. Financial award application deadline: 4/1; financial award applicants required to submit FAFSA. In 2008, 489 master's, 42 doctorates, 24 other advanced degrees awarded. *Degree program information:* Part-time and evening/weekend programs available. Postbaccalaureate distance learning degree programs offered (no on-campus study). Offers career technical teacher education (M Ed, MA, Ed S); community counseling (M Ed, MA); counseling (Ed S); counseling and human development services (PhD); cultural foundations (M Ed, MA, PhD); curriculum and instruction (M Ed, MA, PhD, Ed S); early childhood education (M Ed, MA, MAT); education, health, and human services (M Ed, MA, MAT, MPH, MS, Au D, PhD, Ed S); educational administration (PhD, Ed S); educational psychology (M Ed, MA, PhD); evaluation and measurement (M Ed, MA, PhD); health education and promotion (M Ed, MA, PhD); higher education administration and student personnel (M Ed, MA); instructional technology (M Ed, MA); intervention specialist (M Ed, MA); junior high/middle school (M Ed, MA); K-12 leadership (M Ed, MA, PhD, Ed S); math specialization (M Ed, MA); public health (MPH); reading (M Ed, MA); rehabilitation counseling (M Ed, MA, Ed S); school counseling (M Ed, MA); school psychology (M Ed, PhD, Ed S); secondary education (MAT); special education (PhD, Ed S). *Application deadline:* Applications are processed on a rolling basis. *Application fee:* $30. Electronic applications accepted. *Application Contact:* Nancy Miller, Academic Program Coordinator, Office of Graduate Student Services, 330-672-2576, Fax: 330-672-9162, E-mail: nmiller1@kent.edu. *Dean,* Dr. Daniel Mahony, 330-672-2202, Fax: 330-672-3407, E-mail: dmahony@kent.edu.

School of Exercise, Leisure and Sport Students: 78 full-time (37 women), 17 part-time (8 women); includes 13 minority (10 African Americans, 1 Asian American or Pacific Islander, 2 Hispanic Americans). 79 applicants, 59% accepted. *Faculty:* 24 full-time (10 women), 7 part-time/adjunct (2 women). Expenses: Contact institution. *Financial support:* In 2008–09, fellowships with full tuition reimbursements (averaging $10,952 per year), research assistantships with full tuition reimbursements (averaging $9,632 per year) were awarded; teaching assistantships with full tuition reimbursements, career-related internships or fieldwork, Federal Work-Study, institutionally sponsored loans, and tuition waivers (full) also available. Financial award application deadline: 3/15. In 2008, 29 master's, 2 doctorates awarded. Offers exercise, leisure and sport (MA, PhD); exercise, leisure, and sport (MA); physical education (PhD). *Application deadline:* For fall admission, 7/18 for domestic students; for spring admission, 11/29 for domestic students. Applications are processed on a rolling basis. *Application fee:* $30. Electronic applications accepted. *Application Contact:* Nancy Miller, Academic Program Coordinator, 330-672-2576, Fax: 330-672-9162, E-mail: ogs@kent.edu. *Director,* Wayne Munson, 330-672-2012, Fax: 330-672-4106, E-mail: wmunson@kent.edu.

School of Family and Consumer Studies Students: 37 full-time (34 women), 9 part-time (all women); includes 1 minority (African American). 37 applicants, 59% accepted. *Faculty:* 13 full-time (10 women). Expenses: Contact institution. *Financial support:* In 2008–09, 4 students received support, including 4 research assistantships with full tuition reimbursements available (averaging $8,313 per year); Federal Work-Study, scholarships/grants, and unspecified assistantships also available. Financial award application deadline: 2/1; financial award applicants required to submit FAFSA. In 2008, 10 master's awarded. *Degree program information:* Part-time programs available. Offers family and consumer studies (MA, MS); family studies (MA); nutrition (MS). *Application deadline:* Applications are processed on a rolling basis. *Application fee:* $30. Electronic applications accepted. *Application Contact:* Nancy Miller, Academic Program Coordinator, 330-672-2576, Fax: 330-672-9162, E-mail: ogs@kent.edu. *Director,* Dr. Rhonda Richardson, 330-672-2197, Fax: 330-672-2194, E-mail: rrichard@kent.edu.

School of Speech Pathology and Audiology Students: 117 full-time (115 women), 4 part-time (all women); includes 8 minority (3 African Americans, 3 Asian Americans or Pacific Islanders, 2 Hispanic Americans), 1 international. Average age 23. 210 applicants, 21% accepted. *Faculty:* 11 full-time (7 women), 7 part-time/adjunct (1 woman). Expenses: Contact institution. *Financial support:* In 2008–09, fellowships with full tuition reimbursements (averaging $11,330 per year), research assistantships with full tuition reimbursements (averaging $5,665 per year) were awarded; teaching assistantships with full tuition reimbursements, career-related internships or fieldwork, Federal Work-Study, scholarships/grants, and tuition waivers (full) also available. Financial award application deadline: 3/1. In 2008, 32 master's awarded. Offers audiology (Au D, PhD); speech pathology and audiology (MA, Au D, PhD). *Application deadline:* For fall admission, 3/1 for domestic students; for spring admission, 10/15 for domestic students. Applications are processed on a rolling basis. *Application fee:* $30. Electronic applications accepted. *Application Contact:* Nancy Miller, Academic Program Coordinator, 330-672-2576, Fax: 330-672-9162, E-mail: ogs@kent.edu. *Director,* Dr. Lynne B. Rowan, 330-672-2672, Fax: 330-672-2643, E-mail: lrowan@kent.edu.

Graduate School of Management Students: 182 full-time (77 women), 171 part-time (78 women); includes 22 minority (9 African Americans, 2 American Indian/Alaska Native, 9 Asian Americans or Pacific Islanders, 2 Hispanic Americans), 65 international. Average age 29. 397 applicants, 69% accepted, 116 enrolled. *Faculty:* 54 full-time (13 women), 8 part-time/adjunct (5 women). Expenses: Contact institution. *Financial support:* In 2008–09, 85 students received support, including 52 research assistantships with full tuition reimbursements available (averaging $5,025 per year), 33 teaching assistantships with full tuition reimbursements available (averaging $15,000 per year); fellowships with full tuition reimbursements available, career-related internships or fieldwork, Federal Work-Study, scholarships/grants, and tuition waivers (full) also available. Financial award applicants required to submit FAFSA. In 2008, 128 master's, 9 doctorates awarded. *Degree program information:* Part-time and evening/weekend programs available. Offers accounting (MS, PhD); business administration (MBA); economics (MA); finance (PhD); financial engineering (MSFE); management (MA, MBA, MS, MSFE, PhD); management systems (PhD); marketing (PhD). *Application fee:* $30 ($60 for international students). Electronic applications accepted. *Application Contact:* Louise M. Ditchey, Director, 330-672-2282, Fax: 330-672-7303, E-mail: gradbus@kent.edu. *Associate Dean,* Dr. Frederick W. Schroath, 330-672-2282, Fax: 330-672-7303, E-mail: fschroat@kent.edu.

School of Biomedical Sciences Offers biological anthropology (PhD); biomedical sciences (MS, PhD); cellular and molecular biology (MS, PhD); neuroscience (MS, PhD); pharmacology (MS, PhD); physiology (MS, PhD). Electronic applications accepted.

KENT STATE UNIVERSITY, STARK CAMPUS, Canton, OH 44720-7599

General Information State-supported, coed, comprehensive institution.

GRADUATE UNITS

Graduate School of Education

Professional MBA Program Offers business administration (MBA).

KENTUCKY CHRISTIAN UNIVERSITY, Grayson, KY 41143-2205

General Information Independent-religious, coed, comprehensive institution. *Graduate housing:* Rooms and/or apartments available on a first-come, first-served basis to single and married students.

GRADUATE UNITS

Graduate School *Degree program information:* Part-time programs available. Offers Christian leadership (MA); New Testament (MA). Electronic applications accepted.

KENTUCKY STATE UNIVERSITY, Frankfort, KY 40601

General Information State-related, coed, comprehensive institution. *Enrollment:* 2,659 graduate, professional, and undergraduate students; 58 full-time matriculated graduate/professional students (29 women), 104 part-time matriculated graduate/professional students

(51 women). *Enrollment by degree level:* 162 master's. *Graduate faculty:* 19 full-time (3 women), 1 (woman) part-time/adjunct. Tuition, state resident: full-time $5400; part-time $325 per credit hour. Tuition, nonresident: full-time $13,230; part-time $760 per credit hour. *Required fees:* $450. Tuition and fees vary according to course load. *Graduate housing:* Room and/or apartments available on a first-come, first-served basis to single students; on-campus housing not available to married students. Typical cost: $3240 per year ($6392 including board). Room and board charges vary according to board plan and housing facility selected. Housing application deadline: 6/30. *Student services:* Campus employment opportunities, campus safety program, career counseling, exercise/wellness program, free psychological counseling, grant writing training, international student services, low-cost health insurance, multicultural affairs office, services for students with disabilities, teacher training. *Library facilities:* Blazer Library. *Online resources:* library catalog. *Collection:* 462,703 titles, 922 serial subscriptions, 6,249 audiovisual materials.

Computer facilities: 306 computers available on campus for general student use. A campuswide network can be accessed from student residence rooms and from off campus. Online class registration is available. *Web address:* http://www.kysu.edu/.

General Application Contact: Cedric Cunningham, Coordinator, Office of Graduate Studies, 502-597-6536, E-mail: cedric.cunningham@kysu.edu.

GRADUATE UNITS

College of Mathematics, Sciences, Technology and Health Students: 10 full-time (2 women), 24 part-time (9 women); includes 8 minority (6 African Americans, 1 Asian American or Pacific Islander, 1 Hispanic American), 5 international. Average age 34. 26 applicants, 62% accepted, 15 enrolled. *Faculty:* 7 full-time (1 woman). Expenses: Contact institution. *Financial support:* In 2008–09, 23 students received support, including 11 research assistantships (averaging $6,495 per year); scholarships/grants, tuition waivers (partial), and unspecified assistantships also available. Financial award application deadline: 4/15; financial award applicants required to submit FAFSA. In 2008, 10 master's awarded. *Degree program information:* Part-time and evening/weekend programs available. Postbaccalaureate distance learning degree programs offered (minimal on-campus study). Offers aquaculture (MS); computer science (MS). *Application deadline:* For fall admission, 7/1 priority date for domestic students, 4/1 priority date for international students; for spring admission, 11/15 priority date for domestic students, 8/15 priority date for international students. Applications are processed on a rolling basis. *Application fee:* $30 ($100 for international students). Electronic applications accepted. *Application Contact:* Cedric Cunningham, Coordinator, Office of Graduate Studies, 502-597-6536, E-mail: cedric.cunningham@kysu.edu. *Dean,* Dr. Charles Bennett, 502-597-6926, E-mail: charles.bennett@kysu.edu.

College of Professional Studies Students: 48 full-time (27 women), 75 part-time (39 women); includes 68 minority (66 African Americans, 2 Asian Americans or Pacific Islanders), 5 international. Average age 34. 90 applicants, 73% accepted, 45 enrolled. *Faculty:* 12 full-time (2 women), 1 (woman) part-time/adjunct. Expenses: Contact institution. *Financial support:* In 2008–09, 103 students received support. Scholarships/grants, tuition waivers (partial), and unspecified assistantships available. Financial award application deadline: 4/15; financial award applicants required to submit FAFSA. In 2008, 37 master's awarded. *Degree program information:* Part-time and evening/weekend programs available. Postbaccalaureate distance learning degree programs offered (minimal on-campus study). Offers business administration (MBA); public administration (MPA); special education (MA). *Application deadline:* For fall admission, 7/1 priority date for domestic students, 4/1 priority date for international students; for spring admission, 11/15 priority date for domestic students, 8/15 priority date for international students. Applications are processed on a rolling basis. *Application fee:* $30 ($100 for international students). Electronic applications accepted. *Application Contact:* Cedric Cunningham, Coordinator, Office of Graduate Studies, 502-597-6536, E-mail: cedric.cunningham@kysu.edu. *Dean,* Dr. Gashaw Lake, E-mail: gashaw.lake@kysu.edu.

KETTERING UNIVERSITY, Flint, MI 48504-4898

General Information Independent, coed, primarily men, comprehensive institution. *Enrollment:* 2,600 graduate, professional, and undergraduate students; 13 full-time matriculated graduate/professional students (4 women), 453 part-time matriculated graduate/professional students (140 women). *Enrollment by degree level:* 466 master's. *Graduate faculty:* 27 full-time (4 women), 5 part-time/adjunct (0 women). *Tuition:* Full-time $10,784; part-time $674 per credit hour. *Graduate housing:* Room and/or apartments available on a first-come, first-served basis to single students; on-campus housing not available to married students. Typical cost: $3272 per year ($5662 including board). Housing application deadline: 7/15. *Student services:* Campus employment opportunities, exercise/wellness program, free psychological counseling, international student services, low-cost health insurance, multicultural affairs office, services for students with disabilities. *Library facilities:* Kettering University Library plus 1 other. *Online resources:* library catalog, web page, access to other libraries' catalogs. *Collection:* 130,000 titles, 400 serial subscriptions, 1,200 audiovisual materials. *Research affiliation:* Southern California Edison (Air curtain energy optimization), TRW (Automotive seat testing), MTA (Hybrid vehicle development), Global Testing & Engineering (Crash testing and research), Signal Medical Corporation (Medical instrumentation), Delphi (Automotive).

Computer facilities: 450 computers available on campus for general student use. A campuswide network can be accessed from student residence rooms and from off campus. Online class registration is available. *Web address:* http://www.kettering.edu/.

General Application Contact: Allison Fleming, Graduate Admissions Officer, 810-762-7953, Fax: 810-762-9935, E-mail: afleming@kettering.edu.

GRADUATE UNITS

Graduate School Students: 13 full-time (4 women), 453 part-time (140 women); includes 104 minority (59 African Americans, 2 American Indian/Alaska Native, 11 Asian Americans or Pacific Islanders, 32 Hispanic Americans), 44 international. Average age 33. 223 applicants, 73% accepted, 93 enrolled. *Faculty:* 27 full-time (4 women), 5 part-time/adjunct (0 women). Expenses: Contact institution. *Financial support:* In 2008–09, fellowships with full tuition reimbursements (averaging $13,000 per year), research assistantships with full tuition reimbursements (averaging $13,000 per year), teaching assistantships with full tuition reimbursements (averaging $13,000 per year) were awarded; Federal Work-Study, scholarships/grants, and tuition waivers (partial) also available. Support available to part-time students. Financial award application deadline: 7/15; financial award applicants required to submit CSS PROFILE or FAFSA. In 2008, 137 master's awarded. *Degree program information:* Part-time and evening/weekend programs available. Postbaccalaureate distance learning degree programs offered (no on-campus study). Offers automotive systems (MS Eng); business administration (MBA); computer aided engineering simulation (MS Eng); electrical and computer engineering (MS Eng); engineering management (MSEM); information technology (MSIT); manufacturing management (MSMM); manufacturing operations (MSMO); manufacturing systems engineering (MS Eng); mechanical cognate (MS Eng); mechanical design (MS Eng); operations management (MSOM). *Application deadline:* For fall admission, 9/15 for domestic students, 6/15 priority date for international students; for winter admission, 12/15 for domestic students, 9/15 for international students; for spring admission, 3/15 for domestic students, 12/15 for international students. Applications are processed on a rolling basis. *Application fee:* $0. Electronic applications accepted. *Application Contact:* Allison Fleming, Graduate Admissions Officer, 810-762-7953, Fax: 810-762-9935, E-mail: afleming@kettering.edu. *Vice President of Graduate Studies and Corporate Connections,* Dr. Tony Hain, 810-762-9616, Fax: 810-762-9935, E-mail: thain@kettering.edu.

KEUKA COLLEGE, Keuka Park, NY 14478-0098

General Information Independent-religious, coed, comprehensive institution. *Enrollment:* 1,613 graduate, professional, and undergraduate students; 91 full-time matriculated graduate/professional students (69 women), 40 part-time matriculated graduate/professional students (29 women). *Enrollment by degree level:* 131 master's. *Graduate faculty:* 8 full-time (4 women), 26 part-time/adjunct (10 women). *Graduate housing:* On-campus housing not available. *Student services:* Career counseling, grant writing training, services for students with disabilities, teacher training, writing training. *Library facilities:* Lightner Library. *Online resources:* library catalog. *Collection:* 112,541 titles, 384 serial subscriptions, 3,551 audiovisual materials.

Computer facilities: 120 computers available on campus for general student use. A campuswide network can be accessed from student residence rooms and from off campus. *Web address:* http://www.keuka.edu/.

General Application Contact: Jack Farrel, Director of Admissions, 315-279-5434, Fax: 315-279-5386, E-mail: admissions@mail.keuka.edu.

GRADUATE UNITS

Program in Childhood Education/Literacy Students: 7 part-time (all women). 9 applicants, 100% accepted, 9 enrolled. *Faculty:* 5 part-time/adjunct (3 women). Expenses: Contact institution. *Degree program information:* Part-time and evening/weekend programs available. Offers childhood education/literacy (MS). *Application deadline:* For fall admission, 8/15 priority date for domestic students; for winter admission, 12/15 priority date for domestic students; for spring admission, 4/15 priority date for domestic students. Applications are processed on a rolling basis. *Application fee:* $30. *Application Contact:* Dr. Diane Burke, Director of Graduate Program in Education, 315-279-5688. *Director of Graduate Program in Education,* Dr. Diane Burke, 315-279-5688.

Program in Criminal Justice Administration Students: 9 full-time (6 women), 18 part-time (9 women); includes 8 minority (5 African Americans, 2 Asian Americans or Pacific Islanders, 1 Hispanic American). 89 applicants, 100% accepted, 80 enrolled. *Faculty:* 6 part-time/adjunct (2 women). Expenses: Contact institution. In 2008, 9 master's awarded. *Degree program information:* Part-time and evening/weekend programs available. Offers criminal justice administration (MS). *Application deadline:* For fall admission, 8/15 for domestic students; for winter admission, 12/15 for domestic students; for spring admission, 4/15 for domestic students. *Application fee:* $30. *Application Contact:* Claudine Ninestine, Director of Admissions, 315-279-5413, Fax: 315-279-5386, E-mail: admissions@mail.keuka.edu. *Program Director,* Dr. Tom Tremer, 315-279-5672, E-mail: ttremer@mail.keuka.edu.

Program in Management Students: 60 full-time (42 women), 15 part-time (13 women); includes 9 minority (5 African Americans, 1 American Indian/Alaska Native, 2 Asian Americans or Pacific Islanders, 1 Hispanic American). 31 applicants, 100% accepted, 31 enrolled. *Faculty:* 3 full-time (1 woman), 15 part-time/adjunct (5 women). Expenses: Contact institution. In 2008, 54 master's awarded. *Degree program information:* Evening/weekend programs available. Offers management (MS). *Application deadline:* For fall admission, 8/15 priority date for domestic students; for winter admission, 12/15 priority date for domestic students; for spring admission, 4/15 priority date for domestic students. Applications are processed on a rolling basis. *Application fee:* $30. *Application Contact:* Claudine Ninestine, Director of Admissions, 315-279-5413, Fax: 315-279-5386, E-mail: admissions@mail.keuka.edu. *Chair, Division of Business and Management,* Gary M. Smith, 315-279-5352, E-mail: gsmith@mail.keuka.edu.

Program in Occupational Therapy Students: 22 full-time (21 women); includes 1 minority (American Indian/Alaska Native). Average age 23. 15 applicants, 100% accepted. *Faculty:* 5 full-time (3 women). Expenses: Contact institution. In 2008, 13 master's awarded. Offers occupational therapy (MS). *Application deadline:* For fall admission, 8/15 priority date for domestic students; for winter admission, 12/15 priority date for domestic students; for spring admission, 4/15 priority date for domestic students. Applications are processed on a rolling basis. *Application fee:* $30. *Application Contact:* Claudine Ninestine, Director of Admissions, 315-279-5413, Fax: 315-279-5386, E-mail: admissions@mail.keuka.edu. *Associate Professor and Chair,* Dr. Vicki Smith, 315-279-5666, Fax: 315-279-5439, E-mail: vlsmith@mail.keuka.edu.

KING COLLEGE, Bristol, TN 37620-2699

General Information Independent-religious, coed, comprehensive institution. *Enrollment:* 1,703 graduate, professional, and undergraduate students; 188 part-time matriculated graduate/professional students (104 women). *Enrollment by degree level:* 188 master's. *Graduate faculty:* 14 full-time (3 women), 3 part-time/adjunct. *Graduate housing:* Room and/or apartments available on a first-come, first-served basis to single students; on-campus housing not available to married students. *Student services:* Campus employment opportunities, campus safety program, exercise/wellness program, free psychological counseling, international student services, writing training. *Library facilities:* E. W. King Library. *Online resources:* library catalog, web page, access to other libraries' catalogs. *Collection:* 113,933 titles, 468 serial subscriptions, 5,803 audiovisual materials.

Computer facilities: 90 computers available on campus for general student use. A campuswide network can be accessed from student residence rooms and from off campus. Online class registration is available. *Web address:* http://www.king.edu/.

General Application Contact: Ramona D Salyer, Interim Director, Graduate and Professional Studies, 423-652-4339, Fax: 423-968-4456, E-mail: rdsalyer@king.edu.

GRADUATE UNITS

School of Business and Economics Students: 188 part-time (104 women). Average age 37. 22 applicants, 91% accepted, 18 enrolled. *Faculty:* 14 full-time (3 women), 3 part-time/adjunct (0 women). Expenses: Contact institution. *Financial support:* In 2008–09, 39 students received support. Applicants required to submit FAFSA. In 2008, 39 master's awarded. *Degree program information:* Part-time and evening/weekend programs available. Postbaccalaureate distance learning degree programs offered (no on-campus study). Offers business and economics (MBA). *Application deadline:* Applications are processed on a rolling basis. *Application fee:* $25. Electronic applications accepted. *Application Contact:* Ramona D. Salyer, Interim Director of Recruitment for Graduate and Professional Studies, 423-652-4339, Fax: 423-968-4727, E-mail: rdsalyer@king.edu. *Interim Dean of School of Business,* Dr. Wen-Yuan William Teng, 423-652-4816, Fax: 423-968-4456, E-mail: wyteng@king.edu.

KING'S COLLEGE, Wilkes-Barre, PA 18711-0801

General Information Independent-religious, coed, comprehensive institution. *Enrollment:* 2,673 graduate, professional, and undergraduate students; 65 full-time matriculated graduate/professional students (51 women), 269 part-time matriculated graduate/professional students (209 women). *Enrollment by degree level:* 334 master's. *Graduate faculty:* 14 full-time (8 women), 16 part-time/adjunct (10 women). *Graduate housing:* On-campus housing not available. *Student services:* Career counseling, free psychological counseling, multicultural affairs office, services for students with disabilities. *Library facilities:* D. Leonard Corgan Library. *Online resources:* library catalog, web page, access to other libraries' catalogs. *Collection:* 178,158 titles, 12,658 serial subscriptions, 2,483 audiovisual materials.

Computer facilities: Computer purchase and lease plans are available. 470 computers available on campus for general student use. A campuswide network can be accessed from student residence rooms and from off campus. Online class registration is available. *Web address:* http://www.kings.edu/.

General Application Contact: Dr. Elizabeth S. Lott, Director of Graduate Programs, 570-208-5991, Fax: 570-208-8027, E-mail: elizabethlott@kings.edu.

GRADUATE UNITS

Program in Physician Assistant Studies Students: 65 full-time (51 women); includes 3 minority (2 African Americans, 1 Hispanic American). Average age 25. *Faculty:* 7 full-time (6 women), 6 part-time/adjunct (4 women). Expenses: Contact institution. In 2008, 38 master's awarded. Offers physician assistant studies (MSPAS). *Application deadline:* For fall admission, 11/1 priority date for domestic and international students. *Application fee:* $30. Electronic applications accepted. *Application Contact:* Dr. Elizabeth S. Lott, Director of Graduate Programs, 570-208-5991, Fax: 570-208-8027, E-mail: elizabethlott@kings.edu. *Director of Graduate Programs,* Dr. Elizabeth S. Lott, 570-208-5991, Fax: 570-208-8027, E-mail: elizabethlott@kings.edu.

Program in Reading Students: 88 part-time (78 women); includes 3 minority (1 African American, 2 Hispanic Americans). Average age 27. *Faculty:* 3 full-time (2 women), 9 part-time/adjunct (6 women). Expenses: Contact institution. In 2008, 24 master's awarded. *Degree program information:* Part-time and evening/weekend programs available. Offers reading (M Ed). *Application deadline:* Applications are processed on a rolling basis. *Application fee:* $35. *Application Contact:* Dr. Elizabeth S. Lott, Director of Graduate Programs, 570-208-5991, Fax: 570-825-9049, E-mail: eslott@kings.edu. *Director of Graduate Programs,* Dr. Elizabeth S. Lott, 570-208-5991, Fax: 570-825-9049, E-mail: eslott@kings.edu.

King's College (continued)

William G. McGowan School of Business Students: 54 part-time (32 women); includes 1 minority (African American). Average age 28. *Faculty:* 4 full-time (1 woman), 1 part-time/adjunct (0 women). Expenses: Contact institution. In 2008, 17 master's awarded. *Degree program information:* Part-time programs available. Offers health care administration (MS). *Application deadline:* Applications are processed on a rolling basis. *Application fee:* $35. *Application Contact:* Dr. Elizabeth S. Lott, Director of Graduate Programs, 570-208-5991, Fax: 570-208-8027, E-mail: elizabethlott@kings.edu. *Director,* Dr. John J. Ryan, 570-208-5932, Fax: 570-826-5989, E-mail: jjryan@kings.edu.

KNOWLEDGE SYSTEMS INSTITUTE, Skokie, IL 60076

General Information Independent, coed, graduate-only institution. *Enrollment by degree level:* 72 master's. *Graduate faculty:* 3 full-time (0 women), 6 part-time/adjunct (0 women). *Graduate housing:* On-campus housing not available. *Student services:* Campus employment opportunities, career counseling, international student services, low-cost health insurance, writing training. *Library facilities:* Knowledge Systems Institute Library. *Online resources:* library catalog, web page. *Collection:* 2,900 titles, 2,100 serial subscriptions.

Computer facilities: 73 computers available on campus for general student use. A campuswide network can be accessed from student residence rooms and from off campus. *Web address:* http://www.ksi.edu/.

General Application Contact: Judy Pan, Executive Director, 847-679-3135, Fax: 847-679-3166, E-mail: office@ksi.edu.

GRADUATE UNITS

Program in Computer and Information Sciences Students: 85 full-time (18 women), 10 part-time (3 women); includes 16 minority (2 African Americans, 11 Asian Americans or Pacific Islanders, 3 Hispanic Americans), 62 international. Average age 32. 15 applicants, 73% accepted. *Faculty:* 3 full-time (0 women), 6 part-time/adjunct (0 women). Expenses: Contact institution. *Financial support:* Career-related internships or fieldwork available. Financial award applicants required to submit FAFSA. In 2008, 15 master's awarded. *Degree program information:* Part-time and evening/weekend programs available. Postbaccalaureate distance learning degree programs offered (minimal on-campus study). Offers computer and information sciences (MS). *Application deadline:* Applications are processed on a rolling basis. *Application fee:* $40. Electronic applications accepted. *Application Contact:* Omasan Etuwewe, Office Manager, 847-679-3135, Fax: 847-679-3166, E-mail: oetuwewe@ksi.edu. *Executive Director,* Judy Pan, 847-679-3135, Fax: 847-679-3166, E-mail: office@ksi.edu.

KNOX COLLEGE, Toronto, ON M5S 2E6, Canada

General Information Independent-religious, coed, graduate-only institution. *Graduate housing:* Room and/or apartments available on a first-come, first-served basis to single students; on-campus housing not available to married students. Housing application deadline: 5/31.

GRADUATE UNITS

College of Theology *Degree program information:* Part-time programs available. Offers theology (M Div, MRE, MTS, Th M, D Min, Th D). Applicants for D Min, Th M, and Th D must apply to Toronto School of Theology.

KNOX THEOLOGICAL SEMINARY, Fort Lauderdale, FL 33308

General Information Independent-religious, coed, primarily men, graduate-only institution. *Enrollment by degree level:* 62 first professional, 48 master's, 10 doctoral. *Graduate faculty:* 4 full-time (0 women), 2 part-time/adjunct (0 women). *Tuition:* Full-time $7080; part-time $295 per credit hour. *Required fees:* $25 per semester. *Graduate housing:* On-campus housing not available. *Student services:* Campus employment opportunities, career counseling, international student services. *Library facilities:* Knox Seminary Library. *Collection:* 32,000 titles, 100 serial subscriptions, 2,000 audiovisual materials.

Computer facilities: 9 computers available on campus for general student use. A campuswide network can be accessed from off campus. *Web address:* http://www.knoxseminary.edu/.

General Application Contact: Jim Dietz, Director of Student Services, 800-344-5669, Fax: 954-351-3343, E-mail: jdietz@knoxseminary.edu.

GRADUATE UNITS

Graduate Programs Students: 26 full-time (2 women), 94 part-time (20 women); includes 38 minority (24 African Americans, 2 Asian Americans or Pacific Islanders, 12 Hispanic Americans), 1 international. Average age 40. *Faculty:* 4 full-time (0 women), 2 part-time/adjunct (0 women). Expenses: Contact institution. *Financial support:* Scholarships/grants available. Support available to part-time students. In 2008, 5 first professional degrees, 10 master's, 2 doctorates awarded. *Degree program information:* Part-time programs available. Offers Biblical studies (CBS); Christianity and culture (MA); divinity (M Div); evangelism (ME); ministry (D Min); New and Old Testament (MBT). *Application deadline:* For fall admission, 7/1 priority date for domestic students, 6/1 priority date for international students; for winter admission, 12/1 priority date for domestic students, 10/1 priority date for international students; for spring admission, 1/1 priority date for domestic students, 11/1 priority date for international students. Applications are processed on a rolling basis. *Application fee:* $50. *Application Contact:* Jim Dietz, Director of Student Services, 800-344-5669, Fax: 954-351-3343, E-mail: jdietz@knoxseminary.edu.

KOL YAAKOV TORAH CENTER, Monsey, NY 10952-2954

General Information Independent-religious, men only, comprehensive institution. *Graduate housing:* Room and/or apartments available to single students; on-campus housing not available to married students.

GRADUATE UNITS

Graduate Program *Degree program information:* Part-time and evening/weekend programs available.

KUTZTOWN UNIVERSITY OF PENNSYLVANIA, Kutztown, PA 19530-0730

General Information State-supported, coed, comprehensive institution. CGS member. *Enrollment:* 10,393 graduate, professional, and undergraduate students; 301 full-time matriculated graduate/professional students (203 women), 565 part-time matriculated graduate/professional students (435 women). *Enrollment by degree level:* 722 master's, 144 other advanced degrees. *Graduate faculty:* 86 full-time (42 women), 7 part-time/adjunct (4 women). Tuition, state resident: full-time $6430; part-time $357 per credit. Tuition, nonresident: full-time $10,288; part-time $572 per credit. *Required fees:* $1360; $72 per credit. $67 per semester. *Graduate housing:* Rooms and/or apartments available on a first-come, first-served basis to single and married students. *Student services:* Campus employment opportunities, campus safety program, career counseling, child daycare facilities, exercise/wellness program, free psychological counseling, international student services, low-cost health insurance, multicultural affairs office, services for students with disabilities. *Library facilities:* Rohrbach Library. *Online resources:* library catalog, web page, access to other libraries' catalogs. *Collection:* 500,484 titles, 15,600 serial subscriptions, 15,058 audiovisual materials.

Computer facilities: Computer purchase and lease plans are available. 950 computers available on campus for general student use. A campuswide network can be accessed from student residence rooms. Online class registration is available. *Web address:* http://www.kutztown.edu/.

General Application Contact: Dr. Linda Matthews, Interim Dean of Graduate Studies, 610-683-4201, Fax: 610-683-1393, E-mail: graduate@kutztown.edu.

GRADUATE UNITS

College of Graduate Studies and Extended Learning Students: 301 full-time (203 women), 565 part-time (435 women); includes 40 minority (17 African Americans, 3 American Indian/Alaska Native, 5 Asian Americans or Pacific Islanders, 15 Hispanic Americans), 19 international. Average age 30. 555 applicants, 72% accepted, 198 enrolled. *Faculty:* 86 full-time (42 women), 7 part-time/adjunct (4 women). Expenses: Contact institution. *Financial support:* Career-related internships or fieldwork, Federal Work-Study, scholarships/grants, tuition waivers, and unspecified assistantships available. Financial award application deadline: 3/1; financial award applicants required to submit FAFSA. In 2008, 278 degrees awarded. *Degree program information:* Part-time and evening/weekend programs available. Offers agency counseling (MA); counselor education (M Ed); marital and family therapy (MA); student affairs in higher education (M Ed). *Application deadline:* For fall admission, 8/15 priority date for domestic and international students; for spring admission, 12/15 priority date for domestic and international students. Applications are processed on a rolling basis. *Application fee:* $35. Electronic applications accepted. *Application Contact:* Dr. Linda Matthews, Interim Dean of Graduate Studies, 610-683-4201, Fax: 610-683-1393, E-mail: graduate@kutztown.edu. *Interim Dean of Graduate Studies,* Dr. Linda Matthews, 610-683-4201, Fax: 610-683-1393, E-mail: graduate@kutztown.edu.

College of Business Students: 16 full-time (8 women), 49 part-time (23 women); includes 3 minority (1 African American, 2 Hispanic Americans), 8 international. Average age 32. 50 applicants, 54% accepted, 10 enrolled. *Faculty:* 9 full-time (1 woman), 2 part-time/adjunct (0 women). Expenses: Contact institution. *Financial support:* Career-related internships or fieldwork, Federal Work-Study, scholarships/grants, tuition waivers, and unspecified assistantships available. Financial award application deadline: 3/1; financial award applicants required to submit FAFSA. In 2008, 43 master's awarded. *Degree program information:* Part-time and evening/weekend programs available. Offers business (MBA); business administration (MBA). *Application deadline:* For fall admission, 8/15 priority date for domestic and international students; for spring admission, 12/15 priority date for domestic and international students. Applications are processed on a rolling basis. *Application fee:* $35. Electronic applications accepted. *Application Contact:* Dr. Linda Matthews, Interim Dean of Graduate Studies, 610-683-4201, Fax: 610-683-1393, E-mail: graduate@kutztown.edu. *Dean,* Dr. William Dempsey, 610-683-4575, Fax: 610-683-4573, E-mail: dempsey@kutztown.edu.

College of Education Students: 117 full-time (73 women), 302 part-time (245 women); includes 11 minority (6 African Americans, 1 American Indian/Alaska Native, 3 Asian Americans or Pacific Islanders, 1 Hispanic American), 3 international. Average age 31. 230 applicants, 82% accepted, 92 enrolled. *Faculty:* 25 full-time (18 women), 4 part-time/adjunct (all women). Expenses: Contact institution. *Financial support:* Career-related internships or fieldwork, Federal Work-Study, scholarships/grants, and unspecified assistantships available. Financial award application deadline: 3/1; financial award applicants required to submit FAFSA. In 2008, 132 master's awarded. *Degree program information:* Part-time and evening/weekend programs available. Offers biology (M Ed); curriculum and instruction (M Ed); early childhood education (Certificate); education (M Ed, MLS, Certificate); elementary education (M Ed, Certificate); English (M Ed); instructional technology (M Ed, Certificate); library science (MLS, Certificate); mathematics (M Ed); reading (M Ed); secondary education (Certificate); social studies (M Ed); special education (Certificate). *Application deadline:* For fall admission, 8/15 priority date for domestic and international students; for spring admission, 12/15 priority date for domestic and international students. Applications are processed on a rolling basis. *Application fee:* $35. Electronic applications accepted. *Application Contact:* Dr. Linda Matthews, Interim Dean of Graduate Studies, 610-683-4201, Fax: 610-683-1393, E-mail: graduate@kutztown.edu. *Dean,* Dr. Darrell Garber, 610-683-4253, Fax: 610-683-4255, E-mail: garber@kutztown.edu.

College of Liberal Arts and Sciences Students: 62 full-time (42 women), 73 part-time (49 women); includes 14 minority (4 African Americans, 2 American Indian/Alaska Native, 1 Asian American or Pacific Islander, 7 Hispanic Americans), 7 international. Average age 30. 129 applicants, 70% accepted, 50 enrolled. *Faculty:* 30 full-time (13 women), 1 part-time/adjunct (0 women). Expenses: Contact institution. *Financial support:* Career-related internships or fieldwork, Federal Work-Study, scholarships/grants, and unspecified assistantships available. Financial award application deadline: 3/1; financial award applicants required to submit FAFSA. In 2008, 49 master's awarded. *Degree program information:* Part-time and evening/weekend programs available. Offers computer science (MS); electronic media (MS); English (MA); liberal arts and sciences (MA, MPA, MS, MSN, MSW, Certificate); public administration (MPA); school nursing (MSN, Certificate); social work (MSW). *Application deadline:* For fall admission, 8/15 priority date for domestic and international students; for spring admission, 12/15 priority date for domestic and international students. Applications are processed on a rolling basis. *Application fee:* $35. Electronic applications accepted. *Application Contact:* Dr. Linda Matthews, Interim Dean of Graduate Studies, 610-683-4201, Fax: 610-683-1393, E-mail: graduate@kutztown.edu. *Acting Dean,* Dr. Anne E. Zayaitz, 610-683-4315, Fax: 610-683-4633, E-mail: zayaitz@kutztown.edu.

College of Visual and Performing Arts Students: 26 full-time (18 women), 51 part-time (39 women); includes 4 minority (2 African Americans, 1 Asian American or Pacific Islander, 1 Hispanic American), 1 international. Average age 30. 40 applicants, 88% accepted, 22 enrolled. *Faculty:* 8 full-time (3 women). Expenses: Contact institution. *Financial support:* Career-related internships or fieldwork, Federal Work-Study, scholarships/grants, and unspecified assistantships available. Financial award application deadline: 3/1; financial award applicants required to submit FAFSA. In 2008, 18 master's awarded. *Degree program information:* Part-time programs available. Offers art education (M Ed, Certificate); music education (Certificate); visual and performing arts (M Ed, Certificate). *Application deadline:* For fall admission, 8/15 priority date for domestic and international students; for spring admission, 12/15 priority date for domestic and international students. Applications are processed on a rolling basis. *Application fee:* $35. Electronic applications accepted. *Application Contact:* Dr. Linda Matthews, Interim Dean of Graduate Studies, 610-683-4201, Fax: 610-683-1393, E-mail: graduate@kutztown.edu. *Dean,* Dr. William Mowder, 610-683-4500, Fax: 610-683-4547, E-mail: mowder@kutztown.edu.

LAGRANGE COLLEGE, LaGrange, GA 30240-2999

General Information Independent-religious, coed, comprehensive institution. *Graduate housing:* Room and/or apartments available on a first-come, first-served basis to single students; on-campus housing not available to married students. Housing application deadline: 5/1.

GRADUATE UNITS

Graduate Programs *Degree program information:* Part-time and evening/weekend programs available. Offers curriculum and instruction (M Ed); middle grades (MAT); organizational leadership (MA); secondary education (MAT). Electronic applications accepted.

LAGUNA COLLEGE OF ART & DESIGN, Laguna Beach, CA 92651-1136

General Information Independent, coed, comprehensive institution.

GRADUATE UNITS

Graduate Program Electronic applications accepted.

LAKE ERIE COLLEGE, Painesville, OH 44077-3389

General Information Independent, coed, comprehensive institution. *Enrollment:* 1,054 graduate, professional, and undergraduate students; 22 full-time matriculated graduate/professional students (10 women), 352 part-time matriculated graduate/professional students (282 women). *Enrollment by degree level:* 274 master's. *Graduate faculty:* 14 full-time (7 women), 10 part-time/adjunct (3 women). Tuition and fees vary according to course load and program. *Graduate housing:* On-campus housing not available. *Student services:* Campus employment opportunities, campus safety program, career counseling, exercise/wellness program, free psychological counseling, international student services, services for students with disabilities, teacher training. *Library facilities:* Lincoln Library. *Online resources:* library catalog, web page. *Collection:* 80,000 titles, 10,000 serial subscriptions, 1,230 audiovisual materials.

Computer facilities: 104 computers available on campus for general student use. A campuswide network can be accessed from student residence rooms and from off campus. Online class registration is available. *Web address:* http://www.lec.edu/.

General Application Contact: Hendrik Wolfert, Graduate School Admissions Office, 800-916-0904, Fax: 440-375-7005, E-mail: admissions@lec.edu.

GRADUATE UNITS

Division of Education Students: 2 full-time (1 woman), 170 part-time (162 women); includes 16 minority (12 African Americans, 2 Asian Americans or Pacific Islanders, 2 Hispanic Americans). Average age 37. 14 applicants, 71% accepted, 9 enrolled. *Faculty:* 4 full-time (3 women), 4 part-time/adjunct (3 women). Expenses: Contact institution. *Financial support:* Applicants required to submit FAFSA. In 2008, 22 master's awarded. *Degree program information:* Part-time and evening/weekend programs available. Offers curriculum and instruction (MS Ed); education (MS Ed); educational leadership (MS Ed); reading (MS Ed). *Application deadline:* For fall admission, 8/1 priority date for domestic students, 6/1 for international students; for spring admission, 12/15 for domestic students, 10/1 for international students. Applications are processed on a rolling basis. *Application fee:* $25 ($50 for international students). Electronic applications accepted. *Application Contact:* Hendrik Wolfert, Graduate School Admissions Officer, 800-916.0904, Fax: 440-375-7005, E-mail: admissions@lec.edu. *Associate Dean*, Dr. Richard Bonde, 440-375-7156, Fax: 440-375-7005, E-mail: rbonde@lec.edu.

Division of Management Studies Students: 20 full-time (9 women), 182 part-time (95 women); includes 10 minority (8 African Americans, 2 Asian Americans or Pacific Islanders). Average age 33. 69 applicants, 83% accepted, 51 enrolled. *Faculty:* 10 full-time (4 women), 6 part-time/adjunct (0 women). Expenses: Contact institution. *Financial support:* Career-related internships or fieldwork and unspecified assistantships available. Financial award applicants required to submit FAFSA. In 2008, 34 master's awarded. *Degree program information:* Part-time and evening/weekend programs available. Offers general management (MBA); management healthcare administration (MBA). *Application deadline:* For fall admission, 8/1 priority date for domestic students, 6/1 for international students; for spring admission, 12/15 for domestic students, 10/1 for international students. Applications are processed on a rolling basis. *Application fee:* $25 ($50 for international students). Electronic applications accepted. *Application Contact:* Hendrik Wolfert, Graduate Admissions Officer, 800-533-4996, Fax: 440-375-7005, E-mail: admissions@lec.edu. *Associate Dean*, Prof. Robert Trebar, 440-375-7115, Fax: 440-375-7005, E-mail: rtrebar@lec.edu.

LAKE ERIE COLLEGE OF OSTEOPATHIC MEDICINE, Erie, PA 16509-1025

General Information Independent, coed, graduate-only institution. *Graduate housing:* On-campus housing not available. *Research affiliation:* West Virginia University (neurology), Neuro Structural Research Laboratories (neurology), Cornelli Consulting (CORCON, Italy) (neurology), University of Maryland (neurology), Duke University (neurology).

GRADUATE UNITS

Professional Programs Offers biomedical sciences (Postbaccalaureate Certificate); medical education (MS); osteopathic medicine (DO); pharmacy (Pharm D). Electronic applications accepted.

LAKE FOREST COLLEGE, Lake Forest, IL 60045-2399

General Information Independent, coed, comprehensive institution. *Graduate housing:* On-campus housing not available. *Research affiliation:* Newberry Library (Medieval history), Argonne National Laboratory (physics), Merck (undergraduate research), National Science Foundation, Lake Forest Hospital (genomes).

GRADUATE UNITS

Graduate Program in Liberal Studies *Degree program information:* Part-time and evening/weekend programs available. Offers liberal studies (MLS).

LAKE FOREST GRADUATE SCHOOL OF MANAGEMENT, Lake Forest, IL 60045

General Information Independent, coed, graduate-only institution. *Enrollment by degree level:* 809 master's. *Graduate faculty:* 136 part-time/adjunct (31 women). *Tuition:* Part-time $675 per quarter hour. *Graduate housing:* On-campus housing not available. *Library facilities:* Members of online Electric Library and OCLC Library.

Computer facilities: 11 computers available on campus for general student use. A campuswide network can be accessed. *Web address:* http://www.lakeforestmba.edu/.

General Application Contact: Angel Fournier, Director of Admissions Operations, 800-737-4MBA, Fax: 847-295-3656, E-mail: admiss@lfgsm.edu.

GRADUATE UNITS

MBA Program Students: 809 part-time (310 women); includes 232 minority (62 African Americans, 1 American Indian/Alaska Native, 140 Asian Americans or Pacific Islanders, 29 Hispanic Americans). Average age 38. *Faculty:* 136 part-time/adjunct (31 women). Expenses: Contact institution. *Financial support:* In 2008–09, 290 students received support. Scholarships/grants available. Support available to part-time students. Financial award applicants required to submit FAFSA. In 2008, 196 master's awarded. *Degree program information:* Part-time and evening/weekend programs available. Offers management (MBA). *Application deadline:* For fall admission, 8/13 for domestic students; for spring admission, 1/15 for domestic students. Applications are processed on a rolling basis. *Application fee:* $0. Electronic applications accepted. *Application Contact:* Angel Fournier, Director of Admissions Operations, 800-737-4MBA, Fax: 847-295-3656, E-mail: admiss@lfgsm.edu. *Vice President and Degree Programs Dean*, Arlene Mayzel, 847-574-5198, Fax: 847-574-5199, E-mail: amayzel@lfgsm.edu.

LAKEHEAD UNIVERSITY, Thunder Bay, ON P7B 5E1, Canada

General Information Province-supported, coed, comprehensive institution. *Enrollment:* 7,768 graduate, professional, and undergraduate students; 228 full-time matriculated graduate/professional students (126 women), 95 part-time matriculated graduate/professional students (59 women). *Enrollment by degree level:* 309 master's, 14 doctoral. *Graduate faculty:* 178 full-time (46 women), 28 part-time/adjunct (6 women). *Graduate tuition:* Tuition charges are reported in Canadian dollars. *International tuition:* $13,700 Canadian dollars full-time. *Tuition, area resident:* Full-time $6500 Canadian dollars. *Graduate housing:* Rooms and/or apartments available to single students and available on a first-come, first-served basis to married students. Housing application deadline: 3/10. *Student services:* Campus employment opportunities, campus safety program, career counseling, child daycare facilities, exercise/wellness program, free psychological counseling, grant writing training, international student services, low-cost health insurance, multicultural affairs office, services for students with disabilities, teacher training, writing training. *Library facilities:* Chancellor Norman M. Paterson Library plus 1 other. *Online resources:* library catalog, web page. *Collection:* 613,047 titles, 33,396 serial subscriptions, 1,080 audiovisual materials. *Research affiliation:* Falcon bridge (biology), Placer Dome (biology), Bowater Inc. (engineering), Centre for Northern Forest Ecosystem Research (biology, forestry, tourism), Thunder Bay Regional Cancer Centre (psychosocial oncology), Bowater Inc. (chemistry).

Computer facilities: 594 computers available on campus for general student use. A campuswide network can be accessed from student residence rooms and from off campus. Online class registration is available. *Web address:* http://www.lakeheadu.ca/.

General Application Contact: Elena Arena, Graduate Admissions Officer, 807-343-8527, Fax: 807-346-7705, E-mail: gstudent@lakeheadu.ca.

GRADUATE UNITS

Graduate Studies Tuition charges are reported in Canadian dollars. *Degree program information:* Part-time and evening/weekend programs available. Offers clinical psychology (PhD); experimental psychology (MA); geology (M Sc); gerontology (MA); history (MA); physics (M Sc); specialization gerontology (M Ed, M Sc, MA, MSW); women's studies (MA).

Faculty of Education Tuition charges are reported in Canadian dollars. *Degree program information:* Part-time and evening/weekend programs available. Offers educational studies (PhD); gerontology (M Ed); women's studies (M Ed).

Faculty of Engineering Tuition charges are reported in Canadian dollars. *Degree program information:* Part-time programs available. Offers control engineering (M Sc Engr); electrical/computer engineering (M Sc Engr); environmental engineering (M Sc Engr).

Faculty of Forestry Tuition charges are reported in Canadian dollars. *Degree program information:* Part-time programs available. Offers forest sciences (PhD); forestry (M Sc F, MF).

Faculty of Social Sciences and Humanities Tuition charges are reported in Canadian dollars. *Degree program information:* Part-time and evening/weekend programs available. Offers biology (M Sc); chemistry (M Sc); economics (MA); English (MA); gerontology (MA); health services and policy research (MA); social sciences and humanities (M Sc, MA, MSW, PhD); sociology (MA); women's studies (MA).

School of Kinesiology Tuition charges are reported in Canadian dollars. *Degree program information:* Part-time programs available. Offers kinesiology (M Sc); kinesiology and gerontology (M Sc).

School of Mathematical Sciences Tuition charges are reported in Canadian dollars. *Degree program information:* Part-time and evening/weekend programs available. Offers computer science (M Sc); mathematical science (MA).

School of Social Work Tuition charges are reported in Canadian dollars. *Degree program information:* Part-time programs available. Offers gerontology (MSW); social work (MSW); women's studies (MSW).

LAKELAND COLLEGE, Sheboygan, WI 53082-0359

General Information Independent-religious, coed, comprehensive institution. *Graduate housing:* On-campus housing not available.

GRADUATE UNITS

Graduate Studies Division *Degree program information:* Part-time and evening/weekend programs available. Offers accounting (MBA); counseling (MA); education (M Ed); finance (MBA); healthcare management (MBA); project management (MBA); theology (MAT).

LAMAR UNIVERSITY, Beaumont, TX 77710

General Information State-supported, coed, university. CGS member. *Enrollment:* 13,465 graduate, professional, and undergraduate students; 715 full-time matriculated graduate/professional students (266 women), 3,757 part-time matriculated graduate/professional students (2,731 women). *Enrollment by degree level:* 4,358 master's, 114 doctoral. *Graduate faculty:* 185 full-time (61 women), 20 part-time/adjunct (4 women). Tuition, state resident: full-time $5000; part-time $195 per credit. Tuition, nonresident: full-time $12,376; part-time $476 per credit. *Required fees:* $1570. *Graduate housing:* Room and/or apartments available to single students; on-campus housing not available to married students. Typical cost: $6290 (including board). Room and board charges vary according to board plan. Housing application deadline: 9/1. *Student services:* Campus employment opportunities, campus safety program, career counseling, child daycare facilities, exercise/wellness program, free psychological counseling, grant writing training, international student services, low-cost health insurance, multicultural affairs office, services for students with disabilities, teacher training, writing training. *Library facilities:* Mary and John Gray Library. *Online resources:* library catalog, web page. *Collection:* 698,285 titles, 2,900 serial subscriptions, 6,572 audiovisual materials. *Research affiliation:* Grants Resource Center, National Council of Research Administrators, BASF.

Computer facilities: 120 computers available on campus for general student use. A campuswide network can be accessed from student residence rooms and from off campus. *Web address:* http://www.lamar.edu/.

General Application Contact: Sandy Drane, Coordinator of Graduate Admissions, 409-880-8356, Fax: 409-880-8414, E-mail: gradmissions@hal.lamar.edu.

GRADUATE UNITS

College of Graduate Studies Students: 715 full-time (266 women), 3,757 part-time (2,731 women); includes 1,029 minority (430 African Americans, 21 American Indian/Alaska Native, 57 Asian Americans or Pacific Islanders, 521 Hispanic Americans), 539 international. Average age 34. 3,324 applicants, 76% accepted, 674 enrolled. *Faculty:* 185 full-time (61 women), 20 part-time/adjunct (4 women). Expenses: Contact institution. *Financial support:* Fellowships with partial tuition reimbursements, research assistantships, teaching assistantships, career-related internships or fieldwork, Federal Work-Study, institutionally sponsored loans, scholarships/grants, and tuition waivers (partial) available. Support available to part-time students. Financial award application deadline: 4/1; financial award applicants required to submit FAFSA. In 2008, 450 master's, 34 doctorates awarded. *Degree program information:* Part-time and evening/weekend programs available. *Application deadline:* For fall admission, 5/15 for domestic students; for spring admission, 10/1 for domestic students. Applications are processed on a rolling basis. *Application fee:* $25 ($50 for international students). *Application Contact:* Sandy Drane, Coordinator of Graduate Admissions, 409-880-8356, Fax: 409-880-8414, E-mail: gradmissions@hal.lamar.edu.

College of Arts and Sciences Students: 135 full-time (40 women), 71 part-time (37 women); includes 19 minority (10 African Americans, 2 Asian Americans or Pacific Islanders, 7 Hispanic Americans), 100 international. Average age 28. 338 applicants, 33% accepted, 64 enrolled. *Faculty:* 67 full-time (18 women), 1 part-time/adjunct (0 women). Expenses: Contact institution. *Financial support:* Fellowships, research assistantships, teaching assistantships with tuition reimbursements, career-related internships or fieldwork, Federal Work-Study, institutionally sponsored loans, scholarships/grants, and tuition waivers (partial) available. Support available to part-time students. Financial award application deadline: 4/1. In 2008, 68 master's awarded. *Degree program information:* Part-time and evening/weekend programs available. Offers applied criminology (MS); arts and sciences (MA, MPA, MS, MSN); biology (MS); chemistry (MS); community/clinical psychology (MS); computer science (MS); English (MA); history (MA); industrial/organizational psychology (MS); mathematics (MS); nursing administration (MSN); nursing education (MSN); public administration (MPA). *Application deadline:* For fall admission, 8/1 priority date for domestic students; for spring admission, 12/1 priority date for domestic students. Applications are processed on a rolling basis. *Application fee:* $25 ($50 for international students). *Application Contact:* Dr. James W. Westgate, Assistant Dean, 409-880-7978, E-mail: westgate@hal.lamar.edu. *Dean*, Dr. Brenda S. Nichols, 409-880-8508, Fax: 409-880-8007.

College of Business Students: 45 full-time (18 women), 46 part-time (12 women); includes 10 minority (4 African Americans, 2 Asian Americans or Pacific Islanders, 4 Hispanic Americans), 18 international. Average age 29. 177 applicants, 50% accepted, 20 enrolled. *Faculty:* 10 full-time (3 women), 5 part-time/adjunct (0 women). Expenses: Contact institution. *Financial support:* In 2008–09, 12 students received support, including 4 research assistantships with partial tuition reimbursements available; fellowships with tuition reimbursements available, career-related internships or fieldwork, Federal Work-Study, institutionally sponsored loans, scholarships/grants, and tuition waivers (partial) also available. Support available to part-time students. Financial award application deadline: 4/1; financial award applicants required to submit FAFSA. In 2008, 33 master's awarded. *Degree program information:* Part-time and evening/weekend programs available. Offers accounting (MBA); experiential business and entrepreneurship (MBA); financial management (MBA); healthcare administration (MBA); information systems (MBA); management (MBA). *Application deadline:* For fall admission, 3/15 priority date for domestic students; for spring admission, 10/1 priority date for domestic students. Applications are processed on a rolling basis. *Application fee:* $25 ($50 for international students). *Application Contact:* Dr. Brad Mayer, Professor and Associate Dean, 409-880-2383, Fax: 409-880-8605, E-mail: bradley.mayer@lamar.edu. *Dean*, Dr. Enrique R. Venta, 409-880-8604, Fax: 409-880-8088, E-mail: henry.venta@lamar.edu.

College of Education and Human Development Students: 120 full-time (91 women), 3,507 part-time (2,638 women); includes 963 minority (395 African Americans, 20 American Indian/Alaska Native, 45 Asian Americans or Pacific Islanders, 503 Hispanic Americans), 13 international. Average age 39. 2,174 applicants, 93% accepted, 401 enrolled. *Faculty:* 28 full-time (18 women), 6 part-time/adjunct (1 woman). Expenses: Contact institution. *Financial support:* Fellowships, research assistantships, teaching assistantships, career-related internships or fieldwork, Federal Work-Study, institutionally sponsored loans, and scholarships/grants available. Support available to part-time students. Financial award application deadline: 4/1. In 2008, 89 master's, 21 doctorates awarded. *Degree program information:* Part-time and evening/weekend programs available. Postbaccalaureate distance

Lamar University (continued)

learning degree programs offered. Offers counseling and development (M Ed, Certificate); education administration (M Ed); education and human development (M Ed, MS, DE, Ed D, Certificate); educational leadership (DE); family and consumer science (MS); kinesiology (MS); principal (Certificate); professional pedagogy (Ed D); school superintendent (Certificate); supervision (M Ed); technology application (Certificate); vocational home economics (Certificate). *Application deadline:* For fall admission, 8/1 for domestic students; for spring admission, 12/1 for domestic students. Applications are processed on a rolling basis. *Application fee:* $25 ($50 for international students). *Application Contact:* Dr. Lula Henry, Director of Professional Service, 409-880-8218. *Dean*, Dr. H. Lowery-Moore, 409-880-8661.

College of Engineering Students: 338 full-time (50 women), 98 part-time (18 women); includes 10 minority (5 African Americans, 5 Asian Americans or Pacific Islanders), 405 international. Average age 24. 656 applicants, 35% accepted, 152 enrolled. *Faculty:* 42 full-time (3 women), 3 part-time/adjunct (0 women). Expenses: Contact institution. *Financial support:* In 2008–09, fellowships with partial tuition reimbursements (averaging $6,000 per year), research assistantships with partial tuition reimbursements (averaging $7,500 per year), teaching assistantships with partial tuition reimbursements (averaging $7,500 per year) were awarded; career-related internships or fieldwork, Federal Work-Study, institutionally sponsored loans, scholarships/grants, tuition waivers (full and partial), and laboratory assistantships, graders also available. Support available to part-time students. Financial award application deadline: 4/1. In 2008, 228 master's, 9 doctorates awarded. *Degree program information:* Part-time and evening/weekend programs available. Offers chemical engineering (ME, MES, DE, PhD); civil engineering (ME, MES, DE); electrical engineering (ME, MES, DE); engineering (ME, MEM, MES, MS, DE, PhD); engineering management (MEM); environmental engineering (MS); environmental studies (MS); industrial engineering (ME, MES, DE); mechanical engineering (ME, MES, DE). *Application deadline:* For fall admission, 5/15 priority date for domestic students; for spring admission, 10/1 priority date for domestic students. Applications are processed on a rolling basis. *Application fee:* $25 ($50 for international students). *Application Contact:* Sandy Drane, Coordinator of Graduate Admissions, 409-880-8356, Fax: 409-880-8414, E-mail: gradmissions@hal.lamar.edu. *Chair*, Dr. Jack Hopper, 409-880-8784, Fax: 409-880-2197, E-mail: che_dept@hal.lamar.edu.

College of Fine Arts and Communication Students: 77 full-time (67 women), 35 part-time (26 women); includes 27 minority (16 African Americans, 1 American Indian/Alaska Native, 3 Asian Americans or Pacific Islanders, 7 Hispanic Americans), 3 international. Average age 30. 116 applicants, 56% accepted, 31 enrolled. *Faculty:* 30 full-time (16 women), 4 part-time/adjunct (2 women). Expenses: Contact institution. *Financial support:* Fellowships, research assistantships, teaching assistantships, career-related internships or fieldwork, Federal Work-Study, institutionally sponsored loans, and tuition waivers (partial) available. Support available to part-time students. Financial award application deadline: 4/1. In 2008, 46 master's, 4 doctorates awarded. *Degree program information:* Part-time and evening/weekend programs available. Offers art history (MA); audiology (MS, Au D); deaf studies and deaf education (MS, Ed D); fine arts and communication (MA, MM, MM Ed, MS, Au D, Ed D); music education (MM Ed); music performance (MM); photography (MA); speech language pathology (MS); studio art (MA); theatre (MS); visual design (MA). *Application deadline:* For fall admission, 8/1 for domestic students; for spring admission, 12/1 for domestic students. Applications are processed on a rolling basis. *Application fee:* $25 ($50 for international students). *Application Contact:* Debbie Piper, Coordinator of Graduate Admissions, 409-880-8356, Fax: 409-880-8414, E-mail: gradmissions@hal.lamar.edu. *Dean*, Dr. Russ A. Schultz, 409-880-8137, Fax: 409-880-2286, E-mail: russ.schultz@lamar.edu.

LANCASTER BIBLE COLLEGE, Lancaster, PA 17608-3403

General Information Independent-religious, coed, comprehensive institution. *Graduate housing:* On-campus housing not available.

GRADUATE UNITS

Graduate School *Degree program information:* Part-time and evening/weekend programs available. Offers Bible (MA); consulting resource teacher (M Ed); counseling (MA); ministry (MA); school counseling (M Ed).

LANCASTER THEOLOGICAL SEMINARY, Lancaster, PA 17603-2812

General Information Independent-religious, coed, graduate-only institution. *Graduate housing:* Rooms and/or apartments available on a first-come, first-served basis to single and married students. Housing application deadline: 8/1.

GRADUATE UNITS

Graduate and Professional Programs Offers biblical studies (M Div, MAR); church life and work (M Div, MAR); historical studies (M Div, MAR); integrated ministry studies (M Div, MAR); lay leadership (Certificate); theological studies (M Div, MAR); theology (D Min).

LANDER UNIVERSITY, Greenwood, SC 29649-2099

General Information State-supported, coed, primarily women, comprehensive institution. *Graduate housing:* Room and/or apartments available on a first-come, first-served basis to single students; on-campus housing not available to married students.

GRADUATE UNITS

School of Education *Degree program information:* Part-time programs available. Offers elementary education (M Ed); teaching (MAT). Electronic applications accepted.

LANGSTON UNIVERSITY, Langston, OK 73050-0907

General Information State-supported, coed, comprehensive institution. CGS member. *Graduate housing:* Rooms and/or apartments available on a first-come, first-served basis to single and married students.

GRADUATE UNITS

School of Education and Behavioral Sciences *Degree program information:* Part-time programs available. Offers bilingual/multicultural (M Ed); elementary education (M Ed); English as a second language (M Ed); rehabilitation counseling (M Sc); urban education (M Ed).

School of Physical Therapy Offers physical therapy (DPT).

LA ROCHE COLLEGE, Pittsburgh, PA 15237-5898

General Information Independent-religious, coed, comprehensive institution. *Enrollment:* 1,425 graduate, professional, and undergraduate students; 56 full-time matriculated graduate/professional students (35 women), 76 part-time matriculated graduate/professional students (64 women). *Enrollment by degree level:* 111 master's, 21 other advanced degrees. *Graduate faculty:* 6 full-time (4 women), 6 part-time/adjunct (2 women). *Tuition:* Full-time $9450; part-time $525 per credit. *Graduate housing:* On-campus housing not available. *Student services:* Campus employment opportunities, career counseling, free psychological counseling, international student services, low-cost health insurance, multicultural affairs office, services for students with disabilities. *Library facilities:* John J. Wright Library. *Online resources:* library catalog, web page. *Collection:* 115,215 titles, 582 serial subscriptions.

Computer facilities: Computer purchase and lease plans are available. 186 computers available on campus for general student use. A campuswide network can be accessed. Online class registration is available. *Web address:* http://www.laroche.edu/.

General Application Contact: Hope Schiffgens, Director of Graduate Studies and Adult Education, 412-536-1266, Fax: 412-536-1283, E-mail: schombh1@laroche.edu.

GRADUATE UNITS

School of Graduate Studies and Adult Education Students: 56 full-time (35 women), 73 part-time (62 women); includes 8 minority (7 African Americans, 1 Hispanic American), 13 international. Average age 33. 48 applicants, 96% accepted, 43 enrolled. *Faculty:* 6 full-time (4 women), 8 part-time/adjunct (3 women). Expenses: Contact institution. *Financial support:* Unspecified assistantships available. Financial award application deadline: 3/31; financial award applicants required to submit FAFSA. In 2008, 71 master's awarded. *Degree program information:* Part-time and evening/weekend programs available. Offers human resources management (MS, Certificate); nurse anesthesia (MS); nursing education (MSN); nursing management (MSN). *Application deadline:* For fall admission, 8/15 for domestic and international students; for spring admission, 12/15 for domestic and international students. Applications are processed on a rolling basis. *Application fee:* $50. Electronic applications accepted. *Application Contact:* Hope Schiffgens, Director of Graduate Studies and Adult Education, 412-536-1266, Fax: 412-536-1283, E-mail: schombh1@laroche.edu. *Interim Dean*, Dr. Jean Forti, PhD, 412-536-1193, Fax: 412-536-1179, E-mail: fortij1@laroche.edu.

LA SALLE UNIVERSITY, Philadelphia, PA 19141-1199

General Information Independent-religious, coed, comprehensive institution. *Graduate housing:* Room and/or apartments available on a first-come, first-served basis to single students; on-campus housing not available to married students. Housing application deadline: 7/1.

GRADUATE UNITS

Program in Instructional Technology Management Offers instructional technology management (MS). Electronic applications accepted.

School of Arts and Sciences *Degree program information:* Part-time and evening/weekend programs available. Offers arts and sciences (MA, MS, Psy D); bilingual/bicultural studies (Spanish) (MA); Central and Eastern European studies (MA); clinical psychology (Psy D); clinical-counseling psychology (MA); computer information science (MS); education (MA); family psychology (Psy D); history (MA); information technology leadership (MS); pastoral studies (MA); professional communication (MA); rehabilitation psychology (Psy D); religion (MA); theological studies (MA).

School of Business *Degree program information:* Part-time and evening/weekend programs available. Offers business (MBA, MS, Certificate). Electronic applications accepted.

School of Nursing and Health Sciences Offers nursing (MSN, Certificate); nursing and health sciences (MS, MSN, Certificate); speech-language-hearing science (MS).

LASELL COLLEGE, Newton, MA 02466-2709

General Information Independent, coed, comprehensive institution. *Enrollment:* 1,469 graduate, professional, and undergraduate students; 19 full-time matriculated graduate/professional students (17 women), 63 part-time matriculated graduate/professional students (46 women). *Enrollment by degree level:* 80 master's, 2 other advanced degrees. *Graduate faculty:* 5 full-time (4 women), 9 part-time/adjunct (6 women). *Tuition:* Full-time $4500; part-time $500 per credit hour. *Required fees:* $55 per term. *Graduate housing:* On-campus housing not available. *Student services:* Campus safety program, career counseling, low-cost health insurance, services for students with disabilities. *Library facilities:* Brennan Library. *Online resources:* library catalog, web page, access to other libraries' catalogs. *Collection:* 55,147 titles, 169 serial subscriptions, 2,492 audiovisual materials. *Research affiliation:* The RoseMary B. Fuss Center for Research on Aging and Intergenerational Studies (Elder Care), Lasell Village (Elder Care).

Computer facilities: Computer purchase and lease plans are available. 150 computers available on campus for general student use. A campuswide network can be accessed from student residence rooms and from off campus. Online class registration is available. *Web address:* http://www.lasell.edu/.

General Application Contact: Adrienne Franciosi, Director of Graduate Admission, 617-243-2400, Fax: 617-243-2450, E-mail: gradinfo@lasell.edu.

GRADUATE UNITS

Graduate and Professional Studies in Communication Expenses: Contact institution. *Financial support:* Institutionally sponsored loans available. Support available to part-time students. Financial award application deadline: 8/30; financial award applicants required to submit FAFSA. *Degree program information:* Part-time and evening/weekend programs available. Postbaccalaureate distance learning degree programs offered (minimal on-campus study). Offers integrated marketing communication (MSC, Graduate Certificate); public relations (MSC, Graduate Certificate). *Application deadline:* For fall admission, 8/30 priority date for domestic and international students; for winter admission, 11/30 priority date for domestic and international students; for spring admission, 12/30 priority date for domestic and international students. Applications are processed on a rolling basis. *Application fee:* $40. Electronic applications accepted. *Application Contact:* Adrienne Franciosi, Director of Graduate Admission, 617-243-2400, Fax: 617-243-2450, E-mail: gradinfo@lasell.edu. *Chair, Department of Communication*, Dr. Janice Barrett, 617-243-2400, E-mail: gradinfo@lasell.edu.

Graduate and Professional Studies in Management Students: 19 full-time (17 women), 63 part-time (46 women); includes 17 minority (10 African Americans, 1 Asian American or Pacific Islander, 6 Hispanic Americans), 12 international. Average age 30. 52 applicants, 69% accepted, 26 enrolled. *Faculty:* 5 full-time (4 women), 9 part-time/adjunct (6 women). Expenses: Contact institution. *Financial support:* In 2008–09, 68 students received support. Loans available. Support available to part-time students. Financial award application deadline: 8/30; financial award applicants required to submit FAFSA. In 2008, 23 master's awarded. *Degree program information:* Part-time and evening/weekend programs available. Postbaccalaureate distance learning degree programs offered (no on-campus study). Offers elder care administration (MSM, Graduate Certificate); elder care marketing (MSM, Graduate Certificate); fundraising management (Graduate Certificate); human resource management (Graduate Certificate); management (MSM, Graduate Certificate); marketing (MSM, Graduate Certificate); non-profit management (MSM, Graduate Certificate); project management (Graduate Certificate). *Application deadline:* For fall admission, 8/30 priority date for domestic and international students; for winter admission, 11/30 priority date for domestic and international students; for spring admission, 12/30 priority date for domestic and international students. Applications are processed on a rolling basis. *Application fee:* $40. Electronic applications accepted. *Application Contact:* Adrienne Franciosi, Director of Graduate Admission, 617-243-2400, Fax: 617-243-2450, E-mail: gradinfo@lasell.edu. *Chair of Marketing and Management*, Dr. Nancy Waldron, 617-243-2400, Fax: 617-243-2450, E-mail: gradinfo@lasell.edu.

LA SIERRA UNIVERSITY, Riverside, CA 92515

General Information Independent-religious, coed, comprehensive institution. CGS member. *Graduate housing:* Rooms and/or apartments available on a first-come, first-served basis to single students and available to married students.

GRADUATE UNITS

College of Arts and Sciences *Degree program information:* Part-time programs available. Offers arts and sciences (MA); communication (MA); English (MA).

School of Business and Management Offers accounting (MBA); finance (MBA); general management (MBA); human resources management (MBA); leadership, values, and ethics for business and management (Certificate); marketing (MBA).

School of Education *Degree program information:* Part-time and evening/weekend programs available. Offers administration and leadership (MA, Ed D, Ed S); counseling (MA); curriculum and instruction (MA, Ed D, Ed S); education (MA, MAT, Ed D, Ed S); educational psychology (Ed S); school psychology (Ed S); teaching (MAT).

School of Religion *Degree program information:* Part-time programs available. Offers pastoral ministry (M Div); religion (MA); religious education (MA); religious studies (MA).

LAURA AND ALVIN SIEGAL COLLEGE OF JUDAIC STUDIES, Beachwood, OH 44122-7116

General Information Independent, coed, comprehensive institution. *Graduate housing:* On-campus housing not available.

GRADUATE UNITS

Graduate Programs *Degree program information:* Part-time and evening/weekend programs available. Postbaccalaureate distance learning degree programs offered (no on-campus study). Offers humanities (MA); Jewish education (MAJS); Judaic studies (MAJS); religious education (MAJS).

LAURENTIAN UNIVERSITY, Sudbury, ON P3E 2C6, Canada

General Information Province-supported, coed, comprehensive institution. *Graduate housing:* Rooms and/or apartments available on a first-come, first-served basis to single and married students.

GRADUATE UNITS

School of Graduate Studies and Research *Degree program information:* Part-time and evening/weekend programs available. Offers analytical chemistry (M Sc); applied physics (M Sc); applied psychology (MA); applied social research (MA); biochemistry (M Sc); biology (M Sc); boreal ecology (PhD); environmental chemistry (M Sc); European history (MA); experimental psychology (MA); geology (M Sc); history of Northern Ontario (MA); human development (M Sc, MA); humanities: interpretation and values (MA); mineral deposits and precambrian geology (PhD); mineral exploration (M Sc); North American history (MA); nursing (M Sc N); organic chemistry (M Sc); physical/theoretical chemistry (M Sc); rural and Northern health (PhD); science communication (G Dip).

School of Commerce and Administration *Degree program information:* Part-time and evening/weekend programs available. Offers commerce and administration (MBA).

School of Engineering *Degree program information:* Part-time programs available. Offers mineral resources engineering (M Eng, MA Sc); natural resources engineering (PhD).

School of Social Work *Degree program information:* Part-time programs available. Offers social service (MSS). Open only to French-speaking students.

LAWRENCE TECHNOLOGICAL UNIVERSITY, Southfield, MI 48075-1058

General Information Independent, coed, university. *Enrollment:* 4,417 graduate, professional, and undergraduate students; 63 full-time matriculated graduate/professional students (15 women), 1,335 part-time matriculated graduate/professional students (446 women). *Enrollment by degree level:* 1,308 master's, 90 doctoral. *Graduate faculty:* 57 full-time (18 women), 91 part-time/adjunct (21 women). *Tuition:* Part-time $763 per credit hour. *Required fees:* $115 per semester. Tuition and fees vary according to course level, degree level, campus/location and program. *Graduate housing:* Rooms and/or apartments available on a first-come, first-served basis to single and married students. Housing application deadline: 5/1. *Student services:* Campus employment opportunities, career counseling, exercise/wellness program, free psychological counseling, international student services, low-cost health insurance, services for students with disabilities, writing training. *Library facilities:* Lawrence Technological University Library plus 1 other. *Online resources:* library catalog, web page, access to other libraries' catalogs. *Collection:* 129,721 titles, 62,000 serial subscriptions, 170 audiovisual materials. *Research affiliation:* The U.S. Army Tank Automotive Research, Development and Engineering Center (TARDEC) (durability of composite armor structures), Army Research Labs (development of armor structures), U.S. Department of Transportation (development of long-lasting, corrosion-free bridges), Michigan Department of Transportation (use of carbon fiber in box beam highway bridges), National Renewable Energy Laboratory (NREL) (solar design), William Beaumont Hospital (biomedical engineering).

Computer facilities: Computer purchase and lease plans are available. 60 computers available on campus for general student use. A campuswide network can be accessed from student residence rooms and from off campus. Online class registration, degree audit, Blackboard, SCT Banner (student information) are available. *Web address:* http://www.ltu.edu/.

General Application Contact: Director of Admissions, 248-204-3160, Fax: 248-204-3188, E-mail: admissions@ltu.edu.

GRADUATE UNITS

College of Architecture and Design Students: 17 full-time (12 women), 105 part-time (44 women); includes 19 minority (8 African Americans, 1 American Indian/Alaska Native, 6 Asian Americans or Pacific Islanders, 4 Hispanic Americans), 13 international. Average age 30. 66 applicants, 83% accepted, 17 enrolled. *Faculty:* 9 full-time (2 women), 12 part-time/adjunct (3 women). Expenses: Contact institution. *Financial support:* In 2008–09, 105 students received support. Federal Work-Study available. Financial award application deadline: 4/1; financial award applicants required to submit FAFSA. In 2008, 36 master's awarded. *Degree program information:* Part-time and evening/weekend programs available. Offers architecture (M Arch); interior design (MID). *Application deadline:* For fall admission, 2/1 priority date for domestic students, 2/1 for international students; for winter admission, 11/1 priority date for domestic students, 11/1 for international students; for spring admission, 2/1 priority date for domestic students, 2/1 for international students. Applications are processed on a rolling basis. *Application fee:* $50. Electronic applications accepted. *Application Contact:* Jane Rohrback, Director of Admissions, 248-204-3160, Fax: 248-204-3188, E-mail: admissions@ltu.edu. *Dean*, Glen LeRoy, 248-204-2800, Fax: 248-204-2900, E-mail: archdean@ltu.edu.

College of Arts and Sciences Students: 2 full-time (0 women), 90 part-time (53 women); includes 11 minority (5 African Americans, 6 Asian Americans or Pacific Islanders), 18 international. Average age 30. 86 applicants, 78% accepted, 21 enrolled. *Faculty:* 14 full-time (6 women), 14 part-time/adjunct (4 women). Expenses: Contact institution. *Financial support:* Federal Work-Study available. Financial award application deadline: 4/1; financial award applicants required to submit FAFSA. In 2008, 35 master's awarded. *Degree program information:* Part-time and evening/weekend programs available. Offers computer science (MS); educational technology (MET); science education (MSE); technical communication (MS). *Application deadline:* For fall admission, 8/1 priority date for domestic students, 6/1 for international students; for winter admission, 12/1 priority date for domestic students, 10/1 for international students; for spring admission, 5/1 priority date for domestic students, 3/1 for international students. Applications are processed on a rolling basis. *Application fee:* $50. Electronic applications accepted. *Application Contact:* Jane Rohrback, Director of Admissions, 248-204-3160, Fax: 248-204-3188, E-mail: admissions@ltu.edu. *Dean*, Dr. Hsiao-Ping Moore, 248-204-3500, Fax: 248-204-3518, E-mail: scidean@ltu.edu.

College of Engineering Students: 25 full-time (2 women), 407 part-time (53 women); includes 38 minority (14 African Americans, 19 Asian Americans or Pacific Islanders, 5 Hispanic Americans), 181 international. Average age 30. 384 applicants, 70% accepted, 94 enrolled. *Faculty:* 20 full-time (4 women), 12 part-time/adjunct (0 women). Expenses: Contact institution. *Financial support:* Federal Work-Study and institutionally sponsored loans available. Support available to part-time students. Financial award application deadline: 4/1; financial award applicants required to submit FAFSA. In 2008, 126 master's, 4 doctorates awarded. *Degree program information:* Part-time and evening/weekend programs available. Offers automotive engineering (MAE); civil engineering (MCE); construction engineering management (MS); electrical and computer engineering (MS); engineering management (ME); manufacturing systems (MEMS, DE); mechanical engineering (MS); mechatronic systems engineering (MS). *Application deadline:* For fall admission, 8/1 priority date for domestic students, 6/1 for international students; for winter admission, 12/1 priority date for domestic students, 10/1 for international students; for spring admission, 5/1 priority date for domestic students, 3/1 for international students. Applications are processed on a rolling basis. *Application fee:* $50. Electronic applications accepted. *Application Contact:* Jane Rohrback, Director of Admissions, 248-204-3160, Fax: 248-204-3188, E-mail: admissions@ltu.edu. *Dean*, Dr. Devdas Shetty, 248-204-2500, Fax: 248-204-2509, E-mail: engrdean@ltu.edu.

College of Management Students: 40 full-time (10 women), 709 part-time (286 women); includes 172 minority (101 African Americans, 2 American Indian/Alaska Native, 59 Asian Americans or Pacific Islanders, 10 Hispanic Americans), 124 international. Average age 33. 341 applicants, 88% accepted, 167 enrolled. *Faculty:* 14 full-time (6 women), 53 part-time/adjunct (14 women). Expenses: Contact institution. *Financial support:* Federal Work-Study and institutionally sponsored loans available. Support available to part-time students. Financial award application deadline: 4/1; financial award applicants required to submit FAFSA. In 2008, 275 master's, 11 doctorates awarded. *Degree program information:* Part-time and evening/weekend programs available. Offers business administration (MBA, DBA); information systems (MS); information technology (DM); operations management (MS). *Application deadline:* For fall admission, 8/1 priority date for domestic students, 6/1 for international students; for winter admission, 12/1 priority date for domestic students, 10/1 for international students; for spring admission, 5/1 priority date for domestic students, 3/1 for international students. Applications are processed on a rolling basis. *Application fee:* $50. Electronic applications accepted. *Application Contact:* Jane Rohrback, Director of Admissions, 248-204-3160, Fax: 248-204-3188, E-mail: admissions@ltu.edu. *Dean*, Dr. Lou DeGennaro, 248-204-3050, E-mail: degennaro@ltu.edu.

LEADERSHIP INSTITUTE OF SEATTLE, Kenmore, WA 98028-4966

General Information Independent, coed, graduate-only institution. *Graduate housing:* On-campus housing not available.

GRADUATE UNITS

School of Applied Behavioral Science Offers consulting and coaching in organizations (MA); systems counseling (MA).

LEBANESE AMERICAN UNIVERSITY, Beirut, Lebanon

General Information Private, comprehensive institution.

GRADUATE UNITS

School of Arts and Sciences Offers computer science (MS); international affairs (MA).

School of Business Offers business (MBA).

School of Pharmacy Offers pharmacy (Pharm D).

LEBANON VALLEY COLLEGE, Annville, PA 17003-1400

General Information Independent-religious, coed, comprehensive institution. *Enrollment:* 1,965 graduate, professional, and undergraduate students; 45 full-time matriculated graduate/professional students (35 women), 114 part-time matriculated graduate/professional students (60 women). *Enrollment by degree level:* 114 master's, 45 doctoral. *Graduate faculty:* 14 full-time (6 women), 23 part-time/adjunct (5 women). *Tuition:* Full-time $31,510; part-time $400 per credit hour. *Required fees:* $600. *Graduate housing:* On-campus housing not available. *Student services:* Career counseling, services for students with disabilities. *Library facilities:* Bishop Library. *Online resources:* library catalog, web page, access to other libraries' catalogs. *Collection:* 192,239 titles, 3,100 serial subscriptions, 16,399 audiovisual materials.

Computer facilities: Computer purchase and lease plans are available. 187 computers available on campus for general student use. A campuswide network can be accessed from student residence rooms and from off campus. Online class registration is available. *Web address:* http://www.lvc.edu/.

General Application Contact: Elaine D. Feather, Director of Graduate Studies and Continuing Education, 717-867-6213, Fax: 717-867-6018, E-mail: feather@lvc.edu.

GRADUATE UNITS

Graduate Studies and Continuing Education Students: 114 part-time (60 women); includes 7 minority (5 African Americans, 2 Asian Americans or Pacific Islanders). Average age 34. *Faculty:* 5 full-time (2 women), 12 part-time/adjunct (2 women). Expenses: Contact institution. *Financial support:* Application deadline: 5/1. In 2008, 22 master's awarded. *Degree program information:* Part-time and evening/weekend programs available. Offers business administration (MBA); music education (MME); science education (MSE). *Application deadline:* Applications are processed on a rolling basis. *Application fee:* $30. Electronic applications accepted. *Application Contact:* Elaine D. Feather, Director of Graduate Studies and Continuing Education, 717-867-6213, Fax: 717-867-6018, E-mail: feather@lvc.edu. *Director of Graduate Studies and Continuing Education*, Elaine D. Feather, 717-867-6213, Fax: 717-867-6018, E-mail: feather@lvc.edu.

Physical Therapy Department Students: 45 full-time (35 women); includes 4 minority (3 African Americans, 1 Hispanic American). 33 applicants, 30% accepted, 5 enrolled. *Faculty:* 9 full-time (4 women), 11 part-time/adjunct (3 women). Expenses: Contact institution. *Financial support:* In 2008–09, 45 students received support. Scholarships/grants available. Financial award application deadline: 5/1; financial award applicants required to submit FAFSA. In 2008, 8 doctorates awarded. Offers physical therapy (DPT). *Application fee:* $30. Electronic applications accepted. *Application Contact:* Susan Jones, Director of Admission, 866-582-4236, Fax: 717-867-6026, E-mail: sjones@lvc.edu. *Chairperson and Associate Professor of Physical Therapy*, Dr. Stan M. Dacko, 717-867-6843, Fax: 717-867-6849, E-mail: dacko@lvc.edu.

LEE UNIVERSITY, Cleveland, TN 37320-3450

General Information Independent-religious, coed, comprehensive institution. *Enrollment:* 4,147 graduate, professional, and undergraduate students; 116 full-time matriculated graduate/professional students (83 women), 190 part-time matriculated graduate/professional students (122 women). *Enrollment by degree level:* 306 master's. *Graduate faculty:* 60 full-time (19 women), 16 part-time/adjunct (7 women). *Tuition:* Full-time $10,824; part-time $451 per credit. *Required fees:* $270; $200 per semester. Tuition and fees vary according to course load and program. *Graduate housing:* Rooms and/or apartments available on a first-come, first-served basis to single and married students. Typical cost: $2720 per year ($5650 including board) for single students. Room and board charges vary according to board plan and housing facility selected. Housing application deadline: 9/1. *Student services:* Campus employment opportunities, campus safety program, career counseling, exercise/wellness program, free psychological counseling, international student services, services for students with disabilities, teacher training, writing training. *Library facilities:* William G. Squires Library plus 3 others. *Online resources:* library catalog, web page, access to other libraries' catalogs. *Collection:* 147,863 titles, 28,255 serial subscriptions, 8,453 audiovisual materials.

Computer facilities: 450 computers available on campus for general student use. A campuswide network can be accessed from off campus. Online class registration is available. *Web address:* http://www.leeuniversity.edu/.

General Application Contact: Vicki Glasscock, Graduate Admissions Director, 423-614-8059, E-mail: vglasscock@leeuniversity.edu.

GRADUATE UNITS

College of Arts and Sciences Students: 40 full-time (33 women), 22 part-time (18 women); includes 4 minority (2 Asian Americans or Pacific Islanders, 2 Hispanic Americans), 1 international. Average age 28. 36 applicants, 67% accepted, 17 enrolled. *Faculty:* 11 full-time (5 women), 3 part-time/adjunct (1 woman). Expenses: Contact institution. *Financial support:* Teaching assistantships, career-related internships or fieldwork, Federal Work-Study, institutionally sponsored loans, scholarships/grants, and unspecified assistantships available. Financial award application deadline: 3/1; financial award applicants required to submit FAFSA. In 2008, 33 master's awarded. *Degree program information:* Part-time programs available. Offers mental health counseling (MS); school counseling (MS). *Application deadline:* For fall admission, 4/1 priority date for domestic and international students; for spring admission, 10/1 priority date for domestic and international students. Applications are processed on a rolling basis. *Application fee:* $25. *Application Contact:* Vicki Glasscock, Graduate Admissions Director, 423-614-8059, E-mail: vglasscock@leeuniversity.edu. *Director*, Dr. Doyle Goff, 423-614-8126, Fax: 423-614-8129, E-mail: drgoff@leeuniversity.edu.

Program in Education Students: 46 full-time (34 women), 87 part-time (59 women); includes 11 minority (7 African Americans, 1 American Indian/Alaska Native, 3 Hispanic Americans), 7 international. Average age 33. 72 applicants, 96% accepted, 56 enrolled. *Faculty:* 19 full-time (6 women), 5 part-time/adjunct (3 women). Expenses: Contact institution. *Financial support:* Career-related internships or fieldwork, Federal Work-Study, institutionally sponsored loans, scholarships/grants, and unspecified assistantships available. Financial award application deadline: 3/1; financial award applicants required to submit FAFSA. In 2008, 78 master's awarded. *Degree program information:* Part-time programs available. Offers classroom teaching (M Ed); education specialist (Ed S); educational leadership (M Ed); elementary/secondary education (MAT); special education (elementary) (M Ed); special education (secondary) (M Ed, MAT); special education (severe disabilities) (M Ed). *Application deadline:* For fall admission,

Lee University (continued)

4/1 priority date for domestic students; for spring admission, 10/1 priority date for domestic students. Applications are processed on a rolling basis. *Application fee:* $25. *Application Contact:* Vicki Glasscock, Graduate Admissions Director, 423-614-8059, E-mail: vglasscock@leeuniversity.edu. *Director,* Dr. Gary Riggins, 423-614-8193.

Program in Music Students: 12 full-time (6 women), 15 part-time (7 women); includes 3 minority (all African Americans), 2 international. Average age 29. 8 applicants, 100% accepted, 8 enrolled. *Faculty:* 31 full-time (6 women), 6 part-time/adjunct (3 women). Expenses: Contact institution. *Financial support:* In 2008–09, teaching assistantships (averaging $2,275 per year); career-related internships or fieldwork, Federal Work-Study, institutionally sponsored loans, and scholarships/grants also available. Financial award application deadline: 3/1; financial award applicants required to submit FAFSA. In 2008, 7 master's awarded. *Degree program information:* Part-time programs available. Offers church music (MCM); music education (MME); performance (MMMP). *Application deadline:* For fall admission, 4/1 for domestic students; for spring admission, 10/1 for domestic students. Applications are processed on a rolling basis. *Application fee:* $25. *Application Contact:* Vicki Glasscock, Graduate Admissions Director, 423-614-8059, E-mail: vglasscock@leeuniversity.edu. *Director,* Dr. Jim W. Burns, 423-614-8240, Fax: 423-614-8242, E-mail: gradmusic@leeuniversity.edu.

Program in Religion Students: 11 full-time (6 women), 8 part-time (4 women); includes 1 minority (American Indian/Alaska Native). Average age 25. 6 applicants, 100% accepted, 4 enrolled. *Faculty:* 10 full-time (3 women), 2 part-time/adjunct (0 women). Expenses: Contact institution. *Financial support:* Career-related internships or fieldwork, Federal Work-Study, institutionally sponsored loans, scholarships/grants, and unspecified assistantships available. Financial award application deadline: 3/1; financial award applicants required to submit FAFSA. In 2008, 11 master's awarded. *Degree program information:* Part-time programs available. Offers biblical studies (MA); theological studies (MA); youth and family ministry (MA). *Application deadline:* For fall admission, 4/1 priority date for domestic students; for spring admission, 10/1 priority date for domestic students. Applications are processed on a rolling basis. *Application fee:* $25. *Application Contact:* Vicki Glasscock, Graduate Admissions Director, 423-614-8059, E-mail: vglasscock@leeuniversity.edu. *Director,* Dr. Michael Fuller, 423-614-8338, E-mail: mfuller@leeuniversity.edu.

LEHIGH UNIVERSITY, Bethlehem, PA 18015-3094

General Information Independent, coed, university. CGS member. *Enrollment:* 6,994 graduate, professional, and undergraduate students; 954 full-time matriculated graduate/professional students (414 women), 954 part-time matriculated graduate/professional students (481 women). *Enrollment by degree level:* 1,207 master's, 681 doctoral, 20 other advanced degrees. *Graduate faculty:* 331 full-time (78 women), 65 part-time/adjunct (23 women). *Graduate housing:* Rooms and/or apartments available on a first-come, first-served basis to single and married students. *Student services:* Campus employment opportunities, campus safety program, career counseling, child daycare facilities, exercise/wellness program, free psychological counseling, international student services, low-cost health insurance, multicultural affairs office, services for students with disabilities, teacher training, writing training. *Library facilities:* E. W. Fairchild-Martindale Library plus 1 other. *Online resources:* library catalog, web page, access to other libraries' catalogs. *Collection:* 1.2 million titles, 49,500 serial subscriptions, 6,142 audiovisual materials.

Computer facilities: Computer purchase and lease plans are available. 588 computers available on campus for general student use. A campuswide network can be accessed from student residence rooms and from off campus. Online class registration is available. *Web address:* http://www.lehigh.edu/.

General Application Contact: Information Contact, 610-758-3000.

GRADUATE UNITS

College of Arts and Sciences Students: 276 full-time (137 women), 190 part-time (107 women); includes 27 minority (6 African Americans, 10 Asian Americans or Pacific Islanders, 11 Hispanic Americans), 92 international. Average age 29. 585 applicants, 38% accepted, 134 enrolled. *Faculty:* 155 full-time (42 women), 6 part-time/adjunct (4 women). Expenses: Contact institution. *Financial support:* In 2008–09, 10 fellowships with full tuition reimbursements (averaging $22,000 per year), 21 research assistantships with full tuition reimbursements (averaging $18,500 per year), 119 teaching assistantships with full tuition reimbursements (averaging $16,500 per year) were awarded; career-related internships or fieldwork, Federal Work-Study, institutionally sponsored loans, scholarships/grants, tuition waivers (full and partial), and unspecified assistantships also available. Support available to part-time students. Financial award application deadline: 1/15. In 2008, 124 master's, 30 doctorates awarded. *Degree program information:* Part-time programs available. Postbaccalaureate distance learning degree programs offered (no on-campus study). Offers American studies (MA); applied mathematics (MS, PhD); arts and sciences (MA, MS, PhD); biochemistry (PhD); chemistry (MS, PhD); earth and environmental sciences (MS, PhD); English (MA, PhD); environmental policy design (MA); history (MA, PhD); human cognition and development (MS, PhD); integrative biology and neuroscience (PhD); mathematics (MS, PhD); molecular biology (MS, PhD); photonics (MS); physics (MS, PhD); politics and policy (MA); polymer science (MS, PhD); polymer science and engineering (MS, PhD); sociology (MA); statistics (MS). *Application deadline:* For fall admission, 7/15 for domestic and international students; for spring admission, 12/1 for domestic and international students. Applications are processed on a rolling basis. *Application fee:* $65. Electronic applications accepted. *Application Contact:* Heather Sohara, Administrative Clerk, 610-758-4281, Fax: 610-758-6232, E-mail: incas@lehigh.edu. *Associate Dean of Graduate Studies,* Dr. Michael Stavola, 610-758-4282, Fax: 610-758-6232, E-mail: mjsa@lehigh.edu.

College of Business and Economics Students: 150 full-time (74 women), 231 part-time (69 women); includes 15 minority (6 African Americans, 7 Asian Americans or Pacific Islanders, 2 Hispanic Americans), 115 international. Average age 30. 702 applicants, 43% accepted, 105 enrolled. *Faculty:* 38 full-time (7 women), 20 part-time/adjunct (3 women). Expenses: Contact institution. *Financial support:* In 2008–09, 2 fellowships with full tuition reimbursements (averaging $13,200 per year), 7 research assistantships with full and partial tuition reimbursements (averaging $2,863 per year), 16 teaching assistantships with full tuition reimbursements (averaging $13,840 per year) were awarded; career-related internships or fieldwork, scholarships/grants, health care benefits, tuition waivers (full and partial), and unspecified assistantships also available. Support available to part-time students. Financial award application deadline: 1/15. In 2008, 106 master's, 2 doctorates awarded. *Degree program information:* Part-time and evening/weekend programs available. Postbaccalaureate distance learning degree programs offered (minimal on-campus study). Offers accounting (MS); accounting and information analysis (MS); analytical finance (MS); business administration (MBA); economics (MS, PhD); entrepreneurship (Certificate); finance (MS); health and bio-pharmaceutical economics (MS); project management (Certificate); supply chain management (Certificate). *Application deadline:* For fall admission, 7/15 for domestic students, 5/1 for international students; for spring admission, 12/1 for domestic and international students. Applications are processed on a rolling basis. *Application fee:* $100. Electronic applications accepted. *Application Contact:* Corinn McBride, Director of Recruitment and Admissions, 610-758-3418, Fax: 610-758-5283, E-mail: com207@lehigh.edu. *Graduate Business Programs,* Martin K. Saffer, 610-758-4450, Fax: 610-758-5283, E-mail: mks207@lehigh.edu.

College of Education Students: 158 full-time (122 women), 385 part-time (274 women); includes 49 minority (22 African Americans, 3 American Indian/Alaska Native, 11 Asian Americans or Pacific Islanders, 13 Hispanic Americans), 78 international. Average age 32. 370 applicants, 37% accepted, 129 enrolled. *Faculty:* 30 full-time (16 women), 31 part-time/adjunct (16 women). Expenses: Contact institution. *Financial support:* Fellowships with full and partial tuition reimbursements, research assistantships with full and partial tuition reimbursements, teaching assistantships with full and partial tuition reimbursements, career-related internships or fieldwork, Federal Work-Study, institutionally sponsored loans, scholarships/grants, tuition waivers (full and partial), and unspecified assistantships available. Financial award application deadline: 2/9. In 2008, 160 master's, 11 doctorates awarded. *Degree program information:* Part-time and evening/weekend programs available. Postbaccalaureate distance learning degree programs offered (minimal on-campus study). Offers counseling and human services (M Ed); counseling psychology (PhD); education (M Ed, MS, Ed D, PhD, Certificate, Ed S); educational leadership (M Ed, Ed D, Certificate); elementary and secondary school counseling (M Ed); elementary education (M Ed); globalization and educational change (M Ed); instructional technology (MS); international counseling (M Ed, Certificate); learning sciences and technology (PhD); school psychology (M Ed, PhD, Ed S); secondary education (M Ed); secondary school counseling (M Ed); special education (M Ed, PhD); technology use in schools (Certificate); TESOL (Certificate). *Application deadline:* For fall admission, 1/1 for domestic and international students; for spring admission, 11/1 for domestic and international students. Applications are processed on a rolling basis. *Application fee:* $65. Electronic applications accepted. *Application Contact:* Donna M. Johnson, Coordinator, 610-758 Ext. 3231, Fax: 610-758-6223, E-mail: dmj4@lehigh.edu. *Dean,* Dr. Gary M. Sasso, 610-758-3221, Fax: 610-758-6223, E-mail: gary.sasso@lehigh.edu.

P.C. Rossin College of Engineering and Applied Science Students: 370 full-time (81 women), 148 part-time (31 women); includes 18 minority (5 African Americans, 6 Asian Americans or Pacific Islanders, 7 Hispanic Americans), 291 international. Average age 28. 1,200 applicants, 23% accepted, 167 enrolled. *Faculty:* 110 full-time (14 women), 9 part-time/adjunct (0 women). Expenses: Contact institution. *Financial support:* In 2008–09, 310 students received support, including 26 fellowships with full and partial tuition reimbursements available (averaging $20,400 per year), 197 research assistantships with full and partial tuition reimbursements available (averaging $19,200 per year), 41 teaching assistantships with full and partial tuition reimbursements available (averaging $20,400 per year); career-related internships or fieldwork, institutionally sponsored loans, scholarships/grants, and tuition waivers (full and partial) also available. Support available to part-time students. Financial award application deadline: 1/15. In 2008, 132 master's, 55 doctorates awarded. *Degree program information:* Part-time and evening/weekend programs available. Postbaccalaureate distance learning degree programs offered (no on-campus study). Offers analytical finance (MS); applied mathematics (MS, PhD); biological chemical engineering (M Eng); chemical engineering (M Eng, PhD); civil engineering (M Eng, MS, PhD); computational engineering and mechanics (MS, PhD); computer engineering (M Eng, MS, PhD); computer science (M Eng, MS, PhD); electrical engineering (M Eng, MS, PhD); engineering and applied science (M Eng, MS, PhD); environmental engineering (MS, PhD); industrial engineering (M Eng, MS, PhD); information and systems engineering (M Eng, MS); management science (MS); manufacturing systems engineering (MS); materials science and engineering (M Eng, MS, PhD); mechanical engineering (M Eng, MS, PhD); photonics (MS); polymer science/engineering (M Eng, MS, PhD); quality engineering (MS); structural engineering (M Eng, MS, PhD); wireless network engineering (MS). *Application deadline:* For fall admission, 7/15 for domestic and international students; for spring admission, 12/1 for domestic and international students. Applications are processed on a rolling basis. *Application fee:* $65. Electronic applications accepted. *Application Contact:* Brianne Lisk, Administrative Coordinator of Graduate Studies and Research, 610-758-6310, Fax: 610-758-5623, E-mail: brc3@lehigh.edu. *Associate Dean of Graduate Studies and Research,* Dr. John P. Coulter, 610-758-6310, Fax: 610-758-5623, E-mail: john.coulter@lehigh.edu.

Center for Polymer Science and Engineering Students: 5 full-time (1 woman), 5 part-time (2 women), 4 international. Average age 33. *Faculty:* 1 part-time/adjunct (0 women). Expenses: Contact institution. *Financial support:* In 2008–09, fellowships (averaging $17,667 per year), research assistantships (averaging $17,667 per year), teaching assistantships (averaging $17,667 per year) were awarded. Financial award application deadline: 1/15. In 2008, 6 master's, 2 doctorates awarded. *Degree program information:* Part-time and evening/weekend programs available. Postbaccalaureate distance learning degree programs offered (no on-campus study). Offers polymer science and engineering (M Eng, MS, PhD). Programs are interdisciplinary. *Application deadline:* For fall admission, 7/15 for domestic students, 1/15 for international students; for spring admission, 12/1 for domestic and international students. Applications are processed on a rolling basis. *Application fee:* $65. Electronic applications accepted. *Application Contact:* James E. Roberts, Chair, Polymer Education Committee, 610-758-4841, Fax: 610-758-6536, E-mail: jer1@lehigh.edu. *Director,* Dr. Raymond A. Pearson, 610-758-3857, Fax: 610-758-3526, E-mail: rp02@lehigh.edu.

LEHMAN COLLEGE OF THE CITY UNIVERSITY OF NEW YORK, Bronx, NY 10468-1589

General Information State and locally supported, coed, comprehensive institution. *Graduate housing:* On-campus housing not available. *Research affiliation:* New York Botanical Gardens, Montefiore Hospital and Medical Center.

GRADUATE UNITS

Division of Arts and Humanities *Degree program information:* Part-time and evening/weekend programs available. Offers art (MA, MFA); arts and humanities (MA, MAT, MFA); English (MA); history (MA); music (MAT); Spanish (MA); speech-language pathology and audiology (MA).

Division of Education *Degree program information:* Part-time and evening/weekend programs available. Offers bilingual special education (MS Ed); business education (MS Ed); early childhood education (MS Ed); early special education (MS Ed); education (MA, MS Ed); elementary education (MS Ed); emotional handicaps (MS Ed); English education (MS Ed); guidance and counseling (MS Ed); learning disabilities (MS Ed); mathematics 7–12 (MS Ed); mental retardation (MS Ed); music education (MS Ed); reading teacher (MS Ed); science education (MS Ed); social studies 7–12 (MA); teachers of special education (MS Ed); teaching English to speakers of other languages (MS Ed).

Division of Natural and Social Sciences *Degree program information:* Part-time and evening/weekend programs available. Offers accounting (MS); adult health nursing (MS); biology (MA); clinical nutrition (MS); community nutrition (MS); computer science (MS); dietetic internship (MS); health education and promotion (MA); health N–12 teacher (MS Ed); mathematics (MA); natural and social sciences (MA, MS, MS Ed, PhD); nursing of older adults (MS); nutrition (MS); parent-child nursing (MS); pediatric nurse practitioner (MS); plant sciences (PhD); recreation (MA, MS Ed); recreation education (MA, MS Ed).

LE MOYNE COLLEGE, Syracuse, NY 13214

General Information Independent-religious, coed, comprehensive institution. *Enrollment:* 3,479 graduate, professional, and undergraduate students; 122 full-time matriculated graduate/professional students (97 women), 377 part-time matriculated graduate/professional students (251 women). *Enrollment by degree level:* 499 master's. *Graduate faculty:* 40 full-time (18 women), 60 part-time/adjunct (30 women). *Tuition:* Full-time $10,800; part-time $600 per credit hour. *Required fees:* $25 per semester. *Graduate housing:* On-campus housing not available. *Student services:* Campus employment opportunities, campus safety program, career counseling, free psychological counseling, international student services, low-cost health insurance, multicultural affairs office, services for students with disabilities, teacher training. *Library facilities:* Noreen Reale Falcone Library. *Online resources:* library catalog, web page, access to other libraries' catalogs. *Collection:* 282,975 titles, 57,438 serial subscriptions, 12,929 audiovisual materials.

Computer facilities: Computer purchase and lease plans are available. 325 computers available on campus for general student use. A campuswide network can be accessed from student residence rooms and from off campus. Online class registration, ECHO (campus-wide portal) are available. *Web address:* http://www.lemoyne.edu/.

General Application Contact: Kristen P. Trapasso, Director of Graduate Admission, 315-445-4265, Fax: 315-445-6027, E-mail: trapaskp@lemoyne.edu.

GRADUATE UNITS

Department of Education Students: 45 full-time (42 women), 271 part-time (198 women); includes 21 minority (12 African Americans, 1 American Indian/Alaska Native, 3 Asian Americans or Pacific Islanders, 5 Hispanic Americans). Average age 31. 125 applicants, 100% accepted, 119 enrolled. *Faculty:* 12 full-time (8 women), 44 part-time/adjunct (27 women). Expenses: Contact institution. *Financial support:* In 2008–09, 23 students received support. Career-related internships or fieldwork, health care benefits, and unspecified assistantships available. Support available to part-time students. Financial award applicants required to submit FAFSA. In 2008, 199 master's awarded. *Degree program information:* Part-time and evening/

weekend programs available. Offers adolescent education (MS Ed, MST); adolescent education/special education (MS Ed, MST); childhood education (MS Ed); childhood education/special education (MS Ed); elementary education (MS Ed); general professional education (MS Ed); inclusive childhood education (MST); middle child specialist/special education (MS Ed); middle childhood specialist (MS Ed); school building leadership (MS Ed, CAS); school district business leader (MS Ed, CAS); school district leadership (MS Ed, CAS); secondary education (MS Ed); special education (MS Ed). *Application deadline:* For fall admission, 4/1 priority date for domestic and international students; for spring admission, 10/1 priority date for domestic and international students. Applications are processed on a rolling basis. *Application fee:* $50. *Application Contact:* Kristen P Trapasso, Director of Graduate Admission, 315-445-4265, Fax: 315-445-6027, E-mail: trapaskp@lemoyne.edu. *Visiting Chair, Education Department and Director of Graduate Education,* Dr. William D. Silky, 315-445-4376, Fax: 315-445-4744, E-mail: silkywd@lemoyne.edu.

Department of Nursing Students: 16 part-time (15 women). Average age 44. 8 applicants, 100% accepted, 8 enrolled. *Faculty:* 2 full-time (both women), 1 (woman) part-time/adjunct. Expenses: Contact institution. *Financial support:* In 2008–09, 11 students received support. Career-related internships or fieldwork, scholarships/grants, health care benefits, and unspecified assistantships available. Support available to part-time students. Financial award applicants required to submit FAFSA. In 2008, 4 master's awarded. *Degree program information:* Part-time and evening/weekend programs available. Offers nursing administration (MS); nursing education (CAS). *Application deadline:* For fall admission, 6/1 priority date for domestic and international students; for spring admission, 11/1 priority date for domestic and international students. Applications are processed on a rolling basis. *Application fee:* $50. *Application Contact:* Kristen P. Trapasso, Director of Graduate Admission, 315-445-4265, Fax: 315-445-6027, E-mail: trapaskp@lemoyne.edu. *Clinical Assistant Professor and Interim Chair of Department of Nursing,* Barbara M. Carranti, 315-445-5437, Fax: 315-445-6024, E-mail: carranbm@lemoyne.edu.

Department of Physician Assistant Studies Students: 66 full-time (50 women), 6 part-time (4 women); includes 6 minority (1 African American, 4 Asian Americans or Pacific Islanders, 1 Hispanic American), 1 international. Average age 28. 288 applicants, 18% accepted, 35 enrolled. *Faculty:* 8 full-time (6 women), 11 part-time/adjunct (2 women). Expenses: Contact institution. *Financial support:* In 2008–09, 9 students received support. Career-related internships or fieldwork and health care benefits available. Financial award applicants required to submit FAFSA. In 2008, 34 master's awarded. Offers physician assistant studies (MS). *Application deadline:* For fall admission, 10/1 priority date for domestic and international students. Electronic applications accepted. *Application Contact:* Kristen P. Trapasso, Director of Graduate Admission, 315-445-4265, Fax: 315-445-6027, E-mail: trapaskp@lemoyne.edu. *Clinical Assistant Professor and Director of Department of Physician Assistant Studies,* Mary E. Springston, 315-445-4163, Fax: 315-445-4602, E-mail: springme@lemoyne.edu.

Division of Management Students: 11 full-time (5 women), 84 part-time (34 women); includes 2 minority (1 African American, 1 Hispanic American). Average age 30. 49 applicants, 80% accepted, 36 enrolled. *Faculty:* 18 full-time (2 women), 4 part-time/adjunct (0 women). Expenses: Contact institution. *Financial support:* In 2008–09, 9 students received support. Career-related internships or fieldwork, scholarships/grants, health care benefits, and unspecified assistantships available. Support available to part-time students. Financial award applicants required to submit FAFSA. In 2008, 38 master's awarded. *Degree program information:* Part-time and evening/weekend programs available. Offers management (MBA). *Application deadline:* For fall admission, 7/1 priority date for domestic and international students; for spring admission, 11/1 priority date for domestic and international students. Applications are processed on a rolling basis. *Application fee:* $0. *Application Contact:* Kristen P. Trapasso, Director of Graduate Admission, 315-445-4265, Fax: 315-445-6027, E-mail: trapaskp@lemoyne.edu. *Director of MBA Program,* Dr. George Kulick, 315-445-4786, Fax: 315-445-4787, E-mail: kulick@lemoyne.edu.

LENOIR-RHYNE UNIVERSITY, Hickory, NC 28601

General Information Independent-religious, coed, comprehensive institution. *Graduate housing:* Room and/or apartments available on a first-come, first-served basis to single students; on-campus housing not available to married students.

GRADUATE UNITS

Graduate Programs *Degree program information:* Part-time and evening/weekend programs available. Electronic applications accepted.

Charles M. Snipes School of Business *Degree program information:* Part-time and evening/weekend programs available. Offers accounting (MBA); entrepreneurship (MBA); global leadership (MBA); leadership development (MBA). Electronic applications accepted.

School of Counseling and Human Services *Degree program information:* Part-time and evening/weekend programs available. Offers agency counseling (MA); community counseling (MA); counseling and human services (MA); school counseling (MA). Electronic applications accepted.

School of Education *Degree program information:* Part-time and evening/weekend programs available. Offers birth through kindergarten education (MA); education (MA). Electronic applications accepted.

School of Health, Exercise and Sport Science Offers athletic training (MS).

School of Occupational Therapy Offers occupational therapy (MS).

LESLEY UNIVERSITY, Cambridge, MA 02138-2790

General Information Independent, coed, comprehensive institution. CGS member. *Enrollment:* 6,686 graduate, professional, and undergraduate students; 1,159 full-time matriculated graduate/professional students (991 women), 3,801 part-time matriculated graduate/professional students (3,331 women). *Enrollment by degree level:* 4,663 master's, 125 doctoral, 172 other advanced degrees. *Graduate faculty:* 84 full-time (62 women), 427 part-time/adjunct (294 women). *Tuition:* Full-time $13,770; part-time $765 per credit hour. *Required fees:* $150. Tuition and fees vary according to course load, degree level, campus/location and program. *Graduate housing:* On-campus housing not available. *Student services:* Campus employment opportunities, campus safety program, career counseling, free psychological counseling, international student services, services for students with disabilities, teacher training, writing training. *Library facilities:* Eleanor DeWolfe Ludcke Library plus 2 others. *Online resources:* library catalog, web page, access to other libraries' catalogs. *Collection:* 118,729 titles, 1,150 serial subscriptions, 49,943 audiovisual materials. *Research affiliation:* TERC (education research and development).

Computer facilities: 175 computers available on campus for general student use. A campuswide network can be accessed from student residence rooms and from off campus. Online class registration is available. *Web address:* http://www.lesley.edu/.

General Application Contact: Graduate Studies, 800-LESLEYU, E-mail: info@lesley.edu.

GRADUATE UNITS

Graduate School of Arts and Social Sciences *Degree program information:* Part-time and evening/weekend programs available. Postbaccalaureate distance learning degree programs offered (minimal on-campus study). Offers clinical mental health counseling (MA); counseling psychology (MA, CAGS); creative arts in learning (CAGS); creative writing (MFA); ecological teaching and learning (MS); environmental education (MS); expressive therapies (MA, PhD, CAGS); independent studies (CAGS); independent study (MA); individualized studies (MA); integrative holistic health (MA); intercultural relations (MA, CAGS); interdisciplinary studies (MA); professional counseling (MA); school counseling (MA); urban environmental leadership (MA); visual arts (MFA); women's studies (MA). Electronic applications accepted.

Division of Expressive Therapies Offers art (MA); dance (MA); expressive therapies (MA, PhD, CAGS); music (MA).

School of Education *Degree program information:* Part-time and evening/weekend programs available. Postbaccalaureate distance learning degree programs offered (no on-campus study). Offers curriculum and instruction (M Ed, CAGS); early childhood education (M Ed); educational studies (PhD); elementary education (M Ed); individually designed (M Ed); middle school education (M Ed); moderate special needs (M Ed); reading (M Ed, CAGS); science in education (M Ed); severe special needs (M Ed); special needs (CAGS); technology in education (M Ed, CAGS). Electronic applications accepted.

LETOURNEAU UNIVERSITY, Longview, TX 75607-7001

General Information Independent-religious, coed, comprehensive institution. *Graduate housing:* Room and/or apartments available on a first-come, first-served basis to married students; on-campus housing not available to single students.

GRADUATE UNITS

Graduate and Professional Studies *Degree program information:* Part-time and evening/weekend programs available. Postbaccalaureate distance learning degree programs offered (no on-campus study). Offers business administration (MBA); educational leadership (MEL). Electronic applications accepted.

LEWIS & CLARK COLLEGE, Portland, OR 97219-7899

General Information Independent, coed, comprehensive institution. *Enrollment:* 3,565 graduate, professional, and undergraduate students; 239 full-time matriculated graduate/professional students (195 women), 265 part-time matriculated graduate/professional students (198 women). *Enrollment by degree level:* 430 master's, 34 doctoral, 40 other advanced degrees. *Graduate faculty:* 36 full-time (25 women), 75 part-time/adjunct (48 women). *Tuition:* Full-time $5087; part-time $677 per credit hour. Tuition and fees vary according to course level and campus/location. *Graduate housing:* On-campus housing not available. *Student services:* Campus employment opportunities, campus safety program, career counseling, free psychological counseling, international student services, low-cost health insurance, multicultural affairs office, services for students with disabilities, writing training. *Library facilities:* Aubrey Watzek Library plus 1 other. *Online resources:* library catalog, web page, access to other libraries' catalogs. *Collection:* 312,679 titles, 3,603 serial subscriptions, 17,841 audiovisual materials.

Computer facilities: Computer purchase and lease plans are available. 158 computers available on campus for general student use. A campuswide network can be accessed from student residence rooms and from off campus. Online class registration is available. *Web address:* http://www.lclark.edu/.

General Application Contact: Becky Haas, Director of Admissions, 503-768-6200, Fax: 503-768-6205, E-mail: gseadmit@lclark.edu.

GRADUATE UNITS

Graduate School of Education and Counseling Students: 239 full-time (195 women), 265 part-time (198 women); includes 44 minority (10 African Americans, 3 American Indian/Alaska Native, 11 Asian Americans or Pacific Islanders, 20 Hispanic Americans), 2 international. Average age 33. 492 applicants, 79% accepted, 249 enrolled. *Faculty:* 36 full-time (25 women), 75 part-time/adjunct (48 women). Expenses: Contact institution. *Financial support:* In 2008–09, 382 students received support. Career-related internships or fieldwork, Federal Work-Study, institutionally sponsored loans, scholarships/grants, health care benefits, and tuition waivers (partial) available. Support available to part-time students. Financial award applicants required to submit FAFSA. In 2008, 223 master's, 6 doctorates, 13 other advanced degrees awarded. *Degree program information:* Part-time and evening/weekend programs available. Offers addictions treatment (MA, MS); community counseling (MA, MS); early childhood/elementary education (MAT); education (M Ed, MAT, Ed D); education and counseling (M Ed, MA, MAT, MS, Ed D, Ed S); educational leadership (M Ed, Ed D); marriage, couple and family therapy (MA, MS); middle level/high school education (MAT); psychological and cultural studies (MA, MS); school counseling (M Ed); school psychology (Ed S); special education (M Ed). *Application deadline:* For fall admission, 2/1 for domestic students; for spring admission, 10/1 for domestic students. *Application fee:* $50. Electronic applications accepted. *Application Contact:* Becky Haas, Director of Admissions, 503-768-6200, Fax: 503-768-6205, E-mail: gseadmit@lclark.edu. *Dean,* Dr. Scott Fletcher, 503-768-6004, Fax: 503-768-6005, E-mail: graddean@lclark.edu.

Lewis & Clark Law School *Degree program information:* Part-time and evening/weekend programs available. Offers environmental and natural resources law (LL M); law (JD). Electronic applications accepted.

LEWIS UNIVERSITY, Romeoville, IL 60446

General Information Independent-religious, coed, comprehensive institution. CGS member. *Enrollment:* 5,536 graduate, professional, and undergraduate students; 330 full-time matriculated graduate/professional students (210 women), 1,281 part-time matriculated graduate/professional students (861 women). *Enrollment by degree level:* 1,394 master's, 37 doctoral, 35 other advanced degrees. *Graduate faculty:* 70 full-time (37 women), 124 part-time/adjunct (59 women). *Graduate housing:* Room and/or apartments available on a first-come, first-served basis to single students; on-campus housing not available to married students. Housing application deadline: 7/1. *Student services:* Campus employment opportunities, campus safety program, career counseling, exercise/wellness program, free psychological counseling, international student services, low-cost health insurance, multicultural affairs office, services for students with disabilities, teacher training, writing training. *Library facilities:* Lewis University Library. *Online resources:* library catalog, web page, access to other libraries' catalogs. *Collection:* 149,870 titles, 1,990 serial subscriptions.

Computer facilities: Computer purchase and lease plans are available. 310 computers available on campus for general student use. A campuswide network can be accessed from student residence rooms and from off campus. Online class registration, online help, online billing, online financial aid, online application, online housing application are available. *Web address:* http://www.lewisu.edu/.

General Application Contact: Julie Nickel, Assistant Director, Graduate and Adult Admission, 800-897-9000, Fax: 815-836-5578, E-mail: grad@lewisu.edu.

GRADUATE UNITS

College of Arts and Sciences Students: 134 full-time (90 women), 511 part-time (311 women); includes 174 minority (118 African Americans, 1 American Indian/Alaska Native, 5 Asian Americans or Pacific Islanders, 50 Hispanic Americans), 6 international. Average age 34. *Faculty:* 23 full-time (9 women), 50 part-time/adjunct (16 women). Expenses: Contact institution. *Financial support:* Federal Work-Study, scholarships/grants, tuition waivers (partial), and unspecified assistantships available. Financial award application deadline: 5/1; financial award applicants required to submit FAFSA. In 2008, 227 master's awarded. *Degree program information:* Part-time and evening/weekend programs available. Offers arts and sciences (MA, MS); aviation and transportation (MS); child and adolescent counseling (MA); criminal/social justice (MS); higher education/student services (MA); mental health counseling (MA); organizational management (MA); public administration (MA); public safety administration (MS); school counseling and guidance (MA); training and development (MA). *Application deadline:* For fall admission, 5/1 priority date for international students; for spring admission, 11/15 priority date for international students. Applications are processed on a rolling basis. *Application fee:* $40. Electronic applications accepted. *Application Contact:* Julie Nickel, Assistant Director, Graduate and Adult Admission, 800-897-9000, Fax: 815-836-5578, E-mail: grad@lewisu.edu. *Dean,* Dr. Bonnie Bondavalli, 815-838-0500 Ext. 5240, Fax: 815-836-5995, E-mail: bondavbo@lewisu.edu.

College of Business Students: 82 full-time (35 women), 228 part-time (108 women); includes 76 minority (50 African Americans, 7 Asian Americans or Pacific Islanders, 19 Hispanic Americans), 13 international. Average age 33. *Faculty:* 17 full-time (2 women), 30 part-time/adjunct (12 women). Expenses: Contact institution. *Financial support:* Career-related internships or fieldwork, Federal Work-Study, scholarships/grants, tuition waivers (full), and unspecified assistantships available. Support available to part-time students. Financial award application deadline: 5/1; financial award applicants required to submit FAFSA. In 2008, 86 master's awarded. *Degree program information:* Part-time and evening/weekend programs available. Offers accounting (MBA); business (MBA, MS); business administration (MBA); custom elective option (MBA); e-business (MBA); finance (MBA, MS); healthcare management (MBA); human resources management (MBA); information security (MS); international business (MBA); management (MS); management information systems (MBA); marketing (MBA); project management (MBA); technology and operations management (MBA). *Application deadline:* For fall admission, 5/1 priority date for international students; for spring admis-

Lewis University (continued)

sion, 11/15 priority date for international students. Applications are processed on a rolling basis. *Application fee:* $40. Electronic applications accepted. *Application Contact:* Michele King, Director of Admission, 815-836 Ext. 5384, E-mail: gsm@lewisu.edu. *Dean,* Dr. Rami Khasawneh, 800-838-0500 Ext. 5360, E-mail: khasawra@lewisu.edu.

College of Education Students: 97 full-time (68 women), 318 part-time (241 women); includes 66 minority (44 African Americans, 1 American Indian/Alaska Native, 6 Asian Americans or Pacific Islanders, 15 Hispanic Americans), 3 international. Average age 34. *Faculty:* 23 full-time (17 women), 36 part-time/adjunct (23 women). Expenses: Contact institution. *Financial support:* Federal Work-Study, scholarships/grants, tuition waivers (partial), and unspecified assistantships available. Financial award application deadline: 5/1; financial award applicants required to submit FAFSA. In 2008, 156 master's awarded. *Degree program information:* Part-time and evening/weekend programs available. Offers advanced study in education (CAS); biology (MA); chemistry (MA); curriculum and teacher leadership (MA Ed); educational leadership (M Ed, MA); educational leadership for teaching and learning (Ed D); elementary education (MA); English (MA); English as a second language (M Ed); general administrative (CAS); history (MA); instructional technology (M Ed); math (MA); physics (MA); psychology and social science (MA); reading and literacy (M Ed, MA); secondary education (MA); special education (MA); superintendent endorsement (CAS). *Application deadline:* For fall admission, 5/1 priority date for international students; for spring admission, 11/15 priority date for international students. Applications are processed on a rolling basis. *Application fee:* $40. Electronic applications accepted. *Application Contact:* Julie Nickel, Assistant Director, Graduate and Adult Admission, 815-838-0500 Ext. 5610, E-mail: grad@lewisu.edu. *Dean,* Dr. Jeanette Mines, 815-838-0500 Ext. 5316, Fax: 815-836-5879, E-mail: minesje@lewisu.edu.

College of Nursing and Health Professions Students: 17 full-time (all women), 189 part-time (180 women); includes 56 minority (33 African Americans, 14 Asian Americans or Pacific Islanders, 9 Hispanic Americans), 2 international. Average age 42. *Faculty:* 9 full-time (all women), 10 part-time/adjunct (all women). Expenses: Contact institution. *Financial support:* Federal Work-Study, scholarships/grants, tuition waivers (full and partial), and unspecified assistantships available. Financial award application deadline: 5/1; financial award applicants required to submit FAFSA. In 2008, 20 master's awarded. *Degree program information:* Part-time and evening/weekend programs available. Postbaccalaureate distance learning degree programs offered (no on-campus study). Offers adult nurse practitioner (MSN); nursing administration (MSN); nursing and health professions (MSN); nursing education (MSN). *Application deadline:* For fall admission, 5/1 priority date for international students; for spring admission, 11/15 priority date for international students. Applications are processed on a rolling basis. *Application fee:* $40. Electronic applications accepted. *Application Contact:* Kathy Lisak, 815-836-5355, E-mail: lisakka@lewisu.edu. *Dean,* Dr. Peggy Rice, 815-838-0500 Ext. 5245, E-mail: ricema@lewisu.edu.

LEXINGTON THEOLOGICAL SEMINARY, Lexington, KY 40508-3218

General Information Independent-religious, coed, graduate-only institution. *Graduate housing:* Rooms and/or apartments available on a first-come, first-served basis to single and married students. Housing application deadline: 6/15.

GRADUATE UNITS

Graduate and Professional Programs *Degree program information:* Part-time and evening/weekend programs available. Offers theology (M Div, MA, MAPS, D Min).

LIBERTY UNIVERSITY, Lynchburg, VA 24502

General Information Independent-religious, coed, comprehensive institution. *Enrollment:* 33,604 graduate, professional, and undergraduate students; 4,609 full-time matriculated graduate/professional students (2,324 women), 7,349 part-time matriculated graduate/professional students (3,731 women). *Enrollment by degree level:* 1,382 first professional, 10,576 master's. *Tuition:* Part-time $1779 per semester. *Required fees:* $150 per semester. *Graduate housing:* Room and/or apartments guaranteed to single students; on-campus housing not available to married students. Typical cost: $5996 (including board). *Student services:* Campus employment opportunities, career counseling, free psychological counseling, international student services, multicultural affairs office. *Library facilities:* A. Pierre Guillermin Integrated Learning Resource Center plus 1 other. *Online resources:* library catalog, web page. *Collection:* 291,243 titles, 67,234 serial subscriptions, 7,372 audiovisual materials.

Computer facilities: 600 computers available on campus for general student use. A campuswide network can be accessed from student residence rooms and from off campus. Online class registration is available. *Web address:* http://www.liberty.edu/.

General Application Contact: Kyle A Falce, Director of Graduate Admissions, 800-424-9596, Fax: 800-628-7977, E-mail: gradadmissions@liberty.edu.

GRADUATE UNITS

College of Arts and Sciences *Degree program information:* Part-time programs available. Postbaccalaureate distance learning degree programs offered (minimal on-campus study). Offers counseling (MA); nursing (MSN); pastoral care and counseling (PhD); professional counseling (PhD). Electronic applications accepted.

Liberty Theological Seminary and Graduate School *Degree program information:* Part-time programs available. Postbaccalaureate distance learning degree programs offered (minimal on-campus study). Offers religious studies (M Div, MA, MAR, MRE, D Min); theology (Th M). Electronic applications accepted.

School of Business *Degree program information:* Part-time programs available. Postbaccalaureate distance learning degree programs offered (minimal on-campus study). Offers business (MBA, MS). Electronic applications accepted.

School of Communications *Degree program information:* Part-time programs available. Offers communications (MA). Electronic applications accepted.

School of Education *Degree program information:* Part-time programs available. Postbaccalaureate distance learning degree programs offered (minimal on-campus study). Offers administration and supervision (M Ed); curriculum and instruction (M Ed); early childhood education (M Ed); education specialist (Ed S); educational leadership (Ed D); elementary education (M Ed); gifted education (M Ed); reading specialist (M Ed); school counseling (M Ed); secondary education (M Ed); special education (M Ed). Electronic applications accepted.

School of Law Offers law (JD). Electronic applications accepted.

LIFE CHIROPRACTIC COLLEGE WEST, Hayward, CA 94545

General Information Independent, coed, graduate-only institution. *Enrollment by degree level:* 411 first professional. *Graduate faculty:* 33 full-time (11 women), 30 part-time/adjunct (10 women). *Tuition:* Full-time $18,405; part-time $306.75 per credit. *Graduate housing:* On-campus housing not available. *Student services:* Campus employment opportunities, campus safety program, free psychological counseling, international student services, services for students with disabilities. *Library facilities:* Life West Library plus 1 other. *Online resources:* library catalog. *Collection:* 22,000 titles, 1,100 serial subscriptions. *Research affiliation:* NCCAM (National Center for Complimentary Medicine), NCCAM/UCRF, ARF (Atlas Research Foundation), University of Illinois, Chicago, Case Western Reserve University, BAER (Bay Area Research Roundtable).

Computer facilities: 50 computers available on campus for general student use. A campuswide network can be accessed from student residence rooms and from off campus. WIFI available. *Web address:* http://www.lifewest.edu/.

General Application Contact: Bonnie Seeley, Admissions Counselor, 800-788-4476 Ext. 2520, Fax: 510-780-4525, E-mail: admissions@lifewest.edu.

GRADUATE UNITS

Professional Program Students: 411 full-time (184 women). *Faculty:* 33 full-time (11 women), 30 part-time/adjunct (10 women). Expenses: Contact institution. *Financial support:* Research assistantships, teaching assistantships, career-related internships or fieldwork, Federal Work-Study, and scholarships/grants available. Financial award application deadline: 4/1; financial award applicants required to submit FAFSA. Offers chiropractic (DC). *Application deadline:* For fall admission, 8/1 priority date for domestic students, 7/1 priority date for international students; for winter admission, 10/1 priority date for domestic and international students; for spring admission, 2/1 priority date for domestic students, 1/1 priority date for international students. Applications are processed on a rolling basis. *Application fee:* $45. *Application Contact:* Bonnie Seeley, Admissions Counselor, 800-788-4476 Ext. 2520, Fax: 510-780-4525, E-mail: admissions@lifewest.edu. *President,* Dr. Gerard W. Clum, 800-788-4476 Ext. 2350, E-mail: gclum@lifewest.edu.

LIFE UNIVERSITY, Marietta, GA 30060-2903

General Information Independent, coed, comprehensive institution. *Enrollment:* 2,171 graduate, professional, and undergraduate students; 1,473 full-time matriculated graduate/professional students (881 women), 101 part-time matriculated graduate/professional students (34 women). *Enrollment by degree level:* 1,474 first professional, 100 master's. *Graduate faculty:* 74 full-time (24 women), 21 part-time/adjunct (10 women). *Tuition:* Full-time $7911; part-time $199 per credit hour. *Required fees:* $249. *Graduate housing:* Rooms and/or apartments available on a first-come, first-served basis to single and married students. Typical cost: $12,480 (including board) for single students. *Student services:* Campus employment opportunities, campus safety program, career counseling, exercise/wellness program, free psychological counseling, international student services, services for students with disabilities. *Library facilities:* Library & Learning Services plus 1 other. *Online resources:* library catalog, web page. *Collection:* 56,199 titles, 22,816 serial subscriptions, 8,533 audiovisual materials.

Computer facilities: 118 computers available on campus for general student use. A campuswide network can be accessed from student residence rooms and from off campus. Online class registration is available. *Web address:* http://www.life.edu/.

General Application Contact: Dr. Mary Flannery, Director of Enrollment Services, 800-543-3202, Fax: 770-426-2895, E-mail: mflannery@life.edu.

GRADUATE UNITS

College of Arts and Sciences *Degree program information:* Part-time programs available. Offers chiropractic sport science (MS); exercise and sport science (MS); sport coaching (MS); sport health science (MS); sport injury management (MS). Electronic applications accepted.

College of Chiropractic *Degree program information:* Part-time programs available. Offers chiropractic (DC). Electronic applications accepted.

LIM COLLEGE, New York, NY 10022-5268

General Information Proprietary, coed, primarily women, comprehensive institution.

GRADUATE UNITS

MBA Program Offers entrepreneurship (MBA); fashion management (MBA).

LINCOLN CHRISTIAN SEMINARY, Lincoln, IL 62656-2167

General Information Independent-religious, coed, graduate-only institution. *Enrollment by degree level:* 100 first professional, 229 master's, 10 doctoral. *Graduate faculty:* 12 full-time (2 women), 13 part-time/adjunct (3 women). *Tuition:* Full-time $7962; part-time $434 per credit hour. *Graduate housing:* Rooms and/or apartments available on a first-come, first-served basis to single and married students. *Student services:* Campus employment opportunities, career counseling, exercise/wellness program, free psychological counseling, low-cost health insurance, services for students with disabilities. *Library facilities:* Jessie C. Eury Library. *Online resources:* library catalog, web page, access to other libraries' catalogs. *Collection:* 90,000 titles, 500 serial subscriptions.

Computer facilities: 45 computers available on campus for general student use. A campuswide network can be accessed from student residence rooms and from off campus. Online class registration is available. *Web address:* http://www.lccs.edu/.

General Application Contact: David Harmon, Director of Admissions, 217-732-3168 Ext. 2275, Fax: 217-732-5914, E-mail: semadmis@lccs.edu.

GRADUATE UNITS

Graduate and Professional Programs *Degree program information:* Part-time programs available. Offers Bible and theology (MA); Bible translation (MA); counseling ministry (MA); divinity (M Div); leadership ministry (MA, D Min). MA in Bible translation offered jointly with Pioneer Bible Translators (Dallas, TX). Electronic applications accepted.

LINCOLN MEMORIAL UNIVERSITY, Harrogate, TN 37752-1901

General Information Independent, coed, comprehensive institution. *Enrollment:* 3,365 graduate, professional, and undergraduate students; 480 full-time matriculated graduate/professional students (249 women), 1,147 part-time matriculated graduate/professional students (845 women). *Enrollment by degree level:* 319 first professional, 420 master's, 888 other advanced degrees. *Tuition:* Full-time $5580; part-time $310 per credit hour. Tuition and fees vary according to degree level and program. *Graduate housing:* Rooms and/or apartments available on a first-come, first-served basis to single and married students. Typical cost: $9740 (including board) for single students; $9740 (including board) for married students. Room and board charges vary according to board plan and housing facility selected. *Student services:* Campus employment opportunities, career counseling, free psychological counseling, international student services, low-cost health insurance, services for students with disabilities, teacher training. *Library facilities:* Carnegie-Vincent Library. *Online resources:* library catalog, web page. *Collection:* 199,892 titles, 334 serial subscriptions, 4,064 audiovisual materials.

Computer facilities: A campuswide network can be accessed from student residence rooms. Online class registration is available. *Web address:* http://www.lmunet.edu/.

GRADUATE UNITS

Carter and Moyers School of Education Students: 190 full-time (151 women), 1,299 part-time (959 women); includes 144 minority (128 African Americans, 1 American Indian/Alaska Native, 5 Asian Americans or Pacific Islanders, 10 Hispanic Americans), 4 international. 1,562 applicants, 96% accepted, 1489 enrolled. *Faculty:* 29 full-time (13 women), 17 part-time/adjunct (8 women). Expenses: Contact institution. *Financial support:* In 2008–09, 973 students received support. Career-related internships or fieldwork, health care benefits, and unspecified assistantships available. Support available to part-time students. Financial award application deadline: 4/1; financial award applicants required to submit FAFSA. In 2008, 173 master's, 901 Ed Ss awarded. *Degree program information:* Part-time and evening/weekend programs available. Postbaccalaureate distance learning degree programs offered. Offers administration and supervision (M Ed, Ed S); counseling and guidance (M Ed); curriculum and instruction (M Ed, Ed S); English (M Ed). *Application deadline:* For fall admission, 8/10 for domestic and international students; for spring admission, 1/10 for domestic and international students. *Application fee:* $25. *Application Contact:* Terri Knuckles, Office Manager, Graduate Education, 423-869-6223, Fax: 423-869-6261, E-mail: terri.knuckles@lmunet.edu. *Dean, School of Education,* Dr. Fred Bedelle, 423-869-6259, Fax: 423-869-6261, E-mail: fred.bedelle@lmunet.edu.

Caylor School of Nursing Students: 40 full-time (33 women), 3 part-time (2 women). Average age 30. 66 applicants, 91% accepted, 43 enrolled. *Faculty:* 5 full-time (3 women), 2 part-time/adjunct (both women). Expenses: Contact institution. *Financial support:* Applicants required to submit FAFSA. In 2008, 6 master's awarded. *Degree program information:* Part-time programs available. Offers family nurse practitioner (MSN); nurse anesthesia (MSN). *Application deadline:* For fall admission, 2/1 for domestic students. *Application fee:* $25. *Application Contact:* Sherry Pearman, Director of Nursing Recruitment and Advising, 423-869-6283, E-mail: sherry.pearman@lmunet.edu. *Dean,* Dr. Mary Anne Modrcin, 423-869-6319, Fax: 423-869-6244, E-mail: maryanne.modrcin@lmunet.edu.

DeBusk College of Osteopathic Medicine Students: 168 full-time (79 women); includes 17 minority (2 African Americans, 13 Asian Americans or Pacific Islanders, 2 Hispanic Americans). Average age 26. 2,039 applicants, 15% accepted, 160 enrolled. *Faculty:* 28 full-time (13 women), 562 part-time/adjunct. Expenses: Contact institution. *Financial support:* In 2008–09, 5 students received support. Applicants required to submit FAFSA. Offers osteopathic medicine

(DO). *Application deadline:* For fall admission, 4/1 for domestic students. Applications are processed on a rolling basis. *Application fee:* $50. *Application Contact:* Janette Martin, Director of Admissions, 423-869-7102, Fax: 423-869-7172, E-mail: janette.martin@lmunet.edu. *Vice President and Dean*, Dr. Ray Stowers, 423-869-7077, E-mail: ray.stowers@lmunet.edu.

School of Business Students: 7 full-time (1 woman), 99 part-time (43 women). Average age 27. 51 applicants, 78% accepted, 37 enrolled. *Faculty:* 6 full-time (0 women), 1 part-time/adjunct (0 women). Expenses: Contact institution. *Financial support:* Career-related internships or fieldwork, health care benefits, and unspecified assistantships available. Support available to part-time students. Financial award applicants required to submit FAFSA. In 2008, 23 master's awarded. *Degree program information:* Part-time and evening/weekend programs available. Offers business (MBA). *Application deadline:* For fall admission, 7/15 for domestic and international students; for spring admission, 12/1 for domestic and international students. Applications are processed on a rolling basis. *Application fee:* $25. *Application Contact:* Dr. Michael E Dillon, Director, MBA Program, 423-869-7141, E-mail: michael.dillon@lmunet.edu. *Dean*, Dr. Jack McCann, 423-869-7085, Fax: 423-869-6298, E-mail: jack.mccann@lmunet.edu.

LINCOLN UNIVERSITY, Oakland, CA 94612

General Information Independent, coed, comprehensive institution. *Enrollment:* 331 full-time matriculated graduate/professional students (142 women), 3 part-time matriculated graduate/professional students. *Enrollment by degree level:* 334 master's. *Graduate faculty:* 7 full-time (2 women), 12 part-time/adjunct (1 woman). *Tuition:* Full-time $6570. *Student services:* Campus employment opportunities, campus safety program, career counseling, international student services, low-cost health insurance, writing training. *Library facilities:* Lincoln Library. *Collection:* 17,752 titles, 762 serial subscriptions.

Computer facilities: 20 computers available on campus for general student use. *Web address:* http://www.lincolnuca.edu/.

General Application Contact: Peggy Au, Director of Admissions and Records, 510-628-8010, Fax: 510-628-8012, E-mail: admissions@lincolnuca.edu.

GRADUATE UNITS

Master of Business Administration Program Students: 331 full-time (142 women), 3 part-time (0 women); includes 3 minority (1 African American, 2 Asian Americans or Pacific Islanders), 330 international. Average age 27. 389 applicants, 97% accepted, 122 enrolled. *Faculty:* 7 full-time (2 women), 12 part-time/adjunct (1 woman). Expenses: Contact institution. *Financial support:* In 2008–09, 1 teaching assistantship was awarded; career-related internships or fieldwork and scholarships/grants also available. In 2008, 81 master's awarded. *Degree program information:* Part-time and evening/weekend programs available. Offers finance management and investment banking (MBA); general business (MBA); human resource management (MBA); international business (MBA); management information systems (MBA). *Application deadline:* For fall admission, 8/19 priority date for domestic students; for spring admission, 1/10 priority date for domestic students. Applications are processed on a rolling basis. *Application fee:* $75. Electronic applications accepted. *Application Contact:* Peggy Au, Director of Admissions and Records, 510-628-8010, Fax: 510-628-8012, E-mail: admissions@lincolnuca.edu. *President and Rector*, Dr. Mikhail Brodsky, 510-208-2803, Fax: 510-208-2826, E-mail: president@lincolnuca.edu.

LINCOLN UNIVERSITY, Jefferson City, MO 65102

General Information State-supported, coed, comprehensive institution. *Enrollment:* 3,109 graduate, professional, and undergraduate students; 47 full-time matriculated graduate/professional students (31 women), 102 part-time matriculated graduate/professional students (76 women). *Enrollment by degree level:* 143 master's, 6 other advanced degrees. *Graduate faculty:* 27 full-time (9 women), 9 part-time/adjunct (3 women). Tuition, state resident: full-time $4185; part-time $232.50 per credit hour. Tuition, nonresident: full-time $7767; part-time $431.50 per credit hour. *Required fees:* $270; $15 per credit hour. One-time fee: $20. Tuition and fees vary according to course load. *Graduate housing:* Room and/or apartments available on a first-come, first-served basis to single students; on-campus housing not available to married students. Typical cost: $4040 per year ($6068 including board). Room and board charges vary according to board plan and housing facility selected. Housing application deadline: 7/1. *Student services:* Campus employment opportunities, campus safety program, career counseling, free psychological counseling, international student services, low-cost health insurance, services for students with disabilities. *Library facilities:* Inman Page Library. *Online resources:* library catalog, web page, access to other libraries' catalogs. *Collection:* 204,948 titles, 368 serial subscriptions, 5,497 audiovisual materials. *Research affiliation:* U.S. Department of Defense (defense/government), U.S. Department of Agriculture (agriculture/government).

Computer facilities: Computer purchase and lease plans are available. 250 computers available on campus for general student use. A campuswide network can be accessed from student residence rooms. Online class registration is available. *Web address:* http://www.lincolnu.edu/.

General Application Contact: Dr. Linda S. Bickel, Dean of the School of Graduate Studies and Continuing Education, 573-681-5247, Fax: 573-681-5106, E-mail: gradschool@lincolnu.edu.

GRADUATE UNITS

School of Graduate Studies and Continuing Education Students: 47 full-time (31 women), 102 part-time (76 women); includes 28 minority (all African Americans), 20 international. Average age 34. 48 applicants, 98% accepted, 29 enrolled. *Faculty:* 27 full-time (9 women), 9 part-time/adjunct (3 women). Expenses: Contact institution. *Financial support:* Federal Work-Study and scholarships/grants available. Financial award application deadline: 4/1; financial award applicants required to submit FAFSA. In 2008, 66 master's, 4 other advanced degrees awarded. *Degree program information:* Part-time and evening/weekend programs available. *Application deadline:* For fall admission, 7/1 priority date for domestic and international students; for spring admission, 12/1 priority date for domestic and international students. Applications are processed on a rolling basis. *Application fee:* $20. *Application Contact:* Irasema Steck, Administrative Assistant, 573-681-5247, Fax: 573-681-5106, E-mail: gradschool@lincolnu.edu. *Dean of the School of Graduate Studies and Continuing Education*, Dr. Linda S. Bickel, 573-681-5247, Fax: 573-681-5106, E-mail: gradschool@lincolnu.edu.

College of Business and Professional Studies Students: 20 full-time (11 women), 13 part-time (8 women); includes 10 minority (all African Americans), 6 international. Average age 31. *Faculty:* 7 full-time (1 woman), 1 part-time/adjunct (0 women). Expenses: Contact institution. *Financial support:* Federal Work-Study and scholarships/grants available. Financial award application deadline: 4/1; financial award applicants required to submit FAFSA. In 2008, 19 master's awarded. *Degree program information:* Part-time and evening/weekend programs available. Offers business administration (MBA); business and professional studies (MBA). *Application deadline:* For fall admission, 7/1 priority date for domestic and international students; for spring admission, 12/1 priority date for domestic and international students. Applications are processed on a rolling basis. *Application fee:* $20. *Application Contact:* Irasema Steck, Administrative Assistant, 573-681-5247, Fax: 573-681-5106, E-mail: gradschool@lincolnu.edu. *Dean*, Dr. Linda S. Bickel, 573-681-5489, Fax: 573-681-5488, E-mail: gradschool@lincolnu.edu.

College of Liberal Arts, Education and Journalism Students: 27 full-time (20 women), 89 part-time (68 women); includes 18 minority (all African Americans), 11 international. Average age 35. 38 applicants, 100% accepted, 32 enrolled. *Faculty:* 20 full-time (8 women), 8 part-time/adjunct (3 women). Expenses: Contact institution. *Financial support:* Federal Work-Study and scholarships/grants available. Financial award application deadline: 4/1; financial award applicants required to submit FAFSA. In 2008, 47 master's awarded. *Degree program information:* Part-time and evening/weekend programs available. Offers educational leadership (Ed S); guidance and counseling (M Ed); history (MA); liberal arts, education and journalism (M Ed, MA, Ed S); school administration and supervision (M Ed); school teaching (M Ed); social science (MA); sociology (MA); sociology/criminal justice (MA). *Application deadline:* For fall admission, 7/1 priority date for domestic and international students; for spring admission, 12/1 priority date for domestic and international students. Applications are processed on a rolling basis. *Application fee:* $20. *Application Contact:* Irasema Steck, Administrative Assistant, 573-681-5247, Fax: 573-681-5106, E-mail: gradschool@lincolnu.edu. *Dean*, Dr. Ann Harris, 573-681-5300, Fax: 573-681-5144, E-mail: harrisa@lincolnu.edu.

LINCOLN UNIVERSITY, Lincoln University, PA 19352

General Information State-related, coed, comprehensive institution. *Graduate housing:* On-campus housing not available.

GRADUATE UNITS

Graduate Center *Degree program information:* Evening/weekend programs available. Offers administration (MSA); early childhood education (M Ed); elementary education (M Ed); human services (M Hum Svcs); reading (MSR).

LINDENWOOD UNIVERSITY, St. Charles, MO 63301-1695

General Information Independent-religious, coed, comprehensive institution. *Enrollment:* 10,085 graduate, professional, and undergraduate students; 1,440 full-time matriculated graduate/professional students (953 women), 2,302 part-time matriculated graduate/professional students (1,697 women). *Enrollment by degree level:* 3,351 master's, 313 doctoral, 78 other advanced degrees. *Graduate faculty:* 91 full-time (39 women), 317 part-time/adjunct (139 women). *Tuition:* Full-time $12,700; part-time $360 per credit hour. *Graduate housing:* Rooms and/or apartments available on a first-come, first-served basis to single students and available to married students. Typical cost: $3400 per year ($6500 including board) for married students. Housing application deadline: 8/30. *Student services:* Campus employment opportunities, campus safety program, career counseling, free psychological counseling, international student services, low-cost health insurance, services for students with disabilities, teacher training, writing training. *Library facilities:* Butler Library. *Online resources:* library catalog, web page, access to other libraries' catalogs. *Collection:* 89,807 titles, 402 serial subscriptions, 1,960 audiovisual materials.

Computer facilities: Computer purchase and lease plans are available. 160 computers available on campus for general student use. A campuswide network can be accessed from student residence rooms and from off campus. Online class registration, WebCT are available. *Web address:* http://www.lindenwood.edu/.

General Application Contact: Brett Barger, Dean of Evening Admissions and Extension Campuses, 636-949-4934, Fax: 636-949-4109, E-mail: adultadmissions@lindenwood.edu.

GRADUATE UNITS

Graduate Programs Students: 1,440 full-time (953 women), 2,302 part-time (1,697 women); includes 847 minority (792 African Americans, 10 American Indian/Alaska Native, 25 Asian Americans or Pacific Islanders, 20 Hispanic Americans), 137 international. Average age 36. *Faculty:* 91 full-time (39 women), 317 part-time/adjunct (139 women). Expenses: Contact institution. *Financial support:* Career-related internships or fieldwork, Federal Work-Study, institutionally sponsored loans, tuition waivers (partial), and unspecified assistantships available. Financial award application deadline: 6/30; financial award applicants required to submit FAFSA. In 2008, 1,410 master's, 11 doctorates, 48 other advanced degrees awarded. *Degree program information:* Part-time and evening/weekend programs available. *Application deadline:* For fall admission, 8/30 priority date for domestic and international students; for winter admission, 12/30 priority date for domestic and international students; for spring admission, 12/30 priority date for domestic and international students. Applications are processed on a rolling basis. *Application fee:* $30 ($100 for international students). Electronic applications accepted. *Application Contact:* Brett Barger, Dean of Evening Admissions and Extension Campuses, 636-949-4934, Fax: 636-949-4109, E-mail: adultadmissions@lindenwood.edu. *Vice President of Academic Affairs and Provost*, Dr. Jann Weitzel, 636-949-4708, Fax: 636-949-4992, E-mail: jweitzel@lindenwood.edu.

College of Individualized Education Students: 750 full-time (489 women), 138 part-time (91 women); includes 196 minority (182 African Americans, 1 American Indian/Alaska Native, 5 Asian Americans or Pacific Islanders, 8 Hispanic Americans), 14 international. Average age 34. *Faculty:* 14 full-time (7 women), 119 part-time/adjunct (50 women). Expenses: Contact institution. *Financial support:* Career-related internships or fieldwork, institutionally sponsored loans, tuition waivers (partial), and unspecified assistantships available. Financial award application deadline: 6/30; financial award applicants required to submit FAFSA. In 2008, 349 master's awarded. *Degree program information:* Part-time and evening/weekend programs available. Offers administration (MSA); business administration (MBA); communication (MS); communications (MA); criminal justice and administration (MS); gerontology (MA); health management (MS); human resource management (MS); information technology (MBA, Certificate); management (MSA); managing information technology (MS); marketing (MSA); writing (MFA). *Application deadline:* For fall admission, 9/30 priority date for domestic and international students; for winter admission, 12/30 priority date for domestic and international students; for spring admission, 3/30 priority date for domestic and international students. Applications are processed on a rolling basis. *Application fee:* $30 ($100 for international students). *Application Contact:* Brett Barger, Dean of Evening Admissions and Extension Campuses, 636-949-4934, Fax: 636-949-4109, E-mail: adultadmissions@lindenwood.edu. *Dean of Lindenwood College for Individual Education*, Dan Kemper, 636-949-4501, Fax: 636-949-4505, E-mail: dkemper@lindenwood.edu.

School of Business and Entrepreneurship Students: 198 full-time (91 women), 162 part-time (67 women); includes 23 minority (17 African Americans, 1 American Indian/Alaska Native, 4 Asian Americans or Pacific Islanders, 1 Hispanic American), 107 international. Average age 31. *Faculty:* 19 full-time (7 women), 17 part-time/adjunct (5 women). Expenses: Contact institution. *Financial support:* Career-related internships or fieldwork, Federal Work-Study, institutionally sponsored loans, and tuition waivers (partial) available. Financial award application deadline: 6/30; financial award applicants required to submit FAFSA. In 2008, 158 master's awarded. *Degree program information:* Part-time and evening/weekend programs available. Offers accounting (MBA, MS); business administration (MBA); entrepreneurial studies (MBA, MS); finance (MBA, MS); human resource management (MBA); human resources (MS); international business (MBA, MS); management (MBA, MS); management information systems (MBA, MS); marketing (MBA, MS); public management (MBA, MS); sport management (MA). *Application deadline:* For fall admission, 7/30 priority date for domestic students, 9/30 priority date for international students; for winter admission, 12/30 priority date for domestic and international students; for spring admission, 2/28 priority date for domestic and international students. Applications are processed on a rolling basis. *Application fee:* $30 ($100 for international students). Electronic applications accepted. *Application Contact:* Brett Barger, Dean of Evening Admissions and Extension Campuses, 636-949-4934, Fax: 636-949-4109, E-mail: adultadmissions@lindenwood.edu. *Dean of Management*, Ed Morris, 636-949-4832, E-mail: emorris@lindenwood.edu.

School of Education Students: 460 full-time (352 women), 1,975 part-time (1,518 women); includes 620 minority (585 African Americans, 8 American Indian/Alaska Native, 16 Asian Americans or Pacific Islanders, 11 Hispanic Americans), 9 international. Average age 37. *Faculty:* 33 full-time (13 women), 176 part-time/adjunct (83 women). Expenses: Contact institution. *Financial support:* Career-related internships or fieldwork, institutionally sponsored loans, tuition waivers (partial), and unspecified assistantships available. Financial award applicants required to submit FAFSA. In 2008, 883 master's, 11 doctorates, 51 other advanced degrees awarded. *Degree program information:* Part-time and evening/weekend programs available. Offers education (MA); educational administration (MA, Ed D, Ed S); instructional leadership (Ed D, Ed S); library media (MA); professional and school counseling (MA); professional counseling (MA); school counseling (MA); teaching (MA). *Application deadline:* For fall admission, 8/30 priority date for domestic and international students; for spring admission, 12/30 priority date for domestic and international students. Applications are processed on a rolling basis. *Application fee:* $30 ($100 for international students). Electronic applications accepted. *Application Contact:* Brett Barger, Dean of Evening Admissions and Extension Campuses, 636-949-4934, Fax: 636-949-4109, E-mail: adultadmissions@lindenwood.edu. *Dean of Education*, Dr. Cynthia Bice, 636-949-4618, Fax: 636-949-4197, E-mail: cbice@lindenwood.edu.

Lindenwood University (continued)

School of Fine and Performing Arts Students: 28 full-time (18 women), 27 part-time (21 women); includes 8 minority (all African Americans), 7 international. Average age 35. *Faculty:* 21 full-time (10 women). Expenses: Contact institution. *Financial support:* Career-related internships or fieldwork, institutionally sponsored loans, tuition waivers (partial), and unspecified assistantships available. Financial award application deadline: 6/30; financial award applicants required to submit FAFSA. In 2008, 16 master's awarded. *Degree program information:* Part-time programs available. Offers arts management (MA); communication arts (MA); studio art (MA, MFA); theatre (MA, MFA). *Application deadline:* For fall admission, 8/30 priority date for domestic and international students; for spring admission, 12/30 priority date for domestic and international students. Applications are processed on a rolling basis. *Application fee:* $30 ($100 for international students). Electronic applications accepted. *Application Contact:* Brett Barger, Dean of Evening Admissions and Extension Campuses, 636-949-4934, Fax: 636-949-4109, E-mail: adultadmissions@lindenwood.edu. *Dean of Fine Arts*, Donnell Walsh, 636-949-4853, Fax: 636-949-4910, E-mail: dwalsh@lindenwood.edu.

School of Humanities Students: 4 full-time (3 women). Average age 32. *Faculty:* 4 full-time (2 women), 5 part-time/adjunct (1 woman). Expenses: Contact institution. *Financial support:* Career-related internships or fieldwork, institutionally sponsored loans, tuition waivers (partial), and unspecified assistantships available. Financial award application deadline: 6/30; financial award applicants required to submit FAFSA. In 2008, 1 master's awarded. *Degree program information:* Part-time programs available. Offers American studies (MA). *Application deadline:* For fall admission, 8/30 priority date for domestic and international students; for spring admission, 12/30 for domestic students, 12/30 priority date for international students. Applications are processed on a rolling basis. *Application fee:* $30 ($100 for international students). Electronic applications accepted. *Application Contact:* Brett Barger, Dean of Evening Admissions and Extension Campuses, 636-949-4934, Fax: 636-949-4109, E-mail: adultadmissions@lindenwood.edu. *Dean of Humanities*, Dr. Ana Schnellmann, 636-949-4873, E-mail: aschnellmann@lindenwood.edu.

LINDSEY WILSON COLLEGE, Columbia, KY 42728-1298

General Information Independent-religious, coed, comprehensive institution. *Graduate housing:* Rooms and/or apartments available on a first-come, first-served basis to single and married students.

GRADUATE UNITS

School of Professional Counseling *Degree program information:* Part-time and evening/weekend programs available. Offers counseling and human development (M Ed).

LIPSCOMB UNIVERSITY, Nashville, TN 37204-3951

General Information Independent-religious, coed, comprehensive institution. CGS member. *Graduate housing:* Rooms and/or apartments available on a first-come, first-served basis to single and married students. Housing application deadline: 7/15.

GRADUATE UNITS

Hazelip School of Theology *Degree program information:* Part-time and evening/weekend programs available. Offers biblical studies (MA); Christian studies (MA); divinity (M Div); ministry (MA); New Testament (MA); Old Testament (MA); theological studies (MTS); theology (MA). Electronic applications accepted.

Institute for Conflict Management *Degree program information:* Part-time and evening/weekend programs available. Offers conflict management (MA, Certificate).

MBA Program *Degree program information:* Part-time and evening/weekend programs available. Offers accounting (MBA); business administration (general) (MBA); conflict management (MBA); financial services (MBA); healthcare management (MBA); leadership (MBA); nonprofit management (MBA); sustainable practice (MBA). Electronic applications accepted.

Program in Accountancy *Degree program information:* Part-time and evening/weekend programs available. Offers accountancy (M Acc).

Program in Counseling *Degree program information:* Part-time and evening/weekend programs available. Postbaccalaureate distance learning degree programs offered (minimal on-campus study). Offers counseling psychology (Certificate); professional counseling (MS); psychology (MS). Electronic applications accepted.

Program in Education *Degree program information:* Part-time and evening/weekend programs available. Offers English language learners (MAT); instructional leadership (M Ed); learning and teaching (MALT); school administration and supervision (M Ed); special education instruction, K-12 (MASE).

Program in Pharmacy Offers pharmacy (Pharm D).

LOCK HAVEN UNIVERSITY OF PENNSYLVANIA, Lock Haven, PA 17745-2390

General Information State-supported, coed, comprehensive institution. *Enrollment:* 5,266 graduate, professional, and undergraduate students; 120 full-time matriculated graduate/professional students (89 women), 130 part-time matriculated graduate/professional students (85 women). *Enrollment by degree level:* 250 master's. *Graduate faculty:* 12 full-time (5 women), 6 part-time/adjunct (1 woman). Tuition, state resident: full-time $6430; part-time $357 per credit hour. Tuition, nonresident: full-time $10,288; part-time $572 per credit hour. *Required fees:* $1988; $144 per credit hour. One-time fee: $25. Tuition and fees vary according to course load. *Graduate housing:* Room and/or apartments available on a first-come, first-served basis to single students; on-campus housing not available to married students. Typical cost: $3520 per year ($6448 including board). Room and board charges vary according to board plan, campus/location and housing facility selected. Housing application deadline: 6/1. *Student services:* Campus employment opportunities, campus safety program, career counseling, child daycare facilities, exercise/wellness program, free psychological counseling, international student services, low-cost health insurance, multicultural affairs office, services for students with disabilities, teacher training. *Library facilities:* Stevenson Library. *Online resources:* library catalog, web page, access to other libraries' catalogs.

Computer facilities: 290 computers available on campus for general student use. A campuswide network can be accessed from student residence rooms and from off campus. Online class registration is available. *Web address:* http://www.lhup.edu/.

General Application Contact: Jerry Falco, Assistant Director of Admissions, 570-484-3869, Fax: 570-484-2734, E-mail: jfalco@lhup.edu.

LOGAN UNIVERSITY–COLLEGE OF CHIROPRACTIC, Chesterfield, MO 63006-1065

General Information Independent, coed, upper-level institution. *Enrollment:* 1,143 graduate, professional, and undergraduate students; 957 full-time matriculated graduate/professional students (356 women), 112 part-time matriculated graduate/professional students (37 women). *Enrollment by degree level:* 1,033 first professional, 36 master's. *Graduate faculty:* 51 full-time (15 women), 52 part-time/adjunct (21 women). *Tuition:* Full-time $14,304; part-time $450 per credit hour. *Required fees:* $270; $135 per term. *Graduate housing:* On-campus housing not available. *Student services:* Campus employment opportunities, career counseling, exercise/wellness program, free psychological counseling, international student services, low-cost health insurance, multicultural affairs office, services for students with disabilities. *Library facilities:* Learning Resources Center. *Online resources:* library catalog, web page, access to other libraries' catalogs. *Collection:* 14,281 titles, 18,178 serial subscriptions, 1,577 audiovisual materials. *Research affiliation:* Spine force (rehabilitation), BTE—Multi-Cervical Unit (cervical spine analysis and rehabilitation), ProAdjuster (chiropractic), NanoGreen (nutrition), Biofreeze (topical analgesic), Foot Levelers (orthotics).

Computer facilities: 85 computers available on campus for general student use. A campuswide network can be accessed. Online class registration, on-line classes, course homepages, wireless technologies, Academic Software Solutions for teaching and learning are available. *Web address:* http://www.logan.edu/.

General Application Contact: Dr. Elisabeth Goodman, Interim Vice President, Enrollment Management, 636-227-2100 Ext. 1752, Fax: 636-207-2425, E-mail: loganadm@logan.edu.

GRADUATE UNITS

Chiropractic Program Students: 944 full-time (350 women), 89 part-time (28 women); includes 85 minority (34 African Americans, 5 American Indian/Alaska Native, 21 Asian Americans or Pacific Islanders, 25 Hispanic Americans), 35 international. Average age 26. 215 applicants, 100% accepted, 135 enrolled. *Faculty:* 51 full-time (15 women), 44 part-time/adjunct (19 women). Expenses: Contact institution. *Financial support:* In 2008–09, 100 students received support. Federal Work-Study and scholarships/grants available. Support available to part-time students. Financial award applicants required to submit FAFSA. In 2008, 277 DCs awarded. Offers chiropractic (DC). *Application deadline:* For fall admission, 7/15 priority date for domestic and international students; for winter admission, 11/15 priority date for domestic and international students; for spring admission, 3/15 priority date for domestic students, 3/15 for international students. Applications are processed on a rolling basis. *Application fee:* $50. Electronic applications accepted. *Application Contact:* Dr. Elisabeth Goodman, PhD, Interim Vice President, Enrollment Management, 636-227-2100 Ext. 1752, Fax: 636-207-2425, E-mail: loganadm@logan.edu. *Vice President, Academic Affairs*, Dr. George T White, EdD, 636-227-2100 Ext. 1745, Fax: 636-207-2431, E-mail: george.white@logan.edu.

University Programs Students: 13 full-time (6 women), 23 part-time (9 women); includes 3 minority (all African Americans), 4 international. Average age 31. 34 applicants, 100% accepted, 18 enrolled. *Faculty:* 7 full-time (2 women), 8 part-time/adjunct (2 women). Expenses: Contact institution. *Financial support:* Federal Work-Study available. Support available to part-time students. Financial award applicants required to submit FAFSA. In 2008, 6 master's awarded. Offers chiropractic (MS). *Application deadline:* For fall admission, 7/15 priority date for domestic and international students; for winter admission, 11/15 priority date for domestic and international students; for spring admission, 3/15 priority date for domestic students, 3/15 for international students. *Application fee:* $50. *Application Contact:* Felicia Linear, Assistant Director, Admissions, 636-227-2100 Ext. 1754, Fax: 636-207-2425, E-mail: loganadm@logan.edu. *Vice President, Academic Affairs*, Dr. George T White, EdD, 636-227-2100, Fax: 636-207-2431, E-mail: george.white@logan.edu.

LOGOS EVANGELICAL SEMINARY, El Monte, CA 91731

General Information Independent-religious, coed, graduate-only institution. *Graduate housing:* Rooms and/or apartments available on a first-come, first-served basis to single students and guaranteed to married students.

GRADUATE UNITS

Graduate Programs *Degree program information:* Part-time programs available. Offers theology (M Div, MA, Th M, D Min). Electronic applications accepted.

LOMA LINDA UNIVERSITY, Loma Linda, CA 92350

General Information Independent-religious, coed, upper-level institution. CGS member. *Graduate housing:* Room and/or apartments available on a first-come, first-served basis to single students; on-campus housing not available to married students. *Research affiliation:* Children's Hospital Los Angeles (cancer research), Children's Hospital Orange County (cancer research), City of Hope Hospital (cancer research).

GRADUATE UNITS

Department of Graduate Nursing *Degree program information:* Part-time programs available. Offers adult and aging family nursing (MS); growing family nursing (MS); nursing administration (MS). Electronic applications accepted.

Faculty of Religion Offers biomedical and clinical ethics (MA, Certificate); clinical ministry (MA, Certificate); religion (MA, Certificate); religion and science (MA). Electronic applications accepted.

School of Allied Health Professions Offers allied health professions (MHIS, MOT, MPT, MS, D Sc, DPT, DPTSc, OTD); occupational therapy (MOT, OTD); physical therapy (MPT, D Sc, DPT, DPTSc); physician assistant (MS); speech-language pathology and audiology (MS). Electronic applications accepted.

School of Dentistry Offers dentistry (DDS, MS, Certificate); endodontics (MS, Certificate); implant dentistry (MS, Certificate); oral and maxillofacial surgery (MS, Certificate); orthodontics (MS, Certificate); periodontics (MS).

School of Medicine Offers biochemistry/microbiology (MS, PhD); medicine (MD, MS, PhD); pathology and human anatomy (MS, PhD); physiology/pharmacology (MS, PhD).

School of Pharmacy Offers pharmacy (Pharm D).

School of Public Health *Degree program information:* Part-time programs available. Offers environmental and occupational health (MPH, MSPH); epidemiology and biostatistics (MPH, MSPH, Dr PH, Postbaccalaureate Certificate); global health (MPH); health administration (MBA, MHA, MPH); health promotion and education (MPH, Dr PH); public health (MBA, MHA, MPH, MSPH, Dr PH, Postbaccalaureate Certificate); public health nutrition (MPH, Dr PH). Electronic applications accepted.

School of Science and Technology Offers biological and earth sciences (MS, PhD); counseling and family science (MA, MS, DMFT, PhD, Certificate); psychology (PhD, Psy D); science and technology (MA, MS, MSW, DMFT, PhD, Psy D, Certificate); social policy and research (PhD); social work (MSW). Electronic applications accepted.

LONG ISLAND UNIVERSITY AT RIVERHEAD, Riverhead, NY 11901

General Information Independent, coed, graduate-only institution. *Enrollment by degree level:* 218 master's, 13 other advanced degrees. *Graduate faculty:* 3 full-time (0 women), 21 part-time/adjunct (8 women). *Graduate housing:* On-campus housing not available. *Student services:* Campus employment opportunities, campus safety program, career counseling, international student services, low-cost health insurance, services for students with disabilities. *Library facilities:* Long Island University at Riverhead Library plus 1 other. *Online resources:* library catalog, web page. *Collection:* 1.2 million titles.

Computer facilities: 30 computers available on campus for general student use. A campuswide network can be accessed from off campus. Online class registration, Online Bill Pay are available. *Web address:* http://www.southampton.liu.edu/riverhead/.

General Application Contact: Andrea Borra, Admissions Counselor, 631-287-8010 Ext. 8326, Fax: 631-287-8253, E-mail: andrea.borra@liu.edu.

GRADUATE UNITS

Education Division Students: 29 full-time (25 women), 90 part-time (82 women); includes 2 African Americans, 1 Hispanic American. Average age 30. 48 applicants, 69% accepted, 33 enrolled. *Faculty:* 1 full-time (0 women), 11 part-time/adjunct (7 women). Expenses: Contact institution. *Financial support:* In 2008–09, 105 students received support. Scholarships/grants and tuition waivers (partial) available. Support available to part-time students. Financial award applicants required to submit FAFSA. In 2008, 38 master's awarded. *Degree program information:* Part-time and evening/weekend programs available. Offers applied behavior analysis (Advanced Certificate); childhood education (MS Ed); elementary education (MS Ed); literacy education (MS Ed); teaching students with disabilities (MS Ed). *Application deadline:* Applications are processed on a rolling basis. Electronic applications accepted. *Application Contact:* Andrea Borra, Director of Graduate Admissions and Program Administration, 631-287-8010 Ext. 8326, Fax: 631-287-8253, E-mail: andrea.borra@liu.edu. *Director*, Dr. R. Lawrence McCann, 631-287-8211, E-mail: admissions@southampton.liu.edu.

Homeland Security Management Institute Students: 5 full-time (0 women), 107 part-time (17 women); includes 16 minority (8 African Americans, 1 American Indian/Alaska Native, 2 Asian Americans or Pacific Islanders, 5 Hispanic Americans). 48 applicants, 56% accepted, 23 enrolled. *Faculty:* 2 full-time (0 women), 10 part-time/adjunct (1 woman). Expenses: Contact institution. *Financial support:* In 2008–09, 105 students received support. Career-related internships or fieldwork and scholarships/grants available. Support available to part-time students. Financial award applicants required to submit FAFSA. In 2008, 11 master's, 36 other advanced degrees awarded. *Degree program information:* Part-time programs available. Postbaccalaureate distance learning degree programs offered (no on-campus study). Offers homeland security management (MS, Advanced Certificate). *Application deadline:* Applications are processed on a rolling basis. *Application fee:* $0. Electronic applications accepted. *Application Contact:* Andrea Borra, Admissions Counselor, 631-287-8010 Ext. 8326, Fax: 631-287-8253, E-mail: andrea.borra@liu.edu. *Unit Head,* Dr. Vincent E. Henry, 631-287-8010, Fax: 631-287-8130, E-mail: vincent.henry@liu.edu.

LONG ISLAND UNIVERSITY, BRENTWOOD CAMPUS, Brentwood, NY 11717

General Information Independent, coed, upper-level institution. *Graduate housing:* On-campus housing not available.

GRADUATE UNITS

School of Education *Degree program information:* Part-time and evening/weekend programs available. Offers childhood education (MS); early childhood education (MS); literacy (MS); mental health counseling (MS); school counseling (MS); special education (MS).

School of Public Service *Degree program information:* Part-time and evening/weekend programs available. Offers criminal justice (MS).

LONG ISLAND UNIVERSITY, BROOKLYN CAMPUS, Brooklyn, NY 11201-8423

General Information Independent, coed, university. *Graduate housing:* Rooms and/or apartments available to single and married students. Housing application deadline: 9/1.

GRADUATE UNITS

Arnold and Marie Schwartz College of Pharmacy and Health Sciences *Degree program information:* Part-time and evening/weekend programs available. Offers cosmetic science (MS); drug regulatory affairs (MS); industrial pharmacy (MS); pharmaceutical sciences (MS, PhD); pharmaceutics (PhD); pharmacology/toxicology (MS); pharmacy administration (MS); pharmacy and health sciences (MS, PhD); social and administrative sciences (MS).

Richard L. Conolly College of Liberal Arts and Sciences *Degree program information:* Part-time and evening/weekend programs available. Offers biology (MS); chemistry (MS); clinical psychology (PhD); economics (MA); English literature (MA); history (MS); liberal arts and sciences (MA, MS, PhD, Certificate); media arts (MA); political science (MA); professional and creative writing (MA); psychology (MA, PhD); speech-language pathology (MS); teaching of writing (MA); United Nations studies (Certificate); urban studies (MA). Electronic applications accepted.

School of Business, Public Administration and Information Sciences *Degree program information:* Part-time and evening/weekend programs available. Offers accounting (MS); business administration (MBA); business, public administration and information sciences (MBA, MPA, MS); computer science (MS); human resources management (MS); public administration (MPA); taxation (MS). Electronic applications accepted.

School of Education *Degree program information:* Part-time and evening/weekend programs available. Offers bilingual education (MS Ed); computers in education (MS); counseling and development (MS, MS Ed, Certificate); education (MS, MS Ed, Certificate); elementary education (MS Ed); leadership and policy (MS); mathematics education (MS Ed); reading (MS Ed); school psychology (MS Ed); secondary education (MS Ed); special education (MS Ed); teaching English to speakers of other languages (MS Ed). Electronic applications accepted.

School of Health Professions *Degree program information:* Part-time and evening/weekend programs available. Offers adapted physical education (MS); athletic training and sports sciences (MS); community mental health (MS); exercise physiology (MS); family health (MS); health management (MS); health professions (MS, DPT, TDPT); health sciences (MS); physical therapy (DPT, TDPT). Electronic applications accepted.

School of Nursing Offers adult nurse practitioner (MS, Certificate); nurse executive (MS); nursing (MS, Certificate). Electronic applications accepted.

LONG ISLAND UNIVERSITY, C.W. POST CAMPUS, Brookville, NY 11548-1300

General Information Independent, coed, comprehensive institution. *Graduate housing:* Room and/or apartments available on a first-come, first-served basis to single students; on-campus housing not available to married students. Housing application deadline: 6/1.

GRADUATE UNITS

College of Information and Computer Science Students: 133 full-time (87 women), 440 part-time (331 women); includes 83 minority (29 African Americans, 1 American Indian/Alaska Native, 28 Asian Americans or Pacific Islanders, 25 Hispanic Americans), 25 international. Average age 38. 592 applicants, 75% accepted, 136 enrolled. *Faculty:* 17 full-time (9 women), 37 part-time/adjunct (10 women). Expenses: Contact institution. *Financial support:* Fellowships, research assistantships, career-related internships or fieldwork, Federal Work-Study, institutionally sponsored loans, and tuition waivers (partial) available. Support available to part-time students. Financial award applicants required to submit CSS PROFILE or FAFSA. In 2008, 161 master's, 1 doctorate, 1 other advanced degree awarded. *Degree program information:* Part-time and evening/weekend programs available. Postbaccalaureate distance learning degree programs offered. Offers information and computer science (MS, PhD, Certificate); information systems (MS); information technology education (MS); management engineering (MS). *Application deadline:* For fall admission, 6/1 priority date for international students; for spring admission, 11/1 priority date for international students. Applications are processed on a rolling basis. *Application fee:* $30. Electronic applications accepted. *Application Contact:* Beth Carson, Director of Graduate and International Admissions, 516-299-2900 Ext. 3952, Fax: 516-299-2137, E-mail: enroll@cwpost.liu.edu. *Acting Dean,* Dr. Mary Westermann-Cicio, 516-299-2178, Fax: 516-299-4168, E-mail: mary.westermann-cicio@liu.edu.

Palmer School of Library and Information Science Students: 104 full-time (81 women), 390 part-time (304 women); includes 68 minority (26 African Americans, 1 American Indian/Alaska Native, 20 Asian Americans or Pacific Islanders, 21 Hispanic Americans), 2 international. Average age 39. 257 applicants, 88% accepted, 106 enrolled. *Faculty:* 13 full-time (8 women), 30 part-time/adjunct (10 women). Expenses: Contact institution. *Financial support:* Fellowships, research assistantships, career-related internships or fieldwork, Federal Work-Study, institutionally sponsored loans, and tuition waivers (partial) available. Support available to part-time students. Financial award application deadline: 5/15; financial award applicants required to submit CSS PROFILE or FAFSA. In 2008, 115 master's awarded. *Degree program information:* Part-time and evening/weekend programs available. Postbaccalaureate distance learning degree programs offered (minimal on-campus study). Offers archives and records management (Certificate); information studies (PhD); library and information science (MS); library media specialist (MS); public library management (Certificate). *Application fee:* $30. Electronic applications accepted. *Application Contact:* Rosemary Chu, Graduate Admissions, 516-299-2866, Fax: 516-299-4168, E-mail: palmer@cwpost.liu.edu.

College of Liberal Arts and Sciences Students: 116 full-time (83 women), 155 part-time (95 women); includes 45 minority (9 African Americans, 1 American Indian/Alaska Native, 12 Asian Americans or Pacific Islanders, 23 Hispanic Americans), 16 international. Average age 31. 431 applicants, 41% accepted, 82 enrolled. *Faculty:* 45 full-time (16 women), 31 part-time/adjunct (6 women). Expenses: Contact institution. *Financial support:* In 2008–09, 10 fellowships, 12 research assistantships, 7 teaching assistantships were awarded; career-related internships or fieldwork, Federal Work-Study, institutionally sponsored loans, tuition waivers (full and partial), and unspecified assistantships also available. Support available to part-time students. Financial award application deadline: 5/15; financial award applicants required to submit CSS PROFILE or FAFSA. In 2008, 52 master's, 9 doctorates awarded. *Degree program information:* Part-time and evening/weekend programs available. Offers applied mathematics (MS); biology (MS); biology education (MS); clinical psychology (Psy D); earth science (MS); earth science education (MS); English (MA); English for adolescence education (MS); environmental studies (MS); history (MA); interdisciplinary studies (MA, MS); liberal arts and sciences (MA, MS, Psy D); mathematics education (MS); mathematics for secondary school teachers (MS); political science/international studies (MA); psychology (MA); Spanish (MA); Spanish education (MS). *Application deadline:* Applications are processed on a rolling basis. *Application fee:* $30. Electronic applications accepted. *Application Contact:* Beth Carson, Director of Graduate and International Admissions, 516-299-2900 Ext. 3952, Fax: 516-299-2137, E-mail: enroll@cwpost.liu.edu. *Dean,* Dr. Katherine Hill-Miller, 516-299-2710, Fax: 516-299-4140.

College of Management Students: 221 full-time (123 women), 251 part-time (132 women); includes 107 minority (48 African Americans, 27 Asian Americans or Pacific Islanders, 32 Hispanic Americans), 76 international. Average age 31. 586 applicants, 59% accepted, 121 enrolled. *Faculty:* 35 full-time (10 women), 79 part-time/adjunct (22 women). Expenses: Contact institution. *Financial support:* Fellowships, research assistantships, teaching assistantships, career-related internships or fieldwork, Federal Work-Study, institutionally sponsored loans, scholarships/grants, tuition waivers (partial), and unspecified assistantships available. Support available to part-time students. Financial award application deadline: 5/15; financial award applicants required to submit CSS PROFILE or FAFSA. In 2008, 307 master's, 1 other advanced degree awarded. *Degree program information:* Part-time and evening/weekend programs available. Offers criminal justice (MS); fraud examination (MS); gerontology (Certificate); health care administration (MPA); health care administration/gerontology (MPA); management (MBA, MPA, MS, MSW, Certificate); nonprofit management (MPA, Certificate); public administration (MPA); security administration (MS); social work (MSW). *Application deadline:* Applications are processed on a rolling basis. *Application fee:* $30. Electronic applications accepted. *Application Contact:* Beth Carson, Director of Graduate and International Admissions, 516-299-2900 Ext. 3952, Fax: 516-299-2137, E-mail: enroll@cwpost.liu.edu. *Dean,* Francis Bonsignore, 516-299-3017, Fax: 516-299-2786, E-mail: francis.bonsignore@liu.edu.

School of Business *Degree program information:* Part-time and evening/weekend programs available. Offers accounting and taxation (Certificate); business administration (Certificate); finance (MBA, Certificate); general business administration (MBA); international business (MBA, Certificate); management (MBA, Certificate); management information systems (MBA, Certificate); marketing (MBA, Certificate). Electronic applications accepted.

School of Professional Accountancy Students: 16 full-time (9 women), 25 part-time (12 women); includes 6 minority (2 African Americans, 1 Asian American or Pacific Islander, 3 Hispanic Americans), 3 international. Average age 30. 40 applicants, 68% accepted, 12 enrolled. *Faculty:* 3 full-time (1 woman), 5 part-time/adjunct (2 women). Expenses: Contact institution. *Financial support:* Career-related internships or fieldwork, Federal Work-Study, institutionally sponsored loans, and unspecified assistantships available. Support available to part-time students. Financial award application deadline: 5/15; financial award applicants required to submit CSS PROFILE or FAFSA. In 2008, 27 master's awarded. *Degree program information:* Part-time and evening/weekend programs available. Offers accounting (MS); taxation (MS). *Application deadline:* Applications are processed on a rolling basis. *Application fee:* $30. Electronic applications accepted. *Application Contact:* Fred Tobias, Advisor, 516-299-2098, Fax: 516-299-2297, E-mail: ftobias@liu.edu. *Director,* Dr. Charles Barragato, 516-299-3279, Fax: 516-299-3221, E-mail: charles.barragato@liu.edu.

School of Education Students: 546 full-time (451 women), 827 part-time (645 women); includes 155 minority (55 African Americans, 3 American Indian/Alaska Native, 32 Asian Americans or Pacific Islanders, 65 Hispanic Americans), 14 international. Average age 31. 873 applicants, 70% accepted, 299 enrolled. *Faculty:* 60 full-time (28 women), 131 part-time/adjunct (49 women). Expenses: Contact institution. *Financial support:* In 2008–09, 29 research assistantships were awarded; teaching assistantships, career-related internships or fieldwork and Federal Work-Study also available. Support available to part-time students. Financial award application deadline: 5/15; financial award applicants required to submit CSS PROFILE or FAFSA. In 2008, 871 master's, 92 other advanced degrees awarded. *Degree program information:* Part-time and evening/weekend programs available. Offers adolescence education (MS); adolescence education: biology (MS); adolescence education: earth science (MS); adolescence education: English (MS); adolescence education: mathematics (MS); adolescence education: social studies (MS); adolescence education: Spanish (MS); art education (MS); bilingual education (MS); childhood education (MS); childhood education/literacy (MS); childhood education/special education (MS); computers in education (MS); early childhood education (MS); education (MA, MS, MS Ed, AC); literacy (MS Ed); mental health counseling (MS); middle childhood education (MS); music education (MS); school administration and supervision (MS Ed); school building leader (AC); school counseling (MS); school district business leader (AC); school district leader (AC); special education (MS Ed); speech language pathology (MA); teaching English to speakers of other languages (MS). *Application deadline:* Applications are processed on a rolling basis. *Application fee:* $30. Electronic applications accepted. *Application Contact:* Beth Carson, Director of Graduate and International Admissions, 516-299-2900 Ext. 3952, Fax: 516-299-2137, E-mail: enroll@cwpost.liu.edu. *Dean,* Dr. Robert Manheimer, 516-299-2210, Fax: 516-299-4167, E-mail: robert.manheimer@liu.edu.

School of Health Professions and Nursing Students: 143 full-time (78 women), 137 part-time (118 women); includes 58 minority (21 African Americans, 1 American Indian/Alaska Native, 26 Asian Americans or Pacific Islanders, 10 Hispanic Americans), 89 international. Average age 31. 344 applicants, 74% accepted, 98 enrolled. *Faculty:* 8 full-time (6 women), 38 part-time/adjunct (25 women). Expenses: Contact institution. *Financial support:* In 2008–09, 45 students received support, including 4 fellowships with partial tuition reimbursements available, 6 teaching assistantships with partial tuition reimbursements available; career-related internships or fieldwork, Federal Work-Study, institutionally sponsored loans, tuition waivers (partial), and unspecified assistantships also available. Support available to part-time students. Financial award application deadline: 5/15; financial award applicants required to submit CSS PROFILE or FAFSA. In 2008, 31 master's awarded. *Degree program information:* Part-time and evening/weekend programs available. Postbaccalaureate distance learning degree programs offered. Offers cardiovascular perfusion (MS); clinical laboratory management (MS); clinical nurse specialist (MS); dietetic internship (Certificate); family nurse practitioner (MS, Certificate); health professions and nursing (MS, Certificate); medical biology (MS); nutrition (MS). *Application deadline:* Applications are processed on a rolling basis. *Application fee:* $30. Electronic applications accepted. *Application Contact:* Beth Carson, Director of Graduate and International Admissions, 516-299-2900 Ext. 3952, Fax: 516-299-2137, E-mail: enroll@cwpost.liu.edu. *Dean,* Dr. Theodora T. Grauer, 516-299-2486, Fax: 516-299-2527, E-mail: healprof@cwpost.liu.edu.

School of Visual and Performing Arts Students: 87 full-time (68 women), 46 part-time (31 women); includes 11 minority (4 African Americans, 5 Asian Americans or Pacific Islanders, 2 Hispanic Americans), 26 international. Average age 31. 113 applicants, 67% accepted, 39 enrolled. *Faculty:* 16 full-time (9 women), 34 part-time/adjunct (18 women). Expenses: Contact institution. *Financial support:* Fellowships, teaching assistantships, career-related internships or fieldwork, Federal Work-Study, institutionally sponsored loans, scholarships/grants, and unspecified assistantships available. Support available to part-time students. Financial award application deadline: 5/15; financial award applicants required to submit CSS PROFILE or FAFSA. In 2008, 81 master's awarded. *Degree program information:* Part-time and evening/weekend programs available. Offers art (MA); art education (MS); clinical art therapy (MA); fine art and design (MFA); interactive multimedia (MA); music (MA); music education (MS); theatre (MA); visual and performing arts (MA, MFA, MS). *Application deadline:* Applications are processed on a rolling basis. *Application fee:* $30. Electronic applications accepted. *Application Contact:* Beth Carson, Director of Graduate and International Admissions, 516-299-2900 Ext. 3952, Fax: 516-299-2137, E-mail: enroll@cwpost.liu.edu. *Acting Dean,* Rhoda Grauer, 516-299-2395, Fax: 516-299-4180.

LONG ISLAND UNIVERSITY, ROCKLAND GRADUATE CAMPUS, Orangeburg, NY 10962

General Information Independent, coed, graduate-only institution. *Enrollment by degree level:* 473 master's. *Graduate faculty:* 11 full-time (5 women), 35 part-time/adjunct (15 women). *Tuition:* Part-time $882 per credit. *Required fees:* $100 per semester. *Graduate housing:* On-campus housing not available. *Student services:* Campus employment opportunities,

Long Island University, Rockland Graduate Campus (continued)

teacher training. *Library facilities:* Long Island University, Rockland Campus Library. *Online resources:* library catalog. *Collection:* 9,200 titles, 550 serial subscriptions, 1,000 audiovisual materials.

Computer facilities: 55 computers available on campus for general student use. A campuswide network can be accessed from off campus. Online class registration is available. *Web address:* http://www.liu.edu/rockland/.

General Application Contact: Peter S. Reiner, Director of Admissions and Marketing, 845-359-7200, Fax: 845-359-7248, E-mail: peter.reiner@liu.edu.

GRADUATE UNITS

Graduate School *Degree program information:* Part-time and evening/weekend programs available. Offers adolescence education (MS Ed); business administration (MBA, Post Master's Certificate); childhood education (MS); childhood/literacy (MS); childhood/special education (MS); cosmetic science (MS); gerontology (Advanced Certificate); health administration (MPA); industrial pharmacy (MS); literacy (MS Ed); mental health counseling (MS); public administration (MPA); school building leader (MS Ed, Advanced Certificate); school counselor (MS); school district business leader (Advanced Certificate); school district leader (Advanced Certificate); special education (MS Ed).

LONG ISLAND UNIVERSITY, WESTCHESTER GRADUATE CAMPUS, Purchase, NY 10577

General Information Independent, coed, graduate-only institution. *Graduate housing:* On-campus housing not available.

GRADUATE UNITS

Program in Business Administration *Degree program information:* Part-time and evening/weekend programs available. Offers business administration (MBA).

Program in Library and Information Science *Degree program information:* Part-time and evening/weekend programs available. Offers library and information science (MS).

Program in Mental Health Counseling Offers mental health counseling (MS).

Programs in Education-School Counselor and School Psychology *Degree program information:* Part-time and evening/weekend programs available. Offers school counselor (MS Ed); school psychologist (MS Ed).

Programs in Education-Teaching *Degree program information:* Part-time and evening/weekend programs available. Offers early childhood education (MS Ed, Advanced Certificate); elementary education (MS Ed, Advanced Certificate); literacy education (MS Ed, Advanced Certificate); second language, TESOL, bilingual education (MS Ed, Advanced Certificate); special education and secondary education (MS Ed, Advanced Certificate).

Program in Second Language, TESOL, Bilingual Education *Degree program information:* Part-time and evening/weekend programs available. Offers second language, TESOL, bilingual education (MS Ed, Advanced Certificate).

LONGWOOD UNIVERSITY, Farmville, VA 23909

General Information State-supported, coed, comprehensive institution. CGS member. *Graduate housing:* On-campus housing not available.

GRADUATE UNITS

Office of Graduate Studies *Degree program information:* Part-time and evening/weekend programs available. Offers 6-12 initial teaching/licensure (MA); creative writing (MA); criminal justice (MS); English education and writing (MA); literature (MA).

College of Business and Economics Offers retail management (MBA).

College of Education and Human Services *Degree program information:* Part-time and evening/weekend programs available. Offers communication sciences and disorders (MS); community and college counseling (MS); curriculum and instruction specialist-elementary (MS); curriculum and instruction specialist-secondary (MS); educational leadership (MS); guidance and counseling (MS); literacy and culture (MS); school library media (MS).

LONGY SCHOOL OF MUSIC, Cambridge, MA 02138

General Information Independent, coed, graduate-only institution. *Graduate housing:* On-campus housing not available.

GRADUATE UNITS

Conservatory at Longy *Degree program information:* Part-time programs available. Offers chamber ensemble (Artist Diploma); collaborative piano (MM, Artist Diploma, GPD); composition (MM); Dalcroze eurhythmics (MM); early music (MM, Artist Diploma, GPD); instrumental performance (MM, Artist Diploma, GPD); modern American music (MM, GPD); opera performance (MM, GPD); organ performance (MM, Artist Diploma, GPD); piano performance (MM, Artist Diploma, GPD); vocal performance (MM, Artist Diploma, GPD).

LORAS COLLEGE, Dubuque, IA 52004-0178

General Information Independent-religious, coed, comprehensive institution. *Graduate housing:* On-campus housing not available.

GRADUATE UNITS

Graduate Division *Degree program information:* Part-time and evening/weekend programs available. Offers applied psychology (MA); educational leadership (MA); instructional strategist I K-6 and 7-12 (MA); ministry (MA); theology (MA).

LOUISIANA STATE UNIVERSITY AND AGRICULTURAL AND MECHANICAL COLLEGE, Baton Rouge, LA 70803

General Information State-supported, coed, university. CGS member. *Enrollment:* 28,628 graduate, professional, and undergraduate students; 3,477 full-time matriculated graduate/professional students (1,763 women), 1,051 part-time matriculated graduate/professional students (605 women). *Enrollment by degree level:* 329 first professional, 2,256 master's, 1,943 doctoral. *Graduate faculty:* 1,282 full-time (330 women), 14 part-time/adjunct (2 women). *Graduate housing:* Rooms and/or apartments available on a first-come, first-served basis to single and married students. Typical cost: $4610 per year ($7722 including board) for single students. Room and board charges vary according to board plan, campus/location and housing facility selected. Housing application deadline: 3/15. *Student services:* Campus employment opportunities, campus safety program, career counseling, child daycare facilities, exercise/wellness program, free psychological counseling, grant writing training, international student services, low-cost health insurance, multicultural affairs office, services for students with disabilities, teacher training, writing training. *Library facilities:* Troy H. Middleton Library plus 4 others. *Online resources:* library catalog, web page, access to other libraries' catalogs. *Collection:* 4.1 million titles, 104,545 serial subscriptions, 28,538 audiovisual materials. *Research affiliation:* Albert Einstein Institute, Arctic Research Consortium of the U. S., Organization for Tropical Studies, Coalition for Academic Scientific Computing, Inter-University Consortium for Political and Social Research, Laser Interferometer Gravitational Wave Observatory.

Computer facilities: 7,000 computers available on campus for general student use. A campuswide network can be accessed from student residence rooms and from off campus. Online class registration, free software for download, personal Web sites, storage, discounts on hardware, virtual computer lab are available. *Web address:* http://www.lsu.edu/.

General Application Contact: Dr. Renee Renegar, Office of Graduate Admissions, 225-578-1641, Fax: 225-578-1370, E-mail: rreneg1@lsu.edu.

GRADUATE UNITS

Graduate School Students: 3,477 full-time (1,763 women), 1,051 part-time (605 women); includes 536 minority (350 African Americans, 18 American Indian/Alaska Native, 87 Asian Americans or Pacific Islanders, 81 Hispanic Americans), 1,111 international. Average age 29. 4,113 applicants, 46% accepted, 1037 enrolled. *Faculty:* 1,282 full-time (330 women), 14 part-time/adjunct (2 women). Expenses: Contact institution. *Financial support:* In 2008–09, 3,603 students received support, including 170 fellowships with full tuition reimbursements available (averaging $24,857 per year), 985 research assistantships with partial tuition reimbursements available (averaging $16,979 per year), 1,092 teaching assistantships with partial tuition reimbursements available (averaging $14,158 per year); career-related internships or fieldwork, Federal Work-Study, institutionally sponsored loans, scholarships/grants, traineeships, health care benefits, tuition waivers (full and partial), and unspecified assistantships also available. Support available to part-time students. Financial award application deadline: 1/15; financial award applicants required to submit FAFSA. In 2008, 928 master's, 218 doctorates, 17 other advanced degrees awarded. *Degree program information:* Part-time and evening/weekend programs available. Postbaccalaureate distance learning degree programs offered. *Application deadline:* For fall admission, 5/15 priority date for domestic students, 5/15 for international students; for winter admission, 10/15 priority date for domestic students; for spring admission, 10/15 for domestic and international students. Applications are processed on a rolling basis. *Application fee:* $50 ($70 for international students). Electronic applications accepted. *Application Contact:* Dr. Renee Renegar, Director of Graduate Admissions, 225-578-1641, Fax: 225-578-1370. *Interim Dean,* Dr. David Constant, 225-578-3885, Fax: 225-578-1370, E-mail: hscons@lsu.edu.

College of Agriculture Students: 314 full-time (164 women), 127 part-time (65 women); includes 39 minority (27 African Americans, 7 Asian Americans or Pacific Islanders, 5 Hispanic Americans), 149 international. Average age 31. 226 applicants, 54% accepted, 103 enrolled. Expenses: Contact institution. *Financial support:* In 2008–09, 348 students received support, including 7 fellowships with full tuition reimbursements available (averaging $19,900 per year), 217 research assistantships with partial tuition reimbursements available (averaging $16,996 per year), 42 teaching assistantships with partial tuition reimbursements available (averaging $12,531 per year); career-related internships or fieldwork, Federal Work-Study, institutionally sponsored loans, health care benefits, tuition waivers (full), and unspecified assistantships also available. Support available to part-time students. Financial award applicants required to submit FAFSA. In 2008, 81 master's, 20 doctorates awarded. *Degree program information:* Part-time programs available. Offers agricultural economics and agribusiness (MS, PhD); agriculture (M App St, MS, MSBAE, PhD); agriculture and extension education and youth development (MS, PhD); agronomy (MS, PhD); animal sciences (MS, PhD); applied statistics (M App St); biological and agricultural engineering (MSBAE); career and technical education (MS, PhD); comprehensive vocational education (MS, PhD); engineering science (MS, PhD); entomology (MS, PhD); extension and international education (MS, PhD); fisheries (MS); food science (MS, PhD); forestry (MS, PhD); horticulture (MS, PhD); human ecology (MS, PhD); human resource and leadership development (MS, PhD); industrial education (MS); plant health (MS, PhD); plant, environmental and soil science (MS, PhD); vocational agriculture education (MS, PhD); vocational business education (MS); vocational home economics education (MS); wildlife (MS); wildlife and fisheries science (PhD). *Application deadline:* For fall admission, 5/15 for domestic and international students; for spring admission, 10/15 for domestic and international students. Applications are processed on a rolling basis. *Application fee:* $50 ($70 for international students). Electronic applications accepted. *Application Contact:* Paula Beecher, Recruiting Coordinator, 225-578-2468, E-mail: pbeeche@lsu.edu. *Dean,* Dr. Kenneth Koonce, 225-578-2362, Fax: 225-578-2526, E-mail: kkoonce@lsu.edu.

College of Art and Design Students: 122 full-time (69 women), 6 part-time (4 women); includes 14 minority (4 African Americans, 7 Asian Americans or Pacific Islanders, 3 Hispanic Americans), 13 international. Average age 29. 164 applicants, 39% accepted, 43 enrolled. Expenses: Contact institution. *Financial support:* In 2008–09, 100 students received support, including 26 research assistantships with partial tuition reimbursements available (averaging $6,826 per year), 43 teaching assistantships with partial tuition reimbursements available (averaging $7,029 per year); fellowships, career-related internships or fieldwork, Federal Work-Study, institutionally sponsored loans, scholarships/grants, health care benefits, tuition waivers (full and partial), and unspecified assistantships also available. Support available to part-time students. Financial award applicants required to submit FAFSA. In 2008, 35 master's awarded. *Degree program information:* Part-time programs available. Offers architecture (M Arch); art and design (M Arch, MA, MFA, MLA); art history (MA); ceramics (MFA); graphic design (MFA); landscape architecture (MLA); painting and drawing (MFA); photography (MFA); printmaking (MFA); sculpture (MFA); studio art (MFA). *Application deadline:* For fall admission, 1/25 priority date for domestic students, 5/15 for international students; for spring admission, 10/15 for international students. Applications are processed on a rolling basis. *Application fee:* $50 ($70 for international students). Electronic applications accepted. *Application Contact:* Theresa Mooney, Academic Counselor, 225-578-5400, Fax: 225-578-1445, E-mail: deacon1@lsu.edu. *Dean,* David Cronrath, 225-578-5400, Fax: 225-578-5040, E-mail: dc1@lsu.edu.

College of Arts and Sciences Students: 610 full-time (332 women), 136 part-time (71 women); includes 67 minority (32 African Americans, 8 American Indian/Alaska Native, 10 Asian Americans or Pacific Islanders, 17 Hispanic Americans), 109 international. Average age 30. 882 applicants, 39% accepted, 166 enrolled. Expenses: Contact institution. *Financial support:* In 2008–09, 626 students received support, including 38 fellowships with full tuition reimbursements available (averaging $24,528 per year), 58 research assistantships with full and partial tuition reimbursements available (averaging $17,020 per year), 364 teaching assistantships with full and partial tuition reimbursements available (averaging $14,589 per year); career-related internships or fieldwork, Federal Work-Study, institutionally sponsored loans, scholarships/grants, traineeships, health care benefits, tuition waivers (full), and unspecified assistantships also available. Support available to part-time students. Financial award applicants required to submit FAFSA. In 2008, 103 master's, 56 doctorates awarded. *Degree program information:* Part-time and evening/weekend programs available. Offers anthropology (MA); arts and sciences (MA, MALA, MFA, MS, PhD); biological psychology (MA, PhD); clinical psychology (MA, PhD); cognitive psychology (MA, PhD); communication sciences and disorders (MA, PhD); communication studies (MA, PhD); comparative literature (MA, PhD); creative writing (MFA); developmental psychology (MA, PhD); English (MA, PhD); French literature and linguistics (MA, PhD); geography (MA, MS, PhD); Hispanic studies (MA); history (MA, PhD); industrial/organizational psychology (MA, PhD); liberal arts (MALA); linguistics (MA, PhD); mathematics (MS, PhD); philosophy (MA); political science (MA, PhD); school psychology (MA, PhD); sociology (MA, PhD). *Application deadline:* For fall admission, 5/15 priority date for domestic students, 5/15 for international students; for spring admission, 10/15 priority date for domestic students, 10/15 for international students. *Application fee:* $50 ($70 for international students). Electronic applications accepted. *Application Contact:* Dr. Robin Roberts, Associate Dean, 225-578-8273, Fax: 225-587-6447, E-mail: rrobert@lsu.edu. *Dean,* Dr. Guillermo Ferreya, 225-578-8273, Fax: 225-578-6447, E-mail: dnferr@lsu.edu.

College of Basic Sciences Students: 492 full-time (174 women), 51 part-time (13 women); includes 71 minority (50 African Americans, 1 American Indian/Alaska Native, 15 Asian Americans or Pacific Islanders, 5 Hispanic Americans), 243 international. Average age 29. 604 applicants, 39% accepted, 121 enrolled. Expenses: Contact institution. *Financial support:* In 2008–09, 521 students received support, including 74 fellowships with full and partial tuition reimbursements available (averaging $25,637 per year), 185 research assistantships with full and partial tuition reimbursements available (averaging $20,345 per year), 232 teaching assistantships with full and partial tuition reimbursements available (averaging $19,078 per year); career-related internships or fieldwork, Federal Work-Study, institutionally sponsored loans, health care benefits, tuition waivers (full and partial), and unspecified assistantships also available. Support available to part-time students. Financial award applicants required to submit FAFSA. In 2008, 52 master's, 50 doctorates awarded. *Degree program information:* Part-time programs available. Offers astronomy (PhD); astrophysics (PhD); basic sciences (MNS, MS, MSSS, PhD); biochemistry (MS, PhD); biological science (MS, PhD); chemistry (MS, PhD); computer science (MSSS, PhD); geology and geophysics (MS, PhD); medical physics (MS); natural sciences (MNS); physics (MS, PhD); systems science (MSSS). *Application deadline:* For fall admission, 5/15 for international students; for spring admission, 10/15 for international students. Applications are processed on a rolling basis. *Application fee:* $50 ($70 for international students). Electronic applications accepted. *Application Contact:* Dr. Fred Rainey, Associate Dean, 225-578-4200, Fax: 225-578-8826, E-mail: frainey@lsu.edu. *Dean,* Dr. Kevin Carman, 225-578-8859, Fax: 225-578-8826, E-mail: bascdean@lsu.edu.

College of Education Students: 200 full-time (133 women), 207 part-time (155 women); includes 71 minority (66 African Americans, 2 Asian Americans or Pacific Islanders, 3 Hispanic Americans), 13 international. Average age 32. 188 applicants, 48% accepted, 59 enrolled. Expenses: Contact institution. *Financial support:* In 2008–09, 251 students received support, including 2 fellowships (averaging $29,836 per year), 25 research assistantships with partial tuition reimbursements available (averaging $9,520 per year), 44 teaching assistantships with partial tuition reimbursements available (averaging $10,701 per year); career-related internships or fieldwork, Federal Work-Study, institutionally sponsored loans, health care benefits, tuition waivers (partial), and unspecified assistantships also available. Support available to part-time students. Financial award applicants required to submit FAFSA. In 2008, 94 master's, 23 doctorates, 15 other advanced degrees awarded. *Degree program information:* Part-time and evening/weekend programs available. Offers counseling (M Ed, MA, Ed S); education (M Ed, MA, MS, PhD, Ed S); educational administration (M Ed, MA, PhD, Ed S); educational technology (MA); elementary education (M Ed); higher education (PhD); kinesiology (MS, PhD); research methodology (PhD); secondary education (M Ed). *Application deadline:* For fall admission, 1/25 priority date for domestic students, 5/15 for international students; for spring admission, 10/15 for international students. Applications are processed on a rolling basis. *Application fee:* $50 ($70 for international students). Electronic applications accepted. *Application Contact:* Dr. Patricia Exner, Associate Dean, 225-578-2208, Fax: 225-578-2267, E-mail: pexner@lsu.edu. *Dean*, Dr. Jayne Fleener, 225-578-1258, Fax: 225-578-2267, E-mail: fleener@lsu.edu.

College of Engineering Students: 425 full-time (21 women), 92 part-time (21 women); includes 33 minority (18 African Americans, 1 American Indian/Alaska Native, 9 Asian Americans or Pacific Islanders, 5 Hispanic Americans), 377 international. Average age 28. 817 applicants, 39% accepted, 97 enrolled. Expenses: Contact institution. *Financial support:* In 2008–09, 433 students received support, including 27 fellowships with full and partial tuition reimbursements available (averaging $22,818 per year), 261 research assistantships with full and partial tuition reimbursements available (averaging $16,365 per year), 98 teaching assistantships with full and partial tuition reimbursements available (averaging $12,799 per year); career-related internships or fieldwork, Federal Work-Study, institutionally sponsored loans, scholarships/grants, health care benefits, tuition waivers (full and partial), and unspecified assistantships also available. Financial award applicants required to submit FAFSA. In 2008, 89 master's, 33 doctorates awarded. *Degree program information:* Part-time and evening/weekend programs available. Offers chemical engineering (MS Ch E, PhD); electrical and computer engineering (MSEE, PhD); engineering (MS Ch E, MS Pet E, MSCE, MSEE, MSES, MSIE, MSME, PhD); engineering science (MSES, PhD); environmental engineering (MSCE, PhD); geotechnical engineering (MSCE, PhD); industrial engineering (MSIE); mechanical engineering (MSME, PhD); petroleum engineering (MS Pet E, PhD); structural engineering and mechanics (MSCE, PhD); transportation engineering (MSCE, PhD); water resources (MSCE, PhD). *Application deadline:* For fall admission, 1/25 priority date for domestic students, 5/15 for international students; for spring admission, 10/15 for international students. Applications are processed on a rolling basis. *Application fee:* $50 ($70 for international students). Electronic applications accepted. *Application Contact:* Dr. Kelly A Rusch, Associate Dean for Research and Graduate Studies, 225-578-8528, Fax: 225-578-9162, E-mail: krusch@lsu.edu. *Dean*, Dr. Richard Koubek, 225-578-5701, Fax: 225-578-9162, E-mail: koubek@lsu.edu.

College of Music and Dramatic Arts Students: 180 full-time (96 women), 40 part-time (26 women); includes 28 minority (14 African Americans, 8 Asian Americans or Pacific Islanders, 6 Hispanic Americans), 34 international. Average age 29. 199 applicants, 47% accepted, 63 enrolled. Expenses: Contact institution. *Financial support:* In 2008–09, 175 students received support, including 7 fellowships with full and partial tuition reimbursements available (averaging $26,957 per year), 3 research assistantships with full and partial tuition reimbursements available (averaging $15,166 per year), 107 teaching assistantships with full and partial tuition reimbursements available (averaging $11,145 per year); Federal Work-Study, scholarships/grants, health care benefits, tuition waivers (full and partial), and unspecified assistantships also available. Support available to part-time students. Financial award applicants required to submit FAFSA. In 2008, 24 master's, 7 doctorates awarded. *Degree program information:* Part-time programs available. Offers acting (MFA); directing (MFA); music (MM, DMA, PhD); music and dramatic arts (MFA, MM, DMA, PhD); music education (PhD); theatre (PhD); theatre design/technology (MFA). *Application deadline:* For fall admission, 3/15 priority date for domestic students, 5/15 for international students; for spring admission, 10/15 for international students. Applications are processed on a rolling basis. *Application fee:* $50 ($70 for international students). *Application Contact:* Dr. Lawrence Kaptain, Interim Dean, 225-578-3261, Fax: 225-578-2562. *Interim Dean*, Dr. Lawrence Kaptain, 225-578-3261, Fax: 225-578-2562.

E. J. Ourso College of Business Students: 450 full-time (188 women), 181 part-time (85 women); includes 91 minority (65 African Americans, 2 American Indian/Alaska Native, 15 Asian Americans or Pacific Islanders, 9 Hispanic Americans), 98 international. Average age 29. 586 applicants, 54% accepted, 248 enrolled. Expenses: Contact institution. *Financial support:* In 2008–09, 410 students received support, including 7 fellowships (averaging $19,900 per year), 83 research assistantships with full and partial tuition reimbursements available (averaging $13,917 per year), 93 teaching assistantships with full and partial tuition reimbursements available (averaging $11,274 per year); career-related internships or fieldwork, Federal Work-Study, institutionally sponsored loans, scholarships/grants, health care benefits, and unspecified assistantships also available. Support available to part-time students. Financial award applicants required to submit FAFSA. In 2008, 260 master's, 8 doctorates awarded. *Degree program information:* Part-time and evening/weekend programs available. Offers accounting (MS, PhD); business (EMBA, MBA, MPA, MS, PMBA, PhD); business administration (PhD); economics (MS, PhD); finance (MS); information systems and decision sciences (MS, PhD); public administration (MPA). *Application deadline:* For fall admission, 1/25 priority date for domestic students, 5/15 for international students; for spring admission, 10/15 for international students. Applications are processed on a rolling basis. *Application fee:* $50 ($70 for international students). Electronic applications accepted. *Application Contact:* Dr. Eli Jones, Interim Dean, 225-578-5297, Fax: 225-578-5256. *Interim Dean*, Dr. Eli Jones, 225-578-5297, Fax: 225-578-5256.

Manship School of Mass Communication Students: 43 full-time (27 women), 19 part-time (13 women); includes 12 minority (9 African Americans, 1 American Indian/Alaska Native, 2 Hispanic Americans), 11 international. Average age 31. 76 applicants, 45% accepted, 23 enrolled. *Faculty:* 28 full-time (14 women). Expenses: Contact institution. *Financial support:* In 2008–09, 48 students received support, including 30 research assistantships with full and partial tuition reimbursements available (averaging $16,333 per year), 2 teaching assistantships with full and partial tuition reimbursements available (averaging $24,000 per year); fellowships, career-related internships or fieldwork, Federal Work-Study, institutionally sponsored loans, scholarships/grants, health care benefits, tuition waivers (full and partial), and unspecified assistantships also available. Support available to part-time students. Financial award application deadline: 3/1; financial award applicants required to submit FAFSA. In 2008, 8 master's, 5 doctorates awarded. *Degree program information:* Part-time programs available. Postbaccalaureate distance learning degree programs offered (minimal on-campus study). Offers mass communication (MMC, PhD). *Application deadline:* For fall admission, 1/25 priority date for domestic students, 5/15 for international students; for spring admission, 10/15 for international students. Applications are processed on a rolling basis. *Application fee:* $50 ($70 for international students). Electronic applications accepted. *Application Contact:* Dr. Margaret DeFleur, Associate Dean of Graduate Studies and Research, 225-578-9294, Fax: 225-578-2125, E-mail: defleur@lsu.edu. *Dean*, Dr. John Maxwell Hamilton, 225-578-2002, Fax: 225-578-2125, E-mail: jhamilt@lsu.edu.

School of Library and Information Science Students: 66 full-time (51 women), 109 part-time (94 women); includes 22 minority (13 African Americans, 2 Asian Americans or Pacific Islanders, 7 Hispanic Americans), 6 international. Average age 33. 74 applicants, 81% accepted, 35 enrolled. *Faculty:* 11 full-time (8 women). Expenses: Contact institution. *Financial support:* In 2008–09, 95 students received support, including 6 research assistantships with partial tuition reimbursements available (averaging $12,200 per year), 17 teaching assistantships with partial tuition reimbursements available (averaging $12,294 per year); fellowships, career-related internships or fieldwork, Federal Work-Study, institutionally sponsored loans, scholarships/grants, health care benefits, and unspecified assistantships also available. Support available to part-time students. Financial award applicants required to submit FAFSA. In 2008, 47 master's awarded. *Degree program information:* Part-time and evening/weekend programs available. Postbaccalaureate distance learning degree programs offered (no on-campus study). Offers library and information science (MLIS, CAS). *Application deadline:* For fall admission, 1/25 priority date for domestic students, 5/15 for international students; for spring admission, 10/15 for international students. Applications are processed on a rolling basis. *Application fee:* $50 ($70 for international students). Electronic applications accepted. *Application Contact:* LaToya Joseph, Administrative Assistant, 225-578-3150, Fax: 225-578-4581, E-mail: lcjoseph@lsu.edu. *Dean*, Dr. Beth M. Paskoff, 225-578-3158, Fax: 225-578-4581, E-mail: bpaskoff@lsu.edu.

School of Social Work Students: 150 full-time (132 women), 47 part-time (42 women); includes 45 minority (42 African Americans, 1 American Indian/Alaska Native, 2 Asian Americans or Pacific Islanders), 3 international. Average age 33. 122 applicants, 77% accepted, 73 enrolled. *Faculty:* 15 full-time (10 women). Expenses: Contact institution. *Financial support:* In 2008–09, 149 students received support, including 5 research assistantships with partial tuition reimbursements available (averaging $15,420 per year), 22 teaching assistantships with partial tuition reimbursements available (averaging $24,495 per year); fellowships, career-related internships or fieldwork, Federal Work-Study, scholarships/grants, health care benefits, and unspecified assistantships also available. Support available to part-time students. Financial award applicants required to submit FAFSA. In 2008, 95 master's, 1 doctorate awarded. *Degree program information:* Part-time programs available. Offers social work (MSW, PhD). *Application deadline:* For fall admission, 2/15 for domestic and international students. *Application fee:* $50 ($70 for international students). Electronic applications accepted. *Application Contact:* Denise Chiasson, Assistant Dean, 225-578-1234, Fax: 225-578-1357, E-mail: dchiass@lsu.edu. *Dean*, Dr. Christian Molidor, 225-578-5875, Fax: 225-578-1357, E-mail: cmolidor@lsu.edu.

School of the Coast and Environment Students: 65 full-time (30 women), 18 part-time (8 women); includes 1 minority (Hispanic American), 20 international. Average age 29. 57 applicants, 42% accepted, 14 enrolled. Expenses: Contact institution. *Financial support:* In 2008–09, 72 students received support, including 7 fellowships with full tuition reimbursements available (averaging $30,637 per year), 52 research assistantships with full and partial tuition reimbursements available (averaging $17,840 per year), 5 teaching assistantships with full and partial tuition reimbursements available (averaging $13,890 per year); career-related internships or fieldwork, Federal Work-Study, institutionally sponsored loans, health care benefits, and unspecified assistantships also available. Financial award applicants required to submit FAFSA. In 2008, 15 master's, 6 doctorates awarded. *Degree program information:* Part-time programs available. Offers environmental planning and management (MS); environmental toxicology (MS); oceanography and coastal sciences (MS, PhD); the coast and environment (MS, PhD). *Application deadline:* For fall admission, 1/25 priority date for domestic students, 5/15 for international students; for spring admission, 10/15 for international students. Applications are processed on a rolling basis. *Application fee:* $50 ($70 for international students). Electronic applications accepted. *Application Contact:* Dr. Ed Laws, Dean, 225-578-6316, Fax: 225-578-5328. *Dean*, Dr. Ed Laws, 225-578-6316, Fax: 225-578-5328.

Paul M. Hebert Law Center Students: 575 full-time (264 women), 9 part-time (3 women); includes 67 minority (31 African Americans, 5 American Indian/Alaska Native, 7 Asian Americans or Pacific Islanders, 24 Hispanic Americans), 8 international. Average age 26. 1,343 applicants, 37% accepted, 211 enrolled. *Faculty:* 41 full-time (12 women), 48 part-time/adjunct (5 women). Expenses: Contact institution. *Financial support:* Scholarships/grants and tuition waivers (full and partial) available. Financial award applicants required to submit FAFSA. In 2008, 7 master's awarded. Offers law (LL M, MCL). *Application deadline:* For fall admission, 3/1 priority date for domestic students, 2/1 priority date for international students. Applications are processed on a rolling basis. *Application fee:* $25. Electronic applications accepted. *Application Contact:* Michele Forbes, Director of Student Affairs and Registrar, 225-578-8646, Fax: 225-578-8647, E-mail: michele.forbes@law.lsu.edu. *Chancellor*, Jack M. Weiss, 225-578-8491, Fax: 225-578-8202, E-mail: jack.weiss@law.lsu.edu.

School of Veterinary Medicine Students: 370 full-time (277 women), 18 part-time (8 women); includes 31 minority (3 African Americans, 4 American Indian/Alaska Native, 8 Asian Americans or Pacific Islanders, 16 Hispanic Americans), 27 international. Average age 32. 118 applicants, 88% accepted, 11 enrolled. *Faculty:* 69 full-time (17 women). Expenses: Contact institution. *Financial support:* In 2008–09, 347 students received support, including 85 fellowships with full tuition reimbursements available (averaging $26,755 per year), 37 research assistantships with full and partial tuition reimbursements available (averaging $24,495 per year); teaching assistantships with full and partial tuition reimbursements available, career-related internships or fieldwork, Federal Work-Study, institutionally sponsored loans, scholarships/grants, health care benefits, tuition waivers (full and partial), and unspecified assistantships also available. Financial award applicants required to submit FAFSA. In 2008, 3 master's, 6 doctorates awarded. Offers comparative biomedical sciences (MS, PhD); pathobiological sciences (MS, PhD); veterinary clinical sciences (MS, PhD); veterinary medicine (DVM, MS, PhD). *Application deadline:* For fall admission, 3/1 priority date for domestic students, 5/15 for international students; for spring admission, 10/15 for international students. Applications are processed on a rolling basis. *Application fee:* $50 ($70 for international students). Electronic applications accepted. *Application Contact:* Dr. Peter Haynes, Dean, 225-578-9903, Fax: 225-578-9916, E-mail: pfhaynes@vetmed.lsu.edu. *Dean*, Dr. Peter Haynes, 225-578-9903, Fax: 225-578-9916, E-mail: pfhaynes@vetmed.lsu.edu.

LOUISIANA STATE UNIVERSITY HEALTH SCIENCES CENTER, New Orleans, LA 70112-2223

General Information State-supported, coed, university. CGS member. *Graduate housing:* Rooms and/or apartments available to single and married students. Housing application deadline: 6/1.

GRADUATE UNITS

School of Allied Health Professions *Degree program information:* Part-time and evening/weekend programs available. Offers allied health professions (MCD, MHS, MOT, Au D, DPT); audiology (Au D); clinical concepts (MHS); education (MHS); management administration (MHS); occupational therapy (MOT); physical therapy (DPT); rehabilitation counseling (MHS); speech pathology (MCD).

School of Dentistry Offers dentistry (DDS).

School of Graduate Studies in New Orleans *Degree program information:* Part-time and evening/weekend programs available. Offers biostatistics (MPH, MS, PhD); cell biology and anatomy (MS, PhD); human genetics (MS, PhD); medicine (MPH, MS, PhD); microbiology and immunology (MS, PhD); neuroscience (MS, PhD); pathology (MS, PhD); pharmacology and experimental therapeutics (MS, PhD); physiology (MS, PhD).

School of Medicine in New Orleans Offers medicine (MD, MPH). Open only to Louisiana residents. Electronic applications accepted.

School of Nursing *Degree program information:* Part-time programs available. Offers advanced public/community health nursing (MN); clinical nurse specialist (MN); nurse anesthesia (MN); nurse practitioner (MN); nursing (DNS).

LOUISIANA STATE UNIVERSITY HEALTH SCIENCES CENTER AT SHREVEPORT, Shreveport, LA 71130-3932

General Information State-supported, coed, university.

GRADUATE UNITS

Department of Biochemistry and Molecular Biology Offers biochemistry and molecular biology (MS, PhD).

Department of Cellular Biology and Anatomy Offers cellular biology and anatomy (MS, PhD).

Department of Microbiology and Immunology Offers microbiology and immunology (MS, PhD).

Louisiana State University Health Sciences Center at Shreveport (continued)

Department of Molecular and Cellular Physiology Offers physiology (MS, PhD).

Department of Pharmacology, Toxicology and Neuroscience Offers pharmacology (PhD).

School of Medicine Offers medicine (MD).

LOUISIANA STATE UNIVERSITY IN SHREVEPORT, Shreveport, LA 71115-2399

General Information State-supported, coed, comprehensive institution. *Enrollment:* 105 full-time matriculated graduate/professional students (72 women), 283 part-time matriculated graduate/professional students (189 women). *Enrollment by degree level:* 369 master's, 19 other advanced degrees. Tuition, state resident: full-time $2385; part-time $132 per credit hour. Tuition, nonresident: full-time $6697; part-time $372 per credit hour. *Required fees:* $42 per credit hour. Tuition and fees vary according to course load. *Graduate housing:* Rooms and/or apartments available on a first-come, first-served basis to single and married students. *Student services:* Campus employment opportunities, career counseling, exercise/wellness program, free psychological counseling, services for students with disabilities, teacher training. *Library facilities:* Noel Memorial Library. *Online resources:* library catalog, web page, access to other libraries' catalogs. *Collection:* 279,821 titles, 1,190 serial subscriptions. *Research affiliation:* Micromanufacturing Institute (manufacturing technology), Department of Agriculture (crop science), Louisiana Manufacturing Science Center (robotics), Biomedical Research Institute, Cotton, Inc. (plant physiology).

Computer facilities: A campuswide network can be accessed. Online class registration is available. *Web address:* http://www.lsus.edu/.

General Application Contact: Yvonne Yarbrough, Secretary, Graduate Studies, 318-797-5247, Fax: 318-798-4120, E-mail: yyarbrou@lsus.edu.

GRADUATE UNITS

College of Business Administration Offers business administration (MBA).

College of Education and Human Development Offers counseling psychology (MS); education (M Ed); education and human development (M Ed, MS, SSP); education curriculum and instruction (M Ed); educational leadership (M Ed); school psychology (SSP).

College of Liberal Arts Offers health administration (MHA); human services administration (MS); liberal arts (MA, MHA, MS).

College of Sciences Offers computer systems technology (MS); sciences (MS).

LOUISIANA TECH UNIVERSITY, Ruston, LA 71272

General Information State-supported, coed, university. *Graduate housing:* Rooms and/or apartments guaranteed to single students and available on a first-come, first-served basis to married students. Housing application deadline: 7/15.

GRADUATE UNITS

Graduate School *Degree program information:* Part-time programs available.

College of Applied and Natural Sciences *Degree program information:* Part-time programs available. Offers applied and natural sciences (MS); biological sciences (MS); dietetics (MS); human ecology (MS).

College of Business *Degree program information:* Part-time programs available. Offers business (MBA, MPA, DBA); business administration (MBA, DBA); business economics (MBA, DBA); finance (MBA, DBA); marketing (MBA, DBA); professional accountancy (MBA, MPA, DBA).

College of Education *Degree program information:* Part-time programs available. Offers counseling (MA); counseling psychology (PhD); curriculum and instruction (MS, Ed D); education (M Ed, MA, MS, Ed D, PhD); educational leadership (Ed D); health and exercise sciences (MS); industrial/organizational psychology (MA); secondary education (M Ed); special education (MA).

College of Engineering and Science *Degree program information:* Part-time programs available. Offers applied computational analysis and modeling (PhD); biomedical engineering (MS, PhD); chemical engineering (MS, PhD); chemistry (MS); civil engineering (MS, PhD); computer science (MS); electrical engineering (MS, PhD); engineering (PhD); engineering and science (MS, PhD); industrial engineering (MS); mathematics and statistics (MS); mechanical engineering (MS, PhD); physics (MS).

College of Liberal Arts *Degree program information:* Part-time programs available. Offers art and graphic design (MFA); English (MA); history (MA); interior design (MFA); liberal arts (MA, MFA); photography (MFA); speech (MA); speech pathology and audiology (MA); studio art (MFA).

LOUISVILLE PRESBYTERIAN THEOLOGICAL SEMINARY, Louisville, KY 40205-1798

General Information Independent-religious, coed, graduate-only institution. *Enrollment by degree level:* 103 first professional, 45 master's, 54 doctoral. *Graduate faculty:* 21 full-time (10 women), 30 part-time/adjunct (11 women). *Tuition:* Full-time $9660; part-time $322 per credit hour. *Required fees:* $118 per semester. *Graduate housing:* Rooms and/or apartments available on a first-come, first-served basis to single and married students. Typical cost: $3933 per year ($5433 including board) for single students; $3933 per year ($5433 including board) for married students. Housing application deadline: 4/15. *Student services:* Campus employment opportunities, career counseling, free psychological counseling, international student services, low-cost health insurance, services for students with disabilities, writing training. *Library facilities:* Ernest White Library. *Online resources:* library catalog, access to other libraries' catalogs. *Collection:* 133,581 titles, 561 serial subscriptions, 2,781 audiovisual materials. *Research affiliation:* Louisville Institute (American religion).

Computer facilities: 13 computers available on campus for general student use. A campuswide network can be accessed from student residence rooms. *Web address:* http://www.lpts.edu/.

General Application Contact: Cheri Harper, Director of Admissions, 502-895-3411 Ext. 371, Fax: 502-895-1096, E-mail: charper@lpts.edu.

GRADUATE UNITS

Graduate and Professional Programs Students: 148 full-time (81 women), 62 part-time (34 women); includes 37 minority (30 African Americans, 1 American Indian/Alaska Native, 2 Asian Americans or Pacific Islanders, 4 Hispanic Americans), 7 international. Average age 37. 121 applicants, 78% accepted, 62 enrolled. *Faculty:* 21 full-time (10 women), 30 part-time/adjunct (11 women). Expenses: Contact institution. *Financial support:* Career-related internships or fieldwork, Federal Work-Study, institutionally sponsored loans, and scholarships/grants available. Financial award application deadline: 4/15; financial award applicants required to submit CSS PROFILE or FAFSA. In 2008, 22 first professional degrees, 10 master's, 6 doctorates awarded. *Degree program information:* Part-time programs available. Offers Bible (MAR); divinity (M Div); ministry (D Min); religious thought (MAR); theology (Th M). *Application deadline:* For fall admission, 6/15 priority date for domestic students, 6/1 priority date for international students; for spring admission, 11/15 priority date for domestic and international students. Applications are processed on a rolling basis. *Application fee:* $60. Electronic applications accepted. *Application Contact:* Cheri Harper, Director of Admission, 502-895-3411 Ext. 371, Fax: 502-895-1096, E-mail: charper@lpts.edu. *Dean,* Dr. David C. Hester, 502-894-2282, Fax: 502-895-1096, E-mail: dhester@lpts.edu.

LOURDES COLLEGE, Sylvania, OH 43560-2898

General Information Independent-religious, coed, comprehensive institution. CGS member. *Graduate housing:* On-campus housing not available.

GRADUATE UNITS

School of Graduate and Professional Studies *Degree program information:* Evening/weekend programs available. Offers endorsement in computer technology (M Ed); organizational leadership (MOL).

LOYOLA MARYMOUNT UNIVERSITY, Los Angeles, CA 90045-2659

General Information Independent-religious, coed, comprehensive institution. CGS member. *Enrollment:* 9,011 graduate, professional, and undergraduate students; 2,491 full-time matriculated graduate/professional students (1,447 women), 844 part-time matriculated graduate/professional students (463 women). *Enrollment by degree level:* 1,371 first professional, 1,757 master's, 52 doctoral, 155 other advanced degrees. *Graduate faculty:* 297 full-time (116 women), 92 part-time/adjunct (53 women). *Tuition:* Part-time $872 per credit hour. Tuition and fees vary according to degree level and campus/location. *Graduate housing:* Room and/or apartments available on a first-come, first-served basis to single students; on-campus housing not available to married students. *Student services:* Campus employment opportunities, career counseling, child daycare facilities, exercise/wellness program, free psychological counseling, international student services, low-cost health insurance, multicultural affairs office, services for students with disabilities, teacher training. *Library facilities:* William H. Hannon Library. *Online resources:* library catalog, web page, access to other libraries' catalogs. *Collection:* 566,000 titles, 19,500 serial subscriptions, 40,000 audiovisual materials.

Computer facilities: Computer purchase and lease plans are available. 56 computers available on campus for general student use. A campuswide network can be accessed from student residence rooms and from off campus. Online class registration is available. *Web address:* http://www.lmu.edu/.

General Application Contact: Chake H. Kouyoumjian, Associate Dean of the Graduate Division, 310-338-2721, Fax: 310-338-6086, E-mail: ckouyoum@lmu.edu.

GRADUATE UNITS

College of Business Administration Expenses: Contact institution. Offers business administration (MBA); executive business administration (MBA). *Application Contact:* Dr. Dennis Draper, Dean, 310-338-2848, Fax: 310-338-2899. *Dean,* Dr. Dennis Draper, 310-338-2848, Fax: 310-338-2899.

College of Fine Arts Expenses: Contact institution. Offers fine arts (MA); marital and family therapy (MA). *Application Contact:* Barbara J. Busse, Dean, 310-338-7430. *Dean,* Barbara J. Busse, 310-338-7430.

College of Liberal Arts Expenses: Contact institution. Offers English (MA); liberal arts (MA); pastoral theology (MA); philosophy (MA); theology (MA). *Application Contact:* Dr. Michael Engh, Dean, 310-338-2716, Fax: 310-338-2704, E-mail: mengh@lmu.edu. *Dean,* Dr. Michael Engh, 310-338-2716, Fax: 310-338-2704, E-mail: mengh@lmu.edu.

The Bioethics Institute Expenses: Contact institution. Offers bioethics (MA). *Application Contact:* Dr. James J. Walter, Chair, 310-258-8621, Fax: 310-258-8642, E-mail: jwalter@lmu.edu. *Chair,* Dr. James J. Walter, 310-258-8621, Fax: 310-258-8642, E-mail: jwalter@lmu.edu.

College of Science and Engineering Expenses: Contact institution. Offers civil engineering (MS, MSE); computer science (MS); electrical engineering (MSE); environmental engineering (MSE); environmental science (MS); mechanical engineering (MSE); science and engineering (MAT, MS, MSE); systems engineering and leadership (MS); teaching mathematics (MAT). *Application Contact:* Dr. Michael Manoogian, Chair, 310-338-2827, E-mail: mmanoogi@lmu.edu. *Chair,* Dr. Michael Manoogian, 310-338-2827, E-mail: mmanoogi@lmu.edu.

Loyola Law School Los Angeles Students: 992 full-time (497 women), 295 part-time (129 women); includes 519 minority (48 African Americans, 5 American Indian/Alaska Native, 311 Asian Americans or Pacific Islanders, 155 Hispanic Americans). Average age 23. 4,879 applicants, 33% accepted, 410 enrolled. *Faculty:* 74 full-time (35 women), 55 part-time/adjunct (13 women). Expenses: Contact institution. *Financial support:* In 2008–09, 322 students received support; research assistantships, Federal Work-Study and scholarships/grants available. Financial award application deadline: 3/16; financial award applicants required to submit FAFSA. In 2008, 396 JDs, 60 master's awarded. *Degree program information:* Part-time and evening/weekend programs available. Offers law (JD); taxation (LL M). *Application deadline:* For fall admission, 2/1 priority date for domestic and international students. Applications are processed on a rolling basis. *Application fee:* $65. Electronic applications accepted. *Application Contact:* Janell Lundy Roberts, Assistant Dean, Admissions, 213-736-1074, Fax: 213-736-6523, E-mail: admissions@lls.edu. *Dean,* Victor Gold, 213-736-1062, Fax: 213-487-6736, E-mail: victor.gold@lls.edu.

School of Education Expenses: Contact institution. *Financial support:* Research assistantships, Federal Work-Study and scholarships/grants available. Support available to part-time students. Financial award application deadline: 6/1; financial award applicants required to submit FAFSA. *Degree program information:* Part-time and evening/weekend programs available. Offers bilingual elementary education (MA); bilingual secondary education (MA); biliteracy, leadership, and intercultural education (MA); Catholic inclusive education (MA); Catholic school administration (MA); child/adolescent literacy (MA); counseling (MA); early childhood education (MA); education (MA, Ed D); educational leadership in social justice (Ed D); elementary education (MA); general education (MA); guidance and counseling (MA); literacy education (MA); literacy/language arts (MA); school administration (MA); school psychology (MA); secondary education (MA); special education (MA); teaching English as a second language (MA); urban education (MA). *Application deadline:* For fall admission, 7/15 for domestic students; for spring admission, 11/15 for domestic students. *Application fee:* $50. Electronic applications accepted. *Application Contact:* Chake H. Kouyoumjian, Director, Graduate Admissions, 310-338-2721, Fax: 310-338-6086, E-mail: ckouyoum@lmu.edu. *Dean,* Dr. Shane Martin, 310-338-2863, Fax: 310-338-1976, E-mail: smartin@lmu.edu.

School of Film and Television Expenses: Contact institution. *Financial support:* Research assistantships, teaching assistantships, career-related internships or fieldwork and scholarships/grants available. Support available to part-time students. Financial award application deadline: 6/1; financial award applicants required to submit FAFSA. Offers film and television (MFA); production (film and television) (MFA); screenwriting (MFA). *Application deadline:* For fall admission, 3/15 for domestic students. *Application fee:* $50. Electronic applications accepted. *Application Contact:* Dr. Eric Xavier, Graduate Director, 310-338-2779, Fax: 310-338-3030, E-mail: exavier@lmu.edu. *Dean,* Teri Schwartz, 310-338-3089, Fax: 310-338-3089, E-mail: tschwartz@lmu.edu.

See Close-Up on page 937.

LOYOLA UNIVERSITY CHICAGO, Chicago, IL 60611-2196

General Information Independent-religious, coed, university. CGS member. *Enrollment:* 15,670 graduate, professional, and undergraduate students; 4,113 full-time matriculated graduate/professional students (2,482 women), 1,433 part-time matriculated graduate/professional students (1,006 women). *Enrollment by degree level:* 1,487 first professional, 3,024 master's, 918 doctoral, 117 other advanced degrees. *Graduate faculty:* 975 full-time (384 women), 698 part-time/adjunct (230 women). *Tuition:* Full-time $13,500; part-time $750 per credit hour. *Required fees:* $60 per semester. Full-time tuition and fees vary according to program. *Graduate housing:* Room and/or apartments available on a first-come, first-served basis to single students; on-campus housing not available to married students. Typical cost: $10,490 (including board). Housing application deadline: 5/1. *Student services:* Campus employment opportunities, campus safety program, career counseling, free psychological counseling, international student services, low-cost health insurance, services for students with disabilities, teacher training. *Library facilities:* Cudahy Library plus 7 others. *Online resources:* library catalog, web page. *Collection:* 1.4 million titles, 13,939 serial subscriptions, 15,174 audiovisual materials. *Research affiliation:* Chicago Public Schools (Behavioral Intervention), University of Oregon (Student Behavior), Erikson Institute for Early Education (Child Development), Illinois Children's Mental Health Partnership & Illinois State Board of Education (Children's Mental Health), Ford Foundation (Urban Research & Learning), Kellogg Foundation (Urban Research & Learning).

Computer facilities: Computer purchase and lease plans are available. 800 computers available on campus for general student use. A campuswide network can be accessed from student residence rooms and from off campus. Online class registration is available. *Web address:* http://www.luc.edu/.

General Application Contact: Janice K. Atkinson, Director, Graduate and Professional Enrollment Management, 312-915-8902, Fax: 312-915-8905, E-mail: gradapp@luc.edu.

GRADUATE UNITS

Graduate School Students: 1,079 full-time (640 women), 341 part-time (178 women); includes 200 minority (82 African Americans, 5 American Indian/Alaska Native, 60 Asian Americans or Pacific Islanders, 53 Hispanic Americans), 122 international. Average age 33. 4,642 applicants, 47% accepted, 1162 enrolled. *Faculty:* 477 full-time (168 women), 144 part-time/adjunct (81 women). Expenses: Contact institution. *Financial support:* In 2008–09, 325 students received support, including 90 fellowships with full tuition reimbursements available (averaging $19,000 per year), 130 research assistantships with full tuition reimbursements available (averaging $18,000 per year), 105 teaching assistantships with full and partial tuition reimbursements available (averaging $13,000 per year); career-related internships or fieldwork, Federal Work-Study, institutionally sponsored loans, scholarships/grants, and unspecified assistantships also available. Support available to part-time students. Financial award application deadline: 2/1; financial award applicants required to submit FAFSA. In 2008, 286 master's, 109 doctorates awarded. *Degree program information:* Part-time and evening/weekend programs available. Postbaccalaureate distance learning degree programs offered (no on-campus study). Offers applied social psychology (MA, PhD); applied sociology (MA); applied statistics (MS); biochemistry (MS, PhD); biology (MA, MS); cell and molecular physiology (MS, PhD); cell biology, neurobiology and anatomy (MS, PhD); chemistry (MS, PhD); clinical psychology (MA, PhD); computer science (MS); criminal justice (MA); developmental psychology (MA, PhD); English (MA, PhD); health care ethics (MA); history (MA, PhD); human perception (MS); immunology (PhD); information technology (MS); mathematics and statistics (MS); microbiology (MS); molecular biology (PhD); neuroscience (MS, PhD); pharmacology and experimental therapeutics (MS, PhD); philosophy (MA, PhD); political science (MA, PhD); public history (MA); public policy (MPP); social philosophy (MA); sociology (MA, PhD); software technology (MS); Spanish (MA); theology (MA, PhD). Application is free if done online. *Application deadline:* Applications are processed on a rolling basis. *Application fee:* $50. Electronic applications accepted. *Application Contact:* Ron Martin, Assistant Director of Enrollment Management, 312-915-8950, Fax: 312-915-8905, E-mail: gradapp@luc.edu. *Dean,* Dr. Samuel Attoh, 773-508-3459, Fax: 773-508-2460, E-mail: sattoh@luc.edu.

Marcella Niehoff School of Nursing Students: 48 full-time (46 women), 301 part-time (284 women); includes 59 minority (20 African Americans, 30 Asian Americans or Pacific Islanders, 9 Hispanic Americans), 1 international. Average age 37. 143 applicants, 69% accepted, 91 enrolled. *Faculty:* 26 full-time (25 women), 58 part-time/adjunct (50 women). Expenses: Contact institution. *Financial support:* In 2008–09, 10 students received support, including 1 fellowship with tuition reimbursement available, 4 research assistantships with tuition reimbursements available, 1 teaching assistantship with tuition reimbursement available; career-related internships or fieldwork, Federal Work-Study, institutionally sponsored loans, traineeships, and unspecified assistantships also available. Support available to part-time students. Financial award applicants required to submit FAFSA. In 2008, 50 master's, 7 doctorates awarded. *Degree program information:* Part-time and evening/weekend programs available. Postbaccalaureate distance learning degree programs offered (minimal on-campus study). Offers acute care (Certificate); acute care clinical nurse specialist (MSN); acute care nurse practitioner (MSN); adult clinical nurse specialist (MSN, Certificate); adult nurse practitioner (MSN); cardiac health (Certificate); cardiovascular health (Certificate); cardiovascular health and disease management clinical nurse specialist (MSN, Certificate); critical care/trauma (MSN); emergency nurse practitioner (Certificate); family nurse practitioner (MSN); family practice nurse practitioner (Certificate); informatics (Certificate); manager care (Certificate); nursing (MSN, DNP, PhD, Certificate); nursing oncology (Certificate); nursing practice (DNP); oncology clinical nurse specialist (MSN); oncology nursing (Certificate); outcomes performance management (Certificate); population-based infection control and environmental safety (MSN, Certificate); women's health nurse practitioner (MSN). *Application deadline:* For fall admission, 8/1 priority date for domestic and international students; for spring admission, 12/15 priority date for domestic students, 12/1 priority date for international students. Applications are processed on a rolling basis. *Application fee:* $50. Electronic applications accepted. *Application Contact:* Dr. Vicki A. Keough, Associate Professor/Master's Program Director, 708-216-3582, Fax: 708-216-9555, E-mail: vkeough@luc.edu. *Dean,* Dr. Mary K. Walker, 708-216-5448, Fax: 708-216-9555, E-mail: mwalker1@luc.edu.

Graduate School of Business *Degree program information:* Part-time and evening/weekend programs available. Offers accountancy (MS, MSA); business administration (MBA); finance (MS); healthcare management (MBA); human resources and employee relations (MS, MSHR); information systems and operations management (MS); information systems management (MS); integrated marketing communications (MS); marketing (MS, MSIMC); strategic financial services (MBA). Electronic applications accepted.

Institute of Human Resources and Employee Relations *Degree program information:* Part-time programs available. Offers human resources and employee relations (MSHR).

Institute of Pastoral Studies Students: 137 full-time (88 women), 111 part-time (79 women); includes 28 minority (18 African Americans, 3 Asian Americans or Pacific Islanders, 7 Hispanic Americans), 11 international. Average age 42. 105 applicants, 88% accepted, 64 enrolled. *Faculty:* 6 full-time (1 woman), 33 part-time/adjunct (16 women). Expenses: Contact institution. *Financial support:* In 2008–09, 84 students received support. Career-related internships or fieldwork, Federal Work-Study, institutionally sponsored loans, scholarships/grants, and tuition waivers (partial) available. Support available to part-time students. Financial award application deadline: 3/1; financial award applicants required to submit FAFSA. In 2008, 6 first professional degrees, 53 master's awarded. *Degree program information:* Part-time and evening/weekend programs available. Offers divinity (M Div); pastoral care and counseling (MA); pastoral counseling (MA, Certificate); pastoral studies (MA); religious education (MA, Certificate); social justice (MA, Certificate); spiritual direction (Certificate); spirituality (MA). *Application deadline:* Applications are processed on a rolling basis. *Application fee:* $50. Electronic applications accepted. *Application Contact:* Randy Gibbons, Administrative Assistant, 312-915-7450, Fax: 312-915-7410, E-mail: rgibbon@luc.edu. *Director,* Dr. Robert A. Ludwig, 312-915-7467, Fax: 312-915-7410, E-mail: rludwig@luc.edu.

School of Education Students: 321 full-time (229 women), 536 part-time (378 women); includes 163 minority (67 African Americans, 1 American Indian/Alaska Native, 28 Asian Americans or Pacific Islanders, 67 Hispanic Americans), 2 international. Average age 36. 718 applicants, 59% accepted, 226 enrolled. *Faculty:* 47 full-time (32 women), 53 part-time/adjunct (37 women). Expenses: Contact institution. *Financial support:* In 2008–09, 8 fellowships with full tuition reimbursements (averaging $11,000 per year), 37 research assistantships with full tuition reimbursements (averaging $11,000 per year), 4 teaching assistantships (averaging $2,000 per year) were awarded; career-related internships or fieldwork, Federal Work-Study, institutionally sponsored loans, scholarships/grants, tuition waivers (partial), and unspecified assistantships also available. Support available to part-time students. Financial award application deadline: 2/15; financial award applicants required to submit FAFSA. In 2008, 233 master's, 52 doctorates, 38 other advanced degrees awarded. *Degree program information:* Part-time and evening/weekend programs available. Offers administration and supervision (M Ed, Ed D, Certificate); community counseling (M Ed, MA); counseling psychology (PhD); cultural and educational policy studies (M Ed, MA, Ed D, PhD); curriculum and instruction (M Ed, Ed D); education (M Ed, MA, Ed D, PhD, Certificate, Ed S); educational psychology (M Ed); elementary education (M Ed); higher education (M Ed, PhD); instructional leadership (M Ed); reading specialist (M Ed); research methods (M Ed, MA, PhD); school counseling (M Ed, Certificate); school psychology (M Ed, PhD, Ed S); school technology (M Ed); science education (M Ed); secondary education (M Ed); special education (M Ed). *Application deadline:* For fall admission, 7/1 for domestic and international students; for spring admission, 11/1 for domestic and international students. Applications are processed on a rolling basis. *Application fee:* $50. Electronic applications accepted. *Application Contact:* Marie Rosin-Dittmar, Information Contact, 312-915-6800, E-mail: schleduc@luc.edu. *Dean,* Dr. David Prasse, 312-915-6992, Fax: 312-915-6980, E-mail: dprasse@luc.edu.

School of Law Students: 631 full-time (332 women), 331 part-time (188 women); includes 154 minority (48 African Americans, 6 American Indian/Alaska Native, 60 Asian Americans or Pacific Islanders, 40 Hispanic Americans), 9 international. Average age 25. 4,269 applicants, 32% accepted, 275 enrolled. *Faculty:* 46 full-time (19 women), 107 part-time/adjunct (51 women). Expenses: Contact institution. *Financial support:* In 2008–09, 817 students received support; fellowships, research assistantships, teaching assistantships, Federal Work-Study, scholarships/grants, tuition waivers (partial), and unspecified assistantships available. Support available to part-time students. Financial award application deadline: 3/1; financial award applicants required to submit FAFSA. In 2008, 276 first professional degrees, 28 master's awarded. *Degree program information:* Part-time programs available. Offers business law (LL M, MJ); child and family law (LL M, MJ); health law (LL M, MJ, D Law, SJD); law (JD). *Application deadline:* For fall admission, 3/1 for domestic and international students. Applications are processed on a rolling basis. *Application fee:* $50. Electronic applications accepted. *Application Contact:* Pamela A. Bloomquist, Assistant Dean, Law Admission and Financial Assistance, 312-915-7170, Fax: 312-915-7906, E-mail: law-admissions@luc.edu. *Dean,* David N. Yellen, 312-815-7120.

School of Social Work *Degree program information:* Part-time programs available. Postbaccalaureate distance learning degree programs offered (minimal on-campus study). Offers social work (MSW, PhD, PGC). Electronic applications accepted.

Stritch School of Medicine Offers medicine (MD).

See Close-Up on page 939.

LOYOLA UNIVERSITY MARYLAND, Baltimore, MD 21210-2699

General Information Independent-religious, coed, comprehensive institution. CGS member. *Enrollment:* 6,080 graduate, professional, and undergraduate students; 646 full-time matriculated graduate/professional students (444 women), 1,718 part-time matriculated graduate/professional students (1,021 women). *Enrollment by degree level:* 2,156 master's, 87 doctoral, 121 other advanced degrees. *Graduate faculty:* 262 full-time (134 women), 144 part-time/adjunct (71 women). *Graduate housing:* On-campus housing not available. *Student services:* Campus employment opportunities, campus safety program, career counseling, exercise/wellness program, international student services, low-cost health insurance, multicultural affairs office, services for students with disabilities. *Library facilities:* Loyola/Notre Dame Library. *Online resources:* library catalog, web page, access to other libraries' catalogs. *Collection:* 293,639 titles, 2,126 serial subscriptions.

Computer facilities: Computer purchase and lease plans are available. A campuswide network can be accessed from student residence rooms and from off campus. Online class registration is available. *Web address:* http://www.loyola.edu/.

General Application Contact: Maureen Faux, Interim Director, Graduate Admissions, 410-617-5020, Fax: 410-617-2002, E-mail: graduate@loyola.edu.

GRADUATE UNITS

Graduate Programs Students: 646 full-time (444 women), 1,718 part-time (1,021 women); includes 409 minority (285 African Americans, 6 American Indian/Alaska Native, 79 Asian Americans or Pacific Islanders, 39 Hispanic Americans). Average age 33. *Faculty:* 262 full-time (134 women), 144 part-time/adjunct (71 women). Expenses: Contact institution. *Financial support:* Research assistantships, career-related internships or fieldwork, scholarships/grants, and college/university gift aid from institutional funds available. Financial award applicants required to submit FAFSA. In 2008, 803 master's, 17 doctorates, 6 other advanced degrees awarded. *Degree program information:* Part-time and evening/weekend programs available. *Application deadline:* For fall admission, 8/20 priority date for domestic students. Applications are processed on a rolling basis. *Application fee:* $50. *Application Contact:* Maureen Faux, Interim Director, Graduate Admissions, 410-617-5020, Fax: 410-617-2002, E-mail: graduate@loyola.edu. *President,* Rev. Brian Linnane, 410-617-2201.

College of Arts and Sciences Students: 450 full-time (365 women), 962 part-time (735 women); includes 293 minority (221 African Americans, 6 American Indian/Alaska Native, 41 Asian Americans or Pacific Islanders, 25 Hispanic Americans). Average age 33. *Faculty:* 227 full-time (118 women), 119 part-time/adjunct (66 women). Expenses: Contact institution. *Financial support:* Research assistantships, career-related internships or fieldwork available. Financial award applicants required to submit FAFSA. In 2008, 688 master's, 17 doctorates, 6 other advanced degrees awarded. *Degree program information:* Part-time and evening/weekend programs available. Offers administration and supervision (M Ed, MA, CAS); arts and sciences (M Ed, MA, MMS, MS, PhD, Psy D, CAS); clinical psychology (MS, Psy D, CAS); computer science (MS); counseling psychology (MS, CAS); curriculum and instruction (M Ed, MA, CAS); educational technology (M Ed); liberal studies (MMS); Montessori education (M Ed, CAS); pastoral counseling (MS, PhD, CAS); reading (M Ed, CAS); school counseling (M Ed, CAS); software engineering (MS); special education (M Ed, CAS); speech-language pathology and audiology (MS, CAS); spiritual and pastoral care (MA). *Application deadline:* Applications are processed on a rolling basis. *Application fee:* $50. *Application Contact:* Maureen Faux, Interim Director, Graduate Admissions, 410-617-5020, Fax: 410-617-2002, E-mail: graduate@loyola.edu. *Dean,* Dr. James Buckley, 410-617-2563, E-mail: jbuckley@loyola.edu.

Sellinger School of Business and Management Students: 196 full-time (79 women), 756 part-time (286 women); includes 116 minority (64 African Americans, 38 Asian Americans or Pacific Islanders, 14 Hispanic Americans). Average age 31. *Faculty:* 67 full-time (17 women), 26 part-time/adjunct (5 women). Expenses: Contact institution. *Financial support:* Career-related internships or fieldwork, institutionally sponsored loans, and scholarships/grants available. Financial award applicants required to submit FAFSA. In 2008, 296 master's awarded. *Degree program information:* Part-time and evening/weekend programs available. Offers accounting (MBA); business and management (MBA, MSF); executive business administration (MBA); finance (MBA); general business (MBA); international business (MBA); management (MBA); management information systems (MBA); marketing (MBA). *Application deadline:* For fall admission, 8/15 priority date for domestic students; for spring admission, 11/20 priority date for domestic students. Applications are processed on a rolling basis. *Application fee:* $50. *Application Contact:* Maureen Faux, Interim Director, Graduate Admissions, 410-617-5020, Fax: 410-617-2002, E-mail: graduate@loyola.edu. *Dean,* Dr. Karyl Leggio, 410-617-2301, E-mail: kbleggio@loyola.edu.

LOYOLA UNIVERSITY NEW ORLEANS, New Orleans, LA 70118-6195

General Information Independent-religious, coed, comprehensive institution. *Enrollment:* 4,474 graduate, professional, and undergraduate students; 836 full-time matriculated graduate/professional students (453 women), 968 part-time matriculated graduate/professional students (756 women). *Enrollment by degree level:* 841 first professional, 963 master's. *Tuition:* Full-time $13,146; part-time $626 per credit hour. *Required fees:* $876; $229 per semester. *Graduate housing:* Room and/or apartments available on a first-come, first-served basis to single students; on-campus housing not available to married students. Typical cost: $5814 per year ($6814 including board). Housing application deadline: 8/1. *Student services:* Campus employment opportunities, campus safety program, career counseling, child daycare facilities, free psychological counseling, international student services, low-cost health insurance, multicultural affairs office, services for students with disabilities. *Library facilities:* University Library plus 1 other. *Online resources:* library catalog, web page, access to other libraries' catalogs. *Collection:* 612,163 titles, 40,662 serial subscriptions, 14,916 audiovisual materials. *Research affiliation:* New Orleans Museum of Art (communications, history, visual arts).

Computer facilities: Computer purchase and lease plans are available. 525 computers available on campus for general student use. A campuswide network can be accessed from student residence rooms and from off campus. Online class registration is available. *Web address:* http://www.loyno.edu/.

General Application Contact: Salvadore A. Liberto, Vice President for Enrollment Management and Associate Provost, 504-865-3240, Fax: 504-865-3383, E-mail: admit@loyno.edu.

GRADUATE UNITS

College of Law Students: 695 full-time (347 women), 146 part-time (77 women); includes 204 minority (99 African Americans, 5 American Indian/Alaska Native, 34 Asian Americans or Pacific Islanders, 66 Hispanic Americans), 3 international. Average age 27. 1,611 applicants, 50% accepted, 249 enrolled. Expenses: Contact institution. *Financial support:* In 2008–09, 31 research assistantships (averaging $1,452 per year), 19 teaching assistantships (averaging

Loyola University New Orleans (continued)

$2,053 per year) were awarded; career-related internships or fieldwork and scholarships/grants also available. Support available to part-time students. Financial award application deadline: 5/1; financial award applicants required to submit FAFSA. In 2008, 249 JDs awarded. *Degree program information:* Part-time and evening/weekend programs available. Offers law (JD, LL M). *Application deadline:* For fall admission, 2/1 priority date for domestic and international students. Applications are processed on a rolling basis. *Application fee:* $40. Electronic applications accepted. *Application Contact:* Michele K. Allison-Davis, Assistant Dean, Admissions, 504-861-5575, Fax: 504-861-5772, E-mail: maldavis@loyno.edu. *Dean,* Brian Bromberger, 504-861-5405, Fax: 504-861-5739, E-mail: bbromber@loyno.edu.

College of Music and Fine Arts Students: 11 full-time (5 women), 4 part-time (all women); includes 4 minority (2 African Americans, 2 Hispanic Americans), 1 international. Average age 27. 10 applicants, 60% accepted, 5 enrolled. Expenses: Contact institution. *Financial support:* Career-related internships or fieldwork, Federal Work-Study, institutionally sponsored loans, scholarships/grants, and unspecified assistantships available. Support available to part-time students. Financial award application deadline: 5/1; financial award applicants required to submit FAFSA. In 2008, 2 master's awarded. *Degree program information:* Part-time programs available. Offers music therapy (MMT); performance (MM). *Application deadline:* For fall admission, 8/15 priority date for domestic and international students; for spring admission, 1/1 priority date for domestic and international students. Applications are processed on a rolling basis. *Application fee:* $20. Electronic applications accepted. *Application Contact:* Anthony A. Decuir, PhD, Associate Dean, 504-865-3037, Fax: 504-865-2852, E-mail: decuir@loyno.edu. *Dean,* Donald R. Boomgaarden, PhD, 504-865-3039, Fax: 504-865-2852, E-mail: deancmfa@loyno.edu.

College of Social Sciences Students: 67 full-time (58 women), 759 part-time (635 women); includes 180 minority (119 African Americans, 1 American Indian/Alaska Native, 15 Asian Americans or Pacific Islanders, 45 Hispanic Americans), 5 international. Average age 43. 457 applicants, 95% accepted, 323 enrolled. Expenses: Contact institution. *Financial support:* Application deadline: 5/1. In 2008, 178 master's, 1 other advanced degree awarded. *Degree program information:* Part-time and evening/weekend programs available. Offers counseling (MS); criminal justice (MCJ); social sciences (MCJ, MPS, MRE, MS, MSN, Certificate). *Application deadline:* For fall admission, 8/1 priority date for domestic and international students; for winter admission, 12/15 priority date for international students; for spring admission, 1/5 priority date for domestic and international students. Applications are processed on a rolling basis. *Application fee:* $20. Electronic applications accepted. *Application Contact:* Salvadore A. Liberto, Vice President for Enrollment Management and Associate Provost, 504-865-3240, Fax: 504-865-3383, E-mail: admit@loyno.edu. *Dean,* Luis F. Miron, PhD, 504-865-2497, Fax: 504-865-3883, E-mail: lmiron@loyno.edu.

Loyola Institute for Ministry Students: 3 full-time (2 women), 284 part-time (207 women); includes 44 minority (8 African Americans, 1 American Indian/Alaska Native, 4 Asian Americans or Pacific Islanders, 31 Hispanic Americans), 4 international. Average age 48. 156 applicants, 96% accepted, 88 enrolled. Expenses: Contact institution. *Financial support:* Career-related internships or fieldwork, scholarships/grants, health care benefits, tuition waivers (partial), and room and board assistance available. Support available to part-time students. Financial award application deadline: 5/1; financial award applicants required to submit FAFSA. In 2008, 78 master's, 1 other advanced degree awarded. *Degree program information:* Part-time and evening/weekend programs available. Postbaccalaureate distance learning degree programs offered (no on-campus study). Offers pastoral studies (MPS); religious education (MRE); theology and ministry (Certificate). *Application deadline:* Applications are processed on a rolling basis. *Application fee:* $20. Electronic applications accepted. *Application Contact:* Cecelia M. Bennett, Associate Director, 504-865-3398, Fax: 504-865-2066, E-mail: abennett@loyno.edu. *Director,* Tom Ryan, PhD, 504-865-2069, Fax: 504-865-2066, E-mail: tfryan@loyno.edu.

School of Nursing Students: 57 full-time (51 women), 454 part-time (414 women); includes 126 minority (103 African Americans, 11 Asian Americans or Pacific Islanders, 12 Hispanic Americans), 1 international. Average age 43. 282 applicants, 94% accepted, 218 enrolled. Expenses: Contact institution. *Financial support:* Traineeships and Incumbent Workers Training Program grants available. Financial award application deadline: 5/1; financial award applicants required to submit FAFSA. In 2008, 80 master's awarded. *Degree program information:* Part-time and evening/weekend programs available. Postbaccalaureate distance learning degree programs offered. Offers adult nurse practitioner (MSN); family nurse practitioner (MSN); health care systems management (MSN); nursing (MSN). *Application deadline:* For fall admission, 8/1 priority date for domestic and international students; for winter admission, 12/15 priority date for domestic and international students; for spring admission, 5/15 priority date for domestic and international students. Applications are processed on a rolling basis. *Application fee:* $20. Electronic applications accepted. *Application Contact:* Deborah Smith, Assistant to the Director, 504-865-2823, Fax: 504-865-3254, E-mail: dhsmith@loyno.edu. *Director,* Ann H. Cary, PhD, 800-488-6257, Fax: 504-865-3254, E-mail: nursing@loyno.edu.

Joseph A. Butt, S.J., College of Business Students: 32 full-time (17 women), 37 part-time (21 women); includes 18 minority (7 African Americans, 2 Asian Americans or Pacific Islanders, 9 Hispanic Americans), 3 international. Average age 27. 66 applicants, 85% accepted, 28 enrolled. Expenses: Contact institution. *Financial support:* In 2008–09, 14 research assistantships (averaging $3,600 per year) were awarded; scholarships/grants, tuition waivers (partial), and unspecified assistantships also available. Financial award application deadline: 5/1; financial award applicants required to submit FAFSA. In 2008, 27 master's awarded. *Degree program information:* Part-time and evening/weekend programs available. Postbaccalaureate distance learning degree programs offered (minimal on-campus study). Offers business (MBA); business administration (MBA). *Application deadline:* For fall admission, 6/15 priority date for domestic and international students; for spring admission, 11/15 priority date for domestic and international students. Applications are processed on a rolling basis. *Application fee:* $50. Electronic applications accepted. *Application Contact:* Stephanie Mansfield, Assistant Director, Graduate Programs, 504-864-7965, Fax: 504-864-7970, E-mail: smans@loyno.edu. *Dean,* William B. Locander, PhD, 504-864-7990, Fax: 504-864-7970, E-mail: locander@loyno.edu.

LUBBOCK CHRISTIAN UNIVERSITY, Lubbock, TX 79407-2099

General Information Independent-religious, coed, comprehensive institution. *Graduate housing:* Rooms and/or apartments available to single and married students. Housing application deadline: 8/15.

GRADUATE UNITS

Graduate Biblical Studies *Degree program information:* Part-time programs available. Offers Bible and ministry (MS); biblical interpretation (MA).

LUTHERAN SCHOOL OF THEOLOGY AT CHICAGO, Chicago, IL 60615-5199

General Information Independent-religious, coed, graduate-only institution. *Enrollment by degree level:* 188 first professional, 53 master's, 71 doctoral, 23 other advanced degrees. *Graduate faculty:* 22 full-time, 15 part-time/adjunct. *Tuition:* Full-time $11,700; part-time $1300 per course. *Required fees:* $25 per semester. Tuition and fees vary according to degree level. *Graduate housing:* Rooms and/or apartments available on a first-come, first-served basis to single and married students. Typical cost: $3195 per year for single students; $6210 per year for married students. *Student services:* Career counseling, exercise/wellness program, international student services, low-cost health insurance. *Library facilities:* Jesuit-Krauss-McCormick Library. *Collection:* 334,388 titles. *Research affiliation:* Chicago Center for Public Ministry, Zygon Center for Religion and Science. *Web address:* http://www.lstc.edu/.

General Application Contact: Dorothy C. Dominiak, Director of Admissions and Financial Aid, 773-256-0726, Fax: 773-256-0782, E-mail: ddominia@lstc.edu.

GRADUATE UNITS

Graduate and Professional Programs Students: 231 full-time (116 women), 104 part-time (58 women); includes 18 African Americans, 5 Asian Americans or Pacific Islanders, 13 Hispanic Americans, 57 international. *Faculty:* 22 full-time, 15 part-time/adjunct. Expenses: Contact institution. *Financial support:* Career-related internships or fieldwork and scholarships/grants available. Support available to part-time students. *Degree program information:* Part-time programs available. Offers ministry (MAM, D Min); ministry, pastoral care, and counseling (D Min PCC); theological studies (MATS, PhD); theology (M Div, Th M). *Application deadline:* Applications are processed on a rolling basis. *Application fee:* $50. *Application Contact:* Dorothy C. Dominiak, Director of Admissions and Financial Aid, 773-256-0726, Fax: 773-256-0782, E-mail: ddominia@lstc.edu. *Dean,* Dr. Kathleen Billman, 773-256-0721, Fax: 773-256-0782, E-mail: kbillman@lstc.edu.

LUTHERAN THEOLOGICAL SEMINARY, Saskatoon, SK S7N 0X3, Canada

General Information Independent-religious, coed, graduate-only institution. *Graduate housing:* Room and/or apartments available to single students; on-campus housing not available to married students. Housing application deadline: 4/30.

GRADUATE UNITS

Graduate and Professional Programs *Degree program information:* Part-time programs available. Offers Biblical studies (MTS); church history (MTS); ethics/church and society (MTS); history of Christianity (STM); New Testament (STM); Old Testament (STM); pastoral studies (STM); pastoral theology (MTS); systematic theology (MTS); systematic theology and philosophy of religion (STM); theology (M Div, D Div).

LUTHERAN THEOLOGICAL SEMINARY AT GETTYSBURG, Gettysburg, PA 17325-1795

General Information Independent-religious, coed, graduate-only institution. *Graduate housing:* Rooms and/or apartments available on a first-come, first-served basis to single and married students. Housing application deadline: 4/1.

GRADUATE UNITS

Graduate and Professional Programs *Degree program information:* Part-time programs available. Postbaccalaureate distance learning degree programs offered (no on-campus study). Offers divinity (M Div); ministerial studies (MAMS); outdoor ministry (MAR); parish ministry (D Min); theology (STM). Electronic applications accepted.

THE LUTHERAN THEOLOGICAL SEMINARY AT PHILADELPHIA, Philadelphia, PA 19119-1794

General Information Independent-religious, coed, graduate-only institution. *Graduate housing:* Rooms and/or apartments available on a first-come, first-served basis to single and married students. Housing application deadline: 4/15.

GRADUATE UNITS

Graduate School *Degree program information:* Part-time and evening/weekend programs available. Offers divinity (M Div); ministry (D Min); religion (MAR); social ministry (Certificate); theology (STM). Electronic applications accepted.

LUTHERAN THEOLOGICAL SOUTHERN SEMINARY, Columbia, SC 29203

General Information Independent-religious, coed, graduate-only institution. *Graduate housing:* Rooms and/or apartments available on a first-come, first-served basis to single and married students. Housing application deadline: 5/1.

GRADUATE UNITS

Graduate and Professional Programs *Degree program information:* Part-time programs available. Offers theology (M Div, MAR, STM, D Min).

LUTHER RICE UNIVERSITY, Lithonia, GA 30038-2454

General Information Independent-religious, coed, comprehensive institution. *Graduate housing:* On-campus housing not available.

GRADUATE UNITS

Graduate Programs *Degree program information:* Part-time programs available. Postbaccalaureate distance learning degree programs offered (no on-campus study). Offers Bible/theology (M Div); Christian education (M Div); Christian studies (MA); church ministry (D Min); counseling (M Div); discipleship counseling (MA); ministry (M Div, MA); missions/evangelism (M Div).

LUTHER SEMINARY, St. Paul, MN 55108-1445

General Information Independent-religious, coed, graduate-only institution. *Graduate housing:* Rooms and/or apartments available on a first-come, first-served basis to single and married students.

GRADUATE UNITS

Graduate and Professional Programs Offers theology (M Div, M Th, MA, MSM, D Min, PhD). Electronic applications accepted.

LYNCHBURG COLLEGE, Lynchburg, VA 24501-3199

General Information Independent-religious, coed, comprehensive institution. *Enrollment:* 2,572 graduate, professional, and undergraduate students; 110 full-time matriculated graduate/professional students (76 women), 189 part-time matriculated graduate/professional students (133 women). *Enrollment by degree level:* 299 master's. *Graduate faculty:* 35 full-time (17 women), 9 part-time/adjunct (4 women). *Tuition:* Full-time $6750; part-time $375 per credit. *Graduate housing:* Room and/or apartments available on a first-come, first-served basis to single students; on-campus housing not available to married students. Typical cost: $3820 per year ($6770 including board). Housing application deadline: 8/1. *Student services:* Campus employment opportunities, career counseling, exercise/wellness program, free psychological counseling, grant writing training, international student services, multicultural affairs office, services for students with disabilities, teacher training, writing training. *Library facilities:* Knight-Capron Library. *Online resources:* library catalog, web page. *Collection:* 238,000 titles, 473 serial subscriptions, 7,258 audiovisual materials.

Computer facilities: 300 computers available on campus for general student use. A campuswide network can be accessed from student residence rooms. Online class registration is available. *Web address:* http://www.lynchburg.edu/.

General Application Contact: Dr. Edward Polloway, Vice President for Community Advancement and Dean of Graduate Studies, 434-544-8655, E-mail: polloway@lynchburg.edu.

GRADUATE UNITS

Graduate Studies Students: 110 full-time (76 women), 189 part-time (133 women); includes 28 minority (24 African Americans, 1 Asian American or Pacific Islander, 3 Hispanic Americans), 12 international. Average age 33. 156 applicants, 74% accepted, 81 enrolled. *Faculty:* 35 full-time (17 women), 9 part-time/adjunct (4 women). Expenses: Contact institution. *Financial support:* Career-related internships or fieldwork, Federal Work-Study, scholarships/grants, and unspecified assistantships available. Financial award applicants required to submit FAFSA. In 2008, 116 master's awarded. *Degree program information:* Part-time and evening/weekend programs available. *Application deadline:* For fall admission, 7/31 for domestic students, 6/1 for international students; for spring admission, 11/30 for domestic students, 10/1 for international students. *Application fee:* $30. Electronic applications accepted. *Application Contact:* Vice President for Graduate and Community Advancement. *Vice President for Graduate and Community Advancement,* Dr. Edward Polloway, 434-544-8655, E-mail: polloway@lynchburg.edu.

School of Business and Economics Students: 15 full-time (5 women), 41 part-time (16 women); includes 7 minority (6 African Americans, 1 Asian American or Pacific Islander), 5 international. Average age 35. 25 applicants, 72% accepted, 17 enrolled. *Faculty:* 5 full-time (1 woman), 2 part-time/adjunct (0 women). Expenses: Contact institution. *Financial* *support:* Federal Work-Study, institutionally sponsored loans, and scholarships/grants available. Financial award applicants required to submit FAFSA. In 2008, 19 master's awarded. *Degree program information:* Part-time and evening/weekend programs available. Offers business (MBA). *Application deadline:* For fall admission, 7/31 for domestic students, 6/1 for international students; for spring admission, 11/30 for domestic students, 10/1 for international students. *Application fee:* $30. *Application Contact:* Dr. Sally Selden, MBA Program Director, 434-544-8266, E-mail: selden@lynchburg.edu. *Dean, School of Business and Economics,* Dr. Joe Turek, 434-522-8542, E-mail: turek@lynchburg.edu.

School of Communications and the Arts Students: 3 part-time (all women); includes 1 minority (African American). Average age 38. 3 applicants, 67% accepted, 2 enrolled. *Faculty:* 2 full-time (1 woman), 1 part-time/adjunct (0 women). Expenses: Contact institution. *Financial support:* Career-related internships or fieldwork, scholarships/grants, and unspecified assistantships available. *Degree program information:* Part-time and evening/weekend programs available. Offers music (MA). *Application deadline:* For fall admission, 7/31 for domestic students, 6/1 for international students; for spring admission, 11/30 for domestic students, 10/1 for international students. *Application fee:* $30. *Application Contact:* Dr. Jong H. Kim, Program Coordinator, 434-544 Ext. 8443, E-mail: kim@lynchburg.edu. *Vice President for Graduate and Community Advancement,* Dr. Edward Polloway, 434-544-8655, E-mail: polloway@lynchburg.edu.

School of Education and Human Development Students: 76 full-time (60 women), 127 part-time (103 women); includes 20 minority (17 African Americans, 3 Hispanic Americans), 6 international. Average age 33. 99 applicants, 75% accepted, 49 enrolled. *Faculty:* 19 full-time (11 women), 5 part-time/adjunct (4 women). Expenses: Contact institution. *Financial support:* Career-related internships or fieldwork, scholarships/grants, and unspecified assistantships available. Financial award applicants required to submit FAFSA. In 2008, 96 master's awarded. *Degree program information:* Part-time and evening/weekend programs available. Offers community counseling (M Ed); counselor education (M Ed); curriculum and instruction (M Ed); educational leadership (M Ed); English education (M Ed); reading (M Ed); school counseling (M Ed); science education (M Ed); special education (M Ed). *Application deadline:* For fall admission, 7/31 for domestic students, 6/1 for international students; for spring admission, 11/30 for domestic students, 10/1 for international students. *Application fee:* $30. *Application Contact:* Dr. Edward Polloway, Vice President for Graduate and Community Advancement, 434-544-8655, E-mail: polloway@lynchburg.edu. *Dean,* Dr. Jan Stenette, 434-544-8662.

School of Humanities and Social Sciences Students: 19 full-time (11 women), 18 part-time (11 women), 1 international. Average age 33. 30 applicants, 73% accepted, 13 enrolled. *Faculty:* 7 full-time (4 women), 1 part-time/adjunct (0 women). Expenses: Contact institution. *Financial support:* Career-related internships or fieldwork, Federal Work-Study, scholarships/grants, and unspecified assistantships available. In 2008, 1 master's awarded. *Degree program information:* Part-time programs available. Offers English (MA); history (MA). *Application deadline:* For fall admission, 7/31 for domestic students, 6/1 for international students; for spring admission, 11/30 for domestic students, 10/1 for international students. *Application fee:* $30. *Application Contact:* Dr. Kim McCabe, Dean, School of Humanities and Social Sciences, 434-544-8129, E-mail: McCabe@lynchburg.edu. *Vice President for Graduate and Community Advancement,* Dr. Edward Polloway, 434-544-8655, E-mail: polloway@lynchburg.edu.

LYNDON STATE COLLEGE, Lyndonville, VT 05851-0919

General Information State-supported, coed, comprehensive institution. *Graduate housing:* On-campus housing not available.

GRADUATE UNITS

Graduate Programs in Education *Degree program information:* Part-time and evening/weekend programs available. Offers curriculum and instruction (M Ed); education (M Ed); natural sciences (MST); reading specialist (M Ed); science education (MST); special education (M Ed); teaching and counseling (M Ed).

LYNN UNIVERSITY, Boca Raton, FL 33431-5598

General Information Independent, coed, comprehensive institution. *Graduate housing:* Room and/or apartments available on a first-come, first-served basis to single students; on-campus housing not available to married students.

GRADUATE UNITS

College of Arts and Sciences *Degree program information:* Part-time and evening/weekend programs available. Postbaccalaureate distance learning degree programs offered. Offers applied psychology (MS); criminal justice administration (MS); emergency planning and administration (MS, Certificate).

College of Business and Management *Degree program information:* Part-time and evening/weekend programs available. Postbaccalaureate distance learning degree programs offered. Offers aviation management (MBA); financial valuation and investment management (MBA); global leadership (PhD); hospitality management (MBA); international business (MBA); marketing (MBA); mass communication and media management (MBA); sports and athletics administration (MBA). Electronic applications accepted.

Conservatory of Music *Degree program information:* Part-time and evening/weekend programs available. Offers music performance (MM); professional performance (Certificate).

Donald and Helen Ross College of Education *Degree program information:* Part-time and evening/weekend programs available. Offers exceptional student education (M Ed); global leadership (PhD). Electronic applications accepted.

Eugene M. and Christine E. Lynn College of International Communication *Degree program information:* Part-time and evening/weekend programs available. Offers mass communication (MS).

MACHZIKEI HADATH RABBINICAL COLLEGE, Brooklyn, NY 11204-1805

General Information Independent-religious, men only, comprehensive institution. *Graduate housing:* Room and/or apartments available to single students; on-campus housing not available to married students.

GRADUATE UNITS

Graduate Programs

MADONNA UNIVERSITY, Livonia, MI 48150-1173

General Information Independent-religious, coed, comprehensive institution. *Graduate housing:* Room and/or apartments available on a first-come, first-served basis to single students; on-campus housing not available to married students. Housing application deadline: 4/29.

GRADUATE UNITS

Department of English *Degree program information:* Part-time and evening/weekend programs available. Offers teaching English to speakers of other languages (MATESOL). Electronic applications accepted.

Department of Psychology *Degree program information:* Part-time and evening/weekend programs available. Offers clinical psychology (MSCP). Electronic applications accepted.

Program in Health Services *Degree program information:* Part-time programs available. Offers health services (MSHS). Electronic applications accepted.

Program in Hospice *Degree program information:* Part-time and evening/weekend programs available. Offers hospice (MSH). Electronic applications accepted.

Program in Liberal Studies Offers liberal studies (MALS).

Program in Nursing *Degree program information:* Part-time programs available. Offers adult health: chronic health conditions (MSN); adult nurse practitioner (MSN); nursing administration (MSN). Electronic applications accepted.

Program in Religious Studies Offers pastoral ministry (MA).

Programs in Education *Degree program information:* Part-time and evening/weekend programs available. Offers Catholic school leadership (MSA); educational leadership (MSA); learning disabilities (MAT); literacy education (MAT); teaching and learning (MAT). Electronic applications accepted.

School of Business *Degree program information:* Part-time and evening/weekend programs available. Postbaccalaureate distance learning degree programs offered (minimal on-campus study). Offers business administration (MBA); international business (MSBA); leadership studies (MSBA); leadership studies in criminal justice (MSBA); quality and operations management (MSBA). Electronic applications accepted.

MAHARISHI UNIVERSITY OF MANAGEMENT, Fairfield, IA 52557

General Information Independent, coed, university. *Graduate housing:* Room and/or apartments guaranteed to single students; on-campus housing not available to married students. Housing application deadline: 8/1.

GRADUATE UNITS

Graduate Studies *Degree program information:* Evening/weekend programs available. Postbaccalaureate distance learning degree programs offered (minimal on-campus study). Offers accounting (MBA); business administration (PhD); computer science (MS); Maharishi Vedic science (MA, PhD); sustainability (MBA); teaching elementary education (MA); teaching secondary education (MA). Electronic applications accepted.

MAINE COLLEGE OF ART, Portland, ME 04101

General Information Independent, coed, comprehensive institution. *Graduate housing:* Room and/or apartments available to single students; on-campus housing not available to married students.

GRADUATE UNITS

Program in Studio Arts Offers studio arts (MFA). Electronic applications accepted.

MAINE MARITIME ACADEMY, Castine, ME 04420

General Information State-supported, coed, primarily men, comprehensive institution. *Graduate housing:* Rooms and/or apartments available on a first-come, first-served basis to single and married students. Housing application deadline: 3/15.

GRADUATE UNITS

Department of Graduate Studies *Degree program information:* Part-time and evening/weekend programs available. Postbaccalaureate distance learning degree programs offered (no on-campus study). Offers global supply chain management (MS, Certificate, Diploma); international business (MS, Certificate, Diploma); maritime management (MS, Certificate, Diploma). Electronic applications accepted.

MALONE UNIVERSITY, Canton, OH 44709-3897

General Information Independent-religious, coed, comprehensive institution. *Enrollment:* 2,442 graduate, professional, and undergraduate students; 45 full-time matriculated graduate/professional students (32 women), 357 part-time matriculated graduate/professional students (232 women). *Enrollment by degree level:* 402 master's. *Graduate faculty:* 37 full-time (20 women), 36 part-time/adjunct (18 women). *Tuition:* Part-time $435 per semester hour. Tuition and fees vary according to program. *Graduate housing:* On-campus housing not available. *Student services:* Career counseling, multicultural affairs office, services for students with disabilities, writing training. *Library facilities:* Everett L. Cattell Library. *Online resources:* library catalog, web page, access to other libraries' catalogs. *Collection:* 178,992 titles, 47,942 serial subscriptions, 10,710 audiovisual materials.

Computer facilities: Computer purchase and lease plans are available. 200 computers available on campus for general student use. A campuswide network can be accessed from student residence rooms and from off campus. Online class registration, online advising, online financial aid information, and online credit card payments are available. *Web address:* http://www.malone.edu/.

General Application Contact: David L. Kleffman, Assistant Director of Enrollment, 330-471-8447, Fax: 330-471-8343, E-mail: dkleffman@malone.edu.

GRADUATE UNITS

Graduate Program in Business Students: 7 full-time (4 women), 117 part-time (39 women); includes 13 minority (10 African Americans, 2 Asian Americans or Pacific Islanders, 1 Hispanic American), 2 international. Average age 36. *Faculty:* 10 full-time (4 women), 8 part-time/adjunct (2 women). Expenses: Contact institution. *Financial support:* Tuition waivers (partial) available. Support available to part-time students. Financial award application deadline: 6/30. In 2008, 19 master's awarded. *Degree program information:* Part-time and evening/weekend programs available. Offers business (MBA). *Application deadline:* Applications are processed on a rolling basis. *Application fee:* $25. *Application Contact:* David L. Kleffman, Assistant Director of Enrollment, 330-471-8447, Fax: 330-471-8343, E-mail: dkleffman@malone.edu. *Director,* Dr. Julia A. Frankland, 330-471-8552, Fax: 330-471-8563, E-mail: jfrankland@malone.edu.

Graduate Program in Christian Ministries Students: 3 full-time (1 woman), 29 part-time (10 women); includes 8 minority (7 African Americans, 1 American Indian/Alaska Native). Average age 37. *Faculty:* 7 full-time (1 woman), 4 part-time/adjunct (0 women). Expenses: Contact institution. *Financial support:* Tuition waivers (partial) and unspecified assistantships available. Support available to part-time students. Financial award application deadline: 6/30. In 2008, 10 master's awarded. *Degree program information:* Part-time and evening/weekend programs available. Offers Christian leadership in sports ministry (MA); Christian ministries (MA); leadership in the Christian church (MA). *Application deadline:* Applications are processed on a rolling basis. *Application fee:* $25. *Application Contact:* David L. Kleffman, Assistant Director of Enrollment, 330-471-8447, Fax: 330-471-8343, E-mail: dkleffman@malone.edu. *Interim Director,* Dr. D. Nathan Phinney, 330-471-8194, Fax: 330-471-8477, E-mail: dphinney@malone.edu.

Graduate Program in Counselor and Guidance Education Students: 33 full-time (25 women), 95 part-time (78 women); includes 17 minority (15 African Americans, 1 Asian American or Pacific Islander, 1 Hispanic American). Average age 34. *Faculty:* 4 full-time (3 women), 4 part-time/adjunct (1 woman). Expenses: Contact institution. *Financial support:* Tuition waivers (partial) available. Support available to part-time students. Financial award application deadline: 6/30. In 2008, 28 master's awarded. *Degree program information:* Part-time and evening/weekend programs available. Offers clinical counseling (MA); school counseling (MA). *Application deadline:* Applications are processed on a rolling basis. *Application fee:* $25. *Application Contact:* David L. Kleffman, Assistant Director of Enrollment, 330-471-8447, Fax: 330-471-8343, E-mail: dkleffman@malone.edu. *Associate Dean of Graduate Studies/Director of the Graduate Program in Counselor and Guidance Education,* Dr. Brock M. Reiman, 330-471-8404, Fax: 330-471-8343, E-mail: breiman@malone.edu.

Graduate Program in Education Students: 2 full-time (both women), 67 part-time (58 women); includes 2 minority (1 Asian American or Pacific Islander, 1 Hispanic American). Average age 34. *Faculty:* 7 full-time (3 women), 8 part-time/adjunct (7 women). Expenses: Contact institution. *Financial support:* Tuition waivers (partial) available. Support available to part-time students. Financial award application deadline: 6/30. In 2008, 46 master's awarded. *Degree program information:* Part-time and evening/weekend programs available. Offers curriculum and instruction (MA); curriculum, instruction, and professional development (MA); instructional technology (MA); intervention specialist (MA); reading (MA). *Application deadline:* Applications are processed on a rolling basis. *Application fee:* $25. *Application Contact:* David L. Kleffman, Assistant Director of Enrollment, 330-471-8447, Fax: 330-471-8343, E-mail: dkleffman@malone.edu. *Director,* Dr. Alice E. Christie, 330-478-8541, Fax: 330-471-8563, E-mail: achristie@malone.edu.

Graduate Program in Nursing Students: 49 part-time (47 women); includes 2 minority (both African Americans). Average age 37. 56 applicants, 75% accepted, 35 enrolled. *Faculty:* 9 full-time (all women), 12 part-time/adjunct (8 women). Expenses: Contact institution. *Financial*

Malone University (continued)

support: Tuition waivers (partial) available. Support available to part-time students. Financial award application deadline: 6/30. In 2008, 19 master's awarded. *Degree program information:* Part-time and evening/weekend programs available. Offers clinical nurse specialist (MSN); family nurse practitioner (MSN). *Application deadline:* Applications are processed on a rolling basis. *Application fee:* $25. *Application Contact:* David L. Kleffman, Assistant Director of Enrollment, 330-471-8447, Fax: 330-471-8343, E-mail: dkleffman@malone.edu. *Interim Director,* Dr. Loretta M. Reinhart, 330-471-8168, Fax: 330-471-8607, E-mail: loreinhart@malone.edu.

MANHATTAN COLLEGE, Riverdale, NY 10471

General Information Independent-religious, coed, comprehensive institution. *Graduate housing:* On-campus housing not available.

GRADUATE UNITS

Graduate Division *Degree program information:* Part-time and evening/weekend programs available.

School of Education *Degree program information:* Part-time and evening/weekend programs available. Offers 5 year dual childhood/special education (MS Ed); counseling (MA, Diploma); dual childhood/special education (MS Ed); mental health counseling (MA); school building leadership (MS Ed, Diploma); school counseling (MA); special education (MS Ed).

School of Engineering *Degree program information:* Part-time and evening/weekend programs available. Offers chemical engineering (MS); civil engineering (MS); computer engineering (MS); electrical engineering (MS); environmental engineering (ME, MS); mechanical engineering (MS).

MANHATTAN SCHOOL OF MUSIC, New York, NY 10027-4698

General Information Independent, coed, comprehensive institution. *Enrollment:* 969 graduate, professional, and undergraduate students; 541 full-time matriculated graduate/professional students (310 women), 6 part-time matriculated graduate/professional students (4 women). *Enrollment by degree level:* 447 master's, 64 doctoral, 36 other advanced degrees. *Graduate faculty:* 50 full-time (0 women), 162 part-time/adjunct (74 women). *Tuition:* Full-time $29,975; part-time $1300 per credit. Tuition and fees vary according to course load. *Graduate housing:* Room and/or apartments available on a first-come, first-served basis to single students; on-campus housing not available to married students. Typical cost: $11,500 per year ($15,900 including board). Room and board charges vary according to board plan. Housing application deadline: 6/15. *Student services:* Campus employment opportunities, campus safety program, career counseling, international student services, low-cost health insurance. *Library facilities:* Peter J. Sharp Library.

Computer facilities: 20 computers available on campus for general student use. A campuswide network can be accessed from student residence rooms and from off campus. *Web address:* http://www.msmnyc.edu/.

General Application Contact: Amy A. Anderson, Associate Dean for Enrollment Management, 917-493-4501, Fax: 212-749-3025, E-mail: aanderson@msmnyc.edu.

GRADUATE UNITS

Graduate Programs Students: 505 full-time (286 women), 6 part-time (4 women); includes 77 minority (11 African Americans, 1 American Indian/Alaska Native, 46 Asian Americans or Pacific Islanders, 19 Hispanic Americans), 198 international. Average age 22. 1,439 applicants, 38% accepted, 265 enrolled. *Faculty:* 50 full-time (0 women), 162 part-time/adjunct (74 women). Expenses: Contact institution. *Financial support:* In 2008–09, 244 students received support, including 14 teaching assistantships with partial tuition reimbursements available (averaging $4,700 per year); Federal Work-Study, scholarships/grants, and tuition waivers (full and partial) also available. Support available to part-time students. Financial award application deadline: 3/1; financial award applicants required to submit FAFSA. In 2008, 135 master's, 10 doctorates awarded. Offers composition (MM, DMA); jazz (MM, DMA); music performance (MM, DMA); orchestral performance (MM). *Application deadline:* For fall admission, 12/1 for domestic and international students. *Application fee:* $100. Electronic applications accepted. *Application Contact:* Amy A. Anderson, Associate Dean for Enrollment Management, 917-493-4501, Fax: 212-749-3025, E-mail: aanderson@msmnyc.edu. *Dean of Academic Affairs,* Dr. Marjorie Merryman, 212-749-2802 Ext. 4584, Fax: 212-749-5471, E-mail: mmerryman@msmnyc.edu.

Professional Studies Certificate Program Students: 35 full-time (24 women); includes 3 minority (1 African American, 2 Asian Americans or Pacific Islanders), 20 international. Average age 24. 139 applicants, 71% accepted, 33 enrolled. *Faculty:* 50 full-time (0 women), 162 part-time/adjunct (74 women). Expenses: Contact institution. *Financial support:* In 2008–09, 20 students received support. Federal Work-Study, scholarships/grants, and tuition waivers (full and partial) available. Support available to part-time students. Financial award application deadline: 3/1; financial award applicants required to submit FAFSA. In 2008, 30 CPSs awarded. Offers instrumental music (CPS); vocal music (CPS). *Application deadline:* For fall admission, 12/1 for domestic and international students. *Application fee:* $100. Electronic applications accepted. *Application Contact:* Amy A. Anderson, Associate Dean for Enrollment Management, 917-493-4501, Fax: 212-749-3025, E-mail: aanderson@msmnyc.edu. *Dean of Academic Affairs,* Dr. Marjorie Merryman, 212-749-2802 Ext. 4584, Fax: 212-749-5471, E-mail: mmerryman@msmnyc.edu.

MANHATTANVILLE COLLEGE, Purchase, NY 10577-2132

General Information Independent, coed, comprehensive institution. *Enrollment by degree level:* 1,032 master's. *Tuition:* Full-time $13,680; part-time $760 per credit. *Required fees:* $45 per semester. *Graduate housing:* Rooms and/or apartments available to single and married students. Typical cost: $7740 per year ($13,040 including board) for single students; $7740 per year ($13,040 including board) for married students. Housing application deadline: 7/1. *Student services:* Campus employment opportunities, campus safety program, career counseling, free psychological counseling, international student services, multicultural affairs office, services for students with disabilities, teacher training, writing training. *Library facilities:* Manhattanville College Library. *Online resources:* library catalog, web page, access to other libraries' catalogs. *Collection:* 239,202 titles, 27,838 serial subscriptions.

Computer facilities: Computer purchase and lease plans are available. 240 computers available on campus for general student use. A campuswide network can be accessed from student residence rooms and from off campus. Online class registration is available. *Web address:* http://www.manhattanville.edu/.

General Application Contact: Graduate Admissions, 914-323-5464, Fax: 914-323-, E-mail: admissions@mville.edu.

GRADUATE UNITS

Graduate Programs Students: 355 full-time (232 women), 677 part-time (470 women); includes 85 minority (30 African Americans, 10 Asian Americans or Pacific Islanders, 45 Hispanic Americans), 8 international. Expenses: Contact institution. *Financial support:* Career-related internships or fieldwork, Federal Work-Study, institutionally sponsored loans, scholarships/grants, tuition waivers (partial), and unspecified assistantships available. Support available to part-time students. Financial award application deadline: 3/1; financial award applicants required to submit FAFSA. In 2008, 375 master's awarded. *Degree program information:* Part-time and evening/weekend programs available. Offers finance (MS); integrated marketing communications (MS); international management (MS); leadership and strategic management (MS); liberal studies (MA); organizational management and human resource development (MS); sport business management (MS); writing (MA). *Application deadline:* Applications are processed on a rolling basis. *Application fee:* $65. *Application Contact:* Office of Graduate Admissions, 914-323-5464, E-mail: admissions@mville.edu. *Interim Provost,* Dr. Edgar Schick, 914-323-5262, E-mail: provost@mville.edu.

School of Education Students: 321 full-time (225 women), 590 part-time (429 women); includes 76 minority (26 African Americans, 9 Asian Americans or Pacific Islanders, 41 Hispanic Americans), 5 international. Expenses: Contact institution. *Financial support:* Career-related internships or fieldwork, Federal Work-Study, institutionally sponsored loans, and unspecified assistantships available. Financial award application deadline: 3/1; financial award applicants required to submit FAFSA. In 2008, 295 master's awarded. *Degree program information:* Part-time and evening/weekend programs available. Offers biology (MAT); biology and special education (MPS); chemistry (MAT); chemistry and special education (MPS); child and early childhood education (MAT, MPS); childhood and early childhood education (MAT); childhood and special education (MPS); childhood education (MAT); early childhood education (birth-grade 2) (MAT); education (M Ed, MAT, MPS); educational leadership (MPS); English (MAT); English and special education (MPS); English as a second language (MAT); literacy (MPS); literacy (birth-grade 6) (MPS); literacy (birth-grade 6) and special education (grades 1-6) (MPS); literacy and special education (MPS); math (MAT); math and special education (MPS); music education (MAT); physical education and sport pedagogy (MAT); second language (MAT); social studies (MAT); social studies and special education (MPS); special education (MPS); special education (birth-grade 2) (MPS); special education (birth-grade 6) (MPS); special education childhood (MPS); teaching English as a second language (MPS); visual arts education (MAT). *Application deadline:* Applications are processed on a rolling basis. *Application fee:* $65. Electronic applications accepted. *Application Contact:* Jeanine Pardey-Levine, Director of Admissions, 914-323-3208, Fax: 914-694-1732, E-mail: edschool@mville.edu. *Dean,* Dr. Shelley Wepner, 914-323-5192, Fax: 914-694-2386, E-mail: wepners@mville.edu.

See Close-Up on page 941.

MANSFIELD UNIVERSITY OF PENNSYLVANIA, Mansfield, PA 16933

General Information State-supported, coed, comprehensive institution. *Enrollment:* 69 full-time matriculated graduate/professional students (46 women), 409 part-time matriculated graduate/professional students (367 women). *Enrollment by degree level:* 478 master's. *Graduate faculty:* 23 full-time (16 women), 14 part-time/adjunct (12 women). *Graduate housing:* Room and/or apartments available on a first-come, first-served basis to single students; on-campus housing not available to married students. *Student services:* Campus employment opportunities, campus safety program, career counseling, child daycare facilities, exercise/wellness program, free psychological counseling, grant writing training, international student services, low-cost health insurance, multicultural affairs office, services for students with disabilities, teacher training. *Library facilities:* North Hall Library. *Online resources:* library catalog, web page, access to other libraries' catalogs. *Collection:* 246,141 titles, 2,948 serial subscriptions, 26,742 audiovisual materials.

Computer facilities: 661 computers available on campus for general student use. A campuswide network can be accessed from student residence rooms and from off campus. Online class registration is available. *Web address:* http://www.mansfield.edu/.

General Application Contact: Christina Hale, Assistant Director of Enrollment Services/Graduate Admissions, 570-662-4806, Fax: 570-662-4121, E-mail: chale@mansfield.edu.

GRADUATE UNITS

Graduate Studies Students: 69 full-time (46 women), 409 part-time (367 women); includes 32 minority (18 African Americans, 3 American Indian/Alaska Native, 2 Asian Americans or Pacific Islanders, 9 Hispanic Americans). Average age 36. 453 applicants, 76% accepted, 210 enrolled. *Faculty:* 23 full-time (16 women), 14 part-time/adjunct (12 women). Expenses: Contact institution. *Financial support:* In 2008–09, 50 students received support. Career-related internships or fieldwork and unspecified assistantships available. Support available to part-time students. Financial award application deadline: 5/1; financial award applicants required to submit FAFSA. In 2008, 137 degrees awarded. *Degree program information:* Part-time and evening/weekend programs available. Postbaccalaureate distance learning degree programs offered (no on-campus study). Offers art education (M Ed); band conducting (MA); choral conducting (MA); elementary education (M Ed); library science (M Ed); nursing (MSN); performance (MA); secondary education (MS). *Application deadline:* For fall admission, 8/1 priority date for domestic students, 6/1 for international students. Applications are processed on a rolling basis. *Application fee:* $25. Electronic applications accepted. *Application Contact:* Christina Hale, Assistant Director of Enrollment Management/Graduate Admissions, 570-662-4812, Fax: 570-662-4121, E-mail: chale@mansfield.edu. *Associate Provost,* Dr. Deborah Erickson, 570-662-4806, Fax: 570-662-4121, E-mail: denckso@mansfield.edu.

MAPLE SPRINGS BAPTIST BIBLE COLLEGE AND SEMINARY, Capitol Heights, MD 20743

General Information Independent-religious, coed, comprehensive institution. *Graduate housing:* On-campus housing not available.

GRADUATE UNITS

Graduate and Professional Programs Offers biblical studies (MA, Certificate); Christian counseling (MA); church administration (MA); divinity (M Div); ministry (D Min); religious education (MRE).

MARANATHA BAPTIST BIBLE COLLEGE, Watertown, WI 53094

General Information Independent-religious, coed, comprehensive institution. *Enrollment:* 865 graduate, professional, and undergraduate students; 21 full-time matriculated graduate/professional students (7 women), 27 part-time matriculated graduate/professional students (5 women). *Enrollment by degree level:* 48 master's. *Graduate faculty:* 5 full-time (0 women), 2 part-time/adjunct (0 women). *Tuition:* Full-time $3840; part-time $240 per credit hour. *Required fees:* $20 per credit hour. *Graduate housing:* On-campus housing not available. *Student services:* Campus employment opportunities. *Library facilities:* Cedarholm Library and Resource Center. *Online resources:* library catalog, access to other libraries' catalogs. *Collection:* 122,251 titles, 502 serial subscriptions.

Computer facilities: 120 computers available on campus for general student use. A campuswide network can be accessed from student residence rooms and from off campus. *Web address:* http://www.mbbc.edu/.

General Application Contact: Dr. Jim Harrison, Director of Admissions, 920-206-2327, Fax: 920-261-9109, E-mail: admissions@mbbc.edu.

GRADUATE UNITS

Program in Biblical Counseling Students: 7 full-time (5 women), 5 part-time (3 women). Average age 24. 7 applicants, 100% accepted, 7 enrolled. *Faculty:* 5 full-time (0 women), 2 part-time/adjunct (0 women). Expenses: Contact institution. *Financial support:* In 2008–09, 2 students received support. Scholarships/grants and tuition waivers (full and partial) available. Support available to part-time students. In 2008, 2 master's awarded. *Degree program information:* Part-time programs available. Offers biblical counseling (MA). *Application deadline:* Applications are processed on a rolling basis. *Application fee:* $50. *Application Contact:* Dr. Jim Harrison, Director of Admissions, 920-206-2327, Fax: 920-261-9109, E-mail: admissions@mbbc.edu. *Dean of Maranatha Baptist Seminary,* Dr. Larry Oats, 920-206-2324, Fax: 920-261-9109, E-mail: loats@mbbc.edu.

Program in Biblical Studies Students: 10 full-time (0 women), 9 part-time (0 women). Average age 27. 6 applicants, 100% accepted, 6 enrolled. *Faculty:* 5 full-time (0 women), 2 part-time/adjunct (0 women). Expenses: Contact institution. *Financial support:* In 2008–09, 8 students received support. Scholarships/grants and tuition waivers (full and partial) available. Support available to part-time students. In 2008, 8 master's awarded. *Degree program information:* Part-time programs available. Offers biblical studies (MA). *Application deadline:* Applications are processed on a rolling basis. *Application fee:* $50. *Application Contact:* Dr. Jim Harrison, Director of Admissions, 920-206-2327, Fax: 920-261-9109, E-mail: admissions@mbbc.edu. *Dean of Maranatha Baptist Seminary,* Dr. Larry Oats, 920-206-2324, Fax: 920-261-9109, E-mail: loats@mbbc.edu.

Program in Cross-Cultural Studies Students: 3 full-time (all women), 1 part-time (0 women). Average age 23. 3 applicants, 100% accepted, 3 enrolled. *Faculty:* 5 full-time (0 women), 2 part-time/adjunct (0 women). Expenses: Contact institution. *Financial support:* Scholarships/grants and tuition waivers (full and partial) available. Support available to part-time students. *Degree program information:* Part-time programs available. Offers cross-cultural studies

(MA). *Application deadline:* Applications are processed on a rolling basis. *Application fee:* $50. *Application Contact:* Dr. Jim Harrison, Director of Admissions, 920-206-2327, Fax: 920-261-9109, E-mail: admissions@mbbc.edu. *Dean of Maranatha Baptist Seminary*, Dr. Larry Oats, 920-206-2324, Fax: 920-261-9109, E-mail: loats@mbbc.edu.

Program in Theology Students: 3 full-time (0 women), 2 part-time (0 women). Average age 27. *Faculty:* 5 full-time (0 women), 2 part-time/adjunct (0 women). Expenses: Contact institution. In 2008, 1 master's awarded. *Degree program information:* Part-time programs available. Offers theology (MA). *Application Contact:* Dr. Jim Harrison, Director of Admissions, 920-206-2327, Fax: 920-261-9109, E-mail: admissions@mbbc.edu. *Dean of Maranatha Baptist Seminary*, Dr. Larry Oats, 920-206-2324, Fax: 920-261-9109, E-mail: loats@mbbc.edu.

MARIAN UNIVERSITY, Indianapolis, IN 46222-1997

General Information Independent-religious, coed, comprehensive institution. *Enrollment:* 2,143 graduate, professional, and undergraduate students; 14 full-time matriculated graduate/professional students (9 women), 158 part-time matriculated graduate/professional students (94 women). *Enrollment by degree level:* 172 master's. *Graduate faculty:* 13 full-time (11 women), 10 part-time/adjunct (all women). *Tuition:* Full-time $9400; part-time $350 per credit hour. *Student services:* Campus safety program, career counseling, exercise/wellness program, free psychological counseling, low-cost health insurance, services for students with disabilities, teacher training. *Library facilities:* Mother Theresa Hackelmeier Memorial Library. *Online resources:* library catalog, web page, access to other libraries' catalogs. *Collection:* 102,237 titles, 337 serial subscriptions, 2,517 audiovisual materials.

Computer facilities: 225 computers available on campus for general student use. A campuswide network can be accessed from student residence rooms. Online class registration is available. *Web address:* http://www.marian.edu/.

General Application Contact: Dr. Karen Bevis, Director of Special Programs, 317-955-6089, Fax: 317-955-6448, E-mail: kbevis@marian.edu.

GRADUATE UNITS

School of Education Students: 14 full-time (9 women), 158 part-time (94 women); includes 32 minority (21 African Americans, 1 American Indian/Alaska Native, 2 Asian Americans or Pacific Islanders, 8 Hispanic Americans). Average age 31. *Faculty:* 13 full-time (11 women), 10 part-time/adjunct (all women). Expenses: Contact institution. *Financial support:* Applicants required to submit FAFSA. In 2008, 18 master's awarded. *Degree program information:* Part-time and evening/weekend programs available. Offers education (MAT). *Application deadline:* For fall admission, 2/1 priority date for domestic students. Applications are processed on a rolling basis. *Application fee:* $0. *Application Contact:* Cheryl Hertzer, Chair, 317-955-6087, Fax: 317-955-6448, E-mail: chertzer@marian.edu. *Dean of the School of Education*, Dr. Lindan Hill, 317-955-6089, Fax: 317-955-6448, E-mail: lhill@marian.edu.

MARIAN UNIVERSITY, Fond du Lac, WI 54935-4699

General Information Independent-religious, coed, comprehensive institution. CGS member. *Enrollment:* 2,891 graduate, professional, and undergraduate students; 76 full-time matriculated graduate/professional students (57 women), 819 part-time matriculated graduate/professional students (557 women). *Enrollment by degree level:* 765 master's, 50 doctoral, 80 other advanced degrees. *Graduate faculty:* 22 full-time (13 women), 67 part-time/adjunct (43 women). *Tuition:* Part-time $380 per credit hour. Tuition and fees vary according to program. *Graduate housing:* On-campus housing not available. *Student services:* Campus employment opportunities, campus safety program, career counseling, child daycare facilities, exercise/wellness program, free psychological counseling, multicultural affairs office, services for students with disabilities, teacher training, writing training. *Library facilities:* Cardinal Meyer Library. *Online resources:* library catalog, web page, access to other libraries' catalogs. *Collection:* 105,015 titles, 1,357 serial subscriptions, 1,512 audiovisual materials.

Computer facilities: Computer purchase and lease plans are available. 315 computers available on campus for general student use. A campuswide network can be accessed from student residence rooms and from off campus. Online class registration is available. *Web address:* http://www.mariancollege.edu/.

General Application Contact: Dr. Deborah Golias, Interim Vice President for Academic Affairs, 920-923-7604, E-mail: dgolais94@marianuniversity.edu.

GRADUATE UNITS

Business Division Students: 4 full-time (all women), 78 part-time (51 women); includes 14 minority (9 African Americans, 1 American Indian/Alaska Native, 1 Asian American or Pacific Islander, 3 Hispanic Americans). Average age 38. 25 applicants, 92% accepted, 23 enrolled. *Faculty:* 10 part-time/adjunct (2 women). Expenses: Contact institution. *Financial support:* In 2008–09, 25 students received support. Institutionally sponsored loans available. Support available to part-time students. Financial award application deadline: 3/1; financial award applicants required to submit FAFSA. In 2008, 24 master's awarded. *Degree program information:* Part-time and evening/weekend programs available. Offers organizational leadership and quality (MS). *Application deadline:* Applications are processed on a rolling basis. *Application fee:* $25. Electronic applications accepted. *Application Contact:* Tracy Qualman, Director of Marketing and Admission, 920-923-7159, Fax: 920-923-7167, E-mail: tqualmann@marianuniversity.edu. *Assistant Provost and Dean of PACE*, Donna Innes, 920-923-8760, Fax: 920-923-7167, E-mail: dinnes@marianuniversity.edu.

School of Education Students: 44 full-time (26 women), 719 part-time (484 women); includes 24 minority (8 African Americans, 3 American Indian/Alaska Native, 3 Asian Americans or Pacific Islanders, 10 Hispanic Americans), 2 international. Average age 36. *Faculty:* 16 full-time (8 women), 52 part-time/adjunct (37 women). Expenses: Contact institution. *Financial support:* In 2008–09, 213 students received support. Federal Work-Study and institutionally sponsored loans available. Support available to part-time students. Financial award application deadline: 3/1; financial award applicants required to submit FAFSA. In 2008, 315 master's, 3 doctorates awarded. *Degree program information:* Part-time programs available. Offers educational leadership (MA, PhD); teacher development (MA). *Application deadline:* Applications are processed on a rolling basis. *Application fee:* $50. *Application Contact:* Robert Bohnsack, Graduate Education Admissions, 920-923-8100, Fax: 920-923-7154, E-mail: bbohnsack@marianuniversity.edu. *Dean, School of Education*, Donna Innes, 920-923-8099, Fax: 920-923-7663, E-mail: dinnes@marianuniversity.edu.

School of Nursing Students: 28 full-time (27 women), 22 part-time (all women). Average age 39. 14 applicants, 100% accepted, 14 enrolled. *Faculty:* 6 full-time (5 women), 5 part-time/adjunct (4 women). Expenses: Contact institution. *Financial support:* In 2008–09, 25 students received support. Institutionally sponsored loans and scholarships/grants available. Support available to part-time students. Financial award application deadline: 3/1; financial award applicants required to submit FAFSA. In 2008, 9 master's awarded. *Degree program information:* Part-time and evening/weekend programs available. Offers adult nurse practitioner (MSN); nurse educator (MSN). *Application deadline:* Applications are processed on a rolling basis. *Application fee:* $50. Electronic applications accepted. *Application Contact:* Dr. Greta Kostac, Director, 920-923-7603, Fax: 920-923-8770, E-mail: gmkostac@marianuniversity.edu. *Dean, School of Nursing*, Dr. James C. McCann, 920-923-8094, Fax: 920-923-8770, E-mail: jcmccann70@marianuniversity.edu.

MARIETTA COLLEGE, Marietta, OH 45750-4000

General Information Independent, coed, comprehensive institution. *Enrollment:* 1,602 graduate, professional, and undergraduate students; 66 full-time matriculated graduate/professional students (49 women), 48 part-time matriculated graduate/professional students (29 women). *Enrollment by degree level:* 114 master's. *Graduate faculty:* 15 full-time (8 women), 4 part-time/adjunct (1 woman). *Graduate housing:* On-campus housing not available. *Student services:* Campus safety program, career counseling, free psychological counseling, international student services, services for students with disabilities, teacher training, writing training. *Library facilities:* Legacy Library. *Online resources:* library catalog, web page, access to other libraries' catalogs. *Collection:* 246,706 titles, 28,188 serial subscriptions, 6,147 audiovisual materials.

Computer facilities: 350 computers available on campus for general student use. A campuswide network can be accessed from student residence rooms and from off campus. Online class registration is available. *Web address:* http://www.marietta.edu/.

General Application Contact: Cathy J. Brown, Director of Graduate and Continuing Studies, 740-376-4740, Fax: 740-376-4423, E-mail: ce@marietta.edu.

GRADUATE UNITS

Program in Corporate Media Students: 10 full-time (6 women), 8 part-time (3 women). *Faculty:* 5 full-time (4 women), 2 part-time/adjunct (0 women). Expenses: Contact institution. Offers corporate media (MCM). *Application Contact:* Cathy J. Brown, Director of Graduate and Continuing Studies, 740-376-4740, Fax: 740-376-4423, E-mail: ce@marietta.edu. *Director*, Marilee Morrow, 740-376-4828, E-mail: marilee.morrow@marietta.edu.

Program in Education Students: 8 full-time (7 women), 30 part-time (19 women). Average age 35. *Faculty:* 2 full-time (1 woman), 2 part-time/adjunct (1 woman). Expenses: Contact institution. *Financial support:* Available to part-time students. *Degree program information:* Part-time and evening/weekend programs available. Offers education (MA). *Application deadline:* For fall admission, 8/23 priority date for domestic students. *Application fee:* $25. *Application Contact:* Cathy J. Brown, Director of Graduate and Continuing Studies, 740-376-4740, Fax: 740-376-4423, E-mail: ce@marietta.edu. *Chair*, Dr. Dorothy Erb, 740-376-4761.

Program in Physician Assistant Studies Students: 38 full-time (28 women). Average age 25. *Faculty:* 3 full-time (2 women), 1 part-time/adjunct (0 women). Expenses: Contact institution. Offers physician assistant studies (MS). *Application Contact:* Cathy J. Brown, Director of Graduate and Continuing Studies, 740-376-4740, Fax: 740-376-4423, E-mail: ce@marietta.edu. *Director*, Dr. Gloria M. Stewart, 740-370-4458.

Program in Psychology Students: 10 full-time (8 women), 9 part-time (7 women). Average age 22. *Faculty:* 3 full-time (1 woman). Expenses: Contact institution. Offers psychology (MAP). *Application Contact:* Cathy J. Brown, Director of Graduate and Continuing Studies, 740-376-4740, Fax: 740-376-4423, E-mail: ce@marietta.edu. *Chair*, Dr. Mark E. Sibicky, 740-376-4762, E-mail: sibickym@marietta.edu.

MARIST COLLEGE, Poughkeepsie, NY 12601-1387

General Information Independent, coed, comprehensive institution. *Graduate housing:* On-campus housing not available. *Research affiliation:* Hudson River Psychiatric Center, St. Francis Hospital, Dutchess County Community Mental Health Center, Center for Advanced Brain Imaging Psychology, NYSTAR (New York State Office of Technology and Academic Research), HVTDC (Hudson Valley Technology Development Corp.).

GRADUATE UNITS

Graduate Programs *Degree program information:* Part-time and evening/weekend programs available. Postbaccalaureate distance learning degree programs offered (minimal on-campus study). Electronic applications accepted.

School of Communication and the Arts *Degree program information:* Part-time programs available. Postbaccalaureate distance learning degree programs offered (no on-campus study). Offers organizational communication and leadership (MA). Electronic applications accepted.

School of Computer Science and Mathematics *Degree program information:* Part-time and evening/weekend programs available. Postbaccalaureate distance learning degree programs offered (minimal on-campus study). Offers information systems (MS, Adv C); software development (MS); technology management (MS). Electronic applications accepted.

School of Management *Degree program information:* Part-time and evening/weekend programs available. Postbaccalaureate distance learning degree programs offered (no on-campus study). Offers business administration (MBA, Adv C); executive leadership (Adv C); public administration (MPA); technology management (MS). Electronic applications accepted.

School of Social and Behavioral Sciences *Degree program information:* Part-time and evening/weekend programs available. Offers counseling psychology (MA); education (M Ed); education psychology (MA); school psychology (MA, Adv C). Electronic applications accepted.

MARLBORO COLLEGE, Marlboro, VT 05344

General Information Independent, coed, comprehensive institution. *Enrollment:* 330 graduate, professional, and undergraduate students; 4 full-time matriculated graduate/professional students (1 woman), 11 part-time matriculated graduate/professional students (4 women). *Enrollment by degree level:* 15 master's. *Graduate faculty:* 2 full-time (0 women), 20 part-time/adjunct (10 women). *Graduate housing:* On-campus housing not available. *Student services:* Low-cost health insurance, teacher training. *Library facilities:* Rice-Aron Library. *Online resources:* library catalog.

Computer facilities: 47 computers available on campus for general student use. A campuswide network can be accessed from student residence rooms and from off campus. *Web address:* http://www.marlboro.edu/.

General Application Contact: Joe Heslin, Associate Director of Admissions, 802-258-9209, Fax: 802-258-9201, E-mail: jheslin@marlboro.edu.

GRADUATE UNITS

Graduate School Students: 4 full-time (1 woman), 11 part-time (4 women). Average age 37. 10 applicants, 100% accepted, 8 enrolled. *Faculty:* 3 full-time (0 women), 20 part-time/adjunct (10 women). Expenses: Contact institution. *Financial support:* Applicants required to submit FAFSA. In 2008, 20 master's awarded. *Degree program information:* Part-time and evening/weekend programs available. Postbaccalaureate distance learning degree programs offered (minimal on-campus study). Offers (management) healthcare administration (MS); information technologies (MS); managing for sustainability (MBA); teaching with technology (MAT). *Application deadline:* Applications are processed on a rolling basis. *Application fee:* $0. Electronic applications accepted. *Application Contact:* Joe Heslin, Associate Director of Admissions, 802-258-9209, Fax: 802-258-9201, E-mail: jheslin@marlboro.edu. *Academic Director*, Peter Crowell, 802-258-9203, Fax: 802-258-9201, E-mail: pcrowell@marlboro.edu.

MARQUETTE UNIVERSITY, Milwaukee, WI 53201-1881

General Information Independent-religious, coed, university. CGS member. *Enrollment:* 11,633 graduate, professional, and undergraduate students; 2,068 full-time matriculated graduate/professional students (1,060 women), 1,428 part-time matriculated graduate/professional students (686 women). *Enrollment by degree level:* 1,071 first professional, 1,716 master's, 643 doctoral, 66 other advanced degrees. *Graduate faculty:* 652 full-time (252 women), 444 part-time/adjunct (183 women). *Tuition:* Full-time $15,120; part-time $840 per credit hour. *Graduate housing:* Rooms and/or apartments available on a first-come, first-served basis to single and married students. *Student services:* Campus employment opportunities, campus safety program, career counseling, child daycare facilities, exercise/wellness program, free psychological counseling, grant writing training, international student services, low-cost health insurance, multicultural affairs office, services for students with disabilities, teacher training, writing training. *Library facilities:* Raynor Memorial Libraries plus 1 other. *Online resources:* library catalog, web page, access to other libraries' catalogs. *Collection:* 1.6 million titles, 24,242 serial subscriptions. *Research affiliation:* NASA, Milwaukee Museum, Argonne National Laboratory, American Educational Research Association.

Computer facilities: 1,200 computers available on campus for general student use. A campuswide network can be accessed from student residence rooms and from off campus. Online class registration, AV Software are available. *Web address:* http://www.marquette.edu/.

General Application Contact: Erin Fox, Assistant Director for Recruitment, 414-288-5319, Fax: 414-288-1902, E-mail: erin.fox@marquette.edu.

GRADUATE UNITS

Graduate School Students: 995 full-time (606 women), 791 part-time (481 women); includes 167 minority (65 African Americans, 10 American Indian/Alaska Native, 51 Asian Americans or Pacific Islanders, 41 Hispanic Americans), 201 international. Average age 30. 2,006 applicants, 60% accepted, 478 enrolled. *Faculty:* 431 full-time (178 women), 386 part-time/adjunct (169 women). Expenses: Contact institution. *Financial support:* Fellowships, research assistantships with full tuition reimbursements, teaching assistantships with full tuition reimbursements, career-related internships or fieldwork, Federal Work-Study, institutionally

Marquette University (continued)

sponsored loans, scholarships/grants, and tuition waivers (full and partial) available. Support available to part-time students. Financial award application deadline: 2/15. In 2008, 610 master's, 126 doctorates awarded. *Degree program information:* Part-time and evening/weekend programs available. Offers interdisciplinary studies (PhD); public service (MAPS); transfusion medicine (MS). *Application deadline:* Applications are processed on a rolling basis. *Application fee:* $40. Electronic applications accepted. *Application Contact:* Erin Fox, Assistant Director for Recruitment, 414-288-5319, Fax: 414-288-1902, E-mail: erin.fox@marquette.edu. *Vice Provost for Research/Dean,* Dr. William Wiener, 414-288-1532, Fax: 414-288-1578.

College of Arts and Sciences Students: 365 full-time (149 women), 171 part-time (58 women); includes 37 minority (9 African Americans, 2 American Indian/Alaska Native, 13 Asian Americans or Pacific Islanders, 13 Hispanic Americans), 98 international. Average age 30. 848 applicants, 45% accepted, 114 enrolled. *Faculty:* 257 full-time (93 women), 90 part-time/adjunct (35 women). Expenses: Contact institution. *Financial support:* In 2008–09, 9 fellowships, 48 research assistantships, 196 teaching assistantships were awarded; career-related internships or fieldwork, Federal Work-Study, institutionally sponsored loans, scholarships/grants, and tuition waivers (full and partial) also available. Support available to part-time students. Financial award application deadline: 2/15. In 2008, 85 master's, 41 doctorates awarded. *Degree program information:* Part-time programs available. Offers American literature (PhD); analytical chemistry (MS, PhD); ancient philosophy (MA, PhD); arts and sciences (MA, MAT, MS, PhD); bioanalytical chemistry (MS, PhD); bioinformatics (MS); biophysical chemistry (MS, PhD); British and American literature (MA); British empiricism and analytic philosophy (MA, PhD); British literature (PhD); cell biology (MS, PhD); chemical physics (MS, PhD); Christian philosophy (MA, PhD); clinical psychology (MS); computational sciences (PhD); computers (MS); computing (MS); developmental biology (MS, PhD); early modern European philosophy (MA, PhD); ecology (MS, PhD); endocrinology (MS, PhD); ethics (MA, PhD); European history (MA, PhD); evolutionary biology (MS, PhD); genetics (MS, PhD); German philosophy (MA, PhD); historical theology (MA, PhD); inorganic chemistry (MS, PhD); international affairs (MA); mathematics education (MS); medieval history (MA); medieval philosophy (MA, PhD); microbiology (MS, PhD); molecular biology (MS, PhD); muscle and exercise physiology (MS, PhD); neurobiology (MS, PhD); organic chemistry (MS, PhD); phenomenology and existentialism (MA, PhD); philosophy of religion (MA, PhD); physical chemistry (MS, PhD); political science (MA); psychology (PhD); religious studies (PhD); Renaissance and Reformation (MA); reproductive physiology (MS, PhD); social and applied philosophy (MA); Spanish (MA, MAT); systematic theology (MA, PhD); theology (MA); theology and society (PhD); United States history (MA, PhD). *Application fee:* $40. *Application Contact:* Erin Fox, Assistant Director for Recruitment, 414-288-5319, Fax: 414-288-1902, E-mail: erin.fox@marquette.edu. *Dean,* Dr. Jeanne Hossenlopp, 414-288-7472.

College of Communication Students: 29 full-time (20 women), 24 part-time (19 women); includes 6 minority (1 African American, 2 American Indian/Alaska Native, 2 Asian Americans or Pacific Islanders, 1 Hispanic American), 10 international. Average age 26. 85 applicants, 52% accepted, 16 enrolled. *Faculty:* 31 full-time (17 women), 35 part-time/adjunct (16 women). Expenses: Contact institution. *Financial support:* In 2008–09, 6 research assistantships, 12 teaching assistantships were awarded; career-related internships or fieldwork, Federal Work-Study, institutionally sponsored loans, scholarships/grants, and tuition waivers (full and partial) also available. Support available to part-time students. Financial award application deadline: 2/15. In 2008, 17 master's awarded. *Degree program information:* Part-time and evening/weekend programs available. Offers advertising and public relations (MA); broadcasting and electronic communications (MA); communications studies (MA); journalism (MA); mass communications (MA); religious communications (MA); science, health and environmental communications (MA). *Application fee:* $40. *Application Contact:* Erin Fox, Assistant Director for Recruitment, 414-288-5319, Fax: 414-288-1902, E-mail: erin.fox@marquette.edu. *Dean,* Dr. Ana Garner, 414-288-3588, Fax: 414-288-1578.

College of Education Students: 119 full-time (96 women), 148 part-time (98 women); includes 31 minority (16 African Americans, 1 American Indian/Alaska Native, 8 Asian Americans or Pacific Islanders, 6 Hispanic Americans), 4 international. Average age 31. 275 applicants, 52% accepted, 75 enrolled. *Faculty:* 23 full-time (14 women), 23 part-time/adjunct (14 women). Expenses: Contact institution. *Financial support:* In 2008–09, 5 research assistantships, 5 teaching assistantships were awarded; Federal Work-Study, institutionally sponsored loans, scholarships/grants, and tuition waivers (full and partial) also available. Support available to part-time students. Financial award application deadline: 2/15. In 2008, 47 master's, 6 doctorates awarded. *Degree program information:* Part-time programs available. Offers education (MA, Ed D, PhD, Spec). *Application fee:* $40. *Application Contact:* Dr. Joan Whipp, Assistant Dean, 414-288-1421, Fax: 414-288-5333. *Dean,* Dr. Bill Henk, 414-288-7376.

College of Engineering Students: 125 full-time (41 women), 111 part-time (20 women); includes 15 minority (4 African Americans, 9 Asian Americans or Pacific Islanders, 2 Hispanic Americans), 81 international. Average age 27. 281 applicants, 64% accepted, 47 enrolled. *Faculty:* 61 full-time (8 women), 23 part-time/adjunct (14 women). Expenses: Contact institution. *Financial support:* In 2008–09, 115 students received support, including 30 fellowships with tuition reimbursements available (averaging $16,866 per year), 53 research assistantships with tuition reimbursements available (averaging $14,861 per year), 32 teaching assistantships with tuition reimbursements available (averaging $13,790 per year); Federal Work-Study, institutionally sponsored loans, scholarships/grants, and tuition waivers (full and partial) also available. Support available to part-time students. Financial award application deadline: 2/15. In 2008, 66 master's, 8 doctorates awarded. *Degree program information:* Part-time and evening/weekend programs available. Offers bioinstrumentation/computers (MS, PhD); biomechanics/biomaterials (MS, PhD); computing (MS); construction and public works management (MS, PhD); electrical engineering (MS, PhD); engineering (MS, PhD); engineering management (MS); environmental/water resources engineering (MS, PhD); functional imaging (PhD); healthcare technologies management (MS); mechanical engineering (MS, PhD); structural/geotechnical engineering (MS, PhD); systems physiology (MS, PhD); transportation planning and engineering (MS, PhD). *Application deadline:* Applications are processed on a rolling basis. *Application fee:* $40. Electronic applications accepted. *Application Contact:* Craig Pierce, Director of Admissions, 414-288-7137, Fax: 414-288-1902, E-mail: mugs@vms.csd.mu.edu. *Dean,* Dr. Stan V. Jaskolski, 414-288-6591, Fax: 414-288-7082, E-mail: stan.jaskolski@marquette.edu.

College of Health Sciences Students: 222 full-time (185 women), 5 part-time (all women); includes 25 minority (4 African Americans, 2 American Indian/Alaska Native, 10 Asian Americans or Pacific Islanders, 9 Hispanic Americans), 2 international. Average age 24. 367 applicants, 34% accepted, 94 enrolled. *Faculty:* 30 full-time (19 women), 17 part-time/adjunct (9 women). Expenses: Contact institution. In 2008, 61 master's, 68 doctorates awarded. Offers health sciences (MS, DPT); physical therapy (DPT); physician assistant studies (MS); speech-language pathology (MS). *Application Contact:* Erin Fox, Assistant Director for Recruitment, 414-288-5319, Fax: 414-288-1902, E-mail: erin.fox@marquette.edu. *Dean,* Dr. Jack C. Brooks, 414-288-5053, E-mail: jack.brooks@mu.edu.

College of Nursing Students: 114 full-time (101 women), 200 part-time (191 women); includes 26 minority (13 African Americans, 2 American Indian/Alaska Native, 6 Asian Americans or Pacific Islanders, 5 Hispanic Americans), 2 international. Average age 32. 174 applicants, 82% accepted, 102 enrolled. *Faculty:* 29 full-time (27 women), 43 part-time/adjunct (all women). Expenses: Contact institution. *Financial support:* In 2008–09, 6 research assistantships, 1 teaching assistantship were awarded; career-related internships or fieldwork, Federal Work-Study, institutionally sponsored loans, scholarships/grants, and tuition waivers (full and partial) also available. Support available to part-time students. Financial award application deadline: 2/15. In 2008, 46 master's awarded. *Degree program information:* Part-time and evening/weekend programs available. Offers adult nurse practitioner (Certificate); advanced practice nursing (MSN); gerontological nurse practitioner (Certificate); neonatal nurse practitioner (Certificate); nurse-midwifery (Certificate); nursing (PhD); pediatric nurse practitioner (Certificate). *Application fee:* $40. *Application Contact:* Dr. Judy Miller, Director of Graduate Studies, 414-288-3810, Fax: 414-288-1578. *Dean,* Dr. Lea Acord, 414-288-3812, Fax: 414-288-1578.

Graduate School of Management Students: 128 full-time (51 women), 479 part-time (132 women); includes 53 minority (8 African Americans, 1 American Indian/Alaska Native, 36 Asian Americans or Pacific Islanders, 8 Hispanic Americans), 54 international. Average age 30. 341 applicants, 81% accepted, 155 enrolled. *Faculty:* 67 full-time (18 women), 37 part-time/adjunct (8 women). Expenses: Contact institution. *Financial support:* In 2008–09, 4 research assistantships, 13 teaching assistantships were awarded; Federal Work-Study, institutionally sponsored loans, scholarships/grants, and tuition waivers (full and partial) also available. Support available to part-time students. Financial award application deadline: 2/15. In 2008, 231 master's awarded. *Degree program information:* Part-time and evening/weekend programs available. Offers accounting (MSA); business administration (MBA); business economics (MSAE); entrepreneurship (Graduate Certificate); financial economics (MSAE); human resources (MSHR); international economics (MSAE); management (MBA, MSA, MSAE, MSHR, Graduate Certificate). *Application fee:* $40. *Application Contact:* Erin Fox, Assistant Director for Recruitment, 414-288-5319, Fax: 414-288-1902, E-mail: erin.fox@marquette.edu. *Dean,* Dr. David Shrock, 414-288-7141, Fax: 414-288-1578.

Law School *Degree program information:* Part-time and evening/weekend programs available. Offers law (JD). Electronic applications accepted.

School of Dentistry Offers advanced training in general dentistry (MS); dental biomaterials (MS); dentistry (DDS, MS); endodontics (MS); orthodontics (MS); prosthodontics (MS).

MARSHALL UNIVERSITY, Huntington, WV 25755

General Information State-supported, coed, university. CGS member. *Enrollment:* 13,573 graduate, professional, and undergraduate students; 1,721 full-time matriculated graduate/professional students (1,015 women), 1,726 part-time matriculated graduate/professional students (1,252 women). *Enrollment by degree level:* 277 first professional, 2,877 master's, 219 doctoral, 74 other advanced degrees. *Graduate faculty:* 369 full-time (145 women), 147 part-time/adjunct (101 women). *Graduate housing:* Rooms and/or apartments available on a first-come, first-served basis to single and married students. *Student services:* Campus employment opportunities, campus safety program, career counseling, child daycare facilities, exercise/wellness program, free psychological counseling, grant writing training, international student services, low-cost health insurance, multicultural affairs office, services for students with disabilities, teacher training, writing training. *Library facilities:* John Deaver Drinko Library plus 2 others. *Online resources:* library catalog, web page. *Collection:* 1.6 million titles, 37,178 serial subscriptions, 209,256 audiovisual materials. *Research affiliation:* Bayer Corporation (field research), Kanawha Valley Local Port District (field research), Greenbrier County Commission (field research), Dominion Power (field research), Wyeth Ayerst Pharmaceutical (clinical pharmaceutical study).

Computer facilities: 1,461 computers available on campus for general student use. A campuswide network can be accessed from student residence rooms and from off campus. Online class registration is available. *Web address:* http://www.marshall.edu/.

General Application Contact: Graduate Admissions, 304-746-1900, Fax: 304-746-1902, E-mail: services@marshall.edu.

GRADUATE UNITS

Academic Affairs Division Students: 1,444 full-time (883 women), 1,726 part-time (1,252 women); includes 128 minority (81 African Americans, 12 American Indian/Alaska Native, 24 Asian Americans or Pacific Islanders, 11 Hispanic Americans), 192 international. Average age 33. *Faculty:* 369 full-time (145 women), 147 part-time/adjunct (101 women). Expenses: Contact institution. *Financial support:* Fellowships, research assistantships, teaching assistantships, career-related internships or fieldwork, Federal Work-Study, tuition waivers (full and partial), and unspecified assistantships available. Support available to part-time students. In 2008, 852 master's, 15 doctorates, 4 other advanced degrees awarded. *Degree program information:* Part-time and evening/weekend programs available. *Application deadline:* Applications are processed on a rolling basis. *Application fee:* $40 ($100 for international students). *Application Contact:* Graduate Admissions, 304-746-1900, Fax: 304-746-1902, E-mail: services@marshall.edu. *Provost and Senior Vice President for Academic Affairs,* Dr. Gayle Ormiston, 304-696-3716, E-mail: Ormiston@marshall.edu.

College of Education and Human Services Students: 545 full-time (382 women), 1,189 part-time (935 women); includes 65 minority (50 African Americans, 4 American Indian/Alaska Native, 8 Asian Americans or Pacific Islanders, 3 Hispanic Americans), 64 international. Average age 35. *Faculty:* 45 full-time (24 women), 40 part-time/adjunct (24 women). Expenses: Contact institution. *Financial support:* Career-related internships or fieldwork, Federal Work-Study, tuition waivers (full and partial), and unspecified assistantships available. Support available to part-time students. In 2008, 414 master's, 12 doctorates, 4 other advanced degrees awarded. *Degree program information:* Evening/weekend programs available. Offers adult and technical education (MS); counseling (MA, Ed S); early childhood education (MA); education (MAT); education and human services (MA, MAT, MS, Ed D, Ed S); education and professional development (MA, Ed D, Ed S); elementary education (MA); exercise science (MS); exercise science, sport and recreation (MS); family and consumer sciences (MA); human development and allied technology (MA, MS); leadership studies (MA, Ed D, Ed S); reading education (MA, Ed S); school psychology (Ed S); secondary education (MA); special education (MA); sport administration (MS). *Application deadline:* Applications are processed on a rolling basis. *Application fee:* $40 ($100 for international students). *Application Contact:* Graduate Admissions, 304-746-1900, Fax: 304-746-1902, E-mail: services@marshall.edu. *Executive Dean,* Dr. Rosalyn Anstine Templeton, 304-696-3131, E-mail: templetonr@marshall.edu.

College of Fine Arts Students: 22 full-time (12 women), 13 part-time (6 women); includes 2 minority (1 American Indian/Alaska Native, 1 Asian American or Pacific Islander), 4 international. Average age 29. *Faculty:* 29 full-time (10 women), 11 part-time/adjunct (10 women). Expenses: Contact institution. In 2008, 12 master's awarded. *Degree program information:* Evening/weekend programs available. Offers art (MA); fine arts (MA); music (MA). *Application fee:* $40. *Application Contact:* Information Contact, 304-746-1900, Fax: 304-746-1902, E-mail: services@marshall.edu. *Dean,* Dr. Donald Van Horn, 304-696-2964, E-mail: vanhorn@marshall.edu.

College of Health Professions Students: 69 full-time (66 women), 98 part-time (89 women); includes 3 minority (1 African American, 1 American Indian/Alaska Native, 1 Hispanic American). Average age 33. *Faculty:* 41 full-time (37 women), 16 part-time/adjunct (13 women). Expenses: Contact institution. In 2008, 57 master's awarded. Offers communication disorders (MA); dietetics (MS); health professions (MA, MS, MSN); nursing (MSN). *Application fee:* $40. *Application Contact:* Information Contact, 304-746-1900, Fax: 304-746-1902, E-mail: services@marshall.edu. *Dean,* Dr. Shortie McKinney, 304-696-5270, E-mail: mckinnes@marshall.edu.

College of Information Technology and Engineering Students: 72 full-time (21 women), 114 part-time (26 women); includes 5 minority (4 African Americans, 1 Hispanic American), 35 international. Average age 33. *Faculty:* 23 full-time (3 women), 9 part-time/adjunct (0 women). Expenses: Contact institution. *Financial support:* Fellowships, tuition waivers (full) available. Support available to part-time students. Financial award application deadline: 8/1; financial award applicants required to submit FAFSA. In 2008, 42 master's awarded. *Degree program information:* Part-time and evening/weekend programs available. Offers applied science and technology (MS); engineering (MSE); environmental science (MS); information systems (MS); information technology and engineering (MS, MSE); safety (MS); technology management (MS). *Application fee:* $40. *Application Contact:* Information Contact, 304-746-1900, Fax: 304-746-1902, E-mail: services@marshall.edu. *Dean,* Dr. Betsy Dulin, 304-746-2087, E-mail: bdulin@marshall.edu.

College of Liberal Arts Students: 250 full-time (156 women), 90 part-time (53 women); includes 14 minority (8 African Americans, 2 American Indian/Alaska Native, 1 Asian American or Pacific Islander, 3 Hispanic Americans), 19 international. Average age 29. *Faculty:* 100 full-time (40 women), 127 part-time/adjunct (65 women). Expenses: Contact institution. *Financial support:* Fellowships, teaching assistantships with tuition reimbursements available. In 2008, 92 master's, 3 doctorates awarded. *Degree program information:* Evening/weekend programs available. Offers clinical psychology (MA); communication studies (MA); criminal justice (MS); English (MA); general psychology (MA); geography (MA, MS); history (MA); humanities (MA); industrial and organizational psychology (MA);

Latin (MA); liberal arts (MA, MS, Psy D); political science (MA); psychology (Psy D); sociology (MA); Spanish (MA). *Application fee:* $40. *Application Contact:* Graduate Admissions, 304-746-1900, Fax: 304-746-1902, E-mail: services@marshall.edu. *Dean,* Dr. David J. Pittenger, 304-696-2530.

College of Science Students: 76 full-time (30 women), 11 part-time (7 women); includes 5 minority (2 African Americans, 3 American Indian/Alaska Native), 18 international. Average age 26. *Faculty:* 61 full-time (16 women), 32 part-time/adjunct (12 women). Expenses: Contact institution. *Financial support:* Career-related internships or fieldwork available. In 2008, 35 master's awarded. Offers biological science (MA, MS); chemistry (MS); mathematics (MA, MS); physical science (MS); science (MA, MS). *Application fee:* $40. *Application Contact:* Graduate Admissions, 304-746-1900, Fax: 304-746-1902, E-mail: services@marshall.edu. *Interim Dean,* Dr. Wayne Elmore, 304-696-3638, E-mail: elmore@marshall.edu.

Lewis College of Business Students: 301 full-time (150 women), 106 part-time (57 women); includes 32 minority (15 African Americans, 14 Asian Americans or Pacific Islanders, 3 Hispanic Americans), 44 international. Average age 29. *Faculty:* 48 full-time (15 women), 10 part-time/adjunct (3 women). Expenses: Contact institution. *Financial support:* Career-related internships or fieldwork and tuition waivers (full) available. Support available to part-time students. Financial award applicants required to submit FAFSA. In 2008, 192 master's, 5 doctorates awarded. *Degree program information:* Part-time and evening/weekend programs available. Offers business (IMBA, MBA, MS, DMPNA, Graduate Certificate); business administration (IMBA, MBA); business management foundations (Graduate Certificate); health care administration (MS, DMPNA); human resource management (MS); management (IMBA, MBA, MS, DMPNA, Graduate Certificate). *Application deadline:* Applications are processed on a rolling basis. *Application fee:* $40. *Application Contact:* Dr. Uday Tate, Information Contact, 304-696-2672, Fax: 304-746-1902, E-mail: tate@marshall.edu. *Dean,* Dr. Chong Kim, 304-696-2862, Fax: 304-696-4344, E-mail: kim@marshall.edu.

School of Journalism and Mass Communications Students: 18 full-time (12 women), 6 part-time (4 women); includes 2 minority (1 African American, 1 American Indian/Alaska Native), 8 international. Average age 28. *Faculty:* 3 full-time (0 women), 4 part-time/adjunct (1 woman). Expenses: Contact institution. In 2008, 8 master's awarded. Offers journalism and mass communications (MAJ). *Application fee:* $40. *Application Contact:* Janet Dooley, Assistant Dean, 304-696-2734, Fax: 304-746-1902, E-mail: dooley@marshall.edu. *Dean,* Dr. Corley F. Dennison, 304-696-2809, E-mail: dennisoc@marshall.edu.

Joan C. Edwards School of Medicine Offers biomedical sciences (MS, PhD); medicine (MD, MS, PhD). Electronic applications accepted.

MARS HILL GRADUATE SCHOOL, Seattle, WA 98121

General Information Independent-religious, coed, graduate-only institution.

GRADUATE UNITS

Graduate Programs *Degree program information:* Part-time programs available.

MARTIN UNIVERSITY, Indianapolis, IN 46218-3867

General Information Independent, coed, comprehensive institution. *Graduate housing:* On-campus housing not available.

GRADUATE UNITS

Division of Psychology *Degree program information:* Part-time and evening/weekend programs available. Offers community psychology (MS).

Graduate School of Urban Ministry *Degree program information:* Part-time and evening/weekend programs available. Offers urban ministry studies (MA).

MARY BALDWIN COLLEGE, Staunton, VA 24401-3610

General Information Independent, Undergraduate: women only; graduate: coed, comprehensive institution. *Graduate housing:* On-campus housing not available.

GRADUATE UNITS

Graduate Studies *Degree program information:* Part-time and evening/weekend programs available. Postbaccalaureate distance learning degree programs offered (minimal on-campus study). Offers acting (M Litt); directing (M Litt); elementary education (MAT); middle grades education (MAT); Shakespeare and Renaissance literature in performance (M Litt, MFA); teaching (M Litt, MAT).

MARYGROVE COLLEGE, Detroit, MI 48221-2599

General Information Independent-religious, coed, primarily women, comprehensive institution. *Graduate housing:* Room and/or apartments available to single students; on-campus housing not available to married students.

GRADUATE UNITS

Graduate Division *Degree program information:* Part-time and evening/weekend programs available. Postbaccalaureate distance learning degree programs offered (no on-campus study). Offers art of teaching (MAT); educational leadership (MA); English (MA); Griot (M Ed); human resource management (MA); modern language translation (Certificate); reading and literacy (M Ed); Sage (M Ed); social justice (MA). Electronic applications accepted.

MARYLAND INSTITUTE COLLEGE OF ART, Baltimore, MD 21217

General Information Independent, coed, comprehensive institution. *Enrollment:* 1,847 graduate, professional, and undergraduate students; 145 full-time matriculated graduate/professional students (86 women), 69 part-time matriculated graduate/professional students (57 women). *Enrollment by degree level:* 194 master's, 20 other advanced degrees. *Graduate faculty:* 20 full-time (16 women), 28 part-time/adjunct (12 women). *Tuition:* Full-time $31,640; part-time $1318 per credit. *Required fees:* $1040; $520 per semester. *Graduate housing:* Room and/or apartments available on a first-come, first-served basis to single students; on-campus housing not available to married students. Typical cost: $5850 per year ($8090 including board). Room and board charges vary according to board plan and housing facility selected. Housing application deadline: 5/1. *Student services:* Campus employment opportunities, campus safety program, career counseling, exercise/wellness program, free psychological counseling, grant writing training, international student services, low-cost health insurance, multicultural affairs office, services for students with disabilities, teacher training, writing training. *Library facilities:* Decker Library plus 1 other. *Online resources:* library catalog, web page, access to other libraries' catalogs. *Collection:* 84,200 titles, 317 serial subscriptions, 5,100 audiovisual materials.

Computer facilities: 440 computers available on campus for general student use. A campuswide network can be accessed from student residence rooms and from off campus. Online class registration, campus Portal, online gallery space, network storage space, personal websites are available. *Web address:* http://www.mica.edu/.

General Application Contact: Scott G. Kelly, Associate Dean of Graduate Admission, 410-225-2256, Fax: 410-225-2408, E-mail: graduate@mica.edu.

GRADUATE UNITS

Graduate Studies Students: 145 full-time (86 women), 69 part-time (57 women); includes 24 minority (11 African Americans, 1 American Indian/Alaska Native, 8 Asian Americans or Pacific Islanders, 4 Hispanic Americans), 15 international. Average age 30. *Faculty:* 20 full-time (16 women), 28 part-time/adjunct (12 women). Expenses: Contact institution. *Financial support:* In 2008–09, 208 students received support, including 18 fellowships (averaging $15,820 per year), 109 teaching assistantships (averaging $1,500 per year); career-related internships or fieldwork and scholarships/grants also available. Financial award application deadline: 3/1; financial award applicants required to submit FAFSA. In 2008, 111 master's, 21 other advanced degrees awarded. *Degree program information:* Part-time programs available. Offers art education (MA, MAT); community arts (MA); fine arts (Certificate); graphic design (MFA); photographic and electronic media (MFA); studio art (MFA). *Application deadline:* For fall admission, 2/15 for domestic and international students. *Application fee:* $50. *Application Contact:* Scott G. Kelly, Associate Dean of Graduate Admission, 410-225-2256, Fax: 410-225-2408, E-mail: graduate@mica.edu. *Assistant Dean of Graduate Studies,* Erin Jakowski, 410-225-5273, Fax: 410-225-5275, E-mail: graduate@mica.edu.

Hoffberger School of Painting Students: 14 full-time (11 women); includes 1 minority (African American), 3 international. Average age 31. *Faculty:* 1 (woman) full-time, 3 part-time/adjunct (1 woman). Expenses: Contact institution. *Financial support:* In 2008–09, 14 students received support, including 1 fellowship (averaging $15,820 per year), 12 teaching assistantships (averaging $1,500 per year); career-related internships or fieldwork and scholarships/grants also available. Financial award application deadline: 3/1; financial award applicants required to submit FAFSA. In 2008, 6 master's awarded. Offers painting (MFA). *Application deadline:* For fall admission, 2/15 for domestic and international students. *Application fee:* $50. *Application Contact:* Scott G. Kelly, Associate Dean of Graduate Admission, 410-225-2256, Fax: 410-225-2408, E-mail: graduate@mica.edu. *Director,* Joyce Kozloff, 410-225-5273, Fax: 410-225-5275, E-mail: graduate@mica.edu.

Mount Royal School of Art Students: 25 full-time (10 women); includes 5 minority (2 African Americans, 1 Asian American or Pacific Islander, 2 Hispanic Americans), 2 international. Average age 27. *Faculty:* 1 (woman) full-time, 3 part-time/adjunct (1 woman). Expenses: Contact institution. *Financial support:* In 2008–09, 25 students received support, including 4 fellowships (averaging $15,820 per year), 21 teaching assistantships (averaging $1,500 per year); career-related internships or fieldwork and scholarships/grants also available. Financial award application deadline: 3/1; financial award applicants required to submit FAFSA. In 2008, 12 master's awarded. Offers painting (MFA). *Application deadline:* For fall admission, 2/15 for domestic and international students. *Application fee:* $50. *Application Contact:* Scott G. Kelly, Associate Dean of Graduate Admission, 410-225-2256, Fax: 410-225-2408, E-mail: graduate@mica.edu. *Director,* Frances Barth, 410-230-9479, Fax: 410-225-5275, E-mail: graduate@mica.edu.

Rinehart School of Sculpture Students: 11 full-time (7 women); includes 2 minority (1 Asian American or Pacific Islander, 1 Hispanic American). Average age 31. *Faculty:* 1 (woman) full-time. Expenses: Contact institution. *Financial support:* In 2008–09, 11 students received support, including 2 fellowships (averaging $15,820 per year), 9 teaching assistantships (averaging $1,500 per year); career-related internships or fieldwork and scholarships/grants also available. Financial award application deadline: 3/1; financial award applicants required to submit FAFSA. In 2008, 3 master's awarded. Offers sculpture (MFA). *Application deadline:* For fall admission, 2/15 for domestic and international students. *Application fee:* $50. *Application Contact:* Scott G. Kelly, Associate Dean of Graduate Admission, 410-225-2256, Fax: 410-225-2408, E-mail: graduate@mica.edu. *Director,* Maren Hassinger, 410-225-2534, Fax: 410-225-2408.

MARYLHURST UNIVERSITY, Marylhurst, OR 97036-0261

General Information Independent-religious, coed, primarily women, comprehensive institution. *Enrollment:* 1,802 graduate, professional, and undergraduate students; 161 full-time matriculated graduate/professional students (119 women), 695 part-time matriculated graduate/professional students (449 women). *Enrollment by degree level:* 27 first professional, 829 master's. *Graduate faculty:* 12 full-time (8 women), 73 part-time/adjunct (41 women). *Tuition:* Full-time $11,988; part-time $444 per quarter hour. *Required fees:* $297; $11 per quarter hour. *Graduate housing:* On-campus housing not available. *Student services:* Career counseling, international student services, low-cost health insurance, services for students with disabilities, writing training. *Online resources:* library catalog, access to other libraries' catalogs. *Collection:* 97,747 titles, 18,234 serial subscriptions, 4,617 audiovisual materials.

Computer facilities: 40 computers available on campus for general student use. A campuswide network can be accessed. Online class registration is available. *Web address:* http://www.marylhurst.edu/.

General Application Contact: Office of Admissions, 503-636-8141 Ext. 6268, Fax: 503-635-6585, E-mail: admissions@marylhurst.edu.

GRADUATE UNITS

Department of Art Therapy Counseling Students: 48 full-time (46 women), 5 part-time (all women); includes 2 minority (1 African American, 1 Asian American or Pacific Islander). Average age 32. 26 applicants, 96% accepted, 21 enrolled. *Faculty:* 3 full-time (all women), 4 part-time/adjunct (all women). Expenses: Contact institution. *Financial support:* Federal Work-Study and scholarships/grants available. Support available to part-time students. Financial award applicants required to submit FAFSA. In 2008, 19 master's awarded. *Degree program information:* Part-time programs available. Offers art therapy (PGC); art therapy counseling (MA); counseling (PGC). *Application deadline:* For fall admission, 1/31 priority date for domestic and international students. Applications are processed on a rolling basis. *Application fee:* $40 ($50 for international students). *Application Contact:* Kathleen Schneff, Admissions Specialist, 800-634-9982 Ext. 3322, Fax: 503-635-6585, E-mail: admissions@marylhurst.edu. *Chair,* Christine Turner, 503-636-8141, Fax: 503-636-9526, E-mail: cturner@marylhurst.edu.

Department of Business Administration Students: 20 full-time (11 women), 452 part-time (255 women); includes 31 minority (12 African Americans, 12 Asian Americans or Pacific Islanders, 7 Hispanic Americans), 13 international. Average age 37. 213 applicants, 83% accepted, 149 enrolled. *Faculty:* 2 full-time (1 woman), 28 part-time/adjunct (5 women). Expenses: Contact institution. *Financial support:* Federal Work-Study and scholarships/grants available. Support available to part-time students. Financial award applicants required to submit FAFSA. In 2008, 98 master's awarded. *Degree program information:* Part-time and evening/weekend programs available. Postbaccalaureate distance learning degree programs offered (no on-campus study). Offers finance (MBA); general management (MBA); health care management (MBA); marketing (MBA); nonprofit management (MBA); organizational behavior (MBA); real estate (MBA); sustainable business (MBA). *Application deadline:* For fall admission, 9/11 priority date for domestic and international students; for winter admission, 12/15 priority date for domestic and international students; for spring admission, 3/17 priority date for domestic and international students. Applications are processed on a rolling basis. *Application fee:* $40 ($50 for international students). Electronic applications accepted. *Application Contact:* Kathleen Schneff, Admissions Specialist, 800-634-9982 Ext. 3322, Fax: 503-635-6585, E-mail: admissions@marylhurst.edu. *Director of Business and Real Estate Programs,* Bob Hanks, 503-636-8141, Fax: 503-697-5597, E-mail: mba@marylhurst.edu.

Department of Education Students: 76 full-time (48 women), 17 part-time (11 women); includes 1 minority (Hispanic American). Average age 35. 61 applicants, 97% accepted, 53 enrolled. *Faculty:* 4 full-time (2 women), 30 part-time/adjunct (26 women). Expenses: Contact institution. *Financial support:* Federal Work-Study and scholarships/grants available. Support available to part-time students. Financial award applicants required to submit FAFSA. *Degree program information:* Part-time programs available. Offers education (M Ed, MA). *Application deadline:* For fall admission, 3/1 priority date for domestic and international students. Applications are processed on a rolling basis. *Application fee:* $40 ($50 for international students). *Application Contact:* Kathleen Schneff, Admissions Specialist, 800-634-9982 Ext. 3322, Fax: 503-635-6585, E-mail: admissions@marylhurst.edu. *Chair,* Dr. Thomas Ruhl, 503-636-8141, Fax: 503-636-9526, E-mail: truhl@marylhurst.edu.

Department of Interdisciplinary Studies Students: 1 (woman) full-time, 30 part-time (21 women); includes 1 minority (Hispanic American). Average age 47. 11 applicants, 82% accepted, 9 enrolled. *Faculty:* 2 full-time (both women), 2 part-time/adjunct (1 woman). Expenses: Contact institution. *Financial support:* Federal Work-Study and scholarships/grants available. Support available to part-time students. Financial award applicants required to submit FAFSA. In 2008, 10 master's awarded. *Degree program information:* Part-time and evening/weekend programs available. Offers interdisciplinary studies (MA). *Application deadline:* Applications are processed on a rolling basis. *Application fee:* $40 ($50 for international students). Electronic applications accepted. *Application Contact:* Kathleen Schneff, Admissions Specialist, 800-634-9982 Ext. 3322, Fax: 503-635-6585, E-mail: admissions@marylhurst.edu. *Chair,* Dr. Debrah B. Bokowski, 503-636-8141, Fax: 503-697-5597, E-mail: dbokowski@marylhurst.edu.

Department of Religious StudiesûApplied Theology Program Students: 3 full-time (all women), 24 part-time (17 women). Average age 48. 6 applicants, 100% accepted, 6 enrolled.

Marylhurst University (continued)

Faculty: 1 full-time (0 women), 9 part-time/adjunct (5 women). Expenses: Contact institution. *Financial support:* Fellowships, research assistantships, teaching assistantships, Federal Work-Study and scholarships/grants available. Support available to part-time students. Financial award applicants required to submit FAFSA. In 2008, 9 master's awarded. *Degree program information:* Part-time and evening/weekend programs available. Offers applied theology (MA). *Application deadline:* For fall admission, 6/30 priority date for domestic students, 6/30 for international students; for winter admission, 11/30 priority date for domestic students, 11/30 for international students; for spring admission, 3/30 priority date for domestic students, 3/30 for international students. Applications are processed on a rolling basis. *Application fee:* $40 ($50 for international students). Electronic applications accepted. *Application Contact:* Kathleen Schneff, Admissions Specialist, 800-634-9982 Ext. 3322, Fax: 503-635-6585, E-mail: admissions@marylhurst.edu. *Chair,* Dr. Jerry Roussell, 503-636-8141, Fax: 503-697-5597, E-mail: jroussell@marylhurst.edu.

Department of Religious StudiesûDivinity Program Students: 11 full-time (9 women), 16 part-time (13 women). Average age 48. 9 applicants, 89% accepted, 8 enrolled. *Faculty:* 1 full-time (0 women), 9 part-time/adjunct (5 women). Expenses: Contact institution. *Financial support:* Fellowships, research assistantships, teaching assistantships, Federal Work-Study and scholarships/grants available. Support available to part-time students. Financial award applicants required to submit FAFSA. In 2008, 6 M Divs awarded. *Degree program information:* Part-time and evening/weekend programs available. Offers divinity (M Div). *Application deadline:* For fall admission, 6/30 for domestic students; for winter admission, 11/30 for domestic students; for spring admission, 3/30 for domestic students. Applications are processed on a rolling basis. *Application fee:* $40 ($50 for international students). Electronic applications accepted. *Application Contact:* Kathleen Schneff, Admissions Specialist, 800-634-9982 Ext. 3322, Fax: 503-635-6585, E-mail: admissions@marylhurst.edu. *Chair,* Dr. Jerry Roussell, 503-636-8141, Fax: 503-697-5597, E-mail: jroussell@marylhurst.edu.

MARYMOUNT UNIVERSITY, Arlington, VA 22207-4299

General Information Independent-religious, coed, comprehensive institution. CGS member. *Enrollment:* 3,548 graduate, professional, and undergraduate students; 487 full-time matriculated graduate/professional students (395 women), 792 part-time matriculated graduate/professional students (622 women). *Enrollment by degree level:* 1,046 master's, 162 doctoral, 71 other advanced degrees. *Graduate faculty:* 70 full-time (48 women), 55 part-time/adjunct (31 women). *Tuition:* Full-time $12,420; part-time $690 per credit hour. *Required fees:* $126; $7 per credit hour. Tuition and fees vary according to degree level. *Graduate housing:* On-campus housing not available. *Student services:* Campus employment opportunities, campus safety program, career counseling, free psychological counseling, international student services, low-cost health insurance, services for students with disabilities, teacher training. *Library facilities:* Emerson C. Reinsch Library plus 1 other. *Online resources:* library catalog, web page, access to other libraries' catalogs. *Collection:* 187,097 titles, 1,048 serial subscriptions.

Computer facilities: 260 computers available on campus for general student use. A campuswide network can be accessed from student residence rooms. Online class registration, online drive space are available. *Web address:* http://www.marymount.edu/.

General Application Contact: Francesca Reed, Director, Graduate Admissions, 703-284-5901, Fax: 703-527-3815, E-mail: grad.admissions@marymount.edu.

GRADUATE UNITS

Academic Outreach Program Students: 20 part-time (15 women); includes 7 minority (5 African Americans, 2 Asian Americans or Pacific Islanders). Average age 41. *Faculty:* 1 part-time/adjunct (0 women). Expenses: Contact institution. *Financial support:* In 2008–09, 7 students received support. Career-related internships or fieldwork, Federal Work-Study, scholarships/grants, and unspecified assistantships available. Support available to part-time students. Financial award applicants required to submit FAFSA. *Degree program information:* Part-time and evening/weekend programs available. Offers health care management (MS); management studies (Certificate); organization development (Certificate). *Application deadline:* For fall admission, 7/1 for international students; for spring admission, 10/15 for international students. Applications are processed on a rolling basis. *Application fee:* $40. Electronic applications accepted. *Application Contact:* Francesca Reed, Director, Graduate Admissions, 703-284-5901, Fax: 703-527-3815, E-mail: grad.admissions@marymount.edu. *Assistant Vice President for Graduate and Adult Education,* Dr. Donald Shandler, 703-284-5716, E-mail: donald.shandler@marymount.edu.

School of Arts and Sciences Students: 28 full-time (all women), 52 part-time (46 women); includes 20 minority (13 African Americans, 3 Asian Americans or Pacific Islanders, 4 Hispanic Americans), 2 international. Average age 34. 33 applicants, 100% accepted, 19 enrolled. *Faculty:* 10 full-time (8 women), 3 part-time/adjunct (2 women). Expenses: Contact institution. *Financial support:* In 2008–09, 49 students received support; research assistantships with full and partial tuition reimbursements available, career-related internships or fieldwork, Federal Work-Study, scholarships/grants, and unspecified assistantships available. Support available to part-time students. Financial award applicants required to submit FAFSA. In 2008, 26 master's awarded. *Degree program information:* Part-time and evening/weekend programs available. Offers arts and sciences (MA); humanities (MA); interior design (MA); literature and languages (MA). *Application deadline:* For fall admission, 7/1 for international students; for spring admission, 10/15 for international students. Applications are processed on a rolling basis. *Application fee:* $40. Electronic applications accepted. *Application Contact:* Francesca Reed, Director, Graduate Admissions, 703-284-5901, Fax: 703-527-3815, E-mail: grad.admissions@marymount.edu. *Dean,* Dr. Teresa Reed, 703-284-1560, Fax: 703-284-3859, E-mail: teresa.reed@marymount.edu.

School of Business Administration Students: 95 full-time (54 women), 301 part-time (199 women); includes 162 minority (95 African Americans, 1 American Indian/Alaska Native, 33 Asian Americans or Pacific Islanders, 33 Hispanic Americans), 40 international. Average age 32. 191 applicants, 95% accepted, 113 enrolled. *Faculty:* 25 full-time (14 women), 20 part-time/adjunct (6 women). Expenses: Contact institution. *Financial support:* Research assistantships with full tuition reimbursements, career-related internships or fieldwork, Federal Work-Study, scholarships/grants, and unspecified assistantships available. Support available to part-time students. Financial award applicants required to submit FAFSA. In 2008, 140 master's, 12 other advanced degrees awarded. *Degree program information:* Part-time and evening/weekend programs available. Offers business administration (MA, MBA, MS, Certificate); computer security and information assurance (Certificate); forensic computing (Certificate); health care informatics (Certificate); health care management (MS); human resource management (MA, Certificate); information technology (MS, Certificate); information technology project management: technology leadership (Certificate); instructional design (Certificate); leadership (Certificate); legal administration (MA); management (MS); organization development (Certificate); paralegal studies (Certificate); project management (Certificate). *Application deadline:* For fall admission, 7/15 for international students; for spring admission, 10/15 for international students. Applications are processed on a rolling basis. *Application fee:* $40. Electronic applications accepted. *Application Contact:* Francesca Reed, Director, Graduate Admissions, 703-284-5901, Fax: 703-527-3815, E-mail: grad.admissions@marymount.edu. *Dean,* James Ryerson, 703-284-5910, Fax: 703-527-3830, E-mail: james.ryerson@marymount.edu.

School of Education and Human Services Students: 255 full-time (219 women), 280 part-time (248 women); includes 72 minority (38 African Americans, 1 American Indian/Alaska Native, 14 Asian Americans or Pacific Islanders, 19 Hispanic Americans), 7 international. Average age 31. 338 applicants, 91% accepted, 196 enrolled. *Faculty:* 21 full-time (14 women), 29 part-time/adjunct (22 women). Expenses: Contact institution. *Financial support:* In 2008–09, 359 students received support; research assistantships with full tuition reimbursements available, career-related internships or fieldwork, Federal Work-Study, scholarships/grants, and unspecified assistantships available. Support available to part-time students. Financial award applicants required to submit FAFSA. In 2008, 218 master's, 1 other advanced degree awarded. *Degree program information:* Part-time and evening/weekend programs available. Postbaccalaureate distance learning degree programs offered (minimal on-campus study). Offers Catholic school leadership (M Ed, Certificate); community counseling (MA, Certificate); community counseling and forensic psychologyeducation and human services (M Ed, MA, Certificate); elementary education (M Ed); English as a second language (M Ed); forensic psychology (MA); learning disabilities (M Ed); pastoral and spiritual care (MA); pastoral counseling (MA, Certificate); professional studies (M Ed); school counseling (MA); secondary education (M Ed). *Application deadline:* For fall admission, 7/1 for international students; for spring admission, 10/15 for international students. Applications are processed on a rolling basis. *Application fee:* $40. Electronic applications accepted. *Application Contact:* Francesca Reed, Director, Graduate Admissions, 703-284-5901, Fax: 703-527-3815, E-mail: grad.admissions@marymount.edu. *Dean,* Dr. Wayne Lesko, 703-284-1620, Fax: 703-284-1631, E-mail: wayne.lesko@marymount.edu.

School of Health Professions Students: 109 full-time (94 women), 139 part-time (114 women); includes 67 minority (46 African Americans, 13 Asian Americans or Pacific Islanders, 8 Hispanic Americans), 7 international. Average age 34. 177 applicants, 90% accepted, 70 enrolled. *Faculty:* 14 full-time (12 women), 3 part-time/adjunct (1 woman). Expenses: Contact institution. *Financial support:* In 2008–09, 120 students received support; research assistantships with full and partial tuition reimbursements available, career-related internships or fieldwork, Federal Work-Study, scholarships/grants, and unspecified assistantships available. Support available to part-time students. Financial award applicants required to submit FAFSA. In 2008, 31 master's, 80 doctorates, 1 other advanced degree awarded. *Degree program information:* Part-time and evening/weekend programs available. Offers family nurse practitioner (MSN, Certificate); health professions (MS, MSN, DPT, Certificate); health promotion management (MS); nursing education (MSN, Certificate); physical therapy (DPT); RN to MSN (MSN). *Application deadline:* For fall admission, 7/1 for international students; for spring admission, 10/15 for international students. Applications are processed on a rolling basis. *Application fee:* $40. Electronic applications accepted. *Application Contact:* Francesca Reed, Director, Graduate Admissions, 703-284-5901, Fax: 703-527-3815, E-mail: grad.admissions@marymount.edu. *Dean,* Dr. Tess Cappello, 703-284-1580, Fax: 703-284-3819, E-mail: tess.cappello@marymount.edu.

MARYVILLE UNIVERSITY OF SAINT LOUIS, St. Louis, MO 63141-7299

General Information Independent, coed, comprehensive institution. *Enrollment:* 3,517 graduate, professional, and undergraduate students; 118 full-time matriculated graduate/professional students (98 women), 501 part-time matriculated graduate/professional students (367 women). *Enrollment by degree level:* 491 master's, 128 doctoral. *Graduate faculty:* 45 full-time (30 women), 38 part-time/adjunct (23 women). *Tuition:* Full-time $19,650; part-time $605 per credit hour. *Required fees:* $100 per semester. Part-time tuition and fees vary according to degree level and program. *Graduate housing:* Room and/or apartments available on a first-come, first-served basis to single students; on-campus housing not available to married students. *Student services:* Campus employment opportunities, campus safety program, career counseling, exercise/wellness program, free psychological counseling, international student services, low-cost health insurance, multicultural affairs office, services for students with disabilities, teacher training, writing training. *Library facilities:* Maryville University Library. *Online resources:* library catalog, web page, access to other libraries' catalogs. *Collection:* 156,073 titles, 15,923 serial subscriptions, 10,779 audiovisual materials. *Research affiliation:* Southwestern Bell Foundation (secondary education curriculum and teacher education), Monsanto Fund (early childhood, science, mathematics curriculum development and teacher enrichment).

Computer facilities: Computer purchase and lease plans are available. 489 computers available on campus for general student use. A campuswide network can be accessed from student residence rooms and from off campus. Online class registration, specialized software, university catalog are available. *Web address:* http://www.maryville.edu/.

General Application Contact: Denise Evans, Assistant Vice President, Adult and Continuing Education, 314-529-9676, Fax: 314-529-9927, E-mail: devans1@maryville.edu.

GRADUATE UNITS

College of Arts and Sciences Students: 7 full-time (4 women), 4 part-time (3 women); includes 2 minority (both Asian Americans or Pacific Islanders), 4 international. Average age 28. Expenses: Contact institution. In 2008, 5 master's awarded. *Degree program information:* Part-time and evening/weekend programs available. Offers actuarial science (MS); arts and sciences (MS). *Application deadline:* Applications are processed on a rolling basis. *Application fee:* $40 ($60 for international students). Electronic applications accepted. *Application Contact:* Denise Evans, Assistant Vice President, Adult and Continuing Education, 314-529-9676, Fax: 314-529-9927, E-mail: devans1@maryville.edu. *Dean,* Dr. Dan Sparling, 314-529-9436, E-mail: dsparling@maryville.edu.

The John E. Simon School of Business Students: 16 full-time (8 women), 164 part-time (97 women); includes 13 minority (7 African Americans, 1 American Indian/Alaska Native, 3 Asian Americans or Pacific Islanders, 2 Hispanic Americans), 4 international. Average age 32. Expenses: Contact institution. *Financial support:* Career-related internships or fieldwork, Federal Work-Study, tuition waivers (partial), and campus employment available. Financial award application deadline: 7/31; financial award applicants required to submit FAFSA. In 2008, 70 master's awarded. *Degree program information:* Part-time and evening/weekend programs available. Offers accounting (MBA, PGC); business studies (PGC); e-marketing (MBA, PGC); management (MBA, PGC); marketing (MBA, PGC). *Application deadline:* Applications are processed on a rolling basis. *Application fee:* $40 ($60 for international students). Electronic applications accepted. *Application Contact:* Kathy Dougherty, Director of MBA Admissions and Enrollment, 314-529-9382, Fax: 314-529-9975, E-mail: business@maryville.edu. *Dean,* Dr. Pamela Horwitz, 314-529-9418, Fax: 314-529-9975, E-mail: horwitz@maryville.edu.

School of Education Students: 19 full-time (15 women), 227 part-time (173 women); includes 38 minority (30 African Americans, 3 American Indian/Alaska Native, 4 Asian Americans or Pacific Islanders, 1 Hispanic American). Average age 36. Expenses: Contact institution. *Financial support:* Career-related internships or fieldwork, Federal Work-Study, tuition waivers (partial), and professional educator discounts available. Financial award application deadline: 7/31; financial award applicants required to submit FAFSA. In 2008, 46 master's, 35 doctorates awarded. *Degree program information:* Part-time and evening/weekend programs available. Offers art education (MA Ed); early childhood education (MA Ed); educational leadership (Ed D); educational leadership: principal certification (MA Ed); elementary education (MA Ed); elementary education/English (MA Ed); elementary education/psychology (MA Ed); environmental education (MA Ed); gifted education (MA Ed); literacy specialist (MA Ed); middle grades education (MA Ed); secondary teaching and inquiry (MA Ed); teacher as leader (MA Ed). *Application deadline:* Applications are processed on a rolling basis. *Application fee:* $40 ($60 for international students). Electronic applications accepted. *Application Contact:* Dr. Lillian Curtis, Graduate Admissions Coordinator, 314-529-9542, Fax: 314-529-9921, E-mail: teachered@maryville.edu. *Dean,* Dr. Sam Hausfather, 314-529-9466, Fax: 314-529-9921, E-mail: shausfather@maryville.edu.

School of Health Professions Students: 76 full-time (71 women), 106 part-time (94 women); includes 26 minority (17 African Americans, 5 Asian Americans or Pacific Islanders, 4 Hispanic Americans), 2 international. Average age 33. Expenses: Contact institution. *Financial support:* Career-related internships or fieldwork, Federal Work-Study, and campus employment available. Financial award application deadline: 7/31. In 2008, 102 master's awarded. *Degree program information:* Part-time and evening/weekend programs available. Offers adult nurse practitioner (MSN); family nurse practitioner (MSN); health professions (MARC, MMT, MOT, MSN, DPT); marriage and family therapy (MARC); music therapy (MARC); nursing education (MSN); occupational therapy (MOT); physical therapy (DPT); substance abuse (MARC). *Application deadline:* Applications are processed on a rolling basis. *Application fee:* $40 ($60 for international students). Electronic applications accepted. *Application Contact:* Dr. Charles Gulas, Dean, 314-529-9625, Fax: 314-529-9139, E-mail: hlthprofessions@maryville.edu. *Dean,* Dr. Charles Gulas, 314-529-9625, Fax: 314-529-9139, E-mail: hlthprofessions@maryville.edu.

MARYWOOD UNIVERSITY, Scranton, PA 18509-1598

General Information Independent-religious, coed, comprehensive institution. CGS member. *Graduate housing:* Room and/or apartments available to single students; on-campus housing not available to married students.

GRADUATE UNITS

Academic Affairs *Degree program information:* Part-time and evening/weekend programs available. Electronic applications accepted.

College of Education and Human Development Offers addiction (MA); child/clinical school psychology (MA); clinical psychology (Psy D); clinical services (MA); counseling (Certificate); early childhood intervention (MS); education (M Ed); education and human development (M Ed, MA, MAT, MS, PhD, Psy D, Certificate, Ed S); educational administration (PhD); elementary education (MAT); elementary school counseling (MS); general (MA); general theoretical psychology (MA); health promotion (PhD); higher education administration (MS, PhD); human development (PhD); instructional leadership (M Ed, PhD); mental health counseling (MA); pastoral (MA); psychology (MA); reading education (MS); school leadership (MS); school psychology (Ed S); secondary education (MAT); secondary school counseling (MS); social work (PhD); special education (MS); special education administration and supervision (MS); speech-language pathology (MS).

College of Health and Human Services Offers clinical physician assistant (MS); criminal justice (MPA); dietetic internships (Certificate); gerontology (MS, Certificate); health and human services (MHSA, MPA, MS, MSW, Certificate); health services administration (MHSA); long-term care management (MHSA); managed care (MHSA); nursing administration (MS); nutrition (MS); physician assistant studies (MS); public administration (MPA); social work (MSW); sports nutrition and exercise science (MS).

College of Liberal Arts and Sciences Offers biotechnology (MS); criminal justice (MS); liberal arts and sciences (MS).

Insalaco College of Creative Arts and Management Offers advertising design (MA, MFA); art education (MA); art therapy (MA, Certificate); ceramics (MA); clay (MA, MFA); communication arts (MA, Certificate); corporate communication (MS, Certificate); creative arts and management (MA, MBA, MFA, MMT, MS, Certificate); e-business (MS, Certificate); fibers (MFA); finance and investments (MBA); general management (MBA); graphic design (MA, MFA); health communication (MS, Certificate); illustration (MA, MFA); information sciences (MS); instructional technology (MS, Certificate); interdisciplinary (MA); interior architecture (MA); library science/information science (MS); library science/information specialist (Certificate); management information systems (MBA); media management (MA); metals (MFA); music education (MA); music therapy (MMT, Certificate); painting (MA, MFA); photography (MA, MFA); printmaking (MA, MFA); production (MA); sculpture (MA); studio art (MA); visual arts (MFA); vocal pedagogy (Certificate); weaving (MA).

School of Architecture Offers architecture (M Arch).

MASSACHUSETTS COLLEGE OF ART AND DESIGN, Boston, MA 02115-5882

General Information State-supported, coed, comprehensive institution. *Enrollment:* 2,349 graduate, professional, and undergraduate students; 83 full-time matriculated graduate/professional students (53 women), 43 part-time matriculated graduate/professional students (32 women). *Enrollment by degree level:* 126 master's. *Graduate faculty:* 11 full-time (6 women), 9 part-time/adjunct (7 women). Tuition, state resident: full-time $17,100; part-time $570 per credit. Tuition and fees vary according to program. *Graduate housing:* On-campus housing not available. *Student services:* Campus employment opportunities, campus safety program, career counseling, free psychological counseling, international student services, low-cost health insurance. *Library facilities:* Morton R. Godine Library. *Online resources:* library catalog, web page, access to other libraries' catalogs. *Collection:* 258,675 titles, 557 serial subscriptions.

Computer facilities: Computer purchase and lease plans are available. 370 computers available on campus for general student use. A campuswide network can be accessed from student residence rooms and from off campus. *Web address:* http://www.massart.edu/.

General Application Contact: George Creamer, Director of Graduate Programs, 617-879-7163.

GRADUATE UNITS

Graduate Programs Students: 83 full-time (53 women), 43 part-time (32 women); includes 10 minority (1 African American, 1 American Indian/Alaska Native, 4 Asian Americans or Pacific Islanders, 4 Hispanic Americans), 16 international. Average age 34. 304 applicants, 26% accepted, 47 enrolled. *Faculty:* 11 full-time (6 women), 9 part-time/adjunct (7 women). Expenses: Contact institution. *Financial support:* In 2008–09, 53 research assistantships (averaging $2,000 per year), 31 teaching assistantships (averaging $2,000 per year) were awarded; career-related internships or fieldwork, Federal Work-Study, unspecified assistantships, and clerical/technical assistantships also available. Support available to part-time students. Financial award application deadline: 3/1; financial award applicants required to submit FAFSA. In 2008, 50 master's awarded. *Degree program information:* Part-time programs available. Postbaccalaureate distance learning degree programs offered (minimal on-campus study). Offers architecture (MA); art education (MSAE); ceramics (MFA); design (MFA); fibers (MFA); film (MFA); glass (MFA); media and performing arts (MFA); metals (MFA); painting (MFA); photography (MFA); printmaking (MFA); sculpture (MFA); teaching (MA). *Application deadline:* For fall admission, 1/15 for domestic and international students. Applications are processed on a rolling basis. *Application fee:* $75. Electronic applications accepted. *Application Contact:* George Creamer, Director, 617-879-7163. *Director,* George Creamer, 617-879-7163, Fax: 617-879-7171, E-mail: creamer@massart.edu.

MASSACHUSETTS COLLEGE OF LIBERAL ARTS, North Adams, MA 01247-4100

General Information State-supported, coed, comprehensive institution. *Graduate housing:* On-campus housing not available.

GRADUATE UNITS

Program in Education *Degree program information:* Part-time and evening/weekend programs available. Offers curriculum (M Ed); educational administration (M Ed); reading (M Ed); special education (M Ed).

MASSACHUSETTS COLLEGE OF PHARMACY AND HEALTH SCIENCES, Boston, MA 02115-5896

General Information Independent, coed, university. *Enrollment:* 3,909 graduate, professional, and undergraduate students; 2,549 full-time matriculated graduate/professional students (1,666 women), 109 part-time matriculated graduate/professional students (72 women). *Enrollment by degree level:* 2,335 first professional, 306 master's, 17 doctoral. *Tuition:* Full-time $27,000; part-time $840 per credit hour. *Required fees:* $180 per semester. Tuition and fees vary according to campus/location, program and student level. *Graduate housing:* Room and/or apartments available on a first-come, first-served basis to single students; on-campus housing not available to married students. Typical cost: $11,600 (including board). Room and board charges vary according to campus/location. Housing application deadline: 5/1. *Student services:* Campus employment opportunities, campus safety program, career counseling, exercise/wellness program, free psychological counseling, grant writing training, international student services, low-cost health insurance, multicultural affairs office, services for students with disabilities, teacher training, writing training. *Library facilities:* Henrietta DeBenedictis Library plus 2 others. *Online resources:* library catalog, web page, access to other libraries' catalogs. *Research affiliation:* Center for Brain Sciences (neuropharmacology), Center for Analytical Science (analytical medicinal chemistry).

Computer facilities: 479 computers available on campus for general student use. A campuswide network can be accessed from student residence rooms and from off campus. *Web address:* http://www.mcphs.edu/.

General Application Contact: Tara Hennesey, Coordinator of Graduate Admission, 617-732-2850, E-mail: admissions@mcphs.edu.

GRADUATE UNITS

Graduate Studies Expenses: Contact institution. *Financial support:* Fellowships with partial tuition reimbursements, research assistantships with partial tuition reimbursements, teaching assistantships with partial tuition reimbursements, scholarships/grants, tuition waivers (partial), unspecified assistantships, and animal caretaker available. Financial award application deadline: 3/15. In 2008, 20 master's, 2 doctorates awarded. *Degree program information:* Part-time programs available. Offers applied natural products (MANP); chemistry (MS, PhD); drug discovery and development (MS); drug regulatory affairs and health policy (MS); pharmaceutics/industrial pharmacy (MS, PhD); pharmacology (MS, PhD); pharmacy and health sciences (Pharm D, MANP, MPAS, MS, PhD). *Application Contact:* Tara Hennesey, Coordinator of Graduate Admission, 617-732-2850, E-mail: admissions@mcphs.edu. *Assistant Dean of Graduate Studies,* Dr. Barbara LeDuc, 617-732-2939, E-mail: divisionofgraduatestudies@mcphs.edu.

School of Pharmacy–Boston Expenses: Contact institution. Offers 6-year (Pharm D); non-traditional (Pharm D); pharmacy (Pharm D, MANP). *Application Contact:* Tara Hennesey, Coordinator of Graduate Admission, 617-732-2850, E-mail: admissions@mcphs.edu. *Assistant Dean of Graduate Studies,* Dr. Barbara LeDuc, 617-732-2939, E-mail: divisionofgraduatestudies@mcphs.edu.

School of Pharmacy–Worcester/Manchester Students: 564 full-time (360 women), 17 part-time (10 women); includes 226 minority (58 African Americans, 1 American Indian/Alaska Native, 154 Asian Americans or Pacific Islanders, 13 Hispanic Americans), 27 international. Average age 25. 1,111 applicants, 25% accepted, 221 enrolled. Expenses: Contact institution. In 2008, 154 first professional degrees awarded. Offers pharmacy (Pharm D, MPAS). *Application Contact:* Bryan Witham, Admissions, 617-732-5623, E-mail: bryan.witham@mcphs.edu. *Dean, School of Pharmacy (Worcester/Manchester),* Dr. Michael Malloy, 508-373-5603, E-mail: bryan.witham@mcphs.edu.

School of Physician Assistant Studies Expenses: Contact institution. Offers physician assistant studies (MPAS). *Application Contact:* Tara Hennesey, Coordinator of Graduate Admission, 617-732-2850, E-mail: admissions@mcphs.edu. *Assistant Dean of Graduate Studies,* Dr. Barbara LeDuc, 617-732-2939, E-mail: divisionofgraduatestudies@mcphs.edu.

MASSACHUSETTS INSTITUTE OF TECHNOLOGY, Cambridge, MA 02139-4307

General Information Independent, coed, university. CGS member. *Enrollment:* 10,299 graduate, professional, and undergraduate students; 5,974 full-time matriculated graduate/professional students (1,858 women), 36 part-time matriculated graduate/professional students (13 women). *Enrollment by degree level:* 2,420 master's, 3,590 doctoral. *Graduate faculty:* 998 full-time (195 women), 11 part-time/adjunct (3 women). *Tuition:* Full-time $36,140; part-time $565 per unit. *Required fees:* $250. *Graduate housing:* Rooms and/or apartments available to single and married students. Typical cost: $15,224 (including board) for single students. Room and board charges vary according to board plan and housing facility selected. Housing application deadline: 5/16. *Student services:* Campus employment opportunities, campus safety program, career counseling, child daycare facilities, exercise/wellness program, free psychological counseling, grant writing training, international student services, low-cost health insurance, services for students with disabilities, teacher training, writing training. *Library facilities:* MIT Libraries plus 11 others. *Online resources:* library catalog, web page. *Collection:* 2.7 million titles, 22,103 serial subscriptions, 38,798 audiovisual materials. *Research affiliation:* Novartis (pharmaceutical manufacturing), Singapore National Research Foundation (infectious diseases, environmental sensing, biosystems), Woods Hole Oceanographic Institute (applied ocean science and engineering), Howard Hughes Medical Institute (biomedical research), Whitehead Institute (developmental biology), Dupont (bio-technology, materials, chemical and biological sciences).

Computer facilities: Computer purchase and lease plans are available. 1,100 computers available on campus for general student use. A campuswide network can be accessed from student residence rooms and from off campus. Online class registration is available. *Web address:* http://www.mit.edu/.

General Application Contact: Stuart Schmill, Dean of Admissions, 617-253-2917, Fax: 617-258-8304, E-mail: mitgrad@mit.edu.

GRADUATE UNITS

MIT Sloan School of Management Students: 788 full-time (254 women); includes 167 minority (21 African Americans, 4 American Indian/Alaska Native, 109 Asian Americans or Pacific Islanders, 33 Hispanic Americans), 284 international. Average age 28. 3,896 applicants, 15% accepted, 391 enrolled. *Faculty:* 98 full-time (19 women). Expenses: Contact institution. *Financial support:* In 2008–09, 369 students received support; fellowships with tuition reimbursements available, research assistantships with tuition reimbursements available, teaching assistantships with tuition reimbursements available, Federal Work-Study, institutionally sponsored loans, scholarships/grants, health care benefits, and unspecified assistantships available. Support available to part-time students. In 2008, 472 master's, 13 doctorates awarded. Offers management (M Fin, MBA, MS, SM, PhD). *Application deadline:* For fall admission, 1/13 for domestic and international students. *Application fee:* $230. Electronic applications accepted. *Application Contact:* Rod Garcia, Director of Admissions, MBA Program, 617-253-5434, Fax: 617-253-6405, E-mail: mbaadmissions@sloan.mit.edu. *Dean,* David C Schmittlein, 617-253-2804, Fax: 617-258-6617, E-mail: dschmitt@mit.edu.

Operations Research Center Offers operations research (SM, PhD). Electronic applications accepted.

School of Architecture and Planning Students: 580 full-time (248 women), 1 (woman) part-time; includes 81 minority (16 African Americans, 3 American Indian/Alaska Native, 40 Asian Americans or Pacific Islanders, 22 Hispanic Americans), 220 international. Average age 28. 1,695 applicants, 23% accepted, 263 enrolled. *Faculty:* 80 full-time (21 women), 1 (woman) part-time/adjunct. Expenses: Contact institution. *Financial support:* In 2008–09, 469 students received support, including 230 fellowships with tuition reimbursements available (averaging $17,647 per year), 195 research assistantships with tuition reimbursements available (averaging $26,799 per year), 44 teaching assistantships with tuition reimbursements available (averaging $27,593 per year); Federal Work-Study, institutionally sponsored loans, scholarships/grants, health care benefits, and unspecified assistantships also available. In 2008, 198 master's, 35 doctorates awarded. Offers architecture (M Arch, PhD); architecture and planning (M Arch, MCP, SM, SM Arch S, SM Vis S, SMBT, SMRED, PhD); architecture studies (SM Arch S); building technology (SMBT); city planning (MCP); media arts and sciences (SM, PhD); media technology (SM); urban and regional planning (PhD); urban and regional studies (PhD); urban studies and planning (SM); visual studies (SM Vis S). *Application fee:* $75. Electronic applications accepted. *Application Contact:* Graduate Admissions, 617-253-2917, Fax: 617-258-8304, E-mail: mitgrad@mit.edu. *Dean,* Prof. Ad??le Naud?? Santos, 617-253-4401, Fax: 617-253-9417, E-mail: sap-info@mit.edu.

Center for Real Estate Offers real estate (MSRED). Electronic applications accepted.

School of Engineering Students: 2,695 full-time (687 women), 11 part-time (2 women); includes 437 minority (58 African Americans, 6 American Indian/Alaska Native, 295 Asian Americans or Pacific Islanders, 78 Hispanic Americans), 1,161 international. Average age 27. 6,971 applicants, 23% accepted, 1002 enrolled. *Faculty:* 366 full-time (50 women), 2 part-time/adjunct (0 women). Expenses: Contact institution. *Financial support:* In 2008–09, 2,346 students received support, including 629 fellowships with tuition reimbursements available (averaging $25,205 per year), 1,462 research assistantships with tuition reimbursements available (averaging $27,112 per year), 255 teaching assistantships with tuition reimbursements available (averaging $28,528 per year); career-related internships or fieldwork, Federal Work-Study, institutionally sponsored loans, scholarships/grants, traineeships, health care benefits, and unspecified assistantships also available. In 2008, 748 master's, 304 doctorates, 11 other advanced degrees awarded. Offers aeronautics and astronautics (SM, PhD, Sc D, EAA); aerospace computational engineering (PhD, Sc D); air transportation systems (PhD, Sc D); air-breathing propulsion (PhD, Sc D); aircraft systems engineering (PhD, Sc D); applied biosciences (PhD, Sc D); archaeological materials (PhD, Sc D); autonomous systems (Sc D); bio- and polymeric materials (PhD, Sc D); bioengineering (PhD, Sc D); biological oceanography (PhD, Sc D); biomedical engineering (M Eng); chemical engineering (SM, PhD, Sc D); chemical engineering practice (SM, PhD); chemical oceanography (PhD, Sc D); civil and environmental engineering (M Eng, SM, PhD, Sc D, CE); civil and environmental systems (PhD, Sc D); civil engineering (PhD, Sc D); coastal engineering (PhD, Sc D); communications and networks (PhD, Sc D); computation for design and optimization (SM);

Massachusetts Institute of Technology (continued)

computational and systems biology (PhD); computer science (PhD, Sc D, ECS); construction engineering and management (PhD, Sc D); controls (Sc D); electrical engineering (PhD, Sc D, EE); electrical engineering and computer science (M Eng, SM, PhD, Sc D); electronic, photonic and magnetic materials (PhD, Sc D); emerging, fundamental and computational studies in materials science (Sc D); emerging, fundamental, and computational studies in materials science (PhD); engineering (M Eng, SM, PhD, Sc D, CE, EAA, ECS, EE, Mat E, Mech E, Met E, NE, Naval E); environmental biology (PhD, Sc D); environmental chemistry (PhD, Sc D); environmental engineering (PhD, Sc D); environmental fluid mechanics (PhD, Sc D); genetic toxicology (PhD, Sc D); geotechnical and geoenvironmental engineering (PhD, Sc D); humans in aerospace (PhD, Sc D); hydrology (PhD, Sc D); information technology (PhD, Sc D); manufacturing (M Eng); materials and structures (Sc D); materials engineering (Mat E); materials science and engineering (M Eng, SM, PhD, Sc D); mechanical engineering (SM, PhD, Sc D, Mech E); metallurgical engineering (Met E); molecular and systems bacterial pathogenesis (PhD, Sc D); molecular and systems toxicology and pharmacology (PhD, Sc D); molecular systems toxicology (PhD, Sc D); naval architecture and marine engineering (SM, PhD, Sc D); naval engineering (Naval E); nuclear science and engineering (SM, PhD, Sc D, NE); ocean engineering (SM, PhD, Sc D); oceanographic engineering (SM, PhD, Sc D); space propulsion (PhD, Sc D); space systems (PhD, Sc D); structural and environmental materials (PhD, Sc D); structures and materials (PhD, Sc D); toxicology (SM, PhD, Sc D); transportation (PhD, Sc D). *Application fee:* $75. Electronic applications accepted. *Application Contact:* Graduate Admissions, 617-253-2917, Fax: 617-258-8304, E-mail: mitgrad@mit.edu. *Dean*, Prof. Subra Suresh, 617-253-3291, Fax: 617-253-8549.

Engineering Systems Division Students: 277 full-time (74 women); includes 40 minority (8 African Americans, 1 American Indian/Alaska Native, 24 Asian Americans or Pacific Islanders, 7 Hispanic Americans), 109 international. Average age 30. 486 applicants, 47% accepted, 168 enrolled. *Faculty:* 6 full-time (0 women). Expenses: Contact institution. *Financial support:* In 2008–09, 155 students received support, including 53 fellowships with tuition reimbursements available (averaging $17,599 per year), 87 research assistantships with tuition reimbursements available (averaging $26,218 per year), 15 teaching assistantships with tuition reimbursements available (averaging $24,161 per year); career-related internships or fieldwork, Federal Work-Study, institutionally sponsored loans, scholarships/grants, health care benefits, and unspecified assistantships also available. In 2008, 157 master's, 11 doctorates awarded. Offers engineering and management (SM); engineering systems (SM, PhD); logistics (M Eng); technology and policy (SM); technology, management and policy (PhD). *Application fee:* $75. *Application Contact:* Graduate Admissions, 617-253-1182, E-mail: esdgrad@mit.edu. *Director*, Prof. Yossi Sheffi, 617-253-1764, E-mail: esdinquiries@mit.edu.

School of Humanities, Arts, and Social Sciences Students: 310 full-time (132 women); includes 30 minority (2 African Americans, 3 American Indian/Alaska Native, 18 Asian Americans or Pacific Islanders, 7 Hispanic Americans), 118 international. Average age 28. 1,728 applicants, 8% accepted, 69 enrolled. *Faculty:* 157 full-time (50 women), 3 part-time/adjunct (1 woman). Expenses: Contact institution. *Financial support:* In 2008–09, 252 students received support, including 128 fellowships with tuition reimbursements available (averaging $31,740 per year), 54 research assistantships with tuition reimbursements available (averaging $28,496 per year), 70 teaching assistantships with tuition reimbursements available (averaging $34,245 per year); Federal Work-Study, institutionally sponsored loans, scholarships/grants, health care benefits, and unspecified assistantships also available. In 2008, 28 master's, 45 doctorates awarded. Offers comparative media studies (SM); economics (SM, PhD); history, anthropology, and science, technology and society (PhD); humanities, arts, and social sciences (SM, PhD); linguistics (PhD); philosophy (PhD); political science (SM, PhD); science writing (SM). *Application fee:* $75. Electronic applications accepted. *Application Contact:* Graduate Admissions Office, 617-253-2917, Fax: 617-258-8304, E-mail: mitgrad@mit.edu. *Dean*, Prof. Deborah Fitzgerald, 617-253-3450, E-mail: www-shass@mit.edu.

School of Science Students: 1,060 full-time (383 women); includes 177 minority (18 African Americans, 4 American Indian/Alaska Native, 103 Asian Americans or Pacific Islanders, 52 Hispanic Americans), 332 international. Average age 26. 2,943 applicants, 17% accepted, 199 enrolled. *Faculty:* 279 full-time (48 women), 2 part-time/adjunct (0 women). Expenses: Contact institution. *Financial support:* In 2008–09, 973 students received support, including 340 fellowships with tuition reimbursements available (averaging $28,855 per year), 477 research assistantships with tuition reimbursements available (averaging $29,161 per year), 156 teaching assistantships with tuition reimbursements available (averaging $29,791 per year); Federal Work-Study, institutionally sponsored loans, scholarships/grants, health care benefits, and unspecified assistantships also available. In 2008, 31 master's, 176 doctorates awarded. Offers atmospheric chemistry (PhD, Sc D); atmospheric science (SM, PhD, Sc D); biochemistry (PhD); biological chemistry (PhD, Sc D); biological oceanography (PhD); biology (PhD); biophysical chemistry and molecular structure (PhD); cell biology (PhD); climate physics and chemistry (PhD, Sc D); cognitive science (PhD); computational and systems biology (PhD); developmental biology (PhD); earth and planetary sciences (SM); genetics (PhD); geochemistry (PhD, Sc D); geology (PhD, Sc D); geophysics (PhD, Sc D); geosystems (SM); immunology (PhD); inorganic chemistry (PhD, Sc D); marine geology and geophysics (SM); mathematics (PhD); microbiology (PhD); molecular biology (PhD); neurobiology (PhD); neuroscience (PhD); oceanography (SM); organic chemistry (PhD, Sc D); physical chemistry (PhD, Sc D); physical oceanography (PhD, Sc D); physics (SM, PhD); planetary sciences (PhD, Sc D); science (SM, PhD, Sc D). *Application fee:* $75. Electronic applications accepted. *Application Contact:* Graduate Admissions Office, 617-253-2917, Fax: 617-258-8304, E-mail: mitgrad@mit.edu. *Dean*, Prof. Marc A. Kastner, 617-253-8900, Fax: 617-253-8901, E-mail: scnc@mit.edu.

Whitaker College of Health Sciences and Technology Expenses: Contact institution. *Financial support:* Fellowships with full tuition reimbursements, research assistantships with full tuition reimbursements, teaching assistantships with full tuition reimbursements, Federal Work-Study, institutionally sponsored loans, scholarships/grants, traineeships, and health care benefits available. Support available to part-time students. Financial award application deadline: 12/15. Offers biomedical engineering (M Eng); biomedical enterprise (SM); biomedical informatics (SM); health sciences and technology (MD, M Eng, SM, PhD, Sc D); medical engineering (PhD); medical engineering and medical physics (Sc D); medical physics (PhD); medical sciences (MD); speech and hearing bioscience and technology (PhD, Sc D). *Application deadline:* For fall admission, 12/15 for domestic students. *Application fee:* $70. *Application Contact:* Charlene Placido, Assistant Provost for Research, 617-253-1975, Fax: 617-253-8388, E-mail: placido@mit.edu. *Director*, Dr. Ram Sasisekharan, E-mail: rams@mit.edu.

MASSACHUSETTS MARITIME ACADEMY, Buzzards Bay, MA 02532-1803

General Information State-supported, coed, primarily men, comprehensive institution.

GRADUATE UNITS

Program in Emergency Management Offers emergency management (MS).

Program in Facilities Management *Degree program information:* Part-time and evening/weekend programs available. Offers facilities management (MS).

MASSACHUSETTS SCHOOL OF LAW AT ANDOVER, Andover, MA 01810

General Information Independent, coed, graduate-only institution. *Graduate housing:* On-campus housing not available.

GRADUATE UNITS

Professional Program *Degree program information:* Part-time and evening/weekend programs available. Offers law (JD). Electronic applications accepted.

MASSACHUSETTS SCHOOL OF PROFESSIONAL PSYCHOLOGY, Boston, MA 02132

General Information Independent, coed, primarily women, graduate-only institution. *Graduate housing:* On-campus housing not available.

GRADUATE UNITS

Graduate Programs Offers clinical psychology (Psy D); clinical psychopharmacology (Post-Doctoral MS); counseling psychology (MA); executive coaching (Graduate Certificate); forensic psychology (MA); organizational psychology (MA); respecialization in clinical psychology (Certificate). Electronic applications accepted.

THE MASTER'S COLLEGE AND SEMINARY, Santa Clarita, CA 91321-1200

General Information Independent-religious, coed, comprehensive institution. *Graduate housing:* On-campus housing not available.

GRADUATE UNITS

The Master's Seminary *Degree program information:* Part-time programs available. Offers biblical counseling (MABC); New Testament (Th D); Old Testament (Th D); preaching (D Min); theology (M Div, M Th, Th D).

MAYO GRADUATE SCHOOL, Rochester, MN 55905

General Information Independent, coed, graduate-only institution. *Graduate housing:* On-campus housing not available.

GRADUATE UNITS

Graduate Programs in Biomedical Sciences Offers biochemistry and structural biology (PhD); biomedical engineering (PhD); biomedical sciences (PhD); cell biology and genetics (PhD); immunology (PhD); molecular biology (PhD); molecular neuroscience (PhD); molecular pharmacology and experimental therapeutics (PhD); tumor biology (PhD); virology and gene therapy (PhD). Electronic applications accepted.

MAYO MEDICAL SCHOOL, Rochester, MN 55905

General Information Independent, coed, graduate-only institution. *Graduate housing:* On-campus housing not available.

GRADUATE UNITS

Professional Program Offers medicine (MD). MD offered through the Mayo Foundation's Division of Education. Electronic applications accepted.

MAYO SCHOOL OF HEALTH SCIENCES, Rochester, MN 55905

General Information Independent, coed, graduate-only institution. *Enrollment:* 171 full-time matriculated graduate/professional students (118 women). *Enrollment by degree level:* 88 master's, 83 doctoral. *Graduate faculty:* 6 full-time (1 woman), 4 part-time/adjunct (3 women). *Student services:* Campus employment opportunities, campus safety program, exercise/wellness program, multicultural affairs office, services for students with disabilities. *Library facilities:* Venables Library plus 5 others.

Computer facilities: A campuswide network can be accessed from off campus. *Web address:* http://www.mayo.edu/mshs/.

General Application Contact: Troy Tynsky, Director, Enrollment and Student Services, 507-266-4077, Fax: 507-284-0656, E-mail: tynsky.troy@mayo.edu.

GRADUATE UNITS

Program in Nurse Anesthesia Students: 88 full-time (54 women); includes 5 minority (1 African American, 1 American Indian/Alaska Native, 2 Asian Americans or Pacific Islanders, 1 Hispanic American). Average age 30. 83 applicants, 36% accepted, 30 enrolled. *Faculty:* 1 (woman) full-time, 2 part-time/adjunct (1 woman). Expenses: Contact institution. *Financial support:* Scholarships/grants, health care benefits, and stipends available. Financial award applicants required to submit FAFSA. In 2008, 30 master's awarded. Offers nurse anesthesia (MNA). *Application deadline:* For fall admission, 10/15 for domestic students. *Application fee:* $50. Electronic applications accepted. *Application Contact:* Tammy Neis, Administrative Assistant, 507-284-8331, Fax: 507-284-0656, E-mail: neis.tamra@mayo.edu. *Director*, Mary E. Marienau, 507-284-3293, Fax: 507-284-0656, E-mail: marienau.mary@mayo.edu.

Program in Physical Therapy Students: 83 full-time (64 women); includes 2 minority (1 African American, 1 Asian American or Pacific Islander). Average age 25. 145 applicants, 30% accepted, 28 enrolled. *Faculty:* 5 full-time (0 women), 3 part-time/adjunct (all women). Expenses: Contact institution. *Financial support:* In 2008–09, 83 students received support. Scholarships/grants available. Financial award applicants required to submit FAFSA. Offers physical therapy (DPT). *Application deadline:* For winter admission, 2/1 for domestic and international students. Applications are processed on a rolling basis. Electronic applications accepted. *Application Contact:* Carol Cooper, Secretary, 507-284-2054, Fax: 507-284-0656, E-mail: cooper.carol@mayo.edu. *Director*, Dr. John Hollman, 507-284-8487, Fax: 507-284-0656, E-mail: hollman.john@mayo.edu.

McCORMICK THEOLOGICAL SEMINARY, Chicago, IL 60615

General Information Independent-religious, coed, graduate-only institution. *Graduate housing:* Rooms and/or apartments available on a first-come, first-served basis to single and married students. Housing application deadline: 7/1.

GRADUATE UNITS

Graduate and Professional Programs *Degree program information:* Part-time and evening/weekend programs available. Offers ministry (D Min); theological studies (MATS, Certificate); theology (M Div).

McDANIEL COLLEGE, Westminster, MD 21157-4390

General Information Independent, coed, comprehensive institution. *Graduate housing:* On-campus housing not available.

GRADUATE UNITS

Graduate and Professional Studies *Degree program information:* Part-time and evening/weekend programs available. Offers curriculum and instruction (MS); education of the deaf (MS); educational administration (MS); elementary education (MS); guidance and counseling (MS); human resources development (MS); human services management in special education (MS); liberal studies (MLA); media/library science (MS); physical education (MS); reading education (MS); secondary education (MS); special education (MS).

McGILL UNIVERSITY, Montréal, QC H3A 2T5, Canada

General Information Province-supported, coed, university. CGS member. *Graduate housing:* Room and/or apartments available to married students; on-campus housing not available to single students.

GRADUATE UNITS

Faculty of Graduate and Postdoctoral Studies

Desautels Faculty of Management Offers administration (PhD); entrepreneurial studies (MBA); finance (MBA); general management (Post Master's Certificate); information systems (MBA); international business (exchange program) (MBA); international Master's program in practicing management (MM); management (MBA); management for development (MBA); manufacturing management (MMM); marketing (MBA); operations management (MBA); public accountancy (Diploma); strategic management (MBA).

Faculty of Agricultural and Environmental Sciences Offers agricultural and environmental sciences (M Sc, M Sc A, PhD, Certificate, Graduate Diploma); agricultural economics (M Sc); animal science (M Sc, M Sc A, PhD); biotechnology (M Sc A, Certificate); computer applications (M Sc, M Sc A, PhD); dietetics (M Sc A, Graduate Diploma); entomology (M Sc, PhD); environmental assessment (M Sc, PhD); food engineering (M Sc, M Sc A, PhD); food science and agricultural chemistry (M Sc, PhD); forest science (M Sc, PhD); grain drying (M Sc, M Sc A, PhD); human nutrition (M Sc, M Sc A, PhD); irrigation and drainage (M Sc, M Sc A, PhD); machinery (M Sc, M Sc A, PhD); microbiology (M Sc, PhD); micrometeorology (M Sc, PhD); neotropical environment (M Sc, PhD); parasitology (M Sc, PhD); plant science (M Sc, M Sc A, PhD, Certificate); pollution control (M Sc, M Sc A, PhD); post-harvest technology (M Sc, M Sc A, PhD); soil dynamics (M Sc, M Sc A, PhD); soil science (M Sc, PhD); structure and environment (M Sc, M Sc A, PhD); vegetable and fruit storage (M Sc, M Sc A, PhD); wildlife biology (M Sc, PhD).

Faculty of Arts Offers anthropology (MA, PhD); art history and communication studies (MA, PhD); arts (MA, MSW, PhD, Diploma); bioethics (MA); East Asian studies (MA, PhD); economics (MA, PhD); English (MA, PhD); French language and literature (MA, PhD); German studies (MA, PhD); Hispanic studies (MA, PhD); history (MA, PhD); history of medicine (MA); Islamic studies (MA, PhD, Diploma); Italian studies (MA, PhD); Jewish studies (MA); language acquisition (PhD); linguistics (MA, PhD); medical anthropology (MA); medical sociology (MA); neo-tropical environment (MA); philosophy (PhD); political science (MA, PhD); Russian literature (MA, PhD); social statistics (MA); social work (MSW, PhD, Diploma); sociology (MA, PhD, Diploma).

Faculty of Dentistry Offers forensic dentistry (Certificate); oral and maxillofacial surgery (M Sc, PhD).

Faculty of Education Offers counseling psychology (MA, PhD); culture and values in education (MA, PhD); curriculum studies (MA); education (M Ed, M Sc, MA, MLIS, PhD, Certificate, Diploma); educational leadership (MA, Certificate); educational psychology (M Ed, MA, PhD); educational studies (PhD); information studies (MLIS, PhD, Certificate, Diploma); integrated studies in education (M Ed); kinesiology and physical education (M Sc, MA, PhD, Certificate, Diploma); school/applied child psychology and applied developmental psychology (M Ed, MA, PhD, Diploma); second language education (MA, PhD).

Faculty of Engineering Offers aerospace (M Eng); affordable homes (M Arch II, Diploma); architectural history and theory (M Arch II); architecture (PhD); chemical engineering (M Eng, PhD); domestic environment (M Arch II); domestic environments (Diploma); electrical and computer engineering (M Eng, PhD); engineering (M Arch I, M Arch II, M Eng, M Sc, MMM, MUP, PhD, Diploma); environmental engineering (M Eng, M Sc, PhD); environmental planning (MUP); fluid mechanics (M Sc); fluid mechanics and hydraulic engineering (M Eng, PhD); housing (MUP); manufacturing management (MMM); materials engineering (M Eng, PhD); mechanical engineering (M Eng, M Sc, PhD); minimum cost housing in developing countries (M Arch II, Diploma); mining engineering (M Eng, M Sc, PhD, Diploma); professional architecture (M Arch I); rehabilitation of urban infrastructure (M Eng, PhD); soil behavior (M Eng, PhD); soil mechanics and foundations (M Eng, PhD); structures and structural mechanics (M Eng, PhD); transportation (MUP); urban design (MUP); urban planning, policy and design (PhD); water resources (M Sc); water resources engineering (M Eng, PhD).

Faculty of Law Offers air and space law (LL M, DCL, Graduate Certificate); bioethics (LL M); comparative law (LL M, DCL, Graduate Certificate); law (LL M, DCL). Applications for LL M with specialization in bioethics are made initially through the Biomedical Ethics Unit in the Faculty of Medicine.

Faculty of Medicine Offers anatomy and cell biology (M Sc, PhD); assessing driving capability (PGC); biochemistry (M Sc, PhD); biomedical engineering (M Eng, PhD); communication science and disorders (M Sc); communication sciences and disorders (PhD); community health (M Sc); environmental health (M Sc); epidemiology and biostatistics (M Sc, PhD, Diploma); experimental medicine (M Sc, PhD); genetic counseling (M Sc); health care evaluation (M Sc); human genetics (M Sc, PhD); medical anthropology (MA, PhD); medical history (MA, PhD); medical physics (M Sc, PhD); medical sociology (MA, PhD); medical statistics (M Sc); medicine (M Eng, M Sc, M Sc A, MA, PhD, Diploma, Graduate Diploma, PGC); microbiology and immunology (M Sc, M Sc A, PhD); neurology and neurosurgery (M Sc, PhD); nurse practitioner (Graduate Diploma); nursing (M Sc A, PhD); occupational health (M Sc, PhD); otolaryngology (M Sc); pathology (M Sc, PhD); pharmacology and therapeutics (M Sc, PhD); physiology (M Sc, PhD); psychiatry (M Sc); rehabilitation science (M Sc, PhD); speech-language pathology (M Sc A); surgery (M Sc, PhD).

Faculty of Religious Studies Offers religious studies (MA, STM, PhD).

Faculty of Science Offers atmospheric science (M Sc, PhD); bioinformatics (M Sc, PhD); chemical biology (M Sc, PhD); chemistry (M Sc, PhD); clinical psychology (PhD); computational science and engineering (M Sc); computer science (M Sc, PhD); earth and planetary sciences (M Sc, PhD); environment (M Sc, PhD); experimental psychology (M Sc, MA, PhD); geography (M Sc, MA, PhD); mathematics and statistics (M Sc, MA, PhD); neo-tropical environment (M Sc, MA, PhD); physical oceanography (M Sc, PhD); physics (M Sc, PhD); science (M Sc, MA, PhD); social statistics (MA).

Schulich School of Music Offers composition (M Mus, D Mus, PhD); music education (MA, PhD); music technology (MA, PhD); musicology (MA, PhD); performance (M Mus); performance studies (D Mus); sound recording (M Mus, PhD); theory (MA, PhD).

Professional Program in Dentistry Offers dentistry (DMD). Electronic applications accepted.

Professional Program in Law Offers law (JD).

Professional Program in Medicine Offers medicine.

McKENDREE UNIVERSITY, Lebanon, IL 62254-1299

General Information Independent-religious, coed, comprehensive institution. *Enrollment:* 3,327 graduate, professional, and undergraduate students; 179 full-time matriculated graduate/professional students (131 women), 774 part-time matriculated graduate/professional students (538 women). *Enrollment by degree level:* 953 master's. *Graduate faculty:* 31 full-time (14 women), 70 part-time/adjunct (33 women). *Tuition:* Full-time $6300; part-time $350 per credit hour. *Student services:* Career counseling, free psychological counseling, multicultural affairs office, services for students with disabilities, teacher training. *Library facilities:* Holman Library. *Online resources:* library catalog, web page, access to other libraries' catalogs. *Collection:* 109,000 titles, 450 serial subscriptions, 6,637 audiovisual materials.

Computer facilities: Computer purchase and lease plans are available. 140 computers available on campus for general student use. A campuswide network can be accessed from student residence rooms and from off campus. Online class registration is available. *Web address:* http://www.mckendree.edu/.

General Application Contact: Sabrina Storner, Director of Graduate Admission, 618-537-6477, Fax: 618-537-6410, E-mail: skstorner@mckendree.edu.

GRADUATE UNITS

Graduate Programs Students: 179 full-time (131 women), 774 part-time (538 women); includes 82 minority (64 African Americans, 3 American Indian/Alaska Native, 5 Asian Americans or Pacific Islanders, 10 Hispanic Americans), 2 international. Average age 35. 529 applicants, 73% accepted, 252 enrolled. *Faculty:* 31 full-time (14 women), 70 part-time/adjunct (33 women). Expenses: Contact institution. *Financial support:* In 2008–09, 1 student received support. Application deadline: 6/30. In 2008, 300 master's awarded. *Degree program information:* Part-time and evening/weekend programs available. Offers business administration (MBA); certification (MA Ed); educational administration and leadership (MA Ed); educational studies (MA Ed); human resource management (MBA); international business (MBA); music education (MA Ed); nursing education (MSN); nursing management/administration (MSN); professional counseling (MA); special education (MA Ed). *Application deadline:* Applications are processed on a rolling basis. Electronic applications accepted. *Application Contact:* Sabrina K. Storner, Director of Graduate Admission, 618-537-6477, Fax: 618-537-6410, E-mail: skstorner@mckendree.edu. *Administrative Director of Graduate Studies,* Dr. Joseph J. Cipfl, 618-537-6462, Fax: 618-537-6417, E-mail: jjcipfl@mckendree.edu.

McMASTER UNIVERSITY, Hamilton, ON L8S 4M2, Canada

General Information Province-supported, coed, university. CGS member. *Graduate housing:* Room and/or apartments available to single students; on-campus housing not available to married students. Housing application deadline: 6/30. *Research affiliation:* Commonwealth Development (telecommunications), Canadian Centre for Inland Waters (chemical and civil engineering).

GRADUATE UNITS

Faculty of Health Sciences *Degree program information:* Part-time programs available. Postbaccalaureate distance learning degree programs offered (minimal on-campus study). Offers biochemistry and biomedical sciences (M Sc, PhD); blood and vascular (M Sc, PhD); genetics and cancer (M Sc, PhD); health research methodology (course-based) (M Sc); health research methodology (thesis) (M Sc, PhD); health sciences (M Sc, PhD); immunity and infection (M Sc, PhD); metabolism and nutrition (M Sc, PhD); neurosciences and behavioral sciences (M Sc, PhD); nursing (M Sc, PhD); occupational therapy (M Sc); physiology/pharmacology (M Sc, PhD); physiotherapy (M Sc); rehabilitation science (M Sc, PhD); rehabilitation science (course-based) (M Sc).

McMaster Divinity College *Degree program information:* Part-time programs available. Offers Biblical studies (MA, MTS, Diploma); biblical studies (M Div); Christian interpretation/history (M Div, MA, MTS, Diploma); Christian ministry (M Div, MA, MTS, Diploma); Christian Studies (Certificate); Christian theology (PhD). Affiliated with the Toronto School of Theology.

School of Graduate Studies *Degree program information:* Part-time programs available.

Faculty of Business *Degree program information:* Part-time programs available. Offers business (MBA, PhD); human resources and management (MBA, PhD); information systems (PhD).

Faculty of Engineering *Degree program information:* Part-time programs available. Offers chemical engineering (M Eng, MA Sc, PhD); civil engineering (M Eng, MA Sc, PhD); computer science (M Sc, PhD); electrical engineering (M Eng, MA Sc, PhD); engineering (M Eng, M Sc, MA Sc, PhD); engineering physics (M Eng, MA Sc, PhD); materials engineering (M Eng, MA Sc, PhD); materials science (M Eng, PhD); mechanical engineering (M Eng, MA Sc, PhD); nuclear engineering (PhD); software engineering (M Eng, MA Sc, PhD).

Faculty of Humanities *Degree program information:* Part-time and evening/weekend programs available. Offers classics (MA, PhD); cultural studies and critical theory (MA); English (MA, PhD); French (MA); globalization studies (MA); history (MA, PhD); humanities (MA, PhD); philosophy (MA, PhD).

Faculty of Science *Degree program information:* Part-time and evening/weekend programs available. Offers analytical chemistry (M Sc, PhD); applied statistics (M Sc); astrophysics (PhD); biology (M Sc, PhD); chemical physics (M Sc, PhD); chemistry (M Sc, PhD); geochemistry (PhD); geology (M Sc, PhD); health and radiation physics (M Sc); human geography (MA, PhD); inorganic chemistry (M Sc, PhD); mathematics (M Sc, PhD); medical physics (M Sc, PhD); medical statistics (M Sc); organic chemistry (M Sc, PhD); physical chemistry (M Sc, PhD); physical geography (M Sc, PhD); physics (PhD); polymer chemistry (M Sc, PhD); psychology (M Sc, PhD); science (M Sc, MA, PhD); statistical theory (M Sc); statistics (M Sc).

Faculty of Social Sciences *Degree program information:* Part-time and evening/weekend programs available. Offers analysis of social welfare policy (MSW); analysis of social work practice (MSW); anthropology (MA, PhD); economics (MA, PhD); human biodynamics (M Sc, PhD); international relations (PhD); political science (MA); public and the global economy (MA); public policy (PhD); public policy and administration (MA); religious studies (MA, PhD); social sciences (M Sc, MA, MSW, PhD); sociology (MA, PhD); work and society (MA).

McNEESE STATE UNIVERSITY, Lake Charles, LA 70609

General Information State-supported, coed, comprehensive institution. *Enrollment:* 8,283 graduate, professional, and undergraduate students; 338 full-time matriculated graduate/professional students (172 women), 444 part-time matriculated graduate/professional students (340 women). *Enrollment by degree level:* 776 master's, 6 other advanced degrees. *Graduate faculty:* 115 full-time (38 women), 6 part-time/adjunct (4 women). Tuition, state resident: full-time $2386. *Required fees:* $885. Tuition and fees vary according to course load. *Graduate housing:* Room and/or apartments available on a first-come, first-served basis to single students. Typical cost: $2000 per year ($4050 including board). Housing application deadline: 8/15. *Student services:* Campus employment opportunities, campus safety program, career counseling, exercise/wellness program, free psychological counseling, grant writing training, international student services, low-cost health insurance, multicultural affairs office, services for students with disabilities, teacher training, writing training. *Library facilities:* Frazer Memorial Library plus 2 others. *Collection:* 332,521 titles, 22,177 serial subscriptions.

Computer facilities: 700 computers available on campus for general student use. A campuswide network can be accessed from student residence rooms and from off campus. Online class registration is available. *Web address:* http://www.mcneese.edu/.

General Application Contact: Dr. George F. Mead, Interim Dean of Dore' School of Graduate Studies, 337-475-5396, Fax: 337-475-5397, E-mail: admissions@mcneese.edu.

GRADUATE UNITS

Doré School of Graduate Studies Students: 338 full-time (172 women), 444 part-time (340 women); includes 105 minority (86 African Americans, 1 American Indian/Alaska Native, 7 Asian Americans or Pacific Islanders, 11 Hispanic Americans), 136 international. Average age 31. *Faculty:* 115 full-time (38 women), 6 part-time/adjunct (4 women). Expenses: Contact institution. *Financial support:* Fellowships, research assistantships, teaching assistantships, career-related internships or fieldwork, Federal Work-Study, institutionally sponsored loans, and unspecified assistantships available. Support available to part-time students. Financial award application deadline: 5/1. In 2008, 299 master's awarded. *Degree program information:* Part-time and evening/weekend programs available. *Application deadline:* For fall admission, 5/15 priority date for domestic and international students; for spring admission, 10/15 priority date for domestic and international students. Applications are processed on a rolling basis. *Application fee:* $20 ($30 for international students). *Application Contact:* Dr. George F. Mead, Interim Dean of Dore' School of Graduate Studies, 337-475-5396, Fax: 337-475-5397, E-mail: admissions@mcneese.edu. *Interim Dean,* Dr. George F. Mead, 337-475-5394, Fax: 337-475-5397, E-mail: mead@mcneese.edu.

Burton College of Education Students: 124 full-time (95 women), 302 part-time (252 women); includes 76 minority (65 African Americans, 1 American Indian/Alaska Native, 2 Asian Americans or Pacific Islanders, 8 Hispanic Americans), 15 international. *Faculty:* 33 full-time (16 women), 5 part-time/adjunct (4 women). Expenses: Contact institution. *Financial support:* Fellowships, research assistantships, teaching assistantships, Federal Work-Study available. Support available to part-time students. Financial award application deadline: 5/1. In 2008, 137 master's awarded. *Degree program information:* Part-time and evening/weekend programs available. Offers addiction treatment (MA); applied behavior analysis (MA); counseling psychology (MA); curriculum and instruction (M Ed); early childhood education (M Ed); education (M Ed, MA, MAT, MS, Ed S); educational leadership (M Ed, Ed S); educational technology (Ed S); educational technology leadership (M Ed); elementary education (M Ed); elementary education grades 1-5 (MAT); exercise physiology (MS); general/experimental psychology (MA); health promotion (MS); instructional technology (MS); nutrition and wellness (MS); school counseling (M Ed); secondary education (M Ed); secondary education grades 6-12 (MAT); special education—mild/moderate grades 1-12 (MAT); special education mild/moderate grades 1-12 (M Ed); teaching (MAT). *Application deadline:* For fall admission, 5/15 priority date for domestic and international students; for spring admission, 10/15 priority date for domestic and international students. Applications are processed on a rolling basis. *Application fee:* $20 ($30 for international students). *Application Contact:* Dr. George F. Mead, Interim Dean of Dore' School of Graduate Studies, 337-475-5396, Fax: 337-475-5397, E-mail: admissions@mcneese.edu. *Dean,* Dr. Wayne R Fetter, 337-475-5432, Fax: 337-475-5467, E-mail: wfetter@mcneese.edu.

College of Business Students: 54 full-time (23 women), 45 part-time (19 women); includes 4 minority (1 African American, 2 Asian Americans or Pacific Islanders, 1 Hispanic American), 29 international. *Faculty:* 11 full-time (0 women). Expenses: Contact institution. *Financial support:* Research assistantships, teaching assistantships, Federal Work-Study available. Support available to part-time students. Financial award application deadline: 5/1. In 2008, 28 master's awarded. *Degree program information:* Part-time and evening/weekend programs available. Offers accounting (MBA); business (MBA). *Application deadline:* For fall admission, 5/15 priority date for domestic and international students; for spring admission, 10/15 priority date for domestic and international students. Applications are processed on a rolling basis. *Application fee:* $20 ($30 for international students). *Application Contact:* Dr. Akm Rahman, Interim MBA Director, 337-475-5573, Fax: 337-475-5010, E-mail: mrahman@mcneese.edu. *Dean,* Dr. Mitchell Adrian, 337-475-5514, Fax: 337-475-5010, E-mail: madrian@mcneese.edu.

McNEESE STATE UNIVERSITY (CONTINUED)

College of Engineering and Engineering Technology Students: 61 full-time (6 women), 10 part-time (2 women); includes 1 minority (African American), 61 international. *Faculty:* 12 full-time (0 women). Expenses: Contact institution. *Financial support:* Federal Work-Study available. Support available to part-time students. Financial award application deadline: 5/1. In 2008, 42 master's awarded. *Degree program information:* Part-time and evening/weekend programs available. Offers chemical engineering (M Eng); civil engineering (M Eng); electrical engineering (M Eng); engineering management (M Eng); mechanical engineering (M Eng). *Application deadline:* For fall admission, 5/15 priority date for domestic and international students; for spring admission, 10/15 priority date for domestic and international students. Applications are processed on a rolling basis. *Application fee:* $20 ($30 for international students). *Application Contact:* Dr. Jay O. Uppot, Director of Engineering Graduate Program, 337-475-5868, Fax: 337-475-5286, E-mail: juppot@mcneese.edu. *Dean,* Dr. Nikos Kiritsis, 337-475-5875, Fax: 337-475-5237, E-mail: nikosk@mcneese.edu.

College of Liberal Arts Students: 30 full-time (13 women), 8 part-time (7 women); includes 6 minority (3 African Americans, 2 Asian Americans or Pacific Islanders, 1 Hispanic American). *Faculty:* 29 full-time (12 women). Expenses: Contact institution. *Financial support:* Teaching assistantships, Federal Work-Study available. Support available to part-time students. Financial award application deadline: 5/1. In 2008, 14 master's awarded. *Degree program information:* Part-time and evening/weekend programs available. Offers creative writing (MFA); English (MA); Kodaly studies (MM Ed); liberal arts (MA, MFA, MM Ed); music education (MM Ed); vocal (MM Ed). *Application deadline:* For fall admission, 5/15 priority date for domestic and international students; for spring admission, 10/15 priority date for domestic and international students. Applications are processed on a rolling basis. *Application fee:* $20 ($30 for international students). *Application Contact:* Dr. George F. Mead, Interim Dean of Dore' School of Graduate Studies, 337-475-5396, Fax: 337-475-5397, E-mail: admissions@mcneese.edu. *Dean,* Dr. Ray Miles, 337-475-5192, Fax: 337-475-5594, E-mail: rmiles@mcneese.edu.

College of Nursing Students: 26 full-time (21 women), 62 part-time (51 women); includes 15 minority (14 African Americans, 1 Hispanic American). *Faculty:* 4 full-time (all women), 1 part-time/adjunct (0 women). Expenses: Contact institution. *Financial support:* Application deadline: 5/1. In 2008, 23 master's awarded. Offers clinical nurse specialist (MSN); nurse educator (MSN); nurse practitioner (MSN); nursing leadership and administration (MSN). *Application deadline:* For fall admission, 5/15 priority date for domestic and international students; for spring admission, 10/15 priority date for domestic and international students. Applications are processed on a rolling basis. *Application fee:* $20 ($30 for international students). *Application Contact:* Valarie Waldmeier, Coordinator of Graduate Nursing, 337-475-5285, Fax: 337-475-5707, E-mail: vwaldmeier@mcneese.edu. *Dean,* Dr. Peggy L. Wolfe, 337-475-5820, Fax: 337-475-5924, E-mail: pwolfe@mcneese.edu.

College of Science Students: 43 full-time (14 women), 17 part-time (9 women); includes 3 minority (2 African Americans, 1 Asian American or Pacific Islander), 31 international. *Faculty:* 26 full-time (6 women). Expenses: Contact institution. *Financial support:* Teaching assistantships, Federal Work-Study available. Support available to part-time students. Financial award application deadline: 5/1. In 2008, 55 master's awarded. *Degree program information:* Part-time and evening/weekend programs available. Offers agricultural sciences (MS); chemistry (MS); chemistry education (MS); environmental and chemical science (MS); environmental and chemical sciences (MS); environmental science education (MS); environmental sciences (MS); mathematical science (MS); science (MS). *Application deadline:* For fall admission, 5/15 priority date for domestic and international students; for spring admission, 10/15 priority date for domestic and international students. Applications are processed on a rolling basis. *Application fee:* $20 ($30 for international students). *Application Contact:* Dr. George F. Mead, Interim Dean of Dore' School of Graduate Studies, 337-475-5396, Fax: 337-475-5397, E-mail: admissions@mcneese.edu. *Dean,* Dr. George F. Mead, 337-475-5785, Fax: 337-475-5249, E-mail: mead@mcneese.edu.

MEADVILLE LOMBARD THEOLOGICAL SCHOOL, Chicago, IL 60637-1602

General Information Independent-religious, coed, graduate-only institution. *Graduate housing:* Rooms and/or apartments available on a first-come, first-served basis to single and married students. Housing application deadline: 3/15.

GRADUATE UNITS

Graduate and Professional Programs *Degree program information:* Part-time programs available. Postbaccalaureate distance learning degree programs offered (minimal on-campus study). Offers divinity (M Div); ministry (D Min); religion (MA).

MEDAILLE COLLEGE, Buffalo, NY 14214-2695

General Information Independent, coed, comprehensive institution. *Enrollment:* 2,917 graduate, professional, and undergraduate students; 1,128 full-time matriculated graduate/professional students, 64 part-time matriculated graduate/professional students. *Enrollment by degree level:* 1,192 master's. *Graduate faculty:* 41 full-time (25 women), 101 part-time/adjunct (58 women). *Tuition:* Full-time $15,480; part-time $645 per credit hour. *Graduate housing:* Rooms and/or apartments available on a first-come, first-served basis to single and married students. Typical cost: $8845 (including board) for single students; $8845 (including board) for married students. Housing application deadline: 8/15. *Student services:* Campus employment opportunities, campus safety program, career counseling, exercise/wellness program, free psychological counseling, low-cost health insurance, multicultural affairs office, services for students with disabilities, teacher training, writing training. *Library facilities:* Medaille College Library. *Online resources:* library catalog, web page, access to other libraries' catalogs. *Collection:* 56,854 titles, 240 serial subscriptions.

Computer facilities: 120 computers available on campus for general student use. A campuswide network can be accessed from student residence rooms and from off campus. Online class registration is available. *Web address:* http://www.medaille.edu/.

General Application Contact: Jacqueline Matheny, Executive Director of Marketing and Enrollment, 716-932-2541, Fax: 716-632-1811, E-mail: jmatheny@medaille.edu.

GRADUATE UNITS

Program in Business Administration—Amherst Students: 235 full-time (144 women); includes 64 minority (49 African Americans, 2 American Indian/Alaska Native, 2 Asian Americans or Pacific Islanders, 11 Hispanic Americans). Average age 35. 130 applicants, 96% accepted, 120 enrolled. *Faculty:* 4 full-time (1 woman), 30 part-time/adjunct (15 women). Expenses: Contact institution. *Financial support:* In 2008–09, 180 students received support. Federal Work-Study available. Financial award applicants required to submit FAFSA. In 2008, 89 master's awarded. *Degree program information:* Evening/weekend programs available. Offers business administration (MBA); organizational leadership (MA). *Application deadline:* Applications are processed on a rolling basis. *Application fee:* $100. *Application Contact:* Jacqueline Matheny, Executive Director of Marketing and Enrollment, 716-932-2541, Fax: 716-632-1811, E-mail: jmatheny@medaille.edu. *Associate Dean for Special Programs,* Jennifer Bavifard, 716-631-1061 Ext. 150, Fax: 716-631-1380, E-mail: jbavifar@medaille.edu.

Program in Business Administration—Rochester Students: 37 full-time (26 women); includes 14 minority (9 African Americans, 5 Hispanic Americans). Average age 36. 31 applicants, 90% accepted, 25 enrolled. *Faculty:* 3 full-time (2 women), 40 part-time/adjunct (20 women). Expenses: Contact institution. *Financial support:* In 2008–09, 37 students received support. Federal Work-Study available. Financial award applicants required to submit FAFSA. In 2008, 27 master's awarded. *Degree program information:* Evening/weekend programs available. Offers business administration (MBA); organizational leadership (MA). *Application deadline:* Applications are processed on a rolling basis. *Application fee:* $100. *Application Contact:* Jane Rowlands, Marketing Support, 585-272-0030, Fax: 585-272-0057, E-mail: jrowlands@medaille.edu. *Branch Campus Director,* Jennifer Bavifard, 716-932-2591, Fax: 716-631-1380, E-mail: jbavifard@medaille.edu.

Program in Education Students: 809 full-time (717 women), 64 part-time (50 women); includes 21 minority (13 African Americans, 4 American Indian/Alaska Native, 1 Asian American or Pacific Islander, 3 Hispanic Americans), 569 international. Average age 26. 730 applicants, 92% accepted, 600 enrolled. *Faculty:* 28 full-time (19 women), 21 part-time/adjunct (15 women). Expenses: Contact institution. *Financial support:* In 2008–09, 501 students received support. Federal Work-Study available. Financial award applicants required to submit FAFSA. In 2008, 677 master's awarded. *Degree program information:* Part-time and evening/weekend programs available. Offers curriculum and instruction (MS Ed); education preparation (MS Ed); literacy (MS Ed); special education (MS). *Application deadline:* For fall admission, 8/15 priority date for domestic students; for spring admission, 1/15 priority date for domestic students. Applications are processed on a rolling basis. *Application fee:* $35. Electronic applications accepted. *Application Contact:* Jacqueline Matheny, Executive Director of Marketing and Enrollment, 716-932-2541, Fax: 716-632-1811, E-mail: jmatheny@medaille.edu. *Director of Graduate Programs,* Dr. Robert DiSibio, 716-932-2548, Fax: 716-631-1380, E-mail: rdisibio@medaille.edu.

Programs in Psychology Students: 148 full-time (118 women); includes 30 minority (29 African Americans, 1 Hispanic American). Average age 34. 85 applicants, 94% accepted, 75 enrolled. *Faculty:* 6 full-time (3 women), 10 part-time/adjunct (8 women). Expenses: Contact institution. *Financial support:* In 2008–09, 90 students received support. Federal Work-Study available. Financial award applicants required to submit FAFSA. In 2008, 37 master's awarded. *Degree program information:* Part-time and evening/weekend programs available. Offers mental health counseling (MA); psychology (MA). *Application deadline:* Applications are processed on a rolling basis. *Application fee:* $35. Electronic applications accepted. *Application Contact:* Jacqueline Matheny, Executive Director of Marketing and Enrollment, 716-932-2541, Fax: 716-632-1811, E-mail: jmatheny@medaille.edu. *Dean of Adult and Graduate Studies,* Dr. Judith Horowitz, 716-880-2229, Fax: 716-884-0291, E-mail: jhorowitz@medaille.edu.

MEDICAL COLLEGE OF GEORGIA, Augusta, GA 30912

General Information State-supported, coed, upper-level institution. CGS member. *Enrollment:* 2,443 graduate, professional, and undergraduate students; 1,715 full-time matriculated graduate/professional students (988 women), 138 part-time matriculated graduate/professional students (114 women). *Enrollment by degree level:* 1,002 first professional, 413 master's, 436 doctoral, 2 other advanced degrees. *Graduate faculty:* 664 full-time (240 women), 144 part-time/adjunct (64 women). *Graduate housing:* Rooms and/or apartments available on a first-come, first-served basis to single and married students. *Student services:* Campus employment opportunities, campus safety program, career counseling, child daycare facilities, exercise/wellness program, free psychological counseling, international student services, low-cost health insurance, multicultural affairs office. *Library facilities:* Robert B. Greenblatt MD Library. *Online resources:* library catalog, web page, access to other libraries' catalogs. *Collection:* 165,433 titles, 1,823 serial subscriptions, 952 audiovisual materials. *Research affiliation:* Georgia Center of Innovation for Life Sciences (research commercialization and economic development), Georgia Research Alliance (science and technology development), Georgia Cancer Coalition (cancer research programs), Advanced Technology Development Center (biotechnology transfer), Medical College of Georgia Research Institute, Inc. (biomedical research).

Computer facilities: 323 computers available on campus for general student use. A campuswide network can be accessed. Online class registration is available. *Web address:* http://www.mcg.edu/.

General Application Contact: Dr. Beverly Boggs, Executive Director of Financial Aid and Academic Admissions, 706-721-2725, Fax: 706-721-7279, E-mail: bboggs@mail.mcg.edu.

GRADUATE UNITS

School of Dentistry Students: 252 full-time (111 women); includes 63 minority (21 African Americans, 1 American Indian/Alaska Native, 32 Asian Americans or Pacific Islanders, 9 Hispanic Americans), 1 international. Average age 25. 314 applicants, 24% accepted, 66 enrolled. *Faculty:* 69 full-time (11 women), 32 part-time/adjunct (5 women). Expenses: Contact institution. *Financial support:* Federal Work-Study and scholarships/grants available. Financial award application deadline: 5/1; financial award applicants required to submit FAFSA. In 2008, 59 DMDs awarded. Offers dentistry (DMD). *Application deadline:* For fall admission, 10/15 for domestic students. *Application fee:* $30. Electronic applications accepted. *Application Contact:* Dr. Carole M. Hanes, Associate Dean for Student and Alumni Affairs, 706-721-3587, Fax: 706-721-6276, E-mail: chanes@mcg.edu. *Dean,* Connie Drisko, 706-721-2117, Fax: 706-721-6276, E-mail: cdrisko@mcg.edu.

School of Graduate Studies Students: 308 full-time (210 women), 120 part-time (98 women); includes 89 minority (52 African Americans, 1 American Indian/Alaska Native, 27 Asian Americans or Pacific Islanders, 9 Hispanic Americans), 70 international. Average age 33. 451 applicants, 44% accepted, 125 enrolled. *Faculty:* 225 full-time (74 women), 7 part-time/adjunct (4 women). Expenses: Contact institution. *Financial support:* In 2008–09, 10 fellowships with partial tuition reimbursements (averaging $26,000 per year), 111 research assistantships with partial tuition reimbursements (averaging $23,000 per year) were awarded; teaching assistantships, career-related internships or fieldwork, Federal Work-Study, institutionally sponsored loans, scholarships/grants, traineeships, and unspecified assistantships also available. Support available to part-time students. Financial award application deadline: 5/31; financial award applicants required to submit FAFSA. In 2008, 68 master's, 48 doctorates awarded. *Degree program information:* Part-time programs available. Postbaccalaureate distance learning degree programs offered (no on-campus study). Offers adult acute/critical care advanced practice nursing (MSN); allied health sciences (MS); biochemistry and molecular biology (PhD); biostatistics (MS, PhD); cellular biology and anatomy (PhD); clinical and translational science (MCTS, CCTS); clinical nurse leader (MSN); family nurse practitioner (MSN); genomic medicine (PhD); medical illustration (MS); molecular medicine (PhD); neuroscience (PhD); nursing (PhD); nursing anesthesia (MSN); nursing practice (DNP); oral biology and maxillofacial pathology (MS, PhD); pediatric nurse practitioner (MSN); pharmacology (PhD); physiology (PhD); public health–informatics (MPH); vascular biology (PhD). *Application fee:* $30. Electronic applications accepted. *Application Contact:* Dr. Beverly A. Boggs, Executive Director of Academic Admissions and Student Financial Aid, 706-721-2725, Fax: 706-721-7279, E-mail: bbogs@mcg.edu. *Dean,* Dr. Gretchen B. Caughman, 706-721-3278, Fax: 706-721-6829, E-mail: gcaughma@mail.mcg.edu.

School of Medicine Students: 749 full-time (340 women), 1 (woman) part-time; includes 211 minority (44 African Americans, 4 American Indian/Alaska Native, 148 Asian Americans or Pacific Islanders, 15 Hispanic Americans), 1 international. Average age 25. 2,102 applicants, 13% accepted, 190 enrolled. *Faculty:* 504 full-time (128 women), 83 part-time/adjunct (35 women). Expenses: Contact institution. *Financial support:* In 2008–09, 599 students received support; fellowships with tuition reimbursements available, career-related internships or fieldwork, Federal Work-Study, institutionally sponsored loans, and scholarships/grants available. Support available to part-time students. Financial award application deadline: 5/1; financial award applicants required to submit FAFSA. In 2008, 170 MDs awarded. Offers medicine (MD). *Application deadline:* For fall admission, 11/1 for domestic students. Applications are processed on a rolling basis. *Application fee:* $0. *Application Contact:* Dr. Mason P. Thompson, Associate Dean for Admissions and Student Affairs, 706-721-3186, Fax: 706-721-0959, E-mail: mthomps@mail.mcg.edu. *Dean,* Dr. David M. Stern, 706-721-2231, Fax: 706-721-7035, E-mail: dstern@mcg.edu.

MEDICAL COLLEGE OF WISCONSIN, Milwaukee, WI 53226-0509

General Information Independent, coed, graduate-only institution. CGS member. *Graduate housing:* On-campus housing not available. *Research affiliation:* General Electric Medical Systems (biophysics, radiology).

GRADUATE UNITS

Graduate School of Biomedical Sciences *Degree program information:* Part-time and evening/weekend programs available. Postbaccalaureate distance learning degree programs offered (minimal on-campus study). Offers biochemistry (PhD); bioethics (MA); bioinformatics (MS); biomedical sciences (MA, MPH, MS, PhD, Graduate Certificate); biophysics (PhD); biostatistics (PhD); epidemiology (MS); functional imaging (PhD); health care technologies (MS); medical informatics (MS); microbiology and molecular genetics (MS, PhD); neuroscience (PhD); pathology (MS, PhD); pharmacology and toxicology (PhD); physiology (MS, PhD); public and community health (PhD); public health (MPH, PhD, Graduate Certificate).

Medical School *Degree program information:* Part-time programs available. Postbaccalaureate distance learning degree programs offered (no on-campus study). Offers medicine (MD, MPH); occupational health and medicine (MPH); public and community health (MPH).

MEDICAL UNIVERSITY OF SOUTH CAROLINA, Charleston, SC 29425-0002

General Information State-supported, coed, upper-level institution. CGS member. *Enrollment:* 2,531 graduate, professional, and undergraduate students; 2,013 full-time matriculated graduate/professional students (1,196 women), 199 part-time matriculated graduate/professional students (143 women). *Enrollment by degree level:* 1,098 first professional, 602 master's, 528 doctoral, 16 other advanced degrees. *Graduate faculty:* 1,213 full-time (494 women), 251 part-time/adjunct (129 women). *Graduate housing:* On-campus housing not available. *Student services:* Campus employment opportunities, campus safety program, exercise/wellness program, free psychological counseling, grant writing training, international student services, low-cost health insurance, multicultural affairs office, services for students with disabilities, writing training. *Library facilities:* Medical University of South Carolina Library plus 1 other. *Online resources:* library catalog, web page, access to other libraries' catalogs. *Collection:* 178,542 titles, 1,587 serial subscriptions, 6,112 audiovisual materials. *Research affiliation:* GlaxoSmithKline (cancer), United Therapeutics (cardiovascular diseases), Elan Pharmaceuticals (neurosciences), Arena Pharmaceuticals, Inc (lipidomics), Actelion Pharmaceuticals (immunology and inflammatory diseases), Eli Lilly (substance abuse).

Computer facilities: 200 computers available on campus for general student use. A campuswide network can be accessed from off campus. Online class registration is available. *Web address:* http://www.musc.edu/.

General Application Contact: George W. Ohlandt, Director of Admissions, 843-792-3281, Fax: 843-792-6615, E-mail: ohlandtg@musc.edu.

GRADUATE UNITS

College of Dental Medicine Students: 225 full-time (86 women); includes 17 minority (6 African Americans, 1 American Indian/Alaska Native, 8 Asian Americans or Pacific Islanders, 2 Hispanic Americans), 1 international. Average age 26. 814 applicants, 8% accepted, 56 enrolled. *Faculty:* 50 full-time (8 women), 30 part-time/adjunct (8 women). Expenses: Contact institution. *Financial support:* In 2008–09, 29 students received support. Federal Work-Study, scholarships/grants, and tuition waivers (partial) available. Support available to part-time students. Financial award application deadline: 3/10; financial award applicants required to submit FAFSA. In 2008, 54 DMDs awarded. Offers dental medicine (DMD). *Application deadline:* For spring admission, 1/15 for domestic and international students. *Application fee:* $75. Electronic applications accepted. *Application Contact:* William H. Liner, Dental Admissions Counselor, 843-792-4892, Fax: 843-792-6615, E-mail: linerw@musc.edu. *Dean,* Dr. John J. Sanders, 843-792-3811, Fax: 843-792-1376, E-mail: sandersjj@musc.edu.

College of Graduate Studies Students: 146 full-time (82 women), 37 part-time (16 women); includes 12 African Americans, 5 Asian Americans or Pacific Islanders, 6 Hispanic Americans, 28 international. Average age 30. 80 applicants, 60% accepted, 37 enrolled. *Faculty:* 324 full-time, 176 part-time/adjunct. Expenses: Contact institution. *Financial support:* In 2008–09, 183 students received support, including fellowships with partial tuition reimbursements available (averaging $21,000 per year); Federal Work-Study and scholarships/grants also available. Support available to part-time students. Financial award application deadline: 3/10; financial award applicants required to submit FAFSA. In 2008, 26 master's, 41 doctorates awarded. Offers biochemistry and molecular biology (MS, PhD); bioinformatics (MS, PhD); biostatistics (MS, PhD); cancer biology (PhD); cardiovascular biology (MS, PhD); cell and molecular pharmacology and experimental therapeutics (MS, PhD); cell regulation (MS, PhD); clinical research (MS); epidemiology (MS, PhD); genetics and development (MS, PhD); marine biomedicine (PhD); microbiology and immunology (MS, PhD); molecular biology (MS, PhD); neurosciences (MS, PhD); nursing (PhD); pathology and laboratory medicine (MS, PhD); pharmaceutical sciences (PhD); structural biology (MS, PhD). *Application deadline:* For fall admission, 1/15 priority date for domestic and international students. Applications are processed on a rolling basis. *Application fee:* $75 for international students. Electronic applications accepted. *Application Contact:* Dr. Cynthia F. Wright, Assistant Dean for Admissions, 843-792-3391, Fax: 843-792-6590, E-mail: wrightcf@musc.edu. *Dean,* Dr. Perry V. Halushka, 843-792-3012, Fax: 843-792-6590, E-mail: halushpv@musc.edu.

College of Health Professions Students: 614 full-time (482 women), 47 part-time (30 women); includes 75 minority (44 African Americans, 1 American Indian/Alaska Native, 16 Asian Americans or Pacific Islanders, 14 Hispanic Americans), 2 international. Average age 28. 1,183 applicants, 35% accepted, 298 enrolled. *Faculty:* 39 full-time (17 women), 6 part-time/adjunct (4 women). Expenses: Contact institution. *Financial support:* In 2008–09, 32 students received support. Career-related internships or fieldwork, Federal Work-Study, scholarships/grants, and tuition waivers (partial) available. Support available to part-time students. Financial award application deadline: 3/10; financial award applicants required to submit FAFSA. In 2008, 194 master's, 127 doctorates awarded. *Degree program information:* Part-time programs available. Offers anesthesia for nurses (MS); health administration (DHA); health administration-executive (MHA); health administration-residential (MHA); health and rehabilitation science (PhD); health professions (MHA, MRA, MS, DHA, DPT, PhD); occupational therapy (MS); physical therapy (DPT); physician assistant (MS); research administration (MRA). *Application fee:* $75. Electronic applications accepted. *Application Contact:* Lauren Smith, Recruitment and Student Affairs Coordinator, 843-792-8476, Fax: 843-792-0253, E-mail: smilau@musc.edu. *Dean,* Dr. Mark S. Sothmann, 843-792-3328, Fax: 843-792-3322, E-mail: sothmann@musc.edu.

College of Medicine Students: 642 full-time (270 women); includes 143 minority (77 African Americans, 7 American Indian/Alaska Native, 42 Asian Americans or Pacific Islanders, 17 Hispanic Americans), 10 international. Average age 26. 2,496 applicants, 7% accepted, 156 enrolled. *Faculty:* 1,085 full-time (400 women), 152 part-time/adjunct (68 women). Expenses: Contact institution. *Financial support:* In 2008–09, 583 students received support. Federal Work-Study and scholarships/grants available. Financial award application deadline: 3/10; financial award applicants required to submit FAFSA. In 2008, 131 MDs awarded. Offers medicine (MD). MSCR is achieved through successful completion of Southeastern Predoctoral Training in Clinical Research program. *Application deadline:* For fall admission, 12/1 for domestic students. Applications are processed on a rolling basis. *Application fee:* $75. Electronic applications accepted. *Application Contact:* Wanda L. Taylor, Director of Admissions, 843-792-2055, Fax: 843-792-0204, E-mail: taylorwl@musc.edu. *Dean,* Dr. Jerry G. Reves, 843-792-2842, Fax: 843-792-2967, E-mail: revesj@musc.edu.

College of Nursing Students: 49 full-time (47 women), 69 part-time (65 women); includes 13 minority (8 African Americans, 1 American Indian/Alaska Native, 3 Asian Americans or Pacific Islanders, 1 Hispanic American). Average age 35. 94 applicants, 52% accepted, 31 enrolled. *Faculty:* 27 full-time (26 women), 14 part-time/adjunct (12 women). Expenses: Contact institution. *Financial support:* In 2008–09, 109 students received support. Federal Work-Study, scholarships/grants, and traineeships available. Support available to part-time students. Financial award application deadline: 3/10; financial award applicants required to submit FAFSA. In 2008, 51 master's awarded. *Degree program information:* Part-time programs available. Postbaccalaureate distance learning degree programs offered (minimal on-campus study). Offers adult nurse practitioner (MSN); family nurse practitioner (MSN); nurse administrator (MSN); nurse educator (MSN); nursing (MSN, DNP); pediatric nurse practitioner (MSN); post-master's for advanced practice nurses (DNP). *Application deadline:* For fall admission, 2/1 for domestic and international students; for spring admission, 9/15 for domestic and international students. *Application fee:* $75. Electronic applications accepted. *Application Contact:* Carolyn F. Page, Director, Student Services, 843-792-3844, Fax: 843-792-9258, E-mail: pagecf@musc.edu. *Dean,* Dr. Gail W. Stuart, 843-792-3941, Fax: 843-792-0504, E-mail: stuartg@musc.edu.

South Carolina College of Pharmacy Students: 313 full-time (214 women), 1 (woman) part-time; includes 49 minority (19 African Americans, 2 American Indian/Alaska Native, 21 Asian Americans or Pacific Islanders, 7 Hispanic Americans), 1 international. Average age 25. 584 applicants, 36% accepted, 192 enrolled. *Faculty:* 59 full-time (24 women), 1 part-time/adjunct (0 women). Expenses: Contact institution. *Financial support:* In 2008–09, 76 students received support. Career-related internships or fieldwork, Federal Work-Study, institutionally sponsored loans, and scholarships/grants available. Financial award application deadline: 3/10; financial award applicants required to submit FAFSA. In 2008, 78 Pharm Ds awarded. Offers pharmacy (Pharm D). *Application deadline:* For fall admission, 1/1 for domestic and international students. *Application fee:* $75. Electronic applications accepted. *Application Contact:* Dr. Philip D. Hall, Associate Dean, 843-792-8979, Fax: 843-792-9081, E-mail: hallpd@sccp.sc.edu. *Executive Dean,* Dr. Joseph T. DiPiro, 843-792-8452, Fax: 843-792-9081, E-mail: jdipiro@sccp.sc.edu.

MEHARRY MEDICAL COLLEGE, Nashville, TN 37208-9989

General Information Independent-religious, coed, graduate-only institution. CGS member. *Graduate faculty:* 273 full-time (69 women), 46 part-time/adjunct (11 women). *Graduate housing:* Rooms and/or apartments available on a first-come, first-served basis to single and married students. *Student services:* Campus employment opportunities, campus safety program, career counseling, child daycare facilities, exercise/wellness program, free psychological counseling, international student services, low-cost health insurance. *Library facilities:* Meharry Medical College Library. *Online resources:* library catalog, web page. *Collection:* 98,000 titles, 1,011 serial subscriptions, 382 audiovisual materials.

Computer facilities: 100 computers available on campus for general student use. A campuswide network can be accessed from student residence rooms and from off campus. *Web address:* http://www.mmc.edu/.

General Application Contact: Allen D. Mosley, Director of Admissions and Recruitment, 615-327-6223, Fax: 615-327-6228, E-mail: amosley@mmc.edu.

GRADUATE UNITS

School of Dentistry Students: 248 full-time (138 women); includes 227 minority (187 African Americans, 3 American Indian/Alaska Native, 21 Asian Americans or Pacific Islanders, 16 Hispanic Americans). Average age 26. 1,976 applicants, 4% accepted, 51 enrolled. *Faculty:* 39 full-time (10 women), 16 part-time/adjunct (5 women). Expenses: Contact institution. *Financial support:* Career-related internships or fieldwork, Federal Work-Study, and institutionally sponsored loans available. Financial award application deadline: 4/15; financial award applicants required to submit FAFSA. In 2008, 60 DDSs awarded. Offers dentistry (DDS). *Application deadline:* For winter admission, 1/15 for domestic and international students. Applications are processed on a rolling basis. *Application fee:* $65. *Application Contact:* Allen D. Mosley, Director of Admissions and Recruitment, 615-327-6223, Fax: 615-327-6228, E-mail: amosley@mmc.edu. *Dean,* Dr. William B. Butler, 615-327-6207, Fax: 615-327-6213.

School of Graduate Studies Students: 85 full-time (63 women); includes 83 minority (82 African Americans, 1 Asian American or Pacific Islander). Average age 30. 161 applicants, 25% accepted, 30 enrolled. *Faculty:* 32 full-time (11 women). Expenses: Contact institution. *Financial support:* In 2008–09, 23 students received support, including 52 fellowships (averaging $22,000 per year); research assistantships, teaching assistantships, career-related internships or fieldwork, Federal Work-Study, institutionally sponsored loans, scholarships/grants, and tuition waivers (full) also available. Support available to part-time students. Financial award applicants required to submit FAFSA. In 2008, 10 master's, 13 doctorates awarded. Postbaccalaureate distance learning degree programs offered (minimal on-campus study). Offers cancer biology (PhD); interdisciplinary studiesmicrobiology and immunology (PhD); neuroscience (PhD); occupational medicine (MSPH); pharmacology (PhD); public health administration (MSPH). *Application deadline:* For fall admission, 6/1 for domestic students. Applications are processed on a rolling basis. *Application fee:* $65. *Application Contact:* Dr. Maria F. Lima, Interim Director, 615-327-6533, Fax: 615-327-2933, E-mail: mflima@mmc.edu. *Interim Director,* Dr. Maria F. Lima, 615-327-6533, Fax: 615-327-2933, E-mail: mflima@mmc.edu.

School of Medicine Students: 422 full-time (248 women); includes 392 minority (348 African Americans, 6 American Indian/Alaska Native, 25 Asian Americans or Pacific Islanders, 13 Hispanic Americans). 4,577 applicants, 4% accepted, 100 enrolled. Expenses: Contact institution. *Financial support:* Federal Work-Study, institutionally sponsored loans, and tuition waivers (partial) available. Financial award applicants required to submit FAFSA. Offers medicine (MD). *Application deadline:* For fall admission, 12/15 for domestic students. Applications are processed on a rolling basis. *Application fee:* $65. Electronic applications accepted. *Application Contact:* Allen D. Mosley, Director of Admissions and Recruitment, 615-327-6223, Fax: 615-327-6228, E-mail: amosley@mmc.edu. *Dean,* Dr. Valerie Montgomery Rice, 615-327-6204, Fax: 615-327-6568.

MEMORIAL UNIVERSITY OF NEWFOUNDLAND, St. John's, NL A1C 5S7, Canada

General Information Province-supported, coed, university. *Graduate housing:* Rooms and/or apartments available on a first-come, first-served basis to single and married students. *Research affiliation:* Eastern Regional Health Authority (health research).

GRADUATE UNITS

Faculty of Medicine *Degree program information:* Part-time programs available. Postbaccalaureate distance learning degree programs offered (no on-campus study). Offers medicine (M Sc, PhD, Diploma). Electronic applications accepted.

Graduate Programs in Medicine *Degree program information:* Part-time programs available. Offers applied health services research (M Sc); cancer (M Sc, PhD); cardiovascular (M Sc, PhD); clinical epidemiology (M Sc, PhD, Diploma); community health (M Sc, PhD, Diploma); human genetics (M Sc, PhD); immunology (M Sc, PhD); medicine (M Sc, PhD, Diploma); neuroscience (M Sc, PhD). Electronic applications accepted.

School of Graduate Studies *Degree program information:* Part-time and evening/weekend programs available. Postbaccalaureate distance learning degree programs offered (minimal on-campus study). Offers applied social psychology (MASP); aquaculture (M Sc); archaeology and physical anthropology (MA, PhD); atomic and molecular physics (M Sc, PhD); biochemistry (M Sc, PhD); biology (M Sc, PhD); chemistry (M Sc, PhD); classics (MA); cognitive and behavioral ecology (M Sc, PhD); computational science (M Sc); computational science (cooperative) (M Sc); computer engineering (MA Sc); computer science (M Sc, PhD); condensed matter physics (M Sc, PhD); economics (MA); employment relations (MER); English language and literature (MA, PhD); environmental science (M Env Sc, M Sc); environmental systems engineering and management (MA Sc); ethnomusicology (MA, PhD); experimental psychology (M Sc, PhD); fisheries resource management (MMS, Advanced Diploma); folklore (MA, PhD); food science (M Sc, PhD); French studies (MA); gender (PhD); geography (M Sc, MA, PhD); geology (M Sc, PhD); geophysics (M Sc, PhD); German language and literature (M Phil, MA); history (MA, PhD); humanities (M Phil); instrumental analysis (M Sc); linguistics (MA, PhD); marine biology (M Sc, PhD); maritime sociology (PhD); mathematics (M Sc, PhD); philosophy (MA); physical oceanography (M Sc, PhD); physics (M Sc); political science (MA); religious studies (MA); social and cultural anthropology (MA, PhD); sociology (M Phil, MA); statistics (M Sc, MAS, PhD); women's studies (MWS); work and development (PhD). Electronic applications accepted.

Faculty of Business Administration *Degree program information:* Part-time programs available. Offers business administration (EMBA, MBA). Electronic applications accepted.

Faculty of Education *Degree program information:* Part-time programs available. Offers counseling psychology (M Ed); curriculum, teaching, and learning studies (M Ed); education (PhD); educational leadership studies (M Ed); information technology (M Ed); post-secondary studies (M Ed, Diploma). Electronic applications accepted.

Faculty of Engineering and Applied Science *Degree program information:* Part-time programs available. Offers civil engineering (M Eng, PhD); electrical and computer engineering (M Eng, PhD); mechanical engineering (M Eng, PhD); ocean and naval architecture engineering (M Eng, PhD). Electronic applications accepted.

School of Human Kinetics and Recreation *Degree program information:* Part-time programs available. Offers administration, curriculum and supervision (MPE); biomechanics/ergonomics (MS Kin); exercise and work physiology (MS Kin); sport psychology (MS Kin). Electronic applications accepted.

School of Music Offers conducting (MMus); performance pedagogy (MMus); performing (MMus). Electronic applications accepted.

Memorial University of Newfoundland (continued)

School of Nursing *Degree program information:* Part-time programs available. Offers nursing (MN, PMD). Electronic applications accepted.

School of Pharmacy *Degree program information:* Part-time programs available. Offers pharmacy (MSCPharm, PhD). Electronic applications accepted.

School of Social Work *Degree program information:* Part-time and evening/weekend programs available. Offers social work (MSW). Electronic applications accepted.

MEMPHIS COLLEGE OF ART, Memphis, TN 38104-2764

General Information Independent, coed, comprehensive institution. *Enrollment:* 403 graduate, professional, and undergraduate students; 19 full-time matriculated graduate/professional students (10 women), 62 part-time matriculated graduate/professional students (41 women). *Enrollment by degree level:* 81 master's. *Graduate faculty:* 25 full-time (13 women), 4 part-time/adjunct (2 women). *Tuition:* Full-time $22,000; part-time $958 per credit hour. *Required fees:* $560; $280 per semester. Tuition and fees vary according to program. *Graduate housing:* Room and/or apartments available on a first-come, first-served basis to single students; on-campus housing not available to married students. Typical cost: $5800 per year. Room charges vary according to housing facility selected. Housing application deadline: 8/15. *Student services:* Campus employment opportunities, campus safety program, career counseling, international student services, teacher training. *Library facilities:* G. Pillow Lewis Library plus 1 other. *Online resources:* web page. *Collection:* 14,500 titles, 108 serial subscriptions, 175 audiovisual materials.

Computer facilities: Computer purchase and lease plans are available. 70 computers available on campus for general student use. *Web address:* http://www.mca.edu/.

General Application Contact: Annette James Moore, Director of Admissions, 800-727-1088, Fax: 901-272-5158, E-mail: info@mca.edu.

GRADUATE UNITS

Graduate Programs Students: 19 full-time (10 women), 62 part-time (41 women); includes 18 minority (15 African Americans, 1 Asian American or Pacific Islander, 2 Hispanic Americans). Average age 29. 74 applicants, 59% accepted, 24 enrolled. *Faculty:* 25 full-time (13 women), 4 part-time/adjunct (2 women). Expenses: Contact institution. *Financial support:* In 2008–09, 5 teaching assistantships with partial tuition reimbursements (averaging $2,000 per year) were awarded; career-related internships or fieldwork, Federal Work-Study, institutionally sponsored loans, scholarships/grants, tuition waivers (partial), unspecified assistantships, and merit awards also available. Support available to part-time students. Financial award application deadline: 8/1; financial award applicants required to submit FAFSA. In 2008, 4 master's awarded. *Degree program information:* Part-time programs available. Offers art education (MA, MAT); computer arts (MFA); painting (MFA); photography (MFA); printmaking (MFA); sculpture (MFA); studio art (MFA). *Application deadline:* For fall admission, 3/1 priority date for domestic and international students; for spring admission, 11/1 priority date for domestic and international students. *Application fee:* $50. Electronic applications accepted. *Application Contact:* Annette James Moore, Director of Admissions, 800-727-1088, Fax: 901-272-5158, E-mail: info@mca.edu. *Vice President for Academic Affairs*, Ken Strickland, 901-272-5100, Fax: 901-272-5104, E-mail: info@mca.edu.

MEMPHIS THEOLOGICAL SEMINARY, Memphis, TN 38104-4395

General Information Independent-religious, coed, graduate-only institution. *Graduate housing:* Rooms and/or apartments available on a first-come, first-served basis to single and married students. Housing application deadline: 7/15. *Research affiliation:* Lilly Foundation (technology/religion), Wabash Center for Teaching and Learning (theology, religion).

GRADUATE UNITS

Graduate and Professional Programs *Degree program information:* Part-time programs available. Offers theology (M Div, MAR, D Min).

MENNONITE BRETHREN BIBLICAL SEMINARY, Fresno, CA 93727-5097

General Information Independent-religious, coed, graduate-only institution. *Graduate housing:* Rooms and/or apartments available on a first-come, first-served basis to single and married students.

GRADUATE UNITS

School of Theology *Degree program information:* Part-time programs available. Post-baccalaureate distance learning degree programs offered (minimal on-campus study). Offers Christian ministry (MA); divinity (M Div); intercultural mission (MA); marriage, family, and child counseling (MAMFCC, Diploma); New Testament (MA); Old Testament (MA); theology (MA).

MERCER UNIVERSITY, Macon, GA 31207-0003

General Information Independent-religious, coed, university. *Enrollment:* 5,464 graduate, professional, and undergraduate students; 2,172 full-time matriculated graduate/professional students (1,287 women), 936 part-time matriculated graduate/professional students (620 women). *Enrollment by degree level:* 1,522 first professional, 1,360 master's, 163 doctoral, 63 other advanced degrees. *Graduate faculty:* 126 full-time (57 women), 27 part-time/adjunct (10 women). Tuition and fees vary according to degree level, campus/location, program and student level. *Graduate housing:* Rooms and/or apartments available on a first-come, first-served basis to single and married students. *Student services:* Campus employment opportunities, campus safety program, career counseling, free psychological counseling, international student services, low-cost health insurance, services for students with disabilities. *Library facilities:* Jack Tarver Library plus 3 others. *Online resources:* library catalog, web page. *Collection:* 692,225 titles, 28,163 serial subscriptions, 64,319 audiovisual materials. *Research affiliation:* MedCen Foundation (basic clinical investigations), Central State Hospital of Milledgeville, Georgia (schizophrenia, treatment of psychosis, tumor necrosis).

Computer facilities: 500 computers available on campus for general student use. A campuswide network can be accessed from student residence rooms and from off campus. Online class registration is available. *Web address:* http://www.mercer.edu/.

General Application Contact: 478-301-2700.

GRADUATE UNITS

Graduate Studies, Cecil B. Day Campus Students: 1,242 full-time (807 women), 737 part-time (527 women); includes 806 minority (627 African Americans, 2 American Indian/Alaska Native, 146 Asian Americans or Pacific Islanders, 31 Hispanic Americans), 69 international. Average age 31. *Faculty:* 82 full-time (42 women), 23 part-time/adjunct (8 women). Expenses: Contact institution. *Financial support:* Teaching assistantships, career-related internships or fieldwork, Federal Work-Study, and scholarships/grants available. Support available to part-time students. In 2008, 188 first professional degrees, 322 master's, 19 doctorates, 13 other advanced degrees awarded. *Degree program information:* Part-time and evening/weekend programs available. Postbaccalaureate distance learning degree programs offered (no on-campus study). *Application Contact:* Andrew I. Horn, Director of Admissions/Marketing, 678-547-6206, E-mail: horn_ai@mercer.edu. *Senior Vice President*, Richard V Swindle, 678-547-6397, E-mail: swindle_rv@mercer.edu.

College of Pharmacy and Health Sciences Students: 637 full-time (422 women), 7 part-time (4 women); includes 202 minority (81 African Americans, 1 American Indian/Alaska Native, 106 Asian Americans or Pacific Islanders, 14 Hispanic Americans), 35 international. Average age 26. 2,250 applicants, 13% accepted, 155 enrolled. *Faculty:* 19 full-time (12 women), 3 part-time/adjunct (1 woman). Expenses: Contact institution. *Financial support:* In 2008–09, 350 students received support; teaching assistantships with tuition reimbursements available, career-related internships or fieldwork, Federal Work-Study, institutionally sponsored loans, scholarships/grants, and tuition waivers available. Support available to part-time students. Financial award application deadline: 5/1; financial award applicants required to submit FAFSA. In 2008, 137 first professional degrees, 12 doctorates awarded. Offers medical sciences (MS); pharmacy (Pharm D, PhD). *Application deadline:* For fall admission, 1/1 for domestic students. Applications are processed on a rolling basis. *Application fee:* $25. Electronic applications accepted. *Application Contact:* Dr. James W. Bartling, Associate Dean for Student Affairs and Admissions, 678-547-6181, Fax: 678-547-6063, E-mail: bartling_jw@mercer.edu. *Dean*, Dr. Hewitt W. Matthews, 678-547-6304, Fax: 678-547-6315, E-mail: matthews_h@mercer.edu.

Eugene W. Stetson School of Business and Economics (Atlanta) Students: 183 full-time (78 women), 104 part-time (46 women); includes 104 minority (84 African Americans, 12 Asian Americans or Pacific Islanders, 8 Hispanic Americans), 18 international. Average age 33. *Faculty:* 17 full-time (5 women), 4 part-time/adjunct (0 women). Expenses: Contact institution. *Financial support:* Federal Work-Study available. In 2008, 135 master's awarded. *Degree program information:* Part-time and evening/weekend programs available. Offers business administration (MBA, XMBA). *Application deadline:* For fall admission, 7/1 priority date for domestic students; for spring admission, 11/1 priority date for domestic students. Applications are processed on a rolling basis. *Application fee:* $50 ($100 for international students). Electronic applications accepted. *Application Contact:* Jim W. Westbrook, Coordinator for Academic Affairs, 678-547-6173, E-mail: westbrook_j@mercer.edu. *Coordinator for Academic Affairs*, Jim W. Westbrook, 678-547-6173, E-mail: westbrook_j@mercer.edu.

Georgia Baptist College of Nursing Students: 4 full-time (all women), 10 part-time (all women); includes 3 minority (all African Americans). Average age 39. 8 applicants, 88% accepted, 6 enrolled. *Faculty:* 19 full-time (18 women). Expenses: Contact institution. *Financial support:* In 2008–09, 10 students received support. Institutionally sponsored loans, scholarships/grants, and traineeships available. Support available to part-time students. Financial award application deadline: 5/1; financial award applicants required to submit FAFSA. In 2008, 2 master's awarded. *Degree program information:* Part-time programs available. Offers nurse education (Certificate); nursing (MSN, PhD). *Application deadline:* For fall admission, 6/1 for domestic students, 4/1 for international students; for winter admission, 11/1 for domestic students, 9/1 for international students; for spring admission, 4/1 for domestic students, 2/1 for international students. Applications are processed on a rolling basis. *Application fee:* $50. *Application Contact:* Lynn Vines, Director of Admissions, 678-547-6700, Fax: 678-547-6794, E-mail: vines_ml@mercer.edu. *Dean/Professor*, Dr. Susan S. Gunby, 678-547-6793, Fax: 678-547-6796, E-mail: gunby_ss@mercer.edu.

James and Carolyn McAfee School of Theology Students: 156 full-time (81 women), 69 part-time (34 women); includes 85 minority (80 African Americans, 3 Asian Americans or Pacific Islanders, 2 Hispanic Americans), 3 international. Average age 34. 114 applicants, 78% accepted, 48 enrolled. *Faculty:* 11 full-time (3 women), 10 part-time/adjunct (4 women). Expenses: Contact institution. *Financial support:* In 2008–09, 30 students received support. Career-related internships or fieldwork, Federal Work-Study, institutionally sponsored loans, scholarships/grants, and merit based scholarships available. Support available to part-time students. Financial award applicants required to submit FAFSA. In 2008, 51 first professional degrees, 7 doctorates awarded. *Degree program information:* Part-time programs available. Offers theology (M Div, MACM, D Min). *Application deadline:* For fall admission, 7/1 for domestic students, 2/1 for international students; for spring admission, 1/4 for domestic students. Applications are processed on a rolling basis. *Application fee:* $35. *Application Contact:* Dr. Ryan A. Clark, Director of Admissions, 678-547-6451, Fax: 678-547-6478, E-mail: clark_ra@mercer.edu. *Dean*, Dr. R. Alan Culpepper, 678-547-6470, Fax: 678-547-6478, E-mail: culpepper_ra@mercer.edu.

Tift College of Education (Atlanta) Students: 202 full-time (174 women), 464 part-time (358 women); includes 333 minority (305 African Americans, 1 American Indian/Alaska Native, 21 Asian Americans or Pacific Islanders, 6 Hispanic Americans), 8 international. Average age 33. *Faculty:* 21 full-time (10 women), 5 part-time/adjunct (3 women). Expenses: Contact institution. *Financial support:* Federal Work-Study available. Support available to part-time students. Financial award application deadline: 5/1. In 2008, 149 master's, 13 other advanced degrees awarded. *Degree program information:* Part-time and evening/weekend programs available. Offers curriculum and instruction (PhD); early childhood education (M Ed, MAT); educational leadership (PhD, Ed S); middle grades education (M Ed, MAT); reading education (M Ed); secondary education (M Ed, MAT); teacher leadership (Ed S). *Application deadline:* For fall admission, 8/1 for domestic and international students; for spring admission, 12/1 for domestic and international students. Applications are processed on a rolling basis. *Application fee:* $25. *Application Contact:* Dr. Allison Gilmore, Associate Dean for Graduate Teacher Education, 678-547-6330, Fax: 678-547-6055, E-mail: gilmore_a@mercer.edu. *Dean*, Dr. Carl R. Martray, 478-301-5397, Fax: 478-301-2280, E-mail: martray_cr@mercer.edu.

Graduate Studies, Macon Campus Students: 88 full-time (71 women), 183 part-time (80 women); includes 81 minority (45 African Americans, 23 Asian Americans or Pacific Islanders, 13 Hispanic Americans), 13 international. Average age 33. *Faculty:* 42 full-time (15 women), 4 part-time/adjunct (2 women). Expenses: Contact institution. *Financial support:* Career-related internships or fieldwork, Federal Work-Study, and institutionally sponsored loans available. Support available to part-time students. In 2008, 81 master's awarded. *Degree program information:* Part-time and evening/weekend programs available. *Application Contact:* Director, 912-301-2700.

Eugene W. Stetson School of Business and Economics (Macon) Students: 7 full-time (4 women), 23 part-time (12 women); includes 8 minority (4 African Americans, 2 Asian Americans or Pacific Islanders, 2 Hispanic Americans), 3 international. Average age 26. 20 applicants, 95% accepted, 19 enrolled. *Faculty:* 9 full-time (5 women). Expenses: Contact institution. In 2008, 16 master's awarded. *Degree program information:* Part-time and evening/weekend programs available. Offers business and economics (MBA). *Application deadline:* For fall admission, 8/1 for domestic students; for spring admission, 12/1 for domestic students. Applications are processed on a rolling basis. *Application fee:* $50 ($100 for international students). *Application Contact:* Robert Holland, Director/Academic Administrator, 478-301-2835, Fax: 478-301-2635, E-mail: holland_r@mercer.edu. *Dean*, Dr. William S. Mounts, 478-301-2837, Fax: 478-301-2635, E-mail: mounts_ws@mercer.edu.

School of Engineering Students: 9 full-time (3 women), 91 part-time (19 women); includes 32 minority (4 African Americans, 20 Asian Americans or Pacific Islanders, 8 Hispanic Americans), 5 international. Average age 32. 35 applicants, 74% accepted, 22 enrolled. *Faculty:* 20 full-time (4 women), 1 part-time/adjunct (0 women). Expenses: Contact institution. *Financial support:* Federal Work-Study available. In 2008, 42 master's awarded. *Degree program information:* Part-time and evening/weekend programs available. Postbaccalaureate distance learning degree programs offered (no on-campus study). Offers biomedical engineering (MSE); computer engineering (MSE); electrical engineering (MSE); engineering management (MSE); environmental engineering (MSE); environmental systems (MS); mechanical engineering (MSE); software engineering (MSE); software systems (MS); technical communications management (MS); technical management (MS). *Application deadline:* For fall admission, 7/1 for domestic students; for spring admission, 11/15 for domestic students. Applications are processed on a rolling basis. *Application fee:* $35 ($50 for international students). Electronic applications accepted. *Application Contact:* Greg Lofton, Graduate Program Coordinator, 478-301-5480, Fax: 478-301-5434, E-mail: lofton_g@mercer.edu. *Interim Dean*, Dr. Michael S. Leonard, 478-301-2459, Fax: 478-301-5593, E-mail: leonard_ms@mercer.edu.

School of Music Students: 16 full-time (12 women), 2 part-time (1 woman), 4 international. Average age 29. *Faculty:* 1 full-time (0 women). Expenses: Contact institution. In 2008, 7 master's awarded. Offers choral conducting (MM); church music (MM); performance (MM). *Application fee:* $50. *Application Contact:* Gina Cook Nelson, Director of Admissions, 478-301-2307, E-mail: nelson_gc@mercer.edu. *Director of Graduate Studies*, John E. Simon, 478-301-4012, E-mail: simons_je@mercer.edu.

Tift College of Education (Macon) Students: 56 full-time (52 women), 67 part-time (48 women); includes 41 minority (37 African Americans, 1 Asian American or Pacific Islander, 3 Hispanic Americans), 1 international. Average age 33. *Faculty:* 12 full-time (6 women), 3 part-time/adjunct (2 women). Expenses: Contact institution. *Financial support:* Federal Work-Study and institutionally sponsored loans available. Support available to part-time students. Financial award application deadline: 5/1. In 2008, 23 master's awarded. *Degree program information:* Part-time and evening/weekend programs available. Offers collaborative education (M Ed); curriculum and instruction (PhD); educational leadership (PhD, Ed S). *Application deadline:* For fall admission, 8/1 for domestic students; for spring admission, 12/1 for domestic students. Applications are processed on a rolling basis. *Application fee:* $25. *Application Contact:* Dr. Penny Elkins, Associate Dean, 678-547-6556, Fax: 678-547-6389, E-mail: elkins_pl@mercer.edu. *Dean,* Dr. Carl R. Martray, 478-301-5397, Fax: 478-301-2280, E-mail: martray_cr@mercer.edu.

School of Medicine Offers medicine (MD, MFT, MPH, MSA).

Walter F. George School of Law Students: 443 full-time (192 women); includes 76 minority (47 African Americans, 4 American Indian/Alaska Native, 15 Asian Americans or Pacific Islanders, 10 Hispanic Americans). Average age 25. 1,314 applicants, 37% accepted, 150 enrolled. *Faculty:* 33 full-time (12 women), 20 part-time/adjunct (6 women). Expenses: Contact institution. *Financial support:* In 2008–09, 403 students received support, including 20 fellowships (averaging $5,500 per year), 23 research assistantships (averaging $452 per year); career-related internships or fieldwork, Federal Work-Study, institutionally sponsored loans, scholarships/grants, tuition waivers (partial), and institutional work-study, federal student loans also available. Support available to part-time students. Financial award application deadline: 4/1; financial award applicants required to submit FAFSA. In 2008, 144 JDs awarded. *Degree program information:* Part-time programs available. Offers law (JD). *Application deadline:* For fall admission, 3/15 priority date for domestic students. Applications are processed on a rolling basis. *Application fee:* $50. Electronic applications accepted. *Application Contact:* Susan Martin, Admissions Assistant, 478-301-2605, Fax: 478-301-2989, E-mail: martin_sv@law.mercer.edu. *Dean,* Daisy H. Floyd, 478-301-2602, Fax: 478-301-2101, E-mail: floyd_dh@law.mercer.edu.

MERCY COLLEGE, Dobbs Ferry, NY 10522-1189

General Information Independent, coed, comprehensive institution. CGS member. *Enrollment:* 9,043 graduate, professional, and undergraduate students; 1,229 full-time matriculated graduate/professional students (994 women), 2,261 part-time matriculated graduate/professional students (1,781 women). *Enrollment by degree level:* 3,378 master's, 71 doctoral, 41 other advanced degrees. *Graduate faculty:* 82 full-time (45 women), 211 part-time/adjunct (113 women). *Tuition:* Full-time $12,330; part-time $685 per credit. *Required fees:* $240; $120 per semester. Tuition and fees vary according to program. *Graduate housing:* Room and/or apartments available on a first-come, first-served basis to single students; on-campus housing not available to married students. Typical cost: $7438 per year ($10,588 including board). Room and board charges vary according to board plan. Housing application deadline: 7/1. *Student services:* Campus employment opportunities, career counseling, child daycare facilities, exercise/wellness program, free psychological counseling, international student services, services for students with disabilities, teacher training, writing training. *Library facilities:* Mercy College Library. *Online resources:* library catalog, web page, access to other libraries' catalogs. *Collection:* 304,396 titles, 1,820 serial subscriptions, 19,017 audiovisual materials.

Computer facilities: 680 computers available on campus for general student use. A campuswide network can be accessed from student residence rooms and from off campus. Online class registration is available. *Web address:* http://www.mercy.edu/.

General Application Contact: Allison Rickards, Senior Associate Director of Recruitment, 877-MERCY-GO, Fax: 914-674-7608, E-mail: admissions@mercy.edu.

GRADUATE UNITS

School of Business Students: 117 full-time (73 women), 199 part-time (134 women); includes 173 minority (122 African Americans, 2 American Indian/Alaska Native, 12 Asian Americans or Pacific Islanders, 37 Hispanic Americans), 13 international. Average age 36. 186 applicants, 74% accepted, 54 enrolled. *Faculty:* 12 full-time (2 women), 39 part-time/adjunct (18 women). Expenses: Contact institution. *Financial support:* In 2008–09, 137 students received support. Career-related internships or fieldwork, Federal Work-Study, scholarships/grants, and unspecified assistantships available. Support available to part-time students. Financial award applicants required to submit FAFSA. In 2008, 190 master's awarded. *Degree program information:* Part-time and evening/weekend programs available. Postbaccalaureate distance learning degree programs offered (minimal on-campus study). Offers business administration (MBA); human resource management (MS); organizational leadership (MS); public accounting (MS). *Application deadline:* For fall admission, 8/1 for international students. Applications are processed on a rolling basis. *Application fee:* $40. Electronic applications accepted. *Application Contact:* Saira Vargas, Coordinator, 914-674-7481, E-mail: svargas@mercy.edu. *Dean,* Dr. Geofrey Mills, 914-674-7482, E-mail: gmills@mercy.edu.

School of Education Students: 553 full-time (460 women), 1,399 part-time (1,097 women); includes 744 minority (365 African Americans, 6 American Indian/Alaska Native, 33 Asian Americans or Pacific Islanders, 340 Hispanic Americans), 6 international. Average age 32. 640 applicants, 88% accepted, 498 enrolled. *Faculty:* 32 full-time (19 women), 120 part-time/adjunct (77 women). Expenses: Contact institution. *Financial support:* In 2008–09, 1,217 students received support. Career-related internships or fieldwork, Federal Work-Study, scholarships/grants, and unspecified assistantships available. Support available to part-time students. Financial award applicants required to submit FAFSA. In 2008, 1,006 master's, 3 other advanced degrees awarded. Offers adolescence education, grades 7-12 (MS); applied behavior analysis (Post Master's Certificate); bilingual education (MS); childhood education, grade 1-6 (MS); early childhood education, birth-grade 2 (MS); early childhood education/students with disabilities (MS); individualized certification plan for teachers (ICPT) (MS); middle childhood education, grades 5-9 (MS); school building leadership (MS, Advanced Certificate); teaching English to speakers of other languages (TESOL) (MS); teaching literacy (MS); urban education (MS). *Application deadline:* For fall admission, 8/1 for international students. Applications are processed on a rolling basis. *Application fee:* $40. Electronic applications accepted. *Application Contact:* Mary ellen Hoffman, Interim Associate Dean, 914-674-7334, E-mail: mehoffman@mercy.edu. *Interim Dean,* Dr. Andrew Peiser, 914-674-7489, E-mail: apeiser@mercy.edu.

School of Health and Natural Sciences Students: 324 full-time (263 women), 192 part-time (167 women); includes 188 minority (90 African Americans, 1 American Indian/Alaska Native, 45 Asian Americans or Pacific Islanders, 52 Hispanic Americans), 17 international. Average age 33. 586 applicants, 34% accepted, 102 enrolled. *Faculty:* 25 full-time (21 women), 19 part-time/adjunct (17 women). Expenses: Contact institution. *Financial support:* In 2008–09, 122 students received support. Career-related internships or fieldwork, Federal Work-Study, scholarships/grants, and unspecified assistantships available. Financial award applicants required to submit FAFSA. In 2008, 155 master's, 14 doctorates, 2 other advanced degrees awarded. *Degree program information:* Part-time and evening/weekend programs available. Postbaccalaureate distance learning degree programs offered (minimal on-campus study). Offers communication disorders (MS); nursing (MS); nursing administration (MS); nursing education (MS, Certificate); occupational therapy (MS); physical therapy (MS, DPT); physician assistant (MS); physician assistant studies (MS). *Application fee:* $65. *Application Contact:* Dr. Pat Chute, Dean, 914-674-7746, E-mail: pchute@mercy.edu. *Dean,* Dr. Pat Chute, 914-674-7746, E-mail: pchute@mercy.edu.

School of Liberal Arts Students: 14 full-time (5 women), 87 part-time (61 women); includes 16 African Americans, 2 Asian Americans or Pacific Islanders, 11 Hispanic Americans, 14 international. Average age 34. 73 applicants, 75% accepted, 29 enrolled. *Faculty:* 7 full-time (1 woman), 4 part-time/adjunct (0 women). Expenses: Contact institution. *Financial support:* In 2008–09, 43 students received support. Career-related internships or fieldwork, Federal Work-Study, scholarships/grants, and unspecified assistantships available. Financial award applicants required to submit FAFSA. In 2008, 13 master's awarded. *Degree program information:* Part-time and evening/weekend programs available. Postbaccalaureate distance learning degree programs offered (minimal on-campus study). Offers English literature (MA); information assurance and security (MS); Internet business systems (MS). *Application fee:* $40. *Application Contact:* Sean Dugan, Interim Dean for the School of Liberal Arts, 914-674-7356, E-mail: sdugan@mercy.edu. *Interim Dean for the School of Liberal Arts,* Sean Dugan, 914-674-7356, E-mail: sdugan@mercy.edu.

School of Social and Behavioral Sciences Students: 221 full-time (193 women), 384 part-time (322 women); includes 375 minority (181 African Americans, 3 American Indian/Alaska Native, 14 Asian Americans or Pacific Islanders, 177 Hispanic Americans), 7 international. Average age 34. 391 applicants, 66% accepted, 161 enrolled. *Faculty:* 16 full-time (10 women), 48 part-time/adjunct (28 women). Expenses: Contact institution. *Financial support:* In 2008–09, 184 students received support. Career-related internships or fieldwork, Federal Work-Study, scholarships/grants, and unspecified assistantships available. Support available to part-time students. Financial award applicants required to submit FAFSA. In 2008, 111 master's, 7 other advanced degrees awarded. *Degree program information:* Part-time and evening/weekend programs available. Postbaccalaureate distance learning degree programs offered (minimal on-campus study). Offers alcohol and substance abuse counseling (Certificate); counseling (MS, Certificate); health services management (MPA, MS); marriage and family therapy (MS); mental health counseling (MS); psychology (MS); retirement counseling (Certificate); school counseling (Certificate); school counseling and bilingual extension (Certificate); school psychology (MS). *Application deadline:* For fall admission, 8/1 for international students. Applications are processed on a rolling basis. *Application fee:* $40. Electronic applications accepted. *Application Contact:* Hind Rassam Culhane, Interim Dean, 914-674-7376, E-mail: hculhane@mercy.edu. *Interim Dean,* Hind Rassam Culhane, 914-674-7376, E-mail: hculhane@mercy.edu.

MERCYHURST COLLEGE, Erie, PA 16546

General Information Independent-religious, coed, comprehensive institution. *Graduate housing:* Room and/or apartments available on a first-come, first-served basis to single students; on-campus housing not available to married students. Housing application deadline: 8/15.

GRADUATE UNITS

Graduate Program *Degree program information:* Part-time and evening/weekend programs available. Offers administration of justice (MS); applied intelligence (MS, Certificate); bilingual/bicultural special education (MS); educational leadership (Certificate); forensic and biological anthropology (MS); organizational leadership (MS, Certificate); special education (MS). Electronic applications accepted.

MEREDITH COLLEGE, Raleigh, NC 27607-5298

General Information Independent, Undergraduate: women only; graduate: coed, comprehensive institution. *Graduate housing:* On-campus housing not available.

GRADUATE UNITS

John E. Weems Graduate School *Degree program information:* Part-time and evening/weekend programs available. Offers music (MM); nutrition (MS). Electronic applications accepted.

School of Business *Degree program information:* Part-time and evening/weekend programs available. Offers business administration (MBA). Electronic applications accepted.

School of Education *Degree program information:* Part-time and evening/weekend programs available. Offers education (M Ed). Electronic applications accepted.

MERITUS UNIVERSITY, Fredricton, NB E3C 2R2, Canada

General Information Proprietary, coed, comprehensive institution.

GRADUATE UNITS

School of Business Offers business (MBA).

MERRIMACK COLLEGE, North Andover, MA 01845-5800

General Information Independent-religious, coed, comprehensive institution. *Graduate housing:* On-campus housing not available.

GRADUATE UNITS

Department of Education *Degree program information:* Part-time and evening/weekend programs available. Offers education (M Ed).

MESA STATE COLLEGE, Grand Junction, CO 81501-3122

General Information State-supported, coed, comprehensive institution. *Graduate housing:* Room and/or apartments available on a first-come, first-served basis to single students; on-campus housing not available to married students. Housing application deadline: 6/1.

GRADUATE UNITS

Center for Teacher Education *Degree program information:* Evening/weekend programs available. Offers teacher education (MAEd). Electronic applications accepted.

Department of Business *Degree program information:* Part-time and evening/weekend programs available. Offers business (MBA). Electronic applications accepted.

MESIVTA OF EASTERN PARKWAY–YESHIVA ZICHRON MEILECH, Brooklyn, NY 11218-5559

General Information Independent-religious, men only, comprehensive institution.

GRADUATE UNITS

Graduate Programs

MESIVTA TIFERETH JERUSALEM OF AMERICA, New York, NY 10002-6301

General Information Independent-religious, men only, comprehensive institution.

GRADUATE UNITS

Graduate Programs

MESIVTA TORAH VODAATH RABBINICAL SEMINARY, Brooklyn, NY 11218-5299

General Information Independent-religious, men only, comprehensive institution.

GRADUATE UNITS

Graduate Programs

METHODIST THEOLOGICAL SCHOOL IN OHIO, Delaware, OH 43015-8004

General Information Independent-religious, coed, graduate-only institution. *Graduate housing:* Rooms and/or apartments available on a first-come, first-served basis to single students and available to married students. Housing application deadline: 8/15.

GRADUATE UNITS

Graduate and Professional Programs *Degree program information:* Part-time programs available. Offers theology (M Div, MACE, MACM, MTS, D Min).

METHODIST UNIVERSITY, Fayetteville, NC 28311-1498

General Information Independent-religious, coed, comprehensive institution.

GRADUATE UNITS

School of Graduate Studies Offers business administration (MBA); justice administration (MJA); physician assistant studies (MMS).

METROPOLITAN COLLEGE OF NEW YORK, New York, NY 10013

General Information Independent, coed, primarily women, comprehensive institution. *Graduate housing:* On-campus housing not available. *Research affiliation:* U.S. Department of Homeland Security (homeland security), U.S. Federal Emergency Management Administration (higher education).

GRADUATE UNITS

Program in Childhood Education Offers childhood education (MS).

Metropolitan College of New York (continued)

Program in General Management *Degree program information:* Evening/weekend programs available. Offers general management (MBA). Electronic applications accepted.

Program in Media Management *Degree program information:* Evening/weekend programs available. Offers media management (MBA). Electronic applications accepted.

Program in Public Administration *Degree program information:* Evening/weekend programs available. Offers public administration (MPA). Electronic applications accepted.

METROPOLITAN STATE UNIVERSITY, St. Paul, MN 55106-5000

General Information State-supported, coed, comprehensive institution. *Graduate housing:* On-campus housing not available.

GRADUATE UNITS

College of Arts and Sciences *Degree program information:* Part-time and evening/weekend programs available. Offers computer science (MS); liberal studies (MA); technical communication (MS).

College of Management *Degree program information:* Part-time and evening/weekend programs available. Offers business administration (MBA); information management (MMIS); MIS generalist (Graduate Certificate); MIS systems analysis (Graduate Certificate); nonprofit management (MPNA); project management (Graduate Certificate); public administration (MPNA); systems management (MMIS).

College of Nursing and Health Sciences *Degree program information:* Part-time programs available. Offers nursing (MSN, DNP).

College of Professional Studies *Degree program information:* Part-time and evening/weekend programs available. Offers psychology (MA).

MGH INSTITUTE OF HEALTH PROFESSIONS, Boston, MA 02129

General Information Independent, coed, primarily women, graduate-only institution. *Enrollment by degree level:* 383 master's, 281 doctoral, 99 other advanced degrees. *Graduate faculty:* 64 full-time (53 women), 20 part-time/adjunct (17 women). *Tuition:* Part-time $916 per credit. *Graduate housing:* On-campus housing not available. *Student services:* Campus employment opportunities, campus safety program, career counseling, child daycare facilities, international student services, low-cost health insurance, services for students with disabilities, teacher training, writing training. *Library facilities:* Treadwell Library. *Online resources:* library catalog, web page, access to other libraries' catalogs. *Collection:* 50,000 titles, 700 serial subscriptions, 75 audiovisual materials. *Research affiliation:* Brigham and Women's Hospital, Partners Health Care System, Inc., McLean Psychiatric Hospital, Spaulding Rehabilitation Hospital, Massachusetts General Hospital.

Computer facilities: 50 computers available on campus for general student use. A campuswide network can be accessed from off campus. Online class registration, online billing are available. *Web address:* http://www.mghihp.edu/.

General Application Contact: Maureen Rika Judd, Manager of Admissions, 617-726-6069, Fax: 617-726-8010, E-mail: admissions@mghihp.edu.

GRADUATE UNITS

Graduate Programs Students: 452 full-time (386 women), 311 part-time (244 women); includes 104 minority (27 African Americans, 1 American Indian/Alaska Native, 61 Asian Americans or Pacific Islanders, 15 Hispanic Americans), 1 international. Average age 31. 801 applicants, 62% accepted, 274 enrolled. *Faculty:* 58 full-time (49 women), 29 part-time/adjunct (20 women). Expenses: Contact institution. *Financial support:* In 2008–09, 173 students received support, including 37 research assistantships; teaching assistantships, career-related internships or fieldwork, scholarships/grants, traineeships, tuition waivers (partial), and unspecified assistantships also available. Support available to part-time students. Financial award application deadline: 3/1; financial award applicants required to submit FAFSA. In 2008, 119 master's, 115 doctorates, 37 other advanced degrees awarded. *Degree program information:* Part-time and evening/weekend programs available. Postbaccalaureate distance learning degree programs offered (no on-campus study). Offers medical imaging (Certificate); physical therapy (MS, DPT, Certificate); reading (Certificate); speech-language pathology (MS). *Application deadline:* For fall admission, 1/1 priority date for domestic students, 3/1 for international students; for winter admission, 11/1 priority date for domestic students, 7/1 for international students; for spring admission, 3/1 priority date for domestic students, 11/1 for international students. *Application fee:* $50. Electronic applications accepted. *Application Contact:* Maureen Rika Judd, Manager of Admissions, 617-726-6069, Fax: 617-726-8010, E-mail: admissions@mghihp.edu. *President,* Dr. Janis P. Bellack, 617-726-8002, Fax: 617-726-3716, E-mail: jbellack@mghihp.edu.

School of Nursing Students: 262 full-time (227 women), 63 part-time (57 women); includes 43 minority (18 African Americans, 1 American Indian/Alaska Native, 16 Asian Americans or Pacific Islanders, 8 Hispanic Americans). Average age 31. 339 applicants, 59% accepted, 93 enrolled. *Faculty:* 33 full-time (31 women), 10 part-time/adjunct (8 women). Expenses: Contact institution. *Financial support:* In 2008–09, 47 students received support, including 1 research assistantship (averaging $1,200 per year), 2 teaching assistantships (averaging $1,200 per year); career-related internships or fieldwork, scholarships/grants, traineeships, tuition waivers (full and partial), and unspecified assistantships also available. Support available to part-time students. Financial award application deadline: 3/1; financial award applicants required to submit FAFSA. In 2008, 64 master's, 2 other advanced degrees awarded. Offers advanced practice nursing (MSN); gerontological nursing (MSN); nursing (DNP); pediatric nursing (MSN); psychiatric nursing (MSN); teaching and learning for health care education (Certificate); women's health nursing (MSN). *Application deadline:* For fall admission, 1/10 for domestic and international students. *Application fee:* $50. Electronic applications accepted. *Application Contact:* Maureen Rika Judd, Manager of Admissions, 617-726-6069, Fax: 617-726-8010, E-mail: admissions@mghihp.edu. *Director,* Margery Chisholm, 617-724-0480, Fax: 617-726-8022, E-mail: mchisholm@mghihp.edu.

MIAMI INTERNATIONAL UNIVERSITY OF ART & DESIGN, Miami, FL 33132-1418

General Information Proprietary, coed, comprehensive institution.

GRADUATE UNITS

Program in Computer Animation Postbaccalaureate distance learning degree programs offered. Offers computer animation (MFA).

Program in Film Postbaccalaureate distance learning degree programs offered. Offers film (MFA).

Program in Graphic Design Postbaccalaureate distance learning degree programs offered. Offers graphic design (MFA).

Program in Interior Design Offers interior design (MFA).

Program in Visual Arts Postbaccalaureate distance learning degree programs offered. Offers visual arts (MFA).

MIAMI UNIVERSITY, Oxford, OH 45056

General Information State-related, coed, university. CGS member. *Graduate housing:* Rooms and/or apartments available on a first-come, first-served basis to single and married students. Housing application deadline: 3/1.

GRADUATE UNITS

Graduate School *Degree program information:* Part-time programs available. Electronic applications accepted.

College of Arts and Sciences *Degree program information:* Part-time programs available. Offers analytical chemistry (MS, PhD); arts and sciences (MA, MAT, MGS, MS, MS Stat, MTSC, PhD); biochemistry (MS, PhD); biological sciences (MAT); botany (MA, MAT, MS, PhD); chemical education (MS, PhD); chemistry (MS, PhD); clinical psychology (PhD); comparative religion (MA); composition and rhetoric (MA, PhD); creative writing (MA); criticism (PhD); English and American literature and language (PhD); English education (MAT); experimental psychology (PhD); French (MA); geography (MA); geology (MA, MS, PhD); gerontology (MGS); history (MA, PhD); inorganic chemistry (MS, PhD); library theory (PhD); literature (MA, MAT, PhD); mass communication (MA); mathematics (MA, MAT, MS); mathematics/operations research (MS); microbiology (MS, PhD); organic chemistry (MS, PhD); philosophy (MA); physical chemistry (MS, PhD); physics (MAT, MS); political science (MA, MAT, PhD); social gerontology (PhD); social psychology (PhD); Spanish (MA); speech communication (MA); speech pathology and audiology (MA, MS); statistics (MS Stat); technical and scientific communication (MTSC); zoology (MA, MS, PhD).

Farmer School of Business *Degree program information:* Part-time programs available. Offers accountancy (M Acc); business administration (MBA); economics (MA); finance (MBA); general management (MBA); management information systems (MBA); marketing (MBA); quality and process improvement (MBA).

Institute of Environmental Sciences *Degree program information:* Part-time programs available. Offers environmental sciences (M En S). Electronic applications accepted.

School of Education and Allied Professions *Degree program information:* Part-time programs available. Offers adolescent education (MAT); child and family studies (MS); college student personnel services (MS); curriculum and teacher leadership (M Ed); education and allied professions (M Ed, MAT, MS, Ed D, PhD, Ed S); educational administration (Ed D, PhD); educational leadership (M Ed, MS); educational psychology (M Ed); elementary education (M Ed, MAT); elementary mathematics education (M Ed); exercise and health studies (MS); reading education (M Ed); school psychology (MS, Ed S); secondary education (M Ed, MAT); special education (M Ed); sport studies (MS).

School of Engineering and Applied Science Offers computer science (MCS); computer science and systems analysis (MCS); paper science and engineering (MS); software development (Certificate).

School of Fine Arts *Degree program information:* Part-time programs available. Offers architecture (M Arch); art education (MA); fine arts (M Arch, MA, MFA, MM); music education (MM); music performance (MM); studio art (MFA); theatre (MA).

MICHIGAN SCHOOL OF PROFESSIONAL PSYCHOLOGY, Farmington Hills, MI 48334

General Information Independent, coed, graduate-only institution. *Enrollment by degree level:* 40 master's, 69 doctoral. *Graduate faculty:* 3 full-time (1 woman), 20 part-time/adjunct (11 women). *Graduate housing:* On-campus housing not available. *Library facilities:* Center for Humanistic Studies Library. *Collection:* 10,272 titles, 52 serial subscriptions, 185 audiovisual materials.

Computer facilities: 16 computers available on campus for general student use. A campuswide network can be accessed from off campus. *Web address:* http://www.mispp.edu/.

General Application Contact: Linda Potter-Gallant, Admissions Advisor, 248-476-1122 Ext. 117, Fax: 248-476-1125, E-mail: lpgallant@mispp.edu.

GRADUATE UNITS

Programs in Humanistic and Clinical Psychology Students: 109 full-time (86 women); includes 20 minority (13 African Americans, 7 Asian Americans or Pacific Islanders). Average age 38. 200 applicants, 40% accepted, 69 enrolled. *Faculty:* 3 full-time (1 woman), 20 part-time/adjunct (11 women). Expenses: Contact institution. *Financial support:* In 2008–09, 39 students received support. Application deadline: 6/30. In 2008, 39 master's, 11 doctorates awarded. Offers humanistic and clinical psychology (MA, Psy D). *Application deadline:* For fall admission, 1/15 priority date for domestic students. Applications are processed on a rolling basis. *Application fee:* $75. Electronic applications accepted. *Application Contact:* Linda Potter-Gallant, Admissions Advisor, 248-476-1122 Ext. 117, Fax: 248-476-1125, E-mail: lpgallant@mispp.edu. *President,* Dr. Kerry Moustakas, 248-476-1122, Fax: 248-476-1125, E-mail: kmoustakas@mispp.edu.

MICHIGAN STATE UNIVERSITY, East Lansing, MI 48824

General Information State-supported, coed, university. CGS member. *Enrollment:* 46,648 graduate, professional, and undergraduate students; 7,123 full-time matriculated graduate/professional students (3,687 women), 1,846 part-time matriculated graduate/professional students (1,238 women). *Enrollment by degree level:* 1,823 first professional, 3,822 master's, 3,324 doctoral, 8,969 other advanced degrees. *Graduate faculty:* 1,992 full-time (638 women), 18 part-time/adjunct (6 women). Tuition, state resident: part-time $434 per credit hour. Tuition, nonresident: part-time $892.75 per credit hour. *Required fees:* $312 per term. *Graduate housing:* Rooms and/or apartments available on a first-come, first-served basis to single and married students. *Student services:* Campus employment opportunities, campus safety program, career counseling, child daycare facilities, exercise/wellness program, free psychological counseling, grant writing training, international student services, low-cost health insurance, multicultural affairs office, services for students with disabilities, teacher training, writing training. *Library facilities:* Main Library plus 14 others. *Online resources:* library catalog, web page, access to other libraries' catalogs. *Collection:* 4.9 million titles, 74,177 serial subscriptions, 71,316 audiovisual materials. *Research affiliation:* Argonne National Laboratory (high-energy physics and structural biology), Association of Sea Grant Programs (fresh water ecosystems), Fraunhofer Center (manufacturing), Michigan Economic Development Corporation (life sciences, homeland security, automotive technologies), Oak Ridge Associate Universities (scientific research and education), Southern Astrophysical Research (SOAR) Telescope (astronomy).

Computer facilities: Computer purchase and lease plans are available. 2,100 computers available on campus for general student use. A campuswide network can be accessed from student residence rooms and from off campus. Online class registration is available. *Web address:* http://www.msu.edu/.

General Application Contact: Dr. Karen Klomparens, Dean of the Graduate School and Associate Provost for Graduate Education, 517-353-0301, Fax: 517-353-3355.

GRADUATE UNITS

College of Human Medicine Students: 580 full-time (313 women), 30 part-time (22 women); includes 170 minority (45 African Americans, 5 American Indian/Alaska Native, 91 Asian Americans or Pacific Islanders, 29 Hispanic Americans), 28 international. Average age 26. 389 applicants, 77% accepted. *Faculty:* 85 full-time (28 women). Expenses: Contact institution. *Financial support:* In 2008–09, 37 research assistantships with tuition reimbursements (averaging $14,560 per year), 1 teaching assistantship with tuition reimbursement (averaging $15,885 per year) were awarded. In 2008, 95 first professional degrees, 14 master's, 4 doctorates awarded. Offers biochemistry and molecular biology (MS, PhD); epidemiology (MS, PhD); human medicine (MD, MPH, MS, PhD); human medicine/medical scientist training program (MD); microbiology (MS); microbiology and molecular genetics (PhD); pharmacology and toxicology (MS, PhD); physiology (MS, PhD); public health (MPH). *Application Contact:* CHM Admissions Officer, 517-353-9620, Fax: 517-432-0021, E-mail: mdadmissions@msu.edu. *Dean,* Dr. Marsha D. Rappley, 517-353-1730, E-mail: rappley@msu.edu.

College of Osteopathic Medicine Students: 832 full-time (411 women), 34 part-time (25 women); includes 175 minority (31 African Americans, 3 American Indian/Alaska Native, 128 Asian Americans or Pacific Islanders, 13 Hispanic Americans), 3 international. Average age 26. 25 applicants, 64% accepted. *Faculty:* 61 full-time (23 women). Expenses: Contact institution. *Financial support:* In 2008–09, 17 research assistantships with tuition reimbursements (averaging $16,303 per year) were awarded. In 2008, 138 first professional degrees, 1 master's, 1 doctorate awarded. Offers biochemistry and molecular biology (MS, PhD); integrative pharmacology (MS); microbiology (MS); microbiology and molecular genetics (PhD); osteopathic medicine (DO, MS, PhD); pharmacology and toxicology (MS, PhD); pharmacology and toxicology-environmental toxicology (PhD); physiology (MS, PhD). *Dean,* Dr. William D. Strampel, 517-355-9616, Fax: 517-432-2125, E-mail: strampe3@msu.edu.

College of Veterinary Medicine Students: 483 full-time (384 women), 86 part-time (52 women); includes 76 minority (20 African Americans, 6 American Indian/Alaska Native, 31

Asian Americans or Pacific Islanders, 19 Hispanic Americans), 49 international. Average age 27. 159 applicants, 87% accepted. *Faculty:* 91 full-time (33 women), 1 part-time/adjunct (0 women). Expenses: Contact institution. *Financial support:* In 2008–09, 31 research assistantships with tuition reimbursements (averaging $17,244 per year), 1 teaching assistantship with tuition reimbursement (averaging $15,300 per year) were awarded. In 2008, 109 first professional degrees, 17 master's, 12 doctorates awarded. Offers animal science–environmental toxicology (PhD); biochemistry and molecular biology–environmental toxicology (PhD); chemistry–environmental toxicology (PhD); comparative medicine and integrative biology (MS, PhD); comparative medicine and integrative biology–environmental toxicology (PhD); crop and soil sciences–environmental toxicology (PhD); environmental engineering–environmental toxicology (PhD); environmental geosciences–environmental toxicology (PhD); fisheries and wildlife–environmental toxicology (PhD); food safety (MS); food safety and toxicology (MS); food science–environmental toxicology (PhD); forestry–environmental toxicology (PhD); genetics–environmental toxicology (PhD); human nutrition–environmental toxicology (PhD); industrial microbiology (MS, PhD); integrative toxicology (PhD); large animal clinical sciences (MS, PhD); microbiology (MS, PhD); microbiology and molecular genetics (MS, PhD); microbiology–environmental toxicology (PhD); pathobiology and diagnostic investigation (MS, PhD); pathology (MS, PhD); pathology–environmental toxicology (PhD); pharmacology and toxicology (MS, PhD); pharmacology and toxicology–environmental toxicology (PhD); physiology (MS, PhD); small animal clinical sciences (MS); veterinary medicine (DVM); veterinary medicine/medical scientist training program (DVM); zoology–environmental toxicology (PhD). *Dean,* Dr. Christopher M. Brown, 517-355-6509, Fax: 517-432-1037, E-mail: browncm@cvm.msu.edu.

The Graduate School Expenses: Contact institution. *Financial support:* Fellowships with tuition reimbursements, research assistantships with tuition reimbursements, teaching assistantships with tuition reimbursements, career-related internships or fieldwork, Federal Work-Study, institutionally sponsored loans, scholarships/grants, traineeships, health care benefits, and unspecified assistantships available. Support available to part-time students. Financial award applicants required to submit FAFSA. *Degree program information:* Part-time and evening/weekend programs available. Postbaccalaureate distance learning degree programs offered. *Application deadline:* For fall admission, 12/28 priority date for domestic students. Applications are processed on a rolling basis. *Application fee:* $50. Electronic applications accepted. *Dean of the Graduate School and Associate Provost for Graduate Education,* Dr. Karen Klomparens, 517-353-0301, Fax: 517-353-3355.

College of Agriculture and Natural Resources Students: 513 full-time (264 women), 120 part-time (48 women); includes 37 minority (14 African Americans, 2 American Indian/Alaska Native, 12 Asian Americans or Pacific Islanders, 9 Hispanic Americans), 270 international. Average age 30. 570 applicants, 40% accepted. *Faculty:* 302 full-time (75 women), 3 part-time/adjunct (2 women). Expenses: Contact institution. *Financial support:* In 2008–09, 316 research assistantships with tuition reimbursements (averaging $14,099 per year), 48 teaching assistantships with tuition reimbursements (averaging $14,087 per year) were awarded; career-related internships or fieldwork, Federal Work-Study, institutionally sponsored loans, scholarships/grants, tuition waivers (partial), and unspecified assistantships also available. Support available to part-time students. In 2008, 100 master's, 47 doctorates awarded. Offers agricultural economics (MS, PhD); agricultural, food, and resource economics (MS, PhD); agriculture and natural resources (MA, MIPS, MS, MURP, PhD); animal science (MS, PhD); animal science-environmental toxicology (PhD); biosystems engineering (MS, PhD); community, agriculture, recreation, and resource studies (MS, PhD); construction management (MS, PhD); crop and soil sciences (MS, PhD); crop and soil sciences-environmental toxicology (PhD); entomology (MS, PhD); environmental design (MA); fisheries and wildlife (MS, PhD); fisheries and wildlife—environmental toxicology (PhD); food science (MS, PhD); food science—environmental toxicology (PhD); forestry (MS, PhD); forestry-environmental toxicology (PhD); horticulture (MS, PhD); human nutrition (MS, PhD); human nutrition-environmental toxicology (PhD); integrated pest management (MS); interior design and facilities management (MA); international planning studies (MIPS); packaging (MS, PhD); plant breeding and genetics (MS, PhD); plant breeding and genetics-crop and soil sciences (MS); plant breeding, genetics and biotechnology-crop and soil sciences (PhD); plant breeding, genetics and biotechnology-forestry (MS, PhD); plant breeding, genetics and biotechnology-horticulture (MS, PhD); plant pathology (MS, PhD); urban and regional planning (MURP). *Application Contact:* Janell Kebler, Graduate Secretary, 517-353-8588, Fax: 517-353-9896, E-mail: jkebler@msu.edu. *Dean,* Dr. Jeffrey D. Armstrong, 517-355-0232, Fax: 517-353-9896, E-mail: armstroj@msu.edu.

College of Arts and Letters Students: 189 full-time (24 women), 48 part-time (29 women); includes 89 minority (43 African Americans, 8 American Indian/Alaska Native, 10 Asian Americans or Pacific Islanders, 28 Hispanic Americans), 112 international. Average age 32. 479 applicants, 37% accepted. *Faculty:* 187 full-time (89 women). Expenses: Contact institution. *Financial support:* In 2008–09, 56 research assistantships with tuition reimbursements (averaging $13,180 per year), 221 teaching assistantships with tuition reimbursements (averaging $12,912 per year) were awarded. In 2008, 53 master's, 40 doctorates awarded. Offers African American and African studies (MA, PhD); American studies (MA, PhD); applied Spanish linguistics (MA); arts and letters (MA, MFA, PhD); critical studies in literacy and pedagogy (MA); digital rhetoric and professional writing (MA); English (PhD); French (MA); French language and literature (PhD); German studies (MA, PhD); Hispanic cultural studies (PhD); Hispanic literatures (MA); history (MA, PhD); history-secondary school teaching (MA); linguistics (MA, PhD); literature in English (MA); philosophy (MA, PhD); rhetoric and writing (PhD); second language studies (PhD); studio art (MFA); teaching English to speakers of other languages (MA); theatre (MA, MFA). Electronic applications accepted. *Application Contact:* Janet Roe-Darden, Assistant for Graduate Studies, 517-355-5360, Fax: 517-432-0129, E-mail: jroe@msu.edu. *Dean,* Dr. Karin A. Wurst, 517-355-4597, Fax: 517-355-0159, E-mail: wurst@msu.edu.

College of Communication Arts and Sciences Students: 277 full-time (195 women), 116 part-time (62 women); includes 38 minority (14 African Americans, 1 American Indian/Alaska Native, 15 Asian Americans or Pacific Islanders, 8 Hispanic Americans), 155 international. Average age 28. 732 applicants, 33% accepted. *Faculty:* 68 full-time (27 women). Expenses: Contact institution. *Financial support:* In 2008–09, 49 research assistantships with tuition reimbursements (averaging $13,617 per year), 48 teaching assistantships with tuition reimbursements (averaging $14,573 per year) were awarded. In 2008, 122 master's, 16 doctorates awarded. Offers advertising (MA); communication (MA, PhD); communication arts and sciences (MA, MS, PhD); communication arts and sciences–media and information studies (PhD); communicative sciences and disorders (MA, PhD); health communication (MA); journalism (MA); public relations (MA); retailing (MS, PhD); telecommunication, information studies, and media (MA). *Interim Dean,* Dr. Bradley S. Greenberg, 517-355-3410, Fax: 517-432-1244, E-mail: bradg@msu.edu.

College of Education Students: 677 full-time (447 women), 629 part-time (447 women); includes 174 minority (96 African Americans, 9 American Indian/Alaska Native, 32 Asian Americans or Pacific Islanders, 37 Hispanic Americans), 178 international. Average age 32. 796 applicants, 54% accepted. *Faculty:* 123 full-time (68 women). Expenses: Contact institution. *Financial support:* In 2008–09, 294 research assistantships with tuition reimbursements (averaging $14,352 per year), 195 teaching assistantships with tuition reimbursements (averaging $14,553 per year) were awarded. In 2008, 442 master's, 83 doctorates awarded. Offers ccurriculum, instruction and teacher education (PhD); counseling (MA); curriculum, instruction and teacher education (Ed S); education (MA, MS, PhD, Ed S); education for professional teachers (MA); educational policy (PhD); educational psychology and educational technology (PhD); educational technology (MA); higher, adult and lifelong education (MA, PhD); K–12 educational administration (MA, PhD, Ed S); kinesiology (MS, PhD); literacy instruction (MA); measurement and quantitative methods (PhD); rehabilitation counseling (MA); rehabilitation counselor education (PhD); school psychology (MA, PhD, Ed S); special education (MA, PhD); student affairs administration (MA); teaching and curriculum (MA). Electronic applications accepted. *Dean,* Dr. Carole Ames, 517-355-1734, Fax: 517-353-6393, E-mail: cames@msu.edu.

College of Engineering Students: 538 full-time (112 women), 46 part-time (9 women); includes 51 minority (17 African Americans, 1 American Indian/Alaska Native, 13 Asian Americans or Pacific Islanders, 20 Hispanic Americans), 362 international. Average age 27. 1,436 applicants, 11% accepted. *Faculty:* 146 full-time (16 women), 2 part-time/adjunct (0 women). Expenses: Contact institution. *Financial support:* In 2008–09, 317 research assistantships with tuition reimbursements (averaging $16,470 per year), 133 teaching assistantships with tuition reimbursements (averaging $15,937 per year) were awarded. In 2008, 91 master's, 4 doctorates awarded. *Degree program information:* Part-time programs available. Offers chemical engineering (MS, PhD); civil engineering (MS, PhD); computer science (MS, PhD); electrical engineering (MS, PhD); engineering (MS, PhD); engineering mechanics (MS, PhD); environmental engineering (MS, PhD); environmental engineering-environmental toxicology (PhD); materials science and engineering (MS, PhD); mechanical engineering (MS, PhD). Electronic applications accepted. *Dean,* Dr. Satish Udpa, 517-355-5113, Fax: 517-355-2288, E-mail: udpa@egr.msu.edu.

College of Music Students: 232 full-time (131 women), 42 part-time (27 women); includes 24 minority (6 African Americans, 4 American Indian/Alaska Native, 9 Asian Americans or Pacific Islanders, 5 Hispanic Americans), 112 international. Average age 29. 336 applicants, 29% accepted. *Faculty:* 59 full-time (14 women), 1 part-time/adjunct (0 women). Expenses: Contact institution. *Financial support:* In 2008–09, 14 research assistantships with tuition reimbursements (averaging $13,013 per year), 85 teaching assistantships with tuition reimbursements (averaging $12,666 per year) were awarded. In 2008, 66 master's, 31 doctorates awarded. Offers collaborative piano (M Mus); jazz studies (M Mus); music (PhD); music composition (M Mus, DMA); music conducting (M Mus, DMA); music education (M Mus); music performance (M Mus, DMA); music theory (M Mus); music therapy (M Mus); musicology (MA); piano pedagogy (M Mus). Electronic applications accepted. *Application Contact:* Anne Simon, Assistant to the Associate Dean for Graduate Studies and Research, 517-353-9122, Fax: 517-432-2880, E-mail: musgrad@msu.edu. *Dean,* Prof. James B. Forger, 517-355-4583, Fax: 517-432-2880, E-mail: forger@msu.edu.

College of Natural Science Students: 970 full-time (418 women), 60 part-time (31 women); includes 59 minority (14 African Americans, 2 American Indian/Alaska Native, 26 Asian Americans or Pacific Islanders, 17 Hispanic Americans), 468 international. Average age 28. 1,382 applicants, 20% accepted. *Faculty:* 295 full-time (58 women), 3 part-time/adjunct (1 woman). Expenses: Contact institution. *Financial support:* In 2008–09, 385 research assistantships with tuition reimbursements (averaging $15,925 per year), 397 teaching assistantships with tuition reimbursements (averaging $15,237 per year) were awarded. In 2008, 123 master's, 95 doctorates awarded. Offers applied mathematics (MS, PhD); applied statistics (MS); astrophysics and astronomy (MS, PhD); biochemistry and molecular biology (MS, PhD); biochemistry and molecular biology/environmental toxicology (PhD); biological, physical and general science for teachers (MAT, MS); biomedical laboratory operations (MS); cell and molecular biology (MS, PhD); cell and molecular biology/environmental toxicology (PhD); chemical physics (PhD); chemistry (MS, PhD); chemistry-environmental toxicology (PhD); clinical laboratory sciences (MS); computational chemistry (MS); ecology, evolutionary biology and behavior (PhD); environmental geosciences (MS, PhD); environmental geosciences-environmental toxicology (PhD); genetics (MS, PhD); genetics–environmental toxicology (PhD); geological sciences (MS, PhD); industrial mathematics (MS); mathematics (MAT, MS, PhD); mathematics education (MS, PhD); natural science (MAT, MS, PhD); neuroscience (MS, PhD); physics (MS, PhD); physiology (MS, PhD); plant biology (MS, PhD); plant breeding, genetics and biotechnology—plant biology (MS, PhD); quantitative biology (PhD); statistics (MS, PhD); zoo and aquarium management (MS); zoology (MS, PhD); zoology-environmental toxicology (PhD). Electronic applications accepted. *Dean,* Dr. R. James Kirkpatrick, 517-355-4473, Fax: 517-432-1054, E-mail: cnsdean@msu.edu.

College of Nursing Students: 53 full-time (50 women), 162 part-time (154 women); includes 14 minority (5 African Americans, 1 American Indian/Alaska Native, 4 Asian Americans or Pacific Islanders, 4 Hispanic Americans), 4 international. Average age 38. 171 applicants, 43% accepted. *Faculty:* 18 full-time (16 women). Expenses: Contact institution. *Financial support:* In 2008–09, 2 research assistantships with tuition reimbursements (averaging $12,636 per year), 3 teaching assistantships with tuition reimbursements (averaging $12,426 per year) were awarded. In 2008, 43 master's, 1 doctorate awarded. *Degree program information:* Part-time programs available. Postbaccalaureate distance learning degree programs offered (no on-campus study). Offers nursing (MSN, PhD). *Application deadline:* For fall admission, 11/1 priority date for domestic students. Electronic applications accepted. *Application Contact:* Information Contact, 517-353-4827, Fax: 517-432-8251, E-mail: nurse@hc.msu.edu. *Dean,* Dr. Mary Mundt, 517-355-6527, Fax: 517-353-9553, E-mail: mary.mundt@hc.msu.edu.

College of Social Science Students: 903 full-time (551 women), 436 part-time (321 women); includes 214 minority (94 African Americans, 17 American Indian/Alaska Native, 41 Asian Americans or Pacific Islanders, 62 Hispanic Americans), 231 international. Average age 30. 1,814 applicants, 34% accepted. *Faculty:* 327 full-time (126 women), 3 part-time/adjunct (1 woman). Expenses: Contact institution. *Financial support:* In 2008–09, 192 research assistantships with tuition reimbursements (averaging $13,605 per year), 257 teaching assistantships with tuition reimbursements (averaging $13,591 per year) were awarded; career-related internships or fieldwork, Federal Work-Study, institutionally sponsored loans, scholarships/grants, and unspecified assistantships also available. Support available to part-time students. In 2008, 344 master's, 66 doctorates awarded. Offers anthropology (MA, PhD); Chicano/Latino studies (PhD); child development (MA); clinical social work (MSW); community services (MS); criminal justice (MS, PhD); economics (MA, PhD); family and child ecology (PhD); family studies (MA); forensic science (MS); geographic information science (MS); geography (MS, PhD); human resources and labor relations (MLRHR); industrial relations and human resources (PhD); law enforcement intelligence and analysis (MS); marriage and family therapy (MA); organizational and community practice (MSW); political science (MA, PhD); professional applications in anthropology (MA); psychology (MA, PhD); public policy (MPP); social science (MA, MIPS, MLRHR, MPP, MS, MSW, MURP, PhD); social work (PhD); sociology (MA, PhD); youth development (MA). Electronic applications accepted. *Application Contact:* Jeanne Kalin, Executive Secretary, 517-353-4823, Fax: 517-355-1912, E-mail: kalin@msu.edu. *Dean,* Dr. Marietta L. Baba, 517-355-6675, Fax: 517-355-1912, E-mail: mbaba@msu.edu.

Eli Broad Graduate School of Management Students: 745 full-time (214 women), 43 part-time (15 women); includes 117 minority (35 African Americans, 63 Asian Americans or Pacific Islanders, 19 Hispanic Americans), 195 international. Average age 30. 779 applicants, 47% accepted. *Faculty:* 108 full-time (25 women), 1 part-time/adjunct (0 women). Expenses: Contact institution. *Financial support:* In 2008–09, 127 research assistantships with tuition reimbursements (averaging $13,836 per year), 27 teaching assistantships with tuition reimbursements (averaging $13,018 per year) were awarded. In 2008, 431 master's, 16 doctorates awarded. *Degree program information:* Evening/weekend programs available. Offers accounting (MS); business administration (MBA, PhD); business research (MBA); corporate business administration (MBA); finance (MS); foodservice business management (MS); hospitality business management (MS); integrative management (MBA); management (MBA, MS, PhD); marketing (MBA, PhD); supply chain management (MS). Electronic applications accepted. *Application Contact:* Deb North, Executive Secretary, 517-432-3196, Fax: 517-353-6395, E-mail: north@bus.msu.edu. *Acting Dean,* Dr. Elvin C. Lashbrooke, 517-355-8377, Fax: 517-353-6395, E-mail: lashbrooke@bus.msu.edu.

See Close-Up on page 943.

MICHIGAN STATE UNIVERSITY COLLEGE OF LAW, East Lansing, MI 48824-1300

General Information Independent, coed, graduate-only institution. *Enrollment by degree level:* 955 first professional, 3 other advanced degrees. *Graduate faculty:* 52 full-time (23 women), 73 part-time/adjunct (17 women). *Graduate housing:* Rooms and/or apartments available on a first-come, first-served basis to single and married students. Housing application deadline: 4/1. *Student services:* Campus employment opportunities, campus safety program, career counseling, exercise/wellness program, international student services, low-cost health insurance, multicultural affairs office, services for students with disabilities, writing training. *Library facilities:* Michigan State University College of Law Library plus 5 others. *Online resources:* library catalog, access to other libraries' catalogs. *Collection:* 136,094 titles, 15,009 serial subscriptions, 1,024 audiovisual materials.

Michigan State University College of Law (continued)

Computer facilities: 72 computers available on campus for general student use. A campuswide network can be accessed from student residence rooms and from off campus. Online class registration is available. *Web address:* http://www.law.msu.edu/.

General Application Contact: Charles Roboski, Assistant Dean of Admissions, 517-432-0222, Fax: 517-432-0098, E-mail: roboski@law.msu.edu.

GRADUATE UNITS

Professional Program Students: 814 full-time (305 women), 144 part-time (71 women); includes 106 minority (39 African Americans, 12 American Indian/Alaska Native, 33 Asian Americans or Pacific Islanders, 22 Hispanic Americans), 52 international. Average age 28. 1,999 applicants, 55% accepted, 306 enrolled. *Faculty:* 52 full-time (23 women), 73 part-time/adjunct (17 women). Expenses: Contact institution. *Financial support:* In 2008–09, 288 students received support, including 313 fellowships (averaging $21,893 per year); career-related internships or fieldwork, Federal Work-Study, institutionally sponsored loans, scholarships/grants, and tuition waivers (full) also available. Support available to part-time students. Financial award application deadline: 4/15; financial award applicants required to submit FAFSA. In 2008, 319 JDs awarded. *Degree program information:* Part-time and evening/weekend programs available. Offers American legal system (LL M); intellectual property (LL M); law (JD). *Application deadline:* For fall admission, 3/15 priority date for domestic students, 7/1 priority date for international students. Applications are processed on a rolling basis. *Application fee:* $60. Electronic applications accepted. *Application Contact:* Charles Roboski, Assistant Dean of Admissions, 517-432-0222, Fax: 517-432-0098, E-mail: roboski@law.msu.edu. *Dean and Professor of Law,* Joan W. Howarth, 517-432-6993, Fax: 517-432-6801, E-mail: howarth@law.msu.edu.

MICHIGAN TECHNOLOGICAL UNIVERSITY, Houghton, MI 49931-1295

General Information State-supported, coed, university. CGS member. *Graduate housing:* Rooms and/or apartments available on a first-come, first-served basis to single and married students.

GRADUATE UNITS

Graduate School *Degree program information:* Part-time programs available. Postbaccalaureate distance learning degree programs offered (minimal on-campus study). Electronic applications accepted.

College of Engineering *Degree program information:* Part-time programs available. Postbaccalaureate distance learning degree programs offered (minimal on-campus study). Offers biomedical engineering (PhD); chemical engineering (MS, PhD); civil engineering (ME, MS, PhD); computational science and engineering (PhD); electrical engineering (MS, PhD); engineering (ME, MS, PhD); engineering mechanics (MS); environmental engineering (ME, MS, PhD); environmental engineering science (MS); geological engineering (MS, PhD); geology (MS, PhD); geophysics (MS); materials science and engineering (MS, PhD); mechanical engineering (MS, PhD); mechanical engineering-engineering mechanics (PhD); mining engineering (MS, PhD). Electronic applications accepted.

College of Sciences and Arts *Degree program information:* Part-time programs available. Offers applied science education (MS); atmospheric sciences (PhD); biological sciences (MS, PhD); chemistry (MS, PhD); computational science and engineering (PhD); computer science (MS, PhD); engineering physics (PhD); environmental policy (MS); industrial archaeology (MS); industrial heritage and archeology (PhD); mathematical sciences (MS, PhD); physics (MS, PhD); rhetoric and technical communication (MS, PhD); sciences and arts (MS, PhD). Electronic applications accepted.

School of Business and Economics *Degree program information:* Part-time programs available. Offers applied natural resource economics (MS); business administration (MBA); business and economics (MBA, MS). Electronic applications accepted.

School of Forest Resources and Environmental Science *Degree program information:* Part-time programs available. Offers applied ecology (MS); forest ecology and management (MS); forest molecular genetics and biotechnology (MS, PhD); forest resources and environmental science (MF, MS, PhD); forest science (PhD); forestry (MF, MS). Electronic applications accepted.

Sustainable Futures Institute *Degree program information:* Part-time programs available. Offers sustainability (Certificate).

See Close-Up on page 945.

MICHIGAN THEOLOGICAL SEMINARY, Plymouth, MI 48170

General Information Independent-religious, coed, graduate-only institution. *Graduate housing:* On-campus housing not available.

GRADUATE UNITS

Graduate Programs *Degree program information:* Part-time and evening/weekend programs available. Offers Bible (Graduate Certificate); Christian education (MA); counseling psychology (MA); divinity (M Div); theological studies (MA).

MID-AMERICA BAPTIST THEOLOGICAL SEMINARY, Cordova, TN 38016

General Information Independent-religious, coed, primarily men. *Graduate housing:* Rooms and/or apartments available on a first-come, first-served basis to single and married students.

GRADUATE UNITS

Graduate and Professional Programs Offers theology (M Div, MACE, MCE, MM, D Min, PhD). Electronic applications accepted.

MID-AMERICA BAPTIST THEOLOGICAL SEMINARY NORTHEAST BRANCH, Schenectady, NY 12303-3463

General Information Independent-religious, coed, primarily men, graduate-only institution. *Graduate housing:* Rooms and/or apartments available on a first-come, first-served basis to single and married students.

GRADUATE UNITS

Program in Theology *Degree program information:* Part-time and evening/weekend programs available. Offers theology (M Div). Electronic applications accepted.

MIDAMERICA NAZARENE UNIVERSITY, Olathe, KS 66062-1899

General Information Independent-religious, coed, comprehensive institution. *Enrollment:* 1,743 graduate, professional, and undergraduate students; 203 full-time matriculated graduate/professional students (113 women), 148 part-time matriculated graduate/professional students (121 women). *Enrollment by degree level:* 326 master's, 25 other advanced degrees. *Graduate faculty:* 18 full-time (6 women), 39 part-time/adjunct (19 women). *Graduate housing:* On-campus housing not available. *Student services:* Campus safety program, career counseling, free psychological counseling, international student services, multicultural affairs office, teacher training. *Library facilities:* Mabee Library. *Online resources:* library catalog, web page, access to other libraries' catalogs. *Collection:* 132,991 titles, 1,250 serial subscriptions, 11,427 audiovisual materials.

Computer facilities: 85 computers available on campus for general student use. A campuswide network can be accessed from student residence rooms and from off campus. *Web address:* http://www.mnu.edu/.

General Application Contact: Kevin Mokhtarian, Admissions Coordinator, 913-971-3436, E-mail: khmokhtarian@mnu.edu.

GRADUATE UNITS

Graduate Studies in Counseling Students: 62 full-time (44 women), 28 part-time (all women); includes 9 minority (5 African Americans, 2 American Indian/Alaska Native, 2 Hispanic Americans). Average age 35. 42 applicants, 64% accepted. *Faculty:* 6 full-time (2 women), 7 part-time/adjunct (4 women). Expenses: Contact institution. In 2008, 22 master's awarded. *Degree program information:* Evening/weekend programs available. Offers counseling (MAC); play therapy (PMC). *Application deadline:* For fall admission, 6/15 for domestic students. *Application fee:* $75. *Application Contact:* Aileen Douglas, Secretary, 913-791-3449, Fax: 913-791-3402, E-mail: adouglas@mnu.edu. *Director,* Dr. Todd Frye, 913-971-3449, Fax: 913-791-3402, E-mail: tmfrye@mnu.edu.

Graduate Studies in Education Students: 2 full-time (both women), 112 part-time (88 women); includes 6 minority (4 African Americans, 2 Hispanic Americans). Average age 35. 64 applicants, 91% accepted, 56 enrolled. *Faculty:* 6 full-time (2 women), 14 part-time/adjunct (8 women). Expenses: Contact institution. *Financial support:* Applicants required to submit FAFSA. In 2008, 151 master's awarded. *Degree program information:* Part-time and evening/weekend programs available. Postbaccalaureate distance learning degree programs offered (no on-campus study). Offers ESOL (M Ed); professional teaching (M Ed); special education (MA); technology enhanced teaching (M Ed). *Application deadline:* Applications are processed on a rolling basis. *Application fee:* $25. *Application Contact:* Glenna Murray, Administrative Assistant, 913-971-3292, Fax: 913-971-3407, E-mail: gkmurray@mnu.edu. *Director,* Dr. Martin Dunlap, 913-971-3292, Fax: 913-971-3407, E-mail: mhdunlap@mnu.edu.

Graduate Studies in Management Students: 139 full-time (67 women), 8 part-time (5 women); includes 33 minority (22 African Americans, 1 American Indian/Alaska Native, 2 Asian Americans or Pacific Islanders, 8 Hispanic Americans), 1 international. Average age 35. 85 applicants, 96% accepted. *Faculty:* 6 full-time (2 women), 18 part-time/adjunct (7 women). Expenses: Contact institution. *Financial support:* Application deadline: 5/1. In 2008, 63 master's awarded. *Degree program information:* Evening/weekend programs available. Offers management (MBA); organizational administration (MA). *Application deadline:* For fall admission, 9/1 priority date for domestic students; for spring admission, 5/1 priority date for domestic students. Applications are processed on a rolling basis. *Application fee:* $100. Electronic applications accepted. *Application Contact:* Melanie Sutherland, Administrative Assistant, 913-971-3276, Fax: 913-971-3409, E-mail: mba@mnu.edu. *Director,* Dr. Willadee Wehmeyer, 913-971-3276, Fax: 913-791-3409, E-mail: wwehmeye@mnu.edu.

MID-AMERICA REFORMED SEMINARY, Dyer, IN 46311

General Information Independent-religious, men only, graduate-only institution.

GRADUATE UNITS

Graduate Programs Offers theology (M Div, MTS).

MIDDLEBURY COLLEGE, Middlebury, VT 05753-6002

General Information Independent, coed, comprehensive institution. *Enrollment:* 2,455 graduate, professional, and undergraduate students; 1,427 full-time matriculated graduate/professional students. *Graduate faculty:* 192 full-time. *Graduate housing:* Room and/or apartments guaranteed to single students; on-campus housing not available to married students. *Student services:* Campus safety program, career counseling, free psychological counseling, international student services, services for students with disabilities, teacher training. *Library facilities:* Main Library plus 3 others. *Online resources:* library catalog, web page, access to other libraries' catalogs. *Collection:* 853,000 titles, 2,908 serial subscriptions, 45,024 audiovisual materials.

Computer facilities: 494 computers available on campus for general student use. A campuswide network can be accessed from student residence rooms and from off campus. Online class registration, help-line, personal Web pages, file servers are available. *Web address:* http://www.middlebury.edu/.

General Application Contact: Admissions Office, 802-443-3000, Fax: 802-443-2056, E-mail: admissions@middlebury.edu.

GRADUATE UNITS

Bread Loaf School of English Students: 496 full-time; includes 19 minority (12 African Americans, 1 American Indian/Alaska Native, 4 Asian Americans or Pacific Islanders, 2 Hispanic Americans). Average age 30. *Faculty:* 54 full-time. Expenses: Contact institution. *Financial support:* In 2008–09, 242 students received support, including 36 fellowships; scholarships/grants also available. Support available to part-time students. In 2008, 72 master's awarded. Offers English (M Litt, MA). Offered during summer only. *Application deadline:* Applications are processed on a rolling basis. *Application fee:* $55. Electronic applications accepted. *Application Contact:* Language Schools Office, 802-443-5510, Fax: 802-443-2075. *Director,* Dr. James Maddox, 802-443-5418, Fax: 802-443-2060, E-mail: blse@breadnet.middlebury.edu.

Language Schools Students: 390 full-time (281 women); includes 67 minority (6 African Americans, 1 American Indian/Alaska Native, 19 Asian Americans or Pacific Islanders, 41 Hispanic Americans). Average age 33. 772 applicants, 69% accepted, 420 enrolled. *Faculty:* 86 full-time (33 women). Expenses: Contact institution. *Financial support:* Fellowships, scholarships/grants available. In 2008, 151 master's, 6 doctorates awarded. Offers French (MA, DML); German (MA, DML); Italian (MA, DML); language (MA, DML); Russian (MA, DML); Spanish (MA, DML). *Application deadline:* Applications are processed on a rolling basis. *Application fee:* $55. Electronic applications accepted. *Application Contact:* Kara Gennarelli, Language Schools Office, 802-443-5727, Fax: 802-443-2075, E-mail: languages@middlebury.edu. *Vice President for Language Schools, Schools Abroad and Graduate Programs,* Dr. Michael E. Geisler, 802-443-5508, Fax: 802-443-2075.

Chinese School Students: 21 full-time (17 women); includes 12 minority (all Asian Americans or Pacific Islanders). Average age 34. 37 applicants, 65% accepted, 22 enrolled. *Faculty:* 3 full-time (1 woman). Expenses: Contact institution. *Financial support:* Fellowships, scholarships/grants available. Financial award applicants required to submit FAFSA. In 2008, 1 master's awarded. Offers Chinese (MA). *Application deadline:* Applications are processed on a rolling basis. *Application fee:* $55. Electronic applications accepted. *Application Contact:* Anna Sun, Coordinator, 802-443-5520, Fax: 802-443-2075, E-mail: sun@middlebury.edu. *Director,* Dr. Jianhua Bai, 802-443-5520, Fax: 802-443-2075, E-mail: jbai@middlebury.edu.

MIDDLE TENNESSEE SCHOOL OF ANESTHESIA, Madison, TN 37116

General Information Independent-religious, coed, graduate-only institution. *Graduate housing:* On-campus housing not available.

GRADUATE UNITS

Program in Nurse Anesthesia Offers nurse anesthesia (MS).

MIDDLE TENNESSEE STATE UNIVERSITY, Murfreesboro, TN 37132

General Information State-supported, coed, university. CGS member. *Enrollment:* 23,872 graduate, professional, and undergraduate students; 252 full-time matriculated graduate/professional students (117 women), 2,096 part-time matriculated graduate/professional students (1,385 women). *Graduate faculty:* 416 full-time (175 women), 10 part-time/adjunct (3 women). *Graduate housing:* Rooms and/or apartments available on a first-come, first-served basis to single and married students. *Student services:* Campus employment opportunities, campus safety program, career counseling, exercise/wellness program, free psychological counseling, international student services, low-cost health insurance, multicultural affairs office, services for students with disabilities. *Library facilities:* James E. Walker Library. *Online resources:* library catalog, web page, access to other libraries' catalogs. *Collection:* 936,172 titles, 4,144 serial subscriptions.

Computer facilities: 2,400 computers available on campus for general student use. A campuswide network can be accessed from student residence rooms and from off campus. Online class registration is available. *Web address:* http://www.mtsu.edu/.

General Application Contact: Dr. Michael Allen, Dean and Vice Provost for Research, 615-898-2840, Fax: 615-904-8020, E-mail: mallen@mtsu.edu.

GRADUATE UNITS

College of Graduate Studies Students: 252 full-time (117 women), 2,096 part-time (1,385 women); includes 482 minority (316 African Americans, 7 American Indian/Alaska Native, 129 Asian Americans or Pacific Islanders, 30 Hispanic Americans). Average age 29. 2,173 applicants, 69% accepted, 1493 enrolled. *Faculty:* 416 full-time (175 women), 10 part-time/adjunct (3 women). Expenses: Contact institution. *Financial support:* In 2008–09, 348 students received support. Career-related internships or fieldwork and institutionally sponsored loans available. Support available to part-time students. Financial award application deadline: 5/1; financial award applicants required to submit FAFSA. In 2008, 672 master's, 24 doctorates, 94 other advanced degrees awarded. *Degree program information:* Part-time and evening/weekend programs available. Postbaccalaureate distance learning degree programs offered. Offers gerontology (Graduate Certificate); health care management (Graduate Certificate). *Application deadline:* For fall admission, 6/1 for domestic and international students. Applications are processed on a rolling basis. *Application fee:* $25 ($30 for international students). Electronic applications accepted. *Dean and Vice Provost for Research*, Dr. Michael Allen, 615-898-2840, Fax: 615-904-8020, E-mail: mallen@mtsu.edu.

College of Basic and Applied Sciences Students: 30 full-time (11 women), 299 part-time (168 women); includes 84 minority (41 African Americans, 2 American Indian/Alaska Native, 38 Asian Americans or Pacific Islanders, 3 Hispanic Americans). Average age 30. 298 applicants, 58% accepted, 172 enrolled. *Faculty:* 102 full-time (44 women). Expenses: Contact institution. *Financial support:* In 2008–09, 98 students received support. Institutionally sponsored loans available. Support available to part-time students. Financial award application deadline: 5/1; financial award applicants required to submit FAFSA. In 2008, 74 master's, 1 doctorate awarded. *Degree program information:* Part-time and evening/weekend programs available. Postbaccalaureate distance learning degree programs offered. Offers aerospace education (M Ed); aviation administration (MS); basic and applied sciences (M Ed, MS, MSN, MST, DA, Graduate Certificate); biology (MS); biostatistics (MS); biotechnology (MS); chemistry (MS, DA); computer science (MS); engineering technology and industrial studies (MS); family nurse practitioner (MSN, Graduate Certificate); health care informatics (MS); mathematics (MS, MST); nursing (MSN, Graduate Certificate). *Application deadline:* For fall admission, 6/1 for domestic and international students. Applications are processed on a rolling basis. *Application fee:* $25 ($30 for international students). Electronic applications accepted. *Dean*, Dr. Thomas Cheatham, 615-898-2613, Fax: 615-898-2615.

College of Continuing Education and Distance Learning Students: 1 full-time (0 women), 45 part-time (34 women); includes 13 minority (12 African Americans, 1 Hispanic American). 41 applicants, 78% accepted, 32 enrolled. Expenses: Contact institution. *Financial support:* In 2008–09, 4 students received support. Application deadline: 5/1. In 2008, 4 degrees awarded. *Degree program information:* Part-time and evening/weekend programs available. Postbaccalaureate distance learning degree programs offered. Offers social sciences (MPS). *Application deadline:* For fall admission, 6/1 for domestic and international students. Applications are processed on a rolling basis. *Application fee:* $25 ($30 for international students). *Program Director*, Dr. David Gotcher, 615-904-8042, E-mail: dgotcher@mtsu.edu.

College of Education and Behavioral Science Students: 66 full-time (38 women), 1,039 part-time (822 women); includes 184 minority (146 African Americans, 1 American Indian/Alaska Native, 24 Asian Americans or Pacific Islanders, 13 Hispanic Americans). Average age 31. 715 applicants. *Faculty:* 109 full-time (56 women), 7 part-time/adjunct (2 women). Expenses: Contact institution. *Financial support:* In 2008–09, 79 students received support. Career-related internships or fieldwork and institutionally sponsored loans available. Support available to part-time students. Financial award application deadline: 5/1; financial award applicants required to submit FAFSA. In 2008, 338 master's, 11 doctorates, 94 other advanced degrees awarded. *Degree program information:* Part-time and evening/weekend programs available. Postbaccalaureate distance learning degree programs offered. Offers administration and supervision (M Ed, Ed S); child development and family studies (MS); clinical psychology (MA); criminal justice administration (MCJ); curriculum and instruction (M Ed, Ed S); dyslexic studies (Graduate Certificate); early childhood education (M Ed); education and behavioral science (M Ed, MA, MCJ, MS, PhD, Ed S, Graduate Certificate); elementary education (M Ed, Ed S); English as a second language (M Ed, Ed S); exercise science (MS); health, physical education and recreation (MS); human performance (PhD); industrial/organizational psychology (MA); literacy studies (PhD); mental health counseling (M Ed); middle school education (M Ed); nutrition and food science (MS); professional counseling (M Ed, Ed S); psychology (MA); reading (M Ed); school counseling (M Ed); school psychology (Ed S); secondary education (M Ed); special education (M Ed); teaching and learning (M Ed); technology and curriculum design (Ed S). *Application deadline:* For fall admission, 6/1 for domestic and international students. Applications are processed on a rolling basis. *Application fee:* $25 ($30 for international students). Electronic applications accepted. *Interim Dean*, Dr. Terry Whiteside, 615-898-2874, Fax: 615-898-2530, E-mail: whitesid@mtsu.edu.

College of Liberal Arts Students: 15 full-time (9 women), 221 part-time (133 women); includes 26 minority (14 African Americans, 1 American Indian/Alaska Native, 7 Asian Americans or Pacific Islanders, 4 Hispanic Americans). Average age 28. 162 applicants, 76% accepted, 123 enrolled. *Faculty:* 106 full-time (55 women), 3 part-time/adjunct (1 woman). Expenses: Contact institution. *Financial support:* In 2008–09, 99 students received support. Career-related internships or fieldwork and institutionally sponsored loans available. Support available to part-time students. Financial award application deadline: 5/1; financial award applicants required to submit FAFSA. In 2008, 33 master's, 6 doctorates awarded. *Degree program information:* Part-time and evening/weekend programs available. Postbaccalaureate distance learning degree programs offered. Offers English (MA, PhD); English as a second language (M Ed); foreign language (MAT); geosciences (Graduate Certificate); history (MA, PhD); liberal arts (M Ed, MA, MAT, MSW, PhD, Graduate Certificate); music (MA); public history (MA, PhD); social work (MSW); sociology (MA). *Application deadline:* For fall admission, 6/1 for domestic and international students. Applications are processed on a rolling basis. *Application fee:* $25 ($30 for international students). Electronic applications accepted. *Dean*, Dr. John McDaniel, 615-898-2534, Fax: 615-898-5907, E-mail: mcdaniel@mtsu.edu.

College of Mass Communication Students: 16 full-time (2 women), 60 part-time (38 women); includes 28 minority (20 African Americans, 6 Asian Americans or Pacific Islanders, 2 Hispanic Americans). Average age 27. 75 applicants, 56% accepted, 42 enrolled. *Faculty:* 32 full-time (3 women). Expenses: Contact institution. *Financial support:* In 2008–09, 12 students received support. Institutionally sponsored loans available. Support available to part-time students. Financial award application deadline: 5/1; financial award applicants required to submit FAFSA. In 2008, 25 degrees awarded. *Degree program information:* Part-time and evening/weekend programs available. Postbaccalaureate distance learning degree programs offered. Offers mass communication (MFA, MS); recording arts and technologies (MFA). *Application deadline:* For fall admission, 6/1 for domestic and international students. Applications are processed on a rolling basis. *Application fee:* $25 ($30 for international students). Electronic applications accepted. *Interim Dean*, Dr. John Omachionu, 615-898-2813, Fax: 615-898-5682.

Jennings A. Jones College of Business Students: 124 full-time (57 women), 423 part-time (182 women); includes 142 minority (79 African Americans, 2 American Indian/Alaska Native, 54 Asian Americans or Pacific Islanders, 7 Hispanic Americans). Average age 29. 326 applicants, 67% accepted, 217 enrolled. *Faculty:* 67 full-time (17 women). Expenses: Contact institution. *Financial support:* In 2008–09, 57 students received support. Institutionally sponsored loans available. Support available to part-time students. Financial award application deadline: 5/1; financial award applicants required to submit FAFSA. In 2008, 190 master's, 6 doctorates awarded. *Degree program information:* Part-time and evening/weekend programs available. Postbaccalaureate distance learning degree programs offered. Offers accounting (MS); business (MA, MBA, MBE, MS, PhD); business education (MBE); computer information systems (MS); economics (MA, PhD); information systems (MS); management and marketing (MBA). *Application deadline:* For fall admission, 6/1 for domestic and international students. Applications are processed on a rolling basis. *Application fee:* $25 ($30 for international students). Electronic applications accepted. *Dean*, Dr. E. James Burton, 615-898-2764, Fax: 615-898-4736, E-mail: eburton@mtsu.edu.

MIDWEST COLLEGE OF ORIENTAL MEDICINE, Racine, WI 53403-9747

General Information Proprietary, coed, graduate-only institution. *Graduate housing:* On-campus housing not available. *Research affiliation:* Guangzhou University of Traditional Chinese Medicine (pharmacology).

GRADUATE UNITS

Graduate Programs *Degree program information:* Part-time and evening/weekend programs available. Offers acupuncture (Certificate); oriental medicine (MSOM).

Graduate Programs-Chicago *Degree program information:* Part-time and evening/weekend programs available.

MIDWESTERN BAPTIST THEOLOGICAL SEMINARY, Kansas City, MO 64118-4697

General Information Independent-religious, coed, graduate-only institution. *Graduate housing:* Rooms and/or apartments guaranteed to single and married students.

GRADUATE UNITS

Graduate and Professional Programs *Degree program information:* Part-time programs available. Postbaccalaureate distance learning degree programs offered (minimal on-campus study). Offers Biblical archaeology (MA); Biblical languages (MA); Christian education (M Div, MACE); Christian foundations—lay ministry (Graduate Certificate); collegiate ministries (M Div); counseling (MA); educational ministry (D Ed Min); international church planting (M Div); ministry (M Div, D Min); North American church planting (M Div); sacred music (MCM); urban ministry (M Div); worship leadership (M Div); youth ministry (M Div). Electronic applications accepted.

MIDWESTERN STATE UNIVERSITY, Wichita Falls, TX 76308

General Information State-supported, coed, comprehensive institution. *Graduate housing:* Rooms and/or apartments available on a first-come, first-served basis to single and married students.

GRADUATE UNITS

Graduate Studies *Degree program information:* Part-time and evening/weekend programs available. Electronic applications accepted.

College of Business Administration *Degree program information:* Part-time and evening/weekend programs available. Offers business administration (MBA); health services administration (MBA). Electronic applications accepted.

College of Education *Degree program information:* Part-time and evening/weekend programs available. Offers curriculum and instruction (ME); education (M Ed, MA, ME); educational leadership and technology (ME); general counseling (MA); human resource development (MA); reading education (M Ed); school counseling (M Ed); special education (M Ed); training and development (MA). Electronic applications accepted.

College of Health Sciences and Human Services *Degree program information:* Part-time and evening/weekend programs available. Offers family nurse practitioner (MSN); health sciences and human services (MHA, MPA, MSK, MSN, MSR); health services administration (MHA, MSN); kinesiology (MSK); nurse educator (MSN); public administration (MPA); public administration (administrative justice) (MPA); public administration (health services administration) with certificate (MPA); public administration (health services) (MPA); radiologic administration (MSR); radiologic education (MSR); radiologic sciences (MSR); radiologist assistant (MSR). Electronic applications accepted.

College of Humanities and Social Sciences *Degree program information:* Part-time and evening/weekend programs available. Offers English (MA); history (MA); humanities and social sciences (MA); political science (MA); psychology (MA). Electronic applications accepted.

College of Science and Mathematics *Degree program information:* Part-time and evening/weekend programs available. Offers biology (MS); computer science (MS); science and mathematics (MS). Electronic applications accepted.

MIDWESTERN UNIVERSITY, DOWNERS GROVE CAMPUS, Downers Grove, IL 60515-1235

General Information Independent, coed, graduate-only institution. *Enrollment by degree level:* 1,443 first professional, 324 master's, 231 doctoral. *Graduate faculty:* 126 full-time (78 women), 359 part-time/adjunct (87 women). *Graduate housing:* Rooms and/or apartments available on a first-come, first-served basis to single and married students. *Student services:* Campus employment opportunities, campus safety program, career counseling, exercise/wellness program, free psychological counseling, low-cost health insurance. *Library facilities:* Alumni Memorial Library plus 2 others. *Online resources:* web page. *Collection:* 84,097 titles, 1,450 serial subscriptions.

Computer facilities: 190 computers available on campus for general student use. A campuswide network can be accessed from student residence rooms and from off campus. Black Board Learning Software available. *Web address:* http://www.midwestern.edu/.

General Application Contact: Michael Laken, Director of Admissions, 630-515-6171, Fax: 630-971-6086, E-mail: admissil@midwestern.edu.

GRADUATE UNITS

Chicago College of Osteopathic Medicine Students: 680 full-time (351 women); includes 101 minority (3 African Americans, 96 Asian Americans or Pacific Islanders, 2 Hispanic Americans), 1 international. Average age 26. 4,930 applicants, 8% accepted, 176 enrolled. *Faculty:* 44 full-time (18 women), 248 part-time/adjunct (54 women). Expenses: Contact institution. *Financial support:* In 2008–09, 568 students received support; fellowships with partial tuition reimbursements available, career-related internships or fieldwork, Federal Work-Study, institutionally sponsored loans, and tuition waivers (full and partial) available. Financial award application deadline: 6/1; financial award applicants required to submit FAFSA. In 2008, 178 DOs awarded. Offers osteopathic medicine (DO). *Application deadline:* For fall admission, 1/1 for domestic students. Applications are processed on a rolling basis. *Application fee:* $50. *Application Contact:* Michael Laken, Director of Admissions, 630-515-6171, Fax: 630-971-6086, E-mail: admissil@midwestern.edu. *Dean*, Dr. Karen J. Nichols, 630-515-6159, E-mail: knicho@midwestern.edu.

Chicago College of Pharmacy Students: 735 full-time (448 women), 28 part-time (17 women); includes 255 minority (9 African Americans, 1 American Indian/Alaska Native, 229 Asian Americans or Pacific Islanders, 16 Hispanic Americans), 11 international. Average age 25. 2,499 applicants, 19% accepted, 201 enrolled. *Faculty:* 49 full-time (36 women), 16 part-time/adjunct (9 women). Expenses: Contact institution. *Financial support:* Federal Work-Study and institutionally sponsored loans available. Support available to part-time students. Financial award applicants required to submit FAFSA. In 2008, 217 Pharm Ds awarded. *Degree program information:* Part-time programs available. Postbaccalaureate distance learning degree programs offered (minimal on-campus study). Offers pharmacy (Pharm D). *Application deadline:* For fall admission, 2/3 for domestic students. *Application fee:* $50. *Application Contact:* Michael Laken, Director of Admissions, 630-515-6171, Fax: 630-971-6086, E-mail: admissil@midwestern.edu. *Dean*, Dr. Nancy Fjortoft, 630-971-6408.

College of Health Sciences, Illinois Campus Students: 539 full-time (435 women), 16 part-time (8 women); includes 60 minority (10 African Americans, 33 Asian Americans or Pacific Islanders, 17 Hispanic Americans), 4 international. Average age 25. 1,425 applicants, 33% accepted, 221 enrolled. *Faculty:* 33 full-time (24 women), 92 part-time/adjunct (24 women). Expenses: Contact institution. *Financial support:* In 2008–09, 229 students received support. Federal Work-Study, institutionally sponsored loans, and scholarships/grants available. Financial award applicants required to submit FAFSA. In 2008, 96 master's, 28 doctorates awarded. Offers biomedical sciences (MBS); clinical psychology (MA, Psy D); health sciences (MA, MBS, MMS, MOT, DPT, Psy D); occupational therapy (MOT); physical therapy (DPT); physician assistant studies (MMS). *Application deadline:* Applications are processed on a rolling basis. *Application fee:* $50. *Application Contact:* Michael Laken, Director of

Midwestern University, Downers Grove Campus (continued)

Admissions, 630-515-6171, Fax: 630-971-6086, E-mail: admissil@midwestern.edu. *Dean,* Dr. Jacquelyn J. Smith, 630-515-6388.

MIDWESTERN UNIVERSITY, GLENDALE CAMPUS, Glendale, AZ 85308

General Information Independent, coed, upper-level institution. *Enrollment:* 1,745 full-time matriculated graduate/professional students (862 women), 18 part-time matriculated graduate/professional students (13 women). *Enrollment by degree level:* 1,335 first professional, 366 master's, 62 other advanced degrees. *Graduate faculty:* 101 full-time (45 women), 903 part-time/adjunct (161 women). *Graduate housing:* Rooms and/or apartments available on a first-come, first-served basis to single and married students. *Student services:* Exercise/wellness program. *Web address:* http://www.midwestern.edu/.

General Application Contact: James Walter, Director of Admissions, 888-247-9277, Fax: 623-572-3229, E-mail: admissaz@midwestern.edu.

GRADUATE UNITS

Arizona College of Osteopathic Medicine Students: 704 full-time (278 women), 2 part-time (1 woman); includes 55 minority (1 African American, 3 American Indian/Alaska Native, 42 Asian Americans or Pacific Islanders, 9 Hispanic Americans), 6 international. Average age 27. 2,992 applicants, 19% accepted, 252 enrolled. *Faculty:* 47 full-time (16 women), 780 part-time/adjunct (122 women). Expenses: Contact institution. *Financial support:* Fellowships with partial tuition reimbursements, career-related internships or fieldwork, Federal Work-Study, institutionally sponsored loans, and tuition waivers (full and partial) available. Financial award application deadline: 6/12; financial award applicants required to submit FAFSA. In 2008, 135 DOs awarded. Offers osteopathic medicine (DO). *Application deadline:* For fall admission, 11/1 priority date for domestic students; for winter admission, 2/1 for domestic students. Applications are processed on a rolling basis. *Application fee:* $50. Electronic applications accepted. *Application Contact:* James Walter, Director of Admissions, 888-247-9277, Fax: 623-572-3229, E-mail: admissaz@midwestern.edu. *Dean,* Dr. Lori Kemper, 623-572-3202.

College of Dental Medicine 1,878 applicants, 11% accepted, 111 enrolled. *Faculty:* 3 full-time (0 women), 2 part-time/adjunct (0 women). Expenses: Contact institution. Offers dental medicine (DMD). *Application Contact:* James Walter, Director of Admissions, 888-247-9277, Fax: 623-572-3229, E-mail: admissaz@midwestern.edu. *Dean,* Dr. Richard Simonsen, 623-572-3801.

College of Health Sciences, Arizona Campus Students: 538 full-time (329 women), 11 part-time (8 women); includes 83 minority (24 African Americans, 3 American Indian/Alaska Native, 40 Asian Americans or Pacific Islanders, 16 Hispanic Americans), 11 international. Average age 27. 1,349 applicants, 31% accepted, 230 enrolled. *Faculty:* 26 full-time (11 women), 115 part-time/adjunct (37 women). Expenses: Contact institution. *Financial support:* Federal Work-Study available. In 2008, 107 master's awarded. *Degree program information:* Part-time programs available. Offers bioethics (MA, Certificate); biomedical sciences (MBS); cardiovascular science (MCVS); clinical psychology (Psy D); health professions education (MHPE); health sciences (DPM, MA, MBS, MCVS, MHPE, MMS, MOT, MS, Psy D, Certificate); nurse anesthesia (MS); occupational therapy (MOT); physician assistant studies (MMS); podiatric medicine (DPM). *Application deadline:* For fall admission, 6/4 for domestic students. Applications are processed on a rolling basis. *Application fee:* $50. *Application Contact:* James Walter, Director of Admissions, 888-247-9277, Fax: 623-572-3229, E-mail: admissaz@midwestern.edu. *Dean,* Dr. Jacquelyn Smith, 623-572-3601, Fax: 623-572-3601.

College of Pharmacy-Glendale Students: 392 full-time (201 women), 5 part-time (4 women); includes 121 minority (3 African Americans, 3 American Indian/Alaska Native, 96 Asian Americans or Pacific Islanders, 19 Hispanic Americans), 8 international. Average age 27. 1,841 applicants, 11% accepted, 130 enrolled. *Faculty:* 23 full-time (15 women), 7 part-time/adjunct (2 women). Expenses: Contact institution. *Financial support:* Applicants required to submit FAFSA. In 2008, 133 Pharm Ds awarded. Offers pharmacy (Pharm D). *Application deadline:* For fall admission, 2/1 for domestic students. *Application fee:* $50. *Application Contact:* James Walter, Director of Admissions, 888-247-9277, Fax: 623-572-3229, E-mail: admissaz@midwestern.edu. *Interim Dean,* Dr. Dennis McCallian, 623-572-3501.

MIDWEST UNIVERSITY, Wentzville, MO 63385

General Information Independent-religious, coed, university. *Graduate housing:* Rooms and/or apartments available on a first-come, first-served basis to single and married students. Housing application deadline: 1/21.

GRADUATE UNITS

Graduate Programs *Degree program information:* Part-time programs available. Postbaccalaureate distance learning degree programs offered (minimal on-campus study). Offers social work (DSW); teaching English to speakers of other languages (MA); theology (M Div, MA, D Min).

MIDWIVES COLLEGE OF UTAH, Orem, UT 84058

General Information Independent, women only, comprehensive institution.

GRADUATE UNITS

Graduate Program

MILLERSVILLE UNIVERSITY OF PENNSYLVANIA, Millersville, PA 17551-0302

General Information State-supported, coed, comprehensive institution. CGS member. *Enrollment:* 8,319 graduate, professional, and undergraduate students; 152 full-time matriculated graduate/professional students (120 women), 517 part-time matriculated graduate/professional students (392 women). *Enrollment by degree level:* 669 master's. *Graduate faculty:* 204 full-time (105 women), 93 part-time/adjunct (55 women). Tuition, state resident: full-time $6430; part-time $357 per credit. Tuition, nonresident: full-time $10,288; part-time $572 per credit. *Required fees:* $1937; $73.50 per credit. One-time fee: $88 part-time. Tuition and fees vary according to course load. *Graduate housing:* On-campus housing not available. *Student services:* Campus employment opportunities, campus safety program, career counseling, exercise/wellness program, free psychological counseling, international student services, low-cost health insurance, services for students with disabilities, teacher training. *Library facilities:* Helen A. Ganser Library. *Online resources:* library catalog, web page, access to other libraries' catalogs. *Collection:* 564,648 titles, 16,487 serial subscriptions, 15,425 audiovisual materials. *Research affiliation:* Marine Science Consortium at Wallops Island, Virginia (Biology).

Computer facilities: 705 computers available on campus for general student use. A campuswide network can be accessed from student residence rooms and from off campus. Online class registration is available. *Web address:* http://www.millersville.edu/.

General Application Contact: Dr. Victor S. DeSantis, Dean of Graduate and Professional Studies, 717-872-3099, Fax: 717-872-3453, E-mail: victor.desantis@millersville.edu.

GRADUATE UNITS

Graduate School Students: 152 full-time (120 women), 517 part-time (392 women); includes 37 minority (20 African Americans, 1 American Indian/Alaska Native, 5 Asian Americans or Pacific Islanders, 11 Hispanic Americans), 7 international. Average age 31. 219 applicants, 73% accepted, 121 enrolled. *Faculty:* 204 full-time (105 women), 93 part-time/adjunct (55 women). Expenses: Contact institution. *Financial support:* In 2008–09, 106 students received support, including 106 research assistantships with full and partial tuition reimbursements available (averaging $4,610 per year); institutionally sponsored loans and unspecified assistantships also available. Support available to part-time students. Financial award application deadline: 3/15; financial award applicants required to submit FAFSA. In 2008, 235 master's awarded. *Degree program information:* Part-time and evening/weekend programs available. Postbaccalaureate distance learning degree programs offered (no on-campus study). *Application deadline:* For fall admission, 2/1 priority date for domestic and international students; for winter admission, 10/1 priority date for domestic and international students; for spring admission, 10/1 priority date for domestic and international students. Applications are processed on a rolling basis. *Application fee:* $40. Electronic applications accepted. *Application Contact:* Dr. Victor S. DeSantis, Dean of Graduate and Professional Studies, 717-872-3099, Fax: 717-872-3453, E-mail: victor.desantis@millersville.edu. *Dean of Graduate and Professional Studies,* Dr. Victor S. DeSantis, 717-872-3099, Fax: 717-872-3453, E-mail: victor.desantis@millersville.edu.

School of Education Students: 104 full-time (83 women), 313 part-time (235 women); includes 23 minority (13 African Americans, 3 Asian Americans or Pacific Islanders, 7 Hispanic Americans), 2 international. Average age 30. 133 applicants, 58% accepted, 53 enrolled. *Faculty:* 91 full-time (47 women), 52 part-time/adjunct (27 women). Expenses: Contact institution. *Financial support:* In 2008–09, 68 students received support, including 68 research assistantships with full and partial tuition reimbursements available (averaging $4,772 per year); institutionally sponsored loans and unspecified assistantships also available. Support available to part-time students. Financial award application deadline: 3/15; financial award applicants required to submit FAFSA. In 2008, 153 master's awarded. *Degree program information:* Part-time and evening/weekend programs available. Offers athletic coaching (M Ed); athletic management (M Ed); clinical psychology (MS); early childhood education (M Ed); education (M Ed, MS); elementary education (M Ed); gifted education (M Ed); language and literacy education (M Ed); language and literacy education-ESL option (M Ed); leadership for teaching and learning (M Ed); psychology (MS); school counseling (M Ed); school psychology (MS); special education (M Ed); sport management (M Ed); technology education (M Ed). *Application deadline:* For fall admission, 2/1 priority date for domestic and international students; for winter admission, 10/1 priority date for domestic and international students; for spring admission, 10/1 priority date for domestic and international students. Applications are processed on a rolling basis. *Application fee:* $40. Electronic applications accepted. *Application Contact:* Dr. Victor S. DeSantis, Dean of Graduate and Professional Studies, 717-872-3099, Fax: 717-872-3453, E-mail: victor.desantis@millersville.edu. *Dean,* Dr. Jane S. Bray, 717-872-3379, Fax: 717-872-3856, E-mail: jane.bray@millersville.edu.

School of Humanities and Social Sciences Students: 46 full-time (35 women), 146 part-time (106 women); includes 10 minority (5 African Americans, 1 Asian American or Pacific Islander, 4 Hispanic Americans), 5 international. Average age 31. 70 applicants, 99% accepted, 56 enrolled. *Faculty:* 66 full-time (39 women), 31 part-time/adjunct (20 women). Expenses: Contact institution. *Financial support:* In 2008–09, 34 students received support, including 34 research assistantships with full and partial tuition reimbursements available (averaging $4,440 per year); institutionally sponsored loans and unspecified assistantships also available. Support available to part-time students. Financial award application deadline: 3/15; financial award applicants required to submit FAFSA. In 2008, 67 master's awarded. *Degree program information:* Part-time and evening/weekend programs available. Postbaccalaureate distance learning degree programs offered (no on-campus study). Offers art education (M Ed); emergency management (MS); English (MA); English education (M Ed); French (M Ed, MA); German (M Ed, MA); history (MA); humanities and social sciences (M Ed, MA, MS, MSW); social work (MSW); Spanish (M Ed, MA). *Application deadline:* For fall admission, 2/1 priority date for domestic and international students; for winter admission, 10/1 priority date for domestic and international students; for spring admission, 10/1 priority date for domestic and international students. Applications are processed on a rolling basis. *Application fee:* $40. Electronic applications accepted. *Application Contact:* Dr. Victor S. DeSantis, Dean of Graduate and Professional Studies, 717-872-3099, Fax: 717-872-3453, E-mail: victor.desantis@millersville.edu. *Dean,* Dr. John N. Short, 717-872-3553, Fax: 717-871-2003, E-mail: john.short@millersville.edu.

School of Science and Mathematics Students: 2 full-time (both women), 58 part-time (51 women); includes 4 minority (2 African Americans, 1 American Indian/Alaska Native, 1 Asian American or Pacific Islander). Average age 31. 16 applicants, 88% accepted, 12 enrolled. *Faculty:* 47 full-time (19 women), 10 part-time/adjunct (8 women). Expenses: Contact institution. *Financial support:* In 2008–09, 4 students received support, including 4 research assistantships with full and partial tuition reimbursements available (averaging $3,276 per year); institutionally sponsored loans and unspecified assistantships also available. Support available to part-time students. Financial award application deadline: 3/15; financial award applicants required to submit FAFSA. In 2008, 15 master's awarded. *Degree program information:* Part-time and evening/weekend programs available. Offers biology (MS); mathematics (M Ed); nursing (MSN); science and mathematics (M Ed, MS, MSN). *Application deadline:* For fall admission, 2/1 priority date for domestic and international students; for winter admission, 10/1 priority date for domestic and international students; for spring admission, 10/1 priority date for domestic and international students. Applications are processed on a rolling basis. *Application fee:* $40. Electronic applications accepted. *Application Contact:* Dr. Victor S. DeSantis, Dean of Graduate and Professional Studies, 717-872-3099, Fax: 717-872-3453, E-mail: victor.desantis@millersville.edu. *Dean,* Dr. Edward C. Shane, 717-872-3407, Fax: 717-872-3985, E-mail: Edward.Shane@millersville.edu.

MILLIGAN COLLEGE, Milligan College, TN 37682

General Information Independent-religious, coed, comprehensive institution. *Graduate housing:* Rooms and/or apartments available on a first-come, first-served basis to single and married students. Housing application deadline: 4/1.

GRADUATE UNITS

Area of Teacher Education *Degree program information:* Part-time programs available. Offers teacher education (M Ed). Electronic applications accepted.

Program in Business Administration Offers business administration (MBA).

Program in Occupational Therapy Students: 75 full-time (66 women), 3 part-time (all women). Average age 28. 53 applicants, 60% accepted, 27 enrolled. *Faculty:* 5 full-time (3 women), 4 part-time/adjunct (3 women). Expenses: Contact institution. *Financial support:* In 2008–09, 1 teaching assistantship (averaging $6,000 per year) was awarded; career-related internships or fieldwork and institutionally sponsored loans also available. Financial award application deadline: 4/15; financial award applicants required to submit FAFSA. In 2008, 23 master's awarded. Offers occupational therapy (MSOT). *Application deadline:* For spring admission, 4/15 for domestic students, 4/15 priority date for international students. Applications are processed on a rolling basis. *Application fee:* $30. Electronic applications accepted. *Application Contact:* Karyn Garland, Office Manager and Admissions Representative, 423-975-8010, Fax: 423-975-8019, E-mail: kngarland@milligan.edu. *Program Director and Associate Professor,* Dr. Jeff Snodgrass, PhD, 423-975-8010, Fax: 423-975-8019, E-mail: jsnodgrass@milligan.edu.

MILLIKIN UNIVERSITY, Decatur, IL 62522-2084

General Information Independent-religious, coed, comprehensive institution. *Enrollment:* 2,344 graduate, professional, and undergraduate students; 44 full-time matriculated graduate/professional students (20 women), 4 part-time matriculated graduate/professional students (3 women). *Enrollment by degree level:* 48 master's. *Graduate faculty:* 13 full-time (8 women), 8 part-time/adjunct (1 woman). *Tuition:* Full-time $23,940; part-time $630 per credit hour. *Student services:* Campus employment opportunities, career counseling, exercise/wellness program, international student services, writing training. *Library facilities:* Staley Library. *Online resources:* library catalog, web page, access to other libraries' catalogs. *Collection:* 216,883 titles, 430 serial subscriptions, 2,734 audiovisual materials.

Computer facilities: 198 computers available on campus for general student use. A campuswide network can be accessed from student residence rooms. Online class registration, online degree audit; online financials (view and pay bills; view financial aid) are available. *Web address:* http://www.millikin.edu/.

GRADUATE UNITS

School of Nursing Students: 15 full-time (all women), 4 part-time (3 women); includes 1 minority (African American). Average age 43. *Faculty:* 9 full-time (8 women), 1 (woman) part-time/adjunct. Expenses: Contact institution. *Financial support:* Institutionally sponsored loans and Nickey Awards available. Financial award applicants required to submit FAFSA. In 2008, 8 master's awarded. *Degree program information:* Part-time programs available. Offers clinical nurse leader (MSN); nurse educator (MSN). *Application deadline:* For spring admission, 11/1 priority date for domestic students. Applications are processed on a rolling basis. *Application fee:* $0. Electronic applications accepted. *Application Contact:* Dr. Sally Pflaum, Administrative Assistant, Master of Science in Nursing Program, 800-373-7733 Ext. 5034, Fax: 217-420-6677, E-mail: spflaum@millikin.edu. *Director, School of Nursing*, Dr. Deborah Slayton, 217-424-6348, Fax: 217-420-6731, E-mail: dslayton@millikin.edu.

Tabor School of Business Students: 29 full-time (5 women); includes 6 minority (3 African Americans, 3 Asian Americans or Pacific Islanders), 3 international. Average age 35. 200 applicants, 17% accepted, 29 enrolled. *Faculty:* 4 full-time (0 women), 7 part-time/adjunct (0 women). Expenses: Contact institution. *Financial support:* Applicants required to submit FAFSA. In 2008, 26 master's awarded. *Degree program information:* Evening/weekend programs available. Offers business (MBA). *Application deadline:* For spring admission, 11/1 priority date for domestic students, 8/1 priority date for international students. Applications are processed on a rolling basis. *Application fee:* $0. Electronic applications accepted. *Application Contact:* Dr. Anthony Liberatore, Director of MBA Program, 217-424-6338, E-mail: aliberatore@millikin.edu. *Dean*, Dr. James G. Dahl, 217-420-6634, Fax: 217-424-6286, E-mail: jdahl@millikin.edu.

MILLSAPS COLLEGE, Jackson, MS 39210-0001

General Information Independent-religious, coed, comprehensive institution. *Graduate housing:* Room and/or apartments available to single students; on-campus housing not available to married students. Housing application deadline: 6/1.

GRADUATE UNITS

Else School of Management *Degree program information:* Part-time programs available. Offers accounting (M Acc); business administration (MBA). Electronic applications accepted.

MILLS COLLEGE, Oakland, CA 94613-1000

General Information Independent, Undergraduate: women only; graduate: coed, comprehensive institution. *Enrollment:* 1,476 graduate, professional, and undergraduate students; 427 full-time matriculated graduate/professional students (336 women), 66 part-time matriculated graduate/professional students (58 women). *Enrollment by degree level:* 385 master's, 49 doctoral, 59 other advanced degrees. *Graduate faculty:* 96 full-time (59 women), 103 part-time/adjunct (73 women). *Tuition:* Full-time $25,072; part-time $6272 per course. *Required fees:* $880. *Graduate housing:* Rooms and/or apartments available on a first-come, first-served basis to single and married students. Typical cost: $7960 per year ($13,200 including board) for single students; $9272 per year ($14,512 including board) for married students. Room and board charges vary according to board plan and housing facility selected. Housing application deadline: 9/1. *Student services:* Campus employment opportunities, campus safety program, career counseling, exercise/wellness program, free psychological counseling, international student services, low-cost health insurance, multicultural affairs office, services for students with disabilities, teacher training, writing training. *Library facilities:* F. W. Olin Library plus 1 other. *Online resources:* library catalog, web page, access to other libraries' catalogs. *Collection:* 243,317 titles, 24,721 serial subscriptions, 10,598 audiovisual materials.

Computer facilities: Computer purchase and lease plans are available. 336 computers available on campus for general student use. A campuswide network can be accessed from student residence rooms and from off campus. Online class registration, online degree audit are available. *Web address:* http://www.mills.edu/.

General Application Contact: Mariko Benko, Graduate Admission Specialist, 510-430-3309, Fax: 510-430-2159, E-mail: grad-studies@mills.edu.

GRADUATE UNITS

Graduate Studies Students: 427 full-time (336 women), 66 part-time (58 women); includes 148 minority (71 African Americans, 1 American Indian/Alaska Native, 40 Asian Americans or Pacific Islanders, 36 Hispanic Americans), 13 international. Average age 31. 762 applicants, 79% accepted, 269 enrolled. *Faculty:* 96 full-time (59 women), 103 part-time/adjunct (73 women). Expenses: Contact institution. *Financial support:* In 2008–09, 418 students received support, including 363 fellowships (averaging $6,690 per year), 101 teaching assistantships with partial tuition reimbursements available (averaging $5,838 per year); career-related internships or fieldwork, institutionally sponsored loans, and scholarships/grants also available. Support available to part-time students. Financial award application deadline: 2/1; financial award applicants required to submit FAFSA. In 2008, 187 master's, 7 doctorates, 53 other advanced degrees awarded. *Degree program information:* Part-time and evening/weekend programs available. Offers book art and creative writing (MFA); ceramics (MFA); composition (MA); computer science (Certificate); creative writing, poetry (MFA); creative writing, prose (MFA); dance (MA, MFA); electronic music and recording media (MFA); English and American literature (MA); interdisciplinary computer science (MA); intermedia (MFA); music performance and literature (MFA); painting (MFA); photography (MFA); pre-medical studies (Certificate); public policy (MPP); sculpture (MFA). *Application deadline:* For fall admission, 2/1 for domestic and international students; for spring admission, 11/1 for domestic and international students. Applications are processed on a rolling basis. *Application fee:* $50. *Application Contact:* Marika Benko, Graduate Admission Specialist, 510-430-3309, Fax: 510-430-2159, E-mail: grad-studies@mills.edu. *Administrative Dean for Graduate Recruitment and Enrollment*, Carol Langlois, 510-430-3118, Fax: 510-430-2159, E-mail: clangloi@mills.edu.

Lori I. Lokey Graduate School of Business Students: 65 full-time (all women), 3 part-time (all women); includes 32 minority (18 African Americans, 9 Asian Americans or Pacific Islanders, 5 Hispanic Americans), 5 international. Average age 30. 60 applicants, 97% accepted, 36 enrolled. *Faculty:* 6 full-time (2 women), 12 part-time/adjunct (7 women). Expenses: Contact institution. *Financial support:* In 2008–09, 76 students received support, including 81 fellowships (averaging $7,858 per year); scholarships/grants also available. Support available to part-time students. Financial award applicants required to submit FAFSA. In 2008, 44 master's awarded. Offers management (MBA). *Application deadline:* For fall admission, 2/1 for domestic and international students. *Application fee:* $50. *Application Contact:* Marika Benko, Graduate Admission Specialist, 510-430-3309, Fax: 510-430-2159, E-mail: grad-studies@mills.edu. *Dean*, Nancy Thornborrow, 510-430-2344, Fax: 510-430-3314, E-mail: nancy@mills.edu.

School of Education Students: 128 full-time (116 women), 47 part-time (41 women); includes 64 minority (36 African Americans, 10 Asian Americans or Pacific Islanders, 18 Hispanic Americans), 2 international. Average age 35. 183 applicants, 95% accepted, 88 enrolled. *Faculty:* 10 full-time (8 women), 13 part-time/adjunct (11 women). Expenses: Contact institution. *Financial support:* In 2008–09, 160 students received support, including 149 fellowships (averaging $5,782 per year), 17 teaching assistantships with partial tuition reimbursements available (averaging $2,857 per year); career-related internships or fieldwork and scholarships/grants also available. Support available to part-time students. Financial award application deadline: 2/1; financial award applicants required to submit FAFSA. In 2008, 55 master's, 7 doctorates awarded. *Degree program information:* Part-time and evening/weekend programs available. Offers child life in hospitals (MA); early childhood education (MA); education (MA); educational leadership (MA, Ed D); infant mental health (MA). *Application deadline:* For fall admission, 2/1 for domestic and international students; for spring admission, 11/1 for domestic and international students. Applications are processed on a rolling basis. *Application fee:* $50. Electronic applications accepted. *Application Contact:* Marika Benko, Graduate Admission Specialist, 510-430-3309, Fax: 510-430-2159, E-mail: grad-studies@mills.edu. *Chairperson*, Joseph Kahne, 510-430-3190, Fax: 510-430-3314, E-mail: grad-studies@mills.edu.

MILWAUKEE SCHOOL OF ENGINEERING, Milwaukee, WI 53202-3109

General Information Independent, coed, primarily men, comprehensive institution. *Enrollment:* 2,622 graduate, professional, and undergraduate students; 12 full-time matriculated graduate/professional students (4 women), 192 part-time matriculated graduate/professional students (48 women). *Enrollment by degree level:* 204 master's. *Graduate faculty:* 11 full-time (1 woman), 31 part-time/adjunct (7 women). *Tuition:* Part-time $575 per credit. *Graduate housing:* Room and/or apartments available on a first-come, first-served basis to single students; on-campus housing not available to married students. Typical cost: $4380 per year ($6825 including board). Housing application deadline: 7/1. *Student services:* Campus employment opportunities, campus safety program, career counseling, exercise/wellness program, free psychological counseling, international student services, low-cost health insurance, multicultural affairs office, services for students with disabilities, writing training. *Library facilities:* Walter Schroeder Library. *Online resources:* library catalog, web page, access to other libraries' catalogs. *Collection:* 79,275 titles, 378 serial subscriptions, 1,538 audiovisual materials. *Research affiliation:* Kern Foundation (entrepreneurship), National Fluid Power Association (hydralics and pneumatics), 3DMD (biomolecular modeling), The Procter & Gamble Company (rapid tooling), Caterpillar, Inc. (electrohydraulics), Medical College of Wisconsin (physics).

Computer facilities: Computer purchase and lease plans are available. 125 computers available on campus for general student use. A campuswide network can be accessed from student residence rooms and from off campus. Online class registration is available. *Web address:* http://www.msoe.edu/.

General Application Contact: David E. Tietyen, Director of Graduate Admissions, 800-332-6763, Fax: 414-277-7475, E-mail: tietyen@msoe.edu.

GRADUATE UNITS

Department of Architectural Engineering and Building Construction Students: 2 full-time (1 woman), 20 part-time (8 women); includes 1 minority (Asian American or Pacific Islander). Average age 22. 10 applicants, 30% accepted, 1 enrolled. *Faculty:* 2 full-time (0 women), 6 part-time/adjunct (1 woman). Expenses: Contact institution. *Financial support:* In 2008–09, 7 students received support; research assistantships, career-related internships or fieldwork available. Support available to part-time students. Financial award applicants required to submit FAFSA. In 2008, 2 master's awarded. *Degree program information:* Part-time and evening/weekend programs available. Offers environmental engineering (MS); structural engineering (MS). *Application deadline:* Applications are processed on a rolling basis. *Application fee:* $30. Electronic applications accepted. *Application Contact:* David E. Tietyen, Graduate Admissions Director, 800-332-6763, Fax: 414-277-7475, E-mail: wp@msoe.edu. *Chair*, Dr. Deborah J. Jackman, 414-277-7472, Fax: 414-277-7479, E-mail: jackman@msoe.edu.

Department of Electrical Engineering and Computer Science Students: 6 full-time (0 women), 42 part-time (6 women); includes 3 minority (2 Asian Americans or Pacific Islanders, 1 Hispanic American), 1 international. Average age 27. 44 applicants, 55% accepted, 18 enrolled. *Faculty:* 3 full-time (0 women), 7 part-time/adjunct (2 women). Expenses: Contact institution. *Financial support:* In 2008–09, 22 students received support, including 4 research assistantships (averaging $15,000 per year); career-related internships or fieldwork also available. Support available to part-time students. Financial award applicants required to submit FAFSA. In 2008, 10 master's awarded. *Degree program information:* Part-time and evening/weekend programs available. Offers cardiovascular studies (MS); engineering (MS); perfusion (MS). *Application deadline:* Applications are processed on a rolling basis. *Application fee:* $30. Electronic applications accepted. *Application Contact:* David E. Tietyen, Graduate Admissions Director, 800-332-6763, Fax: 414-277-7475, E-mail: wp@msoe.edu. *Chairman*, Dr. Owe Petersen, 414-277-7114, Fax: 414-277-7465, E-mail: petersen@msoe.edu.

Department of Nursing Expenses: Contact institution. Offers clinical nurse leadership (MS). *Application deadline:* Applications are processed on a rolling basis. *Application fee:* $30. Electronic applications accepted. *Application Contact:* David E. Tietyen, Graduate Admissions Director, 800-332-6763, Fax: 414-277-7475, E-mail: wp@msoe.edu. *Director*, Dr. Debra Jenks, 414-277-4516.

Rader School of Business Students: 2 full-time (1 woman), 132 part-time (34 women); includes 8 minority (1 African American, 1 American Indian/Alaska Native, 4 Asian Americans or Pacific Islanders, 2 Hispanic Americans). Average age 26. 51 applicants, 78% accepted, 30 enrolled. *Faculty:* 6 full-time (1 woman), 17 part-time/adjunct (3 women). Expenses: Contact institution. *Financial support:* In 2008–09, 19 students received support, including 2 research assistantships (averaging $15,000 per year); career-related internships or fieldwork also available. Support available to part-time students. Financial award applicants required to submit FAFSA. In 2008, 52 master's awarded. *Degree program information:* Part-time and evening/weekend programs available. Offers engineering management (MS); marketing and export management (MS); medical informatics (MS); new product management (MS). *Application deadline:* Applications are processed on a rolling basis. *Application fee:* $30. Electronic applications accepted. *Application Contact:* Dr. Steven Bialek, Chairman, 414-277-7364, Fax: 414-277-7479, E-mail: bialek@msoe.edu. *Chairman*, Dr. Steven Bialek, 414-277-7364, Fax: 414-277-7479, E-mail: bialek@msoe.edu.

MINNEAPOLIS COLLEGE OF ART AND DESIGN, Minneapolis, MN 55404-4347

General Information Independent, coed, comprehensive institution. *Enrollment:* 772 graduate, professional, and undergraduate students; 32 full-time matriculated graduate/professional students (15 women), 31 part-time matriculated graduate/professional students (18 women). *Enrollment by degree level:* 33 master's, 30 other advanced degrees. *Graduate faculty:* 32 full-time (12 women). *Tuition:* Full-time $28,400; part-time $813 per credit. *Graduate housing:* On-campus housing not available. *Student services:* Campus employment opportunities, campus safety program, career counseling, exercise/wellness program, free psychological counseling, grant writing training, international student services, low-cost health insurance, teacher training, writing training. *Library facilities:* Minneapolis College of Art and Design Library. *Online resources:* web page. *Collection:* 47,166 titles, 196 serial subscriptions, 139,245 audiovisual materials.

Computer facilities: Computer purchase and lease plans are available. 110 computers available on campus for general student use. A campuswide network can be accessed from student residence rooms and from off campus. *Web address:* http://www.mcad.edu/.

General Application Contact: William Mullen, Vice President of Enrollment Management, 612-874-3762, Fax: 612-874-3701, E-mail: william_mullen@mcad.edu.

GRADUATE UNITS

Program in Arts Students: 32 full-time (15 women), 31 part-time (18 women); includes 5 minority (2 African Americans, 1 American Indian/Alaska Native, 2 Hispanic Americans), 4 international. Average age 24. 172 applicants, 27% accepted, 19 enrolled. *Faculty:* 23 full-time (7 women), 9 part-time/adjunct (4 women). Expenses: Contact institution. *Financial support:* Career-related internships or fieldwork and scholarships/grants available. Financial award application deadline: 3/15; financial award applicants required to submit FAFSA. In 2008, 15 Certificates awarded. *Degree program information:* Part-time programs available. Postbaccalaureate distance learning degree programs offered. Offers design (Certificate); fine arts (Certificate); media (Certificate); sustainable design (Certificate). *Application deadline:* For fall admission, 1/15 for domestic and international students. *Application fee:* $50. Electronic applications accepted. *Application Contact:* William Mullen, Vice President, Enrollment Management, 612-874-3762, Fax: 612-874-3701, E-mail: william_mullen@mcad.edu. *Graduate Director*, Carole Fisher, 612-874-3629, E-mail: carole_fisher@mcad.edu.

Program in Visual Studies Students: 40 full-time (21 women), 1 (woman) part-time; includes 1 minority (American Indian/Alaska Native). Average age 27. 172 applicants, 24% accepted, 15 enrolled. *Faculty:* 23 full-time (7 women), 9 part-time/adjunct (4 women). Expenses: Contact institution. *Financial support:* In 2008–09, 23 students received support, including 15 teaching assistantships (averaging $6,000 per year); career-related internships or fieldwork, Federal Work-Study, scholarships/grants, and unspecified assistantships also available. Support available to part-time students. Financial award application deadline: 3/15; financial award applicants required to submit FAFSA. In 2008, 7 master's awarded. *Degree program information:* Part-time programs available. Offers animation (MFA); comic art (MFA); drawing (MFA); filmmaking (MFA); fine arts (MFA); furniture design (MFA); graphic design (MFA); illustration (MFA); interactive media (MFA); painting (MFA); photography (MFA); printmaking (MFA); sculpture (MFA). *Application deadline:* For fall admission, 1/15 for domestic and international students. *Application fee:* $50. Electronic applications accepted. *Application Contact:* William Mullen, Vice President of Enrollment Management, 612-874-3762, Fax: 612-874-3701, E-mail: william_mullen@mcad.edu. *Graduate Director*, Carole Fisher, 612-874-3629, E-mail: carole_fisher@mcad.edu.

MINNESOTA STATE UNIVERSITY MANKATO, Mankato, MN 56001

General Information State-supported, coed, university. CGS member. *Enrollment:* 14,515 graduate, professional, and undergraduate students; 557 full-time matriculated graduate/professional students (332 women), 1,305 part-time matriculated graduate/professional students (834 women). *Enrollment by degree level:* 1,862 master's. *Graduate housing:* Room and/or apartments available on a first-come, first-served basis to single students; on-campus housing not available to married students. *Student services:* Campus employment opportunities, campus safety program, career counseling, child daycare facilities, exercise/wellness program, free psychological counseling, international student services, low-cost health insurance, multicultural affairs office, services for students with disabilities, teacher training, writing training. *Library facilities:* Memorial Library. *Online resources:* library catalog, web page. *Collection:* 1.2 million titles, 20,000 serial subscriptions.

Computer facilities: Computer purchase and lease plans are available. 900 computers available on campus for general student use. A campuswide network can be accessed from student residence rooms and from off campus. Online class registration is available. *Web address:* http://www.mnsu.edu/.

General Application Contact: Information Contact, 507-389-2321, E-mail: grad@mnsu.edu.

GRADUATE UNITS

College of Graduate Studies Students: 557 full-time (332 women), 1,305 part-time (834 women). Average age 32. Expenses: Contact institution. *Financial support:* In 2008–09, research assistantships with full and partial tuition reimbursements (averaging $9,000 per year), teaching assistantships with full and partial tuition reimbursements (averaging $10,800 per year) were awarded; fellowships with full tuition reimbursements, career-related internships or fieldwork, Federal Work-Study, institutionally sponsored loans, scholarships/grants, and unspecified assistantships also available. Support available to part-time students. Financial award application deadline: 3/15; financial award applicants required to submit FAFSA. In 2008, 460 master's, 62 other advanced degrees awarded. *Degree program information:* Part-time programs available. Postbaccalaureate distance learning degree programs offered. Offers cross-disciplinary studies (MS). *Application deadline:* For fall admission, 7/1 for domestic students, 5/1 for international students; for spring admission, 11/1 for domestic students, 10/1 for international students. Applications are processed on a rolling basis. *Application fee:* $40. Electronic applications accepted. *Application Contact:* 507-389-2321, E-mail: grad@mnsu.edu. *Dean,* Dean Anne Blackhurst, 507-389-2321.

College of Allied Health and Nursing Students: 141 full-time (86 women), 222 part-time (166 women). Expenses: Contact institution. *Financial support:* Research assistantships with full tuition reimbursements, teaching assistantships with full tuition reimbursements, career-related internships or fieldwork, Federal Work-Study, institutionally sponsored loans, and unspecified assistantships available. Support available to part-time students. Financial award application deadline: 3/15; financial award applicants required to submit FAFSA. *Degree program information:* Part-time programs available. Offers allied health and nursing (MA, MS, MSN, MT, DNP, SP); communication disorders (MS); community health (MS); family nursing (MSN); health science (MS, MT); human performance (MA, MS, MT, SP); managed care (MSN); nursing (DNP); rehabilitation counseling (MS); school health (MS). *Application deadline:* Applications are processed on a rolling basis. *Application fee:* $40. Electronic applications accepted. *Application Contact:* 507-389-2321, E-mail: grad@mnsu.edu. *Dean,* Dr. Kaye Herth, 507-389-6315.

College of Arts and Humanities Students: 72 full-time (43 women), 154 part-time (104 women). Expenses: Contact institution. *Financial support:* Research assistantships with full tuition reimbursements, teaching assistantships with full tuition reimbursements, career-related internships or fieldwork, Federal Work-Study, institutionally sponsored loans, and unspecified assistantships available. Support available to part-time students. Financial award application deadline: 3/15; financial award applicants required to submit FAFSA. *Degree program information:* Part-time and evening/weekend programs available. Offers art education (MS); arts and humanities (MA, MAT, MFA, MM, MS, MT, Certificate); creative writing (MFA); design/technology (MFA); English (MA, MS); English literature (MA); forensics (MFA); French (MAT, MS); music (MM, MT); performance (MFA); Spanish (MAT, MS); speech communication (MA, MS, MT); studio art (MA); teaching art (MAT, MT); teaching English (MS, MT); teaching English as a second language (MA, Certificate); technical communication (Certificate); theatre arts (MA, MFA). *Application deadline:* For fall admission, 7/1 for domestic students, 5/1 for international students; for spring admission, 11/1 for domestic students, 10/1 for international students. Applications are processed on a rolling basis. *Application fee:* $40. *Application Contact:* 507-389-2321, E-mail: grad@mnsu.edu. *Interim Dean,* Dr. Terrance Flaherty, 507-389-2117.

College of Business Students: 5 full-time (1 woman), 43 part-time (12 women). Expenses: Contact institution. Offers accounting and business law (MBA); finance (MBA); management (MBA); marketing and international business (MBA). *Application deadline:* For fall admission, 7/1 for domestic students, 5/1 for international students; for spring admission, 11/1 for domestic students, 10/1 for international students. Electronic applications accepted. *Application Contact:* Dr. Kevin Elliott, Graduate Coordinator, 507-389-5420. *Graduate Coordinator,* Dr. Kevin Elliott, 507-389-5420.

College of Education Students: 117 full-time (87 women), 469 part-time (338 women). Expenses: Contact institution. *Financial support:* Fellowships with partial tuition reimbursements, research assistantships with full tuition reimbursements, teaching assistantships with full tuition reimbursements, career-related internships or fieldwork, Federal Work-Study, institutionally sponsored loans, and unspecified assistantships available. Support available to part-time students. Financial award application deadline: 3/15; financial award applicants required to submit FAFSA. In 2008, 46 other advanced degrees awarded. *Degree program information:* Part-time and evening/weekend programs available. Offers college student affairs (MS); computer services administration (MS); counselor education and supervision (Ed D); curriculum and instruction (SP); early education for exceptional children (MS); education (MAT, MS, Ed D, Certificate, SP); educational administration (Certificate); educational leadership (MS, Ed D); educational technology (MS); elementary and early childhood education (MS); elementary school administration (MS, SP); emotional/behavioral disorders (MS, Certificate); experiential education (MS, Certificate, SP); general school administration (MS); higher education administration (MS); learning disabilities (MS, Certificate); library media education (MS, Certificate, SP); marriage and family counseling (Certificate); professional community counseling (MS); professional school counseling (MS); secondary administration (MS, SP); talent development and gifted education (MS, Certificate, SP); teaching and learning (MAT, MS, Certificate); vocational-technical administration (MS). *Application deadline:* Applications are processed on a rolling basis. *Application fee:* $40. Electronic applications accepted. *Application Contact:* 507-389-2321, E-mail: grad@mnsu.edu. *Dean,* Dr. Michael Miller, 507-389-5445.

College of Science, Engineering and Technology Students: 47 full-time (9 women), 102 part-time (36 women). Expenses: Contact institution. *Financial support:* Fellowships with full tuition reimbursements, research assistantships with full tuition reimbursements, teaching assistantships with full tuition reimbursements, career-related internships or fieldwork, Federal Work-Study, institutionally sponsored loans, and unspecified assistantships available. Support available to part-time students. Financial award application deadline: 3/15; financial award applicants required to submit FAFSA. In 2008, 37 master's awarded. *Degree program information:* Part-time programs available. Offers biology (MS); biology education (MS); computer science (MS, Graduate Certificate); database technologies (Certificate); electrical and computer engineering and technology (MSE); environmental sciences (MS); manufacturing engineering technology (MS); mathematics (MA, MS); mathematics education (MAT, MS); physics (MS); physics and astronomy (MT); science, engineering and technology (MA, MAT, MS, MSE, MT, Certificate, Graduate Certificate); statistics (MS). *Application deadline:* For fall admission, 7/1 priority date for domestic students; for spring admission, 11/1 for domestic students. Applications are processed on a rolling basis. *Application fee:* $40. Electronic applications accepted. *Application Contact:* 507-389-2321, E-mail: grad@mnsu.edu. *Dean,* Dean John Knox.

College of Social and Behavioral Sciences Students: 158 full-time (93 women), 175 part-time (86 women). Expenses: Contact institution. *Financial support:* Fellowships with partial tuition reimbursements, research assistantships with full tuition reimbursements, teaching assistantships with full tuition reimbursements, career-related internships or fieldwork, Federal Work-Study, institutionally sponsored loans, and unspecified assistantships available. Support available to part-time students. Financial award application deadline: 3/15; financial award applicants required to submit FAFSA. *Degree program information:* Part-time programs available. Offers anthropology (MS); clinical psychology (MA); ethnic studies (MS); geography (MS); geography education (MT); gerontology (MS, Certificate); history (MA, MS); industrial/organizational psychology (MA); local government (Certificate); psychology (MT); public administration (MAPA); school psychology (Psy D); social and behavioral sciences (MA, MAPA, MS, MT, Psy D, Certificate); social studies (MS); sociology (MA); sociology: corrections (MS); sociology: human services planning and administration (MS); teaching history (MS, MT); urban and regional studies (MA); urban planning (Certificate); women's studies (MS, Certificate). *Application deadline:* Applications are processed on a rolling basis. *Application fee:* $40. Electronic applications accepted. *Application Contact:* 507-389-2321, E-mail: grad@mnsu.edu. *Dean,* Dr. John Alessio, 507-389-6307.

MINNESOTA STATE UNIVERSITY MOORHEAD, Moorhead, MN 56563-0002

General Information State-supported, coed, comprehensive institution. *Graduate housing:* Room and/or apartments available to single students; on-campus housing not available to married students. Housing application deadline: 3/1. *Research affiliation:* West Central Minnesota Business Innovation Center.

GRADUATE UNITS

Graduate Studies *Degree program information:* Part-time and evening/weekend programs available. Postbaccalaureate distance learning degree programs offered (minimal on-campus study). Electronic applications accepted.

College of Arts and Humanities *Degree program information:* Part-time programs available. Offers arts and humanities (MFA, MLA); creative writing (MFA); liberal studies (MLA). Electronic applications accepted.

College of Education and Human Services *Degree program information:* Part-time and evening/weekend programs available. Offers counseling and student affairs (MS); curriculum and instruction (MS); educational leadership (MS, Ed S); nursing (MS); reading (MS); special education (MS); speech-language pathology (MS). Electronic applications accepted.

College of Social and Natural Sciences *Degree program information:* Part-time and evening/weekend programs available. Offers public, human services, and health administration (MS); school psychology (MS, Psy S); social and natural sciences (MS, Psy S). Electronic applications accepted.

MINOT STATE UNIVERSITY, Minot, ND 58707-0002

General Information State-supported, coed, comprehensive institution. *Enrollment:* 3,432 graduate, professional, and undergraduate students; 54 full-time matriculated graduate/professional students (31 women), 206 part-time matriculated graduate/professional students (117 women). *Enrollment by degree level:* 260 master's. *Tuition, area resident:* Full-time $5527; part-time $230.30 per credit hour. Tuition, state resident: full-time $8291; part-time $345.45 per credit hour. Tuition, nonresident: full-time $14,758; part-time $614.90 per credit hour. *Required fees:* $865; $36.03 per credit hour. Tuition and fees vary according to course load and reciprocity agreements. *Graduate housing:* Rooms and/or apartments available on a first-come, first-served basis to single and married students. Typical cost: $2700 per year ($4450 including board) for single students; $2700 per year ($4450 including board) for married students. Housing application deadline: 6/30. *Student services:* Campus employment opportunities, campus safety program, career counseling, exercise/wellness program, free psychological counseling, international student services, multicultural affairs office, services for students with disabilities, writing training. *Library facilities:* Gordon B. Olson Library. *Online resources:* library catalog, web page, access to other libraries' catalogs. *Research affiliation:* Rural Crime & Justice Center (Criminal Justice Research), NDCPD (North Dakota Center for Persons with Disabilities- Research and Aid).

Computer facilities: Computer purchase and lease plans are available. 460 computers available on campus for general student use. A campuswide network can be accessed from student residence rooms and from off campus. Online class registration is available. *Web address:* http://www.minotstateu.edu/.

General Application Contact: Administrative Assistant, 701-858-3250 Ext. 3150, Fax: 701-858-4286, E-mail: graduate@minotstateu.edu.

GRADUATE UNITS

Graduate School Students: 112 full-time (89 women), 148 part-time (117 women); includes 10 minority (2 African Americans, 5 American Indian/Alaska Native, 3 Hispanic Americans), 48 international. Average age 35. 107 applicants, 78% accepted, 71 enrolled. *Faculty:* 108 part-time/adjunct (49 women). Expenses: Contact institution. *Financial support:* In 2008–09, 111 students received support, including 40 research assistantships with partial tuition reimbursements available (averaging $1,250 per year); career-related internships or fieldwork, institutionally sponsored loans, scholarships/grants, traineeships, tuition waivers (partial), and unspecified assistantships also available. Support available to part-time students. Financial award application deadline: 4/1; financial award applicants required to submit FAFSA. In 2008, 95 master's, 1 other advanced degree awarded. Postbaccalaureate distance learning degree programs offered. Offers audiology (MS); criminal justice (MS); education of the deaf (MS); elementary education (M Ed); information systems (MSIS); learning disabilities (MS); management (MS); mathematics (MAT); school psychology (Ed Sp); science (MAT); special education strategist (MS); speech-language pathology (MS). *Application deadline:* Applications are processed on a rolling basis. *Application fee:* $35. *Application Contact:* Dr. Linda Cresap, Dean, 701-858-3250, E-mail: linda.cresap@minotstateu.edu. *Dean,* Dr. Linda Cresap, 701-858-3250, E-mail: linda.cresap@minotstateu.edu.

Division of Music *Faculty:* 3 full-time (all women). Expenses: Contact institution. *Financial support:* Research assistantships with partial tuition reimbursements, teaching assistantships with partial tuition reimbursements, career-related internships or fieldwork, institutionally sponsored loans, scholarships/grants, traineeships, tuition waivers (partial), and unspecified assistantships available. Support available to part-time students. Financial award application deadline: 4/1. Offers music education (MME). Program offered during summer only. *Application deadline:* Applications are processed on a rolling basis. *Application fee:* $35. *Application Contact:* Sandra Starr, Chairperson, 701-858-3185, Fax: 701-839-6933. *Chairperson,* Sandra Starr, 701-858-3185, Fax: 701-839-6933.

MIRRER YESHIVA, Brooklyn, NY 11223-2010

General Information Independent-religious, men only, comprehensive institution.

GRADUATE UNITS

Graduate Programs

MISERICORDIA UNIVERSITY, Dallas, PA 18612-1098

General Information Independent-religious, coed, primarily women, comprehensive institution. *Enrollment:* 2,501 graduate, professional, and undergraduate students; 73 full-time matriculated graduate/professional students (62 women), 304 part-time matriculated graduate/professional students (213 women). *Enrollment by degree level:* 319 master's, 58 doctoral. *Graduate faculty:* 24 full-time (16 women), 29 part-time/adjunct (15 women). *Tuition:* Part-time $525 per credit. *Graduate housing:* On-campus housing not available. *Student services:* Campus employment opportunities, campus safety program, career counseling, free psychological counseling, international student services, low-cost health insurance, multicultural affairs office, services for students with disabilities, writing training. *Library facilities:* Mary Kintz Bevevino Library. *Online resources:* library catalog, web page, access to other libraries' catalogs. *Collection:* 79,612 titles, 373 serial subscriptions, 10,695 audiovisual materials.

Computer facilities: Computer purchase and lease plans are available. 100 computers available on campus for general student use. A campuswide network can be accessed from student residence rooms and from off campus. Online class registration, Student Leadership Transcript are available. *Web address:* http://www.misericordia.edu/.

General Application Contact: Larree Brown, Coordinator of Part-Time Undergraduate and Graduate Programs, 570-674-6451, Fax: 570-674-6232, E-mail: lbrown@misericordia.edu.

GRADUATE UNITS

College of Health Sciences Students: 73 full-time (62 women), 104 part-time (89 women); includes 1 minority (African American). Average age 29. *Faculty:* 17 full-time (12 women), 11 part-time/adjunct (9 women). Expenses: Contact institution. *Financial support:* In 2008–09, 95 students received support; teaching assistantships, career-related internships or fieldwork, Federal Work-Study, scholarships/grants, traineeships, and tuition waivers (partial) available. Support available to part-time students. Financial award application deadline: 6/30; financial award applicants required to submit FAFSA. In 2008, 104 master's, 36 doctorates awarded. *Degree program information:* Part-time and evening/weekend programs available. Offers health sciences (MSN, MSOT, MSPT, MSSLP, DPT, OTD); nursing (MSN); occupational therapy (MSOT, OTD); physical therapy (MSPT, DPT); speech-language pathology (MSSLP). *Application deadline:* Applications are processed on a rolling basis. *Application fee:* $25. Electronic applications accepted. *Application Contact:* Larree Brown, Coordinator of Part-Time Undergraduate and Graduate Programs, 570-674-6451, Fax: 570-674-6232, E-mail: lbrown@misericordia.edu. *Dean of Health Sciences,* Dr. Jean A Dyer, 570-674-8152, E-mail: jdyer@misericordia.edu.

College of Professional Studies and Social Sciences Students: 200 part-time (124 women); includes 2 minority (1 African American, 1 Hispanic American). Average age 35. *Faculty:* 8 full-time (5 women), 19 part-time/adjunct (6 women). Expenses: Contact institution. *Financial support:* In 2008–09, 86 students received support. Career-related internships or fieldwork and scholarships/grants available. Support available to part-time students. Financial award application deadline: 6/30; financial award applicants required to submit FAFSA. In 2008, 57 master's awarded. *Degree program information:* Part-time and evening/weekend programs available. Offers business administration (MBA); education/curriculum (MS); organizational management (MS). *Application deadline:* For fall admission, 8/1 priority date for domestic students. Applications are processed on a rolling basis. *Application fee:* $25. Electronic applications accepted. *Application Contact:* Larree Brown, Coordinator of Part-Time Undergraduate and Graduate Programs, 570-674-6451, Fax: 570-674-6232, E-mail: lbrown@misericordia.edu. *Dean of Adult and Continuing Education,* Tom O'Neill, 570-674-6331, E-mail: toneill@misericordia.edu.

MISSISSIPPI COLLEGE, Clinton, MS 39058

General Information Independent-religious, coed, comprehensive institution. *Enrollment:* 4,741 graduate, professional, and undergraduate students; 944 full-time matriculated graduate/professional students (429 women), 758 part-time matriculated graduate/professional students (545 women). *Enrollment by degree level:* 550 first professional, 1,104 master's, 14 doctoral, 34 other advanced degrees. *Graduate faculty:* 103 full-time (40 women), 85 part-time/adjunct (32 women). *Tuition:* Full-time $7830; part-time $435 per hour. *Required fees:* $98 per semester. Tuition and fees vary according to course load, campus/location, program and student level. *Graduate housing:* Room and/or apartments available on a first-come, first-served basis to single students; on-campus housing not available to married students. Typical cost: $4800 per year ($5800 including board). Room and board charges vary according to housing facility selected. Housing application deadline: 8/15. *Student services:* Campus employment opportunities, career counseling, free psychological counseling, international student services, multicultural affairs office, services for students with disabilities, writing training. *Library facilities:* Leland Speed Library plus 1 other. *Online resources:* library catalog, web page, access to other libraries' catalogs. *Collection:* 376,719 titles, 15,834 audiovisual materials. *Research affiliation:* Gulf Coast Research Laboratory (Marine Biology).

Computer facilities: 340 computers available on campus for general student use. A campuswide network can be accessed from student residence rooms and from off campus. Online class registration is available. *Web address:* http://www.mc.edu/.

General Application Contact: Dr. Debbie C. Norris, Graduate Dean, 601-925-3260, Fax: 601-925-3889, E-mail: dnorris@mc.edu.

GRADUATE UNITS

Graduate School Students: 404 full-time (214 women), 706 part-time (512 women); includes 364 minority (334 African Americans, 4 American Indian/Alaska Native, 21 Asian Americans or Pacific Islanders, 5 Hispanic Americans), 180 international. Average age 30. *Faculty:* 86 full-time (30 women), 46 part-time/adjunct (17 women). Expenses: Contact institution. *Financial support:* Teaching assistantships, career-related internships or fieldwork, Federal Work-Study, tuition waivers (partial), and unspecified assistantships available. Support available to part-time students. Financial award application deadline: 4/1; financial award applicants required to submit FAFSA. In 2008, 402 master's awarded. *Degree program information:* Part-time and evening/weekend programs available. Postbaccalaureate distance learning degree programs offered (no on-campus study). Offers health services administration (MHSA); liberal studies (MLS). *Application fee:* $30. Electronic applications accepted. *Application Contact:* Elnora Lewis, Secretary, 601-925-3225, Fax: 601-925-3889, E-mail: lewis09@mc.edu. *Graduate Dean,* Dr. Debbie C. Norris, 601-925-3260, Fax: 601-925-3889, E-mail: dnorris@mc.edu.

College of Arts and Sciences Students: 157 full-time (82 women), 147 part-time (95 women); includes 74 minority (54 African Americans, 1 American Indian/Alaska Native, 16 Asian Americans or Pacific Islanders, 3 Hispanic Americans), 70 international. Average age 27. *Faculty:* 52 full-time (16 women), 13 part-time/adjunct (6 women). Expenses: Contact institution. *Financial support:* Teaching assistantships, career-related internships or fieldwork, Federal Work-Study, scholarships/grants, tuition waivers (partial), and unspecified assistantships available. Support available to part-time students. Financial award application deadline: 4/1; financial award applicants required to submit FAFSA. In 2008, 111 master's awarded. *Degree program information:* Part-time and evening/weekend programs available. Offers administration of justice (MSS); applied communication (MSC); applied music performance (MM); art (M Ed, MA, MFA); arts and sciences (M Ed, MA, MCS, MFA, MM, MS, MSC, MSS, Certificate); biological science (M Ed); biology (MCS); biology-biological sciences (MS); biology-medical sciences (MS); chemistry and biochemistry (MCS, MS); Christian studies and the arts (M Ed, MA, MFA, MM, MSC); computer science (M Ed, MS); conducting (MM); English (M Ed, MA); history (M Ed, MA, MSS); humanities and social sciences (M Ed, MA, MS, MSS, Certificate); mathematics (M Ed, MCS, MS); music education (MM); music performance: organ (MM); paralegal studies (Certificate); political science (MSS); public relations and corporate communication (MSC); science and mathematics (M Ed, MCS, MS); social sciences (M Ed, MSS); teaching English to speakers of other languages (MA, MS); vocal pedagogy (MM). *Application deadline:* For fall admission, 8/15 priority date for domestic students. Applications are processed on a rolling basis. *Application fee:* $30. Electronic applications accepted. *Application Contact:* Elnora Lewis, Secretary, 601-925-3225, Fax: 601-925-3889, E-mail: lewis09@mc.edu. *Dean,* Dr. Ron Howard, 601-925-3327, Fax: 601-925-3499, E-mail: howard@mc.edu.

School of Business Students: 100 full-time (33 women), 140 part-time (87 women); includes 52 minority (47 African Americans, 4 Asian Americans or Pacific Islanders, 1 Hispanic American), 69 international. Average age 29. *Faculty:* 12 full-time (2 women), 5 part-time/adjunct (0 women). Expenses: Contact institution. *Financial support:* Federal Work-Study and unspecified assistantships available. Support available to part-time students. Financial award application deadline: 4/1; financial award applicants required to submit FAFSA. In 2008, 54 master's awarded. *Degree program information:* Part-time and evening/weekend programs available. Offers accounting (Certificate); business administration (MBA); business education (M Ed); finance (MBA, Certificate). *Application deadline:* For fall admission, 8/15 priority date for domestic students. Applications are processed on a rolling basis. *Application fee:* $30. Electronic applications accepted. *Application Contact:* Elnora Lewis, Secretary, 601-925-3225, Fax: 601-925-3889, E-mail: lewis09@mc.edu. *Dean,* Dr. Marcelo Eduardo, 601-925-3420, E-mail: eduardo@mc.edu.

School of Education Students: 105 full-time (76 women), 395 part-time (315 women); includes 214 minority (209 African Americans, 3 American Indian/Alaska Native, 1 Asian American or Pacific Islander, 1 Hispanic American), 15 international. Average age 33. *Faculty:* 21 full-time (11 women), 21 part-time/adjunct (8 women). Expenses: Contact institution. *Financial support:* Teaching assistantships, career-related internships or fieldwork, Federal Work-Study, scholarships/grants, and unspecified assistantships available. Support available to part-time students. Financial award application deadline: 4/1; financial award applicants required to submit FAFSA. In 2008, 197 master's awarded. *Degree program information:* Part-time and evening/weekend programs available. Postbaccalaureate distance learning degree programs offered (no on-campus study). Offers art (M Ed); athletic administration (MS); biological science (M Ed); business education (M Ed); computer science (M Ed); counseling (Ed S); dyslexia therapy (M Ed); education (M Ed, MS, Ed D, Ed S); educational leadership (M Ed, Ed D, Ed S); elementary education (M Ed, Ed S); English (M Ed); higher education administration (MS); marriage and family counseling (MS); mathematics (M Ed); mental health counseling (MS); school counseling (M Ed); secondary education (M Ed); social studies (history) (M Ed); teaching arts (M Ed). *Application fee:* $30. Electronic applications accepted. *Application Contact:* Elnora Lewis, Secretary, 601-925-3225, Fax: 601-925-3889, E-mail: lewis09@mc.edu. *Dean,* Dr. Don Locke, 601-925-3250, E-mail: locke@mc.edu.

School of Law Offers civil law studies (Certificate); law (JD). Electronic applications accepted.

MISSISSIPPI STATE UNIVERSITY, Mississippi State, MS 39762

General Information State-supported, coed, university. CGS member. *Enrollment:* 17,824 graduate, professional, and undergraduate students; 1,468 full-time matriculated graduate/professional students (650 women), 1,598 part-time matriculated graduate/professional students (882 women). *Enrollment by degree level:* 1,994 master's, 976 doctoral, 96 other advanced degrees. *Graduate faculty:* 558 full-time (137 women), 51 part-time/adjunct (24 women). *International tuition:* $12,833 full-time. Tuition, state resident: full-time $5151; part-time $286.25 per hour. Tuition, nonresident: full-time $12,503; part-time $408.50 per hour. Tuition and fees vary according to course load. *Graduate housing:* Rooms and/or apartments available on a first-come, first-served basis to single and married students. Typical cost: $5616 per year for single students; $4980 per year for married students. Housing application deadline: 8/1. *Student services:* Campus employment opportunities, campus safety program, career counseling, child daycare facilities, exercise/wellness program, free psychological counseling, grant writing training, international student services, low-cost health insurance, multicultural affairs office, services for students with disabilities, teacher training, writing training. *Library facilities:* Mitchell Memorial Library plus 2 others. *Online resources:* library catalog, web page, access to other libraries' catalogs. *Collection:* 2.1 million titles, 57,007 serial subscriptions, 296,087 audiovisual materials. *Research affiliation:* Southeastern Universities Research Association (interdisciplinary research), Oak Ridge Associated Universities (energy related research–interdisciplinary), Mississippi Research and Technology Park (engineering—interdisciplinary), Mississippi Mineral Resources Institute (geology–sciences and engineering), NASA John C. Stennis Space Center (interdisciplinary research), Mississippi Research Consortium (interdisciplinary research).

Computer facilities: 1,000 computers available on campus for general student use. A campuswide network can be accessed from student residence rooms and from off campus. Online class registration, campus-wide wireless Internet access are available. *Web address:* http://www.msstate.edu/.

General Application Contact: Karin Lee, Manager, Graduate Programs, 662-325-8095, Fax: 662-325-1967, E-mail: grad@grad.msstate.edu.

GRADUATE UNITS

Bagley College of Engineering Students: 317 full-time (66 women), 165 part-time (35 women); includes 57 minority (35 African Americans, 19 Asian Americans or Pacific Islanders, 3 Hispanic Americans), 207 international. Average age 29. 633 applicants, 35% accepted, 106 enrolled. *Faculty:* 104 full-time (13 women), 6 part-time/adjunct (0 women). Expenses: Contact institution. *Financial support:* In 2008–09, 239 research assistantships with full tuition reimbursements (averaging $13,945 per year), 43 teaching assistantships with full tuition reimbursements (averaging $13,257 per year) were awarded; fellowships, Federal Work-Study, institutionally sponsored loans, scholarships/grants, and unspecified assistantships also available. Financial award application deadline: 4/1; financial award applicants required to submit FAFSA. In 2008, 93 master's, 22 doctorates awarded. *Degree program information:* Part-time programs available. Postbaccalaureate distance learning degree programs offered (no on-campus study). Offers aerospace engineering (MS); civil engineering (MS); computer engineering (MS, PhD); computer science (MS, PhD); electrical engineering (MS, PhD); engineering (PhD); industrial engineering (MS); mechanical engineering (MS). *Application deadline:* For fall admission, 7/1 for domestic students, 5/1 for international students; for spring admission, 11/1 for domestic students, 9/1 for international students. Applications are processed on a rolling basis. *Application fee:* $30 ($40 for international students). Electronic applications accepted. *Application Contact:* Dr. Lori Bruce, Associate Dean for Research and Graduate Studies, 662-325-2270, Fax: 662-325-8573, E-mail: bruce@bagley.msstate.edu. *Dean,* Dr. Sarah A. Rajala, 662-325-2270, Fax: 662-325-8573, E-mail: rajala@bagley.msstate.edu.

David C. Swalm School of Chemical Engineering Students: 25 full-time (8 women), 7 part-time (0 women); includes 4 minority (3 African Americans, 1 Asian American or Pacific Islander), 13 international. Average age 28. 20 applicants, 5% accepted, 1 enrolled. *Faculty:* 12 full-time (4 women). Expenses: Contact institution. *Financial support:* In 2008–09, 21 research assistantships with full tuition reimbursements (averaging $15,147 per year) were awarded; Federal Work-Study, institutionally sponsored loans, and unspecified assistantships also available. Financial award application deadline: 4/1; financial award applicants required to submit FAFSA. In 2008, 2 master's, 5 doctorates awarded. Offers chemical engineering (MS); engineering (PhD). *Application deadline:* For fall admission, 4/1 priority date for domestic students, 5/1 for international students; for spring admission, 8/1 priority date for domestic students, 9/1 for international students. Applications are processed on a rolling basis. *Application fee:* $30 ($40 for international students). Electronic applications accepted. *Application Contact:* Dr. Mark White, Director, 662-325-2480, Fax: 662-325-2482, E-mail: white@che.msstate.edu. *Director,* Dr. Mark White, 662-325-2480, Fax: 662-325-2482, E-mail: white@che.msstate.edu.

College of Agriculture and Life Sciences Students: 197 full-time (87 women), 122 part-time (57 women); includes 40 minority (29 African Americans, 1 American Indian/Alaska Native, 5 Asian Americans or Pacific Islanders, 5 Hispanic Americans), 73 international. Average age 30. 237 applicants, 46% accepted, 78 enrolled. *Faculty:* 107 full-time (17 women), 5 part-time/adjunct (3 women). Expenses: Contact institution. *Financial support:* In 2008–09, 132 research assistantships with full tuition reimbursements (averaging $13,342 per year), 17 teaching assistantships with full tuition reimbursements (averaging $11,190 per year) were awarded; career-related internships or fieldwork, Federal Work-Study, institutionally sponsored loans, scholarships/grants, tuition waivers (partial), and unspecified assistantships also available. Financial award application deadline: 4/1; financial award applicants required to submit FAFSA. In 2008, 65 master's, 18 doctorates awarded. Postbaccalaureate distance learning degree programs offered (no on-campus study). Offers agribusiness management (MABM); agricultural life sciences (MS, PhD); agricultural science (PhD); agriculture (MS); agriculture and life sciences (MABM, MLA, MS, PhD, Ed S); agriculture life sciences (MS); agriculture sciences (PhD); biological engineering (MS); biomedical engineering (MS, PhD); engineering (PhD); food science, nutrition and health promotion (MS, PhD); landscape architecture (MLA); life sciences (PhD); molecular biology (PhD). *Application deadline:* For fall admission, 7/1 for domestic students, 5/1 for international students; for spring admission, 11/1 for domestic students, 9/1 for international students. Applications are processed on a rolling basis. *Application fee:* $30 ($40 for international students). Electronic applications accepted. *Application Contact:* Forest Sparks, Admissions Manager, 662-325-7400, Fax: 662-325-1967, E-mail: grad@grad.msstate.edu. *Interim Dean and Vice President,* Dr. Melissa Mixon, 662-325-3006, E-mail: mixon@dafvm.msstate.edu.

School of Human Sciences Students: 8 full-time (5 women), 42 part-time (25 women); includes 11 minority (all African Americans). Average age 35. 13 applicants, 85% accepted, 9 enrolled. *Faculty:* 8 full-time (3 women). Expenses: Contact institution. *Financial support:*

Mississippi State University (continued)

In 2008–09, 3 research assistantships (averaging $11,441 per year), 5 teaching assistantships with full tuition reimbursements (averaging $10,830 per year) were awarded; Federal Work-Study, institutionally sponsored loans, and unspecified assistantships also available. Financial award application deadline: 4/1; financial award applicants required to submit FAFSA. In 2008, 6 master's, 3 doctorates awarded. *Degree program information:* Part-time programs available. Offers agricultural sciences (PhD); agriculture and extension education (MS); education (Ed S). *Application deadline:* For fall admission, 7/1 for domestic students, 5/1 for international students; for spring admission, 11/1 for domestic students, 9/1 for international students. Applications are processed on a rolling basis. *Application fee:* $30 ($40 for international students). Electronic applications accepted. *Application Contact:* Dr. Jacquelyn Deeds, Professor and Graduate Coordinator, 662-325-7834, E-mail: jdeeds@ais.msstate.edu. *Director*, Dr. Gary Jackson, 662-325-8593, E-mail: gjackson@humansci.msstate.edu.

College of Architecture, Art and Design Students: 15 full-time (8 women), 2 part-time (both women); includes 2 minority (both African Americans), 5 international. Average age 27. 14 applicants, 57% accepted, 5 enrolled. *Faculty:* 10 full-time (2 women), 3 part-time/adjunct (0 women). Expenses: Contact institution. *Financial support:* In 2008–09, 5 research assistantships with full tuition reimbursements (averaging $9,000 per year) were awarded; career-related internships or fieldwork, Federal Work-Study, institutionally sponsored loans, and unspecified assistantships also available. Financial award application deadline: 4/1; financial award applicants required to submit FAFSA. In 2008, 9 master's awarded. Offers architecture, art and design (MS). *Application deadline:* For fall admission, 7/1 for domestic students, 5/1 for international students; for spring admission, 11/1 for domestic students, 9/1 for international students. Applications are processed on a rolling basis. *Application fee:* $30 ($40 for international students). Electronic applications accepted. *Application Contact:* James L. West, Dean, 662-325-2202, Fax: 662-325-8872, E-mail: jwest@coa.msstate.edu. *Dean*, James L. West, 662-325-2202, Fax: 662-325-8872, E-mail: jwest@coa.msstate.edu.

School of Architecture Students: 15 full-time (8 women), 2 part-time (both women); includes 2 minority (both African Americans), 5 international. Average age 27. 14 applicants, 57% accepted, 5 enrolled. *Faculty:* 5 full-time (1 woman), 3 part-time/adjunct (0 women). Expenses: Contact institution. *Financial support:* In 2008–09, 5 research assistantships with full tuition reimbursements (averaging $9,000 per year) were awarded; Federal Work-Study, institutionally sponsored loans, scholarships/grants, and unspecified assistantships also available. Financial award application deadline: 4/1; financial award applicants required to submit FAFSA. In 2008, 8 master's awarded. Offers architecture (MS). *Application deadline:* For fall admission, 7/1 for domestic students, 5/1 for international students; for spring admission, 11/1 for domestic students, 9/1 for international students. Applications are processed on a rolling basis. *Application fee:* $30 ($40 for international students). Electronic applications accepted. *Application Contact:* Sarah Pittman, Manager, Graduate Studies Program, 662-325-7400, Fax: 662-325-1967, E-mail: spittman@caad.msstate.edu. *Director*, Dr. Larry Barrow, 662-325-2541, Fax: 662-325-8872, E-mail: lbarrow@caad.msstate.edu.

College of Arts and Sciences Students: 351 full-time (182 women), 441 part-time (236 women); includes 101 minority (71 African Americans, 4 American Indian/Alaska Native, 11 Asian Americans or Pacific Islanders, 15 Hispanic Americans), 93 international. Average age 33. 727 applicants, 62% accepted, 343 enrolled. *Faculty:* 168 full-time (49 women), 10 part-time/adjunct (3 women). Expenses: Contact institution. *Financial support:* In 2008–09, 47 research assistantships with full tuition reimbursements (averaging $12,540 per year), 221 teaching assistantships with full tuition reimbursements (averaging $11,786 per year) were awarded; Federal Work-Study, institutionally sponsored loans, scholarships/grants, tuition waivers (partial), and unspecified assistantships also available. Financial award applicants required to submit FAFSA. In 2008, 226 master's, 18 doctorates awarded. *Degree program information:* Part-time and evening/weekend programs available. Offers applied anthropology (MA); arts and sciences (MA, MPPA, MS, PhD); biological sciences (MS, PhD); chemistry (MS, PhD); cognitive science (PhD); engineering (PhD); English (MA); foreign language (MA); geosciences (MS); history (MA); mathematical sciences (PhD); mathematics (MS); physics (MS); political science (MA); psychology (MS); public policy and administration (MPPA, PhD); sociology (MS, PhD); statistics (MS). *Application deadline:* For fall admission, 7/1 for domestic students, 5/1 for international students; for spring admission, 11/1 for domestic students, 9/1 for international students. Applications are processed on a rolling basis. *Application fee:* $30 ($40 for international students). Electronic applications accepted. *Application Contact:* Admissions Manager. *Dean/Professor*, Dr. Gary Myers, 662-325-2646, Fax: 662-325-8740, E-mail: gmyers@deanas.msstate.edu.

College of Business Students: 187 full-time (71 women), 234 part-time (64 women); includes 47 minority (28 African Americans, 2 American Indian/Alaska Native, 14 Asian Americans or Pacific Islanders, 3 Hispanic Americans), 43 international. Average age 29. 349 applicants, 54% accepted, 138 enrolled. *Faculty:* 54 full-time (11 women), 2 part-time/adjunct (1 woman). Expenses: Contact institution. *Financial support:* In 2008–09, 37 research assistantships with full tuition reimbursements (averaging $8,345 per year), 30 teaching assistantships with full tuition reimbursements (averaging $12,069 per year) were awarded; career-related internships or fieldwork, Federal Work-Study, institutionally sponsored loans, scholarships/grants, and unspecified assistantships also available. Financial award applicants required to submit FAFSA. In 2008, 180 master's, 7 doctorates awarded. *Degree program information:* Part-time and evening/weekend programs available. Postbaccalaureate distance learning degree programs offered (no on-campus study). Offers applied economics (PhD); business administration (MBA, PhD); business and industry (MA, MBA, MPA, MSBA, MSIS, MTX, PhD); economics (MA); finance (MSBA); information systems (MSIS); marketing (PhD); project management (MBA). *Application deadline:* For fall admission, 3/1 priority date for domestic students, 5/1 for international students; for spring admission, 11/1 for domestic students, 9/1 for international students. Applications are processed on a rolling basis. *Application fee:* $30 ($40 for international students). Electronic applications accepted. *Application Contact:* Dr. Barbara Spencer, Associate Dean, Graduate Studies, 662-325-1891, Fax: 662-325-7360, E-mail: gsb@cobilan.msstate.edu. *Dean*, Dr. Lynne Richardson, 662-325-3580, Fax: 662-325-7360, E-mail: lrichardson@cobilan.msstate.edu.

School of Accountancy Students: 38 full-time (14 women), 2 part-time (0 women); includes 4 minority (3 Asian Americans or Pacific Islanders, 1 Hispanic American), 3 international. Average age 24. 35 applicants, 77% accepted, 22 enrolled. *Faculty:* 9 full-time (2 women), 1 (woman) part-time/adjunct. Expenses: Contact institution. *Financial support:* Career-related internships or fieldwork, Federal Work-Study, institutionally sponsored loans, scholarships/grants, and unspecified assistantships available. Support available to part-time students. Financial award applicants required to submit FAFSA. In 2008, 36 master's awarded. Offers accounting (MPA); taxation (MTX). *Application deadline:* For fall admission, 7/1 for domestic students, 5/1 for international students; for spring admission, 11/1 for domestic students, 9/1 for international students. Applications are processed on a rolling basis. *Application fee:* $30 ($40 for international students). Electronic applications accepted. *Application Contact:* Dr. Barbara Spencer, Associate Dean, Graduate Studies, 662-325-3710, Fax: 662-325-1646, E-mail: sac@cobilan.msstate.edu. *Director*, Dr. Louis Dawkins, 662-325-1633, E-mail: ldawkins@cobilan.msstate.edu.

College of Education Students: 289 full-time (201 women), 607 part-time (480 women); includes 360 minority (351 African Americans, 3 American Indian/Alaska Native, 3 Asian Americans or Pacific Islanders, 3 Hispanic Americans), 14 international. Average age 35. 349 applicants, 61% accepted, 167 enrolled. *Faculty:* 72 full-time (40 women), 23 part-time/adjunct (17 women). Expenses: Contact institution. *Financial support:* In 2008–09, 18 research assistantships (averaging $9,684 per year), 16 teaching assistantships (averaging $9,097 per year) were awarded; career-related internships or fieldwork, Federal Work-Study, institutionally sponsored loans, scholarships/grants, and unspecified assistantships also available. Financial award applicants required to submit FAFSA. In 2008, 209 master's, 45 doctorates, 40 other advanced degrees awarded. *Degree program information:* Part-time and evening/weekend programs available. Postbaccalaureate distance learning degree programs offered (minimal on-campus study). Offers college/postsecondary student counseling and personnel services (PhD); community college education (MAT); community college leadership (PhD); counselor education (MS); counselor education/student counseling and guidance services (PhD); curriculum and instruction (PhD); education (MAT, MS, MSIT, Ed D, PhD, Ed S); educational psychology (MS, PhD); elementary education (MS, PhD); elementary, middle school, and secondary education administration (PhD); instructional systems and workforce development (PhD); instructional technology (MSIT); physical education (MS); school administration (MS); secondary education (MS, PhD); secondary teacher alternate route (MAT); special education (MS); technology (MS); workforce educational leadership (MS). *Application deadline:* For fall admission, 7/1 for domestic students, 5/1 for international students; for spring admission, 11/1 for domestic students, 9/1 for international students. Applications are processed on a rolling basis. *Application fee:* $30 ($40 for international students). Electronic applications accepted. *Application Contact:* Dr. Sue Minshew, Associate Dean and Professor, 662-325-3717, Fax: 662-325-8784, E-mail: sminshew@colled.msstate.edu. *Dean*, Dr. Richard Blackbourn, 662-325-3717, Fax: 662-325-8784, E-mail: rlb277@msstate.edu.

College of Forest Resources Students: 112 full-time (35 women), 27 part-time (8 women); includes 7 minority (3 African Americans, 2 Asian Americans or Pacific Islanders, 2 Hispanic Americans), 30 international. Average age 29. 60 applicants, 62% accepted, 31 enrolled. *Faculty:* 43 full-time (5 women), 2 part-time/adjunct (0 women). Expenses: Contact institution. *Financial support:* In 2008–09, 95 research assistantships with full tuition reimbursements (averaging $13,418 per year), 6 teaching assistantships with full tuition reimbursements (averaging $14,760 per year) were awarded; career-related internships or fieldwork, Federal Work-Study, institutionally sponsored loans, and unspecified assistantships also available. Financial award application deadline: 4/1; financial award applicants required to submit FAFSA. In 2008, 17 master's, 7 doctorates awarded. *Degree program information:* Part-time programs available. Offers forest resources (MS, PhD); forestry (MS); wildlife and fisheries science (MS). *Application deadline:* For fall admission, 7/1 for domestic students, 5/1 for international students; for spring admission, 11/1 for domestic students, 9/1 for international students. Applications are processed on a rolling basis. *Application fee:* $30 ($40 for international students). Electronic applications accepted. *Application Contact:* Interim Associate Vice President for Academic Affairs/Interim Dean of Graduate Studies. *Dean*, Dr. George M. Hopper, 662-325-2696, Fax: 662-325-8726, E-mail: ghopper@cfr.msstate.edu.

College of Veterinary Medicine Offers environmental toxicology (PhD); veterinary medical science (MS, PhD); veterinary medicine (DVM, MS, PhD). Electronic applications accepted.

MISSISSIPPI UNIVERSITY FOR WOMEN, Columbus, MS 39701-9998

General Information State-supported, coed, primarily women, comprehensive institution. *Graduate housing:* Rooms and/or apartments available on a first-come, first-served basis to single and married students.

GRADUATE UNITS

Graduate School *Degree program information:* Part-time programs available.

College of Education and Human Sciences *Degree program information:* Part-time programs available. Offers differentiated instruction (M Ed); gifted studies (M Ed); teaching (MAT).

College of Nursing and Speech-Language Pathology *Degree program information:* Part-time programs available. Offers nursing (MSN, PMC); speech/language pathology (MS).

Division of Health and Kinesiology Offers health education (MS).

MISSISSIPPI VALLEY STATE UNIVERSITY, Itta Bena, MS 38941-1400

General Information State-supported, coed, comprehensive institution. *Graduate housing:* Room and/or apartments available to single students; on-campus housing not available to married students. Housing application deadline: 8/1.

GRADUATE UNITS

Department of Criminal Justice and Social Work *Degree program information:* Part-time and evening/weekend programs available. Offers criminal justice (MS). Electronic applications accepted.

Department of Education Offers education (MAT); elementary education (MA).

Department of Natural Science and Environmental Health *Degree program information:* Part-time and evening/weekend programs available. Offers bioinformatics (MS); environmental health (MS).

MISSOURI BAPTIST UNIVERSITY, St. Louis, MO 63141-8660

General Information Independent-religious, coed, comprehensive institution.

GRADUATE UNITS

Graduate Programs

MISSOURI SOUTHERN STATE UNIVERSITY, Joplin, MO 64801-1595

General Information State-supported, coed, comprehensive institution.

GRADUATE UNITS

Program in Business Administration Postbaccalaureate distance learning degree programs offered. Offers business administration (MBA).

Program in Criminal Justice Administration Postbaccalaureate distance learning degree programs offered. Offers criminal justice administration (MS).

Program in Dental Hygiene *Degree program information:* Part-time programs available. Offers dental hygiene (MS). Electronic applications accepted.

Program in Early Childhood Education Offers early childhood education (MS Ed).

Program in Instructional Technology Offers instructional technology (MS Ed).

Program in Nursing *Degree program information:* Part-time programs available. Offers nursing (MSN). Electronic applications accepted.

Program in Teaching Offers teaching (MAT).

MISSOURI STATE UNIVERSITY, Springfield, MO 65804-0094

General Information State-supported, coed, comprehensive institution. CGS member. *Enrollment:* 19,348 graduate, professional, and undergraduate students; 1,321 full-time matriculated graduate/professional students (726 women), 1,321 part-time matriculated graduate/professional students (801 women). *Enrollment by degree level:* 2,457 master's, 120 doctoral, 65 other advanced degrees. *Graduate faculty:* 426 full-time (132 women), 137 part-time/adjunct (43 women). Tuition, state resident: full-time $3852; part-time $214 per credit hour. Tuition, nonresident: full-time $7524; part-time $418 per credit hour. *Required fees:* $230 per semester. Tuition and fees vary according to course level and course load. *Graduate housing:* Rooms and/or apartments available on a first-come, first-served basis to single and married students. Typical cost: $3850 per year ($5576 including board) for single students; $7716 per year for married students. Room and board charges vary according to board plan. Housing application deadline: 7/1. *Student services:* Campus employment opportunities, campus safety program, career counseling, child daycare facilities, exercise/wellness program, free psychological counseling, grant writing training, international student services, low-cost health insurance, multicultural affairs office, services for students with disabilities, teacher training, writing training. *Library facilities:* Meyer Library plus 3 others. *Online resources:* library catalog, web page, access to other libraries' catalogs. *Collection:* 1.7 million titles, 4,238 serial subscriptions, 33,547 audiovisual materials.

Computer facilities: Computer purchase and lease plans are available. 1,800 computers available on campus for general student use. A campuswide network can be accessed from student residence rooms and from off campus. Online class registration is available. *Web address:* http://www.missouristate.edu/.

General Application Contact: Eric Eckert, Coordinator of Admissions and Recruitment, 417-836-5331, Fax: 417-836-6888, E-mail: ericeckert@missouristate.edu.

GRADUATE UNITS

Graduate College Students: 1,321 full-time (726 women), 1,321 part-time (801 women); includes 113 minority (41 African Americans, 7 American Indian/Alaska Native, 31 Asian Americans or Pacific Islanders, 34 Hispanic Americans), 349 international. Average age 29. 951 applicants, 79% accepted, 537 enrolled. *Faculty:* 426 full-time (132 women), 137 part-time/adjunct (43 women). Expenses: Contact institution. *Financial support:* In 2008–09, 51 research assistantships with full tuition reimbursements (averaging $8,415 per year), 126 teaching assistantships with full tuition reimbursements (averaging $7,990 per year) were awarded; Federal Work-Study, institutionally sponsored loans, scholarships/grants, and unspecified assistantships also available. Financial award application deadline: 3/31; financial award applicants required to submit FAFSA. In 2008, 857 master's, 32 doctorates, 20 other advanced degrees awarded. *Degree program information:* Part-time programs available. Post-baccalaureate distance learning degree programs offered. Offers applied communication (MS); criminal justice (MS); environmental management (MS); project management (MS); sports management (MS). *Application deadline:* For fall admission, 7/20 priority date for domestic students, 5/1 for international students; for spring admission, 12/20 priority date for domestic students, 9/1 for international students. Applications are processed on a rolling basis. *Application fee:* $35 ($50 for international students). Electronic applications accepted. *Application Contact:* Eric Eckert, Coordinator of Admissions and Recruitment, 417-836-5331, Fax: 417-836-6888, E-mail: ericeckert@missouristate.edu. *Associate Provost and Dean of the Graduate College,* Dr. Frank A. Einhellig, 417-836-5335, Fax: 417-836-6888, E-mail: frankeinhellig@missouristate.edu.

College of Arts and Letters Students: 81 full-time (46 women), 112 part-time (70 women); includes 2 minority (1 African American, 1 Hispanic American), 11 international. Average age 28. 81 applicants, 99% accepted, 55 enrolled. *Faculty:* 77 full-time (37 women). Expenses: Contact institution. *Financial support:* In 2008–09, 3 research assistantships with full tuition reimbursements (averaging $7,340 per year), 59 teaching assistantships with full tuition reimbursements (averaging $7,340 per year) were awarded; Federal Work-Study, institutionally sponsored loans, scholarships/grants, and unspecified assistantships also available. Financial award application deadline: 3/31; financial award applicants required to submit FAFSA. In 2008, 80 master's awarded. *Degree program information:* Part-time and evening/weekend programs available. Offers arts and letters (MA, MM, MS Ed); communication and mass media (MA); English and writing (MA); music (MM); secondary education (MS Ed); theatre (MA). *Application deadline:* For fall admission, 7/20 for domestic students, 5/1 for international students; for spring admission, 12/20 for domestic students, 9/1 for international students. Applications are processed on a rolling basis. *Application fee:* $35 ($50 for international students). Electronic applications accepted. *Application Contact:* Eric Eckert, Coordinator of Admissions and Recruitment, 417-836-5331, Fax: 417-836-6888, E-mail: ericeckert@missouristate.edu. *Dean,* Dr. Carey Adams, 417-836-5247, Fax: 417-836-6940, E-mail: careyadams@missouristate.edu.

College of Business Administration Students: 372 full-time (154 women), 277 part-time (133 women); includes 26 minority (11 African Americans, 1 American Indian/Alaska Native, 10 Asian Americans or Pacific Islanders, 4 Hispanic Americans), 204 international. Average age 27. 236 applicants, 90% accepted, 172 enrolled. *Faculty:* 68 full-time (16 women), 1 part-time/adjunct (0 women). Expenses: Contact institution. *Financial support:* In 2008–09, 1 research assistantship with full tuition reimbursement (averaging $7,340 per year), 2 teaching assistantships with full tuition reimbursements (averaging $8,535 per year) were awarded; Federal Work-Study, institutionally sponsored loans, scholarships/grants, and unspecified assistantships also available. Financial award application deadline: 3/31; financial award applicants required to submit FAFSA. In 2008, 273 master's awarded. *Degree program information:* Part-time and evening/weekend programs available. Postbaccalaureate distance learning degree programs offered. Offers accountancy (M Acc); business administration (M Acc, MBA, MHA, MS, MS Ed); computer information systems (MS); health administration (MHA); secondary education (MS Ed); technology and construction management (MS). *Application deadline:* For fall admission, 7/20 priority date for domestic students, 5/1 for international students; for spring admission, 12/20 priority date for domestic students, 9/1 for international students. Applications are processed on a rolling basis. *Application fee:* $35 ($50 for international students). Electronic applications accepted. *Application Contact:* Eric Eckert, Coordinator of Graduate Admissions and Recruitment, 417-836-5331, Fax: 417-836-6888, E-mail: ericeckert@missouristate.edu. *Dean,* Dr. Danny Arnold, 417-836-4408, Fax: 417-836-4407, E-mail: COBA@missouristate.edu.

College of Education Students: 200 full-time (153 women), 586 part-time (430 women); includes 34 minority (9 African Americans, 2 American Indian/Alaska Native, 7 Asian Americans or Pacific Islanders, 16 Hispanic Americans), 6 international. Average age 34. 125 applicants, 94% accepted, 84 enrolled. *Faculty:* 43 full-time (23 women), 25 part-time/adjunct (11 women). Expenses: Contact institution. *Financial support:* In 2008–09, 5 research assistantships with full tuition reimbursements (averaging $7,340 per year), 5 teaching assistantships with full tuition reimbursements (averaging $7,340 per year) were awarded; Federal Work-Study, institutionally sponsored loans, scholarships/grants, and unspecified assistantships also available. Financial award application deadline: 3/31; financial award applicants required to submit FAFSA. In 2008, 203 master's, 20 other advanced degrees awarded. *Degree program information:* Part-time programs available. Offers counseling (MS); early childhood and family development (MS); education (MAT, MS, MS Ed, Ed S); educational administration (MS Ed, Ed S); elementary education (MS Ed); elementary principal (Ed S); instructional media technology (MS Ed); reading (MS Ed); reading education (MS Ed); secondary education (MS Ed); secondary principal (Ed S); special education (MS Ed); student affairs (MS); superintendent (Ed S); teaching (MAT). *Application deadline:* For fall admission, 7/20 for domestic students, 5/1 for international students; for spring admission, 12/20 for domestic students, 9/1 for international students. Applications are processed on a rolling basis. *Application fee:* $35 ($50 for international students). Electronic applications accepted. *Application Contact:* Eric Eckert, Coordinator of Admissions and Recruitment, 417-836-5331, Fax: 417-836-6888, E-mail: ericeckert@missouristate.edu. *Dean,* Dr. Dennis Kear, 417-836-5254, Fax: 417-836-4884, E-mail: coestudentservices@missouristate.edu.

College of Health and Human Services Students: 439 full-time (279 women), 98 part-time (69 women); includes 22 minority (9 African Americans, 1 American Indian/Alaska Native, 5 Asian Americans or Pacific Islanders, 7 Hispanic Americans), 90 international. Average age 27. 305 applicants, 51% accepted, 102 enrolled. *Faculty:* 75 full-time (29 women), 79 part-time/adjunct (27 women). Expenses: Contact institution. *Financial support:* In 2008–09, 16 research assistantships with full tuition reimbursements (averaging $7,638 per year), 14 teaching assistantships with full tuition reimbursements (averaging $8,363 per year) were awarded; Federal Work-Study, institutionally sponsored loans, scholarships/grants, and unspecified assistantships also available. Financial award application deadline: 3/31; financial award applicants required to submit FAFSA. In 2008, 155 master's, 32 doctorates awarded. *Degree program information:* Part-time programs available. Offers audiology (Au D); cell and molecular biology (MS); communication sciences and disorders (MS); family nurse practitioner (MSN); health and human services (MPH, MS, MS Ed, MSN, MSW, Au D, DPT); health promotion and wellness management (MS); nurse anesthesia (MS); nurse educator (MSN); nursing (MSN); physical therapy (DPT); physician assistant studies (MS); psychology (MS); public health (MPH); secondary education (MS Ed); social work (MSW). *Application deadline:* For fall admission, 7/20 for domestic students, 5/1 for international students; for spring admission, 12/20 for domestic students, 9/1 for international students. *Application fee:* $35 ($50 for international students). Electronic applications accepted. *Application Contact:* Eric Eckert, Coordinator of Admissions and Recruitment, 417-836-5331, Fax: 417-836-6888, E-mail: ericeckert@missouristate.edu. *Dean,* Dr. Helen Reid, 417-836-4176, Fax: 417-836-6905.

College of Humanities and Public Affairs Students: 131 full-time (51 women), 115 part-time (46 women); includes 17 minority (6 African Americans, 1 American Indian/Alaska Native, 5 Asian Americans or Pacific Islanders, 5 Hispanic Americans), 12 international. Average age 28. 122 applicants, 97% accepted, 74 enrolled. *Faculty:* 53 full-time (10 women), 25 part-time/adjunct (3 women). Expenses: Contact institution. *Financial support:* In 2008–09, 2 research assistantships with full tuition reimbursements (averaging $8,535 per year), 8 teaching assistantships with full tuition reimbursements (averaging $8,230 per year) were awarded; Federal Work-Study, institutionally sponsored loans, scholarships/grants, and unspecified assistantships also available. Financial award application deadline: 3/31; financial award applicants required to submit FAFSA. In 2008, 65 master's awarded. *Degree program information:* Part-time programs available. Offers criminology (MS); defense and strategic studies (MS); history (MA); humanities and public affairs (MA, MIAA, MPA, MS, MS Ed); international affairs and administration (MIAA); public administration (MPA); religious studies (MA); secondary education (MS Ed). *Application deadline:* For fall admission, 7/20 priority date for domestic students; for spring admission, 12/20 priority date for domestic students. Applications are processed on a rolling basis. *Application fee:* $35 ($50 for international students). Electronic applications accepted. *Application Contact:* Eric Eckert, Coordinator of Admissions and Recruitment, 417-836-5331, Fax: 417-836-6888, E-mail: ericeckert@missouristate.edu. *Dean,* Dr. Victor Matthews, 417-836-5529, Fax: 417-836-8472, E-mail: victormatthews@missouristate.edu.

College of Natural and Applied Sciences Students: 82 full-time (34 women), 77 part-time (28 women); includes 5 minority (1 African American, 2 American Indian/Alaska Native, 2 Asian Americans or Pacific Islanders), 26 international. Average age 27. 71 applicants, 86% accepted, 38 enrolled. *Faculty:* 110 full-time (17 women), 7 part-time/adjunct (2 women). Expenses: Contact institution. *Financial support:* In 2008–09, 24 research assistantships with full tuition reimbursements (averaging $9,330 per year), 34 teaching assistantships with full tuition reimbursements (averaging $8,910 per year) were awarded; Federal Work-Study, institutionally sponsored loans, scholarships/grants, and unspecified assistantships also available. Financial award application deadline: 3/31; financial award applicants required to submit FAFSA. In 2008, 48 master's awarded. *Degree program information:* Part-time and evening/weekend programs available. Offers biology (MS); chemistry (MS); computer science (MNAS); geospatial sciences (MS); materials science (MS); mathematics (MS); natural and applied science (MNAS); natural and applied sciences (MNAS, MS, MS Ed); physics, astronomy, and materials science (MNAS); plant science (MS); secondary education (MS Ed). *Application deadline:* For fall admission, 7/20 for domestic students, 5/1 for international students; for spring admission, 12/20 for domestic students, 9/1 for international students. Applications are processed on a rolling basis. *Application fee:* $35 ($50 for international students). Electronic applications accepted. *Application Contact:* Eric Eckert, Coordinator of Admissions and Recruitment, 417-836-5331, Fax: 417-836-6888, E-mail: ericeckert@missouristate.edu. *Dean,* Dr. Tamera Jahnke, 417-836-5249, Fax: 417-836-6934.

See Close-Up on page 947.

MISSOURI UNIVERSITY OF SCIENCE AND TECHNOLOGY, Rolla, MO 65409

General Information State-supported, coed, primarily men, university. CGS member. *Graduate housing:* Rooms and/or apartments available on a first-come, first-served basis to single and married students.

GRADUATE UNITS

Graduate School *Degree program information:* Part-time and evening/weekend programs available. Offers aerospace engineering (MS, PhD); applied and environmental biology (MS); applied mathematics (MS); business and information technology (MBA); ceramic engineering (MS, DE, PhD); chemical engineering (MS, DE, PhD); chemistry (MS, MST, PhD); civil engineering (MS, DE, PhD); computer science (MS, PhD); construction engineering (MS, DE, PhD); engineering management (MS, DE, PhD); environmental engineering (MS); fluid mechanics (MS, DE, PhD); geological engineering (MS, DE, PhD); geology and geophysics (MS, PhD); geotechnical engineering (MS, DE, PhD); hydrology and hydraulic engineering (MS, DE, PhD); information science and technology (MS); manufacturing engineering (M Eng, MS); mathematics (MST, PhD); mechanical engineering (MS, DE, PhD); metallurgical engineering (MS, PhD); mining engineering (MS, DE, PhD); nuclear engineering (MS, DE, PhD); petroleum engineering (MS, DE, PhD); physics (MS, MST, PhD); systems engineering (MS, PhD). Electronic applications accepted.

School of Engineering *Degree program information:* Part-time and evening/weekend programs available. Offers computer engineering (MS, DE, PhD); electrical engineering (MS, DE, PhD); engineering (M Eng, MS, DE, PhD). Electronic applications accepted.

MOLLOY COLLEGE, Rockville Centre, NY 11571-5002

General Information Independent, coed, comprehensive institution. *Enrollment:* 3,791 graduate, professional, and undergraduate students; 7 full-time matriculated graduate/professional students (all women), 341 part-time matriculated graduate/professional students (322 women). *Enrollment by degree level:* 348 master's. *Graduate faculty:* 18 full-time (all women), 4 part-time/adjunct (3 women). *Tuition:* Full-time $12,870; part-time $715 per credit. *Required fees:* $620; $620 per contact hour. One-time fee: $60 full-time. *Graduate housing:* On-campus housing not available. *Student services:* Campus employment opportunities, campus safety program, career counseling, free psychological counseling, low-cost health insurance, services for students with disabilities, teacher training, writing training. *Library facilities:* James Edward Tobin Library. *Online resources:* library catalog, web page, access to other libraries' catalogs. *Collection:* 115,000 titles, 680 serial subscriptions, 3,860 audiovisual materials.

Computer facilities: 391 computers available on campus for general student use. A campuswide network can be accessed from off campus. Online class registration is available. *Web address:* http://www.molloy.edu/.

General Application Contact: Dr. Mary O'Shaughnessy, Interim Associate Dean/Director, Graduate Program, 516-678-5000 Ext. 6838, Fax: 516-256-2267, E-mail: moshaughnessy@molloy.edu.

GRADUATE UNITS

Department of Nursing *Degree program information:* Part-time and evening/weekend programs available. Offers adult nurse practitioner (Advanced Certificate); clinical nurse specialist- adult health (Advanced Certificate); family nurse practitioner (Advanced Certificate); nurse practitioner psychiatry (Advanced Certificate); nursing (MS); nursing administration (Advanced Certificate); nursing administration with informatics (Advanced Certificate); nursing education (Advanced Certificate); nursing informatics (Advanced Certificate); pediatric nurse practitioner (Advanced Certificate).

MONMOUTH UNIVERSITY, West Long Branch, NJ 07764-1898

General Information Independent, coed, comprehensive institution. *Enrollment:* 6,442 graduate, professional, and undergraduate students; 521 full-time matriculated graduate/professional students (383 women), 1,200 part-time matriculated graduate/professional students (874 women). *Enrollment by degree level:* 1,721 master's. *Graduate faculty:* 134 full-time (66 women), 69 part-time/adjunct (45 women). *Tuition:* Full-time $13,914; part-time $773 per credit. *Required fees:* $628; $157 per semester. *Graduate housing:* On-campus housing not available. *Student services:* Campus employment opportunities, campus safety program, career counseling, exercise/wellness program, free psychological counseling, international student services, low-cost health insurance, multicultural affairs office, services for students with disabilities, writing training. *Library facilities:* Monmouth University Library. *Online resources:* library catalog, web page. *Collection:* 280,000 titles, 25,196 serial subscriptions.

Computer facilities: 695 computers available on campus for general student use. A campuswide network can be accessed from student residence rooms and from off campus. Online class registration is available. *Web address:* http://www.monmouth.edu/.

General Application Contact: Kevin Roane, Director, Office of Graduate Admission, 732-571-3452, Fax: 732-263-5123, E-mail: gradadm@monmouth.edu.

GRADUATE UNITS

Graduate School Students: 521 full-time (383 women), 1,200 part-time (874 women); includes 219 minority (80 African Americans, 5 American Indian/Alaska Native, 70 Asian Americans or Pacific Islanders, 64 Hispanic Americans), 59 international. Average age 32. 1,142 applicants, 92% accepted, 537 enrolled. *Faculty:* 134 full-time (66 women), 69 part-time/adjunct (45 women). Expenses: Contact institution. *Financial support:* In 2008–09, 815 students received support, including 798 fellowships (averaging $1,921 per year), 93 research assistantships (averaging $7,629 per year); career-related internships or fieldwork, scholarships/grants, tuition waivers (full and partial), and unspecified assistantships also available. Support avail-

Monmouth University (continued)

able to part-time students. Financial award application deadline: 3/1; financial award applicants required to submit FAFSA. In 2008, 551 master's awarded. *Degree program information:* Part-time and evening/weekend programs available. Offers community and international development (MSW); computer science (MS); corporate and public communication (MA); criminal justice administration (MA, Certificate); English (MA); history (MA); human resources communication (Certificate); liberal arts (MA); media studies (Certificate); practice with families and children (MSW); professional counseling (PMC); psychological counseling (MA); public policy (MA); public relations (Certificate); software development (Certificate); software engineering (MS, Certificate). *Application deadline:* For fall admission, 7/15 priority date for domestic students, 6/1 for international students; for spring admission, 11/15 priority date for domestic students, 11/1 for international students. Applications are processed on a rolling basis. *Application fee:* $50. Electronic applications accepted. *Application Contact:* Kevin Roane, Director, Office of Graduate Admission, 732-571-3452, Fax: 732-263-5123, E-mail: gradadm@monmouth.edu. *Dean,* Dr. Datta V. Naik, 732-571-7550, Fax: 732-263-5142.

Leon Hess Business School Students: 71 full-time (24 women), 151 part-time (69 women); includes 16 minority (6 African Americans, 4 Asian Americans or Pacific Islanders, 6 Hispanic Americans), 13 international. Average age 30. 151 applicants, 79% accepted, 66 enrolled. *Faculty:* 27 full-time (8 women), 2 part-time/adjunct (0 women). Expenses: Contact institution. *Financial support:* In 2008–09, 156 students received support, including 155 fellowships (averaging $1,685 per year), 12 research assistantships (averaging $9,411 per year); career-related internships or fieldwork, scholarships/grants, tuition waivers (partial), and unspecified assistantships also available. Support available to part-time students. Financial award application deadline: 3/1; financial award applicants required to submit FAFSA. In 2008, 68 master's awarded. *Degree program information:* Part-time and evening/weekend programs available. Offers accounting (MBA); business administration (MBA); health care management (MBA, Certificate). *Application deadline:* For fall admission, 7/15 priority date for domestic students, 6/1 for international students; for spring admission, 11/15 priority date for domestic students, 11/1 for international students. Applications are processed on a rolling basis. *Application fee:* $50. Electronic applications accepted. *Application Contact:* Kevin Roane, Director, Office of Graduate Admission, 732-571-3452, Fax: 732-263-5123, E-mail: gradadm@monmouth.edu. *Program Director,* Donald Smith, 732-571-7536, Fax: 732-263-5517, E-mail: dsmith@monmouth.edu.

The Marjorie K. Unterberg School of Nursing and Health Studies Students: 8 full-time (all women), 211 part-time (206 women); includes 47 minority (10 African Americans, 1 American Indian/Alaska Native, 29 Asian Americans or Pacific Islanders, 7 Hispanic Americans), 1 international. Average age 44. 113 applicants, 100% accepted, 62 enrolled. *Faculty:* 11 full-time (all women), 2 part-time/adjunct (both women). Expenses: Contact institution. *Financial support:* In 2008–09, 113 students received support, including 113 fellowships (averaging $1,340 per year), 3 research assistantships (averaging $5,136 per year); career-related internships or fieldwork, scholarships/grants, tuition waivers (partial), and unspecified assistantships also available. Support available to part-time students. Financial award application deadline: 3/1; financial award applicants required to submit FAFSA. In 2008, 36 master's awarded. *Degree program information:* Part-time and evening/weekend programs available. Offers advanced practice nursing (Post-Master's Certificate); nursing (MSN); school nursing (Certificate); substance awareness coordinator (Certificate). *Application deadline:* For fall admission, 7/15 priority date for domestic students, 6/1 for international students; for spring admission, 11/15 priority date for domestic students, 11/1 for international students. Applications are processed on a rolling basis. *Application fee:* $50. Electronic applications accepted. *Application Contact:* Kevin Roane, Director, Office of Graduate Admission, 732-571-3452, Fax: 732-263-5123, E-mail: gradadm@monmouth.edu. *Director,* Dr. Janet Mahoney, 732-571-3443, Fax: 732-263-5131, E-mail: jmahoney@monmouth.edu.

School of Education Students: 168 full-time (137 women), 348 part-time (276 women); includes 35 minority (13 African Americans, 1 American Indian/Alaska Native, 10 Asian Americans or Pacific Islanders, 11 Hispanic Americans), 2 international. Average age 30. 305 applicants, 95% accepted, 159 enrolled. *Faculty:* 20 full-time (11 women), 31 part-time/adjunct (22 women). Expenses: Contact institution. *Financial support:* In 2008–09, 170 students received support, including 165 fellowships (averaging $1,731 per year), 22 research assistantships (averaging $9,051 per year); career-related internships or fieldwork, scholarships/grants, tuition waivers (partial), and unspecified assistantships also available. Support available to part-time students. Financial award application deadline: 3/1; financial award applicants required to submit FAFSA. In 2008, 207 master's awarded. *Degree program information:* Part-time and evening/weekend programs available. Offers education (M Ed); educational counseling (MS Ed); elementary education (MAT); learning disabilities-teacher consultant (Certificate); principal studies (MS Ed); reading specialist (MS Ed, Certificate); special education (MS Ed); supervisor (Certificate); teacher of the handicapped (Certificate). *Application deadline:* For fall admission, 7/15 priority date for domestic students, 7/1 for international students; for spring admission, 11/15 priority date for domestic students, 11/1 for international students. Applications are processed on a rolling basis. *Application fee:* $50. Electronic applications accepted. *Application Contact:* Kevin Roane, Director, Office of Graduate Admission, 732-571-3452, Fax: 732-263-5123, E-mail: gradadm@monmouth.edu. *Program Director,* Dr. Terri Rothman, 732-571-7507, Fax: 732-263-5277, E-mail: trothman@monmouth.edu.

See Close-Up on page 949.

MONROE COLLEGE, Bronx, NY 10468-5407

General Information Proprietary, coed, comprehensive institution.

GRADUATE UNITS

King School of Business Postbaccalaureate distance learning degree programs offered. Offers business management (MBA). Program also offered in New Rochelle, NY.

MONTANA STATE UNIVERSITY, Bozeman, MT 59717

General Information State-supported, coed, university. CGS member. *Enrollment:* 12,369 graduate, professional, and undergraduate students; 449 full-time matriculated graduate/professional students (222 women), 1,085 part-time matriculated graduate/professional students (537 women). *Enrollment by degree level:* 1,149 master's, 383 doctoral, 415 other advanced degrees. *Graduate faculty:* 553 full-time (195 women), 265 part-time/adjunct (150 women). Tuition, state resident: full-time $4103; part-time $227.95 per credit. Tuition, nonresident: full-time $12,438; part-time $691 per credit. *Required fees:* $1118.60; $98.85 per credit. Tuition and fees vary according to course load and program. *Graduate housing:* Rooms and/or apartments available on a first-come, first-served basis to single and married students. Typical cost: $7000 (including board) for single students; $8000 (including board) for married students. Room and board charges vary according to housing facility selected. *Student services:* Campus employment opportunities, campus safety program, career counseling, child daycare facilities, exercise/wellness program, free psychological counseling, international student services, low-cost health insurance, multicultural affairs office, services for students with disabilities, teacher training, writing training. *Library facilities:* Renne Library plus 2 others. *Online resources:* library catalog, web page, access to other libraries' catalogs. *Collection:* 730,422 titles, 9,924 serial subscriptions, 10,841 audiovisual materials. *Research affiliation:* Phillips Environmental (microbial technology), Microvision (information transmission system), LigoCyte Pharmaceuticals, Inc. (pharmaceuticals), Eli Lilly & Company (antifungal technology), S2 Corporation (instrumentation), ILX Lightwave (laser diodes, electro-optical test equipment).

Computer facilities: 850 computers available on campus for general student use. A campuswide network can be accessed from student residence rooms and from off campus. Online class registration is available. *Web address:* http://www.montana.edu/.

General Application Contact: Dr. Carl A. Fox, Vice Provost for Graduate Education, 406-994-4145, Fax: 406-994-7433, E-mail: gradstudy@montana.edu.

GRADUATE UNITS

College of Graduate Studies Students: 10 full-time (7 women), 202 part-time (124 women); includes 7 minority (4 American Indian/Alaska Native, 2 Asian Americans or Pacific Islanders, 1 Hispanic American). Average age 37. 90 applicants, 53% accepted, 55 enrolled. *Faculty:* 2 full-time (both women), 3 part-time/adjunct (all women). Expenses: Contact institution. *Financial support:* Fellowships with full and partial tuition reimbursements, research assistantships with full and partial tuition reimbursements, teaching assistantships with full and partial tuition reimbursements, career-related internships or fieldwork, Federal Work-Study, institutionally sponsored loans, scholarships/grants, traineeships, tuition waivers (full and partial), and unspecified assistantships available. Support available to part-time students. Financial award application deadline: 3/1; financial award applicants required to submit FAFSA. In 2008, 18 master's awarded. *Degree program information:* Part-time programs available. Postbaccalaureate distance learning degree programs offered (minimal on-campus study). *Application deadline:* For fall admission, 7/15 priority date for domestic students, 5/15 priority date for international students; for spring admission, 12/1 priority date for domestic students, 10/1 priority date for international students. Applications are processed on a rolling basis. *Application fee:* $30. Electronic applications accepted. *Application Contact:* Dr. Carl A. Fox, Vice Provost for Graduate Education, 406-994-4145, Fax: 406-994-7433, E-mail: gradstudy@montana.edu. *Vice Provost for Graduate Education,* Dr. Carl A. Fox, 406-994-4145, Fax: 406-994-7433, E-mail: gradstudy@montana.edu.

College of Agriculture Students: 30 full-time (15 women), 93 part-time (42 women); includes 1 minority (Asian American or Pacific Islander), 18 international. Average age 28. 80 applicants, 36% accepted, 28 enrolled. *Faculty:* 80 full-time (17 women), 17 part-time/adjunct (5 women). Expenses: Contact institution. *Financial support:* Application deadline: 3/1. In 2008, 26 master's, 9 doctorates awarded. *Degree program information:* Part-time programs available. Postbaccalaureate distance learning degree programs offered (minimal on-campus study). Offers agricultural education (MS); agriculture (MS, PhD); animal and range sciences (MS, PhD); ecology and environmental sciences (PhD); land rehabilitation (interdisciplinary) (MS); land resources and environmental sciences (MS); plant pathology (MS); plant sciences (MS, PhD); veterinary molecular biology (MS, PhD). *Application deadline:* For fall admission, 7/15 priority date for domestic students, 5/15 priority date for international students; for spring admission, 12/1 priority date for domestic students, 10/1 priority date for international students. Applications are processed on a rolling basis. *Application fee:* $30. Electronic applications accepted. *Application Contact:* Dr. Carl A. Fox, Vice Provost for Graduate Education, 406-994-4145, Fax: 406-994-7433, E-mail: gradstudy@montana.edu. *Dean,* Dr. Jeffrey S. Jacobsen, 406-994-7060, Fax: 406-994-3933, E-mail: jefj@montana.edu.

College of Arts and Architecture Students: 81 full-time (29 women), 96 part-time (30 women); includes 4 minority (1 American Indian/Alaska Native, 2 Asian Americans or Pacific Islanders, 1 Hispanic American), 7 international. Average age 34. 222 applicants, 68% accepted, 128 enrolled. *Faculty:* 65 full-time (18 women), 26 part-time/adjunct (14 women). Expenses: Contact institution. *Financial support:* Application deadline: 3/1. In 2008, 72 master's awarded. *Degree program information:* Part-time programs available. Offers architecture (M Arch); art (MFA); arts and architecture (M Arch, MFA); science and natural history filmmaking (MFA). *Application deadline:* For fall admission, 7/15 priority date for domestic students, 5/15 priority date for international students; for spring admission, 12/1 priority date for domestic students, 10/1 priority date for international students. Applications are processed on a rolling basis. *Application fee:* $30. Electronic applications accepted. *Application Contact:* Dr. Carl A. Fox, Vice Provost for Graduate Education, 406-994-4145, Fax: 406-994-7433, E-mail: gradstudy@montana.edu. *Dean,* Susan Agre-Kippenhan, 406-994-4405, Fax: 406-994-3680, E-mail: susanak@montana.edu.

College of Business Students: 46 full-time (27 women), 4 part-time (3 women). Average age 26. 26 applicants, 69% accepted, 15 enrolled. *Faculty:* 28 full-time (12 women), 22 part-time/adjunct (10 women). Expenses: Contact institution. *Financial support:* In 2008–09, 9 students received support, including 6 teaching assistantships with partial tuition reimbursements available (averaging $1,950 per year); career-related internships or fieldwork also available. Financial award application deadline: 3/1; financial award applicants required to submit FAFSA. In 2008, 37 master's awarded. *Degree program information:* Part-time programs available. Offers professional accountancy (MP Ac). *Application deadline:* For fall admission, 7/15 priority date for domestic students, 5/15 priority date for international students; for spring admission, 12/1 priority date for domestic students, 10/1 priority date for international students. Applications are processed on a rolling basis. *Application fee:* $30. Electronic applications accepted. *Application Contact:* Dr. Carl A. Fox, Vice Provost for Graduate Education, 406-994-4145, Fax: 406-994-7433, E-mail: gradstudy@montana.edu. *Dean,* Dr. Dan Moshavi, 406-994-4423, Fax: 406-994-6206, E-mail: dmoshavi@montana.edu.

College of Education, Health, and Human Development Students: 75 full-time (59 women), 436 part-time (273 women); includes 47 minority (1 African American, 45 American Indian/Alaska Native, 1 Asian American or Pacific Islander), 2 international. Average age 36. 83 applicants, 35% accepted, 37 enrolled. *Faculty:* 48 full-time (31 women), 32 part-time/adjunct (24 women). Expenses: Contact institution. *Financial support:* Application deadline: 3/1. In 2008, 91 master's, 6 doctorates awarded. *Degree program information:* Part-time programs available. Postbaccalaureate distance learning degree programs offered (minimal on-campus study). Offers adult and higher education (Ed D); curriculum and instruction (Ed D, Ed S); education (M Ed); education, health, and human development (M Ed, MS, Ed D, Ed S); educational leadership (Ed D, Ed S); health and human development (MS). *Application deadline:* For fall admission, 7/15 priority date for domestic students, 5/15 priority date for international students; for spring admission, 12/1 priority date for domestic students, 10/1 priority date for international students. Applications are processed on a rolling basis. *Application fee:* $30. Electronic applications accepted. *Application Contact:* Dr. Carl A. Fox, Vice Provost for Graduate Education, 406-994-4145, Fax: 406-994-7433, E-mail: gradstudy@montana.edu. *Dean,* Larry Baker, 406-994-6752, Fax: 406-994-1854, E-mail: lbaker@montana.edu.

College of Engineering Students: 63 full-time (11 women), 104 part-time (21 women); includes 6 minority (2 American Indian/Alaska Native, 4 Asian Americans or Pacific Islanders), 44 international. Average age 27. 228 applicants, 33% accepted, 42 enrolled. *Faculty:* 66 full-time (5 women), 13 part-time/adjunct (4 women). Expenses: Contact institution. *Financial support:* Application deadline: 3/1. In 2008, 49 master's, 11 doctorates awarded. *Degree program information:* Part-time programs available. Offers chemical engineering (MS); CHMYical engineering (MS); civil engineering (MS); computer science (MS, PhD); construction engineering management (MCEM); electrical engineering (MS); engineering (PhD); environmental engineering (MS); industrial and management engineering (MS); mechanical engineering (MS). *Application deadline:* For fall admission, 7/15 priority date for domestic students, 5/15 priority date for international students; for spring admission, 12/1 priority date for domestic students, 10/1 priority date for international students. Applications are processed on a rolling basis. *Application fee:* $30. Electronic applications accepted. *Application Contact:* Dr. Carl A. Fox, Vice Provost for Graduate Education, 406-994-4145, Fax: 406-994-7433, E-mail: gradstudy@montana.edu. *Dean,* Dr. Robert Marley, 406-994-2272, Fax: 406-994-6665, E-mail: rmarley@coe.montana.edu.

College of Letters and Science Students: 114 full-time (42 women), 338 part-time (154 women); includes 17 minority (1 African American, 8 American Indian/Alaska Native, 4 Asian Americans or Pacific Islanders, 4 Hispanic Americans), 60 international. Average age 30. 352 applicants, 44% accepted, 116 enrolled. *Faculty:* 170 full-time (51 women), 66 part-time/adjunct (35 women). Expenses: Contact institution. *Financial support:* Application deadline: 3/1. In 2008, 98 master's, 27 doctorates awarded. *Degree program information:* Part-time programs available. Postbaccalaureate distance learning degree programs offered (minimal on-campus study). Offers biochemistry (MS, PhD); biological sciences (MS, PhD); chemistry (MS, PhD); earth sciences (MS, PhD); ecological and environmental statistics (MS); ecology and environmental sciences (PhD); English (MA); fish and wildlife biology (PhD); fish and wildlife management (MS); history (MA, PhD); letters and science (MA, MPA, MS, PhD); mathematics (MS, PhD); microbiology (MS, PhD); Native American studies (MA); neuroscience (MS, PhD); physics (MS, PhD); psychology (MS); public administration (MPA); statistics (MS, PhD). *Application deadline:* For fall admission, 7/15 priority date for domestic students, 5/15 priority date for international students; for spring admission, 12/1 priority date for domestic students, 10/1 priority date for international students. Applications are processed on a rolling basis. *Application fee:* $30. Electronic applications accepted. *Application Contact:* Dr. Carl A. Fox, Vice Provost for Graduate Education, 406-994-4145,

Fax: 406-994-7433, E-mail: gradstudy@montana.edu. *Interim Dean*, Dr. Paula Lutz, 406-994-4288, Fax: 406-994-6879, E-mail: plutz@montana.edu.

College of Nursing Students: 40 full-time (39 women), 14 part-time (all women); includes 4 minority (3 American Indian/Alaska Native, 1 Hispanic American). Average age 38. 35 applicants, 57% accepted, 15 enrolled. *Faculty:* 51 full-time (48 women), 33 part-time/adjunct (all women). Expenses: Contact institution. *Financial support:* In 2008–09, 25 students received support, including 8 teaching assistantships with partial tuition reimbursements available (averaging $7,050 per year); institutionally sponsored loans, scholarships/grants, traineeships, and tuition waivers (partial) also available. Financial award application deadline: 3/1; financial award applicants required to submit FAFSA. In 2008, 12 master's awarded. *Degree program information:* Part-time programs available. Postbaccalaureate distance learning degree programs offered (no on-campus study). Offers clinical nurse specialist (CNS) (MN, Post-Master's Certificate); family nurse practitioner (MN, Post-Master's Certificate); nursing education (Certificate). *Application deadline:* For fall admission, 7/15 priority date for domestic students, 5/15 priority date for international students; for spring admission, 12/1 priority date for domestic students, 10/1 priority date for international students. Applications are processed on a rolling basis. *Application fee:* $30. Electronic applications accepted. *Application Contact:* Dr. Carl A. Fox, Vice Provost for Graduate Education, 406-994-4145, Fax: 406-994-7433, E-mail: gradstudy@montana.edu. *Dean*, Dr. Elizabeth Kinion, 406-994-2725, Fax: 406-994-6020, E-mail: ekinion@montana.edu.

MONTANA STATE UNIVERSITY–BILLINGS, Billings, MT 59101-0298

General Information State-supported, coed, comprehensive institution. *Graduate housing:* Rooms and/or apartments available on a first-come, first-served basis to single and married students.

GRADUATE UNITS

College of Allied Health Professions *Degree program information:* Part-time and evening/weekend programs available. Postbaccalaureate distance learning degree programs offered (minimal on-campus study). Offers allied health professions (MHA, MS, MSRC); athletic training (MS); health administration (MHA); rehabilitation and human services (MSRC); sport management (MS).

College of Arts and Sciences *Degree program information:* Part-time programs available. Postbaccalaureate distance learning degree programs offered. Offers arts and sciences (MPA, MS); psychology (MS); public administration (MPA); public relations (MS).

College of Education *Degree program information:* Part-time programs available. Postbaccalaureate distance learning degree programs offered (minimal on-campus study). Offers advanced studies (MS Sp Ed); early childhood education (M Ed); education (M Ed, MS Sp Ed, Certificate); educational technology (M Ed); general curriculum (M Ed); interdisciplinary studies (M Ed); reading (M Ed); school counseling (M Ed); secondary education (M Ed); special education (MS Sp Ed); special education generalist (MS Sp Ed); teaching (Certificate).

MONTANA STATE UNIVERSITY–NORTHERN, Havre, MT 59501-7751

General Information State-supported, coed, comprehensive institution. *Graduate housing:* Rooms and/or apartments available on a first-come, first-served basis to single students and available to married students. Housing application deadline: 8/22.

GRADUATE UNITS

College of Education and Graduate Programs *Degree program information:* Part-time and evening/weekend programs available. Postbaccalaureate distance learning degree programs offered (minimal on-campus study). Offers counselor education (M Ed); learning development (M Ed). Electronic applications accepted.

MONTANA TECH OF THE UNIVERSITY OF MONTANA, Butte, MT 59701-8997

General Information State-supported, coed, comprehensive institution. *Enrollment:* 2,402 graduate, professional, and undergraduate students; 51 full-time matriculated graduate/professional students (18 women), 58 part-time matriculated graduate/professional students (28 women). *Enrollment by degree level:* 109 master's. *Graduate faculty:* 121 full-time (41 women), 61 part-time/adjunct (30 women). Tuition, state resident: full-time $4919; part-time $306 per credit. Tuition, nonresident: full-time $14,141; part-time $819 per credit. *Graduate housing:* Rooms and/or apartments guaranteed to single students and available on a first-come, first-served basis to married students. Housing application deadline: 8/22. *Student services:* Campus employment opportunities, campus safety program, career counseling, exercise/wellness program, grant writing training, international student services, low-cost health insurance, multicultural affairs office, services for students with disabilities. *Library facilities:* Montana Tech Library. *Online resources:* library catalog, web page. *Collection:* 173,644 titles, 28,747 serial subscriptions, 3,962 audiovisual materials. *Research affiliation:* Newmont Mining Inc. USA (Mining and Mineral Processing), Stillwater Mining (Mineral production and training), NorthWestern Energy (Electric efficiency), Edison Welding Institute (Fuel Cell Design), Montana Resources Inc. (Mine Reclamation and Revegetation), QualTech Inc (Battery Monitor technology).

Computer facilities: 491 computers available on campus for general student use. A campuswide network can be accessed from student residence rooms and from off campus. Online class registration is available. *Web address:* http://www.mtech.edu/.

General Application Contact: Cindy Dunstan, Administrator, Graduate School, 406-496-4304, Fax: 406-496-4710, E-mail: cdunstan@mtech.edu.

GRADUATE UNITS

Graduate School Students: 51 full-time (18 women), 58 part-time (28 women); includes 8 minority (3 African Americans, 5 American Indian/Alaska Native), 18 international. 86 applicants, 48% accepted, 34 enrolled. *Faculty:* 121 full-time (41 women), 61 part-time/adjunct (30 women). Expenses: Contact institution. *Financial support:* In 2008–09, 60 students received support, including 43 teaching assistantships with partial tuition reimbursements available (averaging $5,746 per year); research assistantships with full tuition reimbursements available, career-related internships or fieldwork, tuition waivers (full and partial), and unspecified assistantships also available. Financial award application deadline: 4/1; financial award applicants required to submit FAFSA. In 2008, 30 master's awarded. *Degree program information:* Part-time and evening/weekend programs available. Postbaccalaureate distance learning degree programs offered (no on-campus study). Offers electrical engineering (MS); environmental engineering (MS); general engineering (MS); geochemistry (MS); geological engineering (MS); geology (MS); geophysical engineering (MS); hydrogeological engineering (MS); hydrogeology (MS); industrial hygiene (MS); interdisciplinary studies (MS); metallurgical/mineral processing engineering (MS); mining engineering (MS); petroleum engineering (MS); project engineering and management (MPEM); technical communication (MS). *Application deadline:* For fall admission, 4/1 priority date for domestic students, 3/1 priority date for international students; for spring admission, 10/1 priority date for domestic students, 7/1 priority date for international students. Applications are processed on a rolling basis. *Application fee:* $30. Electronic applications accepted. *Application Contact:* Cindy Dunstan, Administrator, Graduate School, 406-496-4304, Fax: 406-496-4710, E-mail: cdunstan@mtech.edu. *Associate Vice Chancellor, Research and Graduate Studies*, Dr. Joseph Figueira, 406-496-4102, Fax: 406-496-4334.

MONTCLAIR STATE UNIVERSITY, Montclair, NJ 07043-1624

General Information State-supported, coed, comprehensive institution. CGS member. *Enrollment:* 17,475 graduate, professional, and undergraduate students; 738 full-time matriculated graduate/professional students (521 women), 1,758 part-time matriculated graduate/professional students (1,202 women). *Enrollment by degree level:* 2,417 master's, 79 doctoral. *Graduate faculty:* 524 full-time (248 women), 873 part-time/adjunct (485 women). *Graduate housing:* Room and/or apartments available on a first-come, first-served basis to single students. Housing application deadline: 3/1. *Student services:* Campus employment opportunities, campus safety program, career counseling, child daycare facilities, exercise/wellness program, free psychological counseling, international student services, low-cost health insurance, services for students with disabilities, teacher training. *Library facilities:* Sprague Library. *Online resources:* library catalog, web page, access to other libraries' catalogs. *Collection:* 495,462 titles, 3,094 serial subscriptions, 14,184 audiovisual materials. *Research affiliation:* Spencer Foundation (education improvement), The International Society for Optical Engineering (optics and photonics), Deafness Research Foundation (heating science).

Computer facilities: Computer purchase and lease plans are available. 218 computers available on campus for general student use. A campuswide network can be accessed from student residence rooms and from off campus. Online class registration is available. *Web address:* http://www.montclair.edu/.

General Application Contact: Ben Enoma, Director of the Office of Graduate Admissions and Support Services, 973-655-5147, Fax: 973-655-7869, E-mail: graduate.school@montclair.edu.

GRADUATE UNITS

The Office of Graduate Admissions and Support Services Students: 739 full-time (521 women), 1,758 part-time (1,202 women); includes 383 minority (179 African Americans, 2 American Indian/Alaska Native, 97 Asian Americans or Pacific Islanders, 105 Hispanic Americans), 118 international. Average age 31. 1,214 applicants, 52% accepted, 467 enrolled. *Faculty:* 524 full-time (248 women), 873 part-time/adjunct (485 women). Expenses: Contact institution. *Financial support:* In 2008–09, 140 research assistantships with full tuition reimbursements (averaging $7,000 per year) were awarded; Federal Work-Study, scholarships/grants, and unspecified assistantships also available. Support available to part-time students. Financial award application deadline: 3/1; financial award applicants required to submit FAFSA. In 2008, 836 master's, 8 doctorates, 66 other advanced degrees awarded. *Degree program information:* Part-time and evening/weekend programs available. *Application deadline:* For fall admission, 6/1 for international students; for spring admission, 10/1 for international students. Applications are processed on a rolling basis. *Application fee:* $60. Electronic applications accepted. *Application Contact:* Amy Aiello, Associate Director of Admissions, 973-655-5147, Fax: 973-655-7869, E-mail: graduate.school@montclair.edu. *Vice Provost for Academic Affairs*, Dr. Joan Ficke, 973-655-5147, Fax: 973-655-7869, E-mail: graduate.school@montclair.edu.

College of Education and Human Services Students: 356 full-time (269 women), 934 part-time (728 women); includes 177 minority (92 African Americans, 29 Asian Americans or Pacific Islanders, 56 Hispanic Americans), 20 international. Average age 31. 346 applicants, 62% accepted, 176 enrolled. *Faculty:* 84 full-time (56 women), 169 part-time/adjunct (116 women). Expenses: Contact institution. *Financial support:* In 2008–09, 72 research assistantships with full tuition reimbursements (averaging $7,000 per year) were awarded; Federal Work-Study, scholarships/grants, and unspecified assistantships also available. Support available to part-time students. Financial award application deadline: 3/1; financial award applicants required to submit FAFSA. In 2008, 456 master's, 1 doctorate, 14 other advanced degrees awarded. *Degree program information:* Part-time and evening/weekend programs available. Offers administration and supervision (MA); advanced counseling (Certificate); American Dietetic Association (Certificate); counseling and guidance (MA); counselor education (PhD); critical thinking (M Ed); early childhood education and teaching students with disabilities (MAT); early childhood special education (M Ed, Certificate); early childhood/elementary education (M Ed); education (M Ed); education and human services (M Ed, MA, MAT, MS, Ed D, PhD, Certificate); educational technology (M Ed); elementary education with disabilities (MAT); elementary school teacher (Certificate); food safety instructor (Certificate); health and physical education (Certificate); health education (MA); learning disabilities (Certificate); learning disabled teacher consultant (Certificate); mathematics education (Ed D); nutrition and exercise science (MS, Certificate); nutrition and food science (MS); philosophy for children (M Ed, Ed D, Certificate); physical education (MA, Certificate); principal (Certificate); reading (MA, Certificate); reading specialist (Certificate); school administrator (Certificate); school business administrator (Certificate); school counselor (Certificate); school library media specialist (Certificate); substance awareness coordinator (Certificate); teaching (MAT, Certificate). *Application deadline:* For fall admission, 6/1 for international students; for spring admission, 10/1 for international students. Applications are processed on a rolling basis. *Application fee:* $60. Electronic applications accepted. *Application Contact:* Amy Aiello, Associate Director of Admissions. *Dean*, Dr. Ada Beth Cutler, 973-655-5167, E-mail: cutler@mail.montclair.edu.

College of Humanities and Social Sciences Students: 153 full-time (125 women), 233 part-time (182 women); includes 66 minority (34 African Americans, 2 American Indian/Alaska Native, 15 Asian Americans or Pacific Islanders, 15 Hispanic Americans), 13 international. Average age 31. 438 applicants, 35% accepted, 101 enrolled. *Faculty:* 144 full-time (80 women), 219 part-time/adjunct (138 women). Expenses: Contact institution. *Financial support:* In 2008–09, 32 research assistantships with full tuition reimbursements (averaging $7,000 per year) were awarded; Federal Work-Study, scholarships/grants, and unspecified assistantships also available. Support available to part-time students. Financial award application deadline: 3/1; financial award applicants required to submit FAFSA. In 2008, 123 master's, 4 doctorates, 30 other advanced degrees awarded. *Degree program information:* Part-time and evening/weekend programs available. Offers applied linguistics (MA); applied sociology (MA); audiology (Sc D); child advocacy (MA, Certificate); conflict management in the workplace (Certificate); dispute resolution (MA); educational psychology (MA); English (MA, Certificate); French (MA, Certificate); governance, compliance and regulation (MA); humanities and social sciences (MA, Sc D, Certificate); intellectual property (MA); Italian (Certificate); law and governance (MA); legal management, information and technology (MA); paralegal studies (Certificate); psychology (MA, Certificate); public child welfare (MA); school psychologist (Certificate); social sciences (MA); social studies (Certificate); Spanish (MA, Certificate); speech/language pathology (MA); teacher of English as a second language (Certificate); translating and interpreting Spanish (Certificate). *Application deadline:* For fall admission, 6/1 for international students; for spring admission, 10/1 for international students. Applications are processed on a rolling basis. *Application fee:* $60. Electronic applications accepted. *Application Contact:* Amy Aiello, Associate Director of Admissions, 973-655-5147, Fax: 973-655-7869, E-mail: graduate.school@montclair.edu. *Dean*, Dr. Morrissey, 973-655-4000.

College of Science and Mathematics Students: 92 full-time (44 women), 221 part-time (120 women); includes 48 minority (18 African Americans, 14 Asian Americans or Pacific Islanders, 16 Hispanic Americans), 36 international. Average age 31. 119 applicants, 71% accepted, 56 enrolled. *Faculty:* 90 full-time (25 women), 95 part-time/adjunct (43 women). Expenses: Contact institution. *Financial support:* In 2008–09, 36 research assistantships with full tuition reimbursements were awarded; Federal Work-Study, scholarships/grants, and unspecified assistantships also available. Support available to part-time students. Financial award application deadline: 3/1; financial award applicants required to submit FAFSA. In 2008, 95 master's, 3 doctorates, 14 other advanced degrees awarded. *Degree program information:* Part-time and evening/weekend programs available. Offers applied mathematics (MS); applied statistics (MS); biology (MS); chemical business (MS); chemistry (MS); CISCO (Certificate); earth science (Certificate); environmental management (MA, D Env M, PhD); environmental studies (MS); geographic information science (Certificate); geoscience (MS, Certificate); informatics (MS); math pedagogy (Ed D); mathematics (MS); molecular biology (Certificate); object oriented computing (Certificate); physical science (Certificate); science and mathematics (MA, MS, D Env M, Ed D, PhD, Certificate); teaching middle grades math (MS, Certificate). *Application deadline:* For fall admission, 6/1 for international students; for spring admission, 10/1 for international students. Applications are processed on a rolling basis. *Application fee:* $60. Electronic applications accepted. *Application Contact:* Amy Aiello, Associate Director of Admissions, 973-655-5147, Fax: 973-655-7869, E-mail: graduate.school@montclair.edu. *Dean*, Dr. Robert Prezant, 973-655-5108.

School of Business Students: 81 full-time (43 women), 274 part-time (104 women); includes 71 minority (22 African Americans, 36 Asian Americans or Pacific Islanders, 13 Hispanic Americans), 37 international. Average age 30. 213 applicants, 53% accepted, 86 enrolled.

Montclair State University (continued)

Faculty: 75 full-time (24 women), 42 part-time/adjunct (9 women). Expenses: Contact institution. *Financial support:* In 2008–09, 28 students received support, including 17 research assistantships with full tuition reimbursements available (averaging $7,000 per year); Federal Work-Study, scholarships/grants, and unspecified assistantships also available. Support available to part-time students. Financial award application deadline: 3/1; financial award applicants required to submit FAFSA. In 2008, 116 master's, 1 other advanced degree awarded. *Degree program information:* Part-time and evening/weekend programs available. Offers accounting (MBA, Certificate); business (MBA, Certificate); business economics (MBA); finance (MBA, Certificate); international business (MBA, Certificate); management (MBA, Certificate); management information systems (MBA, Certificate); marketing (Certificate). *Application deadline:* For fall admission, 6/1 for international students; for spring admission, 10/1 for international students. Applications are processed on a rolling basis. *Application fee:* $60. Electronic applications accepted. *Application Contact:* Amy Aiello, Associate Director of Admissions, 973-655-5147, Fax: 973-655-7869, E-mail: graduate.school@montclair.edu. *Dean,* Dr. William Turner, 973-655-4304, E-mail: oppenheima@mail.montclair.edu.

School of the Arts Students: 56 full-time (40 women), 96 part-time (68 women); includes 21 minority (13 African Americans, 3 Asian Americans or Pacific Islanders, 5 Hispanic Americans), 12 international. Average age 32. 98 applicants, 61% accepted, 46 enrolled. *Faculty:* 67 full-time (29 women), 211 part-time/adjunct (105 women). Expenses: Contact institution. *Financial support:* In 2008–09, 8 research assistantships with full tuition reimbursements (averaging $7,000 per year) were awarded; Federal Work-Study, scholarships/grants, and unspecified assistantships also available. Support available to part-time students. Financial award application deadline: 3/1; financial award applicants required to submit FAFSA. In 2008, 46 master's, 7 other advanced degrees awarded. *Degree program information:* Part-time and evening/weekend programs available. Offers art education (MA, Certificate); art history (MA); arts (MA, MFA, AD, Certificate); music (AD); music education (MA); music therapy (MA); organizational communication (MA); performance (MA, Certificate); public relations (MA); speech communication (MA); studio arts (MA, MFA); theatre (MA); theory/composition (MA). *Application deadline:* For fall admission, 2/1 for domestic students, 6/1 for international students; for spring admission, 10/1 for international students. Applications are processed on a rolling basis. *Application fee:* $60. Electronic applications accepted. *Application Contact:* Amy Aiello, Associate Director of Admissions, 973-655-5147, Fax: 973-655-7869, E-mail: graduate.school@montclair.edu. *Dean,* Dr. Geoffrey Newman, 973-655-5104, E-mail: newmang@mail.montclair.edu.

See Close-Up on page 951.

MONTEREY INSTITUTE OF INTERNATIONAL STUDIES, Monterey, CA 93940-2691

General Information Independent, coed, graduate-only institution. *Enrollment:* 726 full-time matriculated graduate/professional students (453 women), 78 part-time matriculated graduate/professional students (50 women). *Enrollment by degree level:* 801 master's, 3 other advanced degrees. *Tuition:* Full-time $29,300; part-time $1400 per credit. *Required fees:* $56. *Graduate housing:* On-campus housing not available. *Student services:* Campus employment opportunities, career counseling, exercise/wellness program, international student services, low-cost health insurance, services for students with disabilities, writing training. *Library facilities:* William Tell Coleman Library. *Online resources:* library catalog, web page, access to other libraries' catalogs. *Collection:* 100,579 titles, 559 serial subscriptions.

Computer facilities: 105 computers available on campus for general student use. A campuswide network can be accessed from off campus. *Web address:* http://www.miis.edu/.

General Application Contact: Admissions Office, 831-647-4123, Fax: 831-647-6405, E-mail: admit@miis.edu.

GRADUATE UNITS

Fisher Graduate School of International Business Students: 101 full-time (41 women), 3 part-time (2 women); includes 12 minority (3 African Americans, 4 Asian Americans or Pacific Islanders, 5 Hispanic Americans), 31 international. Average age 27. 120 applicants, 92% accepted, 53 enrolled. Expenses: Contact institution. *Financial support:* In 2008–09, 129 students received support. Career-related internships or fieldwork, Federal Work-Study, institutionally sponsored loans, scholarships/grants, tuition waivers (partial), and unspecified assistantships available. Support available to part-time students. Financial award application deadline: 3/15; financial award applicants required to submit FAFSA. In 2008, 50 master's awarded. Offers international business (MBA). *Application deadline:* For fall admission, 3/15 priority date for domestic students, 3/5 priority date for international students; for spring admission, 10/1 priority date for domestic and international students. Applications are processed on a rolling basis. *Application fee:* $50. Electronic applications accepted. *Application Contact:* 831-647-4123, Fax: 831-647-6405, E-mail: admit@miis.edu. *Dean,* Dr. Ernest J. Scalberg, 831-647-4140, Fax: 831-647-6506, E-mail: fgsib@miis.edu.

Graduate School of International Policy Studies Students: 397 full-time (235 women), 10 part-time (7 women); includes 57 minority (12 African Americans, 2 American Indian/Alaska Native, 23 Asian Americans or Pacific Islanders, 20 Hispanic Americans), 87 international. Average age 27. 469 applicants, 96% accepted, 190 enrolled. Expenses: Contact institution. *Financial support:* In 2008–09, 419 students received support. Career-related internships or fieldwork, Federal Work-Study, institutionally sponsored loans, scholarships/grants, and tuition waivers (partial) available. Support available to part-time students. Financial award application deadline: 3/15; financial award applicants required to submit FAFSA. In 2008, 182 master's awarded. Offers international environmental policy (MA); international management (MPA); international policy studies (MA, MPA); international trade policy (MA). *Application deadline:* For fall admission, 3/15 priority date for domestic and international students; for spring admission, 10/1 priority date for domestic and international students. Applications are processed on a rolling basis. *Application fee:* $50. Electronic applications accepted. *Application Contact:* 831-647-4123, Fax: 831-647-6405, E-mail: admit@miis.edu. *Dean,* Dr. Edward J. Laurance, 831-647-4155, Fax: 831-647-4199, E-mail: gsips@miis.edu.

Graduate School of Language and Educational Linguistics Students: 44 full-time (37 women), 60 part-time (39 women); includes 17 minority (3 African Americans, 12 Asian Americans or Pacific Islanders, 2 Hispanic Americans), 30 international. Average age 35. 67 applicants, 87% accepted, 26 enrolled. Expenses: Contact institution. *Financial support:* In 2008–09, 132 students received support. Career-related internships or fieldwork, Federal Work-Study, institutionally sponsored loans, scholarships/grants, tuition waivers (partial), and unspecified assistantships available. Support available to part-time students. Financial award application deadline: 3/15; financial award applicants required to submit FAFSA. In 2008, 41 master's awarded. Offers language and educational linguistics (MATESOL, MATFL); teaching English to speakers of other languages (MATESOL); teaching foreign language (MATFL). *Application deadline:* For fall admission, 3/15 priority date for domestic and international students; for spring admission, 10/1 priority date for domestic and international students. Applications are processed on a rolling basis. *Application fee:* $50. Electronic applications accepted. *Application Contact:* 831-647-4123, Fax: 831-647-6405, E-mail: admit@miis.edu. *Dean,* Dr. Renee Jourdenais, 831-647-4185, Fax: 831-647-6650, E-mail: gslel@miis.edu.

Graduate School of Translation and Interpretation Students: 184 full-time (140 women), 5 part-time (2 women); includes 32 minority (3 African Americans, 13 Asian Americans or Pacific Islanders, 16 Hispanic Americans), 108 international. Average age 27. 236 applicants, 72% accepted, 122 enrolled. Expenses: Contact institution. *Financial support:* In 2008–09, 177 students received support. Career-related internships or fieldwork, Federal Work-Study, institutionally sponsored loans, scholarships/grants, tuition waivers (partial), and unspecified assistantships available. Support available to part-time students. Financial award application deadline: 3/15; financial award applicants required to submit FAFSA. In 2008, 86 master's awarded. Offers conference interpretation (MA); translation (MA); translation and interpretation (MA); translation and localization management (MA). *Application deadline:* For fall admission, 3/15 priority date for domestic and international students; for spring admission, 10/1 priority date for domestic and international students. Applications are processed on a rolling basis. *Application fee:* $50. Electronic applications accepted. *Application Contact:* 831-647-4123, Fax: 831-647-6405, E-mail: admit@miis.edu. *Dean,* Dr. Chuanyun Bao, 831-647-4170, Fax: 831-647-3560, E-mail: gsti@miis.edu.

MONTREAT COLLEGE, Montreat, NC 28757-1267

General Information Independent-religious, coed, comprehensive institution. *Graduate housing:* On-campus housing not available.

GRADUATE UNITS

School of Professional and Adult Studies *Degree program information:* Evening/weekend programs available. Postbaccalaureate distance learning degree programs offered. Offers business administration (MBA); K-6 education (MA Ed).

MOODY BIBLE INSTITUTE, Chicago, IL 60610-3284

General Information Independent-religious, coed, comprehensive institution. *Graduate housing:* Rooms and/or apartments guaranteed to single students and available on a first-come, first-served basis to married students. Housing application deadline: 6/1.

GRADUATE UNITS

Graduate School *Degree program information:* Part-time programs available. Offers biblical studies (MABS, Graduate Certificate); intercultural studies (MAIS, Graduate Certificate); ministry (M Div, M Min); spiritual formation and discipleship (MASF, Graduate Certificate); urban studies (MA, Graduate Certificate).

MORAVIAN COLLEGE, Bethlehem, PA 18018-6650

General Information Independent-religious, coed, comprehensive institution. *Enrollment:* 5 full-time matriculated graduate/professional students (2 women), 175 part-time matriculated graduate/professional students (116 women). *Enrollment by degree level:* 180 master's. *Graduate housing:* On-campus housing not available. *Student services:* Career counseling, international student services, multicultural affairs office, services for students with disabilities, teacher training, writing training. *Library facilities:* Reeves Library. *Online resources:* library catalog, web page, access to other libraries' catalogs. *Collection:* 260,363 titles, 3,274 serial subscriptions, 4,740 audiovisual materials.

Computer facilities: Computer purchase and lease plans are available. 263 computers available on campus for general student use. A campuswide network can be accessed from student residence rooms and from off campus. *Web address:* http://www.moravian.edu/.

General Application Contact: Dr. William A. Kleintop, Associate Dean for Business and Management Programs, 610-861-1400, Fax: 610-861-1400, E-mail: comenius@moravian.edu.

GRADUATE UNITS

The Moravian College Comenius Center Students: 5 full-time (2 women), 175 part-time (116 women). Expenses: Contact institution. In 2008, 37 master's awarded. *Degree program information:* Part-time and evening/weekend programs available. Offers business and management (MBA, MSHRM); clinical nurse leader (MSN); general management (MBA); health care management (MBA); leadership (MSHRM); nurse educator (MSN); supply chain management (MBA); training and development (MSHRM). *Application deadline:* Applications are processed on a rolling basis. *Application Contact:* Dr. Florence Kimball, Dean, Continuing and Graduate Studies, 610-861-1400, Fax: 610-861-1466, E-mail: comenius@moravian.edu. *Dean, Continuing and Graduate Studies,* Dr. Florence Kimball, 610-861-1400, Fax: 610-861-1466, E-mail: comenius@moravian.edu.

MORAVIAN THEOLOGICAL SEMINARY, Bethlehem, PA 18018-6614

General Information Independent-religious, coed, graduate-only institution. *Graduate housing:* Rooms and/or apartments available to single and married students. Housing application deadline: 2/15.

GRADUATE UNITS

Graduate and Professional Programs *Degree program information:* Part-time programs available. Offers theology (M Div, MAPC, MATS).

MOREHEAD STATE UNIVERSITY, Morehead, KY 40351

General Information State-supported, coed, comprehensive institution. *Enrollment:* 8,981 graduate, professional, and undergraduate students; 309 full-time matriculated graduate/professional students (190 women), 941 part-time matriculated graduate/professional students (630 women). *Enrollment by degree level:* 1,217 master's, 33 other advanced degrees. *Graduate faculty:* 151 full-time (57 women), 15 part-time/adjunct (5 women). Tuition, state resident: full-time $6084; part-time $338 per credit hour. Tuition, nonresident: full-time $15,804; part-time $878 per credit hour. *Graduate housing:* Rooms and/or apartments available on a first-come, first-served basis to single and married students. Typical cost: $5852 (including board) for single students. Housing application deadline: 8/1. *Student services:* Campus employment opportunities, campus safety program, career counseling, child daycare facilities, exercise/wellness program, free psychological counseling, grant writing training, international student services, low-cost health insurance, multicultural affairs office, services for students with disabilities, teacher training, writing training. *Library facilities:* Camden Carroll Library. *Online resources:* library catalog, web page. *Collection:* 529,130 titles, 2,006 serial subscriptions, 26,347 audiovisual materials.

Computer facilities: Computer purchase and lease plans are available. 2,045 computers available on campus for general student use. A campuswide network can be accessed from student residence rooms and from off campus. Online class registration is available. *Web address:* http://www.moreheadstate.edu/.

General Application Contact: Michelle Barber, Graduate Admissions Counselor, 606-783-2039, Fax: 606-783-5061, E-mail: m.barber@moreheadstate.edu.

GRADUATE UNITS

Graduate Programs Students: 309 full-time (190 women), 941 part-time (630 women); includes 68 minority (44 African Americans, 3 American Indian/Alaska Native, 9 Asian Americans or Pacific Islanders, 12 Hispanic Americans), 21 international. Average age 32. 834 applicants, 66% accepted, 359 enrolled. *Faculty:* 151 full-time (57 women), 15 part-time/adjunct (5 women). Expenses: Contact institution. *Financial support:* In 2008–09, 28 research assistantships (averaging $6,000 per year), 57 teaching assistantships (averaging $6,000 per year) were awarded; career-related internships or fieldwork, Federal Work-Study, and unspecified assistantships also available. Financial award application deadline: 4/1; financial award applicants required to submit FAFSA. In 2008, 386 master's, 2 other advanced degrees awarded. *Degree program information:* Part-time and evening/weekend programs available. Postbaccalaureate distance learning degree programs offered (minimal on-campus study). *Application deadline:* For fall admission, 7/1 priority date for domestic and international students; for spring admission, 12/1 priority date for domestic and international students. Applications are processed on a rolling basis. *Application fee:* $30 ($55 for international students). Electronic applications accepted. *Application Contact:* Michelle Barber, Graduate Admissions Counselor, 606-783-2039, Fax: 606-783-5061, E-mail: m.barber@moreheadstate.edu. *Associate Vice President for Graduate and Undergraduate Programs,* Susan Maxey, 606-783-2004, Fax: 606-783-5061, E-mail: d.abell@moreheadstate.edu.

Caudill College of Humanities Students: 53 full-time (31 women), 82 part-time (58 women); includes 9 minority (7 African Americans, 1 Asian American or Pacific Islander, 1 Hispanic American), 5 international. Average age 32. 85 applicants, 74% accepted, 51 enrolled. *Faculty:* 52 full-time (15 women), 6 part-time/adjunct (2 women). Expenses: Contact institution. *Financial support:* In 2008–09, 31 teaching assistantships (averaging $6,000 per year) were awarded; career-related internships or fieldwork, Federal Work-Study, and unspecified assistantships also available. Financial award application deadline: 4/1; financial award applicants required to submit FAFSA. In 2008, 33 master's awarded. *Degree program information:* Part-time and evening/weekend programs available. Postbaccalaureate distance learning degree programs offered. Offers art education (MA); communication (MA); criminology (MA); English (MA); general sociology (MA); gerontology (MA); humanities (MA, MM); music education (MM); music performance (MM); studio art (MA). *Application deadline:* For fall admission, 8/1 priority date for domestic and international students; for spring admission, 12/1 priority date for domestic and international students. Applications are processed on a rolling basis. *Application fee:* $30 ($55 for international students). Electronic applications accepted. *Application Contact:* Michelle Barber, Graduate Admissions Counselor, 606-783-2039, Fax: 606-783-5061, E-mail: m.barber@moreheadstate.edu. *Interim Dean*, Dr. Scott McBride, 606-783-2650, Fax: 606-783-5046, E-mail: s.mcbride@moreheadstate.edu.

College of Business Students: 34 full-time (19 women), 170 part-time (89 women); includes 21 minority (11 African Americans, 7 Asian Americans or Pacific Islanders, 3 Hispanic Americans), 5 international. Average age 32. 101 applicants, 62% accepted, 58 enrolled. *Faculty:* 21 full-time (7 women). Expenses: Contact institution. *Financial support:* In 2008–09, 6 teaching assistantships (averaging $6,000 per year) were awarded; career-related internships or fieldwork, Federal Work-Study, and unspecified assistantships also available. Financial award application deadline: 4/1; financial award applicants required to submit FAFSA. In 2008, 56 master's awarded. *Degree program information:* Part-time and evening/weekend programs available. Postbaccalaureate distance learning degree programs offered (minimal on-campus study). Offers business (MBA, MSIS); information systems (MSIS). *Application deadline:* For fall admission, 8/1 for domestic and international students; for spring admission, 12/1 for domestic and international students. Applications are processed on a rolling basis. *Application fee:* $30 ($55 for international students). Electronic applications accepted. *Application Contact:* Michelle Barber, Graduate Admissions Counselor, 606-783-2039, Fax: 606-783-5061, E-mail: m.barber@moreheadstate.edu. *Dean*, Dr. Robert L. Albert, 606-783-2174, Fax: 606-783-5025, E-mail: r.albert@moreheadstate.edu.

College of Education Students: 158 full-time (105 women), 647 part-time (462 women); includes 34 minority (22 African Americans, 3 American Indian/Alaska Native, 1 Asian American or Pacific Islander, 8 Hispanic Americans), 2 international. Average age 33. 488 applicants, 69% accepted, 221 enrolled. *Faculty:* 46 full-time (26 women), 8 part-time/adjunct (3 women). Expenses: Contact institution. *Financial support:* In 2008–09, 6 teaching assistantships (averaging $6,000 per year) were awarded; research assistantships, career-related internships or fieldwork, Federal Work-Study, and unspecified assistantships also available. Financial award application deadline: 4/1; financial award applicants required to submit FAFSA. In 2008, 258 master's, 5 other advanced degrees awarded. *Degree program information:* Part-time and evening/weekend programs available. Offers adult and higher education (MA, Ed S); counseling (MA Ed, Ed S); curriculum and instruction (Ed S); education (MA, MA Ed, MAT, Ed S); elementary education (MA Ed); exercise physiology (MA); health and physical education (MA); instructional leadership (Ed S); school administration (MA); secondary education (MA Ed); special education (MA Ed); sports management (MA); teaching (MAT). *Application deadline:* For fall admission, 8/1 priority date for domestic and international students; for spring admission, 12/1 priority date for domestic and international students. Applications are processed on a rolling basis. *Application fee:* $30 ($55 for international students). Electronic applications accepted. *Application Contact:* Michelle Barber, Graduate Admissions Counselor, 606-783-2039, Fax: 606-783-5061, E-mail: m.barber@moreheadstate.edu. *Dean*, Dr. Cathy Gunn, 606-783-2040, Fax: 606-783-5029, E-mail: c.gunn@moreheadstate.edu.

College of Science and Technology Students: 46 full-time (26 women), 35 part-time (15 women); includes 1 minority (African American), 9 international. Average age 30. 45 applicants, 60% accepted, 19 enrolled. *Faculty:* 30 full-time (8 women). Expenses: Contact institution. *Financial support:* In 2008–09, 28 research assistantships (averaging $6,000 per year), 4 teaching assistantships (averaging $6,000 per year) were awarded; career-related internships or fieldwork and Federal Work-Study also available. Financial award application deadline: 4/1; financial award applicants required to submit FAFSA. In 2008, 27 master's awarded. *Degree program information:* Part-time and evening/weekend programs available. Offers biology (MS); clinical psychology (MS); counseling psychology (MS); experimental/general psychology (MS); industrial technology (MS); regional analysis and public policy (MS); science and technology (MS). *Application deadline:* For fall admission, 8/1 priority date for domestic and international students; for spring admission, 12/1 priority date for domestic and international students. Applications are processed on a rolling basis. *Application fee:* $30 ($55 for international students). Electronic applications accepted. *Application Contact:* Michelle Barber, Graduate Admissions Counselor, 606-783-2039, Fax: 606-783-5061, E-mail: m.barber@moreheadstate.edu. *Dean*, Dr. Gerald DeMoss, 606-783-2158, Fax: 606-783-5039, E-mail: g.demoss@moreheadstate.edu.

Institute for Regional Analysis and Public Policy Students: 18 full-time (9 women), 7 part-time (6 women); includes 2 minority (both African Americans). Average age 28. 49 applicants, 31% accepted, 10 enrolled. *Faculty:* 2 full-time (1 woman), 1 part-time/adjunct (0 women). Expenses: Contact institution. *Financial support:* In 2008–09, 10 teaching assistantships (averaging $6,000 per year) were awarded. In 2008, 6 master's awarded. Offers public administration (MPA). *Application deadline:* For fall admission, 8/1 priority date for domestic and international students; for spring admission, 12/1 priority date for domestic and international students. Applications are processed on a rolling basis. *Application fee:* $30 ($55 for international students). Electronic applications accepted. *Application Contact:* Michelle Barber, Graduate Admissions Counselor, 606-783-2039, Fax: 606-783-5061, E-mail: m.barber@moreheadstate.edu. *Dean*, Dr. David Rudy, 606-783-5419, Fax: 606-783-5092, E-mail: d.rudy@moreheadstate.edu.

MOREHOUSE SCHOOL OF MEDICINE, Atlanta, GA 30310-1495

General Information Independent, coed, graduate-only institution. *Enrollment by degree level:* 216 first professional, 56 master's, 28 doctoral. *Graduate faculty:* 210 full-time (103 women), 32 part-time/adjunct (12 women). *Tuition:* Part-time $425 per credit hour. *Required fees:* $2000 per degree program. Tuition and fees vary according to course load, degree level and program. *Graduate housing:* On-campus housing not available. *Student services:* Campus employment opportunities, career counseling, exercise/wellness program, free psychological counseling, international student services. *Library facilities:* Library plus 1 other. *Online resources:* library catalog. *Collection:* 40,000 titles, 350 serial subscriptions, 490 audiovisual materials. *Research affiliation:* Merck (hypotension), CareStat (renal insufficiency), Wyeth (helicobacter pylori study), Bristol Myers Squibb (pharmacokinetics), Parke-Davis (cardiovascular risk factors), NitroMel, Inc. (heart failure).

Computer facilities: 142 computers available on campus for general student use. A campuswide network can be accessed from off campus. Online class registration is available. *Web address:* http://www.msm.edu/.

General Application Contact: Dr. Sterling Roaf, Director of Admissions, 404-752-1650, Fax: 404-752-1512, E-mail: sroaf@msm.edu.

GRADUATE UNITS

Graduate Programs in Biomedical Sciences Students: 31 full-time (19 women); includes 18 minority (all African Americans). Average age 28. 21 applicants, 38% accepted, 6 enrolled. *Faculty:* 52 full-time (17 women), 7 part-time/adjunct (2 women). Expenses: Contact institution. *Financial support:* Fellowships with full and partial tuition reimbursements, career-related internships or fieldwork, institutionally sponsored loans, scholarships/grants, traineeships, health care benefits, and tuition waivers (full) available. Financial award application deadline: 5/1; financial award applicants required to submit FAFSA. In 2008, 3 degrees awarded. Offers biomedical research (MS); biomedical sciences (PhD); biomedical technology (MS). *Application deadline:* For fall admission, 10/1 for domestic and international students; for spring admission, 2/1 for domestic and international students. *Application fee:* $50. Electronic applications accepted. *Application Contact:* Dr. Sterling Roaf, Director of Admissions, 404-752-1650, Fax: 404-752-1512, E-mail: phdadmissions@msm.edu. *Director*, Dr. Douglas Paulsen, 404-752-1559.

Master of Public Health Program Students: 42 full-time (25 women), 3 part-time (2 women); includes 15 minority (all African Americans). Average age 28. 62 applicants, 48% accepted, 29 enrolled. *Faculty:* 17 full-time (9 women), 10 part-time/adjunct (5 women). Expenses: Contact institution. *Financial support:* In 2008–09, 32 students received support, including 3 research assistantships with partial tuition reimbursements available (averaging $10,000 per year); teaching assistantships, career-related internships or fieldwork, Federal Work-Study, and institutionally sponsored loans also available. Support available to part-time students. Financial award application deadline: 5/1; financial award applicants required to submit FAFSA. In 2008, 10 degrees awarded. *Degree program information:* Part-time programs available. Offers public health (MPH). *Application deadline:* For fall admission, 3/1 for domestic and international students. *Application fee:* $50. Electronic applications accepted. *Application Contact:* Dr. Sterling Roaf, Director of Admissions, 404-752-1650, Fax: 404-752-1512, E-mail: mphadmissions@msm.edu. *Director*, Dr. Patricia Rodney, 404-752-1944, Fax: 404-752-1051.

Master of Science in Clinical Research Program Students: 5 full-time (2 women); all minorities (all African Americans). Average age 32. 5 applicants, 60% accepted, 3 enrolled. *Faculty:* 15 full-time (3 women), 10 part-time/adjunct (2 women). Expenses: Contact institution. In 2008, 1 master's awarded. Offers clinical research (MS). *Application deadline:* For fall admission, 4/6 for domestic students. *Application fee:* $0. *Application Contact:* Dr. Sterling Roaf, Director of Admissions, 404-752-1650, Fax: 404-752-1512, E-mail: sroaf@msm.edu. *Director*, Dr. Elizabeth Ofili, 404-752-1192, E-mail: ofilie@msm.edu.

Professional Program Students: 217 full-time (133 women); includes 196 minority (156 African Americans, 22 American Indian/Alaska Native, 11 Asian Americans or Pacific Islanders, 7 Hispanic Americans). Average age 26. 3,753 applicants, 4% accepted, 56 enrolled. *Faculty:* 220 full-time (105 women), 41 part-time/adjunct (16 women). Expenses: Contact institution. *Financial support:* In 2008–09, 200 students received support. Career-related internships or fieldwork, Federal Work-Study, institutionally sponsored loans, and scholarships/grants available. Financial award application deadline: 5/1; financial award applicants required to submit FAFSA. In 2008, 52 degrees awarded. Offers medicine (MD). *Application deadline:* For fall admission, 12/1 for domestic students. Applications are processed on a rolling basis. *Application fee:* $50. Electronic applications accepted. *Application Contact:* Dr. Sterling Roaf, Director of Admissions, 404-752-1650, Fax: 404-752-1512, E-mail: mdadmission@msm.edu. *Senior Associate Dean for Education/Faculty Affairs*, Dr. Martha Elks, 404-752-1881, Fax: 404-752-1594, E-mail: melks@msm.edu.

MORNINGSIDE COLLEGE, Sioux City, IA 51106

General Information Independent-religious, coed, comprehensive institution. *Graduate housing:* Rooms and/or apartments available to single and married students. Housing application deadline: 7/1. *Research affiliation:* Iowa Public Service Company (biology, chemistry, physics).

GRADUATE UNITS

Graduate Division *Degree program information:* Part-time and evening/weekend programs available. Offers professional educator (MAT); special education: instructional strategist I: mild/moderate elementary (K-6) (MAT); special education: instructional strategist II-mild/moderate secondary (7-12) (MAT); special education: K-12 instructional strategist II-behavior disorders/learning disabilities (MAT); special education: K-12 instructional strategist II-mental disabilities (MAT).

MORRISON UNIVERSITY, Reno, NV 89521

General Information Proprietary, coed, comprehensive institution. *Graduate housing:* On-campus housing not available.

GRADUATE UNITS

Graduate School *Degree program information:* Part-time and evening/weekend programs available. Electronic applications accepted.

MOUNTAIN STATE UNIVERSITY, Beckley, WV 25802-9003

General Information Independent, coed, comprehensive institution. *Enrollment:* 5,108 graduate, professional, and undergraduate students; 589 full-time matriculated graduate/professional students (331 women), 38 part-time matriculated graduate/professional students (27 women). *Enrollment by degree level:* 627 master's. *Graduate faculty:* 23 full-time (12 women), 56 part-time/adjunct (25 women). *Tuition:* Full-time $4020; part-time $335 per contact hour. *Graduate housing:* Room and/or apartments available on a first-come, first-served basis to single students; on-campus housing not available to married students. *Student services:* Campus employment opportunities, campus safety program, career counseling, exercise/wellness program, grant writing training, international student services, multicultural affairs office, services for students with disabilities, writing training. *Library facilities:* Mountain State University Library. *Online resources:* library catalog. *Collection:* 113,613 titles, 157 serial subscriptions, 4,464 audiovisual materials.

Computer facilities: Computer purchase and lease plans are available. 185 computers available on campus for general student use. A campuswide network can be accessed from student residence rooms and from off campus. Online class registration is available. *Web address:* http://www.mountainstate.edu/.

General Application Contact: Dinah Rock, Coordinator of Graduate Academic Services, 304-929-1588, Fax: 304-929-1637, E-mail: drock@mountainstate.edu.

GRADUATE UNITS

Graduate Studies Students: 589 full-time (331 women), 38 part-time (27 women); includes 109 minority (69 African Americans, 3 American Indian/Alaska Native, 25 Asian Americans or Pacific Islanders, 12 Hispanic Americans), 21 international. Average age 35. 701 applicants, 64% accepted, 351 enrolled. *Faculty:* 23 full-time (12 women), 56 part-time/adjunct (25 women). Expenses: Contact institution. *Financial support:* In 2008–09, 7 research assistantships (averaging $2,000 per year) were awarded; career-related internships or fieldwork, Federal Work-Study, scholarships/grants, tuition waivers (partial), and unspecified assistantships also available. Support available to part-time students. Financial award applicants required to submit FAFSA. In 2008, 259 master's awarded. *Degree program information:* Part-time and evening/weekend programs available. Postbaccalaureate distance learning degree programs offered (no on-campus study). Offers administration/education (MSN); criminal justice administration (MCJA); family nurse practitioner (MSN); health science (MHS); interdisciplinary studies (MA, MS); nurse anesthesia (MSN); physician assistant (MSPA); registered nurse anesthetist (Certificate); strategic leadership (MSSL). *Application deadline:* For fall admission, 5/31 priority date for domestic and international students. Applications are processed on a rolling basis. *Application fee:* $25 ($50 for international students). Electronic applications accepted. *Application Contact:* Dinah Rock, Coordinator of Graduate Academic Services, 304-929-1690, Fax: 304-929-1637, E-mail: drock@mountainstate.edu. *Dean, School of Graduate Studies*, Dr. Brian Holloway, 304-929-1690, Fax: 304-929-1637, E-mail: holloway@mountainstate.edu.

MOUNT ALLISON UNIVERSITY, Sackville, NB E4L 1E4, Canada

General Information Province-supported, coed, comprehensive institution. *Graduate housing:* Room and/or apartments available to single students; on-campus housing not available to married students. Housing application deadline: 5/15. *Research affiliation:* Atlantic Cancer Institute (medical research), Moncton Hospital (medical research), Huntsman Marine Science Centre (marine biology).

GRADUATE UNITS

Department of Biology Offers biology (M Sc).

Department of Chemistry Offers chemistry (M Sc).

MOUNT ALOYSIUS COLLEGE, Cresson, PA 16630-1999

General Information Independent-religious, coed, comprehensive institution.

GRADUATE UNITS

Program in Correctional Administration Offers correctional administration (MA).

Program in Health and Human Services Administration Offers health and human services administration (MS).

Program in Psychology Offers psychology (MS).

MOUNT ANGEL SEMINARY, Saint Benedict, OR 97373

General Information Independent-religious, Undergraduate: men only; graduate: coed, comprehensive institution. *Graduate housing:* Room and/or apartments guaranteed to single students; on-campus housing not available to married students.

GRADUATE UNITS

Program in Theology *Degree program information:* Part-time programs available. Offers theology (M Div, MA).

MOUNT CARMEL COLLEGE OF NURSING, Columbus, OH 43222

General Information Independent, coed, primarily women, comprehensive institution. *Graduate housing:* Room and/or apartments available on a first-come, first-served basis to single students; on-campus housing not available to married students. Housing application deadline: 4/1.

GRADUATE UNITS

Nursing Program *Degree program information:* Part-time programs available. Offers adult health CNS (clinical nurse specialist) (MS); nursing administration (MS); nursing education (MS).

MOUNT HOLYOKE COLLEGE, South Hadley, MA 01075

General Information Independent, women only, comprehensive institution.

GRADUATE UNITS

Department of Psychology and Education Offers psychology and education (MA).

MOUNT MARTY COLLEGE, Yankton, SD 57078-3724

General Information Independent-religious, coed, comprehensive institution. *Graduate housing:* On-campus housing not available.

GRADUATE UNITS

Graduate Studies Division Offers business administration (MBA); nurse anesthesia (MS); pastoral ministries (MPM). Electronic applications accepted.

MOUNT MARY COLLEGE, Milwaukee, WI 53222-4597

General Information Independent-religious, Undergraduate: women only; graduate: coed, comprehensive institution. CGS member. *Enrollment:* 1,862 graduate, professional, and undergraduate students; 279 full-time matriculated graduate/professional students (264 women), 120 part-time matriculated graduate/professional students (116 women). *Enrollment by degree level:* 399 master's. *Graduate faculty:* 15 full-time (13 women), 47 part-time/adjunct (35 women). *Tuition:* Part-time $545 per credit. *Graduate housing:* Room and/or apartments available on a first-come, first-served basis to single students; on-campus housing not available to married students. *Student services:* Campus employment opportunities, campus safety program, career counseling, child daycare facilities, exercise/wellness program, free psychological counseling, international student services, multicultural affairs office, services for students with disabilities, teacher training, writing training. *Library facilities:* The Patrick and Beatrice Haggerty Library. *Online resources:* library catalog, web page, access to other libraries' catalogs. *Collection:* 696,609 titles, 28,163 serial subscriptions, 27,288 audiovisual materials.

Computer facilities: 80 computers available on campus for general student use. A campuswide network can be accessed from student residence rooms and from off campus. Online class registration is available. *Web address:* http://www.mtmary.edu/.

General Application Contact: Dr. Douglas J. Mickelson, Associate Dean for Graduate and Continuing Education, 414-256-1252, Fax: 414-256-0167, E-mail: mickelsd@mtmary.edu.

GRADUATE UNITS

Graduate Programs Students: 279 full-time (264 women), 120 part-time (116 women); includes 61 minority (42 African Americans, 2 American Indian/Alaska Native, 4 Asian Americans or Pacific Islanders, 13 Hispanic Americans), 1 international. Average age 35. 231 applicants, 59% accepted, 116 enrolled. *Faculty:* 15 full-time (13 women), 47 part-time/adjunct (35 women). Expenses: Contact institution. *Financial support:* In 2008–09, 5 students received support. Career-related internships or fieldwork, Federal Work-Study, and unspecified assistantships available. Support available to part-time students. Financial award application deadline: 5/1; financial award applicants required to submit FAFSA. In 2008, 45 master's awarded. *Degree program information:* Part-time and evening/weekend programs available. Offers administrative dietetics (MS); art therapy (MS); business administration (MBA); clinical dietetics (MS); community counseling (MS); education (MA); English (MA); nutrition education (MS); occupational therapy (MS); professional development (MA). *Application deadline:* For fall admission, 8/1 priority date for domestic and international students; for spring admission, 12/1 priority date for domestic and international students. Applications are processed on a rolling basis. *Application fee:* $35 ($75 for international students). Electronic applications accepted. *Application Contact:* Dr. Douglas J. Mickelson, Associate Dean for Graduate and Continuing Education, 414-256-1252, Fax: 414-256-0167, E-mail: mickelsd@mtmary.edu. *Associate Dean for Graduate and Continuing Education,* Dr. Douglas J. Mickelson, 414-256-1252, Fax: 414-256-0167, E-mail: mickelsd@mtmary.edu.

MOUNT SAINT MARY COLLEGE, Newburgh, NY 12550-3494

General Information Independent, coed, comprehensive institution. *Enrollment:* 2,629 graduate, professional, and undergraduate students; 90 full-time matriculated graduate/professional students (72 women), 403 part-time matriculated graduate/professional students (315 women). *Enrollment by degree level:* 493 master's. *Graduate faculty:* 24 full-time (15 women), 22 part-time/adjunct (15 women). *Tuition:* Full-time $13,356; part-time $742 per credit. *Required fees:* $50 per semester. *Graduate housing:* On-campus housing not available. *Student services:* Campus employment opportunities, campus safety program, career counseling, free psychological counseling, international student services. *Library facilities:* Curtin Memorial Library plus 1 other. *Online resources:* library catalog, web page, access to other libraries' catalogs. *Collection:* 100,031 titles, 25,128 serial subscriptions, 7,247 audiovisual materials.

Computer facilities: Computer purchase and lease plans are available. 570 computers available on campus for general student use. A campuswide network can be accessed from student residence rooms and from off campus. Online class registration, intranet are available. *Web address:* http://www.msmc.edu/.

General Application Contact: Graduate Coordinator, 845-561-0800, Fax: 845-562-6762.

GRADUATE UNITS

Division of Business Students: 26 full-time (14 women), 78 part-time (47 women); includes 50 minority (10 African Americans, 30 Asian Americans or Pacific Islanders, 10 Hispanic Americans). Average age 31. 46 applicants, 91% accepted, 41 enrolled. *Faculty:* 7 full-time (1 woman), 3 part-time/adjunct (0 women). Expenses: Contact institution. *Financial support:* In 2008–09, 22 students received support. Unspecified assistantships available. Financial award application deadline: 4/15; financial award applicants required to submit FAFSA. In 2008, 31 master's awarded. *Degree program information:* Part-time and evening/weekend programs available. Offers business (MBA); financial planning (MBA). *Application deadline:* Applications are processed on a rolling basis. *Application fee:* $40. *Application Contact:* Janice Banker, Secretary, 845-569-3582, Fax: 845-569-3885, E-mail: banker@msmc.edu. *Coordinator,* Dr. Moira Tolan, 845-569-3288, Fax: 845-562-6762, E-mail: tolan@msmc.edu.

Division of Education Students: 61 full-time (55 women), 279 part-time (226 women); includes 28 minority (7 African Americans, 4 Asian Americans or Pacific Islanders, 17 Hispanic Americans). Average age 31. 150 applicants, 56% accepted, 60 enrolled. *Faculty:* 14 full-time (12 women), 18 part-time/adjunct (14 women). Expenses: Contact institution. *Financial support:* In 2008–09, 146 students received support. Unspecified assistantships available. Financial award application deadline: 4/15; financial award applicants required to submit FAFSA. In 2008, 140 master's awarded. *Degree program information:* Part-time and evening/weekend programs available. Offers adolescence and special education (MS Ed); adolescence education (MS Ed); childhood and special education (MS Ed); childhood education (MS Ed); literacy and special education (MS Ed); literacy/childhood (MS Ed); middle school (5-6) (MS Ed); middle school (7-9) (MS Ed); special education (1-6) (MS Ed); special education (7-12) (MS Ed). *Application deadline:* Applications are processed on a rolling basis. *Application fee:* $40. *Application Contact:* Dr. Theresa Lewis, Coordinator, 845-569-3149, Fax: 845-569-3535, E-mail: tlewis@msmc.edu. *Coordinator,* Dr. Theresa Lewis, 845-569-3149, Fax: 845-569-3535, E-mail: tlewis@msmc.edu.

Division of Nursing Students: 3 full-time (all women), 46 part-time (42 women); includes 11 minority (5 African Americans, 3 Asian Americans or Pacific Islanders, 3 Hispanic Americans). Average age 40. 25 applicants, 100% accepted, 23 enrolled. *Faculty:* 3 full-time (2 women), 1 (woman) part-time/adjunct. Expenses: Contact institution. *Financial support:* In 2008–09, 2 students received support. Unspecified assistantships and nursing lab assistant available. Financial award application deadline: 4/15; financial award applicants required to submit FAFSA. In 2008, 8 master's awarded. *Degree program information:* Part-time and evening/weekend programs available. Offers adult nurse practitioner (MS); clinical nurse specialist-adult health (MS). *Application deadline:* For fall admission, 6/3 priority date for domestic students; for spring admission, 10/31 priority date for domestic students. Applications are processed on a rolling basis. *Application fee:* $40. *Application Contact:* Graduate Coordinator, 845-561-0800, Fax: 845-562-6762. *Coordinator,* Dr. Karen Baldwin, 845-569-3512, Fax: 845-562-6762, E-mail: baldwin@msmc.edu.

MOUNT ST. MARY'S COLLEGE, Los Angeles, CA 90049-1599

General Information Independent-religious, coed, comprehensive institution. *Enrollment:* 2,343 graduate, professional, and undergraduate students; 109 full-time matriculated graduate/professional students (83 women), 212 part-time matriculated graduate/professional students (163 women). *Enrollment by degree level:* 366 master's, 89 doctoral. *Graduate faculty:* 16 full-time (all women), 23 part-time/adjunct (19 women). *Tuition:* Full-time $16,992; part-time $708 per unit. *Required fees:* $313. One-time fee: $110 full-time. Tuition and fees vary according to course load and program. *Graduate housing:* On-campus housing not available. *Student services:* Free psychological counseling, services for students with disabilities.

Computer facilities: 350 computers available on campus for general student use. A campuswide network can be accessed from student residence rooms and from off campus. Online class registration is available. *Web address:* http://www.msmc.la.edu/.

General Application Contact: Jessica M. Bibeau, Director of Graduate Admission, 213-477-2800 Ext. 2798, Fax: 213-477-2797, E-mail: jbibeau@msmc.la.edu.

GRADUATE UNITS

Graduate Division Students: 245 full-time (191 women), 218 part-time (173 women); includes 153 minority (28 African Americans, 1 American Indian/Alaska Native, 37 Asian Americans or Pacific Islanders, 87 Hispanic Americans), 1 international. Average age 34. *Faculty:* 21 full-time (14 women), 71 part-time/adjunct (46 women). Expenses: Contact institution. *Financial support:* Career-related internships or fieldwork, Federal Work-Study, institutionally sponsored loans, and tuition waivers (full and partial) available. Support available to part-time students. Financial award application deadline: 3/15; financial award applicants required to submit FAFSA. In 2008, 67 master's awarded. *Degree program information:* Part-time and evening/weekend programs available. Offers administrative studies (MS); business administration (MBA); counseling psychology (MS); elementary education (MS); humanities (MA); nursing (MS); physical therapy (DPT); religious studies (MA); secondary education (MS); special education (MS). *Application deadline:* Applications are processed on a rolling basis. *Application fee:* $50. Electronic applications accepted. *Application Contact:* Jessica M. Bibeau, Director of Graduate Admission, 213-477-2800 Ext. 2798, Fax: 213-477-2797, E-mail: jbibeau@msmc.la.edu.

MOUNT ST. MARY'S UNIVERSITY, Emmitsburg, MD 21727-7799

General Information Independent-religious, coed, comprehensive institution. *Enrollment:* 2,079 graduate, professional, and undergraduate students; 205 full-time matriculated graduate/professional students (34 women), 233 part-time matriculated graduate/professional students (124 women). *Enrollment by degree level:* 116 first professional, 322 master's. *Graduate faculty:* 25 full-time (6 women), 18 part-time/adjunct (9 women). *Tuition:* Full-time $7938; part-time $441 per credit hour. Tuition and fees vary according to program. *Graduate housing:* Room and/or apartments available on a first-come, first-served basis to single students; on-campus housing not available to married students. Typical cost: $4784 per year ($9520 including board). Room and board charges vary according to board plan. *Student services:* Campus employment opportunities, campus safety program, career counseling, exercise/wellness program, free psychological counseling, international student services, low-cost health insurance, multicultural affairs office, services for students with disabilities, teacher training, writing training. *Library facilities:* Phillips Library. *Online resources:* library catalog, web page, access to other libraries' catalogs. *Collection:* 215,076 titles, 901 serial subscriptions, 5,108 audiovisual materials.

Computer facilities: 150 computers available on campus for general student use. A campuswide network can be accessed from student residence rooms and from off campus. Online class registration, tuition payment, course management system are available. *Web address:* http://www.msmary.edu/.

General Application Contact: David Rehm, Vice President for Academic Affairs, 301-447-5218, Fax: 301-447-5863, E-mail: rehm@msmary.edu.

GRADUATE UNITS

Graduate Seminary Students: 143 full-time (0 women), 2 part-time (0 women); includes 11 minority (5 Asian Americans or Pacific Islanders, 6 Hispanic Americans), 13 international. Average age 30. 57 applicants, 74% accepted, 42 enrolled. *Faculty:* 10 full-time (0 women), 4 part-time/adjunct (2 women). Expenses: Contact institution. *Financial support:* In 2008–09, 49 students received support. Career-related internships or fieldwork and scholarships/grants available. Financial award applicants required to submit FAFSA. In 2008, 36 first professional degrees, 10 master's awarded. Offers theology (M Div, MA). *Application deadline:* For fall admission, 8/1 for domestic and international students. *Application fee:* $0. *Application Contact:* Susan Nield, Seminary Admissions, 301-447-7423, Fax: 301-447-7402, E-mail: Nield@msmary.edu. *Vice President/Rector,* Rev. Steven P. Rohlfs, 301-447-5295, Fax: 301-447-5636, E-mail: rohlfs@msmary.edu.

Program in Business Administration Students: 33 full-time (16 women), 169 part-time (74 women); includes 27 minority (14 African Americans, 6 Asian Americans or Pacific Islanders, 7 Hispanic Americans), 6 international. Average age 32. 69 applicants, 97% accepted, 43 enrolled. *Faculty:* 10 full-time (2 women), 7 part-time/adjunct (4 women). Expenses: Contact institution. *Financial support:* In 2008–09, 71 students received support. Career-related internships or fieldwork and unspecified assistantships available. Financial award applicants required to submit FAFSA. In 2008, 99 master's awarded. *Degree program information:* Part-time and evening/weekend programs available. Offers business administration (MBA). *Application deadline:* Applications are processed on a rolling basis. *Application fee:* $35. *Application Contact:* Dr. Carolyn Jacobson, Director, MBA Program, 301-447-5326, Fax: 301-447-5335, E-mail: jacobson@msmary.edu. *Director, MBA Program,* Dr. Carolyn Jacobson, 301-447-5326, Fax: 301-447-5335, E-mail: jacobson@msmary.edu.

Program in Education Students: 28 full-time (18 women), 62 part-time (50 women); includes 4 minority (1 Asian American or Pacific Islander, 3 Hispanic Americans), 1 international. Average age 33. 25 applicants, 72% accepted, 14 enrolled. *Faculty:* 5 full-time (4 women), 7 part-time/adjunct (3 women). Expenses: Contact institution. *Financial support:* In 2008–09, 63 students received support. Career-related internships or fieldwork and unspecified assistantships available. Financial award applicants required to submit FAFSA. In 2008, 17 master's awarded. *Degree program information:* Part-time and evening/weekend programs available. Offers education (M Ed, MAT). *Application deadline:* For fall admission, 8/15 for domestic and international students. Applications are processed on a rolling basis. *Application fee:* $35. *Application Contact:* Laura Frazier, Director, 301-447-5371, Fax: 301-447-5250, E-mail: frazier@msmary.edu. *Director,* Laura Frazier, 301-447-5371, Fax: 301-447-5250, E-mail: frazier@msmary.edu.

MOUNT SAINT VINCENT UNIVERSITY, Halifax, NS B3M 2J6, Canada

General Information Province-supported, coed, primarily women, comprehensive institution. *Graduate housing:* Room and/or apartments available on a first-come, first-served basis to single students; on-campus housing not available to married students. Housing application deadline: 5/15.

GRADUATE UNITS

Graduate Programs *Degree program information:* Part-time and evening/weekend programs available. Postbaccalaureate distance learning degree programs offered (minimal on-campus study). Offers applied human nutrition (M Sc AHN, MAHN); child and youth study (MA); family studies and gerontology (MA); women's studies (MA). Electronic applications accepted.

Faculty of Education *Degree program information:* Part-time and evening/weekend programs available. Postbaccalaureate distance learning degree programs offered (minimal on-campus study). Offers adult education (M Ed, MA Ed, MA-R); curriculum studies (M Ed, MA Ed, MA-R); education of the blind or visually impaired (M Ed, MA Ed); education of the deaf or hard of hearing (M Ed, MA Ed); education of young adolescents (M Ed, MA Ed, MA-R); educational foundations (M Ed, MA Ed, MA-R); educational psychology (M Ed, MA Ed, MA-R); elementary education (M Ed, MA Ed, MA-R); general studies (M Ed, MA Ed, MA-R); human relations (M Ed, MA Ed); literacy education (M Ed, MA Ed, MA-R); school psychology (MASP); teaching English as a second language (M Ed, MA Ed, MA-R). Electronic applications accepted.

MOUNT SINAI SCHOOL OF MEDICINE OF NEW YORK UNIVERSITY, New York, NY 10029-6504

General Information Independent, coed, graduate-only institution. *Enrollment by degree level:* 504 first professional, 139 master's, 259 doctoral. *Graduate faculty:* 1,269 full-time. *Tuition:* Full-time $23,175. *Required fees:* $100. Full-time tuition and fees vary according to course load, degree level, program and student level. *Graduate housing:* Rooms and/or apartments guaranteed to single and married students. Typical cost: $8400 per year for single students; $10,500 per year for married students. Room charges vary according to housing facility selected. Housing application deadline: 7/1. *Student services:* Campus employment opportunities, campus safety program, career counseling, free psychological counseling, grant writing training, international student services, low-cost health insurance, multicultural affairs office, services for students with disabilities, teacher training, writing training. *Library facilities:* Levy Library. *Online resources:* web page. *Collection:* 156,000 titles, 2,600 serial subscriptions.

Computer facilities: 75 computers available on campus for general student use. A campuswide network can be accessed from student residence rooms and from off campus. Online class registration is available. *Web address:* http://www.mssm.edu/.

General Application Contact: Jessica Maysonet, Assistant Director, Admissions, 212-241-6696, Fax: 212-876-4658, E-mail: admissions@mssm.edu.

GRADUATE UNITS

Graduate School of Biological Sciences Students: 498 full-time (259 women); includes 123 minority (27 African Americans, 3 American Indian/Alaska Native, 76 Asian Americans or Pacific Islanders, 17 Hispanic Americans), 95 international. 859 applicants, 30% accepted, 102 enrolled. *Faculty:* 126 full-time (40 women). Expenses: Contact institution. *Financial support:* In 2008–09, fellowships with full tuition reimbursements (averaging $28,000 per year), research assistantships with full tuition reimbursements (averaging $28,000 per year) were awarded; Federal Work-Study, institutionally sponsored loans, scholarships/grants, health care benefits, and unspecified assistantships also available. Financial award application deadline: 4/30; financial award applicants required to submit FAFSA. In 2008, 60 master's, 27 doctorates awarded. Offers bioethics (MS); biological sciences (PhD); clinical research (MS); community medicine (MPH); genetic counseling (MS); neurosciences (PhD). *Application deadline:* For fall admission, 12/15 for domestic and international students. Applications are processed on a rolling basis. *Application fee:* $75. Electronic applications accepted. *Application Contact:* Lily Recanati, Manager, 212-241-2793, Fax: 212-241-0651, E-mail: lily.recanati@mssm.edu. *Dean,* Dr. John Morrison, 212-241-6546, Fax: 212-241-0651, E-mail: john.morrison@mssm.edu.

Medical School Students: 504 full-time (261 women); includes 219 minority (32 African Americans, 6 American Indian/Alaska Native, 107 Asian Americans or Pacific Islanders, 74 Hispanic Americans), 19 international. Average age 25. 6,745 applicants, 5% accepted, 140 enrolled. *Faculty:* 1,269 full-time. Expenses: Contact institution. *Financial support:* In 2008–09, 403 students received support. Career-related internships or fieldwork, Federal Work-Study, institutionally sponsored loans, and scholarships/grants available. Financial award application deadline: 4/30; financial award applicants required to submit FAFSA. In 2008, 147 MDs awarded. Offers medicine (MD). *Application deadline:* For fall admission, 12/15 for domestic and international students. *Application fee:* $105. *Application Contact:* Jessica Maysonet, Assistant Director of Admissions, 212-241-2260, Fax: 212-828-4135, E-mail: jessica.maysonet@mssm.edu. *Dean for Medical Education,* David Muller, MD, 212-241-8716, Fax: 212-369-6013, E-mail: david.muller@mssm.edu.

MOUNT VERNON NAZARENE UNIVERSITY, Mount Vernon, OH 43050-9500

General Information Independent-religious, coed, comprehensive institution. *Graduate housing:* On-campus housing not available.

GRADUATE UNITS

Department of Education *Degree program information:* Part-time and evening/weekend programs available. Offers education (MA Ed); professional educator's license (MA Ed).

Program in Management *Degree program information:* Part-time and evening/weekend programs available. Offers management (MSM).

Program in Ministry *Degree program information:* Part-time and evening/weekend programs available. Offers ministry (M Min).

MULTNOMAH UNIVERSITY, Portland, OR 97220-5898

General Information Independent-religious, coed, comprehensive institution. *Enrollment:* 840 graduate, professional, and undergraduate students; 154 full-time matriculated graduate/professional students (39 women), 104 part-time matriculated graduate/professional students (42 women). *Enrollment by degree level:* 113 first professional, 94 master's, 51 other advanced degrees. *Tuition:* Full-time $12,690; part-time $423 per hour. *Graduate housing:* Rooms and/or apartments available on a first-come, first-served basis to single and married students. Housing application deadline: 7/1. *Student services:* Campus employment opportunities, career counseling, free psychological counseling, international student services. *Library facilities:* John Mitchell Library. *Online resources:* library catalog, access to other libraries' catalogs. *Collection:* 109,480 titles, 372 serial subscriptions, 5,990 audiovisual materials.

Computer facilities: 42 computers available on campus for general student use. A campuswide network can be accessed from student residence rooms and from off campus. Online class registration is available. *Web address:* http://www.multnomah.edu/.

General Application Contact: Penny Rader, Seminary Admissions Counselor, 503-251-6485, Fax: 503-254-1268, E-mail: admiss@multnomah.edu.

GRADUATE UNITS

Multnomah Bible College Graduate Degree Programs Students: 11 full-time (4 women), 12 part-time (9 women); includes 4 minority (1 African American, 2 Asian Americans or Pacific Islanders, 1 Hispanic American), 1 international. Average age 32. 25 applicants, 22 enrolled. *Faculty:* 6 full-time (all women), 8 part-time/adjunct (2 women). Expenses: Contact institution. Offers counseling (MA); teaching (MA). *Application deadline:* For fall admission, 7/15 for domestic and international students; for spring admission, 11/15 for domestic and international students. *Application Contact:* Penny Rader, Seminary Admissions Counselor, 503-251-6485, Fax: 503-254-1268, E-mail: admiss@multnomah.edu. *Academic Dean,* Dr. Wayne Strickland, 503-251-6401.

Multnomah Biblical Seminary Students: 143 full-time (35 women), 92 part-time (33 women); includes 33 minority (9 African Americans, 1 American Indian/Alaska Native, 15 Asian Americans or Pacific Islanders, 8 Hispanic Americans), 15 international. Average age 34. 147 applicants, 83% accepted, 94 enrolled. *Faculty:* 10 full-time (1 woman), 13 part-time/adjunct (2 women). Expenses: Contact institution. *Financial support:* Career-related internships or fieldwork and scholarships/grants available. Support available to part-time students. Financial award application deadline: 7/15; financial award applicants required to submit FAFSA. In 2008, 23 first professional degrees, 34 master's awarded. *Degree program information:* Part-time programs available. Offers theology (M Div, MABS, MAPS, Th M, Certificate). *Application deadline:* For fall admission, 7/15 priority date for domestic and international students; for spring admission, 11/15 priority date for domestic and international students. Applications are processed on a rolling basis. *Application fee:* $40. *Application Contact:* Penny Rader, Seminary Admissions Counselor, 503-251-6485, Fax: 503-254-1268, E-mail: admiss@multnomah.edu. *Dean,* Dr. Robert R Redman, 503-255-0332, Fax: 503-251-6444, E-mail: rredman@multnomah.edu.

MURRAY STATE UNIVERSITY, Murray, KY 42071

General Information State-supported, coed, comprehensive institution. CGS member. *Graduate housing:* Rooms and/or apartments available on a first-come, first-served basis to single and married students.

GRADUATE UNITS

College of Business and Public Affairs *Degree program information:* Part-time and evening/weekend programs available. Offers business administration (MBA); business and public affairs (MA, MBA, MPAC, MS); economics (MS); mass communications (MA, MS); organizational communication (MA, MS); professional accountancy (MPAC); telecommunications systems management (MS).

College of Education *Degree program information:* Part-time programs available. Offers advanced learning behavior disorders (MA Ed); community and agency counseling (Ed S); early childhood education (MA Ed); education (MA Ed, MS, Ed D, PhD, Ed S); elementary education (MA Ed, Ed S); elementary education/reading and writing (MA Ed, Ed S); health, physical education, and recreation (MA); human development and leadership (MS); industrial and technical education (MS); learning disabilities (MA Ed); middle school education (MA Ed, Ed S); moderate/severe disorders (MA Ed); reading and writing (MA Ed); school administration (MA Ed, Ed S); school guidance and counseling (MA Ed, Ed S); secondary education (MA Ed, Ed S); special education (MA Ed).

College of Health Sciences and Human Services *Degree program information:* Part-time programs available. Offers clinical nurse specialist (MSN); environmental science (MS); exercise and leisure studies (MS); family nurse practitioner (MSN); health sciences and human services (MS, MSN); industrial hygiene (MS); nurse anesthesia (MSN); safety management (MS); speech-language pathology (MS).

College of Humanities and Fine Arts *Degree program information:* Part-time programs available. Offers clinical psychology (MA, MS); creative writing (MFA); English (MA); history (MA); humanities and fine arts (MA, MFA, MME, MPA, MS); music education (MME); psychology (MA, MS); public administration (MPA); public affairs (MPA); teaching English to speakers of other languages (MA).

College of Science, Engineering and Technology *Degree program information:* Part-time programs available. Offers biological sciences (MAT, MS, PhD); chemistry (MS); geosciences (MS); management of technology (MS); mathematics (MA, MAT, MS); science, engineering and technology (MA, MAT, MS, PhD); water science (MS).

School of Agriculture *Degree program information:* Evening/weekend programs available. Postbaccalaureate distance learning degree programs offered (minimal on-campus study). Offers agriculture (MS); agriculture education (MS).

MUSKINGUM UNIVERSITY, New Concord, OH 43762

General Information Independent-religious, coed, comprehensive institution. *Graduate housing:* On-campus housing not available.

GRADUATE UNITS

Graduate Programs in Education *Degree program information:* Part-time programs available. Offers education (MAE, MAT).

NAROPA UNIVERSITY, Boulder, CO 80302-6697

General Information Independent, coed, comprehensive institution. *Enrollment:* 1,075 graduate, professional, and undergraduate students; 379 full-time matriculated graduate/professional students (262 women), 226 part-time matriculated graduate/professional students (176 women). *Enrollment by degree level:* 605 master's. *Graduate faculty:* 52 full-time (29 women), 158 part-time/adjunct (106 women). *Tuition:* Full-time $14,767; part-time $726 per credit hour. *Required fees:* $45 per term. *Graduate housing:* On-campus housing not available. *Student services:* Campus employment opportunities, campus safety program, career counseling, free psychological counseling, international student services, low-cost health insurance, multicultural affairs office, services for students with disabilities, writing training. *Library facilities:* Allen Ginsberg Library. *Online resources:* library catalog, web page. *Collection:* 29,175 titles, 81 serial subscriptions.

Computer facilities: 75 computers available on campus for general student use. A campuswide network can be accessed from student residence rooms and from off campus. Online class registration is available. *Web address:* http://www.naropa.edu/.

General Application Contact: Office of Admissions, 303-546-3572, Fax: 303-546-3583, E-mail: admissions@naropa.edu.

GRADUATE UNITS

Graduate Programs Students: 379 full-time (262 women), 226 part-time (176 women); includes 57 minority (8 African Americans, 9 American Indian/Alaska Native, 13 Asian Americans or Pacific Islanders, 27 Hispanic Americans), 37 international. Average age 33. 649 applicants, 61% accepted, 237 enrolled. *Faculty:* 52 full-time (29 women), 158 part-time/adjunct (106 women). Expenses: Contact institution. *Financial support:* In 2008–09, 259 students received support, including 52 research assistantships with partial tuition reimbursements available (averaging $3,000 per year), 20 teaching assistantships with partial tuition reimbursements available (averaging $3,000 per year); career-related internships or fieldwork, Federal Work-Study, scholarships/grants, health care benefits, tuition waivers (partial), and unspecified assistantships also available. Support available to part-time students. Financial award application deadline: 3/1; financial award applicants required to submit FAFSA. In 2008, 208 master's awarded. *Degree program information:* Part-time and evening/weekend programs available. Postbaccalaureate distance learning degree programs offered (minimal on-campus study). Offers art therapy (MA); body psychotherapy (MA); contemplative education (MA); contemplative psychotherapy (MA); counseling psychology (MA); creative writing (MFA); dance/movement therapy (MA); divinity (M Div); ecopsychology (MA); environmental leadership (MA); Indo-Tibetan Buddhism (MA); Indo-Tibetan Buddhism with language (MA); religious studies (MA); religious studies with language (MA); theater: contemporary performance (MFA); theater: Lecoq-based actor-created theater (MFA); transpersonal psychology (MA); wilderness therapy (MA); writing and poetics (MFA). *Application deadline:* For fall admission, 1/15 priority date for domestic and international students; for spring admission, 10/15 priority date for domestic and international students. Applications are processed on a rolling basis. *Application fee:* $60. Electronic applications accepted. *Application Contact:* Office of Admissions, 303-546-3572, Fax: 303-546-3583, E-mail: admissions@naropa.edu. *Dean of Admissions,* Susan Boyle, 303-546-3517, Fax: 303-546-3583, E-mail: sboyle@naropa.edu.

NASHOTAH HOUSE, Nashotah, WI 53058-9793

General Information Independent-religious, coed, primarily men, graduate-only institution. *Graduate housing:* Rooms and/or apartments available on a first-come, first-served basis to single and married students. Housing application deadline: 8/15.

Nashotah House (continued)

GRADUATE UNITS

School of Theology *Degree program information:* Part-time programs available. Offers theology (M Div, MTS, STM, Certificate).

NATIONAL AMERICAN UNIVERSITY, Rapid City, SD 57701

General Information Proprietary, coed, comprehensive institution. *Graduate housing:* Room and/or apartments available on a first-come, first-served basis to single students. Housing application deadline: 6/1.

GRADUATE UNITS

Graduate Programs *Degree program information:* Part-time and evening/weekend programs available. Postbaccalaureate distance learning degree programs offered. Offers business (MBA, MM). Programs also offered in Wichita, KS; Albuquerque, NM; Bloomington, MN; Brooklyn Center, MN; Colorado Springs, CO; Denver, CO; Independence, MO; Overland Park, KS; Rio Rancho, NM; Roseville, MN; Zona Rosa, MO. Electronic applications accepted.

NATIONAL COLLEGE OF MIDWIFERY, Taos, NM 87571

General Information Independent, women only, comprehensive institution.

GRADUATE UNITS

Graduate Programs *Degree program information:* Part-time and evening/weekend programs available. Postbaccalaureate distance learning degree programs offered (no on-campus study). Offers midwifery (MS, PhD). Electronic applications accepted.

NATIONAL COLLEGE OF NATURAL MEDICINE, Portland, OR 97201

General Information Independent, coed, primarily women, graduate-only institution. *Enrollment by degree level:* 113 master's, 399 doctoral. *Graduate faculty:* 27 full-time (11 women), 88 part-time/adjunct (47 women). *Graduate housing:* On-campus housing not available. *Student services:* Campus employment opportunities, campus safety program, career counseling, free psychological counseling, grant writing training, international student services, low-cost health insurance, services for students with disabilities. *Library facilities:* Natural College of Naturopathic Medicine Library. *Collection:* 10,000 titles, 125 serial subscriptions. *Research affiliation:* Oregon College of Oriental Medicine, Kaiser Center for Health Research, Oregon Health and Science University.

Computer facilities: 20 computers available on campus for general student use. A campuswide network can be accessed. VRS Software Programs, WIFI available. *Web address:* http://www.ncnm.edu/.

General Application Contact: Hang Nguyen, Admissions Coordinator, 503-552-1660, Fax: 503-499-0027, E-mail: admissions@ncmn.edu.

GRADUATE UNITS

Classical Chinese Medicine School Students: 111 full-time (63 women), 2 part-time (both women); includes 7 minority (1 African American, 4 Asian Americans or Pacific Islanders, 2 Hispanic Americans), 1 international. Average age 29. 51 applicants, 88% accepted, 34 enrolled. *Faculty:* 8 full-time (2 women), 27 part-time/adjunct (10 women). Expenses: Contact institution. *Financial support:* In 2008–09, 77 students received support. Federal Work-Study and scholarships/grants available. Financial award application deadline: 4/30; financial award applicants required to submit FAFSA. In 2008, 26 master's awarded. Offers classical Chinese medicine (MSOM). *Application deadline:* For fall admission, 11/1 priority date for domestic and international students; for winter admission, 2/1 priority date for domestic and international students. Applications are processed on a rolling basis. *Application fee:* $75. *Application Contact:* Hang Nguyen, Admissions Coordinator, 503-552-1660, Fax: 503-499-0027, E-mail: admissions@ncmn.edu. *Dean,* Dr. Laurie Regan, 503-552-1775, Fax: 503-499-0027, E-mail: admissions@ncnm.edu.

Naturopathic School Students: 394 full-time (321 women), 5 part-time (all women); includes 44 minority (8 African Americans, 1 American Indian/Alaska Native, 21 Asian Americans or Pacific Islanders, 14 Hispanic Americans), 12 international. Average age 29. 220 applicants, 60% accepted, 104 enrolled. *Faculty:* 18 full-time (9 women), 62 part-time/adjunct (37 women). Expenses: Contact institution. *Financial support:* In 2008–09, 308 students received support. Federal Work-Study and scholarships/grants available. Financial award application deadline: 4/30; financial award applicants required to submit FAFSA. In 2008, 60 doctorates awarded. Offers naturopathic medicine (ND). *Application deadline:* For fall admission, 11/1 priority date for domestic and international students; for winter admission, 2/1 priority date for domestic and international students. Applications are processed on a rolling basis. *Application fee:* $75. *Application Contact:* Hang Nguyen, Admissions Coordinator, 503-552-1660, Fax: 503-499-0027, E-mail: admissions@ncmn.edu. *Dean,* Dr. Rita Bettenburg, 503-552-1761, Fax: 503-499-0022, E-mail: rbettenburg@ncnm.edu.

NATIONAL DEFENSE UNIVERSITY, Washington, DC 20319-5066

General Information Federally supported, coed, graduate-only institution. *Enrollment by degree level:* 588 master's, 408 other advanced degrees. *Graduate faculty:* 417 full-time (68 women). *Graduate housing:* On-campus housing not available. *Student services:* Exercise/wellness program, international student services. *Library facilities:* NDU Library plus 1 other. *Online resources:* library catalog, web page, access to other libraries' catalogs. *Collection:* 650,000 titles, 52,400 serial subscriptions, 7,000 audiovisual materials.

Computer facilities: 1,500 computers available on campus for general student use. A campuswide network can be accessed from off campus. Online class registration, Laptops are issued to ICAF and NWC students for the duration of their programs are available. *Web address:* http://www.ndu.edu/.

General Application Contact: Dr. John Deegan, Provost and Vice President for Academic Affairs, 202-685-2649, E-mail: DeeganJ@ndu.edu.

GRADUATE UNITS

College of International Security Affairs Students: 33 full-time (2 women), 305 part-time (75 women). Average age 30. 133 applicants, 100% accepted, 133 enrolled. *Faculty:* 13 full-time (3 women), 14 part-time/adjunct (2 women). Expenses: Contact institution. In 2008, 39 master's awarded. *Degree program information:* Part-time and evening/weekend programs available. Offers strategic security studies (MA). *Application Contact:* Dr. R. Joseph DeSutter, Director, 202-685-3871. *Director,* Dr. R. Joseph DeSutter, 202-685-3871.

Industrial College of the Armed Forces Students: 320 full-time (70 women); includes 54 minority (33 African Americans, 1 American Indian/Alaska Native, 9 Asian Americans or Pacific Islanders, 11 Hispanic Americans). Average age 46. 339 applicants, 94% accepted, 320 enrolled. *Faculty:* 102 full-time. Expenses: Contact institution. In 2008, 296 master's awarded. Offers national resource strategy (MS). Open only to Department of Defense employees and specific federal agencies. *Application deadline:* For fall admission, 3/15 for domestic students. *Application Contact:* Rear Adm. Garry E. Hall, Commandant, 202-685-4333. *Commandant,* Rear Adm. Garry E. Hall, 202-685-4333.

Joint Advanced Warfighting School Students: 41 full-time (3 women); includes 8 minority (4 African Americans, 2 Asian Americans or Pacific Islanders, 2 Hispanic Americans). Average age 42. 41 applicants, 100% accepted, 41 enrolled. *Faculty:* 10 full-time (1 woman). Expenses: Contact institution. In 2008, 41 master's awarded. Offers joint campaign planning and strategy (MS). Open only to Department of Defense employees and specific federal agencies. *Application deadline:* For spring admission, 4/15 for domestic and international students. *Application fee:* $0. *Application Contact:* Shirley A. Wallace, Chief of Plans and Policy/Registrar, 757-443-6189, Fax: 757-443-6034, E-mail: wallaces@jfsc.ndu.edu. *Academic Dean,* Dr. Linda B. McCluney, 757-443-6185, Fax: 757-443-6034, E-mail: mccluneyl@jfsc.ndu.edu.

National War College Students: 223 full-time (29 women); includes 28 minority (11 African Americans, 10 Asian Americans or Pacific Islanders, 7 Hispanic Americans). Average age 45. 227 applicants, 98% accepted, 223 enrolled. *Faculty:* 62 full-time (10 women). Expenses: Contact institution. Offers national security strategy (MS). Open only to Department of Defense employees and specific federal agencies. *Application deadline:* For fall admission, 3/15 for domestic students. *Application fee:* $0. *Application Contact:* Brig. Gen. Robert P. Steel, Commandant, 202-685-2128, Fax: 202-685-3993. *Commandant,* Brig. Gen. Robert P. Steel, 202-685-2128, Fax: 202-685-3993.

THE NATIONAL GRADUATE SCHOOL OF QUALITY MANAGEMENT, Falmouth, MA 02541

General Information Independent, coed, graduate-only institution.

GRADUATE UNITS

Program in Quality Systems Management Offers e-commerce (MS); management (MS); six sigma (MS).

NATIONAL-LOUIS UNIVERSITY, Chicago, IL 60603

General Information Independent, coed, university. *Enrollment:* 7,056 graduate, professional, and undergraduate students; 1,054 full-time matriculated graduate/professional students (830 women), 4,253 part-time matriculated graduate/professional students (3,438 women). *Enrollment by degree level:* 4,712 master's, 275 doctoral, 320 other advanced degrees. *Graduate faculty:* 254 full-time (173 women), 856 part-time/adjunct (574 women). *Graduate housing:* On-campus housing not available. *Student services:* Campus employment opportunities, career counseling, international student services, low-cost health insurance, services for students with disabilities, teacher training, writing training. *Library facilities:* NLU Library plus 5 others. *Online resources:* library catalog. *Collection:* 4,857 audiovisual materials.

Computer facilities: A campuswide network can be accessed from off campus. Online class registration is available. *Web address:* http://www.nl.edu/.

General Application Contact: Dr. Larry Poselli, Vice President of Enrollment Management, 312-261-3550, Fax: 312-261-3550, E-mail: polselli@nl.edu.

GRADUATE UNITS

College of Arts and Sciences Students: 27 full-time (20 women), 603 part-time (499 women); includes 268 minority (212 African Americans, 3 American Indian/Alaska Native, 9 Asian Americans or Pacific Islanders, 44 Hispanic Americans), 3 international. Average age 38. Expenses: Contact institution. *Financial support:* Career-related internships or fieldwork, Federal Work-Study, institutionally sponsored loans, scholarships/grants, and tuition waivers available. Support available to part-time students. Financial award applicants required to submit FAFSA. In 2008, 176 master's, 5 other advanced degrees awarded. *Degree program information:* Part-time and evening/weekend programs available. Postbaccalaureate distance learning degree programs offered (minimal on-campus study). Offers addictions counseling (Certificate); addictions treatment (Certificate); arts and sciences (M Ed, MA, MS, Ed D, Certificate); career counseling and development studies (Certificate); community counseling (MS); community wellness and prevention (Certificate); counseling (Certificate); cultural psychology (MA); eating disorders counseling (Certificate); employee assistance programs (MS, Certificate); gerontology administration (Certificate); gerontology counseling (MS, Certificate); health psychology (MA); human development (MA); human services administration (MS, Certificate); long-term care administration (Certificate); organizational psychology (MA); psychology (Certificate); school counseling (MS); written communication (MS). *Application Contact:* Dr. Larry Poselli, Vice President of Enrollment and Student Services, 800-443-5522 Ext. 5718, Fax: 312-261-.3550, E-mail: larry.polselli@nl.edu.

Division of Language and Academic Development Students: 1 (woman) full-time, 29 part-time (27 women); includes 7 minority (6 African Americans, 1 Hispanic American). Average age 40. Expenses: Contact institution. *Financial support:* Fellowships, research assistantships, career-related internships or fieldwork, Federal Work-Study, institutionally sponsored loans, scholarships/grants, and tuition waivers available. Support available to part-time students. Financial award application deadline: 4/15; financial award applicants required to submit FAFSA. In 2008, 10 master's awarded. *Degree program information:* Part-time programs available. Postbaccalaureate distance learning degree programs offered (minimal on-campus study). Offers adult education (Ed D); adult literacy and developmental studies (M Ed, Certificate); adult, continuing, and literacy education (M Ed, Certificate). *Application Contact:* Dr. Larry Poselli, Vice President of Enrollment and Student Services, 800-443-5522 Ext. 5718, Fax: 312-261-.3550, E-mail: larry.polselli@nl.edu. *Associate Professor,* Judith Kent, 312-261-3535.

College of Management and Business Students: 190 full-time (130 women), 9 part-time (7 women); includes 96 minority (49 African Americans, 1 American Indian/Alaska Native, 8 Asian Americans or Pacific Islanders, 38 Hispanic Americans), 1 international. Average age 37. *Faculty:* 26 full-time (9 women), 352 part-time/adjunct (102 women). Expenses: Contact institution. *Financial support:* Federal Work-Study, institutionally sponsored loans, and scholarships/grants available. Support available to part-time students. Financial award applicants required to submit FAFSA. In 2008, 134 master's awarded. *Degree program information:* Part-time and evening/weekend programs available. Offers business administration (MBA); human resource management and development (MS); management (MS); management and business (MBA, MS). *Application deadline:* Applications are processed on a rolling basis. *Application Contact:* Dr. Larry Poselli, Vice President of Enrollment and Student Services, 800-443-5522 Ext. 5718, Fax: 312-261-.3550, E-mail: larry.polselli@nl.edu. *Executive Dean,* Chrisopher Multhauf, 312-261-3073, Fax: 312-261-3073, E-mail: chris.multhauf@nl.edu.

National College of Education Students: 832 full-time (676 women), 2,724 part-time (2,085 women); includes 722 minority (413 African Americans, 7 American Indian/Alaska Native, 86 Asian Americans or Pacific Islanders, 216 Hispanic Americans). Average age 35. *Faculty:* 163 full-time (118 women), 588 part-time/adjunct (416 women). Expenses: Contact institution. *Financial support:* Fellowships, research assistantships, teaching assistantships, career-related internships or fieldwork, Federal Work-Study, institutionally sponsored loans, and scholarships/grants available. Support available to part-time students. Financial award applicants required to submit FAFSA. In 2008, 1,706 master's, 37 doctorates, 128 other advanced degrees awarded. *Degree program information:* Part-time and evening/weekend programs available. Offers administration and supervision (M Ed, CAS, Ed S); adult education (Ed D); curriculum and instruction (M Ed, MS Ed, CAS); curriculum and social inquiry (Ed D); early childhood administration (M Ed, CAS); early childhood curriculum and instruction specialist (M Ed, MS Ed, CAS); early childhood education (M Ed, MAT, CAS); education (M Ed, MAT, MS Ed, Ed D, CAS, Ed S); educational leadership (Ed D); educational leadership/superintendent endorsement (Ed D); educational psychology (CAS, Ed S); educational psychology/human learning and development (M Ed, MS Ed); educational psychology/school psychology (Ed D); elementary education (MAT); general special education (M Ed, MAT, CAS); human learning and development (Ed D); interdisciplinary studies in curriculum and instruction (M Ed); language and literacy (M Ed, MS Ed, CAS); learning disabilities (M Ed, CAS); learning disabilities/behavior disorders (M Ed, MAT, CAS); mathematics education (M Ed, MS Ed, CAS); reading and language (M Ed, MS Ed, Ed D, CAS); reading recovery (CAS); reading specialist (M Ed, MS Ed, CAS); school psychology (M Ed, Ed S); science education (M Ed, MS Ed, CAS); secondary education (MAT); technology in education (M Ed, MS Ed, CAS). *Application deadline:* Applications are processed on a rolling basis. *Application Contact:* Dr. Larry Poselli, Vice President of Enrollment and Student Services, 800-443-5522 Ext. 5718, Fax: 312-261-.3550, E-mail: larry.polselli@nl.edu. *Dean,* Dr. Alison Hilsbeck, 312-361-3580, Fax: 312-261-2580, E-mail: ahilsabeck@nl.edu.

NATIONAL THEATRE CONSERVATORY, Denver, CO 80204-2157

General Information Independent, coed, graduate-only institution. *Graduate housing:* On-campus housing not available.

GRADUATE UNITS

Department of Acting Offers acting (MFA, Certificate).

NATIONAL UNIVERSITY, La Jolla, CA 92037-1011

General Information Independent, coed, comprehensive institution. CGS member. *Enrollment:* 26,417 graduate, professional, and undergraduate students; 6,764 full-time matriculated graduate/professional students (4,572 women), 12,080 part-time matriculated graduate/professional students (7,830 women). *Enrollment by degree level:* 18,844 master's. *Graduate faculty:* 237 full-time (113 women), 2,626 part-time/adjunct (1,333 women). *Tuition:* Full-time $8694; part-time $322 per credit hour. Tuition and fees vary according to course load. *Graduate housing:* On-campus housing not available. *Student services:* Campus employment opportunities, campus safety program, career counseling, international student services, multicultural affairs office, services for students with disabilities, teacher training, writing training. *Library facilities:* National University Library. *Online resources:* library catalog, web page. *Collection:* 303,000 titles, 22,700 serial subscriptions, 9,700 audiovisual materials.

Computer facilities: Computer purchase and lease plans are available. 3,100 computers available on campus for general student use. A campuswide network can be accessed from off campus. Online class registration is available. *Web address:* http://www.nu.edu/.

General Application Contact: Dominick Giovanniello, Associate Regional Dean—San Diego, 800-NAT-UNIV, Fax: 858-541-7792, E-mail: dgiovann@nu.edu.

GRADUATE UNITS

Academic Affairs Students: 6,764 full-time (4,572 women), 12,080 part-time (7,830 women); includes 5,700 minority (1,648 African Americans, 151 American Indian/Alaska Native, 957 Asian Americans or Pacific Islanders, 2,944 Hispanic Americans), 568 international. Average age 36. 10,760 applicants, 10760 enrolled. *Faculty:* 237 full-time (113 women), 2,626 part-time/adjunct (1,333 women). Expenses: Contact institution. *Financial support:* Career-related internships or fieldwork, institutionally sponsored loans, scholarships/grants, and tuition waivers (partial) available. Support available to part-time students. Financial award application deadline: 6/30; financial award applicants required to submit FAFSA. In 2008, 3,424 master's awarded. *Degree program information:* Part-time and evening/weekend programs available. Postbaccalaureate distance learning degree programs offered (no on-campus study). *Application deadline:* Applications are processed on a rolling basis. *Application fee:* $60 ($65 for international students). Electronic applications accepted. *Application Contact:* Dominick Giovanniello, Associate Regional Dean—San Diego, 800-NAT-UNIV, Fax: 858-541-7792, E-mail: dgiovann@nu.edu. *Provost,* Dr. Thomas M. Green, 858-642-8130, Fax: 858-642-8719, E-mail: acooper@nu.edu.

College of Letters and Sciences Students: 896 full-time (662 women), 1,304 part-time (920 women); includes 723 minority (292 African Americans, 17 American Indian/Alaska Native, 105 Asian Americans or Pacific Islanders, 309 Hispanic Americans), 15 international. Average age 36. 1,420 applicants, 1420 enrolled. *Faculty:* 68 full-time (28 women), 681 part-time/adjunct (305 women). Expenses: Contact institution. *Financial support:* Career-related internships or fieldwork, institutionally sponsored loans, scholarships/grants, and tuition waivers (partial) available. Support available to part-time students. Financial award application deadline: 6/30; financial award applicants required to submit FAFSA. In 2008, 560 master's awarded. *Degree program information:* Part-time and evening/weekend programs available. Postbaccalaureate distance learning degree programs offered (no on-campus study). Offers counseling psychology (MA); creative writing (MFA); English (MA); forensic science (MFS); history (MA); human behavior (MA); letters and sciences (MA, MFA, MFS, MPA); public administration (MPA). *Application deadline:* Applications are processed on a rolling basis. *Application fee:* $60 ($65 for international students). Electronic applications accepted. *Application Contact:* Dominick Giovanniello, Associate Regional Dean—San Diego, 800-NAT-UNIV, Fax: 858-541-7792, E-mail: dgiovann@nu.edu. *Dean,* Dr. Michael Mcanear, 858-642-8450, Fax: 858-642-8715, E-mail: mcanear@nu.edu.

School of Business and Management Students: 616 full-time (310 women), 966 part-time (476 women); includes 588 minority (193 African Americans, 15 American Indian/Alaska Native, 169 Asian Americans or Pacific Islanders, 211 Hispanic Americans), 270 international. Average age 35. 938 applicants, 100% accepted, 938 enrolled. *Faculty:* 31 full-time (6 women), 249 part-time/adjunct (68 women). Expenses: Contact institution. *Financial support:* Career-related internships or fieldwork, scholarships/grants, and tuition waivers (partial) available. Support available to part-time students. Financial award application deadline: 6/30; financial award applicants required to submit FAFSA. In 2008, 385 master's awarded. *Degree program information:* Part-time and evening/weekend programs available. Postbaccalaureate distance learning degree programs offered (no on-campus study). Offers accountancy (MS); alternative dispute resolution (MBA); business and management (MA, MBA, MS); corporate and international finance (MS); e-business (MBA, MS); financial management (MBA); human resource management (MBA); human resources management (MA); international business (MBA); knowledge management (MS); management (MA); marketing (MBA); organizational leadership (MBA, MS); technology management (MBA). *Application deadline:* Applications are processed on a rolling basis. *Application fee:* $60 ($65 for international students). Electronic applications accepted. *Application Contact:* Dominick Giovanniello, Associate Regional Dean—San Diego, 800-NAT-UNIV, Fax: 858-541-7792, E-mail: dgiovann@nu.edu. *Interim Dean,* Dr. Thomas M Green, 858-642-8401, Fax: 858-642-8406, E-mail: acooper@nu.edu.

School of Education Students: 4,903 full-time (3,492 women), 8,772 part-time (5,856 women); includes 4,098 minority (1,055 African Americans, 114 American Indian/Alaska Native, 641 Asian Americans or Pacific Islanders, 2,288 Hispanic Americans), 60 international. Average age 36. 7,322 applicants, 100% accepted, 7322 enrolled. *Faculty:* 91 full-time (55 women), 1,293 part-time/adjunct (792 women). Expenses: Contact institution. *Financial support:* Career-related internships or fieldwork, institutionally sponsored loans, scholarships/grants, and tuition waivers (partial) available. Support available to part-time students. Financial award application deadline: 6/30. In 2008, 2,329 master's awarded. *Degree program information:* Part-time and evening/weekend programs available. Postbaccalaureate distance learning degree programs offered (no on-campus study). Offers applied school leadership (MS); best practices (MA); cross-cultural teaching (M Ed); deaf and hard of hearing education (MS); education (M Ed, MA, MS); educational administration (MS); educational counseling (MS); exceptional student education (MS); school psychology (MS); special education (MS); teacher leadership (MA); teaching (MA); teaching/learning in global society (MA). *Application deadline:* Applications are processed on a rolling basis. *Application fee:* $60 ($65 for international students). Electronic applications accepted. *Application Contact:* Dominick Giovanniello, Associate Regional Dean—San Diego, 800-NAT-UNIV, Fax: 858-541-7792, E-mail: dgiovann@nu.edu. *Interim Dean,* Dr. Carl Kalani Beyer, 858-642-8320, Fax: 858-642-8724, E-mail: cbeyer@nu.edu.

School of Engineering and Technology Students: 230 full-time (48 women), 217 part-time (49 women); includes 99 minority (26 African Americans, 2 American Indian/Alaska Native, 45 Asian Americans or Pacific Islanders, 26 Hispanic Americans), 211 international. Average age 32. 254 applicants, 100% accepted, 254 enrolled. *Faculty:* 14 full-time (2 women), 200 part-time/adjunct (38 women). Expenses: Contact institution. *Financial support:* Career-related internships or fieldwork, institutionally sponsored loans, scholarships/grants, and tuition waivers (partial) available. Support available to part-time students. Financial award application deadline: 6/30; financial award applicants required to submit FAFSA. In 2008, 85 master's awarded. *Degree program information:* Part-time and evening/weekend programs available. Postbaccalaureate distance learning degree programs offered (no on-campus study). Offers computer science (MS); database administration (MS); engineering and technology (MS); engineering management (MS); environmental engineering (MS); homeland security and safety engineering (MS); information systems (MS); software engineering (MS); system engineering (MS); technology management (MS); wireless communications (MS). *Application deadline:* Applications are processed on a rolling basis. *Application fee:* $60 ($65 for international students). Electronic applications accepted. *Application Contact:* Dominick Giovanniello, Associate Regional Dean—San Diego, 800-NAT-UNIV, Fax: 858-642-8709, E-mail: dgiovann@nu.edu. *Dean,* Dr. Howard Evans, 858-309-3413, Fax: 858-309-3420, E-mail: hevans@nu.edu.

School of Health and Human Services Students: 2 full-time (both women), 19 part-time (10 women); includes 5 minority (3 African Americans, 1 Asian American or Pacific Islander, 1 Hispanic American), 7 international. Average age 31. 21 applicants, 100% accepted, 21 enrolled. *Faculty:* 19 full-time (16 women), 118 part-time/adjunct (101 women). Expenses: Contact institution. *Financial support:* Career-related internships or fieldwork, institutionally sponsored loans, and scholarships/grants available. Support available to part-time students. Financial award application deadline: 6/30; financial award applicants required to submit FAFSA. In 2008, 3 master's awarded. *Degree program information:* Part-time and evening/weekend programs available. Postbaccalaureate distance learning degree programs offered (no on-campus study). Offers health and human services (MHA, MHCA, MIH, MS); integrative health (MIH). *Application deadline:* Applications are processed on a rolling basis. *Application fee:* $60 ($65 for international students). Electronic applications accepted. *Application Contact:* Dominick Giovanniello, Associate Regional Dean—San Diego, 800-NAT-UNIV, Fax: 858-541-7792, E-mail: dgiovann@nu.edu. *Dean,* Dr. Michael Lacourse, 858-309-3472, Fax: 858-309-3480, E-mail: mlacourse@nu.edu.

School of Media and Communication Students: 70 full-time (26 women), 153 part-time (70 women); includes 71 minority (31 African Americans, 1 American Indian/Alaska Native, 13 Asian Americans or Pacific Islanders, 26 Hispanic Americans). Average age 39. 138 applicants, 100% accepted, 138 enrolled. *Faculty:* 14 full-time (6 women), 85 part-time/adjunct (29 women). Expenses: Contact institution. *Financial support:* Career-related internships or fieldwork, institutionally sponsored loans, scholarships/grants, and tuition waivers (partial) available. Support available to part-time students. Financial award application deadline: 6/30; financial award applicants required to submit FAFSA. In 2008, 62 master's awarded. *Degree program information:* Part-time and evening/weekend programs available. Postbaccalaureate distance learning degree programs offered (no on-campus study). Offers digital cinema (MFA); educational and instructional technology (MS); media and communication (MA, MFA, MS); strategic communication (MA); video game production and design (MFA). *Application deadline:* Applications are processed on a rolling basis. *Application fee:* $60 ($65 for international students). Electronic applications accepted. *Application Contact:* Dominick Giovanniello, Associate Regional Dean—San Diego, 800-NAT-UNIV, Fax: 858-541-7792, E-mail: dgiovann@nu.edu. *Dean,* Karla Berry, 858-309-3442, Fax: 858-309-3450, E-mail: kberry@nu.edu.

NATIONAL UNIVERSITY OF HEALTH SCIENCES, Lombard, IL 60148-4583

General Information Independent, coed, graduate-only institution. *Enrollment:* 421 full-time matriculated graduate/professional students (200 women), 75 part-time matriculated graduate/professional students (51 women). *Enrollment by degree level:* 421 first professional, 23 master's. *Graduate faculty:* 57 full-time (16 women), 66 part-time/adjunct (28 women). *Tuition:* Full-time $19,224; part-time $356 per hour. *Required fees:* $334. *Graduate housing:* Rooms and/or apartments available on a first-come, first-served basis to single and married students. *Student services:* Campus employment opportunities, campus safety program, career counseling, international student services, services for students with disabilities. *Library facilities:* NUHS—Learning Resource Center. *Online resources:* library catalog. *Collection:* 28,373 titles, 256 serial subscriptions, 2,220 audiovisual materials.

Computer facilities: 65 computers available on campus for general student use. A campuswide network can be accessed from student residence rooms. Online class registration, student email, course documents are available. *Web address:* http://www.nuhs.edu/.

General Application Contact: Teri Hatfield, Assistant Director of Admissions, 800-826-6285 Ext. 6572, Fax: 630-889-6566, E-mail: thatfield@nuhs.edu.

GRADUATE UNITS

Chiropractic Program in Florida Expenses: Contact institution. *Financial support:* Fellowships, research assistantships, teaching assistantships, Federal Work-Study, scholarships/grants, and tuition waivers (partial) available. Support available to part-time students. Financial award applicants required to submit FAFSA. Offers chiropractic (DC). *Application deadline:* For fall admission, 8/15 for domestic students, 8/1 for international students; for winter admission, 12/12 for domestic students, 12/1 for international students; for spring admission, 4/17 for domestic students, 4/1 for international students. Applications are processed on a rolling basis. *Application fee:* $55. Electronic applications accepted. *Application Contact:* Teri Hatfield, Assistant Director of Admissions, 800-826-6285, Fax: 630-889-6566, E-mail: thatfield@nuhs.edu. *Dean, College of Professional Studies—Florida,* Dr. Joseph Stiefel, 727-394-6058, Fax: 727-394-6210, E-mail: jstiefel@nuhs.edu.

College of Professional Studies Students: 421 full-time (200 women), 75 part-time (51 women); includes 110 minority (33 African Americans, 1 American Indian/Alaska Native, 54 Asian Americans or Pacific Islanders, 22 Hispanic Americans), 16 international. Average age 25. 282 applicants, 78% accepted, 115 enrolled. *Faculty:* 57 full-time (16 women), 66 part-time/adjunct (28 women). Expenses: Contact institution. *Financial support:* In 2008–09, 101 students received support; fellowships, research assistantships, teaching assistantships, Federal Work-Study, scholarships/grants, and tuition waivers (partial) available. Support available to part-time students. Financial award applicants required to submit FAFSA. In 2008, 290 DCs awarded. Offers acupuncture (MSAC); chiropractic medicine (DC); naturopathic medicine (ND); Oriental medicine (MSOM). *Application deadline:* For fall admission, 8/15 for domestic students, 8/1 for international students; for winter admission, 12/12 for domestic students, 12/1 for international students; for spring admission, 4/17 for domestic students, 4/1 for international students. Applications are processed on a rolling basis. *Application fee:* $55. Electronic applications accepted. *Application Contact:* Teri Hatfield, Assistant Director of Admissions, 800-826-6285, Fax: 630-889-6566, E-mail: thatfield@nuhs.edu. *Dean, College of Professional Studies,* Dr. Nicholas A. Trongale, 630-889-6673, Fax: 630-889-6499, E-mail: ntrongale@nuhs.edu.

NAVAL POSTGRADUATE SCHOOL, Monterey, CA 93943

General Information Federally supported, coed, graduate-only institution. CGS member. *Graduate housing:* Rooms and/or apartments available to single and married students.

GRADUATE UNITS

Graduate Programs *Degree program information:* Part-time programs available. Postbaccalaureate distance learning degree programs offered (minimal on-campus study). Offers applied mathematics (MS, PhD); applied physics (MS); applied science (MS); computer science (MS, PhD); defense analysis (MS); electrical and computer engineering (MS, PhD, Eng); electrical engineering (MS); engineering acoustics (MS); information sciences (MS); intelligence (MA); international relations (MA); joint information operations (MS); knowledge superiority (MS, Certificate); mechanical and astronautical engineering (MS, D Eng, PhD, Eng); meteorology (MS, PhD); modeling of virtual environments and simulations (MS, PhD); oceanography (MS, PhD); operations research (MS, PhD); physical oceanography (MS); physics (MS, PhD); political science (MA); regional security education (MA); security building (MA); security studies (MA); software engineering (MS, PhD); space systems operations (MS); special operations (MS); systems engineering (MS, PhD, Certificate); systems engineering and analysis (MS); systems engineering management (MS). Programs only open to commissioned officers of the United States and friendly nations and selected United States federal civilian employees.

School of Business and Public Policy *Degree program information:* Part-time programs available. Postbaccalaureate distance learning degree programs offered (minimal on-campus study). Offers contract management (MS); defense-focused business administration (MBA); executive business administration (MBA); leadership and human resource development (MS); management (MS); program management (MS); systems engineering management (MS). Program only open to commissioned officers of the United States and friendly nations and selected United States federal civilian employees.

NAVAL WAR COLLEGE, Newport, RI 02841-1207

General Information Federally supported, coed, primarily men, graduate-only institution.

GRADUATE UNITS

Program in National Security and Strategic Studies Offers national security and strategic studies (MA). Program open only to full-time military personnel.

NAZARENE THEOLOGICAL SEMINARY, Kansas City, MO 64131-1263

General Information Independent-religious, coed, graduate-only institution. *Graduate housing:* On-campus housing not available. *Research affiliation:* University of Missouri-Kansas City (religious studies).

Nazarene Theological Seminary (continued)

GRADUATE UNITS

Graduate and Professional Programs *Degree program information:* Part-time programs available. Offers Christian education (MA); intercultural studies (MA); theological studies (MA); theology (M Div, D Min). Electronic applications accepted.

NAZARETH COLLEGE OF ROCHESTER, Rochester, NY 14618-3790

General Information Independent, coed, comprehensive institution. *Graduate housing:* Room and/or apartments available on a first-come, first-served basis to single students; on-campus housing not available to married students. Housing application deadline: 5/15.

GRADUATE UNITS

Graduate Studies *Degree program information:* Part-time and evening/weekend programs available. Postbaccalaureate distance learning degree programs offered. Offers art education (MS Ed); art therapy (MS); business education (MS Ed); communication sciences and disorders (MS); educational technology/computer education (MS Ed); gerontological nurse practitioner (MS); human resource management (MS); inclusive education-adolescence level (MS Ed); inclusive education-childhood level (MS Ed); inclusive education-early childhood level (MS Ed); liberal studies (MA); literacy education (MS Ed); management (MS); music education (MS Ed); music therapy (MS); physical therapy (MS, DPT); social work (MSW); teaching English to speakers of other languages (MS Ed).

NEBRASKA METHODIST COLLEGE, Omaha, NE 68114

General Information Independent-religious, coed, primarily women, comprehensive institution. *Enrollment:* 589 graduate, professional, and undergraduate students; 59 full-time matriculated graduate/professional students (50 women), 24 part-time matriculated graduate/professional students (23 women). *Enrollment by degree level:* 83 master's. *Graduate faculty:* 1 (woman) full-time, 24 part-time/adjunct (16 women). *Tuition:* Full-time $9828; part-time $546 per credit hour. *Required fees:* $450; $25 per credit hour. *Graduate housing:* Room and/or apartments available on a first-come, first-served basis to single students; on-campus housing not available to married students. Typical cost: $6580 per year. Housing application deadline: 4/1. *Student services:* Campus employment opportunities, campus safety program, career counseling, exercise/wellness program, free psychological counseling, international student services, low-cost health insurance, services for students with disabilities, teacher training, writing training.

Computer facilities: 45 computers available on campus for general student use. A campuswide network can be accessed. *Web address:* http://www.methodistcollege.edu/.

General Application Contact: Sara Bonney, Director of Admissions, 402-354-7111, Fax: 402-354-7020, E-mail: admissions@methodistcollege.edu.

GRADUATE UNITS

Program in Health Promotion Management Students: 21 full-time; includes 1 minority (Hispanic American). Average age 28. 26 applicants, 65% accepted, 13 enrolled. *Faculty:* 7 part-time/adjunct (6 women). Expenses: Contact institution. *Financial support:* In 2008–09, 7 students received support; research assistantships with full and partial tuition reimbursements available, scholarships/grants available. Support available to part-time students. Financial award applicants required to submit FAFSA. In 2008, 17 master's awarded. *Degree program information:* Evening/weekend programs available. Postbaccalaureate distance learning degree programs offered (no on-campus study). Offers health promotion management (MS). *Application deadline:* Applications are processed on a rolling basis. *Application fee:* $25. *Application Contact:* Sara Bonney, Director of Admissions, 402-354-7111, Fax: 402-354-7020, E-mail: admissions@methodistcollege.edu. *Program Development Officer,* Beth Pernie, 402-354-7138, Fax: 402-354-7020, E-mail: Beth.Pirnie@methodistcollege.edu.

Program in Medical Group Administration Students: 11 full-time (4 women). Average age 45. *Faculty:* 9 part-time/adjunct (2 women). Expenses: Contact institution. *Financial support:* In 2008–09, 3 students received support. Scholarships/grants available. *Degree program information:* Evening/weekend programs available. Postbaccalaureate distance learning degree programs offered (no on-campus study). Offers medical group administration (MS). *Application fee:* $25. *Application Contact:* Sara Bonney, Director of Admissions, 402-354-7111, Fax: 402-354-7020, E-mail: admissions@methodistcollege.edu. *Program Development Officer,* Beth Pernie, 402-354-7138, Fax: 402-354-7020, E-mail: beth.pernie@methodistcollege.edu.

Program in Nursing Students: 24 full-time (all women), 24 part-time (all women); includes 3 minority (all African Americans). Average age 41. *Faculty:* 1 (woman) full-time, 8 part-time/adjunct (all women). Expenses: Contact institution. *Financial support:* In 2008–09, 10 students received support; research assistantships with full and partial tuition reimbursements available, scholarships/grants available. Support available to part-time students. Financial award applicants required to submit FAFSA. In 2008, 15 master's awarded. *Degree program information:* Evening/weekend programs available. Postbaccalaureate distance learning degree programs offered (no on-campus study). Offers nursing (MSN). *Application deadline:* For spring admission, 11/1 for domestic and international students. Applications are processed on a rolling basis. *Application fee:* $25. *Application Contact:* Sara Bonney, Director of Admissions, 402-354-7111, Fax: 402-354-7020, E-mail: admissions@methodistcollege.edu. *Coordinator, Graduate Nursing Programs,* Linda Foley, 402-354-7050, Fax: 402-354-7020, E-mail: linda.foley@methodistcollege.edu.

NEBRASKA WESLEYAN UNIVERSITY, Lincoln, NE 68504-2796

General Information Independent-religious, coed, comprehensive institution.

GRADUATE UNITS

University College *Degree program information:* Part-time programs available. Offers forensic science (MFS); historical studies (MA); nursing (MSN).

NER ISRAEL RABBINICAL COLLEGE, Baltimore, MD 21208

General Information Independent-religious, men only, comprehensive institution. *Graduate housing:* Rooms and/or apartments guaranteed to single students and available on a first-come, first-served basis to married students.

GRADUATE UNITS

Graduate Programs Offers rabbinics (MTL, DTL, Professional Certificate).

NER ISRAEL YESHIVA COLLEGE OF TORONTO, Thornhill, ON L4J 8A7, Canada

General Information Independent-religious, men only, comprehensive institution.

GRADUATE UNITS

Graduate Programs

NEUMANN UNIVERSITY, Aston, PA 19014-1298

General Information Independent-religious, coed, comprehensive institution. *Enrollment:* 3,037 graduate, professional, and undergraduate students; 119 full-time matriculated graduate/professional students (78 women), 434 part-time matriculated graduate/professional students (310 women). *Enrollment by degree level:* 431 master's, 122 doctoral. *Graduate faculty:* 22 full-time (17 women), 58 part-time/adjunct (35 women). *Graduate housing:* On-campus housing not available. *Student services:* Campus employment opportunities, campus safety program, career counseling, child daycare facilities, exercise/wellness program, free psychological counseling, multicultural affairs office, services for students with disabilities, teacher training, writing training. *Library facilities:* Neumann College Library. *Online resources:* library catalog, web page, access to other libraries' catalogs. *Collection:* 75,000 titles, 400 serial subscriptions, 2,000 audiovisual materials.

Computer facilities: Computer purchase and lease plans are available. 400 computers available on campus for general student use. A campuswide network can be accessed from student residence rooms and from off campus. Online class registration is available. *Web address:* http://www.neumann.edu/.

General Application Contact: Kittie D. Pain, Associate Director of Admissions, Graduate and Adult Programs, 610-558-5613, Fax: 610-558-5652, E-mail: paink@neumann.edu.

GRADUATE UNITS

Program in Education Students: 36 full-time (25 women), 198 part-time (152 women); includes 21 minority (18 African Americans, 1 American Indian/Alaska Native, 2 Asian Americans or Pacific Islanders). Average age 34. 100 applicants, 100% accepted, 75 enrolled. *Faculty:* 2 full-time (1 woman), 31 part-time/adjunct (15 women). Expenses: Contact institution. *Financial support:* Available to part-time students. Application deadline: 3/15. In 2008, 60 master's awarded. *Degree program information:* Part-time programs available. Offers education (MS). *Application deadline:* Applications are processed on a rolling basis. *Application fee:* $50. *Application Contact:* Kittie D. Pain, Associate Director of Admissions, Graduate and Adult Programs, 610-558-5613, Fax: 610-558-5652, E-mail: paink@neumann.edu. *Coordinator, Division of Education and Human Services,* Dr. Andrew DeSanto, 610-558-5404, Fax: 610-459-1370, E-mail: desantoa@neumann.edu.

Program in Nursing and Health Sciences Students: 17 part-time (15 women); includes 1 minority (Hispanic American). Average age 46. 10 applicants, 100% accepted, 8 enrolled. *Faculty:* 6 full-time (all women), 1 (woman) part-time/adjunct. Expenses: Contact institution. *Financial support:* Available to part-time students. Application deadline: 3/15. In 2008, 2 master's awarded. *Degree program information:* Part-time programs available. Offers nursing and health sciences (MS). *Application deadline:* Applications are processed on a rolling basis. *Application fee:* $50. *Application Contact:* Kittie D. Pain, Associate Director of Admissions, Graduate and Adult Programs, 610-558-5613, Fax: 610-558-5652, E-mail: paink@neumann.edu. *Dean, Division of Nursing and Health Services,* Dr. Kathleen Hoover, 610-558-5560, Fax: 610-459-1370, E-mail: hooverk@neumann.edu.

Program in Pastoral Counseling Students: 9 full-time (4 women), 101 part-time (78 women); includes 17 minority (10 African Americans, 1 American Indian/Alaska Native, 3 Asian Americans or Pacific Islanders, 3 Hispanic Americans). Average age 49. 50 applicants, 100% accepted, 45 enrolled. *Faculty:* 3 full-time (2 women), 7 part-time/adjunct (5 women). Expenses: Contact institution. *Financial support:* In 2008–09, 8 students received support. Available to part-time students. Application deadline: 3/15. In 2008, 23 master's awarded. *Degree program information:* Part-time and evening/weekend programs available. Offers pastoral counseling (MS, CAS); spiritual direction (CSD). *Application deadline:* Applications are processed on a rolling basis. *Application fee:* $50. *Application Contact:* Kittie D. Pain, Associate Director of Admissions, Graduate and Adult Programs, 610-558-5613, Fax: 610-558-5652, E-mail: paink@neumann.edu. *Executive Director,* Dr. Leonard DiPaul, 610-558-5220, Fax: 610-459-1370, E-mail: dipall@neumann.edu.

Program in Physical Therapy Students: 70 full-time (48 women), 5 part-time (3 women); includes 12 minority (2 African Americans, 3 Asian Americans or Pacific Islanders, 7 Hispanic Americans). Average age 34. 96 applicants, 47% accepted, 35 enrolled. *Faculty:* 6 full-time (4 women), 6 part-time/adjunct (5 women). Expenses: Contact institution. *Financial support:* Available to part-time students. Application deadline: 3/15. In 2008, 33 doctorates awarded. *Degree program information:* Evening/weekend programs available. Offers physical therapy (DPT). *Application deadline:* For fall admission, 12/1 for domestic students. *Application fee:* $50. *Application Contact:* Kittie D. Pain, Associate Director of Admissions, Graduate and Adult Programs, 610-558-5613, Fax: 610-558-5652, E-mail: paink@neumann.edu. *Director,* Dr. Robert Post, 610-558-5233, Fax: 610-459-1370, E-mail: postr@neumann.edu.

Program in Sports Management Students: 3 full-time (0 women), 11 part-time (5 women); includes 2 minority (both African Americans). Average age 28. 10 applicants, 100% accepted, 8 enrolled. *Faculty:* 2 full-time (both women), 3 part-time/adjunct (2 women). Expenses: Contact institution. *Financial support:* Available to part-time students. Application deadline: 3/15. In 2008, 11 master's awarded. *Degree program information:* Part-time programs available. Offers sports management (MS). *Application deadline:* Applications are processed on a rolling basis. *Application fee:* $50. *Application Contact:* Kittie D. Pain, Associate Director of Admissions, Graduate and Adult Programs, 610-558-5613, Fax: 610-558-5652, E-mail: paink@neumann.edu. *Coordinator,* Dr. Sandra L. Slabik, 610-361-5291, Fax: 610-558-5574, E-mail: slabiks@neumann.edu.

Program in Strategic Leadership Students: 56 part-time (33 women); includes 12 minority (11 African Americans, 1 Hispanic American). Average age 39. 40 applicants, 100% accepted, 35 enrolled. *Faculty:* 1 full-time (0 women), 6 part-time/adjunct (3 women). Expenses: Contact institution. *Financial support:* Available to part-time students. Application deadline: 3/15. In 2008, 33 master's awarded. Offers strategic leadership (MS). *Application fee:* $50. *Application Contact:* Kittie D. Pain, Associate Director of Admissions, Graduate and Adult Programs, 610-558-5613, Fax: 610-558-5652, E-mail: paink@neumann.edu. *Coordinator, Division of Continuing Adult and Professional Studies,* Dr. Frederick Loomis, 610-361-5292, E-mail: loomisf@neumann.edu.

Programs in Education Students: 1 (woman) full-time, 46 part-time (24 women); includes 4 minority (3 African Americans, 1 Asian American or Pacific Islander). Average age 39. *Faculty:* 4 full-time (2 women), 1 (woman) part-time/adjunct. Expenses: Contact institution. Offers education (Ed D). *Application Contact:* Kittie D. Pain, Associate Director of Admissions, Graduate and Adult Programs, 610-558-5613, Fax: 610-558-5652, E-mail: paink@neumann.edu. *Dean of Studies,* Jannay Morrow, 914-437-5257.

NEW BRUNSWICK THEOLOGICAL SEMINARY, New Brunswick, NJ 08901-1196

General Information Independent-religious, coed, graduate-only institution. *Graduate housing:* Rooms and/or apartments available on a first-come, first-served basis to single students and available to married students.

GRADUATE UNITS

Graduate and Professional Programs *Degree program information:* Part-time and evening/weekend programs available. Offers metro-urban ministry (D Min); theological studies (M Div, MA, D Min). Electronic applications accepted.

NEW ENGLAND COLLEGE, Henniker, NH 03242-3293

General Information Independent, coed, comprehensive institution. *Graduate housing:* Room and/or apartments available on a first-come, first-served basis to single students; on-campus housing not available to married students. Housing application deadline: 5/1.

GRADUATE UNITS

Program in Community Mental Health Counseling *Degree program information:* Part-time and evening/weekend programs available. Offers human services (MS); mental health counseling (MS).

Program in Creative Writing *Degree program information:* Part-time and evening/weekend programs available. Offers poetry (MFA). Electronic applications accepted.

Program in Education *Degree program information:* Part-time and evening/weekend programs available. Offers literacy and language arts (M Ed); meeting the needs of all learners/special education (M Ed); teacher leadership/school reform (M Ed).

Program in Management *Degree program information:* Part-time and evening/weekend programs available. Offers healthcare administration (MS); nonprofit leadership (MS); organizational leadership (MS). Electronic applications accepted.

Program in Public Policy *Degree program information:* Part-time and evening/weekend programs available. Postbaccalaureate distance learning degree programs offered (no on-campus study). Offers public policy (MA). Electronic applications accepted.

THE NEW ENGLAND COLLEGE OF OPTOMETRY, Boston, MA 02115-1100

General Information Independent, coed, graduate-only institution. *Graduate housing:* On-campus housing not available. *Research affiliation:* Vistakon Johnson and Johnson (contact lens study), Boston University School of Medicine (vision science).

GRADUATE UNITS

Professional Program Offers optometry (OD); vision science (MS). Electronic applications accepted.

NEW ENGLAND CONSERVATORY OF MUSIC, Boston, MA 02115-5000

General Information Independent, coed, comprehensive institution. *Enrollment:* 714 graduate, professional, and undergraduate students; 339 full-time matriculated graduate/professional students (171 women), 19 part-time matriculated graduate/professional students (14 women). *Enrollment by degree level:* 274 master's, 23 doctoral, 61 other advanced degrees. *Graduate faculty:* 89 full-time (30 women), 127 part-time/adjunct (39 women). *Tuition:* Full-time $32,900; part-time $2100 per credit. *Required fees:* $425. *Graduate housing:* Room and/or apartments available on a first-come, first-served basis to single students; on-campus housing not available to married students. Typical cost: $11,600 (including board). Housing application deadline: 6/15. *Student services:* Campus employment opportunities, career counseling, free psychological counseling, international student services, low-cost health insurance, services for students with disabilities. *Library facilities:* Spaulding Library plus 3 others. *Online resources:* library catalog, web page, access to other libraries' catalogs. *Collection:* 91,418 titles, 305 serial subscriptions, 61,416 audiovisual materials.

Computer facilities: 70 computers available on campus for general student use. A campuswide network can be accessed. *Web address:* http://www.newenglandconservatory.edu/.

General Application Contact: Christina Daly, Director of Admissions, 617-585-1101, Fax: 617-585-1115, E-mail: christina.daly@newenglandconservatory.edu.

GRADUATE UNITS

Graduate Program in Music Students: 339 full-time (171 women), 19 part-time (14 women); includes 39 minority (9 African Americans, 2 American Indian/Alaska Native, 21 Asian Americans or Pacific Islanders, 7 Hispanic Americans), 138 international. Average age 25. 1,319 applicants, 30% accepted, 173 enrolled. *Faculty:* 89 full-time (30 women), 127 part-time/adjunct (39 women). Expenses: Contact institution. *Financial support:* In 2008–09, 342 students received support, including 330 fellowships with partial tuition reimbursements available (averaging $15,120 per year); teaching assistantships, Federal Work-Study, scholarships/grants, and tuition waivers (partial) also available. Support available to part-time students. Financial award application deadline: 12/1; financial award applicants required to submit FAFSA. In 2008, 148 master's, 167 doctorates, 35 other advanced degrees awarded. Offers music (MM, DMA, Diploma). *Application deadline:* For fall admission, 12/1 priority date for domestic and international students; for spring admission, 11/1 for domestic and international students. Applications are processed on a rolling basis. *Application fee:* $100. *Application Contact:* Christina Daly, Director of Admissions, 617-585-1101, Fax: 617-585-1115, E-mail: christina.daly@newenglandconservatory.edu. *Dean of the College,* Tom Novak, 617-585-1304, Fax: 617-585-1303, E-mail: tnovak@newenglandconservatory.edu.

NEW ENGLAND SCHOOL OF ACUPUNCTURE, Newton, MA 02458

General Information Independent, coed, graduate-only institution. *Graduate housing:* On-campus housing not available.

GRADUATE UNITS

Program in Acupuncture and Oriental Medicine *Degree program information:* Part-time programs available. Offers acupuncture (M Ac); acupuncture and Oriental medicine (MAOM).

NEW ENGLAND SCHOOL OF LAW, Boston, MA 02116-5687

General Information Independent, coed, graduate-only institution. *Enrollment by degree level:* 1,103 first professional. *Graduate faculty:* 37 full-time (14 women), 72 part-time/adjunct (27 women). Tuition and fees vary according to program. *Graduate housing:* On-campus housing not available. *Student services:* Campus employment opportunities, career counseling, low-cost health insurance, services for students with disabilities, writing training. *Library facilities:* New England Law [B]oston Law Library. *Online resources:* library catalog, web page, access to other libraries' catalogs. *Collection:* 202,689 titles, 1,552 serial subscriptions, 911 audiovisual materials.

Computer facilities: 74 computers available on campus for general student use. A campuswide network can be accessed from off campus. Online class registration is available. *Web address:* http://www.nesl.edu/.

General Application Contact: Michelle L'Etoile, Director of Admissions, 617-422-7210, Fax: 617-422-7201, E-mail: admit@nesl.edu.

GRADUATE UNITS

Professional Program Students: 703 full-time (403 women), 374 part-time (176 women); includes 113 minority (18 African Americans, 3 American Indian/Alaska Native, 72 Asian Americans or Pacific Islanders, 20 Hispanic Americans). Average age 27. 2,569 applicants, 58% accepted, 255 enrolled. *Faculty:* 37 full-time (14 women), 72 part-time/adjunct (27 women). Expenses: Contact institution. *Financial support:* In 2008–09, 534 students received support. Federal Work-Study, scholarships/grants, and tuition waivers (full and partial) available. Support available to part-time students. Financial award application deadline: 4/9; financial award applicants required to submit FAFSA. In 2008, 315 JDs awarded. *Degree program information:* Part-time and evening/weekend programs available. Offers law (JD, LL M). *Application deadline:* For fall admission, 3/15 for domestic students. Applications are processed on a rolling basis. *Application fee:* $65. Electronic applications accepted. *Application Contact:* Michelle L'Etoile, Director of Admissions, 617-422-7210, Fax: 617-422-7201, E-mail: admit@nesl.edu. *Dean,* John F. O'Brien, 617-422-7221, Fax: 617-422-7333, E-mail: jobrien@nesl.edu.

NEW JERSEY CITY UNIVERSITY, Jersey City, NJ 07305-1597

General Information State-supported, coed, comprehensive institution. *Graduate housing:* On-campus housing not available.

GRADUATE UNITS

Graduate Studies and Continuing Education *Degree program information:* Part-time and evening/weekend programs available.

College of Arts and Sciences *Degree program information:* Part-time and evening/weekend programs available. Offers art (MFA); art education (MA); arts and sciences (MA, MFA, MM, PD); counseling (MA); educational psychology (MA, PD); mathematics education (MA); music education (MA); performance (MM); school psychology (PD); studio art (MFA).

College of Education Offers basics and urban studies (MA); bilingual/bicultural education and English as a second language (MA); early childhood education (MA); education (MA, MAT); educational administration and supervision (MA); educational technology (MA); elementary education (MAT); elementary school reading (MA); reading specialist (MA); secondary education (MAT); secondary school reading (MA); special education (MA).

College of Professional Studies *Degree program information:* Part-time and evening/weekend programs available. Offers accounting (MS); community health education (MS); criminal justice (MS); finance (MS); health administration (MS); law enforcement (MS); school health education (MS).

NEW JERSEY INSTITUTE OF TECHNOLOGY, Newark, NJ 07102

General Information State-supported, coed, university. CGS member. *Enrollment:* 8,398 graduate, professional, and undergraduate students; 1,497 full-time matriculated graduate/professional students (467 women), 1,201 part-time matriculated graduate/professional students (325 women). *Enrollment by degree level:* 2,147 master's, 439 doctoral, 112 other advanced degrees. *Graduate faculty:* 396 full-time (67 women), 263 part-time/adjunct (48 women). Tuition, state resident: full-time $13,780; part-time $750 per credit. Tuition, nonresident: full-time $19,580; part-time $1033 per credit. *Required fees:* $1956; $197 per credit. *Graduate housing:* Room and/or apartments available on a first-come, first-served basis to single students; on-campus housing not available to married students. Typical cost: $9209 (including board). Housing application deadline: 3/31. *Student services:* Campus employment opportunities, campus safety program, career counseling, child daycare facilities, exercise/wellness program, free psychological counseling, international student services, low-cost health insurance, services for students with disabilities, teacher training, writing training. *Library facilities:* Van Houten Library plus 1 other. *Online resources:* library catalog, web page, access to other libraries' catalogs. *Collection:* 160,000 titles, 1,100 serial subscriptions.

Computer facilities: Computer purchase and lease plans are available. 1,938 computers available on campus for general student use. A campuswide network can be accessed from student residence rooms and from off campus. Online class registration is available. *Web address:* http://www.njit.edu/.

General Application Contact: Kathryn Kelly, Director of Admissions, 973-596-3300, Fax: 973-596-3461, E-mail: admissions@njit.edu.

GRADUATE UNITS

Office of Graduate Studies Students: 1,497 full-time (467 women), 1,201 part-time (325 women); includes 706 minority (169 African Americans, 11 American Indian/Alaska Native, 344 Asian Americans or Pacific Islanders, 182 Hispanic Americans), 1,302 international. Average age 29. 5,034 applicants, 20% accepted, 904 enrolled. *Faculty:* 396 full-time (67 women), 263 part-time/adjunct (48 women). Expenses: Contact institution. *Financial support:* Fellowships with full and partial tuition reimbursements, research assistantships with full and partial tuition reimbursements, teaching assistantships with full and partial tuition reimbursements, career-related internships or fieldwork, Federal Work-Study, institutionally sponsored loans, and unspecified assistantships available. Financial award application deadline: 3/15. In 2008, 983 master's, 56 doctorates awarded. *Degree program information:* Part-time and evening/weekend programs available. *Application deadline:* For fall admission, 6/5 priority date for domestic students, 4/1 for international students; for spring admission, 11/15 for domestic and international students. Applications are processed on a rolling basis. *Application fee:* $60. Electronic applications accepted. *Application Contact:* Kathryn Kelly, Director of Admissions, 973-596-3300, Fax: 973-596-3461, E-mail: admissions@njit.edu. *Dean of Graduate Studies,* Dr. Ronald Kane, 973-596-3462, E-mail: ronald.kane@njit.edu.

College of Computing Science Students: 362 full-time (107 women), 268 part-time (67 women); includes 154 minority (30 African Americans, 3 American Indian/Alaska Native, 84 Asian Americans or Pacific Islanders, 37 Hispanic Americans), 351 international. Average age 28. 1,424 applicants, 63% accepted, 630 enrolled. *Faculty:* 51 full-time (5 women), 19 part-time/adjunct (1 woman). Expenses: Contact institution. *Financial support:* Fellowships with full and partial tuition reimbursements, research assistantships with full and partial tuition reimbursements, teaching assistantships with full and partial tuition reimbursements, career-related internships or fieldwork, Federal Work-Study, institutionally sponsored loans, and unspecified assistantships available. Financial award application deadline: 3/15. In 2008, 314 master's, 17 doctorates awarded. *Degree program information:* Part-time and evening/weekend programs available. Offers bioInformatics (MS); business and information systems (MS); computer science (MS, PhD); computing and business (MS); computing science (MS, PhD); emergency management and business continuity (MS); information systems (MS, PhD); software engineering (MS). *Application deadline:* For fall admission, 6/5 priority date for domestic students, 4/1 for international students; for spring admission, 11/15 for domestic and international students. Applications are processed on a rolling basis. *Application fee:* $60. Electronic applications accepted. *Application Contact:* Kathryn Kelly, Director of Admissions, 973-596-3300, Fax: 973-596-3461, E-mail: admissions@njit.edu. *Chairperson,* Dr. Narain Gehani, 973-542-5488, Fax: 973-596-5777, E-mail: narain.gehani@njit.edu.

College of Science and Liberal Arts Students: 144 full-time (66 women), 125 part-time (56 women); includes 77 minority (24 African Americans, 3 American Indian/Alaska Native, 39 Asian Americans or Pacific Islanders, 11 Hispanic Americans), 106 international. Average age 31. 474 applicants, 58% accepted, 86 enrolled. *Faculty:* 149 full-time (33 women), 73 part-time/adjunct (22 women). Expenses: Contact institution. *Financial support:* Fellowships with full tuition reimbursements, research assistantships with full tuition reimbursements, teaching assistantships with full tuition reimbursements available. Financial award application deadline: 3/15. In 2008, 68 master's, 19 doctorates awarded. *Degree program information:* Part-time and evening/weekend programs available. Offers applied mathematics (MS); applied physics (MS, PhD); applied statistics (MS); biology (MS, PhD); biostatistics (MS); chemistry (MS, PhD); computational biology (MS); computing biology (MS); environmental policy studies (MS); environmental science (MS, PhD); history (MA, MAT); material science and engineering (MS); materials science and engineering (PhD); mathematics science (PhD); professional and technical communication (MS); science and liberal arts (MA, MAT, MS, PhD). *Application deadline:* For fall admission, 6/5 priority date for domestic students, 4/1 for international students; for spring admission, 11/15 for domestic and international students. Applications are processed on a rolling basis. *Application fee:* $60. Electronic applications accepted. *Application Contact:* Kathryn Kelly, Director of Admissions, 973-596-3300, Fax: 973-596-3461, E-mail: admissions@njit.edu. *Dean,* Dr. Fadi P. Deek, 973-596-3676, Fax: 973-565-0586, E-mail: fadi.deek@njit.edu.

Newark College of Engineering Students: 749 full-time (210 women), 578 part-time (132 women); includes 321 minority (73 African Americans, 3 American Indian/Alaska Native, 149 Asian Americans or Pacific Islanders, 96 Hispanic Americans), 720 international. Average age 28. 2,593 applicants, 68% accepted, 482 enrolled. *Faculty:* 138 full-time (15 women), 96 part-time/adjunct (6 women). Expenses: Contact institution. *Financial support:* Fellowships with full and partial tuition reimbursements, research assistantships with full and partial tuition reimbursements, teaching assistantships with full and partial tuition reimbursements available. Financial award application deadline: 3/15. In 2008, 454 master's, 23 doctorates awarded. *Degree program information:* Part-time and evening/weekend programs available. Offers biomedical engineering (MS, PhD); chemical engineering (MS, PhD); civil engineering (MS, PhD); computer engineering (MS, PhD); electrical engineering (MS, PhD); engineering (MS, PhD, Engineer); engineering management (MS); engineering science (MS); environmental engineering (MS, PhD); industrial engineering (MS, PhD); Internet engineering (MS); manufacturing engineering (MS); mechanical engineering (MS, PhD, Engineer); occupational safety and health engineering (MS); pharmaceutical engineering (MS); power and energy systems (MS); transportation (MS, PhD). *Application deadline:* For fall admission, 6/5 priority date for domestic students, 4/1 for international students; for spring admission, 11/15 for domestic and international students. Applications are processed on a rolling basis. *Application fee:* $60. Electronic applications accepted. *Application Contact:* Kathryn Kelly, Director of Admissions, 973-596-3300, Fax: 973-596-3461, E-mail: admissions@njit.edu. *Dean,* Dr. Sunil Saigal, 973-596-5443, E-mail: sunil.saigal@njit.edu.

School of Architecture Students: 92 full-time (51 women), 30 part-time (14 women); includes 33 minority (14 African Americans, 1 American Indian/Alaska Native, 11 Asian Americans or Pacific Islanders, 7 Hispanic Americans), 25 international. Average age 33. 163 applicants, 56% accepted, 34 enrolled. *Faculty:* 29 full-time (7 women), 58 part-time/adjunct (17 women). Expenses: Contact institution. *Financial support:* Fellowships with full and partial tuition reimbursements, research assistantships with full and partial tuition reimbursements, teaching assistantships with full and partial tuition reimbursements, career-related internships or fieldwork, Federal Work-Study, institutionally sponsored loans, and unspecified assistantships available. Financial award application deadline: 3/15. In 2008, 36 master's awarded. *Degree program information:* Part-time and evening/weekend programs available. Offers architecture (M Arch, MIP, MS, PhD); infrastructure planning (MIP); urban systems (PhD). *Application deadline:* For fall admission, 6/5 priority date for domestic students, 4/1 for international students; for spring admission, 11/15 for domestic and international students. Applications are processed on a rolling basis. *Application fee:* $60. Electronic applications accepted. *Application Contact:* Kathryn Kelly, Director of Admissions, 973-596-3300, Fax: 973-596-3461, E-mail: admissions@njit.edu. *Dean,* Urs P. Gauchat, 973-596-3079, E-mail: urs.p.gauchat@njit.edu.

School of Management Students: 120 full-time (23 women), 87 part-time (22 women); includes 70 minority (18 African Americans, 1 American Indian/Alaska Native, 35 Asian Americans or Pacific Islanders, 16 Hispanic Americans), 77 international. Average age 32. 326 applicants, 53% accepted, 76 enrolled. *Faculty:* 29 full-time (8 women), 14 part-time/adjunct (1 woman). Expenses: Contact institution. *Financial support:* Fellowships with full

New Jersey Institute of Technology (continued)

and partial tuition reimbursements, research assistantships with full and partial tuition reimbursements, teaching assistantships with full and partial tuition reimbursements, career-related internships or fieldwork, Federal Work-Study, institutionally sponsored loans, and unspecified assistantships available. Financial award application deadline: 3/15. In 2008, 109 master's, 1 doctorate awarded. *Degree program information:* Part-time and evening/weekend programs available. Offers management of business administration (MBA); management of technology (MS). *Application deadline:* For fall admission, 6/5 priority date for domestic students, 4/1 for international students; for spring admission, 11/15 for domestic and international students. Applications are processed on a rolling basis. *Application fee:* $60. Electronic applications accepted. *Application Contact:* Kathryn Kelly, Director of Admissions, 973-596-3300, Fax: 973-596-3461, E-mail: admissions@njit.edu. *Interim Dean,* Dr. Robert English, 973-596-3224, Fax: 973-596-3074, E-mail: robert.english@njit.edu.

NEW LIFE THEOLOGICAL SEMINARY, Charlotte, NC 28206-7901

General Information Independent-religious, coed, comprehensive institution.

GRADUATE UNITS

Graduate Program *Degree program information:* Part-time and evening/weekend programs available. Electronic applications accepted.

NEWMAN THEOLOGICAL COLLEGE, Edmonton, AB T6V 1H3, Canada

General Information Independent-religious, coed, graduate-only institution. *Graduate housing:* On-campus housing not available.

GRADUATE UNITS

Religious Education Program *Degree program information:* Part-time programs available. Postbaccalaureate distance learning degree programs offered (no on-campus study). Offers Catholic school administration (CCSA); religious education (MRE, GDRE).

Theology Program *Degree program information:* Part-time programs available. Offers theology (M Div, M Th, MTS).

NEWMAN UNIVERSITY, Wichita, KS 67213-2097

General Information Independent-religious, coed, comprehensive institution. *Enrollment:* 2,435 graduate, professional, and undergraduate students; 164 full-time matriculated graduate/professional students (109 women), 465 part-time matriculated graduate/professional students (333 women). *Enrollment by degree level:* 396 master's, 233 other advanced degrees. *Graduate faculty:* 19 full-time (5 women), 36 part-time/adjunct (27 women). *Graduate housing:* Rooms and/or apartments available on a first-come, first-served basis to single and married students. Housing application deadline: 8/1. *Student services:* Campus employment opportunities, campus safety program, career counseling, exercise/wellness program, free psychological counseling, international student services, low-cost health insurance, services for students with disabilities, teacher training, writing training. *Library facilities:* Dungan Library and Campus Center. *Online resources:* library catalog, web page, access to other libraries' catalogs. *Collection:* 110,167 titles, 156 serial subscriptions, 1,952 audiovisual materials.

Computer facilities: 130 computers available on campus for general student use. A campuswide network can be accessed from student residence rooms. Online class registration is available. *Web address:* http://www.newmanu.edu/.

General Application Contact: Linda Kay Sabala, Director of Graduate Admissions, 316-942-4291 Ext. 2230, Fax: 316-942-4483, E-mail: sabalal@newmanu.edu.

GRADUATE UNITS

School of Business Students: 71 full-time (34 women), 92 part-time (32 women); includes 30 minority (12 African Americans, 2 American Indian/Alaska Native, 12 Asian Americans or Pacific Islanders, 4 Hispanic Americans), 26 international. Average age 31. 119 applicants, 74% accepted, 70 enrolled. *Faculty:* 7 full-time (1 woman), 6 part-time/adjunct (1 woman). Expenses: Contact institution. *Financial support:* In 2008–09, 3 students received support. Federal Work-Study and tuition waivers (full) available. Financial award application deadline: 8/15; financial award applicants required to submit FAFSA. In 2008, 72 master's awarded. *Degree program information:* Part-time programs available. Offers international business (MBA); leadership (MBA); management (MBA); technology (MBA). *Application deadline:* For fall admission, 8/1 priority date for domestic students, 7/15 priority date for international students; for winter admission, 1/1 priority date for domestic students; for spring admission, 1/1 priority date for domestic students, 11/15 priority date for international students. Applications are processed on a rolling basis. *Application fee:* $25 ($40 for international students). Electronic applications accepted. *Application Contact:* Linda Kay Sabala, Director of Graduate Admissions, 316-942-4291 Ext. 2230, Fax: 316-942-4483, E-mail: sabalal@newmanu.edu. *Dean of the College of Professional Studies and Director of the School of Business,* Dr. Joe Goetz, 316-942-4291 Ext. 2111, Fax: 316-942-4486, E-mail: goetzj@newmanu.edu.

School of Education Students: 9 full-time (all women), 287 part-time (228 women); includes 27 minority (6 African Americans, 1 American Indian/Alaska Native, 2 Asian Americans or Pacific Islanders, 18 Hispanic Americans), 2 international. Average age 38. 48 applicants, 85% accepted, 39 enrolled. *Faculty:* 3 full-time (0 women), 21 part-time/adjunct (all women). Expenses: Contact institution. *Financial support:* In 2008–09, 8 students received support. Federal Work-Study and tuition waivers (full) available. Financial award application deadline: 8/15; financial award applicants required to submit FAFSA. In 2008, 55 master's awarded. *Degree program information:* Part-time programs available. Postbaccalaureate distance learning degree programs offered (no on-campus study). Offers building leadership (MS Ed); curriculum and instruction (MS Ed). *Application deadline:* For fall admission, 8/15 priority date for domestic students, 7/15 priority date for international students; for spring admission, 1/10 priority date for domestic students, 11/15 priority date for international students. Applications are processed on a rolling basis. *Application fee:* $25 ($40 for international students). Electronic applications accepted. *Application Contact:* Linda Kay Sabala, Director of Graduate Admissions, 316-942-4291 Ext. 2230, Fax: 316-942-4483, E-mail: sabalal@newmanu.edu. *Director,* Dr. Guy Glidden, 316-942-4291 Ext. 2331, Fax: 316-942-4483, E-mail: gliddeng@newmanu.edu.

School of Nursing and Allied Health Students: 35 full-time (21 women), 1 part-time (0 women); includes 4 minority (2 African Americans, 1 Asian American or Pacific Islander, 1 Hispanic American). Average age 33. 108 applicants, 18% accepted, 18 enrolled. *Faculty:* 3 full-time (2 women), 3 part-time/adjunct (2 women). Expenses: Contact institution. *Financial support:* Federal Work-Study and tuition waivers (full) available. Financial award application deadline: 8/15; financial award applicants required to submit FAFSA. In 2008, 12 master's awarded. Offers nurse anesthesia (MS). *Application deadline:* For fall admission, 12/1 for domestic and international students. Applications are processed on a rolling basis. *Application fee:* $25 ($40 for international students). Electronic applications accepted. *Application Contact:* Linda Kay Sabala, Director of Graduate Admissions, 316-942-4291 Ext. 2230, Fax: 316-942-4483, E-mail: sabalal@newmanu.edu. *Director,* Dr. Sharon Niemann, 316-942-4291 Ext. 2272, Fax: 316-942-4483, E-mail: niemanns@newmanu.edu.

School of Social Work Students: 49 full-time (45 women), 85 part-time (73 women); includes 36 minority (17 African Americans, 3 American Indian/Alaska Native, 2 Asian Americans or Pacific Islanders, 14 Hispanic Americans), 1 international. Average age 35. 91 applicants, 79% accepted, 58 enrolled. *Faculty:* 6 full-time (2 women), 6 part-time/adjunct (3 women). Expenses: Contact institution. *Financial support:* In 2008–09, 7 students received support. Federal Work-Study, scholarships/grants, and tuition waivers (full) available. Financial award application deadline: 8/15; financial award applicants required to submit FAFSA. In 2008, 72 master's awarded. Postbaccalaureate distance learning degree programs offered (no on-campus study). Offers social work (MSW). *Application deadline:* For fall admission, 8/15 for domestic students, 7/15 priority date for international students. Applications are processed on a rolling basis. *Application fee:* $25 ($40 for international students). *Application Contact:* Linda Kay Sabala, Director of Graduate Admissions, 316-942-4291 Ext. 2230, Fax: 316-942-4483, E-mail: sabalal@newmanu.edu. *Director,* Dr. Kevin Brown, 316-942-4291 Ext. 2458, Fax: 316-942-4483.

NEW MEXICO HIGHLANDS UNIVERSITY, Las Vegas, NM 87701

General Information State-supported, coed, comprehensive institution. CGS member. *Enrollment:* 3,524 graduate, professional, and undergraduate students; 524 full-time matriculated graduate/professional students (371 women), 530 part-time matriculated graduate/professional students (368 women). *Enrollment by degree level:* 1,054 master's. *Graduate faculty:* 152 full-time (72 women). *International tuition:* $5645 full-time. Tuition, state resident: full-time $2880; part-time $120 per credit hour. Tuition, nonresident: full-time $4234; part-time $176 per credit hour. One-time fee: $20. *Graduate housing:* Rooms and/or apartments guaranteed to single and married students. Typical cost: $4330 per year for single students. *Student services:* Career counseling, child daycare facilities, exercise/wellness program, free psychological counseling, international student services, low-cost health insurance, services for students with disabilities, teacher training, writing training. *Library facilities:* Donnelly Library. *Online resources:* library catalog, web page, access to other libraries' catalogs. *Collection:* 434,927 titles, 33,231 serial subscriptions, 1,039 audiovisual materials. *Research affiliation:* Spectra Gases, Inc. (chemistry), Los Alamos National Laboratory (Chemistry), Sigma Aldrich (Chemistry).

Computer facilities: 500 computers available on campus for general student use. A campuswide network can be accessed from student residence rooms and from off campus. Online class registration is available. *Web address:* http://www.nmhu.edu/.

General Application Contact: Diane Trujillo, Administrative Assistant, Graduate Studies, 505-454-3266, Fax: 505-426-2117, E-mail: dtrujillo@nmhu.edu.

GRADUATE UNITS

Graduate Studies Students: 524 full-time (371 women), 530 part-time (368 women); includes 581 minority (31 African Americans, 70 American Indian/Alaska Native, 15 Asian Americans or Pacific Islanders, 465 Hispanic Americans), 69 international. Average age 36. 757 applicants, 87% accepted, 448 enrolled. *Faculty:* 152 full-time (72 women). Expenses: Contact institution. *Financial support:* In 2008–09, 563 students received support, including 20 research assistantships with full and partial tuition reimbursements available (averaging $6,500 per year), 71 teaching assistantships with full and partial tuition reimbursements available (averaging $6,500 per year); fellowships, career-related internships or fieldwork, Federal Work-Study, institutionally sponsored loans, scholarships/grants, tuition waivers (full and partial), and unspecified assistantships also available. Support available to part-time students. Financial award application deadline: 3/1. In 2008, 345 master's awarded. *Degree program information:* Part-time programs available. *Application deadline:* For fall admission, 8/1 priority date for domestic students. Applications are processed on a rolling basis. *Application fee:* $15. *Application Contact:* Diane Trujillo, Administrative Assistant, Graduate Studies, 505-454-3266, Fax: 505-426-2117, E-mail: dtrujillo@nmhu.edu. *Vice President for Academic Affairs,* Dr. Gilbert Rivera, 505-426-2250, Fax: 505-454-3558, E-mail: gilbertrivera@nmhu.edu.

College of Arts and Sciences Students: 92 full-time (49 women), 55 part-time (25 women); includes 57 minority (2 African Americans, 1 American Indian/Alaska Native, 2 Asian Americans or Pacific Islanders, 52 Hispanic Americans), 30 international. Average age 31. 93 applicants, 59% accepted. *Faculty:* 38 full-time (18 women). Expenses: Contact institution. *Financial support:* In 2008–09, 77 students received support, including research assistantships with full and partial tuition reimbursements available (averaging $6,500 per year), teaching assistantships with full and partial tuition reimbursements available (averaging $6,500 per year); career-related internships or fieldwork, Federal Work-Study, institutionally sponsored loans, scholarships/grants, tuition waivers (full and partial), and unspecified assistantships also available. Support available to part-time students. Financial award application deadline: 3/1. In 2008, 32 master's awarded. *Degree program information:* Part-time programs available. Offers anthropology (MA); applied sociology (MA); arts and sciences (MA, MS); chemistry (MS); English (MA); life science (MS); media arts and computer science (MS); psychology (MS). *Application deadline:* For fall admission, 8/1 priority date for domestic students. Applications are processed on a rolling basis. *Application fee:* $15. Electronic applications accepted. *Application Contact:* Diane Trujillo, Administrative Assistant, Graduate Studies, 505-454-3266, Fax: 505-454-3558, E-mail: dtrujillo@nmhu.edu. *Dean,* Dr. Roy Lujan, 505-454-3080, Fax: 505-454-3389, E-mail: rlujana@nmhu.edu.

School of Business Students: 50 full-time (28 women), 113 part-time (77 women); includes 106 minority (3 African Americans, 18 American Indian/Alaska Native, 7 Asian Americans or Pacific Islanders, 78 Hispanic Americans), 26 international. Average age 34. 131 applicants, 80% accepted, 35 enrolled. *Faculty:* 17 full-time (6 women). Expenses: Contact institution. *Financial support:* In 2008–09, 60 students received support, including 8 teaching assistantships with full and partial tuition reimbursements available (averaging $6,500 per year); career-related internships or fieldwork, Federal Work-Study, institutionally sponsored loans, scholarships/grants, tuition waivers (full and partial), and unspecified assistantships also available. Support available to part-time students. Financial award application deadline: 3/1; financial award applicants required to submit FAFSA. In 2008, 55 master's awarded. Offers business administration (MBA). *Application deadline:* For fall admission, 8/1 priority date for domestic students. Applications are processed on a rolling basis. *Application fee:* $15. *Application Contact:* Diane Trujillo, Administrative Assistant, Graduate Studies, 505-454-3266, Fax: 505-426-2117, E-mail: dtrujillo@nmhu.edu. *Dean,* Dr. Charles Swim, 505-454-3344, Fax: 505-454-3354, E-mail: charlesswim@nmhu.edu.

School of Education Students: 108 full-time (83 women), 245 part-time (183 women); includes 221 minority (7 African Americans, 19 American Indian/Alaska Native, 3 Asian Americans or Pacific Islanders, 192 Hispanic Americans), 5 international. Average age 39. 89 applicants, 88% accepted, 63 enrolled. *Faculty:* 30 full-time (23 women). Expenses: Contact institution. *Financial support:* In 2008–09, 180 students received support, including 16 teaching assistantships with full and partial tuition reimbursements available (averaging $6,500 per year); career-related internships or fieldwork, Federal Work-Study, institutionally sponsored loans, scholarships/grants, traineeships, tuition waivers (partial), and unspecified assistantships also available. Support available to part-time students. Financial award application deadline: 3/1; financial award applicants required to submit FAFSA. In 2008, 117 master's awarded. *Degree program information:* Part-time programs available. Offers curriculum and instruction (MA); education (MA); educational leadership (MA); exercise and sport sciences (MA); guidance and counseling (MA); human performance and sport (MA); special education (MA); sports administration (MA); teacher education (MA). *Application deadline:* For fall admission, 8/1 priority date for domestic students. Applications are processed on a rolling basis. *Application fee:* $15. *Application Contact:* Diane Trujillo, Administrative Assistant for Graduate Studies, 505-454-3266, Fax: 505-426-2117, E-mail: dtrujillo@nmhu.edu. *Interim Dean,* Dr. Michael Anderson, 505-454-3213, E-mail: mfanderson@nmhu.edu.

School of Social Work Students: 249 full-time (197 women), 73 part-time (61 women); includes 163 minority (10 African Americans, 32 American Indian/Alaska Native, 1 Asian American or Pacific Islander, 120 Hispanic Americans), 6 international. Average age 38. 210 applicants, 90% accepted, 145 enrolled. *Faculty:* 19 full-time (8 women). Expenses: Contact institution. *Financial support:* In 2008–09, 223 students received support. Career-related internships or fieldwork, Federal Work-Study, institutionally sponsored loans, scholarships/grants, tuition waivers (partial), and unspecified assistantships available. Support available to part-time students. Financial award application deadline: 3/1; financial award applicants required to submit FAFSA. In 2008, 121 master's awarded. *Degree program information:* Part-time programs available. Offers bilingual/bicultural social work practice (MSW); clinical practice (MSW); government non-profit management (MSW). *Application deadline:* For fall admission, 8/1 priority date for domestic students. Applications are processed on a rolling basis. *Application fee:* $15. *Application Contact:* LouAnn Romero, Administrative Assistant, Graduate Studies, 505-454-3087, E-mail: laromero@nmhu.edu. *Dean,* Dr. Alfredo Garcia, 505-891-9053, Fax: 505-454-3290, E-mail: a_garcia@nmhu.edu.

NEW MEXICO INSTITUTE OF MINING AND TECHNOLOGY, Socorro, NM 87801

General Information State-supported, coed, university. *Graduate housing:* Rooms and/or apartments available on a first-come, first-served basis to single and married students. Housing application deadline: 6/1. *Research affiliation:* National Center for Atmospheric Research (atmosphere research), National Radio Astronomy Observatory (astronomy), Joint Center for Materials Research (materials engineering/metallurgy), Gas Technology Institute (natural gas recovery), Optical Surface Technologies LLC (custom optical components).

GRADUATE UNITS

Graduate Studies Offers advanced mechanics (MS); applied math (PhD); astrophysics (MS, PhD); atmospheric physics (MS, PhD); biochemistry (MS); biology (MS); chemistry (MS); computer science (MS, PhD); electrical engineering (MS); engineering management (MEM); environmental chemistry (PhD); environmental engineering (MS); explosives engineering (MS); explosives technology and atmospheric chemistry (PhD); geochemistry (MS, PhD); geology (MS, PhD); geology and geochemistry (MS, PhD); geophysics (MS, PhD); hydrology (MS, PhD); instrumentation (MS); materials engineering (MS, PhD); mathematical physics (PhD); mathematics (MS); mining and mineral engineering (MS); operations research (MS); petroleum engineering (MS, PhD); science teaching (MST). Electronic applications accepted.

See Close-Up on page 953.

NEW MEXICO STATE UNIVERSITY, Las Cruces, NM 88003-8001

General Information State-supported, coed, university. CGS member. *Enrollment:* 17,200 graduate, professional, and undergraduate students; 1,816 full-time matriculated graduate/professional students (958 women), 1,674 part-time matriculated graduate/professional students (994 women). *Enrollment by degree level:* 2,748 master's, 679 doctoral, 72 other advanced degrees. *Graduate faculty:* 413 full-time (164 women), 64 part-time/adjunct (31 women). Tuition, state resident: full-time $3890; part-time $212.85 per credit. Tuition, nonresident: full-time $13,916; part-time $630.55 per credit. *Required fees:* $1218; $609 per semester. *Graduate housing:* Rooms and/or apartments available on a first-come, first-served basis to single students and available to married students. Typical cost: $3422 per year ($5976 including board) for single students; $0 per year for married students. *Student services:* Campus employment opportunities, campus safety program, career counseling, child daycare facilities, free psychological counseling, grant writing training, international student services, low-cost health insurance, multicultural affairs office, services for students with disabilities, teacher training, writing training. *Library facilities:* New Mexico State University Library plus 2 others. *Online resources:* library catalog, web page, access to other libraries' catalogs. *Collection:* 1.8 million titles, 4,402 serial subscriptions, 13,880 audiovisual materials. *Research affiliation:* Los Alamos National Laboratory (Energy research, environmental sciences, information sciences), Sandia National Laboratories (Energy research, information sciences), General Electric (Water resources research), United States Army Research Laboratories (Information Sciences), Northrop Grumman (Aerospace), Sapphire Energy (Bio-fuel research).

Computer facilities: Computer purchase and lease plans are available. 751 computers available on campus for general student use. A campuswide network can be accessed from student residence rooms and from off campus. Online class registration, online financial aid are available. *Web address:* http://www.nmsu.edu/.

General Application Contact: Elena Luna, Coordinator, 575-646-3498, Fax: 575-646-7721, E-mail: rosluna@nmsu.edu.

GRADUATE UNITS

Graduate School Students: 1,816 full-time (958 women), 1,674 part-time (994 women); includes 1,139 minority (84 African Americans, 77 American Indian/Alaska Native, 38 Asian Americans or Pacific Islanders, 940 Hispanic Americans), 731 international. Average age 33. 2,883 applicants, 82% accepted, 1300 enrolled. *Faculty:* 413 full-time (164 women), 64 part-time/adjunct (31 women). Expenses: Contact institution. *Financial support:* In 2008–09, 1,242 students received support, including 295 research assistantships (averaging $13,466 per year), 714 teaching assistantships (averaging $10,900 per year); career-related internships or fieldwork, Federal Work-Study, scholarships/grants, traineeships, health care benefits, and unspecified assistantships also available. Support available to part-time students. In 2008, 835 master's, 61 doctorates, 30 other advanced degrees awarded. *Degree program information:* Part-time and evening/weekend programs available. Postbaccalaureate distance learning degree programs offered (no on-campus study). Offers interdisciplinary studies (MA, MS, PhD); molecular biology (MS, PhD). *Application fee:* $30 ($50 for international students). Electronic applications accepted. *Application Contact:* Elena Luna, Coordinator, 575-646-3498, Fax: 575-646-7721, E-mail: rosluna@nmsu.edu. *Dean*, Dr. Linda Lacey, 575-646-5746, Fax: 575-646-7721, E-mail: lacey@nmsu.edu.

College of Agriculture, Consumer and Environmental Sciences Students: 138 full-time (71 women), 68 part-time (35 women); includes 54 minority (2 African Americans, 4 American Indian/Alaska Native, 1 Asian American or Pacific Islander, 47 Hispanic Americans), 42 international. Average age 29. 105 applicants, 90% accepted, 64 enrolled. *Faculty:* 48 full-time (23 women), 1 part-time/adjunct (0 women). Expenses: Contact institution. *Financial support:* In 2008–09, 138 students received support, including 48 research assistantships (averaging $19,174 per year), 50 teaching assistantships (averaging $13,089 per year); career-related internships or fieldwork, Federal Work-Study, and health care benefits also available. Support available to part-time students. Financial award application deadline: 3/1. In 2008, 72 master's, 3 doctorates awarded. *Degree program information:* Part-time and evening/weekend programs available. Offers agribusiness (M Ag, MBA); agricultural and extension education (MA); agricultural biology (MS); agricultural economics (MS); agriculture, consumer and environmental sciences (M Ag, MA, MBA, MS, DED, PhD); animal science (M Ag, MS, PhD); economics (MA); family and consumer sciences (MS); horticulture (MS); plant and environmental sciences (MS, PhD); range science (M Ag, MS, PhD); wildlife science (MS). *Application deadline:* For fall admission, 7/1 priority date for domestic students; for spring admission, 11/1 for domestic students. Applications are processed on a rolling basis. *Application fee:* $30 ($50 for international students). Electronic applications accepted. *Application Contact:* Dr. Lowell Catlett, Interim Dean, 575-646-1806, Fax: 575-646-5975, E-mail: agdean@nmsu.edu. *Interim Dean*, Dr. Lowell Catlett, 575-646-1806, Fax: 575-646-5975, E-mail: agdean@nmsu.edu.

College of Arts and Sciences Students: 697 full-time (322 women), 296 part-time (141 women); includes 210 minority (20 African Americans, 16 American Indian/Alaska Native, 8 Asian Americans or Pacific Islanders, 166 Hispanic Americans), 275 international. Average age 31. 870 applicants, 71% accepted, 298 enrolled. *Faculty:* 163 full-time (62 women), 16 part-time/adjunct (6 women). Expenses: Contact institution. *Financial support:* In 2008–09, 634 students received support, including 117 research assistantships (averaging $15,101 per year), 375 teaching assistantships (averaging $12,292 per year); career-related internships or fieldwork, Federal Work-Study, scholarships/grants, and health care benefits also available. Support available to part-time students. In 2008, 199 master's, 16 doctorates awarded. *Degree program information:* Part-time programs available. Postbaccalaureate distance learning degree programs offered. Offers anthropology (MA); art history (MA); arts and sciences (MA, MAG, MCJ, MFA, MM, MPA, MS, PhD); astronomy (MS, PhD); biology (MS, PhD); ceramics (MA, MFA); chemistry and biochemistry (MS, PhD); communication studies (MA); computer science (MS, PhD); conducting (MM); creative writing (MFA); criminal justice (MCJ); design (MA, MFA); drawing (MFA); English (MA); geography (MAG); geological sciences (MS); government (MA, MPA); history (MA); mathematical sciences (MS, PhD); metals (MA, MFA); music education (MM); painting (MFA); performance (MM); photography (MFA); physics (MS, PhD); printmaking (MA, MFA); psychology (MA, PhD); public history (MA); rhetoric and professional communication (PhD); sculpture (MA, MFA); sociology (MA); Spanish (MA). *Application fee:* $30 ($50 for international students). Electronic applications accepted. *Application Contact:* Elena Luna, Coordinator, 575-646-3498, Fax: 575-646-7721, E-mail: rosluna@nmsu.edu. *Interim Dean*, Dr. Pamela Jansma, 575-646-2001, Fax: 575-646-6096, E-mail: pjansma@nmsu.edu.

College of Business Students: 209 full-time (88 women), 188 part-time (82 women); includes 151 minority (9 African Americans, 6 American Indian/Alaska Native, 6 Asian Americans or Pacific Islanders, 130 Hispanic Americans), 78 international. Average age 31. 330 applicants, 89% accepted, 199 enrolled. *Faculty:* 41 full-time (5 women), 2 part-time/adjunct (1 woman). Expenses: Contact institution. *Financial support:* In 2008–09, 140 students received support, including 32 research assistantships (averaging $10,617 per year), 76 teaching assistantships (averaging $10,677 per year); fellowships, career-related internships or fieldwork, Federal Work-Study, institutionally sponsored loans, scholarships/grants, health care benefits, and unspecified assistantships also available. Support available to part-time students. Financial award application deadline: 3/1. In 2008, 121 master's, 4 doctorates awarded. *Degree program information:* Part-time programs available. Offers accounting and information systems (M Acct); business (M Acct, MA, MBA, MS, DED, PhD); business administration (MBA, PhD); economic development (DED); economics (MA); experimental statistics (MS). *Application deadline:* For fall admission, 7/1 priority date for domestic students; for spring admission, 11/1 for domestic students. Applications are processed on a rolling basis. *Application fee:* $30 ($50 for international students). Electronic applications accepted. *Application Contact:* Dr. Garrey Carruthers, Dean, 575-646-2821, Fax: 575-646-6155, E-mail: garrey@nmsu.edu. *Dean*, Dr. Garrey Carruthers, 575-646-2821, Fax: 575-646-6155, E-mail: garrey@nmsu.edu.

College of Education Students: 269 full-time (210 women), 557 part-time (404 women); includes 373 minority (20 African Americans, 26 American Indian/Alaska Native, 9 Asian Americans or Pacific Islanders, 318 Hispanic Americans), 58 international. Average age 38. 505 applicants, 90% accepted, 264 enrolled. *Faculty:* 49 full-time (27 women), 24 part-time/adjunct (13 women). Expenses: Contact institution. *Financial support:* In 2008–09, 216 students received support, including 13 research assistantships (averaging $10,731 per year), 76 teaching assistantships (averaging $9,393 per year); fellowships, career-related internships or fieldwork, Federal Work-Study, and health care benefits also available. Support available to part-time students. Financial award application deadline: 3/1. In 2008, 193 master's, 27 doctorates, 14 other advanced degrees awarded. *Degree program information:* Part-time and evening/weekend programs available. Postbaccalaureate distance learning degree programs offered (minimal on-campus study). Offers communication disorders (MA); counseling and guidance (MA); counseling psychology (PhD); curriculum and instruction (MAT, Ed D, PhD, Ed S); education (MA, MAT, Ed D, PhD, Ed S); educational administration (MA, PhD); educational management and development (Ed D); general education (MA); school psychology (Ed S); special education (MA, Ed D, PhD). *Application deadline:* Applications are processed on a rolling basis. *Application fee:* $30 ($50 for international students). Electronic applications accepted. *Application Contact:* Elena Luna, Coordinator, 575-646-3498, Fax: 575-646-7721, E-mail: rosluna@nmsu.edu. *Dean*, Dr. Michael Morehead, 575-646-3404, Fax: 575-646-6032, E-mail: mmorehea@nmsu.edu.

College of Engineering Students: 242 full-time (55 women), 186 part-time (44 women); includes 91 minority (12 African Americans, 2 American Indian/Alaska Native, 5 Asian Americans or Pacific Islanders, 72 Hispanic Americans), 229 international. Average age 32. 525 applicants, 73% accepted, 133 enrolled. *Faculty:* 45 full-time (5 women), 3 part-time/adjunct (0 women). Expenses: Contact institution. *Financial support:* In 2008–09, 213 students received support, including 70 research assistantships (averaging $8,916 per year), 96 teaching assistantships (averaging $7,833 per year); fellowships, career-related internships or fieldwork, Federal Work-Study, and health care benefits also available. Support available to part-time students. Financial award application deadline: 3/1. In 2008, 128 master's, 11 doctorates awarded. *Degree program information:* Part-time programs available. Offers chemical engineering (MS Ch E, PhD); civil engineering (MSCE, PhD); electrical and computer engineering (MSEE, PhD); engineering (MS Ch E, MS Env E, MSCE, MSEE, MSIE, MSME, PhD); environmental engineering (MS Env E); industrial engineering (MSIE, PhD); mechanical engineering (MSME, PhD). *Application deadline:* For fall admission, 7/1 priority date for domestic students; for spring admission, 11/1 for domestic students. Applications are processed on a rolling basis. *Application fee:* $30 ($50 for international students). Electronic applications accepted. *Application Contact:* Elena Luna, Coordinator, 575-646-3498, Fax: 575-646-7721, E-mail: rosluna@nmsu.edu. *Dean*, Dr. Steven Castillo, 575-646-2914, Fax: 575-646-3549, E-mail: scastill@nmsu.edu.

College of Health and Social Services Students: 220 full-time (188 women), 166 part-time (138 women); includes 153 minority (12 African Americans, 18 American Indian/Alaska Native, 3 Asian Americans or Pacific Islanders, 120 Hispanic Americans), 30 international. Average age 37. 272 applicants, 95% accepted, 162 enrolled. *Faculty:* 33 full-time (18 women), 7 part-time/adjunct (4 women). Expenses: Contact institution. *Financial support:* In 2008–09, 81 students received support, including 5 research assistantships (averaging $8,840 per year), 37 teaching assistantships (averaging $5,654 per year); fellowships, career-related internships or fieldwork, Federal Work-Study, scholarships/grants, traineeships, and health care benefits also available. Financial award application deadline: 3/1. In 2008, 118 master's awarded. *Degree program information:* Part-time and evening/weekend programs available. Postbaccalaureate distance learning degree programs offered. Offers community health education (MPH); community/public health (MSN); health and social services (MPH, MSN, MSW); medical-surgical (adult health) (MSN); nursing administration (MSN); psychiatric/mental health (MSN); social work (MSW). *Application deadline:* For fall admission, 7/1 priority date for domestic students. Applications are processed on a rolling basis. *Application fee:* $30 ($50 for international students). Electronic applications accepted. *Application Contact:* Associate Dean. *Interim Dean*, Dr. Robert Rhodes, 575-646-3526, Fax: 575-646-6166, E-mail: rorhodes@nmsu.edu.

NEW ORLEANS BAPTIST THEOLOGICAL SEMINARY, New Orleans, LA 70126-4858

General Information Independent-religious, coed, primarily men, comprehensive institution. *Graduate housing:* Rooms and/or apartments available to single and married students.

GRADUATE UNITS

Graduate and Professional Programs *Degree program information:* Evening/weekend programs available. Offers biblical studies (MA); Christian education (M Div, MACE, D Min, DEM, PhD); church music ministries (MMCM, DMA); pastoral ministries (M Div, MAMFC, D Min, PhD); theological and historical studies (M Div, D Min, PhD); theology (M Div, MA, MACE, MAMFC, MMCM, D Min, DEM, DMA, PhD).

THE NEW SCHOOL: A UNIVERSITY, New York, NY 10011

General Information Independent, coed, university. *Enrollment by degree level:* 2,695 master's, 608 doctoral, 147 other advanced degrees. *Graduate faculty:* 177 full-time (72 women), 304 part-time/adjunct (121 women). *Tuition:* Full-time $27,144; part-time $1508 per credit. *Required fees:* $355 per semester. *Graduate housing:* Room and/or apartments available on a first-come, first-served basis to single students; on-campus housing not available to married students. Typical cost: $12,260 per year ($15,260 including board). Room and board charges vary according to board plan and housing facility selected. Housing application deadline: 5/1. *Student services:* Campus employment opportunities, campus safety program, career counseling, free psychological counseling, grant writing training, international student services, low-cost health insurance, multicultural affairs office, services for students with disabilities, teacher training, writing training. *Research affiliation:* The Goldman Sachs Group, Inc., Siemens Corporation, Raytheon Corporation, National Geospatial-Intelligence Agency, Environmental Systems Research Institute, Dow Jones & Company, Inc. *Web address:* http://www.newschool.edu/.

General Application Contact: Christy Kalan, Assistant Vice President for Enrollment Operations, 212-229-5155 Ext. 3580, E-mail: kalanc@newschool.edu.

GRADUATE UNITS

Mannes College The New School for Music Students: 188 full-time (120 women), 4 part-time (3 women); includes 20 minority (1 African American, 10 Asian Americans or Pacific Islanders, 9 Hispanic Americans), 108 international. Average age 25. 813 applicants, 30% accepted, 97 enrolled. *Faculty:* 7 full-time (1 woman), 112 part-time/adjunct (44 women). Expenses: Contact institution. *Financial support:* Fellowships with partial tuition reimbursements, research assistantships with partial tuition reimbursements, teaching assistantships with partial tuition reimbursements, career-related internships or fieldwork, Federal Work-Study, scholarships/grants, and tuition waivers (partial) available. Support available to part-time students. Financial award application deadline: 3/1; financial award applicants required

The New School: A University (continued)

to submit FAFSA. In 2008, 59 master's, 16 other advanced degrees awarded. Offers music performance (MM, PD). *Application deadline:* For fall admission, 11/15 for domestic students. *Application fee:* $100. *Application Contact:* Director of Admissions, 212-580-0210 Ext. 263. *Dean*, Joel Lester, 212-580-0210 Ext. 4848.

Milano The New School for Management and Urban Policy Students: 228 full-time (166 women), 277 part-time (200 women); includes 182 minority (90 African Americans, 3 American Indian/Alaska Native, 32 Asian Americans or Pacific Islanders, 57 Hispanic Americans), 38 international. Average age 32. 393 applicants, 82% accepted, 148 enrolled. *Faculty:* 18 full-time (4 women), 45 part-time/adjunct (16 women). Expenses: Contact institution. *Financial support:* Fellowships with full and partial tuition reimbursements, research assistantships, career-related internships or fieldwork, Federal Work-Study, scholarships/grants, and tuition waivers (full and partial) available. Support available to part-time students. Financial award application deadline: 3/1; financial award applicants required to submit FAFSA. In 2008, 117 master's, 3 doctorates, 3 other advanced degrees awarded. *Degree program information:* Part-time and evening/weekend programs available. Postbaccalaureate distance learning degree programs offered (minimal on-campus study). Offers health services management and policy (MS); human resources management (MS, Adv C); management and urban policy (MS, PhD, Adv C); medical group practice management (Adv C); nonprofit management (MS); organizational change management (MS); public and urban policy (PhD); urban policy analysis and management (MS). *Application deadline:* For fall admission, 9/1 priority date for domestic students. Applications are processed on a rolling basis. *Application fee:* $50. *Application Contact:* Merida Escandon, Director of Admissions, 212-229-5462 Ext. 1108, Fax: 212-229-5354, E-mail: milanoadmissions@newschool.edu. *Dean*, Dr. Lisa Servon, 212-229-5400 Ext. 1202, Fax: 212-229-8935, E-mail: servonL@newschool.edu.

The New School for Drama Students: 124 full-time (73 women), 7 part-time (6 women); includes 19 minority (14 African Americans, 5 Hispanic Americans), 21 international. Average age 27. 358 applicants, 20% accepted, 50 enrolled. *Faculty:* 5 full-time (2 women), 37 part-time/adjunct (20 women). Expenses: Contact institution. *Financial support:* Federal Work-Study and scholarships/grants available. Financial award application deadline: 3/1; financial award applicants required to submit FAFSA. In 2008, 52 master's awarded. Offers acting (MFA); directing (MFA); playwriting (MFA). *Application deadline:* For fall admission, 1/10 priority date for domestic students. *Application fee:* $50. *Application Contact:* Matthew Kelty, Director of Admissions, 212-229-5859, Fax: 212-229-5150, E-mail: keltym@newschool.edu. *Director*, Robert LuPone, 212-229-5859 Ext. 2636, E-mail: luponer@newschool.edu.

The New School for General Studies Students: 600 full-time (405 women), 496 part-time (326 women); includes 216 minority (66 African Americans, 3 American Indian/Alaska Native, 59 Asian Americans or Pacific Islanders, 88 Hispanic Americans), 153 international. Average age 30. 1,404 applicants, 62% accepted, 390 enrolled. *Faculty:* 35 full-time (16 women), 124 part-time/adjunct (57 women). Expenses: Contact institution. *Financial support:* Fellowships with partial tuition reimbursements, teaching assistantships with partial tuition reimbursements, career-related internships or fieldwork, Federal Work-Study, scholarships/grants, tuition waivers (full and partial), and unspecified assistantships available. Support available to part-time students. Financial award application deadline: 3/1; financial award applicants required to submit FAFSA. In 2008, 320 master's awarded. *Degree program information:* Part-time and evening/weekend programs available. Postbaccalaureate distance learning degree programs offered (no on-campus study). Offers communication theory (MA); creative writing (MFA); general studies (MA, MFA, MS); global management, trade, and finance (MA, MS); international development (MA, MS); international media and communication (MA, MS); international politics and diplomacy (MA, MS); media studies (MA); service, civic, and non-profit management (MS); teaching English to speakers of other languages (MA). *Application deadline:* Applications are processed on a rolling basis. *Application fee:* $50. *Application Contact:* David Norris, Director of Admissions, 212-229-5630, Fax: 212-989-3887, E-mail: nsadmissions@newschool.edu. *Dean*, Dr. Linda Dunne, 212-229-5613, Fax: 212-645-0661, E-mail: dunnel@newschool.edu.

The New School for Social Research Students: 785 full-time (407 women), 315 part-time (173 women); includes 166 minority (52 African Americans, 3 American Indian/Alaska Native, 44 Asian Americans or Pacific Islanders, 67 Hispanic Americans), 301 international. Average age 31. 1,125 applicants, 72% accepted, 257 enrolled. *Faculty:* 67 full-time (27 women), 28 part-time/adjunct (4 women). Expenses: Contact institution. *Financial support:* Fellowships with tuition reimbursements, research assistantships with tuition reimbursements, teaching assistantships with tuition reimbursements, career-related internships or fieldwork, Federal Work-Study, scholarships/grants, tuition waivers (full and partial), and unspecified assistantships available. Financial award application deadline: 3/1; financial award applicants required to submit FAFSA. In 2008, 180 master's, 60 doctorates awarded. *Degree program information:* Part-time and evening/weekend programs available. Offers anthropology (MA, DS Sc, PhD); clinical psychology (PhD); economics (MA, DS Sc, PhD); general psychology (MA, PhD); global finance (MS); historical studies (MA, PhD); liberal studies (MA); philosophy (MA, DS Sc, PhD); political science (MA, DS Sc, PhD); social research (MA, MS, DS Sc, PhD); sociology (MA, DS Sc, PhD). *Application deadline:* For fall admission, 1/15 priority date for domestic students. Applications are processed on a rolling basis. *Application fee:* $50. *Application Contact:* Robert MacDonald, Director of Admissions, 800-523-5710 Ext. 3007, Fax: 212-989-7102, E-mail: macdonar@newschool.edu. *Dean*, Dr. Michael Schober, 212-229-5777, E-mail: schober@newschool.edu.

Parsons The New School for Design Students: 344 full-time (215 women), 82 part-time (69 women); includes 65 minority (11 African Americans, 1 American Indian/Alaska Native, 42 Asian Americans or Pacific Islanders, 11 Hispanic Americans), 114 international. Average age 28. 1,068 applicants, 47% accepted, 177 enrolled. *Faculty:* 47 full-time (18 women), 182 part-time/adjunct (66 women). Expenses: Contact institution. *Financial support:* Fellowships with partial tuition reimbursements, research assistantships with partial tuition reimbursements, teaching assistantships with partial tuition reimbursements, Federal Work-Study, scholarships/grants, and tuition waivers (partial) available. Financial award application deadline: 3/1; financial award applicants required to submit FAFSA. In 2008, 152 master's awarded. Offers architecture (M Arch); design (M Arch, MA, MFA); design and technology (MFA); fine arts (MFA); history of decorative arts (MA); interior design (MFA); lighting design (MFA); photography (MFA). *Application deadline:* For fall admission, 3/1 priority date for domestic students. Applications are processed on a rolling basis. *Application fee:* $50. *Application Contact:* David Norris, Director of Admissions, 212-229-8989, Fax: 212-229-8975, E-mail: norrisd@newschool.edu. *Dean*.

See Close-Up on page 955.

NEWSCHOOL OF ARCHITECTURE & DESIGN, San Diego, CA 92101-6634

General Information Proprietary, coed, primarily men, comprehensive institution. *Graduate housing:* On-campus housing not available. *Research affiliation:* Center City Development Corporation.

GRADUATE UNITS

Program in Architecture *Degree program information:* Part-time and evening/weekend programs available. Offers architecture (M Arch, MS).

NEW YORK ACADEMY OF ART, New York, NY 10013-2911

General Information Independent, coed, graduate-only institution. *Graduate housing:* On-campus housing not available.

GRADUATE UNITS

Program in Figurative Art Offers figurative art (MFA).

NEW YORK CHIROPRACTIC COLLEGE, Seneca Falls, NY 13148-0800

General Information Independent, coed, graduate-only institution. *Enrollment by degree level:* 658 first professional, 158 master's. *Graduate faculty:* 59 full-time (26 women), 27 part-time/adjunct (8 women). *Tuition:* Full-time $17,120; part-time $426 per credit. *Required fees:* $680; $290 per term. *Graduate housing:* Rooms and/or apartments available on a first-come, first-served basis to single and married students. Typical cost: $4780 per year ($4780 including board) for single students; $6540 per year ($6540 including board) for married students. Room and board charges vary according to board plan, campus/location and housing facility selected. *Student services:* Campus employment opportunities, campus safety program, career counseling, exercise/wellness program, free psychological counseling, services for students with disabilities. *Library facilities:* New York Chiropractic College Library. *Online resources:* library catalog, web page, access to other libraries' catalogs. *Collection:* 16,521 titles, 320 serial subscriptions, 38,463 audiovisual materials. *Research affiliation:* Foot Levelers, Inc. (orthotics research), Isagenix International (Nutrition).

Computer facilities: 137 computers available on campus for general student use. A campuswide network can be accessed from student residence rooms and from off campus. *Web address:* http://www.nycc.edu/.

General Application Contact: Michael Lynch, Director of Admissions, 315-568-3040, Fax: 315-568-3087, E-mail: mlynch@nycc.edu.

GRADUATE UNITS

Acupuncture and Oriental Medicine Programs Students: 51 full-time (44 women), 27 part-time (17 women); includes 9 minority (1 African American, 1 American Indian/Alaska Native, 7 Asian Americans or Pacific Islanders). Average age 33. 42 applicants, 90% accepted, 33 enrolled. *Faculty:* 8 full-time (6 women), 6 part-time/adjunct (3 women). Expenses: Contact institution. *Financial support:* In 2008–09, 58 students received support, including 1 fellowship with tuition reimbursement available (averaging $30,000 per year); Federal Work-Study and scholarships/grants also available. Financial award applicants required to submit FAFSA. In 2008, 43 master's awarded. Offers acupuncture (MS); acupuncture and oriental medicine (MS). *Application deadline:* Applications are processed on a rolling basis. *Application fee:* $60. Electronic applications accepted. *Application Contact:* Michael Lynch, Director of Admissions, 315-568-3040, Fax: 315-568-3087, E-mail: mlynch@nycc.edu. *Dean of School of Acupuncture and Oriental Medicine*, Shaune Ralph, 315-568-3268, E-mail: sralph@nycc.edu.

Doctor of Chiropractic Program Students: 658 full-time (281 women); includes 69 minority (14 African Americans, 1 American Indian/Alaska Native, 30 Asian Americans or Pacific Islanders, 24 Hispanic Americans), 98 international. Average age 26. 331 applicants, 82% accepted, 191 enrolled. *Faculty:* 51 full-time (20 women), 20 part-time/adjunct (5 women). Expenses: Contact institution. *Financial support:* In 2008–09, 608 students received support, including 5 fellowships with full tuition reimbursements available (averaging $30,000 per year), 1 research assistantship with full tuition reimbursement available (averaging $30,000 per year); Federal Work-Study and scholarships/grants also available. Financial award applicants required to submit FAFSA. In 2008, 187 DCs awarded. Offers chiropractic (DC). *Application deadline:* Applications are processed on a rolling basis. *Application fee:* $60. Electronic applications accepted. *Application Contact:* Michael Lynch, Director of Admissions, 315-568-3040, Fax: 315-568-3087, E-mail: mlynch@nycc.edu. *Dean*, Dr. Karen A. Bobak, 315-568-3864, Fax: 315-568-3087.

Program in Applied Clinical Nutrition Students: 77 part-time (43 women); includes 6 minority (1 American Indian/Alaska Native, 4 Asian Americans or Pacific Islanders, 1 Hispanic American), 9 international. Average age 32. 56 applicants, 86% accepted, 40 enrolled. *Faculty:* 3 part-time/adjunct (1 woman). Expenses: Contact institution. *Financial support:* In 2008–09, 63 students received support. Federal Work-Study and scholarships/grants available. Financial award applicants required to submit FAFSA. In 2008, 40 master's awarded. *Degree program information:* Part-time and evening/weekend programs available. Offers applied clinical nutrition (MS). *Application deadline:* Applications are processed on a rolling basis. *Application fee:* $60. Electronic applications accepted. *Application Contact:* Michael Lynch, Director of Admissions, 315-568-3040, Fax: 315-568-3087, E-mail: mlynch@nycc.edu. *Director*, Dr. Anna R. Kelles, 315-568-3310.

Program in Clinical Anatomy Students: 2 full-time (both women). Average age 30. 10 applicants, 10% accepted, 1 enrolled. *Faculty:* 8 full-time (4 women). Expenses: Contact institution. *Financial support:* In 2008–09, 2 students received support, including 2 fellowships. Financial award application deadline: 7/31. Offers clinical anatomy (MS). *Application deadline:* For fall admission, 7/31 priority date for domestic and international students. *Application fee:* $0. Electronic applications accepted. *Application Contact:* Michael Lynch, Director of Admissions, 315-568-3040, Fax: 315-568-3087, E-mail: mlynch@nycc.edu. *Director, Clinical Anatomy Program*, Dr. Robert A. Walker, 315-568-3210, E-mail: rwalker@nycc.edu.

Program in Diagnostic Imaging Students: 2 part-time (1 woman). 3 applicants, 33% accepted, 1 enrolled. *Faculty:* 1 full-time (0 women), 6 part-time/adjunct (2 women). Expenses: Contact institution. *Financial support:* In 2008–09, 1 student received support, including 2 fellowships. Financial award applicants required to submit FAFSA. In 2008, 1 master's awarded. Offers diagnostic imaging (MS). *Application deadline:* Applications are processed on a rolling basis. *Application fee:* $0. *Application Contact:* Director of Admissions. *Director*, Dr. Jean-Nicolas Poirier, 315-568-3197, E-mail: npoirier@nycc.edu.

NEW YORK COLLEGE OF HEALTH PROFESSIONS, Syosset, NY 11791-4413

General Information Independent, coed. *Graduate housing:* On-campus housing not available. *Research affiliation:* North Shore Hospital (acupuncture).

GRADUATE UNITS

Graduate School of Oriental Medicine *Degree program information:* Part-time programs available. Offers acupuncture (MS); Oriental medicine (MS).

NEW YORK COLLEGE OF PODIATRIC MEDICINE, New York, NY 10035

General Information Independent, coed, graduate-only institution. *Graduate housing:* Rooms and/or apartments available on a first-come, first-served basis to single and married students. Housing application deadline: 8/15. *Research affiliation:* Cyberlogics (ultrasound use), Novartis (fungal diseases of nail), Prescription Dispensing Laboratories (topical verapamil), Anodyne Corporation (light energy applications).

GRADUATE UNITS

Professional Program Offers podiatric medicine (DPM).

NEW YORK COLLEGE OF TRADITIONAL CHINESE MEDICINE, Mineola, NY 11501

General Information Independent, coed, graduate-only institution.

GRADUATE UNITS

Graduate Programs

NEW YORK FILM ACADEMY, Los Angeles, CA 90068

General Information Independent, coed.

GRADUATE UNITS

Program in Filmmaking–Hollywood Offers acting for film (MFA); filmmaking (MFA); producing (MFA); screenwriting (MFA).

Program in Filmmaking–New York Offers acting for film (MFA); filmmaking (MFA); producing (MFA); screenwriting (MFA).

Program in Filmmaking–United Arab Emirates Offers acting for film (MFA); filmmaking (MFA); producing (MFA); screenwriting (MFA).

NEW YORK INSTITUTE OF TECHNOLOGY, Old Westbury, NY 11568-8000

General Information Independent, coed, university. CGS member. *Enrollment:* 11,505 graduate, professional, and undergraduate students; 2,779 full-time matriculated graduate/

professional students (1,313 women), 1,554 part-time matriculated graduate/professional students (624 women). *Enrollment by degree level:* 1,179 first professional, 3,016 master's, 112 doctoral, 26 other advanced degrees. *Tuition:* Part-time $783 per credit. *Graduate housing:* Room and/or apartments available on a first-come, first-served basis to single students; on-campus housing not available to married students. Typical cost: $6420 per year ($10,520 including board). Room and board charges vary according to board plan and campus/location. *Student services:* Campus employment opportunities, career counseling, exercise/wellness program, free psychological counseling, international student services, low-cost health insurance, multicultural affairs office, services for students with disabilities, teacher training, writing training. *Library facilities:* George and Gertrude Wisser Memorial Library plus 4 others. *Online resources:* library catalog, web page. *Collection:* 272,227 titles, 13,827 serial subscriptions.

Computer facilities: 815 computers available on campus for general student use. A campuswide network can be accessed from student residence rooms and from off campus. E-mail available. *Web address:* http://www.nyit.edu/.

General Application Contact: Dr. Jacquelyn Nealon, Vice President for Enrollment Services, 516-686-7925, Fax: 516-686-7597, E-mail: jnealon@nyit.edu.

GRADUATE UNITS

Graduate Division Students: 1,600 full-time (706 women), 1,554 part-time (624 women); includes 388 minority (163 African Americans, 2 American Indian/Alaska Native, 126 Asian Americans or Pacific Islanders, 97 Hispanic Americans), 858 international. Average age 29. Expenses: Contact institution. *Financial support:* Fellowships with partial tuition reimbursements, research assistantships with partial tuition reimbursements, career-related internships or fieldwork, Federal Work-Study, institutionally sponsored loans, tuition waivers (full and partial), and unspecified assistantships available. Support available to part-time students. Financial award applicants required to submit FAFSA. In 2008, 1,459 master's, 47 doctorates, 18 other advanced degrees awarded. *Degree program information:* Part-time and evening/weekend programs available. Postbaccalaureate distance learning degree programs offered (minimal on-campus study). *Application deadline:* For fall admission, 7/1 priority date for domestic students; for spring admission, 12/1 priority date for domestic students. Applications are processed on a rolling basis. *Application fee:* $50. Electronic applications accepted. *Application Contact:* Dr. Jacquelyn Nealon, Vice President for Enrollment Services, 516-686-7925, Fax: 516-686-7597, E-mail: jnealon@nyit.edu. *Provost and Vice President for Academic Affairs*, Dr. Richard Pizer, 516-686-7630, Fax: 516-686-7631, E-mail: rpizer@nyit.edu.

School of Architecture and Design Students: 11 full-time (8 women), 4 part-time (1 woman); includes 2 minority (1 Asian American or Pacific Islander, 1 Hispanic American), 10 international. Average age 31. Expenses: Contact institution. *Financial support:* Research assistantships with partial tuition reimbursements, institutionally sponsored loans and tuition waivers (full and partial) available. Support available to part-time students. Financial award applicants required to submit FAFSA. In 2008, 5 master's awarded. *Degree program information:* Part-time programs available. Offers urban and regional design (M Arch). *Application deadline:* For fall admission, 7/1 priority date for domestic students; for spring admission, 12/1 priority date for domestic students. Applications are processed on a rolling basis. *Application fee:* $50. Electronic applications accepted. *Application Contact:* Dr. Jacquelyn Nealon, Vice President for Enrollment Services, 516-686-7925, Fax: 516-686-7597, E-mail: jnealon@nyit.edu. *Dean*, Judith DiMaio, 516-686-7594, Fax: 516-686-7921, E-mail: jdimaio@nyit.edu.

School of Arts and Sciences Students: 101 full-time (69 women), 103 part-time (60 women); includes 39 minority (14 African Americans, 10 Asian Americans or Pacific Islanders, 15 Hispanic Americans), 74 international. Average age 29. Expenses: Contact institution. *Financial support:* Research assistantships with partial tuition reimbursements, career-related internships or fieldwork, Federal Work-Study, institutionally sponsored loans, tuition waivers (partial), and unspecified assistantships available. Support available to part-time students. Financial award applicants required to submit FAFSA. In 2008, 108 master's awarded. *Degree program information:* Part-time and evening/weekend programs available. Offers arts and sciences (MA); communication arts (MA). *Application deadline:* For fall admission, 7/1 priority date for domestic students; for spring admission, 12/1 priority date for domestic students. Applications are processed on a rolling basis. *Application fee:* $50. Electronic applications accepted. *Application Contact:* Dr. Jacquelyn Nealon, Vice President for Enrollment Services, 516-686-7925, Fax: 516-686-7597, E-mail: jnealon@nyit.edu. *Dean*, Dr. Roger Yu, 516-686-7700, Fax: 516-686-1192, E-mail: ryu@nyit.edu.

School of Education Students: 19 full-time (9 women), 453 part-time (206 women); includes 94 minority (52 African Americans, 1 American Indian/Alaska Native, 18 Asian Americans or Pacific Islanders, 23 Hispanic Americans), 9 international. Average age 35. Expenses: Contact institution. *Financial support:* Research assistantships with partial tuition reimbursements, career-related internships or fieldwork, institutionally sponsored loans, and tuition waivers (full and partial) available. Support available to part-time students. Financial award applicants required to submit FAFSA. In 2008, 113 master's, 1 other advanced degree awarded. *Degree program information:* Part-time and evening/weekend programs available. Postbaccalaureate distance learning degree programs offered. Offers distance learning (Advanced Certificate); district leadership and technology (Professional Diploma); education (MS, Advanced Certificate, Professional Diploma); elementary education (MS); instructional technology (MS); mental health counseling and school counseling (MS); multimedia (Advanced Certificate); school counseling (MS); school leadership and technology (Professional Diploma). *Application deadline:* For fall admission, 7/1 priority date for domestic students; for spring admission, 12/1 priority date for domestic students. Applications are processed on a rolling basis. *Application fee:* $50. Electronic applications accepted. *Application Contact:* Dr. Jacquelyn Nealon, Vice President for Enrollment Services, 516-686-7925, Fax: 516-686-7597, E-mail: jnealon@nyit.edu. *Dean*, Dr. Michael Uttendorfer, 516-686-7706, Fax: 516-686-7655, E-mail: muttendo@nyit.edu.

School of Engineering and Computing Sciences Students: 368 full-time (77 women), 307 part-time (62 women); includes 67 minority (29 African Americans, 22 Asian Americans or Pacific Islanders, 16 Hispanic Americans), 401 international. Average age 28. Expenses: Contact institution. *Financial support:* Fellowships, research assistantships with partial tuition reimbursements, career-related internships or fieldwork, institutionally sponsored loans, tuition waivers (full and partial), and unspecified assistantships available. Support available to part-time students. Financial award applicants required to submit FAFSA. In 2008, 268 master's, 10 other advanced degrees awarded. *Degree program information:* Part-time and evening/weekend programs available. Postbaccalaureate distance learning degree programs offered. Offers computer science (MS); electrical engineering and computer engineering (MS); energy management (MS); energy technology (Advanced Certificate); engineering and computing sciences (MS, Advanced Certificate); environmental management (Advanced Certificate); environmental technology (MS); facilities management (Advanced Certificate). *Application deadline:* For fall admission, 7/1 priority date for domestic students; for spring admission, 12/1 priority date for domestic students. Applications are processed on a rolling basis. *Application fee:* $50. Electronic applications accepted. *Application Contact:* Dr. Jacquelyn Nealon, Vice President for Enrollment Services, 516-686-7925, Fax: 516-686-7597, E-mail: jnealon@nyit.edu. *Dean*, Dr. Nada Anid, 516-686-7931, Fax: 516-625-7933, E-mail: nanid@nyit.edu.

School of Health Professions, Behavioral, and Life Sciences Students: 309 full-time (216 women), 61 part-time (42 women); includes 74 minority (21 African Americans, 33 Asian Americans or Pacific Islanders, 20 Hispanic Americans), 9 international. Average age 27. Expenses: Contact institution. *Financial support:* Fellowships, research assistantships with partial tuition reimbursements, career-related internships or fieldwork, institutionally sponsored loans, tuition waivers (full and partial), and unspecified assistantships available. Support available to part-time students. Financial award applicants required to submit FAFSA. In 2008, 49 master's, 47 doctorates awarded. *Degree program information:* Part-time and evening/weekend programs available. Postbaccalaureate distance learning degree programs offered. Offers clinical nutrition (MS); health professions, behavioral, and life sciences (MPS, MS, DPT); human relations (MPS); occupational therapy (MS); physical therapy (MS, DPT); physician assistant (MS). *Application deadline:* For fall admission, 7/1 priority date for domestic students; for spring admission, 12/1 priority date for domestic students. Applications are processed on a rolling basis. *Application fee:* $50. Electronic applications accepted. *Application Contact:* Dr. Jacquelyn Nealon, Vice President for Enrollment Services, 516-686-7925, Fax: 516-686-7597, E-mail: jnealon@nyit.edu. *Dean*, Dr. Chukuka Enwemeka, 516-686-3939, Fax: 516-686-3795, E-mail: enwemeka@nyit.edu.

School of Management Students: 711 full-time (292 women), 625 part-time (252 women); includes 72 minority (26 African Americans, 32 Asian Americans or Pacific Islanders, 14 Hispanic Americans), 355 international. Average age 29. Expenses: Contact institution. *Financial support:* Fellowships, research assistantships with partial tuition reimbursements, career-related internships or fieldwork, institutionally sponsored loans, tuition waivers (full and partial), and unspecified assistantships available. Support available to part-time students. Financial award applicants required to submit FAFSA. In 2008, 900 master's, 7 other advanced degrees awarded. *Degree program information:* Part-time and evening/weekend programs available. Postbaccalaureate distance learning degree programs offered. Offers accounting (Advanced Certificate); business administration (MBA); finance (Advanced Certificate); human resources administration (Advanced Certificate); human resources management and labor relations (MS); international business (Advanced Certificate); labor relations (Advanced Certificate); management (MBA, MS, Advanced Certificate); management of information systems (Advanced Certificate); marketing (Advanced Certificate). *Application deadline:* For fall admission, 7/1 priority date for domestic students; for spring admission, 12/1 priority date for domestic students. Applications are processed on a rolling basis. *Application fee:* $50. Electronic applications accepted. *Application Contact:* Dr. Jacquelyn Nealon, Vice President for Enrollment Services, 516-686-7925, Fax: 516-686-7597, E-mail: jnealon@nyit.edu. *Dean*, Dr. Jess Boronico, 516-686-7838, Fax: 516-686-7430, E-mail: jboronic@nyit.edu.

New York College of Osteopathic Medicine Students: 1,179 full-time (607 women); includes 495 minority (74 African Americans, 366 Asian Americans or Pacific Islanders, 55 Hispanic Americans). Average age 27. *Faculty:* 49 full-time (14 women), 41 part-time/adjunct. Expenses: Contact institution. *Financial support:* In 2008–09, 914 students received support, including fellowships with partial tuition reimbursements available (averaging $17,200 per year); tuition waivers (full and partial) also available. Financial award application deadline: 4/1; financial award applicants required to submit FAFSA. In 2008, 273 DOs awarded. Offers osteopathic medicine (DO). *Application deadline:* For fall admission, 2/1 for domestic students. *Application fee:* $60. *Application Contact:* Rodika Zaika, Director of Admissions, 516-686-3792, Fax: 516-686-3831, E-mail: rzaika@nyit.edu. *Dean*, Dr. Thomas Scandalis, 516-686-3722, Fax: 516-686-3830, E-mail: tscandal@nyit.edu.

NEW YORK LAW SCHOOL, New York, NY 10013

General Information Independent, coed, graduate-only institution. *Graduate housing:* Room and/or apartments available on a first-come, first-served basis to single students; on-campus housing not available to married students. Housing application deadline: 6/1.

GRADUATE UNITS

Graduate Programs *Degree program information:* Part-time and evening/weekend programs available. Postbaccalaureate distance learning degree programs offered. Offers law (JD); mental disability law (MA); real estate (LL M); taxation (LL M). Electronic applications accepted.

NEW YORK MEDICAL COLLEGE, Valhalla, NY 10595-1691

General Information Independent, coed, graduate-only institution. CGS member. *Graduate housing:* Rooms and/or apartments available on a first-come, first-served basis to single and married students. *Research affiliation:* Westchester Medical Center (disaster medicine), Danbury Hospital (behavioral sciences and epidemiology), Westchester Institute for Human Development (disability and human development).

GRADUATE UNITS

Graduate School of Basic Medical Sciences *Degree program information:* Part-time and evening/weekend programs available. Offers basic medical sciences (MS, PhD); biochemistry and molecular biology (MS, PhD); cell biology and neuroscience (MS, PhD); experimental pathology (MS, PhD); microbiology and immunology (MS, PhD); pharmacology (MS, PhD); physiology (MS, PhD).

Professional Program Offers medicine (MD). Electronic applications accepted.

School of Health Sciences and Practice *Degree program information:* Part-time and evening/weekend programs available. Offers behavioral sciences and health promotion (MPH, Dr PH); biostatistics (MPH); disability and human development (MPH); environmental health science (MPH); epidemiology (MPH, Dr PH); global health (MPH); health policy and management (MPH, MS, Dr PH); physical therapy (DPT); public health (MPH, MS, DPT, Dr PH); speech-language pathology (MS). Electronic applications accepted.

NEW YORK SCHOOL OF INTERIOR DESIGN, New York, NY 10021-5110

General Information Independent, coed, primarily women, comprehensive institution. *Enrollment:* 721 graduate, professional, and undergraduate students; 16 full-time matriculated graduate/professional students (13 women). *Enrollment by degree level:* 16 master's. *Graduate faculty:* 9 part-time/adjunct (5 women). *Tuition:* Full-time $21,750. One-time fee: $75 full-time. *Graduate housing:* On-campus housing not available. *Student services:* Campus employment opportunities, career counseling, free psychological counseling, international student services, low-cost health insurance. *Research affiliation:* Metropolitan New York Library Council–Research Consortium.

Computer facilities: 135 computers available on campus for general student use. A campuswide network can be accessed from off campus. Online class registration is available. *Web address:* http://www.nysid.edu/.

General Application Contact: Scott Ageloff, Dean, 212-472-1500 Ext. 301, Fax: 212-288-6577, E-mail: sageloff@nysid.edu.

GRADUATE UNITS

Program in Interior Design Students: 16 full-time (13 women); includes 9 minority (1 African American, 7 Asian Americans or Pacific Islanders, 1 Hispanic American), 1 international. Average age 25. 86 applicants, 24% accepted, 8 enrolled. *Faculty:* 9 part-time/adjunct (5 women). Expenses: Contact institution. *Financial support:* In 2008–09, 6 students received support, including 6 fellowships (averaging $10,000 per year); career-related internships or fieldwork, Federal Work-Study, institutionally sponsored loans, and scholarships/grants also available. Financial award application deadline: 5/1; financial award applicants required to submit FAFSA. In 2008, 6 master's awarded. Offers interior design (MFA). *Application deadline:* For fall admission, 3/1 priority date for domestic and international students. Applications are processed on a rolling basis. *Application fee:* $50 ($75 for international students). Electronic applications accepted. *Application Contact:* David T. Sprouls, Director of Admissions, 212-472-1500 Ext. 202, Fax: 212-472-1867, E-mail: dsprouls@nysid.edu. *Dean*, Scott Ageloff, 212-472-1500 Ext. 301, Fax: 212-288-6577, E-mail: sageloff@nysid.edu.

NEW YORK STUDIO SCHOOL OF DRAWING, PAINTING AND SCULPTURE, New York, NY 10011

General Information Comprehensive institution.

GRADUATE UNITS

Certificate Program Offers studio art (Certificate).

MFA Program Offers painting (MFA); sculpture (MFA).

NEW YORK THEOLOGICAL SEMINARY, New York, NY 10115

General Information Independent-religious, coed, graduate-only institution. *Graduate housing:* On-campus housing not available. *Research affiliation:* Bellevue Hospital Center, Goldwater Memorial Hospital, Institutes of Religion and Health, Lutheran Medical Center, Postgraduate Center for Mental Health.

New York Theological Seminary (continued)

GRADUATE UNITS

Graduate and Professional Programs *Degree program information:* Part-time programs available. Offers theology (M Div, MPS, MSW, D Min).

NEW YORK UNIVERSITY, New York, NY 10012-1019

General Information Independent, coed, university. CGS member. *Enrollment:* 42,189 graduate, professional, and undergraduate students; 12,236 full-time matriculated graduate/professional students (7,114 women), 8,167 part-time matriculated graduate/professional students (4,618 women). *Enrollment by degree level:* 3,466 first professional, 14,321 master's, 2,094 doctoral, 522 other advanced degrees. *Graduate faculty:* 3,695 full-time (1,442 women), 3,540 part-time/adjunct (1,615 women). *Tuition:* Full-time $28,944; part-time $1206 per credit. *Required fees:* $2094. Part-time tuition and fees vary according to course load and program. *Graduate housing:* Room and/or apartments available on a first-come, first-served basis to single students; on-campus housing not available to married students. Typical cost: $17,355 (including board). Room and board charges vary according to board plan. Housing application deadline: 5/1. *Student services:* Campus employment opportunities, campus safety program, career counseling, exercise/wellness program, free psychological counseling, grant writing training, international student services, low-cost health insurance, multicultural affairs office, services for students with disabilities, teacher training, writing training. *Library facilities:* Elmer H. Bobst Library plus 11 others. *Online resources:* library catalog, web page, access to other libraries' catalogs. *Collection:* 5.2 million titles, 48,958 serial subscriptions. *Research affiliation:* Smithsonian Institute, Metropolitan Museum of Art, Inter-University Doctoral Consortium, American Museum of Natural History, Center for American Archaeology, New York Botanical Gardens.

Computer facilities: 4,500 computers available on campus for general student use. A campuswide network can be accessed from student residence rooms and from off campus. Online class registration is available. *Web address:* http://www.nyu.edu/.

General Application Contact: New York University Information, 212-998-1212.

GRADUATE UNITS

College of Dentistry Offers clinical research (MS); dentistry (DDS, MS, PhD, Advanced Certificate); endodontics (Advanced Certificate); oral and maxillofacial surgery (Advanced Certificate); orthodontics (Advanced Certificate); pediatric dentistry (Advanced Certificate); periodontics (Advanced Certificate); prosthodontics (Advanced Certificate); prosthodontics (implantology) (Advanced Certificate).

College of Nursing Students: 25 full-time (21 women), 508 part-time (473 women); includes 223 minority (85 African Americans, 111 Asian Americans or Pacific Islanders, 27 Hispanic Americans). 205 applicants, 88% accepted, 128 enrolled. *Faculty:* 53 full-time (47 women), 85 part-time/adjunct (74 women). Expenses: Contact institution. *Financial support:* In 2008–09, 2 research assistantships with full and partial tuition reimbursements were awarded; fellowships with full and partial tuition reimbursements, career-related internships or fieldwork, institutionally sponsored loans, scholarships/grants, and tuition waivers (partial) also available. Support available to part-time students. Financial award application deadline: 2/1; financial award applicants required to submit FAFSA. In 2008, 113 master's, 6 doctorates, 2 other advanced degrees awarded. *Degree program information:* Part-time and evening/weekend programs available. Offers advanced practice nursing: adult acute care (MS, Advanced Certificate); advanced practice nursing: adult primary care (MS, Advanced Certificate); advanced practice nursing: adult primary care/geriatrics (MS); advanced practice nursing: children with special needs (Advanced Certificate); advanced practice nursing: geriatrics (MS, Advanced Certificate); advanced practice nursing: holistic nursing (MS, Advanced Certificate); advanced practice nursing: home health nursing (Advanced Certificate); advanced practice nursing: mental health (MS); advanced practice nursing: mental health nursing (Advanced Certificate); advanced practice nursing: pediatrics (MS, Advanced Certificate); advanced practice nursing: pediatrics/children with special needs (MS); midwifery (MS, Advanced Certificate); nursing (MS, PhD, Advanced Certificate); nursing administration (MS, Advanced Certificate); nursing education (MS, Advanced Certificate); nursing informatics (MS, Advanced Certificate); palliative care (MS, Advanced Certificate); research and theory development in nursing science (PhD). *Application deadline:* Applications are processed on a rolling basis. *Application fee:* $75. *Application Contact:* Amy Knowles, Assistant Dean for Student Affairs and Admissions, 212-998-5333, Fax: 212-995-4302, E-mail: ak96@nyu.edu. *Dean,* Dr. Terry Fulmer, 212-998-5303, Fax: 212-995-3143.

Gallatin School of Individualized Study Students: 44 full-time (34 women), 172 part-time (130 women); includes 58 minority (29 African Americans, 1 American Indian/Alaska Native, 15 Asian Americans or Pacific Islanders, 13 Hispanic Americans), 16 international. Average age 34. 197 applicants, 48% accepted, 48 enrolled. *Faculty:* 34 full-time (17 women), 40 part-time/adjunct (23 women). Expenses: Contact institution. *Financial support:* In 2008–09, 72 students received support, including 5 fellowships (averaging $50,000 per year), 2 research assistantships with full tuition reimbursements available (averaging $16,500 per year); Federal Work-Study, scholarships/grants, and unspecified assistantships also available. Support available to part-time students. Financial award application deadline: 2/1; financial award applicants required to submit FAFSA. In 2008, 44 master's awarded. *Degree program information:* Part-time and evening/weekend programs available. Offers individualized study (MA). *Application deadline:* For fall admission, 2/1 priority date for domestic students, 2/1 for international students; for spring admission, 11/1 for domestic and international students. Applications are processed on a rolling basis. *Application fee:* $50. Electronic applications accepted. *Application Contact:* Frances R. Levin, Director of Graduate Admissions, 212-998-7370, Fax: 212-995-4150, E-mail: gallatin.gradadmissions@nyu.edu. *Dean,* Dr. Susanne L. Wofford, 212-998-7370.

Graduate School of Arts and Science Students: 3,270 full-time (1,823 women), 1,194 part-time (655 women); includes 575 minority (120 African Americans, 9 American Indian/Alaska Native, 275 Asian Americans or Pacific Islanders, 171 Hispanic Americans), 1,453 international. Average age 29. 11,452 applicants, 26% accepted, 1260 enrolled. *Faculty:* 597 full-time (159 women), 393 part-time/adjunct. Expenses: Contact institution. *Financial support:* Fellowships with tuition reimbursements, research assistantships with tuition reimbursements, teaching assistantships with tuition reimbursements, career-related internships or fieldwork, Federal Work-Study, institutionally sponsored loans, scholarships/grants, health care benefits, tuition waivers (partial), unspecified assistantships, and instructorships available. Financial award applicants required to submit FAFSA. In 2008, 979 master's, 259 doctorates awarded. *Degree program information:* Part-time and evening/weekend programs available. Offers African diaspora (PhD); African history (PhD); Africana studies (MA); American studies (MA, PhD); anthropology (MA, PhD); anthropology and French studies (PhD); applied economic analysis (Advanced Certificate); archival management and historical editing (Advanced Certificate); arts and science (MA, MFA, MS, PhD, Advanced Certificate); Atlantic history (PhD); bioethics (MA); biology (PhD); biomaterials science (MS); biomedical journalism (MS); cancer and molecular biology (PhD); chemistry (MS, PhD); classics (MA, PhD); cognition and perception (PhD); community psychology (PhD); comparative literature (MA, PhD); composition and theory (MA, PhD); computational biology (PhD); computers in biological research (MS); creative writing (MA, MFA); cultural reporting and criticism (MA); culture and mediadevelopmental genetics (PhD); early music performance (Advanced Certificate); East Asian studies (MA, PhD); economics (MA, PhD); English and American literature (MA, PhD); environmental health sciences (MS, PhD); ethnomusicology (MA, PhD); French studies and sociology (PhD); French studies/history (PhD); French studies/journalism (MA); general biology (MS); general psychology (MA); German studies and critical thought (MA, PhD); Hebrew and Judaic studies (MA, PhD); Hebrew and Judaic studies/history (PhD); Hebrew and Judaic studies/museum studies (MA); history (MA, PhD); humanities and social thought (MA); immunology and microbiology (PhD); industrial/organizational psychology (MA); Irish and Irish American studies (MA); Italian (MA, PhD); Italian studies (MA); journalism (MA); Latin American and Caribbean studies/journalism (MA); linguistics (MA, PhD); Middle Eastern history (MA); Middle Eastern studies/history (PhD); molecular genetics (PhD); museum studies (MA, Advanced Certificate); Near Eastern studies/journalism (MA); neurobiology (PhD); oral biology (MS); philosophy (MA, PhD); physics (MS, PhD); plant biology (PhD); poetics and theory (Advanced Certificate); political campaign management (MA); politics (MA, PhD); Portuguese (MA, PhD); psychotherapy and psychoanalysis (Advanced Certificate); public history (Advanced Certificate); recombinant DNA technology (MS); religion (Advanced Certificate); religious studies (MA); Russian literature (MA); science and environmental reporting (Advanced Certificate); Slavic literature (MA); social theory (Advanced Certificate); social/personality psychology (PhD); sociology (MA, PhD); Spanish (PhD); Spanish and Latin American literatures and cultures (MA); Spanish language and translation (MA); trauma and violence transdisciplinary studies (MA, Advanced Certificate); world history (MA). *Application fee:* $85. Electronic applications accepted. *Application Contact:* Roberta Popik, Associate Dean of Enrollment, 212-998-8050, Fax: 212-995-4557, E-mail: gsas.admissions@nyu.edu. *Dean,* Catharine R. Stimpson, 212-998-8040.

Center for European Studies Students: 12 full-time (9 women), 1 (woman) part-time; includes 1 minority (African American), 4 international. Average age 25. 21 applicants, 90% accepted, 6 enrolled. *Faculty:* 4 full-time (0 women). Expenses: Contact institution. *Financial support:* Fellowships with tuition reimbursements, teaching assistantships with tuition reimbursements, career-related internships or fieldwork, Federal Work-Study, institutionally sponsored loans, and scholarships/grants available. Financial award application deadline: 1/4; financial award applicants required to submit FAFSA. In 2008, 7 master's awarded. Offers European studies (MA). *Application deadline:* For fall admission, 1/4 priority date for domestic students. *Application fee:* $55. Electronic applications accepted. *Application Contact:* Jennifer Denbo, Department Graduate Administrator, 212-998-3838, Fax: 212-995-4188. *Director,* Katherine Fleming, 212-998-3838, Fax: 212-995-4188, E-mail: european.studies@nyu.edu.

Center for French Civilization and Culture Students: 99 full-time (71 women), 9 part-time (5 women); includes 7 minority (4 African Americans, 2 Asian Americans or Pacific Islanders, 1 Hispanic American), 29 international. Average age 30. 124 applicants, 61% accepted, 30 enrolled. Expenses: Contact institution. *Financial support:* Fellowships with tuition reimbursements, research assistantships with tuition reimbursements, teaching assistantships with tuition reimbursements, Federal Work-Study, institutionally sponsored loans, scholarships/grants, traineeships, unspecified assistantships, and instructorships available. Financial award application deadline: 1/4; financial award applicants required to submit FAFSA. In 2008, 37 master's, 7 doctorates awarded. *Degree program information:* Part-time and evening/weekend programs available. Offers French (PhD); French civilization (PhD); French civilization and culture (MA, PhD, Advanced Certificate); French language and civilization (MA); French literature (MA); French studies (MA, PhD, Advanced Certificate); French studies and anthropology (PhD); French studies and history (PhD); French studies and journalism (MA); French studies and sociology (PhD); Romance languages and literatures (MA). *Application deadline:* For fall admission, 1/4 for domestic students. *Application fee:* $85. *Application Contact:* Brett Underhill, Graduate Secretary, 212-998-8700, Fax: 212-995-3539, E-mail: french.grad@nyu.edu. *Chair,* Judith Miller, 212-998-8700, Fax: 212-995-3539, E-mail: french.grad@nyu.edu.

Center for Latin American and Caribbean Studies Students: 31 full-time (23 women), 10 part-time (5 women); includes 12 minority (2 African Americans, 10 Hispanic Americans), 5 international. Average age 27. 59 applicants, 68% accepted, 16 enrolled. *Faculty:* 2 full-time (0 women), 5 part-time/adjunct. Expenses: Contact institution. *Financial support:* Fellowships with tuition reimbursements, teaching assistantships with tuition reimbursements, Federal Work-Study, institutionally sponsored loans, scholarships/grants, health care benefits, and unspecified assistantships available. Financial award application deadline: 1/4; financial award applicants required to submit FAFSA. In 2008, 14 master's awarded. *Degree program information:* Part-time programs available. Offers Latin American and Caribbean studies (MA). *Application deadline:* For fall admission, 1/4 priority date for domestic students. *Application fee:* $85. *Application Contact:* Maritza Colon, Department Administrator, 212-998-8686, Fax: 212-995-4163, E-mail: clacs.info@nyu.edu. *Director,* Tom Abercrombie, 212-998-8686, Fax: 212-995-4163, E-mail: clacs.info@nyu.edu.

Center for Neural Science Students: 28 full-time (13 women), 2 part-time (1 woman); includes 6 minority (2 African Americans, 3 Asian Americans or Pacific Islanders, 1 Hispanic American), 2 international. Average age 27. 168 applicants, 17% accepted, 4 enrolled. *Faculty:* 15 full-time (3 women), 4 part-time/adjunct. Expenses: Contact institution. *Financial support:* Fellowships with tuition reimbursements, research assistantships with tuition reimbursements, career-related internships or fieldwork, Federal Work-Study, institutionally sponsored loans, scholarships/grants, health care benefits, and unspecified assistantships available. Financial award application deadline: 12/18; financial award applicants required to submit FAFSA. In 2008, 4 doctorates awarded. Offers neural science (PhD). *Application deadline:* For fall admission, 12/18 for domestic students. *Application fee:* $85. *Application Contact:* Lynne Kiorpes, Director of Graduate Studies, 212-998-7780, Fax: 212-995-4011, E-mail: cns@nyu.edu. *Chair,* J. Anthony Movshon, 212-998-7780, Fax: 212-995-4011, E-mail: cns@nyu.edu.

Courant Institute of Mathematical Sciences Students: 362 full-time (87 women), 258 part-time (44 women); includes 70 minority (4 African Americans, 60 Asian Americans or Pacific Islanders, 6 Hispanic Americans), 352 international. Average age 29. 1,965 applicants, 27% accepted, 169 enrolled. *Faculty:* 76 full-time (1 woman). Expenses: Contact institution. *Financial support:* Fellowships with tuition reimbursements, research assistantships with tuition reimbursements, teaching assistantships with tuition reimbursements, career-related internships or fieldwork, Federal Work-Study, institutionally sponsored loans, scholarships/grants, health care benefits, tuition waivers (full and partial), and unspecified assistantships available. Financial award application deadline: 1/4; financial award applicants required to submit FAFSA. In 2008, 172 master's, 35 doctorates awarded. *Degree program information:* Part-time and evening/weekend programs available. Offers atmosphere ocean science and mathematics (PhD); computer science (MS, PhD); information systems (MS); mathematics (MS, PhD); mathematics and statistics/operations research (MS); mathematics in finance (MS); scientific computing (MS). *Application deadline:* For fall admission, 1/4 for domestic students. *Application fee:* $85. *Application Contact:* Tamar Arnon, Application Contact, 212-998-3238, Fax: 212-995-4195, E-mail: admissions@math.nyu.edu. *Director of Graduate Studies,* Fedor Bogomolov, 212-998-3238, Fax: 212-995-4121, E-mail: admissions@math.nyu.edu.

Hagop Kevorkian Center for Near Eastern Studies Students: 71 full-time (44 women), 3 part-time (0 women); includes 10 minority (9 Asian Americans or Pacific Islanders, 1 Hispanic American), 26 international. Average age 29. 272 applicants, 19% accepted, 24 enrolled. *Faculty:* 32 full-time (11 women). Expenses: Contact institution. *Financial support:* Fellowships with tuition reimbursements, teaching assistantships with tuition reimbursements, Federal Work-Study and institutionally sponsored loans available. Financial award application deadline: 1/4; financial award applicants required to submit FAFSA. In 2008, 9 master's, 3 doctorates awarded. *Degree program information:* Part-time and evening/weekend programs available. Offers Middle Eastern and Islamic studies (MA, PhD); Middle Eastern and Islamic studies/history (PhD); Near Eastern studies (MA, PhD); Near Eastern studies (museum studies) (MA); Near Eastern studies/journalism (MA). *Application deadline:* For fall admission, 1/4 for domestic students. *Application fee:* $85. *Application Contact:* Roberta Popik, Associate Dean of Enrollment, 212-998-8050, Fax: 212-995-4557, E-mail: gsas.admissions@nyu.edu. *Chair,* Timothy Mitchell, 212-998-8877, Fax: 212-995-4144, E-mail: kevorkian.center@nyu.edu.

Institute for Law and Society Students: 20 full-time (14 women), 1 (woman) part-time; includes 2 minority (1 African American, 1 Asian American or Pacific Islander), 5 international. Average age 31. 50 applicants, 12% accepted, 3 enrolled. *Faculty:* 3 full-time (1 woman). Expenses: Contact institution. *Financial support:* Fellowships with tuition reimbursements, teaching assistantships with tuition reimbursements, career-related internships or fieldwork, Federal Work-Study, institutionally sponsored loans, scholarships/grants, health care benefits, and unspecified assistantships available. Financial award application deadline: 12/18; financial award applicants required to submit FAFSA. In 2008, 2 doctorates awarded. Offers law and society (MA, PhD). *Application deadline:* For fall admission, 12/18 for domestic students. *Application fee:* $85. *Application Contact:* Jo Dixon, Director of Graduate Studies, 212-998-8536, Fax: 212-995-4034, E-mail: law.society@nyu.edu. *Director,* Lewis Kornhauser, 212-998-8536, Fax: 212-995-4034, E-mail: law.society@nyu.edu.

Institute of Fine Arts Students: 287 full-time (178 women), 59 part-time (50 women); includes 24 minority (15 Asian Americans or Pacific Islanders, 9 Hispanic Americans), 30 international. Average age 32. 336 applicants, 30% accepted, 49 enrolled. *Faculty:* 19

full-time (5 women). Expenses: Contact institution. *Financial support:* Fellowships with tuition reimbursements, research assistantships with tuition reimbursements, teaching assistantships with tuition reimbursements, career-related internships or fieldwork, Federal Work-Study, institutionally sponsored loans, and tuition waivers (partial) available. Financial award application deadline: 12/18; financial award applicants required to submit FAFSA. In 2008, 39 master's, 17 doctorates awarded. *Degree program information:* Part-time programs available. Offers architectural studies (PhD); art history and archaeology (MA, PhD); classical art and archaeology (PhD); conservation trainingcuratorial studies (PhD); East and South Asian art (PhD); Near Eastern art and archaeology (PhD). *Application deadline:* For fall admission, 12/18 for domestic students. *Application fee:* $85. *Application Contact:* Priscilla Saucek, Director of Graduate Studies, 212-992-5800, Fax: 212-992-5807, E-mail: ifa.program@nyu.edu. *Chair,* Mariet Westermann, 212-992-5800, E-mail: ifa.program@nyu.edu.

Leonard N. Stern School of Business *Degree program information:* Part-time and evening/weekend programs available. Offers accounting (MBA, PhD); economics (MBA, PhD); entertainment, media and technology (MBA); finance (MBA, PhD); general marketing (MBA); information systems (MBA, PhD); information, operations and management sciences (MBA, PhD); management and organizations (MBA, PhD, APC); management organizations (MBA); marketing (MBA, PhD); operations management (MBA, PhD); organization theory (PhD); organizational behavior (PhD); product management (MBA); statistics (MBA, PhD); strategy (PhD). Electronic applications accepted.

NYU in Madrid Offers creative writing in Spanish (MFA); Spanish (PhD); Spanish and Latin American literatures and cultures (MA); Spanish language and translation (MA).

NYU in Paris Offers teaching French as a foreign language (MA).

Robert F. Wagner Graduate School of Public Service Students: 478 full-time (358 women), 438 part-time (317 women); includes 171 minority (53 African Americans, 3 American Indian/Alaska Native, 76 Asian Americans or Pacific Islanders, 39 Hispanic Americans), 121 international. Average age 30. 1,463 applicants, 60% accepted, 322 enrolled. *Faculty:* 31 full-time (14 women), 68 part-time/adjunct (34 women). Expenses: Contact institution. *Financial support:* In 2008–09, 302 fellowships (averaging $7,802 per year), 8 research assistantships with full tuition reimbursements (averaging $16,000 per year) were awarded; career-related internships or fieldwork, Federal Work-Study, institutionally sponsored loans, scholarships/grants, health care benefits, and unspecified assistantships also available. Support available to part-time students. Financial award application deadline: 1/15; financial award applicants required to submit FAFSA. In 2008, 360 master's, 7 doctorates, 4 other advanced degrees awarded. *Degree program information:* Part-time and evening/weekend programs available. Offers health finance (MPA); health policy analysis (MPA); health policy and management (Advanced Certificate); health services management (MPA); housing (Advanced Certificate); international health (MPA); international public service organizations management (MS); management (MS); public administration (PhD); public and nonprofit management and policy (MPA, Advanced Certificate); public economics (Advanced Certificate); public service (MPA, MS, MUP, PhD, Advanced Certificate); quantitative analysis and computer applications for policy and planning (Advanced Certificate); urban planning (MUP). *Application deadline:* For fall admission, 6/1 for domestic students, 1/15 for international students; for spring admission, 11/15 for domestic students, 10/1 for international students. Applications are processed on a rolling basis. *Application fee:* $70. Electronic applications accepted. *Application Contact:* Peter King, Director, Admissions and Recruitment, 212-998-7414, Fax: 212-995-4164, E-mail: wagner.admissions@nyu.edu. *Dean,* Prof. Ellen Schall, 212-998-7400, Fax: 212-995-4161.

School of Continuing and Professional Studies Students: 485 full-time (202 women), 1,644 part-time (844 women); includes 325 minority (114 African Americans, 128 Asian Americans or Pacific Islanders, 83 Hispanic Americans), 206 international. Average age 30. 1,619 applicants, 58% accepted, 607 enrolled. *Faculty:* 49 full-time (14 women), 310 part-time/adjunct (92 women). Expenses: Contact institution. *Financial support:* In 2008–09, 818 students received support, including 808 fellowships (averaging $2,027 per year), 5 research assistantships with partial tuition reimbursements available (averaging $9,000 per year); career-related internships or fieldwork, Federal Work-Study, institutionally sponsored loans, scholarships/grants, and tuition waivers (partial) also available. Support available to part-time students. Financial award application deadline: 3/1; financial award applicants required to submit FAFSA. In 2008, 558 master's, 121 other advanced degrees awarded. *Degree program information:* Part-time and evening/weekend programs available. Postbaccalaureate distance learning degree programs offered (no on-campus study). *Application deadline:* For fall admission, 3/15 priority date for domestic and international students; for spring admission, 10/15 priority date for domestic students, 8/15 priority date for international students. Applications are processed on a rolling basis. *Application fee:* $75. Electronic applications accepted. *Application Contact:* Office of Admissions, 212-998-7100, Fax: 212-995-4674. *Dean,* Robert Lapiner, 212-998-7000, Fax: 212-995-4130.

Center for Advanced Digital Applications Students: 45 full-time (20 women), 37 part-time (11 women); includes 11 minority (4 African Americans, 3 Asian Americans or Pacific Islanders, 4 Hispanic Americans), 9 international. Average age 30. 48 applicants, 69% accepted, 23 enrolled. *Faculty:* 4 full-time (1 woman), 21 part-time/adjunct (2 women). Expenses: Contact institution. *Financial support:* In 2008–09, 46 students received support, including 46 fellowships with tuition reimbursements available (averaging $2,663 per year); career-related internships or fieldwork and scholarships/grants also available. Support available to part-time students. Financial award application deadline: 3/1; financial award applicants required to submit FAFSA. In 2008, 50 master's awarded. *Degree program information:* Part-time programs available. Offers digital imaging and design (MS). *Application deadline:* For fall admission, 3/15 priority date for domestic and international students; for spring admission, 10/15 priority date for domestic students, 8/15 priority date for international students. Applications are processed on a rolling basis. *Application fee:* $75. Electronic applications accepted. *Application Contact:* Assistant Director, 212-992-3370, Fax: 212-992-3377, E-mail: cada@nyu.edu. *Director,* Michael Hosenfeld, 212-992-3647, Fax: 212-992-3377, E-mail: michael.hosenfeld@nyu.edu.

Center for Global Affairs Students: 92 full-time (65 women), 163 part-time (120 women); includes 33 minority (11 African Americans, 10 Asian Americans or Pacific Islanders, 12 Hispanic Americans), 29 international. Average age 31. 309 applicants, 63% accepted, 109 enrolled. *Faculty:* 8 full-time (7 women), 31 part-time/adjunct (14 women). Expenses: Contact institution. *Financial support:* In 2008–09, 144 students received support, including 144 fellowships (averaging $2,556 per year); institutionally sponsored loans, scholarships/grants, and tuition waivers (partial) also available. Support available to part-time students. Financial award application deadline: 3/1; financial award applicants required to submit FAFSA. In 2008, 115 master's awarded. *Degree program information:* Part-time and evening/weekend programs available. Offers global affairs (MS). *Application deadline:* For fall admission, 3/15 priority date for domestic and international students; for spring admission, 10/15 priority date for domestic students, 8/15 priority date for international students. Applications are processed on a rolling basis. *Application fee:* $75. Electronic applications accepted. *Application Contact:* Mykellan Ledden, Associate Director, 212-992-8380, Fax: 212-995-4597, E-mail: mykellan.ledden@nyu.edu. *Assistant Dean and Director,* Dr. Vera Jelinek, 212-992-8380, Fax: 212-995-4597, E-mail: vera.jelinek@nyu.edu.

Division for Media Industry Studies and Design Students: 99 full-time (69 women), 173 part-time (107 women); includes 38 minority (11 African Americans, 1 American Indian/Alaska Native, 15 Asian Americans or Pacific Islanders, 11 Hispanic Americans), 27 international. Average age 29. 168 applicants, 69% accepted, 67 enrolled. *Faculty:* 6 full-time (3 women), 67 part-time/adjunct (26 women). Expenses: Contact institution. *Financial support:* In 2008–09, 182 students received support, including 182 fellowships (averaging $2,245 per year). Financial award application deadline: 3/1; financial award applicants required to submit FAFSA. In 2008, 110 master's awarded. *Degree program information:* Part-time and evening/weekend programs available. Offers graphic communications management and technology (MA); publishing (MS). *Application deadline:* For fall admission, 3/15 priority date for domestic and international students; for spring admission, 10/15 priority date for domestic and international students. Applications are processed on a rolling basis. *Application fee:* $75. Electronic applications accepted. *Application Contact:* Office of Admissions, 212-998-7100, Fax: 212-995-4674. *Dean,* Bonnie Blake, 212-998-7000, Fax: 212-995-4130.

Division of Programs in Business Students: 119 full-time (94 women), 589 part-time (372 women); includes 150 minority (61 African Americans, 54 Asian Americans or Pacific Islanders, 35 Hispanic Americans), 80 international. Average age 30. 540 applicants, 55% accepted, 187 enrolled. *Faculty:* 9 full-time (2 women), 87 part-time/adjunct (29 women). Expenses: Contact institution. *Financial support:* In 2008–09, 171 students received support, including 171 fellowships (averaging $1,859 per year); career-related internships or fieldwork, institutionally sponsored loans, and scholarships/grants also available. Support available to part-time students. Financial award application deadline: 3/1; financial award applicants required to submit FAFSA. In 2008, 42 master's, 10 other advanced degrees awarded. *Degree program information:* Part-time and evening/weekend programs available. Postbaccalaureate distance learning degree programs offered (minimal on-campus study). Offers benefits and compensation (Advanced Certificate); brand management (MS); corporate and organizational communications (MS); database technologies (MS); digital marketing (MS); enterprise and risk management (Advanced Certificate); enterprise risk management (MS); human resource development (MS); human resource management (MS, Advanced Certificate); information technologies (Advanced Certificate); interactive marketing (MS); leadership and human capital management (MS, Advanced Certificate); management and systems (MS, Advanced Certificate); marketing analytics (MS); organizational and executive coaching (Advanced Certificate); organizational effectiveness (MS); public relations and corporate communications (MS); public relations management (MS); strategy and leadership (MS, Advanced Certificate); systems management (MS). *Application deadline:* For fall admission, 3/15 priority date for domestic and international students; for spring admission, 10/15 priority date for domestic students, 8/15 priority date for international students. Applications are processed on a rolling basis. *Application fee:* $75. Electronic applications accepted. *Application Contact:* Dr. Anthony Davidson, Assistant Dean, 212-992-3600, Fax: 212-995-3650, E-mail: anthony.davidson@nyu.edu. *Assistant Dean,* Dr. Anthony Davidson, 212-992-3600, Fax: 212-995-3650, E-mail: anthony.davidson@nyu.edu.

The George Heyman Jr. Center for Philanthropy and Fundraising Students: 5 full-time (3 women), 33 part-time (28 women); includes 6 minority (3 African Americans, 3 Hispanic Americans), 2 international. Average age 34. 21 applicants, 71% accepted, 9 enrolled. *Faculty:* 1 (woman) full-time, 10 part-time/adjunct (6 women). Expenses: Contact institution. *Financial support:* In 2008–09, 12 students received support, including 12 fellowships (averaging $2,028 per year); scholarships/grants also available. Financial award application deadline: 3/1; financial award applicants required to submit FAFSA. In 2008, 5 master's awarded. *Degree program information:* Part-time and evening/weekend programs available. Offers fundraising (MS). *Application deadline:* For fall admission, 3/15 priority date for domestic and international students; for spring admission, 10/15 priority date for domestic students, 8/15 priority date for international students. Applications are processed on a rolling basis. *Application fee:* $75. Electronic applications accepted. *Director,* Lewis Brindle, 212-998-6790, Fax: 212-995-4784, E-mail: lcb@nyu.edu.

The Preston Robert Tisch Center for Hospitality, Tourism, and Sports Management Students: 50 full-time (27 women), 98 part-time (44 women); includes 16 minority (4 African Americans, 8 Asian Americans or Pacific Islanders, 4 Hispanic Americans), 34 international. Average age 28. 200 applicants, 38% accepted, 53 enrolled. *Faculty:* 14 full-time (6 women), 27 part-time/adjunct (5 women). Expenses: Contact institution. *Financial support:* In 2008–09, 75 students received support, including 75 fellowships (averaging $2,609 per year), 5 research assistantships with partial tuition reimbursements available (averaging $9,000 per year); career-related internships or fieldwork, Federal Work-Study, institutionally sponsored loans, and scholarships/grants also available. Support available to part-time students. Financial award application deadline: 3/1; financial award applicants required to submit FAFSA. In 2008, 72 master's, 10 other advanced degrees awarded. *Degree program information:* Part-time and evening/weekend programs available. Offers customer relationship management (MS); hospitality industry studies (MS, Advanced Certificate); sports business (MS, Advanced Certificate); tourism and travel management (MS, Advanced Certificate); tourism development (MS); tourism planning and analysis (MS). *Application deadline:* For fall admission, 3/15 priority date for domestic and international students; for spring admission, 10/15 priority date for domestic students, 8/15 priority date for international students. Applications are processed on a rolling basis. *Application fee:* $75. Electronic applications accepted. *Application Contact:* Office of Admissions, 212-998-7100, Fax: 212-995-4674. *Associate Dean,* Dr. Lalia Rach, 212-998-9100, Fax: 212-995-4676.

Schack Institute of Real Estate Students: 120 full-time (25 women), 590 part-time (134 women); includes 86 minority (24 African Americans, 42 Asian Americans or Pacific Islanders, 20 Hispanic Americans), 44 international. Average age 32. 381 applicants, 64% accepted, 172 enrolled. *Faculty:* 10 full-time (2 women), 87 part-time/adjunct (10 women). Expenses: Contact institution. *Financial support:* In 2008–09, 173 students received support, including 173 fellowships (averaging $1,276 per year); scholarships/grants also available. Support available to part-time students. Financial award application deadline: 3/1; financial award applicants required to submit FAFSA. In 2008, 217 master's, 77 other advanced degrees awarded. *Degree program information:* Part-time and evening/weekend programs available. Offers construction management (MS, Advanced Certificate); construction management for the development process (MS); development (MS); finance and investment (MS); project management (MS); real estate (MS, Advanced Certificate); strategic real estate management (MS). *Application deadline:* For fall admission, 3/15 priority date for domestic and international students; for spring admission, 10/15 priority date for domestic students, 8/15 priority date for international students. Applications are processed on a rolling basis. *Application fee:* $75. Electronic applications accepted. *Application Contact:* Marcie Burros, Director of Administration and Student Services, 212-992-3335, Fax: 212-992-3686, E-mail: gradadmissions@nyu.edu. *Divisional Dean,* D. Kenneth Patton, 212-992-3335, Fax: 212-992-3686, E-mail: dk.patton@nyu.edu.

School of Law Students: 1,423 full-time (658 women); includes 317 minority (90 African Americans, 2 American Indian/Alaska Native, 141 Asian Americans or Pacific Islanders, 84 Hispanic Americans), 42 international. 7,074 applicants, 448 enrolled. *Faculty:* 126 full-time (38 women), 64 part-time/adjunct (18 women). Expenses: Contact institution. *Financial support:* Fellowships, research assistantships, teaching assistantships, career-related internships or fieldwork, Federal Work-Study, institutionally sponsored loans, scholarships/grants, tuition waivers (partial), and loan repayment assistance available. Financial award application deadline: 4/15; financial award applicants required to submit FAFSA. In 2008, 485 first professional degrees, 460 master's, 4 doctorates awarded. *Degree program information:* Part-time programs available. Offers law (JD, LL M, JSD); law and business (Advanced Certificate); taxation (Advanced Certificate). *Application deadline:* For fall admission, 2/1 for domestic students. *Application fee:* $85. Electronic applications accepted. *Application Contact:* Kenneth J. Kleinrock, Assistant Dean for Admissions, 212-998-6060, Fax: 212-995-4527. *Dean,* Richard L. Revesz, 212-998-6000, Fax: 212-995-3150.

School of Medicine Offers biomedical sciences (PhD); clinical investigation (MS); medicine (MD, MS, PhD).

Sackler Institute of Graduate Biomedical Sciences Offers cellular and molecular biology (PhD); computational biology (PhD); developmental genetics (PhD); immunology (PhD); medical and molecular parasitology (PhD); microbiology (PhD); molecular oncology (PhD); molecular oncology and immunology (PhD); molecular pharmacology (PhD); neuroscience and physiology (PhD); pathobiology (PhD); pharmacology (PhD); structural biology (PhD). Electronic applications accepted.

Silver School of Social Work Students: 810 full-time, 336 part-time; includes 342 minority (110 African Americans, 2 American Indian/Alaska Native, 100 Asian Americans or Pacific Islanders, 130 Hispanic Americans). Average age 27. 1,309 applicants, 80% accepted, 432 enrolled. *Faculty:* 41 full-time (33 women), 145 part-time/adjunct (108 women). Expenses: Contact institution. *Financial support:* In 2008–09, 841 students received support, including 5 research assistantships with full and partial tuition reimbursements available (averaging $20,000 per year); career-related internships or fieldwork, Federal Work-Study, scholarships/grants, health care benefits, tuition waivers (partial), and unspecified assistantships also available. Support available to part-time students. Financial award application deadline: 3/1; financial award applicants required to submit FAFSA. In 2008, 468 master's, 11 doctorates

New York University (continued)

awarded. *Degree program information:* Part-time and evening/weekend programs available. Offers social work (MSW, PhD). *Application deadline:* For fall admission, 3/1 priority date for domestic and international students; for spring admission, 11/2 priority date for domestic and international students. Applications are processed on a rolling basis. *Application fee:* $50. Electronic applications accepted. *Application Contact:* Robert W. Sommo, Assistant Dean for Enrollment Services, 212-998-5910, Fax: 212-995-4171, E-mail: ssw.admissions@nyu.edu. *Dean,* Dr. Suzanne England, 212-998-5959, Fax: 212-995-4172.

Steinhardt School of Culture, Education, and Human Development Students: 2,325 full-time (1,568 women), 1,423 part-time (895 women); includes 768 minority (256 African Americans, 5 American Indian/Alaska Native, 280 Asian Americans or Pacific Islanders, 227 Hispanic Americans), 577 international. Average age 29. 4,708 applicants, 55% accepted, 1163 enrolled. *Faculty:* 305 full-time (169 women), 574 part-time/adjunct (369 women). Expenses: Contact institution. *Financial support:* Fellowships with full and partial tuition reimbursements, research assistantships with full and partial tuition reimbursements, teaching assistantships with full and partial tuition reimbursements, career-related internships or fieldwork, Federal Work-Study, institutionally sponsored loans, scholarships/grants, traineeships, tuition waivers (partial), and unspecified assistantships available. Support available to part-time students. Financial award application deadline: 2/1; financial award applicants required to submit FAFSA. In 2008, 1,369 master's, 102 doctorates, 19 other advanced degrees awarded. *Degree program information:* Part-time programs available. Offers advanced occupational therapy (MA); art education (MA); art therapy (MA); bilingual education (MA, PhD, Advanced Certificate); biology grades 7-12 (MA); business education (MA, Advanced Certificate); business education in higher education (MA); chemistry grades 7-12 (MA); childhood education (MA, PhD, Advanced Certificate); childhood special education (MA); clinical nutrition (MS); communication sciences and disorders (MA, PhD); community health (MPH); community public health (MPH, PhD); counseling and guidance (MA, Advanced Certificate); counseling for mental health and wellness (MA); counseling psychology (PhD); counselor education (MA, PhD, Advanced Certificate); culture, education, and human development (MA, MFA, MM, MPH, MS, DPS, DPT, Ed D, PhD, Advanced Certificate); dance education (MA); drama therapy (MA); dual certification: educational theatre and social studies (MA); dual degree: educational theatre and social studies (MA); early childhood and childhood education (MA, PhD, Advanced Certificate); early childhood education (MA, PhD, Advanced Certificate); early childhood special education (MA); education and Jewish studies (MA, PhD); education and jewish studies (MA); education and Jewish studies (PhD); education and social policy (MA); educational and developmental psychology (MA, PhD); educational communication and technology (MA, PhD, Advanced Certificate); educational leadership (MA, Ed D, PhD, Advanced Certificate); educational psychology (MA); educational theatre (MA, Ed D, PhD, Advanced Certificate); educational theatre for colleges and communities (MA, PhD); educational theatre with English 7-12 (MA); English education (MA, PhD, Advanced Certificate); environmental conservation education (MA); food studies (MA); food studies and food management (MA, PhD); foods and nutrition (MS); for-profit sector (MA); foreign language education (MA, Advanced Certificate); foreign language education/TESOL (MA); higher and postsecondary education (Ed D, PhD); higher education (MA, Ed D, PhD); higher education administration (Ed D); higher education/student personnel administration (MA); history of education (MA, PhD); instrumental performance (MM); international community health (MPH); international education (MA, PhD, Advanced Certificate); literacy education (MA); mathematics education (MA); media, culture, and communication (MA, PhD); multilingual/multicultural studies (MA, PhD, Advanced Certificate); music business (MA); music education (MA, Ed D, PhD, Advanced Certificate); music performance and composition (MM, PhD); music technology (MM); music theory and composition (MM); music therapy (MA); not-for-profit sector (MA); nutrition and dietetics (MS, PhD); occupational therapy (MA, MS, DPS); orthopedic physical therapy (Advanced Certificate); performing arts administration (MA); physical therapists pathokinesiology (MA); physical therapy (DPT); physics grades 7-12 (MA); piano performance (MM); politics and advocacy (MA); practicing physical therapist (DPT); psychological development (PhD); psychology and social intervention (PhD); public health (PhD); public health nutrition (MPH); research in occupational therapy (PhD); research in physical therapy (PhD); school building leader (MA); school district leader (Advanced Certificate); science education (MA); social studies education (MA); sociology of education (MA, PhD); special education (MA); studio art (MA, MFA); teaching and learning (Ed D, PhD); teaching educational theatre, all grades (MA); teaching English to speakers of other languages (MA, PhD, Advanced Certificate); visual arts administration (MA); visual culture (MA, PhD); visual culture and education (PhD); visual culture: costume studies (MA); visual culture: theory (MA, PhD); vocal performance (MM); workplace learning (Advanced Certificate). *Application deadline:* For fall admission, 12/15 priority date for domestic students, 12/15 for international students; for spring admission, 1/1 for domestic and international students. Applications are processed on a rolling basis. *Application fee:* $75. Electronic applications accepted. *Application Contact:* John Myers, Director of Enrollment Management, 212-998-5030, Fax: 212-995-4328, E-mail: steinhardt.gradadmissions@nyu.edu. *Dean,* Dr. Mary Brabeck, 212-998-5000.

Tisch School of the Arts Students: 784 full-time (397 women), 27 part-time (16 women); includes 181 minority (50 African Americans, 2 American Indian/Alaska Native, 89 Asian Americans or Pacific Islanders, 40 Hispanic Americans). Average age 25. 2,785 applicants, 26% accepted, 428 enrolled. *Faculty:* 112 full-time, 131 part-time/adjunct. Expenses: Contact institution. *Financial support:* Fellowships, career-related internships or fieldwork, Federal Work-Study, institutionally sponsored loans, scholarships/grants, and tuition waivers (full and partial) available. Support available to part-time students. Financial award application deadline: 2/1; financial award applicants required to submit CSS PROFILE or FAFSA. In 2008, 286 master's, 15 doctorates awarded. Offers acting (MFA); arts (MA, MFA, MPS, PhD); arts politics (MA); cinema studies (MA, PhD); dance (MFA); design for stage and film (MFA); dramatic writing (MFA); interactive telecommunications (MPS); moving image archiving and preservation (MA); musical theatre writing (MFA); performance studies (MA, PhD). *Application fee:* $75. Electronic applications accepted. *Application Contact:* Dan Sandford, Director of Graduate Admissions, 212-998-1918, Fax: 212-995-4060, E-mail: tisch.gradadmissions@nyu.edu. *Dean,* Dr. Mary Schmidt Campbell, 212-998-1800.

Tisch School of the Arts Asia Students: 76 full-time (40 women); includes 21 minority (7 African Americans, 11 Asian Americans or Pacific Islanders, 3 Hispanic Americans). Average age 25. 280 applicants, 32% accepted, 42 enrolled. *Faculty:* 24 full-time (6 women), 1 part-time/adjunct (0 women). Expenses: Contact institution. *Financial support:* Fellowships with full and partial tuition reimbursements, research assistantships, teaching assistantships, Federal Work-Study, institutionally sponsored loans, and unspecified assistantships available. Financial award application deadline: 2/15; financial award applicants required to submit FAFSA. Offers animation and digital arts (MFA); dramatic writing (MFA); film production (MFA). *Application deadline:* For fall admission, 2/1 priority date for domestic and international students. *Application fee:* $60. Electronic applications accepted. *Application Contact:* NYU Tisch School of the Arts Asia, 212-998-1212, E-mail: tisch.asia@nyu.edu. *Vice Dean/President,* Dean Pari Sara Shirazi.

Kanbar Institute of Film and Television Students: 111 full-time (53 women), 76 part-time (35 women); includes 67 minority (23 African Americans, 2 American Indian/Alaska Native, 36 Asian Americans or Pacific Islanders, 6 Hispanic Americans). Average age 25. 707 applicants, 8% accepted, 36 enrolled. *Faculty:* 19 full-time, 20 part-time/adjunct. Expenses: Contact institution. *Financial support:* In 2008–09, 60 students received support, including 16 fellowships with full and partial tuition reimbursements available, 6 teaching assistantships with tuition reimbursements available; Federal Work-Study, institutionally sponsored loans, scholarships/grants, tuition waivers (full and partial), and unspecified assistantships also available. Financial award application deadline: 2/15; financial award applicants required to submit FAFSA. In 2008, 30 master's awarded. Offers film and television (MFA). *Application deadline:* For fall admission, 12/1 for domestic and international students. *Application fee:* $60. Electronic applications accepted. *Application Contact:* Dan Sandford, Director of Graduate Admissions, 212-998-1918, Fax: 212-995-4060, E-mail: tisch.gradadmissions@nyu.edu. *Chair,* John Tintori, 212-998-1780, E-mail: jt42@nyu.edu.

See Close-Up on page 957.

NIAGARA UNIVERSITY, Niagara Falls, Niagara University, NY 14109

General Information Independent-religious, coed, comprehensive institution. *Enrollment:* 4,255 graduate, professional, and undergraduate students; 591 full-time matriculated graduate/professional students (410 women), 259 part-time matriculated graduate/professional students (179 women). *Enrollment by degree level:* 827 master's, 23 other advanced degrees. *Graduate faculty:* 36 full-time (16 women), 44 part-time/adjunct (20 women). *Tuition:* Full-time $12,330; part-time $685 per contact hour. *Required fees:* $25 per semester. Tuition and fees vary according to program. *Graduate housing:* Room and/or apartments available to single students; on-campus housing not available to married students. Typical cost: $9750 (including board). Housing application deadline: 8/1. *Student services:* Campus employment opportunities, campus safety program, career counseling, free psychological counseling, international student services, low-cost health insurance, multicultural affairs office, services for students with disabilities. *Library facilities:* Our Lady of Angels. *Online resources:* library catalog. *Collection:* 297,813 titles, 164 serial subscriptions. *Research affiliation:* Roswell Park Memorial Institute.

Computer facilities: 175 computers available on campus for general student use. A campuswide network can be accessed from student residence rooms. Online class registration is available. *Web address:* http://www.niagara.edu/.

General Application Contact: Carlos Tejada, Associate Dean for Graduate Recruitment, 716-286-8769, Fax: 716-286-8170.

GRADUATE UNITS

Graduate Division of Arts and Sciences Students: 21 full-time (16 women), 23 part-time (14 women); includes 3 minority (2 African Americans, 1 American Indian/Alaska Native), 2 international. Average age 29. *Faculty:* 7 full-time (2 women). Expenses: Contact institution. *Financial support:* Fellowships, career-related internships or fieldwork and Federal Work-Study available. Support available to part-time students. In 2008, 28 master's awarded. *Degree program information:* Part-time and evening/weekend programs available. Offers arts and sciences (MA, MS); criminal justice administration (MS); interdisciplinary studies (MA). *Application deadline:* For fall admission, 8/1 for domestic students. Applications are processed on a rolling basis. *Application fee:* $30. *Application Contact:* Dr. Talia Harmon, Director, 716-286-8093, Fax: 716-286-8061, E-mail: tharmon@niagara.edu. *Dean,* Dr. Nancy McGlen, 716-286-8060, Fax: 716-286-8061, E-mail: nmcglen@niagara.edu.

Graduate Division of Business Administration Students: 88 full-time (33 women), 58 part-time (24 women); includes 14 minority (4 African Americans, 3 American Indian/Alaska Native, 5 Asian Americans or Pacific Islanders, 2 Hispanic Americans), 23 international. Average age 33. 89 applicants, 73% accepted. *Faculty:* 6 full-time (1 woman), 7 part-time/adjunct (1 woman). Expenses: Contact institution. *Financial support:* In 2008–09, 3 fellowships, 2 research assistantships were awarded; career-related internships or fieldwork and Federal Work-Study also available. Support available to part-time students. Financial award application deadline: 8/1; financial award applicants required to submit FAFSA. In 2008, 66 master's awarded. *Degree program information:* Part-time and evening/weekend programs available. Offers business (MBA); commerce (MBA). *Application deadline:* For fall admission, 8/1 for domestic students; for spring admission, 11/1 for domestic students. Applications are processed on a rolling basis. *Application fee:* $30. *Application Contact:* Carlos Tejada, Associate Dean for Graduate Recruitment, 716-286-8769, Fax: 716-286-8170. *Director,* Dr. PEGGY CHOONG, 716-286-8178, Fax: 716-286-8206.

Graduate Division of Education Students: 482 full-time (361 women), 178 part-time (141 women); includes 13 minority (4 African Americans, 5 American Indian/Alaska Native, 2 Asian Americans or Pacific Islanders, 2 Hispanic Americans), 311 international. Average age 28. 382 applicants, 75% accepted. *Faculty:* 26 full-time (16 women), 36 part-time/adjunct (17 women). Expenses: Contact institution. *Financial support:* In 2008–09, 2 fellowships, 3 research assistantships were awarded; career-related internships or fieldwork, Federal Work-Study, scholarships/grants, and unspecified assistantships also available. Support available to part-time students. Financial award application deadline: 3/15. In 2008, 355 master's, 22 other advanced degrees awarded. *Degree program information:* Part-time and evening/weekend programs available. Offers administration/supervision (Certificate); early childhood and childhood education (MS Ed); educational administration/supervision (MS Ed); educational leadership (MS Ed, Certificate); educational leadership school district building (MS Ed); foundations of teaching (MA, MS Ed); literacy instruction (MS Ed); mental health counseling (MS, Certificate); middle and adolescence education (MS Ed); school business administration (Certificate); school business leadership (MS Ed); school counseling (MS Ed, Certificate); school district administration (Certificate); school psychology (MS, Certificate); special education (grades 1-12) (MS Ed); teacher education (Certificate). *Application deadline:* For fall admission, 8/1 for domestic students. Applications are processed on a rolling basis. *Application fee:* $30. *Application Contact:* Carlos Tejada, Associate Dean for Graduate Recruitment, 716-286-8769, Fax: 716-286-8170. *Dean,* Dr. Debra A. Colley, 716-286-8560, Fax: 716-286-8561, E-mail: dcolley@niagara.edu.

NICHOLLS STATE UNIVERSITY, Thibodaux, LA 70310

General Information State-supported, coed, comprehensive institution. *Graduate housing:* Rooms and/or apartments available on a first-come, first-served basis to single and married students. Housing application deadline: 4/13.

GRADUATE UNITS

Graduate Studies *Degree program information:* Part-time and evening/weekend programs available. Postbaccalaureate distance learning degree programs offered (minimal on-campus study).

College of Arts and Sciences *Degree program information:* Part-time and evening/weekend programs available. Offers arts and sciences (MS); community/technical college mathematics (MS); marine and environmental biology (MS). Electronic applications accepted.

College of Business Administration *Degree program information:* Part-time and evening/weekend programs available. Offers business administration (MBA). Electronic applications accepted.

College of Education *Degree program information:* Part-time and evening/weekend programs available. Offers administration and supervision (M Ed); counselor education (M Ed); curriculum and instruction (M Ed); education (M Ed, MA, SSP); psychological counseling (MA); school psychology (SSP). Electronic applications accepted.

NICHOLS COLLEGE, Dudley, MA 01571-5000

General Information Independent, coed, comprehensive institution. *Enrollment:* 1,532 graduate, professional, and undergraduate students; 45 full-time matriculated graduate/professional students (18 women), 229 part-time matriculated graduate/professional students (117 women). *Enrollment by degree level:* 274 master's. *Graduate faculty:* 33 part-time/adjunct (8 women). *Tuition:* Part-time $540 per credit. *Graduate housing:* On-campus housing not available. *Student services:* Campus employment opportunities, career counseling, free psychological counseling, low-cost health insurance, services for students with disabilities. *Library facilities:* Conant Library plus 1 other. *Online resources:* library catalog, web page. *Collection:* 76,374 titles, 137 serial subscriptions, 2,016 audiovisual materials.

Computer facilities: Computer purchase and lease plans are available. 69 computers available on campus for general student use. A campuswide network can be accessed from student residence rooms and from off campus. Online class registration is available. *Web address:* http://www.nichols.edu/.

General Application Contact: Nora Luquer, Assistant Director of Enrollment Services, 508-213-2295, Fax: 508-213-2490, E-mail: nora.luquer@nichols.edu.

GRADUATE UNITS

Graduate Program in Business Administration Students: 45 full-time (18 women), 229 part-time (117 women); includes 21 minority (11 African Americans, 5 Asian Americans or Pacific Islanders, 5 Hispanic Americans), 1 international. Average age 34. 310 applicants, 38% accepted, 42 enrolled. *Faculty:* 33 part-time/adjunct (8 women). Expenses: Contact institution. *Financial support:* Career-related internships or fieldwork available. Support available to part-time students. Financial award applicants required to submit FAFSA. In 2008, 72 master's awarded. *Degree program information:* Part-time and evening/weekend programs available. Postbaccalaureate distance learning degree programs offered (no on-campus study). Offers business administration (MBA, MOL); security management (MBA); sport management (MBA). *Application deadline:* Applications are processed on a rolling basis. *Application fee:* $25. Electronic applications accepted. *Application Contact:* Nora Luquer, Assistant Director of Enrollment Services, 508-213-2295, Fax: 800-243-3844, E-mail: nora.luquer@nichols.edu. *Dean, Graduate and Professional Studies,* Laurie Albert, 508-213-2440, Fax: 800-243-3844, E-mail: laurie.albert@nichols.edu.

THE NIGERIAN BAPTIST THEOLOGICAL SEMINARY, Ogbomoso, Oyo, Nigeria

General Information Independent-religious, coed, primarily men, comprehensive institution. *Graduate housing:* Rooms and/or apartments available to single and married students.

GRADUATE UNITS

Graduate Studies *Degree program information:* Part-time programs available. Offers church music (M Div, M Th, Diploma); divinity (M Div); ministry (D Min); religious education (M Div, M Th, PhD); theological studies (MATS); theology (M Th, PhD).

NIPISSING UNIVERSITY, North Bay, ON P1B 8L7, Canada

General Information Province-supported, coed, comprehensive institution. *Graduate housing:* Room and/or apartments available to single students; on-campus housing not available to married students. Housing application deadline: 6/13. *Research affiliation:* Canada Space Agency (CSA) & MacDonald, Dettwiler and Associates Ltd (MDA)—RADARSAT-2 (remote sensing), Education Quality and Accountability Office (EQAO) (assessing educational quality), Ontario Association of Deans of Education (OADE) (assessing pre-service practicum processes), Tembec (forestry restoration), Metals in the Human Environment Research Network (MITHE-RN) (assessing environmental pollutants on aquatic ecosystems).

GRADUATE UNITS

Faculty of Education *Degree program information:* Part-time and evening/weekend programs available. Offers education (M Ed, Certificate).

NORFOLK STATE UNIVERSITY, Norfolk, VA 23504

General Information State-supported, coed, comprehensive institution. CGS member. *Graduate housing:* Room and/or apartments available to single students; on-campus housing not available to married students. Housing application deadline: 3/1. *Research affiliation:* Department of Energy NASA, National Science (fundamental and applied research studies), NASA Langley Research Center (NASA interests; aerospace applications; lidan application), National Science Foundation (fundamental and applied research studies), Department of Education (Title III projects; no child left behind initiative), University of Virginia's IGERT (science and engineering interactions with matter), Applied Research Center (technology transfer).

GRADUATE UNITS

School of Graduate Studies *Degree program information:* Part-time programs available. Electronic applications accepted.

School of Education *Degree program information:* Part-time programs available. Offers early childhood education (MAT); education (MA, MAT); pre-elementary education (MA); principal preparation (MA); secondary education (MAT); severe disabilities (MA); teaching (MA); urban education/administration (MA).

School of Liberal Arts *Degree program information:* Part-time programs available. Offers applied sociology (MS); community/clinical psychology (MA); criminal justice (MA); liberal arts (MA, MFA, MM, MS, Psy D); media and communication (MA); music (MM); music education (MM); performance (MM); psychology (Psy D); theory and composition (MM); urban affairs (MA); visual studies (MA, MFA).

School of Science and Technology Offers computer science (MS); electronics engineering (MS); materials science (MS); optical engineering (MS); science and technology (MS).

School of Social Work *Degree program information:* Part-time programs available. Offers social work (MSW, PhD).

NORTH CAROLINA AGRICULTURAL AND TECHNICAL STATE UNIVERSITY, Greensboro, NC 27411

General Information State-supported, coed, university. CGS member. *Graduate housing:* Room and/or apartments available on a first-come, first-served basis to single students; on-campus housing not available to married students. Housing application deadline: 5/8. *Research affiliation:* North Carolina Biotechnology Research Center (biotechnology research), The Boeing Company (aerospace engineering), Northrop Grumman Corporation (high performance computing), Research Triangle Institute (environmental protection, advanced technology), Rockwell Inc. (avionics technology, communications technology), Honeywell (industrial automation control).

GRADUATE UNITS

Graduate School *Degree program information:* Part-time and evening/weekend programs available.

College of Arts and Sciences *Degree program information:* Part-time and evening/weekend programs available. Offers art education (MS); arts and sciences (MA, MAT, MS, MSW); biology (MS); biology education (MAT); chemistry (MS); English (MA); English and Afro-American literature (MA); English education (MS); history education (MAT, MS); mathematics education (MS); social studies education (MS); sociology and social work (MSW).

College of Engineering *Degree program information:* Part-time programs available. Offers chemical engineering (MS Ch E); civil engineering (MSCE); computer science (MSCS); electrical engineering (MSEE, PhD); engineering (MS Ch E, MSCE, MSCS, MSE, MSEE, MSIE, MSME, PhD); industrial engineering (MSIE, PhD); mechanical engineering (MSME, PhD).

School of Agriculture and Environmental Sciences *Degree program information:* Part-time and evening/weekend programs available. Offers agricultural economics (MS); agricultural education (MS); agriculture and environmental sciences (MS); animal health science (MS); food and nutrition (MS); plant, soil and environmental science (MS).

School of Education *Degree program information:* Part-time and evening/weekend programs available. Offers adult education (MS); counselor education (MS); education (MA Ed, MAT, MS); elementary education (MA Ed); human resources-agency counseling (MS); human resources-rehabilitation counseling (MS); instructional technology (MS); leadership studies (PhD); physical education (MAT, MS); reading (MA Ed); school administration (MS); teaching (MAT).

School of Technology *Degree program information:* Part-time and evening/weekend programs available. Offers construction management (MSIT); electronics and computer technology (MSIT); industrial arts education (MS); industrial technology (MS, MSIT); occupational safety and health (MSIT); safety and driver education (MS); technology (MS, MSIT, PhD); technology education (MS); technology management (PhD); vocational-industrial education (MS); workforce development director (MS).

NORTH CAROLINA CENTRAL UNIVERSITY, Durham, NC 27707-3129

General Information State-supported, coed, comprehensive institution. CGS member. *Graduate housing:* Room and/or apartments available to single students; on-campus housing not available to married students. Housing application deadline: 7/1.

GRADUATE UNITS

Division of Academic Affairs *Degree program information:* Part-time and evening/weekend programs available.

College of Behavioral and Social Sciences Offers athletic administration (MS); behavioral and social sciences (MA, MPA, MS); criminal justice (MS); family and consumer sciences (MS); physical education (MS); psychology (MA); public administration (MPA); recreation administration (MS); sociology (MA); therapeutic recreation (MS).

College of Liberal Arts *Degree program information:* Part-time and evening/weekend programs available. Offers English (MA); history (MA); jazz studies (MM); liberal arts (MA, MM).

College of Science and Technology Offers applied mathematics (MS); biology (MS); chemistry (MS); earth sciences (MS); mathematics education (MS); physics (MS); pure mathematics (MS); science and technology (MS).

School of Business *Degree program information:* Part-time and evening/weekend programs available. Offers business (MBA).

School of Education *Degree program information:* Part-time and evening/weekend programs available. Offers career counseling (MA); communication disorders (M Ed); community agency counseling (MA); curriculum and instruction (MA); education (M Ed, MA, MAT, MSA); educational technology (MA); instructional technology (M Ed); school administration (MSA); school counseling (MA); special education (M Ed, MAT).

School of Law *Degree program information:* Part-time and evening/weekend programs available. Offers law (JD).

School of Library and Information Sciences *Degree program information:* Part-time and evening/weekend programs available. Offers library and information sciences (MIS, MLS).

NORTH CAROLINA STATE UNIVERSITY, Raleigh, NC 27695

General Information State-supported, coed, university. CGS member. *Graduate housing:* Rooms and/or apartments available on a first-come, first-served basis to single and married students. *Research affiliation:* Triangle Universities Nuclear Laboratory, Research Triangle Institute, Highlands Biological Station, National Humanities Center, Microelectronics Center of North Carolina, North Carolina-Japan Center.

GRADUATE UNITS

College of Veterinary Medicine *Degree program information:* Part-time programs available. Offers cell biology (MS, PhD); infectious disease (MS, PhD); pathology (MS, PhD); pharmacology (MS, PhD); population medicine (MS, PhD); specialized veterinary medicine (MSpVM); veterinary medicine (DVM, MS, MSpVM, MVPH, PhD); veterinary public health (MVPH). Electronic applications accepted.

Graduate School *Degree program information:* Part-time and evening/weekend programs available. Postbaccalaureate distance learning degree programs offered. Electronic applications accepted.

College of Agriculture and Life Sciences *Degree program information:* Part-time programs available. Offers agricultural and extension education (Ed D); agricultural and resource economics (MS); agricultural education (MAE, MS, Certificate); agriculture and life sciences (M Tox, MAE, MB, MBAE, MFG, MFM, MFS, MG, MMB, MN, MP, MS, MZS, Ed D, PhD, Certificate); animal and poultry science (PhD); animal science (MS); biochemistry (PhD); bioinformatics (MB, PhD); biological and agricultural engineering (MBAE, MS, PhD, Certificate); crop science (MS, PhD); entomology (MS, PhD); environmental and molecular toxicology (M Tox, MS, PhD); extension education (MS); financial mathematics (MFM); food science (MFS, MS, PhD); functional genomics (MFG, MS, PhD); genetics (MG, MS, PhD); genomic sciences (MS, PhD); horticultural science (MS, PhD, Certificate); immunology (MS, PhD); microbial biotechnology (MMB); microbiology (MMB, MS, PhD); nutrition (MN, MS, PhD); physiology (MP, MS, PhD); plant biology (MS, PhD); plant pathology (MS, PhD); poultry science (MS); soil science (MS, PhD); zoology (MS, MZS, PhD). Electronic applications accepted.

College of Design *Degree program information:* Part-time programs available. Offers architecture (M Arch); art and design (MAD); design (M Arch, MAD, MGD, MID, MLA, PhD); graphic design (MGD); industrial design (MID); landscape architecture (MLA). Electronic applications accepted.

College of Education *Degree program information:* Part-time programs available. Offers adult and community college education (M Ed, MS, Ed D); agency counseling (M Ed, MS); business and marketing education (M Ed, MS); counselor education (M Ed, MS, PhD); curriculum and instruction (M Ed, MS, MS Ed, PhD); education (M Ed, MS, MS Ed, MSA, Ed D, PhD, Certificate); educational administration and supervision (Ed D); educational research and policy analysis (PhD); elementary education (M Ed); higher education administration (M Ed, MS, Ed D); human resource development (MS); instructional technology (M Ed, MS); mathematics education (M Ed, MS, PhD); middle grades education (M Ed, MS); school administration (MSA); science education (M Ed, MS, PhD); secondary English education (M Ed, MS Ed); social studies education (M Ed); special education (M Ed, MS); technology education (M Ed, MS, Ed D); training and development (M Ed, Ed D, Certificate). Electronic applications accepted.

College of Engineering *Degree program information:* Part-time programs available. Offers aerospace engineering (MS, PhD); biomedical engineering (MS, PhD); chemical engineering (M Ch E, MS, PhD); civil engineering (MCE, MS, PhD); computer engineering (MS, PhD); computer networking (MS); computer science (MC Sc, MS, PhD); electrical engineering (MS, PhD); engineering (M Ch E, M Eng, MC Sc, MCE, MIE, MIMS, MMSE, MNE, MOR, MS, PhD); industrial engineering (MIE, MS, PhD); integrated manufacturing systems engineering (MIMS); materials science and engineering (MMSE, MS, PhD); mechanical engineering (MS, PhD); nuclear engineering (MNE, MS, PhD); operations research (MOR, MS, PhD). Electronic applications accepted.

College of Humanities and Social Sciences *Degree program information:* Part-time and evening/weekend programs available. Offers anthropology (MA); bioarchaeology (MA); communication (MS); communication, rhetoric, and digital media (PhD); creative writing (MFA); cultural anthropology (MA); developmental psychology (PhD); English (MA, MFA, MS); environmental anthropology (MA); ergonomics and experimental psychology (PhD); French language and literature (MA); history (MA); humanities and social sciences (M Soc, MA, MFA, MIS, MPA, MS, MSW, PhD, Certificate); industrial/organizational psychology (PhD); international studies (MIS); liberal studies (MA); nonprofit management (Certificate); psychology in the public interest (PhD); public administration (MPA, PhD); public history (MA); school psychology (PhD); social work (MSW); sociology (M Soc, MS, PhD); Spanish language and literature (MA); technical communication (MS). Electronic applications accepted.

College of Management *Degree program information:* Part-time programs available. Offers accounting (MAC); analytics (MS); biosciences management (MBA); economics (M Econ, MA, PhD); entrepreneurship and technology commercialization (MBA); financial management (MBA); innovation management (MBA); management (M Econ, MA, MAC, MBA, MS, PhD); marketing management (MBA); services management and consulting (MBA); supply chain management (MBA). Electronic applications accepted.

College of Natural Resources *Degree program information:* Part-time programs available. Offers fisheries and wildlife sciences (MFWS, MS, PhD); forestry and environmental resources (MF, MS, PhD); natural resource management (MPRTM, MS); natural resources (MF, MFWS, MNR, MPRTM, MS, MWPS, PhD); park and recreation management (MPRTM, MS); parks, recreation and tourism management (PhD); recreational sport management (MPRTM, MS); spatial information science (MPRTM, MS); tourism policy and development (MPRTM, MS); wood and paper science (MS, MWPS, PhD). Electronic applications accepted.

College of Physical and Mathematical Sciences *Degree program information:* Part-time programs available. Offers applied mathematics (MS, PhD); biomathematics (M Biomath, MS, PhD); chemistry (MS, PhD); marine, earth, and atmospheric sciences (MS, PhD); mathematics (MS, PhD); meteorology (MS, PhD); oceanography (MS, PhD); physical and mathematical sciences (M Biomath, M Stat, MS, PhD); physics (MS, PhD); statistics (M Stat, MS, PhD). Electronic applications accepted.

College of Textiles *Degree program information:* Part-time and evening/weekend programs available. Postbaccalaureate distance learning degree programs offered. Offers fiber and polymer science (PhD); textile and apparel technology and management (MS, MT); textile chemistry (MS); textile engineering (MS); textile technology management (PhD); textiles (MS, MT, PhD). Electronic applications accepted.

NORTH CENTRAL COLLEGE, Naperville, IL 60566-7063

General Information Independent-religious, coed, comprehensive institution. *Graduate housing:* Room and/or apartments available on a first-come, first-served basis to single students; on-campus housing not available to married students.

GRADUATE UNITS

Graduate Programs *Degree program information:* Part-time and evening/weekend programs available. Offers business administration (MBA); computer science (MS); curriculum and instruction (MA Ed); leadership and administration (MA Ed); leadership studies (MLD); liberal studies (MALS); management information systems (MS). Electronic applications accepted.

NORTHCENTRAL UNIVERSITY, Prescott Valley, AZ 86314

General Information Proprietary, coed, comprehensive institution.

GRADUATE UNITS

Graduate Studies

NORTH DAKOTA STATE UNIVERSITY, Fargo, ND 58105

General Information State-supported, coed, university. CGS member. *Enrollment:* 13,229 graduate, professional, and undergraduate students; 985 full-time matriculated graduate/professional students (460 women), 625 part-time matriculated graduate/professional students (306 women). *Enrollment by degree level:* 1,068 master's, 542 doctoral. *Graduate faculty:* 510 full-time (140 women), 21 part-time/adjunct (6 women). *Graduate housing:* Rooms and/or apartments available on a first-come, first-served basis to single and married students. *Student services:* Career counseling, child daycare facilities, free psychological counseling, international student services, low-cost health insurance, multicultural affairs office, services for students with disabilities. *Library facilities:* North Dakota State University Library plus 3 others. *Online resources:* library catalog, web page, access to other libraries' catalogs. *Collection:* 136,912 titles, 2,499 serial subscriptions, 3,767 audiovisual materials. *Research affiliation:* U.S. Department of Agriculture–Metabolism and Radiation Laboratory.

Computer facilities: Computer purchase and lease plans are available. 500 computers available on campus for general student use. A campuswide network can be accessed from student residence rooms. Online class registration is available. *Web address:* http://www.ndsu.edu/.

General Application Contact: Dr. David A. Wittrock, Dean, 701-231-7033, Fax: 701-231-6524.

GRADUATE UNITS

College of Graduate and Interdisciplinary Studies Students: 985 full-time (460 women), 625 part-time (306 women). Average age 25. 1,081 applicants, 65% accepted, 399 enrolled. *Faculty:* 510 full-time (140 women), 21 part-time/adjunct (6 women). Expenses: Contact institution. *Financial support:* Fellowships with full tuition reimbursements, research assistantships with full tuition reimbursements, teaching assistantships with full tuition reimbursements, career-related internships or fieldwork, Federal Work-Study, institutionally sponsored loans, scholarships/grants, traineeships, tuition waivers (full and partial), and unspecified assistantships available. Support available to part-time students. Financial award applicants required to submit FAFSA. In 2008, 281 master's, 59 doctorates, 8 other advanced degrees awarded. *Degree program information:* Part-time and evening/weekend programs available. Postbaccalaureate distance learning degree programs offered (minimal on-campus study). Offers cellular and molecular biology (PhD); environmental and conservation sciences (MS, PhD); food safety (MS, PhD); genomics and bioinformatics (MS, PhD); materials and nanotechnology (PhD); natural resources management (MS, PhD); transportation and logistics (PhD). *Application deadline:* For fall admission, 7/31 priority date for domestic students, 5/1 priority date for international students; for spring admission, 12/15 priority date for domestic students, 8/1 priority date for international students. *Application fee:* $45 ($60 for international students). Electronic applications accepted. *Application Contact:* Dr. David A. Wittrock, Dean, 701-231-7033, Fax: 701-231-6524. *Dean,* Dr. David A. Wittrock, 701-231-7033, Fax: 701-231-6524.

College of Agriculture, Food Systems, and Natural Resources Students: 92 full-time (39 women), 45 part-time (19 women); includes 31 minority (4 African Americans, 1 American Indian/Alaska Native, 17 Asian Americans or Pacific Islanders, 9 Hispanic Americans), 30 international. *Faculty:* 126. Expenses: Contact institution. *Financial support:* Fellowships with full tuition reimbursements, research assistantships with full tuition reimbursements, teaching assistantships with full tuition reimbursements, career-related internships or fieldwork, Federal Work-Study, and institutionally sponsored loans available. Support available to part-time students. *Degree program information:* Part-time programs available. Offers agribusiness and applied economics (MS); agriculture, food systems, and natural resources (MS, PhD); animal science (MS, PhD); cereal science (MS, PhD); crop and weed sciences (MS); entomology (MS, PhD); environment and conservation science (MS, PhD); environmental and conservation science (PhD); environmental conservation science (MS); food safety (MS); horticulture (MS); international agribusiness (MS); microbiology (MS); molecular pathogenesis (PhD); natural resource management (MS, PhD); plant pathology (MS, PhD); plant sciences (PhD); range sciences (MS, PhD); soil sciences (MS, PhD). *Application deadline:* Applications are processed on a rolling basis. *Application fee:* $45 ($60 for international students). Electronic applications accepted. *Application Contact:* Dr. Kenneth F. Grafton, Dean, 701-231-8790, Fax: 701-231-8520, E-mail: k.grafton@ndsu.edu. *Dean,* Dr. Kenneth F. Grafton, 701-231-8790, Fax: 701-231-8520, E-mail: k.grafton@ndsu.edu.

College of Arts, Humanities and Social Sciences Students: 43 full-time (22 women), 138 part-time (98 women). *Faculty:* 77 full-time (26 women). Expenses: Contact institution. *Financial support:* In 2008–09, 3 fellowships with full tuition reimbursements (averaging $12,150 per year), 93 teaching assistantships with full tuition reimbursements (averaging $8,000 per year) were awarded; research assistantships with full tuition reimbursements, career-related internships or fieldwork, Federal Work-Study, institutionally sponsored loans, scholarships/grants, and tuition waivers (full) also available. Support available to part-time students. In 2008, 20 master's, 5 doctorates awarded. *Degree program information:* Part-time and evening/weekend programs available. Offers arts, humanities and social sciences (M Ed, MA, MM, MS, DMA, PhD); communication (PhD); criminal justice (MS, PhD); emergency management (MS, PhD); English (MA, MS); history (MA, MS, PhD); mass communication (MA, MS); music (M Ed, MM, DMA); social science (MA, MS); sociology (MS); speech communication (MA, MS). *Application deadline:* Applications are processed on a rolling basis. *Application fee:* $45 ($60 for international students). *Application Contact:* Dr. Thomas J. Riley, Dean, 701-231-9588, Fax: 701-231-1047, E-mail: thomas.riley@ndsu.edu. *Dean,* Dr. Thomas J. Riley, 701-231-9588, Fax: 701-231-1047, E-mail: thomas.riley@ndsu.edu.

College of Business Students: 52 full-time (26 women), 23 part-time (11 women); includes 4 minority (1 African American, 2 Asian Americans or Pacific Islanders, 1 Hispanic American), 18 international. Average age 29. 55 applicants, 76% accepted, 38 enrolled. *Faculty:* 25 full-time (5 women). Expenses: Contact institution. *Financial support:* In 2008–09, 14 students received support, including 13 research assistantships, 1 teaching assistantship; institutionally sponsored loans and tuition waivers (partial) also available. Support available to part-time students. Financial award application deadline: 5/15; financial award applicants required to submit FAFSA. In 2008, 26 master's awarded. *Degree program information:* Part-time and evening/weekend programs available. Offers business (MBA). *Application deadline:* For fall admission, 7/15 priority date for domestic students; for spring admission, 11/15 for domestic students. Applications are processed on a rolling basis. *Application fee:* $45 ($60 for international students). *Application Contact:* Paul R. Brown, Director, 701-231-7681, Fax: 701-231-7508, E-mail: paul.brown@ndsu.edu. *Dean,* Dr. Ron Johnson, 701-231-8805.

College of Engineering and Architecture Students: 49 full-time (10 women), 105 part-time (11 women); includes 72 minority (1 African American, 8 American Indian/Alaska Native, 62 Asian Americans or Pacific Islanders, 1 Hispanic American), 47 international. Average age 27. 225 applicants, 47% accepted. *Faculty:* 72 full-time (9 women), 11 part-time/adjunct (0 women). Expenses: Contact institution. *Financial support:* In 2008–09, 150 students received support, including fellowships with full tuition reimbursements available (averaging $15,000 per year), research assistantships with full tuition reimbursements available (averaging $9,000 per year), teaching assistantships with full tuition reimbursements available (averaging $8,000 per year); career-related internships or fieldwork, Federal Work-Study, institutionally sponsored loans, scholarships/grants, and tuition waivers (full) also available. Support available to part-time students. Financial award application deadline: 4/15. In 2008, 32 master's, 5 doctorates awarded. *Degree program information:* Part-time programs available. Offers agricultural and biosystems engineering (MS, PhD); civil engineering (MS, PhD); construction management (MS); electrical and computer engineering (MS, PhD); engineering (PhD); engineering and architecture (MS, PhD); environmental engineering (MS, PhD); industrial and manufacturing engineering (PhD); industrial engineering and management (MS); manufacturing engineering (MS); mechanical engineering and applied mechanics (MS, PhD); natural resource management (MS); natural resources management (PhD); transportation and logistics (PhD). *Application deadline:* For fall admission, 4/1 priority date for domestic and international students; for spring admission, 10/1 priority date for domestic and international students. Applications are processed on a rolling basis. *Application fee:* $45 ($60 for international students). *Application Contact:* Dr. David A. Wittrock, Dean, 701-231-7033, Fax: 701-231-6524. *Dean,* Dr. Gary R. Smith, 701-231-7494, Fax: 701-231-8957, E-mail: gary.smith@ndsu.edu.

College of Human Development and Education Students: 22 full-time (14 women), 16 part-time (12 women); includes 8 minority (1 African American, 5 American Indian/Alaska Native, 1 Asian American or Pacific Islander, 1 Hispanic American), 1 international. Average age 32. Expenses: Contact institution. *Financial support:* Fellowships, research assistantships, teaching assistantships, career-related internships or fieldwork, Federal Work-Study, institutionally sponsored loans, and tuition waivers (full) available. Support available to part-time students. In 2008, 6 master's, 9 doctorates awarded. *Degree program information:* Part-time and evening/weekend programs available. Postbaccalaureate distance learning degree programs offered (minimal on-campus study). Offers agricultural education (M Ed, MS); agricultural extension education (MS); child development and family science (MS); counseling (M Ed, MS, PhD); couple and family therapy (MS); curriculum and instruction (M Ed, MS); dietetics (MS); education (PhD); educational leadership (M Ed, MS, Ed S); entry level athletic training (MS); exercise science (MS); family and consumer sciences education (M Ed, MS); family financial planning (MS); gerontology (MS, PhD); history education (M Ed, MS); human development (PhD); human development and education (M Ed, MS, Ed D, PhD, Ed S); institutional analysis (Ed D); mathematics education (M Ed, MS); music education (M Ed, MS); nutrition science (MS); occupational and adult education (Ed D); pedagogy (M Ed, MS); physical education and athletic administration (M Ed, MS); public health (MS); science education (M Ed, MS); sport pedagogy (MS); sports recreation management (MS). *Application deadline:* Applications are processed on a rolling basis. *Application fee:* $45 ($60 for international students). *Application Contact:* Dr. Virginia Clark Johnson, Dean, 701-231-8211, Fax: 701-231-7174, E-mail: virginia.clark@ndsu.edu. *Dean,* Dr. Virginia Clark Johnson, 701-231-8211, Fax: 701-231-7174, E-mail: virginia.clark@ndsu.edu.

College of Pharmacy, Nursing and Allied Sciences Students: 45 full-time (34 women), 14 part-time (13 women); includes 1 American Indian/Alaska Native, 1 Asian American or Pacific Islander, 20 international. Expenses: Contact institution. *Financial support:* Research assistantships with full tuition reimbursements, career-related internships or fieldwork, Federal Work-Study, institutionally sponsored loans, and scholarships/grants available. Financial award application deadline: 4/1. In 2008, 3 master's, 13 doctorates awarded. *Degree program information:* Part-time programs available. Offers nursing (MS, DNP); pharmaceutical sciences (MS, PhD); pharmacy, nursing and allied sciences (MS, DNP, PhD). *Application deadline:* For fall admission, 4/1 for domestic students. Applications are processed on a rolling basis. *Application fee:* $45 ($60 for international students). *Application Contact:* Dr. Jonathan Sheng, Assistant Professor, 701-231-6140, Fax: 701-231-8333, E-mail: jonathan.sheng@ndsu.edu. *Dean,* Dr. Charles D. Peterson, 701-231-7609, Fax: 701-231-7606.

College of Science and Mathematics Students: 32 full-time (11 women), 12 part-time (5 women); includes 1 African American, 2 Asian Americans or Pacific Islanders, 18 international. Expenses: Contact institution. *Financial support:* Fellowships with full tuition reimbursements, research assistantships with full tuition reimbursements, teaching assistantships with full tuition reimbursements, career-related internships or fieldwork, Federal Work-Study, institutionally sponsored loans, scholarships/grants, traineeships, tuition waivers (full and partial), and unspecified assistantships available. Support available to part-time students. Financial award applicants required to submit FAFSA. In 2008, 9 master's, 2 doctorates awarded. *Degree program information:* Part-time programs available. Offers applied mathematics (MS, PhD); applied statistics (MS, Certificate); biochemistry (MS, PhD); biology (MS); botany (MS, PhD); cellular and molecular biology (PhD); chemistry (MS, PhD); clinical psychology (MS); coatings and polymeric materials (MS, PhD); cognitive and visual neuroscience (PhD); computer science (MS, PhD); environmental and conservation sciences (MS, PhD); genomics (PhD); health and social psychology (PhD); mathematics (MS, PhD); natural resources management (MS, PhD); operations research (MS); physics (MS, PhD); psychology (MS); science and mathematics (MS, PhD, Certificate); software engineering (MS, PhD, Certificate); statistics (PhD); zoology (MS, PhD). *Application deadline:* Applications are processed on a rolling basis. *Application fee:* $45 ($60 for international students). Electronic applications accepted. *Application Contact:* Dr. Kevin McCaul, Dean, 701-231-7411, E-mail: kevin.mccaul@ndsu.edu. *Dean,* Dr. Kevin McCaul, 701-231-7411, E-mail: kevin.mccaul@ndsu.edu.

See Close-Up on page 959.

NORTHEASTERN ILLINOIS UNIVERSITY, Chicago, IL 60625-4699

General Information State-supported, coed, comprehensive institution. CGS member. *Graduate housing:* On-campus housing not available. *Research affiliation:* Advocate Health Care Network (health care cost containment), Lutheran General Hospital (clinical cardiology), Advocate Medical Group (health care outcomes research).

GRADUATE UNITS

Graduate College *Degree program information:* Part-time and evening/weekend programs available. Electronic applications accepted.

College of Arts and Sciences *Degree program information:* Part-time and evening/weekend programs available. Offers arts and sciences (MA, MS); biology (MS); chemistry (MS); communication, media and theatre (MA); composition/writing (MA); computer science (MS); earth science (MS); English (MA); geography and environmental studies (MA); gerontology (MA); history (MA); linguistics (MA); literature (MA); mathematics (MA, MS); mathematics for elementary school teachers (MA); music (MA); political science (MA). Electronic applications accepted.

College of Business and Management *Degree program information:* Part-time and evening/weekend programs available. Offers accounting (MBA); finance (MBA); management (MBA); marketing (MBA). Electronic applications accepted.

College of Education *Degree program information:* Part-time and evening/weekend programs available. Offers bilingual/bicultural education (MAT, MSI); early childhood special education (MA); educating children with behavior disorders (MA); educating individuals with mental retardation (MA); education (MA, MAT, MSI); educational administration and supervision (MA); educational leadership (MA); gifted education (MA); guidance and counseling (MA); human resource development (MA); inner city studies (MA); instruction (MSI); language arts (MAT, MSI); reading (MA); special education (MA); teaching (MAT); teaching children with learning disabilities (MA). Electronic applications accepted.

NORTHEASTERN OHIO UNIVERSITIES COLLEGE OF MEDICINE AND PHARMACY, Rootstown, OH 44272-0095

General Information State-supported, coed, graduate-only institution. *Enrollment by degree level:* 602 first professional. *Graduate faculty:* 344 full-time (100 women), 1,939 part-time/adjunct (318 women). Tuition, state resident: full-time $26,884. Tuition, nonresident: full-time

$51,943. *Required fees:* $2145. Full-time tuition and fees vary according to program and student level. *Graduate housing:* On-campus housing not available. *Student services:* Campus employment opportunities, campus safety program, career counseling, free psychological counseling, low-cost health insurance, multicultural affairs office, services for students with disabilities. *Library facilities:* Oliver Ocasek Regional Medical Information Center. *Online resources:* library catalog, web page, access to other libraries' catalogs. *Collection:* 121,625 titles, 4,118 serial subscriptions, 830 audiovisual materials. *Research affiliation:* Pathogen Systems, Inc. (microbiology), Health Resources and Services Administration (human health), National Science Foundation (anatomy), National Institutes of Health (anatomy, biochemistry, immunology, neurobiology, microbiology), American Heart Association (physiology, biochemistry), Musculoskeletal Transplant Foundation (anatomy).

Computer facilities: 50 computers available on campus for general student use. A campuswide network can be accessed from student residence rooms and from off campus. Online class registration is available. *Web address:* http://www.neoucom.edu/.

General Application Contact: Michelle Cassetty Collins, Director, Admissions and Student Services, 330-325-6270, E-mail: admission@neoucom.edu.

GRADUATE UNITS

College of Medicine Students: 460 full-time (227 women); includes 174 minority (15 African Americans, 1 American Indian/Alaska Native, 145 Asian Americans or Pacific Islanders, 13 Hispanic Americans). Average age 23. 2,018 applicants, 8% accepted, 115 enrolled. *Faculty:* 340 full-time (100 women), 1,670 part-time/adjunct (367 women). Expenses: Contact institution. *Financial support:* In 2008–09, 135 students received support. Institutionally sponsored loans and scholarships/grants available. Financial award application deadline: 4/15; financial award applicants required to submit FAFSA. In 2008, 101 MDs awarded. Offers medicine (MD). *Application deadline:* For fall admission, 10/1 for domestic students. Applications are processed on a rolling basis. *Application fee:* $40. Electronic applications accepted. *Application Contact:* Julie Groves, Assistant Director of Admissions, 330-325-6270, E-mail: admission@neoucom.edu. *President and Dean of Medicine,* Dr. Lois Margaret Nora, 330-325-6255.

College of Pharmacy Students: 142 full-time (81 women); includes 31 minority (9 African Americans, 1 American Indian/Alaska Native, 19 Asian Americans or Pacific Islanders, 2 Hispanic Americans). Average age 25. 245 applicants, 36% accepted, 73 enrolled. *Faculty:* 19 full-time (8 women), 1 part-time/adjunct (0 women). Expenses: Contact institution. *Financial support:* In 2008–09, 26 students received support. Application deadline: 4/15. Offers pharmacy (Pharm D). *Application deadline:* For fall admission, 1/4 for domestic students. Applications are processed on a rolling basis. *Application fee:* $50. Electronic applications accepted. *Application Contact:* Julie Groves, Assistant Director of Admissions, 330-325-6270, E-mail: admission@neoucom.edu. *Dean,* Dr. David D. Allen, 330-325-6467, Fax: 330-325-5930.

NORTHEASTERN SEMINARY AT ROBERTS WESLEYAN COLLEGE, Rochester, NY 14624

General Information Independent-religious, coed, graduate-only institution. *Graduate housing:* On-campus housing not available.

GRADUATE UNITS

Graduate and Professional Programs *Degree program information:* Evening/weekend programs available. Offers ministry (D Min); theological studies (MA); theology (M Div). Electronic applications accepted.

NORTHEASTERN STATE UNIVERSITY, Tahlequah, OK 74464-2399

General Information State-supported, coed, comprehensive institution. *Enrollment:* 8,833 graduate, professional, and undergraduate students; 325 full-time matriculated graduate/professional students (213 women), 668 part-time matriculated graduate/professional students (456 women). *Enrollment by degree level:* 105 first professional, 888 master's. *Graduate faculty:* 121 full-time (35 women), 10 part-time/adjunct (5 women). *Graduate housing:* Rooms and/or apartments available to single and married students. Housing application deadline: 6/1. *Student services:* Campus employment opportunities, career counseling, free psychological counseling, international student services, low-cost health insurance, multicultural affairs office, services for students with disabilities, teacher training. *Library facilities:* John Vaughn Library. *Online resources:* library catalog, web page. *Collection:* 415,000 titles, 19,785 serial subscriptions, 8,306 audiovisual materials.

Computer facilities: Computer purchase and lease plans are available. 897 computers available on campus for general student use. A campuswide network can be accessed from student residence rooms and from off campus. *Web address:* http://www.nsuok.edu/.

General Application Contact: Donna Trout, Graduate Program Coordinator, 918-449-6000 Ext. 6123, Fax: 918-449-6120, E-mail: troutdk@nsuok.edu.

GRADUATE UNITS

College of Optometry Students: 106 full-time (55 women); includes 25 minority (3 African Americans, 11 American Indian/Alaska Native, 10 Asian Americans or Pacific Islanders, 1 Hispanic American). Average age 26. 112 applicants, 35% accepted, 28 enrolled. *Faculty:* 29 full-time (14 women), 9 part-time/adjunct (3 women). Expenses: Contact institution. *Financial support:* In 2008–09, 83 students received support. Federal Work-Study, institutionally sponsored loans, scholarships/grants, tuition waivers (partial), and residencies available. Financial award application deadline: 5/1; financial award applicants required to submit FAFSA. In 2008, 26 ODs awarded. Offers optometry (OD). Applicants must be residents of Oklahoma, Arkansas, Kansas, Colorado, New Mexico, Missouri, Texas, or Nebraska. *Application deadline:* For fall admission, 2/1 for domestic students. Applications are processed on a rolling basis. *Application fee:* $45. *Application Contact:* Natalie Batt, Student and Alumni Affairs, 918-456-5511 Ext. 4036, Fax: 918-458-2104, E-mail: batt@nsuok.edu. Natalie Batt.

Graduate College Students: 294 full-time (219 women), 561 part-time (390 women); includes 234 minority (45 African Americans, 166 American Indian/Alaska Native, 2 Asian Americans or Pacific Islanders, 21 Hispanic Americans), 12 international. Average age 35. *Faculty:* 121 full-time (35 women), 10 part-time/adjunct (5 women). Expenses: Contact institution. *Financial support:* Research assistantships, teaching assistantships, career-related internships or fieldwork, Federal Work-Study, scholarships/grants, and tuition waivers (partial) available. Financial award application deadline: 3/1. In 2008, 285 master's awarded. *Degree program information:* Part-time and evening/weekend programs available. *Application deadline:* Applications are processed on a rolling basis. *Application fee:* $0. Electronic applications accepted. *Application Contact:* Margie Railey, Administrative Assistant, 918-456-5511 Ext. 2093, Fax: 918-458-2061, E-mail: railey@nsuok.edu. *Dean,* Dr. Thomas L. Jackson, 918-456-5511 Ext. 2220, Fax: 918-458-2061, E-mail: jacks009@nsuok.edu.

College of Business and Technology Students: 31 full-time (18 women), 120 part-time (58 women); includes 44 minority (7 African Americans, 33 American Indian/Alaska Native, 1 Asian American or Pacific Islander, 3 Hispanic Americans), 7 international. *Faculty:* 12 full-time (2 women). Expenses: Contact institution. *Financial support:* Teaching assistantships, Federal Work-Study available. Financial award application deadline: 3/1. In 2008, 30 master's awarded. *Degree program information:* Part-time and evening/weekend programs available. Offers accounting and financial analysis (MS); business administration (MBA); business and technology (MBA, MS); industrial management (MS). *Application deadline:* For fall admission, 6/1 priority date for domestic students. Applications are processed on a rolling basis. *Application fee:* $0 ($25 for international students). *Application Contact:* Dr. John Schleede, Dean, 918-456-5511 Ext. 2910, Fax: 918-458-2337, E-mail: schleede@nsuok.edu. *Dean,* Dr. John Schleede, 918-456-5511 Ext. 2910, Fax: 918-458-2337, E-mail: schleede@nsuok.edu.

College of Education Students: 188 full-time (147 women), 350 part-time (264 women); includes 211 minority (32 African Americans, 166 American Indian/Alaska Native, 1 Asian American or Pacific Islander, 12 Hispanic Americans), 5 international. *Faculty:* 26 full-time (11 women). Expenses: Contact institution. *Financial support:* Teaching assistantships, career-related internships or fieldwork and Federal Work-Study available. Financial award application deadline: 3/1. In 2008, 207 master's awarded. *Degree program information:* Part-time and evening/weekend programs available. Offers collegiate scholarship and services (MS); counseling psychology (MS); early childhood education (M Ed); education (M Ed, MS, MS Ed); health and kinesiology (MS Ed); higher education administration and services (MS); library media and information technology (MS Ed); mathematics education (M Ed); reading (M Ed); school administration (M Ed); school counseling (M Ed); teaching (M Ed). *Application deadline:* For fall admission, 6/1 priority date for domestic students. Applications are processed on a rolling basis. *Application fee:* $0 ($25 for international students). Electronic applications accepted. *Application Contact:* Margie Railey, Administrative Assistant, 918-456-5511 Ext. 2093, Fax: 918-458-2061, E-mail: railey@nsuok.edu. *Head,* Dr. Kay Grant, 918-456-5511 Ext. 3700.

College of Liberal Arts Students: 41 full-time (21 women), 84 part-time (61 women); includes 17 minority (6 African Americans, 7 American Indian/Alaska Native, 4 Hispanic Americans). *Faculty:* 26 full-time (6 women). Expenses: Contact institution. *Financial support:* Teaching assistantships, Federal Work-Study available. Financial award application deadline: 3/1. In 2008, 29 master's awarded. *Degree program information:* Part-time and evening/weekend programs available. Offers American studies (MA); communication (MA); criminal justice (MS); English (MA); liberal arts (MA, MS). *Application deadline:* For fall admission, 6/1 priority date for domestic students. Applications are processed on a rolling basis. *Application fee:* $0 ($25 for international students). Electronic applications accepted. *Application Contact:* Margie Railey, Administrative Assistant, 918-456-5511 Ext. 2093, Fax: 918-458-2061, E-mail: railey@nsuok.edu. *Interim Dean,* Dr. Paul Westbrook, 918-456-5511 Ext. 3600, Fax: 918-458-2348, E-mail: westbroo@nsuok.edu.

College of Science and Health Professions Students: 34 full-time (33 women), 7 part-time (all women); includes 6 minority (4 American Indian/Alaska Native, 2 Hispanic Americans). Expenses: Contact institution. In 2008, 19 master's awarded. Offers science and health professions (M Ed, MS); science education (M Ed); speech-language pathology (MS). *Application Contact:* Margie Railey, Administrative Assistant, 918-456-5511 Ext. 2093, Fax: 918-458-2061, E-mail: railey@nsuok.edu. *Interim Dean,* Dr. Doug Penisten, 918-456-5511 Ext. 3800.

NORTHEASTERN UNIVERSITY, Boston, MA 02115-5096

General Information Independent, coed, university. CGS member. *Graduate housing:* Room and/or apartments available on a first-come, first-served basis to single students; on-campus housing not available to married students. *Research affiliation:* BBN Technologies (information technology), Analog Devices, Inc. (electronics), General Electric Company (engineering), Jobs for America's Graduates (labor studies), Cytyc Corporation (medical technology).

GRADUATE UNITS

Bouvé College of Health Sciences Graduate School *Degree program information:* Part-time and evening/weekend programs available. Offers applied behavior analysis (MS); applied educational psychology (MS); audiology (Au D); biotechnology (PSM); clinical exercise physiology (MS); college student development and counseling (MS); counseling psychology (MS, PhD, CAGS); health sciences (Pharm D, MS, MS Ed, PSM, Au D, DPT, PhD, CAGS, CAS); pharmaceutical sciences (PhD); pharmacology (MS); pharmacy (Pharm D); physician assistant (MS); school counseling (MS); school psychology (MS, PhD, CAGS); special needs and intensive special needs (MS Ed); speech-language pathology (MS); toxicology (MS).

School of Nursing *Degree program information:* Part-time programs available. Offers critical care-acute care nurse practitioner (MS, CAS); critical care-neonatal nurse practitioner (MS, CAS); nurse anesthesia (MS, CAGS); nursing (MS, PhD, CAGS, CAS); nursing administration (MS); primary care nursing (MS, CAS); psychiatric-mental health nursing (MS, CAS).

College of Arts and Sciences *Degree program information:* Part-time and evening/weekend programs available. Offers analytical chemistry (PhD); applied mathematics (MS); arts and sciences (M Arch, MA, MAW, MPA, MS, MSOR, PMS, PSM, PhD, Certificate); bioinformatics (PMS); biology (MS, PhD); biotechnology (MS); chemistry (MS, PhD); cinema studies (Certificate); development administration (MPA); economics (MA, PhD); English (MA, PhD); experimental psychology (MA, PhD); health administration and policy (MPA); history (MA); inorganic chemistry (PhD); law, policy, and society (MS, PhD); marine biology (MS); mathematics (MS, PhD); operations research (MSOR); organic chemistry (PhD); physical chemistry (PhD); physics (MS, PhD); political science (MA); public administration (MPA, Certificate); public and international affairs (PhD); public history (MA); sociology (MA, PhD); state and local government (MPA); urban studies (Certificate); women's studies (Certificate); world history (PhD). Electronic applications accepted.

School of Journalism *Degree program information:* Part-time and evening/weekend programs available. Offers journalism (MA). Electronic applications accepted.

College of Computer and Information Science *Degree program information:* Part-time and evening/weekend programs available. Offers computer and information science (PhD); computer science (MS); health informatics (MS); information assurance (MS); telecommunication systems management (MS). Electronic applications accepted.

College of Criminal Justice *Degree program information:* Part-time and evening/weekend programs available. Offers criminal justice (MS, PhD). Electronic applications accepted.

College of Engineering *Degree program information:* Part-time programs available. Offers chemical engineering (MS, PhD); civil and environmental engineering (MS, PhD); computer engineering (PhD); computer systems engineering (MS); electrical engineering (MS, PhD); engineering (MS, PSM, PhD, Certificate); engineering management (MS); industrial engineering (MS, PhD); information systems (MS, Certificate); mechanical engineering (MS, PhD); operations research (MS); telecommunication systems management (MS). Electronic applications accepted.

Graduate School of Business Administration *Degree program information:* Part-time and evening/weekend programs available. Offers business administration (EMBA, MBA, MSF, MST, CAGS); finance (MSF). Electronic applications accepted.

Graduate School of Professional Accounting Offers professional accounting (MST, CAGS); taxation (MST, CAGS). Electronic applications accepted.

School of Architecture Offers architecture (M Arch). Electronic applications accepted.

School of Law Offers law (JD). Electronic applications accepted.

School of Technological Entrepreneurship Offers technological entrepreneurship (MS).

NORTHERN ARIZONA UNIVERSITY, Flagstaff, AZ 86011

General Information State-supported, coed, university. CGS member. *Graduate housing:* Rooms and/or apartments available to single and married students. *Research affiliation:* Museum of Northern Arizona, Lowell Observatory, Rocky Mountain Forest and Range Experiment Station, U.S. Naval Observatory, U.S. Geological Survey, W. L. Gore and Associates, Inc.

GRADUATE UNITS

Graduate College *Degree program information:* Part-time and evening/weekend programs available. Electronic applications accepted.

College of Arts and Letters *Degree program information:* Part-time programs available. Offers applied linguistics (PhD); arts and letters (MA, MAT, MM, PhD, Certificate); choral conducting (MM); creative writing (MA); English (MA); general English (MA); history (MA, PhD); instrumental conducting (MM); instrumental performance (MM); literacy, technology and professional writing (MA); literature (MA); music education (MM); musicology (MM); secondary English education (MA); Spanish (MAT); sustainable communities (MA); teaching English as a second language (MA); teaching English as a second language/applied linguistics (MA, PhD, Certificate); teaching English as a second language/English as a second language (Certificate); theory and composition (MM); vocal performance (MM).

College of Education *Degree program information:* Part-time and evening/weekend programs available. Offers bilingual education (M Ed); career and technical education (M Ed); community college/higher education (M Ed); community counseling (MA); counseling psychology (PhD); curriculum and instruction (Ed D); early childhood education (M Ed); education (M Ed, MA, Ed D, PhD, Certificate); educational foundations (M Ed); educational leadership (Ed D); educational technology (M Ed, Certificate); elementary education (M Ed);

Northern Arizona University (continued)

human relations (M Ed); learning and instruction (PhD); multicultural education (M Ed); school counseling (M Ed); school leadership (M Ed); school psychology (PhD); secondary education (M Ed); special education (M Ed); student affairs (M Ed).

College of Engineering, Forestry and Natural Sciences Offers applied physics (MS); biological sciences (MS, PhD); chemistry (MS); civil engineering (MSE); computer science (MSE); earth science (MAT, MS); electrical engineering (MSE); engineering (M Eng, MSE); engineering, forestry and natural sciences (M Eng, MAT, MF, MS, MSE, MSF, PhD); environmental engineering (MSE); environmental sciences and policy (MS); forestry (MF, MSF, PhD); geology (MAT, MS); mathematics (MAT, MS); mechanical engineering (MSE); quaternary sciences (MS); science education (MAT); statistics (MS).

College of Health and Human Services *Degree program information:* Part-time programs available. Offers clinical speech pathology (MS); family nurse practitioner (MSN); health and human services (M Ad, MPH, MS, MSN, DPT); health sciences (M Ad, MPH); nursing (MSN); nursing education (MSN); physical therapy (DPT).

College of Social and Behavioral Sciences *Degree program information:* Part-time programs available. Offers applied communication (MA); applied criminology (MS); applied geographic information science (MS); applied health psychology (MA); applied sociology (MA); archaeology (MA); clinical psychology (MA); criminal justice policy and planning (Certificate); cultural anthropology (MA); general psychology (MA); geographic information systems (Certificate); linguistic anthropology (MA); political science (MA, PhD, Certificate); public administration (MPA); public management (Certificate); rural geography (MA); social and behavioral sciences (MA, MPA, MS, PhD, Certificate); sociology (MA); teaching of psychology (MA).

The W. A. Franke College of Business *Degree program information:* Part-time programs available. Offers business (MBA).

NORTHERN BAPTIST THEOLOGICAL SEMINARY, Lombard, IL 60148-5698

General Information Independent-religious, coed, primarily men, graduate-only institution. *Enrollment by degree level:* 93 first professional, 25 master's, 27 doctoral, 2 other advanced degrees. *Graduate faculty:* 6 full-time (1 woman), 30 part-time/adjunct (5 women). *Tuition:* Part-time $440 per credit. *Required fees:* $100 per quarter. Tuition and fees vary according to degree level. *Graduate housing:* Rooms and/or apartments available on a first-come, first-served basis to single and married students. Typical cost: $9300 per year for single students; $9300 per year for married students. Room charges vary according to housing facility selected. Housing application deadline: 6/30. *Student services:* Campus employment opportunities, low-cost health insurance. *Library facilities:* Brimsom-Grow Library. *Online resources:* library catalog, web page, access to other libraries' catalogs. *Collection:* 53,200 titles, 282 serial subscriptions, 1,397 audiovisual materials.

Computer facilities: 18 computers available on campus for general student use. A campuswide network can be accessed from student residence rooms. Online class registration is available. *Web address:* http://www.seminary.edu/.

General Application Contact: Greg Henson, Executive Director of External Relations, 630-620-2180, Fax: 630-620-2190, E-mail: admissions@seminary.edu.

GRADUATE UNITS

Graduate and Professional Programs Students: 127 full-time (38 women), 20 part-time (13 women); includes 67 minority (51 African Americans, 12 Asian Americans or Pacific Islanders, 4 Hispanic Americans), 3 international. Average age 40. *Faculty:* 6 full-time (1 woman), 30 part-time/adjunct (5 women). Expenses: Contact institution. *Financial support:* Career-related internships or fieldwork and scholarships/grants available. Support available to part-time students. Financial award application deadline: 9/1. *Degree program information:* Part-time programs available. Offers Biblical studies (MA); Christian ministries (MACM); divinity (M Div); ministry (D Min); missional church (MA); theology (MA). *Application deadline:* For fall admission, 9/1 priority date for domestic students, 2/1 priority date for international students; for winter admission, 12/1 priority date for domestic students; for spring admission, 3/1 priority date for domestic students. Applications are processed on a rolling basis. *Application fee:* $35. Electronic applications accepted. *Application Contact:* Greg Henson, Executive Director of External Relations, 630-620-2180, Fax: 630-620-2190, E-mail: admissions@seminary.edu. *Dean,* Alistair Brown, 630-620-2103, Fax: 630-620-2190.

NORTHERN ILLINOIS UNIVERSITY, De Kalb, IL 60115-2854

General Information State-supported, coed, university. CGS member. *Graduate housing:* Rooms and/or apartments available on a first-come, first-served basis to single and married students. *Research affiliation:* Argonne National Laboratory, Fermi National Accelerator Laboratory, Field Museum of Natural History, Burpee Museum of Natural History.

GRADUATE UNITS

College of Law *Degree program information:* Part-time programs available. Offers law (JD). Electronic applications accepted.

Graduate School *Degree program information:* Part-time and evening/weekend programs available. Postbaccalaureate distance learning degree programs offered (minimal on-campus study). Electronic applications accepted.

College of Business *Degree program information:* Part-time and evening/weekend programs available. Offers accountancy (MAS, MST); business (MAS, MBA, MS, MST); business administration (MBA); management information systems (MS). Electronic applications accepted.

College of Education *Degree program information:* Part-time and evening/weekend programs available. Postbaccalaureate distance learning degree programs offered (minimal on-campus study). Offers adult and higher education (MS Ed, Ed D); counseling (MS Ed, Ed D); curriculum and instruction (MS Ed, Ed D); early childhood education (MS Ed); education (MS, MS Ed, Ed D, Ed S); educational administration (MS Ed, Ed D, Ed S); educational psychology (MS Ed, Ed D); educational research and evaluation (MS); elementary education (MS Ed); foundations of education (MS Ed); instructional technology (MS Ed, Ed D); literacy education (MS Ed); physical education (MS Ed); school business management (MS Ed); special education (MS Ed); sport management (MS). Electronic applications accepted.

College of Engineering and Engineering Technology *Degree program information:* Part-time and evening/weekend programs available. Offers electrical engineering (MS); engineering and engineering technology (MS); industrial engineering (MS); industrial management (MS); mechanical engineering (MS). Electronic applications accepted.

College of Health and Human Sciences *Degree program information:* Part-time and evening/weekend programs available. Offers applied family and child studies (MS); communicative disorders (MA, Au D); health and human sciences (MA, MPH, MPT, MS, Au D); nursing (MS); nutrition and dietetics (MS); physical therapy (MPT); public health (MPH). Electronic applications accepted.

College of Liberal Arts and Sciences *Degree program information:* Part-time and evening/weekend programs available. Offers anthropology (MA); biological sciences (MS, PhD); chemistry (MS, PhD); communication studies (MA); computer science (MS); economics (MA, PhD); English (MA, PhD); French (MA); geography (MS); geology (MS, PhD); history (MA, PhD); liberal arts and sciences (MA, MPA, MS, PhD); mathematical sciences (PhD); mathematics (MS); philosophy (MA); physics (MS, PhD); political science (MA, PhD); psychology (MA, PhD); public administration (MPA); sociology (MA); Spanish (MA); statistics (MS). Electronic applications accepted.

College of Visual and Performing Arts *Degree program information:* Part-time and evening/weekend programs available. Offers art (MA, MFA, MS); music (MM, Performer's Certificate); theatre and dance (MFA); visual and performing arts (MA, MFA, MM, MS, Performer's Certificate). Electronic applications accepted.

NORTHERN KENTUCKY UNIVERSITY, Highland Heights, KY 41099

General Information State-supported, coed, comprehensive institution. CGS member. *Enrollment:* 15,082 graduate, professional, and undergraduate students; 522 full-time matriculated graduate/professional students (285 women), 1,441 part-time matriculated graduate/professional students (942 women). *Enrollment by degree level:* 570 first professional, 1,296 master's, 11 doctoral, 86 other advanced degrees. *Graduate faculty:* 150 full-time (72 women), 67 part-time/adjunct (35 women). Tuition, state resident: full-time $6642. Tuition, nonresident: full-time $11,682. *Graduate housing:* Room and/or apartments available on a first-come, first-served basis to single students; on-campus housing not available to married students. Typical cost: $1510 per year ($2755 including board). Room and board charges vary according to campus/location and housing facility selected. Housing application deadline: 5/1. *Student services:* Campus employment opportunities, campus safety program, career counseling, child daycare facilities, exercise/wellness program, free psychological counseling, international student services, low-cost health insurance, multicultural affairs office, services for students with disabilities. *Library facilities:* W. Frank Steely Library plus 1 other. *Online resources:* library catalog, web page, access to other libraries' catalogs. *Collection:* 850,752 titles, 1,579 serial subscriptions, 6,971 audiovisual materials.

Computer facilities: 500 computers available on campus for general student use. A campuswide network can be accessed from student residence rooms and from off campus. Online class registration, course specific software, office software are available. *Web address:* http://www.nku.edu/.

General Application Contact: Dr. Peg Griffin, Director of Graduate Programs, 859-572-5224, Fax: 859-572-6670, E-mail: griffinp@nku.edu.

GRADUATE UNITS

Office of Graduate Programs Students: 175 full-time (120 women), 1,218 part-time (841 women); includes 108 minority (64 African Americans, 3 American Indian/Alaska Native, 28 Asian Americans or Pacific Islanders, 13 Hispanic Americans), 27 international. Average age 33. 826 applicants, 62% accepted, 420 enrolled. *Faculty:* 117 full-time (59 women), 50 part-time/adjunct (27 women). Expenses: Contact institution. *Financial support:* Traineeships and unspecified assistantships available. Financial award applicants required to submit FAFSA. In 2008, 502 master's awarded. *Degree program information:* Part-time and evening/weekend programs available. Postbaccalaureate distance learning degree programs offered (no on-campus study). *Application deadline:* For fall admission, 6/1 for international students; for spring admission, 10/1 for international students. Applications are processed on a rolling basis. *Application fee:* $40. Electronic applications accepted. *Application Contact:* Dr. Peg Griffin, Director of Graduate Programs, 859-572-6934, Fax: 859-572-6670, E-mail: griffinp@nku.edu. *Graduate Dean/Associate Provost for Research,* Dr. Salina Shrofel, 859-572-5224, Fax: 859-572-5565, E-mail: shrofels1@nku.edu.

College of Arts and Sciences Students: 20 full-time (15 women), 192 part-time (127 women); includes 23 minority (17 African Americans, 3 Asian Americans or Pacific Islanders, 3 Hispanic Americans), 2 international. Average age 35. 144 applicants, 67% accepted, 86 enrolled. *Faculty:* 24 full-time (12 women), 6 part-time/adjunct (2 women). Expenses: Contact institution. *Financial support:* Unspecified assistantships available. Financial award applicants required to submit FAFSA. In 2008, 65 master's awarded. *Degree program information:* Part-time and evening/weekend programs available. Postbaccalaureate distance learning degree programs offered (minimal on-campus study). Offers arts and sciences (MA, MPA, MS, Certificate); civic engagement (Certificate); English (MA); industrial psychology (Certificate); industrial-organizational psychology (MS); integrative studies (MA); nonprofit management (Certificate); occupational health psychology (Certificate); organizational psychology (Certificate); public administration (MPA). *Application deadline:* For fall admission, 8/1 for domestic students, 6/1 for international students; for spring admission, 12/1 for domestic students, 10/1 for international students. *Application fee:* $40. Electronic applications accepted. *Application Contact:* Dr. Peg Griffin, Director of Graduate Programs, 859-572-6934, Fax: 859-572-6670, E-mail: griffinp@nku.edu. *Dean,* Dr. Kevin Corcoran, 859-572-5495, Fax: 859-572-6185, E-mail: corcorank1@nku.edu.

College of Business Students: 52 full-time (27 women), 264 part-time (120 women); includes 33 minority (19 African Americans, 1 American Indian/Alaska Native, 11 Asian Americans or Pacific Islanders, 2 Hispanic Americans), 13 international. Average age 32. 174 applicants, 55% accepted, 84 enrolled. *Faculty:* 19 full-time (9 women), 12 part-time/adjunct (3 women). Expenses: Contact institution. *Financial support:* Unspecified assistantships available. Financial award applicants required to submit FAFSA. In 2008, 126 master's awarded. *Degree program information:* Part-time and evening/weekend programs available. Offers accountancy (M Acc); advanced taxation (Certificate); business (M Acc, MBA, MS, Certificate); business administration (MBA); entrepreneurship (Certificate); executive leadership and organizational change (MS); finance (Certificate); international business (Certificate); marketing (Certificate); project management (Certificate). *Application deadline:* For fall admission, 8/1 priority date for domestic students, 6/1 priority date for international students; for spring admission, 12/1 priority date for domestic students, 10/1 priority date for international students. *Application fee:* $40. *Application Contact:* Dr. Carol Cornell, Director, 859-442-4281, Fax: 859-572-6177, E-mail: cornellc1@nku.edu. *Dean,* Dr. John Beehler, 859-572-5551, Fax: 859-572-6177, E-mail: beehlerj1@nku.edu.

College of Education and Human Services Students: 53 full-time (42 women), 462 part-time (366 women); includes 20 minority (8 African Americans, 2 American Indian/Alaska Native, 3 Asian Americans or Pacific Islanders, 7 Hispanic Americans), 1 international. Average age 32. 207 applicants, 54% accepted, 98 enrolled. *Faculty:* 38 full-time (21 women), 14 part-time/adjunct (9 women). Expenses: Contact institution. *Financial support:* Unspecified assistantships available. Financial award applicants required to submit FAFSA. In 2008, 247 master's awarded. *Degree program information:* Part-time and evening/weekend programs available. Offers college student development administration (Certificate); community counseling (MS, Certificate); education (MA); educational leadership (Ed D); instructional leadership (MA); school counseling (MA, Certificate); school superintendent (Certificate); special education (Certificate); teacher as a leader (MA); teaching (MA, Certificate); temporary school counseling provision (Certificate). *Application deadline:* For fall admission, 8/1 priority date for domestic students, 6/1 for international students; for spring admission, 12/1 priority date for domestic students, 10/1 for international students. Applications are processed on a rolling basis. *Application fee:* $40. Electronic applications accepted. *Application Contact:* Dr. Peg Griffin, Director of Graduate Programs, 859-572-6934, Fax: 859-572-6670, E-mail: griffinp@nku.edu. *Dean,* Dr. Elaine McNally Jarchow, 859-572-7976, Fax: 859-572-6623, E-mail: jarchowe1@nku.edu.

College of Informatics Students: 28 full-time (14 women), 118 part-time (56 women); includes 18 minority (11 African Americans, 7 Asian Americans or Pacific Islanders), 10 international. Average age 33. 96 applicants, 72% accepted, 54 enrolled. *Faculty:* 21 full-time (2 women), 4 part-time/adjunct (0 women). Expenses: Contact institution. *Financial support:* Unspecified assistantships available. Financial award applicants required to submit FAFSA. In 2008, 26 master's awarded. *Degree program information:* Part-time and evening/weekend programs available. Offers business informatics (MS, Certificate); communication (MA); computer science (MSCS); corporate information security (Certificate); enterprise resource planning (Certificate); health informatics (MS, Certificate); informatics (MA, MS, MSCS, Certificate); secure software engineering (Certificate). *Application deadline:* For fall admission, 8/1 priority date for domestic students, 6/1 priority date for international students; for spring admission, 12/1 priority date for domestic students, 10/1 priority date for international students. Applications are processed on a rolling basis. *Application fee:* $40. Electronic applications accepted. *Application Contact:* Dr. Peg Griffin, Director of Graduate Programs, 859-572-6934, Fax: 859-572-6670, E-mail: griffinp@nku.edu. *Dean,* Dr. Douglas Perry, 859-572-5666, Fax: 859-572-6097, E-mail: perryd1@nku.edu.

School of Nursing and Health Professions Students: 22 full-time (all women), 182 part-time (172 women); includes 14 minority (9 African Americans, 4 Asian Americans or Pacific Islanders, 1 Hispanic American), 1 international. Average age 39. 108 applicants, 38% accepted, 31 enrolled. *Faculty:* 15 full-time (all women), 14 part-time/adjunct (13 women). Expenses: Contact institution. *Financial support:* Traineeships and unspecified assistantships available. Financial award applicants required to submit FAFSA. In 2008, 38 master's awarded. *Degree program information:* Part-time and evening/weekend programs available. Postbaccalaureate distance learning degree programs offered (no on-campus study). Offers nurse practitioner advancement (Certificate); nursing (MSN, Post-Master's Certificate). *Application deadline:* For fall admission, 2/1 for domestic and international students; for spring admission, 10/15 for domestic and international students. *Application fee:* $40.

Electronic applications accepted. *Application Contact:* Dr. Peg Griffin, Director of Graduate Programs, 859-572-6934, Fax: 859-572-6670, E-mail: griffinp@nku.edu. *Program Director,* Dr. Denise C. Robinson, 859-572-5688, Fax: 859-572-6098, E-mail: robinson@nku.edu.

Salmon P. Chase College of Law Students: 323 full-time (153 women), 215 part-time (103 women); includes 44 minority (24 African Americans, 2 American Indian/Alaska Native, 10 Asian Americans or Pacific Islanders, 8 Hispanic Americans). Average age 24. 1,130 applicants, 45% accepted, 216 enrolled. *Faculty:* 33 full-time (13 women), 16 part-time/adjunct (6 women). Expenses: Contact institution. *Financial support:* In 2008–09, 150 students received support, including 15 fellowships (averaging $3,500 per year), 26 research assistantships (averaging $1,000 per year); career-related internships or fieldwork, Federal Work-Study, scholarships/grants, and unspecified assistantships also available. Support available to part-time students. Financial award application deadline: 3/1; financial award applicants required to submit FAFSA. In 2008, 156 JDs awarded. *Degree program information:* Part-time and evening/weekend programs available. Offers law (JD). *Application deadline:* For fall admission, 4/1 priority date for domestic and international students. Applications are processed on a rolling basis. *Application fee:* $40. Electronic applications accepted. *Application Contact:* Ashley Folger Gray, Director of Admissions, 859-572-5841, Fax: 859-572-6081, E-mail: folger@nku.edu. *Dean,* Dennis R. Honabach, 859-572-6406, Fax: 859-572-6183, E-mail: honabachd1@nku.edu.

NORTHERN MICHIGAN UNIVERSITY, Marquette, MI 49855-5301

General Information State-supported, coed, comprehensive institution. CGS member. *Graduate housing:* Rooms and/or apartments available to single and married students.

GRADUATE UNITS

College of Graduate Studies *Degree program information:* Part-time and evening/weekend programs available. Postbaccalaureate distance learning degree programs offered. Electronic applications accepted.

College of Arts and Sciences *Degree program information:* Part-time programs available. Postbaccalaureate distance learning degree programs offered (minimal on-campus study). Offers arts and sciences (MA, MFA, MPA, MS); biology (MS); creative writing (MFA); literature (MA); pedagogy (MA); psychology (MS); public administration (MPA); writing (MA).

College of Professional Studies *Degree program information:* Part-time programs available. Offers administration and supervision (MA Ed, Ed S); criminal justice (MS); elementary education (MA Ed); exercise science (MS); learning disabilities (MA Ed); literacy leadership (Ed S); nursing (MSN); reading (MA Ed); reading education (MA Ed, Ed S); reading specialist (MA Ed); school guidance counseling (MA Ed); science education (MS); secondary education (MA Ed).

NORTHERN STATE UNIVERSITY, Aberdeen, SD 57401-7198

General Information State-supported, coed, comprehensive institution. *Graduate housing:* Room and/or apartments available on a first-come, first-served basis to single students; on-campus housing not available to married students. *Research affiliation:* AASCU-Grants Resource Center.

GRADUATE UNITS

Division of Graduate Studies in Education *Degree program information:* Part-time and evening/weekend programs available. Offers education (MS, MS Ed); educational studies (MS Ed); elementary classroom teaching (MS Ed); elementary school administration (MS Ed); guidance and counseling (MS Ed); health, physical education, and coaching (MS Ed); language and literacy (MS Ed); secondary classroom teaching (MS Ed); secondary school administration (MS Ed); special education (MS Ed). Electronic applications accepted.

Center for Statewide E-Learning *Degree program information:* Part-time and evening/weekend programs available. Offers e-learning design and instruction (MS Ed); e-learning technology and administration (MS). Electronic applications accepted.

NORTH GEORGIA COLLEGE & STATE UNIVERSITY, Dahlonega, GA 30597

General Information State-supported, coed, comprehensive institution. *Graduate housing:* Room and/or apartments available on a first-come, first-served basis to single students; on-campus housing not available to married students. Housing application deadline: 1/1. *Research affiliation:* Northeast Georgia Medical Center, Morehouse School of Medicine, St. Joseph's Hospital, Mettler Electronic Corporation.

GRADUATE UNITS

Graduate Studies *Degree program information:* Part-time and evening/weekend programs available. Postbaccalaureate distance learning degree programs offered. Offers community counseling (MS); early childhood education (M Ed); educational leadership (Ed S); family nurse practitioner (MSN); middle grades education (M Ed); nursing education (MSN); physical therapy (DPT); public administration (MPA); secondary education (M Ed); special education (M Ed). Electronic applications accepted.

NORTH GREENVILLE UNIVERSITY, Tigerville, SC 29688-1892

General Information Independent-religious, coed, comprehensive institution. *Enrollment:* 2,160 graduate, professional, and undergraduate students; 51 full-time matriculated graduate/professional students (21 women), 60 part-time matriculated graduate/professional students (22 women). *Enrollment by degree level:* 111 master's. *Graduate faculty:* 3 full-time (1 woman), 9 part-time/adjunct (1 woman). *Tuition:* Full-time $4500; part-time $750 per course. One-time fee: $150. *Graduate housing:* Room and/or apartments available on a first-come, first-served basis to single students; on-campus housing not available to married students. Typical cost: $6720 (including board). Housing application deadline: 8/1. *Student services:* Campus employment opportunities, campus safety program, career counseling, exercise/wellness program, free psychological counseling, international student services, low-cost health insurance, services for students with disabilities, writing training. *Library facilities:* Hester Memorial Library. *Online resources:* library catalog, web page. *Collection:* 49,000 titles, 536 serial subscriptions, 5,644 audiovisual materials.

Computer facilities: 78 computers available on campus for general student use. A campuswide network can be accessed from student residence rooms and from off campus. *Web address:* http://www.ngu.edu/.

General Application Contact: Tawana P. Scott, Director of Graduate Enrollment, 864-877-1598, Fax: 864-877-1653, E-mail: tscott@ngu.edu.

GRADUATE UNITS

T. Walter Brashier Graduate School Students: 51 full-time (21 women), 60 part-time (22 women); includes 17 minority (14 African Americans, 3 Hispanic Americans), 4 international. Average age 32. 135 applicants, 85% accepted, 111 enrolled. *Faculty:* 3 full-time (1 woman), 9 part-time/adjunct (1 woman). Expenses: Contact institution. *Financial support:* In 2008–09, 35 students received support. Federal Work-Study, institutionally sponsored loans, scholarships/grants, and tuition waivers (partial) available. Support available to part-time students. Financial award applicants required to submit FAFSA. In 2008, 39 master's awarded. *Degree program information:* Part-time and evening/weekend programs available. Postbaccalaureate distance learning degree programs offered (no on-campus study). Offers business administration (MBA); Christian ministry (MCM). *Application deadline:* For fall admission, 8/1 for domestic students, 6/1 for international students; for winter admission, 1/1 for domestic students, 10/1 for international students; for spring admission, 3/1 for domestic students, 1/1 for international students. Applications are processed on a rolling basis. *Application fee:* $30. Electronic applications accepted. *Application Contact:* Tawana P. Scott, Director of Graduate Enrollment, 864-877-1598, Fax: 864-877-1653, E-mail: tscott@ngu.edu. *Vice President for Graduate Studies,* Dr. Joseph Samuel Isgett, 864-877-3052, Fax: 864-877-1653, E-mail: sisgett@ngu.edu.

NORTH PARK THEOLOGICAL SEMINARY, Chicago, IL 60625-4895

General Information Independent-religious, coed, graduate-only institution. *Graduate housing:* Rooms and/or apartments available to single and married students. Housing application deadline: 9/1. *Research affiliation:* Northside Chicago Theological Institute, Covenant Archives and Historical Society, American Theological Library Association.

GRADUATE UNITS

Graduate and Professional Programs *Degree program information:* Part-time programs available. Offers adult ministry (Certificate); camping and retreat ministry (Certificate); children and family ministry (Certificate); Christian formation (MA); Christian formation-all ages (Certificate); Christian ministry (MACM); Christian spirituality (Certificate); faith and health (Certificate); justice ministry (Certificate); leadership and administration (Certificate); preaching (D Min); spiritual direction (Certificate); theological studies (MATS); theology (M Div); youth ministry (Certificate).

NORTH PARK UNIVERSITY, Chicago, IL 60625-4895

General Information Independent-religious, coed, comprehensive institution. *Graduate housing:* Rooms and/or apartments available to single and married students.

GRADUATE UNITS

School of Business and Nonprofit Management *Degree program information:* Part-time and evening/weekend programs available. Offers business and nonprofit management (MBA, MHEA, MHRM, MM, MNA).

School of Education Offers education (MA).

School of Nursing *Degree program information:* Part-time and evening/weekend programs available. Offers advanced practice nursing (MS); leadership and management (MS).

NORTH SHORE–LIJ GRADUATE SCHOOL OF MOLECULAR MEDICINE, Manhasset, NY 11030

General Information Independent, coed, graduate-only institution. *Graduate housing:* On-campus housing not available. *Research affiliation:* Feinstein Institute for Medical Research (medicine and medical research).

GRADUATE UNITS

Graduate Program Offers molecular medicine (PhD).

NORTHWEST BAPTIST SEMINARY, Tacoma, WA 98407

General Information Independent-religious, coed, primarily men, graduate-only institution. *Graduate housing:* On-campus housing not available.

GRADUATE UNITS

Programs in Theology *Degree program information:* Part-time and evening/weekend programs available. Offers theology (M Div, M Min, MTS, STM, Th M, D Min, Certificate).

NORTHWEST CHRISTIAN UNIVERSITY, Eugene, OR 97401-3745

General Information Independent-religious, coed, comprehensive institution. *Graduate housing:* Rooms and/or apartments available on a first-come, first-served basis to single students and available to married students.

GRADUATE UNITS

School of Business and Management *Degree program information:* Part-time and evening/weekend programs available. Offers business and management (MBA).

School of Education and Counseling *Degree program information:* Part-time and evening/weekend programs available. Postbaccalaureate distance learning degree programs offered (minimal on-campus study). Offers community counseling (MA); education (M Ed); school counseling (MA). Electronic applications accepted.

NORTHWESTERN HEALTH SCIENCES UNIVERSITY, Bloomington, MN 55431-1599

General Information Independent, coed, graduate-only institution. *Enrollment by degree level:* 704 first professional, 104 master's. *Graduate housing:* On-campus housing not available. *Student services:* Campus employment opportunities, campus safety program, career counseling, exercise/wellness program, free psychological counseling, international student services, low-cost health insurance, services for students with disabilities. *Library facilities:* Greenwalt Library. *Online resources:* library catalog, web page. *Collection:* 12,000 titles, 400 serial subscriptions, 450 audiovisual materials. *Research affiliation:* University of Minnesota, School of Medicine (orthopedic surgery), Pain Assessment and Rehabilitation Center (pain management), Berman Center for Outcomes and Clinical Research (outcomes and clinical research).

Computer facilities: 76 computers available on campus for general student use. A campuswide network can be accessed from off campus. Online class registration is available. *Web address:* http://www.nwhealth.edu/.

General Application Contact: Lynn Heieie, Associate Director of Admissions, 952-888-4777 Ext. 409, Fax: 952-888-6713, E-mail: admit@nwhealth.edu.

GRADUATE UNITS

Minnesota College of Acupuncture and Oriental Medicine Offers acupuncture (M Ac); oriental medicine (MOM). Electronic applications accepted.

Northwestern College of Chiropractic Offers chiropractic (DC). Electronic applications accepted.

School of Massage Therapy Offers massage therapy (Professional Certificate).

NORTHWESTERN OKLAHOMA STATE UNIVERSITY, Alva, OK 73717-2799

General Information State-supported, coed, comprehensive institution. *Enrollment:* 46 full-time matriculated graduate/professional students (28 women), 133 part-time matriculated graduate/professional students (107 women). *Enrollment by degree level:* 179 master's. *Graduate faculty:* 48 full-time (25 women), 24 part-time/adjunct (17 women). *Required fees:* $152 per hour. *Graduate housing:* Room and/or apartments available to single students; on-campus housing not available to married students. *Student services:* Campus employment opportunities, career counseling, exercise/wellness program, free psychological counseling, international student services. *Library facilities:* J. W. Martin Library plus 1 other. *Online resources:* library catalog, web page, access to other libraries' catalogs. *Collection:* 344,640 titles, 3,990 serial subscriptions, 3,609 audiovisual materials.

Computer facilities: 172 computers available on campus for general student use. A campuswide network can be accessed from student residence rooms and from off campus. Online class registration is available. *Web address:* http://www.nwosu.edu/.

General Application Contact: Debbie Skinner, Coordinator of Graduate Studies, 580-327-8410, E-mail: dgskinner@nwosu.edu.

GRADUATE UNITS

School of Professional Studies Students: 46 full-time (28 women), 133 part-time (107 women); includes 20 minority (3 African Americans, 10 American Indian/Alaska Native, 1 Asian American or Pacific Islander, 6 Hispanic Americans), 1 international. Average age 31. 137 applicants, 100% accepted. *Faculty:* 48 full-time (25 women), 24 part-time/adjunct (17 women). Expenses: Contact institution. *Financial support:* Federal Work-Study available. Support available to part-time students. Financial award application deadline: 5/1; financial award applicants required to submit FAFSA. In 2008, 63 master's awarded. *Degree program information:* Part-time programs available. Offers counseling psychology (MCP); elementary education (M Ed); guidance and counseling K–12 (M Ed); reading specialist (M Ed); secondary education (M Ed). *Application deadline:* Applications are processed on a rolling basis.

Northwestern Oklahoma State University (continued)

Application fee: $15. *Application Contact:* Debbie Skinner, Coordinator of Graduate Studies, 580-327-8410, E-mail: dgskinner@nwosu.edu. *Dean,* Dr. James Bowen, 580-327-8455.

NORTHWESTERN POLYTECHNIC UNIVERSITY, Fremont, CA 94539-7482

General Information Independent, coed, comprehensive institution. *Enrollment:* 824 graduate, professional, and undergraduate students; 685 full-time matriculated graduate/professional students (238 women), 65 part-time matriculated graduate/professional students (29 women). *Enrollment by degree level:* 689 master's, 61 doctoral. *Graduate faculty:* 17 full-time (1 woman), 43 part-time/adjunct (2 women). *Tuition:* Full-time $12,150; part-time $450 per unit. *Required fees:* $210; $70 per trimester. *Graduate housing:* Room and/or apartments available on a first-come, first-served basis to single students; on-campus housing not available to married students. Typical cost: $4800 per year. Room charges vary according to housing facility selected. Housing application deadline: 7/15. *Student services:* Campus employment opportunities, career counseling, exercise/wellness program, free psychological counseling, international student services, low-cost health insurance, multicultural affairs office, services for students with disabilities, writing training. *Library facilities:* Northwest Polytechnic University Library. *Online resources:* library catalog, web page. *Collection:* 12,000 titles, 200 serial subscriptions.

Computer facilities: 200 computers available on campus for general student use. A campuswide network can be accessed from student residence rooms and from off campus. Online class registration, online learning resource services are available. *Web address:* http://www.npu.edu/.

General Application Contact: Michael Tang, Director of Admissions, 510-592-9688 Ext. 15, Fax: 510-657-8975, E-mail: Michael@npu.edu.

GRADUATE UNITS

School of Business and Information Technology Students: 261 full-time (138 women), 32 part-time (16 women). Average age 28. 423 applicants, 94% accepted, 103 enrolled. *Faculty:* 10 full-time (1 woman), 16 part-time/adjunct (2 women). Expenses: Contact institution. *Financial support:* In 2008–09, 8 teaching assistantships with partial tuition reimbursements (averaging $2,400 per year) were awarded; career-related internships or fieldwork and unspecified assistantships also available. In 2008, 91 master's awarded. *Degree program information:* Part-time and evening/weekend programs available. Offers business and information technology (MBA). *Application deadline:* For fall admission, 8/31 priority date for domestic students, 8/3 priority date for international students; for spring admission, 1/4 priority date for domestic students, 12/6 priority date for international students. Applications are processed on a rolling basis. *Application fee:* $60 ($30 for international students). *Application Contact:* Michael Tang, Director of Admissions, 510-592-9688 Ext. 15, Fax: 510-657-8975, E-mail: Michael@npu.edu. *Dean,* Paul Jensen, 510-592-9688 Ext. 16, Fax: 510-657-8975, E-mail: npuadm@npu.edu.

School of Engineering Students: 424 full-time (100 women), 33 part-time (13 women). Average age 28. 1,357 applicants, 96% accepted, 191 enrolled. *Faculty:* 9 full-time (0 women), 27 part-time/adjunct (0 women). Expenses: Contact institution. *Financial support:* In 2008–09, 160 teaching assistantships with full and partial tuition reimbursements (averaging $1,000 per year) were awarded; career-related internships or fieldwork and unspecified assistantships also available. In 2008, 268 master's awarded. *Degree program information:* Part-time and evening/weekend programs available. Offers computer science (MS); computer systems engineering (MS); electrical engineering (MS). *Application deadline:* For fall admission, 8/31 priority date for domestic students, 8/3 priority date for international students; for spring admission, 1/4 priority date for domestic students, 12/6 priority date for international students. Applications are processed on a rolling basis. *Application fee:* $60. *Application Contact:* Michael Tang, Director of Admissions, 510-592-9688 Ext. 15, Fax: 510-657-8975, E-mail: Michael@npu.edu. *Dean,* Dr. Pochang Hsu, 510-592-9688 Ext. 16, Fax: 510-657-8975, E-mail: npuadm@npu.edu.

NORTHWESTERN STATE UNIVERSITY OF LOUISIANA, Natchitoches, LA 71497

General Information State-supported, coed, comprehensive institution. CGS member. *Enrollment:* 9,111 graduate, professional, and undergraduate students; 207 full-time matriculated graduate/professional students (146 women), 674 part-time matriculated graduate/professional students (551 women). *Enrollment by degree level:* 793 master's, 88 other advanced degrees. *Graduate housing:* Rooms and/or apartments available on a first-come, first-served basis to single and married students. Housing application deadline: 7/30. *Student services:* Campus employment opportunities, campus safety program, career counseling, exercise/wellness program, free psychological counseling, low-cost health insurance, services for students with disabilities. *Library facilities:* Eugene P. Watson Memorial Library. *Online resources:* library catalog, web page, access to other libraries' catalogs. *Collection:* 778,085 titles, 1,183 serial subscriptions, 3,397 audiovisual materials. *Research affiliation:* NASA (strategic defense initiative), Central State Hospital, Federal Records and Archives Services.

Computer facilities: A campuswide network can be accessed from student residence rooms and from off campus. Online class registration is available. *Web address:* http://www.nsula.edu/.

General Application Contact: Dr. Steven G. Horton, Associate Provost/Dean, Graduate Studies, Research, and Information Systems, 318-357-5851, Fax: 318-357-5019, E-mail: gradschool@nsula.edu.

GRADUATE UNITS

Graduate Studies and Research Students: 207 full-time (146 women), 674 part-time (551 women); includes 179 minority (167 African Americans, 6 American Indian/Alaska Native, 2 Asian Americans or Pacific Islanders, 4 Hispanic Americans), 5 international. Average age 34. 367 applicants, 99% accepted, 275 enrolled. *Faculty:* 80 full-time (40 women), 20 part-time/adjunct (16 women). Expenses: Contact institution. *Financial support:* Fellowships, research assistantships with tuition reimbursements, teaching assistantships with tuition reimbursements, career-related internships or fieldwork, Federal Work-Study, and tuition waivers (partial) available. Support available to part-time students. Financial award application deadline: 7/15. In 2008, 222 master's, 16 other advanced degrees awarded. *Degree program information:* Part-time and evening/weekend programs available. Postbaccalaureate distance learning degree programs offered (no on-campus study). Offers clinical psychology (MS); English (MA); health and human performance (MS); heritage resources (MA). *Application deadline:* For fall admission, 8/1 priority date for domestic students; for spring admission, 1/10 for domestic students. Applications are processed on a rolling basis. *Application fee:* $20 ($30 for international students). Electronic applications accepted. *Application Contact:* Dr. Steven G. Horton, Associate Provost/Dean, Graduate Studies, Research, and Information Systems, 318-357-5851, Fax: 318-357-5019, E-mail: grad_school@nsula.edu. *Associate Provost/Dean, Graduate Studies, Research, and Information Systems,* Dr. Steven G. Horton, 318-357-5851, Fax: 318-357-5019, E-mail: grad_school@nsula.edu.

College of Education Students: 74 full-time (66 women), 461 part-time (379 women); includes 120 minority (117 African Americans, 2 American Indian/Alaska Native, 1 Asian American or Pacific Islander), 1 international. Average age 35. 196 applicants, 100% accepted, 147 enrolled. *Faculty:* 25 full-time (14 women), 9 part-time/adjunct (6 women). Expenses: Contact institution. *Financial support:* Career-related internships or fieldwork and Federal Work-Study available. Financial award application deadline: 7/15. In 2008, 144 master's, 16 other advanced degrees awarded. Offers adult and continuing education (M Ed); business and distributive education (M Ed); counseling (M Ed, Ed S); counseling and guidance (M Ed, Ed S); curriculum and instruction (M Ed); early childhood education (M Ed); early childhood education and teaching (M Ed); education (M Ed, MA, MAT, Ed S); education leadership (M Ed); educational leadership (Ed S); educational technology (M Ed, Ed S); educational technology leadership (M Ed); elementary education (MAT); elementary teaching (M Ed, Ed S); English education (M Ed); home economics education (M Ed); mathematics education (M Ed); middle school education (MAT); reading (M Ed, Ed S); school counseling (MA); science education (M Ed); secondary education (MAT); secondary teaching (M Ed, Ed S); social sciences education (M Ed); special education (MA); student personnel services (MA); teacher education and professional development, specific levels and methods (M Ed). *Application deadline:* For fall admission, 8/1 priority date for domestic students; for spring admission, 1/10 for domestic students. Applications are processed on a rolling basis. *Application fee:* $20 ($30 for international students). *Application Contact:* Dr. Steven G. Horton, Associate Provost/Dean, Graduate Studies, Research, and Information Systems, 318-357-5851, Fax: 318-357-5019, E-mail: grad_school@nsula.edu. *Chair,* Dr. Vickie Gentry, 318-357-6288, Fax: 318-357-6275, E-mail: education@nsula.edu.

College of Nursing Students: 18 full-time (all women), 165 part-time (143 women); includes 26 minority (22 African Americans, 2 American Indian/Alaska Native, 1 Asian American or Pacific Islander, 1 Hispanic American). Average age 34. 77 applicants, 100% accepted, 60 enrolled. *Faculty:* 10 full-time (all women), 7 part-time/adjunct (all women). Expenses: Contact institution. *Financial support:* Career-related internships or fieldwork and Federal Work-Study available. Support available to part-time students. Financial award application deadline: 7/15. In 2008, 37 master's awarded. *Degree program information:* Part-time programs available. Offers nursing (MSN). *Application deadline:* For fall admission, 8/1 priority date for domestic students; for spring admission, 1/10 for domestic students. Applications are processed on a rolling basis. *Application fee:* $20 ($30 for international students). *Application Contact:* Dr. Steven G. Horton, Associate Provost/Dean, Graduate Studies, Research, and Information Systems, 318-357-5851, Fax: 318-357-5019, E-mail: grad_school@nsula.edu. *Director,* Dr. Norann Planchock, 318-677-3100, Fax: 318-676-7887, E-mail: planchockn@alpha.nsula.edu.

School of Creative and Performing Arts Students: 21 full-time (4 women), 1 (woman) part-time; includes 6 minority (all African Americans), 3 international. Average age 30. 9 applicants, 100% accepted, 5 enrolled. *Faculty:* 20 full-time (3 women), 1 (woman) part-time/adjunct. Expenses: Contact institution. *Financial support:* Career-related internships or fieldwork and Federal Work-Study available. Support available to part-time students. Financial award application deadline: 7/15. In 2008, 9 master's awarded. Offers art (MA); fine and graphic arts (MA); music (MM). *Application deadline:* For fall admission, 8/1 priority date for domestic students; for spring admission, 1/10 for domestic students. Applications are processed on a rolling basis. *Application fee:* $20 ($30 for international students). *Application Contact:* Dr. Steven G. Horton, Associate Provost/Dean, Graduate Studies, Research, and Information Systems, 318-357-5851, Fax: 318-357-5019, E-mail: grad_school@nsula.edu. *Chairman,* William E. Brent, 318-357-4522, Fax: 318-357-5906, E-mail: brent@alpha.nsula.edu.

NORTHWESTERN UNIVERSITY, Evanston, IL 60208

General Information Independent, coed, university. CGS member. *Graduate housing:* Rooms and/or apartments available on a first-come, first-served basis to single students and available to married students. Housing application deadline: 9/1. *Research affiliation:* Amoco Oil Company (materials science and engineering), Dow Chemical Company (materials science and engineering), E. I. du Pont de Nemours and Company (physics), Exxon Chemical Company (chemical engineering), Ford Motor Company (mechanical engineering), Medtronics, Inc. (cardiology).

GRADUATE UNITS

The Graduate School *Degree program information:* Part-time and evening/weekend programs available. Offers African studies (Certificate); biochemistry, molecular biology, and cell biology (PhD); biotechnology (PhD); cell and molecular biology (PhD); clinical investigation (MSCI, Certificate); clinical psychology (PhD); counseling psychology (MA); developmental biology and genetics (PhD); genetic counseling (MS); hormone action and signal transduction (PhD); law and social science (Certificate); liberal studies (MA); literature (MA); management and organizations and sociology (PhD); marital and family therapy (MS); mathematical methods in social science (MS); neuroscience (PhD); public health (MPH); structural biology, biochemistry, and biophysics (PhD). DPT offered through the Medical School; MSC offered through the School of Speech. Electronic applications accepted.

Center for International and Comparative Studies Offers international and comparative studies (Certificate).

Institute for Neuroscience Offers neuroscience (PhD). Admissions and degree offered through The Graduate School.

Judd A. and Marjorie Weinberg College of Arts and Sciences *Degree program information:* Part-time and evening/weekend programs available. Offers anthropology (PhD); art history (PhD); arts and sciences (MA, MFA, MS, PhD, Certificate); astrophysics (PhD); brain, behavior and cognition (PhD); chemistry (PhD); clinical psychology (PhD); cognitive psychology (PhD); comparative literary studies (PhD); economics (MA, PhD); eighteenth-century studies (Certificate); English (MA, PhD); French (PhD); French and comparative literature (PhD); geological sciences (MS, PhD); German literature and critical thought (PhD); history (PhD); Italian studies (Certificate); linguistics (MA, PhD); mathematics (PhD); neurobiology and physiology (MS); personality (PhD); philosophy (PhD); physics (MS, PhD); political science (MA, PhD); Slavic languages and literature (PhD); social psychology (PhD); sociology (PhD); statistics (MS, PhD); visual arts (MFA).

Kellogg School of Management *Degree program information:* Part-time and evening/weekend programs available. Offers accounting (PhD); business administration (MBA); finance (PhD); management (MBA, PhD); management and organizations (PhD); managerial economics and strategy (PhD); marketing (PhD). PhD admissions and degree offered through The Graduate School. Electronic applications accepted.

School of Communication *Degree program information:* Part-time programs available. Offers audiology and hearing sciences (MA, PhD); clinical audiology (Au D); communication (MA, MFA, MSC, Au D, PhD); communication studies (MA, PhD); communication systems strategy and management (MSC); directing (MFA); learning disabilities (MA, PhD); managerial communication (MSC); performance studies (MA, PhD); radio/television/film (MA, MFA, PhD); speech and language pathology (MA, PhD); speech and language pathology and learning disabilities (MA); stage design (MFA); theatre (MA); theatre and drama (PhD). MA, MFA, and PhD admissions and degrees offered through The Graduate School; MSC admissions and degrees offered through the School of Speech.

School of Education and Social Policy Students: 156 full-time (117 women), 159 part-time (127 women); includes 56 minority (16 African Americans, 1 American Indian/Alaska Native, 30 Asian Americans or Pacific Islanders, 9 Hispanic Americans), 13 international. *Faculty:* 43 full-time (15 women), 64 part-time/adjunct (34 women). Expenses: Contact institution. *Financial support:* In 2008–09, 41 fellowships with full tuition reimbursements (averaging $25,308 per year), 17 research assistantships with full tuition reimbursements (averaging $25,308 per year), 15 teaching assistantships with full tuition reimbursements (averaging $25,308 per year) were awarded; career-related internships or fieldwork, Federal Work-Study, institutionally sponsored loans, scholarships/grants, and tuition waivers (partial) also available. Financial award application deadline: 1/15; financial award applicants required to submit FAFSA. In 2008, 88 master's, 11 doctorates awarded. *Degree program information:* Part-time and evening/weekend programs available. Offers advanced teaching (MS); education and social policy (MS); elementary education and policy (MS); higher education administration (MS); human development and social policy (PhD); learning and organizational change (MS); learning sciences (MA, PhD); secondary teaching (MS). MA and PhD admissions and degrees offered through The Graduate School. Electronic applications accepted. *Application Contact:* 847-491-3790, Fax: 847-491-4664, E-mail: sesp@northwestern.edu. *Graduate Student Administrative Liaison,* Mark P. Hoffman, 847-491-3790, Fax: 847-491-4664, E-mail: markhoffman@northwestern.edu.

Henry and Leigh Bienen School of Music Offers collaborative arts (DM); conducting (MM, DM); jazz (MM); music (MM, DM, PhD, CP); music composition (DM); music education (MM, PhD); music technology (MM); music technology/new media (DM); music theory (MM, PhD); musicology (MM, PhD); performance (MM); piano performance (MM, DM, CP); piano performance and collaborative arts (MM); piano performance and pedagogy (MM); string performance and pedagogy (MM); strings (MM, DM); strings, winds and percussion (CP); voice (MM, DM, CP); winds and percussion (MM, DM). PhD admissions and degree offered through The Graduate School. Electronic applications accepted.

Law School Students: 781 full-time (347 women); includes 302 minority (72 African Americans, 9 American Indian/Alaska Native, 145 Asian Americans or Pacific Islanders, 76 Hispanic Americans), 50 international. Average age 26. 4,868 applicants, 18% accepted, 242 enrolled. *Faculty:* 100 full-time (43 women), 68 part-time/adjunct (13 women). Expenses: Contact institution. *Financial support:* In 2008–09, 771 students received support, including 246 fellowships (averaging $20,000 per year); career-related internships or fieldwork, Federal Work-Study, institutionally sponsored loans, and scholarships/grants also available. Financial award application deadline: 2/15; financial award applicants required to submit FAFSA. In 2008, 254 JDs awarded. Offers executive (LL M); international human rights (LL M); law (JD, LL M); tax (LL M in Tax); two-year accelerated (JD). *Application deadline:* For fall admission, 2/15 for domestic students, 2/1 for international students. Applications are processed on a rolling basis. *Application fee:* $100. Electronic applications accepted. *Application Contact:* Johann H. Lee, Assistant Dean of Admissions and Financial Aid, 312-503-8465, Fax: 312-503-0178, E-mail: johann@law.northwestern.edu. *Dean,* David Van Zandt, 312-503-3100, Fax: 847-467-1035.

McCormick School of Engineering and Applied Science *Degree program information:* Part-time and evening/weekend programs available. Offers applied mathematics (MS, PhD); biomedical engineering (MS, PhD); chemical engineering (MS, PhD); computational biology and bioinformatics (MS); computer science (MS, PhD); electrical and computer engineering (MS, PhD); electronic materials (MS, PhD, Certificate); engineering and applied science (MEM, MIT, MME, MMM, MPD, MS, PhD, Certificate); engineering management (MEM); environmental engineering and science (MS, PhD); fluid mechanics (MS, PhD); geotechnical engineering (MS, PhD); industrial engineering and management science (MS, PhD); information technology (MIT); manufacturing engineering (MME); materials science and engineering (MS, PhD); mechanical engineering (MS, PhD); mechanics of materials and solids (MS, PhD); operations research (MS, PhD); project management (MS); solid mechanics (MS, PhD); structural engineering and materials (MS, PhD); theoretical and applied mechanics (MS, PhD); transportation systems analysis and planning (MS, PhD). MS and PhD admissions and degrees offered through The Graduate School. Electronic applications accepted.

Segal Design Institute Offers engineering design and innovation (MS).

Medill School of Journalism Offers advertising/sales promotion (MSIMC); broadcast journalism (MSJ); direct database and e-commerce marketing (MSIMC); general studies (MSIMC); integrated marketing communications (MSIMC); magazine publishing (MSJ); new media (MSJ); public relations (MSIMC); reporting and writing (MSJ). Electronic applications accepted.

Northwestern University Feinberg School of Medicine Offers cancer biology (PhD); cell biology (PhD); clinical investigation (MSCI); developmental biology (PhD); evolutionary biology (PhD); immunology and microbial pathogenesis (PhD); medicine (MD, MS, MSCI, DPT, PhD); molecular biology and genetics (PhD); movement and rehabilitation science (PhD); neurobiology (PhD); pharmacology and toxicology (PhD); physical therapy (DPT); structural biology and biochemistry (PhD). Electronic applications accepted.

NORTHWEST MISSOURI STATE UNIVERSITY, Maryville, MO 64468-6001

General Information State-supported, coed, comprehensive institution. *Graduate housing:* Room and/or apartments available on a first-come, first-served basis to single students; on-campus housing not available to married students. Housing application deadline: 7/1.

GRADUATE UNITS

Graduate School *Degree program information:* Part-time programs available. Electronic applications accepted.

College of Arts and Sciences *Degree program information:* Part-time programs available. Offers arts and sciences (MA, MS, MS Ed, Certificate); biology (MS); English (MA); English with speech emphasis (MA); geographic information sciences (MS, Certificate); history (MA); teaching English (option 1) (MS Ed); teaching English with speech emphasis (MS Ed); teaching history (MS Ed); teaching mathematics (MS Ed); teaching music (MS Ed); teaching: science (MS Ed). Electronic applications accepted.

College of Education and Human Services *Degree program information:* Part-time programs available. Offers applied health science (MS); education and human services (MS, MS Ed, Certificate, Ed S); educational leadership (MS Ed, Ed S); educational leadership: elementary (MS Ed); educational leadership: secondary (MS Ed); elementary principalship (Ed S); English language learners (Certificate); guidance and counseling (MS Ed); health and physical education (MS Ed); higher education leadership (MS); reading (MS Ed); recreation (MS); secondary individualized prescribed programs (MS Ed); secondary principalship (Ed S); special education (MS Ed); superintendency (Ed S); teaching secondary (MS Ed); teaching: early childhood (MS Ed); teaching: elementary self contained (MS Ed); teaching: English language learners (MS Ed); teaching: middle school (MS Ed). Electronic applications accepted.

Melvin and Valorie Booth College of Business and Professional Studies *Degree program information:* Part-time programs available. Offers accounting (MBA); agricultural economics (MBA); agriculture (MS); applied computer science (MS); business administration (MBA); business and professional studies (MBA, MS, MS Ed, Certificate); health management (MBA); information technology management (MBA); instructional technology (Certificate); quality (MBA, MS); quality management (Certificate); teaching agriculture (MS Ed); teaching instructional technology (MS Ed). Electronic applications accepted.

NORTHWEST NAZARENE UNIVERSITY, Nampa, ID 83686-5897

General Information Independent-religious, coed, comprehensive institution. *Enrollment:* 1,939 graduate, professional, and undergraduate students; 478 full-time matriculated graduate/professional students (251 women), 137 part-time matriculated graduate/professional students (92 women). *Enrollment by degree level:* 55 first professional, 560 master's. *Graduate faculty:* 48 full-time (19 women), 72 part-time/adjunct (25 women). *Graduate housing:* Rooms and/or apartments available on a first-come, first-served basis to single students and available to married students. Housing application deadline: 4/1. *Student services:* Career counseling, free psychological counseling, multicultural affairs office, teacher training. *Library facilities:* John E. Riley Library. *Online resources:* library catalog, web page, access to other libraries' catalogs. *Collection:* 10,026 titles, 821 serial subscriptions.

Computer facilities: Computer purchase and lease plans are available. 400 computers available on campus for general student use. A campuswide network can be accessed from student residence rooms and from off campus. Online class registration, various software packages are available. *Web address:* http://www.nnu.edu/.

General Application Contact: Dr. Mark Maddix, Director, Graduate Studies, 208-467-8817, Fax: 208-467-8252, E-mail: mamaddix@nnu.edu.

GRADUATE UNITS

Graduate Studies Students: 467 full-time (243 women), 117 part-time (76 women); includes 43 minority (11 African Americans, 5 American Indian/Alaska Native, 10 Asian Americans or Pacific Islanders, 17 Hispanic Americans), 2 international. Average age 34. *Faculty:* 45 full-time (18 women), 72 part-time/adjunct (25 women). Expenses: Contact institution. *Financial support:* In 2008–09, 193 students received support. Career-related internships or fieldwork available. In 2008, 158 master's awarded. *Degree program information:* Part-time and evening/weekend programs available. Offers business administration (MBA); Christian education (MA); community counseling (MS); curriculum and instruction (M Ed); educational leadership (M Ed); exceptional child (M Ed); marriage and family counseling (MS); missional leadership (MA); pastoral ministry (MA); reading education (M Ed); religion (M Div); school counseling (M Ed, MS); social work (MSW); spiritual formation (MA). *Application deadline:* Applications are processed on a rolling basis. *Application fee:* $50. Electronic applications accepted. *Application Contact:* Jill Jones, Program Assistant, 208-467-8368, Fax: 208-467-8252, E-mail: jdjones@nnu.edu. *Director, Graduate Studies,* Dr. Mark Maddix, 208-467-8817, Fax: 208-467-8252, E-mail: mamaddix@nnu.edu.

NORTHWEST UNIVERSITY, Kirkland, WA 98033

General Information Independent-religious, coed, comprehensive institution. *Enrollment:* 1,290 graduate, professional, and undergraduate students; 140 full-time matriculated graduate/professional students (97 women), 36 part-time matriculated graduate/professional students (20 women). *Enrollment by degree level:* 176 master's. *Graduate faculty:* 1 full-time (0 women), 21 part-time/adjunct (8 women). *Graduate housing:* Rooms and/or apartments available on a first-come, first-served basis to single and married students. *Student services:* Campus employment opportunities, campus safety program, career counseling, free psychological counseling, international student services, low-cost health insurance, services for students with disabilities. *Library facilities:* D. V. Hurst Library. *Online resources:* library catalog, web page. *Collection:* 129,721 titles, 12,458 serial subscriptions, 1,446 audiovisual materials.

Computer facilities: 88 computers available on campus for general student use. A campuswide network can be accessed from student residence rooms and from off campus. Online class registration is available. *Web address:* http://www.northwestu.edu/.

General Application Contact: Roy Rowland, Director of Graduate and Professional Studies Enrollment, 425-889-7787, Fax: 425-803-3059, E-mail: gpse@northwestu.edu.

GRADUATE UNITS

College of Social and Behavioral Sciences Students: 82 full-time (70 women), 6 part-time (5 women); includes 9 minority (5 African Americans, 2 Asian Americans or Pacific Islanders, 2 Hispanic Americans), 2 international. 108 applicants, 69% accepted, 54 enrolled. *Faculty:* 1 full-time (0 women), 7 part-time/adjunct (4 women). Expenses: Contact institution. *Financial support:* In 2008–09, 2 students received support. Career-related internships or fieldwork, health care benefits, and interational student scholarships available. Financial award application deadline: 6/30. In 2008, 28 master's awarded. *Degree program information:* Evening/weekend programs available. Offers counseling psychology (MA); international care and community development (MA). *Application deadline:* For fall admission, 12/1 priority date for domestic and international students; for spring admission, 4/1 priority date for domestic and international students. Applications are processed on a rolling basis. *Application fee:* $75. *Application Contact:* Sara Bickerstaff, Student Services Coordinator, 425-889-5249, Fax: 425-739-4602, E-mail: sara.bickerstaff@northwestu.edu. *Dean,* Dr. William Herkelrath, 425-889-5328, Fax: 425-739-4602, E-mail: william.herkelrath@northwestu.edu.

School of Business and Management Students: 25 full-time (6 women), 3 part-time (1 woman); includes 6 minority (2 African Americans, 3 Asian Americans or Pacific Islanders, 1 Hispanic American), 2 international. Average age 34. 15 applicants, 73% accepted, 8 enrolled. *Faculty:* 4 part-time/adjunct (3 women). Expenses: Contact institution. *Financial support:* Federal Work-Study, scholarships/grants, health care benefits, and tuition waivers (full) available. Financial award applicants required to submit FAFSA. In 2008, 11 master's awarded. *Degree program information:* Evening/weekend programs available. Offers business and management (MBA). *Application deadline:* For fall admission, 8/1 for domestic and international students; for spring admission, 12/1 for domestic and international students. Applications are processed on a rolling basis. *Application fee:* $75. Electronic applications accepted. *Application Contact:* Roy Rowland, Director of Graduate and Professional Studies Enrollment, 425-889-5213, Fax: 425-803-3059, E-mail: roy.rowland@northwestu.edu. *Dean,* Dr. Teresa Gillespie, 425-889-5290, E-mail: teresa.gillespie@northwestu.edu.

School of Education Students: 24 full-time (19 women), 9 part-time (all women); includes 6 minority (1 African American, 5 Asian Americans or Pacific Islanders). 53 applicants, 83% accepted, 32 enrolled. *Faculty:* 5 part-time/adjunct (2 women). Expenses: Contact institution. *Financial support:* Federal Work-Study and health care benefits available. In 2008, 25 master's awarded. *Degree program information:* Part-time and evening/weekend programs available. Offers education (M Ed); teaching (MIT). *Application deadline:* For fall admission, 3/1 priority date for domestic students. Applications are processed on a rolling basis. *Application fee:* $75. *Application Contact:* Pam Skolrud, Coordinator and Certification Specialist, 425-889-5299, Fax: 425-889-6332, E-mail: pam.skolrud@northwestu.edu. *Dean,* Dr. Gary Newbill, 425-889-5272, E-mail: gary.newbill@northwestu.edu.

NORTHWOOD UNIVERSITY, Midland, MI 48640-2398

General Information Independent, coed, comprehensive institution. *Graduate housing:* Room and/or apartments available on a first-come, first-served basis to single students. Housing application deadline: 8/30. *Research affiliation:* Motor & Equipment Manufacturers Association (automotive), Specialized Equipment Manufacturers Association (automotive), Automotive Aftermarket Industry Association (automotive), Automotive Warehouse Distributors Association (automotive).

GRADUATE UNITS

Richard DeVos Graduate School of Management *Degree program information:* Part-time and evening/weekend programs available. Offers management (EMBA, MBA, MMBA). Electronic applications accepted.

NORWICH UNIVERSITY, Northfield, VT 05663

General Information Independent, coed, primarily men, comprehensive institution. *Enrollment:* 1,250 full-time matriculated graduate/professional students (438 women), 3 part-time matriculated graduate/professional students (1 woman). *Enrollment by degree level:* 1,228 master's, 1,253 other advanced degrees. *Graduate faculty:* 2 full-time (0 women), 173 part-time/adjunct (34 women). *Tuition:* Full-time $16,000. Full-time tuition and fees vary according to degree level and program. *Graduate housing:* On-campus housing not available. *Student services:* Services for students with disabilities. *Library facilities:* Kreitzberg Library. *Online resources:* library catalog, web page, access to other libraries' catalogs. *Collection:* 280,000 titles, 904 serial subscriptions, 1,501 audiovisual materials.

Computer facilities: 200 computers available on campus for general student use. A campuswide network can be accessed from student residence rooms and from off campus. *Web address:* http://www.norwich.edu/.

General Application Contact: Sally Burkart, Administrative Assistant, 802-485-2567, Fax: 802-485-2533, E-mail: sburkart@norwich.edu.

GRADUATE UNITS

School of Graduate Studies Students: 1,477 full-time (407 women), 28 part-time (6 women); includes 176 minority (68 African Americans, 7 American Indian/Alaska Native, 47 Asian Americans or Pacific Islanders, 54 Hispanic Americans), 1 international. Average age 36. 1,895 applicants, 95% accepted, 1250 enrolled. *Faculty:* 2 full-time (0 women), 199 part-time/adjunct (31 women). Expenses: Contact institution. *Financial support:* Scholarships/grants available. Financial award applicants required to submit FAFSA. In 2008, 802 master's awarded. *Degree program information:* Evening/weekend programs available. Offers business administration (MBA); civil engineering (MCE); corrections administration (MJA); information assurance (MS); international commerce (MA); international conflict management (MA); international terrorism (MA); justice administration (MJA); law administration (MJA); military history (MA); nursing administration (MSN); organizational leadership (MSOL); public administration (MPA). *Application deadline:* For fall admission, 8/10 for domestic and international students; for winter admission, 11/7 for domestic and international students; for spring admission, 2/6 for domestic and international students. *Application fee:* $50. Electronic applications accepted. *Application Contact:* Shelley W. Brown, Administrative Director of Admissions and Marketing, 802-485-2784, Fax: 802-485-2533, E-mail: sbrown@norwich.edu. *Dean,* Dr. William Clemments, 802-485-2730.

NOTRE DAME COLLEGE, South Euclid, OH 44121-4293

General Information Independent-religious, coed, comprehensive institution. *Graduate housing:* On-campus housing not available.

GRADUATE UNITS

Graduate Studies *Degree program information:* Part-time and evening/weekend programs available. Offers accounting (Certificate); creative critical thinking (M Ed); financial services management (Certificate); information systems (Certificate); learning disabilities (M Ed); management (Certificate); paralegal (Certificate); pastoral ministry (Certificate); reading (M Ed); teacher education (Certificate).

NOTRE DAME DE NAMUR UNIVERSITY, Belmont, CA 94002-1908

General Information Independent-religious, coed, comprehensive institution. *Enrollment:* 1,478 graduate, professional, and undergraduate students; 153 full-time matriculated graduate/professional students (121 women), 524 part-time matriculated graduate/professional students (410 women). *Enrollment by degree level:* 471 master's, 206 other advanced degrees. *Graduate faculty:* 28 full-time (13 women), 63 part-time/adjunct (44 women). *Tuition:* Part-time $699 per unit. *Required fees:* $3 per unit. $35 per semester. *Graduate housing:* Rooms and/or apartments available on a first-come, first-served basis to single and married students. Housing application deadline: 7/1. *Student services:* Campus employment opportunities, campus safety program, career counseling, free psychological counseling, international student services, low-cost health insurance, multicultural affairs office, services for students with disabilities, teacher training, writing training. *Library facilities:* The Carl Gellert and Celia Berta Gellert Library. *Online resources:* library catalog, web page, access to other libraries' catalogs. *Collection:* 91,389 titles, 12,500 serial subscriptions, 9,122 audiovisual materials.

Computer facilities: 80 computers available on campus for general student use. A campuswide network can be accessed from student residence rooms. Online class registration is available. *Web address:* http://www.ndnu.edu/.

General Application Contact: Candace Hallmark, Assistant Director of Graduate Admissions, 650-508-3592, Fax: 650-508-3426, E-mail: grad.admit@ndnu.edu.

GRADUATE UNITS

Division of Academic Affairs Students: 153 full-time (121 women), 524 part-time (410 women); includes 169 minority (13 African Americans, 1 American Indian/Alaska Native, 73 Asian Americans or Pacific Islanders, 82 Hispanic Americans), 31 international. Average age 35. 310 applicants, 77% accepted, 182 enrolled. *Faculty:* 28 full-time (13 women), 63 part-time/adjunct (44 women). Expenses: Contact institution. *Financial support:* Career-related internships or fieldwork and scholarships/grants available. Support available to part-time students. Financial award applicants required to submit FAFSA. In 2008, 182 master's, 109 other advanced degrees awarded. *Degree program information:* Part-time and evening/weekend programs available. *Application deadline:* For fall admission, 8/1 priority date for domestic students; for spring admission, 12/1 priority date for domestic students. Applications are processed on a rolling basis. *Application fee:* $60. Electronic applications accepted. *Application Contact:* Candace Hallmark, Director of Graduate Admissions, 650-508-3592, Fax: 650-508-3426, E-mail: grad.admit@ndnu.edu. *Interim Provost,* Dr. Richard Giardina, 650-508-3506, Fax: 650-508-3495, E-mail: rgiardina@ndnu.edu.

School of Arts and Humanities Students: 11 full-time (9 women), 20 part-time (15 women); includes 6 minority (2 Asian Americans or Pacific Islanders, 4 Hispanic Americans), 2 international. Average age 35. 12 applicants, 100% accepted, 9 enrolled. *Faculty:* 8 full-time (4 women), 13 part-time/adjunct (7 women). Expenses: Contact institution. *Financial support:* Applicants required to submit FAFSA. In 2008, 19 master's awarded. *Degree program information:* Part-time programs available. Offers arts and humanities (MA, MFA, MM, Certificate); English (MA); music (MFA, MM); pedagogy (MM); performance (MM); teaching English to speakers of other languages (Certificate). *Application deadline:* For fall admission, 8/1 for domestic students; for spring admission, 12/1 for domestic students. *Application fee:* $60. *Application Contact:* Candace Hallmark, Assistant Director of Graduate Admissions, 650-508-3592, Fax: 650-508-3426, E-mail: grad.admit@ndnu.edu. *Dean,* Dr. Arnell R. Etherington, 650-508-3485, E-mail: aetherington@ndnu.edu.

School of Business and Management Students: 28 full-time (22 women), 144 part-time (89 women); includes 78 minority (4 African Americans, 4 American Indian/Alaska Native, 32 Asian Americans or Pacific Islanders, 38 Hispanic Americans), 12 international. Average age 33. 56 applicants, 100% accepted, 40 enrolled. *Faculty:* 8 full-time (1 woman), 8 part-time/adjunct (2 women). Expenses: Contact institution. *Financial support:* Scholarships/grants available. Support available to part-time students. In 2008, 60 master's awarded. *Degree program information:* Part-time programs available. Offers business administration (MBA); business and management (MBA, MPA, MSM); finance (MBA); human resource management (MBA); management (MSM); managing with information technology (MSM); marketing (MBA); operations management (MSM); project and program management (MSM); public administration (MPA); public affairs administration (MPA). *Application deadline:* For fall admission, 8/1 for domestic students; for spring admission, 12/1 for domestic students. *Application fee:* $60. *Application Contact:* Candace Hallmark, Director of Graduate Admissions, 650-508-3592, Fax: 650-508-3426, E-mail: grad.admit@ndnu.edu. *Dean,* Dr. James Fogal, 650-508-3601, E-mail: jfogal@ndnu.edu.

School of Education and Leadership Students: 98 full-time (75 women), 236 part-time (184 women); includes 53 minority (6 African Americans, 2 American Indian/Alaska Native, 17 Asian Americans or Pacific Islanders, 28 Hispanic Americans), 2 international. Average age 36. 142 applicants, 98% accepted, 123 enrolled. *Faculty:* 8 full-time (5 women), 16 part-time/adjunct (13 women). Expenses: Contact institution. *Financial support:* Applicants required to submit FAFSA. In 2008, 49 master's, 109 other advanced degrees awarded. *Degree program information:* Part-time programs available. Offers education (MA); education and leadership (MA, MAT, Certificate); multiple subject teaching credential (Certificate); reading (MA, Certificate); school administration (MA, Certificate); single subject teaching credential (Certificate); special education (MA, Certificate); teaching (MAT). *Application deadline:* For fall admission, 8/1 for domestic students; for spring admission, 12/1 for domestic students. *Application fee:* $60. *Application Contact:* Candace Hallmark, Director of Graduate Admissions, 650-508-3592, Fax: 650-508-3426, E-mail: grad.admit@ndnu.edu. *Dean,* Dr. Joanne Rossi, 650-508-3613, E-mail: jrossi@ndnu.edu.

School of Sciences Students: 73 full-time (68 women), 127 part-time (115 women); includes 53 minority (7 African Americans, 24 Asian Americans or Pacific Islanders, 22 Hispanic Americans), 5 international. Average age 34. 69 applicants, 90% accepted, 45 enrolled. *Faculty:* 4 full-time (3 women), 14 part-time/adjunct (12 women). Expenses: Contact institution. *Financial support:* Available to part-time students. Applicants required to submit FAFSA. In 2008, 54 master's, 3 other advanced degrees awarded. *Degree program information:* Part-time programs available. Offers art therapy psychology (MAAT, MAMFT); clinical gerontology (Certificate); clinical psychology (MA); marital and family therapy (MAMFT); premedical studies (Certificate); sciences (MA, MAAT, MACP, MAMFT, Certificate). *Application deadline:* For fall admission, 8/1 for domestic students; for spring admission, 12/1 for domestic students. *Application fee:* $60. *Application Contact:* Candace Hallmark, Assistant Director of Graduate Admissions, 650-508-3592, Fax: 650-508-3426, E-mail: grad.admit@ndnu.edu. *Dean,* Dr. Arnell Etherington, 650-508-3485, E-mail: aetherington@ndnu.edu.

NOTRE DAME SEMINARY, New Orleans, LA 70118-4391

General Information Independent-religious, coed, primarily men, graduate-only institution.

GRADUATE UNITS

Graduate School of Theology *Degree program information:* Part-time programs available. Offers theology (M Div, MA).

NOVA SCOTIA AGRICULTURAL COLLEGE, Truro, NS B2N 5E3, Canada

General Information Province-supported, coed, comprehensive institution. *Enrollment:* 65 full-time matriculated graduate/professional students (36 women), 13 part-time matriculated graduate/professional students (8 women). *Enrollment by degree level:* 78 master's. *Graduate faculty:* 56 full-time (11 women), 23 part-time/adjunct (1 woman). *Graduate housing:* Room and/or apartments available on a first-come, first-served basis to single students; on-campus housing not available to married students. Typical cost: $7272 Canadian dollars per year. Housing application deadline: 6/30. *Student services:* Campus employment opportunities, campus safety program, career counseling, child daycare facilities, exercise/wellness program, free psychological counseling, international student services, low-cost health insurance, services for students with disabilities, teacher training, writing training. *Library facilities:* MacRae Library. *Collection:* 23,000 titles, 800 serial subscriptions. *Research affiliation:* Atlantic BioVenture Centre (bio-products, bio-resources, value-added), Bio-Environmental Engineering Centre (resource and environmental sciences), Performance Genomics, Inc. (animal genomics), Organic Agriculture Centre of Canada (organic agriculture), Atlantic Poultry Research Institute (poultry), Crop Development Institute (crop physiology/horticulture).

Computer facilities: 110 computers available on campus for general student use. A campuswide network can be accessed. Online class registration is available. *Web address:* http://www.nsac.ns.ca/.

General Application Contact: Heather A Hughes, Manager, Research and Graduate Studies, 902-893-6360, Fax: 902-893-3430, E-mail: hhughes@nsac.ca.

GRADUATE UNITS

Research and Graduate Studies Students: 65 full-time (36 women), 13 part-time (8 women); includes 26 minority (25 Asian Americans or Pacific Islanders, 1 Hispanic American). Average age 25. *Faculty:* 56 full-time (11 women), 23 part-time/adjunct (1 woman). Expenses: Contact institution. *Financial support:* In 2008–09, 61 students received support, including 18 fellowships (averaging $16,500 per year), 43 research assistantships (averaging $16,500 per year), 16 teaching assistantships (averaging $1,200 per year); career-related internships or fieldwork, scholarships/grants, health care benefits, and unspecified assistantships also available. In 2008, 17 master's awarded. *Degree program information:* Part-time programs available. Offers agriculture (M Sc). *Application deadline:* For fall admission, 6/1 for domestic students, 4/1 priority date for international students; for winter admission, 10/31 for domestic students, 8/31 priority date for international students; for spring admission, 2/28 for domestic students, 12/31 priority date for international students. Applications are processed on a rolling basis. *Application fee:* $70. *Application Contact:* Marie Law, Administrative Assistant, 902-893-6502, Fax: 902-893-3430, E-mail: mlaw@nsac.ca. *Manager,* Heather A Hughes, 902-893-6360, Fax: 902-893-3430, E-mail: hhughes@nsac.ca.

NOVA SOUTHEASTERN UNIVERSITY, Fort Lauderdale, FL 33314-7796

General Information Independent, coed, university. CGS member. *Enrollment:* 28,378 graduate, professional, and undergraduate students; 9,891 full-time matriculated graduate/professional students (6,859 women), 12,588 part-time matriculated graduate/professional students (9,052 women). *Enrollment by degree level:* 3,617 first professional, 10,962 master's, 6,314 doctoral, 1,577 other advanced degrees. *Graduate housing:* Rooms and/or apartments guaranteed to single and married students. *Student services:* Campus employment opportunities, campus safety program, career counseling, exercise/wellness program, free psychological counseling, international student services, low-cost health insurance, services for students with disabilities, teacher training. *Library facilities:* Alvin Sherman Library, Research, and Information Technology Center plus 4 others. *Online resources:* library catalog, web page, access to other libraries' catalogs. *Collection:* 725,000 titles, 22,295 serial subscriptions, 23,738 audiovisual materials.

Computer facilities: 2,708 computers available on campus for general student use. A campuswide network can be accessed from student residence rooms and from off campus. Online class registration is available. *Web address:* http://www.nova.edu/.

General Application Contact: Information Contact, 800-541-6682, E-mail: nsuinfo@nsu.nova.edu.

GRADUATE UNITS

Center for Psychological Studies Students: 827 full-time (706 women), 662 part-time (591 women); includes 631 minority (283 African Americans, 5 American Indian/Alaska Native, 31 Asian Americans or Pacific Islanders, 312 Hispanic Americans), 27 international. 1,433 applicants, 49% accepted, 520 enrolled. *Faculty:* 34 full-time (11 women), 68 part-time/adjunct (32 women). Expenses: Contact institution. *Financial support:* In 2008–09, 5 research assistantships, 34 teaching assistantships (averaging $1,000 per year) were awarded; career-related internships or fieldwork, Federal Work-Study, institutionally sponsored loans, scholarships/grants, and unspecified assistantships also available. Support available to part-time students. Financial award application deadline: 4/1. In 2008, 340 master's, 77 doctorates, 20 other advanced degrees awarded. Postbaccalaureate distance learning degree programs offered. Offers clinical pharmacology (MS); clinical psychology (PhD, Psy D, SPS); mental health counseling (MS); psychological studies (MS, PhD, Psy D, Psy S, SPS); school guidance and counseling (MS); school psychology (Psy S). *Application deadline:* Applications are processed on a rolling basis. *Application fee:* $50. Electronic applications accepted. *Application Contact:* Carlos Perez, Enrollment Management, 954-262-5790, Fax: 954-262-3893, E-mail: cpsinfo@cps.nova.edu. *Dean,* Karen Grosby, 954-262-5701, Fax: 954-262-3859, E-mail: grosby@nova.edu.

Criminal Justice Institute Students: 15 full-time (12 women), 191 part-time (133 women); includes 140 minority (104 African Americans, 2 American Indian/Alaska Native, 2 Asian Americans or Pacific Islanders, 32 Hispanic Americans), 1 international. 41 applicants, 73% accepted, 30 enrolled. *Faculty:* 41 part-time/adjunct (7 women). Expenses: Contact institution. In 2008, 51 master's awarded. *Degree program information:* Part-time and evening/weekend programs available. Offers criminal justice (MHS, MS). *Application deadline:* For fall admission, 7/8 for domestic and international students; for winter admission, 1/8 for domestic and international students; for spring admission, 3/8 for domestic and international students. Applications are processed on a rolling basis. *Application fee:* $50. Electronic applications accepted. *Application Contact:* Russell Garner, Administrative Assistant, 954-262-7001, E-mail: cji@nova.edu. *Director,* Dr. Tammy Kushner, 954-262-7001, Fax: 954-937-7005, E-mail: kushner@nova.edu.

Fischler School of Education and Human Services Students: 4,031 full-time (3,175 women), 6,099 part-time (5,075 women); includes 5,366 minority (3,997 African Americans, 33 American Indian/Alaska Native, 114 Asian Americans or Pacific Islanders, 1,222 Hispanic Americans), 227 international. Average age 38. 4,354 applicants, 65% accepted, 2078 enrolled. *Faculty:* 105 full-time (55 women), 438 part-time/adjunct (266 women). Expenses: Contact institution. *Financial support:* In 2008–09, 6,903 students received support, including 2 fellowships with full tuition reimbursements available (averaging $30,000 per year); career-related internships or fieldwork, Federal Work-Study, and tuition waivers (full) also available. Support available to part-time students. Financial award application deadline: 4/15; financial award applicants required to submit FAFSA. In 2008, 2,044 master's, 579 doctorates, 682 other advanced degrees awarded. *Degree program information:* Part-time and evening/weekend programs available. Offers adult education (Ed D); athletic administration (MS); brain research (MS, Ed S); charter school education/leadership (MS); child and youth studies (Ed D); child protection (MHS); cognitive and behavioral disabilities (MS); computer science education (Ed S); computer science education (K-12) (MS); computing and information technology (Ed D); curriculum and teaching (Ed S); curriculum, instruction and technology (MS); curriculum, instruction, management and administration (Ed S); early childhood education (MS); early literacy and reading (Ed S); early literacy education (MS); education (MS); education and human services (MA, MHS, MS, Ed D, SLPD, Ed S); education technology (MS); educational leaders (Ed D); educational leadership (Ed D); educational leadership (administration K–12) (MS, Ed S); educational media (Ed S); educational media (K-12) (MS); elementary education (MS, Ed S); English education (MS, Ed S); environmental education (MS); exceptional student education (MS); gifted education (MS, Ed S); health care education (Ed D); health professions education (MS); higher education (Ed D); higher education leadership (Ed D); human services administration (Ed D); instructional leadership (Ed D); instructional technology and distance education (MS, Ed D); interdisciplinary arts education (MS); leadership (MS); management and administration of educational programs (MS); mathematics (MS); mathematics education (Ed S); multicultural early intervention (MS); organizational leadership (Ed D); pre-kindergarten/primary (MS); preschool education (MS); reading (MS); reading and TESOL (MS); reading education (Ed S); science (MS); science education (Ed S); secondary education (MS); social studies (MS, Ed S); Spanish language (MS); special education (Ed D); special education and reading (MS); speech language pathology (Ed D); speech-language pathology (MS, SLPD); substance abuse counseling and education (MS); teaching and learning (MA, MS); teaching English to speakers of other languages (MS, Ed S); technology management and administration (Ed S); urban studies education (MS); vocational, occupational and technical education (Ed D). *Application deadline:* Applications are processed on a rolling basis. *Application fee:* $50. Electronic applications accepted. *Application Contact:* Dr. Jennifer Quinones Nottingham, Dean of Student Affairs, 800-986-3223 Ext. 8500, E-mail: jlquinon@nova.edu. *Provost/Dean*, Dr. H. Wells Singleton, 954-262-8730, Fax: 954-262-3894, E-mail: singlew@nova.edu.

Graduate School of Computer and Information Sciences Students: 92 full-time (27 women), 823 part-time (222 women); includes 336 minority (155 African Americans, 6 American Indian/Alaska Native, 71 Asian Americans or Pacific Islanders, 104 Hispanic Americans), 41 international. Average age 41. *Faculty:* 20 full-time (5 women), 21 part-time/adjunct (3 women). Expenses: Contact institution. *Financial support:* Federal Work-Study, scholarships/grants, and unspecified assistantships available. Support available to part-time students. Financial award application deadline: 5/1. In 2008, 180 master's, 32 doctorates awarded. *Degree program information:* Part-time and evening/weekend programs available. Postbaccalaureate distance learning degree programs offered (no on-campus study). Offers computer information systems (MS, PhD); computer science (MS, PhD); computing technology in education (PhD); information security (MS); information systems (MS, PhD); management information systems (MS). *Application deadline:* Applications are processed on a rolling basis. *Application fee:* $50. Electronic applications accepted. *Application Contact:* 954-262-2000, Fax: 954-262-2752, E-mail: scisinfo@nova.edu. *Interim Dean*, Dr. Amon Seagull, PhD, 954-262-7300.

Graduate School of Humanities and Social Sciences Students: 313 full-time (238 women), 277 part-time (211 women); includes 293 minority (187 African Americans, 2 American Indian/Alaska Native, 15 Asian Americans or Pacific Islanders, 89 Hispanic Americans), 34 international. Average age 37. 250 applicants, 89% accepted, 147 enrolled. *Faculty:* 18 full-time (10 women), 13 part-time/adjunct (4 women). Expenses: Contact institution. *Financial support:* In 2008–09, 393 students received support, including 15 research assistantships (averaging $15,600 per year), 3 teaching assistantships (averaging $1,000 per year); career-related internships or fieldwork, Federal Work-Study, scholarships/grants, unspecified assistantships, and clinical assistantships also available. Financial award application deadline: 4/1; financial award applicants required to submit CSS PROFILE. In 2008, 87 master's, 18 doctorates awarded. *Degree program information:* Part-time and evening/weekend programs available. Postbaccalaureate distance learning degree programs offered (minimal on-campus study). Offers college student affairs (MS); college student personnel administration (Certificate); conflict analysis and resolution (MS, PhD); conflict analysis and resolution studies (Certificate); cross-disciplinary studies (MA); family studies (Certificate); family systems healthcare (Certificate); family therapy (MS, DMFT, PhD, Certificate); health care conflict resolution (Certificate); humanities and social sciences (MA, MS, DMFT, PhD, Certificate); marriage and family therapy (DMFT); peace studies (Certificate); qualitative research (Certificate). *Application deadline:* For fall admission, 7/1 priority date for domestic and international students; for winter admission, 11/1 priority date for domestic and international students; for spring admission, 3/1 priority date for domestic and international students. Applications are processed on a rolling basis. *Application fee:* $50. Electronic applications accepted. *Application Contact:* Marcia Arango, Student Recruitment Coordinator, 954-262-3006, Fax: 954-262-3968, E-mail: marango@nsu.nova.edu. *Dean*, Honggang Yang, PhD, 954-262-3016, Fax: 954-262-3968, E-mail: yangh@nova.edu.

Health Professions Division Students: 3,188 full-time (1,890 women), 790 part-time (573 women); includes 1,664 minority (276 African Americans, 12 American Indian/Alaska Native, 688 Asian Americans or Pacific Islanders, 688 Hispanic Americans), 78 international. Expenses: Contact institution. *Financial support:* Fellowships, teaching assistantships, career-related internships or fieldwork, Federal Work-Study, institutionally sponsored loans, scholarships/grants, and unspecified assistantships available. Support available to part-time students. In 2008, 638 first professional degrees, 128 master's, 122 doctorates awarded. Postbaccalaureate distance learning degree programs offered (minimal on-campus study). Offers health professions (DMD, DO, OD, Pharm D, MBS, MH Sc, MMS, MOT, MPH, MS, MSN, Au D, DHSc, DPT, OTD, PhD, TDPT). *Application deadline:* Applications are processed on a rolling basis. *Application fee:* $50. *Application Contact:* Information Contact, 800-541-6682, E-mail: nsuinfo@nsu.nova.edu. *Chancellor*, Dr. Frederick Lippman, 954-262-1100 Ext. 1507.

College of Allied Health and Nursing Students: 618 full-time (456 women), 534 part-time (390 women); includes 338 minority (132 African Americans, 3 American Indian/Alaska Native, 84 Asian Americans or Pacific Islanders, 119 Hispanic Americans), 17 international. *Faculty:* 43 full-time (25 women), 8 part-time/adjunct (4 women). Expenses: Contact institution. *Financial support:* Teaching assistantships, institutionally sponsored loans and unspecified assistantships available. In 2008, 80 master's, 122 doctorates awarded. Postbaccalaureate distance learning degree programs offered (minimal on-campus study). Offers allied health and nursing (MH Sc, MMS, MOT, MSN, Au D, DHSc, DPT, OTD, PhD, TDPT); audiology (Au D); health science (MH Sc, DHSc); medical science/physician assistant (MMS); nursing (MSN, PhD); occupational therapy (MOT, OTD, PhD); physical therapy (DPT, PhD, TDPT). *Application deadline:* Applications are processed on a rolling basis. *Application fee:* $50. *Application Contact:* Marla Frolinger, Admissions Counselor, 954-262-1100, E-mail: marlaf@nova.edu. *Dean*, Dr. Richard Davis, 954-262-1203, E-mail: redavis@nova.edu.

College of Dental Medicine Students: 498 full-time (237 women), 4 part-time (1 woman); includes 189 minority (12 African Americans, 1 American Indian/Alaska Native, 76 Asian Americans or Pacific Islanders, 100 Hispanic Americans), 24 international. Average age 24. 2,774 applicants, 6% accepted, 105 enrolled. *Faculty:* 83 full-time (23 women), 200 part-time/adjunct (44 women). Expenses: Contact institution. *Financial support:* In 2008–09, 372 students received support, including 1 fellowship with full tuition reimbursement available, 11 teaching assistantships with full tuition reimbursements available. Financial award application deadline: 4/3; financial award applicants required to submit FAFSA. In 2008, 92 first professional degrees, 3 master's awarded. Offers dental medicine (DMD); dentistry (MS). *Application deadline:* For fall admission, 1/15 for domestic students, 2/15 for international students. Applications are processed on a rolling basis. *Application fee:* $50. *Application Contact:* Su-Ann Zarrett, Associate Director, 954-262-1108, Fax: 954-262-2282, E-mail: zarrett@nsu.nova.edu. *Dean*, Dr. Robert A. Uchin, 954-262-7312, Fax: 954-262-1782, E-mail: ruchin@nova.edu.

College of Medical Sciences Students: 27 full-time (17 women), 2 part-time (1 woman); includes 22 minority (6 African Americans, 7 Asian Americans or Pacific Islanders, 9 Hispanic Americans). Average age 27. 108 applicants, 23% accepted. *Faculty:* 32 full-time (13 women), 4 part-time/adjunct (1 woman). Expenses: Contact institution. *Financial support:* Applicants required to submit FAFSA. In 2008, 9 master's awarded. Offers biomedical sciences (MBS). *Application deadline:* For spring admission, 4/15 for domestic students. Applications are processed on a rolling basis. *Application fee:* $50. *Application Contact:* Richard Wilson, Admissions Counselor, 954-262-1111, Fax: 954-262-1802, E-mail: rwilson@nsu.nova.edu. *Dean*, Dr. Harold E. Laubach, 954-262-1303, Fax: 954-262-1802, E-mail: harold@nsu.nova.edu.

College of Optometry Students: 341 full-time (226 women), 109 part-time (79 women); includes 184 minority (16 African Americans, 121 Asian Americans or Pacific Islanders, 47 Hispanic Americans), 18 international. Average age 23. 772 applicants, 25% accepted, 103 enrolled. *Faculty:* 44 full-time (28 women), 14 part-time/adjunct (10 women). Expenses: Contact institution. *Financial support:* In 2008–09, 378 students received support. Federal Work-Study, institutionally sponsored loans, and scholarships/grants available. In 2008, 90 first professional degrees, 5 master's awarded. Postbaccalaureate distance learning degree programs offered (no on-campus study). Offers clinical vision research (MS); optometry (OD). *Application deadline:* For fall admission, 4/1 for domestic and international students. Applications are processed on a rolling basis. *Application fee:* $50. Electronic applications accepted. *Application Contact:* Fran Franconeri, Admissions Counselor, 954-262-1132, Fax: 954-262-2282. *Dean*, Dr. David Loshin, 954-262-1404, Fax: 954-262-1818.

College of Osteopathic Medicine Students: 935 full-time (459 women), 45 part-time (32 women); includes 348 minority (43 African Americans, 5 American Indian/Alaska Native, 196 Asian Americans or Pacific Islanders, 104 Hispanic Americans), 7 international. 3,386 applicants, 11% accepted, 232 enrolled. *Faculty:* 74 full-time (29 women), 887 part-time/adjunct (177 women). Expenses: Contact institution. *Financial support:* In 2008–09, 598 students received support, including 12 fellowships with partial tuition reimbursements available; research assistantships, teaching assistantships, career-related internships or fieldwork, Federal Work-Study, institutionally sponsored loans, and scholarships/grants also available. Financial award application deadline: 6/1; financial award applicants required to submit FAFSA. In 2008, 207 first professional degrees, 34 master's awarded. Offers osteopathic medicine (DO); public health (MPH). *Application deadline:* For fall admission, 1/15 for domestic students. Applications are processed on a rolling basis. *Application fee:* $50. Electronic applications accepted. *Application Contact:* Rachel Weiner, Associate Director of Admissions, 954-262-1113. *Dean*, Dr. Anthony J. Silavgni, 954-262-1407, E-mail: silvagni@hpd.nova.edu.

College of Pharmacy Students: 690 full-time (458 women), 66 part-time (54 women); includes 535 minority (54 African Americans, 3 American Indian/Alaska Native, 186 Asian Americans or Pacific Islanders, 292 Hispanic Americans), 10 international. Average age 25. 1,177 applicants, 22% accepted, 189 enrolled. *Faculty:* 52 full-time (32 women), 9 part-time/adjunct (3 women). Expenses: Contact institution. *Financial support:* Career-related internships or fieldwork, Federal Work-Study, institutionally sponsored loans, and scholarships/grants available. Financial award application deadline: 4/15; financial award applicants required to submit FAFSA. In 2008, 249 Pharm Ds awarded. Postbaccalaureate distance learning degree programs offered (minimal on-campus study). Offers pharmacy (Pharm D). *Application deadline:* For fall admission, 3/1 for domestic students, 2/1 for international students. Applications are processed on a rolling basis. *Application fee:* $50. Electronic applications accepted. *Application Contact:* Tracy Templin, Admissions Counselor, 954-262-1112, Fax: 954-262-2282, E-mail: dpetracy@nsu.nova.edu. *Dean*, Dr. Andres Malave, 954-262-1300, Fax: 954-262-2278.

H. Wayne Huizenga School of Business and Entrepreneurship Students: 379 full-time (235 women), 3,561 part-time (2,116 women); includes 2,451 minority (1,206 African Americans, 9 American Indian/Alaska Native, 164 Asian Americans or Pacific Islanders, 1,072 Hispanic Americans), 186 international. Average age 38. 1,062 applicants, 73% accepted, 545 enrolled. *Faculty:* 44 full-time (13 women), 137 part-time/adjunct (32 women). Expenses: Contact institution. *Financial support:* In 2008–09, 2 students received support. Federal Work-Study and scholarships/grants available. Support available to part-time students. Financial award applicants required to submit FAFSA. In 2008, 976 master's, 52 doctorates awarded. *Degree program information:* Part-time and evening/weekend programs available. Postbaccalaureate distance learning degree programs offered (minimal on-campus study). Offers accounting (DBA); business administration (MBA); business and entrepreneurship (M Acc, M Tax, MBA, MIBA, MPA, MS, MSHRM, DBA); entrepreneurship (MBA); finance (DBA); human resource management (DBA); human resources management (MSHRM); international business (DBA); international business administration (MIBA); leadership (MS); management (DBA); operations management (DBA); public administration (MPA); real estate development (MS); taxation (M Tax). *Application deadline:* Applications are processed on a rolling basis. *Application fee:* $50. Electronic applications accepted. *Application Contact:* Karen Goldberg, Assistant Director, 954-262-5039, Fax: 954-262-3822, E-mail: karen@nova.edu. *Dean*, Dr. Randolph A. Pohlman, 954-262-5005, E-mail: pohlman@huizenga.nova.edu.

Oceanographic Center Students: 72 full-time (43 women), 100 part-time (68 women); includes 13 minority (2 African Americans, 1 American Indian/Alaska Native, 2 Asian Americans or Pacific Islanders, 8 Hispanic Americans), 3 international. Average age 30. 82 applicants, 91% accepted, 49 enrolled. *Faculty:* 15 full-time (1 woman), 5 part-time/adjunct (0 women). Expenses: Contact institution. *Financial support:* In 2008–09, 6 research assistantships (averaging $4,000 per year), 3 teaching assistantships (averaging $3,500 per year) were awarded; career-related internships or fieldwork, Federal Work-Study, scholarships/grants, tuition waivers (partial), and unspecified assistantships also available. Support available to part-time students. Financial award applicants required to submit FAFSA. In 2008, 31 master's, 1 doctorate awarded. *Degree program information:* Part-time and evening/weekend programs available. Offers coastal zone management (MS); marine biology (MS, PhD); marine biology and oceanography (PhD); marine environmental science (MS); oceanography (PhD); physical oceanography (MS). *Application deadline:* Applications are processed on a rolling basis. *Application fee:* $50. *Application Contact:* Dr. Richard Spieler, Director of Academic Programs, 954-262-3600, Fax: 954-262-4020, E-mail: spieler@nova.edu. *Dean*, Dr. Richard Dodge, 954-262-3600, Fax: 954-262-4020, E-mail: dodge@nsu.nova.edu.

Shepard Broad Law Center Students: 967 full-time (529 women), 122 part-time (93 women); includes 309 minority (71 African Americans, 7 American Indian/Alaska Native, 41 Asian Americans or Pacific Islanders, 190 Hispanic Americans), 15 international. 2,855 applicants, 45% accepted, 384 enrolled. *Faculty:* 63 full-time (35 women), 48 part-time/adjunct (18 women). Expenses: Contact institution. *Financial support:* In 2008–09, 58 fellowships were awarded; research assistantships, teaching assistantships, Federal Work-Study, scholarships/grants, tuition waivers (full and partial), and unspecified assistantships also available. Support available to part-time students. Financial award application deadline: 4/15; financial award applicants required to submit FAFSA. In 2008, 253 first professional degrees, 23 master's awarded. *Degree program information:* Part-time and evening/weekend programs available. Postbaccalaureate distance learning degree programs offered (minimal on-campus study). Offers education law (MS, Certificate); employment law (MS); health law (MS); law (JD). *Application deadline:* For fall admission, 3/1 priority date for domestic students. Applications are processed on a rolling basis. *Application fee:* $50. Electronic applications accepted. *Application Contact:* Beth Hall, Assistant Dean of Admissions, 954-262-6121, Fax: 954-262-3844, E-mail: hallb@nsu.law.nova.edu. *Dean*, Joseph D. Harbaugh, 954-262-6105, Fax: 954-262-3834, E-mail: harbaughj@nsu.law.nova.edu.

NSCAD UNIVERSITY, Halifax, NS B3J 3J6, Canada

General Information Province-supported, coed, comprehensive institution. *Graduate housing:* On-campus housing not available.

GRADUATE UNITS

Program in Fine Arts Offers craft (MFA); design (M Des); fine and media arts (MFA).

NYACK COLLEGE, Nyack, NY 10960-3698

General Information Independent-religious, coed, comprehensive institution. *Graduate housing:* Rooms and/or apartments available on a first-come, first-served basis to single and married students. Housing application deadline: 9/1.

GRADUATE UNITS

Alliance Graduate School of Counseling Offers counseling (MA).

School of Education *Degree program information:* Part-time and evening/weekend programs available. Offers childhood education (MS); childhood special education (MS); inclusive education (MS).

School of Adult and Distance Education Offers organizational leadership (MS).

School of Business *Degree program information:* Evening/weekend programs available. Offers accounting (MBA); business administration (MBA).

OAKLAND CITY UNIVERSITY, Oakland City, IN 47660-1099

General Information Independent-religious, coed, comprehensive institution. *Graduate housing:* Rooms and/or apartments guaranteed to single students and available on a first-come, first-served basis to married students. Housing application deadline: 7/1.

GRADUATE UNITS

Chapman Seminary *Degree program information:* Part-time programs available. Offers religious studies (M Div, D Min).

School of Adult and Extended Learning *Degree program information:* Part-time and evening/weekend programs available. Offers management (MS Mgt).

School of Education and Technology Offers educational leadership (Ed D); teaching (MA).

OAKLAND UNIVERSITY, Rochester, MI 48309-4401

General Information State-supported, coed, university. CGS member. *Enrollment:* 18,169 graduate, professional, and undergraduate students; 1,224 full-time matriculated graduate/professional students (826 women), 2,307 part-time matriculated graduate/professional students (1,479 women). *Enrollment by degree level:* 2,699 master's, 722 doctoral, 107 other advanced degrees. *Graduate faculty:* 225 full-time (88 women), 86 part-time/adjunct (47 women).

Oakland University (continued)

Graduate housing: Rooms and/or apartments available on a first-come, first-served basis to single and married students. Housing application deadline: 9/1. *Student services:* Campus employment opportunities, campus safety program, career counseling, child daycare facilities, exercise/wellness program, free psychological counseling, international student services, low-cost health insurance, multicultural affairs office, services for students with disabilities. *Library facilities:* Kresge Library. *Online resources:* library catalog, web page, access to other libraries' catalogs. *Collection:* 856,760 titles, 20,490 serial subscriptions, 21,323 audiovisual materials. *Research affiliation:* Beaumont Hospital Corporation (eye research, nursing), Henry Ford Health Systems (medical physics).

Computer facilities: A campuswide network can be accessed from student residence rooms and from off campus. Online class registration is available. *Web address:* http://www.oakland.edu/.

General Application Contact: Katherine Z. Rowley, Associate Director of Graduate Study and Lifelong Learning, 248-370-3167, Fax: 248-370-4114, E-mail: kzrowley@oakland.edu.

GRADUATE UNITS

Graduate Study and Lifelong Learning Students: 1,224 full-time (826 women), 2,307 part-time (1,479 women); includes 429 minority (198 African Americans, 21 American Indian/Alaska Native, 147 Asian Americans or Pacific Islanders, 63 Hispanic Americans), 275 international. Average age 33. 1,897 applicants, 70% accepted, 1026 enrolled. *Faculty:* 225 full-time (88 women), 86 part-time/adjunct (47 women). Expenses: Contact institution. *Financial support:* Fellowships, research assistantships, teaching assistantships, career-related internships or fieldwork, Federal Work-Study, institutionally sponsored loans, and tuition waivers (full) available. Financial award application deadline: 3/1; financial award applicants required to submit FAFSA. In 2008, 930 master's, 62 doctorates, 159 other advanced degrees awarded. *Degree program information:* Part-time and evening/weekend programs available. *Application deadline:* For fall admission, 5/1 for international students; for winter admission, 9/1 for international students. Applications are processed on a rolling basis. *Application fee:* $0. Electronic applications accepted. *Application Contact:* Katherine Z. Rowley, Director of Graduate Admissions, 248-370-3167, Fax: 248-370-4114, E-mail: kzrowley@oakland.edu. *Executive Director*, Claire K. Rammel, 248-370-3159, Fax: 248-370-4114, E-mail: rammel@oakland.edu.

College of Arts and Sciences Students: 164 full-time (87 women), 171 part-time (105 women); includes 37 minority (16 African Americans, 3 American Indian/Alaska Native, 12 Asian Americans or Pacific Islanders, 6 Hispanic Americans), 41 international. Average age 33. 198 applicants, 74% accepted, 105 enrolled. *Faculty:* 64 full-time (16 women), 11 part-time/adjunct (7 women). Expenses: Contact institution. *Financial support:* Fellowships, research assistantships, teaching assistantships, career-related internships or fieldwork, Federal Work-Study, institutionally sponsored loans, and tuition waivers (full) available. Financial award application deadline: 3/1; financial award applicants required to submit FAFSA. In 2008, 85 master's, 8 doctorates, 1 other advanced degree awarded. *Degree program information:* Part-time and evening/weekend programs available. Offers applied mathematical sciences (PhD); applied statistics (MS); arts and sciences (MA, MM, MPA, MS, PhD, Certificate); biological sciences (MA, MS); biological sciences: health and environmental chemistry (PhD); biomedical sciences: biological communications (PhD); chemistry (MS); English (MA); history (MA); industrial applied mathematics (MS); liberal studies (MA); linguistics (MA); mathematics (MA); medical physics (PhD); music (MM); music education (PhD); physics (MS); public administration (MPA); statistical methods (Certificate); teaching English as a second language (Certificate). *Application deadline:* Applications are processed on a rolling basis. *Application fee:* $0. Electronic applications accepted. *Application Contact:* Katherine Z. Rowley, Director, Graduate Admissions, 248-370-3167, Fax: 248-370-4114, E-mail: kzrowley@oakland.edu. *Dean*, Ronald A. Sudol, 248-370-2140, Fax: 248-370-4280, E-mail: sudol@oakland.edu.

School of Business Administration Students: 103 full-time (41 women), 414 part-time (121 women); includes 75 minority (12 African Americans, 4 American Indian/Alaska Native, 47 Asian Americans or Pacific Islanders, 12 Hispanic Americans), 45 international. Average age 31. 175 applicants, 86% accepted, 142 enrolled. *Faculty:* 29 full-time (5 women), 10 part-time/adjunct (1 woman). Expenses: Contact institution. *Financial support:* Career-related internships or fieldwork, Federal Work-Study, institutionally sponsored loans, and tuition waivers (full) available. Financial award application deadline: 3/1; financial award applicants required to submit FAFSA. In 2008, 187 master's, 9 other advanced degrees awarded. *Degree program information:* Part-time and evening/weekend programs available. Offers accounting (M Acc, Certificate); business administration (M Acc, MBA, MS, Certificate); economics (Certificate); entrepreneurship (Certificate); finance (Certificate); general management (Certificate); human resource management (Certificate); information technology management (MS); international business (Certificate); management information systems (Certificate); marketing (Certificate); production and operations management (Certificate). *Application deadline:* For fall admission, 8/15 priority date for domestic students, 5/1 priority date for international students; for winter admission, 12/1 priority date for domestic students, 9/1 priority date for international students; for spring admission, 4/15 priority date for domestic students. Applications are processed on a rolling basis. *Application fee:* $35. Electronic applications accepted. *Application Contact:* Donna Free, Coordinator, 248-370-3281. *Dean*, Dr. Jonathan Silberman, 248-370-3286, Fax: 248-370-4974.

School of Education and Human Services Students: 484 full-time (418 women), 1,231 part-time (1,034 women); includes 199 minority (135 African Americans, 9 American Indian/Alaska Native, 26 Asian Americans or Pacific Islanders, 29 Hispanic Americans), 16 international. Average age 34. 685 applicants, 88% accepted, 495 enrolled. *Faculty:* 60 full-time (35 women), 49 part-time/adjunct (34 women). Expenses: Contact institution. *Financial support:* Career-related internships or fieldwork, Federal Work-Study, institutionally sponsored loans, and tuition waivers (full) available. Financial award application deadline: 3/1; financial award applicants required to submit FAFSA. In 2008, 443 master's, 13 doctorates, 139 other advanced degrees awarded. *Degree program information:* Part-time and evening/weekend programs available. Offers advanced microcomputer applications (Certificate); counseling (MA, PhD, Certificate); early childhood education (M Ed, PhD, Certificate); early mathematics education (Certificate); education and human services (M Ed, MA, MAT, MTD, PhD, Certificate, Ed S); education studies (M Ed); educational leadership (M Ed, PhD); higher education (Certificate); higher education administration (Certificate); human resource development (MTD); microcomputer applications (Certificate); reading (Certificate); reading and language arts (MAT); reading education (PhD); reading, language arts and literature (Certificate); school administration (Ed S); secondary education (MAT); special education (M Ed, Certificate). *Application deadline:* Applications are processed on a rolling basis. *Application fee:* $35. Electronic applications accepted. *Application Contact:* Christina J. Grabowski, Associate Director of Graduate Study and Lifelong Learning, 248-370-3167, Fax: 248-370-4114, E-mail: grabowsk@oakland.edu. *Dean*, Dr. Mary L. Otto, 248-370-3050, Fax: 248-370-4202, E-mail: otto@oakland.edu.

School of Engineering and Computer Science Students: 179 full-time (46 women), 283 part-time (51 women); includes 60 minority (7 African Americans, 2 American Indian/Alaska Native, 47 Asian Americans or Pacific Islanders, 4 Hispanic Americans), 120 international. Average age 32. 223 applicants, 84% accepted, 123 enrolled. *Faculty:* 29 full-time (6 women), 7 part-time/adjunct (0 women). Expenses: Contact institution. *Financial support:* Federal Work-Study, institutionally sponsored loans, and tuition waivers (full) available. Financial award application deadline: 3/1; financial award applicants required to submit FAFSA. In 2008, 149 master's, 13 doctorates awarded. *Degree program information:* Part-time and evening/weekend programs available. Offers computer science (MS); electrical and computer engineering (MS); embedded systems (MS); engineering and computer science (MS, PhD); engineering management (MS); information systems engineering (MS); mechanical engineering (MS, PhD); software engineering (MS); systems engineering (MS, PhD). *Application deadline:* For fall admission, 8/1 priority date for domestic students, 5/1 priority date for international students; for winter admission, 12/1 priority date for domestic students, 9/1 priority date for international students; for spring admission, 4/1 priority date for domestic students. Applications are processed on a rolling basis. *Application fee:* $0. Electronic applications accepted. *Application Contact:* Information Contact, 248-370-2233. *Dean*, Dr. Pieter A. Frick, 248-370-2217, Fax: 248-370-2217, E-mail: frick@oakland.edu.

School of Health Sciences Students: 191 full-time (142 women), 79 part-time (46 women); includes 20 minority (7 African Americans, 11 Asian Americans or Pacific Islanders, 2 Hispanic Americans), 51 international. Average age 28. 373 applicants, 36% accepted, 81 enrolled. *Faculty:* 16 full-time (8 women), 4 part-time/adjunct (1 woman). Expenses: Contact institution. *Financial support:* Fellowships, Federal Work-Study, institutionally sponsored loans, and tuition waivers (full) available. Financial award application deadline: 3/1; financial award applicants required to submit FAFSA. In 2008, 12 master's, 38 doctorates, 28 other advanced degrees awarded. Offers complimentary medicine and wellness (Certificate); exercise science (MS, Certificate); health sciences (MS, MSPT, DPT, Dr Sc PT, Certificate); neurological rehabilitation (Certificate); orthopedic manual physical therapy (Certificate); orthopedic physical therapy (Certificate); pediatric rehabilitation (Certificate); physical therapy (MSPT, DPT, Dr Sc PT); safety management (MS); teaching and learning for rehabilitation professionals (Certificate). *Application deadline:* For fall admission, 10/15 for domestic and international students. Applications are processed on a rolling basis. *Application fee:* $0. Electronic applications accepted. *Application Contact:* Christina J. Grabowski, Associate Director of Graduate Study and Lifelong Learning, 248-370-3167, Fax: 248-370-4114, E-mail: grabowsk@oakland.edu. *Dean*, Dr. Kenneth R. Hightower, 248-370-3562, Fax: 248-370-4227, E-mail: hightower@oakland.edu.

School of Nursing Students: 103 full-time (92 women), 129 part-time (122 women); includes 38 minority (21 African Americans, 3 American Indian/Alaska Native, 4 Asian Americans or Pacific Islanders, 10 Hispanic Americans), 2 international. Average age 39. 243 applicants, 46% accepted, 80 enrolled. *Faculty:* 21 full-time (18 women), 4 part-time/adjunct (3 women). Expenses: Contact institution. *Financial support:* Federal Work-Study, institutionally sponsored loans, and tuition waivers (full) available. Financial award application deadline: 3/1; financial award applicants required to submit FAFSA. In 2008, 39 master's, 22 doctorates, 3 other advanced degrees awarded. *Degree program information:* Part-time and evening/weekend programs available. Offers adult gerontological nurse practitioner (MSN, Certificate); adult health (MSN); family nurse practitioner (MSN, Certificate); nurse anesthetist (MSN, Certificate); nursing (MSN, DNP, Certificate); nursing education (MSN, Certificate); nursing practice (DNP). *Application fee:* $0. Electronic applications accepted. *Application Contact:* Mary Bray, Graduate Program Coordinator, 248-370-4482. *Dean*, Dr. Linda Thompson, 248-370-4081, Fax: 248-370-4279.

See Close-Up on page 961.

OAKWOOD UNIVERSITY, Huntsville, AL 35896

General Information Independent-religious, coed, upper-level institution.

GRADUATE UNITS

Program in Pastoral Studies Offers pastoral studies (MA).

OBERLIN COLLEGE, Oberlin, OH 44074

General Information Independent, coed, comprehensive institution. *Graduate housing:* Room and/or apartments available on a first-come, first-served basis to single students; on-campus housing not available to married students. Housing application deadline: 6/15.

GRADUATE UNITS

Conservatory of Music Offers music (MM, MMT, AD). Electronic applications accepted.

Graduate Teacher Education Program Offers early childhood education (M Ed); middle childhood education (M Ed).

OBLATE SCHOOL OF THEOLOGY, San Antonio, TX 78216-6693

General Information Independent-religious, coed, graduate-only institution. *Enrollment by degree level:* 74 first professional, 38 master's, 27 doctoral, 8 other advanced degrees. *Graduate faculty:* 24 full-time (7 women), 6 part-time/adjunct (1 woman). *Tuition:* Full-time $11,570; part-time $445 per credit hour. *Required fees:* $170 per semester. One-time fee: $85 full-time. Part-time tuition and fees vary according to course level and course load. *Graduate housing:* On-campus housing not available. *Student services:* Campus employment opportunities, international student services, writing training. *Collection:* 90,000 titles, 360 serial subscriptions.

Computer facilities: 10 computers available on campus for general student use. A campuswide network can be accessed from student residence rooms and from off campus. *Web address:* http://www.ost.edu/.

General Application Contact: James Oberhausen, Registrar, 210-341-1366 Ext. 212, Fax: 210-341-4519, E-mail: registrar@ost.edu.

GRADUATE UNITS

Graduate and Professional Programs Students: 91 full-time (5 women), 56 part-time (25 women); includes 62 minority (7 African Americans, 3 American Indian/Alaska Native, 13 Asian Americans or Pacific Islanders, 39 Hispanic Americans), 29 international. Average age 39. 33 applicants, 100% accepted, 33 enrolled. *Faculty:* 24 full-time (7 women), 6 part-time/adjunct (1 woman). Expenses: Contact institution. *Financial support:* Scholarships/grants available. Support available to part-time students. Financial award application deadline: 8/1; financial award applicants required to submit FAFSA. In 2008, 16 first professional degrees, 8 master's, 5 Certificates awarded. *Degree program information:* Part-time programs available. Offers divinity (M Div); Hispanic ministry (D Min); pastoral ministry (MAP Min); pastoral studies (Certificate); spirituality (MA Sp); supervision (D Min); theology (MA Th). *Application deadline:* For fall admission, 6/15 priority date for domestic and international students; for spring admission, 12/30 for domestic and international students. Applications are processed on a rolling basis. *Application fee:* $45. *Application Contact:* James Oberhausen, Director of Admission/Registrar, 210-341-1366 Ext. 212, Fax: 210-341-4519, E-mail: registrar@ost.edu. *Academic Dean*, Sr. Elaine Brothers, 210-341-1366, Fax: 214-341-4519, E-mail: ebrothers@ost.edu.

OCCIDENTAL COLLEGE, Los Angeles, CA 90041-3314

General Information Independent, coed, comprehensive institution. *Graduate housing:* On-campus housing not available.

GRADUATE UNITS

Graduate Studies *Degree program information:* Part-time programs available. Offers biology (MA); elementary education (MAT); English and comparative literary studies (MAT); history (MAT); liberal studies (MAT); life science (MAT); mathematics (MAT); physical science (MAT); secondary education (MAT); social science (MAT); Spanish (MAT).

OGI SCHOOL OF SCIENCE & ENGINEERING AT OREGON HEALTH & SCIENCE UNIVERSITY, Beaverton, OR 97006-8921

General Information State-related, coed, graduate-only institution. *Graduate housing:* On-campus housing not available. *Research affiliation:* Biospeech dnc (center for spoken language), GeoSyntech (environmental and biomolecular systems), Intel (computer science), Calpine Corporation (coastal land), HemCon Inc. (biomedical), Medical Research Foundation (biomedical spoken language, environmental and biomolecular).

GRADUATE UNITS

Graduate Studies *Degree program information:* Part-time and evening/weekend programs available. Offers biochemistry and molecular biology (MS, PhD); biomedical engineering (MS, PhD); computer science (PhD); computer science and engineering (MS, PhD); electrical engineering (MS, PhD); environmental health systems (MS); environmental information technology (MS, PhD); environmental science and engineering (MS, PhD); health care management (Certificate); management in science and technology (MS, Certificate). Electronic applications accepted.

Science and Technology Center for Coastal and Land Margin Research *Degree program information:* Part-time programs available. Offers coastal and land margin research (M Sc, PhD). Electronic applications accepted.

OGLALA LAKOTA COLLEGE, Kyle, SD 57752-0490

General Information State and locally supported, coed, comprehensive institution. *Graduate housing:* On-campus housing not available.

GRADUATE UNITS

Graduate Studies *Degree program information:* Part-time and evening/weekend programs available. Offers educational administration (MA); Lakota leadership and management (MA).

OGLETHORPE UNIVERSITY, Atlanta, GA 30319-2797

General Information Independent, coed, comprehensive institution. *Graduate housing:* On-campus housing not available.

GRADUATE UNITS

Division of Education *Degree program information:* Part-time programs available. Offers early childhood education (MAT).

OHIO COLLEGE OF PODIATRIC MEDICINE, Independence, OH 44131

General Information Independent, coed, graduate-only institution. *Enrollment by degree level:* 390 first professional. *Graduate faculty:* 14 full-time (5 women), 12 part-time/adjunct (5 women). *Tuition:* Full-time $26,000; part-time $1300 per credit hour. *Required fees:* $1200; $1200 per semester hour. $600 per semester. *Graduate housing:* On-campus housing not available. *Student services:* Campus employment opportunities, campus safety program, career counseling, exercise/wellness program, free psychological counseling, international student services, low-cost health insurance, services for students with disabilities. *Library facilities:* Morton & Norma Seidman Memorial Medical Library. *Online resources:* library catalog, web page. *Collection:* 19,496 titles, 96 serial subscriptions, 788 audiovisual materials. *Research affiliation:* N/A.

Computer facilities: 66 computers available on campus for general student use. A campuswide network can be accessed from off campus. Academic catalog, student handbook available. *Web address:* http://www.ocpm.edu/.

General Application Contact: Lois Lott, Dean of Student Affairs, 216-231-3300 Ext. 7485, Fax: 216-447-0210, E-mail: llott@ocpm.edu.

GRADUATE UNITS

Ohio College of Podiatric Medicine Students: 389 full-time (176 women), 1 part-time (0 women); includes 100 minority (72 African Americans, 1 American Indian/Alaska Native, 16 Asian Americans or Pacific Islanders, 11 Hispanic Americans), 3 international. Average age 27. 467 applicants, 32% accepted, 113 enrolled. *Faculty:* 14 full-time (5 women), 12 part-time/adjunct (5 women). Expenses: Contact institution. *Financial support:* In 2008–09, 46 students received support. Career-related internships or fieldwork, Federal Work-Study, institutionally sponsored loans, and scholarships/grants available. Financial award application deadline: 6/30; financial award applicants required to submit FAFSA. In 2008, 47 DPMs awarded. Offers podiatric medicine (DPM). *Application deadline:* For fall admission, 4/1 priority date for domestic students. Applications are processed on a rolling basis. *Application fee:* $50. Electronic applications accepted. *Application Contact:* Lois Lott, Dean of Student Affairs, 216-231-3300 Ext. 7485, Fax: 216-447-0210, E-mail: llott@ocpm.edu. *President,* Dr. Thomas Melillo, 216-231-3300.

OHIO DOMINICAN UNIVERSITY, Columbus, OH 43219-2099

General Information Independent-religious, coed, comprehensive institution. *Graduate housing:* Room and/or apartments available on a first-come, first-served basis to single students; on-campus housing not available to married students.

GRADUATE UNITS

Graduate Programs *Degree program information:* Part-time and evening/weekend programs available. Offers liberal studies (MA); TESOL (MA).

Division of Business *Degree program information:* Part-time and evening/weekend programs available. Offers business (MBA). Program also offered in Dayton, OH.

Division of Education *Degree program information:* Part-time and evening/weekend programs available. Offers education (M Ed).

Division of Theology, Arts and Ideas *Degree program information:* Part-time and evening/weekend programs available. Offers theology (MA).

OHIO NORTHERN UNIVERSITY, Ada, OH 45810-1599

General Information Independent-religious, coed, comprehensive institution. *Graduate housing:* Room and/or apartments available on a first-come, first-served basis to single students; on-campus housing not available to married students.

GRADUATE UNITS

Claude W. Pettit College of Law Offers law (JD, LL M). Electronic applications accepted.

Raabe College of Pharmacy Students: 1,046 full-time (629 women), 42 part-time; includes 57 minority (14 African Americans, 1 American Indian/Alaska Native, 38 Asian Americans or Pacific Islanders, 4 Hispanic Americans), 19 international. Average age 21. 915 applicants, 30% accepted, 175 enrolled. *Faculty:* 33 full-time (13 women), 30 part-time/adjunct. Expenses: Contact institution. *Financial support:* In 2008–09, 900 students received support. Federal Work-Study, institutionally sponsored loans, and scholarships/grants available. Financial award application deadline: 5/1; financial award applicants required to submit FAFSA. In 2008, 162 Pharm Ds awarded. Offers pharmacy (Pharm D). Students enter the program as undergraduates. *Application deadline:* For fall admission, 11/1 priority date for domestic students, 2/1 priority date for international students. *Application fee:* $30. Electronic applications accepted. *Application Contact:* Dr. Robert McCurdy, Assistant Dean and Director of Pharmacy Student Services, 419-772-2278, Fax: 419-772-3554, E-mail: r-mccurdy@onu.edu. *Dean,* Dr. Jon E Sprague, 419-772-2275, Fax: 419-772-3554, E-mail: j-sprague@onu.edu.

THE OHIO STATE UNIVERSITY, Columbus, OH 43210

General Information State-supported, coed, university. CGS member. *Graduate housing:* Rooms and/or apartments available to single students and available on a first-come, first-served basis to married students. *Research affiliation:* Children's Hospital (pediatrics), Transportation Research Center, Midwest Universities Consortium for International Activities, Science and Technology Campus, Ohio Learning Network (education).

GRADUATE UNITS

College of Dentistry Offers dentistry (DDS, MS, PhD); oral biology (PhD). Electronic applications accepted.

College of Medicine Offers medicine (MD, MOT, MPT, MS, PhD). Electronic applications accepted.

School of Allied Medical Professions *Degree program information:* Part-time programs available. Offers allied medicine (MS); circulation technology (MS); occupational therapy (MOT); physical therapy (MPT). Electronic applications accepted.

School of Biomedical Science Offers anatomy (MS, PhD); biomedical science (MD, MS, PhD); experimental pathobiology (MS); immunology (PhD); medical genetics (PhD); medical science (PhD); medicine (MD); molecular virology (PhD); molecular virology, immunology and medical genetics (MS, PhD); neuroscience (PhD); pathology assistant (MS); pharmacology (PhD). Electronic applications accepted.

College of Optometry Offers optometry (OD, MS, PhD); vision science (MS, PhD). Electronic applications accepted.

College of Pharmacy Expenses: Contact institution. *Financial support:* Fellowships with full tuition reimbursements, research assistantships with full tuition reimbursements, teaching assistantships with full tuition reimbursements, career-related internships or fieldwork, Federal Work-Study, institutionally sponsored loans, scholarships/grants, and traineeships available. *Degree program information:* Part-time programs available. Offers medicinal chemistry and pharmacognosy (MS, PhD); pharmaceutical administration (MS, PhD); pharmaceutics (MS, PhD); pharmacology (PhD); pharmacy (Pharm D, MS, PhD); pharmacy practice and administration (MS, PhD). *Application deadline:* For fall admission, 1/1 priority date for domestic students. *Application fee:* $40 ($50 for international students). Electronic applications accepted. *Application Contact:* Kathy I. Brooks, Graduate Program Coordinator, 614-292-6822, Fax: 614-292-2588, E-mail: brooks@pharmacy.ohio-state.edu. *Dean,* Dr. Robert W. Brueggemeier, 614-292-5711, Fax: 614-292-2435, E-mail: brueggemeier@pharmacy.ohio-state.edu.

College of Public Health Offers public health (MHA, MHROD, MPH, MS, PhD). Electronic applications accepted.

College of Veterinary Medicine Offers anatomy and cellular biology (MS, PhD); pathobiology (MS, PhD); pharmacology (MS, PhD); toxicology (MS, PhD); veterinary clinical sciences (MS, PhD); veterinary medicine (DVM, MS, PhD); veterinary physiology (MS, PhD); veterinary preventive medicine (MS, PhD). Electronic applications accepted.

Graduate School *Degree program information:* Part-time and evening/weekend programs available. Electronic applications accepted.

College of Biological Sciences *Degree program information:* Part-time programs available. Offers biochemistry (MS); biological sciences (MS, PhD); biophysics (MS, PhD); cell and developmental biology (MS, PhD); entomology (MS, PhD); environmental science (MS, PhD); evolution, ecology, and organismal biology (MS, PhD); genetics (MS, PhD); microbiology (MS, PhD); molecular biology (MS, PhD); molecular, cellular and developmental biology (MS, PhD); plant biology (MS, PhD). Electronic applications accepted.

College of Education and Human Ecology Offers education and human ecology (M Ed, MA, MS, PhD); educational policy and leadership (M Ed, MA, PhD); family and consumer sciences education (M Ed, MS); family resource management (MS, PhD); food service management (MS, PhD); foods (MS, PhD); higher education and student affairs (MA); hospitality management (MS, PhD); human development and family science (M Ed, MS, PhD); nutrition (MS, PhD); physical activity and educational services (M Ed, MA, PhD); teaching and learning (M Ed, MA, PhD); textiles and clothing (MS, PhD). Electronic applications accepted.

College of Engineering *Degree program information:* Part-time and evening/weekend programs available. Offers aeronautical and astronautical engineering (MS, PhD); architecture (M Arch, M Land Arch, MAS, MCRP, PhD); biomedical engineering (MS, PhD); chemical engineering (MS, PhD); city and regional planning (MCRP, PhD); civil engineering (MS, PhD); computer and information science (MS, PhD); computer science and engineering (MS); electrical engineering (MS, PhD); engineering (M Arch, M Land Arch, MAS, MCRP, MS, MWE, PhD); engineering mechanics (MS, PhD); engineering physics (MS, PhD); geodetic science and surveying (MS, PhD); industrial and systems engineering (MS, PhD); landscape architecture (M Land Arch); materials science and engineering (MS, PhD); mechanical engineering (MS, PhD); nuclear engineering (MS, PhD); welding engineering (MS, MWE, PhD). Electronic applications accepted.

College of Food, Agricultural, and Environmental Sciences *Degree program information:* Part-time programs available. Offers agricultural economics and rural sociology (MS, PhD); animal sciences (MS, PhD); environment and natural resources (MS, PhD); food science and nutrition (MS, PhD); food, agricultural, and biological engineering (MS, PhD); food, agricultural, and environmental sciences (M Ed, MS, PhD); horticulture and crop science (MS, PhD); human and community resource development (M Ed, MS, PhD); human dimensions in natural resources (MS, PhD); natural resources (MS, PhD); plant pathology (MS, PhD); rural sociology (MS, PhD); soil science (MS, PhD); vocational education (PhD). Electronic applications accepted.

College of Humanities *Degree program information:* Part-time programs available. Offers African-American and African studies (MA); ancient Greek (MA); Chinese (MA, PhD); classics (MA, PhD); comparative studies (MA, PhD); English (MA, MFA, PhD); French (MA, PhD); Germanic languages and literatures (MA, PhD); Greek studies (MA, PhD); history (MA, PhD); humanities (MA, MFA, PhD); Italian (MA); Japanese (MA, PhD); Latin studies (MA, PhD); linguistics (MA, PhD); modern Greek (MA, PhD); Near Eastern languages and cultures (MA, PhD); philosophy (MA, PhD); Slavic and East European studies (MA); Slavic languages and literatures (MA, PhD); Spanish and Portuguese (MA, PhD); women's studies (MA, PhD). Electronic applications accepted.

College of Mathematical and Physical Sciences *Degree program information:* Part-time programs available. Offers astronomy (MS, PhD); biostatistics (PhD); chemical physics (MS, PhD); chemistry (MS, PhD); earth sciences (MS, PhD); geodetic science (MS); geological sciences (MS, PhD); mathematical and physical sciences (M Appl Stat, MA, MS, PhD); mathematics (MA, MS, PhD); physics (MS, PhD); statistics (M Appl Stat, MS, PhD). Electronic applications accepted.

College of Nursing *Degree program information:* Part-time programs available. Offers nursing (MS, PhD). Electronic applications accepted.

College of Social and Behavioral Sciences *Degree program information:* Part-time programs available. Offers anthropology (MA, PhD); atmospheric sciences (MS, PhD); audiology (Au D); behavioral neuroscience (PhD); clinical psychology (PhD); cognitive psychology (PhD); communication (MA, PhD); developmental psychology (PhD); economics (MA, PhD); geography (MA, PhD); hearing science (PhD); journalism and communication (MA); mental retardation and developmental disabilities (PhD); political science (MA, PhD); psychology (MA); quantitative psychology (PhD); social and behavioral science (MA, MS, Au D, PhD); social and behavioral sciences (MA, MS, Au D, PhD); social psychology (PhD); sociology (MA, PhD); speech hearing science (MA); speech-language pathology (MA, PhD); speech-language science (PhD). Electronic applications accepted.

College of Social Work *Degree program information:* Part-time programs available. Offers social work (MSW, PhD). Electronic applications accepted.

College of the Arts *Degree program information:* Part-time programs available. Offers art (MFA); art education (MA, PhD); arts (M Mus, MA, MFA, DMA, PhD, CAL); arts policy and administration (MA); choreography (MFA); dance (MA, MFA, PhD); dance and technology (MFA); dance studies (PhD); history of art (MA, PhD); industrial, interior, and visual communication design (MA, MFA); Labanotation (MFA); lighting (MFA); music (M Mus, MA, DMA, PhD); performance (MFA); photography and cinema (MA); theatre (MA, MFA, PhD). Electronic applications accepted.

Max M. Fisher College of Business *Degree program information:* Part-time programs available. Offers accounting (M Acc, MA, MS); accounting and MIS (PhD); business (M Acc, MA, MBA, MBLE, MLHR, PhD); business administration (MA, MBA, PhD); business logistics engineering (MBLE); finance (MA, PhD); labor and human resources (MLHR, PhD). Electronic applications accepted.

John Glenn School of Public Affairs *Degree program information:* Part-time programs available. Offers public affairs (MA, MPA, PhD). Electronic applications accepted.

Moritz College of Law Offers law (JD, LL M, MSL). Electronic applications accepted.

THE OHIO STATE UNIVERSITY AT LIMA, Lima, OH 45804

General Information State-supported, coed, comprehensive institution.

GRADUATE UNITS

Graduate Programs Electronic applications accepted.

THE OHIO STATE UNIVERSITY AT MARION, Marion, OH 43302-5695

General Information State-supported, coed, comprehensive institution.

GRADUATE UNITS

Graduate Programs Electronic applications accepted.

THE OHIO STATE UNIVERSITY–MANSFIELD CAMPUS, Mansfield, OH 44906-1599

General Information State-supported, coed, comprehensive institution.

The Ohio State University–Mansfield Campus (continued)

GRADUATE UNITS

Graduate Programs Electronic applications accepted.

THE OHIO STATE UNIVERSITY–NEWARK CAMPUS, Newark, OH 43055-1797

General Information State-supported, coed, comprehensive institution.

GRADUATE UNITS

Graduate Programs Electronic applications accepted.

OHIO UNIVERSITY, Athens, OH 45701-2979

General Information State-supported, coed, university. CGS member. *Graduate housing:* Rooms and/or apartments available on a first-come, first-served basis to single and married students. Housing application deadline: 5/1.

GRADUATE UNITS

College of Osteopathic Medicine Students: 445 full-time (244 women); includes 116 minority (49 African Americans, 6 American Indian/Alaska Native, 40 Asian Americans or Pacific Islanders, 21 Hispanic Americans). Average age 24. 3,167 applicants, 6% accepted, 120 enrolled. *Faculty:* 83 full-time (26 women), 35 part-time/adjunct (11 women). Expenses: Contact institution. *Financial support:* In 2008–09, 423 students received support, including 10 fellowships with full tuition reimbursements available (averaging $40,775 per year); career-related internships or fieldwork, Federal Work-Study, institutionally sponsored loans, scholarships/grants, and tuition waivers (partial) also available. Financial award applicants required to submit FAFSA. In 2008, 106 DOs awarded. Offers osteopathic medicine (DO). *Application deadline:* For fall admission, 2/1 for domestic students. Applications are processed on a rolling basis. *Application fee:* $40. Electronic applications accepted. *Application Contact:* Dr. John D. Schriner, Director of Admissions, 740-593-4313, Fax: 740-593-2256, E-mail: admissions@exchange.oucom.ohiou.edu. *Dean,* Dr. John A. Brose, 740-593-9350, Fax: 740-593-0761, E-mail: blue@ohio.edu.

Graduate College *Degree program information:* Part-time and evening/weekend programs available. Electronic applications accepted.

Center for International Studies Offers African studies (MA); communications and development studies (MA); development studies (MA); international studies (MA); Latin American studies (MA); Southeast Asian studies (MA).

College of Arts and Sciences *Degree program information:* Part-time programs available. Offers applied economics (MA); applied linguistics/TESOL (MA); arts and sciences (MA, MFE, MPA, MS, MSS, MSW, PhD); astronomy (MS, PhD); biological sciences (MS, PhD); cell biology and physiology (MS, PhD); chemistry and biochemistry (MS, PhD); clinical psychology (PhD); ecology and evolutionary biology (MS, PhD); English language and literature (MA, PhD); environmental and plant biology (MS, PhD); environmental geochemistry (MS); environmental geology (MS); environmental studies (MS); environmental/hydrology (MS); exercise physiology and muscle biology (MS, PhD); experimental psychology (PhD); financial economics (MFE); French (MA); geography (MA); geology (MS); geology education (MS); geomorphology/surficial processes (MS); geophysics (MS); history (MA, PhD); hydrogeology (MS); mathematics (MS, PhD); microbiology (MS, PhD); molecular and cellular biology (MS, PhD); neuroscience (MS, PhD); organizational psychology (PhD); philosophy (MA); physics (MS, PhD); political science (MA); public administration (MPA); sedimentology (MS); social sciences (MSS); social work (MSW); sociology (MA); Spanish (MA); structure/tectonics (MS). Electronic applications accepted.

College of Business *Degree program information:* Part-time and evening/weekend programs available. Offers business (EMBA, MBA); business administration (EMBA, MBA). Electronic applications accepted.

College of Education *Degree program information:* Part-time and evening/weekend programs available. Offers adolescent to young adult education (M Ed); college student personnel (M Ed); community/agency counseling (M Ed); computer education and technology (M Ed); counselor education (PhD); cultural studies in education (PhD); curriculum and instruction (M Ed, PhD); early childhood/special education (M Ed); education (M Ed, Ed D, PhD); educational administration (M Ed, Ed D); educational research and evaluation (M Ed, PhD); higher education (M Ed, PhD); instructional technology (PhD); mathematics education (PhD); middle child education (M Ed); reading and language arts (PhD); reading education (M Ed); rehabilitation counseling (M Ed); school counseling (M Ed); social studies education (PhD); special education (M Ed, PhD). Electronic applications accepted.

College of Fine Arts *Degree program information:* Part-time programs available. Postbaccalaureate distance learning degree programs offered (minimal on-campus study). Offers accompanying (MM); art history (MA); ceramics (MFA); composition (MM); conducting (MM); film (MFA); film studies (MA); fine arts (MA, MFA, MM, PhD, Certificate); graphic design (MFA); history/literature (MM); interdisciplinary arts (PhD); music education (MM); music therapy (MM); painting (MFA); performance (MM, Certificate); performance/pedagogy (MM); photography (MFA); printmaking (MFA); sculpture (MFA); theater (MA, MFA); theory (MM). Electronic applications accepted.

College of Health and Human Services *Degree program information:* Part-time programs available. Offers athletic training education (MS); audiology (Au D); child development and family life (MS); coaching education (MS); early childhood education (MS); family studies (MS); food and nutrition (MS); health and human services (MA, MHA, MPH, MS, MSA, Au D, DPT, PhD); health sciences (MHA, MPH); hearing science (PhD); physical therapy (DPT); physiology of exercise (MS); recreation studies (MS); speech language pathology (MA); speech-language science (PhD); sports administration and facility management (MSA). Electronic applications accepted.

Russ College of Engineering and Technology *Degree program information:* Part-time programs available. Offers biomedical engineering (MS); chemical engineering (MS, PhD); civil (PhD); computer science (MS); construction (MS); electrical engineering (MS, PhD); engineering and technology (MS, PhD); environmental (MS); geotechnical and environmental engineering (MS); industrial (PhD); industrial and manufacturing systems engineering (MS); integrated engineering (PhD); manufacturing engineering (MS); mechanical (PhD); mechanical engineering (MS, PhD); structures (MS); transportation (MS); water resources and structures (MS). Electronic applications accepted.

Scripps College of Communication *Degree program information:* Part-time programs available. Offers communication (MA, MCTP, MS, PhD); communication studies (PhD); information and telecommunication systems (MCTP); journalism (MS, PhD); mass communication (PhD); media arts and studies (MA); visual communication (MA). Electronic applications accepted.

OHR HAMEIR THEOLOGICAL SEMINARY, Peekskill, NY 10566

General Information Independent-religious, men only, comprehensive institution.

GRADUATE UNITS

Graduate Programs

OKLAHOMA CHRISTIAN UNIVERSITY, Oklahoma City, OK 73136-1100

General Information Independent-religious, coed, comprehensive institution. *Enrollment:* 2,161 graduate, professional, and undergraduate students; 12 full-time matriculated graduate/professional students (2 women), 30 part-time matriculated graduate/professional students (4 women). *Enrollment by degree level:* 15 first professional, 25 master's, 2 other advanced degrees. *Graduate faculty:* 11 full-time (0 women). *Graduate housing:* Rooms and/or apartments available on a first-come, first-served basis to single and married students. Typical cost: $4560 per year ($5412 including board) for single students; $5480 per year ($6430 including board) for married students. *Student services:* Campus employment opportunities, campus safety program, exercise/wellness program, free psychological counseling, international student services, low-cost health insurance, writing training. *Library facilities:* Tom and Ada Beam Library. *Online resources:* library catalog, web page, access to other libraries' catalogs. *Collection:* 129,324 titles, 8,694 serial subscriptions, 6,775 audiovisual materials.

Computer facilities: 101 computers available on campus for general student use. A campuswide network can be accessed from student residence rooms and from off campus. Online class registration is available. *Web address:* http://www.oc.edu/.

General Application Contact: Dustin Crawford, Graduate School of Theology Admissions Counselor, 405-425-5485, Fax: 405-425-5076, E-mail: dustin.crawford@oc.edu.

GRADUATE UNITS

Graduate School of Theology Students: 12 full-time (2 women), 30 part-time (4 women); includes 3 minority (2 African Americans, 1 American Indian/Alaska Native), 3 international. *Faculty:* 11 full-time (0 women). Expenses: Contact institution. *Financial support:* Career-related internships or fieldwork, Federal Work-Study, scholarships/grants, and tuition waivers (partial) available. Support available to part-time students. Financial award application deadline: 3/1. *Degree program information:* Part-time programs available. Postbaccalaureate distance learning degree programs offered (minimal on-campus study). Offers family life ministry (MA); ministry (M Div, MA); youth ministry (MA). *Application deadline:* For fall admission, 8/15 priority date for domestic and international students; for spring admission, 1/3 priority date for domestic and international students. Applications are processed on a rolling basis. *Application fee:* $25. Electronic applications accepted. *Application Contact:* Dustin Crawford, Admissions Counselor, 405-425-5485, Fax: 405-425-5076, E-mail: dustin.crawford@oc.edu. *Chair,* Dr. John Harrison, 405-425-5377, Fax: 405-425-5076, E-mail: john.harrison@oc.edu.

OKLAHOMA CITY UNIVERSITY, Oklahoma City, OK 73106-1402

General Information Independent-religious, coed, comprehensive institution. *Graduate housing:* Rooms and/or apartments available on a first-come, first-served basis to single and married students. Housing application deadline: 8/15.

GRADUATE UNITS

Kramer School of Nursing Offers nursing (MSN).

Margaret E. Petree College of Performing Arts Offers costume design (MA); performing arts (MA, MFA, MM); technical theater (MA); theater (MA); theater for young audiences (MA).

Ann Lacy School of American Dance and Arts Management Offers dance (MFA).

Wanda L. Bass School of Music *Degree program information:* Part-time programs available. Offers composition (MM); conducting (MM); musical theatre (MM); opera performance (MM); performance (MM).

Meinders School of Business *Degree program information:* Part-time and evening/weekend programs available. Offers accounting (MSA); business (MBA, MSA); finance (MBA); health administration (MBA); information technology (MBA); integrated marketing communications (MBA); international business (MBA); marketing (MBA).

Petree College of Arts and Sciences *Degree program information:* Part-time and evening/weekend programs available. Offers art (MLA); arts and sciences (M Ed, MA, MCJ, MLA, MS); general studies (MLA); leadership/management (MLA); literature (MLA); mass communications (MLA); philosophy (MLA); writing (MLA).

Division of Computer Science *Degree program information:* Part-time and evening/weekend programs available. Offers computer science (MS).

Division of Education and Kinesiology Exercise Studies *Degree program information:* Part-time and evening/weekend programs available. Offers applied behavioral studies (M Ed); early childhood education (M Ed); education and kinesiology exercise studies (M Ed, MA); elementary education (M Ed); teaching English to speakers of other languages (MA).

Division of Sociology and Justice Studies *Degree program information:* Part-time and evening/weekend programs available. Offers criminal justice (MCJ).

School of Law *Degree program information:* Part-time and evening/weekend programs available. Offers law (JD). Electronic applications accepted.

Wimberly School of Religion and Graduate Theological Center *Degree program information:* Part-time and evening/weekend programs available. Offers religion and theology (M Rel, MAR).

OKLAHOMA STATE UNIVERSITY, Stillwater, OK 74078

General Information State-supported, coed, university. CGS member. *Enrollment:* 22,768 graduate, professional, and undergraduate students; 1,515 full-time matriculated graduate/professional students (651 women), 2,516 part-time matriculated graduate/professional students (1,155 women). *Enrollment by degree level:* 2,598 master's, 1,419 doctoral, 14 other advanced degrees. *Graduate faculty:* 1,030 full-time (320 women), 212 part-time/adjunct (103 women). Tuition, state resident: part-time $154.85 per credit hour. Tuition, nonresident: part-time $602 per credit hour. *Required fees:* $73.85 per credit hour. One-time fee: $50 part-time. Tuition and fees vary according to course load and campus/location. *Graduate housing:* Rooms and/or apartments available on a first-come, first-served basis to single and married students. Typical cost: $3402 per year ($6502 including board) for single students; $8748 per year for married students. Room and board charges vary according to board plan and housing facility selected. *Student services:* Campus employment opportunities, campus safety program, career counseling, exercise/wellness program, free psychological counseling, grant writing training, international student services, low-cost health insurance, multicultural affairs office, services for students with disabilities, teacher training. *Library facilities:* Edmon Low Library plus 3 others. *Online resources:* library catalog, web page, access to other libraries' catalogs. *Research affiliation:* Coskata, Inc. (agriculture engineering), American Heart Association (physiological sciences), The Institute for Study Abroad (IFSA) Foundation (Agriculture), National Cattlemen's Beef Assoc. (animal science), Cotton, Inc. (plant and soil sciences), Howard Hughes Foundation (biological sciences).

Computer facilities: Computer purchase and lease plans are available. A campuswide network can be accessed from student residence rooms and from off campus. Online class registration is available. *Web address:* http://www.okstate.edu/.

General Application Contact: Dr. Gordon Emslie, Dean, 405-744-6368, Fax: 405-744-0355, E-mail: grad_i@okstate.edu.

GRADUATE UNITS

Center for Veterinary Health Sciences Postbaccalaureate distance learning degree programs offered. Offers veterinary biomedical sciences (MS, PhD); veterinary health sciences (DVM, MS, PhD); veterinary medicine (DVM).

College of Agricultural Science and Natural Resources Students: 155 full-time (67 women), 299 part-time (138 women); includes 34 minority (3 African Americans, 21 American Indian/Alaska Native, 5 Asian Americans or Pacific Islanders, 5 Hispanic Americans), 167 international. Average age 29. 445 applicants, 33% accepted, 99 enrolled. *Faculty:* 250 full-time (53 women), 11 part-time/adjunct (0 women). Expenses: Contact institution. *Financial support:* In 2008–09, 283 research assistantships (averaging $15,534 per year), 26 teaching assistantships (averaging $14,475 per year) were awarded; fellowships, career-related internships or fieldwork, Federal Work-Study, scholarships/grants, health care benefits, tuition waivers (partial), and unspecified assistantships also available. Support available to part-time students. Financial award application deadline: 3/1; financial award applicants required to submit FAFSA. In 2008, 80 master's, 28 doctorates awarded. Offers agricultural economics (M Ag, MS, PhD); agricultural education, communications and leadership (M Ag, MS, PhD); agricultural science and natural resources (M Ag, MS, PhD); animal breeding and reproduction (PhD); animal nutrition (PhD); animal sciences (M Ag, MS); biochemistry and molecular biology (MS, PhD); biomechanical engineering (MS, PhD); bioprocessing and biotechnology (MS, PhD); crop science (PhD); entomology (MS, PhD); environmental and natural resources (MS, PhD); environmental science (PhD); food processing (MS, PhD); food science (MS, PhD); horticulture (M Ag, MS); international agriculture (M Ag); natural resource ecology and management (M Ag, MS, PhD); plant and soil sciences (M Ag, MS); plant pathology (PhD); plant science (PhD); soil science (PhD). *Application deadline:* For fall admission, 3/1 priority date for international students; for spring admission, 8/1 priority date for international students. Applications are processed on a rolling basis. *Application fee:* $40 ($75 for international students).

Electronic applications accepted. *Application Contact:* Dr. Gordon Emslie, Dean, 405-744-6368, Fax: 405-744-0355, E-mail: grad_i@okstate.edu. *Dean,* Dr. Robert E. Whitson, 405-744-5398, Fax: 405-744-2480.

College of Arts and Sciences Students: 278 full-time (138 women), 553 part-time (237 women); includes 88 minority (21 African Americans, 40 American Indian/Alaska Native, 14 Asian Americans or Pacific Islanders, 13 Hispanic Americans), 226 international. Average age 31. 1,284 applicants, 35% accepted, 211 enrolled. *Faculty:* 399 full-time (131 women), 51 part-time/adjunct (25 women). Expenses: Contact institution. *Financial support:* In 2008–09, 99 research assistantships (averaging $15,327 per year), 434 teaching assistantships (averaging $14,502 per year) were awarded; fellowships, career-related internships or fieldwork, Federal Work-Study, scholarships/grants, health care benefits, tuition waivers (full and partial), and unspecified assistantships also available. Support available to part-time students. Financial award application deadline: 3/1; financial award applicants required to submit FAFSA. In 2008, 157 master's, 38 doctorates awarded. Offers applied history (MA); applied mathematics (MS); arts and sciences (MA, MFA, MM, MS, PhD); botany (MS); chemistry (MS, PhD); clinical psychology (PhD); communications sciences and disorders (MS); computer science (MS, PhD); creative writing (MA); English (MFA); environmental science (PhD); fire and emergency management administration (MS, PhD); general psychology (MS); geography (MS, PhD); history (PhD); lifespan development psychology (PhD); literature (PhD); mathematics (pure and applied) (PhD); mathematics (pure) (MS); mathematics education (MS, PhD); microbiology and molecular genetics (MS, PhD); pedagogy and performance (MM); philosophy (MA); photonics (MS, PhD); physics (MS, PhD); plant science (PhD); political science (MA); sociology (MS, PhD); statistics (MS, PhD); theatre (MA); zoology (MS, PhD). *Application deadline:* For fall admission, 3/1 priority date for international students; for spring admission, 8/1 priority date for international students. Applications are processed on a rolling basis. *Application fee:* $40 ($75 for international students). Electronic applications accepted. *Application Contact:* Dr. Gordon Emslie, Dean, 405-744-6368, Fax: 405-744-0355, E-mail: grad_i@okstate.edu. *Dean,* Dr. Peter M. A. Sherwood, 405-744-5663, Fax: 405-744-1797.

School of Geology Students: 27 full-time (13 women), 21 part-time (6 women); includes 7 minority (2 African Americans, 3 American Indian/Alaska Native, 1 Asian American or Pacific Islander, 1 Hispanic American), 6 international. Average age 28. 50 applicants, 66% accepted, 17 enrolled. *Faculty:* 10 full-time (2 women), 1 part-time/adjunct (0 women). Expenses: Contact institution. *Financial support:* In 2008–09, 4 research assistantships (averaging $9,015 per year), 20 teaching assistantships (averaging $9,135 per year) were awarded; career-related internships or fieldwork, Federal Work-Study, scholarships/grants, health care benefits, tuition waivers (partial), and unspecified assistantships also available. Support available to part-time students. Financial award application deadline: 3/1; financial award applicants required to submit FAFSA. In 2008, 7 master's awarded. Offers geology (MS, PhD). *Application deadline:* For fall admission, 3/1 priority date for international students; for spring admission, 8/1 priority date for international students. Applications are processed on a rolling basis. *Application fee:* $40 ($75 for international students). Electronic applications accepted. *Application Contact:* Dr. Gordon Emslie, Dean, 405-744-6368, Fax: 405-744-0355, E-mail: grad_i@okstate.edu. *Head,* Dr. Jay Gregg, 405-744-6358, Fax: 405-744-7841.

School of Journalism and Broadcasting Students: 9 full-time (7 women), 19 part-time (6 women); includes 2 minority (both American Indian/Alaska Native), 3 international. Average age 30. 28 applicants, 57% accepted, 11 enrolled. *Faculty:* 18 full-time (5 women), 3 part-time/adjunct (1 woman). Expenses: Contact institution. *Financial support:* In 2008–09, 4 teaching assistantships (averaging $11,655 per year) were awarded; career-related internships or fieldwork, Federal Work-Study, scholarships/grants, health care benefits, tuition waivers (partial), and unspecified assistantships also available. Support available to part-time students. Financial award application deadline: 3/1; financial award applicants required to submit FAFSA. In 2008, 6 master's awarded. Offers mass communication (MS). *Application deadline:* For fall admission, 3/1 priority date for international students; for spring admission, 8/1 priority date for international students. Applications are processed on a rolling basis. *Application fee:* $40 ($75 for international students). Electronic applications accepted. *Application Contact:* Dr. Gordon Emslie, Dean, 405-744-6368, Fax: 405-744-0355, E-mail: grad_i@okstate.edu. *Director,* Dr. Derina Holtzhausen, 405-744-6354, Fax: 405-744-7104.

College of Education Students: 242 full-time (179 women), 566 part-time (385 women); includes 130 minority (53 African Americans, 52 American Indian/Alaska Native, 11 Asian Americans or Pacific Islanders, 14 Hispanic Americans), 65 international. Average age 37. 506 applicants, 42% accepted, 165 enrolled. *Faculty:* 101 full-time (60 women), 68 part-time/adjunct (40 women). Expenses: Contact institution. *Financial support:* In 2008–09, 64 research assistantships (averaging $8,430 per year), 74 teaching assistantships (averaging $9,629 per year) were awarded; career-related internships or fieldwork, Federal Work-Study, scholarships/grants, health care benefits, tuition waivers (partial), and unspecified assistantships also available. Support available to part-time students. Financial award application deadline: 3/1; financial award applicants required to submit FAFSA. In 2008, 141 master's, 48 doctorates awarded. *Degree program information:* Part-time programs available. Postbaccalaureate distance learning degree programs offered. Offers education (MS, Ed D, PhD, Ed S). *Application deadline:* For fall admission, 3/1 priority date for international students; for spring admission, 8/1 priority date for international students. Applications are processed on a rolling basis. *Application fee:* $40 ($75 for international students). Electronic applications accepted. *Application Contact:* Dr. Gordon Emslie, Dean, 405-744-6368, Fax: 405-744-0355, E-mail: grad_i@okstate.edu. *Dean,* Dr. Pamela Fry, 405-744-3373, Fax: 405-744-6399.

School of Applied Health and Educational Psychology Students: 169 full-time (127 women), 198 part-time (130 women); includes 59 minority (26 African Americans, 18 American Indian/Alaska Native, 6 Asian Americans or Pacific Islanders, 9 Hispanic Americans), 30 international. Average age 34. 263 applicants, 38% accepted, 73 enrolled. *Faculty:* 36 full-time (17 women), 18 part-time/adjunct (11 women). Expenses: Contact institution. *Financial support:* In 2008–09, 35 research assistantships (averaging $7,124 per year), 57 teaching assistantships (averaging $8,792 per year) were awarded; career-related internships or fieldwork, Federal Work-Study, scholarships/grants, health care benefits, tuition waivers (partial), and unspecified assistantships also available. Support available to part-time students. Financial award application deadline: 3/1; financial award applicants required to submit FAFSA. In 2008, 65 master's, 27 doctorates awarded. *Degree program information:* Part-time programs available. Postbaccalaureate distance learning degree programs offered. Offers applied behavioral studies (Ed D). *Application deadline:* For fall admission, 3/1 priority date for international students; for spring admission, 8/1 priority date for international students. Applications are processed on a rolling basis. *Application fee:* $40 ($75 for international students). Electronic applications accepted. *Application Contact:* Dr. Gordon Emslie, Dean, 405-744-6368, Fax: 405-744-0355, E-mail: grad_i@okstate.edu. *Head,* Dr. John Romans, 405-744-6040, Fax: 405-744-6779.

School of Educational Studies Students: 27 full-time (14 women), 198 part-time (127 women); includes 38 minority (15 African Americans, 20 American Indian/Alaska Native, 1 Asian American or Pacific Islander, 2 Hispanic Americans), 24 international. Average age 39. 138 applicants, 49% accepted, 56 enrolled. *Faculty:* 32 full-time (15 women), 23 part-time/adjunct (5 women). Expenses: Contact institution. *Financial support:* In 2008–09, 15 research assistantships (averaging $9,723 per year), 7 teaching assistantships (averaging $9,954 per year) were awarded; career-related internships or fieldwork, Federal Work-Study, scholarships/grants, health care benefits, tuition waivers (partial), and unspecified assistantships also available. Support available to part-time students. Financial award application deadline: 3/1; financial award applicants required to submit FAFSA. In 2008, 31 master's, 15 doctorates awarded. *Degree program information:* Part-time programs available. Postbaccalaureate distance learning degree programs offered. Offers higher education (Ed D). *Application deadline:* For fall admission, 3/1 priority date for international students; for spring admission, 8/1 priority date for international students. Applications are processed on a rolling basis. *Application fee:* $40 ($75 for international students). Electronic applications accepted. *Application Contact:* Dr. Gordon Emslie, Dean, 405-744-6368, Fax: 405-744-0355, E-mail: grad_i@okstate.edu. *Head,* Dr. Bert Jacobson, 405-744-6275, Fax: 405-744-7758.

School of Teaching and Curriculum Leadership Students: 46 full-time (38 women), 170 part-time (128 women); includes 33 minority (12 African Americans, 14 American Indian/Alaska Native, 4 Asian Americans or Pacific Islanders, 3 Hispanic Americans), 11 international. Average age 40. 105 applicants, 41% accepted, 36 enrolled. *Faculty:* 32 full-time (27 women), 27 part-time/adjunct (24 women). Expenses: Contact institution. *Financial support:* In 2008–09, 12 research assistantships (averaging $9,989 per year), 10 teaching assistantships (averaging $14,175 per year) were awarded; career-related internships or fieldwork, Federal Work-Study, scholarships/grants, health care benefits, tuition waivers (partial), and unspecified assistantships also available. Support available to part-time students. Financial award application deadline: 3/1; financial award applicants required to submit FAFSA. In 2008, 45 master's, 6 doctorates awarded. *Degree program information:* Part-time programs available. Postbaccalaureate distance learning degree programs offered. Offers teaching and curriculum leadership (MS, PhD). *Application deadline:* For fall admission, 3/1 priority date for international students; for spring admission, 8/1 priority date for international students. Applications are processed on a rolling basis. *Application fee:* $40 ($75 for international students). Electronic applications accepted. *Application Contact:* Dr. Gordon Emslie, Dean, 405-744-6368, Fax: 405-744-0355, E-mail: grad_i@okstate.edu. *Head,* Dr. Christine Ormsbee, 405-744-7125, Fax: 405-744-6290.

College of Engineering, Architecture and Technology Students: 328 full-time (45 women), 370 part-time (59 women); includes 46 minority (11 African Americans, 12 American Indian/Alaska Native, 15 Asian Americans or Pacific Islanders, 8 Hispanic Americans), 427 international. Average age 29. 1,234 applicants, 38% accepted, 191 enrolled. *Faculty:* 108 full-time (11 women), 14 part-time/adjunct (1 woman). Expenses: Contact institution. *Financial support:* In 2008–09, 217 research assistantships (averaging $10,594 per year), 170 teaching assistantships (averaging $8,366 per year) were awarded; fellowships, career-related internships or fieldwork, Federal Work-Study, scholarships/grants, health care benefits, tuition waivers (partial), and unspecified assistantships also available. Support available to part-time students. Financial award application deadline: 3/1; financial award applicants required to submit FAFSA. In 2008, 183 master's, 14 doctorates awarded. Postbaccalaureate distance learning degree programs offered. Offers engineering, architecture and technology (MS, PhD). *Application deadline:* For fall admission, 3/1 priority date for international students; for spring admission, 8/1 priority date for international students. Applications are processed on a rolling basis. *Application fee:* $40 ($75 for international students). Electronic applications accepted. *Application Contact:* Dr. Gordon Emslie, Dean, 405-744-6368, Fax: 405-744-0355, E-mail: grad_i@okstate.edu. *Dean,* Dr. Karl N. Reid, 405-744-5140.

School of Chemical Engineering Students: 16 full-time (4 women), 21 part-time (5 women); includes 2 minority (1 African American, 1 American Indian/Alaska Native), 34 international. Average age 27. 82 applicants, 41% accepted, 14 enrolled. *Faculty:* 12 full-time (2 women), 2 part-time/adjunct (0 women). Expenses: Contact institution. *Financial support:* In 2008–09, 30 research assistantships (averaging $12,004 per year), 18 teaching assistantships (averaging $12,260 per year) were awarded; fellowships, career-related internships or fieldwork, Federal Work-Study, scholarships/grants, health care benefits, tuition waivers (partial), and unspecified assistantships also available. Support available to part-time students. Financial award application deadline: 3/1; financial award applicants required to submit FAFSA. In 2008, 12 master's, 1 doctorate awarded. Offers chemical engineering (MS, PhD). *Application deadline:* For fall admission, 3/1 priority date for international students; for spring admission, 8/1 priority date for international students. Applications are processed on a rolling basis. *Application fee:* $40 ($75 for international students). Electronic applications accepted. *Application Contact:* Dr. Gordon Emslie, Dean, 405-744-6368, Fax: 405-744-0355, E-mail: grad_i@okstate.edu. *Head,* Dr. Khaled A.M. Gasem, 405-744-5280, Fax: 405-744-6338.

School of Civil and Environmental Engineering Students: 38 full-time (13 women), 20 part-time (1 woman); includes 4 minority (1 American Indian/Alaska Native, 3 Asian Americans or Pacific Islanders), 34 international. Average age 29. 107 applicants, 31% accepted, 16 enrolled. *Faculty:* 16 full-time (1 woman), 2 part-time/adjunct (0 women). Expenses: Contact institution. *Financial support:* In 2008–09, 24 research assistantships (averaging $11,740 per year), 11 teaching assistantships (averaging $9,736 per year) were awarded; career-related internships or fieldwork, Federal Work-Study, scholarships/grants, health care benefits, tuition waivers (partial), and unspecified assistantships also available. Support available to part-time students. Financial award application deadline: 3/1; financial award applicants required to submit FAFSA. In 2008, 11 master's, 2 doctorates awarded. Offers civil engineering (MS); environmental engineering (PhD). *Application deadline:* For fall admission, 3/1 priority date for international students; for spring admission, 8/1 priority date for international students. Applications are processed on a rolling basis. *Application fee:* $40 ($75 for international students). Electronic applications accepted. *Application Contact:* Dr. Gordon Emslie, Dean, 405-744-6368, Fax: 405-744-0355, E-mail: grad_i@okstate.edu. *Head,* Dr. John Veenstra, 405-744-5190, Fax: 405-744-7554.

School of Electrical and Computer Engineering Students: 86 full-time (10 women), 80 part-time (10 women); includes 13 minority (1 African American, 4 American Indian/Alaska Native, 5 Asian Americans or Pacific Islanders, 3 Hispanic Americans), 108 international. Average age 29. 389 applicants, 32% accepted, 38 enrolled. *Faculty:* 26 full-time (3 women). Expenses: Contact institution. *Financial support:* In 2008–09, 46 research assistantships (averaging $9,801 per year), 39 teaching assistantships (averaging $8,274 per year) were awarded; career-related internships or fieldwork, Federal Work-Study, scholarships/grants, health care benefits, tuition waivers (partial), and unspecified assistantships also available. Support available to part-time students. Financial award application deadline: 3/1; financial award applicants required to submit FAFSA. In 2008, 35 master's, 5 doctorates awarded. Postbaccalaureate distance learning degree programs offered. Offers electrical and computer engineering (MS, PhD). *Application deadline:* For fall admission, 3/1 priority date for international students; for spring admission, 8/1 priority date for international students. Applications are processed on a rolling basis. *Application fee:* $40 ($75 for international students). Electronic applications accepted. *Application Contact:* Dr. Gordon Emslie, Dean, 405-744-6368, Fax: 405-744-0355, E-mail: grad_i@okstate.edu. *Head,* Dr. Keith Teague, 405-744-5151, Fax: 405-744-9198.

School of Industrial Engineering and Management Students: 72 full-time (10 women), 186 part-time (33 women); includes 26 minority (9 African Americans, 5 American Indian/Alaska Native, 7 Asian Americans or Pacific Islanders, 5 Hispanic Americans), 100 international. Average age 31. 379 applicants, 41% accepted, 61 enrolled. *Faculty:* 11 full-time (1 woman), 3 part-time/adjunct (1 woman). Expenses: Contact institution. *Financial support:* In 2008–09, 33 research assistantships (averaging $8,240 per year), 32 teaching assistantships (averaging $7,517 per year) were awarded; career-related internships or fieldwork, Federal Work-Study, scholarships/grants, health care benefits, tuition waivers (partial), and unspecified assistantships also available. Support available to part-time students. Financial award application deadline: 3/1; financial award applicants required to submit FAFSA. In 2008, 91 master's, 3 doctorates awarded. Postbaccalaureate distance learning degree programs offered. Offers industrial engineering and management (PhD). *Application deadline:* For fall admission, 3/1 priority date for international students; for spring admission, 8/1 priority date for international students. Applications are processed on a rolling basis. *Application fee:* $40 ($75 for international students). Electronic applications accepted. *Application Contact:* Dr. Gordon Emslie, Dean, 405-744-6368, Fax: 405-744-0355, E-mail: grad_i@okstate.edu. *Head,* Dr. William J. Kolarik, 405-744-6055, Fax: 405-744-4654.

School of Mechanical and Aerospace Engineering Students: 116 full-time (8 women), 63 part-time (10 women); includes 1 minority (American Indian/Alaska Native), 151 international. Average age 25. 277 applicants, 45% accepted, 62 enrolled. *Faculty:* 25 full-time (1 woman), 4 part-time/adjunct (0 women). Expenses: Contact institution. *Financial support:* In 2008–09, 83 research assistantships (averaging $11,155 per year), 68 teaching assistantships (averaging $7,625 per year) were awarded; career-related internships or fieldwork, Federal Work-Study, scholarships/grants, health care benefits, tuition waivers (partial), and unspecified assistantships also available. Support available to part-time students. Financial award application deadline: 3/1; financial award applicants required to submit FAFSA. In 2008, 34 master's, 3 doctorates awarded. Postbaccalaureate distance learning degree programs offered. Offers mechanical engineering (MS, PhD). *Application deadline:* For fall admission, 3/1 priority date for international students; for spring admission, 8/1 priority date for international students. Applications are processed on a rolling basis. *Application fee:* $40 ($75 for international students). Electronic applications accepted. *Application Contact:*

Oklahoma State University (continued)

Dr. Gordon Emslie, Dean, 405-744-6368, Fax: 405-744-0355, E-mail: grad_i@okstate.edu. *Head,* Dr. Lawrence L. Hoberock, 405-744-5900, Fax: 405-744-7873.

College of Human Environmental Sciences Students: 100 full-time (76 women), 138 part-time (98 women); includes 30 minority (6 African Americans, 13 American Indian/Alaska Native, 3 Asian Americans or Pacific Islanders, 8 Hispanic Americans), 73 international. Average age 32. 190 applicants, 52% accepted, 60 enrolled. *Faculty:* 83 full-time (56 women), 13 part-time/adjunct (9 women). Expenses: Contact institution. *Financial support:* In 2008–09, 88 research assistantships (averaging $10,615 per year), 47 teaching assistantships (averaging $9,398 per year) were awarded; career-related internships or fieldwork, Federal Work-Study, scholarships/grants, health care benefits, tuition waivers (partial), and unspecified assistantships also available. Support available to part-time students. Financial award application deadline: 3/1; financial award applicants required to submit FAFSA. In 2008, 55 master's, 1 doctorate awarded. Postbaccalaureate distance learning degree programs offered. Offers design, housing and merchandising (MS, PhD); human development and family science (MS, PhD); human environmental sciences (MS); nutritional sciences (MS, PhD). *Application deadline:* For fall admission, 3/1 priority date for international students; for spring admission, 8/1 priority date for international students. Applications are processed on a rolling basis. *Application fee:* $40 ($75 for international students). Electronic applications accepted. *Application Contact:* Dr. Gordon Emslie, Dean, 405-744-6368, Fax: 405-744-0355, E-mail: grad_i@okstate.edu. *Dean,* Dr. Stephan Wilson, 405-744-5053, Fax: 405-744-7113.

School of Hotel and Restaurant Administration Students: 28 full-time (20 women), 30 part-time (13 women); includes 11 minority (1 African American, 5 American Indian/Alaska Native, 5 Hispanic Americans), 33 international. Average age 36. 32 applicants, 47% accepted, 6 enrolled. *Faculty:* 13 full-time (3 women), 3 part-time/adjunct (0 women). Expenses: Contact institution. *Financial support:* In 2008–09, 14 research assistantships (averaging $9,035 per year), 11 teaching assistantships (averaging $9,932 per year) were awarded; career-related internships or fieldwork, Federal Work-Study, scholarships/grants, health care benefits, tuition waivers (partial), and unspecified assistantships also available. Support available to part-time students. Financial award application deadline: 3/1; financial award applicants required to submit FAFSA. In 2008, 6 master's, 1 doctorate awarded. Offers hotel and restaurant administration (MS, PhD). *Application deadline:* For fall admission, 3/1 priority date for international students; for spring admission, 8/1 priority date for international students. Applications are processed on a rolling basis. *Application fee:* $40 ($75 for international students). Electronic applications accepted. *Application Contact:* Dr. Gordon Emslie, Dean, 405-744-6368, Fax: 405-744-0355, E-mail: grad_i@okstate.edu. *Head,* Dr. Richard Ghiselli, 405-744-6713, Fax: 405-744-6299.

Graduate College Students: 74 full-time (34 women), 173 part-time (95 women); includes 49 minority (16 African Americans, 16 American Indian/Alaska Native, 8 Asian Americans or Pacific Islanders, 9 Hispanic Americans), 57 international. Average age 33. 681 applicants, 67% accepted, 64 enrolled. *Faculty:* 2 full-time (0 women), 1 part-time/adjunct (0 women). Expenses: Contact institution. *Financial support:* In 2008–09, 2 research assistantships (averaging $9,600 per year) were awarded; career-related internships or fieldwork, Federal Work-Study, scholarships/grants, health care benefits, tuition waivers (partial), and unspecified assistantships also available. Support available to part-time students. Financial award application deadline: 3/1; financial award applicants required to submit FAFSA. In 2008, 78 master's, 11 doctorates awarded. Offers environmental science (MS); natural and applied science (MS); photonics (PhD); plant science (PhD). Programs are interdisciplinary. *Application deadline:* For fall admission, 3/1 priority date for international students; for spring admission, 8/1 priority date for international students. Applications are processed on a rolling basis. *Application fee:* $40 ($75 for international students). Electronic applications accepted. *Application Contact:* Dr. Craig Satterfield, Director of Student Services, 405-744-6368, Fax: 405-744-0355, E-mail: grad_i@okstate.edu. *Dean,* Dr. Gordon Emslie, 405-744-6368, Fax: 405-744-0355, E-mail: grad_i@okstate.edu.

William S. Spears School of Business Students: 338 full-time (112 women), 417 part-time (143 women); includes 87 minority (22 African Americans, 38 American Indian/Alaska Native, 15 Asian Americans or Pacific Islanders, 12 Hispanic Americans), 185 international. Average age 30. 950 applicants, 38% accepted, 217 enrolled. *Faculty:* 108 full-time (26 women), 33 part-time/adjunct (11 women). Expenses: Contact institution. *Financial support:* In 2008–09, 33 research assistantships (averaging $10,217 per year), 143 teaching assistantships (averaging $8,768 per year) were awarded; career-related internships or fieldwork, Federal Work-Study, scholarships/grants, health care benefits, tuition waivers (partial), and unspecified assistantships also available. Support available to part-time students. Financial award application deadline: 3/1; financial award applicants required to submit FAFSA. In 2008, 254 master's, 9 doctorates awarded. *Degree program information:* Part-time programs available. Postbaccalaureate distance learning degree programs offered. Offers business (MBA, MS, PhD); business administration (MBA, PhD); economics and legal studies in business (MS, PhD); finance (PhD); management (MS, PhD); management information systems (MS); management science and information systems (PhD); marketing (MBA, PhD); quantitative financial economics (MS); telecommunications management (MS). *Application deadline:* For fall admission, 3/1 priority date for international students; for spring admission, 8/1 priority date for international students. Applications are processed on a rolling basis. *Application fee:* $40 ($75 for international students). Electronic applications accepted. *Application Contact:* Jan Analla, Assistant Director, 405-744-2951, E-mail: jan.analla@okstate.edu. *Dean,* Dr. Sara M. Freedman, 405-744-5064, Fax: 405-744-8956.

School of Accounting Students: 43 full-time (22 women), 24 part-time (16 women); includes 7 minority (2 African Americans, 4 American Indian/Alaska Native, 1 Asian American or Pacific Islander), 13 international. Average age 29. 83 applicants, 30% accepted, 10 enrolled. *Faculty:* 16 full-time (7 women), 4 part-time/adjunct (0 women). Expenses: Contact institution. *Financial support:* In 2008–09, 2 research assistantships (averaging $14,238 per year), 30 teaching assistantships (averaging $8,990 per year) were awarded; career-related internships or fieldwork, Federal Work-Study, scholarships/grants, health care benefits, tuition waivers (partial), and unspecified assistantships also available. Support available to part-time students. Financial award application deadline: 3/1; financial award applicants required to submit FAFSA. In 2008, 44 master's, 1 doctorate awarded. *Degree program information:* Part-time programs available. Offers accounting (MS, PhD). *Application deadline:* For fall admission, 3/1 priority date for international students; for spring admission, 8/1 priority date for international students. Applications are processed on a rolling basis. *Application fee:* $40 ($75 for international students). Electronic applications accepted. *Application Contact:* Dr. Gordon Emslie, Dean, 405-744-6368, Fax: 405-744-0355, E-mail: grad_i@okstate.edu. *Head,* Dr. Don Hansen, 405-744-5123, Fax: 405-744-1680.

OKLAHOMA STATE UNIVERSITY CENTER FOR HEALTH SCIENCES, Tulsa, OK 74107-1898

General Information State-supported, coed, graduate-only institution. *Graduate housing:* On-campus housing not available. *Research affiliation:* Sun River, Inc. (cognitive rehabilitation), Merck and Company (pharmaceutical sciences), Viropharma (pharmaceutical sciences), Ingenex (pharmaceutical sciences), Proctor & Gamble (pharmaceutical sciences), Glaxo-Smith Kline (pharmaceutical sciences).

GRADUATE UNITS

College of Osteopathic Medicine Offers osteopathic medicine (DO).

Graduate Program in Forensic Sciences *Degree program information:* Part-time and evening/weekend programs available. Postbaccalaureate distance learning degree programs offered (no on-campus study). Offers forensic DNA/molecular biology (MS); forensic examination of questioned documents (MFSA, Certificate); forensic pathology (MS); forensic psychology (MS); forensic sciences (MFSA); forensic toxicology (MS).

Program in Biomedical Sciences Offers biomedical sciences (MS, PhD).

OLD DOMINION UNIVERSITY, Norfolk, VA 23529

General Information State-supported, coed, university. CGS member. *Enrollment:* 23,086 graduate, professional, and undergraduate students; 1,407 full-time matriculated graduate/professional students (961 women), 2,667 part-time matriculated graduate/professional students (1,500 women). *Enrollment by degree level:* 2,975 master's, 1,036 doctoral, 63 other advanced degrees. *Graduate faculty:* 589 full-time (208 women), 128 part-time/adjunct (69 women). Tuition, state resident: full-time $7704; part-time $321 per credit. Tuition, nonresident: full-time $19,104; part-time $796 per credit. *Required fees:* $99 per semester. One-time fee: $40. *Graduate housing:* Room and/or apartments available on a first-come, first-served basis to single students; on-campus housing not available to married students. Typical cost: $4234 per year ($7092 including board). Housing application deadline: 5/1. *Student services:* Campus employment opportunities, campus safety program, career counseling, exercise/wellness program, free psychological counseling, grant writing training, international student services, low-cost health insurance, multicultural affairs office, services for students with disabilities, teacher training. *Library facilities:* Patricia W. and Douglas Perry Library plus 3 others. *Online resources:* library catalog, web page, access to other libraries' catalogs. *Collection:* 1.2 million titles, 17,967 serial subscriptions, 50,413 audiovisual materials. *Research affiliation:* Thomas Jefferson National Accelerator Facility (high energy physics and laser processing), NASA-Langley Research Center (aerodynamic testing and evaluation), Eastern Virginia Medical Center (medicine), Mid Atlantic Institue for Space and Technology (aerospace engineering), Virginia Commerical Space Flight Authority (aerospace engineering), Joint Forces Command (modelling, simulation, and technology development).

Computer facilities: Computer purchase and lease plans are available. 2,035 computers available on campus for general student use. A campuswide network can be accessed from student residence rooms and from off campus. Online class registration, online courses are available. *Web address:* http://www.odu.edu/.

General Application Contact: Lakeisha Phelps, Director of Admissions, 757-683-3648, Fax: 757-683-3255, E-mail: gradadmit@odu.edu.

GRADUATE UNITS

College of Arts and Letters Students: 150 full-time (91 women), 221 part-time (144 women); includes 52 minority (39 African Americans, 6 Asian Americans or Pacific Islanders, 7 Hispanic Americans), 31 international. Average age 32. 276 applicants, 66% accepted, 117 enrolled. *Faculty:* 137 full-time (57 women), 11 part-time/adjunct (5 women). Expenses: Contact institution. *Financial support:* In 2008–09, 214 students received support, including 6 fellowships with full and partial tuition reimbursements available (averaging $15,000 per year), 16 research assistantships with full and partial tuition reimbursements available (averaging $11,000 per year), 58 teaching assistantships with full and partial tuition reimbursements available (averaging $10,000 per year); career-related internships or fieldwork, institutionally sponsored loans, scholarships/grants, tuition waivers (partial), and unspecified assistantships also available. Support available to part-time students. Financial award application deadline: 2/15; financial award applicants required to submit CSS PROFILE or FAFSA. In 2008, 88 master's, 5 doctorates awarded. *Degree program information:* Part-time and evening/weekend programs available. Offers applied linguistics (MA); applied sociology (MA); arts and letters (MA, MFA, MME, PhD); conflict and cooperation (PhD); creative writing (MFA); criminology and criminal justice (PhD); English (MA, PhD); history (MA); humanities (MA); music education (MME); U.S. foreign policy (MA). *Application deadline:* For fall admission, 6/1 priority date for domestic students, 2/15 for international students; for spring admission, 11/1 priority date for domestic students, 10/1 for international students. *Application fee:* $40. Electronic applications accepted. *Application Contact:* Dr. Robert Wojtowicz, Associate Dean, 757-683-6077, Fax: 757-683-5746, E-mail: rwojtowi@odu.edu. *Dean,* Dr. Chandra deSilva, 757-683-3925, Fax: 757-683-5746, E-mail: cdesilva@odu.edu.

College of Business and Public Administration Students: 151 full-time (72 women), 386 part-time (189 women); includes 117 minority (81 African Americans, 5 American Indian/Alaska Native, 25 Asian Americans or Pacific Islanders, 6 Hispanic Americans), 82 international. Average age 32. 368 applicants, 75% accepted. *Faculty:* 73 full-time (17 women), 12 part-time/adjunct (3 women). Expenses: Contact institution. *Financial support:* In 2008–09, 230 students received support, including 6 fellowships with partial tuition reimbursements available (averaging $15,000 per year), 55 research assistantships with full and partial tuition reimbursements available (averaging $10,972 per year), 18 teaching assistantships with full and partial tuition reimbursements available (averaging $10,500 per year); career-related internships or fieldwork, Federal Work-Study, scholarships/grants, tuition waivers (partial), and unspecified assistantships also available. Support available to part-time students. Financial award application deadline: 2/15; financial award applicants required to submit FAFSA. In 2008, 159 master's, 13 doctorates awarded. *Degree program information:* Part-time and evening/weekend programs available. Postbaccalaureate distance learning degree programs offered (no on-campus study). Offers accounting (MS); business and economic forecasting (MBA); business and public administration (MA, MBA, MPA, MS, PhD); economics (MA); finance (PhD); financial analysis and valuation (MBA); information technology (PhD); information technology and enterprise integration (MBA); international business (MBA); maritime and port management (MBA); marketing (PhD); public administration (MPA); public administration and urban policy (PhD); strategic management (PhD). *Application deadline:* For fall admission, 6/1 priority date for domestic and international students; for winter admission, 11/1 priority date for domestic and international students. Applications are processed on a rolling basis. *Application fee:* $40. Electronic applications accepted. *Application Contact:* Dr. Ali Ardalan, Associate Dean, 757-683-3520, Fax: 757-683-4076, E-mail: aardalan@odu.edu. *Dean,* Dr. Nancy Bagranoff, 757-683-3520, Fax: 757-683-4076, E-mail: nbagranoff@odu.edu.

College of Health Sciences Students: 284 full-time (240 women), 155 part-time (139 women); includes 101 minority (65 African Americans, 1 American Indian/Alaska Native, 24 Asian Americans or Pacific Islanders, 11 Hispanic Americans), 11 international. Average age 33. 335 applicants, 73% accepted, 110 enrolled. *Faculty:* 42 full-time (31 women), 15 part-time/adjunct (13 women). Expenses: Contact institution. *Financial support:* In 2008–09, 210 students received support, including 5 fellowships with full tuition reimbursements available (averaging $15,000 per year), 10 research assistantships with tuition reimbursements available (averaging $10,000 per year), 10 teaching assistantships with tuition reimbursements available (averaging $10,000 per year); career-related internships or fieldwork, institutionally sponsored loans, scholarships/grants, traineeships, tuition waivers (partial), and unspecified assistantships also available. Support available to part-time students. Financial award application deadline: 2/15; financial award applicants required to submit FAFSA. In 2008, 92 master's, 31 doctorates awarded. *Degree program information:* Part-time and evening/weekend programs available. Postbaccalaureate distance learning degree programs offered (minimal on-campus study). Offers community health professions (MS); environmental health (MS); health care administration (MS); health sciences (MPH, MS, MSN, DNP, DPT, PhD); health services research (PhD); long-term care administration (MS); nursing practice (DNP); public health (MPH); wellness and promotion (MS). *Application deadline:* Applications are processed on a rolling basis. *Application fee:* $40. Electronic applications accepted. *Application Contact:* Dr. Andrew Balas, Dean, 757-683-4960, Fax: 757-683-3674, E-mail: abalas@odu.edu. *Dean,* Dr. Andrew Balas, 757-683-4960, Fax: 757-683-3674, E-mail: abalas@odu.edu.

School of Dental Hygiene Students: 7 full-time (all women), 6 part-time (all women); includes 5 minority (3 African Americans, 2 Asian Americans or Pacific Islanders), 3 international. Average age 34. 5 applicants, 80% accepted, 4 enrolled. *Faculty:* 8 full-time (all women). Expenses: Contact institution. *Financial support:* In 2008–09, 4 students received support, including 3 teaching assistantships with partial tuition reimbursements available (averaging $10,000 per year); fellowships, research assistantships, career-related internships or fieldwork, scholarships/grants, tuition waivers, and unspecified assistantships also available. Support available to part-time students. Financial award application deadline: 2/15; financial award applicants required to submit CSS PROFILE or FAFSA. In 2008, 1 master's awarded. *Degree program information:* Part-time programs available. Offers dental hygiene (MS). *Application deadline:* For fall admission, 7/1 for domestic students, 4/15 for international students; for spring admission, 12/1 for domestic students, 10/1 for international students. Applications are processed on a rolling basis. *Application fee:* $40. Electronic applications accepted. *Application Contact:* Prof. Michele L. Darby, Graduate Program Director, 757-683-5232, Fax: 757-683-5329, E-mail: mdarby@odu.edu. *Graduate Program Director,* Prof. Michele L. Darby, 757-683-5232, Fax: 757-683-5329, E-mail: mdarby@odu.edu.

School of Nursing Students: 115 full-time (101 women), 106 part-time (102 women); includes 42 minority (21 African Americans, 15 Asian Americans or Pacific Islanders, 6 Hispanic Americans), 1 international. Average age 38. 169 applicants, 81% accepted, 122 enrolled. *Faculty:* 10 full-time (8 women), 15 part-time/adjunct (14 women). Expenses: Contact institution. *Financial support:* In 2008–09, 18 students received support, including 2 research assistantships with tuition reimbursements available (averaging $10,000 per year); teaching assistantships, career-related internships or fieldwork, scholarships/grants, traineeships, and tuition waivers (partial) also available. Support available to part-time students. Financial award application deadline: 2/15; financial award applicants required to submit FAFSA. In 2008, 72 master's awarded. *Degree program information:* Part-time programs available. Postbaccalaureate distance learning degree programs offered (no on-campus study). Offers family nurse practitioner (MSN); nurse anesthesia (MSN); nurse educator (MSN); nurse midwifery (MSN); women's health nurse practitioner (MSN). *Application deadline:* For fall admission, 6/1 for domestic students. Applications are processed on a rolling basis. *Application fee:* $40. Electronic applications accepted. *Application Contact:* Sue Parker, Graduate Program Assistant, 757-683-4298, Fax: 757-683-5253, E-mail: sparker@odu.edu. *Graduate Program Director,* Dr. Laurel Garzon, 757-683-5250, Fax: 757-683-5253, E-mail: nursgpd@odu.edu.

School of Physical Therapy Students: 125 full-time (101 women), 2 part-time (both women); includes 23 minority (15 African Americans, 4 Asian Americans or Pacific Islanders, 4 Hispanic Americans), 1 international. Average age 24. 170 applicants, 48% accepted, 49 enrolled. *Faculty:* 9 full-time (6 women), 6 part-time/adjunct (4 women). Expenses: Contact institution. *Financial support:* In 2008–09, 4 students received support, including 1 fellowship (averaging $15,000 per year), 1 research assistantship with partial tuition reimbursement available (averaging $7,500 per year), 2 teaching assistantships (averaging $5,000 per year); career-related internships or fieldwork also available. Financial award applicants required to submit FAFSA. In 2008, 29 doctorates awarded. Offers physical therapy (DPT). *Application deadline:* For fall admission, 11/1 for domestic and international students. Applications are processed on a rolling basis. *Application fee:* $40. *Application Contact:* Dr. Martha Walker, Graduate Program Director, 757-683-4519, Fax: 757-683-4410, E-mail: ptgpd@odu.edu. *Graduate Program Director,* Dr. Martha Walker, 757-683-4519, Fax: 757-683-4410, E-mail: ptgpd@odu.edu.

College of Sciences Students: 166 full-time (82 women), 295 part-time (144 women); includes 41 minority (16 African Americans, 1 American Indian/Alaska Native, 16 Asian Americans or Pacific Islanders, 8 Hispanic Americans), 179 international. Average age 29. *Faculty:* 130 full-time (32 women), 3 part-time/adjunct (1 woman). Expenses: Contact institution. *Financial support:* In 2008–09, 3 fellowships (averaging $5,000 per year), 158 research assistantships with tuition reimbursements (averaging $18,000 per year), 101 teaching assistantships with tuition reimbursements (averaging $16,000 per year) were awarded; career-related internships or fieldwork, scholarships/grants, and tuition waivers (partial) also available. Support available to part-time students. Financial award application deadline: 2/15; financial award applicants required to submit FAFSA. In 2008, 88 master's, 25 doctorates awarded. *Degree program information:* Part-time and evening/weekend programs available. Offers analytical chemistry (MS); applied experimental psychology (PhD); biochemistry (MS); biology (MS); biomedical sciences (PhD); chemistry (PhD); clinical psychology (Psy D); computational and applied mathematics (MS, PhD); computer science (MS, PhD); ecological sciences (PhD); environmental chemistry (MS); human factors psychology (PhD); industrial/organizational psychology (PhD); ocean and earth sciences (MS); oceanography (PhD); organic chemistry (MS); physical chemistry (MS); physics (MS, PhD); psychology (MS, PhD); sciences (MS, PhD, Psy D). *Application fee:* $40. Electronic applications accepted. *Application Contact:* Dr. Chris Platsoucas, Dean, 757-683-3274, Fax: 757-683-3034, E-mail: cplatsoucas@odu.edu. *Dean,* Dr. Chris Platsoucas, 757-683-3274, Fax: 757-683-3034, E-mail: cplatsoucas@odu.edu.

Darden College of Education Students: 546 full-time (445 women), 1,013 part-time (778 women); includes 315 minority (240 African Americans, 8 American Indian/Alaska Native, 31 Asian Americans or Pacific Islanders, 36 Hispanic Americans), 21 international. Average age 34. 1,125 applicants, 72% accepted. *Faculty:* 100 full-time (56 women), 74 part-time/adjunct (45 women). Expenses: Contact institution. *Financial support:* In 2008–09, 141 students received support, including 9 fellowships with full and partial tuition reimbursements available (averaging $15,000 per year), 60 research assistantships with full and partial tuition reimbursements available (averaging $15,000 per year), 72 teaching assistantships with full and partial tuition reimbursements available (averaging $15,000 per year); career-related internships or fieldwork, Federal Work-Study, institutionally sponsored loans, scholarships/grants, tuition waivers (partial), and unspecified assistantships also available. Support available to part-time students. Financial award application deadline: 2/15; financial award applicants required to submit CSS PROFILE or FAFSA. In 2008, 581 master's, 11 doctorates, 17 other advanced degrees awarded. *Degree program information:* Part-time and evening/weekend programs available. Postbaccalaureate distance learning degree programs offered (no on-campus study). Offers athletic training (MS Ed); biology (MS Ed); business and industry training (MS); career and technical education (MS, PhD); chemistry (MS Ed); community college leadership (PhD); community college teaching (MS); counseling (MS Ed, PhD, Ed S); curriculum and instruction (MS Ed); early childhood education (MS Ed, PhD); education (MS, MS Ed, PhD, Ed S); educational leadership (MS Ed, PhD, Ed S); educational media (MS Ed); educational training (MS Ed); elementary education (MS Ed); English (MS Ed); exercise and wellness (MS Ed); higher education (MS Ed, PhD, Ed S); human movement science (PhD); human resources training (PhD); instructional design and technology (PhD); instructional technology (MS Ed); library science (MS Ed); literacy leadership (PhD); middle school education (MS Ed); physical education (MS Ed); principal preparation (MS Ed); reading education (MS Ed); recreation and tourism studies (MS Ed); secondary education (MS Ed); special education (MS Ed, PhD); speech-language pathology (MS Ed); sport management (MS Ed); technology education (PhD). *Application deadline:* For fall admission, 6/1 priority date for domestic and international students; for spring admission, 11/1 priority date for domestic and international students. Applications are processed on a rolling basis. *Application fee:* $40. Electronic applications accepted. *Application Contact:* Alice McAdory, Director of Admissions, 757-683-3685, Fax: 757-683-3255, E-mail: gradadmit@odu.edu. *Dean,* Dr. William H. Graves, 757-683-3938, Fax: 757-683-5083, E-mail: wgraves@odu.edu.

Frank Batten College of Engineering and Technology Students: 110 full-time (31 women), 597 part-time (106 women); includes 88 minority (41 African Americans, 3 American Indian/Alaska Native, 29 Asian Americans or Pacific Islanders, 15 Hispanic Americans), 224 international. Average age 32. 558 applicants, 63% accepted, 144 enrolled. *Faculty:* 93 full-time (12 women), 13 part-time/adjunct (2 women). Expenses: Contact institution. *Financial support:* In 2008–09, 168 students received support, including 8 fellowships with full and partial tuition reimbursements available (averaging $15,000 per year), 92 research assistantships with full and partial tuition reimbursements available (averaging $15,000 per year), 68 teaching assistantships with full and partial tuition reimbursements available (averaging $15,000 per year); career-related internships or fieldwork, Federal Work-Study, institutionally sponsored loans, scholarships/grants, and unspecified assistantships also available. Support available to part-time students. Financial award applicants required to submit FAFSA. In 2008, 253 master's, 21 doctorates awarded. *Degree program information:* Part-time and evening/weekend programs available. Postbaccalaureate distance learning degree programs offered. Offers aerospace engineering (ME, MS, D Eng, PhD); civil and environmental engineering (D Eng); civil engineering (ME, MS, PhD); computer engineering (ME, MS); design and manufacturing (ME); electrical and computer engineering (PhD); electrical engineering (ME, MS); engineering and technology (ME, MEM, MS, D Eng, PhD); engineering management (MEM, MS, PhD); engineering management and systems engineering (D Eng); environmental engineering (ME, MS, PhD); mechanical engineering (ME, MS, D Eng, PhD); modeling and simulation (ME, MS, D Eng, PhD); motorsports (ME); systems engineering (ME). *Application deadline:* For fall admission, 6/1 for domestic students, 2/15 priority date for international students; for spring admission, 11/1 for domestic students, 10/1 for international students. Applications are processed on a rolling basis. *Application fee:* $40. Electronic applications accepted. *Application Contact:* Dr. Linda Vahala, Associate Dean, 757-683-3789, Fax: 757-683-4898, E-mail: lvahala@odu.edu. *Dean,* Dr. Oktay Baysal, 757-683-3789, Fax: 757-683-4898, E-mail: obaysal@odu.edu.

OLIVET COLLEGE, Olivet, MI 49076-9701

General Information Independent-religious, coed, comprehensive institution.

GRADUATE UNITS

Program in Education Offers education (MAT). Electronic applications accepted.

OLIVET NAZARENE UNIVERSITY, Bourbonnais, IL 60914-2271

General Information Independent-religious, coed, comprehensive institution. *Graduate housing:* Room and/or apartments available to single students; on-campus housing not available to married students. Housing application deadline: 8/15.

GRADUATE UNITS

Graduate School *Degree program information:* Part-time and evening/weekend programs available. Offers business administration (MBA); practical ministries (MPM).

Division of Education *Degree program information:* Evening/weekend programs available. Offers curriculum and instruction (MAE); elementary education (MAT); library information specialist (MAE); reading specialist (MAE); school leadership (MAE); secondary education (MAT).

Division of Religion *Degree program information:* Part-time programs available. Offers biblical literature (MA); religion (MA); theology (MA).

Program in Organizational Leadership Offers organizational leadership (MOL).

ORAL ROBERTS UNIVERSITY, Tulsa, OK 74171-0001

General Information Independent-religious, coed, comprehensive institution. *Graduate housing:* Room and/or apartments available on a first-come, first-served basis to single students; on-campus housing not available to married students.

GRADUATE UNITS

School of Business *Degree program information:* Part-time programs available. Postbaccalaureate distance learning degree programs offered (minimal on-campus study). Offers accounting (MBA); entrepreneurship (MBA); finance (MBA); international business (MBA); management (MBA); marketing (MBA); non-profit management (M Man, MBA); organizational dynamics (M Man); sales marketing (M Man).

School of Education *Degree program information:* Part-time programs available. Postbaccalaureate distance learning degree programs offered (minimal on-campus study). Offers Christian school administration (K-12) (MA Ed, Ed D); Christian school curriculum development (MA Ed); college and higher education administration (MA Ed, Ed D); public school administration (K-12) (MA Ed, Ed D); public school teaching (MA Ed); teaching English as a second language (MA Ed).

School of Theology and Missions *Degree program information:* Part-time programs available. Postbaccalaureate distance learning degree programs offered (minimal on-campus study). Offers biblical literature (MA); Christian counseling (MA); Christian education (MA); divinity (M Div); missions (MA); practical theology (MA); theological/historical studies (MA); theology (D Min). Electronic applications accepted.

OREGON COLLEGE OF ORIENTAL MEDICINE, Portland, OR 97216

General Information Independent, coed, graduate-only institution. *Graduate housing:* On-campus housing not available.

GRADUATE UNITS

Graduate Program in Acupuncture and Oriental Medicine *Degree program information:* Part-time programs available. Offers acupuncture and Oriental medicine (M Ac OM, MAcOM, DAOM).

OREGON HEALTH & SCIENCE UNIVERSITY, Portland, OR 97239-3098

General Information State-related, coed, upper-level institution. *Enrollment:* 2,424 graduate, professional, and undergraduate students; 1,367 full-time matriculated graduate/professional students (720 women), 453 part-time matriculated graduate/professional students (250 women). *Enrollment by degree level:* 803 first professional, 421 master's, 305 doctoral, 291 other advanced degrees. *Graduate faculty:* 820. *Graduate housing:* On-campus housing not available. *Student services:* Campus safety program, career counseling, exercise/wellness program, free psychological counseling, low-cost health insurance, multicultural affairs office, services for students with disabilities. *Library facilities:* OHSU Main Library plus 7 others. *Online resources:* library catalog, web page, access to other libraries' catalogs. *Collection:* 275,230 titles, 12,865 serial subscriptions, 1,119 audiovisual materials. *Research affiliation:* Oregon Regional Primate Research Center.

Computer facilities: 49 computers available on campus for general student use. A campuswide network can be accessed from student residence rooms and from off campus. *Web address:* http://www.ohsu.edu/.

General Application Contact: Registrar's Office, 503-494-7800.

GRADUATE UNITS

OGI School of Science and Engineering Offers biochemistry and molecular biology (MS, PhD); biomedical engineering (MS, PhD); computer science and engineering (MS, PhD); electrical engineering (MS, PhD); environmental science and engineering (MS, PhD); management in science and technology (MS); science and engineering (MS, PhD).

School of Dentistry Offers biomaterials and biomechanics (MS); dentistry (DMD, MS, Certificate); endodontics (Certificate); oral and maxillofacial surgery (Certificate); oral molecular biology (MS); orthodontics (MS, Certificate); pediatric dentistry (Certificate); periodontology (MS, Certificate); restorative dentistry (MS). Electronic applications accepted.

School of Medicine *Degree program information:* Part-time programs available. Offers epidemiology and biostatistics (MPH); medicine (MD, MPH, MS, PhD, Certificate).

Graduate Programs in Medicine *Degree program information:* Part-time programs available. Offers behavioral neuroscience (MS, PhD); biochemistry and molecular biology (PhD); biomedical informatics (MS, PhD, Certificate); cell and developmental biology (PhD); clinical nutrition (MS); medicine (MS, PhD, Certificate); molecular and medical genetics (PhD); molecular microbiology and immunology (PhD); neuroscience (PhD); pharmacology (PhD); physiology (PhD).

School of Nursing *Degree program information:* Part-time programs available. Offers gerontological nursing (Post Master's Certificate); mental health nursing (MN, MS, Post Master's Certificate); nurse anesthesia (MN, MS); nurse midwifery (MN, MS, Post Master's Certificate); nurse practitioner (MN, MS, Post Master's Certificate); nursing (MN, MPH, MS, DNP, PhD, Post Master's Certificate); nursing education (MN, MS, Post Master's Certificate); primary care and disparities (MPH); public health (MPH, Post Master's Certificate). Electronic applications accepted.

OREGON STATE UNIVERSITY, Corvallis, OR 97331

General Information State-supported, coed, university. CGS member. *Enrollment:* 20,320 graduate, professional, and undergraduate students; 2,542 full-time matriculated graduate/professional students (1,260 women), 1,105 part-time matriculated graduate/professional students (594 women). *Enrollment by degree level:* 552 first professional, 1,492 master's, 1,099 doctoral. *Graduate faculty:* 1,148 full-time (431 women), 237 part-time/adjunct (131 women). Tuition, state resident: full-time $9396; part-time $348 per credit. Tuition, nonresident: full-time $15,228; part-time $564 per credit. *Graduate housing:* Rooms and/or apartments available on a first-come, first-served basis to single and married students. Housing application deadline: 9/10. *Student services:* Campus employment opportunities, campus safety program, career counseling, child daycare facilities, exercise/wellness program, free psychological counseling, international student services, low-cost health insurance, multicultural affairs office, services for students with disabilities, teacher training, writing training. *Library facilities:* Valley Library. *Online resources:* library catalog, web page, access to other libraries' catalogs.

Oregon State University (continued)

Collection: 689,119 titles, 12,254 serial subscriptions. *Research affiliation:* David and Lucille Packard Foundation (science, environmental science), W.M. Keck Foundation (science, engineering), William and Flora Hewett Foundation (science, engineering), George and Betty Moore Foundation (medical research, science education), Comer Science and Educational Foundation (science).

Computer facilities: Computer purchase and lease plans are available. 1,300 computers available on campus for general student use. A campuswide network can be accessed from student residence rooms and from off campus. Online class registration is available. *Web address:* http://www.oregonstate.edu/.

General Application Contact: Dr. Sally K. Francis, Dean of the Graduate School, 541-737-4881, Fax: 541-737-3313, E-mail: franciss@orst.edu.

GRADUATE UNITS

College of Pharmacy Students: 347 full-time (190 women), 9 part-time (8 women); includes 114 minority (6 African Americans, 102 Asian Americans or Pacific Islanders, 6 Hispanic Americans), 46 international. Average age 27. *Faculty:* 32 full-time (15 women). Expenses: Contact institution. *Financial support:* Fellowships, research assistantships, teaching assistantships, career-related internships or fieldwork, Federal Work-Study, and institutionally sponsored loans available. Support available to part-time students. Financial award application deadline: 2/1. In 2008, 78 first professional degrees, 5 master's, 2 doctorates awarded. *Degree program information:* Part-time programs available. Offers pharmacy (Pharm D, MS, PhD). *Application deadline:* For fall admission, 3/1 for domestic students. Applications are processed on a rolling basis. *Application fee:* $50. *Application Contact:* Terri L. Allen, Office Specialist I, 541-737-5677, Fax: 541-737-3999. *Dean,* Dr. Wayne A. Kradjan, 541-737-3424, Fax: 541-737-3424, E-mail: wayne.kradjan@orst.edu.

College of Veterinary Medicine Students: 195 full-time (160 women), 1 (woman) part-time; includes 6 minority (1 American Indian/Alaska Native, 3 Asian Americans or Pacific Islanders, 2 Hispanic Americans), 7 international. Average age 27. *Faculty:* 40 full-time (21 women), 5 part-time/adjunct (all women). Expenses: Contact institution. *Financial support:* Fellowships, research assistantships, Federal Work-Study, institutionally sponsored loans, and scholarships/grants available. Support available to part-time students. Financial award application deadline: 2/1. In 2008, 44 first professional degrees, 2 master's awarded. *Degree program information:* Part-time programs available. Offers comparative veterinary medicine (PhD); veterinary medicine (DVM, MS, PhD). DVM admissions open only to residents of Oregon and other states participating in the Western Interstate Commission for Higher Education (WICHE). *Application deadline:* For fall admission, 11/1 for domestic students. *Application fee:* $50. *Application Contact:* Dr. Susan J. Tornquist, Associate Dean, 541-737-2098, Fax: 541-737-4245, E-mail: susan.tornquist@oregonstate.edu. *Dean,* Dr. Cyril Clarke, 541-737-0811.

Graduate School Students: 1,918 full-time (876 women), 635 part-time (321 women); includes 248 minority (30 African Americans, 26 American Indian/Alaska Native, 103 Asian Americans or Pacific Islanders, 89 Hispanic Americans), 569 international. Average age 31. Expenses: Contact institution. *Financial support:* Fellowships, research assistantships, teaching assistantships, career-related internships or fieldwork, Federal Work-Study, institutionally sponsored loans, and unspecified assistantships available. Support available to part-time students. Financial award application deadline: 2/1. In 2008, 665 master's, 172 doctorates awarded. *Degree program information:* Part-time programs available. Offers environmental sciences (MA, MS, PhD); interdisciplinary studies (MAIS); molecular and cellular biology (MS, PhD); plant physiology (MS, PhD); water resources engineering (MS, PhD). *Application fee:* $50. *Application Contact:* Rosemary Garagnani, Assistant Dean, 541-737-1465, Fax: 541-737-3313. *Dean,* Dr. Sally K. Francis, 541-737-4881, Fax: 541-737-3313, E-mail: franciss@orst.edu.

College of Agricultural Sciences Students: 241 full-time (124 women), 21 part-time (10 women); includes 27 minority (7 American Indian/Alaska Native, 10 Asian Americans or Pacific Islanders, 10 Hispanic Americans), 76 international. Average age 31. *Faculty:* 225 full-time (58 women), 19 part-time/adjunct (8 women). Expenses: Contact institution. *Financial support:* Fellowships, research assistantships, teaching assistantships, career-related internships or fieldwork, Federal Work-Study, and institutionally sponsored loans available. Support available to part-time students. Financial award application deadline: 2/1. In 2008, 60 master's, 24 doctorates awarded. *Degree program information:* Part-time programs available. Offers agricultural and resource economics (M Agr, MAIS, MS, PhD); agricultural education (M Agr, MAIS, MAT, MS); agricultural sciences (M Ag, M Agr, MA, MAIS, MAT, MS, PhD); animal science (M Agr, MAIS, MS, PhD); crop science (M Agr, MAIS, MS, PhD); economics (MS, PhD); fisheries science (M Agr, MAIS, MS, PhD); food science and technology (M Agr, MAIS, MS, PhD); genetics (MA, MAIS, MS, PhD); horticulture (M Ag, MAIS, MS, PhD); poultry science (M Agr, MAIS, MS, PhD); rangeland ecology and management (M Agr, MAIS, MS, PhD); soil science (M Agr, MAIS, MS, PhD); toxicology (MS, PhD); wildlife science (MAIS, MS, PhD). *Application fee:* $50. *Application Contact:* Dr. Stella Coakley, Associate Dean, 541-737-5264, Fax: 541-737-3178, E-mail: stella.coakley@oregonstate.edu. *Dean,* Dr. Thayne R. Dutson, 541-737-5812, Fax: 541-737-4574, E-mail: thayne.dutson@orst.edu.

College of Business Students: 69 full-time (22 women), 19 part-time (11 women); includes 6 minority (1 African American, 1 American Indian/Alaska Native, 4 Asian Americans or Pacific Islanders), 15 international. Average age 29. *Faculty:* 37 full-time (9 women), 9 part-time/adjunct (3 women). Expenses: Contact institution. *Financial support:* Fellowships, teaching assistantships, career-related internships or fieldwork, Federal Work-Study, and institutionally sponsored loans available. Financial award application deadline: 2/1. In 2008, 43 master's awarded. *Degree program information:* Part-time programs available. Offers business (MAIS, MBA, Certificate). *Application deadline:* For fall admission, 3/15 for domestic students. Applications are processed on a rolling basis. *Application fee:* $50. *Application Contact:* Brenda R. Sallee, Head Advisor, 541-737-3716, Fax: 541-737-4890, E-mail: brenda.sallee@bus.oregonstate.edu. *Dean,* Dr. Ilene K. Kleinsorge, 541-737-6024, Fax: 541-737-3033, E-mail: ilene@bus.oregonstate.edu.

College of Education Students: 116 full-time (95 women), 233 part-time (161 women); includes 56 minority (11 African Americans, 6 American Indian/Alaska Native, 11 Asian Americans or Pacific Islanders, 28 Hispanic Americans), 11 international. Average age 39. *Faculty:* 53 full-time (37 women), 26 part-time/adjunct (19 women). Expenses: Contact institution. *Financial support:* Fellowships, research assistantships, teaching assistantships, career-related internships or fieldwork, Federal Work-Study, and institutionally sponsored loans available. Support available to part-time students. Financial award application deadline: 2/1. In 2008, 125 master's, 25 doctorates awarded. *Degree program information:* Part-time programs available. Offers adult education and higher education leadership (Ed M, MAIS); college student service administration (Ed M, MS); counseling (MS, PhD); education (Ed M, MAIS, MAT, MS, Ed D, PhD); elementary education (MAT); family and consumer sciences education (MAT, MS); general education (Ed M, MAIS, MS, Ed D, PhD); language arts education (MAT); music education (MAT). *Application fee:* $50. *Application Contact:* Rosemary Garagnani, Assistant Dean, 541-737-1465, Fax: 541-737-3313. *Dean,* Dr. Sam Stern, 541-737-6392, Fax: 541-737-8971, E-mail: sam.stern@oregonstate.edu.

College of Engineering Students: 482 full-time (98 women), 154 part-time (31 women); includes 58 minority (8 African Americans, 1 American Indian/Alaska Native, 35 Asian Americans or Pacific Islanders, 14 Hispanic Americans), 244 international. Average age 30. *Faculty:* 111 full-time (18 women), 14 part-time/adjunct (5 women). Expenses: Contact institution. *Financial support:* In 2008–09, 20 fellowships with full tuition reimbursements (averaging $11,608 per year), 192 research assistantships with full tuition reimbursements (averaging $12,639 per year), 129 teaching assistantships with full tuition reimbursements (averaging $9,965 per year) were awarded; career-related internships or fieldwork, Federal Work-Study, institutionally sponsored loans, and instructorships also available. Support available to part-time students. Financial award application deadline: 2/1. In 2008, 125 master's, 25 doctorates awarded. *Degree program information:* Part-time programs available. Offers biological and ecological engineering (M Eng, MS, PhD); chemical engineering (M Eng, MS, PhD); chemical, biological and environmental engineering (M Eng, MS, PhD); civil engineering (MS, PhD); coastal and ocean engineering (M Oc E, PhD); coastal engineering (MS); computer science (M Eng, MAIS, MS, PhD); construction engineering management (MBE, PhD); electrical and computer engineering (M Eng, MS, PhD); engineering (M Eng, M Engr, M Oc E, MA, MAIS, MBE, MHP, MS, PhD); geotechnical engineering (MS, PhD); human systems engineering (MS, PhD); industrial engineering (MS, PhD); information systems engineering (MS, PhD); manufacturing engineering (M Engr); manufacturing systems engineering (MS, PhD); materials science (MAIS, MS, PhD); mechanical engineering (MS, PhD); nano/micro fabrication (MS, PhD); nuclear engineering (M Eng, MS, PhD); radiation health physics (MA, MHP, MS, PhD); structural engineering (MS, PhD); transportation engineering (MS, PhD); water engineering (MS, PhD). *Application deadline:* Applications are processed on a rolling basis. *Application fee:* $50. *Application Contact:* Chris A. Bell, Associate Dean, 541-737-1598, Fax: 541-737-1805, E-mail: chris.a.bell@oregonstate.edu. *Dean,* Dr. Ronald L. Adams, 541-737-7722, Fax: 541-737-1805, E-mail: ronald.lynn.adams@orst.edu.

College of Forestry Students: 109 full-time (48 women), 29 part-time (8 women); includes 9 minority (1 African American, 4 Asian Americans or Pacific Islanders, 4 Hispanic Americans), 38 international. Average age 32. *Faculty:* 61 full-time (9 women), 6 part-time/adjunct (3 women). Expenses: Contact institution. *Financial support:* Fellowships, research assistantships, teaching assistantships, career-related internships or fieldwork, Federal Work-Study, institutionally sponsored loans, and unspecified assistantships available. Support available to part-time students. Financial award application deadline: 2/1. In 2008, 30 master's, 11 doctorates awarded. *Degree program information:* Part-time programs available. Offers forest ecosystems and society (MAIS, MF, MS, PhD); forest engineering (MF, MS); forest hydrology (MF, MS, PhD); forest operations (MF); forest products (MAIS, MF, MS, PhD); forest soil science (MF, MS, PhD); forestry (MAIS, MF, MS, PhD); timber harvesting (PhD); wood science and technology (MF, MS, PhD). *Application deadline:* Applications are processed on a rolling basis. *Application fee:* $50. *Application Contact:* Clay W. Torset, Head Advisor, 541-737-1542, Fax: 541-737-2668, E-mail: clay.torset@oregonstate.edu. *Dean,* Hal J. Salwasser, 541-737-5704, Fax: 541-737-2906, E-mail: hal.salwasser@oregonstate.edu.

College of Health and Human Sciences Students: 190 full-time (146 women), 46 part-time (30 women); includes 27 minority (4 African Americans, 4 American Indian/Alaska Native, 11 Asian Americans or Pacific Islanders, 8 Hispanic Americans), 35 international. Average age 33. *Faculty:* 96 full-time (74 women), 43 part-time/adjunct (27 women). Expenses: Contact institution. *Financial support:* Fellowships, research assistantships, teaching assistantships, career-related internships or fieldwork, Federal Work-Study, and institutionally sponsored loans available. Support available to part-time students. Financial award application deadline: 2/1. In 2008, 52 master's, 13 doctorates awarded. Offers design and human environment (MA, MAIS, MS, PhD); environmental health and occupational safety management (MAIS, MS); exercise and sport science (MS, PhD); gerontology (MAIS); health and human sciences (MA, MAIS, MAT, MPH, MS, PhD); health management and policy (MS, PhD); health promotion and health behavior (MAIS, MAT, MS, PhD); human development and family studies (MS, PhD); movement studies in disabilities (MAIS, MS); nutrition and exercise sciences (MAIS); nutrition and food management (MS); physical education teacher education (MAT, MS); public health (MPH, PhD). *Application deadline:* Applications are processed on a rolling basis. *Application fee:* $50. *Application Contact:* Dr. Tammy Bray, Dean, 541-737-3220, Fax: 541-737-3220. *Dean,* Dr. Tammy Bray, 541-737-3220, Fax: 541-737-3220.

College of Liberal Arts Students: 110 full-time (61 women), 19 part-time (14 women); includes 14 minority (2 African Americans, 2 American Indian/Alaska Native, 5 Asian Americans or Pacific Islanders, 5 Hispanic Americans), 13 international. Average age 32. *Faculty:* 67 full-time (28 women), 14 part-time/adjunct (6 women). Expenses: Contact institution. *Financial support:* Fellowships, research assistantships, teaching assistantships, career-related internships or fieldwork, Federal Work-Study, and institutionally sponsored loans available. Support available to part-time students. Financial award application deadline: 2/1. In 2008, 45 master's, 2 doctorates awarded. *Degree program information:* Part-time programs available. Offers anthropology (MAIS); applied anthropology (MA); applied ethics (MA); contemporary Hispanic studies (MA); economics (MA, MS, PhD); English (MA, MAIS, MFA); foreign language education (MAT); history of science (MA, PhD); interdisciplinary studies (MAIS); interdisciplinary study (MAIS); liberal arts (MA, MAIS, MAT, MFA, MS, PhD); music education (MAT). *Application deadline:* Applications are processed on a rolling basis. *Application fee:* $50. *Application Contact:* Polly Jeneva, Head Adviser, 541-737-0561, Fax: 541-737-2434, E-mail: polly.jeneva@oregonstate.edu. *Dean,* Dr. Kay F. Schaffer, 541-737-0561, Fax: 541-737-2434, E-mail: kschaffer@orst.edu.

College of Oceanic and Atmospheric Sciences Students: 84 full-time (41 women), 10 part-time (6 women); includes 7 minority (1 American Indian/Alaska Native, 3 Asian Americans or Pacific Islanders, 3 Hispanic Americans), 14 international. Average age 30. *Faculty:* 61 full-time (10 women), 4 part-time/adjunct (2 women). Expenses: Contact institution. *Financial support:* Fellowships, research assistantships, teaching assistantships, career-related internships or fieldwork, Federal Work-Study, and institutionally sponsored loans available. Support available to part-time students. Financial award application deadline: 2/1. In 2008, 19 master's, 7 doctorates awarded. Offers atmospheric sciences (MA, MS, PhD); geophysics (MA, MS, PhD); marine resource management (MA, MS); oceanic and atmospheric sciences (MA, MS, PhD); oceanography (MA, MS, PhD). *Application deadline:* For fall admission, 2/1 priority date for domestic students. Applications are processed on a rolling basis. *Application fee:* $50. *Application Contact:* Dr. Robert S. Allan, Assistant Director, Student Programs, 541-737-1340, Fax: 541-737-2064, E-mail: rallan@coas.oregonstate.edu. *Dean,* Dr. Mark R. Abbott, 541-737-5195, Fax: 541-737-2064, E-mail: mark@coas.oregonstate.edu.

College of Science Students: 381 full-time (165 women), 62 part-time (32 women); includes 24 minority (3 African Americans, 2 American Indian/Alaska Native, 12 Asian Americans or Pacific Islanders, 7 Hispanic Americans), 95 international. Average age 30. *Faculty:* 132 full-time (30 women), 20 part-time/adjunct (8 women). Expenses: Contact institution. *Financial support:* Fellowships, research assistantships, teaching assistantships, career-related internships or fieldwork, Federal Work-Study, and institutionally sponsored loans available. Support available to part-time students. Financial award application deadline: 2/1. In 2008, 104 master's, 51 doctorates awarded. *Degree program information:* Part-time programs available. Offers analytical chemistry (MS, PhD); applied physics (MS); biochemistry and biophysics (MA, MAIS, MS, PhD); biology education (MS); chemistry (MA, MAIS); chemistry education (MS); ecology (MA, MAIS, MS, PhD); general science (MA, MS, PhD); genetics (MA, MAIS, MS, PhD); geography (MA, MAIS, MS, PhD); geology (MA, MAIS, MS, PhD); inorganic chemistry (MS, PhD); integrated science education (MS); mathematics (MA, MAIS, MS, PhD); mathematics education (MA, MS, PhD); microbiology (MA, MAIS, MS, PhD); molecular and cellular biology (MA, MAIS, MS, PhD); mycology (MA, MAIS, MS, PhD); nuclear and radiation chemistry (MS, PhD); operations research (MA, MS); organic chemistry (MS, PhD); physical chemistry (MS, PhD); physics (MA, MS, PhD); physics education (MS); plant pathology (MA, MAIS, MS, PhD); plant physiology (MA, MAIS, MS, PhD); science (MA, MAIS, MAT, MS, PhD); science education (MA, MS, PhD); statistics (MA, MS, PhD); structural botany (MA, MAIS, MS, PhD); systematics (MA, MAIS, MS, PhD); zoology (MA, MAIS, MS, PhD). *Application deadline:* Applications are processed on a rolling basis. *Application fee:* $50. *Application Contact:* Dr. Mary Ann Matzke, Head Advisor, 541-737-3880, Fax: 541-737-1009, E-mail: maryann.matzke@oregonstate.edu. *Dean,* Dr. Sherman H. Bloomer, 541-737-3877, E-mail: sherman.bloomer@oregonstate.edu.

OREGON STATE UNIVERSITY–CASCADES, Bend, OR 97701

General Information State-supported, coed, comprehensive institution.

GRADUATE UNITS

Program in Counseling Offers community counseling (MS); school counseling (MS).

Program in Education Offers education (MAT).

OTIS COLLEGE OF ART AND DESIGN, Los Angeles, CA 90045-9785

General Information Independent, coed, comprehensive institution. *Enrollment:* 1,206 graduate, professional, and undergraduate students; 41 full-time matriculated graduate/professional students (28 women), 15 part-time matriculated graduate/professional students (9 women). *Enrollment by degree level:* 56 master's. *Graduate faculty:* 2 full-time (1 woman), 20 part-time/adjunct (9 women). *Tuition:* Full-time $30,464. *Required fees:* $700. *Graduate housing:* On-campus housing not available. *Student services:* Campus employment opportunities, campus safety program, career counseling, free psychological counseling, international student services, low-cost health insurance, writing training. *Library facilities:* Milliard Sheets Library. *Online resources:* library catalog, web page, access to other libraries' catalogs. *Collection:* 42,000 titles, 150 serial subscriptions.

Computer facilities: 240 computers available on campus for general student use. A campuswide network can be accessed. Online class registration is available. *Web address:* http://www.otis.edu/.

General Application Contact: Graduate Studies, 310-665-6820, E-mail: admissions@otis.edu.

GRADUATE UNITS

Program in Fine Arts Students: 17 full-time (8 women); includes 6 minority (1 African American, 1 American Indian/Alaska Native, 2 Asian Americans or Pacific Islanders, 2 Hispanic Americans), 1 international. Average age 32. 129 applicants, 21% accepted, 8 enrolled. *Faculty:* 1 (woman) full-time, 8 part-time/adjunct (3 women). Expenses: Contact institution. *Financial support:* Career-related internships or fieldwork, Federal Work-Study, scholarships/grants, and tuition waivers (partial) available. Financial award applicants required to submit FAFSA. In 2008, 12 master's awarded. Offers new genres (MFA); painting (MFA); photography (MFA); sculpture (MFA). *Application deadline:* For fall admission, 2/15 for domestic and international students. *Application fee:* $50. Electronic applications accepted. *Application Contact:* Information Contact, 310-665-6820, Fax: 310-665-6821, E-mail: admissions@otis.edu. *Chair,* Roy Dowell, 310-665-6893, Fax: 310-665-6998, E-mail: grads@otis.edu.

Program in Graphic Design Students: 7 full-time (5 women); includes 2 African Americans, 4 Asian Americans or Pacific Islanders. 38 applicants, 24% accepted, 7 enrolled. *Faculty:* 3. Expenses: Contact institution. Offers graphic design (MFA). *Application deadline:* For fall admission, 2/15 for domestic and international students. Electronic applications accepted. *Application Contact:* Information Contact, 310-665-6820, Fax: 310-665-6821, E-mail: admissions@otis.edu. *Chair, Graduate Studies,* Kali Nikitas, 310-665-6820, Fax: 310-665-6843, E-mail: jhayes@otis.edu.

Program in Public Practice Students: 11 full-time (10 women); includes 8 minority (3 Asian Americans or Pacific Islanders, 5 Hispanic Americans). 37 applicants, 57% accepted, 11 enrolled. *Faculty:* 7 part-time/adjunct (5 women). Expenses: Contact institution. Offers public practice (MFA). *Application deadline:* For fall admission, 2/15 for domestic and international students. *Application fee:* $50. Electronic applications accepted. *Application Contact:* Information Contact, 310-665-6820, Fax: 310-665-6821, E-mail: admissions@otis.edu. *Chair, Graduate Studies,* Suzanne Lacy, 310-665-6820, Fax: 310-846-2612, E-mail: cvelasco@otis.edu.

Program in Writing Students: 11 full-time (8 women), 13 part-time (7 women); includes 15 minority (3 African Americans, 7 Asian Americans or Pacific Islanders, 5 Hispanic Americans). Average age 34. 44 applicants, 61% accepted, 11 enrolled. *Faculty:* 1 full-time (0 women), 5 part-time/adjunct (1 woman). Expenses: Contact institution. *Financial support:* Federal Work-Study, scholarships/grants, and tuition waivers (partial) available. Financial award applicants required to submit FAFSA. In 2008, 6 master's awarded. Offers writing (MFA). *Application deadline:* For fall admission, 2/15 for domestic and international students. *Application fee:* $50. Electronic applications accepted. *Application Contact:* Information Contact, 310-665-6820, Fax: 310-665-6821, E-mail: admissions@otis.edu. *Chair,* Paul Vangelisti, 310-665-6891, Fax: 310-665-6890, E-mail: pvangel@otis.edu.

OTTAWA UNIVERSITY, Ottawa, KS 66067-3399

General Information Independent-religious, coed, comprehensive institution. *Graduate housing:* On-campus housing not available.

GRADUATE UNITS

Graduate Studies-Arizona *Degree program information:* Part-time and evening/weekend programs available. Postbaccalaureate distance learning degree programs offered. Offers business administration (MBA); Christian counseling (MA); community college counseling (MA); curriculum and instruction (MA); early childhood (MA); education intervention (MA); education leadership (MA); education technology (MA); expressive arts therapy (MA); finance (MBA); human resources (MA, MBA); leadership (MBA); marketing (MBA); marriage and family therapy (MA); Montessori early childhood education (MA); Montessori elementary education (MA); professional development (MA); school guidance counseling (MA); special education—cross categorical (MA); treatment of trauma, abuse and deprivation (MA). Electronic applications accepted.

Graduate Studies-International Postbaccalaureate distance learning degree programs offered (minimal on-campus study). Offers business administration (MBA). Electronic applications accepted.

Graduate Studies-Kansas City *Degree program information:* Part-time and evening/weekend programs available. Postbaccalaureate distance learning degree programs offered (minimal on-campus study). Offers business administration (MBA); human resources (MA). Electronic applications accepted.

Graduate Studies-Wisconsin *Degree program information:* Part-time and evening/weekend programs available. Postbaccalaureate distance learning degree programs offered. Offers business administration (MBA). Electronic applications accepted.

OTTERBEIN COLLEGE, Westerville, OH 43081

General Information Independent-religious, coed, comprehensive institution. *Graduate housing:* On-campus housing not available.

GRADUATE UNITS

Department of Business, Accounting and Economics *Degree program information:* Part-time and evening/weekend programs available. Offers business, accounting and economics (MBA).

Department of Education Offers education (MAE, MAT).

Department of Nursing *Degree program information:* Part-time and evening/weekend programs available. Postbaccalaureate distance learning degree programs offered (minimal on-campus study). Offers adult nurse practitioner (MSN, Certificate); clinical nurse leader (MSN); family nurse practitioner (MSN, Certificate); nurse service administration (MSN).

OUR LADY OF HOLY CROSS COLLEGE, New Orleans, LA 70131-7399

General Information Independent-religious, coed, comprehensive institution. *Graduate housing:* On-campus housing not available.

GRADUATE UNITS

Program in Education and Counseling *Degree program information:* Part-time and evening/weekend programs available. Offers administration and supervision (M Ed); curriculum and instruction (M Ed); marriage and family counseling (MA); school counseling (M Ed, MA).

OUR LADY OF THE LAKE UNIVERSITY OF SAN ANTONIO, San Antonio, TX 78207-4689

General Information Independent-religious, coed, comprehensive institution. *Enrollment:* 2,642 graduate, professional, and undergraduate students; 235 full-time matriculated graduate/professional students (201 women), 844 part-time matriculated graduate/professional students (613 women). *Enrollment by degree level:* 853 master's, 209 doctoral, 16 other advanced degrees. *Tuition:* Full-time $11,970; part-time $665 per credit hour. *Required fees:* $500; $250 per term. *Graduate housing:* Room and/or apartments available on a first-come, first-served basis to single students; on-campus housing not available to married students. Typical cost: $3638 per year ($6449 including board). Room and board charges vary according to board plan. Housing application deadline: 7/15. *Student services:* Campus employment opportunities, career counseling, exercise/wellness program, free psychological counseling, international student services, low-cost health insurance, services for students with disabilities, teacher training. *Library facilities:* The Sueltenfuss Library. *Online resources:* library catalog, web page. *Collection:* 93,551 titles, 600 serial subscriptions, 7,140 audiovisual materials.

Computer facilities: 230 computers available on campus for general student use. A campuswide network can be accessed from student residence rooms and from off campus. Online class registration is available. *Web address:* http://www.ollusa.edu/.

General Application Contact: Information Contact, 210-434-6711 Ext. 2314, Fax: 210-431-4036, E-mail: gradadm@lake.ollusa.edu.

GRADUATE UNITS

College of Arts and Sciences Students: 12 full-time (11 women), 7 part-time (all women); includes 14 minority (1 African American, 13 Hispanic Americans). Expenses: Contact institution. *Financial support:* Research assistantships, teaching assistantships, career-related internships or fieldwork, Federal Work-Study, institutionally sponsored loans, and tuition waivers (partial) available. Support available to part-time students. Financial award application deadline: 4/15. In 2008, 5 master's awarded. *Degree program information:* Part-time and evening/weekend programs available. Offers English (MA); English and communication arts (MA); English and literature (MA); English education (MA); writing (MA). *Application deadline:* Applications are processed on a rolling basis. *Application fee:* $25 ($50 for international students). Electronic applications accepted. *Application Contact:* 210-434-6711, Fax: 210-431-4036, E-mail: gradadm@lake.ollusa.edu. *Dean,* Dr. Mary Francine Danis, 210-434-6711 Ext. 2240.

School of Business and Leadership Students: 34 full-time (23 women), 486 part-time (301 women); includes 318 minority (51 African Americans, 2 American Indian/Alaska Native, 7 Asian Americans or Pacific Islanders, 258 Hispanic Americans), 6 international. Average age 35. Expenses: Contact institution. *Financial support:* In 2008–09, 40 students received support; fellowships available. Financial award application deadline: 4/15. In 2008, 121 master's, 23 doctorates awarded. *Degree program information:* Part-time and evening/weekend programs available. Offers accounting/finance (MBA); healthcare management (MBA); information systems and security (MS); leadership studies (PhD); management (MBA); nonprofit management (MS); organizational leadership (MS). *Application deadline:* Applications are processed on a rolling basis. *Application fee:* $25 ($50 for international students). Electronic applications accepted. *Application Contact:* 210-434-6711, Fax: 210-436-2314. *Dean,* Dr. Robert Bisking, 210-434-6711, Fax: 210-434-0821.

School of Professional Studies Students: 150 full-time (131 women), 308 part-time (272 women); includes 276 minority (44 African Americans, 1 American Indian/Alaska Native, 6 Asian Americans or Pacific Islanders, 225 Hispanic Americans), 4 international. Average age 36. Expenses: Contact institution. *Financial support:* Research assistantships, teaching assistantships, career-related internships or fieldwork, Federal Work-Study, institutionally sponsored loans, scholarships/grants, and tuition waivers (partial) available. Support available to part-time students. In 2008, 160 master's, 3 doctorates awarded. *Degree program information:* Part-time and evening/weekend programs available. Offers bilingual (M Ed); communication and learning disorders (MA); counseling psychology (MS, Psy D); curriculum and instruction (M Ed); early childhood education (M Ed); early elementary education (M Ed); English as a second language (M Ed); generic special education (M Ed); human sciences (MA); integrated math teaching (M Ed); integrated science teaching (M Ed); intermediate education (M Ed); learning resources specialist (M Ed); marriage and family therapy (MS); master technology teacher (M Ed); principal (M Ed); psychology (MS, Psy D); reading specialist (M Ed); school counseling (M Ed); school psychology (MS); secondary education (M Ed). *Application deadline:* Applications are processed on a rolling basis. *Application fee:* $25 ($50 for international students). Electronic applications accepted. *Application Contact:* 210-434-6711 Ext. 2314, Fax: 210-431-4036, E-mail: gradadm@lake.ollusa.edu. *Dean,* Dr. Teresita Aguilar, 210-434-6711 Ext. 2291, Fax: 210-431-3927, E-mail: secs@lake.ollusa.edu.

Worden School of Social Service Students: 38 full-time (35 women), 17 part-time (16 women); includes 28 minority (9 African Americans, 19 Hispanic Americans), 1 international. Average age 34. Expenses: Contact institution. *Financial support:* In 2008–09, 11 research assistantships were awarded; career-related internships or fieldwork, Federal Work-Study, institutionally sponsored loans, and tuition waivers (partial) also available. Financial award application deadline: 4/15. In 2008, 32 master's awarded. *Degree program information:* Part-time programs available. Offers social service (MSW). *Application deadline:* For fall admission, 4/2 priority date for domestic and international students; for spring admission, 11/1 priority date for domestic and international students. Applications are processed on a rolling basis. *Application fee:* $25 ($50 for international students). Electronic applications accepted. *Application Contact:* 210-434-6711 Ext. 2314, Fax: 210-431-4036, E-mail: gradadm@lake.ollusa.edu. *Director,* Dr. Walter Calvo, 210-431-3969, Fax: 210-431-4028, E-mail: wecalvo@lake.ollusa.edu.

OXFORD GRADUATE SCHOOL, Dayton, TN 37321-6736

General Information Independent-religious, coed, graduate-only institution. *Graduate housing:* Rooms and/or apartments guaranteed to single students and available to married students.

GRADUATE UNITS

Graduate Programs Offers family life education (M Litt); organizational leadership in nonprofits (M Litt); religion and society (D Phil).

PACE UNIVERSITY, New York, NY 10038

General Information Independent, coed, university. CGS member. *Enrollment:* 12,704 graduate, professional, and undergraduate students; 921 full-time matriculated graduate/professional students (585 women), 3,121 part-time matriculated graduate/professional students (1,872 women). *Enrollment by degree level:* 3,678 master's, 313 doctoral, 51 other advanced degrees. Tuition and fees vary according to course load, degree level and program. *Graduate housing:* Room and/or apartments available on a first-come, first-served basis to single students; on-campus housing not available to married students. *Student services:* Campus employment opportunities, career counseling, free psychological counseling, international student services, low-cost health insurance, multicultural affairs office, teacher training, writing training. *Library facilities:* Henry Birnbaum Library plus 3 others. *Online resources:* library catalog, web page, access to other libraries' catalogs. *Collection:* 816,086 titles, 31,983 serial subscriptions, 2,319 audiovisual materials.

Computer facilities: Computer purchase and lease plans are available. 250 computers available on campus for general student use. A campuswide network can be accessed from student residence rooms and from off campus. Online class registration is available. *Web address:* http://www.pace.edu/.

General Application Contact: Donna Hoyt, Dean of Admissions, 212-346-1531, Fax: 212-346-1585, E-mail: gradnyc@pace.edu.

GRADUATE UNITS

Dyson College of Arts and Sciences Students: 416 full-time (328 women), 297 part-time (241 women); includes 202 minority (106 African Americans, 2 American Indian/Alaska Native, 37 Asian Americans or Pacific Islanders, 57 Hispanic Americans), 38 international. Average age 28. 789 applicants, 60% accepted, 218 enrolled. Expenses: Contact institution. *Financial support:* Research assistantships, teaching assistantships, career-related internships or fieldwork, Federal Work-Study, and tuition waivers (partial) available. Support available to part-time students. Financial award application deadline: 5/15; financial award applicants required to submit FAFSA. In 2008, 152 master's, 19 doctorates awarded. *Degree program information:* Part-time and evening/weekend programs available. Offers acting (MFA); arts and sciences (MA, MFA, MPA, MS, MS Ed, Psy D); counseling-substance abuse (MS); directing (MFA); environmental science (MS); forensic science (MS); government management (MPA); health care administration (MPA); loss and grief (MS); mental health (MS); nonprofit management (MPA); physician assistant (MS); playwriting (MFA); psychology (MA, MS, MS Ed, Psy D); publishing (MS); school psychology (MS Ed); school-clinical child psychology (MS Ed, Psy D); school-clinical psychology (Psy D); substance abuse (MS). *Application deadline:* Applications are processed on a rolling basis. *Application fee:* $70. Electronic

Pace University (continued)

applications accepted. *Application Contact:* Joanna Broda, Director of Admissions, 212-346-1652, Fax: 212-346-1585, E-mail: gradnyc@pace.edu. *Dean,* Dr. Nira Hermann, 212-346-1517.

Lienhard School of Nursing Students: 40 full-time (37 women), 265 part-time (242 women); includes 124 minority (63 African Americans, 37 Asian Americans or Pacific Islanders, 24 Hispanic Americans), 8 international. Average age 36. 361 applicants, 61% accepted, 90 enrolled. *Faculty:* 7 full-time (all women), 13 part-time/adjunct (10 women). Expenses: Contact institution. *Financial support:* Research assistantships, career-related internships or fieldwork, Federal Work-Study, and tuition waivers (partial) available. Support available to part-time students. Financial award applicants required to submit FAFSA. In 2008, 77 master's, 5 other advanced degrees awarded. *Degree program information:* Part-time and evening/weekend programs available. Offers family nurse practitioner (MS); nursing (Advanced Certificate); nursing education (MA); nursing practice (DNP). *Application deadline:* For fall admission, 7/31 priority date for domestic students, 4/30 priority date for international students; for spring admission, 10/14 for domestic students, 9/14 for international students. Applications are processed on a rolling basis. *Application fee:* $70. Electronic applications accepted. *Application Contact:* Joanna Broda, Director of Graduate Admissions, 914-422-4283, Fax: 914-422-4287, E-mail: gradwp@pace.edu. *Dean,* Dr. Harriet Feldman, 914-773-3341.

Lubin School of Business Students: 236 full-time (109 women), 812 part-time (351 women); includes 203 minority (46 African Americans, 1 American Indian/Alaska Native, 116 Asian Americans or Pacific Islanders, 40 Hispanic Americans), 361 international. Average age 30. 1,306 applicants, 65% accepted, 329 enrolled. Expenses: Contact institution. *Financial support:* Research assistantships, career-related internships or fieldwork, Federal Work-Study, and tuition waivers (full and partial) available. Support available to part-time students. Financial award applicants required to submit FAFSA. In 2008, 389 master's, 2 doctorates, 5 other advanced degrees awarded. *Degree program information:* Part-time and evening/weekend programs available. Postbaccalaureate distance learning degree programs offered (minimal on-campus study). Offers banking and finance (MBA); business (MBA, MS, DPS, APC); corporate economic planning (MBA); corporate financial management (MBA); financial economics (MBA); financial management (MBA); information systems (MBA); international business (MBA); international economics (MBA); investment management (MBA, MS); management (MBA); management science (MBA); managerial accounting (MBA); marketing management (MBA); marketing research (MBA); operations management (MBA); professional studies (DPS); public accounting (MBA, MS); taxation (MBA, MS). *Application deadline:* For fall admission, 7/31 priority date for domestic students; for spring admission, 11/30 for domestic students. Applications are processed on a rolling basis. *Application fee:* $70. Electronic applications accepted. *Application Contact:* Susan Ford-Goldschein, Director of Admissions, 212-346-1652, Fax: 212-346-1585, E-mail: gradnyc@pace.edu. *Dean,* Joseph R. Baczko, 212-346-1963.

School of Education Students: 112 full-time (84 women), 1,358 part-time (907 women); includes 161 minority (63 African Americans, 1 American Indian/Alaska Native, 38 Asian Americans or Pacific Islanders, 59 Hispanic Americans), 7 international. Average age 27. 414 applicants, 89% accepted, 251 enrolled. Expenses: Contact institution. *Financial support:* Research assistantships, career-related internships or fieldwork and Federal Work-Study available. Support available to part-time students. Financial award applicants required to submit FAFSA. In 2008, 672 master's, 37 other advanced degrees awarded. *Degree program information:* Part-time and evening/weekend programs available. Offers administration and supervision (MS Ed); curriculum and instruction (MS); education (MST); school business management (Certificate). *Application deadline:* For fall admission, 7/31 priority date for domestic students; for spring admission, 11/30 for domestic students. Applications are processed on a rolling basis. *Application fee:* $70. Electronic applications accepted. *Application Contact:* Susan Ford-Goldschein, Director of Admissions, 212-346-1652, Fax: 212-346-1585, E-mail: gradnyc@pace.edu. *Interim Dean,* Dr. Harriet Feldman, 212-346-1512.

School of Law *Degree program information:* Part-time and evening/weekend programs available. Offers comparative legal studies (LL M); environmental law (LL M, SJD); law (JD); real estate law (LL M). Electronic applications accepted.

Seidenberg School of Computer Science and Information Systems Students: 117 full-time (27 women), 389 part-time (131 women); includes 174 minority (64 African Americans, 1 American Indian/Alaska Native, 64 Asian Americans or Pacific Islanders, 45 Hispanic Americans), 96 international. Average age 34. 373 applicants, 87% accepted, 146 enrolled. Expenses: Contact institution. *Financial support:* Research assistantships, career-related internships or fieldwork available. Support available to part-time students. Financial award applicants required to submit FAFSA. In 2008, 72 master's, 4 doctorates awarded. *Degree program information:* Part-time and evening/weekend programs available. Offers computer communications and networks (Certificate); computer science (MS); computing studies (DPS); information systems (MS); object-oriented programming (Certificate); telecommunications (MS, Certificate). *Application deadline:* For fall admission, 7/31 priority date for domestic students; for spring admission, 11/30 for domestic students. Applications are processed on a rolling basis. *Application fee:* $70. Electronic applications accepted. *Application Contact:* Joanna Broda, Director of Graduate Admissions, 914-422-4283, Fax: 914-422-4287, E-mail: gradwp@pace.edu. *Interim Dean,* Dr. Constance Knapp, 914-773-3750, Fax: 914-773-3533, E-mail: cknapp@pace.edu.

PACIFICA GRADUATE INSTITUTE, Carpinteria, CA 93013

General Information Proprietary, coed, graduate-only institution. *Graduate housing:* Rooms and/or apartments guaranteed to single and married students. Housing application deadline: 8/15. *Research affiliation:* EBSCO—Elton B. Stevens Company (journal management), American Psychological Association (psychology-research), North California consortium of Psychology Libraries (psychology).

GRADUATE UNITS

Graduate Programs Offers clinical psychology (PhD); counseling psychology (MA); depth psychology (MA, PhD); mythological studies (MA, PhD).

PACIFIC COLLEGE OF ORIENTAL MEDICINE, San Diego, CA 92108

General Information Proprietary, coed, graduate-only institution. *Graduate housing:* On-campus housing not available. *Research affiliation:* National Institutes of Health (complementary and alternative medicine).

GRADUATE UNITS

Graduate Program *Degree program information:* Part-time and evening/weekend programs available. Offers Oriental medicine (MSTOM, DAOM).

PACIFIC COLLEGE OF ORIENTAL MEDICINE-CHICAGO, Chicago, IL 60613

General Information Proprietary, coed, graduate-only institution. *Graduate housing:* On-campus housing not available. *Research affiliation:* Children's Memorial Hospital of Chicago (pediatric research).

GRADUATE UNITS

Graduate Program *Degree program information:* Part-time and evening/weekend programs available. Offers oriental medicine (MTOM).

PACIFIC COLLEGE OF ORIENTAL MEDICINE-NEW YORK, New York, NY 10010

General Information Proprietary, coed, graduate-only institution. *Graduate housing:* On-campus housing not available.

GRADUATE UNITS

Graduate Program *Degree program information:* Part-time and evening/weekend programs available. Offers Oriental medicine (MSTOM).

PACIFIC LUTHERAN THEOLOGICAL SEMINARY, Berkeley, CA 94708-1597

General Information Independent-religious, coed, graduate-only institution. *Graduate housing:* Rooms and/or apartments available on a first-come, first-served basis to single and married students. Housing application deadline: 8/1.

GRADUATE UNITS

Graduate and Professional Programs *Degree program information:* Part-time programs available. Offers theology (M Div, MA, MCM, MTS, PhD, Th D, Certificate).

PACIFIC LUTHERAN UNIVERSITY, Tacoma, WA 98447

General Information Independent-religious, coed, comprehensive institution. *Graduate housing:* Rooms and/or apartments available on a first-come, first-served basis to single and married students. Housing application deadline: 5/1.

GRADUATE UNITS

Division of Graduate Studies *Degree program information:* Part-time and evening/weekend programs available. Electronic applications accepted.

Division of Humanities *Degree program information:* Part-time programs available. Offers creative writing (MFA). Offered during summer only. Electronic applications accepted.

Division of Social Sciences Offers marriage and family therapy (MA); social sciences (MA). Electronic applications accepted.

School of Business *Degree program information:* Part-time and evening/weekend programs available. Offers business administration (MBA).

School of Education *Degree program information:* Part-time and evening/weekend programs available. Offers education (MAE); educational leadership (MAE); initial teaching certification (MAE).

School of Nursing *Degree program information:* Part-time and evening/weekend programs available. Offers client systems management (MSN); entry level nursing (MSN); family nurse practitioner (MSN); health care systems management (MSN); nursing (MSN).

See Close-Up on page 963.

PACIFIC OAKS COLLEGE, Pasadena, CA 91103

General Information Independent, coed, primarily women, upper-level institution. *Graduate housing:* Room and/or apartments available to single students; on-campus housing not available to married students.

GRADUATE UNITS

Graduate School *Degree program information:* Part-time and evening/weekend programs available. Postbaccalaureate distance learning degree programs offered (minimal on-campus study). Offers human development (MA); marriage, family and child counseling (MA).

PACIFIC SCHOOL OF RELIGION, Berkeley, CA 94709-1323

General Information Independent, coed, graduate-only institution. *Graduate housing:* Rooms and/or apartments guaranteed to single and married students. Housing application deadline: 4/1. *Research affiliation:* Center for Women and Religion (women's studies), Center for Ethics and Social Policy (business ethics), Disciples Seminary Foundation (theology), Swedenborgean House of Studies (theology), Bay Area Faith and Health Consortium (public health).

GRADUATE UNITS

Graduate and Professional Programs *Degree program information:* Part-time programs available. Offers religion (M Div, MA, MTS, D Min, PhD, Th D, CAPS, CMS, CSS, CTS). Electronic applications accepted.

PACIFIC STATES UNIVERSITY, Los Angeles, CA 90006

General Information Independent, coed, comprehensive institution. *Graduate housing:* Room and/or apartments available on a first-come, first-served basis to single students; on-campus housing not available to married students.

GRADUATE UNITS

College of Business *Degree program information:* Part-time and evening/weekend programs available. Postbaccalaureate distance learning degree programs offered (no on-campus study). Offers accounting (MBA); business administration (DBA); finance (MBA); international business (MBA); management of information technology (MBA); real estate management (MBA).

College of Computer Science *Degree program information:* Part-time and evening/weekend programs available. Offers computer science (MSCS); information systems (MSCS).

PACIFIC UNION COLLEGE, Angwin, CA 94508-9707

General Information Independent-religious, coed, comprehensive institution. *Enrollment:* 1,278 graduate, professional, and undergraduate students; 2 full-time matriculated graduate/professional students (both women), 15 part-time matriculated graduate/professional students (11 women). *Enrollment by degree level:* 17 master's. *Graduate faculty:* 3 full-time (1 woman). *Tuition:* Full-time $22,560; part-time $656 per quarter hour. Tuition and fees vary according to student's religious affiliation. *Graduate housing:* Rooms and/or apartments guaranteed to single students and available on a first-come, first-served basis to married students. Typical cost: $3765 per year ($6315 including board) for single students. Room and board charges vary according to housing facility selected. Housing application deadline: 8/31. *Library facilities:* Nelson Memorial Library plus 1 other.

Computer facilities: Computer purchase and lease plans are available. 150 computers available on campus for general student use. A campuswide network can be accessed from student residence rooms and from off campus. Online class registration is available. *Web address:* http://www.puc.edu/.

General Application Contact: Marsha Crow, Credential Analyst/Associate Professor of Education, 707-965-6643, Fax: 707-965-6645, E-mail: mcrow@puc.edu.

GRADUATE UNITS

Department of Education Students: 2 full-time (both women), 15 part-time (11 women); includes 3 minority (all Asian Americans or Pacific Islanders). Average age 30. 3 applicants, 100% accepted. *Faculty:* 3 full-time (1 woman). Expenses: Contact institution. *Financial support:* In 2008–09, 2 students received support, including 2 teaching assistantships with full tuition reimbursements available (averaging $2,600 per year); scholarships/grants and unspecified assistantships also available. Financial award application deadline: 3/1. In 2008, 2 master's awarded. *Degree program information:* Part-time programs available. Offers education (M Ed). Program runs during summer only. *Application deadline:* For fall admission, 7/1 priority date for domestic students; for winter admission, 11/1 priority date for domestic students; for spring admission, 2/1 priority date for domestic students. Applications are processed on a rolling basis. *Application fee:* $0. *Application Contact:* Marsha Crow, Credential Analyst/Associate Professor, 707-965-6643, Fax: 707-965-6645, E-mail: mcrow@puc.edu. *Chair/Professor,* Dr. Jim Roy, 707-965-6644, Fax: 707-965-6645, E-mail: jroy@puc.edu.

PACIFIC UNIVERSITY, Forest Grove, OR 97116-1797

General Information Independent, coed, comprehensive institution. *Enrollment:* 3,167 graduate, professional, and undergraduate students; 1,300 full-time matriculated graduate/professional students (816 women), 202 part-time matriculated graduate/professional students (151 women). *Enrollment by degree level:* 522 first professional, 681 master's, 299 doctoral. *Graduate faculty:* 104 full-time (58 women), 105 part-time/adjunct (61 women). *Graduate housing:* On-campus housing not available. *Student services:* Campus employment opportunities, campus safety program, career counseling, free psychological counseling, international student services, low-cost health insurance, services for students with disabilities, teacher training. *Library facilities:* Pacific University Library. *Online resources:* library catalog, web page, access to other libraries' catalogs. *Collection:* 206,198 titles, 20,908 serial subscriptions, 8,580 audiovisual materials. *Research affiliation:* Jacob Lieberman, O.D. (contact lens, vision research, sports vision), NEI/PEDIG—JAEB Center of Health Research (amblyopia treatment study), BSK (student thesis projects), CIBA Vision (contact lens), Cooper Vision (contact lens), Ohio State University/Vistakon Johnson & Johnson (achieve study, adolescent and child vision care).

Computer facilities: Computer purchase and lease plans are available. 315 computers available on campus for general student use. A campuswide network can be accessed from student residence rooms and from off campus. Web space, printing, student and academic information, WebCT, computer peripherals available. *Web address:* http://www.pacificu.edu/.

General Application Contact: Jon-Erik Larsen, Director of Graduate and Professional Admissions, 503-352-7221, Fax: 503-352-7290, E-mail: admissions@pacificu.edu.

GRADUATE UNITS

College of Education *Degree program information:* Part-time and evening/weekend programs available. Offers early childhood education (MAT); education (MAE); elementary education (MAT); high school education (MAT); middle school education (MAT); special education (MAT); visual function in learning (M Ed). Electronic applications accepted.

College of Optometry Offers optometry (OD, MS). Electronic applications accepted.

School of Occupational Therapy Offers occupational therapy (MOT). Electronic applications accepted.

School of Pharmacy Offers pharmacy (Pharm D). Electronic applications accepted.

School of Physical Therapy Offers entry level (DPT); post-professional (DPT). Electronic applications accepted.

School of Physician Assistant Studies Students: 85 full-time; includes 16 minority (3 African Americans, 1 American Indian/Alaska Native, 7 Asian Americans or Pacific Islanders, 5 Hispanic Americans). Average age 29. 600 applicants, 42 enrolled. *Faculty:* 11 full-time. Expenses: Contact institution. *Financial support:* Fellowships, research assistantships, teaching assistantships, career-related internships or fieldwork, Federal Work-Study, and scholarships/grants available. Financial award applicants required to submit FAFSA. In 2008, 42 master's awarded. Offers physician assistant studies (MHS, MS). *Application deadline:* For fall admission, 10/1 for domestic and international students. *Application fee:* $25. *Application Contact:* Leah Pelto, Assistant Director of Graduate and Professional Admissions, 503-352-7224, Fax: 503-352-7290, E-mail: gradadmissions@pacificu.edu. *Director,* Randy Randolph, 800-933-9308, Fax: 503-352-7290, E-mail: gradadmissions@pacificu.edu.

School of Professional Psychology *Degree program information:* Part-time programs available. Offers clinical psychology (MS, Psy D); counseling psychology (MA). Electronic applications accepted.

PALM BEACH ATLANTIC UNIVERSITY, West Palm Beach, FL 33416-4708

General Information Independent-religious, coed, comprehensive institution. *Enrollment:* 3,211 graduate, professional, and undergraduate students; 538 full-time matriculated graduate/professional students (373 women), 264 part-time matriculated graduate/professional students (156 women). *Enrollment by degree level:* 303 first professional, 499 master's. *Graduate faculty:* 35 full-time (20 women), 13 part-time/adjunct (5 women). *Tuition:* Full-time $8010; part-time $445 per credit hour. *Required fees:* $99 per semester. Tuition and fees vary according to course load, degree level and campus/location. *Graduate housing:* On-campus housing not available. *Student services:* Campus safety program, career counseling, exercise/wellness program, free psychological counseling, international student services, low-cost health insurance, multicultural affairs office, services for students with disabilities, writing training. *Library facilities:* Warren Library. *Online resources:* library catalog, web page. *Collection:* 147,514 titles, 332 serial subscriptions, 4,540 audiovisual materials.

Computer facilities: 460 computers available on campus for general student use. A campuswide network can be accessed from student residence rooms and from off campus. Online class registration is available. *Web address:* http://www.pba.edu/.

General Application Contact: Joe Sharp, Dean of Admissions, 888-468-6722, Fax: 561-803-2115, E-mail: grad@pba.edu.

GRADUATE UNITS

Gregory School of Pharmacy Students: 287 full-time (182 women), 16 part-time (11 women); includes 97 minority (16 African Americans, 1 American Indian/Alaska Native, 39 Asian Americans or Pacific Islanders, 41 Hispanic Americans), 14 international. Average age 26. 801 applicants, 25% accepted, 74 enrolled. *Faculty:* 14 full-time (10 women), 4 part-time/adjunct (2 women). Expenses: Contact institution. *Financial support:* Unspecified assistantships available. Financial award applicants required to submit FAFSA. In 2008, 65 Pharm Ds awarded. Offers pharmacy (Pharm D). *Application deadline:* For fall admission, 5/31 priority date for domestic and international students. Applications are processed on a rolling basis. *Application fee:* $80. Electronic applications accepted. *Application Contact:* Joe Sharp, Assistant Director of Graduate and Evening Admissions, 888-468-6722, Fax: 561-803-2115, E-mail: grad@pba.edu. *Dean,* Dr. Daniel Brown, 561-803-2702, E-mail: daniel_brown@pba.edu.

MacArthur School of Leadership Students: 1 full-time (0 women), 89 part-time (44 women); includes 39 minority (24 African Americans, 2 Asian Americans or Pacific Islanders, 13 Hispanic Americans), 2 international. Average age 38. 48 applicants, 75% accepted, 28 enrolled. *Faculty:* 4 full-time (2 women), 4 part-time/adjunct (1 woman). Expenses: Contact institution. *Financial support:* Tuition waivers (partial) and unspecified assistantships available. Financial award applicants required to submit FAFSA. In 2008, 21 master's awarded. *Degree program information:* Part-time and evening/weekend programs available. Offers organizational leadership (MS). *Application deadline:* For fall admission, 7/15 priority date for domestic students; for spring admission, 11/15 priority date for domestic students. Applications are processed on a rolling basis. *Application fee:* $45. Electronic applications accepted. *Application Contact:* Joe Sharp, Dean of Admissions, 888-468-6722, Fax: 561-803-2115, E-mail: grad@pba.edu. *Dean,* Dr. Jim Laub, 561-803-2318, Fax: 561-803-2306, E-mail: jim_laub@pba.edu.

Rinker School of Business Students: 41 full-time (20 women), 73 part-time (33 women); includes 33 minority (14 African Americans, 1 American Indian/Alaska Native, 1 Asian American or Pacific Islander, 17 Hispanic Americans), 18 international. Average age 32. 70 applicants, 61% accepted, 35 enrolled. *Faculty:* 6 full-time (2 women), 1 part-time/adjunct (0 women). Expenses: Contact institution. *Financial support:* Career-related internships or fieldwork and unspecified assistantships available. Support available to part-time students. Financial award applicants required to submit FAFSA. In 2008, 33 master's awarded. *Degree program information:* Part-time and evening/weekend programs available. Offers business (MBA). *Application deadline:* For fall admission, 7/15 priority date for domestic students; for spring admission, 11/15 priority date for domestic students. Applications are processed on a rolling basis. *Application fee:* $45. Electronic applications accepted. *Application Contact:* Joe Sharp, Assistant Director of Graduate and Evening Admissions, 888-468-6722, Fax: 561-803-2115, E-mail: grad@pba.edu. *Dean,* Dr. Edgar Langlois, 561-803-2462, E-mail: edgar_langlois@pba.edu.

School of Education and Behavioral Studies Students: 210 full-time (172 women), 79 part-time (61 women); includes 117 minority (67 African Americans, 3 Asian Americans or Pacific Islanders, 47 Hispanic Americans), 11 international. Average age 37. 113 applicants, 89% accepted, 77 enrolled. *Faculty:* 12 full-time (5 women), 5 part-time/adjunct (2 women). Expenses: Contact institution. *Financial support:* Career-related internships or fieldwork and unspecified assistantships available. Support available to part-time students. Financial award applicants required to submit FAFSA. In 2008, 84 master's awarded. *Degree program information:* Part-time and evening/weekend programs available. Offers counseling psychology (MSCP). *Application deadline:* For fall admission, 7/15 priority date for domestic students; for spring admission, 11/15 priority date for domestic students. Applications are processed on a rolling basis. *Application fee:* $45. Electronic applications accepted. *Application Contact:* Joe Sharp, Assistant Director of Graduate and Evening Admissions, 888-468-6722, Fax: 561-803-2115, E-mail: grad@pba.edu. *Program Director,* Dr. Phillip Henry, 561-803-2350, Fax: 561-803-2186, E-mail: phillip_henry@pba.edu.

PALMER COLLEGE OF CHIROPRACTIC, Davenport, IA 52803-5287

General Information Independent, coed, comprehensive institution. *Graduate housing:* On-campus housing not available.

GRADUATE UNITS

Division of Graduate Studies Offers anatomy (MS); clinical research (MS). Electronic applications accepted.

Professional Program *Degree program information:* Part-time programs available. Offers chiropractic (DC).

Professional Program–Florida Campus Offers chiropractic (DC).

Professional Program–West Campus Offers chiropractic (DC). Electronic applications accepted.

PALO ALTO UNIVERSITY, Palo Alto, CA 94303-4232

General Information Independent, coed, graduate-only institution. *Graduate housing:* On-campus housing not available.

GRADUATE UNITS

Distance Learning Program in Psychology Postbaccalaureate distance learning degree programs offered (no on-campus study). Offers psychology (MS). Electronic applications accepted.

PGSP-Stanford Psy D Consortium Program Offers psychology (Psy D). Electronic applications accepted.

Program in Clinical Psychology Offers clinical psychology (PhD). Electronic applications accepted.

PARKER COLLEGE OF CHIROPRACTIC, Dallas, TX 75229-5668

General Information Independent, coed, graduate-only institution. *Graduate housing:* On-campus housing not available.

GRADUATE UNITS

First Professional Degree Program *Degree program information:* Part-time programs available. Offers chiropractic (DC). Electronic applications accepted.

PARK UNIVERSITY, Parkville, MO 64152-3795

General Information Independent, coed, comprehensive institution. CGS member. *Graduate housing:* Room and/or apartments available on a first-come, first-served basis to single students; on-campus housing not available to married students.

GRADUATE UNITS

College of Graduate and Professional Studies *Degree program information:* Part-time and evening/weekend programs available. Postbaccalaureate distance learning degree programs offered (no on-campus study). Offers adult education (M Ed); at-risk students (M Ed); disaster and emergency management (MPA); educational administration (M Ed); entrepreneurship (MBA); general business (MBA); general education (M Ed); government/business relations (MPA); healthcare/services management (MBA, MPA); international business (MBA); K-12 certification (MAT); management information systems (MBA); management of information systems (MPA); middle school certification (MAT); multi-cultural education (M Ed); nonprofit management (MPA); public management (MPA); school law (M Ed); secondary school certification (MAT); special education (M Ed). Electronic applications accepted.

PAYNE THEOLOGICAL SEMINARY, Wilberforce, OH 45384-3474

General Information Independent-religious, coed, graduate-only institution. *Graduate housing:* Rooms and/or apartments available on a first-come, first-served basis to single and married students. Housing application deadline: 8/15.

GRADUATE UNITS

Program in Theology *Degree program information:* Part-time and evening/weekend programs available. Postbaccalaureate distance learning degree programs offered (minimal on-campus study). Offers theology (M Div).

PENN STATE DICKINSON SCHOOL OF LAW, Carlisle, PA 17013-2899

General Information State-related, coed, graduate-only institution. *Enrollment by degree level:* 636 first professional, 6 master's. *Graduate housing:* On-campus housing not available. *Student services:* Campus employment opportunities, campus safety program, career counseling, international student services, low-cost health insurance, services for students with disabilities, teacher training, writing training. *Library facilities:* The H. Laddie Montague, Jr. Law Library of The Dickinson School of Law. *Online resources:* library catalog, web page, access to other libraries' catalogs.

Computer facilities: A campuswide network can be accessed from student residence rooms and from off campus. Online class registration is available. *Web address:* http://www.dsl.psu.edu/.

General Application Contact: Barbara W. Guillaume, Director, Law Admissions, 717-240-5207, Fax: 717-241-3503, E-mail: bwg1@psu.edu.

GRADUATE UNITS

Graduate and Professional Programs Students: 554 full-time (244 women), 88 part-time (32 women); includes 126 minority (48 African Americans, 2 American Indian/Alaska Native, 36 Asian Americans or Pacific Islanders, 40 Hispanic Americans), 24 international. Average age 25. Expenses: Contact institution. *Financial support:* In 2008–09, 519 students received support; research assistantships, Federal Work-Study, institutionally sponsored loans, and scholarships/grants available. Support available to part-time students. Financial award application deadline: 3/1; financial award applicants required to submit FAFSA. In 2008, 190 JDs, 12 master's awarded. *Degree program information:* Part-time programs available. Offers comparative law (LL M); law (JD). *Application deadline:* For fall admission, 3/1 priority date for domestic students. Applications are processed on a rolling basis. *Application fee:* $60. Electronic applications accepted. *Application Contact:* Barbara W. Guillaume, Director, Law Admissions, 717-240-5207, Fax: 717-241-3503, E-mail: bwg1@psu.edu. *Dean,* Philip J. McConnaughay, 814-863-1521, E-mail: pjm30@psu.edu.

PENN STATE ERIE, THE BEHREND COLLEGE, Erie, PA 16563-0001

General Information State-related, coed, comprehensive institution. *Enrollment:* 4,334 graduate, professional, and undergraduate students; 71 full-time matriculated graduate/professional students (22 women), 75 part-time matriculated graduate/professional students (14 women). Tuition, state resident: part-time $709 per credit. Tuition, nonresident: part-time $1099 per credit. *Graduate housing:* Room and/or apartments available on a first-come, first-served basis to single students; on-campus housing not available to married students. *Student services:* Campus employment opportunities, campus safety program, career counseling, child daycare facilities, exercise/wellness program, free psychological counseling, grant writing training, international student services, low-cost health insurance, multicultural affairs office, services for students with disabilities. *Library facilities:* John M. Lilley Library. *Online resources:* library catalog, web page, access to other libraries' catalogs. *Collection:* 5.1 million titles, 71,230 serial subscriptions, 163,643 audiovisual materials.

Computer facilities: Computer purchase and lease plans are available. 700 computers available on campus for general student use. A campuswide network can be accessed from student residence rooms and from off campus. Online class registration is available. *Web address:* http://www.pserie.psu.edu/.

General Application Contact: Ann M. Burbules, Graduate Admissions Counselor, 814-898-7255, Fax: 814-898-6044, E-mail: amb29@psu.edu.

Penn State Erie, The Behrend College (continued)

GRADUATE UNITS

Graduate School Students: 71 full-time (22 women), 45 part-time (14 women); includes 7 minority (2 African Americans, 4 Asian Americans or Pacific Islanders, 1 Hispanic American), 7 international. Average age 28. 52 applicants, 73% accepted, 33 enrolled. Expenses: Contact institution. *Financial support:* In 2008–09, 75 students received support. Federal Work-Study available. Financial award application deadline: 2/15; financial award applicants required to submit FAFSA. *Degree program information:* Part-time programs available. Offers business (MBA); project management (MPM). *Application deadline:* Applications are processed on a rolling basis. *Application fee:* $65. Electronic applications accepted. *Application Contact:* Ann M. Burbules, Graduate Admissions Counselor, 814-898-7255, Fax: 814-898-6044, E-mail: amb29@psu.edu. *CEO and Dean*, Dr. John D. Burke, 814-898-6160, Fax: 814-898-6461, E-mail: jdb1@psu.edu.

PENN STATE GREAT VALLEY, Malvern, PA 19355-1488

General Information State-related, coed, graduate-only institution. *Graduate housing:* On-campus housing not available.

GRADUATE UNITS

Graduate Studies Students: 100 full-time (40 women), 933 part-time (422 women); includes 174 minority (46 African Americans, 2 American Indian/Alaska Native, 101 Asian Americans or Pacific Islanders, 25 Hispanic Americans), 17 international. Average age 33. 443 applicants, 77% accepted, 232 enrolled. Expenses: Contact institution. *Financial support:* In 2008–09, 319 students received support; fellowships, research assistantships, teaching assistantships, Federal Work-Study, scholarships/grants, health care benefits, and unspecified assistantships available. Support available to part-time students. Financial award application deadline: 2/15; financial award applicants required to submit FAFSA. In 2008, 393 master's awarded. *Degree program information:* Evening/weekend programs available. *Application deadline:* Applications are processed on a rolling basis. *Application fee:* $65. Electronic applications accepted. *Application Contact:* 610-648-3242, Fax: 610-889-1334. *Chancellor*, Dr. Craig Edelbrock, 610-648-3202, E-mail: cse1@psu.edu.

Education Division Expenses: Contact institution. Offers curriculum and instruction (M Ed); instructional leadership (M Ed); science education (M Ed); special education (M Ed, MS); technology integration for educators (M Ed); training design for corporations (M Ed). *Application Contact:* Dr. Roy Clariana, Division Head, 610-648-3253, Fax: 610-725-5253, E-mail: rbc4@psu.edu. *Division Head*, Dr. Roy Clariana, 610-648-3253, Fax: 610-725-5253, E-mail: rbc4@psu.edu.

Engineering Division Expenses: Contact institution. Offers engineering management (MEM); information science (MS); software engineering (MSE). *Application Contact:* Dr. James A. Nemes, Division Head, 610-648-3335 Ext. 610, Fax: 648-648-3377, E-mail: jan16@psu.edu. *Division Head*, Dr. James A. Nemes, 610-648-3335 Ext. 610, Fax: 648-648-3377, E-mail: jan16@psu.edu.

Management Division Expenses: Contact institution. Offers biotechnology and health industry management (MBA); business administration (MBA); finance (M Fin); leadership development (MLD); management of information technology (MBA); new ventures and entrepreneurial studies (MBA). *Application Contact:* Dr. Daniel Indro, Division Head, 610-725-5283, Fax: 610-725-5224, E-mail: dci1@psu.edu. *Division Head*, Dr. Daniel Indro, 610-725-5283, Fax: 610-725-5224, E-mail: dci1@psu.edu.

PENN STATE HARRISBURG, Middletown, PA 17057-4898

General Information State-related, coed, comprehensive institution. *Graduate housing:* Room and/or apartments available on a first-come, first-served basis to single students; on-campus housing not available to married students.

GRADUATE UNITS

Graduate School Students: 199 full-time (115 women), 1,167 part-time (742 women); includes 141 minority (76 African Americans, 3 American Indian/Alaska Native, 37 Asian Americans or Pacific Islanders, 25 Hispanic Americans), 20 international. Average age 31. 756 applicants, 76% accepted, 413 enrolled. Expenses: Contact institution. *Financial support:* In 2008–09, 541 students received support; fellowships, research assistantships, teaching assistantships, career-related internships or fieldwork, Federal Work-Study, and unspecified assistantships available. Support available to part-time students. Financial award application deadline: 2/15; financial award applicants required to submit FAFSA. In 2008, 494 master's, 12 doctorates awarded. *Degree program information:* Part-time and evening/weekend programs available. *Application deadline:* Applications are processed on a rolling basis. *Application fee:* $65. Electronic applications accepted. *Application Contact:* Robert Coffman, Director of Admissions, 717-948-6250, Fax: 717-948-6325, E-mail: ric1@psu.edu. *Chancellor*, Dr. Madlyn L. Hanes, 717-948-6000, Fax: 717-948-6100, E-mail: mqh3@psu.edu.

School of Behavioral Sciences and Education Expenses: Contact institution. *Financial support:* Career-related internships or fieldwork available. *Degree program information:* Part-time and evening/weekend programs available. Offers applied behavior analysis (MA); applied clinical psychology (MA); applied psychological research (MA); community psychology and social change (MA); health education (M Ed); literacy education (M Ed); teaching and curriculum (M Ed); training and development (M Ed). *Application Contact:* Dr. Robert W. Coffman, Director of Admissions, 717-948-6214, E-mail: rwc11@psu.edu. *Director*, Dr. William D. Milheim, 717-948-6205, Fax: 717-948-6209, E-mail: wdm2@psu.edu.

School of Business Administration Expenses: Contact institution. Offers business administration (MBA, MS); information systems (MS). *Application Contact:* Dr. Stephen P. Schappe, Acting Director, 717-948-6142. *Acting Director*, Dr. Stephen P. Schappe, 717-948-6142.

School of Humanities Expenses: Contact institution. *Degree program information:* Evening/weekend programs available. Offers American studies (MA, PhD); humanities (MA). *Application Contact:* Robert Coffman, Director of Admissions, 717-948-6250, Fax: 717-948-6325, E-mail: ric1@psu.edu. *Director*, Dr. Kathryn Robinson, 717-948-6470, E-mail: kdr12@psu.edu.

School of Public Affairs Expenses: Contact institution. Offers criminal justice (MA); health administration (MHA); public administration (MPA, PhD). *Application Contact:* Robert Coffman, Director of Admissions, 717-948-6250, Fax: 717-948-6325, E-mail: ric1@psu.edu. *Director*, Dr. Steven A. Peterson, 717-948-6154, E-mail: sap12@psu.edu.

School of Science, Engineering and Technology Expenses: Contact institution. *Degree program information:* Evening/weekend programs available. Offers computer science (MS); electrical engineering (M Eng); engineering management (MPS); engineering science (M Eng); environmental engineering (M Eng); environmental pollution control (MEPC, MS). *Application Contact:* Robert Coffman, Director of Admissions, 717-948-6250, Fax: 717-948-6325, E-mail: ric1@psu.edu. *Director*, Dr. Omid Ansary, 717-948-6353, E-mail: axa8@psu.edu.

See Close-Up on page 965.

PENN STATE HERSHEY MEDICAL CENTER, Hershey, PA 17033-2360

General Information State-related, coed, graduate-only institution. *Graduate faculty:* 203 full-time. *Graduate housing:* Rooms and/or apartments available on a first-come, first-served basis to single and married students. Typical cost: $768 per year for married students. Room charges vary according to housing facility selected. *Student services:* Campus safety program, career counseling, child daycare facilities, exercise/wellness program, free psychological counseling, grant writing training, international student services, low-cost health insurance, multicultural affairs office, services for students with disabilities, teacher training, writing training. *Library facilities:* George T. Harrell Library. *Collection:* 100,836 titles, 1,717 serial subscriptions.

Computer facilities: A campuswide network can be accessed from student residence rooms and from off campus. Online class registration is available. *Web address:* http://www.hmc.psu.edu/college/.

General Application Contact: Dr. Michael F. Verderame, Associate Dean of Graduate Studies, 717-531-8892, Fax: 717-531-0786, E-mail: grad-hmc@psu.edu.

GRADUATE UNITS

College of Medicine Students: 215. Average age 0. *Faculty:* 203. Expenses: Contact institution. *Financial support:* In 2008–09, 99 students received support, including research assistantships with full tuition reimbursements available (averaging $22,260 per year); fellowships with full tuition reimbursements available, career-related internships or fieldwork, scholarships/grants, health care benefits, and unspecified assistantships also available. Offers medicine (MD, MS, PhD). *Application deadline:* Applications are processed on a rolling basis. *Application fee:* $65 ($0 for international students). Electronic applications accepted. *Application Contact:* Dr. Michael Verderame, Assistant Dean for Graduate Studies, 717-531-8892, Fax: 717-531-0786, E-mail: GRAD-HMC@PSU.EDU. *Assistant Dean for Graduate Studies*, Dr. Michael Verderame, 717-531-8892, Fax: 717-531-0786, E-mail: GRAD-HMC@PSU.EDU.

Graduate School Programs in the Biomedical Sciences Students: 215. Average age 24. *Faculty:* 203. Expenses: Contact institution. *Financial support:* In 2008–09, 3 fellowships with full tuition reimbursements (averaging $26,500 per year), 37 research assistantships with full tuition reimbursements (averaging $22,250 per year) were awarded; career-related internships or fieldwork, scholarships/grants, health care benefits, tuition waivers (full), and unspecified assistantships also available. Financial award applicants required to submit FAFSA. Offers anatomy (MS, PhD); biochemistry and molecular biology (MS, PhD); bioengineering (MS, PhD); biomedical sciences (MS, PhD); cell and molecular biology (MS, PhD); genetics (PhD); immunology (MS, PhD); integrative biosciences (MS, PhD); laboratory animal medicine (MS); life sciences (MS, PhD); microbiology (MS); microbiology/virology (PhD); molecular biology (PhD); molecular medicine (MS, PhD); molecular toxicology (MS, PhD); neuroscience (MS, PhD); pharmacology (MS, PhD); physiology (MS, PhD); public health sciences (MS). *Application deadline:* For fall admission, 1/31 priority date for domestic students, 2/1 priority date for international students. Applications are processed on a rolling basis. *Application fee:* $65. Electronic applications accepted. *Application Contact:* Kathleen M. Simon, Administrative Assistant, 717-531-8892, Fax: 717-531-0786, E-mail: grad-hmc@psu.edu. *Associate Dean of Graduate Studies*, Dr. Michael F. Verderame, 717-531-8892, Fax: 717-531-0786, E-mail: grad-hmc@psu.edu.

PENN STATE UNIVERSITY PARK, State College, University Park, PA 16802-1503

General Information State-related, coed, university. CGS member. *Graduate housing:* Rooms and/or apartments available on a first-come, first-served basis to single and married students.

GRADUATE UNITS

Graduate School Students: 4,758 full-time (2,079 women), 667 part-time (333 women); includes 479 minority (163 African Americans, 13 American Indian/Alaska Native, 163 Asian Americans or Pacific Islanders, 140 Hispanic Americans), 2,091 international. Average age 37. 11,898 applicants, 28% accepted, 1588 enrolled. *Faculty:* 4,758 full-time (2,079 women), 667 part-time/adjunct (333 women). Expenses: Contact institution. *Financial support:* In 2008–09, 1,664 students received support; fellowships, research assistantships, teaching assistantships, Federal Work-Study, traineeships, health care benefits, tuition waivers (full), and unspecified assistantships available. Support available to part-time students. Financial award application deadline: 2/15; financial award applicants required to submit FAFSA. *Degree program information:* Part-time programs available. Postbaccalaureate distance learning degree programs offered. Offers acoustics (M Eng, MS, PhD); bioengineering (MS, PhD); biogeochemistry (dual) (PhD); business administration (MBA); cell and developmental biology (PhD); demography (dual) (MA); ecology (MS, PhD); environmental pollution control (MEPC, MS); genetics (MS, PhD); human dimensions of natural resources and the environment (dual) (MA, MS, PhD); immunology and infectious diseases (MS); integrative biosciences (MS, PhD); materials science and engineering (PhD); operations research (dual) (M Eng, MA, MS, PhD); physiology (MS, PhD); plant physiology (MS, PhD); quality and manufacturing management (MMM). *Application deadline:* Applications are processed on a rolling basis. *Application fee:* $45. Electronic applications accepted. *Application Contact:* Cynthia E. Nicosia, Director, Graduate Enrollment Services, 814-865-1795, Fax: 814-865-4627, E-mail: cey1@psu.edu. *Vice President, Research and Dean of the Graduate School*, Dr. Eva J. Pell, 814-863-9580, Fax: 814-863-9659, E-mail: ejp@psu.edu.

College of Agricultural Sciences Students: 310 full-time (172 women), 45 part-time (23 women); includes 24 minority (6 African Americans, 7 Asian Americans or Pacific Islanders, 11 Hispanic Americans), 137 international. Average age 28. 459 applicants, 32% accepted, 84 enrolled. *Faculty:* 310 full-time (172 women), 45 part-time/adjunct (23 women). Expenses: Contact institution. *Financial support:* In 2008–09, 111 students received support; fellowships, research assistantships, teaching assistantships available. Financial award applicants required to submit FAFSA. In 2008, 61 master's, 51 doctorates awarded. Offers agricultural and biological engineering (MS, PhD); agricultural and extension education (M Ed, MS, PhD); agricultural sciences (M Agr, M Ed, MFR, MS, PhD); agricultural, environmental and regional economics (M Agr, MS, PhD); agronomy (M Agr, MS, PhD); animal science (M Agr, MS, PhD); entomology (MS, PhD); food science (MS, PhD); forest resources (MFR, MS, PhD); horticulture (M Agr, MS, PhD); pathobiology (PhD); plant pathology (MS, PhD); rural sociology (M Agr, MS, PhD); soil science (M Agr, PhD); wildlife and fisheries sciences (MFR, MS, PhD); youth and family education (M Ed). *Application deadline:* Applications are processed on a rolling basis. *Application fee:* $65. Electronic applications accepted. *Application Contact:* Cynthia E. Nicosia, Director, Graduate Enrollment Services, 814-865-1834, E-mail: cey1@psu.edu. *Dean*, Dr. Bruce A. McPheron, 814-865-2541, Fax: 814-865-3103, E-mail: bam10@psu.edu.

College of Arts and Architecture Students: 185 full-time (116 women), 24 part-time (16 women); includes 21 minority (8 African Americans, 2 American Indian/Alaska Native, 5 Asian Americans or Pacific Islanders, 6 Hispanic Americans), 43 international. Average age 29. 354 applicants, 43% accepted, 81 enrolled. Expenses: Contact institution. *Financial support:* In 2008–09, 77 students received support; fellowships, research assistantships, teaching assistantships available. Financial award applicants required to submit FAFSA. In 2008, 76 master's, 4 doctorates awarded. Offers architecture (M Arch); art (MFA); art education (M Ed, MS, PhD); art history (MA, PhD); arts and architecture (M Arch, M Ed, M Mus, MA, MFA, MLA, MME, MS, PhD); composition/theory (M Mus); conducting (M Mus); landscape architecture (MLA, MS); music education (MME, PhD); music theory (MA); music theory and history (MA); musicology (MA); performance (M Mus); piano performance (PhD); piano, pedagogy and performance (M Mus); theatre (MFA); voice performance and pedagogy (M Mus). *Application deadline:* Applications are processed on a rolling basis. *Application fee:* $65. Electronic applications accepted. *Application Contact:* Cynthia E. Nicosia, Director, Graduate Enrollment Services, 814-865-1834, E-mail: cey1@psu.edu. *Dean*, Dr. Barbara O. Korner, 814-865-2591, Fax: 814-865-2018, E-mail: bok2@psu.edu.

College of Communications Students: 65 full-time (36 women), 14 part-time (9 women); includes 11 minority (5 African Americans, 3 Asian Americans or Pacific Islanders, 3 Hispanic Americans), 19 international. Average age 31. 157 applicants, 39% accepted, 20 enrolled. Expenses: Contact institution. *Financial support:* In 2008–09, 19 students received support; fellowships, research assistantships, teaching assistantships available. Financial award applicants required to submit FAFSA. In 2008, 12 master's, 10 doctorates awarded. Offers communications (MA, PhD); mass communications (PhD); media studies (MA); telecommunications studies (MA). *Application deadline:* Applications are processed on a rolling basis. *Application fee:* $65. Electronic applications accepted. *Application Contact:* Cynthia E. Nicosia, Director, Graduate Enrollment Services, 814-865-1834, E-mail: cey1@psu.edu. *Dean*, Dr. Douglas A. Anderson, 814-863-1484, Fax: 814-863-8044, E-mail: douganderson@psu.edu.

College of Earth and Mineral Sciences Students: 357 full-time (123 women), 34 part-time (7 women); includes 29 minority (10 African Americans, 1 American Indian/Alaska Native, 4 Asian Americans or Pacific Islanders, 14 Hispanic Americans), 149 international. Average age 29. 500 applicants, 40% accepted, 87 enrolled. Expenses: Contact institution. *Financial support:* In 2008–09, 131 students received support; fellowships, research assistantships, teaching assistantships available. Financial award applicants required to submit FAFSA. In

2008, 77 master's, 50 doctorates awarded. Offers earth and mineral sciences (MS, PhD); energy and geo-environmental engineering (MS, PhD); geography (MS, PhD); geosciences (MS, PhD); materials science and engineering (MS, PhD); meteorology (MS, PhD). *Application deadline:* Applications are processed on a rolling basis. *Application fee:* $65. Electronic applications accepted. *Application Contact:* Cynthia E. Nicosia, Director, Graduate Enrollment Services, 814-865-1834, E-mail: cey1@psu.edu. *Dean*, Dr. William E. Easterling, 814-865-6546, Fax: 814-863-7708, E-mail: wee2@psu.edu.

College of Education Students: 484 full-time (324 women), 258 part-time (149 women); includes 85 minority (47 African Americans, 4 American Indian/Alaska Native, 17 Asian Americans or Pacific Islanders, 17 Hispanic Americans), 142 international. Average age 35. 731 applicants, 43% accepted, 185 enrolled. Expenses: Contact institution. *Financial support:* In 2008–09, 324 students received support; fellowships, research assistantships, teaching assistantships available. Financial award applicants required to submit FAFSA. In 2008, 196 master's, 101 doctorates awarded. Offers adult education (M Ed, D Ed, PhD); college student affairs (M Ed); counseling psychology (PhD); counselor education (M Ed, MS); counselor education, counseling psychology and rehabilitation services (D Ed); curriculum and supervision (M Ed, MS, D Ed, PhD); early childhood education (M Ed, MS, D Ed, PhD); education (M Ed, MA, MS, D Ed, PhD); educational leadership (M Ed, MS, D Ed, PhD); educational psychology (MS, PhD); educational theory and policy (MA, PhD); elementary education (M Ed, MS, D Ed, PhD); higher education (M Ed, D Ed, PhD); instructional systems (M Ed, MS, D Ed, PhD); language and literacy education (M Ed, MS, D Ed, PhD); mathematics education (M Ed, MS, D Ed, PhD); school psychology (M Ed, MS, PhD); science education (M Ed, MS, D Ed, PhD); social studies education (M Ed, MS, PhD); special education (M Ed, MS, PhD); workforce education and development (M Ed, MS, D Ed, PhD); world language education (M Ed, MS, D Ed, PhD). *Application deadline:* Applications are processed on a rolling basis. *Application fee:* $65. Electronic applications accepted. *Application Contact:* Cynthia E. Nicosia, Director, Graduate Enrollment Services, 814-865-1834, E-mail: cey1@psu.edu. *Dean*, Dr. David H. Monk, 814-865-2526, Fax: 814-865-0555, E-mail: dhm6@psu.edu.

College of Engineering Students: 1,144 full-time (229 women), 129 part-time (21 women); includes 70 minority (15 African Americans, 1 American Indian/Alaska Native, 37 Asian Americans or Pacific Islanders, 17 Hispanic Americans), 793 international. Average age 27. 3,110 applicants, 34% accepted, 352 enrolled. Expenses: Contact institution. *Financial support:* In 2008–09, 417 students received support; fellowships, research assistantships, teaching assistantships available. Financial award applicants required to submit FAFSA. In 2008, 262 master's, 119 doctorates awarded. Offers aerospace engineering (M Eng, MS, PhD); architectural engineering (M Eng, MS, PhD); chemical engineering (MS, PhD); civil engineering (M Eng, MS, PhD); computer science and engineering (M Eng, MS, PhD); electrical engineering (MS, PhD); engineering (M Eng, MMM, MS, PhD); engineering mechanics (M Eng, MS, PhD); engineering science (M Eng, MS, PhD); engineering science and mechanics (M Eng, MS, PhD); environmental engineering (M Eng, MS, PhD); industrial engineering (M Eng, MS, PhD); manufacturing engineering (M Eng); mechanical engineering (M Eng, MS, PhD); nuclear engineering (M Eng, MS, PhD); structural engineering (M Eng, MS, PhD); transportation and highway engineering (M Eng, MS, PhD); water resources engineering (M Eng, MS, PhD). *Application deadline:* Applications are processed on a rolling basis. *Application fee:* $65. Electronic applications accepted. *Application Contact:* Cynthia E. Nicosia, Director, Graduate Enrollment Services, 814-865-1834, E-mail: cey1@psu.edu. *Dean*, Dr. David N. Wormley, 814-865-7537, Fax: 814-865-8767, E-mail: dnw2@engr.psu.edu.

College of Health and Human Development Students: 346 full-time (254 women), 68 part-time (53 women); includes 28 minority (11 African Americans, 11 Asian Americans or Pacific Islanders, 6 Hispanic Americans), 106 international. Average age 28. 441 applicants, 38% accepted, 83 enrolled. Expenses: Contact institution. *Financial support:* In 2008–09, 98 students received support; fellowships, research assistantships, teaching assistantships available. Financial award applicants required to submit FAFSA. In 2008, 64 master's, 45 doctorates awarded. Offers biobehavioral health (MS, PhD); communication sciences and disorders (MS, PhD); health and human development (M Ed, MHA, MS, PhD); health policy and administration (MHA, MS, PhD); hospitality management (MS, PhD); hotel, restaurant, and institutional management (MHRIM, MS, PhD); human development and family studies (MS, PhD); human nutrition (M Ed); kinesiology (MS, PhD); leisure studies (MS, PhD); nursing (MS, PhD); nutrition (MS, PhD); recreation, park and tourism management (M Ed). *Application deadline:* Applications are processed on a rolling basis. *Application fee:* $65. Electronic applications accepted. *Application Contact:* Cynthia E. Nicosia, Director, Graduate Enrollment Services, 814-865-1795, Fax: 814-865-4627, E-mail: cey1@psu.edu. *Dean*, Dr. Ann C. Crouter, 814-865-1428, Fax: 814-865-3282, E-mail: ac1@psu.edu.

College of Information Sciences and Technology Students: 89 full-time (37 women), 7 part-time (1 woman); includes 7 minority (2 African Americans, 4 Asian Americans or Pacific Islanders, 1 Hispanic American), 58 international. Average age 30. 112 applicants, 34% accepted, 27 enrolled. Expenses: Contact institution. *Financial support:* In 2008–09, 12 students received support; fellowships, research assistantships, teaching assistantships available. Financial award applicants required to submit FAFSA. In 2008, 4 master's, 9 doctorates awarded. Offers information sciences and technology (MS, PhD). *Application deadline:* Applications are processed on a rolling basis. *Application fee:* $65. Electronic applications accepted. *Application Contact:* Dr. Henry Foley, Dean, 814-863-3528, Fax: 814-865-5604, E-mail: hcf2@psu.edu. *Dean*, Dr. Henry Foley, 814-863-3528, Fax: 814-865-5604, E-mail: hcf2@psu.edu.

College of the Liberal Arts Students: 733 full-time (417 women), 59 part-time (39 women); includes 97 minority (33 African Americans, 3 American Indian/Alaska Native, 28 Asian Americans or Pacific Islanders, 33 Hispanic Americans), 210 international. Average age 28. 2,509 applicants, 16% accepted, 206 enrolled. Expenses: Contact institution. *Financial support:* In 2008–09, 204 students received support; fellowships, research assistantships, teaching assistantships available. Financial award applicants required to submit FAFSA. In 2008, 113 master's, 109 doctorates awarded. Offers anthropology (MA, PhD); applied linguistics (PhD); classical American philosophy (MA, PhD); clinical psychology (MS, PhD); cognitive psychology (MS, PhD); communication arts and sciences (MA, PhD); comparative literature (MA, PhD); contemporary European philosophy (MA, PhD); crime, law, and justice (MA, PhD); developmental psychology (MS, PhD); economics (MA, PhD); English (MA, MFA, PhD); French (MA, PhD); German (MA, PhD); history (MA, PhD); history of philosophy (MA, PhD); industrial relations and human resources (MS); industrial/organizational psychology (MS, PhD); liberal arts (MA, MFA, MPS, MS, PhD); political science (MA, PhD); psychobiology (MS, PhD); Russian and comparative literature (MA); social psychology (MS, PhD); sociology (MA, PhD); Spanish (MA, PhD); teaching English as a second language (MA). *Application fee:* $65. *Application Contact:* Cynthia E. Nicosia, Director, Graduate Enrollment Services, 814-865-1795, Fax: 814-865-4627, E-mail: cey1@psu.edu. *Dean*, Dr. Susan Welch, 814-865-7691, Fax: 814-863-2085, E-mail: swelch@psu.edu.

Eberly College of Science Students: 705 full-time (262 women), 26 part-time (14 women); includes 51 minority (4 African Americans, 24 Asian Americans or Pacific Islanders, 23 Hispanic Americans), 333 international. Average age 26. 1,338 applicants, 21% accepted, 164 enrolled. Expenses: Contact institution. *Financial support:* In 2008–09, 144 students received support; fellowships, research assistantships, teaching assistantships available. Financial award applicants required to submit FAFSA. In 2008, 49 master's, 93 doctorates awarded. Offers applied statistics (MAS); astronomy and astrophysics (MS, PhD); biochemistry, microbiology, and molecular biology (MS, PhD); biology (MS, PhD); biotechnology (MS); cell and developmental biology (MS, PhD); chemistry (MS, PhD); mathematics (M Ed, MA, D Ed, PhD); molecular evolutionary biology (MS, PhD); physics (M Ed, MS, D Ed, PhD); science (M Ed, MA, MAS, MS, D Ed, PhD); statistics (MA, MAS, MS, PhD). *Application deadline:* Applications are processed on a rolling basis. *Application fee:* $65. Electronic applications accepted. *Application Contact:* Cynthia E. Nicosia, Director, Graduate Enrollment Services, 814-865-1795, Fax: 814-865-4627, E-mail: cey1@psu.edu. *Dean*, Dr. Daniel J. Larson, 814-865-9591, Fax: 814-863-0491, E-mail: sciencedean@psu.edu.

The Mary Jean and Frank P. Smeal College of Business Administration Students: 340 full-time (109 women), 3 part-time (1 woman); includes 56 minority (22 African Americans, 2 American Indian/Alaska Native, 23 Asian Americans or Pacific Islanders, 9 Hispanic Americans), 101 international. Average age 31. 1,090 applicants, 24% accepted, 161 enrolled. Expenses: Contact institution. *Financial support:* In 2008–09, 127 students received support; fellowships, research assistantships, teaching assistantships available. Financial award applicants required to submit FAFSA. In 2008, 98 master's, 16 doctorates awarded. Offers business (MBA); business administration (MBA); supply chain management (MPS). *Application deadline:* Applications are processed on a rolling basis. *Application fee:* $65. Electronic applications accepted. *Application Contact:* Cynthia E. Nicosia, Director, Graduate Enrollment Services, 814-865-1795, Fax: 814-865-4627, E-mail: cey1@psu.edu. *Dean*, Dr. James B. Thomas, 814-863-0448, Fax: 814-865-7064, E-mail: j2t@psu.edu.

See Close-Up on page 967.

PENNSYLVANIA ACADEMY OF THE FINE ARTS, Philadelphia, PA 19102

General Information Independent, coed, graduate-only institution. *Graduate housing:* On-campus housing not available.

GRADUATE UNITS

Graduate School Offers drawing (MFA, Postbaccalaureate Certificate); painting (MFA, Postbaccalaureate Certificate); printmaking (MFA, Postbaccalaureate Certificate); sculpture (MFA, Postbaccalaureate Certificate). Electronic applications accepted.

PEPPERDINE UNIVERSITY, Los Angeles, CA 90045

General Information Independent-religious, coed, upper-level institution. *Enrollment by degree level:* 2,283 master's, 577 doctoral. *Graduate faculty:* 147 full-time (43 women), 155 part-time/adjunct (75 women). *Graduate housing:* On-campus housing not available. *Student services:* Campus employment opportunities, career counseling, exercise/wellness program, international student services, low-cost health insurance, services for students with disabilities, teacher training. *Web address:* http://www.pepperdine.edu/.

General Application Contact: Information Contact, 310-568-5500.

GRADUATE UNITS

Graduate School of Education and Psychology Students: 1,356 full-time (1,043 women), 131 part-time (104 women); includes 463 minority (162 African Americans, 11 American Indian/Alaska Native, 119 Asian Americans or Pacific Islanders, 171 Hispanic Americans), 51 international. *Faculty:* 64 full-time (28 women), 108 part-time/adjunct (64 women). Expenses: Contact institution. *Financial support:* Research assistantships, teaching assistantships, career-related internships or fieldwork, Federal Work-Study, institutionally sponsored loans, scholarships/grants, and unspecified assistantships available. Support available to part-time students. Financial award application deadline: 7/1; financial award applicants required to submit FAFSA. In 2008, 466 master's, 90 doctorates awarded. *Degree program information:* Part-time and evening/weekend programs available. Postbaccalaureate distance learning degree programs offered (minimal on-campus study). Offers education and psychology (MA, MS, Ed D, Psy D). *Application deadline:* For fall admission, 6/2 for domestic students; for spring admission, 11/3 for domestic students. Applications are processed on a rolling basis. *Application fee:* $45. *Application Contact:* Admissions Specialist, 310-258-2850, E-mail: anne.mclintock@pepperdine.edu. *Dean*, Dr. Margaret J. Weber, 310-568-5600, E-mail: margaret.weber@pepperdine.edu.

Division of Education Students: 594 full-time (382 women), 33 part-time (22 women); includes 211 minority (86 African Americans, 4 American Indian/Alaska Native, 54 Asian Americans or Pacific Islanders, 67 Hispanic Americans), 13 international. *Faculty:* 32 full-time (17 women), 32 part-time/adjunct (22 women). Expenses: Contact institution. *Financial support:* Research assistantships, teaching assistantships, career-related internships or fieldwork, institutionally sponsored loans, and scholarships/grants available. Support available to part-time students. Financial award application deadline: 7/1; financial award applicants required to submit FAFSA. In 2008, 330 master's, 68 doctorates awarded. *Degree program information:* Part-time and evening/weekend programs available. Postbaccalaureate distance learning degree programs offered (minimal on-campus study). Offers administration and preliminary administrative services credential (MS); education (MA); educational leadership, administration, and policy (Ed D); learning technologies (MA, Ed D); organization change (Ed D); organizational leadership (Ed D). *Application deadline:* Applications are processed on a rolling basis. *Application fee:* $45. *Application Contact:* Brenden Wysocki, Admissions Manager, 310-568-5786. *Associate Dean*, Dr. Chester McCall, 310-568-2323, E-mail: chester.mccall@pepperdine.edu.

Division of Psychology Students: 762 full-time (661 women), 98 part-time (82 women); includes 252 minority (76 African Americans, 7 American Indian/Alaska Native, 65 Asian Americans or Pacific Islanders, 104 Hispanic Americans), 38 international. *Faculty:* 32 full-time (11 women), 76 part-time/adjunct (42 women). Expenses: Contact institution. *Financial support:* Research assistantships, teaching assistantships, career-related internships or fieldwork and scholarships/grants available. Support available to part-time students. Financial award application deadline: 7/1; financial award applicants required to submit FAFSA. In 2008, 313 master's, 22 doctorates awarded. *Degree program information:* Part-time and evening/weekend programs available. Offers clinical psychology (MA, Psy D); clinical psychology (daytime) (MA); clinical psychology (evening) (MA); psychology (MA). *Application deadline:* For fall admission, 2/1 for domestic students. Applications are processed on a rolling basis. *Application fee:* $55. *Application Contact:* Brenden Wysocki, Admissions Manager, 310-568-5786. *Associate Dean*, Dr. Robert deMayo, 310-568-5747, E-mail: robert.demayo@pepperdine.edu.

Graziadio School of Business and Management Students: 547 full-time, 826 part-time; includes 505 minority (68 African Americans, 8 American Indian/Alaska Native, 295 Asian Americans or Pacific Islanders, 134 Hispanic Americans), 44 international. 1,032 applicants, 50% accepted. *Faculty:* 83 full-time (15 women), 47 part-time/adjunct (11 women). Expenses: Contact institution. *Financial support:* Career-related internships or fieldwork, institutionally sponsored loans, scholarships/grants, and unspecified assistantships available. Support available to part-time students. Financial award applicants required to submit FAFSA. In 2008, 586 master's awarded. *Degree program information:* Part-time and evening/weekend programs available. Offers applied finance (MS); business administration (MBA); fully-employed (MBA); international business administration (IMBA); management and leadership (MS); organizational development (MSOD); presidential and key executive business administration (Exec MBA). *Application deadline:* For fall admission, 6/28 for domestic students. Applications are processed on a rolling basis. *Application fee:* $45. *Application Contact:* Darrell Eriksen, Director of Admission and Student Accounts, 310-568-5525, E-mail: darrell.eriksen@pepperdine.edu. *Dean*, Dr. Linda A. Livingstone, 310-568-5689, Fax: 310-568-5766, E-mail: linda.livingstone@pepperdine.edu.

PEPPERDINE UNIVERSITY, Malibu, CA 90263

General Information Independent-religious, coed, university. CGS member. *Enrollment:* 7,614 graduate, professional, and undergraduate students; 1,149 full-time matriculated graduate/professional students (551 women), 137 part-time matriculated graduate/professional students (75 women). *Enrollment by degree level:* 607 first professional, 679 master's. *Graduate faculty:* 41 full-time (11 women), 43 part-time/adjunct (10 women). *Tuition:* Full-time $36,442; part-time $1273 per unit. Tuition and fees vary according to degree level and program. *Graduate housing:* Rooms and/or apartments available on a first-come, first-served basis to single and married students. Typical cost: $11,000 per year for single students; $12,740 per year for married students. *Student services:* Campus employment opportunities, campus safety program, career counseling, exercise/wellness program, free psychological counseling, international student services, low-cost health insurance, multicultural affairs office, services for students with disabilities, teacher training. *Library facilities:* Payson Library plus 2 others. *Online resources:* library catalog, web page.

Computer facilities: Computer purchase and lease plans are available. 292 computers available on campus for general student use. A campuswide network can be accessed from student residence rooms and from off campus. Online class registration is available. *Web address:* http://www.pepperdine.edu/.

Pepperdine University (continued)

General Application Contact: Kristin A. Collins, Director of Admission, 310-506-4392, Fax: 310-506-4861, E-mail: admission-seaver@pepperdine.edu.

GRADUATE UNITS

Graduate School of Education and Psychology Students: 85 full-time (67 women); includes 15 minority (2 African Americans, 1 American Indian/Alaska Native, 6 Asian Americans or Pacific Islanders, 6 Hispanic Americans), 6 international. *Faculty:* 4 full-time (2 women). Expenses: Contact institution. Offers clinical psychology (MA); education and psychology (MA, MS, Ed D, Psy D). *Application deadline:* For fall admission, 2/2 for domestic and international students. Applications are processed on a rolling basis. *Application fee:* $55. Electronic applications accepted. *Application Contact:* Fionnbarr Kelly, Director, Recruitment and Admissions, 310-568-5744, E-mail: fionnbarr.kelly@pepperdine.edu. *Dean,* Dr. Margaret J. Weber, 310-568-5000, E-mail: margaret.weber@pepperdine.edu.

Malibu Graduate Business Programs Students: 333 full-time (122 women), 2 part-time (0 women); includes 48 minority (3 African Americans, 36 Asian Americans or Pacific Islanders, 9 Hispanic Americans), 125 international. 576 applicants, 62% accepted, 172 enrolled. *Faculty:* 10 full-time (4 women). Expenses: Contact institution. *Financial support:* Career-related internships or fieldwork, institutionally sponsored loans, scholarships/grants, and unspecified assistantships available. Financial award application deadline: 6/1; financial award applicants required to submit FAFSA. In 2008, 86 master's awarded. Offers business administration (MBA); international business (MIB). *Application deadline:* For fall admission, 5/1 for domestic and international students. Applications are processed on a rolling basis. *Application fee:* $45. Electronic applications accepted. *Application Contact:* Paul E. Pinckley, Executive Director, Recruitment, 310-506-4858, Fax: 310-506-4126, E-mail: paul.pinckley@pepperdine.edu. *Director, Full-Time Programs,* Dr. Mark Mallinger, 310-506-6962, Fax: 310-506-4126, E-mail: mark.mallinger@pepperdine.edu.

School of Law Students: 627 full-time (306 women), 40 part-time (23 women); includes 111 minority (25 African Americans, 6 American Indian/Alaska Native, 52 Asian Americans or Pacific Islanders, 28 Hispanic Americans), 16 international. 2,795 applicants, 32% accepted, 251 enrolled. *Faculty:* 40 full-time (11 women), 36 part-time/adjunct (11 women). Expenses: Contact institution. *Financial support:* Fellowships, research assistantships, teaching assistantships, career-related internships or fieldwork, Federal Work-Study, institutionally sponsored loans, and scholarships/grants available. Support available to part-time students. Financial award application deadline: 4/1; financial award applicants required to submit FAFSA. In 2008, 204 JDs, 36 master's awarded. Offers dispute resolution (LL M, MDR); law (JD, LL M, MDR). *Application deadline:* For fall admission, 2/1 for domestic students, 3/1 for international students. Applications are processed on a rolling basis. *Application fee:* $50. Electronic applications accepted. *Application Contact:* Shannon Phillips, Director of Admissions/Records, 310-506-4631, Fax: 310-506-4266, E-mail: shannon.phillips@pepperdine.edu. *Dean,* Kenneth W. Starr, 310-506-4621, Fax: 310-506-4266, E-mail: ken.starr@pepperdine.edu.

School of Public Policy Students: 86 full-time (46 women), 3 part-time (2 women); includes 18 minority (4 African Americans, 2 American Indian/Alaska Native, 6 Asian Americans or Pacific Islanders, 6 Hispanic Americans), 4 international. 149 applicants, 74% accepted, 45 enrolled. *Faculty:* 6 full-time (1 woman), 5 part-time/adjunct (1 woman). Expenses: Contact institution. *Financial support:* Research assistantships, teaching assistantships, institutionally sponsored loans and scholarships/grants available. Financial award application deadline: 5/1; financial award applicants required to submit FAFSA. In 2008, 27 master's awarded. Offers American politics (MPP); economics (MPP); international relations (MPP); public policy (MPP); state and local policy (MPP). *Application deadline:* For fall admission, 4/15 for domestic students. Applications are processed on a rolling basis. *Application fee:* $50. Electronic applications accepted. *Application Contact:* Melinda E. van Hemert, Director of Recruitment and Career Services, 310-506-7492, Fax: 310-506-7494, E-mail: melinda.vanhemert@pepperdine.edu. *Dean,* Dr. James R. Wilburn, 310-506-7490, Fax: 310-506-7494, E-mail: james.wilburn@pepperdine.edu.

Seaver College Students: 18 full-time (10 women), 92 part-time (50 women); includes 8 minority (3 African Americans, 3 Asian Americans or Pacific Islanders, 2 Hispanic Americans), 1 international. 97 applicants, 63% accepted, 39 enrolled. *Faculty:* 36 full-time (7 women). Expenses: Contact institution. *Financial support:* Fellowships, research assistantships, teaching assistantships, career-related internships or fieldwork, Federal Work-Study, institutionally sponsored loans, scholarships/grants, and tuition waivers (partial) available. Support available to part-time students. Financial award application deadline: 2/15; financial award applicants required to submit FAFSA. In 2008, 27 master's awarded. *Degree program information:* Part-time and evening/weekend programs available. Offers American studies (MA); communication (MA); history (MA); ministry (MS); religion (M Div, MA). *Application deadline:* For fall admission, 5/1 for domestic students. Applications are processed on a rolling basis. *Application fee:* $55. *Application Contact:* Paul A. Long, Dean of Admission and Enrollment Management, 310-506-6165, Fax: 310-506-4861, E-mail: admission-seaver@pepperdine.edu. *Dean,* Dr. David W. Baird, 310-506-4280, E-mail: david.baird@pepperdine.edu.

PERU STATE COLLEGE, Peru, NE 68421

General Information State-supported, coed, comprehensive institution. *Graduate housing:* Rooms and/or apartments available to single and married students.

GRADUATE UNITS

Graduate Programs *Degree program information:* Part-time programs available. Postbaccalaureate distance learning degree programs offered. Offers curriculum and instruction (MS Ed); organizational management (MS).

PFEIFFER UNIVERSITY, Misenheimer, NC 28109-0960

General Information Independent-religious, coed, comprehensive institution. *Graduate housing:* On-campus housing not available.

GRADUATE UNITS

Program in Business Administration *Degree program information:* Part-time and evening/weekend programs available. Postbaccalaureate distance learning degree programs offered (minimal on-campus study). Offers business administration (MBA); organizational management (MS).

Program in Health Administration Offers health administration (MHA).

Program in Organizational Change and Leadership Offers organizational change and leadership (MS).

School of Education Offers elementary education (MS); teaching (MAT).

School of Religion and Christian Education *Degree program information:* Part-time and evening/weekend programs available. Offers religion and Christian education (MACE).

PHILADELPHIA BIBLICAL UNIVERSITY, Langhorne, PA 19047-2990

General Information Independent-religious, coed, comprehensive institution. *Enrollment:* 1,373 graduate, professional, and undergraduate students; 43 full-time matriculated graduate/professional students (13 women), 269 part-time matriculated graduate/professional students (154 women). *Enrollment by degree level:* 54 first professional, 258 master's. *Graduate faculty:* 16 full-time (5 women), 18 part-time/adjunct (9 women). *Tuition:* Full-time $9450; part-time $525 per credit. *Required fees:* $10; $10 per year. Tuition and fees vary according to program. *Graduate housing:* Rooms and/or apartments available on a first-come, first-served basis to single and married students. Typical cost: $3790 per year ($7350 including board) for single students. Room and board charges vary according to board plan and housing facility selected. *Student services:* Campus employment opportunities, campus safety program, career counseling, exercise/wellness program, international student services, low-cost health insurance, services for students with disabilities, teacher training. *Library facilities:* Masland Learning Resource Center. *Online resources:* library catalog, web page. *Collection:* 109,085 titles, 803 serial subscriptions, 8,452 audiovisual materials.

Computer facilities: Computer purchase and lease plans are available. 90 computers available on campus for general student use. A campuswide network can be accessed from student residence rooms and from off campus. Online class registration is available. *Web address:* http://www.pbu.edu/.

General Application Contact: Binu Abraham, Assistant Director, Graduate Admissions, 800-572-2472, Fax: 215-702-4248, E-mail: babraham@pbu.edu.

GRADUATE UNITS

School of Biblical Studies Students: 18 full-time (2 women), 76 part-time (18 women); includes 33 minority (26 African Americans, 6 Asian Americans or Pacific Islanders, 1 Hispanic American), 3 international. Average age 39. 59 applicants, 47% accepted, 28 enrolled. *Faculty:* 5 full-time (0 women), 6 part-time/adjunct (0 women). Expenses: Contact institution. *Financial support:* In 2008–09, 50 students received support. Scholarships/grants available. Support available to part-time students. Financial award applicants required to submit FAFSA. In 2008, 1 M Div, 9 master's awarded. *Degree program information:* Part-time and evening/weekend programs available. Offers biblical studies (M Div, MSB). *Application deadline:* Applications are processed on a rolling basis. *Application fee:* $25. Electronic applications accepted. *Application Contact:* Binu Abraham, Assistant Director, Graduate Admissions, 800-572-2472, Fax: 215-702-4248, E-mail: babraham@pbu.edu. *Dean,* Dr. O. Herbert Hirt, 215-702-4354, Fax: 215-702-4359, E-mail: bible@pbu.edu.

School of Business and Leadership Students: 1 (woman) full-time, 23 part-time (9 women); includes 9 minority (all African Americans), 2 international. Average age 39. 23 applicants, 39% accepted, 8 enrolled. *Faculty:* 1 full-time (0 women), 3 part-time/adjunct (1 woman). Expenses: Contact institution. *Financial support:* In 2008–09, 11 students received support. Scholarships/grants available. Support available to part-time students. Financial award applicants required to submit FAFSA. In 2008, 18 master's awarded. *Degree program information:* Part-time and evening/weekend programs available. Offers organizational leadership (MSOL). *Application deadline:* Applications are processed on a rolling basis. *Application fee:* $25. Electronic applications accepted. *Application Contact:* Binu Abraham, Assistant Director, Graduate Admissions, 800-572-2472, Fax: 215-702-4248, E-mail: babraham@pbu.edu. *Dean,* Ron Ferner, 215-702-9260, Fax: 215-702-4248.

School of Church and Community Ministries Students: 5 full-time (all women), 124 part-time (90 women); includes 38 minority (31 African Americans, 6 Asian Americans or Pacific Islanders, 1 Hispanic American). Average age 37. 77 applicants, 61% accepted, 38 enrolled. *Faculty:* 4 full-time (1 woman), 9 part-time/adjunct (6 women). Expenses: Contact institution. *Financial support:* In 2008–09, 63 students received support. Scholarships/grants available. Support available to part-time students. Financial award applicants required to submit FAFSA. In 2008, 39 master's awarded. *Degree program information:* Part-time and evening/weekend programs available. Offers Christian counseling (MSCC). *Application deadline:* Applications are processed on a rolling basis. *Application fee:* $25. Electronic applications accepted. *Application Contact:* Gwen Dorsey, Enrollment Counselor, Graduate Counseling, 800-572-2472, Fax: 215-702-4248, E-mail: gdorsey@pbu.edu. *Dean,* Donald Cheyney, 215-702-4546, E-mail: dcheyney@pbu.edu.

School of Education Students: 13 full-time (9 women), 59 part-time (38 women); includes 17 minority (10 African Americans, 6 Asian Americans or Pacific Islanders, 1 Hispanic American), 2 international. Average age 36. 26 applicants, 58% accepted, 15 enrolled. *Faculty:* 8 full-time (6 women), 3 part-time/adjunct (2 women). Expenses: Contact institution. *Financial support:* In 2008–09, 27 students received support. Scholarships/grants available. Support available to part-time students. Financial award applicants required to submit FAFSA. In 2008, 26 master's awarded. *Degree program information:* Part-time and evening/weekend programs available. Offers educational leadership and administration (MS El); teacher education (MS Ed). *Application deadline:* Applications are processed on a rolling basis. *Application fee:* $25. Electronic applications accepted. *Application Contact:* Katerina Penkova, Enrollment Counselor, Graduate Education, 800-572-2472, Fax: 215-702-4248, E-mail: kpenkova@pbu.edu. *Dean,* Dr. Martha MacCullough, 215-702-4387, E-mail: teacher.ed@pbu.edu.

PHILADELPHIA COLLEGE OF OSTEOPATHIC MEDICINE, Philadelphia, PA 19131-1694

General Information Independent, coed, graduate-only institution. *Graduate housing:* On-campus housing not available. *Research affiliation:* Medical College of Georgia (coronary artery disease), Lankenau Institute for Medical Research (cell differentiation), Albert Einstein Medical Center (clinical pain studies, chronic inflammation), Neuromuscular Engineering (exercise), Mount Sinai School of Medicine (joint and bone disease).

GRADUATE UNITS

Graduate and Professional Programs Offers biomedical sciences (MS, Certificate); clinical psychology (Psy D); counseling and clinical health psychology (MS); forensic medicine (MS); health sciences (MS); organizational leadership and development (MS); osteopathic medicine (DO); psychology (Certificate); school psychology (MS, Psy D, Ed S).

PHILADELPHIA UNIVERSITY, Philadelphia, PA 19144-5497

General Information Independent, coed, comprehensive institution. *Graduate housing:* On-campus housing not available.

GRADUATE UNITS

School of Architecture Offers architecture (MS); construction management (MS); sustainable design (MS).

School of Business Administration *Degree program information:* Part-time and evening/weekend programs available. Postbaccalaureate distance learning degree programs offered (no on-campus study). Offers business (MBA, MS, PhD); business administration (MBA); finance (MBA); health care management (MBA); international business (MBA); marketing (MBA); taxation (MS). Electronic applications accepted.

School of Design and Media *Degree program information:* Part-time and evening/weekend programs available. Offers design and media (MS); digital design (MS).

School of Engineering and Textiles *Degree program information:* Part-time programs available. Offers engineering and textiles (MS, PhD); fashion apparel studies (MS); textile design (MS); textile engineering (MS, PhD). Electronic applications accepted.

School of Science and Health *Degree program information:* Part-time and evening/weekend programs available. Postbaccalaureate distance learning degree programs offered (minimal on-campus study). Offers disaster medicine and management (MS); midwifery (MS); nurse midwifery (Postbaccalaureate Certificate); occupational therapy (MS); physician assistant studies (MS); science and health (MS, Postbaccalaureate Certificate). Electronic applications accepted.

PHILLIPS GRADUATE INSTITUTE, Encino, CA 91316-1509

General Information Independent, coed, graduate-only institution. *Graduate housing:* On-campus housing not available.

GRADUATE UNITS

Program in Clinical Family Psychology and Organizational Consulting *Degree program information:* Evening/weekend programs available. Offers clinical psychology (Psy D); organizational consulting (Psy D).

Programs in Marriage and Family Therapy, School Counseling and School Psychology *Degree program information:* Evening/weekend programs available. Offers marital and family therapy (MA); organizational consulting (MA); school counseling (MA).

PHILLIPS THEOLOGICAL SEMINARY, Tulsa, OK 74116

General Information Independent-religious, coed, graduate-only institution. *Graduate housing:* On-campus housing not available.

GRADUATE UNITS

Programs in Theology *Degree program information:* Part-time programs available. Postbaccalaureate distance learning degree programs offered (minimal on-campus study). Offers administration of church agencies (M Div); campus ministry (M Div); church-related social work (M Div); college and seminary teaching (M Div); global mission work (M Div); institutional chaplaincy (M Div); ministerial vocations in Christian education (M Div); ministry (D Min); ministry and culture (MAMC); ministry of music (M Div); parish ministry (D Min); pastoral care and counseling (M Div); pastoral counseling (D Min); pastoral ministry (M Div); practices of ministry (D Min); theological studies (MTS).

PHOENIX SEMINARY, Scottsdale, AZ 85254

General Information Independent-religious, coed, graduate-only institution.

GRADUATE UNITS

Graduate Programs

PIEDMONT BAPTIST COLLEGE AND GRADUATE SCHOOL, Winston-Salem, NC 27101-5197

General Information Independent-religious, coed, comprehensive institution. *Graduate housing:* Rooms and/or apartments available on a first-come, first-served basis to single and married students. Housing application deadline: 5/1.

GRADUATE UNITS

Piedmont Baptist Graduate School *Degree program information:* Part-time programs available. Postbaccalaureate distance learning degree programs offered (no on-campus study). Offers chaplaincy track (MABS); non-language track (MABS); PhD preparation track (MABS); theology (M Min, PhD). Electronic applications accepted.

PIEDMONT COLLEGE, Demorest, GA 30535-0010

General Information Independent-religious, coed, comprehensive institution. CGS member. *Graduate housing:* On-campus housing not available.

GRADUATE UNITS

School of Business Offers business (MBA).

School of Education *Degree program information:* Part-time and evening/weekend programs available. Offers early childhood education (MA, MAT); instruction (Ed S); secondary education (MA, MAT).

PIKEVILLE COLLEGE, Pikeville, KY 41501

General Information Independent-religious, coed, comprehensive institution. *Graduate housing:* Room and/or apartments available on a first-come, first-served basis to married students; on-campus housing not available to single students.

GRADUATE UNITS

School of Osteopathic Medicine Offers osteopathic medicine (DO).

PITTSBURGH THEOLOGICAL SEMINARY, Pittsburgh, PA 15206-2596

General Information Independent-religious, coed, graduate-only institution. *Enrollment by degree level:* 168 first professional, 39 master's, 111 doctoral. *Graduate faculty:* 18 full-time (3 women), 8 part-time/adjunct (1 woman). *Tuition:* Part-time $295 per credit. *Required fees:* $46 per term. *Graduate housing:* Rooms and/or apartments available on a first-come, first-served basis to single and married students. Typical cost: $3555 per year for single students; $5940 per year for married students. Housing application deadline: 6/1. *Student services:* Campus employment opportunities, career counseling, child daycare facilities, exercise/wellness program, free psychological counseling, international student services, low-cost health insurance, services for students with disabilities, writing training. *Library facilities:* Clifford E. Barbour Library. *Online resources:* library catalog, web page. *Collection:* 290,000 titles, 870 serial subscriptions, 12,777 audiovisual materials.

Computer facilities: 11 computers available on campus for general student use. A campuswide network can be accessed from student residence rooms. *Web address:* http://www.pts.edu/.

General Application Contact: Sherry Sparks, Director of Admissions, 412-362-5610 Ext. 2115, Fax: 412-363-3260, E-mail: ssparks@pts.edu.

GRADUATE UNITS

Graduate and Professional Programs Students: 254 full-time (87 women), 64 part-time (31 women); includes 52 minority (46 African Americans, 1 American Indian/Alaska Native, 4 Asian Americans or Pacific Islanders, 1 Hispanic American), 13 international. Average age 36. 135 applicants, 70% accepted, 78 enrolled. *Faculty:* 18 full-time (3 women), 8 part-time/adjunct (1 woman). Expenses: Contact institution. *Financial support:* In 2008–09, 137 students received support. Career-related internships or fieldwork, scholarships/grants, and institutional work-study available. Financial award application deadline: 4/15; financial award applicants required to submit FAFSA. In 2008, 46 first professional degrees, 8 master's, 12 doctorates awarded. *Degree program information:* Part-time and evening/weekend programs available. Offers divinity (M Div); ministry (D Min); theology (MA, STM). *Application deadline:* For fall admission, 6/31 priority date for domestic students, 12/1 for international students; for winter admission, 10/15 priority date for domestic students; for spring admission, 1/15 priority date for domestic students. Applications are processed on a rolling basis. *Application fee:* $40. *Application Contact:* Sherry Sparks, Director of Admissions, 412-362-5610 Ext. 2115, Fax: 412-363-3260, E-mail: ssparks@pts.edu. *Dean of Faculty and Vice President for Academic Affairs,* Dr. Byron H. Jackson, 412-362-5610 Ext. 2118, Fax: 412-363-3260, E-mail: bjackson@pts.edu.

PITTSBURG STATE UNIVERSITY, Pittsburg, KS 66762

General Information State-supported, coed, comprehensive institution. CGS member. *Graduate housing:* Rooms and/or apartments available on a first-come, first-served basis to single students and available to married students. *Research affiliation:* Cargill Inc. (vegetable oil).

GRADUATE UNITS

Graduate School *Degree program information:* Part-time and evening/weekend programs available. Postbaccalaureate distance learning degree programs offered (no on-campus study). Electronic applications accepted.

College of Arts and Sciences Offers applied communication (MA); applied physics (MS); art education (MA); arts and sciences (MA, MM, MS, MSN); biology (MS); chemistry (MS); communication education (MA); English (MA); history (MA); instrumental music education (MM); mathematics (MS); music history/music literature (MM); nursing (MSN); performance (MM); physics (MS); professional physics (MS); studio art (MA); theatre (MA); theory and composition (MM); vocal music education (MM).

College of Education Offers behavioral disorders (MS); classroom reading teacher (MS); community college and higher education (Ed S); community counseling (MS); counselor education (MS); early childhood education (MS); education (MAT, MS, Ed S); educational leadership (MS); educational technology (MS); elementary education (MS); learning disabilities (MS); mentally retarded (MS); physical education (MS); psychology (MS); reading (MS); reading specialist (MS); school counseling (MS); school psychology (Ed S); secondary education (MS); special education teaching (MS); teaching (MAT).

College of Technology Offers engineering technology (MET); human resource development (MS); industrial education (Ed S); technical teacher education (MS); technology (MS); technology education (MS).

Kelce College of Business Offers accounting (MBA); business (MBA); general administration (MBA).

PLYMOUTH STATE UNIVERSITY, Plymouth, NH 03264-1595

General Information State-supported, coed, comprehensive institution. *Graduate housing:* Rooms and/or apartments available on a first-come, first-served basis to single students and guaranteed to married students. Housing application deadline: 5/1. *Research affiliation:* Hubbard Brook Experimental Forest (science), NH Department of Environmental Services (science), White Mountain National Forest (science), National Oceanic and Atmospheric Admdu (NOAA) (science).

GRADUATE UNITS

College of Graduate Studies *Degree program information:* Part-time and evening/weekend programs available. Postbaccalaureate distance learning degree programs offered (minimal on-campus study). Offers business (MBA).

POINT LOMA NAZARENE UNIVERSITY, San Diego, CA 92106-2899

General Information Independent-religious, coed, comprehensive institution. *Graduate housing:* On-campus housing not available.

GRADUATE UNITS

Graduate Studies *Degree program information:* Part-time and evening/weekend programs available. Postbaccalaureate distance learning degree programs offered (minimal on-campus study). Offers biology (MA, MS); business administration (MBA); education (MA, Ed S); nursing (MSN); religion (M Min, MA).

POINT PARK UNIVERSITY, Pittsburgh, PA 15222-1984

General Information Independent, coed, comprehensive institution. *Enrollment:* 3,846 graduate, professional, and undergraduate students; 215 full-time matriculated graduate/professional students (144 women), 305 part-time matriculated graduate/professional students (178 women). *Enrollment by degree level:* 520 master's. *Graduate faculty:* 34 full-time, 49 part-time/adjunct. *Tuition:* Full-time $11,880; part-time $660 per credit. *Required fees:* $486; $27 per credit. *Graduate housing:* Room and/or apartments available on a first-come, first-served basis to single students; on-campus housing not available to married students. Typical cost: $4300 per year ($9020 including board). Housing application deadline: 7/31. *Student services:* Campus employment opportunities, career counseling, child daycare facilities, free psychological counseling, international student services, services for students with disabilities. *Library facilities:* Point Park University Library. *Online resources:* library catalog, web page, access to other libraries' catalogs. *Collection:* 125,000 titles, 230 serial subscriptions, 3,300 audiovisual materials.

Computer facilities: 247 computers available on campus for general student use. A campuswide network can be accessed from student residence rooms. Online class registration is available. *Web address:* http://www.pointpark.edu/.

General Application Contact: Kathy Ballas, Associate Director, Graduate and Adult Enrollment, 412-392-3812, Fax: 412-392-6164, E-mail: kballas@pointpark.edu.

GRADUATE UNITS

Conservatory of Performing Arts Students: 6 full-time (3 women), 1 international. Average age 40. 17 applicants, 35% accepted, 6 enrolled. *Faculty:* 4 full-time, 2 part-time/adjunct. Expenses: Contact institution. *Financial support:* In 2008–09, 5 students received support, including 5 teaching assistantships with full tuition reimbursements available (averaging $6,400 per year); Federal Work-Study and scholarships/grants also available. Support available to part-time students. Financial award application deadline: 5/1; financial award applicants required to submit FAFSA. In 2008, 1 master's awarded. Offers theatre arts-acting (MFA). *Application deadline:* Applications are processed on a rolling basis. *Application fee:* $30. Electronic applications accepted. *Application Contact:* Lynn C. Ribar, Associate Director, Adult and Graduate Enrollment, 412-392-3908, Fax: 412-392-6164, E-mail: lribar@pointpark.edu. *Dean/Artistic Producing Director,* Ronald Allan-Lindblom, 412-392-3454, Fax: 412-392-2424, E-mail: rlindblom@pointpark.edu.

School of Arts and Sciences Students: 76 full-time (60 women), 97 part-time (63 women); includes 46 minority (42 African Americans, 1 American Indian/Alaska Native, 2 Asian Americans or Pacific Islanders, 1 Hispanic American), 5 international. Average age 31. 213 applicants, 55% accepted, 74 enrolled. *Faculty:* 18 full-time, 30 part-time/adjunct. Expenses: Contact institution. *Financial support:* In 2008–09, 11 students received support, including 11 teaching assistantships with full tuition reimbursements available (averaging $6,400 per year); Federal Work-Study and scholarships/grants also available. Support available to part-time students. Financial award application deadline: 5/1; financial award applicants required to submit FAFSA. In 2008, 59 master's awarded. *Degree program information:* Part-time and evening/weekend programs available. Offers arts and sciences (MA, MS); criminal justice administration (MS); curriculum and instruction (MA); educational administration (MA); engineering management (MS); journalism and mass communication (MA). *Application deadline:* Applications are processed on a rolling basis. *Application fee:* $30. Electronic applications accepted. *Application Contact:* Dr. Karen McIntyre, Dean, 412-392-3976, E-mail: kmcintyre@pointpark.edu. *Dean,* Dr. Karen McIntyre, 412-392-3976, E-mail: kmcintyre@pointpark.edu.

School of Business Students: 133 full-time (81 women), 208 part-time (115 women); includes 94 minority (85 African Americans, 2 American Indian/Alaska Native, 5 Asian Americans or Pacific Islanders, 2 Hispanic Americans), 35 international. Average age 31. 361 applicants, 64% accepted, 152 enrolled. *Faculty:* 12 full-time, 17 part-time/adjunct. Expenses: Contact institution. *Financial support:* In 2008–09, 7 students received support, including 7 teaching assistantships with full tuition reimbursements available (averaging $5,400 per year); Federal Work-Study and scholarships/grants also available. Support available to part-time students. Financial award application deadline: 5/1; financial award applicants required to submit FAFSA. In 2008, 141 master's awarded. *Degree program information:* Part-time and evening/weekend programs available. Offers business (MBA); organizational leadership (MA). *Application deadline:* Applications are processed on a rolling basis. *Application fee:* $30. Electronic applications accepted. *Application Contact:* Marty M. Paonessa, Associate Director, Graduate and Adult Enrollment, 412-392-3915, Fax: 412-392-6164, E-mail: mpaonessa@pointpark.edu. *Dean,* Dr. Soren Hogsgaard, 412-392-3940, Fax: 412-765-2570, E-mail: shogsgaard@pointpark.edu.

POLYTECHNIC INSTITUTE OF NYU, Brooklyn, NY 11201-2990

General Information Independent, coed, university. CGS member. *Graduate housing:* Room and/or apartments available on a first-come, first-served basis to single students; on-campus housing not available to married students. Housing application deadline: 6/30.

GRADUATE UNITS

Department of Chemical and Biological Sciences Offers bioinformatics (MS); biomedical engineering (MS, PhD); biotechnology (MS); biotechnology and entrepreneurship (MS); chemistry (MS); materials chemistry (PhD); polymer science and engineering (MS).

Department of Civil Engineering *Degree program information:* Part-time and evening/weekend programs available. Offers civil engineering (MS, PhD); construction management (MS); environmental engineering (MS); environmental science (MS); transportation management (MS); transportation planning and engineering (MS, PhD). Electronic applications accepted.

Department of Computer and Information Science *Degree program information:* Part-time and evening/weekend programs available. Offers computer science (MS, PhD); cyber security (Graduate Certificate); software engineering (Graduate Certificate). Electronic applications accepted.

Department of Electrical and Computer Engineering *Degree program information:* Part-time and evening/weekend programs available. Offers computer engineering (MS, Certificate); electrical engineering (MS, PhD); electrophysics (MS); image processing (Certificate); systems engineering (MS); telecommunication networks (MS); wireless communications (Certificate). Electronic applications accepted.

Department of Finance and Risk Engineering *Degree program information:* Part-time and evening/weekend programs available. Offers financial engineering (MS, Advanced Certificate); financial technology management (Advanced Certificate); risk management (Advanced Certificate). Electronic applications accepted.

Department of Humanities and Social Sciences *Degree program information:* Part-time and evening/weekend programs available. Offers environment-behavior studies (MS); history

Polytechnic Institute of NYU (continued)
of science (MS); integrated digital media (MS, Graduate Certificate); technical communication (Graduate Certificate); technical writing and specialized journalism (MS). Electronic applications accepted.

Department of Management *Degree program information:* Part-time and evening/weekend programs available. Offers management (MBA, MS, PhD); management of technology (MS); organizational behavior (MS); technology management (MBA, PhD); telecommunications and information management (MS). Electronic applications accepted.

Department of Mathematics *Degree program information:* Part-time and evening/weekend programs available. Offers mathematics (MS, PhD). Electronic applications accepted.

Department of Mechanical and Aerospace Engineering *Degree program information:* Part-time and evening/weekend programs available. Offers industrial engineering (MS); manufacturing engineering (MS); materials science (MS); mechanical engineering (MS, PhD). Electronic applications accepted.

Department of Physics *Degree program information:* Part-time and evening/weekend programs available. Offers physics (MS, PhD). Electronic applications accepted.

Othmer-Jacobs Department of Chemical and Biological Engineering *Degree program information:* Part-time and evening/weekend programs available. Offers chemical engineering (MS, PhD). Electronic applications accepted.

POLYTECHNIC INSTITUTE OF NYU, LONG ISLAND GRADUATE CENTER, Melville, NY 11747

General Information Independent, coed, graduate-only institution. *Graduate housing:* Room and/or apartments available to single students; on-campus housing not available to married students.

GRADUATE UNITS

Graduate Programs *Degree program information:* Part-time and evening/weekend programs available. Offers aeronautics and astronautics (MS); bioinstrumentation (Certificate); biomedical engineering (MS, PhD); biomedical materials (Certificate); biotechnology (MS); biotechnology and entrepreneurship (MS); chemical engineering (MS, PhD); chemistry (MS, PhD); civil engineering (MS, PhD); computer engineering (MS); computer science (MS, PhD); distributed information systems engineering (MS); electrical engineering (MS, PhD); electrophysics (MS); environmental engineering (MS); financial engineering (MS, AC); industrial engineering (MS); management (MS); manufacturing engineering (MS); materials chemistry (PhD); mechanical engineering (MS, PhD); software engineering (MS); systems engineering (MS); telecommunication networks (MS); transportation planning and engineering (MS); wireless innovation (M Engr). Electronic applications accepted.

POLYTECHNIC INSTITUTE OF NYU, WESTCHESTER GRADUATE CENTER, Hawthorne, NY 10532-1507

General Information Independent, coed, graduate-only institution. *Graduate housing:* Room and/or apartments available to single students; on-campus housing not available to married students.

GRADUATE UNITS

Graduate Programs *Degree program information:* Part-time and evening/weekend programs available. Offers chemical engineering (MS); chemistry (MS); computer engineering (MS); computer science (MS, PhD); electrical engineering (MS, PhD); information systems engineering (MS); materials chemistry (PhD); telecommunication networks (MS). Electronic applications accepted.

Department of Management *Degree program information:* Part-time and evening/weekend programs available. Offers capital markets (MS); computational finance (MS); financial engineering (MS, AC); financial technology (MS); financial technology management (AC); information management (AC); management (MS, AC); management of technology (MS). Electronic applications accepted.

POLYTECHNIC UNIVERSITY OF PUERTO RICO, Hato Rey, PR 00919

General Information Independent, coed, primarily men, comprehensive institution. CGS member. *Graduate housing:* On-campus housing not available. *Research affiliation:* University of Missouri-Columbia (engineering, mathematics and science), University of Puerto Rico-Mayagüez (electrical engineering), Virginia Polytechnic Institute (mechanical/electrical engineering), Navy Research Laboratories (mechanical/electrical engineering), Department of Energy Laboratories (electrical engineering).

GRADUATE UNITS

Graduate School *Degree program information:* Part-time and evening/weekend programs available.

POLYTECHNIC UNIVERSITY OF THE AMERICAS–MIAMI CAMPUS, Miami, FL 33166

General Information Independent, comprehensive institution.

GRADUATE UNITS

Graduate School *Degree program information:* Part-time and evening/weekend programs available. Postbaccalaureate distance learning degree programs offered (no on-campus study). Electronic applications accepted.

POLYTECHNIC UNIVERSITY OF THE AMERICAS–ORLANDO CAMPUS, Winter Park, FL 32792

General Information Independent, comprehensive institution. *Graduate housing:* On-campus housing not available.

GRADUATE UNITS

Graduate School *Degree program information:* Part-time and evening/weekend programs available. Postbaccalaureate distance learning degree programs offered (no on-campus study). Electronic applications accepted.

PONCE SCHOOL OF MEDICINE, Ponce, PR 00732-7004

General Information Independent, coed, graduate-only institution. *Enrollment by degree level:* 280 first professional, 46 master's, 224 doctoral, 52 other advanced degrees. *Graduate faculty:* 200 full-time (81 women), 211 part-time/adjunct (63 women). *Graduate housing:* On-campus housing not available. *Student services:* Career counseling, free psychological counseling, low-cost health insurance. *Library facilities:* Fundación Angel Ramos Library. *Online resources:* library catalog, access to other libraries' catalogs. *Collection:* 40,962 titles, 556 serial subscriptions, 1,398 audiovisual materials. *Research affiliation:* H.L. Moffit Comprehensive Cancer Center (cancer biology/oncology), University of Kentucky (biomedical sciences), University of Puerto Rico, Mayagüez Campus (cancer biology, molecular genetics), University of Puerto Rico, Medical Sciences Campus (translational research), University of Maryland—Institute of Virology (HIV/AIDS research).

Computer facilities: 40 computers available on campus for general student use. A campuswide network can be accessed from student residence rooms and from off campus. *Web address:* http://www.psm.edu/.

General Application Contact: Maria Colon, Admissions Officer, 787-840-2575 Ext. 2143, E-mail: mcolon@psm.edu.

GRADUATE UNITS

Professional Program Students: 315 full-time (151 women). Average age 32. 1,306 applicants, 14% accepted, 68 enrolled. *Faculty:* 159 full-time (60 women), 194 part-time/adjunct (54 women). Expenses: Contact institution. *Financial support:* In 2008–09, 280 students received support; fellowships, scholarships/grants available. Financial award application deadline: 4/30; financial award applicants required to submit FAFSA. In 2008, 69 MDs awarded. Offers medicine (MD). *Application deadline:* For fall admission, 12/15 for domestic and international students. Applications are processed on a rolling basis. *Application fee:* $100. Electronic applications accepted. *Application Contact:* Maria Colon, Admissions Officer, 787-840-2575 Ext. 2143, E-mail: mcolon@psm.edu. *President and Dean,* Dr. Joxel Garcia, 787-844-3710, Fax: 787-840-9756, E-mail: jgarcia@psm.edu.

Program in Biomedical Sciences Students: 30 full-time (24 women); includes 21 minority (all Hispanic Americans). Average age 29. 8 applicants, 63% accepted, 5 enrolled. *Faculty:* 8 full-time (1 woman). Expenses: Contact institution. *Financial support:* In 2008–09, 25 students received support, including 4 fellowships with full tuition reimbursements available (averaging $6,560 per year), 17 research assistantships with full tuition reimbursements available (averaging $9,208 per year); scholarships/grants also available. Financial award application deadline: 4/30; financial award applicants required to submit FAFSA. In 2008, 2 doctorates awarded. Offers biomedical sciences (PhD). *Application deadline:* For fall admission, 4/15 for domestic and international students. *Application fee:* $100. *Application Contact:* Dr. Jose Torres, Associate Dean for Graduate Studies and Research, 787-840-2158, E-mail: jtorres@psm.edu. *Associate Dean for Graduate Studies and Research,* Dr. Jose Torres, 787-840-2158, E-mail: jtorres@psm.edu.

Program in Clinical Psychology Students: 186 full-time (157 women); all minorities (all Hispanic Americans). Average age 28. 92 applicants, 34% accepted, 31 enrolled. *Faculty:* 26 full-time (9 women), 5 part-time/adjunct (2 women). Expenses: Contact institution. *Financial support:* In 2008–09, 153 students received support; fellowships, scholarships/grants available. Financial award application deadline: 4/30; financial award applicants required to submit FAFSA. In 2008, 37 doctorates awarded. Offers clinical psychology (Psy D). *Application deadline:* For fall admission, 4/15 for domestic and international students. *Application fee:* $100. *Application Contact:* Maria Colon, Admissions Officer, 787-840-2575 Ext. 2143, E-mail: mcolon@psm.edu. *Head,* Dr. Jose Pons, 787-840-2575, E-mail: jpons@psm.edu.

Program in Public Health Students: 71 full-time (54 women); includes 62 minority (all Hispanic Americans). Average age 33. 34 applicants, 74% accepted, 19 enrolled. *Faculty:* 7 full-time (3 women), 12 part-time/adjunct (6 women). Expenses: Contact institution. *Financial support:* In 2008–09, 46 students received support. Scholarships/grants available. Financial award application deadline: 5/30; financial award applicants required to submit FAFSA. In 2008, 21 master's awarded. Offers public health (MPH). *Application deadline:* For fall admission, 5/15 for domestic students, 4/15 for international students. *Application fee:* $100. *Application Contact:* Maria Colon, Admissions Officer, 787-840-2575 Ext. 2143, E-mail: mcolon@psm.edu. *Head,* Dr. Manuel Bayona, 787-840-2575 Ext. 2232, E-mail: mbayona@psm.edu.

PONTIFICAL CATHOLIC UNIVERSITY OF PUERTO RICO, Ponce, PR 00717-0777

General Information Independent-religious, coed, university. *Graduate housing:* Room and/or apartments available to single students; on-campus housing not available to married students. Housing application deadline: 7/15.

GRADUATE UNITS

College of Arts and Humanities *Degree program information:* Part-time and evening/weekend programs available. Offers arts and humanities (MA, Professional Certificate); grammar and writing (Professional Certificate); Hispanic studies (MA); history (MA); theology and philosophy (M Div).

College of Business Administration *Degree program information:* Part-time and evening/weekend programs available. Offers accounting (MBA); business administration (MBA, PhD); finance (MBA); general business (MBA); human resources (MBA); international business (MBA); management (MBA); management information systems (MBA); marketing (MBA); office administration (MBA).

College of Education *Degree program information:* Part-time and evening/weekend programs available. Offers business teacher education (M Ed, PhD); counselor education (M Ed); curriculum and instruction (M Ed, PhD); education (M Ed, MA Ed, MRE, PhD); education-general (M Ed, MA Ed); educational leadership and administration (PhD); educational psychology (M Ed); English as a second language (M Ed).

College of Sciences *Degree program information:* Part-time and evening/weekend programs available. Offers chemistry (MS); environmental sciences (MS); medical technology (Certificate); medical-surgical nursing (MS); mental health and psychiatric nursing (MS); sciences (MS, Certificate).

Institute of Graduate Studies in Behavioral Science and Community Affairs *Degree program information:* Part-time and evening/weekend programs available. Offers clinical psychology (MA, MS, PhD); clinical social work (MSW); criminology (MA); industrial psychology (MS, PhD); psychology (PhD); public administration (MA); vocational rehabilitation counseling (MSS).

School of Law *Degree program information:* Part-time and evening/weekend programs available. Offers law (JD).

PONTIFICAL COLLEGE JOSEPHINUM, Columbus, OH 43235-1498

General Information Independent-religious, men only, comprehensive institution. *Enrollment:* 164 graduate, professional, and undergraduate students; 49 full-time matriculated graduate/professional students, 2 part-time matriculated graduate/professional students. *Enrollment by degree level:* 51 master's. *Graduate faculty:* 15 full-time (1 woman), 7 part-time/adjunct (1 woman). *Tuition:* Full-time $20,053; part-time $630 per credit hour. *Required fees:* $707. *Graduate housing:* Room and/or apartments guaranteed to single students; on-campus housing not available to married students. Typical cost: $3899 per year ($7798 including board). Housing application deadline: 8/15. *Student services:* Campus employment opportunities, free psychological counseling, international student services, low-cost health insurance. *Library facilities:* Wehrle Memorial Library. *Online resources:* web page. *Collection:* 137,883 titles, 465 serial subscriptions.

Computer facilities: 10 computers available on campus for general student use. A campuswide network can be accessed from student residence rooms. *Web address:* http://www.pcj.edu/.

General Application Contact: Dr. Perry Cahall, Director of Admissions, 614-885-5585, Fax: 614-885-2307, E-mail: pcahall@pcj.edu.

GRADUATE UNITS

School of Theology Students: 49 full-time (0 women), 2 part-time (0 women); includes 5 minority (2 Asian Americans or Pacific Islanders, 3 Hispanic Americans), 10 international. Average age 28. 16 applicants, 88% accepted, 14 enrolled. *Faculty:* 17 full-time (1 woman), 5 part-time/adjunct (2 women). Expenses: Contact institution. *Financial support:* Career-related internships or fieldwork and Federal Work-Study available. Financial award application deadline: 8/15; financial award applicants required to submit FAFSA. In 2008, 9 master's awarded. *Degree program information:* Part-time programs available. Offers theology (M Div, MA). *Application deadline:* For fall admission, 8/15 for domestic students. Applications are processed on a rolling basis. *Application fee:* $35. *Application Contact:* Dr. Perry Cahall, Director of Admissions, 614-885-5585, Fax: 614-885-2307, E-mail: pcahall@pcj.edu. *Vice Rector-School of Theology,* Rev. Msgr. Nevin Klinger, 614-885-5585, Fax: 614-885-2307, E-mail: nklinger@pcj.edu.

PORTLAND STATE UNIVERSITY, Portland, OR 97207-0751

General Information State-supported, coed, university. CGS member. *Enrollment:* 26,382 graduate, professional, and undergraduate students; 2,478 full-time matriculated graduate/professional students (1,537 women), 2,659 part-time matriculated graduate/professional students (1,571 women). *Enrollment by degree level:* 4,014 master's, 535 doctoral, 588 other advanced degrees. *Graduate faculty:* 724 full-time (317 women), 583 part-time/adjunct (298 women). Tuition and fees vary according to course load and program. *Graduate housing:*

Rooms and/or apartments available on a first-come, first-served basis to single and married students. Typical cost: $6687 per year ($9486 including board) for single students; $6687 per year ($9486 including board) for married students. Room and board charges vary according to board plan, campus/location and housing facility selected. *Student services:* Campus employment opportunities, campus safety program, career counseling, child daycare facilities, exercise/wellness program, free psychological counseling, international student services, low-cost health insurance, multicultural affairs office, services for students with disabilities, teacher training. *Library facilities:* Branford P. Millar Library plus 2 others. *Online resources:* library catalog, web page, access to other libraries' catalogs. *Collection:* 1.8 million titles, 18,900 serial subscriptions, 89,607 audiovisual materials. *Research affiliation:* Bonneville Power Administration (civil and mechanical engineering, geology, urban studies), Battelle Pacific Northwest Laboratories (computer science, geographic information systems, mechanical engineering, science education), Intel Corporation (electronic cooling, engineering), City of Portland (civil engineering, urban planning), Tri-County Metropolitan Transportation District of Oregon, Tektronix (electrical engineering).

Computer facilities: 875 computers available on campus for general student use. A campuswide network can be accessed from student residence rooms and from off campus. Online class registration is available. *Web address:* http://www.pdx.edu/.

General Application Contact: Information Contact, 503-725-3511, Fax: 503-725-5525, E-mail: admissions@pdx.edu.

GRADUATE UNITS

Graduate Studies Students: 2,478 full-time (1,537 women), 2,659 part-time (1,571 women); includes 656 minority (113 African Americans, 54 American Indian/Alaska Native, 228 Asian Americans or Pacific Islanders, 261 Hispanic Americans), 599 international. Average age 33. 3,060 applicants, 63% accepted, 1468 enrolled. *Faculty:* 800 full-time (352 women), 665 part-time/adjunct (344 women). Expenses: Contact institution. *Financial support:* In 2008–09, 124 research assistantships with full tuition reimbursements (averaging $10,918 per year), 164 teaching assistantships with full tuition reimbursements (averaging $9,912 per year) were awarded; fellowships, career-related internships or fieldwork, Federal Work-Study, scholarships/grants, tuition waivers (partial), and unspecified assistantships also available. Support available to part-time students. Financial award application deadline: 3/1; financial award applicants required to submit FAFSA. In 2008, 1,506 master's, 46 doctorates awarded. *Degree program information:* Part-time and evening/weekend programs available. Postbaccalaureate distance learning degree programs offered (minimal on-campus study). Offers computational intelligence (Certificate); computer modeling and simulation (Certificate); systems science (MS); systems science/anthropology (PhD); systems science/business administration (PhD); systems science/civil engineering (PhD); systems science/economics (PhD); systems science/engineering management (PhD); systems science/general (PhD); systems science/mathematical sciences (PhD); systems science/mechanical engineering (PhD); systems science/psychology (PhD); systems science/sociology (PhD). *Application deadline:* For fall admission, 6/1 for domestic students, 3/1 for international students; for winter admission, 10/1 for domestic students, 7/1 for international students; for spring admission, 2/1 for domestic students, 11/1 for international students. Applications are processed on a rolling basis. *Application fee:* $50. *Application Contact:* 503-725-3511, Fax: 503-725-5525. *Vice Provost for Sponsored Research/Dean of Graduate Studies*, Dr. William H. Feyerherm, 503-725-3423, Fax: 503-725-3416.

College of Liberal Arts and Sciences Students: 681 full-time (427 women), 495 part-time (298 women); includes 117 minority (20 African Americans, 16 American Indian/Alaska Native, 39 Asian Americans or Pacific Islanders, 42 Hispanic Americans), 116 international. Average age 33. 890 applicants, 56% accepted, 365 enrolled. *Faculty:* 368 full-time (165 women), 231 part-time/adjunct (126 women). Expenses: Contact institution. *Financial support:* In 2008–09, 37 research assistantships with full tuition reimbursements (averaging $11,535 per year), 145 teaching assistantships with full tuition reimbursements (averaging $9,905 per year) were awarded; career-related internships or fieldwork, Federal Work-Study, scholarships/grants, and tuition waivers (partial) also available. Support available to part-time students. Financial award application deadline: 3/1; financial award applicants required to submit FAFSA. In 2008, 282 master's, 7 doctorates awarded. *Degree program information:* Part-time and evening/weekend programs available. Offers anthropology (MA); applied economics (MA, MS); biology (MA, MS, PhD); chemistry (MA, MS, PhD); conflict resolution (MA, MS); economics (PhD); English (MA); environmental management (MEM); environmental sciences and resources (PhD); environmental sciences/biology (PhD); environmental sciences/chemistry (PhD); environmental sciences/civil engineering (PhD); environmental sciences/geography (PhD); environmental sciences/geology (PhD); environmental sciences/physics (PhD); environmental studies (MS); foreign literature and language (MA); French (MA); general arts and letters education (MAT, MST); general economics (MA, MS); general science education (MAT, MST); general social science education (MAT, MST); general speech communication (MA, MS, Certificate); geography (MA, MAT, MS, MST, PhD); geology (MA, MS); German (MA); history (MA); Japanese (MA); liberal arts and sciences (MA, MAT, MEM, MS, MST, PhD, Certificate); mathematical sciences (PhD); mathematics education (PhD); physics (MA, MS, PhD); psychology (MA, MS, PhD); science/environmental science (MST); science/geology (MAT, MST); sociology (MA, MS, PhD); Spanish (MA); speech-language pathology (MA, MS); statistics (MS); teaching English to speakers of other languages (MA). *Application deadline:* Applications are processed on a rolling basis. *Application fee:* $50. *Application Contact:* Dr. Marvin Kaiser, Dean, 503-725-3514, Fax: 503-725-3693, E-mail: marvin@clas.pdx.edu. *Dean*, Dr. Marvin Kaiser, 503-725-3514, Fax: 503-725-3693, E-mail: marvin@clas.pdx.edu.

College of Urban and Public Affairs Students: 282 full-time (193 women), 313 part-time (180 women); includes 65 minority (16 African Americans, 10 American Indian/Alaska Native, 17 Asian Americans or Pacific Islanders, 22 Hispanic Americans), 33 international. Average age 33. 434 applicants, 54% accepted, 167 enrolled. *Faculty:* 74 full-time (32 women), 89 part-time/adjunct (39 women). Expenses: Contact institution. *Financial support:* In 2008–09, 22 research assistantships with full tuition reimbursements (averaging $9,050 per year), 5 teaching assistantships with full tuition reimbursements (averaging $8,445 per year) were awarded; fellowships, career-related internships or fieldwork, Federal Work-Study, scholarships/grants, tuition waivers (partial), and unspecified assistantships also available. Support available to part-time students. Financial award application deadline: 3/1; financial award applicants required to submit FAFSA. In 2008, 202 master's, 18 doctorates awarded. *Degree program information:* Part-time and evening/weekend programs available. Offers aging (Certificate); criminology and criminal justice (MS, PhD); government (MA, MAT, MPA, MS, MST, PhD); health administration (MPA, MPH); health education (MA, MS); health education and health promotion (MPH); health studies (MPA, MPH); political science (MA, MAT, MS, MST, PhD); public administration (MPA); public administration and policy (PhD); urban and public affairs (MA, MAT, MPA, MPH, MS, MST, MURP, MUS, PhD, Certificate); urban and regional planning (MURP); urban studies (MUS, PhD); urban studies and planning (MURP, MUS, PhD). *Application fee:* $50. *Application Contact:* Rod Johnson, Admissions Officer, 503-725-4044, Fax: 503-725-5199, E-mail: rod@pdx.edu. *Dean*, Dr. Lawrence Wallack, 503-725-4043, Fax: 503-725-5199, E-mail: wallackl@pdx.edu.

Graduate School of Social Work Students: 389 full-time (336 women), 168 part-time (144 women); includes 93 minority (25 African Americans, 13 American Indian/Alaska Native, 12 Asian Americans or Pacific Islanders, 43 Hispanic Americans), 13 international. Average age 35. 586 applicants, 51% accepted, 221 enrolled. *Faculty:* 40 full-time (28 women), 18 part-time/adjunct (13 women). Expenses: Contact institution. *Financial support:* In 2008–09, 10 research assistantships with full tuition reimbursements (averaging $11,972 per year), 1 teaching assistantship with full tuition reimbursement (averaging $13,692 per year) were awarded; career-related internships or fieldwork, Federal Work-Study, scholarships/grants, tuition waivers (partial), and unspecified assistantships also available. Support available to part-time students. Financial award application deadline: 3/1; financial award applicants required to submit FAFSA. In 2008, 158 master's, 4 doctorates awarded. *Degree program information:* Part-time programs available. Offers social work (MSW); social work and social research (PhD). *Application deadline:* For fall admission, 2/1 for domestic and international students. *Application fee:* $50. *Application Contact:* Janet Putnam, Director of Student Affairs, 503-725-4712, Fax: 503-725-5545, E-mail: putnamj@pdx.edu. *Dean*, Dr. Kristine E. Nelson, 503-725-4712, Fax: 503-725-5545, E-mail: nelsonk@pdx.edu.

Maseeh College of Engineering and Computer Science Students: 303 full-time (77 women), 340 part-time (71 women); includes 86 minority (8 African Americans, 3 American Indian/Alaska Native, 57 Asian Americans or Pacific Islanders, 18 Hispanic Americans), 314 international. Average age 29. 424 applicants, 76% accepted, 175 enrolled. *Faculty:* 83 full-time (12 women), 16 part-time/adjunct (2 women). Expenses: Contact institution. *Financial support:* In 2008–09, 32 research assistantships with full tuition reimbursements (averaging $14,238 per year), 4 teaching assistantships with full tuition reimbursements (averaging $11,440 per year) were awarded; career-related internships or fieldwork, Federal Work-Study, scholarships/grants, and unspecified assistantships also available. Support available to part-time students. Financial award application deadline: 3/1; financial award applicants required to submit FAFSA. In 2008, 149 master's, 5 doctorates awarded. *Degree program information:* Part-time and evening/weekend programs available. Offers civil and environmental engineering (M Eng, MS, PhD); civil and environmental engineering management (M Eng); computer science (MS, PhD); electrical and computer engineering (M Eng, MS, PhD); engineering and computer science (M Eng, ME, MS, MSE, PhD, Certificate); engineering and technology management (M Eng); engineering management (MS); environmental sciences and resources (PhD); manufacturing engineering (ME); manufacturing management (M Eng); mechanical engineering (M Eng, MS, PhD); software engineering (MSE); systems engineering (M Eng); systems engineering fundamentals (Certificate); systems science (PhD); systems science/engineering management (PhD). *Application deadline:* For fall admission, 4/1 for domestic students, 3/1 for international students; for winter admission, 9/1 for domestic and international students; for spring admission, 2/1 for domestic and international students. Applications are processed on a rolling basis. *Application fee:* $50. *Application Contact:* Marcia Fischer, Assistant Dean for Enrollment, 503-725-4289, Fax: 503-725-4298, E-mail: fischerm@cecs.pdx.edu. *Interim Dean*, Richard I. Knight, 503-725-2820, Fax: 503-725-2825, E-mail: dknight@cecs.pdx.edu.

School of Business Administration Students: 256 full-time (113 women), 280 part-time (89 women); includes 72 minority (5 African Americans, 2 American Indian/Alaska Native, 47 Asian Americans or Pacific Islanders, 18 Hispanic Americans), 80 international. Average age 31. 384 applicants, 71% accepted, 147 enrolled. *Faculty:* 66 full-time (27 women), 52 part-time/adjunct (11 women). Expenses: Contact institution. *Financial support:* Research assistantships with full tuition reimbursements, teaching assistantships with full tuition reimbursements, career-related internships or fieldwork, Federal Work-Study, scholarships/grants, tuition waivers (partial), and unspecified assistantships available. Support available to part-time students. Financial award application deadline: 3/1; financial award applicants required to submit FAFSA. In 2008, 206 master's awarded. *Degree program information:* Part-time and evening/weekend programs available. Offers business administration (MBA, MIM, MSFA, PhD); financial analysis (MSFA); human resource management (MBA); international management (MIM). *Application deadline:* For fall admission, 4/1 priority date for domestic students, 3/1 priority date for international students. Applications are processed on a rolling basis. *Application fee:* $50. *Application Contact:* Pam Mitchell, Administrator, 503-725-3730, Fax: 503-725-5850, E-mail: pamm@sba.pdx.edu. *Dean*, Dr. Scott Dawson, 503-725-3714, Fax: 503-725-5850, E-mail: scottd@sba.pdx.edu.

School of Education Students: 458 full-time (339 women), 887 part-time (678 women); includes 182 minority (29 African Americans, 7 American Indian/Alaska Native, 43 Asian Americans or Pacific Islanders, 103 Hispanic Americans), 27 international. Average age 36. 616 applicants, 81% accepted, 410 enrolled. *Faculty:* 56 full-time (36 women), 142 part-time/adjunct (94 women). Expenses: Contact institution. *Financial support:* In 2008–09, 19 research assistantships with full tuition reimbursements (averaging $6,342 per year), 1 teaching assistantship with full tuition reimbursement (averaging $10,408 per year) were awarded; career-related internships or fieldwork, Federal Work-Study, institutionally sponsored loans, scholarships/grants, and unspecified assistantships also available. Support available to part-time students. Financial award application deadline: 3/1; financial award applicants required to submit FAFSA. In 2008, 487 master's, 4 doctorates awarded. *Degree program information:* Part-time and evening/weekend programs available. Offers counselor education (MA, MS); early childhood education (MA, MS); education (M Ed, MA, MAT, MS, MST, Ed D); educational leadership (MA, MS, Ed D); educational leadership: curriculum and instruction (Ed D); educational media/school librarianship (MA, MS); elementary education (M Ed, MAT, MST); postsecondary, adult and continuing education (Ed D); reading (MA, MS); secondary education (M Ed, MAT, MST); special and counselor education (Ed D); special education (MA, MS). *Application deadline:* For fall admission, 4/1 for domestic and international students; for winter admission, 9/1 for domestic and international students; for spring admission, 11/1 for domestic and international students. *Application fee:* $50. *Application Contact:* Tasa Lehman, Information Contact, 503-725-4619, Fax: 503-725-5599, E-mail: lehmant@pdx.edu. *Dean*, Dr. Randy Hitz, 503-725-4619, Fax: 503-725-5399.

School of Fine and Performing Arts Students: 52 full-time (30 women), 16 part-time (12 women); includes 8 minority (1 African American, 4 Asian Americans or Pacific Islanders, 3 Hispanic Americans), 2 international. Average age 30. 109 applicants, 30% accepted, 23 enrolled. *Faculty:* 69 full-time (30 women), 88 part-time/adjunct (43 women). Expenses: Contact institution. *Financial support:* In 2008–09, 1 research assistantship with full tuition reimbursement (averaging $9,437 per year) was awarded; teaching assistantships with full tuition reimbursements, career-related internships or fieldwork, Federal Work-Study, scholarships/grants, tuition waivers (partial), and unspecified assistantships also available. Support available to part-time students. Financial award application deadline: 3/1; financial award applicants required to submit FAFSA. In 2008, 20 master's awarded. *Degree program information:* Part-time programs available. Offers conducting (MMC); drawing (MFA); fine and performing arts (MA, MAT, MFA, MMC, MMP, MS, MST); mixed media (MFA); music education (MAT, MST); painting (MFA); performance (MMP); printmaking (MFA); sculpture (MFA); theater arts (MA, MS). *Application deadline:* For fall admission, 3/1 for domestic and international students. Applications are processed on a rolling basis. *Application fee:* $50. *Application Contact:* Barbara Sestak, Dean, 503-725-3105, Fax: 503-725-3351. *Dean*, Barbara Sestak, 503-725-3105, Fax: 503-725-3351.

PRAIRIE VIEW A&M UNIVERSITY, Prairie View, TX 77446-0519

General Information State-supported, coed, comprehensive institution. *Graduate housing:* Room and/or apartments available on a first-come, first-served basis to single students; on-campus housing not available to married students. Housing application deadline: 4/16. *Research affiliation:* Science and Engineering Alliance, NASA (space radiation on material systems and devices), Lawrence Livermore National Laboratory (engineering and sciences), Sandia National Laboratories (engineering and chemistry), U.S. Department of Defense (engineering), U.S. Department of Energy (engineering and sciences).

GRADUATE UNITS

College of Agriculture and Human Sciences *Degree program information:* Part-time and evening/weekend programs available. Offers agricultural economics (MS); animal sciences (MS); interdisciplinary human sciences (MS); soil science (MS).

College of Arts and Sciences *Degree program information:* Part-time and evening/weekend programs available. Offers arts and sciences (MA, MS); biology (MS); chemistry (MS); English (MA); mathematics (MS). Electronic applications accepted.

Division of Social Work, Behavioral and Political Science *Degree program information:* Part-time and evening/weekend programs available. Offers sociology (MA).

College of Business *Degree program information:* Part-time and evening/weekend programs available. Offers accounting (MS); general business administration (MBA). Electronic applications accepted.

College of Education *Degree program information:* Part-time and evening/weekend programs available. Postbaccalaureate distance learning degree programs offered (no on-campus study). Offers counseling (MA, MS Ed); curriculum and instruction (M Ed, MS Ed); education (M Ed, MA, MS, MS Ed, PhD); educational administration (M Ed, MS Ed); educational leader-

Prairie View A&M University (continued)
ship (PhD); health education (M Ed, MS); physical education (M Ed, MS); special education (M Ed, MS Ed). Electronic applications accepted.

College of Engineering *Degree program information:* Part-time and evening/weekend programs available. Offers computer information systems (MSCIS); computer science (MSCS); electrical engineering (MSEE, PhDEE); engineering (MS Engr). Electronic applications accepted.

College of Juvenile Justice and Psychology *Degree program information:* Part-time and evening/weekend programs available. Offers clinical adolescent psychology (PhD); juvenile forensic psychology (MSJFP); juvenile justice (MSJJ, PhD).

College of Nursing *Degree program information:* Part-time programs available. Offers family nurse practitioner (MSN); nursing administration (MSN); nursing education (MSN).

School of Architecture *Degree program information:* Part-time and evening/weekend programs available. Offers architecture (M Arch); community development (MCD). Electronic applications accepted.

PRATT INSTITUTE, Brooklyn, NY 11205-3899

General Information Independent, coed, comprehensive institution. *Enrollment:* 4,763 graduate, professional, and undergraduate students; 1,351 full-time matriculated graduate/professional students (965 women), 288 part-time matriculated graduate/professional students (223 women). *Enrollment by degree level:* 1,639 master's. *Graduate faculty:* 57 full-time (22 women), 362 part-time/adjunct (164 women). *Tuition:* Full-time $20,412; part-time $1134 per credit. *Required fees:* $1190; $1190 per year. *Graduate housing:* Rooms and/or apartments available on a first-come, first-served basis to single and married students. Typical cost: $12,384 per year ($15,984 including board) for single students; $12,384 per year ($15,984 including board) for married students. Housing application deadline: 5/1. *Student services:* Campus employment opportunities, campus safety program, career counseling, exercise/wellness program, free psychological counseling, grant writing training, international student services, low-cost health insurance, multicultural affairs office, services for students with disabilities, teacher training, writing training. *Library facilities:* Pratt Institute Library. *Online resources:* library catalog, web page, access to other libraries' catalogs. *Collection:* 172,000 titles, 540 serial subscriptions. *Research affiliation:* General Motors Corporation (transportation), The Procter & Gamble Company (product design), Ford Motor Company (transportation).

Computer facilities: 250 computers available on campus for general student use. A campuswide network can be accessed from student residence rooms and from off campus. Online class registration is available. *Web address:* http://www.pratt.edu/.

General Application Contact: Young Hah, Director of Graduate Admissions, 718-636-3683, Fax: 718-399-4242, E-mail: yhah@pratt.edu.

GRADUATE UNITS

School of Architecture Students: 272 full-time (139 women), 27 part-time (14 women); includes 53 minority (16 African Americans, 21 Asian Americans or Pacific Islanders, 16 Hispanic Americans), 71 international. Average age 27. 788 applicants, 57% accepted, 142 enrolled. *Faculty:* 13 full-time (5 women), 74 part-time/adjunct (27 women). Expenses: Contact institution. *Financial support:* Career-related internships or fieldwork, Federal Work-Study, institutionally sponsored loans, scholarships/grants, health care benefits, and unspecified assistantships available. Support available to part-time students. Financial award application deadline: 2/1; financial award applicants required to submit FAFSA. In 2008, 96 master's awarded. *Degree program information:* Part-time programs available. Offers architecture (M Arch, MS, MS Arch, MSCRP, MSUESM); architecture (first-professional) (M Arch); architecture (post-professional) (MS Arch); architecture and urban design (post-profession) (MS); city and regional planning (MSCRP); facilities management (MS); historic preservation (MS); urban environmental systems management (MSUESM). *Application deadline:* For fall admission, 2/1 for domestic and international students; for spring admission, 10/1 for domestic and international students. Applications are processed on a rolling basis. *Application fee:* $50 ($90 for international students). Electronic applications accepted. *Application Contact:* Young Hah, Director of Graduate Admissions, 718-636-3683, Fax: 718-399-4242, E-mail: yhah@pratt.edu. *Dean,* Thomas Hanrahan, 718-399-4304, Fax: 718-399-4315, E-mail: hanrahan@pratt.edu.

School of Art and Design Students: 937 full-time (713 women), 53 part-time (43 women); includes 142 minority (40 African Americans, 3 American Indian/Alaska Native, 60 Asian Americans or Pacific Islanders, 39 Hispanic Americans), 331 international. Average age 28. 1,553 applicants, 44% accepted, 334 enrolled. *Faculty:* 41 full-time (17 women), 200 part-time/adjunct (99 women). Expenses: Contact institution. *Financial support:* Career-related internships or fieldwork, Federal Work-Study, institutionally sponsored loans, scholarships/grants, health care benefits, and unspecified assistantships available. Support available to part-time students. Financial award application deadline: 2/1; financial award applicants required to submit FAFSA. In 2008, 381 master's awarded. *Degree program information:* Part-time programs available. Offers art and design (MFA, MID, MPS, MS, Adv C); art and design education (MS, Adv C); art history (MS); art therapy and creativity development (MPS); art therapy-special education (MPS); arts and cultural management (MPS); communications design (MS); dance/movement therapy (MS); design management (MPS); digital arts (MFA); industrial design (MID); interior design (MS); new forms (MFA); package design (MS); painting and drawing (MFA); photography (MFA); printmaking (MFA); sculpture (MFA); theory and criticism (MS). *Application deadline:* For fall admission, 2/1 for domestic and international students; for spring admission, 10/1 for domestic and international students. *Application fee:* $50 ($90 for international students). Electronic applications accepted. *Application Contact:* Young Hah, Director of Graduate Admissions, 718-636-3683, Fax: 718-399-4242, E-mail: yhah@pratt.edu. *Chairperson,* Concetta Stewart.

School of Information and Library Science Students: 142 full-time (113 women), 208 part-time (166 women); includes 60 minority (12 African Americans, 1 American Indian/Alaska Native, 23 Asian Americans or Pacific Islanders, 24 Hispanic Americans), 6 international. Average age 32. 309 applicants, 76% accepted, 117 enrolled. *Faculty:* 9 full-time (6 women), 27 part-time/adjunct (15 women). Expenses: Contact institution. *Financial support:* Career-related internships or fieldwork, Federal Work-Study, institutionally sponsored loans, scholarships/grants, health care benefits, and unspecified assistantships available. Support available to part-time students. Financial award application deadline: 2/1; financial award applicants required to submit FAFSA. In 2008, 179 master's awarded. *Degree program information:* Part-time programs available. Offers archives (Adv C); library and information science (MS, Adv C); library and information science/media specialist (MS, Adv C); museum libraries (Adv C). *Application deadline:* For fall admission, 2/1 for domestic and international students; for spring admission, 10/1 for domestic and international students. *Application fee:* $50 ($90 for international students). Electronic applications accepted. *Application Contact:* Young Hah, Director of Graduate Admissions, 718-636-3683, Fax: 718-399-4242, E-mail: yhah@pratt.edu. *Dean,* Dr. Tula Giannini, 212-647-7682, E-mail: giannini@pratt.edu.

PRESCOTT COLLEGE, Prescott, AZ 86301

General Information Independent, coed, comprehensive institution. *Enrollment:* 1,065 graduate, professional, and undergraduate students; 218 full-time matriculated graduate/professional students (155 women), 126 part-time matriculated graduate/professional students (95 women). *Enrollment by degree level:* 269 master's, 42 doctoral, 33 other advanced degrees. *Graduate faculty:* 4 full-time (2 women), 206 part-time/adjunct (113 women). *Tuition:* Full-time $13,608; part-time $567 per credit. *Required fees:* $50 per term. One-time fee: $182. Tuition and fees vary according to degree level. *Graduate housing:* On-campus housing not available. *Student services:* Campus employment opportunities, career counseling, free psychological counseling, international student services, low-cost health insurance, services for students with disabilities. *Library facilities:* Prescott College Library. *Online resources:* library catalog, web page, access to other libraries' catalogs. *Collection:* 35,293 titles, 16,424 serial subscriptions, 2,015 audiovisual materials. *Research affiliation:* Packard Foundation (Kino Bay Research), Marshall Foundation (Youth & Wilderness), US Department of Agriculture (Agro-ecology), National Park Service (Forest Health).

Computer facilities: 50 computers available on campus for general student use. A campuswide network can be accessed from student residence rooms and from off campus. *Web address:* http://www.prescott.edu/.

General Application Contact: Lea Detweiler, Admissions Counselor, 928-350-2112, Fax: 928-776-5242, E-mail: admissions@prescott.edu.

GRADUATE UNITS

Graduate Programs Students: 218 full-time (155 women), 126 part-time (95 women); includes 53 minority (18 African Americans, 8 American Indian/Alaska Native, 6 Asian Americans or Pacific Islanders, 21 Hispanic Americans), 13 international. Average age 38. 180 applicants, 77% accepted, 98 enrolled. *Faculty:* 4 full-time (2 women), 203 part-time/adjunct (111 women). Expenses: Contact institution. *Financial support:* Career-related internships or fieldwork, Federal Work-Study, and scholarships/grants available. Financial award applicants required to submit FAFSA. In 2008, 99 master's awarded. *Degree program information:* Part-time programs available. Postbaccalaureate distance learning degree programs offered (minimal on-campus study). Offers adventure education (MA); adventure-based psychotherapy (MA); counseling psychology (MA); early childhood special education (MA); ecopsychology (MA); ecotherapy (MA); education (MA); elementary education (MA); environmental education leadership and admininstration (MA); environmental studies (MA); equine-assisted experiential learning (MA); equine-assisted mental health (MA); expressive arts therapy (MA); humanities (MA); school guidance counseling (MA); secondary education (MA); somatic psychology (MA); special education: learning disability (MA); special education: mental retardation (MA); special education: serious emotional disability (MA); student-directed independent study (MA); sustainability education (PhD). *Application deadline:* For fall admission, 3/15 priority date for domestic and international students; for spring admission, 9/15 priority date for domestic and international students. Applications are processed on a rolling basis. *Application fee:* $40. Electronic applications accepted. *Application Contact:* Kerstin Alicki, Admissions Counselor, 877-350-2102, Fax: 928-776-5242, E-mail: admissions@prescott.edu. *Dean, Adult Degree and Graduate Programs,* Paul Burkhardt, PhD, 928-350-3210, Fax: 928-776-5151, E-mail: pburkhardt@prescott.edu.

PRINCETON THEOLOGICAL SEMINARY, Princeton, NJ 08542-0803

General Information Independent-religious, coed, graduate-only institution. *Graduate housing:* Rooms and/or apartments available on a first-come, first-served basis to single and married students. *Research affiliation:* Center of Theological Inquiry.

GRADUATE UNITS

Graduate and Professional Programs *Degree program information:* Part-time programs available. Offers theology (M Div, MA, Th M, D Min, PhD). Electronic applications accepted.

PRINCETON UNIVERSITY, Princeton, NJ 08544-1019

General Information Independent, coed, university. CGS member. *Graduate housing:* Rooms and/or apartments available to single and married students. Housing application deadline: 4/15. *Research affiliation:* Institute for Advanced Study (physics and mathematics), Brookhaven National Laboratory (experimental physics), Textile Research Institute (polymer research), NOAA-GFD Laboratory (weather prediction).

GRADUATE UNITS

Graduate School Offers anthropology (PhD); applied and computational mathematics (PhD); applied physics (M Eng, MSE, PhD); astronomy (PhD); atmospheric and oceanic sciences (PhD); chemical engineering (M Eng, MSE, PhD); chemistry (PhD); civil and environmental engineering (MSE); classical and hellenic studies (PhD); classical art and archaeology (PhD); classical philosophy (PhD); comparative literature (PhD); composition (PhD); computational methods (M Eng, MSE); computer science (MSE, PhD); demography (PhD, Certificate); dynamics and control systems (M Eng, MSE, PhD); East Asian art and archaeology (PhD); East Asian studies (PhD); ecology and evolutionary biology (PhD); economics (PhD); economics and demography (PhD); electrical engineering (M Eng, PhD); energy and environmental policy (M Eng, MSE, PhD); energy conversion, propulsion, and combustion (M Eng, MSE, PhD); English (PhD); environmental engineering and water resources (M Eng, PhD); financial engineering (M Eng, MSE); flight science and technology (M Eng, MSE, PhD); fluid mechanics (M Eng, MSE, PhD); French language and literature (PhD); geosciences (PhD); German (PhD); history (PhD); history (the ancient world) (PhD); history of science (PhD); industrial chemistry (MS); literature and philology (PhD); mathematics (PhD); mechanics, materials, and structures (PhD); molecular biology (PhD); musicology (PhD); Near Eastern studies (MA, PhD); neuroscience (PhD); ocean sciences and marine biology (PhD); operations research and financial engineering (PhD); philosophy (PhD); philosophy of science (PhD); physics (PhD); plasma physics (PhD); political philosophy (PhD); politics (PhD); psychology (PhD); public affairs and demography (PhD); religion (PhD); Russian and Slavic linguistics (PhD); Russian literature (PhD); sociology (PhD); sociology and demography (PhD); Spanish and Portuguese languages and cultures (PhD); structural engineering (M Eng). Electronic applications accepted.

Bendheim Center for Finance Offers finance (M Fin). Electronic applications accepted.

School of Architecture Offers architecture (M Arch, PhD). Electronic applications accepted.

Woodrow Wilson School of Public and International Affairs Offers public affairs (MPA, PhD); public policy (MPP). Electronic applications accepted.

Princeton Institute for the Science and Technology of Materials (PRISM) Offers materials (PhD).

Princeton Neuroscience Institute Offers neuroscience (PhD). Electronic applications accepted.

THE PROTESTANT EPISCOPAL THEOLOGICAL SEMINARY IN VIRGINIA, Alexandria, VA 22304

General Information Independent-religious, coed, graduate-only institution. *Graduate housing:* Room and/or apartments available on a first-come, first-served basis to single students; on-campus housing not available to married students. Housing application deadline: 5/1.

GRADUATE UNITS

Graduate and Professional Programs *Degree program information:* Part-time programs available. Offers theology (M Div, MACE, MTS, D Min).

PROVIDENCE COLLEGE, Providence, RI 02918

General Information Independent-religious, coed, comprehensive institution. *Enrollment:* 4,673 graduate, professional, and undergraduate students; 139 full-time matriculated graduate/professional students (78 women), 325 part-time matriculated graduate/professional students (210 women). *Enrollment by degree level:* 464 master's. *Graduate faculty:* 42 full-time (13 women), 53 part-time/adjunct (27 women). *Tuition:* Part-time $333 per credit hour. One-time fee: $170 part-time. Tuition and fees vary according to program. *Graduate housing:* On-campus housing not available. *Student services:* Campus employment opportunities, career counseling, exercise/wellness program, international student services, low-cost health insurance, multicultural affairs office, services for students with disabilities, teacher training, writing training. *Library facilities:* Phillips Memorial Library. *Online resources:* library catalog, web page, access to other libraries' catalogs. *Collection:* 424,229 titles, 43,632 serial subscriptions.

Computer facilities: Computer purchase and lease plans are available. 278 computers available on campus for general student use. A campuswide network can be accessed from student residence rooms and from off campus. Online class registration is available. *Web address:* http://www.providence.edu/.

General Application Contact: Dr. Thomas F. Flaherty, Dean, Graduate Studies, 401-865-2247, Fax: 401-865-1147, E-mail: tflahert@providence.edu.

GRADUATE UNITS

Graduate Studies Students: 139 full-time (78 women), 325 part-time (210 women); includes 14 minority (7 African Americans, 1 American Indian/Alaska Native, 1 Asian American or Pacific Islander, 5 Hispanic Americans), 5 international. Average age 31. 174 applicants, 97%

accepted. *Faculty:* 42 full-time (13 women), 53 part-time/adjunct (27 women). Expenses: Contact institution. *Financial support:* In 2008–09, 62 research assistantships with full tuition reimbursements (averaging $8,400 per year) were awarded; career-related internships or fieldwork, Federal Work-Study, institutionally sponsored loans, and unspecified assistantships also available. Support available to part-time students. Financial award application deadline: 8/1; financial award applicants required to submit FAFSA. In 2008, 208 master's awarded. *Degree program information:* Part-time and evening/weekend programs available. Offers administration (M Ed); American history (MA); biblical studies (MABS); counseling (M Ed); early Christian studies (MA Th); elementary administration (M Ed); elementary special education (M Ed); European history (MA); literacy (M Ed); mathematics (MAT); secondary administration (M Ed); special education (M Ed); St. Thomas Aquinas studies (MA Th, MTS). *Application deadline:* For fall admission, 8/1 priority date for domestic and international students; for spring admission, 12/1 priority date for domestic and international students. Applications are processed on a rolling basis. *Application fee:* $55. *Application Contact:* Carol A. Daniels, Coordinator of Graduate Faculty and Administrative Services, 401-865-2247, Fax: 401-865-1147, E-mail: daniels@providence.edu. *Dean, Graduate Studies,* Dr. Thomas F. Flaherty, 401-865-2247, Fax: 401-865-1147, E-mail: tflahert@providence.edu.

School of Business Students: 49 full-time (15 women), 46 part-time (23 women); includes 4 minority (2 African Americans, 1 Asian American or Pacific Islander, 1 Hispanic American), 2 international. Average age 27. 56 applicants, 93% accepted, 50 enrolled. *Faculty:* 9 full-time (2 women), 9 part-time/adjunct (2 women). Expenses: Contact institution. *Financial support:* In 2008–09, 34 research assistantships with full tuition reimbursements (averaging $8,400 per year) were awarded; Federal Work-Study, institutionally sponsored loans, and unspecified assistantships also available. Support available to part-time students. Financial award application deadline: 8/1; financial award applicants required to submit FAFSA. In 2008, 40 master's awarded. *Degree program information:* Part-time and evening/weekend programs available. Offers accountancy (MBA); economics (MBA); entrepreneurship (MBA); finance (MBA); international business (MBA); management (MBA); marketing (MBA); not-for-profit (MBA); quantitative (MBA). *Application deadline:* For fall admission, 8/1 priority date for domestic and international students; for spring admission, 12/1 priority date for domestic and international students. Applications are processed on a rolling basis. *Application fee:* $55. *Application Contact:* Katherine A. Follett, Administrative Coordinator, 401-865-2333, Fax: 401-865-2978, E-mail: kfollett@providence.edu. *Director, MBA Program,* Dr. MaryJane Lenon, 401-865-2566, Fax: 401-865-2978, E-mail: mjlenon@providence.edu.

PROVIDENCE COLLEGE AND THEOLOGICAL SEMINARY, Otterburne, MB R0A 1G0, Canada

General Information Independent-religious, coed, comprehensive institution. *Graduate housing:* Rooms and/or apartments guaranteed to single students and available on a first-come, first-served basis to married students. Housing application deadline: 8/15.

GRADUATE UNITS

Theological Seminary *Degree program information:* Part-time programs available. Offers children's ministry (Certificate); Christian studies (MA, Certificate); counseling (MA); cross-cultural discipleship (Certificate); divinity (M Div); educational studies (MA); global studies (MA); lay counseling (Diploma); ministry (D Min); teaching English to speakers of other languages (Certificate); theological studies (MA); training teacher of English to speakers of other languages (Certificate); youth ministry (Certificate).

PURCHASE COLLEGE, STATE UNIVERSITY OF NEW YORK, Purchase, NY 10577-1400

General Information State-supported, coed, comprehensive institution. *Enrollment:* 4,251 graduate, professional, and undergraduate students; 127 full-time matriculated graduate/professional students (69 women), 18 part-time matriculated graduate/professional students (17 women). *Enrollment by degree level:* 145 master's. *Graduate faculty:* 97. Tuition, state resident: full-time $6900; part-time $288 per credit. Tuition, nonresident: full-time $10,920; part-time $455 per credit. *Required fees:* $1461; $0.85 per credit. One-time fee: $75 full-time. *Graduate housing:* Rooms and/or apartments available on a first-come, first-served basis to single and married students. *Student services:* Campus employment opportunities, campus safety program, career counseling, child daycare facilities, exercise/wellness program, free psychological counseling, international student services, low-cost health insurance, services for students with disabilities. *Library facilities:* Purchase College Library. *Online resources:* library catalog, web page, access to other libraries' catalogs. *Collection:* 281,686 titles, 1,990 serial subscriptions.

Computer facilities: 600 computers available on campus for general student use. A campuswide network can be accessed from student residence rooms and from off campus. Online class registration is available. *Web address:* http://www.purchase.edu/.

General Application Contact: Sabrina Johnston, Admissions Counselor, 914-251-6479, Fax: 914-251-6314, E-mail: admissn@purchase.edu.

GRADUATE UNITS

Conservatory of Dance Students: 13 full-time (11 women), 1 (woman) part-time; includes 3 minority (1 African American, 1 American Indian/Alaska Native, 1 Asian American or Pacific Islander), 5 international. Average age 29. 31 applicants, 35% accepted, 8 enrolled. Expenses: Contact institution. *Financial support:* Fellowships, teaching assistantships, Federal Work-Study, scholarships/grants, and tuition waivers (partial) available. Support available to part-time students. Financial award application deadline: 3/15; financial award applicants required to submit FAFSA. In 2008, 1 master's awarded. Offers dance (MFA). *Application deadline:* For fall admission, 3/15 priority date for domestic students. Applications are processed on a rolling basis. *Application fee:* $50. Electronic applications accepted. *Application Contact:* Sabrina Johnston, Counselor, 914-251-6479, Fax: 914-251-6314, E-mail: admissn@purchase.edu. *Interim Associate Dean,* Stacey-Jo Marine, 914-251-6800, Fax: 914-251-6806.

Conservatory of Music Students: 90 full-time (40 women), 5 part-time (all women); includes 6 minority (2 African Americans, 2 Asian Americans or Pacific Islanders, 2 Hispanic Americans), 27 international. Average age 30. 146 applicants, 37% accepted, 29 enrolled. Expenses: Contact institution. *Financial support:* Fellowships, teaching assistantships, career-related internships or fieldwork, Federal Work-Study, scholarships/grants, and tuition waivers (partial) available. Support available to part-time students. Financial award application deadline: 3/15; financial award applicants required to submit FAFSA. In 2008, 33 master's awarded. Offers composition (MM); instrumental performance (MM); jazz studies (MM); studio composition (MM); voice and opera studies (MM). *Application deadline:* For fall admission, 3/1 for domestic students. *Application fee:* $50. Electronic applications accepted. *Application Contact:* Sabrina Johnston, Counselor, 914-251-6479, Fax: 914-251-6314, E-mail: admissn@purchase.edu. *Interim Dean,* Robert Thompson, 914-251-6700, Fax: 914-251-6739, E-mail: robert.thompson@purchase.edu.

Conservatory of Theatre Arts and Film Students: 6 full-time (all women), 2 international. Average age 26. 9 applicants, 33% accepted, 3 enrolled. Expenses: Contact institution. *Financial support:* Fellowships, teaching assistantships, career-related internships or fieldwork, Federal Work-Study, scholarships/grants, and tuition waivers (partial) available. Support available to part-time students. Financial award application deadline: 3/15; financial award applicants required to submit FAFSA. In 2008, 3 master's awarded. Offers theatre design (MFA); theatre technology (MFA). *Application deadline:* For fall admission, 3/1 for domestic students. *Application fee:* $50. Electronic applications accepted. *Application Contact:* Sabrina Johnston, Counselor, 914-251-6479, Fax: 914-251-6314, E-mail: admissn@purchase.edu. *Interim Dean,* Gregory Taylor, 914-251-6831, E-mail: gregory.taylor@purchase.edu.

Division of Humanities Students: 6 full-time (all women), 12 part-time (11 women); includes 1 minority (Asian American or Pacific Islander), 1 international. Average age 31. 17 applicants, 41% accepted, 3 enrolled. Expenses: Contact institution. *Financial support:* In 2008–09, 1 fellowship (averaging $5,000 per year) was awarded; Federal Work-Study, scholarships/grants, and tuition waivers (partial) also available. Support available to part-time students. Financial award application deadline: 3/15; financial award applicants required to submit FAFSA. In 2008, 8 master's awarded. Offers art history (MA). *Application deadline:* For fall admission, 3/15 for domestic students. *Application fee:* $50. *Application Contact:* Sabrina Johnston, Counselor, 914-251-6479, Fax: 914-251-6314, E-mail: admissn@purchase.edu. *Dean, Division of Humanities,* Louise Yelin, 914-251-6000, E-mail: Louise.Yelin@purchase.edu.

School of Art and Design Students: 12 full-time (6 women); includes 1 minority (Hispanic American), 1 international. Average age 32. 68 applicants, 10% accepted, 6 enrolled. Expenses: Contact institution. *Financial support:* Fellowships, teaching assistantships, Federal Work-Study, scholarships/grants, and tuition waivers (partial) available. Support available to part-time students. Financial award application deadline: 3/15; financial award applicants required to submit FAFSA. In 2008, 2 master's awarded. Offers art and design (MFA). *Application deadline:* For fall admission, 3/1 for domestic students. Applications are processed on a rolling basis. *Application fee:* $50. Electronic applications accepted. *Application Contact:* Sabrina Johnston, Counselor, 914-251-6479, Fax: 914-251-6314, E-mail: admissn@purchase.edu. *Dean,* Denise Mullen, 914-251-6750, Fax: 914-251-6793.

PURDUE UNIVERSITY, West Lafayette, IN 47907

General Information State-supported, coed, university. CGS member. *Enrollment:* 40,090 graduate, professional, and undergraduate students; 6,350 full-time matriculated graduate/professional students (2,716 women), 1,700 part-time matriculated graduate/professional students (657 women). *Enrollment by degree level:* 902 first professional, 2,906 master's, 4,133 doctoral, 109 other advanced degrees. *Graduate faculty:* 1,779 full-time (447 women), 334 part-time/adjunct (76 women). *Graduate housing:* Rooms and/or apartments available on a first-come, first-served basis to single and married students. Housing application deadline: 3/1. *Student services:* Campus employment opportunities, campus safety program, career counseling, child daycare facilities, exercise/wellness program, free psychological counseling, grant writing training, international student services, low-cost health insurance, multicultural affairs office, services for students with disabilities, teacher training, writing training. *Library facilities:* Hicks Undergraduate Library plus 13 others. *Online resources:* library catalog, web page, access to other libraries' catalogs. *Collection:* 2.5 million titles, 40,073 serial subscriptions.

Computer facilities: Computer purchase and lease plans are available. 5,783 computers available on campus for general student use. A campuswide network can be accessed from student residence rooms and from off campus. Online class registration is available. *Web address:* http://www.purdue.edu/.

General Application Contact: Marcia Fritzlen, Graduate School Admissions, 765-494-2600, Fax: 765-494-0136, E-mail: gradinfo@purdue.edu.

GRADUATE UNITS

College of Engineering Students: 1,701 full-time (324 women), 630 part-time (111 women); includes 185 minority (50 African Americans, 3 American Indian/Alaska Native, 85 Asian Americans or Pacific Islanders, 47 Hispanic Americans), 1,255 international. 5,223 applicants, 33% accepted, 587 enrolled. *Faculty:* 348 full-time (50 women), 39 part-time/adjunct (8 women). Expenses: Contact institution. *Financial support:* Fellowships with full tuition reimbursements, research assistantships with partial tuition reimbursements, teaching assistantships with partial tuition reimbursements, career-related internships or fieldwork, health care benefits, and unspecified assistantships available. Financial award applicants required to submit FAFSA. In 2008, 425 master's, 194 doctorates awarded. *Degree program information:* Part-time programs available. Postbaccalaureate distance learning degree programs offered (no on-campus study). Offers agricultural and biological engineering (MS, MSABE, MSE, PhD); biomedical engineering (MSBME, PhD); engineering (MS, MSAAE, MSABE, MSBME, MSCE, MSChE, MSE, MSECE, MSIE, MSME, MSMSE, MSNE, PhD, Certificate); engineering professional education (MS, MSE). *Application deadline:* Applications are processed on a rolling basis. *Application fee:* $55. Electronic applications accepted. *Application Contact:* Susan K. Fisher, Graduate School Admissions, 765-494-0600, E-mail: engrgrad@purdue.edu. *Associate Dean,* Dr. Audeen Fentiman, 765-494-5340, E-mail: engrgrad@purdue.edu.

School of Aeronautics and Astronautics Engineering Students: 218 full-time (35 women), 52 part-time (8 women); includes 22 minority (6 African Americans, 1 American Indian/Alaska Native, 11 Asian Americans or Pacific Islanders, 4 Hispanic Americans), 113 international. 260 applicants, 75% accepted, 80 enrolled. *Faculty:* 26 full-time (4 women), 4 part-time/adjunct (0 women). Expenses: Contact institution. *Financial support:* Fellowships with full tuition reimbursements, research assistantships with full tuition reimbursements, teaching assistantships with full tuition reimbursements, career-related internships or fieldwork, scholarships/grants, health care benefits, and unspecified assistantships available. In 2008, 49 master's, 12 doctorates awarded. *Degree program information:* Part-time programs available. Postbaccalaureate distance learning degree programs offered (no on-campus study). Offers aeronautics and astronautics engineering (MS, MSAAE, MSE, PhD). *Application deadline:* For fall admission, 1/1 priority date for domestic and international students; for spring admission, 9/1 priority date for domestic and international students. Applications are processed on a rolling basis. *Application fee:* $55. Electronic applications accepted. *Application Contact:* Linda Flack, Administrative Assistant, 765-494-5152, Fax: 765-494-0307, E-mail: flack@ecn.purdue.edu. *Graduate Chair,* Prof. Anastansios Lyrintzis, 765-494-5152, E-mail: lyrintzi@purdue.edu.

School of Chemical Engineering Students: 92 full-time (25 women), 9 part-time (1 woman); includes 9 minority (3 African Americans, 5 Asian Americans or Pacific Islanders, 1 Hispanic American), 56 international. 326 applicants, 17% accepted, 21 enrolled. *Faculty:* 24 full-time (3 women), 1 part-time/adjunct (0 women). Expenses: Contact institution. *Financial support:* Fellowships with partial tuition reimbursements, research assistantships with partial tuition reimbursements, teaching assistantships with partial tuition reimbursements, career-related internships or fieldwork, health care benefits, and unspecified assistantships available. Support available to part-time students. Financial award applicants required to submit FAFSA. In 2008, 4 master's, 22 doctorates awarded. Offers chemical engineering (MSChE, PhD). *Application deadline:* For fall admission, 1/15 priority date for domestic students, 1/15 for international students; for spring admission, 9/15 priority date for domestic students, 9/15 for international students. Applications are processed on a rolling basis. *Application fee:* $55. Electronic applications accepted. *Application Contact:* Debra Bowman, Graduate Administrator, 765-494-4057, Fax: 765-494-0805, E-mail: chegrad@ecn.purdue.edu. *Director, Graduate Studies,* Dr. James D. Lister, 765-494-4057, Fax: 765-494-0805.

School of Civil Engineering Students: 211 full-time (40 women), 37 part-time (9 women); includes 18 minority (4 African Americans, 4 Asian Americans or Pacific Islanders, 10 Hispanic Americans), 136 international. 445 applicants, 66% accepted. *Faculty:* 51 full-time (7 women). Expenses: Contact institution. *Financial support:* Fellowships with full and partial tuition reimbursements, research assistantships with partial tuition reimbursements, teaching assistantships with partial tuition reimbursements, scholarships/grants, health care benefits, and unspecified assistantships available. Support available to part-time students. Financial award application deadline: 6/30; financial award applicants required to submit FAFSA. In 2008, 63 master's, 26 doctorates awarded. *Degree program information:* Part-time programs available. Offers civil engineering (MS, MSCE, MSE, PhD). *Application deadline:* For fall admission, 1/1 priority date for domestic and international students; for spring admission, 9/15 priority date for domestic and international students. Applications are processed on a rolling basis. *Application fee:* $55. Electronic applications accepted. *Application Contact:* Graduate Office, 765-494-2436, Fax: 765-494-0395, E-mail: cegrad@purdue.edu. *Director of Academic Programs,* Dr. Timothy M. Whalen, 765-494-2225, E-mail: cegrad@purdue.edu.

School of Electrical and Computer Engineering Students: 454 full-time (72 women), 189 part-time (31 women); includes 33 minority (10 African Americans, 15 Asian Americans or Pacific Islanders, 8 Hispanic Americans), 479 international. 1,619 applicants, 28% accepted. *Faculty:* 83 full-time (8 women), 14 part-time/adjunct (4 women). Expenses: Contact institution. *Financial support:* Fellowships with full tuition reimbursements, research assistantships with partial tuition reimbursements, teaching assistantships with partial tuition reimbursements, health care benefits and unspecified assistantships available. Financial award application deadline: 1/5. In 2008, 85 master's, 58 doctorates awarded. *Degree program information:* Part-time programs available. Postbaccalaureate distance learning degree programs offered (no on-campus study). Offers electrical and computer engineering (MS, MSE, MSECE, PhD). MS and PhD degree programs in biomedical engineering offered

Purdue University (continued)

jointly with School of Mechanical Engineering and School of Chemical Engineering. *Application deadline:* For fall admission, 1/5 priority date for domestic and international students; for spring admission, 9/15 for domestic and international students. *Application fee:* $55. Electronic applications accepted. *Application Contact:* Karen Jurss, Admissions Representative, 765-494-3392, Fax: 765-494-3393, E-mail: ecegrad@ecn.purdue.edu. *Graduate Coordinator*, Stan Zak, 765-496-6162, Fax: 765-494-3393, E-mail: ecegrad@purdue.edu.

School of Engineering Education Students: 25 full-time (13 women), 5 part-time (3 women); includes 4 minority (1 Asian American or Pacific Islander, 3 Hispanic Americans), 12 international. 21 applicants, 38% accepted. *Faculty:* 17 full-time (8 women), 1 (woman) part-time/adjunct. Expenses: Contact institution. *Financial support:* Fellowships with full and partial tuition reimbursements, research assistantships with full tuition reimbursements, teaching assistantships with full tuition reimbursements, health care benefits and unspecified assistantships available. Financial award applicants required to submit FAFSA. Offers engineering education (PhD). *Application deadline:* For fall admission, 5/1 priority date for domestic and international students; for spring admission, 11/1 priority date for domestic and international students. Applications are processed on a rolling basis. *Application fee:* $55. Electronic applications accepted. *Application Contact:* Graduate Secretary, 765-496-3374, Fax: 765-494-5819, E-mail: engr-info@purdue.edu. *Graduate Chair*, David Radcliffe, 765-494-3374.

School of Industrial Engineering Students: 112 full-time (24 women), 29 part-time (6 women); includes 11 minority (2 African Americans, 7 Asian Americans or Pacific Islanders, 2 Hispanic Americans), 111 international. 347 applicants, 34% accepted. *Faculty:* 20 full-time (2 women), 1 (woman) part-time/adjunct. Expenses: Contact institution. *Financial support:* Fellowships with full and partial tuition reimbursements, research assistantships with partial tuition reimbursements, teaching assistantships with partial tuition reimbursements, health care benefits and unspecified assistantships available. Financial award application deadline: 3/15; financial award applicants required to submit FAFSA. In 2008, 39 master's, 11 doctorates awarded. *Degree program information:* Part-time programs available. Postbaccalaureate distance learning degree programs offered (no on-campus study). Offers industrial engineering (MS, MSIE, PhD). *Application deadline:* For fall admission, 3/15 for domestic and international students; for spring admission, 9/1 for domestic and international students. Applications are processed on a rolling basis. *Application fee:* $55. Electronic applications accepted. *Application Contact:* Sandra Morgeson, Graduate Program Coordinator, 765-494-5434, E-mail: sandy@purdue.edu. *Graduate Committee Chair*, Dr. C. Richard Liu, 765-494-5413, E-mail: engi@ecn.purdue.edu.

School of Materials Engineering Students: 49 full-time (17 women), 8 part-time (4 women); includes 2 minority (1 American Indian/Alaska Native, 1 Asian American or Pacific Islander), 29 international. 222 applicants, 14% accepted. *Faculty:* 20 full-time (2 women), 3 part-time/adjunct (0 women). Expenses: Contact institution. *Financial support:* Fellowships with full and partial tuition reimbursements, research assistantships with partial tuition reimbursements, teaching assistantships with partial tuition reimbursements, career-related internships or fieldwork, scholarships/grants, health care benefits, and unspecified assistantships available. Support available to part-time students. Financial award applicants required to submit FAFSA. In 2008, 8 master's, 14 doctorates awarded. *Degree program information:* Part-time programs available. Offers materials engineering (MSMSE, PhD). *Application deadline:* For fall admission, 1/1 priority date for domestic students, 1/1 for international students. Applications are processed on a rolling basis. *Application fee:* $55. Electronic applications accepted. *Application Contact:* Vicki Cline, Academic Program Administrator, 765-494-4103, E-mail: msegrad@purdue.edu. *Graduate Coordinator*, Dr. Carol Handwerker, 765-494-0147, E-mail: msegrad@purdue.edu.

School of Mechanical Engineering Students: 306 full-time (39 women), 89 part-time (7 women); includes 34 minority (7 African Americans, 19 Asian Americans or Pacific Islanders, 8 Hispanic Americans), 179 international. 448 applicants, 45% accepted, 77 enrolled. *Faculty:* 57 full-time (5 women), 8 part-time/adjunct (1 woman). Expenses: Contact institution. *Financial support:* Fellowships with full and partial tuition reimbursements, research assistantships with partial tuition reimbursements, teaching assistantships with partial tuition reimbursements, career-related internships or fieldwork, scholarships/grants, health care benefits, and unspecified assistantships available. Financial award applicants required to submit FAFSA. In 2008, 64 master's, 37 doctorates awarded. *Degree program information:* Part-time programs available. Postbaccalaureate distance learning degree programs offered (no on-campus study). Offers mechanical engineering (MS, MSE, MSME, PhD, Certificate). MS and PhD degree programs in biomedical engineering offered jointly with School of Electrical and Computer Engineering and School of Chemical Engineering. *Application deadline:* For fall admission, 1/31 priority date for domestic and international students; for spring admission, 11/1 for domestic students, 9/15 for international students. Applications are processed on a rolling basis. *Application fee:* $55. Electronic applications accepted. *Application Contact:* Julayne Moser, Graduate Administrator, 765-494-5729, Fax: 765-494-0539, E-mail: purdueme@ecn.purdue.edu. *Associate Head*, Anil K. Bajaj, 765-494-5730, Fax: 765-494-0539.

School of Nuclear Engineering Students: 50 full-time (0 women), 6 part-time (1 woman); includes 1 minority (Hispanic American), 32 international. 47 applicants, 81% accepted. *Faculty:* 12 full-time (2 women), 5 part-time/adjunct (1 woman). Expenses: Contact institution. *Financial support:* Fellowships with full and partial tuition reimbursements, research assistantships with partial tuition reimbursements, teaching assistantships with partial tuition reimbursements, career-related internships or fieldwork, scholarships/grants, and unspecified assistantships available. Support available to part-time students. Financial award application deadline: 5/1; financial award applicants required to submit FAFSA. In 2008, 6 master's, 5 doctorates awarded. *Degree program information:* Part-time programs available. Offers nuclear engineering (MS, MSNE, PhD). *Application deadline:* For fall admission, 2/28 priority date for domestic and international students; for spring admission, 9/30 priority date for domestic and international students. Applications are processed on a rolling basis. *Application fee:* $55. Electronic applications accepted. *Application Contact:* Erica Timmerman, Graduate Administrator, 765-494-7463, Fax: 765-494-9570, E-mail: etimmer@purdue.edu.

College of Pharmacy and Pharmacal Sciences *Degree program information:* Part-time programs available. Offers pharmacy and pharmacal sciences (Pharm D, MS, PhD, Certificate). Electronic applications accepted.

Graduate Programs in Pharmacy and Pharmacal Sciences *Degree program information:* Part-time programs available. Offers analytical medicinal chemistry (PhD); clinical pharmacy (MS, PhD); computational and biophysical medicinal chemistry (PhD); industrial and physical pharmacy (MS, PhD, Certificate); medicinal and bioorganic chemistry (PhD); medicinal biochemistry and molecular biology (PhD); medicinal chemistry and molecular pharmacology (MS, PhD); molecular pharmacology and toxicology (PhD); natural products and pharmacognosy (PhD); nuclear pharmacy (MS); pharmaceutics (PhD); pharmacy administration (MS, PhD); pharmacy practice (MS, PhD); radiopharmaceutical chemistry and nuclear pharmacy (PhD); regulatory quality compliance (MS, Certificate). Electronic applications accepted.

Graduate School *Degree program information:* Part-time and evening/weekend programs available. Postbaccalaureate distance learning degree programs offered (no on-campus study). Offers life sciences (PhD). Electronic applications accepted.

Center for Education and Research in Information Assurance and Security (CERIAS) Offers information security (MS).

College of Agriculture Students: 437 full-time (193 women), 128 part-time (54 women); includes 34 minority (16 African Americans, 4 American Indian/Alaska Native, 4 Asian Americans or Pacific Islanders, 10 Hispanic Americans), 214 international. 591 applicants, 35% accepted, 134 enrolled. *Faculty:* 296 full-time (49 women), 60 part-time/adjunct (13 women). Expenses: Contact institution. *Financial support:* Fellowships with tuition reimbursements, research assistantships with tuition reimbursements, teaching assistantships with tuition reimbursements, career-related internships or fieldwork and tuition waivers (partial) available. Support available to part-time students. Financial award applicants required to submit FAFSA. In 2008, 85 master's, 59 doctorates awarded. *Degree program information:* Part-time programs available. Offers agricultural economics (MS, PhD); agriculture (EMBA, M Agr, MA, MS, MSF, PhD); agronomy (MS, PhD); animal sciences (MS, PhD); aquaculture, fisheries, aquatic science (MSF); aquaculture, fisheries, aquatic sciences (MS, PhD); biochemistry (MS, PhD); botany and plant pathology (MS, PhD); entomology (MS, PhD); food and agricultural business (EMBA); food science (MS, PhD); forest biology (MS, MSF, PhD); horticulture (M Agr, MS, PhD); natural resources and environmental policy (MS, MSF); natural resources environmental policy (PhD); quantitative resource analysis (MS, MSF, PhD); wildlife science (MS, MSF, PhD); wood science and technology (MS, MSF, PhD); youth development and agricultural education (MA, PhD). *Application deadline:* Applications are processed on a rolling basis. *Application fee:* $55. Electronic applications accepted. *Application Contact:* Graduate School Admissions, 765-494-2600, Fax: 765-494-0136, E-mail: gradinfo@purdue.edu. *Dean*, Dr. Victor L. Lechtenberg, 765-494-8392.

College of Consumer and Family Sciences *Degree program information:* Part-time programs available. Offers consumer and family sciences (MS, PhD); consumer behavior (MS, PhD); developmental studies (MS, PhD); family and consumer economics (MS, PhD); family studies (MS, PhD); hospitality and tourism management (MS, PhD); marriage and family therapy (MS, PhD); nutrition (MS, PhD); retail management (MS, PhD); textile science (MS, PhD). Electronic applications accepted.

College of Liberal Arts *Degree program information:* Part-time and evening/weekend programs available. Offers American studies (MA, PhD); anthropology (MS, PhD); art and design (MA); audiology (MS, Au D, PhD); communication (MA, MS, PhD); comparative literature (MA, PhD); creative writing (MFA); exercise, human physiology of movement and sport (PhD); French (MA, MAT, PhD); German (MA, MAT, PhD); health and fitness (MS); health promotion (MS); health promotion and disease prevention (PhD); history (MA, PhD); liberal arts (MA, MAT, MFA, MS, Au D, PhD); linguistics (MS, PhD); literature (MA, PhD); movement and sport science (MS); pedagogy and administration (MS); pedagogy of physical activity and health (PhD); philosophy (MA, PhD); political science (MA, PhD); psychological sciences (PhD); psychology of sport and exercise, and motor behavior (PhD); sociology (MS, PhD); Spanish (MA, MAT, PhD); speech and hearing science (MS, PhD); speech-language pathology (MS, PhD); theatre (MA, MFA). Electronic applications accepted.

College of Science *Degree program information:* Part-time programs available. Offers analytical chemistry (MS, PhD); biochemistry (MS, PhD); biophysics (PhD); cell and developmental biology (PhD); chemical education (MS, PhD); computer sciences (MS, PhD); earth and atmospheric sciences (MS, PhD); ecology, evolutionary and population biology (MS, PhD); genetics (MS, PhD); inorganic chemistry (MS, PhD); mathematics (MS, PhD); microbiology (MS, PhD); molecular biology (PhD); neurobiology (MS, PhD); organic chemistry (MS, PhD); physical chemistry (MS, PhD); physics (MS, PhD); plant physiology (PhD); science (MS, PhD, Certificate); statistics (MS, PhD, Certificate). Electronic applications accepted.

College of Technology Postbaccalaureate distance learning degree programs offered. Offers industrial technology (MS); technology (MS). Electronic applications accepted.

Krannert School of Management Offers business administration (MBA); economics (PhD); finance (MSF); general business (MBA); human resource management (MSHRM); industrial administration (MSIA); international management (MBA); management (EMBA, MBA, MS, MSF, MSHRM, MSIA, PhD); organizational behavior and human resource management (PhD). Electronic applications accepted.

School of Education *Degree program information:* Part-time and evening/weekend programs available. Offers administration (MS Ed, PhD, Ed S); agricultural and extension education (PhD, Ed S); agriculture and extension education (MS, MS Ed); art education (PhD); consumer and family sciences and extension education (MS Ed, PhD, Ed S); counseling and development (MS Ed, PhD); curriculum studies (MS Ed, PhD, Ed S); education (MS, MS Ed, PhD, Ed S); education of the gifted (MS Ed); educational psychology (MS Ed, PhD); educational technology (MS Ed, PhD, Ed S); elementary education (MS Ed); foreign language education (MS Ed, PhD, Ed S); foundations of education (MS Ed, PhD); higher education administration (MS Ed, PhD); industrial technology (PhD, Ed S); language arts (MS Ed, PhD, Ed S); literacy (MS Ed, PhD, Ed S); mathematics/science education (MS, MS Ed, PhD, Ed S); social studies (MS Ed, PhD); social studies education (Ed S); special education (MS Ed, PhD); vocational/industrial education (MS Ed, PhD, Ed S); vocational/technical education (MS Ed, PhD, Ed S). Electronic applications accepted.

School of Health Sciences *Degree program information:* Part-time programs available. Offers health sciences (MS, PhD). Electronic applications accepted.

School of Veterinary Medicine *Degree program information:* Part-time and evening/weekend programs available. Offers anatomy (MS, PhD); basic medical sciences (MS, PhD); comparative epidemiology and public health (MS); comparative epidemiology and public heath (PhD); comparative microbiology and immunology (MS, PhD); comparative pathobiology (MS, PhD); interdisciplinary studies (PhD); lab animal medicine (MS); pharmacology (MS, PhD); physiology (MS, PhD); veterinary anatomic pathology (MS); veterinary clinical pathology (MS); veterinary clinical sciences (MS, PhD); veterinary medicine (DVM, MS, PhD).

PURDUE UNIVERSITY CALUMET, Hammond, IN 46323-2094

General Information State-supported, coed, comprehensive institution. *Graduate housing:* On-campus housing not available.

GRADUATE UNITS

Graduate School *Degree program information:* Part-time and evening/weekend programs available. Electronic applications accepted.

School of Education Offers counseling (MS Ed); educational administration (MS Ed); human services (MS Ed); instructional technology (MS Ed); mental health counseling (MS Ed); school counseling (MS Ed); special education (MS Ed).

School of Engineering, Mathematics, and Science *Degree program information:* Part-time and evening/weekend programs available. Postbaccalaureate distance learning degree programs offered (minimal on-campus study). Offers biology (MS); biology teaching (MS); biotechnology (MS); computer engineering (MSE); electrical engineering (MSE); engineering (MS); engineering, mathematics, and science (MAT, MS, MSE); mathematics (MAT, MS); mechanical engineering (MSE). Electronic applications accepted.

School of Liberal Arts and Social Sciences *Degree program information:* Part-time programs available. Offers communication (MA); English (MA); history (MA); liberal arts and social sciences (MA, MS); marriage and family therapy (MS).

School of Management *Degree program information:* Part-time and evening/weekend programs available. Offers accountancy (M Acc); business administration (MBA); business administration for executives (EMBA). Electronic applications accepted.

School of Nursing *Degree program information:* Part-time programs available. Postbaccalaureate distance learning degree programs offered (minimal on-campus study). Offers nursing (MS). Electronic applications accepted.

PURDUE UNIVERSITY NORTH CENTRAL, Westville, IN 46391-9542

General Information State-supported, coed, comprehensive institution. *Graduate housing:* On-campus housing not available.

GRADUATE UNITS

Program in Education *Degree program information:* Part-time and evening/weekend programs available. Offers elementary education (MS Ed). Electronic applications accepted.

QUEENS COLLEGE OF THE CITY UNIVERSITY OF NEW YORK, Flushing, NY 11367-1597

General Information State and locally supported, coed, comprehensive institution. CGS member. *Enrollment:* 19,572 graduate, professional, and undergraduate students; 436 full-time matriculated graduate/professional students (349 women), 3,403 part-time matriculated graduate/professional students (2,433 women). *Enrollment by degree level:* 3,839 master's. *Graduate faculty:* 628 full-time (267 women), 693 part-time/adjunct (344 women). *Graduate housing:* Room and/or apartments available on a first-come, first-served basis to single students; on-campus housing not available to married students. Typical cost: $8500 per year. Housing application deadline: 6/1. *Student services:* Campus employment opportunities, career counseling, child daycare facilities, free psychological counseling, international student services, low-cost health insurance, multicultural affairs office, services for students with disabilities, teacher training, writing training. *Library facilities:* Main library plus 1 other. *Online resources:* library catalog, web page, access to other libraries' catalogs. *Collection:* 1.1 million titles, 2,689 serial subscriptions, 35,721 audiovisual materials. *Research affiliation:* The New York Times, Brookhaven National Laboratory/SUNY Stony Brook (physics).

Computer facilities: Computer purchase and lease plans are available. 2,300 computers available on campus for general student use. A campuswide network can be accessed from off campus. Online class registration is available. *Web address:* http://www.qc.cuny.edu/.

General Application Contact: Mario Caruso, Director of Graduate Admissions, 718-997-5200, Fax: 718-997-5193, E-mail: graduate_admissions@qc.edu.

GRADUATE UNITS

Division of Graduate Studies Students: 436 full-time (349 women), 3,405 part-time (2,435 women); includes 1,422 minority (431 African Americans, 74 American Indian/Alaska Native, 410 Asian Americans or Pacific Islanders, 507 Hispanic Americans). Average age 26. 3,314 applicants, 71% accepted, 1741 enrolled. *Faculty:* 628 full-time (267 women), 693 part-time/adjunct (344 women). Expenses: Contact institution. *Financial support:* Career-related internships or fieldwork, Federal Work-Study, institutionally sponsored loans, tuition waivers (partial), unspecified assistantships, and adjunct lectureships available. Support available to part-time students. Financial award application deadline: 4/1; financial award applicants required to submit FAFSA. In 2008, 1,182 master's awarded. *Degree program information:* Part-time and evening/weekend programs available. *Application deadline:* For fall admission, 4/1 priority date for domestic students, 3/1 priority date for international students; for winter admission, 11/1 priority date for domestic students, 10/1 priority date for international students; for spring admission, 11/1 priority date for domestic students, 10/1 priority date for international students. Applications are processed on a rolling basis. *Application fee:* $125. *Application Contact:* Mario Caruso, Director of Graduate Admissions, 718-997-5200, Fax: 718-997-5193, E-mail: graduate_admissions@qc.edu. *Acting Dean of Research and Graduate Services,* Dr. Richard Bodnar, 718-997-5190, Fax: 718-997-5493, E-mail: richard.bodnar@qc.cuny.edu.

Arts and Humanities Division Students: 67 full-time (59 women), 388 part-time (252 women). Average age 26. 786 applicants, 47% accepted, 242 enrolled. *Faculty:* 136 full-time (61 women). Expenses: Contact institution. *Financial support:* Career-related internships or fieldwork, Federal Work-Study, institutionally sponsored loans, tuition waivers (partial), and adjunct lectureships available. Support available to part-time students. Financial award application deadline: 4/1; financial award applicants required to submit FAFSA. In 2008, 108 master's awarded. *Degree program information:* Part-time and evening/weekend programs available. Offers applied linguistics (MA); art history (MA); arts and humanities (MA, MFA, MS Ed); creative writing (MA); English language and literature (MA); fine arts (MFA); French (MA); Italian (MA); music (MA); Spanish (MA); speech pathology (MA); teaching English to speakers of other languages (MS Ed). *Application deadline:* Applications are processed on a rolling basis. *Application fee:* $125. *Application Contact:* Mario Caruso, Director of Graduate Admissions, 718-997-5200, Fax: 718-997-5193, E-mail: graduate_admissions@qc.edu. *Dean,* Dr. Tamara Evans, 718-997-5790, E-mail: tamara_evans@qc.edu.

Division of Education Students: 341 full-time (211 women), 995 part-time (494 women). 1,527 applicants, 74% accepted, 889 enrolled. *Faculty:* 73 full-time (50 women). Expenses: Contact institution. *Financial support:* Career-related internships or fieldwork, Federal Work-Study, institutionally sponsored loans, and tuition waivers (partial) available. Support available to part-time students. Financial award application deadline: 4/1; financial award applicants required to submit FAFSA. In 2008, 638 master's, 124 other advanced degrees awarded. *Degree program information:* Part-time and evening/weekend programs available. Offers art (MS Ed); bilingual education (MS Ed); biology (MS Ed, AC); chemistry (MS Ed, AC); childhood education (MA); counselor education (MS Ed); early childhood education (MA); earth sciences (MS Ed, AC); education (MA, MS Ed, AC); educational leadership (AC); elementary education (MS Ed, AC); English (MS Ed, AC); French (MS Ed, AC); Italian (MS Ed, AC); literacy (MS Ed); mathematics (MS Ed, AC); music (MS Ed, AC); physics (MS Ed, AC); school psychology (MS Ed, AC); social studies (MS Ed, AC); Spanish (MS Ed, AC); special education (MS Ed). *Application deadline:* For fall admission, 4/1 for domestic students; for spring admission, 11/1 for domestic students. Applications are processed on a rolling basis. *Application fee:* $125. *Application Contact:* Mario Caruso, Director of Graduate Admissions, 718-997-5200, Fax: 718-997-5193, E-mail: graduate_admissions@qc.edu. *Dean,* Dr. Penny Hammrich, 718-997-5220.

Mathematics and Natural Sciences Division Students: 33 full-time (22 women), 289 part-time (171 women). Average age 26. 376 applicants, 80% accepted, 175 enrolled. *Faculty:* 149 full-time (46 women). Expenses: Contact institution. *Financial support:* Career-related internships or fieldwork, Federal Work-Study, institutionally sponsored loans, tuition waivers (partial), unspecified assistantships, and adjunct lectureships available. Support available to part-time students. Financial award application deadline: 4/1; financial award applicants required to submit FAFSA. In 2008, 119 master's awarded. *Degree program information:* Part-time and evening/weekend programs available. Offers biochemistry (MA); biology (MA); chemistry (MA); clinical behavioral applications in mental health settings (MA); computer science (MA); earth and environmental sciences (MA); home economics (MS Ed); mathematics (MA); mathematics and natural sciences (MA, MS Ed, PhD); physical education and exercise sciences (MS Ed); physics (MA, PhD); psychology (MA). *Application deadline:* For fall admission, 4/1 for domestic students; for spring admission, 11/1 for domestic students. Applications are processed on a rolling basis. *Application fee:* $125. *Application Contact:* Mario Caruso, Director of Graduate Admissions, 718-997-5200, Fax: 718-997-5193, E-mail: graduate_admissions@qc.edu. *Dean,* Dr. Thomas Strekas, 718-997-4105, E-mail: thomas_strekas@qc.edu.

Social Science Division Students: 78 full-time (57 women), 731 part-time (516 women). 625 applicants, 88% accepted, 435 enrolled. *Faculty:* 98 full-time (37 women). Expenses: Contact institution. *Financial support:* Career-related internships or fieldwork, Federal Work-Study, institutionally sponsored loans, and tuition waivers (partial) available. Support available to part-time students. Financial award application deadline: 4/1; financial award applicants required to submit FAFSA. In 2008, 317 master's awarded. *Degree program information:* Part-time and evening/weekend programs available. Offers accounting (MS); history (MA); liberal studies (MALS); library and information studies (MLS, AC); social science (MA, MALS, MASS, MLS, MS, AC); social sciences (MASS); sociology (MA); urban studies (MA). *Application deadline:* For fall admission, 4/1 for domestic students; for spring admission, 11/1 for domestic students. Applications are processed on a rolling basis. *Application fee:* $125. *Application Contact:* Mario Caruso, Director of Graduate Admissions, 718-997-5200, Fax: 718-997-5193, E-mail: graduate_admissions@qc.edu. *Dean,* Dr. Elizabeth Hendrey, 718-997-5210.

See Close-Up on page 969.

QUEEN'S UNIVERSITY AT KINGSTON, Kingston, ON K7L 3N6, Canada

General Information Province-supported, coed, university. *Graduate housing:* Rooms and/or apartments available to single students and available on a first-come, first-served basis to married students. Housing application deadline: 6/15.

GRADUATE UNITS

Faculty of Law *Degree program information:* Part-time programs available. Offers law (JD, LL M).

Queens School of Business Offers business (M Sc, MBA, PhD); consulting and project management (MBA); finance (MBA); innovation and entrepreneurship (MBA); marketing (MBA).

Queen's Theological College *Degree program information:* Part-time programs available. Offers theology (M Div, MTS, Certificate).

School of Graduate Studies and Research *Degree program information:* Part-time programs available.

Faculty of Applied Science *Degree program information:* Part-time programs available. Offers applied science (M Eng, M Sc, M Sc Eng, PhD); chemical engineering (M Sc, PhD); civil engineering (M Eng, M Sc Eng, PhD); electrical and computer engineering (M Eng, M Sc, M Sc Eng, PhD); mechanical and materials engineering (M Eng, M Sc, M Sc Eng, PhD); mining engineering (M Eng, M Sc, M Sc Eng, PhD). Electronic applications accepted.

Faculty of Arts and Sciences *Degree program information:* Part-time programs available. Offers arts and sciences (M Sc, M Sc Eng, MA, PhD); biology (M Sc, PhD); brain behavior and cognitive science (MA, PhD); Canadian politics (PhD); chemistry (M Sc, PhD); classics, Greek, Latin (MA); clinical psychology (MA, PhD); communication and information technology (MA, PhD); comparative politics (PhD); computing (M Sc, PhD); developmental psychology (MA, PhD); English language and literature (MA, PhD); feminist sociology (MA, PhD); French studies (MA, PhD); gender and politics (PhD); geography (M Sc, MA, PhD); geological sciences and geological engineering (M Sc, M Sc Eng, PhD); German language and literature (MA, PhD); international relations (PhD); mathematics (M Sc, M Sc Eng, PhD); philosophy (MA, PhD); physics (M Sc, M Sc Eng, PhD); political theory (PhD); religious studies (MA); social personality psychology (MA, PhD); socio-legal studies (MA, PhD); sociological theory (MA, PhD); Spanish language and literature (MA); statistics (M Sc, M Sc Eng, PhD). Electronic applications accepted.

Faculty of Education *Degree program information:* Part-time programs available. Offers education (M Ed, PhD).

Faculty of Health Sciences *Degree program information:* Part-time programs available. Offers biochemistry (M Sc, PhD); biology of reproduction (M Sc, PhD); cancer (M Sc, PhD); cardiovascular pathophysiology (M Sc, PhD); cell and molecular biology (M Sc, PhD); drug metabolism (M Sc, PhD); endocrinology (M Sc, PhD); epidemiology (PhD); epidemiology and population health (M Sc); health and chronic illness (M Sc); health sciences (M Sc, M Sc OT, M Sc PT, MPH, PhD, Certificate); health services (M Sc); microbiology and immunology (M Sc, PhD); motor control (M Sc, PhD); neural regeneration (M Sc, PhD); neurophysiology (M Sc, PhD); nurse scientist (PhD); occupational therapy (M Sc OT); pathology and molecular medicine (M Sc, PhD); pharmacology and toxicology (M Sc, PhD); physical therapy (M Sc PT); physiology (M Sc, PhD); policy research and clinical epidemiology (M Sc); primary health care nurse practitioner (Certificate); public health (MPH); rehabilitation science (M Sc, PhD); women's and children's health (M Sc). Electronic applications accepted.

School of Industrial Relations *Degree program information:* Part-time programs available. Offers industrial relations (MIR).

School of Kinesiology and Health Studies *Degree program information:* Part-time programs available. Offers applied exercise science (PhD); biomechanics/ergonomics (M Sc); exercise physiology (M Sc); social psychology of sport and exercise rehabilitation (MA); sociology of sport (MA). Electronic applications accepted.

School of Policy Studies *Degree program information:* Part-time programs available. Offers policy studies (MIR, MPA).

School of Urban and Regional Planning *Degree program information:* Part-time programs available. Offers urban and regional planning (M Pl).

School of Medicine Offers medicine (MD). Electronic applications accepted.

QUEENS UNIVERSITY OF CHARLOTTE, Charlotte, NC 28274-0002

General Information Independent-religious, coed, comprehensive institution. *Enrollment:* 2,302 graduate, professional, and undergraduate students; 202 full-time matriculated graduate/professional students (126 women), 343 part-time matriculated graduate/professional students (226 women). *Enrollment by degree level:* 545 master's. *Graduate faculty:* 31 full-time (11 women), 11 part-time/adjunct (8 women). *Graduate housing:* On-campus housing not available. *Student services:* Campus safety program, international student services, multicultural affairs office, services for students with disabilities, teacher training. *Library facilities:* Everett Library. *Online resources:* library catalog, web page, access to other libraries' catalogs. *Collection:* 126,242 titles, 592 serial subscriptions.

Computer facilities: Computer purchase and lease plans are available. 125 computers available on campus for general student use. A campuswide network can be accessed from student residence rooms and from off campus. *Web address:* http://www.queens.edu/.

General Application Contact: Robert Mobley, Director of Graduate Admissions, McColl School of Business, 704-337-2224, Fax: 704-337-2594.

GRADUATE UNITS

College of Arts and Sciences Students: 81 full-time (58 women), 1 part-time (0 women); includes 16 minority (12 African Americans, 2 Asian Americans or Pacific Islanders, 2 Hispanic Americans). 21 applicants, 95% accepted, 19 enrolled. *Faculty:* 4 full-time (1 woman), 2 part-time/adjunct (1 woman). Expenses: Contact institution. In 2008, 46 master's awarded. *Degree program information:* Part-time programs available. Postbaccalaureate distance learning degree programs offered (minimal on-campus study). Offers creative writing (MFA). *Application deadline:* Applications are processed on a rolling basis. *Application fee:* $45. Electronic applications accepted. *Application Contact:* Melissa Marshall, MFA Coordinator, 704-337-2499, Fax: 704-337-2325. *Dean,* Dr. Betty J. Powell, 704-337-2463, Fax: 704-337-2325.

McColl School of Business Students: 86 full-time (36 women), 207 part-time (104 women); includes 55 minority (35 African Americans, 10 Asian Americans or Pacific Islanders, 10 Hispanic Americans), 8 international. Average age 27. 158 applicants, 91% accepted, 121 enrolled. *Faculty:* 18 full-time (4 women), 3 part-time/adjunct (1 woman). Expenses: Contact institution. *Financial support:* In 2008–09, 104 fellowships were awarded; institutionally sponsored loans also available. Support available to part-time students. In 2008, 61 master's awarded. *Degree program information:* Part-time and evening/weekend programs available. Offers business administration (EMBA, MBA). *Application deadline:* Applications are processed on a rolling basis. *Application fee:* $75. Electronic applications accepted. *Application Contact:* Robert Mobley, Director of Graduate Admissions, 704-337-2224, Fax: 704-337-2594. *Dean,* Terry Broderick, 704-337-2234.

Presbyterian School of Nursing Students: 3 full-time (all women), 29 part-time (27 women); includes 5 minority (all African Americans), 1 international. Average age 27. 15 applicants, 67% accepted, 10 enrolled. *Faculty:* 2 full-time (both women), 3 part-time/adjunct (all women). Expenses: Contact institution. In 2008, 13 master's awarded. Offers nursing management (MSN). *Application deadline:* Applications are processed on a rolling basis. *Application fee:* $40. Electronic applications accepted. *Application Contact:* Danielle Dupree, Director, Admissions, 704-688-2780, Fax: 704-337-2477. *Dean,* Dr. William K. Cody, 704-337-2276, Fax: 704-337-2477.

School of Communication Students: 2 full-time (1 woman), 27 part-time (23 women); includes 10 minority (4 African Americans, 2 Asian Americans or Pacific Islanders, 4 Hispanic Americans), 4 international. Average age 28. 11 applicants, 73% accepted, 7 enrolled. *Faculty:* 2 full-time (1 woman), 3 part-time/adjunct (all women). Expenses: Contact institution. *Financial support:* In 2008–09, 5 fellowships were awarded. In 2008, 9 master's awarded. *Degree program information:* Part-time and evening/weekend programs available. Offers organizational and strategic communication (MA). *Application fee:* $40. *Application Contact:* Gilda McGee, Assistant Director, Graduate Admissions, 704-337-2313, Fax: 704-337-2403. *Dean,* Van King, 704-337-2397, Fax: 704-688-2767.

Wayland H. Cato, Jr. School of Education Students: 30 full-time (28 women), 79 part-time (72 women); includes 14 minority (11 African Americans, 1 Asian American or Pacific Islander, 2 Hispanic Americans). Average age 27. 34 applicants, 68% accepted, 23 enrolled. *Faculty:* 5 full-time (3 women). Expenses: Contact institution. *Financial support:* Institutionally sponsored loans available. In 2008, 41 master's awarded. *Degree program information:* Part-time and evening/weekend programs available. Offers education in literacy (M Ed); elementary education (MAT); school administration (MSA). *Application deadline:* Applications are processed on a rolling basis. *Application fee:* $40. *Application Contact:* Gilda McGee, Assistant Director, Graduate Admissions, 704-337-2313, Fax: 704-337-2403. *Dean,* Dr. Darrel L. Miller, 704-337-2574, Fax: 704-688-2770.

QUINCY UNIVERSITY, Quincy, IL 62301-2699

General Information Independent-religious, coed, comprehensive institution. *Enrollment:* 1,424 graduate, professional, and undergraduate students; 121 full-time matriculated graduate/professional students (77 women), 89 part-time matriculated graduate/professional students (57 women). *Enrollment by degree level:* 210 master's. *Graduate faculty:* 8 full-time (3 women), 17 part-time/adjunct (13 women). *Tuition:* Full-time $8400; part-time $350 per semester hour. *Required fees:* $15 per semester hour. Tuition and fees vary according to course load and program. *Graduate housing:* On-campus housing not available. *Student services:* Campus employment opportunities, campus safety program, career counseling, exercise/wellness program, free psychological counseling, international student services, teacher training. *Library facilities:* Brenner Library. *Online resources:* library catalog, web page, access to other libraries' catalogs. *Collection:* 204,557 titles, 365 serial subscriptions, 9,293 audiovisual materials.

Computer facilities: 190 computers available on campus for general student use. A campuswide network can be accessed from student residence rooms and from off campus. Online class registration is available. *Web address:* http://www.quincy.edu/.

General Application Contact: Jennifer O'Donnell, Coordinator of Adult Studies, 217-228-5404, Fax: 217-228-5479, E-mail: admissions@quincy.edu.

GRADUATE UNITS

Program in Business Administration Students: 11 full-time, 27 part-time. *Faculty:* 3 full-time (2 women). Expenses: Contact institution. *Financial support:* Available to part-time students. Applicants required to submit FAFSA. In 2008, 33 master's awarded. *Degree program information:* Part-time and evening/weekend programs available. Offers business administration (MBA). *Application deadline:* Applications are processed on a rolling basis. *Application fee:* $25. Electronic applications accepted. *Application Contact:* Jennifer O'Donnell, Coordinator of Adult Studies, 217-228-5404, Fax: 217-228-5479, E-mail: admissions@quincy.edu. *Director,* Dr. John Palmer, 217-228-5432 Ext. 3070, E-mail: palmejo@quincy.edu.

Program in Counseling Students: 8 full-time, 28 part-time. *Faculty:* 2 full-time (0 women), 1 part-time/adjunct (0 women). Expenses: Contact institution. *Financial support:* Available to part-time students. Applicants required to submit FAFSA. In 2008, 14 master's awarded. *Degree program information:* Part-time and evening/weekend programs available. Offers counseling (MS Ed). *Application deadline:* Applications are processed on a rolling basis. *Application fee:* $25. Electronic applications accepted. *Application Contact:* Jennifer O'Donnell, Coordinator of Adult Studies, 217-228-5404, Fax: 217-228-5479, E-mail: admissions@quincy.edu. *Director,* Dr. Duncan Sylvester, 217-228-5432 Ext. 3114, E-mail: sylvedu@quincy.edu.

Program in Education Students: 102 full-time, 34 part-time. *Faculty:* 3 full-time (1 woman), 16 part-time/adjunct (13 women). Expenses: Contact institution. *Financial support:* Available to part-time students. Applicants required to submit FAFSA. In 2008, 26 master's awarded. *Degree program information:* Part-time programs available. Postbaccalaureate distance learning degree programs offered. Offers education (MS Ed). *Application deadline:* Applications are processed on a rolling basis. *Application fee:* $25. Electronic applications accepted. *Application Contact:* Jennifer O'Donnell, Coordinator of Adult Studies, 217-228-5404, Fax: 217-228-5479, E-mail: admissions@quincy.edu. *Interim Dean of the School of Education,* Dr. Ann Behrens, 217-228-5432 Ext. 3106, E-mail: behrean@quincy.edu.

Program in Theological Studies Expenses: Contact institution. *Financial support:* Applicants required to submit FAFSA. In 2008, 1 master's awarded. *Degree program information:* Part-time and evening/weekend programs available. Offers theological studies (MTS). *Application deadline:* Applications are processed on a rolling basis. *Application fee:* $25. Electronic applications accepted. *Application Contact:* Jennifer O'Donnell, Coordinator of Adult Studies, 217-228-5404, Fax: 217-228-5479, E-mail: admissions@quincy.edu. *Director,* Dr. Ed Maniscalco, 217-228-5432 Ext. 3201, E-mail: manised@quincy.edu.

QUINNIPIAC UNIVERSITY, Hamden, CT 06518-1940

General Information Independent, coed, comprehensive institution. *Enrollment:* 7,434 graduate, professional, and undergraduate students; 654 full-time matriculated graduate/professional students (467 women), 392 part-time matriculated graduate/professional students (250 women). *Enrollment by degree level:* 929 master's, 117 doctoral. *Graduate faculty:* 101 full-time (42 women), 92 part-time/adjunct (41 women). *Tuition:* Full-time $14,600; part-time $730 per credit. *Required fees:* $630; $30 per credit. *Graduate housing:* On-campus housing not available. *Student services:* Campus employment opportunities, campus safety program, career counseling, exercise/wellness program, free psychological counseling, international student services, low-cost health insurance, multicultural affairs office. *Library facilities:* Arnold Bernhard Library plus 1 other. *Online resources:* library catalog, web page, access to other libraries' catalogs. *Collection:* 285,000 titles, 5,500 serial subscriptions.

Computer facilities: Computer purchase and lease plans are available. 600 computers available on campus for general student use. A campuswide network can be accessed from student residence rooms and from off campus. Online class registration, e-commerce 'Q' card for local merchants, food service, dorm card access are available. *Web address:* http://www.quinnipiac.edu/.

General Application Contact: Information Contact, 800-462-1944, Fax: 203-582-3443, E-mail: graduate@quinnipiac.edu.

GRADUATE UNITS

Division of Education Students: 85 full-time (65 women), 64 part-time (57 women); includes 6 minority (1 African American, 1 Asian American or Pacific Islander, 4 Hispanic Americans). Average age 24. 137 applicants, 99% accepted, 123 enrolled. *Faculty:* 8 full-time (5 women), 23 part-time/adjunct (14 women). Expenses: Contact institution. *Financial support:* Career-related internships or fieldwork, tuition waivers (partial), and unspecified assistantships available. Financial award application deadline: 4/15; financial award applicants required to submit FAFSA. In 2008, 73 master's awarded. Offers biology (MAT); education (MAT); elementary education (MAT); English (MAT); history/social studies (MAT); mathematics (MAT); Spanish (MAT). *Application deadline:* For fall admission, 5/1 priority date for domestic students; for spring admission, 12/15 priority date for domestic students. Applications are processed on a rolling basis. *Application fee:* $45. Electronic applications accepted. *Application Contact:* Jennifer Boutin, Associate Director of Graduate Admissions, 800-462-1944, Fax: 203-582-3443, E-mail: jennifer.boutin@quinnipiac.edu. *Dean,* Dr. Cynthia Dubea, 203-582-8730, Fax: 203-582-8709, E-mail: cynthia.dubea@quinnipiac.edu.

School of Business Students: 79 full-time (28 women), 151 part-time (56 women); includes 25 minority (7 African Americans, 10 Asian Americans or Pacific Islanders, 8 Hispanic Americans), 14 international. Average age 28. 157 applicants, 80% accepted, 93 enrolled. *Faculty:* 26 full-time (4 women), 6 part-time/adjunct (2 women). Expenses: Contact institution. *Financial support:* In 2008–09, 177 students received support. Career-related internships or fieldwork, tuition waivers (partial), and unspecified assistantships available. Support available to part-time students. Financial award application deadline: 4/15; financial award applicants required to submit FAFSA. In 2008, 90 master's awarded. *Degree program information:* Part-time and evening/weekend programs available. Offers accounting (MBA); business (MBA, MS); chartered financial analyst (MBA); finance (MBA); health care management (MBA); healthcare management (MBA); information systems management (MS); international business (MBA); management (MBA); marketing (MBA). *Application deadline:* For fall admission, 7/30 priority date for domestic students, 4/30 priority date for international students; for spring admission, 12/15 priority date for domestic students, 9/15 priority date for international students. Applications are processed on a rolling basis. *Application fee:* $45. Electronic applications accepted. *Application Contact:* Jennifer Boutin, Associate Director of Graduate Admissions, 800-462-1944, Fax: 203-582-3443, E-mail: jennifer.boutin@quinnipiac.edu. *Director of Master of Business Administration,* Dr. Kim McKeage, 203-582-3676, Fax: 203-582-8664, E-mail: Kim.McKeage@quinnipiac.edu.

School of Communications Students: 44 full-time (24 women), 62 part-time (38 women); includes 17 minority (10 African Americans, 1 Asian American or Pacific Islander, 6 Hispanic Americans), 1 international. Average age 29. 61 applicants, 95% accepted, 42 enrolled. *Faculty:* 9 full-time (2 women), 14 part-time/adjunct (3 women). Expenses: Contact institution. *Financial support:* In 2008–09, 1 fellowship with full tuition reimbursement was awarded; career-related internships or fieldwork, tuition waivers (partial), and unspecified assistantships also available. Support available to part-time students. Financial award application deadline: 4/15; financial award applicants required to submit FAFSA. In 2008, 43 master's awarded. *Degree program information:* Part-time and evening/weekend programs available. Offers communications (MS); interactive communications (MS); journalism (MS); public relations (MS). *Application deadline:* For fall admission, 7/30 priority date for domestic students, 4/30 priority date for international students; for spring admission, 12/15 priority date for domestic students, 9/15 priority date for international students. Applications are processed on a rolling basis. *Application fee:* $45. Electronic applications accepted. *Application Contact:* Scott Farber, Information Contact, E-mail: graduate@quinnipiac.edu. *Graduate Admissions Office,* 800-462-1944, Fax: 203-582-3443, E-mail: graduate@quinnipiac.edu.

School of Health Sciences Students: 446 full-time (350 women), 115 part-time (99 women); includes 75 minority (17 African Americans, 32 Asian Americans or Pacific Islanders, 26 Hispanic Americans), 11 international. Average age 26. 973 applicants, 32% accepted, 252 enrolled. *Faculty:* 58 full-time (31 women), 49 part-time/adjunct (22 women). Expenses: Contact institution. *Financial support:* Career-related internships or fieldwork, traineeships, tuition waivers (partial), and unspecified assistantships available. Support available to part-time students. Financial award application deadline: 4/15; financial award applicants required to submit FAFSA. In 2008, 180 master's awarded. Offers adult nurse practitioner (MSN, Post Master's Certificate); biomedical sciences (MHS); cardiovascular perfusion (MHS); family nurse practitioner (MSN, Post Master's Certificate); health sciences (MHS, MHS, MOT, MPT, MS, MSN, DPT, Post Master's Certificate); laboratory management (MHS); microbiology (MHS); molecular and cell biology (MS); occupational therapy (MOT); pathologists' assistant (MHS); physical therapy (MPT, DPT); physician assistant (MHS); radiologist assistant (MHS). *Application deadline:* For fall admission, 4/30 priority date for international students; for spring admission, 9/15 priority date for international students. Applications are processed on a rolling basis. *Application fee:* $45. Electronic applications accepted. *Application Contact:* Kristin Parent, Assistant Director of Graduate Health Sciences Admissions, 800-462-1944, Fax: 203-582-3443, E-mail: kristin.parent@quinnipiac.edu. *Dean,* Dr. Edward O'Connor, 203-582-8710, Fax: 203-582-8706.

School of Law Students: 247 full-time (126 women), 140 part-time (73 women); includes 38 minority (13 African Americans, 3 American Indian/Alaska Native, 8 Asian Americans or Pacific Islanders, 14 Hispanic Americans), 9 international. Average age 25. 2,560 applicants, 31% accepted, 133 enrolled. *Faculty:* 33 full-time (13 women), 36 part-time/adjunct (14 women). Expenses: Contact institution. *Financial support:* In 2008–09, 354 students received support, including 23 fellowships (averaging $1,560 per year), 38 research assistantships (averaging $680 per year); career-related internships or fieldwork, Federal Work-Study, and scholarships/grants also available. Support available to part-time students. Financial award application deadline: 4/15; financial award applicants required to submit FAFSA. In 2008, 120 JDs awarded. *Degree program information:* Part-time and evening/weekend programs available. Offers health law (LL M); law (JD). *Application deadline:* For fall admission, 3/1 priority date for domestic students. Applications are processed on a rolling basis. *Application fee:* $40. Electronic applications accepted. *Application Contact:* Edwin Wilkes, Executive Dean of Law School Admissions, 203-582-3400, Fax: 203-582-3339, E-mail: ladm@quinnipiac.edu. *Dean,* Brad Saxton, 203-582-3200, Fax: 203-582-3209, E-mail: ladm@quinnipiac.edu.

RABBI ISAAC ELCHANAN THEOLOGICAL SEMINARY, New York, NY 10033-2807

General Information Independent-religious, men only, graduate-only institution. *Graduate housing:* Rooms and/or apartments guaranteed to single students and available on a first-come, first-served basis to married students. Housing application deadline: 6/1.

GRADUATE UNITS

Graduate Program Offers theology (Certificate of Advanced Ordination, Certificate of Ordination).

RABBINICAL ACADEMY MESIVTA RABBI CHAIM BERLIN, Brooklyn, NY 11230-4715

General Information Independent-religious, men only, comprehensive institution. *Graduate housing:* Room and/or apartments available to single students; on-campus housing not available to married students. Housing application deadline: 9/30.

GRADUATE UNITS

Graduate Program Offers Talmudic law and rabbinics (Advanced Talmudic Degree, Second Talmudic Degree).

RABBINICAL COLLEGE BETH SHRAGA, Monsey, NY 10952-3035

General Information Independent-religious, men only, comprehensive institution.

GRADUATE UNITS

Graduate Programs Offers theology.

RABBINICAL COLLEGE BOBOVER YESHIVA B'NEI ZION, Brooklyn, NY 11219

General Information Independent-religious, men only, comprehensive institution. *Graduate housing:* Room and/or apartments available to single students; on-campus housing not available to married students.

GRADUATE UNITS

Graduate Programs Offers theology.

RABBINICAL COLLEGE CH'SAN SOFER, Brooklyn, NY 11204

General Information Independent-religious, men only, comprehensive institution.

GRADUATE UNITS

Graduate Programs Offers theology.

RABBINICAL COLLEGE OF LONG ISLAND, Long Beach, NY 11561-3305

General Information Independent-religious, men only, comprehensive institution.

GRADUATE UNITS

Graduate Programs Offers theology.

RABBINICAL SEMINARY M'KOR CHAIM, Brooklyn, NY 11219

General Information Independent-religious, men only, comprehensive institution.

GRADUATE UNITS

Graduate Programs Offers theology.

RABBINICAL SEMINARY OF AMERICA, Flushing, NY 11367

General Information Independent-religious, men only, comprehensive institution. *Graduate housing:* Room and/or apartments available to single students; on-campus housing not available to married students. Housing application deadline: 6/15.

GRADUATE UNITS

Graduate Programs School offers a master's and first professional degree.

RADFORD UNIVERSITY, Radford, VA 24142

General Information State-supported, coed, comprehensive institution. CGS member. *Enrollment:* 9,157 graduate, professional, and undergraduate students; 431 full-time matriculated graduate/professional students (314 women), 466 part-time matriculated graduate/professional students (348 women). *Enrollment by degree level:* 869 master's, 5 doctoral, 23 other advanced degrees. *Graduate faculty:* 222 full-time (109 women), 44 part-time/adjunct

(34 women). Tuition, state resident: full-time $4845; part-time $202 per credit. Tuition, nonresident: full-time $11,483; part-time $478 per credit. *Required fees:* $2349; $98 per credit. *Graduate housing:* Room and/or apartments guaranteed to single students; on-campus housing not available to married students. Typical cost: $6716 (including board). Room and board charges vary according to board plan and housing facility selected. Housing application deadline: 5/1. *Student services:* Campus employment opportunities, campus safety program, career counseling, exercise/wellness program, free psychological counseling, grant writing training, international student services, low-cost health insurance, multicultural affairs office, services for students with disabilities, teacher training, writing training. *Library facilities:* McConnell Library. *Online resources:* library catalog, web page, access to other libraries' catalogs. *Collection:* 382,048 titles, 11,069 serial subscriptions, 18,011 audiovisual materials. *Research affiliation:* National Science Foundation (Communication Sciences and Disorders, Nursing, Criminal Justice, Psychology, Mathematics, Biology, Computer Science), U.S. Department of Health and Human Services (Nursing), Virginia Department of Social Services (Social Work), Virginia Department of Education (School of Teacher Education and Leadership), Verizon Foundation (Communication Sciences and Disorders), U.S. Department of Education (School of Teacher Education and Leadership).

Computer facilities: 756 computers available on campus for general student use. A campuswide network can be accessed from student residence rooms and from off campus. Online class registration, online financial aid status and student accounts payable are available. *Web address:* http://www.radford.edu/.

General Application Contact: Graduate Admissions, 540-831-5431, Fax: 540-831-6061, E-mail: gradcollege@radford.edu.

GRADUATE UNITS

College of Graduate and Professional Studies Students: 431 full-time (314 women), 466 part-time (348 women); includes 69 minority (45 African Americans, 1 American Indian/Alaska Native, 11 Asian Americans or Pacific Islanders, 12 Hispanic Americans), 16 international. Average age 32. 638 applicants, 70% accepted, 289 enrolled. *Faculty:* 222 full-time (109 women), 44 part-time/adjunct (34 women). Expenses: Contact institution. *Financial support:* In 2008–09, 509 students received support, including 201 research assistantships with partial tuition reimbursements available (averaging $8,000 per year), 48 teaching assistantships with partial tuition reimbursements available (averaging $8,700 per year); career-related internships or fieldwork, Federal Work-Study, institutionally sponsored loans, scholarships/grants, and unspecified assistantships also available. Financial award application deadline: 3/1; financial award applicants required to submit FAFSA. In 2008, 426 master's, 12 other advanced degrees awarded. *Degree program information:* Part-time and evening/weekend programs available. *Application deadline:* For fall admission, 3/1 priority date for domestic students, 12/1 for international students; for spring admission, 10/1 for domestic students, 7/1 for international students. Applications are processed on a rolling basis. *Application fee:* $40. Electronic applications accepted. *Application Contact:* Graduate Admissions, 540-831-5431, Fax: 540-831-6061, E-mail: gradcollege@radford.edu. *Dean,* Dr. Dennis Grady, 540-831-7163, Fax: 540-831-6061, E-mail: dgrady4@radford.edu.

College of Business and Economics Students: 28 full-time (10 women), 50 part-time (23 women); includes 7 minority (5 African Americans, 1 Asian American or Pacific Islander, 1 Hispanic American), 6 international. Average age 29. 49 applicants, 78% accepted, 35 enrolled. *Faculty:* 32 full-time (5 women). Expenses: Contact institution. *Financial support:* In 2008–09, 34 students received support, including 23 research assistantships with partial tuition reimbursements available (averaging $8,000 per year); career-related internships or fieldwork, Federal Work-Study, institutionally sponsored loans, scholarships/grants, and unspecified assistantships also available. Financial award application deadline: 3/1; financial award applicants required to submit FAFSA. In 2008, 39 master's awarded. *Degree program information:* Part-time and evening/weekend programs available. Offers business administration (MBA); business and economics (MBA). *Application deadline:* For fall admission, 3/1 priority date for domestic students, 12/1 for international students; for spring admission, 10/1 for domestic students, 7/1 for international students. Applications are processed on a rolling basis. *Application fee:* $40. Electronic applications accepted. *Application Contact:* Graduate Admissions, 540-831-5431, Fax: 540-831-6061, E-mail: gradcollege@radford.edu. *Dean,* Dr. Faye W Gilbert, 540-831-5187, Fax: 540-831-6103, E-mail: fwgilbert@radford.edu.

College of Education and Human Development Students: 118 full-time (94 women), 286 part-time (225 women); includes 21 minority (17 African Americans, 1 Asian American or Pacific Islander, 3 Hispanic Americans), 3 international. Average age 34. 174 applicants, 86% accepted, 98 enrolled. *Faculty:* 38 full-time (26 women), 14 part-time/adjunct (9 women). Expenses: Contact institution. *Financial support:* In 2008–09, 230 students received support, including 49 research assistantships with partial tuition reimbursements available (averaging $8,000 per year), 1 teaching assistantship with partial tuition reimbursement available (averaging $8,700 per year); career-related internships or fieldwork, Federal Work-Study, institutionally sponsored loans, scholarships/grants, and unspecified assistantships also available. Financial award application deadline: 3/1; financial award applicants required to submit FAFSA. In 2008, 221 master's awarded. *Degree program information:* Part-time programs available. Offers community counseling (MS); content area studies (MS); curriculum and instruction (MS); deaf and hard of hearing (MS); early childhood education (MS); early childhood special education (MS); education (MS); education and human development (MS); educational leadership (MS); educational technology (MS); high incidence disabilities (MS); library media (MS); literacy education (MS); school counseling (MS); severe disabilities (MS); special education (MS); student administration counseling (MS); student affairs counseling (MS). *Application deadline:* For fall admission, 3/1 priority date for domestic students, 12/1 for international students; for spring admission, 10/1 for domestic students, 7/1 for international students. Applications are processed on a rolling basis. *Application fee:* $40. Electronic applications accepted. *Application Contact:* Graduate Admissions, 540-831-5431, Fax: 540-831-6061, E-mail: gradcollege@radford.edu. *Dean,* Dr. Patricia Shoemaker, 540-831-5439, Fax: 540-831-5440, E-mail: pshoemak@radford.edu.

College of Humanities and Behavioral Sciences Students: 127 full-time (78 women), 45 part-time (29 women); includes 10 minority (5 African Americans, 1 American Indian/Alaska Native, 2 Asian Americans or Pacific Islanders, 2 Hispanic Americans), 5 international. Average age 28. 219 applicants, 59% accepted, 75 enrolled. *Faculty:* 64 full-time (29 women), 2 part-time/adjunct (both women). Expenses: Contact institution. *Financial support:* In 2008–09, 131 students received support, including 66 research assistantships with partial tuition reimbursements available (averaging $8,000 per year), 29 teaching assistantships with partial tuition reimbursements available (averaging $8,700 per year); career-related internships or fieldwork, Federal Work-Study, institutionally sponsored loans, scholarships/grants, and unspecified assistantships also available. Financial award application deadline: 3/1; financial award applicants required to submit FAFSA. In 2008, 76 master's, 12 other advanced degrees awarded. *Degree program information:* Part-time and evening/weekend programs available. Offers clinical psychology (MA, MS); corporate and professional communication (MS); counseling psychology (Psy D); criminal justice (MA, MS); English (MA, MS); experimental psychology (MA); general psychology (MS); humanities and behavioral sciences (MA, MS, Psy D, Ed S); industrial/organizational psychology (MA, MS); school psychology (Ed S). *Application deadline:* For fall admission, 3/1 priority date for domestic students, 12/1 for international students; for spring admission, 10/1 priority date for domestic students, 7/1 for international students. Applications are processed on a rolling basis. *Application fee:* $40. Electronic applications accepted. *Application Contact:* Graduate Admissions, 540-831-5431, Fax: 540-831-6061, E-mail: gradcollege@radford.edu. *Dean,* Dr. Brian Conniff, 540-831-6571, Fax: 540-831-5970, E-mail: bpconniff@radford.edu.

College of Visual and Performing Arts Students: 32 full-time (21 women), 5 part-time (1 woman); includes 9 minority (5 African Americans, 4 Asian Americans or Pacific Islanders), 2 international. Average age 29. 33 applicants, 73% accepted, 14 enrolled. *Faculty:* 24 full-time (8 women), 6 part-time/adjunct (all women). Expenses: Contact institution. *Financial support:* In 2008–09, 28 students received support, including 17 research assistantships with partial tuition reimbursements available (averaging $8,000 per year), 6 teaching assistantships with partial tuition reimbursements available (averaging $8,700 per year); career-related internships or fieldwork, Federal Work-Study, institutionally sponsored loans, scholarships/grants, and unspecified assistantships also available. Financial award application deadline: 3/1; financial award applicants required to submit FAFSA. In 2008, 17 master's awarded. *Degree program information:* Part-time programs available. Offers art (MFA); music (MA); music education (MS); music therapy (MS); visual and performing arts (MA, MFA, MS). *Application deadline:* For fall admission, 3/15 priority date for domestic students, 12/1 for international students; for spring admission, 10/1 for domestic students, 7/1 for international students. Applications are processed on a rolling basis. *Application fee:* $40. Electronic applications accepted. *Application Contact:* Graduate Admissions, 540-831-5431, Fax: 540-831-6061, E-mail: gradcollege@radford.edu. *Dean,* Dr. Joseph P. Scartelli, 540-831-5265, Fax: 540-831-6313, E-mail: jscartel@radford.edu.

Waldron College of Health and Human Services Students: 126 full-time (111 women), 76 part-time (68 women); includes 22 minority (13 African Americans, 3 Asian Americans or Pacific Islanders, 6 Hispanic Americans). Average age 32. 163 applicants, 65% accepted, 62 enrolled. *Faculty:* 32 full-time (30 women), 18 part-time/adjunct (15 women). Expenses: Contact institution. *Financial support:* In 2008–09, 153 students received support, including 51 research assistantships with partial tuition reimbursements available (averaging $8,000 per year), 9 teaching assistantships with partial tuition reimbursements available (averaging $8,700 per year); career-related internships or fieldwork, Federal Work-Study, institutionally sponsored loans, scholarships/grants, and unspecified assistantships also available. Financial award application deadline: 3/1; financial award applicants required to submit FAFSA. In 2008, 73 master's awarded. *Degree program information:* Part-time and evening/weekend programs available. Offers adult clinical nurse specialist (MSN); family nurse practitioner (MSN); health and human services (MA, MS, MSN, MSW); social work (MSW); speech-language pathology (MS). *Application deadline:* For fall admission, 3/1 priority date for domestic students, 12/1 for international students; for spring admission, 10/1 for domestic students, 7/1 for international students. Applications are processed on a rolling basis. *Application fee:* $40. Electronic applications accepted. *Application Contact:* Graduate Admissions Office, 540-831-5431, Fax: 540-831-6061, E-mail: gradcollege@radford.edu. *Dean,* Dr. Raymond Linville, 540-831-7600, Fax: 540-831-7604, E-mail: rlinvill@radford.edu.

RAMAPO COLLEGE OF NEW JERSEY, Mahwah, NJ 07430-1680

General Information State-supported, coed, comprehensive institution. *Enrollment:* 5,847 graduate, professional, and undergraduate students; 12 full-time matriculated graduate/professional students (7 women), 25 part-time matriculated graduate/professional students (14 women). *Enrollment by degree level:* 371 master's. *Graduate faculty:* 9 full-time (6 women), 25 part-time/adjunct (14 women). Tuition, state resident: part-time $472.20 per credit. Tuition, nonresident: part-time $606.85 per credit. *Required fees:* $43.80 per credit. Part-time tuition and fees vary according to reciprocity agreements. *Graduate housing:* On-campus housing not available. *Student services:* Campus safety program, career counseling, exercise/wellness program, free psychological counseling, international student services, services for students with disabilities. *Library facilities:* George T. Potter Library. *Online resources:* library catalog, web page, access to other libraries' catalogs. *Collection:* 265,187 titles, 600 serial subscriptions, 9,333 audiovisual materials.

Computer facilities: 1,058 computers available on campus for general student use. A campuswide network can be accessed from student residence rooms and from off campus. Online class registration is available. *Web address:* http://www.ramapo.edu/.

General Application Contact: Dr. Beth E. Barnett, Vice President of Academic Affairs and Provost, Office Of The Provost, 201-684-7529, E-mail: bbarnett@ramapo.edu.

GRADUATE UNITS

Master of Science in Educational Technology Program Students: 8 full-time (6 women), 133 part-time (97 women); includes 8 minority (4 African Americans, 4 Hispanic Americans), 3 international. Average age 35. 107 applicants, 100% accepted, 44 enrolled. *Faculty:* 4 full-time (3 women), 17 part-time/adjunct (9 women). Expenses: Contact institution. *Financial support:* Scholarships/grants available. Financial award application deadline: 3/1; financial award applicants required to submit FAFSA. In 2008, 84 master's awarded. *Degree program information:* Part-time programs available. Offers educational technology (MS). *Application deadline:* Applications are processed on a rolling basis. *Application fee:* $60. *Application Contact:* Joyce Wilson, Administrative Assistant, 201-684-7721, Fax: 201-684-6699, E-mail: mlafayette@ramapo.edu. *Dean of the Masters in Educational Technology Program/Executive Director of Special Programs, Office Of The Provost,* Dr. Angela Cristini, 201-684-7721, Fax: 201-684-6699, E-mail: acristin@ramapo.edu.

Master of Science in Nursing Program Students: 39 part-time (all women); includes 8 minority (4 African Americans, 2 Asian Americans or Pacific Islanders, 2 Hispanic Americans). 18 applicants, 100% accepted, 8 enrolled. *Faculty:* 7 part-time/adjunct (5 women). Expenses: Contact institution. *Financial support:* In 2008–09, 10 students received support. Traineeships available. Financial award applicants required to submit FAFSA. In 2008, 22 degrees awarded. *Degree program information:* Part-time programs available. Postbaccalaureate distance learning degree programs offered (minimal on-campus study). Offers nursing education (MSN). *Application deadline:* Applications are processed on a rolling basis. *Application fee:* $60. *Application Contact:* Ulysses Simpkins, Program Assistant, Nursing, 201-684-7749, E-mail: usimpkin@ramapo.edu. *Assistant Dean,* Dr. Kathleen M. Burke, 201-684-7737, E-mail: kmburke@ramapo.edu.

Program in Liberal Studies Students: 36 part-time (26 women); includes 3 minority (1 African American, 2 Hispanic Americans), 2 international. 15 applicants, 100% accepted, 12 enrolled. *Faculty:* 4 part-time/adjunct (3 women). Expenses: Contact institution. *Financial support:* Tuition waivers (full) available. Financial award applicants required to submit FAFSA. In 2008, 4 degrees awarded. *Degree program information:* Part-time and evening/weekend programs available. Offers liberal studies (MALS). *Application deadline:* For fall admission, 9/1 priority date for domestic and international students; for spring admission, 1/30 priority date for domestic and international students. Applications are processed on a rolling basis. *Application fee:* $55. Electronic applications accepted. *Application Contact:* Melissa C. Kupfer, MALS Secretary, 201-684-7709, Fax: 201-684-7973, E-mail: mkupfer@ramapo.edu. *Director,* Dr. Anthony T. Padovano, 201-684-7430, Fax: 201-684-7973, E-mail: apadovan@ramapo.edu.

RECONSTRUCTIONIST RABBINICAL COLLEGE, Wyncote, PA 19095-1898

General Information Independent-religious, coed, graduate-only institution. *Graduate housing:* On-campus housing not available.

GRADUATE UNITS

Graduate Program *Degree program information:* Part-time programs available. Offers rabbinical studies (MAHL, MAJS, DHL, Certificate).

REED COLLEGE, Portland, OR 97202-8199

General Information Independent, coed, comprehensive institution. *Enrollment:* 1,471 graduate, professional, and undergraduate students; 37 part-time matriculated graduate/professional students (20 women). *Enrollment by degree level:* 37 master's. *Graduate faculty:* 11 part-time/adjunct (5 women). *Tuition:* Part-time $3440 per unit. *Graduate housing:* On-campus housing not available. *Student services:* Campus employment opportunities, campus safety program, career counseling, exercise/wellness program, free psychological counseling, low-cost health insurance, multicultural affairs office, services for students with disabilities, writing training. *Library facilities:* Hauser Library. *Online resources:* library catalog, web page, access to other libraries' catalogs. *Collection:* 592,335 titles, 6,705 serial subscriptions, 24,050 audiovisual materials.

Computer facilities: Computer purchase and lease plans are available. 424 computers available on campus for general student use. A campuswide network can be accessed from student residence rooms and from off campus. Online class registration is available. *Web address:* http://www.reed.edu/.

Reed College (continued)

General Application Contact: Barbara A. Amen, Director, Graduate Studies, 503-777-7259, Fax: 503-517-7345, E-mail: bamen@reed.edu.

GRADUATE UNITS

Graduate Program in Liberal Studies Students: 37 part-time (20 women); includes 7 minority (2 African Americans, 3 Asian Americans or Pacific Islanders, 2 Hispanic Americans). Average age 39. 17 applicants, 41% accepted, 5 enrolled. *Faculty:* 11 part-time/adjunct (5 women). Expenses: Contact institution. *Financial support:* In 2008–09, 5 students received support. Scholarships/grants and health care benefits available. Support available to part-time students. Financial award application deadline: 5/1; financial award applicants required to submit CSS PROFILE or FAFSA. In 2008, 5 master's awarded. *Degree program information:* Part-time and evening/weekend programs available. Offers liberal studies (MALS). *Application deadline:* For fall admission, 7/1 priority date for domestic students; for spring admission, 12/1 priority date for domestic students. Applications are processed on a rolling basis. *Application fee:* $60. *Application Contact:* Barbara A. Amen, Director, Graduate Studies, 503-777-7259, Fax: 503-517-7345, E-mail: bamen@reed.edu. *Director, Graduate Studies,* Barbara A. Amen, 503-777-7259, Fax: 503-517-7345, E-mail: bamen@reed.edu.

REFORMED PRESBYTERIAN THEOLOGICAL SEMINARY, Pittsburgh, PA 15208-2594

General Information Independent-religious, coed, primarily men, graduate-only institution. *Graduate housing:* Rooms and/or apartments available on a first-come, first-served basis to single and married students.

GRADUATE UNITS

Graduate and Professional Programs *Degree program information:* Part-time and evening/weekend programs available. Offers theology (M Div, MTS, D Min). Electronic applications accepted.

REFORMED THEOLOGICAL SEMINARY–CHARLOTTE CAMPUS, Charlotte, NC 28226-6318

General Information Independent-religious, coed, primarily men, graduate-only institution. *Graduate housing:* On-campus housing not available.

GRADUATE UNITS

Graduate and Professional Programs *Degree program information:* Part-time programs available. Offers biblical studies (MA); ministry (M Div, D Min); theological studies (MA). Electronic applications accepted.

REFORMED THEOLOGICAL SEMINARY–JACKSON CAMPUS, Jackson, MS 39209-3099

General Information Independent-religious, coed, primarily men, graduate-only institution. *Graduate housing:* Rooms and/or apartments available on a first-come, first-served basis to single and married students.

GRADUATE UNITS

Graduate and Professional Programs Offers Bible, theology, and missions (Certificate); biblical studies (MA); Christian education (M Div, MA); counseling (M Div); divinity (M Div, Diploma); marriage and family therapy (MA); ministry (D Min); missions (M Div, MA, D Min); New Testament (Th M); Old Testament (Th M); theological studies (MA); theology (Th M).

REFORMED THEOLOGICAL SEMINARY–ORLANDO CAMPUS, Oviedo, FL 32765-7197

General Information Independent-religious, coed, primarily men, graduate-only institution. *Enrollment by degree level:* 175 first professional, 126 master's, 68 doctoral, 1 other advanced degree. *Graduate faculty:* 15 full-time (0 women), 5 part-time/adjunct (0 women). *Tuition:* Full-time $12,190; part-time $345 per semester hour. *Required fees:* $70 per semester. Tuition and fees vary according to degree level. *Graduate housing:* On-campus housing not available. *Student services:* Campus employment opportunities, career counseling, free psychological counseling, international student services, low-cost health insurance, writing training. *Library facilities:* Reformed Theological Seminary Library. *Online resources:* library catalog, web page, access to other libraries' catalogs. *Collection:* 70,000 titles, 250 serial subscriptions, 500 audiovisual materials.

Computer facilities: 5 computers available on campus for general student use. A campuswide network can be accessed from off campus. Online class registration is available. *Web address:* http://www.rts.edu/.

General Application Contact: Marcia Davis, Admissions Assistant, 407-366-9493 Ext. 258, Fax: 407-366-9425, E-mail: mdavis@rts.edu.

GRADUATE UNITS

Graduate Program Students: 370. 203 applicants, 75% accepted, 107 enrolled. *Faculty:* 15 full-time (0 women), 5 part-time/adjunct (0 women). Expenses: Contact institution. *Degree program information:* Part-time programs available. Postbaccalaureate distance learning degree programs offered (minimal on-campus study). Offers biblical studies (MA); counseling (MA); ministry (D Min); reformation studies (Th M); theological studies (MA); theology (M Div). *Application deadline:* For fall admission, 5/21 priority date for domestic students; for winter admission, 10/3 priority date for domestic students; for spring admission, 11/5 priority date for domestic students. Applications are processed on a rolling basis. *Application fee:* $60. Electronic applications accepted. *Application Contact:* Thomas G. Nelson, Director of Admissions, 407-366-9493 Ext. 225, Fax: 407-366-9425, E-mail: tnelson@rts.edu. *Interim President,* Dr. Michael A. Milton, 407-366-9493, Fax: 407-366-9425.

REFORMED THEOLOGICAL SEMINARY–WASHINGTON D.C., McLean, VA 22101

General Information Independent-religious, coed, primarily men, graduate-only institution. *Graduate housing:* On-campus housing not available.

GRADUATE UNITS

Graduate and Professional Programs *Degree program information:* Part-time and evening/weekend programs available. Offers bible (M Div); practical theology (M Div); religion (MA); theology (M Div). Electronic applications accepted.

REGENT COLLEGE, Vancouver, BC V6T 2E4, Canada

General Information Independent-religious, coed, graduate-only institution. *Enrollment by degree level:* 183 first professional, 273 master's, 100 other advanced degrees. *Graduate faculty:* 21 full-time (4 women), 17 part-time/adjunct (6 women). *Graduate tuition:* Tuition and fees charges are reported in Canadian dollars. *Tuition:* Full-time $14,940 Canadian dollars; part-time $475 Canadian dollars per credit. *Required fees:* $135 Canadian dollars per term. One-time fee: $210.21 Canadian dollars. *Graduate housing:* On-campus housing not available. *Student services:* Campus employment opportunities, campus safety program, career counseling, international student services, low-cost health insurance, services for students with disabilities, writing training. *Library facilities:* The John Richard Allison Library plus 3 others. *Online resources:* library catalog, web page, access to other libraries' catalogs. *Collection:* 126,787 titles, 372 serial subscriptions, 10,390 audiovisual materials.

Computer facilities: 8 computers available on campus for general student use. A campuswide network can be accessed from off campus. *Web address:* http://www.regent-college.edu/.

General Application Contact: Cindy Y. Aalders, Assistant Registrar, 604-224-3245 Ext. 335, Fax: 604-224-3097, E-mail: admissions@regent-college.edu.

GRADUATE UNITS

Program in Theology Students: 269 full-time (92 women), 293 part-time (111 women); includes 166 minority (4 African Americans, 1 American Indian/Alaska Native, 152 Asian Americans or Pacific Islanders, 9 Hispanic Americans). Average age 33. 263 applicants, 86% accepted, 135 enrolled. *Faculty:* 21 full-time (4 women), 17 part-time/adjunct (6 women). Expenses: Contact institution. *Financial support:* In 2008–09, 71 students received support, including 150 teaching assistantships (averaging $2,500 per year); career-related internships or fieldwork, scholarships/grants, and health care benefits also available. Financial award application deadline: 3/1. In 2008, 46 first professional degrees, 96 master's, 61 Dip CSs awarded. *Degree program information:* Part-time and evening/weekend programs available. Offers theology (M Div, MCS, Th M, Dip CS). *Application deadline:* For fall admission, 2/1 priority date for domestic students, 1/1 priority date for international students; for winter admission, 7/1 priority date for domestic and international students; for spring admission, 2/1 priority date for domestic students, 1/1 priority date for international students. *Application fee:* $60 Canadian dollars. *Application Contact:* Cindy Y. Aalders, Director of Admissions, 604-224-3245 Ext. 335, Fax: 604-224-3097, E-mail: admissions@regent-college.edu. *President,* Dr. Rod Wilson, 604-221-3318, Fax: 604-224-3097, E-mail: presidentsoffice@regent-college.edu.

REGENT UNIVERSITY, Virginia Beach, VA 23464-9800

General Information Independent, coed, comprehensive institution. CGS member. *Enrollment:* 4,560 graduate, professional, and undergraduate students; 1,152 full-time matriculated graduate/professional students (693 women), 1,903 part-time matriculated graduate/professional students (1,109 women). *Enrollment by degree level:* 675 first professional, 1,605 master's, 775 doctoral. *Graduate faculty:* 179 full-time (59 women), 397 part-time/adjunct (192 women). *Tuition:* Full-time $15,141; part-time $721 per credit hour. *Required fees:* $200; $100 per semester. Tuition and fees vary according to course level, course load, degree level and program. *Graduate housing:* Rooms and/or apartments available on a first-come, first-served basis to single and married students. Typical cost: $4800 per year for single students; $8700 per year for married students. Room charges vary according to housing facility selected. Housing application deadline: 8/30. *Student services:* Campus employment opportunities, campus safety program, career counseling, free psychological counseling, international student services, low-cost health insurance, services for students with disabilities, teacher training, writing training. *Library facilities:* Regent University Library plus 1 other. *Online resources:* library catalog, web page, access to other libraries' catalogs. *Collection:* 409,942 titles, 4,307 serial subscriptions, 18,674 audiovisual materials.

Computer facilities: 200 computers available on campus for general student use. A campuswide network can be accessed from student residence rooms and from off campus. Online class registration is available. *Web address:* http://www.regent.edu/.

General Application Contact: Matthew Chadwick, Director of Admissions, 800-373-5504, Fax: 757-352-4381, E-mail: admissions@regent.edu.

GRADUATE UNITS

Graduate School Students: 1,152 full-time (693 women), 1,903 part-time (1,109 women); includes 902 minority (719 African Americans, 20 American Indian/Alaska Native, 73 Asian Americans or Pacific Islanders, 90 Hispanic Americans), 118 international. Average age 35. 2,386 applicants, 56% accepted, 952 enrolled. *Faculty:* 179 full-time (59 women), 397 part-time/adjunct (192 women). Expenses: Contact institution. *Financial support:* Fellowships with full and partial tuition reimbursements, research assistantships with full and partial tuition reimbursements, teaching assistantships with full and partial tuition reimbursements, career-related internships or fieldwork, scholarships/grants, and tuition waivers (full and partial) available. Support available to part-time students. Financial award application deadline: 9/1; financial award applicants required to submit FAFSA. In 2008, 183 first professional degrees, 520 master's, 195 doctorates awarded. *Degree program information:* Part-time and evening/weekend programs available. Postbaccalaureate distance learning degree programs offered (minimal on-campus study). *Application deadline:* Applications are processed on a rolling basis. *Application fee:* $50. Electronic applications accepted. *Application Contact:* Matthew Chadwick, Director of Admissions, 800-373-5504, Fax: 757-352-4381, E-mail: admissions@regent.edu. *Vice President for Academic Affairs,* Dr. Carlos Campo, 757-352-4320, Fax: 757-352-4448, E-mail: ccampo@regent.edu.

Robertson School of Government Students: 60 full-time (33 women), 69 part-time (34 women); includes 29 minority (22 African Americans, 1 Asian American or Pacific Islander, 6 Hispanic Americans), 3 international. Average age 30. 136 applicants, 54% accepted, 54 enrolled. *Faculty:* 6 full-time (1 woman), 11 part-time/adjunct (1 woman). Expenses: Contact institution. *Financial support:* Career-related internships or fieldwork, scholarships/grants, tuition waivers (full and partial), and unspecified assistantships available. Support available to part-time students. Financial award application deadline: 9/1; financial award applicants required to submit FAFSA. In 2008, 48 master's awarded. *Degree program information:* Part-time and evening/weekend programs available. Postbaccalaureate distance learning degree programs offered (minimal on-campus study). Offers health care policy and administration (MA); international politics (MA); law and public policy (MA); Mid-East Politics (MA); political leadership and management (MA); political management (MA); public administration (MA); public policy (MA); terrorism and homeland defense (MA); world economies and political development (MA). *Application deadline:* For fall admission, 5/1 priority date for domestic students; for spring admission, 11/1 priority date for domestic students. Applications are processed on a rolling basis. *Application fee:* $50. Electronic applications accepted. *Application Contact:* Matthew Chadwick, Director of Admissions, 800-373-5504, Fax: 757-352-4381, E-mail: admissions@regent.edu. *Dean,* Dr. Charles W. Dunn, 757-352-4322, Fax: 757-352-4643, E-mail: cwdunn@regent.edu.

School of Communication and the Arts Students: 136 full-time (77 women), 163 part-time (90 women); includes 83 minority (59 African Americans, 3 American Indian/Alaska Native, 5 Asian Americans or Pacific Islanders, 16 Hispanic Americans), 15 international. Average age 32. 230 applicants, 63% accepted, 102 enrolled. *Faculty:* 26 full-time (3 women), 15 part-time/adjunct (3 women). Expenses: Contact institution. *Financial support:* Fellowships with full and partial tuition reimbursements, career-related internships or fieldwork, scholarships/grants, tuition waivers (full and partial), and unspecified assistantships available. Support available to part-time students. Financial award application deadline: 9/1; financial award applicants required to submit FAFSA. In 2008, 53 master's, 16 doctorates awarded. *Degree program information:* Part-time programs available. Postbaccalaureate distance learning degree programs offered (minimal on-campus study). Offers acting (MFA); acting and directing (MFA); cinema arts/television arts (MA); communication (MA, PhD); digital media (MA); directing for cinema/TV (MA); journalism (MA); producing for cinema/TV (MA); script and screenwriting (MFA); theatre (MA). *Application deadline:* For fall admission, 3/1 priority date for domestic students; for spring admission, 10/1 priority date for domestic students. Applications are processed on a rolling basis. *Application fee:* $50. Electronic applications accepted. *Application Contact:* Matthew Chadwick, Director of Admissions, 800-373-5504, Fax: 757-352-4381, E-mail: admissions@regent.edu. *Dean,* Michael Patrick, 757-352-4970, Fax: 757-352-4279, E-mail: michpat@regent.edu.

School of Divinity Students: 194 full-time (90 women), 391 part-time (164 women); includes 249 minority (217 African Americans, 3 American Indian/Alaska Native, 11 Asian Americans or Pacific Islanders, 18 Hispanic Americans), 19 international. Average age 38. 320 applicants, 65% accepted, 137 enrolled. *Faculty:* 21 full-time (4 women), 24 part-time/adjunct (5 women). Expenses: Contact institution. *Financial support:* Fellowships with full and partial tuition reimbursements, career-related internships or fieldwork, scholarships/grants, tuition waivers (full and partial), and unspecified assistantships available. Support available to part-time students. Financial award application deadline: 9/1; financial award applicants required to submit FAFSA. In 2008, 39 first professional degrees, 36 master's, 29 doctorates awarded. *Degree program information:* Part-time programs available. Postbaccalaureate distance learning degree programs offered (minimal on-campus study). Offers Biblical studies (MA); leadership and renewal (D Min); missiology (M Div, MA); practical theology (M Div, MA); renewal studies (PhD). *Application deadline:* For fall admission, 5/1 priority date for domestic students. Applications are processed on a rolling basis. *Application fee:* $50. Electronic applications accepted. *Application Contact:* Matthew Chadwick, Director of Admissions, 800-373-5504, Fax: 757-352-4381, E-mail: admissions@regent.edu. *Dean,* Dr. Michael Palmer, 757-352-4406, Fax: 757-352-4597, E-mail: mpalmer@regent.edu.

School of Education Students: 153 full-time (132 women), 647 part-time (505 women); includes 244 minority (209 African Americans, 3 American Indian/Alaska Native, 19 Asian

Americans or Pacific Islanders, 13 Hispanic Americans), 11 international. Average age 39. 534 applicants, 73% accepted, 339 enrolled. *Faculty:* 31 full-time (15 women), 148 part-time/adjunct (111 women). Expenses: Contact institution. *Financial support:* Fellowships, career-related internships or fieldwork, scholarships/grants, tuition waivers (full and partial), and unspecified assistantships available. Support available to part-time students. Financial award application deadline: 4/1; financial award applicants required to submit FAFSA. In 2008, 178 master's, 11 doctorates awarded. *Degree program information:* Part-time and evening/weekend programs available. Postbaccalaureate distance learning degree programs offered (minimal on-campus study). Offers career switcher (M Ed); Christian school program (M Ed); cross-categorical special education (M Ed); education (M Ed, Ed D); education licensure (M Ed); educational leadership (M Ed); elementary education (M Ed); individualized degree plan (M Ed); leadership in character education (M Ed); master teacher (M Ed); mathematics education (M Ed); special education leadership (Ed S); student affairs (M Ed); TESOL (M Ed). *Application deadline:* For fall admission, 4/1 priority date for domestic students; for spring admission, 10/15 priority date for domestic students. Applications are processed on a rolling basis. *Application fee:* $50. Electronic applications accepted. *Application Contact:* Matthew Chadwick, Director of Admissions, 800-373-5504, Fax: 757-352-4381, E-mail: admissions@regent.edu. *Dean,* Dr. Alan A. Arroyo, 757-352-4261, Fax: 757-352-4318, E-mail: alanarr@regent.edu.

School of Global Leadership and Entrepreneurship Students: 28 full-time (14 women), 431 part-time (164 women); includes 140 minority (109 African Americans, 5 American Indian/Alaska Native, 7 Asian Americans or Pacific Islanders, 19 Hispanic Americans), 47 international. Average age 40. 169 applicants, 50% accepted, 61 enrolled. *Faculty:* 22 full-time (5 women), 7 part-time/adjunct (0 women). Expenses: Contact institution. *Financial support:* Career-related internships or fieldwork, scholarships/grants, and tuition waivers (full and partial) available. Support available to part-time students. Financial award application deadline: 9/1. In 2008, 103 master's, 58 doctorates awarded. *Degree program information:* Part-time and evening/weekend programs available. Postbaccalaureate distance learning degree programs offered (minimal on-campus study). Offers business administration (MBA); management (MA); organizational leadership (MA, PhD, Certificate); strategic foresight (MA); strategic leadership (DSL). *Application deadline:* For fall admission, 5/1 priority date for domestic students; for spring admission, 10/1 priority date for domestic students. Applications are processed on a rolling basis. *Application fee:* $50. Electronic applications accepted. *Application Contact:* Matthew Chadwick, Director of Admissions, 800-373-5504, Fax: 757-352-4381, E-mail: admissions@regent.edu. *Dean,* Dr. Bruce Winston, 757-352-4306, Fax: 757-352-4634, E-mail: brucwin@regent.edu.

School of Law Students: 405 full-time (205 women), 10 part-time (8 women); includes 52 minority (20 African Americans, 4 American Indian/Alaska Native, 20 Asian Americans or Pacific Islanders, 8 Hispanic Americans), 10 international. Average age 27. 680 applicants, 43% accepted, 147 enrolled. *Faculty:* 27 full-time (7 women), 48 part-time/adjunct (11 women). Expenses: Contact institution. *Financial support:* Career-related internships or fieldwork, scholarships/grants, and tuition waivers (full and partial) available. Support available to part-time students. Financial award application deadline: 2/1; financial award applicants required to submit FAFSA. In 2008, 158 JDs awarded. *Degree program information:* Part-time and evening/weekend programs available. Offers American legal studies (LL M); law (JD). *Application deadline:* For fall admission, 3/1 for domestic students. Applications are processed on a rolling basis. *Application fee:* $50. Electronic applications accepted. *Application Contact:* Matthew Chadwick, Director of Admissions, 800-373-5504, Fax: 757-352-4381, E-mail: admissions@regent.edu. *Dean,* Jeffrey Brauch, 757-352-4040, Fax: 757-352-4595, E-mail: jeffbra@regent.edu.

School of Psychology and Counseling Students: 176 full-time (142 women), 192 part-time (144 women); includes 100 minority (78 African Americans, 2 American Indian/Alaska Native, 10 Asian Americans or Pacific Islanders, 10 Hispanic Americans), 13 international. Average age 32. 317 applicants, 47% accepted, 112 enrolled. *Faculty:* 25 full-time (12 women), 19 part-time/adjunct (9 women). Expenses: Contact institution. *Financial support:* Research assistantships with full and partial tuition reimbursements, teaching assistantships with full and partial tuition reimbursements, career-related internships or fieldwork, scholarships/grants, and tuition waivers (full and partial) available. Support available to part-time students. Financial award application deadline: 9/1; financial award applicants required to submit FAFSA. In 2008, 129 master's, 22 doctorates awarded. *Degree program information:* Part-time and evening/weekend programs available. Postbaccalaureate distance learning degree programs offered (minimal on-campus study). Offers clinical psychology (MA, Psy D); counseling (MA); counseling studies (CAGS); counselor education and supervision (PhD). PhD program offered online only. *Application deadline:* For fall admission, 4/1 priority date for domestic students; for spring admission, 11/1 priority date for domestic students. Applications are processed on a rolling basis. *Application fee:* $50. Electronic applications accepted. *Application Contact:* Matthew Chadwick, Director of Admissions, 800-373-5504, Fax: 757-352-4381, E-mail: admissions@regent.edu. *Dean,* Dr. Rosemarie Hughes, 757-352-4269, Fax: 757-352-4282, E-mail: rosehug@regent.edu.

REGIS COLLEGE, Toronto, ON M4Y 2R5, Canada

General Information Independent-religious, coed, graduate-only institution. *Enrollment by degree level:* 66 first professional, 59 master's, 32 doctoral, 62 other advanced degrees. *Graduate faculty:* 15 full-time (4 women), 12 part-time/adjunct (2 women). *Graduate housing:* Room and/or apartments available on a first-come, first-served basis to single students; on-campus housing not available to married students. *Student services:* Campus employment opportunities, campus safety program, career counseling, exercise/wellness program, free psychological counseling, international student services, low-cost health insurance, multicultural affairs office, services for students with disabilities, teacher training, writing training. *Library facilities:* Regis College Library. *Online resources:* library catalog, access to other libraries' catalogs. *Collection:* 119,321 titles, 367 serial subscriptions.

Computer facilities: 10 computers available on campus for general student use. A campuswide network can be accessed from off campus. Online class registration is available. *Web address:* http://www.regiscollege.ca/.

General Application Contact: Elaine Chu, Registrar, 416-922-5474 Ext. 226, Fax: 416-922-2898, E-mail: regis.registrar@utoronto.ca.

GRADUATE UNITS

Graduate and Professional Programs Students: 88 full-time (30 women), 131 part-time (78 women); includes 74 minority (16 African Americans, 1 American Indian/Alaska Native, 48 Asian Americans or Pacific Islanders, 9 Hispanic Americans). Average age 45. 73 applicants, 88% accepted, 52 enrolled. *Faculty:* 15 full-time (4 women), 12 part-time/adjunct (2 women). Expenses: Contact institution. *Financial support:* In 2008–09, 58 students received support. Career-related internships or fieldwork and scholarships/grants available. Support available to part-time students. Financial award application deadline: 3/15. In 2008, 10 first professional degrees, 13 master's, 5 other advanced degrees awarded. Offers ministry (D Min); ministry and spirituality (MAMS); sacred theology (STB, STM, STD, STL); theological study (MTS); theology (M Div, MA, Th M, PhD, Th D). *Application deadline:* For fall admission, 3/15 priority date for domestic and international students; for winter admission, 12/1 for domestic and international students; for spring admission, 3/15 for domestic and international students. Applications are processed on a rolling basis. *Application fee:* $25. *Application Contact:* Elaine Chu, Registrar, 416-922-5474 Ext. 226, Fax: 416-922-2898, E-mail: regis.registrar@utoronto.ca. *Dean,* Dr. Gordon Rixon, 416-922-5474 Ext. 225, Fax: 416-922-2898, E-mail: gordon.rixon@utoronto.ca.

REGIS COLLEGE, Weston, MA 02493

General Information Independent-religious, coed, comprehensive institution. *Tuition:* Part-time $676 per credit. *Graduate housing:* Room and/or apartments available on a first-come, first-served basis to single students; on-campus housing not available to married students. *Student services:* Campus employment opportunities, campus safety program, career counseling, exercise/wellness program, low-cost health insurance, multicultural affairs office, teacher training. *Library facilities:* Regis College Library. *Online resources:* library catalog, web page, access to other libraries' catalogs. *Collection:* 135,458 titles, 607 serial subscriptions, 7,670 audiovisual materials. *Research affiliation:* Beth Israel Deaconess Medical Center (nursing), Caritas Norwood Hospital (nursing), Boston Medical Center (nursing), Lahey Clinic Medical Center (nursing).

Computer facilities: 201 computers available on campus for general student use. A campuswide network can be accessed from student residence rooms and from off campus. Online class registration is available. *Web address:* http://www.regiscollege.edu/.

General Application Contact: Christine Petherick, Administrative Coordinator, Planning and Enrollment, 866-438-7330, Fax: 781-768-7071, E-mail: christine.petherick@regiscollege.edu.

GRADUATE UNITS

Department of Education Students: 2 full-time (both women), 65 part-time (58 women); includes 5 minority (all Asian Americans or Pacific Islanders). Average age 36. 8 applicants, 88% accepted, 4 enrolled. *Faculty:* 2 full-time (both women), 5 part-time/adjunct (all women). Expenses: Contact institution. *Financial support:* In 2008–09, 1 student received support, including 1 fellowship with full tuition reimbursement available (averaging $11,970 per year); Federal Work-Study and scholarships/grants also available. Financial award applicants required to submit FAFSA. In 2008, 11 master's awarded. *Degree program information:* Part-time and evening/weekend programs available. Offers education (MAT). *Application deadline:* Applications are processed on a rolling basis. *Application fee:* $50. Electronic applications accepted. *Application Contact:* Christine Petherick, Administrative Coordinator, Graduate Admission, 866-438-7344, Fax: 781-768-7071, E-mail: christine.petherick@regiscollege.edu. *Program Director,* Dr. Leona McCaughey-Oreszak, 781-768-7421, Fax: 781-768-7159, E-mail: leona.mccaughey-oreszak@regiscollege.edu.

Department of Health Product Regulation Students: 1 (woman) full-time, 24 part-time (20 women); includes 2 minority (both Asian Americans or Pacific Islanders). Average age 37. 5 applicants, 100% accepted, 3 enrolled. *Faculty:* 4 part-time/adjunct (1 woman). Expenses: Contact institution. *Financial support:* In 2008–09, 7 students received support. Career-related internships or fieldwork and scholarships/grants available. Financial award applicants required to submit FAFSA. In 2008, 15 master's awarded. *Degree program information:* Part-time and evening/weekend programs available. Offers health product regulation (MS). *Application deadline:* Applications are processed on a rolling basis. *Application fee:* $50. *Application Contact:* Christine Petherick, Administrative Coordinator, Graduate Admission, 866-438-7344, Fax: 781-768-7071, E-mail: christine.petherick@regiscollege.edu. *Director,* Charles Burr, 781-768-7008, E-mail: charles.burr@regiscollege.edu.

Department of Management and Leadership Students: 14 part-time (13 women); includes 1 minority (Asian American or Pacific Islander). Average age 36. 3 applicants, 100% accepted, 3 enrolled. *Faculty:* 1 full-time (0 women), 3 part-time/adjunct (0 women). Expenses: Contact institution. *Financial support:* Fellowships with partial tuition reimbursements, tuition waivers (partial) available. Financial award applicants required to submit FAFSA. In 2008, 2 master's awarded. *Degree program information:* Part-time and evening/weekend programs available. Offers leadership and organizational change (MS). *Application deadline:* Applications are processed on a rolling basis. *Application fee:* $50. *Application Contact:* Christine Petherick, Administrative Coordinator, Graduate Admission, 866-438-7344, Fax: 781-768-7071, E-mail: christine.petherick@regiscollege.edu. *Director,* Dr. Phillip Jutras, 781-768-7436, Fax: 781-768-7159, E-mail: phillip.jutras@regiscollege.edu.

Department of Organizational and Professional Communication Students: 12 part-time (all women); includes 2 minority (1 Asian American or Pacific Islander, 1 Hispanic American). Average age 34. 5 applicants, 100% accepted, 5 enrolled. *Faculty:* 1 (woman) full-time, 3 part-time/adjunct (1 woman). Expenses: Contact institution. *Financial support:* In 2008–09, 9 students received support. Scholarships/grants available. Financial award applicants required to submit FAFSA. In 2008, 13 master's awarded. *Degree program information:* Part-time and evening/weekend programs available. Offers organizational and professional communication (MS). *Application deadline:* Applications are processed on a rolling basis. *Application fee:* $50. *Application Contact:* Christine Petherick, Administrative Coordinator, Graduate Admission, 866-438-7344, Fax: 781-768-7071, E-mail: christine.petherick@regiscollege.edu. *Director,* Dr. Joan Murray, 781-768-7416, Fax: 781-768-7159, E-mail: joan.murray@regiscollege.edu.

Program in Public Administration Students: 5 part-time (4 women); includes 1 minority (Hispanic American). Average age 31. 5 applicants, 100% accepted, 5 enrolled. *Faculty:* 1 (woman) full-time, 2 part-time/adjunct (both women). Expenses: Contact institution. *Degree program information:* Part-time programs available. Postbaccalaureate distance learning degree programs offered. Offers nonprofit administration (Graduate Certificate); public administration (MPA); public policymaking (Graduate Certificate). *Application fee:* $50. *Application Contact:* Christine Petherick, Administrative Coordinator, Graduate Admission, 866-438-7344, Fax: 781-768-7071, E-mail: christine.petherick@regiscollege.edu. *Director of Graduate Admission,* Claudia Pouravelis, 781-768-7058, E-mail: claudia.pouravelis@regiscollege.edu.

School of Nursing and Health Professions Students: 152 full-time (139 women), 324 part-time (299 women); includes 50 minority (29 African Americans, 1 American Indian/Alaska Native, 15 Asian Americans or Pacific Islanders, 5 Hispanic Americans). Average age 38. 300 applicants, 73% accepted, 151 enrolled. *Faculty:* 18 full-time (all women), 12 part-time/adjunct (all women). Expenses: Contact institution. *Financial support:* In 2008–09, 28 students received support, including 13 research assistantships; Federal Work-Study, scholarships/grants, traineeships, and unspecified assistantships also available. Support available to part-time students. Financial award applicants required to submit FAFSA. In 2008, 47 master's, 7 other advanced degrees awarded. *Degree program information:* Part-time and evening/weekend programs available. Offers nurse educator (Certificate); nurse practitioner (Certificate); nursing (MS). *Application deadline:* Applications are processed on a rolling basis. *Application fee:* $50. Electronic applications accepted. *Application Contact:* Christine Petherick, Administrative Coordinator, Graduate Admission, 866-438-7344, Fax: 781-768-7071, E-mail: christine.petherick@regiscollege.edu. *Dean,* Dr. Antoinette Hays, 781-768-7091, Fax: 781-768-8339, E-mail: antoinette.hays@regiscollege.edu.

REGIS UNIVERSITY, Denver, CO 80221-1099

General Information Independent-religious, coed, comprehensive institution. *Graduate housing:* On-campus housing not available. *Research affiliation:* Commission for Accelerated Programs (accelerated advit programs), Transparency By Design (online programs/best practices), Learning Anytime Anywhere Partnership (Internet based technology).

GRADUATE UNITS

College for Professional Studies *Degree program information:* Part-time and evening/weekend programs available. Postbaccalaureate distance learning degree programs offered (no on-campus study). Offers accounting (MS); adult learning, training, and development (M Ed); business administration (MBA); community counseling (MAC); computer information technology (MSOL); counseling children and adolescents (Post-Graduate Certificate); criminology (MA); curriculum, instruction, and assessment (M Ed); early childhood (M Ed); educational technology (Certificate); elementary (M Ed); ESL (M Ed); executive internal management (Certificate); executive leadership (Certificate); finance (MBA); finance and accounting (MBA); fine arts (M Ed); fine arts administration (Certificate); human resource management (MSOL); instructional technology (M Ed); international business (MBA); language and communication (MA); leadership (Certificate); marketing (MBA); marriage and family therapy (Post-Graduate Certificate); mediation (Certificate); nonprofit management (MNM); operations management (MBA); organization leadership (MS); organizational leadership (MSOL); professional leadership (M Ed); program management (Certificate); project leadership and management (MSOL, Certificate); project management (Certificate); psychology (MA); reading (M Ed); resource development (Certificate); secondary (M Ed); self-designed (M Ed); self-designed major (MA); social justice, peace, and reconciliation (Certificate); social science (MA); space studies (M Ed); special education (M Ed); strategic business (Certificate); strategic human resource (Certificate); teacher licensure (M Ed); technical communication (Certificate); technical management (Certificate). Electronic applications accepted.

School of Computer and Information Sciences *Degree program information:* Part-time and evening/weekend programs available. Postbaccalaureate distance learning degree programs offered (no on-campus study). Offers database administration with IBM DB2 (Certificate); database administration with Oracle (Certificate); database development

Regis University (continued)

(Certificate); database technologies (MA); enterprise Java software development (Certificate); executive information technologies (Certificate); information assurance (MA, Certificate); information technology management (MA); software and information systems (M Sc); software engineering (MA, Certificate); storage area networks (Certificate); systems engineering (MA, Certificate). Offered at Boulder Campus, Northwest Denver Campus, Southeast Denver Campus, Fort Collins Campus, Colorado Springs Campus, and Broomfield Campus. Electronic applications accepted.

Regis College *Degree program information:* Part-time and evening/weekend programs available. Offers education (MA). Offered at Northwest Denver Campus.

Rueckert-Hartman School for Health Professions Offers clinical leadership for physician assistants (MS); family nurse practitioner (MSN); health informatics (Postbaccalaureate Certificate); health services administration (MS); healthcare education (Certificate); leadership in healthcare systems (MSN); neonatal nurse practitioner (MSN); nursing (MSN); pharmacy (Pharm D); physical therapy (DPT, TDPT). Electronic applications accepted.

REINHARDT COLLEGE, Waleska, GA 30183-2981

General Information Independent-religious, coed, comprehensive institution. *Enrollment:* 1,051 graduate, professional, and undergraduate students; 25 full-time matriculated graduate/professional students (16 women), 1 (woman) part-time matriculated graduate/professional student. *Enrollment by degree level:* 26 master's. *Graduate faculty:* 5 full-time (2 women), 1 part-time/adjunct (0 women). *Tuition:* Full-time $4200; part-time $300 per credit hour. *Required fees:* $70; $35 per term. Tuition and fees vary according to course load and program. *Graduate housing:* On-campus housing not available. *Student services:* Career counseling, exercise/wellness program, free psychological counseling, international student services, low-cost health insurance, services for students with disabilities, writing training. *Library facilities:* Hill Freeman Library/Spruill Learning Center plus 1 other. *Online resources:* library catalog, web page, access to other libraries' catalogs. *Collection:* 54,000 titles, 117,200 serial subscriptions, 12,000 audiovisual materials. *Research affiliation:* N/A.

Computer facilities: Computer purchase and lease plans are available. 164 computers available on campus for general student use. A campuswide network can be accessed from student residence rooms and from off campus. Online class registration is available. *Web address:* http://www.reinhardt.edu/.

General Application Contact: Ray Schumacher, Admissions Counselor, 770-993-6971, Fax: 770-475-0263, E-mail: res@reinhardt.edu.

GRADUATE UNITS

Program in Business Administration (Alpharetta Campus) Students: 25 full-time (16 women), 1 (woman) part-time; includes 3 minority (1 African American, 1 Asian American or Pacific Islander, 1 Hispanic American). 15 applicants, 87% accepted, 13 enrolled. *Faculty:* 5 full-time (2 women), 1 part-time/adjunct (0 women). Expenses: Contact institution. *Financial support:* In 2008–09, 12 students received support. Application deadline: 5/1. In 2008, 9 master's awarded. *Degree program information:* Part-time and evening/weekend programs available. Offers business administration (MBA). *Application deadline:* For fall admission, 5/7 for domestic and international students; for spring admission, 8/9 for domestic and international students. Applications are processed on a rolling basis. *Application fee:* $25. Electronic applications accepted. *Application Contact:* Ray Schumacher, Admissions Counselor, 770-993-6971, Fax: 770-475-0263, E-mail: res@reinhardt.edu. *Admissions Counselor,* Ray Schumacher, 770-993-6971, Fax: 770-475-0263, E-mail: res@reinhardt.edu.

Program in Early Childhood Education Offers early childhood education (MAT).

Program in Music Offers conducting (MM); music education (MM); piano pedagogy (MM).

RENSSELAER AT HARTFORD, Hartford, CT 06120-2991

General Information Independent, coed, graduate-only institution. *Graduate housing:* On-campus housing not available.

GRADUATE UNITS

Department of Computer and Information Science *Degree program information:* Part-time and evening/weekend programs available. Offers computer science (MS); information technology (MS). Electronic applications accepted.

Department of Engineering *Degree program information:* Part-time and evening/weekend programs available. Offers computer and systems engineering (ME); electrical engineering (MS); engineering (ME, MS); mechanical engineering (MS). Electronic applications accepted.

Lally School of Management and Technology *Degree program information:* Part-time and evening/weekend programs available. Postbaccalaureate distance learning degree programs offered (no on-campus study). Offers management and technology (MBA, MS). Electronic applications accepted.

RENSSELAER POLYTECHNIC INSTITUTE, Troy, NY 12180-3590

General Information Independent, coed, university. CGS member. *Enrollment:* 7,521 graduate, professional, and undergraduate students; 1,127 full-time matriculated graduate/professional students (303 women), 886 part-time matriculated graduate/professional students (227 women). *Enrollment by degree level:* 1,145 master's, 868 doctoral. *Graduate faculty:* 401 full-time (87 women), 95 part-time/adjunct (19 women). *Graduate housing:* Rooms and/or apartments available on a first-come, first-served basis to single and married students. *Student services:* Campus employment opportunities, campus safety program, career counseling, exercise/wellness program, free psychological counseling, grant writing training, international student services, low-cost health insurance, multicultural affairs office, services for students with disabilities, teacher training, writing training. *Library facilities:* Folsom Library plus 1 other. *Online resources:* library catalog, web page, access to other libraries' catalogs. *Collection:* 309,171 titles, 10,210 serial subscriptions. *Research affiliation:* New York State Energy Research and Development Authority (fuel cells, polymer membranes, renewable energy sources), Cleveland Clinic Foundation (tissue engineering and regenerative medicine, imaging, bio-nano materials), Semiconductor Research Corporation (high density magnetic storage devices), Lockheed Martin (advanced sensors systems, THz detection technologies), IBM (broadband technologies, modeling and simulation of complex systems).

Computer facilities: Computer purchase and lease plans are available. 1,081 computers available on campus for general student use. A campuswide network can be accessed from student residence rooms and from off campus. Online class registration, billing are available. *Web address:* http://www.rpi.edu/.

General Application Contact: James G. Nondorf, Vice President for Enrollment, 518-276-6216, Fax: 518-276-4072, E-mail: admissions@rpi.edu.

GRADUATE UNITS

Graduate School Students: 1,127 full-time (303 women), 886 part-time (227 women); includes 297 minority (76 African Americans, 2 American Indian/Alaska Native, 136 Asian Americans or Pacific Islanders, 83 Hispanic Americans), 584 international. Average age 28. 3,042 applicants, 36% accepted, 430 enrolled. *Faculty:* 401 full-time (87 women), 95 part-time/adjunct (19 women). Expenses: Contact institution. *Financial support:* In 2008–09, 867 students received support, including 103 fellowships with full tuition reimbursements available (averaging $22,000 per year), 424 research assistantships with full tuition reimbursements available (averaging $20,000 per year), 335 teaching assistantships with full tuition reimbursements available (averaging $16,500 per year); career-related internships or fieldwork, institutionally sponsored loans, scholarships/grants, health care benefits, tuition waivers (partial), and unspecified assistantships also available. Financial award application deadline: 1/15. In 2008, 672 master's, 158 doctorates awarded. *Degree program information:* Part-time and evening/weekend programs available. Postbaccalaureate distance learning degree programs offered (no on-campus study). *Application deadline:* For fall admission, 1/1 priority date for domestic and international students; for spring admission, 8/15 priority date for domestic and international students. Applications are processed on a rolling basis. *Application fee:* $75. Electronic applications accepted. *Application Contact:* Paul Marthers, 518-276-6216, Fax: 518-276-4072, E-mail: admissions@rpi.edu. *Vice Provost and Dean of Graduate Education,* Dr. Stanley M. Dunn, 518-276-8433, Fax: 518-276-8062, E-mail: dunns6@rpi.edu.

Lally School of Management and Technology Students: 128 full-time (37 women), 416 part-time (126 women); includes 129 minority (36 African Americans, 1 American Indian/Alaska Native, 69 Asian Americans or Pacific Islanders, 23 Hispanic Americans), 53 international. Average age 28. 253 applicants, 80% accepted, 167 enrolled. *Faculty:* 35 full-time (8 women), 4 part-time/adjunct (0 women). Expenses: Contact institution. *Financial support:* In 2008–09, 53 students received support; fellowships with partial tuition reimbursements available, career-related internships or fieldwork, institutionally sponsored loans, scholarships/grants, and teaching and research assistantships (for PhD students only), tuition scholarships (for qualified MBA students) available. Financial award application deadline: 3/15; financial award applicants required to submit FAFSA. In 2008, 265 master's, 9 doctorates awarded. *Degree program information:* Part-time and evening/weekend programs available. Offers business (MBA); financial engineering and risk analytics (MS); management (MS, PhD); technology commercialization and entrepreneurship (MS). *Application deadline:* For fall admission, 3/15 priority date for domestic and international students. Applications are processed on a rolling basis. *Application fee:* $75. Electronic applications accepted. *Application Contact:* Michele M. Martens, Manager of Graduate Programs, 518-276-6586, Fax: 518-276-2665, E-mail: lallymba@rpi.edu. *Dean,* Dr. David A. Gautschi, 518-276-6586, Fax: 518-276-2665, E-mail: lallymba@rpi.edu.

School of Architecture *Degree program information:* Part-time programs available. Offers architectural acoustics (MS); architectural sciences (PhD); architectural sciences (built ecologies) (MS); architecture (M Arch, MS, PhD); lighting (MS). Electronic applications accepted.

School of Engineering *Degree program information:* Part-time and evening/weekend programs available. Postbaccalaureate distance learning degree programs offered (no on-campus study). Offers aerospace engineering (M Eng, MS, PhD); biomedical engineering (MS, PhD); ceramics and glass science (M Eng, MS, PhD); chemical and biological engineering (M Eng, MS, PhD); civil engineering (M Eng, MS, D Eng, PhD); composites (M Eng, MS, PhD); computer and systems engineering (M Eng, MS, D Eng, PhD); decision sciences and engineering systems (PhD); electric power engineering (M Eng, MS, D Eng, PhD); electrical engineering (M Eng, MS, D Eng, PhD); electronic materials (M Eng, MS, PhD); engineering (M Eng, MS, D Eng, PhD); engineering physics (MS, PhD); environmental engineering (M Eng, MS, D Eng, PhD); geotechnical engineering (M Eng, MS, D Eng, PhD); industrial and management engineering (M Eng, MS, PhD); mechanical engineering (M Eng, MS, PhD); mechanics of composite materials and structures (M Eng, MS, D Eng, PhD); metallurgy (M Eng, MS, PhD); nuclear engineering (M Eng, MS, PhD); nuclear engineering and science (PhD); polymers (M Eng, MS, PhD); structural engineering (M Eng, MS, D Eng, PhD); transportation engineering (M Eng, MS, D Eng, PhD). Electronic applications accepted.

School of Humanities and Social Sciences *Degree program information:* Part-time and evening/weekend programs available. Postbaccalaureate distance learning degree programs offered (no on-campus study). Offers cognitive science (PhD); communication and rhetoric (MS, PhD); ecological economics (PhD); ecological economics, values, and policy (MS); economics (MS); electronic arts (MFA, PhD); human-computer interaction (MS); humanities and social sciences (MFA, MS, PhD); science and technology studies (MS, PhD); technical communication (MS). Electronic applications accepted.

School of Science *Degree program information:* Part-time and evening/weekend programs available. Postbaccalaureate distance learning degree programs offered (no on-campus study). Offers analytical chemistry (MS, PhD); applied mathematics (MS); applied science (MS); biochemistry (MS, PhD); biophysics (MS, PhD); cell biology (MS, PhD); computer science (MS, PhD); developmental biology (MS, PhD); geochemistry (PhD); geology (MS, PhD); geophysics (PhD); hydrogeology (MS, PhD); information technology (MS); inorganic chemistry (MS, PhD); mathematics (MS, PhD); microbiology (MS, PhD); molecular biology (MS, PhD); multidisciplinary science (MS, PhD); natural sciences (MS); organic chemistry (MS, PhD); petrology (PhD); physical chemistry (MS, PhD); physics (MS, PhD); polymer chemistry (MS, PhD); science (MS, PhD). Electronic applications accepted.

RESEARCH COLLEGE OF NURSING, Kansas City, MO 64132

General Information Independent, coed, primarily women, comprehensive institution. *Enrollment:* 382 graduate, professional, and undergraduate students; 3 full-time matriculated graduate/professional students (all women), 63 part-time matriculated graduate/professional students (60 women). *Enrollment by degree level:* 66 master's. *Graduate faculty:* 7 full-time (all women), 4 part-time/adjunct (all women). *Tuition:* Part-time $380 per credit hour. *Required fees:* $25 per credit hour. $50 per semester. *Graduate housing:* Rooms and/or apartments available on a first-come, first-served basis to single and married students. Typical cost: $1975 per year for single students; $2962 per year for married students. *Student services:* Campus safety program, child daycare facilities, low-cost health insurance, services for students with disabilities, writing training. *Library facilities:* Greenlease Library. *Online resources:* library catalog, web page, access to other libraries' catalogs. *Collection:* 150,000 titles, 675 serial subscriptions.

Computer facilities: 125 computers available on campus for general student use. A campuswide network can be accessed from student residence rooms and from off campus. Online class registration is available. *Web address:* http://www.researchcollege.edu/.

General Application Contact: Leslie Mendenhall, Director of Transfer and Graduate Recruitment, 816-995-2820, Fax: 816-995-2813, E-mail: leslie.mendenhall@researchcollege.edu.

GRADUATE UNITS

Nursing Program Students: 3 full-time (all women), 63 part-time (60 women). Average age 30. *Faculty:* 7 full-time (all women), 4 part-time/adjunct (all women). Expenses: Contact institution. *Financial support:* Applicants required to submit FAFSA. In 2008, 23 master's awarded. *Degree program information:* Part-time programs available. Postbaccalaureate distance learning degree programs offered (no on-campus study). Offers executive nurse practitioner (MSN); family nurse practitioner (MSN); nursing education (MSN). *Application deadline:* For spring admission, 10/1 priority date for domestic students. Applications are processed on a rolling basis. *Application fee:* $50. *Application Contact:* Leslie Mendenhall, Director of Transfer and Graduate Recruitment, 816-995-2820, Fax: 816-995-2813, E-mail: leslie.mendenhall@researchcollege.edu. *President and Dean,* Dr. Nancy O. De Basio, 816-995-2815, Fax: 816-995-2817, E-mail: nancy.debasio@researchcollege.edu.

RHODE ISLAND COLLEGE, Providence, RI 02908-1991

General Information State-supported, coed, comprehensive institution. *Enrollment:* 9,085 graduate, professional, and undergraduate students; 244 full-time matriculated graduate/professional students (200 women), 517 part-time matriculated graduate/professional students (402 women). *Enrollment by degree level:* 631 master's, 52 doctoral, 78 other advanced degrees. *Graduate faculty:* 128 full-time (62 women), 50 part-time/adjunct (35 women). Tuition, state resident: full-time $6816; part-time $284 per credit hour. Tuition, nonresident: full-time $13,920; part-time $580 per credit hour. *Required fees:* $454; $16 per credit. $68 per term. *Graduate housing:* On-campus housing not available. *Student services:* Campus employment opportunities, career counseling, free psychological counseling, international student services, low-cost health insurance, multicultural affairs office, services for students with disabilities. *Library facilities:* Adams Library. *Online resources:* library catalog, web page, access to other libraries' catalogs. *Collection:* 650,538 titles, 6,558 audiovisual materials.

Computer facilities: Computer purchase and lease plans are available. 675 computers available on campus for general student use. A campuswide network can be accessed from student residence rooms and from off campus. Online class registration is available. *Web address:* http://www.ric.edu/.

General Application Contact: Graduate Studies, 401-456-8700.

GRADUATE UNITS

School of Graduate Studies Students: 244 full-time (200 women), 517 part-time (402 women); includes 65 minority (27 African Americans, 2 American Indian/Alaska Native, 10 Asian Americans or Pacific Islanders, 26 Hispanic Americans), 3 international. Average age 35. *Faculty:* 136 full-time (64 women), 45 part-time/adjunct (28 women). Expenses: Contact institution. *Financial support:* In 2008–09, 2 teaching assistantships with full tuition reimbursements (averaging $4,000 per year) were awarded; research assistantships with partial tuition reimbursements, career-related internships or fieldwork, Federal Work-Study, traineeships, health care benefits, tuition waivers (partial), and unspecified assistantships also available. Support available to part-time students. Financial award application deadline: 5/15; financial award applicants required to submit FAFSA. In 2008, 249 master's, 7 doctorates, 24 other advanced degrees awarded. *Degree program information:* Part-time and evening/weekend programs available. *Application deadline:* For fall admission, 4/1 priority date for domestic students; for spring admission, 11/1 for domestic students. Applications are processed on a rolling basis. *Application fee:* $50. *Application Contact:* Graduate Studies, 401-456-8700. *Graduate Studies*, 401-456-8700.

Faculty of Arts and Sciences Students: 24 full-time (15 women), 65 part-time (40 women); includes 5 minority (3 African Americans, 1 Asian American or Pacific Islander, 1 Hispanic American). Average age 34. *Faculty:* 75 full-time (33 women), 8 part-time/adjunct (6 women). Expenses: Contact institution. *Financial support:* In 2008–09, 2 teaching assistantships with full tuition reimbursements (averaging $3,900 per year) were awarded; research assistantships with tuition reimbursements, career-related internships or fieldwork, Federal Work-Study, scholarships/grants, health care benefits, and unspecified assistantships also available. Support available to part-time students. Financial award application deadline: 5/15; financial award applicants required to submit FAFSA. In 2008, 36 master's awarded. *Degree program information:* Part-time and evening/weekend programs available. Offers art education (MA, MAT); arts and sciences (MA, MAT, MFA, MM Ed, MPA); biology (MA); creative writing (MA); English (MA); history (MA); mathematics (MA); media studies (MA); music education (MAT, MM Ed); psychology (MA); public administration (MPA); theatre (MFA). *Application deadline:* For fall admission, 4/1 for domestic students; for spring admission, 11/1 for domestic students. Applications are processed on a rolling basis. *Application fee:* $50. *Application Contact:* Graduate Studies, 401-456-8700. *Interim Dean*, Dr. Earl Simson, 401-456-8107, E-mail: esimson@ric.edu.

Feinstein School of Education and Human Development Students: 73 full-time (59 women), 358 part-time (285 women); includes 24 minority (5 African Americans, 2 American Indian/Alaska Native, 5 Asian Americans or Pacific Islanders, 12 Hispanic Americans), 2 international. Average age 36. *Faculty:* 37 full-time (17 women), 37 part-time/adjunct (25 women). Expenses: Contact institution. *Financial support:* Teaching assistantships with full tuition reimbursements, career-related internships or fieldwork, Federal Work-Study, scholarships/grants, health care benefits, and unspecified assistantships available. Support available to part-time students. Financial award application deadline: 5/15; financial award applicants required to submit FAFSA. In 2008, 158 master's, 7 doctorates, 24 other advanced degrees awarded. *Degree program information:* Part-time and evening/weekend programs available. Offers counseling (MA); early childhood education (M Ed); education (PhD); education and human development (M Ed, MA, MAT, PhD, CAGS, CGS); educational leadership (M Ed); elementary education (M Ed, MAT); English (MAT); French (MAT); health education (M Ed); history (MAT); math (MAT); physical education (CGS); reading (M Ed); school administration (M Ed); school counseling (CAGS); secondary education (MAT); Spanish (MAT); special education (M Ed, CAGS); teaching English as a second language (M Ed); technology education (M Ed). *Application deadline:* For fall admission, 3/15 for domestic students; for spring admission, 11/1 for domestic students. Applications are processed on a rolling basis. *Application fee:* $50. *Application Contact:* Graduate Studies, 401-456-8700. *Interim Dean*, Dr. Roger Eldridge, 401-456-8591, E-mail: reldridge@ric.edu.

School of Management Students: 2 full-time (0 women), 16 part-time (8 women); includes 2 minority (1 Asian American or Pacific Islander, 1 Hispanic American), 1 international. Average age 32. *Faculty:* 4 full-time (2 women). Expenses: Contact institution. *Financial support:* Federal Work-Study, scholarships/grants, health care benefits, and unspecified assistantships available. Support available to part-time students. Financial award application deadline: 5/15; financial award applicants required to submit FAFSA. In 2008, 4 master's awarded. *Degree program information:* Part-time and evening/weekend programs available. Offers accounting (MP Ac); financial planning (CGS); management (MP Ac, CGS). *Application deadline:* For fall admission, 4/1 for domestic students; for spring admission, 11/1 for domestic students. Applications are processed on a rolling basis. *Application fee:* $50. *Application Contact:* Graduate Studies, 401-456-8700. *Interim Dean*, David Blanchette, 401-456-8009, E-mail: dblanchette@ric.edu.

School of Nursing Students: 2 full-time (both women), 22 part-time (all women); includes 1 minority (Hispanic American). Average age 45. *Faculty:* 5 full-time (all women). Expenses: Contact institution. *Financial support:* Federal Work-Study, scholarships/grants, health care benefits, and unspecified assistantships available. Support available to part-time students. Financial award application deadline: 5/15; financial award applicants required to submit FAFSA. *Degree program information:* Part-time programs available. Offers nursing (MSN). *Application deadline:* For fall admission, 2/15 for domestic students. Applications are processed on a rolling basis. *Application fee:* $50. *Application Contact:* Graduate Studies, 401-456-8700. *Dean*, Dr. Jane Williams, 401-456-8013, Fax: 401-456-9608, E-mail: jwilliams@ric.edu.

School of Social Work Students: 145 full-time (126 women), 54 part-time (47 women); includes 33 minority (19 African Americans, 3 Asian Americans or Pacific Islanders, 11 Hispanic Americans). Average age 32. *Faculty:* 7 full-time (5 women), 5 part-time/adjunct (4 women). Expenses: Contact institution. *Financial support:* Career-related internships or fieldwork, Federal Work-Study, scholarships/grants, health care benefits, and unspecified assistantships available. Support available to part-time students. Financial award application deadline: 5/15; financial award applicants required to submit FAFSA. In 2008, 51 master's awarded. *Degree program information:* Part-time programs available. Offers social work (MSW). *Application deadline:* For fall admission, 2/15 for domestic students. Applications are processed on a rolling basis. *Application fee:* $50. *Application Contact:* Graduate Studies, 401-456-8700. *Interim Dean*, Sue Pearlmutter, 401-456-8042, E-mail: spearlmutter@ric.edu.

RHODE ISLAND SCHOOL OF DESIGN, Providence, RI 02903-2784

General Information Independent, coed, comprehensive institution. *Graduate housing:* Room and/or apartments available on a first-come, first-served basis to single students; on-campus housing not available to married students.

GRADUATE UNITS

Graduate Studies Offers art education (MA, MAT); digital media (MFA). Electronic applications accepted.

Division of Architecture and Design Offers architecture (M Arch); architecture and design (M Arch, MFA, MIA, MID, MLA); furniture design (MFA); graphic design (MFA); industrial design (MID); interior architecture (MIA); landscape architecture (MLA).

Division of Fine Arts Offers ceramics (MFA); glass (MFA); jewelry and light metals (MFA); painting (MFA); photography (MFA); printmaking (MFA); sculpture (MFA); textiles (MFA).

RHODES COLLEGE, Memphis, TN 38112-1690

General Information Independent-religious, coed, comprehensive institution. *Enrollment:* 1,673 graduate, professional, and undergraduate students; 9 full-time matriculated graduate/professional students (3 women). *Enrollment by degree level:* 9 master's. *Graduate faculty:* 5 full-time (2 women), 1 part-time/adjunct (0 women). *Tuition:* Full-time $32,136; part-time $1350 per credit. *Required fees:* $310. *Graduate housing:* Room and/or apartments available on a first-come, first-served basis to single students; on-campus housing not available to married students. Typical cost: $7842 (including board). Housing application deadline: 3/1. *Student services:* Campus employment opportunities, campus safety program, career counseling, free psychological counseling, international student services, multicultural affairs office, services for students with disabilities. *Library facilities:* Burrow Library. *Online resources:* library catalog, web page, access to other libraries' catalogs. *Collection:* 281,099 titles, 873 serial subscriptions, 9,615 audiovisual materials.

Computer facilities: 220 computers available on campus for general student use. A campuswide network can be accessed from student residence rooms and from off campus. Online class registration is available. *Web address:* http://www.rhodes.edu/.

General Application Contact: Dr. Pamela H. Church, Program Director, 901-843-3863, Fax: 901-843-3798, E-mail: church@rhodes.edu.

GRADUATE UNITS

Department of Economics and Business Administration Students: 9 full-time (3 women). Average age 22. *Faculty:* 5 full-time (2 women), 1 part-time/adjunct (0 women). Expenses: Contact institution. *Financial support:* Career-related internships or fieldwork and scholarships/grants available. Support available to part-time students. Financial award application deadline: 3/1; financial award applicants required to submit FAFSA. *Degree program information:* Part-time programs available. Offers accounting (MS). *Application deadline:* For fall admission, 3/1 for domestic students. *Application fee:* $25. *Application Contact:* Dr. Pamela H. Church, Program Director, 901-843-3863, Fax: 901-843-3798, E-mail: church@rhodes.edu. *Program Director*, Dr. Pamela H. Church, 901-843-3863, Fax: 901-843-3798, E-mail: church@rhodes.edu.

RICE UNIVERSITY, Houston, TX 77251-1892

General Information Independent, coed, university. CGS member. *Graduate housing:* Rooms and/or apartments available on a first-come, first-served basis to single and married students. Housing application deadline: 7/15. *Research affiliation:* Fermi National Accelerator Laboratory, Los Alamos National Laboratory, Brookhaven National Laboratory, Arecibo Observatory, Houston Area Research Center.

GRADUATE UNITS

Graduate Programs *Degree program information:* Part-time programs available. Offers education (MAT). Electronic applications accepted.

George R. Brown School of Engineering *Degree program information:* Part-time programs available. Offers bioengineering (MS, PhD); biostatistics (PhD); chemical and biomolecular engineering (MS, PhD); chemical engineering (M Ch E); circuits, controls, and communication systems (MS, PhD); civil engineering (MCE, MS, PhD); computational and applied mathematics (MA, MCAM, PhD); computational finance (PhD); computational science and engineering (MCSE, PhD); computer science (MCS, MS, PhD); computer science and engineering (MS, PhD); computer science in bioinformatics (MCS); electrical engineering (MEE); engineering (M Ch E, M Stat, MA, MBE, MCAM, MCE, MCS, MCSE, MEE, MEE, MES, MME, MMS, MS, PhD); environmental engineering (MEE, MES, MS, PhD); environmental science (MEE, MES, MS, PhD); lasers, microwaves, and solid-state electronics (MS, PhD); materials science (MMS, MS, PhD); mechanical engineering (MME, MS, PhD); statistics (M Stat, MA, PhD). Electronic applications accepted.

Jesse H. Jones Graduate School of Management *Degree program information:* Evening/weekend programs available. Offers business administration (EMBA, MBA, PMBA). Electronic applications accepted.

School of Architecture Offers architecture (M Arch, D Arch); urban design (M Arch UD).

School of Humanities Offers English (MA, PhD); French studies (MA, PhD); history (MA, PhD); humanities (MA, PhD); linguistics (MA, PhD); philosophy (MA, PhD); religious studies (PhD); Spanish (MA).

School of Social Sciences Offers anthropology (MA, PhD); cognitive sciences (MA, PhD); economics (MA, PhD); industrial-organizational/social psychology (MA, PhD); political science (MA, PhD); psychology (MA, PhD); social sciences (MA, PhD).

Shepherd School of Music Offers composition (MM, DMA); conducting (MM); history (MM); performance (MM, DMA); theory (MM). Electronic applications accepted.

Wiess School of Natural Sciences *Degree program information:* Part-time programs available. Offers biochemistry and cell biology (MA, PhD); chemistry (MA); earth science (MA, PhD); ecology and evolutionary biology (MA, MS, PhD); inorganic chemistry (PhD); mathematics (MA, PhD); natural sciences (MA, MS, MST, PhD); organic chemistry (PhD); physical chemistry (PhD); physics (MA); physics and astronomy (MS, MST, PhD). Electronic applications accepted.

Wiess School–Professional Science Master's Programs Offers environmental analysis and decision making (MS); geophysics (MS); nanoscale physics (MS); professional science (MS).

Rice Quantum Institute Offers quantum physics (MS, PhD). Electronic applications accepted.

THE RICHARD STOCKTON COLLEGE OF NEW JERSEY, Pomona, NJ 08240-0195

General Information State-supported, coed, comprehensive institution. CGS member. *Enrollment:* 7,307 graduate, professional, and undergraduate students; 144 full-time matriculated graduate/professional students (108 women), 389 part-time matriculated graduate/professional students (293 women). *Enrollment by degree level:* 397 master's, 136 doctoral. *Graduate faculty:* 46 full-time (27 women), 16 part-time/adjunct (12 women). Tuition, state resident: full-time $8526; part-time $474 per credit. Tuition, nonresident: full-time $13,125; part-time $729 per course. *Required fees:* $2030; $113 per credit. *Graduate housing:* Room and/or apartments available to single students; on-campus housing not available to married students. Typical cost: $7295 per year ($10,204 including board). Housing application deadline: 4/1. *Student services:* Campus employment opportunities, campus safety program, career counseling, child daycare facilities, exercise/wellness program, free psychological counseling, international student services, low-cost health insurance, services for students with disabilities, teacher training, writing training. *Library facilities:* The Richard Stockton College of New Jersey Library. *Online resources:* library catalog, web page. *Collection:* 283,028 titles, 34,748 serial subscriptions, 13,367 audiovisual materials. *Research affiliation:* Aviation Research & Technology Park (aviation research), Nature Conservancy of NJ (environmental studies), Association of State Colleges (civic engagement), Jewish Foundation (Holocaust studies), Wetlands Institute (marine biology).

Computer facilities: 865 computers available on campus for general student use. A campuswide network can be accessed from student residence rooms and from off campus. Online class registration is available. *Web address:* http://www.stockton.edu/.

General Application Contact: Ann Mari Tarsitano, Director of Graduate Recruitment and Marketing, 609-652-4298, E-mail: gradschool@stockton.edu.

GRADUATE UNITS

School of Graduate and Continuing Education Students: 144 full-time (108 women), 389 part-time (293 women); includes 60 minority (21 African Americans, 18 Asian Americans or Pacific Islanders, 21 Hispanic Americans), 3 international. Average age 33. 397 applicants, 50% accepted, 172 enrolled. *Faculty:* 46 full-time (27 women), 16 part-time/adjunct (12 women). Expenses: Contact institution. *Financial support:* In 2008–09, 13 fellowships, 101 research assistantships were awarded; career-related internships or fieldwork, Federal Work-Study, and scholarships/grants also available. Support available to part-time students. Financial award application deadline: 3/1; financial award applicants required to submit FAFSA. In 2008, 143 master's awarded. *Degree program information:* Part-time programs available. Offers business administration (MBA); criminal justice (MA); education (MA); Holocaust and genocide studies (MA); instructional technology (MA); nursing (MSN); occupational therapy (MSOT); paralegal (Certificate); physical therapy (DPT). *Application deadline:* For fall admission, 8/1 for domestic and international students. Applications are processed on a rolling basis. *Application fee:* $50. Electronic applications accepted. *Application Contact:* John Iacovelli, Dean of Enrollment Management, 866-RSC-2885, Fax: 609-748-5541, E-mail: admissions@stockton.edu. *Dean of Graduate Studies*, Dr. Deborah M. Figart, 609-652-4298, E-mail: graduatestudies@stockton.edu.

RICHMOND, THE AMERICAN INTERNATIONAL UNIVERSITY IN LONDON, Richmond, Surrey TW10 6JP, United Kingdom

General Information Independent, coed, comprehensive institution. *Enrollment:* 1,043 graduate, professional, and undergraduate students; 10 full-time matriculated graduate/professional students (9 women). *Enrollment by degree level:* 10 master's. *Graduate faculty:* 1 full-time (0

Richmond, The American International University in London (continued)

women), 6 part-time/adjunct (3 women). *Tuition:* Full-time $28,500. *Graduate housing:* Room and/or apartments available on a first-come, first-served basis to single students; on-campus housing not available to married students. Typical cost: $12,600 per year ($18,000 including board). Housing application deadline: 8/1. *Student services:* Campus safety program, international student services, low-cost health insurance, multicultural affairs office, services for students with disabilities, writing training. *Library facilities:* Taylor Library plus 2 others. *Online resources:* library catalog, web page, access to other libraries' catalogs. *Collection:* 70,000 titles, 300 serial subscriptions.

Computer facilities: 420 computers available on campus for general student use. A campuswide network can be accessed from student residence rooms and from off campus. *Web address:* http://www.richmond.ac.uk/.

General Application Contact: Mark Kopenski, Vice President and Dean of Enrollment, 44-208-332-8252, Fax: 44-208-332-1596, E-mail: ma@richmond.ac.uk.

GRADUATE UNITS

Program in Art History Students: 10 full-time (9 women). Average age 24. 24 applicants, 83% accepted, 8 enrolled. *Faculty:* 1 full-time (0 women), 6 part-time/adjunct (3 women). Expenses: Contact institution. *Financial support:* Career-related internships or fieldwork, scholarships/grants, and tuition waivers (partial) available. Support available to part-time students. Financial award application deadline: 6/30; financial award applicants required to submit FAFSA. In 2008, 8 master's awarded. *Degree program information:* Part-time programs available. Offers art history (MA). *Application deadline:* For fall admission, 3/31 priority date for domestic and international students. *Application fee:* $50. Electronic applications accepted. *Application Contact:* Mark Kopenski, Vice President and Dean of Enrollment, 44-208-332-8252, Fax: 44-208-332-1596, E-mail: ma@richmond.ac.uk. *Associate Director,* Dr. Robert Wallis, 44-208-332-9000, Fax: 44-208-332-1596, E-mail: ma@richmond.ac.uk.

RICHMONT GRADUATE UNIVERSITY, Atlanta, GA 30327

General Information Independent-religious, coed, graduate-only institution.

GRADUATE UNITS

Graduate Programs

RIDER UNIVERSITY, Lawrenceville, NJ 08648-3001

General Information Independent, coed, comprehensive institution. *Graduate housing:* Room and/or apartments available on a first-come, first-served basis to single students; on-campus housing not available to married students. Housing application deadline: 5/1.

GRADUATE UNITS

College of Business Administration *Degree program information:* Part-time and evening/weekend programs available. Offers accountancy (M Acc); business administration (M Acc, MBA). Electronic applications accepted.

Department of Graduate Education, Leadership and Counseling *Degree program information:* Part-time and evening/weekend programs available. Offers alternative route in special education (Certificate); business education (Certificate); counseling services (MA, Certificate, Ed S); curriculum, instruction and supervision (MA, Certificate); director of school counseling (Certificate); educational administration (MA, Certificate); elementary education (Certificate); English as a second language (Certificate); English education (Certificate); mathematics education (Certificate); organizational leadership (MA); preschool to grade 3 (Certificate); principal (Certificate); reading specialist (Certificate); reading/language arts (MA, Certificate); school administrator (Certificate); school counseling services (Certificate); school psychology (Certificate, Ed S); science education (Certificate); social studies education (Certificate); special education (MA, Certificate); supervisor (Certificate); teacher certification (Certificate); teacher of students with disabilities (Certificate); teacher of the handicapped (Certificate); teaching (MA); world languages (Certificate). Electronic applications accepted.

RIVIER COLLEGE, Nashua, NH 03060

General Information Independent-religious, coed, comprehensive institution. *Enrollment:* 2,231 graduate, professional, and undergraduate students; 139 full-time matriculated graduate/professional students (111 women), 615 part-time matriculated graduate/professional students (480 women). *Enrollment by degree level:* 631 master's, 35 doctoral, 88 other advanced degrees. *Graduate faculty:* 36 full-time (18 women), 64 part-time/adjunct (34 women). *Tuition:* Full-time $5208; part-time $434 per credit. *Graduate housing:* On-campus housing not available. *Student services:* Campus safety program, career counseling, free psychological counseling, international student services, low-cost health insurance, multicultural affairs office, services for students with disabilities, teacher training.

Computer facilities: 93 computers available on campus for general student use. A campuswide network can be accessed from student residence rooms and from off campus. *Web address:* http://www.rivier.edu/.

General Application Contact: Mat Kittredge, Director of Graduate Admissions, 603-897-8129, Fax: 603-897-8810, E-mail: gradadm@rivier.edu.

GRADUATE UNITS

School of Graduate Studies Students: 139 full-time (111 women), 615 part-time (480 women); includes 49 minority (10 African Americans, 31 Asian Americans or Pacific Islanders, 8 Hispanic Americans), 2 international. Average age 38. 236 applicants, 95% accepted, 198 enrolled. *Faculty:* 36 full-time (18 women), 64 part-time/adjunct (34 women). Expenses: Contact institution. *Financial support:* Available to part-time students. Application deadline: 2/1. In 2008, 350 master's, 18 other advanced degrees awarded. *Degree program information:* Part-time programs available. Offers business administration (MBA); computer information systems (MS); computer science (MS); curriculum and instruction (M Ed); early childhood education (M Ed); educational administration (M Ed); educational studies (M Ed); elementary education (M Ed); elementary education and general special education (M Ed); emotional and behavioral disorders (M Ed); English (MA, MAT); general social education (M Ed); leadership and learning (Ed D, CAGS); learning disabilities (M Ed); learning disabilities and reading (M Ed); mathematics (MAT); mental health counseling (MA); organizational leadership (EMBA); reading (M Ed); school counseling (M Ed); social studies education (MAT); Spanish (MAT); writing and literature (MA). *Application deadline:* Applications are processed on a rolling basis. *Application fee:* $25. Electronic applications accepted. *Application Contact:* Mathew Kittredge, Director of Graduate Admissions, 603-897-8129, Fax: 603-897-8810, E-mail: mkittredge@rivier.edu. *Vice President of Academic Affairs,* Sr. Therese LaRochelle, 603-888-1311.

Division of Nursing Students: 4 full-time (all women), 36 part-time (34 women); includes 1 minority (African American). Average age 41. 13 applicants, 85% accepted, 11 enrolled. *Faculty:* 4 full-time (3 women). Expenses: Contact institution. *Financial support:* Available to part-time students. Application deadline: 2/1. In 2008, 20 master's awarded. *Degree program information:* Part-time and evening/weekend programs available. Offers family nurse practitioner (MS); nursing education (MS). *Application deadline:* Applications are processed on a rolling basis. *Application fee:* $25. Electronic applications accepted. *Application Contact:* Mathew Kittredge, Director of Graduate Admissions, 603-897-8129, Fax: 603-897-8810, E-mail: mkittredge@rivier.edu. *Head,* Dr. Paula Williams, 603-897-8529.

ROBERT MORRIS COLLEGE, Chicago, IL 60605

General Information Independent, coed, comprehensive institution. *Enrollment:* 4,590 graduate, professional, and undergraduate students; 40 full-time matriculated graduate/professional students (31 women), 310 part-time matriculated graduate/professional students (209 women). *Enrollment by degree level:* 350 master's. *Graduate faculty:* 13 full-time (5 women), 19 part-time/adjunct (7 women). *Tuition:* Part-time $1700 per course. *Graduate housing:* Rooms and/or apartments available on a first-come, first-served basis to single and married students. Typical cost: $9900 (including board) for single students; $9900 (including board) for married students. Room and board charges vary according to campus/location and housing facility selected. Housing application deadline: 5/1. *Student services:* Campus employment opportunities, career counseling, exercise/wellness program, free psychological counseling, international student services, services for students with disabilities, writing training. *Library facilities:* Thomas Jefferson Library plus 6 others. *Online resources:* library catalog, web page, access to other libraries' catalogs. *Collection:* 145,170 titles, 40,684 audiovisual materials.

Computer facilities: 1,702 computers available on campus for general student use. A campuswide network can be accessed from student residence rooms and from off campus. Online billing, Individual Student Assessment available. *Web address:* http://www.robertmorris.edu/.

General Application Contact: Office of Graduate Admissions, 800-762-5960.

GRADUATE UNITS

Morris Graduate School of Management Students: 40 full-time (31 women), 310 part-time (209 women); includes 216 minority (137 African Americans, 1 American Indian/Alaska Native, 15 Asian Americans or Pacific Islanders, 63 Hispanic Americans), 7 international. Average age 32. 193 applicants, 79% accepted, 94 enrolled. *Faculty:* 13 full-time (5 women), 19 part-time/adjunct (7 women). Expenses: Contact institution. *Financial support:* Career-related internships or fieldwork, Federal Work-Study, scholarships/grants, and tuition waivers (partial) available. Support available to part-time students. Financial award applicants required to submit FAFSA. In 2008, 92 master's awarded. *Degree program information:* Part-time and evening/weekend programs available. Offers accounting (MBA); accounting and finance (MBA); human resource management (MBA); information technology (MIS); management (MBA); management and finance (MBA). *Application deadline:* Applications are processed on a rolling basis. *Application fee:* $30 ($100 for international students). Electronic applications accepted. *Application Contact:* Courtney A. Kohn, Dean of Graduate Admissions, 312-935-4240, Fax: 312-935-4248, E-mail: ckohn@robertmorris.edu. *Dean Morris Graduate School of Management,* Kayed Akkawi, 312-935-4244, E-mail: kakkawi@robertmorris.edu.

ROBERT MORRIS UNIVERSITY, Moon Township, PA 15108-1189

General Information Independent, coed, university. *Enrollment:* 4,815 graduate, professional, and undergraduate students; 1,042 part-time matriculated graduate/professional students (560 women). *Enrollment by degree level:* 788 master's, 180 doctoral, 74 other advanced degrees. *Tuition:* Part-time $730 per credit hour. *Required fees:* $15 per credit hour. Part-time tuition and fees vary according to degree level, campus/location and program. *Graduate housing:* Room and/or apartments available on a first-come, first-served basis to single students; on-campus housing not available to married students. Typical cost: $5010 per year ($10,370 including board). Housing application deadline: 5/1. *Student services:* Campus employment opportunities, campus safety program, career counseling, international student services, services for students with disabilities. *Library facilities:* Robert Morris University Library plus 1 other. *Online resources:* library catalog, access to other libraries' catalogs. *Collection:* 122,650 titles, 582 serial subscriptions, 3,156 audiovisual materials.

Computer facilities: Computer purchase and lease plans are available. 300 computers available on campus for general student use. A campuswide network can be accessed from student residence rooms and from off campus. Online class registration, online payment are available. *Web address:* http://www.rmu.edu/.

General Application Contact: Edward J. Lamm, Assistant Dean, Graduate Admissions, 412-397-5200, Fax: 412-397-2425, E-mail: graduateadmissions@rmu.edu.

GRADUATE UNITS

Graduate Studies Expenses: Contact institution. *Financial support:* Research assistantships with partial tuition reimbursements, Federal Work-Study, institutionally sponsored loans, and unspecified assistantships available. Support available to part-time students. Financial award application deadline: 5/1; financial award applicants required to submit FAFSA. *Degree program information:* Part-time and evening/weekend programs available. *Application deadline:* For fall admission, 7/1 priority date for domestic and international students; for spring admission, 11/1 priority date for domestic and international students. Applications are processed on a rolling basis. *Application fee:* $35. Electronic applications accepted. *Application Contact:* Kellie L. Laurenzi, Dean of Admissions, 412-262-8235, Fax: 412-397-2425, E-mail: laurenzi@rmu.edu. *Provost/Senior Vice President for Academic Affairs,* Dr. David L. Jamison, 412-262-8641, Fax: 412-397-2528, E-mail: jamison@rmu.edu.

School of Business Students: 231 part-time (106 women); includes 16 minority (13 African Americans, 1 Asian American or Pacific Islander, 2 Hispanic Americans), 5 international. Average age 31. 126 applicants, 81% accepted, 66 enrolled. *Faculty:* 21 full-time (7 women), 3 part-time/adjunct (1 woman). Expenses: Contact institution. *Financial support:* Research assistantships with partial tuition reimbursements, Federal Work-Study, institutionally sponsored loans, and unspecified assistantships available. Support available to part-time students. Financial award application deadline: 5/1; financial award applicants required to submit FAFSA. In 2008, 131 master's awarded. *Degree program information:* Part-time and evening/weekend programs available. Offers business administration and management (MBA); human resource management (MS); nonprofit management (MS); taxation (MS). *Application deadline:* For fall admission, 7/1 priority date for domestic and international students; for spring admission, 11/1 priority date for domestic and international students. Applications are processed on a rolling basis. *Application fee:* $35. Electronic applications accepted. *Application Contact:* Edward J. Lamm, Assistant Dean, Graduate Admissions, 412-397-5200, Fax: 412-397-2425, E-mail: graduateadmissions@rmu.edu. *Dean,* Dr. Derya A. Jacobs, 412-262-8451, Fax: 412-262-8494, E-mail: jacobs@rmu.edu.

School of Communications and Information Systems Students: 248 part-time (79 women); includes 49 minority (32 African Americans, 14 Asian Americans or Pacific Islanders, 3 Hispanic Americans), 19 international. Average age 33. 95 applicants, 94% accepted, 66 enrolled. *Faculty:* 26 full-time (9 women), 9 part-time/adjunct (2 women). Expenses: Contact institution. *Financial support:* Research assistantships with partial tuition reimbursements, institutionally sponsored loans and unspecified assistantships available. Support available to part-time students. Financial award application deadline: 5/1. In 2008, 160 master's, 9 doctorates awarded. *Degree program information:* Part-time and evening/weekend programs available. Offers communication and information systems (MS); competitive intelligence systems (MS); information security and assurance (MS); information systems and communications (D Sc); information systems management (MS); information technology project management (MS); Internet information systems (MS); organizational studies (MS). *Application deadline:* For fall admission, 7/1 priority date for domestic and international students; for spring admission, 11/1 priority date for domestic and international students. Applications are processed on a rolling basis. *Application fee:* $35. Electronic applications accepted. *Application Contact:* Edward J. Lamm, Assistant Dean, Graduate Admissions, 412-397-5200, Fax: 412-397-2425, E-mail: graduateadmissions@rmu.edu. *Acting Dean,* Dr. Barbara J. Levine, 412-397-2591, Fax: 412-397-2481, E-mail: levine@rmu.edu.

School of Education and Social Sciences Students: 310 part-time (203 women); includes 24 minority (20 African Americans, 1 Asian American or Pacific Islander, 3 Hispanic Americans), 2 international. Average age 31. 77 applicants, 99% accepted, 51 enrolled. *Faculty:* 6 full-time (1 woman), 8 part-time/adjunct (3 women). Expenses: Contact institution. In 2008, 88 master's, 6 doctorates, 124 other advanced degrees awarded. *Degree program information:* Part-time and evening/weekend programs available. Offers business education (MS); education (Postbaccalaureate Certificate); instructional leadership (MS); instructional management and leadership (PhD). *Application deadline:* For fall admission, 7/1 priority date for domestic and international students; for spring admission, 11/1 priority date for domestic and international students. Applications are processed on a rolling basis. *Application fee:* $35. Electronic applications accepted. *Application Contact:* Edward J. Lamm, Assistant Dean, Graduate Admissions, 412-397-5200, Fax: 412-397-2425, E-mail: graduateadmissions@rmu.edu. *Dean,* Dr. John E. Graham, 412-397-3228, Fax: 412-397-2524, E-mail: graham@rmu.edu.

School of Engineering, Mathematics and Science Students: 47 part-time (6 women); includes 2 minority (1 African American, 1 American Indian/Alaska Native), 16 international. Average age 33. 11 applicants, 73% accepted, 7 enrolled. *Faculty:* 3 full-time (0 women). Expenses: Contact institution. *Financial support:* Federal Work-Study, institutionally sponsored loans, and unspecified assistantships available. Financial award application deadline: 5/1; financial award applicants required to submit FAFSA. In 2008, 12 master's awarded. *Degree program information:* Part-time and evening/weekend programs available. Offers engineering management (MS). *Application deadline:* For fall admission, 7/1 priority date for domestic and international students; for spring admission, 11/1 priority date for domestic and international students. Applications are processed on a rolling basis. *Application fee:* $35. Electronic applications accepted. *Application Contact:* Edward J. Lamm, Assistant Dean, Graduate Admissions, 412-397-5200, Fax: 412-397-2425, E-mail: graduateadmissions@rmu.edu. *Department Head, Engineering,* Dr. Joe Iannelli, 412-397-2514, Fax: 412-397-2593, E-mail: iannelli@rmu.edu.

School of Nursing and Health Sciences Students: 106 part-time (96 women); includes 8 minority (6 African Americans, 1 Asian American or Pacific Islander, 1 Hispanic American), 1 international. Average age 38. 71 applicants, 100% accepted, 59 enrolled. *Faculty:* 4 full-time (3 women). Expenses: Contact institution. *Financial support:* Federal Work-Study, institutionally sponsored loans, and unspecified assistantships available. Financial award application deadline: 5/1; financial award applicants required to submit FAFSA. In 2008, 1 master's awarded. *Degree program information:* Part-time and evening/weekend programs available. Offers nursing (MS, DNP). *Application deadline:* For fall admission, 7/1 priority date for domestic and international students; for spring admission, 11/1 priority date for domestic and international students. Applications are processed on a rolling basis. *Application fee:* $35. Electronic applications accepted. *Application Contact:* Edward J. Lamm, Assistant Dean, Graduate Admissions, 412-397-5200, Fax: 412-397-2425, E-mail: graduateadmissions@rmu.edu. *Dean,* Dr. Lynda J. Davidson, 412-397-3859, Fax: 412-397-3277, E-mail: davidson@rmu.edu.

See Close-Up on page 971.

ROBERTS WESLEYAN COLLEGE, Rochester, NY 14624-1997

General Information Independent-religious, coed, comprehensive institution. *Graduate housing:* Room and/or apartments available on a first-come, first-served basis to single students; on-campus housing not available to married students.

GRADUATE UNITS

Division of Adult Professional Studies *Degree program information:* Evening/weekend programs available. Offers health administration (MS).

Division of Business *Degree program information:* Evening/weekend programs available. Offers nonprofit leadership (Certificate); strategic leadership (MS); strategic marketing (MS).

Division of Nursing Offers nursing administration (MSN); nursing education (MSN).

Division of Social Sciences Offers counseling in ministry (MA); school counseling (MS); school psychology (MS).

Division of Social Work Offers child and family practice (MSW); congregational and community practice (MSW); mental health practice (MSW).

Division of Teacher Education *Degree program information:* Part-time and evening/weekend programs available. Offers adolescence education (M Ed); childhood and special education (M Ed); literacy education (M Ed); urban education (M Ed).

ROCHESTER INSTITUTE OF TECHNOLOGY, Rochester, NY 14623-5603

General Information Independent, coed, comprehensive institution. CGS member. *Enrollment:* 16,494 graduate, professional, and undergraduate students; 1,458 full-time matriculated graduate/professional students (524 women), 1,057 part-time matriculated graduate/professional students (337 women). *Enrollment by degree level:* 2,376 master's, 118 doctoral, 21 other advanced degrees. *Tuition:* Full-time $30,174; part-time $848 per credit hour. *Required fees:* $207. Tuition and fees vary according to course load. *Graduate housing:* Rooms and/or apartments available on a first-come, first-served basis to single and married students. Typical cost: $5421 per year ($9381 including board) for single students; $5421 per year ($9381 including board) for married students. Room and board charges vary according to board plan, campus/location and housing facility selected. *Student services:* Campus employment opportunities, campus safety program, career counseling, child daycare facilities, exercise/wellness program, free psychological counseling, grant writing training, international student services, low-cost health insurance, multicultural affairs office, services for students with disabilities, teacher training, writing training. *Library facilities:* Wallace Memorial Library. *Online resources:* library catalog, web page, access to other libraries' catalogs. *Collection:* 452,355 titles, 23,325 serial subscriptions, 9,719 audiovisual materials.

Computer facilities: Computer purchase and lease plans are available. 2,500 computers available on campus for general student use. A campuswide network can be accessed from student residence rooms and from off campus. Online class registration, student account information are available. *Web address:* http://www.rit.edu/.

General Application Contact: Diane Ellison, Assistant Vice President, Graduate Enrollment Services, 585-475-2229, Fax: 585-475-7164, E-mail: gradinfo@rit.edu.

GRADUATE UNITS

Graduate Enrollment Services Students: 1,458 full-time (524 women), 1,057 part-time (337 women); includes 220 minority (84 African Americans, 11 American Indian/Alaska Native, 79 Asian Americans or Pacific Islanders, 46 Hispanic Americans), 925 international. 3,327 applicants, 56% accepted, 855 enrolled. Expenses: Contact institution. *Financial support:* Fellowships, research assistantships, teaching assistantships, career-related internships or fieldwork, Federal Work-Study, scholarships/grants, tuition waivers (full and partial), and unspecified assistantships available. Support available to part-time students. Financial award applicants required to submit FAFSA. In 2008, 892 master's, 15 doctorates, 42 other advanced degrees awarded. *Degree program information:* Part-time and evening/weekend programs available. Postbaccalaureate distance learning degree programs offered (no on-campus study). *Application deadline:* Applications are processed on a rolling basis. *Application fee:* $50. Electronic applications accepted. *Application Contact:* Diane Ellison, Assistant Vice President, Graduate Enrollment Services, 585-475-2229, Fax: 585-475-7164, E-mail: gradinfo@rit.edu. *Assistant Vice President, Graduate Enrollment Services,* Diane Ellison, 585-475-2229, Fax: 585-475-7164, E-mail: gradinfo@rit.edu.

B. Thomas Golisano College of Computing and Information Sciences Students: 356 full-time (73 women), 238 part-time (43 women); includes 39 minority (11 African Americans, 3 American Indian/Alaska Native, 16 Asian Americans or Pacific Islanders, 9 Hispanic Americans), 289 international. 815 applicants, 71% accepted, 221 enrolled. Expenses: Contact institution. *Financial support:* Research assistantships with partial tuition reimbursements, teaching assistantships with partial tuition reimbursements, career-related internships or fieldwork, scholarships/grants, health care benefits, and unspecified assistantships available. Support available to part-time students. Financial award applicants required to submit FAFSA. In 2008, 146 master's, 8 other advanced degrees awarded. *Degree program information:* Part-time and evening/weekend programs available. Postbaccalaureate distance learning degree programs offered (no on-campus study). Offers computer science (MS); computing and information sciences (MS, PhD, AC); database administration (AC); game design and development (MS); human computer interaction (MS); information assurance (AC); information technology (MS, AC); interactive multimedia development (AC); network planning and design (AC); networking and systems administration (MS, AC); security and information assurance (MS); software development and management (MS); software engineering (MS). *Application deadline:* For fall admission, 2/1 priority date for domestic and international students; for winter admission, 11/1 for domestic and international students; for spring admission, 2/1 for domestic and international students. Applications are processed on a rolling basis. *Application fee:* $50. Electronic applications accepted. *Application Contact:* Diane Ellison, Assistant Vice President, Graduate Enrollment Services, 585-475-2229, Fax: 585-475-7164, E-mail: gradinfo@rit.edu. *Dean,* Dr. Jorge Diaz-Herrera, 585-475-7203, Fax: 585-475-4775, E-mail: jdiaz@gccis.rit.edu.

College of Applied Science and Technology Students: 157 full-time (72 women), 286 part-time (137 women); includes 57 minority (31 African Americans, 3 American Indian/Alaska Native, 12 Asian Americans or Pacific Islanders, 11 Hispanic Americans), 134 international. 356 applicants, 58% accepted, 125 enrolled. Expenses: Contact institution. *Financial support:* Research assistantships with partial tuition reimbursements, teaching assistantships with partial tuition reimbursements, career-related internships or fieldwork, scholarships/grants, and unspecified assistantships available. Support available to part-time students. Financial award applicants required to submit FAFSA. In 2008, 169 master's, 16 other advanced degrees awarded. *Degree program information:* Part-time and evening/weekend programs available. Postbaccalaureate distance learning degree programs offered (no on-campus study). Offers applied science and technology (MS, AC); elements of health care leadership (AC); environmental management (MS); facility management (MS); health information resources (AC); health systems administration (MS, AC); health systems administration executive leader (MS); health systems-finance (AC); hospitality-tourism management (MS); human resources development (MS); manufacturing and mechanical systems integration (MS); multidisciplinary studies (MS, AC); packaging science (MS); professional studies (MS); service leadership and innovation (MS); technical information design (AC); telecommunications engineering technology (MS). *Application deadline:* For fall admission, 2/15 priority date for domestic and international students; for winter admission, 11/1 priority date for domestic students, 10/1 priority date for international students; for spring admission, 2/1 priority date for domestic students, 1/1 priority date for international students. Applications are processed on a rolling basis. *Application fee:* $50. Electronic applications accepted. *Application Contact:* Diane Ellison, Assistant Vice President, Graduate Enrollment Services, 585-475-2229, Fax: 585-475-7164, E-mail: gradinfo@rit.edu. *Dean,* Dr. H. Fred Walker, 585-475-4399, Fax: 585-475-7080, E-mail: cast@rit.edu.

College of Imaging Arts and Sciences Students: 229 full-time (111 women), 74 part-time (39 women); includes 24 minority (4 African Americans, 2 American Indian/Alaska Native, 11 Asian Americans or Pacific Islanders, 7 Hispanic Americans), 125 international. 485 applicants, 44% accepted, 118 enrolled. Expenses: Contact institution. *Financial support:* Fellowships with partial tuition reimbursements, research assistantships with partial tuition reimbursements, teaching assistantships with partial tuition reimbursements, career-related internships or fieldwork, institutionally sponsored loans, scholarships/grants, tuition waivers (partial), and unspecified assistantships available. Support available to part-time students. Financial award application deadline: 8/30; financial award applicants required to submit FAFSA. In 2008, 96 master's awarded. *Degree program information:* Part-time programs available. Offers ceramics (MFA); computer graphics design (MFA); fine arts (MFA, MST); fine arts studio (MST); glass (MFA); graphic design (MFA); imaging arts (MFA); imaging arts and sciences (MFA, MS, MST); industrial design (MFA); medical illustration (MFA); metal crafts and jewelry (MFA); painting (MFA); print media (MS); printmaking (MFA); visual art (MST); woodworking and furniture design (MFA). *Application deadline:* For fall admission, 2/15 priority date for domestic and international students. Applications are processed on a rolling basis. *Application fee:* $50. Electronic applications accepted. *Application Contact:* Diane Ellison, Assistant Vice President, Graduate Enrollment Services, 585-475-2229, Fax: 585-475-7164, E-mail: gradinfo@rit.edu. *Interim Dean,* Frank Cost, 585-475-2733, E-mail: fjcppr@rit.edu.

College of Liberal Arts Students: 85 full-time (65 women), 31 part-time (19 women); includes 10 minority (6 African Americans, 4 Asian Americans or Pacific Islanders), 9 international. 103 applicants, 65% accepted, 40 enrolled. Expenses: Contact institution. *Financial support:* Research assistantships with partial tuition reimbursements, teaching assistantships with partial tuition reimbursements, career-related internships or fieldwork, scholarships/grants, and unspecified assistantships available. Support available to part-time students. Financial award applicants required to submit FAFSA. In 2008, 34 master's, 11 other advanced degrees awarded. *Degree program information:* Part-time programs available. Offers communication and media technologies (MS); liberal arts (MS, AC); psychology (MS); school psychology (MS, AC); science, technology and public policy (MS). *Application deadline:* For fall admission, 2/1 priority date for domestic and international students; for winter admission, 11/1 for domestic and international students; for spring admission, 2/1 for domestic and international students. Applications are processed on a rolling basis. *Application fee:* $50. Electronic applications accepted. *Application Contact:* Diane Ellison, Assistant Vice President, Graduate Enrollment Services, 585-475-2229, Fax: 585-475-7164, E-mail: gradinfo@rit.edu. *Dean,* Dr. Robert Ulin, 585-475-2929, Fax: 585-475-7120, E-mail: libarts@rit.edu.

College of Science Students: 126 full-time (38 women), 66 part-time (11 women); includes 17 minority (3 African Americans, 2 American Indian/Alaska Native, 7 Asian Americans or Pacific Islanders, 5 Hispanic Americans), 69 international. 247 applicants, 49% accepted, 65 enrolled. Expenses: Contact institution. *Financial support:* Fellowships with full and partial tuition reimbursements, research assistantships with full and partial tuition reimbursements, teaching assistantships with full and partial tuition reimbursements, career-related internships or fieldwork, scholarships/grants, tuition waivers (full and partial), and unspecified assistantships available. Support available to part-time students. Financial award applicants required to submit FAFSA. In 2008, 37 master's, 12 doctorates awarded. *Degree program information:* Part-time and evening/weekend programs available. Offers astrophysical sciences and technology (MS, PhD); bioinformatics (MS); chemistry (MS); clinical chemistry (MS); color science (MS, PhD); environmental science (MS); imaging science (MS, PhD); industrial and applied mathematics (MS); materials science and engineering (MS); science (MS, PhD). *Application deadline:* For fall admission, 2/15 priority date for domestic and international students. Applications are processed on a rolling basis. *Application fee:* $50. Electronic applications accepted. *Application Contact:* Diane Ellison, Assistant Vice President, Graduate Enrollment Services, 585-475-2229, Fax: 585-475-7164, E-mail: gradinfo@rit.edu. *Interim Dean,* Dr. Sophia Maggelakis, 585-475-2484, E-mail: cos@rit.edu.

E. Philip Saunders College of Business Students: 191 full-time (77 women), 131 part-time (44 women); includes 27 minority (14 African Americans, 10 Asian Americans or Pacific Islanders, 3 Hispanic Americans), 90 international. 446 applicants, 53% accepted, 121 enrolled. Expenses: Contact institution. *Financial support:* Research assistantships with partial tuition reimbursements, teaching assistantships with partial tuition reimbursements, career-related internships or fieldwork, scholarships/grants, and unspecified assistantships available. Support available to part-time students. Financial award applicants required to submit FAFSA. In 2008, 173 master's awarded. *Degree program information:* Part-time and evening/weekend programs available. Postbaccalaureate distance learning degree programs offered (minimal on-campus study). Offers accounting (MBA); business (Exec MBA, MBA, MS); business administration (MBA); executive business administration (Exec MBA); finance (MS); innovation management (MS); management (MS). *Application deadline:* For fall admission, 2/15 priority date for domestic and international students; for winter admission, 11/1 priority date for domestic students, 10/1 priority date for international students; for spring admission, 2/1 priority date for domestic students, 1/1 priority date for international students. Applications are processed on a rolling basis. *Application fee:* $50. *Application Contact:* Diane Ellison, Assistant Vice President, 585-475-2229, Fax: 585-475-7164, E-mail: gradinfo@rit.edu. *Dean,* Dr. Ashok Rao, 585-475-7935, E-mail: arao@saunders.rit.edu.

Golisano Institute for Sustainability Expenses: Contact institution. Offers sustainability (PhD). *Application deadline:* For fall admission, 1/15 priority date for domestic and international students. *Application fee:* $50. *Application Contact:* Diane Ellison, Assistant Vice President, Graduate Enrollment Services, 585-475-2229, Fax: 585-475-7164, E-mail: gradinfo@rit.edu. *Assistant Provost and Director,* Dr. Nabil Nasr, 585-475-2602, E-mail: info@sustainability.rit.edu.

Kate Gleason College of Engineering Students: 274 full-time (59 women), 224 part-time (38 women); includes 38 minority (11 African Americans, 1 American Indian/Alaska Native, 15 Asian Americans or Pacific Islanders, 11 Hispanic Americans), 206 international. 836 applicants, 50% accepted, 138 enrolled. Expenses: Contact institution. *Financial support:* Fellowships with partial tuition reimbursements, research assistantships with partial tuition reimbursements, teaching assistantships with partial tuition reimbursements, career-related internships or fieldwork, institutionally sponsored loans, scholarships/grants, tuition waivers (partial), and unspecified assistantships available. Support available to part-time students. Financial award applicants required to submit FAFSA. In 2008, 209 master's, 3 doctorates, 4 other advanced degrees awarded. *Degree program information:* Part-time and evening/weekend programs available. Offers applied statistics (MS); computer engineering (MS); electrical engineering (MSEE); engineering (ME, MS, MSEE, PhD, AC); engineering management (ME); industrial engineering (ME, MS); manufacturing engineering (ME, MS); manufacturing leadership (MS); mechanical engineering (ME, MS); microelectronic

Rochester Institute of Technology (continued)

engineering (MS); microelectronic manufacturing engineering (ME); microsystems engineering (PhD); product development (MS); statistical quality (AC); systems engineering (ME). *Application deadline:* For fall admission, 2/15 priority date for domestic and international students. Applications are processed on a rolling basis. *Application fee:* $50. Electronic applications accepted. *Application Contact:* Diane Ellison, Assistant Vice President, Graduate Enrollment Services, 585-475-2229, Fax: 585-475-7164, E-mail: gradinfo@rit.edu. *Dean,* Dr. Harvey Palmer, 585-475-2145, Fax: 585-475-6879, E-mail: coe@rit.edu.

National Technical Institute for the Deaf Students: 40 full-time (29 women), 7 part-time (6 women); includes 8 minority (4 African Americans, 4 Asian Americans or Pacific Islanders), 3 international. 39 applicants, 77% accepted, 27 enrolled. Expenses: Contact institution. *Financial support:* Fellowships with partial tuition reimbursements, research assistantships with partial tuition reimbursements, teaching assistantships with partial tuition reimbursements, career-related internships or fieldwork, scholarships/grants, and unspecified assistantships available. Support available to part-time students. Financial award applicants required to submit FAFSA. In 2008, 28 master's awarded. Offers deaf studies (MS); secondary education (MS). *Application deadline:* For fall admission, 2/15 priority date for domestic and international students. Applications are processed on a rolling basis. *Application fee:* $50. *Application Contact:* Diane Ellison, Assistant Vice President, Graduate Enrollment Services, 585-475-2229, Fax: 585-475-7164, E-mail: gradinfo@rit.edu. *Vice President and Dean,* Dr. Alan Hurwitz, 585-475-6400, Fax: 585-475-5978, E-mail: ntidmc@rit.edu.

See Close-Up on page 973.

THE ROCKEFELLER UNIVERSITY, New York, NY 10021-6399

General Information Independent, coed, graduate-only institution. CGS member. *Enrollment by degree level:* 19 master's, 207 doctoral. *Graduate faculty:* 104 full-time (25 women), 160 part-time/adjunct (40 women). *Graduate housing:* Rooms and/or apartments guaranteed to single and married students. Housing application deadline: 6/1. *Student services:* Campus safety program, child daycare facilities, exercise/wellness program, free psychological counseling, low-cost health insurance. *Library facilities:* Rita & Frits Markus Library and Scientific Information Center. *Online resources:* library catalog, web page, access to other libraries' catalogs. *Collection:* 52,676 titles, 2,973 serial subscriptions, 13 audiovisual materials.

Computer facilities: 19 computers available on campus for general student use. A campuswide network can be accessed from student residence rooms and from off campus. *Web address:* http://www.rockefeller.edu/.

General Application Contact: Dr. Sidney Strickland, Dean of Graduate Studies, 212-327-8086, Fax: 212-327-8505, E-mail: phd@rockefeller.edu.

GRADUATE UNITS

Program in Biomedical Sciences Students: 226 full-time (98 women); includes 40 minority (13 African Americans, 1 American Indian/Alaska Native, 18 Asian Americans or Pacific Islanders, 8 Hispanic Americans), 89 international. Average age 28. 558 applicants, 15% accepted, 30 enrolled. *Faculty:* 104 full-time (25 women), 160 part-time/adjunct (40 women). Expenses: Contact institution. *Financial support:* In 2008–09, 226 students received support, including 226 fellowships with full tuition reimbursements available (averaging $31,000 per year); institutionally sponsored loans, scholarships/grants, traineeships, and health care benefits also available. In 2008, 26 doctorates awarded. Offers biomedical sciences (PhD). *Application deadline:* For winter admission, 12/7 for domestic and international students. *Application fee:* $80. Electronic applications accepted. *Application Contact:* Kristen Cullen, Admissions and Records Administrator, 212-327-8088, Fax: 212-327-8505, E-mail: cullenk@rockefeller.edu. *Dean of Graduate Studies,* Dr. Sidney Strickland, 212-327-8086, Fax: 212-327-8505, E-mail: phd@rockefeller.edu.

ROCKFORD COLLEGE, Rockford, IL 61108-2393

General Information Independent, coed, comprehensive institution. *Enrollment:* 1,391 graduate, professional, and undergraduate students; 37 full-time matriculated graduate/professional students (24 women), 147 part-time matriculated graduate/professional students (102 women). *Enrollment by degree level:* 184 master's. *Graduate faculty:* 16 full-time (5 women), 61 part-time/adjunct (39 women). *Tuition:* Full-time $11,250; part-time $625 per credit hour. *Required fees:* $30 per semester. Tuition and fees vary according to course load and program. *Graduate housing:* Room and/or apartments available on a first-come, first-served basis to single students; on-campus housing not available to married students. Typical cost: $5170 per year ($8070 including board). Room and board charges vary according to board plan and housing facility selected. *Student services:* Campus employment opportunities, campus safety program, career counseling, free psychological counseling, grant writing training, international student services, low-cost health insurance, multicultural affairs office, services for students with disabilities, teacher training, writing training. *Library facilities:* Howard Colman Library. *Online resources:* library catalog, web page. *Collection:* 140,000 titles, 831 serial subscriptions.

Computer facilities: 75 computers available on campus for general student use. A campuswide network can be accessed from student residence rooms and from off campus. *Web address:* http://www.rockford.edu/.

General Application Contact: Michele Mehren, Office Manager for Graduate Studies, 815-226-4041, Fax: 815-394-3706, E-mail: MMehren@rockford.edu.

GRADUATE UNITS

Graduate Studies Students: 37 full-time (24 women), 147 part-time (102 women); includes 17 minority (7 African Americans, 3 Asian Americans or Pacific Islanders, 7 Hispanic Americans), 4 international. Average age 35. *Faculty:* 16 full-time (5 women), 61 part-time/adjunct (39 women). Expenses: Contact institution. *Financial support:* In 2008–09, 70 students received support. Scholarships/grants and unspecified assistantships available. Support available to part-time students. Financial award application deadline: 3/1; financial award applicants required to submit FAFSA. In 2008, 117 master's awarded. *Degree program information:* Part-time and evening/weekend programs available. Offers business administration (MBA); education (MAT); elementary education (MAT); instructional strategies (MAT); reading (MAT); secondary education (MAT); special education (MAT). *Application deadline:* Applications are processed on a rolling basis. *Application fee:* $50. Electronic applications accepted. *Application Contact:* Michele Mehren, Office Manager for Graduate Studies, 815-226-4041, Fax: 815-394-3706, E-mail: MMehren@rockford.edu. *MAT Director,* Dr. Michelle M. McReynolds, 815-226-3390, Fax: 815-394-3706, E-mail: mmcreynolds@rockford.edu.

ROCKHURST UNIVERSITY, Kansas City, MO 64110-2561

General Information Independent-religious, coed, comprehensive institution. CGS member. *Enrollment:* 3,086 graduate, professional, and undergraduate students; 406 full-time matriculated graduate/professional students (282 women), 438 part-time matriculated graduate/professional students (223 women). *Enrollment by degree level:* 720 master's, 124 doctoral. *Graduate faculty:* 59 full-time (31 women), 23 part-time/adjunct (9 women). Tuition and fees vary according to program. *Graduate housing:* Room and/or apartments available on a first-come, first-served basis to single students; on-campus housing not available to married students. Typical cost: $3800 per year ($6800 including board). Housing application deadline: 6/10. *Student services:* Campus employment opportunities, campus safety program, career counseling, free psychological counseling, international student services, multicultural affairs office, services for students with disabilities, teacher training. *Library facilities:* Greenlease Library. *Online resources:* library catalog, web page, access to other libraries' catalogs. *Collection:* 189,527 titles, 42,563 serial subscriptions, 1,663 audiovisual materials.

Computer facilities: Computer purchase and lease plans are available. 227 computers available on campus for general student use. A campuswide network can be accessed from student residence rooms and from off campus. Online class registration, wireless network are available. *Web address:* http://www.rockhurst.edu/.

General Application Contact: Cheryl Hooper, Director of Graduate Recruitment, 816-501-4097, Fax: 816-501-4241, E-mail: graduate.admission@rockhurst.edu.

GRADUATE UNITS

Helzberg School of Management Students: 123 full-time (50 women), 251 part-time (87 women); includes 33 minority (11 African Americans, 2 American Indian/Alaska Native, 11 Asian Americans or Pacific Islanders, 9 Hispanic Americans). Average age 30. 171 applicants, 61% accepted, 98 enrolled. *Faculty:* 20 full-time (5 women), 9 part-time/adjunct (4 women). Expenses: Contact institution. *Financial support:* Career-related internships or fieldwork available. Support available to part-time students. Financial award application deadline: 4/1; financial award applicants required to submit FAFSA. In 2008, 169 master's awarded. *Degree program information:* Part-time and evening/weekend programs available. Offers management (MBA). *Application deadline:* For fall admission, 7/25 priority date for domestic students; for spring admission, 12/15 for domestic students. Applications are processed on a rolling basis. *Application fee:* $0. Electronic applications accepted. *Application Contact:* Michele Haggerty, Director of MBA Admission, 816-4823, E-mail: michele.haggerty@rockhurst.edu. *Dean,* Dr. James Daley, 816-501-4201, Fax: 816-501-4650, E-mail: james.daley@rockhurst.edu.

School of Graduate and Professional Studies Students: 283 full-time (232 women), 172 part-time (124 women); includes 47 minority (21 African Americans, 2 American Indian/Alaska Native, 7 Asian Americans or Pacific Islanders, 17 Hispanic Americans), 1 international. Average age 28. 501 applicants, 47% accepted, 160 enrolled. *Faculty:* 26 full-time (18 women), 14 part-time/adjunct (12 women). Expenses: Contact institution. *Financial support:* In 2008–09, 10 research assistantships, 20 teaching assistantships were awarded; career-related internships or fieldwork, institutionally sponsored loans, and unspecified assistantships also available. Financial award applicants required to submit FAFSA. In 2008, 122 master's, 29 doctorates awarded. *Degree program information:* Part-time and evening/weekend programs available. Offers arts and sciences (M Ed, MOT, MS, DPT); communication sciences and disorders (MS); education (M Ed); occupational therapy (MOT); physical therapy (DPT). *Application deadline:* Applications are processed on a rolling basis. *Application fee:* $25. Electronic applications accepted. *Application Contact:* Cheryl Hooper, Director of Graduate Admission, 816-501-4097, Fax: 816-501-4241, E-mail: cheryl.hooper@rockhurst.edu. *Dean,* Dr. Donna Calvert, 816-501-4104, E-mail: donna.calvert@rockhurst.edu.

ROCKY MOUNTAIN COLLEGE, Billings, MT 59102-1796

General Information Independent-religious, coed, comprehensive institution.

GRADUATE UNITS

Graduate Programs

ROGER WILLIAMS UNIVERSITY, Bristol, RI 02809

General Information Independent, coed, comprehensive institution. *Enrollment:* 5,159 graduate, professional, and undergraduate students; 620 full-time matriculated graduate/professional students (323 women), 195 part-time matriculated graduate/professional students (126 women). *Enrollment by degree level:* 551 first professional, 228 master's, 36 other advanced degrees. *Graduate faculty:* 34 full-time (15 women), 30 part-time/adjunct (8 women). *Tuition:* Full-time $33,450; part-time $1251 per credit hour. *Required fees:* $570. Tuition and fees vary according to class time, program and reciprocity agreements. *Graduate housing:* Room and/or apartments available on a first-come, first-served basis to single students; on-campus housing not available to married students. Typical cost: $6390 per year ($11,880 including board). Room and board charges vary according to board plan, campus/location and housing facility selected. *Student services:* Campus employment opportunities, campus safety program, career counseling, exercise/wellness program, free psychological counseling, international student services, low-cost health insurance, multicultural affairs office, services for students with disabilities, teacher training, writing training. *Library facilities:* Roger Williams University Library plus 1 other. *Online resources:* library catalog, web page. *Collection:* 224,278 titles, 31,904 serial subscriptions, 96,138 audiovisual materials.

Computer facilities: 410 computers available on campus for general student use. A campuswide network can be accessed from student residence rooms and from off campus. Online class registration is available. *Web address:* http://www.rwu.edu/.

General Application Contact: Lori Vales, Graduate Admission Coordinator, 401-254-6200, Fax: 401-254-3557, E-mail: lvales@rwu.edu.

GRADUATE UNITS

Feinstein College of Arts and Sciences Students: 35 full-time (28 women), 37 part-time (23 women); includes 7 minority (2 African Americans, 1 American Indian/Alaska Native, 1 Asian American or Pacific Islander, 3 Hispanic Americans), 1 international. Average age 31. 80 applicants, 76% accepted, 34 enrolled. *Faculty:* 15 full-time (2 women). Expenses: Contact institution. *Financial support:* In 2008–09, 39 students received support. Application deadline: 6/15. In 2008, 25 master's awarded. *Degree program information:* Part-time and evening/weekend programs available. Postbaccalaureate distance learning degree programs offered (minimal on-campus study). Offers arts and sciences (MA, MPA); forensic psychology (MA); public administration (MPA). *Application deadline:* Applications are processed on a rolling basis. *Application fee:* $50. Electronic applications accepted. *Application Contact:* Lori Vales, Graduate Admission Coordinator, 401-254-6200, Fax: 401-254-3557, E-mail: gradadmit@rwu.edu. *Dean,* Dean Robert Cole, 401-254-3149, E-mail: rcole@rwu.edu.

School of Architecture, Art and Historic Preservation Students: 53 full-time (16 women), 8 part-time (2 women); includes 1 minority (Hispanic American), 2 international. Average age 23. 38 applicants, 87% accepted, 31 enrolled. *Faculty:* 9 full-time (1 woman), 2 part-time/adjunct (1 woman). Expenses: Contact institution. *Financial support:* In 2008–09, 61 students received support. Application deadline: 6/15. In 2008, 5 master's awarded. Offers architecture (M Arch). Students often begin 5-6 year dual degree sequence as undergraduates. *Application deadline:* For fall admission, 3/1 priority date for domestic students. *Application fee:* $50. Electronic applications accepted. *Application Contact:* Lori Vales, Graduate Admission Coordinator, 401-254-6600, Fax: 401-254-3557, E-mail: gradadmit@rwu.edu. *Dean,* Dean Stephen White, 401-254-3607, E-mail: swhite@rwu.edu.

School of Education Students: 11 full-time (10 women), 62 part-time (54 women); includes 3 minority (1 African American, 1 Asian American or Pacific Islander, 1 Hispanic American). Average age 33. 60 applicants, 92% accepted, 48 enrolled. *Faculty:* 7 full-time (6 women), 5 part-time/adjunct (3 women). Expenses: Contact institution. *Financial support:* In 2008–09, 19 students received support. Application deadline: 6/15. In 2008, 30 master's awarded. *Degree program information:* Part-time and evening/weekend programs available. Offers education (MA, MAT); elementary education (MAT); literacy (MA). *Application deadline:* Applications are processed on a rolling basis. *Application fee:* $50. Electronic applications accepted. *Application Contact:* Lori Vales, Graduate Admission Coordinator, 401-254-6600, Fax: 401-254-3557, E-mail: gradadmit@rwu.edu. *Dean of the School of Education,* Dr. Mieko Kamii, 401-254-3422, Fax: 401-254-3710, E-mail: mkamii@rwu.edu.

School of Engineering, Computing and Construction Management Offers construction management (MSCM).

School of Justice Studies Students: 8 full-time (4 women), 41 part-time (14 women); includes 1 minority (African American). Average age 31. 17 applicants, 76% accepted, 10 enrolled. *Faculty:* 7 full-time (5 women). Expenses: Contact institution. *Financial support:* In 2008–09, 11 students received support. Application deadline: 6/15. In 2008, 20 master's awarded. *Degree program information:* Part-time and evening/weekend programs available. Offers criminal justice (MS). *Application deadline:* Applications are processed on a rolling basis. *Application fee:* $50. Electronic applications accepted. *Application Contact:* Lori Vales, Graduate Admission Coordinator, 401-254-6600, Fax: 401-254-3557, E-mail: gradadmit@rwu.edu. *Dean,* Dr. Stephanie Manzi, 401-254-3715, Fax: 401-254-3431, E-mail: smanzi@rwu.edu.

School of Law Offers law (JD). Electronic applications accepted.

ROLLINS COLLEGE, Winter Park, FL 32789-4499

General Information Independent, coed, comprehensive institution. *Enrollment:* 2,511 graduate, professional, and undergraduate students; 392 full-time matriculated graduate/professional students (193 women), 334 part-time matriculated graduate/professional students (211 women).

Enrollment by degree level: 726 master's. *Graduate faculty:* 26 full-time (6 women). *Graduate housing:* On-campus housing not available. *Student services:* Campus employment opportunities, campus safety program, career counseling, exercise/wellness program, free psychological counseling, international student services, low-cost health insurance, multicultural affairs office, services for students with disabilities. *Library facilities:* Olin Library. *Online resources:* library catalog, web page, access to other libraries' catalogs. *Collection:* 306,243 titles, 36,989 serial subscriptions, 5,923 audiovisual materials.

Computer facilities: 240 computers available on campus for general student use. A campuswide network can be accessed from student residence rooms and from off campus. Online class registration is available. *Web address:* http://www.rollins.edu/.

General Application Contact: Information Contact, 407-646-2000.

GRADUATE UNITS

Crummer Graduate School of Business Students: 321 full-time (128 women), 152 part-time (70 women); includes 106 minority (37 African Americans, 3 American Indian/Alaska Native, 26 Asian Americans or Pacific Islanders, 40 Hispanic Americans), 13 international. Average age 30. *Faculty:* 22 full-time (3 women). Expenses: Contact institution. *Financial support:* Fellowships, research assistantships, career-related internships or fieldwork, Federal Work-Study, scholarships/grants, and tuition waivers (full) available. In 2008, 207 master's awarded. *Degree program information:* Part-time and evening/weekend programs available. Offers business (MBA). *Application deadline:* For fall admission, 4/1 priority date for domestic students; for spring admission, 12/1 for domestic students. Applications are processed on a rolling basis. *Application fee:* $50. Electronic applications accepted. *Application Contact:* Student Admissions Office, 407-646-2405, Fax: 407-646-1550. *Dean,* Dr. Craig M. McAllaster, 407-646-2249, Fax: 407-646-1550, E-mail: cmcallaster@rollins.edu.

Hamilton Holt School Students: 71 full-time (65 women), 182 part-time (141 women); includes 49 minority (22 African Americans, 1 American Indian/Alaska Native, 5 Asian Americans or Pacific Islanders, 21 Hispanic Americans), 2 international. Average age 31. Expenses: Contact institution. *Financial support:* Teaching assistantships, institutionally sponsored loans and scholarships/grants available. Support available to part-time students. In 2008, 70 master's awarded. *Degree program information:* Part-time and evening/weekend programs available. Offers elementary education (M Ed, MAT); human resources (MA); liberal studies (MLS); mental health counseling (MA); secondary education (MAT). *Application deadline:* Applications are processed on a rolling basis. *Application fee:* $50. Electronic applications accepted. *Application Contact:* Graduate Program Admission, 407-646-2232, Fax: 407-646-1551. *Acting Dean,* Dr. James C. Eck, 407-646-2292, Fax: 407-646-1551, E-mail: jeck@ollins.edu.

ROOSEVELT UNIVERSITY, Chicago, IL 60605-1394

General Information Independent, coed, comprehensive institution. CGS member. *Enrollment:* 7,692 graduate, professional, and undergraduate students; 1,127 full-time matriculated graduate/professional students (804 women), 2,086 part-time matriculated graduate/professional students (1,497 women). *Enrollment by degree level:* 3,125 master's, 144 doctoral. *Graduate faculty:* 210 full-time (86 women), 543 part-time/adjunct (247 women). *Tuition:* Full-time $14,730; part-time $709 per credit. *Required fees:* $175 per semester. Tuition and fees vary according to course load and program. *Graduate housing:* Room and/or apartments available on a first-come, first-served basis to single students; on-campus housing not available to married students. Typical cost: $3258 per year ($10,806 including board). Room and board charges vary according to board plan, campus/location and housing facility selected. Housing application deadline: 7/1. *Student services:* Campus employment opportunities, campus safety program, career counseling, child daycare facilities, exercise/wellness program, free psychological counseling, international student services, low-cost health insurance, services for students with disabilities, teacher training, writing training. *Library facilities:* Murray-Green Library plus 4 others. *Online resources:* library catalog, web page, access to other libraries' catalogs. *Collection:* 202,000 titles, 1,300 serial subscriptions.

Computer facilities: 300 computers available on campus for general student use. A campuswide network can be accessed from student residence rooms and from off campus. Online class registration is available. *Web address:* http://www.roosevelt.edu/.

General Application Contact: Joanne Canyon-Heller, Coordinator of Graduate Admission, 877-APPLY RU, Fax: 312-281-3356, E-mail: applyru@roosevelt.edu.

GRADUATE UNITS

Graduate Division Students: 1,049 full-time (762 women), 2,086 part-time (1,481 women); includes 1,025 minority (665 African Americans, 8 American Indian/Alaska Native, 168 Asian Americans or Pacific Islanders, 184 Hispanic Americans), 200 international. Average age 32. 2,772 applicants, 47% accepted, 831 enrolled. *Faculty:* 216 full-time (86 women), 415 part-time/adjunct (193 women). Expenses: Contact institution. *Financial support:* In 2008–09, 175 students received support, including 52 research assistantships with full tuition reimbursements available (averaging $5,200 per year); career-related internships or fieldwork, Federal Work-Study, scholarships/grants, tuition waivers (full and partial), and unspecified assistantships also available. Support available to part-time students. Financial award application deadline: 5/1; financial award applicants required to submit FAFSA. In 2008, 1,063 master's, 14 doctorates awarded. *Degree program information:* Part-time and evening/weekend programs available. *Application deadline:* For fall admission, 6/1 priority date for domestic students; for spring admission, 12/1 for domestic students. Applications are processed on a rolling basis. *Application fee:* $25 ($35 for international students). Electronic applications accepted. *Application Contact:* Joanne Canyon-Heller, Coordinator of Graduate Admission, 877-APPLY RU, Fax: 312-281-3356, E-mail: applyru@roosevelt.edu. *Dean of Graduate Studies,* Dr. Janett Trubatch, 312-341-2440, Fax: 312-341-2013.

Chicago College of Performing Arts Students: 128 full-time (68 women), 6 part-time (2 women); includes 8 African Americans, 3 American Indian/Alaska Native. Average age 25. 618 applicants, 33% accepted, 64 enrolled. Expenses: Contact institution. *Financial support:* Research assistantships, career-related internships or fieldwork, Federal Work-Study, scholarships/grants, and tuition waivers (full and partial) available. Support available to part-time students. In 2008, 67 master's awarded. *Degree program information:* Part-time and evening/weekend programs available. Offers directing and dramaturgy (MFA); music (MM); musical theatre (MFA); performing arts (MA, MFA, MM, Diploma); piano pedagogy (Diploma); theatre (MA, MFA); theatre-directing (MA); theatre-performance (MFA). *Application deadline:* For fall admission, 6/1 priority date for domestic students. Applications are processed on a rolling basis. *Application fee:* $25 ($35 for international students). *Application Contact:* Joanne Canyon-Heller, Coordinator of Graduate Admission, 877-APPLY RU, Fax: 312-281-3356, E-mail: applyru@roosevelt.edu. *Interim Dean,* Rudy Marcozzi, 312-341-3782.

College of Arts and Sciences Students: 435 full-time (331 women), 613 part-time (425 women); includes 323 minority (209 African Americans, 2 American Indian/Alaska Native, 53 Asian Americans or Pacific Islanders, 59 Hispanic Americans), 72 international. Average age 31. Expenses: Contact institution. *Financial support:* Research assistantships, teaching assistantships, career-related internships or fieldwork, Federal Work-Study, institutionally sponsored loans, scholarships/grants, and tuition waivers (full and partial) available. Support available to part-time students. Financial award application deadline: 2/15. In 2008, 310 master's, 8 doctorates awarded. *Degree program information:* Part-time and evening/weekend programs available. Offers anthropology (MA); applied economics (MA); arts and sciences (MA, MFA, MPA, MS, MSC, MSIMC, MSJ, MST, Psy D, Certificate); biotechnology and chemical science (MS); clinical professional psychology (MA, Psy D); computer science (MSC); creative writing (MFA); economics (MA); English (MA); history (MA); industrial/organizational psychology (MA); integrated marketing communications (MSIMC); journalism (MSJ); mathematical sciences (MS); mathematics (MS); political science (MA); psychology (Psy D); public administration (MPA); sociology (MA); Spanish (MA); telecommunications (MST); women's and gender studies (MA, Certificate). *Application deadline:* For fall admission, 6/1 priority date for domestic students. Applications are processed on a rolling basis. *Application fee:* $25 ($35 for international students). *Application Contact:* Joanne Canyon-Heller, Coordinator of Graduate Admission, 877-APPLY RU, Fax: 312-281-3356, E-mail: applyru@roosevelt.edu. *Dean,* Lynn Weiner, 312-341-2134, E-mail: lweiner@roosevelt.edu.

College of Education Students: 309 full-time (266 women), 574 part-time (451 women); includes 270 minority (172 African Americans, 3 American Indian/Alaska Native, 32 Asian Americans or Pacific Islanders, 63 Hispanic Americans), 4 international. Average age 37. 1,474 applicants, 51% accepted, 259 enrolled. Expenses: Contact institution. *Financial support:* Federal Work-Study available. Support available to part-time students. Financial award application deadline: 2/15. In 2008, 371 master's, 10 doctorates awarded. *Degree program information:* Part-time and evening/weekend programs available. Offers counseling and human services (MA); early childhood education (MA); education (MA, Ed D); educational leadership (MA, Ed D); elementary education (MA); reading teacher education (MA); secondary education (MA); special education (MA); teacher leadership (MA). *Application deadline:* For fall admission, 6/1 priority date for domestic students. Applications are processed on a rolling basis. *Application fee:* $25 ($35 for international students). *Application Contact:* Joanne Canyon-Heller, Coordinator of Graduate Admission, 877-APPLY RU, Fax: 312-281-3356, E-mail: applyru@roosevelt.edu. *Interim Dean,* George Olson, 312-341-3700.

College of Professional Studies Students: 47 full-time (41 women), 231 part-time (193 women); includes 98 minority (84 African Americans, 2 American Indian/Alaska Native, 6 Asian Americans or Pacific Islanders, 6 Hispanic Americans), 23 international. Average age 37. 300 applicants, 56% accepted, 73 enrolled. *Faculty:* 68. Expenses: Contact institution. *Financial support:* Federal Work-Study available. Support available to part-time students. Financial award application deadline: 2/15. In 2008, 55 master's awarded. *Degree program information:* Part-time and evening/weekend programs available. Offers hospitality management (MS); training and development (MA). *Application deadline:* For fall admission, 6/1 priority date for domestic students. Applications are processed on a rolling basis. *Application fee:* $25 ($35 for international students). *Application Contact:* Joanne Canyon-Heller, Coordinator of Graduate Admission, 877-APPLY RU, Fax: 312-281-3356, E-mail: applyru@roosevelt.edu. *Dean,* John Cicero, 312-281-3376.

Walter E. Heller College of Business Administration Students: 175 full-time (93 women), 710 part-time (422 women); includes 313 minority (178 African Americans, 1 American Indian/Alaska Native, 71 Asian Americans or Pacific Islanders, 63 Hispanic Americans), 54 international. Average age 32. 1,468 applicants, 56% accepted, 293 enrolled. Expenses: Contact institution. *Financial support:* Career-related internships or fieldwork, Federal Work-Study, and tuition waivers (partial) available. Support available to part-time students. Financial award application deadline: 2/15. In 2008, 281 master's awarded. *Degree program information:* Part-time and evening/weekend programs available. Offers accounting (MSA); business administration (MBA, MS, MSA, MSHRM, MSIB, MSIS, Certificate); commercial real estate development (Certificate); human resource management (MSHRM); information systems (MSIS); international business (MSIB); real estate (MBA, MS). *Application deadline:* For fall admission, 6/1 priority date for domestic students. Applications are processed on a rolling basis. *Application fee:* $25 ($35 for international students). *Application Contact:* Joanne Canyon-Heller, Coordinator of Graduate Admission, 877-APPLY RU, Fax: 312-281-3356, E-mail: applyru@roosevelt.edu. *Interim Dean,* Joe Chan, 312-281-3254.

See Close-Up on page 975.

ROSALIND FRANKLIN UNIVERSITY OF MEDICINE AND SCIENCE, North Chicago, IL 60064-3095

General Information Independent, coed, graduate-only institution. *Enrollment:* 1,687 matriculated graduate/professional students. *Graduate faculty:* 829. *Graduate housing:* Rooms and/or apartments available on a first-come, first-served basis to single and married students. Typical cost: $8863 per year for single students; $11,700 per year for married students. Room charges vary according to housing facility selected. Housing application deadline: 3/13. *Student services:* Campus employment opportunities, free psychological counseling, low-cost health insurance, multicultural affairs office. *Library facilities:* Boxer University Library plus 1 other. *Online resources:* library catalog, web page. *Collection:* 120,000 titles, 2,296 serial subscriptions, 222 audiovisual materials. *Research affiliation:* Argonne National Laboratory (medical physics), Veterans Administration Hospital (pulmonary medicine).

Computer facilities: 200 computers available on campus for general student use. A campuswide network can be accessed from student residence rooms and from off campus. Online class registration is available. *Web address:* http://www.rosalindfranklin.edu/.

General Application Contact: Caryn F. Wickersheim, IGPBS Coordinator, 866-984-4727, E-mail: IGPBS@rosalindfranklin.edu.

GRADUATE UNITS

The Chicago Medical School Offers medicine (MD).

College of Health Professions *Faculty:* 39 full-time (26 women), 48 part-time/adjunct (22 women). Expenses: Contact institution. *Financial support:* Fellowships, research assistantships, teaching assistantships, career-related internships or fieldwork, Federal Work-Study, institutionally sponsored loans, scholarships/grants, and tuition waivers (partial) available. Support available to part-time students. Financial award applicants required to submit FAFSA. *Degree program information:* Part-time programs available. Postbaccalaureate distance learning degree programs offered (minimal on-campus study). Offers biomedical sciences (MS); clinical counseling (MS); clinical laboratory science (MS); clinical nutrition (MS); health professions (MS, D Sc, DPT, PhD, TDPT, Certificate); healthcare administration and management (MS, Certificate); interprofessional healthcare (D Sc, PhD); interprofessional studies (D Sc); medical radiation physics (MS); nurse anesthesia (MS); nutrition education (MS); pathologists' assistant (MS); physical therapy (MS, DPT, TDPT); physician assistant (MS); psychology (MS, PhD); women's healthcare studies (MS, Certificate). *Application deadline:* Applications are processed on a rolling basis. *Application fee:* $25. *Application Contact:* Caryn Wickersheim, Admissions Officer, 847-578-3209. *Dean,* Dr. Wendy Rheault, 847-578-8805, E-mail: wendy.rheault@rosalindfranklin.edu.

The Dr. William M. Scholl College of Podiatric Medicine Offers podiatric medicine (DPM).

School of Graduate and Postdoctoral Studies—Interdisciplinary Graduate Program in Biomedical Sciences Expenses: Contact institution. *Financial support:* In 2008–09, fellowships (averaging $23,665 per year), research assistantships (averaging $23,665 per year) were awarded; teaching assistantships, career-related internships or fieldwork, scholarships/grants, and tuition waivers (full and partial) also available. Financial award applicants required to submit FAFSA. Offers biochemistry and molecular biology (MS, PhD); cell biology and anatomy (MS, PhD); cellular and molecular pharmacology (MS, PhD); microbiology and immunology (MS, PhD); neuroscience (PhD); physiology and biophysics (MS, PhD). *Application deadline:* For fall admission, 1/15 priority date for domestic and international students. *Application Contact:* Caryn F. Wickersheim, IGPBS Coordinator, 866-984-4727, E-mail: IGPBS@rosalindfranklin.edu. *Dean/Vice President for Research,* Dr. Michael P. Sarras, 847-578-3251, E-mail: Michael.Sarras@rosalindfranklin.edu.

ROSE-HULMAN INSTITUTE OF TECHNOLOGY, Terre Haute, IN 47803-3999

General Information Independent, coed, primarily men, comprehensive institution. *Enrollment:* 1,923 graduate, professional, and undergraduate students; 39 full-time matriculated graduate/professional students (10 women), 52 part-time matriculated graduate/professional students (8 women). *Enrollment by degree level:* 91 master's. *Graduate faculty:* 94 full-time (21 women), 3 part-time/adjunct (1 woman). *Tuition:* Full-time $33,000; part-time $987 per credit hour. *Graduate housing:* On-campus housing not available. *Student services:* Campus employment opportunities, career counseling, exercise/wellness program, free psychological counseling, international student services, low-cost health insurance, services for students with disabilities. *Library facilities:* John A. Logan Library. *Online resources:* library catalog, web page, access to other libraries' catalogs. *Collection:* 80,301 titles, 23,498 serial subscriptions, 930 audiovisual materials.

Computer facilities: Computer purchase and lease plans are available. 45 computers available on campus for general student use. A campuswide network can be accessed from student residence rooms and from off campus. Online class registration is available. *Web address:* http://www.rose-hulman.edu/.

Rose-Hulman Institute of Technology (continued)

General Application Contact: Dr. Daniel J. Moore, Associate Dean of the Faculty, 812-877-8110, Fax: 812-877-8061, E-mail: daniel.j.moore@rose-hulman.edu.

GRADUATE UNITS

Faculty of Engineering and Applied Sciences Students: 39 full-time (10 women), 52 part-time (8 women); includes 5 minority (1 African American, 4 Asian Americans or Pacific Islanders), 30 international. Average age 28. 55 applicants, 96% accepted, 25 enrolled. *Faculty:* 94 full-time (21 women), 3 part-time/adjunct (1 woman). Expenses: Contact institution. *Financial support:* In 2008–09, 22 students received support; fellowships with full and partial tuition reimbursements available, research assistantships with full and partial tuition reimbursements available, institutionally sponsored loans, scholarships/grants, and tuition waivers (full and partial) available. In 2008, 41 master's awarded. *Degree program information:* Part-time and evening/weekend programs available. Postbaccalaureate distance learning degree programs offered (minimal on-campus study). Offers biomedical engineering (MS); chemical engineering (MS); civil engineering (MS); electrical engineering (MS); engineering and applied sciences (MS); engineering management (MS); environmental engineering (MS); mechanical engineering (MS); optical engineering (MS). *Application deadline:* For fall admission, 2/1 priority date for domestic students. Applications are processed on a rolling basis. *Application fee:* $0. *Application Contact:* Dr. Daniel J. Moore, Associate Dean of the Faculty, 812-877-8110, Fax: 812-877-8061, E-mail: daniel.j.moore@rose-hulman.edu. *Associate Dean of the Faculty*, Dr. Daniel J. Moore, 812-877-8110, Fax: 812-877-8061, E-mail: daniel.j.moore@rose-hulman.edu.

ROSEMONT COLLEGE, Rosemont, PA 19010-1699

General Information Independent-religious, coed, comprehensive institution. *Graduate housing:* Room and/or apartments available to single students; on-campus housing not available to married students.

GRADUATE UNITS

Schools of Graduate and Professional Studies Students: 83 full-time (72 women), 302 part-time (251 women); includes 70 minority (56 African Americans, 6 Asian Americans or Pacific Islanders, 8 Hispanic Americans), 5 international. Average age 35. 101 applicants, 90% accepted, 86 enrolled. *Faculty:* 2 full-time (both women), 61 part-time/adjunct (35 women). Expenses: Contact institution. *Financial support:* In 2008–09, 49 students received support. Career-related internships or fieldwork and unspecified assistantships available. Support available to part-time students. Financial award applicants required to submit FAFSA. In 2008, 139 master's awarded. *Degree program information:* Part-time and evening/weekend programs available. Offers business administration (MBA); creative writing (MFA); elementary certification (MA); English and publishing (MA); English literature (MA); human services (MA); management (MSM); school counseling (MA). *Application deadline:* For fall admission, 8/1 for domestic and international students; for spring admission, 12/1 for domestic and international students. Applications are processed on a rolling basis. *Application fee:* $0. Electronic applications accepted. *Application Contact:* Karen Scales, Director, Enrollment and Student Services, 610-527-0200 Ext. 2187, Fax: 610-526-2964, E-mail: gradstudies@rosemont.edu. *Dean of Graduate Studies*, Dr. Judith Renyi, 610-527-0200 Ext. 2381, Fax: 610-526-2964, E-mail: jrenyi@rosemont.edu.

See Close-Up on page 977.

ROWAN UNIVERSITY, Glassboro, NJ 08028-1701

General Information State-supported, coed, comprehensive institution. CGS member. *Enrollment:* 10,271 graduate, professional, and undergraduate students; 229 full-time matriculated graduate/professional students (149 women), 601 part-time matriculated graduate/professional students (404 women). *Enrollment by degree level:* 696 master's, 134 doctoral. *Graduate faculty:* 116 full-time (50 women), 56 part-time/adjunct (24 women). Tuition, state resident: full-time $10,624; part-time $590 per credit. Tuition, nonresident: full-time $10,624; part-time $590 per credit. *Required fees:* $2258; $124.90 per credit. *Graduate housing:* Room and/or apartments available on a first-come, first-served basis to single students; on-campus housing not available to married students. Typical cost: $9616 (including board). Housing application deadline: 5/1. *Student services:* Campus employment opportunities, campus safety program, career counseling, child daycare facilities, exercise/wellness program, free psychological counseling, international student services, low-cost health insurance, multicultural affairs office, services for students with disabilities, teacher training, writing training. *Library facilities:* Keith and Shirley Campbell Library plus 2 others. *Online resources:* library catalog, web page, access to other libraries' catalogs. *Collection:* 430,903 titles, 35,610 serial subscriptions, 11,725 audiovisual materials.

Computer facilities: 1,200 computers available on campus for general student use. A campuswide network can be accessed from student residence rooms and from off campus. Online class registration, online library are available. *Web address:* http://www.rowan.edu/.

General Application Contact: Dr. Mira Lalovic-Hand, Dean, College of Professional and Continuing Education, 856-256-5120, Fax: 856-256-4436, E-mail: lalovic-hand@rowan.edu.

GRADUATE UNITS

Graduate School Students: 229 full-time (149 women), 601 part-time (404 women); includes 129 minority (60 African Americans, 2 American Indian/Alaska Native, 41 Asian Americans or Pacific Islanders, 26 Hispanic Americans). Average age 32. 433 applicants, 61% accepted, 198 enrolled. *Faculty:* 116 full-time (50 women), 56 part-time/adjunct (24 women). Expenses: Contact institution. *Financial support:* In 2008–09, 97 students received support. Career-related internships or fieldwork, Federal Work-Study, scholarships/grants, health care benefits, and unspecified assistantships available. Support available to part-time students. In 2008, 317 master's, 28 doctorates awarded. *Degree program information:* Part-time and evening/weekend programs available. *Application deadline:* Applications are processed on a rolling basis. *Application fee:* $50. Electronic applications accepted. *Application Contact:* Karen Haynes, Director of Graduate Admissions, 856-256-4052, Fax: 856-256-4436, E-mail: haynesk@rowan.edu. *Assistant Provost/Director of the Graduate School*, Dr. Mira Lalovic-Hand, 856-256-5120, E-mail: Lalovic-hand@rowan.edu.

College of Communication Students: 19 full-time (14 women), 31 part-time (20 women); includes 5 minority (2 African Americans, 1 Asian American or Pacific Islander, 2 Hispanic Americans). Average age 31. 29 applicants, 79% accepted, 15 enrolled. *Faculty:* 12 full-time (4 women), 3 part-time/adjunct (2 women). Expenses: Contact institution. *Financial support:* Career-related internships or fieldwork and unspecified assistantships available. Support available to part-time students. In 2008, 21 master's awarded. *Degree program information:* Part-time and evening/weekend programs available. Offers communication (MA); public relations (MA); writing (MA). *Application deadline:* For fall admission, 10/15 for domestic students; for spring admission, 2/15 for domestic students. Applications are processed on a rolling basis. *Application fee:* $50. Electronic applications accepted. *Application Contact:* Karen Haynes, Adviser, 856-256-4052, E-mail: haynesk@rowan.edu. *Interim Associate Provost/Director of Graduate School*, Dr. Mira Lalovic-Hand, 856-256-5120.

College of Education Students: 122 full-time (93 women), 431 part-time (326 women); includes 80 minority (47 African Americans, 2 American Indian/Alaska Native, 13 Asian Americans or Pacific Islanders, 18 Hispanic Americans). Average age 34. 217 applicants, 66% accepted, 115 enrolled. *Faculty:* 34 full-time (23 women), 36 part-time/adjunct (18 women). Expenses: Contact institution. *Financial support:* Career-related internships or fieldwork, Federal Work-Study, scholarships/grants, health care benefits, and unspecified assistantships available. Support available to part-time students. In 2008, 198 master's, 28 doctorates awarded. *Degree program information:* Part-time and evening/weekend programs available. Offers business administration (MA); collaborative teaching (MST); counseling in educational settings (MA); education (M Ed, MA, MST, MST, Ed D, Ed S); educational leadership (MA, Ed D); elementary education (MST); elementary school teaching (MA); higher education administration (MA); learning disabilities (MA); music education (MA); principal preparation (MA); reading education (MA); school administration (MA); school and public librarianship (MA); school business administration (MA); school psychology (MA, Ed S); secondary education (MST); special education (MA); standards-based practice (M Ed); subject matter teaching (MA); supervision and curriculum development (MA); teacher leadership (M Ed). *Application deadline:* For fall admission, 10/15 for domestic students; for spring admission, 2/15 for domestic students. Applications are processed on a rolling basis. *Application fee:* $50. Electronic applications accepted. *Application Contact:* Karen Haynes, Graduate Coordinator, 856-256-4052, Fax: 856-256-4436, E-mail: Haynes@rowan.edu. *Interim Associate Provost/Director of Graduate School*, Dr. Mira Lalovic-Hand, 856-256-5120.

College of Engineering Students: 26 full-time (7 women), 34 part-time (5 women); includes 17 minority (2 African Americans, 13 Asian Americans or Pacific Islanders, 2 Hispanic Americans). Average age 26. 44 applicants, 70% accepted, 27 enrolled. *Faculty:* 21 full-time (6 women), 4 part-time/adjunct (0 women). Expenses: Contact institution. *Financial support:* Career-related internships or fieldwork, Federal Work-Study, and unspecified assistantships available. Support available to part-time students. In 2008, 15 master's awarded. *Degree program information:* Part-time and evening/weekend programs available. Offers engineering (MEM, MS); engineering management (MEM). *Application deadline:* Applications are processed on a rolling basis. *Application fee:* $50. Electronic applications accepted. *Application Contact:* Dr. Ralph Dusseau, Program Adviser, 856-256-5332. *Dean*, Dr. Dianne Dorland, 856-256-5301.

College of Fine and Performing Arts Students: 9 full-time (4 women), 5 part-time (1 woman). Average age 31. 14 applicants, 36% accepted, 4 enrolled. *Faculty:* 14 full-time (2 women), 5 part-time/adjunct (1 woman). Expenses: Contact institution. *Financial support:* Career-related internships or fieldwork, scholarships/grants, health care benefits, and unspecified assistantships available. In 2008, 4 master's awarded. *Degree program information:* Part-time and evening/weekend programs available. Offers fine and performing arts (MA, MM, MST); performance (MM); theatre (MA); theatre education (MST). *Application deadline:* Applications are processed on a rolling basis. *Application fee:* $50. Electronic applications accepted. *Application Contact:* Karen Haynes, Graduate Coordinator, 856-256-4052, Fax: 856-256-4436, E-mail: Haynes@rowan.edu. *Interim Associate Provost/Director of Graduate School*, Dr. Mira Lalovic-Hand, 856-256-5120, E-mail: Lalovic-hand@rowan.edu.

College of Liberal Arts and Sciences Students: 27 full-time (17 women), 35 part-time (24 women); includes 8 minority (3 African Americans, 3 Asian Americans or Pacific Islanders, 2 Hispanic Americans). Average age 28. 58 applicants, 45% accepted, 19 enrolled. *Faculty:* 27 full-time (13 women), 5 part-time/adjunct (2 women). Expenses: Contact institution. *Financial support:* Career-related internships or fieldwork, Federal Work-Study, scholarships/grants, health care benefits, and unspecified assistantships available. Support available to part-time students. In 2008, 10 master's awarded. *Degree program information:* Part-time and evening/weekend programs available. Offers criminal justice (MA); liberal arts and sciences (MA); mathematics (MA); mental health counseling (MA); mental health counseling and applied psychology (MA). *Application deadline:* Applications are processed on a rolling basis. *Application fee:* $50. Electronic applications accepted. *Application Contact:* Karen Haynes, Graduate Coordinator, 856-256-4052, Fax: 856-256-4436, E-mail: Haynes@rowan.edu. *Interim Associate Provost/Director of Graduate School*, Dr. Mira Lalovic-Hand, 856-256-5120, E-mail: Lalovic-hand@rowan.edu.

William G. Rohrer College of Business Students: 26 full-time (14 women), 65 part-time (28 women); includes 19 minority (6 African Americans, 11 Asian Americans or Pacific Islanders, 2 Hispanic Americans). Average age 30. 81 applicants, 42% accepted, 18 enrolled. *Faculty:* 8 full-time (2 women), 3 part-time/adjunct (1 woman). Expenses: Contact institution. *Financial support:* Career-related internships or fieldwork, Federal Work-Study, scholarships/grants, health care benefits, and unspecified assistantships available. In 2008, 29 master's awarded. *Degree program information:* Part-time and evening/weekend programs available. Offers business (MBA). *Application deadline:* Applications are processed on a rolling basis. *Application fee:* $50. Electronic applications accepted. *Application Contact:* Karen Haynes, Graduate Coordinator, 856-256-4052, E-mail: Haynes@rowan.edu. *Interim Associate Provost/Director of Graduate School*, Dr. Mira Lalovic-Hand, 856-256-5120, E-mail: Lalovic-hand@rowan.edu.

ROYAL MILITARY COLLEGE OF CANADA, Kingston, ON K7K 7B4, Canada

General Information Federally supported, coed, comprehensive institution. *Enrollment:* 340 full-time matriculated graduate/professional students (76 women), 261 part-time matriculated graduate/professional students (57 women). *Enrollment by degree level:* 530 master's, 71 doctoral. *Graduate faculty:* 172 full-time. *Graduate tuition:* Tuition charges are reported in Canadian dollars. *Tuition, area resident:* Part-time $950 Canadian dollars per course. Tuition and fees vary according to program. *Library facilities:* Massey Library plus 1 other. *Online resources:* library catalog, web page. *Collection:* 300,000 titles, 1,100 serial subscriptions, 2,510 audiovisual materials.

Computer facilities: A campuswide network can be accessed from student residence rooms and from off campus. *Web address:* http://www.rmc.ca/.

General Application Contact: Suzanne Paquette, Administrative Assistant, Division of Graduate Studies, 613-541-6000 Ext. 3728, Fax: 613-542-8612, E-mail: suzanne.paquette@rmc.ca.

GRADUATE UNITS

Division of Graduate Studies and Research Students: 340 full-time (76 women), 261 part-time (57 women). Expenses: Contact institution. *Financial support:* Fellowships with full tuition reimbursements, research assistantships with partial tuition reimbursements, teaching assistantships with partial tuition reimbursements, tuition waivers (partial) available. *Degree program information:* Part-time programs available. Postbaccalaureate distance learning degree programs offered (minimal on-campus study). *Application deadline:* For fall admission, 5/1 priority date for domestic students; for winter admission, 9/1 priority date for domestic students. Applications are processed on a rolling basis. *Application fee:* $50. Electronic applications accepted. *Application Contact:* Suzanne Paquette, Administrative Assistant, Graduate Studies, 613-541-6000 Ext. 3728, Fax: 613-542-8612, E-mail: suzanne.paquette@rmc.ca. *Dean*, Dr. B. J. Fugere, 613-541-6000 Ext. 3854, Fax: 613-542-8612, E-mail: fugere-j@rmc.ca.

Continuing Studies Expenses: Contact institution. Offers business administration (MBA); defense management and policy (MA); history (PhD); war studies (MA). *Application deadline:* For fall admission, 5/1 priority date for domestic students; for winter admission, 9/1 priority date for domestic students. Applications are processed on a rolling basis. *Application fee:* $50. Electronic applications accepted. *Application Contact:* Suzanne Paquette, Administrative Assistant, Graduate Studies, 613-541-6000 Ext. 3728, Fax: 613-542-8612, E-mail: suzanne.paquette@rmc.ca. *Dean*, Dr. M. A. Hennessy, 613-541-6000 Ext. 6845, Fax: 613-542-8612, E-mail: hennessy-m@rmc.ca.

Engineering Division Expenses: Contact institution. Offers chemical and materials (M Eng); chemical and materials science (M Sc, PhD); chemistry (M Eng); civil engineering (M Eng, MA Sc, PhD); computer engineering (M Eng, PhD); electrical engineering (M Eng, PhD); engineering (M Eng, M Sc, MA Sc, PhD); environmental (PhD); environmental engineering (M Eng, PhD); environmental science (M Sc, PhD); mechanical engineering (M Eng, MA Sc, PhD); nuclear (PhD); nuclear engineering (M Eng, MA Sc, PhD); nuclear science (M Sc, PhD); software engineering (M Eng, PhD). *Application deadline:* For fall admission, 5/1 priority date for domestic students; for winter admission, 9/1 priority date for domestic students. Applications are processed on a rolling basis. *Application fee:* $50. Electronic applications accepted. *Application Contact:* Suzanne Paquette, Administrative Assistant, Graduate Studies, 613-541-6000 Ext. 3728, Fax: 613-542-8612, E-mail: suzanne.paquette@rmc.ca. *Dean*, Dr. Allen A. Stewart, 613-541-6000 Ext. 6371, Fax: 613-542-8612, E-mail: stewart-j@rmc.ca.

Science Division Expenses: Contact institution. Offers chemical engineering (M Eng, MA Sc, PhD); chemistry (M Sc, PhD); computer science (M Sc); mathematics (M Sc); physics (M Sc); science (M Eng, M Sc, MA Sc, PhD). *Application deadline:* For fall admission, 5/1 priority date for domestic students; for winter admission, 9/1 priority date for domestic students. Applications are processed on a rolling basis. *Application fee:* $50. Electronic applications accepted. *Application Contact:* Suzanne Paquette, Administrative Assistant, Graduate Studies, 613-541-6000 Ext. 3728, Fax: 613-542-8612, E-mail: suzanne.paquette@

rmc.ca. *Dean of Science*, Dr. Richard Marsden, 613-541-6000 Ext. 6413, Fax: 613-542-8612, E-mail: marsden-r@rmc.ca.

ROYAL ROADS UNIVERSITY, Victoria, BC V9B 5Y2, Canada

General Information Province-supported, coed, upper-level institution. *Graduate housing:* Room and/or apartments available on a first-come, first-served basis to single students; on-campus housing not available to married students.

GRADUATE UNITS

Graduate Studies Postbaccalaureate distance learning degree programs offered (minimal on-campus study). Offers conflict analysis (G Dip); conflict analysis and management (MA); destination development (Graduate Certificate); disaster and emergency management (MA); environment and management (M Sc, MA); environmental education and communication (MA, G Dip, Graduate Certificate); executive coaching (Graduate Certificate); health systems leadership (Graduate Certificate); human security and peacebuilding (MA); international hotel management (MA); project management (Graduate Certificate); public relations management (Graduate Certificate); strategic human resources management (Graduate Certificate); sustainable tourism (Graduate Certificate); tourism leadership (Graduate Certificate); tourism management (MA). Electronic applications accepted.

Faculty of Management Postbaccalaureate distance learning degree programs offered (minimal on-campus study). Offers digital technologies management (MBA); executive management (MBA); human resources management (MBA). Electronic applications accepted.

RUSH UNIVERSITY, Chicago, IL 60612-3832

General Information Independent, coed, upper-level institution. CGS member. *Graduate housing:* Rooms and/or apartments available on a first-come, first-served basis to single and married students. Housing application deadline: 6/1.

GRADUATE UNITS

College of Health Sciences *Degree program information:* Part-time and evening/weekend programs available. Offers audiology (Au D); clinical laboratory management (MS); clinical laboratory science (MS); clinical nutrition (MS); health sciences (MA, MS, Au D, DHSc, Graduate Certificate); health systems management (MS, DHSc); healthcare ethics (MA, Graduate Certificate); occupational therapy (MS); speech-language pathology (MS). Electronic applications accepted.

College of Nursing *Degree program information:* Part-time programs available. Postbaccalaureate distance learning degree programs offered (minimal on-campus study). Offers acute care nurse practitioner (MSN, Post-Master's Certificate); adult health nursing (DNP, PhD); adult nurse practitioner (MSN, Post-Master's Certificate); adult/gerontological nurse practitioner (MSN); anesthesia nurse practitioner (MSN, Post-Master's Certificate); community and mental health nursing (DNP, PhD); critical care clinical specialist (MSN); family nurse practitioner (MSN, Post-Master's Certificate); gerontological nurse practitioner (MSN, Post-Master's Certificate); medical surgical clinical specialist (MSN); neonatal nurse practitioner (MSN, Post-Master's Certificate); nursing (MSN, DNP, PhD, Post-Master's Certificate); pediatric acute/chronic care nurse practitioner (MSN); pediatric clinical nurse specialist (MSN); pediatric nurse practitioner (MSN, Post-Master's Certificate); psychiatric clinical specialist (MSN); psychiatric nurse practitioner—adult (MSN); psychiatric nurse practitioner—family (MSN); psychiatric-mental health clinical specialist (Post-Master's Certificate); psychiatric-mental health nurse practitioner (Post-Master's Certificate); public health nursing (MSN); women's and children's health nursing (DNP, PhD). Electronic applications accepted.

Graduate College *Degree program information:* Part-time programs available. Offers anatomy and cell biology (MS, PhD); biochemistry (PhD); clinical research (MS); immunology (MS, PhD); medical physics (MS, PhD); microbiology (PhD); pharmacology (MS, PhD); physiology (PhD); virology (MS, PhD). Electronic applications accepted.

Division of Neuroscience Offers neuroscience (MS, PhD). Electronic applications accepted.

Rush Medical College Offers medicine (MD). Electronic applications accepted.

RUTGERS, THE STATE UNIVERSITY OF NEW JERSEY, CAMDEN, Camden, NJ 08102-1401

General Information State-supported, coed, university. *Graduate housing:* Rooms and/or apartments available to single and married students.

GRADUATE UNITS

Graduate School of Arts and Sciences *Degree program information:* Part-time and evening/weekend programs available. Offers American and public history (MA); biology (MS); chemistry (MS); childhood studies (MA, PhD); computer science (MS); creative writing (MFA); criminal justice (MA); education policy and leadership (MPA); English (MA); international public service and development (MPA); liberal studies (MALS); mathematics (MS); physical therapy (DPT); psychology (MA); public management (MPA). Electronic applications accepted.

School of Business *Degree program information:* Part-time and evening/weekend programs available. Offers business (MBA). Electronic applications accepted.

School of Law *Degree program information:* Part-time and evening/weekend programs available. Offers law (JD). Electronic applications accepted.

RUTGERS, THE STATE UNIVERSITY OF NEW JERSEY, NEWARK, Newark, NJ 07102

General Information State-supported, coed, university. CGS member. *Graduate housing:* Room and/or apartments available to single students; on-campus housing not available to married students. Housing application deadline: 5/15.

GRADUATE UNITS

Graduate School *Degree program information:* Part-time and evening/weekend programs available. Offers accounting (PhD); accounting information systems (PhD); American political system (MA); American studies (MA, PhD); analytical chemistry (MS, PhD); applied physics (MS, PhD); biochemistry (MS, PhD); biology (MS, PhD); cognitive neuroscience (PhD); cognitive science (PhD); computational biology (MS); computer information systems (PhD); creative writing (MFA); economics (MA); English (MA); environmental geology (MS); environmental science (MS, PhD); finance (PhD); health care administration (MPA); history (MA, MAT); human resources administration (MPA); information technology (PhD); inorganic chemistry (MS, PhD); integrative neuroscience (PhD); international business (PhD); international relations (MA); jazz history and research (MA); liberal studies (MALS); management science (PhD); marketing (PhD); mathematical sciences (PhD); nursing (MS); organic chemistry (MS, PhD); organization management (PhD); perception (PhD); physical chemistry (MS, PhD); psychobiology (PhD); public administration (PhD); public management (MPA); public policy analysis (MPA); social cognition (PhD); urban systems (PhD); urban systems and issues (MPA). Electronic applications accepted.

Division of Global Affairs *Degree program information:* Part-time and evening/weekend programs available. Offers global affairs (MS, PhD). Electronic applications accepted.

School of Criminal Justice Offers criminal justice (MA, PhD). Electronic applications accepted.

Rutgers Business SchoolûNewark and New Brunswick *Degree program information:* Part-time and evening/weekend programs available. Offers accounting (PhD); accounting information systems (PhD); business (M Accy, MBA, MQF, PhD, Certificate); business environment (MBA); customized concentration (MBA); finance (PhD); finance and economics (MBA, MQF); global business (MBA); government financial management (Certificate); governmental accounting (M Accy); individualized study (PhD); information technology (PhD); international business (PhD); management and business strategy (MBA); management science (PhD); management science and information systems (MBA); marketing (MBA); organizational management (PhD); professional accounting (MBA); supply chain management (PhD); taxation (M Accy). Electronic applications accepted.

School of Law *Degree program information:* Part-time and evening/weekend programs available. Offers law (JD).

See Close-Up on page 979.

RUTGERS, THE STATE UNIVERSITY OF NEW JERSEY, NEW BRUNSWICK, Piscataway, NJ 08854-8097

General Information State-supported, coed, university. CGS member. *Graduate housing:* Rooms and/or apartments available to single and married students.

GRADUATE UNITS

Edward J. Bloustein School of Planning and Public Policy *Degree program information:* Part-time and evening/weekend programs available. Offers planning and public policy (MCRP, MCRS, MPAP, MPH, MPP, Dr PH, PhD); public health (MPH, Dr PH, PhD); public policy (MPAP, MPP); urban planning and policy development (MCRP, MCRS, PhD). Electronic applications accepted.

Ernest Mario School of Pharmacy Offers medicinal chemistry (MS, PhD); pharamceutical science (PhD); pharmaceutical science (MS); pharmacy (Pharm D). Electronic applications accepted.

Graduate School *Degree program information:* Part-time and evening/weekend programs available. Postbaccalaureate distance learning degree programs offered. Offers African-American history (PhD); air pollution and resources (MS, PhD); American politics (PhD); anthropology (MA, PhD); applied mathematics (MS, PhD); applied microbiology (MS, PhD); applied statistics (MS); aquatic biology (MS, PhD); aquatic chemistry (MS, PhD); art history (MA, PhD); astronomy (MS, PhD); atmospheric science (MS, PhD); behavioral neuroscience (PhD); bilingualism and second language acquisition (MA, PhD); biochemistry (PhD); biological chemistry (MS, PhD); biomedical engineering (MS, PhD); biophysics (PhD); biostatistics (MS); cell and developmental biology (MS, PhD); cellular and molecular pharmacology (PhD); chemical and biochemical engineering (MS, PhD); chemistry and physics of aerosol and hydrosol systems (MS, PhD); civil and environmental engineering (MS, PhD); classics (MA, MAT, PhD); clinical microbiology (MS, PhD); clinical psychology (PhD); cognitive psychology (PhD); communications and solid-state electronics (MS, PhD); comparative literature (MA, PhD); comparative politics (PhD); computational biology and molecular biophysics (PhD); computational molecular biology (PhD); computer engineering (MS, PhD); computer science (MS, PhD); condensed matter physics (MS, PhD); control systems (MS, PhD); curatorial studies (Certificate); data mining (MS); design and control (MS, PhD); digital signal processing (MS, PhD); early American history (PhD); early modern European history (PhD); east Asian history (PhD); ecology and evolution (MS, PhD); economics (MA, PhD); elementary particle physics (MS, PhD); endocrinology and animal biosciences (MS, PhD); entomology (MS, PhD); environmental chemistry (MS, PhD); environmental microbiology (MS, PhD); environmental toxicology (MS, PhD); exposure assessment (PhD); fate and effects of pollutants (MS, PhD); fluid mechanics (MS, PhD); food and business economics (MS); food science (M Phil, MS, PhD); French (MA, PhD); French studies (MAT); geography (MA, MS, PhD); geological sciences (MS, PhD); German (MAT, PhD); German literature (MA, PhD); global and comparative history (PhD); historic preservation (Certificate); history (PhD); history of diplomacy and foreign relations (PhD); history of technology, environment and health (PhD); history of the Atlantic cultures and African diaspora (PhD); horticulture and plant technology (MS, PhD); immunology (MS, PhD); industrial and systems engineering (MS, PhD); industrial-occupational toxicology (MS, PhD); information technology (MS); inorganic chemistry (MS, PhD); interdisciplinary classical studies and ancient history (MA, PhD); interdisciplinary health psychology (PhD); intermediate energy nuclear physics (MS); international relations (PhD); Italian (MA, PhD); Italian literature and literary criticism (MA); language, literature and culture (MAT); Latin American history (PhD); linguistics (PhD); literatures in English (PhD); manufacturing systems engineering (MS); materials science and engineering (MS, PhD); mathematics (MS, PhD); mechanics (MS, PhD); medieval history (PhD); microbial biochemistry (MS, PhD); microbiology and molecular genetics (MS, PhD); modern European history (PhD); molecular and cellular biology (MS, PhD); molecular genetics (MS, PhD); neuroscience (PhD); nineteenth and twentieth century American history (PhD); nuclear physics (MS, PhD); nutritional sciences (MS, PhD); nutritional toxicology (MS, PhD); oceanography (MS, PhD); operations research (PhD); organic chemistry (MS, PhD); organismal and population biology (MS, PhD); pharmaceutical toxicology (MS, PhD); philosophy (PhD); physical chemistry (MS, PhD); physics (MST); plant pathology (MS, PhD); political theory (PhD); pollution prevention and control (MS, PhD); public law (PhD); quality and productivity management (MS); quality and reliability engineering (MS); social psychology (PhD); sociology (MA, PhD); solid mechanics (MS, PhD); Spanish (MA, MAT, PhD); Spanish literature (MA, PhD); statistics (MS, PhD); surface science (PhD); theoretical physics (MS, PhD); thermal sciences (MS, PhD); translation (MA); virology (MS, PhD); water and wastewater treatment (MS, PhD); water resources (MS, PhD); women and politics (PhD); women's and gender history (PhD); women's and gender studies (MA, PhD).

Graduate School of Applied and Professional Psychology Offers applied and professional psychology (Psy M, Psy D); clinical psychology (Psy M, Psy D); organizational psychology (Psy M, Psy D); school psychology (Psy M, Psy D). Electronic applications accepted.

Graduate School of Education *Degree program information:* Part-time and evening/weekend programs available. Offers counseling psychology (Ed M); early childhood/elementary education (Ed M, Ed D); education (Ed M, Ed D, PhD); educational administration and supervision (Ed M, Ed D); educational policy (PhD); educational psychology (PhD); educational statistics, measurement and evaluation (Ed M); English as a second language education (Ed M); English education (Ed M); language education (Ed M, Ed D); learning, cognition and development (Ed M); literacy education (Ed M, Ed D); mathematics education (Ed M, Ed D, PhD); reading education (Ed M); science education (Ed M, Ed D); social and philosophical foundations of education (Ed M, Ed D); social studies education (Ed M, Ed D); special education (Ed M, Ed D). Electronic applications accepted.

Mason Gross School of the Arts *Degree program information:* Part-time programs available. Offers acting (MFA); arts (MFA, MM, DMA, AD); collaborative piano (MM, DMA); conducting: choral (MM, DMA); conducting: instrumental (MM, DMA); conducting: orchestral (MM, DMA); design (MFA); directing (MFA); drawing (MFA); jazz studies (MM); music (DMA, AD); music education (MM, DMA); music performance (MM); painting (MFA); playwriting (MFA); sculpture (MFA); stage management (MFA).

School of Communication, Information and Library Studies *Degree program information:* Part-time programs available. Postbaccalaureate distance learning degree programs offered (no on-campus study). Offers communication and information studies (MCIS); communication, information and library studies (MCIS, MLS, PhD); communication, library and information science and media studies (PhD); library and information science (MLS). Electronic applications accepted.

School of Management and Labor Relations *Degree program information:* Part-time and evening/weekend programs available. Offers human resource management (MHRM); industrial relations and human resources (PhD); labor and employment relations (MLER). Electronic applications accepted.

School of Social Work *Degree program information:* Part-time programs available. Offers social work (MSW, PhD). Electronic applications accepted.

RYERSON UNIVERSITY, Toronto, ON M5B 2K3, Canada

General Information Province-supported, coed, comprehensive institution. CGS member.

GRADUATE UNITS

School of Graduate Studies Offers photographic preservation and collections management (MA).

SACRED HEART MAJOR SEMINARY, Detroit, MI 48206-1799

General Information Independent-religious, coed, comprehensive institution. *Graduate housing:* Room and/or apartments guaranteed to single students; on-campus housing not available to married students. Housing application deadline: 8/1.

Sacred Heart Major Seminary (continued)

GRADUATE UNITS

School of Theology *Degree program information:* Part-time and evening/weekend programs available. Offers pastoral studies (MAPS); theology (M Div, MA).

SACRED HEART SCHOOL OF THEOLOGY, Hales Corners, WI 53130-0429

General Information Independent-religious, coed, primarily men, graduate-only institution. *Graduate housing:* Room and/or apartments guaranteed to single students; on-campus housing not available to married students.

GRADUATE UNITS

Graduate and Professional Programs *Degree program information:* Part-time programs available. Offers theology (M Div, MA).

SACRED HEART UNIVERSITY, Fairfield, CT 06825-1000

General Information Independent-religious, coed, comprehensive institution. *Graduate housing:* On-campus housing not available.

GRADUATE UNITS

Graduate Programs *Degree program information:* Part-time and evening/weekend programs available. Postbaccalaureate distance learning degree programs offered (minimal on-campus study). Electronic applications accepted.

College of Arts and Sciences *Degree program information:* Part-time and evening/weekend programs available. Offers arts and sciences (MA, MS, CPS); chemistry (MS); computer science (MS); criminal justice (MA); database (CPS); information technology (MS, CPS); information technology and network security (CPS); interactive multimedia (CPS); religious studies (MA); Web development (CPS). Electronic applications accepted.

College of Education and Health Professions *Degree program information:* Part-time and evening/weekend programs available. Postbaccalaureate distance learning degree programs offered (minimal on-campus study). Offers administration (CAS); clinical nurse leader (MSN); education and health professions (MAT, MS, MSN, MSOT, DPT, CAS); educational technology (MAT); elementary education (MAT); exercise science and nutrition (MS); family nurse practitioner (MSN); geriatric health and wellness (MS); occupational therapy (MSOT); patient care services administration (MSN); physical therapy (DPT); reading (CAS); secondary education (MAT); teaching (CAS). Electronic applications accepted.

John F. Welch College of Business *Degree program information:* Part-time and evening/weekend programs available. Offers business (MBA). Electronic applications accepted.

SAGE GRADUATE SCHOOL, Troy, NY 12180-4115

General Information Independent, coed, graduate-only institution. *Enrollment by degree level:* 776 master's, 155 doctoral, 32 other advanced degrees. *Graduate faculty:* 50 full-time (42 women), 58 part-time/adjunct (40 women). *Tuition:* Full-time $10,080; part-time $560 per credit hour. *Graduate housing:* Room and/or apartments available on a first-come, first-served basis to single students; on-campus housing not available to married students. Typical cost: $4700 per year ($9200 including board). Housing application deadline: 5/1. *Student services:* Career counseling, low-cost health insurance. *Library facilities:* James Wheelock Clark Library plus 1 other. *Online resources:* library catalog, web page. *Collection:* 240,916 titles, 488 serial subscriptions, 35,188 audiovisual materials. *Research affiliation:* Samuel Stratton Veterans Administration Hospital (nursing), Ellis Hospital (nursing), Samaritan Hospital (nursing), Albany Medical College (occupational therapy), Enlarged City School District of Troy (education).

Computer facilities: 340 computers available on campus for general student use. A campuswide network can be accessed from student residence rooms and from off campus. Online class registration is available. *Web address:* http://www.sage.edu/.

General Application Contact: Wendy D. Diefendorf, Director of Graduate and Adult Admission, 518-244-2443, Fax: 518-244-6880, E-mail: sgsadm@sage.edu.

GRADUATE UNITS

Graduate School Students: 338 full-time (289 women), 625 part-time (517 women); includes 84 minority (35 African Americans, 3 American Indian/Alaska Native, 18 Asian Americans or Pacific Islanders, 28 Hispanic Americans), 3 international. Average age 31. 563 applicants, 63% accepted, 240 enrolled. *Faculty:* 50 full-time (42 women), 58 part-time/adjunct (40 women). Expenses: Contact institution. *Financial support:* Fellowships, research assistantships, Federal Work-Study, scholarships/grants, tuition waivers (partial), and unspecified assistantships available. Support available to part-time students. Financial award application deadline: 3/1; financial award applicants required to submit FAFSA. In 2008, 292 master's, 42 doctorates, 22 other advanced degrees awarded. *Degree program information:* Part-time and evening/weekend programs available. Offers adult health (MS); adult nurse practitioner (MS, Post Master's Certificate); applied behavior analysis and autism (MS); applied nutrition (MS); art education (MAT); business administration (MBA); business strategy (MBA); child care and children's services (MA); childhood education (MS Ed); childhood education/literacy (MS); childhood special education (MS Ed); clinical nurse leader/specialist (Post Master's Certificate); community counseling (MA); community health (MS); community health education (MA); community psychology (MA); counseling and community psychology (MA); dietetic internship (Certificate); education and leadership (DNS); educational leadership (Ed D); English (MAT); family nurse practitioner (MS, Post Master's Certificate); finance (MBA); forensic mental health (MS, Certificate); forensic psychology (Certificate); general psychology (MA); gerontological nurse practitioner (Post Master's Certificate); gerontology (MS); guidance and counseling (MS, Post Master's Certificate); health services administration (MS, Certificate); human resources (MBA); literacy (MS Ed); literacy/childhood special education (MS Ed); marketing (MBA); mathematics (MAT); nurse administrator/executive (Post Master's Certificate); nursing (Post Master's Certificate); nutrition (MS); occupational therapy (MS); organizational management (MS); physical therapy (DPT); psychiatric mental health (MS, Post Master's Certificate); psychiatric mental health nurse practitioner (MS, Post Master's Certificate); public administration (MS); school health education (MS); social studies (MAT); teaching (MAT). *Application deadline:* Applications are processed on a rolling basis. *Application fee:* $40. *Application Contact:* Wendy D. Diefendorf, Director of Graduate and Adult Admission, 518-244-2443, Fax: 518-244-6880, E-mail: diefew@sage.edu. *Dean,* Dr. John A. Tribble, 518-244-2264, E-mail: tribbj@sage.edu.

SAGINAW VALLEY STATE UNIVERSITY, University Center, MI 48710

General Information State-supported, coed, comprehensive institution. *Enrollment:* 9,837 graduate, professional, and undergraduate students; 239 full-time matriculated graduate/professional students (148 women), 1,408 part-time matriculated graduate/professional students (1,072 women). *Enrollment by degree level:* 1,574 master's, 73 other advanced degrees. *Graduate faculty:* 154 full-time (92 women), 74 part-time/adjunct (47 women). Tuition, state resident: full-time $8620; part-time $359.15 per credit hour. Tuition, nonresident: full-time $16,526; part-time $688.60 per credit hour. *Required fees:* $350.40; $14.60 per credit hour. Tuition and fees vary according to campus/location. *Graduate housing:* Room and/or apartments available on a first-come, first-served basis to single students; on-campus housing not available to married students. Typical cost: $3510 per year ($6240 including board). Room and board charges vary according to board plan and housing facility selected. Housing application deadline: 6/5. *Student services:* Campus employment opportunities, career counseling, exercise/wellness program, free psychological counseling, international student services, multicultural affairs office, services for students with disabilities, writing training. *Library facilities:* Zahnow Library. *Online resources:* library catalog, web page, access to other libraries' catalogs. *Collection:* 241,661 titles, 23,741 serial subscriptions, 25,099 audiovisual materials.

Computer facilities: 1,033 computers available on campus for general student use. A campuswide network can be accessed from student residence rooms and from off campus. Online class registration is available. *Web address:* http://www.svsu.edu/.

General Application Contact: P. Laine Blasch, Graduate Recruitment Coordinator, 989-964-2182, Fax: 989-790-0180, E-mail: blasch@svsu.edu.

GRADUATE UNITS

College of Arts and Behavioral Sciences Students: 34 full-time (20 women), 63 part-time (37 women); includes 17 minority (12 African Americans, 1 Asian American or Pacific Islander, 4 Hispanic Americans), 22 international. Average age 34. 50 applicants, 90% accepted, 29 enrolled. *Faculty:* 9 full-time (2 women), 8 part-time/adjunct (3 women). Expenses: Contact institution. *Financial support:* Federal Work-Study available. Support available to part-time students. Financial award applicants required to submit FAFSA. In 2008, 22 master's awarded. *Degree program information:* Part-time and evening/weekend programs available. Offers administrative science (MA); arts and behavioral sciences (MA); communication and digital media design (MA). *Application deadline:* Applications are processed on a rolling basis. *Application fee:* $25. Electronic applications accepted. *Application Contact:* Dr. Mary Hedberg, Dean, 989-964-4062, Fax: 989-964-7232, E-mail: hedberg@svsu.edu. *Dean,* Dr. Mary Hedberg, 989-964-4062, Fax: 989-964-7232, E-mail: hedberg@svsu.edu.

College of Business and Management Students: 70 full-time (30 women), 61 part-time (32 women); includes 7 minority (4 African Americans, 2 American Indian/Alaska Native, 1 Hispanic American), 67 international. Average age 29. 96 applicants, 93% accepted, 33 enrolled. *Faculty:* 23 full-time (4 women), 1 part-time/adjunct (0 women). Expenses: Contact institution. *Financial support:* Federal Work-Study and scholarships/grants available. Support available to part-time students. Financial award application deadline: 4/1; financial award applicants required to submit FAFSA. In 2008, 28 master's awarded. *Degree program information:* Part-time and evening/weekend programs available. Offers business administration (MBA); business and management (MBA). *Application deadline:* Applications are processed on a rolling basis. *Application fee:* $25. Electronic applications accepted. *Application Contact:* Dr. Marwan A. Wafa, Dean, 989-964-4064, Fax: 989-964-7497, E-mail: cbmdean@svsu.edu. *Dean,* Dr. Marwan A. Wafa, 989-964-4064, Fax: 989-964-7497, E-mail: cbmdean@svsu.edu.

College of Education Students: 63 full-time (41 women), 1,167 part-time (895 women); includes 51 minority (28 African Americans, 2 American Indian/Alaska Native, 6 Asian Americans or Pacific Islanders, 15 Hispanic Americans), 7 international. Average age 34. 258 applicants, 99% accepted, 205 enrolled. *Faculty:* 94 full-time (69 women), 53 part-time/adjunct (36 women). Expenses: Contact institution. *Financial support:* Federal Work-Study and scholarships/grants available. Support available to part-time students. Financial award applicants required to submit FAFSA. In 2008, 358 master's, 37 other advanced degrees awarded. *Degree program information:* Part-time and evening/weekend programs available. Offers adapted physical activity (MAT); chief business officers (M Ed); e-learning (MA); early childhood education (MAT); education (M Ed, MA, MAT, Ed S); education leadership (Ed S); educational administration and supervision (M Ed); elementary (MAT); elementary classroom teaching (MAT); instructional technology (MAT); learning and behavioral disorders (MAT); middle school (MAT); middle school classroom teaching (MAT); principalship (M Ed); reading education (MAT); secondary classroom teaching (MAT); secondary school (MAT); special education (MAT); superintendency (M Ed). *Application deadline:* Applications are processed on a rolling basis. *Application fee:* $25. Electronic applications accepted. *Application Contact:* Kathy Lopez, Certification Officer, 989-964-4661, Fax: 989-964-4385, E-mail: klopez@svsu.edu. *Dean,* Dr. Steve P. Barbus, 989-964-6067, Fax: 989-790-4385, E-mail: barbus@svsu.edu.

Crystal M. Lange College of Nursing and Health Sciences Students: 72 full-time (57 women), 117 part-time (108 women); includes 9 minority (4 African Americans, 2 Asian Americans or Pacific Islanders, 3 Hispanic Americans), 4 international. Average age 33. 48 applicants, 96% accepted, 37 enrolled. *Faculty:* 22 full-time (16 women), 8 part-time/adjunct (all women). Expenses: Contact institution. *Financial support:* Federal Work-Study and scholarships/grants available. Support available to part-time students. Financial award application deadline: 4/1; financial award applicants required to submit FAFSA. In 2008, 41 master's awarded. *Degree program information:* Part-time and evening/weekend programs available. Offers clinical nurse specialist (MSN); health leadership (MS); health system nurse specialist (MSN); nurse practitioner (MSN); nursing (MSN); nursing and health sciences (MS, MSN, MSOT); occupational therapy (MSOT). *Application deadline:* Applications are processed on a rolling basis. *Application fee:* $25. Electronic applications accepted. *Application Contact:* Dr. Janalou Blecke, Dean, 989-964-4145, Fax: 989-964-4024, E-mail: blecke@svsu.edu. *Dean,* Dr. Janalou Blecke, 989-964-4145, Fax: 989-964-4024, E-mail: blecke@svsu.edu.

ST. AMBROSE UNIVERSITY, Davenport, IA 52803-2898

General Information Independent-religious, coed, comprehensive institution. *Enrollment:* 3,794 graduate, professional, and undergraduate students; 291 full-time matriculated graduate/professional students (224 women), 554 part-time matriculated graduate/professional students (311 women). *Enrollment by degree level:* 705 master's, 140 doctoral. *Graduate faculty:* 63 full-time (26 women), 44 part-time/adjunct (20 women). *Tuition:* Part-time $672 per contact hour. Tuition and fees vary according to degree level, program and reciprocity agreements. *Graduate housing:* Room and/or apartments available on a first-come, first-served basis to single students; on-campus housing not available to married students. Typical cost: $3988 per year ($7825 including board). Room and board charges vary according to board plan and housing facility selected. Housing application deadline: 3/1. *Student services:* Campus employment opportunities, campus safety program, career counseling, free psychological counseling, international student services, multicultural affairs office, services for students with disabilities, teacher training, writing training. *Library facilities:* SAU Library plus 1 other. *Online resources:* library catalog, web page, access to other libraries' catalogs. *Collection:* 169,549 titles, 728 serial subscriptions, 3,822 audiovisual materials.

Computer facilities: 276 computers available on campus for general student use. A campuswide network can be accessed from student residence rooms and from off campus. Online class registration, online course syllabi, online class listings, and online payments are available. *Web address:* http://www.sau.edu/.

General Application Contact: Elizabeth Loveless, Director of Graduate Student Recruitment, 563-333-6271, Fax: 563-333-6268, E-mail: lovelesselizabethb@sau.edu.

GRADUATE UNITS

College of Arts and Sciences Students: 53 full-time (44 women), 39 part-time (26 women); includes 14 minority (5 African Americans, 2 American Indian/Alaska Native, 1 Asian American or Pacific Islander, 6 Hispanic Americans), 1 international. Average age 31. 76 applicants, 75% accepted, 41 enrolled. *Faculty:* 10 full-time (5 women), 9 part-time/adjunct (6 women). Expenses: Contact institution. *Financial support:* In 2008–09, 78 students received support, including 11 research assistantships with partial tuition reimbursements available (averaging $3,346 per year); career-related internships or fieldwork, scholarships/grants, tuition waivers (partial), and unspecified assistantships also available. Financial award application deadline: 8/15; financial award applicants required to submit FAFSA. In 2008, 56 master's awarded. *Degree program information:* Part-time and evening/weekend programs available. Offers arts and sciences (MCJ, MOL, MPS, MSW); criminal justice (MCJ); juvenile justice education (MCJ); pastoral studies (MPS); social work (MSW). *Application deadline:* For fall admission, 8/1 priority date for domestic students; for winter admission, 12/15 priority date for domestic students; for spring admission, 1/1 priority date for domestic students. Applications are processed on a rolling basis. *Application fee:* $25. Electronic applications accepted. *Application Contact:* Elizabeth Loveless, Director of Graduate Student Recruitment, 563-333-6271, Fax: 563-333-6268, E-mail: lovelesselizabethb@sau.edu. *Dean,* Dr. Aron R. Aji, 563-333-6053, Fax: 563-333-6052, E-mail: aronajir@sau.edu.

College of Business Students: 87 full-time (44 women), 420 part-time (219 women); includes 47 minority (23 African Americans, 1 American Indian/Alaska Native, 12 Asian Americans or Pacific Islanders, 11 Hispanic Americans), 4 international. Average age 34. 215 applicants, 85% accepted, 113 enrolled. *Faculty:* 29 full-time (5 women), 19 part-time/adjunct (5 women). Expenses: Contact institution. *Financial support:* In 2008–09, 124 students received support, including 12 research assistantships with partial tuition reimbursements available (averaging $3,450 per year); career-related internships or fieldwork, scholarships/grants, tuition waivers (partial), and unspecified assistantships also available. Financial award application deadline: 3/15; financial award applicants required to submit FAFSA. In 2008, 203 master's, 6 doctorates awarded. *Degree program information:* Part-time and evening/weekend programs available. Offers accounting (MAC); business (MAC, MBA, MOL, MSITM, DBA); business administration (DBA); health care (MBA); human resources (MBA); information technology management (MSITM); organizational leadership (MOL). *Application deadline:* For fall admission, 8/15 priority date for domestic students; for winter admission, 12/15 for domestic students; for spring admission, 1/1 for domestic students. Applications are processed on a rolling basis. *Application fee:* $25. Electronic applications accepted. *Application Contact:* Elizabeth Loveless, Director of Graduate Student Recruitment, 563-333-6271, Fax: 563-333-6268, E-mail: lovelesselizabethb@sau.edu. *Dean,* Dr. John P. Byrne, 563-333-6406, Fax: 563-333-6268, E-mail: byrnejohnp@sau.edu.

College of Education and Health Sciences Students: 151 full-time (136 women), 95 part-time (66 women); includes 6 minority (1 African American, 1 Asian American or Pacific Islander, 4 Hispanic Americans), 3 international. Average age 29. 225 applicants, 44% accepted, 78 enrolled. *Faculty:* 25 full-time (16 women), 15 part-time/adjunct (9 women). Expenses: Contact institution. *Financial support:* In 2008–09, 163 students received support, including 20 research assistantships with partial tuition reimbursements available (averaging $3,555 per year); career-related internships or fieldwork, scholarships/grants, tuition waivers (full and partial), and unspecified assistantships also available. Financial award application deadline: 3/15; financial award applicants required to submit FAFSA. In 2008, 78 master's, 44 doctorates awarded. *Degree program information:* Part-time and evening/weekend programs available. Postbaccalaureate distance learning degree programs offered (no on-campus study). Offers education and health sciences (M Ed, MEA, MOT, MSN, DPT); educational administration (MEA); nursing (MSN); occupational therapy (MOT); physical therapy (DPT); special education (M Ed); teaching (M Ed). *Application deadline:* For fall admission, 8/15 priority date for domestic students; for winter admission, 12/15 priority date for domestic students; for spring admission, 1/1 priority date for domestic students. Applications are processed on a rolling basis. *Application fee:* $25. Electronic applications accepted. *Application Contact:* Elizabeth Loveless, Director of Graduate Student Recruitment, 563-333-6271, Fax: 563-333-6268, E-mail: lovelesselizabethb@sau.edu. *Dean,* Dr. Robert Ristow, 563-333-6078, Fax: 563-333-6297, E-mail: ristowrobert@sau.edu.

ST. ANDREW'S COLLEGE, Saskatoon, SK S7N 0W3, Canada

General Information Independent-religious, coed, graduate-only institution.

GRADUATE UNITS

Graduate Programs in Theology Offers theology (M Div, MTS, STM).

ST. ANDREW'S COLLEGE IN WINNIPEG, Winnipeg, MB R3T 2M7, Canada

General Information Independent-religious, coed, primarily men, graduate-only institution. *Graduate housing:* Rooms and/or apartments available to single and married students. Housing application deadline: 7/31.

GRADUATE UNITS

Graduate Programs Offers theology (M Div).

ST. AUGUSTINE'S SEMINARY OF TORONTO, Scarborough, ON M1M 1M3, Canada

General Information Independent-religious, coed, primarily men, graduate-only institution. *Graduate housing:* On-campus housing not available.

GRADUATE UNITS

Graduate and Professional Programs *Degree program information:* Part-time and evening/weekend programs available. Offers divinity (M Div); lay ministry (Diploma); religious education (MRE); theological studies (MTS, Diploma).

SAINT BERNARD'S SCHOOL OF THEOLOGY AND MINISTRY, Rochester, NY 14618

General Information Independent-religious, coed, graduate-only institution. *Enrollment by degree level:* 23 first professional, 94 master's, 9 other advanced degrees. *Graduate faculty:* 3 full-time (2 women), 3 part-time/adjunct (1 woman). *Tuition:* Full-time $8400; part-time $1400 per course. *Required fees:* $30 per semester. *Graduate housing:* On-campus housing not available. *Student services:* Writing training. *Library facilities:* Rush Rhees Library at University of Rochester. *Online resources:* library catalog, access to other libraries' catalogs. *Collection:* 66,334 titles, 328 serial subscriptions, 335 audiovisual materials. *Research affiliation:* Colgate Rochester Divinity School.

Computer facilities: 2 computers available on campus for general student use. Word processing, scanning, image editing, chat utilities available. *Web address:* http://www.stbernards.edu/.

General Application Contact: Charmel Trinidad, Director of Admissions and Financial Aid, 585-271-3657 Ext. 289, Fax: 585-271-2045, E-mail: ctrinidad@stbernards.edu.

GRADUATE UNITS

Graduate and Professional Programs Students: 3 full-time (2 women), 126 part-time (55 women); includes 13 minority (7 African Americans, 1 American Indian/Alaska Native, 2 Asian Americans or Pacific Islanders, 3 Hispanic Americans). Average age 50. 40 applicants, 50% accepted, 20 enrolled. *Faculty:* 7 full-time (3 women), 4 part-time/adjunct (1 woman). Expenses: Contact institution. *Financial support:* In 2008–09, 33 students received support; fellowships, research assistantships, teaching assistantships, career-related internships or fieldwork, scholarships/grants, and tuition waivers (partial) available. Support available to part-time students. Financial award application deadline: 4/15; financial award applicants required to submit FAFSA. In 2008, 4 first professional degrees, 37 master's awarded. *Degree program information:* Part-time and evening/weekend programs available. Offers pastoral studies (MA, Certificate); theological studies (MA); theology (M Div). *Application deadline:* Applications are processed on a rolling basis. *Application fee:* $75. *Application Contact:* Charmel Trinidad, Director of Admissions and Financial Aid, 585-271-3657 Ext. 289, Fax: 585-271-2045, E-mail: strinidad@stbernards.edu. *President,* Dr. Patricia Schoelles, 585-271-3657 Ext. 276, Fax: 585-271-2045, E-mail: pschoelles@stbernards.edu.

ST. BONAVENTURE UNIVERSITY, St. Bonaventure, NY 14778-2284

General Information Independent-religious, coed, comprehensive institution. CGS member. *Graduate housing:* Room and/or apartments available to single students; on-campus housing not available to married students. Housing application deadline: 3/19.

GRADUATE UNITS

School of Graduate Studies *Degree program information:* Part-time and evening/weekend programs available.

School of Arts and Sciences *Degree program information:* Part-time and evening/weekend programs available. Offers arts and sciences (MA); English (MA).

School of Business *Degree program information:* Part-time and evening/weekend programs available. Offers accounting and finance (MBA); general business (MBA); international business (MBA); management and marketing (MBA); professional leadership (MS).

School of Education *Degree program information:* Part-time and evening/weekend programs available. Offers community mental health counselor (Adv C); counseling education-school (MS Ed); education (MS, MS Ed, Adv C); educational leadership (MS Ed); literacy (MS Ed); school building leader (Adv C); school counselor (Adv C); school district leader (Adv C); supervisor of curriculum and instruction (Adv C).

School of Franciscan Studies *Degree program information:* Part-time programs available. Offers Franciscan studies (MA, Adv C).

ST. CATHERINE UNIVERSITY, St. Paul, MN 55105-1789

General Information Independent-religious, Undergraduate: women only; graduate: coed, comprehensive institution. CGS member. *Enrollment:* 5,201 graduate, professional, and undergraduate students; 771 full-time matriculated graduate/professional students (695 women), 703 part-time matriculated graduate/professional students (645 women). *Enrollment by degree level:* 1,355 master's, 119 doctoral. *Graduate faculty:* 93 full-time (74 women). *Tuition:* Part-time $687 per credit. *Required fees:* $20 per term. Tuition and fees vary according to course load and program. *Graduate housing:* Rooms and/or apartments available on a first-come, first-served basis to single and married students. Typical cost: $7560 per year ($8320 including board) for single students; $4730 per year ($6470 including board) for married students. Room and board charges vary according to board plan and housing facility selected. Housing application deadline: 5/1. *Student services:* Campus employment opportunities, campus safety program, career counseling, free psychological counseling, international student services, low-cost health insurance, multicultural affairs office, writing training. *Library facilities:* St. Catherine Library plus 2 others. *Online resources:* library catalog, web page, access to other libraries' catalogs. *Collection:* 263,495 titles, 1,141 serial subscriptions.

Computer facilities: Computer purchase and lease plans are available. 350 computers available on campus for general student use. A campuswide network can be accessed from student residence rooms and from off campus. Transcript available. *Web address:* http://www.stkate.edu/.

General Application Contact: Sylvia Alexander-Sedey, Senior Admissions Counselor, 651-690-6933, Fax: 651-690-6064, E-mail: graduate_study@stkate.edu.

GRADUATE UNITS

Graduate Programs Students: 771 full-time (695 women), 703 part-time (645 women); includes 89 minority (33 African Americans, 4 American Indian/Alaska Native, 29 Asian Americans or Pacific Islanders, 23 Hispanic Americans), 19 international. Average age 35. 825 applicants, 69% accepted, 427 enrolled. *Faculty:* 93 full-time (74 women). Expenses: Contact institution. *Financial support:* In 2008–09, 552 students received support; research assistantships with tuition reimbursements available, career-related internships or fieldwork and institutionally sponsored loans available. Support available to part-time students. Financial award application deadline: 4/1; financial award applicants required to submit FAFSA. In 2008, 346 master's, 25 doctorates awarded. *Degree program information:* Part-time and evening/weekend programs available. Offers education–curriculum and instruction (MA); holistic health studies (MA); library and information science (MLIS); nursing (MA, DNP); occupational therapy (MA); organizational leadership (MA); physical therapy (DPT); social work (MSW); theology (MA). *Application fee:* $35. *Application Contact:* 651-690-6933, Fax: 651-690-6064. *Dean of Professional Studies,* Susan Cochrane, 651-690-6500, Fax: 651-690-6024.

ST. CHARLES BORROMEO SEMINARY, OVERBROOK, Wynnewood, PA 19096

General Information Independent-religious, Undergraduate: men only; graduate: coed, comprehensive institution. *Enrollment:* 243 graduate, professional, and undergraduate students; 58 full-time matriculated graduate/professional students, 46 part-time matriculated graduate/professional students (23 women). *Enrollment by degree level:* 47 first professional, 57 master's. *Graduate faculty:* 11 full-time (3 women), 12 part-time/adjunct (3 women). *Tuition:* Full-time $14,705; part-time $1351 per course. *Graduate housing:* Room and/or apartments guaranteed to single students; on-campus housing not available to married students. Typical cost: $8931 (including board). Housing application deadline: 7/15. *Student services:* Campus employment opportunities, career counseling. *Library facilities:* Ryan Memorial Library. *Online resources:* web page. *Collection:* 128,738 titles, 575 serial subscriptions, 17,187 audiovisual materials.

Computer facilities: 60 computers available on campus for general student use. A campuswide network can be accessed. Online class registration is available. *Web address:* http://www.scs.edu/.

General Application Contact: Rev. David E. Diamond, Vice Rector, 610-785-6271, Fax: 610-617-9267, E-mail: frdd@adphila.org.

GRADUATE UNITS

Graduate and Professional Programs Students: 58 full-time (0 women), 46 part-time (23 women); includes 9 minority (2 African Americans, 1 American Indian/Alaska Native, 3 Asian Americans or Pacific Islanders, 3 Hispanic Americans), 3 international. Average age 39. 27 applicants, 100% accepted, 26 enrolled. *Faculty:* 11 full-time (3 women), 12 part-time/adjunct (3 women). Expenses: Contact institution. *Financial support:* In 2008–09, 74 students received support. Federal Work-Study and scholarships/grants available. Financial award application deadline: 7/15; financial award applicants required to submit CSS PROFILE. In 2008, 13 first professional degrees, 32 master's awarded. *Degree program information:* Part-time programs available. Offers religious studies (MA); theology (M Div, MA). *Application deadline:* For fall admission, 7/15 for domestic students, 3/15 priority date for international students. Applications are processed on a rolling basis. *Application fee:* $0. *Application Contact:* Rev. David E. Diamond, Vice Rector, 610-785-6271, Fax: 610-617-9267, E-mail: frdd@adphila.org. *Rector and President,* Msgr. Joseph G. Prior, 610-785-6200, Fax: 610-667-7635, E-mail: igprior@adphila.org.

ST. CLOUD STATE UNIVERSITY, St. Cloud, MN 56301-4498

General Information State-supported, coed, comprehensive institution. CGS member. *Enrollment:* 16,921 graduate, professional, and undergraduate students; 671 full-time matriculated graduate/professional students (430 women), 1,200 part-time matriculated graduate/professional students (737 women). *Enrollment by degree level:* 1,849 master's, 22 doctoral. *Graduate faculty:* 540 full-time (194 women), 34 part-time/adjunct (16 women). Tuition, state resident: full-time $4404.20; part-time $275.20 per credit. Tuition, nonresident: full-time $6885; part-time $430.35 per credit. *Required fees:* $29.58 per credit. Tuition and fees vary according to course level, degree level, campus/location and reciprocity agreements. *Graduate housing:* Room and/or apartments available on a first-come, first-served basis to single students; on-campus housing not available to married students. Housing application deadline: 4/15. *Student services:* Campus employment opportunities, campus safety program, career counseling, child daycare facilities, exercise/wellness program, free psychological counseling, international student services, low-cost health insurance, multicultural affairs office, services for students with disabilities, writing training. *Library facilities:* James W. Miller Learning Resources Center. *Online resources:* library catalog, web page, access to other libraries' catalogs. *Collection:* 947,787 titles, 955 serial subscriptions, 26,927 audiovisual materials.

Computer facilities: Computer purchase and lease plans are available. 1,489 computers available on campus for general student use. A campuswide network can be accessed from student residence rooms and from off campus. Online class registration is available. *Web address:* http://www.stcloudstate.edu/.

General Application Contact: Annette Day, Director of Graduate Admissions, 320-308-2113, Fax: 320-308-5371, E-mail: aeday@stcloudstate.edu.

GRADUATE UNITS

School of Graduate Studies Students: 671 full-time (430 women), 1,200 part-time (737 women); includes 143 minority (46 African Americans, 12 American Indian/Alaska Native, 65 Asian Americans or Pacific Islanders, 20 Hispanic Americans), 242 international. Average age 31. 767 applicants, 64% accepted. *Faculty:* 540 full-time (194 women), 34 part-time/adjunct (16 women). Expenses: Contact institution. *Financial support:* In 2008–09, 250 research assistantships with partial tuition reimbursements (averaging $10,300 per year), 75 teaching assistantships with partial tuition reimbursements (averaging $10,300 per year) were awarded; career-related internships or fieldwork, Federal Work-Study, scholarships/grants, and unspecified assistantships also available. Financial award application deadline: 3/1; financial award applicants required to submit FAFSA. In 2008, 499 master's awarded. *Degree program information:* Part-time and evening/weekend programs available. Postbaccalaureate distance learning degree programs offered (no on-campus study). *Application deadline:* Applications are processed on a rolling basis. *Application fee:* $35. *Application Contact:* Linda Lou Krueger, School of Graduate Studies, 320-308-2113, Fax: 320-308-5371, E-mail: lekrueger@stcloudstate.edu. *Dean,* Dr. Dennis Nunes, 320-308-2113, Fax: 320-308-5371, E-mail: dlnunes@stcloudstate.edu.

St. Cloud State University (continued)

College of Education Students: 272 full-time (205 women), 480 part-time (364 women); includes 57 minority (16 African Americans, 8 American Indian/Alaska Native, 24 Asian Americans or Pacific Islanders, 9 Hispanic Americans), 25 international. 390 applicants, 60% accepted. *Faculty:* 96 full-time (52 women), 18 part-time/adjunct (14 women). Expenses: Contact institution. *Financial support:* Career-related internships or fieldwork, Federal Work-Study, scholarships/grants, and unspecified assistantships available. Financial award application deadline: 3/1. In 2008, 294 master's awarded. *Degree program information:* Part-time and evening/weekend programs available. Postbaccalaureate distance learning degree programs offered (no on-campus study). Offers applied behavior analysis (MS); child and family studies (MS); college counseling and student development (MS); community counseling (MS); curriculum and instruction (MS); educable mentally handicapped (MS); education (MS, Ed D, Spt); educational administration and leadership (MS); educational leadership and community psychology (Spt); emotionally disturbed (MS); exercise science (MS); gifted and talented (MS); higher education administration (MS, Ed D); information media (MS); learning disabled (MS); marriage and family therapy (MS); physical education (MS); rehabilitation counseling (MS); school counseling (MS); social responsibility (MS); special education (MS); sports management (MS); trainable mentally retarded (MS). *Application deadline:* Applications are processed on a rolling basis. *Application fee:* $35. *Application Contact:* Linda Lou Krueger, School of Graduate Studies, 320-308-2113, Fax: 320-308-5371, E-mail: lekrueger@stcloudstate.edu. *Interim Dean,* Dr. Glen Palm, 320-308-3023, Fax: 320-308-4237, E-mail: gfpalm@stcloudstate.edu.

College of Fine Arts and Humanities Students: 110 full-time (88 women), 86 part-time (62 women); includes 11 minority (4 African Americans, 2 American Indian/Alaska Native, 4 Asian Americans or Pacific Islanders, 1 Hispanic American), 23 international. 76 applicants, 80% accepted. *Faculty:* 80 full-time (38 women), 2 part-time/adjunct (1 woman). Expenses: Contact institution. *Financial support:* Federal Work-Study, scholarships/grants, and unspecified assistantships available. Financial award application deadline: 3/1. In 2008, 49 master's awarded. Offers communication sciences and disorders (MS); conducting and literature (MM); English (MA, MS); fine arts and humanities (MA, MM, MS); mass communication (MS); music education (MM); piano pedagogy (MM); teaching English as a second language (MA). *Application fee:* $35. *Application Contact:* Linda Lou Krueger, School of Graduate Studies, 320-308-2113, Fax: 320-308-5371, E-mail: lekrueger@stcloudstate.edu. *Dean,* Todd DeVriese, 320-308-3093, Fax: 320-308-4716.

College of Science and Engineering Students: 98 full-time (15 women), 108 part-time (52 women); includes 15 minority (1 African American, 12 Asian Americans or Pacific Islanders, 2 Hispanic Americans), 117 international. 144 applicants, 41% accepted. *Faculty:* 85 full-time (19 women). Expenses: Contact institution. *Financial support:* Federal Work-Study and unspecified assistantships available. Financial award application deadline: 3/1. In 2008, 44 master's awarded. Offers applied statistics (MS); biological sciences (MA, MS); computer science (MS); electrical engineering (MS); engineering management (MEM); environmental and technological studies (MS); mathematics (MS); mechanical engineering (MS); regulatory affairs and services (MS); science and engineering (MA, MEM, MS). *Application fee:* $35. Electronic applications accepted. *Application Contact:* Linda Lou Krueger, School of Graduate Studies, 320-308-2113, Fax: 320-308-5371, E-mail: lekrueger@stcloudstate.edu. *Chairperson,* Dr. David DeGroote, 320-308-2036, Fax: 320-308-4166.

College of Social Sciences Students: 122 full-time (66 women), 98 part-time (60 women); includes 16 minority (12 African Americans, 1 American Indian/Alaska Native, 1 Asian American or Pacific Islander, 2 Hispanic Americans), 43 international. 51 applicants, 96% accepted. *Faculty:* 81 full-time (32 women), 16 part-time/adjunct (2 women). Expenses: Contact institution. *Financial support:* Federal Work-Study and unspecified assistantships available. Financial award application deadline: 3/1. In 2008, 46 master's awarded. *Degree program information:* Part-time programs available. Offers applied economics (MS); criminal justice administration (MS); criminal justice counseling (MS); cultural resource management archeology (MS); geography (MS); gerontology (MS); history (MA, MS); industrial-organizational psychology (MS); public and nonprofit institutions (MS); public safety executive leadership (MS); social sciences (MA, MS, MSW); social work (MSW). *Application deadline:* Applications are processed on a rolling basis. *Application fee:* $35. Electronic applications accepted. *Application Contact:* Linda Lou Krueger, School of Graduate Studies, 320-308-2113, Fax: 320-308-5371, E-mail: lekrueger@stcloudstate.edu. *Interim Dean,* Dr. Sharon Cogdill, 320-308-4790, E-mail: scogdill@stcloudstate.edu.

G.R. Herberger College of Business Students: 60 full-time (21 women), 133 part-time (56 women); includes 16 minority (4 African Americans, 1 American Indian/Alaska Native, 11 Asian Americans or Pacific Islanders), 33 international. 64 applicants, 89% accepted, 50 enrolled. *Faculty:* 62 full-time (17 women), 4 part-time/adjunct (1 woman). Expenses: Contact institution. *Financial support:* Federal Work-Study, scholarships/grants, and unspecified assistantships available. Financial award application deadline: 3/1. In 2008, 80 master's awarded. *Degree program information:* Part-time and evening/weekend programs available. Offers management and finance (MBA); marketing and general business (MBA). *Application deadline:* For fall admission, 6/1 priority date for domestic students, 4/1 for international students; for spring admission, 10/1 priority date for domestic students, 8/1 for international students. Applications are processed on a rolling basis. *Application fee:* $35. Electronic applications accepted. *Application Contact:* Linda Lou Krueger, School of Graduate Studies, 320-308-2113, Fax: 320-308-5371, E-mail: lekrueger@stcloudstate.edu. *Graduate Director,* Michele Mumm, 320-308-3212, E-mail: michelem@stcloudstate.edu.

ST. EDWARD'S UNIVERSITY, Austin, TX 78704

General Information Independent-religious, coed, comprehensive institution. *Enrollment:* 5,348 graduate, professional, and undergraduate students; 166 full-time matriculated graduate/professional students (115 women), 783 part-time matriculated graduate/professional students (472 women). *Enrollment by degree level:* 949 master's. *Graduate faculty:* 51 full-time (15 women), 73 part-time/adjunct (29 women). *Tuition:* Full-time $13,752; part-time $764 per credit hour. *Required fees:* $50 per semester. Full-time tuition and fees vary according to course load and program. *Graduate housing:* On-campus housing not available. *Student services:* Campus employment opportunities, campus safety program, career counseling, exercise/wellness program, free psychological counseling, international student services, low-cost health insurance, services for students with disabilities, writing training. *Library facilities:* Scarborough-Phillips Library. *Online resources:* library catalog, web page. *Collection:* 190,633 titles, 1,733 serial subscriptions, 3,752 audiovisual materials.

Computer facilities: 649 computers available on campus for general student use. A campuswide network can be accessed from student residence rooms and from off campus. Online class registration is available. *Web address:* http://www.gotostedwards.com/.

General Application Contact: Bridget S. Davidson, Director, Center for Academic Progress, 512-428-1061, Fax: 512-428-1032, E-mail: bridgets@stedwards.edu.

GRADUATE UNITS

New College Students: 91 full-time (72 women), 237 part-time (170 women); includes 76 minority (19 African Americans, 3 American Indian/Alaska Native, 7 Asian Americans or Pacific Islanders, 47 Hispanic Americans), 2 international. Average age 34. 133 applicants, 77% accepted, 87 enrolled. *Faculty:* 24 full-time (6 women), 30 part-time/adjunct (15 women). Expenses: Contact institution. *Financial support:* In 2008–09, 8 students received support. Scholarships/grants available. In 2008, 89 master's awarded. *Degree program information:* Part-time and evening/weekend programs available. Offers college student development (MA); counseling (MA); global issues (MLA); humanities (MLA); liberal arts (Certificate); social sciences (MLA). *Application deadline:* For fall admission, 8/1 for domestic students, 7/1 for international students; for spring admission, 12/1 for domestic students, 11/1 for international students. Applications are processed on a rolling basis. *Application fee:* $45 ($50 for international students). Electronic applications accepted. *Application Contact:* Bridget S. Davidson, Director, Center for Academic Progress, 512-428-1061, Fax: 512-428-1032, E-mail: bridgets@stedwards.edu. *Dean,* Dr. H. Ramsey Fowler, 512-448-8648, Fax: 512-448-8492, E-mail: ramseyf@stedwards.edu.

School of Education Students: 7 full-time (4 women), 33 part-time (20 women); includes 9 minority (2 African Americans, 7 Hispanic Americans), 1 international. Average age 30. 21 applicants, 67% accepted, 10 enrolled. *Faculty:* 3 full-time (0 women), 3 part-time/adjunct (2 women). Expenses: Contact institution. *Financial support:* In 2008–09, 4 students received support. Scholarships/grants available. In 2008, 4 master's awarded. *Degree program information:* Part-time and evening/weekend programs available. Offers curriculum leadership (Certificate); education (MA, Certificate); instructional technology (Certificate); mentoring and supervision (Certificate); sports management (Certificate); teaching (MA). *Application deadline:* For fall admission, 8/1 for domestic students, 7/1 for international students; for spring admission, 12/1 for domestic students, 11/1 for international students. Applications are processed on a rolling basis. *Application fee:* $45 ($50 for international students). Electronic applications accepted. *Application Contact:* Kay L. Arnold, Graduate Admissions Coordinator, 512-233-1636, Fax: 512-428-1032, E-mail: kayla@stedwards.edu. *Dean,* Dr. Karen Jenlink, 512-448-8655, Fax: 512-428-1372, E-mail: karenj@stedwards.edu.

School of Management and Business Students: 68 full-time (39 women), 513 part-time (282 women); includes 201 minority (53 African Americans, 1 American Indian/Alaska Native, 38 Asian Americans or Pacific Islanders, 109 Hispanic Americans), 12 international. Average age 34. 241 applicants, 78% accepted, 157 enrolled. *Faculty:* 24 full-time (9 women), 40 part-time/adjunct (12 women). Expenses: Contact institution. *Financial support:* In 2008–09, 18 students received support. Scholarships/grants available. In 2008, 204 master's awarded. *Degree program information:* Part-time and evening/weekend programs available. Offers accounting (M Ac); administration (Certificate); business management (MBA); computer information systems (MS); conflict resolution (Certificate); corporate finance (MBA, Certificate); digital media management (MBA); entrepreneurship (MBA, Certificate); family mediation (Certificate); global business (MBA, Certificate); human resource management (MBA, Certificate); human services (MA); management and business (M Ac, MA, MBA, MS, Certificate); management information systems (MBA, Certificate); marketing (MBA, Certificate); mediation (Certificate); operations management (MBA, Certificate); organization development and training (Certificate); organizational leadership and ethics (MS); project management (MS). *Application deadline:* For fall admission, 8/1 for domestic students, 7/1 for international students; for spring admission, 12/1 for domestic students, 11/1 for international students. Applications are processed on a rolling basis. *Application fee:* $45 ($50 for international students). Electronic applications accepted. *Application Contact:* Kelly Luna, 512-233-1697, Fax: 512-428-1032, E-mail: kellyl@stedwards.edu. *Dean,* Marsha Kelliher, 512-448-8588, Fax: 512-448-8492, E-mail: marshak@stedwards.edu.

SAINT FRANCIS MEDICAL CENTER COLLEGE OF NURSING, Peoria, IL 61603-3783

General Information Independent-religious, coed, primarily women, upper-level institution. *Enrollment:* 452 graduate, professional, and undergraduate students; 10 full-time matriculated graduate/professional students (all women), 109 part-time matriculated graduate/professional students (103 women). *Enrollment by degree level:* 119 master's. *Graduate faculty:* 1 (woman) full-time, 9 part-time/adjunct (all women). *Tuition:* Full-time $5460; part-time $455 per credit hour. *Required fees:* $260. Part-time tuition and fees vary according to course load. *Graduate housing:* Room and/or apartments guaranteed to single students; on-campus housing not available to married students. Typical cost: $2000 per year. Housing application deadline: 3/14. *Student services:* Campus safety program, exercise/wellness program, free psychological counseling. *Library facilities:* Sister Mary Ludgera Pieperbeck Learning and Resource Center.

Computer facilities: 52 computers available on campus for general student use. A campuswide network can be accessed from student residence rooms and from off campus. Online class registration is available. *Web address:* http://www.sfmccon.edu/.

General Application Contact: Dr. Janice F. Boundy, Associate Dean, 309-655-2230, Fax: 309-624-8973, E-mail: jan.f.boundy@osfhealthcare.org.

GRADUATE UNITS

Graduate Program Students: 10 full-time (all women), 109 part-time (103 women); includes 6 minority (1 African American, 4 Asian Americans or Pacific Islanders, 1 Hispanic American). Average age 28. 24 applicants, 79% accepted, 19 enrolled. *Faculty:* 1 (woman) full-time, 9 part-time/adjunct (all women). Expenses: Contact institution. *Financial support:* In 2008–09, 6 students received support. Scholarships/grants and tuition waivers (partial) available. Support available to part-time students. Financial award application deadline: 6/15; financial award applicants required to submit FAFSA. In 2008, 13 master's awarded. *Degree program information:* Part-time programs available. Postbaccalaureate distance learning degree programs offered (minimal on-campus study). Offers child and family nursing (MSN); clinical nurse leader (MSN); medical-surgical nursing (MSN); nurse clinician (Post-Graduate Certificate); nurse educator (Post-Graduate Certificate). *Application deadline:* For fall admission, 6/1 priority date for domestic and international students; for spring admission, 11/15 priority date for domestic and international students. Applications are processed on a rolling basis. *Application fee:* $50. Electronic applications accepted. *Application Contact:* Dr. Janice F. Boundy, Associate Dean, 309-655-2230, Fax: 309-624-8973, E-mail: jan.f.boundy@osfhealthcare.org. *Dean,* Dr. Lois J. Hamilton, 309-655-2201, Fax: 309-624-8973, E-mail: lois.j.hamilton@osfhealthcare.org.

SAINT FRANCIS SEMINARY, St. Francis, WI 53235-3795

General Information Independent-religious, coed, graduate-only institution. *Graduate housing:* Room and/or apartments available to single students; on-campus housing not available to married students. Housing application deadline: 7/15.

GRADUATE UNITS

Graduate and Professional Programs *Degree program information:* Part-time programs available. Offers theology (M Div, MAPS).

SAINT FRANCIS UNIVERSITY, Loretto, PA 15940-0600

General Information Independent-religious, coed, comprehensive institution. *Graduate housing:* Rooms and/or apartments available on a first-come, first-served basis to single and married students.

GRADUATE UNITS

Department of Occupational Therapy Students: 29 full-time (28 women). Average age 22. 21 applicants, 100% accepted, 21 enrolled. *Faculty:* 5 full-time (3 women). Expenses: Contact institution. In 2008, 19 master's awarded. Offers occupational therapy (MOT). *Application Contact:* Dr. Peter Raymond Skoner, Associate Vice President for Academic Affairs, 814-472-3085, Fax: 814-472-3365, E-mail: pskoner@francis.edu. *Chair,* Dr. Donald Walkovich, 814-472-3899, Fax: 814-472-3950, E-mail: dwalkovich@francis.edu.

Department of Physical Therapy Students: 92 full-time (62 women); includes 2 minority (1 African American, 1 Asian American or Pacific Islander). Average age 24. 50 applicants, 30% accepted, 5 enrolled. *Faculty:* 8 full-time (4 women), 16 part-time/adjunct (9 women). Expenses: Contact institution. *Financial support:* In 2008–09, 11 students received support, including 11 teaching assistantships with partial tuition reimbursements available; unspecified assistantships also available. Offers physical therapy (DPT). *Application deadline:* For winter admission, 1/15 for domestic and international students. *Application fee:* $30. Electronic applications accepted. *Application Contact:* Dr. Kay Malek, Interim Department Chair/Assistant Professor, 814-472-3123, Fax: 814-472-3140, E-mail: kmalek@francis.edu. *Interim Department Chair/Assistant Professor,* Dr. Kay Malek, 814-472-3123, Fax: 814-472-3140, E-mail: kmalek@francis.edu.

Department of Physician Assistant Sciences Students: 111 full-time (86 women); includes 5 minority (3 African Americans, 2 Asian Americans or Pacific Islanders). Average age 25. 478 applicants, 9% accepted, 10 enrolled. *Faculty:* 11 full-time (9 women), 3 part-time/adjunct (0 women). Expenses: Contact institution. *Financial support:* Applicants required to submit FAFSA. In 2008, 51 master's awarded. Offers health science (MHS); medical science (MMS); physician assistant sciences (MPAS). *Application deadline:* For fall admission, 11/1 for domestic and international students. Applications are processed on a rolling basis. *Application fee:* $170. Electronic applications accepted. *Application Contact:* Marie S. Link, Director of

Research and MPAS Graduate Admission, 814-472-3138, Fax: 814-472-3137, E-mail: mlink@francis.edu. *Director*, Donna L. Yeisley, 814-472-3131, Fax: 814-472-3137, E-mail: dyeisley@francis.edu.

Graduate Education Program Students: 10 full-time (7 women), 145 part-time (103 women); includes 1 minority (African American), 1 international. Average age 30. 26 applicants, 100% accepted, 26 enrolled. *Faculty:* 27 part-time/adjunct (8 women). Expenses: Contact institution. In 2008, 46 master's awarded. *Degree program information:* Part-time and evening/weekend programs available. Offers education (M Ed); leadership (M Ed); reading (M Ed). *Application deadline:* Applications are processed on a rolling basis. *Application fee:* $30. *Application Contact:* Sherri L. Toth, Coordinator of Education Programs, 814-472-3058, Fax: 814-472-3864, E-mail: stoth@francis.edu. *Director, Graduate Education*, Dr. Janette D. Kelly, 814-472-3068, Fax: 814-472-3864, E-mail: jkelly@francis.edu.

Graduate School of Business and Human Resource Management *Degree program information:* Part-time and evening/weekend programs available. Offers business administration (MBA); business and human resource management (MBA, MHRM); human resource management (MHRM).

ST. FRANCIS XAVIER UNIVERSITY, Antigonish, NS B2G 2W5, Canada

General Information Independent-religious, coed, comprehensive institution. *Graduate housing:* Room and/or apartments available on a first-come, first-served basis to single students; on-campus housing not available to married students. Housing application deadline: 7/1.

GRADUATE UNITS

Graduate Studies *Degree program information:* Part-time programs available. Postbaccalaureate distance learning degree programs offered (minimal on-campus study). Offers adult education (M Ad Ed); biology (M Sc); Celtic studies (MA); chemistry (M Sc); computer science (M Sc); curriculum and instruction (M Ed); earth sciences (M Sc); educational administration and leadership (M Ed); physics (M Sc).

ST. JOHN FISHER COLLEGE, Rochester, NY 14618-3597

General Information Independent-religious, coed, comprehensive institution. *Enrollment:* 3,832 graduate, professional, and undergraduate students; 292 full-time matriculated graduate/professional students (127 women), 629 part-time matriculated graduate/professional students (365 women). *Enrollment by degree level:* 189 first professional, 670 master's, 62 doctoral. *Graduate faculty:* 75 full-time (38 women), 34 part-time/adjunct (19 women). *Tuition:* Part-time $655 per credit hour. *Required fees:* $25 per semester. *Graduate housing:* On-campus housing not available. *Student services:* Campus employment opportunities, campus safety program, career counseling, child daycare facilities, exercise/wellness program, free psychological counseling, low-cost health insurance, multicultural affairs office, services for students with disabilities, teacher training, writing training. *Library facilities:* Charles J. Lavery Library. *Online resources:* library catalog, web page, access to other libraries' catalogs. *Collection:* 214,834 titles, 22,428 serial subscriptions, 6,830 audiovisual materials.

Computer facilities: 525 computers available on campus for general student use. A campuswide network can be accessed from student residence rooms and from off campus. Online class registration is available. *Web address:* http://www.sjfc.edu/.

General Application Contact: Holly Smith, Assistant Director of Graduate Admissions, 585-385-8161, Fax: 585-385-8344, E-mail: hsmith@sjfc.edu.

GRADUATE UNITS

Ralph C. Wilson Jr. School of Education Students: 106 full-time (53 women), 317 part-time (194 women); includes 69 minority (48 African Americans, 3 American Indian/Alaska Native, 2 Asian Americans or Pacific Islanders, 16 Hispanic Americans). Average age 31. 307 applicants, 87% accepted, 175 enrolled. *Faculty:* 29 full-time (15 women), 27 part-time/adjunct (19 women). Expenses: Contact institution. *Financial support:* In 2008–09, 305 students received support. Federal Work-Study and scholarships/grants available. Financial award applicants required to submit FAFSA. In 2008, 241 master's, 1 other advanced degree awarded. *Degree program information:* Part-time and evening/weekend programs available. Offers adolescence English (MS Ed); adolescence French (MS Ed); adolescence social studies (MS Ed); adolescence Spanish (MS Ed); childhood education/special education (MS Ed); education (MS, MS Ed, Ed D, Certificate); educational leadership (MS Ed); executive leadership (Ed D); literacy birth to grade 6 (MS); literacy grades 5 to 12 (MS); organizational learning and human resource development (MS); special education (MS, Certificate). *Application deadline:* Applications are processed on a rolling basis. *Application fee:* $30. Electronic applications accepted. *Application Contact:* Jose Perales, Director of Graduate Admissions, 585-385-8067, E-mail: jperales@sjfc.edu. *Acting Dean of the School of Education*, Dr. Julius G. Adams, 585-385-3813, E-mail: jadams@sjfc.edu.

Ronald L. Bittner School of Business Students: 8 full-time (5 women), 49 part-time (23 women); includes 6 minority (3 African Americans, 3 Asian Americans or Pacific Islanders). Average age 31. 29 applicants, 83% accepted, 15 enrolled. *Faculty:* 7 full-time (0 women). Expenses: Contact institution. *Financial support:* In 2008–09, 47 students received support. Federal Work-Study and scholarships/grants available. Financial award applicants required to submit FAFSA. In 2008, 38 master's awarded. *Degree program information:* Part-time and evening/weekend programs available. Offers business (MBA); business administration and management (MBA). *Application deadline:* For fall admission, 7/1 for domestic students; for spring admission, 10/30 for domestic students. Applications are processed on a rolling basis. *Application fee:* $30. Electronic applications accepted. *Application Contact:* Jose Perales, Interim Director of Graduate Admissions, 585-385-8067, E-mail: jperales@sjfc.edu. *Dean*, Dr. Selim Ilter, 585-385-8079, Fax: 585-385-8094, E-mail: silter@sjfc.edu.

School of Arts and Sciences Students: 13 full-time (5 women), 87 part-time (51 women); includes 7 minority (5 African Americans, 1 Asian American or Pacific Islander, 1 Hispanic American). Average age 30. 39 applicants, 87% accepted, 25 enrolled. *Faculty:* 8 full-time (1 woman), 4 part-time/adjunct (0 women). Expenses: Contact institution. *Financial support:* In 2008–09, 66 students received support. Federal Work-Study and scholarships/grants available. Financial award applicants required to submit FAFSA. In 2008, 46 master's awarded. *Degree program information:* Part-time and evening/weekend programs available. Offers arts and sciences (MS); international studies (MS); mathematics/science/technology education (MS). *Application deadline:* For fall admission, 7/1 for domestic students; for spring admission, 10/30 for domestic students. Applications are processed on a rolling basis. *Application fee:* $30. Electronic applications accepted. *Application Contact:* Jose Perales, Director of Graduate Admissions, 585-385-8067, E-mail: jperales@sjfc.edu. *Dean of the School of Arts and Sciences*, Dr. David Pate, 585-385-8034, E-mail: dpate@sjfc.edu.

Wegmans School of Nursing Students: 43 full-time (41 women), 109 part-time (97 women); includes 11 minority (8 African Americans, 1 American Indian/Alaska Native, 2 Hispanic Americans). Average age 37. 118 applicants, 78% accepted, 61 enrolled. *Faculty:* 15 full-time (14 women), 3 part-time/adjunct (0 women). Expenses: Contact institution. *Financial support:* In 2008–09, 131 students received support. Scholarships/grants available. Financial award applicants required to submit FAFSA. In 2008, 27 master's awarded. *Degree program information:* Part-time and evening/weekend programs available. Offers advanced practice nursing (MS); clinical nurse specialist (Certificate); family nurse practitioner (Certificate); mental health counseling (MS); nurse educator (Certificate); nursing (MS, DNP, Certificate); nursing practice (DNP). *Application deadline:* Applications are processed on a rolling basis. Electronic applications accepted. *Application Contact:* Jose Perales, Director of Graduate Admissions, 585-385-8067, E-mail: jperales@sjfc.edu. *Dean of the Wegmans School of Nursing*, Dr. Diane Cooney-Miner, 585-385-8241, Fax: 585-385-8466, E-mail: dcooney-miner@sjfc.edu.

Wegmans School of Pharmacy Students: 189 full-time (90 women); includes 26 minority (2 African Americans, 20 Asian Americans or Pacific Islanders, 4 Hispanic Americans), 5 international. Average age 25. 1,288 applicants, 12% accepted, 72 enrolled. *Faculty:* 17 full-time (9 women). Expenses: Contact institution. *Financial support:* In 2008–09, 175 students received support. Federal Work-Study and scholarships/grants available. Offers pharmacy (Pharm D). *Application deadline:* For fall admission, 2/2 for domestic students. Applications are processed on a rolling basis. *Application fee:* $50. Electronic applications accepted. *Application Contact:* Jose Perales, Director of Graduate Admissions, 585-385-8067, E-mail: jperales@sjfc.edu. *Dean*, Dr. Scott A. Swigart, 585-385-8201, Fax: 585-385-8453, E-mail: sswigart@sjfc.edu.

ST. JOHN'S COLLEGE, Annapolis, MD 21404

General Information Independent, coed, comprehensive institution. *Graduate housing:* On-campus housing not available.

GRADUATE UNITS

Graduate Institute in Liberal Education *Degree program information:* Evening/weekend programs available. Offers liberal arts (MALA).

ST. JOHN'S COLLEGE, Santa Fe, NM 87505-4599

General Information Independent, coed, comprehensive institution. *Graduate housing:* Rooms and/or apartments available on a first-come, first-served basis to single and married students. Housing application deadline: 4/1.

GRADUATE UNITS

Graduate Institute in Liberal Education *Degree program information:* Evening/weekend programs available. Offers Eastern classics (MA); liberal arts (MA); liberal education (MA).

ST. JOHN'S SEMINARY, Camarillo, CA 93012-2598

General Information Independent-religious, coed, primarily men, graduate-only institution. *Enrollment by degree level:* 64 first professional, 15 master's. *Graduate faculty:* 19 full-time (4 women), 8 part-time/adjunct (1 woman). *Tuition:* Full-time $12,750; part-time $425 per unit. One-time fee: $3421 full-time; $25 part-time. Full-time tuition and fees vary according to course load and program. *Graduate housing:* Room and/or apartments guaranteed to single students; on-campus housing not available to married students. Typical cost: $10,500 (including board). *Student services:* Campus employment opportunities, career counseling, free psychological counseling, international student services, low-cost health insurance, writing training. *Library facilities:* Edward Laurence Doheny Memorial Library plus 1 other. *Online resources:* library catalog, web page. *Collection:* 55,640 titles, 247 serial subscriptions, 3,388 audiovisual materials.

Computer facilities: 25 computers available on campus for general student use. A campuswide network can be accessed from student residence rooms and from off campus. Class schedules by e-mail available. *Web address:* http://www.stjohnsem.edu.

General Application Contact: Dr. Mark F. Fischer, Director of Admissions, 805-482-2755 Ext. 1063, Fax: 805-482-3470, E-mail: fischer@stjohnsem.edu.

GRADUATE UNITS

Graduate and Professional Programs Students: 69 full-time (0 women), 10 part-time (5 women); includes 46 minority (1 African American, 25 Asian Americans or Pacific Islanders, 20 Hispanic Americans), 11 international. Average age 34. 13 applicants, 100% accepted, 13 enrolled. *Faculty:* 19 full-time (4 women), 8 part-time/adjunct (1 woman). Expenses: Contact institution. In 2008, 17 first professional degrees, 6 master's awarded. *Degree program information:* Part-time programs available. Offers divinity (M Div); pastoral ministry (MAPM); theology (MA). *Application deadline:* For fall admission, 7/15 priority date for domestic students. Applications are processed on a rolling basis. *Application fee:* $0. Electronic applications accepted. *Application Contact:* Esme M. Takahashi, Registrar, 805-482-2755 Ext. 1014, Fax: 805-482-3470, E-mail: registrar-sjs@stjohnsem.edu. *Academic Dean*, Rev. Richard Benson, CM, 805-482-2755, Fax: 805-482-3470, E-mail: rbensoncm@stjohnsem.edu.

SAINT JOHN'S SEMINARY, Brighton, MA 02135

General Information Independent-religious, coed, graduate-only institution. *Graduate housing:* Room and/or apartments available to single students; on-campus housing not available to married students. Housing application deadline: 8/1.

GRADUATE UNITS

Graduate Programs Offers theology (M Div, MA Th, MAM).

SAINT JOHN'S UNIVERSITY, Collegeville, MN 56321

General Information Independent-religious, coed, primarily men, comprehensive institution. *Graduate housing:* Rooms and/or apartments available on a first-come, first-served basis to single and married students. *Research affiliation:* Hill Monastic Manuscript Library (monastic studies, liturgy, spirituality), Center for Ecumenical and Cultural Research, Arca Artium (visual and book arts).

GRADUATE UNITS

Saint John's School of Theology and Seminary *Degree program information:* Part-time programs available. Postbaccalaureate distance learning degree programs offered (no on-campus study). Offers divinity (M Div); liturgical music (MA); liturgical studies (MA); pastoral ministry (MA); theology (MA). Electronic applications accepted.

ST. JOHN'S UNIVERSITY, Queens, NY 11439

General Information Independent-religious, coed, university. CGS member. *Enrollment:* 20,109 graduate, professional, and undergraduate students; 1,996 full-time matriculated graduate/professional students (1,193 women), 3,297 part-time matriculated graduate/professional students (2,213 women). *Enrollment by degree level:* 1,408 first professional, 3,270 master's, 537 doctoral, 78 other advanced degrees. *Graduate faculty:* 696 full-time (291 women), 824 part-time/adjunct (334 women). *Tuition:* Full-time $20,760; part-time $865 per credit. *Required fees:* $300; $150 per semester. Tuition and fees vary according to program. *Graduate housing:* On-campus housing not available. *Student services:* Campus employment opportunities, campus safety program, career counseling, exercise/wellness program, free psychological counseling, international student services, low-cost health insurance, services for students with disabilities, writing training. *Library facilities:* St. John's University Library plus 1 other. *Online resources:* library catalog, web page, access to other libraries' catalogs. *Collection:* 570,457 titles, 14,277 serial subscriptions, 14,364 audiovisual materials. *Research affiliation:* Merck & Co., Inc. (Pharmaceutical research), Chinese American Medical Society (Medical science), Children's Hospital of the Kings Daughters (Medical services), Medical University of South Carolina (Medical science), American Cancer Society (Chemical research), Columbia University (Social science).

Computer facilities: Computer purchase and lease plans are available. 13,107 computers available on campus for general student use. A campuswide network can be accessed from student residence rooms and from off campus. Online class registration, various software packages are available. *Web address:* http://www.stjohns.edu/.

General Application Contact: Kathleen Davis, Director of Graduate Admissions, 718-990-2790, E-mail: gradhelp@stjohns.edu.

GRADUATE UNITS

College of Pharmacy and Allied Health Professions Students: 534 full-time (348 women), 274 part-time (139 women); includes 342 minority (20 African Americans, 1 American Indian/Alaska Native, 309 Asian Americans or Pacific Islanders, 12 Hispanic Americans), 252 international. Average age 25. 842 applicants, 31% accepted, 97 enrolled. *Faculty:* 80 full-time (39 women), 18 part-time/adjunct (7 women). Expenses: Contact institution. *Financial support:* In 2008–09, 147 students received support, including 32 fellowships with full and partial tuition reimbursements available (averaging $10,348 per year), 6 research assistantships with full and partial tuition reimbursements available (averaging $11,833 per year), 3 teaching assistantships with full and partial tuition reimbursements available (averaging $7,333 per year); career-related internships or fieldwork, scholarships/grants, and unspecified assistantships also available. Support available to part-time students. Financial award application deadline: 3/1; financial award applicants required to submit FAFSA. In 2008, 267 first professional degrees, 39 master's, 5 doctorates awarded. *Degree program information:* Part-time and evening/weekend programs available. Offers pharmaceutical sciences (MS, PhD); pharmacy (Pharm D, MS, PhD); pharmacy administration (MS); pharmacy and allied

St. John's University (continued)

health professions (Pharm D, MS, PhD); toxicology (MS). *Application deadline:* For fall admission, 3/1 for domestic students, 5/1 priority date for international students; for spring admission, 11/1 for domestic students, 11/1 priority date for international students. Applications are processed on a rolling basis. *Application fee:* $70. Electronic applications accepted. *Application Contact:* Kathleen Davis, Director of Graduate Admission, 718-990-2790, E-mail: gradhelp@stjohns.edu. *Dean,* Dr. Robert Mangione, 718-990-6411, Fax: 718-990-1871, E-mail: mangionr@stjohns.edu.

College of Professional Studies Students: 10 full-time (5 women), 88 part-time (49 women); includes 37 minority (18 African Americans, 5 Asian Americans or Pacific Islanders, 14 Hispanic Americans), 2 international. Average age 28. 90 applicants, 61% accepted, 33 enrolled. *Faculty:* 27 full-time (8 women), 40 part-time/adjunct (11 women). Expenses: Contact institution. *Financial support:* In 2008–09, 81 students received support, including research assistantships (averaging $10,000 per year), teaching assistantships (averaging $8,000 per year). Financial award application deadline: 3/1. In 2008, 27 master's awarded. Offers criminal justice and legal studies (MPS); sport management (MPS). *Application deadline:* For fall admission, 5/1 priority date for domestic and international students; for spring admission, 11/1 priority date for domestic and international students. Applications are processed on a rolling basis. *Application fee:* $70. Electronic applications accepted. *Application Contact:* Kathleen Davis, Director of Graduate Admission, 718-990-2790, Fax: 718-990-5686, E-mail: gradhelp@stjohns.edu. *Dean,* Dr. Kathleen Voute MacDonald, 718-990-6435, Fax: 718-990-1882, E-mail: macdonk@stjohns.edu.

Institute for Biotechnology Students: 1 (woman) full-time, 14 part-time (6 women); includes 2 minority (1 African American, 1 Asian American or Pacific Islander), 11 international. Average age 25. 102 applicants, 21% accepted, 6 enrolled. Expenses: Contact institution. *Financial support:* In 2008–09, 7 students received support, including 3 teaching assistantships with full tuition reimbursements available (averaging $4,723 per year). Financial award application deadline: 4/1. In 2008, 1 master's awarded. Offers biological/pharmaceutical biotechnology (MS). *Application deadline:* For fall admission, 5/1 for domestic and international students; for spring admission, 11/1 for domestic and international students. Applications are processed on a rolling basis. *Application fee:* $70. Electronic applications accepted. *Application Contact:* Kathleen Davis, Director of Graduate Admission, 718-990-2790, E-mail: gradhelp@stjohns.edu. *Director,* Dr. Diana Bartelt, 718-990-1654, E-mail: barteltd@stjohns.edu.

The Peter J. Tobin College of Business Students: 280 full-time (137 women), 473 part-time (216 women); includes 182 minority (61 African Americans, 87 Asian Americans or Pacific Islanders, 34 Hispanic Americans), 255 international. Average age 27. 684 applicants, 74% accepted, 325 enrolled. *Faculty:* 94 full-time (20 women), 38 part-time/adjunct (10 women). Expenses: Contact institution. *Financial support:* In 2008–09, 367 students received support, including 40 research assistantships with full and partial tuition reimbursements available (averaging $17,301 per year); scholarships/grants also available. Support available to part-time students. Financial award application deadline: 3/1; financial award applicants required to submit FAFSA. In 2008, 332 master's awarded. *Degree program information:* Part-time and evening/weekend programs available. Offers accounting (MBA, MS, Adv C); business (MBA, MS, Adv C); computer information systems and decision sciences (MBA, Adv C); finance (MBA, MS, Adv C); international business (MBA, Adv C); management (MBA, Adv C); marketing (MBA, Adv C); taxation (MBA, MS, Adv C). *Application deadline:* For fall admission, 5/1 priority date for domestic and international students; for spring admission, 11/1 priority date for domestic and international students. Applications are processed on a rolling basis. *Application fee:* $70. Electronic applications accepted. *Application Contact:* Nicole T. Bryan, Assistant Dean, 718-990-2599, Fax: 718-990-5242, E-mail: tcbgradadmissions@stjohns.edu. *Dean,* Dr. Steven Papamarcos, 718-990-6800, Fax: 718-990-5966, E-mail: papamars@stjohns.edu.

School of Risk Management and Actuarial Science Students: 30 full-time (13 women), 59 part-time (30 women); includes 11 minority (8 African Americans, 3 Asian Americans or Pacific Islanders), 54 international. Average age 27. 86 applicants, 74% accepted, 41 enrolled. Expenses: Contact institution. *Financial support:* Research assistantships available. In 2008, 34 master's awarded. Offers risk management and actuarial science (MBA, MS). *Application deadline:* For fall admission, 5/1 priority date for domestic and international students; for spring admission, 11/1 priority date for domestic and international students. Applications are processed on a rolling basis. *Application fee:* $70. Electronic applications accepted. *Application Contact:* Nicole T. Bryan, Assistant Dean, 718-990-2599, Fax: 718-990-5242, E-mail: TCBgradadmissions@stjohns.edu. *Chair,* Dr. James Barrese, 212-277-5191, E-mail: barresej@stjohns.edu.

St. John's College of Liberal Arts and Sciences Students: 292 full-time (234 women), 810 part-time (569 women); includes 256 minority (80 African Americans, 2 American Indian/Alaska Native, 65 Asian Americans or Pacific Islanders, 109 Hispanic Americans), 98 international. Average age 34. 1,518 applicants, 41% accepted, 307 enrolled. *Faculty:* 261 full-time (103 women), 351 part-time/adjunct (157 women). Expenses: Contact institution. *Financial support:* In 2008–09, 778 students received support, including 107 fellowships with full and partial tuition reimbursements available (averaging $14,182 per year), 82 research assistantships with full and partial tuition reimbursements available (averaging $16,538 per year), 29 teaching assistantships with full and partial tuition reimbursements available (averaging $16,279 per year); career-related internships or fieldwork, scholarships/grants, and unspecified assistantships also available. Support available to part-time students. Financial award application deadline: 3/1; financial award applicants required to submit FAFSA. In 2008, 1 first professional degree, 274 master's, 30 doctorates, 28 other advanced degrees awarded. *Degree program information:* Part-time and evening/weekend programs available. Offers algebra (MA); analysis (MA); applied mathematics (MA); biological sciences (MS, PhD); chemistry (MS); clinical psychology (PhD); clinical psychology-child (PhD); clinical psychology-general (PhD); computer science (MA); criminology and justice (MA); English (MA, DA); general experimental psychology (MA); geometry-topology (MA); government and politics (MA, Adv C); government information specialisthistory (MA); international law and diplomacy (Adv C); languages and literatures (Adv C); liberal arts and sciences (M Div, MA, MLS, MS, Au D, DA, PhD, Psy D, Adv C, Advanced Diploma, Certificate); liberal studies (MA); library and information science (MLS, Adv C); logic and foundations (MA); modern world history (DA); pastoral ministry (Certificate); philosophy (MA); priestly studies (M Div); probability and statistics (MA); school psychology (MS, Psy D); sociology (MA); Spanish (MA); speech, communication sciences and theatre (MA, Au D, Advanced Diploma); theology (MA, Certificate). *Application deadline:* For fall admission, 5/1 priority date for domestic and international students; for spring admission, 11/1 priority date for domestic and international students. Applications are processed on a rolling basis. *Application fee:* $70. Electronic applications accepted. *Application Contact:* Kathleen Davis, Associate Vice President and Executive Director, Enrollment Management, 718-990-2790, Fax: 718-990-5686, E-mail: gradhelp@stjohns.edu. *Dean,* Dr. Jeffrey Fagen, 718-990-6068, Fax: 718-990-6593, E-mail: fagenj@stjohns.edu.

Institute of Asian Studies Students: 6 full-time (4 women), 5 part-time (3 women); includes 3 minority (2 Asian Americans or Pacific Islanders, 1 Hispanic American), 7 international. Average age 25. 13 applicants, 100% accepted, 4 enrolled. Expenses: Contact institution. *Financial support:* Research assistantships, scholarships/grants available. Support available to part-time students. Financial award application deadline: 3/1; financial award applicants required to submit FAFSA. In 2008, 5 master's awarded. *Degree program information:* Part-time and evening/weekend programs available. Offers Asian and African cultural studies (Adv C); Asian studies (Adv C); Chinese studies (MA, Adv C); East Asian culture studies (Adv C); East Asian studies (MA). *Application deadline:* For fall admission, 5/1 priority date for domestic and international students; for spring admission, 11/1 priority date for domestic and international students. Applications are processed on a rolling basis. *Application fee:* $70. Electronic applications accepted. *Application Contact:* Kathleen Davis, Director of Graduate Admission, 718-990-2790, Fax: 718-990-5686, E-mail: gradhelp@stjohns.edu. *Chair,* Dr. Bernadette Li, 718-990-1657, E-mail: lib@stjohns.edu.

The School of Education Students: 136 full-time (116 women), 1,450 part-time (1,137 women); includes 413 minority (170 African Americans, 54 Asian Americans or Pacific Islanders, 189 Hispanic Americans), 40 international. Average age 33. 1,077 applicants, 77% accepted, 464 enrolled. *Faculty:* 45 full-time (28 women), 121 part-time/adjunct (59 women). Expenses: Contact institution. *Financial support:* In 2008–09, 1,310 students received support, including 147 fellowships with full and partial tuition reimbursements available (averaging $14,085 per year), 2 research assistantships with full and partial tuition reimbursements available (averaging $12,975 per year), 3 teaching assistantships with full and partial tuition reimbursements available (averaging $13,836 per year); career-related internships or fieldwork, scholarships/grants, and unspecified assistantships also available. Support available to part-time students. Financial award application deadline: 3/1; financial award applicants required to submit FAFSA. In 2008, 431 master's, 22 doctorates, 13 other advanced degrees awarded. *Degree program information:* Part-time and evening/weekend programs available. Post-baccalaureate distance learning degree programs offered (no on-campus study). Offers administration and supervision (Ed D, PD); adolescent education (MS Ed); bilingual school counseling (MS Ed, PD); bilingual/multicultural education/teaching English to speakers of other languages (MS Ed); childhood education (MS Ed); early childhood education (MS Ed); education (MS Ed, Ed D, PhD, PD); educational administration and supervision (Ed D, PD); instructional leadership (Ed D, PD); literacy (MS Ed, PhD); mental health counseling (MS Ed); school building leadership (MS Ed, PD); school counseling (MS Ed, PD); school district leadership (PD); teaching children with disabilities in childhood education (MS Ed); teaching literacy 5-12 (MS Ed); teaching literacy B-12 (MS Ed); teaching literacy B-6 (MS Ed). *Application deadline:* For fall admission, 4/1 priority date for domestic students, 5/1 for international students; for spring admission, 11/1 for domestic and international students. Applications are processed on a rolling basis. *Application fee:* $70. Electronic applications accepted. *Application Contact:* Kelly K. Ronayne, Assistant Dean, 718-990-2303, Fax: 718-990-2343, E-mail: graded@stjohns.edu. *Dean,* Dr. Jerrold Ross, 718-990-1305, Fax: 718-990-6096, E-mail: rossj@stjohns.edu.

School of Law Students: 743 full-time (352 women), 188 part-time (97 women); includes 219 minority (54 African Americans, 1 American Indian/Alaska Native, 95 Asian Americans or Pacific Islanders, 69 Hispanic Americans), 18 international. Average age 25. 3,934 applicants, 38% accepted, 308 enrolled. *Faculty:* 57 full-time (27 women), 51 part-time/adjunct (10 women). Expenses: Contact institution. *Financial support:* In 2008–09, 816 students received support; research assistantships, career-related internships or fieldwork and scholarships/grants available. Support available to part-time students. Financial award application deadline: 3/1; financial award applicants required to submit FAFSA. In 2008, 276 JDs awarded. *Degree program information:* Part-time and evening/weekend programs available. Offers bankruptcy (LL M); law (JD, LL M); U.S. legal studies (LL M). *Application deadline:* For fall admission, 4/1 priority date for domestic and international students. Applications are processed on a rolling basis. *Application fee:* $60. Electronic applications accepted. *Application Contact:* Robert Harrison, Assistant Dean and Director of Admissions, 718-990-2310, Fax: 718-990-6699, E-mail: lawinfo@stjohns.edu. *Dean,* Michael A. Simons, 718-990-6013, Fax: 718-990-6694, E-mail: simonsm@stjohns.edu.

SAINT JOSEPH COLLEGE, West Hartford, CT 06117-2700

General Information Independent-religious, Undergraduate: women only; graduate: coed, comprehensive institution. *Enrollment:* 1,926 graduate, professional, and undergraduate students; 140 full-time matriculated graduate/professional students (121 women), 523 part-time matriculated graduate/professional students (449 women). *Enrollment by degree level:* 663 master's. *Tuition:* Part-time $560 per credit. *Required fees:* $30 per credit. *Student services:* Campus employment opportunities, campus safety program, career counseling, exercise/wellness program, free psychological counseling, low-cost health insurance, multicultural affairs office, services for students with disabilities, teacher training. *Library facilities:* Pope Pius XII Library. *Online resources:* library catalog, web page, access to other libraries' catalogs.

Computer facilities: A campuswide network can be accessed from student residence rooms and from off campus. Online class registration is available. *Web address:* http://www.sjc.edu/.

General Application Contact: Graduate Admissions Office, 860-231-5261, E-mail: graduate@sjc.edu.

GRADUATE UNITS

Institute in Gerontology Students: 4 full-time (3 women), 15 part-time (14 women). Expenses: Contact institution. *Financial support:* Career-related internships or fieldwork, health care benefits, and unspecified assistantships available. Support available to part-time students. Financial award applicants required to submit FAFSA. *Degree program information:* Part-time and evening/weekend programs available. Offers human development/gerontology (MA, Certificate). *Application deadline:* Applications are processed on a rolling basis. *Application fee:* $50. Electronic applications accepted. *Application Contact:* Graduate Admissions Office, 860-231-5261, E-mail: graduate@sjc.edu.

SAINT JOSEPH'S COLLEGE, Rensselaer, IN 47978

General Information Independent-religious, coed, comprehensive institution. *Graduate housing:* Rooms and/or apartments available on a first-come, first-served basis to single students and available to married students. Housing application deadline: 6/20.

GRADUATE UNITS

Rensselaer Program of Church Music and Liturgy *Degree program information:* Part-time programs available. Offers church music and liturgy (MA); pastoral liturgy and music (Diploma). Offered during summer only.

ST. JOSEPH'S COLLEGE, LONG ISLAND CAMPUS, Patchogue, NY 11772-2399

General Information Independent, coed, comprehensive institution. *Graduate housing:* On-campus housing not available.

GRADUATE UNITS

Executive MBA Program Offers business administration (EMBA).

Program in Accounting Offers accounting (MBA).

Program in Infant/Toddler Early Childhood Special Education *Degree program information:* Part-time and evening/weekend programs available. Offers infant/toddler early childhood special education (MA).

Program in Literacy and Cognition Offers literacy and cognition (MA).

Program in Management Offers health care (AC); health care management (MS); human resource management (AC); human resources management (MS); organizational management (MS).

Program in Nursing Offers nursing (MS).

ST. JOSEPH'S COLLEGE, NEW YORK, Brooklyn, NY 11205-3688

General Information Independent, coed, comprehensive institution.

GRADUATE UNITS

Graduate Programs Offers accounting (MBA); executive business administration (EMBA); infant/toddler early childhood special education (MA); literacy and cognition (MA); management (MS); nursing (MS); severe and multiple disabilities (MA); special education (MA).

SAINT JOSEPH'S COLLEGE OF MAINE, Standish, ME 04084-5263

General Information Independent-religious, coed, comprehensive institution. *Graduate housing:* On-campus housing not available.

GRADUATE UNITS

Department of Nursing *Degree program information:* Part-time programs available. Post-baccalaureate distance learning degree programs offered (minimal on-campus study). Offers nursing (MS); nursing administration and leadership (Certificate); nursing and health care education (Certificate). MS degree offered only through faculty-directed independent study. Electronic applications accepted.

Program in Business Administration *Degree program information:* Part-time programs available. Offers quality leadership (MBA).

Program in Health Services Administration *Degree program information:* Part-time programs available. Postbaccalaureate distance learning degree programs offered (minimal on-campus study). Offers health services administration (MHSA). Degree program is external; available only by correspondence and online. Electronic applications accepted.

Program in Teacher Education *Degree program information:* Part-time programs available. Postbaccalaureate distance learning degree programs offered (minimal on-campus study). Offers teacher education (MS). Program available by correspondence. Electronic applications accepted.

ST. JOSEPH'S SEMINARY, Yonkers, NY 10704

General Information Independent-religious, coed, graduate-only institution. *Graduate housing:* Room and/or apartments guaranteed to single students; on-campus housing not available to married students.

GRADUATE UNITS

Institute of Religious Studies *Degree program information:* Part-time and evening/weekend programs available. Offers religious studies (MA). Electronic applications accepted.

Professional Program Offers divinity (M Div); theology (MA).

SAINT JOSEPH'S UNIVERSITY, Philadelphia, PA 19131-1395

General Information Independent-religious, coed, comprehensive institution. *Enrollment:* 7,900 graduate, professional, and undergraduate students; 240 full-time matriculated graduate/professional students (120 women), 1,902 part-time matriculated graduate/professional students (1,093 women). *Enrollment by degree level:* 2,094 master's, 48 doctoral. *Graduate faculty:* 140 full-time (49 women), 130 part-time/adjunct (45 women). *Tuition:* Part-time $745 per credit. Tuition and fees vary according to course load, degree level and program. *Graduate housing:* On-campus housing not available. *Student services:* Campus employment opportunities, campus safety program, career counseling, free psychological counseling, international student services, low-cost health insurance, multicultural affairs office, services for students with disabilities, teacher training, writing training. *Library facilities:* Francis A. Drexel Library plus 1 other. *Online resources:* library catalog, web page, access to other libraries' catalogs. *Collection:* 352,000 titles, 16,600 serial subscriptions, 4,800 audiovisual materials.

Computer facilities: Computer purchase and lease plans are available. 670 computers available on campus for general student use. A campuswide network can be accessed from student residence rooms and from off campus. Online class registration is available. *Web address:* http://www.sju.edu/.

General Application Contact: Coralee Dixon, Assistant Director, Graduate Admissions, 610-660-1101, Fax: 610-660-1224, E-mail: graduate@sju.edu.

GRADUATE UNITS

College of Arts and Sciences Students: 104 full-time (59 women), 1,185 part-time (794 women); includes 274 minority (217 African Americans, 1 American Indian/Alaska Native, 31 Asian Americans or Pacific Islanders, 25 Hispanic Americans), 74 international. Average age 33. *Faculty:* 75 full-time (35 women), 96 part-time/adjunct (40 women). Expenses: Contact institution. *Financial support:* In 2008–09, 91 students received support, including fellowships (averaging $24,000 per year), research assistantships with full and partial tuition reimbursements available (averaging $14,000 per year), teaching assistantships with full and partial tuition reimbursements available (averaging $7,200 per year); scholarships/grants and unspecified assistantships also available. Financial award applicants required to submit FAFSA. In 2008, 481 master's, 5 doctorates awarded. *Degree program information:* Part-time and evening/weekend programs available. Postbaccalaureate distance learning degree programs offered. Offers administration/police executive (MS); adult learning and training (MS, Certificate); arts and sciences (MA, MS, Ed D, Certificate, Post-Master's Certificate); behavior analysis (MS, Post-Master's Certificate); biology (MA, MS); computer science (MS); criminal justice (MS, Post-Master's Certificate); criminology (MS); educational leadership (Ed D); elementary education (MS); environmental protection and safety management (MS, Post-Master's Certificate); federal law (MS); gerontological counseling (MS); gerontological services (Post-Master's Certificate); health administration (MS, Post-Master's Certificate); health education (MS, Post-Master's Certificate); health informatics (Post-Master's Certificate); healthcare ethics (Certificate); homeland security (MS, Certificate); human services administration (MS); instructional technology (MS); intelligence and crime (MS); mathematics and computer science (Post-Master's Certificate); nurse anesthesia (MS); organization dynamics and leadership (MS, Certificate); organizational psychology and development (MS, Certificate); probation, parole, and corrections (MS); professional education (MS); psychology (MS); public safety (Post-Master's Certificate); public safety management (MS, Certificate); reading specialist (MS); school nurse certification (MS); secondary education (MS); special education (MS); training and organizational development (MS); writing studies (MA). *Application deadline:* For fall admission, 7/15 priority date for domestic students, 4/15 for international students; for winter admission, 4/15 for domestic students, 1/15 for international students; for spring admission, 11/15 priority date for domestic students, 10/15 for international students. Applications are processed on a rolling basis. *Application fee:* $35. Electronic applications accepted. *Application Contact:* Coralee Dixon, Assistant Director of Graduate Admissions, 610-660-1102, Fax: 610-660-1224, E-mail: coralee.dixon@sju.edu. *Associate Dean/Executive Director of Graduate Programs,* Dr. Sabrina DeTurk, 610-660-1289, Fax: 610-660-3230, E-mail: sdeturk@sju.edu.

Erivan K. Haub School of Business Students: 168 full-time (70 women), 716 part-time (304 women); includes 119 minority (66 African Americans, 40 Asian Americans or Pacific Islanders, 13 Hispanic Americans), 57 international. Average age 32. *Faculty:* 65 full-time (14 women), 34 part-time/adjunct (5 women). Expenses: Contact institution. *Financial support:* In 2008–09, research assistantships with full and partial tuition reimbursements (averaging $4,000 per year), teaching assistantships with full and partial tuition reimbursements (averaging $4,000 per year) were awarded; fellowships, scholarships/grants and unspecified assistantships also available. Financial award application deadline: 5/1; financial award applicants required to submit FAFSA. In 2008, 352 master's awarded. *Degree program information:* Part-time and evening/weekend programs available. Postbaccalaureate distance learning degree programs offered (minimal on-campus study). Offers accounting (MBA); business (MBA, MS, Post Master's Certificate); business intelligence (MS); executive business administration (MBA); executive pharmaceutical marketing (Post Master's Certificate); finance (MBA); financial services (MS); food marketing (MBA, MS); general business (MBA); health and medical services administration (MBA); human resource management (MBA, MS); international business (MBA); international marketing (MS); management (MBA); marketing (MBA); pharmaceutical marketing (MBA). *Application deadline:* For fall admission, 7/15 priority date for domestic students, 4/15 priority date for international students; for spring admission, 11/15 priority date for domestic students, 10/15 priority date for international students. Applications are processed on a rolling basis. *Application fee:* $35. Electronic applications accepted. *Application Contact:* Coralee Dixon, Assistant Director of Graduate Admissions, 610-660-1102, Fax: 610-660-1224, E-mail: cdixon01@sju.edu. *Dean,* Dr. Joseph A. DiAngelo, 610-660-1645, Fax: 610-660-1649, E-mail: jodiange@sju.edu.

ST. LAWRENCE UNIVERSITY, Canton, NY 13617-1455

General Information Independent, coed, comprehensive institution. *Graduate housing:* Room and/or apartments available on a first-come, first-served basis to single students; on-campus housing not available to married students. Housing application deadline: 4/1.

GRADUATE UNITS

Department of Education *Degree program information:* Part-time and evening/weekend programs available. Offers combined school building leadership/school district leadership (CAS); counseling and human development (M Ed, MS, CAS); educational leadership (M Ed, CAS); general studies in education (M Ed); mental health counseling (MS); school building leadership (M Ed); school counseling (M Ed, CAS); school district leadership (CAS).

SAINT LEO UNIVERSITY, Saint Leo, FL 33574-6665

General Information Independent-religious, coed, comprehensive institution. *Graduate housing:* Room and/or apartments available on a first-come, first-served basis to single students; on-campus housing not available to married students. *Research affiliation:* American Jewish Committee (religion).

GRADUATE UNITS

Graduate Business Studies *Degree program information:* Part-time and evening/weekend programs available. Postbaccalaureate distance learning degree programs offered (no on-campus study). Offers accounting (MBA); business (MBA); criminal justice (MBA); health services management (MBA); human resource administration (MBA); information security management (MBA); sport business (MBA). Electronic applications accepted.

Graduate Pastoral Studies *Degree program information:* Part-time and evening/weekend programs available. Offers pastoral studies (MA). Electronic applications accepted.

Graduate Studies in Criminal Justice *Degree program information:* Part-time and evening/weekend programs available. Postbaccalaureate distance learning degree programs offered (no on-campus study). Offers criminal justice (MS); critical incident management (MS). Electronic applications accepted.

Graduate Studies in Education *Degree program information:* Part-time and evening/weekend programs available. Postbaccalaureate distance learning degree programs offered (minimal on-campus study). Offers education (MAT); educational leadership (M Ed); exceptional student education (M Ed); instructional design (MS); instructional leadership (M Ed); reading (M Ed). Electronic applications accepted.

ST. LOUIS COLLEGE OF PHARMACY, St. Louis, MO 63110-1088

General Information Independent, coed, comprehensive institution. *Graduate housing:* Rooms and/or apartments available on a first-come, first-served basis to single and married students. Housing application deadline: 5/1.

GRADUATE UNITS

Professional Program in Pharmacy Offers pharmacy (Pharm D). Electronic applications accepted.

SAINT LOUIS UNIVERSITY, St. Louis, MO 63103-2097

General Information Independent-religious, coed, university. CGS member. *Graduate housing:* Rooms and/or apartments available to single and married students. Housing application deadline: 5/1. *Research affiliation:* National Center for Atmospheric Research (earth and atmospheric sciences), Argonne National Laboratory (energy/physics/chemistry/mathematics and computer science), Small Business Administration (business, administration and entrepreneurship), Monsanto Chemical Corporation (chemistry), Missouri Botanical Garden (biology/plant science), ATT Foundation (communication).

GRADUATE UNITS

Graduate School *Degree program information:* Part-time and evening/weekend programs available. Postbaccalaureate distance learning degree programs offered (minimal on-campus study). Offers anatomy (MS-R, PhD); biochemistry and molecular biology (PhD); biomedical sciences (MS-R, PhD); molecular microbiology and immunology (PhD); pathology (PhD); pharmacological and physiological science (PhD). Electronic applications accepted.

Center for Advanced Dental Education Offers endodontics (MSD); orthodontics (MSD); periodontics (MSD). Electronic applications accepted.

Center for Health Care Ethics Offers clinical health care ethics (Certificate); health care ethics (PhD). Electronic applications accepted.

College of Arts and Sciences *Degree program information:* Part-time and evening/weekend programs available. Offers American studies (MA, MA-R, PhD); arts and sciences (M Pr Met, MA, MA-R, MS, MS-R, PhD); biology (MS, MS-R, PhD); chemistry (MS, MS-R, PhD); clinical psychology (MS-R, PhD); communication (MA, MA-R); communication sciences and disorders (MA, MA-R); English (MA, MA-R, PhD); experimental psychology (MS-R, PhD); French (MA); geophysics (PhD); geoscience (MS); historical theology (MA, PhD); history (MA, MA-R, PhD); industrial-organizational psychology (PhD); mathematics (MA, MA-R, PhD); meteorology (M Pr Met, MS-R, PhD); philosophy (MA, MA-R, PhD); political science (MA); psychology (PhD); Spanish (MA); theology (MA). Electronic applications accepted.

College of Education and Public Service *Degree program information:* Part-time programs available. Offers Catholic school leadership (MA); counseling and family therapy (PhD); curriculum and instruction (MA, Ed D, PhD); education and public service (MA, MA-R, MAPA, MAT, MAUA, MSW, MUPRED, Ed D, PhD, Certificate, Ed S); educational administration (MA, Ed D, PhD, Ed S); educational foundations (MA, Ed D, PhD); geographic information systems (Certificate); higher education (MA, Ed D, PhD); human development counseling (MA); marriage and family therapy (Certificate); organizational development (Certificate); public administration (MAPA); public policy analysis (PhD); school counseling (MA, MA-R); social work (MSW); special education (MA); student personnel administration (MA); teaching (MAT); urban affairs (MAUA); urban planning and real estate development (MUPRED). Electronic applications accepted.

Doisy College of Health Sciences *Degree program information:* Part-time programs available. Offers athletic training (MAT); health sciences (MAT, MMS, MOT, MS, MSN, MSN-R, DNP, DPT, PhD, Certificate); medical dietetics (MS); nursing (MSN, MSN-R, DNP, PhD, Certificate); nutrition and physical performance (MS); occupational science and occupational therapy (MOT); physical therapy (DPT); physician assistant education (MMS).

John Cook School of Business *Degree program information:* Part-time and evening/weekend programs available. Offers accounting (M Acct, MBA); business (EMIB, M Acct, MBA, MSF, PhD); business administration (MBA); executive international business (EMIB); finance (MBA, MSF); international business (MBA). Electronic applications accepted.

Parks College of Engineering, Aviation, and Technology *Degree program information:* Part-time programs available. Postbaccalaureate distance learning degree programs offered (minimal on-campus study). Offers biomedical engineering (MS, MS-R, PhD); engineering, aviation, and technology (MS, MS-R, PhD).

School of Medicine Offers medicine (MD). Electronic applications accepted.

School of Public Health *Degree program information:* Part-time programs available. Offers biosecurity (Certificate); community health (MPH, MS, MSPH); health administration (MHA); health management and policy (MHA, MPH, PhD); health policy (MPH); public health (PhD); public health studies (PhD).

School of Law *Degree program information:* Part-time and evening/weekend programs available. Offers law (JD, LL M). Electronic applications accepted.

See Close-Up on page 981.

SAINT LOUIS UNIVERSITY–MADRID CAMPUS, 28003 Madrid, Spain

General Information Independent-religious, coed, comprehensive institution. *Enrollment:* 16 full-time matriculated graduate/professional students (13 women), 15 part-time matriculated graduate/professional students (9 women). *Enrollment by degree level:* 31 master's. *Graduate faculty:* 73 full-time (44 women), 5 part-time/adjunct (3 women). *Graduate tuition:* Tuition and fees charges are reported in euros. *Tuition:* Full-time 4920 euros; part-time 410 euros per credit. One-time fee: 200 euros. Tuition and fees vary according to course load. *Graduate housing:* Room and/or apartments available on a first-come, first-served basis to single students; on-campus housing not available to married students. Typical cost: 3000 euros per year (7000 euros including board). Room and board charges vary according to board plan and housing facility selected. *Student services:* Campus employment opportunities, career counseling, exercise/wellness program, free psychological counseling, international student services, low-cost health insurance, teacher training, writing training. *Library facilities:* Main

Saint Louis University–Madrid Campus (continued)

library plus 1 other. *Online resources:* library catalog. *Collection:* 8,000 titles, 75 serial subscriptions. *Research affiliation:* Universidad Autónoma de Madrid (Filologìa Inglesa).

Computer facilities: 72 computers available on campus for general student use. A campuswide network can be accessed from student residence rooms. Online class registration is available. *Web address:* http://www.spain.slu.edu/.

General Application Contact: Stephanie Reina, Admissions Counselor and Graduate Programs Coordinator, 34-91-554-58-58, Fax: 34-91-554-62-02, E-mail: graduate_admissions@madrid.slu.edu.

GRADUATE UNITS

Graduate Programs Students: 16 full-time (13 women), 15 part-time (9 women). Average age 34. 33 applicants, 82% accepted, 21 enrolled. *Faculty:* 73 full-time (44 women), 5 part-time/adjunct (3 women). Expenses: Contact institution. *Financial support:* In 2008–09, 11 students received support, including 2 research assistantships with partial tuition reimbursements available (averaging $2,000 per year), 1 teaching assistantship with full tuition reimbursement available (averaging $7,200 per year); career-related internships or fieldwork, Federal Work-Study, scholarships/grants, health care benefits, tuition waivers (full and partial), and unspecified assistantships also available. Support available to part-time students. Financial award application deadline: 5/30; financial award applicants required to submit FAFSA. In 2008, 8 master's awarded. *Degree program information:* Part-time programs available. Offers English (MA); Spanish language and literature (MA). *Application deadline:* For fall admission, 4/30 for domestic and international students; for winter admission, 12/1 for domestic and international students; for spring admission, 10/30 for domestic and international students. Applications are processed on a rolling basis. *Application fee:* $40. *Application Contact:* Stephanie Reina, Admissions Counselor and Graduate Programs Coordinator, 34-91-554-58-58 Ext. 232, Fax: 34-91-554-62-02, E-mail: graduate_admissions@madrid.slu.edu. *Chair,* Dr. Paul Anthony Vita, 34-91-554-58-58, Fax: 34-91-554-62-02, E-mail: vitap@.slu.edu.

SAINT MARTIN'S UNIVERSITY, Lacey, WA 98503-1297

General Information Independent-religious, coed, comprehensive institution. *Graduate housing:* Room and/or apartments available on a first-come, first-served basis to single students; on-campus housing not available to married students. Housing application deadline: 3/15.

GRADUATE UNITS

Graduate Programs *Degree program information:* Part-time and evening/weekend programs available. Offers administration (M Ed); civil engineering (MCE); counseling psychology (MAC); engineering management (M Eng Mgt); English as a second language (M Ed); guidance and counseling (M Ed); reading (M Ed); special education (M Ed); teaching (MIT); technology in education (M Ed).

Division of Economics and Business Administration *Degree program information:* Part-time and evening/weekend programs available. Offers economics and business administration (MBA).

SAINT MARY-OF-THE-WOODS COLLEGE, Saint Mary-of-the-Woods, IN 47876

General Information Independent-religious, coed, primarily women, comprehensive institution. *Graduate housing:* Rooms and/or apartments guaranteed to single students and available to married students.

GRADUATE UNITS

Program in Art Therapy *Degree program information:* Part-time and evening/weekend programs available. Postbaccalaureate distance learning degree programs offered (minimal on-campus study). Offers art therapy (MA, Post-Master's Certificate). Electronic applications accepted.

Program in Earth Literacy *Degree program information:* Part-time programs available. Postbaccalaureate distance learning degree programs offered (minimal on-campus study). Offers earth literacy (MA). Electronic applications accepted.

Program in Leadership Development Offers leadership development (MLD).

Program in Music Therapy *Degree program information:* Part-time programs available. Postbaccalaureate distance learning degree programs offered (minimal on-campus study). Offers music therapy (MA). Electronic applications accepted.

Program in Pastoral Theology *Degree program information:* Part-time and evening/weekend programs available. Postbaccalaureate distance learning degree programs offered (minimal on-campus study). Offers pastoral theology (MA); youth ministry (Graduate Certificate).

SAINT MARY'S COLLEGE OF CALIFORNIA, Moraga, CA 94575

General Information Independent-religious, coed, comprehensive institution. CGS member. *Graduate housing:* On-campus housing not available.

GRADUATE UNITS

Graduate Business Programs *Degree program information:* Part-time and evening/weekend programs available. Offers business (MBA); business administration (MBA); executive business administration (MBA).

Kalmanovitz School of Education *Degree program information:* Part-time and evening/weekend programs available. Offers early childhood education and Montessori teacher training (M Ed, MA); education (M Ed, MA, MAT, PhD); educational leadership (MA, PhD); general counseling (MA); instruction (M Ed); marital and family therapy (MA); reading leadership (MA); school counseling (MA); special education (M Ed, MA); teachers for tomorrow (MAT); teaching leadership (MA).

School of Liberal Arts *Degree program information:* Part-time programs available. Offers creative writing (MFA); kinesiology (MA); leadership (MA); liberal arts (MA, MFA); liberal studies (MA).

SAINT MARY SEMINARY AND GRADUATE SCHOOL OF THEOLOGY, Wickliffe, OH 44092-2527

General Information Independent-religious, coed, primarily men, graduate-only institution. *Graduate housing:* Room and/or apartments available to single students; on-campus housing not available to married students.

GRADUATE UNITS

School of Theology *Degree program information:* Part-time programs available. Offers theology (M Div, MA, D Min).

ST. MARY'S SEMINARY AND UNIVERSITY, Baltimore, MD 21210-1994

General Information Independent-religious, coed, primarily men, graduate-only institution. *Graduate housing:* Room and/or apartments guaranteed to single students; on-campus housing not available to married students. Housing application deadline: 8/15.

GRADUATE UNITS

Ecumenical Institute of Theology *Degree program information:* Part-time and evening/weekend programs available. Offers church ministries (MA); theology (MA Th, Certificate).

School of Theology *Degree program information:* Part-time programs available. Offers theology (M Div, STB, MA Th, STD, STL).

SAINT MARY'S UNIVERSITY, Halifax, NS B3H 3C3, Canada

General Information Province-supported, coed, comprehensive institution. *Graduate housing:* Rooms and/or apartments available on a first-come, first-served basis to single students and available to married students. Housing application deadline: 3/30.

GRADUATE UNITS

Faculty of Arts *Degree program information:* Part-time and evening/weekend programs available. Offers arts (MA); Atlantic Canada studies (MA); criminology (MA); history (MA); international development studies (MA); philosophy (MA); women and gender studies (MA).

Faculty of Commerce *Degree program information:* Part-time and evening/weekend programs available. Offers business administration (MBA); finance (MF); management (PhD).

Faculty of Science *Degree program information:* Part-time programs available. Offers applied psychology (M Sc, PhD); astronomy (M Sc, PhD); science (M Sc, PhD).

ST. MARY'S UNIVERSITY, San Antonio, TX 78228-8507

General Information Independent-religious, coed, comprehensive institution. *Enrollment:* 3,889 graduate, professional, and undergraduate students; 995 full-time matriculated graduate/professional students (498 women), 522 part-time matriculated graduate/professional students (265 women). *Enrollment by degree level:* 827 first professional, 611 master's, 79 doctoral. *Graduate faculty:* 47 full-time (18 women), 55 part-time/adjunct (18 women). *Tuition:* Full-time $12,006; part-time $667 per credit hour. *Required fees:* $440; $220 per semester. *Graduate housing:* Room and/or apartments available on a first-come, first-served basis to single students; on-campus housing not available to married students. Typical cost: $4812 per year ($7230 including board). Housing application deadline: 5/1. *Student services:* Campus employment opportunities, career counseling, exercise/wellness program, free psychological counseling, international student services, low-cost health insurance, services for students with disabilities. *Library facilities:* Louis J. Blume Library plus 1 other. *Online resources:* library catalog, web page, access to other libraries' catalogs. *Collection:* 595,259 titles, 415 serial subscriptions, 5,558 audiovisual materials. *Research affiliation:* Southeast Research Consortium (behavioral science, biomedical engineering, social science).

Computer facilities: Computer purchase and lease plans are available. 100 computers available on campus for general student use. A campuswide network can be accessed from student residence rooms and from off campus. Online class registration is available. *Web address:* http://www.stmarytx.edu/.

General Application Contact: Dr. Henry Flores, Dean of the Graduate School, 210-436-3101, Fax: 210-431-2220, E-mail: hflores@stmarytx.edu.

GRADUATE UNITS

Graduate School Students: 995 full-time (498 women), 522 part-time (265 women); includes 529 minority (63 African Americans, 6 American Indian/Alaska Native, 53 Asian Americans or Pacific Islanders, 407 Hispanic Americans), 67 international. Average age 29. 1,805 applicants, 67% accepted, 550 enrolled. *Faculty:* 47 full-time (18 women), 55 part-time/adjunct (18 women). Expenses: Contact institution. *Financial support:* In 2008–09, 113 fellowships (averaging $4,523 per year), 22 research assistantships (averaging $6,250 per year) were awarded; career-related internships or fieldwork, Federal Work-Study, institutionally sponsored loans, scholarships/grants, health care benefits, tuition waivers, unspecified assistantships, and employer tuition benefit also available. Financial award application deadline: 3/31; financial award applicants required to submit FAFSA. In 2008, 241 master's, 14 doctorates awarded. *Degree program information:* Part-time and evening/weekend programs available. Postbaccalaureate distance learning degree programs offered (minimal on-campus study). Offers Catholic principalship (Certificate); Catholic school administrators (Certificate); Catholic school leadership (MA, Certificate); Catholic school teachers (Certificate); clinical psychology (MA, MS); communication studies (MA); community counseling (MA); computer information systems (MS); computer science (MS); counseling (Sp C); counseling education and supervision (PhD); educational leadership (MA, Certificate); electrical engineering (MS); electrical/computer engineering (MS); engineering administration (MS); engineering computer applications (MS); engineering management (MS); engineering systems management (MS); English literature and language (MA); industrial engineering (MS); industrial/organizational psychology (MA, MS); inter-American administration (MPA); international relations (MA); marriage and family relations (Certificate); marriage and family therapy (MA, PhD); mental health (MA); mental health and substance abuse counseling (Certificate); operations research (MS); pastoral ministry (MA); political communications and applied science (MA); political science (MA); principalship (mid-management) (Certificate); public administration (MPA); public management (MPA); reading (MA); software engineering (MS); substance abuse (MA); theology (MA). *Application deadline:* Applications are processed on a rolling basis. Electronic applications accepted. *Application Contact:* Dr. Henry Flores, Dean of the Graduate School, 210-436-3101, Fax: 210-431-2220, E-mail: hflores@stmarytx.edu. *Dean of the Graduate School,* Dr. Henry Flores, 210-436-3101, Fax: 210-431-2220, E-mail: hflores@stmarytx.edu.

Bill Greehey School of Business Students: 23 full-time (15 women), 33 part-time (12 women); includes 17 minority (2 African Americans, 1 American Indian/Alaska Native, 14 Hispanic Americans), 12 international. Average age 29. 53 applicants, 53% accepted, 22 enrolled. Expenses: Contact institution. *Financial support:* In 2008–09, 12 students received support, including 12 fellowships (averaging $9,918 per year); career-related internships or fieldwork, Federal Work-Study, institutionally sponsored loans, scholarships/grants, health care benefits, and unspecified assistantships also available. Financial award application deadline: 3/31. In 2008, 42 master's awarded. *Degree program information:* Part-time and evening/weekend programs available. Postbaccalaureate distance learning degree programs offered (minimal on-campus study). Offers accounting (M Acc); business administration (MBA); finance (MBA); international business (MBA); management (MBA); taxation (M Acc). *Application deadline:* Applications are processed on a rolling basis. *Application fee:* $0. Electronic applications accepted. *Application Contact:* Dr. Henry Flores, Dean of the Graduate School, 210-436-3101, Fax: 210-431-2220, E-mail: hflores@stmarytx.edu. *Interim Dean,* Dr. Orion J Welch, 210-436-2031, E-mail: owelch@stmarytx.edu.

School of Law Students: 739 full-time (327 women), 88 part-time (37 women); includes 272 minority (29 African Americans, 4 American Indian/Alaska Native, 33 Asian Americans or Pacific Islanders, 206 Hispanic Americans), 3 international. 1,354 applicants, 66% accepted, 323 enrolled. *Faculty:* 38 full-time (14 women), 36 part-time/adjunct (13 women). Expenses: Contact institution. *Financial support:* In 2008–09, 68 research assistantships (averaging $1,900 per year), 58 teaching assistantships (averaging $1,250 per year) were awarded; career-related internships or fieldwork, Federal Work-Study, institutionally sponsored loans, scholarships/grants, and health care benefits also available. Financial award application deadline: 2/15; financial award applicants required to submit FAFSA. In 2008, 235 JDs awarded. Offers law (JD). *Application deadline:* For fall admission, 3/1 for domestic students. *Application fee:* $55. Electronic applications accepted. *Application Contact:* Dr. William Charles Wilson, Assistant Dean and Director of Admissions, 210-436-3523, Fax: 210-431-4202. *Interim Dean,* Dr. Charles Cantu, 210-436-3424, Fax: 210-436-3515.

SAINT MARY'S UNIVERSITY OF MINNESOTA, Winona, MN 55987-1399

General Information Independent-religious, coed, comprehensive institution. *Enrollment:* 5,611 graduate, professional, and undergraduate students; 575 full-time matriculated graduate/professional students (334 women), 2,730 part-time matriculated graduate/professional students (1,814 women). *Enrollment by degree level:* 2,768 master's, 202 doctoral, 335 other advanced degrees. *Graduate faculty:* 9 full-time (2 women), 386 part-time/adjunct (196 women). Tuition and fees vary according to degree level and program. *Student services:* Campus safety program, services for students with disabilities, teacher training, writing training. *Library facilities:* Fitzgerald Library plus 1 other. *Online resources:* library catalog, web page, access to other libraries' catalogs. *Collection:* 241,470 titles, 39,650 serial subscriptions, 10,087 audiovisual materials.

Computer facilities: 200 computers available on campus for general student use. A campuswide network can be accessed from student residence rooms and from off campus. Online class registration is available. *Web address:* http://www.smumn.edu/.

General Application Contact: Becky Copper, Director of Admissions for Graduate and Professional Programs, 612-728-5207, Fax: 612-728-5121, E-mail: bcopper@smumn.edu.

GRADUATE UNITS

Schools of Graduate and Professional Programs Students: 575 full-time (334 women), 2,730 part-time (1,814 women); includes 333 minority (202 African Americans, 7 American

Indian/Alaska Native, 81 Asian Americans or Pacific Islanders, 43 Hispanic Americans), 101 international. Average age 35. *Faculty:* 9 full-time (2 women), 386 part-time/adjunct (196 women). Expenses: Contact institution. *Application Contact:* Becky Copper, Director of Admissions for Graduate and Professional Programs, 612-728-5207, Fax: 612-728-5121, E-mail: bcopper@smumn.edu. *Vice President, Schools of Graduate and Professional Programs,* James M. Bedtke, 507-457-1458, Fax: 507-457-1752, E-mail: jbedtke@smumn.edu.

Graduate School of Business and Technology Offers arts and cultural management (MA); business administration (MBA); business and technology (MA, MBA, MS, Certificate); geographic information science (MS, Certificate); human development (MA); human resource management (MA); information technology management (MS); international business (MA); management (MA); organizational leadership (MA); philanthropy and development (MA); project management (MS, Certificate); public safety administration (MA).

Graduate School of Education Offers behavioral disorders (Certificate); Catholic school leadership (MA); curriculum, assessment and instruction (Ed S); education (MA); education-Wisconsin (MA); educational administration (Ed S); educational leadership (MA); gifted and talented instruction (Certificate); instruction (MA, Certificate); K-12 reading teacher (Certificate); learning disabilities (Certificate); literacy education (MA); special education (MA); teaching and learning (M Ed).

Graduate School of Health and Human Services Offers Canon law (Certificate); counseling and psychological services (MA, Psy D); health and human services (MA, MS, Psy D, Certificate); health and human services administration (MA); marriage and family therapy (MA, Certificate); nurse anesthesia (MS); pastoral administration (MA); pastoral ministries (MA).

SAINT MEINRAD SCHOOL OF THEOLOGY, Saint Meinrad, IN 47577

General Information Independent-religious, coed, primarily men, graduate-only institution. *Graduate housing:* Room and/or apartments guaranteed to single students; on-campus housing not available to married students. Housing application deadline: 7/15.

GRADUATE UNITS

Professional Program Offers theology (M Div).

Program in Catholic Philosophical Studies Offers Catholic philosophical studies (MA).

Program in Catholic Thought and Life *Degree program information:* Part-time and evening/weekend programs available. Offers Catholic thought and life (MA).

Program in Theological Studies *Degree program information:* Part-time and evening/weekend programs available. Offers theological studies (MTS).

SAINT MICHAEL'S COLLEGE, Colchester, VT 05439

General Information Independent-religious, coed, comprehensive institution. *Graduate housing:* On-campus housing not available.

GRADUATE UNITS

Graduate Programs *Degree program information:* Part-time and evening/weekend programs available. Offers administration (M Ed, CAGS); administration and management (MSA, CAMS); arts in education (CAGS); clinical psychology (MA); curriculum and instruction (M Ed, CAGS); information technology (CAGS); reading (M Ed); special education (M Ed, CAGS); teaching English as a second language (MATESL, Certificate); technology (M Ed); theology (MA, CAS, Certificate). Electronic applications accepted.

ST. NORBERT COLLEGE, De Pere, WI 54115-2099

General Information Independent-religious, coed, comprehensive institution. *Enrollment:* 2,137 graduate, professional, and undergraduate students; 78 part-time matriculated graduate/professional students (58 women). *Enrollment by degree level:* 78 master's. *Graduate faculty:* 6 full-time (3 women), 6 part-time/adjunct (4 women). *Tuition:* Part-time $350 per credit hour. *Graduate housing:* On-campus housing not available. *Student services:* Campus employment opportunities, campus safety program, career counseling, child daycare facilities, exercise/wellness program, free psychological counseling, international student services, low-cost health insurance, multicultural affairs office, services for students with disabilities, teacher training, writing training. *Library facilities:* Todd Wehr Library. *Online resources:* library catalog, web page, access to other libraries' catalogs. *Collection:* 229,958 titles, 485 serial subscriptions, 6,971 audiovisual materials.

Computer facilities: Computer purchase and lease plans are available. 233 computers available on campus for general student use. A campuswide network can be accessed from student residence rooms and from off campus. Online class registration is available. *Web address:* http://www.snc.edu/.

General Application Contact: Dinah Grassel, Program Coordinator, 920-403-3957, Fax: 920-403-4086.

GRADUATE UNITS

Program in Education Students: 17 part-time (14 women); includes 3 minority (1 African American, 2 American Indian/Alaska Native). 17 applicants, 100% accepted, 17 enrolled. *Faculty:* 1 (woman) full-time, 3 part-time/adjunct (2 women). Expenses: Contact institution. *Financial support:* Scholarships/grants and tuition waivers (partial) available. Support available to part-time students. In 2008, 16 master's awarded. *Degree program information:* Part-time and evening/weekend programs available. Offers education (MS). *Application fee:* $35. Electronic applications accepted. *Application Contact:* Karen L. Cleereman, Office Manager, Fax: 920-403-4078, E-mail: karen.cleereman@snc.edu. *Director/Professor,* Dr. Susan M. Landt, 920-403-1328, Fax: 920-403-4078, E-mail: susan.landt@snc.edu.

Program in Liberal Studies Expenses: Contact institution. Offers liberal studies (MA). *Application Contact:* Program Coordinator, Fax: 920-403-4086, E-mail: deette.radant@snc.edu. *Director,* Dr. Howard Ebert, 920-403-3956, Fax: 920-403-4086, E-mail: howard.ebert@snc.edu.

Program in Theological Studies Students: 61 part-time (44 women); includes 7 minority (1 Asian American or Pacific Islander, 6 Hispanic Americans). 4 applicants, 125% accepted, 5 enrolled. *Faculty:* 5 full-time (2 women), 3 part-time/adjunct (2 women). Expenses: Contact institution. *Financial support:* In 2008–09, 9 students received support. Scholarships/grants available. Support available to part-time students. In 2008, 4 master's awarded. *Degree program information:* Part-time programs available. Offers theological studies (MTS). *Application deadline:* Applications are processed on a rolling basis. *Application fee:* $50. Electronic applications accepted. *Application Contact:* Dinah Grassel, Program Coordinator, 920-403-3957, Fax: 920-403-4086, E-mail: dinah.grassel@snc.edu. *Director,* Dr. Howard Ebert, 920-403-3956, Fax: 920-403-4086, E-mail: howard.ebert@snc.edu.

ST. PATRICK'S SEMINARY & UNIVERSITY, Menlo Park, CA 94025-3596

General Information Independent-religious, coed, primarily men, graduate-only institution. *Graduate housing:* Room and/or apartments guaranteed to single students; on-campus housing not available to married students. Housing application deadline: 8/15.

GRADUATE UNITS

School of Theology *Degree program information:* Part-time programs available. Offers theology (M Div, STB, MA).

SAINT PAUL SCHOOL OF THEOLOGY, Kansas City, MO 64127-2440

General Information Independent-religious, coed, graduate-only institution. *Graduate housing:* Rooms and/or apartments available to single and married students. Housing application deadline: 5/31.

GRADUATE UNITS

Graduate and Professional Programs *Degree program information:* Part-time programs available. Offers theology (M Div, MA, MTS, D Min).

SAINT PAUL UNIVERSITY, Ottawa, ON K1S 1C4, Canada

General Information Province-supported, coed, university. *Graduate housing:* Room and/or apartments available to single students; on-campus housing not available to married students.

GRADUATE UNITS

Faculty of Canon Law Students: 46 full-time (8 women), 8 part-time (4 women); includes 25 minority (12 African Americans, 12 Asian Americans or Pacific Islanders, 1 Hispanic American). Average age 40. 40 applicants, 70% accepted, 16 enrolled. *Faculty:* 9 full-time (1 woman), 6 part-time/adjunct (1 woman). Expenses: Contact institution. *Financial support:* Scholarships/grants and bursaries available. In 2008, 6 master's, 8 doctorates, 36 other advanced degrees awarded. *Degree program information:* Part-time programs available. Offers canon law (MCL, JCD, PhD, Graduate Certificate, JCL); canonical practice (Graduate Certificate); ecclesiastical administration (Graduate Certificate). *Application deadline:* For fall admission, 8/15 priority date for domestic students, 9/15 priority date for international students. Applications are processed on a rolling basis. *Application fee:* $65 Canadian dollars. *Application Contact:* Beverly Ruth Kavanaugh, Administrative Assistant, 613-751-4018, Fax: 613-751-4036, E-mail: bkavanaugh@ustpaul.ca. *Dean,* Dr. Roland Jacques, 613-751-4035, Fax: 613-751-4036, E-mail: canonlaw@ustpaul.ca.

Faculty of Human Sciences Offers conflict studies (MA); counseling and spirituality (MA); individual and/or marital/couple counseling (MA Past St); individual or marital/couple counseling (MA); mission and interreligious studies (MA); pastoral care in health care services (MA Past St); spiritual care (MA). Programs offered in French and English.

Faculty of Theology Students: 62 full-time (21 women), 9 part-time (6 women), 20 international. *Faculty:* 25 full-time (8 women), 4 part-time/adjunct (0 women). Expenses: Contact institution. In 2008, 7 master's, 2 doctorates, 2 other advanced degrees awarded. Offers theology (MA Th, MP Th, MRE, D Min, D Th, PhD, L Th). *Application deadline:* For fall admission, 6/15 priority date for domestic students; for winter admission, 10/15 for domestic students. Applications are processed on a rolling basis. *Application fee:* $60. *Application Contact:* Francine Forgues, Associate Registrar, 613-236-1393 Ext. 2237, Fax: 613-782-3014, E-mail: fforgues@ustpaul.ca. *Dean,* Dr. Andrea Spatafora, 613-236-1393 Ext. 2277, Fax: 613-751-4016, E-mail: doyenFTdean@ustapaul.ca.

ST. PETERSBURG THEOLOGICAL SEMINARY, St. Petersburg, FL 33708

General Information Independent-religious, coed, upper-level institution. *Graduate housing:* On-campus housing not available.

GRADUATE UNITS

Graduate Programs *Degree program information:* Part-time and evening/weekend programs available. Postbaccalaureate distance learning degree programs offered (minimal on-campus study). Electronic applications accepted.

SAINT PETER'S COLLEGE, Jersey City, NJ 07306-5997

General Information Independent-religious, coed, comprehensive institution. *Graduate housing:* On-campus housing not available.

GRADUATE UNITS

Graduate Programs in Education *Degree program information:* Part-time and evening/weekend programs available. Offers administration and supervision (MA); elementary teacher (Certificate); reading specialist (MA); special education (MA); supervisor of instruction (Certificate); teaching (MA, Certificate).

MBA Programs *Degree program information:* Part-time and evening/weekend programs available. Offers finance (MBA); international business (MBA); management (MBA); management information systems (MBA); marketing (MBA).

Nursing Program *Degree program information:* Part-time and evening/weekend programs available. Offers adult nurse practitioner (MSN); case management (MSN); RN to MSN bridge (MSN).

Program in Accountancy *Degree program information:* Part-time and evening/weekend programs available. Offers accountancy (MS).

See Close-Up on page 983.

ST. PETER'S SEMINARY, London, ON N6A 3Y1, Canada

General Information Independent-religious, coed, primarily men, graduate-only institution.

GRADUATE UNITS

Department of Theology Offers theology (M Div, MTS).

SAINTS CYRIL AND METHODIUS SEMINARY, Orchard Lake, MI 48324

General Information Independent-religious, coed, graduate-only institution. *Graduate housing:* Room and/or apartments guaranteed to single students; on-campus housing not available to married students. Housing application deadline: 7/1.

GRADUATE UNITS

Graduate and Professional Programs *Degree program information:* Part-time programs available. Offers pastoral ministry (MAPM); religious education (MARE); theology (M Div, MA).

ST. STEPHEN'S COLLEGE, Edmonton, AB T6G 2J6, Canada

General Information Independent-religious, coed, graduate-only institution. *Graduate housing:* On-campus housing not available.

GRADUATE UNITS

Programs in Theology *Degree program information:* Part-time and evening/weekend programs available. Postbaccalaureate distance learning degree programs offered (minimal on-campus study). Offers ministry (D Min); pastoral counseling (MA); social transformation ministry (MA); spirituality and liturgy (MA); theological studies (MTS); theology (M Th). Electronic applications accepted.

ST. THOMAS AQUINAS COLLEGE, Sparkill, NY 10976

General Information Independent, coed, comprehensive institution. *Graduate housing:* On-campus housing not available. *Research affiliation:* Lederle Laboratories (science education), Lamont Doherty Laboratories (science education).

GRADUATE UNITS

Division of Business Administration *Degree program information:* Part-time and evening/weekend programs available. Offers business administration (MBA); finance (MBA); management (MBA); marketing (MBA). Electronic applications accepted.

Division of Teacher Education *Degree program information:* Part-time and evening/weekend programs available. Offers adolescence education (MST); childhood and special education (MST); childhood education (MST); educational leadership (MS Ed); reading (MS Ed, PMC); special education (MS Ed, PMC); teaching (MS Ed). Electronic applications accepted.

ST. THOMAS UNIVERSITY, Miami Gardens, FL 33054-6459

General Information Independent-religious, coed, comprehensive institution. *Graduate housing:* Room and/or apartments available on a first-come, first-served basis to single students; on-campus housing not available to married students. Housing application deadline: 7/1.

GRADUATE UNITS

Biscayne College Offers guidance and counseling (MS, Post-Master's Certificate); marriage and family therapy (MS, Post-Master's Certificate); mental health counseling (MS).

St. Thomas University (continued)

School of Business Offers accounting (MBA); business (M Acc, MBA, MIB, MS, MSM, Certificate); business administration (M Acc, MBA, Certificate); general management (MSM, Certificate); health management (MBA, MSM, Certificate); human resource management (MBA, MSM, Certificate); international business (MBA, MIB, MSM, Certificate); justice administration (MSM, Certificate); management accounting (MSM, Certificate); public management (MSM, Certificate); sports administration (MS).

School of Law Postbaccalaureate distance learning degree programs offered (no on-campus study). Offers international human rights (LL M); international taxation (LL M); law (JD). Electronic applications accepted.

School of Leadership Studies *Degree program information:* Part-time and evening/weekend programs available. Offers art management (MA); electronic media (MA); executive management (MPS); Hispanic media (MA, Certificate); leadership studies (MA, MPS, MS, Ed D, Certificate).

Institute for Education *Degree program information:* Part-time and evening/weekend programs available. Offers earth/space science (Certificate); educational administration (MS, Certificate); educational leadership (Ed D); elementary education (MS); ESOL (Certificate); gifted education (Certificate); instructional technology (MS, Certificate); professional/studies (Certificate); reading (MS, Certificate); special education (MS). Electronic applications accepted.

School of Theology and Ministry Offers theology and ministry (MA, PhD, Certificate).

Institute for Pastoral Ministries *Degree program information:* Part-time and evening/weekend programs available. Offers pastoral ministries (MA, Certificate); practical theology (PhD). Electronic applications accepted.

ST. TIKHON'S ORTHODOX THEOLOGICAL SEMINARY, South Canaan, PA 18459

General Information Independent-religious, men only, graduate-only institution. *Enrollment by degree level:* 55 first professional. *Graduate faculty:* 8 full-time (1 woman), 6 part-time/adjunct (0 women). *Tuition:* Part-time $85 per credit. *Required fees:* $10 per semester. One-time fee: $100 part-time. *Graduate housing:* Room and/or apartments guaranteed to single students; on-campus housing not available to married students. Typical cost: $1880 (including board). *Student services:* Career counseling. *Library facilities:* Patriarch St Tikhon Library. *Online resources:* library catalog, web page, access to other libraries' catalogs. *Collection:* 49,000 titles, 250 serial subscriptions, 550 audiovisual materials.

Computer facilities: 25 computers available on campus for general student use. A campuswide network can be accessed from student residence rooms and from off campus. *Web address:* http://www.stots.edu/.

General Application Contact: Fr. Michael Dahulich, Dean and Director of Admissions, 570-937-4411 Ext. 113, Fax: 570-937-3100, E-mail: fr.michael@stots.edu.

GRADUATE UNITS

Divinity Program Students: 48 full-time (0 women), 7 part-time (0 women); includes 3 minority (1 African American, 2 Hispanic Americans), 4 international. 35 applicants, 80% accepted, 28 enrolled. *Faculty:* 8 full-time (1 woman), 6 part-time/adjunct (0 women). Expenses: Contact institution. *Financial support:* Fellowships with partial tuition reimbursements, career-related internships or fieldwork, institutionally sponsored loans, scholarships/grants, and tuition waivers (partial) available. Offers divinity (M Div). *Application deadline:* For fall admission, 7/30 for domestic students, 6/30 for international students. Applications are processed on a rolling basis. *Application fee:* $15. *Application Contact:* Fr. Michael Dahulich, Dean and Director of Admissions, 570-937-4411 Ext. 113, Fax: 570-937-3100, E-mail: fr.michael@stots.edu. *Rector*, Bp. Tikhon Mollard, 570-937-4411, Fax: 570-937-4139, E-mail: bp.tikhon@stots.edu.

SAINT VINCENT COLLEGE, Latrobe, PA 15650-2690

General Information Independent-religious, coed, comprehensive institution. *Graduate housing:* Room and/or apartments available on a first-come, first-served basis to single students; on-campus housing not available to married students.

GRADUATE UNITS

Program in Education *Degree program information:* Part-time and evening/weekend programs available. Offers curriculum and instruction (MS); environmental education (MS); library media management (MS); school administration (MS); special education (MS).

Program in Health Services Offers nurse anesthesia (MS).

Program in Health Services Leadership Offers health services leadership (MS).

SAINT VINCENT DE PAUL REGIONAL SEMINARY, Boynton Beach, FL 33436-4899

General Information Independent-religious, coed, primarily men, graduate-only institution. *Graduate housing:* Room and/or apartments guaranteed to single students; on-campus housing not available to married students.

GRADUATE UNITS

Graduate and Professional Programs *Degree program information:* Part-time programs available. Offers theology (M Div, MA Th).

SAINT VINCENT SEMINARY, Latrobe, PA 15650-2690

General Information Independent-religious, coed, primarily men, graduate-only institution. *Graduate housing:* Room and/or apartments guaranteed to single students; on-campus housing not available to married students. Housing application deadline: 8/1.

GRADUATE UNITS

School of Theology *Degree program information:* Part-time programs available. Offers theology (M Div, MA). Electronic applications accepted.

ST. VLADIMIR'S ORTHODOX THEOLOGICAL SEMINARY, Crestwood, NY 10707-1699

General Information Independent-religious, coed, primarily men, graduate-only institution. *Graduate housing:* Rooms and/or apartments available on a first-come, first-served basis to single and married students. Housing application deadline: 5/1.

GRADUATE UNITS

Graduate School of Theology *Degree program information:* Part-time programs available. Offers general theological studies (MA); liturgical music (MA); religious education (MA); theology (M Div, M Th, D Min). MA in general theological studies, M Div offered jointly with St. Nersess Seminary.

SAINT XAVIER UNIVERSITY, Chicago, IL 60655-3105

General Information Independent-religious, coed, comprehensive institution. *Graduate housing:* Room and/or apartments available on a first-come, first-served basis to single students; on-campus housing not available to married students. Housing application deadline: 8/15. *Research affiliation:* Alexian Brothers Hospital, Holy Cross Hospital, Little Company of Mary Hospital, Mercy Center for Health Care Services.

GRADUATE UNITS

Graduate Studies *Degree program information:* Part-time and evening/weekend programs available. Electronic applications accepted.

Graham School of Management *Degree program information:* Part-time and evening/weekend programs available. Offers e-commerce (MBA); employee health benefits (Certificate); finance (MBA, MS); financial analysis and investments (MBA); financial planning (MBA, Certificate); financial trading and practice (MBA, Certificate); generalist/administration (MBA); health administration (MBA, MS); managed care (Certificate); management (MBA, MS); marketing (MBA); public and non-profit management (MBA); public health (MPH); service management (MBA); training and performance management (MBA). Electronic applications accepted.

School of Arts and Sciences *Degree program information:* Part-time and evening/weekend programs available. Offers adult counseling (Certificate); applied computer science in Internet information systems (MS); arts and sciences (MA, MS, CAS, Certificate); child/adolescent counseling (Certificate); core counseling (Certificate); counseling psychology (MA); English (CAS); literary studies (MA); mathematics and computer science (MA); speech-language pathology (MS); teaching of writing (MA); writing pedagogy (CAS).

School of Education *Degree program information:* Part-time and evening/weekend programs available. Offers counseling (MA); counselor education (MA); curriculum and instruction (MA); early childhood education (MA); education (CAS); educational administration (MA); elementary education (MA); field-based education (MA); general educational studies (MA); individualized program (MA); learning disabilities (MA); reading (MA); secondary education (MA).

School of Nursing *Degree program information:* Part-time and evening/weekend programs available. Offers adult health clinical nurse specialist (MS); family nurse practitioner (MS, PMC); leadership in community health nursing (MS); psychiatric-mental health clinical nurse specialist (MS); psychiatric-mental health clinical specialist (PMC).

SALEM COLLEGE, Winston-Salem, NC 27101

General Information Independent-religious, Undergraduate: women only; graduate: coed, comprehensive institution. *Graduate housing:* On-campus housing not available.

GRADUATE UNITS

Department of Education *Degree program information:* Part-time and evening/weekend programs available. Offers early education and leadership (MAT); elementary education (MAT); English as a second language (MAT); language and literacy (M Ed); middle school education (MAT); secondary education (MAT); special education (MAT).

SALEM INTERNATIONAL UNIVERSITY, Salem, WV 26426-0500

General Information Independent, coed, comprehensive institution. *Graduate housing:* Rooms and/or apartments available on a first-come, first-served basis to single students and available to married students.

GRADUATE UNITS

School of Business *Degree program information:* Part-time programs available. Postbaccalaureate distance learning degree programs offered (no on-campus study). Offers information security (MBA); international business (MBA). Electronic applications accepted.

School of Education *Degree program information:* Part-time and evening/weekend programs available. Postbaccalaureate distance learning degree programs offered. Offers curriculum and instruction (M Ed); educational leadership (M Ed). Electronic applications accepted.

SALEM STATE COLLEGE, Salem, MA 01970-5353

General Information State-supported, coed, comprehensive institution. CGS member. *Enrollment:* 10,157 graduate, professional, and undergraduate students; 283 full-time matriculated graduate/professional students (216 women), 1,174 part-time matriculated graduate/professional students (922 women). *Enrollment by degree level:* 1,457 master's. *Graduate faculty:* 338 full-time (173 women), 433 part-time/adjunct (242 women). *Graduate housing:* On-campus housing not available. *Student services:* Campus employment opportunities, campus safety program, career counseling, child daycare facilities, exercise/wellness program, free psychological counseling, international student services, low-cost health insurance, services for students with disabilities, teacher training, writing training. *Library facilities:* Salem State College Library. *Online resources:* library catalog, web page, access to other libraries' catalogs. *Collection:* 277,985 titles, 1,914 serial subscriptions, 3,811 audiovisual materials.

Computer facilities: Computer purchase and lease plans are available. 426 computers available on campus for general student use. A campuswide network can be accessed from student residence rooms and from off campus. Online class registration is available. *Web address:* http://www.salemstate.edu/.

General Application Contact: Dr. Marc Glasser, Dean of the Graduate School, 978-542-6323, Fax: 978-542-7215.

GRADUATE UNITS

School of Graduate Studies Students: 283 full-time (216 women), 1,174 part-time (922 women); includes 59 minority (22 African Americans, 1 American Indian/Alaska Native, 8 Asian Americans or Pacific Islanders, 28 Hispanic Americans), 40 international. Average age 35. Expenses: Contact institution. *Financial support:* Fellowships with partial tuition reimbursements, research assistantships with full tuition reimbursements, career-related internships or fieldwork and Federal Work-Study available. Support available to part-time students. In 2008, 649 master's, 46 other advanced degrees awarded. *Degree program information:* Part-time and evening/weekend programs available. Offers advanced practice in rehabilitation (MSN); art (MAT); bilingual education (M Ed); biology (MAT); business administration (MBA); chemistry (MAT); counseling and psychological services (MS); criminal justice (MS); direct entry nursing (MSN); early childhood education (M Ed); educational leadership (CAGS); elementary education (M Ed); English (MA, MAT); English as a second language (MAT); field-based education (M Ed); general science (MAT); geo-information science (MS); higher education in student affairs (M Ed); history (MA, MAT); humanities (M Ed); innovative practices (CAGS); library media studies (M Ed); mathematics (MAT, MS); middle school (MAT); nursing (MSN); occupational therapy (MS); physical education 5-12 (M Ed); physical education K-9 (M Ed); reading (M Ed, CAGS); reading, literacy and language (CAGS); school business officer (M Ed); school counseling (M Ed); secondary education (M Ed); social work (MSW); Spanish (MAT); special education (M Ed, MAT); teaching English as a second language (MAT); technology in education (M Ed). *Application deadline:* Applications are processed on a rolling basis. *Application fee:* $35. *Application Contact:* Dr. Marc Glasser, Dean of the School of Graduate Studies, 978-542-7044, Fax: 978-542-7215, E-mail: mglasser@salemstate.edu. *Dean of the School of Graduate Studies*, Dr. Marc Glasser, 978-542-7044, Fax: 978-542-7215, E-mail: mglasser@salemstate.edu.

SALISBURY UNIVERSITY, Salisbury, MD 21801-6837

General Information State-supported, coed, comprehensive institution. *Enrollment:* 7,868 graduate, professional, and undergraduate students; 242 full-time matriculated graduate/professional students (168 women), 345 part-time matriculated graduate/professional students (249 women). *Enrollment by degree level:* 587 master's. *Graduate faculty:* 88 full-time (43 women), 21 part-time/adjunct (15 women). *Tuition, area resident:* Part-time $270 per credit hour. Tuition, state resident: part-time $270 per credit hour. Tuition, nonresident: part-time $566 per credit hour. *Required fees:* $52 per credit hour. *Graduate housing:* On-campus housing not available. *Student services:* Campus employment opportunities, campus safety program, career counseling, exercise/wellness program, free psychological counseling, international student services, multicultural affairs office, services for students with disabilities, writing training. *Library facilities:* Blackwell Library plus 1 other. *Online resources:* library catalog, web page, access to other libraries' catalogs. *Collection:* 271,328 titles, 1,153 serial subscriptions, 1,325 audiovisual materials. *Research affiliation:* NASA (mathematics, physics).

Computer facilities: Computer purchase and lease plans are available. 423 computers available on campus for general student use. A campuswide network can be accessed from student residence rooms and from off campus. Online class registration, accounts for all students are available. *Web address:* http://www.salisbury.edu/.

General Application Contact: Melissa Boog, Associate Director of Admissions, 410-543-6161, Fax: 410-546-6016, E-mail: admissions@salisbury.edu.

GRADUATE UNITS

Graduate Division Students: 242 full-time (168 women), 345 part-time (249 women); includes 65 minority (49 African Americans, 3 American Indian/Alaska Native, 6 Asian Americans or Pacific Islanders, 7 Hispanic Americans), 17 international. Average age 31. 341 applicants,

60% accepted, 165 enrolled. *Faculty:* 88 full-time (43 women), 21 part-time/adjunct (15 women). Expenses: Contact institution. *Financial support:* In 2008–09, 350 students received support. Career-related internships or fieldwork, institutionally sponsored loans, scholarships/grants, and unspecified assistantships available. Support available to part-time students. Financial award application deadline: 2/1; financial award applicants required to submit FAFSA. In 2008, 222 master's awarded. *Degree program information:* Part-time and evening/weekend programs available. Postbaccalaureate distance learning degree programs offered (minimal on-campus study). Offers accounting track (MBA); applied health physiology (MS); composition, language and rhetoric (MA); educational leadership (M Ed); general track (MBA); geographic information systems and public administration (MS); history (MA); literature (MA); mathematics education (MSME); nursing (MS); reading specialist (M Ed); social work (MSW); teaching (MA); teaching English to speakers of other languages (MA). *Application deadline:* Applications are processed on a rolling basis. *Application fee:* $45. Electronic applications accepted. *Application Contact:* Melissa Boog, Associate Director of Admissions, 410-543-6161, Fax: 410-546-6016, E-mail: admissions@salisbury.edu. *Associate Director of Admissions*, Melissa Boog, 410-543-6161, Fax: 410-546-6016, E-mail: admissions@salisbury.edu.

SALUS UNIVERSITY, Elkins Park, PA 19027-1598

General Information Independent, coed, graduate-only institution. *Graduate housing:* Rooms and/or apartments available to single and married students. *Research affiliation:* Charles River Laboratories (photobiology).

GRADUATE UNITS

Graduate Studies in Vision Impairment and Audiology *Degree program information:* Part-time programs available. Offers audiology (Au D); education of children and youth with visual and multiple impairments (M Ed, Certificate); low vision rehabilitation (MS, Certificate); orientation and mobility therapy (MS, Certificate); rehabilitation teaching (MS, Certificate).

Professional Program Postbaccalaureate distance learning degree programs offered. Offers optometry (OD). Electronic applications accepted.

SALVE REGINA UNIVERSITY, Newport, RI 02840-4192

General Information Independent-religious, coed, comprehensive institution. *Enrollment:* 2,691 graduate, professional, and undergraduate students; 116 full-time matriculated graduate/professional students (65 women), 447 part-time matriculated graduate/professional students (250 women). *Enrollment by degree level:* 500 master's, 63 doctoral. *Graduate faculty:* 19 full-time (9 women), 47 part-time/adjunct (19 women). *Tuition:* Part-time $395 per credit. *Required fees:* $40 per term. Tuition and fees vary according to degree level. *Graduate housing:* On-campus housing not available. *Student services:* Campus employment opportunities, campus safety program, career counseling, free psychological counseling, international student services, multicultural affairs office, services for students with disabilities, writing training. *Library facilities:* McKillop Library. *Online resources:* library catalog, web page, access to other libraries' catalogs.

Computer facilities: Computer purchase and lease plans are available. 163 computers available on campus for general student use. A campuswide network can be accessed from student residence rooms and from off campus. Online class registration is available. *Web address:* http://www.salve.edu/.

General Application Contact: Kelly Alverson, Graduate Admissions Counselor, 401-341-2153, Fax: 401-341-2973, E-mail: kelly.alverson@salve.edu.

GRADUATE UNITS

Graduate Studies Students: 116 full-time (65 women), 447 part-time (250 women); includes 17 minority (5 African Americans, 1 American Indian/Alaska Native, 3 Asian Americans or Pacific Islanders, 8 Hispanic Americans), 11 international. Average age 38. 285 applicants, 71% accepted, 176 enrolled. *Faculty:* 19 full-time (9 women), 47 part-time/adjunct (19 women). Expenses: Contact institution. *Financial support:* Career-related internships or fieldwork and Federal Work-Study available. Support available to part-time students. Financial award application deadline: 3/1; financial award applicants required to submit FAFSA. In 2008, 165 master's, 5 doctorates, 15 other advanced degrees awarded. *Degree program information:* Part-time and evening/weekend programs available. Postbaccalaureate distance learning degree programs offered (minimal on-campus study). Offers business administration (MBA); business studies (Certificate); expressive and creative arts (CAGS); healthcare administration and management (MS, Certificate); holistic counseling (MA); holistic leadership (MA, CAGS); homeland security (Certificate); human resources management (Certificate); humanities (MA, PhD, CAGS); international relations (MA, Certificate); justice and homeland security (MS); law enforcement leadership (MS); management (Certificate); mental health (CAGS); mental health counseling (CAGS); organizational development (Certificate); rehabilitation counseling (MA). *Application deadline:* For fall admission, 3/15 priority date for domestic and international students; for spring admission, 9/15 priority date for domestic and international students. Applications are processed on a rolling basis. *Application fee:* $60. Electronic applications accepted. *Application Contact:* Kelly Alverson, Graduate Admissions Counselor, 401-341-2153, Fax: 401-341-2973, E-mail: kelly.alverson@salve.edu. *Dean of Graduate Studies and Continuing Education*, Dr. Thomas M. Sabbagh, 401-341-2477, Fax: 401-341-2973, E-mail: thomas.sabbagh@salve.edu.

SAMFORD UNIVERSITY, Birmingham, AL 35229

General Information Independent-religious, coed, university. *Enrollment:* 4,469 graduate, professional, and undergraduate students; 1,344 full-time matriculated graduate/professional students (694 women), 243 part-time matriculated graduate/professional students (153 women). *Enrollment by degree level:* 1,132 first professional, 294 master's, 138 doctoral, 23 other advanced degrees. *Graduate faculty:* 144 full-time (60 women), 38 part-time/adjunct (14 women). *Tuition:* Full-time $24,800; part-time $1007 per credit. *Required fees:* $110 per semester. *Graduate housing:* Room and/or apartments available on a first-come, first-served basis to single students; on-campus housing not available to married students. Typical cost: $2735 per year ($5323 including board). Room and board charges vary according to board plan, campus/location and housing facility selected. Housing application deadline: 5/1. *Student services:* Campus employment opportunities, campus safety program, career counseling, exercise/wellness program, free psychological counseling, international student services, low-cost health insurance, services for students with disabilities. *Library facilities:* Samford University Library plus 5 others. *Online resources:* library catalog, web page, access to other libraries' catalogs. *Collection:* 439,760 titles, 3,724 serial subscriptions. *Research affiliation:* Southern Research Institute (SRI) of Birmingham, College of Pharmacy, Yanbian University, Yanji, China (Pharmacy), College of Pharmacy, Meijo University, Nagoya, Japan (Pharmacy), University of Alabama at Birmingham Medical School, Vulcan Materials Center (Risk Science and Management), Clinical Research Institute, Wallace Memorial Baptist Hospital, Pusan, Korea.

Computer facilities: 330 computers available on campus for general student use. A campuswide network can be accessed from student residence rooms. Online class registration is available. *Web address:* http://www.samford.edu/.

General Application Contact: Brian E Willett, Director of Admissions, 205-726-2902, Fax: 205-726-2171, E-mail: bewillet@samford.edu.

GRADUATE UNITS

Beeson School of Divinity Students: 174 full-time (32 women), 11 part-time (4 women); includes 28 minority (27 African Americans, 1 Hispanic American). Average age 31. 74 applicants, 73% accepted, 43 enrolled. *Faculty:* 18 full-time (3 women), 4 part-time/adjunct (0 women). Expenses: Contact institution. *Financial support:* In 2008–09, 158 students received support. Scholarships/grants and tuition waivers (full and partial) available. Financial award applicants required to submit FAFSA. In 2008, 46 first professional degrees, 11 master's, 8 doctorates awarded. Offers divinity (M Div, MTS, D Min). *Application deadline:* For fall admission, 3/1 for domestic and international students; for spring admission, 10/1 for domestic and international students. *Application fee:* $25. Electronic applications accepted. *Application Contact:* Dr. Timothy George, Dean, 205-726-2632, E-mail: tfgeorge@samford.edu. *Dean*, Dr. Timothy George, 205-726-2632, E-mail: tfgeorge@samford.edu.

Brock School of Business Students: 67 full-time (28 women), 13 part-time (3 women); includes 9 minority (7 African Americans, 2 Hispanic Americans), 2 international. Average age 28. 71 applicants, 80% accepted, 46 enrolled. *Faculty:* 13 full-time (2 women). Expenses: Contact institution. *Financial support:* In 2008–09, 18 students received support. Career-related internships or fieldwork and institutionally sponsored loans available. Support available to part-time students. Financial award applicants required to submit FAFSA. In 2008, 57 master's awarded. *Degree program information:* Part-time and evening/weekend programs available. Offers business (M Acc, MBA). *Application deadline:* For fall admission, 7/31 priority date for domestic students, 6/1 for international students; for spring admission, 12/31 priority date for domestic students, 10/1 for international students. Applications are processed on a rolling basis. *Application fee:* $25. *Application Contact:* Larron Harper, Director of Graduate Programs, 205-726-2931, Fax: 205-726-4555, E-mail: lcharper@samford.edu. *Dean*, Dr. Beck Taylor, 205-726-2364, Fax: 205-726-2464, E-mail: btaylor@samford.edu.

Cumberland School of Law Students: 479 full-time (216 women), 13 part-time (9 women); includes 37 minority (30 African Americans, 3 American Indian/Alaska Native, 2 Asian Americans or Pacific Islanders, 2 Hispanic Americans), 3 international. Average age 25. 1,105 applicants, 47% accepted, 162 enrolled. *Faculty:* 27 full-time (9 women), 13 part-time/adjunct (7 women). Expenses: Contact institution. *Financial support:* In 2008–09, 169 students received support. Career-related internships or fieldwork, Federal Work-Study, institutionally sponsored loans, and scholarships/grants available. Financial award application deadline: 3/1; financial award applicants required to submit FAFSA. In 2008, 159 first professional degrees, 1 master's awarded. *Degree program information:* Part-time programs available. Offers law (JD, MCL). *Application deadline:* For fall admission, 2/28 priority date for domestic and international students. Applications are processed on a rolling basis. *Application fee:* $50. Electronic applications accepted. *Application Contact:* Jennifer Y. Sims, Director of Admissions, 205-726-2702, Fax: 205-726-2057, E-mail: law.admissions@samford.edu. *Dean*, John L. Carroll, 205-726-2704, Fax: 205-726-4107, E-mail: jlcarrol@samford.edu.

Howard College of Arts and Sciences Students: 7 full-time (2 women), 18 part-time (10 women); includes 4 minority (all African Americans), 2 international. Average age 35. 12 applicants, 100% accepted, 12 enrolled. *Faculty:* 5 full-time (0 women), 6 part-time/adjunct (0 women). Expenses: Contact institution. *Financial support:* In 2008–09, 2 students received support. In 2008, 9 master's awarded. *Degree program information:* Part-time and evening/weekend programs available. Offers arts and sciences (MSEM). *Application deadline:* For fall admission, 8/1 for domestic and international students; for spring admission, 1/2 for domestic students, 12/14 for international students. *Application fee:* $25. *Application Contact:* Dr. Ron Hunsinger, Head, 205-726-2944, Fax: 205-726-2479, E-mail: rnhunsin@samford.edu. *Dean*, Dr. David W. Chapman, 205-726-2771, Fax: 205-726-2279.

Ida V. Moffett School of Nursing Students: 107 full-time (87 women), 23 part-time (14 women); includes 19 minority (16 African Americans, 1 Asian American or Pacific Islander, 2 Hispanic Americans). Average age 34. 14 applicants, 79% accepted, 9 enrolled. *Faculty:* 15 full-time (all women), 1 part-time/adjunct (0 women). Expenses: Contact institution. *Financial support:* In 2008–09, 3 students received support. Institutionally sponsored loans, scholarships/grants, and traineeships available. Financial award application deadline: 3/1; financial award applicants required to submit FAFSA. In 2008, 41 master's awarded. *Degree program information:* Part-time programs available. Postbaccalaureate distance learning degree programs offered (minimal on-campus study). Offers advance practice (DNP); anesthesia (MSN); education (MSN); family nurse practitioner (MSN); management (MSN); nurse educator (DNP); nurse manager (DNP). *Application deadline:* For fall admission, 7/7 priority date for domestic and international students; for spring admission, 6/1 priority date for domestic and international students. Applications are processed on a rolling basis. *Application fee:* $35. *Application Contact:* Marian Carter, Director of Graduate Student Services, 205-726-2047, Fax: 205-726-4269, E-mail: mwcarter@samford.edu. *Dean*, Dr. Nena F. Sanders, 205-726-2629, E-mail: nfsander@samford.edu.

McWhorter School of Pharmacy Students: 486 full-time (314 women), 14 part-time (7 women); includes 45 minority (19 African Americans, 5 American Indian/Alaska Native, 16 Asian Americans or Pacific Islanders, 5 Hispanic Americans), 7 international. Average age 24. 1,171 applicants, 14% accepted, 123 enrolled. *Faculty:* 39 full-time (18 women), 1 (woman) part-time/adjunct. Expenses: Contact institution. *Financial support:* In 2008–09, 224 students received support. Career-related internships or fieldwork, Federal Work-Study, and institutionally sponsored loans available. Financial award application deadline: 5/2; financial award applicants required to submit FAFSA. In 2008, 114 Pharm Ds awarded. Postbaccalaureate distance learning degree programs offered (minimal on-campus study). Offers pharmacy (Pharm D). *Application deadline:* For winter admission, 2/1 for domestic students. Applications are processed on a rolling basis. *Application fee:* $50. Electronic applications accepted. *Application Contact:* C. Bruce Foster, Director of External Relations and Pharmacy Admissions, 205-726-2982, Fax: 205-726-4141, E-mail: cbfoster@samford.edu. *Dean*, Dr. Bobby G. Bryant, 205-726-2820, Fax: 205-726-2759, E-mail: bgbryant@samford.edu.

Orlean Bullard Beeson School of Education and Professional Studies Students: 9 full-time (8 women), 146 part-time (103 women); includes 34 minority (32 African Americans, 1 American Indian/Alaska Native, 1 Asian American or Pacific Islander), 1 international. Average age 40. 44 applicants, 100% accepted, 44 enrolled. *Faculty:* 15 full-time (11 women), 4 part-time/adjunct (2 women). Expenses: Contact institution. *Financial support:* In 2008–09, 146 students received support; research assistantships, career-related internships or fieldwork, Federal Work-Study, scholarships/grants, and tuition waivers (partial) available. Support available to part-time students. Financial award applicants required to submit FAFSA. In 2008, 28 master's, 15 doctorates, 26 other advanced degrees awarded. *Degree program information:* Part-time programs available. Offers early childhood education (Ed S); early childhood/elementary education (MS Ed); educational administration (Ed S); educational leadership (Ed D); elementary education (Ed S); gifted education (MS Ed); instructional leadership (MS Ed); secondary collaboration (MS Ed). *Application deadline:* Applications are processed on a rolling basis. *Application fee:* $25. *Application Contact:* Dr. Maurice Persall, Director, Graduate Office, 205-726-2019, E-mail: jmpersal@samford.edu. *Dean*, Dr. Jean Ann Box, 205-726-2559, E-mail: jabox@samford.edu.

School of the Arts Students: 15 full-time (7 women), 5 part-time (3 women); includes 3 minority (1 African American, 1 American Indian/Alaska Native, 1 Asian American or Pacific Islander). Average age 26. 10 applicants, 80% accepted, 6 enrolled. *Faculty:* 12 full-time (2 women), 9 part-time/adjunct (4 women). Expenses: Contact institution. *Financial support:* In 2008–09, 19 students received support, including research assistantships (averaging $4,000 per year); Federal Work-Study, scholarships/grants, and tuition waivers (partial) also available. Financial award application deadline: 9/1. In 2008, 3 master's awarded. *Degree program information:* Part-time programs available. Offers church music (MM); music (MME); piano pedagogy (MM). *Application deadline:* For fall admission, 5/1 priority date for domestic students; for spring admission, 12/1 priority date for domestic students. Applications are processed on a rolling basis. *Application fee:* $35. *Application Contact:* Dr. Moya Nordlund, Director, Graduate Studies, 205-726-2651, Fax: 205-726-2165, E-mail: mlnordlu@samford.edu. *Dean*, Dr. Joseph H. Hopkins, 205-726-2165, E-mail: jhhopkin@samford.edu.

SAM HOUSTON STATE UNIVERSITY, Huntsville, TX 77341

General Information State-supported, coed, university. CGS member. *Enrollment:* 16,663 graduate, professional, and undergraduate students; 622 full-time matriculated graduate/professional students (374 women), 1,738 part-time matriculated graduate/professional students (1,249 women). *Enrollment by degree level:* 1,867 master's, 244 doctoral. *Graduate faculty:* 222 full-time (84 women), 41 part-time/adjunct (20 women). Tuition, state resident: full-time $3564; part-time $198 per credit hour. Tuition, nonresident: full-time $8622; part-time $479 per credit hour. *Required fees:* $1290. Tuition and fees vary according to course load and campus/location. *Graduate housing:* Room and/or apartments available on a first-come, first-served basis to single students; on-campus housing not available to married students. Typical cost: $3460 per year ($6046 including board). Room and board charges vary according to board plan and housing facility selected. Housing application deadline: 8/20. *Student services:* Campus employment opportunities, campus safety program, career counseling, child daycare facilities, exercise/wellness program, free psychological counseling, grant writing training, international student services, multicultural affairs office, services for students with disabilities, writing training. *Library facilities:* Newton Gresham Library. *Online resources:*

Sam Houston State University (continued)

library catalog. *Collection:* 1.3 million titles, 13,821 serial subscriptions, 14,283 audiovisual materials. *Research affiliation:* Texas Criminal Justice Division, Texas Department of Corrections, Research Division.

Computer facilities: 600 computers available on campus for general student use. A campuswide network can be accessed from student residence rooms and from off campus. Online class registration is available. *Web address:* http://www.shsu.edu/.

General Application Contact: Dr. Mitchell Muehsam, Dean of Graduate Studies and Associate Vice President for Academic Affairs, 936-294-1971, Fax: 936-294-1271, E-mail: graduate@shsu.edu.

GRADUATE UNITS

College of Arts and Sciences Students: 93 full-time (36 women), 82 part-time (42 women); includes 23 minority (6 African Americans, 2 Asian Americans or Pacific Islanders, 15 Hispanic Americans), 49 international. Average age 29. 116 applicants, 89% accepted, 81 enrolled. *Faculty:* 47 full-time (11 women), 3 part-time/adjunct (0 women). Expenses: Contact institution. *Financial support:* Research assistantships, teaching assistantships, career-related internships or fieldwork, Federal Work-Study, institutionally sponsored loans, scholarships/grants, and tuition waivers (partial) available. Support available to part-time students. Financial award application deadline: 5/31; financial award applicants required to submit FAFSA. In 2008, 57 master's awarded. *Degree program information:* Part-time and evening/weekend programs available. Offers agriculture (MS); arts and sciences (MA, MFA, MM, MS); biology (MA, MS); chemistry (MS); computing and information science (MS); dance (MFA); industrial technology (MA); mathematics (MA, MS); statistics (MS). *Application deadline:* For fall admission, 8/1 for domestic and international students; for spring admission, 12/1 for domestic and international students. Applications are processed on a rolling basis. *Application fee:* $20. Electronic applications accepted. *Application Contact:* Tammy Gray, Advisor, 936-294-1230, E-mail: dca_tag@shsu.edu. *Dean*, Dr. Jaimie Hebert, 936-294-1401, Fax: 936-294-1598, E-mail: mth_jlh@shsu.edu.

School of Music Students: 13 full-time (4 women), 10 part-time (5 women); includes 5 minority (1 African American, 4 Hispanic Americans), 2 international. Average age 30. 15 applicants, 93% accepted, 11 enrolled. *Faculty:* 9 full-time (0 women), 1 part-time/adjunct (0 women). Expenses: Contact institution. *Financial support:* Teaching assistantships, Federal Work-Study and scholarships/grants available. Financial award application deadline: 5/31; financial award applicants required to submit FAFSA. In 2008, 5 master's awarded. *Degree program information:* Part-time programs available. Offers music (MM); music education (MM). *Application deadline:* For fall admission, 8/1 for domestic and international students; for spring admission, 12/1 for domestic and international students. Applications are processed on a rolling basis. *Application fee:* $20. *Application Contact:* Scott Plugge, Advisor, 936-294-1393, E-mail: plugge@shsu.edu. *Chair*, Dr. James Bankhead, 936-294-3808, Fax: 936-294-3765, E-mail: bankhead@shsu.edu.

College of Business Administration Students: 118 full-time (49 women), 114 part-time (55 women); includes 34 minority (13 African Americans, 7 Asian Americans or Pacific Islanders, 14 Hispanic Americans), 21 international. Average age 30. 139 applicants, 83% accepted, 85 enrolled. *Faculty:* 30 full-time (9 women). Expenses: Contact institution. *Financial support:* Research assistantships, Federal Work-Study, institutionally sponsored loans, and unspecified assistantships available. Financial award application deadline: 5/31; financial award applicants required to submit FAFSA. In 2008, 65 master's awarded. *Degree program information:* Part-time and evening/weekend programs available. Offers accounting (MS); business administration (MBA); finance (MS); general business and finance (MS). *Application deadline:* For fall admission, 8/1 for domestic students; for spring admission, 12/1 for domestic students. Applications are processed on a rolling basis. *Application fee:* $20. *Application Contact:* Dr. Leroy Ashorn, Acting Dean, 936-294-1246, Fax: 936-294-3612, E-mail: lashorn@shsu.edu. *Acting Dean*, Dr. Leroy Ashorn, 936-294-1246, Fax: 936-294-3612, E-mail: lashorn@shsu.edu.

College of Criminal Justice Students: 76 full-time (40 women), 119 part-time (53 women); includes 26 minority (6 African Americans, 1 American Indian/Alaska Native, 5 Asian Americans or Pacific Islanders, 14 Hispanic Americans), 45 international. Average age 32. 102 applicants, 73% accepted, 67 enrolled. *Faculty:* 25 full-time (4 women), 1 part-time/adjunct (0 women). Expenses: Contact institution. *Financial support:* Fellowships, research assistantships, teaching assistantships, career-related internships or fieldwork, Federal Work-Study, institutionally sponsored loans, and unspecified assistantships available. Support available to part-time students. Financial award application deadline: 5/31; financial award applicants required to submit FAFSA. In 2008, 34 master's, 15 doctorates awarded. Offers criminal justice (MS, PhD); criminal justice and criminology (MA); criminal justice management (MS); forensic science (MS); security studies (MS); victim services management (MS). *Application deadline:* For fall admission, 8/1 for domestic students; for spring admission, 12/1 for domestic students. Applications are processed on a rolling basis. *Application fee:* $20. *Application Contact:* Doris Powell-Pratt, Advisor, 936-294-3637, Fax: 936-294-4055, E-mail: icc_dcp@shsu.edu. *Dean*, Dr. Vincent Webb, 936-294-1632, Fax: 936-294-1653, E-mail: vwebb@shsu.edu.

College of Education and Applied Science Students: 202 full-time (147 women), 1,233 part-time (997 women); includes 431 minority (170 African Americans, 6 American Indian/Alaska Native, 16 Asian Americans or Pacific Islanders, 239 Hispanic Americans), 20 international. Average age 35. 517 applicants, 97% accepted, 398 enrolled. *Faculty:* 65 full-time (40 women), 36 part-time/adjunct (20 women). Expenses: Contact institution. *Financial support:* Research assistantships, teaching assistantships, career-related internships or fieldwork, Federal Work-Study, institutionally sponsored loans, and tuition waivers (partial) available. Support available to part-time students. Financial award application deadline: 5/31; financial award applicants required to submit FAFSA. In 2008, 313 master's, 11 doctorates awarded. *Degree program information:* Part-time and evening/weekend programs available. Offers administration (M Ed, MA); counseling (M Ed, MA); counselor education (MA, PhD); curriculum and instruction (M Ed, MA); education and applied science (M Ed, MA, MLS, Ed D, PhD); educational leadership (Ed D); health and kinesiology (M Ed, MA); instructional leadership (M Ed, MA); instructional technology (M Ed); library science (MLS); reading (M Ed, MA, Ed D); special education (M Ed, MA). *Application deadline:* For fall admission, 8/1 for domestic students; for spring admission, 12/1 for domestic students. *Application fee:* $20. *Application Contact:* Molly Doughtie, Advisor, 936-294-1105, E-mail: edu_mxd@shsu.edu. *Dean*, Dr. Genevieve Brown, 936-294-1101, Fax: 936-294-1102, E-mail: edu_gxb@shsu.edu.

College of Humanities and Social Sciences Students: 124 full-time (96 women), 148 part-time (79 women); includes 40 minority (9 African Americans, 1 American Indian/Alaska Native, 13 Asian Americans or Pacific Islanders, 17 Hispanic Americans), 7 international. Average age 30. 239 applicants, 52% accepted, 103 enrolled. *Faculty:* 53 full-time (19 women), 1 part-time/adjunct (0 women). Expenses: Contact institution. In 2008, 43 master's, 4 doctorates awarded. Offers clinical psychology (PhD); dietetics (MS); English (MA); family and consumer sciences (MS); history (MA); humanities and social sciences (MA, MPA, MS, PhD); political science (MA); psychology (MA); public administration (MPA); sociology (MA). *Application deadline:* For fall admission, 8/1 for domestic students; for spring admission, 12/1 for domestic students. *Application fee:* $20. *Application Contact:* Dr. Mitchell Muehsam, Dean of Graduate Studies and Associate Vice President for Academic Affairs, 936-294-1971, Fax: 936-294-1271, E-mail: graduate@shsu.edu. *Dean*, Dr. John deCastro, 936-294-2200, Fax: 936-294-2207, E-mail: jmd018@shsu.edu.

SAMRA UNIVERSITY OF ORIENTAL MEDICINE, Los Angeles, CA 90015

General Information Independent, coed, graduate-only institution. *Graduate housing:* On-campus housing not available.

GRADUATE UNITS

Program in Oriental Medicine *Degree program information:* Part-time and evening/weekend programs available. Offers Oriental medicine (MS, DAOM).

SAMUEL MERRITT UNIVERSITY, Oakland, CA 94609-3108

General Information Independent, coed, primarily women, upper-level institution. *Graduate housing:* Room and/or apartments available to single students; on-campus housing not available to married students. *Research affiliation:* Summit Medical Center (nursing).

GRADUATE UNITS

Department of Occupational Therapy Offers occupational therapy (MOT).

Department of Physical Therapy Offers physical therapy (DPT).

Department of Physician Assistant Studies Offers physician assistant studies (MPA).

School of Nursing *Degree program information:* Part-time and evening/weekend programs available. Offers case management (MSN); family nurse practitioner (MSN, Certificate); nurse anesthetist (MSN, Certificate); nursing (MSN).

SAN DIEGO STATE UNIVERSITY, San Diego, CA 92182

General Information State-supported, coed, university. CGS member. *Graduate housing:* Room and/or apartments available on a first-come, first-served basis to single students; on-campus housing not available to married students. Housing application deadline: 5/1. *Research affiliation:* Children's Hospital and Research Center (children's health), Qualcomm (wireless and telecommunications), Robert Wood Johnson Foundation (public health), General Atomics Corporation (technical student services), William and Flora Hewlit Foundation (teacher education), American Heart Association (biology).

GRADUATE UNITS

Graduate and Research Affairs *Degree program information:* Part-time and evening/weekend programs available. Offers interdisciplinary studies (MA, MS). Electronic applications accepted.

College of Arts and Letters *Degree program information:* Part-time and evening/weekend programs available. Offers anthropology (MA); applied linguistics and English as a second language (CAL); arts and letters (MA, MFA, PhD, CAL); Asian studies (MA); computational linguistics (MA); creative writing (MFA); economics (MA); English (MA); English as a second language/applied linguistics (MA); European studies (MA); general linguistics (MA); geography (MA, PhD); history (MA); Latin American studies (MA); liberal arts and sciences (MA); philosophy (MA); political science (MA); rhetoric and writing (MA); sociology (MA); Spanish (MA); women's studies (MA). Electronic applications accepted.

College of Business Administration *Degree program information:* Part-time and evening/weekend programs available. Offers accountancy (MS); business administration (MBA, MS); entrepreneurship (MS); finance (MS); human resources management (MS); information and decision systems (MS); international business (MS); management science (MS); marketing (MS); production and operations management (MS); sports business management (MBA). Electronic applications accepted.

College of Education *Degree program information:* Part-time and evening/weekend programs available. Offers child development (MS); counseling and school psychology (MS); education (MA, MS, Ed D, PhD); educational leadership (MA); educational leadership in post-secondary education (MA); educational technology (MA); educational technology and teaching and learning (Ed D); elementary curriculum and instruction (MA); multi-cultural emphasis (PhD); policy studies in language and cross cultural education (MA); reading education (MA); rehabilitation counseling (MS); secondary curriculum and instruction (MA); special education (MA). Electronic applications accepted.

College of Engineering *Degree program information:* Part-time and evening/weekend programs available. Offers aerospace engineering (MS); civil engineering (MS); electrical engineering (MS); engineering (MS, PhD); engineering mechanics (MS); engineering sciences and applied mechanics (PhD); flight dynamics (MS); fluid dynamics (MS); manufacture and design (MS); mechanical engineering (MS). Electronic applications accepted.

College of Health and Human Services *Degree program information:* Part-time and evening/weekend programs available. Offers audiology (Au D); biometry (MPH); communicative disorders (MA); environmental health (MPH); epidemiology (MPH, PhD); gerontology (MS); global emergency preparedness and response (MS); global health (PhD); health and human services (MA, MPH, MS, MSW, Au D, PhD); health behavior (PhD); health promotion (MPH); health services administration (MPH); language and communicative disorders (PhD); nursing (MS); social work (MSW); toxicology (MS). Electronic applications accepted.

College of Professional Studies and Fine Arts *Degree program information:* Part-time programs available. Offers advertising and public relations (MA); art history (MA); city planning (MCP); composition (acoustic and electronic) (MM); conducting (MM); criminal justice administration (MPA); criminal justice and criminology (MS); critical-cultural studies (MA); ethnomusicology (MA); exercise physiology (MS); interaction studies (MA); intercultural and international studies (MA); jazz studies (MM); musicology (MA); new media studies (MA); news and information studies (MA); nutritional science (MS); nutritional sciences (MS); performance (MM); physical education/kinesiology (MS); piano pedagogy (MA); professional studies and fine arts (MA, MCP, MFA, MM, MPA, MS); public administration (MPA); studio arts (MA, MFA); telecommunications and media management (MA); television, film, and new media production (MA); theatre arts (MA, MFA); theory (MA).

College of Sciences *Degree program information:* Part-time programs available. Offers applied mathematics (MS); astronomy (MS); biology (MA, MS); cell and molecular biology (PhD); chemistry (MA, MS, PhD); clinical psychology (MS, PhD); computational science (MS, PhD); computer science (MS); ecology (MS, PhD); geological sciences (MS); industrial and organizational psychology (MS); mathematics (MA); mathematics and science education (PhD); microbiology (MS); molecular biology (MA, MS); physics (MA, MS); program evaluation (MS); psychology (MA); radiological physics (MS); regulatory affairs (MS); sciences (MA, MS, PhD); statistics (MS). Electronic applications accepted.

SAN FRANCISCO ART INSTITUTE, San Francisco, CA 94133

General Information Independent, coed, comprehensive institution. *Graduate housing:* Room and/or apartments available on a first-come, first-served basis to single students; on-campus housing not available to married students. *Research affiliation:* Exploratorium (museum of science, art, and human perception).

GRADUATE UNITS

Graduate Program *Degree program information:* Part-time programs available. Offers design and technology (MFA, Certificate); exhibition and museum studies (MA); film (MFA, Certificate); fine arts (MA, MFA, Certificate); history and theory of contemporary art (MA); new genres (Certificate); painting (MFA, Certificate); performance/video (MFA); photography (MFA, Certificate); printmaking (MFA, Certificate); sculpture (MFA, Certificate); urban studies (MA). Electronic applications accepted.

SAN FRANCISCO CONSERVATORY OF MUSIC, San Francisco, CA 94102

General Information Independent, coed, comprehensive institution. *Graduate housing:* On-campus housing not available.

GRADUATE UNITS

Graduate Division *Degree program information:* Part-time programs available. Offers chamber music (MM); classical guitar (MM); composition (MM); conducting (MM); keyboards (MM); orchestral instruments (MM); voice (MM). Electronic applications accepted.

SAN FRANCISCO STATE UNIVERSITY, San Francisco, CA 94132-1722

General Information State-supported, coed, comprehensive institution. CGS member. *Graduate housing:* Room and/or apartments available on a first-come, first-served basis to single students; on-campus housing not available to married students.

GRADUATE UNITS

Division of Graduate Studies *Degree program information:* Part-time and evening/weekend programs available.

College of Behavioral and Social Sciences *Degree program information:* Part-time and evening/weekend programs available. Offers anthropology (MA); behavioral and social sciences (MA, MPA, MS); economics (MA); geography (MA); history (MA); human sexuality studies (MA); integrated and collaborative services (MPA); international relations (MA); nonprofit administration (MPA); policy analysis (MPA); political science (MA); psychology (MA, MS); public management (MPA); urban administration (MPA).

College of Business Offers business (MBA, MSBA); business administration (MBA).

College of Creative Arts Offers art (MFA); art history (MA); chamber music (MM); cinema (MFA); cinema studies (MA); classical performance (MM); composition (MA); conducting (MM); creative arts (MA, MFA, MM); drama (MA); industrial arts (MA); music education (MA); music history (MA); radio and television (MA); theatre arts (MFA).

College of Education Offers adult education (MA Ed, AC); communicative disorders (MS); early childhood education (MA); education (MA, MA Ed, MS, PhD, AC); educational administration (MA, AC); educational technology (MA); elementary education (MA); equity and social justice (AC); equity and social justice in education (MA Ed); language and literacy education (MA); mathematics education (MA); secondary education (MA Ed); special education (MA, PhD, AC); special interest (MA Ed); training systems development (AC).

College of Ethnic Studies *Degree program information:* Part-time programs available. Offers Asian American studies (MA); ethnic studies (MA).

College of Health and Human Services *Degree program information:* Part-time programs available. Offers case management (MS); counseling (MS); family and consumer sciences (MA); geriatric care management (MA); health and human services (MA, MPH, MS, MSC, MSW, DPT, Dr Sc PT); health education (MPH); health, wellness and aging (MA); kinesiology (MS); long-term care administration (MA); marriage, family, and child counseling (MSC); nursing administration (MS); nursing education (MS); physical therapy (MS, DPT, Dr Sc PT); recreation (MS); rehabilitation counseling (MS); social work (MSW).

College of Humanities *Degree program information:* Part-time and evening/weekend programs available. Offers Chinese (MA); classics (MA); communication studies (MA); comparative literature (MA); composition (MA, Certificate); creative writing (MA, MFA); French (MA); German (MA); humanities (MA, MFA, Certificate); Italian (MA); Japanese (MA); linguistics (MA); literature (MA); museum studies (MA); philosophy (MA); Spanish (MA); teaching composition (Certificate); teaching critical thinking (Certificate); teaching English to speakers of other languages (MA); teaching post-secondary reading (Certificate); women studies (MA).

College of Science and Engineering *Degree program information:* Part-time programs available. Offers applied geosciences (MS); biomedical laboratory science (MS); cell and molecular biology (MS); chemistry (MS); computer science (MS); computer science: computing and business (MS); computer science: computing for life sciences (MS); computer science: software and engineering (MS); conservation biology (MS); ecology and systematic biology (MS); embedded electrical and computer systems (MS); engineering (MS); marine biology (MS); marine science (MS); mathematics (MA); microbiology (MS); physics (MS); physiology and behavioral biology (MS); science and engineering (MA, MS); structural/earthquake engineering (MS). Electronic applications accepted.

SAN FRANCISCO THEOLOGICAL SEMINARY, San Anselmo, CA 94960-2997

General Information Independent-religious, coed, graduate-only institution. *Graduate housing:* Rooms and/or apartments available on a first-come, first-served basis to single and married students. Housing application deadline: 5/1.

GRADUATE UNITS

Graduate and Professional Programs *Degree program information:* Part-time programs available. Offers theology (M Div, MA, MATS, D Min, PhD, Th D).

SAN JOAQUIN COLLEGE OF LAW, Clovis, CA 93612-1312

General Information Independent, coed, graduate-only institution. *Graduate housing:* On-campus housing not available.

GRADUATE UNITS

Law Program *Degree program information:* Part-time and evening/weekend programs available. Offers law (JD).

SAN JOSE STATE UNIVERSITY, San Jose, CA 95192-0001

General Information State-supported, coed, comprehensive institution. CGS member. *Graduate housing:* Room and/or apartments available on a first-come, first-served basis to single students; on-campus housing not available to married students. *Research affiliation:* Moss Landing Marine Laboratories.

GRADUATE UNITS

Graduate Studies and Research *Degree program information:* Part-time and evening/weekend programs available. Postbaccalaureate distance learning degree programs offered (minimal on-campus study). Offers interdisciplinary studies (MA, MS). Electronic applications accepted.

College of Applied Sciences and Arts *Degree program information:* Part-time and evening/weekend programs available. Offers applied sciences and arts (MA, MLIS, MPH, MS, MSW, PhD, Certificate); applied social gerontology (Certificate); community health education (MPH); gerontology nurse practitioner (MS); justice studies (MS); kinesiology (MA); library and information science (MLIS, PhD); mass communications (MS); nursing (Certificate); nursing administration (MS); nursing education (MS); nutritional science (MS); occupational therapy (MS); recreation (MS); social work (MSW, Certificate). Electronic applications accepted.

College of Education *Degree program information:* Evening/weekend programs available. Offers child and adolescent development (MA); counselor education (MA); education (MA, Certificate); educational administration (MA); elementary education (MA, Certificate); higher education administration (MA); instructional technology (MA, Certificate); school business management (Certificate); secondary education (Certificate); special education (MA, Certificate); speech language pathology (MA). Electronic applications accepted.

College of Engineering *Degree program information:* Part-time programs available. Offers aerospace engineering (MS); chemical engineering (MS); civil engineering (MS); computer engineering (MS); electrical engineering (MS); engineering (MS); general engineering (MS); human factors and ergonomics (MS); industrial and systems engineering (MS); materials engineering (MS); mechanical engineering (MS); quality assurance (MS); software engineering (MS). Electronic applications accepted.

College of Humanities and the Arts Offers art education (MA); art history (MA); computational linguistics (Certificate); creative writing (MFA); digital media (MFA); digital media in art history and education (MA); French (MA); humanities and the arts (MA, MFA, Certificate); linguistics (MA, Certificate); literature (MA); music (MA); philosophy (MA, Certificate); photography (MFA); pictorial arts (MFA); secondary English education (Certificate); Spanish (MA); spatial arts (MFA); teaching English to speakers of other languages (MA, Certificate); theatre arts (MA). Electronic applications accepted.

College of Science *Degree program information:* Part-time and evening/weekend programs available. Offers applied mathematics (MS); biological sciences (MA, MS); chemistry (MA, MS); computational physics (MS); computer science (MS); geology (MS); marine science (MS); mathematics (MA, MS); mathematics education (MA); meteorology (MS); molecular biology and microbiology (MS); organismal biology, conservation and ecology (MS); physics (MS); physiology (MS); science (MA, MS); statistics (MA). Electronic applications accepted.

College of Social Sciences *Degree program information:* Part-time and evening/weekend programs available. Offers applied anthropology (MA); applied economics (MA); clinical psychology (MS); communication studies (MA); economics (MA); environmental studies (MS); experimental psychology (MA); geographic information science (Certificate); geography (MA); history (MA); history education (MA); industrial/organizational psychology (MS); Mexican-American studies (MA); psychology (MA); public administration (MPA); social sciences (MA, MPA, MS, MUP, Certificate); sociology (MA); urban and regional planning (MUP, Certificate). Electronic applications accepted.

Lucas Graduate School of Business *Degree program information:* Part-time and evening/weekend programs available. Postbaccalaureate distance learning degree programs offered (minimal on-campus study). Offers accounting (MS); business (MBA, MS); business administration (MBA); taxation (MS); transportation management (MS). Electronic applications accepted.

SAN JUAN BAUTISTA SCHOOL OF MEDICINE, Caguas, PR 00726-4968

General Information Independent, coed, graduate-only institution. *Graduate housing:* On-campus housing not available.

GRADUATE UNITS

Professional Program Offers medicine (MD).

SANTA CLARA UNIVERSITY, Santa Clara, CA 95053

General Information Independent-religious, coed, university. CGS member. *Enrollment:* 8,758 graduate, professional, and undergraduate students; 1,414 full-time matriculated graduate/professional students (659 women), 1,798 part-time matriculated graduate/professional students (738 women). *Enrollment by degree level:* 941 first professional, 1,934 master's, 49 doctoral, 288 other advanced degrees. *Graduate faculty:* 218 full-time (75 women), 131 part-time/adjunct (43 women). *Tuition:* Full-time $6849; part-time $761 per credit hour. Tuition and fees vary according to course load and program. *Graduate housing:* On-campus housing not available. *Student services:* Campus employment opportunities, campus safety program, career counseling, child daycare facilities, exercise/wellness program, free psychological counseling, international student services, multicultural affairs office. *Library facilities:* University Library plus 1 other. *Online resources:* library catalog, web page, access to other libraries' catalogs. *Collection:* 797,312 titles, 4,400 serial subscriptions, 10,803 audiovisual materials.

Computer facilities: Computer purchase and lease plans are available. 800 computers available on campus for general student use. A campuswide network can be accessed from student residence rooms and from off campus. Online class registration is available. *Web address:* http://www.scu.edu/.

General Application Contact: Richard Toomey, Associate Vice Provost, Enrollment Management, 408-554-4966, E-mail: rtoomey@scu.edu.

GRADUATE UNITS

Leavey School of Business Students: 242 full-time (82 women), 875 part-time (273 women); includes 395 minority (13 African Americans, 5 American Indian/Alaska Native, 346 Asian Americans or Pacific Islanders, 31 Hispanic Americans), 246 international. Average age 33. 493 applicants, 77% accepted, 245 enrolled. *Faculty:* 88 full-time (21 women), 20 part-time/adjunct (3 women). Expenses: Contact institution. *Financial support:* Fellowships, research assistantships, career-related internships or fieldwork, Federal Work-Study, institutionally sponsored loans, and scholarships/grants available. Support available to part-time students. Financial award application deadline: 3/1; financial award applicants required to submit FAFSA. In 2008, 328 master's awarded. *Degree program information:* Part-time and evening/weekend programs available. Offers business (EMBA, MBA, MSIS); business administration (EMBA, MBA); information systems (MSIS). *Application deadline:* For fall admission, 6/1 for domestic students; for winter admission, 9/1 for domestic students; for spring admission, 1/15 for domestic students. Applications are processed on a rolling basis. *Application fee:* $75 ($100 for international students). Electronic applications accepted. *Application Contact:* Elizabeth Ford, Assistant Dean, 408-554-2752, Fax: 408-554-4571. *Dean,* Dr. Barry Posner, 408-554-4523.

School of Education, Counseling Psychology, and Pastoral Ministries Students: 153 full-time (137 women), 449 part-time (349 women); includes 155 minority (6 African Americans, 1 American Indian/Alaska Native, 65 Asian Americans or Pacific Islanders, 83 Hispanic Americans), 21 international. Average age 34. 333 applicants, 78% accepted, 209 enrolled. *Faculty:* 30 full-time (12 women), 32 part-time/adjunct (19 women). Expenses: Contact institution. *Financial support:* Fellowships, teaching assistantships, career-related internships or fieldwork, Federal Work-Study, institutionally sponsored loans, and scholarships/grants available. Support available to part-time students. Financial award application deadline: 3/1; financial award applicants required to submit FAFSA. In 2008, 147 master's, 174 other advanced degrees awarded. *Degree program information:* Part-time and evening/weekend programs available. Offers catechetics (MA); counseling (MA); counseling psychology (MA); education, counseling psychology, and pastoral ministries (MA, Certificate); educational administration (MA); interdisciplinary education (MA); liturgical music (MA); multiple subject teaching (Certificate); pastoral liturgy (MA); single subject teaching (Certificate); special education (MA, Certificate); spirituality (MA); teacher education (Certificate). *Application deadline:* Applications are processed on a rolling basis. *Application fee:* $50. *Application Contact:* Dr. Dale Larson, Interim Dean, 408-554-4320. *Interim Dean,* Dr. Dale Larson, 408-554-4320.

School of Engineering Students: 131 full-time (33 women), 411 part-time (86 women); includes 209 minority (4 African Americans, 1 American Indian/Alaska Native, 181 Asian Americans or Pacific Islanders, 23 Hispanic Americans), 129 international. Average age 31. 398 applicants, 60% accepted, 153 enrolled. *Faculty:* 39 full-time (10 women), 48 part-time/adjunct (7 women). Expenses: Contact institution. *Financial support:* Fellowships, research assistantships, teaching assistantships, career-related internships or fieldwork, Federal Work-Study, institutionally sponsored loans, and scholarships/grants available. Support available to part-time students. Financial award application deadline: 3/1; financial award applicants required to submit FAFSA. In 2008, 198 master's, 6 doctorates, 11 other advanced degrees awarded. *Degree program information:* Part-time and evening/weekend programs available. Offers analog circuit design (Certificate); applied mathematics (MSAM); ASIC design and test (Certificate); civil engineering (MSCE); computer science and engineering (MSCSE, PhD, Engineer); controls (Certificate); data storage technologies (Certificate); digital signal processing (Certificate); dynamics (Certificate); electrical engineering (MSEE, PhD, Engineer); engineering (MS, MSAM, MSCE, MSCSE, MSE, MSE Mgt, MSEE, MSME, PhD, Certificate, Engineer); engineering management (MSE Mgt); fundamentals of electrical engineering (Certificate); grid computing (Certificate); information assurance (Certificate); materials engineering (Certificate); mechanical design analysis (Certificate); mechanical engineering (MSME, PhD, Engineer); mechatronics systems engineering (Certificate); networking (Certificate); software engineering (MS, Certificate); technology jump-start (Certificate); telecommunications management (Certificate); thermofluids (Certificate). *Application deadline:* For fall admission, 7/18 for domestic students; for spring admission, 2/1 for domestic students. Applications are processed on a rolling basis. *Application fee:* $60. Electronic applications accepted. *Application Contact:* Diana McDonald, Assistant Director for Admissions and Recruiting, 408-554-4313, Fax: 408-554-5474, E-mail: engrgrad@engr.scu.edu. *Dean,* Godfrey Mungal, 408-554-2375.

School of Law Students: 888 full-time (407 women), 69 part-time (35 women); includes 360 minority (41 African Americans, 3 American Indian/Alaska Native, 235 Asian Americans or Pacific Islanders, 81 Hispanic Americans), 23 international. Average age 28. 3,857 applicants, 47% accepted, 351 enrolled. *Faculty:* 61 full-time (32 women), 31 part-time/adjunct (14 women). Expenses: Contact institution. *Financial support:* Fellowships, research assistantships, career-related internships or fieldwork, Federal Work-Study, institutionally sponsored loans, and scholarships/grants available. Support available to part-time students. Financial award application deadline: 2/1; financial award applicants required to submit FAFSA. In 2008, 281 first professional degrees, 10 master's awarded. *Degree program information:* Part-time and evening/weekend programs available. Offers high technology law (Certificate); intellectual property law (LL M); international and comparative law (LL M); international law (Certificate); law (JD); public interest and social justice law (Certificate); US law for foreign lawyers (LL M). *Application deadline:* For fall admission, 2/1 for domestic students. *Application fee:* $75. *Application Contact:* Julia Yaffee, Director of Admissions, 408-554-4800, Fax: 408-554-7897. *Dean,* Donald Polden, 408-554-4361.

SARAH LAWRENCE COLLEGE, Bronxville, NY 10708-5999

General Information Independent, coed, comprehensive institution. CGS member. *Enrollment:* 224 full-time matriculated graduate/professional students (207 women), 81 part-time matriculated graduate/professional students (71 women). *Enrollment by degree level:* 326 master's. *Graduate faculty:* 134 part-time/adjunct (78 women). *Tuition:* Full-time $26,544; part-time $1106 per credit. *Required fees:* $450. Tuition and fees vary according to program. *Graduate housing:* On-campus housing not available. *Student services:* Campus employment opportunities, career counseling, exercise/wellness program, free psychological counseling, grant writing training, international student services, low-cost health insurance, multicultural affairs office, services for students with disabilities, teacher training, writing training. *Library facilities:* Esther Rauschenbush Library plus 2 others. *Online resources:* library catalog, web page, access to other libraries' catalogs. *Collection:* 298,611 titles, 917 serial subscriptions, 10,251 audiovisual materials. *Research affiliation:* Westchester/New York Medical College, New York Hospital–Cornell Medical Center, Albert Einstein College of Medicine of Yeshiva University, New York University Medical Center, Columbia University Medical Center.

Computer facilities: Computer purchase and lease plans are available. 110 computers available on campus for general student use. A campuswide network can be accessed from student residence rooms and from off campus. *Web address:* http://www.sarahlawrence.edu/.

General Application Contact: Susan Guma, Dean of Graduate Studies, 914-395-2373, E-mail: sguma@mail.slc.edu.

GRADUATE UNITS

Graduate Studies Students: 245 full-time (207 women), 81 part-time (71 women); includes 45 minority (15 African Americans, 14 Asian Americans or Pacific Islanders, 16 Hispanic Americans), 27 international. Average age 31. 699 applicants, 49% accepted, 124 enrolled. *Faculty:* 134 part-time/adjunct (78 women). Expenses: Contact institution. *Financial support:* In 2008–09, 217 students received support, including 165 fellowships (averaging $5,659 per year); career-related internships or fieldwork, Federal Work-Study, scholarships/grants, and unspecified assistantships also available. Support available to part-time students. Financial award application deadline: 3/1; financial award applicants required to submit CSS PROFILE or FAFSA. In 2008, 131 master's awarded. *Degree program information:* Part-time programs available. Offers art of teaching (MS Ed); child development (MA); creative non-fiction (MFA); dance (MFA); fiction (MFA); health advocacy (MA); human genetics (MS); individualized study (MA); poetry (MFA); theater (MFA); women's history (MA). *Application fee:* $60. Electronic applications accepted. *Application Contact:* Susan Guma, Dean of Graduate Studies, 914-395-2373, E-mail: sguma@mail.slc.edu. *Dean of Graduate Studies*, Susan Guma, 914-395-2373, E-mail: sguma@mail.slc.edu.

See Close-Up on page 985.

SAVANNAH COLLEGE OF ART AND DESIGN, Savannah, GA 31402-3146

General Information Independent, coed, comprehensive institution. CGS member. *Enrollment:* 9,332 graduate, professional, and undergraduate students; 1,151 full-time matriculated graduate/professional students (652 women), 326 part-time matriculated graduate/professional students (199 women). *Enrollment by degree level:* 1,447 master's. *Graduate faculty:* 284 full-time (115 women), 79 part-time/adjunct (30 women). *Tuition:* Full-time $28,215; part-time $3135 per course. One-time fee: $500. *Graduate housing:* Room and/or apartments available on a first-come, first-served basis to single students; on-campus housing not available to married students. Typical cost: $11,710 (including board). Room and board charges vary according to board plan and housing facility selected. Housing application deadline: 4/1. *Student services:* Campus employment opportunities, campus safety program, career counseling, exercise/wellness program, free psychological counseling, international student services, multicultural affairs office, services for students with disabilities, teacher training, writing training. *Library facilities:* Jen Library plus 1 other. *Online resources:* library catalog, web page. *Collection:* 189,357 titles, 1,247 serial subscriptions, 6,075 audiovisual materials.

Computer facilities: Computer purchase and lease plans are available. 3,400 computers available on campus for general student use. A campuswide network can be accessed from student residence rooms and from off campus. Online class registration is available. *Web address:* http://www.scad.edu/.

General Application Contact: Darrell Tutchton, Director of Graduate and International Enrollment, 912-525-5961, Fax: 912-525-5985, E-mail: admission@scad.edu.

GRADUATE UNITS

Graduate School *Degree program information:* Part-time programs available. Postbaccalaureate distance learning degree programs offered (no on-campus study). Offers advertising design (MA, MFA); animation (MA, MFA); architectural history (MA, MFA); architecture (M Arch); art history (MA, MFA); arts administration (MA); broadcast design (MA, MFA); cinema studies (MA); commercial photography (MA); digital photography (MA); documentary photography (MA); fashion (MA, MFA); fibers (MA, MFA); film and television (MA, MFA); furniture design (MA, MFA); graphic design (MA, MFA); historic preservation (MA, MFA); illustration (MA, MFA); illustration design (MA); industrial design (MA, MFA); interactive design and game development (MA, MFA); interior design (MA, MFA); metals and jewelry (MA, MFA); painting (MA, MFA); performing arts (MA, MFA); photography (MA, MFA); printmaking (MA, MFA); production design (MA, MFA); professional education (MA); professional writing (MFA); sculpture (MA, MFA); sequential art (MA, MFA); sound design (MA, MFA); urban design and development (MA); visual effects (MA, MFA). Electronic applications accepted.

SAVANNAH STATE UNIVERSITY, Savannah, GA 31404

General Information State-supported, coed, comprehensive institution. *Graduate housing:* Room and/or apartments available to single students; on-campus housing not available to married students.

GRADUATE UNITS

Program in Business Administration Offers business administration (MBA). Electronic applications accepted.

Program in Marine Science *Degree program information:* Part-time programs available. Offers marine science (MS). Electronic applications accepted.

Program in Public Administration Offers public administration (MPA).

Program in Social Work Offers social work (MSW).

Program in Urban Studies *Degree program information:* Part-time programs available. Offers urban studies (MS).

SAYBROOK GRADUATE SCHOOL AND RESEARCH CENTER, San Francisco, CA 94111-1920

General Information Independent, coed, graduate-only institution. *Graduate housing:* On-campus housing not available. *Research affiliation:* Rollo May Center for Humanistic Studies.

GRADUATE UNITS

Programs in Psychology, Human Science and Organizational Systems Postbaccalaureate distance learning degree programs offered (minimal on-campus study). Offers clinical psychology (PhD); creativity studies (MA); human science (MA, PhD); marriage and family therapy (MA); organizational systems (MA, PhD); psychology (MA, PhD). Electronic applications accepted.

SCHILLER INTERNATIONAL UNIVERSITY, D-69121 Heidelberg, Germany

General Information Independent, coed, comprehensive institution. *Graduate housing:* Room and/or apartments available on a first-come, first-served basis to single students; on-campus housing not available to married students.

GRADUATE UNITS

MBA Programs, Heidelberg, Germany *Degree program information:* Part-time and evening/weekend programs available. Offers international business (MBA, MIM); management of information technology (MBA).

SCHILLER INTERNATIONAL UNIVERSITY, F-75015 Paris, France

General Information Independent, coed, comprehensive institution. *Graduate housing:* On-campus housing not available.

GRADUATE UNITS

MBA Program Paris, France *Degree program information:* Part-time and evening/weekend programs available. Postbaccalaureate distance learning degree programs offered (no on-campus study). Offers international business (MBA). Bilingual French/English MBA available for native French speakers.

Program in International Relations and Diplomacy *Degree program information:* Part-time and evening/weekend programs available. Offers international relations and diplomacy (MA).

SCHILLER INTERNATIONAL UNIVERSITY, 28015 Madrid, Spain

General Information Independent, coed, comprehensive institution. *Graduate housing:* On-campus housing not available.

GRADUATE UNITS

MBA Program, Madrid, Spain *Degree program information:* Part-time programs available. Offers international business (MBA).

SCHILLER INTERNATIONAL UNIVERSITY, F-67000 Strasbourg, France

General Information Independent, coed, graduate-only institution. *Graduate housing:* Rooms and/or apartments available to single and married students. Housing application deadline: 8/1.

GRADUATE UNITS

MBA Program, Strasbourg, France Campus *Degree program information:* Part-time and evening/weekend programs available. Postbaccalaureate distance learning degree programs offered (no on-campus study). Offers international business (MBA).

SCHILLER INTERNATIONAL UNIVERSITY, London SE1 8TX, United Kingdom

General Information Independent, coed, comprehensive institution. *Graduate housing:* Room and/or apartments available on a first-come, first-served basis to single students; on-campus housing not available to married students. Housing application deadline: 8/1.

GRADUATE UNITS

Graduate Programs, London *Degree program information:* Part-time and evening/weekend programs available. Postbaccalaureate distance learning degree programs offered (no on-campus study). Offers business communication (MA); international business (MBA); international hotel and tourism management (MA, MBA); international management (MIM); international relations and diplomacy (MA); management of information technology (MBA).

SCHILLER INTERNATIONAL UNIVERSITY, Largo, FL 33770

General Information Independent, coed, comprehensive institution. *Graduate housing:* Room and/or apartments available on a first-come, first-served basis to single students; on-campus housing not available to married students. Housing application deadline: 8/1.

GRADUATE UNITS

MBA Programs, Florida *Degree program information:* Part-time and evening/weekend programs available. Postbaccalaureate distance learning degree programs offered (no on-campus study). Offers financial planning (MBA); information technology (MBA); international business (MBA); international hotel and tourism management (MBA).

SCHOOL OF ADVANCED AIR AND SPACE STUDIES, Maxwell AFB, AL 36112-6424

General Information Federally supported, coed, primarily men, graduate-only institution.

GRADUATE UNITS

Program in Airpower Art and Science Offers airpower art and science (MA). Available to active duty military officers only.

THE SCHOOL OF PROFESSIONAL PSYCHOLOGY AT FOREST INSTITUTE, Springfield, MO 65807

General Information Independent, coed, graduate-only institution. *Enrollment by degree level:* 30 master's, 212 doctoral. *Graduate faculty:* 18 full-time (9 women), 28 part-time/adjunct (15 women). *Tuition:* Full-time $22,500. *Graduate housing:* Rooms and/or apartments available on a first-come, first-served basis to single and married students. *Student services:* Campus employment opportunities, exercise/wellness program, international student services, low-cost health insurance, multicultural affairs office, services for students with disabilities, writing training. *Library facilities:* Francis D. Jones Library. *Online resources:* library catalog, web page, access to other libraries' catalogs. *Collection:* 8,209 titles, 7 serial subscriptions, 525 audiovisual materials.

Computer facilities: 54 computers available on campus for general student use. A campuswide network can be accessed from student residence rooms and from off campus. *Web address:* http://www.forest.edu/.

General Application Contact: Dawn Medley, Director of Admissions, 417-823-3477, Fax: 417-823-3442, E-mail: dmedley@forest.edu.

GRADUATE UNITS

Graduate Programs Students: 208 full-time (141 women), 34 part-time (27 women). 153 applicants, 42% accepted, 40 enrolled. *Faculty:* 18 full-time (9 women), 28 part-time/adjunct (15 women). Expenses: Contact institution. *Financial support:* In 2008–09, 91 students received support. Career-related internships or fieldwork, Federal Work-Study, and scholarships/grants also available. Support available to part-time students. Financial award applicants required to submit FAFSA. In 2008, 36 master's, 36 doctorates awarded. Offers clinical psychology (Psy D); counseling psychology (MA); marriage and family therapy (MA, PGC). *Application deadline:* For fall admission, 1/15 priority date for domestic and international students; for spring admission, 8/1 priority date for domestic and international students. Applications are processed on a rolling basis. *Application fee:* $50. Electronic applications accepted. *Application Contact:* Dawn Medley, Director of Enrollment Management, 417-823-3477, Fax: 417-823-3442, E-mail: dmedley@forest.edu. *President*, Dr. Mark E. Skrade, 417-823-3477, Fax: 417-823-3442, E-mail: mskrade@forest.edu.

SCHOOL OF THE ART INSTITUTE OF CHICAGO, Chicago, IL 60603-3103

General Information Independent, coed, comprehensive institution. *Graduate housing:* Room and/or apartments available on a first-come, first-served basis to single students; on-campus housing not available to married students. Housing application deadline: 3/21.

GRADUATE UNITS

Graduate Division *Degree program information:* Part-time programs available. Offers architecture (M Arc); art and technology studies (MFA); art education and art teaching (MAAE, MAT); art therapy (MAAT); arts administration (MAAAP); ceramics (MFA); design for emerging technologies (MFA); designed objects (M Des); fashion, body, and garment (M Des, Certificate); fiber and material studies (MFA); film, video, and new media (MFA); historic preservation (MSHP); interior architecture (M Arc); modern art history, theory, and criticism (MA, Certificate); new arts journalism (MA); painting and drawing (MFA); performance (MFA); photography (MFA); printmaking (MFA); sculpture (MFA); sound (MFA); visual and critical studies (MA); visual communication (MFA); writing (MFA, Certificate).

SCHOOL OF THE MUSEUM OF FINE ARTS, BOSTON, Boston, MA 02115

General Information Independent, coed, comprehensive institution. *Graduate housing:* On-campus housing not available.

GRADUATE UNITS

Graduate Program Offers fine arts (MAT, MFA).

SCHOOL OF VISUAL ARTS, New York, NY 10010-3994

General Information Proprietary, coed, comprehensive institution. *Graduate housing:* Room and/or apartments available on a first-come, first-served basis to single students; on-campus housing not available to married students.

GRADUATE UNITS

Graduate Programs Offers art criticism and writing (MFA); art education (MAT); art therapy (MPS); computer art (MFA); design (MFA); design criticism (MFA); digital photography (MPS); illustration (MFA); painting (MFA); photography, video and related media (MFA); printmaking (MFA); sculpture (MFA). Electronic applications accepted.

SCHREINER UNIVERSITY, Kerrville, TX 78028-5697

General Information Independent-religious, coed, comprehensive institution. *Enrollment:* 974 graduate, professional, and undergraduate students; 21 full-time matriculated graduate/professional students (15 women). *Enrollment by degree level:* 21 master's. *Graduate faculty:* 2 full-time (1 woman), 4 part-time/adjunct (3 women). *Tuition:* Full-time $14,400. *Student services:* Campus employment opportunities, campus safety program, career counseling, exercise/wellness program, free psychological counseling, international student services, services for students with disabilities, teacher training. *Library facilities:* W. M. Logan Library. *Online resources:* library catalog, web page, access to other libraries' catalogs. *Collection:* 110,000 titles, 225 serial subscriptions, 700 audiovisual materials.

Computer facilities: Computer purchase and lease plans are available. 120 computers available on campus for general student use. A campuswide network can be accessed from student residence rooms. Online class registration is available. *Web address:* http://www.schreiner.edu/.

General Application Contact: Betty Lavonne Miller, Administrative Assistant, 830-792-7455 Ext. 455, Fax: 830-792-7382, E-mail: lmiller@schreiner.edu.

GRADUATE UNITS

Program in Education Students: 21 full-time (15 women); includes 3 minority (all Hispanic Americans). Average age 35. *Faculty:* 3 full-time (2 women), 4 part-time/adjunct (3 women). Expenses: Contact institution. *Financial support:* Institutionally sponsored loans available. Support available to part-time students. Financial award application deadline: 8/1; financial award applicants required to submit FAFSA. *Degree program information:* Evening/weekend programs available. Offers education (M Ed, MET). *Application deadline:* For fall admission, 7/1 priority date for domestic students, 7/1 for international students. Applications are processed on a rolling basis. *Application fee:* $25. Electronic applications accepted. *Application Contact:* Betty Lavonne Miller, Administrative Assistant, 830-792-7455, Fax: 830-792-7382, E-mail: lmiller@schreiner.edu. *Director, Teacher Education and Graduate Studies,* Dr. Carole Diane Errett, 830-792-7445, Fax: 830-792-7382, E-mail: cderrett@schreiner.edu.

THE SCRIPPS RESEARCH INSTITUTE, La Jolla, CA 92037

General Information Independent, coed, graduate-only institution. *Graduate housing:* On-campus housing not available.

GRADUATE UNITS

Kellogg School of Science and Technology Offers science and technology (PhD). Electronic applications accepted.

SEABURY-WESTERN THEOLOGICAL SEMINARY, Evanston, IL 60201-2976

General Information Independent-religious, coed, graduate-only institution. *Graduate housing:* Rooms and/or apartments available to single students and available on a first-come, first-served basis to married students. Housing application deadline: 5/30.

GRADUATE UNITS

School of Theology *Degree program information:* Part-time programs available. Offers advanced theological studies (Certificate); church music and liturgy (MTS); congregational development (D Min); preaching (D Min); theological studies (MA); theology (M Div, L Th). D Min in congregational development offered in summer only.

SEATTLE INSTITUTE OF ORIENTAL MEDICINE, Seattle, WA 98115

General Information Proprietary, coed, primarily women, graduate-only institution. *Graduate housing:* On-campus housing not available.

GRADUATE UNITS

Graduate Program Offers Oriental medicine (M Ac OM).

SEATTLE PACIFIC UNIVERSITY, Seattle, WA 98119-1997

General Information Independent-religious, coed, comprehensive institution. *Enrollment:* 3,891 graduate, professional, and undergraduate students; 242 full-time matriculated graduate/professional students (167 women), 576 part-time matriculated graduate/professional students (389 women). *Enrollment by degree level:* 666 master's, 152 doctoral. *Graduate faculty:* 31 full-time (11 women). *Tuition:* Part-time $659 per credit hour. One-time fee: $50 part-time. Tuition and fees vary according to program. *Graduate housing:* Rooms and/or apartments available on a first-come, first-served basis to single and married students. Housing application deadline: 8/1. *Student services:* Campus employment opportunities, campus safety program, career counseling, exercise/wellness program, free psychological counseling, international student services, low-cost health insurance, multicultural affairs office, services for students with disabilities, teacher training, writing training. *Library facilities:* Seattle Pacific University Library. *Online resources:* library catalog, web page, access to other libraries' catalogs. *Collection:* 191,807 titles, 1,230 serial subscriptions, 4,408 audiovisual materials. *Research affiliation:* Battelle Research Center (business marketing), Washington Research Center/Gates Foundation (education effectiveness), Fred Hutchinson Cancer Research Center (cancer and tumors).

Computer facilities: 150 computers available on campus for general student use. A campuswide network can be accessed from student residence rooms and from off campus. Online class registration is available. *Web address:* http://www.spu.edu/.

General Application Contact: John Glancy, Director, Graduate Admissions/Marketing, 206-281-2325, Fax: 206-281-2877, E-mail: jglancy@spu.edu.

GRADUATE UNITS

Educational Leadership Program Students: 2 full-time (1 woman), 19 part-time (15 women); includes 5 minority (2 African Americans, 1 American Indian/Alaska Native, 1 Asian American or Pacific Islander, 1 Hispanic American), 2 international. Average age 37. 10 applicants, 50% accepted, 5 enrolled. *Faculty:* 2 full-time (1 woman). Expenses: Contact institution. *Financial support:* Career-related internships or fieldwork available. Financial award applicants required to submit FAFSA. In 2008, 4 master's awarded. *Degree program information:* Part-time and evening/weekend programs available. Offers educational leadership (M Ed, Ed D); principal (Certificate); superintendent (Certificate). *Application deadline:* For fall admission, 7/1 priority date for domestic students; for spring admission, 3/1 priority date for domestic students. Applications are processed on a rolling basis. *Application fee:* $50. Electronic applications accepted. *Application Contact:* Grad Center The, 206-281-2091. *Chair,* Dr. Richard Smith, 206-281-2375, Fax: 206-281-2756, E-mail: rsmith@spu.edu.

Industrial Organizational Psychology Program Students: 28 full-time (21 women), 20 part-time (14 women); includes 7 minority (2 African Americans, 4 Asian Americans or Pacific Islanders, 1 Hispanic American), 2 international. Average age 28. 74 applicants, 35% accepted, 24 enrolled. *Faculty:* 6 full-time (all women), 1 (woman) part-time/adjunct. Expenses: Contact institution. In 2008, 27 master's awarded. Offers industrial organizational psychology (MA, PhD). *Application fee:* $50. Electronic applications accepted. *Application Contact:* Grad Center The, 206-281-2091. *Chair,* Dr. Robert B McKenna, 206-281-2629, E-mail: rmckenna@spu.edu.

Literacy Program Students: 13 part-time (12 women); includes 1 Asian American or Pacific Islander. Average age 32. 4 applicants, 50% accepted, 2 enrolled. *Faculty:* 12 full-time (5 women), 8 part-time/adjunct (4 women). Expenses: Contact institution. *Financial support:* In 2008–09, 10 students received support. Scholarships/grants available. Offers literacy (M Ed). *Application Contact:* Grad Center The, 206-281-2091. *Co-Chair,* Dr. William Nagy, 206-281-2253, E-mail: wnagy@spu.edu.

MA in Teaching English to Speakers of Other Languages Program Students: 11 full-time (6 women), 11 part-time (10 women); includes 4 minority (all Asian Americans or Pacific Islanders), 2 international. Average age 35. 17 applicants, 35% accepted, 6 enrolled. *Faculty:* 6 full-time (3 women), 3 part-time/adjunct (2 women). Expenses: Contact institution. *Financial support:* In 2008–09, 11 students received support. Career-related internships or fieldwork available. Financial award applicants required to submit FAFSA. In 2008, 14 master's awarded. *Degree program information:* Part-time programs available. Offers K-12 certification (MA); teaching English to speakers of other languages (MA). *Application deadline:* For fall admission, 8/11 priority date for domestic students; for winter admission, 12/1 for domestic students; for spring admission, 3/11 for domestic students. Applications are processed on a rolling basis. *Application fee:* $50. Electronic applications accepted. *Application Contact:* Grad Center The, 206-281-2091. *Chair,* Dr. Kathryn Bartholomew, 206-281-3533, Fax: 206-281-2500.

Master's Degree in Business Administration (MBA) Program Students: 12 full-time (2 women), 114 part-time (40 women); includes 23 minority (6 African Americans, 15 Asian Americans or Pacific Islanders, 2 Hispanic Americans), 13 international. Average age 32. 69 applicants, 46% accepted, 32 enrolled. *Faculty:* 15 full-time (6 women), 6 part-time/adjunct (15 women). Expenses: Contact institution. *Financial support:* In 2008–09, 38 students received support. Scholarships/grants available. In 2008, 38 master's awarded. Offers business administration (MBA). *Application deadline:* Applications are processed on a rolling basis. Electronic applications accepted. *Application Contact:* Grad Center The, 206-281-2091. *Graduate Director,* Gary Karns, 206-281-2948, Fax: 206-281-2733.

Master's Degree in Information Systems Management (MS-ISM) Program Students: 1 (woman) full-time, 13 part-time (3 women); includes 1 minority (Hispanic American), 1 international. Average age 30. 10 applicants, 50% accepted, 5 enrolled. *Faculty:* 3 full-time (0 women), 1 part-time/adjunct (0 women). Expenses: Contact institution. In 2008, 40 master's awarded. Offers information systems management (MS). *Application deadline:* Applications are processed on a rolling basis. *Application fee:* $50. Electronic applications accepted. *Application Contact:* Grad Center The, 206-281-2091. *Graduate Director,* Gary Karns, 206-281-2948, Fax: 206-281-2733.

Master of Arts in Teaching Program Students: 44 full-time (24 women), 70 part-time (50 women); includes 9 minority (2 African Americans, 2 American Indian/Alaska Native, 2 Asian Americans or Pacific Islanders, 3 Hispanic Americans), 1 international. Average age 31. 61 applicants, 51% accepted, 31 enrolled. *Faculty:* 14 full-time (6 women), 7 part-time/adjunct (4 women). Expenses: Contact institution. *Financial support:* In 2008–09, 96 students received support. Scholarships/grants available. Financial award applicants required to submit FAFSA. In 2008, 77 master's awarded. *Degree program information:* Part-time and evening/weekend programs available. Offers alternate routes to certification (Certificate); teaching (MAT). *Application deadline:* For fall admission, 9/24 for domestic students; for spring admission, 4/15 for domestic students. *Application fee:* $50. Electronic applications accepted. *Application Contact:* Grad Center The, 206-281-2091. *Chair,* Dr. Richard Schuerman, 206-281-2186, Fax: 206-281-2756.

Masters of Fine Arts in Creative Writing Program Students: 22 part-time (13 women); includes 6 minority (2 African Americans, 2 Asian Americans or Pacific Islanders, 2 Hispanic Americans), 1 international. Average age 37. *Faculty:* 1 full-time (0 women), 6 part-time/adjunct (4 women). Expenses: Contact institution. *Financial support:* In 2008–09, 15 students received support. Applicants required to submit FAFSA. In 2008, 10 master's awarded. *Degree program information:* Part-time programs available. Offers creative writing (MFA). *Application deadline:* For fall admission, 2/15 for domestic students; for spring admission, 10/1 for domestic students. *Application fee:* $50. Electronic applications accepted. *Application Contact:* Grad Center The, 206-281-2091. *Director,* Dr. Gregory Wolfe, 206-281-2109, E-mail: gwolfe@spu.edu.

Medical Family Therapy Certificate Program Students: 3 full-time (2 women), 3 part-time (all women). 7 applicants, 86% accepted, 5 enrolled. *Faculty:* 1 (woman) full-time. Expenses: Contact institution. Offers medical family therapy (Certificate). *Application fee:* $50. *Application Contact:* Grad Center The, 206-281-2091. *Chair,* Dr. Claudia Grauf-Grounds, 206-281-2632, Fax: 206-281-2695, E-mail: claudiagg@spu.edu.

M Ed in Curriculum and Instruction Program Students: 1 (woman) full-time, 60 part-time (46 women); includes 4 minority (2 Asian Americans or Pacific Islanders, 2 Hispanic Americans), 1 international. Average age 34. 33 applicants, 70% accepted, 23 enrolled. *Faculty:* 12 full-time (5 women), 8 part-time/adjunct (4 women). Expenses: Contact institution. *Financial support:* In 2008–09, 32 students received support. Applicants required to submit FAFSA. In 2008, 18 master's awarded. *Degree program information:* Part-time and evening/weekend programs available. Offers reading/language arts education (M Ed). *Application deadline:* For fall admission, 7/1 priority date for domestic students; for spring admission, 3/1 priority date for domestic students. Applications are processed on a rolling basis. *Application fee:* $50. Electronic applications accepted. *Application Contact:* Grad Center The, 206-281-2091. *Chair,* Dr. Andrew Lumpe, 206-281-2369.

MS in Marriage and Family Therapy Program Students: 51 full-time (41 women), 18 part-time (12 women); includes 8 minority (1 African American, 1 American Indian/Alaska Native, 4 Asian Americans or Pacific Islanders, 2 Hispanic Americans), 4 international. Average age 32. 92 applicants, 36% accepted, 29 enrolled. *Faculty:* 6 full-time (3 women), 3 part-time/adjunct (2 women). Expenses: Contact institution. *Financial support:* In 2008–09, 50 students received support; fellowships, Federal Work-Study available. Financial award applicants required to submit FAFSA. In 2008, 18 master's awarded. *Degree program information:* Part-time programs available. Offers marriage and family therapy (MS). *Application deadline:* For fall admission, 3/1 for domestic students. Applications are processed on a rolling basis. *Application fee:* $50. Electronic applications accepted. *Application Contact:* Grad Center The, 206-281-2091. *Chair,* Dr. Claudia Grauf-Grounds, 206-281-2632, Fax: 206-281-2695, E-mail: claudiagg@spu.edu.

MS in Nursing Program Students: 15 full-time (11 women), 43 part-time (40 women); includes 10 minority (1 American Indian/Alaska Native, 7 Asian Americans or Pacific Islanders, 2 Hispanic Americans). Average age 43. 50 applicants, 74% accepted, 37 enrolled. *Faculty:* 7 full-time (all women), 1 part-time/adjunct (0 women). Expenses: Contact institution. *Financial support:* Fellowships, scholarships/grants available. In 2008, 10 master's awarded. Offers administration (MSN); adult/gerontology nurse practitioner (MSN); clinical nurse specialist (MSN); family nurse practitioner (MSN); informatics (MSN); nurse educator (MSN). *Application deadline:* For fall admission, 9/1 priority date for domestic students. Applications are processed on a rolling basis. *Application fee:* $50. Electronic applications accepted. *Application Contact:* Grad Center The, 206-281-2091. *Director,* Dr. Susan Casey, 206-281-2769, Fax: 206-281-2767, E-mail: caseys@spu.edu.

PhD in Clinical Psychology Program Students: 49 full-time (36 women), 29 part-time (27 women); includes 11 minority (1 African American, 1 American Indian/Alaska Native, 5 Asian

Seattle Pacific University (continued)

Americans or Pacific Islanders, 4 Hispanic Americans). Average age 29. 107 applicants, 10% accepted, 11 enrolled. *Faculty:* 9 full-time (5 women), 3 part-time/adjunct (0 women). Expenses: Contact institution. *Financial support:* In 2008–09, 63 students received support; fellowships, scholarships/grants available. Financial award applicants required to submit FAFSA. In 2008, 16 doctorates awarded. Offers clinical psychology (PhD). *Application deadline:* For fall admission, 2/1 for domestic students. Electronic applications accepted. *Application Contact:* Grad Center The, 206-281-2091. *Chair,* Dr. Jay Skidmore, 706-281-2916.

Post-Master's Family Nurse Practitioner Certificate Program Students: 1 (woman) part-time; minority (Asian American or Pacific Islander). Average age 47. 4 applicants, 0% accepted. Expenses: Contact institution. *Financial support:* Applicants required to submit FAFSA. *Degree program information:* Part-time and evening/weekend programs available. Offers adult/gerontological nurse practitioner (Certificate); family nurse practitioner (Certificate). *Application deadline:* For fall admission, 9/1 priority date for domestic students. Applications are processed on a rolling basis. *Application fee:* $50. Electronic applications accepted. *Application Contact:* Grad Center The, 206-281-2091. *Associate Dean,* Susan Casey, 206-281-2649.

School Counseling Program Students: 20 full-time (18 women), 33 part-time (31 women); includes 4 minority (1 African American, 1 American Indian/Alaska Native, 1 Asian American or Pacific Islander, 1 Hispanic American), 1 international. 59 applicants, 22% accepted, 13 enrolled. *Faculty:* 2 full-time (1 woman). Expenses: Contact institution. *Financial support:* In 2008–09, 39 students received support. Scholarships/grants available. Financial award applicants required to submit FAFSA. In 2008, 12 master's awarded. *Degree program information:* Part-time programs available. Offers school counseling (M Ed, PhD, Certificate). *Application deadline:* For fall admission, 7/1 priority date for domestic students; for spring admission, 3/1 priority date for domestic students. *Application fee:* $50. Electronic applications accepted. *Application Contact:* Grad Center The, 206-281-2091. *Chair,* Dr. Cher Edwards, 206-281-2286, Fax: 206-281-2756.

SEATTLE UNIVERSITY, Seattle, WA 98122-1090

General Information Independent-religious, coed, comprehensive institution. *Graduate housing:* Room and/or apartments available on a first-come, first-served basis to single students; on-campus housing not available to married students. *Research affiliation:* Swedish Medical Centers (nursing).

GRADUATE UNITS

Albers School of Business and Economics *Degree program information:* Part-time and evening/weekend programs available. Offers business administration (MBA, MIB, Certificate); business and economics (EMBA, MBA, MIB, MPAC, MSF, Certificate); finance (MSF, Certificate); professional accounting (MPAC).

Center for Leadership Formation Offers leadership formation (EMBA, Certificate).

College of Arts and Sciences Offers arts and sciences (MA Psych, MACJ, MNPL, MPA, MSAL); criminal justice (MACJ); existential and phenomenological therapeutic psychology (MA Psych).

The Center for Nonprofit and Social Enterprise Management Offers nonprofit and social enterprise management (MNPL).

Center for the Study of Sport and Exercise Offers sport and exercise (MSAL).

Institute of Public Service Offers public service (MPA).

College of Education *Degree program information:* Part-time and evening/weekend programs available. Offers adult education and training (M Ed, MA, Certificate); counseling and school psychology (MA, Certificate, Ed S); curriculum and instruction (M Ed, MA, Certificate); education (M Ed, MA, MIT, Ed D, Certificate, Ed S, Post-Master's Certificate); educational administration (M Ed, MA, Certificate, Ed S); educational leadership (Ed D); literacy (M Ed, Post-Master's Certificate); special education (M Ed, MA, Certificate); student development administration (M Ed, MA); teacher education (MIT); teaching English to speakers of other languages (M Ed, MA, Certificate).

College of Nursing *Degree program information:* Part-time and evening/weekend programs available. Offers advanced practice nursing immersion (MSN); leadership in community nursing (MSN); nursing (MSN); primary care nurse practitioner (MSN).

College of Science and Engineering *Degree program information:* Part-time and evening/weekend programs available. Offers science and engineering (MSE); software engineering (MSE).

School of Law Students: 807 full-time (425 women), 232 part-time (112 women); includes 269 minority (39 African Americans, 10 American Indian/Alaska Native, 163 Asian Americans or Pacific Islanders, 57 Hispanic Americans), 14 international. Average age 27. 2,907 applicants, 35% accepted, 328 enrolled. *Faculty:* 59 full-time (23 women), 54 part-time/adjunct (18 women). Expenses: Contact institution. *Financial support:* In 2008–09, 532 students received support. Career-related internships or fieldwork, Federal Work-Study, institutionally sponsored loans, and scholarships/grants available. Support available to part-time students. Financial award application deadline: 4/1; financial award applicants required to submit FAFSA. In 2008, 357 JDs awarded. *Degree program information:* Part-time programs available. Offers law (JD, JD/MATL). *Application deadline:* For fall admission, 3/1 priority date for domestic and international students. Applications are processed on a rolling basis. *Application fee:* $60. Electronic applications accepted. *Application Contact:* Carol T. Cochran, Assistant Dean for Admission, 206-398-4206, Fax: 206-398-4058, E-mail: ccochran@seattleu.edu. *Dean,* Kellye Y. Testy, 206-398-4300, Fax: 206-398-4310, E-mail: ktesty@seattleu.edu.

School of Theology and Ministry *Degree program information:* Part-time and evening/weekend programs available. Offers divinity (M Div); pastoral counseling (MA); pastoral studies (MAPS); theology and ministry (M Div, MA, MAPS, MATS, Certificate); transforming spirituality (MATS, Certificate).

SEMINARY OF THE IMMACULATE CONCEPTION, Huntington, NY 11743-1696

General Information Independent-religious, coed, graduate-only institution. *Graduate housing:* Room and/or apartments guaranteed to single students; on-campus housing not available to married students. Housing application deadline: 8/30.

GRADUATE UNITS

School of Theology *Degree program information:* Part-time and evening/weekend programs available. Offers pastoral studies (MA); theology (M Div, MA, D Min, Certificate).

SEMINARY OF THE SOUTHWEST, Austin, TX 78768-2247

General Information Independent-religious, coed, graduate-only institution. *Enrollment by degree level:* 36 first professional, 37 master's, 4 other advanced degrees. *Graduate faculty:* 10 full-time (3 women), 31 part-time/adjunct (11 women). *Tuition:* Full-time $13,150; part-time $390 per credit hour. One-time fee: $75 full-time; $20 part-time. *Graduate housing:* Rooms and/or apartments available on a first-come, first-served basis to single and married students. Typical cost: $4800 per year ($5450 including board) for single students; $9000 per year ($9650 including board) for married students. Housing application deadline: 8/1. *Student services:* Campus employment opportunities, international student services, low-cost health insurance, writing training. *Library facilities:* Episcopal Theological Seminary of the Southwest Library plus 1 other. *Online resources:* library catalog, web page, access to other libraries' catalogs. *Collection:* 137,373 titles, 284 serial subscriptions, 2,407 audiovisual materials.

Computer facilities: 8 computers available on campus for general student use. A campuswide network can be accessed from student residence rooms. *Web address:* http://www.ssw.edu/.

General Application Contact: Jennielle Strother, Director of Admissions, 512-472-4133 Ext. 375, Fax: 512-472-3098, E-mail: jstrother@ssw.edu.

GRADUATE UNITS

Graduate and Professional Programs Students: 46 full-time (29 women), 31 part-time (23 women); includes 7 minority (4 African Americans, 1 Asian American or Pacific Islander, 2 Hispanic Americans), 2 international. Average age 46. 28 applicants, 96% accepted, 22 enrolled. *Faculty:* 10 full-time (3 women), 31 part-time/adjunct (11 women). Expenses: Contact institution. *Financial support:* Career-related internships or fieldwork and scholarships/grants available. Support available to part-time students. Financial award application deadline: 6/17. In 2008, 23 first professional degrees, 13 master's, 5 other advanced degrees awarded. *Degree program information:* Part-time and evening/weekend programs available. Offers Anglican studies (Advanced Diploma); chaplaincy (MCPC); counseling (MAC); divinity (M Div); religion (MAR); spiritual formation (MAPM); theological studies (Advanced Diploma). *Application deadline:* For fall admission, 7/1 for domestic students; for spring admission, 11/1 for domestic students. Applications are processed on a rolling basis. *Application fee:* $50. *Application Contact:* Jennielle Strother, Director of Admissions, 512-472-4133 Ext. 375, Fax: 512-472-3098, E-mail: jstrother@ssw.edu. *Dean and President,* Very Rev. Douglas Travis, 512-472-4133 Ext. 307, Fax: 512-472-3098, E-mail: dtravis@ssw.edu.

SETON HALL UNIVERSITY, South Orange, NJ 07079-2697

General Information Independent-religious, coed, university. CGS member. *Enrollment:* 1,900 full-time matriculated graduate/professional students (1,014 women), 2,079 part-time matriculated graduate/professional students (1,150 women). *Enrollment by degree level:* 1,185 first professional, 2,130 master's, 519 doctoral, 145 other advanced degrees. *Graduate housing:* On-campus housing not available. *Student services:* Campus employment opportunities, career counseling, exercise/wellness program, free psychological counseling, international student services, low-cost health insurance, services for students with disabilities, teacher training, writing training. *Library facilities:* Walsh Library plus 1 other. *Online resources:* library catalog, web page, access to other libraries' catalogs. *Collection:* 506,042 titles, 1,475 serial subscriptions, 2,225 audiovisual materials.

Computer facilities: Computer purchase and lease plans are available. 300 computers available on campus for general student use. A campuswide network can be accessed from student residence rooms and from off campus. Online class registration is available. *Web address:* http://www.shu.edu/.

General Application Contact: Sarah Caron, Director, Graduate Admissions, 973-275-2892, Fax: 973-275-2993, E-mail: shugrad@shu.edu.

GRADUATE UNITS

College of Arts and Sciences Students: 227 full-time (150 women), 334 part-time (181 women); includes 122 minority (69 African Americans, 4 American Indian/Alaska Native, 29 Asian Americans or Pacific Islanders, 20 Hispanic Americans), 43 international. Average age 33. 393 applicants, 87% accepted, 184 enrolled. *Faculty:* 94 full-time (36 women), 26 part-time/adjunct (12 women). Expenses: Contact institution. *Financial support:* Research assistantships with full tuition reimbursements, teaching assistantships with full tuition reimbursements, career-related internships or fieldwork, Federal Work-Study, institutionally sponsored loans, scholarships/grants, and unspecified assistantships available. Financial award applicants required to submit FAFSA. In 2008, 215 master's, 3 doctorates awarded. *Degree program information:* Part-time and evening/weekend programs available. Postbaccalaureate distance learning degree programs offered (minimal on-campus study). Offers analytical chemistry (MS, PhD); arts and sciences (MA, MHA, MPA, MS, PhD, Graduate Certificate); Asian languages (MA); Asian studies (MA); biochemistry (MS, PhD); biology (MS); biology/business administration (MS); chemistry (MS); corporate and professional communication (MA); English (MA); experimental psychology (MS); healthcare administration (MHA, Graduate Certificate); history (MA); Holocaust studies (MA); inorganic chemistry (MS, PhD); intercultural communication (MA); Jewish-Christian Studies (MA); microbiology (MS); molecular bioscience (PhD); molecular bioscience/neuroscience (PhD); museum professions (MA); nonprofit organization management (MPA); organic chemistry (MS, PhD); organizational communication (MA); physical chemistry (MS, PhD); public administration (MPA, Graduate Certificate); public relations (MA); strategic communication and leadership (MA); strategic communication planning (MA); teaching Chinese language and culture (MA). *Application deadline:* For fall admission, 7/1 priority date for domestic and international students; for spring admission, 11/1 priority date for domestic and international students. Applications are processed on a rolling basis. *Application fee:* $50. Electronic applications accepted. *Application Contact:* Sarah Caron, Director, Graduate Admissions, 973-275-2892, Fax: 973-275-2993, E-mail: shugrad@shu.edu. *Dean,* Dr. Joseph R. Marbach, 973-761-9022, Fax: 973-761-9596, E-mail: artsci@shu.edu.

College of Education and Human Services Students: 396 full-time (282 women), 742 part-time (463 women); includes 110 minority (71 African Americans, 2 American Indian/Alaska Native, 10 Asian Americans or Pacific Islanders, 27 Hispanic Americans), 11 international. Average age 35. 449 applicants, 89% accepted, 171 enrolled. *Faculty:* 39 full-time (21 women), 116 part-time/adjunct (32 women). Expenses: Contact institution. *Financial support:* In 2008–09, 13 students received support; fellowships, research assistantships, career-related internships or fieldwork, institutionally sponsored loans, and unspecified assistantships available. Financial award application deadline: 2/1. In 2008, 276 master's, 45 doctorates, 53 other advanced degrees awarded. *Degree program information:* Part-time and evening/weekend programs available. Offers bilingual education (Ed S); Catholic school teaching EPICS (MA); college student personnel administration (MA); counseling psychology (MA, PhD); education and human services (MA, MS, Ed D, Exec Ed D, PhD, Ed S); education media specialist (MA); higher education administration (Ed D, PhD); human resource training and development (MA); instructional design (MA); K–12 administration and supervision (Ed D, Exec Ed D, Ed S); K–12 leadership, management and policy (Ed D, Exec Ed D, Ed S); marriage and family therapy (MS, PhD, Ed S); professional development (MA); psychological studies (MA); school psychology (Ed S). *Application deadline:* Applications are processed on a rolling basis. *Application fee:* $50. Electronic applications accepted. *Application Contact:* Dr. Manina Urgolo Huckvale, Associate Dean, 973-761-9668, Fax: 973-275-2187, E-mail: huckvama@shu.edu. *Dean,* Dr. Joseph V. De Pierro, 973-761-9025.

College of Nursing *Degree program information:* Part-time programs available. Postbaccalaureate distance learning degree programs offered (minimal on-campus study). Offers acute care nurse practitioner (MSN); adult nurse practitioner (MSN); advanced practice in acute care nursing (MSN); advanced practice in primary health care (MSN); gerontological nurse practitioner (MSN); health systems administration (MSN); nursing (MA, MSN, PhD); nursing case management (MSN); nursing education (MA); pediatric nurse practitioner (MSN); school nurse (MSN); women's health nurse practitioner (MSN). Electronic applications accepted.

Immaculate Conception Seminary School of Theology *Degree program information:* Part-time and evening/weekend programs available. Offers pastoral ministry (M Div, MA); theology (MA). Electronic applications accepted.

School of Health and Medical Sciences *Degree program information:* Part-time and evening/weekend programs available. Offers athletic training (MS); health and medical sciences (MS, DPT, PhD); health sciences (MS, PhD); occupational therapy (MS); physician assistant (MS); professional physical therapy (DPT); speech-language pathology (MS). Electronic applications accepted.

School of Law *Degree program information:* Part-time and evening/weekend programs available. Offers law (JD, LL M, MSJ). Electronic applications accepted.

Stillman School of Business Students: 70 full-time (19 women), 404 part-time (165 women); includes 52 minority (20 African Americans, 19 Asian Americans or Pacific Islanders, 13 Hispanic Americans). Average age 27. 271 applicants, 49% accepted, 77 enrolled. *Faculty:* 57 full-time (13 women), 30 part-time/adjunct (3 women). Expenses: Contact institution. *Financial support:* In 2008–09, 60 students received support, including research assistantships with full and partial tuition reimbursements available (averaging $5,400 per year); career-related internships or fieldwork, Federal Work-Study, scholarships/grants, health care benefits, and unspecified assistantships also available. Support available to part-time students. Financial award application deadline: 6/1; financial award applicants required to submit FAFSA. In 2008, 195 master's awarded. *Degree program information:* Part-time and evening/weekend programs available. Offers accounting (MBA, MS); business (MBA, MS, Certificate); finance (MBA); financial markets, institutions and instruments (MBA); healthcare management (MBA); information systems (MBA); international business (MS, Certificate); management (MBA); marketing (MBA); pharmaceutical management (MBA); professional accounting (MS); sport management (MBA); taxation (MS). *Application deadline:* For fall admission, 6/1 priority date for domestic students, 5/1 for international students; for spring admission, 11/1 priority date for domestic students, 10/1 for international students. Applications are processed on a rolling basis. *Application fee:* $75 ($100 for international students). Electronic applications accepted. *Application Contact:* Catherine Bianchi, Director of Graduate Admissions, 973-761-9220, Fax: 973-761-9208, E-mail: biancha@shu.edu. *Dean,* Dr. Karen E. Boroff, 973-761-9013, Fax: 973-275-2465, E-mail: boroffka@shu.edu.

Whitehead School of Diplomacy and International Relations Average age 26. 360 applicants, 58% accepted. *Faculty:* 14 full-time (3 women), 17 part-time/adjunct (6 women). Expenses: Contact institution. *Financial support:* Research assistantships with full and partial tuition reimbursements, career-related internships or fieldwork, scholarships/grants, tuition waivers (full and partial), and unspecified assistantships available. In 2008, 106 master's awarded. *Degree program information:* Part-time and evening/weekend programs available. Offers diplomacy and international relations (MA). *Application deadline:* For fall admission, 5/1 priority date for domestic students; for winter admission, 10/1 priority date for domestic students. Applications are processed on a rolling basis. *Application fee:* $50. Electronic applications accepted. *Application Contact:* Catherine Ruby, Director of Graduate Admissions, 973-275-2142, Fax: 973-275-2519, E-mail: rubycath@shu.edu. *Assistant Dean of Graduate Studies,* Ursula Sanjamino, 973-313-6210, Fax: 973-275-2519, E-mail: sanjamur@shu.edu.

SETON HILL UNIVERSITY, Greensburg, PA 15601

General Information Independent-religious, coed, comprehensive institution. *Enrollment:* 2,093 graduate, professional, and undergraduate students; 155 full-time matriculated graduate/professional students (128 women), 272 part-time matriculated graduate/professional students (191 women). *Enrollment by degree level:* 427 master's. *Graduate faculty:* 23 full-time (12 women), 23 part-time/adjunct (12 women). *Tuition:* Full-time $12,510; part-time $695 per credit hour. *Required fees:* $200; $100 per semester. Tuition and fees vary according to course load and program. *Graduate housing:* Room and/or apartments guaranteed to single students; on-campus housing not available to married students. Typical cost: $8170 (including board). Housing application deadline: 8/15. *Student services:* Campus employment opportunities, campus safety program, career counseling, exercise/wellness program, free psychological counseling, international student services, multicultural affairs office, services for students with disabilities, teacher training, writing training. *Library facilities:* Reeves Memorial Library. *Online resources:* library catalog, web page, access to other libraries' catalogs. *Collection:* 123,538 titles, 423 serial subscriptions, 6,684 audiovisual materials.

Computer facilities: Computer purchase and lease plans are available. 300 computers available on campus for general student use. A campuswide network can be accessed from student residence rooms and from off campus. Online class registration is available. *Web address:* http://www.setonhill.edu/.

General Application Contact: Tracey Bartos, Director of Graduate and Adult Studies, 724-838-4283, Fax: 724-830-1891, E-mail: bartos@setonhill.edu.

GRADUATE UNITS

Program in Art Therapy *Degree program information:* Part-time programs available. Offers art therapy (MA, Certificate). Electronic applications accepted.

Program in Business Administration *Degree program information:* Part-time and evening/weekend programs available. Offers business administration (MBA). Electronic applications accepted.

Program in Elementary Education *Degree program information:* Part-time and evening/weekend programs available. Offers elementary education (MA, Teaching Certificate). Electronic applications accepted.

Program in Genocide and Holocaust Studies Offers genocide and Holocaust studies (Certificate).

Program in Inclusive Education *Degree program information:* Part-time and evening/weekend programs available. Postbaccalaureate distance learning degree programs offered (no on-campus study). Offers inclusive education (MA).

Program in Marriage and Family Therapy *Degree program information:* Part-time and evening/weekend programs available. Offers marriage and family therapy (MA). Electronic applications accepted.

Program in Physician Assistant Offers physician assistant (MS). Electronic applications accepted.

Program in Special Education *Degree program information:* Part-time and evening/weekend programs available. Offers special education (MA, Teaching Certificate). Electronic applications accepted.

Program in Writing Popular Fiction *Degree program information:* Part-time programs available. Postbaccalaureate distance learning degree programs offered (minimal on-campus study). Offers writing popular fiction (MA). Electronic applications accepted.

SEWANEE: THE UNIVERSITY OF THE SOUTH, Sewanee, TN 37383-1000

General Information Independent-religious, coed, comprehensive institution. *Enrollment:* 1,562 graduate, professional, and undergraduate students; 106 full-time matriculated graduate/professional students (46 women), 15 part-time matriculated graduate/professional students (9 women). *Enrollment by degree level:* 62 first professional, 59 master's. *Graduate faculty:* 13 full-time (6 women), 10 part-time/adjunct (4 women). *Tuition:* Full-time $15,804; part-time $660 per credit hour. *Required fees:* $576. *Graduate housing:* Rooms and/or apartments available on a first-come, first-served basis to single and married students. Typical cost: $432 per year for single students; $844 per year for married students. Housing application deadline: 4/1. *Student services:* Campus employment opportunities, campus safety program, career counseling, child daycare facilities, free psychological counseling, international student services, multicultural affairs office. *Library facilities:* Jessie Ball duPont Library. *Online resources:* library catalog, web page. *Collection:* 648,459 titles, 3,444 serial subscriptions.

Computer facilities: Computer purchase and lease plans are available. 340 computers available on campus for general student use. A campuswide network can be accessed from student residence rooms and from off campus. Online class registration is available. *Web address:* http://www.sewanee.edu/.

GRADUATE UNITS

School of Theology Students: 70 full-time (26 women), 9 part-time (7 women); includes 6 minority (5 African Americans, 1 Hispanic American), 1 international. Average age 44. 50 applicants, 72% accepted. *Faculty:* 11 full-time (4 women), 11 part-time/adjunct (4 women). Expenses: Contact institution. *Financial support:* Institutionally sponsored loans and scholarships/grants available. Support available to part-time students. Financial award application deadline: 5/1; financial award applicants required to submit FAFSA. In 2008, 28 first professional degrees, 3 master's, 5 doctorates awarded. *Degree program information:* Part-time programs available. Offers theology (M Div, MA, STM, D Min). *Application deadline:* For fall admission, 4/1 priority date for domestic students, 4/1 for international students. Applications are processed on a rolling basis. *Application fee:* $25. *Application Contact:* Roslyn Dianne Weaver, Director of Admissions/Registrar, 931-598-1283, Fax: 931-598-1852, E-mail: rweaver@sewanee.edu. *Dean,* Very Rev. William S. Stafford, 931-598-1288, Fax: 931-598-1412, E-mail: wstafford@sewanee.edu.

Sewanee School of Letters Students: 36 full-time (20 women), 6 part-time (2 women); includes 3 minority (2 African Americans, 1 Asian American or Pacific Islander). Average age 31. 20 applicants, 95% accepted, 12 enrolled. *Faculty:* 8 full-time (3 women). Expenses: Contact institution. *Financial support:* Application deadline: 4/1. *Degree program information:* Part-time programs available. Offers American literature and English literature (MA); creative writing (MFA). Programs offered only during the summer. *Application deadline:* For spring admission, 2/1 priority date for domestic and international students. Applications are processed on a rolling basis. *Application fee:* $40. Electronic applications accepted. *Application Contact:* Margaret D Binnicker, Coordinator, 931-598-1636, Fax: 931-598-3303, E-mail: mbinnick@sewanee.edu. *Director,* Dr. John M Grammer, 931-598-1483, Fax: 931-598-3303, E-mail: jgrammer@sewanee.edu.

SHASTA BIBLE COLLEGE, Redding, CA 96002

General Information Independent-religious, coed, comprehensive institution. *Graduate housing:* Rooms and/or apartments available on a first-come, first-served basis to single and married students.

GRADUATE UNITS

Program in Biblical Counseling *Degree program information:* Part-time programs available. Offers biblical counseling and Christian family life education (MA).

Program in Christian Ministry *Degree program information:* Part-time programs available. Postbaccalaureate distance learning degree programs offered (minimal on-campus study). Offers Christian ministry (MA).

Program in School and Church Administration *Degree program information:* Part-time and evening/weekend programs available. Offers school and church administration (MS).

SHAW UNIVERSITY, Raleigh, NC 27601-2399

General Information Independent-religious, coed, comprehensive institution. *Graduate housing:* Room and/or apartments available on a first-come, first-served basis to single students; on-campus housing not available to married students. *Research affiliation:* UNC (end of life in African American community), Old North State Medical Society (health and spirituality), The University of North Carolina at Chapel Hill (health disparities in the African American community), General Baptist State Convention (domestic violence prevention), Wabash Center (philosophy of religious education).

GRADUATE UNITS

Department of Education *Degree program information:* Part-time and evening/weekend programs available. Offers curriculum and instruction (MS). Electronic applications accepted.

Divinity School *Degree program information:* Part-time and evening/weekend programs available. Offers divinity (M Div, MRE). Electronic applications accepted.

SHENANDOAH UNIVERSITY, Winchester, VA 22601-5195

General Information Independent-religious, coed, comprehensive institution. *Enrollment:* 740 full-time matriculated graduate/professional students (504 women), 777 part-time matriculated graduate/professional students (537 women). *Enrollment by degree level:* 420 first professional, 661 master's, 377 doctoral, 59 other advanced degrees. *Graduate faculty:* 115 full-time (65 women), 56 part-time/adjunct (34 women). *Tuition:* Full-time $16,900; part-time $670 per credit. *Graduate housing:* Room and/or apartments available on a first-come, first-served basis to single students; on-campus housing not available to married students. Typical cost: $3715 (including board). Room and board charges vary according to board plan. Housing application deadline: 7/1. *Student services:* Campus employment opportunities, campus safety program, career counseling, child daycare facilities, exercise/wellness program, free psychological counseling, international student services, low-cost health insurance, multicultural affairs office, services for students with disabilities. *Library facilities:* Alson H. Smith Jr. Library plus 1 other. *Online resources:* library catalog, web page, access to other libraries' catalogs. *Collection:* 131,174 titles, 19,479 serial subscriptions, 31,143 audiovisual materials.

Computer facilities: Computer purchase and lease plans are available. 175 computers available on campus for general student use. A campuswide network can be accessed from student residence rooms and from off campus. Online class registration, online student account information are available. *Web address:* http://www.su.edu/.

General Application Contact: David Anthony, Dean of Admissions, 540-665-4581, Fax: 540-665-4627, E-mail: admit@su.edu.

GRADUATE UNITS

Byrd School of Business Students: 41 full-time (21 women), 10 part-time (8 women); includes 12 minority (3 African Americans, 1 American Indian/Alaska Native, 8 Asian Americans or Pacific Islanders), 11 international. Average age 35. 26 applicants, 96% accepted, 19 enrolled. *Faculty:* 9 full-time (2 women), 1 part-time/adjunct (0 women). Expenses: Contact institution. *Financial support:* In 2008–09, 28 students received support, including 8 teaching assistantships with partial tuition reimbursements available (averaging $4,519 per year); fellowships, career-related internships or fieldwork, institutionally sponsored loans, and unspecified assistantships also available. Support available to part-time students. Financial award application deadline: 3/15; financial award applicants required to submit FAFSA. In 2008, 24 master's, 3 other advanced degrees awarded. *Degree program information:* Part-time and evening/weekend programs available. Offers business administration (MBA); health care management (Certificate); information systems and computer technology (Certificate). *Application deadline:* Applications are processed on a rolling basis. *Application fee:* $30. Electronic applications accepted. *Application Contact:* David Anthony, Dean of Admissions, 540-665-4581, Fax: 540-665-4627, E-mail: admit@su.edu. *Dean,* Dr. Randy Boxx, 540-665-4572, Fax: 540-665-5437, E-mail: rboxx@su.edu.

School of Education and Human Development Students: 17 full-time (13 women), 336 part-time (251 women); includes 18 minority (10 African Americans, 1 American Indian/Alaska Native, 1 Asian American or Pacific Islander, 6 Hispanic Americans), 24 international. Average age 40. 202 applicants, 86% accepted, 131 enrolled. *Faculty:* 15 full-time (9 women), 25 part-time/adjunct (18 women). Expenses: Contact institution. *Financial support:* Career-related internships or fieldwork, institutionally sponsored loans, and unspecified assistantships available. Support available to part-time students. Financial award application deadline: 3/15; financial award applicants required to submit FAFSA. In 2008, 82 master's, 6 doctorates, 19 other advanced degrees awarded. *Degree program information:* Part-time and evening/weekend programs available. Postbaccalaureate distance learning degree programs offered (minimal on-campus study). Offers advanced professional teaching English to speakers of other languages (Certificate); education (MSE); elementary education (Certificate); ESL (Certificate); middle school education (Certificate); organizational leadership (D Ed); professional studies (Certificate); professional studies for VA licensure (Certificate); professional teaching English to speakers of other languages (Certificate); public management (Certificate); secondary education (Certificate). *Application deadline:* For fall admission, 7/1 for domestic and international students; for spring admission, 10/15 for domestic and international students. *Application fee:* $30. Electronic applications accepted. *Application Contact:* David Anthony, Dean of Admissions, 540-665-4581, Fax: 540-665-4627, E-mail: admit@su.edu. *Dean,* Dr. Steven E. Humphries, 540-535-3574, E-mail: shumphri@su.edu.

School of Health Professions Students: 611 full-time (428 women), 281 part-time (198 women); includes 77 minority (14 African Americans, 1 American Indian/Alaska Native, 49 Asian Americans or Pacific Islanders, 13 Hispanic Americans), 21 international. Average age 32. 1,254 applicants, 21% accepted, 145 enrolled. *Faculty:* 49 full-time (32 women), 7 part-time/adjunct (5 women). Expenses: Contact institution. *Financial support:* Application deadline: 3/15. In 2008, 77 master's, 54 doctorates, 3 other advanced degrees awarded. *Degree program information:* Part-time programs available. Postbaccalaureate distance learning degree programs offered. Offers health professions (MS, MSN, DPT, Certificate). *Application deadline:* Applications are processed on a rolling basis. *Application fee:* $30. Electronic applications accepted. *Application Contact:* Information Contact, 540-665-5500, Fax: 540-665-5519.

Division of Athletic Training Students: 16 full-time (13 women), 3 part-time (all women); includes 1 minority (African American), 2 international. Average age 22. *Faculty:* 3 full-time (1 woman). Expenses: Contact institution. *Financial support:* In 2008–09, 13 students received support. Institutionally sponsored loans available. Support available to part-time students. Financial award application deadline: 3/15; financial award applicants required to submit FAFSA. In 2008, 12 master's awarded. Offers athletic training (MS). *Application deadline:* Applications are processed on a rolling basis. *Application fee:* $30. Electronic applications accepted. *Application Contact:* David Anthony, Dean of Admissions, 540-665-4581, Fax: 540-665-4627, E-mail: admit@su.edu. *Director,* Dr. Rose A. Schmieg, 540-665-5534, Fax: 540-545-7387, E-mail: rschmieg@su.edu.

Shenandoah University (continued)

Division of Nursing Students: 18 full-time (17 women), 53 part-time (50 women); includes 3 minority (1 African American, 1 Asian American or Pacific Islander, 1 Hispanic American). Average age 39. 68 applicants, 87% accepted, 41 enrolled. *Faculty:* 10 full-time (all women), 2 part-time/adjunct (both women). Expenses: Contact institution. *Financial support:* In 2008–09, 22 students received support, including 2 teaching assistantships with partial tuition reimbursements available (averaging $2,000 per year); fellowships, institutionally sponsored loans and scholarships/grants also available. Support available to part-time students. Financial award application deadline: 3/15; financial award applicants required to submit FAFSA. In 2008, 15 master's awarded. *Degree program information:* Part-time programs available. Offers family nurse practitioner (Certificate); health systems management (Certificate); nurse-midwifery (Certificate); nursing (MSN); psychiatric mental health nurse practitioner (Certificate). *Application deadline:* For fall admission, 6/15 priority date for domestic and international students. Applications are processed on a rolling basis. *Application fee:* $30. Electronic applications accepted. *Application Contact:* David Anthony, Dean of Admissions, 540-665-4581, Fax: 540-665-4627, E-mail: admit@su.edu. *Director,* Dr. Kathryn Ganske, 540-678-4381, Fax: 540-665-5519.

Division of Occupational Therapy Students: 42 full-time (38 women), 9 part-time (all women); includes 1 minority (Hispanic American). Average age 29. 74 applicants, 61% accepted, 28 enrolled. *Faculty:* 3 full-time (all women), 2 part-time/adjunct (both women). Expenses: Contact institution. *Financial support:* In 2008–09, 40 students received support. Institutionally sponsored loans and scholarships/grants available. Support available to part-time students. Financial award application deadline: 3/15; financial award applicants required to submit FAFSA. In 2008, 20 master's awarded. Offers occupational therapy (MS). *Application deadline:* For fall admission, 7/1 for domestic students. Applications are processed on a rolling basis. *Application fee:* $30. Electronic applications accepted. *Application Contact:* David Anthony, Dean of Admissions, 540-665-4581, Fax: 540-665-4627, E-mail: admit@su.edu. *Director,* Dr. Deborah A. Marr, 540-678-4312, Fax: 540-665-5564, E-mail: dmarr@su.edu.

Division of Physical Therapy Students: 117 full-time (86 women), 107 part-time (75 women); includes 11 minority (5 African Americans, 6 Hispanic Americans), 3 international. Average age 34. 276 applicants, 37% accepted, 78 enrolled. *Faculty:* 7 full-time (4 women), 2 part-time/adjunct (0 women). Expenses: Contact institution. *Financial support:* In 2008–09, 76 students received support. Institutionally sponsored loans and scholarships/grants available. Support available to part-time students. Financial award application deadline: 3/15; financial award applicants required to submit FAFSA. In 2008, 54 doctorates awarded. *Degree program information:* Part-time programs available. Postbaccalaureate distance learning degree programs offered. Offers physical therapy and non-traditional physical therapy (DPT). *Application deadline:* For fall admission, 7/31 for domestic students; for spring admission, 5/15 for domestic students. Applications are processed on a rolling basis. *Application fee:* $30. Electronic applications accepted. *Application Contact:* David Anthony, Dean of Admissions, 540-665-4581, Fax: 540-665-4627, E-mail: admit@su.edu. *Director,* Dr. Karen Abraham-Justice, 540-665-5520, Fax: 540-545-7387, E-mail: kabraham@su.edu.

Division of Physician Assistant Studies Students: 100 full-time (85 women), 4 part-time (3 women); includes 5 minority (1 African American, 3 Asian Americans or Pacific Islanders, 1 Hispanic American), 2 international. Average age 28. 349 applicants, 19% accepted, 40 enrolled. *Faculty:* 4 full-time (2 women). Expenses: Contact institution. *Financial support:* In 2008–09, 64 students received support. Institutionally sponsored loans and scholarships/grants available. Support available to part-time students. Financial award application deadline: 3/15; financial award applicants required to submit FAFSA. In 2008, 30 master's awarded. Offers physician assistant studies (MS). *Application deadline:* For fall admission, 1/15 for domestic students. Applications are processed on a rolling basis. *Application fee:* $30. Electronic applications accepted. *Application Contact:* David Anthony, Dean of Admissions, 540-665-4581, Fax: 540-665-4627, E-mail: admit@su.edu. *Director,* Anthony A. Miller, 540-545-7257, Fax: 540-542-6210, E-mail: amiller@su.edu.

School of Pharmacy Students: 318 full-time (189 women), 102 part-time (55 women); includes 56 minority (6 African Americans, 1 American Indian/Alaska Native, 45 Asian Americans or Pacific Islanders, 4 Hispanic Americans), 12 international. Average age 31. 1,187 applicants, 17% accepted, 104 enrolled. *Faculty:* 22 full-time (12 women), 1 (woman) part-time/adjunct. Expenses: Contact institution. *Financial support:* In 2008–09, 298 students received support. Institutionally sponsored loans and scholarships/grants available. Support available to part-time students. Financial award application deadline: 3/15; financial award applicants required to submit FAFSA. *Degree program information:* Part-time programs available. Postbaccalaureate distance learning degree programs offered (minimal on-campus study). Offers pharmacy and non-traditional pharmacy (Pharm D). *Application deadline:* For fall admission, 2/1 for domestic and international students. Applications are processed on a rolling basis. *Application fee:* $30. Electronic applications accepted. *Application Contact:* David Anthony, Dean of Admissions, 540-665-4581, Fax: 540-665-4627, E-mail: admit@su.edu. *Dean,* Dr. Alan McKay, 540-665-1280, Fax: 540-665-1283, E-mail: amckay@su.edu.

Shenandoah Conservatory Students: 71 full-time (42 women), 150 part-time (80 women); includes 14 minority (9 African Americans, 2 Asian Americans or Pacific Islanders, 3 Hispanic Americans), 32 international. Average age 40. 76 applicants, 96% accepted, 49 enrolled. *Faculty:* 39 full-time (19 women), 21 part-time/adjunct (9 women). Expenses: Contact institution. *Financial support:* In 2008–09, 154 students received support, including 26 teaching assistantships with partial tuition reimbursements available (averaging $5,870 per year); fellowships, career-related internships or fieldwork, institutionally sponsored loans, scholarships/grants, and unspecified assistantships also available. Support available to part-time students. Financial award application deadline: 3/15; financial award applicants required to submit FAFSA. In 2008, 24 master's, 10 doctorates, 7 other advanced degrees awarded. *Degree program information:* Part-time and evening/weekend programs available. Offers arts administration (MS); church music (MM, Certificate); composition (MM); conducting (MM); dance (MA, MFA, MS); dance accompanying (MM); music (MS); music education (MME, DMA); music therapy (MMT, Certificate); pedagogy (MM, DMA); performance (MM, DMA, Artist Diploma); piano accompanying (MM). *Application deadline:* Applications are processed on a rolling basis. *Application fee:* $30. Electronic applications accepted. *Application Contact:* David Anthony, Dean of Admissions, 540-665-4581, Fax: 540-665-4627, E-mail: admit@su.edu. *Dean,* Dr. Laurence A. Kaptain, 540-665-4600, Fax: 540-665-5402, E-mail: lkaptain@su.edu.

SHEPHERD UNIVERSITY, Shepherdstown, WV 25443-3210

General Information State-supported, coed, comprehensive institution. CGS member.

GRADUATE UNITS

Program in Curriculum and Instruction Offers curriculum and instruction (MA).

SHERMAN COLLEGE OF STRAIGHT CHIROPRACTIC, Spartanburg, SC 29304-1452

General Information Independent, coed, graduate-only institution. *Graduate housing:* On-campus housing not available. *Research affiliation:* Foundation for Chiropractic Education and Research, American Public Health Service (chiropractic research).

GRADUATE UNITS

Professional Program Offers chiropractic (DC). Electronic applications accepted.

SHIPPENSBURG UNIVERSITY OF PENNSYLVANIA, Shippensburg, PA 17257-2299

General Information State-supported, coed, comprehensive institution. CGS member. *Enrollment:* 7,942 graduate, professional, and undergraduate students; 270 full-time matriculated graduate/professional students (159 women), 773 part-time matriculated graduate/professional students (503 women). *Enrollment by degree level:* 1,043 master's. *Graduate faculty:* 155 full-time (60 women), 24 part-time/adjunct (15 women). Tuition, state resident: full-time $6430; part-time $357 per credit. Tuition, nonresident: full-time $10,288; part-time $572 per credit. *Required fees:* $1127; $38 per credit. One-time fee: $44 part-time. *Graduate housing:* On-campus housing not available. *Student services:* Campus employment opportunities, campus safety program, career counseling, child daycare facilities, exercise/wellness program, free psychological counseling, grant writing training, international student services, low-cost health insurance, multicultural affairs office, services for students with disabilities, teacher training, writing training. *Library facilities:* Ezra Lehman Memorial Library plus 1 other. *Online resources:* library catalog, web page, access to other libraries' catalogs. *Collection:* 457,371 titles, 1,225 serial subscriptions, 72,732 audiovisual materials.

Computer facilities: 1,100 computers available on campus for general student use. A campuswide network can be accessed from student residence rooms and from off campus. Online class registration, personal Web pages are available. *Web address:* http://www.ship.edu/.

General Application Contact: Renee Payne, Associate Dean of Graduate Admissions, 717-477-1231, Fax: 717-477-4016, E-mail: rmpayn@ship.edu.

GRADUATE UNITS

School of Graduate Studies Students: 270 full-time (159 women), 773 part-time (503 women); includes 87 minority (48 African Americans, 2 American Indian/Alaska Native, 27 Asian Americans or Pacific Islanders, 10 Hispanic Americans), 24 international. Average age 30. 623 applicants, 64% accepted, 241 enrolled. *Faculty:* 155 full-time (60 women), 24 part-time/adjunct (15 women). Expenses: Contact institution. *Financial support:* In 2008–09, 144 research assistantships with full tuition reimbursements (averaging $5,000 per year) were awarded; career-related internships or fieldwork, scholarships/grants, unspecified assistantships, and residence hall directors, student payroll positions also available. Support available to part-time students. Financial award application deadline: 3/1; financial award applicants required to submit FAFSA. In 2008, 337 master's awarded. *Degree program information:* Part-time and evening/weekend programs available. Postbaccalaureate distance learning degree programs offered (minimal on-campus study). *Application deadline:* For fall admission, 3/1 for international students; for spring admission, 7/1 for international students. Applications are processed on a rolling basis. *Application fee:* $30. Electronic applications accepted. *Application Contact:* Renee Payne, Associate Dean of Graduate Admissions, 717-477-1231, Fax: 717-477-4016, E-mail: rmpayn@ship.edu. *Dean of Graduate Studies/Associate Provost,* Dr. Tracy Schoolcraft, 717-477-1148, Fax: 717-477-4038, E-mail: tascho@ship.edu.

College of Arts and Sciences Students: 135 full-time (57 women), 148 part-time (79 women); includes 23 minority (10 African Americans, 10 Asian Americans or Pacific Islanders, 3 Hispanic Americans), 15 international. Average age 29. 229 applicants, 72% accepted, 87 enrolled. *Faculty:* 86 full-time (25 women), 6 part-time/adjunct (3 women). Expenses: Contact institution. *Financial support:* In 2008–09, 74 research assistantships with full tuition reimbursements (averaging $5,000 per year) were awarded; career-related internships or fieldwork, scholarships/grants, unspecified assistantships, and residence hall directors, student payroll positions also available. Support available to part-time students. Financial award application deadline: 3/1; financial award applicants required to submit FAFSA. In 2008, 115 master's awarded. *Degree program information:* Part-time and evening/weekend programs available. Offers applied history (MA, Certificate); arts and sciences (MA, MPA, MS, Certificate); biology (MS); communication studies (MS); computer science (MS); geoenvironmental studies (MS); organizational development and leadership (MS); psychology (MS); public administration (MPA). *Application deadline:* For fall admission, 3/1 for international students; for spring admission, 7/1 for international students. Applications are processed on a rolling basis. *Application fee:* $30. Electronic applications accepted. *Application Contact:* Renee Payne, Associate Dean of Graduate Admissions, 717-477-1231, Fax: 717-477-4016, E-mail: rmpayn@ship.edu. *Dean,* Dr. James Mike, 717-477-1151, Fax: 717-477-4026, E-mail: jhmike@ship.edu.

College of Education and Human Services Students: 119 full-time (97 women), 464 part-time (361 women); includes 44 minority (29 African Americans, 1 American Indian/Alaska Native, 9 Asian Americans or Pacific Islanders, 5 Hispanic Americans), 4 international. Average age 30. 256 applicants, 54% accepted, 94 enrolled. *Faculty:* 48 full-time (25 women), 16 part-time/adjunct (10 women). Expenses: Contact institution. *Financial support:* In 2008–09, 57 research assistantships with full tuition reimbursements (averaging $5,000 per year) were awarded; career-related internships or fieldwork, scholarships/grants, unspecified assistantships, and resident hall directors, student payroll positions also available. Support available to part-time students. Financial award application deadline: 3/1; financial award applicants required to submit FAFSA. In 2008, 182 master's awarded. *Degree program information:* Part-time and evening/weekend programs available. Offers Adlerian studies (Certificate); administration of justice (MS); advanced study in counseling (Certificate); aging (Certificate); alcohol and drug counseling (Certificate); counseling (M Ed, MS); couple and family counseling (Certificate); curriculum and instruction (M Ed); education and human services (M Ed, MS, MSW, Certificate); reading (M Ed); school administration principal K-12 (M Ed); social work (MSW); special education (M Ed). *Application deadline:* For fall admission, 3/1 for international students; for spring admission, 7/1 for international students. Applications are processed on a rolling basis. *Application fee:* $30. Electronic applications accepted. *Application Contact:* Renee Payne, Associate Dean of Graduate Admissions, 717-477-1231, Fax: 717-477-4016, E-mail: rmpayn@ship.edu. *Dean,* Dr. James R. Johnson, 717-477-1373, Fax: 717-477-4012, E-mail: jrjohnson@ship.edu.

John L. Grove College of Business Students: 16 full-time (5 women), 161 part-time (63 women); includes 20 minority (9 African Americans, 1 American Indian/Alaska Native, 8 Asian Americans or Pacific Islanders, 2 Hispanic Americans), 5 international. Average age 31. 138 applicants, 69% accepted, 60 enrolled. *Faculty:* 21 full-time (10 women), 2 part-time/adjunct (both women). Expenses: Contact institution. *Financial support:* In 2008–09, 13 research assistantships with full tuition reimbursements (averaging $5,000 per year) were awarded; career-related internships or fieldwork, scholarships/grants, unspecified assistantships, and resident hall directors, student payroll positions also available. Support available to part-time students. Financial award application deadline: 3/1; financial award applicants required to submit FAFSA. In 2008, 40 master's awarded. *Degree program information:* Part-time and evening/weekend programs available. Postbaccalaureate distance learning degree programs offered (minimal on-campus study). Offers advanced studies in business (Certificate); business administration (MBA). *Application deadline:* For fall admission, 3/1 for international students; for spring admission, 7/1 for international students. Applications are processed on a rolling basis. *Application fee:* $30. Electronic applications accepted. *Application Contact:* Renee Payne, Associate Dean of Graduate Admissions, 717-477-1231, Fax: 717-477-4016, E-mail: rmpayn@ship.edu. *Director/Assistant Dean,* Dr. Patricia Wolf, 717-477-1483, Fax: 717-477-4003, E-mail: pdwolf@ship.edu.

See Close-Up on page 987.

SHORTER COLLEGE, Rome, GA 30165

General Information Independent-religious, coed, comprehensive institution. *Enrollment by degree level:* 300 master's. *Graduate faculty:* 10 full-time (1 woman), 23 part-time/adjunct (10 women). *Tuition:* Full-time $8450. *Required fees:* $384. *Graduate housing:* On-campus housing not available. *Student services:* Career counseling. *Library facilities:* Livingston Library. *Online resources:* library catalog, web page, access to other libraries' catalogs. *Collection:* 213,297 titles, 8,511 serial subscriptions, 12,134 audiovisual materials.

Computer facilities: 100 computers available on campus for general student use. A campuswide network can be accessed from student residence rooms. Online class registration is available. *Web address:* http://www.shorter.edu/.

General Application Contact: Patrick McElhaney, Director of Admissions, 800-868-6980, E-mail: pmcelhaney@shorter.edu.

GRADUATE UNITS

School of Business *Degree program information:* Evening/weekend programs available. Offers business administration (MBA); leadership (MA).

SH'OR YOSHUV RABBINICAL COLLEGE, Lawrence, NY 11559-1714

General Information Independent-religious, men only, comprehensive institution.

SIENA HEIGHTS UNIVERSITY, Adrian, MI 49221-1796

General Information Independent-religious, coed, comprehensive institution. *Graduate housing:* Room and/or apartments available on a first-come, first-served basis to single students; on-campus housing not available to married students. Housing application deadline: 4/1.

GRADUATE UNITS

Graduate College *Degree program information:* Part-time and evening/weekend programs available. Offers early childhood education (MA); educational leadership (MA); elementary education (MA); elementary education/reading (MA); mathematics education (MA); middle school education (MA); Montessori education (MA); secondary education (MA); secondary education/reading (MA).

SIERRA NEVADA COLLEGE, Incline Village, NV 89451

General Information Independent, coed, comprehensive institution. *Graduate housing:* On-campus housing not available.

GRADUATE UNITS

Teacher Education Program *Degree program information:* Part-time and evening/weekend programs available. Offers elementary education (MAT); secondary education (MAT).

SILICON VALLEY UNIVERSITY, San Jose, CA 95131

General Information Proprietary, coed, comprehensive institution.

GRADUATE UNITS

Graduate Programs

SILVER LAKE COLLEGE, Manitowoc, WI 54220-9319

General Information Independent-religious, coed, primarily women, comprehensive institution. *Enrollment:* 853 graduate, professional, and undergraduate students; 15 full-time matriculated graduate/professional students (14 women), 93 part-time matriculated graduate/professional students (61 women). *Enrollment by degree level:* 108 master's. *Graduate faculty:* 7 full-time (all women), 63 part-time/adjunct (36 women). *Tuition:* Part-time $395 per credit. *Student services:* Campus employment opportunities, campus safety program, career counseling, international student services, services for students with disabilities, teacher training, writing training. *Library facilities:* The Erma M. and Theodore M. Zigmunt Library. *Online resources:* library catalog, access to other libraries' catalogs. *Collection:* 62,465 titles, 250 serial subscriptions, 7,112 audiovisual materials.

Computer facilities: 50 computers available on campus for general student use. A campuswide network can be accessed from off campus. Online class registration is available. *Web address:* http://www.sl.edu/.

General Application Contact: Jamie Grant, Associate Director of Admissions, 800-236-4752 Ext. 186, Fax: 920-686-6322, E-mail: jgrant@silver.sl.edu.

GRADUATE UNITS

Division of Graduate Studies Students: 15 full-time (14 women), 93 part-time (61 women); includes 7 minority (1 African American, 5 American Indian/Alaska Native, 1 Hispanic American). Average age 38. 60 applicants, 70% accepted, 25 enrolled. *Faculty:* 7 full-time (all women), 63 part-time/adjunct (36 women). Expenses: Contact institution. *Financial support:* In 2008–09, 19 students received support. Career-related internships or fieldwork, Federal Work-Study, and scholarships/grants available. Support available to part-time students. Financial award applicants required to submit FAFSA. In 2008, 56 master's awarded. *Degree program information:* Part-time and evening/weekend programs available. Postbaccalaureate distance learning degree programs offered (minimal on-campus study). Offers administrative leadership (MA Ed); management and organizational behavior (MS); music education-Kodaly emphasis (MM); special education (MASE); teacher leadership (MA Ed). *Application deadline:* For fall admission, 8/1 for domestic and international students; for spring admission, 12/1 for domestic and international students. Applications are processed on a rolling basis. *Application fee:* $35. Electronic applications accepted. *Application Contact:* Jamie Grant, Associate Director of Admissions, 800-236-4752 Ext. 186, Fax: 920-686-6322, E-mail: jgrant@silver.sl.edu.

SIMMONS COLLEGE, Boston, MA 02115

General Information Independent, Undergraduate: women only; graduate: coed, university. CGS member. *Graduate housing:* Room and/or apartments available on a first-come, first-served basis to single students; on-campus housing not available to married students. Housing application deadline: 7/15. *Student services:* Campus employment opportunities, campus safety program, career counseling, exercise/wellness program, free psychological counseling, international student services, low-cost health insurance, multicultural affairs office, services for students with disabilities. *Library facilities:* Beatley Library plus 1 other. *Online resources:* library catalog, web page, access to other libraries' catalogs. *Collection:* 207,823 titles, 44,734 serial subscriptions, 8,785 audiovisual materials.

Computer facilities: Computer purchase and lease plans are available. 350 computers available on campus for general student use. A campuswide network can be accessed from student residence rooms and from off campus. Online class registration is available. *Web address:* http://www.simmons.edu/.

General Application Contact: Donna M. Dolan, Registrar, 617-521-2111, Fax: 617-521-3144, E-mail: donna.dolan@simmons.edu.

GRADUATE UNITS

College of Arts and Sciences Graduate Studies Students: 149 full-time (136 women), 820 part-time (721 women); includes 106 minority (51 African Americans, 3 American Indian/Alaska Native, 25 Asian Americans or Pacific Islanders, 27 Hispanic Americans), 3 international. Average age 28. 457 applicants, 77% accepted, 249 enrolled. *Faculty:* 59 full-time (42 women), 72 part-time/adjunct (42 women). Expenses: Contact institution. *Financial support:* Career-related internships or fieldwork, scholarships/grants, and unspecified assistantships available. Financial award application deadline: 3/1; financial award applicants required to submit FAFSA. In 2008, 410 master's, 33 other advanced degrees awarded. *Degree program information:* Part-time and evening/weekend programs available. Offers applied behavior analysis (PhD); arts and sciences (MA, MAT, MFA, MS, MS Ed, PhD, CAGS, Ed S); assistive technology (MS Ed, Ed S); behavioral education (MS Ed, Ed S); children's literature (MA); communications management (MS); educational leadership (MS Ed, CAGS); elementary education (MAT, CAGS); English (MA); gender/cultural studies (MA); general education (CAGS); general purposes (MS); health professions education (PhD); language and literacy (MS Ed, Ed S); middle school education (MAT, CAGS); moderate disabilities (Ed S); moderate special needs (MS Ed); professional license (CAGS); professional license: elementary (MS Ed); professional license: middle/high (MS Ed); secondary education (MAT, CAGS); severe disabilities (Ed S); severe special needs (MS Ed); Spanish (MA); special education (MS Ed, PhD, Ed S); special education administration (MS Ed, PhD, Ed S); teacher preparation (MAT, MS, MS Ed, CAGS); teaching English as a second language (MAT, CAGS); urban education (MS Ed, CAGS); writing for children (MFA). *Application deadline:* For fall admission, 8/1 priority date for domestic and international students; for winter admission, 12/15 priority date for domestic students, 12/1 priority date for international students; for spring admission, 5/1 priority date for domestic and international students. Applications are processed on a rolling basis. *Application fee:* $35. Electronic applications accepted. *Application Contact:* Kristen Haack, Director, Graduate Studies Admission, 617-521-2917, Fax: 617-521-3058, E-mail: gsa@simmons.edu. *Dean,* Dr. Diane Raymond, 617-521-2212, Fax: 617-521-3058, E-mail: gsa@simmons.edu.

Graduate School of Library and Information Science Students: 18 full-time (16 women), 655 part-time (525 women); includes 53 minority (11 African Americans, 3 American Indian/Alaska Native, 25 Asian Americans or Pacific Islanders, 14 Hispanic Americans), 8 international. Average age 33. 417 applicants, 92% accepted, 229 enrolled. *Faculty:* 21 full-time (13 women), 35 part-time/adjunct (22 women). Expenses: Contact institution. *Financial support:* In 2008–09, 104 students received support, including 11 fellowships (averaging $8,017 per year); scholarships/grants also available. Financial award application deadline: 3/1; financial award applicants required to submit FAFSA. In 2008, 270 master's, 1 doctorate awarded. *Degree program information:* Part-time and evening/weekend programs available. Offers history and archives managementlibrary and information science (PhD); school library teacher (MS, Certificate). MS/DA and MS/MA offered jointly with Department of History. *Application deadline:* For fall admission, 3/1 priority date for domestic students, 3/1 for international students; for spring admission, 7/1 priority date for domestic students. Applications are processed on a rolling basis. *Application fee:* $50. Electronic applications accepted. *Application Contact:* Sarah Petrakos, Assistant Dean, Admission and Recruitment, 617-521-2868, Fax: 617-521-3192, E-mail: gslisadm@simmons.edu. *Dean,* Dr. Michele V. Cloonan, 617-521-2806, Fax: 617-521-3192, E-mail: cloonan@simmons.edu.

School of Health Sciences Students: 129 full-time (119 women), 300 part-time (274 women); includes 44 minority (15 African Americans, 23 Asian Americans or Pacific Islanders, 6 Hispanic Americans), 1 international. Average age 27. *Faculty:* 47 full-time (40 women), 194 part-time/adjunct (171 women). Expenses: Contact institution. *Financial support:* Application deadline: 3/1. In 2008, 39 master's, 49 doctorates, 39 other advanced degrees awarded. *Degree program information:* Part-time and evening/weekend programs available. Postbaccalaureate distance learning degree programs offered (no on-campus study). Offers didactic program in dietetics (Certificate); health care administration (MHA, CAGS); health professions education (PhD, CAGS); health sciences (MHA, MS, DPT, PhD, CAGS, Certificate); nursing practice (PhD); nutrition (dietetic internship) (Certificate); nutrition and health promotion (MS); physical therapy (DPT); primary health care nursing (MS, CAGS); sports nutrition (Certificate). Electronic applications accepted. *Application Contact:* Carmen Fortin, Assistant Dean/Director of Admission, 617-521-2651, Fax: 617-521-3137, E-mail: shs@simmons.edu. *Dean,* Dr. Gerald P. Koocher, 617-521-2605, Fax: 617-521-3137, E-mail: gerald.koocher@simmons.edu.

School of Management Students: 31 full-time (all women), 114 part-time (all women); includes 28 minority (12 African Americans, 14 Asian Americans or Pacific Islanders, 2 Hispanic Americans). Average age 31. 102 applicants, 75% accepted, 58 enrolled. *Faculty:* 28 full-time (23 women), 9 part-time/adjunct (7 women). Expenses: Contact institution. *Financial support:* In 2008–09, 92 students received support. Institutionally sponsored loans and scholarships/grants available. Financial award application deadline: 3/1; financial award applicants required to submit FAFSA. In 2008, 70 master's, 5 other advanced degrees awarded. *Degree program information:* Part-time and evening/weekend programs available. Offers entrepreneurship (Certificate); management (MBA). *Application deadline:* For fall admission, 5/1 priority date for domestic students, 4/1 priority date for international students; for spring admission, 11/3 priority date for domestic and international students. Applications are processed on a rolling basis. *Application fee:* $75. Electronic applications accepted. *Application Contact:* Kerri Brophy, Senior Director of Admissions and Marketing, 617-521-3818, Fax: 617-521-3880, E-mail: somadm@simmons.edu. *Dean,* Dr. Deborah Merrill-Sands, 617-521-3873, Fax: 617-521-3881.

School of Social Work Students: 281 full-time (255 women), 154 part-time (139 women); includes 70 minority (45 African Americans, 8 Asian Americans or Pacific Islanders, 17 Hispanic Americans), 3 international. Average age 27. 573 applicants, 89% accepted, 185 enrolled. *Faculty:* 26 full-time (19 women), 53 part-time/adjunct (41 women). Expenses: Contact institution. *Financial support:* In 2008–09, 102 students received support. Scholarships/grants available. Financial award application deadline: 3/1; financial award applicants required to submit FAFSA. In 2008, 120 master's, 1 doctorate awarded. *Degree program information:* Part-time programs available. Offers clinical social work (MSW, PhD). *Application deadline:* For fall admission, 12/15 priority date for domestic students, 2/15 priority date for international students; for spring admission, 10/15 for domestic students. Applications are processed on a rolling basis. *Application fee:* $45. Electronic applications accepted. *Application Contact:* Carlos Frontado, Director of Admissions, 617-521-3920, Fax: 617-521-3980, E-mail: carlos.frontado@simmons.edu. *Dean,* Dr. Stefan Krug, 617-521-3929, Fax: 617-521-3980, E-mail: stefan.krug@simmons.edu.

SIMON FRASER UNIVERSITY, Burnaby, BC V5A 1S6, Canada

General Information Province-supported, coed, university. CGS member. *Graduate housing:* Rooms and/or apartments available on a first-come, first-served basis to single and married students. Housing application deadline: 1/2. *Research affiliation:* Bamfield Marine Research Station.

GRADUATE UNITS

Graduate Studies *Degree program information:* Part-time and evening/weekend programs available.

Faculty of Applied Sciences Offers applied sciences (M Eng, M Sc, MA, MA Sc, MRM, PhD); communication (MA, PhD); computing science (M Sc, PhD); engineering science (M Eng, MA Sc, PhD); information technology (M Sc, PhD); interactive arts (M Sc, PhD); kinesiology (M Sc, PhD); resource and environmental management (MRM, PhD).

Faculty of Arts and Social Sciences *Degree program information:* Part-time and evening/weekend programs available. Offers anthropology (MA, PhD); archaeology (MA, PhD); arts and social sciences (M Pub, M Sc, MA, MALS, MFA, MPP, MUS, PhD, Graduate Diploma); contemporary arts (MFA); criminology (MA, PhD); economics (MA, PhD); English (MA, PhD); French (MA); geography (M Sc, MA, PhD); gerontology (MA, PhD); history (MA, PhD); Latin American studies (MA); liberal studies (MALS); linguistics (MA, PhD); philosophy (MA, PhD); political science (MA, PhD); psychology (MA, PhD); public policy (MPP); publishing (M Pub); sociology (MA, PhD); urban studies (MUS, Graduate Diploma); women's studies (MA, PhD).

Faculty of Business Administration Postbaccalaureate distance learning degree programs offered. Offers business administration (EMBA, PhD); financial management (MA); general business (MBA); global asset and wealth management (MBA); management of technology/biotechnology (MBA).

Faculty of Education Offers administrative leadership (M Ed, MA, Ed D); arts education (M Ed, MA, PhD); counseling psychology (M Ed, MA); curriculum theory and implementation (PhD); education (M Ed, M Sc, MA, Ed D, PhD); educational psychology (M Ed, MA, PhD); educational technology and learning design (M Ed, MA, PhD); foundations (M Ed, MA); mathematics education (M Ed, M Sc, PhD); philosophy of education (PhD); teaching English as a second/foreign language (M Ed).

Faculty of Health Sciences Offers population and public health (M Sc).

Faculty of Science *Degree program information:* Part-time programs available. Offers applied and computational mathematics (M Sc, PhD); biological sciences (M Sc, PhD); biophysics (M Sc, PhD); chemical physics (M Sc, PhD); chemistry (PhD); earth sciences (M Sc, PhD); environmental toxicology (MET); mathematics (M Sc, PhD); molecular biology and biochemistry (M Sc, PhD); pest management (MPM); physics (M Sc, PhD); science (M Sc, MET, MPM, PhD); statistics and actuarial science (M Sc, PhD).

SIMPSON UNIVERSITY, Redding, CA 96003-8606

General Information Independent-religious, coed, comprehensive institution. *Graduate housing:* On-campus housing not available.

GRADUATE UNITS

A.W. Tozer Theological Seminary *Degree program information:* Part-time and evening/weekend programs available. Postbaccalaureate distance learning degree programs offered (minimal on-campus study). Offers Christian leadership (MA); Christian studies (MA); intercultural studies (MA); ministry (M Div). Electronic applications accepted.

School of Education *Degree program information:* Part-time and evening/weekend programs available. Offers education (MA); education and preliminary administrative services (MA); education and preliminary teaching (MA); teaching (MA). Electronic applications accepted.

SINTE GLESKA UNIVERSITY, Mission, SD 57555

General Information Independent, coed, comprehensive institution. *Graduate housing:* Rooms and/or apartments available on a first-come, first-served basis to single and married students.

GRADUATE UNITS

Graduate Education Program *Degree program information:* Part-time and evening/weekend programs available. Offers elementary education (M Ed).

SIOUX FALLS SEMINARY, Sioux Falls, SD 57105-1599

General Information Independent-religious, coed, graduate-only institution. *Graduate faculty:* 10 full-time (1 woman), 11 part-time/adjunct (2 women). *Graduate housing:* Rooms and/or apartments available to single and married students. Housing application deadline: 7/1. *Student services:* Campus employment opportunities, career counseling, exercise/wellness program, free psychological counseling, international student services, low-cost health insurance. *Library facilities:* Kaiser-Ramaker Library. *Collection:* 66,978 titles, 590 serial subscriptions, 9,128 audiovisual materials. *Web address:* http://sfseminary.edu/.

General Application Contact: Bryce H. Eben, Director of Enrollment Development, 605-336-6588, Fax: 605-335-9090, E-mail: beben@sfseminary.edu.

GRADUATE UNITS

Graduate and Professional Programs *Degree program information:* Part-time programs available. Offers Bible and theology (MA); Christian leadership (MA); counseling (MA); marriage and family therapy (MA); ministry (D Min); pastoral ministry (M Div); religious studies (MA); theological studies (Certificate).

SIT GRADUATE INSTITUTE, Brattleboro, VT 05302-0676

General Information Independent, coed, graduate-only institution. *Enrollment by degree level:* 623 master's. *Graduate faculty:* 27 full-time (12 women), 19 part-time/adjunct (8 women). *Graduate housing:* Rooms and/or apartments available on a first-come, first-served basis to single and married students. *Student services:* Campus employment opportunities, campus safety program, career counseling, exercise/wellness program, free psychological counseling, international student services, low-cost health insurance, multicultural affairs office, services for students with disabilities, teacher training, writing training. *Library facilities:* Donald B. Watt Library. *Collection:* 32,000 titles, 450 serial subscriptions.

Computer facilities: 55 computers available on campus for general student use. A campuswide network can be accessed from student residence rooms and from off campus. *Web address:* http://www.sit.edu/.

General Application Contact: Information Contact, 800-336-1616, Fax: 802-258-3500, E-mail: admissions@sit.edu.

GRADUATE UNITS

Graduate Programs Students: 224 full-time (161 women), 399 part-time (277 women); includes 73 minority (31 African Americans, 3 American Indian/Alaska Native, 14 Asian Americans or Pacific Islanders, 25 Hispanic Americans), 143 international. Average age 32. 657 applicants, 74% accepted, 224 enrolled. *Faculty:* 27 full-time (12 women), 19 part-time/adjunct (8 women). Expenses: Contact institution. *Financial support:* In 2008–09, 397 students received support. Career-related internships or fieldwork, Federal Work-Study, institutionally sponsored loans, and scholarships/grants available. Financial award application deadline: 3/1; financial award applicants required to submit FAFSA. In 2008, 251 master's awarded. *Degree program information:* Part-time programs available. Postbaccalaureate distance learning degree programs offered (minimal on-campus study). Offers conflict transformation (MA); English for speakers of other languages (MAT); French (MAT); global management (MGM); intercultural service, leadership, and management (MA); international education (MA); management (MS); social justice in intercultural relations (MA); Spanish (MAT); sustainable development (MA). *Application deadline:* Applications are processed on a rolling basis. *Application fee:* $50. Electronic applications accepted. *Application Contact:* Information Contact, 800-336-1616, Fax: 802-258-3500, E-mail: admissions@sit.edu. *President/CEO of World Learning and SIT*, Adam Weinberg, 802-258-3357, Fax: 802-258-3110, E-mail: adam.weinberg@sit.edu.

SKIDMORE COLLEGE, Saratoga Springs, NY 12866-1632

General Information Independent, coed, comprehensive institution. *Enrollment:* 2,777 graduate, professional, and undergraduate students; 60 part-time matriculated graduate/professional students (48 women). *Enrollment by degree level:* 60 master's. *Graduate faculty:* 46 full-time (28 women), 27 part-time/adjunct (9 women). *Graduate housing:* On-campus housing not available. *Student services:* Career counseling. *Library facilities:* Scribner Library plus 1 other. *Online resources:* library catalog, web page, access to other libraries' catalogs. *Collection:* 376,682 titles, 959 serial subscriptions, 11,078 audiovisual materials.

Computer facilities: Computer purchase and lease plans are available. 230 computers available on campus for general student use. A campuswide network can be accessed from student residence rooms and from off campus. Online class registration is available. *Web address:* http://www.skidmore.edu/.

General Application Contact: Dr. John Anzalone, Director, 518-580-5480, Fax: 518-580-5486.

GRADUATE UNITS

Liberal Studies Program Students: 60 part-time (48 women); includes 5 minority (2 African Americans, 3 Hispanic Americans). Average age 42. 37 applicants, 73% accepted, 21 enrolled. *Faculty:* 46 full-time (28 women), 27 part-time/adjunct (9 women). Expenses: Contact institution. *Financial support:* In 2008–09, 6 students received support. Career-related internships or fieldwork and scholarships/grants available. Support available to part-time students. Financial award applicants required to submit FAFSA. In 2008, 14 master's awarded. *Degree program information:* Part-time programs available. Postbaccalaureate distance learning degree programs offered (minimal on-campus study). Offers liberal studies (MA). *Application deadline:* For fall admission, 6/1 priority date for domestic and international students; for spring admission, 10/1 priority date for domestic and international students. Applications are processed on a rolling basis. *Application fee:* $60. Electronic applications accepted. *Application Contact:* Information Contact, 518-580-5480, Fax: 518-580-5486, E-mail: mals@skidmore.edu. *Director*, Dr. John Anzalone, 518-580-5480, Fax: 518-580-5486, E-mail: mals@skidmore.edu.

SLIPPERY ROCK UNIVERSITY OF PENNSYLVANIA, Slippery Rock, PA 16057-1383

General Information State-supported, coed, comprehensive institution. *Enrollment:* 8,458 graduate, professional, and undergraduate students; 376 full-time matriculated graduate/professional students (254 women), 391 part-time matriculated graduate/professional students (272 women). *Enrollment by degree level:* 583 master's, 128 doctoral, 56 other advanced degrees. *Graduate faculty:* 67 full-time (37 women), 9 part-time/adjunct (7 women). Tuition, state resident: full-time $6430; part-time $357 per credit. Tuition, nonresident: full-time $10,288; part-time $572 per credit. *Required fees:* $2062; $158 per credit. *Graduate housing:* Room and/or apartments available on a first-come, first-served basis to single students; on-campus housing not available to married students. Typical cost: $5730 per year ($8066 including board). *Student services:* Campus employment opportunities, campus safety program, career counseling, child daycare facilities, exercise/wellness program, free psychological counseling, international student services, multicultural affairs office, services for students with disabilities, writing training. *Library facilities:* Bailey Library. *Online resources:* library catalog, web page, access to other libraries' catalogs. *Collection:* 513,194 titles, 500 serial subscriptions, 11,181 audiovisual materials.

Computer facilities: Computer purchase and lease plans are available. 1,323 computers available on campus for general student use. A campuswide network can be accessed from student residence rooms and from off campus. Online class registration is available. *Web address:* http://www.sru.edu/.

General Application Contact: Angela Piverotto, Director of Graduate Admissions, 724-738-2051, Fax: 724-738-2146, E-mail: graduate.admissions@sru.edu.

GRADUATE UNITS

Graduate Studies (Recruitment) Students: 369 full-time (248 women), 342 part-time (236 women); includes 30 minority (19 African Americans, 3 American Indian/Alaska Native, 3 Asian Americans or Pacific Islanders, 5 Hispanic Americans), 7 international. Average age 28. 851 applicants, 52% accepted, 347 enrolled. *Faculty:* 67 full-time (37 women), 9 part-time/adjunct (7 women). Expenses: Contact institution. *Financial support:* In 2008–09, 175 students received support. Career-related internships or fieldwork, Federal Work-Study, institutionally sponsored loans, scholarships/grants, tuition waivers (full), and unspecified assistantships available. Support available to part-time students. Financial award application deadline: 5/1; financial award applicants required to submit FAFSA. In 2008, 193 master's, 51 doctorates awarded. *Degree program information:* Part-time and evening/weekend programs available. Postbaccalaureate distance learning degree programs offered (no on-campus study). *Application deadline:* For fall admission, 7/1 priority date for domestic students, 5/1 priority date for international students; for spring admission, 11/1 priority date for domestic students, 9/1 priority date for international students. Applications are processed on a rolling basis. *Application fee:* $25 ($30 for international students). Electronic applications accepted. *Application Contact:* Angela Piverotto, Director of Graduate Studies, 724-738-2051, Fax: 724-738-2146, E-mail: graduate.admissions@sru.edu. *Director of Graduate Studies*, Angela Piverotto, 724-738-2051, Fax: 724-738-2146, E-mail: graduate.admissions@sru.edu.

College of Education Expenses: Contact institution. *Financial support:* Career-related internships or fieldwork, Federal Work-Study, scholarships/grants, and unspecified assistantships available. Support available to part-time students. Financial award application deadline: 5/1; financial award applicants required to submit FAFSA. *Degree program information:* Part-time and evening/weekend programs available. Offers community counseling (MA); education (M Ed, MA, MS); elementary guidance and counseling (M Ed); master teacher (M Ed); physical education (M Ed); reading (M Ed); secondary education in math/science (M Ed); secondary guidance and counseling (M Ed); sport management (MS); student personnel (MA); supervision (M Ed). *Application deadline:* For fall admission, 7/1 priority date for domestic and international students; for spring admission, 11/1 priority date for domestic and international students. Applications are processed on a rolling basis. *Application fee:* $25. Electronic applications accepted. *Application Contact:* Angela Piverotto, Director of Graduate Admissions, 724-738-2051, Fax: 724-738-2146, E-mail: graduate.admissions@sru.edu. *Dean*, Dr. Jay Hertzog, 724-738-2685, Fax: 724-738-2880, E-mail: jay.hertzog@sru.edu.

College of Health, Environment, and Science Expenses: Contact institution. *Financial support:* Career-related internships or fieldwork, Federal Work-Study, institutionally sponsored loans, scholarships/grants, and unspecified assistantships available. Support available to part-time students. Financial award application deadline: 5/1; financial award applicants required to submit FAFSA. *Degree program information:* Part-time and evening/weekend programs available. Offers environmental education (M Ed); health, environment, and science (M Ed, MS, DPT); physical therapy (DPT); resource management (MS); sustainable systems (MS). *Application deadline:* For fall admission, 7/1 priority date for domestic and international students; for spring admission, 11/1 priority date for domestic and international students. Applications are processed on a rolling basis. *Application fee:* $25. Electronic applications accepted. *Application Contact:* Angela Piverotto, Director of Graduate Admissions, 724-738-2051, Fax: 724-738-2146, E-mail: graduate.admissions@sru.edu. *Dean*, Dr. Susan Hannam, 724-738-4862, Fax: 724-738-2881, E-mail: susan.hannam@sru.edu.

College of Humanities, Fine and Performing Arts Expenses: Contact institution. *Financial support:* Career-related internships or fieldwork, scholarships/grants, and unspecified assistantships available. Support available to part-time students. Financial award application deadline: 5/1; financial award applicants required to submit FAFSA. *Degree program information:* Part-time and evening/weekend programs available. Offers history (MA); humanities, fine and performing arts (MA); literature and composition (MA); professional writing (MA). *Application deadline:* For fall admission, 7/1 priority date for domestic and international students; for spring admission, 11/1 priority date for domestic and international students. Applications are processed on a rolling basis. *Application fee:* $25. Electronic applications accepted. *Application Contact:* Angela Piverotto, Director of Graduate Admissions, 724-738-2051, Fax: 724-738-2146, E-mail: graduate.admissions@sru.edu. *Interim Dean*, Dr. Diana Dreyer, 724-738-4863, Fax: 724-738-2188, E-mail: diana.dreyer@sru.edu.

See Close-Up on page 989.

SMITH COLLEGE, Northampton, MA 01063

General Information Independent, women only, comprehensive institution. *Enrollment:* 3,065 graduate, professional, and undergraduate students; 56 full-time matriculated graduate/professional students (48 women), 22 part-time matriculated graduate/professional students (21 women). *Enrollment by degree level:* 71 master's, 7 other advanced degrees. *Graduate faculty:* 278 full-time (150 women), 27 part-time/adjunct (13 women). *Graduate housing:* Room and/or apartments available on a first-come, first-served basis to single students; on-campus housing not available to married students. Typical cost: $6030 per year ($12,050 including board). Housing application deadline: 5/1. *Student services:* Campus employment opportunities, campus safety program, career counseling, child daycare facilities, exercise/wellness program, international student services, low-cost health insurance, multicultural affairs office, services for students with disabilities, teacher training, writing training. *Library facilities:* Neilson Library plus 3 others. *Online resources:* library catalog, web page, access to other libraries' catalogs. *Collection:* 1.5 million titles, 37,414 serial subscriptions, 74,858 audiovisual materials.

Computer facilities: Computer purchase and lease plans are available. 624 computers available on campus for general student use. A campuswide network can be accessed from student residence rooms and from off campus. Online class registration is available. *Web address:* http://www.smith.edu/.

General Application Contact: Danielle Ramdath, Director, 413-585-3050, Fax: 413-585-3054, E-mail: dramdath@smith.edu.

GRADUATE UNITS

Graduate and Special Programs Students: 56 full-time (48 women), 22 part-time (21 women); includes 6 minority (3 African Americans, 1 Asian American or Pacific Islander, 2 Hispanic Americans), 3 international. Average age 28. 140 applicants, 64% accepted, 69 enrolled. *Faculty:* 278 full-time (150 women), 27 part-time/adjunct (13 women). Expenses: Contact institution. *Financial support:* In 2008–09, 77 students received support, including 7 fellowships with full tuition reimbursements available (averaging $11,910 per year), 8 research assistantships with full tuition reimbursements available (averaging $11,910 per year), 17 teaching assistantships with full tuition reimbursements available (averaging $11,910 per year); career-related internships or fieldwork, institutionally sponsored loans, scholarships/grants, and tuition waivers (full and partial) also available. Support available to part-time students. Financial award application deadline: 1/15; financial award applicants required to submit CSS PROFILE or FAFSA. In 2008, 49 master's, 6 other advanced degrees awarded. *Degree program information:* Part-time programs available. Offers biological sciences (MAT, MS); biological sciences education (MAT); chemistry (MAT); chemistry education (MAT); dance (MFA); education of the deaf (MED); elementary education (MAT); English education (MAT); English language and literature (MAT); exercise and sport studies (MS); French education (MAT); French language and literature (MAT); geology education (MAT); government education (MAT); history (MAT); history education (MAT); mathematics (MAT); mathematics education (MAT); middle school education (MAT); physics education (MAT); playwriting (MFA); secondary education (MAT); Spanish (MAT); Spanish education (MAT); women in mathematics (Postbaccalaureate Certificate). *Application deadline:* For fall admission, 1/15 for domestic and international students; for spring admission, 12/1 for domestic students. *Application fee:* $60. *Application Contact:* Ruth Morgan, Administrative Assistant, 413-585-3050, Fax: 413-585-3054, E-mail: gradstdy@smith.edu. *Director*, Danielle Ramdath, 413-585-3050, Fax: 413-585-3054, E-mail: dramdath@smith.edu.

School for Social Work Students: 359 full-time (317 women), 39 part-time (32 women); includes 90 minority (41 African Americans, 3 American Indian/Alaska Native, 22 Asian

Americans or Pacific Islanders, 24 Hispanic Americans), 9 international. Average age 33. 350 applicants, 71% accepted, 125 enrolled. *Faculty:* 15 full-time (11 women), 98 part-time/adjunct (72 women). Expenses: Contact institution. *Financial support:* In 2008–09, 204 students received support. Career-related internships or fieldwork, institutionally sponsored loans, and scholarships/grants available. Financial award application deadline: 3/20; financial award applicants required to submit FAFSA. In 2008, 101 master's, 6 doctorates awarded. Offers social work (MSW, PhD). *Application deadline:* For fall admission, 2/21 for domestic students. Applications are processed on a rolling basis. *Application fee:* $60. *Application Contact:* Irene Rodriguez Martin, Director of Enrollment Management and Continuing Education, 413-585-7960, Fax: 413-585-7994, E-mail: imartin@smith.edu. *Director of Graduate Enrollment*, Irene Rodriguez Martin, 413-585-7960, E-mail: sswadm@smith.edu.

SOJOURNER-DOUGLASS COLLEGE, Baltimore, MD 21205-1814

General Information Independent, coed, primarily women, comprehensive institution.

GRADUATE UNITS

Graduate Program *Degree program information:* Part-time and evening/weekend programs available.

SONOMA STATE UNIVERSITY, Rohnert Park, CA 94928-3609

General Information State-supported, coed, comprehensive institution. *Enrollment:* 8,921 graduate, professional, and undergraduate students; 455 full-time matriculated graduate/professional students (341 women), 272 part-time matriculated graduate/professional students (203 women). *Enrollment by degree level:* 727 master's. *Graduate faculty:* 60 full-time (32 women), 20 part-time/adjunct (13 women). *Required fees:* $1701 per semester. *Graduate housing:* Room and/or apartments available on a first-come, first-served basis to single students; on-campus housing not available to married students. Typical cost: $10,115 (including board). Housing application deadline: 1/1. *Student services:* Campus employment opportunities, career counseling, child daycare facilities, exercise/wellness program, free psychological counseling, international student services, multicultural affairs office, services for students with disabilities. *Library facilities:* Jean and Charles Schultz Information Center. *Online resources:* library catalog, web page, access to other libraries' catalogs. *Collection:* 678,474 titles, 21,117 serial subscriptions. *Research affiliation:* Kenwood Vineyards Kenwood, CA (Science), Bimimetica Shantee CA (Biology), Gallo Family Vineyards Sonoma County CA (Science), Natural Industries Inc. Houston TX (Sudden Oak Death Research), Clean Filtration Technologies Saratoga CA (Environmental Microbiology Fund).

Computer facilities: 400 computers available on campus for general student use. A campuswide network can be accessed from student residence rooms and from off campus. Online class registration is available. *Web address:* http://www.sonoma.edu/.

General Application Contact: Elaine Sundberg, Associate Vice Provost, Academic Programs/Graduate Studies, 707-664-2215, Fax: 707-664-4060, E-mail: elaine.sundberg@sonoma.edu.

GRADUATE UNITS

Institute of Interdisciplinary Studies/Special Major Students: 10 full-time (8 women), 8 part-time (7 women); includes 2 minority (1 African American, 1 Asian American or Pacific Islander). Average age 43. *Faculty:* 3 full-time (2 women). Expenses: Contact institution. *Financial support:* Career-related internships or fieldwork, Federal Work-Study, and institutionally sponsored loans available. Support available to part-time students. Financial award applicants required to submit FAFSA. In 2008, 8 master's awarded. *Degree program information:* Part-time programs available. Offers special major (MA, MS). *Application deadline:* For fall admission, 1/31 for domestic students; for spring admission, 10/31 for domestic students. *Application fee:* $55. *Application Contact:* Elaine Sundberg, Associate Vice Provost, Academic Programs/Graduate Studies, 707-664-2215, Fax: 707-664-4060, E-mail: elaine.sundberg@sonoma.edu. *Coordinator*, Dr. Ellen Carlton, 707-664-3918, E-mail: ellen.carlton@sonoma.edu.

School of Arts and Humanities *Degree program information:* Part-time and evening/weekend programs available. Offers American literature (MA); arts and humanities (MA); creative writing (MA); English literature (MA); world literature (MA).

School of Business and Economics Students: 15 full-time (7 women), 20 part-time (7 women); includes 2 minority (both Hispanic Americans), 1 international. Average age 31. 47 applicants, 55% accepted, 7 enrolled. *Faculty:* 6 full-time (3 women). Expenses: Contact institution. *Financial support:* Career-related internships or fieldwork, Federal Work-Study, institutionally sponsored loans, and scholarships/grants available. Support available to part-time students. Financial award application deadline: 3/2; financial award applicants required to submit FAFSA. In 2008, 11 master's awarded. *Degree program information:* Part-time and evening/weekend programs available. Offers business administration (MBA); business and economics (MBA). *Application deadline:* For fall admission, 1/31 priority date for domestic students; for spring admission, 8/31 for domestic students. Applications are processed on a rolling basis. *Application fee:* $55. *Application Contact:* Elaine Sundberg, Associate Vice Provost, Academic Programs/Graduate Studies, 707-664-2215, Fax: 707-664-4060, E-mail: elaine.sundberg@sonoma.edu. *Coordinator*, Sandra Newton, 707-664-3296, E-mail: newtonsa@sonoma.edu.

School of Education Students: 85 full-time (61 women), 112 part-time (83 women); includes 25 minority (2 African Americans, 1 American Indian/Alaska Native, 4 Asian Americans or Pacific Islanders, 18 Hispanic Americans), 3 international. Average age 38. 156 applicants, 67% accepted, 5 enrolled. *Faculty:* 11 full-time (6 women), 7 part-time/adjunct (3 women). Expenses: Contact institution. *Financial support:* Fellowships, career-related internships or fieldwork and Federal Work-Study available. Support available to part-time students. Financial award application deadline: 3/2; financial award applicants required to submit FAFSA. In 2008, 46 master's awarded. *Degree program information:* Part-time and evening/weekend programs available. Offers education (MA); education—curriculum, teaching and learning (MA); educational leadership (MA); literacy studies and elementary education (MA); special education (MA). *Application fee:* $55. *Application Contact:* Elaine Sundberg, Associate Vice Provost, Academic Programs/Graduate Studies, 707-664-2215, Fax: 707-664-4060, E-mail: elaine.sundberg@sonoma.edu. *Dean*, Dr. Mary Gendernalik-Cooper, 707-664-2132, E-mail: gendernm@sonoma.edu.

School of Science and Technology *Degree program information:* Part-time programs available. Offers environmental biology (MA); family nurse practitioner (MS); general biology (MA); kinesiology (MA); science and technology (MA, MS).

School of Social Sciences *Degree program information:* Part-time and evening/weekend programs available. Offers counseling (MA); cultural resources management (MA); history (MA); marriage, family, and child counseling (MA); public administration (MPA); pupil personnel services (MA); social sciences (MA, MPA).

SOUTH BAYLO UNIVERSITY, Anaheim, CA 92801-1701

General Information Independent, coed, graduate-only institution. *Graduate housing:* On-campus housing not available. *Research affiliation:* University of California Irvine College of Medicine (complimentary and alternative medicine), National Nutritional Foods Association (herbs and nutritional supplements), Henan College of Traditional Chinese Medicine, China (herbology and acupuncture), Kaiser Permanente (patient care: acupuncture and oriental medicine), University of Illinois at Chicago (testing of herbal formulations).

GRADUATE UNITS

Program in Oriental Medicine and Acupuncture *Degree program information:* Evening/weekend programs available. Offers Oriental medicine and acupuncture (MS). Electronic applications accepted.

SOUTH CAROLINA STATE UNIVERSITY, Orangeburg, SC 29117-0001

General Information State-supported, coed, comprehensive institution. CGS member. *Enrollment:* 4,888 graduate, professional, and undergraduate students; 285 full-time matriculated graduate/professional students (237 women), 367 part-time matriculated graduate/professional students (287 women). *Enrollment by degree level:* 407 master's, 113 doctoral, 132 other advanced degrees. *Graduate faculty:* 51 full-time (28 women), 22 part-time/adjunct (10 women). Tuition, state resident: full-time $7806; part-time $434 per credit hour. Tuition, nonresident: full-time $15,298; part-time $850 per credit hour. *Graduate housing:* On-campus housing not available. *Student services:* Campus employment opportunities, career counseling, exercise/wellness program, free psychological counseling, international student services, low-cost health insurance, services for students with disabilities, teacher training, writing training. *Library facilities:* Miller F. Whittaker Library. *Online resources:* library catalog, web page, access to other libraries' catalogs. *Collection:* 313,329 titles, 3,031 serial subscriptions.

Computer facilities: 300 computers available on campus for general student use. A campuswide network can be accessed. Online class registration is available. *Web address:* http://www.scsu.edu/.

General Application Contact: Dr. Thomas Thompson, Dean of the School of Graduate Studies, 803-516-4734, Fax: 803-536-8812, E-mail: tthompson@scsu.edu.

GRADUATE UNITS

School of Graduate Studies Students: 285 full-time (237 women), 367 part-time (287 women); includes 572 minority (565 African Americans, 4 Asian Americans or Pacific Islanders, 3 Hispanic Americans). Average age 35. 340 applicants, 93% accepted, 194 enrolled. *Faculty:* 51 full-time (28 women), 22 part-time/adjunct (10 women). Expenses: Contact institution. *Financial support:* In 2008–09, 51 fellowships (averaging $5,317 per year) were awarded; career-related internships or fieldwork, Federal Work-Study, institutionally sponsored loans, scholarships/grants, and unspecified assistantships also available. Financial award application deadline: 6/1. In 2008, 98 master's, 13 doctorates, 40 other advanced degrees awarded. *Degree program information:* Part-time and evening/weekend programs available. Offers agribusiness (MS); agribusiness and entrepreneurship (MBA); early childhood and special education (M Ed); early childhood education (MAT); educational leadership (Ed D, Ed S); elementary counselor education (M Ed); elementary education (M Ed, MAT); engineering (MAT); general science (MAT); individual and family development (MS); mathematics (MAT); nutritional sciences (MS); rehabilitation counseling (MA); secondary counselor education (M Ed); secondary education (M Ed); special education (M Ed); speech/language pathology (MA); transportation (MS). *Application deadline:* For fall admission, 6/15 for domestic and international students; for spring admission, 11/1 for domestic and international students. *Application fee:* $25. Electronic applications accepted. *Application Contact:* Annette Hazzard-Jones, Program Coordinator II, 803-536-8809, Fax: 803-536-8812, E-mail: zs_ahazzard@scsu.edu. *Dean of the School of Graduate Studies*, Dr. Thomas Thompson, 803-516-4734, Fax: 803-536-8812, E-mail: tthompson@scsu.edu.

SOUTH DAKOTA SCHOOL OF MINES AND TECHNOLOGY, Rapid City, SD 57701-3995

General Information State-supported, coed, university. CGS member. *Graduate housing:* Room and/or apartments available on a first-come, first-served basis to single students; on-campus housing not available to married students. *Research affiliation:* CEA USA, Inc. (radium/nickel extraction), Black Hills Corporation (wind power), EG & G Idaho, Inc. (ground-probing radar), RE/SPEC, Inc. (preparation of new plant growth regulators), Horizons, Inc. (interferometric synthetic aperture radar).

GRADUATE UNITS

Graduate Division *Degree program information:* Part-time programs available. Offers biomedical engineering (MS, PhD); chemical and biological engineering (PhD); chemical engineering (MS); chemistry (MS); civil engineering (MS); electrical engineering (MS); engineering (MS, PhD); geology and geological engineering (MS, PhD); materials engineering and science (MS, PhD); mechanical engineering (MS); metallurgical engineering (MS); nanoscience and nanoengineering (PhD); paleontology (MS); physics (MS); technology management (MS). Electronic applications accepted.

College of Science and Letters Offers atmospheric and environmental sciences (PhD); atmospheric sciences (MS); computer science (MS); science and letters (MS, PhD).

SOUTH DAKOTA STATE UNIVERSITY, Brookings, SD 57007

General Information State-supported, coed, university. CGS member. *Enrollment:* 11,995 graduate, professional, and undergraduate students; 572 full-time matriculated graduate/professional students (236 women), 709 part-time matriculated graduate/professional students (466 women). *Graduate housing:* Rooms and/or apartments available to single and married students. *Student services:* Campus employment opportunities, campus safety program, career counseling, child daycare facilities, exercise/wellness program, free psychological counseling, grant writing training, international student services, low-cost health insurance, multicultural affairs office, services for students with disabilities, teacher training, writing training. *Library facilities:* H. M. Briggs Library. *Online resources:* library catalog, web page, access to other libraries' catalogs. *Collection:* 987,599 titles, 44,599 serial subscriptions, 3,280 audiovisual materials.

Computer facilities: Computer purchase and lease plans are available. 692 computers available on campus for general student use. A campuswide network can be accessed from student residence rooms and from off campus. Online class registration is available. *Web address:* http://www.sdstate.edu/.

General Application Contact: Linda Winkler, Registration Officer, 605-688-4182, Fax: 605-688-6167, E-mail: linda.winkler@sdstate.edu.

GRADUATE UNITS

Graduate School Students: 572 full-time (236 women), 709 part-time (466 women); includes 247 minority (32 African Americans, 11 American Indian/Alaska Native, 196 Asian Americans or Pacific Islanders, 8 Hispanic Americans). Expenses: Contact institution. *Financial support:* Fellowships with tuition reimbursements, research assistantships with partial tuition reimbursements, teaching assistantships with partial tuition reimbursements, career-related internships or fieldwork, Federal Work-Study, and unspecified assistantships available. *Degree program information:* Part-time and evening/weekend programs available. Postbaccalaureate distance learning degree programs offered (no on-campus study). *Application deadline:* For fall admission, 4/15 priority date for international students; for spring admission, 8/15 priority date for international students. Applications are processed on a rolling basis. *Application fee:* $35. *Application Contact:* Rabbi Diane Rickerl, Associate Dean, 605-688-4181, E-mail: diane.rickerl@sdstate.edu. *Dean*, Dr. Kevin Kephart, 605-688-4181, Fax: 605-688-6167, E-mail: kevin.kephart@sdstate.edu.

College of Agriculture and Biological Sciences Students: 128 full-time (45 women), 118 part-time (51 women); includes 62 minority (6 African Americans, 4 American Indian/Alaska Native, 48 Asian Americans or Pacific Islanders, 4 Hispanic Americans). Expenses: Contact institution. *Financial support:* Fellowships, research assistantships, teaching assistantships, career-related internships or fieldwork, Federal Work-Study, and unspecified assistantships available. *Degree program information:* Part-time programs available. Offers agriculture and biological sciences (MS, PhD); agriculture and biosystems engineering (MS, PhD); agronomy (PhD); animal science (MS, PhD); animal sciences (MS, PhD); biological sciences (MS, PhD); economics (MS); plant science (MS); rural sociology (MS); sociology (PhD); wildlife and fisheries sciences (MS, PhD). *Application deadline:* Applications are processed on a rolling basis. *Application fee:* $35. *Application Contact:* Dr. Donald Marshall, Acting Dean, 605-688-4148. *Acting Dean*, Dr. Donald Marshall, 605-688-4148.

College of Arts and Science Students: 53 full-time (23 women), 318 part-time (242 women); includes 29 minority (11 African Americans, 2 American Indian/Alaska Native, 14 Asian Americans or Pacific Islanders, 2 Hispanic Americans). Expenses: Contact institution. *Financial support:* Research assistantships, teaching assistantships, career-related internships or fieldwork, Federal Work-Study, and unspecified assistantships available. *Degree program information:* Part-time programs available. Offers arts and science (MA, MS, PhD); chemistry (MS, PhD); communication studies and journalism (MS); English (MA); geography (MS); health, physical education and recreation (MS). *Application deadline:* Applications are processed on a rolling basis. *Application fee:* $35. *Application Contact:* Dr. Daniel Landes, Assistant Dean, 605-688-4723, Fax: 605-688-6750, E-mail: daniel.

South Dakota State University (continued)

landes@sdstate.edu. *Dean*, Dr. Jerry Jorgensen, 605-688-4723, Fax: 605-688-6750, E-mail: jerry.jorgensen@sdstate.edu.

College of Engineering Students: 201 full-time (39 women), 26 part-time (8 women); includes 12 African Americans, 125 Asian Americans or Pacific Islanders. 213 applicants, 56% accepted, 91 enrolled. *Faculty:* 63 full-time (5 women). Expenses: Contact institution. *Financial support:* Fellowships, research assistantships, teaching assistantships, career-related internships or fieldwork, Federal Work-Study, and unspecified assistantships available. In 2008, 43 master's awarded. *Degree program information:* Part-time programs available. Offers biological sciences (MS, PhD); computational science and statistics (PhD); electrical engineering (PhD); engineering (MS); geospatial science and engineering (PhD); industrial management (MS); mathematics (MS). *Application deadline:* Applications are processed on a rolling basis. *Application fee:* $35. *Application Contact:* Dr. Richard Reid, Assistant Dean, 605-688-4161, E-mail: richard.reid@sdstate.edu. *Dean*, Dr. Lewis Brown, 605-688-4161, E-mail: lewis.brown@sdstate.edu.

College of Family and Consumer Sciences Students: 5 full-time (3 women), 33 part-time (28 women); includes 5 Asian Americans or Pacific Islanders. Expenses: Contact institution. *Financial support:* Research assistantships, teaching assistantships, Federal Work-Study and unspecified assistantships available. In 2008, 15 master's awarded. Offers apparel merchandising and interior design (MFCS); family and consumer sciences (MFCS); human development, consumer and family sciences (MFCS); nutrition, food science and hospitality (MFCS). *Application deadline:* Applications are processed on a rolling basis. *Application fee:* $35. *Application Contact:* The Graduate School, 605-688-4181, E-mail: sdsu_gradschool@sdstate.edu. *Acting Dean*, Dr. Jane Hegland, 605-688-6181, Fax: 605-688-4439, E-mail: jane.hegland@sdstate.edu.

College of Nursing Students: 6 full-time (all women), 181 part-time (174 women); includes 1 African American. 83 applicants, 83% accepted, 69 enrolled. *Faculty:* 19 full-time (17 women). Expenses: Contact institution. *Financial support:* In 2008–09, 2 fellowships, 1 research assistantship, 3 teaching assistantships were awarded; career-related internships or fieldwork, Federal Work-Study, scholarships/grants, and unspecified assistantships also available. In 2008, 24 master's, 1 doctorate awarded. *Degree program information:* Part-time and evening/weekend programs available. Postbaccalaureate distance learning degree programs offered. Offers nursing (MS, PhD). *Application deadline:* For fall admission, 3/1 priority date for domestic students. *Application fee:* $35. *Application Contact:* Emily Mosley, Senior Secretary, 605-688-4114, Fax: 605-688-5827, E-mail: emily.mosely@sdstate.edu. *Department Head, Graduate Nursing*, Dr. Sandra J. Bunkers, 605-688-4114, Fax: 605-688-5827.

College of Pharmacy Students: 136 full-time (84 women), 7 part-time (2 women); includes 1 Hispanic American. Expenses: Contact institution. *Financial support:* Research assistantships, teaching assistantships, Federal Work-Study available. Financial award application deadline: 3/1; financial award applicants required to submit FAFSA. Offers biological science (MS); pharmaceutical sciences (PhD); pharmacy (Pharm D, MS, PhD). *Application deadline:* For fall admission, 3/1 for domestic students. Applications are processed on a rolling basis. *Application fee:* $15. *Application Contact:* Dr. Chandradhar Dwivedi, Coordinator of Graduate Studies, 605-688-4247. *Dean*, Dr. Dennis Hedge, 605-688-4238, Fax: 605-688-6232, E-mail: dennis.hedge@sdstate.edu.

SOUTHEASTERN BAPTIST THEOLOGICAL SEMINARY, Wake Forest, NC 27588-1889

General Information Independent-religious, coed, primarily men. *Graduate housing:* Rooms and/or apartments available on a first-come, first-served basis to single and married students.

GRADUATE UNITS

Graduate and Professional Programs Offers advanced biblical studies (M Div); Christian education (M Div, MACE); Christian ethics (PhD); Christian ministry (M Div); Christian planting (M Div); church music (MACM); counseling (MACO); evangelism (PhD); language (M Div); ministry (D Min); New Testament (PhD); Old Testament (PhD); philosophy (PhD); theology (Th M, PhD); women's studies (M Div).

SOUTHEASTERN LOUISIANA UNIVERSITY, Hammond, LA 70402

General Information State-supported, coed, comprehensive institution. CGS member. *Enrollment:* 15,224 graduate, professional, and undergraduate students; 390 full-time matriculated graduate/professional students (272 women), 599 part-time matriculated graduate/professional students (453 women). *Enrollment by degree level:* 956 master's, 33 doctoral. *Graduate faculty:* 142 full-time (60 women). Tuition, state resident: full-time $2376. Tuition, nonresident: full-time $6876. *Required fees:* $1105. *Graduate housing:* Room and/or apartments available on a first-come, first-served basis to single students; on-campus housing not available to married students. Typical cost: $1950 per year ($2945 including board). Room and board charges vary according to board plan and housing facility selected. Housing application deadline: 6/15. *Student services:* Campus employment opportunities, campus safety program, career counseling, exercise/wellness program, free psychological counseling, international student services, low-cost health insurance, multicultural affairs office, services for students with disabilities, teacher training, writing training. *Library facilities:* Sims Memorial Library. *Online resources:* library catalog, web page, access to other libraries' catalogs. *Collection:* 716,268 titles, 4,008 serial subscriptions, 11,542 audiovisual materials. *Research affiliation:* Hotchalk Inc. (Education), Freeport McMoran (wetland ecology and water quality), Entergy (Biology), Lake Ponchartrain Basin Foundation (water quality and wetland ecology), Petroleum Research Fund (chemistry).

Computer facilities: 1,603 computers available on campus for general student use. A campuswide network can be accessed from student residence rooms and from off campus. Online class registration, campus Webmail, student newspaper, transcripts, bookstore are available. *Web address:* http://www.selu.edu/.

General Application Contact: Sandra Meyers, Graduate Admissions Analyst, 985-549-2066, Fax: 985-549-5632, E-mail: admissions@selu.edu.

GRADUATE UNITS

College of Arts, Humanities and Social Sciences Students: 72 full-time (40 women), 127 part-time (77 women); includes 33 minority (all African Americans), 8 international. Average age 29. 73 applicants, 97% accepted, 55 enrolled. *Faculty:* 45 full-time (17 women). Expenses: Contact institution. *Financial support:* Career-related internships or fieldwork, Federal Work-Study, institutionally sponsored loans, scholarships/grants, unspecified assistantships, and administrative assistantship available. Support available to part-time students. Financial award application deadline: 5/1; financial award applicants required to submit FAFSA. In 2008, 50 master's awarded. *Degree program information:* Part-time programs available. Offers applied sociology (MS); arts, humanities and social sciences (M Mus, MA, MS); English (MA); history (MA); music (M Mus); organizational communication (MA); psychology (MA). *Application deadline:* For fall admission, 7/15 priority date for domestic students, 6/1 priority date for international students; for spring admission, 12/1 priority date for domestic students, 10/1 priority date for international students. Applications are processed on a rolling basis. *Application fee:* $20 ($30 for international students). Electronic applications accepted. *Application Contact:* Sandra Meyers, Graduate Admissions Analyst, 985-549-2066, Fax: 985-549-5632, E-mail: admissions@selu.edu. *Interim Dean*, Dr. Bryan DePoy, 985-549-2101, Fax: 985-549-5014, E-mail: tbourg@selu.edu.

College of Business Students: 116 full-time (57 women), 33 part-time (19 women); includes 12 minority (8 African Americans, 4 Asian Americans or Pacific Islanders), 16 international. Average age 26. 57 applicants, 96% accepted, 43 enrolled. *Faculty:* 20 full-time (4 women). Expenses: Contact institution. *Financial support:* Career-related internships or fieldwork, Federal Work-Study, institutionally sponsored loans, scholarships/grants, unspecified assistantships, and administrative assistantships available. Support available to part-time students. Financial award application deadline: 5/1; financial award applicants required to submit FAFSA. In 2008, 102 master's awarded. *Degree program information:* Part-time and evening/weekend programs available. Offers business administration (MBA). *Application deadline:* For fall admission, 7/15 priority date for domestic students, 6/1 priority date for international students; for spring admission, 12/1 priority date for domestic students, 10/1 priority date for international students. Applications are processed on a rolling basis. *Application fee:* $20 ($30 for international students). Electronic applications accepted. *Application Contact:* Sandra Meyers, Graduate Admissions Analyst, 985-549-2066, Fax: 985-549-5632, E-mail: admissions@selu.edu. *Dean*, Dr. Randy Settoon, 985-549-2258, Fax: 985-549-5038, E-mail: rsettoon@selu.edu.

College of Education and Human Development Students: 78 full-time (74 women), 305 part-time (255 women); includes 52 minority (44 African Americans, 3 Asian Americans or Pacific Islanders, 5 Hispanic Americans), 2 international. Average age 35. 77 applicants, 99% accepted, 53 enrolled. *Faculty:* 24 full-time (15 women). Expenses: Contact institution. *Financial support:* Career-related internships or fieldwork, Federal Work-Study, institutionally sponsored loans, scholarships/grants, unspecified assistantships, and administrative assistantships available. Support available to part-time students. Financial award application deadline: 5/1; financial award applicants required to submit FAFSA. In 2008, 136 master's awarded. *Degree program information:* Part-time programs available. Offers counselor education (M Ed); curriculum and instruction (M Ed); education and human development (M Ed, MAT, Ed D); educational leadership (M Ed, Ed D); educational technology leadership (M Ed); elementary education (MAT); special education (M Ed). *Application deadline:* For fall admission, 7/15 priority date for domestic students, 6/1 priority date for international students; for spring admission, 12/1 priority date for domestic students, 10/1 priority date for international students. Applications are processed on a rolling basis. *Application fee:* $20 ($30 for international students). Electronic applications accepted. *Application Contact:* Sandra Meyers, Graduate Admissions Analyst, 985-549-2066, Fax: 985-549-5632, E-mail: admissions@selu.edu. *Dean*, Dr. Diane Allen, 985-549-2217, Fax: 985-549-2070, E-mail: dallen@selu.edu.

College of Nursing and Health Sciences Students: 99 full-time (87 women), 108 part-time (93 women); includes 25 minority (21 African Americans, 2 Asian Americans or Pacific Islanders, 2 Hispanic Americans), 10 international. Average age 31. 71 applicants, 94% accepted, 47 enrolled. *Faculty:* 21 full-time (15 women). Expenses: Contact institution. *Financial support:* Career-related internships or fieldwork, Federal Work-Study, institutionally sponsored loans, scholarships/grants, unspecified assistantships, and administrative assistantship available. Support available to part-time students. Financial award application deadline: 5/1; financial award applicants required to submit FAFSA. In 2008, 41 master's awarded. *Degree program information:* Part-time programs available. Offers communication sciences and disorders (MS); health and kinesiology (MA); nursing and health sciences (MA, MS, MSN). *Application deadline:* For fall admission, 7/15 priority date for domestic students, 6/1 priority date for international students; for spring admission, 12/1 priority date for domestic students, 10/1 priority date for international students. Applications are processed on a rolling basis. *Application fee:* $20 ($30 for international students). Electronic applications accepted. *Application Contact:* Sandra Meyers, Graduate Admissions Analyst, 985-549-2066, Fax: 985-549-5632, E-mail: admissions@selu.edu. *Dean*, Dr. Donnie Booth, 985-549-5045, Fax: 985-549-5087, E-mail: dbooth@selu.edu.

School of Nursing Students: 11 full-time (10 women), 63 part-time (54 women); includes 6 minority (all African Americans), 1 international. Average age 39. 14 applicants, 86% accepted, 12 enrolled. *Faculty:* 9 full-time (all women). Expenses: Contact institution. *Financial support:* In 2008–09, 1 student received support, including 1 fellowship with full tuition reimbursement available (averaging $11,400 per year); career-related internships or fieldwork, Federal Work-Study, institutionally sponsored loans, scholarships/grants, unspecified assistantships, and administrative assistantship also available. Support available to part-time students. Financial award application deadline: 5/1; financial award applicants required to submit FAFSA. In 2008, 16 master's awarded. *Degree program information:* Part-time programs available. Offers nursing (MSN). *Application deadline:* For fall admission, 7/15 priority date for domestic students, 6/1 priority date for international students; for spring admission, 12/1 priority date for domestic students, 10/1 priority date for international students. Applications are processed on a rolling basis. *Application fee:* $20 ($30 for international students). Electronic applications accepted. *Application Contact:* Sandra Meyers, Graduate Admissions Analyst, 985-549-2066, Fax: 985-549-5632, E-mail: admissions@selu.edu. *Director*, Dr. Barbara Moffett, 985-549-2156, Fax: 985-549-2869, E-mail: bmoffett@selu.edu.

College of Science and Technology Students: 25 full-time (14 women), 26 part-time (9 women); includes 4 minority (3 African Americans, 1 Asian American or Pacific Islander), 17 international. Average age 29. 13 applicants, 92% accepted, 10 enrolled. *Faculty:* 32 full-time (8 women). Expenses: Contact institution. *Financial support:* In 2008–09, 2 students received support, including 2 research assistantships with full tuition reimbursements available (averaging $10,100 per year); career-related internships or fieldwork, Federal Work-Study, institutionally sponsored loans, unspecified assistantships, and administrative assistantships also available. Support available to part-time students. Financial award application deadline: 5/1; financial award applicants required to submit FAFSA. In 2008, 13 master's awarded. *Degree program information:* Part-time programs available. Offers biology (MS); integrated science and technology (MS); science and technology (MS). *Application deadline:* For fall admission, 7/15 priority date for domestic students, 6/1 priority date for international students; for spring admission, 12/1 priority date for domestic students, 10/1 priority date for international students. Applications are processed on a rolling basis. *Application fee:* $20 ($30 for international students). Electronic applications accepted. *Application Contact:* Sandra Meyers, Graduate Admissions Analyst, 985-549-2066, Fax: 985-549-5632, E-mail: admissions@selu.edu. *Dean*, Dr. Daniel McCarthy, 985-549-2055, Fax: 985-549-3396, E-mail: dmccarthy@selu.edu.

SOUTHEASTERN OKLAHOMA STATE UNIVERSITY, Durant, OK 74701-0609

General Information State-supported, coed, comprehensive institution. *Enrollment:* 3,889 graduate, professional, and undergraduate students; 92 full-time matriculated graduate/professional students (50 women), 208 part-time matriculated graduate/professional students (104 women). *Enrollment by degree level:* 300 master's. *Graduate faculty:* 97 full-time (33 women), 8 part-time/adjunct (3 women). *Graduate housing:* Room and/or apartments available on a first-come, first-served basis to single students; on-campus housing not available to married students. Housing application deadline: 8/1. *Student services:* Campus employment opportunities, campus safety program, career counseling, exercise/wellness program, free psychological counseling, international student services, low-cost health insurance, multicultural affairs office, services for students with disabilities. *Library facilities:* Henry G. Bennett Memorial Library. *Online resources:* library catalog. *Collection:* 307,939 titles, 730 serial subscriptions, 9,895 audiovisual materials. *Research affiliation:* Virginia Polytechnic Institute (physical sciences), United States Department of Agriculture (biological sciences), J. J. Keller Foundation (occupational safety research), Oklahoma Small Business Development Center (business development).

Computer facilities: 518 computers available on campus for general student use. A campuswide network can be accessed from student residence rooms. Online class registration, campus Blackboard classes are available. *Web address:* http://www.sosu.edu/.

General Application Contact: Carrie Williamson, Graduate Secretary, 580-745-2200, Fax: 580-745-7474, E-mail: cwilliamson@se.edu.

GRADUATE UNITS

Department of Aviation Science Students: 40 full-time (13 women), 98 part-time (22 women); includes 26 minority (10 African Americans, 4 American Indian/Alaska Native, 4 Asian Americans or Pacific Islanders, 8 Hispanic Americans). Average age 30. 58 applicants, 100% accepted, 58 enrolled. Expenses: Contact institution. *Financial support:* Federal Work-Study and institutionally sponsored loans available. Support available to part-time students. Financial award application deadline: 6/15. In 2008, 50 master's awarded. *Degree program information:* Part-time and evening/weekend programs available. Offers aerospace administration and logistics (MS). *Application deadline:* For fall admission, 8/1 for domestic students, 6/1 for international students; for spring admission, 1/5 for domestic students, 11/1 for international students. *Application fee:* $20 ($55 for international students). Electronic applications accepted. *Application Contact:* Carrie Williamson, Graduate Secretary, 580-745-2200, Fax: 580-745-

7474, E-mail: cwilliamson@se.edu. *Director*, Dr. David Conway, 580-745-3240, Fax: 580-924-0741, E-mail: dconway@se.edu.

School of Arts and Sciences Students: 4 full-time (2 women), 2 part-time (1 woman); includes 2 minority (both American Indian/Alaska Native), 1 international. Average age 28. 1 applicant, 100% accepted, 1 enrolled. *Faculty:* 12 full-time (4 women), 1 part-time/adjunct (0 women). Expenses: Contact institution. *Financial support:* In 2008–09, 8 students received support; fellowships, research assistantships, teaching assistantships, Federal Work-Study and institutionally sponsored loans available. Support available to part-time students. Financial award application deadline: 6/15; financial award applicants required to submit FAFSA. In 2008, 7 master's awarded. *Degree program information:* Part-time and evening/weekend programs available. Offers technology (MT). *Application deadline:* For fall admission, 8/1 for domestic students, 6/1 for international students; for spring admission, 1/5 for domestic students, 11/1 for international students. *Application fee:* $20 ($55 for international students). Electronic applications accepted. *Application Contact:* Carrie Williamson, Graduate Secretary, 580-745-2200, Fax: 580-745-7474, E-mail: cwilliamson@se.edu. *Graduate Coordinator*, Dr. Teresa Golden, 580-745-2286, E-mail: tgolden@se.edu.

School of Behavioral Sciences Students: 17 full-time (15 women), 18 part-time (15 women); includes 9 minority (8 American Indian/Alaska Native, 1 Hispanic American). Average age 35. 11 applicants, 100% accepted, 11 enrolled. *Faculty:* 10 full-time (3 women). Expenses: Contact institution. *Financial support:* Fellowships, research assistantships, teaching assistantships, Federal Work-Study available. Support available to part-time students. Financial award application deadline: 6/15. In 2008, 12 master's awarded. *Degree program information:* Part-time and evening/weekend programs available. Offers community counseling (MBS). *Application deadline:* For fall admission, 8/1 for domestic students, 6/1 for international students; for spring admission, 1/5 for domestic students, 11/1 for international students. *Application fee:* $20 ($55 for international students). Electronic applications accepted. *Application Contact:* Carrie Williamson, Graduate Secretary, 580-745-2200, Fax: 580-745-7474, E-mail: cwilliamson@se.edu. *Program Coordinator*, Dr. Daniel Weigel, 580-745-2632, E-mail: dweigel@se.edu.

School of Business Students: 15 full-time (10 women), 20 part-time (10 women); includes 9 minority (8 American Indian/Alaska Native, 1 Asian American or Pacific Islander), 2 international. Average age 35. 232 applicants, 10% accepted, 23 enrolled. *Faculty:* 13 full-time (6 women), 5 part-time/adjunct (0 women). Expenses: Contact institution. *Financial support:* In 2008–09, 30 students received support, including 3 teaching assistantships with full tuition reimbursements available (averaging $5,000 per year); Federal Work-Study, institutionally sponsored loans, and tuition waivers (partial) also available. Support available to part-time students. Financial award application deadline: 6/15; financial award applicants required to submit FAFSA. In 2008, 9 master's awarded. *Degree program information:* Part-time and evening/weekend programs available. Offers business (MBA, MS). *Application deadline:* For fall admission, 8/1 for domestic students, 6/1 for international students; for spring admission, 1/5 for domestic students, 11/1 for international students. *Application fee:* $20 ($55 for international students). Electronic applications accepted. *Application Contact:* Carrie Williamson, Graduate Secretary, 580-745-2200, Fax: 580-745-7474, E-mail: cwilliamson@se.edu. *Dean*, Dr. Buddy Gaster, 580-745-2030, Fax: 580-970-7479, E-mail: bgaster@se.edu.

School of Education Students: 16 full-time (10 women), 70 part-time (56 women); includes 15 minority (all American Indian/Alaska Native). Average age 35. 46 applicants, 100% accepted, 46 enrolled. *Faculty:* 52 full-time (19 women), 1 (woman) part-time/adjunct. Expenses: Contact institution. *Financial support:* In 2008–09, 1 teaching assistantship with full tuition reimbursement (averaging $5,000 per year) was awarded; Federal Work-Study, institutionally sponsored loans, and tuition waivers (partial) also available. Support available to part-time students. Financial award application deadline: 6/15; financial award applicants required to submit FAFSA. In 2008, 61 master's awarded. *Degree program information:* Part-time and evening/weekend programs available. Offers elementary education (M Ed); math specialist (M Ed); reading specialist (M Ed); school administration (M Ed); school counseling (M Ed). *Application deadline:* For fall admission, 8/1 for domestic students, 6/1 for international students; for spring admission, 1/5 for domestic students, 11/1 for international students. *Application fee:* $20 ($55 for international students). Electronic applications accepted. *Application Contact:* Carrie Williamson, Graduate Secretary, 580-745-2200, Fax: 580-745-7474, E-mail: cwilliamson@se.edu. *Chair*, Dr. Muhammad Betz, 580-745-2262, Fax: 580-745-7474, E-mail: mbetz@se.edu.

SOUTHEAST MISSOURI STATE UNIVERSITY, Cape Girardeau, MO 63701-4799

General Information State-supported, coed, comprehensive institution. CGS member. *Enrollment:* 10,814 graduate, professional, and undergraduate students; 209 full-time matriculated graduate/professional students (133 women), 1,224 part-time matriculated graduate/professional students (998 women). *Enrollment by degree level:* 1,344 master's, 89 other advanced degrees. *Graduate faculty:* 212 full-time (86 women). *Tuition, area resident:* Part-time $213.30 per credit hour. Tuition, state resident: part-time $213.30 per credit hour. Tuition, nonresident: part-time $393.30 per credit hour. *Required fees:* $23.70 per credit hour. *Graduate housing:* Room and/or apartments available on a first-come, first-served basis to single students; on-campus housing not available to married students. Typical cost: $3673 per year ($5935 including board). Room and board charges vary according to board plan and housing facility selected. Housing application deadline: 12/15. *Student services:* Campus employment opportunities, campus safety program, career counseling, child daycare facilities, exercise/wellness program, free psychological counseling, international student services, multicultural affairs office, services for students with disabilities, teacher training, writing training. *Library facilities:* Kent Library. *Online resources:* library catalog, web page, access to other libraries' catalogs. *Collection:* 503,242 titles, 49,866 serial subscriptions, 15,554 audiovisual materials.

Computer facilities: 1,311 computers available on campus for general student use. A campuswide network can be accessed from student residence rooms. Online class registration is available. *Web address:* http://www.semo.edu/.

General Application Contact: Dr. Fred Janzow, Dean of the School of Graduate Studies, 573-651-2192, Fax: 573-651-2001, E-mail: graduateschool@semo.edu.

GRADUATE UNITS

School of Graduate Studies Students: 209 full-time (133 women), 1,224 part-time (998 women); includes 57 minority (28 African Americans, 7 American Indian/Alaska Native, 5 Asian Americans or Pacific Islanders, 17 Hispanic Americans), 45 international. Average age 35. 376 applicants, 80% accepted. *Faculty:* 212 full-time (86 women). Expenses: Contact institution. *Financial support:* In 2008–09, 177 students received support, including 85 research assistantships with full tuition reimbursements available (averaging $7,600 per year), 92 teaching assistantships with full tuition reimbursements available (averaging $7,600 per year); unspecified assistantships also available. Financial award applicants required to submit FAFSA. In 2008, 233 master's, 27 other advanced degrees awarded. *Degree program information:* Part-time and evening/weekend programs available. Postbaccalaureate distance learning degree programs offered. Offers applied chemistry (MNS); biology (MNS); communication disorders (MA); community wellness and leisure (MPA); counseling (MA, Ed S); counseling education (Ed S); criminal justice and sociology (MS); educational administration (MA, Ed S); educational studies (MA); elementary education (MA); English (MA); exceptional child education (MA); higher education (MA); history (MA); human environmental studies (MA); mathematics (MNS); mental health counseling (MA); middle level education (MA); music education (MME); nursing (MSN); nutrition and exercise science (MS); public administration (MPA); school counseling (MA); teaching English to speakers of other languages (MA); technology management (MS). *Application deadline:* For fall admission, 8/1 for domestic students, 7/1 for international students; for spring admission, 11/21 for domestic students, 11/1 for international students. Applications are processed on a rolling basis. *Application fee:* $25 ($100 for international students). Electronic applications accepted. *Application Contact:* Marsha L. Arant, Senior Administrative Assistant, School of Graduate Studies, 573-651-2192, Fax: 573-651-2001, E-mail: marant@semo.edu. *Vice Provost and Dean of the School of Graduate Studies*, Dr. Fred Janzow, 573-651-2192, Fax: 573-651-2001, E-mail: fjanzow@semo.edu.

Godwin Center for Science and Mathematics Education Students: 1 (woman) full-time, 3 part-time (2 women). Average age 29. 1 applicant, 100% accepted, 1 enrolled. *Faculty:* 4 full-time (3 women). Expenses: Contact institution. *Financial support:* In 2008–09, 1 student received support, including 1 teaching assistantship with full tuition reimbursement available (averaging $7,600 per year); scholarships/grants and unspecified assistantships also available. Financial award application deadline: 3/15; financial award applicants required to submit FAFSA. In 2008, 4 master's awarded. *Degree program information:* Part-time programs available. Postbaccalaureate distance learning degree programs offered (minimal on-campus study). Offers science education (MNS). *Application deadline:* For fall admission, 8/1 for domestic students, 7/1 for international students; for spring admission, 11/21 for domestic students, 11/1 for international students. Applications are processed on a rolling basis. *Application fee:* $25 ($100 for international students). Electronic applications accepted. *Application Contact:* Marsha L. Arant, Senior Administrative Assistant, School of Graduate Studies, 573-651-2192, Fax: 573-651-2001, E-mail: marant@semo.edu. *Director of Graduate Program in Science Education*, Dr. Rachel Morgan Theall, 573-651-2372, Fax: 573-986-6792, E-mail: rmtheall@semo.edu.

Harrison College of Business Students: 40 full-time (17 women), 66 part-time (35 women); includes 5 minority (2 African Americans, 1 Asian American or Pacific Islander, 2 Hispanic Americans), 21 international. Average age 28. 68 applicants, 78% accepted. *Faculty:* 31 full-time (10 women). Expenses: Contact institution. *Financial support:* In 2008–09, 37 students received support, including 24 research assistantships with full tuition reimbursements available (averaging $7,600 per year), 3 teaching assistantships with full tuition reimbursements available (averaging $7,600 per year); unspecified assistantships also available. Financial award applicants required to submit FAFSA. In 2008, 29 master's awarded. *Degree program information:* Part-time and evening/weekend programs available. Postbaccalaureate distance learning degree programs offered (no on-campus study). Offers accounting (MBA); entrepreneurship (MBA); environmental management (MBA); financial management (MBA); general management (MBA); health administration (MBA); industrial management (MBA); international business (MBA); sport management (MBA). *Application deadline:* For fall admission, 8/1 for domestic students, 7/1 for international students; for spring admission, 11/21 for domestic students, 11/1 for international students. Applications are processed on a rolling basis. *Application fee:* $25 ($35 for international students). *Application Contact:* Marsha L. Arant, Senior Administrative Assistant, School of Graduate Studies, 573-651-2192, Fax: 573-651-2001, E-mail: marant@semo.edu. *Director, Graduate Programs in Business*, Dr. Kenneth A. Heischmidt, PhD, 573-651-5116, Fax: 573-651-5032, E-mail: kheischmidt@semo.edu.

SOUTHERN ADVENTIST UNIVERSITY, Collegedale, TN 37315-0370

General Information Independent-religious, coed, comprehensive institution. *Enrollment:* 2,640 graduate, professional, and undergraduate students; 112 full-time matriculated graduate/professional students (45 women), 91 part-time matriculated graduate/professional students (92 women). *Enrollment by degree level:* 203 master's. *Graduate faculty:* 4 full-time (3 women), 20 part-time/adjunct (4 women). *Tuition:* Full-time $25,728; part-time $464 per credit hour. *Graduate housing:* Rooms and/or apartments available on a first-come, first-served basis to single and married students. Typical cost: $6000 per year ($9000 including board) for single students. *Student services:* Campus employment opportunities, campus safety program, career counseling, exercise/wellness program, free psychological counseling, international student services, low-cost health insurance, multicultural affairs office, services for students with disabilities, teacher training, writing training. *Library facilities:* McKee Library. *Online resources:* library catalog, web page. *Collection:* 1,750 serial subscriptions, 4,483 audiovisual materials.

Computer facilities: 200 computers available on campus for general student use. A campuswide network can be accessed from student residence rooms and from off campus. Online class registration is available. *Web address:* http://www.southern.edu/.

General Application Contact: Melodie Lopez, Administrative Assistant, 423-236-2964, Fax: 423-236-1694, E-mail: graduatestudies@southern.edu.

GRADUATE UNITS

School of Business and Management *Degree program information:* Part-time and evening/weekend programs available. Postbaccalaureate distance learning degree programs offered (no on-campus study). Offers accounting (MBA); administration (MS); financial services (MFS); health care administration (MBA); human resource management (MBA); management (MBA); marketing (MBA). Electronic applications accepted.

School of Education and Psychology *Degree program information:* Part-time and evening/weekend programs available. Offers curriculum and instruction (MS Ed); educational administration and supervision (MS Ed); inclusive education (MS Ed); literacy education (MS Ed); outdoor teacher education (MS Ed); professional counseling (MS); school counseling (MS). Electronic applications accepted.

School of Nursing *Degree program information:* Part-time programs available. Offers adult nurse practitioner (MSN); family nurse practitioner (MSN); nurse educator (MSN). Electronic applications accepted.

School of Religion *Degree program information:* Part-time programs available. Offers Biblical and theological studies (MA); church leadership and management (MA); church ministry and homiletics (MA); evangelism and world mission (MA); religious studies (MA). Summer program only.

SOUTHERN ARKANSAS UNIVERSITY–MAGNOLIA, Magnolia, AR 71753

General Information State-supported, coed, comprehensive institution. *Enrollment:* 3,117 graduate, professional, and undergraduate students; 104 full-time matriculated graduate/professional students (73 women), 343 part-time matriculated graduate/professional students (252 women). *Enrollment by degree level:* 447 master's. *Graduate faculty:* 35 full-time (19 women), 15 part-time/adjunct (8 women). Tuition, state resident: full-time $3564; part-time $198 per credit hour. Tuition, nonresident: full-time $5238; part-time $291 per credit hour. *Required fees:* $512. *Graduate housing:* Rooms and/or apartments available on a first-come, first-served basis to single and married students. Typical cost: $2130 per year ($4250 including board) for single students; $2130 per year ($4250 including board) for married students. Housing application deadline: 6/1. *Student services:* Campus employment opportunities, campus safety program, career counseling, exercise/wellness program, free psychological counseling, international student services, low-cost health insurance, multicultural affairs office, services for students with disabilities. *Library facilities:* Magale Library. *Online resources:* library catalog, web page. *Collection:* 151,166 titles, 1,065 serial subscriptions.

Computer facilities: 194 computers available on campus for general student use. A campuswide network can be accessed from student residence rooms and from off campus. Online class registration is available. *Web address:* http://www.saumag.edu/.

General Application Contact: Dr. Kim Bloss, Dean, Graduate Studies, 870-235-4150, Fax: 870-235-5227, E-mail: kkbloss@saumag.edu.

GRADUATE UNITS

Graduate Programs Students: 104 full-time (73 women), 343 part-time (252 women); includes 113 minority (108 African Americans, 3 American Indian/Alaska Native, 2 Asian Americans or Pacific Islanders), 12 international. Average age 34. *Faculty:* 35 full-time (19 women), 15 part-time/adjunct (8 women). Expenses: Contact institution. *Financial support:* Career-related internships or fieldwork, Federal Work-Study, scholarships/grants, tuition waivers (full), and unspecified assistantships available. Financial award applicants required to submit FAFSA. In 2008, 77 master's awarded. *Degree program information:* Part-time and evening/weekend programs available. Offers agriculture (MS); business administration (MBA); computer and information sciences (MS); counseling (MS); education (M Ed); kinesiology (MS); library media and information specialist (M Ed); public administration (EMPA); school counseling (M Ed); teaching (MAT). *Application deadline:* For fall admission, 8/15 for domestic students; for winter admission, 1/8 for domestic students; for spring admission, 1/8 for domestic students. Applications are processed on a rolling basis. *Application fee:* $0. *Application*

Southern Arkansas University–Magnolia (continued)

Contact: Dr. Kim Bloss, Dean, Graduate Studies, 870-235-4150, Fax: 870-235-5227, E-mail: kkbloss@saumag.edu. *Dean, Graduate Studies,* Dr. Kim Bloss, 870-235-4150, Fax: 870-235-5227, E-mail: kkbloss@saumag.edu.

SOUTHERN BAPTIST THEOLOGICAL SEMINARY, Louisville, KY 40280-0004

General Information Independent-religious, coed, comprehensive institution. *Graduate housing:* Rooms and/or apartments available on a first-come, first-served basis to single and married students.

GRADUATE UNITS

Billy Graham School of Missions, Evangelism and Church Growth *Degree program information:* Part-time and evening/weekend programs available. Postbaccalaureate distance learning degree programs offered (minimal on-campus study). Offers Christian mission/world religion (PhD); evangelism/church growth (PhD); ministry (D Min); missiology (MA, D Miss); missions, evangelism and church growth (M Div); religion (Th M); theological studies (MA).

School of Church Music and Worship Offers church music (M Div, MCM, MM); church music and worship (DMA, DMM); worship (M Div, MAW).

School of Leadership and Church Ministry *Degree program information:* Part-time programs available. Postbaccalaureate distance learning degree programs offered (minimal on-campus study). Offers advanced youth ministry (M Div); Christian education (M Div, MACE); leadership (Ed D); leadership and church ministry (PhD); ministry (D Ed Min); women's leadership (M Div); youth ministry (M Div, MAYM).

School of Theology *Degree program information:* Part-time and evening/weekend programs available. Postbaccalaureate distance learning degree programs offered (minimal on-campus study). Offers biblical and theological studies (M Div); biblical counseling (M Div, MA, D Min); biblical spirituality (D Min); Christian ministry (M Div); expository preaching (D Min); pastoral studies (M Div); theological studies (MA); theology (Th M, PhD); theology and arts (MA); theology and law (MA); worldview and apologetics (M Div).

SOUTHERN CALIFORNIA COLLEGE OF OPTOMETRY, Fullerton, CA 92831-1615

General Information Independent, coed, graduate-only institution. *Graduate housing:* On-campus housing not available. *Research affiliation:* Alcon Laboratories (ophthalmic products), Essilor (spectacle lenses), Allergan (ophthalmic products).

GRADUATE UNITS

Professional Program Offers optometry (OD). Electronic applications accepted.

SOUTHERN CALIFORNIA INSTITUTE OF ARCHITECTURE, Los Angeles, CA 90013

General Information Independent, coed, comprehensive institution. *Graduate housing:* On-campus housing not available.

GRADUATE UNITS

Graduate Program in Architecture Offers architecture (M Arch).

SOUTHERN CALIFORNIA SEMINARY, El Cajon, CA 92019

General Information Independent-religious, coed, comprehensive institution. *Graduate housing:* Rooms and/or apartments available on a first-come, first-served basis to single and married students.

GRADUATE UNITS

Graduate and Professional Programs *Degree program information:* Part-time and evening/weekend programs available. Postbaccalaureate distance learning degree programs offered (minimal on-campus study). Offers biblical studies (MA); counseling psychology (MACP); psychology (Psy D); religious studies (MRS); theology (M Div). Electronic applications accepted.

SOUTHERN CALIFORNIA UNIVERSITY OF HEALTH SCIENCES, Whittier, CA 90609-1166

General Information Independent, coed, graduate-only institution. *Graduate housing:* On-campus housing not available.

GRADUATE UNITS

College of Acupuncture and Oriental Medicine *Degree program information:* Part-time and evening/weekend programs available. Offers acupuncture and Oriental medicine (MAOM). Electronic applications accepted.

Los Angeles College of Chiropractic Offers chiropractic (DC). Electronic applications accepted.

SOUTHERN COLLEGE OF OPTOMETRY, Memphis, TN 38104-2222

General Information Independent, coed, graduate-only institution. *Graduate housing:* On-campus housing not available.

GRADUATE UNITS

Professional Program Offers optometry (OD).

SOUTHERN CONNECTICUT STATE UNIVERSITY, New Haven, CT 06515-1355

General Information State-supported, coed, comprehensive institution. CGS member. *Graduate housing:* Room and/or apartments available on a first-come, first-served basis to single students; on-campus housing not available to married students.

GRADUATE UNITS

School of Graduate Studies *Degree program information:* Part-time and evening/weekend programs available. Postbaccalaureate distance learning degree programs offered (no on-campus study). Electronic applications accepted.

School of Arts and Sciences Offers art education (MS); arts and sciences (MA, MS, Diploma); biology (MS); biology for nurse anesthetists (MS); chemistry (MS); English (MA, MS); environmental education (MS); history (MA, MS); mathematics (MS); multicultural-bilingual education/teaching English to speakers of other languages (MS); political science (MS); psychology (MA); science education (MS, Diploma); sociology (MS); urban studies (MS); women's studies (MA). Electronic applications accepted.

School of Business *Degree program information:* Evening/weekend programs available. Offers business (MBA); business administration (MBA). Electronic applications accepted.

School of Communication, Information and Library Science *Degree program information:* Part-time and evening/weekend programs available. Postbaccalaureate distance learning degree programs offered (no on-campus study). Offers communication, information and library science (MLS, MS, Diploma); computer science (MS); library science (MLS); library/information studies (Diploma). Electronic applications accepted.

School of Education *Degree program information:* Part-time programs available. Offers classroom teacher specialist (Diploma); community counseling (MS); counseling (Diploma); education (MS, MS Ed, Ed D, Diploma); educational foundations (Diploma); educational leadership (Ed D, Diploma); elementary education (MS); foundational studies (Diploma); human performance (MS); physical education (MS); reading (MS, Diploma); research, statistics, and measurement (MS); school counseling (MS); school health education (MS); school psychology (MS, Diploma); special education (MS Ed, Diploma); sport psychology (MS). Electronic applications accepted.

School of Health and Human Services *Degree program information:* Part-time and evening/weekend programs available. Offers audiology (MS); health and human services (MFT, MPH, MS, MSN, MSW); marriage and family therapy (MFT); nursing administration (MSN); nursing education (MSN); public health (MPH); recreation and leisure studies (MS); social work (MSW); speech pathology (MS). Electronic applications accepted.

Announcement: The University maintains a high standard of excellence in its programs and seeks to instill in its students a desire for continuing self-education and self-development. Each school of the University has developed its graduate programs in accordance with the highest national standards for the respective fields.

See Close-Up on page 991.

SOUTHERN EVANGELICAL SEMINARY, Matthews, NC 28105

General Information Independent-religious, coed, primarily men, graduate-only institution. *Graduate housing:* On-campus housing not available.

GRADUATE UNITS

Graduate School of Ministry and Missions *Degree program information:* Part-time and evening/weekend programs available. Postbaccalaureate distance learning degree programs offered. Offers apologetics (Certificate); Christian education (MA); church ministry (MA, Certificate); divinity (Certificate); Islamic studies (Certificate); theology (M Div); youth ministry (MA).

Veritas Graduate School of Apologetics and Counter-Cult Ministry *Degree program information:* Part-time and evening/weekend programs available. Postbaccalaureate distance learning degree programs offered (minimal on-campus study). Offers apologetics (MA, D Min, PhD, Certificate); Islamic studies (MA); Jewish studies (MA); philosophy (MA); religion (MA).

SOUTHERN ILLINOIS UNIVERSITY CARBONDALE, Carbondale, IL 62901-4701

General Information State-supported, coed, university. CGS member. *Graduate housing:* Rooms and/or apartments available on a first-come, first-served basis to single and married students. *Research affiliation:* Argonne National Laboratory, NASA–Ames Research Center.

GRADUATE UNITS

Graduate School *Degree program information:* Part-time programs available. Offers molecular, cellular and systemic physiology (MS); pharmacology (MS, PhD); physiology (MS, PhD).

College of Agriculture *Degree program information:* Part-time programs available. Offers agribusiness economics (MS); agriculture (MS); animal science (MS); food and nutrition (MS); forestry (MS); horticultural science (MS); plant and soil science (MS).

College of Applied Science Offers applied science (M Arch, MSPA); architecture (M Arch); physician assistant studies (MSPA).

College of Business and Administration *Degree program information:* Part-time programs available. Offers accountancy (M Acc, PhD); business administration (MBA, PhD); business and administration (M Acc, MBA, PhD).

College of Education *Degree program information:* Part-time programs available. Offers behavior analysis and therapy (MS); behavioral analysis and therapy (MS); communication disorders and sciences (MS); community health education (MPH); counselor education (MS Ed, PhD); curriculum and instruction (MS Ed, PhD); education (MPH, MS, MS Ed, MSW, PhD, Rh D); educational administration (MS Ed, PhD); educational psychology (MS Ed, PhD); health education (MS Ed, PhD); higher education (MS Ed); human learning and development (MS Ed); measurement and statistics (PhD); physical education (MS Ed); recreation (MS Ed); rehabilitation (Rh D); rehabilitation administration and services (MS); rehabilitation counseling (MS); social work (MSW); special education (MS Ed); workforce education and development (MS Ed, PhD).

College of Engineering Offers biomedical engineering (ME, MS); civil engineering (MS); electrical and computer engineering (MS, PhD); electrical systems (PhD); engineering (ME, MS, PhD); fossil energy (PhD); manufacturing systems (MS); mechanical engineering and energy processes (MS); mechanics (PhD); mining engineering (MS).

College of Liberal Arts *Degree program information:* Part-time programs available. Offers administration of justice (MA); anthropology (MA, PhD); applied linguistics (MA); ceramics (MFA); clinical psychology (MA, MS, PhD); composition (MA, PhD); composition and theory (MM); counseling psychology (MA, MS, PhD); creative writing (MFA); drawing (MFA); economics (MA, MS, PhD); experimental psychology (MA, MS, PhD); fiber/weaving (MFA); foreign languages and literatures (MA); geography (MS, PhD); glass (MFA); history (MA, PhD); history and literature (MM); jewelry (MFA); liberal arts (MA, MFA, MM, MPA, MS, PhD); metalsmithing/blacksmithing (MFA); music education (MM); opera/music theater (MM); painting (MFA); performance (MM); philosophy (MA, PhD); piano pedagogy (MM); political science (MA, PhD); printmaking (MFA); public administration (MPA); sculpture (MFA); sociology (MA, PhD); speech communication (MA, MS, PhD); speech/theater (PhD); teaching English to speakers of other languages (MA); theater (MFA).

College of Mass Communication and Media Arts *Degree program information:* Part-time programs available. Offers journalism (PhD); mass communication and media arts (MA, MFA, PhD); media theory and research (MA); professional media and media management studies (MA).

College of Science *Degree program information:* Part-time programs available. Offers biological sciences (MS); chemistry and biochemistry (MS, PhD); computer science (MS, PhD); environmental resources and policy (PhD); geology (MS, PhD); mathematics (MA, MS, PhD); molecular biology, microbiology, and biochemistry (MS, PhD); physics (MS, PhD); plant biology (MS, PhD); science (MA, MS, PhD); statistics (MS); zoology (MS, PhD).

School of Law *Degree program information:* Part-time programs available. Offers general law (LL M, MLS); health law and policy (LL M, MLS); law (JD); legal studies (MLS). Electronic applications accepted.

SOUTHERN ILLINOIS UNIVERSITY EDWARDSVILLE, Edwardsville, IL 62026-0001

General Information State-supported, coed, comprehensive institution. CGS member. *Enrollment:* 13,602 graduate, professional, and undergraduate students; 1,078 full-time matriculated graduate/professional students (598 women), 1,196 part-time matriculated graduate/professional students (757 women). *Enrollment by degree level:* 443 first professional. *Graduate faculty:* 462 full-time (178 women). Tuition, state resident: full-time $5838. Tuition, nonresident: full-time $14,596. *Required fees:* $1525. *Graduate housing:* Rooms and/or apartments available on a first-come, first-served basis to single and married students. Housing application deadline: 5/1. *Student services:* Campus employment opportunities, campus safety program, career counseling, child daycare facilities, exercise/wellness program, free psychological counseling, grant writing training, international student services, low-cost health insurance, multicultural affairs office, services for students with disabilities, teacher training, writing training. *Library facilities:* Lovejoy Library. *Online resources:* library catalog, web page, access to other libraries' catalogs. *Collection:* 847,631 titles, 24,530 serial subscriptions, 30,078 audiovisual materials. *Research affiliation:* Amsted Rail (Mechanical Engineering), Chestnut Health Systems (Public Administration), Nutracea, Inc. Fermentation Lab (National Corn to Ethanol Research Center), G.S. Robins and Co. (Engineering (Map Development for manufacturing)), Ag-Defense Systems, Inc. (Engineering), JETRO New York (Business).

Computer facilities: 600 computers available on campus for general student use. A campuswide network can be accessed from student residence rooms and from off campus. Online class registration, online job finder are available. *Web address:* http://www.siue.edu/.

General Application Contact: Michelle Robinson, Coordinator of Graduate Recruitment, 618-650-2811, Fax: 618-650-3523, E-mail: michero@siue.edu.

GRADUATE UNITS

Graduate Studies and Research Students: 689 full-time (404 women), 1,248 part-time (793 women); includes 180 minority (129 African Americans, 4 American Indian/Alaska Native, 26

Asian Americans or Pacific Islanders, 21 Hispanic Americans), 223 international. Average age 26. 2,047 applicants, 40% accepted. *Faculty:* 426 full-time (174 women). Expenses: Contact institution. *Financial support:* In 2008–09, 19 fellowships with full tuition reimbursements (averaging $8,370 per year), 46 research assistantships with full tuition reimbursements (averaging $8,064 per year), 472 teaching assistantships with full tuition reimbursements (averaging $8,064 per year) were awarded; career-related internships or fieldwork, Federal Work-Study, institutionally sponsored loans, scholarships/grants, traineeships, tuition waivers (full), and unspecified assistantships also available. Support available to part-time students. Financial award application deadline: 3/1; financial award applicants required to submit FAFSA. In 2008, 706 master's, 16 other advanced degrees awarded. *Degree program information:* Part-time programs available. *Application deadline:* For fall admission, 7/20 for domestic students, 6/1 for international students; for spring admission, 12/8 for domestic students, 10/1 for international students. Applications are processed on a rolling basis. *Application fee:* $30. Electronic applications accepted. *Application Contact:* Michelle Robinson, Coordinator of Graduate Recruitment, 618-650-2811, Fax: 618-650-3523, E-mail: michero@siue.edu. *Associate Provost for Research and Dean of Graduate School,* Dr. Stephen L. Hansen, 618-650-3010, Fax: 618-650-3523, E-mail: gradsch@siue.edu.

College of Arts and Sciences Students: 270 full-time (173 women), 357 part-time (235 women); includes 98 minority (74 African Americans, 2 American Indian/Alaska Native, 14 Asian Americans or Pacific Islanders, 8 Hispanic Americans), 45 international. Average age 26. 717 applicants, 47% accepted. *Faculty:* 231 full-time (92 women). Expenses: Contact institution. *Financial support:* In 2008–09, 7 fellowships with full tuition reimbursements (averaging $8,370 per year), 7 research assistantships with full tuition reimbursements (averaging $8,064 per year), 254 teaching assistantships with full tuition reimbursements (averaging $8,064 per year) were awarded; career-related internships or fieldwork, Federal Work-Study, institutionally sponsored loans, scholarships/grants, traineeships, and unspecified assistantships also available. Support available to part-time students. Financial award application deadline: 3/1; financial award applicants required to submit FAFSA. In 2008, 154 master's, 12 other advanced degrees awarded. *Degree program information:* Part-time programs available. Offers American and English literature (MA, Postbaccalaureate Certificate); art therapy counseling (MA); arts and sciences (MA, MFA, MM, MPA, MS, MSW, Postbaccalaureate Certificate); biology (MA, MS); biotechnology management (MS); chemistry (MS); corporate and organizational communication (Postbaccalaureate Certificate); creative writing (MA); environmental science management (MS); environmental sciences (MS); geography (MS); history (MA); mass communications (MS, Postbaccalaureate Certificate); mathematics (MS); media literacy (Postbaccalaureate Certificate); museum studies (Postbaccalaureate Certificate); music education (MM); music performance (MM); physics (MS); piano pedagogy (Postbaccalaureate Certificate); public administration and policy analysis (MPA); school social work (MSW); sociology and criminal justice studies (MA); speech communication (MA, Postbaccalaureate Certificate); studio art (MFA); teaching English as a second language (MA, Postbaccalaureate Certificate); teaching of writing (MA, Postbaccalaureate Certificate); vocal pedagogy (Postbaccalaureate Certificate). *Application deadline:* For fall admission, 7/20 for domestic students, 6/1 for international students; for spring admission, 12/14 for domestic students, 10/1 for international students. Applications are processed on a rolling basis. *Application fee:* $30. Electronic applications accepted. *Application Contact:* Michelle Robinson, Coordinator of Graduate Recruitment, 618-650-2811, Fax: 618-650-3523, E-mail: michero@siue.edu. *Acting Dean,* Dr. John Danley, 618-650-5047, E-mail: College_Arts_Sciences@siue.edu.

School of Business Students: 104 full-time (37 women), 215 part-time (84 women); includes 18 minority (13 African Americans, 1 American Indian/Alaska Native, 2 Asian Americans or Pacific Islanders, 2 Hispanic Americans), 34 international. Average age 26. 245 applicants, 44% accepted. *Faculty:* 46 full-time (16 women). Expenses: Contact institution. *Financial support:* In 2008–09, 4 fellowships with full tuition reimbursements (averaging $8,370 per year), 25 research assistantships with full tuition reimbursements (averaging $8,064 per year), 41 teaching assistantships with full tuition reimbursements (averaging $8,064 per year) were awarded; career-related internships or fieldwork, Federal Work-Study, institutionally sponsored loans, traineeships, and unspecified assistantships also available. Support available to part-time students. Financial award application deadline: 3/1; financial award applicants required to submit FAFSA. In 2008, 161 master's awarded. *Degree program information:* Part-time programs available. Offers accounting (MSA); business (MA, MBA, MMR, MS, MSA); computer management and information systems (MS); economics and finance (MA, MS); general business (MBA); management information systems (MBA); marketing research (MMR); project management (MBA). *Application deadline:* For fall admission, 7/20 for domestic students, 6/1 for international students; for spring admission, 12/14 for domestic students, 10/1 for international students. Applications are processed on a rolling basis. *Application fee:* $30. Electronic applications accepted. *Application Contact:* Dr. Gary Giamartino, Dean, 618-650-3822, E-mail: ggiamar@siue.edu. *Dean,* Dr. Gary Giamartino, 618-650-3822, E-mail: ggiamar@siue.edu.

School of Education Students: 159 full-time (130 women), 438 part-time (327 women); includes 42 minority (32 African Americans, 2 Asian Americans or Pacific Islanders, 8 Hispanic Americans), 7 international. Average age 26. 517 applicants, 40% accepted. *Faculty:* 76 full-time (40 women). Expenses: Contact institution. *Financial support:* In 2008–09, 4 fellowships with full tuition reimbursements (averaging $8,370 per year), 2 research assistantships with full tuition reimbursements (averaging $8,064 per year), 97 teaching assistantships with full tuition reimbursements (averaging $8,064 per year) were awarded; career-related internships or fieldwork, Federal Work-Study, institutionally sponsored loans, traineeships, and unspecified assistantships also available. Support available to part-time students. Financial award application deadline: 3/1; financial award applicants required to submit FAFSA. In 2008, 221 master's, 25 other advanced degrees awarded. *Degree program information:* Part-time programs available. Offers art (MS Ed); biology (MS Ed); chemistry (MS Ed); clinical child and school psychology (MS); clinical-adult psychology (MA); curriculum and instruction (MS Ed); earth and space sciences (MS Ed); education (MA, MAT, MS, MS Ed, Ed S, Post-Master's Certificate, Postbaccalaureate Certificate, SD); educational administration (MS Ed, Ed S); English/language arts (MS Ed); exercise physiology (Postbaccalaureate Certificate); foreign languages (MS Ed); history (MS Ed); industrial-organizational psychology (MA); instructional technology (MS Ed); kinesiology (MS Ed); learning, culture, and society (MS Ed); literacy education (MS Ed); literacy specialist (Post-Master's Certificate); mathematics (MS Ed); pedagogy administration (Postbaccalaureate Certificate); physics (MS Ed); school psychology (SD); secondary education (MS Ed); special education (MS Ed); speech language pathology (MS); sport and exercise behavior (Postbaccalaureate Certificate); teaching (MAT); web-based learning (Postbaccalaureate Certificate). *Application deadline:* For fall admission, 7/20 for domestic students, 6/1 for international students; for spring admission, 12/14 for domestic students, 10/1 for international students. Applications are processed on a rolling basis. *Application fee:* $30. Electronic applications accepted. *Application Contact:* Dr. Mary Weishaar, Associate Dean, 618-650-3491, E-mail: mweisha@siue.edu. *Interim Dean,* Dr. Bette Bergeron, 618-650-3350, E-mail: bberger@siue.edu.

School of Engineering Students: 101 full-time (27 women), 103 part-time (20 women); includes 7 minority (3 African Americans, 4 Asian Americans or Pacific Islanders), 137 international. Average age 26. 441 applicants, 26% accepted. *Faculty:* 43 full-time (2 women). Expenses: Contact institution. *Financial support:* In 2008–09, 3 fellowships with full tuition reimbursements (averaging $8,370 per year), 12 research assistantships with full tuition reimbursements (averaging $8,064 per year), 80 teaching assistantships with full tuition reimbursements (averaging $8,064 per year) were awarded; career-related internships or fieldwork, Federal Work-Study, institutionally sponsored loans, scholarships/grants, traineeships, and unspecified assistantships also available. Support available to part-time students. Financial award application deadline: 3/1; financial award applicants required to submit FAFSA. In 2008, 81 master's awarded. *Degree program information:* Part-time programs available. Offers civil engineering (MS); computer science (MS); electrical engineering (MS); engineering (MS); industrial engineering (MS); mechanical engineering (MS). *Application deadline:* For fall admission, 7/20 for domestic students, 6/1 for international students; for spring admission, 12/14 for domestic students, 10/1 for international students. Applications are processed on a rolling basis. *Application fee:* $30. Electronic applications accepted. *Application Contact:* Dr. Hasan Sevim, Dean, 618-650-2541, E-mail: hsevim@siue.edu. *Dean,* Dr. Hasan Sevim, 618-650-2541, E-mail: hsevim@siue.edu.

School of Nursing Students: 55 full-time (37 women), 135 part-time (127 women); includes 15 minority (7 African Americans, 1 American Indian/Alaska Native, 4 Asian Americans or Pacific Islanders, 3 Hispanic Americans). Average age 26. 127 applicants, 39% accepted. *Faculty:* 26 full-time (23 women). Expenses: Contact institution. *Financial support:* In 2008–09, 1 fellowship with full tuition reimbursement (averaging $8,370 per year) was awarded; research assistantships, teaching assistantships, career-related internships or fieldwork, Federal Work-Study, institutionally sponsored loans, scholarships/grants, traineeships, and unspecified assistantships also available. Support available to part-time students. Financial award application deadline: 3/1; financial award applicants required to submit FAFSA. In 2008, 64 master's, 4 other advanced degrees awarded. Offers family nurse practitioner (MS, Post-Master's Certificate); health care and nursing administration (MS, Post-Master's Certificate); nurse anesthesia (MS, Post-Master's Certificate); nurse educator (MS, Post-Master's Certificate); nursing (MS, Post-Master's Certificate). *Application deadline:* For fall admission, 3/13 for domestic and international students. *Application fee:* $30. Electronic applications accepted. *Application Contact:* Dr. Jacquelyn Clement, Director, 618-650-3923, E-mail: jclemen@siue.edu. *Dean,* Dr. Marcia Maurer, 618-650-3959, E-mail: mamaure@siue.edu.

School of Dental Medicine Students: 194 full-time (88 women); includes 34 minority (14 African Americans, 2 American Indian/Alaska Native, 11 Asian Americans or Pacific Islanders, 7 Hispanic Americans). Average age 25. *Faculty:* 20 full-time (1 woman). Expenses: Contact institution. *Financial support:* Application deadline: 3/1. In 2008, 54 DMDs awarded. Offers dental medicine (DMD). *Application deadline:* For fall admission, 6/1 priority date for domestic students, 6/1 for international students. *Application fee:* $20. Electronic applications accepted. *Application Contact:* Dr. Ann Boyle, Dean, 618-474-7120, E-mail: sdmapps@siue.edu. *Dean,* Dr. Ann Boyle, 618-474-7120, E-mail: sdmapps@siue.edu.

School of Pharmacy Students: 318 full-time (181 women); includes 34 minority (12 African Americans, 18 Asian Americans or Pacific Islanders, 4 Hispanic Americans), 1 international. Average age 26. *Faculty:* 16 full-time (3 women). Expenses: Contact institution. *Financial support:* Application deadline: 3/1. Offers pharmacy (Pharm D). *Application deadline:* For fall admission, 8/1 for domestic and international students. *Application fee:* $40. Electronic applications accepted. *Application Contact:* Dr. Philip J. Medon, Head, 618-650-5150, E-mail: pharmacy@siue.edu. *Head,* Dr. Philip J. Medon, 618-650-5150, E-mail: pharmacy@siue.edu.

See Close-Up on page 993.

SOUTHERN METHODIST UNIVERSITY, Dallas, TX 75275

General Information Independent-religious, coed, university. CGS member. *Enrollment:* 10,965 graduate, professional, and undergraduate students; 2,145 full-time matriculated graduate/professional students (885 women), 2,250 part-time matriculated graduate/professional students (977 women). *Enrollment by degree level:* 1,204 first professional, 2,768 master's, 423 doctoral. *Graduate faculty:* 656 full-time (232 women), 378 part-time/adjunct (147 women). *Graduate housing:* Rooms and/or apartments available on a first-come, first-served basis to single and married students. Housing application deadline: 5/31. *Student services:* Campus employment opportunities, campus safety program, career counseling, child daycare facilities, exercise/wellness program, free psychological counseling, grant writing training, international student services, low-cost health insurance, multicultural affairs office, services for students with disabilities, teacher training. *Library facilities:* Central University Library plus 7 others. *Online resources:* library catalog, web page, access to other libraries' catalogs. *Collection:* 2.8 million titles, 11,701 serial subscriptions, 45,168 audiovisual materials.

Computer facilities: 758 computers available on campus for general student use. A campuswide network can be accessed from student residence rooms and from off campus. Online class registration, online billing/payment processing are available. *Web address:* http://www.smu.edu/.

General Application Contact: Dr. James E. Quick, Associate Vice President for Research and Dean of Graduate Studies, 214-768-4345.

GRADUATE UNITS

Annette Caldwell Simmons School of Education and Human Development Students: 43 full-time (36 women), 750 part-time (609 women); includes 210 minority (87 African Americans, 5 American Indian/Alaska Native, 19 Asian Americans or Pacific Islanders, 99 Hispanic Americans), 19 international. Average age 36. *Faculty:* 26 full-time (16 women), 61 part-time/adjunct (40 women). Expenses: Contact institution. In 2008, 167 master's, 38 other advanced degrees awarded. Offers bilingual/ESL education (MBE); counseling (MS); dispute resolution (MA, Certificate); dispute resolution and counseling (MA, Certificate); education (M Ed, PhD); educational preparation (Certificate); gifted and talented focus (MBE); learning therapist (Certificate); liberal studies (MLS); teaching and learning (MBE, PhD, Certificate). *Application fee:* $75. *Application Contact:* Associate Vice President for Research and Dean of Graduate Studies. *Leon Simmons Endowed Dean,* Prof. David J. Chard, PhD, 214-768-7587, Fax: 214-768-1797.

Bobby B. Lyle School of Engineering Students: 174 full-time (46 women), 771 part-time (174 women); includes 266 minority (74 African Americans, 7 American Indian/Alaska Native, 116 Asian Americans or Pacific Islanders, 69 Hispanic Americans), 208 international. Average age 32. 672 applicants, 54% accepted, 226 enrolled. *Faculty:* 52 full-time (5 women), 54 part-time/adjunct (3 women). Expenses: Contact institution. *Financial support:* In 2008–09, 72 students received support, including 35 research assistantships with full tuition reimbursements available (averaging $16,800 per year), 33 teaching assistantships with full tuition reimbursements available (averaging $12,600 per year); fellowships, career-related internships or fieldwork, Federal Work-Study, institutionally sponsored loans, scholarships/grants, and tuition waivers (full and partial) also available. Financial award applicants required to submit FAFSA. In 2008, 351 master's, 19 doctorates awarded. *Degree program information:* Part-time and evening/weekend programs available. Postbaccalaureate distance learning degree programs offered (no on-campus study). Offers applied science (MS, PhD); civil engineering (MS, PhD); computer engineering (MS Cp E, PhD); computer science (MS, PhD); electrical engineering (MSEE, PhD); electronic and optical packaging (MS); engineering (MS, MS Cp E, MSEE, MSEM, MSIEM, MSME, DE, PhD); engineering management (MSEM, DE); environmental engineering (MS); environmental science (MS); facilities management (MS); information engineering and management (MSIEM); manufacturing systems management (MS); mechanical engineering (MSME, PhD); operations research (MS, PhD); security engineering (MS); software engineering (MS); systems engineering (MS); telecommunications (MS). *Application deadline:* For fall admission, 7/1 for domestic students, 5/15 for international students; for spring admission, 11/15 for domestic students, 9/1 for international students. Applications are processed on a rolling basis. *Application fee:* $75. *Application Contact:* Marc Valerin, Director of Graduate and Executive Admissions, 214-768-3042, E-mail: valerin@engr.smu.edu. *Dean,* Dr. Geoffrey Orsak, 214-768-3050, Fax: 214-768-3845.

Cox School of Business Students: 462 full-time (131 women), 396 part-time (105 women); includes 186 minority (40 African Americans, 4 American Indian/Alaska Native, 92 Asian Americans or Pacific Islanders, 50 Hispanic Americans), 100 international. Average age 31. 973 applicants, 54% accepted, 417 enrolled. *Faculty:* 38 full-time (8 women), 11 part-time/adjunct (1 woman). Expenses: Contact institution. *Financial support:* In 2008–09, 10 research assistantships (averaging $2,800 per year) were awarded; unspecified assistantships also available. Financial award application deadline: 3/1; financial award applicants required to submit FAFSA. In 2008, 547 master's awarded. *Degree program information:* Part-time and evening/weekend programs available. Offers accounting (MBA, MSA); business (Exec MBA); business administration (MBA); entrepreneurship (MS); finance (MBA); information technology and operations management (MBA); management (MSM); marketing (MBA); strategy and entrepreneurship (MBA). *Application deadline:* Applications are processed on a rolling basis. *Application fee:* $75. Electronic applications accepted. *Application Contact:* Patti Cudney, Director of MBA Admissions, 214-768-3001, Fax: 214-768-3956, E-mail: pcudney@cox.smu.edu. *Dean,* Dr. Albert W. Niemi, 214-768-3012, Fax: 214-768-3713, E-mail: aniemi@mail.cox.smu.edu.

Southern Methodist University (continued)

Dedman College Students: 165 full-time (82 women), 187 part-time (86 women); includes 43 minority (7 African Americans, 5 American Indian/Alaska Native, 7 Asian Americans or Pacific Islanders, 24 Hispanic Americans), 103 international. Average age 30. 555 applicants, 37% accepted, 90 enrolled. *Faculty:* 280 full-time (101 women), 64 part-time/adjunct (35 women). Expenses: Contact institution. *Financial support:* In 2008–09, 194 students received support, including research assistantships with full tuition reimbursements available (averaging $16,000 per year), teaching assistantships with full tuition reimbursements available (averaging $16,000 per year); fellowships, career-related internships or fieldwork, Federal Work-Study, institutionally sponsored loans, scholarships/grants, tuition waivers (full and partial), and unspecified assistantships also available. Support available to part-time students. Financial award applicants required to submit FAFSA. In 2008, 68 master's, 23 doctorates awarded. *Degree program information:* Part-time and evening/weekend programs available. Offers anthropology (PhD); applied economics (MA); applied geophysics (MS); biological sciences (MA, MS, PhD); chemistry (MS, PhD); clinical psychology (PhD); computational and applied mathematics (MS, PhD); economics (MA, PhD); English (MA, PhD); geology (MS, PhD); geophysics (MS, PhD); history (MA, PhD); medical anthropology (MA); medieval studies (MA); physics (MS, PhD); religious studies (MA, PhD); statistical science (MS, PhD). *Application deadline:* For fall admission, 2/1 priority date for domestic and international students; for winter admission, 11/30 priority date for domestic and international students. Applications are processed on a rolling basis. *Application fee:* $75. Electronic applications accepted. *Application Contact:* Barbara Phillips, Assistant Dean, 214-768-4202, Fax: 214-768-4235, E-mail: bphillips@smu.edu. Dr. R. Hal Williams, 214-768-4336.

Dedman School of Law Students: 967 full-time (427 women), 82 part-time (33 women); includes 214 minority (50 African Americans, 9 American Indian/Alaska Native, 84 Asian Americans or Pacific Islanders, 71 Hispanic Americans), 81 international. Average age 27. 2,355 applicants, 27% accepted, 282 enrolled. *Faculty:* 43 full-time (17 women), 48 part-time/adjunct (11 women). Expenses: Contact institution. *Financial support:* Career-related internships or fieldwork, Federal Work-Study, and scholarships/grants available. Financial award application deadline: 2/15; financial award applicants required to submit FAFSA. In 2008, 308 JDs, 56 master's awarded. *Degree program information:* Part-time and evening/weekend programs available. Offers foreign law school graduates (LL M); law (JD, SJD); law-general (LL M); taxation (LL M). *Application deadline:* For fall admission, 2/15 priority date for domestic students. Applications are processed on a rolling basis. *Application fee:* $75. Electronic applications accepted. *Application Contact:* Virginia Keehan, Assistant Dean for Admissions, 214-768-2550, Fax: 214-768-2549, E-mail: lawadmit@smu.edu. *Dean,* John B. Attanasio, 214-768-8999, Fax: 214-768-2182, E-mail: jba@mail.smu.edu.

Meadows School of the Arts Students: 96 full-time (62 women), 115 part-time (69 women); includes 33 minority (11 African Americans, 1 American Indian/Alaska Native, 7 Asian Americans or Pacific Islanders, 14 Hispanic Americans), 44 international. Average age 28. 219 applicants, 62% accepted, 89 enrolled. *Faculty:* 112 full-time (45 women), 73 part-time/adjunct (30 women). Expenses: Contact institution. *Financial support:* In 2008–09, 136 teaching assistantships (averaging $4,400 per year) were awarded; research assistantships, scholarships/grants and unspecified assistantships also available. Financial award application deadline: 3/1; financial award applicants required to submit FAFSA. In 2008, 58 master's, 13 other advanced degrees awarded. *Degree program information:* Evening/weekend programs available. Offers acting (MFA); art history (MA); arts (MA, MFA, MM, MSM, Certificate); conducting (MM); dance (MFA); design (MFA); music composition (MM); music education (MM); music history (MM); music theory (MM); performance (MM, Certificate); piano performance and pedagogy (MM); sacred music (MSM); studio art (MFA). *Application fee:* $75. *Application Contact:* Jean Cherry, Director of Graduate Admissions and Records, 214-768-3765, Fax: 214-768-3272, E-mail: jcherry@smu.edu. *Dean,* Jose Antonio Bowen, 214-768-2880.

Division of Arts Administration Students: 24 full-time (21 women); includes 2 minority (1 Asian American or Pacific Islander, 1 Hispanic American), 1 international. Average age 26. 18 applicants, 72% accepted, 7 enrolled. *Faculty:* 1 (woman) full-time, 1 (woman) part-time/adjunct. Expenses: Contact institution. Offers arts administration. *Application deadline:* For fall admission, 1/15 priority date for domestic and international students. Applications are processed on a rolling basis. *Application fee:* $75. Electronic applications accepted. *Application Contact:* Lynette Hilliard, Assistant Director, 214-768-3425, E-mail: ihilliar@smu.edu. *Interim Chair,* Dr. P. Gregory Warden, 214-768-3425, E-mail: lhilliar@smu.edu.

Division of Communication Arts Students: 12 full-time (7 women), 1 part-time (0 women); includes 2 minority (1 American Indian/Alaska Native, 1 Hispanic American), 5 international. Average age 30. 9 applicants, 78% accepted, 4 enrolled. *Faculty:* 9 full-time (3 women), 6 part-time/adjunct (1 woman). Expenses: Contact institution. *Financial support:* In 2008–09, 7 students received support, including 7 teaching assistantships (averaging $6,500 per year); research assistantships, scholarships/grants, tuition waivers (full), and unspecified assistantships also available. Financial award application deadline: 3/15. In 2008, 6 master's awarded. *Degree program information:* Part-time and evening/weekend programs available. Offers communication arts (MA). *Application deadline:* For fall admission, 3/1 priority date for domestic and international students. *Application fee:* $75. *Application Contact:* Jean Cherry, Director of Graduate Admissions and Records, 214-768-3765, Fax: 214-768-3272, E-mail: jcherry@smu.edu. *Chair,* Rick Worland, 214-768-3708, Fax: 214-768-2784, E-mail: rworland@smu.edu.

Perkins School of Theology Students: 172 full-time (90 women), 192 part-time (109 women); includes 88 minority (60 African Americans, 2 American Indian/Alaska Native, 5 Asian Americans or Pacific Islanders, 21 Hispanic Americans), 6 international. Average age 39. 141 applicants, 77% accepted, 75 enrolled. *Faculty:* 31 full-time (12 women), 13 part-time/adjunct (3 women). Expenses: Contact institution. *Financial support:* In 2008–09, 188 students received support, including 3 fellowships with full tuition reimbursements available (averaging $5,000 per year); career-related internships or fieldwork, Federal Work-Study, scholarships/grants, and minister's family tuition awards also available. Support available to part-time students. Financial award application deadline: 3/1; financial award applicants required to submit FAFSA. In 2008, 68 first professional degrees, 29 master's, 15 doctorates awarded. *Degree program information:* Part-time programs available. Offers theology (M Div, CMM, MSM, MTS, D Min). *Application deadline:* For fall admission, 5/1 for domestic students, 12/15 for international students; for spring admission, 11/1 for domestic students. Applications are processed on a rolling basis. *Application fee:* $50. *Application Contact:* Rev. Herbert S. Coleman, Director, Recruitment and Admissions, 214-768-2139, Fax: 214-768-4245, E-mail: theology@smu.edu. *Dean,* Dr. William B. Lawrence, 214-768-2534, Fax: 214-768-2966.

SOUTHERN NAZARENE UNIVERSITY, Bethany, OK 73008

General Information Independent-religious, coed, comprehensive institution. *Graduate housing:* Rooms and/or apartments available on a first-come, first-served basis to single and married students. Housing application deadline: 8/1.

GRADUATE UNITS

Graduate College *Degree program information:* Part-time and evening/weekend programs available. Offers theology (MA). Electronic applications accepted.

School of Business *Degree program information:* Part-time and evening/weekend programs available. Offers business (MBA, MS Mgt). Electronic applications accepted.

School of Education *Degree program information:* Part-time and evening/weekend programs available. Offers curriculum and instruction (MA); educational leadership (MA).

School of Nursing *Degree program information:* Part-time and evening/weekend programs available. Offers nursing education (MS); nursing leadership (MS).

School of Psychology Offers counseling psychology (MSCP); marriage and family therapy (MA).

SOUTHERN NEW ENGLAND SCHOOL OF LAW, North Dartmouth, MA 02747-1252

General Information Independent, coed, graduate-only institution. *Enrollment by degree level:* 234 first professional. *Graduate faculty:* 12 full-time (5 women), 25 part-time/adjunct (9 women). *Tuition:* Full-time $21,200; part-time $715 per credit. *Required fees:* $375; $375 per year. *Graduate housing:* On-campus housing not available. *Student services:* Campus employment opportunities, career counseling, free psychological counseling, low-cost health insurance, writing training. *Library facilities:* Southern New England School of Law Library. *Online resources:* library catalog, web page. *Collection:* 48,225 titles, 1,100 serial subscriptions, 246 audiovisual materials.

Computer facilities: 30 computers available on campus for general student use. A campuswide network can be accessed. Online class registration, email, listserves, financial aid are available. *Web address:* http://www.snesl.edu/.

General Application Contact: Nancy Fitzsimmons Hebert, Director of Admissions, 508-998-9400 Ext. 113, Fax: 508-998-9561, E-mail: nhebert@snesl.edu.

GRADUATE UNITS

Professional Program Students: 110 full-time (50 women), 124 part-time (77 women); includes 68 minority (41 African Americans, 15 Asian Americans or Pacific Islanders, 12 Hispanic Americans), 7 international. *Faculty:* 12 full-time (5 women), 25 part-time/adjunct (9 women). Expenses: Contact institution. *Financial support:* Research assistantships, scholarships/grants, tuition waivers (full and partial), and summer stipends available. Support available to part-time students. Financial award application deadline: 6/30; financial award applicants required to submit FAFSA. *Degree program information:* Part-time and evening/weekend programs available. Offers law (JD). *Application deadline:* For fall admission, 6/30 for domestic students. Applications are processed on a rolling basis. *Application fee:* $50. *Application Contact:* Nancy Fitzsimmons Hebert, Director of Admission, 508-998-9400 Ext. 113, Fax: 508-998-9561, E-mail: nhebert@snesl.edu. *Dean,* Robert V. Ward, 508-998-9600 Ext. 170, Fax: 508-998-9561, E-mail: rward@snesl.edu.

SOUTHERN NEW HAMPSHIRE UNIVERSITY, Manchester, NH 03106-1045

General Information Independent, coed, comprehensive institution. *Graduate housing:* Room and/or apartments available on a first-come, first-served basis to single students; on-campus housing not available to married students.

GRADUATE UNITS

School of Business *Degree program information:* Part-time and evening/weekend programs available. Postbaccalaureate distance learning degree programs offered (no on-campus study). Offers accounting (MS); business administration (MBA, Certificate); finance (MS); hospitality and tourism leadership (Certificate); information technology (MS, Certificate); information technology/international business (Certificate); integrated marketing communications (Certificate); international business (MS, DBA); marketing (MS); operations and project management (MS); organizational leadership (MS); project management (Certificate); sport management (MS). Electronic applications accepted.

School of Community Economic Development *Degree program information:* Part-time and evening/weekend programs available. Offers community economic development (MA, MBA, MS, PhD). Electronic applications accepted.

School of Education *Degree program information:* Part-time and evening/weekend programs available. Postbaccalaureate distance learning degree programs offered (no on-campus study). Offers business education (MS); child development (M Ed); computer technology education (Certificate); curriculum and instruction (M Ed); education (M Ed, CAS); elementary education (M Ed); general special education (Certificate); school business administrator (Certificate); secondary education (M Ed); training and development (Certificate). Electronic applications accepted.

School of Liberal Arts *Degree program information:* Part-time and evening/weekend programs available. Offers clinical services for adults psychiatric disabilities (Certificate); clinical services for children and adolescents with psychiatric disabilities (Certificate); clinical services for persons with co-occurring substance abuse and psychiatric disabilities (Certificate); community mental health (MS); fiction writing (MFA); non-fiction writing (MFA); teaching English as a foreign language (MS). Electronic applications accepted.

SOUTHERN OREGON UNIVERSITY, Ashland, OR 97520

General Information State-supported, coed, comprehensive institution. *Graduate housing:* Rooms and/or apartments available on a first-come, first-served basis to single and married students. *Research affiliation:* U.S. Forest Service (biology, ecology studies), U.S. Fish and Wildlife Service (forensics), Oregon Shakespeare Festival, Crater Lake National Park (scientific studies), Bureau of Land Management (ecological studies), Bear Creek Corporation (environmental studies).

GRADUATE UNITS

Graduate Studies *Degree program information:* Part-time programs available. Electronic applications accepted.

School of Arts and Letters Offers music (MA, MS). Electronic applications accepted.

School of Business Offers business (MA Ed, MIM, MS Ed). Electronic applications accepted.

School of Sciences *Degree program information:* Part-time programs available. Offers environmental education (MA, MS); mathematics/computer science (MA, MS); science (MA, MS).

School of Social Sciences Offers applied psychology (MAP); elementary education (MA Ed, MS Ed); human service-organizational training and development (MA, MS); secondary education (MA Ed, MS Ed); social science (MA, MS); social science, health and physical education (MA, MA Ed, MAP, MAT, MS, MS Ed); teaching (MAT).

SOUTHERN POLYTECHNIC STATE UNIVERSITY, Marietta, GA 30060-2896

General Information State-supported, coed, comprehensive institution. *Enrollment:* 4,818 graduate, professional, and undergraduate students; 197 full-time matriculated graduate/professional students (67 women), 357 part-time matriculated graduate/professional students (122 women). *Enrollment by degree level:* 515 master's, 39 other advanced degrees. *Graduate faculty:* 62 full-time (21 women), 17 part-time/adjunct (7 women). Tuition, state resident: full-time $2752; part-time $172 per semester hour. Tuition, nonresident: full-time $10,992; part-time $687 per semester hour. *Required fees:* $365 per semester. *Graduate housing:* Room and/or apartments available on a first-come, first-served basis to single students; on-campus housing not available to married students. Typical cost: $5520 per year ($7990 including board). Room and board charges vary according to housing facility selected. Housing application deadline: 8/1. *Student services:* Campus employment opportunities, campus safety program, career counseling, exercise/wellness program, free psychological counseling, international student services, low-cost health insurance, multicultural affairs office, services for students with disabilities. *Library facilities:* Lawrence V. Johnson Library. *Online resources:* library catalog, web page, access to other libraries' catalogs. *Collection:* 125,636 titles, 1,016 serial subscriptions, 290 audiovisual materials. *Research affiliation:* Cyber Object (information technology), Microsoft (software security).

Computer facilities: 1,300 computers available on campus for general student use. A campuswide network can be accessed from student residence rooms and from off campus. Online class registration is available. *Web address:* http://www.spsu.edu/.

General Application Contact: Nikki Palamiotis, Director of Graduate Studies, 678-915-4276, Fax: 678-915-7292, E-mail: npalamio@spsu.edu.

GRADUATE UNITS

Division of Engineering Students: 1 full-time (0 women), 38 part-time (11 women); includes 14 minority (9 African Americans, 2 Asian Americans or Pacific Islanders, 3 Hispanic Americans). Average age 36. 27 applicants, 85% accepted, 17 enrolled. *Faculty:* 3 full-time (2 women), 2 part-time/adjunct (1 woman). Expenses: Contact institution. *Financial support:* In 2008–09, 6 students received support. In 2008, 6 master's awarded. *Degree program information:* Part-time and evening/weekend programs available. Offers systems engineering (MS, Graduate Certificate). *Application deadline:* For fall admission, 7/1 priority date for domestic students, 5/1 priority date for international students; for spring admission, 11/1 priority date for domestic students, 9/1 priority date for international students. Applications are processed on a rolling basis. *Application fee:* $20. Electronic applications accepted. *Application Contact:* Nikki Palamiotis, Director of Graduate Studies, 678-915-4276, Fax: 678-915-7292, E-mail: npalamio@spsu.edu. *Associate Dean*, Dr. Tom Currin, 678-915-7482, Fax: 678-915-5527, E-mail: tcurrin@spsu.edu.

School of Architecture, Civil Engineering Technology and Construction Students: 35 full-time (9 women), 21 part-time (4 women); includes 17 minority (13 African Americans, 3 Asian Americans or Pacific Islanders, 1 Hispanic American), 21 international. Average age 34. 50 applicants, 52% accepted, 17 enrolled. *Faculty:* 7 full-time (0 women), 1 part-time/adjunct (0 women). Expenses: Contact institution. *Financial support:* In 2008–09, 16 students received support, including 12 research assistantships with tuition reimbursements available (averaging $1,500 per year); career-related internships or fieldwork, scholarships/grants, and unspecified assistantships also available. Support available to part-time students. Financial award application deadline: 5/1; financial award applicants required to submit FAFSA. In 2008, 17 master's awarded. *Degree program information:* Part-time and evening/weekend programs available. Offers architecture, civil engineering technology and construction (MS); construction management (MS). *Application deadline:* For fall admission, 7/1 priority date for domestic students, 5/1 priority date for international students; for spring admission, 11/1 priority date for domestic students, 9/1 priority date for international students. Applications are processed on a rolling basis. *Application fee:* $20. Electronic applications accepted. *Application Contact:* Nikki Palamiotis, Director of Graduate Studies, 678-915-4276, Fax: 678-915-7292, E-mail: npalamio@spsu.edu. *Dean*, Dr. Wilson Barnes, 678-915-5481, Fax: 678-915-3945, E-mail: wbarnes@spsu.edu.

School of Arts and Sciences Students: 5 full-time (4 women), 38 part-time (25 women); includes 13 minority (12 African Americans, 1 Hispanic American), 3 international. Average age 38. 38 applicants, 68% accepted, 23 enrolled. *Faculty:* 4 full-time (3 women), 1 part-time/adjunct (0 women). Expenses: Contact institution. *Financial support:* In 2008–09, 14 students received support, including 1 research assistantship with full tuition reimbursement available (averaging $4,000 per year); career-related internships or fieldwork, Federal Work-Study, scholarships/grants, and unspecified assistantships also available. Support available to part-time students. Financial award application deadline: 5/1; financial award applicants required to submit FAFSA. In 2008, 10 master's awarded. *Degree program information:* Part-time and evening/weekend programs available. Postbaccalaureate distance learning degree programs offered (minimal on-campus study). Offers arts and sciences (MS, Graduate Certificate); communications management (Graduate Certificate); content development (Graduate Certificate); information design and communication (MS); instructional design (Graduate Certificate); technical and professional communication (Graduate Certificate); visual communication and graphics (Graduate Certificate). *Application deadline:* For fall admission, 7/1 priority date for domestic students, 5/1 priority date for international students; for spring admission, 11/1 priority date for domestic students, 9/1 priority date for international students. Applications are processed on a rolling basis. *Application fee:* $20. Electronic applications accepted. *Application Contact:* Nikki Palamiotis, Director of Graduate Studies, 678-915-4276, Fax: 678-915-7292, E-mail: npalamio@spsu.edu. *Dean*, Dr. Alan Gabrielli, 678-915-7464, Fax: 678-915-7292, E-mail: agabriel@spsu.edu.

School of Computing and Software Engineering Students: 81 full-time (26 women), 90 part-time (30 women); includes 44 minority (27 African Americans, 16 Asian Americans or Pacific Islanders, 1 Hispanic American), 72 international. Average age 32. 133 applicants, 63% accepted, 58 enrolled. *Faculty:* 22 full-time (7 women), 4 part-time/adjunct (2 women). Expenses: Contact institution. *Financial support:* In 2008–09, 44 students received support, including research assistantships with full tuition reimbursements available (averaging $1,500 per year), teaching assistantships with full and partial tuition reimbursements available (averaging $1,500 per year); career-related internships or fieldwork, scholarships/grants, and unspecified assistantships also available. Support available to part-time students. Financial award application deadline: 5/1; financial award applicants required to submit FAFSA. In 2008, 70 master's awarded. *Degree program information:* Part-time and evening/weekend programs available. Postbaccalaureate distance learning degree programs offered. Offers business continuity (Graduate Certificate); computer science (MS, Graduate Certificate, Graduate Transition Certificate); computing and software engineering (MS, MS SwE, MSIT, Graduate Certificate, Graduate Transition Certificate); information security and assurance (Graduate Certificate); information technology (MSIT, Graduate Certificate, Graduate Transition Certificate); software engineering (MSSWE, Graduate Certificate). *Application deadline:* For fall admission, 7/1 priority date for domestic students, 5/1 priority date for international students; for spring admission, 11/1 priority date for domestic students, 9/1 priority date for international students. Applications are processed on a rolling basis. *Application fee:* $20. Electronic applications accepted. *Application Contact:* Nikki Palamiotis, Director of Graduate Studies, 678-915-4276, Fax: 678-915-7292, E-mail: npalamio@spsu.edu. *Dean*, Dr. Han Reichgelt, 678-915-7399, Fax: 678-915-5577, E-mail: hreichge@spsu.edu.

School of Engineering Technology and Management Students: 75 full-time (28 women), 170 part-time (52 women); includes 82 minority (67 African Americans, 11 Asian Americans or Pacific Islanders, 4 Hispanic Americans), 73 international. Average age 34. 167 applicants, 65% accepted, 81 enrolled. *Faculty:* 26 full-time (9 women), 9 part-time/adjunct (4 women). Expenses: Contact institution. *Financial support:* In 2008–09, 60 students received support, including 13 research assistantships with tuition reimbursements available (averaging $1,500 per year); teaching assistantships with partial tuition reimbursements available, career-related internships or fieldwork, scholarships/grants, and unspecified assistantships also available. Support available to part-time students. Financial award application deadline: 5/1; financial award applicants required to submit FAFSA. In 2008, 78 master's awarded. *Degree program information:* Part-time and evening/weekend programs available. Postbaccalaureate distance learning degree programs offered. Offers accounting (MSA); business administration (MBA, Graduate Certificate); engineering technology and management (MBA, MS, MSA, Graduate Certificate); engineering technology/electrical (MS); quality assurance (MS, Graduate Certificate). *Application deadline:* For fall admission, 7/1 priority date for domestic students, 5/1 priority date for international students; for spring admission, 11/1 priority date for domestic students, 9/1 priority date for international students. Applications are processed on a rolling basis. *Application fee:* $20. Electronic applications accepted. *Application Contact:* Nikki Palamiotis, Director of Graduate Studies, 678-915-4276, Fax: 678-915-7292, E-mail: npalamio@spsu.edu. *Dean*, Dr. Jeff Ray, 678-915-7205, Fax: 678-915-7134, E-mail: jray@spsu.edu.

SOUTHERN UNIVERSITY AND AGRICULTURAL AND MECHANICAL COLLEGE, Baton Rouge, LA 70813

General Information State-supported, coed, university. CGS member. *Graduate housing:* Room and/or apartments available on a first-come, first-served basis to single students; on-campus housing not available to married students. Housing application deadline: 6/30. *Research affiliation:* NASA (mechanical engineering), Michigan State University (language screening of African-Americans), University of Georgia at Athens (substance abuse prevention), University of Alabama (diabetes), NASA (drinking water remote sensing), Livingston Observatory (gravitational waves/cosmic gravity waves/black waves).

GRADUATE UNITS

College of Business Offers business (MBA).

Graduate School *Degree program information:* Part-time programs available. Offers science/mathematics education (PhD); special education (M Ed, PhD).

College of Agricultural, Family and Consumer Sciences Offers urban forestry (MS).

College of Arts and Humanities Offers arts and humanities (MA); mass communications (MA); social sciences (MA).

College of Education Offers administration and supervision (M Ed); counselor education (MA); education (M Ed, MA, MS, PhD); educational leadership (M Ed); elementary education (M Ed); media (M Ed); mental health counseling (MA); secondary education (M Ed); therapeutic recreation (MS).

College of Engineering Offers engineering (ME).

College of Sciences *Degree program information:* Part-time programs available. Offers analytical chemistry (MS); biochemistry (MS); biology (MS); environmental sciences (MS); information systems (MS); inorganic chemistry (MS); mathematics (MS); micro/minicomputer architecture (MS); operating systems (MS); organic chemistry (MS); physical chemistry (MS); physics (MS); rehabilitation counseling (MS); sciences (MA, MS).

Nelson Mandela School of Public Policy and Urban Affairs Offers criminal justice (MS); public administration (MPA); public policy (PhD); public policy and urban affairs (MA, MPA, MS, PhD); social sciences (MA).

School of Nursing *Degree program information:* Part-time programs available. Offers educator/administrator (PhD); family health nursing (MSN); family nurse practitioner (Post Master's Certificate); geriatric nurse practitioner/gerontology (PhD).

Southern University Law Center *Degree program information:* Part-time and evening/weekend programs available. Offers law (JD). Electronic applications accepted.

SOUTHERN UNIVERSITY AT NEW ORLEANS, New Orleans, LA 70126-1009

General Information State-supported, coed, primarily women, comprehensive institution. *Graduate housing:* On-campus housing not available.

GRADUATE UNITS

School of Social Work *Degree program information:* Part-time and evening/weekend programs available. Offers social work (MSW).

SOUTHERN UTAH UNIVERSITY, Cedar City, UT 84720-2498

General Information State-supported, coed, comprehensive institution. *Graduate housing:* Room and/or apartments available on a first-come, first-served basis to single students; on-campus housing not available to married students.

GRADUATE UNITS

College of Education *Degree program information:* Part-time programs available. Offers education (M Ed, MS); sports conditioning (MS).

College of Humanities and Social Sciences Offers communication (MA); humanities and social sciences (MA, MS); public administration (MS).

College of Performing and Visual Arts Offers arts administration (MFA); performing and visual arts (MFA).

College of Science Offers forensic science (MS); science (MS).

School of Business *Degree program information:* Part-time programs available. Offers accounting (M Acc); business (M Acc, MBA); business administration (MBA).

SOUTHERN WESLEYAN UNIVERSITY, Central, SC 29630-1020

General Information Independent-religious, coed, comprehensive institution. *Graduate housing:* On-campus housing not available.

GRADUATE UNITS

Program in Business Administration *Degree program information:* Evening/weekend programs available. Offers business administration (MBA).

Program in Christian Ministries *Degree program information:* Evening/weekend programs available. Offers Christian ministries (M Min).

Program in Education *Degree program information:* Evening/weekend programs available. Offers education (M Ed). Program also offered at Greenville, SC site.

Program in Management *Degree program information:* Evening/weekend programs available. Offers management (MSM).

SOUTH TEXAS COLLEGE OF LAW, Houston, TX 77002-7000

General Information Independent, coed, graduate-only institution. *Enrollment by degree level:* 1,267 first professional. *Graduate faculty:* 59 full-time (21 women), 65 part-time/adjunct (19 women). *Student services:* Campus employment opportunities, campus safety program, career counseling, international student services, services for students with disabilities. *Library facilities:* The Fred Parks Law Library. *Online resources:* library catalog, web page, access to other libraries' catalogs. *Collection:* 241,948 titles, 123,535 serial subscriptions, 772 audiovisual materials.

Computer facilities: 92 computers available on campus for general student use. A campuswide network can be accessed from off campus. Online class registration is available. *Web address:* http://www.stcl.edu/.

General Application Contact: Alicia K. Cramer, Assistant Dean of Admissions, 713-646-1810, Fax: 713-646-2906, E-mail: admissions@stcl.edu.

GRADUATE UNITS

Professional Program Students: 953 full-time (442 women), 314 part-time (134 women); includes 305 minority (53 African Americans, 8 American Indian/Alaska Native, 124 Asian Americans or Pacific Islanders, 120 Hispanic Americans), 4 international. Average age 27. 2,360 applicants, 45% accepted, 410 enrolled. *Faculty:* 60 full-time (22 women), 64 part-time/adjunct (18 women). Expenses: Contact institution. *Financial support:* In 2008–09, 1,224 students received support. Federal Work-Study, scholarships/grants, and tuition waivers (full and partial) available. Support available to part-time students. Financial award application deadline: 5/1; financial award applicants required to submit FAFSA. In 2008, 362 JDs awarded. *Degree program information:* Part-time and evening/weekend programs available. Offers law (JD). *Application deadline:* For fall admission, 2/15 for domestic and international students; for spring admission, 10/1 for domestic and international students. *Application fee:* $50. Electronic applications accepted. *Application Contact:* Alicia K. Cramer, Assistant Dean of Admissions, 713-646-1810, Fax: 713-646-2906, E-mail: admissions@stcl.edu. *President and Dean*, James J. Alfini, 713-646-1819, Fax: 713-646-2909, E-mail: jalfini@stcl.edu.

SOUTH UNIVERSITY, Montgomery, AL 36116-1120

General Information Proprietary, coed, comprehensive institution.

GRADUATE UNITS

Program in Business Administration Offers business administration (MBA); healthcare administration (MBA).

Program in Professional Counseling Offers professional counseling (MA).

SOUTH UNIVERSITY, West Palm Beach, FL 33409

General Information Proprietary, coed, comprehensive institution.

GRADUATE UNITS

Program in Business Administration Offers business administration (MBA); healthcare administration (MBA).

Program in Professional Counseling Offers professional counseling (MA).

SOUTH UNIVERSITY, Savannah, GA 31406

General Information Proprietary, coed, comprehensive institution.

GRADUATE UNITS

Graduate Programs

College of Arts and Sciences Offers arts and sciences (MA); professional counseling (MA).

College of Business Offers business (MBA).

College of Health Professions Offers anesthesiologist assistant (MM Sc); health professions (MM Sc, MS); physician assistant studies (MS).

School of Pharmacy Offers pharmacy (Pharm D).

SOUTH UNIVERSITY, Columbia, SC 29203

General Information Proprietary, coed, comprehensive institution.

South University (continued)

GRADUATE UNITS

Program in Business Administration Offers business administration (MBA); healthcare administration (MBA).

Program in Professional Counseling Offers professional counseling (MA).

SOUTHWEST ACUPUNCTURE COLLEGE, Santa Fe, NM 87505

General Information Private, coed, primarily women, graduate-only institution. *Graduate housing:* On-campus housing not available.

GRADUATE UNITS

Program in Oriental Medicine, Albuquerque Campus Students: 78 full-time (63 women), 5 part-time (3 women); includes 11 minority (2 African Americans, 3 American Indian/Alaska Native, 2 Asian Americans or Pacific Islanders, 4 Hispanic Americans). Average age 38. 22 applicants, 95% accepted, 14 enrolled. *Faculty:* 20 part-time/adjunct (6 women). Expenses: Contact institution. *Financial support:* In 2008–09, 90 students received support. Scholarships/grants available. Financial award applicants required to submit FAFSA. In 2008, 19 master's awarded. *Degree program information:* Part-time programs available. Offers Oriental medicine (MS). *Application deadline:* Applications are processed on a rolling basis. *Application fee:* $100. Electronic applications accepted. *Application Contact:* Dr. Li Xu, E-mail: drding@acupuncturecollege.edu. *Campus Director,* Dr. Li Xu, 505-888-8898, Fax: 505-888-1380, E-mail: drlixu@acupuncturecollege.edu.

Program in Oriental Medicine, Boulder Campus *Degree program information:* Part-time programs available. Offers Oriental medicine (MS).

Program in Oriental Medicine, Santa Fe Campus Students: 52 full-time (42 women), 4 part-time (all women); includes 4 minority (1 African American, 1 American Indian/Alaska Native, 2 Hispanic Americans). Average age 38. 28 applicants, 89% accepted, 17 enrolled. *Faculty:* 23 part-time/adjunct (10 women). Expenses: Contact institution. *Financial support:* Scholarships/grants available. Financial award applicants required to submit FAFSA. In 2008, 18 master's awarded. *Degree program information:* Part-time programs available. Offers Oriental medicine (MS). *Application deadline:* Applications are processed on a rolling basis. *Application fee:* $100. Electronic applications accepted. *Application Contact:* Dr. Dawei Shao, Academic Dean, 505-438-8884, Fax: 505-438-8883, E-mail: drshao@acupuncturecollege.edu. *Campus Director,* Richard Shcolnik, 505-438-8884, Fax: 505-438-8883, E-mail: Richard@acupuncturecollege.edu.

SOUTHWEST BAPTIST UNIVERSITY, Bolivar, MO 65613-2597

General Information Independent-religious, coed, comprehensive institution. *Enrollment:* 3,656 graduate, professional, and undergraduate students; 347 full-time matriculated graduate/professional students (235 women), 158 part-time matriculated graduate/professional students (113 women). *Enrollment by degree level:* 349 master's, 113 doctoral, 43 other advanced degrees. *Graduate faculty:* 15 full-time (7 women), 49 part-time/adjunct (30 women). *Graduate housing:* Room and/or apartments available on a first-come, first-served basis to single students; on-campus housing not available to married students. Typical cost: $2666 per year ($5166 including board). Room and board charges vary according to board plan. *Student services:* Campus employment opportunities, campus safety program, career counseling, free psychological counseling, international student services, low-cost health insurance, services for students with disabilities, teacher training. *Library facilities:* Harriett K. Hutchens Library plus 3 others. *Online resources:* library catalog, web page, access to other libraries' catalogs. *Collection:* 185,703 titles, 22,388 serial subscriptions, 11,553 audiovisual materials.

Computer facilities: 261 computers available on campus for general student use. A campuswide network can be accessed from student residence rooms and from off campus. Online class registration is available. *Web address:* http://www.sbuniv.edu/.

General Application Contact: Dr. Gordon Dutile, Provost, 417-328-1601, Fax: 417-328-1514, E-mail: gdutile@sbuniv.edu.

SOUTHWEST COLLEGE OF NATUROPATHIC MEDICINE AND HEALTH SCIENCES, Tempe, AZ 85282

General Information Independent, coed, graduate-only institution. *Enrollment by degree level:* 330 doctoral. *Graduate faculty:* 19 full-time (7 women), 49 part-time/adjunct (27 women). *Tuition:* Full-time $24,000; part-time $4682 per quarter. *Required fees:* $809; $238 per credit. $15 per quarter. One-time fee: $749. *Graduate housing:* On-campus housing not available. *Student services:* Campus employment opportunities, career counseling, free psychological counseling, low-cost health insurance. *Library facilities:* SCNM Library plus 1 other. *Online resources:* library catalog, web page, access to other libraries' catalogs. *Collection:* 15,500 titles, 100 serial subscriptions, 3,804 audiovisual materials. *Research affiliation:* University of Arizona (biochemistry/herbal medicine), Translational Genomics Research Institute (genomics/herbal medicine), Arizona State University, Biodesign Institute (genomics/herbal medicine).

Computer facilities: 23 computers available on campus for general student use. A campuswide network can be accessed. *Web address:* http://www.scnm.edu/.

General Application Contact: Alison Scott, Assistant Director of Admissions, 480-858-9100 Ext. 213, Fax: 480-858-9116, E-mail: a.scott@scnm.edu.

GRADUATE UNITS

Program in Naturopathic Medicine Students: 325 full-time (246 women), 5 part-time (3 women); includes 73 minority (36 African Americans, 4 American Indian/Alaska Native, 18 Asian Americans or Pacific Islanders, 15 Hispanic Americans), 13 international. Average age 31. 227 applicants, 65% accepted, 73 enrolled. *Faculty:* 19 full-time (7 women), 49 part-time/adjunct (27 women). Expenses: Contact institution. *Financial support:* Federal Work-Study and scholarships/grants available. Support available to part-time students. Financial award application deadline: 7/1; financial award applicants required to submit FAFSA. In 2008, 69 doctorates awarded. Offers naturopathic medicine (ND). *Application deadline:* For fall admission, 2/1 priority date for domestic students; for spring admission, 11/1 priority date for domestic students. Applications are processed on a rolling basis. *Application fee:* $65 ($90 for international students). *Application Contact:* Alison Scott, Assistant Director of Admissions, 480-8589100 Ext. 213, Fax: 480-8589116, E-mail: a.scott@scnm.edu. *Executive Vice President of Academic and Clinical Affairs,* Dr. Christine Girard, 480-858-9100 Ext. 114, Fax: 480-222-9860, E-mail: c.girard@scnm.edu.

SOUTHWESTERN ADVENTIST UNIVERSITY, Keene, TX 76059

General Information Independent-religious, coed, comprehensive institution. *Graduate housing:* Rooms and/or apartments available on a first-come, first-served basis to single and married students. Housing application deadline: 8/31.

GRADUATE UNITS

Business Department, Graduate Program *Degree program information:* Part-time and evening/weekend programs available. Offers accounting (MBA); finance (MBA); management / leadership (MBA).

Education Department, Graduate Program *Degree program information:* Part-time and evening/weekend programs available. Offers curriculum and instruction with reading emphasis (M Ed); educational leadership (M Ed).

SOUTHWESTERN ASSEMBLIES OF GOD UNIVERSITY, Waxahachie, TX 75165-5735

General Information Independent-religious, coed, comprehensive institution. *Graduate housing:* Room and/or apartments guaranteed to single students.

GRADUATE UNITS

Thomas F. Harrison School of Graduate Studies *Degree program information:* Part-time and evening/weekend programs available. Postbaccalaureate distance learning degree programs offered (minimal on-campus study). Offers Bible and theology (MS); Biblical studies (M Div); Christian school administration (MS); counseling (M Div); counseling psychology (clinical) (MCP); cross cultural missions (M Div); curriculum development (MS); early education administration (M Ed); history (MA); human services counseling (MS); middle and secondary education (M Ed); practical theology (M Div); theological studies (M Div). Electronic applications accepted.

SOUTHWESTERN BAPTIST THEOLOGICAL SEMINARY, Fort Worth, TX 76122-0000

General Information Independent-religious, coed, primarily men, graduate-only institution. *Enrollment by degree level:* 2,067 first professional, 462 doctoral, 142 other advanced degrees. *Graduate faculty:* 145 full-time (20 women), 64 part-time/adjunct (12 women). *Tuition:* Full-time $3460. *Required fees:* $626. *Graduate housing:* Rooms and/or apartments available on a first-come, first-served basis to single and married students. Typical cost: $1920 per year ($4200 including board) for single students; $4980 per year ($4980 including board) for married students. Room and board charges vary according to board plan, campus/location and housing facility selected. *Student services:* Campus employment opportunities, campus safety program, career counseling, exercise/wellness program, free psychological counseling, international student services, low-cost health insurance. *Library facilities:* A. Webb Roberts Library plus 3 others. *Online resources:* library catalog, web page, access to other libraries' catalogs. *Collection:* 858,831 titles, 2,150 serial subscriptions, 49,000 audiovisual materials. *Research affiliation:* Campus Crusade for Christ/Jesus Film Project (evangelical missions), DAWN Disciple A Whole Nation (evangelical missions).

Computer facilities: A campuswide network can be accessed from off campus. *Web address:* http://www.swbts.edu/.

General Application Contact: Adam Groza, Director of Admissions, 817-923-1921 Ext. 2700, Fax: 817-921-8757, E-mail: admissions@swbts.edu.

GRADUATE UNITS

School of Church Music Expenses: Contact institution. *Financial support:* Teaching assistantships, career-related internships or fieldwork, institutionally sponsored loans, and scholarships/grants available. Support available to part-time students. Financial award application deadline: 11/1. *Degree program information:* Part-time programs available. Offers church music (MACM, MAWSHP, MM, DMA, PhD, SPCM). *Application deadline:* For fall admission, 7/15 priority date for domestic students, 6/15 priority date for international students; for spring admission, 12/15 priority date for domestic students, 11/15 priority date for international students. Applications are processed on a rolling basis. Electronic applications accepted. *Application Contact:* Adam Groza, Director of Admissions, 817-923-1921 Ext. 2700, Fax: 817-921-8757, E-mail: admissions@swbts.edu. *Dean,* Dr. Stephen Johnson, 817-923-1921 Ext. 3111, Fax: 817-921-8762, E-mail: sjohnson@swbts.edu.

School of Educational Ministries Expenses: Contact institution. *Financial support:* Teaching assistantships, career-related internships or fieldwork, institutionally sponsored loans, scholarships/grants, and tuition waivers (partial) available. Support available to part-time students. Financial award application deadline: 11/1. *Degree program information:* Part-time and evening/weekend programs available. Offers educational ministries (MA Comm, MACC, MACCM, MACE, MACSE, MAMFC, DEM, PhD, SPEM). *Application deadline:* For fall admission, 7/15 priority date for domestic students, 6/15 priority date for international students; for spring admission, 12/15 priority date for domestic students, 11/15 priority date for international students. Applications are processed on a rolling basis. Electronic applications accepted. *Application Contact:* Adam Groza, Director of Admissions, 817-923-1921 Ext. 2700, Fax: 817-921-8757, E-mail: admissions@swbts.edu. *Dean,* Dr. Wes Black, 817-923-1921 Ext. 2140, Fax: 817-921-8763, E-mail: wblack@swbts.edu.

School of Theology Expenses: Contact institution. *Financial support:* Teaching assistantships, career-related internships or fieldwork, institutionally sponsored loans, scholarships/grants, and tuition waivers (partial) available. Support available to part-time students. Financial award application deadline: 11/1. *Degree program information:* Part-time and evening/weekend programs available. Offers theology (M Div, MA Islamic, MA Miss, MA Th, Th M, D Min, PhD, SPTH). *Application deadline:* For fall admission, 7/15 priority date for domestic students, 6/15 priority date for international students; for spring admission, 12/15 priority date for domestic students, 11/15 priority date for international students. Applications are processed on a rolling basis. Electronic applications accepted. *Application Contact:* Adam Groza, Director of Admissions, 817-923-1921 Ext. 2700, Fax: 817-921-8757, E-mail: admissions@swbts.edu. *Dean,* Dr. David Allen, 817-923-1921 Ext. 4200, Fax: 817-921-8767, E-mail: dallen@swbts.edu.

SOUTHWESTERN CHRISTIAN UNIVERSITY, Bethany, OK 73008-0340

General Information Independent-religious, coed, comprehensive institution.

GRADUATE UNITS

Program in Ministry *Degree program information:* Part-time programs available. Offers church planting (M Min); church revitalization and renewal (M Min); intercultural studies (M Min); leadership (M Min); life coaching (M Min); pastoral ministries (M Min); work place ministries (M Min). Electronic applications accepted.

SOUTHWESTERN COLLEGE, Winfield, KS 67156-2499

General Information Independent-religious, coed, comprehensive institution. *Enrollment:* 1,823 graduate, professional, and undergraduate students; 131 full-time matriculated graduate/professional students (51 women), 168 part-time matriculated graduate/professional students (96 women). *Enrollment by degree level:* 299 master's. *Graduate faculty:* 7 full-time (2 women), 35 part-time/adjunct (18 women). *Tuition:* Full-time $6970; part-time $387 per credit. Tuition and fees vary according to class time, course load, campus/location and program. *Graduate housing:* Rooms and/or apartments available on a first-come, first-served basis to single and married students. Typical cost: $2586 per year ($5620 including board) for single students; $3693 per year for married students. Room and board charges vary according to board plan and housing facility selected. Housing application deadline: 6/1. *Student services:* Campus employment opportunities, career counseling, services for students with disabilities, teacher training. *Library facilities:* Harold and Mary Ellen Deets Library plus 1 other. *Online resources:* library catalog, web page. *Collection:* 81,621 titles, 33,234 serial subscriptions, 9,597 audiovisual materials.

Computer facilities: 30 computers available on campus for general student use. A campuswide network can be accessed from student residence rooms and from off campus. Online class registration is available. *Web address:* http://www.sckans.edu/.

General Application Contact: Office of Graduate Admissions, 620-229-6000.

GRADUATE UNITS

Fifth-Year Graduate Programs Students: 20 full-time (7 women), 12 part-time (5 women); includes 10 minority (7 African Americans, 1 American Indian/Alaska Native, 2 Hispanic Americans), 1 international. Average age 24. 33 applicants, 94% accepted, 28 enrolled. *Faculty:* 9 part-time/adjunct (4 women). Expenses: Contact institution. *Financial support:* In 2008–09, 27 students received support. Federal Work-Study, tuition waivers (partial), and unspecified assistantships available. Financial award application deadline: 4/1; financial award applicants required to submit FAFSA. In 2008, 15 master's awarded. *Degree program information:* Part-time programs available. Offers leadership (MS); management (MBA); specialized ministries (MA). *Application deadline:* For fall admission, 8/24 priority date for domestic students; for spring admission, 12/1 priority date for domestic students. Applications are processed on a rolling basis. *Application fee:* $25. Electronic applications accepted. *Application Contact:* Marla Sexson, Director of Admissions, 800-846-1543 Ext. 6364, Fax: 620-229-6344, E-mail: marla.sexson@sckans.edu. *Vice President for Academic Affairs,* Dr. James Sheppard, 620-229-6227, Fax: 620-229-6224, E-mail: james.sheppard@sckans.edu.

Master of Education Programs Students: 9 full-time (8 women), 72 part-time (50 women); includes 13 minority (6 African Americans, 3 American Indian/Alaska Native, 4 Hispanic Americans), 1 international. Average age 38. 32 applicants, 100% accepted, 27 enrolled. *Faculty:* 2 full-time (0 women), 7 part-time/adjunct (6 women). Expenses: Contact institution. *Financial support:* In 2008–09, 41 students received support. Tuition waivers (partial) and unspecified assistantships available. Financial award application deadline: 4/1; financial award applicants required to submit FAFSA. In 2008, 16 master's awarded. *Degree program information:* Part-time and evening/weekend programs available. Postbaccalaureate distance learning degree programs offered (minimal on-campus study). Offers curriculum and instruction (M Ed); special education (M Ed); teaching (MA). *Application deadline:* For fall admission, 8/24 priority date for domestic students; for spring admission, 1/24 priority date for domestic students. Applications are processed on a rolling basis. *Application fee:* $25. Electronic applications accepted. *Application Contact:* Lindy Kralicek, Education Program Representative, 888-684-5335 Ext. 130, Fax: 316-688-5218, E-mail: lindy.kralicek@sckans.edu. *Director of Teacher Education*, Dr. David Hofmeister, 800-846-1543 Ext. 6115, Fax: 620-229-6341, E-mail: david.hofmeister@sckans.edu.

Professional Studies Programs Students: 100 full-time (36 women), 84 part-time (40 women); includes 27 minority (17 African Americans, 1 Asian American or Pacific Islander, 9 Hispanic Americans). Average age 37. 48 applicants, 100% accepted, 39 enrolled. *Faculty:* 2 full-time (0 women), 25 part-time/adjunct (12 women). Expenses: Contact institution. *Financial support:* In 2008–09, 133 students received support. Tuition waivers (partial) and unspecified assistantships available. Financial award application deadline: 4/1; financial award applicants required to submit FAFSA. In 2008, 64 master's awarded. *Degree program information:* Part-time and evening/weekend programs available. Postbaccalaureate distance learning degree programs offered (minimal on-campus study). Offers business administration (MBA); leadership (MS); management (MS); security administration (MS); specialized ministries (MA). *Application deadline:* Applications are processed on a rolling basis. *Application fee:* $0. Electronic applications accepted. *Application Contact:* Gail Cullen, Director of Academic Affairs, 888-684-5335 Ext. 203, Fax: 316-688-5218, E-mail: gail.cullen@sckans.edu. *Director of Academic Affairs*, Gail Cullen, 888-684-5335 Ext. 203, Fax: 316-688-5218, E-mail: gail.cullen@sckans.edu.

SOUTHWESTERN COLLEGE, Santa Fe, NM 87502-4788

General Information Independent, coed, primarily women, graduate-only institution. *Graduate housing:* On-campus housing not available.

GRADUATE UNITS

Program in Art Therapy/Counseling *Degree program information:* Part-time and evening/weekend programs available. Offers art therapy/counseling (MA).

Program in Counseling *Degree program information:* Part-time and evening/weekend programs available. Offers counseling (MA).

Program in Grief, Loss and Trauma Counseling *Degree program information:* Part-time and evening/weekend programs available. Postbaccalaureate distance learning degree programs offered (minimal on-campus study). Offers grief, loss and trauma counseling (MA, Certificate).

Program in Integral Somatic Psychology Offers integral somatic psychology (Certificate).

Program in Psychodrama and Action Methods Offers psychodrama and action methods (Certificate).

Program in Transformational Ecopsychology Offers transformational ecopsychology (Certificate).

SOUTHWESTERN LAW SCHOOL, Los Angeles, CA 90010

General Information Independent, coed, graduate-only institution. *Graduate housing:* On-campus housing not available.

GRADUATE UNITS

Graduate Program *Degree program information:* Part-time and evening/weekend programs available. Offers entertainment and media law (LL M); general studies (LL M); law (JD). Electronic applications accepted.

SOUTHWESTERN OKLAHOMA STATE UNIVERSITY, Weatherford, OK 73096-3098

General Information State-supported, coed, comprehensive institution. *Graduate housing:* Rooms and/or apartments available on a first-come, first-served basis to single and married students. Housing application deadline: 8/19. *Research affiliation:* Gulf Coast Research Laboratory.

GRADUATE UNITS

College of Arts and Sciences *Degree program information:* Part-time programs available. Offers art education (M Ed); arts and sciences (M Ed, MM); English (M Ed); mathematics (M Ed); music education (MM); natural sciences (M Ed); performance (MM); social sciences (M Ed).

College of Pharmacy Offers pharmacy (Pharm D).

College of Professional and Graduate Studies *Degree program information:* Part-time and evening/weekend programs available. Postbaccalaureate distance learning degree programs offered (minimal on-campus study).

School of Behavioral Sciences and Education *Degree program information:* Part-time and evening/weekend programs available. Postbaccalaureate distance learning degree programs offered (minimal on-campus study). Offers community counseling (M Ed); early childhood education (M Ed); educational administration (M Ed); elementary education (M Ed); health sciences and microbiology (M Ed); kinesiology (M Ed); parks and recreation management (M Ed); school counseling (M Ed); school psychology (MS); school psychometry (M Ed); secondary education (M Ed); special education (M Ed).

School of Business and Technology *Degree program information:* Part-time and evening/weekend programs available. Postbaccalaureate distance learning degree programs offered (minimal on-campus study). Offers business and technology (MBA). MBA distance learning degree program offered to Oklahoma residents only.

SOUTHWEST MINNESOTA STATE UNIVERSITY, Marshall, MN 56258

General Information State-supported, coed, comprehensive institution. *Enrollment:* 6,502 graduate, professional, and undergraduate students; 224 full-time matriculated graduate/professional students (158 women), 164 part-time matriculated graduate/professional students (98 women). *Enrollment by degree level:* 388 master's. *Graduate faculty:* 6 full-time (3 women), 16 part-time/adjunct (9 women). Tuition, state resident: full-time $5462; part-time $288 per credit. Tuition, nonresident: full-time $5462; part-time $288 per credit. *Required fees:* $36 per credit. Tuition and fees vary according to campus/location and program. *Graduate housing:* Room and/or apartments available to single students; on-campus housing not available to married students. Typical cost: $5462 (including board). Room and board charges vary according to board plan. *Student services:* Campus employment opportunities, campus safety program, career counseling, child daycare facilities, exercise/wellness program, free psychological counseling, international student services, low-cost health insurance, multicultural affairs office, services for students with disabilities, teacher training, writing training. *Library facilities:* Southwest Minnesota State University. *Online resources:* library catalog, web page, access to other libraries' catalogs. *Collection:* 394,508 titles, 301 serial subscriptions, 11,239 audiovisual materials.

Computer facilities: 420 computers available on campus for general student use. A campuswide network can be accessed from student residence rooms and from off campus. Online class registration is available. *Web address:* http://www.smsu.edu/.

General Application Contact: LeAnn Thooft, Interim Admissions Director, 507-537-6286, E-mail: LeAnn.Thooft@smsu.edu.

GRADUATE UNITS

Department of Business and Public Affairs Students: 10 full-time (5 women), 80 part-time (47 women); includes 10 minority (4 African Americans, 2 American Indian/Alaska Native, 3 Asian Americans or Pacific Islanders, 1 Hispanic American), 16 international. Average age 31. 38 applicants, 20 enrolled. *Faculty:* 7 full-time (2 women). Expenses: Contact institution. *Financial support:* Institutionally sponsored loans and unspecified assistantships available. Support available to part-time students. Financial award applicants required to submit FAFSA. In 2008, 33 master's awarded. *Degree program information:* Part-time and evening/weekend programs available. Postbaccalaureate distance learning degree programs offered (no on-campus study). Offers business administration (MBA); management (MS). *Application deadline:* For fall admission, 6/15 for international students; for spring admission, 11/15 for international students. Applications are processed on a rolling basis. *Application fee:* $20. Electronic applications accepted. *Application Contact:* CoriAnn Dahlager, Graduate Office Coordinator, 507-537-6819, Fax: 507-537-6227, E-mail: CoriAnn.Dahlager@smsu.edu. *Professor*, Dr. William Thomas, 507-537-7392, E-mail: Will.Thomas@smsu.edu.

Department of Education Students: 214 full-time (155 women), 84 part-time (64 women); includes 5 minority (1 African American, 2 Asian Americans or Pacific Islanders, 2 Hispanic Americans). Average age 34. 194 applicants, 172 enrolled. *Faculty:* 6 full-time (3 women), 9 part-time/adjunct (7 women). Expenses: Contact institution. *Financial support:* Institutionally sponsored loans and unspecified assistantships available. Support available to part-time students. Financial award applicants required to submit FAFSA. In 2008, 136 master's awarded. *Degree program information:* Part-time and evening/weekend programs available. Postbaccalaureate distance learning degree programs offered (no on-campus study). Offers education (MS); special education (MS). *Application deadline:* For fall admission, 6/15 for international students; for spring admission, 11/15 for international students. Applications are processed on a rolling basis. *Application fee:* $20. *Application Contact:* CoriAnn Dahlager, Graduate Office Coordinator, 507-537-6819, E-mail: CoriAnn.Dahlager@smsu.edu. *Dean of Business, Education and Professional Studies*, Dr. Donna Burgraff, 507-537-6218, E-mail: Donna.Burgraff@smsu.edu.

SPALDING UNIVERSITY, Louisville, KY 40203-2188

General Information Independent-religious, coed, comprehensive institution. CGS member. *Enrollment:* 1,712 graduate, professional, and undergraduate students; 368 full-time matriculated graduate/professional students (292 women), 277 part-time matriculated graduate/professional students (190 women). *Enrollment by degree level:* 423 master's, 219 doctoral, 3 other advanced degrees. *Graduate faculty:* 28 full-time (20 women), 27 part-time/adjunct (20 women). *Tuition:* Full-time $11,340; part-time $630 per credit hour. Tuition and fees vary according to program. *Graduate housing:* Room and/or apartments available on a first-come, first-served basis to single students; on-campus housing not available to married students. Typical cost: $3060 per year ($4560 including board). Room and board charges vary according to board plan. *Student services:* Campus employment opportunities, campus safety program, career counseling, exercise/wellness program, free psychological counseling, international student services, low-cost health insurance, services for students with disabilities, teacher training, writing training. *Library facilities:* Spalding Library. *Online resources:* library catalog, web page. *Collection:* 87,856 titles, 1,735 audiovisual materials.

Computer facilities: 80 computers available on campus for general student use. A campuswide network can be accessed. Online class registration is available. *Web address:* http://www.spalding.edu/.

General Application Contact: Admissions Office, 502-585-7111, E-mail: admissions@spalding.edu.

GRADUATE UNITS

Graduate Studies Students: 368 full-time (292 women), 277 part-time (190 women); includes 125 minority (105 African Americans, 4 American Indian/Alaska Native, 9 Asian Americans or Pacific Islanders, 7 Hispanic Americans), 39 international. Average age 35. 1,106 applicants, 80% accepted, 181 enrolled. *Faculty:* 28 full-time (20 women), 27 part-time/adjunct (20 women). Expenses: Contact institution. *Financial support:* In 2008–09, 282 students received support, including 48 research assistantships with partial tuition reimbursements available; career-related internships or fieldwork, Federal Work-Study, scholarships/grants, traineeships, and unspecified assistantships also available. Support available to part-time students. Financial award application deadline: 3/15; financial award applicants required to submit FAFSA. In 2008, 222 master's, 33 doctorates awarded. *Degree program information:* Part-time and evening/weekend programs available. *Application fee:* $30. *Application Contact:* Admissions Office, 502-585-7111, E-mail: admissions@spalding.edu. *Senior Vice President for Academic Affairs*, Dr. Randy Strickland, 502-585-9911 Ext. 2101, E-mail: rstrickland@spalding.edu.

College of Business and Communication Students: 29 full-time (22 women), 32 part-time (25 women); includes 12 minority (11 African Americans, 1 American Indian/Alaska Native). Average age 36. 48 applicants, 71% accepted, 18 enrolled. *Faculty:* 6 full-time (2 women). Expenses: Contact institution. *Financial support:* In 2008–09, 28 students received support. Application deadline: 3/15. In 2008, 18 master's awarded. *Degree program information:* Part-time and evening/weekend programs available. Offers business communication (MS). *Application deadline:* Applications are processed on a rolling basis. *Application fee:* $30. Electronic applications accepted. *Application Contact:* Debbie Pierce, Administrative Assistant, 502-585-9911 Ext. 2120, E-mail: cbc@spalding.edu. *Dean*, Dr. Diane Tobin, 502-585-9911 Ext. 2747, E-mail: dtobin@spalding.edu.

College of Education Students: 76 full-time (56 women), 152 part-time (93 women); includes 70 minority (66 African Americans, 1 American Indian/Alaska Native, 2 Asian Americans or Pacific Islanders, 1 Hispanic American), 35 international. Average age 37. 273 applicants, 86% accepted, 47 enrolled. *Faculty:* 6 full-time (3 women), 10 part-time/adjunct (8 women). Expenses: Contact institution. *Financial support:* In 2008–09, 68 students received support, including 7 research assistantships with partial tuition reimbursements available (averaging $3,810 per year); scholarships/grants, traineeships, and unspecified assistantships also available. Financial award application deadline: 3/15; financial award applicants required to submit FAFSA. In 2008, 66 master's, 14 doctorates awarded. *Degree program information:* Part-time and evening/weekend programs available. Offers education (MA, MAT, Ed D); elementary school education (MAT); general education (MA); high school education (MAT); leadership education (Ed D); middle school education (MAT); school administration (MA); special education (learning and behavioral disorders) (MAT). *Application deadline:* Applications are processed on a rolling basis. *Application fee:* $30. Electronic applications accepted. *Application Contact:* Admissions Office, 502-585-7111, E-mail: admissions@spalding.edu. *Dean*, Dr. Beverly Keepers, 502-588-7121, Fax: 502-585-7123, E-mail: bkeepers@spalding.edu.

College of Health and Natural Sciences Students: 97 full-time (90 women), 15 part-time (13 women); includes 9 minority (6 African Americans, 1 Asian American or Pacific Islander, 2 Hispanic Americans), 2 international. Average age 35. 172 applicants, 74% accepted, 40 enrolled. *Faculty:* 7 full-time (6 women), 2 part-time/adjunct (both women). Expenses: Contact institution. *Financial support:* In 2008–09, 66 students received support, including 4 research assistantships with partial tuition reimbursements available (averaging $2,869 per year); career-related internships or fieldwork, scholarships/grants, traineeships, and unspecified assistantships also available. Support available to part-time students. Financial award application deadline: 3/15; financial award applicants required to submit FAFSA. In 2008, 54 master's awarded. *Degree program information:* Part-time and evening/weekend programs available. Offers adult nurse practitioner (MSN); family nurse practitioner (MSN); health and natural sciences (MS, MSN); leadership in nursing and healthcare (MSN); occupational therapy (advanced-level) (MS); occupational therapy (entry-level) (MS); pediatric nurse practitioner (MSN). *Application Contact:* Admissions Office, 502-585-7111, E-mail: admissions@spalding.edu. *Interim Dean*, Dr. John James, 502-585-9911 Ext. 2434, E-mail: jjames@spalding.edu.

College of Social Sciences and Humanities Students: 166 full-time (124 women), 78 part-time (59 women); includes 34 minority (22 African Americans, 2 American Indian/Alaska Native, 6 Asian Americans or Pacific Islanders, 4 Hispanic Americans), 2 international. Average age 33. 486 applicants, 79% accepted, 66 enrolled. *Faculty:* 11 full-time (7 women), 11 part-time/adjunct (6 women). Expenses: Contact institution. *Financial support:* In 2008–09, 120 students received support, including 37 research assistantships with partial tuition reimbursements available (averaging $5,505 per year); career-related internships or fieldwork, Federal Work-Study, scholarships/grants, and unspecified assistantships also available. Financial award application deadline: 3/15; financial award applicants required to submit FAFSA. In 2008, 84 master's, 19 doctorates awarded. *Degree program*

Spalding University (continued)

information: Part-time and evening/weekend programs available. Postbaccalaureate distance learning degree programs offered (minimal on-campus study). Offers applied behavior analysis (MA); clinical psychology (MA, Psy D); social sciences and humanities (MA, MFA, MSW, Psy D); social work (MSW); writing (MFA). *Application fee:* $30. *Application Contact:* Admissions Office, 502-585-7111, E-mail: admissions@spalding.edu. *Dean,* Dr. John James, 502-585-9911 Ext. 2434, E-mail: jjames@spalding.edu.

SPERTUS INSTITUTE OF JEWISH STUDIES, Chicago, IL 60605-1901

General Information Independent, coed, graduate-only institution. *Enrollment by degree level:* 288 master's, 38 doctoral. *Graduate faculty:* 35 part-time/adjunct (12 women). *Graduate housing:* On-campus housing not available. *Student services:* Career counseling, grant writing training, international student services, writing training. *Library facilities:* Asher Library. *Online resources:* web page. *Collection:* 100,000 titles, 800 serial subscriptions.

Computer facilities: 10 computers available on campus for general student use. *Web address:* http://www.spertus.edu/.

General Application Contact: Natasha Tribble, Assistant Director of Recruitment and Alumni Affairs, 312-322-1707, Fax: 312-994-5360, E-mail: nwhiteside@spertus.edu.

GRADUATE UNITS

Graduate Programs *Degree program information:* Part-time and evening/weekend programs available. Postbaccalaureate distance learning degree programs offered (minimal on-campus study). Offers Jewish education (MAJ Ed); Jewish studies (MAJS, MSJE, MSJS, DJS, DSJS); nonprofit management (MSNM).

SPRING ARBOR UNIVERSITY, Spring Arbor, MI 49283-9799

General Information Independent-religious, coed, comprehensive institution. *Enrollment:* 3,973 graduate, professional, and undergraduate students; 714 full-time matriculated graduate/professional students (555 women), 522 part-time matriculated graduate/professional students (408 women). *Enrollment by degree level:* 1,236 master's. *Graduate faculty:* 28 full-time (10 women), 119 part-time/adjunct (53 women). *Tuition:* Full-time $5280; part-time $440 per credit hour. *Required fees:* $240; $150. Tuition and fees vary according to program. *Graduate housing:* Rooms and/or apartments available on a first-come, first-served basis to single and married students. Typical cost: $3250 per year ($6950 including board) for single students; $3250 per year ($6950 including board) for married students. Housing application deadline: 5/1. *Student services:* Campus employment opportunities, campus safety program, career counseling, services for students with disabilities. *Library facilities:* Hugh A. White Library. *Online resources:* library catalog, web page, access to other libraries' catalogs. *Collection:* 111,736 titles, 665 serial subscriptions, 3,775 audiovisual materials.

Computer facilities: 230 computers available on campus for general student use. A campuswide network can be accessed from student residence rooms and from off campus. Online class registration is available. *Web address:* http://www.arbor.edu/.

General Application Contact: John Ball, Coordinator of Admissions, 517-750-1459, E-mail: jball@arbor.edu.

GRADUATE UNITS

School of Arts and Sciences Students: 104 full-time (64 women), 38 part-time (24 women); includes 8 minority (7 African Americans, 1 Hispanic American), 1 international. Average age 42. *Faculty:* 6 full-time (1 woman), 11 part-time/adjunct (5 women). Expenses: Contact institution. *Financial support:* Applicants required to submit FAFSA. In 2008, 3 master's awarded. *Degree program information:* Part-time programs available. Postbaccalaureate distance learning degree programs offered (no on-campus study). Offers communication (MA); spiritual formation and leadership (MA). *Application fee:* $40. *Application Contact:* Dale Glinz, Lead Recruitment Specialist/Trainer, Graduate and Professional Studies, 517-750-6703, E-mail: dglinz@arbor.edu. *Chair of the Department of Communication,* Dr. Wally Metts, 517-750-1200 Ext. 1491, E-mail: wmetts@arbor.edu.

School of Business and Management Students: 65 full-time (37 women), 27 part-time (12 women); includes 19 minority (11 African Americans, 3 Asian Americans or Pacific Islanders, 5 Hispanic Americans), 3 international. Average age 36. 63 applicants, 63% accepted, 21 enrolled. *Faculty:* 7 full-time (1 woman), 5 part-time/adjunct (2 women). Expenses: Contact institution. *Financial support:* Career-related internships or fieldwork, scholarships/grants, and tuition waivers (partial) available. Support available to part-time students. Financial award application deadline: 8/25; financial award applicants required to submit FAFSA. In 2008, 17 master's awarded. *Degree program information:* Part-time and evening/weekend programs available. Postbaccalaureate distance learning degree programs offered. Offers business and management (MBA). *Application deadline:* Applications are processed on a rolling basis. *Application fee:* $40. *Application Contact:* Greg Bentle, Coordinator of Graduate Recruitment, GPS Undergraduate Programs, 517-750-6763, Fax: 517-750-6624, E-mail: gbentle@arbor.edu. *Dean, School of Business Management,* Dr. James Coe, 517-750-1200 Ext. 1569, Fax: 517-750-6624, E-mail: jcoe@arbor.edu.

School of Education Students: 36 full-time (27 women), 151 part-time (127 women); includes 9 minority (5 African Americans, 2 American Indian/Alaska Native, 2 Hispanic Americans), 1 international. Average age 36. *Faculty:* 8 full-time (5 women), 4 part-time/adjunct (1 woman). Expenses: Contact institution. *Financial support:* Applicants required to submit FAFSA. In 2008, 53 master's awarded. *Degree program information:* Part-time programs available. Offers education (MAE); special education (MSE). *Application deadline:* For fall admission, 9/1 priority date for domestic students; for winter admission, 2/1 priority date for domestic students; for spring admission, 2/1 priority date for domestic students. Applications are processed on a rolling basis. *Application fee:* $40. Electronic applications accepted. *Application Contact:* Terri Reeves, Coordinator of Graduate Recruitment, GPS Undergraduate Programs, 517-750-6554, Fax: 517-750-6629, E-mail: treeves@arbor.edu. *Dean of Education,* Dr. Linda Sherrill, 517-750-1200 Ext. 1562, Fax: 517-750-6629, E-mail: lsherril@arbor.edu.

School of Graduate and Professional Studies Students: 509 full-time (427 women), 306 part-time (245 women); includes 208 minority (179 African Americans, 2 American Indian/Alaska Native, 9 Asian Americans or Pacific Islanders, 18 Hispanic Americans), 3 international. Average age 39. *Faculty:* 8 full-time (3 women), 99 part-time/adjunct (45 women). Expenses: Contact institution. *Financial support:* Scholarships/grants available. Support available to part-time students. Financial award applicants required to submit FAFSA. In 2008, 249 master's awarded. *Degree program information:* Part-time and evening/weekend programs available. Postbaccalaureate distance learning degree programs offered (no on-campus study). Offers counseling (MAC); family studies (MAFS); nursing (MSN); organizational management (MAOM). *Application deadline:* Applications are processed on a rolling basis. *Application fee:* $40. Electronic applications accepted. *Application Contact:* John Ball, Coordinator of Admissions, GPS Undergraduate Programs, 517-750-6459, Fax: 517-750-6602, E-mail: jball@arbor.edu. *Dean of Graduate and Professional Studies,* Dr. Robert Hamill, 517-750-1200 Ext. 1343, Fax: 517-750-6602, E-mail: rhamill@arbor.edu.

SPRINGFIELD COLLEGE, Springfield, MA 01109-3797

General Information Independent, coed, comprehensive institution. *Enrollment:* 1,049 full-time matriculated graduate/professional students, 361 part-time matriculated graduate/professional students. *Enrollment by degree level:* 1,370 master's, 40 doctoral. *Graduate faculty:* 171 full-time (75 women), 151 part-time/adjunct (75 women). *Tuition:* Full-time $9132; part-time $761 per semester hour. *Required fees:* $150. Tuition and fees vary according to course load. *Graduate housing:* Rooms and/or apartments available on a first-come, first-served basis to single and married students. Typical cost: $3650 per year ($6480 including board) for single students; $5100 per year for married students. Room and board charges vary according to board plan. Housing application deadline: 5/1. *Student services:* Campus employment opportunities, campus safety program, career counseling, child daycare facilities, exercise/wellness program, free psychological counseling, international student services, low-cost health insurance, multicultural affairs office, services for students with disabilities, teacher training, writing training. *Library facilities:* Babson Library. *Collection:* 125,000 titles, 850 serial subscriptions.

Computer facilities: Computer purchase and lease plans are available. 95 computers available on campus for general student use. A campuswide network can be accessed from student residence rooms and from off campus. *Web address:* http://www.spfldcol.edu/.

General Application Contact: Donald James Shaw, Director of Graduate Admissions, 413-748-3479, Fax: 413-748-3694, E-mail: donald_shaw_jr@spfldcol.edu.

GRADUATE UNITS

Graduate Programs Students: 1,049 full-time, 361 part-time; includes 458 minority (333 African Americans, 7 American Indian/Alaska Native, 18 Asian Americans or Pacific Islanders, 100 Hispanic Americans), 2 international. Average age 29. 808 applicants, 76% accepted, 354 enrolled. *Faculty:* 171 full-time (75 women), 151 part-time/adjunct (75 women). Expenses: Contact institution. *Financial support:* In 2008–09, 4 fellowships with partial tuition reimbursements, 196 teaching assistantships with partial tuition reimbursements were awarded; career-related internships or fieldwork, Federal Work-Study, institutionally sponsored loans, scholarships/grants, traineeships, and unspecified assistantships also available. Financial award application deadline: 3/1; financial award applicants required to submit FAFSA. In 2008, 657 master's, 2 doctorates, 7 other advanced degrees awarded. *Degree program information:* Part-time and evening/weekend programs available. Offers adapted physical education (M Ed, MPE, MS); advanced level coaching (M Ed, MPE, MS); alcohol rehabilitation/substance abuse counseling (M Ed, MS); art therapy (M Ed, MS, CAGS); athletic administration (M Ed, MPE, MS); athletic counseling (M Ed, MS, CAGS); athletic training (MS); counseling and secondary education (M Ed, MS); deaf counseling (M Ed, MS); developmental disabilities (M Ed, MS); early childhood education (M Ed, MS); education (M Ed, MS); educational administration (M Ed, MS); educational studies (M Ed, MS); elementary education (M Ed, MS); exercise physiology (MS); exercise science and sport studies (PhD); general counseling and casework (M Ed, MS); general physical education (PhD, CAGS); health care management (M Ed, MS); health education licensure (MPE, MS); health education licensure program (M Ed); health promotion and disease prevention (MS); human services (MS); industrial/organizational psychology (M Ed, MS, CAGS); marriage and family therapy (M Ed, MS, CAGS); mental health counseling (M Ed, MS, CAGS); occupational therapy (M Ed, MS, CAGS); physical education licensure (MPE, MS); physical education licensure program (M Ed); physical therapy (DPT); physician assistant (MS); psychiatric rehabilitation/mental health counseling (M Ed, MS); recreational management (M Ed, MS); school guidance and counseling (M Ed, MS, CAGS); secondary education (M Ed, MS); special education (M Ed, MS); special services (M Ed, MS); sport management (M Ed, MS); sport psychology (MS); student personnel in higher education (M Ed, MS, CAGS); teaching and administration (MS); therapeutic recreational management (M Ed, MS). *Application deadline:* For fall admission, 1/15 priority date for domestic and international students; for winter admission, 11/1 priority date for domestic and international students; for spring admission, 11/1 priority date for domestic and international students. Applications are processed on a rolling basis. *Application fee:* $50. Electronic applications accepted. *Application Contact:* Donald James Shaw, Director of Graduate Admissions, 413-748-3225, Fax: 413-748-3694, E-mail: graduate@spfldcol.edu. *Assistant Vice President for Academic Affairs,* Dr. Mary Ann Coughlin, 413-748-3125, Fax: 413-748-3764.

School of Social Work Students: 198 full-time, 91 part-time. Average age 30. 262 applicants, 77% accepted, 133 enrolled. *Faculty:* 10 full-time (4 women), 3 part-time/adjunct (all women). Expenses: Contact institution. *Financial support:* Fellowships with partial tuition reimbursements, teaching assistantships with partial tuition reimbursements, career-related internships or fieldwork, Federal Work-Study, institutionally sponsored loans, and unspecified assistantships available. Financial award application deadline: 3/1; financial award applicants required to submit FAFSA. In 2008, 89 master's awarded. *Degree program information:* Part-time programs available. Offers advanced generalist (weekday and weekend) (MSW); advanced standing (MSW). *Application deadline:* For fall admission, 3/1 for domestic and international students. Applications are processed on a rolling basis. *Application fee:* $50. Electronic applications accepted. *Application Contact:* Donald James Shaw, Director of Graduate Admissions, 413-748-3479, Fax: 413-748-3694, E-mail: donald_shaw_jr@spfldcol.edu. *Dean,* Dr. Francine Vecchiolla, 413-748-3057, Fax: 413-748-3069, E-mail: fvecchiolla@spfldcol.edu.

See Close-Up on page 995.

SPRING HILL COLLEGE, Mobile, AL 36608-1791

General Information Independent-religious, coed, comprehensive institution. *Enrollment:* 1,534 graduate, professional, and undergraduate students; 22 full-time matriculated graduate/professional students (19 women), 156 part-time matriculated graduate/professional students (91 women). *Enrollment by degree level:* 178 master's. *Graduate faculty:* 22 full-time (7 women), 11 part-time/adjunct (6 women). *Tuition:* Full-time $4860; part-time $270 per credit hour. Tuition and fees vary according to program. *Graduate housing:* On-campus housing not available. *Student services:* Campus safety program, career counseling, exercise/wellness program, writing training. *Library facilities:* Marnie and John Burke Memorial Library plus 1 other. *Online resources:* library catalog, web page, access to other libraries' catalogs. *Collection:* 185,926 titles, 889 serial subscriptions, 946 audiovisual materials.

Computer facilities: 194 computers available on campus for general student use. A campuswide network can be accessed from student residence rooms and from off campus. Online class registration is available. *Web address:* http://www.shc.edu/.

General Application Contact: Donna B. Tarasavage, Director of Marketing and Recruiting, Graduate and Continuing Studies, 251-380-3094, Fax: 251-460-2190, E-mail: grad@shc.edu.

GRADUATE UNITS

Graduate Programs Students: 22 full-time (19 women), 156 part-time (91 women); includes 36 minority (27 African Americans, 3 American Indian/Alaska Native, 1 Asian American or Pacific Islander, 5 Hispanic Americans), 2 international. Average age 39. 169 applicants, 44% accepted, 34 enrolled. *Faculty:* 22 full-time (7 women), 11 part-time/adjunct (6 women). Expenses: Contact institution. *Financial support:* In 2008–09, 113 students received support. Career-related internships or fieldwork, scholarships/grants, and loans available. Support available to part-time students. Financial award applicants required to submit FAFSA. In 2008, 61 master's awarded. *Degree program information:* Part-time and evening/weekend programs available. Offers business administration (MBA); clinical nurse leader (MSN); early childhood education (MAT, MS Ed); elementary education (MAT, MS Ed); liberal arts (MLA); secondary education (MAT, MS Ed); theology (MA, MPS, MTS). *Application deadline:* For fall admission, 8/1 priority date for domestic and international students; for spring admission, 12/1 priority date for domestic and international students. Applications are processed on a rolling basis. *Application fee:* $25 ($35 for international students). Electronic applications accepted. *Application Contact:* Donna B. Tarasavage, Director of Marketing and Recruiting, Graduate and Continuing Studies, 251-380-3094, Fax: 251-460-2190, E-mail: grad@shc.edu. *Associate Provost of Graduate and Continuing Studies,* Ramona Marsalis Hill, 251-380-3094, Fax: 251-460-2190, E-mail: grad@shc.edu.

STANFORD UNIVERSITY, Stanford, CA 94305-9991

General Information Independent, coed, university. CGS member. *Graduate housing:* Rooms and/or apartments guaranteed to single and married students. Housing application deadline: 5/5.

GRADUATE UNITS

Graduate School of Business Offers business (MBA, PhD). Electronic applications accepted.

Law School Offers law (JD, JSM, MLS, JSD). Electronic applications accepted.

School of Earth Sciences Offers earth sciences (MS, PhD, Eng); earth systems (MS); geological and environmental sciences (MS, PhD, Eng); geophysics (MS, PhD); petroleum engineering (MS, PhD, Eng). Electronic applications accepted.

School of Education Offers administration and policy analysis (Ed D, PhD); anthropology of education (PhD); art education (MA, PhD); child and adolescent development (PhD); counseling psychology (PhD); dance education (MA); economics of education (PhD); education (MA, Ed D, PhD); educational linguistics (PhD); educational psychology (PhD); English education (MA, PhD); evaluation (MA); general curriculum studies (MA, PhD); higher education (PhD); history of education (PhD); interdisciplinary studies (PhD); international comparative education (MA, PhD); international education administration and policy analysis (MA); languages education (MA); learning, design, and technology (MA, PhD); mathematics education (MA, PhD); philosophy of education (PhD); policy analysis (MA); prospective principal's program (MA); science education (MA, PhD); social studies education (MA, PhD); sociology of education (PhD); symbolic systems in education (PhD); teacher education (MA, PhD). Electronic applications accepted.

School of Engineering Offers aeronautics and astronautics (MS, PhD, Eng); biomechanical engineering (MS); chemical engineering (MS, PhD, Eng); civil and environmental engineering (MS, PhD, Eng); computer science (MS, PhD); electrical engineering (MS, PhD, Eng); engineering (MS, PhD, Eng); management science and engineering (MS, PhD); materials science and engineering (MS, PhD, Eng); mechanical engineering (MS, PhD, Eng); product design (MS); scientific computing and computational mathematics (MS, PhD). Electronic applications accepted.

School of Humanities and Sciences Offers anthropological sciences (MA, MS, PhD); applied physics (MS, PhD); art history (PhD); art practice (MFA); biological sciences (MS, PhD); biophysics (PhD); chemistry (PhD); Chinese (MA, PhD); classics (MA, PhD); communication (journalism specialization) (MA); communication theory and research (PhD); comparative literature (PhD); computer-based music theory and acoustics (MA, PhD); cultural and social anthropology (MA, PhD); drama (PhD); economics (PhD); English (MA, PhD); financial mathematics (MS); French (MA, PhD); German studies (MA, PhD); history (MA, PhD); humanities (MA); humanities and sciences (MA, MFA, MS, DMA, PhD); international policy studies (MA); Italian (MA, PhD); Japanese (MA, PhD); linguistics (MA, PhD); mathematics (MS, PhD); modern thought and literature (PhD); music composition (MA, DMA); music history (MA); music, science, and technology (MA); musicology (PhD); philosophy (MA, PhD); physics (PhD); political science (MA, PhD); psychology (PhD); religious studies (MA, PhD); Russian (MA); Slavic languages and literatures (PhD); sociology (PhD); Spanish (MA, PhD); statistics (MS, PhD). Electronic applications accepted.

Center for East Asian Studies Offers East Asian studies (MA). Electronic applications accepted.

Center for Russian and East European Studies Offers Russian and East European studies (MA). Electronic applications accepted.

School of Medicine Offers bioengineering (MS, PhD); medicine (MD, MS, PhD). Electronic applications accepted.

Graduate Programs in Medicine Offers biochemistry (PhD); biomedical informatics (MS, PhD); cancer biology (PhD); developmental biology (PhD); epidemiology (MS, PhD); genetics (PhD); health services research (MS); immunology (PhD); medicine (MS, PhD); microbiology and immunology (PhD); molecular and cellular physiology (PhD); molecular pharmacology (PhD); neurosciences (PhD); structural biology (PhD). Electronic applications accepted.

STARR KING SCHOOL FOR THE MINISTRY, Berkeley, CA 94709-1209

General Information Independent-religious, coed, graduate-only institution. *Graduate housing:* On-campus housing not available.

GRADUATE UNITS

Professional Program Offers theology (M Div).

STATE UNIVERSITY OF NEW YORK AT BINGHAMTON, Binghamton, NY 13902-6000

General Information State-supported, coed, university. CGS member. *Enrollment:* 14,898 graduate, professional, and undergraduate students; 1,668 full-time matriculated graduate/professional students (784 women), 1,048 part-time matriculated graduate/professional students (545 women). *Enrollment by degree level:* 1,470 master's, 1,246 doctoral. *Graduate faculty:* 461 full-time (162 women), 211 part-time/adjunct (92 women). Tuition, state resident: full-time $6900; part-time $288 per credit. Tuition, nonresident: full-time $10,920; part-time $455 per credit. *Required fees:* $1130. Part-time tuition and fees vary according to course load, program and student level. *Graduate housing:* On-campus housing not available. *Student services:* Campus employment opportunities, career counseling, child daycare facilities, exercise/wellness program, free psychological counseling, grant writing training, international student services, low-cost health insurance, services for students with disabilities, teacher training. *Library facilities:* Glenn G. Bartle Library plus 2 others. *Online resources:* library catalog, web page, access to other libraries' catalogs. *Collection:* 2.4 million titles, 76,166 serial subscriptions, 128,055 audiovisual materials. *Research affiliation:* Universal Instruments (engineering), Lockheed Martin Corporation (engineering, management, mathematics), Matco Company (engineering), IBM (engineering).

Computer facilities: 992 computers available on campus for general student use. A campuswide network can be accessed from student residence rooms and from off campus. Online class registration, course management system, personal Web space are available. *Web address:* http://www.binghamton.edu/.

General Application Contact: Dr. Nancy E. Stamp, Vice Provost and Dean of the Graduate School, 607-777-2070, Fax: 607-777-2501, E-mail: nstamp@binghamton.edu.

GRADUATE UNITS

Graduate School Students: 1,773 full-time (819 women), 1,099 part-time (576 women); includes 305 minority (105 African Americans, 9 American Indian/Alaska Native, 98 Asian Americans or Pacific Islanders, 93 Hispanic Americans), 995 international. Average age 30. 3,644 applicants, 35% accepted, 867 enrolled. *Faculty:* 461 full-time (162 women), 211 part-time/adjunct (92 women). Expenses: Contact institution. *Financial support:* In 2008–09, 1,169 students received support, including 138 fellowships with full tuition reimbursements available (averaging $6,332 per year), 188 research assistantships with full tuition reimbursements available (averaging $7,370 per year), 612 teaching assistantships with full tuition reimbursements available (averaging $8,074 per year); career-related internships or fieldwork, Federal Work-Study, institutionally sponsored loans, traineeships, tuition waivers (full and partial), and unspecified assistantships also available. Support available to part-time students. Financial award application deadline: 2/15; financial award applicants required to submit FAFSA. In 2008, 663 master's, 124 doctorates, 28 other advanced degrees awarded. *Degree program information:* Part-time and evening/weekend programs available. *Application deadline:* For fall admission, 4/5 priority date for domestic students, 1/15 for international students; for spring admission, 11/1 priority date for domestic students, 10/1 for international students. Applications are processed on a rolling basis. *Application fee:* $60. Electronic applications accepted. *Application Contact:* Victoria Williams, Recruiting and Admissions Coordinator, 607-777-2151, Fax: 607-777-2501, E-mail: vwilliam@binghamton.edu. *Vice Provost and Dean of the Graduate School*, Dr. Nancy E. Stamp, 607-777-2070, Fax: 607-777-2501, E-mail: nstamp@binghamton.edu.

College of Community and Public Affairs Students: 146 full-time (97 women), 121 part-time (88 women); includes 48 minority (26 African Americans, 1 American Indian/Alaska Native, 9 Asian Americans or Pacific Islanders, 12 Hispanic Americans), 8 international. Average age 33. 229 applicants, 67% accepted, 102 enrolled. *Faculty:* 2 full-time (0 women), 1 part-time/adjunct (0 women). Expenses: Contact institution. *Financial support:* In 2008–09, 20 students received support, including 2 fellowships with full tuition reimbursements available (averaging $10,000 per year), teaching assistantships with full tuition reimbursements available (averaging $10,000 per year); career-related internships or fieldwork, Federal Work-Study, institutionally sponsored loans, scholarships/grants, health care benefits, and unspecified assistantships also available. Financial award application deadline: 2/15; financial award applicants required to submit FAFSA. In 2008, 102 master's awarded. *Degree program information:* Part-time and evening/weekend programs available. Offers community and public affairs (MPA, MSW); public administration (MPA); social work (MSW). *Application deadline:* For fall admission, 4/15 priority date for domestic students, 1/15 priority date for international students; for spring admission, 11/1 for domestic students, 10/1 priority date for international students. Applications are processed on a rolling basis. *Application fee:* $60. Electronic applications accepted. *Application Contact:* Victoria Williams, Recruiting and Admissions Coordinator, 607-777-2151, Fax: 607-777-2501, E-mail: vwilliam@binghamton.edu. *Dean*, Dr. Patricia Ingraham, 607-777-5572, Fax: 607-777-2406, E-mail: pingraham@binghamton.edu.

Decker School of Nursing Students: 55 full-time (47 women), 61 part-time (55 women); includes 11 minority (8 African Americans, 2 Asian Americans or Pacific Islanders, 1 Hispanic American), 9 international. Average age 38. 64 applicants, 83% accepted, 31 enrolled. *Faculty:* 30 full-time (28 women), 9 part-time/adjunct (8 women). Expenses: Contact institution. *Financial support:* In 2008–09, 29 students received support, including 18 fellowships with partial tuition reimbursements available (averaging $8,250 per year), 3 research assistantships with full tuition reimbursements available (averaging $10,000 per year), 3 teaching assistantships with full tuition reimbursements available (averaging $10,000 per year); career-related internships or fieldwork, Federal Work-Study, institutionally sponsored loans, traineeships, health care benefits, and unspecified assistantships also available. Financial award application deadline: 2/15; financial award applicants required to submit FAFSA. In 2008, 23 master's, 4 doctorates, 19 other advanced degrees awarded. *Degree program information:* Part-time and evening/weekend programs available. Offers nursing (MS, PhD, Certificate). *Application deadline:* For fall admission, 4/15 priority date for domestic students, 1/15 priority date for international students; for spring admission, 11/1 for domestic students, 10/1 priority date for international students. Applications are processed on a rolling basis. *Application fee:* $60. Electronic applications accepted. *Application Contact:* Theresa Grabo, Director of Graduate Studies, 607-777-6163, Fax: 607-777-4440, E-mail: tgrabo@binghamton.edu. *Dean*, Dr. Joyce Ferrario, 607-777-2311, Fax: 607-777-4440, E-mail: jferrari@binghamton.edu.

School of Arts and Sciences Students: 715 full-time (377 women), 454 part-time (251 women); includes 142 minority (43 African Americans, 4 American Indian/Alaska Native, 39 Asian Americans or Pacific Islanders, 56 Hispanic Americans), 336 international. Average age 31. 1,434 applicants, 44% accepted, 242 enrolled. *Faculty:* 301 full-time (92 women), 141 part-time/adjunct (55 women). Expenses: Contact institution. *Financial support:* In 2008–09, 607 students received support, including 62 fellowships with full tuition reimbursements available (averaging $14,100 per year), 47 research assistantships with full tuition reimbursements available (averaging $14,100 per year), 444 teaching assistantships with full tuition reimbursements available (averaging $14,100 per year); career-related internships or fieldwork, Federal Work-Study, institutionally sponsored loans, scholarships/grants, health care benefits, and unspecified assistantships also available. Financial award application deadline: 2/15; financial award applicants required to submit FAFSA. In 2008, 171 master's, 84 doctorates, 4 other advanced degrees awarded. *Degree program information:* Part-time and evening/weekend programs available. Offers analytical chemistry (PhD); anthropology (MA, PhD); applied physics (MS); art history (MA, PhD); arts and sciences (MA, MM, MS, PhD, Certificate); behavioral neuroscience (MA, PhD); biological sciences (MA, PhD); chemistry (MA, MS); clinical psychology (MA, PhD); cognitive and behavioral science (MA, PhD); comparative literature (MA, PhD); computer science (MA, PhD); economics (MA, PhD); economics and finance (MA, PhD); English (MA, PhD); French (MA); geography (MA); geological sciences (MA, PhD); history (MA, PhD); inorganic chemistry (PhD); Italian (MA); music (MA, MM); organic chemistry (PhD); philosophy (MA, PhD); philosophy, interpretation and culture (MA, PhD); physical chemistry (PhD); physics (MA, MS); political science (MA, PhD); probability and statistics (MA, PhD); public policy (MA, PhD); social, political, ethical and legal philosophy (MA, PhD); sociology (MA, PhD); Spanish (MA, Certificate); theater (MA); translation (Certificate); translation research and instruction (Certificate). *Application deadline:* For fall admission, 4/15 priority date for domestic students, 1/15 priority date for international students; for spring admission, 11/1 for domestic students, 10/1 priority date for international students. Applications are processed on a rolling basis. *Application fee:* $60. Electronic applications accepted. *Application Contact:* Victoria Williams, Recruiting and Admissions Coordinator, 607-777-2151, Fax: 607-777-2501, E-mail: vwilliam@binghamton.edu. *Dean*, Dr. Jean-Pierre Mileur, 607-777-2144, E-mail: jpmileur@binghamton.edu.

School of Education Students: 151 full-time (94 women), 143 part-time (107 women); includes 12 minority (3 African Americans, 1 American Indian/Alaska Native, 4 Asian Americans or Pacific Islanders, 4 Hispanic Americans), 6 international. Average age 32. 201 applicants, 73% accepted, 112 enrolled. *Faculty:* 23 full-time (14 women), 18 part-time/adjunct (13 women). Expenses: Contact institution. *Financial support:* In 2008–09, 37 students received support, including 8 fellowships with full tuition reimbursements available (averaging $12,000 per year), 1 research assistantship with full tuition reimbursement available (averaging $12,000 per year), 15 teaching assistantships with full tuition reimbursements available (averaging $12,000 per year); career-related internships or fieldwork, Federal Work-Study, institutionally sponsored loans, scholarships/grants, health care benefits, tuition waivers (full and partial), and unspecified assistantships also available. Financial award application deadline: 2/15; financial award applicants required to submit FAFSA. In 2008, 95 master's, 5 doctorates awarded. *Degree program information:* Part-time and evening/weekend programs available. Offers biology education (MAT, MS Ed, MST); childhood education (MS Ed); earth science education (MAT, MS Ed, MST); education (MAT, MS Ed, MST, Ed D); educational theory and practice (Ed D); English education (MAT, MS Ed, MST); French education (MAT, MST); literacy education (MS Ed); mathematical sciences education (MAT, MS Ed, MST); physics (MAT, MS Ed, MST); social studies (MAT, MS Ed, MST); Spanish education (MAT, MST); special education (MS Ed). *Application deadline:* For fall admission, 4/15 priority date for domestic students, 1/15 priority date for international students; for spring admission, 11/1 for domestic students, 10/1 priority date for international students. Applications are processed on a rolling basis. *Application fee:* $60. Electronic applications accepted. *Application Contact:* Victoria Williams, Recruiting and Admissions Coordinator, 607-777-2151, Fax: 607-777-2501, E-mail: vwilliam@binghamton.edu. *Interim Dean*, Dr. Susan Strahle, 607-777-7329, E-mail: sstrahle@binghamton.edu.

School of Management Students: 282 full-time (126 women), 39 part-time (15 women); includes 29 minority (4 African Americans, 1 American Indian/Alaska Native, 17 Asian Americans or Pacific Islanders, 7 Hispanic Americans), 150 international. Average age 26. 678 applicants, 53% accepted, 191 enrolled. *Faculty:* 38 full-time (8 women), 15 part-time/adjunct (2 women). Expenses: Contact institution. *Financial support:* In 2008–09, 44 students received support, including 11 fellowships with full tuition reimbursements available (averaging $17,000 per year), 17 teaching assistantships with full tuition reimbursements available (averaging $17,000 per year); career-related internships or fieldwork, Federal Work-Study, institutionally sponsored loans, scholarships/grants, health care benefits, tuition waivers (partial), and unspecified assistantships also available. Financial award application deadline: 2/15; financial award applicants required to submit FAFSA. In 2008, 117 master's, 4 doctorates awarded. *Degree program information:* Part-time and evening/weekend programs available. Offers accounting (MS, PhD); business administration (MBA, PhD); health care professional executive (MBA); management (MBA, MS, PhD). *Application deadline:* For fall admission, 4/15 priority date for domestic students, 1/15 priority date for international students; for spring admission, 11/1 for domestic students, 10/1 priority date for international students. Applications are processed on a rolling basis. *Application fee:* $60. Electronic applications accepted. *Application Contact:* Victoria Williams, Recruiting and Admissions Coordinator, 607-777-2151, Fax: 607-777-2501, E-mail: vwilliam@binghamton.edu. *Dean*, Dr. Upinder S. Dhillon, 607-777-2314, E-mail: dhillon@binghamton.edu.

Thomas J. Watson School of Engineering and Applied Science Students: 424 full-time (78 women), 281 part-time (60 women); includes 51 minority (13 African Americans, 27 Asian Americans or Pacific Islanders, 11 Hispanic Americans), 484 international. Average age 27. 1,038 applicants, 63% accepted, 189 enrolled. *Faculty:* 50 full-time (6 women), 24 part-time/adjunct (6 women). Expenses: Contact institution. *Financial support:* In 2008–09, 212 students received support, including 10 fellowships with full tuition reimbursements available (averaging $16,500 per year), 122 research assistantships with full tuition reimbursements available (averaging $16,500 per year), 72 teaching assistantships with full tuition reimbursements available (averaging $16,500 per year); career-related internships or fieldwork, Federal Work-Study, institutionally sponsored loans, scholarships/grants, health

State University of New York at Binghamton (continued)
care benefits, tuition waivers (full and partial), and unspecified assistantships also available. Financial award application deadline: 2/15; financial award applicants required to submit FAFSA. In 2008, 153 master's, 27 doctorates awarded. *Degree program information:* Part-time and evening/weekend programs available. Offers computer science (M Eng, MS, PhD); electrical and computer engineering (M Eng, MS, PhD); engineering and applied science (M Eng, MS, MSAT, PhD); materials science and engineering (MS, PhD); mechanical engineering (M Eng, MS, PhD); systems science and industrial engineering (M Eng, MS, MSAT, PhD). *Application deadline:* For fall admission, 4/15 priority date for domestic students, 1/15 priority date for international students; for spring admission, 11/1 for domestic students, 10/1 priority date for international students. Applications are processed on a rolling basis. *Application fee:* $60. Electronic applications accepted. *Application Contact:* Victoria Williams, Recruiting and Admissions Coordinator, 607-777-2151, Fax: 607-777-2501, E-mail: vwilliam@binghamton.edu. *Dean,* Dr. Seshu Desu, 607-777-2871, E-mail: sdesu@binghamton.edu.

STATE UNIVERSITY OF NEW YORK AT FREDONIA, Fredonia, NY 14063-1136

General Information State-supported, coed, comprehensive institution. CGS member. *Enrollment:* 5,573 graduate, professional, and undergraduate students; 193 full-time matriculated graduate/professional students (157 women), 202 part-time matriculated graduate/professional students (141 women). *Enrollment by degree level:* 345 master's, 38 other advanced degrees. *Graduate faculty:* 50 full-time (26 women), 24 part-time/adjunct (12 women). Tuition, state resident: full-time $8370; part-time $349 per credit hour. Tuition, nonresident: full-time $13,250; part-time $552 per credit hour. *Required fees:* $1289; $53.55 per credit hour. *Graduate housing:* Room and/or apartments available on a first-come, first-served basis to single students;, on-campus housing not available to married students. Housing application deadline: 7/15. *Student services:* Campus employment opportunities, campus safety program, career counseling, child daycare facilities, exercise/wellness program, free psychological counseling, international student services, low-cost health insurance, multicultural affairs office, services for students with disabilities. *Library facilities:* Reed Library. *Online resources:* library catalog, web page, access to other libraries' catalogs. *Collection:* 396,000 titles, 2,270 serial subscriptions.

Computer facilities: Computer purchase and lease plans are available. 500 computers available on campus for general student use. A campuswide network can be accessed from student residence rooms and from off campus. Online class registration is available. *Web address:* http://www.fredonia.edu/.

General Application Contact: Dr. Kevin P Kearns, Associate Vice President of Graduate Studies and Research, 716-673-3808, Fax: 716-673-3338, E-mail: Kevin.Kearns@fredonia.edu.

GRADUATE UNITS

Graduate Studies *Degree program information:* Part-time and evening/weekend programs available. Offers accounting (MS); biology (MS, MS Ed); chemistry (MS); curriculum and instruction science education (MS Ed); English (MA, MS Ed); interdisciplinary studies (MA, MS); mathematical sciences (MS Ed); speech pathology and audiology (MS, MS Ed). Electronic applications accepted.

College of Education *Degree program information:* Part-time and evening/weekend programs available. Offers educational administration (CAS); elementary education (MS Ed); literacy (MS Ed); secondary education (MS Ed); teaching English to speakers of other languages (MS Ed).

School of Music *Degree program information:* Part-time and evening/weekend programs available. Offers music (MM); music education (MM).

STATE UNIVERSITY OF NEW YORK AT NEW PALTZ, New Paltz, NY 12561

General Information State-supported, coed, comprehensive institution. *Enrollment:* 8,205 graduate, professional, and undergraduate students; 522 full-time matriculated graduate/professional students (321 women), 729 part-time matriculated graduate/professional students (534 women). *Enrollment by degree level:* 1,110 master's, 141 other advanced degrees. *Graduate faculty:* 144 full-time (81 women), 49 part-time/adjunct (31 women). *Graduate housing:* On-campus housing not available. *Student services:* Campus employment opportunities, campus safety program, career counseling, child daycare facilities, free psychological counseling, international student services, low-cost health insurance, services for students with disabilities. *Library facilities:* Sojourner Truth Library. *Online resources:* library catalog, web page. *Collection:* 527,765 titles, 43,209 serial subscriptions, 4,330 audiovisual materials.

Computer facilities: 600 computers available on campus for general student use. A campuswide network can be accessed from student residence rooms and from off campus. Online class registration is available. *Web address:* http://www.newpaltz.edu/.

General Application Contact: Caroline Murphy, Graduate Admissions Advisor, 845-257-3285, Fax: 845-257-3284, E-mail: gradschool@newpaltz.edu.

GRADUATE UNITS

Graduate School Students: 522 full-time (321 women), 729 part-time (534 women); includes 115 minority (23 African Americans, 1 American Indian/Alaska Native, 45 Asian Americans or Pacific Islanders, 46 Hispanic Americans), 187 international. Average age 30. 1,041 applicants, 49% accepted, 324 enrolled. *Faculty:* 144 full-time (81 women), 49 part-time/adjunct (31 women). Expenses: Contact institution. *Financial support:* In 2008–09, 100 students received support, including research assistantships with partial tuition reimbursements available (averaging $5,000 per year), teaching assistantships with partial tuition reimbursements available (averaging $5,000 per year); fellowships with partial tuition reimbursements available, career-related internships or fieldwork, Federal Work-Study, institutionally sponsored loans, scholarships/grants, traineeships, health care benefits, tuition waivers (full and partial), and unspecified assistantships also available. Support available to part-time students. Financial award application deadline: 8/1; financial award applicants required to submit FAFSA. In 2008, 484 master's, 49 other advanced degrees awarded. *Degree program information:* Part-time and evening/weekend programs available. *Application deadline:* For fall admission, 5/15 priority date for domestic students, 5/15 for international students; for spring admission, 11/15 for domestic and international students. Applications are processed on a rolling basis. *Application fee:* $50. Electronic applications accepted. *Application Contact:* Vika F. Shock, Director of Graduate Admissions, 845-257-3286, Fax: 845-257-3284, E-mail: gradschool@newpaltz.edu. *Associate Provost for Academic Affairs/Dean of the Graduate School,* Dr. Laurel M. Garrick Duhaney, 845-257-3287, Fax: 845-257-3284, E-mail: gradschool@newpaltz.edu.

School of Business Students: 63 full-time (31 women), 44 part-time (24 women); includes 13 minority (1 African American, 9 Asian Americans or Pacific Islanders, 3 Hispanic Americans), 28 international. Average age 30. 67 applicants, 36% accepted, 14 enrolled. *Faculty:* 18 full-time (5 women), 1 (woman) part-time/adjunct. Expenses: Contact institution. *Financial support:* In 2008–09, 13 students received support, including 2 fellowships (averaging $8,000 per year), 7 research assistantships with partial tuition reimbursements available (averaging $5,000 per year), 1 teaching assistantship with partial tuition reimbursement available (averaging $5,000 per year); career-related internships or fieldwork, scholarships/grants, traineeships, tuition waivers (full), and unspecified assistantships also available. Financial award application deadline: 8/1; financial award applicants required to submit FAFSA. In 2008, 42 master's awarded. *Degree program information:* Part-time and evening/weekend programs available. Offers business administration (MBA); public accountancy (MBA). *Application deadline:* For fall admission, 5/15 priority date for domestic students, 5/15 for international students; for spring admission, 11/15 for domestic and international students. Applications are processed on a rolling basis. *Application fee:* $50. Electronic applications accepted. *Application Contact:* Aaron Hines, Coordinator, 845-257-2968, E-mail: mba@newpaltz.edu. *Dean,* Dr. Hadi Salavitabar, 845-257-2930, E-mail: mba@newpaltz.edu.

School of Education Students: 182 full-time (131 women), 488 part-time (372 women); includes 55 minority (15 African Americans, 7 Asian Americans or Pacific Islanders, 33 Hispanic Americans), 4 international. Average age 32. 316 applicants, 61% accepted, 161 enrolled. *Faculty:* 40 full-time (28 women), 25 part-time/adjunct (17 women). Expenses: Contact institution. *Financial support:* In 2008–09, 12 students received support. Career-related internships or fieldwork, Federal Work-Study, institutionally sponsored loans, scholarships/grants, and tuition waivers (full) available. Financial award application deadline: 8/1; financial award applicants required to submit FAFSA. In 2008, 310 master's, 85 other advanced degrees awarded. *Degree program information:* Part-time and evening/weekend programs available. Offers adolescence (7-12) (MS Ed); adolescence education: biology (MS Ed); adolescence education: English (MS Ed); adolescence education: social studies (MS Ed); adolescence special education and literacy education (MS Ed); alternative certificate: school district leader (transition D) (CAS); childhood (1-6) (MS Ed); childhood education (MS Ed); childhood education (1-6) (MST); childhood special education and literacy education (MS Ed); early childhood (B-2) (MS Ed); education (MAT, MPS, MS Ed, MST, CAS); English as a second language (MS Ed); humanistic/multicultural education (MPS); literacy education (5-12) (MS Ed); literacy education (B-6) (MS Ed); literacy education and adolescence special education (MS Ed); literacy education and childhood education and childhood special education (MS Ed); school business leadership (CAS); school leadership (MS Ed, CAS); second language education (MS Ed); special education (MS Ed). *Application deadline:* For fall admission, 3/1 priority date for domestic and international students; for spring admission, 10/1 priority date for domestic and international students. Applications are processed on a rolling basis. *Application fee:* $50. Electronic applications accepted. *Application Contact:* Caroline Murphy, Graduate Admissions Advisor, 845-257-3285, Fax: 845-257-3284, E-mail: gradschool@newpaltz.edu. *Dean,* Dr. Robert Michael, 845-257-2800, E-mail: michaelr@newpaltz.edu.

School of Fine and Performing Arts Students: 62 full-time (51 women), 56 part-time (42 women); includes 12 minority (1 African American, 8 Asian Americans or Pacific Islanders, 3 Hispanic Americans), 11 international. Average age 30. 112 applicants, 40% accepted, 32 enrolled. *Faculty:* 29 full-time (21 women), 10 part-time/adjunct (6 women). Expenses: Contact institution. *Financial support:* In 2008–09, 15 students received support, including 3 fellowships (averaging $8,000 per year), 3 research assistantships with partial tuition reimbursements available (averaging $5,000 per year), 8 teaching assistantships with partial tuition reimbursements available (averaging $5,000 per year); Federal Work-Study, institutionally sponsored loans, scholarships/grants, traineeships, tuition waivers (full), and unspecified assistantships also available. Financial award application deadline: 8/1; financial award applicants required to submit FAFSA. In 2008, 40 master's awarded. *Degree program information:* Part-time and evening/weekend programs available. Offers ceramics (MFA); fine and performing arts (MA, MFA, MS, MS Ed); interdisciplinary (MA); metal (MFA); music therapy (MS); painting/drawing (MFA); printmaking (MFA); sculpture (MFA); visual arts education (MS Ed). *Application deadline:* For fall admission, 2/15 priority date for domestic students, 2/15 for international students. Applications are processed on a rolling basis. *Application fee:* $50. Electronic applications accepted. *Application Contact:* Caroline Murphy, Graduate Admissions Advisor, 845-257-3285, Fax: 845-257-3284, E-mail: gradschool@newpaltz.edu. *Dean,* Dr. Mary Haefeli, 845-257-3860, E-mail: dawk@newpaltz.edu.

School of Liberal Arts and Sciences Students: 86 full-time (76 women), 86 part-time (63 women); includes 15 minority (5 African Americans, 7 Asian Americans or Pacific Islanders, 3 Hispanic Americans), 1 international. Average age 30. 215 applicants, 49% accepted, 65 enrolled. *Faculty:* 37 full-time (24 women), 9 part-time/adjunct (7 women). Expenses: Contact institution. *Financial support:* In 2008–09, 36 students received support, including 1 fellowship (averaging $8,000 per year), 2 research assistantships with partial tuition reimbursements available (averaging $5,000 per year), 31 teaching assistantships with partial tuition reimbursements available (averaging $5,000 per year); career-related internships or fieldwork, Federal Work-Study, institutionally sponsored loans, scholarships/grants, traineeships, tuition waivers (full), and unspecified assistantships also available. Financial award application deadline: 8/1; financial award applicants required to submit FAFSA. In 2008, 59 master's awarded. *Degree program information:* Part-time and evening/weekend programs available. Offers communication disorders (MS); English (MA); liberal arts and sciences (MA, MS); mental health counseling (MS); psychology (MA); school counseling (MS). *Application deadline:* For fall admission, 5/15 for domestic and international students; for spring admission, 11/15 for domestic and international students. Applications are processed on a rolling basis. *Application fee:* $50. Electronic applications accepted. *Application Contact:* Caroline Murphy, Graduate Admissions Advisor, 845-257-3285, Fax: 845-257-3284, E-mail: gradschool@newpaltz.edu. *Dean,* Dr. James Schiffer, 845-257-3520, E-mail: schiffej@newpaltz.edu.

School of Science and Engineering Students: 129 full-time (32 women), 55 part-time (33 women); includes 16 minority (1 African American, 1 American Indian/Alaska Native, 14 Asian Americans or Pacific Islanders), 143 international. Average age 24. 331 applicants, 44% accepted, 52 enrolled. *Faculty:* 20 full-time (3 women), 4 part-time/adjunct (0 women). Expenses: Contact institution. *Financial support:* In 2008–09, 18 students received support, including 7 teaching assistantships with partial tuition reimbursements available (averaging $5,000 per year); traineeships, tuition waivers (partial), and unspecified assistantships also available. In 2008, 82 master's awarded. *Degree program information:* Part-time and evening/weekend programs available. Offers biology (MA); computer science (MS); electrical engineering (MS); science and engineering (MA, MS). *Application deadline:* For fall admission, 5/15 priority date for domestic students, 5/15 for international students; for spring admission, 11/15 for domestic and international students. Applications are processed on a rolling basis. *Application fee:* $50. Electronic applications accepted. *Application Contact:* Caroline Murphy, Graduate Admissions Advisor, 845-257-3285, Fax: 845-257-3284, E-mail: gradschool@newpaltz.edu. *Dean,* Dr. Daniel Jelski, 845-257-3728, E-mail: jelskid@newpaltz.edu.

STATE UNIVERSITY OF NEW YORK AT OSWEGO, Oswego, NY 13126

General Information State-supported, coed, comprehensive institution. CGS member. *Graduate housing:* Room and/or apartments available on a first-come, first-served basis to single students; on-campus housing not available to married students. Housing application deadline: 4/1. *Research affiliation:* IBM (research and education), Sun Microsystems, Inc. (research and education), Alcan (research and education), Merck (research and education), Entergy (research and education), Intel (research and education).

GRADUATE UNITS

Graduate Studies *Degree program information:* Part-time programs available.

College of Arts and Sciences *Degree program information:* Part-time programs available. Offers art (MA); arts and sciences (MA, MS); chemistry (MS); English (MA); history (MA); human computer interaction (MA).

School of Business *Degree program information:* Part-time and evening/weekend programs available. Offers business (MBA); business administration (MBA).

School of Education *Degree program information:* Part-time programs available. Offers agriculture (MS Ed); art education (MAT); business and marketing (MS Ed); counseling services (MS, CAS); education (MAT, MS, MS Ed, CAS); educational administration and supervision (CAS); elementary education (MS Ed); family and consumer sciences (MS Ed); health careers (MS Ed); human services/counseling (MS); literacy education (MS Ed); school building leadership (CAS); school psychology (MS, CAS); secondary education (MS Ed); special education (MS Ed); technical education (MS Ed); technology (MS Ed); trade education (MS Ed).

STATE UNIVERSITY OF NEW YORK AT PLATTSBURGH, Plattsburgh, NY 12901-2681

General Information State-supported, coed, comprehensive institution. *Enrollment:* 6,358 graduate, professional, and undergraduate students; 279 full-time matriculated graduate/professional students (211 women), 236 part-time matriculated graduate/professional students (159 women). *Enrollment by degree level:* 419 master's, 96 other advanced degrees. *Gradu-*

ate faculty: 72 full-time (38 women), 56 part-time/adjunct (30 women). Tuition, state resident: full-time $7880; part-time $328 per credit hour. *Required fees:* $1060. *Graduate housing:* Room and/or apartments available on a first-come, first-served basis to single students; on-campus housing not available to married students. Typical cost: $5350 per year ($8250 including board). Housing application deadline: 5/1. *Student services:* Campus employment opportunities, campus safety program, career counseling, child daycare facilities, free psychological counseling, international student services, low-cost health insurance, multicultural affairs office, services for students with disabilities, teacher training, writing training. *Library facilities:* Feinberg Library. *Online resources:* library catalog, web page, access to other libraries' catalogs. *Collection:* 592,765 titles, 4,052 serial subscriptions, 24,573 audiovisual materials. *Research affiliation:* New York State Sea Grant (environmental science), Miner Agricultural Research Institute (environmental science).

Computer facilities: Computer purchase and lease plans are available. 343 computers available on campus for general student use. A campuswide network can be accessed from student residence rooms and from off campus. Online class registration, online library databases are available. *Web address:* http://www.plattsburgh.edu/.

General Application Contact: Marguerite Adelman, Assistant Director of Graduate Admissions, 518-564-4723, Fax: 518-564-4722, E-mail: adelmaml@plattsburgh.edu.

GRADUATE UNITS

Division of Education, Health, and Human Services Students: 251 full-time (191 women), 206 part-time (142 women); includes 11 minority (2 African Americans, 2 American Indian/Alaska Native, 3 Asian Americans or Pacific Islanders, 4 Hispanic Americans), 4 international. Average age 30. 254 applicants, 70% accepted, 134 enrolled. *Faculty:* 43 full-time (26 women), 51 part-time/adjunct (27 women). Expenses: Contact institution. *Financial support:* In 2008–09, 1 teaching assistantship was awarded; research assistantships, career-related internships or fieldwork and Federal Work-Study also available. Support available to part-time students. Financial award application deadline: 4/15; financial award applicants required to submit FAFSA. In 2008, 242 master's, 31 other advanced degrees awarded. *Degree program information:* Part-time programs available. Offers adolescence education (MST); biology 7-12 (MST); birth to grade 2 (MS Ed); birth-grade 6 (MS Ed); chemistry 7-12 (MST); childhood education (grades 1-6) (MST); college/agency counseling (MS); earth science 7-12 (MST); education, health, and human services (MA, MS, MS Ed, MST, CAS); educational leadership (CAS); English 7-12 (MST); French 7-12 (MST); grades 1 to 6 (MS Ed); grades 5-12 (MS Ed); grades 7 to 12 (MS Ed); mathematics 7-12 (MST); physics 7-12 (MST); school counselor (MS Ed, CAS); social studies 7-12 (MST); Spanish 7-12 (MST); speech-language pathology (MA); teacher education: curriculum and instruction (MS Ed). *Application deadline:* For fall admission, 2/15 priority date for domestic and international students. Applications are processed on a rolling basis. *Application fee:* $75. *Application Contact:* Marguerite Adelman, Assistant Director, Graduate Admissions, 518-564-4723, Fax: 518-564-4722, E-mail: adelmaml@plattsburgh.edu. *Dean*, Dr. David Hill, 518-564-3066, E-mail: david.hill@plattsburgh.edu.

Faculty of Arts and Science Students: 21 full-time (14 women), 7 part-time (5 women); includes 3 minority (1 Asian American or Pacific Islander, 2 Hispanic Americans), 1 international. Average age 25. 25 applicants, 76% accepted, 11 enrolled. *Faculty:* 2 full-time (1 woman), 3 part-time/adjunct (2 women). Expenses: Contact institution. *Financial support:* Federal Work-Study available. Support available to part-time students. Financial award application deadline: 4/15; financial award applicants required to submit FAFSA. In 2008, 8 master's, 8 other advanced degrees awarded. *Degree program information:* Part-time programs available. Offers arts and science (MA, MS, CAS); natural science (MS); school psychology (MA, CAS). *Application deadline:* For fall admission, 2/15 priority date for domestic students. Applications are processed on a rolling basis. *Application fee:* $75. *Application Contact:* Marguerite Adelman, Assistant Director, Graduate Admissions, 518-564-4723, Fax: 518-564-4722, E-mail: adelmaml@plattsburgh.edu. *Dean*, Dr. Kathleen Lavoie, 518-564-3150.

School of Business and Economics Students: 7 full-time (6 women), 23 part-time (12 women). Average age 37. 11 applicants, 100% accepted, 9 enrolled. *Faculty:* 5 full-time (2 women), 2 part-time/adjunct (0 women). Expenses: Contact institution. In 2008, 27 master's awarded. *Degree program information:* Part-time and evening/weekend programs available. Offers business and economics (MA); liberal studies (MA). *Application deadline:* For fall admission, 2/15 priority date for domestic students; for spring admission, 10/15 priority date for domestic students. *Application fee:* $75. *Application Contact:* Marguerite Adelman, Assistant Director, Graduate Admissions, 518-564-4723, Fax: 518-564-4722, E-mail: adelmaml@plattsburgh.edu. *Interim Dean*, Dr. Raymond Guydosh, 518-564-4185, E-mail: guydosrm@plattsburgh.edu.

STATE UNIVERSITY OF NEW YORK COLLEGE AT CORTLAND, Cortland, NY 13045

General Information State-supported, coed, comprehensive institution. *Graduate housing:* On-campus housing not available.

GRADUATE UNITS

Graduate Studies *Degree program information:* Part-time and evening/weekend programs available.

School of Arts and Sciences *Degree program information:* Part-time and evening/weekend programs available. Offers American civilization and culture (CAS); arts and sciences (MA, MAT, MS Ed, CAS); biology (MAT, MS Ed); chemistry (MAT, MS Ed); earth science (MAT, MS Ed); English (MA, MAT, MS Ed); French (MS Ed); history (MA, MS Ed); mathematics (MAT, MS Ed); physics (MAT, MS Ed); second language education (MS Ed); social studies (MS Ed); Spanish (MS Ed).

School of Education *Degree program information:* Part-time and evening/weekend programs available. Offers childhood/early child education (MS Ed, MST); educational leadership (CAS); literacy (MS Ed); teaching students with disabilities (MS Ed).

School of Professional Studies *Degree program information:* Part-time and evening/weekend programs available. Offers exercise science and sport studies (MS); health education (MS Ed, MST); international sport management (MS); physical education (MS Ed); professional studies (MS, MS Ed, MST); recreation and leisure studies (MS, MS Ed); sport management (MS).

STATE UNIVERSITY OF NEW YORK COLLEGE AT GENESEO, Geneseo, NY 14454-1401

General Information State-supported, coed, comprehensive institution. *Enrollment:* 5,585 graduate, professional, and undergraduate students; 53 full-time matriculated graduate/professional students (46 women), 68 part-time matriculated graduate/professional students (59 women). *Enrollment by degree level:* 121 master's. *Graduate faculty:* 38 full-time (18 women), 12 part-time/adjunct (7 women). Tuition, state resident: full-time $7635; part-time $349 per credit hour. Tuition, nonresident: full-time $12,085; part-time $552 per credit hour. One-time fee: $28.28 part-time. *Graduate housing:* On-campus housing not available. *Student services:* Campus employment opportunities, campus safety program, career counseling, child daycare facilities, exercise/wellness program, free psychological counseling, international student services, low-cost health insurance, multicultural affairs office, services for students with disabilities, teacher training. *Library facilities:* Milne Library. *Online resources:* library catalog, web page, access to other libraries' catalogs. *Collection:* 647,100 titles, 54,864 serial subscriptions, 28,134 audiovisual materials. *Research affiliation:* Mt. Hope Family Center (psychology), Center for Nanomaterials and Nanoelectronics (chemistry), Rochester National Technical Institute for the Deaf (communicative disorders), Great Lakes Research Consortium (biology), Rochester Laboratory for Laser Energetics (nuclear physics), Armor Dynamics, Inc. (physics).

Computer facilities: Computer purchase and lease plans are available. 900 computers available on campus for general student use. A campuswide network can be accessed from student residence rooms and from off campus. Online class registration is available. *Web address:* http://www.geneseo.edu/.

General Application Contact: Dr. Terence Bazzett, Associate Dean of the College, 585-245-5541, Fax: 585-245-5032, E-mail: bazzett@geneseo.edu.

GRADUATE UNITS

Graduate Studies Students: 53 full-time (46 women), 68 part-time (59 women); includes 4 minority (2 African Americans, 1 Asian American or Pacific Islander, 1 Hispanic American). Average age 26. 140 applicants, 61% accepted, 56 enrolled. *Faculty:* 38 full-time (18 women), 12 part-time/adjunct (7 women). Expenses: Contact institution. *Financial support:* In 2008–09, 6 students received support. Career-related internships or fieldwork, institutionally sponsored loans, scholarships/grants, health care benefits, and unspecified assistantships available. Support available to part-time students. Financial award application deadline: 4/1; financial award applicants required to submit FAFSA. In 2008, 87 master's awarded. *Degree program information:* Part-time and evening/weekend programs available. Offers communicative disorders and sciences (MA). *Application deadline:* For fall admission, 3/1 for domestic students; for spring admission, 10/1 for domestic students. *Application fee:* $50. *Application Contact:* Dr. Mary Radosh, Dean of the College, 585-245-5541, Fax: 585-245-5032, E-mail: radosh@geneseo.edu. *Dean of the College*, Dr. Mary Radosh, 585-245-5541, Fax: 585-245-5032, E-mail: radosh@geneseo.edu.

School of Business Students: 5 full-time (2 women). Average age 23. 9 applicants, 100% accepted, 5 enrolled. *Faculty:* 3 full-time (0 women), 1 part-time/adjunct (0 women). Expenses: Contact institution. *Financial support:* Application deadline: 4/1. In 2008, 5 master's awarded. Offers accounting (MS). *Application deadline:* For fall admission, 2/1 for domestic students; for spring admission, 9/1 priority date for domestic students. *Application fee:* $50. *Application Contact:* Dr. Harry Howe, Director, 585-245-5465, Fax: 585-245-5467, E-mail: howeh@geneseo.edu. *Interim Dean*, Dr. Michael Schinski, 585-245-5367, Fax: 585-245-5467, E-mail: schinski@geneseo.edu.

School of Education Students: 19 full-time (16 women), 61 part-time (52 women); includes 5 minority (2 African Americans, 2 Asian Americans or Pacific Islanders, 1 Hispanic American). Average age 26. 60 applicants, 100% accepted, 42 enrolled. *Faculty:* 23 full-time (13 women). Expenses: Contact institution. *Financial support:* In 2008–09, 6 students received support. Scholarships/grants, health care benefits, and unspecified assistantships available. Support available to part-time students. Financial award application deadline: 4/1; financial award applicants required to submit FAFSA. In 2008, 61 master's awarded. *Degree program information:* Part-time and evening/weekend programs available. Offers childhood multicultural education (1-6) (MS Ed); early childhood education (MS Ed); elementary education (MS Ed); reading (MS Ed); secondary education (MS Ed). *Application deadline:* For fall admission, 3/1 priority date for domestic students; for spring admission, 10/1 for domestic students. *Application fee:* $50. *Application Contact:* Dr. Susan Salmon, Graduate Liaison, 585-245-5560, Fax: 585-245-5220, E-mail: salmon@geneseo.edu. *Chairperson*, Dr. Osman Alawiye, 585-245-5560, Fax: 585-245-5220, E-mail: alawiyeo@geneseo.edu.

STATE UNIVERSITY OF NEW YORK COLLEGE AT OLD WESTBURY, Old Westbury, NY 11568-0210

General Information State-supported, coed, comprehensive institution. *Graduate housing:* Room and/or apartments available to single students; on-campus housing not available to married students.

GRADUATE UNITS

Program in Accounting *Degree program information:* Part-time and evening/weekend programs available. Offers accounting (MS); taxation and finance (MS). Electronic applications accepted.

STATE UNIVERSITY OF NEW YORK COLLEGE AT ONEONTA, Oneonta, NY 13820-4015

General Information State-supported, coed, comprehensive institution. *Enrollment:* 5,757 graduate, professional, and undergraduate students; 77 full-time matriculated graduate/professional students (62 women), 102 part-time matriculated graduate/professional students (71 women). *Enrollment by degree level:* 167 master's, 12 other advanced degrees. Tuition, state resident: full-time $6900. Tuition, nonresident: full-time $10,920. Part-time tuition and fees vary according to program. *Graduate housing:* Room and/or apartments available on a first-come, first-served basis to single students; on-campus housing not available to married students. Typical cost: $4866 per year ($8106 including board). Room and board charges vary according to board plan and housing facility selected. Housing application deadline: 5/1. *Student services:* Campus employment opportunities, campus safety program, career counseling, child daycare facilities, exercise/wellness program, free psychological counseling, grant writing training, international student services, low-cost health insurance, multicultural affairs office, services for students with disabilities, teacher training, writing training. *Library facilities:* Milne Library. *Online resources:* library catalog, web page, access to other libraries' catalogs. *Collection:* 554,493 titles, 36,800 serial subscriptions, 11,416 audiovisual materials. *Research affiliation:* New York State Historical Association (history museum studies).

Computer facilities: Computer purchase and lease plans are available. 700 computers available on campus for general student use. A campuswide network can be accessed from student residence rooms and from off campus. Online class registration is available. *Web address:* http://www.oneonta.edu/.

General Application Contact: Dean, 607-436-2523, Fax: 607-436-3084, E-mail: gradoffice@oneonta.edu.

GRADUATE UNITS

Graduate Education Students: 77 full-time (62 women), 102 part-time (71 women); includes 9 minority (2 African Americans, 3 Asian Americans or Pacific Islanders, 4 Hispanic Americans). Average age 27. 45 applicants, 100% accepted, 45 enrolled. Expenses: Contact institution. *Financial support:* In 2008–09, 12 students received support; fellowships, teaching assistantships, Federal Work-Study and scholarships/grants available. Financial award applicants required to submit FAFSA. In 2008, 52 master's, 5 other advanced degrees awarded. *Degree program information:* Part-time and evening/weekend programs available. Postbaccalaureate distance learning degree programs offered (no on-campus study). Offers biology (MA); earth sciences (MA); history museum studies (MA); nutrition and dietetics (MS). *Application deadline:* Applications are processed on a rolling basis. *Application fee:* $50. *Application Contact:* Dean, 607-436-2523, Fax: 607-436-3084, E-mail: gradoffice@oneonta.edu. *Dean*, 607-436-2523, Fax: 607-436-3084, E-mail: gradoffice@oneonta.edu.

Division of Education Students: 6 full-time (4 women). Expenses: Contact institution. In 2008, 6 master's awarded. *Degree program information:* Part-time and evening/weekend programs available. Offers adolescence education (MS Ed); childhood education (MS Ed); educational psychology and counseling (MS Ed, CAS); elementary education and reading (MS Ed); family and consumer science education (MS Ed); literacy education (MS Ed); school counselor K-12 (MS Ed, CAS); secondary education (MS Ed). *Application deadline:* For fall admission, 3/25 priority date for domestic students; for spring admission, 10/1 priority date for domestic students. Applications are processed on a rolling basis. *Application fee:* $50. *Application Contact:* Dean, 607-436-2523, Fax: 607-436-3084, E-mail: gradoffice@oneonta.edu. *Associate Dean*, Dr. Joanne Curran, 607-436-2541, Fax: 607-436-2554, E-mail: curranjm@oneonta.edu.

STATE UNIVERSITY OF NEW YORK COLLEGE AT POTSDAM, Potsdam, NY 13676

General Information State-supported, coed, comprehensive institution. *Enrollment:* 4,325 graduate, professional, and undergraduate students; 484 full-time matriculated graduate/professional students (364 women), 172 part-time matriculated graduate/professional students (132 women). *Enrollment by degree level:* 656 master's. *Graduate faculty:* 59 full-time (29 women), 16 part-time/adjunct (13 women). Tuition, state resident: full-time $7390; part-time $328 per credit hour. Tuition, nonresident: full-time $12,085; part-time $552 per credit hour. *Required fees:* $952; $43.70 per credit hour. *Graduate housing:* Room and/or apartments available on a first-come, first-served basis to single students; on-campus housing not available to married students. *Student services:* Campus employment opportunities, campus safety program, career counseling, child daycare facilities, exercise/wellness program, free psychological counseling, grant writing training, international student services, low-cost health insurance, multicultural affairs office, services for students with disabilities, teacher training,

State University of New York College at Potsdam (continued)

writing training. *Library facilities:* F. W. Crumb Memorial Library plus 1 other. *Online resources:* library catalog, web page, access to other libraries' catalogs. *Collection:* 467,878 titles, 10,000 serial subscriptions, 13,083 audiovisual materials.

Computer facilities: Computer purchase and lease plans are available. 470 computers available on campus for general student use. A campuswide network can be accessed from student residence rooms and from off campus. Online class registration, online access to financial aid status, unofficial transcripts, billing, meal plan and housing sign ups are available. *Web address:* http://www.potsdam.edu/.

General Application Contact: Peter Cutler, Graduate Admissions Counselor, 315-267-3154, Fax: 315-267-4802, E-mail: cutlerpj@potsdam.edu.

GRADUATE UNITS

Crane School of Music Students: 21 full-time (12 women), 4 part-time (1 woman); includes 2 minority (1 African American, 1 Asian American or Pacific Islander), 3 international. 32 applicants, 56% accepted, 18 enrolled. *Faculty:* 10 full-time (3 women). Expenses: Contact institution. *Financial support:* In 2008–09, 1 student received support; teaching assistantships with full tuition reimbursements available, career-related internships or fieldwork, Federal Work-Study, scholarships/grants, and unspecified assistantships available. Support available to part-time students. Financial award application deadline: 3/1; financial award applicants required to submit FAFSA. In 2008, 10 master's awarded. *Degree program information:* Part-time programs available. Offers composition (MM); history and literature (MM); music education (MM); music theory (MM); performance (MM). *Application deadline:* For fall admission, 3/1 for domestic and international students. Applications are processed on a rolling basis. *Application fee:* $50. *Application Contact:* Peter Cutler, Graduate Admissions Counselor, 315-267-3154, Fax: 315-267-4802, E-mail: cutlerpj@potsdam.edu. *Dean,* Dr. Alan Solomon, 315-267-2415, Fax: 315-267-2413, E-mail: solomon@potsdam.edu.

School of Arts and Sciences Students: 17 full-time (9 women), 9 part-time (7 women), 1 international. 16 applicants, 81% accepted, 10 enrolled. *Faculty:* 12 full-time (5 women), 1 (woman) part-time/adjunct. Expenses: Contact institution. *Financial support:* In 2008–09, 2 students received support; teaching assistantships with full tuition reimbursements available, Federal Work-Study and unspecified assistantships available. Support available to part-time students. Financial award application deadline: 3/1; financial award applicants required to submit FAFSA. In 2008, 9 master's awarded. *Degree program information:* Part-time and evening/weekend programs available. Offers arts and sciences (MA); English and communication (MA); mathematics (MA). *Application deadline:* For fall admission, 4/1 priority date for domestic and international students; for spring admission, 10/15 priority date for domestic and international students. Applications are processed on a rolling basis. *Application fee:* $50. *Application Contact:* Peter Cutler, Graduate Admissions Counselor, 315-267-3154, Fax: 315-267-4802, E-mail: cutlerpj@potsdam.edu. *Dean,* Dr. Galen K. Pletcher, 315-267-2231, Fax: 315-267-3140, E-mail: pletchgk@potsdam.edu.

School of Education and Professional Studies Students: 446 full-time (343 women), 159 part-time (124 women); includes 10 minority (2 African Americans, 5 American Indian/Alaska Native, 2 Asian Americans or Pacific Islanders, 1 Hispanic American), 248 international. 276 applicants, 83% accepted, 175 enrolled. *Faculty:* 37 full-time (21 women), 15 part-time/adjunct (12 women). Expenses: Contact institution. *Financial support:* In 2008–09, 3 students received support; fellowships, teaching assistantships with full tuition reimbursements available, career-related internships or fieldwork, Federal Work-Study, scholarships/grants, tuition waivers (full), and unspecified assistantships available. Support available to part-time students. Financial award application deadline: 3/1; financial award applicants required to submit FAFSA. In 2008, 426 master's awarded. *Degree program information:* Part-time programs available. Postbaccalaureate distance learning degree programs offered (minimal on-campus study). Offers birth-grade 2 (MS Ed); childhood education (grades 1-6) (MST); childhood instruction (MST); curriculum and instruction (MS Ed); education and professional studies (MS Ed, MST); educational technology specialist (MS Ed); English (MST); grades 1-6 (MS Ed); grades 5-9 (MS Ed); grades 7-12 (MS Ed); human performance technology (MS Ed); information technology (MS Ed); literacy educator (MS Ed); literacy specialist (MS Ed); mathematics (with grades 5-6 extension) (MST); organizational leadership (MS Ed); science (MST); social studies (MS Ed); Social Studies (with grades 5-6 extension) (MST); technology educator (MS Ed). *Application deadline:* For fall admission, 4/1 priority date for domestic and international students; for spring admission, 10/15 priority date for domestic and international students. Applications are processed on a rolling basis. *Application fee:* $50. *Application Contact:* Peter Cutler, Graduate Admissions Counselor, 315-267-3154, Fax: 315-267-4802, E-mail: cutlerpj@potsdam.edu. *Dean,* Dr. William Amoriell, 315-267-2515, Fax: 315-267-4802, E-mail: amoriewj@potsdam.edu.

STATE UNIVERSITY OF NEW YORK COLLEGE OF ENVIRONMENTAL SCIENCE AND FORESTRY, Syracuse, NY 13210-2779

General Information State-supported, coed, university. CGS member. *Graduate housing:* Rooms and/or apartments available to single and married students. Housing application deadline: 5/1. *Research affiliation:* NYS Department Env. Conservation (NYSDEC), Honeywell International, Department of Commerce, U.S. Department of Agriculture (CREES), NASA.

GRADUATE UNITS

Department of Chemistry Offers biochemistry (MPS, MS, PhD); environmental and forest chemistry (MPS, MS, PhD); organic chemistry (MPS); organic chemistry of natural products (MS, PhD); polymer chemistry (MPS, MS, PhD). Electronic applications accepted.

Department of Construction Management and Wood Products Engineering Offers environmental and resources engineering (MPS, MS, PhD).

Department of Environmental and Forest Biology Offers applied ecology (MPS); chemical ecology (MPS, MS, PhD); conservation biology (MPS, MS, PhD); ecology (MPS, MS, PhD); entomology (MPS, MS, PhD); environmental interpretation (MPS, MS, PhD); environmental physiology (MPS, MS, PhD); fish and wildlife biology (MPS, MS, PhD); forest pathology and mycology (MPS, MS, PhD); plant biotechnology (MPS); plant science and biotechnology (MPS, MS, PhD).

Department of Environmental Resources and Forest Engineering Offers environmental and resources engineering (MPS, MS, PhD).

Department of Environmental Studies Offers environmental studies (MPS, MS).

Department of Forest and Natural Resources Management Offers environmental and natural resource policy (MS, PhD); environmental and natural resources policy (MPS); forest management and operations (MF); forestry ecosystems science and applications (MPS, MS, PhD); natural resources management (MPS, MS, PhD); quantitative methods and management in forest science (MPS, MS, PhD); recreation and resource management (MPS, MS, PhD); watershed management and forest hydrology (MPS, MS, PhD).

Department of Landscape Architecture Offers community design and planning (MLA, MS); cultural landscape studies and conservation (MLA, MS); landscape and urban ecology (MLA, MS).

Department of Paper and Bioprocess Engineering Offers environmental and resources engineering (MPS, MS, PhD).

Program in Environmental Science *Degree program information:* Part-time programs available. Offers environmental and community land planning (MPS, MS, PhD); environmental and natural resources policy (PhD); environmental communication and participatory processes (MPS, MS, PhD); environmental policy and democratic processes (MPS, MS, PhD); environmental systems and risk management (MPS, MS, PhD); water and wetland resource studies (MPS, MS, PhD).

STATE UNIVERSITY OF NEW YORK COLLEGE OF OPTOMETRY, New York, NY 10036

General Information State-supported, coed, graduate-only institution. *Graduate housing:* On-campus housing not available. *Research affiliation:* Schnurmacher Institute for Vision Research (vision science).

GRADUATE UNITS

Graduate Programs *Degree program information:* Part-time programs available. Offers vision science (MS, PhD).

Professional Program Offers optometry (OD). Electronic applications accepted.

STATE UNIVERSITY OF NEW YORK DOWNSTATE MEDICAL CENTER, Brooklyn, NY 11203-2098

General Information State-supported, coed, upper-level institution. *Graduate housing:* Rooms and/or apartments available on a first-come, first-served basis to single and married students. Housing application deadline: 5/29. *Research affiliation:* Polytechnic University Brooklyn (biomedical engineering), Brooklyn Veterans Administration Medical Center.

GRADUATE UNITS

College of Medicine Offers medicine (MD, MPH); urban and immigrant health (MPH).

College of Nursing *Degree program information:* Part-time and evening/weekend programs available. Offers clinical nurse specialist (MS, Post Master's Certificate); nurse anesthesia (MS); nurse midwifery (MS, Post Master's Certificate); nurse practitioner (MS, Post Master's Certificate); nursing (MS, Post Master's Certificate).

School of Graduate Studies Offers bioimaging and neuroengineering (PhD); biomedical engineering (MS); molecular and cellular biology (PhD); neural and behavioral science (PhD).

STATE UNIVERSITY OF NEW YORK EMPIRE STATE COLLEGE, Saratoga Springs, NY 12866-4391

General Information State-supported, coed, comprehensive institution. *Graduate housing:* On-campus housing not available.

GRADUATE UNITS

Graduate Studies *Degree program information:* Part-time and evening/weekend programs available. Postbaccalaureate distance learning degree programs offered (minimal on-campus study). Offers business administration (MBA); business and policy studies (MA); labor and policy studies (MA); liberal studies (MA); social policy (MA); teaching (MA). Electronic applications accepted.

STATE UNIVERSITY OF NEW YORK INSTITUTE OF TECHNOLOGY, Utica, NY 13504-3050

General Information State-supported, coed, comprehensive institution. *Graduate housing:* Room and/or apartments available on a first-come, first-served basis to single students; on-campus housing not available to married students. *Research affiliation:* Wyle Laboratories-Reliability Information Analysis Center (reliability analysis and information).

GRADUATE UNITS

School of Arts and Sciences *Degree program information:* Part-time and evening/weekend programs available. Offers applied sociology (MS); information design and technology (MS).

School of Business *Degree program information:* Part-time and evening/weekend programs available. Postbaccalaureate distance learning degree programs offered (no on-campus study). Offers accountancy (MS); business administration in technology management (MBA); health services administration (MS); technology management (MBA).

School of Information Systems and Engineering Technology *Degree program information:* Part-time and evening/weekend programs available. Offers advanced technology (MS); computer and information science (MS); telecommunications (MS).

School of Nursing and Health Systems *Degree program information:* Part-time programs available. Offers adult nurse practitioner (MS, CAS); family nurse practitioner (MS, CAS); gerontological nurse practitioner (MS, CAS); nursing administration (MS, CAS); nursing education (MS, CAS).

See Close-Up on page 997.

STATE UNIVERSITY OF NEW YORK MARITIME COLLEGE, Throggs Neck, NY 10465-4198

General Information State-supported, coed, primarily men, comprehensive institution. *Graduate housing:* Room and/or apartments available to single students; on-campus housing not available to married students. *Research affiliation:* Port Authority of New York and New Jersey (transportation), Transportation Infrastructure Research Consortium, Transportation Research Board (maritime transportation).

GRADUATE UNITS

Program in International Transportation Management *Degree program information:* Part-time and evening/weekend programs available. Offers international transportation management (MS).

STATE UNIVERSITY OF NEW YORK UPSTATE MEDICAL UNIVERSITY, Syracuse, NY 13210-2334

General Information State-supported, coed, upper-level institution. CGS member. *Graduate housing:* Rooms and/or apartments available on a first-come, first-served basis to single and married students. Housing application deadline: 8/1.

GRADUATE UNITS

College of Graduate Studies Students: 123 full-time (72 women), 4 part-time (3 women); includes 16 minority (2 African Americans, 11 Asian Americans or Pacific Islanders, 3 Hispanic Americans), 39 international. Average age 28. 165 applicants, 30% accepted, 24 enrolled. *Faculty:* 80 full-time (15 women), 15 part-time/adjunct (2 women). Expenses: Contact institution. *Financial support:* In 2008–09, 118 students received support, including fellowships (averaging $21,514 per year), research assistantships (averaging $21,514 per year); Federal Work-Study, institutionally sponsored loans, health care benefits, tuition waivers (full), and unspecified assistantships also available. Financial award application deadline: 4/15; financial award applicants required to submit FAFSA. In 2008, 4 master's, 20 doctorates awarded. Offers anatomy (MS); anatomy and cell biology (PhD); biochemistry (MS); biochemistry and molecular biology (PhD); microbiology (MS); microbiology and immunology (PhD); neuroscience (PhD); pharmacology (PhD); physiology (MS, PhD). *Application deadline:* Applications are processed on a rolling basis. *Application fee:* $40. Electronic applications accepted. *Application Contact:* Sandra Tillotson, Coordinator of Graduate Recruitment, 315-464-7655, Fax: 315-464-4544, E-mail: tillotss@upstate.edu. *Dean, College of Graduate Studies,* Dr. Steven R. Goodman, 315-464-4538.

College of Medicine Students: 646 full-time (314 women); includes 187 minority (70 African Americans, 2 American Indian/Alaska Native, 112 Asian Americans or Pacific Islanders, 3 Hispanic Americans), 42 international. Average age 26. 5,270 applicants, 8% accepted, 160 enrolled. *Faculty:* 366 full-time (74 women), 182 part-time/adjunct (37 women). Expenses: Contact institution. *Financial support:* In 2008–09, 545 students received support; research assistantships, teaching assistantships, career-related internships or fieldwork, Federal Work-Study, institutionally sponsored loans, scholarships/grants, and tuition waivers (full and partial) available. Support available to part-time students. Financial award application deadline: 3/1; financial award applicants required to submit FAFSA. In 2008, 157 MDs awarded. Offers medicine (MD). *Application deadline:* For fall admission, 12/1 for domestic and international students. Applications are processed on a rolling basis. *Application fee:* $100. Electronic applications accepted. *Application Contact:* Jennifer Welch, Director of Admissions, 315-

464-4570, Fax: 315-464-8867, E-mail: welchj@upstate.edu. *Dean,* Dr. Steven J. Scheinman, 315-464-9720, E-mail: scheinms@upstate.edu.

College of Nursing *Degree program information:* Part-time programs available. Offers nurse practitioner (Post Master's Certificate); nursing (MS). Electronic applications accepted.

Department of Physical Therapy *Degree program information:* Part-time and evening/weekend programs available. Postbaccalaureate distance learning degree programs offered (minimal on-campus study).

Program in Medical Technology Offers medical technology (MS).

STEPHEN F. AUSTIN STATE UNIVERSITY, Nacogdoches, TX 75962

General Information State-supported, coed, comprehensive institution. *Graduate housing:* Rooms and/or apartments available on a first-come, first-served basis to single students and available to married students. Housing application deadline: 6/1. *Research affiliation:* University Health Center at Tyler (biotechnology, environmental science).

GRADUATE UNITS

Graduate School *Degree program information:* Part-time and evening/weekend programs available. Postbaccalaureate distance learning degree programs offered. Electronic applications accepted.

College of Applied Arts and Science *Degree program information:* Part-time programs available. Offers applied arts and science (MA, MIS, MSW); communication (MA); interdisciplinary studies (MIS); mass communication (MA); social work (MSW).

College of Business *Degree program information:* Part-time and evening/weekend programs available. Offers business (MBA, MPAC, MS); computer science (MS); management and marketing (MBA); professional accountancy (MPAC).

College of Education *Degree program information:* Part-time and evening/weekend programs available. Offers athletic training (MS); counseling (MA); early childhood education (M Ed); education (M Ed, MA, MS, Ed D); educational leadership (Ed D); elementary education (M Ed); human sciences (MS); kinesiology (M Ed); school psychology (MA); secondary education (M Ed); special education (M Ed); speech pathology (MS).

College of Fine Arts *Degree program information:* Part-time programs available. Offers art (MA); design (MFA); drawing (MFA); fine arts (MA, MFA, MM); music (MA, MM); painting (MFA); sculpture (MFA).

College of Forestry and Agriculture Offers agriculture (MS); forestry (MF, MS, PhD); forestry and agriculture (MF, MS, PhD).

College of Liberal Arts *Degree program information:* Part-time and evening/weekend programs available. Offers English (MA); history (MA); liberal arts (MA, MPA); psychology (MA); public administration (MPA).

College of Sciences and Mathematics *Degree program information:* Part-time programs available. Offers biology (MS); biotechnology (MS); chemistry (MS); environmental science (MS); geology (MS, MSNS); mathematics (MS); mathematics education (MS); physics (MS); sciences and mathematics (MS, MSNS); statistics (MS).

STEPHENS COLLEGE, Columbia, MO 65215-0002

General Information Independent, Undergraduate: women only; graduate: coed, comprehensive institution. *Enrollment:* 1,147 graduate, professional, and undergraduate students; 168 full-time matriculated graduate/professional students (146 women), 32 part-time matriculated graduate/professional students (28 women). *Enrollment by degree level:* 200 master's. *Graduate faculty:* 8 full-time (6 women), 19 part-time/adjunct (11 women). *Tuition:* Part-time $335 per credit hour. *Required fees:* $15 per credit hour. *Graduate housing:* On-campus housing not available. *Student services:* Teacher training. *Library facilities:* Hugh Stephens Library. *Online resources:* library catalog, web page, access to other libraries' catalogs. *Collection:* 133,581 titles, 21,375 serial subscriptions, 1,548 audiovisual materials.

Computer facilities: Computer purchase and lease plans are available. 104 computers available on campus for general student use. A campuswide network can be accessed from student residence rooms and from off campus. *Web address:* http://www.stephens.edu/.

General Application Contact: Jennifer Deaver, Director of Recruitment for Graduate and Continuing Studies, 800-388-7579, E-mail: online@stephens.edu.

GRADUATE UNITS

Division of Graduate and Continuing Studies Students: 168 full-time (146 women), 32 part-time (28 women); includes 10 minority (7 African Americans, 1 American Indian/Alaska Native, 1 Asian American or Pacific Islander, 1 Hispanic American). Average age 35. 57 applicants, 91% accepted, 48 enrolled. *Faculty:* 8 full-time (6 women), 19 part-time/adjunct (11 women). Expenses: Contact institution. *Financial support:* In 2008–09, 41 students received support, including 6 fellowships with full tuition reimbursements available (averaging $9,000 per year); scholarships/grants and unspecified assistantships also available. Financial award applicants required to submit FAFSA. In 2008, 59 master's awarded. *Degree program information:* Part-time and evening/weekend programs available. Postbaccalaureate distance learning degree programs offered (minimal on-campus study). Offers business administration (MBA); counseling (M Ed); curriculum and instruction (M Ed). *Application deadline:* For fall admission, 7/25 priority date for domestic and international students; for winter admission, 12/1 priority date for domestic and international students; for spring admission, 4/25 priority date for domestic and international students. Applications are processed on a rolling basis. *Application fee:* $40. Electronic applications accepted. *Application Contact:* Jennifer Deaver, Director of Marketing and Recruitment, 800-388-7579, E-mail: online@stephens.edu. *Dean of Graduate and Continuing Studies,* Dean Suzanne Sharp, 573-876-7123, Fax: 573-876-7237, E-mail: online@stephens.edu.

STETSON UNIVERSITY, DeLand, FL 32723

General Information Independent, coed, comprehensive institution. *Enrollment:* 3,696 graduate, professional, and undergraduate students; 1,019 full-time matriculated graduate/professional students (571 women), 426 part-time matriculated graduate/professional students (233 women). *Enrollment by degree level:* 1,081 first professional, 357 master's, 7 other advanced degrees. *Graduate faculty:* 80 full-time (34 women), 65 part-time/adjunct (24 women). *Graduate housing:* Rooms and/or apartments available to single and married students. *Student services:* Campus employment opportunities, campus safety program, career counseling, free psychological counseling, international student services, multicultural affairs office, teacher training. *Library facilities:* DuPont-Ball Library plus 1 other. *Online resources:* library catalog, web page. *Collection:* 393,753 titles, 31,000 serial subscriptions, 20,236 audiovisual materials.

Computer facilities: 458 computers available on campus for general student use. A campuswide network can be accessed from student residence rooms and from off campus. Online class registration is available. *Web address:* http://www.stetson.edu/.

General Application Contact: Office of Graduate Studies, 386-822-7075, Fax: 386-822-7388.

GRADUATE UNITS

College of Arts and Sciences Students: 104 full-time (86 women), 43 part-time (39 women); includes 33 minority (14 African Americans, 3 American Indian/Alaska Native, 16 Hispanic Americans). Average age 33. Expenses: Contact institution. *Financial support:* Career-related internships or fieldwork, Federal Work-Study, institutionally sponsored loans, scholarships/grants, and tuition waivers (partial) available. Support available to part-time students. In 2008, 95 master's awarded. *Degree program information:* Part-time and evening/weekend programs available. Offers arts and sciences (M Ed, MA, MS); education (M Ed, MS); educational leadership (M Ed); marriage and family therapy (MS); mental health counseling (MS); reading education (M Ed); school guidance and family consultation (MS). *Application deadline:* For fall admission, 3/1 priority date for domestic students; for spring admission, 11/1 for domestic students. Applications are processed on a rolling basis. *Application fee:* $25. *Application Contact:* Diana Belian, Office of Graduate Studies, 386-822-7075, Fax: 386-822-7388, E-mail: dbelian@stetson.edu. *Dean,* Dr. Grady Ballenger, 386-822-7515.

Division of Humanities Students: 4 part-time (all women). Average age 27. Expenses: Contact institution. In 2008, 4 master's awarded. Offers English (MA); humanities (MA). *Application deadline:* For fall admission, 3/1 priority date for domestic students; for spring admission, 11/1 for domestic students. Applications are processed on a rolling basis. *Application fee:* $25. *Application Contact:* Diana Belian, Office of Graduate Studies, 386-822-7075, Fax: 386-822-7388, E-mail: dbelian@stetson.edu. *Dean,* Dr. Grady Ballenger, 386-822-7515.

College of Law Students: 828 full-time (437 women), 253 part-time (132 women); includes 199 minority (69 African Americans, 9 American Indian/Alaska Native, 36 Asian Americans or Pacific Islanders, 85 Hispanic Americans), 18 international. Average age 28. Expenses: Contact institution. *Financial support:* Research assistantships, teaching assistantships, career-related internships or fieldwork, institutionally sponsored loans, and scholarships/grants available. Financial award application deadline: 4/1; financial award applicants required to submit FAFSA. In 2008, 300 JDs awarded. Offers law (JD, LL M). *Application deadline:* For fall admission, 3/1 priority date for domestic students; for spring admission, 9/1 for domestic students. *Application fee:* $50. *Application Contact:* Pamela Coleman, Assistant Dean and Director of Admissions, 727-562-7802, E-mail: lawadmit@law.stetson.edu. *Dean,* Dr. Darby Dickerson, 727-562-7810.

School of Business Administration Students: 87 full-time (48 women), 130 part-time (62 women); includes 25 minority (12 African Americans, 7 Asian Americans or Pacific Islanders, 6 Hispanic Americans), 8 international. Average age 29. Expenses: Contact institution. *Financial support:* In 2008–09, 3 research assistantships were awarded; Federal Work-Study and institutionally sponsored loans also available. Support available to part-time students. Financial award application deadline: 3/15. In 2008, 142 master's awarded. *Degree program information:* Part-time and evening/weekend programs available. Offers accounting (M Acc); business administration (M Acc, MBA). *Application deadline:* For fall admission, 7/1 for domestic students. *Application fee:* $25. *Application Contact:* Jeanne Bosco, Administrative Assistant, 386-822-7410, Fax: 386-822-7413, E-mail: jbosco@stetson.edu. *Dean,* Dr. James Scheiner, 386-822-7415.

STEVENS INSTITUTE OF TECHNOLOGY, Hoboken, NJ 07030

General Information Independent, coed, university. CGS member. *Graduate housing:* Room and/or apartments available on a first-come, first-served basis to single students.

GRADUATE UNITS

Graduate School *Degree program information:* Part-time and evening/weekend programs available. Postbaccalaureate distance learning degree programs offered (no on-campus study). Electronic applications accepted.

Charles V. Schaefer Jr. School of Engineering *Degree program information:* Part-time and evening/weekend programs available. Postbaccalaureate distance learning degree programs offered. Offers advanced manufacturing (Certificate); air pollution technology (Certificate); analytical chemistry (PhD, Certificate); applied mathematics (MS); applied optics (Certificate); applied statistics (Certificate); armament engineering (M Eng); bioinformatics (PhD, Certificate); biomedical chemistry (Certificate); biomedical engineering (M Eng, Certificate); chemical biology (MS, PhD, Certificate); chemical engineering (M Eng, PhD, Engr); chemical physiology (Certificate); chemistry (MS, PhD); civil engineering (M Eng, PhD, Certificate, Engr); computational fluid mechanics and heat transfer (Certificate); computer and electrical engineering (M Eng); computer architecture and digital system design (M Eng); computer engineering (M Eng, PhD, Certificate); computer graphics (Certificate); computer science (MS, PhD); computer systems (M Eng, Certificate); construction accounting/estimating (Certificate); construction engineering (Certificate); construction law/disputes (Certificate); construction management (MS, Certificate); construction/quality management (Certificate); data communications and networks (M Eng); database management systems (Certificate); design and production management (Certificate); digital signal processing (Certificate); digital systems design (M Eng); distributed systems (Certificate); electrical engineering (M Eng, PhD, Certificate); elements of computer science (Certificate); engineered software systems (M Eng); engineering (M Eng, MS, PhD, Certificate, Engr); engineering physics (M Eng); enterprise computing (Certificate); enterprise security and information assurance (Certificate); environmental compatibility in engineering (Certificate); environmental engineering (M Eng, PhD, Certificate); environmental processes (M Eng, Certificate); geotechnical engineering (Certificate); geotechnical/geoenvironmental engineering (M Eng, Engr); groundwater and soil pollution control (M Eng, Certificate); health informatics (Certificate); hydrologic modeling (M Eng); image processing and multimedia (M Eng); information system security (M Eng); information systems (M Eng); inland and coastal environmental hydrodynamics (M Eng, Certificate); integrated product development (M Eng); manufacturing technologies (M Eng); maritime systems (MS); materials science (M Eng, PhD); mathematics (MS, PhD); mechanical engineering (M Eng, PhD); microdevices and microsystems (Certificate); microelectronics and photonics (Certificate); microelectronics and photonics science and technology (M Eng); multimedia experience and management (Certificate); networks and systems administration (Certificate); ocean engineering (M Eng, PhD); organic chemistry (PhD); pharmaceutical manufacturing (M Eng, MS, Certificate); physical chemistry (PhD); physics (MS, PhD); plasma and surface physics (Certificate); polymer chemistry (PhD, Certificate); power generation (Certificate); product architecture and engineering (M Eng); real-time and embedded systems (Certificate); robotics and control (Certificate); security and privacy (Certificate); service oriented computing (Certificate); signal processing for communications (M Eng); software design (Certificate); stochastic systems (MS, Certificate); stormwater management (M Eng); structural analysis and design (Certificate); structural engineering (M Eng, Engr); systems reliability and design (M Eng); telecommunications systems engineering (M Eng); theoretical computer science (Certificate); vibration and noise control (Certificate); water quality control (Certificate); water resources engineering (M Eng); wireless communications (M Eng, Certificate). Electronic applications accepted.

School of Systems and Enterprises Offers agile systems and enterprises (Certificate); engineering management (M Eng, PhD); enterprise systems (MS, PhD); financial engineering (MS); software engineering (MS); space systems engineering (M Eng, Certificate); systems and enterprises (M Eng, MS, PhD, Certificate); systems and supportability engineering (Certificate); systems design and operational effectiveness (M Eng); systems engineering (M Eng, PhD); systems engineering management (Certificate).

Wesley J. Howe School of Technology Management *Degree program information:* Part-time and evening/weekend programs available. Postbaccalaureate distance learning degree programs offered. Offers business (MS); computer science (MS); e-commerce (MS); engineering management (MBA); enterprise systems (MS); entrepreneurial information technology (MS); financial engineering (MBA); general management (MS); global innovation management (MS); human resource management (MS); information architecture (MS); information management (MBA, MS, PhD, Certificate); information security (MS); information technology in financial services (MBA); information technology in financial services industry (MS); information technology in the pharmaceutical industry (MBA, MS); information technology outsourcing (MBA); information technology outsourcing management (MS); management of wireless networks (MS); online security, technology and business (MS); pharmaceutical management (MBA); professional communications (Certificate); project management (MBA, MS, Certificate); software engineering (MS); technical management (MS); technology commercialization (MS); technology management (EMBA, EMTM, MBA, MS, PhD, Certificate); technology management for experienced professionals (EMTM, MS, Certificate); telecommunications (MS); telecommunications management (MBA, PhD, Certificate). Electronic applications accepted.

STEVENSON UNIVERSITY, Stevenson, MD 21153

General Information Independent, coed, comprehensive institution. *Enrollment:* 3,409 graduate, professional, and undergraduate students; 75 full-time matriculated graduate/professional students (51 women), 183 part-time matriculated graduate/professional students (115 women). *Enrollment by degree level:* 258 master's. *Graduate faculty:* 4 full-time (2 women), 4 part-time/adjunct (2 women). *Tuition:* Part-time $495 per credit. *Required fees:* $75 per term. *Graduate housing:* On-campus housing not available. *Student services:* Campus employment opportunities, campus safety program, career counseling, exercise/wellness program,

Stevenson University (continued)

international student services, multicultural affairs office, services for students with disabilities. *Library facilities:* Villa Julie College Library. *Online resources:* library catalog, web page, access to other libraries' catalogs. *Collection:* 81,802 titles, 1,058 serial subscriptions, 2,727 audiovisual materials.

Computer facilities: 300 computers available on campus for general student use. A campuswide network can be accessed from student residence rooms and from off campus. *Web address:* http://www.stevenson.edu/.

General Application Contact: Nicole Metzger, Enrollment Counselor, 443-352-4417, E-mail: nmetzger@stevenson.edu.

GRADUATE UNITS

Graduate and Professional Studies Programs Students: 75 full-time (51 women), 183 part-time (115 women); includes 77 minority (60 African Americans, 5 Asian Americans or Pacific Islanders, 12 Hispanic Americans), 1 international. Average age 31. 560 applicants. *Faculty:* 4 full-time (2 women), 4 part-time/adjunct (2 women). Expenses: Contact institution. In 2008, 85 master's awarded. *Degree program information:* Part-time and evening/weekend programs available. Postbaccalaureate distance learning degree programs offered (minimal on-campus study). Offers advanced information technologies (MS); business and technology management (MS); forensic accounting (MS); forensic legal professional (MS); forensic science (MS); information technology (MS); interdisciplinary track (MS); investigations (MS). *Application deadline:* For fall admission, 8/1 for domestic students; for spring admission, 12/31 for domestic students. Applications are processed on a rolling basis. *Application fee:* $25. *Application Contact:* Nicole Metzger, Enrollment Counselor, 443-352-4417, E-mail: nmetzger@stevenson.edu. *Director of Enrollment for Graduate and Professional Studies,* Allison Jones, 410-486-7001, Fax: 443-352-4440, E-mail: adm-alli@mail.vjc.edu.

STONY BROOK UNIVERSITY, STATE UNIVERSITY OF NEW YORK, Stony Brook, NY 11794

General Information State-supported, coed, university. CGS member. *Enrollment:* 23,994 graduate, professional, and undergraduate students; 4,442 full-time matriculated graduate/professional students (2,309 women), 2,395 part-time matriculated graduate/professional students (1,583 women). *Enrollment by degree level:* 630 first professional, 3,287 master's, 2,369 doctoral, 551 other advanced degrees. *Graduate faculty:* 1,298 full-time (417 women), 480 part-time/adjunct (193 women). *Graduate housing:* Rooms and/or apartments available to single and married students. Typical cost: $11,328 per year for single students; $15,408 per year for married students. *Student services:* Campus employment opportunities, campus safety program, career counseling, child daycare facilities, exercise/wellness program, free psychological counseling, grant writing training, international student services, low-cost health insurance, multicultural affairs office, services for students with disabilities, teacher training, writing training. *Library facilities:* Frank Melville, Jr. Building Library plus 6 others. *Online resources:* library catalog, web page, access to other libraries' catalogs. *Collection:* 2 million titles, 59,198 serial subscriptions, 50,043 audiovisual materials. *Research affiliation:* Veterans Affairs Medical Center (Northport, NY), Nassau University Medical Center, Winthrop University Hospital, Cold Spring Harbor Laboratory, Brookhaven National Laboratory.

Computer facilities: Computer purchase and lease plans are available. 2,600 computers available on campus for general student use. A campuswide network can be accessed from student residence rooms and from off campus. Online class registration is available. *Web address:* http://www.sunysb.edu/.

General Application Contact: Dr. Kent Marks, Assistant Dean, Admissions and Records, 631-632-4723, Fax: 631-632-7243, E-mail: kmarks@notes.cc.sunysb.edu.

GRADUATE UNITS

Graduate School Expenses: Contact institution. *Financial support:* Fellowships, research assistantships, teaching assistantships, career-related internships or fieldwork, Federal Work-Study, institutionally sponsored loans, scholarships/grants, traineeships, health care benefits, tuition waivers (full), and unspecified assistantships available. *Degree program information:* Part-time and evening/weekend programs available. *Application deadline:* For fall admission, 1/15 for domestic and international students; for spring admission, 10/1 for domestic and international students. *Application fee:* $60. *Application Contact:* Dr. Kent Marks, Assistant Dean, Admissions and Records, 631-632-4723, Fax: 631-632-7243, E-mail: kmarks@notes.cc.sunysb.edu. *Dean,* Dr. Lawrence B. Martin, 631-632-7035, Fax: 631-632-7243.

College of Arts and Sciences Students: 1,722 full-time (869 women), 192 part-time (128 women); includes 244 minority (45 African Americans, 3 American Indian/Alaska Native, 96 Asian Americans or Pacific Islanders, 100 Hispanic Americans), 679 international. 3,738 applicants, 25% accepted. *Faculty:* 450 full-time (125 women), 67 part-time/adjunct (27 women). Expenses: Contact institution. *Financial support:* In 2008–09, 327 research assistantships, 699 teaching assistantships were awarded; fellowships, career-related internships or fieldwork, Federal Work-Study, scholarships/grants, traineeships, health care benefits, and unspecified assistantships also available. In 2008, 244 master's, 217 doctorates, 6 other advanced degrees awarded. *Degree program information:* Part-time and evening/weekend programs available. Offers Africana studies (MA); anthropology (MA, PhD); applied ecology (MA); art history and criticism (MA, PhD); arts and sciences (MA, MAPP, MAT, MFA, MM, MS, DMA, PhD, Certificate); astronomy (PhD); biochemistry and molecular biology (PhD); biochemistry and structural biology (PhD); biological sciences (MA); biopsychology (PhD); cellular and developmental biology (PhD); chemistry (MS, PhD); clinical psychology (PhD); cognitive/experimental psychology (PhD); comparative literature (MA, PhD); composition studies (Certificate); cultural studies (PhD); dramaturgy (MFA); earth science (MAT); ecology and evolution (PhD); economics (MA, PhD); English (MA, PhD); English education (MAT); ethnomusicology (MA, PhD); French (MA); genetics (PhD); geosciences (MS, PhD); Hispanic languages and literature (MA, PhD); history (MA, PhD); immunology and pathology (PhD); Italian (MA); linguistics (MA, PhD); mathematics (MA, MAT, PhD); modern research instrumentation (MS); molecular and cellular biology (MA, PhD); music history/theory (MA, PhD); music performance (MM, DMA); neuroscience (PhD); philosophy (MA, PhD); physics (MA, MAT, MS, PhD); physics education (MAT); political science (MA, PhD); public policy (MAPP); Romance languages (MA); social and health psychology (PhD); sociology (MA, PhD); studio art (MFA); teaching English to speakers of other languages (MA); theatre arts (MA, MFA). *Application deadline:* For fall admission, 1/15 for domestic students. *Application fee:* $60. *Application Contact:* Dr. Kent Marks, Assistant Dean, Admissions and Records, 631-632-4723, Fax: 631-632-7243, E-mail: kmarks@notes.cc.sunysb.edu. *Interim Dean,* Dr. Nancy Squires, 631-632-6999, Fax: 631-632-6900.

College of Business Students: 134 full-time (64 women), 112 part-time (44 women); includes 54 minority (8 African Americans, 1 American Indian/Alaska Native, 35 Asian Americans or Pacific Islanders, 10 Hispanic Americans), 56 international. Average age 29. 222 applicants, 55% accepted. *Faculty:* 17 full-time (2 women), 25 part-time/adjunct (5 women). Expenses: Contact institution. *Financial support:* In 2008–09, 2 teaching assistantships were awarded; research assistantships. In 2008, 173 master's, 5 other advanced degrees awarded. Offers business (MBA, MS, Certificate); finance (MBA, Certificate); health care management (MBA, Certificate); human resource management (Certificate); human resources (MBA); information systems management (MBA, Certificate); management (MBA); marketing (MBA); technology management (MS). *Application deadline:* For fall admission, 1/15 for domestic and international students; for spring admission, 10/1 for domestic and international students. *Application fee:* $60. *Application Contact:* Aristotle Lekacos, Director, Graduate Program, 631-632-7171, E-mail: aristotle.lekacost@notes.cc.sunysb.edu. *Interim Dean,* Joseph McDonnell, 631-632-7180.

College of Engineering and Applied Sciences Students: 735 full-time (213 women), 223 part-time (74 women); includes 102 minority (17 African Americans, 71 Asian Americans or Pacific Islanders, 14 Hispanic Americans), 665 international. 2,318 applicants, 36% accepted. *Faculty:* 140 full-time (26 women), 20 part-time/adjunct (2 women). Expenses: Contact institution. *Financial support:* In 2008–09, 211 research assistantships, 139 teaching assistantships were awarded; fellowships, career-related internships or fieldwork also available. In 2008, 250 master's, 82 doctorates awarded. *Degree program information:* Part-time and evening/weekend programs available. Offers applied mathematics and statistics (MS, PhD); biomedical engineering (MS, PhD, Certificate); computer science (MS, PhD); educational technology (MS); electrical and computer engineering (MS, PhD); energy and environmental systems (MS, Advanced Certificate); engineering and applied sciences (MS, PhD, Advanced Certificate, Certificate); global operations management (MS); information systems (Certificate); information systems engineering (MS); materials science and engineering (MS, PhD); mechanical engineering (MS, PhD); medical physics (MS, PhD); software engineering (Certificate); technology, policy, and innovation (PhD). *Application deadline:* For fall admission, 1/15 for domestic students. *Application fee:* $60. *Application Contact:* Dr. Kent Marks, Assistant Dean, Admissions and Records, 631-632-4723, Fax: 631-632-7243, E-mail: kmarks@notes.cc.sunysb.edu. *Dean,* Dr. Yacov Shamash, 631-632-8380.

School of Marine and Atmospheric Sciences Students: 112 full-time (65 women), 6 part-time (2 women); includes 10 minority (1 African American, 3 Asian Americans or Pacific Islanders, 6 Hispanic Americans), 38 international. Average age 28. 110 applicants, 54% accepted. *Faculty:* 38 full-time (6 women), 2 part-time/adjunct (both women). Expenses: Contact institution. *Financial support:* In 2008–09, 42 research assistantships, 49 teaching assistantships were awarded; fellowships, career-related internships or fieldwork and tuition waivers (full) also available. In 2008, 9 master's, 12 doctorates awarded. *Degree program information:* Evening/weekend programs available. Offers atmospheric sciences (MS, PhD); marine and atmospheric sciences (MS, PhD); marine sciences (MS, PhD). *Application fee:* $60. *Application Contact:* Dr. Glenn R. Lopez, Assistant Director, 631-632-8660, Fax: 631-632-8200, E-mail: glopez@notes.cc.sunysb.edu. *Dean and Director,* Dr. David O. Conover, 631-632-8700, Fax: 631-632-8200, E-mail: dconover@notes.cc.sunnysb.edu.

School of Professional Development Students: 317 full-time (187 women), 1,200 part-time (773 women); includes 187 minority (77 African Americans, 2 American Indian/Alaska Native, 22 Asian Americans or Pacific Islanders, 86 Hispanic Americans), 11 international. Average age 28. *Faculty:* 5 full-time (3 women), 131 part-time/adjunct (53 women). Expenses: Contact institution. *Financial support:* Fellowships, research assistantships, teaching assistantships, career-related internships or fieldwork available. Support available to part-time students. In 2008, 597 master's, 234 other advanced degrees awarded. *Degree program information:* Part-time and evening/weekend programs available. Postbaccalaureate distance learning degree programs offered. Offers biology -grade 7-12 (MAT); chemistry-grade 7-12 (MAT); coaching (Graduate Certificate); computer integrated engineering (Graduate Certificate); earth science-grade 7-12 (MAT); educational computing (Graduate Certificate); educational leadership (Advanced Certificate); English-grade 7-12 (MAT); environmental management (Graduate Certificate); environmental/occupational health and safety (Graduate Certificate); French-grade 7-12 (MAT); German-grade 7-12 (MAT); human resource management (Graduate Certificate); information systems management (Graduate Certificate); Italian-grade 7-12 (MAT); liberal studies (MA); liberal studies online (MA); mathematics-grade 7-12 (MAT); operation research (Graduate Certificate); physics-grade 7-12 (MAT); school administration and supervision (Graduate Certificate); school building leadership (Graduate Certificate); school district administration (Graduate Certificate); school district business leadership (Advanced Certificate); school district leadership (Graduate Certificate); social science and the professions (MPS); social studies-grade 7-12 (MAT); Spanish-grade 7-12 (MAT); waste management (Graduate Certificate). *Application deadline:* Applications are processed on a rolling basis. *Application fee:* $62. *Application Contact:* Dr. Paul J. Edelson, Dean, 631-632-7052, Fax: 631-632-9046, E-mail: paul.edelson@stonybrook.edu. *Dean,* Dr. Paul J. Edelson, 631-632-7052, Fax: 631-632-9046, E-mail: paul.edelson@stonybrook.edu.

Stony Brook Southampton Students: 6 full-time (4 women), 27 part-time (19 women); includes 2 minority (1 African American, 1 Asian American or Pacific Islander). 28 applicants, 68% accepted. *Faculty:* 1 (woman) full-time, 12 part-time/adjunct (6 women). Expenses: Contact institution. *Financial support:* In 2008–09, 6 teaching assistantships were awarded. In 2008, 5 master's awarded. Offers fiction (MFA); poetry (MFA); scientific writing (MFA); scriptwriting (MFA). *Application Contact:* Dr. Robert Reeves, Director, 631-632-5030, Fax: 631-632-2576, E-mail: southamptonwriters@notes.cc.sunysb.edu. *Director,* Dr. Robert Reeves, 631-632-5030, Fax: 631-632-2576, E-mail: southamptonwriters@notes.cc.sunysb.edu.

Stony Brook University Medical Center Expenses: Contact institution. In 2008, 147 first professional degrees, 433 master's, 102 doctorates, 42 other advanced degrees awarded. Offers medicine (DDS, MD, MPH, MS, MSW, DNP, DPT, PhD, Advanced Certificate, Certificate). *Application Contact:* Dr. Kent Marks, Assistant Dean, Admissions and Records, 631-632-4723, Fax: 631-632-7243, E-mail: kmarks@notes.cc.sunysb.edu. *Chief Executive Officer,* Steven L. Strongwater, 631-444-4000.

Health Sciences Center Students: 1,416 full-time (907 women), 636 part-time (544 women); includes 657 minority (207 African Americans, 6 American Indian/Alaska Native, 323 Asian Americans or Pacific Islanders, 121 Hispanic Americans), 44 international. 5,812 applicants, 14% accepted. *Faculty:* 701 full-time (265 women), 224 part-time/adjunct (98 women). Expenses: Contact institution. *Financial support:* In 2008–09, 95 research assistantships were awarded; fellowships, teaching assistantships, career-related internships or fieldwork, Federal Work-Study, institutionally sponsored loans, traineeships, and tuition waivers (full) also available. Financial award applicants required to submit FAFSA. In 2008, 147 first professional degrees, 433 master's, 102 doctorates, 42 other advanced degrees awarded. *Degree program information:* Part-time programs available. Offers adult health nurse practitioner (Certificate); adult health/primary care nursing (MS); child health nurse practitioner (Certificate); child health nursing (MS); dental medicine (DDS, MS, PhD, Certificate); endodontics (Certificate); family nurse practitioner (MS, Certificate); health care management (Advanced Certificate); health care policy and management (MS); health sciences (DDS, MD, MS, MSW, DNP, DPT, PhD, Advanced Certificate, Certificate); mental health/psychiatric nursing (MS, Certificate); neonatal nurse practitioner (Certificate); neonatal nursing (MS); nurse midwifery (MS, Certificate); nursing (MS, DNP, Certificate); nursing practice (DNP); occupational therapy (MS); oral biology and pathology (MS, PhD); orthodontics (Certificate); perinatal women's health nursing (MS, Certificate); periodontics (Certificate); physical therapy (DPT); physician assistant (MS); social welfare (PhD); social work (MSW). *Application fee:* $60. *Application Contact:* Dr. Kent Marks, Assistant Dean, Admissions and Records, 631-632-4723, Fax: 631-632-7243, E-mail: kmarks@notes.cc.sunysb.edu. *Interim Executive Dean,* Dr. Craig A. Lehmann, 631-444-2251, Fax: 631-444-6032.

School of Medicine Students: 588 full-time (287 women), 29 part-time (24 women); includes 259 minority (52 African Americans, 3 American Indian/Alaska Native, 175 Asian Americans or Pacific Islanders, 29 Hispanic Americans), 28 international. 3,699 applicants, 8% accepted. *Faculty:* 572 full-time (182 women), 93 part-time/adjunct (43 women). Expenses: Contact institution. *Financial support:* Fellowships, research assistantships, teaching assistantships, career-related internships or fieldwork, Federal Work-Study, and tuition waivers (full) available. In 2008, 108 first professional degrees, 19 master's, 19 doctorates awarded. Offers anatomical sciences (PhD); community health (MPH); evaluation sciences (MPH); family violence (MPH); health economics (MPH); medical scientistmedicine (MD, MPH, PhD); molecular and cellular pharmacology (PhD); molecular microbiology (PhD); physiology and biophysics (PhD); population health (MPH); population health and clinical outcomes research (PhD); substance abuse (MPH). *Application deadline:* For fall admission, 1/15 for domestic students. *Application Contact:* Dr. Richard N. Fine, Dean, 631-444-2113. *Dean,* Dr. Richard N. Fine, 631-444-2113.

STRATFORD UNIVERSITY, Falls Church, VA 22043

General Information Proprietary, coed, comprehensive institution. *Enrollment:* 944 full-time matriculated graduate/professional students (430 women), 15 part-time matriculated graduate/professional students (5 women). *Enrollment by degree level:* 959 master's. *Graduate faculty:* 35 full-time, 115 part-time/adjunct. *Tuition:* Full-time $10,125; part-time $375 per credit. One-time fee: $100 full-time. *Graduate housing:* On-campus housing not available. *Student services:* Campus employment opportunities, career counseling, exercise/wellness program, international student services, multicultural affairs office, writing training. *Library facilities:* Stratford University Library. *Collection:* 1,800 titles, 75 serial subscriptions, 283 audiovisual materials.

Computer facilities: 7 computers available on campus for general student use. A campuswide network can be accessed. Online class registration is available. *Web address:* http://www.stratford.edu/.

General Application Contact: James W. Ray, Director of Admissions, 703-821-8570 Ext. 3021, Fax: 703-734-5339, E-mail: jray@stratford.edu.

GRADUATE UNITS

School of Graduate Studies Students: 944 full-time (430 women), 15 part-time (5 women). Average age 26. 950 applicants, 45% accepted, 415 enrolled. *Faculty:* 32 full-time (14 women), 112 part-time/adjunct (25 women). Expenses: Contact institution. *Financial support:* Federal Work-Study available. Financial award applicants required to submit FAFSA. In 2008, 412 master's awarded. *Degree program information:* Part-time and evening/weekend programs available. Postbaccalaureate distance learning degree programs offered (no on-campus study). Offers accounting (MS); business administration (IMBA, MBA); enterprise business management (MS); information systems (MS); software engineering (MS). *Application deadline:* Applications are processed on a rolling basis. *Application fee:* $50. Electronic applications accepted. *Application Contact:* James Ray, Director of Admissions, 703-8218570 Ext. 3021, Fax: 703-7345339, E-mail: jray@stratford.edu. *Chief Academic Officer*, Dr. Habib Khan, 703-821-8570 Ext. 3305, Fax: 703-734-5335, E-mail: hkhan@stratford.edu.

STRAYER UNIVERSITY, Washington, DC 20005-2603

General Information Proprietary, coed, comprehensive institution. *Graduate housing:* On-campus housing not available.

GRADUATE UNITS

Graduate Studies *Degree program information:* Part-time and evening/weekend programs available. Postbaccalaureate distance learning degree programs offered (minimal on-campus study). Offers accounting (MS); acquisition (MBA); business administration (MBA); communications technology (MS); educational management (M Ed); finance (MBA); health services administration (MHSA); hospitality and tourism management (MBA); human resource management (MBA); information systems (MS); management (MBA); management information systems (MS); marketing (MBA); professional accounting (MS); public administration (MPA); supply chain management (MBA); technology in education (M Ed). Programs also offered at campus locations in Birmingham, AL; Chamblee, GA; Cobb County, GA; Morrow, GA; White Marsh, MD; Charleston, SC; Columbia, SC; Greensboro, NC; Greenville, SC; Lexington, KY; Louisville, KY; Nashville, TN; North Raleigh, NC; Washington, DC. Electronic applications accepted.

SUFFOLK UNIVERSITY, Boston, MA 02108-2770

General Information Independent, coed, comprehensive institution. *Enrollment:* 9,435 graduate, professional, and undergraduate students; 1,816 full-time matriculated graduate/professional students (1,106 women), 1,749 part-time matriculated graduate/professional students (941 women). *Enrollment by degree level:* 1,652 first professional, 1,773 master's, 59 doctoral, 81 other advanced degrees. *Graduate faculty:* 243 full-time (94 women), 115 part-time/adjunct (43 women). *Tuition:* Full-time $31,550; part-time $1052 per credit. *Required fees:* $10 per year. Tuition and fees vary according to program. *Graduate housing:* On-campus housing not available. *Student services:* Campus employment opportunities, campus safety program, career counseling, exercise/wellness program, free psychological counseling, grant writing training, international student services, low-cost health insurance, multicultural affairs office, services for students with disabilities, teacher training, writing training. *Library facilities:* Mildred Sawyer Library plus 2 others. *Online resources:* library catalog, web page, access to other libraries' catalogs. *Collection:* 129,647 titles, 23,183 serial subscriptions, 699 audiovisual materials.

Computer facilities: Computer purchase and lease plans are available. 539 computers available on campus for general student use. A campuswide network can be accessed from student residence rooms and from off campus. Online class registration is available. *Web address:* http://www.suffolk.edu/.

General Application Contact: Judith Reynolds, Director of Graduate Admissions, 617-573-8302, Fax: 617-305-1733, E-mail: grad.admission@suffolk.edu.

GRADUATE UNITS

College of Arts and Sciences Students: 266 full-time (199 women), 323 part-time (248 women); includes 50 minority (25 African Americans, 2 American Indian/Alaska Native, 12 Asian Americans or Pacific Islanders, 11 Hispanic Americans), 78 international. Average age 28. 981 applicants, 51% accepted, 240 enrolled. *Faculty:* 131 full-time (63 women), 35 part-time/adjunct (16 women). Expenses: Contact institution. *Financial support:* In 2008–09, 408 students received support, including 251 fellowships with full and partial tuition reimbursements available (averaging $8,985 per year); career-related internships or fieldwork, Federal Work-Study, institutionally sponsored loans, scholarships/grants, and unspecified assistantships also available. Support available to part-time students. Financial award application deadline: 4/1; financial award applicants required to submit FAFSA. In 2008, 200 master's, 11 doctorates, 3 other advanced degrees awarded. *Degree program information:* Part-time and evening/weekend programs available. Offers administration of higher education (M Ed, CAGS); arts and sciences (M Ed, MA, MAC, MS, MSCJS, MSCS, MSE, MSEP, MSIE, MSPS, PhD, CAGS, Graduate Certificate); clinical psychology (PhD); communication studies (MAC); crime and justice studies (MSCJS); economic policy (MSEP); economics (MSE, PhD); ethics and public policy (MS); foundations of education (M Ed); global human resources (Graduate Certificate); human resource, learning and performance (MS, CAGS, Graduate Certificate); human resources (MS, Graduate Certificate); integrated marketing communication (MAC); international economics (MSIE); international relations (MSPS); leadership (CAGS); mental health counseling (MS, CAGS); middle school teaching (M Ed); organizational communication (MAC); organizational development (CAGS, Graduate Certificate); organizational learning and development (MS, Graduate Certificate); political science (MSPS); professional politics (MSPS, CAGS); public relations and advertising (MAC); school counseling (M Ed, CAGS); school teaching (M Ed, CAGS); secondary school teaching (M Ed); software engineering and databases (MSCS); women's health (MA). *Application deadline:* For fall admission, 6/15 priority date for domestic students, 6/15 for international students; for spring admission, 11/1 priority date for domestic students, 11/1 for international students. Applications are processed on a rolling basis. *Application fee:* $50. Electronic applications accepted. *Application Contact:* Judith Reynolds, Director of Graduate Admissions, 617-573-8302, Fax: 617-305-1733, E-mail: grad.admission@suffolk.edu. *Dean*, Dr. Kenneth S. Greenberg, 617-573-8265, Fax: 617-573-8513, E-mail: kgreenbe@suffolk.edu.

Law School *Degree program information:* Part-time and evening/weekend programs available. Offers business law and financial services (JD); civil litigation (JD); global law and technology (LL M); health care and biotechnology law (JD); intellectual property law (JD); international law (JD); U.S. law for international business lawyers (LL M). Electronic applications accepted.

New England School of Art and Design Students: 54 full-time (52 women), 68 part-time (60 women); includes 9 minority (1 African American, 5 Asian Americans or Pacific Islanders, 3 Hispanic Americans), 19 international. Average age 29. 76 applicants, 89% accepted, 38 enrolled. *Faculty:* 22 full-time (12 women), 7 part-time/adjunct (2 women). Expenses: Contact institution. *Financial support:* In 2008–09, 72 students received support, including 10 fellowships with partial tuition reimbursements available (averaging $7,636 per year). Financial award application deadline: 4/1. In 2008, 30 master's awarded. *Degree program information:* Part-time and evening/weekend programs available. Offers graphic design (MA); interior design (MA). *Application deadline:* For fall admission, 6/15 priority date for domestic students, 6/15 for international students; for spring admission, 11/1 priority date for domestic students, 11/1 for international students. Applications are processed on a rolling basis. *Application fee:* $50. Electronic applications accepted. *Application Contact:* Judith Reynolds, Director of Graduate Admissions, 617-573-8302, Fax: 617-305-1733, E-mail: grad.admission@suffolk.edu. *Director*, William Davis, 617-994-4264, Fax: 617-994-4250, E-mail: wdavis@suffolk.edu.

Sawyer Business School Students: 271 full-time (147 women), 805 part-time (407 women); includes 105 minority (38 African Americans, 3 American Indian/Alaska Native, 46 Asian Americans or Pacific Islanders, 18 Hispanic Americans), 199 international. Average age 31. 1,117 applicants, 69% accepted, 353 enrolled. *Faculty:* 110 full-time (31 women), 80 part-time/adjunct (27 women). Expenses: Contact institution. *Financial support:* In 2008–09, 567 students received support, including 264 fellowships with partial tuition reimbursements available (averaging $11,637 per year); career-related internships or fieldwork, Federal Work-Study, and institutionally sponsored loans also available. Support available to part-time students. Financial award application deadline: 4/1; financial award applicants required to submit FAFSA. In 2008, 486 master's, 4 other advanced degrees awarded. *Degree program information:* Part-time and evening/weekend programs available. Postbaccalaureate distance learning degree programs offered (no on-campus study). Offers accounting (MBA, MSA, GDPA); business (EMBA, GMBA, MBA, MBAH, MHA, MPA, MSA, MSF, MSFSB, MST, APC, CASPA, CPASF, GDPA); business administration (APC); corporate financial executive track (MBA); entrepreneurship (MBA); executive business administration (EMBA); finance (MSF, MSFSB, CPASF); global business administration (GMBA); health administration (MBA); international business (MBA); marketing (MBA); nonprofit management (MPA); organizational behavior (MBA); public administration (CASPA); state and local government (MPA); strategic management (MBA); taxation (MBA, MST). *Application deadline:* For fall admission, 6/15 priority date for domestic students, 6/15 for international students; for spring admission, 11/1 for domestic and international students. Applications are processed on a rolling basis. *Application fee:* $50. Electronic applications accepted. *Application Contact:* Judith Reynolds, Director of Graduate Admissions, 617-573-8302, Fax: 617-305-1733, E-mail: grad.admission@suffolk.edu. *Dean*, Dr. William J. O'Neill, 617-573-2665, Fax: 617-573-8704, E-mail: woneill@suffolk.edu.

SULLIVAN UNIVERSITY, Louisville, KY 40205

General Information Proprietary, coed, comprehensive institution. *Enrollment:* 291 full-time matriculated graduate/professional students (88 women), 319 part-time matriculated graduate/professional students (211 women). *Graduate faculty:* 13 full-time (7 women), 11 part-time/adjunct (4 women). *Graduate housing:* On-campus housing not available. *Student services:* Campus employment opportunities, campus safety program, career counseling, exercise/wellness program, international student services, services for students with disabilities. *Library facilities:* McWhorter Library. *Online resources:* library catalog, web page, access to other libraries' catalogs. *Collection:* 22,500 titles, 16,500 serial subscriptions.

Computer facilities: 225 computers available on campus for general student use. A campuswide network can be accessed from student residence rooms and from off campus. *Web address:* http://www.sullivan.edu/.

General Application Contact: Beverly Horsley, Admissions Officer, 502-456-6505, Fax: 502-456-0040, E-mail: bhorsley@sullivan.edu.

GRADUATE UNITS

School of Business Students: 291 full-time (188 women), 319 part-time (211 women); includes 181 minority (143 African Americans, 1 American Indian/Alaska Native, 31 Asian Americans or Pacific Islanders, 6 Hispanic Americans), 9 international. *Faculty:* 13 full-time (7 women), 11 part-time/adjunct (4 women). Expenses: Contact institution. In 2008, 126 master's awarded. *Degree program information:* Part-time programs available. Postbaccalaureate distance learning degree programs offered (no on-campus study). Offers business administration (MBA); collaborative leadership (MSCL); conflict management (MSCM); dispute resolution (MSDR); executive business administration (EMBA); human resource leadership (MSHRL); information technology (MSMIT); management and information technology (MBIT); pharmacy (Pharm D). *Application deadline:* Applications are processed on a rolling basis. *Application fee:* $100. *Application Contact:* Beverly Horsley, Admissions Officer, 502-456-6505, Fax: 502-456-0040, E-mail: bhorsley@sullivan.edu. *Dean of Graduate School*, Dr. Eric S Harter, 502-456-6504, Fax: 502-456-0040, E-mail: eharter@sullivan.edu.

SUL ROSS STATE UNIVERSITY, Alpine, TX 79832

General Information State-supported, coed, comprehensive institution. *Graduate housing:* Rooms and/or apartments available to single and married students. *Research affiliation:* Chihuahuan Desert Research Institute (biology, geology), Big Bend National Park (biology, geology).

GRADUATE UNITS

Division of Agricultural and Natural Resource Science *Degree program information:* Part-time programs available. Offers agricultural and natural resource science (M Ag, MS); animal science (M Ag, MS); range and wildlife management (M Ag, MS).

Rio Grande College of Sul Ross State University *Degree program information:* Part-time and evening/weekend programs available. Offers business administration (MBA); teacher education (M Ed).

School of Arts and Sciences *Degree program information:* Part-time and evening/weekend programs available. Offers art education (M Ed); art history (M Ed); arts and sciences (M Ed, MA, MS); biology (MS); Earth and physical sciences (MS); English (MA); history (MA); political science (MA); psychology (MA); public administration (MA); studio art (M Ed).

School of Professional Studies *Degree program information:* Part-time and evening/weekend programs available. Offers bilingual education (M Ed); business administration (MBA); counseling (M Ed); criminal justice (MS); educational diagnostics (M Ed); elementary education (M Ed); physical education (M Ed); professional studies (M Ed, MBA, MS); reading specialist (M Ed); school administration (M Ed); secondary education (M Ed); supervision (M Ed).

SWEDISH INSTITUTE, COLLEGE OF HEALTH SCIENCES, New York, NY 10001-6700

General Information Proprietary, coed, comprehensive institution. *Graduate housing:* On-campus housing not available.

GRADUATE UNITS

Graduate Program *Degree program information:* Part-time and evening/weekend programs available.

SWEET BRIAR COLLEGE, Sweet Briar, VA 24595

General Information Independent, women only, comprehensive institution. *Enrollment:* 828 graduate, professional, and undergraduate students; 11 full-time matriculated graduate/professional students (all women), 3 part-time matriculated graduate/professional students (2 women). *Enrollment by degree level:* 14 master's. *Graduate faculty:* 3 full-time (2 women), 4 part-time/adjunct (all women). *Tuition:* Part-time $450 per credit hour. Tuition and fees vary according to program. *Graduate housing:* Room and/or apartments available on a first-come, first-served basis to single students; on-campus housing not available to married students. *Student services:* Campus employment opportunities, campus safety program, career counseling, exercise/wellness program, free psychological counseling, international student services, services for students with disabilities, teacher training, writing training. *Library facilities:* Mary Helen Cochran Library plus 3 others. *Online resources:* library catalog, web page, access to other libraries' catalogs. *Collection:* 282,324 titles, 56,272 serial subscriptions, 10,776 audiovisual materials.

Computer facilities: Computer purchase and lease plans are available. 128 computers available on campus for general student use. A campuswide network can be accessed from student residence rooms and from off campus. Online class registration is available. *Web address:* http://www.sbc.edu/.

General Application Contact: Jill E. Gavitt, Assistant Director of Admissions/Special Programs, 434-381-6240, Fax: 434-381-6152, E-mail: jgavitt@sbc.edu.

GRADUATE UNITS

Department of Education Students: 11 full-time (all women), 3 part-time (2 women); includes 1 minority (Hispanic American). Average age 26. 17 applicants, 94% accepted, 14 enrolled. *Faculty:* 3 full-time (2 women), 4 part-time/adjunct (all women). Expenses: Contact institution. *Financial support:* Available to part-time students. Applicants required to submit FAFSA. In 2008, 10 master's awarded. *Degree program information:* Part-time programs available. Offers education (M Ed, MAT). *Application deadline:* For fall admission, 2/1 for domestic students. *Application fee:* $40. Electronic applications accepted. *Application Contact:* Jill E. Gavitt, Assistant Director of Admissions-Special Programs, 434-381-6240, Fax: 434-381-6152, E-mail: jgavitt@sbc.edu. *Director of Graduate Program—Education*, Dr. James L. Alouf, 434-381-6130, E-mail: alouf@sbc.edu.

SYRACUSE UNIVERSITY, Syracuse, NY 13244

General Information Independent, coed, university. CGS member. *Enrollment:* 19,366 graduate, professional, and undergraduate students; 3,830 full-time matriculated graduate/professional students (1,912 women), 1,516 part-time matriculated graduate/professional students (831 women). *Enrollment by degree level:* 640 first professional, 3,230 master's, 1,380 doctoral, 96 other advanced degrees. *Graduate faculty:* 959 full-time (343 women), 550 part-time/adjunct (270 women). *Tuition:* Full-time $19,242; part-time $1069 per credit hour. *Required fees:* $1218. *Graduate housing:* Rooms and/or apartments available on a first-come, first-served basis to single and married students. Typical cost: $6670 per year for single students; $6670 per year for married students. Room charges vary according to housing facility selected. Housing application deadline: 5/1. *Student services:* Campus employment opportunities, campus safety program, career counseling, child daycare facilities, exercise/wellness program, free psychological counseling, grant writing training, international student services, low-cost health insurance, multicultural affairs office, services for students with disabilities, teacher training, writing training. *Library facilities:* E. S. Bird Library plus 7 others. *Online resources:* library catalog, web page, access to other libraries' catalogs. *Collection:* 3.2 million titles, 23,285 serial subscriptions, 436,119 audiovisual materials. *Research affiliation:* Center of Excellence (Environmental & Energy Systems), Say Yes to Education Inc. (High School Support for Higher Education).

Computer facilities: Computer purchase and lease plans are available. 2,955 computers available on campus for general student use. A campuswide network can be accessed from student residence rooms and from off campus. Online class registration, online services, networked client and server computing are available. *Web address:* http://www.syracuse.edu/.

General Application Contact: Diana Hahn, Associate Director, Graduate Recruitment and Retention, 315-443-4492, Fax: 315-443-3423, E-mail: grad@syr.edu.

GRADUATE UNITS

College of Law Students: 634 full-time (266 women), 6 part-time (5 women); includes 130 minority (21 African Americans, 4 American Indian/Alaska Native, 77 Asian Americans or Pacific Islanders, 28 Hispanic Americans), 17 international. Average age 25. 1,842 applicants, 226 enrolled. *Faculty:* 62 full-time (30 women), 16 part-time/adjunct (3 women). Expenses: Contact institution. *Financial support:* In 2008–09, 487 students received support; fellowships, research assistantships, career-related internships or fieldwork, Federal Work-Study, institutionally sponsored loans, scholarships/grants, and tuition waivers (partial) available. Support available to part-time students. Financial award application deadline: 2/15; financial award applicants required to submit FAFSA. In 2008, 223 JDs awarded. *Degree program information:* Part-time programs available. Offers law (JD). *Application deadline:* For fall admission, 4/1 priority date for domestic and international students. Applications are processed on a rolling basis. *Application fee:* $70. Electronic applications accepted. *Application Contact:* Nikki Laubenstein, Director of Admissions, 315-443-1962, Fax: 315-443-9568, E-mail: admissions@law.syr.edu. *Dean,* Hannah Arterian, 315-443-2524, Fax: 315-443-4213.

Graduate School *Degree program information:* Part-time and evening/weekend programs available. Postbaccalaureate distance learning degree programs offered. Electronic applications accepted.

College of Arts and Sciences *Degree program information:* Part-time programs available. Offers applied statistics (MS); art history (MA); arts and sciences (MA, MFA, MFS, MS, Au D, PhD); audiology (Au D, PhD); biology (MS, PhD); chemistry (MS, PhD); clinical psychology (PhD); college science teaching (PhD); composition and cultural rhetoric (PhD); creative writing (MFA); English (MA, PhD); experimental psychology (PhD); forensic science (MFS); French and Francophone studies (MA); geology (MA, MS, PhD); linguistic studies (MA); mathematics (MS, PhD); Pan-African studies (MA); philosophy (MA, PhD); physics (MS, PhD); religion (MA, PhD); school psychology (PhD); social psychology (PhD); Spanish language, literature and culture (MA); speech language pathology (MS, PhD); structural biology, biochemistry and biophysics (PhD). Electronic applications accepted.

College of Human Ecology *Degree program information:* Part-time and evening/weekend programs available. Offers child and family studies (MA, MS, PhD); human ecology (MA, MS, MSW, PhD); marriage and family therapy (MA, PhD); nutrition science and food management (MA, MS); social work (MSW). Electronic applications accepted.

College of Visual and Performing Arts *Degree program information:* Part-time and evening/weekend programs available. Postbaccalaureate distance learning degree programs offered (minimal on-campus study). Offers art photography (MFA); art video (MFA); ceramics (MFA); communication and rhetorical studies (MA, MS); composition (M Mus); computer art (MFA); conducting (M Mu); fiber arts/material studies (MFA); film (MFA); illustration (MFA); jewelry and metalsmithing (MFA); museum studies (MA); organ (M Mus); painting (MFA); percussion (M Mus); piano (M Mus); printmaking (MFA); sculpture (MFA); strings (M Mus); visual and performing arts (M Mu, M Mus, MA, MFA, MS); voice (M Mus); wind instruments (M Mus). Electronic applications accepted.

L. C. Smith College of Engineering and Computer Science *Degree program information:* Part-time and evening/weekend programs available. Offers bioengineering (ME, MS, PhD); chemical engineering (MS), civil engineering (MS, PhD); computer and information science and engineering (PhD); computer engineering (MS); computer science (MS); electrical and computer engineering (PhD); electrical engineering (MS, EE); engineering and computer science (ME, MS, PhD, CE, EE); engineering management (MS); environmental engineering (MS); mechanical and aerospace engineering (MS, PhD); microwave engineering (MS, PhD). Electronic applications accepted.

Maxwell School of Citizenship and Public Affairs *Degree program information:* Part-time and evening/weekend programs available. Postbaccalaureate distance learning degree programs offered. Offers anthropology (MA, PhD); citizenship and public affairs (EMPA, MA, MPA, MS Sc, PhD, CAS); conflict resolutioneconomics (MA, PhD); geography (MA, PhD); health services management and policy (CAS); history (MA, PhD); political science (MA, PhD); public administration (EMPA, MPA, PhD, CAS); public diplomacy (MA); social sciences (MS Sc, PhD); sociology (MA, PhD). Electronic applications accepted.

School of Architecture Offers architecture (M Arch I, M Arch II). Electronic applications accepted.

School of Education Offers art education (CAS); art education/professional certification (MS); art education: preparation (MS); childhood education: (1-6) preparation (MS); community counseling (MS); counselor education (PhD); cultural foundations of education (MS, PhD); disabilities studies (CAS); early childhood special education (MS); education (M Mus, MS, Ed D, PhD, CAS); educational leadership (MS, Ed D, CAS); educational technology (MS); English education (PhD); English education: preparation 7-12 (MS); exercise science (MS); higher education (MS, PhD); inclusive special education (grades 1-6) (MS); inclusive special education (grades 7-12) (MS); inclusive special education: severe/multiple disabilities (MS); instructional design, development, and evaluation (MS, PhD, CAS); lifelong learning and continuing education (MS, PhD); literacy education: birth-grade 6 (MS); literacy education: grades 5-12 (MS); mathematics education (PhD); mathematics education: preparation 7-12 (MS); music education/professional certification (M Mus, MS); music education: teacher preparation (MS); professional practice in educational technology (MS); reading education (PhD); rehabilitation and community counseling (MS); rehabilitation counseling (MS); school counseling (MS, CAS); science education (PhD); science/biology education: preparation 7-12 (MS); science/chemistry education: preparation 7-12 (MS); science/earth science education: preparation 7-12 (MS); science/physics education: preparation 7-12 (MS); social studies education: preparation 7-12 (MS); special education (PhD); student affairs counseling (MS); teaching and curriculum (MS, PhD, CAS); teaching English language learners (MS). Electronic applications accepted.

School of Information Studies *Degree program information:* Part-time and evening/weekend programs available. Postbaccalaureate distance learning degree programs offered (minimal on-campus study). Offers digital libraries (CAS); information management (MS); information science and technology (PhD); information security management (CAS); information systems and telecommunications management (CAS); library and information science (MS); library and information science: school media (MS); school library media (CAS); telecommunications and network management (MS). Electronic applications accepted.

S. I. Newhouse School of Public Communications Postbaccalaureate distance learning degree programs offered (minimal on-campus study). Offers advertising (MA); arts journalism (MA); broadcast journalism (MS); communications management (MS); documentary film and history (MA); magazine, newspaper and online journalism (MA); mass communications (PhD); media management (MS); media studies (MA); photography (MS); public communications (MA, MS, PhD); public relations (MS); television, radio, and film (MA). Electronic applications accepted.

Martin J. Whitman School of Management *Degree program information:* Part-time programs available. Postbaccalaureate distance learning degree programs offered (minimal on-campus study). Offers accounting (MBA, PhD); entrepreneurship (MBA); finance (MBA, PhD); management (MBA, MS Acct, MSF, PhD); management information systems (PhD); managerial statistics (PhD); marketing (MBA, PhD); operations management (PhD); organizational behavior (PhD); strategy and human resources (PhD); supply chain management (MBA, PhD). Electronic applications accepted.

TABOR COLLEGE, Hillsboro, KS 67063

General Information Independent-religious, coed, comprehensive institution.

GRADUATE UNITS

Graduate Program Offers accounting (MBA). Program offered at the Wichita campus only.

TAI SOPHIA INSTITUTE, Laurel, MD 20723

General Information Independent, coed, primarily women, graduate-only institution. *Graduate housing:* On-campus housing not available. *Research affiliation:* Maryland State Department of Public Safety and Corrections (acupuncture detox services).

GRADUATE UNITS

Chinese Herb Certificate Program *Degree program information:* Part-time and evening/weekend programs available. Offers Chinese herb (Certificate).

Program in Acupuncture Offers acupuncture (M Ac).

Program in Applied Healing Arts Offers applied healing arts (MA).

Program in Herbal Medicine Offers herbal medicine (MS).

TALMUDICAL ACADEMY OF NEW JERSEY, Adelphia, NJ 07710

General Information Independent-religious, men only, comprehensive institution.

GRADUATE UNITS

Graduate Program

TALMUDIC COLLEGE OF FLORIDA, Miami Beach, FL 33139

General Information Independent-religious, men only, comprehensive institution. *Graduate housing:* Rooms and/or apartments available on a first-come, first-served basis to single and married students.

GRADUATE UNITS

Program in Talmudic Law Offers Talmudic law (MRE, Master of Talmudic Law, Doctor of Talmudic Law).

TARLETON STATE UNIVERSITY, Stephenville, TX 76402

General Information State-supported, coed, comprehensive institution. *Enrollment:* 9,634 graduate, professional, and undergraduate students; 317 full-time matriculated graduate/professional students (194 women), 1,431 part-time matriculated graduate/professional students (988 women). *Enrollment by degree level:* 1,679 master's, 69 doctoral. *Graduate faculty:* 140 full-time (49 women), 42 part-time/adjunct (21 women). Tuition, state resident: full-time $2853; part-time $158.50 per credit hour. Tuition, nonresident: full-time $7551; part-time $419.50 per credit hour. *Required fees:* $1040; $42 per credit hour. $124 per semester. Tuition and fees vary according to course load and campus/location. *Graduate housing:* Rooms and/or apartments available on a first-come, first-served basis to single and married students. Typical cost: $3270 per year ($6140 including board) for single students; $6900 per year ($9771 including board) for married students. Room and board charges vary according to board plan and housing facility selected. Housing application deadline: 8/1. *Student services:* Campus employment opportunities, campus safety program, career counseling, child daycare facilities, exercise/wellness program, free psychological counseling, grant writing training, international student services, low-cost health insurance, multicultural affairs office, services for students with disabilities, teacher training, writing training. *Library facilities:* Dick Smith Library plus 1 other. *Online resources:* library catalog, web page, access to other libraries' catalogs. *Collection:* 400,000 titles, 25,800 serial subscriptions.

Computer facilities: 1,000 computers available on campus for general student use. A campuswide network can be accessed from student residence rooms and from off campus. Online class registration is available. *Web address:* http://www.tarleton.edu/.

General Application Contact: Dr. Linda M. Jones, Dean, 254-968-9104, Fax: 254-968-9670, E-mail: ljones@tarleton.edu.

GRADUATE UNITS

College of Graduate Studies Students: 317 full-time (194 women), 1,431 part-time (988 women); includes 435 minority (268 African Americans, 11 American Indian/Alaska Native, 23 Asian Americans or Pacific Islanders, 133 Hispanic Americans), 20 international. Average age 36. 709 applicants, 83% accepted, 454 enrolled. *Faculty:* 140 full-time (49 women), 42 part-time/adjunct (21 women). Expenses: Contact institution. *Financial support:* In 2008–09, 120 research assistantships (averaging $12,687 per year) were awarded; teaching assistantships, career-related internships or fieldwork, Federal Work-Study, institutionally sponsored loans, scholarships/grants, and tuition waivers (partial) also available. Support available to part-time students. Financial award application deadline: 5/1; financial award applicants required to submit FAFSA. In 2008, 443 master's, 14 doctorates awarded. *Degree program information:* Part-time and evening/weekend programs available. Postbaccalaureate distance learning degree programs offered (minimal on-campus study). Offers liberal studies (MS). *Application deadline:* For fall admission, 8/5 priority date for domestic students; for spring admission, 12/1 for domestic students. *Application fee:* $30 ($130 for international students). Electronic applications accepted. *Application Contact:* Information Contact, 254-968-9104, Fax: 254-968-9670, E-mail: gradoffice@tarleton.edu. *Dean,* Dr. Linda M. Jones, 254-968-9104, Fax: 254-968-9670, E-mail: ljones@tarleton.edu.

College of Agriculture and Human Sciences Students: 34 full-time (20 women), 28 part-time (14 women); includes 4 African Americans, 2 Asian Americans or Pacific Islanders, 2 international. Average age 26. 28 applicants, 75% accepted, 13 enrolled. *Faculty:* 23 full-time (6 women), 1 part-time/adjunct (0 women). Expenses: Contact institution. *Financial support:* In 2008–09, 27 research assistantships (averaging $11,556 per year) were awarded; teaching assistantships, career-related internships or fieldwork, Federal Work-Study, and institutionally sponsored loans also available. Support available to part-time students. Financial award application deadline: 5/1; financial award applicants required to submit FAFSA. In 2008, 27 master's awarded. *Degree program information:* Part-time and evening/weekend programs available. Postbaccalaureate distance learning degree programs offered (minimal on-campus study). Offers agriculture (MS); agriculture and human sciences (MS); agriculture education (MS). *Application deadline:* For fall admission, 8/5 priority date for domestic students; for spring admission, 12/1 for domestic students. Applications are processed on a rolling basis. *Application fee:* $30 ($130 for international students). Electronic applications accepted. *Application Contact:* Information Contact, 254-968-9104, Fax: 254-968-9670, E-mail: gradoffice@tarleton.edu. *Dean,* Dr. Don Cawthon, 254-968-9277, Fax: 254-968-9655, E-mail: cawthon@tarleton.edu.

College of Business Administration Students: 79 full-time (36 women), 408 part-time (212 women); includes 128 minority (78 African Americans, 2 American Indian/Alaska Native, 11 Asian Americans or Pacific Islanders, 37 Hispanic Americans), 13 international. Average age 33. 277 applicants, 88% accepted, 185 enrolled. *Faculty:* 29 full-time (3 women), 7 part-time/adjunct (4 women). Expenses: Contact institution. *Financial support:* In 2008–09, 10 research assistantships (averaging $12,667 per year) were awarded; teaching assistantships, career-related internships or fieldwork, Federal Work-Study, and institutionally sponsored loans also available. Support available to part-time students. Financial award application deadline: 5/1; financial award applicants required to submit FAFSA. In 2008, 105 master's awarded. *Degree program information:* Part-time and evening/weekend programs available. Postbaccalaureate distance learning degree programs offered (minimal on-campus study). Offers business administration (MBA, MS); human resource management (MS); information systems (MS); management and leadership (MS). *Application deadline:* For fall admission, 8/5 priority date for domestic students; for spring admission, 12/1 for domestic students. Applications are processed on a rolling basis. *Application fee:* $30 ($130 for international students). Electronic applications accepted. *Application Contact:* Information Contact, 254-968-9104, Fax: 254-968-9670, E-mail: gradoffice@tarleton.edu. Dr. Raja Iyer, Fax: 254-968-9328, E-mail: iyer@tarleton.edu.

College of Education Students: 121 full-time (89 women), 899 part-time (703 women); includes 258 minority (163 African Americans, 7 American Indian/Alaska Native, 8 Asian Americans or Pacific Islanders, 80 Hispanic Americans), 3 international. Average age 36. 291 applicants, 80% accepted, 182 enrolled. *Faculty:* 52 full-time (27 women), 27 part-time/adjunct (14 women). Expenses: Contact institution. *Financial support:* In 2008–09, 14 research assistantships (averaging $13,524 per year) were awarded; teaching assistantships with partial tuition reimbursements, career-related internships or fieldwork, Federal Work-Study, institutionally sponsored loans, and tuition waivers (partial) also available. Support available to part-time students. Financial award application deadline: 5/1; financial award applicants required to submit FAFSA. In 2008, 276 master's, 14 doctorates awarded. *Degree program information:* Part-time and evening/weekend programs available. Postbaccalaureate distance learning degree programs offered (minimal on-campus study). Offers counseling and psychology (M Ed); curriculum and instruction (M Ed); education (M Ed, Ed D, Certificate); educational administration (M Ed); educational leadership (Ed D, Certificate); physical education (M Ed); secondary education (Certificate); special education (Certificate). *Application deadline:* For fall admission, 8/5 priority date for domestic students; for spring admission, 12/1 for domestic students. Applications are processed on a rolling basis. *Application fee:* $30 ($130 for international students). Electronic applications accepted. *Application Contact:* Information Contact, 254-968-9104, Fax: 254-968-9670, E-mail: gradoffice@tarleton.edu. *Dean,* Dr. Jill Burk, 254-968-9089, Fax: 254-968-9525, E-mail: burk@tarleton.edu.

College of Liberal and Fine Arts Students: 21 full-time (8 women), 46 part-time (27 women); includes 15 minority (10 African Americans, 5 Hispanic Americans). Average age 34. 45 applicants, 69% accepted, 25 enrolled. *Faculty:* 20 full-time (9 women), 1 part-time/adjunct (0 women). Expenses: Contact institution. *Financial support:* In 2008–09, 12 research assistantships (averaging $13,492 per year) were awarded; teaching assistantships. Financial award application deadline: 5/1; financial award applicants required to submit FAFSA. In 2008, 22 master's awarded. *Degree program information:* Part-time and evening/weekend programs available. Offers criminal justice (MCJ); English (MA); history (MA); liberal and fine arts (MA, MCJ, MM); music education (MM); political science (MA). *Application deadline:* For fall admission, 8/5 priority date for domestic students; for spring admission, 12/1 for domestic students. Applications are processed on a rolling basis. *Application fee:* $30 ($130 for international students). Electronic applications accepted. *Application Contact:* Information Contact, 254-968-9104, Fax: 254-968-9670, E-mail: gradoffice@tarleton.edu. *Dean,* Dr. Dean A. Minix, 254-968-9141, Fax: 254-968-9784, E-mail: minix@tarleton.edu.

College of Science and Technology Students: 16 full-time (11 women), 30 part-time (14 women); includes 6 minority (4 African Americans, 2 Hispanic Americans), 2 international. Average age 30. 23 applicants, 83% accepted, 17 enrolled. *Faculty:* 17 full-time (5 women), 5 part-time/adjunct (2 women). Expenses: Contact institution. *Financial support:* In 2008–09, 19 research assistantships (averaging $13,263 per year) were awarded; teaching assistantships, career-related internships or fieldwork, Federal Work-Study, and tuition waivers (partial) also available. Support available to part-time students. Financial award application deadline: 5/1; financial award applicants required to submit FAFSA. In 2008, 13 master's awarded. *Degree program information:* Part-time and evening/weekend programs available. Postbaccalaureate distance learning degree programs offered (minimal on-campus study). Offers biology (MS); environmental science (MS); mathematics (MS); science and technology (MS). *Application deadline:* For fall admission, 8/5 priority date for domestic students; for spring admission, 12/1 for domestic students. Applications are processed on a rolling basis. *Application fee:* $30 ($130 for international students). Electronic applications accepted. *Application Contact:* Information Contact, 254-968-9104, Fax: 254-968-9670, E-mail: gradoffice@tarleton.edu. *Dean,* Dr. James Pierce, 254-968-9781, Fax: 254-968-0549, E-mail: jrpierce@tarleton.edu.

TAYLOR COLLEGE AND SEMINARY, Edmonton, AB T6J 4T3, Canada

General Information Independent-religious, coed, comprehensive institution. *Graduate housing:* Room and/or apartments available on a first-come, first-served basis to single students; on-campus housing not available to married students. Housing application deadline: 8/1.

GRADUATE UNITS

Graduate and Professional Programs *Degree program information:* Part-time programs available. Offers Christian studies (Diploma); intercultural studies (MA, Diploma); theology (M Div, MTS).

TAYLOR UNIVERSITY, Upland, IN 46989-1001

General Information Independent-religious, coed, comprehensive institution. *Enrollment:* 1,871 graduate, professional, and undergraduate students; 120 full-time matriculated graduate/professional students (46 women), 10 part-time matriculated graduate/professional students (4 women). *Enrollment by degree level:* 130 master's. *Graduate faculty:* 1 full-time (0 women), 21 part-time/adjunct (0 women). *Tuition:* Full-time $10,530; part-time $390 per credit. *Required fees:* $495 per semester. *Graduate housing:* On-campus housing not available. *Student services:* Campus employment opportunities, campus safety program, career counseling, exercise/wellness program, free psychological counseling, international student services, multicultural affairs office, services for students with disabilities, writing training. *Library facilities:* Zondervan Library. *Online resources:* library catalog, web page, access to other libraries' catalogs. *Collection:* 188,986 titles, 30,449 serial subscriptions, 9,837 audiovisual materials.

Computer facilities: Computer purchase and lease plans are available. 339 computers available on campus for general student use. A campuswide network can be accessed from student residence rooms and from off campus. Online class registration is available. *Web address:* http://www.taylor.edu/.

General Application Contact: Sherri Blair, Assistant to the Dean of Professional and Graduate Studies, 765-998-5108, Fax: 765-998-4389, E-mail: shblair@taylor.edu.

GRADUATE UNITS

Master of Arts in Higher Education Program Students: 33 full-time (16 women), 1 (woman) part-time; includes 2 African Americans, 1 American Indian/Alaska Native, 1 Hispanic American. Average age 26. 28 applicants, 89% accepted, 16 enrolled. *Faculty:* 5 part-time/adjunct. Expenses: Contact institution. *Financial support:* In 2008–09, 22 students received support, including 32 fellowships (averaging $5,000 per year). Financial award applicants required to submit FAFSA. *Degree program information:* Part-time programs available. Offers higher education (MA). *Application deadline:* For fall admission, 2/1 for domestic students, 1/1 for international students. Applications are processed on a rolling basis. *Application fee:* $100. *Application Contact:* Cindi Carder, MAHE Program Assistant, 765-998-5373, Fax: 765-998-4577, E-mail: jccarder@taylor.edu. *Graduate Chair, Master of Arts in Higher Education,* Dr. Tim Herrmann, 765-998-5142, E-mail: tmherrmann@taylor.edu.

Master of Arts in Religious Studies Program Students: 5 part-time (1 woman); includes 1 African American. Average age 25. 3 applicants, 100% accepted, 3 enrolled. *Faculty:* 4 part-time/adjunct. Expenses: Contact institution. *Financial support:* In 2008–09, 2 students received support, including 3 fellowships (averaging $2,000 per year). Financial award applicants required to submit FAFSA. *Degree program information:* Part-time programs available. Offers biblical studies (MA); world religions (MA). *Application deadline:* Applications are processed on a rolling basis. *Application Contact:* Kari Manganello, Program Assistant, 765-998-5148, Fax: 765-998-4930, E-mail: krmangane@taylor.edu. *Graduate Chair, Master of Arts in Religious Studies,* Dr. Sheri Klouda, 765-998-4786, Fax: 765-998-4930, E-mail: shklouda@taylor.edu.

Master of Environmental Science Program Students: 19 full-time (8 women). Average age 25. 10 applicants, 90% accepted, 9 enrolled. *Faculty:* 3 part-time/adjunct (0 women). Expenses: Contact institution. *Financial support:* In 2008–09, 15 students received support, including 10 fellowships; scholarships/grants also available. Financial award applicants required to submit FAFSA. In 2008, 5 master's awarded. Offers environmental science (MES). *Application deadline:* Applications are processed on a rolling basis. *Application fee:* $0. *Application Contact:* Becky Taylor, Program Assistant, 765-998-4960, Fax: 765-998-4976, E-mail: mes@taylor.edu. *Graduate Chair, Master of Environmental Science,* Dr. Edwin Richard Squiers, 765-998-5386, Fax: 765-998-4976, E-mail: rcsquiers@taylor.edu.

Masters of Business Administration Program Students: 68 full-time (22 women), 4 part-time (2 women); includes 4 African Americans, 1 Asian American or Pacific Islander, 1 Hispanic American, 2 international. Average age 36. 36 applicants, 100% accepted, 32 enrolled. *Faculty:* 1 full-time, 9 part-time/adjunct. Expenses: Contact institution. *Financial support:* In 2008–09, 29 students received support. Applicants required to submit FAFSA. In 2008, 32 master's awarded. *Degree program information:* Part-time programs available. Offers emerging business strategies (MA); global leadership (MA). *Application deadline:* Applications are processed on a rolling basis. *Application fee:* $100. *Application Contact:* Wendy Speakman, Program Director, 866-471-6062, Fax: 260-492-0452, E-mail: wnspeakman@taylor.edu. *Graduate Chair, Master of Business Administration,* Dr. Larry Rottmeyer, 260-399-1622, E-mail: Lrrottmeyer@taylor.edu.

TEACHERS COLLEGE, COLUMBIA UNIVERSITY, New York, NY 10027-6696

General Information Independent, coed, graduate-only institution. *Enrollment by degree level:* 3,532 master's, 1,584 doctoral. *Graduate faculty:* 152 full-time (90 women), 260 part-time/adjunct. *Tuition:* Full-time $26,040; part-time $1085 per credit. *Required fees:* $720. *Graduate housing:* Rooms and/or apartments available on a first-come, first-served basis to single and married students. Typical cost: $7200 per year for single students. Housing application deadline: 2/1. *Student services:* Campus employment opportunities, campus safety program, career counseling, child daycare facilities, exercise/wellness program, free psychological counseling, grant writing training, international student services, low-cost health insurance, multicultural affairs office, services for students with disabilities, teacher training, writing training. *Library facilities:* Milbank Memorial Library. *Online resources:* library catalog, web page, access to other libraries' catalogs. *Collection:* 585,901 titles, 2,095 serial subscriptions, 3,987 audiovisual materials.

Computer facilities: 482 computers available on campus for general student use. A campuswide network can be accessed from student residence rooms and from off campus. Online class registration is available. *Web address:* http://www.tc.columbia.edu/.

General Application Contact: Thomas Rock, Director of Admissions, 212-678-3083, Fax: 212-678-4171, E-mail: rock@tc.edu.

GRADUATE UNITS

Graduate Faculty of Education Students: 1,627 full-time (1,266 women), 3,489 part-time (2,653 women); includes 1,321 minority (447 African Americans, 547 Asian Americans or Pacific Islanders, 327 Hispanic Americans), 620 international. Average age 32. 4,754 applicants, 55% accepted, 1202 enrolled. *Faculty:* 152 full-time (90 women). Expenses: Contact institution. *Financial support:* Fellowships, research assistantships, teaching assistantships, career-related internships or fieldwork, Federal Work-Study, institutionally sponsored loans, traineeships, tuition waivers (full and partial), and unspecified assistantships available. Support available to part-time students. Financial award application deadline: 2/1. In 2008, 1,572 master's, 213 doctorates awarded. *Degree program information:* Part-time and evening/weekend programs available. Offers administration and supervision in special education (Ed M, MA, Ed D, PhD); adult education (MA, Ed D); anthropology (Ed M, MA, Ed D, PhD); applied educational psychology–school psychology (Ed M, MA, Ed D, PhD); applied linguistics (Ed M, MA, Ed D); art and art education (Ed M, MA, Ed D, Ed DCT); arts administration (MA); behavioral disorders (MA, Ed D, PhD); bilingual and bicultural education (MA); blind and visual impairment (MA, Ed D); childhood/disabilities (Certificate); clinical psychology (PhD); communications (Ed M, MA, Ed D); comparative and international education (Ed M, MA, Ed D, PhD); computing in education (MA); counseling psychology (Ed M, Ed D, PhD); curriculum and teaching (Ed M, MA, Ed D, Certificate); curriculum and teaching in physical education (Ed M, MA, Ed D); developmental psychology (MA, Ed D, PhD); early childhood education (Ed M, MA, Ed D); early childhood special education (Ed M, MA); economics and education (Ed M, MA, Ed D, PhD); education (Ed M, MA, MS, Ed D, Ed DCT, PhD, Certificate); education leadership (Ed M, MA, Ed D, PhD); education leadership studies (Ed M, MA, Ed D); educational administration (Ed M, MA, Ed D, PhD); educational media/instructional technology (Ed M, MA, Ed D); educational psychology-human cognition and learning (Ed M, MA, Ed D, PhD); elementary/childhood education, preservice (MA); giftedness (MA, Ed D); health education (MA, MS, Ed D); hearing impairment (MA, Ed D); higher education (Ed M, MA, Ed D, PhD); history and education (Ed M, MA, Ed D, PhD); inquiry in education leadership (Ed D); interdisciplinary studies (Ed M, MA, Ed D); international educational development (Ed M, MA, Ed D, PhD); leadership, policy and politics (Ed M, MA, Ed D, PhD); learning disabilities (Ed M, MA, Ed D); literacy specialist (MA); mathematics education (Ed M, MA, MS, Ed D, Ed DCT, PhD); measurement, evaluation, and statistics (MA, MS, Ed D, PhD); mental retardation (MA, Ed D, PhD); motor learning/movement science (Ed M, MA, Ed D); music and music education (Ed M, MA, Ed D, Ed DCT); neuroscience and education (Ed M, Ed D); nurse executive (Ed M, MA, Ed D); nursing, professional role (Ed M, MA, Ed D); nutrition and education (Ed M, MS, Ed D); nutrition education (Ed M, MS, Ed D); nutrition education and public health nutrition (Ed M, MS, Ed D); organizational psychology (MA, Ed D, PhD); philosophy and education (Ed M, MA, Ed D, PhD); physical disabilities (MA, Ed D, PhD); politics and education (Ed M, MA, Ed D, PhD); private school leadership (Ed M, MA, Ed D); public school and school district leadership (Ed M, MA, Ed D); reading specialist (MA); religion and education (Ed M, MA, Ed D); research in special education (Ed D); science education (Ed M, MA, MS, Ed D, Ed DCT, PhD); severe or multiple disabilities (Ed M); social and organizational psychology (MA, Ed D, PhD); social psychology (Ed D, PhD); social studies education (Ed M, MA, Ed D, PhD); sociology and education (Ed M, MA, Ed D, PhD); special education (Ed M, MA, Ed D); speech-language pathology (Ed M, MS, Ed D, PhD); student personnel administration (Ed M, MA, Ed D); teaching English to speakers of other languages (Ed M, MA, Ed D); teaching of English and English education (Ed M, MA, Ed D, PhD); teaching of sign language (MA); teaching of Spanish (Ed M, MA, Ed D, Ed DCT, PhD). *Application fee:* $75. Electronic applications accepted. *Application Contact:* Thomas Rock, Director of Admissions, 212-678-3083, Fax: 212-678-4171, E-mail: rock@tc.edu. *President,* Susan Furhman, 212-678-3050.

See Close-Up on page 999.

TÉLÉ-UNIVERSITÉ, Québec, QC G1K 9H5, Canada

General Information Province-supported, coed, comprehensive institution. *Graduate housing:* On-campus housing not available.

GRADUATE UNITS

Graduate Programs *Degree program information:* Part-time programs available. Offers computer science (PhD); corporate finance (MS); distance learning (MS).

TELSHE YESHIVA–CHICAGO, Chicago, IL 60625-5598

General Information Independent-religious, men only, comprehensive institution.

GRADUATE UNITS

Graduate Program

TEMPLE BAPTIST SEMINARY, Chattanooga, TN 37404-3530

General Information Independent-religious, coed, primarily men, graduate-only institution. *Graduate housing:* On-campus housing not available.

GRADUATE UNITS

Program in Theology *Degree program information:* Part-time and evening/weekend programs available. Postbaccalaureate distance learning degree programs offered (minimal on-campus study). Offers biblical languages (M Div); Biblical studies (MABS); Christian education (MACE); English Bible û language tools (M Div); theology (MM, D Min).

TEMPLE UNIVERSITY, Philadelphia, PA 19122-6096

General Information State-related, coed, university. CGS member. *Graduate housing:* Rooms and/or apartments available on a first-come, first-served basis to single and married students. Housing application deadline: 5/1.

GRADUATE UNITS

Ambler College Offers community and regional planning (MS). Electronic applications accepted.

Graduate School *Degree program information:* Part-time and evening/weekend programs available. Electronic applications accepted.

College of Education *Degree program information:* Part-time and evening/weekend programs available. Offers adult and organizational development (Ed M); applied behavioral analysis (MS Ed); career and technical education (MS Ed); counseling psychology (Ed M, PhD); early childhood education and elementary education (MS Ed); education (Ed M, MS Ed, Ed D, PhD); educational administration (Ed M, Ed D); educational psychology (Ed M, PhD); English education (MS Ed); language arts education (Ed D); math/science education (Ed D); mathematics education (MS Ed); school psychology (Ed M, PhD); science education (MS Ed); second and foreign language education (MS Ed); special education (MS Ed); teaching English as a second language (MS Ed); urban education (Ed M, Ed D). Electronic applications accepted.

College of Engineering *Degree program information:* Part-time programs available. Offers civil engineering (MSE); electrical engineering (MSE); engineering (MS, MSE, PhD); mechanical engineering (MSE). Electronic applications accepted.

College of Liberal Arts *Degree program information:* Part-time and evening/weekend programs available. Offers African American studies (MA, PhD); anthropology (PhD); clinical psychology (PhD); cognitive psychology (PhD); creative writing (MA); criminal justice (MA, PhD); developmental psychology (PhD); English (MA, PhD); geography (MA); history (MA, PhD); liberal arts (MA, MLA, PhD); philosophy (MA, PhD); political science (MA, PhD); religion (MA, PhD); social psychology (PhD); sociology (MA, PhD); Spanish (MA, PhD); urban studies (MA). Electronic applications accepted.

College of Science and Technology *Degree program information:* Part-time and evening/weekend programs available. Offers applied mathematics (MA); biology (MS, PhD); chemistry (MA, PhD); computer and information sciences (MS, PhD); geology (MS); mathematics (PhD); physics (MA, PhD); pure mathematics (MA); science and technology (MA, MS, PhD). Electronic applications accepted.

Esther Boyer College of Music and Dance *Degree program information:* Part-time and evening/weekend programs available. Offers choral activities (MM); composition (MM, DMA); dance (Ed M, MFA, PhD); instrumental studies (MM, DMA); keyboard instruction (MM, DMA); music and dance (Ed M, MFA, MM, MMT, DMA, PhD); music education (MM, PhD); music history (MM); music theory (MM); music therapy (MMT, PhD); voice and opera (MM, DMA). Electronic applications accepted.

Fox School of Business Students: 432 full-time (182 women), 372 part-time (131 women); includes 62 minority (22 African Americans, 33 Asian Americans or Pacific Islanders, 7 Hispanic Americans), 231 international. Average age 31. 1,081 applicants, 47% accepted, 253 enrolled. *Faculty:* 87 full-time (16 women), 26 part-time/adjunct (3 women). Expenses: Contact institution. *Financial support:* Fellowships with full and partial tuition reimbursements, research assistantships with full and partial tuition reimbursements, teaching assistantships with full and partial tuition reimbursements, career-related internships or fieldwork, Federal Work-Study, scholarships/grants, health care benefits, tuition waivers (full and partial), and unspecified assistantships available. Financial award applicants required to submit FAFSA. In 2008, 214 master's, 35 doctorates awarded. *Degree program information:* Part-time and evening/weekend programs available. Postbaccalaureate distance learning degree programs offered (minimal on-campus study). Offers accounting (MBA, PhD); accounting and financial management (MS); actuarial science (MS); business (EMBA, IMBA, MBA, MHM, MS, PhD); business management (MBA); entrepreneurship (PhD); finance (MS, PhD); financial engineering (MS); financial management (MBA); healthcare and life sciences innovation (MBA); healthcare financial management (MS); healthcare management (MHM); human resource administration (PhD); human resource management (MBA, MS); international business (IMBA, PhD); IT management (MBA); management information systems (MS, PhD); marketing (MS, PhD); marketing management (MBA); pharmaceutical management (MBA); risk management and insurance (PhD); statistics (MS, PhD); strategic management (EMBA, MBA, PhD); tourism and sport (PhD). *Application deadline:* For fall admission, 6/1 for domestic students, 3/15 for international students; for spring admission, 9/30 for domestic students, 9/1 for international students. Applications are processed on a rolling basis. *Application fee:* $60. Electronic applications accepted. *Application Contact:* Phyllis Tutora, Director, Enrollment Management, 215-204-1184, Fax: 215-204-1632, E-mail: ptutora@temple.edu. *Dean,* Dr. M. Moshe Porat, 215-204-1836, Fax: 215-204-8705, E-mail: porat@temple.edu.

School of Communications and Theater *Degree program information:* Part-time and evening/weekend programs available. Offers acting (MFA); broadcasting, telecommunications and mass media (MA); communication management (MS); communications and theater (MA, MFA, MJ, MS, PhD); design (MFA); directing (MFA); film and media arts (MFA); journalism (MJ); mass media and communication (PhD). Electronic applications accepted.

School of Social Administration *Degree program information:* Part-time and evening/weekend programs available. Offers social administration (MSW); social work (MSW). Electronic applications accepted.

School of Tourism and Hospitality Management *Degree program information:* Part-time and evening/weekend programs available. Offers sport and recreation administration (Ed M); tourism and hospitality management (Ed M, MTHM). Electronic applications accepted.

Tyler School of Art *Degree program information:* Part-time and evening/weekend programs available. Offers art (Ed M, MA, MFA, PhD); art and art education (Ed M); art history (MA, PhD); ceramics/glass (MFA); fibers and fabric design (MFA); graphic and interactive design (MFA); metals/jewelry/CAD-CAM (MFA); painting (MFA); photography (MFA); printmaking (MFA); sculpture (MFA). Electronic applications accepted.

Health Sciences Center *Degree program information:* Part-time and evening/weekend programs available. Offers health sciences (DMD, DPM, MD, Pharm D, Ed M, MA, MOT, MPH, MS, MSN, DPT, PhD, Certificate). Electronic applications accepted.

College of Health Professions *Degree program information:* Part-time and evening/weekend programs available. Postbaccalaureate distance learning degree programs offered (minimal on-campus study). Offers communication sciences (PhD); community health education (MPH); environmental health (MS); epidemiology (MS); health professions (Ed M, MA, MOT, MPH, MS, MSN, DPT, PhD); health studies (PhD); kinesiology (Ed M, PhD); linguistics (MA); nursing (MSN); occupational therapy (MOT, MS); physical therapy (DPT, PhD); public health (Ed M, MPH, MS, PhD); school health education (Ed M); speech-language-hearing (MA); therapeutic recreation (Ed M).

School of Dentistry Offers advanced education in general dentistry (Certificate); dentistry (DMD, MS, Certificate); endodontology (Certificate); oral biology (MS); orthodontics (Certificate); periodontology (Certificate). Electronic applications accepted.

School of Medicine Offers anatomy and cell biology (MS, PhD); biochemistry (MS, PhD); medicine (MD, MS, PhD); microbiology and immunology (MS, PhD); molecular biology and genetics (PhD); neuroscience (MS, PhD); pathology and laboratory medicine (PhD); pharmacology (PhD); physiology (PhD). Electronic applications accepted.

School of Pharmacy *Degree program information:* Part-time and evening/weekend programs available. Postbaccalaureate distance learning degree programs offered (minimal on-campus study). Offers medicinal chemistry (MS, PhD); pharmaceutics (MS, PhD); pharmacodynamics (MS, PhD); pharmacy (Pharm D, MS, PhD); quality assurance/regulatory affairs (MS). Electronic applications accepted.

School of Podiatric Medicine Offers podiatric medicine (DPM).

James E. Beasley School of Law *Degree program information:* Part-time and evening/weekend programs available. Offers law (JD); legal education (SJD); taxation (LL M); transnational law (LL M); trial advocacy (LL M). Electronic applications accepted.

Announcement: Located in the sixth-largest U.S. city, Temple University is as diverse academically as it is culturally. With more than 5,000 graduate students (over 37,000 students total), Temple offers 81 doctoral and 165 master's programs that range from fine arts and sciences to professional degrees. While housed in selective schools, these programs are immersed in the cultural wealth of a comprehensive university.

See Close-Up on page 1001.

TENNESSEE STATE UNIVERSITY, Nashville, TN 37209-1561

General Information State-supported, coed, comprehensive institution. CGS member. *Enrollment:* 8,254 graduate, professional, and undergraduate students; 612 full-time matriculated graduate/professional students (424 women), 1,211 part-time matriculated graduate/professional students (856 women). *Enrollment by degree level:* 1,166 master's, 307 doctoral, 350 other advanced degrees. *Graduate faculty:* 151 full-time (63 women), 20 part-time/adjunct (11 women). *Graduate housing:* Rooms and/or apartments available on a first-come, first-served basis to single and married students. Housing application deadline: 8/1. *Student services:* Campus employment opportunities, campus safety program, career counseling, child daycare facilities, exercise/wellness program, free psychological counseling, international student services, low-cost health insurance, services for students with disabilities, teacher training, writing training. *Library facilities:* Martha M. Brown/Lois H. Daniel Library plus 1 other. *Online resources:* library catalog, web page. *Collection:* 630,890 titles.

Computer facilities: 1,025 computers available on campus for general student use. A campuswide network can be accessed from student residence rooms and from off campus. Online class registration is available. *Web address:* http://www.tnstate.edu/.

General Application Contact: Deborah Chisom, Director of Graduate School Admissions, 615-963-5962, Fax: 615-963-5963, E-mail: gradschool@tnstate.edu.

GRADUATE UNITS

The School of Graduate Studies and Research Students: 53 full-time (38 women), 234 part-time (180 women); includes 174 minority (167 African Americans, 1 American Indian/Alaska Native, 5 Asian Americans or Pacific Islanders, 1 Hispanic American), 1 international. Average age 34. 110 applicants, 91% accepted, 94 enrolled. *Faculty:* 179 full-time (73 women), 48 part-time/adjunct (30 women). Expenses: Contact institution. *Financial support:* In 2008–09, 60 students received support, including 7 fellowships, 19 research assistantships (averaging $5,500 per year), 24 teaching assistantships (averaging $5,500 per year); career-related internships or fieldwork, institutionally sponsored loans, scholarships/grants, traineeships, and unspecified assistantships also available. Support available to part-time students. Financial award applicants required to submit FAFSA. *Application deadline:* For fall admission, 4/1 priority date for domestic students. *Application fee:* $25. *Application Contact:* Deborah Chisom, Director of Graduate Admissions, 615-963-5962, Fax: 615-963-5963, E-mail: dchiscom@tnstate.edu. *Dean,* Dr. Helen Barrett, 615-963-5139, Fax: 615-963-5963, E-mail: hbarrett@tnstate.edu.

College of Arts and Sciences Students: 85 full-time (52 women), 89 part-time (58 women); includes 121 minority (113 African Americans, 5 Asian Americans or Pacific Islanders, 3 Hispanic Americans), 12 international. Average age 31. 144 applicants, 42% accepted, 31 enrolled. *Faculty:* 55 full-time (17 women), 22 part-time/adjunct (14 women). Expenses: Contact institution. *Financial support:* Fellowships, research assistantships, teaching assistantships, unspecified assistantships available. Support available to part-time students. Financial award application deadline: 4/1. In 2008, 16 master's awarded. *Degree program information:* Part-time and evening/weekend programs available. Offers arts and sciences (MA, MCJ, MS, PhD); biological sciences (MS, PhD); chemistry (MS); criminal justice (MCJ); English (MA); mathematical sciences (MS); music education (MS). *Application deadline:* For fall admission, 4/1 priority date for domestic and international students. Applications are processed on a rolling basis. *Application fee:* $25. Electronic applications accepted. *Application Contact:* Deborah Chisom, Director of Graduate Admissions, 615-963-5962, Fax: 615-963-5963, E-mail: dchisom@tnstate.edu. *Interim Dean,* Dr. Gloria Johnson, 615-963-7519, E-mail: gjohnson@tnstate.edu.

College of Business Students: 35 full-time (18 women), 55 part-time (28 women); includes 51 minority (40 African Americans, 1 American Indian/Alaska Native, 9 Asian Americans or Pacific Islanders, 1 Hispanic American), 13 international. Average age 30. 115 applicants, 43% accepted, 32 enrolled. *Faculty:* 11 full-time (1 woman), 3 part-time/adjunct (2 women). Expenses: Contact institution. *Financial support:* In 2008–09, 2 research assistantships (averaging $10,595 per year), teaching assistantships (averaging $5,800 per year) were awarded. In 2008, 25 master's awarded. *Degree program information:* Part-time and evening/weekend programs available. Postbaccalaureate distance learning degree programs offered. Offers business (MBA). *Application deadline:* For fall admission, 4/1 priority date for domestic and international students. Applications are processed on a rolling basis. *Application fee:* $25. Electronic applications accepted. *Application Contact:* Dr. Raovl Russell, Director, 615-963-7170, Fax: 615-963-7139, E-mail: rrussell3@tnstate.edu. *Dean,* Dr. Tilden J. Curry, 615-963-7121, Fax: 615-963-7139, E-mail: tcurry@tnstate.edu.

College of Education Students: 273 full-time (209 women), 626 part-time (459 women); includes 537 minority (519 African Americans, 2 American Indian/Alaska Native, 9 Asian Americans or Pacific Islanders, 7 Hispanic Americans), 7 international. 634 applicants, 56% accepted, 211 enrolled. *Faculty:* 56 full-time (30 women), 11 part-time/adjunct (6 women). Expenses: Contact institution. *Financial support:* In 2008–09, 2 teaching assistantships (averaging $6,089 per year) were awarded; fellowships, research assistantships, career-related internships or fieldwork and institutionally sponsored loans also available. Support available to part-time students. Financial award application deadline: 5/1; financial award applicants required to submit FAFSA. In 2008, 190 master's, 43 doctorates, 35 other advanced degrees awarded. *Degree program information:* Part-time and evening/weekend programs available. Offers administration and supervision (M Ed, Ed D, Ed S); counseling and guidance (MS); counseling psychology (PhD); curriculum and instruction (M Ed, Ed D); education (M Ed, MA Ed, MS, Ed D, PhD, Ed S); elementary education (M Ed, MA Ed, Ed D); human performance and sports science (MA Ed); psychology (MS, PhD); school psychology (MS, PhD); special education (M Ed, MA Ed, Ed D). *Application deadline:* Applications are processed on a rolling basis. *Application fee:* $25. *Application Contact:* Dr. Helen Barrett, Dean, 615-963-5139, Fax: 615-963-5963, E-mail: hbarrett@tnstate.edu. *Dean,* Dr. Peter Millett, 615-963-5451, E-mail: pmillett@tnstate.edu.

College of Engineering, Technology, and Computer Science Students: 23 full-time (7 women), 41 part-time (5 women); includes 54 minority (45 African Americans, 9 Asian Americans or Pacific Islanders). Average age 32. 93 applicants, 46% accepted, 29 enrolled. *Faculty:* 17 full-time (0 women), 3 part-time/adjunct (1 woman). Expenses: Contact institution. *Financial support:* In 2008–09, 4 research assistantships (averaging $59,216 per year), 3 teaching assistantships (averaging $26,896 per year) were awarded. In 2008, 20 master's awarded. *Degree program information:* Part-time and evening/weekend programs available. Offers computer and information systems engineering (MS, PhD); engineering (ME). *Application deadline:* For fall admission, 4/1 priority date for domestic students. *Application fee:* $25. *Application Contact:* Dr. Mohan J. Malkani, Associate Dean, 615-963-5400, Fax: 615-963-5397, E-mail: mmalkani@tnstate.edu. *Dean,* Dr. Lonnie Sharpe, 615-963-5409, Fax: 615-963-5397, E-mail: lsharpe@tnstate.edu.

College of Health Sciences Students: 144 full-time (115 women), 41 part-time (39 women); includes 60 minority (53 African Americans, 2 American Indian/Alaska Native, 3 Asian Americans or Pacific Islanders, 2 Hispanic Americans), 2 international. 220 applicants, 46% accepted, 52 enrolled. *Faculty:* 13 full-time (9 women), 4 part-time/adjunct (3 women).

Expenses: Contact institution. *Financial support:* Fellowships, research assistantships, teaching assistantships, scholarships/grants available. Financial award application deadline: 3/15. In 2008, 33 master's awarded. *Degree program information:* Part-time and evening/weekend programs available. Offers health sciences (MPT, MS, DPT); physical therapy (MPT, DPT); speech and hearing science (MS). *Application deadline:* For fall admission, 4/1 for domestic students. Applications are processed on a rolling basis. *Application fee:* $25. Electronic applications accepted. *Application Contact:* Dr. Harold R. Mitchell, Head, Department of Speech Pathology and Audiology, 615-963-7009, Fax: 615-963-7119, E-mail: hmitchell@tnstate.edu. *Dean,* Dr. Kathleen McEnerney, 615-963-5924, Fax: 615-963-5926, E-mail: kmcenerney@tnstate.edu.

Institute of Government Students: 26 full-time (18 women), 96 part-time (59 women); includes 33 minority (31 African Americans, 1 Asian American or Pacific Islander, 1 Hispanic American). Average age 36. 111 applicants, 60% accepted, 25 enrolled. *Faculty:* 5 full-time (1 woman), 2 part-time/adjunct (1 woman). Expenses: Contact institution. *Financial support:* In 2008–09, 3 research assistantships (averaging $4,185 per year), teaching assistantships (averaging $4,185 per year) were awarded. Support available to part-time students. In 2008, 19 master's, 3 doctorates awarded. *Degree program information:* Part-time and evening/weekend programs available. Offers public administration (MPA, PhD). *Application deadline:* For fall admission, 3/1 priority date for domestic students. *Application fee:* $25. *Application Contact:* Dr. Rodney Stonley, Coordinator of Graduate Studies, 615-963-7249, Fax: 615-963-7245, E-mail: rstonleyl@tnstate.edu. *Director,* Dr. Ann-Marie Rizzo, 615-963-7250, Fax: 615-963-7245, E-mail: arizzo@tnstate.edu.

School of Agriculture and Consumer Sciences Students: 11 full-time (9 women), 6 part-time (1 woman); includes 12 minority (9 African Americans, 3 Asian Americans or Pacific Islanders). Average age 31. 9 applicants, 56% accepted, 3 enrolled. *Faculty:* 6 full-time (0 women). Expenses: Contact institution. *Financial support:* In 2008–09, 2 research assistantships (averaging $9,511 per year), 1 teaching assistantship (averaging $9,511 per year) were awarded. In 2008, 10 master's awarded. *Degree program information:* Part-time and evening/weekend programs available. Offers agricultural sciences (MS). *Application deadline:* For fall admission, 4/1 priority date for domestic students. *Application fee:* $25. *Application Contact:* Deborah Chisom, Director of Graduate Admissions, 615-963-5962, Fax: 615-963-5963, E-mail: dchiscom@tnstate.edu. *Dean,* Dr. Chandra Reddy, 615-963-7620, Fax: 615-963-5888.

School of Nursing Students: 41 full-time (38 women), 95 part-time (88 women); includes 55 minority (51 African Americans, 1 Asian American or Pacific Islander, 3 Hispanic Americans). Average age 37. 66 applicants, 68% accepted, 32 enrolled. *Faculty:* 7 full-time (6 women). Expenses: Contact institution. *Financial support:* In 2008–09, research assistantships (averaging $6,500 per year), 3 teaching assistantships (averaging $6,500 per year) were awarded. In 2008, 8 master's awarded. Offers family nurse practitioner (MSN); holistic nursing (MSN); nursing administration (MSN); nursing education (MSN); nursing informatics (MSN). *Application deadline:* For fall admission, 4/1 priority date for domestic students. Applications are processed on a rolling basis. *Application fee:* $25. *Application Contact:* Deborah Chisom, Director of Graduate Admissions, 615-963-5962, Fax: 615-963-5963, E-mail: dchiscom@tnstate.edu. *Interim Dean,* Dr. Bernadeen Fleming, 615-963-7106, Fax: 615-963-5049, E-mail: bfleming@tnstate.edu.

TENNESSEE TECHNOLOGICAL UNIVERSITY, Cookeville, TN 38505

General Information State-supported, coed, university. CGS member. *Graduate housing:* Rooms and/or apartments available on a first-come, first-served basis to single students and available to married students. Housing application deadline: 6/1. *Research affiliation:* Center for Excellence in Teacher Evaluation, Appalachian Center for Crafts, Center of Excellence in Water Resources, Center of Excellence in Manufacturing Resources, Center of Excellence in Electric Power.

GRADUATE UNITS

Graduate School *Degree program information:* Part-time and evening/weekend programs available. Electronic applications accepted.

College of Arts and Sciences *Degree program information:* Part-time programs available. Offers arts and sciences (MA, MS, PhD); chemistry (MS); computer science (MS); English (MA); environmental biology (MS); environmental sciences (PhD); fish, game, and wildlife management (MS); mathematics (MS). Electronic applications accepted.

College of Business *Degree program information:* Part-time and evening/weekend programs available. Offers business (MBA).

College of Education *Degree program information:* Part-time and evening/weekend programs available. Offers curriculum (MA, Ed S); early childhood education (MA, Ed S); education (MA, PhD, Ed S); educational psychology (MA, Ed S); educational psychology and student personnel (MA, Ed S); elementary education (MA, Ed S); exceptional learning (PhD); exercise science, physical education and wellness (MA); instructional leadership (MA, Ed S); library science (MA, Ed S); reading (MA, Ed S); secondary education (MA, Ed S); special education (MA, Ed S). Electronic applications accepted.

College of Engineering *Degree program information:* Part-time programs available. Offers chemical engineering (MS, PhD); civil engineering (MS, PhD); electrical engineering (MS, PhD); engineering (MS, PhD); mechanical engineering (MS, PhD).

School of Nursing Offers nursing (MSN).

TENNESSEE TEMPLE UNIVERSITY, Chattanooga, TN 37404-3587

General Information Independent-religious, coed, comprehensive institution. *Graduate housing:* Rooms and/or apartments available to single students and available on a first-come, first-served basis to married students. Housing application deadline: 6/1.

GRADUATE UNITS

Graduate Studies in Education *Degree program information:* Part-time programs available. Offers education (M Ed); educational leadership (M Ed); instructional effectiveness (M Ed).

TEXAS A&M HEALTH SCIENCE CENTER, College Station, TX 77840

General Information State-supported, coed, upper-level institution. *Graduate housing:* On-campus housing not available.

GRADUATE UNITS

Baylor College of Dentistry Offers dentistry (DDS, MD, MS, PhD, Certificate).

Graduate Division *Degree program information:* Part-time programs available. Offers biomaterials science (MS); biomedical sciences (MS, PhD); dental hygiene (MS); endodontics (MS, PhD, Certificate); health professions education (MS); oral and maxillofacial pathology (MS, PhD, Certificate); oral and maxillofacial surgery (MD, Certificate); oral biology (MS, PhD); orthodontics (MS, Certificate); pediatric dentistry (MS, Certificate); periodontics (MS, Certificate); prosthodontics (MS, Certificate).

College of Medicine Offers medicine (MD, PhD). Electronic applications accepted.

Graduate School of Biomedical Sciences Offers cell and molecular biology (PhD); immunology (PhD); microbial and molecular pathogenesis (PhD); microbiology (PhD); molecular and cellular medicine (PhD); molecular biology (PhD); neuroscience and experimental therapeutics (PhD); systems biology and translational medicine (PhD); virology (PhD).

Institute of Biosciences and Technology Offers medical sciences (PhD). Degree awarded by the Graduate School for Biomedical Sciences.

School of Rural Public Health *Degree program information:* Part-time programs available. Postbaccalaureate distance learning degree programs offered (no on-campus study). Offers environmental/occupational health (MPH); epidemiology/biostatistics (MPH); health policy/management (MPH); social and behavioral health (MPH). Electronic applications accepted.

TEXAS A&M INTERNATIONAL UNIVERSITY, Laredo, TX 78041-1900

General Information State-supported, coed, comprehensive institution. *Enrollment:* 5,856 graduate, professional, and undergraduate students; 187 full-time matriculated graduate/professional students (101 women), 876 part-time matriculated graduate/professional students (549 women). *Enrollment by degree level:* 1,033 master's, 30 doctoral. *Graduate faculty:* 79 full-time (21 women), 13 part-time/adjunct (3 women). *Graduate housing:* Rooms and/or apartments available on a first-come, first-served basis to single and married students. *Student services:* Campus employment opportunities, campus safety program, career counseling, exercise/wellness program, free psychological counseling, international student services, low-cost health insurance, multicultural affairs office, services for students with disabilities, teacher training, writing training. *Library facilities:* Sue and Radcliff Killam Library. *Online resources:* library catalog, web page, access to other libraries' catalogs. *Collection:* 310,366 titles, 8,149 serial subscriptions, 4,504 audiovisual materials.

Computer facilities: 410 computers available on campus for general student use. A campuswide network can be accessed from student residence rooms and from off campus. Online class registration is available. *Web address:* http://www.tamiu.edu/.

General Application Contact: Dr. Jeff Brown, Dean, Office of Graduate Studies, 956-326-2596, Fax: 956-326-3021, E-mail: jbrown@tamiu.edu.

GRADUATE UNITS

Office of Graduate Studies and Research Students: 187 full-time (101 women), 876 part-time (549 women); includes 850 minority (4 African Americans, 5 Asian Americans or Pacific Islanders, 841 Hispanic Americans), 168 international. Average age 32. 760 applicants, 76% accepted, 359 enrolled. *Faculty:* 79 full-time (21 women), 13 part-time/adjunct (3 women). Expenses: Contact institution. *Financial support:* In 2008–09, 227 students received support, including 8 fellowships with partial tuition reimbursements available, 13 research assistantships, 8 teaching assistantships; Federal Work-Study, institutionally sponsored loans, and scholarships/grants also available. Support available to part-time students. Financial award application deadline: 11/1; financial award applicants required to submit FAFSA. In 2008, 314 master's, 1 doctorate awarded. *Degree program information:* Part-time and evening/weekend programs available. Offers educational administration (MS Ed); generic special education (MS Ed); school counseling (MS). *Application deadline:* For fall admission, 4/30 priority date for domestic students, 4/30 for international students; for spring admission, 11/3 priority date for domestic students, 10/1 for international students. Applications are processed on a rolling basis. *Application fee:* $25. *Application Contact:* Rosie Espinoza-Dickinson, Director of Admissions, 956-326-2200, Fax: 956-326-2199, E-mail: enroll@tamiu.edu. *Dean,* Dr. Jeff Brown, 956-326-2596, Fax: 956-326-3021, E-mail: jbrown@tamiu.edu.

College of Arts and Sciences Students: 34 full-time (20 women), 175 part-time (104 women); includes 188 minority (all Hispanic Americans), 8 international. Average age 32. 129 applicants, 94% accepted, 71 enrolled. *Faculty:* 29 full-time (8 women), 3 part-time/adjunct (1 woman). Expenses: Contact institution. *Financial support:* In 2008–09, 51 students received support, including 2 fellowships with tuition reimbursements available, 5 research assistantships (averaging $9,100 per year), 11 teaching assistantships (averaging $9,100 per year); Federal Work-Study and institutionally sponsored loans also available. Support available to part-time students. Financial award application deadline: 11/1; financial award applicants required to submit FAFSA. In 2008, 51 master's awarded. *Degree program information:* Part-time and evening/weekend programs available. Postbaccalaureate distance learning degree programs offered (no on-campus study). Offers arts and sciences (MA, MACP, MPA, MS, PhD); biology (MS); counseling psychology (MACP); criminal justice (MS); English (MA); Hispanic studies (PhD); history (MA); mathematical and physical science (MA); political science (MA); psychology (MS); public administration (MPA); sociology (MA); Spanish (MA). *Application deadline:* For fall admission, 4/30 priority date for domestic students, 4/30 for international students; for spring admission, 11/30 for domestic students, 10/1 for international students. Applications are processed on a rolling basis. *Application fee:* $25. *Application Contact:* Rosie Espinoza-Dickinson, Director of Admissions, 956-326-2200, Fax: 956-326-2199, E-mail: enroll@tamiu.edu. *Interim Dean,* Dr. Thomas R. Mitchell, 956-326-2633, Fax: 956-326-2459, E-mail: tmitchell@tamiu.edu.

College of Business Administration Students: 115 full-time (44 women), 244 part-time (102 women); includes 187 minority (1 African American, 3 Asian Americans or Pacific Islanders, 183 Hispanic Americans), 159 international. Average age 30. 363 applicants, 60% accepted, 146 enrolled. *Faculty:* 26 full-time (1 woman), 6 part-time/adjunct (0 women). Expenses: Contact institution. *Financial support:* In 2008–09, 27 students received support, including 7 research assistantships, 1 teaching assistantship; fellowships, Federal Work-Study and institutionally sponsored loans also available. Support available to part-time students. Financial award application deadline: 11/1; financial award applicants required to submit FAFSA. In 2008, 139 master's awarded. *Degree program information:* Part-time and evening/weekend programs available. Offers accounting (MP Acc); business administration (MBA, MP Acc, MSIS); information systems (MSIS); international banking (MBA); international trade (MBA). *Application deadline:* For fall admission, 4/30 priority date for domestic students; for spring admission, 11/30 for domestic students. Applications are processed on a rolling basis. *Application fee:* $25. *Application Contact:* Imelda Lopez, Graduate Admissions Counselor, 956-326-2485, Fax: 956-326-2459, E-mail: lopez@tamiu.edu. *Associate Dean,* Dr. Antonio Rodriguez, 956-326-2517, E-mail: rodriguez@tamiu.edu.

College of Education Students: 38 full-time (37 women), 427 part-time (324 women); includes 447 minority (3 African Americans, 1 Asian American or Pacific Islander, 443 Hispanic Americans), 1 international. Average age 35. 246 applicants, 93% accepted, 130 enrolled. *Faculty:* 21 full-time (9 women), 3 part-time/adjunct (1 woman). Expenses: Contact institution. *Financial support:* In 2008–09, 101 students received support, including 5 fellowships, 3 research assistantships; Federal Work-Study and institutionally sponsored loans also available. Support available to part-time students. Financial award application deadline: 11/1; financial award applicants required to submit FAFSA. In 2008, 117 master's awarded. *Degree program information:* Part-time and evening/weekend programs available. Offers bilingual education (PhD); curriculum and instruction (MS, PhD); early childhood education (PhD); education (MS, MS Ed, PhD); reading (MS). *Application deadline:* For fall admission, 4/30 priority date for domestic students; for spring admission, 11/30 for domestic students. Applications are processed on a rolling basis. *Application fee:* $25. *Application Contact:* Rosie Espinoza-Dickinson, Director of Admissions, 956-326-2200, Fax: 956-326-2199, E-mail: enroll@tamiu.edu. *Dean,* Dr. Humberto Gonzalez, 956-326-2420, E-mail: hgonzalez@tamiu.edu.

College of Nursing and Health Sciences Students: 30 part-time (19 women); includes 28 minority (1 Asian American or Pacific Islander, 27 Hispanic Americans). Average age 36. 14 applicants, 93% accepted, 12 enrolled. *Faculty:* 3 full-time (all women), 1 (woman) part-time/adjunct. Expenses: Contact institution. *Financial support:* In 2008–09, 12 students received support, including 1 fellowship. Offers nursing and health sciences (MSN). *Application fee:* $25. *Application Contact:* Rosie Espinoza, Director, Office of Admissions, 956-326-2200, Fax: 956-326-2269, E-mail: enroll@tamiu.edu. *Interim Dean,* Natalie Burkhalter, 956-326-2579, E-mail: natalie@tamiu.edu.

TEXAS A&M UNIVERSITY, College Station, TX 77843

General Information State-supported, coed, university. CGS member. *Enrollment:* 48,039 graduate, professional, and undergraduate students; 7,506 full-time matriculated graduate/professional students (3,024 women), 2,103 part-time matriculated graduate/professional students (1,073 women). *Enrollment by degree level:* 503 first professional, 5,799 master's, 3,307 doctoral. *Graduate faculty:* 1,633. Tuition, state resident: full-time $3838.50. Tuition, nonresident: full-time $8897. *Required fees:* $2359.60. *Graduate housing:* Rooms and/or apartments available on a first-come, first-served basis to single and married students. *Student services:* Campus employment opportunities, campus safety program, career counseling, child daycare facilities, exercise/wellness program, free psychological counseling, grant writing training, international student services, low-cost health insurance, multicultural affairs office, services for students with disabilities, teacher training, writing training. *Library facilities:* Sterling C. Evans Library plus 6 others. *Online resources:* library catalog, web page, access to other libraries' catalogs. *Collection:* 3.8 million titles, 61,717 serial subscriptions, 55,193

Texas A&M University (continued)

audiovisual materials. *Research affiliation:* Texas Department of Transportation (transportation), US Department of Agriculture (agriculture), National Science Foundation (geosciences), Joint Oceanographic Institutions, Inc. (geosciences).

Computer facilities: 1,483 computers available on campus for general student use. A campuswide network can be accessed from student residence rooms and from off campus. Online class registration is available. *Web address:* http://www.tamu.edu/.

General Application Contact: Graduate Admissions, 979-458-0427, E-mail: admissions@tamu.edu.

GRADUATE UNITS

College of Agriculture and Life Sciences Students: 973 full-time (496 women), 307 part-time (138 women); includes 151 minority (36 African Americans, 6 American Indian/Alaska Native, 13 Asian Americans or Pacific Islanders, 96 Hispanic Americans), 410 international. Average age 29. *Faculty:* 317. Expenses: Contact institution. *Financial support:* Fellowships, research assistantships, teaching assistantships, career-related internships or fieldwork, Federal Work-Study, institutionally sponsored loans, scholarships/grants, tuition waivers (partial), and unspecified assistantships available. Support available to part-time students. Financial award applicants required to submit FAFSA. In 2008, 163 master's, 91 doctorates awarded. *Degree program information:* Part-time programs available. Postbaccalaureate distance learning degree programs offered (minimal on-campus study). Offers agricultural economics (MAB, MS, PhD); agricultural education (M Ed, MS, Ed D, PhD); agriculture (M Agr); agriculture and life sciences (M Agr, M Ed, M Eng, MAB, MS, DE, Ed D, PhD); agronomy (M Agr, MS, PhD); animal breeding (MS, PhD); animal science (M Agr, MS, PhD); biochemistry (MS, PhD); biological and agricultural engineering (M Agr, M Eng, MS, DE, PhD); biophysics (MS); dairy science (M Agr, MS); entomology (M Agr, MS, PhD); forestry (MS, PhD); genetics (PhD); horticulture (PhD); horticulture and floriculture (M Agr, MS); molecular and environmental plant sciences (MS, PhD); natural resources development (M Agr); nutrition and food science (M Agr, MS, PhD); physiology of reproduction (MS, PhD); plant pathology (MS, PhD); plant protection (M Agr); poultry science (M Agr, MS, PhD); recreation resources development (M Agr); recreation, park, and tourism sciences (MS, PhD); soil science (MS, PhD); wildlife and fisheries sciences (M Agr, MS, PhD). *Application deadline:* For fall admission, 7/21 priority date for domestic students, 6/1 priority date for international students; for spring admission, 12/1 priority date for domestic students, 10/1 priority date for international students. Applications are processed on a rolling basis. *Application fee:* $50 ($75 for international students). Electronic applications accepted. *Application Contact:* Graduate Admissions, 979-845-1044, E-mail: admissions@tamu.edu. *Interim Vice Chancellor*, Dr. Mark Hussey, 979-845-4747, Fax: 979-845-9938, E-mail: mhussey@tamu.edu.

College of Architecture Students: 442 full-time (166 women), 75 part-time (24 women); includes 48 minority (7 African Americans, 1 American Indian/Alaska Native, 16 Asian Americans or Pacific Islanders, 24 Hispanic Americans), 268 international. Average age 29. *Faculty:* 94. Expenses: Contact institution. *Financial support:* In 2008–09, fellowships with partial tuition reimbursements (averaging $1,000 per year), research assistantships with partial tuition reimbursements (averaging $8,139 per year), teaching assistantships with partial tuition reimbursements (averaging $7,650 per year) were awarded; career-related internships or fieldwork, Federal Work-Study, institutionally sponsored loans, scholarships/grants, and unspecified assistantships also available. Financial award application deadline: 1/15; financial award applicants required to submit FAFSA. In 2008, 138 master's, 8 doctorates awarded. Offers architecture (M Arch, MS Arch, PhD); construction management (MS); land development (MSLD); landscape architecture (MLA); urban and regional science (PhD); urban planning (MUP); visualization science (MS). *Application deadline:* For fall admission, 1/15 priority date for domestic and international students. Applications are processed on a rolling basis. *Application fee:* $50 ($75 for international students). Electronic applications accepted. *Application Contact:* 979-845-6582, Fax: 979-862-7119, E-mail: gradoff@archone.tamu.edu. *Interim Dean*, Jorge Vanegas, 979-845-1221, Fax: 979-845-4491, E-mail: jvanegas@tamu.edu.

College of Education and Human Development Students: 552 full-time (376 women), 806 part-time (581 women); includes 387 minority (162 African Americans, 8 American Indian/Alaska Native, 29 Asian Americans or Pacific Islanders, 188 Hispanic Americans), 139 international. Average age 36. *Faculty:* 141. Expenses: Contact institution. *Financial support:* In 2008–09, fellowships with partial tuition reimbursements (averaging $12,000 per year), research assistantships with partial tuition reimbursements (averaging $10,000 per year), teaching assistantships with partial tuition reimbursements (averaging $10,000 per year) were awarded; career-related internships or fieldwork, Federal Work-Study, institutionally sponsored loans, scholarships/grants, tuition waivers (partial), and unspecified assistantships also available. Financial award applicants required to submit FAFSA. In 2008, 238 master's, 94 doctorates awarded. *Degree program information:* Part-time and evening/weekend programs available. Postbaccalaureate distance learning degree programs offered (no on-campus study). Offers counseling psychology (PhD); curriculum and instruction (M Ed, MS, PhD); education and human development (M Ed, MS, Ed D, PhD); educational administration and human resource development (M Ed, MS, Ed D, PhD); educational psychology (PhD); educational technology (M Ed); gifted and talented education (M Ed, MS); health education (M Ed, MS, Ed D, PhD); Hispanic bilingual education (M Ed, PhD); human learning and development (MS); intelligence, creativity, and giftedness (PhD); kinesiology (M Ed, MS, Ed D, PhD); learning, development, and instruction (PhD); mathematics education (M Ed, MS, PhD); multicultural/urban/ESL/international education (M Ed, MS, PhD); reading/language arts (M Ed, MS, PhD); research, measurement and statistics (MS); research, measurement, and statistics (PhD); school counseling (M Ed); school psychology (PhD); science education (M Ed, MS, PhD); social studies education (M Ed, MS, PhD); special education (M Ed, PhD). *Application fee:* $50 ($75 for international students). Electronic applications accepted. *Application Contact:* Becky Carr, Assistant Dean, 979-845-5311, Fax: 979-845-6129, E-mail: bcarr@tamu.edu. *Dean*, Doug Palmer, 979-845-5311, E-mail: dpalmer@tamu.edu.

College of Engineering Students: 2,283 full-time (451 women), 376 part-time (70 women); includes 224 minority (43 African Americans, 4 American Indian/Alaska Native, 81 Asian Americans or Pacific Islanders, 96 Hispanic Americans), 1,815 international. *Faculty:* 359. Expenses: Contact institution. *Financial support:* Fellowships, research assistantships, teaching assistantships, career-related internships or fieldwork, institutionally sponsored loans, scholarships/grants, and unspecified assistantships available. Financial award applicants required to submit FAFSA. In 2008, 503 master's, 177 doctorates awarded. *Degree program information:* Part-time programs available. Postbaccalaureate distance learning degree programs offered (minimal on-campus study). Offers aerospace engineering (M Eng, MS, PhD); biomedical engineering (M Eng, MS, D Eng, PhD); chemical engineering (M Eng, MS, PhD); computer engineering (M En, M Eng, MS, PhD); computer science (MCS, MS, PhD); construction engineering and management (M Eng, MS, D Eng, PhD); electrical engineering (MS, PhD); engineering (M En, M Eng, MCS, MID, MS, D Eng, PhD); engineering technology and industrial distribution (MID); environmental engineering (M Eng, MS, D Eng, PhD); geotechnical engineering (M Eng, MS, D Eng, PhD); health physics (MS); industrial and systems engineering (M Eng, MS); industrial engineering (D Eng, PhD); materials engineering (M Eng, MS, D Eng, PhD); mechanical engineering (M Eng, MS, D Eng, PhD); nuclear engineering (M Eng, MS, PhD); ocean engineering (M Eng, MS, D Eng, PhD); petroleum engineering (M Eng, MS, PhD); structural engineering (M Eng, MS, D Eng, PhD); transportation engineering (M Eng, MS, D Eng, PhD); water resources engineering (M Eng, MS, D Eng, PhD). *Application fee:* $50 ($75 for international students). Electronic applications accepted. *Application Contact:* Karen Butler-Purry, Assistant Dean, 979-845-7200, Fax: 979-847-8654, E-mail: eapo@tamu.edu. *Dean*, Dr. G. Kemble Bennett, 979-845-7203, Fax: 979-845-8986, E-mail: kem-bennett@tamu.edu.

College of Geosciences Students: 255 full-time (99 women), 57 part-time (23 women); includes 19 minority (4 African Americans, 2 American Indian/Alaska Native, 4 Asian Americans or Pacific Islanders, 9 Hispanic Americans), 123 international. Average age 30. *Faculty:* 82. Expenses: Contact institution. *Financial support:* Fellowships with partial tuition reimbursements, research assistantships, teaching assistantships, career-related internships or fieldwork, Federal Work-Study, institutionally sponsored loans, scholarships/grants, tuition waivers (partial), and unspecified assistantships available. Financial award application deadline: 3/1; financial award applicants required to submit FAFSA. In 2008, 30 master's, 18 doctorates awarded. *Degree program information:* Part-time programs available. Offers atmospheric sciences (MS, PhD); geography (MS, PhD); geology (MS, PhD); geophysics (MS, PhD); geosciences (MS, PhD); oceanography (MS, PhD). *Application deadline:* For fall admission, 3/1 priority date for domestic students; for spring admission, 12/1 for domestic students. Applications are processed on a rolling basis. *Application fee:* $50 ($75 for international students). Electronic applications accepted. *Application Contact:* Graduate Admissions, 979-845-1044, E-mail: admissions@tamu.edu. *Dean*, Dr. Bjorn Kjerfve, 979-845-3651, E-mail: kjerfve@tamu.edu.

College of Liberal Arts Students: 635 full-time (333 women), 188 part-time (99 women); includes 171 minority (42 African Americans, 5 American Indian/Alaska Native, 23 Asian Americans or Pacific Islanders, 101 Hispanic Americans), 184 international. *Faculty:* 216. Expenses: Contact institution. *Financial support:* Fellowships, research assistantships with partial tuition reimbursements, teaching assistantships with partial tuition reimbursements, career-related internships or fieldwork, Federal Work-Study, institutionally sponsored loans, unspecified assistantships, and assistant lecturer positions available. Financial award applicants required to submit FAFSA. In 2008, 93 master's, 61 doctorates awarded. *Degree program information:* Part-time programs available. Offers anthropology (MA, PhD); behavioral and cellular neuroscience (MS, PhD); clinical psychology (MS, PhD); cognitive psychology (MS, PhD); communication (MA, PhD); developmental psychology (MS, PhD); economics (MS, PhD); English (MA, PhD); Hispanic studies (MA, PhD); history (MA, PhD); industrial/organizational psychology (MS, PhD); liberal arts (MA, MS, PhD); philosophy (MA, PhD); political science (MA, PhD); social psychology (MS, PhD); sociology (MS, PhD). *Application fee:* $50 ($75 for international students). Electronic applications accepted. *Application Contact:* Dr. Larry J. Oliver, Associate Dean, 979-845-8541, Fax: 979-845-5164, E-mail: l-oliver@tamu.edu. *Dean*, Dr. Charles A. Johnson, 979-845-5141, Fax: 979-845-5164, E-mail: cjohnson@tamu.edu.

College of Science Students: 693 full-time (235 women), 97 part-time (39 women); includes 87 minority (11 African Americans, 5 American Indian/Alaska Native, 27 Asian Americans or Pacific Islanders, 44 Hispanic Americans), 366 international. *Faculty:* 204. Expenses: Contact institution. *Financial support:* Fellowships, research assistantships, teaching assistantships, career-related internships or fieldwork, institutionally sponsored loans, and scholarships/grants available. Financial award applicants required to submit FAFSA. In 2008, 69 master's, 68 doctorates awarded. *Degree program information:* Part-time programs available. Offers applied physics (PhD); biology (MS, PhD); botany (MS, PhD); chemistry (MS, PhD); mathematics (MS, PhD); microbiology (MS, PhD); molecular and cell biology (PhD); neuroscience (MS, PhD); physics (MS, PhD); science (MS, PhD); statistics (MS, PhD); zoology (MS, PhD). *Application Contact:* James C. Holste, Associate Dean for Graduate Studies, 979-845-7362, Fax: 979-845-6077, E-mail: j-holste@tamu.edu. *Dean*, H. Joseph Newton, 979-845-7361, Fax: 979-845-6077, E-mail: jnewton@tamu.edu.

College of Veterinary Medicine Students: 611 full-time (442 women), 44 part-time (33 women); includes 75 minority (5 African Americans, 3 American Indian/Alaska Native, 23 Asian Americans or Pacific Islanders, 44 Hispanic Americans), 45 international. *Faculty:* 69. Expenses: Contact institution. *Financial support:* Fellowships, research assistantships, teaching assistantships, career-related internships or fieldwork, Federal Work-Study, institutionally sponsored loans, tuition waivers (partial), and clinical associateships available. Support available to part-time students. Financial award applicants required to submit FAFSA. In 2008, 129 first professional degrees, 26 master's, 25 doctorates awarded. *Degree program information:* Part-time programs available. Offers epidemiology (MS); food safety/toxicology (MS); genetics (MS, PhD); physiology and pharmacology (MS, PhD); toxicology (MS, PhD); veterinary anatomy (MS, PhD); veterinary medicine (DVM, MS, PhD); veterinary medicine and surgery (MS); veterinary microbiology (MS, PhD); veterinary parasitology (MS); veterinary pathology (MS, PhD); veterinary public health (MS). *Application Contact:* Graduate Admissions, 979-845-1044, E-mail: admissions@tamu.edu. *Dean*, Dr. H. Richard Adams, 979-845-5051, Fax: 979-845-5088, E-mail: radams@tamu.edu.

George Bush School of Government and Public Service Students: 188 full-time (80 women), 101 part-time (37 women); includes 40 minority (10 African Americans, 5 Asian Americans or Pacific Islanders, 25 Hispanic Americans), 22 international. Average age 24. *Faculty:* 43. Expenses: Contact institution. *Financial support:* In 2008–09, fellowships (averaging $11,000 per year), research assistantships (averaging $11,250 per year) were awarded; career-related internships or fieldwork, Federal Work-Study, and institutionally sponsored loans also available. Financial award application deadline: 2/1; financial award applicants required to submit FAFSA. In 2008, 64 master's awarded. Offers advanced international affairs (Certificate); homeland security (Certificate); international affairs (MPIA); nonprofit management (Certificate); public service and administration (MPSA). *Application deadline:* For fall admission, 1/24 for domestic and international students. *Application fee:* $50 ($75 for international students). Electronic applications accepted. *Application Contact:* Kathryn Meyer, Recruitment/Placement Officer, 979-458-4767, Fax: 979-845-4155, E-mail: admissions@bushschool.tamu.edu. *Dean*, A. Benton Cocanougher, 979-862-8842, E-mail: bushschool@tamu.edu.

Mays Business School Offers accounting (MS, PhD); business (EMBA, MBA, MLERE, MS, PhD); business administration (EMBA, MBA); finance (MS, PhD); human resource management (MS); management (PhD); management information systems (MS, PhD); management science (PhD); marketing (MS, PhD); production and operations management (PhD); real estate (MLERE). Electronic applications accepted.

TEXAS A&M UNIVERSITY AT GALVESTON, Galveston, TX 77553-1675

General Information State-supported, coed, comprehensive institution. CGS member. *Enrollment:* 1,612 graduate, professional, and undergraduate students; 26 full-time matriculated graduate/professional students (20 women), 20 part-time matriculated graduate/professional students (12 women). *Enrollment by degree level:* 41 master's, 5 doctoral. *Graduate faculty:* 33 full-time (7 women). *Graduate housing:* Room and/or apartments available on a first-come, first-served basis to single students; on-campus housing not available to married students. *Student services:* Campus employment opportunities, career counseling, international student services, services for students with disabilities. *Library facilities:* Jack K. Williams Library. *Online resources:* library catalog, web page, access to other libraries' catalogs. *Collection:* 56,589 titles, 640 serial subscriptions.

Computer facilities: 122 computers available on campus for general student use. A campuswide network can be accessed from student residence rooms and from off campus. Online class registration, degree plan progress, billing statement are available. *Web address:* http://www.tamug.edu/.

General Application Contact: Nicole Wilkins, Administrative Coordinator for Graduate Studies, 409-740-4937, Fax: 409-740-4754, E-mail: wilkinsn@tamug.edu.

GRADUATE UNITS

Department of Marine Biology Students: 1 full-time (0 women); minority (Hispanic American). Average age 23. 5 applicants, 60% accepted, 1 enrolled. *Faculty:* 33 full-time (7 women). Expenses: Contact institution. *Financial support:* In 2008–09, 1 student received support, including 1 research assistantship; teaching assistantships, scholarships/grants, health care benefits, and unspecified assistantships also available. Financial award applicants required to submit FAFSA. Offers marine biology (MS, PhD). *Application deadline:* Applications are processed on a rolling basis. *Application fee:* $50 ($75 for international students). Electronic applications accepted. *Application Contact:* Nicole Wilkins, Administrative Coordinator for Graduate Studies, 409-740-4937, Fax: 409-740-4754, E-mail: wilkinsn@tamug.edu. *Professor/Chair of Marine Biology Interdisciplinary Program*, Dr. Bernd Wursig, 409-740-4413, E-mail: wursigb@tamug.edu.

Department of Marine Sciences Students: 23 full-time (20 women), 7 part-time (5 women); includes 7 minority (2 African Americans, 2 Asian Americans or Pacific Islanders, 3 Hispanic Americans). Average age 23. 20 applicants, 45% accepted, 8 enrolled. *Faculty:* 33 full-time (7 women). Expenses: Contact institution. *Financial support:* In 2008–09, 14 students received support, including 1 research assistantship, 2 teaching assistantships; scholarships/grants, health care benefits, and unspecified assistantships also available. Financial award application deadline: 4/1; financial award applicants required to submit FAFSA. In 2008, 5 master's awarded. Offers marine resources management (MMRM). *Application deadline:* Applications are processed on a rolling basis. *Application fee:* $50 ($75 for international students). Electronic applications accepted. *Application Contact:* Dr. Frederick C. Schlemmer, Associate Professor/Graduate Advisor, 409-740-4518, Fax: 409-740-4429, E-mail: schlemme@tamug.edu. *Head,* Dr. Ernest Estes, 409-710-4599.

TEXAS A&M UNIVERSITY–COMMERCE, Commerce, TX 75429-3011

General Information State-supported, coed, university. CGS member. *Graduate housing:* Rooms and/or apartments available on a first-come, first-served basis to single and married students. *Research affiliation:* A&M–Commerce Regional Division of Texas Engineering Experiment Station.

GRADUATE UNITS

Graduate School *Degree program information:* Part-time programs available. Electronic applications accepted.

College of Arts and Sciences *Degree program information:* Part-time programs available. Offers agricultural education (M Ed, MS); agricultural sciences (M Ed, MS); art (MA, MS); art history (MA); arts and sciences (M Ed, MA, MFA, MM, MS, PhD); biological and earth sciences (M Ed, MS); chemistry (M Ed, MS); college teaching of English (PhD); computer science (MS); English (MA, MS); fine arts (MFA); history (MA, MS); mathematics (MA, MS); music (MA, MS); music composition (MA, MM); music education (MA, MM, MS); music literature (MA); music performance (MA, MM); music theory (MA, MM); physics (M Ed, MS); social sciences (M Ed, MS); sociology (MA, MS); Spanish (MA); studio art (MA); theatre (MA, MS). Electronic applications accepted.

College of Business and Technology *Degree program information:* Part-time programs available. Offers business administration (MBA); business and technology (MA, MBA, MS); economics (MA, MS); industrial technology (MS); technology management (MS). Electronic applications accepted.

College of Education and Human Services *Degree program information:* Part-time programs available. Offers bilingual/ESL education (M Ed, MS); cognition and instruction (PhD); counseling (M Ed, MS, PhD); early childhood education (M Ed, MS); education and human services (M Ed, MA, MS, MSW, Ed D, PhD); educational administration (M Ed, Ed D); educational technology (M Ed, MS); elementary education (M Ed, MS); exercise physiology (MS); health and human performance (M Ed); health promotion (MS); health, kinesiology and sports studies (Ed D); higher education (MS, Ed D); learning technology and information systems (M Ed, MS); motor performance (MS); psychology (MA, MS); reading (M Ed, MS); secondary education (M Ed, MS); social work (MSW); special education (M Ed, MA, MS); sport studies (MS); supervision, curriculum and instruction: elementary education (Ed D); supervision, curriculum, and instruction (Ed D); training and development (MS). Electronic applications accepted.

TEXAS A&M UNIVERSITY–CORPUS CHRISTI, Corpus Christi, TX 78412-5503

General Information State-supported, coed, comprehensive institution. CGS member. *Graduate housing:* Room and/or apartments available on a first-come, first-served basis to single students; on-campus housing not available to married students. Housing application deadline: 5/1.

GRADUATE UNITS

Graduate Studies and Research *Degree program information:* Part-time and evening/weekend programs available. Postbaccalaureate distance learning degree programs offered (minimal on-campus study). Electronic applications accepted.

College of Business *Degree program information:* Part-time and evening/weekend programs available. Offers accounting (M Acc); health care administration (MBA); international business (MBA). Electronic applications accepted.

College of Education *Degree program information:* Part-time and evening/weekend programs available. Offers counseling (MS, PhD); counselor education (PhD); curriculum and instruction (MS, Ed D); early childhood education (MS); educational administration (MS); educational leadership (Ed D); educational technology (MS); elementary education (MS); kinesiology (MS); reading (MS); secondary education (MS); special education (MS). Electronic applications accepted.

College of Liberal Arts *Degree program information:* Part-time and evening/weekend programs available. Offers English (MA); history (MA); psychology (MA); public administration (MPA); studio arts (MA, MFA). Electronic applications accepted.

College of Nursing and Health Sciences *Degree program information:* Part-time and evening/weekend programs available. Offers clinical nurse specialist (MSN); family nurse practitioner (MSN); health care administration (MSN); leadership in nursing systems (MSN). Electronic applications accepted.

College of Science and Technology *Degree program information:* Part-time and evening/weekend programs available. Offers applied and computational mathematics (MS); biology (MS); coastal and marine system science (PhD); computer science (MS); curriculum content (MS); environmental science (MS); mariculture (MS); science and technology (MS, PhD). Electronic applications accepted.

TEXAS A&M UNIVERSITY–KINGSVILLE, Kingsville, TX 78363

General Information State-supported, coed, university. *Graduate housing:* Rooms and/or apartments available on a first-come, first-served basis to single and married students. Housing application deadline: 8/1. *Research affiliation:* Gas Research Institute (engineering), U.S. Filters (engineering), Texas A&M University (biology), University of Texas Health Science Center–Houston (biology), University of Texas Health Science Center–San Antonio (biology), Institute of Biosciences and Technology (biology).

GRADUATE UNITS

College of Graduate Studies *Degree program information:* Part-time and evening/weekend programs available. Postbaccalaureate distance learning degree programs offered (minimal on-campus study).

College of Agriculture and Home Economics *Degree program information:* Part-time and evening/weekend programs available. Offers agribusiness (MS); agricultural education (MS); agriculture and home economics (MS, PhD); animal sciences (MS); human sciences (MS); plant and soil sciences (MS, PhD); range and wildlife management (MS); wildlife science (PhD).

College of Arts and Sciences *Degree program information:* Part-time and evening/weekend programs available. Offers applied geology (MS); art (MA, MS); arts and sciences (MA, MM, MS); biology (MS); chemistry (MS); communication (MS); English (MA, MS); gerontology (MS); history and political science (MA, MS); mathematics (MS); music education (MM); psychology (MA, MS); sociology (MA, MS); Spanish (MA).

College of Business Administration *Degree program information:* Part-time and evening/weekend programs available. Offers business administration (MBA, MS).

College of Education *Degree program information:* Part-time and evening/weekend programs available. Offers adult education (M Ed); bilingual education (MA, MS, Ed D); early childhood education (M Ed); education (M Ed, MA, MS, Ed D, PhD); elementary education (MA, MS); English as a second language (M Ed); guidance and counseling (MA, MS); health and kinesiology (MA, MS); higher education administration leadership (PhD); reading (MS); school administration (MA, MS, Ed D); secondary education (MA, MS); special education (M Ed); supervision (MA, MS).

College of Engineering *Degree program information:* Part-time and evening/weekend programs available. Offers chemical engineering (ME, MS); civil engineering (ME, MS); computer science (MS); electrical engineering (ME, MS); engineering (ME, MS, PhD); environmental engineering (ME, MS, PhD); industrial engineering (ME, MS); mechanical engineering (ME, MS); natural gas engineering (ME, MS).

TEXAS A&M UNIVERSITY–TEXARKANA, Texarkana, TX 75505-5518

General Information State-supported, coed, upper-level institution. *Graduate housing:* On-campus housing not available.

GRADUATE UNITS

Graduate Studies and Research *Degree program information:* Part-time and evening/weekend programs available. Electronic applications accepted.

College of Arts and Sciences and Education *Degree program information:* Part-time and evening/weekend programs available. Offers adult education (MS); curriculum and instruction (MS); education (MS); educational administration (M Ed); English (MA); history (MS); instructional technology (MS); interdisciplinary studies (MS); special education (M Ed, MS). Electronic applications accepted.

College of Business *Degree program information:* Part-time and evening/weekend programs available. Offers accounting (MSA); business administration (MBA, MS). Electronic applications accepted.

College of Health and Behavioral Sciences *Degree program information:* Part-time and evening/weekend programs available. Offers counseling psychology (MS). Electronic applications accepted.

TEXAS CHIROPRACTIC COLLEGE, Pasadena, TX 77505-1699

General Information Independent, coed, graduate-only institution. *Enrollment by degree level:* 341 first professional. *Graduate faculty:* 28 full-time (6 women), 11 part-time/adjunct (2 women). *Tuition:* Full-time $22,125; part-time $633 per credit hour. *Required fees:* $450. *Graduate housing:* On-campus housing not available. *Student services:* Campus employment opportunities, career counseling, exercise/wellness program, free psychological counseling, international student services, low-cost health insurance. *Library facilities:* The Mae Hilty Memorial Library. *Online resources:* library catalog. *Collection:* 17,400 titles, 170 serial subscriptions, 1,057 audiovisual materials.

Computer facilities: 68 computers available on campus for general student use. A campuswide network can be accessed from off campus. Online class registration is available. *Web address:* http://www.txchiro.edu/.

General Application Contact: Dr. Sandra Hughes, Director of Admissions, 281-998-6098, Fax: 281-991-4871, E-mail: shughes@txchiro.edu.

GRADUATE UNITS

Professional Program Students: 374 full-time (132 women), 5 part-time (3 women); includes 111 minority (31 African Americans, 5 American Indian/Alaska Native, 33 Asian Americans or Pacific Islanders, 42 Hispanic Americans). Average age 30. 198 applicants, 84% accepted, 131 enrolled. *Faculty:* 28 full-time (6 women), 3 part-time/adjunct (0 women). Expenses: Contact institution. *Financial support:* Career-related internships or fieldwork, Federal Work-Study, institutionally sponsored loans, and tuition waivers (partial) available. Support available to part-time students. Financial award application deadline: 4/15; financial award applicants required to submit FAFSA. In 2008, 120 DCs awarded. *Degree program information:* Part-time programs available. Offers chiropractic (DC). *Application deadline:* For fall admission, 9/1 priority date for domestic students; for spring admission, 12/1 priority date for domestic students. Applications are processed on a rolling basis. *Application fee:* $50. *Application Contact:* Dr. Sandra Hughes, Director of Admissions, 281-998-6098, Fax: 281-991-4871, E-mail: shughes@txchiro.edu. *President,* Dr. Richard G. Brassard, 281-487-1170, Fax: 281-487-0329, E-mail: rbrassard@txchiro.edu.

TEXAS CHRISTIAN UNIVERSITY, Fort Worth, TX 76129-0002

General Information Independent-religious, coed, university. CGS member. *Enrollment:* 8,696 graduate, professional, and undergraduate students; 502 full-time matriculated graduate/professional students (256 women), 723 part-time matriculated graduate/professional students (400 women). *Enrollment by degree level:* 978 master's, 233 doctoral, 14 other advanced degrees. *Graduate faculty:* 506 full-time (209 women), 305 part-time/adjunct (150 women). *Tuition:* Full-time $17,640. *Graduate housing:* Rooms and/or apartments available on a first-come, first-served basis to single and married students. Housing application deadline: 5/1. *Student services:* Campus employment opportunities, campus safety program, career counseling, exercise/wellness program, free psychological counseling, international student services, low-cost health insurance, multicultural affairs office, services for students with disabilities, teacher training, writing training. *Library facilities:* Mary Couts Burnett Library. *Online resources:* library catalog, web page, access to other libraries' catalogs. *Collection:* 1.4 million titles, 32,935 serial subscriptions. *Research affiliation:* Bell Helicopter (engineering), Lockheed Martin (engineering), Botanical Research Institute of Texas, Inc. (biology), Aberdeen Proving Ground (engineering), TXU (engineering), Laerdal Corporation (engineering).

Computer facilities: A campuswide network can be accessed from student residence rooms and from off campus. Online class registration is available. *Web address:* http://www.tcu.edu/.

General Application Contact: Admissions, TCU Graduate Studies Office, 817-257-7515, Fax: 817-257-7484, E-mail: frogmail@tcu.edu.

GRADUATE UNITS

AddRan College of Liberal Arts Expenses: Contact institution. *Financial support:* Unspecified assistantships available. Financial award application deadline: 3/1. *Degree program information:* Part-time and evening/weekend programs available. Offers English (MA, PhD); history (MA, PhD); liberal arts (MA, PhD). *Application deadline:* For fall admission, 3/1 for domestic students; for spring admission, 12/1 for domestic students. Applications are processed on a rolling basis. *Application fee:* $0. *Application Contact:* Admissions, TCU Graduate Studies Office, 817-257-7515, Fax: 817-257-7484, E-mail: frogmail@tcu.edu. *Dean,* Dr. Andrew Schoolmaster, 817-257-7160, E-mail: a.schoolmaster@tcu.edu.

College of Communication Expenses: Contact institution. *Financial support:* Unspecified assistantships available. Financial award application deadline: 3/1. *Degree program information:* Part-time and evening/weekend programs available. Offers communication (MS); communication in human relations (MS). *Application deadline:* For fall admission, 3/1 for domestic students; for spring admission, 12/1 for domestic students. Applications are processed on a rolling basis. *Application fee:* $0. *Application Contact:* Dr. John Burton, Director of Graduate Studies, 817-257-7603, Fax: 817-257-7703, E-mail: j.burton@tcu.edu. *Dean,* Dr. David Whillock, 817-257-5918, E-mail: d.whillock@tcu.edu.

Schieffer School of Journalism Expenses: Contact institution. *Financial support:* Application deadline: 3/1. *Degree program information:* Part-time and evening/weekend programs available. Offers advertising/public relations (MS); news-editorial (MS). *Application deadline:* For fall admission, 3/1 for domestic students; for spring admission, 12/1 for domestic students. Applications are processed on a rolling basis. *Application fee:* $0. *Application Contact:* Dr. John Tisdale, Director, 817-257-6554, E-mail: j.tisdale@tcu.edu. *Director,* Dr. John Tisdale, 817-257-6554, E-mail: j.tisdale@tcu.edu.

College of Education *Faculty:* 21. Expenses: Contact institution. *Financial support:* Career-related internships or fieldwork and unspecified assistantships available. Financial award application deadline: 3/1. *Degree program information:* Part-time and evening/weekend programs available. Offers counseling (M Ed); curriculum studies (M Ed); education (M Ed, PhD, Certificate); educational administration (M Ed); educational studies: science education (PhD); elementary education (M Ed, Certificate); middle school education (M Ed); school counseling (Certificate); science education (M Ed); secondary education (M Ed); special education (M Ed). *Application deadline:* For fall admission, 3/1 for domestic students; for spring admission, 12/1 for domestic students. Applications are processed on a rolling basis. *Application fee:* $50. *Application Contact:* Director of Graduate Studies, 817-257-7664. *Dean,* Dr. Mary M. Patton, 817-257-7663, E-mail: m.patton@tcu.edu.

College of Fine Arts Expenses: Contact institution. *Financial support:* Application deadline: 3/1. *Degree program information:* Part-time and evening/weekend programs available. Offers art history (MA); fine arts (M Mus, MA, MFA, MM Ed, Artist Diploma); studio art (MFA). *Application deadline:* For fall admission, 3/1 for domestic students; for spring admission, 12/1

Texas Christian University (continued)

for domestic students. Applications are processed on a rolling basis. *Application fee:* $0. *Application Contact:* Admissions, TCU Graduate Studies Office, 817-257-7515, Fax: 817-257-7484, E-mail: frogmail@tcu.edu. *Dean,* Dr. Scott Sullivan, 817-257-7601, E-mail: s.sullivan@tcu.edu.

School of Music Expenses: Contact institution. *Financial support:* Unspecified assistantships available. Financial award application deadline: 3/1. *Degree program information:* Part-time and evening/weekend programs available. Offers conducting (M Mus); music education (MM Ed); musicology (M Mus); organ performance (M Mus); piano (Artist Diploma); piano pedagogy (M Mus); piano performance (M Mus); string performance (M Mus); theory/composition (M Mus); vocal performance (M Mus); voice pedagogy (M Mus); wind and percussion performance (M Mus). *Application deadline:* For fall admission, 3/1 for domestic students; for spring admission, 12/1 for domestic students. Applications are processed on a rolling basis. *Application fee:* $0. *Application Contact:* Dr. Joseph Butler, Associate Dean, College of Fine Arts, E-mail: j.butler@tcu.edu. *Director,* Dr. Richard Gipson, 817-257-7602.

College of Science and Engineering Expenses: Contact institution. *Financial support:* Fellowships, teaching assistantships, unspecified assistantships available. Financial award application deadline: 3/1. *Degree program information:* Part-time and evening/weekend programs available. Offers biology (MA, MS); chemistry (MA, MS, PhD); earth sciences (MS); ecology (MS); geology (MS); mathematics (MAT); physics (MA, MS, PhD); psychology (MA, MS, PhD); science and engineering (MA, MAT, MS, PhD). *Application deadline:* For fall admission, 3/1 for domestic students; for spring admission, 12/1 for domestic students. Applications are processed on a rolling basis. *Application fee:* $0. *Application Contact:* Admissions, TCU Graduate Studies Office, 817-257-7515, Fax: 817-257-7484, E-mail: frogmail@tcu.edu. *Dean,* Dr. Demetrius Kouris, 817-257-7727, E-mail: d.kouris@tcu.edu.

Graduate Studies Expenses: Contact institution. *Financial support:* Application deadline: 3/1. *Degree program information:* Part-time and evening/weekend programs available. Offers liberal arts (MLA). *Application deadline:* For fall admission, 3/1 for domestic students; for spring admission, 12/1 for domestic students. Applications are processed on a rolling basis. *Application fee:* $0. *Application Contact:* Dr. Bonnie Melhart, Associate Provost for Academic Affairs, 817-257-7104, E-mail: b.melhart@tcu.edu. *Associate Provost for Academic Affairs,* Dr. Bonnie Melhart, 817-257-7104, E-mail: b.melhart@tcu.edu.

Harris College of Nursing and Health Sciences Expenses: Contact institution. *Financial support:* Application deadline: 3/1. *Degree program information:* Part-time and evening/weekend programs available. Offers adult nursing (MSN); kinesiology (MS); nursing (DNP); nursing and health sciences (MS, MSN, MSNA, DNP); speech-language pathology (MS). *Application deadline:* For fall admission, 3/1 for domestic students; for spring admission, 12/1 for domestic students. Applications are processed on a rolling basis. *Application fee:* $0. *Application Contact:* Admissions, TCU Graduate Studies Office, 817-257-7515, Fax: 817-257-7484, E-mail: frogmail@tcu.edu. *Dean,* Dr. Paulette Burns, 817-257-7621.

School of Nurse Anesthesia Expenses: Contact institution. Offers nurse anesthesia (MSNA). *Application Contact:* Admissions, TCU Graduate Studies Office, 817-257-7515, Fax: 817-257-7484, E-mail: frogmail@tcu.edu. *Director,* Dr. Kay K. Sanders, 817-257-7887, E-mail: k.sanders@tcu.edu.

The Neeley School of Business at TCU Expenses: Contact institution. *Financial support:* Career-related internships or fieldwork, Federal Work-Study, institutionally sponsored loans, and unspecified assistantships available. Support available to part-time students. Financial award application deadline: 5/1; financial award applicants required to submit FAFSA. *Degree program information:* Part-time and evening/weekend programs available. Offers accounting (M Ac); business administration (MBA); international management (MIM). *Application deadline:* For fall admission, 4/30 priority date for domestic students. Applications are processed on a rolling basis. *Application fee:* $50. Electronic applications accepted. *Application Contact:* Peggy Conway, Director, MBA Admissions, 817-257-7531, Fax: 817-257-6431, E-mail: mbainfo@tcu.edu. *Dean,* Dr. Homer Erekson, 817-257-7526, Fax: 817-257-7227, E-mail: h.erekson@tcu.edu.

TEXAS COLLEGE OF TRADITIONAL CHINESE MEDICINE, Austin, TX 78704

General Information Private, coed, graduate-only institution.

GRADUATE UNITS

Program in Acupuncture and Oriental Medicine *Degree program information:* Part-time and evening/weekend programs available. Offers acupuncture and Oriental medicine (MAOM). Electronic applications accepted.

TEXAS SOUTHERN UNIVERSITY, Houston, TX 77004-4584

General Information State-supported, coed, university. CGS member. *Enrollment:* 9,102 graduate, professional, and undergraduate students; 1,186 full-time matriculated graduate/professional students (690 women), 739 part-time matriculated graduate/professional students (501 women). *Enrollment by degree level:* 1,039 first professional, 735 master's, 151 doctoral. *Graduate faculty:* 179 full-time (77 women), 37 part-time/adjunct (13 women). Tuition, state resident: full-time $1912; part-time $96 per credit hour. Tuition, nonresident: full-time $6302; part-time $343 per credit hour. *Required fees:* $3542. *Graduate housing:* Room and/or apartments available on a first-come, first-served basis to single students; on-campus housing not available to married students. Housing application deadline: 7/15. *Student services:* Campus employment opportunities, campus safety program, career counseling, child daycare facilities, exercise/wellness program, free psychological counseling, international student services, multicultural affairs office, services for students with disabilities. *Library facilities:* Robert J. Terry Library plus 2 others. *Online resources:* library catalog, access to other libraries' catalogs. *Collection:* 264,254 titles, 1,774 serial subscriptions. *Research affiliation:* Texas Space Grant Consortium (Airway Science), Lockheed Missile Company, Inc, Texas Space Grant Consortium.

Computer facilities: 500 computers available on campus for general student use. A campuswide network can be accessed from student residence rooms and from off campus. Online class registration, Blackboard Learning and Community Portal System (E-education) are available. *Web address:* http://www.tsu.edu/.

General Application Contact: Dr. Gregory Maddox, Interim Dean of the Graduate School, 713-313-7011 Ext. 4410, Fax: 713-639-1876, E-mail: maddox_gh@tsu.edu.

GRADUATE UNITS

College of Education Students: 98 full-time (72 women), 212 part-time (173 women); includes 290 minority (272 African Americans, 4 Asian Americans or Pacific Islanders, 14 Hispanic Americans), 2 international. Average age 36. 101 applicants, 94% accepted, 69 enrolled. *Faculty:* 28 full-time (13 women), 1 part-time/adjunct (0 women). Expenses: Contact institution. *Financial support:* In 2008–09, 2 research assistantships (averaging $8,626 per year) were awarded; fellowships, teaching assistantships, career-related internships or fieldwork, Federal Work-Study, and institutionally sponsored loans also available. Financial award application deadline: 5/1. In 2008, 89 master's, 13 doctorates awarded. *Degree program information:* Part-time and evening/weekend programs available. Offers bilingual education (M Ed); counseling (M Ed); counselor education (Ed D); curriculum and instruction (Ed D); education (M Ed, MS, Ed D); educational administration (M Ed, Ed D); health education (MS); human performance (MS); secondary education (M Ed). *Application deadline:* For fall admission, 7/15 priority date for domestic students. Applications are processed on a rolling basis. *Application fee:* $50 ($75 for international students). *Application Contact:* Dr. Gregory Maddox, Interim Dean of the Graduate School, 713-313-7011 Ext. 4410, Fax: 713-639-1876, E-mail: maddox_gh@tsu.edu. Dr. Jay Cummings, E-mail: cummings_jr@tsu.edu.

College of Pharmacy and Health Sciences Students: 282 full-time (157 women), 238 part-time (144 women); includes 435 minority (237 African Americans, 171 Asian Americans or Pacific Islanders, 27 Hispanic Americans), 50 international. Average age 28. 130 applicants, 98% accepted, 114 enrolled. *Faculty:* 14 full-time (6 women). Expenses: Contact institution. *Financial support:* In 2008–09, 5 research assistantships (averaging $15,687 per year), 1 teaching assistantship (averaging $8,100 per year) were awarded; fellowships, career-related internships or fieldwork, scholarships/grants, and tuition waivers (partial) also available. Financial award application deadline: 5/1; financial award applicants required to submit FAFSA. In 2008, 126 first professional degrees, 2 master's awarded. Postbaccalaureate distance learning degree programs offered. Offers pharmacy and health sciences (Pharm D, MS, PhD). *Application deadline:* For fall admission, 3/15 for domestic students. *Application fee:* $50 ($75 for international students). *Application Contact:* LaJoy Kay, Director, 713-313-1880, E-mail: kay_lj@tsu.edu. *Dean,* Dr. Barbara Hayes, 713-313-7164, Fax: 713-313-1091, E-mail: hayes_bc@tsu.edu.

College of Liberal Arts and Behavioral Sciences Students: 53 full-time (48 women), 91 part-time (73 women); includes 141 minority (135 African Americans, 2 Asian Americans or Pacific Islanders, 4 Hispanic Americans). Average age 33. 51 applicants, 100% accepted, 39 enrolled. *Faculty:* 27 full-time (13 women), 1 (woman) part-time/adjunct. Expenses: Contact institution. *Financial support:* Fellowships, research assistantships, teaching assistantships, career-related internships or fieldwork, Federal Work-Study, and institutionally sponsored loans available. Financial award application deadline: 5/1. In 2008, 30 master's awarded. *Degree program information:* Part-time and evening/weekend programs available. Offers English (MA); fine arts (MA); history (MA); human services and consumer sciences (MS); liberal arts and behavioral sciences (MA, MS); music (MA); psychology (MA); sociology (MA). *Application deadline:* For fall admission, 7/15 priority date for domestic students. Applications are processed on a rolling basis. *Application fee:* $50 ($75 for international students). *Application Contact:* Dr. Gregory Maddox, Interim Dean of the Graduate School, 713-313-7011 Ext. 4410, Fax: 713-639-1876, E-mail: maddox_gh@tsu.edu. *Dean,* Dr. Merline Pitre, 713-313-7210, E-mail: pitre_mx@tsu.edu.

Jesse H. Jones School of Business Students: 44 full-time (25 women), 39 part-time (22 women); includes 77 minority (71 African Americans, 4 Asian Americans or Pacific Islanders, 2 Hispanic Americans), 4 international. Average age 31. 50 applicants, 92% accepted, 34 enrolled. *Faculty:* 14 full-time (2 women), 2 part-time/adjunct (both women). Expenses: Contact institution. *Financial support:* In 2008–09, 5 research assistantships (averaging $5,700 per year), 3 teaching assistantships (averaging $2,367 per year) were awarded; fellowships, career-related internships or fieldwork, tuition waivers (partial), and unspecified assistantships also available. Financial award application deadline: 5/1. In 2008, 26 master's awarded. *Degree program information:* Part-time and evening/weekend programs available. Offers business (MBA, MS); business administration (MBA); management information systems (MS). *Application deadline:* For fall admission, 7/15 priority date for domestic students; for spring admission, 11/15 for domestic students. Applications are processed on a rolling basis. *Application fee:* $50 ($75 for international students). *Application Contact:* Bobbie J. Richardson, Executive Secretary, 713-313-7309, Fax: 713-313-7705, E-mail: richardson_bj@tsu.edu. *Dean,* Dr. Joseph Boyd, 713-313-7215, Fax: 713-313-7701, E-mail: boyd_jl@tsu.edu.

School of Public Affairs Students: 84 full-time (48 women), 63 part-time (36 women); includes 130 African Americans, 2 Asian Americans or Pacific Islanders, 6 Hispanic Americans, 4 international. Average age 36. 64 applicants, 95% accepted, 55 enrolled. *Faculty:* 14 full-time (3 women), 4 part-time/adjunct (1 woman). Expenses: Contact institution. *Financial support:* In 2008–09, 4 research assistantships (averaging $9,350 per year), 2 teaching assistantships (averaging $3,955 per year) were awarded; fellowships, career-related internships or fieldwork, Federal Work-Study, institutionally sponsored loans, and unspecified assistantships also available. Financial award application deadline: 5/1; financial award applicants required to submit FAFSA. In 2008, 22 master's, 4 doctorates awarded. *Degree program information:* Part-time programs available. Offers administration of justice (MS, PhD); public administration (MPA); public affairs (MPA, MS, PhD); urban planning and environmental policy (MS, PhD). *Application deadline:* For fall admission, 7/15 priority date for domestic students. Applications are processed on a rolling basis. *Application fee:* $50 ($75 for international students). *Application Contact:* Pinkie Cotton, Administrative Assistant, 713-313-7311, E-mail: cotton_pe@tsu.edu. *Dean,* Dr. Theophilus Herrington, 713-313-7447, E-mail: herrington_tx@tsu.edu.

School of Science and Technology Students: 62 full-time (45 women), 60 part-time (30 women); includes 102 minority (74 African Americans, 1 American Indian/Alaska Native, 23 Asian Americans or Pacific Islanders, 4 Hispanic Americans), 16 international. Average age 32. 46 applicants, 96% accepted, 33 enrolled. *Faculty:* 34 full-time (10 women), 2 part-time/adjunct (0 women). Expenses: Contact institution. *Financial support:* In 2008–09, 8 research assistantships (averaging $11,463 per year), 24 teaching assistantships (averaging $7,001 per year) were awarded; fellowships, career-related internships or fieldwork, Federal Work-Study, institutionally sponsored loans, scholarships/grants, tuition waivers (partial), and unspecified assistantships also available. Financial award application deadline: 5/1. In 2008, 29 master's, 7 doctorates awarded. *Degree program information:* Part-time and evening/weekend programs available. Offers biology (MS); chemistry (MS); computer science (MS); environmental toxicology (MS, PhD); industrial technology (MS); mathematics (MS); science and technology (MS, PhD); transportation, planning and management (MS). *Application deadline:* For fall admission, 7/15 priority date for domestic students. Applications are processed on a rolling basis. *Application fee:* $50 ($75 for international students). *Application Contact:* Lulueua Nasser, Administrative Secretary, 713-313-7679, E-mail: nasser_la@tsu.edu. *Interim Dean,* Dr. John Sapp, 713-313-7008, E-mail: sapp_jb@tsu.edu.

Tavis Smiley School of Communication Students: 15 full-time (11 women), 34 part-time (22 women); includes 46 African Americans, 1 Hispanic American, 2 international. Average age 30. 16 applicants, 100% accepted, 13 enrolled. *Faculty:* 4 full-time (2 women). Expenses: Contact institution. *Financial support:* Fellowships, research assistantships, teaching assistantships, career-related internships or fieldwork, Federal Work-Study, and institutionally sponsored loans available. Financial award application deadline: 5/1. In 2008, 15 master's awarded. *Degree program information:* Part-time programs available. Offers communication (MA). *Application deadline:* For fall admission, 7/15 priority date for domestic students. Applications are processed on a rolling basis. *Application fee:* $50 ($75 for international students). *Application Contact:* Dr. Louis Browne, Graduate Adviser, 713-313-7024. *Dean,* Dr. James Ward, 713-313-7740, E-mail: ward_jw@tsu.edu.

Thurgood Marshall School of Law Students: 548 full-time (284 women), 2 part-time (1 woman); includes 437 minority (277 African Americans, 2 American Indian/Alaska Native, 36 Asian Americans or Pacific Islanders, 122 Hispanic Americans), 20 international. Average age 28. 314 applicants, 99% accepted, 202 enrolled. *Faculty:* 41 full-time (20 women), 8 part-time/adjunct (2 women). Expenses: Contact institution. *Financial support:* In 2008–09, 75 students received support, including 37 research assistantships (averaging $1,703 per year), 3 teaching assistantships (averaging $6,300 per year); fellowships, career-related internships or fieldwork, Federal Work-Study, institutionally sponsored loans, scholarships/grants, and tuition waivers (partial) also available. Financial award application deadline: 4/1; financial award applicants required to submit FAFSA. In 2008, 181 JDs awarded. Offers law (JD). *Application deadline:* For fall admission, 4/1 priority date for domestic students. Applications are processed on a rolling basis. *Application fee:* $55. Electronic applications accepted. *Application Contact:* Edward Rene, Director of Admissions, 713-313-7115 Ext. 1004, Fax: 713-313-1049, E-mail: erene@tsulaw.edu. *Dean,* Dr. McKen V. Carrington, 713-313-1076, Fax: 713-313-1049, E-mail: carrington_mv@tsulaw.edu.

TEXAS STATE UNIVERSITY–SAN MARCOS, San Marcos, TX 78666

General Information State-supported, coed, university. CGS member. *Enrollment:* 29,105 graduate, professional, and undergraduate students; 1,690 full-time matriculated graduate/professional students (1,072 women), 2,056 part-time matriculated graduate/professional students (1,306 women). *Enrollment by degree level:* 40 first professional, 3,475 master's, 231 doctoral. *Graduate faculty:* 377 full-time (163 women), 81 part-time/adjunct (42 women). *Tuition, area resident:* Full-time $5280; part-time $220 per credit hour. Tuition, state resident: full-time $5280; part-time $220 per credit hour. Tuition, nonresident: full-time $12,024; part-time $501 per credit hour. *Required fees:* $1576; $42 per credit hour. $302 per semester. Tuition and fees vary according to course load. *Graduate housing:* Rooms and/or apartments available on a first-come, first-served basis to single and married students. Typical cost:

$3846 per year ($6012 including board) for single students; $7800 per year ($9948 including board) for married students. Room and board charges vary according to board plan and housing facility selected. Housing application deadline: 7/1. *Student services:* Campus employment opportunities, campus safety program, career counseling, exercise/wellness program, free psychological counseling, international student services, low-cost health insurance, multicultural affairs office, services for students with disabilities, teacher training, writing training. *Library facilities:* Alkek Library. *Online resources:* library catalog, web page, access to other libraries' catalogs. *Collection:* 1.4 million titles, 8,330 serial subscriptions, 277,806 audiovisual materials. *Research affiliation:* Lower Colorado River Authority (Environmental Conservation), Edwards Aquifer Authority (Conservation), ITT Corporation (Engineering), Advanced Materials and Processes (Environmental & Industrial Scienc), New Vectors (Risk Assessment), Nanohmics (Nano Technology).

Computer facilities: Computer purchase and lease plans are available. 1,453 computers available on campus for general student use. A campuswide network can be accessed from student residence rooms and from off campus. Online class registration is available. *Web address:* http://www.txstate.edu/.

General Application Contact: Dr. J. Michael Willoughby, Dean of Graduate School, 512-245-2581, Fax: 512-245-8365, E-mail: gradcollege@txstate.edu.

GRADUATE UNITS

Graduate School Students: 1,690 full-time (1,072 women), 2,056 part-time (1,306 women); includes 1,045 minority (198 African Americans, 18 American Indian/Alaska Native, 141 Asian Americans or Pacific Islanders, 688 Hispanic Americans), 184 international. Average age 31. 2,048 applicants, 72% accepted, 1057 enrolled. *Faculty:* 429 full-time (196 women), 74 part-time/adjunct (43 women). Expenses: Contact institution. *Financial support:* In 2008–09, 2,104 students received support, including 236 research assistantships (averaging $6,245 per year), 652 teaching assistantships (averaging $5,618 per year); fellowships, career-related internships or fieldwork, Federal Work-Study, institutionally sponsored loans, scholarships/grants, unspecified assistantships, and laboratory instructorships, stipends also available. Support available to part-time students. Financial award application deadline: 4/1; financial award applicants required to submit FAFSA. In 2008, 1,155 master's, 9 doctorates awarded. *Degree program information:* Part-time and evening/weekend programs available. Postbaccalaureate distance learning degree programs offered (minimal on-campus study). Offers applied sociology (MAIS); biology (MSIS); criminal justice (MSIS); educational administration and psychological services (MAIS); elementary mathematics, science, and technology (MSIS); health, physical education, and recreation (MAIS); interdisciplinary studies in political science (MAIS); international studies (MA); modern languages (MAIS); occupational education (MAIS, MSIS); psychology (MAIS). *Application deadline:* For fall admission, 6/15 for domestic students, 6/1 for international students; for spring admission, 10/15 for domestic students, 10/1 for international students. Applications are processed on a rolling basis. *Application fee:* $40 ($90 for international students). Electronic applications accepted. *Application Contact:* Dr. J. Michael Willoughby, Dean of Graduate School, 512-245-2581, Fax: 512-245-8365, E-mail: gradcollege@txstate.edu. *Dean,* Dr. J. Michael Willoughby, 512-245-2581, Fax: 512-245-8365, E-mail: gradcollege@txstate.edu.

College of Applied Arts Students: 89 full-time (58 women), 154 part-time (81 women); includes 89 minority (20 African Americans, 2 American Indian/Alaska Native, 3 Asian Americans or Pacific Islanders, 64 Hispanic Americans), 3 international. Average age 32. 91 applicants, 99% accepted, 60 enrolled. *Faculty:* 18 full-time (10 women), 9 part-time/adjunct (2 women). Expenses: Contact institution. *Financial support:* In 2008–09, 170 students received support, including 15 research assistantships (averaging $6,330 per year), 39 teaching assistantships (averaging $4,871 per year); career-related internships or fieldwork, Federal Work-Study, and institutionally sponsored loans also available. Support available to part-time students. Financial award application deadline: 4/1; financial award applicants required to submit FAFSA. In 2008, 36 master's awarded. *Degree program information:* Part-time and evening/weekend programs available. Offers agriculture (M Ed); applied arts (M Ed, MS, MSCJ, MSW); criminal justice (MSCJ); family and child studies (MS); human nutrition (MS); management of technical education (M Ed); social work (MSW). *Application deadline:* For fall admission, 6/15 priority date for domestic students; for spring admission, 10/15 priority date for domestic students. Applications are processed on a rolling basis. *Application fee:* $40 ($90 for international students). Electronic applications accepted. *Application Contact:* Dr. J. Michael Willoughby, Dean of Graduate School, 512-245-2581, Fax: 512-245-8365, E-mail: gradcollege@txstate.edu. *Dean,* Dr. Jaime Chahin, 512-245-3333, Fax: 512-245-3338, E-mail: tc03@txstate.edu.

College of Education Students: 453 full-time (345 women), 801 part-time (620 women); includes 336 minority (67 African Americans, 4 American Indian/Alaska Native, 21 Asian Americans or Pacific Islanders, 244 Hispanic Americans), 17 international. Average age 32. 535 applicants, 77% accepted, 307 enrolled. *Faculty:* 82 full-time (53 women), 39 part-time/adjunct (29 women). Expenses: Contact institution. *Financial support:* In 2008–09, 870 students received support, including 67 research assistantships (averaging $5,524 per year), 80 teaching assistantships (averaging $5,101 per year); fellowships, career-related internships or fieldwork, Federal Work-Study, and institutionally sponsored loans also available. Support available to part-time students. Financial award application deadline: 4/1; financial award applicants required to submit FAFSA. In 2008, 385 master's, 2 doctorates awarded. *Degree program information:* Part-time and evening/weekend programs available. Offers athletic training (MS); counseling and guidance (M Ed); developmental and adult education (MA, PhD); early childhood education (M Ed, MA); education (M Ed, MA, MSRLS, PhD); educational administration (M Ed, MA); elementary education (M Ed, MA); elementary education-bilingual/bicultural (M Ed, MA); health education (M Ed); physical education (M Ed); professional counseling (MA); reading education (M Ed); recreation and leisure services (MSRLS); school psychology (MA); secondary education (M Ed, MA); special education (M Ed). *Application deadline:* For fall admission, 6/15 priority date for domestic students; for spring admission, 10/15 priority date for domestic students. Applications are processed on a rolling basis. *Application fee:* $40 ($90 for international students). Electronic applications accepted. *Application Contact:* Dr. J. Michael Willoughby, Dean of Graduate School, 512-245-2581, Fax: 512-245-8365, E-mail: gradcollege@txstate.edu. *Dean,* Dr. Rosalinda Barrera, 512-245-2150, Fax: 512-245-8345, E-mail: rb43@txstate.edu.

College of Fine Arts and Communication Students: 129 full-time (82 women), 80 part-time (52 women); includes 53 minority (9 African Americans, 11 Asian Americans or Pacific Islanders, 33 Hispanic Americans), 14 international. Average age 30. 96 applicants, 88% accepted, 61 enrolled. *Faculty:* 44 full-time (18 women), 7 part-time/adjunct (5 women). Expenses: Contact institution. *Financial support:* In 2008–09, 168 students received support, including 10 research assistantships (averaging $4,863 per year), 68 teaching assistantships (averaging $4,094 per year); career-related internships or fieldwork, Federal Work-Study, institutionally sponsored loans, scholarships/grants, and unspecified assistantships also available. Support available to part-time students. Financial award application deadline: 4/1; financial award applicants required to submit FAFSA. In 2008, 78 master's awarded. *Degree program information:* Part-time and evening/weekend programs available. Offers communication design (MFA); communication studies (MA); fine arts and communication (MA, MFA, MM); journalism and mass communication (MA); music education (MM); music performance (MM); theatre arts (MA). *Application deadline:* For fall admission, 6/15 priority date for domestic students; for spring admission, 10/15 priority date for domestic students. Applications are processed on a rolling basis. *Application fee:* $40 ($90 for international students). Electronic applications accepted. *Application Contact:* Dr. J. Michael Willoughby, Dean of Graduate School, 512-245-2581, Fax: 512-245-8365, E-mail: gradcollege@txstate.edu. *Dean,* Dr. T. Richard Cheatham, 512-245-2308, Fax: 512-245-8334, E-mail: tc02@txstate.edu.

College of Health Professions Students: 198 full-time (163 women), 173 part-time (131 women); includes 119 minority (28 African Americans, 3 American Indian/Alaska Native, 9 Asian Americans or Pacific Islanders, 79 Hispanic Americans), 12 international. Average age 29. 411 applicants, 46% accepted, 148 enrolled. *Faculty:* 44 full-time (30 women), 6 part-time/adjunct (4 women). Expenses: Contact institution. *Financial support:* In 2008–09, 306 students received support, including 14 research assistantships (averaging $3,363 per year), 30 teaching assistantships (averaging $2,542 per year); fellowships, career-related internships or fieldwork, Federal Work-Study, institutionally sponsored loans, scholarships/grants, and stipends also available. Support available to part-time students. Financial award application deadline: 4/1; financial award applicants required to submit FAFSA. In 2008, 169 master's awarded. *Degree program information:* Part-time and evening/weekend programs available. Offers communication disorders (MA, MSCD); health administration (MHA, MS); health professions (MA, MHA, MS, MSCD, DPT); health services research (MS); healthcare human resources (MS); physical therapy (DPT). *Application deadline:* For fall admission, 6/15 for domestic students, 6/1 for international students; for spring admission, 10/15 priority date for domestic students, 10/1 for international students. Applications are processed on a rolling basis. *Application fee:* $40 ($90 for international students). Electronic applications accepted. *Application Contact:* Dr. J. Michael Willoughby, Dean of Graduate School, 512-245-2581, Fax: 512-245-8365, E-mail: gradcollege@txstate.edu. *Dean,* Dr. Ruth Welborn, 512-245-3300, Fax: 512-245-3791, E-mail: mw01@txstate.edu.

College of Liberal Arts Students: 406 full-time (231 women), 461 part-time (262 women); includes 248 minority (44 African Americans, 3 American Indian/Alaska Native, 17 Asian Americans or Pacific Islanders, 184 Hispanic Americans), 27 international. Average age 31. 507 applicants, 70% accepted, 243 enrolled. *Faculty:* 134 full-time (56 women), 7 part-time/adjunct (2 women). Expenses: Contact institution. *Financial support:* In 2008–09, 663 students received support, including 46 research assistantships (averaging $7,012 per year), 198 teaching assistantships (averaging $5,170 per year); fellowships, career-related internships or fieldwork, Federal Work-Study, institutionally sponsored loans, and scholarships/grants also available. Support available to part-time students. Financial award application deadline: 4/1; financial award applicants required to submit FAFSA. In 2008, 207 master's, 7 doctorates awarded. *Degree program information:* Part-time and evening/weekend programs available. Offers anthropology (MA); applied geography (MAG); creative writing (MFA); environmental geography (PhD); environmental geography, geography education, and geography information science (PhD); geographic information science (MAG); geography (MAG, MS); geography education (PhD); health psychology (MA); history (M Ed, MA); information science (PhD); land/area studies (MAG); legal studies (MA); liberal arts (M Ed, MA, MAG, MFA, MPA, MS, PhD); literature (MA); political science (MA, MPA); public administration (MPA); resource and environmental studies (MAG); rhetoric and composition (MA); sociology (MA, MS); Spanish (MA); technical communication (MA). *Application deadline:* For fall admission, 6/15 priority date for domestic students; for spring admission, 10/15 priority date for domestic students. Applications are processed on a rolling basis. *Application fee:* $40 ($90 for international students). Electronic applications accepted. *Application Contact:* Dr. J. Michael Willoughby, Dean of Graduate School, 512-245-2581, Fax: 512-245-8365, E-mail: gradcollege@txstate.edu. *Dean,* Dr. Ann Marrie Ellis, 512-245-2317, Fax: 512-245-8291, E-mail: ae02@txstate.edu.

College of Science Students: 243 full-time (108 women), 164 part-time (66 women); includes 114 minority (14 African Americans, 2 American Indian/Alaska Native, 53 Asian Americans or Pacific Islanders, 45 Hispanic Americans), 55 international. Average age 30. 198 applicants, 90% accepted, 105 enrolled. *Faculty:* 75 full-time (14 women), 4 part-time/adjunct (1 woman). Expenses: Contact institution. *Financial support:* In 2008–09, 207 students received support, including 49 research assistantships (averaging $5,654 per year), 162 teaching assistantships (averaging $6,075 per year); career-related internships or fieldwork, Federal Work-Study, institutionally sponsored loans, and laboratory instructorships also available. Support available to part-time students. Financial award application deadline: 4/1; financial award applicants required to submit FAFSA. In 2008, 102 master's awarded. *Degree program information:* Part-time and evening/weekend programs available. Offers aquatic resources (MS, PhD); biochemistry (MS); biology (M Ed, MA, MS); chemistry (MA, MS); computer science (MA, MS); industrial mathematics (MS); industrial technology (MST); mathematics (M Ed, MS, PhD); mathematics education (PhD); middle school mathematics teaching (M Ed); physics (MS); population and conservation biology (MS); science (M Ed, MA, MS, MST, PhD); software engineering (MS); wildlife ecology (MS). *Application deadline:* For fall admission, 6/15 priority date for domestic students, 6/1 priority date for international students; for spring admission, 10/15 priority date for domestic students, 10/1 priority date for international students. Applications are processed on a rolling basis. *Application fee:* $40 ($90 for international students). Electronic applications accepted. *Application Contact:* Dr. J. Michael Willoughby, Dean of Graduate School, 512-245-2581, Fax: 512-245-8365, E-mail: gradcollege@txstate.edu. *Dean,* Dr. Hector E. Flores, 512-245-2119, Fax: 512-245-8095, E-mail: hf12@txstate.edu.

Emmett and Miriam McCoy College of Business Administration Students: 172 full-time (85 women), 223 part-time (94 women); includes 86 minority (16 African Americans, 4 American Indian/Alaska Native, 27 Asian Americans or Pacific Islanders, 39 Hispanic Americans), 56 international. Average age 29. 162 applicants, 81% accepted, 107 enrolled. *Faculty:* 32 full-time (15 women), 1 part-time/adjunct (0 women). Expenses: Contact institution. *Financial support:* In 2008–09, 200 students received support, including 9 research assistantships (averaging $4,788 per year), 28 teaching assistantships (averaging $5,087 per year); Federal Work-Study and institutionally sponsored loans also available. Support available to part-time students. Financial award application deadline: 4/1; financial award applicants required to submit FAFSA. In 2008, 138 master's awarded. *Degree program information:* Part-time programs available. Offers accounting (M Acy); accounting and information technology (MS); business administration (M Acy, MBA, MS). *Application deadline:* For fall admission, 6/1 for domestic and international students; for spring admission, 10/1 for domestic and international students. Applications are processed on a rolling basis. *Application fee:* $40 ($90 for international students). Electronic applications accepted. *Application Contact:* Dr. J. Michael Willoughby, Dean of Graduate School, 512-245-2581, Fax: 512-245-8365, E-mail: gradcollege@txstate.edu. *Dean,* Dr. Denise Smart, 512-245-2311, Fax: 512-245-8375, E-mail: ds37@txstate.edu.

TEXAS TECH UNIVERSITY, Lubbock, TX 79409

General Information State-supported, coed, university. CGS member. *Enrollment:* 28,422 graduate, professional, and undergraduate students; 3,564 full-time matriculated graduate/professional students (1,567 women), 1,751 part-time matriculated graduate/professional students (943 women). *Enrollment by degree level:* 645 first professional, 2,609 master's, 1,582 doctoral, 479 other advanced degrees. *Graduate faculty:* 725 full-time (217 women), 42 part-time/adjunct (10 women). *Tuition, area resident:* Part-time $194 per credit hour. Tuition, state resident: full-time $4648; part-time $194 per credit hour. Tuition, nonresident: full-time $11,392; part-time $475 per credit hour. *Required fees:* $2206; $69 per credit hour. $389 per semester. *Graduate housing:* Room and/or apartments available on a first-come, first-served basis to single students; on-campus housing not available to married students. Typical cost: $3980 per year ($7310 including board). Room and board charges vary according to board plan and housing facility selected. Housing application deadline: 5/1. *Student services:* Campus employment opportunities, campus safety program, career counseling, exercise/wellness program, free psychological counseling, international student services, low-cost health insurance, multicultural affairs office, services for students with disabilities, teacher training, writing training. *Library facilities:* Texas Tech Library plus 3 others. *Online resources:* library catalog, web page, access to other libraries' catalogs. *Collection:* 2.4 million titles, 42,372 serial subscriptions, 4,898 audiovisual materials. *Research affiliation:* Lawrence Livermore National Laboratory (atomic force microscopy), Cotton Inc. (improvement of cotton), Sandia National Lab (chemistry), Intervet, Inc (consumer meat industry), Meat and Livestock Australia (consumer meat industry), Bayer Crop Science (agriculture genetics).

Computer facilities: Computer purchase and lease plans are available. 3,000 computers available on campus for general student use. A campuswide network can be accessed from student residence rooms and from off campus. Online class registration, online degree plans, accounts, transcripts, schedules are available. *Web address:* http://www.ttu.edu/.

General Application Contact: Dr. Duane Crawford, Assistant Dean of Graduate Admissions and Recruitment, 806-742-2781, Fax: 806-742-4038, E-mail: gradschool@ttu.edu.

GRADUATE UNITS

Center for Biotechnology and Genomics Students: 28 full-time (12 women), 1 (woman) part-time, 25 international. Average age 23. 124 applicants, 45% accepted, 18 enrolled. Expenses: Contact institution. *Financial support:* In 2008–09, 4 students received support;

Texas Tech University (continued)

research assistantships with partial tuition reimbursements available available. Financial award application deadline: 4/15. In 2008, 3 master's awarded. *Degree program information:* Part-time programs available. Offers biotechnology (MS); science and agricultural biotechnology (MS). *Application deadline:* For fall admission, 3/1 priority date for international students; for spring admission, 11/1 priority date for international students. *Application fee:* $50 ($60 for international students). *Application Contact:* Jatindra Tripathy, Senior Research Associate, 806-742-3722 Ext. 229, Fax: 806-742-3788, E-mail: jatindra.tripathy@ttu.edu. *Advisor*, Dr. David B. Knaff, 806-742-0288, Fax: 806-742-1289, E-mail: david.knaff@ttu.edu.

Graduate School Students: 2,930 full-time (1,292 women), 1,740 part-time (939 women); includes 662 minority (142 African Americans, 34 American Indian/Alaska Native, 112 Asian Americans or Pacific Islanders, 374 Hispanic Americans), 967 international. Average age 31. 6,014 applicants, 55% accepted, 1491 enrolled. *Faculty:* 716 full-time (214 women), 37 part-time/adjunct (9 women). Expenses: Contact institution. *Financial support:* In 2008–09, 3,348 students received support, including 469 research assistantships with partial tuition reimbursements available (averaging $13,643 per year), 1,033 teaching assistantships with partial tuition reimbursements available (averaging $12,233 per year); career-related internships or fieldwork, Federal Work-Study, institutionally sponsored loans, scholarships/grants, and health care benefits also available. Support available to part-time students. Financial award application deadline: 4/15; financial award applicants required to submit FAFSA. In 2008, 746 master's, 139 doctorates awarded. *Degree program information:* Part-time and evening/weekend programs available. Postbaccalaureate distance learning degree programs offered (minimal on-campus study). Offers heritage management (MS); interdisciplinary studies (MA, MS); museum science (MA). *Application deadline:* For fall admission, 3/1 for international students; for spring admission, 11/1 for international students. Applications are processed on a rolling basis. *Application fee:* $50 ($60 for international students). Electronic applications accepted. *Application Contact:* Shannon Samson, Coordinator of Graduate School Recruitment, 806-742-2781 Ext. 239, Fax: 806-742-4038, E-mail: gradschool@ttu.edu. *Dean*, Dr. Fred Hartmeister, 806-742-1998 Ext. 226, Fax: 806-742-2179, E-mail: fred.hartmeister@ttu.edu.

College of Agricultural Sciences and Natural Resources Students: 203 full-time (93 women), 87 part-time (33 women); includes 28 minority (5 African Americans, 2 American Indian/Alaska Native, 7 Asian Americans or Pacific Islanders, 14 Hispanic Americans), 54 international. Average age 30. 244 applicants, 61% accepted, 81 enrolled. *Faculty:* 57 full-time (8 women), 7 part-time/adjunct (0 women). Expenses: Contact institution. *Financial support:* In 2008–09, 189 students received support, including 143 research assistantships with partial tuition reimbursements available (averaging $12,506 per year), 12 teaching assistantships with partial tuition reimbursements available (averaging $13,227 per year); career-related internships or fieldwork, Federal Work-Study, and institutionally sponsored loans also available. Support available to part-time students. Financial award application deadline: 4/15; financial award applicants required to submit FAFSA. In 2008, 31 master's, 9 doctorates awarded. *Degree program information:* Part-time and evening/weekend programs available. Offers agribusiness (MAB); agricultural and applied economics (MS, PhD); agricultural communication (MS); agricultural education (MS, Ed D); agricultural sciences and natural resources (M Agr, MAB, MLA, MS, Ed D, PhD); animal science (MS, PhD); crop science (MS); entomology (MS); fisheries science (MS, PhD); food science (MS); horticulture (MS); landscape architecture (MLA); plant and soil science (PhD); range science (MS, PhD); soil science (MS); wildlife science (MS, PhD). *Application deadline:* For fall admission, 3/1 priority date for international students; for spring admission, 11/1 priority date for international students. Applications are processed on a rolling basis. *Application fee:* $50 ($60 for international students). Electronic applications accepted. *Application Contact:* Dr. Cindy Akers, Director, Student Services Center, 806-742-2808, Fax: 806-742-2836, E-mail: cindy.akers@ttu.edu. *Dean*, Dr. John M. Burns, 806-742-2810, E-mail: john.burns@ttu.edu.

College of Architecture Students: 108 full-time (29 women), 18 part-time (4 women); includes 22 minority (1 African American, 1 American Indian/Alaska Native, 4 Asian Americans or Pacific Islanders, 16 Hispanic Americans), 6 international. Average age 26. 93 applicants, 54% accepted, 33 enrolled. *Faculty:* 24 full-time (3 women), 1 part-time/adjunct (0 women). Expenses: Contact institution. *Financial support:* In 2008–09, 87 students received support, including 1 research assistantship with partial tuition reimbursement available (averaging $7,472 per year), 2 teaching assistantships with partial tuition reimbursements available (averaging $10,000 per year); career-related internships or fieldwork, Federal Work-Study, and institutionally sponsored loans also available. Support available to part-time students. Financial award application deadline: 4/15; financial award applicants required to submit FAFSA. In 2008, 44 master's, 1 doctorate awarded. *Degree program information:* Part-time programs available. Offers architecture (M Arch, MS, PhD); land-use planning, management, and design (PhD). *Application deadline:* For fall admission, 3/1 priority date for international students; for spring admission, 11/1 priority date for international students. Applications are processed on a rolling basis. *Application fee:* $50 ($60 for international students). Electronic applications accepted. *Application Contact:* Jess Schwintz, Academic Program Assistant, 806-742-3136 Ext. 272, Fax: 806-742-1400, E-mail: jess.schwintz@ttu.edu. *Dean*, David Andrew Vernooy, 806-742-3136, Fax: 806-742-1400, E-mail: andrew.vernoy@ttu.edu.

College of Arts and Sciences Students: 905 full-time (414 women), 252 part-time (121 women); includes 146 minority (21 African Americans, 6 American Indian/Alaska Native, 33 Asian Americans or Pacific Islanders, 86 Hispanic Americans), 293 international. Average age 30. 1,433 applicants, 44% accepted, 286 enrolled. *Faculty:* 303 full-time (78 women), 11 part-time/adjunct (6 women). Expenses: Contact institution. *Financial support:* In 2008–09, 685 students received support, including 85 research assistantships with partial tuition reimbursements available (averaging $15,878 per year), 656 teaching assistantships with partial tuition reimbursements available (averaging $13,330 per year); career-related internships or fieldwork, Federal Work-Study, and institutionally sponsored loans also available. Support available to part-time students. Financial award application deadline: 4/15; financial award applicants required to submit FAFSA. In 2008, 146 master's, 48 doctorates awarded. *Degree program information:* Part-time and evening/weekend programs available. Offers anthropology (MA); applied linguistics (MA); applied physics (MS); arts and sciences (MA, MPA, MS, PhD); atmospheric sciences (MS); biological informatics (MS); biology (MS, PhD); chemistry (MS, PhD); classics (MA); clinical psychology (PhD); communication studies (MA); counseling psychology (MA, PhD); economics (MA, PhD); English (MA, PhD); environmental toxicology (MS, PhD); exercise and sport sciences (MS); experimental psychology (MA, PhD); geoscience (MS, PhD); German (MA); history (MA, PhD); mathematics (MA, MS, PhD); microbiology (MS); philosophy (MA); physics (MS, PhD); political science (MA, PhD); psychology (MA, PhD); public administration (MPA); Romance language (MA); Romance languages-French (MA); Romance languages-Spanish (MA, PhD); sociology (MA); sports health (MS); statistics (MS); technical communication (MA); technical communication and rhetoric (PhD); zoology (MS, PhD). *Application deadline:* For fall admission, 3/1 priority date for international students; for spring admission, 11/1 priority date for international students. Applications are processed on a rolling basis. *Application fee:* $50 ($60 for international students). Electronic applications accepted. *Application Contact:* Dr. Robert A. Stewart, Associate Dean, 806-742-3833, Fax: 806-742-3893, E-mail: rob.stewart@ttu.edu. *Dean*, Dr. Jane L. Winer, 806-742-3831, Fax: 806-742-3893, E-mail: jane.winer@ttu.edu.

College of Education Students: 318 full-time (233 women), 584 part-time (447 women); includes 189 minority (47 African Americans, 6 American Indian/Alaska Native, 9 Asian Americans or Pacific Islanders, 127 Hispanic Americans), 30 international. Average age 35. 866 applicants, 69% accepted, 248 enrolled. *Faculty:* 52 full-time (37 women), 3 part-time/adjunct (2 women). Expenses: Contact institution. *Financial support:* In 2008–09, 535 students received support, including 2 research assistantships with partial tuition reimbursements available (averaging $10,800 per year), 13 teaching assistantships with partial tuition reimbursements available (averaging $10,800 per year); career-related internships or fieldwork, Federal Work-Study, and institutionally sponsored loans also available. Support available to part-time students. Financial award application deadline: 4/15; financial award applicants required to submit FAFSA. In 2008, 122 master's, 30 doctorates awarded. *Degree program information:* Part-time programs available. Offers bilingual education (M Ed); counselor education (M Ed, PhD); curriculum and instruction (M Ed, PhD); education (M Ed, Ed D, PhD); educational leadership (M Ed, Ed D); educational psychology (M Ed, PhD); elementary education (M Ed); higher education (M Ed, Ed D, PhD); instructional technology (M Ed, Ed D); language and literacy education (M Ed); secondary education (M Ed); special education (M Ed, Ed D). *Application deadline:* For fall admission, 3/1 priority date for international students; for spring admission, 11/1 priority date for international students. Applications are processed on a rolling basis. *Application fee:* $50 ($60 for international students). Electronic applications accepted. *Application Contact:* Patsy Ann Mountz, Administrative Assistant, 806-742-1988 Ext. 434, Fax: 806-742-2179, E-mail: patsy.mountz@ttu.edu. *Interim Dean*, Dr. Charles Ruch, 806-742-1998 Ext. 450, Fax: 806-742-2179, E-mail: charles.ruch@ttu.edu.

College of Engineering Students: 489 full-time (101 women), 184 part-time (22 women); includes 43 minority (9 African Americans, 2 American Indian/Alaska Native, 14 Asian Americans or Pacific Islanders, 18 Hispanic Americans), 381 international. Average age 27. 1,570 applicants, 36% accepted, 218 enrolled. *Faculty:* 94 full-time (16 women), 10 part-time/adjunct (0 women). Expenses: Contact institution. *Financial support:* In 2008–09, 318 students received support, including 142 research assistantships with partial tuition reimbursements available (averaging $14,340 per year), 85 teaching assistantships with partial tuition reimbursements available (averaging $11,261 per year); career-related internships or fieldwork, Federal Work-Study, and institutionally sponsored loans also available. Support available to part-time students. Financial award application deadline: 4/15; financial award applicants required to submit FAFSA. In 2008, 100 master's, 18 doctorates awarded. *Degree program information:* Part-time programs available. Offers chemical engineering (MS Ch E, PhD); civil engineering (MSCE, PhD); computer science (MS, PhD); electrical engineering (MSEE, PhD); engineering (M Engr, MENVEGR, MS, MS Ch E, MSCE, MSEE, MSETM, MSIE, MSME, MSMSE, MSPE, MSSEM, PhD); environmental engineering (MENVEGR); environmental technology and management (MSETM); industrial engineering (MSIE, PhD); manufacturing systems and engineering (MSMSE); mechanical engineering (MSME, PhD); petroleum engineering (MSPE, PhD); software engineering (MS); systems and engineering management (MSSEM, PhD); wind science and engineering (PhD). *Application deadline:* For fall admission, 3/1 priority date for international students; for spring admission, 11/1 priority date for international students. Applications are processed on a rolling basis. *Application fee:* $50 ($60 for international students). Electronic applications accepted. *Application Contact:* Dr. John E. Kobza, Senior Associate Dean, 806-742-3451, Fax: 806-742-3493, E-mail: john.kobza@ttu.edu. *Interim Dean*, Dr. Jon C. Strauss, 806-742-3451, Fax: 806-742-3493.

College of Human Sciences Students: 208 full-time (126 women), 109 part-time (67 women); includes 48 minority (15 African Americans, 4 American Indian/Alaska Native, 12 Asian Americans or Pacific Islanders, 17 Hispanic Americans), 54 international. Average age 32. 301 applicants, 67% accepted, 93 enrolled. *Faculty:* 48 full-time (32 women), 1 (woman) part-time/adjunct. Expenses: Contact institution. *Financial support:* In 2008–09, 207 students received support, including 36 research assistantships with partial tuition reimbursements available (averaging $12,954 per year), 87 teaching assistantships with partial tuition reimbursements available (averaging $12,099 per year); career-related internships or fieldwork, Federal Work-Study, institutionally sponsored loans, and scholarships/grants also available. Support available to part-time students. Financial award application deadline: 4/15; financial award applicants required to submit FAFSA. In 2008, 50 master's, 11 doctorates awarded. *Degree program information:* Part-time and evening/weekend programs available. Postbaccalaureate distance learning degree programs offered (minimal on-campus study). Offers family and consumer sciences education (MS, PhD); gerontology (MS); hospitality administration (PhD); human development and family studies (MS, PhD); human sciences (MS, PhD); interior and environmental design (MS, PhD); marriage and family therapy (MS, PhD); nutritional sciences (MS, PhD); personal financial planning (MS, PhD); restaurant, hotel and institutional management (MS); restaurant, hotel, and institutional management (MS, PhD). *Application deadline:* For fall admission, 3/1 priority date for domestic students; for spring admission, 11/1 priority date for domestic students. Applications are processed on a rolling basis. *Application fee:* $50 ($60 for international students). Electronic applications accepted. *Application Contact:* Dr. Lynn Huffman, Executive Associate Dean, 806-742-3031, Fax: 806-742-1849, E-mail: lynn.huffman@ttu.edu. *Dean*, Dr. Linda C. Hoover, 806-742-3031, Fax: 806-742-1849.

College of Mass Communications Students: 28 full-time (15 women), 8 part-time (4 women); includes 4 minority (1 American Indian/Alaska Native, 3 Hispanic Americans), 6 international. Average age 32. 56 applicants, 41% accepted, 9 enrolled. *Faculty:* 13 full-time (3 women), 1 part-time/adjunct (0 women). Expenses: Contact institution. *Financial support:* In 2008–09, 38 students received support, including 14 teaching assistantships with partial tuition reimbursements available (averaging $17,742 per year); research assistantships with partial tuition reimbursements available, Federal Work-Study and institutionally sponsored loans also available. Support available to part-time students. Financial award application deadline: 4/15; financial award applicants required to submit FAFSA. In 2008, 13 master's, 3 doctorates awarded. *Degree program information:* Part-time programs available. Offers mass communications (MA, PhD). *Application deadline:* For fall admission, 3/1 priority date for international students; for spring admission, 11/1 priority date for international students. Applications are processed on a rolling basis. *Application fee:* $50 ($60 for international students). Electronic applications accepted. *Application Contact:* Dr. Coy Callison, Associate Dean of Graduate Studies, 806-742-3385 Ext. 235, Fax: 806-742-1085, E-mail: coy.callison@ttu.edu. *Dean*, Dr. Jerry C. Hudson, 806-742-3385 Ext. 224, Fax: 806-742-1085, E-mail: jerry.hudson@ttu.edu.

College of Visual and Performing Arts Students: 173 full-time (76 women), 67 part-time (37 women); includes 23 minority (6 African Americans, 2 American Indian/Alaska Native, 1 Asian American or Pacific Islander, 14 Hispanic Americans), 33 international. Average age 36. 212 applicants, 68% accepted, 70 enrolled. *Faculty:* 62 full-time (25 women), 1 part-time/adjunct (0 women). Expenses: Contact institution. *Financial support:* In 2008–09, 190 students received support, including 135 teaching assistantships with partial tuition reimbursements available (averaging $8,167 per year); research assistantships with partial tuition reimbursements available, career-related internships or fieldwork, Federal Work-Study, and institutionally sponsored loans also available. Support available to part-time students. Financial award application deadline: 4/15. In 2008, 37 master's, 10 doctorates awarded. *Degree program information:* Part-time programs available. Offers art (MFA); art education (MAE); arts (PhD); composition (MM, DMA); conducting (DMA); fine arts (PhD); fine arts-art (PhD); fine arts-music (PhD); music (MM Ed, PhD); music theory (MM); musicology (MM); pedagogy (MM); performance (MM, DMA); piano pedagogy (DMA); theatre arts (MA, MFA, PhD); visual and performing arts (MA, MAE, MFA, MM, MM Ed, DMA, PhD). *Application deadline:* For fall admission, 3/1 priority date for international students; for spring admission, 11/1 priority date for international students. Applications are processed on a rolling basis. *Application fee:* $50 ($60 for international students). Electronic applications accepted. *Application Contact:* Shannon Samson, Coordinator of Graduate School Recruitment, 806-742-2781 Ext. 239, Fax: 806-742-4038, E-mail: gradschool@ttu.edu. *Dean*, Dr. Carol Edwards, 806-742-0700, Fax: 806-742-0695.

Jerry S. Rawls College of Business Administration Students: 230 full-time (79 women), 427 part-time (149 women); includes 98 minority (20 African Americans, 10 American Indian/Alaska Native, 15 Asian Americans or Pacific Islanders, 53 Hispanic Americans), 107 international. Average age 28. 656 applicants, 78% accepted, 390 enrolled. *Faculty:* 69 full-time (11 women), 4 part-time/adjunct (0 women). Expenses: Contact institution. *Financial support:* In 2008–09, 130 students received support, including 48 research assistantships (averaging $8,000 per year), 40 teaching assistantships (averaging $17,000 per year); fellowships, career-related internships or fieldwork, Federal Work-Study, scholarships/grants, health care benefits, and unspecified assistantships also available. Financial award applicants required to submit FAFSA. In 2008, 252 master's, 9 doctorates awarded. *Degree program information:* Part-time and evening/weekend programs available. Offers accounting (PhD); agricultural business (MBA); audit/financial reporting (MSA); business administration (IMBA, MBA, MS, MSA, PhD, Certificate); business statistics (MS, PhD); entrepreneurship (MBA); finance (MS, PhD); general business (MBA); health organization management (MBA); international business (MBA); management (PhD); management and leadership skills (MBA);

management information systems (MBA, MS, PhD); marketing (MBA, PhD); production and operations management (MS, PhD); statistics (MBA); taxation (MSA). *Application deadline:* For fall admission, 7/1 priority date for domestic students, 3/1 priority date for international students; for spring admission, 11/1 priority date for domestic students, 9/1 priority date for international students. Applications are processed on a rolling basis. *Application fee:* $50 ($60 for international students). Electronic applications accepted. *Application Contact:* Cynthia D. Barnes, Director, Graduate Services Center, 806-742-3184, Fax: 806-742-3958, E-mail: ba_grad@ttu.edu. *Dean*, Dr. Allen T. McInnes, 806-742-1300, Fax: 806-742-1092, E-mail: allen.mcinnes@ttu.edu.

School of Law Students: 634 full-time (275 women), 11 part-time (4 women); includes 154 minority (25 African Americans, 8 American Indian/Alaska Native, 22 Asian Americans or Pacific Islanders, 99 Hispanic Americans), 1 international. Average age 26. 1,556 applicants, 27% accepted, 210 enrolled. *Faculty:* 9 full-time (3 women), 5 part-time/adjunct (1 woman). Expenses: Contact institution. *Financial support:* In 2008–09, 633 students received support, including 23 teaching assistantships with partial tuition reimbursements available (averaging $7,500 per year); research assistantships with partial tuition reimbursements available, career-related internships or fieldwork, Federal Work-Study, and institutionally sponsored loans also available. Financial award application deadline: 4/15; financial award applicants required to submit FAFSA. In 2008, 215 JDs awarded. Offers law (JD). *Application deadline:* For fall admission, 2/1 priority date for domestic and international students. Applications are processed on a rolling basis. *Application fee:* $50 ($60 for international students). *Application Contact:* Terence Cook, Assistant Dean of Admissions and Recruitment, 806-742-3990, Fax: 806-742-4617, E-mail: terence.cook@ttu.edu. *Dean*, Walter Burl Huffman, 806-742-3990, Fax: 806-742-4014, E-mail: walter.huffman@ttu.edu.

See Close-Up on page 1003.

TEXAS TECH UNIVERSITY HEALTH SCIENCES CENTER, Lubbock, TX 79430

General Information State-supported, coed, graduate-only institution. *Graduate housing:* On-campus housing not available.

GRADUATE UNITS

Graduate School of Biomedical Sciences Offers biochemistry and molecular genetics (MS, PhD); biomedical sciences (MS, PhD); biotechnology (MS); cell and molecular biology (MS, PhD); cell physiology and molecular biophysics (MS, PhD); medical microbiology (MS, PhD); pharmaceutical sciences (MS, PhD); pharmacology and neuroscience (MS, PhD). Electronic applications accepted.

School of Allied Health Sciences Students: 656 full-time (479 women), 70 part-time (46 women); includes 150 minority (37 African Americans, 6 American Indian/Alaska Native, 33 Asian Americans or Pacific Islanders, 74 Hispanic Americans), 6 international. Average age 29. 1,537 applicants, 26% accepted. *Faculty:* 67 full-time (32 women), 1 part-time/adjunct (0 women). Expenses: Contact institution. *Financial support:* Fellowships, research assistantships, teaching assistantships, career-related internships or fieldwork, institutionally sponsored loans, scholarships/grants, and tuition waivers (full) available. Financial award application deadline: 9/1; financial award applicants required to submit FAFSA. In 2008, 158 master's, 19 doctorates awarded. Offers allied health sciences (MAT, MOT, MPAS, MPT, MRC, MS, Au D, DPT, PhD, Sc D); athletic training (MAT); clinical practice management (MS); molecular pathology (MS); occupational therapy (MOT); physical therapy (MPT, DPT, Sc D); physician assistant studies (MPAS); rehabilitation counseling (MRC); rehabilitation sciences (PhD); speech, language and hearing sciences (MS, Au D, PhD). *Application fee:* $35. Electronic applications accepted. *Application Contact:* Jeri Moravcik, Assistant Director of Admissions and Student Affairs, 806-743-3220, Fax: 806-743-2994, E-mail: jeri.moravcik@ttuhsc.edu. Lindsay E Roberts.

School of Medicine Offers medicine (MD). Open only to residents of Texas, eastern New Mexico, and southwestern Oklahoma. Electronic applications accepted.

School of Nursing *Degree program information:* Part-time programs available. Postbaccalaureate distance learning degree programs offered (minimal on-campus study). Offers acute care nurse practitioner (MSN, Certificate); administration (MSN); advanced practice (DNP); education (MSN); executive leadership (DNP); family nurse practitioner (MSN, Certificate); geriatric nurse practitioner (MSN, Certificate); pediatric nurse practitioner (MSN, Certificate).

TEXAS WESLEYAN UNIVERSITY, Fort Worth, TX 76105-1536

General Information Independent-religious, coed, comprehensive institution. *Enrollment:* 3,202 graduate, professional, and undergraduate students; 1,002 full-time matriculated graduate/professional students (559 women), 492 part-time matriculated graduate/professional students (302 women). *Enrollment by degree level:* 811 first professional, 665 master's, 18 doctoral. *Graduate faculty:* 37 full-time (11 women), 40 part-time/adjunct (13 women). Tuition and fees vary according to degree level. *Graduate housing:* Room and/or apartments available on a first-come, first-served basis to single students; on-campus housing not available to married students. Typical cost: $3900 per year. Room charges vary according to housing facility selected. *Student services:* Campus employment opportunities, career counseling, free psychological counseling, international student services, low-cost health insurance, services for students with disabilities, teacher training, writing training. *Library facilities:* Eunice and James L. West Library plus 1 other. *Online resources:* library catalog, web page, access to other libraries' catalogs. *Collection:* 245,092 titles, 619 serial subscriptions, 5,432 audiovisual materials.

Computer facilities: 77 computers available on campus for general student use. A campuswide network can be accessed from student residence rooms. Online class registration is available. *Web address:* http://www.txwes.edu/.

General Application Contact: Holly Kiser, Director of Admissions, 817-531-4458, Fax: 817-531-4231, E-mail: hkiser@txwes.edu.

GRADUATE UNITS

Graduate Programs Students: 1,002 full-time (559 women), 492 part-time (302 women); includes 359 minority (118 African Americans, 17 American Indian/Alaska Native, 88 Asian Americans or Pacific Islanders, 136 Hispanic Americans). Average age 31. 2,740 applicants, 45% accepted, 504 enrolled. *Faculty:* 37 full-time (11 women), 40 part-time/adjunct (13 women). Expenses: Contact institution. *Financial support:* Fellowships with full and partial tuition reimbursements, career-related internships or fieldwork, Federal Work-Study, institutionally sponsored loans, scholarships/grants, and tuition waivers (full and partial) available. Support available to part-time students. Financial award application deadline: 3/15; financial award applicants required to submit FAFSA. In 2008, 233 master's awarded. *Degree program information:* Part-time and evening/weekend programs available. Postbaccalaureate distance learning degree programs offered (no on-campus study). Offers business administration (MBA); education (M Ed); health services administration (MS); management (MiM); mental health/school counseling (MSP); nurse anesthesia (MHS, MSNA, DNAP); professional counseling (MA). *Application deadline:* Applications are processed on a rolling basis. *Application fee:* $50. Electronic applications accepted. *Application Contact:* Dr. Allen Henderson, Provost, 817-531-4405. *Provost*, Dr. Allen Henderson, 817-531-4405.

School of Law Students: 522 full-time (258 women), 289 part-time (145 women); includes 196 minority (51 African Americans, 14 American Indian/Alaska Native, 51 Asian Americans or Pacific Islanders, 80 Hispanic Americans). Average age 29. 2,007 applicants, 46% accepted, 286 enrolled. *Faculty:* 41 full-time (20 women), 34 part-time/adjunct (12 women). Expenses: Contact institution. *Financial support:* Career-related internships or fieldwork, scholarships/grants, and tuition waivers (full and partial) available. Support available to part-time students. Financial award application deadline: 3/15; financial award applicants required to submit FAFSA. In 2008, 204 JDs awarded. *Degree program information:* Part-time and evening/weekend programs available. Offers law (JD). *Application deadline:* For fall admission, 3/31 priority date for domestic students. Applications are processed on a rolling basis. *Application fee:* $55. Electronic applications accepted. *Application Contact:* Sherolyn Hurst, Assistant Dean of Admissions and Scholarships, 817-212-4040, Fax: 817-212-4141, E-mail: lawadmissions@law.txwes.edu. *Dean*, Frederic White, 817-212-4100, Fax: 817-212-4199.

TEXAS WOMAN'S UNIVERSITY, Denton, TX 76201

General Information State-supported, coed, primarily women, university. CGS member. *Enrollment:* 12,465 graduate, professional, and undergraduate students; 1,721 full-time matriculated graduate/professional students (1,466 women), 2,856 part-time matriculated graduate/professional students (2,543 women). *Enrollment by degree level:* 3,657 master's, 920 doctoral. *Graduate faculty:* 308 full-time (224 women), 196 part-time/adjunct (141 women). Tuition, state resident: full-time $3564; part-time $198 per semester hour. Tuition, nonresident: full-time $8622; part-time $479 per semester hour. *Required fees:* $1158; $64 per semester hour. Tuition and fees vary according to course load. *Graduate housing:* Rooms and/or apartments available on a first-come, first-served basis to single and married students. Typical cost: $3278 per year ($6078 including board) for single students; $7820 per year for married students. Room and board charges vary according to board plan, campus/location and housing facility selected. *Student services:* Campus employment opportunities, campus safety program, career counseling, exercise/wellness program, free psychological counseling, grant writing training, international student services, low-cost health insurance, multicultural affairs office, services for students with disabilities, teacher training, writing training. *Library facilities:* Blagg-Huey Library plus 1 other. *Online resources:* library catalog, web page, access to other libraries' catalogs. *Collection:* 643,323 titles, 3,500 serial subscriptions, 18,646 audiovisual materials.

Computer facilities: 800 computers available on campus for general student use. A campuswide network can be accessed from student residence rooms and from off campus. Online class registration is available. *Web address:* http://www.twu.edu/.

General Application Contact: Samuel Wheeler, Assistant Director of Admissions, 940-898-3188, Fax: 940-898-3081, E-mail: wheelersr@twu.edu.

GRADUATE UNITS

Graduate School Students: 1,721 full-time (1,466 women), 2,856 part-time (2,543 women); includes 1,517 minority (797 African Americans, 28 American Indian/Alaska Native, 272 Asian Americans or Pacific Islanders, 420 Hispanic Americans), 240 international. Average age 35. 2,898 applicants, 64% accepted, 1326 enrolled. *Faculty:* 308 full-time (224 women), 196 part-time/adjunct (141 women). Expenses: Contact institution. *Financial support:* In 2008–09, 1,478 students received support, including fellowships (averaging $45 per year), 295 research assistantships (averaging $10,790 per year), 118 teaching assistantships (averaging $10,589 per year); career-related internships or fieldwork, Federal Work-Study, institutionally sponsored loans, scholarships/grants, traineeships, health care benefits, and unspecified assistantships also available. Support available to part-time students. Financial award application deadline: 3/1; financial award applicants required to submit FAFSA. In 2008, 1,674 master's, 94 doctorates awarded. *Degree program information:* Part-time and evening/weekend programs available. Postbaccalaureate distance learning degree programs offered. *Application deadline:* For fall admission, 6/30 for domestic students, 4/1 for international students; for spring admission, 12/1 for domestic students, 8/1 for international students. Applications are processed on a rolling basis. *Application fee:* $30 ($50 for international students). Electronic applications accepted. *Application Contact:* Samuel Wheeler, Assistant Director of Admissions, 940-898-3188, Fax: 940-898-3081, E-mail: wheelersr@twu.edu. *Vice Provost and Dean of the Graduate School*, Dr. Jennifer L. Martin, 940-898-3415, Fax: 940-898-3412, E-mail: jmartin@twu.edu.

College of Arts and Sciences Students: 694 full-time (558 women), 603 part-time (511 women); includes 561 minority (360 African Americans, 7 American Indian/Alaska Native, 87 Asian Americans or Pacific Islanders, 107 Hispanic Americans), 86 international. Average age 35. *Faculty:* 116 full-time (70 women), 59 part-time/adjunct (26 women). Expenses: Contact institution. *Financial support:* In 2008–09, fellowships (averaging $6 per year), 157 research assistantships (averaging $10,982 per year), 85 teaching assistantships (averaging $10,771 per year) were awarded; career-related internships or fieldwork, Federal Work-Study, institutionally sponsored loans, scholarships/grants, traineeships, health care benefits, and unspecified assistantships also available. Support available to part-time students. Financial award application deadline: 3/1; financial award applicants required to submit FAFSA. In 2008, 560 master's, 15 doctorates awarded. *Degree program information:* Part-time and evening/weekend programs available. Postbaccalaureate distance learning degree programs offered (minimal on-campus study). Offers art (MA, MFA); arts (MA, MFA, PhD); arts and sciences (MA, MBA, MFA, MHSM, MS, PhD, SSP); biology (MS); biology teaching (MS); business administration (MBA); chemistry (MS); chemistry teaching (MS); counseling psychology (MA, PhD); dance (MA, MFA, PhD); drama (MA); English (MA); government (MA); health systems management (MHSM); history (MA); mathematics (MA, MS); mathematics teaching (MS); molecular biology (PhD); music (MA); rhetoric (PhD); school psychology (PhD, SSP); science teaching (MS); sociology (MA, PhD); women's studies (MA). *Application deadline:* For fall admission, 6/30 for domestic students, 4/1 for international students; for spring admission, 12/1 for domestic students, 8/1 for international students. Applications are processed on a rolling basis. *Application fee:* $30 ($50 for international students). Electronic applications accepted. *Application Contact:* Samuel Wheeler, Assistant Director of Admissions, 940-898-3188, Fax: 940-898-3081, E-mail: wheelersr@twu.edu. *Dean*, Dr. Ann Staton, 940-898-3326, Fax: 940-898-3366, E-mail: CAS@twu.edu.

College of Health Sciences Students: 709 full-time (613 women), 577 part-time (476 women); includes 357 minority (131 African Americans, 12 American Indian/Alaska Native, 94 Asian Americans or Pacific Islanders, 120 Hispanic Americans), 116 international. Average age 30. *Faculty:* 91 full-time (67 women), 32 part-time/adjunct (29 women). Expenses: Contact institution. *Financial support:* In 2008–09, 1 fellowship (averaging $18,000 per year), 78 research assistantships (averaging $10,682 per year), 18 teaching assistantships (averaging $10,870 per year) were awarded; career-related internships or fieldwork, Federal Work-Study, institutionally sponsored loans, scholarships/grants, traineeships, health care benefits, tuition waivers (partial), and unspecified assistantships also available. Support available to part-time students. Financial award application deadline: 3/1; financial award applicants required to submit FAFSA. In 2008, 496 master's, 23 doctorates awarded. *Degree program information:* Part-time and evening/weekend programs available. Postbaccalaureate distance learning degree programs offered. Offers education of the deaf (MS); exercise and sports nutrition (MS); food science (MS); food systems administration (MS); health care administration (MHA); health sciences (MA, MHA, MOT, MS, DPT, Ed D, PhD); health studies (MS, Ed D, PhD); kinesiology (MS, PhD); nutrition (MS, PhD); occupational therapy (MA, MOT, PhD); physical therapy (MS, DPT, PhD); speech-language pathology (MS). *Application deadline:* For fall admission, 4/1 for international students; for spring admission, 8/1 for international students. Applications are processed on a rolling basis. *Application fee:* $30 ($50 for international students). Electronic applications accepted. *Application Contact:* Samuel Wheeler, Assistant Director of Admissions, 940-898-3188, Fax: 940-898-3081, E-mail: wheelersr@twu.edu. *Dean*, Dr. Jimmy Ishee, 940-898-2852, Fax: 940-898-2853, E-mail: jishee@twu.edu.

College of Nursing Students: 81 full-time (77 women), 466 part-time (438 women); includes 212 minority (111 African Americans, 4 American Indian/Alaska Native, 62 Asian Americans or Pacific Islanders, 35 Hispanic Americans), 7 international. Average age 40. *Faculty:* 44 full-time (43 women), 27 part-time/adjunct (23 women). Expenses: Contact institution. *Financial support:* In 2008–09, 37 fellowships (averaging $14,902 per year), 13 research assistantships (averaging $11,484 per year), 3 teaching assistantships (averaging $11,484 per year) were awarded; career-related internships or fieldwork, Federal Work-Study, institutionally sponsored loans, scholarships/grants, traineeships, health care benefits, and unspecified assistantships also available. Support available to part-time students. Financial award application deadline: 3/1; financial award applicants required to submit FAFSA. In 2008, 132 master's, 27 doctorates awarded. *Degree program information:* Part-time programs available. Postbaccalaureate distance learning degree programs offered. Offers acute care nurse practitioner (MS); adult health clinical nurse specialist (MS); adult health nurse practitioner (MS); child health clinical nurse specialist (MS); community health (MS); family nurse practitioner (MS); health systems management (MS); nursing education (MS); nursing practice (DNP); nursing science (PhD); pediatric nurse practitioner (MS); women's

Texas Woman's University (continued)

health clinical nurse specialist (MS); women's health nurse practitioner (MS). *Application deadline:* For fall admission, 5/1 for domestic students, 4/1 for international students; for spring admission, 9/15 for domestic students, 8/1 for international students. Applications are processed on a rolling basis. *Application fee:* $30 ($50 for international students). Electronic applications accepted. *Application Contact:* Samuel Wheeler, Assistant Director of Admissions, 940-898-3188, Fax: 940-898-3081, E-mail: wheelersr@twu.edu. *Interim Dean*, Dr. Patricia Holden-Huchton, 940-898-2401, Fax: 940-898-2437, E-mail: pholdenhuchton@twu.edu.

College of Professional Education Students: 237 full-time (218 women), 1,210 part-time (1,118 women); includes 387 minority (195 African Americans, 5 American Indian/Alaska Native, 29 Asian Americans or Pacific Islanders, 158 Hispanic Americans), 31 international. Average age 37. *Faculty:* 57 full-time (44 women), 78 part-time/adjunct (63 women). Expenses: Contact institution. *Financial support:* In 2008–09, 1 fellowship, 47 research assistantships (averaging $11,132 per year), 12 teaching assistantships (averaging $10,932 per year) were awarded; career-related internships or fieldwork, Federal Work-Study, institutionally sponsored loans, scholarships/grants, traineeships, health care benefits, tuition waivers (partial), and unspecified assistantships also available. Support available to part-time students. Financial award application deadline: 3/1; financial award applicants required to submit FAFSA. In 2008, 486 master's, 29 doctorates awarded. *Degree program information:* Part-time and evening/weekend programs available. Offers administration (M Ed, MA); child development (MS, PhD); counseling and development (MS); early childhood education (M Ed, MA, MS, Ed D); elementary education (MA); family studies (MS, PhD); family therapy (MS, PhD); library science (MA, MLS, PhD); professional education (M Ed, MA, MAT, MLS, MS, Ed D, PhD); reading education (M Ed, MA, MS, Ed D, PhD); special education (M Ed, MA, PhD); teaching (MAT); teaching, learning, and curriculum (M Ed). *Application deadline:* For fall admission, 4/1 for international students; for spring admission, 8/1 for international students. Applications are processed on a rolling basis. *Application fee:* $30 ($50 for international students). Electronic applications accepted. *Application Contact:* Samuel Wheeler, Assistant Director of Admissions, 940-898-3188, Fax: 940-898-3081, E-mail: wheelersr@twu.edu. *Dean*, Dr. Nan L. Restine, 940-898-2202, Fax: 940-898-2209, E-mail: lrestine@mail.twu.edu.

THOMAS COLLEGE, Waterville, ME 04901-5097

General Information Independent, coed, comprehensive institution. *Graduate housing:* On-campus housing not available.

GRADUATE UNITS

Graduate School *Degree program information:* Part-time and evening/weekend programs available. Offers business (MBA); computer technology education (MS); education (MS); human resource management (MBA). Electronic applications accepted.

THOMAS EDISON STATE COLLEGE, Trenton, NJ 08608-1176

General Information State-supported, coed, comprehensive institution. CGS member. *Enrollment:* 17,369 graduate, professional, and undergraduate students; 573 part-time matriculated graduate/professional students (325 women). *Enrollment by degree level:* 566 master's, 7 other advanced degrees. *Tuition, area resident:* Part-time $465 per credit. Tuition, state resident: part-time $465 per credit. Tuition, nonresident: part-time $465 per credit. *Graduate housing:* On-campus housing not available. *Student services:* Services for students with disabilities.

Computer facilities: A campuswide network can be accessed from off campus. Online class registration, undergraduate and Nursing students are able to schedule appointments online with their advisors are available. *Web address:* http://www.tesc.edu/.

General Application Contact: David Hoftiezer, Director of Admissions, 888-442-8372, Fax: 609-984-8447, E-mail: admissions@tesc.edu.

GRADUATE UNITS

Heavin School of Arts and Sciences Students: 113 part-time (72 women); includes 33 minority (23 African Americans, 3 Asian Americans or Pacific Islanders, 7 Hispanic Americans), 1 international. Average age 42. 107 applicants, 56 enrolled. Expenses: Contact institution. *Financial support:* Applicants required to submit FAFSA. In 2008, 20 master's, 12 other advanced degrees awarded. *Degree program information:* Part-time programs available. Postbaccalaureate distance learning degree programs offered (no on-campus study). Offers arts and sciences (MAEL, MALS, Graduate Certificate); educational leadership (MAEL); homeland security (Graduate Certificate); online learning and teaching (Graduate Certificate). *Application deadline:* For fall admission, 8/15 priority date for domestic and international students; for winter admission, 11/15 priority date for domestic and international students; for spring admission, 2/15 priority date for domestic and international students. Applications are processed on a rolling basis. *Application fee:* $75. Electronic applications accepted. *Application Contact:* David Hoftiezer, Director of Admissions, 888-442-8372, Fax: 609-984-8447, E-mail: admissions@tesc.edu. *Dean, Heavin School of Arts and Sciences*, Dr. Susan Davenport, 609-984-1130, Fax: 609-984-0740, E-mail: info@tesc.edu.

School of Applied Science and Technology 10 applicants, 1 enrolled. Expenses: Contact institution. *Financial support:* Applicants required to submit FAFSA. In 2008, 3 Graduate Certificates awarded. Offers applied science and technology (Graduate Certificate); clinical trials management (Graduate Certificate). *Application deadline:* For fall admission, 8/15 priority date for domestic and international students; for winter admission, 11/15 priority date for domestic and international students; for spring admission, 2/15 priority date for domestic students, 1/15 priority date for international students. Applications are processed on a rolling basis. *Application fee:* $75. Electronic applications accepted. *Application Contact:* David Hoftiezer, Director of Admissions, 888-442-8372, Fax: 609-984-8447, E-mail: admissions@tesc.edu. *Dean, School of Applied Science and Technology*, Dr. Marcus Tillery, 609-984-1130, Fax: 609-984-3898, E-mail: info@tesc.edu.

School of Business and Management Students: 319 part-time (121 women); includes 115 minority (77 African Americans, 3 American Indian/Alaska Native, 7 Asian Americans or Pacific Islanders, 28 Hispanic Americans), 5 international. Average age 42. 165 applicants, 151 enrolled. Expenses: Contact institution. *Financial support:* Applicants required to submit FAFSA. In 2008, 60 master's, 5 other advanced degrees awarded. *Degree program information:* Part-time programs available. Postbaccalaureate distance learning degree programs offered. Offers business and management (MSHRM, MSM, Graduate Certificate); human resource management (MSM); human resources management (MSHRM, Graduate Certificate); organizational management and leadership (Graduate Certificate); public service leadership (Graduate Certificate). *Application deadline:* For fall admission, 8/15 priority date for domestic and international students; for winter admission, 11/15 priority date for domestic and international students; for spring admission, 2/15 priority date for domestic and international students. Applications are processed on a rolling basis. *Application fee:* $75. Electronic applications accepted. *Application Contact:* David Hoftiezer, Director of Admissions, 888-442-8372, Fax: 609-984-8447, E-mail: admissions@tesc.edu. *Dean, School of Business and Management*, Dr. Joseph Santora, 609-984-1130, Fax: 609-984-3898, E-mail: infor@tesc.edu.

School of Nursing Students: 141 part-time (132 women); includes 27 minority (21 African Americans, 1 American Indian/Alaska Native, 2 Asian Americans or Pacific Islanders, 3 Hispanic Americans), 1 international. Average age 47. 61 applicants, 78 enrolled. Expenses: Contact institution. *Financial support:* Applicants required to submit FAFSA. In 2008, 1 other advanced degree awarded. *Degree program information:* Part-time programs available. Postbaccalaureate distance learning degree programs offered (no on-campus study). Offers nurse educator (Post-Master's Certificate); nursing (MSN, Post-Master's Certificate). *Application deadline:* For fall admission, 8/15 for domestic and international students; for winter admission, 11/15 for domestic and international students; for spring admission, 2/15 for domestic and international students. *Application fee:* $75. Electronic applications accepted. *Application Contact:* David Hoftiezer, Director of Admissions, 888-442-8372, Fax: 609-984-8447, E-mail: admissions@tesc.edu. *Dean, School of Nursing*, Dr. Susan O'Brien, 609-633-6460, Fax: 609-292-8279, E-mail: nursing@tesc.edu.

See Close-Up on page 1005.

THOMAS JEFFERSON SCHOOL OF LAW, San Diego, CA 92110-2905

General Information Independent, coed, graduate-only institution. *Graduate housing:* On-campus housing not available.

GRADUATE UNITS

Professional Program *Degree program information:* Part-time and evening/weekend programs available. Offers law (JD). Electronic applications accepted.

THOMAS JEFFERSON UNIVERSITY, Philadelphia, PA 19107

General Information Independent, coed, university. CGS member. *Enrollment:* 1,157 full-time matriculated graduate/professional students (580 women), 153 part-time matriculated graduate/professional students (110 women). *Enrollment by degree level:* 1,040 first professional, 126 master's, 119 doctoral, 25 other advanced degrees. *Tuition:* Full-time $25,950; part-time $855 per credit. *Required fees:* $400; $132 per semester. *Graduate housing:* Rooms and/or apartments available to single and married students. *Student services:* Campus employment opportunities, campus safety program, career counseling, child daycare facilities, exercise/wellness program, free psychological counseling, grant writing training, international student services, low-cost health insurance, multicultural affairs office, services for students with disabilities, writing training. *Library facilities:* Scott Memorial Library plus 1 other. *Online resources:* web page. *Collection:* 170,000 titles, 2,290 serial subscriptions. *Research affiliation:* A.I. DuPont for Children Nemours (biomedical research), University of Delaware (biomedical research), Christiana Care Health Services (biomedical research), Lankenau Institute for Medical Research (biomedical research).

Computer facilities: 100 computers available on campus for general student use. A campuswide network can be accessed from off campus. *Web address:* http://www.jefferson.edu/.

General Application Contact: Marc E. Stearns, Director of Admissions, 215-503-0155, Fax: 215-503-9920, E-mail: jcgs-info@jefferson.edu.

GRADUATE UNITS

Jefferson College of Graduate Studies Students: 117 full-time (69 women), 152 part-time (110 women); includes 53 minority (17 African Americans, 30 Asian Americans or Pacific Islanders, 6 Hispanic Americans), 43 international. Average age 29. 447 applicants, 32% accepted, 108 enrolled. *Faculty:* 181 full-time (46 women), 25 part-time/adjunct (9 women). Expenses: Contact institution. *Financial support:* In 2008–09, 117 students received support, including 117 fellowships with full tuition reimbursements available (averaging $51,850 per year); Federal Work-Study, institutionally sponsored loans, scholarships/grants, and traineeships also available. Support available to part-time students. Financial award application deadline: 5/1; financial award applicants required to submit FAFSA. In 2008, 41 master's, 16 doctorates awarded. *Degree program information:* Part-time and evening/weekend programs available. Postbaccalaureate distance learning degree programs offered (no on-campus study). Offers biochemistry and molecular biology (PhD); biomedical sciences (MS); cell and developmental biology (MS, PhD); clinical research, public health, and research management (Certificate); flexible-entry pathway (PhD); genetics (PhD); immunology and microbial pathogenesis (PhD); microbiology (MS); molecular pharmacology and structural biology (PhD); molecular physiology and biophysics (PhD); neuroscience (PhD); pharmacology (MS); public health (MPH, MS); tissue engineering and regenerative medicine (PhD). *Application deadline:* For fall admission, 1/15 priority date for domestic and international students; for winter admission, 6/1 priority date for international students; for spring admission, 9/1 priority date for international students. Applications are processed on a rolling basis. *Application fee:* $50. Electronic applications accepted. *Application Contact:* Marc E. Stearns, Director of Admissions, 215-503-0155, Fax: 215-503-9920, E-mail: jcgs-info@jefferson.edu. *Dean*, Dr. James H. Keen, 215-503-8982, Fax: 215-503-6690, E-mail: james.keen@jefferson.edu.

Jefferson College of Health Professions Offers bioscience technologies (MS); family therapy (MS); health professions (Pharm D, MS, DPT); nursing (MS); occupational therapy (MS); physical therapy (MS, DPT).

School of Pharmacy Offers pharmacy (Pharm D).

Jefferson Medical College Students: 1,040 full-time (511 women); includes 309 minority (20 African Americans, 4 American Indian/Alaska Native, 245 Asian Americans or Pacific Islanders, 40 Hispanic Americans), 47 international. Average age 26. 9,323 applicants, 5% accepted, 255 enrolled. *Faculty:* 727 full-time (209 women), 42 part-time/adjunct (21 women). Expenses: Contact institution. *Financial support:* In 2008–09, 862 students received support. Federal Work-Study and institutionally sponsored loans available. Financial award application deadline: 3/1; financial award applicants required to submit FAFSA. In 2008, 214 MDs awarded. Offers medicine (MD). *Application deadline:* For fall admission, 11/15 for domestic and international students. Applications are processed on a rolling basis. *Application fee:* $80. Electronic applications accepted. *Application Contact:* Dr. Clara Callahan, Dean for Admissions, 215-955-6983, Fax: 215-923-6939, E-mail: clara.callahan@jefferson.edu. *Interim Dean*, Dr. Mark Tykowcinski, 215-955-6980, Fax: 215-923-6939.

See Close-Up on page 1007.

THOMAS M. COOLEY LAW SCHOOL, Lansing, MI 48901-3038

General Information Independent, coed, graduate-only institution. *Graduate housing:* Rooms and/or apartments available on a first-come, first-served basis to single and married students.

GRADUATE UNITS

Graduate Programs *Degree program information:* Part-time and evening/weekend programs available. Offers corporate law and finance (LL M); intellectual property (LL M); law (JD); taxation (LL M). Electronic applications accepted.

THOMAS MORE COLLEGE, Crestview Hills, KY 41017-3495

General Information Independent-religious, coed, comprehensive institution. *Enrollment:* 1,894 graduate, professional, and undergraduate students; 115 full-time matriculated graduate/professional students (57 women), 28 part-time matriculated graduate/professional students (19 women). *Enrollment by degree level:* 143 master's. *Graduate faculty:* 14 full-time (3 women), 8 part-time/adjunct (4 women). *Tuition:* Full-time $10,555; part-time $499 per credit hour. Tuition and fees vary according to program. *Graduate housing:* On-campus housing not available. *Student services:* Career counseling, exercise/wellness program, free psychological counseling, international student services, multicultural affairs office, services for students with disabilities, teacher training. *Library facilities:* Thomas More Library. *Online resources:* library catalog, web page, access to other libraries' catalogs. *Collection:* 116,839 titles, 479 serial subscriptions, 2,300 audiovisual materials.

Computer facilities: 100 computers available on campus for general student use. A campuswide network can be accessed from student residence rooms and from off campus. Online class registration is available. *Web address:* http://www.thomasmore.edu/.

General Application Contact: Nathan Hartman, Director of Lifelong Learning, 859-344-3602, Fax: 859-344-3686, E-mail: nathan.hartman@thomasmore.edu.

GRADUATE UNITS

Program in Business Administration Students: 110 full-time (54 women); includes 4 minority (2 African Americans, 1 Asian American or Pacific Islander, 1 Hispanic American), 1 international. Average age 33. 64 applicants, 59% accepted, 36 enrolled. *Faculty:* 12 full-time (2 women), 2 part-time/adjunct (0 women). Expenses: Contact institution. *Financial support:* In 2008–09, 86 students received support. Institutionally sponsored loans available. Financial award application deadline: 3/15; financial award applicants required to submit FAFSA. In 2008, 56 master's awarded. Offers business administration (MBA). *Application deadline:* Applications are processed on a rolling basis. *Application fee:* $25. Electronic applications accepted. *Application Contact:* Nathan Hartman, Director of Lifelong Learning, 859-344-3602, Fax: 859-344-3686, E-mail: nathan.hartman@thomasmore.edu. *Director of Lifelong Learning*, Nathan Hartman, 859-344-3602, Fax: 859-344-3686, E-mail: nathan.hartman@thomasmore.edu.

Program in Teaching Students: 5 full-time (3 women), 28 part-time (19 women). Average age 33. 26 applicants, 85% accepted, 14 enrolled. *Faculty:* 3 full-time (2 women), 6 part-time/adjunct (4 women). Expenses: Contact institution. *Financial support:* In 2008–09, 2 students received support. Application deadline: 3/15. Offers teaching (MAT). *Application deadline:* Applications are processed on a rolling basis. Electronic applications accepted. *Application Contact:* Joyce Hamberg, Director, 859-344-3626, Fax: 859-344-3607, E-mail: joyce.hamberg@thomasmore.edu. *Director,* Joyce Hamberg, 859-344-3626, Fax: 859-344-3607, E-mail: joyce.hamberg@thomasmore.edu.

THOMAS UNIVERSITY, Thomasville, GA 31792-7499

General Information Independent, coed, comprehensive institution. *Graduate housing:* Room and/or apartments available on a first-come, first-served basis to single students; on-campus housing not available to married students. Housing application deadline: 8/1.

GRADUATE UNITS

Department of Business Administration *Degree program information:* Part-time programs available. Offers business administration (MBA). Electronic applications accepted.

Department of Education *Degree program information:* Part-time programs available. Offers education (M Ed). Electronic applications accepted.

Department of Human Services *Degree program information:* Part-time programs available. Offers community counseling (MSCC); rehabilitation counseling (MRC). Electronic applications accepted.

Department of Nursing *Degree program information:* Part-time programs available. Offers nursing (MSN). Electronic applications accepted.

THUNDERBIRD SCHOOL OF GLOBAL MANAGEMENT, Glendale, AZ 85306-6000

General Information Independent, coed, graduate-only institution. *Graduate housing:* Room and/or apartments available on a first-come, first-served basis to single students; on-campus housing not available to married students. Housing application deadline: 7/15. *Research affiliation:* Wiley (publishing).

GRADUATE UNITS

Graduate Programs *Degree program information:* Part-time and evening/weekend programs available. Postbaccalaureate distance learning degree programs offered (minimal on-campus study). Offers corporate learning (MBA); global affairs and management (MA); global business administration for Latin American managers (GMBA); global business administration on-demand (GMBA); global management (GMBA, MA, MBA, MS). Electronic applications accepted.

TIFFIN UNIVERSITY, Tiffin, OH 44883-2161

General Information Independent, coed, comprehensive institution. *Graduate housing:* Room and/or apartments available on a first-come, first-served basis to single students; on-campus housing not available to married students. Housing application deadline: 8/1.

GRADUATE UNITS

Program in Business Administration *Degree program information:* Part-time and evening/weekend programs available. Postbaccalaureate distance learning degree programs offered (no on-campus study). Offers general management (MBA); leadership (MBA); safety and security management (MBA); sports management (MBA). Electronic applications accepted.

Program in Criminal Justice *Degree program information:* Part-time and evening/weekend programs available. Postbaccalaureate distance learning degree programs offered (no on-campus study). Offers crime analysis (MSCJ); criminal behavior (MSCJ); forensic psychology (MSCJ); homeland security administration (MSCJ); justice administration (MSCJ). Electronic applications accepted.

Program in Humanities Offers humanities (MH).

TORONTO SCHOOL OF THEOLOGY, Toronto, ON M5S 2C3, Canada

General Information Independent-religious, coed, graduate-only institution. *Enrollment by degree level:* 763 first professional, 116 master's, 310 doctoral. *Graduate faculty:* 102 full-time (24 women), 206 part-time/adjunct (64 women). *Student services:* Career counseling, child daycare facilities, free psychological counseling, grant writing training, international student services, low-cost health insurance, services for students with disabilities, writing training. *Library facilities:* University of Toronto Libraries plus 7 others.

Computer facilities: A campuswide network can be accessed from off campus. *Web address:* http://www.tst.edu/.

General Application Contact: Jonathan Weverink, Advanced Degree Administrator, 416-978-4050, Fax: 416-978-7821, E-mail: inquiries@tst.edu.

GRADUATE UNITS

Graduate Programs Students: 680 full-time (250 women), 509 part-time (274 women). Average age 42. *Faculty:* 102 full-time (24 women), 206 part-time/adjunct (64 women). Expenses: Contact institution. *Financial support:* Career-related internships or fieldwork available. In 2008, 148 first professional degrees, 18 master's, 20 doctorates awarded. Postbaccalaureate distance learning degree programs offered (minimal on-campus study). Offers theology (M Div, M Mus, M Rel, MA, MAMS, MPS, MRE, MTS, Th M, D Min, PhD, Th D). Federation of seven Toronto-area theological colleges; basic degrees offered through the member colleges jointly with the University of Toronto. *Application deadline:* For fall admission, 1/15 priority date for domestic and international students. Applications are processed on a rolling basis. *Application fee:* $100 Canadian dollars. Electronic applications accepted. *Application Contact:* Jonathan Weverink, Advanced Degree Administrator, 416-978-4050, Fax: 416-978-7821, E-mail: inquiries@tst.edu. *Director,* Dr. Alan L. Hayes, 416-978-7822, Fax: 416-978-7821, E-mail: alan.hayes@utoronto.ca.

TOURO COLLEGE, New York, NY 10010

General Information Independent, coed, comprehensive institution.

GRADUATE UNITS

Barry Z. Levine School of Health Sciences Offers acupuncture (MS); occupational therapy (MS); oriental medicine (MSOM); physical therapy (DPT); speech-language pathology (MS).

Graduate School of Jewish Studies *Degree program information:* Part-time programs available. Offers Jewish studies (MA).

Jacob D. Fuchsberg Law Center *Degree program information:* Part-time and evening/weekend programs available. Offers law (JD); U.S. law for foreign lawyers (LL M).

TOURO UNIVERSITY, Vallejo, CA 94592

General Information Independent, coed, graduate-only institution. *Enrollment by degree level:* 897 first professional, 383 master's. *Graduate faculty:* 84 full-time (45 women). *Graduate housing:* On-campus housing not available. *Student services:* Campus safety program, career counseling, exercise/wellness program, free psychological counseling, low-cost health insurance, multicultural affairs office, services for students with disabilities, teacher training. *Library facilities:* Touro Library plus 1 other. *Online resources:* library catalog, web page, access to other libraries' catalogs. *Research affiliation:* Genetech (cancer), Siemans (cancer).

Computer facilities: 50 computers available on campus for general student use. A campuswide network can be accessed from off campus. Online class registration is available. *Web address:* http://www.tu.edu/.

General Application Contact: Dr. Harold Borrero, Registrar, 707-638-5242, Fax: 707-638-5267, E-mail: hborrero@touro.edu.

GRADUATE UNITS

Graduate Programs Students: 995 full-time (610 women), 285 part-time (204 women). *Faculty:* 84 full-time (45 women). Expenses: Contact institution. *Financial support:* Fellowships, Federal Work-Study and scholarships/grants available. Support available to part-time students. Financial award applicants required to submit FAFSA. Offers education (MA); osteopathic medicine (DO); pharmacy (Pharm D); physician assistant studies (MS); public health (MPH). *Application deadline:* For fall admission, 4/1 for domestic students. Applications are processed on a rolling basis. *Application fee:* $100. Electronic applications accepted. *Application Contact:* Steve Davis, Associate Director of Admissions, 707-638-5270, Fax: 707-638-5250, E-mail: steven.davis@tu.edu.

TOWSON UNIVERSITY, Towson, MD 21252-0001

General Information State-supported, coed, university. CGS member.

GRADUATE UNITS

College of Graduate Studies and Research *Degree program information:* Part-time and evening/weekend programs available. Postbaccalaureate distance learning degree programs offered. Offers accounting and business advisory services (MS); applied and industrial mathematics (MS); applied gerontology (MS, Certificate); applied information technology (D Sc); art education (M Ed); audiology (Au D); biology (MS); clinical psychology (MA); clinician-administrator transition (Certificate); communications management (MS); computer science (MS); counseling psychology (CAS); database management (Certificate); early childhood education (M Ed, CAS); elementary education (M Ed); environmental science (MS, Certificate); family-professional collaboration (Certificate); forensic science (MS); geography and environmental planning (MA); health science (MS); human resource development (MS); humanities (MA); information security and assurance (Certificate); information systems management (Certificate); instructional design and training (MS); instructional technology (Ed D); integrated homeland security management (MS); interactive media design (Certificate); Internet application development (Certificate); kinesiology (MS); management and leadership development (Certificate); mathematics education (MS); music education (MS, Certificate); music performance and composition (MM); networking technologies (Certificate); nursing (MS); nursing education (Certificate); occupational science (Sc D); occupational therapy (MS); organizational change (CAS); physician assistant studies (MS); professional studies (MA); professional writing (MS); reading (M Ed); reading education (CAS); school psychology (CAS); science education (MS); secondary education (M Ed); security assessment and management (Certificate); social science (MS); software engineering (Certificate); special education leadership (M Ed); speech-language pathology (MS); strategic public relations and integrated communications (Certificate); studio arts (MFA); teaching (MAT); theatre (MFA); women's studies (MS, Certificate). Electronic applications accepted.

Arts Integration Institute Offers arts integration (Certificate).

Joint University of Baltimore/Towson University (UB/Towson) MBA Program Offers business administration (MBA). Electronic applications accepted.

TRADITIONAL CHINESE MEDICAL COLLEGE OF HAWAII, Kamuela, HI 96743-2288

General Information Proprietary, coed, graduate-only institution.

GRADUATE UNITS

Graduate Programs Offers Oriental medicine (MSOM).

TRENT UNIVERSITY, Peterborough, ON K9J 7B8, Canada

General Information Province-supported, coed, university. *Graduate housing:* Room and/or apartments available to single students; on-campus housing not available to married students. Housing application deadline: 7/10. *Research affiliation:* Watershed Science Centre (watershed studies), Ontario Power Generation, Inc. (acid rain deposition), Enbridge Consumers Gas (ozone depletion), Forensics Laboratory (DNA testing).

GRADUATE UNITS

Graduate Studies *Degree program information:* Part-time programs available. Offers anthropology (MA); applications of modeling in the natural and social sciences (MA); biology (M Sc, PhD); chemistry (M Sc); computer studies (M Sc); cultural studies (PhD); environmental and resource studies (M Sc, PhD); geography (M Sc, PhD); indigenous studies (PhD); materials science (M Sc); physics (M Sc).

The Frost Centre for Canadian Studies and Indigenous Studies *Degree program information:* Part-time programs available. Offers Canadian studies (PhD); Canadian studies and indigenous studies (MA).

TREVECCA NAZARENE UNIVERSITY, Nashville, TN 37210-2877

General Information Independent-religious, coed, comprehensive institution. *Enrollment:* 2,366 graduate, professional, and undergraduate students; 927 full-time matriculated graduate/professional students (671 women), 146 part-time matriculated graduate/professional students (85 women). *Enrollment by degree level:* 951 master's, 122 doctoral. *Graduate faculty:* 43 full-time (19 women), 42 part-time/adjunct (20 women). Tuition and fees vary according to degree level and program. *Graduate housing:* Rooms and/or apartments available to single and married students. Housing application deadline: 6/15. *Student services:* Teacher training. *Library facilities:* Mackey Library. *Online resources:* library catalog, web page, access to other libraries' catalogs. *Collection:* 109,669 titles, 613 serial subscriptions, 4,545 audiovisual materials.

Computer facilities: 200 computers available on campus for general student use. A campuswide network can be accessed from student residence rooms and from off campus. *Web address:* http://www.trevecca.edu/.

General Application Contact: Glenda Bolling, Director of Non-Traditional and Graduate Admissions, 615-248-1320, Fax: 615-248-7406, E-mail: gbolling@trevecca.edu.

GRADUATE UNITS

Graduate Division Students: 927 full-time (671 women), 146 part-time (85 women); includes 214 minority (196 African Americans, 2 American Indian/Alaska Native, 4 Asian Americans or Pacific Islanders, 12 Hispanic Americans), 7 international. Average age 35. *Faculty:* 43 full-time (19 women), 42 part-time/adjunct (20 women). Expenses: Contact institution. *Financial support:* Applicants required to submit FAFSA. In 2008, 396 master's, 25 doctorates awarded. *Degree program information:* Part-time and evening/weekend programs available. Offers biblical studies (MA); business (MBA, MSM); business administration (MBA); clinical counseling (Ed D); counseling (MA); counseling psychology (MA); management (MSM); marriage and family therapy (MMFT); physician assistant (MS); preaching and practical theology (MA); systematic theology/historical theology (MA). *Application deadline:* Applications are processed on a rolling basis. *Application fee:* $25. *Application Contact:* Glenda Bolling, Director of Non-Traditional and Graduate Admissions, 615-248-1320, Fax: 615-248-7406. *Provost and Chief Academic Officer,* Dr. Stephen M. Pusey, 615-248-1258, Fax: 615-248-1435, E-mail: spusey@trevecca.edu.

School of Education Students: 497 full-time (382 women), 61 part-time (43 women); includes 125 minority (114 African Americans, 2 American Indian/Alaska Native, 2 Asian Americans or Pacific Islanders, 7 Hispanic Americans), 5 international. Average age 36. *Faculty:* 18 full-time (14 women), 20 part-time/adjunct (10 women). Expenses: Contact institution. *Financial support:* Applicants required to submit FAFSA. In 2008, 261 master's, 25 doctorates awarded. *Degree program information:* Part-time and evening/weekend programs available. Offers educational leadership (M Ed); English language learners (PreK-12) (M Ed); instructional effectiveness (M Ed); instructional technology (M Ed); leadership and professional practice (Ed D); library and information science (MLI Sc); reading PreK-12 (M Ed); teaching (MAT); teaching 7-12 (MAT); teaching K-6 (MAT). *Application deadline:* Applications are processed on a rolling basis. *Application fee:* $50. *Application Contact:* Admissions Office, 615-248-1201, Fax: 615-248-1597, E-mail: admissions_ged@trevecca.edu. *Dean/Director of Graduate Education Programs,* Dr. Esther Swink, 615-248-1201, Fax: 615-248-1597, E-mail: eswink@trevecca.edu.

TRINE UNIVERSITY, Angola, IN 46703-1764

General Information Independent, coed, comprehensive institution. *Graduate housing:* Room and/or apartments available on a first-come, first-served basis to single students; on-campus housing not available to married students. Housing application deadline: 8/1.

GRADUATE UNITS

Allen School of Engineering and Technology *Degree program information:* Part-time and evening/weekend programs available. Offers civil engineering (ME); mechanical engineering (ME).

Program in Criminal Justice Offers criminal justice (MS).

TRINITY BAPTIST COLLEGE, Jacksonville, FL 32221

General Information Independent-religious, coed, comprehensive institution.

GRADUATE UNITS

Graduate Programs Postbaccalaureate distance learning degree programs offered.

TRINITY COLLEGE, Hartford, CT 06106-3100

General Information Independent, coed, comprehensive institution. *Graduate housing:* On-campus housing not available.

GRADUATE UNITS

Graduate Programs *Degree program information:* Part-time and evening/weekend programs available. Offers American studies (MA); economics (MA); English (MA); public policy studies (MA). Electronic applications accepted.

TRINITY EPISCOPAL SCHOOL FOR MINISTRY, Ambridge, PA 15003-2397

General Information Independent-religious, coed, graduate-only institution. *Graduate housing:* On-campus housing not available.

GRADUATE UNITS

Graduate Programs *Degree program information:* Part-time programs available. Offers Anglican studies (Diploma); basic Christian studies (Diploma); divinity (M Div); ministry (D Min); mission and evangelism (MAME, Diploma); religion (MAR); youth ministry (Diploma).

TRINITY INTERNATIONAL UNIVERSITY, Deerfield, IL 60015-1284

General Information Independent-religious, coed, university. *Graduate housing:* Rooms and/or apartments available on a first-come, first-served basis to single and married students..

GRADUATE UNITS

Trinity Evangelical Divinity School *Degree program information:* Part-time programs available. Postbaccalaureate distance learning degree programs offered (minimal on-campus study). Offers Biblical and Near Eastern archaeology and languages (MA); Christian studies (MA, Certificate); Christian thought (MA); church history (MA, Th M); congregational ministry: pastor-teacher (M Div); congregational ministry: team ministry (M Div); counseling ministries (MA); counseling psychology (MA); cross-cultural ministry (M Div); educational studies (PhD); evangelism (MA); history of Christianity in America (MA); intercultural studies (MA, PhD); leadership and ministry management (D Min); military chaplaincy (D Min); ministry (MA); mission and evangelism (Th M); missions and evangelism (D Min); New Testament (MA, Th M); Old Testament (Th M); Old Testament and Semitic languages (MA); pastoral care (M Div); pastoral care and counseling (D Min); pastoral counseling and psychology (Th M); pastoral theology (Th M); philosophy of religion (MA); preaching (D Min); religion (MA); research ministry (M Div); systematic theology (Th M); theological studies (PhD); urban ministry (MA). Electronic applications accepted.

Trinity Graduate School *Degree program information:* Part-time and evening/weekend programs available. Postbaccalaureate distance learning degree programs offered (minimal on-campus study). Offers bioethics (MA); communication and culture (MA); counseling psychology (MA); instructional leadership (M Ed); teaching (MA). Electronic applications accepted.

Trinity Law School *Degree program information:* Part-time and evening/weekend programs available. Offers law (JD).

TRINITY INTERNATIONAL UNIVERSITY, SOUTH FLORIDA CAMPUS, Miami, FL 33132-1996

General Information Independent-religious, coed, graduate-only institution. *Graduate housing:* On-campus housing not available.

GRADUATE UNITS

Divinity School Offers Christian studies (MA, Certificate).

Graduate School Offers counseling psychology (MA).

TRINITY LUTHERAN SEMINARY, Columbus, OH 43209-2334

General Information Independent-religious, coed, graduate-only institution. *Graduate housing:* Rooms and/or apartments available on a first-come, first-served basis to single and married students. Housing application deadline: 5/15.

GRADUATE UNITS

Graduate and Professional Programs *Degree program information:* Part-time programs available. Offers church music (MA); divinity (M Div); lay ministry (MA); sacred theology (STM); theological studies (MTS).

TRINITY UNIVERSITY, San Antonio, TX 78212-7200

General Information Independent-religious, coed, comprehensive institution. *Enrollment:* 2,703 graduate, professional, and undergraduate students; 122 full-time matriculated graduate/professional students (75 women), 92 part-time matriculated graduate/professional students (58 women). *Enrollment by degree level:* 214 master's. *Graduate faculty:* 21 full-time (10 women), 8 part-time/adjunct. *Graduate housing:* On-campus housing not available. *Student services:* Campus safety program, free psychological counseling, international student services, services for students with disabilities. *Library facilities:* Elizabeth Huth Coates Library. *Online resources:* library catalog, web page, access to other libraries' catalogs. *Collection:* 1.1 million titles, 2,118 serial subscriptions, 29,869 audiovisual materials.

Computer facilities: Computer purchase and lease plans are available. 450 computers available on campus for general student use. A campuswide network can be accessed from student residence rooms and from off campus. Online class registration is available. *Web address:* http://www.trinity.edu/.

General Application Contact: Office of the Registrar, 210-999-7201, Fax: 210-999-7202, E-mail: roffice@trinity.edu.

GRADUATE UNITS

Department of Business Administration Students: 25 full-time (14 women); includes 8 minority (1 African American, 4 Asian Americans or Pacific Islanders, 3 Hispanic Americans), 2 international. Average age 23. *Faculty:* 6 full-time (3 women), 1 part-time/adjunct. Expenses: Contact institution. *Financial support:* In 2008–09, 12 research assistantships were awarded. Financial award application deadline: 4/1. In 2008, 52 master's awarded. *Degree program information:* Part-time programs available. Offers accounting (MS). *Application deadline:* For fall admission, 2/1 priority date for domestic students. *Application fee:* $30. *Application Contact:* Office of the Registrar, 210-999-7201, Fax: 210-999-7202, E-mail: roffice@trinity.edu. *Director of the Accounting Program,* Dr. Petrea K. Sandlin, 210-999-7296, Fax: 210-999-8134, E-mail: psandlin@trinity.edu.

Department of Education Students: 122 full-time (75 women), 92 part-time (58 women); includes 62 minority (12 African Americans, 1 American Indian/Alaska Native, 13 Asian Americans or Pacific Islanders, 36 Hispanic Americans), 2 international. Average age 29. *Faculty:* 8 full-time (2 women), 6 part-time/adjunct. Expenses: Contact institution. *Financial support:* Fellowships, research assistantships, teaching assistantships, career-related internships or fieldwork, Federal Work-Study, institutionally sponsored loans, and scholarships/grants available. Support available to part-time students. Financial award application deadline: 4/1. In 2008, 105 master's awarded. *Degree program information:* Part-time and evening/weekend programs available. Offers school administration (M Ed); school psychology (MA); teacher education (MAT). *Application deadline:* For fall admission, 5/1 priority date for domestic students. *Application fee:* $30. *Application Contact:* Office of the Registrar, 210-999-7201, Fax: 210-999-7202, E-mail: roffice@trinity.edu. *Chair,* Dr. Paul Kelleher, 210-999-7501, Fax: 210-999-7592, E-mail: paul.kelleher@trinity.edu.

Department of Health Care Administration Students: 44 full-time (16 women), 52 part-time (27 women); includes 25 minority (5 African Americans, 8 Asian Americans or Pacific Islanders, 12 Hispanic Americans). Average age 30. *Faculty:* 7 full-time (1 woman), 1 part-time/adjunct. Expenses: Contact institution. *Financial support:* In 2008–09, 9 research assistantships (averaging $9,500 per year) were awarded; career-related internships or fieldwork, institutionally sponsored loans, traineeships, and unspecified assistantships also available. Financial award application deadline: 4/1. In 2008, 33 master's awarded. *Degree program information:* Part-time programs available. Postbaccalaureate distance learning degree programs offered (minimal on-campus study). Offers health care administration (MS). *Application deadline:* For fall admission, 6/1 priority date for domestic students. Applications are processed on a rolling basis. *Application fee:* $30. *Application Contact:* Sharon Hubenak, Director of Recruiting and Residencies, 210-999-8141, Fax: 210-999-8108, E-mail: shubenak@trinity.edu. *Chair,* Dr. Mary E. Stefl, 210-999-7521, Fax: 210-999-8108, E-mail: mstefl@trinity.edu.

TRINITY (WASHINGTON) UNIVERSITY, Washington, DC 20017-1094

General Information Independent-religious, Undergraduate: women only; graduate: coed, comprehensive institution. *Graduate housing:* Room and/or apartments available on a first-come, first-served basis to single students; on-campus housing not available to married students.

GRADUATE UNITS

School of Education *Degree program information:* Part-time and evening/weekend programs available. Offers counseling (MA); early childhood education (MAT); educating for change (M Ed); educational administration (MSA); elementary education (MAT); school counseling (MA); secondary education (MAT); special education (MAT); teaching English as a second language (MAT); teaching English to speakers of other languages (M Ed); the teaching of reading (M Ed).

School of Professional Studies *Degree program information:* Part-time and evening/weekend programs available. Offers business administration (MBA); communication (MA); international security studies (MA); organizational management (MSA).

TRINITY WESTERN UNIVERSITY, Langley, BC V2Y 1Y1, Canada

General Information Independent-religious, coed, comprehensive institution. *Graduate housing:* On-campus housing not available.

GRADUATE UNITS

ACTS Seminaries *Degree program information:* Part-time programs available. Offers Christian studies (MA); church ministries (MA); cross cultural ministries (MA); theology (M Div, M Th, MAMFT, MLE, MTS, D Min).

Faculty of Graduate Studies Offers biblical studies (MA); business (MA, Certificate); Christian ministry (MA); counseling psychology (MA); education (MA, Certificate); general humanities (MAIH); healthcare (MA, Certificate); international business (MBA); linguistics (MA); managing the growing enterprise (MBA); non-profit (MA, Certificate); non-profit and charitable organization management (MBA); specialized (MAIH); teaching English to speakers of other languages (TESOL) (MA).

TRI STATE COLLEGE OF ACUPUNCTURE, New York, NY 10011

General Information Independent, coed, graduate-only institution. *Graduate housing:* On-campus housing not available.

GRADUATE UNITS

Program in Acupuncture *Degree program information:* Evening/weekend programs available. Offers acupuncture (MS); oriental medicine (MS); traditional Chinese herbology (Certificate).

TROY UNIVERSITY, Troy, AL 36082

General Information State-supported, coed, comprehensive institution. *Enrollment:* 28,303 graduate, professional, and undergraduate students; 2,370 full-time matriculated graduate/professional students (1,642 women), 4,789 part-time matriculated graduate/professional students (3,225 women). *Enrollment by degree level:* 6,997 master's, 162 other advanced degrees. *Graduate faculty:* 259 full-time (61 women), 310 part-time/adjunct (112 women). Tuition, state resident: full-time $4800; part-time $200 per credit hour. Tuition, nonresident: full-time $9600; part-time $400 per credit hour. *Required fees:* $140 per term. *Graduate housing:* Rooms and/or apartments available to single and married students. Typical cost: $5286 (including board) for single students; $5286 (including board) for married students. Housing application deadline: 7/31. *Student services:* Campus employment opportunities, campus safety program, career counseling, child daycare facilities, free psychological counseling, international student services, low-cost health insurance, services for students with disabilities, writing training. *Library facilities:* Lurleen B. Wallace Library (Troy Campus) plus 2 others. *Online resources:* library catalog. *Collection:* 571,172 titles, 3,309 serial subscriptions, 34,306 audiovisual materials. *Research affiliation:* Systemics Research Fund (protozoan symbionts), Birmingham Audubon Society (Alabama flora and fauna).

Computer facilities: 1,570 computers available on campus for general student use. A campuswide network can be accessed from student residence rooms and from off campus. Online class registration is available. *Web address:* http://www.troy.edu/.

General Application Contact: Brenda K. Campbell, Director of Graduate Admissions, 334-670-3178, Fax: 334-670-3733, E-mail: bcamp@troy.edu.

GRADUATE UNITS

Graduate School Students: 2,370 full-time (1,642 women), 4,789 part-time (3,225 women); includes 3,798 minority (3,446 African Americans, 65 American Indian/Alaska Native, 91 Asian Americans or Pacific Islanders, 196 Hispanic Americans), 200 international. Average age 33. 2,952 applicants, 79% accepted, 1797 enrolled. Expenses: Contact institution. *Financial support:* Fellowships, career-related internships or fieldwork available. Support available to part-time students. Financial award application deadline: 5/1; financial award applicants required to submit FAFSA. In 2008, 2,728 master's, 93 other advanced degrees awarded. *Degree program information:* Part-time and evening/weekend programs available. *Application deadline:* Applications are processed on a rolling basis. *Application fee:* $50. Electronic applications accepted. *Application Contact:* Brenda K. Campbell, Director of Graduate Admissions, 334-670-3178, Fax: 334-670-3733, E-mail: bcamp@troy.edu. *Associate Provost/Dean of Graduate School,* Dr. Dianne Barron, 334-670-3189, Fax: 334-370-3912, E-mail: dlbarron@troy.edu.

College of Arts and Sciences Students: 444 full-time (245 women), 1,337 part-time (666 women); includes 694 minority (542 African Americans, 14 American Indian/Alaska Native, 52 Asian Americans or Pacific Islanders, 86 Hispanic Americans). Average age 32. 712 applicants, 87% accepted, 465 enrolled. Expenses: Contact institution. *Financial support:* Available to part-time students. Applicants required to submit FAFSA. In 2008, 484 master's awarded. *Degree program information:* Part-time and evening/weekend programs available. Offers arts and sciences (MPA, MS); computer and information science (MS); criminal justice (MS); education (MPA); environmental analysis and management (MS); health care administration (MPA); international relations (MS); justice administration (MPA); management information systems (MPA); national security affairs (MPA); nonprofit management (MPA); public human resources management (MPA); public management (MPA). *Application deadline:* Applications are processed on a rolling basis. *Application fee:* $50. Electronic applications accepted. *Application Contact:* Brenda K. Campbell, Director of Graduate

Admissions, 334-670-3178, Fax: 334-670-3733, E-mail: bcamp@troy.edu. *Dean*, Dr. William S Richardson, 334-670-3399, Fax: 334-670-3673, E-mail: wsrichardson@troy.edu.

College of Business Students: 914 full-time (584 women), 1,831 part-time (1,132 women); includes 1,590 minority (1,448 African Americans, 16 American Indian/Alaska Native, 60 Asian Americans or Pacific Islanders, 66 Hispanic Americans). Average age 33. Expenses: Contact institution. *Financial support:* In 2008–09, 5 research assistantships were awarded; career-related internships or fieldwork also available. Support available to part-time students. Financial award applicants required to submit FAFSA. In 2008, 2,031 master's awarded. *Degree program information:* Part-time and evening/weekend programs available. Postbaccalaureate distance learning degree programs offered. Offers business (EMBA, MBA, MS, MSM); business administration (EMBA, MBA); human resources management (MS); management (MS, MSM). *Application deadline:* Applications are processed on a rolling basis. *Application fee:* $50. Electronic applications accepted. *Application Contact:* Brenda K. Campbell, Director of Graduate Admissions, 334-670-3178, Fax: 334-670-3733, E-mail: bcamp@troy.edu. *Dean*, Dr. Don Hines, 334-670-3143, Fax: 334-670-3708, E-mail: dhines@troy.edu.

College of Communication and Fine Arts Offers communication and fine arts (MS).

College of Education *Degree program information:* Part-time and evening/weekend programs available. Offers adult education (MS); clinical mental health (MS); community counseling (MS, Ed S); counselor education (MS); early childhood education (MS, MSE, Ed S); education (M Ed, MS, MSE, Ed S); educational administration/leadership (MS, Ed S); guidance services (MS); K–6 elementary and collaborative education (MS, MSE, Ed S); postsecondary education (M Ed); rehabilitation counseling (Ed S); school counseling (Ed S); school psychology (MS); secondary education (MS, Ed S); student affairs counseling (MS); teacher education-multiple levels (MS, Ed S). Electronic applications accepted.

College of Health and Human Services Students: 65 full-time (44 women), 114 part-time (83 women). Average age 32. Expenses: Contact institution. *Financial support:* In 2008–09, 4 students received support. Tuition waivers and unspecified assistantships available. Support available to part-time students. Financial award application deadline: 4/5; financial award applicants required to submit FAFSA. In 2008, 47 master's awarded. *Degree program information:* Part-time and evening/weekend programs available. Offers health and human services (MS, MSN); nursing (MSN); sport and fitness management (MS). *Application deadline:* Applications are processed on a rolling basis. *Application fee:* $50. Electronic applications accepted. *Application Contact:* Brenda K. Campbell, Director of Graduate Admissions, 334-670-3178, Fax: 334-670-3733, E-mail: bcamp@troy.edu. *Interim Dean*, Dr. Edith Smith, 334-670-3712, Fax: 334-670-3743, E-mail: esmith@troy.edu.

TRUMAN STATE UNIVERSITY, Kirksville, MO 63501-4221

General Information State-supported, coed, comprehensive institution. CGS member. *Graduate housing:* Rooms and/or apartments available on a first-come, first-served basis to single and married students. Housing application deadline: 5/1. *Research affiliation:* Gulf Coast Research Laboratory (marine science), Kirksville College of Osteopathic Medicine (biology).

GRADUATE UNITS

Graduate School Offers education (MAE). Electronic applications accepted.

College of Arts and Sciences Offers arts and sciences (MA, MS); biology (MS); English (MA); music (MA). Electronic applications accepted.

School of Business Offers accounting (M Ac); business (M Ac). Electronic applications accepted.

School of Health Sciences and Education Offers communication disorders (MA); health sciences and education (MA, MAE). Electronic applications accepted.

TUFTS UNIVERSITY, Medford, MA 02155

General Information Independent, coed, university. CGS member. *Enrollment:* 10,030 graduate, professional, and undergraduate students; 4,094 full-time matriculated graduate/professional students (2,318 women), 510 part-time matriculated graduate/professional students (268 women). *Enrollment by degree level:* 1,735 first professional, 1,893 master's, 839 doctoral, 137 other advanced degrees. *Graduate faculty:* 768 full-time (300 women), 459 part-time/adjunct (217 women). *Tuition:* Full-time $36,632. *Required fees:* $660. Tuition and fees vary according to course level, course load, degree level, program and student level. *Graduate housing:* Room and/or apartments available on a first-come, first-served basis to single students; on-campus housing not available to married students. Typical cost: $6538 per year. Room charges vary according to campus/location and housing facility selected. *Student services:* Campus employment opportunities, campus safety program, career counseling, child daycare facilities, exercise/wellness program, free psychological counseling, international student services, low-cost health insurance, multicultural affairs office, services for students with disabilities, teacher training, writing training. *Library facilities:* Tisch Library plus 1 other. *Online resources:* library catalog, web page, access to other libraries' catalogs. *Collection:* 1.7 million titles, 4,341 serial subscriptions, 40,307 audiovisual materials. *Research affiliation:* Maine Medical Center (medicine), The Stockholm Environmental Institute (environmental science and policy), Caritas St. Elizabeth's Medical Center (medicine), Tufts-New England medical Center (medicine), Lahey Clinic Medical Center (medicine), Baystate Medical Center (medicine).

Computer facilities: Computer purchase and lease plans are available. 300 computers available on campus for general student use. A campuswide network can be accessed from student residence rooms and from off campus. Online class registration is available. *Web address:* http://www.tufts.edu/.

General Application Contact: Information Contact, 617-628-5000.

GRADUATE UNITS

Cummings School of Veterinary Medicine Offers animals and public policy (MS); comparative biomedical sciences (PhD); veterinary medicine (DVM, MS, PhD). Electronic applications accepted.

Fletcher School of Law and Diplomacy Postbaccalaureate distance learning degree programs offered (minimal on-campus study). Offers law and diplomacy (LL M, MA, MAHA, MALD, MIB, PhD). Electronic applications accepted.

The Gerald J. and Dorothy R. Friedman School of Nutrition Science and Policy *Degree program information:* Part-time programs available. Offers humanitarian assistance (MAHA); nutrition (MS, PhD). Electronic applications accepted.

Graduate School of Arts and Sciences Students: 1,004 (682 women); includes 128 minority (45 African Americans, 4 American Indian/Alaska Native, 43 Asian Americans or Pacific Islanders, 36 Hispanic Americans), 127 international. Average age 29. 1,967 applicants, 46% accepted, 368 enrolled. *Faculty:* 295 full-time, 188 part-time/adjunct. Expenses: Contact institution. *Financial support:* Fellowships with full and partial tuition reimbursements, research assistantships with full and partial tuition reimbursements, teaching assistantships with full and partial tuition reimbursements, Federal Work-Study, scholarships/grants, health care benefits, tuition waivers (full and partial), and unspecified assistantships available. Support available to part-time students. Financial award applicants required to submit FAFSA. In 2008, 322 master's, 49 doctorates, 16 other advanced degrees awarded. *Degree program information:* Part-time programs available. Offers analytical chemistry (MS, PhD); art history (MA); arts and sciences (MA, MAT, MFA, MPP, MS, OTD, PhD, CAGS, Certificate); bioengineering (Certificate); biology (MS, PhD); bioorganic chemistry (MS, PhD); biotechnology (Certificate); biotechnology engineering (Certificate); child development (MA, PhD, CAGS); classical archaeology (MA); classics (MA); community development (MA); community environmental studies (Certificate); computer science (Certificate); computer science minor (Certificate); dance (MA, PhD); drama (MA); dramatic literature and criticism (PhD); early childhood education (MAT); economics (MS); education (MA, MAT, MS, PhD); English (MA, PhD); environmental chemistry (MS, PhD); environmental management (Certificate); environmental policy (MA); epidemiology (Certificate); ethnomusicology (MA); French (MA); German (MA); health and human welfare (MA); history (MA, PhD); housing policy (MA); human-computer interaction (Certificate); inorganic chemistry (MS, PhD); international environment/development policy (MA); management of community organizations (Certificate); manufacturing engineering (Certificate); mathematics (MA, MS, PhD); microwave and wireless engineering (Certificate); middle and secondary education (MA, MAT); museum studies (Certificate); music history and literature (MA); music theory and composition (MA); occupational therapy (Certificate); organic chemistry (MS, PhD); philosophy (MA); physical chemistry (MS, PhD); physics (MS, PhD); program evaluation (Certificate); psychology (MS, PhD); public policy (MPP); school psychology (MA, CAGS); secondary education (MA); studio art (MFA); theater history (PhD). *Application deadline:* For fall admission, 1/15 priority date for domestic students, 12/30 for international students. Applications are processed on a rolling basis. *Application fee:* $75. Electronic applications accepted. *Application Contact:* Information Contact, 617-628-5000. *Dean*, Lynne Pepall, 617-327-3395, Fax: 617-627-3016, E-mail: gradschool@ase.tufts.edu.

Sackler School of Graduate Biomedical Sciences Offers biochemistry (PhD); biomedical sciences (MS, PhD); cell, molecular and developmental biology (PhD); cellular and molecular physiology (PhD); genetics (PhD); immunology (PhD); integrated studies (PhD); molecular microbiology (PhD); neuroscience (PhD); pharmacology and experimental therapeutics (PhD). Electronic applications accepted.

Division of Clinical Care Research *Degree program information:* Part-time programs available. Offers clinical care research (MS, PhD). Electronic applications accepted.

School of Dental Medicine Offers dental medicine (DMD, MS, Certificate); dentistry (Certificate).

School of Engineering Students: 503 (148 women); includes 46 minority (5 African Americans, 30 Asian Americans or Pacific Islanders, 11 Hispanic Americans), 113 international. 651 applicants, 48% accepted, 156 enrolled. *Faculty:* 70 full-time, 33 part-time/adjunct. Expenses: Contact institution. *Financial support:* Fellowships with full tuition reimbursements, research assistantships with full and partial tuition reimbursements, teaching assistantships with full and partial tuition reimbursements, Federal Work-Study, scholarships/grants, tuition waivers (partial), and unspecified assistantships available. Financial award application deadline: 1/15; financial award applicants required to submit FAFSA. In 2008, 132 master's, 21 doctorates awarded. *Degree program information:* Part-time programs available. Offers biomedical engineering (ME, MS, PhD); chemical and biological engineering (ME, MS, PhD); civil engineering (ME, MS, PhD); computer science (MS, PhD); electrical engineering (MS, PhD); engineering (ME, MS, MSEM, PhD); environmental engineering (ME, MS, PhD); human factors (MS); mechanical engineering (ME, MS, PhD). *Application deadline:* For fall admission, 1/15 priority date for domestic students, 12/30 for international students; for spring admission, 10/15 for domestic students, 9/15 for international students. Applications are processed on a rolling basis. *Application fee:* $75. Electronic applications accepted. *Application Contact:* Information Contact, 617-628-5000. *Dean*, Linda Abriola, 617-627-3237, Fax: 617-627-3819.

The Gordon Institute Students: 115 (24 women); includes 1 minority (Asian American or Pacific Islander), 6 international. 59 applicants, 80% accepted, 38 enrolled. *Faculty:* 9 part-time/adjunct. Expenses: Contact institution. In 2008, 35 master's awarded. *Degree program information:* Part-time programs available. Offers engineering management (MSEM). *Application deadline:* For fall admission, 3/15 priority date for domestic students. Applications are processed on a rolling basis. *Application fee:* $75. Electronic applications accepted. *Application Contact:* Information Contact, 617-628-5000. *Director*, Robert Hannemann, 617-627-3111, Fax: 617-627-3180.

School of Medicine Expenses: Contact institution. Offers biomedical sciences (MS); health communication (MS); medicine (MD, MPH, MS); pain research, education and policy (MS); public health (MPH). *Application Contact:* Information Contact, 617-628-5000. *Dean*, Dr. Michael Rosenblatt, 617-636-6565.

See Close-Up on page 1009.

TUI UNIVERSITY, Cypress, CA 90630

General Information Independent, coed, university. *Enrollment:* 8,004 graduate, professional, and undergraduate students; 1,333 full-time matriculated graduate/professional students (468 women), 2,893 part-time matriculated graduate/professional students (986 women). *Enrollment by degree level:* 3,774 master's, 452 doctoral. *Graduate faculty:* 223. *Tuition:* Part-time $345 per semester hour. Part-time tuition and fees vary according to degree level. *Library facilities:* Touro Cyber Library. *Online resources:* web page. *Collection:* 30,692 titles, 1,500 serial subscriptions.

Computer facilities: A campuswide network can be accessed from off campus. Online class registration is available. *Web address:* http://www.tuiu.edu/.

General Application Contact: Wei Ren, Registrar, 800-375-9878, Fax: 714-827-7407, E-mail: registration@tuiu.edu.

GRADUATE UNITS

College of Business Administration Students: 741 full-time (200 women), 1,585 part-time (410 women). 379 applicants, 81% accepted, 300 enrolled. Expenses: Contact institution. In 2008, 752 master's, 28 doctorates awarded. *Degree program information:* Part-time and evening/weekend programs available. Postbaccalaureate distance learning degree programs offered (no on-campus study). Offers business administration (MBA, PhD); conflict and negotiation management (MBA); criminal justice administration (MBA); entrepreneurship (MBA); finance (MBA); general management (MBA); government accounting (MBA); human resource management (MBA); information security and digital assurance management (MBA); information technology management (MBA); international business (MBA); logistics management (MBA); marketing (MBA); project management (MBA); public management (MBA); quality management (MBA); strategic leadership (MBA). *Application deadline:* For fall admission, 10/3 for domestic and international students; for winter admission, 12/22 for domestic and international students; for spring admission, 4/3 for domestic and international students. Applications are processed on a rolling basis. *Application fee:* $75. Electronic applications accepted. *Application Contact:* Wei Ren-Finaly, Registrar, 800-375-9878, Fax: 714-827-7407, E-mail: registration@tuiu.edu. *Dean*, Dr. Paul Watkins, 714-816-0366 Ext. 2054, Fax: 714-816-0367, E-mail: infocba@tuiu.edu.

College of Education Students: 173 full-time (86 women), 421 part-time (189 women). 112 applicants, 72% accepted, 81 enrolled. Expenses: Contact institution. In 2008, 227 master's, 16 doctorates awarded. *Degree program information:* Part-time and evening/weekend programs available. Postbaccalaureate distance learning degree programs offered (no on-campus study). Offers adult education (MA Ed); aviation education (MA Ed); children's literacy development (MA Ed); e-learning (MA Ed); e-learning leadership (MA Ed, PhD); early childhood education (MA Ed); education (MA Ed, PhD); educational leadership (MA Ed); enrollment management (MA Ed); higher education (MA Ed); higher education leadership (PhD); K-12 leadership (PhD); teaching and instruction (MA Ed); training and development (MA Ed). *Application deadline:* For fall admission, 10/3 for domestic and international students; for winter admission, 12/22 for domestic and international students; for spring admission, 4/3 for domestic and international students. Applications are processed on a rolling basis. *Application fee:* $75. Electronic applications accepted. *Application Contact:* Wei Ren-Finaly, Registrar, 800-375-9878, Fax: 714-827-7407, E-mail: registration@tuiu.edu. *Dean*, Dr. Michaela Tanasescu, 714-816-0366, Fax: 714-226-9844, E-mail: infocoe@tuiu.edu.

College of Health Sciences Students: 322 full-time (170 women), 709 part-time (357 women). 227 applicants, 80% accepted, 164 enrolled. Expenses: Contact institution. In 2008, 366 master's, 29 doctorates awarded. *Degree program information:* Part-time and evening/weekend programs available. Postbaccalaureate distance learning degree programs offered (no on-campus study). Offers clinical research administration (MS, Certificate); emergency and disaster management (MS, Certificate); environmental health science (Certificate); health care administration (PhD); health care management (MS); health education (MS, Certificate); health informatics (Certificate); health sciences (MS, PhD, Certificate); international health (MS); international health: educator or researcher option (PhD); international health: practitioner option (PhD); law and expert witness studies (MS, Certificate); public health (MS); quality assurance (Certificate). *Application deadline:* For fall admission, 10/3 for domestic and international students; for winter admission, 12/22 for domestic and international students; for spring admission, 4/3 for domestic and international students. Applications are processed on a rolling basis. *Application fee:* $75. Electronic applications accepted. *Application Contact:*

TUI University (continued)

Wei Ren-Finaly, Registrar, 800-375-9878, Fax: 714-827-7407, E-mail: registration@tuiu.edu. *Dean,* Dr. Michaela Tanasescu, 714-816-0366, Fax: 714-226-9844, E-mail: infocoe@tuiu.edu.

College of Information Systems Students: 83 full-time (12 women), 178 part-time (30 women). 67 applicants, 84% accepted, 50 enrolled. Expenses: Contact institution. In 2008, 116 master's awarded. *Degree program information:* Part-time and evening/weekend programs available. Postbaccalaureate distance learning degree programs offered (no on-campus study). Offers business intelligence (Certificate); information technology management (MS). *Application deadline:* For fall admission, 10/3 for domestic and international students; for winter admission, 12/22 for domestic and international students; for spring admission, 4/3 for domestic and international students. Applications are processed on a rolling basis. *Application fee:* $0. Electronic applications accepted. *Application Contact:* Wei Ren-Finaly, Registrar, 800-375-9878, Fax: 714-827-7407, E-mail: registration@tuiu.edu. *Dean,* Dr. Paul Watkins, 800-509-3901, E-mail: infocis@tuiu.edu.

TULANE UNIVERSITY, New Orleans, LA 70118-5669

General Information Independent, coed, university. CGS member. *Graduate housing:* Rooms and/or apartments available on a first-come, first-served basis to single and married students. Housing application deadline: 3/24.

GRADUATE UNITS

A. B. Freeman School of Business *Degree program information:* Part-time and evening/weekend programs available. Offers business (EMBA, M Acct, M Fin, MBA, PMBA, PhD). Electronic applications accepted.

Program in Liberal Arts *Degree program information:* Part-time programs available. Offers liberal arts (MLA).

School of Architecture *Degree program information:* Part-time programs available. Offers architecture (M Arch, MPS).

School of Law Offers admiralty (LL M); American business law (LL M); energy and environment (LL M); international and comparative law (LL M); law (JD, LL M, SJD). Electronic applications accepted.

School of Liberal Arts *Degree program information:* Part-time programs available. Offers anthropology (MA, PhD); art (MFA); art history (MA); classical studies (MA); design and technical production (MFA); economics (MA, PhD); English (MA, PhD); French (MA, PhD); history (MA, PhD); liberal arts (MA, MFA, MS, PhD); music (MA, MFA); philosophy (MA, PhD); political science (MA, PhD); Portuguese (MA); sociology (MA, PhD); Spanish (MA); Spanish and Portuguese (PhD). Electronic applications accepted.

The Payson Center for International Development and Technology Transfer *Degree program information:* Part-time programs available. Offers international development (MS, PhD). Electronic applications accepted.

Roger Thayer Stone Center for Latin American Studies Offers Latin American studies (MA, PhD). Electronic applications accepted.

School of Medicine Offers medicine (MD, MBS, MS, PhD).

Graduate Programs in Biomedical Sciences Offers biochemistry (MS, PhD); biomedical sciences (MBS, MS, PhD); human genetics (MBS, PhD); microbiology and immunology (MS, PhD); molecular and cellular biology (PhD); neuroscience (MS, PhD); pharmacology (MS, PhD); physiology (MS, PhD); structural and cellular biology (MS, PhD).

School of Public Health and Tropical Medicine *Degree program information:* Part-time and evening/weekend programs available. Postbaccalaureate distance learning degree programs offered (no on-campus study). Offers biostatistics (MS, MSPH, PhD, Sc D); clinical tropical medicine and travelers health (Diploma); environmental health sciences (MPH, MSPH, Dr PH, PhD); epidemiology (MPH, MS, Dr PH, PhD); health education and communication (MPH); health systems management (MHA, MMM, MPH, PhD, Sc D); international health and development (MPH, Dr PH, PhD); maternal and child health (MPH, Dr PH); nutrition (MPH); parasitology (MSPH, PhD); public health and tropical medicine (MHA, MMM, MPH, MPHTM, MS, MSPH, Dr PH, PhD, Sc D, Diploma); vector borne infectious diseases (MS, PhD). MS, PhD offered through the Graduate School. Electronic applications accepted.

School of Science and Engineering *Degree program information:* Part-time programs available. Offers applied mathematics (MS); biomedical engineering (MS, PhD); cell and molecular biology (MS, PhD); chemical and biomolecular engineering (PhD); chemistry (MS, PhD); earth and environmental sciences (MS, PhD); ecology and evolutionary biology (MS, PhD); interdisciplinary studies (PhD); mathematics (MS, PhD); neuroscience (MS, PhD); physics (PhD); psychology (MS, PhD); science and engineering (M Eng, MS, PhD); statistics (MS). MS and PhD offered through the Graduate School. Electronic applications accepted.

School of Social Work *Degree program information:* Part-time programs available. Offers social work (MSW). Electronic applications accepted.

TUSCULUM COLLEGE, Greeneville, TN 37743-9997

General Information Independent-religious, coed, comprehensive institution. *Graduate housing:* On-campus housing not available.

GRADUATE UNITS

Graduate School *Degree program information:* Evening/weekend programs available. Offers adult education (MA Ed); K–12 (MA Ed); organizational management (MAOM).

TUSKEGEE UNIVERSITY, Tuskegee, AL 36088

General Information Independent, coed, comprehensive institution. *Enrollment:* 2,994 graduate, professional, and undergraduate students; 431 full-time matriculated graduate/professional students (305 women), 22 part-time matriculated graduate/professional students (10 women). *Enrollment by degree level:* 235 first professional, 163 master's, 24 doctoral. *Graduate faculty:* 112 full-time (17 women), 11 part-time/adjunct (5 women). *Tuition:* Full-time $14,740; part-time $473 per credit hour. *Graduate housing:* Rooms and/or apartments available to single and married students. Housing application deadline: 5/1. *Student services:* Campus employment opportunities, campus safety program, career counseling, child daycare facilities, free psychological counseling, international student services, low-cost health insurance. *Library facilities:* Hollis B. Frissell Library plus 3 others. *Online resources:* library catalog. *Collection:* 623,824 titles, 81,157 serial subscriptions.

Computer facilities: 1,000 computers available on campus for general student use. A campuswide network can be accessed from student residence rooms and from off campus. Online class registration is available. *Web address:* http://www.tuskegee.edu/.

General Application Contact: Dr. Robert L. Laney, Vice President/Director of Admissions and Enrollment Management, 334-727-8580, Fax: 334-727-5750, E-mail: planey@tuskegee.edu.

GRADUATE UNITS

Graduate Programs Students: 431 full-time (305 women), 22 part-time (10 women); includes 268 minority (251 African Americans, 2 American Indian/Alaska Native, 5 Asian Americans or Pacific Islanders, 10 Hispanic Americans), 65 international. Average age 28. 1,197 applicants, 62% accepted, 453 enrolled. *Faculty:* 112 full-time (17 women), 11 part-time/adjunct (5 women). Expenses: Contact institution. *Financial support:* Fellowships, research assistantships, teaching assistantships, career-related internships or fieldwork, Federal Work-Study, institutionally sponsored loans, and scholarships/grants available. Support available to part-time students. Financial award application deadline: 4/15; financial award applicants required to submit FAFSA. In 2008, 50 first professional degrees, 46 master's awarded. *Degree program information:* Part-time programs available. *Application deadline:* For fall admission, 7/15 for domestic students. Applications are processed on a rolling basis. *Application fee:* $25 ($35 for international students). *Application Contact:* Dr. Robert L. Laney, Vice President/Director of Admissions and Enrollment Management, 334-727-8580, Fax: 334-727-5750, E-mail: planey@tuskegee.edu. *Provost,* Dr. Luther S. Williams, 334-727-8164.

College of Agricultural, Environmental and Natural Sciences Students: 91 full-time (61 women), 10 part-time (5 women); includes 73 minority (69 African Americans, 1 American Indian/Alaska Native, 3 Asian Americans or Pacific Islanders), 20 international. Average age 29. 65 applicants, 65% accepted, 23 enrolled. *Faculty:* 26 full-time (12 women), 1 part-time/adjunct (0 women). Expenses: Contact institution. *Financial support:* Fellowships, research assistantships, teaching assistantships, career-related internships or fieldwork, Federal Work-Study, and institutionally sponsored loans available. Support available to part-time students. Financial award application deadline: 4/15. In 2008, 22 master's awarded. Offers agricultural and resource economics (MS); agricultural, environmental and natural sciences (MS, PhD); animal and poultry sciences (MS); biology (MS); chemistry (MS); environmental sciences (MS); food and nutritional sciences (MS); integrative biosciences (PhD); plant and soil sciences (MS). *Application deadline:* For fall admission, 7/15 for domestic students. Applications are processed on a rolling basis. *Application fee:* $25 ($35 for international students). *Application Contact:* Dr. Robert L. Laney, Vice President/Director of Admissions and Enrollment Management, 334-727-8580, Fax: 334-727-5750, E-mail: planey@tuskegee.edu. *Dean,* Dr. Walter A. Hill, 334-727-8157.

College of Engineering, Architecture and Physical Sciences Students: 53 full-time (21 women), 8 part-time (2 women); includes 22 minority (21 African Americans, 1 Asian American or Pacific Islander), 34 international. Average age 28. 104 applicants, 59% accepted. *Faculty:* 19 full-time (0 women). Expenses: Contact institution. *Financial support:* Fellowships, research assistantships, teaching assistantships, career-related internships or fieldwork, Federal Work-Study, and institutionally sponsored loans available. Support available to part-time students. Financial award application deadline: 4/15. In 2008, 15 master's awarded. Offers electrical engineering (MSEE); engineering, architecture and physical sciences (MSEE, MSME, PhD); material science and engineering (PhD); mechanical engineering (MSME). *Application deadline:* For fall admission, 7/15 for domestic students. Applications are processed on a rolling basis. *Application fee:* $25 ($35 for international students). *Application Contact:* Dr. Robert L. Laney, Vice President/Director of Admissions and Enrollment Management, 334-727-8580, Fax: 334-727-5750, E-mail: planey@tuskegee.edu. *Acting Dean,* Dr. Legand L. Burge, 334-727-8356.

College of Veterinary Medicine, Nursing and Allied Health Students: 265 full-time (208 women), 3 part-time (all women); includes 160 minority (148 African Americans, 1 American Indian/Alaska Native, 2 Asian Americans or Pacific Islanders, 9 Hispanic Americans), 10 international. Average age 27. *Faculty:* 62 full-time (6 women). Expenses: Contact institution. *Financial support:* Fellowships, research assistantships, teaching assistantships, career-related internships or fieldwork, Federal Work-Study, institutionally sponsored loans, and scholarships/grants available. Support available to part-time students. Financial award application deadline: 4/15. In 2008, 50 first professional degrees awarded. Offers veterinary medicine (DVM, MS); veterinary medicine, nursing and allied health (DVM, MS). *Application deadline:* For fall admission, 7/15 for domestic students. Applications are processed on a rolling basis. *Application fee:* $25 ($35 for international students). *Application Contact:* Dr. Robert L. Laney, Vice President/Director of Admissions and Enrollment Management, 334-727-8580, Fax: 334-727-5750, E-mail: planey@tuskegee.edu. *Dean,* Dr. Tsegaye Habtemariam, 334-727-8174, Fax: 334-727-8177.

TYNDALE UNIVERSITY COLLEGE & SEMINARY, Toronto, ON M2M 4B3, Canada

General Information Independent-religious, coed, comprehensive institution. *Graduate housing:* Room and/or apartments available on a first-come, first-served basis to single students; on-campus housing not available to married students.

GRADUATE UNITS

Graduate Programs *Degree program information:* Part-time programs available. Postbaccalaureate distance learning degree programs offered (no on-campus study). Offers Biblical studies (M Div); Christian foundations (MTS); Christian studies (Diploma); counseling (M Div); educational ministry (M Div); missions (M Div, Diploma); pastoral and Chinese ministry (M Div); pastoral ministry (M Div); Pentecostal studies (MTS); spiritual formation (M Div, Diploma); theological studies (M Div); theology (Th M); worship and liturgy (M Div, MTS); youth and family ministry (M Div). Electronic applications accepted.

UNIFICATION THEOLOGICAL SEMINARY, Barrytown, NY 12507

General Information Independent-religious, coed, primarily men, graduate-only institution. *Enrollment by degree level:* 52 first professional, 88 master's, 33 doctoral. *Graduate faculty:* 7 full-time (2 women), 16 part-time/adjunct (3 women). *Tuition:* Full-time $10,250; part-time $410 per credit. *Required fees:* $127 per semester. Tuition and fees vary according to course load, degree level and campus/location. *Graduate housing:* Rooms and/or apartments guaranteed to single students and available on a first-come, first-served basis to married students. Typical cost: $6940 (including board) for single students; $6000 per year ($9360 including board) for married students. Room and board charges vary according to board plan, campus/location and housing facility selected. *Student services:* Campus employment opportunities, career counseling, international student services, low-cost health insurance. *Library facilities:* UTS Library plus 1 other. *Online resources:* library catalog, web page, access to other libraries' catalogs. *Collection:* 55,100 titles, 75 serial subscriptions, 2,000 audiovisual materials.

Computer facilities: 14 computers available on campus for general student use. A campuswide network can be accessed from student residence rooms. *Web address:* http://www.uts.edu/.

General Application Contact: Henry Christopher, Director of Admissions, 845-752-3000 Ext. 200, Fax: 845-752-3016, E-mail: admissions@uts.edu.

GRADUATE UNITS

Graduate Program, Main Campus Students: 86 full-time (19 women), 13 part-time (1 woman); includes 25 minority (10 African Americans, 1 American Indian/Alaska Native, 12 Asian Americans or Pacific Islanders, 2 Hispanic Americans), 57 international. Average age 37. *Faculty:* 7 full-time (2 women), 6 part-time/adjunct (1 woman). Expenses: Contact institution. *Financial support:* In 2008–09, 99 students received support; teaching assistantships, career-related internships or fieldwork, institutionally sponsored loans, scholarships/grants, and tuition waivers (partial) available. Financial award applicants required to submit FAFSA. In 2008, 6 first professional degrees, 21 master's awarded. *Degree program information:* Part-time programs available. Offers theology (M Div, MRE, D Min). *Application deadline:* For fall admission, 8/15 priority date for domestic students; for spring admission, 1/15 priority date for domestic students. Applications are processed on a rolling basis. *Application fee:* $30. *Application Contact:* Henry Christopher, Director of Admissions, 845-752-3000 Ext. 200, Fax: 845-752-3016, E-mail: admissions@uts.edu. *Academic Dean,* Dr. Kathy Winings, 845-752-3000 Ext. 228, Fax: 845-752-3014, E-mail: academics@uts.edu.

Graduate Program, New York Extension Students: 21 full-time (9 women), 53 part-time (27 women); includes 65 minority (56 African Americans, 2 American Indian/Alaska Native, 3 Asian Americans or Pacific Islanders, 4 Hispanic Americans), 4 international. Average age 41. *Faculty:* 4 full-time (1 woman), 10 part-time/adjunct (2 women). Expenses: Contact institution. *Financial support:* In 2008–09, 74 students received support. Career-related internships or fieldwork, institutionally sponsored loans, scholarships/grants, and tuition waivers (partial) available. Financial award applicants required to submit FAFSA. In 2008, 3 first professional degrees, 4 master's awarded. *Degree program information:* Part-time and evening/weekend programs available. Offers theology (M Div, MRE). *Application deadline:* For fall admission, 8/15 priority date for domestic students; for spring admission, 1/15 priority date for domestic students. Applications are processed on a rolling basis. *Application fee:* $30. *Application Contact:* Rev. Leander Hardaway, Admissions Officer, 212-563-6647 Ext. 15, Fax: 212-563-6431, E-mail: lwhardaway@aol.com. *Dean of the Extension Center,* Dr. Lonnie McLeod, 212-563-6647 Ext. 104, Fax: 212-563-6431, E-mail: LHOPEC@aol.com.

UNIFORMED SERVICES UNIVERSITY OF THE HEALTH SCIENCES, Bethesda, MD 20814-4799

General Information Federally supported, coed, graduate-only institution. *Graduate housing:* On-campus housing not available. *Research affiliation:* U.S. Armed Forces Radiobiology

Research Institute, National Institutes of Health, National Library of Medicine, Walter Reed Army Institute of Research, Armed Forces Institute of Pathology.

GRADUATE UNITS

Graduate School of Nursing Postbaccalaureate distance learning degree programs offered (no on-campus study). Offers nurse anesthesia (MSN); nurse practitioner (MSN); perioperative clinical nurse specialty (MSN). Available to military officers only. Electronic applications accepted.

School of Medicine Offers medicine (MD, MMH, MPH, MSPH, MTMH, Dr PH, PhD).

Graduate Programs in the Biomedical Sciences and Public Health Offers clinical psychology (PhD); emerging infectious diseases (PhD); environmental health science (PhD); medical and clinical psychology (PhD); medical history (MMH); medical psychology (PhD); medical zoology (PhD); microbiology and immunology (PhD); molecular and cell biology (PhD); neuroscience (PhD); preventive medicine and biometrics (MPH, MSPH, MTMH, Dr PH, PhD); public health (MPH, MSPH, Dr PH); tropical medicine and hygiene (MTMH).

UNION COLLEGE, Barbourville, KY 40906-1499

General Information Independent-religious, coed, comprehensive institution. *Graduate housing:* Rooms and/or apartments available to single and married students.

GRADUATE UNITS

Graduate Programs *Degree program information:* Part-time and evening/weekend programs available. Offers clinical psychology (MA); counseling psychology (MA); elementary education (MA); health (MA Ed); health and physical education (MA); middle grades (MA); music education (MA); principalship (MA); reading specialist (MA); school psychology (MA); secondary education (MA); special education (MA).

UNION COLLEGE, Lincoln, NE 68506-4300

General Information Independent-religious, coed, comprehensive institution. *Graduate housing:* Rooms and/or apartments available on a first-come, first-served basis to single and married students.

GRADUATE UNITS

Program in Physician Assistant Studies Offers physician assistant studies (MPAS). Electronic applications accepted.

UNION GRADUATE COLLEGE, Schenectady, NY 12308-3107

General Information Independent, coed, graduate-only institution. *Enrollment by degree level:* 397 master's, 4 other advanced degrees. *Graduate faculty:* 14 full-time (4 women), 36 part-time/adjunct (15 women). *Tuition:* Part-time $2344 per course. One-time fee: $250. Tuition and fees vary according to course load and program. *Student services:* Campus employment opportunities, campus safety program, career counseling, free psychological counseling, international student services, low-cost health insurance, services for students with disabilities, teacher training. *Library facilities:* Schaeffer Library. *Online resources:* library catalog, web page, access to other libraries' catalogs. *Collection:* 2 million titles, 3,728 serial subscriptions, 9,044 audiovisual materials.

Computer facilities: 50 computers available on campus for general student use. A campuswide network can be accessed from off campus. Online class registration is available. *Web address:* http://www.uniongraduatecollege.edu/.

General Application Contact: Rhonda Sheehan, Director of Admissions and Registrar, 518-388-6148, Fax: 518-388-6686, E-mail: sheehanr@uniongraduatecollege.edu.

GRADUATE UNITS

Center for Bioethics and Clinical Leadership Students: 52 full-time (27 women), 33 part-time (25 women). 28 applicants, 86% accepted, 18 enrolled. *Faculty:* 12 full-time (6 women), 10 part-time/adjunct (5 women). Expenses: Contact institution. *Financial support:* Federal Work-Study, scholarships/grants, health care benefits, and tuition waivers (partial) available. Support available to part-time students. Financial award applicants required to submit FAFSA. In 2008, 18 master's awarded. *Degree program information:* Part-time and evening/weekend programs available. Postbaccalaureate distance learning degree programs offered (minimal on-campus study). Offers bioethics (MS); clinical leadership in health management (MS). *Application deadline:* Applications are processed on a rolling basis. *Application fee:* $60. Electronic applications accepted. *Application Contact:* Ann Nolte, Assistant Director, 518-388-8045, Fax: 518-388-8046, E-mail: noltea@uniongraduatecollege.edu. *Director,* Dr. Robert B. Baker, 518-388-6215, Fax: 518-388-8046, E-mail: bakerr@union.edu.

School of Education Students: 54 full-time (33 women), 22 part-time (15 women). 92 applicants, 62% accepted, 51 enrolled. *Faculty:* 4 full-time (1 woman), 25 part-time/adjunct (10 women). Expenses: Contact institution. *Financial support:* In 2008–09, 12 research assistantships with tuition reimbursements (averaging $3,000 per year) were awarded; Federal Work-Study, scholarships/grants, health care benefits, and tuition waivers (partial) also available. Support available to part-time students. Financial award applicants required to submit FAFSA. In 2008, 62 master's awarded. Offers biology (MAT, MS); chemistry (MAT); earth science (MAT); English (MAT); French (MAT); general science (MAT); German (MAT); languages (MAT); Latin (MAT); mathematics (MAT); mathematics and technology (MS); physical science (MS); physics (MAT); social studies (MAT); Spanish (MAT). *Application deadline:* Applications are processed on a rolling basis. *Application fee:* $60. Electronic applications accepted. *Application Contact:* Christine Angley, Assistant, 518-388-6361, Fax: 518-388-6686, E-mail: angleyc@uniongraduatecollege.edu. *Dean,* Dr. Patrick Allen, 518-388-6361, Fax: 518-388-6686, E-mail: mat@union.edu.

School of Engineering and Computer Science Students: 11 full-time (3 women), 58 part-time (8 women). 31 applicants, 68% accepted, 20 enrolled. *Faculty:* 13 part-time/adjunct (1 woman). Expenses: Contact institution. *Financial support:* Research assistantships, Federal Work-Study, scholarships/grants, health care benefits, and tuition waivers (full and partial) available. Support available to part-time students. Financial award applicants required to submit FAFSA. In 2008, 22 master's awarded. *Degree program information:* Part-time and evening/weekend programs available. Offers computer science (MS); electrical engineering (MS); engineering and management systems (MS); mechanical engineering (MS). *Application deadline:* Applications are processed on a rolling basis. *Application fee:* $60. Electronic applications accepted. *Application Contact:* Diane Trzaskos, Coordinator, Admissions, 518-388-6642, Fax: 518-388-6686, E-mail: trzaskod@uniongraduatecollege.edu. *Dean,* Robert Kozik, 515-388-8068, Fax: 518-388-6789, E-mail: kozikr@union.edu.

School of Management Students: 122 full-time (50 women), 106 part-time (45 women). 148 applicants, 76% accepted, 91 enrolled. *Faculty:* 15 full-time (3 women), 22 part-time/adjunct (5 women). Expenses: Contact institution. *Financial support:* Research assistantships, career-related internships or fieldwork, Federal Work-Study, scholarships/grants, health care benefits, and tuition waivers (partial) available. Support available to part-time students. Financial award applicants required to submit FAFSA. In 2008, 70 master's, 35 other advanced degrees awarded. *Degree program information:* Part-time and evening/weekend programs available. Offers Business Administration (MBA); Financial Management (Certificate); General Management (Certificate); Health Systems Administration (MBA, Certificate); Human Resources (Certificate). *Application deadline:* Applications are processed on a rolling basis. *Application fee:* $60. *Application Contact:* Diane Trzaskos, Admissions Coordinator, 518-388-6642, Fax: 518-388-6686, E-mail: trzaskod@uniongraduatecollege.edu. *Dean,* Eric Lewis, 518-388-7186, Fax: 518-388-6754, E-mail: lewise@uniongraduatecollege.edu.

UNION INSTITUTE & UNIVERSITY, Cincinnati, OH 45206-1925

General Information Independent, coed, university. *Graduate housing:* On-campus housing not available.

GRADUATE UNITS

Doctor of Education Program Offers educational leadership (Ed D); higher education (Ed D).

Online MA Programs *Degree program information:* Part-time programs available. Postbaccalaureate distance learning degree programs offered (no on-campus study). Offers health and wellness (MA); history and culture (MA); leadership (MA); literature and writing (MA); psychology (MA).

PhD Program in Interdisciplinary Studies Postbaccalaureate distance learning degree programs offered (minimal on-campus study). Offers interdisciplinary studies (PhD). Individually-designed interdisciplinary programs.

Program in Clinical Psychology Offers clinical psychology (Psy D).

Program in Education (Florida Campus) Offers education (M Ed, Ed S).

Program in Education (Vermont Campus) Offers education (M Ed).

Program in Psychology and Counseling Offers psychology and counseling (MA).

UNION THEOLOGICAL SEMINARY AND PRESBYTERIAN SCHOOL OF CHRISTIAN EDUCATION, Richmond, VA 23227-4597

General Information Independent-religious, coed, graduate-only institution. *Graduate housing:* Rooms and/or apartments available on a first-come, first-served basis to single and married students.

GRADUATE UNITS

School of Christian Education *Degree program information:* Part-time and evening/weekend programs available. Postbaccalaureate distance learning degree programs offered (minimal on-campus study). Offers Christian education (MA, MATS).

School of Theological Studies Offers theological studies (M Div, Th M, D Min, PhD).

UNION THEOLOGICAL SEMINARY IN THE CITY OF NEW YORK, New York, NY 10027-5710

General Information Independent-religious, coed, graduate-only institution. *Graduate housing:* Rooms and/or apartments available on a first-come, first-served basis to single and married students. Housing application deadline: 5/15.

GRADUATE UNITS

Graduate and Professional Programs *Degree program information:* Part-time programs available. Offers theology (M Div, MA, STM, Ed D, PhD).

UNION UNIVERSITY, Jackson, TN 38305-3697

General Information Independent-religious, coed, comprehensive institution. *Graduate housing:* Rooms and/or apartments available on a first-come, first-served basis to single and married students.

GRADUATE UNITS

Institute for International and Intercultural Studies *Degree program information:* Part-time and evening/weekend programs available. Offers international and intercultural studies (MAIS). Electronic applications accepted.

McAfee School of Business Administration *Degree program information:* Evening/weekend programs available. Offers business administration (MBA). Also available at Germantown campus. Electronic applications accepted.

School of Christian Studies Offers Christian studies (MCS); expository preaching (D Min).

School of Education *Degree program information:* Part-time and evening/weekend programs available. Offers education (M Ed, MA Ed); education administration generalist (Ed S); educational leadership (Ed D); educational supervision (Ed S); higher education (Ed D). M Ed also available at Germantown campus.

School of Nursing Offers executive leadership (DNP); nurse anesthesia (DNP); nurse anesthetist (PMC); nurse practitioner (DNP); nursing education (MSN, PMC). Electronic applications accepted.

UNITED STATES ARMY COMMAND AND GENERAL STAFF COLLEGE, Fort Leavenworth, KS 66027-2301

General Information Federally supported, coed, primarily men, graduate-only institution. *Graduate housing:* Rooms and/or apartments available to single and married students.

GRADUATE UNITS

Graduate Program Offers military art and science (MMAS). Only career military officers are selected to attend United States Army Command and General Staff College; Graduate Program is voluntary for first-year students, but mandatory for second-year students.

UNITED STATES INTERNATIONAL UNIVERSITY, Nairobi 00800, Kenya

General Information Independent, coed, comprehensive institution. *Graduate housing:* Room and/or apartments available on a first-come, first-served basis to single students; on-campus housing not available to married students. Housing application deadline: 7/31.

GRADUATE UNITS

School of Arts and Sciences *Degree program information:* Part-time and evening/weekend programs available. Offers counseling psychology (MA); international relations (MA).

School of Business Administration *Degree program information:* Part-time and evening/weekend programs available. Offers finance (MBA); information technology management (MBA); integrated studies (MBA); management and organizational development (MS); marketing (MBA); strategic management (MBA).

UNITED STATES SPORTS ACADEMY, Daphne, AL 36526-7055

General Information Independent, coed, upper-level institution. *Graduate faculty:* 13 full-time (1 woman), 21 part-time/adjunct (4 women). *Graduate housing:* On-campus housing not available. *Student services:* Campus employment opportunities, campus safety program, career counseling, exercise/wellness program, free psychological counseling, international student services, low-cost health insurance. *Web address:* http://www.ussa.edu/.

General Application Contact: Craig T. Bogar, Associate Dean of Student Services, 251-626-3303 Ext. 7147, Fax: 251-625-1035, E-mail: cbogar@ussa.edu.

GRADUATE UNITS

Graduate Programs *Degree program information:* Part-time programs available. Postbaccalaureate distance learning degree programs offered (no on-campus study). Offers health and fitness management (MSS); sport coaching (MSS); sport management (MSS, DSM, Ed D); sport studies (MSS); sports medicine (MSS). Electronic applications accepted.

UNITED TALMUDICAL SEMINARY, Brooklyn, NY 11211-7900

General Information Independent-religious, men only, comprehensive institution.

GRADUATE UNITS

Graduate Programs

UNITED THEOLOGICAL SEMINARY, Trotwood, OH 45426

General Information Independent-religious, coed, graduate-only institution. *Enrollment by degree level:* 105 first professional, 22 master's, 101 doctoral. *Graduate faculty:* 15 full-time (8 women), 34 part-time/adjunct (6 women). *Tuition:* Full-time $9746; part-time $443 per hour. *Required fees:* $80 per semester. Tuition and fees vary according to course load. *Student services:* Campus employment opportunities, international student services, writing training. *Library facilities:* Memorial Library. *Collection:* 138,384 titles, 518 serial subscriptions, 8,038 audiovisual materials.

Computer facilities: 12 computers available on campus for general student use. A campuswide network can be accessed. *Web address:* http://www.united.edu/.

United Theological Seminary (continued)

General Application Contact: Thomas Miller, Admissions Officer, 937-529-2201 Ext. 3307, Fax: 937-529-2292, E-mail: utsadmis@united.edu.

GRADUATE UNITS

Graduate and Professional Programs Expenses: Contact institution. *Financial support:* In 2008–09, 87 students received support. Career-related internships or fieldwork, Federal Work-Study, and scholarships/grants available. Financial award application deadline: 4/1; financial award applicants required to submit CSS PROFILE or FAFSA. *Degree program information:* Part-time and evening/weekend programs available. Offers theology (M Div, MA, MATS, D Min). *Application deadline:* For fall admission, 8/1 for domestic students, 1/15 for international students; for spring admission, 1/1 for domestic students. Applications are processed on a rolling basis. *Application fee:* $40. Electronic applications accepted. *Application Contact:* Linda Rice, Admissions Officer, 937-529-2201 Ext. 3307, Fax: 937-529-2292, E-mail: utsadmis@united.edu. *Director of Academic and Student Services,* Rev. Julie M. Hostetter, 937-529-2201 Ext. 330, Fax: 937-529-2292, E-mail: jhostetter@united.edu.

UNITED THEOLOGICAL SEMINARY OF THE TWIN CITIES, New Brighton, MN 55112-2598

General Information Independent-religious, coed, graduate-only institution. *Enrollment by degree level:* 88 first professional, 35 master's, 29 doctoral, 1 other advanced degree. *Graduate faculty:* 10 full-time (6 women), 24 part-time/adjunct (12 women). *Tuition:* Full-time $11,070; part-time $410 per credit hour. *Required fees:* $295; $135 per term. One-time fee: $25. Tuition and fees vary according to course load, degree level and program. *Graduate housing:* Rooms and/or apartments available on a first-come, first-served basis to single and married students. Typical cost: $5670 per year for single students; $5670 per year for married students. *Student services:* Campus employment opportunities, free psychological counseling, international student services, multicultural affairs office, services for students with disabilities, writing training. *Library facilities:* Spencer Library. *Online resources:* library catalog, web page. *Collection:* 167,814 titles, 213 serial subscriptions, 550 audiovisual materials.

Computer facilities: 13 computers available on campus for general student use. A campuswide network can be accessed from student residence rooms. Software discount program available. *Web address:* http://www.unitedseminary.edu/.

General Application Contact: Rev. Glen Herrington-Hall, Director of Admissions, 651-255-6107, Fax: 651-633-4315, E-mail: gherrington-hall@unitedseminary.edu.

GRADUATE UNITS

Graduate and Professional Programs Students: 60 full-time (34 women), 93 part-time (60 women); includes 10 minority (5 African Americans, 1 American Indian/Alaska Native, 3 Asian Americans or Pacific Islanders, 1 Hispanic American), 1 international. Average age 47. 39 applicants, 100% accepted, 32 enrolled. *Faculty:* 10 full-time (6 women), 24 part-time/adjunct (12 women). Expenses: Contact institution. *Financial support:* In 2008–09, 98 students received support. Career-related internships or fieldwork, institutionally sponsored loans, and scholarships/grants available. Support available to part-time students. Financial award application deadline: 5/1; financial award applicants required to submit FAFSA. In 2008, 21 first professional degrees, 9 master's awarded. *Degree program information:* Part-time and evening/weekend programs available. Offers advanced theological studies (Diploma); justice and peace studies (M Div); leadership toward racial justice (MA, Certificate); Methodist studies (M Div, MA); ministry (D Min); ministry renewal and professional development (Certificate); pastoral care and counseling (M Div); religion and theology (MA); theological and religious studies (Certificate); theology and the arts (MA); urban ministry (MARL); women's studies: religion, theology and ministry (MA). *Application deadline:* For fall admission, 7/1 priority date for domestic students, 11/1 priority date for international students; for winter admission, 11/1 priority date for domestic students; for spring admission, 11/15 priority date for domestic students. Applications are processed on a rolling basis. *Application fee:* $50. *Application Contact:* Rev. Glen Herrington-Hall, Director of Admissions, 651-255-6107 Ext. 107, Fax: 651-633-4315, E-mail: gherrington-hall@unitedseminary.edu. *Dean of the Seminary,* Dr. Richard D. Weis, 651-255-6108 Ext. 108, Fax: 651-633-4315, E-mail: rweis@unitedseminary.edu.

UNIVERSIDAD ADVENTISTA DE LAS ANTILLAS, Mayagüez, PR 00681-0118

General Information Independent-religious, coed, comprehensive institution. *Graduate housing:* Rooms and/or apartments available on a first-come, first-served basis to single and married students.

GRADUATE UNITS

EGECED Department Electronic applications accepted.

UNIVERSIDAD CENTRAL DEL CARIBE, Bayamón, PR 00960-6032

General Information Independent, coed. *Graduate housing:* On-campus housing not available.

GRADUATE UNITS

Program in Substance Abuse Counseling Offers substance abuse counseling (MHS).

School of Medicine Offers anatomy and cell biology (MA, MS); biomedical sciences (MA); medicine (MD, MA, MS); microbiology and immunology (MA, MS); pharmacology (MS); physiology (MS).

UNIVERSIDAD DE LAS AMERICAS, A.C., 06700 Mexico City, Mexico

General Information Independent, comprehensive institution.

GRADUATE UNITS

Program in Business Administration Offers finance (MBA); marketing research (MBA); production and quality (MBA).

Program in Education Offers education (M Ed).

Program in International Organizations and Institutions Offers international organizations and institutions (MA).

Program in Psychology Offers family therapy (MA).

UNIVERSIDAD DE LAS AMÉRICAS–PUEBLA, 72820 Puebla, Mexico

General Information Independent, coed, comprehensive institution. *Graduate housing:* On-campus housing not available. *Research affiliation:* Empacadora San Marcos S.A. de C.U. (food service), Volkswagen de México S.A. de C.U. (mechanical engineering), Institute Mexicano del Tecnologá del agua (electronic engineering), Frugosa S.A. de C.U. (chemical engineering).

GRADUATE UNITS

Division of Graduate Studies *Degree program information:* Part-time and evening/weekend programs available.

School of Business and Economics *Degree program information:* Part-time and evening/weekend programs available. Offers business administration (MBA); finance (M Adm).

School of Engineering *Degree program information:* Part-time and evening/weekend programs available. Offers chemical engineering (MS); computer science (MS); construction management (M Adm); electronic engineering (MS); engineering (M Adm, MS, PhD); food sciences (MS); food technology (MS); industrial engineering (MS); manufacturing administration (MS); production management (M Adm).

School of Humanities *Degree program information:* Part-time and evening/weekend programs available. Offers humanities (MA); information design (MA); linguistics (MA); literature (MA).

School of Sciences *Degree program information:* Part-time and evening/weekend programs available. Offers biotechnology (MS); clinical analysis (biomedicine) (MS); sciences (MS).

School of Social Sciences *Degree program information:* Part-time and evening/weekend programs available. Offers American studies (MA); anthropology (MA); archaeology (MA); economics (MA); education (MA); finance (M Adm); psychology (MA); social sciences (M Adm, MA).

UNIVERSIDAD DEL ESTE, Carolina, PR 00983

General Information Independent, coed, comprehensive institution.

GRADUATE UNITS

Graduate School

UNIVERSIDAD DEL TURABO, Gurabo, PR 00778-3030

General Information Independent, coed, comprehensive institution. CGS member. *Graduate housing:* On-campus housing not available.

GRADUATE UNITS

Graduate Programs *Degree program information:* Part-time and evening/weekend programs available. Postbaccalaureate distance learning degree programs offered. Offers administration of school libraries (M Ed); athletic training (MPE); bilingual education (MA); coaching (MPE); curriculum and instruction and appropriate environment (D Ed); curriculum and teaching (M Ed); education administration and supervision (MA); educational administration (M Ed); educational leadership (D Ed); environmental analysis (MS); environmental management (MS); environmental sciences (DS); guidance counseling (M Ed); library service and information technology (M Ed); special education (MA); teaching at primary level (M Ed); teaching English as a second language (MA); teaching of fine arts (MFA); wellness (MPE).

School in Business Administration *Degree program information:* Part-time and evening/weekend programs available. Offers accounting (MBA); business administration (MBA, DBA); human resources (MBA); logistics and materials management (MBA); management (MBA, DBA); management of information systems (MBA, DBA); marketing (MBA); materials management (MBA); office systems management (MBA); project management (MBA); quality management (MBA); taxation (MBA).

School of Engineering Offers engineering (MS Eng); telecommunication and network administration (MS Eng).

School of Health Sciences Offers clinical nurse leader (MSN); family nurse practitioner (MSN, Advanced Certificate); family nurse practitioner—adult nursing (MSN); health sciences (MS, MSN, Advanced Certificate); speech and language pathology (MS).

School of Social Sciences and Humanities Offers arts administration (MA); counseling psychology (MSS); criminal justice studies (MPA); forensic science (MSS); human services administration (MPA); school psychology (MSS); social sciences and humanities (MA, MPA, MSS).

UNIVERSIDAD DE MONTERREY, 66238 San Pedro Garza García, NL, Mexico

General Information Independent-religious, coed, comprehensive institution.

GRADUATE UNITS

Graduate Programs

UNIVERSIDAD FLET, Miami, FL 33186

General Information Independent-religious, coed, comprehensive institution.

GRADUATE UNITS

Graduate Program

UNIVERSIDAD METROPOLITANA, San Juan, PR 00928-1150

General Information Independent, coed, comprehensive institution. *Graduate housing:* On-campus housing not available. *Research affiliation:* Berkeley National Laboratories (bioremediation), University Consortium of Atmospheric Research (computer science, atmospheric science), University of Colorado at Boulder (computer science, biology), University of Puerto Rico (physics, chemistry), University of Utah (computational chemistry), Howard University (computational chemistry).

GRADUATE UNITS

Graduate Programs in Education *Degree program information:* Part-time and evening/weekend programs available. Offers administration and supervision (MA); curriculum and teaching (MA); educational administration and supervision (MA); environmental education (MA); fitness management (MA); managing leisure services (MA); pre-school centers administration (MA); pre-school education (MA); special education (MA); teaching of physical education (MA). Electronic applications accepted.

School of Business Administration *Degree program information:* Part-time and evening/weekend programs available. Offers accounting (MBA); finance (MBA); human resources management (MBA); international business (MBA); management (MBA); marketing (MBA); public accounting (Certificate). Electronic applications accepted.

School of Environmental Affairs *Degree program information:* Part-time programs available. Offers conservation and management of natural resources (MEM); environmental education (MA); environmental planning (MEM); environmental risk and assessment management (MEM). Electronic applications accepted.

UNIVERSITÉ DE MONCTON, Moncton, NB E1A 3E9, Canada

General Information Province-supported, coed, comprehensive institution. *Graduate housing:* Rooms and/or apartments available on a first-come, first-served basis to single and married students.

GRADUATE UNITS

Faculty of Administration Students: 41 full-time (13 women), 133 part-time (70 women), 27 international. Average age 28. 77 applicants, 43% accepted, 17 enrolled. *Faculty:* 24 full-time (7 women), 20 part-time/adjunct (1 woman). Expenses: Contact institution. *Financial support:* In 2008–09, 7 fellowships (averaging $2,500 per year) were awarded; teaching assistantships, institutionally sponsored loans also available. Support available to part-time students. Financial award application deadline: 5/30. In 2008, 39 master's awarded. *Degree program information:* Part-time and evening/weekend programs available. Postbaccalaureate distance learning degree programs offered (no on-campus study). Offers administration (MBA). *Application deadline:* For fall admission, 6/1 for domestic students, 2/1 for international students; for winter admission, 11/15 for domestic students, 9/1 for international students; for spring admission, 3/31 for domestic students, 1/1 for international students. Applications are processed on a rolling basis. *Application fee:* $39. *Application Contact:* Natalie Allain, Admission Counselor, 506-858-4273, Fax: 506-858-4093, E-mail: natalie.allain@umoncton.ca. *Director,* Dr. Nha Nguyen, 506-858-4231, Fax: 506-858-4093, E-mail: nha.nguyen@umoncton.ca.

Faculty of Arts and Social Sciences *Degree program information:* Part-time programs available. Offers arts and social sciences (MA, MPA, MSW, PhD); economics (MA); French studies (MA, PhD); history (MA); public administration (MPA). Electronic applications accepted.

School of Social Work Offers social work (MSW).

Faculty of Education *Degree program information:* Part-time programs available. Offers education (M Ed, MA Ed).

Graduate Studies in Education *Degree program information:* Part-time programs available. Offers educational psychology (M Ed, MA Ed); guidance (M Ed, MA Ed); school administration (M Ed, MA Ed); teaching (M Ed, MA Ed).

Faculty of Engineering Offers civil engineering (M Sc A); electrical engineering (M Sc A); industrial engineering (M Sc A); mechanical engineering (M Sc A).

Faculty of Law Students: 106 full-time (57 women). Average age 27. 79 applicants, 76% accepted, 36 enrolled. *Faculty:* 12 full-time (5 women), 10 part-time/adjunct (4 women). Expenses: Contact institution. *Financial support:* In 2008–09, 77 fellowships (averaging $2,100 per year) were awarded; career-related internships or fieldwork also available. Financial award application deadline: 10/31. In 2008, 35 first professional degrees, 1 master's awarded. Offers law (LL B, LL M, Diploma). Programs offered exclusively in French. *Application deadline:* For fall admission, 3/31 priority date for domestic students, 2/1 priority date for international students. Applications are processed on a rolling basis. *Application fee:* $39. *Application Contact:* Robert Le Blanc, Associate Dean, 506-863-2127, Fax: 506-858-4534, E-mail: robert.l.leblanc@umoncton.ca. *Dean,* Marie-France Albert, 506-858-4560, Fax: 506-858-4534, E-mail: marie-france.albert@umoncton.ca.

Faculty of Science *Degree program information:* Part-time programs available. Offers biochemistry (M Sc); biology (M Sc); chemistry (M Sc); information technology (M Sc, Certificate, Diploma); mathematics (M Sc); physics and astronomy (M Sc); science (M Sc, Certificate, Diploma). Electronic applications accepted.

School of Food Science, Nutrition and Family Studies *Degree program information:* Part-time programs available. Offers foods/nutrition (M Sc). Electronic applications accepted.

UNIVERSITÉ DE MONTRÉAL, Montréal, QC H3C 3J7, Canada

General Information Independent, coed, university. CGS member. *Enrollment:* 8,596 full-time matriculated graduate/professional students (5,087 women), 2,199 part-time matriculated graduate/professional students (1,558 women). *Graduate faculty:* 1,809 full-time (581 women), 1,822 part-time/adjunct (682 women). *Graduate housing:* Room and/or apartments available on a first-come, first-served basis to single students; on-campus housing not available to married students. Housing application deadline: 2/1. *Student services:* Campus safety program, career counseling, child daycare facilities, exercise/wellness program, free psychological counseling, international student services, low-cost health insurance, services for students with disabilities. *Library facilities:* Bibliotheque des lettres et sciences humaines plus 18 others. *Online resources:* library catalog, web page. *Collection:* 4 million titles, 18,330 serial subscriptions. *Research affiliation:* Centre Hospitalier Universitaire Mère-Enfant de l'Hôpital Sainte-Justine (pédiatric, urgentologie pédiatrique et périnatalogie), Centre de Recherche de L'Hôpital Sacré-Coeur (maladies cardiovasculaires, maladies rénales, maladies respiratoires, neurobiologie psychiatrique et troubles du sommeil et traumatologie), Institut de recherches cliniques de Montréal (bioéthique, cancer, chimie bioorganique, génétique, hématolgie, immunologie, neurosciences et endocrinologie, systeme cardiovasculaire), Institut de Cardiologie de Montréal (cardiologie, médicine et chirurgie cardiovasculaires, prévention et réadaption), Institut Universitaire de gériatric de Montréal (gérontologie clinique et gériatric neurosciences cognitives, soins et services, nutrition et les troubles sensoriels).

Computer facilities: 1,500 computers available on campus for general student use. A campuswide network can be accessed from student residence rooms and from off campus. Online class registration is available. *Web address:* http://www.umontreal.ca/.

General Application Contact: Louise Beliveau, Dean of Graduate Studies, 514-343-6537, E-mail: louise.beliveau@umontreal.ca.

GRADUATE UNITS

Department of Kinesiology Students: 68 full-time (42 women), 14 part-time (8 women). Average age 26. 103 applicants, 31% accepted, 17 enrolled. *Faculty:* 15 full-time (3 women), 15 part-time/adjunct (3 women). Expenses: Contact institution. *Financial support:* In 2008–09, 3 fellowships (averaging $20,000 per year), 10 research assistantships (averaging $5,000 per year), 6 teaching assistantships (averaging $7,000 per year) were awarded. Financial award application deadline: 2/1. In 2008, 10 master's, 3 doctorates, 2 other advanced degrees awarded. Offers kinesiology (M Sc, Certificate, DESS); physical activity (M Sc, PhD). *Application deadline:* For fall admission, 2/1 priority date for domestic students; for winter admission, 11/1 priority date for domestic students; for spring admission, 2/1 priority date for domestic students. *Application fee:* $100. Electronic applications accepted. *Application Contact:* Francine Normandeau, Information Contact, 514-343-6152, E-mail: francine.normandeau@umontreal.ca. *Director,* Francois Prince, 514-343-6116, Fax: 514-343-2181, E-mail: francois.prince@umontreal.ca.

Faculty of Arts and Sciences Students: 3,573 full-time (2,022 women), 362 part-time (264 women). 3,590 applicants, 33% accepted, 1006 enrolled. *Faculty:* 732 full-time (200 women), 134 part-time/adjunct (43 women). Expenses: Contact institution. *Financial support:* Fellowships, research assistantships, teaching assistantships, career-related internships or fieldwork, Federal Work-Study, institutionally sponsored loans, and tuition waivers (full and partial) available. Support available to part-time students. In 2008, 750 master's, 169 doctorates, 62 other advanced degrees awarded. *Degree program information:* Part-time programs available. Offers anthropology (M Sc, PhD); applied human sciences (PhD); art history (MA, PhD); arts and sciences (M Sc, MA, MBSI, PhD, Certificate, DESS); biological sciences (M Sc, PhD); chemistry (M Sc, PhD); communication (PhD); communication in changing organizations (Certificate); communication sciences (M Sc); comparative literature (MA); computer systems (M Sc, PhD); demography (M Sc, PhD); economic sciences (M Sc, PhD); English studies (MA, PhD); environment and durable development (DESS); film studies (MA, PhD); French literature (MA, PhD); geography (M Sc, PhD, DESS); geomatical and spatial analysis (Certificate); German literature (PhD); German studies (MA); Hispanic literature (PhD); Hispanic studies (MA); history (MA, PhD); linguistics and translation (MA, PhD, DESS); literature (PhD); literature and cinema (PhD); mathematics (M Sc, PhD); museology (MA); philosophy (MA, PhD); physics (M Sc, PhD); political science (M Sc, PhD); psychology (M Sc, PhD); sociology (M Sc, PhD); statistics (M Sc, PhD). *Application deadline:* For fall admission, 2/1 priority date for domestic students; for winter admission, 11/1 priority date for domestic students; for spring admission, 2/1 priority date for domestic students. *Application fee:* $100. Electronic applications accepted. *Application Contact:* Jane Janson, Associate Dean of Graduate Studies, 514-343-7391, E-mail: jane.jenson@umontreal.a. *Dean,* G??rard Boismenu, 514-343-6262, Fax: 514-343-2185.

School of Criminology Students: 69 full-time (56 women), 132 part-time (102 women). 143 applicants, 48% accepted, 62 enrolled. *Faculty:* 24 full-time (6 women). Expenses: Contact institution. *Financial support:* Fellowships, research assistantships, teaching assistantships, career-related internships or fieldwork available. Financial award application deadline: 3/15. In 2008, 28 master's, 5 doctorates awarded. Offers criminology (M Sc, PhD). *Application deadline:* For fall admission, 2/1 for domestic students. Applications are processed on a rolling basis. *Application fee:* $100. Electronic applications accepted. *Application Contact:* Jo-Anne Wemmers, Graduate Student Affairs (M Sc), 514-343-6111 Ext. 4864, Fax: 514-343-5650, E-mail: jo-anne.m.wemmers@umontreal.ca. *Chairman,* Marie-Marthe Cousineau, 514-343-7322, Fax: 514-343-5650, E-mail: mm.cousineau@umontreal.ca.

School of Industrial Relations Students: 42 full-time (32 women), 97 part-time (74 women). 131 applicants, 38% accepted, 44 enrolled. *Faculty:* 22 full-time (5 women), 2 part-time/adjunct (1 woman). Expenses: Contact institution. *Financial support:* Fellowships, research assistantships, teaching assistantships, tuition waivers (full) available. In 2008, 21 master's, 3 doctorates, 11 other advanced degrees awarded. *Degree program information:* Part-time programs available. Offers industrial relations (M Sc, PhD, DESS). *Application deadline:* For fall admission, 2/1 priority date for domestic students; for winter admission, 11/1 priority date for domestic students; for spring admission, 2/1 priority date for domestic students. *Application fee:* $100. Electronic applications accepted. *Application Contact:* Jean Charest, Responsible for Graduate Studies (MSc), 514-343-7743, Fax: 514-343-5764, E-mail: jean.charest@umontreal.ca. *Director and Responsible for Graduate Studies (PhD),* Tania Saba, 514-343-5553, Fax: 514-343-5764, E-mail: tania.saba@umontreal.ca.

School of Library and Information Sciences Students: 140 full-time (95 women), 50 part-time (39 women). 199 applicants, 49% accepted, 89 enrolled. *Faculty:* 17 full-time (6 women), 7 part-time/adjunct (4 women). Expenses: Contact institution. *Financial support:* Fellowships available. In 2008, 68 master's awarded. Offers information sciences (MBSI, PhD). *Application deadline:* For fall admission, 2/1 priority date for domestic students; for winter admission, 11/1 priority date for domestic students; for spring admission, 2/1 priority date for domestic students. *Application fee:* $100. Electronic applications accepted. *Application Contact:* Mich??le Hudon, Professor/Responsible for Graduate Studies (PhD), 514-343-6046, Fax: 514-343-5753, E-mail: michele.hudon@umontreal.ca. *Director and Responsible for Graduate Studies (MSc),* Jean-Michel Salaun, 514-343-7400, Fax: 514-343-5753, E-mail: jean-michel.salaun@umontreal.ca.

School of Psychoeducation Students: 69 full-time (60 women), 51 part-time (47 women). 139 applicants, 36% accepted, 47 enrolled. *Faculty:* 16 full-time (5 women), 4 part-time/adjunct (2 women). Expenses: Contact institution. *Financial support:* Fellowships, research assistantships, teaching assistantships, career-related internships or fieldwork and institutionally sponsored loans available. Support available to part-time students. In 2008, 23 master's awarded. *Degree program information:* Part-time programs available. Offers psychoeducation (M Sc, PhD, Certificate). *Application deadline:* For fall admission, 2/1 priority date for domestic students; for winter admission, 11/1 priority date for domestic students; for spring admission, 2/1 priority date for domestic students. *Application fee:* $100. Electronic applications accepted. *Application Contact:* Lyse Turgeon, Graduate Chairperson (MSc), 514-343-6111 Ext. 2559, Fax: 514-343-6951, E-mail: lyse.turgeon@umontreal.ca. *Chairperson and Responsible for Graduate Studies (PhD),* Sophie Parent, 514-343-7421, Fax: 514-343-6951, E-mail: sophie.parent@umontreal.ca.

School of Social Service Students: 24 full-time (21 women), 120 part-time (99 women). 150 applicants, 26% accepted, 37 enrolled. *Faculty:* 27 full-time (15 women), 7 part-time/adjunct (6 women). Expenses: Contact institution. *Financial support:* Research assistantships, teaching assistantships, career-related internships or fieldwork and institutionally sponsored loans available. Financial award application deadline: 9/1. In 2008, 36 master's, 2 doctorates awarded. *Degree program information:* Part-time programs available. Offers social administration (Certificate, DESS); social work (M Sc, PhD). *Application deadline:* For fall admission, 2/1 priority date for domestic students; for winter admission, 11/1 priority date for domestic students; for spring admission, 2/1 priority date for domestic students. *Application fee:* $100. Electronic applications accepted. *Application Contact:* Gilbert Renaud, Responsible, 514-343-2063, Fax: 514-343-2493, E-mail: gilbert.renaud@umontreal.ca. *Director,* Dominique Damant, 514-343-6596, Fax: 514-343-2493, E-mail: dominique.damant@umontreal.ca.

Faculty of Dental Medicine Students: 33 full-time (18 women). 49 applicants, 18% accepted, 9 enrolled. *Faculty:* 12 full-time (5 women), 33 part-time/adjunct (5 women). Expenses: Contact institution. In 2008, 5 master's, 6 Certificates awarded. Offers dental medicine (M Sc, Certificate); multidisciplinary residency (Certificate); oral and dental sciences (M Sc); orthodontics (M Sc); pediatric dentistry (M Sc); prosthodontics rehabilitation (M Sc); stomatology residency (Certificate). *Application deadline:* For fall admission, 10/1 for domestic students. *Application fee:* $100. Electronic applications accepted. *Application Contact:* Anne Charbonneau, Associate Dean for Research, 514-343-5761, Fax: 514-343-2233, E-mail: anne.charbonneau@umontreal.ca. *Dean,* Gilles Lavigne, 514-343-6005, Fax: 514-343-2233, E-mail: gilles.lavigne@umontreal.ca.

Faculty of Education Students: 325 full-time (196 women), 911 part-time (652 women). 819 applicants, 60% accepted, 375 enrolled. *Faculty:* 71 full-time (39 women), 19 part-time/adjunct (9 women). Expenses: Contact institution. *Financial support:* Fellowships, research assistantships, teaching assistantships available. In 2008, 97 master's, 13 doctorates, 144 other advanced degrees awarded. *Degree program information:* Part-time and evening/weekend programs available. Offers administration and foundations of education (M Ed, MA, PhD, DESS); didactics (M Ed, MA, PhD, Certificate, DESS); education (M Ed, MA, PhD, Certificate, DESS); psychopedagogy and andragogy (M Ed, MA, PhD, Certificate, DESS). *Application deadline:* For fall admission, 2/1 priority date for domestic students; for winter admission, 11/1 priority date for domestic students; for spring admission, 2/1 priority date for domestic students. *Application fee:* $100. Electronic applications accepted. *Application Contact:* Francois Bowen, Graduate Chairman and Vice Dean, 514-343-7491, Fax: 514-343-7276, E-mail: francois.bowen@umontreal.ca. *Dean,* Michel D. Laurier, 514-343-6658, Fax: 514-343-7276, E-mail: michel.d.laurier@umontreal.ca.

Faculty of Environmental Design and Planning Students: 279 full-time (148 women), 179 part-time (100 women). 484 applicants, 36% accepted, 150 enrolled. *Faculty:* 39 full-time (11 women), 27 part-time/adjunct (7 women). Expenses: Contact institution. In 2008, 122 master's, 8 doctorates, 15 other advanced degrees awarded. Offers environmental design and planning (M Sc A, M Urb, PhD, DESS). *Application deadline:* For fall admission, 2/1 priority date for domestic students; for winter admission, 11/1 priority date for domestic students; for spring admission, 2/1 priority date for domestic students. *Application fee:* $100. Electronic applications accepted. *Application Contact:* Tilu Poldma, Associate Dean for Graduate Studies, 514-343-2125, Fax: 514-343-2183, E-mail: tilu.poldma@umontreal.ca. *Dean,* Giovanni de Paoli, 514-343-6001, Fax: 514-343-2183, E-mail: giovanni.de.paoli@umontreal.ca.

Faculty of Law Students: 441 full-time (267 women), 85 part-time (53 women). 794 applicants, 41% accepted, 225 enrolled. *Faculty:* 63 full-time (24 women), 6 part-time/adjunct (4 women). Expenses: Contact institution. *Financial support:* Fellowships, research assistantships, teaching assistantships available. In 2008, 40 master's, 7 doctorates, 105 Certificates awarded. *Degree program information:* Part-time programs available. Offers law (LL B, LL M, LL D, Certificate, DDN, DESS). *Application deadline:* For fall admission, 2/1 priority date for domestic students; for winter admission, 11/1 priority date for domestic students; for spring admission, 2/1 priority date for domestic students. *Application fee:* $100. Electronic applications accepted. *Application Contact:* Guy Lefebvre, Associate Dean for Graduate Studies, 514-343-7202, Fax: 514-343-2199, E-mail: guy.lefebvre@umontreal.ca. *Dean,* Gilles Trudeau, 514-343-6469, Fax: 514-343-2199, E-mail: gilles.trudeau@umontreal.ca.

Faculty of Medicine Students: 2,566 full-time (1,593 women), 393 part-time (234 women). 1,562 applicants, 44% accepted, 565 enrolled. *Faculty:* 641 full-time (208 women), 1,364 part-time/adjunct (512 women). Expenses: Contact institution. *Financial support:* Fellowships, research assistantships, teaching assistantships, career-related internships or fieldwork, institutionally sponsored loans, and tuition waivers (full) available. In 2008, 329 master's, 83 doctorates, 221 other advanced degrees awarded. Offers anesthesia (DESS); biochemistry (M Sc, PhD); bioethics (MA, Certificate, DESS); biomedical sciences (M Sc, PhD); biophysics and molecular physiology (M Sc, PhD, DESS); clinical biochemistry (DEPD); community health (M Sc, Certificate, DESS); diagnostic radiology (DESS); environment and prevention (DESS); environment, health and disaster management (DESS); environmental and occupational health (M Sc, Certificate); ergonomics (DESS); family medicine (DESS); gastroenterology (DESS); general training in insurance medicine and expertise in health sciences (Certificate); geriatry (DESS); health administration (M Sc, Certificate, DESS); insurance medicine and expertise in health sciences (DESS); insurance medicine and medicolegal expertise (Certificate, DESS); intensive care (DESS); medical biochemistry (DESS); medical genetics (DESS); medicine (MD, M Sc, M Sc A, MA, PMS, PhD, Certificate, DEPD, DESS); microbiology and immunology (M Sc, PhD); microbiology and infectious diseases (DESS); molecular biology (M Sc, PhD); neurological sciences (M Sc, PhD); nuclear medicine (DESS); nutrition (M Sc, PhD, Certificate, DESS); obstetrics and gynecology (DESS); ophthalmology (DESS); pathology and cellular biology (M Sc, PhD); pediatrics (DESS); pharmacology (M Sc, PhD); physiology (M Sc, PhD); pneumology (DESS); psychiatry (DESS); public health (PhD, Certificate); radiology-oncology (DESS); rheumatology (DESS); surgery (DESS); toxicology and risk analysis (DESS). *Application deadline:* For fall admission, 2/1 priority date for domestic students; for winter admission, 11/1 priority date for domestic students; for spring admission, 2/1 priority date for domestic students. *Application fee:* $100. Electronic applications accepted. *Application Contact:* Dr. Andre Ferron, Vice Dean of Graduate Studies, 514-343-6111 Ext. 0933, Fax: 514-343-5751, E-mail: andre.ferron@umontreal.ca. *Dean,* Dr. Jean-Lucien Rouleau, 514-343-6351, Fax: 514-343-5850, E-mail: jean.rouleau@umontreal.ca.

Institute of Biomedical Engineering Students: 16 full-time (5 women), 29 part-time (11 women). 37 applicants, 24% accepted, 7 enrolled. Expenses: Contact institution. *Financial support:* In 2008–09, 5 fellowships (averaging $15,000 per year) were awarded; career-related internships or fieldwork also available. In 2008, 8 master's, 2 doctorates, 1 other advanced degree awarded. Offers biomedical engineering (M Sc A, PhD, DESS). *Application deadline:* For fall admission, 2/1 priority date for domestic students; for winter admission, 11/1 priority date for domestic students; for spring admission, 2/1 priority date for domestic students. Applications are processed on a rolling basis. *Application fee:* $100. Electronic applications accepted. *Application Contact:* Louise Belanger, Students Files Management Technician, 514-343-6357, Fax: 514-343-6112, E-mail: louise.belanger@

Université de Montréal (continued)

umontreal.ca. *Graduate Adviser,* Aime Robert Leblanc, 514-343-6111 Ext. 5355, Fax: 514-343-6112, E-mail: aime.robert.leblanc@umontreal.ca.

School of Speech Therapy and Audiology Students: 63 full-time (all women), 26 part-time (23 women). 81 applicants, 77% accepted, 61 enrolled. *Faculty:* 14 full-time (9 women), 5 part-time/adjunct (4 women). Expenses: Contact institution. In 2008, 84 master's awarded. Offers audiology (PMS); orthophony (PMS). *Application deadline:* For fall admission, 2/1 for domestic students. *Application fee:* $100. Electronic applications accepted. *Application Contact:* Ana Ines Ansaldo, Responsible for Graduate Studies, 514-343-6111 Ext. 47490, Fax: 514-343-2115, E-mail: ana.ines.ansaldo@umontreal.ca. *Director,* Louise Getty, 514-343-7672, Fax: 514-343-2115.

Faculty of Music Students: 282 full-time (127 women), 4 part-time (3 women). 232 applicants, 43% accepted, 97 enrolled. *Faculty:* 50 full-time (18 women), 45 part-time/adjunct (17 women). Expenses: Contact institution. In 2008, 54 master's, 21 doctorates, 11 other advanced degrees awarded. Offers composition (M Mus, D Mus); musicology and ethnomusicology (MA, PhD); orchestra conducting (M Mus, D Mus); orchestral repertoire (DESS); performance interpretation (DESS); voice and instruments interpretation (M Mus, D Mus). *Application deadline:* For fall admission, 2/1 priority date for domestic students; for winter admission, 11/1 priority date for domestic students; for spring admission, 2/1 priority date for domestic students. *Application fee:* $100. Electronic applications accepted. *Application Contact:* Sylvain Caron, Associate Dean for Graduate Studies, 514-343-6428, Fax: 514-343-5727, E-mail: sylvain.caron@umontreal.ca. *Dean,* Jacques Boucher, 514-343-6429, Fax: 514-343-5727, E-mail: jacques.boucher.2@umontreal.ca.

Faculty of Nursing Students: 153 full-time (140 women), 201 part-time (188 women). 308 applicants, 55% accepted, 149 enrolled. *Faculty:* 32 full-time (26 women), 24 part-time/adjunct (20 women). Expenses: Contact institution. *Financial support:* Fellowships, research assistantships, teaching assistantships, career-related internships or fieldwork, Federal Work-Study, and institutionally sponsored loans available. In 2008, 32 master's, 2 doctorates, 11 other advanced degrees awarded. *Degree program information:* Part-time programs available. Offers nursing (M Sc, PhD, Certificate, DESS). *Application deadline:* For fall admission, 2/1 priority date for domestic students; for winter admission, 11/1 priority date for domestic students; for spring admission, 2/1 priority date for domestic students. Applications are processed on a rolling basis. *Application fee:* $100. Electronic applications accepted. *Application Contact:* Francine Gratton, Vice Dean of Graduate Studies, 514-343-5835, Fax: 514-343-2306, E-mail: francine.gratton@umontreal.ca. *Dean,* Francine Girard, 514-343-6436, Fax: 514-343-2306, E-mail: francine.d.girard@umontreal.ca.

Faculty of Pharmacy Students: 198 full-time (130 women), 113 part-time (76 women). 299 applicants, 47% accepted, 17 enrolled. *Faculty:* 29 full-time (14 women), 32 part-time/adjunct (16 women). Expenses: Contact institution. *Financial support:* Fellowships, teaching assistantships, career-related internships or fieldwork, Federal Work-Study, and institutionally sponsored loans available. In 2008, 18 master's, 11 doctorates, 45 other advanced degrees awarded. *Degree program information:* Part-time programs available. Offers development of medicine (DESS); master pharmacist (DESS); pharmaceutical cares (DESS); pharmaceutical practice (M Sc); pharmaceutical sciences (M Sc, PhD). *Application deadline:* For fall admission, 2/1 priority date for domestic students; for winter admission, 11/1 priority date for domestic students; for spring admission, 2/1 priority date for domestic students. *Application fee:* $100. Electronic applications accepted. *Application Contact:* Daniel Lamontagne, Associate Dean for Graduate Studies, 514-343-6467, Fax: 514-343-2102, E-mail: daniel.lamontagne@umontreal.ca. *Dean,* Pierre Moreau, 514-343-6440, Fax: 514-343-2102, E-mail: pierre.moreau@umontreal.edu.

Faculty of Theology and Sciences of Religions Students: 83 full-time (20 women), 17 part-time (12 women). 74 applicants, 36% accepted, 24 enrolled. *Faculty:* 23 full-time (7 women), 5 part-time/adjunct (1 woman). Expenses: Contact institution. *Financial support:* Research assistantships, teaching assistantships, institutionally sponsored loans and tuition waivers (partial) available. In 2008, 14 master's, 7 doctorates awarded. Offers theology and sciences of religions (MA, D Th, PhD, Certificate, DESS, L Th). *Application deadline:* For fall admission, 2/1 priority date for domestic students; for winter admission, 11/1 priority date for domestic students; for spring admission, 2/1 priority date for domestic students. *Application fee:* $100. Electronic applications accepted. *Application Contact:* Jean-Fran??ois Roussel, Associate Dean of Graduate Studies, 514-343-6840, Fax: 514-343-5738, E-mail: jean-francois.roussel@umontreal.ca. *Dean,* Jean-Claude Breton, 514-343-7160, Fax: 514-343-5738, E-mail: jean-claude.breton@umontreal.ca.

Faculty of Veterinary Medicine Students: 161 full-time (102 women), 30 part-time (24 women). 69 applicants, 46% accepted, 32 enrolled. *Faculty:* 36 full-time (7 women), 49 part-time/adjunct (15 women). Expenses: Contact institution. *Financial support:* Research assistantships, teaching assistantships, career-related internships or fieldwork and scholarships/grants available. In 2008, 24 master's, 4 doctorates, 33 other advanced degrees awarded. Offers veterinary medicine (DVM, M Sc, DES, PhD, Certificate, DESS); veterinary sciences (M Sc, DES, PhD, Certificate, DESS); virology and immunology (PhD). *Application deadline:* For fall admission, 2/1 priority date for domestic students; for winter admission, 11/1 priority date for domestic students; for spring admission, 2/1 priority date for domestic students. *Application fee:* $100. Electronic applications accepted. *Application Contact:* Mario Jacques, Associate Dean, Graduate Studies, 514-343-6111 Ext. 8348, Fax: 450-778-8105, E-mail: mario.jacques@umontreal.ca. *Dean,* Jean Sirois, 514-343-6111 Ext. 8542, Fax: 450-778-8101, E-mail: jean.sirois@umontreal.ca.

School of Optometry Students: 36 full-time (28 women), 14 part-time (10 women). 42 applicants, 57% accepted, 24 enrolled. *Faculty:* 11 full-time (3 women), 16 part-time/adjunct (7 women). Expenses: Contact institution. *Financial support:* Research assistantships, teaching assistantships, career-related internships or fieldwork available. Support available to part-time students. In 2008, 7 master's, 13 DESSs awarded. *Degree program information:* Part-time programs available. Offers optometry (OD, M Sc, DESS); vision sciences (M Sc). *Application deadline:* For fall admission, 2/1 priority date for domestic students; for winter admission, 11/1 priority date for domestic students; for spring admission, 2/1 priority date for domestic students. *Application fee:* $100. Electronic applications accepted. *Application Contact:* Christian Casanova, Chairperson, 514-343-2407, Fax: 514-343-2382, E-mail: christian.casanova@umontreal.ca. *Director,* Jacques Gresset, 514-343-6948, Fax: 514-343-2382, E-mail: jacques.gresset@umontreal.ca.

UNIVERSITÉ DE SHERBROOKE, Sherbrooke, QC J1K 2R1, Canada

General Information Independent, coed, university. *Graduate housing:* Room and/or apartments available to single students; on-campus housing not available to married students. Housing application deadline: 6/1. *Research affiliation:* Société de Microélectronique Industrielle.

GRADUATE UNITS

Faculty of Administration Students: 252 full-time (119 women), 243 part-time (96 women). *Faculty:* 20 full-time. Expenses: Contact institution. *Financial support:* Career-related internships or fieldwork available. In 2008, 395 master's awarded. *Degree program information:* Part-time and evening/weekend programs available. Offers accounting (M Sc); administration (M Sc, M Tax, MBA, DBA, Diploma); business administration (MBA, DBA); finance (M Sc); international business (M Sc); management information systems (M Sc); marketing (M Sc); organizational change and intervention (M Sc); taxation (M Tax, Diploma). *Application fee:* $30. *Application Contact:* Jacques Carbonneau, Registrar, 819-821-7685, Fax: 819-821-7966. *Dean,* Roch Godbout, 819-821-7311.

Faculty of Education *Degree program information:* Part-time and evening/weekend programs available. Offers education (M Ed, MA, Diploma); elementary education (M Ed, Diploma); postsecondary education training (M Ed, Diploma); school administration (M Ed); sciences of education (MA); special education (M Ed, Diploma).

Faculty of Engineering *Degree program information:* Part-time programs available. Offers chemical engineering (M Sc A, PhD); civil engineering (M Sc A, PhD); electrical engineering (M Sc A, PhD); engineering (M Eng, M Env, M Sc A, PhD, Diploma); engineering management (M Eng, Diploma); environment (M Env); mechanical engineering (M Sc A, PhD). Electronic applications accepted.

Faculty of Law *Degree program information:* Part-time and evening/weekend programs available. Offers alternative dispute resolution (LL M, Diploma); biotechnology (LL B); business administration (LL B); business law (Diploma); health law (LL M, Diploma); law (LL B, LL D); legal management (Diploma); notarial law (DDN); transnational law (Diploma). Electronic applications accepted.

Faculty of Letters and Human Sciences *Degree program information:* Part-time programs available. Offers comparative Canadian literature (MA, PhD); economics (MA); French literature (MA, PhD); geography and remote sensing (M Sc, PhD); gerontology (MA); history (MA); letters and human sciences (M Psych, M Sc, MA, MSS, PhD, Diploma); linguistics (MA); lit&erature de crèation (MA, PhD); philosophy (MA); social service (MSS); theatre (MA).

Institute of Management and Development of Cooperatives Offers management and development of cooperatives (MA, Diploma).

Faculty of Medicine and Health Sciences *Degree program information:* Part-time programs available. Offers medicine (MD); medicine and health sciences (MD, M Sc, PhD). Electronic applications accepted.

Graduate Programs in Medicine *Degree program information:* Part-time programs available. Offers biochemistry (M Sc, PhD); cell biology (M Sc, PhD); clinical sciences (M Sc, PhD); immunology (M Sc, PhD); medicine (M Sc, PhD); microbiology (M Sc, PhD); pharmacology (M Sc, PhD); physiology and biophysics (M Sc, PhD); radiobiology (M Sc, PhD). Electronic applications accepted.

Faculty of Physical Education and Sports *Degree program information:* Part-time programs available. Offers kinanthropology (M Sc); physical activity (Diploma); physical education (M Sc, Diploma).

Faculty of Sciences Offers biology (M Sc, PhD, Diploma); chemistry (M Sc, PhD, Diploma); informatics (M Sc, PhD); mathematics (M Sc, PhD); physics (M Sc, PhD); sciences (M Sc, PhD, Diploma).

Centre de Formation en Technologies de L'information Offers information technologies (M Sc, Diploma). Electronic applications accepted.

Centre Universitaire de Formation en Environnement Postbaccalaureate distance learning degree programs offered (no on-campus study). Offers environment (M Sc, Diploma). Electronic applications accepted.

Faculty of Theology, Ethics and Philosophy *Degree program information:* Part-time and evening/weekend programs available. Postbaccalaureate distance learning degree programs offered. Offers applied ethics (Diploma); human science of religions (MA); intercultural training (Diploma); philosophy (MA, PhD); spiritual anthropology (Diploma); theology (MA, PhD, Diploma).

UNIVERSITÉ DU QUÉBEC À CHICOUTIMI, Chicoutimi, QC G7H 2B1, Canada

General Information Province-supported, coed, university. CGS member. *Graduate housing:* Room and/or apartments available to single students; on-campus housing not available to married students.

GRADUATE UNITS

Graduate Programs *Degree program information:* Part-time programs available. Offers didactics of French-mother tongue (Diploma); earth sciences (M Sc A); education (M Ed, MA, PhD); engineering (M Sc A, PhD); ethics (Diploma); fine arts (MA); genetics (M Sc); linguistics (MA); literary studies (MA); mineral resources (PhD); project management (M Sc); regional studies (MA); renewable resources (M Sc); small and medium-sized organization management (M Sc); theology (pastoral studies) (MA, PhD).

UNIVERSITÉ DU QUÉBEC À MONTRÉAL, Montréal, QC H3C 3P8, Canada

General Information Province-supported, coed, university. CGS member. *Graduate housing:* Room and/or apartments available to single students; on-campus housing not available to married students. *Research affiliation:* Labopharm, Inc. (pharmacology), Hydro-Québec (environmental sciences), Bell (computer sciences), Microcréatif (computer sciences), University Corporation for Atmospheric Resources.

GRADUATE UNITS

Graduate Programs *Degree program information:* Part-time programs available. Offers accounting (M Sc, MPA, Diploma); actuarial sciences (Diploma); art history (PhD); art studies (MA); atmospheric sciences (M Sc); biology (M Sc, PhD); business administration (MBA); business administration (research) (MBA); chemistry (M Sc, PhD); communications (MA, PhD); dance (MA); death (Diploma); Earth and atmospheric sciences (PhD); Earth science (M Sc); earth sciences (M Sc); economics (M Sc, PhD); education (M Ed, MA, PhD); education of the environmental sciences (Diploma); environmental sciences (M Sc, PhD, Certificate); ergonomics in occupational health and safety (Diploma); finance (Diploma); fine arts (MA); geographical information systems (Diploma); geography (M Sc); history (MA, PhD); human movement studies (M Sc); linguistics (MA, PhD); literary studies (MA, PhD); management consultant (Diploma); management information systems (M Sc, M Sc A); mathematics (M Sc, PhD); meteorology (PhD, Diploma); mineral resources (PhD); museology (MA); non-renewable resources (DESS); philosophy (MA, PhD); political science (MA, PhD); project management (MGP, Diploma); psychology (D Ps, PhD); religious sciences (MA, PhD); semiology (PhD); sexology (MA); social and labor law (Certificate); social intervention (MA); sociology (MA, PhD); study and practices of the arts (PhD); urban analysis and management (MA); urban studies (MA, PhD).

UNIVERSITÉ DU QUÉBEC À RIMOUSKI, Rimouski, QC G5L 3A1, Canada

General Information Province-supported, coed, comprehensive institution. CGS member. *Graduate housing:* Rooms and/or apartments available on a first-come, first-served basis to single and married students. *Research affiliation:* ISMER (marine sciences), CRDT (territory development), Centre detudes nordiques (nordicity), Quebec Ocean (oceans), Centre recherche en forestene (forest).

GRADUATE UNITS

Graduate Programs *Degree program information:* Part-time programs available. Offers biology (PhD); business administration (MBA); education (M Ed, MA, PhD, Diploma); engineering (M Sc A); ethics (MA, Diploma); literary studies (MA, PhD); management of marine resources (M Sc, Diploma); management of people in working situation (M Sc, Diploma); nursing studies (M Sc, Diploma); oceanography (M Sc, PhD); project management (M Sc, Diploma); psychosocial studies (MA); regional development (MA, PhD, Diploma); wildlife resources management (M Sc, Diploma).

UNIVERSITÉ DU QUÉBEC À TROIS-RIVIÈRES, Trois-Rivières, QC G9A 5H7, Canada

General Information Province-supported, coed, university. CGS member. *Graduate housing:* Room and/or apartments available to single students; on-campus housing not available to married students. Housing application deadline: 2/1.

GRADUATE UNITS

Graduate Programs *Degree program information:* Part-time programs available. Offers accounting science (MBA); biophysics and cellular biology (M Sc, PhD); business administration (MBA, DBA); chemistry (M Sc); chiropractic (DC); education (M Ed, PhD); educational administration (DESS); electrical engineering (M Sc A, PhD); environmental sciences (M Sc, PhD); finance (DESS); industrial engineering (M Sc, DESS); labor relations (DESS); leisure, culture and tourism sciences (MA, DESS); literary studies (MA); mathematics and computer science (M Sc); matter and energy (MS, PhD); nursing sciences (M Sc, DESS); philosophy

(MA, PhD); physical education (M Sc); psychoeducation (M Ed, PhD); psychology (PhD, Certificate); social communication (MA, DESS).

UNIVERSITÉ DU QUÉBEC, ÉCOLE DE TECHNOLOGIE SUPÉRIEURE, Montréal, QC H3C 1K3, Canada

General Information Province-supported, coed, primarily men, comprehensive institution. CGS member. *Graduate housing:* Rooms and/or apartments available on a first-come, first-served basis to single and married students.

GRADUATE UNITS

Graduate Programs Postbaccalaureate distance learning degree programs offered (minimal on-campus study). Offers engineering (M Eng, PhD, Diploma).

UNIVERSITÉ DU QUÉBEC, ÉCOLE NATIONALE D'ADMINISTRATION PUBLIQUE, Quebec, QC G1K 9E5, Canada

General Information Province-supported, coed, graduate-only institution. CGS member. *Graduate housing:* On-campus housing not available.

GRADUATE UNITS

Graduate Program in Public Administration *Degree program information:* Part-time programs available. Offers international administration (MAP, Diploma); public administration (MAGU, MAP, PhD, Diploma); urban analysis and management (MAGU).

UNIVERSITÉ DU QUÉBEC EN ABITIBI-TÉMISCAMINGUE, Rouyn-Noranda, QC J9X 5E4, Canada

General Information Province-supported, coed, comprehensive institution. CGS member. *Graduate housing:* Room and/or apartments available on a first-come, first-served basis to single students; on-campus housing not available to married students. Housing application deadline: 3/1.

GRADUATE UNITS

Graduate Programs *Degree program information:* Part-time programs available. Offers biology (MS); business administration (MBA); education (M Ed, MA, PhD, DESS); engineering (ME); environmental sciences (PhD); mineral engineering (ME); mining engineering (DESS); organization management (M Sc); project management (M Sc, DESS); social work (MSW); sustainable forest ecosystem management (MS).

UNIVERSITÉ DU QUÉBEC EN OUTAOUAIS, Gatineau, QC J8X 3X7, Canada

General Information Province-supported, coed, university. CGS member. *Enrollment:* 5,391 graduate, professional, and undergraduate students; 457 full-time matriculated graduate/professional students, 634 part-time matriculated graduate/professional students. *Enrollment by degree level:* 1,035 master's, 56 doctoral. *Graduate faculty:* 40. *Graduate housing:* Rooms and/or apartments available on a first-come, first-served basis to single and married students. Typical cost: $420 Canadian dollars per year for single students. *Student services:* Campus employment opportunities, international student services, low-cost health insurance, services for students with disabilities. *Library facilities:* Brault Library plus 1 other. *Online resources:* library catalog, web page. *Collection:* 230,910 titles, 12,351 serial subscriptions.

Computer facilities: 141 computers available on campus for general student use. A campuswide network can be accessed from off campus. Online class registration is available. *Web address:* http://www.uqo.ca/.

General Application Contact: Registrar's Office, 819-773-1850, Fax: 819-773-1835, E-mail: registraire@uqo.ca.

GRADUATE UNITS

Graduate Programs Students: 1,091, 65 international. Expenses: Contact institution. *Financial support:* Fellowships, research assistantships, teaching assistantships available. *Degree program information:* Part-time programs available. Offers accounting (DESS); andragogy (DESS); computer science (M Sc, PhD); education (M Ed, MA, PhD, Diploma); executive certified management accounting (MBA, DESS); financial services (MBA, Diploma); industrial relations (M Sc, MA, PhD, Diploma); localisation (DESS); nursing (M Sc, Diploma); project management (M Sc, MA, Diploma); psychoéducation (M Ed, MA); regional development (MA); social work (MA). *Application deadline:* For fall admission, 6/1 for domestic students, 3/1 for international students; for winter admission, 11/1 for domestic students, 10/1 for international students. *Application fee:* $30 Canadian dollars. Electronic applications accepted. *Application Contact:* Registrar's Office, 819-773-1850, Fax: 819-773-1835, E-mail: registraire@uqo.ca. *Dean,* Denis Hurtubise, 819-595-3985, Fax: 819-595-3985, E-mail: denis.hurtubise@uqo.ca.

UNIVERSITÉ DU QUÉBEC, INSTITUT NATIONAL DE LA RECHERCHE SCIENTIFIQUE, Québec, QC G1K 9A9, Canada

General Information Province-supported, coed, graduate-only institution. CGS member. *Graduate housing:* On-campus housing not available.

GRADUATE UNITS

Graduate Programs *Degree program information:* Part-time programs available.

Research Center—Energy, Materials and Telecommunications *Degree program information:* Part-time programs available. Offers energy and materials science (M Sc, PhD); telecommunications (M Sc, PhD). Programs given in French.

Research Center—INRS—Institut Armand-Frappier—Human Health *Degree program information:* Part-time programs available. Offers applied microbiology (M Sc); biology (PhD); experimental health sciences (M Sc); virology and immunology (M Sc, PhD). Programs given in French.

Research Center—Urbanization, Culture and Society *Degree program information:* Part-time programs available. Offers demography (M Sc, PhD); research and public action (M Sc); urban studies (M Sc, PhD). Programs given in French.

Research Center—Water, Earth and Environment *Degree program information:* Part-time programs available. Offers earth sciences (M Sc, PhD); earth sciences-environmental technologies (M Sc); water sciences (M Sc, PhD).

UNIVERSITÉ LAVAL, Québec, QC G1K 7P4, Canada

General Information Independent, coed, university. *Graduate housing:* Room and/or apartments available on a first-come, first-served basis to single students; on-campus housing not available to married students. *Research affiliation:* Centre Hospitalier Universitaire de Québec (biomedical research), Institut National d'optique (optics and photonics), Centre de Développement de la Geomatique (applied geomatics), Institut Maurice-Lamontagne (oceanography), Forintek Canada (forestry and wood processing), Société des pades de Sciences Naturelles du Québec (biology).

GRADUATE UNITS

Faculty of Administrative Sciences *Degree program information:* Part-time programs available. Postbaccalaureate distance learning degree programs offered (no on-campus study). Offers accounting (MBA); administrative sciences (M Sc, MBA, PhD, Diploma); administrative studies (M Sc, PhD); agri-food management (MBA); electronic business (MBA, Diploma); factory management and logistics (MBA); finance (MBA); financial engineering (M Sc); firm management (MBA); genetic management (MBA); information technology management (MBA); international management (MBA); management (MBA); management accounting (MBA, Diploma); marketing (MBA); modeling and organizational decision (MBA); occupational health and safety management (MBA); organizations management and development (Diploma); pharmacy management (MBA); public accountancy (MBA, Diploma); social and environmental responsibility (MBA); technological entrepreneurship (Diploma). Electronic applications accepted.

Faculty of Agricultural and Food Sciences *Degree program information:* Part-time programs available. Offers agri-food engineering (M Sc); agricultural and food sciences (M Sc, PhD, Diploma); agricultural economics (M Sc); agricultural microbiology (M Sc); agro-food microbiology (PhD); animal sciences (M Sc, PhD); consumer sciences (Diploma); environmental technology (M Sc); food sciences and technology (M Sc, PhD); integrated rural development (Diploma); nutrition (M Sc, PhD); plant biology (M Sc, PhD); soils and environment science (M Sc, PhD). Electronic applications accepted.

Faculty of Architecture, Planning and Visual Arts Offers architecture, planning and visual arts (M Arch, M Sc, MA, MATDR, PhD); planning and regional development (MATDR, PhD). Electronic applications accepted.

School of Architecture *Degree program information:* Part-time programs available. Offers architecture (M Arch, M Sc). Electronic applications accepted.

School of Visual Arts Offers graphic design and multimedia (MA); visual arts (MA). Electronic applications accepted.

Faculty of Dentistry Offers buccal and maxillofacial surgery (DESS); dentistry (DMD, M Sc, DESS); gerodontology (DESS); multidisciplinary dentistry (DESS); periodontics (DESS). Electronic applications accepted.

Faculty of Education *Degree program information:* Part-time programs available. Offers didactics (MA, PhD); education (MA, PhD, Diploma); educational administration and evaluation (MA, PhD); educational pedagogy (Diploma); educational practice (Diploma); educational psychology (MA, PhD); orientation sciences (MA, PhD); pedagogy management and development (Diploma); school adaptation (Diploma); teaching technology (MA, PhD). Electronic applications accepted.

Faculty of Forestry and Geomatics Offers agroforestry (M Sc); forestry and geomatics (M Sc, M Sc Geogr, PhD); forestry sciences (M Sc, PhD); geographical sciences (M Sc Geogr, PhD); geography (M Sc Geogr, PhD); geomatics sciences (M Sc, PhD); wood sciences (M Sc, PhD). Electronic applications accepted.

Faculty of Law *Degree program information:* Part-time programs available. Offers environment, sustainable development and food safety (LL M); international and transnational law (LL M, Diploma); law (LL M, LL D, Diploma); law of business (LL M, Diploma); notarial law (Diploma). Electronic applications accepted.

Faculty of Letters *Degree program information:* Part-time programs available. Offers ancient civilization (MA, PhD); archaeology (MA, PhD); art history (MA, PhD); English literatures (MA, PhD); ethnology of French-speaking people in North America (MA, PhD); history (MA, PhD, Diploma); international journalism (Diploma); letters (MA, PhD, Diploma); linguistics (MA, PhD); literary studies (MA, PhD); literature and arts of the screen and stage (PhD); literature and arts of the screen and stage (MA); museology (Diploma); public communication (MA, PhD); public relations (Diploma); Spanish literature (MA, PhD); terminology and translation (MA, Diploma). Electronic applications accepted.

Faculty of Medicine *Degree program information:* Part-time programs available. Offers accident prevention and occupational health and safety management (Diploma); anatomy and physiology (M Sc, PhD); anatomy–pathology (DESS); anesthesiology (DESS); cardiology (DESS); care of older people (Diploma); cellular and molecular biology (M Sc, PhD); clinical research (DESS); community health (M Sc, PhD, DESS); dermatology (DESS); diagnostic radiology (DESS); emergency medicine (Diploma); epidemiology (M Sc, PhD); experimental medicine (M Sc, PhD); family medicine (DESS); general surgery (DESS); geriatrics (DESS); hematology (DESS); internal medicine (DESS); kinesiology (M Sc, PhD); maternal and fetal medicine (Diploma); medical biochemistry (DESS); medical microbiology and infectious diseases (DESS); medical oncology (DESS); medicine (MD, M Sc, PhD, DESS, Diploma); microbiology-immunology (M Sc, PhD); nephrology (DESS); neurobiology (M Sc, PhD); neurology (DESS); neurosurgery (DESS); obstetrics and gynecology (DESS); ophthalmology (DESS); orthopedic surgery (DESS); oto-rhino-laryngology (DESS); palliative medicine (Diploma); pediatrics (DESS); physiology-endocrinology (M Sc, PhD); plastic surgery (DESS); psychiatry (DESS); pulmonary medicine (DESS); radiology–oncology (DESS); speech therapy (M Sc); thoracic surgery (DESS); urology (DESS). Electronic applications accepted.

Faculty of Music Offers composition (M Mus); instrumental didactics (M Mus); interpretation (M Mus); music (M Mus, PhD); music education (M Mus, PhD); musicology (M Mus, PhD). Electronic applications accepted.

Faculty of Nursing Offers nursing (M Sc, PhD, DESS, Diploma). Electronic applications accepted.

Faculty of Pharmacy *Degree program information:* Part-time programs available. Offers community pharmacy (DESS); hospital pharmacy (M Sc); pharmacy (M Sc, PhD, DESS). Electronic applications accepted.

Faculty of Philosophy Offers philosophy (MA, PhD). Electronic applications accepted.

Faculty of Sciences and Engineering *Degree program information:* Part-time programs available. Offers aerospace engineering (M Sc); biochemistry (M Sc, PhD); biology (M Sc, PhD); chemical engineering (M Sc, PhD); chemistry (M Sc, PhD); civil engineering (M Sc, PhD); computer science (M Sc, PhD); earth sciences (M Sc, PhD); electrical engineering (M Sc, PhD); environmental technologies (M Sc); environmental technology (M Sc); geology (M Sc, PhD); industrial engineering (Diploma); mathematics (M Sc, PhD); mechanical engineering (M Sc, PhD); metallurgical engineering (M Sc, PhD); microbiology (M Sc, PhD); mining engineering (M Sc, PhD); oceanography (PhD); physics (M Sc, PhD); sciences and engineering (M Sc, PhD, Diploma); software engineering (Diploma); statistics (M Sc); urban infrastructure engineering (Diploma). Electronic applications accepted.

Faculty of Social Sciences *Degree program information:* Part-time programs available. Offers anthropology (MA, PhD); economics (MA, PhD); feminist studies (Diploma); industrial relations (MA, PhD); policy analysis (MA); political science (MA, PhD); social sciences (M Serv Soc, MA, PhD, Psy D, Diploma); sociology (MA, PhD). Electronic applications accepted.

School of Psychology Offers clinical psychology (PhD); community psychology (PhD); psychology (PhD, Psy D). Electronic applications accepted.

School of Social Work Offers social work (M Serv Soc, PhD). Electronic applications accepted.

Faculty of Theology and Religious Sciences Offers applied ethics (DESS); human sciences of religion (MA, PhD); practical theology (D Th P); theology (MA, PhD); theology and religious sciences (MA, D Th P, PhD, DESS). Electronic applications accepted.

Québec Institute for Advanced International Studies Offers advanced international studies (MA, PhD); international relations (MA, PhD). Electronic applications accepted.

UNIVERSITY AT ALBANY, STATE UNIVERSITY OF NEW YORK, Albany, NY 12222-0001

General Information State-supported, coed, university. CGS member. *Enrollment:* 18,202 graduate, professional, and undergraduate students; 2,571 full-time matriculated graduate/professional students (1,562 women), 1,947 part-time matriculated graduate/professional students (1,227 women). *Enrollment by degree level:* 2,707 master's, 1,684 doctoral, 127 other advanced degrees. *Graduate faculty:* 652 full-time (238 women), 621 part-time/adjunct (284 women). Tuition, state resident: full-time $7880; part-time $328 per credit. Tuition, nonresident: full-time $13,250; part-time $552 per credit. *Required fees:* $1173. *Graduate housing:* Rooms and/or apartments available on a first-come, first-served basis to single and married students. Typical cost: $6052 per year ($9778 including board) for single students. Housing application deadline: 9/1. *Student services:* Campus employment opportunities, campus safety program, career counseling, child daycare facilities, exercise/wellness program, free psychological counseling, grant writing training, international student services, low-cost health insurance, multicultural affairs office, services for students with disabilities, teacher training, writing training. *Library facilities:* University Library plus 2 others. *Online resources:* library catalog, web page, access to other libraries' catalogs. *Collection:* 2.2 million titles, 54,874 serial subscriptions, 15,801 audiovisual materials. *Research affiliation:* Wadsworth Laboratories, New York State Department of Health (Biomedical Sciences, Epidemiology, Environmental Health), Naval Research Laboratories (Organizational Structures (Public Administration)), General Electric Corporate Research and Development Center (Nanoscale

University at Albany, State University of New York (continued)

Science and Engineering), IBM–Watson Research Laboratories (Artificial Intelligence, Computer Science), Whiteface Mountain Observatory (Earth and Atmospheric Sciences), Woods Hole Oceanographic Institution.

Computer facilities: 500 computers available on campus for general student use. A campuswide network can be accessed from student residence rooms and from off campus. Online class registration is available. *Web address:* http://www.albany.edu/.

General Application Contact: Michael DeRensis, Director, Graduate Admissions, 518-442-3980, Fax: 518-442-3922, E-mail: graduate@uamail.albany.edu.

GRADUATE UNITS

College of Arts and Sciences *Degree program information:* Part-time and evening/weekend programs available. Offers African studies (MA); Afro-American studies (MA); anthropology (MA, PhD); art (MA, MFA); arts and sciences (MA, MFA, MRP, MS, DA, PhD, Certificate); atmospheric science (MS, PhD); autism (Certificate); biodiversity, conservation, and policy (MS); biopsychology (PhD); chemistry (MS, PhD); clinical psychology (PhD); communication (MA); demography (Certificate); ecology, evolution, and behavior (MS, PhD); economics (MA, PhD); English (MA, PhD); forensic molecular biology (MS); French (MA, PhD); general/experimental psychology (PhD); geographic information systems and spatial analysis (Certificate); geography (MA, Certificate); geology (MS, PhD); history (MA, PhD); industrial/organizational psychology (PhD); Italian (MA); Latin American, Caribbean, and US Latino studies (MA, Certificate); liberal studies (MA); mathematics (PhD); molecular, cellular, developmental, and neural biology (MS, PhD); philosophy (MA, PhD); physics (MS, PhD); psychology (MA); public history (Certificate); regional planning (MRP); regulatory economics (Certificate); Russian (MA, Certificate); Russian translation (Certificate); secondary teaching (MA); social/personality psychology (PhD); sociology (MA, PhD); sociology and communication (PhD); Spanish (MA, PhD); statistics (MA); theatre (MA); urban policy (Certificate); women's studies (MA, DA).

College of Computing and Information *Degree program information:* Part-time programs available. Offers computer science (MS, PhD); information science (MS, PhD, CAS); information studies (MS, CAS). Electronic applications accepted.

College of Nanoscale Science and Engineering Offers nanoscale science and engineering (MS, PhD).

Nelson A. Rockefeller College of Public Affairs and Policy *Degree program information:* Part-time programs available. Offers administrative behavior (PhD); comparative and development administration (MPA, PhD); human resources (MPA); legislative administration (MPA); nonprofit leadership and management (Certificate); planning and policy analysis (CAS); policy analysis (MPA); political science (MA, PhD); program analysis and evaluation (PhD); public affairs and policy (MA); public finance (MPA, PhD); public management (MPA, PhD); women and public policy (Certificate). Electronic applications accepted.

School of Business *Degree program information:* Part-time and evening/weekend programs available. Offers accounting (MS); business (MBA, MS); finance (MBA); human resource systems (MBA); information technology management (MBA); marketing (MBA); taxation (MS). Electronic applications accepted.

School of Criminal Justice *Degree program information:* Part-time programs available. Offers criminal justice (MA, PhD). Electronic applications accepted.

School of Education *Degree program information:* Part-time and evening/weekend programs available. Offers counseling psychology (MS, PhD, CAS); curriculum and instruction (MS, Ed D, CAS); curriculum planning and development (MA); education (MA, MS, Ed D, PhD, Psy D, CAS); educational administration and policy studies (MS, PhD, CAS); educational communications (MS, CAS); educational psychology (Ed D); educational psychology and statistics (MS); measurements and evaluation (Ed D); reading (MS, Ed D, CAS); rehabilitation counseling (MS); school counselor (CAS); school psychology (Psy D, CAS); special education (MS); statistics and research design (Ed D). Electronic applications accepted.

School of Public Health Offers biochemistry, molecular biology, and genetics (MS, PhD); cell and molecular structure (MS, PhD); environmental and analytical chemistry (MS, PhD); environmental and occupational health (MS, PhD); epidemiology and biostatistics (MS, PhD); health policy, management, and behavior (MS); immunobiology and immunochemistry (MS, PhD); molecular pathogenesis (MS, PhD); neuroscience (MS, PhD); public health (MPH, MS, Dr PH, PhD, Certificate); toxicology (MS, PhD). Electronic applications accepted.

School of Social Welfare *Degree program information:* Part-time and evening/weekend programs available. Offers social welfare (MSW, PhD). Electronic applications accepted.

UNIVERSITY AT BUFFALO, THE STATE UNIVERSITY OF NEW YORK, Buffalo, NY 14260

General Information State-supported, coed, university. CGS member. *Enrollment:* 28,192 graduate, professional, and undergraduate students; 6,969 full-time matriculated graduate/professional students (3,554 women), 2,036 part-time matriculated graduate/professional students (1,154 women). *Enrollment by degree level:* 2,013 first professional, 4,290 master's, 2,508 doctoral, 194 other advanced degrees. *Graduate faculty:* 1,277 full-time (418 women), 1,122 part-time/adjunct (417 women). *Graduate housing:* Rooms and/or apartments available on a first-come, first-served basis to single students and available to married students. Housing application deadline: 5/1. *Student services:* Campus employment opportunities, campus safety program, career counseling, child daycare facilities, exercise/wellness program, free psychological counseling, international student services, low-cost health insurance, multicultural affairs office, services for students with disabilities, teacher training, writing training. *Library facilities:* Lockwood Library plus 7 others. *Online resources:* library catalog, web page, access to other libraries' catalogs. *Collection:* 3.7 million titles, 71,234 serial subscriptions, 275,743 audiovisual materials. *Research affiliation:* Kaleida Health, Hauptman-Woodward Medical Research Institute, Veterans Administration Medical Center, Calspan–UB Research Center, Roswell Park Cancer Institute.

Computer facilities: Computer purchase and lease plans are available. 2,000 computers available on campus for general student use. A campuswide network can be accessed from student residence rooms and from off campus. Online class registration is available. *Web address:* http://www.buffalo.edu/.

General Application Contact: Christopher S. Connor, Director of Graduate Enrollment Management Services, 716-645-3482, Fax: 716-645-6998, E-mail: cconnor@buffalo.edu.

GRADUATE UNITS

Graduate School Students: 7,248 full-time (3,665 women), 1,643 part-time (923 women); includes 1,061 minority (303 African Americans, 33 American Indian/Alaska Native, 518 Asian Americans or Pacific Islanders, 207 Hispanic Americans), 2,165 international. *Faculty:* 1,277 full-time (418 women), 1,122 part-time/adjunct (417 women). Expenses: Contact institution. *Financial support:* Fellowships with full and partial tuition reimbursements, research assistantships with full and partial tuition reimbursements, teaching assistantships with full and partial tuition reimbursements, career-related internships or fieldwork, Federal Work-Study, institutionally sponsored loans, scholarships/grants, traineeships, tuition waivers (full and partial), unspecified assistantships, and stipends available. Support available to part-time students. Financial award applicants required to submit FAFSA. In 2008, 4 first professional degrees, 177 master's, 82 doctorates awarded. *Degree program information:* Part-time and evening/weekend programs available. Postbaccalaureate distance learning degree programs offered. *Application deadline:* Applications are processed on a rolling basis. *Application fee:* $50. Electronic applications accepted. *Application Contact:* Christopher S. Connor, Director of Graduate Enrollment Management Services, 716-645-3482, Fax: 716-645-6998, E-mail: gradrecruit@buffalo.edu. *Associate Provost and Executive Director of the Graduate School,* Dr. Myron A. Thompson, 716-645-2939, Fax: 716-645-6142, E-mail: gradschl@buffalo.edu.

College of Arts and Sciences Students: 1,736 full-time (879 women), 268 part-time (102 women); includes 173 minority (53 African Americans, 9 American Indian/Alaska Native, 57 Asian Americans or Pacific Islanders, 54 Hispanic Americans), 616 international. Average age 29. 4,247 applicants, 30% accepted, 500 enrolled. *Faculty:* 509 full-time (150 women), 257 part-time/adjunct (103 women). Expenses: Contact institution. *Financial support:* Fellowships with full and partial tuition reimbursements, research assistantships with full tuition reimbursements, teaching assistantships with full tuition reimbursements, career-related internships or fieldwork, Federal Work-Study, institutionally sponsored loans, scholarships/grants, tuition waivers (full and partial), and unspecified assistantships available. Support available to part-time students. Financial award applicants required to submit FAFSA. In 2008, 390 master's, 143 doctorates, 26 other advanced degrees awarded. *Degree program information:* Part-time programs available. Offers American studies (MA, PhD); anthropology (MA, PhD); art (MFA); art history (MA, Certificate); arts and sciences (MA, MFA, MM, MS, Au D, PhD, Certificate); audiology (Au D); behavioral neuroscience (PhD); biological sciences (MA, MS, PhD); chemistry (MA, PhD); classics (MA, PhD); clinical psychology (PhD); cognitive psychology (PhD); communication (MA, PhD); communicative disorders and sciences (MA, PhD); comparative literature (MA, PhD); critical museum studies (Certificate); economics (MA, MS, PhD); English (MA, PhD); evolution, ecology and behavior (MS, PhD, Certificate); financial economics (Certificate); fine arts (MFA); French (MA, PhD); general psychology (MA); geographic information science (Certificate); geography (MA, MS, PhD); geology (MA, MS, PhD); health services (Certificate); historical musicology and music theory (PhD); history (MA, PhD); humanities (film studies concentration) (MA); information and Internet economics (Certificate); international economics (Certificate); law and regulation (Certificate); linguistics (MA, PhD); mathematics (MA, PhD); media arts production (MFA); medicinal chemistry (MS, PhD); music composition (MA, PhD); music history (MA); music performance (MM); music theory (MA); new media design (Certificate); philosophy (MA, PhD); physics (MS, PhD); political science (MA, PhD); social-personality psychology (PhD); sociology (MA, PhD); Spanish (MA, PhD); transportation and business geographics (Certificate); urban and regional economics (Certificate). *Application deadline:* Applications are processed on a rolling basis. *Application fee:* $50. Electronic applications accepted. *Application Contact:* Joseph C. Syracuse, Graduate Enrollment Manager, 716-645-2711, Fax: 716-645-3888, E-mail: jcs32@buffalo.edu. *Dean,* Dr. Bruce D. Mc Combe, 716-645-2711, Fax: 716-645-3888, E-mail: cas-dean@buffalo.edu.

Graduate Programs in Cancer Research and Biomedical Sciences at Roswell Park Cancer Institute Students: 151 full-time (88 women), 33 part-time (11 women); includes 26 minority (8 African Americans, 12 Asian Americans or Pacific Islanders, 6 Hispanic Americans), 55 international. Average age 24. 318 applicants, 35% accepted, 50 enrolled. *Faculty:* 129 full-time (34 women). Expenses: Contact institution. *Financial support:* In 2008–09, 120 students received support, including fellowships with full tuition reimbursements available (averaging $24,000 per year), research assistantships with full tuition reimbursements available (averaging $24,000 per year), teaching assistantships with full tuition reimbursements available (averaging $8,500 per year); Federal Work-Study, institutionally sponsored loans, scholarships/grants, and unspecified assistantships also available. Financial award application deadline: 2/1; financial award applicants required to submit FAFSA. In 2008, 24 master's, 12 doctorates awarded. Offers cancer pathology and prevention (PhD); cellular and molecular biology (PhD); immunology (PhD); interdisciplinary biomedical and natural sciences (MS); molecular and cellular biophysics (PhD); molecular and cellular biophysics and biochemistry (PhD); molecular pharmacology and cancer therapeutics (PhD); natural and biomedical sciences (MS). *Application deadline:* For fall admission, 2/1 priority date for domestic and international students. Applications are processed on a rolling basis. *Application fee:* $50. Electronic applications accepted. *Application Contact:* Craig R. Johnson, Director of Admissions, 716-845-2339, Fax: 716-845-8178, E-mail: craig.johnson@roswellpark.org. *Dean,* Dr. Arthur M. Michalek, 716-845-2339, Fax: 716-845-8178, E-mail: arthur.michalek@roswellpark.org.

Graduate School of Education Students: 797 full-time (595 women), 643 part-time (441 women); includes 157 minority (79 African Americans, 7 American Indian/Alaska Native, 30 Asian Americans or Pacific Islanders, 41 Hispanic Americans), 120 international. Average age 31. 1,687 applicants, 60% accepted, 453 enrolled. *Faculty:* 80 full-time (48 women), 98 part-time/adjunct (68 women). Expenses: Contact institution. *Financial support:* Fellowships with full tuition reimbursements, research assistantships with full tuition reimbursements, teaching assistantships with full tuition reimbursements, career-related internships or fieldwork, Federal Work-Study, institutionally sponsored loans, tuition waivers (full and partial), and unspecified assistantships available. Financial award applicants required to submit FAFSA. In 2008, 487 master's, 62 doctorates, 95 other advanced degrees awarded. *Degree program information:* Part-time programs available. Postbaccalaureate distance learning degree programs offered (minimal on-campus study). Offers adolescence education (Certificate); biology (Ed M); chemistry (Ed M); childhood education (Ed M); counseling/school psychology (PhD); counselor education (PhD); early childhood and childhood education with bilingual extension (Ed M); early childhood education (Ed M); earth science (Ed M); education (Ed M, MA, MLS, MS, Ed D, PhD, Certificate); educational administration (Ed M, Ed D, PhD); educational psychology (MA, PhD); elementary education (Ed D, PhD); English (Ed M); English education (PhD); English for speakers of other languages (Ed M); foreign and second language education (PhD); French (Ed M); general education (Ed M); German (Ed M); higher education (PhD); higher education administration (Ed M); Italian (Ed M); Japanese (Ed M); Latin (Ed M); library and information studies (MLS, Certificate); literary specialist (Ed M); mathematics (Ed M); mathematics education (PhD); mental health counseling (MS); mentoring teachers (Certificate); music education (Ed M, Certificate); physics (Ed M); reading education (PhD); rehabilitation counseling (MS); Russian (Ed M); school administrator and supervisor (Certificate); school business and human resource administration (Certificate); school counseling (Ed M, Certificate); school psychology (MA); science education (PhD); social foundations (PhD); social studies (Ed M); Spanish (Ed M); special education (PhD); specialist in education administration (Certificate); teaching and leading for diversity (Certificate); teaching English to speakers of other languages (Ed M). *Application deadline:* Applications are processed on a rolling basis. *Application fee:* $50. Electronic applications accepted. *Application Contact:* Dr. Radhika Suresh, Director of Graduate Admissions and Student Services, 716-645-2110 Ext. 1209, Fax: 716-645-7937, E-mail: gse-info@buffalo.edu. *Dean,* Dr. Mary H. Gresham, 716-645-6640, Fax: 716-645-2479, E-mail: gse-info@buffalo.edu.

Law School Students: 748 full-time (356 women), 4 part-time (2 women); includes 91 minority (27 African Americans, 3 American Indian/Alaska Native, 31 Asian Americans or Pacific Islanders, 30 Hispanic Americans), 30 international. Average age 26. 2,338 applicants, 32% accepted, 241 enrolled. *Faculty:* 54 full-time (24 women), 51 part-time/adjunct (19 women). Expenses: Contact institution. *Financial support:* In 2008–09, 660 students received support, including 25 fellowships with full and partial tuition reimbursements available (averaging $10,000 per year), 34 research assistantships (averaging $1,135 per year); career-related internships or fieldwork, Federal Work-Study, institutionally sponsored loans, scholarships/grants, tuition waivers (full and partial), and unspecified assistantships also available. Financial award application deadline: 3/1; financial award applicants required to submit FAFSA. In 2008, 250 JDs awarded. Offers criminal law (LL M); general law for international students (LL M); law (JD). *Application deadline:* For fall admission, 3/15 priority date for domestic students. Applications are processed on a rolling basis. *Application fee:* $50. Electronic applications accepted. *Application Contact:* Lillie V. Wiley-Upshaw, Associate Dean and Director of Admissions and Financial Aid, 716-645-2907, Fax: 716-645-6676, E-mail: law-admissions@buffalo.edu. *Dean,* Dr. Makau Mutua, 716-645-2311, Fax: 716-645-2064, E-mail: mutua@buffalo.edu.

School of Architecture and Planning Students: 198 full-time (84 women), 18 part-time (3 women); includes 20 minority (12 African Americans, 3 Asian Americans or Pacific Islanders, 5 Hispanic Americans), 37 international. Average age 27. 315 applicants, 63% accepted, 72 enrolled. *Faculty:* 32 full-time (12 women), 35 part-time/adjunct (9 women). Expenses: Contact institution. *Financial support:* Fellowships with full tuition reimbursements, research assistantships with full tuition reimbursements, teaching assistantships with full and partial tuition reimbursements, career-related internships or fieldwork, Federal Work-Study, institutionally sponsored loans, scholarships/grants, traineeships, tuition waivers (full and partial), and unspecified assistantships available. Support available to part-time students. Financial award applicants required to submit FAFSA. In 2008, 75 master's awarded. *Degree program information:* Part-time programs available. Offers architecture (M Arch); architecture and planning (M Arch, MUP); planning (MUP). *Application deadline:* Applications are processed on a rolling basis. *Application fee:* $50. Electronic applications accepted.

Application Contact: Deborah R. Smith, Assistant to the Chair, 716-829-3485 Ext. 105, Fax: 716-829-3256, E-mail: drs5@buffalo.edu. *Dean,* Brian Carter, 716-829-3485 Ext. 121, Fax: 716-829-2297, E-mail: bcarter@buffalo.edu.

School of Dental Medicine Students: 426 full-time (159 women), 2 part-time (1 woman); includes 91 minority (3 African Americans, 79 Asian Americans or Pacific Islanders, 9 Hispanic Americans), 62 international. Average age 26. 2,253 applicants, 10% accepted, 101 enrolled. *Faculty:* 69 full-time (25 women), 109 part-time/adjunct (26 women). Expenses: Contact institution. *Financial support:* Fellowships with full and partial tuition reimbursements, research assistantships with full and partial tuition reimbursements, career-related internships or fieldwork, institutionally sponsored loans, scholarships/grants, and unspecified assistantships available. Financial award applicants required to submit FAFSA. In 2008, 83 first professional degrees, 23 master's, 3 doctorates awarded. Offers advanced education in general dentistry (Certificate); biomaterials (MS); combined prosthodontics (Certificate); dental medicine (DDS, MS, PhD, Certificate); endodontics (Certificate); general practice residency (Certificate); oral and maxillofacial pathology (Certificate); oral and maxillofacial surgery (Certificate); oral biology (PhD); oral diagnostic sciences (MS); oral sciences (MS); orthodontics (MS, Certificate); pediatric dentistry (Certificate); periodontics (Certificate); temporomandibular disorders and oralfacial pain (Certificate). *Application deadline:* For fall admission, 2/1 for domestic and international students. *Application fee:* $50. Electronic applications accepted. *Application Contact:* Dr. Robert Joynt, Director of Admissions, 716-829-2839, Fax: 716-833-3517, E-mail: joynt@buffalo.edu. *Dean,* Dr. Richard N. Buchanan, 716-829-2836, Fax: 716-833-3517, E-mail: rb26@buffalo.edu.

School of Engineering and Applied Sciences Students: 845 full-time (176 women), 131 part-time (19 women); includes 44 minority (20 African Americans, 1 American Indian/Alaska Native, 17 Asian Americans or Pacific Islanders, 6 Hispanic Americans), 703 international. Average age 27. 3,304 applicants, 52% accepted, 390 enrolled. *Faculty:* 138 full-time (17 women), 36 part-time/adjunct (4 women). Expenses: Contact institution. *Financial support:* In 2008–09, 35 fellowships with full tuition reimbursements (averaging $22,000 per year), 157 research assistantships with full and partial tuition reimbursements (averaging $20,700 per year), 183 teaching assistantships with full tuition reimbursements (averaging $19,600 per year) were awarded; career-related internships or fieldwork, Federal Work-Study, institutionally sponsored loans, scholarships/grants, tuition waivers (full and partial), and unspecified assistantships also available. Support available to part-time students. Financial award applicants required to submit FAFSA. In 2008, 355 master's, 66 doctorates awarded. *Degree program information:* Part-time and evening/weekend programs available. Postbaccalaureate distance learning degree programs offered (minimal on-campus study). Offers aerospace engineering (MS, PhD); chemical and biological engineering (M Eng, MS, PhD); civil engineering (M Eng, MS, PhD); computer science and engineering (MS, PhD); electrical engineering (M Eng, MS, PhD); engineering and applied sciences (M Eng, MS, PhD); engineering science (MS); industrial and systems engineering (M Eng, MS, PhD); mechanical engineering (MS, PhD). *Application deadline:* Applications are processed on a rolling basis. *Application fee:* $50. Electronic applications accepted. *Application Contact:* Dr. Rajan Batta, Associate Dean for Graduate Education, 716-645-2771 Ext. 1105, Fax: 716-645-2495, E-mail: batta@eng.buffalo.edu. *Dean,* Dr. Harvey G. Stenger, 716-645-2771 Ext. 1101, Fax: 716-645-2495, E-mail: dean@eng.buffalo.edu.

School of Management Students: 511 full-time (183 women), 208 part-time (57 women); includes 49 minority (11 African Americans, 1 American Indian/Alaska Native, 31 Asian Americans or Pacific Islanders, 6 Hispanic Americans), 331 international. Average age 27. 1,587 applicants, 40% accepted, 274 enrolled. *Faculty:* 65 full-time (18 women), 30 part-time/adjunct (3 women). Expenses: Contact institution. *Financial support:* In 2008–09, 91 students received support, including 17 fellowships with full and partial tuition reimbursements available (averaging $3,917 per year), 38 research assistantships with full and partial tuition reimbursements available (averaging $11,907 per year), 26 teaching assistantships with full and partial tuition reimbursements available (averaging $7,571 per year); career-related internships or fieldwork, Federal Work-Study, institutionally sponsored loans, scholarships/grants, health care benefits, and unspecified assistantships also available. Financial award application deadline: 2/15; financial award applicants required to submit FAFSA. In 2008, 327 master's, 7 doctorates, 3 other advanced degrees awarded. *Degree program information:* Part-time and evening/weekend programs available. Offers accounting (MS); business administration (MBA); finance (MS); information assurance (Certificate); management (PhD); management information systems (MS); supply chains and operations management (MS). *Application deadline:* For fall admission, 6/1 priority date for domestic students, 3/1 priority date for international students. Applications are processed on a rolling basis. *Application fee:* $50. Electronic applications accepted. *Application Contact:* David W. Frasier, Administrative Director of Graduate Programs and Assistant Dean, 716-645-3204, Fax: 716-645-2341, E-mail: davidf@buffalo.edu. *Dean,* Arjang Assad, 716-645-3221, Fax: 716-645-5926, E-mail: aasad@buffalo.edu.

School of Medicine and Biomedical Sciences Students: 716 full-time (380 women), 16 part-time (10 women); includes 165 minority (15 African Americans, 3 American Indian/Alaska Native, 138 Asian Americans or Pacific Islanders, 9 Hispanic Americans), 60 international. Average age 26. 3,971 applicants, 12% accepted. *Faculty:* 154 full-time (32 women), 351 part-time/adjunct (100 women). Expenses: Contact institution. *Financial support:* In 2008–09, fellowships with full tuition reimbursements (averaging $25,000 per year), research assistantships with full tuition reimbursements (averaging $21,000 per year), teaching assistantships with full tuition reimbursements (averaging $21,000 per year) were awarded; career-related internships or fieldwork, Federal Work-Study, institutionally sponsored loans, scholarships/grants, traineeships, health care benefits, and unspecified assistantships also available. Financial award application deadline: 2/1; financial award applicants required to submit FAFSA. In 2008, 131 first professional degrees, 21 master's, 27 doctorates awarded. Offers anatomical sciences (MA, PhD); biochemical pharmacology (MS); biochemistry (MA, PhD); biomedical sciences (PhD); biophysics (MS, PhD); biotechnology (MS); medicine (MD); medicine and biomedical sciences (MD, MA, MS, PhD); microbiology and immunology (MA, PhD); neuroscience (MS, PhD); pathology (MA, PhD); pharmacology (MA, PhD); physiology (MA, PhD); structural biology (MS, PhD). *Application deadline:* For fall admission, 2/1 priority date for domestic and international students. Applications are processed on a rolling basis. *Application fee:* $50. Electronic applications accepted. *Application Contact:* Amy J. Kuzdale, Staff Associate, 716-829-3398, Fax: 716-829-2437, E-mail: akuzdale@buffalo.edu. *Dean of Medicine,* Dr. Michael E. Cain, 716-829-3955, Fax: 716-829-3395, E-mail: mcain@buffalo.edu.

School of Nursing Students: 127 full-time (103 women), 64 part-time (53 women); includes 32 minority (14 African Americans, 8 Asian Americans or Pacific Islanders, 10 Hispanic Americans), 19 international. Average age 34. 247 applicants, 47% accepted. *Faculty:* 38 full-time (34 women), 15 part-time/adjunct (14 women). Expenses: Contact institution. *Financial support:* In 2008–09, 78 students received support, including 13 fellowships with full tuition reimbursements available (averaging $7,220 per year), 10 research assistantships with tuition reimbursements available (averaging $17,881 per year), 23 teaching assistantships with full tuition reimbursements available (averaging $11,245 per year); Federal Work-Study, scholarships/grants, traineeships, health care benefits, and unspecified assistantships also available. Financial award application deadline: 3/15; financial award applicants required to submit FAFSA. In 2008, 61 master's, 2 doctorates, 4 other advanced degrees awarded. *Degree program information:* Part-time programs available. Postbaccalaureate distance learning degree programs offered. Offers acute care nurse practitioner (MS, Certificate); adult health nursing (MS, Certificate); child health nursing (MS); family nurse practitioner (Certificate); family nursing (MS); geriatric nurse practitioner (MS, Certificate); maternal and women's health nurse practitioner (Certificate); maternal and women's health nursing (MS); nurse anesthetist (MS); nursing (PhD); nursing education (Certificate); pediatric nurse practitioner (Certificate); psychiatric/mental health nurse practitioner (Certificate); psychiatric/mental health nursing (MS). *Application deadline:* For fall admission, 6/1 priority date for domestic students, 3/1 priority date for international students; for spring admission, 11/1 for domestic students, 9/15 priority date for international students. Applications are processed on a rolling basis. *Application fee:* $50. Electronic applications accepted. *Application Contact:* Dr. Elaine R. Cusker, Assistant Dean, 716-829-2537, Fax: 716-829-2021, E-mail: ecusker@buffalo.edu. *Interim Dean,* Dr. Jean K. Brown, 716-829-2533, Fax: 716-829-2566, E-mail: jebrown@buffalo.edu.

School of Pharmacy and Pharmaceutical Sciences Students: 395 full-time (240 women), 3 part-time (all women); includes 99 minority (16 African Americans, 3 American Indian/Alaska Native, 71 Asian Americans or Pacific Islanders, 9 Hispanic Americans), 55 international. Average age 26. 1,469 applicants, 9% accepted, 122 enrolled. *Faculty:* 39 full-time (11 women), 7 part-time/adjunct (3 women). Expenses: Contact institution. *Financial support:* In 2008–09, 27 students received support, including 8 fellowships with full tuition reimbursements available (averaging $22,565 per year), 18 research assistantships with full tuition reimbursements available (averaging $22,565 per year); teaching assistantships, Federal Work-Study, institutionally sponsored loans, scholarships/grants, health care benefits, tuition waivers (full and partial), and unspecified assistantships also available. Financial award application deadline: 2/28; financial award applicants required to submit FAFSA. In 2008, 115 first professional degrees, 5 master's, 6 doctorates awarded. Postbaccalaureate distance learning degree programs offered (minimal on-campus study). Offers pharmaceutical sciences (MS, PhD); pharmacy (Pharm D); pharmacy and pharmaceutical sciences (Pharm D, MS, PhD). *Application deadline:* For fall admission, 2/1 priority date for domestic and international students. Applications are processed on a rolling basis. *Application fee:* $50. Electronic applications accepted. *Application Contact:* Cindy F. Konovitz, Assistant Dean, 716-645-2825, Fax: 716-645-3688, E-mail: pharm-admin@acsu.buffalo.edu. *Dean,* Dr. Wayne K. Anderson, 716-645-2823, Fax: 716-645-3688.

School of Public Health and Health Professions Students: 355 full-time (218 women), 66 part-time (50 women); includes 61 minority (19 African Americans, 2 American Indian/Alaska Native, 32 Asian Americans or Pacific Islanders, 8 Hispanic Americans), 84 international. Average age 30. 502 applicants, 55% accepted, 122 enrolled. *Faculty:* 64 full-time (30 women), 43 part-time/adjunct (26 women). Expenses: Contact institution. *Financial support:* In 2008–09, 15 fellowships with full tuition reimbursements (averaging $2,500 per year), 3 research assistantships with full tuition reimbursements (averaging $15,000 per year), 18 teaching assistantships with full tuition reimbursements (averaging $8,500 per year) were awarded; career-related internships or fieldwork, Federal Work-Study, institutionally sponsored loans, scholarships/grants, tuition waivers (full and partial), and unspecified assistantships also available. Financial award applicants required to submit FAFSA. In 2008, 90 master's, 48 doctorates, 2 other advanced degrees awarded. *Degree program information:* Part-time programs available. Offers assistive and rehabilitation technology (Certificate); biostatistics (MA, PhD); community health (PhD); epidemiology (MS, PhD); exercise science (MS, PhD); nutrition (MS); occupational therapy (MS); physical therapy (DPT); public health (MPH); public health and health professions (MA, MPH, MS, DPT, PhD, Certificate). *Application fee:* $50. Electronic applications accepted. *Application Contact:* Cassandra F. Walker-Whiteside, Senior Advisor, PHHP Student Advisement and Recruitment Services, 716-829-3434 Ext. 410, Fax: 716-829-2034, E-mail: cfwalker@buffalo.edu. *Dean,* Dr. Lynn Kozlowski, 716-829-6951, Fax: 716-829-6040, E-mail: lk22@buffalo.edu.

School of Social Work Students: 251 full-time (219 women), 188 part-time (170 women); includes 66 minority (41 African Americans, 4 American Indian/Alaska Native, 8 Asian Americans or Pacific Islanders, 13 Hispanic Americans), 16 international. Average age 31. 599 applicants, 68% accepted. *Faculty:* 21 full-time (12 women), 40 part-time/adjunct (28 women). Expenses: Contact institution. *Financial support:* In 2008–09, 67 students received support, including 4 fellowships with full tuition reimbursements available (averaging $7,500 per year), 3 research assistantships with full tuition reimbursements available (averaging $15,000 per year), 6 teaching assistantships with full tuition reimbursements available (averaging $15,000 per year); Federal Work-Study, scholarships/grants, health care benefits, tuition waivers (partial), unspecified assistantships, and instructorships and research grants for PhD students also available. Financial award application deadline: 2/1; financial award applicants required to submit FAFSA. In 2008, 259 master's, 2 doctorates awarded. *Degree program information:* Part-time programs available. Offers social work (MSW, PhD). MSW available in Buffalo, Rochester, Jamestown, and Corning, New York. *Application deadline:* For fall admission, 3/1 priority date for domestic and international students. Applications are processed on a rolling basis. *Application fee:* $50. Electronic applications accepted. *Application Contact:* Maria Soos, Admissions Processor, 716-645-3381, Fax: 716-645-3456, E-mail: sw-info@buffalo.edu. *Dean,* Dr. Nancy J. Smyth, 716-645-3381 Ext. 221, Fax: 716-645-3883, E-mail: njsmyth@buffalo.edu.

See Close-Up on page 1011.

UNIVERSITY OF ADVANCING TECHNOLOGY, Tempe, AZ 85283-1042

General Information Proprietary, coed, primarily men, comprehensive institution. *Enrollment:* 1,250 graduate, professional, and undergraduate students; 62 full-time matriculated graduate/professional students (11 women), 3 part-time matriculated graduate/professional students. *Enrollment by degree level:* 65 master's. *Graduate faculty:* 7 full-time (3 women), 1 part-time/adjunct (0 women). *Tuition:* Full-time $16,200. *Graduate housing:* Room and/or apartments available on a first-come, first-served basis to single students; on-campus housing not available to married students. Typical cost: $6948 per year ($10,548 including board). Room and board charges vary according to board plan. *Student services:* Campus employment opportunities, career counseling. *Library facilities:* University of Advancing Computer Technology Library. *Online resources:* library catalog, web page. *Collection:* 27,500 titles, 92 serial subscriptions, 1,200 audiovisual materials.

Computer facilities: Computer purchase and lease plans are available. 400 computers available on campus for general student use. A campuswide network can be accessed from student residence rooms and from off campus. Online class registration is available. *Web address:* http://www.uat.edu/.

General Application Contact: Michelle Wilcox, Admissions Office, 800-658-5744, Fax: 602-383-8222, E-mail: mkable@uat.edu.

GRADUATE UNITS

Master of Science Program in Technology Students: 13 full-time (3 women), 4 part-time (2 women). Average age 25. *Faculty:* 10 full-time (2 women), 1 part-time/adjunct (0 women). Expenses: Contact institution. *Financial support:* Career-related internships or fieldwork, Federal Work-Study, and scholarships/grants available. Financial award applicants required to submit FAFSA. In 2008, 5 master's awarded. Offers advancing computer science (MS); emerging technologies (MS); game production and management (MS); information assurance (MS); technology leadership (MS). *Application deadline:* For fall admission, 8/15 priority date for domestic students, 7/15 priority date for international students; for winter admission, 12/15 priority date for domestic students, 11/15 priority date for international students; for spring admission, 4/1 priority date for domestic students, 3/1 priority date for international students. Applications are processed on a rolling basis. *Application fee:* $100 ($250 for international students). Electronic applications accepted. *Application Contact:* Information Contact, 800-658-5744, Fax: 602-383-8222. *Dean of Graduate Education,* Kathleen Dunley, 602-383-8283, Fax: 602-383-8222, E-mail: kdunley@uat.edu.

THE UNIVERSITY OF AKRON, Akron, OH 44325

General Information State-supported, coed, university. CGS member. *Enrollment:* 24,119 graduate, professional, and undergraduate students; 2,097 full-time matriculated graduate/professional students (1,129 women), 2,205 part-time matriculated graduate/professional students (1,417 women). *Enrollment by degree level:* 497 first professional, 2,791 master's, 728 doctoral, 209 other advanced degrees. *Graduate faculty:* 486 full-time (166 women), 445 part-time/adjunct (225 women). Tuition, state resident: full-time $6164; part-time $342 per credit hour. Tuition, nonresident: full-time $10,574; part-time $588 per credit hour. *Required fees:* $806. *Graduate housing:* Room and/or apartments available on a first-come, first-served basis to single students; on-campus housing not available to married students. Housing application deadline: 3/1. *Student services:* Campus employment opportunities, campus safety program, career counseling, child daycare facilities, exercise/wellness program, free psychological counseling, grant writing training, international student services, low-cost health insurance, multicultural affairs office, services for students with disabilities, teacher training, writing training. *Library facilities:* Bierce Library plus 2 others. *Online resources:* library catalog, web page, access to other libraries' catalogs. *Collection:* 1.3 million titles, 14,765 serial subscriptions, 48,423 audiovisual materials.

The University of Akron (continued)

Computer facilities: Computer purchase and lease plans are available. 3,100 computers available on campus for general student use. A campuswide network can be accessed from student residence rooms and from off campus. Online class registration, library laptops for student checkout are available. *Web address:* http://www.uakron.edu/.

General Application Contact: Dr. Mark Tausig, Associate Dean, 330-972-6266, Fax: 330-972-6475, E-mail: mtausig@uakron.edu.

GRADUATE UNITS

Graduate School Students: 2,097 full-time (1,129 women), 2,205 part-time (1,417 women); includes 364 minority (259 African Americans, 5 American Indian/Alaska Native, 62 Asian Americans or Pacific Islanders, 38 Hispanic Americans), 625 international. Average age 32. 2,631 applicants, 56% accepted, 895 enrolled. *Faculty:* 469 full-time (158 women), 435 part-time/adjunct (212 women). Expenses: Contact institution. *Financial support:* In 2008–09, 58 fellowships with full tuition reimbursements, 470 research assistantships with full and partial tuition reimbursements, 618 teaching assistantships with full and partial tuition reimbursements were awarded; career-related internships or fieldwork, Federal Work-Study, institutionally sponsored loans, scholarships/grants, tuition waivers (full and partial), unspecified assistantships, and administrative assistantships also available. Support available to part-time students. In 2008, 939 master's, 103 doctorates awarded. *Degree program information:* Part-time and evening/weekend programs available. *Application deadline:* Applications are processed on a rolling basis. *Application fee:* $30 ($40 for international students). Electronic applications accepted. *Application Contact:* Dr. Mark Tausig, Associate Dean, 330-972-6266, Fax: 330-972-6475, E-mail: mtausig@uakron.edu. *Vice President for Research and Dean of the Graduate School*, Dr. George R. Newkome, 330-972-6458, Fax: 330-972-2413, E-mail: newkome@uakron.edu.

Buchtel College of Arts and Sciences Students: 501 full-time (239 women), 275 part-time (141 women); includes 103 minority (74 African Americans, 1 American Indian/Alaska Native, 14 Asian Americans or Pacific Islanders, 14 Hispanic Americans), 176 international. Average age 30. 662 applicants, 55% accepted, 180 enrolled. *Faculty:* 194 full-time (53 women), 75 part-time/adjunct (19 women). Expenses: Contact institution. *Financial support:* In 2008–09, 1 fellowship with full tuition reimbursement, 77 research assistantships with full tuition reimbursements, 317 teaching assistantships with full tuition reimbursements were awarded; career-related internships or fieldwork, Federal Work-Study, institutionally sponsored loans, scholarships/grants, tuition waivers (full and partial), and unspecified assistantships also available. Support available to part-time students. In 2008, 176 master's, 36 doctorates awarded. *Degree program information:* Part-time and evening/weekend programs available. Offers applied cognitive aging (MA, PhD); applied mathematics (MS); applied politics (MA); arts and sciences (MA, MFA, MPA, MS, PhD); biology (MS); chemistry (MS, PhD); composition (MA); computer science (MS); counseling psychology (MA, PhD); creative writing (MFA); earth science (MS); economics (MA); environmental geology (MS); geographic information science (MS); geology (MS); geophysics (MS); history (MA, PhD); industrial/gerontological psychology (PhD); industrial/organizational psychology (MA, PhD); integrated bioscience (PhD); literature (MA); mathematics (MS); physics (MS); political science (MA); psychology (MA); public administration (MPA); sociology (MA, PhD); Spanish (MA); statistics (MS); urban planning (MA); urban studies (MA, PhD); urban studies and public affairs (PhD). *Application deadline:* Applications are processed on a rolling basis. *Application fee:* $30 ($40 for international students). Electronic applications accepted. *Application Contact:* Dr. Chand Midha, Interim Dean, 330-972-7882, E-mail: cmidha@uakron.edu. *Interim Dean*, Dr. Chand Midha, 330-972-7882, E-mail: cmidha@uakron.edu.

College of Business Administration Students: 203 full-time (89 women), 298 part-time (114 women); includes 30 minority (13 African Americans, 1 American Indian/Alaska Native, 13 Asian Americans or Pacific Islanders, 3 Hispanic Americans), 120 international. Average age 30. 258 applicants, 71% accepted, 124 enrolled. *Faculty:* 35 full-time (8 women), 42 part-time/adjunct (9 women). Expenses: Contact institution. *Financial support:* In 2008–09, 5 fellowships with full tuition reimbursements, 62 research assistantships with full tuition reimbursements, 6 teaching assistantships with full tuition reimbursements were awarded; career-related internships or fieldwork, Federal Work-Study, and tuition waivers (full) also available. In 2008, 147 master's awarded. *Degree program information:* Part-time and evening/weekend programs available. Offers accountancy (MS); accounting-information systems (MS); business administration (MBA, MS, MSM, MT); electronic business (MBA); entrepreneurship (MBA); finance (MBA); international business (MBA); international business for international executive (MBA); management (MBA); management of technology (MBA); management-health services administration (MSM); management-human resources (MSM); management-information systems (MSM); management-supply chain management (MSM); strategic marketing (MBA); taxation (MT). *Application deadline:* Applications are processed on a rolling basis. *Application fee:* $30 ($40 for international students). Electronic applications accepted. *Application Contact:* Dr. James Divoky, Director of Graduate Business Programs, 330-972-7043, Fax: 330-972-6588, E-mail: jdivoky@uakron.edu. *Dean*, Dr. Raj Aggrawal, 330-972-7442, E-mail: cbadean@uakron.edu.

College of Education Students: 465 full-time (312 women), 965 part-time (737 women); includes 160 minority (129 African Americans, 2 American Indian/Alaska Native, 15 Asian Americans or Pacific Islanders, 14 Hispanic Americans), 38 international. Average age 33. 564 applicants, 68% accepted, 277 enrolled. *Faculty:* 53 full-time (34 women), 135 part-time/adjunct (89 women). Expenses: Contact institution. *Financial support:* In 2008–09, 70 research assistantships with full tuition reimbursements, 46 teaching assistantships with full tuition reimbursements were awarded; fellowships with full tuition reimbursements, career-related internships or fieldwork, Federal Work-Study, tuition waivers (full), and unspecified assistantships also available. In 2008, 313 master's, 19 doctorates awarded. *Degree program information:* Part-time programs available. Offers classroom guidance for teachers (MA, MS); community counseling (MA, MS); counseling psychology (PhD); counselor education and supervision (PhD); education (MA, MS, Ed D, PhD); educational leadership (Ed D); elementary education (MA, MS, PhD); elementary education—literacy (MA); elementary education with licensure (MS); exercise physiology/adult fitness (MA, MS); higher education administration (MA, MS); marriage and family therapy (MA, MS); physical education K–12 (MA, MS); principalship (MA, MS); school counseling (MA, MS); school psychology (MS); secondary education (MA, MS, PhD); secondary education with licensure (MS); special education (MA, MS); sports science/coaching (MA, MS); technical education (MS). *Application deadline:* Applications are processed on a rolling basis. *Application fee:* $30 ($40 for international students). Electronic applications accepted. *Application Contact:* Dr. Cynthia Capers, Interim Dean, 330-972-7680, E-mail: capers@uakron.edu. *Interim Dean*, Dr. Cynthia Capers, 330-972-7680, E-mail: capers@uakron.edu.

College of Engineering Students: 222 full-time (52 women), 94 part-time (21 women); includes 16 minority (3 African Americans, 12 Asian Americans or Pacific Islanders, 1 Hispanic American), 185 international. Average age 27. 412 applicants, 43% accepted, 74 enrolled. *Faculty:* 63 full-time (5 women), 25 part-time/adjunct (1 woman). Expenses: Contact institution. *Financial support:* In 2008–09, 2 fellowships with full tuition reimbursements, 45 research assistantships with full tuition reimbursements, 123 teaching assistantships with full tuition reimbursements were awarded; career-related internships or fieldwork, Federal Work-Study, and tuition waivers (full) also available. In 2008, 64 master's, 16 doctorates awarded. *Degree program information:* Part-time and evening/weekend programs available. Offers biomedical engineering (MS, PhD); chemical and biomolecular engineering (MS, PhD); civil engineering (MS, PhD); electrical and computer engineering (MS, PhD); engineering (MS, PhD); engineering (biomedical engineering specialization) (MS); engineering (management specialization) (MS); engineering (polymer specialization) (MS); engineering applied mathematics (PhD); interdisciplinary engineering (PhD); mechanical engineering (MS, PhD). *Application deadline:* Applications are processed on a rolling basis. *Application fee:* $30 ($40 for international students). Electronic applications accepted. *Application Contact:* Dr. Craig Menzemer, Director of Graduate Studies, 330-972-5536, E-mail: ccmenze@uakron.edu. *Dean*, Dr. George Haritos, 330-972-6978, E-mail: haritos@uakron.edu.

College of Fine and Applied Arts Students: 344 full-time (275 women), 135 part-time (106 women); includes 50 minority (41 African Americans, 4 Asian Americans or Pacific Islanders, 5 Hispanic Americans), 21 international. Average age 31. 397 applicants, 58% accepted, 153 enrolled. *Faculty:* 68 full-time (33 women), 112 part-time/adjunct (76 women). Expenses: Contact institution. *Financial support:* In 2008–09, 44 fellowships with full tuition reimbursements, 62 research assistantships with full tuition reimbursements, 94 teaching assistantships with full tuition reimbursements were awarded; career-related internships or fieldwork, Federal Work-Study, institutionally sponsored loans, tuition waivers (partial), and unspecified assistantships also available. Support available to part-time students. In 2008, 151 master's, 8 doctorates awarded. *Degree program information:* Part-time and evening/weekend programs available. Offers arts administration (MA); audiology (Au D); child and family development (MA); child development (MA); child life (MA); clothing, textiles and interiors (MA); communication (MA); composition (MM); family development (MA); fine and applied arts (MA, MM, MS, Au D); music education (MM); music history and literature (MM); music technology (MM); nutrition and dietetics (MS); performance (MM); social work (MS); speech-language pathology (MA); theatre arts (MA); theory (MM). *Application deadline:* Applications are processed on a rolling basis. *Application fee:* $30 ($40 for international students). Electronic applications accepted. *Application Contact:* Dr. Mark Tausig, Associate Dean, 330-972-6266, Fax: 330-972-6475, E-mail: mtausig@uakron.edu. *Interim Dean*, Dr. James Lynn, 330-972-7543.

College of Nursing Students: 66 full-time (53 women), 248 part-time (213 women); includes 29 minority (18 African Americans, 1 American Indian/Alaska Native, 8 Asian Americans or Pacific Islanders, 2 Hispanic Americans), 5 international. Average age 36. 101 applicants, 88% accepted, 54 enrolled. *Faculty:* 20 full-time (all women), 21 part-time/adjunct (18 women). Expenses: Contact institution. *Financial support:* In 2008–09, 15 fellowships with full tuition reimbursements, 8 research assistantships with full tuition reimbursements, 7 teaching assistantships with full tuition reimbursements were awarded; career-related internships or fieldwork, Federal Work-Study, and tuition waivers (full) also available. In 2008, 79 master's, 2 doctorates awarded. *Degree program information:* Part-time programs available. Offers nursing (MSN, PhD); public health (MPH). *Application deadline:* For fall admission, 1/15 for domestic and international students. Applications are processed on a rolling basis. *Application fee:* $30 ($40 for international students). Electronic applications accepted. *Application Contact:* Dr. Margaret Wineman, Dean, 330-972-7551, E-mail: wineman@uakron.edu. *Dean*, Dr. Margaret Wineman, 330-972-7551, E-mail: wineman@uakron.edu.

College of Polymer Science and Polymer Engineering Students: 147 full-time (40 women), 23 part-time (8 women); includes 3 minority (2 African Americans, 1 Asian American or Pacific Islander), 123 international. Average age 29. 237 applicants, 15% accepted, 33 enrolled. *Faculty:* 26 full-time (3 women), 7 part-time/adjunct (0 women). Expenses: Contact institution. *Financial support:* In 2008–09, 1 fellowship with full tuition reimbursement, 132 research assistantships with full tuition reimbursements, 1 teaching assistantship with full tuition reimbursement were awarded; scholarships/grants and tuition waivers (full) also available. In 2008, 5 master's, 25 doctorates awarded. *Degree program information:* Part-time and evening/weekend programs available. Offers polymer engineering (MS, PhD); polymer science (MS, PhD). *Application deadline:* For fall admission, 2/1 for domestic students, 3/1 for international students. Applications are processed on a rolling basis. *Application fee:* $30 ($40 for international students). Electronic applications accepted. *Application Contact:* Associate Dean. *Dean*, Dr. Stephen Cheng, 330-972-7500, E-mail: scheng@uakron.edu.

School of Law Students: 248 full-time (104 women), 249 part-time (129 women); includes 71 minority (33 African Americans, 3 American Indian/Alaska Native, 25 Asian Americans or Pacific Islanders, 10 Hispanic Americans), 3 international. Average age 26. 1,919 applicants, 38% accepted, 175 enrolled. *Faculty:* 33 full-time (12 women), 29 part-time/adjunct (13 women). Expenses: Contact institution. *Financial support:* In 2008–09, 171 students received support. Career-related internships or fieldwork, scholarships/grants, and tuition waivers (full and partial) available. Support available to part-time students. Financial award applicants required to submit FAFSA. In 2008, 157 JDs awarded. *Degree program information:* Part-time and evening/weekend programs available. Offers law (JD). *Application deadline:* For fall admission, 3/1 priority date for domestic and international students. Applications are processed on a rolling basis. *Application fee:* $0. Electronic applications accepted. *Application Contact:* Lauri S. File, Assistant Dean of Admission and Financial Aid, 330-972-7331, Fax: 330-258-2343, E-mail: lfile@uakron.edu. *Dean*, Martin H. Belsky, 330-972-6359, Fax: 330-258-2343, E-mail: belsky@uakron.edu.

THE UNIVERSITY OF ALABAMA, Tuscaloosa, AL 35487

General Information State-supported, coed, university. CGS member. *Enrollment:* 27,014 graduate, professional, and undergraduate students; 2,828 full-time matriculated graduate/professional students (1,489 women), 1,442 part-time matriculated graduate/professional students (977 women). *Enrollment by degree level:* 613 first professional, 2,356 master's, 1,300 doctoral. *Graduate faculty:* 770 full-time (261 women), 16 part-time/adjunct (10 women). Tuition, state resident: full-time $6400. Tuition, nonresident: full-time $18,000. *Graduate housing:* Rooms and/or apartments available on a first-come, first-served basis to single and married students. Typical cost: $4400 per year ($6430 including board) for single students; $6300 per year ($8330 including board) for married students. Room and board charges vary according to housing facility selected. Housing application deadline: 4/1. *Student services:* Campus employment opportunities, campus safety program, career counseling, child daycare facilities, exercise/wellness program, free psychological counseling, grant writing training, international student services, low-cost health insurance, multicultural affairs office, services for students with disabilities, teacher training, writing training. *Library facilities:* Amelia Gayle Gorgas Library plus 8 others. *Online resources:* library catalog, web page, access to other libraries' catalogs. *Collection:* 2.8 million titles, 47,486 serial subscriptions, 30,664 audiovisual materials. *Research affiliation:* ITIS Corp (Information Technology), Northrup Grumman (Information Technology), DuPont (chemistry), BASF (chemistry), QRxPharma (pharma), Murphy Oil (oil and gas).

Computer facilities: 2,200 computers available on campus for general student use. A campuswide network can be accessed from student residence rooms and from off campus. Online class registration is available. *Web address:* http://www.ua.edu/.

General Application Contact: Louise F. Labosier, Admissions Officer, 205-348-5921, Fax: 205-348-0400, E-mail: labosier@aalan.ua.edu.

GRADUATE UNITS

Graduate School Students: 2,383 full-time (1,321 women), 1,427 part-time (975 women); includes 625 minority (482 African Americans, 21 American Indian/Alaska Native, 62 Asian Americans or Pacific Islanders, 60 Hispanic Americans), 403 international. Average age 30. 3,874 applicants, 51% accepted, 804 enrolled. *Faculty:* 671 full-time (199 women), 13 part-time/adjunct (8 women). Expenses: Contact institution. *Financial support:* In 2008–09, 512 students received support, including fellowships with full and partial tuition reimbursements available (averaging $12,000 per year), research assistantships with full and partial tuition reimbursements available (averaging $9,252 per year), teaching assistantships with full and partial tuition reimbursements available (averaging $10,000 per year); career-related internships or fieldwork, Federal Work-Study, institutionally sponsored loans, scholarships/grants, traineeships, health care benefits, tuition waivers (full and partial), and unspecified assistantships also available. Support available to part-time students. Financial award application deadline: 2/15. In 2008, 1,237 master's, 187 doctorates, 83 other advanced degrees awarded. *Degree program information:* Part-time and evening/weekend programs available. Postbaccalaureate distance learning degree programs offered. *Application deadline:* For fall admission, 7/1 priority date for domestic students, 3/15 for international students; for spring admission, 11/1 priority date for domestic students, 7/1 for international students. Applications are processed on a rolling basis. *Application fee:* $30. Electronic applications accepted. *Application Contact:* Louise F. Labosier, Admissions Officer, 205-348-5921, Fax: 205-348-0400, E-mail: labosier@aalan.ua.edu. *Dean*, Dr. David A. Francko, 205-348-8280, Fax: 205-348-0400, E-mail: dfrancko@ua.edu.

Capstone College of Nursing Students: 29 full-time (26 women), 82 part-time (72 women); includes 36 minority (33 African Americans, 2 Asian Americans or Pacific Islanders, 1 Hispanic American). Average age 43. 96 applicants, 96% accepted, 25 enrolled. *Faculty:* 15 full-time (14 women). Expenses: Contact institution. *Financial support:* In 2008–09, 4 fellowships with full tuition reimbursements (averaging $14,000 per year), 1 research assistantship with tuition reimbursement (averaging $14,000 per year) were awarded;

scholarships/grants and traineeships also available. Financial award application deadline: 8/1. In 2008, 19 master's awarded. *Degree program information:* Part-time programs available. Postbaccalaureate distance learning degree programs offered (no on-campus study). Offers nursing (MSN, DNP). *Application deadline:* For fall admission, 6/1 priority date for domestic students; for winter admission, 1/1 priority date for domestic students; for spring admission, 4/15 priority date for domestic students. *Application fee:* $30. Electronic applications accepted. *Application Contact:* Dr. Marietta Stanton, Director, 205-348-1020, Fax: 205-348-5559, E-mail: mstanton@bama.ua.edu. *Dean,* Dr. Sara E. Barger, 205-348-1040, Fax: 205-348-5559, E-mail: sbarger@bama.ua.edu.

College of Arts and Sciences Students: 799 full-time (429 women), 188 part-time (110 women); includes 124 minority (70 African Americans, 3 American Indian/Alaska Native, 22 Asian Americans or Pacific Islanders, 29 Hispanic Americans), 149 international. Average age 28. 1,194 applicants, 35% accepted, 220 enrolled. *Faculty:* 351 full-time (103 women), 8 part-time/adjunct (5 women). Expenses: Contact institution. *Financial support:* In 2008–09, 555 students received support; fellowships with full tuition reimbursements available, research assistantships with full tuition reimbursements available, teaching assistantships with full and partial tuition reimbursements available, career-related internships or fieldwork, Federal Work-Study, institutionally sponsored loans, scholarships/grants, tuition waivers (full and partial), and unspecified assistantships available. Support available to part-time students. Financial award applicants required to submit FAFSA. In 2008, 200 master's, 69 doctorates awarded. *Degree program information:* Part-time programs available. Postbaccalaureate distance learning degree programs offered. Offers acting (MFA); American studies (MA); anthropology (MA, PhD); applied mathematics (PhD); arranging (MM); art history (MA); arts and sciences (MA, MATESOL, MFA, MM, MPA, MS, DMA, PhD); biological sciences (MS, PhD); chemistry (MS, PhD); choral conducting (MM, DMA); clinical psychology (PhD); composition (MM, DMA); composition and rhetoric (PhD); costume design (MFA); creative writing (MFA); criminal justice (MS); directing (MFA); experimental psychology (PhD); French (MA, PhD); French and Spanish (PhD); geography (MS); geological sciences (MS, PhD); German (MA); history (MA, PhD); literature (MA, PhD); mathematics (MA, PhD); music education (MA, PhD); music history (MM); performance (MM, DMA); physics (MS, PhD); political science (MA, PhD); public administration (MPA); pure mathematics (PhD); rhetoric and composition (MA); Romance languages (MA, PhD); scene design/technical production (MFA); Spanish (MA, PhD); speech language pathology (MS); stage management (MFA); studio art (MA, MFA); teaching English as a second language (MATESOL); theatre (MFA); theatre management/administration (MFA); theory (MM); wind conducting (MM, DMA); women's studies (MA). *Application fee:* $25. Electronic applications accepted. *Application Contact:* Louise F. Labosier, Admissions Officer, 205-348-5921, Fax: 205-348-0400, E-mail: labosier@aalan.ua.edu. *Dean,* Dr. Robert F. Olin, 205-348-7007, Fax: 205-348-0272, E-mail: olin@as.ua.edu.

College of Communication and Information Sciences Students: 195 full-time (132 women), 196 part-time (150 women); includes 39 minority (23 African Americans, 3 American Indian/Alaska Native, 6 Asian Americans or Pacific Islanders, 7 Hispanic Americans), 22 international. Average age 31. 472 applicants, 49% accepted, 87 enrolled. *Faculty:* 51 full-time (21 women), 4 part-time/adjunct (3 women). Expenses: Contact institution. *Financial support:* In 2008–09, 78 students received support, including 3 fellowships with tuition reimbursements available (averaging $15,000 per year), 34 research assistantships with tuition reimbursements available (averaging $13,045 per year), 38 teaching assistantships with tuition reimbursements available (averaging $13,045 per year); career-related internships or fieldwork, Federal Work-Study, institutionally sponsored loans, and health care benefits also available. Financial award application deadline: 2/15. In 2008, 148 master's, 6 doctorates awarded. Offers advertising and public relations (MA); book arts (MFA); communication and information sciences (MA, MFA, MLIS, PhD); communication studies (MA); journalism (MA); library and information studies (MLIS, PhD); mass communications (PhD); telecommunication and film (MA). *Application deadline:* For fall admission, 2/15 priority date for domestic and international students; for winter admission, 11/1 priority date for international students; for spring admission, 11/1 priority date for domestic students. Applications are processed on a rolling basis. *Application fee:* $30. Electronic applications accepted. *Application Contact:* Diane Shaddix, Information Contact, 205-348-8593, Fax: 205-348-6774, E-mail: dshaddix@bama.ua.edu. *Associate Dean for Graduate Studies,* Dr. Jennings Bryant, 205-348-8593, Fax: 205-348-6774.

College of Education Students: 357 full-time (253 women), 544 part-time (375 women); includes 164 minority (144 African Americans, 8 American Indian/Alaska Native, 3 Asian Americans or Pacific Islanders, 9 Hispanic Americans), 24 international. Average age 33. 478 applicants, 65% accepted, 87 enrolled. *Faculty:* 85 full-time (47 women). Expenses: Contact institution. *Financial support:* In 2008–09, 42 research assistantships with full and partial tuition reimbursements were awarded; teaching assistantships with full and partial tuition reimbursements, career-related internships or fieldwork, Federal Work-Study, institutionally sponsored loans, scholarships/grants, and unspecified assistantships also available. Financial award applicants required to submit FAFSA. In 2008, 236 master's, 66 doctorates, 83 other advanced degrees awarded. *Degree program information:* Part-time programs available. Postbaccalaureate distance learning degree programs offered (minimal on-campus study). Offers alternative sport pedagogy (MA); choral music education (MA); collaborative teacher program (M Ed, Ed S); early intervention (M Ed, Ed S); education (M Ed, MA, Ed D, PhD, Ed S); educational administration (Ed D, PhD); educational leadership (MA, Ed S); educational studies in psychology, research methodology and counseling (MA, Ed D, PhD, Ed S); elementary education (MA, Ed D, PhD, Ed S); exercise science (MA, PhD); gifted education (M Ed, Ed S); higher education administration (MA, Ed D, PhD); human performance (MA); instructional leadership (Ed D, PhD); instrumental music education (MA); multiple abilities program (M Ed); music education (Ed D, PhD, Ed S); secondary education (MA, Ed D, PhD, Ed S); special education (Ed D, PhD); sport management (MA); sport pedagogy (MA, PhD). *Application deadline:* For fall admission, 7/1 for domestic and international students; for spring admission, 11/17 for domestic and international students. Applications are processed on a rolling basis. *Application fee:* $30. *Application Contact:* Dr. Kathy S. Wetzel, Assistant Dean for Student Services, 205-348-1154, Fax: 205-348-0080, E-mail: kwetzel@bamaed.ua.edu. *Dean,* Dr. James E. McLean, 205-348-6052.

College of Engineering Students: 197 full-time (46 women), 55 part-time (14 women); includes 25 minority (18 African Americans, 4 Asian Americans or Pacific Islanders, 3 Hispanic Americans), 131 international. Average age 28. 306 applicants, 47% accepted, 47 enrolled. *Faculty:* 96 full-time (14 women), 1 part-time/adjunct (0 women). Expenses: Contact institution. *Financial support:* In 2008–09, 188 students received support, including 23 fellowships with full tuition reimbursements available (averaging $16,022 per year), 85 research assistantships with full tuition reimbursements available (averaging $16,022 per year), 73 teaching assistantships with full tuition reimbursements available (averaging $16,022 per year); career-related internships or fieldwork, Federal Work-Study, and institutionally sponsored loans also available. Financial award application deadline: 2/15. In 2008, 78 master's, 19 doctorates awarded. *Degree program information:* Part-time programs available. Postbaccalaureate distance learning degree programs offered (no on-campus study). Offers aerospace engineering (MAE); chemical and biological engineering (MS Ch E, PhD); civil engineering (MSCE, PhD); computer science (MS, PhD); electrical engineering (MS, PhD); engineering (MAE, MES, MS, MS Ch E, MS Met E, MSCE, MSIE, PhD); engineering science and mechanics (MES, PhD); environmental engineering (MS); industrial engineering (MSIE); materials science (PhD); mechanical engineering (MS, PhD); metallurgical and materials engineering (MS Met E, PhD). *Application deadline:* For fall admission, 7/1 for domestic students, 4/15 for international students; for spring admission, 11/15 for domestic students, 9/1 for international students. Applications are processed on a rolling basis. *Application fee:* $30. Electronic applications accepted. *Application Contact:* Dr. David A. Francko, Dean, 205-348-8280, Fax: 205-348-0400, E-mail: dfrancko@ua.edu. *Dean,* Dr. Charles Karr, 205-348-6405, Fax: 205-348-8573.

College of Human Environmental Sciences Students: 158 full-time (102 women), 235 part-time (169 women); includes 75 minority (61 African Americans, 4 American Indian/Alaska Native, 5 Asian Americans or Pacific Islanders, 5 Hispanic Americans), 6 international. Average age 31. 271 applicants, 78% accepted, 71 enrolled. *Faculty:* 28 full-time (21 women), 1 part-time/adjunct (0 women). Expenses: Contact institution. *Financial support:* In 2008–09, 2 research assistantships with full tuition reimbursements (averaging $9,000 per year) were awarded; fellowships with tuition reimbursements, teaching assistantships with full tuition reimbursements, career-related internships or fieldwork, Federal Work-Study, institutionally sponsored loans, and scholarships/grants also available. In 2008, 152 master's, 2 doctorates awarded. *Degree program information:* Part-time and evening/weekend programs available. Postbaccalaureate distance learning degree programs offered (no on-campus study). Offers clothing, textiles, and interior design (MSHES); consumer sciences (MS); family financial planning and counseling (MS); health education and promotion (PhD); health studies (MA); human development and family studies (MSHES); human environmental sciences (MA, MS, MSHES, PhD); human nutrition and hospitality management (MSHES); interactive technology (MS); quality management (MS); restaurant and meeting management (MS); rural community health (MS); sport management (MS). *Application deadline:* For fall admission, 7/6 for domestic students. Applications are processed on a rolling basis. *Application fee:* $30. Electronic applications accepted. *Application Contact:* Dr. Milla D. Boschung, Dean, 205-348-6250, Fax: 205-348-1786, E-mail: mboschun@ches.ua.edu. *Dean,* Dr. Milla D. Boschung, 205-348-6250, Fax: 205-348-1786, E-mail: mboschun@ches.ua.edu.

Manderson Graduate School of Business Students: 444 full-time (157 women), 49 part-time (20 women); includes 48 minority (27 African Americans, 1 American Indian/Alaska Native, 16 Asian Americans or Pacific Islanders, 4 Hispanic Americans), 65 international. Average age 27. 760 applicants, 51% accepted, 233 enrolled. *Faculty:* 51 full-time (21 women), 4 part-time/adjunct (3 women). Expenses: Contact institution. *Financial support:* In 2008–09, 60 research assistantships with full and partial tuition reimbursements (averaging $20,000 per year), 60 teaching assistantships with full and partial tuition reimbursements (averaging $20,000 per year) were awarded; fellowships with full and partial tuition reimbursements, career-related internships or fieldwork, Federal Work-Study, institutionally sponsored loans, and scholarships/grants also available. Support available to part-time students. In 2008, 209 master's, 25 doctorates awarded. *Degree program information:* Part-time and evening/weekend programs available. Postbaccalaureate distance learning degree programs offered (no on-campus study). Offers accounting (M Acc, PhD); applied statistics (MS, PhD); business (EMBA, M Acc, MA, MBA, MS, MTA, PhD); economics (MA, PhD); finance (MS, PhD); general commerce and business (EMBA, MBA); information systems, statistics, and management science—applied statistics (MS, PhD); information systems, statistics, and management science—operations management (MS, PhD); management (MA, MS, PhD); marketing (MS, PhD); operations management (MS, PhD); tax accounting (MTA). *Application deadline:* For winter admission, 1/2 priority date for domestic and international students; for spring admission, 4/15 for domestic and international students. Applications are processed on a rolling basis. *Application fee:* $30. Electronic applications accepted. *Application Contact:* Blake Bedsole, Coordinator of Graduate Recruiting/Admissions, 205-348-9122, Fax: 205-348-4504, E-mail: bbedsole@cba.ua.edu. *Dean,* Dr. J. Barry Mason, 205-348-8935, Fax: 205-348-5308, E-mail: jbmason@cba.ua.edu.

School of Social Work Students: 200 full-time (174 women), 73 part-time (62 women); includes 111 minority (103 African Americans, 2 American Indian/Alaska Native, 4 Asian Americans or Pacific Islanders, 2 Hispanic Americans), 3 international. Average age 32. 12 applicants, 50% accepted, 5 enrolled. *Faculty:* 17 full-time (10 women). Expenses: Contact institution. *Financial support:* In 2008–09, 113 students received support, including 4 fellowships (averaging $3,750 per year), 9 research assistantships with full tuition reimbursements available (averaging $9,394 per year), 3 teaching assistantships with full tuition reimbursements available (averaging $9,396 per year); career-related internships or fieldwork, scholarships/grants, health care benefits, tuition waivers (partial), and unspecified assistantships also available. Financial award application deadline: 2/1. In 2008, 156 master's awarded. Postbaccalaureate distance learning degree programs offered (no on-campus study). Offers social work (MSW, PhD). *Application deadline:* For fall admission, 2/1 priority date for domestic students; for spring admission, 9/1 priority date for domestic students. Applications are processed on a rolling basis. *Application fee:* $30. Electronic applications accepted. *Application Contact:* Dr. Ginny Raymond, Associate Dean, 205-348-3943, Fax: 205-348-9419, E-mail: graymond@sw.ua.edu. *Dean,* Dr. James P. Adams, 205-348-3924, Fax: 205-348-9419, E-mail: jadams@sw.ua.edu.

School of Law *Faculty:* 4 full-time (0 women). Expenses: Contact institution. *Financial support:* In 2008–09, 383 students received support. Career-related internships or fieldwork, Federal Work-Study, institutionally sponsored loans, scholarships/grants, and tuition waivers (full and partial) available. Financial award application deadline: 5/15. In 2008, 154 JDs, 38 master's awarded. Postbaccalaureate distance learning degree programs offered (no on-campus study). Offers law (JD, LL M, LL M in Tax). *Application deadline:* For fall admission, 3/1 for domestic and international students. Applications are processed on a rolling basis. *Application fee:* $35. Electronic applications accepted. *Application Contact:* Page Thead Pulliam, Assistant Director for Admissions, 205-348-7945, Fax: 205-348-3917, E-mail: ppulliam@law.ua.edu. *Dean,* Kenneth C. Randall, 205-348-5117, Fax: 205-348-3917, E-mail: krandall@law.ua.edu.

THE UNIVERSITY OF ALABAMA AT BIRMINGHAM, Birmingham, AL 35294

General Information State-supported, coed, university. CGS member. *Enrollment:* 16,149 graduate, professional, and undergraduate students; 3,478 full-time matriculated graduate/professional students (1,965 women), 1,822 part-time matriculated graduate/professional students (1,215 women). *Enrollment by degree level:* 1,025 first professional, 2,923 master's, 1,279 doctoral, 73 other advanced degrees. *Graduate housing:* Rooms and/or apartments available on a first-come, first-served basis to single and married students. Housing application deadline: 5/1. *Student services:* Campus employment opportunities, campus safety program, career counseling, child daycare facilities, exercise/wellness program, free psychological counseling, international student services, low-cost health insurance, multicultural affairs office, services for students with disabilities, teacher training. *Library facilities:* Mervyn Sterne Library plus 1 other. *Online resources:* library catalog, web page, access to other libraries' catalogs. *Collection:* 1.4 million titles, 67,902 serial subscriptions.

Computer facilities: 550 computers available on campus for general student use. A campuswide network can be accessed from student residence rooms and from off campus. Online class registration, transcript requests are available. *Web address:* http://www.uab.edu/.

General Application Contact: Julie Bryant, Director of Graduate Admissions, 205-934-8227, Fax: 205-934-8413, E-mail: jbryant@uab.edu.

GRADUATE UNITS

Graduate Programs in Joint Health Sciences Students: 434 full-time (188 women), 15 part-time (7 women); includes 74 minority (40 African Americans, 3 American Indian/Alaska Native, 22 Asian Americans or Pacific Islanders, 9 Hispanic Americans), 130 international. Average age 28. Expenses: Contact institution. *Financial support:* Fellowships, career-related internships or fieldwork available. In 2008, 10 master's, 57 doctorates awarded. Offers basic medical sciences (MSBMS); biochemistry and molecular genetics (PhD); cell biology (PhD); cellular and molecular biology (PhD); cellular and molecular physiology (PhD); genetics (PhD); integrative biomedical sciences (PhD); microbiology (PhD); neurobiology (PhD); neuroscience (PhD); pathology (PhD); pharmacology (PhD); pharmacology and toxicology (PhD); physiology and biophysics (PhD); toxicology (PhD). *Application deadline:* Applications are processed on a rolling basis. *Application fee:* $35 ($60 for international students). Electronic applications accepted. *Application Contact:* Julie Bryant, Director of Graduate Admissions, 205-934-8227, Fax: 205-934-8413, E-mail: jbryant@uab.edu. *Vice President/Dean, School of Medicine,* Dr. Robert R. Rich, 205-934-1111, Fax: 205-934-0333, E-mail: rrich@uab.edu.

School of Arts and Humanities Students: 39 full-time (27 women), 44 part-time (33 women); includes 9 minority (7 African Americans, 2 Hispanic Americans), 2 international. Average age 30. 39 applicants, 69% accepted. Expenses: Contact institution. *Financial support:* In 2008–09, 3 teaching assistantships (averaging $9,500 per year) were awarded; research assistantships, career-related internships or fieldwork, Federal Work-Study, and tuition waivers (partial) also available. Support available to part-time students. In 2008, 25 master's awarded. Offers art history (MA); arts and humanities (MA); communication management (MA); English (MA).

The University of Alabama at Birmingham (continued)

Application deadline: Applications are processed on a rolling basis. *Application fee:* $35 ($60 for international students). Electronic applications accepted. *Application Contact:* Julie Bryant, Director of Graduate Admissions, 205-934-8227, Fax: 205-934-8413, E-mail: jbryant@uab.edu. *Dean*, Bert Brouwer, 205-934-2290, E-mail: bbrouwer@uab.edu.

School of Business Students: 108 full-time (42 women), 237 part-time (78 women); includes 54 minority (28 African Americans, 1 American Indian/Alaska Native, 19 Asian Americans or Pacific Islanders, 6 Hispanic Americans), 26 international. Average age 29. 165 applicants, 72% accepted. Expenses: Contact institution. *Financial support:* Fellowships, career-related internships or fieldwork available. In 2008, 146 master's awarded. Offers accounting and information systems (M Acct); business (M Acct, MBA, PhD); management (MBA). *Application deadline:* Applications are processed on a rolling basis. *Application fee:* $35 ($60 for international students). Electronic applications accepted. *Application Contact:* Director, 205-934-8817. *Dean*, Dr. David R. Klock, 205-934-8800, Fax: 205-934-8886, E-mail: dklock@uab.edu.

School of Dentistry Students: 228 full-time (92 women), 2 part-time (1 woman); includes 34 minority (12 African Americans, 4 American Indian/Alaska Native, 13 Asian Americans or Pacific Islanders, 5 Hispanic Americans), 4 international. Average age 25. Expenses: Contact institution. *Financial support:* Fellowships, Federal Work-Study available. In 2008, 58 first professional degrees, 10 master's awarded. Offers dentistry (DMD, MS, MSBMS, PhD); dentistry and oral biology (MS). *Application deadline:* For fall admission, 2/15 for domestic students. *Application fee:* $145. Electronic applications accepted. *Application Contact:* Dr. Steven J. Filler, Director of Dentistry Admissions, 205-934-5424, Fax: 205-975-6519, E-mail: sfiller@uab.edu. *Dean*, Dr. Huw F. Thomas, 205-934-4720, Fax: 205-934-9283.

School of Education Students: 269 full-time (211 women), 523 part-time (416 women); includes 187 minority (174 African Americans, 2 American Indian/Alaska Native, 4 Asian Americans or Pacific Islanders, 7 Hispanic Americans), 8 international. Average age 33. Expenses: Contact institution. *Financial support:* Fellowships, career-related internships or fieldwork and Federal Work-Study available. Support available to part-time students. In 2008, 272 master's, 17 doctorates, 29 other advanced degrees awarded. *Degree program information:* Part-time and evening/weekend programs available. Offers arts education (MA Ed); counseling (MA); early childhood education (MA Ed, PhD); education (MA, MA Ed, Ed D, PhD, Ed S); educational leadership (MA Ed, Ed D, PhD, Ed S); elementary education (MA Ed); health education (MA Ed); health education and health promotion (PhD); high school education (MA Ed); physical education (MA Ed); special education (MA Ed). *Application deadline:* Applications are processed on a rolling basis. *Application fee:* $35 ($60 for international students). Electronic applications accepted. *Application Contact:* Julie Bryant, Director of Graduate Admissions, 205-934-8227, Fax: 205-934-8413, E-mail: jbryant@uab.edu. *Dean*, Dr. Michael J. Froning, 205-934-5363, Fax: 205-934-4963.

School of Engineering Students: 124 full-time (35 women), 180 part-time (36 women); includes 67 minority (47 African Americans, 1 American Indian/Alaska Native, 14 Asian Americans or Pacific Islanders, 5 Hispanic Americans), 99 international. Average age 31. Expenses: Contact institution. *Financial support:* Fellowships with full tuition reimbursements, research assistantships with full tuition reimbursements, career-related internships or fieldwork, Federal Work-Study, institutionally sponsored loans, and tuition waivers (full and partial) available. Support available to part-time students. In 2008, 76 master's, 15 doctorates awarded. *Degree program information:* Evening/weekend programs available. Offers biomedical engineering (MSBME, PhD); civil engineering (MSCE, PhD); computer engineering (PhD); electrical engineering (MSEE); engineering (MS Mt E, MSBME, MSCE, MSEE, MSME, PhD); environmental health engineering (PhD); materials engineering (MS Mt E, PhD); materials science (PhD); mechanical engineering (MSME, PhD). *Application deadline:* Applications are processed on a rolling basis. *Application fee:* $35 ($60 for international students). Electronic applications accepted. *Application Contact:* Julie Bryant, Director of Graduate Admissions, 205-934-8227, Fax: 205-934-8413, E-mail: jbryant@uab.edu. *Dean*, Dr. Linda C. Lucas, 205-934-8420, Fax: 205-975-4919.

School of Health Professions Students: 638 full-time (446 women), 154 part-time (106 women); includes 108 minority (70 African Americans, 7 American Indian/Alaska Native, 23 Asian Americans or Pacific Islanders, 8 Hispanic Americans), 26 international. Average age 29. Expenses: Contact institution. *Financial support:* Fellowships, research assistantships, teaching assistantships, career-related internships or fieldwork, Federal Work-Study, institutionally sponsored loans, scholarships/grants, traineeships, and unspecified assistantships available. Support available to part-time students. In 2008, 163 master's, 46 doctorates awarded. *Degree program information:* Part-time programs available. Offers administration-health services (PhD); clinical nutrition (MS); clinical nutrition and dietetics (MS, Certificate); dietetic internship (Certificate); health administration (MSHA); health informatics (MS); health professions (MNA, MS, MSHA, DPT, Dr Sc PT, PhD, Certificate); low vision rehabilitation (Certificate); nurse anesthesia (MNA); nutrition sciences (PhD); occupational therapy (MS, Certificate); physical therapy (DPT, Dr Sc PT); physician assistant (MS). *Application fee:* $35 ($60 for international students). Electronic applications accepted. *Application Contact:* Julie Bryant, Director of Graduate Admissions, 205-934-8227, Fax: 205-934-8413, E-mail: jbryant@uab.edu. *Dean*, Dr. Harold P. Jones, 205-934-5149, Fax: 205-934-2412, E-mail: jonesh@uab.edu.

School of Medicine Students: 623 full-time (261 women); includes 126 minority (41 African Americans, 3 American Indian/Alaska Native, 82 Asian Americans or Pacific Islanders). Average age 25. 2,055 applicants, 11% accepted. Expenses: Contact institution. *Financial support:* Fellowships, career-related internships or fieldwork available. Financial award application deadline: 5/1; financial award applicants required to submit FAFSA. In 2008, 152 first professional degrees awarded. Offers medicine (MD, MSBMS, PhD). *Application deadline:* For fall admission, 11/1 for domestic students. *Application fee:* $65. Electronic applications accepted. *Application Contact:* Dr. George S. Hand, Assistant Dean for Admissions, 205-934-2333, Fax: 205-934-8724, E-mail: ghand@uab.edu. *Vice President/Dean, School of Medicine*, Dr. Robert R. Rich, 205-934-1111, Fax: 205-934-0333, E-mail: rrich@uab.edu.

School of Natural Sciences and Mathematics Students: 163 full-time (59 women), 27 part-time (13 women); includes 21 minority (13 African Americans, 4 Asian Americans or Pacific Islanders, 4 Hispanic Americans), 79 international. Average age 28. *Faculty:* 72 full-time (7 women), 32 part-time/adjunct (5 women). Expenses: Contact institution. *Financial support:* Fellowships with full tuition reimbursements, research assistantships with full tuition reimbursements, teaching assistantships with full tuition reimbursements, career-related internships or fieldwork, Federal Work-Study, institutionally sponsored loans, scholarships/grants, traineeships, health care benefits, tuition waivers (full and partial), and unspecified assistantships available. Support available to part-time students. Financial award applicants required to submit FAFSA. In 2008, 37 master's, 21 doctorates awarded. Offers applied mathematics (PhD); biology (MS, PhD); chemistry (MS, PhD); computer and information sciences (MS, PhD); mathematics (MS); natural sciences and mathematics (MS, PhD); physics (MS, PhD). *Application deadline:* Applications are processed on a rolling basis. *Application fee:* $35 ($60 for international students). Electronic applications accepted. *Application Contact:* Julie Bryant, Director of Graduate Admissions, 205-934-8227, Fax: 205-934-8413, E-mail: jbryant@uab.edu. *Dean*, Dr. Lowell E. Wenger, 205-934-5102.

School of Nursing Students: 203 full-time (181 women), 573 part-time (515 women); includes 127 minority (101 African Americans, 3 American Indian/Alaska Native, 15 Asian Americans or Pacific Islanders, 8 Hispanic Americans), 15 international. Average age 36. Expenses: Contact institution. *Financial support:* In 2008–09, 3 fellowships (averaging $12,833 per year), 1 research assistantship, teaching assistantships (averaging $6,760 per year) were awarded; Federal Work-Study also available. Support available to part-time students. In 2008, 83 master's, 1 doctorate awarded. Offers nursing (MSN, PhD). *Application deadline:* Applications are processed on a rolling basis. *Application fee:* $35 ($60 for international students). Electronic applications accepted. *Application Contact:* Dr. Lynda L. Harrison, Associate for Graduate Studies, 205-934-6787. *Dean*, Dr. Doreen C. Harper, 205-934-5360, E-mail: dcharper@uab.edu.

School of Optometry Students: 194 full-time (134 women), 7 part-time (1 woman); includes 42 minority (17 African Americans, 3 American Indian/Alaska Native, 19 Asian Americans or Pacific Islanders, 3 Hispanic Americans), 9 international. Average age 29. Expenses: Contact institution. *Financial support:* In 2008–09, 137 students received support. Federal Work-Study available. Financial award application deadline: 5/1; financial award applicants required to submit FAFSA. In 2008, 39 first professional degrees, 1 doctorate awarded. Offers optometry (OD, MS, PhD); vision science (MS, PhD). *Application deadline:* Applications are processed on a rolling basis. *Application fee:* $40. *Application Contact:* Dr. Gerald Simon, Director, Optometry Student Affairs, 205-935-0739, Fax: 205-934-6758, E-mail: gsimonod@uab.edu. *Dean*, Dr. John F. Amos, 205-934-3036, Fax: 205-975-7052, E-mail: optometrydean@uab.edu.

School of Public Health Students: 311 full-time (188 women), 98 part-time (60 women); includes 102 minority (64 African Americans, 30 Asian Americans or Pacific Islanders, 8 Hispanic Americans), 113 international. Average age 30. Expenses: Contact institution. *Financial support:* In 2008–09, 115 students received support; fellowships, career-related internships or fieldwork, Federal Work-Study, scholarships/grants, and unspecified assistantships available. Support available to part-time students. Financial award application deadline: 2/15. In 2008, 94 master's, 18 doctorates awarded. *Degree program information:* Part-time programs available. Offers biostatistics (MS, PhD); environmental health (PhD); epidemiology (PhD); health care organization and policy (MPH, MSPH); health education and health promotion (PhD); public health (MPH, MS, MSPH, DPH, PhD). *Application deadline:* Applications are processed on a rolling basis. *Application fee:* $35 ($60 for international students). Electronic applications accepted. *Application Contact:* Nancy O. Pinson, Coordinator of Student Admissions, 205-934-4993, Fax: 205-975-5484. *Dean*, Dr. Max Michael, 205-975-7742, Fax: 205-975-5484, E-mail: maxm@uab.edu.

School of Social and Behavioral Sciences Students: 148 full-time (104 women), 72 part-time (42 women); includes 47 minority (37 African Americans, 1 American Indian/Alaska Native, 5 Asian Americans or Pacific Islanders, 4 Hispanic Americans), 7 international. Average age 29. Expenses: Contact institution. *Financial support:* Fellowships, research assistantships, teaching assistantships, career-related internships or fieldwork, Federal Work-Study, and institutionally sponsored loans available. Support available to part-time students. In 2008, 43 master's, 16 doctorates awarded. *Degree program information:* Part-time and evening/weekend programs available. Offers anthropology (MA); criminal justice (MSCJ); forensic science (MSFS); history (MA); medical sociology (PhD); psychology (MA, PhD); public administration (MPA); social and behavioral sciences (MA, MPA, MSCJ, MSFS, PhD); sociology (MA). *Application deadline:* Applications are processed on a rolling basis. *Application fee:* $35 ($60 for international students). Electronic applications accepted. *Application Contact:* Julie Bryant, Director of Graduate Admissions, 205-934-8227, Fax: 205-934-8413, E-mail: jbryant@uab.edu. *Dean*, Dr. Jean Ann Linney, 205-934-5643, Fax: 205-934-5643, E-mail: tsm@uab.edu.

THE UNIVERSITY OF ALABAMA IN HUNTSVILLE, Huntsville, AL 35899

General Information State-supported, coed, university. CGS member. *Enrollment:* 7,431 graduate, professional, and undergraduate students; 460 full-time matriculated graduate/professional students (215 women), 937 part-time matriculated graduate/professional students (346 women). *Enrollment by degree level:* 1,082 master's, 291 doctoral, 24 other advanced degrees. *Graduate faculty:* 196 full-time (51 women), 24 part-time/adjunct (5 women). Tuition, state resident: full-time $5214; part-time $323 per credit hour. Tuition, nonresident: full-time $11,444; part-time $705 per credit hour. *Required fees:* $540; $120 per semester. Tuition and fees vary according to course load. *Graduate housing:* Rooms and/or apartments available on a first-come, first-served basis to single and married students. Typical cost: $3120 per year ($5070 including board) for single students; $5760 per year ($7710 including board) for married students. Room and board charges vary according to board plan and housing facility selected. *Student services:* Campus employment opportunities, campus safety program, career counseling, child daycare facilities, exercise/wellness program, free psychological counseling, international student services, low-cost health insurance, multicultural affairs office, services for students with disabilities, teacher training, writing training. *Library facilities:* University of Alabama in Huntsville Library. *Online resources:* library catalog, web page, access to other libraries' catalogs. *Collection:* 334,612 titles, 926 serial subscriptions. *Research affiliation:* Oak Ridge, Lawrence Livermore & Savannah River National Laboratories;Y12 National Security Complex (neutron science, energy, high-performance computing, systems biology, materials science at the nanoscale, and national security), Cummings Research Park/Boeing/ADTRAN/SAIC/Teledyne Brown Engineering/Lockhead Martin/Dynetics, Inc. (Computer Science, Aerospace Engineering, Information Systems, Space Systems, Defense Systems, Informatics), NOAA—National Oceanic & Atmospheric Administration (weather, climate, oceans, satellites), Hudson Alpha Institute for Biotechnology (medical, biotechnology, genetic research, molecular biology), Department of Defense/U.S. Army Aviation & Missile Command (missile research, development and engineering and manufacturing technology), NASA/Marshall Space Flight Center/Goddard Space Flight Center (space science, earth science, information technology, materials science, optical science).

Computer facilities: 1,153 computers available on campus for general student use. A campuswide network can be accessed from student residence rooms and from off campus. Online class registration is available. *Web address:* http://www.uah.edu/.

General Application Contact: Dr. Debra Moriarity, Dean of Graduate Studies, 256-824-6002, Fax: 256-824-6405, E-mail: deangrad@uah.edu.

GRADUATE UNITS

School of Graduate Studies Students: 460 full-time (215 women), 937 part-time (346 women); includes 168 minority (97 African Americans, 14 American Indian/Alaska Native, 40 Asian Americans or Pacific Islanders, 17 Hispanic Americans), 208 international. Average age 32. 1,319 applicants, 55% accepted, 470 enrolled. *Faculty:* 196 full-time (51 women), 24 part-time/adjunct (5 women). Expenses: Contact institution. *Financial support:* In 2008–09, 306 students received support, including 2 fellowships with full and partial tuition reimbursements available (averaging $18,000 per year), 123 research assistantships with full and partial tuition reimbursements available (averaging $12,697 per year), 143 teaching assistantships with full and partial tuition reimbursements available (averaging $10,334 per year); career-related internships or fieldwork, Federal Work-Study, institutionally sponsored loans, scholarships/grants, traineeships, health care benefits, and unspecified assistantships also available. Support available to part-time students. Financial award application deadline: 4/1; financial award applicants required to submit FAFSA. In 2008, 322 master's, 37 doctorates, 31 other advanced degrees awarded. *Degree program information:* Part-time and evening/weekend programs available. Postbaccalaureate distance learning degree programs offered (minimal on-campus study). *Application deadline:* For fall admission, 7/15 priority date for domestic students, 4/1 priority date for international students; for spring admission, 11/30 priority date for domestic students, 9/1 priority date for international students. Applications are processed on a rolling basis. *Application fee:* $40 ($50 for international students). Electronic applications accepted. *Application Contact:* Kathy Biggs, Graduate Studies Admissions Manager, 256-824-6199, Fax: 256-824-6405, E-mail: biggsk@email.uah.edu. *Dean of Graduate Studies*, Dr. Debra Moriarity, 256-824-6002, Fax: 256-824-6405, E-mail: deangrad@uah.edu.

College of Business Administration Students: 42 full-time (13 women), 199 part-time (83 women); includes 36 minority (20 African Americans, 11 Asian Americans or Pacific Islanders, 5 Hispanic Americans), 12 international. Average age 33. 194 applicants, 72% accepted, 113 enrolled. *Faculty:* 21 full-time (3 women), 5 part-time/adjunct (0 women). Expenses: Contact institution. *Financial support:* In 2008–09, 3 students received support, including 1 research assistantship with full and partial tuition reimbursement available (averaging $16,000 per year); fellowships with full and partial tuition reimbursements available, teaching assistantships with full and partial tuition reimbursements available, career-related internships or fieldwork, Federal Work-Study, institutionally sponsored loans, scholarships/grants, health care benefits, and unspecified assistantships also available. Support available to part-time students. Financial award application deadline: 4/1; financial award applicants required to submit FAFSA. In 2008, 59 master's awarded. *Degree program information:* Part-time and evening/weekend programs available. Offers accounting (M Acc, Certificate); business administration (M Acc, MBA, MSIS, Certificate); economics and information systems (MSIS, Certificate); human resource management (Certificate); management

(MBA). *Application deadline:* For fall admission, 8/1 for domestic students, 4/1 for international students; for spring admission, 12/1 for domestic students, 9/1 for international students. Applications are processed on a rolling basis. *Application fee:* $40 ($50 for international students). Electronic applications accepted. *Application Contact:* Dr. Brent Wren, Director of Graduate Programs, 256-824-6681, Fax: 256-824-7571, E-mail: gradbiz@uah.edu. *Acting Dean*, Dr. James Simpson, 256-824-6408, Fax: 256-824-7571, E-mail: simpsonj@uah.edu.

College of Engineering Students: 124 full-time (28 women), 417 part-time (74 women); includes 54 minority (27 African Americans, 3 American Indian/Alaska Native, 18 Asian Americans or Pacific Islanders, 6 Hispanic Americans), 77 international. Average age 32. 445 applicants, 52% accepted, 143 enrolled. *Faculty:* 57 full-time (9 women), 11 part-time/adjunct (2 women). Expenses: Contact institution. *Financial support:* In 2008–09, 83 students received support, including 34 research assistantships with full and partial tuition reimbursements available (averaging $10,658 per year), 49 teaching assistantships with full and partial tuition reimbursements available (averaging $10,466 per year); career-related internships or fieldwork, Federal Work-Study, institutionally sponsored loans, scholarships/grants, health care benefits, and unspecified assistantships also available. Support available to part-time students. Financial award application deadline: 4/1; financial award applicants required to submit FAFSA. In 2008, 108 master's, 20 doctorates awarded. *Degree program information:* Part-time and evening/weekend programs available. Postbaccalaureate distance learning degree programs offered (minimal on-campus study). Offers aerospace engineering (MSE); chemical engineering (MSE); civil and environmental engineering (PhD); civil engineering (MSE); computer engineering (MSE, PhD); electrical engineering (MSE, PhD); engineering (MSE, MSOR, MSSE, PhD); industrial and systems engineering (PhD); industrial engineering (MSE); mechanical engineering (MSE, PhD); operations research (MSOR); optical science and engineering (PhD); optics and photonics (MSE); software engineering (MSSE). *Application deadline:* For fall admission, 7/15 for domestic students, 4/1 for international students; for spring admission, 11/30 for domestic students, 9/1 for international students. Applications are processed on a rolling basis. *Application fee:* $40 ($50 for international students). Electronic applications accepted. *Application Contact:* Kathy Biggs, Graduate Studies Admissions Manager, 256-824-6199, Fax: 256-824-6405, E-mail: deangrad@uah.edu. *Acting Dean*, Dr. Phillip Farrington, 256-824-6474, Fax: 256-824-6843, E-mail: phillip.farrington@uah.edu.

College of Liberal Arts Students: 34 full-time (25 women), 78 part-time (53 women); includes 17 minority (13 African Americans, 1 American Indian/Alaska Native, 3 Hispanic Americans), 2 international. Average age 31. 66 applicants, 70% accepted, 35 enrolled. *Faculty:* 40 full-time (21 women). Expenses: Contact institution. *Financial support:* In 2008–09, 22 students received support, including 1 research assistantship with full and partial tuition reimbursement available (averaging $8,460 per year), 6 teaching assistantships with full and partial tuition reimbursements available (averaging $8,460 per year); career-related internships or fieldwork, Federal Work-Study, institutionally sponsored loans, scholarships/grants, health care benefits, and unspecified assistantships also available. Support available to part-time students. Financial award application deadline: 4/1; financial award applicants required to submit FAFSA. In 2008, 34 master's, 7 other advanced degrees awarded. *Degree program information:* Part-time and evening/weekend programs available. Offers English (MA); history (MA); liberal arts (MA, Certificate); psychology (MA); public affairs (MA); teaching of English to speakers of other languages (Certificate); technical communications (Certificate). *Application deadline:* For fall admission, 7/18 for domestic students, 4/1 for international students; for spring admission, 11/30 for domestic students, 9/1 for international students. Applications are processed on a rolling basis. *Application fee:* $40 ($50 for international students). Electronic applications accepted. *Application Contact:* Kathy Biggs, Graduate Studies Admissions Manager, 256-824-6199, Fax: 256-824-6405, E-mail: deangrad@uah.edu. *Acting Dean*, Glenn Dasher, 256-824-6200, Fax: 256-824-6949, E-mail: dasherg@uah.edu.

College of Nursing Students: 60 full-time (53 women), 102 part-time (93 women); includes 22 minority (14 African Americans, 5 American Indian/Alaska Native, 2 Asian Americans or Pacific Islanders, 1 Hispanic American), 2 international. Average age 39. 173 applicants, 60% accepted, 85 enrolled. *Faculty:* 12 full-time (10 women), 4 part-time/adjunct (2 women). Expenses: Contact institution. *Financial support:* In 2008–09, 33 students received support, including 8 teaching assistantships with full and partial tuition reimbursements available (averaging $6,123 per year); career-related internships or fieldwork, Federal Work-Study, institutionally sponsored loans, scholarships/grants, traineeships, health care benefits, and unspecified assistantships also available. Support available to part-time students. Financial award application deadline: 4/1; financial award applicants required to submit FAFSA. In 2008, 56 master's, 3 other advanced degrees awarded. *Degree program information:* Part-time and evening/weekend programs available. Postbaccalaureate distance learning degree programs offered (minimal on-campus study). Offers family nurse practitioner (Certificate); nursing (MSN, DNP); nursing education (Certificate). *Application deadline:* For fall admission, 7/15 for domestic students, 4/1 for international students; for spring admission, 11/30 for domestic students, 9/1 for international students. Applications are processed on a rolling basis. *Application fee:* $40 ($50 for international students). Electronic applications accepted. *Application Contact:* Charles Davis, Associate Director of Nursing Student Affairs Graduate Programs, 256-824-6669, Fax: 256-824-6026, E-mail: charles.davis@uah.edu. *Dean, College of Nursing*, Dr. Fay Raines, 256-824-6345, Fax: 256-824-6026, E-mail: rainesc@uah.edu.

College of Science Students: 165 full-time (79 women), 116 part-time (37 women); includes 27 minority (13 African Americans, 4 American Indian/Alaska Native, 9 Asian Americans or Pacific Islanders, 1 Hispanic American), 93 international. Average age 29. 374 applicants, 50% accepted, 78 enrolled. *Faculty:* 66 full-time (8 women), 4 part-time/adjunct (1 woman). Expenses: Contact institution. *Financial support:* In 2008–09, 135 students received support, including 1 fellowship with full and partial tuition reimbursement available (averaging $10,000 per year), 70 research assistantships with full and partial tuition reimbursements available (averaging $12,825 per year), 64 teaching assistantships with full and partial tuition reimbursements available (averaging $10,162 per year); career-related internships or fieldwork, Federal Work-Study, institutionally sponsored loans, scholarships/grants, health care benefits, and unspecified assistantships also available. Support available to part-time students. Financial award application deadline: 4/1; financial award applicants required to submit FAFSA. In 2008, 63 master's, 13 doctorates awarded. *Degree program information:* Part-time and evening/weekend programs available. Offers applied mathematics (PhD); atmospheric and environmental science (MS, PhD); biological sciences (MS); chemistry (MS); computer science (MS, PhD); mathematics (MA, MS); optics and photonics technology (MS); physics (MS, PhD); science (MA, MS, MSSE, PhD, Certificate); software engineering (MSSE, Certificate). *Application deadline:* For fall admission, 7/15 for domestic students, 4/1 for international students; for spring admission, 11/30 for domestic students, 9/1 for international students. Applications are processed on a rolling basis. *Application fee:* $40 ($50 for international students). Electronic applications accepted. *Application Contact:* Kathy Biggs, Graduate Studies Admissions Manager, 256-824-6199, Fax: 256-824-6405, E-mail: deangrad@uah.edu. *Dean*, Dr. Jack Fix, 256-824-6605, Fax: 256-824-6819, E-mail: fixj@uah.edu.

Interdisciplinary Studies Students: 35 full-time (17 women), 25 part-time (6 women); includes 12 minority (10 African Americans, 1 American Indian/Alaska Native, 1 Hispanic American), 22 international. Average age 31. 67 applicants, 31% accepted, 16 enrolled. *Faculty:* 77 full-time (10 women), 2 part-time/adjunct (0 women). Expenses: Contact institution. *Financial support:* In 2008–09, 34 students received support, including 1 fellowship with full tuition reimbursement available (averaging $26,000 per year), 17 research assistantships with full and partial tuition reimbursements available (averaging $11,953 per year), 16 teaching assistantships with full and partial tuition reimbursements available (averaging $11,589 per year); career-related internships or fieldwork, Federal Work-Study, institutionally sponsored loans, scholarships/grants, health care benefits, and unspecified assistantships also available. Support available to part-time students. Financial award application deadline: 4/1; financial award applicants required to submit FAFSA. In 2008, 2 master's, 4 doctorates, 13 other advanced degrees awarded. *Degree program information:* Part-time and evening/weekend programs available. Offers biotechnology science and engineering (PhD); information assurance and cybersecurity (Certificate); interdisciplinary studies (MS, PhD, Certificate); materials science (MS, PhD); modeling and simulation (MS, PhD, Certificate); optical science and engineering (PhD). *Application deadline:* For fall admission, 7/15 for domestic students, 4/1 for international students; for spring admission, 11/30 for domestic students, 9/1 for international students. Applications are processed on a rolling basis. *Application fee:* $40 ($50 for international students). Electronic applications accepted. *Application Contact:* Kathy Biggs, Graduate Studies Admissions Manager, 256-824-6199, Fax: 256-824-6405, E-mail: deangrad@uah.edu. *Dean of Graduate Studies*, Dr. Debra Moriarity, 256-824-6002, Fax: 256-824-6405, E-mail: deangrad@uah.edu.

UNIVERSITY OF ALASKA ANCHORAGE, Anchorage, AK 99508-8060

General Information State-supported, coed, comprehensive institution. CGS member. *Enrollment:* 17,361 graduate, professional, and undergraduate students; 267 full-time matriculated graduate/professional students (166 women), 803 part-time matriculated graduate/professional students (591 women). *Enrollment by degree level:* 841 master's, 61 other advanced degrees. *Graduate faculty:* 140 full-time (82 women). Tuition, state resident: full-time $5418; part-time $301 per credit. Tuition, nonresident: full-time $11,070; part-time $615 per credit. *Required fees:* $580; $56 per semester. Tuition and fees vary according to course level, course load, program, reciprocity agreements and student level. *Graduate housing:* Rooms and/or apartments available on a first-come, first-served basis to single and married students. Typical cost: $2625 per year ($5975 including board) for single students; $2625 per year ($5975 including board) for married students. Room and board charges vary according to board plan, campus/location and housing facility selected. Housing application deadline: 7/1. *Student services:* Campus employment opportunities, campus safety program, career counseling, child daycare facilities, exercise/wellness program, free psychological counseling, grant writing training, international student services, low-cost health insurance, multicultural affairs office, services for students with disabilities, teacher training, writing training. *Library facilities:* Consortium Library. *Collection:* 894,080 titles, 3,833 serial subscriptions. *Research affiliation:* Conoco Phillips (energy), Habitat for Humanity (project management), BP Alaska (energy), Municipality of Anchorage (government), Providence Hospital (health care).

Computer facilities: Computer purchase and lease plans are available. 500 computers available on campus for general student use. A campuswide network can be accessed from student residence rooms and from off campus. Online class registration is available. *Web address:* http://www.uaa.alaska.edu/.

General Application Contact: Elisa Mattison, Director, Graduate School, 907-786-1096, Fax: 907-786-1791, E-mail: aygradstudies@uaa.alaska.edu.

GRADUATE UNITS

College of Arts and Sciences *Degree program information:* Part-time programs available. Offers anthropology (MA); arts and sciences (MA, MFA, MS, PhD); biological sciences (MS); clinical psychology (MS); clinical-community psychology with rural-indigenous emphasis (PhD); creative writing and literary arts (MFA); English (MA); interdisciplinary studies (MA, MS).

College of Business and Public Policy *Degree program information:* Part-time and evening/weekend programs available. Offers business administration (MBA); business and public policy (MBA, MPA, MS, Certificate); global supply chain management (MS); public administration (MPA); supply chain management (Certificate).

College of Education *Degree program information:* Part-time programs available. Offers adult education (M Ed); counseling and guidance (M Ed); early childhood special education (M Ed); education (M Ed, MAT, Certificate); educational leadership (M Ed); master teacher (M Ed); principal licensure (Certificate); special education (M Ed, Certificate); superintendent (Certificate); teaching (MAT).

College of Health and Social Welfare *Degree program information:* Part-time and evening/weekend programs available. Offers health and social welfare (MPH, MS, MSW, Certificate).

Division of Health Sciences *Degree program information:* Part-time programs available. Offers public health practice (MPH).

School of Nursing *Degree program information:* Part-time and evening/weekend programs available. Offers family nurse practitioner (Certificate); nursing (MS); nursing education (Certificate); psychiatric nurse practitioner (Certificate).

School of Social Work *Degree program information:* Part-time and evening/weekend programs available. Postbaccalaureate distance learning degree programs offered (no on-campus study). Offers clinical social work practice (Certificate); social work (MSW); social work management (Certificate). Electronic applications accepted.

School of Engineering *Degree program information:* Part-time and evening/weekend programs available. Offers applied environmental science and technology (M AEST, MS); arctic engineering (MS); civil engineering (MCE, MS); engineering (M AEST, MCE, MS, Certificate); engineering management (MS); port and coastal engineering (Certificate); project management (MS); science management (MS).

UNIVERSITY OF ALASKA FAIRBANKS, Fairbanks, AK 99775-7520

General Information State-supported, coed, university. CGS member. *Enrollment:* 8,579 graduate, professional, and undergraduate students; 578 full-time matriculated graduate/professional students (301 women), 484 part-time matriculated graduate/professional students (304 women). *Enrollment by degree level:* 720 master's, 301 doctoral, 16 other advanced degrees. *Graduate faculty:* 311 full-time (98 women), 91 part-time/adjunct (45 women). Tuition, state resident: full-time $5418; part-time $301 per credit. Tuition, nonresident: full-time $11,070; part-time $615 per credit. *Required fees:* $849; $25 per credit. $78 per semester. Tuition and fees vary according to course load and reciprocity agreements. *Graduate housing:* Rooms and/or apartments available on a first-come, first-served basis to single and married students. Typical cost: $4240 per year ($6435 including board) for single students; $4240 per year ($6435 including board) for married students. Room and board charges vary according to board plan and housing facility selected. Housing application deadline: 8/1. *Student services:* Campus employment opportunities, campus safety program, career counseling, child daycare facilities, exercise/wellness program, free psychological counseling, grant writing training, international student services, low-cost health insurance, multicultural affairs office, services for students with disabilities, teacher training, writing training. *Library facilities:* Rasmuson Library plus 1 other. *Online resources:* library catalog, web page, access to other libraries' catalogs. *Collection:* 825,738 titles, 79,487 serial subscriptions, 50,759 audiovisual materials. *Research affiliation:* Institute of Northern Forestry, Alaska Cooperative Fishery and Wildlife Research Unit.

Computer facilities: Computer purchase and lease plans are available. 125 computers available on campus for general student use. A campuswide network can be accessed from student residence rooms and from off campus. Online class registration, university portal; campus wireless access are available. *Web address:* http://www.uaf.edu/.

General Application Contact: Lael Oldmixon, Interim Director of Admissions, 907-474-7500, Fax: 907-474-5379, E-mail: admissions@uaf.edu.

GRADUATE UNITS

College of Engineering and Mines Students: 82 full-time (26 women), 32 part-time (12 women); includes 7 minority (2 African Americans, 2 American Indian/Alaska Native, 3 Asian Americans or Pacific Islanders), 60 international. Average age 31. 116 applicants, 53% accepted, 46 enrolled. *Faculty:* 50 full-time (7 women), 7 part-time/adjunct (0 women). Expenses: Contact institution. *Financial support:* In 2008–09, 3 fellowships (averaging $10,124 per year), 42 research assistantships (averaging $12,579 per year), 25 teaching assistantships (averaging $7,347 per year) were awarded; career-related internships or fieldwork, Federal Work-Study, scholarships/grants, health care benefits, and unspecified assistantships also available. Support available to part-time students. Financial award application deadline: 7/1; financial award applicants required to submit FAFSA. In 2008, 44 master's, 4 doctorates awarded. *Degree program information:* Part-time programs available. Offers arctic engineering (MS, PhD); civil engineering (MCE, MS, PhD); electrical engineering (MEE, MS, PhD); engineering (PhD); engineering and mines (MCE, MEE, MS, PhD); engineering and

University of Alaska Fairbanks (continued)

science management (MS, PhD); engineering management (MS, PhD); environmental engineering (MS, PhD); environmental quality science (MS); geological engineering (MS, PhD); mechanical engineering (MS); mineral preparation engineering (MS); mining engineering (MS, PhD); petroleum engineering (MS, PhD); science management (MS). *Application deadline:* For fall admission, 6/1 for domestic students, 3/1 for international students; for spring admission, 10/15 for domestic students, 9/1 for international students. Applications are processed on a rolling basis. *Application fee:* $60. Electronic applications accepted. *Application Contact:* Dr. Douglas J. Goering, Dean, 907-474-7730, Fax: 907-474-6994, E-mail: fycem@uaf.edu. *Dean,* Dr. Douglas J. Goering, 907-474-7730, Fax: 907-474-6994, E-mail: fycem@uaf.edu.

College of Liberal Arts Students: 114 full-time (59 women), 123 part-time (89 women); includes 51 minority (4 African Americans, 36 American Indian/Alaska Native, 5 Asian Americans or Pacific Islanders, 6 Hispanic Americans), 14 international. Average age 35. 192 applicants, 49% accepted, 74 enrolled. *Faculty:* 83 full-time (35 women), 31 part-time/adjunct (10 women). Expenses: Contact institution. *Financial support:* In 2008–09, 4 fellowships (averaging $14,680 per year), 19 research assistantships (averaging $14,325 per year), 75 teaching assistantships (averaging $11,122 per year) were awarded; career-related internships or fieldwork, Federal Work-Study, scholarships/grants, health care benefits, and unspecified assistantships also available. Support available to part-time students. Financial award application deadline: 7/1; financial award applicants required to submit FAFSA. In 2008, 52 master's, 8 doctorates awarded. *Degree program information:* Part-time programs available. Postbaccalaureate distance learning degree programs offered. Offers anthropology (MA, PhD); applied linguistics (MA); art (MFA); ceramics (MFA); clinical-community psychology (PhD); computer art (MFA); conducting (MA); creative writing (MFA); cross cultural studies (MA); drawing (MFA); environmental politics and policy (MA); justice (MA); liberal arts (MA, MFA, PhD); literature (MA); music education (MA); music history (MA); music theory/composition (MA); Native arts (MFA); Northern history (MA); painting (MFA); performance (MA); photography (MFA); printmaking (MFA); professional communications (MA); sculpture (MFA). *Application deadline:* For fall admission, 6/1 for domestic students, 3/1 for international students; for spring admission, 10/15 for domestic students, 9/1 for international students. Applications are processed on a rolling basis. *Application fee:* $60. Electronic applications accepted. *Application Contact:* Ron Davis, Dean, 907-474-7231, Fax: 907-474-5817, E-mail: fycla@uaf.edu. *Dean,* Ron Davis, 907-474-7231, Fax: 907-474-5817, E-mail: fycla@uaf.edu.

College of Natural Sciences and Mathematics Students: 232 full-time (122 women), 69 part-time (35 women); includes 30 minority (4 African Americans, 6 American Indian/Alaska Native, 11 Asian Americans or Pacific Islanders, 9 Hispanic Americans), 43 international. Average age 30. 230 applicants, 38% accepted, 81 enrolled. *Faculty:* 86 full-time (23 women), 16 part-time/adjunct (2 women). Expenses: Contact institution. *Financial support:* In 2008–09, 4 fellowships (averaging $15,896 per year), 116 research assistantships (averaging $14,121 per year), 60 teaching assistantships (averaging $12,457 per year) were awarded; career-related internships or fieldwork, Federal Work-Study, scholarships/grants, health care benefits, and unspecified assistantships also available. Support available to part-time students. Financial award application deadline: 7/1; financial award applicants required to submit FAFSA. In 2008, 65 master's, 20 doctorates awarded. *Degree program information:* Part-time programs available. Offers atmospheric science (MS, PhD); biochemistry and molecular biology (MS, PhD); biological sciences (MS, PhD); biology (MAT, MS); chemistry (MA, MS); computational physics (MS); computer science (MS); environmental chemistry (MS, PhD); geology (MS, PhD); geophysics (MS, PhD); mathematics (MAT, PhD); natural sciences and mathematics (MA, MAT, MS, MSE, PhD); physics (MAT, MS, PhD); software engineering (MSE); space physics (MS, PhD); statistics (MS); wildlife biology (MS). *Application deadline:* For fall admission, 6/1 for domestic students, 3/1 for international students; for spring admission, 10/15 for domestic students, 9/1 for international students. Applications are processed on a rolling basis. *Application fee:* $60. Electronic applications accepted. *Application Contact:* Dr. Joan Braddock, Dean, 907-474-7608, Fax: 907-474-5101, E-mail: fycnsm@uaf.edu. *Dean,* Dr. Joan Braddock, 907-474-7608, Fax: 907-474-5101, E-mail: fycnsm@uaf.edu.

College of Rural and Community Development Students: 7 full-time (6 women), 13 part-time (9 women); includes 12 minority (11 American Indian/Alaska Native, 1 Asian American or Pacific Islander). Average age 42. 8 applicants, 75% accepted, 5 enrolled. *Faculty:* 6 full-time (4 women), 1 (woman) part-time/adjunct. Expenses: Contact institution. *Financial support:* Fellowships, Federal Work-Study, scholarships/grants, and health care benefits available. Support available to part-time students. Financial award application deadline: 2/15; financial award applicants required to submit FAFSA. In 2008, 6 master's awarded. *Degree program information:* Part-time programs available. Postbaccalaureate distance learning degree programs offered (no on-campus study). Offers rural and community development (MA); rural development (MA). *Application deadline:* For fall admission, 6/1 for domestic students, 3/1 for international students; for spring admission, 10/15 for domestic students, 9/1 for international students. Applications are processed on a rolling basis. *Application fee:* $60. Electronic applications accepted. *Application Contact:* Jennifer Carroll, Acting Vice Chancellor, 907-474-7143, Fax: 907-474-5824, E-mail: fyrural@uaf.edu. *Acting Vice Chancellor,* Jennifer Carroll, 907-474-7143, Fax: 907-474-5824, E-mail: fyrural@uaf.edu.

Graduate School for Interdisciplinary Studies Students: 2 full-time (both women), 1 part-time (0 women), 1 international. Average age 42. 3 applicants, 0% accepted. *Faculty:* 1 part-time/adjunct (0 women). Expenses: Contact institution. *Financial support:* In 2008–09, 2 research assistantships (averaging $5,236 per year) were awarded; fellowships, teaching assistantships, career-related internships or fieldwork, Federal Work-Study, scholarships/grants, health care benefits, and unspecified assistantships also available. Support available to part-time students. Financial award application deadline: 2/15; financial award applicants required to submit FAFSA. *Degree program information:* Part-time programs available. Offers interdisciplinary studies (MA, MS, PhD). *Application deadline:* For fall admission, 6/1 for domestic students, 3/1 for international students; for spring admission, 10/15 for domestic students, 9/1 for international students. Applications are processed on a rolling basis. *Application fee:* $60. Electronic applications accepted. *Application Contact:* Lawrence Duffy, Interim Dean, 907-474-7716, Fax: 907-474-1984, E-mail: fyinds@uaf.edu. *Interim Dean,* Lawrence Duffy, 907-474-7716, Fax: 907-474-1984, E-mail: fyinds@uaf.edu.

School of Education Students: 35 full-time (28 women), 113 part-time (87 women); includes 31 minority (4 African Americans, 18 American Indian/Alaska Native, 5 Asian Americans or Pacific Islanders, 4 Hispanic Americans), 1 international. Average age 32. 140 applicants, 70% accepted, 68 enrolled. *Faculty:* 23 full-time (13 women), 17 part-time/adjunct (10 women). Expenses: Contact institution. *Financial support:* In 2008–09, 5 teaching assistantships (averaging $12,789 per year) were awarded; fellowships, research assistantships, career-related internships or fieldwork, Federal Work-Study, scholarships/grants, health care benefits, and unspecified assistantships also available. Support available to part-time students. Financial award application deadline: 2/15; financial award applicants required to submit FAFSA. In 2008, 30 master's, 2 doctorates, 45 other advanced degrees awarded. Postbaccalaureate distance learning degree programs offered. Offers counseling (M Ed); curriculum and instruction (M Ed); education (M Ed, PhD); elementary education (M Ed); guidance and counseling (M Ed); language and literacy (M Ed); reading (M Ed); secondary education (M Ed). *Application deadline:* For fall admission, 3/1 for domestic and international students; for spring admission, 10/15 for domestic students, 9/1 for international students. *Application fee:* $60. Electronic applications accepted. *Application Contact:* Dr. Eric C. Madsen, Dean, 907-474-7341, Fax: 907-474-5451, E-mail: fysoed@uaf.edu. *Dean,* Dr. Eric C. Madsen, 907-474-7341, Fax: 907-474-5451, E-mail: fysoed@uaf.edu.

School of Fisheries and Ocean Sciences Students: 61 full-time (35 women), 46 part-time (19 women); includes 10 minority (4 American Indian/Alaska Native, 3 Asian Americans or Pacific Islanders, 3 Hispanic Americans), 5 international. Average age 32. 107 applicants, 29% accepted, 30 enrolled. *Faculty:* 27 full-time (8 women), 5 part-time/adjunct (0 women). Expenses: Contact institution. *Financial support:* In 2008–09, 4 fellowships (averaging $12,182 per year), 39 research assistantships (averaging $11,458 per year), 14 teaching assistantships with tuition reimbursements (averaging $9,411 per year) were awarded; career-related internships or fieldwork, Federal Work-Study, scholarships/grants, health care benefits, and unspecified assistantships also available. Support available to part-time students. Financial award application deadline: 2/15; financial award applicants required to submit FAFSA. In 2008, 24 master's, 3 doctorates awarded. *Degree program information:* Part-time programs available. Offers fisheries (MS, PhD); marine biology (MS, PhD); marine sciences and limnology (MS, PhD); oceanography (PhD); seafood science and nutrition (MS, PhD). *Application deadline:* For fall admission, 6/1 for domestic students, 3/1 for international students; for spring admission, 10/15 for domestic students, 9/1 for international students. Applications are processed on a rolling basis. *Application fee:* $60. Electronic applications accepted. *Application Contact:* Katie Murra, Recruitment and Retention Coordinator, 907-474-6786, Fax: 907-474-7204, E-mail: murra@sfos.uaf.edu. *Dean,* Dr. Denis Wiesenberg, 907-474-7824, Fax: 907-474-7204, E-mail: info@sfos.uaf.edu.

School of Management Students: 21 full-time (5 women), 39 part-time (23 women); includes 6 minority (1 African American, 1 Asian American or Pacific Islander, 4 Hispanic Americans), 7 international. Average age 28. 42 applicants, 64% accepted, 25 enrolled. *Faculty:* 22 full-time (6 women), 14 part-time/adjunct (2 women). Expenses: Contact institution. *Financial support:* In 2008–09, 10 teaching assistantships (averaging $12,616 per year) were awarded; fellowships, research assistantships, career-related internships or fieldwork, Federal Work-Study, scholarships/grants, health care benefits, and unspecified assistantships also available. Support available to part-time students. Financial award application deadline: 7/1; financial award applicants required to submit FAFSA. In 2008, 20 master's awarded. *Degree program information:* Part-time programs available. Offers capital markets (MBA); general management (MBA); management (MBA, MS); resource and applied economics (MS). *Application deadline:* For fall admission, 6/1 priority date for domestic students, 2/15 for international students; for spring admission, 10/15 priority date for domestic students, 9/1 for international students. Applications are processed on a rolling basis. *Application fee:* $60. Electronic applications accepted. *Application Contact:* Dr. Mark Herrmann, Dean, 907-474-7461, Fax: 907-474-5219, E-mail: dean.som@uaf.edu. *Dean,* Dr. Mark Herrmann, 907-474-7461, Fax: 907-474-5219, E-mail: dean.som@uaf.edu.

School of Natural Resources and Agricultural Sciences Students: 19 full-time (15 women), 21 part-time (13 women); includes 4 minority (2 American Indian/Alaska Native, 2 Asian Americans or Pacific Islanders), 3 international. Average age 32. 34 applicants, 44% accepted, 11 enrolled. *Faculty:* 17 full-time (4 women), 3 part-time/adjunct (0 women). Expenses: Contact institution. *Financial support:* In 2008–09, 9 research assistantships (averaging $13,137 per year), 4 teaching assistantships (averaging $10,655 per year) were awarded; fellowships, career-related internships or fieldwork, Federal Work-Study, scholarships/grants, health care benefits, and unspecified assistantships also available. Support available to part-time students. Financial award application deadline: 2/15; financial award applicants required to submit FAFSA. In 2008, 8 master's awarded. *Degree program information:* Part-time programs available. Offers natural resource management (MS). *Application deadline:* For fall admission, 6/1 for domestic students, 3/1 for international students; for spring admission, 10/15 for domestic students, 9/1 for international students. Applications are processed on a rolling basis. *Application fee:* $60. Electronic applications accepted. *Application Contact:* Veazey David, Director of Enrollment Management, 907-474-5276, Fax: 907-474-6567, E-mail: Dave.Veazey@alaska.edu. *Dean,* Dr. Carol E. Lewis, 907-474-7083, Fax: 907-474-6567, E-mail: fysnras@uaf.edu.

UNIVERSITY OF ALASKA SOUTHEAST, Juneau, AK 99801

General Information State-supported, coed, comprehensive institution. *Graduate housing:* Rooms and/or apartments available on a first-come, first-served basis to single and married students. Housing application deadline: 5/1. *Research affiliation:* National Park Service (environmental resources, cultural studies), North Pacific Research Board (marine biology, oceanography), US Department of Education (teaching, early childhood education), Natural Science Foundation (marine biology, undergraduate research), US Department of Agriculture (forest service), Alaska Department of Education (teaching).

GRADUATE UNITS

Graduate Programs *Degree program information:* Part-time and evening/weekend programs available. Postbaccalaureate distance learning degree programs offered (minimal on-campus study). Offers business administration (MBA); early childhood education (M Ed, MAT); educational technology (M Ed); elementary education (MAT); public administration (MPA); reading (M Ed); secondary education (MAT). Electronic applications accepted.

UNIVERSITY OF ALBERTA, Edmonton, AB T6G 2E1, Canada

General Information Province-supported, coed, university. CGS member. *Graduate housing:* Rooms and/or apartments available on a first-come, first-served basis to single and married students.

GRADUATE UNITS

Faculty of Extension Offers communications and technology (MA).

Faculty of Graduate Studies and Research *Degree program information:* Part-time and evening/weekend programs available. Offers accounting (PhD); adult education (M Ed, Ed D, PhD); agricultural economics (M Ag, M Sc, PhD); agricultural, food and nutritional science (M Ag, M Eng, M Sc, PhD); agroforestry (M Ag, M Sc, MF); ancient history (PhD); anthropology (MA, PhD); applied linguistics (Germanic, Romance, Slavic) (MA); applied mathematics (M Sc, PhD); applied music (M Mus); astrophysics (M Sc, PhD); biostatistics (M Sc); business administration (Exec MBA); chemical engineering (M Eng, M Sc, PhD); chemistry (M Sc, PhD); Chinese literature (MA); choral conducting (M Mus); classical archaeology (MA, PhD); classical literature (PhD); classics (MA); communications (M Eng, M Sc, PhD); communications and technology (MACT); composition (M Mus); computer engineering (M Eng, M Sc, PhD); computing science (M Sc, PhD); condensed matter (M Sc, PhD); conservation biology (M Sc, PhD); construction engineering and management (M Eng, M Sc, PhD); counseling psychology (M Ed, PhD); criminal justice (MA); demography (MA, PhD); design (MFA); directing (MFA); drama (MA); drawing (MFA); earth and atmospheric sciences (M Sc, MA, PhD); East Asian interdisciplinary studies (MA); economics (MA, PhD); economics and finance (MA); educational administration and leadership (M Ed, Ed D, PhD, Postgraduate Diploma); educational psychology (M Ed, PhD); electromagnetics (M Eng, M Sc, PhD); elementary education (M Ed, Ed D, PhD); engineering management (M Eng); English (MA, PhD); environmental and natural resource economics (PhD); environmental biology and ecology (M Sc, PhD); environmental engineering (M Eng, M Sc, PhD); environmental science (M Sc, PhD); experimental linguistics (M Sc, PhD); family ecology and practice (M Sc, PhD); finance (PhD); First Nations education (M Ed, Ed D, PhD); forest biology and management (M Sc, PhD); forest economics (M Ag, M Sc, PhD); French language, literatures and linguistics (PhD); French language, literatures, and linguistics (MA); geoenvironmental engineering (M Eng, M Sc, PhD); geophysics (M Sc, PhD); geotechnical engineering (M Eng, M Sc, PhD); Germanic languages, literatures and linguistics (PhD); Germanic languages, literatures, and linguistics (MA); history (MA, PhD); history of art, design, and visual culture (MA); human resources/industrial relations (PhD); industrial design (M Des); instructional technology (M Ed); international business (MBA); Italian studies (MA); Japanese literature (MA); land reclamation and remediation (M Sc, PhD); leisure and sport management (MBA); management science (PhD); marketing (PhD); materials engineering (M Eng, M Sc, PhD); mathematical finance (M Sc, PhD); mathematical physics (M Sc, PhD); mathematics (M Sc, PhD); mechanical engineering (M Eng, M Sc, PhD); medical physics (M Sc, PhD); microbiology and biotechnology (M Sc, PhD); mining engineering (M Eng, M Sc, PhD); molecular biology and genetics (M Sc, PhD); music (PhD); nanotechnology and microdevices (M Eng, M Sc, PhD); natural resources and energy (MBA); occupational therapy (M Sc, PhD); organ and choral conductors (D Mus); organizational analysis (PhD); painting (MFA); petroleum engineering (M Eng, M Sc, PhD); pharmacology (M Sc, PhD); philosophy (MA, PhD); physical therapy (M Sc, PhD); physiology and cell biology (M Sc, PhD); piano (D Mus); plant biology (M Sc, PhD); political science (MA, PhD); power/power electronics (M Eng, M Sc, PhD); printmaking (MFA); process control (M Eng, M Sc, PhD); protected areas and wildlands management (M Sc, PhD); psychology (M Sc, MA, PhD); rural sociology (M Ag, M Sc); school counseling (M Ed); school psychology (M Ed, PhD); sculpture (MFA); secondary education (M Ed, Ed D, PhD); Slavic languages and literatures (Russian, Ukrainian) (MA, PhD); Slavic linguistics (Russian, Ukrainian) (MA, PhD); sociology (MA, PhD); soil science (M Ag, M Sc, PhD); Spanish and Latin American studies (MA, PhD); special education (M Ed, PhD); special education-deafness studies (M Ed); speech pathology and audiology (PhD); speech-language pathology (M Sc); statistics (M Sc, PhD, Postgraduate Diploma); structural engineering (M Eng, M Sc, PhD); subatomic physics (M Sc, PhD); systematics and evolution (M Sc, PhD); systems (M Eng, M Sc, PhD); teaching English as a second language (M Ed); technology commercialization (MBA); textiles and clothing (M Sc, MA, PhD); theoretical, cultural and international studies in education (M Ed, Ed D, PhD); Ukrainian folklore (MA, PhD); visual communication design (M Des); water and land resources (M Ag, M Sc, PhD); water resources (M Eng, M Sc, PhD); welding (M Eng); wildlife ecology and management (M Sc, PhD).

Faculté Saint Jean *Degree program information:* Part-time and evening/weekend programs available. Postbaccalaureate distance learning degree programs offered (minimal on-campus study). Offers education (M Ed).

Faculty of Nursing *Degree program information:* Part-time programs available. Offers nursing (MN, PhD).

Faculty of Pharmacy and Pharmaceutical Sciences Offers pharmacy and pharmaceutical sciences (M Sc, PhD). Electronic applications accepted.

Faculty of Physical Education and Recreation *Degree program information:* Part-time programs available. Offers physical education (M Sc); recreation and physical education (MA, PhD).

Faculty of Rehabilitation Medicine Offers rehabilitation medicine (PhD). Electronic applications accepted.

School of Library and Information Studies Offers library and information studies (MLIS). Electronic applications accepted.

Faculty of Law *Degree program information:* Part-time programs available. Offers law (LL B, LL M). Electronic applications accepted.

Faculty of Medicine and Dentistry Offers dental hygiene (Diploma); dentistry (DDS); medicine and dentistry (DDS, MD, M Sc, PhD, Diploma); orthodontics (M Sc, PhD); TMD/orofacial pain (M Sc). Electronic applications accepted.

Graduate Programs in Medicine *Degree program information:* Part-time programs available. Offers biochemistry (M Sc, PhD); biomedical engineering (M Sc); cell and molecular biology (M Sc, PhD); medical genetics (M Sc, PhD); medical microbiology and immunology (M Sc, PhD); medical sciences (M Sc, PhD); medicine (MD, M Sc, PhD); neuroscience (M Sc, PhD); obstetrics and gynecology (MD); oncology (M Sc, PhD); ophthalmology (M Sc, PhD); pediatrics (M Sc, PhD); physiology (M Sc, PhD); psychiatry (M Sc, PhD); radiology and diagnostic imaging (M Sc); surgery (M Sc, PhD).

School of Public Health Offers clinical epidemiology (M Sc, MPH); environmental and occupational health (MPH); environmental health sciences (M Sc); epidemiology (M Sc); global health (M Sc, MPH); health policy and management (MPH); health policy research (M Sc); health technology assessment (MPH); occupational health (M Sc); population health (M Sc); public health (M Sc, MPH, PhD, Postgraduate Diploma); public health leadership (MPH); public health sciences (PhD); quantitative methods (MPH).

Centre for Health Promotion Studies *Degree program information:* Part-time programs available. Postbaccalaureate distance learning degree programs offered. Offers health promotion (M Sc, Postgraduate Diploma).

THE UNIVERSITY OF ARIZONA, Tucson, AZ 85721

General Information State-supported, coed, university. CGS member. *Enrollment:* 38,057 graduate, professional, and undergraduate students; 5,820 full-time matriculated graduate/professional students (2,963 women), 2,070 part-time matriculated graduate/professional students (1,179 women). *Enrollment by degree level:* 1,389 first professional, 3,116 master's, 3,385 doctoral. *Graduate faculty:* 1,626. Tuition, state resident: full-time $6880; part-time $420 per credit hour. Tuition, nonresident: full-time $21,592; part-time $900 per credit hour. *Graduate housing:* Rooms and/or apartments available on a first-come, first-served basis to single students and available to married students. Typical cost: $8450 per year for single students. Room charges vary according to housing facility selected. Housing application deadline: 5/1. *Student services:* Campus employment opportunities, campus safety program, career counseling, child daycare facilities, exercise/wellness program, free psychological counseling, grant writing training, international student services, low-cost health insurance, multicultural affairs office, services for students with disabilities, teacher training, writing training. *Library facilities:* University of Arizona Main Library plus 5 others. *Online resources:* library catalog, web page, access to other libraries' catalogs. *Collection:* 5.3 million titles, 62,468 serial subscriptions, 54,178 audiovisual materials. *Research affiliation:* Research Corporation (astronomy), Smithsonian Astrophysical Observatory (astronomy), National Center for Atmospheric Research (atmospheric physics), Kitt Peak National Observatory (astronomy), Argonne National Laboratory (physics).

Computer facilities: 3,000 computers available on campus for general student use. A campuswide network can be accessed from student residence rooms and from off campus. Online class registration is available. *Web address:* http://www.arizona.edu/.

General Application Contact: Graduate College Admissions Information Desk, 520-621-3471, Fax: 520-621-4101, E-mail: gradadm@grad.arizona.edu.

GRADUATE UNITS

College of Medicine *Degree program information:* Part-time programs available. Offers biochemistry (MS, PhD); cell biology and anatomy (PhD); immunobiology (MS, PhD); medicine (MD, MPH, MS, PhD). MD program open only to state residents.

College of Optical Sciences Students: 173 full-time (41 women), 87 part-time (7 women); includes 34 minority (3 African Americans, 5 American Indian/Alaska Native, 13 Asian Americans or Pacific Islanders, 13 Hispanic Americans), 74 international. Average age 30. 205 applicants, 37% accepted, 75 enrolled. *Faculty:* 29. Expenses: Contact institution. *Financial support:* In 2008–09, 92 research assistantships with full tuition reimbursements (averaging $16,800 per year), 25 teaching assistantships with full tuition reimbursements (averaging $16,800 per year) were awarded; fellowships, scholarships/grants also available. Financial award application deadline: 1/1. In 2008, 46 master's, 19 doctorates awarded. *Degree program information:* Part-time programs available. Offers optical sciences (MS, PhD). *Application deadline:* For fall admission, 1/1 for domestic students, 12/1 for international students. Applications are processed on a rolling basis. *Application fee:* $65. Electronic applications accepted. *Application Contact:* Gail Varin, 520-626-0888, E-mail: gail@optics.arizona.edu. *Dean,* Dr. James Wyant, 520-621-6997, Fax: 520-621-9613, E-mail: lpalomarez@optics.arizona.edu.

Graduate College Students: 4,493 full-time (2,312 women), 1,945 part-time (1,152 women); includes 1,232 minority (132 African Americans, 202 American Indian/Alaska Native, 310 Asian Americans or Pacific Islanders, 588 Hispanic Americans), 1,352 international. Average age 31. 9,082 applicants, 37% accepted, 1675 enrolled. *Faculty:* 1,338. Expenses: Contact institution. *Financial support:* In 2008–09, 1,214 research assistantships with full tuition reimbursements (averaging $16,451 per year), 1,530 teaching assistantships with full tuition reimbursements (averaging $14,886 per year) were awarded; fellowships, career-related internships or fieldwork, Federal Work-Study, institutionally sponsored loans, scholarships/grants, traineeships, health care benefits, tuition waivers (full and partial), and unspecified assistantships also available. Support available to part-time students. In 2008, 76 first professional degrees, 1,283 master's, 433 doctorates awarded. *Degree program information:* Part-time and evening/weekend programs available. Offers American Indian studies (MA, PhD); applied mathematics (MS, PMS, PhD); biomedical engineering (MS, PhD); cancer biology (PhD); genetics (MS, PhD); insect science (MS, PhD); mathematical sciences (PMS); neuroscience (PhD); physiological sciences (MS, PhD); second language acquisition and teaching (PhD); statistics (MS, PhD). *Application deadline:* For fall admission, 1/1 for domestic students, 12/1 for international students. Applications are processed on a rolling basis. *Application fee:* $65. Electronic applications accepted. *Application Contact:* General Information, 520-621-3471, Fax: 520-621-7112, E-mail: gradadm@grad.arizona.edu. *Dean,* Dr. Andrew Comrie, 520-621-3512, Fax: 520-621-4101, E-mail: gradadm@grad.arizona.edu.

College of Agriculture and Life Sciences Students: 276 full-time (148 women), 142 part-time (76 women); includes 76 minority (10 African Americans, 8 American Indian/Alaska Native, 15 Asian Americans or Pacific Islanders, 43 Hispanic Americans), 118 international. Average age 32. 361 applicants, 34% accepted, 88 enrolled. *Faculty:* 151. Expenses: Contact institution. *Financial support:* In 2008–09, 116 research assistantships with full and partial tuition reimbursements (averaging $17,069 per year), 70 teaching assistantships with full and partial tuition reimbursements (averaging $16,257 per year) were awarded; fellowships with full and partial tuition reimbursements, career-related internships or fieldwork, Federal Work-Study, institutionally sponsored loans, scholarships/grants, traineeships, health care benefits, tuition waivers (full and partial), and unspecified assistantships also available. In 2008, 69 master's, 34 doctorates awarded. *Degree program information:* Part-time programs available. Offers agricultural and biosystems engineering (MS, PhD); agricultural and resource economics (MS); agricultural education (M Ag Ed, MS); agriculture and life sciences (M Ag Ed, MHE Ed, MS, PhD); animal sciences (MS, PhD); arid lands resource sciences (PhD); entomology (MS, PhD); family and consumer sciences (MS, PhD); family and consumer sciences education (MS); family studies and human development (PhD); microbiology (MS, PhD); natural resources (MS, PhD); nutritional sciences (MS, PhD); pathobiology (MS, PhD); plant pathology (PhD); plant sciences (MS, PhD); rangeland science and management (MS, PhD); retailing and consumer sciences (MS, PhD); soil, water and environmental science (MS, PhD); watershed resources (MS, PhD); wildlife, fisheries conservation, and management (MS, PhD). *Application deadline:* For fall admission, 1/1 for domestic students, 12/1 for international students. Applications are processed on a rolling basis. *Application fee:* $65. Electronic applications accepted. *Application Contact:* Dr. David E. Cox, Associate Dean, 520-621-3612, Fax: 520-621-8662. *Dean,* Dr. Eugene G. Sander, 520-621-7621, Fax: 520-621-7196.

College of Architecture and Landscape Architecture Students: 94 full-time (45 women), 34 part-time (19 women); includes 21 minority (3 African Americans, 2 American Indian/Alaska Native, 3 Asian Americans or Pacific Islanders, 13 Hispanic Americans), 20 international. Average age 30. 137 applicants, 58% accepted, 48 enrolled. *Faculty:* 16. Expenses: Contact institution. *Financial support:* In 2008–09, 6 research assistantships with full tuition reimbursements (averaging $10,440 per year), 25 teaching assistantships with full tuition reimbursements (averaging $10,613 per year) were awarded; career-related internships or fieldwork, Federal Work-Study, scholarships/grants, health care benefits, tuition waivers (full), and unspecified assistantships also available. In 2008, 30 master's awarded. *Degree program information:* Part-time programs available. Offers architecture (M Arch); architecture and landscape architecture (M Arch, ML Arch, MS); landscape architecture (ML Arch); planning (MS). *Application deadline:* For fall admission, 3/1 for domestic students, 12/1 for international students; for spring admission, 3/1 priority date for domestic students, 3/1 for international students. Applications are processed on a rolling basis. *Application fee:* $65. *Application Contact:* Susan Moody, Assistant Dean, 520-621-6751, Fax: 520-621-8700, E-mail: skemoody@u.arizona.edu. *Dean,* Janice A. Cervelli, 520-621-6754, Fax: 520-621-8700, E-mail: jcervell@email.arizona.edu.

College of Education Students: 315 full-time (234 women), 409 part-time (293 women); includes 210 minority (32 African Americans, 40 American Indian/Alaska Native, 24 Asian Americans or Pacific Islanders, 114 Hispanic Americans), 54 international. Average age 37. 411 applicants, 56% accepted, 147 enrolled. *Faculty:* 58. Expenses: Contact institution. *Financial support:* In 2008–09, 27 research assistantships with full tuition reimbursements (averaging $12,716 per year), 34 teaching assistantships with full tuition reimbursements (averaging $12,792 per year) were awarded; career-related internships or fieldwork, Federal Work-Study, institutionally sponsored loans, scholarships/grants, health care benefits, tuition waivers (full and partial), and unspecified assistantships also available. Support available to part-time students. Financial award application deadline: 3/1. In 2008, 139 master's, 50 doctorates awarded. *Degree program information:* Part-time programs available. Postbaccalaureate distance learning degree programs offered (no on-campus study). Offers bilingual education (M Ed); bilingual/multicultural education (MA); bilingual/multicultural learning disabilities (MA, Ed D, PhD); deaf and hard of hearing (MA, Ed D, PhD); education (M Ed, MA, MS, Ed D, PhD, Ed S); educational leadership (M Ed, Ed D, Ed S); educational psychology (MA, PhD, Ed S); gifted and talented (MA, Ed D, PhD); higher education (MA, PhD); language, reading and culture (MA, Ed D, PhD, Ed S); learning disabilities (MA, Ed D, PhD); rehabilitation (MA, PhD); school counseling and guidance (M Ed); school psychology (PhD, Ed S); severe and profound multiple disabilities (MA, Ed D, PhD); special education (MA); teaching and teacher education (M Ed, MA, Ed D, PhD); visual impairment (MA, Ed D, PhD). *Application deadline:* For fall admission, 2/1 priority date for domestic and international students; for spring admission, 10/1 priority date for domestic students, 9/1 priority date for international students. Applications are processed on a rolling basis. *Application fee:* $65. Electronic applications accepted. *Application Contact:* General Information, 520-621-3471, Fax: 520-621-4101, E-mail: gradadm@grad.arizona.edu. *Dean,* Dr. Ronald Marx, 520-621-1081, Fax: 520-621-9271, E-mail: ronmarx@email.arizona.edu.

College of Engineering Students: 405 full-time (107 women), 202 part-time (34 women); includes 66 minority (5 African Americans, 11 American Indian/Alaska Native, 23 Asian Americans or Pacific Islanders, 27 Hispanic Americans), 337 international. Average age 29. 851 applicants, 42% accepted, 165 enrolled. *Faculty:* 135. Expenses: Contact institution. *Financial support:* In 2008–09, 191 research assistantships with full tuition reimbursements (averaging $18,411 per year), 60 teaching assistantships with full tuition reimbursements (averaging $18,355 per year) were awarded; institutionally sponsored loans, scholarships/grants, health care benefits, and unspecified assistantships also available. In 2008, 151 master's, 50 doctorates awarded. *Degree program information:* Part-time programs available. Postbaccalaureate distance learning degree programs offered (no on-campus study). Offers aerospace engineering (MS, PhD); chemical engineering (MS, PhD); civil engineering (MS, PhD); electrical and computer engineering (M Eng, MS, PhD); engineering (M Eng, ME, MS, PhD, Certificate); engineering mechanics (MS, PhD); environmental engineering (MS, PhD); geological engineering (MS, PhD); hydrology and water resources (MS, PhD); industrial engineering (MS); materials science and engineering (MS, PhD); mechanical engineering (MS, PhD); mine health and safety (Certificate); mine information and production technology (Certificate); mining engineering (M Eng, Certificate); reliability and quality engineering (MS); rock mechanics (Certificate); systems and industrial engineering (MS, PhD); systems engineering (MS, PhD). *Application fee:* $65. *Application Contact:* General Information, 520-621-3471, Fax: 520-621-7112, E-mail: gradadm@grad.arizona.edu. *Dean,* Dr. Thomas W. Peterson, 520-621-6594, Fax: 520-621-2232, E-mail: twp@engr.arizona.edu.

College of Fine Arts Students: 222 full-time (121 women), 114 part-time (64 women); includes 52 minority (5 African Americans, 2 American Indian/Alaska Native, 15 Asian Americans or Pacific Islanders, 30 Hispanic Americans), 43 international. Average age 31. 425 applicants, 41% accepted, 99 enrolled. *Faculty:* 107. Expenses: Contact institution. *Financial support:* In 2008–09, 1 research assistantship with full tuition reimbursement (averaging $11,650 per year), 119 teaching assistantships with full tuition reimbursements (averaging $12,385 per year) were awarded; career-related internships or fieldwork, Federal Work-Study, institutionally sponsored loans, scholarships/grants, health care benefits, tuition waivers (full and partial), and unspecified assistantships also available. Support available to part-time students. In 2008, 67 master's, 18 doctorates awarded. *Degree program information:* Part-time programs available. Offers art education (MA); art history (MA, PhD); composition (MM, A Mus D); conducting (MM, A Mus D); fine arts (MA, MFA, MM, A Mus D, PhD); history and theory of art (PhD); media arts (MA); music education (MM, PhD); music theory (MM, PhD); musicology (MM); performance (MM, A Mus D); studio art (MFA); theatre arts (MA, MFA). *Application fee:* $65. *Application Contact:* General Information, 520-621-1301, Fax: 520-621-1307, E-mail: finearts@email.arizona.edu. *Dean,* Dr. Maurice Sevigny, 520-621-7886, Fax: 520-621-1307.

College of Humanities Students: 316 full-time (191 women), 86 part-time (61 women); includes 80 minority (3 African Americans, 7 American Indian/Alaska Native, 11 Asian Americans or Pacific Islanders, 59 Hispanic Americans), 55 international. Average age 32. 600 applicants, 29% accepted, 111 enrolled. *Faculty:* 133. Expenses: Contact institution. *Financial support:* In 2008–09, 7 research assistantships with full tuition reimbursements (averaging $15,176 per year), 305 teaching assistantships with full tuition reimbursements (averaging $15,160 per year) were awarded; career-related internships or fieldwork, Federal Work-Study, institutionally sponsored loans, scholarships/grants, health care benefits, tuition waivers (full and partial), and unspecified assistantships also available. Support available to part-time students. In 2008, 89 master's, 25 doctorates awarded. *Degree program information:* Part-time programs available. Offers classics (MA); creative writing (MFA); East Asian studies (MA, PhD); English (MA, PhD); French (MA); German (MA); humanities

The University of Arizona (continued)

(MA, MFA, PhD); rhetoric, composition and the teaching of English (PhD); Russian (MA); Spanish (MA, PhD). *Application deadline:* Applications are processed on a rolling basis. *Application fee:* $65. Electronic applications accepted. *Application Contact:* General Information, 520-621-3471, Fax: 520-621-7112, E-mail: gradadm@grad.arizona.edu. *Interim Dean,* Dr. Mary Wildner-Bassett, 520-621-1044, Fax: 520-621-5594.

College of Nursing Students: 83 full-time (73 women), 75 part-time (69 women); includes 28 minority (7 African Americans, 3 American Indian/Alaska Native, 8 Asian Americans or Pacific Islanders, 10 Hispanic Americans), 10 international. Average age 41. 93 applicants, 63% accepted, 59 enrolled. *Faculty:* 20. Expenses: Contact institution. *Financial support:* In 2008–09, 6 research assistantships with full tuition reimbursements (averaging $16,201 per year), 34 teaching assistantships with full tuition reimbursements (averaging $14,342 per year) were awarded; career-related internships or fieldwork, institutionally sponsored loans, scholarships/grants, traineeships, health care benefits, tuition waivers (full), and unspecified assistantships also available. Financial award application deadline: 6/1. In 2008, 25 master's, 17 doctorates awarded. *Degree program information:* Part-time programs available. Postbaccalaureate distance learning degree programs offered (minimal on-campus study). Offers health care informatics (Certificate); nurse practitioner (MS, Certificate); nursing (DNP, PhD); rural health (Certificate). *Application deadline:* For fall admission, 1/15 for domestic and international students. Applications are processed on a rolling basis. *Application fee:* $65. Electronic applications accepted. *Application Contact:* Sue Rawley, Assistant Dean, Student Affairs, 520-626-3808, Fax: 520-626-6424, E-mail: srawley@nursing.arizona.edu. *Interim Dean,* Dr. Carolyn Murdaugh, 520-626-7124, Fax: 520-626-6424, E-mail: cmurdaugh@nursing.arizona.edu.

College of Pharmacy Students: 425 full-time (268 women), 12 part-time (8 women); includes 140 minority (8 African Americans, 4 American Indian/Alaska Native, 82 Asian Americans or Pacific Islanders, 46 Hispanic Americans), 33 international. Average age 27. 171 applicants, 23% accepted, 16 enrolled. *Faculty:* 29. Expenses: Contact institution. *Financial support:* In 2008–09, 46 research assistantships with full tuition reimbursements (averaging $21,339 per year) were awarded; career-related internships or fieldwork, Federal Work-Study, institutionally sponsored loans, scholarships/grants, health care benefits, tuition waivers (full and partial), and unspecified assistantships also available. Support available to part-time students. In 2008, 76 first professional degrees, 30 master's, 16 doctorates awarded. Offers medical pharmacology (MS, PhD); medicinal and natural products chemistry (MS, PhD); perfusion science (MS); pharmaceutical economics (MS, PhD); pharmaceutics and pharmacokinetics (MS, PhD); pharmacy (Pharm D, MS, PhD). *Application fee:* $65. *Application Contact:* Dr. J. Lyle Bootman, Dean, 520-626-1657. *Dean,* Dr. J. Lyle Bootman, 520-626-1657.

College of Science Students: 692 full-time (295 women), 164 part-time (77 women); includes 98 minority (8 African Americans, 17 American Indian/Alaska Native, 34 Asian Americans or Pacific Islanders, 39 Hispanic Americans), 246 international. Average age 29. 1,481 applicants, 21% accepted, 203 enrolled. *Faculty:* 275. Expenses: Contact institution. *Financial support:* In 2008–09, 278 research assistantships with full tuition reimbursements (averaging $17,506 per year), 295 teaching assistantships with full tuition reimbursements (averaging $16,895 per year) were awarded; career-related internships or fieldwork, Federal Work-Study, institutionally sponsored loans, scholarships/grants, health care benefits, tuition waivers (full and partial), and unspecified assistantships also available. Support available to part-time students. In 2008, 123 master's, 73 doctorates awarded. *Degree program information:* Part-time programs available. Offers applied and industrial physics (PMS); applied biosciences (PSM); applied science and business (PMS); astronomy (MS, PhD); atmospheric sciences (MS, PhD); chemistry (MA, MS, PhD); computer science (MS, PhD); ecology and evolutionary biology (MS, PhD); geosciences (MS, PhD); mathematical sciences (PMS); mathematics (MA, MS, PhD); molecular and cellular biology (MS, PhD); physics (MS, PhD); planetary sciences (MS, PhD); science (MA, MS, PMS, PSM, Au D, PhD); speech, language, and hearing sciences (MS, Au D, PhD). *Application fee:* $65. Electronic applications accepted. *Application Contact:* General Information, 520-621-4090, Fax: 520-621-8389, E-mail: uasci@email.arizona.edu. *Dean,* Dr. Joaquin Ruiz, 520-621-4090, Fax: 520-621-8389, E-mail: jruiz@email.arizona.edu.

College of Social and Behavioral Sciences Students: 664 full-time (382 women), 413 part-time (292 women); includes 186 minority (19 African Americans, 39 American Indian/Alaska Native, 29 Asian Americans or Pacific Islanders, 99 Hispanic Americans), 126 international. Average age 32. 1,467 applicants, 19% accepted, 183 enrolled. *Faculty:* 239. Expenses: Contact institution. *Financial support:* In 2008–09, 89 research assistantships with full tuition reimbursements (averaging $14,456 per year), 357 teaching assistantships (averaging $14,420 per year) were awarded; career-related internships or fieldwork, Federal Work-Study, institutionally sponsored loans, scholarships/grants, health care benefits, tuition waivers (full and partial), and unspecified assistantships also available. Support available to part-time students. In 2008, 252 master's, 68 doctorates awarded. *Degree program information:* Part-time and evening/weekend programs available. Offers anthropology (MA, PhD); communication (MA, PhD); geography (MA, PhD); history (MA, PhD); human language technology (MS); information resources and library science (MA, PhD); Latin American studies (MA); linguistics and anthropology (PhD); Native American linguistics (MA); Near Eastern studies (MA, PhD); philosophy (MA, PhD); political science (MA, PhD); psychology (MA, PhD); social and behavioral sciences (MA, MS, PhD); sociology (PhD); theoretical linguistics (PhD); women's studies (MA, PhD). *Application fee:* $65. Electronic applications accepted. *Application Contact:* General Information, 520-621-3471, Fax: 520-621-7112, E-mail: gradadm@grad.arizona.edu. *Dean,* Dr. Edward Donnerstein, 520-621-1112, Fax: 520-621-9424, E-mail: edonners@u.arizona.edu.

Eller College of Management Students: 644 full-time (229 women), 90 part-time (33 women); includes 118 minority (11 African Americans, 9 American Indian/Alaska Native, 37 Asian Americans or Pacific Islanders, 61 Hispanic Americans), 230 international. Average age 30. 1,361 applicants, 35% accepted, 298 enrolled. *Faculty:* 91. Expenses: Contact institution. *Financial support:* In 2008–09, 45 research assistantships with full tuition reimbursements (averaging $15,238 per year), 158 teaching assistantships with full tuition reimbursements (averaging $12,985 per year) were awarded; career-related internships or fieldwork, Federal Work-Study, scholarships/grants, health care benefits, tuition waivers (partial), and unspecified assistantships also available. Financial award application deadline: 3/15. In 2008, 260 master's, 25 doctorates awarded. *Degree program information:* Evening/weekend programs available. Offers accounting (M Ac); business administration (MBA); economics (MA, PhD); finance (MS, PhD); management (M Ac, MA, MBA, MPA, MS, PhD); management information systems (MS); marketing (MS, PhD); public administration (MPA); public administration and policy (PhD). *Application deadline:* Applications are processed on a rolling basis. *Application fee:* $65. Electronic applications accepted. *Application Contact:* Information Contact, 520-621-2165, Fax: 520-621-8105, E-mail: mbaadmissions@eller.arizona.edu. *Dean,* Dr. Paul R. Portney, 520-621-2125, Fax: 520-621-8105, E-mail: pportney@email.arizona.edu.

Mel and Enid Zuckerman College of Public Health Students: 113 full-time (84 women), 108 part-time (74 women); includes 66 minority (12 African Americans, 16 American Indian/Alaska Native, 13 Asian Americans or Pacific Islanders, 25 Hispanic Americans), 18 international. Average age 31. 346 applicants, 26% accepted, 71 enrolled. *Faculty:* 33. Expenses: Contact institution. *Financial support:* In 2008–09, 23 research assistantships with full tuition reimbursements (averaging $14,025 per year), 23 teaching assistantships with full tuition reimbursements (averaging $14,025 per year) were awarded; health care benefits and unspecified assistantships also available. In 2008, 57 master's, 6 doctorates awarded. Offers biostatistics (PhD); epidemiology (MS, PhD); public health (MPH, Dr PH, PhD). *Application deadline:* Applications are processed on a rolling basis. *Application fee:* $65. Electronic applications accepted. *Application Contact:* Lorraine Varela, Special Assistant to the Dean, 520-626-3201, E-mail: varelal@coph.arizona.edu. *Interim Dean,* Dr. Iman Hakim, 520-626-7083, E-mail: ihakim@email.arizona.edu.

James E. Rogers College of Law Students: 506 full-time (252 women); includes 140 minority (22 African Americans, 22 American Indian/Alaska Native, 40 Asian Americans or Pacific Islanders, 56 Hispanic Americans), 18 international. Average age 26. 2,242 applicants, 34% accepted, 160 enrolled. *Faculty:* 35 full-time (12 women), 40 part-time/adjunct (14 women). Expenses: Contact institution. *Financial support:* In 2008–09, 400 students received support, including fellowships with tuition reimbursements available (averaging $3,400 per year); career-related internships or fieldwork, Federal Work-Study, institutionally sponsored loans, scholarships/grants, and tuition waivers (full and partial) also available. Financial award application deadline: 3/1; financial award applicants required to submit FAFSA. In 2008, 143 JDs, 22 master's awarded. Offers indigenous peoples law and policy (LL M); international trade and business law (LL M); law (JD). *Application deadline:* For fall admission, 11/13 priority date for domestic and international students; for spring admission, 2/15 for domestic and international students. Applications are processed on a rolling basis. *Application fee:* $50. Electronic applications accepted. *Application Contact:* Eric James Eden, Assistant Dean for Admissions and Financial Aid, 520-621-7666, Fax: 520-621-9140, E-mail: eric.eden@law.arizona.edu. *Dean,* Toni M. Massaro, 520-621-1498, Fax: 520-621-9140, E-mail: massaro@law.arizona.edu.

UNIVERSITY OF ARKANSAS, Fayetteville, AR 72701-1201

General Information State-supported, coed, university. CGS member. *Enrollment:* 19,194 graduate, professional, and undergraduate students; 1,138 full-time matriculated graduate/professional students (623 women), 2,053 part-time matriculated graduate/professional students (982 women). *Enrollment by degree level:* 2,108 master's, 1,043 doctoral, 40 other advanced degrees. *Graduate faculty:* 655 full-time (169 women), 13 part-time/adjunct (2 women). *Graduate housing:* Room and/or apartments available on a first-come, first-served basis to single students; on-campus housing not available to married students. *Student services:* Campus employment opportunities, campus safety program, career counseling, exercise/wellness program, free psychological counseling, international student services, low-cost health insurance, multicultural affairs office, services for students with disabilities, teacher training, writing training. *Library facilities:* David W. Mullins Library plus 5 others. *Online resources:* library catalog, web page, access to other libraries' catalogs. *Collection:* 1.8 million titles, 18,576 serial subscriptions. *Research affiliation:* Science Coalition, National Minority Graduate Feeder Project, Southern Regional Education Board, Southeastern Universities Research Association, Southern Regional Education Board Uncommon Facilities Program, Oak Ridge Associated Universities.

Computer facilities: Computer purchase and lease plans are available. 2,457 computers available on campus for general student use. A campuswide network can be accessed from student residence rooms and from off campus. Online class registration is available. *Web address:* http://www.uark.edu/.

General Application Contact: Lynn Mosesso, Director of Graduate and International Recruitment and Admissions, 479-575-6246, Fax: 479-575-5908, E-mail: gradinfo@uark.edu.

GRADUATE UNITS

Graduate School Students: 1,033 full-time (543 women), 1,900 part-time (893 women); includes 363 minority (199 African Americans, 37 American Indian/Alaska Native, 49 Asian Americans or Pacific Islanders, 78 Hispanic Americans), 537 international. Expenses: Contact institution. *Financial support:* In 2008–09, 301 fellowships with tuition reimbursements, 633 research assistantships, 452 teaching assistantships with full tuition reimbursements were awarded; career-related internships or fieldwork, Federal Work-Study, institutionally sponsored loans, scholarships/grants, traineeships, and unspecified assistantships also available. Support available to part-time students. Financial award application deadline: 4/1; financial award applicants required to submit FAFSA. In 2008, 865 master's, 144 doctorates awarded. *Degree program information:* Part-time programs available. Postbaccalaureate distance learning degree programs offered (no on-campus study). Offers cell and molecular biology (MS, PhD); classical studies (MA); comparative literature (PhD); environmental dynamics (PhD); microelectronics and photonics (MS, PhD); public policy (PhD); space and planetary sciences (MS, PhD). *Application deadline:* Applications are processed on a rolling basis. *Application fee:* $40 ($50 for international students). Electronic applications accepted. *Application Contact:* Graduate Admissions, 479-575-6246, Fax: 479-575-5908, E-mail: gradinfo@uark.edu. *Associate Dean,* Dr. Patricia R. Koski, 479-575-4401, Fax: 479-575-5908, E-mail: gradinfo@uark.edu.

College of Education and Health Professions Students: 294 full-time (233 women), 456 part-time (327 women); includes 113 minority (82 African Americans, 11 American Indian/Alaska Native, 12 Asian Americans or Pacific Islanders, 8 Hispanic Americans), 28 international. 461 applicants, 43% accepted. Expenses: Contact institution. *Financial support:* In 2008–09, 30 fellowships with tuition reimbursements, 36 research assistantships, 31 teaching assistantships were awarded; career-related internships or fieldwork and Federal Work-Study also available. Support available to part-time students. Financial award application deadline: 4/1; financial award applicants required to submit FAFSA. In 2008, 226 master's, 37 doctorates awarded. Offers childhood education (MAT); communication disorders (MS); counseling (MS, PhD, Ed S); curriculum and instruction (M Ed, MAT, MS, Ed D, PhD, Ed S); education and health professions (M Ed, MAT, MS, MSN, Ed D, PhD, Ed S); education policy (PhD); educational leadership (M Ed, Ed D, Ed S); educational statistics and research methods (MS, PhD); educational technology (M Ed); elementary education (M Ed, Ed S); health science (MS, PhD); higher education (M Ed, Ed D, Ed S); kinesiology (MS, PhD); middle-level education (MAT); nursing (MSN); physical education (M Ed, MAT); recreation (M Ed, Ed D); rehabilitation (MS, PhD); secondary education (M Ed, MAT, Ed S); special education (M Ed, MAT); vocational education (MAT); workforce development education (M Ed, Ed D). *Application fee:* $40 ($50 for international students). *Application Contact:* Graduate Admissions, 479-575-6246, Fax: 479-575-5908, E-mail: gradinfo@uark.edu. *Dean,* Dr. M. Reed Greenwood, 479-575-3208, Fax: 479-575-3119.

College of Engineering Students: 120 full-time (29 women), 503 part-time (134 women); includes 121 minority (64 African Americans, 5 American Indian/Alaska Native, 16 Asian Americans or Pacific Islanders, 36 Hispanic Americans), 164 international. Expenses: Contact institution. *Financial support:* In 2008–09, 33 fellowships with tuition reimbursements, 162 research assistantships, 23 teaching assistantships were awarded; career-related internships or fieldwork and Federal Work-Study also available. Support available to part-time students. Financial award application deadline: 4/1; financial award applicants required to submit FAFSA. In 2008, 255 master's, 16 doctorates awarded. Offers biological and agricultural engineering (MSE, PhD); biological engineering (MSBE); biomedical engineering (MSBME); chemical engineering (MS Ch E, MSE, PhD); civil engineering (MS En E, MSCE, MSE, MSTE, PhD); computer engineering (MS Cmp E, MSE, PhD); computer science (MS, PhD); electrical engineering (MSEE, PhD); engineering (MS, MS Cmp E, MS Ch E, MS En E, MS Tc E, MSBE, MSBME, MSCE, MSE, MSEE, MSIE, MSME, MSOR, MSTE, PhD); environmental engineering (MS En E, MSE); industrial engineering (MS, MSE, MSIE, MSOR, PhD); mechanical engineering (MSE, MSME, PhD); operations management (MS); operations research (MSE, MSOR); telecommunications engineering (MS Tc E); transportation engineering (MSE, MSTE). *Application fee:* $40 ($50 for international students). *Application Contact:* Graduate Admissions, 479-575-6246, Fax: 479-575-5908, E-mail: gradinfo@uark.edu. *Dean,* Ashok Saxena, 479-575-4153, Fax: 479-575-4346, E-mail: asaxena@uark.edu.

Dale Bumpers College of Agricultural, Food and Life Sciences Students: 77 full-time (36 women), 204 part-time (101 women); includes 16 minority (6 African Americans, 1 American Indian/Alaska Native, 2 Asian Americans or Pacific Islanders, 7 Hispanic Americans), 88 international. Expenses: Contact institution. *Financial support:* In 2008–09, 16 fellowships with tuition reimbursements, 184 research assistantships were awarded; teaching assistantships, career-related internships or fieldwork, Federal Work-Study, scholarships/grants, and unspecified assistantships also available. Support available to part-time students. Financial award application deadline: 4/1; financial award applicants required to submit FAFSA. In 2008, 75 master's, 22 doctorates awarded. Offers agricultural and extension education (MS); agricultural economics (MS); agricultural, food and life sciences (MS, PhD); agronomy (MS, PhD); animal science (MS, PhD); entomology (MS, PhD); food science (MS, PhD); horticulture (MS); human environmental sciences (MS); plant pathology (MS); plant science (PhD); poultry science (MS, PhD). *Application fee:* $40 ($50 for international students). *Application Contact:* Graduate Admissions, 479-575-6246, Fax: 479-575-5908, E-mail: gradinfo@uark.edu. *Dean,* Dr. Lalit Verma, 479-575-2252, Fax: 479-575-7273, E-mail: lverma@uark.edu.

J. William Fulbright College of Arts and Sciences Students: 337 full-time (174 women), 464 part-time (224 women); includes 61 minority (22 African Americans, 16 American Indian/Alaska Native, 8 Asian Americans or Pacific Islanders, 15 Hispanic Americans), 108 international. Expenses: Contact institution. *Financial support:* In 2008–09, 141 fellowships, 151 research assistantships, 373 teaching assistantships with full tuition reimbursements were awarded; career-related internships or fieldwork, Federal Work-Study, institutionally sponsored loans, and traineeships also available. Support available to part-time students. Financial award application deadline: 4/1; financial award applicants required to submit FAFSA. In 2008, 175 master's, 37 doctorates awarded. Offers anthropology (MA, PhD); applied physics (MS); art (MFA); arts and sciences (MA, MFA, MM, MPA, MS, MSW, PhD); biological sciences (MA, MS, PhD); chemistry (MS, PhD); communication (MA); creative writing (MFA); drama (MA, MFA); English (MA, PhD); French (MA); geography (MA); geology (MS); German (MA); history (MA, PhD); journalism (MA); mathematics (MS, PhD); music (MM); philosophy (MA, PhD); physics (MS, PhD); physics education (MA); political science (MA, MPA); psychology (MA, PhD); public administration (MPA); secondary mathematics (MA); social work (MSW); sociology (MA); Spanish (MA); statistics (MS); translation (MFA). *Application fee:* $40 ($50 for international students). *Application Contact:* Graduate Admissions, 479-575-6246, Fax: 479-575-5908, E-mail: gradinfo@uark.edu. *Dean*, Dr. Bill Schwab, 479-575-4801, Fax: 479-575-2642.

Sam M. Walton College of Business Administration Students: 125 full-time (44 women), 123 part-time (38 women); includes 16 minority (5 African Americans, 1 American Indian/Alaska Native, 5 Asian Americans or Pacific Islanders, 5 Hispanic Americans), 58 international. Expenses: Contact institution. *Financial support:* In 2008–09, 42 fellowships, 75 research assistantships, 16 teaching assistantships were awarded; career-related internships or fieldwork and Federal Work-Study also available. Support available to part-time students. Financial award application deadline: 4/1; financial award applicants required to submit FAFSA. In 2008, 114 master's, 10 doctorates awarded. Offers accounting (M Acc); business administration (M Acc, MA, MBA, MIS, PhD); economics (MA, PhD); information systems (MIS). *Application fee:* $40 ($50 for international students). *Application Contact:* Rebel Smith, Assistant Director of Marketing and Recruiting, 479-575-6123, E-mail: gsb@walton.uark.edu. *Dean*, Dr. Dan Worrell, 479-575-5949.

School of Law Students: 412 full-time (172 women); includes 74 minority (49 African Americans, 8 American Indian/Alaska Native, 11 Asian Americans or Pacific Islanders, 6 Hispanic Americans), 2 international. Expenses: Contact institution. *Financial support:* In 2008–09, fellowships with full tuition reimbursements (averaging $6,000 per year), 10 research assistantships (averaging $2,500 per year) were awarded; teaching assistantships, career-related internships or fieldwork, Federal Work-Study, and scholarships/grants also available. Support available to part-time students. Financial award application deadline: 4/1; financial award applicants required to submit FAFSA. In 2008, 130 JDs, 4 master's awarded. Offers agricultural law (LL M); law (JD). *Application deadline:* For fall admission, 4/1 for domestic students. Applications are processed on a rolling basis. *Application fee:* $0. *Application Contact:* James K. Miller, Associate Dean for Students, 479-575-3102, E-mail: jkmiller@uark.edu. *Dean*, Cynthia Nance, 479-575-5601, Fax: 479-575-3320, E-mail: cnance@uark.edu.

UNIVERSITY OF ARKANSAS AT LITTLE ROCK, Little Rock, AR 72204-1099

General Information State-supported, coed, university. CGS member. *Graduate housing:* Room and/or apartments available on a first-come, first-served basis to single students; on-campus housing not available to married students.

GRADUATE UNITS

Graduate School *Degree program information:* Part-time and evening/weekend programs available. Postbaccalaureate distance learning degree programs offered. Electronic applications accepted.

Clinton School of Public Service Offers public service (MPS, Graduate Certificate).

College of Arts, Humanities, and Social Science *Degree program information:* Part-time and evening/weekend programs available. Offers applied psychology (MAP); art education (MA); art history (MA); arts, humanities, and social science (MA, MALS, MAP, Graduate Certificate); gerontology (Graduate Certificate); philosophy and liberal studies (MALS); professional and technical writing (MA); public history (MA); second languages (MA); studio art (MA).

College of Business Administration *Degree program information:* Part-time and evening/weekend programs available. Offers accountancy (M Acc, Graduate Certificate); business administration (MBA); construction management (Graduate Certificate); management (Graduate Certificate); management information system (MIS); management information systems (Graduate Certificate); management information systems leadership (Graduate Certificate); taxation (MS, Graduate Certificate).

College of Education *Degree program information:* Part-time and evening/weekend programs available. Offers adult education (M Ed); college student affairs (MA); counselor education (M Ed); early childhood education (M Ed); education (M Ed, MA, Ed D, Ed S, Graduate Certificate); educational administration (M Ed, Ed D, Ed S); educational administration and supervision (Ed D); higher education administration (Ed D); higher education: two-year college teaching (MA); learning systems technology (M Ed); literacy coach (Graduate Certificate); middle childhood education (M Ed); orientation and mobility of the blind (Graduate Certificate); reading (M Ed, Ed S); reading education (M Ed, Ed S, Graduate Certificate); rehabilitation counseling (MA, Graduate Certificate); rehabilitation of the blind (MA); school counseling (M Ed); secondary education (M Ed); special education (M Ed); teaching advanced placement (Graduate Certificate); teaching deaf and hard of hearing (M Ed); teaching the gifted and talented (M Ed); teaching the visually impaired (M Ed).

College of Professional Studies *Degree program information:* Part-time and evening/weekend programs available. Offers advanced direct practice (MSW); applied communication studies (MA); conflict mediation (Graduate Certificate); criminal justice (MA, MS); health sciences (MS); journalism (MA); management and community practice (MSW); marriage and family therapy (Graduate Certificate); nonprofit management (Graduate Certificate); professional studies (MA, MPA, MS, MSW, Graduate Certificate); public administration (MPA); social work (MSW, Graduate Certificate).

College of Science and Mathematics Offers applied statistics (Graduate Certificate); biology (MS); chemistry (MA, MS); geospatial technology (Graduate Certificate); integrated science and mathematics (MS); mathematical sciences (MS); science and mathematics (MA, MS, Graduate Certificate).

George W. Donughey College of Engineering and Information Technology *Degree program information:* Part-time and evening/weekend programs available. Offers applied science (MS, PhD); bioinformatics (MS, PhD); computer and information science (MS); engineering and information technology (MS, PhD, Graduate Certificate); information quality (MS); systems engineering (Graduate Certificate).

William H. Bowen School of Law *Degree program information:* Part-time and evening/weekend programs available. Offers law (JD). Electronic applications accepted.

UNIVERSITY OF ARKANSAS AT MONTICELLO, Monticello, AR 71656

General Information State-supported, coed, comprehensive institution. *Graduate housing:* Rooms and/or apartments guaranteed to single students and available on a first-come, first-served basis to married students. Housing application deadline: 8/15.

GRADUATE UNITS

School of Education *Degree program information:* Part-time and evening/weekend programs available. Postbaccalaureate distance learning degree programs offered (minimal on-campus study). Offers education (M Ed, MAT); educational leadership (M Ed). Electronic applications accepted.

School of Forest Resources *Degree program information:* Part-time programs available. Offers forest resources (MS). Electronic applications accepted.

UNIVERSITY OF ARKANSAS AT PINE BLUFF, Pine Bluff, AR 71601-2799

General Information State-supported, coed, comprehensive institution. *Graduate housing:* Rooms and/or apartments available to single and married students. Housing application deadline: 8/1.

GRADUATE UNITS

Program in Education *Degree program information:* Part-time and evening/weekend programs available. Offers elementary education (M Ed); secondary education (M Ed).

School of Agriculture, Fisheries and Human Sciences Offers aquaculture and fisheries (MS).

School of Arts and Sciences Offers addiction studies (MS).

UNIVERSITY OF ARKANSAS FOR MEDICAL SCIENCES, Little Rock, AR 72205-7199

General Information State-supported, coed, upper-level institution. *Graduate housing:* Rooms and/or apartments available on a first-come, first-served basis to single students and available to married students. *Research affiliation:* National Center for Toxicological Research, Veterans Administration Hospital, Oak Ridge Associated Universities, Arkansas Children's Hospital.

GRADUATE UNITS

College of Medicine Offers medicine (MD).

College of Pharmacy Offers pharmaceutical evaluation and policy (MS); pharmacy (Pharm D, MS).

Graduate School *Degree program information:* Part-time programs available. Offers clinical nutrition (MS); communicative disorders (MS, PhD); genetic counseling (MS); health systems research (PhD).

College of Nursing *Degree program information:* Part-time programs available. Offers nursing (PhD).

Graduate Programs in Biomedical Sciences Offers biochemistry and molecular biology (MS, PhD); biomedical sciences (MS, PhD); microbiology and immunology (MS, PhD); neurobiology and developmental sciences (MS, PhD); occupational and environmental health (MS); pathology (MS); pharmacology (MS, PhD); physiology and biophysics (MS, PhD); toxicology (MS, PhD).

UNIVERSITY OF ATLANTA, Atlanta, GA 30360

General Information Independent, coed, comprehensive institution.

GRADUATE UNITS

Graduate Programs

UNIVERSITY OF BALTIMORE, Baltimore, MD 21201-5779

General Information State-supported, coed, comprehensive institution. *Enrollment:* 5,843 graduate, professional, and undergraduate students; 1,570 full-time matriculated graduate/professional students (849 women), 1,507 part-time matriculated graduate/professional students (912 women). *Enrollment by degree level:* 1,072 first professional, 1,841 master's, 53 doctoral, 111 other advanced degrees. *Graduate faculty:* 166 full-time (68 women), 186 part-time/adjunct (61 women). Tuition, state resident: part-time $568 per credit. Tuition, nonresident: part-time $824 per credit. *Required fees:* $250 per semester. *Graduate housing:* On-campus housing not available. *Student services:* Campus employment opportunities, campus safety program, career counseling, exercise/wellness program, international student services, low-cost health insurance, multicultural affairs office, services for students with disabilities. *Library facilities:* Langsdale Library plus 1 other. *Online resources:* library catalog, web page, access to other libraries' catalogs. *Collection:* 258,747 titles, 10,738 serial subscriptions.

Computer facilities: Computer purchase and lease plans are available. 135 computers available on campus for general student use. A campuswide network can be accessed from off campus. Online class registration is available. *Web address:* http://www.ubalt.edu/.

General Application Contact: Kevin Nies, Assistant Director, Office of Graduate Admission, 410-837-6780, E-mail: knies@ubalt.edu.

GRADUATE UNITS

Graduate School Students: 498 full-time (301 women), 1,349 part-time (825 women); includes 645 minority (524 African Americans, 6 American Indian/Alaska Native, 77 Asian Americans or Pacific Islanders, 38 Hispanic Americans), 181 international. Average age 31. 1,533 applicants, 53% accepted, 670 enrolled. *Faculty:* 166 full-time (68 women), 186 part-time/adjunct (61 women). Expenses: Contact institution. *Financial support:* In 2008–09, 294 students received support, including 75 research assistantships; fellowships, career-related internships or fieldwork, Federal Work-Study, and scholarships/grants also available. Support available to part-time students. Financial award application deadline: 4/1; financial award applicants required to submit FAFSA. In 2008, 451 master's, 10 doctorates awarded. *Degree program information:* Part-time and evening/weekend programs available. Postbaccalaureate distance learning degree programs offered (no on-campus study). *Application deadline:* For fall admission, 8/1 priority date for domestic students, 6/1 for international students; for spring admission, 12/1 for domestic students, 11/1 for international students. Applications are processed on a rolling basis. *Application fee:* $30. Electronic applications accepted. *Application Contact:* Kevin Nies, Assistant Director, Office of Graduate Admission, 410-837-6565, E-mail: knies@ubalt.edu. *Senior Vice President for Enrollment Management*, Miriam King, 410-837-4611, Fax: 410-837-4249.

Merrick School of Business Students: 165 full-time (85 women), 561 part-time (273 women); includes 170 minority (111 African Americans, 1 American Indian/Alaska Native, 43 Asian Americans or Pacific Islanders, 15 Hispanic Americans), 88 international. Average age 30. 583 applicants, 53% accepted, 256 enrolled. *Faculty:* 54 full-time (11 women), 36 part-time/adjunct (6 women). Expenses: Contact institution. *Financial support:* Fellowships, research assistantships, career-related internships or fieldwork and Federal Work-Study available. Support available to part-time students. Financial award application deadline: 4/1; financial award applicants required to submit FAFSA. In 2008, 169 master's awarded. *Degree program information:* Part-time and evening/weekend programs available. Postbaccalaureate distance learning degree programs offered (no on-campus study). Offers accounting and business advisory services (MS); accounting fundamentals (Graduate Certificate); business (MBA, MS, Graduate Certificate); business/finance (MS); business/marketing and venturing (MS); forensic accounting (Graduate Certificate); taxation (MS). *Application deadline:* For fall admission, 8/1 priority date for domestic students, 6/1 for international students; for spring admission, 12/1 for domestic students, 11/1 for international students. Applications are processed on a rolling basis. *Application fee:* $30. Electronic applications accepted. *Application Contact:* Kevin Nies, Assistant Director, Office of Graduate Admission, 410-837-6565, E-mail: knies@ubalt.edu. *Dean*, Dr. Darlene Smith, 410-837-4955.

The Yale Gordon College of Liberal Arts Students: 333 full-time (216 women), 788 part-time (552 women); includes 475 minority (413 African Americans, 5 American Indian/Alaska Native, 34 Asian Americans or Pacific Islanders, 23 Hispanic Americans), 93 international. Average age 32. 950 applicants, 53% accepted, 414 enrolled. *Faculty:* 62 full-time (26 women), 66 part-time/adjunct (26 women). Expenses: Contact institution. *Financial support:* In 2008–09, 35 research assistantships were awarded; fellowships, career-related internships or fieldwork and Federal Work-Study also available. Support available to part-time students. Financial award application deadline: 4/1; financial award applicants required to submit FAFSA. In 2008, 244 master's, 2 doctorates awarded. *Degree program information:* Part-time and evening/weekend programs available. Offers applied psychology (MS); communications design (DCD); creative writing and publishing arts (MFA); criminal justice (MS); health systems management (MS); human services administration (MS); human-computer interaction (MS); integrated design (MFA); interaction design and information technology (MS); legal and ethical studies (MA); liberal arts (MA, MFA, MPA, MS, DCD, DPA); negotiations and conflict management (MS); public

University of Baltimore (continued)

administration (MPA, DPA); publications design (MA). *Application deadline:* For fall admission, 8/1 priority date for domestic students, 6/1 for international students; for spring admission, 12/1 for domestic students, 11/1 for international students. Applications are processed on a rolling basis. *Application fee:* $30. Electronic applications accepted. *Application Contact:* Kevin Nies, Assistant Director, Office of Graduate Admission, 410-837-6565, E-mail: knies@ubalt.edu. *Dean*, Dr. Larry Thomas, 410-837-5353.

Joint University of Baltimore/Towson University (UB/Towson) MBA Program Students: 131 full-time (63 women), 481 part-time (229 women); includes 142 minority (93 African Americans, 1 American Indian/Alaska Native, 35 Asian Americans or Pacific Islanders, 13 Hispanic Americans), 63 international. Average age 29. 432 applicants, 51% accepted, 172 enrolled. *Faculty:* 44 full-time (12 women), 36 part-time/adjunct (6 women). Expenses: Contact institution. *Financial support:* In 2008–09, 16 research assistantships were awarded; fellowships, career-related internships or fieldwork and Federal Work-Study also available. Support available to part-time students. Financial award application deadline: 4/1; financial award applicants required to submit FAFSA. In 2008, 138 master's awarded. *Degree program information:* Part-time and evening/weekend programs available. Postbaccalaureate distance learning degree programs offered (no on-campus study). Offers business administration (MBA). *Application deadline:* For fall admission, 8/1 priority date for domestic students, 6/1 for international students; for spring admission, 12/1 for domestic students, 11/1 for international students. Applications are processed on a rolling basis. *Application fee:* $30. *Application Contact:* Kevin Nies, Executive Director, Office of Graduate Admission, 410-837-6565, E-mail: knies@ubalt.edu. *Director*, Ron Desi, 410-837-4947, E-mail: rdesi@towson.ubalt.edu.

School of Law Students: 633 full-time (327 women), 444 part-time (223 women); includes 178 minority (86 African Americans, 2 American Indian/Alaska Native, 67 Asian Americans or Pacific Islanders, 23 Hispanic Americans), 4 international. Average age 27. 2,590 applicants, 39% accepted, 344 enrolled. *Faculty:* 61 full-time (27 women), 84 part-time/adjunct (22 women). Expenses: Contact institution. *Financial support:* In 2008–09, 162 students received support; research assistantships, teaching assistantships, career-related internships or fieldwork, Federal Work-Study, institutionally sponsored loans, and scholarships/grants available. Support available to part-time students. Financial award application deadline: 4/1; financial award applicants required to submit FAFSA. In 2008, 282 JDs awarded. *Degree program information:* Part-time and evening/weekend programs available. Offers law (JD); law of the United States (LL M); taxation (LL M). *Application deadline:* For fall admission, 4/1 priority date for domestic students. Applications are processed on a rolling basis. *Application fee:* $60. Electronic applications accepted. *Application Contact:* Jeffrey L. Zavrotny, Director of Law Admissions, 410-837-4454, Fax: 410-837-4450, E-mail: jzavrotny@ubalt.edu. *Dean*, Phillip J. Closius, 410-837-4458.

UNIVERSITY OF BRIDGEPORT, Bridgeport, CT 06604

General Information Independent, coed, comprehensive institution. CGS member. *Enrollment:* 5,323 graduate, professional, and undergraduate students; 1,823 full-time matriculated graduate/professional students (705 women), 1,472 part-time matriculated graduate/professional students (708 women). *Enrollment by degree level:* 209 first professional, 2,840 master's, 144 doctoral, 102 other advanced degrees. *Graduate faculty:* 117 full-time (41 women), 435 part-time/adjunct (188 women). *Tuition:* Full-time $19,820; part-time $595 per credit hour. *Required fees:* $75 per semester. *Graduate housing:* Room and/or apartments guaranteed to single students; on-campus housing not available to married students. Typical cost: $10,600 (including board). Room and board charges vary according to board plan. Housing application deadline: 8/15. *Student services:* Campus employment opportunities, campus safety program, career counseling, exercise/wellness program, free psychological counseling, international student services, low-cost health insurance, multicultural affairs office, services for students with disabilities, teacher training. *Library facilities:* Wahlstrom Library. *Online resources:* library catalog, web page, access to other libraries' catalogs. *Collection:* 272,430 titles, 2,117 serial subscriptions. *Research affiliation:* Connecticut Medicine Research Consortia, Marine Biology Station (Hummingbird Cay, Bahamas), Burndy Library.

Computer facilities: Computer purchase and lease plans are available. 500 computers available on campus for general student use. A campuswide network can be accessed from student residence rooms and from off campus. Online class registration is available. *Web address:* http://www.bridgeport.edu/.

General Application Contact: Barbara L Maryak, Associate Vice President for Admissions, 203-576-4552, Fax: 203-576-4941, E-mail: admit@bridgeport.edu.

GRADUATE UNITS

Acupuncture Institute Students: 18 full-time (14 women), 6 part-time (3 women); includes 8 minority (1 African American, 5 Asian Americans or Pacific Islanders, 2 Hispanic Americans), 3 international. Average age 40. 25 applicants, 56% accepted, 6 enrolled. *Faculty:* 2 full-time (1 woman), 8 part-time/adjunct (2 women). Expenses: Contact institution. In 2008, 7 master's awarded. *Degree program information:* Part-time programs available. Offers acupuncture (MS). *Application deadline:* For fall admission, 8/1 priority date for domestic students, 8/1 for international students; for spring admission, 12/1 priority date for domestic students, 12/1 for international students. Applications are processed on a rolling basis. *Application fee:* $50. Electronic applications accepted. *Application Contact:* Michael B Grandison, Director of Health Sciences Admission, 203-576-4348, Fax: 203-576-4941, E-mail: acup@bridgeport.edu. *Director*, Dr. Jennifer Brett, 203-576-4122, Fax: 203-576-4107, E-mail: acup@bridgeport.edu.

College of Chiropractic Students: 208 full-time (87 women), 1 (woman) part-time; includes 58 minority (20 African Americans, 2 American Indian/Alaska Native, 26 Asian Americans or Pacific Islanders, 10 Hispanic Americans), 13 international. Average age 29. 124 applicants, 50% accepted, 38 enrolled. *Faculty:* 20 full-time (4 women), 16 part-time/adjunct (5 women). Expenses: Contact institution. *Financial support:* In 2008–09, 190 students received support. Federal Work-Study and institutionally sponsored loans available. Support available to part-time students. Financial award application deadline: 6/1; financial award applicants required to submit FAFSA. In 2008, 34 DCs awarded. Offers chiropractic (DC). *Application deadline:* For fall admission, 4/1 priority date for domestic and international students; for spring admission, 11/1 priority date for domestic and international students. Applications are processed on a rolling basis. *Application fee:* $75. Electronic applications accepted. *Application Contact:* Michael B Grandison, Director of Chiropractic Admissions, 203-576-4348, Fax: 203-576-4941, E-mail: chiro@bridgeport.edu. *Dean*, Dr. Francis A. Zolli, 203-576-4279, E-mail: zolli@bridgeport.edu.

College of Naturopathic Medicine Students: 93 full-time (75 women), 6 part-time (5 women); includes 32 minority (20 African Americans, 1 American Indian/Alaska Native, 9 Asian Americans or Pacific Islanders, 2 Hispanic Americans), 10 international. Average age 34. 123 applicants, 33% accepted, 22 enrolled. *Faculty:* 6 full-time (3 women), 19 part-time/adjunct (7 women). Expenses: Contact institution. *Financial support:* In 2008–09, 80 students received support. Federal Work-Study, institutionally sponsored loans, and scholarships/grants available. Financial award application deadline: 4/1; financial award applicants required to submit FAFSA. In 2008, 21 doctorates awarded. Offers naturopathic medicine (ND). *Application deadline:* For fall admission, 8/1 priority date for domestic and international students; for spring admission, 12/1 for domestic students, 2/1 priority date for international students. Applications are processed on a rolling basis. *Application fee:* $75. Electronic applications accepted. *Application Contact:* Michael B Grandison, Director of Admissions, 203-576-4348, Fax: 203-576-4941, E-mail: natmed@bridgeport.edu. *Dean*, Dr. Guru Sandesh Singh Khalsa, 203-576-4110, Fax: 203-574-4107, E-mail: gkhalsa@bridgeport.edu.

Fones School of Dental Hygiene Students: 1 (woman) full-time, 6 part-time (all women); includes 1 minority (Hispanic American). Average age 39. 12 applicants, 50% accepted, 3 enrolled. *Faculty:* 3 full-time (all women), 3 part-time/adjunct (all women). Expenses: Contact institution. *Degree program information:* Part-time and evening/weekend programs available. Postbaccalaureate distance learning degree programs offered (no on-campus study). Offers dental hygiene (MS). *Application deadline:* For fall admission, 8/1 priority date for domestic and international students; for spring admission, 12/1 priority date for domestic and international students. *Application fee:* $40 ($35 for international students). *Application Contact:* Michael B Grandison, Vice President of Enrollment Management, 203-576-4138, Fax: 203-576-4941, E-mail: fones@bridgeport.edu. *Dean*, Dr. Margaret H. Zayan, 203-576-4138, Fax: 203-576-4220, E-mail: mzayan@bridgeport.edu.

International College Students: 12 full-time (7 women), 3 part-time (2 women); includes 3 minority (all African Americans), 7 international. Average age 28. 28 applicants, 75% accepted, 11 enrolled. *Faculty:* 7 full-time (4 women), 8 part-time/adjunct (3 women). Expenses: Contact institution. *Degree program information:* Part-time and evening/weekend programs available. Offers global development and peace (MA). *Application deadline:* For fall admission, 8/1 priority date for domestic and international students; for spring admission, 12/1 priority date for domestic and international students. *Application fee:* $40 ($35 for international students). *Application Contact:* Barbara L Maryak, Vice President of Enrollment Management, 203-576-4552, Fax: 203-576-4941, E-mail: admit@bridgeport.edu. *Dean*, Dr. Thomas J Ward, 203-576-4966, E-mail: ward@bridgeport.edu.

Nutrition Institute Students: 14 full-time (7 women), 219 part-time (170 women); includes 16 minority (8 African Americans, 1 American Indian/Alaska Native, 3 Asian Americans or Pacific Islanders, 4 Hispanic Americans), 21 international. Average age 37. 400 applicants, 43% accepted, 66 enrolled. *Faculty:* 2 full-time (0 women), 12 part-time/adjunct (6 women). Expenses: Contact institution. *Financial support:* In 2008–09, 33 students received support. Available to part-time students. Application deadline: 6/1. In 2008, 76 master's awarded. *Degree program information:* Part-time and evening/weekend programs available. Postbaccalaureate distance learning degree programs offered (no on-campus study). Offers human nutrition (MS). *Application deadline:* For fall admission, 8/1 priority date for domestic and international students; for spring admission, 12/1 priority date for domestic and international students. Applications are processed on a rolling basis. *Application fee:* $40 ($35 for international students). Electronic applications accepted. *Application Contact:* Michael B Grandison, Vice President of Enrollment Management, 203-576-4138, Fax: 203-576-4941, E-mail: nutrition@bridgeport.edu. *Director*, Dr. David M. Brady, 203-576-4667, Fax: 203-576-4591, E-mail: dbrady@bridgeport.edu.

School of Business Students: 302 full-time (145 women), 163 part-time (76 women); includes 43 minority (22 African Americans, 8 Asian Americans or Pacific Islanders, 13 Hispanic Americans), 385 international. Average age 27. 1,209 applicants, 59% accepted, 118 enrolled. *Faculty:* 11 full-time (2 women), 39 part-time/adjunct (8 women). Expenses: Contact institution. *Financial support:* In 2008–09, 69 students received support; fellowships, research assistantships, teaching assistantships, career-related internships or fieldwork, Federal Work-Study, institutionally sponsored loans, and tuition waivers (partial) available. Support available to part-time students. Financial award application deadline: 6/1; financial award applicants required to submit FAFSA. In 2008, 79 master's awarded. *Degree program information:* Part-time and evening/weekend programs available. Offers business (MBA); business administration (MBA). *Application deadline:* For fall admission, 8/1 priority date for domestic and international students; for spring admission, 12/1 priority date for domestic and international students. Applications are processed on a rolling basis. *Application fee:* $40 ($35 for international students). Electronic applications accepted. *Application Contact:* Dr. Ward Thrasher, MBA Director, 203-576-4368, Fax: 203-576-4388, E-mail: mba@bridgeport.edu. *Dean*, Paul Lerman, 203-576-4384, Fax: 203-576-4388, E-mail: plerman@bridgeport.edu.

School of Education and Human Resources Students: 276 full-time (199 women), 408 part-time (295 women); includes 102 minority (62 African Americans, 9 Asian Americans or Pacific Islanders, 31 Hispanic Americans), 36 international. Average age 32. 538 applicants, 52% accepted, 218 enrolled. *Faculty:* 21 full-time (9 women), 125 part-time/adjunct (69 women). Expenses: Contact institution. *Financial support:* In 2008–09, 330 students received support; fellowships, research assistantships, teaching assistantships, career-related internships or fieldwork, Federal Work-Study, and institutionally sponsored loans available. Support available to part-time students. Financial award application deadline: 6/1; financial award applicants required to submit FAFSA. In 2008, 291 master's, 10 doctorates, 35 other advanced degrees awarded. *Degree program information:* Part-time and evening/weekend programs available. Offers education and human resources (MS, Ed D, Diploma). *Application deadline:* For fall admission, 8/1 priority date for domestic and international students; for spring admission, 12/1 priority date for domestic and international students. Applications are processed on a rolling basis. *Application fee:* $40 ($35 for international students). Electronic applications accepted. *Application Contact:* Dr. Paul C. Paese, Dean, 203-576-4192, Fax: 203-576-4102, E-mail: ppaese@bridgeport.edu. *Dean*, Dr. Paul C. Paese, 203-576-4192, Fax: 203-576-4102, E-mail: ppaese@bridgeport.edu.

Division of Education Students: 253 full-time (180 women), 346 part-time (245 women); includes 64 minority (31 African Americans, 8 Asian Americans or Pacific Islanders, 25 Hispanic Americans), 29 international. Average age 32. 477 applicants, 53% accepted, 199 enrolled. *Faculty:* 14 full-time (5 women), 112 part-time/adjunct (62 women). Expenses: Contact institution. *Financial support:* In 2008–09, 303 students received support; fellowships, research assistantships, teaching assistantships, career-related internships or fieldwork, Federal Work-Study, and institutionally sponsored loans available. Support available to part-time students. Financial award application deadline: 6/1; financial award applicants required to submit FAFSA. In 2008, 261 master's, 10 doctorates, 34 other advanced degrees awarded. *Degree program information:* Part-time and evening/weekend programs available. Offers computer specialist (Diploma); early childhood education (MS, Diploma); education (MS, Ed D, Diploma); educational management (Ed D, Diploma); elementary education (MS, Diploma); intermediate administrator or supervisor (Diploma); international education (Diploma); leadership (Ed D); reading specialist (MS, Diploma); secondary education (MS, Diploma). *Application deadline:* For fall admission, 8/1 priority date for domestic and international students; for spring admission, 12/1 priority date for domestic and international students. Applications are processed on a rolling basis. *Application fee:* $40 ($35 for international students). Electronic applications accepted. *Application Contact:* Dr. Paul C Paese, Dean, 203-576-4192, Fax: 203-576-4200, E-mail: ppaese@bridgeport.edu. *Dean*, Dr. Paul C Paese, 203-576-4192, Fax: 203-576-4200, E-mail: ppaese@bridgeport.edu.

Division of Human Resources Students: 23 full-time (19 women), 62 part-time (50 women); includes 38 minority (31 African Americans, 1 Asian American or Pacific Islander, 6 Hispanic Americans), 7 international. Average age 35. 61 applicants, 44% accepted, 19 enrolled. *Faculty:* 7 full-time (4 women), 13 part-time/adjunct (7 women). Expenses: Contact institution. *Financial support:* In 2008–09, 27 students received support; fellowships, research assistantships, teaching assistantships, career-related internships or fieldwork, Federal Work-Study, and institutionally sponsored loans available. Support available to part-time students. Financial award application deadline: 6/1; financial award applicants required to submit FAFSA. In 2008, 30 master's awarded. *Degree program information:* Part-time and evening/weekend programs available. Offers college student personnel (MS); community counseling (MS); human resource development (MS); human service (MS). *Application deadline:* For fall admission, 8/1 priority date for domestic and international students; for spring admission, 12/1 priority date for domestic and international students. Applications are processed on a rolling basis. *Application fee:* $40 ($35 for international students). Electronic applications accepted. *Application Contact:* Barbara L Maryak, 203-576-4552, Fax: 203-576-4941, E-mail: admit@bridgeport.edu. *Director, Division of Counseling and Human Resources*, Dr. Tracy Ryan, 203-576-4170, Fax: 203-576-4200, E-mail: tryan@bridgeport.edu.

School of Engineering Students: 895 full-time (167 women), 582 part-time (102 women); includes 16 minority (4 African Americans, 12 Asian Americans or Pacific Islanders), 1,447 international. Average age 25. 2,680 applicants, 70% accepted, 335 enrolled. *Faculty:* 19 full-time (5 women), 26 part-time/adjunct (2 women). Expenses: Contact institution. *Financial support:* In 2008–09, 106 students received support; fellowships, research assistantships, teaching assistantships, career-related internships or fieldwork, Federal Work-Study, institutionally sponsored loans, and tuition waivers (partial) available. Support available to part-time students. Financial award application deadline: 6/1; financial award applicants required to submit FAFSA. In 2008, 302 master's awarded. *Degree program information:* Part-time and evening/weekend programs available. Postbaccalaureate distance learning degree programs offered (no on-campus study). Offers computer engineering (MS); computer science (MS);

computer science and engineering (PhD); electrical engineering (MS); engineering (MS, PhD); mechanical engineering (MS); technology management (MS). *Application deadline:* For fall admission, 8/1 priority date for domestic and international students; for spring admission, 12/1 priority date for domestic and international students. Applications are processed on a rolling basis. *Application fee:* $40 ($35 for international students). Electronic applications accepted. *Application Contact:* Brabara L Maryak, Vice President of Enrollment Management, 203-576-4552, Fax: 203-576-4941, E-mail: admit@bridgeport.edu. *Vice President for Graduate Studies and Research/Dean, School of Engineering,* Dr. Tarek M. Sobh, 203-576-4111, Fax: 203-576-4766, E-mail: sobh@bridgeport.edu.

THE UNIVERSITY OF BRITISH COLUMBIA, Vancouver, BC V6T 1Z1, Canada

General Information Province-supported, coed, university. CGS member. *Graduate housing:* Rooms and/or apartments available on a first-come, first-served basis to single and married students. Housing application deadline: 3/1. *Student services:* Campus employment opportunities, campus safety program, career counseling, child daycare facilities, exercise/wellness program, free psychological counseling, grant writing training, international student services, low-cost health insurance, multicultural affairs office, services for students with disabilities, teacher training, writing training. *Library facilities:* Walter C. Koerner Library plus 9 others. *Online resources:* library catalog, web page, access to other libraries' catalogs. *Collection:* 5.6 million titles, 778,063 serial subscriptions, 840,987 audiovisual materials. *Research affiliation:* Pulp and Paper Research Institute of Canada (pulp and paper research), Pacific Environment Institute, Pacific Biological Station (Nanaimo) (fisheries and oceanography), British Columbia Research (chemical and biological science technology), Forintek Canada (forest technology), National Research Council of Canada Institute of Machinery Research (machinery research).

Computer facilities: 1,500 computers available on campus for general student use. A campuswide network can be accessed from student residence rooms and from off campus. Online class registration is available. *Web address:* http://www.ubc.ca/.

General Application Contact: Jaime Coffey, Student Academic Services Application Clerk, 604-822-3907, Fax: 604-822-5802, E-mail: grad.admissions@ubc.ca.

GRADUATE UNITS

College for Interdisciplinary Studies

Institute for European Studies Students: 11 full-time (all women), 11 part-time (all women). Expenses: Contact institution. *Financial support:* In 2008–09, 6 research assistantships were awarded. In 2008, 8 master's awarded. Offers European studies (MA). *Application Contact:* Roxana del Rio, Student Academic Services Clerk, 604-822-1452, Fax: 604-8223433, E-mail: europe@interchange.ubc.ca. *Director,* Dr. Kurt Hubner, 604-822-1452, E-mail: europe@interchange.ubc.ca.

Faculty of Applied Science *Degree program information:* Part-time programs available. Offers applied science (M Arch, M Eng, M Sc, MA Sc, MASA, MASLA, MLA, MSN, MSS, PhD); chemical engineering (M Eng, M Sc, MA Sc, PhD); civil engineering (M Eng, MA Sc, PhD); electrical and computer engineering (M Eng, MA Sc, PhD); materials and metallurgy (M Sc, PhD); mechanical engineering (M Eng, MA Sc, PhD); metals and materials engineering (MA Sc, PhD); mining engineering (M Eng, MA Sc, PhD); nursing (MSN, PhD); software systems (MSS). Electronic applications accepted.

School of Architecture and Landscape Architecture Students: 202 full-time (121 women). Average age 27. 444 applicants, 34% accepted, 68 enrolled. *Faculty:* 25 full-time (9 women), 14 part-time/adjunct (3 women). Expenses: Contact institution. *Financial support:* In 2008–09, 49 students received support, including 2 fellowships (averaging $18,000 per year), 5 teaching assistantships; research assistantships, Federal Work-Study, institutionally sponsored loans, scholarships/grants, and tuition waivers (partial) also available. In 2008, 31 master's awarded. Offers architecture (M Arch, MASA); landscape architecture (MASLA, MLA). *Application deadline:* For fall admission, 1/10 for domestic and international students. *Application fee:* $90 Canadian dollars ($150 Canadian dollars for international students). Electronic applications accepted. *Application Contact:* Trish Poehnell, Graduate Admissions, 604-822-2779, Fax: 604-822-3808, E-mail: soaadmit@interchange.ubc.ca. *Director,* Dr. Ray Cole, 604-822-2779, Fax: 604-822-3808, E-mail: raycole@arch.ubc.ca.

Faculty of Arts Expenses: Contact institution. Offers ancient culture, religion, and ethnicity (MA); anthropology (MA, PhD); art history (MA, PhD, Diploma); arts (M Mus, M Sc, MA, MAS, MFA, MJ, MLIS, MSW, DMA, PhD, CAS, Diploma); Asian studies (MA, PhD); behavioral neuroscience (MA, PhD); classical and near eastern archaeology (MA); classics (MA, PhD); clinical psychology (MA, PhD); cognitive science (MA, PhD); creative writing (MFA); creative writing and film (MFA); creative writing and film production (MFA); creative writing and theatre (MFA); critical and curatorial studies (MA); developmental psychology (MA, PhD); economics (MA, PhD); English (MA, PhD); film (MA, MFA, Diploma); film production (MFA, Diploma); film studies (MA); French (MA, PhD); geography (M Sc, MA, PhD); Germanic studies (MA, PhD); health psychology (MA, PhD); Hispanic studies (MA, PhD); history (MA, PhD); linguistics (MA, PhD); philosophy (MA, PhD); political science (MA, PhD); quantitative methods (MA, PhD); religious studies (MA, PhD); social/personality psychology (MA, PhD); sociology (MA, PhD); theatre (MA, MFA, PhD); theatre design (MFA); theatre directing (MFA); visual art (MFA). Electronic applications accepted. *Application Contact:* Dr. Nancy Gallini, Dean, 604-822-3828, Fax: 604-822-6096, E-mail: artsdean@mail.arts.ubc.ca. *Dean,* Dr. Nancy Gallini, 604-822-3828, Fax: 604-822-6096, E-mail: artsdean@mail.arts.ubc.ca.

The School of Journalism Students: 56 full-time (42 women); includes 11 minority (10 Asian Americans or Pacific Islanders, 1 Hispanic American). Average age 24. 140 applicants, 24% accepted, 28 enrolled. *Faculty:* 4 full-time (2 women), 8 part-time/adjunct (2 women). Expenses: Contact institution. *Financial support:* In 2008–09, 28 students received support, including 21 fellowships (averaging $12,200 per year), 6 research assistantships (averaging $3,000 per year), 1 teaching assistantship (averaging $5,500 per year). Financial award application deadline: 1/15. In 2008, 20 master's awarded. Offers journalism (MJ). *Application deadline:* For fall admission, 1/15 for domestic and international students. *Application fee:* $90 Canadian dollars ($150 Canadian dollars for international students). Electronic applications accepted. *Application Contact:* Barbara R. Wallin, Program Assistant, 604-822-6688, Fax: 604-822-6707, E-mail: journal@interchange.ubc.ca. *Director,* Prof. Mary Lynn Young, 604-822-6688, Fax: 604-822-6707.

School of Library, Archival and Information Studies Students: 248 full-time (201 women), 13 part-time (10 women). Average age 33. 300 applicants, 43% accepted, 102 enrolled. *Faculty:* 10 full-time (8 women), 21 part-time/adjunct (12 women). Expenses: Contact institution. *Financial support:* In 2008–09, 75 students received support, including 3 fellowships (averaging $13,700 per year), 30 research assistantships (averaging $1,225 per year); teaching assistantships, Federal Work-Study, institutionally sponsored loans, scholarships/grants, health care benefits, tuition waivers (partial), and unspecified assistantships also available. In 2008, 76 master's awarded. *Degree program information:* Part-time programs available. Offers archival studies (MAS, CAS); archival studies/library and information studieschildren's literature (MA); library and information studies (MLIS, CAS); library, archival and information studies (PhD). *Application deadline:* For fall admission, 2/1 for domestic and international students; for winter admission, 6/1 for domestic and international students. *Application fee:* $90 Canadian dollars ($150 Canadian dollars for international students). Electronic applications accepted. *Application Contact:* Graduate Admissions Secretary, 604-822-2404, Fax: 604-822-6006, E-mail: slais.admissions@ubc.ca. *Interim Director,* Prof. Terry Eastwood, 604-822-2404, Fax: 604-822-6006, E-mail: slais@interchange.ubc.ca.

School of Music Students: 115 full-time (58 women); includes 26 minority (1 American Indian/Alaska Native, 18 Asian Americans or Pacific Islanders, 7 Hispanic Americans), 10 international. Average age 24. 188 applicants, 22% accepted, 24 enrolled. *Faculty:* 29 full-time (7 women), 56 part-time/adjunct (18 women). Expenses: Contact institution. *Financial support:* In 2008–09, 72 students received support, including 9 fellowships with tuition reimbursements available (averaging $16,000 per year), 9 research assistantships (averaging $2,000 per year), 46 teaching assistantships (averaging $3,200 per year); institutionally sponsored loans, scholarships/grants, tuition waivers (partial), and unspecified assistantships also available. Financial award application deadline: 1/30. In 2008, 29 master's, 8 doctorates awarded. *Degree program information:* Part-time programs available. Offers music (M Mus, MA, DMA, PhD). *Application deadline:* For fall admission, 1/31 priority date for domestic and international students. Applications are processed on a rolling basis. *Application fee:* $90 Canadian dollars ($150 Canadian dollars for international students). Electronic applications accepted. *Application Contact:* Miriam Nechemia, Graduate Admissions Secretary, 604-822-5750, Fax: 604-822-4884, E-mail: miriamn@interchange.ubc.ca. *Director,* Dr. Richard B. Kurth, 604-822-2079, Fax: 604-822-4884, E-mail: richard.kurth@ubc.ca.

School of Social Work Students: 83 full-time (68 women), 22 part-time (20 women); includes 30 minority (1 African American, 4 American Indian/Alaska Native, 25 Asian Americans or Pacific Islanders), 5 international. Average age 35. 83 applicants, 48% accepted, 40 enrolled. *Faculty:* 16 full-time (7 women). Expenses: Contact institution. *Financial support:* In 2008–09, 3 fellowships (averaging $20,000 per year), 26 research assistantships (averaging $5,400 per year), 15 teaching assistantships (averaging $6,600 per year) were awarded; career-related internships or fieldwork, Federal Work-Study, institutionally sponsored loans, scholarships/grants, and unspecified assistantships also available. Financial award application deadline: 4/1. In 2008, 40 master's awarded. Offers social work (MSW, PhD). *Application deadline:* For fall admission, 1/15 for domestic and international students. *Application fee:* $90 Canadian dollars ($150 Canadian dollars for international students). Electronic applications accepted. *Application Contact:* Christine Graham, Program Advisor, 604-822-4119, Fax: 604-822-8656, E-mail: sowk.advisor@ubc.ca. *Acting Director,* Dr. Brian O'Neill, 604-822-0782, Fax: 604-822-8656.

Faculty of Dentistry Average age 25. 50 applicants, 18% accepted, 9 enrolled. *Faculty:* 32 full-time (7 women), 3 part-time/adjunct (1 woman). Expenses: Contact institution. *Financial support:* In 2008–09, 3 fellowships with partial tuition reimbursements (averaging $15,000 per year), 2 research assistantships with partial tuition reimbursements (averaging $16,000 per year), 6 teaching assistantships with partial tuition reimbursements (averaging $800 per year) were awarded; career-related internships or fieldwork, Federal Work-Study, scholarships/grants, tuition waivers (full and partial), and unspecified assistantships also available. Financial award application deadline: 12/5. In 2008, 4 master's awarded. *Degree program information:* Part-time programs available. Offers dental science (M Sc, PhD); dentistry (DMD, M Sc, PhD, Certificate, Diploma); periodontics (Diploma). *Application deadline:* For fall admission, 11/2 for domestic students; for spring admission, 6/8 for international students. Applications are processed on a rolling basis. *Application fee:* $200 Canadian dollars ($400 Canadian dollars for international students). Electronic applications accepted. *Application Contact:* Connie A. Reynolds, Manager, Admissions and Academic Progress, 604-822-1847, Fax: 604-822-8279, E-mail: connier@interchange.ubc.ca. *Dean,* Dr. C. Shuler, 604-822-5773, Fax: 604-822-4532, E-mail: cshuler@interchange.ubc.ca.

Faculty of Education Students: 1,160 full-time (837 women), 400 part-time (309 women). Average age 37. 970 applicants, 62% accepted, 466 enrolled. *Faculty:* 153 full-time (79 women). Expenses: Contact institution. *Financial support:* In 2008–09, 200 students received support; fellowships with full and partial tuition reimbursements available, research assistantships with full and partial tuition reimbursements available, teaching assistantships with full and partial tuition reimbursements available, career-related internships or fieldwork, Federal Work-Study, institutionally sponsored loans, scholarships/grants, and unspecified assistantships available. In 2008, 69 master's, 47 doctorates, 4 other advanced degrees awarded. *Degree program information:* Part-time and evening/weekend programs available. Postbaccalaureate distance learning degree programs offered (no on-campus study). Offers adult education (M Ed, MA); adult learning and global change (M Ed); art education (M Ed, MA); business education (MA); counseling psychology (M Ed, MA, PhD); curriculum studies (M Ed, MA, PhD); development, learning and culture (PhD); education (M Ed, M Sc, MA, MET, MHK, Ed D, PhD, Diploma); educational administration (M Ed, MA); educational leadership and policy (Ed D); educational studies (PhD); guidance studies (Diploma); higher education (M Ed, MA); home economics education (M Ed, MA); human development, learning and culture (M Ed, MA); library education (M Ed); literacy education (M Ed, MA, PhD); math education (M Ed, MA); measurement and evaluation and research methodology (M Ed); measurement, evaluation and research methodology (MA); measurement, evaluation, and research methodology (PhD); modern language education (M Ed, MA, PhD); music education (M Ed, MA); physical education (M Ed, MA); school psychology (M Ed, MA, PhD); science education (M Ed, MA); social studies education (M Ed, MA); society, culture and politics in education (M Ed, MA); special education (M Ed, MA, PhD, Diploma); teaching English as a second language (M Ed, MA, PhD); technology studies education (M Ed, MA). *Application deadline:* For fall admission, 12/15 for domestic and international students. *Application fee:* $90 Canadian dollars ($150 Canadian dollars for international students). Electronic applications accepted. *Application Contact:* Dr. Beth Haverkamp, Associate Dean, Graduate Programs and Research, 604-822-5513, Fax: 604-822-8971, E-mail: beth.haverkamp@ubc.ca. *Associate Dean, Graduate Programs and Research,* Dr. Beth Haverkamp, 604-822-5513, Fax: 604-822-8971, E-mail: beth.haverkamp@ubc.ca.

Centre for Cross-Faculty Inquiry in Education Students: 88 full-time, 36 part-time. 41 applicants, 46% accepted, 18 enrolled. *Faculty:* 50 full-time (22 women). Expenses: Contact institution. *Financial support:* In 2008–09, 20 students received support; fellowships with tuition reimbursements available, research assistantships with tuition reimbursements available, teaching assistantships with tuition reimbursements available, institutionally sponsored loans, scholarships/grants, and tuition waivers (full and partial) available. In 2008, 28 master's, 8 doctorates awarded. *Degree program information:* Part-time and evening/weekend programs available. Offers curriculum and instruction (M Ed, MA, PhD); early childhood education (M Ed, MA). *Application deadline:* For fall admission, 1/1 for domestic and international students. *Application fee:* $90 Canadian dollars ($150 Canadian dollars for international students). Electronic applications accepted. *Application Contact:* Oliva dela-Cruz Cordero, Graduate Secretary, 604-822-6502, Fax: 604-822-8234, E-mail: oliva.dela.cruz-cordero@ubc.ca. *Director,* Dr. Graeme Chalmers, 604-822-6502, Fax: 604-822-8234, E-mail: f.graeme.chalmers@ubc.ca.

School of Human Kinetics Students: 93 full-time (56 women), 1 part-time (0 women); includes 1 African American, 14 Asian Americans or Pacific Islanders. Average age 25. 51 applicants, 61% accepted, 25 enrolled. *Faculty:* 22 full-time (6 women), 4 part-time/adjunct (1 woman). Expenses: Contact institution. *Financial support:* In 2008–09, 5 fellowships, 5 research assistantships, 55 teaching assistantships (averaging $5,000 per year) were awarded; career-related internships or fieldwork, Federal Work-Study, institutionally sponsored loans, scholarships/grants, and tuition waivers (full and partial) also available. Financial award application deadline: 3/15. In 2008, 10 master's, 6 doctorates awarded. *Degree program information:* Part-time programs available. Offers human kinetics (M Sc, MA, MHK, PhD). *Application deadline:* For fall admission, 3/1 for domestic students, 2/1 for international students; for winter admission, 8/1 for domestic students, 7/1 for international students. Applications are processed on a rolling basis. *Application fee:* $90 Canadian dollars ($150 Canadian dollars for international students). Electronic applications accepted. *Application Contact:* Susan Townsend, Graduate Secretary, 604-822-2767, Fax: 604-822-6842, E-mail: hkin-gradsec@interchange.ubc.ca. *Director,* Dr. Robert E. Sparks, 604-822-2767, Fax: 604-822-6842, E-mail: robert.sparks@ubc.ca.

Faculty of Forestry Students: 261 full-time (104 women). 93 applicants, 71% accepted. *Faculty:* 67 full-time (10 women), 28 part-time/adjunct (4 women). Expenses: Contact institution. *Financial support:* Fellowships, research assistantships, teaching assistantships, scholarships/grants, health care benefits, tuition waivers (full and partial), and unspecified assistantships available. In 2008, 41 master's, 18 doctorates awarded. *Degree program information:* Part-time programs available. Offers forestry (M Sc, MA Sc, MF, PhD). *Application deadline:* For fall admission, 4/1 for domestic students, 3/1 for international students; for winter admission, 8/1 for domestic students, 7/1 for international students; for spring admission, 1/1 for domestic students, 11/1 for international students. Applications are processed on a rolling basis. *Application fee:* $90 Canadian dollars ($150 Canadian dollars for international students). Electronic applications accepted. *Application Contact:* Gayle Kosh, Manager, Graduate Programs, 604-827-4454, Fax: 604-822-8645, E-mail: gayle.kosh@ubc.ca. *Associate Dean, Graduate Studies and Research,* Dr. Cindy E. Prescott, 604-822-4701, Fax: 604-822-8645, E-mail: cindy.prescott@ubc.ca.

The University of British Columbia (continued)

Faculty of Land and Food Systems Students: 184 full-time (123 women). Average age 30. 158 applicants, 43% accepted, 44 enrolled. *Faculty:* 54 full-time (14 women), 10 part-time/adjunct (4 women). Expenses: Contact institution. *Financial support:* In 2008–09, 13 students received support, including 13 fellowships with full and partial tuition reimbursements available (averaging $17,000 per year), 49 research assistantships with partial tuition reimbursements available, 150 teaching assistantships with partial tuition reimbursements available; career-related internships or fieldwork, Federal Work-Study, institutionally sponsored loans, scholarships/grants, and tuition waivers (full and partial) also available. In 2008, 22 master's, 6 doctorates awarded. Offers agricultural economics (M Sc); animal science (M Sc, PhD); food science (M Sc, MFS, PhD); human nutrition (M Sc, PhD); land and food systems (M Sc, MFS, PhD); plant science (M Sc, PhD); soil science (M Sc, PhD). *Application deadline:* For fall admission, 1/3 for domestic and international students; for winter admission, 6/1 for domestic and international students; for spring admission, 9/1 for domestic and international students. Applications are processed on a rolling basis. *Application fee:* $90 Canadian dollars ($150 Canadian dollars for international students). Electronic applications accepted. *Application Contact:* Lia Maria Dragan, Graduate Programs Assistant, 604-822-8373, Fax: 604-822-4400, E-mail: gradapp@interchange.ubc.ca. *Associate Dean, Graduate Programs,* Dr. Mahesh Upadhyaya, 604-822-6139, Fax: 604-822-4400, E-mail: upadh@interchange.ubc.ca.

Faculty of Law Students: 72 full-time (34 women); includes 27 minority (8 African Americans, 3 American Indian/Alaska Native, 10 Asian Americans or Pacific Islanders, 6 Hispanic Americans), 31 international. Average age 30. 98 applicants, 48% accepted, 39 enrolled. *Faculty:* 44 full-time (11 women), 89 part-time/adjunct. Expenses: Contact institution. *Financial support:* In 2008–09, 43 fellowships (averaging $7,000 per year), 5 research assistantships, 8 teaching assistantships (averaging $10,500 per year) were awarded; Federal Work-Study, scholarships/grants, and unspecified assistantships also available. Financial award application deadline: 9/30. In 2008, 6 master's, 4 doctorates awarded. *Degree program information:* Part-time programs available. Offers law (LL M, LL M CL, PhD). *Application deadline:* For fall admission, 1/15 for domestic and international students. Applications are processed on a rolling basis. *Application fee:* $90 ($150 for international students). Electronic applications accepted. *Application Contact:* Joanne Y. Chung, Graduate Administrator, 604-822-6449, Fax: 604-822-4781, E-mail: graduates@law.ubc.ca. *Associate Dean, Graduate Studies and Research,* Dr. Douglas Harris, 604-822-1991, Fax: 604-822-4781, E-mail: harris@law.ubc.ca.

Faculty of Medicine *Degree program information:* Part-time programs available. Offers anatomy and cell biology (M Sc, PhD); anesthesiology, pharmacology and therapeutics (M Sc, PhD); biochemistry and molecular biology (M Sc, PhD); experimental medicine (M Sc, PhD); experimental pathology (M Sc, PhD); genetic counselling (M Sc); medical genetics (M Sc, PhD); medicine (MD, M Sc, MH Sc, MHA, MOT, MPH, MPT, MRSc, PhD); occupational science and occupational therapy (MOT); physiology (M Sc, PhD); reproductive and developmental sciences (M Sc, PhD); surgery (M Sc). Open only to Canadian residents.

School of Audiology and Speech Sciences Students: 70 full-time (57 women); includes 1 Asian American or Pacific Islander, 1 international. Average age 25. 150 applicants, 25% accepted, 36 enrolled. *Faculty:* 12 full-time (8 women), 3 part-time/adjunct (all women). Expenses: Contact institution. *Financial support:* In 2008–09, 16 students received support, including 3 fellowships (averaging $18,000 per year), 6 research assistantships; teaching assistantships, career-related internships or fieldwork, Federal Work-Study, institutionally sponsored loans, scholarships/grants, and unspecified assistantships also available. Financial award application deadline: 1/15. In 2008, 23 master's awarded. Offers audiology and speech sciences (M Sc, PhD). *Application deadline:* For fall admission, 2/28 for domestic and international students. Applications are processed on a rolling basis. *Application fee:* $90 Canadian dollars ($150 Canadian dollars for international students). Electronic applications accepted. *Application Contact:* Sue Madura Bryant, Graduate Program Assistant, 604-827-5920, Fax: 604-822-6569, E-mail: inquiry@audiospeech.ubc.ca. *Director,* Dr. Valter Ciocca, PhD, 604-822-5795, Fax: 604-822-6569, E-mail: director@audiospeech.ubc.ca.

School of Population and Public Health Students: 175 full-time (106 women). Average age 30. 406 applicants, 30% accepted, 83 enrolled. *Faculty:* 125 full-time (43 women), 73 part-time/adjunct (21 women). Expenses: Contact institution. *Financial support:* In 2008–09, 34 students received support, including 15 research assistantships, 19 teaching assistantships; career-related internships or fieldwork, scholarships/grants, traineeships, and unspecified assistantships also available. In 2008, 56 master's, 3 doctorates awarded. Postbaccalaureate distance learning degree programs offered (minimal on-campus study). Offers health administration (MHA); health care and epidemiology (MH Sc, PhD); public health (MPH). *Application deadline:* For fall admission, 2/1 for domestic and international students. *Application fee:* $90 ($150 for international students). Electronic applications accepted. *Application Contact:* Dr. Moira Thejomayen, Program Manager, 604-822-5405, Fax: 604-822-4994, E-mail: moira.thejomayen@ubc.ca. *Director,* Dr. Martin T. Schechter, 604-822-3910, Fax: 604-822-4994, E-mail: martin.schechter@ubc.ca.

School of Rehabilitation Sciences Offers rehabilitation sciences (M Sc, MOT, MPT, MRSc, PhD). Electronic applications accepted.

Faculty of Pharmaceutical Sciences Students: 71 full-time (38 women). Average age 28. 58 applicants, 38% accepted, 18 enrolled. *Faculty:* 30 full-time (9 women), 26 part-time/adjunct (11 women). Expenses: Contact institution. *Financial support:* In 2008–09, fellowships (averaging $16,000 per year), 39 research assistantships (averaging $13,127 per year), 20 teaching assistantships (averaging $7,503 per year) were awarded; career-related internships or fieldwork, institutionally sponsored loans, scholarships/grants, traineeships, health care benefits, and unspecified assistantships also available. In 2008, 4 master's, 1 doctorate awarded. Offers pharmaceutical sciences (Pharm D, M Sc, PhD). *Application deadline:* For fall admission, 3/15 for domestic students, 2/15 for international students. Applications are processed on a rolling basis. *Application fee:* $90 Canadian dollars ($150 Canadian dollars for international students). Electronic applications accepted. *Application Contact:* Dr. Barb Conway, Research Grants Facilitator and Graduate Program Coordinator, 604-822-2390, Fax: 604-822-3035, E-mail: baconway@interchange.ubc.ca. *Dean,* Dr. Robert D. Sindelar, 604-822-2343, Fax: 604-822-3035, E-mail: sindelar@interchange.ubc.ca.

Faculty of Science *Degree program information:* Part-time programs available. Offers astronomy (M Sc, PhD); atmospheric science (M Sc, PhD); botany (M Sc, PhD); chemistry (M Sc, PhD); computer science (M Sc, PhD); engineering physics (MA Sc); geological engineering (M Eng, MA Sc, PhD); geological sciences (M Sc, PhD); geophysics (M Sc, MA Sc, PhD); mathematics (M Sc, MA, PhD); microbiology and immunology (M Sc, PhD); oceanography (M Sc, PhD); physics (M Sc, PhD); science (M Eng, M Sc, MA, MA Sc, PhD); statistics (M Sc, PhD); zoology (M Sc, PhD). Electronic applications accepted.

Genetics Graduate Program Offers genetics (M Sc, PhD).

Institute of Applied Mathematics Offers applied mathematics (M Sc, PhD).

Institute of Asian Research Students: 20 full-time (10 women); includes 10 Asian Americans or Pacific Islanders. Average age 30. 60 applicants, 38% accepted, 15 enrolled. *Faculty:* 9 full-time (1 woman), 2 part-time/adjunct (0 women). Expenses: Contact institution. *Financial support:* In 2008–09, 4 fellowships with tuition reimbursements, 16 research assistantships (averaging $3,500 per year) were awarded; career-related internships or fieldwork, institutionally sponsored loans, scholarships/grants, and tuition waivers (partial) also available. In 2008, 13 master's awarded. Offers Asian research (MAPPS). *Application deadline:* For fall admission, 1/15 for domestic and international students. *Application fee:* $90 ($150 for international students). Electronic applications accepted. *Application Contact:* Marietta T. Lao, Administrator, 604-822-2746, Fax: 604-822-5207, E-mail: mlao@interchange.ubc.ca. *Director,* Masao Nakamura, 604-822-4686, Fax: 604-822-5207, E-mail: nakamura@interchange.ubc.ca.

Program in Resource Management and Environmental Studies Students: 103 full-time (57 women); includes 34 minority (2 African Americans, 2 American Indian/Alaska Native, 24 Asian Americans or Pacific Islanders, 6 Hispanic Americans), 17 international. Average age 30. 113 applicants, 20% accepted, 17 enrolled. *Faculty:* 12 full-time (3 women), 48 part-time/adjunct (5 women). Expenses: Contact institution. *Financial support:* In 2008–09, 49 students received support, including 41 fellowships with partial tuition reimbursements available (averaging $17,500 per year), 8 research assistantships (averaging $17,500 per year); teaching assistantships, institutionally sponsored loans, scholarships/grants, and unspecified assistantships also available. Financial award application deadline: 9/15. In 2008, 2 master's, 8 doctorates awarded. Offers resource management and environmental studies (M Sc, MA, PhD). *Application deadline:* For fall admission, 12/1 priority date for domestic and international students. *Application fee:* $90 Canadian dollars ($150 Canadian dollars for international students). Electronic applications accepted. *Application Contact:* Beth Hall, Graduate Program Coordinator, 604-822-9249, Fax: 604-822-9250, E-mail: rmesgrad@ires.ubc.ca. *Director,* Dr. Gunilla Oberg, 604-822-3010, Fax: 604-822-9250, E-mail: goberg@ires.ubc.ca.

Sauder School of Business *Degree program information:* Part-time and evening/weekend programs available. Offers accounting (PhD); business (IMBA, M Sc, MBA, MM, PhD); business administration (IMBA, MBA); finance (PhD); international business (PhD); management information systems (PhD); management science (PhD); marketing (PhD); operations research (MM); organizational behavior (PhD); strategy and business economics (PhD); transportation and logistics (PhD); urban land economics (PhD). Electronic applications accepted.

School of Community and Regional Planning Offers community and regional planning (M Sc P, MAP, PhD). Electronic applications accepted.

School of Environmental Health *Degree program information:* Part-time programs available. Offers environmental health (M Sc, PhD). Electronic applications accepted.

UNIVERSITY OF CALGARY, Calgary, AB T2N 1N4, Canada

General Information Province-supported, coed, university. CGS member. *Graduate housing:* Rooms and/or apartments available on a first-come, first-served basis to single and married students. Housing application deadline: 3/31. *Research affiliation:* Alta Telecommunications Research Centre, Alberta Sulphur Research, Calgary Society for Students with Learning Difficulties, Canadian Institute of Resources Law, Canadian Music Centre, Canadian Energy Research Institute.

GRADUATE UNITS

Faculty of Graduate Studies *Degree program information:* Part-time and evening/weekend programs available. Postbaccalaureate distance learning degree programs offered (minimal on-campus study). Offers interdisciplinary research (M Sc, MA, PhD); resources and the environment (M Sc, MA, PhD).

Centre for Military and Strategic Studies *Degree program information:* Part-time programs available. Offers military and strategic studies (MSS, PhD). PhD offered in special cases only.

Faculty of Communication and Culture *Degree program information:* Part-time and evening/weekend programs available. Offers communication and culture (MA, MCS, PhD). Electronic applications accepted.

Faculty of Education *Degree program information:* Part-time and evening/weekend programs available. Postbaccalaureate distance learning degree programs offered (minimal on-campus study). Offers community rehabilitation and disability studies (M Ed, M Sc, Ed D, PhD, Graduate Certificate, Graduate Diploma); counseling psychology (M Ed, M Sc, PhD); curriculum, teaching and learning (M Ed, M Sc, MA, Ed D, PhD, Graduate Certificate, Graduate Diploma); education (M Ed, M Sc, MA, Ed D, PhD, Graduate Certificate, Graduate Diploma); educational contexts (M Ed, MA, Ed D, PhD, Graduate Certificate, Graduate Diploma); educational leadership (M Ed, MA, Ed D, PhD, Graduate Certificate, Graduate Diploma); educational technology (M Ed, M Sc, MA, Ed D, PhD, Graduate Certificate, Graduate Diploma); gifted education (M Sc, MA, Ed D, PhD, Graduate Certificate, Graduate Diploma); higher education administration (Ed D); human development and learning (M Ed, M Sc, PhD); interpretive studies in education (M Ed, M Sc, MA, Ed D, PhD, Graduate Certificate, Graduate Diploma); school psychology (M Ed, M Sc, PhD); second language teaching (M Ed, Ed D, PhD, Graduate Certificate, Graduate Diploma); special education (M Ed, M Sc, PhD); teaching English as a second language (M Ed, M Sc, MA, Ed D, PhD, Graduate Certificate, Graduate Diploma); workplace and adult learning (M Ed, MA, Ed D, PhD, Graduate Certificate, Graduate Diploma). Electronic applications accepted.

Faculty of Environmental Design Offers architecture (M Arch); environmental design (M Env Des, PhD).

Faculty of Fine Arts Offers art (MA, MFA); design and technical theatre (MFA); directing (MFA); fine arts (M Mus, MA, MFA, PhD); music (M Mus, MA, PhD); playwriting (MFA); theatre studies (MFA). Electronic applications accepted.

Faculty of Humanities *Degree program information:* Part-time and evening/weekend programs available. Offers English (MA, PhD); French (MA, PhD); German (MA); Greek and Roman studies (MA, PhD); humanities (MA, PhD); philosophy (MA, PhD); religious studies (MA, PhD); Spanish (MA, PhD). Electronic applications accepted.

Faculty of Kinesiology Offers biomedical engineering (M Sc, PhD); kinesiology (M Kin, M Sc, PhD). Electronic applications accepted.

Faculty of Nursing Students: 80 full-time (70 women), 37 part-time (35 women). Average age 30. 58 applicants, 74% accepted, 34 enrolled. *Faculty:* 32 full-time (29 women). Expenses: Contact institution. *Financial support:* In 2008–09, 46 students received support, including 1 fellowship (averaging $50,000 per year), 23 teaching assistantships (averaging $6,106 per year); institutionally sponsored loans, scholarships/grants, health care benefits, and unspecified assistantships also available. Support available to part-time students. Financial award application deadline: 2/1. In 2008, 29 master's, 6 doctorates, 8 other advanced degrees awarded. *Degree program information:* Part-time programs available. Offers nursing (MN, PhD, PMD). *Application deadline:* For fall admission, 2/1 for domestic and international students; for winter admission, 9/15 for domestic and international students. *Application fee:* $100 ($130 for international students). Electronic applications accepted. *Application Contact:* Marleth Bernardo, Graduate Programs Student Advisor, 403-220-6241, Fax: 403-284-4803, E-mail: mbernard@ucalgary.ca. *Associate Dean, Graduate Programs,* Dr. Carol Ewashen, 403-220-6259, Fax: 403-284-4803, E-mail: ewashen@ucalgary.ca.

Faculty of Science *Degree program information:* Part-time programs available. Offers analytical chemistry (M Sc, PhD); applied chemistry (M Sc, PhD); biological sciences (M Sc, PhD); computer science (M Sc, PhD); geology (M Sc, PhD); geophysics (M Sc, PhD); inorganic chemistry (M Sc, PhD); mathematics and statistics (M Sc, PhD); organic chemistry (M Sc, PhD); physical chemistry (M Sc, PhD); physics and astronomy (M Sc, PhD); polymer chemistry (M Sc, PhD); science (M Sc, PhD); software engineering (M Sc); theoretical chemistry (M Sc, PhD).

Faculty of Social Sciences *Degree program information:* Part-time and evening/weekend programs available. Offers anthropology (MA, PhD); archaeology (MA, PhD); clinical psychology (M Sc, PhD); economics (M Ec, MA, PhD); geography (M Sc, MA, MGIS, PhD); history (MA, PhD); linguistics (MA, PhD); political science (MA, PhD); psychology (M Sc, PhD); social sciences (M Ec, M Sc, MA, MGIS, PhD); sociology (MA, PhD).

Faculty of Social Work Offers social work (MSW, PhD, Postgraduate Diploma). Electronic applications accepted.

Haskayne School of Business *Degree program information:* Part-time and evening/weekend programs available. Offers business (EMBA, MBA, PhD); business administration (EMBA, MBA); management (MBA, PhD).

Schulich School of Engineering *Degree program information:* Part-time and evening/weekend programs available. Offers biomedical engineering (M Eng, M Sc, PhD); chemical and petroleum engineering (M Eng, M Sc, PhD); civil engineering (M Eng, M Sc, MPM, PhD); electrical and computer engineering (M Eng, M Sc, PhD); engineering (M Eng, M Sc, MPM, PhD); geomatics engineering (M Eng, M Sc, PhD); mechanical and manufacturing engineering (M Eng, M Sc, PhD).

Faculty of Law Offers law (LL B, LL M, Post-Graduate Certificate); natural resources, energy and environmental law (LL M, Graduate Certificate).

Faculty of Medicine *Degree program information:* Part-time programs available. Offers biochemistry and molecular biology (M Sc, PhD); biomedical technology (MBT); cancer biology (M Sc, PhD); cardiovascular and respiratory sciences (M Sc, PhD); community health sciences (M Sc, MCM, PhD); gastrointestinal sciences (M Sc, PhD); immunology (M Sc,

PhD); joint injury and arthritis research (M Sc, PhD); medical education (M Sc, PhD); medical science (M Sc, PhD); medicine (MD, M Sc, MBT, MCM, PhD); microbiology and infectious diseases (M Sc, PhD); mountain medicine and high altitude physiology (M Sc); neuroscience (M Sc, PhD). Electronic applications accepted.

UNIVERSITY OF CALIFORNIA, BERKELEY, Berkeley, CA 94720-1500

General Information State-supported, coed, university. CGS member. *Graduate housing:* Rooms and/or apartments available to single and married students.

GRADUATE UNITS

Graduate Division *Degree program information:* Part-time and evening/weekend programs available. Offers ancient history and Mediterranean archaeology (MA, PhD); Asian studies (PhD); bioengineering (PhD); biophysics (PhD); Buddhist studies (PhD); comparative biochemistry (PhD); demography (MA, PhD); East Asian studies (MA); endocrinology (MA, PhD); energy and resources (MA, MS, PhD); ethnic studies (PhD); folklore (MA); French (PhD); international and area studies (MA); Italian (PhD); Jewish studies (PhD); Latin American studies (MA); neuroscience (PhD); Northeast Asian studies (MA); performance studies (PhD); range management (MS); sociology and demography (PhD); South Asian studies (MA); Southeast Asian studies (MA); Spanish (PhD); vision science (MS, PhD).

College of Chemistry Offers chemical engineering (MS, PhD); chemistry (MS, PhD).

College of Engineering Offers applied science and technology (PhD); computer science (MS, PhD); electrical engineering (MS, PhD); engineering (M Eng, MS, D Eng, PhD); engineering and project management (M Eng, MS, D Eng, PhD); engineering science (M Eng, MS, PhD); environmental engineering (M Eng, MS, D Eng, PhD); geoengineering (M Eng, MS, D Eng, PhD); industrial engineering and operations research (M Eng, MS, D Eng, PhD); mechanical engineering (M Eng, MS, D Eng, PhD); nuclear engineering (M Eng, MS, D Eng, PhD); structural engineering, mechanics and materials (M Eng, MS, D Eng, PhD); transportation engineering (M Eng, MS, D Eng, PhD).

College of Environmental Design Offers architecture (M Arch); building science (MS, PhD); building structures, construction and materials (MS, PhD); city and regional planning (MCP, PhD); design (MA); design theories, methods, and practices (MS, PhD); environmental design (M Arch, MA, MCP, MLA, MS, MUD, PhD); environmental design in developing countries (MS, PhD); environmental planning (MLA); history of architecture and urbanism (MS, PhD); landscape architecture (MLA); landscape architecture and environmental planning (PhD); landscape design and site planning (MLA); social and cultural processes in architecture and urbanism (MS, PhD); urban and community design (MLA); urban design (MUD).

College of Letters and Science Offers African American studies (PhD); anthropology (PhD); applied mathematics (PhD); art practice (MFA); astrophysics (PhD); Chinese language (PhD); classical archaeology (MA, PhD); classics (MA, PhD); comparative literature (PhD); composition (PhD); Czech (PhD); economics (PhD); English (PhD); ethnomusicology (PhD); French (PhD); geography (PhD); geology (MA, MS, PhD); geophysics (MA, MS, PhD); German (PhD); Greek (MA); Hindi (MA, PhD); Hispanic languages and literature (PhD); history (PhD); history of art (PhD); Indonesian (MA, PhD); integrative biology (PhD); Italian studies (PhD); Japanese language (PhD); Latin (MA); letters and science (MA, MFA, MS, PhD); linguistics (PhD); logic and the methodology of science (PhD); mathematics (MA, PhD); medical anthropology (PhD); molecular and cell biology (PhD); musicology (PhD); Near Eastern religions (PhD); Near Eastern studies (MA, PhD); philosophy (PhD); physics (PhD); Polish (PhD); political science (PhD); psychology (PhD); rhetoric (PhD); Russian (PhD); Sanskrit (MA, PhD); Scandinavian languages and literatures (PhD); Serbo-Croatian (PhD); sociology (PhD); statistics (MA, PhD); Tamil (MA, PhD). Electronic applications accepted.

College of Natural Resources Offers agricultural and resource economics (PhD); environmental science, policy, and management (MS, PhD); forestry (MF); microbiology (PhD); molecular and biochemical nutrition (PhD); molecular toxicology (PhD); natural resources (MF, MS, PhD); plant biology (PhD).

Graduate School of Journalism Offers journalism (MJ).

Graduate School of Public Policy Offers public policy (MPP, PhD).

Haas School of Business Students: 643 full-time (184 women), 884 part-time (211 women); includes 339 minority (11 African Americans, 297 Asian Americans or Pacific Islanders, 31 Hispanic Americans), 629 international. *Faculty:* 85 full-time (23 women), 149 part-time/adjunct (19 women). Expenses: Contact institution. *Financial support:* Fellowships, research assistantships, teaching assistantships, career-related internships or fieldwork, Federal Work-Study, institutionally sponsored loans, scholarships/grants, tuition waivers (full), and unspecified assistantships available. Support available to part-time students. Financial award application deadline: 3/2; financial award applicants required to submit FAFSA. In 2008, 612 master's, 11 doctorates awarded. *Degree program information:* Part-time and evening/weekend programs available. Offers accounting (PhD); business (MBA, MFE, PhD); business administration (MBA, PhD); business and public policy (PhD); finance (PhD); financial engineering (MFE); marketing (PhD); organizational behavior and industrial relations (PhD); real estate (PhD). *Application fee:* $200. *Application Contact:* MBA Admissions Office, 510-642-1405, Fax: 510-643-6659. *Dean,* Richard K. Lyons, 510-643-2027, Fax: 510-642-9128, E-mail: lyons@haas.berkeley.edu.

School of Education Offers development in mathematics and science (MA); developmental teacher educationeducation (MA, Ed D, PhD); education and single subject credential: English (MA); education in mathematics, science, and technology (MA, PhD); human development and education (MA, PhD); language, literacy, and culture (MA, Ed D, PhD); policy and organizational research (MA, PhD); principal leadership (MA); program evaluation and assessment (Ed D); quantitative methods and evaluation (MA, PhD); science and mathematics educationsocial and cultural studies in education (MA, PhD); special education (PhD).

School of Information Management and Systems Offers information management and systems (MIMS, PhD).

School of Public Health Offers biostatistics (MA, PhD); community health education (MPH); environmental health sciences (MPH, MS, Dr PH, PhD); epidemiology (MPH, MS, PhD); health and social behavior (MPH); health policy and management (MPH); health services and policy analysis (PhD); infectious diseases (MPH, PhD); infectious diseases and immunity (PhD); interdisciplinary (MPH); maternal and child health (MPH); public health (MA, MPH, MS, Dr PH, PhD); public health nutrition (MPH).

School of Social Welfare Offers social welfare (MSW, PhD).

School of Law Students: 874 full-time (474 women); includes 294 minority (46 African Americans, 13 American Indian/Alaska Native, 159 Asian Americans or Pacific Islanders, 76 Hispanic Americans), 15 international. Average age 25. 7,391 applicants, 11% accepted, 273 enrolled. *Faculty:* 70 full-time (27 women), 52 part-time/adjunct (17 women). Expenses: Contact institution. *Financial support:* In 2008–09, 718 students received support, including 44 fellowships with partial tuition reimbursements available (averaging $13,541 per year), 162 research assistantships with partial tuition reimbursements available (averaging $4,393 per year), 23 teaching assistantships (averaging $10,440 per year); career-related internships or fieldwork, Federal Work-Study, institutionally sponsored loans, scholarships/grants, health care benefits, tuition waivers (partial), and unspecified assistantships also available. Financial award application deadline: 3/2; financial award applicants required to submit FAFSA. In 2008, 291 first professional degrees, 83 master's, 8 doctorates awarded. Offers jurisprudence and social policy (PhD); law (JD, LL M, JSD). *Application deadline:* For fall admission, 2/1 for domestic students. Applications are processed on a rolling basis. *Application fee:* $75. *Application Contact:* Edward Tom, Director of Admissions, 510-642-2273, Fax: 510-643-6222, E-mail: admissions@law.berkeley.edu. *Dean,* Christopher J. Edley, 510-642-6483, Fax: 510-642-9893.

School of Optometry Offers optometry (OD, Certificate). Electronic applications accepted.

UNIVERSITY OF CALIFORNIA, DAVIS, Davis, CA 95616

General Information State-supported, coed, university, CGS member. *Graduate housing:* Rooms and/or apartments available to single and married students. Housing application deadline: 4/1.

GRADUATE UNITS

College of Engineering *Degree program information:* Part-time programs available. Offers aeronautical engineering (M Engr, MS, D Engr, PhD, Certificate); applied science (MS, PhD); biological systems engineering (M Engr, MS, D Engr, PhD); biomedical engineering (MS, PhD); chemical engineering (MS, PhD); civil and environmental engineering (M Engr, MS, D Engr, PhD, Certificate); computer science (MS, PhD); electrical and computer engineering (MS, PhD); engineering (M Engr, MS, D Engr, PhD, Certificate); materials science and engineering (MS, PhD); mechanical engineering (M Engr, MS, D Engr, PhD, Certificate); transportation, technology and policy (MS, PhD). Electronic applications accepted.

Graduate School of Management Students: 120 full-time (47 women), 402 part-time (116 women); includes 198 minority (10 African Americans, 2 American Indian/Alaska Native, 168 Asian Americans or Pacific Islanders, 18 Hispanic Americans), 72 international. Average age 30. 670 applicants, 42% accepted, 196 enrolled. *Faculty:* 29 full-time (10 women), 23 part-time/adjunct (3 women). Expenses: Contact institution. *Financial support:* In 2008–09, 113 students received support; research assistantships with partial tuition reimbursements available, teaching assistantships with partial tuition reimbursements available, career-related internships or fieldwork, Federal Work-Study, institutionally sponsored loans, scholarships/grants, health care benefits, tuition waivers (partial), and unspecified assistantships available. Support available to part-time students. Financial award application deadline: 3/1; financial award applicants required to submit FAFSA. *Degree program information:* Part-time and evening/weekend programs available. Offers business administration (MBA); management (MBA). *Application deadline:* Applications are processed on a rolling basis. *Application fee:* $125. Electronic applications accepted. *Application Contact:* Kathy Gleed, Director, Admissions and Student Services, 530-754-5476, Fax: 530-754-9355, E-mail: admissions@gsm.ucdavis.edu. *Dean,* Nicole W. Biggart, 530-752-7366, Fax: 530-752-2924, E-mail: nwbiggart@ucdavis.edu.

Graduate Studies Offers acting (MFA); agricultural and environmental chemistry (MS, PhD); agricultural and resource economics (MS, PhD); animal behavior (PhD); animal biology (MAM, MS, PhD); anthropology (MA, PhD); applied linguistics (MA, PhD); applied mathematics (MS, PhD); art (MFA); art history (MA); atmospheric sciences (MS, PhD); avian sciences (MS); biochemistry and molecular biology (MS, PhD); biophysics (MS, PhD); biostatistics (MS, PhD); cell and developmental biology (MS, PhD); chemistry (MS, PhD); child development (MS); clinical research (MAS); communication (MA); community development (MS); comparative literature (PhD); comparative pathology (MS, PhD); composition (MA, PhD); conducting (MA, PhD); creative writing (MA); cultural studies (MA, PhD); dramatic art (PhD); ecology (MS, PhD); economics (MA, PhD); education (MA, Ed D); English (MA, PhD); entomology (MS, PhD); epidemiology (MS, PhD); exercise science (MS); food science (MS, PhD); forensic science (MS); French (PhD); genetics (MS, PhD); geography (MA, PhD); geology (MS, PhD); German (MA, PhD); health informatics (MS); history (MA, PhD); horticulture and agronomy (MS); human development (PhD); hydrologic sciences (MS, PhD); immunology (MS, PhD); instructional studies (PhD); integrated pest management (MS); international agricultural development (MS); linguistics (MA); mathematics (MA, MAT, PhD); microbiology (MS, PhD); molecular, cellular and integrative physiology (MS, PhD); musicology (MA, PhD); Native American studies (MA, PhD); neuroscience (PhD); nutrition (MS, PhD); pharmacology/toxicology (MS, PhD); philosophy (MA, PhD); physics (MS, PhD); plant biology (MS, PhD); plant pathology (MS, PhD); political science (MA, PhD); population biology (PhD); psychological studies (PhD); psychology (PhD); sociocultural studies (PhD); sociology (MA, PhD); soils and biogeochemistry (MS, PhD); Spanish (MA, PhD); statistics (MS, PhD); textile arts and costume design (MFA); textiles (MS); viticulture and enology (MS, PhD). Electronic applications accepted.

School of Law Offers law (JD, LL M). Electronic applications accepted.

School of Medicine Students: 418 full-time (183 women); includes 222 minority (13 African Americans, 2 American Indian/Alaska Native, 165 Asian Americans or Pacific Islanders, 42 Hispanic Americans). Average age 27. 4,861 applicants, 5% accepted, 105 enrolled. *Faculty:* 625 full-time (189 women), 128 part-time/adjunct (50 women). Expenses: Contact institution. *Financial support:* In 2008–09, 363 students received support, including 15 fellowships with full tuition reimbursements available (averaging $22,367 per year), 9 research assistantships with partial tuition reimbursements available (averaging $20,928 per year), 8 teaching assistantships with partial tuition reimbursements available (averaging $1,821 per year); Federal Work-Study, institutionally sponsored loans, scholarships/grants also available. Support available to part-time students. Financial award application deadline: 3/2; financial award applicants required to submit FAFSA. In 2008, 86 MDs awarded. Offers medicine (MD). *Application deadline:* For fall admission, 11/1 for domestic and international students. Applications are processed on a rolling basis. *Application fee:* $60. Electronic applications accepted. *Application Contact:* Edward D. Dagang, Director of Admissions and Outreach, 916-734-4800, Fax: 916-734-4050, E-mail: ed.dagang@ucdmc.ucdavis.edu. *Dean/Vice Chancellor, Human Health Sciences,* Dr. Claire Pomeroy, 916-734-7131, Fax: 916-734-7055, E-mail: claire.pomeroy@ucdmc.ucdavis.edu.

School of Veterinary Medicine Offers preventive veterinary medicine (MPVM); veterinary medicine (DVM, MPVM, Certificate).

UNIVERSITY OF CALIFORNIA, HASTINGS COLLEGE OF THE LAW, San Francisco, CA 94102-4978

General Information State-supported, coed, graduate-only institution. *Graduate housing:* Rooms and/or apartments available on a first-come, first-served basis to single and married students.

GRADUATE UNITS

Graduate Program Offers law (JD, LL M). Electronic applications accepted.

UNIVERSITY OF CALIFORNIA, IRVINE, Irvine, CA 92697

General Information State-supported, coed, university. CGS member. *Graduate housing:* Rooms and/or apartments available on a first-come, first-served basis to single and married students.

GRADUATE UNITS

Office of Graduate Studies *Degree program information:* Part-time and evening/weekend programs available. Offers educational administration (Ed D); educational administration and leadership (Ed D); elementary and secondary education (MAT). Electronic applications accepted.

Claire Trevor School of the Arts Offers accompanying (MFA); acting (MFA); arts (MFA, PhD); choral conducting (MFA); composition and technology (MFA); dance (MFA); design and stage management (MFA); directing (MFA); drama (MFA); drama and theatre (PhD); guitar/lute performance (MFA); instrumental performance (MFA); jazz instrumental/composition (MFA); piano performance (MFA); studio art (MFA); vocal performance (MFA). Electronic applications accepted.

Donald Bren School of Information and Computer Sciences Offers information and computer science (MS, PhD); networked systems (MS, PhD). Electronic applications accepted.

The Paul Merage School of Business *Degree program information:* Part-time and evening/weekend programs available. Offers business administration (MBA); management (PhD). Electronic applications accepted.

School of Biological Sciences Offers biological science (MS); biological sciences (MS, PhD); biotechnology (MS). Electronic applications accepted.

School of Engineering *Degree program information:* Part-time programs available. Offers biomedical engineering (MS, PhD); chemical and biochemical engineering (MS, PhD); civil and environmental engineering (MS, PhD); electrical engineering and computer science

University of California, Irvine (continued)
(MS, PhD); engineering (MS, PhD); materials science and engineering (MS, PhD); mechanical and aerospace engineering (MS, PhD); networked systems (MS, PhD). Electronic applications accepted.

School of Humanities Offers Chinese (MA, PhD); classics (MA, PhD); comparative literature (MA, PhD); creative writing (MFA); East Asian languages and literatures (MA, PhD); English (MA, PhD); English (summer program) (MA); English and American literature (PhD); French (MA, PhD); German (MA, PhD); history (MA, PhD); humanities (MA, MAT, MFA, PhD); Japanese (MA, PhD); philosophy (MA, PhD); Spanish (MA, MAT, PhD); visual studies (MA, PhD); writing (MFA). Electronic applications accepted.

School of Physical Sciences Offers chemical and material physics (PhD); chemical and materials physics (MS, PhD); chemistry (MS, PhD); earth system science (MS, PhD); mathematics (MS, PhD); physical sciences (MS, PhD); physics (MS, PhD). Electronic applications accepted.

School of Social Ecology Offers criminology, law and society (MAS, PhD); planning, policy and design (PhD); psychology and social behavior (PhD); social ecology (MA, MAS, MURP, PhD); urban and regional planning (MURP). Electronic applications accepted.

School of Social Sciences Offers anthropology (MA, PhD); demographic and social analysis (MA); economics (MA, PhD); philosophy (PhD); political psychology (PhD); political sciences (PhD); psychology (PhD); public choice (MA, PhD); social networks (PhD); social networks-social science (MA); social science (MA, PhD); social sciences (MA, PhD); sociology and social relations-social science (MA, PhD); transportation economics (MA, PhD); transportation science (MA, PhD). Electronic applications accepted.

School of Medicine Offers biological sciences (MS, PhD); epidemiology (MS, PhD); genetic counseling (MS); medicine (MD, MS, PhD); pharmacology and toxicology (MS, PhD); research medical science training. Electronic applications accepted.

UNIVERSITY OF CALIFORNIA, LOS ANGELES, Los Angeles, CA 90095

General Information State-supported, coed, university. CGS member. *Enrollment:* 39,650 graduate, professional, and undergraduate students; 11,768 full-time matriculated graduate/professional students (5,641 women). *Enrollment by degree level:* 2,051 first professional, 5,100 master's, 4,617 doctoral. *Graduate faculty:* 1,835 full-time (475 women). Tuition, nonresident: full-time $14,694. *Required fees:* $9669.50. Full-time tuition and fees vary according to course load, degree level, program and student level. *Graduate housing:* Rooms and/or apartments available on a first-come, first-served basis to single and married students. *Student services:* Campus employment opportunities, campus safety program, career counseling, child daycare facilities, exercise/wellness program, free psychological counseling, international student services, low-cost health insurance, multicultural affairs office, services for students with disabilities, writing training. *Library facilities:* Charles E. Young Research Library plus 13 others. *Online resources:* library catalog, web page, access to other libraries' catalogs. *Collection:* 8.2 million titles, 77,509 serial subscriptions, 291,664 audiovisual materials.

Computer facilities: 4,134 computers available on campus for general student use. A campuswide network can be accessed from student residence rooms and from off campus. Online class registration is available. *Web address:* http://www.ucla.edu/.

General Application Contact: Graduate Admissions Office, 310-825-1711.

GRADUATE UNITS

David Geffen School of Medicine Offers medicine (MD, MS, PhD).

Graduate Programs in Medicine Offers anatomy and cell biology (PhD); biological chemistry (MS, PhD); biomathematics (MS, PhD); biomedical physics (MS, PhD); clinical research (MS); experimental pathology (MS, PhD); human genetics (MS, PhD); medicine (MS, PhD); microbiology, immunology and molecular genetics (MS, PhD); molecular and medical pharmacology (PhD); molecular, cell and developmental biology (PhD); neuroscience (PhD); physiology (PhD).

Graduate Division Students: 8,424 full-time (4,238 women); includes 2,392 minority (331 African Americans, 49 American Indian/Alaska Native, 1,196 Asian Americans or Pacific Islanders, 816 Hispanic Americans), 1,556 international. Average age 28. 19,485 applicants, 28% accepted, 2559 enrolled. Expenses: Contact institution. *Financial support:* Fellowships with full and partial tuition reimbursements, research assistantships with full tuition reimbursements, teaching assistantships with full tuition reimbursements, career-related internships or fieldwork, Federal Work-Study, institutionally sponsored loans, scholarships/grants, health care benefits, tuition waivers (full and partial), and unspecified assistantships available. Support available to part-time students. Financial award application deadline: 3/1; financial award applicants required to submit FAFSA. In 2008, 2,197 master's, 733 doctorates awarded. *Application fee:* $60 ($80 for international students). Electronic applications accepted. *Application Contact:* Graduate Admissions, 310-825-1711. *Dean,* Dr. Claudia Mitchell-Kernan, 310-825-4383.

College of Letters and Science Students: 2,712 full-time (1,356 women); includes 612 minority (92 African Americans, 24 American Indian/Alaska Native, 280 Asian Americans or Pacific Islanders, 216 Hispanic Americans), 462 international. Average age 27. 5,350 applicants, 24% accepted, 530 enrolled. Expenses: Contact institution. *Financial support:* Fellowships with full tuition reimbursements, research assistantships with full tuition reimbursements, teaching assistantships with full tuition reimbursements, Federal Work-Study, institutionally sponsored loans, scholarships/grants, traineeships, health care benefits, tuition waivers (full and partial), and unspecified assistantships available. Financial award application deadline: 3/1; financial award applicants required to submit FAFSA. In 2008, 338 master's, 324 doctorates awarded. Offers African studies (MA); Afro-American studies (MA); American Indian studies (MA); anthropology (MA, PhD); applied linguistics (PhD); applied linguistics and teaching English as a second language (MA); archaeology (MA, PhD); art history (MA, PhD); Asian languages and cultures (MA, PhD); Asian-American studies (MA); astronomy (MAT, MS, PhD); atmospheric sciences (MS, PhD); biochemistry and molecular biology (MS, PhD); biological chemistry (PhD); cellular and molecular pathology (PhD); chemistry (MS, PhD); classics (MA, PhD); comparative literature (MA, PhD); East Asian studies (MA); ecology and evolutionary biology (MA, PhD); economics (MA, PhD); English (MA, PhD); French and Francophone studies (MA, PhD); geochemistry (MS, PhD); geography (MA, PhD); geology (MS, PhD); geophysics and space physics (MS, PhD); Germanic languages (MA, PhD); Greek (MA); Hispanic languages and literature (PhD); history (MA, PhD); human genetics (MS, PhD); Indo-European studies (PhD); Islamic studies (MA, PhD); Italian (MA, PhD); Latin (MA); Latin American studies (MA); letters and science (MA, MAT, MS, PhD, Certificate); linguistics (MA, PhD); mathematics (MA, MAT, PhD); microbiology, immunology, and molecular genetics (PhD); molecular biology (PhD); molecular toxicology (PhD); molecular, cellular and integrative physiology (PhD); musicology (MA, PhD); Near Eastern languages and cultures (MA, PhD); neurobiology (PhD); oral biology (PhD); philosophy (MA, PhD); physics (MAT, MS, PhD); physics education (MAT); physiological science (MS); physiology (PhD); political science (MA, PhD); Portuguese (MA); psychology (MA, PhD); Scandinavian (MA); Slavic languages and literatures (MA, PhD); sociology (MA, PhD); Spanish (MA); statistics (MS, PhD); teaching English as a second language (Certificate); women's studies (MA, PhD). *Application fee:* $60 ($80 for international students). Electronic applications accepted. *Application Contact:* Graduate Division Admissions Office, 310-825-1711. *Vice Provost/Dean,* Dr. Judith L Smith, 310-206-3961.

Graduate School of Education and Information Studies *Degree program information:* Part-time and evening/weekend programs available. Offers archival studies (MLIS); education (M Ed, MA, Ed D, PhD); education and information studies (M Ed, MA, MLIS, Ed D, PhD, Certificate); educational leadership (Ed D); informatics (MLIS); information studies (PhD); library and information science (Certificate); library studies (MLIS); moving image archive studies (MA); special education (PhD). Electronic applications accepted.

Henry Samueli School of Engineering and Applied Science Students: 1,502 full-time (275 women); includes 504 minority (17 African Americans, 1 American Indian/Alaska Native, 423 Asian Americans or Pacific Islanders, 63 Hispanic Americans), 533 international. 3,111 applicants, 39% accepted, 523 enrolled. *Faculty:* 156 full-time (19 women). Expenses: Contact institution. *Financial support:* In 2008–09, 578 fellowships, 1,683 research assistantships, 517 teaching assistantships were awarded; career-related internships or fieldwork, Federal Work-Study, institutionally sponsored loans, and tuition waivers (full and partial) also available. Financial award application deadline: 3/2; financial award applicants required to submit FAFSA. In 2008, 316 master's, 133 doctorates awarded. *Degree program information:* Evening/weekend programs available. Postbaccalaureate distance learning degree programs offered (no on-campus study). Offers aerospace engineering (MS, PhD); biomedical engineering (MS, PhD); chemical and biomolecular engineering (MS, PhD); civil and environmental engineering (MS, PhD); computer science (MS, PhD); electrical engineering (MS, PhD); engineering and applied science (MS, PhD); manufacturing engineering (MS); materials science and engineering (MS, PhD); mechanical engineering (MS, PhD). *Application deadline:* For fall admission, 12/15 for domestic and international students. *Application fee:* $60 ($75 for international students). Electronic applications accepted. *Application Contact:* Jan Labuda, Student Affairs Officer, 310-825-2514, Fax: 301-825-2473, E-mail: jan@ea.ucla.edu. *Associate Dean, Academic and Student Affairs,* Dr. Richard D. Wesel, 310-825-2942.

School of Nursing Students: 364 full-time (336 women); includes 140 minority (27 African Americans, 4 American Indian/Alaska Native, 60 Asian Americans or Pacific Islanders, 49 Hispanic Americans), 3 international. Average age 31. 597 applicants, 33% accepted, 151 enrolled. Expenses: Contact institution. *Financial support:* In 2008–09, 209 fellowships with full and partial tuition reimbursements, 11 research assistantships with full and partial tuition reimbursements, 28 teaching assistantships with full and partial tuition reimbursements were awarded; Federal Work-Study, institutionally sponsored loans, scholarships/grants, health care benefits, tuition waivers (full and partial), and unspecified assistantships also available. Financial award application deadline: 3/1; financial award applicants required to submit FAFSA. In 2008, 168 master's, 8 doctorates awarded. Offers nursing (MSN, PhD). *Application deadline:* For fall admission, 12/1 priority date for domestic and international students. *Application fee:* $60 ($80 for international students). Electronic applications accepted. *Application Contact:* Departmental Office, 310-825-7181, E-mail: sonsaff@sonnet.ucla.edu. *Dean,* Courtney H Lyder, 310-825-7181.

School of Public Affairs Offers public affairs (MA, MPP, MSW, PhD); public policy (MPP); social welfare (MSW, PhD); urban planning (MA, PhD). Electronic applications accepted.

School of Public Health Offers biostatistics (MPH, MS, Dr PH, PhD); environmental health sciences (MS, PhD); environmental science and engineering (D Env); epidemiology (MPH, MS, Dr PH, PhD); health services (MPH, MS, Dr PH, PhD); molecular toxicology (PhD); public health (MPH, MS, D Env, Dr PH, PhD). Electronic applications accepted.

School of the Arts and Architecture Offers architecture and urban design (M Arch, MA, PhD); art (MA, MFA); arts and architecture (M Arch, MA, MFA, MM, DMA, PhD); composition (MA, PhD); culture and performance (MA, PhD); dance (MFA); design/media arts (MFA); ethnomusicology (MA, PhD); performance (MM, DMA). Electronic applications accepted.

School of Theater, Film and Television Students: 391 full-time (203 women); includes 104 minority (25 African Americans, 4 American Indian/Alaska Native, 29 Asian Americans or Pacific Islanders, 46 Hispanic Americans), 33 international. Average age 28. 1,223 applicants, 15% accepted, 121 enrolled. Expenses: Contact institution. *Financial support:* In 2008–09, 376 fellowships with full and partial tuition reimbursements, 25 research assistantships with full and partial tuition reimbursements, 182 teaching assistantships with full and partial tuition reimbursements were awarded; career-related internships or fieldwork, Federal Work-Study, institutionally sponsored loans, scholarships/grants, traineeships, health care benefits, tuition waivers (full and partial), and unspecified assistantships also available. Financial award application deadline: 3/1; financial award applicants required to submit FAFSA. In 2008, 101 master's, 12 doctorates awarded. Offers film and television (MA, MFA, PhD); theater (MA, MFA); theater and performance studies (PhD); theater, film and television (MA, MFA, PhD). *Application fee:* $60 ($80 for international students). Electronic applications accepted. *Application Contact:* Departmental Office, 310-825-8787, E-mail: info@tft.ucla.edu. *Dean,* Robert Rosen, 310-825-8787.

UCLA Anderson School of Management Students: 731 full-time (248 women), 772 part-time (227 women); includes 542 minority (32 African Americans, 4 American Indian/Alaska Native, 432 Asian Americans or Pacific Islanders, 74 Hispanic Americans), 232 international. Average age 28. Expenses: Contact institution. *Financial support:* Fellowships, research assistantships, teaching assistantships, career-related internships or fieldwork, Federal Work-Study, institutionally sponsored loans, scholarships/grants, and tuition waivers (full and partial) available. Financial award application deadline: 3/1. In 2008, 607 master's awarded. *Degree program information:* Part-time programs available. Offers management (MBA, MS, PhD). *Application deadline:* Applications are processed on a rolling basis. *Application fee:* $175. *Application Contact:* Mae Jennifer Shores, Assistant Dean and Director of MBA Admissions and Financial Aid, 310-825-6944, E-mail: mba.admissions@anderson.ucla.edu. *Dean,* Judy D. Olian, 310-825-7982, Fax: 310-206-2073.

School of Dentistry Offers dentistry (DDS, MS, PhD, Certificate); oral biology (MS, PhD).

School of Law Offers law (JD, LL M, SJD). Electronic applications accepted.

UNIVERSITY OF CALIFORNIA, MERCED, Merced, CA 95343

General Information State-supported, coed, university.

GRADUATE UNITS

Division of Graduate Studies

UNIVERSITY OF CALIFORNIA, RIVERSIDE, Riverside, CA 92521-0102

General Information State-supported, coed, university. CGS member. *Enrollment:* 18,079 graduate, professional, and undergraduate students; 2,224 full-time matriculated graduate/professional students (1,177 women), 47 part-time matriculated graduate/professional students (17 women). *Enrollment by degree level:* 563 master's, 1,708 doctoral. *Graduate faculty:* 706 full-time (216 women). Tuition, nonresident: full-time $4898. *Required fees:* $10,362. *Graduate housing:* Rooms and/or apartments available on a first-come, first-served basis to single and married students. Typical cost: $12,000 per year for single students; $6600 per year for married students. Housing application deadline: 6/1. *Student services:* Campus safety program, career counseling, child daycare facilities, exercise/wellness program, free psychological counseling, international student services, low-cost health insurance, multicultural affairs office, services for students with disabilities, teacher training, writing training. *Library facilities:* Tomas Rivera Library plus 6 others. *Online resources:* library catalog, web page, access to other libraries' catalogs. *Collection:* 2.4 million titles, 29,941 serial subscriptions, 27,313 audiovisual materials. *Research affiliation:* Fermi National Accelerator Laboratory (physics), Los Alamos National Laboratory (botany and plant sciences, chemistry, earth sciences, physics), Brookhaven National Lab (chemistry, physics), U.S. Salinity Laboratory (environmental sciences, biochemistry), J. Paul Getty Museum (art history), Lawrence Livermore National Laboratory (archaeology).

Computer facilities: Computer purchase and lease plans are available. 793 computers available on campus for general student use. A campuswide network can be accessed from student residence rooms and from off campus. Online class registration, online viewing of financial information are available. *Web address:* http://www.ucr.edu/.

General Application Contact: Graduate Admissions, 951-827-3313, Fax: 951-827-2238, E-mail: grdadmis@ucr.edu.

GRADUATE UNITS

Graduate Division Students: 2,224 full-time (1,177 women), 47 part-time (17 women); includes 485 minority (53 African Americans, 7 American Indian/Alaska Native, 247 Asian Americans or Pacific Islanders, 178 Hispanic Americans), 698 international. Average age 29. *Faculty:* 706 full-time (216 women). Expenses: Contact institution. *Financial support:* Fellowships with full and partial tuition reimbursements, research assistantships with full and partial tuition reimbursements, teaching assistantships with full and partial tuition reimbursements, career-related internships or fieldwork, Federal Work-Study, institutionally sponsored loans, scholarships/grants, and tuition waivers (full and partial) available. Financial award applicants required to submit FAFSA. In 2008, 346 master's, 189 doctorates awarded. *Degree program information:* Part-time and evening/weekend programs available. Offers anthropology (MA, MS, PhD); applied statistics (PhD); archival management (MA); art history (MA); biochemistry and molecular biology (MS, PhD); bioengineering (MS, PhD); biology (MS, PhD); biomedical sciences (PhD); cell, molecular, and developmental biology (MS, PhD); chemical and environmental engineering (MS, PhD); chemistry (MS, PhD); classics (PhD); comparative literature (MA, PhD); composition (PhD); computer science (MS, PhD); creative writing and writing for the performing arts (MFA); critical dance studies (PhD); economics (MA, PhD); electrical engineering (MS, PhD); English (MA, PhD); entomology (MS, PhD); environmental toxicology (MS, PhD); ethnic studies (PhD); ethnomusicology (MA, PhD); evolution, ecology and organismal biology (MS, PhD); experimental choreography (MFA); genomics and bioinformatics (PhD); geological sciences (MS, PhD); historic preservation (MA); history (MA, PhD); mathematics (MA, MS, PhD); mechanical engineering (MS, PhD); microbiology (MS, PhD); molecular genetics (PhD); museum curatorship (MA); musicology (PhD); neuroscience (PhD); philosophy (MA, PhD); physics (MS, PhD); plant biology (MS, PhD); plant biology (plant genetics) (PhD); plant pathology (MS, PhD); political science (MA, PhD); population and evolutionary genetics (PhD); psychology (MA, PhD); sociology (MA, PhD); soil and water sciences (MS, PhD); Southeast Asian studies (MA); Spanish (MA, PhD); statistics (MS); visual arts (MFA). *Application deadline:* For fall admission, 5/1 for domestic students, 2/1 for international students; for winter admission, 2/1 for domestic students, 7/1 for international students; for spring admission, 12/1 for domestic students, 10/1 for international students. Applications are processed on a rolling basis. *Application fee:* $70 ($85 for international students). Electronic applications accepted. *Application Contact:* Graduate Admissions, 951-827-3313, Fax: 951-827-2238, E-mail: grdadmis@ucr.edu. *Dean,* Dr. Joseph W. Childers, 951-827-3313, Fax: 951-827-2238.

A. Gary Anderson Graduate School of Management Students: 140 full-time (80 women), 11 part-time (3 women); includes 25 minority (21 Asian Americans or Pacific Islanders, 4 Hispanic Americans), 90 international. Average age 26. 363 applicants, 43% accepted, 77 enrolled. *Faculty:* 27 full-time (4 women). Expenses: Contact institution. *Financial support:* In 2008–09, 50 students received support, including 50 fellowships with partial tuition reimbursements available (averaging $16,368 per year), teaching assistantships with partial tuition reimbursements available (averaging $16,500 per year); research assistantships, career-related internships or fieldwork, Federal Work-Study, institutionally sponsored loans, scholarships/grants, and tuition waivers (full) also available. Financial award application deadline: 2/1; financial award applicants required to submit FAFSA. In 2008, 52 master's awarded. *Degree program information:* Part-time and evening/weekend programs available. Offers management (MBA). *Application deadline:* For fall admission, 5/1 for domestic students, 2/1 for international students; for winter admission, 9/1 for domestic students, 7/1 for international students; for spring admission, 12/1 for domestic students, 10/1 for international students. Applications are processed on a rolling basis. *Application fee:* $70 ($85 for international students). *Application Contact:* Dr. Mohsen El Hafsi, Graduate Adviser, 951-827-4557, Fax: 951-827-3970, E-mail: mba@ucr.edu. *Dean,* Dr. David W. Stewart, 951-827-4551, Fax: 951-827-3970, E-mail: mba@ucr.edu.

Graduate School of Education Students: 236 full-time (185 women); includes 104 minority (13 African Americans, 1 American Indian/Alaska Native, 39 Asian Americans or Pacific Islanders, 51 Hispanic Americans), 10 international. Average age 34. 215 applicants, 53% accepted, 88 enrolled. *Faculty:* 23 full-time (11 women), 21 part-time/adjunct (13 women). Expenses: Contact institution. *Financial support:* In 2008–09, 6 fellowships with full and partial tuition reimbursements (averaging $24,143 per year), 23 research assistantships with full and partial tuition reimbursements (averaging $12,000 per year), 2 teaching assistantships with full and partial tuition reimbursements (averaging $11,700 per year) were awarded; career-related internships or fieldwork, Federal Work-Study, institutionally sponsored loans, and tuition waivers (full and partial) also available. Financial award application deadline: 1/5; financial award applicants required to submit FAFSA. In 2008, 66 master's, 18 doctorates awarded. Offers autism (M Ed); curriculum and instruction (MA); educational leadership and policy (MA, PhD); educational psychology (PhD); general education (M Ed); higher education administration and policy (PhD); leadership (M Ed); reading (M Ed); school psychology (PhD); special education (MA, PhD). *Application deadline:* For fall admission, 4/15 for domestic students, 2/1 for international students; for winter admission, 9/1 for domestic students, 7/1 for international students; for spring admission, 12/1 for domestic students, 10/1 for international students. Applications are processed on a rolling basis. *Application fee:* $70 ($85 for international students). Electronic applications accepted. *Application Contact:* Dr. Margaret Nash, Graduate Adviser, 951-827-6362, Fax: 951-827-3942, E-mail: edgrad@ucr.edu. *Dean,* Dr. Steven T. Bossert, 951-827-5802, Fax: 951-827-3942, E-mail: steven.bossert@ucr.edu.

UNIVERSITY OF CALIFORNIA, SAN DIEGO, La Jolla, CA 92093

General Information State-supported, coed, university. CGS member. *Graduate housing:* Rooms and/or apartments available to single and married students. *Research affiliation:* Salk Institute, Veterans Administration Medical Center, Scripps Clinic and Research Foundation, La Jolla Institute.

GRADUATE UNITS

Office of Graduate Studies Offers acting (MFA); aerospace engineering (MS, PhD); anthropology (PhD); applied mathematics (MA); applied mechanics (MS, PhD); applied ocean science (MS, PhD); applied physics (MS, PhD); bilingual education (MA); bioengineering (M Eng, MS, PhD); bioinformatics (PhD); biophysics (MS, PhD); chemical engineering (MS, PhD); chemistry (MS, PhD); clinical psychology (PhD); cognitive science (PhD); cognitive science/anthropology (PhD); cognitive science/communication (PhD); cognitive science/computer science and engineering (PhD); cognitive science/linguistics (PhD); cognitive science/neuroscience (PhD); cognitive science/philosophy (PhD); cognitive science/psychology (PhD); cognitive science/sociology (PhD); communication (MA, PhD); communication theory and systems (MS, PhD); comparative literature (MA, PhD); computer engineering (MS, PhD); computer science (MS, PhD); curriculum design (MA); design (MFA); directing (MFA); drama and theatre (PhD); earth sciences (PhD); economics (PhD); economics and international affairs (PhD); electrical engineering (M Eng); electronic circuits and systems (MS, PhD); engineering physics (MS, PhD); ethnic studies (MA, PhD); French literature (MA); German literature (MA); health law (MAS); history (MA, PhD); intelligent systems, robotics and control (MS, PhD); Judaic studies (MA); language and communicative disorders (PhD); Latin American studies (MA); linguistics (PhD); literature (PhD); literatures in English (MA); marine biodiversity and conservation (MAS); marine biology (PhD); materials science and engineering (MS, PhD); mathematics (MA, PhD); mathematics and science education (PhD); mechanical engineering (MS, PhD); music (MA, DMA, PhD); oceanography (PhD); philosophy (PhD); photonics (MS, PhD); physics (MS, PhD); physics/materials physics (MS); playwriting (MFA); political science (PhD); political science and international affairs (PhD); psychology (PhD); public health and epidemiology (PhD); science studies (PhD); signal and image processing (MS, PhD); sociology (PhD); Spanish literature (MA); stage management (MFA); statistics (MS); structural engineering (MS, PhD); teacher education (M Ed); teaching and learning (Ed D); theatre (PhD); visual arts (MFA, PhD). Electronic applications accepted.

Division of Biological Sciences Offers biochemistry (PhD); biology (MS); cell and developmental biology (PhD); computational neurobiology (PhD); ecology, behavior, and evolution (PhD); genetics and molecular biology (PhD); immunology, virology, and cancer biology (PhD); molecular and cellular biology (PhD); neurobiology (PhD); plant molecular biology (PhD); plant systems biology (PhD); signal transduction (PhD). Offered in association with the Salk Institute. Electronic applications accepted.

Graduate School of International Relations and Pacific Studies Offers economics and international affairs (PhD); Pacific international affairs (MPIA); political science and international affairs (PhD). Electronic applications accepted.

Rady School of Management Offers business administration and management (MBA).

School of Medicine Offers audiology (Au D); bioinformatics (PhD); cancer biology/oncology (PhD); cardiovascular sciences and disease (PhD); clinical research (MAS); leadership in healthcare organizations (MAS); medicine (MD, MAS, Au D, PhD); microbiology (PhD); molecular pathology (PhD); neurological disease (PhD); neurosciences (PhD); stem cell and developmental biology (PhD); structural biology/drug design (PhD).

Graduate Studies in Biomedical Sciences Offers molecular cell biology (PhD); pharmacology (PhD); physiology (PhD); regulatory biology (PhD). Electronic applications accepted.

School of Pharmacy and Pharmaceutical Sciences Offers pharmacy and pharmaceutical sciences (Pharm D).

UNIVERSITY OF CALIFORNIA, SAN FRANCISCO, San Francisco, CA 94143

General Information State-supported, coed, graduate-only institution. CGS member. *Graduate housing:* Rooms and/or apartments available to single and married students.

GRADUATE UNITS

Graduate Division *Degree program information:* Part-time programs available. Offers anatomy (PhD); biochemistry and molecular biology (PhD); bioengineering (PhD); cell biology (PhD); developmental biology (PhD); endocrinology (PhD); experimental pathology (PhD); genetics (PhD); history of health sciences (MA, PhD); medical anthropology (PhD); microbiology and immunology (PhD); neuroscience (PhD); oral and craniofacial sciences (MS, PhD); physical therapy (MS, DPT, DPTSc); physiology (PhD).

School of Nursing Offers nursing (MS, PhD); sociology (PhD).

School of Dentistry Offers dentistry (DDS).

School of Medicine Offers medicine (MD). Electronic applications accepted.

School of Pharmacy Offers biological and medical informatics (PhD); biophysics (PhD); chemistry and chemical biology (PhD); pharmaceutical sciences and pharmacogenomics (PhD); pharmacy (Pharm D, PhD).

UNIVERSITY OF CALIFORNIA, SANTA BARBARA, Santa Barbara, CA 93106-2014

General Information State-supported, coed, university. CGS member. *Enrollment:* 2,975 full-time matriculated graduate/professional students (1,354 women). *Enrollment by degree level:* 8 first professional, 573 master's, 2,394 doctoral. Tuition, nonresident: full-time $25,149. *Required fees:* $10,143. Full-time tuition and fees vary according to campus/location, reciprocity agreements and student level. *Graduate housing:* Rooms and/or apartments available on a first-come, first-served basis to single and married students. Housing application deadline: 5/15. *Student services:* Campus employment opportunities, campus safety program, career counseling, child daycare facilities, exercise/wellness program, free psychological counseling, grant writing training, international student services, low-cost health insurance, multicultural affairs office, services for students with disabilities, teacher training, writing training. *Library facilities:* Davidson Library. *Online resources:* library catalog, web page, access to other libraries' catalogs. *Collection:* 3.3 million titles, 36,902 serial subscriptions, 125,324 audiovisual materials. *Research affiliation:* Mitsubishi Chemical Center for Advanced Materials, Center for Stem Cell Biology and Engineering, California NanoSystems Institute, National Center for Ecological Analysis & Synthesis, Intercampus Research Program on Mexican Literary and Cultural Studies, Orfalea Center for Global and International Studies.

Computer facilities: 3,000 computers available on campus for general student use. A campuswide network can be accessed from student residence rooms and from off campus. *Web address:* http://www.ucsb.edu/.

General Application Contact: Graduate Admissions Coordinator, 805-893-2278, Fax: 805-893-8259, E-mail: prospectivegrad@graddiv.ucsb.edu.

GRADUATE UNITS

Graduate Division Students: 2,975 full-time (1,354 women); includes 543 minority (51 African Americans, 13 American Indian/Alaska Native, 250 Asian Americans or Pacific Islanders, 229 Hispanic Americans), 560 international. Average age 29. 7,437 applicants, 29% accepted, 810 enrolled. Expenses: Contact institution. *Financial support:* In 2008–09, 969 fellowships with full and partial tuition reimbursements (averaging $10,000 per year), 1,116 research assistantships with full and partial tuition reimbursements (averaging $11,400 per year), 1,566 teaching assistantships with full and partial tuition reimbursements (averaging $8,500 per year) were awarded; career-related internships or fieldwork, Federal Work-Study, institutionally sponsored loans, scholarships/grants, traineeships, health care benefits, tuition waivers (full and partial), and unspecified assistantships also available. Support available to part-time students. Financial award applicants required to submit FAFSA. In 2008, 570 master's, 335 doctorates awarded. *Application fee:* $70 ($90 for international students). Electronic applications accepted. *Application Contact:* Graduate Admissions Coordinator, 805-893-2278, Fax: 805-893-8259, E-mail: prospectivegrad@graddiv.ucsb.edu. *Dean,* Dr. Gale M. Morrison, 805-893-2013, Fax: 805-893-8259, E-mail: graddeans@graddiv.ucsb.edu.

College of Engineering Students: 672 full-time (142 women); includes 77 minority (6 African Americans, 2 American Indian/Alaska Native, 56 Asian Americans or Pacific Islanders, 13 Hispanic Americans), 322 international. Average age 26. 2,474 applicants, 21% accepted, 141 enrolled. Expenses: Contact institution. *Financial support:* Fellowships with full and partial tuition reimbursements, research assistantships with full and partial tuition reimbursements, teaching assistantships with partial tuition reimbursements, career-related internships or fieldwork, Federal Work-Study, institutionally sponsored loans, scholarships/grants, traineeships, health care benefits, tuition waivers (full and partial), and unspecified assistantships available. Financial award applicants required to submit FAFSA. In 2008, 92 master's, 90 doctorates awarded. Offers chemical engineering (MS, PhD); computational science and engineering (PhD); computer science (MS, PhD); electrical and computer engineering (PhD); engineering (MS, PhD); materials science and engineering (MS, PhD); mechanical engineering (PhD); mehcanical engineering (MS). *Application fee:* $70 ($90 for international students). Electronic applications accepted. *Application Contact:* 805-893-3207, E-mail: engrdean@engineering.ucsb.edu. *Dean,* Dr. Matthew Tirrell, 805-893-3141.

College of Letters and Sciences Students: 1,726 full-time (797 women); includes 296 minority (30 African Americans, 7 American Indian/Alaska Native, 126 Asian Americans or Pacific Islanders, 133 Hispanic Americans), 208 international. Average age 29. 3,886 applicants, 28% accepted, 394 enrolled. Expenses: Contact institution. *Financial support:* Fellowships with full and partial tuition reimbursements, research assistantships with full and partial tuition reimbursements, teaching assistantships with partial tuition reimbursements, career-related internships or fieldwork, Federal Work-Study, institutionally sponsored loans, scholarships/grants, traineeships, health care benefits, tuition waivers (full and partial), and unspecified assistantships available. Support available to part-time students. Financial award applicants required to submit FAFSA. In 2008, 275 master's, 190 doctorates awarded. Offers ancient history (MA, PhD); applied linguistics (PhD); applied mathematics (MA); art (MFA); Asian studies (MA); Asian Studies (MA); biochemistry and molecular biology (MS, PhD); brass (MM); business economics (MA); chemistry (MA, MS, PhD); Chicana and Chicano studies (PhD); classics (MA); cognitive science (PhD); comparative literature (PhD); composition (MA, PhD); computational science and engineering (PhD); conducting (MM, DMA); East Asian language and cultural studies (PhD); East Asian literatures (PhD); economics (PhD); electronic music and sound design (MA); English (PhD); ethnomusicology (MA, PhD); European archaeology (MA); European Medieval studies (PhD); feminist studies (PhD); film and media studies (PhD); financial mathematics and statistics (PhD); French (MA, MABL, PhD); geography (MA); geological sciences (MS, PhD); geophysics (MS); Germanic languages and literature (MA, PhD); global and international studies (MA); global studies (PhD); Hispanic languages and literature (PhD); history of art and architecture (PhD); human development (PhD); humanities and fine arts (MA, MABL, MFA, MM, MS, DMA, PhD); keyboard (MM, DMA); language, interaction and social organization (PhD); language, interaction, and social organizations (PhD); Latin American and Iberian studies (MA); letters and sciences (MA, MFA, MM, MS, DMA, PhD); literature and theory (PhD); marine science (MS, PhD); mathematics (MA, PhD); mathematics, life, and physical sciences (MA, MS, PhD); media arts and technology (PhD); molecular, cellular, and developmental biology (MA, PhD); multimedia engineering (MS); musicology (MA, PhD); North American archeology (MA); philosophy (PhD); physics (PhD); piano accompanying (MM); political science (MA); Portuguese (MA); psychology (MA, PhD); public history (PhD); quantitative methods in the social sciences (PhD); religous studies (MA, PhD); social sciences (MA, PhD); sociocultural anthropology (MA); South American

University of California, Santa Barbara (continued)

archaeology (MA); Spanish (MA); Spanish and Portuguese (MA); statistics (MA); statistics and applied probability (PhD); strings (MM, DMA); technology and society (PhD); theater studies (MA, PhD); theory (MA, PhD); transportation (PhD); visual and spatial arts (MA); voice (MM, DMA); women's studies (PhD); woodwinds (MM). *Application fee:* $70 ($90 for international students). Electronic applications accepted. *Application Contact:* Dr. David Marshall, Executive Dean, 805-893-4327, E-mail: dmarshall@ltsc.ucsb.edu. *Executive Dean,* Dr. David Marshall, 805-893-4327, E-mail: dmarshall@ltsc.ucsb.edu.

Donald Bren School of Environmental Science and Management Students: 187 full-time (112 women); includes 21 minority (1 African American, 1 American Indian/Alaska Native, 11 Asian Americans or Pacific Islanders, 8 Hispanic Americans), 15 international. Average age 27. 335 applicants, 61% accepted, 89 enrolled. *Faculty:* 18 full-time (4 women), 24 part-time/adjunct (7 women). Expenses: Contact institution. *Financial support:* In 2008–09, 68 students received support, including 44 fellowships with full and partial tuition reimbursements available (averaging $8,400 per year), 20 research assistantships with full and partial tuition reimbursements available (averaging $6,600 per year), 28 teaching assistantships with partial tuition reimbursements available (averaging $6,900 per year); career-related internships or fieldwork, Federal Work-Study, institutionally sponsored loans, scholarships/grants, health care benefits, and unspecified assistantships also available. Financial award application deadline: 12/15; financial award applicants required to submit FAFSA. In 2008, 63 master's, 8 doctorates awarded. Offers environmental science and management (MESM, PhD). *Application deadline:* For fall admission, 1/10 priority date for domestic and international students. *Application fee:* $70 ($90 for international students). Electronic applications accepted. *Application Contact:* Kristen Robinson, Graduate Program Advisor, 805-893-7611, Fax: 805-893-6113, E-mail: gradasst@bren.ucsb.edu. *Acting Dean,* Dr. John Melack, 805-893-3879, Fax: 805-893-6113, E-mail: melack@bren.ucsb.edu.

Gevirtz Graduate School of Education Students: 390 full-time (303 women); includes 149 minority (14 African Americans, 3 American Indian/Alaska Native, 57 Asian Americans or Pacific Islanders, 75 Hispanic Americans), 16 international. Average age 31. 717 applicants, 40% accepted, 170 enrolled. *Faculty:* 42 full-time (20 women), 10 part-time/adjunct (4 women). Expenses: Contact institution. *Financial support:* In 2008–09, 253 students received support, including 206 fellowships with full and partial tuition reimbursements available (averaging $5,000 per year), 62 research assistantships with full and partial tuition reimbursements available (averaging $6,200 per year), 87 teaching assistantships with partial tuition reimbursements available (averaging $6,500 per year); career-related internships or fieldwork, Federal Work-Study, institutionally sponsored loans, scholarships/grants, traineeships, health care benefits, and unspecified assistantships also available. Financial award applicants required to submit FAFSA. In 2008, 140 master's, 46 doctorates awarded. Postbaccalaureate distance learning degree programs offered (minimal on-campus study). Offers counseling, clinical and school psychology (PhD); education (M Ed, MA, PhD); educational leadership (Ed D); school psychology (M Ed). *Application fee:* $70 ($90 for international students). Electronic applications accepted. *Application Contact:* Kathryn Marie Tucciarone, Student Affairs Officer, 805-893-2137, E-mail: katiet@education.ucsb.edu. *Chair,* Dr. Jane Conoley, 805-893-2185, E-mail: jane-conoley@education.ucsb.edu.

Summer Sessions Expenses: Contact institution. *Financial support:* Scholarships/grants available. Financial award applicants required to submit FAFSA. In 2008, 17 master's awarded. Offers French (MA); Spanish (MA). *Application fee:* $70 ($90 for international students). Electronic applications accepted. *Application Contact:* Program Manager, 805-893-7053, Fax: 805-893-7306, E-mail: language.institutes@summersessions.ucsb.edu. *Dean of Summer Sessions,* Dr. Loy Lytle, 805-893-2706, Fax: 805-893-7306, E-mail: low.lytle@els.ucsb.edu.

UNIVERSITY OF CALIFORNIA, SANTA CRUZ, Santa Cruz, CA 95064

General Information State-supported, coed, university. CGS member. *Graduate housing:* Rooms and/or apartments available to single and married students. *Research affiliation:* Stanford Linear Accelerator Center, Fermi National Accelerator Laboratory, Lawrence Livermore National Laboratory, Scripps Institute of Oceanography (earth sciences), University of Texas Marine Science Institute (earth sciences).

GRADUATE UNITS

Division of Graduate Studies Electronic applications accepted.

Division of Humanities Offers history (MA, PhD); history of consciousness (PhD); humanities (MA, PhD); linguistics (MA, PhD); literature (MA, PhD); philosophy (MA, PhD). Electronic applications accepted.

Division of Physical and Biological Sciences Offers astronomy and astrophysics (PhD); chemistry and biochemistry (MS, PhD); earth and planetary sciences (MS, PhD); ecology and evolutionary biology (MA, PhD); environmental toxicology (MS, PhD); mathematics (MA, PhD); molecular, cellular, and developmental biology (MA, PhD); ocean sciences (MS, PhD); physical and biological sciences (MA, MS, PhD, Certificate); physics (MS, PhD); science illustration (Certificate); science writing (Certificate).

Division of Social Sciences Offers anthropological archaeology (PhD); applied economics and finance (MS); cultural anthropology (PhD); education (MA); environmental studies (PhD); international economics (PhD); language and literacy studies (PhD); mathematics and science education (PhD); politics (PhD); psychology (PhD); social context and policy studies of education (PhD); social documentation (MA); social sciences (MA, MS, PhD); sociology (PhD).

Division of the Arts Offers arts (MA, MFA, DMA, PhD, Certificate); digital arts and new media (MFA); music (MA, PhD); music composition (DMA); theater arts (Certificate). Electronic applications accepted.

Jack Baskin School of Engineering Offers bioinformatics (MS, PhD); computer engineering (MS, PhD); computer science (MS, PhD); electrical engineering (MS, PhD); engineering (MS, PhD); network engineering (MS); statistics and applied mathematics (MS, PhD).

UNIVERSITY OF CENTRAL ARKANSAS, Conway, AR 72035-0001

General Information State-supported, coed, university. CGS member. *Graduate housing:* Rooms and/or apartments available on a first-come, first-served basis to single and married students. Housing application deadline: 7/1. *Research affiliation:* Acxiom (math/computers), AETN, 3M Corporation, State Farm Foundation (insurance), Arkansas Game and Fish.

GRADUATE UNITS

Graduate School *Degree program information:* Part-time programs available.

College of Business Administration *Degree program information:* Part-time and evening/weekend programs available. Offers accounting (M Acc); business administration (M Acc, MBA, MS); community and economic development (MS).

College of Education *Degree program information:* Part-time programs available. Offers collaborative instructional specialist (ages 0–8) (MSE); collaborative instructional specialist (grades 4–12) (MSE); college student personnel (MS); early childhood education (MSE); education (MAT, MS, MSE, Ed S); education media and library science (MS); educational leadership—district level (Ed S); elementary school counseling (MS); reading education (MSE); school counseling (MS); school leadership (MS); secondary school counseling (MS); special education (MSE); teaching (MAT); teaching and learning (MSE); training systems (MS).

College of Fine Arts and Communication *Degree program information:* Part-time programs available. Offers choral conducting (MM); digital filmmaking (MFA); fine arts and communication (MFA, MM); instrumental conducting (MM); music education (MM); music theory (MM); performance (MM).

College of Health and Behavioral Sciences Offers clinical nurse specialist (MSN); communication sciences and disorders (PhD); community service counseling (MS); counseling psychology (MS); family and consumer sciences (MS); health and behavioral sciences (MS, MSN, DPT, PhD); health education (MS); health systems (MS); kinesiology (MS); nurse practitioner (MSN); occupational therapy (MS); physical therapy (DPT, PhD); school psychology (MS, PhD); speech-language pathology (MS).

College of Liberal Arts *Degree program information:* Part-time programs available. Offers English (MA); foreign languages (MA); geographic information systems (MGIS, Certificate); history (MA); liberal arts (MA, MGIS, Certificate).

College of Natural Sciences and Math *Degree program information:* Part-time programs available. Offers applied computing (MS); applied mathematics (MS); biological science (MS); math education (MA); natural sciences and math (MA, MS).

UNIVERSITY OF CENTRAL FLORIDA, Orlando, FL 32816

General Information State-supported, coed, university. CGS member. *Enrollment:* 50,254 graduate, professional, and undergraduate students; 3,308 full-time matriculated graduate/professional students (1,785 women), 3,286 part-time matriculated graduate/professional students (2,021 women). *Enrollment by degree level:* 4,532 master's, 1,672 doctoral, 380 other advanced degrees. *Graduate faculty:* 1,137 full-time (423 women), 528 part-time/adjunct (285 women). Tuition, state resident: part-time $384 per credit. Tuition, nonresident: part-time $1076 per credit. *Required fees:* $9 per credit. *Graduate housing:* Room and/or apartments available on a first-come, first-served basis to single students; on-campus housing not available to married students. Housing application deadline: 3/1. *Student services:* Campus employment opportunities, campus safety program, career counseling, child daycare facilities, exercise/wellness program, free psychological counseling, grant writing training, international student services, low-cost health insurance, multicultural affairs office, services for students with disabilities, teacher training, writing training. *Library facilities:* University Library. *Online resources:* library catalog, web page, access to other libraries' catalogs. *Collection:* 1.6 million titles, 18,012 serial subscriptions, 46,784 audiovisual materials.

Computer facilities: Computer purchase and lease plans are available. 3,276 computers available on campus for general student use. A campuswide network can be accessed from student residence rooms and from off campus. Online class registration is available. *Web address:* http://www.ucf.edu/.

General Application Contact: Dr. Patricia Bishop, Vice Provost and Dean of Graduate Studies, 407-823-2766, Fax: 407-823-3299, E-mail: graduate@mail.ucf.edu.

GRADUATE UNITS

College of Arts and Humanities Students: 247 full-time (117 women), 231 part-time (117 women); includes 100 minority (27 African Americans, 9 Asian Americans or Pacific Islanders, 64 Hispanic Americans), 15 international. *Faculty:* 247 full-time (111 women), 109 part-time/adjunct (61 women). Expenses: Contact institution. *Financial support:* In 2008–09, 14 fellowships with partial tuition reimbursements (averaging $11,200 per year), 79 research assistantships with partial tuition reimbursements (averaging $6,500 per year), 71 teaching assistantships with partial tuition reimbursements (averaging $6,000 per year) were awarded; career-related internships or fieldwork, Federal Work-Study, institutionally sponsored loans, tuition waivers (partial), and unspecified assistantships also available. Financial award application deadline: 3/1; financial award applicants required to submit FAFSA. In 2008, 134 master's, 4 doctorates, 15 other advanced degrees awarded. *Degree program information:* Part-time and evening/weekend programs available. Offers acting (MA); arts and humanities (MA, MFA, MS, PhD, Certificate); creative writing (MFA); English (MA, MFA); history (MA); literature (MA); music (MA); professional writing (Certificate); public history (MA); rhetoric and composition (MA); Spanish (MA); studio art and the computer (MFA); teaching English to speakers of other languages (MA, Certificate); technical communication (MA); texts and technology (PhD); theatre for young audiences (MFA). *Application fee:* $30. Electronic applications accepted. *Application Contact:* Dr. Jose Fernandez, Dean, 407-823-2573, E-mail: jfernandez@mail.ucf.edu. *Dean,* Dr. Jose Fernandez, 407-823-2573, E-mail: jfernandez@mail.ucf.edu.

Division of Film and Digital Media Students: 72 full-time (13 women), 42 part-time (6 women); includes 28 minority (10 African Americans, 2 Asian Americans or Pacific Islanders, 16 Hispanic Americans), 6 international. *Faculty:* 28 full-time (10 women), 7 part-time/adjunct (3 women). Expenses: Contact institution. *Financial support:* In 2008–09, 2 fellowships (averaging $10,000 per year), 2 research assistantships (averaging $5,480 per year), 13 teaching assistantships (averaging $7,100 per year) were awarded. In 2008, 59 master's awarded. Offers entrepreneurial digital cinema (MFA); interactive entertainment (MS); visual language and interactive media (MA, MFA). *Application Contact:* Dr. Jose Maunez-Cuadra, Interim Chair, 407-823-6100, E-mail: jmaunez@mail.ucf.edu. *Interim Chair,* Dr. Jose Maunez-Cuadra, 407-823-6100, E-mail: jmaunez@mail.ucf.edu.

College of Business Administration Students: 454 full-time (192 women), 504 part-time (241 women); includes 142 minority (9 African Americans, 2 American Indian/Alaska Native, 63 Asian Americans or Pacific Islanders, 68 Hispanic Americans), 92 international. *Faculty:* 117 full-time (29 women), 16 part-time/adjunct (7 women). Expenses: Contact institution. *Financial support:* In 2008–09, 33 fellowships with partial tuition reimbursements (averaging $8,000 per year), 58 research assistantships with partial tuition reimbursements (averaging $6,700 per year), 63 teaching assistantships with partial tuition reimbursements (averaging $10,000 per year) were awarded; career-related internships or fieldwork, Federal Work-Study, institutionally sponsored loans, tuition waivers (partial), and unspecified assistantships also available. Financial award application deadline: 3/1; financial award applicants required to submit FAFSA. In 2008, 415 master's, 6 doctorates, 5 other advanced degrees awarded. *Degree program information:* Part-time and evening/weekend programs available. Offers business administration (MBA, MS, MSA, MSBM, MSM, MST, PhD, Graduate Certificate); economics (MS, PhD); entrepreneurship (Graduate Certificate); finance (PhD); human resources and change management (MSM); management information systems (MS); marketing (PhD); sport business management (MSBM); technology ventures (Graduate Certificate). *Application deadline:* For spring admission, 11/1 priority date for domestic students. *Application fee:* $30. Electronic applications accepted. *Application Contact:* Judy Ryder, Director, Graduate Admissions, 407-823-2364, Fax: 407-823-0219, E-mail: jryder@bus.ucf.edu. *Dean,* Dr. Thomas L. Keon, 407-823-2183, E-mail: thomas.keon@bus.ucf.edu.

Kenneth G. Dixon School of Accounting Students: 87 full-time (49 women), 125 part-time (68 women); includes 43 minority (10 African Americans, 19 Asian Americans or Pacific Islanders, 14 Hispanic Americans), 19 international. *Faculty:* 22 full-time (10 women), 5 part-time/adjunct (2 women). Expenses: Contact institution. *Financial support:* In 2008–09, 1 fellowship with partial tuition reimbursement (averaging $10,000 per year), 8 research assistantships with partial tuition reimbursements (averaging $4,600 per year), 15 teaching assistantships with partial tuition reimbursements (averaging $5,800 per year) were awarded; career-related internships or fieldwork, Federal Work-Study, institutionally sponsored loans, tuition waivers (partial), and unspecified assistantships also available. Financial award application deadline: 3/1; financial award applicants required to submit FAFSA. In 2008, 71 master's awarded. *Degree program information:* Part-time and evening/weekend programs available. Offers accounting (MSA, MST); taxation (MST). *Application deadline:* For fall admission, 6/15 priority date for domestic students; for spring admission, 11/1 priority date for domestic students. Electronic applications accepted. *Application Contact:* Dr. Robin W. Roberts, Director, 407-823-2876, E-mail: robin.roberts@bus.ucf.edu. *Director,* Dr. Robin W. Roberts, 407-823-2876, E-mail: robin.roberts@bus.ucf.edu.

College of Education Students: 553 full-time (424 women), 918 part-time (745 women); includes 290 minority (128 African Americans, 6 American Indian/Alaska Native, 19 Asian Americans or Pacific Islanders, 137 Hispanic Americans), 37 international. *Faculty:* 128 full-time (81 women), 122 part-time/adjunct (88 women). Expenses: Contact institution. *Financial support:* In 2008–09, 48 fellowships with partial tuition reimbursements (averaging $9,200 per year), 132 research assistantships with partial tuition reimbursements (averaging $6,600 per year), 25 teaching assistantships with partial tuition reimbursements (averaging $6,550 per year) were awarded; career-related internships or fieldwork, Federal Work-Study, institutionally sponsored loans, tuition waivers (partial), and unspecified assistantships also available. Financial award application deadline: 3/1; financial award applicants required to submit FAFSA. In 2008, 448 master's, 53 doctorates, 212 other advanced degrees awarded. *Degree program information:* Part-time and evening/weekend programs available. Offers applied learning and instruction (MA); art education (M Ed, MA); autism spectrum disorders (Certificate); biology (MA); career and technical education (MA); career counseling (Certificate); chemistry (MA); communication sciences and disorders (PhD); community college education (Certificate);

counselor education (M Ed, MA, PhD, Ed S); curriculum and instruction (M Ed, MA, Ed D, Ed S); e-learning (MA); e-learning professional development (Certificate); early childhood development and education (MS); early childhood education (MS); education (M Ed, MA, MS, Ed D, PhD, Certificate, Ed S); educational leadership (M Ed, MA, Ed D, Ed S); educational media (M Ed); educational technology (MA); elementary education (M Ed, MA, PhD); English language arts education (M Ed, MA); exceptional education (M Ed, MA); gifted education (Certificate); global and comparative education (Certificate); health/wellness and applied exercise physiology (MA); higher education (PhD); higher education/community college education (MA); higher education/student personnel (MA); hospitality education (PhD); initial teacher professional preparation (Certificate); instructional design for simulations (Certificate); instructional systems (MA); instructional technology (PhD); instructional technology/media (M Ed, MA, Certificate); instructional technology/media and e-learning (MA); instructional/educational technology (Certificate); K-8 mathematics and science education (M Ed, Certificate); marriage and family therapy (MA, Certificate); mathematics education (M Ed, MA, PhD); mental health counseling (MA); middle school mathematics (MA); middle school science (MA); physics (MA); play therapy (Certificate); pre-kindergarten handicapped endorsement (Certificate); reading education (M Ed, Certificate); school counseling (M Ed, MA, Ed S); school psychology (Ed S); science education (M Ed, MA, PhD); severe and profound disabilities (Certificate); social science education (M Ed, MA); special education (Certificate); sport and fitness (MA); sport leadership and coaching (MA); sports leadership (Certificate); teacher leadership (M Ed); teaching excellence (Certificate); urban education (Certificate). *Application fee:* $30. Electronic applications accepted. *Application Contact:* Dr. Sandra L. Robinson, Dean, 407-823-5529. *Dean*, Dr. Sandra L. Robinson, 407-823-5529.

College of Engineering and Computer Science Students: 552 full-time (110 women), 458 part-time (94 women); includes 199 minority (45 African Americans, 2 American Indian/Alaska Native, 61 Asian Americans or Pacific Islanders, 91 Hispanic Americans), 354 international. *Faculty:* 128 full-time (13 women), 34 part-time/adjunct (1 woman). Expenses: Contact institution. *Financial support:* In 2008–09, 46 fellowships with partial tuition reimbursements (averaging $6,500 per year), 288 research assistantships with partial tuition reimbursements (averaging $13,100 per year), 91 teaching assistantships with partial tuition reimbursements (averaging $9,000 per year) were awarded; career-related internships or fieldwork, Federal Work-Study, institutionally sponsored loans, tuition waivers (partial), and unspecified assistantships also available. Financial award application deadline: 3/1; financial award applicants required to submit FAFSA. In 2008, 238 master's, 68 doctorates, 9 other advanced degrees awarded. *Degree program information:* Part-time and evening/weekend programs available. Offers aerospace engineering (MSAE); applied operations research (Certificate); civil engineering (MS, MSCE, PhD, Certificate); computer-integrated manufacturing (MS); construction engineering (Certificate); design for usability (Certificate); digital forensics (MS); engineering and computer science (MS, MS Cp E, MS Env E, MSAE, MSCE, MSEE, MSIE, MSME, MSMSE, PhD, Certificate); engineering management (MS); environmental engineering (MS, MS Env E, PhD); human engineering/ergonomics (MS); industrial engineering (MSIE, PhD); industrial ergonomics and safety (Certificate); interactive simulation and training systems (MS); manufacturing engineering (MS); materials science and engineering (MSMSE, PhD); mechanical engineering (MSME, PhD, Certificate); operations research (MS); project engineering (Certificate); quality assurance (Certificate); quality engineering (MS); simulation modeling and analysis (MS); structural engineering (Certificate); surface water modeling (Certificate); systems engineering (MS, Certificate); systems simulation for engineers (Certificate); technology (MS); training simulation (Certificate); transportation engineering (Certificate). *Application deadline:* For fall admission, 7/15 for domestic students; for spring admission, 12/1 for domestic students. *Application fee:* $30. Electronic applications accepted. *Application Contact:* Dr. Marwan Simaan, Interim Dean, 407-823-2156, E-mail: simaan@eecs.ucf.edu. *Interim Dean*, Dr. Marwan Simaan, 407-823-2156, E-mail: simaan@eecs.ucf.edu.

School of Electrical Engineering and Computer Science Students: 308 full-time (57 women), 194 part-time (26 women); includes 74 minority (11 African Americans, 33 Asian Americans or Pacific Islanders, 30 Hispanic Americans), 201 international. *Faculty:* 59 full-time (5 women), 7 part-time/adjunct (0 women). Expenses: Contact institution. *Financial support:* In 2008–09, 31 fellowships with partial tuition reimbursements (averaging $9,500 per year), 165 research assistantships with partial tuition reimbursements (averaging $12,000 per year), 49 teaching assistantships with partial tuition reimbursements (averaging $8,300 per year) were awarded; career-related internships or fieldwork, Federal Work-Study, institutionally sponsored loans, tuition waivers (partial), and unspecified assistantships also available. Financial award application deadline: 3/1; financial award applicants required to submit FAFSA. In 2008, 167 master's, 48 doctorates awarded. *Degree program information:* Part-time and evening/weekend programs available. Offers communications systems (Certificate); computer engineering (MS Cp E, PhD); computer science (MS, PhD); digital forensics (MS); electrical engineering (MSEE, PhD, Certificate); electronic circuits (Certificate). *Application deadline:* For fall admission, 7/15 priority date for domestic students; for spring admission, 12/1 priority date for domestic students. *Application fee:* $30. Electronic applications accepted. *Application Contact:* Dr. Issa Batarseh, Director, 407-823-0189, Fax: 407-823-5419, E-mail: batarseh@mail.ucf.edu. *Director*, Dr. Issa Batarseh, 407-823-0189, Fax: 407-823-5419, E-mail: batarseh@mail.ucf.edu.

College of Graduate Studies Students: 51 full-time (18 women), 62 part-time (27 women); includes 27 minority (7 African Americans, 4 Asian Americans or Pacific Islanders, 16 Hispanic Americans), 10 international. Expenses: Contact institution. *Financial support:* In 2008–09, 3 fellowships (averaging $8,700 per year), 25 research assistantships (averaging $14,200 per year), 1 teaching assistantship (averaging $7,000 per year) were awarded. In 2008, 18 master's, 5 doctorates awarded. Offers interdisciplinary studies (MA, MS); modeling and simulation (MS, PhD). *Application Contact:* Dr. Patricia Bishop, Vice Provost and Dean, 407-823-6432, E-mail: pbishop@mail.ucf.edu. *Vice Provost and Dean*, Dr. Patricia Bishop, 407-823-6432, E-mail: pbishop@mail.ucf.edu.

College of Health and Public Affairs Students: 549 full-time (425 women), 540 part-time (372 women); includes 313 minority (152 African Americans, 1 American Indian/Alaska Native, 39 Asian Americans or Pacific Islanders, 121 Hispanic Americans), 32 international. *Faculty:* 102 full-time (46 women), 96 part-time/adjunct (49 women). Expenses: Contact institution. *Financial support:* In 2008–09, 40 fellowships with partial tuition reimbursements (averaging $7,000 per year), 91 research assistantships with partial tuition reimbursements (averaging $6,000 per year), 6 teaching assistantships with partial tuition reimbursements (averaging $5,600 per year) were awarded; career-related internships or fieldwork, Federal Work-Study, institutionally sponsored loans, traineeships, tuition waivers (partial), and unspecified assistantships also available. Financial award application deadline: 3/1; financial award applicants required to submit FAFSA. In 2008, 382 master's, 17 doctorates, 62 other advanced degrees awarded. *Degree program information:* Part-time and evening/weekend programs available. Offers child language disorders (Certificate); communication sciences and disorders (MA); corrections leadership (Certificate); crime analysis (Certificate); criminal justice (MS); emergency management and homeland security (Certificate); health and public affairs (MA, MNM, MPA, MS, MSW, DPT, PhD, Certificate); health services administration (MS, Certificate); juvenile justice leadership (Certificate); medical speech-language pathology (Certificate); multicultural/multilingual speech-language pathology (Certificate); non-profit management (MNM, Certificate); physical therapy (DPT); police leadership (Certificate); public administration (MPA, Certificate); public affairs (PhD); urban and regional planning (Certificate). Electronic applications accepted. *Application Contact:* Dr. Michael Frumkin, Dean, 407-823-0171, E-mail: mfrumkin@mail.ucf.edu. *Dean*, Dr. Michael Frumkin, 407-823-0171, E-mail: mfrumkin@mail.ucf.edu.

School of Social Work Students: 113 full-time (99 women), 79 part-time (64 women); includes 61 minority (35 African Americans, 1 American Indian/Alaska Native, 2 Asian Americans or Pacific Islanders, 23 Hispanic Americans), 2 international. *Faculty:* 15 full-time (11 women), 17 part-time/adjunct (15 women). Expenses: Contact institution. *Financial support:* In 2008–09, 2 fellowships with partial tuition reimbursements (averaging $10,000 per year), 18 research assistantships with partial tuition reimbursements (averaging $6,800 per year) were awarded; teaching assistantships with partial tuition reimbursements, career-related internships or fieldwork, Federal Work-Study, institutionally sponsored loans, and unspecified assistantships also available. Financial award application deadline: 3/1; financial award applicants required to submit FAFSA. In 2008, 80 master's, 15 other advanced degrees awarded. *Degree program information:* Part-time and evening/weekend programs available. Offers addictions (Certificate); aging studies (Certificate); children's services (Certificate); school social work (Certificate); social work (MSW); social work administration (Certificate). *Application deadline:* For fall admission, 3/1 for domestic students. *Application fee:* $30. Electronic applications accepted. *Application Contact:* Dr. John Ronnau, Director, 407-823-2114, Fax: 407-823-5697, E-mail: jronnau@mail.ucf.edu. *Director*, Dr. John Ronnau, 407-823-2114, Fax: 407-823-5697, E-mail: jronnau@mail.ucf.edu.

College of Medicine Students: 100 full-time (61 women), 9 part-time (5 women); includes 11 minority (1 African American, 1 American Indian/Alaska Native, 4 Asian Americans or Pacific Islanders, 5 Hispanic Americans), 44 international. *Faculty:* 31 full-time (6 women), 3 part-time/adjunct (1 woman). Expenses: Contact institution. *Financial support:* In 2008–09, 9 fellowships (averaging $13,200 per year), 55 research assistantships (averaging $13,800 per year), 35 teaching assistantships (averaging $10,200 per year) were awarded. In 2008, 7 master's, 5 doctorates awarded. Offers medicine (MS, PhD). *Application Contact:* Dr. Deborah C. German, Dean, 407-823-1829, E-mail: medical@mail.ucf.edu. *Dean*, Dr. Deborah C. German, 407-823-1829, E-mail: medical@mail.ucf.edu.

Burnett School of Biomedical Sciences Students: 27 full-time (19 women), 6 part-time (4 women); includes 6 minority (1 American Indian/Alaska Native, 3 Asian Americans or Pacific Islanders, 2 Hispanic Americans), 8 international. *Faculty:* 19 full-time (4 women), 2 part-time/adjunct (0 women). Expenses: Contact institution. *Financial support:* In 2008–09, 3 fellowships (averaging $10,000 per year), 7 research assistantships (averaging $5,400 per year), 15 teaching assistantships (averaging $8,800 per year) were awarded. In 2008, 7 master's, 5 doctorates awarded. Offers biomedical sciences (MS, PhD); biotechnology (MS); molecular biology and microbiology (MS). *Application Contact:* Dr. Pappachan E. Kolattukudy, Director, 407-823-1206, Fax: 407-823-0956, E-mail: pk@mail.ucf.edu. *Director*, Dr. Pappachan E. Kolattukudy, 407-823-1206, Fax: 407-823-0956, E-mail: pk@mail.ucf.edu.

College of Nursing Students: 99 full-time (91 women), 271 part-time (261 women); includes 98 minority (42 African Americans, 1 American Indian/Alaska Native, 18 Asian Americans or Pacific Islanders, 37 Hispanic Americans), 4 international. *Faculty:* 40 full-time (26 women), 40 part-time/adjunct (37 women). Expenses: Contact institution. *Financial support:* In 2008–09, 42 fellowships with partial tuition reimbursements (averaging $2,400 per year), 2 teaching assistantships with partial tuition reimbursements (averaging $17,800 per year) were awarded; research assistantships with partial tuition reimbursements, career-related internships or fieldwork, Federal Work-Study, institutionally sponsored loans, traineeships, and unspecified assistantships also available. Financial award application deadline: 3/1; financial award applicants required to submit FAFSA. In 2008, 82 master's, 5 doctorates, 10 other advanced degrees awarded. *Degree program information:* Part-time and evening/weekend programs available. Offers adult nurse practitioner (MSN, Post-Master's Certificate); clinical nurse leader (MSN, Post-Master's Certificate); clinical nurse specialist (MSN, Post-Master's Certificate); family nurse practitioner (MSN, Post-Master's Certificate); leadership and management (MSN); nurse educator (MSN); nursing (PhD); nursing education (Post-Master's Certificate); nursing practice (DNP); pediatric nurse practitioner (MSN, Post-Master's Certificate). *Application deadline:* For fall admission, 2/15 for domestic students; for spring admission, 9/15 for domestic students. *Application fee:* $30. Electronic applications accepted. *Application Contact:* Dr. Jean D. Leuner, Dean, 407-823-5496, Fax: 407-823-5675, E-mail: jleuner@mail.ucf.edu. *Dean*, Dr. Jean D. Leuner, 407-823-5496, Fax: 407-823-5675, E-mail: jleuner@mail.ucf.edu.

College of Optics and Photonics Students: 114 full-time (14 women), 9 part-time (1 woman); includes 13 minority (5 African Americans, 3 Asian Americans or Pacific Islanders, 5 Hispanic Americans), 68 international. *Faculty:* 19 full-time (1 woman). Expenses: Contact institution. *Financial support:* In 2008–09, 7 fellowships with partial tuition reimbursements (averaging $8,500 per year), 88 research assistantships with partial tuition reimbursements (averaging $16,600 per year) were awarded; teaching assistantships with partial tuition reimbursements, career-related internships or fieldwork, Federal Work-Study, institutionally sponsored loans, tuition waivers (partial), and unspecified assistantships also available. Financial award application deadline: 3/1; financial award applicants required to submit FAFSA. In 2008, 39 master's, 12 doctorates awarded. *Degree program information:* Part-time and evening/weekend programs available. Offers optics (MS, PhD). *Application deadline:* For fall admission, 2/1 priority date for domestic students; for spring admission, 12/1 for domestic students. *Application fee:* $30. Electronic applications accepted. *Application Contact:* Dr. Bahaa E. Saleh, Dean and Director, 407-882-3326, E-mail: besaleh@creol.ucf.edu. *Dean and Director*, Dr. Bahaa E. Saleh, 407-882-3326, E-mail: besaleh@creol.ucf.edu.

College of Sciences Students: 582 full-time (317 women), 261 part-time (135 women); includes 141 minority (45 African Americans, 23 Asian Americans or Pacific Islanders, 73 Hispanic Americans), 149 international. *Faculty:* 274 full-time (83 women), 82 part-time/adjunct (29 women). Expenses: Contact institution. *Financial support:* In 2008–09, 56 fellowships (averaging $10,800 per year), 163 research assistantships (averaging $10,600 per year), 271 teaching assistantships (averaging $9,100 per year) were awarded. In 2008, 125 master's, 32 doctorates, 20 other advanced degrees awarded. Offers actuarial science (MS); anthropology (MA); applied experimental and human factors psychology (MA, PhD); applied mathematics (Certificate); applied sociology (MA); biology (MS); chemistry (MS, PhD); clinical psychology (MA, MS, PhD); computer forensics (Certificate); conservation biology (PhD, Certificate); data mining (MS); domestic violence (MA); environmental politics (MA); forensic analysis (MS); forensic biochemistry (MS); industrial chemistry (MS); industrial mathematics (MS); industrial/organizational psychology (MS, PhD); international studies (MA); mathematical science (MS); mathematics (PhD); Maya studies (Certificate); physics (MS, PhD); political analysis and policy (MA); SAS data mining (Certificate); sciences (MA, MS, PhD, Certificate); sociology (PhD); statistical computing (MS). *Application Contact:* Dr. Peter Panousis, Dean, 407-823-1911, E-mail: ppanousis@mail.ucf.edu. *Dean*, Dr. Peter Panousis, 407-823-1911, E-mail: ppanousis@mail.ucf.edu.

Nicholson School of Communication Students: 44 full-time (39 women), 28 part-time (25 women); includes 15 minority (6 African Americans, 3 Asian Americans or Pacific Islanders, 6 Hispanic Americans), 9 international. *Faculty:* 41 full-time (18 women), 36 part-time/adjunct (18 women). Expenses: Contact institution. *Financial support:* In 2008–09, 2 fellowships with partial tuition reimbursements (averaging $10,000 per year), 4 research assistantships with partial tuition reimbursements (averaging $4,400 per year), 16 teaching assistantships with partial tuition reimbursements (averaging $6,400 per year) were awarded; career-related internships or fieldwork, Federal Work-Study, institutionally sponsored loans, tuition waivers (partial), and unspecified assistantships also available. Financial award application deadline: 3/1; financial award applicants required to submit FAFSA. In 2008, 29 master's awarded. *Degree program information:* Part-time and evening/weekend programs available. Offers business communication (MA); interpersonal communication (MA); mass communication (MA). *Application deadline:* For fall admission, 7/15 for domestic students; for spring admission, 12/7 for domestic students. *Application fee:* $30. Electronic applications accepted. *Application Contact:* Dr. Robert Chandler, Director, 407-823-2683, Fax: 407-823-5216, E-mail: rcchandl@mail.ucf.edu. *Director*, Dr. Robert Chandler, 407-823-2683, Fax: 407-823-5216, E-mail: rcchandl@mail.ucf.edu.

Rosen College of Hospitality Management Students: 32 full-time (22 women), 36 part-time (27 women); includes 16 minority (3 African Americans, 6 Asian Americans or Pacific Islanders, 7 Hispanic Americans), 7 international. *Faculty:* 37 full-time (10 women), 26 part-time/adjunct (12 women). Expenses: Contact institution. *Financial support:* In 2008–09, 1 fellowship with partial tuition reimbursement (averaging $10,000 per year), 15 research assistantships with partial tuition reimbursements (averaging $5,400 per year) were awarded. In 2008, 29 master's awarded. Offers hospitality and tourism management (MS). *Application deadline:* For fall admission, 2/1 for domestic students. *Application fee:* $30. Electronic applications accepted. *Application Contact:* Dr. Abraham C. Pizam, Dean, 407-903-8010, E-mail: apizam@mail.ucf.edu. *Dean*, Dr. Abraham C. Pizam, 407-903-8010, E-mail: apizam@mail.ucf.edu.

UNIVERSITY OF CENTRAL MISSOURI, Warrensburg, MO 64093

General Information State-supported, coed, comprehensive institution. CGS member. *Graduate housing:* Rooms and/or apartments available on a first-come, first-served basis to single and married students. Housing application deadline: 8/1.

University of Central Missouri (continued)

GRADUATE UNITS

The Graduate School *Degree program information:* Part-time programs available. Electronic applications accepted.

College of Arts, Humanities and Social Sciences *Degree program information:* Part-time programs available. Offers arts, humanities and social sciences (MA, MS); communication (MA); English (MA); history (MA); music (MA); speech communication (MA); teaching English as a second language (MA); theatre (MA).

College of Education Offers college student personnel administration (MS); counseling (MS); counselor education (MS, Ed S); curriculum and instruction (Ed S); education (MS, MSE, Ed D, Ed S); educational leadership (Ed D); educational technology (MSE); elementary education (MSE); human service/guidance counseling (Ed S); human services/ technology and occupational education (Ed S); human services/learning resources (Ed S); K–12 education (MSE); library science and information services (MS, Ed S); literacy education (MSE); school administration (MSE, Ed S); secondary education (MSE); secondary education/ business and office education (MSE); special education (MSE, Ed S); special education/ human services (Ed S); technology and occupational education (MS).

College of Health and Human Services *Degree program information:* Part-time programs available. Offers criminal justice (MS); fire science (MS); health and human services (MA, MS, Ed S); human services/public services (Ed S); industrial hygiene (MS); industrial safety management (MS); loss control (MS); occupational safety management (MS); physical education/exercise and sports science (MS); psychology (MS); public safety (MS); rural family nursing (MS); security (MS); social gerontology (MS); sociology (MA); speech pathology and audiology (MS); transportation safety (MS).

College of Science and Technology *Degree program information:* Part-time programs available. Offers applied mathematics (MS); aviation safety (MS); biology (MS); industrial management (MS); mathematics (MS); science and technology (MS).

Harmon College of Business Administration *Degree program information:* Part-time programs available. Offers accountancy (MA); business administration (MA, MBA, MS); information technology (MS).

See Close-Up on page 1013.

UNIVERSITY OF CENTRAL OKLAHOMA, Edmond, OK 73034-5209

General Information State-supported, coed, comprehensive institution. CGS member. *Graduate housing:* Rooms and/or apartments available on a first-come, first-served basis to single and married students. Housing application deadline: 7/1. *Research affiliation:* U.S. Department of Agriculture–Agricultural Research Service (grazing lands), National Geographic Society (global positioning system education).

GRADUATE UNITS

College of Graduate Studies and Research *Degree program information:* Part-time and evening/weekend programs available. Electronic applications accepted.

College of Arts, Media, and Design *Degree program information:* Part-time and evening/ weekend programs available. Postbaccalaureate distance learning degree programs offered (minimal on-campus study). Offers arts, media, and design (MFA, MM); design and interior design (MFA); music education (MM); performance (MM). Electronic applications accepted.

College of Business Administration *Degree program information:* Part-time programs available. Postbaccalaureate distance learning degree programs offered (minimal on-campus study). Offers business administration (MBA). Electronic applications accepted.

College of Education *Degree program information:* Part-time programs available. Offers adult education (M Ed); community services (M Ed); counseling psychology (MS); early childhood education (M Ed); education (M Ed, MA, MS); educational administration (M Ed); elementary education (M Ed); family and child studies (MS); family and consumer science education (MS); general education (M Ed); general psychology (MA); gerontology (M Ed); guidance and counseling (M Ed); instructional media (M Ed); interior design (MS); nutrition-food management (MS); professional health occupations (M Ed); reading (M Ed); secondary education (M Ed); special education (M Ed); speech-language pathology (M Ed). Electronic applications accepted.

College of Liberal Arts *Degree program information:* Part-time programs available. Offers composition skills (MA); contemporary literature (MA); creative writing (MA); criminal justice management and administration (MA); history (MA); international affairs (MA); liberal arts (MA); museum studies (MA); political science (MA); social studies teaching (MA); Southwestern studies (MA); teaching English as a second language (MA); traditional studies (MA); urban affairs (MA). Electronic applications accepted.

College of Mathematics and Science *Degree program information:* Part-time programs available. Offers applied mathematical sciences (MS); biology (MS); chemistry (MS); mathematics and science (MS); physics and engineering (MS). Electronic applications accepted.

UNIVERSITY OF CHARLESTON, Charleston, WV 25304-1099

General Information Independent, coed, comprehensive institution. *Graduate housing:* Room and/or apartments available to single students; on-campus housing not available to married students.

GRADUATE UNITS

Accelerated Business Administration Program *Degree program information:* Part-time programs available. Offers business administration (MBA). Electronic applications accepted.

Executive Business Administration Program *Degree program information:* Part-time and evening/weekend programs available. Offers business administration (EMBA). Electronic applications accepted.

Program in Forensic Accounting Offers forensic accounting.

Robert C. Byrd School of Pharmacy Offers pharmacy (Pharm D).

UNIVERSITY OF CHICAGO, Chicago, IL 60637-1513

General Information Independent, coed, university. CGS member. *Enrollment:* 12,787 graduate, professional, and undergraduate students; 4,421 full-time matriculated graduate/ professional students (1,988 women), 2,943 part-time matriculated graduate/professional students (929 women). *Enrollment by degree level:* 1,099 first professional, 5,034 master's, 1,231 doctoral. *Graduate faculty:* 2,160 full-time (683 women), 760 part-time/adjunct (280 women). *Graduate housing:* Rooms and/or apartments available on a first-come, first-served basis to single and married students. *Student services:* Campus employment opportunities, campus safety program, career counseling, exercise/wellness program, free psychological counseling, grant writing training, international student services, low-cost health insurance, multicultural affairs office, services for students with disabilities, teacher training, writing training. *Library facilities:* Joseph Regenstein Library plus 6 others. *Online resources:* library catalog, web page, access to other libraries' catalogs. *Collection:* 7 million titles, 47,000 serial subscriptions. *Research affiliation:* National Opinion Research Center (social science), Smithsonian Tropical Research Institute (biology), Field Museum of Natural History (archaeology, zoology), McDonald Observatory (astronomy), Fermilab (high-energy physics), Argonne National Laboratory (energy, materials).

Computer facilities: 1,000 computers available on campus for general student use. A campuswide network can be accessed from student residence rooms and from off campus. Online class registration is available. *Web address:* http://www.uchicago.edu/.

General Application Contact: Martha Jackson, Manager, Office of Graduate Affairs, 773-702-7813, Fax: 773-702-1194, E-mail: graduate-affairs-admissions@uchicago.edu.

GRADUATE UNITS

Divinity School *Degree program information:* Part-time programs available. Offers divinity (M Div, AM, AMRS, PhD). Electronic applications accepted.

Division of Social Sciences Offers anthropology (PhD); comparative human development (PhD); conceptual and historical studies of science (PhD); economics (PhD); history (PhD); international relations (AM); Latin American and Caribbean studies (AM); Middle Eastern studies (AM); political science (PhD); psychology (PhD); social sciences (AM, PhD); social thought (PhD); sociology (PhD). Electronic applications accepted.

Division of the Biological Sciences Students: 462 full-time (220 women); includes 75 minority (15 African Americans, 2 American Indian/Alaska Native, 44 Asian Americans or Pacific Islanders, 14 Hispanic Americans), 69 international. Average age 27. 1,003 applicants, 20% accepted, 84 enrolled. *Faculty:* 447 full-time (209 women), 16 part-time/adjunct (12 women). Expenses: Contact institution. *Financial support:* In 2008–09, 462 students received support, including fellowships with full tuition reimbursements available (averaging $29,053 per year), research assistantships with full tuition reimbursements available (averaging $29,053 per year); institutionally sponsored loans, scholarships/grants, traineeships, and health care benefits also available. Financial award applicants required to submit FAFSA. In 2008, 11 master's, 54 doctorates awarded. Offers biochemistry and molecular biology (PhD); biological sciences (MD, MS, PhD); cancer biology (PhD); cell and molecular biology (PhD); cell physiology (PhD); cellular and molecular physiology (PhD); cellular differentiation (PhD); computational neuroscience (PhD); developmental biology (PhD); developmental endocrinology (PhD); developmental genetics (PhD); developmental neurobiology (PhD); ecology and evolution (PhD); evolutionary biology (PhD); functional and evolutionary biology (PhD); gene expression (PhD); genetics, genomics and systems biology (PhD); health studies (MS, PhD); human genetics (PhD); immunology (PhD); integrative neuroscience (PhD); interdisciplinary scientist training (PhD); medical physics (PhD); microbiology (PhD); molecular metabolism and nutrition (PhD); neurobiology (PhD); ophthalmology and visual science (PhD); organismal biology and anatomy (PhD); pathology (PhD); pharmacological and physiological sciences (PhD). *Application deadline:* For fall admission, 12/1 priority date for domestic and international students. *Application fee:* $55. Electronic applications accepted. *Application Contact:* Parag M. Shah, Associate Dean of Students, Graduate Affairs, 773-702-5853, Fax: 773-834-1618, E-mail: pshah@bsd.uchicago.edu. *Dean,* Dr. James Madara, 773-702-9000.

Pritzker School of Medicine Students: 451 full-time (218 women); includes 180 minority (39 African Americans, 4 American Indian/Alaska Native, 107 Asian Americans or Pacific Islanders, 30 Hispanic Americans), 19 international. Average age 24. 7,374 applicants, 4% accepted, 100 enrolled. *Faculty:* 870 full-time. Expenses: Contact institution. *Financial support:* In 2008–09, 361 students received support, including 8 fellowships with full tuition reimbursements available (averaging $20,500 per year), 75 teaching assistantships; career-related internships or fieldwork, Federal Work-Study, institutionally sponsored loans, and scholarships/grants also available. Financial award application deadline: 4/1; financial award applicants required to submit FAFSA. In 2008, 98 MDs awarded. Offers medicine (MD). *Application deadline:* For fall admission, 10/15 for domestic students. Applications are processed on a rolling basis. *Application fee:* $75. Electronic applications accepted. *Application Contact:* Sylvia Robertson, Assistant Dean for Admissions and Financial Aid, 773-702-1937, Fax: 773-834-5412, E-mail: sroberts@bsd.uchicago.edu.

Division of the Humanities Offers ancient philosophy (AM, PhD); anthropology and linguistics (PhD); art history (AM, PhD); cinema and media studies (AM, PhD); classical archaeology (AM, PhD); classical languages and literatures (AM, PhD); comparative literature (AM, PhD); East Asian languages and civilizations (AM, PhD); English language and literature (AM, PhD); French (AM, PhD); Germanic languages and literatures (AM, PhD); humanities (AM, MA, MFA, PhD); Italian (AM, PhD); linguistics (AM, PhD); music (AM, PhD); Near Eastern languages and civilizations (AM, PhD); philosophy (AM, PhD); Slavic languages and literatures (AM, PhD); South Asian languages and civilizations (AM, PhD); Spanish (AM, PhD); visual arts (MFA).

Division of the Physical Sciences Offers applied mathematics (SM, PhD); astronomy and astrophysics (MS, PhD); atmospheric sciences (SM, PhD); biophysical science (PhD); chemistry (PhD); computer science (SM, PhD); earth sciences (SM, PhD); financial mathematics (MS); mathematics (SM, PhD); paleobiology (PhD); physical sciences (MS, SM, PhD); physics (PhD); planetary and space sciences (SM, PhD); statistics (SM, PhD). Electronic applications accepted.

Full-time MBA Program Students: 1,144 full-time (403 women); includes 283 minority (55 African Americans, 1 American Indian/Alaska Native, 181 Asian Americans or Pacific Islanders, 46 Hispanic Americans), 394 international. Average age 28. 4,144 applicants, 22% accepted, 577 enrolled. *Faculty:* 138 full-time, 47 part-time/adjunct. Expenses: Contact institution. *Financial support:* In 2008–09, 300 fellowships were awarded. Financial award applicants required to submit FAFSA. In 2008, 553 master's awarded. Offers business (IMBA, MBA, PhD); business administration (MBA); executive business administration (MBA); international business administration (IMBA). *Application deadline:* For fall admission, 10/17 priority date for domestic and international students; for winter admission, 1/9 for domestic and international students; for spring admission, 3/12 for domestic and international students. *Application fee:* $200. Electronic applications accepted. *Application Contact:* Rosemaria Martinelli, Student Recruitment and Admissions, 773-702-7369, Fax: 773-702-9085, E-mail: admissions@chicagobooth.edu. *Deputy Dean of full-time MBA Program,* Stacey Kole, 773-702-7121.

Irving B. Harris Graduate School of Public Policy Studies *Degree program information:* Part-time programs available. Offers environmental science and policy (MS); public policy studies (AM, MPP, PhD). Electronic applications accepted.

The Law School Students: 648 full-time (291 women); includes 166 minority (38 African Americans, 1 American Indian/Alaska Native, 69 Asian Americans or Pacific Islanders, 58 Hispanic Americans), 60 international. Average age 24. 5,032 applicants, 18% accepted, 184 enrolled. *Faculty:* 52 full-time (14 women). Expenses: Contact institution. *Financial support:* In 2008–09, 326 students received support, including 7 fellowships; research assistantships, teaching assistantships, career-related internships or fieldwork, institutionally sponsored loans, and scholarships/grants also available. Financial award application deadline: 3/1; financial award applicants required to submit FAFSA. In 2008, 212 first professional degrees, 53 master's, 3 doctorates awarded. Offers law (JD, LL M, MCL, DCL, JSD). *Application deadline:* For fall admission, 2/1 priority date for domestic students. Applications are processed on a rolling basis. *Application fee:* $75. Electronic applications accepted. *Application Contact:* Ann K. Perry, Dean of Admissions, 773-834-4425, Fax: 773-834-0942, E-mail: admissions@law.uchicago.edu. *Dean,* Saul Levmore, 773-702-9494, Fax: 773-834-4409.

School of Social Service Administration *Degree program information:* Part-time and evening/ weekend programs available. Offers social service administration (PhD); social work (AM). Electronic applications accepted.

UNIVERSITY OF CINCINNATI, Cincinnati, OH 45221

General Information State-supported, coed, university. CGS member. *Graduate housing:* Rooms and/or apartments available on a first-come, first-served basis to single and married students. Housing application deadline: 7/1.

GRADUATE UNITS

College of Law Students: 361 full-time (154 women); includes 60 minority (25 African Americans, 28 Asian Americans or Pacific Islanders, 7 Hispanic Americans). Average age 24. 1,198 applicants, 40% accepted, 123 enrolled. *Faculty:* 31 full-time (16 women), 28 part-time/ adjunct (5 women). Expenses: Contact institution. *Financial support:* In 2008–09, 238 students received support, including 238 fellowships (averaging $8,700 per year); research assistantships, career-related internships or fieldwork, Federal Work-Study, scholarships/grants, tuition waivers (full and partial), and unspecified assistantships also available. Financial award application deadline: 3/1; financial award applicants required to submit FAFSA. In 2008, 122 JDs awarded. Offers law (JD). *Application deadline:* For fall admission, 3/1 priority date for domestic students. Applications are processed on a rolling basis. *Application fee:* $35. Electronic applications accepted. *Application Contact:* Al Watson, Assistant Dean and Director of Admissions, 513-556-0077, Fax: 513-556-2391, E-mail: alfred.watson@uc.edu. *Dean,* Louis D. Bilionis, 513-556-0121, Fax: 513-556-2391, E-mail: louis.bilionis@uc.edu.

College of Pharmacy *Degree program information:* Part-time programs available. Offers pharmacy (Pharm D, MS, PhD).

Division of Pharmaceutical Sciences Offers pharmaceutical sciences (MS, PhD).

Division of Pharmacy Practice Offers pharmacy practice (Pharm D).

Graduate School *Degree program information:* Part-time and evening/weekend programs available. Offers neuroscience (PhD). Electronic applications accepted.

College-Conservatory of Music Offers arts administration (MA); choral conducting (MM, DMA); composition (MM, DMA); directing (MFA); keyboard studies (MM, DMA, AD); music (MA, MFA, MM, DMA, PhD, AD); music education (MM); music history (MM); music theory (MM, PhD); musicology (PhD); orchestral conducting (MM, DMA); performance (MM, DMA, AD); theater design and production (MFA); voice and opera (MM, DMA); wind conducting (MM, DMA). Electronic applications accepted.

College of Allied Health Sciences *Degree program information:* Part-time programs available. Offers allied health sciences (MA, MS, Au D, DPT, PhD); blood transfusion medicine (MS); cellular therapies (MS); communication sciences and disorders (MA, Au D, PhD); medical genetics (MS); nutritional science (MS); rehabilitation science (DPT).

College of Business *Degree program information:* Part-time and evening/weekend programs available. Offers accounting (MS, PhD); business (MBA, MS, PhD); business administration (MBA); finance (PhD); information systems (MS, PhD); management (PhD); marketing (MS, PhD); quantitative analysis (MS); quantitative analysis and operations management (PhD). Electronic applications accepted.

College of Design, Architecture, Art, and Planning *Degree program information:* Part-time programs available. Offers architecture (M Arch); art education (MA); art history (MA); community planning (MCP); design, architecture, art, and planning (M Arch, M Des, MA, MCP, MFA, PhD); fashion design (M Des); fine arts (MFA); graphic design (M Des); industrial design (M Des); interaction design (M Des); planning (MCP); product development (M Des); regional development planning (PhD). Electronic applications accepted.

College of Education, Criminal Justice, and Human Services *Degree program information:* Part-time programs available. Postbaccalaureate distance learning degree programs offered (no on-campus study). Offers community health (MS); counseling (Ed D); counselor education (CAGS); criminal justice (MS, PhD); curriculum and instruction (M Ed, Ed D); deaf studies (Certificate); early childhood education (M Ed); education, criminal justice, and human services (M Ed, MA, MS, Ed D, PhD, CAGS, Certificate, Ed S); educational leadership (M Ed, Ed S); educational studies (M Ed, Ed D, PhD, Ed S); health education (MS, PhD); health promotion and education (M Ed); human services (M Ed, MA, MS, Ed D, PhD, CAGS, Ed S); mental health (MA); middle childhood education (M Ed); postsecondary literacy instruction (Certificate); reading/literacy (M Ed, Ed D); school counseling (M Ed); school psychology (PhD, Ed S); secondary education (M Ed); special education (M Ed, Ed D); teaching English as a second language (M Ed, Ed D, Certificate); teaching science (MS); urban educational leadership (Ed D). Electronic applications accepted.

College of Engineering *Degree program information:* Part-time and evening/weekend programs available. Offers aerospace engineering and engineering mechanics (MS, PhD); bioinformatics (PhD); biomechanics (PhD); ceramic science and engineering (MS, PhD); chemical engineering (MS, PhD); civil engineering (MS, PhD); computer engineering (MS); computer science (MS); computer science and engineering (PhD); electrical engineering (MS, PhD); engineering (MS, PhD); environmental engineering (MS, PhD); environmental sciences (MS, PhD); health physics (MS); industrial engineering (MS, PhD); materials science and engineering (MS, PhD); materials science and metallurgical engineering (MS, PhD); mechanical engineering (MS, PhD); medical imaging (PhD); metallurgical engineering (MS, PhD); nuclear engineering (MS, PhD); polymer science and engineering (MS, PhD); tissue engineering (PhD).

College of Medicine Offers biomedical sciences (MS, PhD); cell and cancer biology (PhD); cell biophysics (PhD); environmental and industrial hygiene (MS, PhD); environmental and occupational medicine (MS); environmental genetics and molecular toxicology (MS, PhD); epidemiology and biostatistics (MS, PhD); immunobiology (MS, PhD); medical physics (MS); medicine (MD, MS, PhD); molecular and developmental biology (PhD); molecular genetics, biochemistry and microbiology (MS, PhD); occupational safety and ergonomics (MS, PhD); pathology (PhD); pharmacology (PhD); physiology (PhD). Electronic applications accepted.

College of Nursing Students: 271 full-time (238 women), 374 part-time (347 women); includes 70 minority (45 African Americans, 6 American Indian/Alaska Native, 12 Asian Americans or Pacific Islanders, 7 Hispanic Americans), 6 international. Average age 34. 385 applicants, 49% accepted, 132 enrolled. *Faculty:* 41 full-time (39 women), 16 part-time/adjunct (15 women). Expenses: Contact institution. *Financial support:* In 2008–09, 164 students received support, including 7 fellowships with full tuition reimbursements available (averaging $13,571 per year), research assistantships with full tuition reimbursements available (averaging $12,000 per year), 8 teaching assistantships with full tuition reimbursements available (averaging $12,000 per year); career-related internships or fieldwork, scholarships/grants, traineeships, tuition waivers (partial), and unspecified assistantships also available. Support available to part-time students. Financial award application deadline: 5/1; financial award applicants required to submit FAFSA. In 2008, 77 master's, 5 doctorates awarded. *Degree program information:* Part-time programs available. Postbaccalaureate distance learning degree programs offered (no on-campus study). Offers clinical nurse specialist (MSN); nurse anesthesia (MSN); nurse midwifery (MSN); nurse practitioner (MSN); nursing (PhD). *Application deadline:* For fall admission, 7/26 priority date for domestic and international students. Applications are processed on a rolling basis. *Application fee:* $40. Electronic applications accepted. *Application Contact:* Loren Carter, Program Coordinator, 513-558-5072, Fax: 513-558-7523, E-mail: loren.carter@uc.edu. *Dean,* Dr. Andrea R. Lindell, 513-558-5330, Fax: 513-558-9030, E-mail: andrea.lindell@uc.edu.

McMicken College of Arts and Sciences *Degree program information:* Part-time and evening/weekend programs available. Offers analytical chemistry (MS, PhD); anthropology (MA); applied economics (MA); applied mathematics (MS, PhD); arts and sciences (MA, MALER, MAT, MS, PhD, Certificate); biochemistry (MS, PhD); biological sciences (MS, PhD); classics (MA, PhD); clinical psychology (PhD); communication (MA); English (MA, MAT, PhD); experimental psychology (PhD); French (MA, PhD); geography (MA, PhD); geology (MS, PhD); German studies (MA, PhD); history (MA, PhD); inorganic chemistry (MS, PhD); interdisciplinary studies (PhD); labor and employment relations (MALER); mathematics education (MAT); organic chemistry (MS, PhD); organizational leadership (MALER); philosophy (MA, PhD); physical chemistry (MS, PhD); physics (MS, PhD); political science (MA, PhD); polymer chemistry (MS, PhD); pure mathematics (MS, PhD); Romance languages and literatures (PhD); sensors (PhD); sociology (MA, PhD); Spanish (MA, PhD); statistics (MS, PhD); women's, gender, and sexuality studies (MA, Certificate).

School of Social Work *Degree program information:* Part-time programs available. Offers social work (MSW). Electronic applications accepted.

UNIVERSITY OF COLORADO AT BOULDER, Boulder, CO 80309

General Information State-supported, coed, university. CGS member. *Graduate housing:* Rooms and/or apartments available to single and married students. *Student services:* Campus employment opportunities, campus safety program, career counseling, child daycare facilities, free psychological counseling, international student services, low-cost health insurance. *Library facilities:* Norlin Library plus 5 others. *Online resources:* library catalog, web page, access to other libraries' catalogs. *Collection:* 3.8 million titles, 50,350 serial subscriptions, 84,097 audiovisual materials. *Research affiliation:* National Center for Atmospheric Research, National Institute of Standards and Technology, National Oceanic and Atmospheric Administration, U.S. West Advanced Technologies, NASA.

Computer facilities: Computer purchase and lease plans are available. 1,855 computers available on campus for general student use. A campuswide network can be accessed from student residence rooms and from off campus. Online class registration, standard and academic software, student government voting are available. *Web address:* http://www.colorado.edu/.

General Application Contact: Philip Distefano, Chancellor, 303-492-8908, E-mail: phil.distefano@colorado.edu.

GRADUATE UNITS

ATLAS Institute (Alliance for Technology, Learning, and Society) Average age 34. 23 applicants, 22% accepted, 5 enrolled. Expenses: Contact institution. *Financial support:* In 2008–09, 2 fellowships (averaging $17,747 per year), 7 research assistantships (averaging $18,440 per year), 2 teaching assistantships (averaging $7,642 per year) were awarded. Financial award application deadline: 1/15. In 2008, 1 degree awarded. Offers technology, media, and society (PhD). *Application deadline:* For fall admission, 1/28 for domestic students, 12/1 for international students. *Application Contact:* Application Contact, E-mail: cuatlas@colorado.edu.

Graduate School Average age 30. 7,882 applicants, 26% accepted, 1025 enrolled. Expenses: Contact institution. *Financial support:* In 2008–09, 845 fellowships with full tuition reimbursements (averaging $8,717 per year), 999 research assistantships with full tuition reimbursements (averaging $16,574 per year), 1,259 teaching assistantships with full tuition reimbursements (averaging $13,563 per year) were awarded; career-related internships or fieldwork, Federal Work-Study, institutionally sponsored loans, scholarships/grants, traineeships, tuition waivers (full and partial), and unspecified assistantships also available. Support available to part-time students. Financial award applicants required to submit FAFSA. In 2008, 934 master's, 297 doctorates awarded. *Degree program information:* Part-time programs available. Postbaccalaureate distance learning degree programs offered. *Application fee:* $50 ($60 for international students). Electronic applications accepted. *Application Contact:* Application Contact, E-mail: gradinfo@colorado.edu.

College of Arts and Sciences Average age 30. 4,802 applicants, 16% accepted, 505 enrolled. Expenses: Contact institution. *Financial support:* In 2008–09, 501 fellowships with full tuition reimbursements (averaging $9,580 per year), 565 research assistantships with full tuition reimbursements (averaging $16,694 per year), 1,022 teaching assistantships (averaging $13,970 per year) were awarded; career-related internships or fieldwork, Federal Work-Study, institutionally sponsored loans, scholarships/grants, traineeships, tuition waivers (full), and unspecified assistantships also available. Support available to part-time students. In 2008, 316 master's, 202 doctorates awarded. *Degree program information:* Part-time programs available. Offers animal behavior (MA); anthropology (MA, PhD); applied mathematics (MS, PhD); art history (MA); arts and sciences (MA, MFA, MS, Au D, PhD); astrophysics (MS, PhD); atmospheric and oceanic sciences (MS, PhD); audiology (Au D, PhD); biochemistry (PhD); biology (MA, PhD); cellular structure and function (MA, PhD); ceramics (MFA); chemical physics (PhD); chemistry (MS); Chinese (MA, PhD); classics (MA, PhD); clinical research and practice in audiology (PhD); communication (MA, PhD); comparative literature and humanities (MA, PhD); dance (MFA); developmental biology (MA, PhD); drawing (MFA); economics (MA, PhD); environmental biology (MA, PhD); environmental studies (MS, PhD); evolutionary biology (MA, PhD); French (MA, PhD); geography (MA, PhD); geology (MS, PhD); geophysics (PhD); German (MA); Hispanic linguistics (MA); history (MA, PhD); integrative physiology (MS, PhD); international affairs (MA); Japanese (MA, PhD); linguistics (MA, PhD); liquid crystal science and technology (PhD); literature (MA, PhD); mathematical physics (PhD); mathematics (MA, MS, PhD); medical physics (PhD); medieval/early modern Hispanic literatures (PhD); molecular biology (MA, PhD); museum and field studies (MS); neurobiology (MA); optical sciences and engineering (PhD); painting (MFA); philosophy (MA, PhD); photography and media arts (MFA); physics (MS, PhD); planetary science (MS, PhD); political science (MA, PhD); population biology (MA); population genetics (PhD); printmaking (MFA); psychology and neuroscience (MA, PhD); public policy (MA); religious studies (MA); sculpture (MFA); sociology (PhD); Spanish literature (MA, PhD); speech, language and hearing science (MA); speech-language pathology (MA, PhD); speech-language-hearing sciences (PhD); theatre (MA, PhD). *Application fee:* $50 ($60 for international students). Electronic applications accepted. *Application Contact:* Kate Secrest, Assistant to the Dean, 303-492-8799, E-mail: kate.secrest@colorado.edu. *Dean,* Todd T. Gleeson, 303-492-7294, E-mail: gleeson@stripe.colorado.edu.

College of Engineering and Applied Science Average age 29. 2,078 applicants, 41% accepted, 292 enrolled. Expenses: Contact institution. *Financial support:* In 2008–09, 151 fellowships with full tuition reimbursements (averaging $13,105 per year), 376 research assistantships with full tuition reimbursements (averaging $16,713 per year), 102 teaching assistantships with full tuition reimbursements (averaging $15,863 per year) were awarded; career-related internships or fieldwork, scholarships/grants, traineeships, and tuition waivers (full) also available. In 2008, 364 master's, 66 doctorates awarded. *Degree program information:* Part-time programs available. Postbaccalaureate distance learning degree programs offered. Offers aerospace engineering sciences (ME, MS, PhD); building systems (MS, PhD); chemical and biological engineering (ME, MS, PhD); computer science (ME, MS, PhD); construction engineering and management (MS, PhD); electrical and computer engineering (ME, MS); electrical engineering (PhD); engineering and applied science (ME, MS, PhD); environmental engineering (MS, PhD); geoenvironmental engineering (MS, PhD); geotechnical engineering (MS, PhD); mechanical engineering (ME, MS, PhD); operations and logistics (ME); quality and process (ME); research and development (ME); structural engineering (MS, PhD); telecommunications (ME, MS); water resources engineering (MS, PhD). *Application fee:* $50 ($60 for international students). Electronic applications accepted. *Dean,* Robert Davis, 303-492-7006, Fax: 303-492-0353, E-mail: robert.davis@colorado.edu.

College of Music Average age 30. 420 applicants, 32% accepted, 67 enrolled. Expenses: Contact institution. *Financial support:* In 2008–09, 118 fellowships (averaging $2,437 per year), 1 research assistantship (averaging $15,284 per year), 100 teaching assistantships (averaging $7,479 per year) were awarded; tuition waivers (full) also available. Financial award application deadline: 3/1. In 2008, 41 master's, 19 doctorates awarded. Offers church music (M Mus); composition (M Mus, D Mus A); conducting (M Mus, D Mus A); music education (M Mus Ed, PhD); music literature (M Mus); musicology (PhD); pedagogy (M Mus, D Mus A); performance (M Mus, D Mus A). *Application deadline:* For fall admission, 3/1 priority date for domestic students, 12/1 for international students. Applications are processed on a rolling basis. *Application fee:* $50 ($60 for international students). *Application Contact:* Application Contact, E-mail: gradmusc@colorado.edu.

School of Education Average age 33. 331 applicants, 49% accepted, 107 enrolled. Expenses: Contact institution. *Financial support:* In 2008–09, 65 fellowships (averaging $3,661 per year), 30 research assistantships (averaging $12,943 per year), 20 teaching assistantships (averaging $11,488 per year) were awarded; career-related internships or fieldwork, Federal Work-Study, scholarships/grants, and tuition waivers (full and partial) also available. Support available to part-time students. In 2008, 172 master's, 6 doctorates awarded. *Degree program information:* Part-time programs available. Offers education (MA, PhD); educational and psychological studies (MA, PhD); instruction and curriculum (MA, PhD); research and evaluation methodologies (PhD); social multicultural and bilingual foundations (MA, PhD). *Application deadline:* For fall admission, 2/1 priority date for domestic students, 12/1 for international students; for spring admission, 9/1 for domestic students, 12/1 for international students. *Application fee:* $50 ($60 for international students). *Application Contact:* Graduate Program Assistant, 303-492-6555, Fax: 303-492-5839, E-mail: edadvise@colorado.edu. *Dean,* Lorrie Shepard, 303-492-6937, Fax: 303-492-7090, E-mail: lorrie.shepard@colorado.edu.

School of Journalism and Mass Communication Average age 31. 167 applicants, 52% accepted, 43 enrolled. Expenses: Contact institution. *Financial support:* In 2008–09, 8 fellowships (averaging $3,350 per year), 19 research assistantships with tuition reimbursements (averaging $15,425 per year), 12 teaching assistantships (averaging $14,410 per year) were awarded; institutionally sponsored loans and unspecified assistantships also available. Financial award application deadline: 3/1. In 2008, 34 master's, 3 doctorates awarded. *Degree program information:* Part-time programs available. Offers communication (PhD); mass communication research (MA); media studies (PhD); newsgathering (MA). *Application deadline:* For fall admission, 2/15 for domestic students, 12/1 for international students. Applications are processed on a rolling basis. *Application fee:* $50 ($60 for international students). *Application Contact:* Application Contact, E-mail: sjmcgrad@colorado.edu.

Leeds School of Business Average age 30. 384 applicants, 53% accepted, 118 enrolled. Expenses: Contact institution. *Financial support:* In 2008–09, 81 fellowships (averaging

University of Colorado at Boulder (continued)

$5,422 per year), 37 research assistantships (averaging $16,608 per year), 18 teaching assistantships (averaging $10,715 per year) were awarded; career-related internships or fieldwork, Federal Work-Study, scholarships/grants, and unspecified assistantships also available. In 2008, 129 master's, 5 doctorates awarded. *Degree program information:* Part-time and evening/weekend programs available. Offers accounting (MS, PhD); business (MBA, MS, PhD); business administration (MBA, MS, PhD); finance (PhD); information systems (PhD); marketing (PhD); operations (PhD); strategic, organizational, and entrepreneurial studies (PhD). *Application deadline:* For fall admission, 3/1 priority date for domestic students, 3/1 for international students. Applications are processed on a rolling basis. *Application fee:* $50 ($60 for international students). Electronic applications accepted. *Application Contact:* Information Contact, 303-492-1809, Fax: 303-492-1727, E-mail: busgrad@spot.colorado.edu. *Dean,* Dennis Ahlburg, 303-492-1809, Fax: 303-492-7676, E-mail: dennis.ahlburg@colorado.edu.

School of Law Average age 27. 665 applicants, 100% accepted, 179 enrolled. Expenses: Contact institution. *Financial support:* Federal Work-Study and institutionally sponsored loans available. Financial award applicants required to submit FAFSA. In 2008, 177 degrees awarded. Offers law (JD). *Application deadline:* For fall admission, 2/15 for domestic students. Applications are processed on a rolling basis. *Application fee:* $50 ($60 for international students). *Application Contact:* Application Contact, E-mail: lawadmin@colorado.edu.

UNIVERSITY OF COLORADO AT COLORADO SPRINGS, Colorado Springs, CO 80933-7150

General Information State-supported, coed, comprehensive institution. *Enrollment:* 8,912 graduate, professional, and undergraduate students; 856 full-time matriculated graduate/professional students (527 women), 461 part-time matriculated graduate/professional students (253 women). *Enrollment by degree level:* 1,212 master's, 93 doctoral, 12 other advanced degrees. *Graduate faculty:* 278 full-time (137 women), 90 part-time/adjunct (48 women). *Graduate housing:* Room and/or apartments available on a first-come, first-served basis to single students; on-campus housing not available to married students. *Student services:* Campus employment opportunities, campus safety program, career counseling, child daycare facilities, exercise/wellness program, free psychological counseling, grant writing training, international student services, low-cost health insurance, multicultural affairs office, services for students with disabilities, teacher training, writing training. *Library facilities:* University of Colorado at Colorado Springs Kraemer Family Library. *Online resources:* library catalog, web page, access to other libraries' catalogs. *Collection:* 391,638 titles, 2,201 serial subscriptions. *Research affiliation:* Omegatech (genetics), Colorado Vintage Companies (radon mitigation), Symetrix (ferroelectronics).

Computer facilities: 250 computers available on campus for general student use. A campuswide network can be accessed from student residence rooms and from off campus. *Web address:* http://www.uccs.edu/.

General Application Contact: Michael Sanderson, Graduate Recruitment Coordinator, 719-255-3072, Fax: 719-255-3045, E-mail: michael.sanderson@uccs.edu.

GRADUATE UNITS

Graduate School Students: 856 full-time (527 women), 461 part-time (253 women); includes 195 minority (37 African Americans, 5 American Indian/Alaska Native, 53 Asian Americans or Pacific Islanders, 100 Hispanic Americans), 22 international. Average age 34. 738 applicants, 88% accepted, 398 enrolled. *Faculty:* 278 full-time (137 women), 90 part-time/adjunct (48 women). Expenses: Contact institution. *Financial support:* Fellowships, research assistantships, teaching assistantships, career-related internships or fieldwork, Federal Work-Study, and institutionally sponsored loans available. Support available to part-time students. Financial award applicants required to submit FAFSA. In 2008, 519 master's, 6 doctorates awarded. *Degree program information:* Part-time and evening/weekend programs available. Postbaccalaureate distance learning degree programs offered (no on-campus study). *Application deadline:* Applications are processed on a rolling basis. *Application fee:* $60 ($75 for international students). *Application Contact:* Michael Sanderson, Graduate Recruitment Coordinator, 719-255-3072, Fax: 719-255-3045, E-mail: michael.sanderson@uccs.edu. *Dean,* Dr. Janenne Nelson, 719-255-3779, Fax: 719-255-3417, E-mail: jnelson@uccs.edu.

Beth-El College of Nursing and Health Sciences Students: 121 full-time (107 women), 44 part-time (36 women); includes 22 minority (2 African Americans, 1 American Indian/Alaska Native, 4 Asian Americans or Pacific Islanders, 15 Hispanic Americans), 2 international. Average age 35. 66 applicants, 85% accepted, 49 enrolled. *Faculty:* 16 full-time (14 women), 12 part-time/adjunct (10 women). Expenses: Contact institution. *Financial support:* Fellowships, career-related internships or fieldwork, Federal Work-Study, and institutionally sponsored loans available. Support available to part-time students. In 2008, 24 master's awarded. *Degree program information:* Part-time programs available. Postbaccalaureate distance learning degree programs offered (minimal on-campus study). Offers adult health nurse practitioner and clinical specialist (MSN); family practitioner (MSN); gerontology (MSN); neonatal nurse practitioner and clinical specialist (MSN); nursing administration (MSN); nursing practice (DNP); women nurse practitioner (MSN). *Application deadline:* For fall admission, 6/1 priority date for domestic students; for spring admission, 11/15 for domestic students. *Application fee:* $60 ($75 for international students). Electronic applications accepted. *Application Contact:* Jackie Crouch, Graduate Recruitment Coordinator, 719-255-4493, Fax: 719-255-4416, E-mail: jcrouch@uccs.edu. *Dean,* Dr. Nancy Smith, 719-255-4411, Fax: 719-255-4416, E-mail: nsmith2@uccs.edu.

College of Education Students: 305 full-time (222 women), 106 part-time (90 women); includes 62 minority (13 African Americans, 2 American Indian/Alaska Native, 12 Asian Americans or Pacific Islanders, 35 Hispanic Americans). Average age 35. 91 applicants, 100% accepted, 62 enrolled. *Faculty:* 22 full-time (15 women), 29 part-time/adjunct (17 women). Expenses: Contact institution. *Financial support:* Fellowships, career-related internships or fieldwork and Federal Work-Study available. In 2008, 195 master's awarded. *Degree program information:* Part-time and evening/weekend programs available. Offers counseling and human services (MA); curriculum and instruction (MA); educational administration (MA); educational leadership (MA, PhD); special education (MA). *Application deadline:* For fall admission, 6/15 for domestic students; for spring admission, 10/15 for domestic students. Applications are processed on a rolling basis. *Application fee:* $60 ($75 for international students). *Application Contact:* Melissa Schecter, Student Services Manager, 719-255-4526, Fax: 719-255-4110, E-mail: mschedte@uccs.edu. *Dean,* Dr. LaVonne Neal, 719-262-4111, Fax: 719-262-4110, E-mail: lneal@uccs.edu.

College of Engineering and Applied Science Students: 84 full-time (15 women), 117 part-time (27 women); includes 36 minority (5 African Americans, 20 Asian Americans or Pacific Islanders, 11 Hispanic Americans), 16 international. Average age 33. 73 applicants, 96% accepted, 54 enrolled. *Faculty:* 37 full-time (1 woman), 7 part-time/adjunct (2 women). Expenses: Contact institution. *Financial support:* Fellowships, research assistantships, teaching assistantships, career-related internships or fieldwork and Federal Work-Study available. In 2008, 41 master's, 4 doctorates awarded. *Degree program information:* Part-time and evening/weekend programs available. Offers computer science (MS); electrical engineering (MS, PhD); engineering (PhD); engineering and applied science (ME, MS, PhD); engineering management (ME); information operations (ME); manufacturing (ME); mechanical engineering (MS); software engineering (ME); space operations (ME); space systems (MS). *Application deadline:* For fall admission, 5/1 for domestic students; for spring admission, 10/1 for domestic students. Applications are processed on a rolling basis. *Application fee:* $60 ($75 for international students). *Application Contact:* Tina Moore, Director, Office of Student Support, 719-255-3347, E-mail: tmoore@uccs.edu. *Dean,* Dr. Ramaswami Dandapani, 719-255-3543, Fax: 719-255-3542, E-mail: rdan@cas.uccs.edu.

College of Letters, Arts and Sciences Students: 147 full-time (90 women), 80 part-time (43 women); includes 36 minority (10 African Americans, 2 American Indian/Alaska Native, 6 Asian Americans or Pacific Islanders, 18 Hispanic Americans), 2 international. Average age 33. 339 applicants, 96% accepted, 248 enrolled. *Faculty:* 141 full-time (77 women), 51 part-time/adjunct (31 women). Expenses: Contact institution. *Financial support:* Fellowships, research assistantships, teaching assistantships, career-related internships or fieldwork, Federal Work-Study, and institutionally sponsored loans available. Support available to part-time students. Financial award applicants required to submit FAFSA. In 2008, 309 master's, 6 doctorates awarded. *Degree program information:* Part-time and evening/weekend programs available. Offers applied mathematics (MS); biology (M Sc); chemistry (M Sc); communications (MA); geography and environmental studies (MA); history (MA); letters, arts and sciences (M Sc, MA, MS, PhD); mathematics (M Sc); physics (M Sc); psychology (MA, PhD); sociology (MA). *Application deadline:* Applications are processed on a rolling basis. *Application Contact:* Information Contact, 719-255-3417, Fax: 719-255-3045, E-mail: gradschl@uocs.edu. *Dean,* Dr. Tom Christensen, 719-255-4550, Fax: 719-255-4200, E-mail: tchriste@uccs.edu.

Graduate School of Business Administration Students: 156 full-time (70 women), 82 part-time (39 women); includes 30 minority (7 African Americans, 9 Asian Americans or Pacific Islanders, 14 Hispanic Americans), 2 international. Average age 33. 126 applicants, 94% accepted, 65 enrolled. *Faculty:* 15 full-time (4 women), 4 part-time/adjunct (0 women). Expenses: Contact institution. *Financial support:* Career-related internships or fieldwork, Federal Work-Study, and institutionally sponsored loans available. Support available to part-time students. Financial award applicants required to submit FAFSA. In 2008, 152 master's awarded. *Degree program information:* Part-time and evening/weekend programs available. Offers accounting (MBA); finance (MBA); general health care administration (MBA); information systems (MBA); international business management (MBA); marketing (MBA); service management/technology management (MBA). *Application deadline:* For fall admission, 6/1 for domestic students; for spring admission, 11/1 for domestic students. *Application fee:* $60 ($75 for international students). *Application Contact:* Windy Haddad, MBA Program Director, 719-255-3401, Fax: 719-255-3100, E-mail: whaddad@uccs.edu. *Dean,* Dr. Venkateshwar Reddy, 719-255-3113, Fax: 719-255-3100, E-mail: vreddy@uccs.edu.

Graduate School of Public Affairs Students: 40 full-time (23 women), 38 part-time (23 women); includes 10 minority (2 Asian Americans or Pacific Islanders, 8 Hispanic Americans). Average age 35. 34 applicants, 91% accepted, 24 enrolled. *Faculty:* 3 full-time (1 woman), 25 part-time/adjunct (15 women). Expenses: Contact institution. *Financial support:* Career-related internships or fieldwork and Federal Work-Study available. Support available to part-time students. In 2008, 32 master's awarded. *Degree program information:* Part-time and evening/weekend programs available. Offers criminal justice (MCJ); public administration (MPA). *Application deadline:* For fall admission, 6/1 priority date for domestic students; for spring admission, 11/1 for domestic students. Applications are processed on a rolling basis. *Application fee:* $60 ($75 for international students). *Application Contact:* Mary Lou Kartis, Program Assistant, 719-255-4182, Fax: 719-255-4183, E-mail: mkartis@uccs.edu. *Dean,* Dr. Terry Schwartz, 719-255-4047, Fax: 719-255-4183, E-mail: tschwart@uccs.edu.

UNIVERSITY OF COLORADO DENVER, Denver, CO 80217-3364

General Information State-supported, coed, university. CGS member. *Enrollment:* 21,903 graduate, professional, and undergraduate students; 3,612 full-time matriculated graduate/professional students (2,145 women), 2,857 part-time matriculated graduate/professional students (1,619 women). *Enrollment by degree level:* 1,377 first professional, 4,243 master's, 694 doctoral, 155 other advanced degrees. *Graduate faculty:* 2,474 full-time (1,199 women), 788 part-time/adjunct (430 women). *Graduate housing:* On-campus housing not available. *Student services:* Campus employment opportunities, campus safety program, career counseling, child daycare facilities, exercise/wellness program, free psychological counseling, international student services, low-cost health insurance, services for students with disabilities, teacher training, writing training. *Online resources:* library catalog, web page, access to other libraries' catalogs. *Research affiliation:* The Children's Hospital (genetic counseling), National Jewish Center (immunology, molecular biology).

Computer facilities: 750 computers available on campus for general student use. A campuswide network can be accessed from student residence rooms and from off campus. Online class registration is available. *Web address:* http://www.cudenver.edu/.

General Application Contact: Graduate School Admissions, 303-556-2400, E-mail: admissions@ucdenver.edu.

GRADUATE UNITS

Business School Students: 278 full-time (129 women), 822 part-time (314 women); includes 158 minority (23 African Americans, 6 American Indian/Alaska Native, 79 Asian Americans or Pacific Islanders, 50 Hispanic Americans), 116 international. Average age 31. 647 applicants, 66% accepted, 238 enrolled. *Faculty:* 62 full-time (22 women), 17 part-time/adjunct (5 women). Expenses: Contact institution. *Financial support:* Research assistantships, career-related internships or fieldwork, Federal Work-Study, institutionally sponsored loans, scholarships/grants, traineeships, and tuition waivers (partial) available. Support available to part-time students. Financial award application deadline: 4/1; financial award applicants required to submit FAFSA. In 2008, 435 master's, 2 doctorates awarded. *Degree program information:* Part-time and evening/weekend programs available. Postbaccalaureate distance learning degree programs offered (minimal on-campus study). Offers accounting (MS); business (MBA, MS, MSIB, PhD); business administration (MBA); computer science and information systems (PhD); finance (MS); health administration (MS); information systems (MS); international business (MSIB); management and organization (MS); marketing (MS). *Application deadline:* For fall admission, 6/1 for domestic students, 3/15 for international students; for spring admission, 11/1 for domestic students, 10/1 for international students. Applications are processed on a rolling basis. *Application fee:* $50 ($75 for international students). Electronic applications accepted. *Application Contact:* Shelly Townley, Admissions Coordinator, 303-556-5956, Fax: 303-556-5904, E-mail: shelly.townley@ucdenver.edu. *Dean,* Dr. Sueann Ambron, 303-556-5802, Fax: 303-556-5914, E-mail: sueann.ambron@ucdenver.edu.

College of Architecture and Planning Students: 431 full-time (188 women), 95 part-time (46 women); includes 43 minority (7 African Americans, 1 American Indian/Alaska Native, 16 Asian Americans or Pacific Islanders, 19 Hispanic Americans), 44 international. Average age 31. 441 applicants, 79% accepted, 157 enrolled. *Faculty:* 45 full-time (13 women), 34 part-time/adjunct (5 women). Expenses: Contact institution. *Financial support:* Fellowships with partial tuition reimbursements, research assistantships, teaching assistantships, career-related internships or fieldwork, Federal Work-Study, institutionally sponsored loans, scholarships/grants, and tuition waivers (full and partial) available. Support available to part-time students. Financial award application deadline: 4/1; financial award applicants required to submit FAFSA. In 2008, 180 master's, 3 doctorates awarded. *Degree program information:* Part-time programs available. Offers architecture (M Arch); architecture and planning (M Arch, MLA, MUD, MURP, PhD); design and planning (PhD); landscape architecture (MLA); urban and regional planning (MURP); urban design (MUD). *Application deadline:* For fall admission, 3/15 for domestic students; for spring admission, 10/1 for domestic students. *Application fee:* $50 ($75 for international students). *Application Contact:* Heather Zertuche, Administrative Assistant II, 303-556-3382, Fax: 303-556-3687, E-mail: anpdeansoffice@storm.cudenver.edu. *Dean,* Mark Gelernter, 303-556-5938, Fax: 303-556-3687, E-mail: mark.gelernter@ucdenver.edu.

College of Arts and Media Students: 3 full-time (0 women), 8 part-time (1 woman); includes 2 minority (1 African American, 1 Hispanic American). Average age 33. 12 applicants, 92% accepted, 8 enrolled. *Faculty:* 34 full-time (9 women), 3 part-time/adjunct (1 woman). Expenses: Contact institution. *Financial support:* Federal Work-Study, institutionally sponsored loans, and scholarships/grants available. Support available to part-time students. Financial award application deadline: 4/1; financial award applicants required to submit FAFSA. In 2008, 3 master's awarded. *Degree program information:* Part-time and evening/weekend programs available. Postbaccalaureate distance learning degree programs offered. Offers arts and media (MS); recording arts (MS). *Application deadline:* For fall admission, 2/15 for domestic students; for spring admission, 11/1 for domestic students. Applications are processed on a rolling basis. *Application fee:* $50 ($75 for international students). Electronic applications accepted. *Application Contact:* Clark Strickland, Assistant Dean for Programs and Resources, 303-556-2279, Fax: 303-556-2335, E-mail: Clark.Strickland.cudenver.edu. *Dean,* Dr. David Dynak, 303-556-2279, Fax: 303-556-2335, E-mail: david.dynak@cudenver.edu.

College of Engineering and Applied Science Students: 63 full-time (11 women), 282 part-time (65 women); includes 47 minority (13 African Americans, 2 American Indian/Alaska Native, 21 Asian Americans or Pacific Islanders, 11 Hispanic Americans), 25 international.

Average age 31. 430 applicants, 64% accepted, 114 enrolled. *Faculty:* 38 full-time (3 women), 17 part-time/adjunct (1 woman). Expenses: Contact institution. *Financial support:* Research assistantships, teaching assistantships, career-related internships or fieldwork and Federal Work-Study available. Financial award application deadline: 4/1; financial award applicants required to submit FAFSA. In 2008, 95 master's, 5 doctorates awarded. *Degree program information:* Part-time and evening/weekend programs available. Offers civil engineering (MS, PhD); computer science and engineering (MS); computer science and information systems (PhD); electrical engineering (M Eng, MS); engineering and applied science (M Eng, MS, PhD); geographic information systems (M Eng); mechanical engineering (M Eng, MS). *Application deadline:* For fall admission, 4/1 for domestic students; for spring admission, 10/1 for domestic students. Applications are processed on a rolling basis. *Application fee:* $50 ($75 for international students). Electronic applications accepted. *Application Contact:* Dr. Paul Rakowski, Assistant Dean of Student Services, 303-556-6771, Fax: 303-556-2511, E-mail: paul.rakowski@ucdenver.edu. *Assistant Dean of Student Services,* Dr. Paul Rakowski, 303-556-6771, Fax: 303-556-2511, E-mail: paul.rakowski@ucdenver.edu.

College of Liberal Arts and Sciences Students: 185 full-time (106 women), 459 part-time (271 women); includes 90 minority (16 African Americans, 5 American Indian/Alaska Native, 27 Asian Americans or Pacific Islanders, 42 Hispanic Americans), 60 international. Average age 33. 520 applicants, 58% accepted, 185 enrolled. *Faculty:* 197 full-time (82 women), 30 part-time/adjunct (17 women). Expenses: Contact institution. *Financial support:* Fellowships, research assistantships, teaching assistantships, career-related internships or fieldwork and Federal Work-Study available. Financial award application deadline: 4/1; financial award applicants required to submit FAFSA. In 2008, 172 master's, 3 doctorates awarded. *Degree program information:* Part-time and evening/weekend programs available. Offers anthropology (MA); applied linguistics (MA); applied mathematics (MS, PhD); applied science (MIS); biology (MS); chemistry (MS); clinical health psychology (PhD); communication (MA); computer science (MIS); economics (MA); English studies (MA); environmental sciences (MS); health and behavioral sciences (PhD); history (MA); humanities (MH); liberal arts and sciences (MA, MH, MIS, MS, MSS, PhD, Certificate); literature (MA); mathematics (MIS); political science (MA); psychology (PhD); social science (MSS); sociology (MA); Spanish (MA); teaching English to speakers of other languages (Certificate); teaching of writing (MA); technical communication (MS). *Application deadline:* Applications are processed on a rolling basis. *Application fee:* $50 ($75 for international students). Electronic applications accepted. *Application Contact:* Dr. Brenda Allen, Associate Dean of Student Affairs, 303-556-6713, E-mail: Brenda.J.Allen@ucdenver.edu. *Dean,* Dr. Daniel Howard, 303-556-2557, Fax: 303-556-4861, E-mail: Dan.Howard@ucdenver.edu.

College of Nursing Students: 190 full-time (182 women), 46 part-time (38 women); includes 27 minority (7 African Americans, 4 American Indian/Alaska Native, 3 Asian Americans or Pacific Islanders, 13 Hispanic Americans), 3 international. Average age 38. *Faculty:* 65 full-time (63 women), 57 part-time/adjunct (52 women). Expenses: Contact institution. *Financial support:* Fellowships, research assistantships, teaching assistantships, career-related internships or fieldwork, Federal Work-Study, and institutionally sponsored loans available. Support available to part-time students. Financial award application deadline: 3/15; financial award applicants required to submit FAFSA. In 2008, 112 master's, 10 doctorates awarded. *Degree program information:* Part-time programs available. Offers nursing (MS, DNP, PhD, Post Master's Certificate); nursing practice (DNP). *Application deadline:* For fall admission, 5/1 priority date for domestic students; for spring admission, 10/1 for domestic students. *Application fee:* $65. *Application Contact:* Dr. Patricia Moritz, Dean, 303-724-1679, E-mail: Pat.Moritz@UCDenver.edu. *Dean,* Dr. Patricia Moritz, 303-724-1679, E-mail: Pat.Moritz@UCDenver.edu.

Colorado School of Public Health Students: 124 full-time (82 women), 26 part-time (16 women); includes 23 minority (6 African Americans, 2 American Indian/Alaska Native, 7 Asian Americans or Pacific Islanders, 8 Hispanic Americans), 6 international. Average age 34. *Faculty:* 45 full-time (31 women), 20 part-time/adjunct (8 women). Expenses: Contact institution. In 2008, 6 master's, 11 doctorates awarded. Offers analytic health sciences (PhD); analytical health sciences (PhD); bioInformatics (PhD); biostatistics (MS); epidemiology (PhD); health services research (PhD); public health (MPH, MS, PhD). *Application Contact:* Information Contact, 303-724-4613, E-mail: Colorado.SPH@ucdenver.edu.

Graduate School of Public Affairs Students: 65 full-time (38 women), 267 part-time (162 women); includes 55 minority (17 African Americans, 1 American Indian/Alaska Native, 7 Asian Americans or Pacific Islanders, 30 Hispanic Americans), 30 international. Average age 35. 246 applicants, 70% accepted, 79 enrolled. *Faculty:* 24 full-time (12 women), 25 part-time/adjunct (12 women). Expenses: Contact institution. *Financial support:* Fellowships with partial tuition reimbursements, research assistantships with partial tuition reimbursements, teaching assistantships with partial tuition reimbursements, career-related internships or fieldwork, Federal Work-Study, institutionally sponsored loans, and scholarships/grants available. Support available to part-time students. Financial award application deadline: 4/1; financial award applicants required to submit FAFSA. In 2008, 149 master's, 4 doctorates awarded. *Degree program information:* Part-time and evening/weekend programs available. Postbaccalaureate distance learning degree programs offered. Offers criminal justice (MCJ); public administration (MPA); public affairs (MCJ, MPA, PhD). *Application fee:* $50 ($60 for international students). *Application Contact:* Antoinette Sandoval, Student Service Specialist, 303-315-2487, Fax: 303-315-2229, E-mail: antoinette.sandoval@ucdenver.edu. *Dean,* Paul Teske, 303-315-2805, Fax: 303-315-2229, E-mail: Paul.Teske@ucdenver.edu.

School of Dental Medicine Students: 200 full-time (80 women); includes 25 minority (20 Asian Americans or Pacific Islanders, 5 Hispanic Americans). Average age 27. *Faculty:* 67 full-time (20 women), 13 part-time/adjunct (4 women). Expenses: Contact institution. *Financial support:* Federal Work-Study and institutionally sponsored loans available. Financial award application deadline: 3/15; financial award applicants required to submit FAFSA. In 2008, 67 DDSs awarded. Offers dental medicine (DDS). *Application deadline:* For fall admission, 1/1 for domestic students, 3/31 for international students. *Application fee:* $50 ($125 for international students). *Application Contact:* Dr. Randy L. Kluender, Assistant Dean for Admissions and Student Affairs, 303-724-7124, E-mail: Randy.Kluender@UCDenver.edu. *Dean,* Dr. Denise K. Kassebaum, 303-724-7100, Fax: 303-724-7109, E-mail: Denise.Kassebaum@ucdenver.edu.

School of Education and Human Development Students: 434 full-time (349 women), 813 part-time (678 women); includes 163 minority (28 African Americans, 6 American Indian/Alaska Native, 38 Asian Americans or Pacific Islanders, 91 Hispanic Americans), 65 international. Average age 34. 492 applicants, 77% accepted, 222 enrolled. *Faculty:* 59 full-time (44 women), 98 part-time/adjunct (80 women). Expenses: Contact institution. *Financial support:* Fellowships, research assistantships, teaching assistantships, Federal Work-Study, institutionally sponsored loans, and scholarships/grants available. Support available to part-time students. Financial award application deadline: 4/1; financial award applicants required to submit FAFSA. In 2008, 419 master's, 13 doctorates, 35 other advanced degrees awarded. *Degree program information:* Part-time and evening/weekend programs available. Offers administrative leadership and professional studies (MA, Ed S); counseling psychology and counselor education (MA); curriculum and instruction (MA); early childhood education (MA); education and human development (MA, PhD, Ed S); educational leadership and innovation (PhD); information and learning technologies (MA). *Application deadline:* For fall admission, 4/15 for domestic students; for spring admission, 9/15 for domestic students. Applications are processed on a rolling basis. *Application fee:* $50 ($75 for international students). Electronic applications accepted. *Application Contact:* Lori Sisneros, Student Services Coordinator, 303-315-4979, Fax: 303-315-6311, E-mail: lori.sisneros@ucdenver.edu. *Dean,* Lynn K Rhodes, 303-315-6345, E-mail: lynn.rhodes@ucdenver.edu.

School of Medicine Students: 1,197 full-time (710 women), 34 part-time (25 women); includes 169 minority (19 African Americans, 9 American Indian/Alaska Native, 84 Asian Americans or Pacific Islanders, 57 Hispanic Americans), 31 international. Average age 28. *Faculty:* 1,708 full-time (856 women), 420 part-time/adjunct (210 women). Expenses: Contact institution. *Financial support:* Fellowships, research assistantships, teaching assistantships, career-related internships or fieldwork, Federal Work-Study, and institutionally sponsored loans available. Support available to part-time students. Financial award application deadline: 3/15; financial award applicants required to submit FAFSA. In 2008, 186 first professional degrees, 83 master's, 41 doctorates awarded. Offers child health associate/physician assistant (MPAS); medicine (MD, MPAS, MS, DPT, PhD); physical therapy (DPT). *Application deadline:* For fall admission, 11/1 for domestic students. *Application fee:* $100. *Application Contact:* Dr. Norma Wagoner, Associate Dean for Admissions, 303-724-8025, E-mail: somadmin@ucdenver.edu. *Dean,* Dr. Richard Krugman, 303-724-0882.

Programs in Biomedical Sciences Students: 316 full-time (184 women), 9 part-time (7 women); includes 36 minority (3 African Americans, 1 American Indian/Alaska Native, 18 Asian Americans or Pacific Islanders, 14 Hispanic Americans), 29 international. Expenses: Contact institution. *Financial support:* Fellowships, research assistantships, teaching assistantships, career-related internships or fieldwork, Federal Work-Study, institutionally sponsored loans, and traineeships available. Support available to part-time students. Financial award applicants required to submit FAFSA. In 2008, 17 master's, 41 doctorates awarded. Offers biochemistry and molecular genetics (PhD); biomedical sciences (MS, PhD); biomolecular structure (PhD); biophysics and genetics (MS, PhD); cancer biology (PhD); cell and developmental biology (PhD); cell biology, stem cells and development (PhD); clinical science (MS, PhD); immunology (PhD); microbiology (PhD); microbiology and immunology (PhD); molecular biology (PhD); neuroscience (PhD); pathology (PhD); pharmacology (PhD); physiology (PhD); reproductive sciences (PhD). *Application fee:* $50. *Application Contact:* Gary Brown, Program Administrator, 303-724-3700, E-mail: Gary.Brown@ucdenver.edu. *Director,* Dr. Steven Anderson, 303-724-3742, Fax: 303-724-3712, E-mail: steve.anderson@ucdenver.edu.

School of Pharmacy Students: 442 full-time (270 women), 5 part-time (3 women); includes 122 minority (33 African Americans, 3 American Indian/Alaska Native, 61 Asian Americans or Pacific Islanders, 25 Hispanic Americans), 18 international. Average age 29. *Faculty:* 92 full-time (38 women), 50 part-time/adjunct (35 women). Expenses: Contact institution. *Financial support:* Fellowships, research assistantships, teaching assistantships, career-related internships or fieldwork, Federal Work-Study, and institutionally sponsored loans available. Support available to part-time students. Financial award application deadline: 3/15; financial award applicants required to submit FAFSA. In 2008, 170 first professional degrees, 6 doctorates awarded. Offers pharmaceutical sciences (PhD); pharmacy (Pharm D, PhD); toxicology (PhD). *Application deadline:* For fall admission, 12/1 for domestic students. *Application fee:* $50. *Application Contact:* Beverly Brunson, Director, 303-724-2881, E-mail: Beverly.Brunson@UCDenver.edu. *Dean,* Ralpha Altiere, 303-724-2631, E-mail: Ralph.Altiere@UCDenver.edu.

UNIVERSITY OF CONNECTICUT, Storrs, CT 06269

General Information State-supported, coed, university. CGS member. *Enrollment:* 24,273 graduate, professional, and undergraduate students; 3,839 full-time matriculated graduate/professional students (2,089 women), 2,284 part-time matriculated graduate/professional students (1,116 women). *Enrollment by degree level:* 3,659 master's, 2,220 doctoral, 244 other advanced degrees. *Graduate faculty:* 1,330 full-time (438 women). Tuition, state resident: full-time $4455; part-time $495 per credit. Tuition, nonresident: full-time $11,565; part-time $1285 per credit. *Required fees:* $842 per semester. *Graduate housing:* Rooms and/or apartments available on a first-come, first-served basis to single and married students. Housing application deadline: 4/1. *Student services:* Campus employment opportunities, campus safety program, career counseling, exercise/wellness program, free psychological counseling, grant writing training, international student services, low-cost health insurance, multicultural affairs office, services for students with disabilities, teacher training, writing training. *Library facilities:* Homer Babbidge Library plus 3 others. *Online resources:* library catalog, web page, access to other libraries' catalogs. *Collection:* 3 million titles, 17,378 serial subscriptions, 61,417 audiovisual materials. *Research affiliation:* U.S. Navy–Submarine Medical Research Laboratory, Haskins Laboratories.

Computer facilities: Computer purchase and lease plans are available. 1,318 computers available on campus for general student use. A campuswide network can be accessed from student residence rooms and from off campus. Online class registration is available. *Web address:* http://www.uconn.edu/.

General Application Contact: Anne K. Lanzit, Associate Director of Graduate Admissions, 860-486-3617, Fax: 860-486-6739, E-mail: anne.lanzit@uconn.edu.

GRADUATE UNITS

Graduate School Students: 3,839 full-time (2,089 women), 2,284 part-time (1,116 women); includes 821 minority (281 African Americans, 13 American Indian/Alaska Native, 271 Asian Americans or Pacific Islanders, 256 Hispanic Americans), 1,270 international. Average age 30. 8,341 applicants, 19% accepted, 1047 enrolled. *Faculty:* 1,330 full-time (438 women). Expenses: Contact institution. *Financial support:* In 2008–09, 1,537 research assistantships with full tuition reimbursements, 1,106 teaching assistantships with full tuition reimbursements were awarded; fellowships, career-related internships or fieldwork and Federal Work-Study also available. Financial award application deadline: 2/1; financial award applicants required to submit FAFSA. In 2008, 1,482 master's, 270 doctorates, 111 other advanced degrees awarded. *Degree program information:* Part-time and evening/weekend programs available. Postbaccalaureate distance learning degree programs offered (minimal on-campus study). *Application deadline:* For fall admission, 2/1 priority date for domestic and international students; for spring admission, 11/1 for domestic students, 10/1 for international students. Applications are processed on a rolling basis. *Application fee:* $55. Electronic applications accepted. *Application Contact:* Anne K. Lanzit, Associate Director of Graduate Admissions, 860-486-3617, Fax: 860-486-6739, E-mail: anne.lanzit@uconn.edu. *Dean and Vice President, Research and Graduate Education,* Suman Singha, 860-486-3619, Fax: 860-486-5381, E-mail: suman.singha@uconn.edu.

Center for Continuing Studies Students: 3 full-time (all women), 99 part-time (57 women); includes 18 minority (8 African Americans, 1 American Indian/Alaska Native, 9 Hispanic Americans), 1 international. Average age 36. 46 applicants, 50% accepted, 23 enrolled. Expenses: Contact institution. In 2008, 22 master's awarded. Postbaccalaureate distance learning degree programs offered. Offers continuing studies (MPS); homeland security leadership (MPS); humanitarian services administration (MPS); labor relations (MPS); occupational safety and health management (MPS); personnel (MPS). *Application Contact:* Peter Diplock, Information Contact, 860-486-2915, E-mail: peter.diplock@uconn.edu. *Director,* Susan W. Nesbitt, 860-486-5941.

College of Agriculture and Natural Resources Students: 175 full-time (85 women), 42 part-time (25 women); includes 20 minority (5 African Americans, 1 American Indian/Alaska Native, 8 Asian Americans or Pacific Islanders, 6 Hispanic Americans), 79 international. Average age 30. 194 applicants, 29% accepted, 37 enrolled. *Faculty:* 101 full-time (29 women). Expenses: Contact institution. *Financial support:* In 2008–09, 137 research assistantships with full tuition reimbursements, 25 teaching assistantships with full tuition reimbursements were awarded; fellowships, Federal Work-Study, scholarships/grants, health care benefits, and unspecified assistantships also available. Financial award application deadline: 2/1; financial award applicants required to submit FAFSA. In 2008, 42 master's, 15 doctorates awarded. Offers agricultural and resource economics (MS, PhD); agriculture and natural resources (MS, PhD); allied health sciences (MS); animal science (MS, PhD); natural resources management and engineering (MS, PhD); nutritional sciencespathobiology (MS, PhD); plant and soil sciences (MS, PhD). *Application deadline:* For fall admission, 2/1 priority date for domestic and international students; for spring admission, 11/1 for domestic students, 10/1 for international students. Applications are processed on a rolling basis. *Application fee:* $55. Electronic applications accepted. *Application Contact:* Kirklyn M. Kerr, Dean, 860-486-2917, Fax: 860-486-5113, E-mail: kirklyn.ker@uconn.edu. *Dean,* Kirklyn M. Kerr, 860-486-2917, Fax: 860-486-5113, E-mail: kirklyn.ker@uconn.edu.

College of Liberal Arts and Sciences Students: 1,616 full-time (868 women), 325 part-time (160 women); includes 219 minority (78 African Americans, 4 American Indian/Alaska Native, 66 Asian Americans or Pacific Islanders, 71 Hispanic Americans), 548 international. Average age 29. 3,614 applicants, 15% accepted, 319 enrolled. *Faculty:* 660 full-time (225 women). Expenses: Contact institution. *Financial support:* In 2008–09, 488 research assistantships with full tuition reimbursements, 935 teaching assistantships with full tuition reimbursements were awarded; fellowships, career-related internships or fieldwork, Federal Work-Study, scholarships/grants, health care benefits, and unspecified assistantships also available. Financial award application deadline: 2/1; financial award applicants required to submit FAFSA. In 2008, 301 master's, 132 doctorates, 37 other advanced degrees awarded. Offers actuarial science (MS, PhD); African studies (MA); anthropology (MA, PhD); applied

University of Connecticut (continued)

financial mathematics (MS); applied genomics (MS, PSM); audiology (Au D, PhD); behavioral neuroscience (PhD); biobehavioral science (PhD); biochemistry (MS, PhD); biophysics and structural biology (MS, PhD); biopsychology (PhD); biotechnology (MS); botany (MS, PhD); cell and developmental biology (MS, PhD); chemistry (MS, PhD); clinical psychology (MA, PhD); cognition and instruction (PhD); communication processes (MA); communication processes and marketing communication (PhD); comparative literature and cultural studies (MA, PhD); comparative physiology (MS, PhD); culture, health and human development (Graduate Certificate); developmental psychology (MA, PhD); ecological psychology (PhD); ecology (MS, PhD); economics (MA, PhD); endocrinology (MS, PhD); English (MA, PhD); entomology (MS, PhD); European studies (MA); experimental psychology (PhD); French (MA, PhD); general psychology (MA, PhD); genetics (MS, PhD); genetics, genomics, and bioinformatics (MS, PhD); geographic information systems (Certificate); geography (MS, PhD); geological sciences (MS, PhD); German (MA, PhD); health psychology (Graduate Certificate); history (MA, PhD); human development and family studies (MA, PhD); industrial/organizational psychology (PhD); international studies (MA, Graduate Certificate); Italian (MA, PhD); Italian history and culture (MA); Judaic studies (MA); language and cognition (PhD); Latin American studies (MA); liberal arts and sciences (MA, MPA, MS, PSM, Au D, PhD, Certificate, Graduate Certificate); linguistics (MA, PhD); marine sciences (MS, PhD); mathematics (MS, PhD); medieval studies (MA, PhD); microbial systems analysis (MS, PSM); microbiology (MS, PhD); neurobiology (MS, PhD); neuroscience (PhD); nonprofit management (Graduate Certificate); occupational health psychology (Graduate Certificate); philosophy (MA, PhD); physics (MS, PhD); plant cell and molecular biology (MS, PhD); political science (MA, PhD); public administration (MPA, Graduate Certificate); public financial management (Graduate Certificate); quantitative research methods (Graduate Certificate); social psychology (MA, PhD); sociology (MA, PhD); Spanish (MA, PhD); speech-language pathology (MA, PhD); statistics (MS, PhD); survey research (MA, Graduate Certificate); zoology (MS, PhD). *Application deadline:* For fall admission, 2/1 priority date for domestic and international students; for spring admission, 11/1 for domestic students, 10/1 for international students. Applications are processed on a rolling basis. *Application fee:* $55. Electronic applications accepted. *Application Contact:* Ross D. MacKinnon, Dean, 860-486-2713, Fax: 860-486-0304. *Dean,* Ross D. MacKinnon, 860-486-2713, Fax: 860-486-0304.

Neag School of Education Students: 497 full-time (365 women), 346 part-time (235 women); includes 96 minority (27 African Americans, 2 American Indian/Alaska Native, 27 Asian Americans or Pacific Islanders, 40 Hispanic Americans), 33 international. Average age 31. 1,011 applicants, 21% accepted, 143 enrolled. *Faculty:* 86 full-time (44 women). Expenses: Contact institution. *Financial support:* In 2008–09, 199 research assistantships with full tuition reimbursements, 28 teaching assistantships with full tuition reimbursements were awarded; fellowships, Federal Work-Study, scholarships/grants, health care benefits, and unspecified assistantships also available. Financial award application deadline: 2/1; financial award applicants required to submit FAFSA. In 2008, 307 master's, 32 doctorates, 71 other advanced degrees awarded. Offers adult learning (MA, PhD); agriculture (MA); bilingual and bicultural education (MA, PhD, Post-Master's Certificate); cognition and instruction (MA, PhD, Post-Master's Certificate); counseling psychology (MA, PhD, Post-Master's Certificate); education (MA, DPT, Ed D, PhD, Post-Master's Certificate); education policy analysis (PhD); educational administration (Ed D, PhD, Post-Master's Certificate); elementary education (MA, PhD, Post-Master's Certificate); English education (MA, PhD, Post-Master's Certificate); exercise science (MA, PhD); gifted and talented education (MA, PhD, Post-Master's Certificate); higher education and student affairs (MA); history and social sciences education (MA, PhD, Post-Master's Certificate); learning technology (MA, PhD, Post-Master's Certificate); mathematics education (MA, PhD, Post-Master's Certificate); measurement, evaluation, and assessment (MA, PhD, Post-Master's Certificate); physical therapy (DPT); reading education (MA, PhD, Post-Master's Certificate); school counseling (MA, Post-Master's Certificate); school psychology (MA, PhD, Post-Master's Certificate); science education (MA, PhD); secondary education (MA, PhD, Post-Master's Certificate); special education (MA, PhD, Post-Master's Certificate); sport management and sociology (MA, PhD); world languages education (PhD). *Application deadline:* For fall admission, 2/1 priority date for domestic and international students; for spring admission, 11/1 for domestic students, 10/1 for international students. Applications are processed on a rolling basis. *Application fee:* $55. Electronic applications accepted. *Application Contact:* Thomas DeFranco, Chairperson, 860-486-3815, Fax: 860-486-0210, E-mail: thomas.defranco@uconn.edu. *Dean,* Richard L. Schwab, 860-486-3815, Fax: 860-486-0210, E-mail: richard.schwab@uconn.edu.

School of Business Students: 379 full-time (138 women), 945 part-time (343 women); includes 178 minority (44 African Americans, 2 American Indian/Alaska Native, 92 Asian Americans or Pacific Islanders, 40 Hispanic Americans), 170 international. Average age 31. 887 applicants, 25% accepted, 210 enrolled. *Faculty:* 76 full-time (14 women). Expenses: Contact institution. *Financial support:* In 2008–09, 129 research assistantships with full tuition reimbursements, 3 teaching assistantships with full tuition reimbursements were awarded; fellowships, career-related internships or fieldwork, Federal Work-Study, scholarships/grants, health care benefits, and unspecified assistantships also available. Financial award application deadline: 2/1; financial award applicants required to submit FAFSA. In 2008, 461 master's, 8 doctorates awarded. Offers accounting (MS, PhD); business administration (Exec MBA, MBA, PhD); finance (PhD); health care management and insurance studies (MBA); management (PhD); management consulting (MBA); marketing (PhD); marketing intelligence (MBA). *Application deadline:* For fall admission, 2/1 priority date for domestic and international students; for spring admission, 11/1 for domestic students, 10/1 for international students. Applications are processed on a rolling basis. Electronic applications accepted. *Application Contact:* Richard Dino, Admissions Chairperson, 860-486-4483, E-mail: rich.dino@uconn.edu. *Dean,* P. Christopher Earley, 860-486-2317, Fax: 860-846-0889, E-mail: paul.earley@uconn.edu.

School of Engineering Students: 446 full-time (114 women), 157 part-time (32 women); includes 60 minority (17 African Americans, 24 Asian Americans or Pacific Islanders, 19 Hispanic Americans), 319 international. Average age 28. 1,248 applicants, 16% accepted, 115 enrolled. *Faculty:* 184 full-time (24 women). Expenses: Contact institution. *Financial support:* In 2008–09, 351 research assistantships with full tuition reimbursements, 51 teaching assistantships with full tuition reimbursements were awarded; fellowships, career-related internships or fieldwork, Federal Work-Study, scholarships/grants, health care benefits, and unspecified assistantships also available. Financial award application deadline: 2/1; financial award applicants required to submit FAFSA. In 2008, 79 master's, 41 doctorates awarded. Offers biomedical engineering (MS, PhD); chemical engineering (MS, PhD); civil engineering (MS, PhD); computer science (MS, PhD); electrical engineering (MS, PhD); engineering (M Eng, MS, PhD); environmental engineering (MS, PhD); materials science and engineering (MS, PhD); mechanical engineering (MS, PhD); metallurgy and materials engineering (MS, PhD). *Application deadline:* For fall admission, 2/1 priority date for domestic and international students; for spring admission, 11/1 for domestic students, 10/1 for international students. Applications are processed on a rolling basis. *Application fee:* $55. Electronic applications accepted. *Application Contact:* Mun Y. Choi, Dean, 860-486-2221, Fax: 860-486-0318, E-mail: choi@engr.uconn.edu. *Dean,* Mun Y. Choi, 860-486-2221, Fax: 860-486-0318, E-mail: choi@engr.uconn.edu.

School of Fine Arts Students: 95 full-time (52 women), 33 part-time (18 women); includes 13 minority (3 African Americans, 1 American Indian/Alaska Native, 5 Asian Americans or Pacific Islanders, 4 Hispanic Americans), 18 international. Average age 29. 152 applicants, 31% accepted, 29 enrolled. *Faculty:* 52 full-time (21 women). Expenses: Contact institution. *Financial support:* In 2008–09, 42 research assistantships with full tuition reimbursements, 34 teaching assistantships with full tuition reimbursements were awarded; fellowships, Federal Work-Study, scholarships/grants, health care benefits, and unspecified assistantships also available. Financial award application deadline: 2/1; financial award applicants required to submit FAFSA. In 2008, 34 master's, 1 doctorate, 2 other advanced degrees awarded. Offers acting (MFA); art history (MA); conducting (M Mus, DMA); costume design (MFA); fine arts (M Mus, MA, MFA, DMA, PhD, Performer's Certificate); historical musicology (MA); lighting design (MFA); music (Performer's Certificate); music education (M Mus, PhD); music theory (MA); music theory and history (PhD); performance (M Mus, DMA); puppetry (MA, MFA); scenic design (MFA); studio art (MFA). *Application deadline:* For fall admission, 2/1 priority date for domestic and international students; for spring admission, 11/1 for domestic students, 10/1 for international students. Applications are processed on a rolling basis. *Application fee:* $55. Electronic applications accepted. *Application Contact:* Ted Yungclas, Associate Dean, 860-486-1485, E-mail: ted.yungclas@uconn.edu. *Dean,* David G. Woods, 860-486-3016, Fax: 860-486-5845, E-mail: david.g.woods@uconn.edu.

School of Nursing Students: 55 full-time (49 women), 100 part-time (89 women); includes 20 minority (6 African Americans, 8 Asian Americans or Pacific Islanders, 6 Hispanic Americans), 2 international. Average age 38. 91 applicants, 56% accepted, 29 enrolled. *Faculty:* 32 full-time (26 women). Expenses: Contact institution. *Financial support:* In 2008–09, 7 research assistantships with full tuition reimbursements, 20 teaching assistantships with full tuition reimbursements were awarded; fellowships, Federal Work-Study, scholarships/grants, health care benefits, and unspecified assistantships also available. Financial award application deadline: 2/1; financial award applicants required to submit FAFSA. In 2008, 31 master's, 1 doctorate, 1 other advanced degree awarded. Offers nursing (MS, PhD, Post-Master's Certificate). *Application deadline:* For fall admission, 2/1 priority date for domestic and international students; for spring admission, 11/1 for domestic students, 10/1 for international students. Applications are processed on a rolling basis. *Application fee:* $55. Electronic applications accepted. *Application Contact:* Elizabeth Anderson, Chairperson, 860-486-0577, E-mail: elizabeth.anderson@uconn.edu. *Dean,* Anne R. Bavier, 860-486-0537, Fax: 860-486-0001, E-mail: anne.bavier@uconn.edu.

School of Pharmacy Students: 41 full-time (23 women), 9 part-time (4 women); includes 7 minority (1 African American, 4 Asian Americans or Pacific Islanders, 2 Hispanic Americans), 24 international. Average age 28. 195 applicants, 2% accepted, 2 enrolled. *Faculty:* 26 full-time (7 women). Expenses: Contact institution. *Financial support:* In 2008–09, 34 research assistantships with full tuition reimbursements, 5 teaching assistantships with full tuition reimbursements were awarded; fellowships, career-related internships or fieldwork, Federal Work-Study, scholarships/grants, traineeships, health care benefits, and unspecified assistantships also available. Financial award application deadline: 2/1; financial award applicants required to submit FAFSA. In 2008, 2 master's, 9 doctorates awarded. Offers medicinal chemistry (MS, PhD); pharmaceutics (MS, PhD); pharmacology (MS, PhD); pharmacology and toxicology (MS, PhD); pharmacy (Pharm D, MS, PhD); toxicology (MS, PhD). *Application deadline:* For fall admission, 2/1 priority date for domestic and international students; for spring admission, 11/1 for domestic students, 10/1 for international students. Applications are processed on a rolling basis. *Application fee:* $55. Electronic applications accepted. *Application Contact:* Robert L. McCarthy, Dean, 860-486-2129, Fax: 860-486-1553, E-mail: r.mccarthy@uconn.edu. *Dean,* Robert L. McCarthy, 860-486-2129, Fax: 860-486-1553, E-mail: r.mccarthy@uconn.edu.

School of Social Work Students: 351 full-time (288 women), 74 part-time (63 women); includes 136 minority (79 African Americans, 1 American Indian/Alaska Native, 8 Asian Americans or Pacific Islanders, 48 Hispanic Americans), 3 international. Average age 31. 473 applicants, 35% accepted, 87 enrolled. *Faculty:* 31 full-time (24 women). Expenses: Contact institution. *Financial support:* In 2008–09, 8 research assistantships with full tuition reimbursements, 4 teaching assistantships with full tuition reimbursements were awarded; Federal Work-Study, health care benefits, and unspecified assistantships also available. Financial award application deadline: 2/1; financial award applicants required to submit FAFSA. In 2008, 166 master's, 1 doctorate awarded. Offers social work (MSW, PhD). *Application deadline:* For fall admission, 2/1 priority date for domestic and international students; for spring admission, 11/1 for domestic students, 10/1 for international students. Applications are processed on a rolling basis. *Application fee:* $55. Electronic applications accepted. *Application Contact:* David E. Cournoyer, Interim Dean, 860-570-9141, Fax: 860-570-9264, E-mail: david.cournoyer@uconn.edu. *Interim Dean,* David E. Cournoyer, 860-570-9141, Fax: 860-570-9264, E-mail: david.cournoyer@uconn.edu.

University of Connecticut Health Center Students: 181 full-time (104 women), 154 part-time (90 women); includes 54 minority (13 African Americans, 1 American Indian/Alaska Native, 29 Asian Americans or Pacific Islanders, 11 Hispanic Americans), 73 international. Average age 31. 430 applicants, 15% accepted, 53 enrolled. *Faculty:* 238 full-time (68 women). Expenses: Contact institution. *Financial support:* In 2008–09, 142 research assistantships with full tuition reimbursements, 1 teaching assistantship with full tuition reimbursement were awarded; fellowships, Federal Work-Study, scholarships/grants, health care benefits, and unspecified assistantships also available. Financial award application deadline: 2/1; financial award applicants required to submit FAFSA. In 2008, 37 master's, 30 doctorates awarded. Offers biomedical science (PhD); clinical and translational research (MS); dental science (M Dent Sc); health (M Dent Sc, MPH, MS, PhD); public health (MPH). *Application deadline:* For fall admission, 2/1 priority date for domestic and international students; for spring admission, 11/1 for domestic students, 10/1 for international students. Applications are processed on a rolling basis. *Application fee:* $55. Electronic applications accepted. *Application Contact:* Tricia Avolt, Graduate Coordinator, 860-679-2175, Fax: 860-679-1899, E-mail: robertson@nso2.uchc.edu. *Associate Dean,* Lawrence Klobutcher, 860-679-2816, Fax: 860-679-3408, E-mail: klobutcher@nso2.uchc.edu.

School of Law Students: 494 full-time (238 women), 245 part-time (100 women); includes 141 minority (41 African Americans, 3 American Indian/Alaska Native, 53 Asian Americans or Pacific Islanders, 44 Hispanic Americans), 32 international. Average age 25. 1,872 applicants, 23% accepted, 192 enrolled. *Faculty:* 45 full-time (14 women), 56 part-time/adjunct (8 women). Expenses: Contact institution. *Financial support:* In 2008–09, 358 students received support; research assistantships, teaching assistantships, career-related internships or fieldwork, Federal Work-Study, scholarships/grants, and tuition waivers (full and partial) available. Support available to part-time students. Financial award application deadline: 3/1; financial award applicants required to submit FAFSA. In 2008, 185 JDs awarded. *Degree program information:* Part-time and evening/weekend programs available. Offers law (JD). *Application deadline:* For fall admission, 3/1 for domestic and international students. Applications are processed on a rolling basis. *Application fee:* $60. Electronic applications accepted. *Application Contact:* Karen L. DeMeola, Assistant Dean for Admissions and Student Finance, 860-570-5162, Fax: 860-570-5153, E-mail: karen.demeola@law.uconn.edu. *Dean,* Jeremy Paul, 860-570-5127, Fax: 860-570-5218.

See Close-Up on page 1015.

UNIVERSITY OF CONNECTICUT HEALTH CENTER, Farmington, CT 06030

General Information State-supported, coed, graduate-only institution. *Enrollment by degree level:* 503 first professional, 165 master's, 160 doctoral, 105 other advanced degrees. *Graduate faculty:* 571. *Graduate housing:* On-campus housing not available. *Student services:* Career counseling, child daycare facilities, free psychological counseling, international student services, low-cost health insurance, services for students with disabilities. *Library facilities:* Lyman Maynard Stowe Library. *Online resources:* library catalog, web page, access to other libraries' catalogs. *Collection:* 200,526 titles, 1,497 serial subscriptions, 1,620 audiovisual materials.

Computer facilities: 66 computers available on campus for general student use. A campuswide network can be accessed from off campus. Online class registration is available. *Web address:* http://www.uchc.edu/.

General Application Contact: Tricia Avolt, Graduate Admissions Coordinator, 860-679-2175, Fax: 860-679-1899, E-mail: robertson@nso2.uchc.edu.

GRADUATE UNITS

Graduate School Students: 194 full-time (108 women), 131 part-time (76 women); includes 50 minority (10 African Americans, 1 American Indian/Alaska Native, 28 Asian Americans or Pacific Islanders, 11 Hispanic Americans), 71 international. Average age 31. *Faculty:* 172. Expenses: Contact institution. *Financial support:* In 2008–09, 160 research assistantships with full tuition reimbursements (averaging $27,000 per year) were awarded. In 2008, 35 master's, 30 doctorates awarded. *Degree program information:* Part-time and evening/weekend programs available. Offers biomedical sciencesclinical and translational research (MS); public health (MPH). *Application deadline:* Applications are processed on a rolling basis. *Application Contact:* Tricia Avolt, Graduate Admissions Coordinator, 860-679-2175, Fax: 860-679-1899, E-mail: robertson@nso2.uchc.edu. Dr. Larry Klobutcher.

Programs in Biomedical Sciences Students: 160 full-time (88 women); includes 16 minority (3 African Americans, 1 American Indian/Alaska Native, 10 Asian Americans or Pacific Islanders, 2 Hispanic Americans), 58 international. Average age 28. 264 applicants, 23% accepted, 18 enrolled. *Faculty:* 172. Expenses: Contact institution. *Financial support:* In 2008–09, 160 students received support, including 160 research assistantships with full tuition reimbursements available (averaging $27,000 per year); Federal Work-Study, traineeships, health care benefits, and unspecified assistantships also available. In 2008, 30 doctorates awarded. Offers biomedical sciences (PhD); cell biology (PhD); cellular and molecular pharmacology (PhD); genetics and developmental biology (PhD); immunology (PhD); molecular biology and biochemistry (PhD); neuroscience (PhD); skeletal, craniofacial and oral biology (PhD). *Application deadline:* For fall admission, 12/15 for domestic students. *Application fee:* $55. Electronic applications accepted. *Application Contact:* Tricia Avolt, Graduate Admissions Coordinator, 860-679-2175, Fax: 860-679-1899, E-mail: robertson@nso2.uchc.edu.

Programs in Biomedical Sciences—Integrated Students: 28 full-time (16 women); includes 5 minority (2 African Americans, 2 Asian Americans or Pacific Islanders, 1 Hispanic American), 9 international. Average age 26. 264 applicants, 23% accepted, 18 enrolled. *Faculty:* 172. Expenses: Contact institution. *Financial support:* In 2008–09, 28 students received support, including 28 research assistantships with tuition reimbursements available (averaging $27,000 per year). Offers biomedical sciences—integrated (PhD). *Application deadline:* For fall admission, 12/15 for domestic students. *Application fee:* $55. Electronic applications accepted. *Application Contact:* Tricia Avolt, Graduate Admissions Coordinator, 860-679-2175, Fax: 860-679-1899, E-mail: robertson@ns02.uchc.edu. Dr. Larry Klobutcher.

School of Dental Medicine Students: 172 full-time (83 women); includes 39 minority (10 African Americans, 1 American Indian/Alaska Native, 17 Asian Americans or Pacific Islanders, 11 Hispanic Americans), 6 international. Average age 26. 1,515 applicants, 6% accepted, 49 enrolled. *Faculty:* 385 full-time. Expenses: Contact institution. *Financial support:* In 2008–09, 161 students received support; fellowships, research assistantships, teaching assistantships, Federal Work-Study and institutionally sponsored loans available. Financial award application deadline: 4/15; financial award applicants required to submit FAFSA. In 2008, 40 first professional degrees awarded. Offers dental medicine (DMD, MDS, Certificate); dental science (MDS). *Application deadline:* For fall admission, 2/1 for domestic students. *Application fee:* $75. Electronic applications accepted. *Application Contact:* Tricia Avolt, Graduate Admissions Coordinator, 860-679-2175, Fax: 860-679-1899, E-mail: robertson@nso2.uchc.edu. *Associate Dean for Dental Academic Affairs*, Dr. R. Lamont MacNeil, 860-679-2207, Fax: 860-679-1899, E-mail: macneil@nso.uchc.edu.

School of Medicine Students: 325 full-time (193 women), 6 part-time (2 women); includes 90 minority (34 African Americans, 3 American Indian/Alaska Native, 49 Asian Americans or Pacific Islanders, 4 Hispanic Americans), 6 international. Average age 26. 2,919 applicants, 6% accepted, 85 enrolled. *Faculty:* 525. Expenses: Contact institution. *Financial support:* In 2008–09, 300 students received support. Institutionally sponsored loans and tuition waivers (partial) available. Financial award application deadline: 4/15; financial award applicants required to submit FAFSA. In 2008, 81 MDs awarded. Offers medicine (MD). *Application deadline:* For fall admission, 12/15 for domestic and international students. *Application fee:* $85. Electronic applications accepted. *Application Contact:* Dr. Keat Sanford, Assistant Dean and Director, 860-679-3874, Fax: 860-679-1282, E-mail: sanford@nso1.uchc.edu. *Dean*, Dr. Cato Laurencin, 860-679-2413, Fax: 860-679-1282.

UNIVERSITY OF DALLAS, Irving, TX 75062-4736

General Information Independent-religious, coed, university. *Enrollment:* 2,977 graduate, professional, and undergraduate students; 390 full-time matriculated graduate/professional students (150 women), 1,288 part-time matriculated graduate/professional students (520 women). *Enrollment by degree level:* 1,546 master's, 75 doctoral, 57 other advanced degrees. *Graduate faculty:* 125 full-time, 101 part-time/adjunct. *Tuition:* Full-time $11,880; part-time $660 per credit hour. *Required fees:* $270; $15 per credit hour. *Graduate housing:* On-campus housing not available. *Student services:* Campus employment opportunities, career counseling, international student services, teacher training. *Library facilities:* William A. Blakley Library. *Online resources:* library catalog, web page, access to other libraries' catalogs. *Collection:* 245,228 titles, 1,310 serial subscriptions, 1,317 audiovisual materials.

Computer facilities: Computer purchase and lease plans are available. 125 computers available on campus for general student use. A campuswide network can be accessed from student residence rooms and from off campus. Online class registration is available. *Web address:* http://www.udallas.edu/.

General Application Contact: Dr. David Sweet, Dean, 972-721-5288, Fax: 972-721-5280, E-mail: dsweet@udallas.edu.

GRADUATE UNITS

Braniff Graduate School of Liberal Arts *Degree program information:* Part-time programs available. Offers American studies (MAS); art (MA, MFA); English literature (MA, MEL); humanities (M Hum, MA); liberal arts (M Hum, M Pol, M Psych, M Th, MA, MAS, MCSL, MEL, MFA, MPM, MRE, MTS, PhD); philosophy (MA); politics (M Pol, MA); psychology (M Psych, MA); theology (M Th, MA).

Institute for Religious and Pastoral Studies *Degree program information:* Part-time and evening/weekend programs available. Postbaccalaureate distance learning degree programs offered (no on-campus study). Offers religious and pastoral studies (MCSL, MPM, MRE, MTS).

Institute of Philosophic Studies Offers literature (PhD); philosophy (PhD); politics (PhD).

Graduate School of Management *Degree program information:* Part-time and evening/weekend programs available. Postbaccalaureate distance learning degree programs offered (no on-campus study). Offers accounting (MBA, MS); business management (MBA, MM); corporate finance (MBA, MM); engineering management (MBA, MM); entrepreneurship (MBA, MM); financial services (MBA, MM); global business (MBA, MM); health services management (MBA, MM); human resource management (MBA, MM, MS); information assurance (MBA, MM, MS); information technology (MBA, MM, MS); information technology service management (MBA, MS); marketing management (MBA, MM); not-for-profit management (MBA); organization development (MBA); project management (MBA, MM); service management (MBA, MM); sports and entertainment management (MBA, MM); strategic leadership (MBA, MM); supply chain management (MBA); supply chain management and market logistics (MM); technologies management (MM). Electronic applications accepted.

UNIVERSITY OF DAYTON, Dayton, OH 45469-1300

General Information Independent-religious, coed, university. CGS member. *Enrollment:* 10,920 graduate, professional, and undergraduate students; 1,642 full-time matriculated graduate/professional students (838 women), 973 part-time matriculated graduate/professional students (592 women). *Enrollment by degree level:* 574 first professional, 1,826 master's, 184 doctoral, 31 other advanced degrees. *Graduate faculty:* 161 full-time (44 women), 9 part-time/adjunct (3 women). *Tuition:* Full-time $6950; part-time $1737.50 per semester. *Required fees:* $25 per semester. Tuition and fees vary according to course level, course load, degree level and program. *Graduate housing:* Room and/or apartments available on a first-come, first-served basis to single students; on-campus housing not available to married students. Typical cost: $8000 per year. Room charges vary according to campus/location and housing facility selected. *Student services:* Campus employment opportunities, campus safety program, career counseling, child daycare facilities, exercise/wellness program, free psychological counseling, grant writing training, international student services, low-cost health insurance, multicultural affairs office, services for students with disabilities, teacher training, writing training. *Library facilities:* Roesch Library plus 2 others. *Online resources:* library catalog, web page, access to other libraries' catalogs. *Collection:* 920,035 titles, 10,481 serial subscriptions, 2,186 audiovisual materials. *Research affiliation:* American Chemical Society (geological research), American Society of Heating, Refrigeration & Air Conditioning (material degradation studies), Dayton Area Graduate Studies Institute (electrical, civil, materials & mechanical engineering research), Wright Brothers Institute (aerospace and electro-optics research), Ohio State University Research Foundation (combustion, polymer & nanomaterials and material research), Society of Plastics Industry, Inc. (combustion studies).

Computer facilities: Computer purchase and lease plans are available. 250 computers available on campus for general student use. A campuswide network can be accessed from student residence rooms and from off campus. Online class registration, applications, admission/enrollment status, virtual orientation, online digital resources, online courses, assistive technology, learning management system, multimedia labs, payment, cyber cafes, centrally-licensed, downloadable software and training are available. *Web address:* http://www.udayton.edu/.

General Application Contact: Angela Jones-Glukhov, Associate Director of Graduate Admissions, 937-229-4305, Fax: 937-229-4729.

GRADUATE UNITS

Graduate School Students: 1,642 full-time (838 women), 973 part-time (592 women); includes 294 minority (185 African Americans, 6 American Indian/Alaska Native, 42 Asian Americans or Pacific Islanders, 61 Hispanic Americans), 192 international. Average age 30. 2,465 applicants, 44% accepted, 590 enrolled. *Faculty:* 308 full-time (100 women), 175 part-time/adjunct (71 women). Expenses: Contact institution. *Financial support:* In 2008–09, 337 students received support, including fellowships with tuition reimbursements available (averaging $9,000 per year), 215 research assistantships with full and partial tuition reimbursements available (averaging $10,094 per year), 122 teaching assistantships with full and partial tuition reimbursements available (averaging $9,912 per year); institutionally sponsored loans, scholarships/grants, traineeships, health care benefits, and unspecified assistantships also available. Support available to part-time students. Financial award applicants required to submit FAFSA. In 2008, 717 master's, 21 doctorates, 10 other advanced degrees awarded. *Degree program information:* Part-time and evening/weekend programs available. Postbaccalaureate distance learning degree programs offered (no on-campus study). *Application deadline:* For fall admission, 3/1 priority date for international students; for winter admission, 7/1 priority date for international students; for spring admission, 1/1 priority date for international students. Applications are processed on a rolling basis. *Application fee:* $0 ($50 for international students). Electronic applications accepted. *Application Contact:* Angela Jones-Glukhov, Associate Director of Graduate Admissions, 937-229-4305, Fax: 937-229-4729, E-mail: jonesgas@notes.udayton.edu. *Dean of the Graduate School*, Dr. F. Thomas Eggemeier, 937-229-2390, Fax: 937-229-2400, E-mail: udgradschool@udayton.edu.

College of Arts and Sciences Students: 203 full-time (121 women), 68 part-time (37 women); includes 30 minority (17 African Americans, 7 Asian Americans or Pacific Islanders, 6 Hispanic Americans), 39 international. Average age 29. 569 applicants, 40% accepted, 83 enrolled. *Faculty:* 117 full-time (37 women), 14 part-time/adjunct (4 women). Expenses: Contact institution. *Financial support:* In 2008–09, 4 fellowships with full tuition reimbursements (averaging $15,814 per year), 22 research assistantships with full and partial tuition reimbursements (averaging $10,500 per year), 67 teaching assistantships with full tuition reimbursements (averaging $12,538 per year) were awarded; career-related internships or fieldwork, Federal Work-Study, institutionally sponsored loans, scholarships/grants, traineeships, health care benefits, tuition waivers (full and partial), and unspecified assistantships also available. Support available to part-time students. Financial award application deadline: 3/1; financial award applicants required to submit FAFSA. In 2008, 87 master's, 1 doctorate awarded. *Degree program information:* Part-time and evening/weekend programs available. Postbaccalaureate distance learning degree programs offered (minimal on-campus study). Offers applied mathematics (MAS); arts and sciences (MA, MAS, MCS, MFM, MME, MPA, MS, PhD); biology (MS, PhD); chemistry (MS); clinical psychology (MA); communication (MA); computer science (MCS); English (MA); financial mathematics (MFM); general psychology (MA); mathematics (MME); pastoral ministry (MA); public administration (MPA); theological studies (MA); theology (PhD). *Application deadline:* For fall admission, 3/1 priority date for domestic and international students; for winter admission, 7/1 priority date for international students; for spring admission, 1/1 priority date for international students. Applications are processed on a rolling basis. *Application fee:* $0 ($50 for international students). Electronic applications accepted. *Application Contact:* Angela Jones-Glukhov, Associate Director of Graduate Admissions, 937-229-4305, Fax: 937-229-4729, E-mail: jonesgas@notes.udayton.edu. *Dean*, Dr. Paul Benson, 937-229-2601, Fax: 937-229-2615.

School of Business Administration Students: 122 full-time (49 women), 101 part-time (27 women); includes 22 minority (11 African Americans, 6 Asian Americans or Pacific Islanders, 5 Hispanic Americans), 19 international. Average age 30. 197 applicants, 50% accepted, 52 enrolled. *Faculty:* 29 full-time (8 women), 15 part-time/adjunct (2 women). Expenses: Contact institution. *Financial support:* In 2008–09, 13 fellowships with partial tuition reimbursements, 17 research assistantships with full and partial tuition reimbursements (averaging $7,020 per year) were awarded; career-related internships or fieldwork, institutionally sponsored loans, scholarships/grants, health care benefits, and unspecified assistantships also available. Support available to part-time students. Financial award application deadline: 3/15; financial award applicants required to submit FAFSA. In 2008, 74 master's awarded. *Degree program information:* Part-time and evening/weekend programs available. Offers accounting (MBA); business intelligence (MBA); entrepreneurship (MBA); finance (MBA); international business (MBA); marketing (MBA); MIS (MBA); operations management (MBA); technology-enhanced business/e-commerce (MBA). *Application deadline:* For fall admission, 3/1 priority date for international students; for winter admission, 7/1 priority date for international students; for spring admission, 1/1 priority date for international students. Applications are processed on a rolling basis. *Application fee:* $0 ($50 for international students). Electronic applications accepted. *Application Contact:* Jeffrey Carter, Assistant Director, MBA Program, 937-229-3733, Fax: 937-229-3882, E-mail: Jeff.Carter@notes.udayton.edu. *Director, MBA Program*, Janice M. Glynn, 937-229-3733, Fax: 937-229-3882, E-mail: glynn@udayton.edu.

School of Education and Allied Professions Students: 572 full-time (425 women), 658 part-time (504 women); includes 137 minority (105 African Americans, 2 American Indian/Alaska Native, 9 Asian Americans or Pacific Islanders, 21 Hispanic Americans), 10 international. Average age 32. 1,015 applicants, 50% accepted, 446 enrolled. *Faculty:* 57 full-time (30 women), 86 part-time/adjunct (55 women). Expenses: Contact institution. *Financial support:* In 2008–09, 32 research assistantships with full tuition reimbursements (averaging $9,378 per year), 2 teaching assistantships with full tuition reimbursements (averaging $9,378 per year) were awarded. Financial award applicants required to submit FAFSA. In 2008, 448 master's, 5 doctorates, 9 other advanced degrees awarded. *Degree program information:* Part-time and evening/weekend programs available. Postbaccalaureate distance learning degree programs offered (no on-campus study). Offers adolescent/young adult (MS Ed); art education (MS Ed); college student personnel (MS Ed); community counseling (MS Ed); early childhood education (MS Ed); education administration (Ed S); education and allied professions (MS Ed, DPT, PhD, Ed S); educational leadership (MS Ed, PhD, Ed S); exercise science (MS Ed); higher education administration (MS Ed); human services (MS Ed); inclusive early childhood (MS Ed); interdisciplinary education (MS Ed); intervention specialist education, mild/moderate (MS Ed); literacy (MS Ed); middle childhood (MS Ed); multi-age education (MS Ed); music education (MS Ed); physical therapy (DPT); school counseling (MS Ed); school psychology (MS Ed, Ed S); teacher as child/youth development specialist (MS Ed); teacher as leader (MS Ed); technology in education (MS Ed). *Application deadline:* For fall admission, 3/15 priority date for domestic students, 3/1 priority date for international students; for winter admission, 7/1 priority date for international students; for spring admission, 1/1 priority date for international students. Applications are processed on a rolling basis. *Application fee:* $0 ($50 for international students). Electronic applications accepted. *Application Contact:* Angela Jones-Glukhov, Associate Director of Graduate Admissions, 937-229-4305, Fax: 937-229-4729. *Dean*, Dr. Thomas J. Lasley, 937-229-3146, Fax: 937-229-3199, E-mail: thomas.lasley@notes.udayton.edu.

School of Engineering Students: 275 full-time (57 women), 132 part-time (21 women); includes 45 minority (26 African Americans, 10 Asian Americans or Pacific Islanders, 9 Hispanic Americans), 119 international. Average age 30. 682 applicants, 38% accepted, 104 enrolled. *Faculty:* 50 full-time (4 women), 36 part-time/adjunct (3 women). Expenses: Contact institution. *Financial support:* In 2008–09, 105 students received support, including 7 fellowships with full tuition reimbursements available (averaging $28,000 per year), 84 research assistantships with full tuition reimbursements available (averaging $15,000 per

University of Dayton (continued)

year), 14 teaching assistantships with full tuition reimbursements available (averaging $9,000 per year); career-related internships or fieldwork, institutionally sponsored loans, health care benefits, tuition waivers (full and partial), and unspecified assistantships also available. Financial award applicants required to submit FAFSA. In 2008, 113 master's, 17 doctorates awarded. *Degree program information:* Part-time and evening/weekend programs available. Postbaccalaureate distance learning degree programs offered (no on-campus study). Offers aerospace engineering (MSAE, DE, PhD); chemical engineering (MS Ch E); electrical and computer engineering (MSEE, DE, PhD); electro-optics (MSEO, PhD); engineering (MS, MS Ch E, MS Mat E, MSAE, MSCE, MSE, MSEE, MSEM, MSEM, MSEO, MSME, MSMS, DE, PhD); engineering management (MSEM); engineering mechanics (MSEM); environmental engineering (MSCE); geotechnical engineering (MSCE); materials engineering (MS Mat E, DE, PhD); mechanical engineering (MSME, DE, PhD); renewable and clean energy (MS); structural engineering (MSCE); transport engineering (MSCE); water resources engineering (MSCE). *Application deadline:* For fall admission, 8/1 priority date for domestic students, 3/1 priority date for international students; for winter admission, 7/1 priority date for international students; for spring admission, 1/1 priority date for international students. Applications are processed on a rolling basis. *Application fee:* $0 ($50 for international students). Electronic applications accepted. *Application Contact:* Angela Jones-Glukhov, Associate Director of Graduate Admissions, 937-229-4305, Fax: 937-229-4729, E-mail: jonesgas@notes.udayton.edu. *Interim Dean*, Dr. Malcolm W. Daniels, 937-229-2736, Fax: 937-229-2756, E-mail: malcolm.daniels@notes.udayton.edu.

School of Law Students: 479 full-time (186 women); includes 63 minority (26 African Americans, 5 American Indian/Alaska Native, 12 Asian Americans or Pacific Islanders, 20 Hispanic Americans), 5 international. Average age 26. 2,230 applicants, 55% accepted, 216 enrolled. *Faculty:* 55 full-time (21 women), 24 part-time/adjunct (7 women). Expenses: Contact institution. *Financial support:* In 2008–09, 290 students received support. Career-related internships or fieldwork, institutionally sponsored loans, scholarships/grants, and tuition waivers (partial) available. Financial award application deadline: 3/1; financial award applicants required to submit FAFSA. In 2008, 184 JDs awarded. Offers law (JD, LL M, MSL). *Application deadline:* For fall admission, 5/1 priority date for domestic and international students; for spring admission, 3/1 priority date for domestic and international students. Applications are processed on a rolling basis. *Application fee:* $50. Electronic applications accepted. *Application Contact:* Janet L. Hein, Assistant Dean/Director of Admissions and Financial Aid, 937-229-3555, Fax: 937-229-4194, E-mail: lawinfo@notes.udayton.edu. *Dean*, Lisa A. Kloppenberg, 937-229-3795, Fax: 937-229-2469.

UNIVERSITY OF DELAWARE, Newark, DE 19716

General Information State-related, coed, university. CGS member. *Graduate housing:* Rooms and/or apartments available to single and married students. Housing application deadline: 3/15. *Research affiliation:* Hagley Museum, Winterthur Museum, Longwood Gardens, Bartol Research Foundation.

GRADUATE UNITS

Alfred Lerner College of Business and Economics *Degree program information:* Part-time and evening/weekend programs available. Offers accounting (MS); business administration (MBA); business and economics (MA, MBA, MS, PhD); economics (MA, MS, PhD); economics for entrepreneurship and educators (MA); finance (MS); hospitality information management (MS); information systems and technology management (MS). Electronic applications accepted.

College of Agriculture and Natural Resources *Degree program information:* Part-time programs available. Offers agricultural economics (MS); agriculture and natural resources (MA, MS, PhD); agriculture and technical education (MA); animal sciences (MS, PhD); bioresources engineering (MS); entomology and applied ecology (MS, PhD); food sciences (MS); operations research (MS, PhD); plant and soil sciences (MS, PhD); public horticulture (MS); statistics (MS). Electronic applications accepted.

College of Arts and Sciences *Degree program information:* Part-time and evening/weekend programs available. Offers acting (MFA); applied mathematics (MS, PhD); art (MA, MFA); art history (MA, PhD); arts and sciences (MA, MALS, MFA, MM, MS, DPT, PhD); behavioral neuroscience (PhD); biochemistry (MA, MS, PhD); biomechanics and movement science (MS, PhD); biotechnology (MS); cancer biology (MS, PhD); cell and extracellular matrix biology (MS, PhD); cell and systems physiology (MS, PhD); chemistry (MA, MS, PhD); climatology (PhD); clinical psychology (PhD); cognitive psychology (PhD); communication (MA); composition (MM); computer and information sciences (MS, PhD); criminology (MA, PhD); developmental biology (MS, PhD); early American culture (MA); ecology and evolution (MS, PhD); English and American literature (MA, PhD); foreign languages and literatures (MA); foreign languages pedagogy (MA); geography (MA, MS); history (MA, PhD); history of technology and industrialization (MA, PhD); liberal studies (MALS); linguistics (MA, PhD); mathematics (MS, PhD); microbiology (MS, PhD); molecular biology and genetics (MS, PhD); music education (MM); performance (MM); physical therapy (DPT); physics and astronomy (MS, PhD); political science and international relations (MA, PhD); practicing art conservation (MS); social psychology (PhD); sociology (MA, PhD); stage management (MFA); technical production (MFA). Electronic applications accepted.

College of Engineering *Degree program information:* Part-time and evening/weekend programs available. Postbaccalaureate distance learning degree programs offered (minimal on-campus study). Offers chemical engineering (M Ch E, PhD); electrical and computer engineering (MSECE, PhD); engineering (M Ch E, MAS, MCE, MEM, MMSE, MSECE, MSME, PhD); environmental engineering (MAS, MCE, PhD); geotechnical engineering (MAS, MCE, PhD); materials science and engineering (MMSE, PhD); mechanical engineering (MEM, MSME, PhD); ocean engineering (MAS, MCE, PhD); structural engineering (MAS, MCE, PhD); transportation engineering (MAS, MCE, PhD); water resource engineering (MAS, MCE, PhD). Electronic applications accepted.

College of Health Sciences *Degree program information:* Part-time and evening/weekend programs available. Postbaccalaureate distance learning degree programs offered. Offers adult nurse practitioner (MSN, PMC); cardiopulmonary clinical nurse specialist (MSN, PMC); cardiopulmonary clinical nurse specialist/adult nurse practitioner (MSN, PMC); exercise science (MS); family nurse practitioner (MSN, PMC); gerontology clinical nurse specialist (MSN, PMC); gerontology clinical nurse specialist geriatric nurse practitioner (PMC); gerontology clinical nurse specialist/geriatric nurse practitioner (MSN); health promotion (MS); health sciences (MS, MSN, PMC); health services administration (MSN, PMC); human nutrition (MS); nursing of children clinical nurse specialist (MSN, PMC); nursing of children clinical nurse specialist/pediatric nurse practitioner (MSN, PMC); oncology/immune deficiency clinical nurse specialist (MSN, PMC); oncology/immune deficiency clinical nurse specialist/adult nurse practitioner (MSN, PMC); perinatal/women's health clinical nurse specialist (MSN, PMC); perinatal/women's health clinical nurse specialist/women's health nurse practitioner (MSN, PMC); psychiatric nursing clinical nurse specialist (MSN, PMC). Electronic applications accepted.

College of Human Services, Education and Public Policy *Degree program information:* Part-time and evening/weekend programs available. Offers counseling in higher education (M Ed, MA); human development and family studies (MS, PhD); human services, education and public policy (M Ed, MA, MEEP, MI, MPA, MS, Ed D, PhD, Ed S). Electronic applications accepted.

Center for Energy and Environmental Policy Offers community development and nonprofit leadership (MA); energy and environmental policy (MA); environmental and energy policy (MEEP, PhD); governance, planning and management (PhD); historic preservation (MA); social and urban policy (PhD); technology, environment and society (PhD); urban affairs and public policy (MA, PhD). Electronic applications accepted.

School of Education *Degree program information:* Part-time and evening/weekend programs available. Offers education (PhD); educational leadership (Ed D); higher education (M Ed); instruction (MI); reading (M Ed); school leadership (M Ed); school psychology (MA, Ed S); teaching English as a second language (TESL) (MA). Electronic applications accepted.

School of Urban Affairs and Public Policy *Degree program information:* Part-time and evening/weekend programs available. Offers public administration (MPA); urban affairs and public policy (MPA). Electronic applications accepted.

College of Marine and Earth Studies Offers geology (MS, PhD); marine policy (MS); marine studies (MMP, MS, PhD); oceanography (MS, PhD). Electronic applications accepted.

UNIVERSITY OF DENVER, Denver, CO 80208

General Information Independent, coed, university. CGS member. *Enrollment:* 11,328 graduate, professional, and undergraduate students; 3,325 full-time matriculated graduate/professional students (1,903 women), 2,196 part-time matriculated graduate/professional students (1,184 women). *Enrollment by degree level:* 1,087 first professional, 3,679 master's, 632 doctoral, 123 other advanced degrees. *Graduate faculty:* 453 full-time (182 women), 497 part-time/adjunct (240 women). *Graduate housing:* Rooms and/or apartments available on a first-come, first-served basis to single and married students. *Student services:* Campus employment opportunities, campus safety program, career counseling, exercise/wellness program, free psychological counseling, international student services, low-cost health insurance, multicultural affairs office, services for students with disabilities. *Library facilities:* Penrose Library. *Online resources:* library catalog, web page, access to other libraries' catalogs. *Collection:* 1.3 million titles, 33,745 serial subscriptions, 12,191 audiovisual materials. *Research affiliation:* National Center for Atmospheric Research (infrared measurements).

Computer facilities: Computer purchase and lease plans are available. 200 computers available on campus for general student use. A campuswide network can be accessed from student residence rooms and from off campus. Online class registration is available. *Web address:* http://www.du.edu/.

General Application Contact: Information Contact, 303-871-2706.

GRADUATE UNITS

College of Education Students: 334 full-time (259 women), 454 part-time (350 women); includes 136 minority (28 African Americans, 8 American Indian/Alaska Native, 14 Asian Americans or Pacific Islanders, 86 Hispanic Americans), 20 international. Average age 34. 851 applicants, 76% accepted, 356 enrolled. *Faculty:* 30 full-time (20 women), 58 part-time/adjunct (40 women). Expenses: Contact institution. *Financial support:* In 2008–09, 74 teaching assistantships with full and partial tuition reimbursements (averaging $6,000 per year) were awarded; career-related internships or fieldwork, Federal Work-Study, institutionally sponsored loans, and scholarships/grants also available. Support available to part-time students. Financial award application deadline: 3/1; financial award applicants required to submit FAFSA. In 2008, 214 master's, 43 doctorates, 85 other advanced degrees awarded. *Degree program information:* Part-time and evening/weekend programs available. Postbaccalaureate distance learning degree programs offered (no on-campus study). Offers counseling psychology (MA, PhD); curriculum and instruction (MA, PhD, Certificate); educational administration and policy studies (Certificate); educational psychology (MA, PhD, Ed S); higher education and adult studies (MA, PhD); library and information science (MLIS); library and information sciences (Certificate); school administration (PhD). *Application deadline:* Applications are processed on a rolling basis. *Application fee:* $50. Electronic applications accepted. *Application Contact:* Linda McCarthy, Student Services Coordinator, 303-871-2509, E-mail: edinfo@du.edu. *Associate Dean*, Dr. Cheryl Lovell, 303-871-2479.

College of Law Students: 1,142 full-time (527 women), 153 part-time (83 women); includes 222 minority (41 African Americans, 25 American Indian/Alaska Native, 65 Asian Americans or Pacific Islanders, 91 Hispanic Americans), 27 international. Average age 29. 3,255 applicants, 33% accepted, 348 enrolled. *Faculty:* 69 full-time (33 women), 74 part-time/adjunct (21 women). Expenses: Contact institution. *Financial support:* Career-related internships or fieldwork, Federal Work-Study, institutionally sponsored loans, and tutorships available. Support available to part-time students. Financial award application deadline: 2/15; financial award applicants required to submit FAFSA. In 2008, 317 first professional degrees, 129 master's awarded. *Degree program information:* Part-time and evening/weekend programs available. Offers American and comparative law (LL M); international natural resources law (LL M, MRLS); law (JD, LL M, MRLS, MSLA, MT, Certificate); legal administration (MSLA, Certificate); taxation (LL M, MT). *Application deadline:* For fall admission, 3/1 priority date for domestic students. Applications are processed on a rolling basis. *Application fee:* $60. Electronic applications accepted. *Application Contact:* Wende Best, Assistant Director of Admissions, 303-871-6135, Fax: 303-871-6992, E-mail: admissions@law.du.edu. *Dean*, Jose Roberto Juarez, 303-871-6135.

Daniels College of Business Students: 588 full-time (208 women), 349 part-time (106 women); includes 88 minority (15 African Americans, 5 American Indian/Alaska Native, 39 Asian Americans or Pacific Islanders, 29 Hispanic Americans), 159 international. Average age 30. 1,050 applicants, 77% accepted, 440 enrolled. *Faculty:* 75 full-time (20 women), 20 part-time/adjunct (12 women). Expenses: Contact institution. *Financial support:* In 2008–09, 87 teaching assistantships with full and partial tuition reimbursements (averaging $1,900 per year) were awarded; career-related internships or fieldwork, Federal Work-Study, institutionally sponsored loans, and scholarships/grants also available. Support available to part-time students. Financial award application deadline: 2/15; financial award applicants required to submit FAFSA. In 2008, 512 master's awarded. *Degree program information:* Part-time and evening/weekend programs available. Offers business (IMBA, M Acc, MBA, MS); business administration (MBA); business intelligence (MS); data mining (MS); finance (IMBA, MBA, MS); general business administration (IMBA, MBA, MS); information technology and electronic commerce (IMBA, MBA); international business/management (IMBA, MBA); management (MS); marketing (IMBA, MBA, MS). *Application deadline:* For fall admission, 1/15 priority date for domestic students. Applications are processed on a rolling basis. *Application fee:* $50. Electronic applications accepted. *Application Contact:* Admissions, 303-871-3416, Fax: 303-571-4466, E-mail: daniels@du.edu. *Dean*, Dr. Chris Riordan, 303-871-4324.

School of Accountancy Students: 29 full-time (19 women), 30 part-time (17 women); includes 7 minority (1 African American, 4 Asian Americans or Pacific Islanders, 2 Hispanic Americans), 25 international. Average age 28. *Faculty:* 12 full-time (4 women), 1 part-time/adjunct (0 women). Expenses: Contact institution. *Financial support:* Career-related internships or fieldwork, Federal Work-Study, institutionally sponsored loans, and scholarships/grants available. Support available to part-time students. Financial award application deadline: 2/15; financial award applicants required to submit FAFSA. In 2008, 36 master's awarded. *Degree program information:* Part-time and evening/weekend programs available. Offers accountancy (M Acc); accounting (MBA). *Application deadline:* For fall admission, 1/15 priority date for domestic students. Applications are processed on a rolling basis. *Application fee:* $50. Electronic applications accepted. *Application Contact:* Information Contact, 303-871-3416, Fax: 303-871-4466, E-mail: daniels@du.edu. *Director*, Dr. Ronald Kucic, 303-871-2017.

School of Real Estate and Construction Management Students: 47 full-time (4 women), 70 part-time (11 women); includes 11 minority (4 African Americans, 1 American Indian/Alaska Native, 2 Asian Americans or Pacific Islanders, 4 Hispanic Americans), 4 international. Average age 32. *Faculty:* 6 full-time (0 women), 3 part-time/adjunct (1 woman). Expenses: Contact institution. *Financial support:* In 2008–09, 70 students received support. Career-related internships or fieldwork, Federal Work-Study, institutionally sponsored loans, and scholarships/grants available. Support available to part-time students. Financial award application deadline: 2/15; financial award applicants required to submit FAFSA. In 2008, 95 master's awarded. *Degree program information:* Part-time programs available. Offers construction management (IMBA, MS); real estate (IMBA, MBA, MS). *Application deadline:* For fall admission, 1/15 priority date for domestic students. Applications are processed on a rolling basis. *Application fee:* $50. Electronic applications accepted. *Application Contact:* Information Contact, 303-871-3416, Fax: 303-871-4466, E-mail: daniels@du.edu. *Director*, Dr. Mark Levine, 303-871-2142.

Division of Arts, Humanities and Social Sciences Students: 207 full-time (144 women), 155 part-time (111 women); includes 39 minority (9 African Americans, 2 American Indian/Alaska Native, 12 Asian Americans or Pacific Islanders, 16 Hispanic Americans), 34 international. Average age 29. 958 applicants, 43% accepted, 166 enrolled. *Faculty:* 126 full-time (58 women), 64 part-time/adjunct (25 women). Expenses: Contact institution. *Financial support:* In 2008–09, 20 research assistantships with full and partial tuition reimbursements (averaging $15,000 per year), 126 teaching assistantships with full and partial tuition reimbursements (averaging $10,000 per year) were awarded; career-related internships or fieldwork, Federal Work-Study, institutionally sponsored loans, and scholarships/grants also available. Support available to part-time students. Financial award applicants required to submit FAFSA. In 2008, 110 master's, 20 doctorates awarded. *Degree program information:* Part-time programs available. Offers anthropology (MA); arts, humanities and social sciences (MA, MFA, MM, MPP, MS, PhD, Certificate); economics (MA); English (MA, PhD); psychology (MA, PhD); public policy (MPP); religious studies (MA). *Application deadline:* Applications are processed on a rolling basis. *Application fee:* $50. Electronic applications accepted. *Application Contact:* Information Contact, 360-871-4449, E-mail: ahss@du.edu. *Dean,* Dr. Anne McCall, 303-871-4449.

Lamont School of Music Students: 27 full-time (16 women), 38 part-time (21 women); includes 4 minority (2 African Americans, 1 Asian American or Pacific Islander, 1 Hispanic American), 9 international. Average age 27. *Faculty:* 24 full-time (6 women), 42 part-time/adjunct (16 women). Expenses: Contact institution. *Financial support:* In 2008–09, 37 teaching assistantships with full and partial tuition reimbursements (averaging $4,500 per year) were awarded; career-related internships or fieldwork, Federal Work-Study, institutionally sponsored loans, and scholarships/grants also available. Support available to part-time students. Financial award application deadline: 4/15; financial award applicants required to submit FAFSA. In 2008, 14 master's, 1 other advanced degree awarded. *Degree program information:* Part-time programs available. Offers composition (MA); conducting (MA); jazz and commercial music (Certificate); music (MM); music education (MA); music history and literature (MA); Orff-Schulwerk (MA); performance (MA); piano pedagogy (MA); Suzuki pedagogy (MA); Suzuki teaching (Certificate); theory (MA). *Application deadline:* Applications are processed on a rolling basis. *Application fee:* $50. Electronic applications accepted. *Application Contact:* Information Contact, 303-871-6400. *Director,* Joseph Docksey, 303-871-6986.

School of Art and Art History Students: 15 full-time (12 women), 10 part-time (all women); includes 2 minority (1 Asian American or Pacific Islander, 1 Hispanic American), 1 international. Average age 29. *Faculty:* 15 full-time (11 women), 6 part-time/adjunct (2 women). Expenses: Contact institution. *Financial support:* Career-related internships or fieldwork, Federal Work-Study, institutionally sponsored loans, and scholarships/grants available. Support available to part-time students. Financial award application deadline: 3/1; financial award applicants required to submit FAFSA. In 2008, 11 master's awarded. *Degree program information:* Part-time programs available. Offers art history (MA); art history/museum studies (MA); electronic media arts and design (MFA). *Application deadline:* Applications are processed on a rolling basis. *Application fee:* $50. Electronic applications accepted. *Application Contact:* Dr. Annabeth Headrick, Graduate Advisor, 303-871-3574, E-mail: saah-interest@du.edu. *Director,* Dr. Annette Stott, 303-871-2846.

School of Communication Students: 63 full-time (46 women), 58 part-time (44 women); includes 14 minority (4 African Americans, 2 Asian Americans or Pacific Islanders, 8 Hispanic Americans), 11 international. Average age 29. *Faculty:* 23 full-time (15 women), 7 part-time/adjunct (3 women). Expenses: Contact institution. *Financial support:* Career-related internships or fieldwork, Federal Work-Study, institutionally sponsored loans, and scholarships/grants available. Support available to part-time students. In 2008, 34 master's, 8 doctorates awarded. *Degree program information:* Part-time programs available. Offers advertising management (MS); communication (MA, MS, PhD); digital media studies (MA); human communication studies (MA, PhD); international and intercultural communication (MA); mass communications (MA); public relations (MS); video production (MA). *Application deadline:* Applications are processed on a rolling basis. *Application fee:* $50. Electronic applications accepted. *Application Contact:* Information Contact, 303-871-2166, E-mail: mcomadm@du.edu. *Chairperson.*

Faculty of Natural Sciences and Mathematics Students: 24 full-time (8 women), 67 part-time (22 women); includes 7 minority (2 Asian Americans or Pacific Islanders, 5 Hispanic Americans), 12 international. Average age 29. 159 applicants, 56% accepted, 35 enrolled. *Faculty:* 67 full-time (18 women), 5 part-time/adjunct (1 woman). Expenses: Contact institution. *Financial support:* In 2008–09, 18 research assistantships with full and partial tuition reimbursements (averaging $17,400 per year), 61 teaching assistantships with full and partial tuition reimbursements (averaging $16,200 per year) were awarded; career-related internships or fieldwork, Federal Work-Study, institutionally sponsored loans, and scholarships/grants also available. Support available to part-time students. Financial award application deadline: 3/1; financial award applicants required to submit FAFSA. In 2008, 24 master's, 5 doctorates awarded. *Degree program information:* Part-time and evening/weekend programs available. Offers applied mathematics (MA, MS); biological sciences (MS, PhD); chemistry (MA, MS, PhD); computer science (MS); geography (MA, MS, PhD); mathematics (PhD); natural sciences and mathematics (MA, MS, PhD); physics and astronomy (MS, PhD). *Application deadline:* Applications are processed on a rolling basis. *Application fee:* $50. Electronic applications accepted. *Application Contact:* Information Contact, 303-871-2693. *Dean,* Dr. Alayne Parson, 303-871-2693.

Graduate School of Professional Psychology Students: 198 full-time (162 women), 25 part-time (15 women); includes 26 minority (6 African Americans, 3 American Indian/Alaska Native, 9 Asian Americans or Pacific Islanders, 8 Hispanic Americans), 8 international. Average age 26. 525 applicants, 36% accepted, 92 enrolled. *Faculty:* 12 full-time (6 women), 31 part-time/adjunct (16 women). Expenses: Contact institution. *Financial support:* In 2008–09, 30 teaching assistantships with full and partial tuition reimbursements (averaging $3,500 per year) were awarded; career-related internships or fieldwork, Federal Work-Study, institutionally sponsored loans, scholarships/grants, and clinical assistantships also available. Support available to part-time students. Financial award application deadline: 3/1; financial award applicants required to submit FAFSA. In 2008, 75 master's, 31 doctorates awarded. Offers clinical psychology (Psy D); psychology (MA). *Application deadline:* For fall admission, 1/5 for domestic students. *Application fee:* $50. Electronic applications accepted. *Application Contact:* Admissions, 303-871-3873, Fax: 303-871-4220, E-mail: gsppinfo@du.edu. *Dean,* Dr. Peter Buirski, 303-871-2382.

Graduate School of Social Work Students: 374 full-time (347 women), 24 part-time (22 women); includes 82 minority (17 African Americans, 8 American Indian/Alaska Native, 16 Asian Americans or Pacific Islanders, 41 Hispanic Americans), 3 international. *Faculty:* 21 full-time (16 women), 67 part-time/adjunct (55 women). Expenses: Contact institution. In 2008, 220 master's, 1 doctorate, 5 other advanced degrees awarded. *Degree program information:* Part-time and evening/weekend programs available. Offers social work (MSW, PhD, Certificate). *Application deadline:* Applications are processed on a rolling basis. *Application fee:* $60. Electronic applications accepted. *Application Contact:* Colin Schneider, Director of Admission and Financial Aid, 303-871-2841, Fax: 303-871-2845, E-mail: gssw-admission@du.edu. *Dean,* Dr. James Herbert Williams, 303-871-2203.

Graduate Studies Students: 77 full-time (26 women), 62 part-time (18 women); includes 16 minority (8 African Americans, 1 American Indian/Alaska Native, 3 Asian Americans or Pacific Islanders, 4 Hispanic Americans), 9 international. Average age 37. 87 applicants, 97% accepted, 53 enrolled. *Faculty:* 1 (woman) full-time, 2 part-time/adjunct (1 woman). Expenses: Contact institution. *Financial support:* Career-related internships or fieldwork, Federal Work-Study, institutionally sponsored loans, and scholarships/grants available. Support available to part-time students. Financial award applicants required to submit FAFSA. In 2008, 25 master's, 5 doctorates awarded. *Degree program information:* Part-time and evening/weekend programs available. Offers religious and theological studies (PhD). *Application deadline:* Applications are processed on a rolling basis. Electronic applications accepted. *Application Contact:* Karen Fennel, Graduate Studies Manager, 303-871-2706, Fax: 303-871-4566, E-mail: gfac@du.edu. *Vice Provost,* Dr. James Moran, 303-871-2706.

Conflict Resolution Institute Students: 13 full-time (7 women), 10 part-time (6 women); includes 4 minority (1 African American, 1 Asian American or Pacific Islander, 2 Hispanic Americans). Average age 27. *Faculty:* 1 (woman) full-time, 2 part-time/adjunct (1 woman). Expenses: Contact institution. *Financial support:* Career-related internships or fieldwork, Federal Work-Study, scholarships/grants, and tuition waivers (partial) available. Financial award application deadline: 2/15; financial award applicants required to submit FAFSA. In 2008, 5 master's awarded. *Degree program information:* Part-time programs available. Offers conflict resolution (MA). *Application deadline:* For fall admission, 2/15 priority date for domestic students; for winter admission, 11/1 priority date for domestic students; for spring admission, 1/15 priority date for domestic students. Applications are processed on a rolling basis. *Application fee:* $50. Electronic applications accepted. *Application Contact:* Information Contact, 303-871-6477, E-mail: cri@du.edu. *Director,* Dr. Karen Feste, 303-871-6477, E-mail: kfeste@du.edu.

Intermodal Transportation Institute Students: 22 full-time (2 women), 17 part-time (1 woman); includes 2 minority (both African Americans), 3 international. Average age 42. Expenses: Contact institution. *Financial support:* Applicants required to submit FAFSA. In 2008, 20 master's awarded. Offers intermodal transportation (MS). *Application fee:* $0. *Application Contact:* Information Contact, 303-871-4702, E-mail: du-iti@du.edu. *Executive Director,* Cathryne C. Johnson, 303-871-4702.

Josef Korbel School of International Studies Students: 344 full-time (205 women), 52 part-time (28 women); includes 35 minority (5 African Americans, 3 American Indian/Alaska Native, 7 Asian Americans or Pacific Islanders, 20 Hispanic Americans), 25 international. Average age 28. 819 applicants, 79% accepted, 213 enrolled. *Faculty:* 27 full-time (7 women), 34 part-time/adjunct (13 women). Expenses: Contact institution. *Financial support:* Career-related internships or fieldwork, Federal Work-Study, institutionally sponsored loans, and scholarships/grants available. Support available to part-time students. Financial award applicants required to submit FAFSA. In 2008, 234 master's, 7 doctorates awarded. *Degree program information:* Part-time programs available. Offers international studies (MA, PhD). *Application deadline:* For fall admission, 1/15 priority date for domestic students, 12/1 priority date for international students; for winter admission, 10/15 priority date for domestic and international students. Applications are processed on a rolling basis. *Application fee:* $60. Electronic applications accepted. *Application Contact:* Office of Graduate Admissions, 303-871-2544, E-mail: korbeladm@du.edu. *Director of Graduate Admissions,* Brad Miller, 303-871-2544.

School of Engineering and Computer Science Students: 9 full-time (2 women), 156 part-time (28 women); includes 21 minority (4 African Americans, 11 Asian Americans or Pacific Islanders, 6 Hispanic Americans), 35 international. Average age 31. 239 applicants, 87% accepted, 92 enrolled. *Faculty:* 25 full-time (3 women), 5 part-time/adjunct (1 woman). Expenses: Contact institution. *Financial support:* In 2008–09, 9 research assistantships with full and partial tuition reimbursements (averaging $15,000 per year), 14 teaching assistantships with full and partial tuition reimbursements (averaging $16,000 per year) were awarded. Financial award applicants required to submit FAFSA. In 2008, 24 master's, 4 doctorates awarded. Offers bioengineering (MS); computer engineering (MS); computer science (MS, PhD); computer science and engineering (MS); electrical engineering (MS); engineering (MS, PhD); engineering and computer science (MS, PhD); materials science (PhD); mechanical engineering (MS); mechatronics (MS). *Application deadline:* Applications are processed on a rolling basis. *Application fee:* $50. Electronic applications accepted. *Application Contact:* Dr. Rahmat Shoureshi, Dean, 303-871-2621. *Dean,* Dr. Rahmat Shoureshi, 303-871-2621.

University College Students: 28 full-time (15 women), 699 part-time (401 women); includes 129 minority (54 African Americans, 8 American Indian/Alaska Native, 22 Asian Americans or Pacific Islanders, 45 Hispanic Americans), 4 international. Average age 36. 845 applicants, 96% accepted, 326 enrolled. *Faculty:* 137 part-time/adjunct (55 women). Expenses: Contact institution. *Financial support:* Applicants required to submit FAFSA. In 2008, 221 master's, 3 Certificates awarded. *Degree program information:* Part-time and evening/weekend programs available. Postbaccalaureate distance learning degree programs offered (no on-campus study). Offers applied communication (MAS, MPS, Certificate); computer information systems (MAS, Certificate); environmental policy and management (MAS, Certificate); geographic information systems (MAS, Certificate); human resource administration (MPS, Certificate); knowledge and information technologies (MAS); liberal studies (MLS, Certificate); modern languages (MLS, Certificate); organizational leadership (MPS, Certificate); security management (Certificate); technology management (MAS, Certificate); telecommunications (MAS, Certificate). *Application deadline:* Applications are processed on a rolling basis. *Application fee:* $75. Electronic applications accepted. *Application Contact:* Information Contact, 303-871-3155. *Dean,* Dr. James Davis, 303-871-2291, Fax: 303-871-4047, E-mail: jdavis@du.edu.

See Close-Up on page 1017.

UNIVERSITY OF DETROIT MERCY, Detroit, MI 48221

General Information Independent-religious, coed, university. *Graduate housing:* Rooms and/or apartments available to single and married students.

GRADUATE UNITS

College of Business Administration *Degree program information:* Part-time and evening/weekend programs available. Offers business administration (EMBA, MBA, MS, MSCIS, Certificate); business turnaround management (MS, Certificate); computer information systems (MSCIS); information assurance (MS).

College of Engineering and Science *Degree program information:* Part-time and evening/weekend programs available. Offers chemistry (MS); civil and environmental engineering (ME, DE); computer engineering (ME, DE); computer science (MSCS); computer science education (MATM); computer systems applications (MSCS); engineering and science (M Eng Mgt, MATM, ME, MS, MSCS, DE); engineering management (M Eng Mgt); mathematics education (MATM); mechanical engineering (ME, DE); mechatronics systems (ME, DE); signals and systems (ME, DE); software engineering (MSCS).

College of Health Professions Offers family nurse practitioner (MSN, Certificate); health professions (MHSA, MS, MSN, Certificate); health services administration (MHSA); health systems management (MSN); nurse anesthesiology (MS); physician assistant (MS).

College of Liberal Arts and Education *Degree program information:* Part-time and evening/weekend programs available. Offers addiction counseling (MA); addiction studies (Certificate); clinical psychology (MA, PhD); community counseling (MA); counseling (MA); criminal justice (MA); curriculum and instruction (MA); educational administration (MA); emotionally impaired (MA); industrial/organizational psychology (MA); intelligence analysis (MS); learning disabilities (MA); liberal arts and education (MA, MALS, MS, PhD, Certificate, Spec); liberal studies (MALS); religious studies (MA); school counseling (MA); school psychology (Spec); security administration (MS); special education (MA).

School of Architecture Offers architecture (M Arch).

School of Dentistry Offers dentistry (DDS, MS, Certificate); endodontics (MS, Certificate); orthodontics (MS, Certificate); periodontics (MS, Certificate).

School of Law *Degree program information:* Part-time programs available. Offers law (JD).

UNIVERSITY OF DUBUQUE, Dubuque, IA 52001-5099

General Information Independent-religious, coed, comprehensive institution. *Graduate housing:* Rooms and/or apartments available on a first-come, first-served basis to single students and available to married students.

GRADUATE UNITS

Program in Business Administration *Degree program information:* Part-time and evening/weekend programs available. Offers business administration (MBA). Electronic applications accepted.

Program in Communication *Degree program information:* Part-time and evening/weekend programs available. Offers information technologies communication (MAC); leadership and management (MAC); strategic and corporate communication (MAC). Electronic applications accepted.

Theological Seminary Postbaccalaureate distance learning degree programs offered (minimal on-campus study). Offers theology (M Div, MAR, D Min).

UNIVERSITY OF EVANSVILLE, Evansville, IN 47722

General Information Independent-religious, coed, comprehensive institution. *Enrollment:* 2,789 graduate, professional, and undergraduate students; 150 full-time matriculated graduate/professional students (104 women), 7 part-time matriculated graduate/professional students

University of Evansville (continued)

(6 women). *Enrollment by degree level:* 90 master's, 67 doctoral. *Graduate faculty:* 17 full-time (6 women), 14 part-time/adjunct (5 women). *Tuition:* Full-time $7212. Tuition and fees vary according to course load, degree level and program. *Graduate housing:* On-campus housing not available. *Student services:* Career counseling, free psychological counseling, international student services, multicultural affairs office, services for students with disabilities. *Online resources:* library catalog, web page, access to other libraries' catalogs. *Collection:* 274,174 titles, 845 serial subscriptions, 12,710 audiovisual materials. *Research affiliation:* Council of Independent Colleges (higher education administration), The New American Colleges & Universities (higher education administration), Independent Colleges of Indiana (higher education administration).

Computer facilities: 385 computers available on campus for general student use. A campuswide network can be accessed from student residence rooms and from off campus. Online class registration is available. *Web address:* http://www.evansville.edu/.

General Application Contact: Carla Doty, Director of Continuing Education, 812-488-2981, Fax: 812-488-2432, E-mail: cd39@evansville.edu.

GRADUATE UNITS

Center for Adult Education Students: 63 full-time (45 women), 1 (woman) part-time; includes 3 minority (2 African Americans, 1 American Indian/Alaska Native), 1 international. Average age 38. 32 applicants, 91% accepted, 21 enrolled. *Faculty:* 6 full-time (2 women), 5 part-time/adjunct (2 women). Expenses: Contact institution. *Financial support:* In 2008–09, 12 students received support. Application deadline: 6/1. In 2008, 26 master's awarded. *Degree program information:* Part-time and evening/weekend programs available. Offers public service administration (MS). *Application deadline:* For fall admission, 7/15 priority date for domestic students; for spring admission, 11/30 priority date for domestic students. Applications are processed on a rolling basis. *Application fee:* $35. *Application Contact:* Carla S. Doty, Director of Continuing Education, 812-488-2981, Fax: 812-488-2432, E-mail: cd39@evansville.edu. *Director of Continuing Education,* Carla S. Doty, 812-488-2981, Fax: 812-488-2432, E-mail: cd39@evansville.edu.

College of Education and Health Sciences Students: 74 full-time (56 women), 4 part-time (all women); includes 1 minority (Asian American or Pacific Islander), 6 international. Average age 24. 84 applicants, 71% accepted, 43 enrolled. *Faculty:* 9 full-time (4 women), 7 part-time/adjunct (3 women). Expenses: Contact institution. *Financial support:* In 2008–09, 67 students received support. Scholarships/grants available. Financial award applicants required to submit FAFSA. In 2008, 15 master's awarded. Offers education and health sciences (MS, DPT); health services administration (MS); physical therapy (DPT). *Application deadline:* Applications are processed on a rolling basis. *Application Contact:* Dr. Lynn Penland, Dean, 812-488-2360, Fax: 812-488-1146, E-mail: lp22@evansville.edu. *Dean,* Dr. Lynn Penland, 812-488-2360, Fax: 812-488-1146, E-mail: lp22@evansville.edu.

College of Engineering and Computer Science Students: 2 part-time (1 woman). Average age 29. 3 applicants, 67% accepted, 0 enrolled. *Faculty:* 1 full-time (0 women), 1 part-time/adjunct (0 women). Expenses: Contact institution. *Financial support:* In 2008–09, 1 student received support. Scholarships/grants available. Financial award application deadline: 6/1; financial award applicants required to submit FAFSA. *Degree program information:* Part-time programs available. Offers electrical engineering and computer science (MS); engineering and computer science (MS). *Application deadline:* For fall admission, 5/1 priority date for domestic and international students. Applications are processed on a rolling basis. *Application fee:* $25 ($50 for international students). *Application Contact:* Dr. Dick Blandford, Department Chair, 812-488-2570, Fax: 812-488-2662, E-mail: blandford@evansville.edu. *Dean,* Dr. Philip Gerhart, 812-488-2651, Fax: 812-488-2780, E-mail: pg3@evansville.edu.

Schroeder Family School of Business Administration Students: 12 full-time (3 women); includes 1 minority (African American). Average age 38. *Faculty:* 2 full-time (0 women), 1 part-time/adjunct (0 women). Expenses: Contact institution. *Financial support:* In 2008–09, 1 student received support. Application deadline: 6/1. *Degree program information:* Part-time and evening/weekend programs available. Offers executive business administration (MBA). *Application deadline:* Applications are processed on a rolling basis. *Application fee:* $75. *Application Contact:* Dr. Gale Blalock, Chair, EMBA Admissions, 812-488-2455, Fax: 812-488-2872, E-mail: emba@evansville.edu. *Dean,* Dr. Robert Clark, 812-488-2851, Fax: 812-488-2872, E-mail: rc60@evansville.edu.

THE UNIVERSITY OF FINDLAY, Findlay, OH 45840-3653

General Information Independent-religious, coed, comprehensive institution. CGS member. *Enrollment:* 5,761 graduate, professional, and undergraduate students; 361 full-time matriculated graduate/professional students (233 women), 1,076 part-time matriculated graduate/professional students (522 women). *Enrollment by degree level:* 52 first professional, 1,317 master's. *Graduate faculty:* 106 full-time, 4 part-time/adjunct. Tuition and fees vary according to course load and program. *Graduate housing:* Room and/or apartments available on a first-come, first-served basis to single students; on-campus housing not available to married students. Typical cost: $4144 per year ($8306 including board). Room and board charges vary according to housing facility selected. *Student services:* Campus employment opportunities, campus safety program, career counseling, exercise/wellness program, free psychological counseling, grant writing training, international student services, low-cost health insurance, multicultural affairs office, services for students with disabilities, teacher training. *Library facilities:* Shafer Library. *Online resources:* library catalog, access to other libraries' catalogs. *Collection:* 132,052 titles, 23,128 serial subscriptions. *Research affiliation:* Ohio State University Research Foundation (biology research), Rollin M. Gerstacker Foundation (environmental research), Department of Agriculture (wildlife research), Department of Education (bilingual teaching research), Department of Education (technology innovation), Department of Health and Human Services (terrorism preparedness).

Computer facilities: Computer purchase and lease plans are available. 200 computers available on campus for general student use. A campuswide network can be accessed from student residence rooms and from off campus. Online class registration is available. *Web address:* http://www.findlay.edu/.

General Application Contact: Heather Riffle, Assistant to the Dean, Graduate and Professional Studies, 419-434-4640, Fax: 419-434-5517, E-mail: riffle@findlay.edu.

GRADUATE UNITS

Graduate and Professional Studies Students: 361 full-time (233 women), 1,076 part-time (522 women); includes 48 minority (20 African Americans, 3 American Indian/Alaska Native, 7 Asian Americans or Pacific Islanders, 18 Hispanic Americans), 615 international. Average age 35. 513 applicants, 88% accepted, 377 enrolled. Expenses: Contact institution. *Financial support:* In 2008–09, 16 research assistantships with full and partial tuition reimbursements (averaging $4,000 per year), 7 teaching assistantships with full and partial tuition reimbursements (averaging $6,000 per year) were awarded; unspecified assistantships also available. Financial award application deadline: 4/1; financial award applicants required to submit FAFSA. In 2008, 625 master's awarded. *Degree program information:* Part-time and evening/weekend programs available. Postbaccalaureate distance learning degree programs offered (no on-campus study). Offers administration (MA Ed); early childhood (MA Ed); elementary education (MA Ed); human resource development (MA Ed); leadership (MA Ed); special education (MA Ed); technology (MA Ed); web instruction (MA Ed). *Application deadline:* Applications are processed on a rolling basis. *Application fee:* $25. Electronic applications accepted. *Application Contact:* Heather Riffle, Assistant to the Dean, Graduate and Professional Studies, 419-434-4640, Fax: 419-434-5517, E-mail: riffle@findlay.edu. *Dean, Graduate and Professional Studies,* Dr. Thomas Dillion, 419-434-4640, Fax: 419-434-5517, E-mail: dillon@findlay.edu.

College of Business Students: 82 full-time (35 women), 633 part-time (248 women); includes 18 minority (10 African Americans, 1 American Indian/Alaska Native, 3 Asian Americans or Pacific Islanders, 4 Hispanic Americans), 507 international. Average age 35. 251 applicants, 87% accepted, 180 enrolled. Expenses: Contact institution. *Financial support:* In 2008–09, 6 research assistantships with full and partial tuition reimbursements (averaging $4,200 per year) were awarded; unspecified assistantships also available. Financial award application deadline: 4/1; financial award applicants required to submit FAFSA. In 2008, 396 master's awarded. *Degree program information:* Part-time and evening/weekend programs available. Postbaccalaureate distance learning degree programs offered (no on-campus study). Offers financial management (MBA); human resource management (MBA); international management (MBA); management (MBA); marketing (MBA); public management (MBA). *Application deadline:* Applications are processed on a rolling basis. *Application fee:* $25 ($0 for international students). Electronic applications accepted. *Application Contact:* Heather Riffle, Assistant to the Dean, Graduate and Professional Studies, 419-434-4640, Fax: 419-434-5517, E-mail: riffle@findlay.edu. *Dean,* Dr. Paul Sears, 419-434-4704, Fax: 419-434-4822.

College of Health Professions Students: 181 full-time (131 women), 12 part-time (10 women); includes 1 minority (Asian American or Pacific Islander), 5 international. Average age 35. 79 applicants, 96% accepted, 74 enrolled. Expenses: Contact institution. *Financial support:* In 2008–09, 4 research assistantships with full and partial tuition reimbursements (averaging $3,600 per year), 4 teaching assistantships with full and partial tuition reimbursements (averaging $6,000 per year) were awarded; unspecified assistantships also available. Financial award applicants required to submit FAFSA. In 2008, 80 master's awarded. *Degree program information:* Evening/weekend programs available. Offers athletic training (MAT); health professions (MAT, MOT, MPT); occupational therapy (MOT); physical therapy (MPT). *Application deadline:* For winter admission, 12/1 for domestic and international students. Applications are processed on a rolling basis. *Application fee:* $25. Electronic applications accepted. *Application Contact:* Heather Riffle, Assistant to the Dean, Graduate and Professional Studies, 419-434-4640, Fax: 419-434-5517, E-mail: riffle@findlay.edu. *Dean,* Dr. Andrea Koepke, 419-434-4677, Fax: 419-434-4822, E-mail: koepke@findlay.edu.

College of Liberal Arts Students: 21 full-time (13 women), 37 part-time (30 women); includes 3 minority (1 American Indian/Alaska Native, 2 Hispanic Americans), 31 international. Average age 35. 21 applicants, 86% accepted, 10 enrolled. Expenses: Contact institution. *Financial support:* In 2008–09, 1 teaching assistantship with full tuition reimbursement (averaging $6,000 per year) was awarded. Financial award application deadline: 4/1; financial award applicants required to submit FAFSA. In 2008, 21 master's awarded. *Degree program information:* Part-time and evening/weekend programs available. Offers bilingual and multicultural education (MA); liberal arts (MA, MALS); liberal studies (MALS); teaching English to speakers of other languages (MA). *Application deadline:* Applications are processed on a rolling basis. *Application fee:* $25. Electronic applications accepted. *Application Contact:* Heather Riffle, Assistant to the Dean, Graduate and Professional Studies, 419-434-4640, Fax: 419-434-5517, E-mail: riffle@findlay.edu. *Dean,* Dr. Gary Johnson, 419-434-4643, Fax: 419-434-4822, E-mail: gjohnson@findlay.edu.

College of Pharmacy Offers pharmacy (Pharm D).

College of Sciences Students: 1 full-time (0 women), 120 part-time (42 women); includes 10 minority (4 African Americans, 1 American Indian/Alaska Native, 2 Asian Americans or Pacific Islanders, 3 Hispanic Americans), 64 international. Average age 25. 39 applicants, 77% accepted, 26 enrolled. Expenses: Contact institution. *Financial support:* In 2008–09, 2 research assistantships with full and partial tuition reimbursements (averaging $4,000 per year), 2 teaching assistantships with full and partial tuition reimbursements (averaging $6,000 per year) were awarded; unspecified assistantships also available. Financial award application deadline: 4/1; financial award applicants required to submit FAFSA. In 2008, 29 master's awarded. *Degree program information:* Part-time and evening/weekend programs available. Postbaccalaureate distance learning degree programs offered (no on-campus study). Offers environmental, safety and health management (MSEM); sciences (MSEM). *Application deadline:* Applications are processed on a rolling basis. *Application fee:* $25. Electronic applications accepted. *Application Contact:* Heather Riffle, Assistant to the Dean, Graduate and Professional Studies, 419-434-4640, Fax: 419-434-5517, E-mail: riffle@findlay.edu. *Dean,* Dr. Terry Schwaner, 419-434-5377, E-mail: schwaner@findlay.edu.

UNIVERSITY OF FLORIDA, Gainesville, FL 32611

General Information State-supported, coed, university. CGS member. *Graduate housing:* Rooms and/or apartments available on a first-come, first-served basis to single and married students. *Research affiliation:* Los Alamos National Laboratory (high magnetic field research), National Center for Automated Information Research (law and business data), Oracle Corporation (database management), IBM (information infrastructure), Association of Universities for Research in Astronomy (Gemini multinational telescope).

GRADUATE UNITS

College of Dentistry Offers dentistry (DMD, MS, PhD, Certificate); endodontics (MS, Certificate); foreign trained dentistry (Certificate); oral biology (PhD); orthodontics (MS, Certificate); periodontology (MS, Certificate); prosthodontics (MS, Certificate).

College of Medicine Offers biochemistry and molecular biology (MS, PhD); biomedical sciences (PhD); clinical investigation (MS); epidemiology (MS); genetics (PhD); imaging science and technology (MS, PhD); immunology and microbiology (PhD); immunology and molecular pathology (PhD); medicine (MD, MPAS, MPH, MS, PhD); molecular cell biology (PhD); molecular genetics and microbiology (MS, PhD); neuroscience (MS, PhD); pharmacology and therapeutics (PhD); physician assistant (MPAS); physiology and functional genomics (PhD); physiology and pharmacology (PhD); public health (MPH). Electronic applications accepted.

College of Pharmacy *Degree program information:* Part-time programs available. Postbaccalaureate distance learning degree programs offered (no on-campus study). Offers clinical pharmaceutical sciences (PhD); forensic DNA and serology (MS, Certificate); forensic drug chemistry (MS, Certificate); forensic toxicology (MS, Certificate); medicinal chemistry (Pharm D, MSP, PhD); pharmaceutical sciences (MSP, PhD); pharmaceutics (PhD); pharmacodynamics (MSP, PhD); pharmacology (PhD); pharmacy (Pharm D, MS, MSP, PhD, Certificate); pharmacy health care administration (MSP, PhD); pharmacy practice (PhD). Electronic applications accepted.

College of Veterinary Medicine *Degree program information:* Part-time programs available. Offers forensic toxicology (Certificate); veterinary medical sciences (MS, PhD); veterinary medicine (DVM, MS, PhD, Certificate).

Graduate School *Degree program information:* Part-time programs available. Electronic applications accepted.

College of Agricultural and Life Sciences *Degree program information:* Part-time programs available. Offers agricultural and life sciences (MAB, MFAS, MFRC, MFYCS, MS, DPM, PhD); agricultural education and communication (MS, PhD); agronomy (MS, PhD); anatomy and development (MS, PhD); animal sciences (MS, PhD); biochemistry and molecular biology (MS, PhD); breeding and genetics (MS, PhD); ecology (MS, PhD); entomology and nematology (MS, PhD); family, youth, and community sciences (MFYCS, MS); fisheries and aquatic sciences (MFAS, MS, PhD); food and resource economics (MAB, MS, PhD); food science (MS, PhD); forest resources and conservation (MFRC, MS, PhD); microbiology and cell science (MS, PhD); nutritional sciences (MS, PhD); plant biotechnology (MS, PhD); plant breeding and genetics (MS, PhD); plant medicine (DPM); plant molecular and cellular biology (MS, PhD); plant pathology (MS, PhD); plant production and nutrient management (MS, PhD); postharvest biology (MS, PhD); soil and water science (MS, PhD); stress physiology (MS, PhD); sustainable/organic practice (MS, PhD); taxonomy (MS, PhD); tissue culture (MS, PhD); weed science (MS, PhD); wildlife ecology and conservation (MS, PhD). Electronic applications accepted.

College of Design, Construction and Planning *Degree program information:* Part-time programs available. Offers architecture (M Arch, MSAS, PhD); building construction (MBC, MICM, MSBC, PhD); design, construction and planning (M Arch, MAURP, MBC, MICM, MID, MLA, MSAS, MSBC, PhD); interior design (MID, PhD); landscape architecture (MLA, PhD); urban and regional planning (MAURP, PhD). Electronic applications accepted.

College of Education *Degree program information:* Part-time programs available. Offers bilingual/ESOL education (M Ed, MAE, Ed D, PhD, Ed S); curriculum and instruction (M Ed, MAE, Ed D, PhD, Ed S); early childhood education (Ed D, PhD, Ed S); education (M Ed, MAE, Ed D, PhD, Ed S); educational leadership (M Ed, MAE, Ed D, PhD, Ed S); educational psychology (M Ed, MAE, Ed D, PhD, Ed S); elementary education (M Ed, MAE); English education (M Ed, MAE); higher education administration (Ed D, PhD, Ed S); marriage and family counseling (M Ed, MAE, Ed D, PhD, Ed S); mathematics education (M Ed, MAE); mental health counseling (M Ed, MAE, Ed D, PhD, Ed S); reading education (M Ed, MAE); research and evaluation methodology (M Ed, MAE, Ed D, PhD, Ed S); school counseling and guidance (M Ed, MAE, Ed D, PhD, Ed S); school psychology (M Ed, MAE, Ed D, PhD, Ed S); science education (M Ed, MAE); social foundations (M Ed, MAE, Ed D, PhD); social studies education (M Ed, MAE); special education (M Ed, MAE, Ed D, PhD, Ed S); student personnel in higher education (M Ed, MAE). Electronic applications accepted.

College of Engineering *Degree program information:* Part-time programs available. Offers aerospace engineering (ME, MS, PhD, Engr); agricultural and biological engineering (ME, MS, PhD, Engr); biomedical engineering (ME, MS, PhD, Certificate); chemical engineering (ME, MS, PhD); civil engineering (MCE, MS, PhD, Engr); coastal and oceanographic engineering (ME, MS, PhD, Engr); computer engineering (ME, MS, PhD); computer science (MS); digital arts and sciences (MS); electrical and computer engineering (ME, MS, PhD, Engr); engineering (MCE, ME, MS, PhD, Certificate, Engr); environmental engineering sciences (ME, MS, PhD, Engr); industrial and systems engineering (ME, MS, PhD, Engr); materials science and engineering (ME, MS, PhD, Engr); mechanical engineering (ME, MS, PhD, Engr); nuclear engineering sciences (ME, MS, PhD, Engr). Electronic applications accepted.

College of Fine Arts *Degree program information:* Part-time programs available. Offers art (MFA); art education (MA); art history (MA, PhD); choral conducting (MM, PhD); composition/theory (MM, PhD); digital arts and sciences (MA); ethnomusicology (PhD); fine arts (MA, MFA, MM, PhD); instrumental conducting (MM, PhD); museology (museum studies) (MA); music (MM, PhD); music education (MM, PhD); music history and literature (MM); musicology (PhD); performance (MM); sacred music (MM); theatre (MFA). Electronic applications accepted.

College of Health and Human Performance *Degree program information:* Part-time programs available. Offers athletic training/sport medicine (MS, PhD); biomechanics (MS, PhD); clinical exercise physiology (MS); exercise physiology (MS, PhD); health and human performance (PhD); health behavior (PhD); health communication (Graduate Certificate); health education and behavior (MS); human performance (MS); motor learning/control (MS, PhD); recreational studies (MS); sport and exercise psychology (MS). Electronic applications accepted.

College of Journalism and Communications *Degree program information:* Part-time programs available. Offers advertising (M Adv); journalism (MAMC); mass communication (MAMC, PhD); public relations (MAMC); telecommunication (MAMC). Electronic applications accepted.

College of Liberal Arts and Sciences *Degree program information:* Part-time programs available. Offers African studies (Certificate); anthropology (MA, PhD); astronomy (MS, PhD); behavior analysis (PhD); behavioral neuroscience (MS, PhD); botany (M Ag, MS, MST, PhD); chemistry (MS, MST, PhD); classical studies (MA, PhD); cognitive and sensory processes (PhD); communication sciences and disorders (MA, Au D, PhD); counseling psychology (PhD); creative writing (MFA); criminology and law (MA, PhD); developmental psychology (PhD); English (MA, PhD); French (MA, PhD); gender and development (Graduate Certificate); geography (MA, MS, PhD); geology (MS, MST, PhD); German (MA, PhD); history (MA, PhD); international development policy and administration (MA, Certificate); international relations (MA, MAT); Latin (MA, MAT, ML); Latin American studies (MA, Certificate); liberal arts and sciences (M Ag, M Stat, MA, MAT, MFA, ML, MS, MS Stat, MST, MWS, Au D, PhD, Certificate, Graduate Certificate); linguistics (MA, PhD); mathematics (MA, MAT, MS, MST, PhD); philosophy (MA, PhD); physics (MS, MST, PhD); political campaigning (MA, Certificate); political science (MA, MAT, PhD); public affairs (MA, Certificate); religion (MA, PhD); social psychology (MS, PhD); sociology (MA, PhD); Spanish (MA, PhD); statistics (M Stat, MS Stat, PhD); teaching English as a second language (Certificate); women's studies (MA, MWS, Graduate Certificate); zoology (MS, MST, PhD). Electronic applications accepted.

College of Nursing *Degree program information:* Part-time programs available. Offers nursing (MSN); nursing sciences (PhD). Electronic applications accepted.

College of Public Health and Health Professions *Degree program information:* Part-time programs available. Offers audiology (Au D); biostatistics (MPH); clinical and health psychology (PhD); environmental health (MPH); epidemiology (MPH); health administration (MHA); health services research (PhD); occupational therapy (MHS, MOT); physical therapy (DPT); public health and health professions (MHA, MHS, MOT, MPH, Au D, DPT, PhD); public health management and policy (MPH); public health practice (MPH); rehabilitation counseling (MHS); rehabilitation science (PhD); social and behavioral sciences (MPH). Electronic applications accepted.

School of Natural Resources and Environment Offers interdisciplinary ecology (MS, PhD). Electronic applications accepted.

Warrington College of Business Administration Offers accounting (MBA); arts administration (MBA); business administration (M Acc, MA, MAIB, MBA, MS, PhD, Certificate); business strategy and public policy (MBA); competitive strategy (MBA); decision and information sciences (MBA, MS, PhD); economics (MA, PhD); electronic commerce (MBA); finance (MBA, PhD); financial services (Certificate); general business (MBA); global management (MBA); Graham-Buffett security analysis (MBA); health administration (MBA); human resources management (MBA); insurance (PhD); international business (MAIB); international studies (MBA); Latin American business (MBA); management (MBA, MS, PhD); marketing (MBA); real estate and urban analysis (PhD); sports administration (MBA); supply chain management (MS).

Interdisciplinary Concentration in Animal Molecular and Cellular Biology Offers animal molecular and cellular biology (MS, PhD). Program offered by College of Agricultural and Life Sciences, College of Liberal Arts and Sciences, College of Medicine, and College of Veterinary Medicine.

Levin College of Law Students: 1,369 full-time (620 women); includes 279 minority (69 African Americans, 8 American Indian/Alaska Native, 77 Asian Americans or Pacific Islanders, 125 Hispanic Americans), 71 international. Average age 24. 3,093 applicants, 31% accepted, 397 enrolled. *Faculty:* 77 full-time (38 women), 39 part-time/adjunct (11 women). Expenses: Contact institution. *Financial support:* In 2008–09, 299 students received support, including 85 research assistantships (averaging $1,050 per year); Federal Work-Study, institutionally sponsored loans, scholarships/grants, health care benefits, and unspecified assistantships also available. Financial award application deadline: 4/7; financial award applicants required to submit FAFSA. In 2008, 497 JDs, 1 doctorate awarded. Offers comparative law (LL M); environmental law (LL M); international taxation (LL M); law (JD); taxation (LL M, SJD). *Application deadline:* For fall admission, 1/15 for domestic and international students. Applications are processed on a rolling basis. *Application fee:* $30. Electronic applications accepted. *Application Contact:* Noemar Castro, Acting Assistant Dean for Admissions, 352-273-0890, Fax: 352-392-4087, E-mail: castro@law.ufl.edu. *Dean,* Robert Jerry, 352-273-0600, Fax: 352-392-8727, E-mail: jerryr@law.ufl.edu.

See Close-Up on page 1019.

UNIVERSITY OF GEORGIA, Athens, GA 30602

General Information State-supported, coed, university. CGS member. *Enrollment:* 34,180 graduate, professional, and undergraduate students; 5,939 full-time matriculated graduate/professional students (3,382 women), 2,181 part-time matriculated graduate/professional students (1,294 women). *Enrollment by degree level:* 1,549 first professional, 3,694 master's, 2,643 doctoral, 234 other advanced degrees. *Graduate faculty:* 1,177 full-time (349 women), 54 part-time/adjunct (13 women). *Graduate housing:* Rooms and/or apartments available to single and married students. *Student services:* Career counseling, free psychological counseling. *Library facilities:* Ilah Dunlap Little Memorial Library plus 2 others. *Online resources:* library catalog, web page, access to other libraries' catalogs. *Collection:* 4.6 million titles, 49,097 serial subscriptions. *Research affiliation:* Skidaway Institute of Oceanography, Southeast Water Laboratory, Russell Research Laboratory, Organization for Tropical Studies.

Computer facilities: 3,100 computers available on campus for general student use. A campuswide network can be accessed from student residence rooms and from off campus. Online class registration is available. *Web address:* http://www.uga.edu/.

General Application Contact: Krista Haynes, Director of Graduate Admissions, 706-425-1789, Fax: 706-425-3094, E-mail: gradadm@uga.edu.

GRADUATE UNITS

College of Pharmacy Students: 554 full-time (340 women), 37 part-time (22 women); includes 119 minority (32 African Americans, 2 American Indian/Alaska Native, 78 Asian Americans or Pacific Islanders, 7 Hispanic Americans), 42 international. 171 applicants, 16% accepted, 26 enrolled. *Faculty:* 21 full-time (6 women), 3 part-time/adjunct (0 women). Expenses: Contact institution. *Financial support:* Fellowships, research assistantships, teaching assistantships, career-related internships or fieldwork, Federal Work-Study, institutionally sponsored loans, tuition waivers, and unspecified assistantships available. Support available to part-time students. Financial award application deadline: 2/15. In 2008, 131 first professional degrees, 2 master's, 10 doctorates awarded. Offers clinical trials design and management (Certificate); pharmaceutical and biomedical regulatory affairs (Certificate); pharmacy (MS, PhD); pharmacy and biomedical regulatory affairs (Certificate). *Application deadline:* For fall admission, 7/1 priority date for domestic students; for spring admission, 11/15 for domestic students. *Application fee:* $50. Electronic applications accepted. *Application Contact:* Dr. Svein Oie, Dean, 706-542-1914, Fax: 706-542-5269, E-mail: soie@rx.uga.edu. *Dean,* Dr. Svein Oie, 706-542-1914, Fax: 706-542-5269, E-mail: soie@rx.uga.edu.

College of Public Health Students: 121 full-time (73 women), 26 part-time (20 women); includes 22 African Americans, 4 Asian Americans or Pacific Islanders, 2 Hispanic Americans, 24 international. 130 applicants, 46% accepted, 51 enrolled. *Faculty:* 13 full-time (4 women), 1 (woman) part-time/adjunct. Expenses: Contact institution. In 2008, 45 master's, 5 doctorates awarded. Offers environmental health science (MS, PhD); health promotion and behavior (MA, MPH, PhD); public health (MA, MPH, MS, PhD, Certificate). *Application deadline:* For fall admission, 7/1 for domestic students; for spring admission, 11/15 for domestic students. *Application fee:* $50. *Application Contact:* Clare Robb, Graduate Coordinator, 706-542-3222, Fax: 706-542-3221, E-mail: crobb@uga.edu. *Dean,* Dr. Phillip L. Williams, 706-542-0939, Fax: 706-542-6730, E-mail: pwilliam@uga.edu.

Institute of Gerontology 3 applicants, 67% accepted, 5 enrolled. *Faculty:* 2 full-time (1 woman). Expenses: Contact institution. Offers gerontology (Certificate). *Application Contact:* Dr. Anne H. Glass, Graduate Coordinator, 706-425-3222, E-mail: aglass@geron.uga.edu. *Director,* Dr. Leonard W. Poon, 706-425-3222, E-mail: lpoon@geron.uga.edu.

College of Veterinary Medicine Students: 475 full-time (339 women), 12 part-time (6 women); includes 33 minority (12 African Americans, 1 American Indian/Alaska Native, 7 Asian Americans or Pacific Islanders, 13 Hispanic Americans), 30 international. 88 applicants, 39% accepted, 27 enrolled. *Faculty:* 73 full-time (25 women), 7 part-time/adjunct (2 women). Expenses: Contact institution. *Financial support:* Fellowships, research assistantships, teaching assistantships, Federal Work-Study, scholarships/grants, and unspecified assistantships available. Financial award applicants required to submit FAFSA. In 2008, 96 first professional degrees, 12 master's, 10 doctorates awarded. Offers food animal medicine (MFAM); infectious diseases (MS, PhD); pathology (MS, PhD); pharmacology (MS, PhD); physiology (MS, PhD); physiology and pharmacology (MS, PhD); population health (MAM, MFAM); toxicology (MS, PhD); veterinary anatomy (MS); veterinary anatomy and radiology (MS); veterinary medicine (DVM, MAM, MFAM, MS, PhD). *Application deadline:* For fall admission, 7/1 priority date for domestic students; for spring admission, 11/15 for domestic students. *Application fee:* $50. Electronic applications accepted. *Application Contact:* Malik McKinley, Director of Graduate Admissions, 706-542-5727, E-mail: dvmadmit@uga.edu. *Dean,* Dr. Sheila W. Allen, 706-542-3461, Fax: 706-542-8254, E-mail: sallen01@uga.edu.

Graduate School *Degree program information:* Part-time programs available. Offers law (LL M). Electronic applications accepted.

Biomedical and Health Sciences Institute Students: 10 full-time (7 women); includes 1 minority (Asian American or Pacific Islander), 2 international. 7 applicants, 57% accepted, 3 enrolled. Expenses: Contact institution. Offers neuroscience (PhD). *Application Contact:* Dr. Gaylen L. Edwards, Graduate Coordinator, 706-542-5854, E-mail: gedwards@uga.edu. *Director,* Dr. Harry A. Dailey, 706-542-5922, Fax: 706-542-5285, E-mail: hdailey@uga.edu.

College of Agricultural and Environmental Sciences Students: 314 full-time (154 women), 94 part-time (40 women); includes 37 minority (22 African Americans, 1 American Indian/Alaska Native, 9 Asian Americans or Pacific Islanders, 5 Hispanic Americans), 150 international. 262 applicants, 57% accepted, 98 enrolled. *Faculty:* 166 full-time (21 women), 17 part-time/adjunct (3 women). Expenses: Contact institution. *Financial support:* Fellowships, research assistantships, teaching assistantships, career-related internships or fieldwork and unspecified assistantships available. In 2008, 62 master's, 32 doctorates awarded. Offers agricultural and environmental sciences (MA Ext, MADS, MAE, MAL, MCCS, MFT, MPPPM, MS, PhD); agricultural economics (MAE, MS, PhD); agricultural engineering (MS); agricultural leadership, education, and communication (MA Ext, MAL); animal and dairy science (PhD); animal and dairy sciences (MADS); animal nutrition (PhD); animal science (MS); biological and agricultural engineering (PhD); biological engineering (MS); crop and soil science (MS, PhD); crop and soil sciences (MCCS); dairy science (MS); entomology (MS, PhD); environmental economics (MS); food science (MS, PhD); food technology (MFT); horticulture (MS, PhD); plant pathology (MS, PhD); plant protection and pest management (MPPPM); poultry science (MS, PhD). *Application deadline:* For fall admission, 7/1 priority date for domestic students; for spring admission, 11/15 for domestic students. *Application fee:* $50. Electronic applications accepted. *Application Contact:* Krista Haynes, Director of Enrolled Student Services, 706-425-1789, Fax: 706-425-3094, E-mail: gradoff@uga.edu. *Dean,* Dr. J. Scott Angle, 706-542-3924, Fax: 706-542-0803, E-mail: caesdean@uga.edu.

College of Arts and Sciences Students: 1,442 full-time (703 women), 239 part-time (124 women); includes 121 minority (52 African Americans, 1 American Indian/Alaska Native, 30 Asian Americans or Pacific Islanders, 38 Hispanic Americans), 416 international. 2,487 applicants, 31% accepted, 443 enrolled. *Faculty:* 507 full-time (143 women), 10 part-time/adjunct (2 women). Expenses: Contact institution. *Financial support:* Fellowships, research assistantships, teaching assistantships, Federal Work-Study, institutionally sponsored loans, and unspecified assistantships available. In 2008, 218 master's, 185 doctorates awarded. Offers analytical chemistry (MS, PhD); anthropology (MA, PhD); applied mathematical science (MAMS); archaeological resource management (MS); art (MFA, PhD); art history (MA); artificial intelligence (MS); arts and sciences (MA, MAMS, MAT, MFA, MM, MS, DMA, PhD, Certificate); biochemistry and molecular biology (MS, PhD); cellular biology (MS, PhD); classical languages (MA); comparative literature (MA, PhD); computer science (MS, PhD); creative writing (MFA, PhD); English (MA, MAT, PhD); French (MA); genetics (MS, PhD); geography (MA, MS, PhD); geology (MS, PhD); German (MA); Greek (MA); history (MA, PhD); inorganic chemistry (MS, PhD); Latin (MA); linguistics (MA, PhD); marine sciences (MS, PhD); mathematics (MA, PhD); microbiology (MS, PhD); music (MA, MM, DMA, PhD); organic chemistry (MS, PhD); philosophy (MA, PhD); physical chemistry (MS, PhD); physics (MS, PhD); plant biology (MS, PhD); psychology (MS, PhD); religion (MA); Romance languages (MA, PhD); sociology (MA, PhD); Spanish (MA, PhD); speech communication (MA, PhD); statistics (MS, PhD); theatre (MFA, PhD); women's studies (Certificate). *Application deadline:* For fall admission, 7/1 priority date for domestic students; for spring admission, 11/15 for domestic students. *Application fee:* $50. Electronic applications accepted. *Application Contact:* Director of Enrolled Student Services. *Dean,* Dr. Garnett Stokes, 706-542-3400, Fax: 706-542-3422, E-mail: gstokes@franklin.uga.edu.

College of Education Students: 884 full-time (617 women), 1,092 part-time (783 women); includes 325 minority (243 African Americans, 6 American Indian/Alaska Native, 38 Asian Americans or Pacific Islanders, 38 Hispanic Americans), 132 international. 1,715 applicants, 52% accepted, 548 enrolled. *Faculty:* 139 full-time (70 women), 1 (woman) part-time/adjunct. Expenses: Contact institution. *Financial support:* Fellowships, research assistantships, teaching assistantships, unspecified assistantships available. In 2008, 450 master's, 133 doctorates, 95 other advanced degrees awarded. Offers adult education (M Ed, Ed D, PhD, Ed S); art education (MA Ed, Ed D, PhD, Ed S); college student affairs administration (M Ed, PhD); communication science and disorders (M Ed, MA, PhD, Ed S); counseling

University of Georgia (continued)

and student personnel (PhD); counseling psychology (PhD); early childhood education (M Ed, MAT, PhD, Ed S); education (M Ed, MA, MA Ed, MAT, MM Ed, MS, Ed D, PhD, Ed S); education of the gifted (Ed D); educational administration and policy (M Ed, PhD, Ed S); educational leadership (Ed D); educational psychology (M Ed, MA, Ed D, PhD, Ed S); elementary education (PhD); English education (M Ed, Ed S); higher education (PhD); human resource and organizational design (M Ed); human resources and organization design (M Ed); instructional technology (M Ed, PhD, Ed S); kinesiology (MS, PhD); language and literacy education (PhD); mathematics education (M Ed, Ed D, PhD, Ed S); middle school education (M Ed, PhD, Ed S); music education (MM Ed, Ed D, Ed S); occupational studies (MAT, Ed D, PhD, Ed S); professional counseling (M Ed); professional school counseling (Ed S); reading education (M Ed, Ed D, Ed S); recreation and leisure studies (M Ed, MA, PhD); science education (M Ed, Ed D, PhD, Ed S); social foundations of education (PhD); social studies education (M Ed, Ed D, PhD, Ed S); special education (M Ed, Ed D, PhD, Ed S); teaching additional languages (M Ed, Ed S). *Application deadline:* For fall admission, 7/1 priority date for domestic students; for spring admission, 11/15 for domestic students. *Application fee:* $50. Electronic applications accepted. *Application Contact:* Krista Haynes, Director of Enrolled Student Services, 706-425-1789, Fax: 706-425-3094, E-mail: gradoff@uga.edu. *Interim Dean,* Dr. Arthur M. Horne, 706-542-6446, Fax: 706-542-0360, E-mail: ahorne@uga.edu.

College of Environment and Design Students: 62 full-time (45 women), 35 part-time (18 women); includes 3 Asian Americans or Pacific Islanders, 1 Hispanic American, 5 international. 240 applicants, 33% accepted, 33 enrolled. *Faculty:* 15 full-time (3 women). Expenses: Contact institution. In 2008, 25 master's awarded. Offers environmental planning and design (MEPD); historic preservation (MHP); landscape architecture (MLA). *Application deadline:* For fall admission, 7/1 priority date for domestic students; for spring admission, 11/15 for domestic students. *Application fee:* $50. *Application Contact:* Prof. Brian J. LaHaie, Director of Enrolled Student Services, 706-542-4704, Fax: 706-542-4236, E-mail: blahaie@uga.edu. *Acting Dean,* Dean Daniels J. Nadenicek, 706-542-1100, Fax: 706-542-4485, E-mail: dnadeni@uga.edu.

College of Family and Consumer Sciences Students: 113 full-time (100 women), 21 part-time (16 women); includes 19 minority (14 African Americans, 2 Asian Americans or Pacific Islanders, 3 Hispanic Americans), 18 international. 149 applicants, 47% accepted, 56 enrolled. *Faculty:* 38 full-time (24 women), 1 (woman) part-time/adjunct. Expenses: Contact institution. *Financial support:* Fellowships, research assistantships, teaching assistantships, unspecified assistantships available. In 2008, 23 master's, 12 doctorates awarded. Offers child and family development (MS, PhD); early childhood education (MAT); family and consumer sciences (MAT, MFCS, MS, PhD); foods and nutrition (MFCS, MS, PhD); historic costume and textiles (MS); housing and consumer economics (MS, PhD); merchandising/international trade (MS); textile analysis (PhD); textile chemical processes (PhD); textile products and standards (PhD); textile science (MS). *Application deadline:* For fall admission, 7/1 priority date for domestic students; for spring admission, 11/15 for domestic students. *Application fee:* $50. Electronic applications accepted. *Application Contact:* Director of Enrolled Student Services. *Dean,* Dr. Laura Dunn Jolly, 706-542-4879, Fax: 706-542-4862, E-mail: dean@fcs.uga.edu.

School of Ecology Students: 72 full-time (42 women), 20 part-time (12 women); includes 2 minority (1 African American, 1 Hispanic American), 4 international. 138 applicants, 19% accepted, 21 enrolled. *Faculty:* 15 full-time (4 women), 6 part-time/adjunct (2 women). Expenses: Contact institution. *Financial support:* Fellowships, research assistantships, teaching assistantships, unspecified assistantships available. In 2008, 5 master's, 14 doctorates awarded. Offers conservation ecology and sustainable development (MS); ecology (MS, PhD). *Application deadline:* For fall admission, 7/1 priority date for domestic students; for spring admission, 11/15 for domestic students. *Application fee:* $50. Electronic applications accepted. *Application Contact:* Dr. C. Ronald Carroll, Graduate Coordinator, 706-3381366, Fax: 706-542-4819, E-mail: rcarroll@uga.edu. *Dean,* Dr. John L. Gittleman, 706-542-2968, Fax: 706-542-4819, E-mail: ecohead@uga.edu.

School of Forestry and Natural Resources Students: 130 full-time (41 women), 31 part-time (14 women); includes 5 minority (3 African Americans, 1 American Indian/Alaska Native, 1 Hispanic American), 19 international. 75 applicants, 60% accepted, 44 enrolled. *Faculty:* 33 full-time (2 women), 8 part-time/adjunct (1 woman). Expenses: Contact institution. *Financial support:* Fellowships, research assistantships, teaching assistantships, unspecified assistantships available. In 2008, 51 master's, 11 doctorates awarded. Offers forestry and natural resources (MFR, MS, PhD). *Application deadline:* For fall admission, 7/1 priority date for domestic students; for spring admission, 11/15 for domestic students. *Application fee:* $50. Electronic applications accepted. *Application Contact:* Dr. Lawrence A. Morris, Graduate Coordinator, 706-542-2532, Fax: 706-542-2281, E-mail: lmorris@uga.edu. *Dean,* Dr. Michael C. Clutter, 706-542-4741, Fax: 706-542-2281, E-mail: mclutter@warnell.uga.edu.

School of Social Work Students: 295 full-time (260 women), 72 part-time (64 women); includes 106 minority (89 African Americans, 1 American Indian/Alaska Native, 2 Asian Americans or Pacific Islanders, 14 Hispanic Americans), 11 international. Average age 34. 351 applicants, 62% accepted, 128 enrolled. *Faculty:* 22 full-time (13 women). Expenses: Contact institution. *Financial support:* In 2008–09, 39 students received support, including 4 fellowships (averaging $25,000 per year), 35 research assistantships with tuition reimbursements available (averaging $7,500 per year); teaching assistantships with tuition reimbursements available, career-related internships or fieldwork, Federal Work-Study, scholarships/grants, tuition waivers (full and partial), and unspecified assistantships also available. Support available to part-time students. Financial award application deadline: 2/10; financial award applicants required to submit FAFSA. In 2008, 164 master's, 2 doctorates awarded. *Degree program information:* Part-time and evening/weekend programs available. Offers non-profit organizations (MA, Certificate); social work (MA, MSW, PhD, Certificate). *Application deadline:* For fall admission, 7/1 priority date for domestic students, 7/1 for international students; for spring admission, 11/15 for domestic and international students. Applications are processed on a rolling basis. *Application fee:* $50. Electronic applications accepted. *Application Contact:* Dr. Brian Bride, Graduate Coordinator, 706-542-5471, Fax: 706-542-3282, E-mail: bbride@uga.edu. *Dean,* Dr. Maurice C. Daniels, 706-542-5424, Fax: 706-542-3282, E-mail: sswdean@uga.edu.

Terry College of Business Students: 477 full-time (179 women), 416 part-time (125 women); includes 144 minority (76 African Americans, 2 American Indian/Alaska Native, 48 Asian Americans or Pacific Islanders, 18 Hispanic Americans), 99 international. 856 applicants, 43% accepted, 282 enrolled. *Faculty:* 58 full-time (12 women). Expenses: Contact institution. *Financial support:* Fellowships, research assistantships, teaching assistantships, unspecified assistantships available. In 2008, 381 master's, 16 doctorates awarded. Offers accounting (M Acc); business (M Acc, MA, MBA, MIT, MMR, PhD); business administration (MA, MBA, PhD); economics (MA, PhD); Internet technology (MIT); marketing research (MMR). *Application deadline:* For fall admission, 7/1 priority date for domestic students; for spring admission, 11/15 for domestic students. *Application fee:* $50. Electronic applications accepted. *Application Contact:* Dr. Rich Daniels, Interim Associate Dean, 404-842-4862, E-mail: rdaniels@terry.uga.edu. *Dean,* Dr. Robert T. Sumichrast, 706-542-8100, Fax: 706-542-3835, E-mail: busdean@terry.uga.edu.

Grady School of Journalism and Mass Communication Students: 81 full-time (49 women), 14 part-time (9 women); includes 8 minority (7 African Americans, 1 Hispanic American), 21 international. 263 applicants, 34% accepted, 38 enrolled. *Faculty:* 33 full-time (13 women). Expenses: Contact institution. *Financial support:* Research assistantships, teaching assistantships, tuition waivers (full) and unspecified assistantships available. In 2008, 37 master's, 6 doctorates awarded. Offers journalism and mass communication (MA); mass communication (PhD). *Application deadline:* For spring admission, 2/15 for domestic students. *Application fee:* $50. Electronic applications accepted. *Application Contact:* Dr. Jeffrey K. Springston, Graduate Coordinator, 706-542-7833, Fax: 706-5422183, E-mail: jspring@grady.uga.edu. *Dean,* Dr. E. Culpepper Clark, 706-542-1704, Fax: 706-542-2183, E-mail: cully@uga.edu.

School of Law Students: 671 full-time (323 women), 3 part-time (0 women); includes 85 African Americans, 31 Asian Americans or Pacific Islanders, 12 Hispanic Americans, 12 international. Expenses: Contact institution. *Financial support:* Fellowships, research assistantships, teaching assistantships, Federal Work-Study, institutionally sponsored loans, tuition waivers (partial), and unspecified assistantships available. Financial award application deadline: 1/31. In 2008, 200 JDs awarded. Offers law (JD). *Application deadline:* For fall admission, 7/1 priority date for domestic students; for spring admission, 11/15 for domestic students. *Application fee:* $50. Electronic applications accepted. *Application Contact:* Gabriel (for LLM) Wilner, Associate Director of Law Admissions, 706-542-5238, E-mail: intlgrad@uga.edu. *Dean,* Dean Rebecca H. White, 706-542-7140, Fax: 706-542-5283, E-mail: rhwhite@uga.edu.

School of Public and International Affairs Students: 198 full-time (87 women), 61 part-time (35 women); includes 10 African Americans, 3 Asian Americans or Pacific Islanders, 9 Hispanic Americans, 44 international. 379 applicants, 34% accepted, 91 enrolled. *Faculty:* 34 full-time (5 women). Expenses: Contact institution. *Financial support:* Fellowships, research assistantships, teaching assistantships, unspecified assistantships available. In 2008, 84 master's, 9 doctorates awarded. Offers political science (MA, PhD); public administration (MPA, PhD); public and international affairs (MA, MPA, PhD). *Application deadline:* For fall admission, 7/1 priority date for domestic students; for spring admission, 11/15 for domestic students. *Application fee:* $50. Electronic applications accepted. *Application Contact:* Director of Graduate Admissions. *Dean,* Dr. Thomas P. Lauth, 706-542-2059, Fax: 706-542-0095, E-mail: tplauth@uga.edu.

UNIVERSITY OF GREAT FALLS, Great Falls, MT 59405

General Information Independent-religious, coed, comprehensive institution. *Graduate housing:* Room and/or apartments available on a first-come, first-served basis to single students; on-campus housing not available to married students. Housing application deadline: 8/1.

GRADUATE UNITS

Graduate Studies Students: 22 full-time (19 women), 58 part-time (42 women); includes 7 minority (6 American Indian/Alaska Native, 1 Hispanic American). Average age 34. *Faculty:* 12 full-time (6 women), 11 part-time/adjunct (7 women). Expenses: Contact institution. *Financial support:* In 2008–09, 44 students received support. Career-related internships or fieldwork and institutionally sponsored loans available. Support available to part-time students. Financial award application deadline: 6/1; financial award applicants required to submit FAFSA. In 2008, 23 master's awarded. *Degree program information:* Part-time programs available. Postbaccalaureate distance learning degree programs offered (no on-campus study). Offers counseling psychology (MSC); criminal justice (MSM); education (M Ed); human development (MSM); management (MSM); secondary teaching (MAT). *Application deadline:* For fall admission, 8/15 priority date for domestic students, 6/15 priority date for international students; for spring admission, 12/15 priority date for domestic students, 10/15 priority date for international students. Applications are processed on a rolling basis. *Application fee:* $50. Electronic applications accepted. *Application Contact:* Greg Stivers, Admissions Counselor, 406-791-5205, Fax: 406-791-5209, E-mail: gstivers01@ugf.edu. *Associate Dean for Graduate Studies,* Dr. Katrina Stark, 406-791-5332, Fax: 406-791-5990, E-mail: kstark01@ugf.edu.

UNIVERSITY OF GUAM, Mangilao, GU 96923

General Information Territory-supported, coed, comprehensive institution. *Graduate housing:* Room and/or apartments available on a first-come, first-served basis to single students; on-campus housing not available to married students. Housing application deadline: 5/1. *Research affiliation:* Cancer Research Center of Hawaii (cancer research), Bernice Pauahi Bishop Museum (science, cultural preservation), Pilar Project, Inc. (salvage of artifacts, archaeology).

GRADUATE UNITS

Office of Graduate Studies *Degree program information:* Part-time programs available.

College of Liberal Arts and Social Sciences *Degree program information:* Part-time programs available. Offers ceramics (MA); English (MA); graphics (MA); liberal arts and social sciences (MA); Micronesian studies (MA); painting (MA).

College of Natural and Applied Sciences Offers environmental science (MS); natural and applied sciences (MS, MSW); social work (MSW); tropical marine biology (MS).

School of Business and Public Administration *Degree program information:* Part-time programs available. Offers business administration (PMBA); business and public administration (MPA, PMBA); public administration (MPA).

School of Education *Degree program information:* Part-time programs available. Offers administration and supervision (M Ed); counseling (MA); education (M Ed, MA); language and literacy (M Ed); secondary education (M Ed); special education (M Ed); teaching English to speakers of other languages (M Ed).

UNIVERSITY OF GUELPH, Guelph, ON N1G 2W1, Canada

General Information Province-supported, coed, university. *Graduate housing:* Rooms and/or apartments available to single and married students. Housing application deadline: 5/28.

GRADUATE UNITS

Graduate Program Services *Degree program information:* Part-time and evening/weekend programs available. Postbaccalaureate distance learning degree programs offered (minimal on-campus study). Offers biophysics (M Sc, PhD). Electronic applications accepted.

Collaborative International Development Studies *Degree program information:* Part-time programs available. Offers international development studies (M Eng, M Sc, MA, MBA, PhD).

College of Arts *Degree program information:* Part-time programs available. Offers arts (MA, MFA, PhD); drama (MA); English (MA); European studies (MA); French studies (MA); history (MA, PhD); literary studies/theatre studies in English (PhD); philosophy (MA, PhD); studio art (MFA).

College of Biological Science *Degree program information:* Part-time programs available. Offers biochemistry (M Sc, PhD); biological science (M Sc, PhD); biophysics (M Sc, PhD); botany (M Sc, PhD); microbiology (M Sc, PhD); molecular biology and genetics (M Sc, PhD); nutritional sciences (M Sc, PhD); zoology (M Sc, PhD). Electronic applications accepted.

College of Management and Economics Offers economics (MA, PhD); food and agribusiness management (MBA); hospitality and tourism management (MBA); leadership (MA); management and economics (M Sc, MA, MBA, PhD); marketing and consumer studies (M Sc).

College of Physical and Engineering Science *Degree program information:* Part-time programs available. Offers applied computer science (M Sc); applied mathematics (PhD); applied statistics (PhD); biological engineering (M Eng, M Sc, MA Sc, PhD); chemistry and biochemistry (M Sc, PhD); computer science (PhD); engineering systems and computing (M Eng, M Sc, MA Sc, PhD); environmental engineering (M Eng, M Sc, MA Sc, PhD); mathematics and statistics (M Sc); physical and engineering science (M Eng, M Sc, MA Sc, PhD); physics (M Sc, PhD); water resources engineering (M Eng, M Sc, MA Sc, PhD).

College of Social and Applied Human Sciences *Degree program information:* Part-time programs available. Offers anthropology (MA); applied nutrition (MAN); applied social psychology (MA, PhD); clinical psychology applied development emphasis (PhD); clinical psychology applied developmental emphasis (MA); comparative politics (MA); crime and criminal justice policy (MA); criminology and criminal justice policy (MA); family relations and human development (M Sc, PhD); geography (M Sc, MA, PhD); industrial/organizational psychology (MA, PhD); international development (MA); neuroscience and applied cognitive science (MA, PhD); political science (MA); public policy and public administration (MA); social and applied human sciences (M Sc, MA, MAN, PhD); sociology (MA, PhD); the Americas (Canada emphasis) (MA).

Ontario Agricultural College *Degree program information:* Part-time programs available. Postbaccalaureate distance learning degree programs offered (minimal on-campus study). Offers agricultural economics (M Sc, PhD); agriculture (M Sc, MLA, PhD, Diploma); animal and poultry science (M Sc, PhD); aquaculture (M Sc); atmospheric science (M Sc, PhD); capacity development and extension (M Sc); collaborative international development studies (M Sc, PhD); entomology (M Sc, PhD); environmental and agricultural earth sciences (M Sc, PhD); environmental microbiology and biotechnology (M Sc, PhD); environmental toxicology (M Sc, PhD); food safety and quality assurance (M Sc); food science (M Sc, PhD); international rural planning and development (M Sc); land resources management (M Sc, PhD); landscape architecture (M Sc, MLA); plant agriculture (M Sc, PhD); plant and forest systems (M Sc, PhD); plant pathology (M Sc, PhD); rural planning and development (M Sc); rural planning and development in Canada (M Sc); rural studies (PhD); soil science (M Sc, PhD).

Ontario Veterinary College Offers toxicology (M Sc, PhD); veterinary medicine (M Sc, DV Sc, PhD, Diploma).

Graduate Programs in Veterinary Sciences Offers anatomic pathology (DV Sc, Diploma); anesthesiology (M Sc, DV Sc); cardiology (DV Sc, Diploma); clinical pathology (Diploma); clinical studies (Diploma); comparative pathology (M Sc, PhD); dermatology (M Sc); diagnostic imaging (M Sc, DV Sc); emergency/critical care (M Sc, DV Sc, Diploma); epidemiology (M Sc, DV Sc, PhD); health management (DV Sc); immunology (M Sc, PhD); laboratory animal science (DV Sc); medicine (M Sc, DV Sc); morphology (M Sc, DV Sc, PhD); neurology (M Sc, DV Sc); neuroscience (M Sc, DV Sc, PhD); ophthalmology (M Sc, DV Sc); pathology (M Sc, PhD, Diploma); pharmacology (M Sc, DV Sc, PhD); physiology (M Sc, DV Sc, PhD); population medicine and health management (M Sc); surgery (M Sc, DV Sc); swine health management (M Sc); theriogenology (M Sc, DV Sc); toxicology (M Sc, DV Sc, PhD); veterinary infectious diseases (M Sc, PhD); veterinary sciences (M Sc, DV Sc, PhD, Diploma); zoo animal/wildlife medicine (DV Sc).

UNIVERSITY OF HARTFORD, West Hartford, CT 06117-1599

General Information Independent, coed, comprehensive institution. CGS member. *Graduate housing:* On-campus housing not available.

GRADUATE UNITS

Barney School of Business *Degree program information:* Part-time and evening/weekend programs available. Offers business (MBA, MSAT, Certificate); business administration (MBA); professional accounting (Certificate); taxation (MSAT). Electronic applications accepted.

College of Arts and Sciences *Degree program information:* Part-time and evening/weekend programs available. Offers arts and sciences (MA, MS, Psy D); biology (MS); clinical practices (MA, Psy D); communication (MA); general experimental psychology (MA); neuroscience (MS); organizational behavior (MS); psychology (MA); school psychology (MS). Electronic applications accepted.

College of Education, Nursing, and Health Professions *Degree program information:* Part-time and evening/weekend programs available. Offers administration and supervision (CAGS); community/public health nursing (MSN); counseling (M Ed, MS, Sixth Year Certificate); early childhood education (M Ed); education, nursing, and health professions (M Ed, MS, MSN, MSPT; DPT, Ed D, CAGS, Sixth Year Certificate); educational leadership (Ed D, CAGS); educational technology (M Ed); elementary education (M Ed); nursing education (MSN); nursing management (MSN); physical therapy (MSPT, DPT). Electronic applications accepted.

College of Engineering, Technology and Architecture *Degree program information:* Part-time and evening/weekend programs available. Offers architecture (M Arch); engineering (M Eng); engineering, technology and architecture (M Arch, M Eng). Electronic applications accepted.

Hartford Art School *Degree program information:* Part-time programs available. Offers art (MFA). Electronic applications accepted.

The Hartt School *Degree program information:* Part-time programs available. Offers choral conducting (MM Ed); composition (MM, DMA, Artist Diploma, Diploma); conducting (MM, DMA, Artist Diploma, Diploma); early childhood education (MM Ed); instrumental conducting (MM Ed); Kodály (MM Ed); music (CAGS); music education (DMA, PhD); music history (MM); music theory (MM); pedagogy (MM Ed); performance (MM, MM Ed, DMA, Artist Diploma, Diploma); research (MM Ed); technology (MM Ed). Electronic applications accepted.

UNIVERSITY OF HAWAII AT HILO, Hilo, HI 96720-4091

General Information State-supported, coed, comprehensive institution.

GRADUATE UNITS

Program in China-US Relations

UNIVERSITY OF HAWAII AT MANOA, Honolulu, HI 96822

General Information State-supported, coed, university. CGS member. *Graduate housing:* Rooms and/or apartments available to single and married students. Housing application deadline: 5/1. *Research affiliation:* Bernice Pauahi Bishop Museum (anthropology, zoology), Hawaiian Volcano Observatory (geology, geophysics), Honolulu Academy of Arts, East-West Center (communication, geography, economics), U.S. Geological Survey, Hawaii Agriculture Research Center.

GRADUATE UNITS

Graduate Division Students: 3,309 full-time (1,848 women), 1,653 part-time (1,029 women); includes 1,924 minority (30 African Americans, 23 American Indian/Alaska Native, 1,757 Asian Americans or Pacific Islanders, 114 Hispanic Americans), 1,049 international. 4,026 applicants, 54% accepted, 1426 enrolled. *Faculty:* 1,472 full-time (493 women), 180 part-time/adjunct (41 women). Expenses: Contact institution. *Financial support:* In 2008–09, 2,171 fellowships (averaging $3,800 per year), 741 research assistantships with full tuition reimbursements (averaging $18,800 per year), 524 teaching assistantships with full tuition reimbursements (averaging $14,850 per year) were awarded; career-related internships or fieldwork, Federal Work-Study, institutionally sponsored loans, scholarships/grants, and tuition waivers (full and partial) also available. Support available to part-time students. Financial award applicants required to submit FAFSA. In 2008, 1,107 master's, 187 doctorates, 38 other advanced degrees awarded. *Degree program information:* Part-time programs available. Offers communication and information sciences (PhD); ecology, evolution and conservation biology (MS, PhD). *Application fee:* $60. Electronic applications accepted. *Application Contact:* Graduate Division, 808-956-8544.

College of Arts and Humanities *Degree program information:* Part-time programs available. Offers American studies (MA, PhD); art (MA); art history (MA); arts and humanities (M Mus, MA, MFA, PhD, Graduate Certificate); dance (MA, MFA); historic preservation (Graduate Certificate); history (MA, PhD); museum studies (Graduate Certificate); music (M Mus, MA, PhD); philosophy (MA, PhD); religion (MA); speech (MA); theatre (MA, MFA, PhD); visual arts (MFA).

College of Education *Degree program information:* Part-time and evening/weekend programs available. Offers counseling and guidance (M Ed); curriculum and instruction (PhD); curriculum studies (M Ed); disability and diversity studies (Graduate Certificate); early childhood education (M Ed); education (M Ed, M Ed T, MS, PhD, Graduate Certificate); educational administration (M Ed); educational foundations (M Ed); educational policy studies (PhD); educational psychology (M Ed, PhD); educational technology (M Ed); exceptionalities (PhD); kinesiology (MS, PhD); special education (M Ed); teaching (M Ed T).

College of Engineering *Degree program information:* Part-time programs available. Offers civil and environmental engineering (MS, PhD); electrical engineering (MS, PhD); engineering (MS, PhD, Graduate Certificate); mechanical engineering (MS, PhD).

College of Language, Linguistics and Literature *Degree program information:* Part-time programs available. Offers Chinese (MA, PhD); English (MA, PhD); English as a second language (MA, Graduate Certificate); French (MA); Japanese (MA, PhD); Korean (MA, PhD); language, linguistics and literature (MA, PhD, Graduate Certificate); linguistics (MA, PhD); second language acquisition (PhD); Spanish (MA).

College of Natural Sciences *Degree program information:* Part-time programs available. Offers advanced library and information science (Graduate Certificate); astronomy (MS, PhD); botany (MS, PhD); chemistry (MS, PhD); computer science (MS, PhD); library and information science (MLI Sc, Graduate Certificate); mathematics (MA, PhD); microbiology (MS, PhD); natural sciences (MA, MLI Sc, MS, PhD, Graduate Certificate); physics (MS, PhD); zoology (MS, PhD).

College of Social Sciences *Degree program information:* Part-time and evening/weekend programs available. Offers advanced women's studies (Graduate Certificate); anthropology (MA, PhD); clinical psychology (PhD); communication (MA); community and cultural psychology (PhD); community and culture (MA); community planning and social policy (MURP); conflict resolution (Graduate Certificate); disaster preparedness and emergency management (Graduate Certificate); economics (MA, PhD); environmental planning and management (MURP); geography (MA, PhD); land use and infrastructure planning (MURP); ocean policy (Graduate Certificate); political science (MA, PhD); psychology (MA, PhD, Graduate Certificate); public administration (MPA, Graduate Certificate); public policy (Graduate Certificate); social sciences (MA, MPA, MURP, PhD, Graduate Certificate); sociology (MA, PhD); telecommunication and information resource management (Graduate Certificate); urban and regional planning (PhD, Graduate Certificate); urban and regional planning in Asia and Pacific (MURP).

College of Tropical Agriculture and Human Resources *Degree program information:* Part-time programs available. Offers animal sciences (MS); bioengineering (MS); entomology (MS, PhD); food science (MS); molecular bioscience and bioengineering (MS); molecular biosciences and bioengineering (PhD); natural resources and environmental management (MS, PhD); nutrition (PhD); nutritional sciences (MS, PhD); tropical agriculture and human resources (MS, PhD); tropical plant and soil sciences (MS, PhD); tropical plant pathology (MS, PhD).

School of Hawaiian Knowledge Students: 13 full-time (9 women), 6 part-time (2 women); includes 15 minority (all Asian Americans or Pacific Islanders). 8 applicants, 88% accepted, 7 enrolled. *Faculty:* 13 full-time (8 women), 58 part-time/adjunct (29 women). Expenses: Contact institution. *Financial support:* In 2008–09, 7 fellowships (averaging $2,528 per year), 1 research assistantship (averaging $15,558 per year), 2 teaching assistantships (averaging $14,382 per year) were awarded. In 2008, 1 master's awarded. *Degree program information:* Part-time programs available. Offers Hawaiian (MA); Hawaiian studies (MA). *Application deadline:* For fall admission, 3/1 for domestic and international students. *Application fee:* $60. *Application Contact:* Marvin Nogelmeier, Graduate Chair, 808-956-6480, Fax: 808-956-4599, E-mail: puakea@hawaii.edu.

School of Nursing and Dental Hygiene Students: 56 full-time (46 women), 109 part-time (99 women); includes 83 minority (2 African Americans, 2 American Indian/Alaska Native, 75 Asian Americans or Pacific Islanders, 4 Hispanic Americans), 4 international. 86 applicants, 60% accepted, 48 enrolled. *Faculty:* 37 full-time (33 women), 1 (woman) part-time/adjunct. Expenses: Contact institution. *Financial support:* In 2008–09, 6 fellowships (averaging $1,587 per year), 2 research assistantships (averaging $16,824 per year) were awarded. In 2008, 29 master's, 1 doctorate awarded. *Degree program information:* Part-time programs available. Postbaccalaureate distance learning degree programs offered (minimal on-campus study). Offers clinical nurse specialist (MS); nurse practitioner (MS); nursing (PhD, Graduate Certificate); nursing administration (MS). *Application deadline:* For fall admission, 2/1 for domestic and international students. *Application fee:* $60. *Application Contact:* Merle Katoaka-Yahiro, Graduate Chair, 808-956-8523, Fax: 808-956-3257, E-mail: merle@hawaii.edu. *Dean,* Mary Boland, 808-956-8522, Fax: 808-956-3257, E-mail: mgboland@hawaii.edu.

School of Ocean and Earth Science and Technology *Degree program information:* Part-time programs available. Offers high-pressure geophysics and geochemistry (MS, PhD); hydrogeology and engineering geology (MS, PhD); marine biology (MS, PhD); marine geology and geophysics (MS, PhD); meteorology (MS, PhD); ocean and earth science and technology (MS, PhD); ocean and resources engineering (MS, PhD); oceanography (MS, PhD); planetary geosciences and remote sensing (MS, PhD); seismology and solid-earth geophysics (MS, PhD); volcanology, petrology, and geochemistry (MS, PhD).

School of Pacific and Asian Studies *Degree program information:* Part-time programs available. Offers Asian studies (MA, Graduate Certificate); Chinese studies (Graduate Certificate); Japanese studies (Graduate Certificate); Korean studies (Graduate Certificate); Pacific and Asian studies (MA, Graduate Certificate); Pacific Island studies (MA, Graduate Certificate); Philippine studies (Graduate Certificate); Southeast Asian studies (Graduate Certificate).

School of Social Work Students: 184 full-time (146 women), 61 part-time (49 women); includes 131 minority (5 African Americans, 1 American Indian/Alaska Native, 114 Asian Americans or Pacific Islanders, 11 Hispanic Americans), 10 international. 206 applicants, 67% accepted, 95 enrolled. *Faculty:* 31 full-time (17 women), 68 part-time/adjunct (34 women). Expenses: Contact institution. *Financial support:* In 2008–09, 32 fellowships with full and partial tuition reimbursements (averaging $2,421 per year), 11 research assistantships with full and partial tuition reimbursements (averaging $16,329 per year) were awarded; career-related internships or fieldwork, Federal Work-Study, institutionally sponsored loans, and tuition waivers (full) also available. Support available to part-time students. Financial award application deadline: 2/1; financial award applicants required to submit FAFSA. In 2008, 77 master's, 3 doctorates awarded. *Degree program information:* Part-time programs available. Offers social welfare (PhD); social work (MSW). *Application deadline:* For fall admission, 1/15 for domestic and international students. Applications are processed on a rolling basis. *Application fee:* $60. *Application Contact:* Crystal Mills, Graduate Chair, 808-956-3831, Fax: 808-956-5964, E-mail: millsc@hawaii.edu. *Dean,* Jon Matsuoka, 808-956-6300, E-mail: jmatsuok@hawaii.edu.

School of Travel Industry Management Students: 10 full-time (7 women), 2 part-time (1 woman); includes 2 minority (1 Asian American or Pacific Islander, 1 Hispanic American), 8 international. Average age 28. 39 applicants, 10% accepted, 1 enrolled. *Faculty:* 14 full-time (5 women), 56 part-time/adjunct (28 women). Expenses: Contact institution. *Financial support:* In 2008–09, 2 fellowships with partial tuition reimbursements (averaging $1,425 per year) were awarded; career-related internships or fieldwork, scholarships/grants, tuition waivers (full and partial), and student assistantships also available. Financial award application deadline: 3/1. In 2008, 6 master's awarded. *Degree program information:* Part-time programs available. Offers travel industry management (MS). *Application deadline:* For fall admission, 3/1 for domestic and international students. Applications are processed on a rolling basis. *Application fee:* $60. Electronic applications accepted. *Application Contact:* Harold Richins, Graduate Chair, 808-956-9840, Fax: 808-956-5378, E-mail: richins@hawaii.edu.

Shidler College of Business *Degree program information:* Part-time and evening/weekend programs available. Offers accounting (M Acc); accounting law (M Acc); Asian business studies (MBA); Asian finance (PhD); business (EMBA, M Acc, MBA, MHRM, MS, PhD); Chinese business studies (MBA); decision sciences (MBA); entrepreneurship (MBA); executive business administration (EMBA); finance (MBA); finance and banking (MBA); financial engineering (MS); global information technology management (PhD); human resources management (MBA); information management (MBA); information systems (M Acc); information technology (MBA); international accounting (PhD); international business (MBA); international marketing (PhD); international organization and strategy (PhD); Japanese business studies (MBA); marketing (MBA); organizational behavior (MBA); organizational management (MBA); real estate (MBA); student-designed track (MBA); taxation (M Acc); Vietnam focused business administration (EMBA).

John A. Burns School of Medicine *Degree program information:* Part-time programs available. Offers cell and molecular biology (MS, PhD); communication sciences and disorders (MS); epidemiology (PhD); global health and population studies (Graduate Certificate); medicine (MD, MPH, MS, Dr PH, PhD, Graduate Certificate); public health (MPH, MS, Dr PH).

Graduate Programs in Biomedical Sciences Students: 5 full-time (4 women), 10 part-time (6 women); includes 8 minority (all Asian Americans or Pacific Islanders). Average age 31. 3 applicants, 33% accepted, 1 enrolled. *Faculty:* 15 full-time (10 women), 2 part-time/adjunct (1 woman). Expenses: Contact institution. *Financial support:* In 2008–09, 6 fellowships (averaging $2,401 per year) were awarded; career-related internships or fieldwork, Federal Work-Study, institutionally sponsored loans, and tuition waivers (full and partial) also available. Support available to part-time students. In 2008, 1 master's, 5 doctorates awarded. *Degree program information:* Part-time programs available. Offers biomedical sciences (MS, PhD); physiology (MS, PhD); tropical medicine (MS, PhD). *Application*

University of Hawaii at Manoa (continued)

deadline: For fall admission, 6/1 for domestic and international students. *Application fee:* $60. *Application Contact:* Sandra Chang, Graduate Chairperson, 808-692-0909, Fax: 808-692-1979, E-mail: sandrac@hawaii.edu.

School of Architecture Offers architecture (D Arch).

William S. Richardson School of Law Offers law (JD, LL M, Graduate Certificate).

UNIVERSITY OF HOUSTON, Houston, TX 77204

General Information State-supported, coed, university. CGS member. *Enrollment:* 37,104 graduate, professional, and undergraduate students; 4,920 full-time matriculated graduate/professional students (2,537 women), 2,384 part-time matriculated graduate/professional students (1,167 women). *Enrollment by degree level:* 1,820 first professional, 3,983 master's, 1,501 doctoral. *Graduate faculty:* 653 full-time (167 women), 416 part-time/adjunct (168 women). Tuition, state resident: full-time $5164; part-time $287 per credit. Tuition, nonresident: full-time $10,222; part-time $568 per credit. *Graduate housing:* Rooms and/or apartments available on a first-come, first-served basis to single and married students. Typical cost: $6935 (including board) for single students. Room and board charges vary according to board plan and housing facility selected. Housing application deadline: 3/1. *Student services:* Campus employment opportunities, campus safety program, career counseling, child daycare facilities, exercise/wellness program, free psychological counseling, international student services, low-cost health insurance, services for students with disabilities, teacher training, writing training. *Library facilities:* M.D. Anderson Library plus 6 others. *Online resources:* library catalog, web page, access to other libraries' catalogs. *Collection:* 2.6 million titles, 72,775 serial subscriptions.

Computer facilities: Computer purchase and lease plans are available. 625 computers available on campus for general student use. A campuswide network can be accessed from student residence rooms and from off campus. Online class registration is available. *Web address:* http://www.uh.edu/.

General Application Contact: Jeff Fuller, Executive Associate Director of Admission, 832-842-9047, Fax: 713-743-7542, E-mail: jfuller@uh.edu.

GRADUATE UNITS

Bauer College of Business Students: 634 full-time (275 women), 650 part-time (225 women); includes 457 minority (103 African Americans, 2 American Indian/Alaska Native, 220 Asian Americans or Pacific Islanders, 132 Hispanic Americans), 218 international. Average age 29. 739 applicants, 75% accepted, 449 enrolled. *Faculty:* 48 full-time (9 women), 35 part-time/adjunct (6 women). Expenses: Contact institution. *Financial support:* In 2008–09, 18 fellowships with full tuition reimbursements (averaging $8,875 per year), 99 teaching assistantships with full tuition reimbursements (averaging $7,250 per year) were awarded; research assistantships with full tuition reimbursements, career-related internships or fieldwork, Federal Work-Study, institutionally sponsored loans, scholarships/grants, health care benefits, and unspecified assistantships also available. Support available to part-time students. Financial award application deadline: 2/1; financial award applicants required to submit FAFSA. In 2008, 482 master's, 8 doctorates awarded. *Degree program information:* Part-time and evening/weekend programs available. Offers accountancy (M Acy); accounting (PhD); business (M Acy, MBA, MS, PhD); decision and information sciences (MBA, PhD); finance (MS); management (PhD); marketing and entrepreneurship (PhD). *Application deadline:* For fall admission, 5/1 for domestic students; for spring admission, 10/1 for domestic students. Applications are processed on a rolling basis. *Application fee:* $75 ($150 for international students). *Application Contact:* Dr. Arthur Warga, Dean, 713-743-4604, Fax: 713-743-4622, E-mail: warga@uh.edu. *Dean,* Dr. Arthur Warga, 713-743-4604, Fax: 713-743-4622, E-mail: warga@uh.edu.

College of Architecture Students: 60 full-time (34 women), 10 part-time (3 women); includes 17 minority (2 African Americans, 8 Asian Americans or Pacific Islanders, 7 Hispanic Americans), 10 international. Average age 28. 97 applicants, 57% accepted, 24 enrolled. *Faculty:* 16 full-time (3 women), 16 part-time/adjunct (1 woman). Expenses: Contact institution. *Financial support:* In 2008–09, 1 fellowship with full tuition reimbursement (averaging $9,900 per year), 1 research assistantship with full tuition reimbursement (averaging $9,900 per year), 2 teaching assistantships with full tuition reimbursements (averaging $9,900 per year) were awarded; career-related internships or fieldwork, Federal Work-Study, institutionally sponsored loans, scholarships/grants, health care benefits, and unspecified assistantships also available. Support available to part-time students. Financial award application deadline: 2/1. In 2008, 32 master's awarded. Offers architecture (M Arch, MS). *Application deadline:* For fall admission, 2/1 priority date for domestic students; for spring admission, 10/1 for domestic students. Applications are processed on a rolling basis. *Application fee:* $10 ($75 for international students). *Application Contact:* Thomas M. Colbert, Director of Graduate Studies, 713-743-2380, Fax: 713-743-2358, E-mail: colbert@bayou.uh.edu. *Dean,* Joseph Mashburn, 713-743-2400, Fax: 713-743-2358, E-mail: mashburn@uh.edu.

College of Education Students: 257 full-time (190 women), 527 part-time (379 women); includes 265 minority (109 African Americans, 68 Asian Americans or Pacific Islanders, 88 Hispanic Americans), 46 international. Average age 34. 470 applicants, 63% accepted, 163 enrolled. *Faculty:* 55 full-time (24 women), 44 part-time/adjunct (32 women). Expenses: Contact institution. *Financial support:* In 2008–09, 14 fellowships with full tuition reimbursements (averaging $9,700 per year), 11 research assistantships with full tuition reimbursements (averaging $9,700 per year), 89 teaching assistantships with full tuition reimbursements (averaging $9,700 per year) were awarded; career-related internships or fieldwork, Federal Work-Study, institutionally sponsored loans, scholarships/grants, health care benefits, and unspecified assistantships also available. Support available to part-time students. Financial award application deadline: 2/1; financial award applicants required to submit FAFSA. In 2008, 231 master's, 61 doctorates awarded. *Degree program information:* Part-time and evening/weekend programs available. Offers allied health (M Ed, Ed D); art education (M Ed); bilingual education (M Ed); counseling psychology (M Ed, PhD); curriculum and instruction (Ed D); early childhood education (M Ed); education (M Ed, MS, Ed D, PhD); education of the gifted (M Ed); educational administration (M Ed, Ed D); educational psychology (M Ed); educational psychology and individual differences (PhD); elementary education (M Ed); exercise science (MS); health education (M Ed); higher education (M Ed); historical, social, and cultural foundations of education (M Ed, Ed D); kinesiology (PhD); mathematics education (M Ed); physical education (M Ed, Ed D); reading and language arts education (M Ed); science education (M Ed); second language education (M Ed); secondary education (M Ed); social studies education (M Ed); special education (M Ed, Ed D); teaching (M Ed). *Application fee:* $35 ($75 for international students). *Application Contact:* Jeff Fuller, Executive Associate Director of Admission, 832-842-9047, Fax: 713-743-7542, E-mail: jfuller@uh.edu. *Dean,* Robert K. Wimpelberg, 713-743-5001, Fax: 713-743-5013, E-mail: rwimpelberg@uh.edu.

College of Liberal Arts and Social Sciences Students: 649 full-time (403 women), 350 part-time (226 women); includes 240 minority (63 African Americans, 7 American Indian/Alaska Native, 41 Asian Americans or Pacific Islanders, 129 Hispanic Americans), 119 international. Average age 31. 1,197 applicants, 37% accepted, 252 enrolled. *Faculty:* 195 full-time (73 women), 75 part-time/adjunct (39 women). Expenses: Contact institution. *Financial support:* In 2008–09, 24 fellowships with full tuition reimbursements (averaging $7,300 per year), 23 research assistantships with full tuition reimbursements (averaging $10,600 per year), 411 teaching assistantships with full tuition reimbursements (averaging $10,600 per year) were awarded; career-related internships or fieldwork, Federal Work-Study, institutionally sponsored loans, scholarships/grants, health care benefits, and unspecified assistantships also available. Support available to part-time students. Financial award application deadline: 2/1; financial award applicants required to submit FAFSA. In 2008, 203 master's, 60 doctorates awarded. *Degree program information:* Part-time and evening/weekend programs available. Postbaccalaureate distance learning degree programs offered. Offers anthropology (MA); applied English linguistics (MA); clinical psychology (PhD); economics (MA, PhD); English and American literature (MA, PhD); French (MA); history (MA, PhD); industrial/organizational psychology (PhD); interior design (MA); liberal arts and social sciences (MA, MFA, MM, DMA, PhD); literature and creative writing (MA, MFA, PhD); painting (MA); philosophy (MA); photography (MA); political science (MA, PhD); psychology (MA); public history (MA); sculpture (MA); social psychology (PhD); sociology (MA); Spanish (MA, PhD); speech language pathology (MA). *Application Contact:* Graduate Analyst. *Interim Dean,* Dr. Joseph Pratt, 713-743-3085, E-mail: joepratt@central.uh.edu.

Moores School of Music Students: 105 full-time (55 women), 47 part-time (22 women); includes 20 minority (7 African Americans, 1 American Indian/Alaska Native, 5 Asian Americans or Pacific Islanders, 7 Hispanic Americans), 25 international. Average age 30. 113 applicants, 60% accepted, 49 enrolled. *Faculty:* 28 full-time (6 women), 24 part-time/adjunct (11 women). Expenses: Contact institution. *Financial support:* In 2008–09, 1 fellowship with full tuition reimbursement (averaging $10,000 per year), 51 teaching assistantships with full tuition reimbursements (averaging $10,000 per year) were awarded; career-related internships or fieldwork, Federal Work-Study, institutionally sponsored loans, scholarships/grants, health care benefits, and unspecified assistantships also available. Support available to part-time students. Financial award application deadline: 2/1. In 2008, 28 master's, 10 doctorates awarded. *Degree program information:* Part-time programs available. Offers accompanying (MM); applied music (MM); composition (MM, DMA); conducting (DMA); music education (MM, DMA); music literature (MM); music performance and pedagogy (MM); music theory (MM); performance (DMA). *Application deadline:* For fall admission, 7/1 priority date for domestic students. Applications are processed on a rolling basis. *Application fee:* $0 ($75 for international students). *Application Contact:* Howard Pollack, Director of Graduate Studies, 713-743-3314, Fax: 713-743-3166. *Chairperson,* David Ashley White, 713-743-3009, Fax: 713-743-3166, E-mail: daw@orpheus.music.uh.edu.

School of Communication Students: 29 full-time (25 women), 62 part-time (52 women); includes 32 minority (19 African Americans, 2 Asian Americans or Pacific Islanders, 11 Hispanic Americans), 13 international. Average age 29. 46 applicants, 85% accepted, 20 enrolled. *Faculty:* 7 full-time (4 women), 2 part-time/adjunct (0 women). Expenses: Contact institution. *Financial support:* In 2008–09, 2 fellowships with full tuition reimbursements (averaging $9,950 per year), 6 teaching assistantships with full tuition reimbursements (averaging $9,950 per year) were awarded; career-related internships or fieldwork, Federal Work-Study, institutionally sponsored loans, scholarships/grants, health care benefits, and unspecified assistantships also available. Support available to part-time students. Financial award application deadline: 2/1. In 2008, 20 master's awarded. *Degree program information:* Part-time and evening/weekend programs available. Offers mass communication studies (MA); public relations studies (MA); speech communication (MA). *Application deadline:* For fall admission, 7/3 priority date for domestic students. Applications are processed on a rolling basis. *Application fee:* $25 ($75 for international students). *Application Contact:* Angela Parrish, Graduate Coordinator, 713-743-2873, Fax: 713-743-2876, E-mail: aparrish@bayou.uh.edu. *Chairperson,* Beth Olson, 713-743-2873, Fax: 713-743-2876, E-mail: bolson@uh.edu.

School of Theatre Students: 39 full-time (19 women), 4 part-time (3 women); includes 11 minority (6 African Americans, 1 Asian American or Pacific Islander, 4 Hispanic Americans), 1 international. Average age 29. 31 applicants, 68% accepted, 18 enrolled. *Faculty:* 6 full-time (1 woman), 3 part-time/adjunct (1 woman). Expenses: Contact institution. *Financial support:* In 2008–09, 35 teaching assistantships with full tuition reimbursements (averaging $9,300 per year) were awarded; career-related internships or fieldwork, Federal Work-Study, institutionally sponsored loans, scholarships/grants, health care benefits, and unspecified assistantships also available. Support available to part-time students. Financial award application deadline: 2/1. In 2008, 4 master's awarded. *Degree program information:* Part-time programs available. Offers theatre (MA, MFA). *Application fee:* $25. *Application Contact:* Steven Wallace, Chairperson, 713-743-3003, Fax: 713-749-1420. *Chairperson,* Steven Wallace, 713-743-3003, Fax: 713-749-1420.

College of Natural Sciences and Mathematics Students: 639 full-time (224 women), 164 part-time (51 women); includes 83 minority (14 African Americans, 1 American Indian/Alaska Native, 42 Asian Americans or Pacific Islanders, 26 Hispanic Americans), 546 international. Average age 29. 495 applicants, 74% accepted, 176 enrolled. *Faculty:* 136 full-time (17 women), 28 part-time/adjunct (7 women). Expenses: Contact institution. *Financial support:* In 2008–09, 137 fellowships with full tuition reimbursements (averaging $17,550 per year), 195 research assistantships with full tuition reimbursements (averaging $13,400 per year), 200 teaching assistantships with full tuition reimbursements (averaging $13,400 per year) were awarded; career-related internships or fieldwork, Federal Work-Study, institutionally sponsored loans, scholarships/grants, health care benefits, and unspecified assistantships also available. Support available to part-time students. Financial award application deadline: 2/1; financial award applicants required to submit FAFSA. In 2008, 127 master's, 72 doctorates awarded. *Degree program information:* Part-time and evening/weekend programs available. Postbaccalaureate distance learning degree programs offered. Offers biochemistry (MA, MS, PhD); biology (MA, MS, PhD); chemistry (MA, MS, PhD); computer science (MA, MS, PhD); geology (MA, MS, PhD); geophysics (MA, MS, PhD); mathematics (MA, MS, PhD); natural sciences and mathematics (MA, MS, PhD); physics (MA, MS, PhD). *Application deadline:* Applications are processed on a rolling basis. *Application fee:* $0 ($75 for international students). Electronic applications accepted. *Application Contact:* Jeff Fuller, Executive Associate Director of Admission, 832-842-9047, Fax: 713-743-7542, E-mail: jfuller@uh.edu. *Dean,* Dr. John L. Bear, 713-743-2618, Fax: 713-743-8630, E-mail: jbear@uh.edu.

College of Optometry Students: 408 full-time (280 women), 18 part-time (10 women); includes 204 minority (18 African Americans, 1 American Indian/Alaska Native, 150 Asian Americans or Pacific Islanders, 35 Hispanic Americans), 24 international. Average age 25. 356 applicants, 34% accepted, 105 enrolled. *Faculty:* 26 full-time (6 women), 20 part-time/adjunct (14 women). Expenses: Contact institution. *Financial support:* In 2008–09, 11 research assistantships with full tuition reimbursements (averaging $13,375 per year), 15 teaching assistantships with full tuition reimbursements (averaging $13,375 per year) were awarded; career-related internships or fieldwork, Federal Work-Study, institutionally sponsored loans, scholarships/grants, health care benefits, and unspecified assistantships also available. Support available to part-time students. Financial award application deadline: 2/1. In 2008, 100 first professional degrees, 3 doctorates awarded. Offers optometry (OD, MS Phys Op, PhD); physiological optics/vision science (MS Phys Op, PhD). *Application deadline:* Applications are processed on a rolling basis. *Application Contact:* Paul Pease, Director, Student Affairs and Admission, 713-743-2040, Fax: 713-743-2046, E-mail: ppease@uh.edu. *Dean,* Earl Smith, 713-743-1899, Fax: 713-743-0965, E-mail: esmith@uh.edu.

College of Pharmacy Students: 547 full-time (345 women), 23 part-time (13 women); includes 279 minority (30 African Americans, 210 Asian Americans or Pacific Islanders, 39 Hispanic Americans), 75 international. Average age 25. 678 applicants, 27% accepted, 128 enrolled. *Faculty:* 22 full-time (5 women), 13 part-time/adjunct (7 women). Expenses: Contact institution. *Financial support:* In 2008–09, 15 research assistantships with full tuition reimbursements (averaging $14,650 per year), 38 teaching assistantships with full tuition reimbursements (averaging $14,650 per year) were awarded; career-related internships or fieldwork, Federal Work-Study, institutionally sponsored loans, scholarships/grants, health care benefits, and unspecified assistantships also available. Support available to part-time students. Financial award application deadline: 2/1. In 2008, 116 first professional degrees, 12 master's, 2 doctorates awarded. *Degree program information:* Part-time programs available. Offers hospital pharmacy (MSPHR); medical chemistry and pharmacology (MS); pharmaceutics (MS, PhD); pharmacology (MS, PhD); pharmacy (Pharm D); pharmacy administration (MSPHR). *Application deadline:* For spring admission, 3/1 for domestic students. Applications are processed on a rolling basis. *Application fee:* $25 ($75 for international students). *Application Contact:* Shara Zatopek, Assistant Dean for Admissions, 713-743-1262, Fax: 713-743-1259, E-mail: szatopek@uh.edu. *Dean,* Dr. Mustafa F Lokhandwala, 713-743-1253, Fax: 713-743-1259, E-mail: mlokhandwala@uh.edu.

College of Technology Students: 98 full-time (44 women), 94 part-time (38 women); includes 47 minority (24 African Americans, 1 American Indian/Alaska Native, 12 Asian Americans or Pacific Islanders, 10 Hispanic Americans), 88 international. Average age 30. 115 applicants, 76% accepted, 60 enrolled. *Faculty:* 15 full-time (7 women), 10 part-time/adjunct (1 woman). Expenses: Contact institution. *Financial support:* In 2008–09, 16 fellowships with full tuition reimbursements (averaging $10,700 per year), 4 research assistantships with full tuition reimbursements (averaging $10,700 per year), 22 teaching assistantships with full tuition reimbursements (averaging $10,700 per year) were awarded; career-related internships or fieldwork, Federal Work-Study, institutionally sponsored loans, scholarships/grants, health care benefits, and unspecified assistantships also available. Support available to part-time students. Financial award application deadline: 2/1. In 2008, 51 master's awarded. *Degree program information:* Part-time and evening/weekend programs available. Offers engineering technology (M Tech); human development and consumer science (MS); information and logistics technology (MS); technology (M Tech, MS). *Application deadline:* For fall admission, 7/1 for domestic students; for spring admission, 11/1 for domestic students. *Application fee:* $35 ($110 for international students). *Application Contact:* Holly Rosenthal, Graduate Academic Adviser, 713-743-4098, Fax: 713-743-4032, E-mail: hrosenthal@uh.edu. *Interim Dean,* William Fitzgibbon, 713-743-3465, Fax: 713-743-5699, E-mail: fitz@uh.edu.

Conrad N. Hilton College of Hotel and Restaurant Management Students: 42 full-time (31 women), 13 part-time (10 women); includes 9 minority (3 African Americans, 4 Asian Americans or Pacific Islanders, 2 Hispanic Americans), 28 international. Average age 27. 47 applicants, 87% accepted, 23 enrolled. *Faculty:* 8 full-time (1 woman), 8 part-time/adjunct (3 women). Expenses: Contact institution. *Financial support:* In 2008–09, 16 fellowships with full tuition reimbursements (averaging $9,400 per year), 7 teaching assistantships with full tuition reimbursements (averaging $9,400 per year) were awarded; career-related internships or fieldwork, Federal Work-Study, institutionally sponsored loans, scholarships/grants, health care benefits, and unspecified assistantships also available. Support available to part-time students. Financial award application deadline: 2/1. In 2008, 26 master's awarded. *Degree program information:* Part-time and evening/weekend programs available. Postbaccalaureate distance learning degree programs offered (minimal on-campus study). Offers hotel and restaurant management (MHM, MS). *Application deadline:* For fall admission, 5/1 for domestic students; for spring admission, 10/1 for domestic students. Applications are processed on a rolling basis. *Application fee:* $25 ($75 for international students). Electronic applications accepted. *Application Contact:* Lilian Sutawan-Binns, Program Manager, 713-743-2457, Fax: 713-743-2591, E-mail: lbinns@uh.edu. *Dean,* John Bowen, 713-743-0209, Fax: 713-743-2482, E-mail: jbowen@uh.edu.

Cullen College of Engineering Students: 504 full-time (114 women), 219 part-time (47 women); includes 95 minority (12 African Americans, 1 American Indian/Alaska Native, 57 Asian Americans or Pacific Islanders, 25 Hispanic Americans), 485 international. Average age 27. 962 applicants, 60% accepted, 227 enrolled. *Faculty:* 76 full-time (5 women), 31 part-time/adjunct (2 women). Expenses: Contact institution. *Financial support:* In 2008–09, 32 fellowships with full tuition reimbursements (averaging $16,900 per year), 149 research assistantships with full tuition reimbursements (averaging $12,750 per year), 128 teaching assistantships with full tuition reimbursements (averaging $12,750 per year) were awarded; career-related internships or fieldwork, Federal Work-Study, institutionally sponsored loans, scholarships/grants, health care benefits, and unspecified assistantships also available. Support available to part-time students. Financial award application deadline: 2/1. In 2008, 143 master's, 51 doctorates awarded. *Degree program information:* Part-time and evening/weekend programs available. Offers aerospace engineering (MS, PhD); biomedical engineering (MS); chemical engineering (M Ch E, MS Ch E, PhD); civil and environmental engineering (MCE, MS Env E, MSCE, PhD); computer and systems engineering (MS, PhD); electrical and computer engineering (MEE, MSEE, PhD); engineering (M Ch E, MCE, MEE, MIE, MME, MS, MS Ch E, MS Env E, MSCE, MSEE, MSIE, MSME, PhD); environmental engineering (MS, PhD); industrial engineering (MIE, MSIE, PhD); materials engineering (MS, PhD); mechanical engineering (MME, MSME); petroleum engineering (MS). *Application Contact:* Dr. Larry Witte, Associate Dean, Graduate Programs, 713-743-4205, Fax: 713-743-4214, E-mail: witte@uh.edu. *Dean,* Dr. Joseph Tedesco, 713-743-4207, Fax: 713-743-4214, E-mail: jtedesco@uh.edu.

Graduate School of Social Work Students: 277 full-time (249 women), 71 part-time (62 women); includes 182 minority (102 African Americans, 1 American Indian/Alaska Native, 19 Asian Americans or Pacific Islanders, 60 Hispanic Americans), 8 international. Average age 33. 307 applicants, 57% accepted, 133 enrolled. *Faculty:* 16 full-time (8 women), 24 part-time/adjunct (19 women). Expenses: Contact institution. *Financial support:* In 2008–09, 23 fellowships with full tuition reimbursements (averaging $13,100 per year), 10 research assistantships with full tuition reimbursements (averaging $8,975 per year), 2 teaching assistantships with full tuition reimbursements (averaging $8,975 per year) were awarded; career-related internships or fieldwork, Federal Work-Study, institutionally sponsored loans, scholarships/grants, health care benefits, and unspecified assistantships also available. Support available to part-time students. Financial award application deadline: 3/10; financial award applicants required to submit FAFSA. In 2008, 129 master's, 2 doctorates awarded. *Degree program information:* Part-time programs available. Offers social work (MSW, PhD). *Application deadline:* For fall admission, 3/1 priority date for domestic students. Applications are processed on a rolling basis. *Application fee:* $50 ($125 for international students). *Application Contact:* Colen Skinner, Admissions Office, 713-743-8078, Fax: 713-743-8149, E-mail: cskinner@mail.uh.edu. *Dean,* Dr. Ira C. Colby, 713-743-8085, Fax: 713-743-3267, E-mail: icolby@uh.edu.

Law Center Students: 805 full-time (348 women), 245 part-time (103 women); includes 280 minority (81 African Americans, 2 American Indian/Alaska Native, 98 Asian Americans or Pacific Islanders, 99 Hispanic Americans), 53 international. Average age 28. 966 applicants, 100% accepted, 340 enrolled. *Faculty:* 38 full-time (9 women), 89 part-time/adjunct (28 women). Expenses: Contact institution. *Financial support:* In 2008–09, 691 students received support, including 1 teaching assistantship with full tuition reimbursement available (averaging $12,550 per year); career-related internships or fieldwork, Federal Work-Study, institutionally sponsored loans, scholarships/grants, health care benefits, and unspecified assistantships also available. Support available to part-time students. Financial award application deadline: 3/10; financial award applicants required to submit FAFSA. In 2008, 301 JDs, 51 master's awarded. *Degree program information:* Part-time and evening/weekend programs available. Offers law (JD, LL M). *Application deadline:* For fall admission, 2/15 priority date for domestic students. Applications are processed on a rolling basis. *Application fee:* $50 ($75 for international students). Electronic applications accepted. *Application Contact:* Sondra B. Tennessee, Assistant Dean for Admissions, 713-743-2181. *Interim Dean,* Raymond Nimmer, 713-743-2100, Fax: 713-743-2122, E-mail: rnimmer@uh.edu.

UNIVERSITY OF HOUSTON–CLEAR LAKE, Houston, TX 77058-1098

General Information State-supported, coed, upper-level institution. CGS member. *Graduate housing:* Rooms and/or apartments available on a first-come, first-served basis to single students and available to married students. *Research affiliation:* Baylor College of Medicine (life sciences), Schlumberger (ergonomic software), NASA–Johnson Space Center (computer science, computer engineering).

GRADUATE UNITS

School of Business *Degree program information:* Part-time and evening/weekend programs available. Offers accounting (MS); business (MA, MBA, MHA, MS); business administration (MBA); environmental management (MS); finance (MS); healthcare administration (MHA); human resource management (MA); management information systems (MS); professional accounting (MS). Electronic applications accepted.

School of Education *Degree program information:* Part-time and evening/weekend programs available. Offers counseling (MS); curriculum and instruction (MS); early childhood education (MS); education (MS, Ed D); educational leadership (Ed D); educational management (MS); instructional technology (MS); multicultural studies (MS); reading (MS); school library and information science (MS). Electronic applications accepted.

School of Human Sciences and Humanities *Degree program information:* Part-time and evening/weekend programs available. Offers behavioral sciences (MA); clinical psychology (MA); criminology (MA); cross cultural studies (MA); family therapy (MA); fitness and human performance (MA); history (MA); human sciences and humanities (MA); humanities (MA); literature (MA); school psychology (MA).

School of Science and Computer Engineering *Degree program information:* Part-time and evening/weekend programs available. Offers biological sciences (MS); biotechnology (MS); chemistry (MS); computer engineering (MS); computer information systems (MS); computer science (MS); environmental science (MS); mathematical sciences (MS); physics (MS); science and computer engineering (MS); software engineering (MS); statistics (MS); system engineering (MS).

UNIVERSITY OF HOUSTON–DOWNTOWN, Houston, TX 77002-1001

General Information State-supported, coed, comprehensive institution. *Enrollment:* 12,283 graduate, professional, and undergraduate students; 12 full-time matriculated graduate/professional students (4 women), 137 part-time matriculated graduate/professional students (81 women). *Enrollment by degree level:* 149 master's. *Graduate faculty:* 28 full-time (16 women), 3 part-time/adjunct (0 women). *International tuition:* $7570 full-time. Tuition, state resident: full-time $3060; part-time $170 per credit hour. Tuition, nonresident: full-time $7488; part-time $416 per credit hour. *Required fees:* $854; $307 per term. Tuition and fees vary according to course load. *Graduate housing:* On-campus housing not available. *Student services:* Campus employment opportunities, campus safety program, career counseling, exercise/wellness program, free psychological counseling, international student services, low-cost health insurance, services for students with disabilities. *Library facilities:* W. I. Dykes Library. *Online resources:* library catalog, web page, access to other libraries' catalogs. *Collection:* 325,000 titles, 1,700 serial subscriptions, 4,223 audiovisual materials.

Computer facilities: 1,266 computers available on campus for general student use. A campuswide network can be accessed from off campus. Online class registration is available. *Web address:* http://www.uhd.edu/.

General Application Contact: Traneshia Parker, Assistant Director, Graduate, International and Residency Admissions, 713-221-8093, Fax: 713-221-8658, E-mail: parkert@uhd.edu.

GRADUATE UNITS

College of Humanities and Social Sciences Students: 3 full-time (2 women), 19 part-time (17 women); includes 10 minority (8 African Americans, 1 Asian American or Pacific Islander, 1 Hispanic American). Average age 37. 6 applicants, 83% accepted, 5 enrolled. *Faculty:* 11 full-time (7 women). Expenses: Contact institution. *Financial support:* Applicants required to submit FAFSA. In 2008, 4 master's awarded. *Degree program information:* Part-time and evening/weekend programs available. Offers humanities and social sciences (MS); professional writing and technical communication (MS). *Application deadline:* For fall admission, 3/15 for domestic and international students; for spring admission, 11/15 for domestic and international students. *Application fee:* $35 ($60 for international students). Electronic applications accepted. *Application Contact:* Dr. Ann Jennings, Coordinator of MS in Professional Writing and Technical Communication and Professor, Department of English, 713-221-8013, Fax: 713-226-5205, E-mail: mspwtc@uhd.edu. *Dean,* Dr. Susan K. Ahern, 713-221-8009, Fax: 713-221-8106, E-mail: AhernS@uhd.edu.

College of Public Service Students: 9 full-time (2 women), 118 part-time (64 women); includes 56 minority (22 African Americans, 3 Asian Americans or Pacific Islanders, 31 Hispanic Americans), 6 international. Average age 37. 63 applicants, 83% accepted, 40 enrolled. *Faculty:* 17 full-time (9 women), 3 part-time/adjunct (0 women). Expenses: Contact institution. *Financial support:* Federal Work-Study and scholarships/grants available. Financial award applicants required to submit FAFSA. In 2008, 27 master's awarded. *Degree program information:* Part-time and evening/weekend programs available. Offers bilingual education (MAT); criminal justice (MS); curriculum and instruction (MAT); elementary education (MAT); public service (MAT, MS, MSM); secondary education (MAT); security management for executives (MSM). *Application deadline:* Applications are processed on a rolling basis. *Application fee:* $35 ($60 for international students). Electronic applications accepted. *Application Contact:* Traneshia Parker, Assistant Director, Graduate, International and Residency Admissions, 713-221-8093, Fax: 713-221-8658, E-mail: parkert@uhd.edu. *Dean, College of Public Service,* Dr. Beth Pelz, 713-221-8194, Fax: 713-226-5274, E-mail: pelzb@uhd.edu.

UNIVERSITY OF HOUSTON–VICTORIA, Victoria, TX 77901-4450

General Information State-supported, coed, upper-level institution. *Enrollment:* 3,174 graduate, professional, and undergraduate students; 240 full-time matriculated graduate/professional students (147 women), 1,135 part-time matriculated graduate/professional students (719 women). *Enrollment by degree level:* 1,375 master's. *Graduate faculty:* 81 full-time (33 women). *Graduate housing:* On-campus housing not available. *Student services:* Campus employment opportunities, campus safety program, career counseling, exercise/wellness program, grant writing training, international student services, low-cost health insurance, services for students with disabilities, teacher training, writing training. *Library facilities:* VC/UHV Library plus 1 other. *Online resources:* library catalog, web page, access to other libraries' catalogs. *Collection:* 50,000 titles, 70,000 serial subscriptions, 12,773 audiovisual materials.

Computer facilities: 150 computers available on campus for general student use. A campuswide network can be accessed from off campus. Online class registration is available. *Web address:* http://www.uhv.edu/.

General Application Contact: Admissions and Records, 361-570-4114, E-mail: admissions@uhv.edu.

GRADUATE UNITS

School of Arts and Sciences *Degree program information:* Part-time and evening/weekend programs available. Postbaccalaureate distance learning degree programs offered (no on-campus study). Offers arts and sciences (MA, MAIS, MS); computer science (MS); counseling psychology (MA); interdisciplinary studies (MAIS); school psychology (MA). Electronic applications accepted.

School of Business Administration *Degree program information:* Part-time and evening/weekend programs available. Postbaccalaureate distance learning degree programs offered (no on-campus study). Offers accounting (MBA); economic development and entrepreneurship (MS); finance (GMBA, MBA); general business (MBA); international business (MBA); management (GMBA, MBA); marketing (MBA). Electronic applications accepted.

School of Education and Human Development *Degree program information:* Part-time and evening/weekend programs available. Postbaccalaureate distance learning degree programs offered. Offers administration and supervision (M Ed); counseling (M Ed); curriculum and instruction (M Ed); special education (M Ed). Electronic applications accepted.

School of Nursing Offers nursing (MSN).

UNIVERSITY OF IDAHO, Moscow, ID 83844-2282

General Information State-supported, coed, university. CGS member. *Enrollment:* 11,791 graduate, professional, and undergraduate students; 1,238 full-time matriculated graduate/professional students (546 women), 1,030 part-time matriculated graduate/professional students (463 women). *Enrollment by degree level:* 326 first professional, 1,328 master's, 493 doctoral, 124 other advanced degrees. *Graduate faculty:* 430 full-time (110 women), 119 part-time/adjunct (20 women). Tuition and fees vary according to program. *Graduate housing:* Rooms and/or apartments available on a first-come, first-served basis to single and married students. Typical cost: $5490 per year for single students; $7000 per year for married students. Room charges vary according to housing facility selected. *Student services:* Campus employment opportunities, campus safety program, career counseling, child daycare facilities, exercise/wellness program, free psychological counseling, grant writing training, international student services, low-cost health insurance, multicultural affairs office, services for students with disabilities, writing training. *Library facilities:* University of Idaho Library plus 1 other. *Online resources:* library catalog, web page, access to other libraries' catalogs. *Collection:* 1.4 million titles, 14,230 serial subscriptions, 8,717 audiovisual materials. *Research affiliation:* Idaho Mining and Materials Resources Research Institute, Idaho Research Foundation, Snake River Conservation Research Center, Battelle Pacific Northwest Laboratories, Idaho Nuclear Environmental Engineering Laboratory, Inland Northwest Research Alliance (INRA).

Computer facilities: 670 computers available on campus for general student use. A campuswide network can be accessed from student residence rooms and from off campus. Online class registration, student evaluations of teaching are available. *Web address:* http://www.uidaho.edu/.

University of Idaho (continued)

General Application Contact: Dr. Margrit von Braun, Dean of the College of Graduate Studies, 208-885-6243, Fax: 208-885-6198, E-mail: uigrad@uidaho.edu.

GRADUATE UNITS

College of Graduate Studies Students: 1,238 full-time (546 women), 1,030 part-time (463 women); includes 142 minority (13 African Americans, 17 American Indian/Alaska Native, 54 Asian Americans or Pacific Islanders, 58 Hispanic Americans), 300 international. *Faculty:* 430 full-time (110 women), 119 part-time/adjunct (20 women). Expenses: Contact institution. *Financial support:* Fellowships, research assistantships, teaching assistantships, career-related internships or fieldwork, Federal Work-Study, institutionally sponsored loans, scholarships/grants, and tuition waivers (full and partial) available. Support available to part-time students. Financial award application deadline: 2/15. In 2008, 564 master's, 88 doctorates, 43 other advanced degrees awarded. Offers bioinformatics and computational biology (MS, PhD); bioregional planning (MS); environmental science (MS, PhD); interdisciplinary studies (MA, MS); neuroscience (MS, PhD); water resources (MS, PhD). *Application deadline:* For fall admission, 8/1 for domestic students; for spring admission, 12/15 for domestic students. Applications are processed on a rolling basis. *Application fee:* $55 ($60 for international students). *Application Contact:* Eric Larson, Director of Graduate Admissions, 208-885-4723, E-mail: gadms@uidaho.edu. *Dean of the College of Graduate Studies,* Dr. Margrit von Braun, 208-885-6243, Fax: 208-885-6198, E-mail: uigrad@uidaho.edu.

College of Agricultural and Life Sciences Students: 88 full-time (47 women), 44 part-time (25 women); includes 5 Hispanic Americans, 41 international. Average age 31. *Faculty:* 66 full-time, 13 part-time/adjunct. Expenses: Contact institution. *Financial support:* Research assistantships, teaching assistantships, career-related internships or fieldwork and Federal Work-Study available. Support available to part-time students. Financial award application deadline: 2/15. In 2008, 29 master's, 15 doctorates awarded. Offers agricultural and life sciences (M Engr, MS, PhD); agricultural economics (MS); agricultural education (MS); animal physiology (PhD); animal science (MS, PhD); applied economics (MS); biochemistry (MS); entomology (MS, PhD); family and consumer sciences (MS); food science (MS, PhD); microbiology, molecular biology and biochemistry (PhD); plant science (MS, PhD); soil and land resources (MS, PhD); soil science (MS, PhD); veterinary science (MS). *Application deadline:* For fall admission, 8/1 for domestic students; for spring admission, 12/15 for domestic students. *Application fee:* $55 ($60 for international students). *Application Contact:* Dr. John Hammel, Dean, 208-885-6681. *Dean,* Dr. John Hammel, 208-885-6681.

College of Art and Architecture Students: 72 full-time (28 women), 15 part-time (9 women). Average age 29. *Faculty:* 21. Expenses: Contact institution. In 2008, 52 master's awarded. Offers architecture and interior design (M Arch, MA, MS); art (MAT, MFA); art and architecture (M Arch, MA, MAT, MFA, MS); landscape architecture (MS). *Application Contact:* Dr. Mark Elison Hoversten, Dean, 208-885-5423. *Dean,* Dr. Mark Elison Hoversten, 208-885-5423.

College of Business and Economics Students: 49 full-time, 5 part-time. Average age 34. *Faculty:* 15 full-time. Expenses: Contact institution. *Financial support:* Research assistantships, teaching assistantships, Federal Work-Study and scholarships/grants available. Support available to part-time students. Financial award application deadline: 2/15. In 2008, 15 master's awarded. Offers accounting (M Acct, MS); business and economics (EMBA, M Acct, MBA, MS). *Application deadline:* For fall admission, 8/1 for domestic students; for spring admission, 12/15 for domestic students. *Application fee:* $55 ($60 for international students). *Application Contact:* Dr. John Morris, Dean, 208-885-6478. *Dean,* Dr. John Morris, 208-885-6478.

College of Education Students: 138 full-time (87 women), 444 part-time (264 women). Average age 41. *Faculty:* 53 full-time (24 women), 49 part-time/adjunct (10 women). Expenses: Contact institution. *Financial support:* Teaching assistantships, Federal Work-Study available. Support available to part-time students. Financial award application deadline: 2/15. In 2008, 190 master's, 32 doctorates, 43 other advanced degrees awarded. Offers adult and organizational learning (M Ed, MS, Ed S); counseling and human services (M Ed, MS, Ed D, PhD, Ed S); curriculum and instruction (Ed D, PhD); education (M Ed, MAT, MS, Ed D, PhD, Ed S, Ed Sp PTE); educational leadership (M Ed, MS, Ed S); physical education (M Ed, MS); professional-technical and technology education (M Ed, MS, Ed D, PhD, Ed Sp PTE); recreation (MS); school psychology (Ed S); special education (M Ed, MS, Ed S). *Application deadline:* For fall admission, 8/1 for domestic students; for spring admission, 12/15 for domestic students. *Application fee:* $55 ($60 for international students). *Application Contact:* Dr. Paul Rowland, Dean, 208-885-6773. *Dean,* Dr. Paul Rowland, 208-885-6773.

College of Engineering Students: 128 full-time (14 women), 226 part-time (23 women). Average age 33. *Faculty:* 83. Expenses: Contact institution. *Financial support:* Fellowships, research assistantships, teaching assistantships, career-related internships or fieldwork and Federal Work-Study available. Support available to part-time students. Financial award application deadline: 2/15. In 2008, 94 master's, 13 doctorates awarded. Offers agricultural engineering (M Engr, MS); biological and agricultural engineering (M Engr, MS, PhD); chemical engineering (M Engr, MA, MS, PhD); Civil Engineering (MS, PhD); computer engineering (M Engr, MS); computer science (MS, PhD); electrical engineering (M Engr, MS, PhD); engineering (MS, PhD); engineering management (M Engr, MS); environmental engineering (M Engr, MS); geological engineering (MS); materials science and engineering (MS, PhD); mechanical engineering (M Engr, MS, PhD); metallurgical engineering (MS); nuclear engineering (M Engr, PhD); systems engineering (M Engr). *Application deadline:* For fall admission, 8/1 for domestic students; for spring admission, 12/15 for domestic students. *Application fee:* $55 ($60 for international students). *Application Contact:* Dr. Donald Blackletter, Dean, 208-885-6470. *Dean,* Dr. Donald Blackletter, 208-885-6470.

College of Letters, Arts and Social Sciences Students: 194 full-time (97 women), 107 part-time (63 women). Average age 32. *Faculty:* 109 full-time (23 women), 22 part-time/adjunct (6 women). Expenses: Contact institution. *Financial support:* Fellowships, research assistantships, teaching assistantships, Federal Work-Study available. Support available to part-time students. Financial award application deadline: 2/15. In 2008, 90 master's, 4 doctorates awarded. Offers anthropology (MA); creative writing (MFA); English (MA, MAT, MFA); history (MA, MAT, PhD); letters, arts and social sciences (M Mus, MA, MAT, MFA, MPA, MS, PhD); music (M Mus, MA); political science (MA, PhD); psychology (MS); public administration (MPA); teaching English as a second language (MA); theatre arts (MFA). *Application deadline:* For fall admission, 8/1 for domestic students; for spring admission, 12/15 for domestic students. *Application fee:* $55 ($60 for international students). *Application Contact:* Dr. Katherine Aiken, Dean, 208-885-6426. *Dean,* Dr. Katherine Aiken, 208-885-6426.

College of Natural Resources Students: 83 full-time (37 women), 74 part-time (32 women). Average age 38. *Faculty:* 53. Expenses: Contact institution. *Financial support:* Fellowships, research assistantships, teaching assistantships, Federal Work-Study available. Support available to part-time students. Financial award application deadline: 2/15. In 2008, 27 master's, 11 doctorates awarded. Offers conservation social sciences (MS); fishery resources (MS); forest products (MS); forest resources (MS); natural resources (MNR, MS, PhD); rangeland ecology and management (MS); wildlife resources (MS). *Application deadline:* For fall admission, 8/1 for domestic students; for spring admission, 12/15 for domestic students. *Application fee:* $55 ($60 for international students). *Application Contact:* Dr. William James McLaughlin, Acting Dean, 208-885-8981, Fax: 208-885-6226. *Acting Dean,* Dr. William James McLaughlin, 208-885-8981, Fax: 208-885-6226.

College of Science Students: 132 full-time (52 women), 62 part-time (23 women). Average age 31. *Faculty:* 65 full-time, 11 part-time/adjunct. Expenses: Contact institution. In 2008, 51 master's, 10 doctorates awarded. Offers biological sciences (M Nat Sci); biology (MS, PhD); chemistry (MAT, MS, PhD); Geography (MS, PhD); geology (MS, PhD); hydrology (MS); mathematics (MAT, MS, PhD); physics (MS, PhD); physics education (MAT); science (M Nat Sci, MAT, MS, PhD); statistics (MS). *Application fee:* $55 ($60 for international students). *Application Contact:* Dr. Scott Wood, Dean, 208-885-6195. *Dean,* Dr. Scott Wood, 208-885-6195.

College of Law Students: 302 full-time, 4 part-time. Average age 29. *Faculty:* 23 full-time, 3 part-time/adjunct. Expenses: Contact institution. *Financial support:* Career-related internships or fieldwork, Federal Work-Study, and institutionally sponsored loans available. Financial award application deadline: 2/15. In 2008, 105 JDs awarded. Offers law (JD). *Application deadline:* For fall admission, 2/1 for domestic students. *Application fee:* $55 ($60 for international students). *Application Contact:* Donald L. Burnett, Dean, 208-885-4977. *Dean,* Donald L. Burnett, 208-885-4977.

UNIVERSITY OF ILLINOIS AT CHICAGO, Chicago, IL 60607-7128

General Information State-supported, coed, university. CGS member. *Graduate housing:* Room and/or apartments available on a first-come, first-served basis to single students; on-campus housing not available to married students. Housing application deadline: 3/1. *Research affiliation:* U.S. Department of Energy National Laboratories (physics, environment, computational science), National Surgical Adjuvant Breast and Bowel Project (prevention of breast cancer), Chicago Manufacturing Technology Extension Center (manufacturing research and development, industrial research), Eastern Cooperative Oncology Group (clinical cancer research).

GRADUATE UNITS

College of Dentistry Offers dentistry (DDS, MS, PhD); oral sciences (MS, PhD). Electronic applications accepted.

College of Medicine *Degree program information:* Part-time programs available. Offers biochemistry and molecular genetics (PhD); cellular and systems neuroscience and cell biology (PhD); medical education (MHPE); medicine (MD, MHPE, MS, PhD); microbiology and immunology (PhD); neuroscience (PhD); pharmacology (PhD); physiology and biophysics (MS, PhD); surgery (MS).

College of Pharmacy Offers biopharmaceutical sciences (PhD); forensic science (MS); medicinal chemistry (MS, PhD); pharmacognosy (MS, PhD); pharmacy (Pharm D, MS, PhD); pharmacy administration (MS, PhD).

Center for Pharmaceutical Biotechnology Offers pharmaceutical biotechnology (PhD).

Graduate College *Degree program information:* Part-time and evening/weekend programs available. Postbaccalaureate distance learning degree programs offered. Offers neuroscience (PhD). Electronic applications accepted.

College of Applied Health Sciences *Degree program information:* Part-time programs available. Offers applied health sciences (MS, DPT, OTD, PhD); biomedical visualization (MS); disability and human development (MS); disability studies (PhD); health informatics (MS); kinesiology (MS, PhD); nutrition (MS, PhD); occupational therapy (MS, OTD); physical therapy (MS, DPT). Electronic applications accepted.

College of Architecture and Art *Degree program information:* Part-time and evening/weekend programs available. Offers architecture (M Arch, MS Arch); architecture and art (M Arch, MA, MFA, MS Arch, PhD); architecture in health design (MS Arch); art history (MA, PhD); electronic visualization (MFA); film animation (MFA); graphic design (MFA); industrial design (MFA); photography (MFA); studio arts (MFA). Electronic applications accepted.

College of Education *Degree program information:* Part-time and evening/weekend programs available. Offers curriculum studies (PhD); education (M Ed, Ed D, PhD); educational psychology (PhD); educational studies (M Ed); elementary education (M Ed); literacy, language and culture (M Ed, PhD); policy studies (M Ed); policy studies in urban education (PhD); secondary education (M Ed); special education (M Ed, PhD); urban education leadership (Ed D). Electronic applications accepted.

College of Engineering *Degree program information:* Part-time and evening/weekend programs available. Offers bioengineering (MS, PhD); chemical engineering (MS, PhD); civil engineering (MS, PhD); computer science (MS, PhD); electrical and computer engineering (MS, PhD); energy engineering (MEE); engineering (M Eng, MEE, MS, PhD); industrial engineering (MS); industrial engineering and operations research (PhD); materials engineering (MS, PhD); mechanical engineering (MS, PhD). Electronic applications accepted.

College of Liberal Arts and Sciences *Degree program information:* Part-time and evening/weekend programs available. Offers anthropology (MA, PhD); applied mathematics (MS, PhD); biological sciences (MS, PhD); chemistry (MS, PhD); communication (MA, PhD); computational finance (MS, PhD); computer science (MS, PhD); criminal justice (MA, PhD); earth and environmental sciences (MS, PhD); economics (MA, PhD); elementary (MST); English (MA, PhD); environmental and urban geography (MA); environmental studies (MA); French (MA); Germanic studies (MA, PhD); Hispanic linguistics (MA, PhD); Hispanic literary and cultural studies (MA, PhD); Hispanic studies (MA, PhD); history (MA, MAT, PhD); liberal arts and sciences (MA, MAT, MS, MST, DA, PhD); linguistics (MA); mathematics (DA); mathematics and information sciences for industry (MS); philosophy (MA, PhD); physics (MS, PhD); political science (MA, PhD); probability and statistics (PhD); psychology (PhD); pure mathematics (MS, PhD); secondary (MST); sociology (MA, PhD); statistics (MS); teaching English to speakers of other languages/applied linguistics (MA); teaching of mathematics (MST); urban geography (MA). Electronic applications accepted.

College of Nursing *Degree program information:* Part-time programs available. Offers acute care clinical nurse specialist (MS); acute care nurse practitioner (MS); administrative studies in nursing (MS); adult nurse practitioner (MS); adult/geriatric nurse practitioner (MS); advanced community health nurse specialist (MS); family nurse practitioner (MS); geriatric clinical nurse specialist (MS); geriatric nurse practitioner (MS); mental health clinical nurse specialist (MS); mental health nurse practitioner (MS); nurse midwifery (MS); nursing (MS, DNP, PhD); nursing practice (DNP); nursing science (PhD); occupational health/advanced community health nurse specialist (MS); occupational health/family nurse practitioner (MS); pediatric clinical nurse specialist (MS); pediatric nurse practitioner (MS); perinatal clinical nurse specialist (MS); school/advanced community health nurse specialist (MS); school/family nurse practitioner (MS); women's health nurse practitioner (MS). Electronic applications accepted.

College of Urban Planning and Public Affairs *Degree program information:* Part-time and evening/weekend programs available. Offers public administration (MPA, PhD); urban planning and policy (MUPP, PhD); urban planning and public affairs (MPA, MUPP, PhD). Electronic applications accepted.

Jane Addams College of Social Work *Degree program information:* Part-time programs available. Offers social work (MSW, PhD). Electronic applications accepted.

Liautaud Graduate School of Business *Degree program information:* Part-time and evening/weekend programs available. Offers accounting (MS); business (MA, MBA, MS, PhD); business administration (MBA, PhD); business statistics (PhD); management information systems (MS, PhD); real estate (MA). Electronic applications accepted.

School of Public Health *Degree program information:* Part-time programs available. Offers biostatistics (MS, PhD); cancer epidemiology (MS, PhD); clinical translational science (MS); community health sciences (MPH, MS, Dr PH, PhD); environmental and occupational health sciences (MPH, MS, Dr PH, PhD); epidemiology (MPH, MS, Dr PH, PhD); health policy (PhD); health policy and administration (Dr PH); health services research (PhD); healthcare (MHA); public health (MHA, MPH, MS, Dr PH, PhD); public health policy management (MPH); quantitative methods (MPH). Electronic applications accepted.

UNIVERSITY OF ILLINOIS AT SPRINGFIELD, Springfield, IL 62703-5407

General Information State-supported, coed, comprehensive institution. CGS member. *Enrollment:* 4,711 graduate, professional, and undergraduate students; 463 full-time matriculated graduate/professional students (243 women), 1,147 part-time matriculated graduate/professional students (660 women). *Enrollment by degree level:* 1,590 master's, 20 doctoral. *Graduate faculty:* 180 full-time (70 women), 68 part-time/adjunct (26 women). Tuition, state resident: full-time $6144; part-time $256 per credit hour. Tuition, nonresident: full-time $13,980; part-time $582.50 per credit hour. *Required fees:* $1800. *Graduate housing:* Rooms and/or apartments available on a first-come, first-served basis to single and married students. *Student services:* Campus employment opportunities, campus safety program, career counseling, child daycare facilities, exercise/wellness program, free psychological counseling, international student services, low-cost health insurance, multicultural affairs office, services for students with disabilities, teacher training, writing training. *Library facilities:*

Norris L. Brookens Library. *Online resources:* library catalog, web page, access to other libraries' catalogs. *Collection:* 554,122 titles, 46,131 serial subscriptions, 42,511 audiovisual materials. *Research affiliation:* Council of Undergraduate Research, Interuniversity Consortium for Political and Social Research.

Computer facilities: 475 computers available on campus for general student use. A campuswide network can be accessed from student residence rooms and from off campus. Online class registration is available. *Web address:* http://www.uis.edu/.

General Application Contact: Dr. Lynn Pardie, Office of Graduate Studies, 800-252-8533, Fax: 217-206-7623, E-mail: pardie.lynn@uis.edu.

GRADUATE UNITS

Graduate Programs Students: 463 full-time (243 women), 1,147 part-time (660 women); includes 188 minority (126 African Americans, 7 American Indian/Alaska Native, 39 Asian Americans or Pacific Islanders, 16 Hispanic Americans), 177 international. Average age 33. 1,686 applicants, 67% accepted, 587 enrolled. *Faculty:* 180 full-time (70 women), 68 part-time/adjunct (26 women). Expenses: Contact institution. *Financial support:* In 2008–09, research assistantships with full tuition reimbursements (averaging $8,109 per year), teaching assistantships with full tuition reimbursements (averaging $8,109 per year) were awarded; career-related internships or fieldwork, Federal Work-Study, scholarships/grants, health care benefits, and unspecified assistantships also available. Support available to part-time students. Financial award application deadline: 11/15; financial award applicants required to submit FAFSA. In 2008, 840 master's awarded. *Degree program information:* Part-time and evening/weekend programs available. Postbaccalaureate distance learning degree programs offered (no on-campus study). *Application deadline:* Applications are processed on a rolling basis. *Application fee:* $50 ($60 for international students). Electronic applications accepted. *Application Contact:* Dr. Lynn Pardie, Office of Graduate Studies, 800-252-8533, Fax: 217-206-7623, E-mail: pardie.lynn@uis.edu. *Office of Graduate Studies,* Dr. Lynn Pardie, 800-252-8533, Fax: 217-206-7623, E-mail: pardie.lynn@uis.edu.

College of Business and Management Students: 121 full-time (66 women), 221 part-time (80 women); includes 54 minority (24 African Americans, 2 American Indian/Alaska Native, 23 Asian Americans or Pacific Islanders, 5 Hispanic Americans), 32 international. Average age 33. 323 applicants, 72% accepted, 123 enrolled. *Faculty:* 20 full-time (4 women), 3 part-time/adjunct (0 women). Expenses: Contact institution. *Financial support:* In 2008–09, research assistantships with full tuition reimbursements (averaging $8,109 per year), teaching assistantships with full tuition reimbursements (averaging $8,109 per year) were awarded; career-related internships or fieldwork, Federal Work-Study, scholarships/grants, health care benefits, and unspecified assistantships also available. Support available to part-time students. Financial award application deadline: 11/15; financial award applicants required to submit FAFSA. In 2008, 117 master's awarded. *Degree program information:* Part-time and evening/weekend programs available. Postbaccalaureate distance learning degree programs offered (no on-campus study). Offers accountancy (MA); business administration (MBA); business and management (MA, MBA, MS); management information systems (MS). *Application deadline:* Applications are processed on a rolling basis. *Application fee:* $50 ($60 for international students). Electronic applications accepted. *Application Contact:* Dr. Lynn Pardie, Office of Graduate Studies, 800-252-8533, Fax: 217-206-7623, E-mail: pardie.lynn@uis.edu. *Dean,* Dr. Ronald McNeil, 217-206-6534, Fax: 217-206-7543, E-mail: mcneil.ronald@uis.edu.

College of Education and Human Services Students: 56 full-time (47 women), 444 part-time (332 women); includes 38 minority (32 African Americans, 2 American Indian/Alaska Native, 2 Asian Americans or Pacific Islanders, 2 Hispanic Americans), 2 international. Average age 35. 173 applicants, 56% accepted, 66 enrolled. *Faculty:* 17 full-time (5 women), 22 part-time/adjunct (14 women). Expenses: Contact institution. *Financial support:* In 2008–09, research assistantships with full tuition reimbursements (averaging $8,109 per year), teaching assistantships with full tuition reimbursements (averaging $8,109 per year) were awarded; career-related internships or fieldwork, Federal Work-Study, scholarships/grants, health care benefits, and unspecified assistantships also available. Support available to part-time students. Financial award application deadline: 11/15; financial award applicants required to submit FAFSA. In 2008, 192 master's awarded. *Degree program information:* Part-time and evening/weekend programs available. Postbaccalaureate distance learning degree programs offered (no on-campus study). Offers alcoholism and substance abuse (MA); child and family services (MA); education and human services (MA); educational leadership (MA); gerontology (MA); human development counseling (MA); social services administration (MA); teacher leadership (MA). *Application fee:* $50 ($60 for international students). Electronic applications accepted. *Application Contact:* Dr. Lynn Pardie, Office of Graduate Studies, 800-252-8533, Fax: 217-206-7623, E-mail: pardie.lynn@uis.edu. *Dean,* Dr. Larry Stonecipher, 217-206-7815, Fax: 217-206-6775, E-mail: stonecipher.larry@uis.edu.

College of Liberal Arts and Sciences Students: 143 full-time (60 women), 203 part-time (84 women); includes 24 minority (13 African Americans, 2 American Indian/Alaska Native, 4 Asian Americans or Pacific Islanders, 5 Hispanic Americans), 123 international. Average age 30. 433 applicants, 63% accepted, 107 enrolled. *Faculty:* 53 full-time (25 women), 15 part-time/adjunct (4 women). Expenses: Contact institution. *Financial support:* In 2008–09, research assistantships with full tuition reimbursements (averaging $8,109 per year), teaching assistantships with full tuition reimbursements (averaging $8,109 per year) were awarded; career-related internships or fieldwork, Federal Work-Study, scholarships/grants, health care benefits, and unspecified assistantships also available. Support available to part-time students. Financial award application deadline: 11/15; financial award applicants required to submit FAFSA. In 2008, 403 master's awarded. *Degree program information:* Part-time and evening/weekend programs available. Postbaccalaureate distance learning degree programs offered (no on-campus study). Offers biology (MS); communication (MA); computer science (MS); English (MA); history (MA); interdisciplinary studies (MA); liberal arts and sciences (MA, MS). *Application fee:* $50 ($60 for international students). Electronic applications accepted. *Application Contact:* Dr. Lynn Pardie, Office of Graduate Studies, 800-252-8533, Fax: 217-206-7623, E-mail: pardie.lynn@uis.edu. *Dean,* Dr. Margot Duley, 217-206-6512, Fax: 217-206-6217, E-mail: duley.margot@uis.edu.

College of Public Affairs and Administration Students: 143 full-time (70 women), 279 part-time (164 women); includes 72 minority (57 African Americans, 1 American Indian/Alaska Native, 10 Asian Americans or Pacific Islanders, 4 Hispanic Americans), 20 international. Average age 33. 383 applicants, 47% accepted, 137 enrolled. *Faculty:* 33 full-time (12 women), 17 part-time/adjunct (3 women). Expenses: Contact institution. *Financial support:* In 2008–09, research assistantships with full tuition reimbursements (averaging $8,109 per year), teaching assistantships with full tuition reimbursements (averaging $8,109 per year) were awarded; career-related internships or fieldwork, Federal Work-Study, scholarships/grants, health care benefits, and unspecified assistantships also available. Support available to part-time students. Financial award application deadline: 11/15; financial award applicants required to submit FAFSA. In 2008, 128 master's awarded. *Degree program information:* Part-time and evening/weekend programs available. Postbaccalaureate distance learning degree programs offered (no on-campus study). Offers environmental science (MS); environmental studies (MA); legal studies (MA); political studies (MA); public administration (MPA, DPA); public affairs and administration (MA, MPA, MPH, MS, DPA); public affairs reporting (MA); public health (MPH). *Application deadline:* Applications are processed on a rolling basis. *Application fee:* $50 ($60 for international students). Electronic applications accepted. *Application Contact:* Dr. Lynn Pardie, Office of Graduate Studies, 800-252-8533, Fax: 217-206-7623, E-mail: pardie.lynn@uis.edu. *Dean,* Dr. Pinky Sue Wassenberg, 217-206-6523, Fax: 217-206-7807, E-mail: wassenberg.pinky@uis.edu.

UNIVERSITY OF ILLINOIS AT URBANA–CHAMPAIGN, Champaign, IL 61820

General Information State-supported, coed, university. CGS member. *Enrollment:* 43,246 graduate, professional, and undergraduate students; 8,957 full-time matriculated graduate/professional students (4,110 women), 2,222 part-time matriculated graduate/professional students (1,248 women). *Graduate faculty:* 2,083 full-time (626 women), 154 part-time/adjunct (54 women). *Graduate housing:* Rooms and/or apartments available to single and married students. *Student services:* Campus employment opportunities, campus safety program, career counseling, exercise/wellness program, free psychological counseling, international student services, low-cost health insurance, multicultural affairs office, services for students with disabilities, teacher training. *Library facilities:* University Library plus 36 others. *Online resources:* library catalog, web page, access to other libraries' catalogs. *Collection:* 10.4 million titles, 63,413 serial subscriptions, 4,245 audiovisual materials. *Research affiliation:* Midwest Universities Research Association, Sandia National Laboratories, Fermi National Accelerator Laboratory, National Center for Atmospheric Research.

Computer facilities: Computer purchase and lease plans are available. 3,400 computers available on campus for general student use. A campuswide network can be accessed from student residence rooms and from off campus. Online class registration is available. *Web address:* http://www.uiuc.edu/.

General Application Contact: William Welburn, Associate Dean, 217-333-6715, Fax: 217-333-8019, E-mail: welburn@illinois.edu.

GRADUATE UNITS

College of Law Students: 618 full-time (270 women), 6 part-time (3 women); includes 146 minority (46 African Americans, 5 American Indian/Alaska Native, 57 Asian Americans or Pacific Islanders, 38 Hispanic Americans), 63 international. 512 applicants, 66% accepted, 249 enrolled. *Faculty:* 46 full-time (16 women), 25 part-time/adjunct (10 women). Expenses: Contact institution. *Financial support:* In 2008–09, 1 fellowship, 5 research assistantships, 16 teaching assistantships were awarded; tuition waivers (full and partial) also available. In 2008, 211 first professional degrees, 42 master's awarded. Offers law (JD, LL M, MCL, JSD). *Application deadline:* Applications are processed on a rolling basis. *Application fee:* $75. Electronic applications accepted. *Application Contact:* Charles Crain, Representative, Admissions and Records, 217-244-6415, Fax: 217-244-1478, E-mail: ccrain@illinois.edu. *Dean,* Bruce Smith, 217-244-8446, Fax: 217-244-1478, E-mail: smithb@illinois.edu.

College of Veterinary Medicine Students: 492 full-time (379 women), 21 part-time (13 women); includes 26 minority (6 African Americans, 2 American Indian/Alaska Native, 13 Asian Americans or Pacific Islanders, 5 Hispanic Americans), 29 international. 314 applicants, 69% accepted, 137 enrolled. *Faculty:* 70 full-time (26 women), 4 part-time/adjunct (3 women). Expenses: Contact institution. *Financial support:* In 2008–09, 13 fellowships, 27 research assistantships, 2 teaching assistantships were awarded; tuition waivers (full and partial) also available. In 2008, 97 first professional degrees, 12 master's, 6 doctorates awarded. Offers pathobiology (MS, PhD); veterinary biosciences (MS, PhD); veterinary clinical medicine (MS, PhD); veterinary medical science (DVM); veterinary medicine (DVM, MS, PhD). *Application fee:* $60 ($75 for international students). Electronic applications accepted. *Application Contact:* Herbert Whiteley, Dean, 217-333-2760, Fax: 217-333-4628, E-mail: hwhitele@illinois.edu. *Dean,* Herbert Whiteley, 217-333-2760, Fax: 217-333-4628, E-mail: hwhitele@illinois.edu.

Graduate College Students: 8,957 full-time (4,110 women), 2,222 part-time (1,248 women); includes 1,381 minority (481 African Americans, 36 American Indian/Alaska Native, 637 Asian Americans or Pacific Islanders, 227 Hispanic Americans), 3,491 international. 17,974 applicants, 29% accepted, 3266 enrolled. *Faculty:* 2,083 full-time (626 women), 154 part-time/adjunct (54 women). Expenses: Contact institution. *Financial support:* Fellowships, research assistantships, teaching assistantships, career-related internships or fieldwork and tuition waivers (full and partial) available. In 2008, 2,655 master's, 759 doctorates, 18 other advanced degrees awarded. *Application deadline:* Applications are processed on a rolling basis. *Application fee:* $60 ($75 for international students). Electronic applications accepted. *Application Contact:* Debasish Dutta, Dean, 217-333-6715, Fax: 217-333-8019, E-mail: ddutta@illinois.edu. *Dean,* Debasish Dutta, 217-333-6715, Fax: 217-333-8019, E-mail: ddutta@illinois.edu.

College of Agricultural, Consumer and Environmental Sciences Students: 472 full-time (247 women), 120 part-time (62 women); includes 46 minority (17 African Americans, 15 Asian Americans or Pacific Islanders, 14 Hispanic Americans), 221 international. 533 applicants, 36% accepted, 135 enrolled. *Faculty:* 220 full-time (50 women), 9 part-time/adjunct (3 women). Expenses: Contact institution. *Financial support:* In 2008–09, 111 fellowships, 400 research assistantships, 114 teaching assistantships were awarded; tuition waivers (full and partial) also available. In 2008, 119 master's, 56 doctorates awarded. Offers agricultural and consumer economics (MS, PhD); agricultural education (MS); agricultural engineering (MS, PhD); agricultural, consumer and environmental sciences (MS, PhD); animal sciences (MS, PhD); bioinformatics: animal sciences (MS); bioinformatics: crop sciences (MS); crop sciences (MS, PhD); food science and human nutrition (MS, PhD); human and community development (MS, PhD); natural resources and environmental science (MS, PhD); nutritional sciences (MS, PhD). *Application deadline:* Applications are processed on a rolling basis. *Application fee:* $60 ($75 for international students). Electronic applications accepted. *Application Contact:* Robert A. Easter, Dean, 217-333-0460, Fax: 217-244-2911, E-mail: reaster@illinois.edu. *Dean,* Robert A. Easter, 217-333-0460, Fax: 217-244-2911, E-mail: reaster@illinois.edu.

College of Applied Health Sciences Students: 236 full-time (164 women), 71 part-time (42 women); includes 51 minority (31 African Americans, 1 American Indian/Alaska Native, 14 Asian Americans or Pacific Islanders, 5 Hispanic Americans), 47 international. 505 applicants, 28% accepted, 123 enrolled. *Faculty:* 65 full-time (35 women), 3 part-time/adjunct (1 woman). Expenses: Contact institution. *Financial support:* In 2008–09, 25 fellowships, 93 research assistantships, 128 teaching assistantships were awarded; tuition waivers (full and partial) also available. In 2008, 58 master's, 22 doctorates awarded. Offers applied health sciences (MA, MPH, MS, MSPH, Au D, PhD); audiology (Au D); community health (MS, MSPH, PhD); kinesiology (MS, PhD); public health (MPH); recreation, sport and tourism (MS, PhD); rehabilitation (MS); speech and hearing science (MA, PhD). *Application deadline:* Applications are processed on a rolling basis. *Application fee:* $60 ($75 for international students). Electronic applications accepted. *Application Contact:* Tanya Gallagher, Dean, 217-333-2131, Fax: 217-333-0404, E-mail: tmgallag@illinois.edu. *Dean,* Tanya Gallagher, 217-333-2131, Fax: 217-333-0404, E-mail: tmgallag@illinois.edu.

College of Business Students: 922 full-time (357 women), 25 part-time (9 women); includes 138 minority (20 African Americans, 100 Asian Americans or Pacific Islanders, 18 Hispanic Americans), 407 international. 2,449 applicants, 35% accepted, 566 enrolled. *Faculty:* 91 full-time (21 women), 18 part-time/adjunct (2 women). Expenses: Contact institution. *Financial support:* In 2008–09, 45 fellowships, 80 research assistantships, 108 teaching assistantships were awarded; tuition waivers (full and partial) also available. In 2008, 659 master's, 9 doctorates awarded. Offers accountancy (MAS, MS, PhD); business (MAS, MBA, MS, PhD); business administration (MS, PhD); finance (MS, PhD); taxation (MS); technology management (MS). *Application deadline:* Applications are processed on a rolling basis. *Application fee:* $60 ($75 for international students). Electronic applications accepted. *Application Contact:* Lawrence M. Debrock, Interim Dean, 217-333-6340, Fax: 217-244-3118, E-mail: ldebrock@illinois.edu. *Interim Dean,* Lawrence M. Debrock, 217-333-6340, Fax: 217-244-3118, E-mail: ldebrock@illinois.edu.

College of Education Students: 400 full-time (267 women), 697 part-time (494 women); includes 242 minority (142 African Americans, 8 American Indian/Alaska Native, 47 Asian Americans or Pacific Islanders, 45 Hispanic Americans), 165 international. 844 applicants, 53% accepted, 254 enrolled. *Faculty:* 91 full-time (51 women), 4 part-time/adjunct (all women). Expenses: Contact institution. *Financial support:* In 2008–09, 83 fellowships, 158 research assistantships, 189 teaching assistantships were awarded; tuition waivers (full and partial) also available. In 2008, 240 master's, 68 doctorates, 16 other advanced degrees awarded. Offers curriculum and instruction (Ed M, MA, MS, Ed D, PhD, CAS); early childhood education (Ed M); education (Ed M, MA, MS, Ed D, PhD, CAS); education, organization and leadership (Ed M, MS, Ed D, PhD, CAS); educational policy studies (Ed M, MA, PhD); educational psychology (Ed M, MA, MS, PhD, CAS); elementary education (Ed M); human resource education (Ed M, MS, Ed D, PhD, CAS); secondary education (Ed M); special education (Ed M, MS, Ed D, PhD, CAS). *Application deadline:* Applications are processed on a rolling basis. *Application fee:* $60 ($75 for international students). Electronic applications accepted. *Application Contact:* Mary A. Kalantzis, Dean, 217-333-0960, Fax: 217-333-5847, E-mail: marykalantzis@illinois.edu. *Dean,* Mary A. Kalantzis, 217-333-0960, Fax: 217-333-5847, E-mail: marykalantzis@illinois.edu.

College of Engineering Students: 2,000 full-time (360 women), 374 part-time (47 women); includes 194 minority (31 African Americans, 1 American Indian/Alaska Native, 147 Asian Americans or Pacific Islanders, 15 Hispanic Americans), 1,268 international. 5,103 applicants,

University of Illinois at Urbana–Champaign (continued)

19% accepted, 519 enrolled. *Faculty:* 389 full-time (37 women), 22 part-time/adjunct (1 woman). Expenses: Contact institution. *Financial support:* In 2008–09, 288 fellowships, 1,631 research assistantships, 704 teaching assistantships were awarded; tuition waivers (full and partial) also available. In 2008, 409 master's, 265 doctorates awarded. Offers aerospace engineering (MS, PhD); bioengineering (MS, PhD); bioinformatics (MS); civil engineering (MS); computer science (MCS, MS, PhD); electrical and computer engineering (MS, PhD); engineering (MCS, MS, PhD); environmental engineering in civil engineering (MS, PhD); environmental science in civil engineering (MS, PhD); industrial engineering (MS, PhD); materials science and engineering (MS, PhD); mechanical engineering (MS, PhD); nuclear engineering (MS, PhD); physics (MS, PhD); systems and entrepreneurial engineering (MS, PhD); teaching of physics (MS); theoretical and applied mechanics (MS, PhD). *Application deadline:* Applications are processed on a rolling basis. *Application fee:* $60 ($75 for international students). Electronic applications accepted. *Application Contact:* Dr. Ilesanmi Adesida, Dean, 217-333-2150, Fax: 217-244-7705, E-mail: iadesida@illinois.edu. *Dean*, Dr. Ilesanmi Adesida, 217-333-2150, Fax: 217-244-7705, E-mail: iadesida@illinois.edu.

College of Fine and Applied Arts Students: 740 full-time (383 women), 124 part-time (72 women); includes 78 minority (23 African Americans, 3 American Indian/Alaska Native, 39 Asian Americans or Pacific Islanders, 13 Hispanic Americans), 234 international. 1,444 applicants, 31% accepted, 267 enrolled. *Faculty:* 206 full-time (67 women), 19 part-time/adjunct (6 women). Expenses: Contact institution. *Financial support:* In 2008–09, 101 fellowships, 102 research assistantships, 311 teaching assistantships were awarded; tuition waivers (full and partial) also available. In 2008, 248 master's, 44 doctorates awarded. Offers architectural studies (MS); architecture (M Arch, PhD); art and design (Ed M, MA, MFA, PhD); art education (Ed M, MA, PhD); art history (MA, PhD); crafts (MFA); dance (MFA); fine and applied arts (Ed M, M Arch, M Mus, MA, MFA, MLA, MME, MS, MUP, DMA, Ed D, PhD, AD, CAS); graphic design (MFA); industrial design (MFA); landscape architecture (MLA, PhD); metals (MFA); music (M Mus, DMA, AD); music education (MME, MS, Ed D, PhD, CAS); musicology (PhD); painting (MFA); photography (MFA); regional planning (PhD); sculpture (MFA); theatre (MA, MFA, PhD); urban planning (MUP). *Application deadline:* Applications are processed on a rolling basis. *Application fee:* $60 ($75 for international students). Electronic applications accepted. *Application Contact:* Robert F. Graves, Dean, 217-333-1660, Fax: 217-244-8381, E-mail: rbgraves@illinois.edu. *Dean*, Robert F. Graves, 217-333-1660, Fax: 217-244-8381, E-mail: rbgraves@illinois.edu.

College of Liberal Arts and Sciences Students: 2,222 full-time (1,045 women), 320 part-time (171 women); includes 251 minority (69 African Americans, 7 American Indian/Alaska Native, 124 Asian Americans or Pacific Islanders, 51 Hispanic Americans), 906 international. 4,576 applicants, 20% accepted, 522 enrolled. *Faculty:* 690 full-time (214 women), 23 part-time/adjunct (7 women). Expenses: Contact institution. *Financial support:* In 2008–09, 652 fellowships, 1,027 research assistantships, 1,445 teaching assistantships were awarded; tuition waivers (full and partial) also available. In 2008, 385 master's, 256 doctorates awarded. Offers African studies (MA); animal biology (ecology, ethology and evolution) (MS, PhD); anthropology (MA, PhD); applied mathematics (MS); applied mathematics: actuarial science (MS); applied statistics (MS); Asian studies (MA); astrochemistry (PhD); astronomy (PhD); atmospheric sciences (MS, PhD); biochemistry (MS, PhD); bioinformatics: chemical and biomolecular engineering (MS); biophysics and computational biology (MS, PhD); cell and developmental biology (PhD); chemical engineering (MS, PhD); chemical physics (PhD); chemical sciences (MA, MS, PhD); chemistry (MA, MS, PhD); classical philology (PhD); classics (MA); communication (MA); comparative literature (MA, PhD); creative writing (MFA); earth, society and environment (MA, MS, PhD); East Asian languages and cultures (PhD); ecology, evolution and conservation biology (MS, PhD); economics (MS, PhD); English (MA, PhD); entomology (MS, PhD); French (MA, PhD); geography (MA, MS, PhD); geology (MS, PhD); German (MA, PhD); history (MA, PhD); integrative biology (MS, MST, PhD); Italian (MA, PhD); Latin American studies (MA); liberal arts and sciences (MA, MFA, MS, MST, PhD); linguistics (MA, PhD); literatures, cultures and linguistics (MA, MS, PhD); mathematics (MA, MS, PhD); microbiology (MS, PhD); molecular and cellular biology (MS, PhD); molecular and integrative physiology (MS, PhD); neuroscience (PhD); philosophy (MA, PhD); physiological and molecular plant biology (PhD); plant biology (MS, PhD); policy economics (MS); political science (MA, PhD); Portuguese (MA, PhD); psychology (MA, MS, PhD); Russian, East European and Eurasian studies (MA); Slavic languages and literatures (MA, PhD); sociology (MA, PhD); Spanish (MA, PhD); statistics (PhD); teaching of chemistry (MS); teaching of earth sciences (MS); teaching of English as a second language (MA); teaching of Latin (MA); teaching of mathematics (MS). *Application deadline:* Applications are processed on a rolling basis. *Application fee:* $60 ($75 for international students). Electronic applications accepted. *Application Contact:* Ruth Watkins, Dean, 217-333-1350, Fax: 217-333-9142, E-mail: rwatkins@illinois.edu. *Dean*, Ruth Watkins, 217-333-1350, Fax: 217-333-9142, E-mail: rwatkins@illlinois.edu.

College of Media Students: 78 full-time (46 women), 25 part-time (16 women); includes 20 minority (9 African Americans, 6 Asian Americans or Pacific Islanders, 5 Hispanic Americans), 34 international. 290 applicants, 13% accepted, 35 enrolled. *Faculty:* 31 full-time (11 women), 3 part-time/adjunct (1 woman). Expenses: Contact institution. *Financial support:* In 2008–09, 16 fellowships, 30 research assistantships, 57 teaching assistantships were awarded; tuition waivers (full and partial) also available. In 2008, 39 master's, 10 doctorates awarded. Offers advertising (MS); communications and media (PhD); journalism (MS); media (MS, PhD). *Application deadline:* Applications are processed on a rolling basis. *Application fee:* $60 ($75 for international students). Electronic applications accepted. *Application Contact:* Ronald E. Yates, Dean, 217-333-2350, Fax: 217-333-9882, E-mail: ryates@illinois.edu. *Dean*, Ronald E. Yates, 217-333-2350, Fax: 217-333-9882, E-mail: ryates@illinois.edu.

Graduate School of Library and Information Science Students: 314 full-time (228 women), 295 part-time (226 women); includes 74 minority (25 African Americans, 4 American Indian/Alaska Native, 36 Asian Americans or Pacific Islanders, 9 Hispanic Americans), 39 international. 703 applicants, 49% accepted, 191 enrolled. *Faculty:* 24 full-time (12 women), 6 part-time/adjunct (4 women). Expenses: Contact institution. *Financial support:* In 2008–09, 42 fellowships, 48 research assistantships, 26 teaching assistantships were awarded; tuition waivers (full and partial) also available. In 2008, 225 master's, 12 doctorates, 2 other advanced degrees awarded. Postbaccalaureate distance learning degree programs offered. Offers bioinformatics: library and information science (MS); library and information science (MS, PhD, CAS); library and information science: digital libraries (CAS). *Application deadline:* Applications are processed on a rolling basis. *Application fee:* $60 ($75 for international students). Electronic applications accepted. *Application Contact:* Valerie Youngen, Representative, Admissions and Records, 217-333-0734, Fax: 217-244-3302, E-mail: vyoungen@llinois.edu. *Dean*, John Unsworth, 217-333-3281, Fax: 217-244-3302, E-mail: unsworth@illinois.edu.

School of Labor and Employment Relations Students: 179 full-time (124 women), 9 part-time (6 women); includes 39 minority (20 African Americans, 1 American Indian/Alaska Native, 16 Asian Americans or Pacific Islanders, 2 Hispanic Americans), 38 international. 239 applicants, 53% accepted, 75 enrolled. *Faculty:* 14 full-time (4 women), 1 (woman) part-time/adjunct. Expenses: Contact institution. *Financial support:* In 2008–09, 39 fellowships, 13 research assistantships, 3 teaching assistantships were awarded; tuition waivers (full and partial) also available. In 2008, 89 master's, 2 doctorates awarded. *Degree program information:* Part-time programs available. Offers human resources and industrial relations (MHRIR, PhD). *Application fee:* $60 ($75 for international students). Electronic applications accepted. *Application Contact:* Becky Barker, Graduate Admissions, 217-333-2381, Fax: 217-244-9290, E-mail: ebarker@illinois.edu. *Dean*, Dr. Joel Cutcher Gershenfeld, 217-333-1480, Fax: 217-244-9290, E-mail: joelcg@illinois.edu.

School of Social Work Students: 239 full-time (209 women), 72 part-time (61 women); includes 62 minority (42 African Americans, 2 American Indian/Alaska Native, 12 Asian Americans or Pacific Islanders, 6 Hispanic Americans), 17 international. 291 applicants, 60% accepted, 123 enrolled. *Faculty:* 19 full-time (12 women), 1 (woman) part-time/adjunct. Expenses: Contact institution. *Financial support:* In 2008–09, 4 fellowships, 16 research assistantships, 6 teaching assistantships were awarded; tuition waivers (full and partial) also available. In 2008, 111 master's, 4 doctorates awarded. Offers advocacy, leadership, and social change (MSW); children, youth and family services (MSW); social work (PhD). *Application deadline:* Applications are processed on a rolling basis. *Application fee:* $60 ($75 for international students). Electronic applications accepted. *Application Contact:* Michele Winfrey, Officer II, 217-333-2261, Fax: 217-244-5220, E-mail: mwinfrey@illinois.edu. *Dean*, Wynne S. Korr, 217-333-2260, Fax: 217-244-5220, E-mail: wkorr@illinois.edu.

Institute of Aviation Students: 11 full-time (5 women), 1 (woman) part-time, 8 international. 17 applicants, 41% accepted, 6 enrolled. *Faculty:* 6 full-time (2 women). Expenses: Contact institution. *Financial support:* In 2008–09, 8 research assistantships, 4 teaching assistantships were awarded; fellowships, tuition waivers (full and partial) also available. In 2008, 4 master's awarded. Offers human factors (MS). *Application deadline:* Applications are processed on a rolling basis. *Application fee:* $60 ($75 for international students). Electronic applications accepted. *Application Contact:* Peter Vlach, Director of Graduate Studies, 217-265-9456, E-mail: pvlach@illinois.edu. *Acting Head*, Alex Kirlik, 217-244-8972, E-mail: kirlik@illinois.edu.

UNIVERSITY OF INDIANAPOLIS, Indianapolis, IN 46227-3697

General Information Independent-religious, coed, comprehensive institution. *Enrollment:* 4,701 graduate, professional, and undergraduate students; 444 full-time matriculated graduate/professional students (354 women), 679 part-time matriculated graduate/professional students (474 women). *Graduate faculty:* 94 full-time (52 women), 53 part-time/adjunct (28 women). *Graduate housing:* Rooms and/or apartments available on a first-come, first-served basis to single and married students. *Student services:* Campus employment opportunities, campus safety program, career counseling, exercise/wellness program, free psychological counseling, international student services, low-cost health insurance, services for students with disabilities, teacher training, writing training. *Library facilities:* Krannert Memorial Library. *Online resources:* library catalog, web page, access to other libraries' catalogs. *Collection:* 173,363 titles, 1,015 serial subscriptions.

Computer facilities: 218 computers available on campus for general student use. A campuswide network can be accessed from student residence rooms and from off campus. *Web address:* http://www.uindy.edu/.

General Application Contact: Dr. E. John McIlvried, Associate Provost for Graduate Programs and International Programs, 317-788-3274, E-mail: jmcilvried@uindy.edu.

GRADUATE UNITS

Graduate Programs Students: 444 full-time (354 women), 679 part-time (474 women); includes 85 minority (55 African Americans, 20 Asian Americans or Pacific Islanders, 10 Hispanic Americans), 78 international. Average age 30. *Faculty:* 94 full-time (52 women), 53 part-time/adjunct (28 women). Expenses: Contact institution. *Financial support:* Teaching assistantships, career-related internships or fieldwork, Federal Work-Study, tuition waivers (full and partial), and unspecified assistantships available. Financial award application deadline: 5/1; financial award applicants required to submit FAFSA. In 2008, 297 master's, 90 doctorates awarded. *Degree program information:* Part-time and evening/weekend programs available. *Application deadline:* Applications are processed on a rolling basis. *Application Contact:* Dr. E. John McIlvried, Associate Provost for Graduate Programs and International Programs, 317-788-3274, E-mail: jmcilvried@uindy.edu. *Associate Provost for Graduate Programs and International Programs*, Dr. E. John McIlvried, 317-788-3274, E-mail: jmcilvried@uindy.edu.

Center for Aging and Community Students: 24 part-time (21 women); includes 3 minority (2 African Americans, 1 Hispanic American), 4 international. Average age 37. *Faculty:* 1 (woman) full-time, 1 (woman) part-time/adjunct. Expenses: Contact institution. *Financial support:* Scholarships/grants available. *Degree program information:* Part-time and evening/weekend programs available. Postbaccalaureate distance learning degree programs offered. Offers gerontology (MS, Certificate). *Application deadline:* Applications are processed on a rolling basis. *Application fee:* $50. *Application Contact:* Tamora Wolske, Academic Program Director, 317-791-5930, Fax: 317-791-5945, E-mail: wolsketl@uindy.edu. *Executive Director*, Dr. Ellen Miller, 317-791-5930, Fax: 317-791-5945, E-mail: emiller@uindy.edu.

College of Arts and Sciences Students: 28 full-time (19 women), 54 part-time (35 women); includes 11 minority (7 African Americans, 1 Asian American or Pacific Islander, 3 Hispanic Americans), 14 international. Average age 31. *Faculty:* 33 full-time (12 women), 7 part-time/adjunct (4 women). Expenses: Contact institution. *Financial support:* Teaching assistantships, Federal Work-Study available. Financial award application deadline: 5/1; financial award applicants required to submit FAFSA. *Degree program information:* Part-time and evening/weekend programs available. Offers applied sociology (MA); art (MA); arts and sciences (MA, MS); English (MA); history (MA); human biology (MS); international relations (MA). *Application deadline:* Applications are processed on a rolling basis. *Application fee:* $30. *Application Contact:* Linda Corn, 317-788-3395, E-mail: lcorn@uindy.edu. *Dean*, Dr. Daniel Briere, 317-788-3395, Fax: 317-788-3480, E-mail: dbriere@uindy.edu.

Krannert School of Physical Therapy Students: 131 full-time (105 women), 89 part-time (69 women); includes 10 minority (4 African Americans, 5 Asian Americans or Pacific Islanders, 1 Hispanic American), 35 international. Average age 28. *Faculty:* 15 full-time (9 women), 7 part-time/adjunct (5 women). Expenses: Contact institution. *Financial support:* Teaching assistantships, career-related internships or fieldwork, Federal Work-Study, scholarships/grants, tuition waivers (full and partial), and unspecified assistantships available. Financial award application deadline: 5/1; financial award applicants required to submit FAFSA. *Degree program information:* Part-time and evening/weekend programs available. Offers physical therapy (MHS, DHS, DPT, TDPT). *Application deadline:* For fall admission, 10/12 for domestic students. *Application fee:* $50. Electronic applications accepted. *Application Contact:* Kelly Wilson, Admissions Counselor, 317-788-4909, Fax: 317-788-3542, E-mail: kwilson@uindy.edu. *Dean of Health Sciences*, Dr. Mary Huer, 317-788-3500, Fax: 317-788-3542, E-mail: huerm@uindy.edu.

School of Business Students: 27 full-time (11 women), 171 part-time (67 women); includes 17 minority (8 African Americans, 8 Asian Americans or Pacific Islanders, 1 Hispanic American), 16 international. Average age 30. *Faculty:* 11 full-time (4 women), 12 part-time/adjunct (2 women). Expenses: Contact institution. *Financial support:* Federal Work-Study and unspecified assistantships available. Financial award application deadline: 5/1; financial award applicants required to submit FAFSA. *Degree program information:* Part-time and evening/weekend programs available. Offers business (EMBA, MBA, Graduate Certificate). *Application deadline:* Applications are processed on a rolling basis. *Application fee:* $50. *Application Contact:* Stephen A. Tokar, Director of Graduate Business Programs, 317-788-4905, E-mail: tokarsa@uindy.edu. *Dean*, Dr. Mitch B. Shapiro, 317-788-3378, E-mail: mshapiro@uindy.edu.

School of Education Students: 27 full-time (13 women), 98 part-time (61 women); includes 10 minority (9 African Americans, 1 Asian American or Pacific Islander), 1 international. Average age 34. *Faculty:* 5 full-time (4 women), 6 part-time/adjunct (3 women). Expenses: Contact institution. *Financial support:* Federal Work-Study available. Financial award application deadline: 5/1; financial award applicants required to submit FAFSA. *Degree program information:* Part-time and evening/weekend programs available. Offers art education (MAT); biology (MAT); chemistry (MAT); curriculum and instruction (MA); earth sciences (MAT); education (MA, MAT); educational leadership (MA); elementary education (MA); English (MAT); French (MAT); math (MAT); physical education (MAT); physics (MAT); secondary education (MA); social studies (MAT); Spanish (MAT). *Application deadline:* Applications are processed on a rolling basis. *Application fee:* $50. *Application Contact:* Dr. Kathy Moran, Dean, 317-788-3285, Fax: 317-788-3300, E-mail: kmoran@uindy.edu. *Dean*, Dr. Kathy Moran, 317-788-3285, Fax: 317-788-3300, E-mail: kmoran@uindy.edu.

School of Nursing Students: 21 full-time (18 women), 108 part-time (103 women); includes 16 minority (15 African Americans, 1 Hispanic American). Average age 39. *Faculty:* 10 full-time (9 women), 7 part-time/adjunct (6 women). Expenses: Contact institution. *Financial support:* Federal Work-Study available. Offers family practice (post-RN) (MSN); gerontological nurse practitioner (MSN); nurse-midwifery (MSN); nursing (MSN); nursing administration (MSN); nursing education (MSN). *Application deadline:* For fall admission, 8/1 for domestic students; for winter admission, 12/15 for domestic students; for spring admission, 4/15 for domestic students. Applications are processed on a rolling basis. *Application fee:* $50. *Application Contact:* T.C. Crum, Information Contact, 317-788-2128, Fax: 317-788-3542, E-mail: tcrum@uindy.edu. *Dean*, Dr. Mary McHugh, 317-788-3206, E-mail: issac@uindy.edu.

School of Occupational Therapy Students: 98 full-time (87 women), 80 part-time (75 women); includes 12 minority (5 African Americans, 4 Asian Americans or Pacific Islanders, 3 Hispanic Americans). Average age 27. *Faculty:* 8 full-time (all women), 8 part-time/adjunct (6 women). Expenses: Contact institution. *Financial support:* Career-related internships or fieldwork, Federal Work-Study, tuition waivers (full and partial), and unspecified assistantships available. Financial award application deadline: 5/1; financial award applicants required to submit FAFSA. *Degree program information:* Part-time and evening/weekend programs available. Offers occupational therapy (MHS, MOT, DHS). *Application deadline:* For fall admission, 11/1 for domestic students, 2/1 for international students. *Application fee:* $55. *Application Contact:* Kelly Wilson, Director, Admissions, 317-788-3457, Fax: 317-788-3542, E-mail: kwilson@uindy.edu. *Dean of Health Sciences*, Dr. Mary Huer, 317-788-3500, Fax: 317-788-3542, E-mail: huerm@uindy.edu.

School of Psychological Sciences Students: 112 full-time (101 women), 55 part-time (43 women); includes 6 minority (5 African Americans, 1 Asian American or Pacific Islander), 8 international. Average age 27. *Faculty:* 10 full-time (4 women), 4 part-time/adjunct (1 woman). Expenses: Contact institution. *Financial support:* Federal Work-Study available. Offers clinical psychology (Psy D); clinical psychology/mental health counseling (MA). *Application deadline:* For fall admission, 2/25 for domestic students. *Application fee:* $50. *Application Contact:* Dr. E. John McIlvried, Associate Provost for Graduate Programs and International Programs, 317-788-3274, E-mail: jmcilvried@uindy.edu. *Dean*, Dr. E. John McIlvried, 317-788-3247, Fax: 317-788-3480, E-mail: jmcilvried@uindy.edu.

THE UNIVERSITY OF IOWA, Iowa City, IA 52242-1316

General Information State-supported, coed, university. CGS member. *Enrollment:* 29,747 graduate, professional, and undergraduate students; 5,871 full-time matriculated graduate/professional students (2,949 women), 3,185 part-time matriculated graduate/professional students (1,614 women). *Enrollment by degree level:* 4,149 first professional, 2,120 master's, 2,764 doctoral, 23 other advanced degrees. *Graduate faculty:* 1,585 full-time (468 women), 87 part-time/adjunct (23 women). Tuition and fees vary according to course load and program. *Graduate housing:* Rooms and/or apartments available on a first-come, first-served basis to single and married students. Typical cost: $5641 per year ($8131 including board) for single students; $3915 per year for married students. Room and board charges vary according to board plan and housing facility selected. *Student services:* Campus employment opportunities, campus safety program, career counseling, child daycare facilities, exercise/wellness program, free psychological counseling, international student services, low-cost health insurance, multicultural affairs office, services for students with disabilities, teacher training, writing training. *Library facilities:* Main Library plus 10 others. *Online resources:* library catalog, web page, access to other libraries' catalogs. *Collection:* 4.1 million titles, 49,279 serial subscriptions, 62,205 audiovisual materials.

Computer facilities: Computer purchase and lease plans are available. 1,200 computers available on campus for general student use. A campuswide network can be accessed from student residence rooms and from off campus. Online class registration, online degree process, financial aid summary, bills are available. *Web address:* http://www.uiowa.edu/.

General Application Contact: Emil Rinderspacher, Senior Associate Director of Admissions, 319-335-1525, Fax: 319-335-1535, E-mail: admissions@uiowa.edu.

GRADUATE UNITS

College of Dentistry Offers dental public health (MS); dentistry (DDS, MS, PhD, Certificate); endodontics (MS, Certificate); operative dentistry (MS, Certificate); oral and maxillofacial pathology (Certificate); oral and maxillofacial radiology (Certificate); oral and maxillofacial surgery (MS, Certificate); oral pathology, radiology and medicine (MS, Certificate); oral science (MS, PhD); orthodontics (MS, Certificate); pediatric dentistry (Certificate); periodontics (MS, Certificate); preventive and community dentistry (MS); prosthodontics (MS, Certificate); stomatology (MS).

College of Law Students: 629 full-time (284 women); includes 106 minority (26 African Americans, 4 American Indian/Alaska Native, 44 Asian Americans or Pacific Islanders, 32 Hispanic Americans), 24 international. Average age 24. 1,502 applicants, 38% accepted, 194 enrolled. *Faculty:* 52 full-time (19 women), 40 part-time/adjunct (14 women). Expenses: Contact institution. *Financial support:* In 2008–09, 453 students received support, including 192 fellowships with full and partial tuition reimbursements available (averaging $16,394 per year), 261 research assistantships with partial tuition reimbursements available (averaging $2,015 per year); career-related internships or fieldwork, Federal Work-Study, institutionally sponsored loans, scholarships/grants, health care benefits, and unspecified assistantships also available. Financial award applicants required to submit FAFSA. In 2008, 229 JDs, 4 master's awarded. Offers law (JD, LL M). *Application deadline:* For fall admission, 3/1 for domestic and international students. Applications are processed on a rolling basis. *Application fee:* $60 ($85 for international students). Electronic applications accepted. *Application Contact:* Collins Byrd, Assistant Dean of Admissions, 319-335-9095, Fax: 319-335-9646, E-mail: law-admissions@uiowa.edu. *Dean*, Carolyn Jones, 319-335-9034, E-mail: carolyn-jones@uiowa.edu.

College of Pharmacy Offers pharmacy (MS, PhD). Electronic applications accepted.

Graduate College *Degree program information:* Part-time and evening/weekend programs available. Postbaccalaureate distance learning degree programs offered (minimal on-campus study). Offers applied mathematical and computational sciences (PhD); bioinformatics and computational biology (Certificate); genetics (PhD); health informatics (MS, PhD, Certificate); human toxicology (MS, PhD); immunology (PhD); information science (MS, PhD, Certificate); molecular and cellular biology (PhD); neuroscience (PhD); second language acquisition (PhD); translational biomedicine (MS, PhD); urban and regional planning (MA, MS). Electronic applications accepted.

College of Education Offers administration and research (PhD); art education (MA, PhD); counseling psychology (PhD); counselor education and supervision (PhD); curriculum and supervision (MA, PhD); curriculum supervision (MA); developmental reading (MA); early childhood and elementary education (MA, PhD); early childhood education and care (MA); education (MA, MAT, PhD, Ed S); educational administration (MA, PhD, Ed S); educational measurement and statistics (MA, PhD); educational psychology (MA, PhD); elementary education (MA, PhD); English education (MA, MAT, PhD); foreign language education (MA, MAT); foreign language/ESL education (PhD); higher education (MA, PhD, Ed S); language, literature and culture (PhD); math education (PhD); mathematics education (MA); music education (MA, PhD); rehabilitation counseling (MA); rehabilitation counselor education (PhD); school counseling (MA); school psychology (PhD, Ed S); secondary education (MA, MAT, PhD); social foundations (MA, PhD); social studies (MA, PhD); special education (MA, PhD); student development (MA, PhD). Electronic applications accepted.

College of Engineering Offers biomedical engineering (MS, PhD); chemical and biochemical engineering (MS, PhD); civil and environmental engineering (MS, PhD); electrical and computer engineering (MS, PhD); engineering (MS, PhD); engineering design and manufacturing (MS, PhD); ergonomics (MS, PhD); information and engineering management (MS, PhD); mechanical engineering (MS, PhD); operations research (MS, PhD); quality engineering (MS, PhD). Electronic applications accepted.

College of Liberal Arts and Sciences *Degree program information:* Part-time programs available. Postbaccalaureate distance learning degree programs offered (minimal on-campus study). Offers African American world studies (MA); American studies (MA, PhD); anthropology (MA, PhD); art (MA, MFA); art history (MA, PhD); Asian languages and literature (MA); astronomy (MS); biology (MS, PhD); cell and developmental biology (MS, PhD); chemistry (MS, PhD); classics (MA, PhD); communication research (MA, PhD); comparative literature (MA, PhD); comparative literature translation (MFA); computer science (MCS, MS, PhD); dance (MFA); English (PhD); evolution (MS, PhD); exercise science (MS); film and video production (MA, MFA); film studies (MA, PhD); French (MA, PhD); genetics (MS, PhD); geography (MA, PhD); geoscience (MS, PhD); German (MA, PhD); history (MA, PhD); integrative physiology (PhD); leisure and recreational sport management (MA); liberal arts and sciences (MA, MCS, MFA, MS, MSW, Au D, DMA, PhD); linguistics (MA, PhD); linguistics with TESL (MA); literary criticism (PhD); literary history (PhD); literary studies (MA); mass communication (PhD); mathematics (MS, PhD); media communication (MA); music (MA, MFA, DMA, PhD); neural and behavioral sciences (PhD); neurobiology (MS, PhD); nonfiction writing (MFA); philosophy (MA, PhD); physics (MS, PhD); plant biology (MS, PhD); political science (MA, PhD); professional journalism (MA); professional speech pathology and audiology (MA, Au D); psychology (MA, PhD); psychology of sport and physical activity (MA, PhD); religious studies (MA, PhD); rhetorical studies (MA, PhD); rhetorical theory and stylistics (PhD); science education (MS, PhD); social work (MSW, PhD); sociology (MA, PhD); Spanish (MA, PhD); speech and hearing science (PhD); sports studies (MA, PhD); statistics and actuarial science (MS, PhD); theatre arts (MFA); therapeutic recreation (MA); women's studies (PhD); writer's workshop (MFA). Electronic applications accepted.

College of Nursing Offers nursing (MSN, PhD). Electronic applications accepted.

College of Public Health Offers biostatistics (MS, PhD); clinical investigation (MS); community and behavioral health (MS, PhD); epidemiology (MS, PhD); health management and policy (MHA, PhD); occupational and environmental health (MS, PhD, Certificate); public health (MHA, MPH, MS, PhD, Certificate). Electronic applications accepted.

School of Library and Information Science Offers library and information science (MA). Electronic applications accepted.

Henry B. Tippie College of Business *Degree program information:* Part-time and evening/weekend programs available. Offers accountancy (M Ac); accounting (PhD); business (M Ac, MBA, PhD); business administration (PhD); economics (PhD). Electronic applications accepted.

Henry B. Tippie School of Management *Degree program information:* Part-time and evening/weekend programs available. Offers accounting (MBA); corporate finance (MBA); entrepreneurship (MBA); finance (MBA); individually designed concentration (MBA); investment management (MBA); management information systems (MBA); marketing (MBA); nonprofit management (MBA); operations management (MBA); strategic management and consulting (MBA). Electronic applications accepted.

Roy J. and Lucille A. Carver College of Medicine Students: 968 full-time (480 women), 7 part-time (5 women); includes 150 minority (31 African Americans, 5 American Indian/Alaska Native, 69 Asian Americans or Pacific Islanders, 45 Hispanic Americans), 39 international. 4,172 applicants, 10% accepted, 234 enrolled. *Faculty:* 521 full-time (95 women), 83 part-time/adjunct (39 women). Expenses: Contact institution. *Financial support:* In 2008–09, 798 students received support; fellowships, research assistantships, teaching assistantships, career-related internships or fieldwork, Federal Work-Study, institutionally sponsored loans, scholarships/grants, health care benefits, and tuition waivers (full and partial) available. Support available to part-time students. Financial award applicants required to submit FAFSA. In 2008, 177 first professional degrees, 31 master's, 28 doctorates awarded. *Degree program information:* Part-time programs available. Offers anatomy and biology (PhD); biochemistry (PhD); biology (PhD); chemistry (PhD); free radical and radiation biology (PhD); genetics (PhD); human toxicology (PhD); immunology (PhD); medicine (MD, MA, MPAS, MS, DPT, PhD); microbiology (PhD); molecular and cellular biology (PhD); molecular physiology and biophysics (PhD); neuroscience (PhD); pharmacology (PhD); speech and hearing (PhD). Electronic applications accepted. *Application Contact:* Betty Wood, Associate Director of Admissions, 319-335-1525, Fax: 319-335-1535, E-mail: admissions@uiowa.edu. *Dean*, Dr. Paul B. Rothman, 319-384-4590, Fax: 319-335-8318, E-mail: paul-rothman@uiowa.edu.

Graduate Programs in Medicine Students: 296 full-time (163 women), 7 part-time (5 women); includes 20 minority (4 African Americans, 2 American Indian/Alaska Native, 10 Asian Americans or Pacific Islanders, 4 Hispanic Americans), 35 international. 942 applicants, 11% accepted, 76 enrolled. Expenses: Contact institution. *Financial support:* In 2008–09, 151 students received support, including fellowships (averaging $23,500 per year), research assistantships (averaging $23,500 per year); teaching assistantships, career-related internships or fieldwork, Federal Work-Study, institutionally sponsored loans, health care benefits, and tuition waivers (full and partial) also available. Support available to part-time students. Financial award applicants required to submit FAFSA. In 2008, 31 master's, 24 doctorates awarded. *Degree program information:* Part-time programs available. Offers anatomy and cell biology (PhD); biochemistry (MS, PhD); free radical and radiation biology (MS, PhD); general microbiology and microbial physiology (MS, PhD); immunology (MS, PhD); medicine (MA, MPAS, MS, DPT, PhD); microbial genetics (MS, PhD); molecular physiology and biophysics (PhD); pathogenic bacteriology (MS, PhD); pathology (MS); pharmacology (MS, PhD); physical therapy (DPT); physician assistant (MPAS); rehabilitation science (PhD); virology (MS, PhD). Electronic applications accepted. *Application Contact:* Dr. Paul B. Rothman, Dean, 319-384-4590, Fax: 319-335-8318, E-mail: paul-rothman@uiowa.edu. *Dean*, Dr. Paul B. Rothman, 319-384-4590, Fax: 319-335-8318, E-mail: paul-rothman@uiowa.edu.

THE UNIVERSITY OF KANSAS, Lawrence, KS 66045

General Information State-supported, coed, university. CGS member. *Enrollment:* 29,365 graduate, professional, and undergraduate students; 7,664 matriculated graduate/professional students (4,266 women). *Enrollment by degree level:* 1,458 first professional, 3,904 master's, 2,270 doctoral, 32 other advanced degrees. *Graduate faculty:* 1,800. Tuition, state resident: full-time $6122; part-time $255.10 per credit hour. Tuition, nonresident: full-time $14,629; part-time $609.55 per credit hour. *Required fees:* $847; $70.56 per credit hour. Tuition and fees vary according to course load and program. *Graduate housing:* Rooms and/or apartments available on a first-come, first-served basis to single and married students. Typical cost: $6474 (including board) for single students; $3560 per year for married students. Room and board charges vary according to board plan and housing facility selected. Housing application deadline: 3/1. *Student services:* Campus employment opportunities, campus safety program, career counseling, child daycare facilities, exercise/wellness program, free psychological counseling, grant writing training, international student services, low-cost health insurance, multicultural affairs office, services for students with disabilities, teacher training, writing training. *Library facilities:* Watson Library plus 11 others. *Online resources:* library catalog, web page, access to other libraries' catalogs. *Collection:* 3.5 million titles, 62,016 serial subscriptions, 64,062 audiovisual materials.

Computer facilities: 1,500 computers available on campus for general student use. A campuswide network can be accessed from student residence rooms and from off campus. Online class registration is available. *Web address:* http://www.ku.edu.

General Application Contact: Graduate Studies, 785-864-8040, Fax: 785-864-7209, E-mail: graduate@ku.edu.

GRADUATE UNITS

Graduate Studies Students: 3,890 full-time (2,069 women), 1,442 part-time (757 women); includes 523 minority (139 African Americans, 72 American Indian/Alaska Native, 166 Asian Americans or Pacific Islanders, 146 Hispanic Americans), 927 international. Average age 31. 4,877 applicants, 49% accepted, 1462 enrolled. *Faculty:* 1,043. Expenses: Contact institution. *Financial support:* Fellowships with full and partial tuition reimbursements, research assistantships with full and partial tuition reimbursements, teaching assistantships with full and partial tuition reimbursements, career-related internships or fieldwork, Federal Work-Study, institutionally sponsored loans, scholarships/grants, traineeships, and unspecified assistantships available. Support available to part-time students. Financial award applicants required to submit FAFSA. In 2008, 1,262 master's, 249 doctorates, 6 other advanced degrees awarded. *Degree program information:* Part-time and evening/weekend programs available. Postbaccalaureate distance learning degree programs offered. *Application fee:* $45 ($55 for international students). Electronic applications accepted. *Application Contact:* Dr. John Augusto, Assistant Dean, 785-864-8040, Fax: 785-864-7209, E-mail: graduate@ku.edu. *Associate Vice Provost and Dean of Graduate Studies*, Dr. Sara Rosen, 785-864-8040, Fax: 785-864-7209, E-mail: graduate@ku.edu.

College of Liberal Arts and Sciences Students: 1,661 full-time (862 women), 312 part-time (155 women); includes 156 minority (37 African Americans, 29 American Indian/Alaska Native, 41 Asian Americans or Pacific Islanders, 49 Hispanic Americans), 368 international. Average age 31. 2,180 applicants, 41% accepted, 469 enrolled. Expenses: Contact institution. *Financial support:* Fellowships, research assistantships with partial tuition reimbursements,

The University of Kansas (continued)

teaching assistantships with full and partial tuition reimbursements, career-related internships or fieldwork, Federal Work-Study, institutionally sponsored loans, scholarships/grants, traineeships, and unspecified assistantships available. Support available to part-time students. Financial award applicants required to submit FAFSA. In 2008, 328 master's, 122 doctorates awarded. *Degree program information:* Part-time and evening/weekend programs available. Offers African and African-American studies (MA); African Studies (Graduate Certificate); American studies (MA, PhD); anthropology (MA, PhD); applied behavioral science (MA); arts (MA); audiology (PhD); behavioral psychology (PhD); biochemistry and biophysics (MA, PhD); biological sciences (MA, PhD); botany (MA, PhD); Brazilian studies (Graduate Certificate); Central American and Mexican studies (Graduate Certificate); chemistry (MS, PhD); child language (MA, PhD); classics (MA); clinical child psychology (MA, PhD); cognitive (PhD); collection conservation (Graduate Certificate); communication studies (MA, PhD); computational physics and astronomy (MS); creative writing (MFA); developmental (PhD); East Asian languages and cultures (MA); ecology and evolutionary biology (MA, PhD); economics (MA, PhD); English (MA, PhD); entomology (MA, PhD); film and media studies (PhD); French (MA, PhD); geography (MA, PhD); geology (MS, PhD); German (MA, PhD); gerontology (MA, PhD, Graduate Certificate); global and international studies (MA); global indigenous nations studies (MA); history (MA, PhD); history of art (MA, PhD); Latin American studies (MA); liberal arts and sciences (MA, MFA, MPA, MS, PhD, Graduate Certificate); linguistics (MA, PhD); mathematics (MA, PhD); microbiology (MA, PhD); molecular, cellular, and developmental biology (MA, PhD); museum studies (MA); philosophy (MA, PhD); physics (MS, PhD); political science (MA, PhD); psychology (MA, PhD); public administration (MPA, PhD); quantitative (PhD); religious studies (MA); Russian, East European and Eurasian studies (MA); Slavic languages and literatures (MA, PhD); sociology (MA, PhD); Spanish (MA, PhD); speech-language pathology (MA, PhD); theatre (MA); theatre design (MFA); visual art education (MA); visual arts education (MA). *Application fee:* $45 ($55 for international students). Electronic applications accepted. *Application Contact:* Dr. Greg B. Simpson, Interim Dean, 785-864-3661, Fax: 785-864-5331. *Interim Dean,* Dr. Greg B. Simpson, 785-864-3661, Fax: 785-864-5331.

School of Architecture, Design, and Planning Students: 139 full-time (61 women), 30 part-time (12 women); includes 17 minority (7 African Americans, 6 Asian Americans or Pacific Islanders, 4 Hispanic Americans), 8 international. Average age 27. 151 applicants, 59% accepted, 42 enrolled. *Faculty:* 25 full-time (7 women), 6 part-time/adjunct (0 women). Expenses: Contact institution. *Financial support:* Fellowships, research assistantships with full and partial tuition reimbursements, teaching assistantships with full and partial tuition reimbursements, career-related internships or fieldwork, scholarships/grants, health care benefits, and unspecified assistantships available. Financial award application deadline: 2/1; financial award applicants required to submit FAFSA. In 2008, 81 master's awarded. *Degree program information:* Part-time programs available. Offers architecture (PhD); architecture, design, and planning (M Arch, MA, MFA, MUP, PhD, AC); design (MA, MFA); design management (MA); facility management (AC); interaction design (MA); management option (M Arch); professional track (M Arch); urban planning (MUP). *Application deadline:* For fall admission, 3/1 priority date for domestic students, 2/1 priority date for international students; for spring admission, 11/1 priority date for domestic and international students. *Application fee:* $45 ($55 for international students). Electronic applications accepted. *Application Contact:* Gera Elliott, Admissions Coordinator, 785-864-3167, Fax: 785-864-5185, E-mail: archku@ku.edu. *Dean,* John C. Gaunt, 785-864-4281, E-mail: jgaunt@ku.edu.

School of Business Students: 307 full-time (108 women), 220 part-time (68 women); includes 66 minority (9 African Americans, 3 American Indian/Alaska Native, 40 Asian Americans or Pacific Islanders, 14 Hispanic Americans), 70 international. Average age 29. 485 applicants, 55% accepted, 224 enrolled. *Faculty:* 61. Expenses: Contact institution. *Financial support:* In 2008–09, 31 students received support; fellowships, research assistantships with full and partial tuition reimbursements, teaching assistantships with full and partial tuition reimbursements available, career-related internships or fieldwork, Federal Work-Study, and unspecified assistantships available. Financial award application deadline: 6/1; financial award applicants required to submit FAFSA. In 2008, 213 master's, 5 doctorates awarded. *Degree program information:* Part-time and evening/weekend programs available. Offers accounting (M Acc); animal health (MBA); business (PhD); finance (MBA); human resources management (MBA); information systems (MBA); international business (MBA); management (MBA); marketing (MBA); strategic management (MBA); supply chain management (MS). *Application deadline:* For fall admission, 6/1 priority date for domestic students, 5/1 for international students; for spring admission, 11/1 for domestic students, 10/1 for international students. Applications are processed on a rolling basis. *Application fee:* $60. Electronic applications accepted. *Application Contact:* Dee Steinle, Student Advising Center, 785-864-4254, Fax: 785-864-5328, E-mail: bschoolgrad@ku.edu. *Dean,* William L. Fuerst, 785-864-3795, E-mail: bschoolgrad@ku.edu.

School of Education Students: 717 full-time (512 women), 444 part-time (341 women); includes 122 minority (41 African Americans, 16 American Indian/Alaska Native, 30 Asian Americans or Pacific Islanders, 35 Hispanic Americans), 114 international. Average age 32. 697 applicants, 59% accepted, 311 enrolled. Expenses: Contact institution. *Financial support:* Fellowships, research assistantships with partial tuition reimbursements, teaching assistantships with full and partial tuition reimbursements, career-related internships or fieldwork, scholarships/grants, and unspecified assistantships available. Financial award application deadline: 2/1. In 2008, 297 master's, 66 doctorates, 6 other advanced degrees awarded. *Degree program information:* Part-time programs available. Offers counseling psychology (MS, PhD); curriculum and instruction (MA, MS Ed, Ed D, PhD); education (MA, MS, MS Ed, Ed D, PhD, Ed S); educational administration (MS Ed, Ed D, PhD); educational policy and leadership (Ed D, PhD); educational psychology and research (MS Ed, PhD); foundations (PhD); foundations of education (MS Ed); health and physical education (MS Ed, Ed D, PhD); higher education (MS Ed, Ed D); higher education administration (MS Ed); historical, philosophical, and social foundations of education (MS Ed); policy studies (PhD); school psychology (PhD, Ed S); special education (MS Ed, Ed D, PhD). *Application fee:* $45 ($55 for international students). Electronic applications accepted. *Application Contact:* Mary Ann Williams, Graduate Admissions Coordinator, 785-864-4510, Fax: 785-864-3566, E-mail: mwilliam@ku.edu. *Dean,* Dr. Rick Ginsberg, 785-864-4297.

School of Engineering Students: 423 full-time (91 women), 248 part-time (54 women); includes 58 minority (11 African Americans, 6 American Indian/Alaska Native, 29 Asian Americans or Pacific Islanders, 12 Hispanic Americans), 255 international. Average age 30. 631 applicants, 51% accepted, 141 enrolled. Expenses: Contact institution. *Financial support:* Fellowships, research assistantships with full and partial tuition reimbursements, teaching assistantships with full and partial tuition reimbursements, career-related internships or fieldwork, Federal Work-Study, scholarships/grants, and unspecified assistantships available. In 2008, 149 master's, 19 doctorates awarded. *Degree program information:* Part-time and evening/weekend programs available. Postbaccalaureate distance learning degree programs offered (no on-campus study). Offers aerospace engineering (ME, MS, DE, PhD); architectural engineering (MS); bioengineering (PhD); chemical engineering (MS); chemical/petroleum engineering (PhD); civil engineering (MCE, MS, DE, PhD); computer engineering (MS); computer science (MS, PhD); construction management (MCM); electrical engineering (MS, DE, PhD); engineering (MCE, MCM, ME, MS, DE, PhD); engineering management (MS); environmental engineering (MS, PhD); environmental science (MS, PhD); information technology (MS); mechanical engineering (MS, DE, PhD); petroleum engineering (MS); water resources science (MS). *Application deadline:* Applications are processed on a rolling basis. *Application fee:* $45 ($55 for international students). Electronic applications accepted. *Application Contact:* Dr. Glen Marotz, Associate Dean, 785-864-2980, Fax: 785-864-5445, E-mail: gama@ku.edu. *Dean,* Dr. Stuart R. Bell, 785-864-3881, E-mail: kuengr@ku.edu.

School of Journalism and Mass Communications Students: 42 full-time (25 women), 48 part-time (37 women); includes 10 minority (3 African Americans, 3 American Indian/Alaska Native, 1 Asian American or Pacific Islander, 3 Hispanic Americans), 11 international. Average age 30. 51 applicants, 82% accepted, 26 enrolled. *Faculty:* 23 full-time (8 women), 7 part-time/adjunct (4 women). Expenses: Contact institution. *Financial support:* Fellowships, research assistantships, teaching assistantships with full and partial tuition reimbursements, career-related internships or fieldwork, scholarships/grants, and unspecified assistantships available. Support available to part-time students. Financial award application deadline: 2/1; financial award applicants required to submit FAFSA. In 2008, 13 master's awarded. *Degree program information:* Part-time programs available. Offers journalism (MS). *Application deadline:* For fall admission, 2/1 for domestic and international students; for spring admission, 11/1 for domestic and international students. *Application fee:* $45 ($55 for international students). Electronic applications accepted. *Application Contact:* Cindy Nesvarba, Graduate Records Coordinator, 785-864-7649, Fax: 785-864-5318, E-mail: cnesvarb@ku.edu. *Dean,* Ann Brill, 785-864-4755, Fax: 785-864-4396, E-mail: abrill@ku.edu.

School of Music Students: 157 full-time (87 women), 40 part-time (22 women); includes 22 minority (3 African Americans, 1 American Indian/Alaska Native, 8 Asian Americans or Pacific Islanders, 10 Hispanic Americans), 34 international. Average age 30. 170 applicants, 51% accepted, 50 enrolled. Expenses: Contact institution. *Financial support:* Fellowships with full tuition reimbursements, research assistantships with full and partial tuition reimbursements, teaching assistantships with full and partial tuition reimbursements, scholarships/grants and unspecified assistantships available. In 2008, 19 master's, 20 doctorates awarded. Offers music (MM, MME, DMA, PhD); music education (MME, PhD); music therapy (MME). *Application fee:* $45 ($50 for international students). Electronic applications accepted. *Application Contact:* Dr. Alicia Ann Clair, Interim Dean, 785-864-3421, Fax: 785-864-5387, E-mail: finearts@ku.edu. *Interim Dean,* Dr. Alicia Ann Clair, 785-864-3421, Fax: 785-864-5387, E-mail: finearts@ku.edu.

School of Pharmacy Students: 109 full-time (49 women), 27 part-time (17 women); includes 12 minority (1 African American, 3 American Indian/Alaska Native, 4 Asian Americans or Pacific Islanders, 4 Hispanic Americans), 43 international. Average age 28. 210 applicants, 22% accepted, 29 enrolled. Expenses: Contact institution. *Financial support:* Fellowships with full tuition reimbursements, research assistantships with full and partial tuition reimbursements, teaching assistantships with full and partial tuition reimbursements, career-related internships or fieldwork, scholarships/grants, traineeships, and unspecified assistantships available. In 2008, 25 master's, 15 doctorates awarded. Offers hospital pharmacy (MS); medicinal chemistry (MS, PhD); neurosciences (MS, PhD); pharmaceutical chemistry (MS, PhD); pharmacology and toxicology (MS, PhD); pharmacy (MS, PhD). *Application fee:* $45 ($55 for international students). Electronic applications accepted. *Application Contact:* Kenneth L. Audus, Dean, 785-864-3591, E-mail: pharmacy@ku.edu. *Dean,* Kenneth L. Audus, 785-864-3591, E-mail: pharmacy@ku.edu.

School of Social Welfare Students: 292 full-time (253 women), 59 part-time (47 women); includes 53 minority (24 African Americans, 10 American Indian/Alaska Native, 4 Asian Americans or Pacific Islanders, 15 Hispanic Americans), 13 international. Average age 32. 302 applicants, 78% accepted, 170 enrolled. *Faculty:* 26. Expenses: Contact institution. *Financial support:* Fellowships, research assistantships with full and partial tuition reimbursements, teaching assistantships with full and partial tuition reimbursements, Federal Work-Study, scholarships/grants, and tuition waivers (partial) available. Support available to part-time students. Financial award applicants required to submit FAFSA. In 2008, 136 master's, 2 doctorates awarded. *Degree program information:* Part-time programs available. Postbaccalaureate distance learning degree programs offered (minimal on-campus study). Offers social welfare (MSW); social work (PhD). *Application deadline:* For fall admission, 2/1 for domestic and international students. *Application fee:* $45 ($55 for international students). Electronic applications accepted. *Application Contact:* Becky Hofer, Director of Admissions, 785-864-8956, Fax: 785-864-5277, E-mail: bhofer@ku.edu. *Dean,* Mary Ellen Kondrat, 785-864-4720, Fax: 785-864-5277.

School of Law Students: 493 full-time (189 women), 3 part-time (0 women); includes 83 minority (15 African Americans, 23 American Indian/Alaska Native, 27 Asian Americans or Pacific Islanders, 18 Hispanic Americans), 29 international. Average age 26. 1,101 applicants, 36% accepted, 162 enrolled. *Faculty:* 41 full-time (18 women), 18 part-time/adjunct (5 women). Expenses: Contact institution. *Financial support:* In 2008–09, 426 students received support, including 41 research assistantships, 9 teaching assistantships; career-related internships or fieldwork, Federal Work-Study, institutionally sponsored loans, and scholarships/grants also available. Financial award application deadline: 3/1; financial award applicants required to submit FAFSA. In 2008, 155 JDs awarded. Offers law (JD). *Application deadline:* For fall admission, 3/15 for domestic and international students. Applications are processed on a rolling basis. *Application fee:* $55. Electronic applications accepted. *Application Contact:* Jacqlene Nance, Director of Admissions, 866-220-3654, E-mail: admitlaw@ku.edu. *Dean,* Gail B Agrawal, 785-864-4550, Fax: 785-864-5054.

University of Kansas Medical Center Students: 1,148 full-time (702 women), 573 part-time (456 women); includes 251 minority (73 African Americans, 21 American Indian/Alaska Native, 108 Asian Americans or Pacific Islanders, 49 Hispanic Americans), 81 international. Average age 30. 3,017 applicants, 22% accepted, 466 enrolled. *Faculty:* 329 full-time (155 women), 38 part-time/adjunct (22 women). Expenses: Contact institution. *Financial support:* In 2008–09, 1,044 students received support; fellowships with full and partial tuition reimbursements available, research assistantships with full and partial tuition reimbursements available, teaching assistantships with full and partial tuition reimbursements available, career-related internships or fieldwork, Federal Work-Study, institutionally sponsored loans, scholarships/grants, traineeships, health care benefits, and unspecified assistantships available. In 2008, 160 first professional degrees, 167 master's, 59 doctorates, 201 other advanced degrees awarded. *Degree program information:* Part-time and evening/weekend programs available. Postbaccalaureate distance learning degree programs offered (minimal on-campus study). Offers medicine (MD, MA, MHSA, MOT, MPH, MS, Au D, DNP, DPT, OTD, PhD, Certificate, PMC). *Application deadline:* For fall admission, 7/1 priority date for domestic and international students; for winter admission, 5/1 for domestic students, 5/1 priority date for international students; for spring admission, 12/1 priority date for domestic and international students. Electronic applications accepted. *Application Contact:* Marcia Jones, Director of Graduate Studies, 913-588-1238, Fax: 913-588-5242, E-mail: mjones@kumc.edu. *Vice Chancellor for Academic Affairs and Dean of Graduate Studies,* Dr. Allen Rawitch, 913-588-1258, Fax: 913-588-5242, E-mail: arawitch@kumc.edu.

School of Allied Health Students: 286 full-time (230 women), 105 part-time (75 women); includes 26 minority (7 African Americans, 2 American Indian/Alaska Native, 13 Asian Americans or Pacific Islanders, 4 Hispanic Americans), 21 international. Average age 28. 430 applicants, 47% accepted, 137 enrolled. *Faculty:* 95 full-time (50 women), 17 part-time/adjunct (14 women). Expenses: Contact institution. *Financial support:* In 2008–09, 259 students received support, including 1 fellowship, 9 teaching assistantships with full tuition reimbursements available (averaging $20,124 per year); health care benefits and unspecified assistantships also available. Financial award applicants required to submit FAFSA. In 2008, 68 master's, 46 doctorates awarded. *Degree program information:* Part-time programs available. Postbaccalaureate distance learning degree programs offered (minimal on-campus study). Offers allied health (MA, MOT, MS, Au D, DPT, OTD, PhD, Certificate); audiology (MA, Au D, PhD); dietetic internship (Certificate); dietetics and nutrition (MS); molecular biotechnology (MS); nurse anesthesia (MS); occupational therapy (MOT, MS, OTD); physical therapy and rehabilitation science (DPT, PhD); speech-language pathology (MA, PhD); therapeutic science (PhD). *Application fee:* $60. Electronic applications accepted. *Application Contact:* Moffett Ferguson, Student Affairs Coordinator, 913-588-5275, Fax: 913-588-5254, E-mail: mfergus1@kumc.edu. *Dean,* Dr. Karen L. Miller, 913-588-5235, Fax: 913-588-5254, E-mail: kmiller@kumc.edu.

School of Medicine Students: 803 full-time (416 women), 159 part-time (96 women); includes 188 minority (49 African Americans, 15 American Indian/Alaska Native, 88 Asian Americans or Pacific Islanders, 36 Hispanic Americans), 50 international. Average age 27. 2,670 applicants, 14% accepted, 270 enrolled. *Faculty:* 177 full-time (53 women), 16 part-time/adjunct (4 women). Expenses: Contact institution. *Financial support:* In 2008–09, 690 students received support. Institutionally sponsored loans available. Financial award application deadline: 2/15; financial award applicants required to submit FAFSA. In 2008, 160 first professional degrees, 51 master's, 11 doctorates awarded. Offers anatomy and cell biology (MA, PhD); biochemistry and molecular biology (MS, PhD); biomedical sciences (MA, MPH, MS, PhD); health policy and management (MHSA); medicine (MD, MA, MHSA,

MPH, MS, PhD); microbiology, molecular genetics and immunology (PhD); molecular and integrative physiology (MS, PhD); neuroscience (MS, PhD); pathology and laboratory medicine (MA, PhD); pharmacology (MS, PhD); preventive medicine (MPH, MS); toxicology (MS, PhD). *Application deadline:* For fall admission, 10/15 for domestic students. Applications are processed on a rolling basis. *Application fee:* $50. Electronic applications accepted. *Application Contact:* Executive Dean. *Executive Dean.*

School of Nursing Students: 59 full-time (56 women), 309 part-time (285 women); includes 37 minority (17 African Americans, 4 American Indian/Alaska Native, 7 Asian Americans or Pacific Islanders, 9 Hispanic Americans), 10 international. Average age 38. 152 applicants, 82% accepted, 88 enrolled. *Faculty:* 57 full-time (52 women), 5 part-time/adjunct (4 women). Expenses: Contact institution. *Financial support:* In 2008–09, 95 students received support, including 7 research assistantships (averaging $24,000 per year), 23 teaching assistantships with full and partial tuition reimbursements available (averaging $24,000 per year); traineeships also available. Financial award application deadline: 2/14; financial award applicants required to submit FAFSA. In 2008, 48 master's, 2 doctorates awarded. *Degree program information:* Part-time programs available. Postbaccalaureate distance learning degree programs offered (minimal on-campus study). Offers family nurse practitioner (PMC); health care informatics (PMC); health professions educator (PMC); nurse midwife (PMC); nursing (MS, DNP, PhD); organizational leadership (PMC); psychiatric/mental health nurse practitioner (PMC); public health nursing (PMC). *Application deadline:* For fall admission, 6/1 for domestic students; for spring admission, 10/1 for domestic students. *Application fee:* $60. Electronic applications accepted. *Application Contact:* Dr. Rita K. Clifford, Associate Dean, Student Affairs, 913-588-1619, Fax: 913-588-1615, E-mail: rcliffor@kumc.edu. *Dean*, Dr. Karen L. Miller, 913-588-1604, Fax: 913-588-1660, E-mail: kmiller@kumc.edu.

UNIVERSITY OF KENTUCKY, Lexington, KY 40506-0032

General Information State-supported, coed, university. CGS member. *Enrollment:* 26,054 graduate, professional, and undergraduate students; 3,811 full-time matriculated graduate/professional students (2,092 women), 1,171 part-time matriculated graduate/professional students (756 women). *Graduate faculty:* 2,027 full-time (603 women), 166 part-time/adjunct (34 women). *Graduate housing:* Rooms and/or apartments available to single and married students. *Student services:* Campus employment opportunities, campus safety program, career counseling, child daycare facilities, exercise/wellness program, free psychological counseling, grant writing training, international student services, low-cost health insurance, multicultural affairs office, services for students with disabilities, teacher training, writing training. *Library facilities:* William T. Young Library plus 15 others. *Online resources:* library catalog, web page, access to other libraries' catalogs. *Collection:* 3.1 million titles, 29,633 serial subscriptions, 86,690 audiovisual materials. *Research affiliation:* Battelle Pacific Northwest Laboratories (environmental sciences), Continuous Electron Beam Accelerator Facility (high-energy physics), Oak Ridge National Laboratory (nuclear physics), National Institute of Occupational Health and Safety (environmental health), National Drug Addiction Center (drug abuse and prevention).

Computer facilities: 1,400 computers available on campus for general student use. A campuswide network can be accessed from student residence rooms and from off campus. Online class registration, various software packages are available. *Web address:* http://www.uky.edu/.

General Application Contact: Dr. Brian Jackson, Senior Associate Dean, 859-257-8176, Fax: 859-323-1928, E-mail: grad.webmaster@email.uky.edu.

GRADUATE UNITS

College of Dentistry Offers dentistry (DMD, MS).

College of Law Offers law (JD). Electronic applications accepted.

College of Medicine Offers medicine (MD, MSNS, PhD); nutritional sciences (MSNS, PhD). Electronic applications accepted.

College of Pharmacy Expenses: Contact institution. Offers pharmaceutical sciences (MS, PhD); pharmacy (Pharm D, MS, PhD). *Application Contact:* Dr. Patrick McNamara, Interim Dean, 859-257-7896, Fax: 859-257-7564, E-mail: pmcnamar@email.uky.edu. *Interim Dean*, Dr. Patrick McNamara, 859-257-7896, Fax: 859-257-7564, E-mail: pmcnamar@email.uky.edu.

Graduate School Students: 3,811 full-time (2,092 women), 1,171 part-time (756 women); includes 385 minority (253 African Americans, 11 American Indian/Alaska Native, 40 Asian Americans or Pacific Islanders, 81 Hispanic Americans), 955 international. Average age 31. 7,332 applicants, 34% accepted, 1397 enrolled. *Faculty:* 2,027 full-time (603 women), 171 part-time/adjunct (34 women). Expenses: Contact institution. *Financial support:* In 2008–09, 2,053 students received support, including 284 fellowships with full tuition reimbursements available (averaging $3,692 per year), 1,040 research assistantships with full tuition reimbursements available (averaging $14,000 per year), 922 teaching assistantships with full tuition reimbursements available (averaging $10,362 per year); career-related internships or fieldwork, Federal Work-Study, institutionally sponsored loans, scholarships/grants, traineeships, health care benefits, tuition waivers (partial), and unspecified assistantships also available. Support available to part-time students. Financial award application deadline: 3/15. In 2008, 1,275 master's, 300 doctorates, 12 other advanced degrees awarded. *Degree program information:* Part-time and evening/weekend programs available. Offers biomedical engineering (MSBE, PBME, PhD); health administration (MHA); public administration (MPA, MPP, PhD). *Application deadline:* For fall admission, 7/17 priority date for domestic students, 2/1 for international students; for spring admission, 12/13 priority date for domestic students, 6/15 for international students. *Application fee:* $50 ($65 for international students). Electronic applications accepted. *Application Contact:* Dr. Brian Jackson, Senior Associate Dean, 859-257-4667, Fax: 859-257-4676, E-mail: brian.jackson@uky.edu. *Dean*, Dr. Jeannine Blackwell, 859-257-1759, Fax: 859-323-1928, E-mail: blackwell@uky.edu.

College of Agriculture Students: 312 full-time (179 women), 64 part-time (36 women); includes 22 minority (14 African Americans, 1 American Indian/Alaska Native, 1 Asian American or Pacific Islander, 6 Hispanic Americans), 99 international. Average age 31. 348 applicants, 32% accepted, 82 enrolled. *Faculty:* 321 full-time (59 women), 41 part-time/adjunct (2 women). Expenses: Contact institution. *Financial support:* In 2008–09, 269 students received support, including 22 fellowships with full tuition reimbursements available (averaging $3,750 per year), 226 research assistantships with full tuition reimbursements available (averaging $15,500 per year), 37 teaching assistantships with full tuition reimbursements available (averaging $4,800 per year); career-related internships or fieldwork, Federal Work-Study, institutionally sponsored loans, scholarships/grants, traineeships, health care benefits, tuition waivers (partial), and unspecified assistantships also available. Support available to part-time students. Financial award application deadline: 3/15. In 2008, 55 master's, 22 doctorates awarded. *Degree program information:* Part-time programs available. Offers agricultural economics (MS, PhD); agriculture (MS, MSFAM, MSFOR, PhD); animal sciences (MS, PhD); biosystems and agricultural engineering (MS, PhD); career, technology and leadership education (MS); crop science (MS, PhD); entomology (MS, PhD); family studies, human development, and resource management (MSFAM, PhD); forestry (MSFOR); hospitality and dietetic administration (MS); plant and soil science (MS); plant pathology (MS, PhD); plant physiology (PhD); soil science (PhD); veterinary science (MS, PhD). *Application deadline:* For fall admission, 7/17 priority date for domestic students, 2/1 priority date for international students; for spring admission, 12/13 priority date for domestic students, 6/15 priority date for international students. *Application fee:* $50 ($65 for international students). Electronic applications accepted. *Application Contact:* Dr. Brian Jackson, Senior Associate Dean, 859-257-4667, Fax: 859-257-4676, E-mail: brian.jackson@uky.edu. *Dean*, Dr. Michael Reed, 859-257-4772, Fax: 859-663-6405, E-mail: mrreed@uky.edu.

College of Arts and Sciences Students: 854 full-time (421 women), 84 part-time (36 women); includes 58 minority (26 African Americans, 10 Asian Americans or Pacific Islanders, 22 Hispanic Americans), 216 international. Average age 31. 1,632 applicants, 25% accepted, 222 enrolled. *Faculty:* 426 full-time (127 women), 41 part-time/adjunct (7 women). Expenses: Contact institution. *Financial support:* In 2008–09, 659 students received support, including 114 fellowships with full tuition reimbursements available (averaging $3,127 per year), 171 research assistantships with full tuition reimbursements available (averaging $8,060 per year), 452 teaching assistantships with full tuition reimbursements available (averaging $11,828 per year); career-related internships or fieldwork, Federal Work-Study, institutionally sponsored loans, scholarships/grants, traineeships, health care benefits, tuition waivers (partial), and unspecified assistantships also available. Support available to part-time students. Financial award application deadline: 3/15. In 2008, 135 master's, 85 doctorates awarded. *Degree program information:* Part-time programs available. Offers anthropology (MA, PhD); applied mathematics (MS); arts and sciences (MA, MS, PhD); biology (MS, PhD); chemistry (MS, PhD); classics (MA); clinical psychology (MA); English (MA, PhD); experimental psychology (MA); French (MA); geography (MA, PhD); geology (MS, PhD); German (MA); Hispanic studies (MA, PhD); history (MA, PhD); mathematics (MA, MS, PhD); philosophy (MA, PhD); physics (MS, PhD); political science (MA, PhD); sociology (MA, PhD); statistics (MS, PhD); teaching world languages (MA). *Application deadline:* For fall admission, 7/17 priority date for domestic students, 2/1 priority date for international students; for spring admission, 12/13 priority date for domestic students, 6/15 priority date for international students. Applications are processed on a rolling basis. *Application fee:* $50 ($65 for international students). Electronic applications accepted. *Application Contact:* Dr. Brian Jackson, Senior Associate Dean, 859-257-4667, Fax: 859-257-4676, E-mail: brian.jackson@uky.edu. *Dean*, Dr. Steven Hoch, 859-257-8354, Fax: 859-323-1073, E-mail: steven-hoch@uky.edu.

College of Communications and Information Studies Students: 139 full-time (98 women), 119 part-time (96 women); includes 12 minority (7 African Americans, 1 Asian American or Pacific Islander, 4 Hispanic Americans), 2 international. Average age 32. 266 applicants, 42% accepted, 64 enrolled. *Faculty:* 37 full-time (10 women), 2 part-time/adjunct (0 women). Expenses: Contact institution. *Financial support:* In 2008–09, 40 students received support, including 8 fellowships (averaging $4,333 per year), 8 research assistantships (averaging $10,500 per year), 29 teaching assistantships (averaging $9,500 per year); career-related internships or fieldwork, Federal Work-Study, institutionally sponsored loans, scholarships/grants, traineeships, health care benefits, and unspecified assistantships also available. Support available to part-time students. Financial award application deadline: 3/15; financial award applicants required to submit FAFSA. In 2008, 88 master's, 2 doctorates awarded. *Degree program information:* Part-time programs available. Offers communication (MA, PhD); communications and information studies (MA, MSLS, PhD); library science (MA, MSLS). *Application deadline:* For fall admission, 7/17 priority date for domestic students, 2/1 for international students; for spring admission, 12/13 priority date for domestic students, 6/15 for international students. Applications are processed on a rolling basis. *Application fee:* $50 ($65 for international students). Electronic applications accepted. *Application Contact:* Dr. Brian Jackson, Senior Associate Dean, 859-257-4667, Fax: 859-257-4676, E-mail: brian.jackson@uky.edu. *Dean*, Dr. Derek R. Lane, 859-257-7805, E-mail: drlane@uky.edu.

College of Design Students: 70 full-time (32 women), 2 part-time (0 women); includes 3 minority (1 Asian American or Pacific Islander, 2 Hispanic Americans). Average age 29. 87 applicants, 57% accepted, 43 enrolled. *Faculty:* 19 full-time (5 women), 2 part-time/adjunct (both women). Expenses: Contact institution. *Financial support:* In 2008–09, 27 students received support, including 17 research assistantships with full tuition reimbursements available (averaging $4,000 per year), 10 teaching assistantships with full tuition reimbursements available (averaging $6,200 per year); fellowships with full tuition reimbursements available, Federal Work-Study, scholarships/grants, traineeships, health care benefits, tuition waivers (partial), and unspecified assistantships also available. Support available to part-time students. Financial award application deadline: 3/15; financial award applicants required to submit FAFSA. In 2008, 17 master's awarded. Offers architecture (M Arch); design (M Arch, MAIDM, MHP, MSIDM); historic preservation (MHP); interior design, merchandising, and textiles (MAIDM, MSIDM). *Application deadline:* For fall admission, 7/17 priority date for domestic students, 2/1 priority date for international students; for spring admission, 12/13 priority date for domestic students, 6/15 priority date for international students. *Application fee:* $50 ($65 for international students). Electronic applications accepted. *Application Contact:* Dr. Brian Jackson, Senior Associate Dean, 859-257-4667, Fax: 859-257-4676, E-mail: brian.jackson@uky.edu. *Dean*, Dr. Allison Carll-White, 859-257-7763, Fax: 859-323-1990, E-mail: hedcarll@uky.edu.

College of Education Students: 474 full-time (323 women), 230 part-time (163 women); includes 102 minority (86 African Americans, 4 American Indian/Alaska Native, 2 Asian Americans or Pacific Islanders, 10 Hispanic Americans), 15 international. Average age 34. 647 applicants, 39% accepted, 167 enrolled. *Faculty:* 95 full-time (49 women), 9 part-time/adjunct (4 women). Expenses: Contact institution. *Financial support:* In 2008–09, 111 students received support, including 19 fellowships with full tuition reimbursements available (averaging $2,850 per year), 39 research assistantships with full tuition reimbursements available (averaging $14,894 per year), 62 teaching assistantships with full tuition reimbursements available (averaging $7,336 per year); career-related internships or fieldwork, Federal Work-Study, institutionally sponsored loans, scholarships/grants, traineeships, health care benefits, tuition waivers (partial), and unspecified assistantships also available. Support available to part-time students. Financial award application deadline: 3/15. In 2008, 195 master's, 48 doctorates, 12 other advanced degrees awarded. *Degree program information:* Part-time and evening/weekend programs available. Offers administration and supervision (Ed S); counseling psychology (MS Ed, PhD, Ed S); curriculum and instruction (MA Ed, Ed D); early childhood special education (MS Ed); education (M Ed, MA Ed, MRC, MS, MS Ed, Ed D, PhD, Ed S); educational and counseling psychology (MS Ed); educational policy studies and evaluation (Ed D); educational psychology (Ed D, PhD, Ed S); exercise science (PhD); higher education (MS Ed, PhD); instruction and administration (Ed D); instruction system design (MS Ed); kinesiology (MS, Ed D); middle school education (MS Ed); rehabilitation counseling (MRC); school administration (M Ed); school psychometrist and school psychology (MA Ed); special education (MS Ed); special education leadership personnel preparation (Ed D). *Application deadline:* For fall admission, 7/17 priority date for domestic students, 2/1 priority date for international students; for spring admission, 12/13 priority date for domestic students, 6/15 priority date for international students. *Application fee:* $50 ($65 for international students). Electronic applications accepted. *Application Contact:* Dr. Brian Jackson, Senior Associate Dean, 859-257-4667, Fax: 859-257-4676, E-mail: brian.jackson@uky.edu. *Dean*, Dr. Roy Remer, 859-257-7877, Fax: 859-323-1046, E-mail: roy.remer@uky.edu.

College of Engineering Students: 404 full-time (90 women), 99 part-time (9 women); includes 16 minority (7 African Americans, 1 American Indian/Alaska Native, 6 Asian Americans or Pacific Islanders, 2 Hispanic Americans), 314 international. Average age 28. 1,163 applicants, 36% accepted, 105 enrolled. *Faculty:* 175 full-time (19 women), 10 part-time/adjunct (0 women). Expenses: Contact institution. *Financial support:* In 2008–09, 262 students received support, including 13 fellowships with full tuition reimbursements available (averaging $5,498 per year), 170 research assistantships with full tuition reimbursements available (averaging $7,600 per year), 97 teaching assistantships with full tuition reimbursements available (averaging $6,750 per year); career-related internships or fieldwork, Federal Work-Study, institutionally sponsored loans, scholarships/grants, traineeships, health care benefits, tuition waivers (partial), and unspecified assistantships also available. Support available to part-time students. Financial award application deadline: 3/15. In 2008, 163 master's, 35 doctorates awarded. *Degree program information:* Part-time programs available. Offers chemical engineering (MS, PhD); civil engineering (MCE, MSCE, PhD); computer science (MS, PhD); electrical engineering (MSEE, PhD); engineering (M Eng, MCE, MME, MS, MS Ch E, MS Min, MSCE, MSEE, MSEM, MSMAE, MSME, MSMSE, PhD); manufacturing systems engineering (MSMSE); materials science and engineering (MSMAE, PhD); mechanical engineering (MSME, PhD); mining engineering (MME, MS Min, PhD). *Application deadline:* For fall admission, 7/17 priority date for domestic students, 2/1 priority date for international students; for spring admission, 12/13 priority date for domestic students, 6/15 priority date for international students. *Application fee:* $50 ($65 for international students). Electronic applications accepted. *Application Contact:* Dr. Brian Jackson, Senior Associate Dean, 859-257-4667, Fax: 859-257-4676, E-mail: brian.jackson@uky.edu. *Dean*, Dr. G. T. Lineberry, 859-257-2833, Fax: 859-323-4922, E-mail: gt.lineberry@uky.edu.

College of Fine Arts Students: 169 full-time (87 women), 26 part-time (16 women); includes 23 minority (14 African Americans, 2 American Indian/Alaska Native, 1 Asian American or

University of Kentucky (continued)

Pacific Islander, 6 Hispanic Americans), 18 international. Average age 33. 240 applicants, 35% accepted, 55 enrolled. *Faculty:* 104 full-time (35 women). Expenses: Contact institution. *Financial support:* In 2008–09, 93 students received support, including 18 fellowships with full tuition reimbursements available (averaging $5,250 per year), 17 research assistantships with full tuition reimbursements available (averaging $5,075 per year), 67 teaching assistantships with full tuition reimbursements available (averaging $9,616 per year); Federal Work-Study, institutionally sponsored loans, scholarships/grants, traineeships, health care benefits, tuition waivers (partial), and unspecified assistantships also available. Support available to part-time students. Financial award application deadline: 3/15. In 2008, 35 master's, 18 doctorates awarded. *Degree program information:* Part-time and evening/weekend programs available. Offers art education (MA); art history (MA); art studio (MFA); fine arts (MA, MFA, MM, DMA, PhD); music (PhD); music composition (MM); music education (MM); music performance (MM); music theory (MA); musical arts (DMA); musicology (MA); theatre (MA). *Application deadline:* For fall admission, 7/17 priority date for domestic students, 2/1 priority date for international students; for spring admission, 12/13 priority date for domestic students, 6/15 priority date for international students. *Application fee:* $50 ($65 for international students). Electronic applications accepted. *Application Contact:* Dr. Brian Jackson, Senior Associate Dean, 859-257-4667, Fax: 859-257-4676, E-mail: brian.jackson@uky.edu. *Dean,* Dr. Robert Shay, 859-257-1707, Fax: 859-323-1050, E-mail: robert.shay@uky.edu.

College of Health Sciences Students: 198 full-time (151 women), 24 part-time (21 women); includes 5 minority (4 African Americans, 1 Hispanic American), 5 international. Average age 30. 116 applicants, 22% accepted, 17 enrolled. *Faculty:* 115 full-time (61 women), 3 part-time/adjunct (2 women). Expenses: Contact institution. *Financial support:* In 2008–09, 11 students received support, including 3 fellowships with full tuition reimbursements available (averaging $7,500 per year), 8 research assistantships with full tuition reimbursements available (averaging $12,000 per year); teaching assistantships with full tuition reimbursements available, career-related internships or fieldwork, Federal Work-Study, institutionally sponsored loans, scholarships/grants, traineeships, health care benefits, tuition waivers (partial), and unspecified assistantships also available. Support available to part-time students. Financial award application deadline: 3/15. In 2008, 120 master's, 2 doctorates awarded. *Degree program information:* Part-time programs available. Offers clinical sciences (MS, DS); communication disorders (MSCD); health physics (MSHP); health sciences (MS, MSCD, MSHP, MSPAS, MSPT, MSRMP, DS, PhD); physical therapy (MSPT); physician assistant studies (MSPAS); radiological medical physics (MSRMP); rehabilitation sciences (PhD). *Application deadline:* For fall admission, 7/17 priority date for domestic students, 2/1 priority date for international students; for spring admission, 12/13 priority date for domestic students, 6/15 priority date for international students. *Application fee:* $50 ($65 for international students). Electronic applications accepted. *Application Contact:* Dr. Brian Jackson, Senior Associate Dean, 859-257-4667, Fax: 859-257-4676, E-mail: brian.jackson@uky.edu. *Dean,* Dr. Patrick Kitzman, 859-323-1100 Ext. 80580, Fax: 859-323-1058, E-mail: phkitz1@uky.edu.

College of Public Health Students: 85 full-time (54 women), 39 part-time (30 women); includes 26 minority (20 African Americans, 1 American Indian/Alaska Native, 3 Asian Americans or Pacific Islanders, 2 Hispanic Americans), 16 international. Average age 31. 224 applicants, 52% accepted, 52 enrolled. *Faculty:* 39 full-time (13 women), 6 part-time/adjunct (4 women). Expenses: Contact institution. *Financial support:* In 2008–09, 26 students received support, including 7 fellowships with full tuition reimbursements available (averaging $4,480 per year), 16 research assistantships with full tuition reimbursements available (averaging $8,252 per year), 3 teaching assistantships with full tuition reimbursements available (averaging $8,060 per year); Federal Work-Study, scholarships/grants, traineeships, health care benefits, tuition waivers (partial), and unspecified assistantships also available. Support available to part-time students. Financial award application deadline: 3/15. In 2008, 40 master's awarded. Offers gerontology (PhD); public health (MPH, PhD). *Application deadline:* For fall admission, 7/17 priority date for domestic students, 2/1 priority date for international students; for spring admission, 12/13 priority date for domestic students, 6/15 priority date for international students. *Application fee:* $50 ($65 for international students). Electronic applications accepted. *Application Contact:* Dr. Brian Jackson, Senior Associate Dean, 859-257-4667, Fax: 859-257-4676, E-mail: brian.jackson@uky.edu. *Dean,* Dr. Bill Pfeifle, 859-257-5678 Ext. 82100, Fax: 859-323-5698, E-mail: pfeifle@email.uky.edu.

College of Social Work Students: 194 full-time (170 women), 152 part-time (127 women); includes 29 minority (25 African Americans, 1 Asian American or Pacific Islander, 3 Hispanic Americans), 3 international. Average age 33. 354 applicants, 57% accepted, 141 enrolled. *Faculty:* 23 full-time (15 women), 1 part-time/adjunct (0 women). Expenses: Contact institution. *Financial support:* In 2008–09, 16 students received support, including 1 fellowship (averaging $1,500 per year), 10 research assistantships (averaging $1,500 per year), 6 teaching assistantships (averaging $3,000 per year); career-related internships or fieldwork, Federal Work-Study, institutionally sponsored loans, scholarships/grants, traineeships, health care benefits, and unspecified assistantships also available. Support available to part-time students. Financial award application deadline: 3/15; financial award applicants required to submit FAFSA. In 2008, 98 master's, 1 doctorate awarded. Offers social work (MSW, PhD). *Application deadline:* For fall admission, 7/17 priority date for domestic students, 2/1 priority date for international students; for spring admission, 12/13 priority date for domestic students, 6/15 priority date for international students. *Application fee:* $50 ($65 for international students). Electronic applications accepted. *Application Contact:* Dr. Brian Jackson, Senior Associate Dean, 859-257-4667, Fax: 859-257-4676, E-mail: brian.jackson@uky.edu. *Dean,* Dr. Janet Ford, 859-257-6660, E-mail: jpford01@uky.edu.

Gatton College of Business and Economics Students: 277 full-time (100 women), 76 part-time (23 women); includes 27 minority (13 African Americans, 7 Asian Americans or Pacific Islanders, 7 Hispanic Americans), 90 international. Average age 29. 766 applicants, 40% accepted, 168 enrolled. *Faculty:* 103 full-time (17 women), 5 part-time/adjunct (0 women). Expenses: Contact institution. *Financial support:* In 2008–09, 80 students received support, including 22 fellowships with full tuition reimbursements available (averaging $3,199 per year), 9 research assistantships with full tuition reimbursements available (averaging $14,500 per year), 65 teaching assistantships with full tuition reimbursements available (averaging $12,700 per year); career-related internships or fieldwork, Federal Work-Study, institutionally sponsored loans, scholarships/grants, traineeships, health care benefits, tuition waivers (partial), and unspecified assistantships also available. Support available to part-time students. Financial award application deadline: 3/15; financial award applicants required to submit FAFSA. In 2008, 165 master's, 13 doctorates awarded. *Degree program information:* Part-time and evening/weekend programs available. Offers accounting (MSACC); business administration (MBA, PhD); business and economics (MBA, MS, MSACC, PhD); economics (MS, PhD). *Application deadline:* For fall admission, 7/17 priority date for domestic students, 2/1 priority date for international students; for spring admission, 12/13 priority date for domestic students, 6/15 priority date for international students. *Application fee:* $50 ($65 for international students). Electronic applications accepted. *Application Contact:* Dr. Brian Jackson, Senior Associate Dean, 859-257-4667, Fax: 859-257-4676, E-mail: brian.jackson@uky.edu. *Dean,* Dr. Devanathan Sudharshan, 859-257-8936, Fax: 859-257-8938, E-mail: sudharshan@uky.edu.

Graduate School Programs from the College of Medicine Students: 194 full-time (108 women), 6 part-time (3 women); includes 13 minority (3 African Americans, 2 Asian Americans or Pacific Islanders, 8 Hispanic Americans), 77 international. Average age 29. 327 applicants, 21% accepted, 55 enrolled. *Faculty:* 167 full-time (35 women), 7 part-time/adjunct (1 woman). Expenses: Contact institution. *Financial support:* In 2008–09, 185 students received support, including 18 fellowships with full tuition reimbursements available (averaging $5,666 per year), 175 research assistantships with full tuition reimbursements available (averaging $23,500 per year), 20 teaching assistantships with full tuition reimbursements available (averaging $11,750 per year); Federal Work-Study, scholarships/grants, traineeships, health care benefits, tuition waivers (partial), and unspecified assistantships also available. Support available to part-time students. Financial award application deadline: 3/15; financial award applicants required to submit FAFSA. In 2008, 10 master's, 46 doctorates awarded. Offers anatomy (PhD); biochemistry (PhD); medical science (MS); medicine (MS, PhD); microbiology (PhD); pharmacology (PhD); physiology (MS, PhD); toxicology (MS, PhD). *Application deadline:* For fall admission, 7/17 priority date for domestic students, 2/1 priority date for international students; for spring admission, 12/13 priority date for domestic students, 6/15 priority date for international students. *Application fee:* $50 ($65 for international students). Electronic applications accepted. *Application Contact:* Dr. Brian Jackson, Senior Associate Dean, 859-257-4667, Fax: 859-257-4676, E-mail: brian.jackson@uky.edu. *Dean of College of Medicine,* Dr. Jeffrey Davidson, 859-323-5207, Fax: 859-323-5946, E-mail: jndavid@uky.edu.

Graduate School Programs in the College of Nursing Students: 80 full-time (73 women), 131 part-time (115 women); includes 13 minority (9 African Americans, 1 American Indian/Alaska Native, 2 Asian Americans or Pacific Islanders, 1 Hispanic American), 7 international. Average age 37. 135 applicants, 52% accepted, 60 enrolled. *Faculty:* 32 full-time (31 women), 2 part-time/adjunct (1 woman). Expenses: Contact institution. *Financial support:* In 2008–09, 20 students received support, including 2 fellowships with full tuition reimbursements available, 10 research assistantships with full tuition reimbursements available (averaging $14,000 per year), 8 teaching assistantships with full tuition reimbursements available (averaging $5,000 per year); Federal Work-Study, institutionally sponsored loans, scholarships/grants, traineeships, health care benefits, tuition waivers (partial), and unspecified assistantships also available. Support available to part-time students. Financial award application deadline: 3/15; financial award applicants required to submit FAFSA. In 2008, 46 master's, 8 doctorates awarded. Offers nursing (MSN, PhD). *Application deadline:* For fall admission, 7/17 priority date for domestic students, 2/1 priority date for international students; for spring admission, 12/13 priority date for domestic students, 6/15 priority date for international students. *Application fee:* $50 ($65 for international students). Electronic applications accepted. *Application Contact:* Dr. Brian Jackson, Senior Associate Dean, 859-257-4667, Fax: 859-257-4676, E-mail: brian.jackson@uky.edu. *Dean,* Dr. Terry Lennie, 859-323-6631, Fax: 859-323-1057, E-mail: talenn2@email.uky.edu.

Patterson School of Diplomacy and International Commerce Students: 59 full-time (26 women), 6 part-time (4 women), 6 international. Average age 26. 124 applicants, 42% accepted, 34 enrolled. *Faculty:* 5 full-time (1 woman), 1 part-time/adjunct (0 women). Expenses: Contact institution. *Financial support:* In 2008–09, 18 students received support, including 13 fellowships (averaging $6,500 per year), 3 research assistantships (averaging $9,900 per year), 3 teaching assistantships (averaging $11,000 per year). Financial award application deadline: 3/15; financial award applicants required to submit FAFSA. In 2008, 41 master's awarded. Offers diplomacy and international commerce (MA). *Application deadline:* For fall admission, 2/1 for domestic students. *Application fee:* $40 ($55 for international students). Electronic applications accepted. *Application Contact:* Dr. Brian Jackson, Senior Associate Dean, 859-257-4667, Fax: 859-257-4676, E-mail: brian.jackson@uky.edu. *Director of Graduate Studies,* Dr. Evan Hillebrand, 859-257-6928, Fax: 859-257-4676, E-mail: evan.hillebrand@uky.edu.

UNIVERSITY OF LA VERNE, La Verne, CA 91750-4443

General Information Independent, coed, university. *Enrollment:* 3,923 graduate, professional, and undergraduate students; 1,701 full-time matriculated graduate/professional students (1,037 women), 1,783 part-time matriculated graduate/professional students (1,255 women). *Enrollment by degree level:* 349 first professional, 2,304 master's, 457 doctoral, 374 other advanced degrees. *Graduate faculty:* 73 full-time (32 women), 149 part-time/adjunct (75 women). *Tuition:* Part-time $575 per credit hour. *Required fees:* $575 per credit hour. Tuition and fees vary according to degree level, campus/location and program. *Graduate housing:* Room and/or apartments available on a first-come, first-served basis to single students; on-campus housing not available to married students. Typical cost: $5620 per year ($10,920 including board). Room and board charges vary according to board plan, campus/location and housing facility selected. *Student services:* Campus employment opportunities, campus safety program, career counseling, exercise/wellness program, free psychological counseling, international student services, low-cost health insurance, multicultural affairs office, services for students with disabilities, teacher training, writing training. *Library facilities:* Wilson Library. *Online resources:* library catalog, web page, access to other libraries' catalogs. *Collection:* 196,842 titles, 531,006 serial subscriptions, 2,721 audiovisual materials. *Research affiliation:* Huntington Memorial Hospital (health services management), Southern California Healthcare Systems, Methodist Hospital of Southern California, San Antonio Community Hospital, Riverside Community Hospital, Presbyterian Intercommunity Hospital.

Computer facilities: 250 computers available on campus for general student use. A campuswide network can be accessed from student residence rooms and from off campus. Online class registration, MyULV (online) are available. *Web address:* http://www.ulv.edu/.

General Application Contact: Connie Hamlow, Admissions Information Specialist, 909-593-3511 Ext. 4244, Fax: 909-392-2761, E-mail: gradadmission@ulv.edu.

GRADUATE UNITS

College of Arts and Sciences Students: 89 full-time (76 women), 106 part-time (94 women); includes 114 minority (23 African Americans, 12 Asian Americans or Pacific Islanders, 79 Hispanic Americans). Average age 29. *Faculty:* 13 full-time (6 women), 22 part-time/adjunct (13 women). Expenses: Contact institution. *Financial support:* Career-related internships or fieldwork, institutionally sponsored loans, and scholarships/grants available. Financial award application deadline: 3/2; financial award applicants required to submit FAFSA. In 2008, 24 master's, 20 doctorates awarded. *Degree program information:* Part-time programs available. Offers arts and sciences (MS, Psy D); clinical-community psychology (Psy D); counseling (MS); general counseling (MS); higher education counseling (MS); marriage and family therapy (MS). *Application deadline:* Applications are processed on a rolling basis. *Application Contact:* Connie Hamlow, Admissions Information Specialist, 909-593-3511 Ext. 4244, Fax: 909-392-2761, E-mail: gradadmission@ulv.edu. *Dean,* Dr. Fred Yaffe, 909-593-3511 Ext. 4198, E-mail: fyaffe@ulv.edu.

College of Business and Public Management Students: 527 full-time (275 women), 320 part-time (179 women); includes 534 minority (75 African Americans, 3 American Indian/Alaska Native, 291 Asian Americans or Pacific Islanders, 165 Hispanic Americans), 27 international. Average age 32. *Faculty:* 31 full-time (14 women), 39 part-time/adjunct (11 women). Expenses: Contact institution. *Financial support:* Career-related internships or fieldwork, institutionally sponsored loans, and scholarships/grants available. Financial award application deadline: 3/2; financial award applicants required to submit FAFSA. In 2008, 274 master's, 11 doctorates awarded. *Degree program information:* Part-time and evening/weekend programs available. Offers accounting (MBA); business (MBIT); business administration (MS); business and public management (MBA, MBA-EP, MBIT, MHA, MPA, MS, DPA, Certificate); counseling (MS); executive management (MBA-EP); finance (MBA, MBA-EP); financial management (MHA); gerontology (Certificate); gerontology administration (MS); health administration (MHA); health services management (MBA, MS); human resources (MHA); information management (MHA); information technology (MBA, MBA-EP); international business (MBA, MBA-EP); leadership (MBA-EP); leadership and management (MHA, MS); managed care (MBA, MHA); management (MBA, MBA-EP); marketing (MBA, MBA-EP); marketing and business development (MHA); nonprofit management (Certificate); organizational leadership (Certificate); public administration (MPA, DPA). *Application deadline:* Applications are processed on a rolling basis. *Application fee:* $50. *Application Contact:* Rina Lazarian, Program and Admission Specialist, 909-593-3511 Ext. 4819, Fax: 909-392-2704, E-mail: cbpm@ulv.edu. *Dean,* Dr. Abe Helou, 909-539-3511 Ext. 4211, Fax: 909-392-2704, E-mail: heloua@ulv.edu.

College of Education and Organizational Leadership Students: 287 full-time (222 women), 715 part-time (547 women); includes 429 minority (74 African Americans, 10 American Indian/Alaska Native, 47 Asian Americans or Pacific Islanders, 298 Hispanic Americans), 2 international. Average age 36. *Faculty:* 19 full-time (13 women), 24 part-time/adjunct (18 women). Expenses: Contact institution. *Financial support:* Institutionally sponsored loans, scholarships/grants, and unspecified assistantships available. Financial award application deadline: 3/2; financial award applicants required to submit FAFSA. In 2008, 216 master's, 62 doctorates awarded. *Degree program information:* Part-time programs available. Offers advanced teaching skills (M Ed); child development (MS); child development/child life (MS); child life (MS); education (M Ed); education (special emphasis) (M Ed); education and organizational leadership (M Ed, MS, Ed D, Certificate, Credential); educational management (M Ed,

Credential); multiple subject (Credential); organizational leadership (Ed D); preliminary administrative services (Credential); professional administrative services (Credential); pupil personnel services (Credential); reading (M Ed, Certificate, Credential); reading and language arts specialist (Credential); school counseling (MS, Credential); single subject (Credential); teacher education (Credential). *Application deadline:* Applications are processed on a rolling basis. *Application fee:* $50. *Application Contact:* Connie Hamlow, Admissions Information Specialist, 909-593-3511 Ext. 4244, Fax: 909-392-2761, E-mail: gradadmission@ulv.edu. *Dean,* Dr. Mark Goor, 909-593-3511 Ext. 4647, E-mail: mgoor@ulv.edu.

College of Law Students: 241 full-time (89 women), 113 part-time (56 women); includes 111 minority (12 African Americans, 2 American Indian/Alaska Native, 41 Asian Americans or Pacific Islanders, 56 Hispanic Americans), 1 international. Average age 26. 1,007 applicants, 43% accepted, 109 enrolled. *Faculty:* 18 full-time (9 women), 10 part-time/adjunct (3 women). Expenses: Contact institution. *Financial support:* In 2008–09, 354 students received support. Federal Work-Study, scholarships/grants, and health care benefits available. Support available to part-time students. Financial award application deadline: 3/2; financial award applicants required to submit FAFSA. In 2008, 77 JDs awarded. *Degree program information:* Part-time and evening/weekend programs available. Offers law (JD). Also available at San Fernando Valley Campus. *Application deadline:* For fall admission, 7/1 priority date for domestic students; for spring admission, 11/1 priority date for domestic students. Applications are processed on a rolling basis. *Application fee:* $60. Electronic applications accepted. *Application Contact:* Alexis E. Thompson, Assistant Dean of Admissions, 909-460-2001, Fax: 909-460-2082, E-mail: lawadm@ulv.edu. *Dean,* Allen K. Easley, 909-460-2000, Fax: 909-460-2081, E-mail: lawadm@ulv.edu.

Regional Campus Administration Students: 436 full-time (302 women), 616 part-time (415 women); includes 482 minority (96 African Americans, 17 American Indian/Alaska Native, 79 Asian Americans or Pacific Islanders, 290 Hispanic Americans), 1 international. Average age 36. *Faculty:* 17 full-time (10 women), 133 part-time/adjunct (56 women). Expenses: Contact institution. *Financial support:* Institutionally sponsored loans available. Support available to part-time students. Financial award application deadline: 3/2; financial award applicants required to submit FAFSA. In 2008, 423 master's awarded. *Degree program information:* Part-time programs available. Offers advanced teaching (M Ed); business (MBA-EP); business administration (MBA); business organizational management (MS); cross cultural language and academic development (Credential); educational management (M Ed); health administration (MHA); leadership and management (MS); multiple subject (Credential); public administration (MPA); reading (M Ed); school counseling (MS); single subject (Credential). *Application deadline:* Applications are processed on a rolling basis. *Application fee:* $50. *Application Contact:* Dr. Stephen E. Lesniak, Dean, 909-593-3511 Ext. 5300, E-mail: lesniaks@ulv.edu. *Dean,* Dr. Stephen E. Lesniak, 909-593-3511 Ext. 5300, E-mail: lesniaks@ulv.edu.

UNIVERSITY OF LETHBRIDGE, Lethbridge, AB T1K 3M4, Canada

General Information Province-supported, coed, university. *Enrollment:* 7,877 graduate, professional, and undergraduate students; 215 full-time matriculated graduate/professional students, 98 part-time matriculated graduate/professional students. *Enrollment by degree level:* 275 master's, 38 doctoral. *Graduate housing:* Rooms and/or apartments available on a first-come, first-served basis to single and married students. Housing application deadline: 4/1. *Student services:* Campus employment opportunities, campus safety program, career counseling, exercise/wellness program, free psychological counseling, grant writing training, international student services, low-cost health insurance, multicultural affairs office, services for students with disabilities, teacher training, writing training. *Library facilities:* The University of Lethbridge Library. *Online resources:* library catalog, web page, access to other libraries' catalogs. *Collection:* 573,058 titles, 1,262 serial subscriptions, 5,929 audiovisual materials. *Research affiliation:* Monsanto Dow Agro-Sciences, Pacific Forestry Institution.

Computer facilities: Computer purchase and lease plans are available. 761 computers available on campus for general student use. A campuswide network can be accessed from student residence rooms and from off campus. Online class registration is available. *Web address:* http://www.uleth.ca/.

General Application Contact: Jennifer Gruninger, Coordinator, Graduate Student Recruitment and Communications, 403-329-5194, Fax: 403-329-2097, E-mail: jennifer.gruninger@uleth.ca.

GRADUATE UNITS

School of Graduate Studies Students: 215 full-time, 98 part-time. Expenses: Contact institution. *Financial support:* Fellowships, research assistantships, teaching assistantships, scholarships/grants, health care benefits, and unspecified assistantships available. In 2008, 87 master's, 1 doctorate awarded. *Degree program information:* Part-time and evening/weekend programs available. Offers accounting (MScM); addictions counseling (M Sc); agricultural biotechnology (M Sc); agricultural studies (M Sc, MA); anthropology (MA); archaeology (MA); art (MA, MFA); biochemistry (M Sc); biological sciences (M Sc); biomolecular science (PhD); biosystems and biodiversity (PhD); Canadian studies (MA); chemistry (M Sc); computer science (M Sc); computer science and geographical information science (M Sc); counseling psychology (M Ed); dramatic arts (MA); earth, space, and physical science (PhD); economics (MA); educational leadership (M Ed); English (MA); environmental science (M Sc); evolution and behavior (PhD); exercise science (M Sc); finance (MScM); French (MA); French/German (MA); French/Spanish (MA); general education (M Ed); general management (MScM); geography (M Sc, MA); German (MA); health science (M Sc); health sciences (MA); history (MA); human resource management and labour relations (MScM); individualized multidisciplinary (M Sc, MA); information systems (MScM); international management (MScM); kinesiology (M Sc, MA); management (M Sc, MA); marketing (MScM); mathematics (M Sc); music (M Mus, MA); Native American studies (MA); neuroscience (M Sc, PhD); new media (MA); nursing (M Sc); philosophy (MA); physics (M Sc); policy and strategy (MScM); political science (MA); psychology (M Sc, MA); religious studies (MA); social sciences (MA); sociology (MA); theatre and dramatic arts (MFA); theoretical and computational science (PhD); urban and regional studies (MA); women's studies (MA). *Application fee:* $60 Canadian dollars. *Application Contact:* Dr. Jo-Anne Fiske, Dean, 403-329-2464, Fax: 403-329-2097. *Dean,* Dr. Jo-Anne Fiske, 403-329-2464, Fax: 403-329-2097.

UNIVERSITY OF LOUISIANA AT LAFAYETTE, Lafayette, LA 70504

General Information State-supported, coed, university. CGS member. *Graduate housing:* Rooms and/or apartments available on a first-come, first-served basis to single and married students. *Research affiliation:* National Wetlands Research Center (biology, wetlands restoration), Louisiana Universities Marine Consortium (marine biology), U.S. Fish and Wildlife Service (ecology), Army Corps of Engineers (wetlands), U.S. Geological Survey, U.S. Department of Agriculture.

GRADUATE UNITS

BI Moody III College of Business Administration MBA Program *Degree program information:* Part-time and evening/weekend programs available. Offers counselor education (MS).

College of Education *Degree program information:* Part-time programs available. Offers administration and supervision (M Ed); curriculum and instruction (M Ed); education (M Ed, Ed D); education of the gifted (M Ed); educational leadership (M Ed, Ed D). Electronic applications accepted.

Graduate Studies and Research in Education Offers administration and supervision (M Ed); curriculum and instruction (M Ed); education of the gifted (M Ed); educational leadership (M Ed, Ed D).

College of Engineering *Degree program information:* Part-time and evening/weekend programs available. Offers chemical engineering (MSE); civil engineering (MSE); computer engineering (MS, PhD); computer science (MS, PhD); engineering (MS, MSE, MSET, MSTC, PhD); engineering and technology management (MSET); mechanical engineering (MSE); petroleum engineering (MSE); telecommunications (MSTC). Electronic applications accepted.

Center for Advanced Computer Studies *Degree program information:* Part-time programs available. Offers computer engineering (MS, PhD); computer science (MS, PhD). Electronic applications accepted.

College of Liberal Arts *Degree program information:* Part-time programs available. Offers British and American literature (MA); communicative disorders (MS, PhD); creative writing (PhD); Francophone studies (PhD); French (MA); history (MA); liberal arts (MA, MS, PhD); literature (PhD); mass communications (MS); psychology (MS); rehabilitation counseling (MS); rhetoric (PhD). Electronic applications accepted.

College of Nursing Offers nursing (MSN). Electronic applications accepted.

College of Sciences *Degree program information:* Part-time programs available. Offers biology (MS); cognitive science (PhD); computer science (MS, PhD); environmental and evolutionary biology (PhD); geology (MS); mathematics (MS, PhD); physics (MS); sciences (MS, PhD). Electronic applications accepted.

Institute of Cognitive Science Offers cognitive science (PhD). Electronic applications accepted.

College of the Arts Offers architecture (M Arch); arts (M Arch, MM); conducting (MM); pedagogy (MM); vocal and instrumental performance (MM). Electronic applications accepted.

School of Architecture Offers architecture (M Arch). Electronic applications accepted.

School of Music Offers conducting (MM); pedagogy (MM); vocal and instrumental performance (MM). Electronic applications accepted.

Department of Counselor Education Offers counselor education (MS). Electronic applications accepted.

UNIVERSITY OF LOUISIANA AT MONROE, Monroe, LA 71209-0001

General Information State-supported, coed, university. *Enrollment:* 8,772 graduate, professional, and undergraduate students; 694 full-time matriculated graduate/professional students (424 women), 327 part-time matriculated graduate/professional students (242 women). *Enrollment by degree level:* 362 first professional, 551 master's, 99 doctoral, 9 other advanced degrees. *Graduate faculty:* 108 full-time (49 women), 29 part-time/adjunct (10 women). *Graduate housing:* Room and/or apartments available on a first-come, first-served basis to single students; on-campus housing not available to married students. Typical cost: $3370 per year ($5520 including board). Room and board charges vary according to board plan. Housing application deadline: 7/28. *Student services:* Campus employment opportunities, career counseling, child daycare facilities, exercise/wellness program, free psychological counseling, international student services. *Library facilities:* University Library. *Online resources:* library catalog, access to other libraries' catalogs. *Collection:* 647,696 titles, 140 serial subscriptions, 660 audiovisual materials. *Research affiliation:* Juvenile Diabetes Research Foundation (pharmacology), Philip Morris, Inc. (medicinal chemistry), Harvard Hughes Medical Institute (biology), Xenoport, Inc. (pharmaceutics), U.S. Army Corps of Engineers (toxicology, environmental science), National Center for Toxicological Research (toxicology).

Computer facilities: A campuswide network can be accessed from student residence rooms and from off campus. Online class registration is available. *Web address:* http://www.ulm.edu/.

General Application Contact: Dr. Lisa Colvin, Interim Graduate Studies and Research Director, 318-342-1036, Fax: 318-342-1042, E-mail: lcolvin@ulm.edu.

GRADUATE UNITS

Graduate School Students: 694 full-time (424 women), 327 part-time (242 women); includes 231 minority (171 African Americans, 4 American Indian/Alaska Native, 37 Asian Americans or Pacific Islanders, 19 Hispanic Americans), 68 international. Average age 29. 638 applicants, 58% accepted, 313 enrolled. *Faculty:* 108 full-time (49 women), 29 part-time/adjunct (10 women). Expenses: Contact institution. *Financial support:* In 2008–09, 81 research assistantships with full tuition reimbursements (averaging $3,459 per year), 68 teaching assistantships with full tuition reimbursements (averaging $3,870 per year) were awarded; career-related internships or fieldwork, Federal Work-Study, institutionally sponsored loans, tuition waivers (full and partial), unspecified assistantships, and laboratory assistantships also available. Support available to part-time students. Financial award application deadline: 4/1; financial award applicants required to submit FAFSA. In 2008, 106 first professional degrees, 239 master's, 9 doctorates, 8 other advanced degrees awarded. *Degree program information:* Part-time and evening/weekend programs available. Offers pharmaceutical sciences (MS); pharmacy (Pharm D, MS, PhD). *Application deadline:* For fall admission, 5/22 priority date for domestic students, 7/1 priority date for international students; for winter admission, 12/12 priority date for domestic students; for spring admission, 1/17 priority date for domestic students, 11/1 priority date for international students. Applications are processed on a rolling basis. *Application fee:* $20 ($30 for international students). Electronic applications accepted. *Application Contact:* Misty Wiggins, Coordinator of Enrollment Services, 318-342-1036, Fax: 318-342-1042, E-mail: mwiggins@ulm.edu. *Interim Graduate Studies and Research Director,* Dr. Lisa Colvin, 318-342-1036, Fax: 318-342-1042, E-mail: lcolvin@ulm.edu.

College of Arts and Sciences Students: 83 full-time (46 women), 56 part-time (34 women); includes 29 minority (26 African Americans, 1 Asian American or Pacific Islander, 2 Hispanic Americans), 10 international. Average age 29. *Faculty:* 42 full-time (17 women), 3 part-time/adjunct (1 woman). Expenses: Contact institution. *Financial support:* In 2008–09, 21 research assistantships with full tuition reimbursements (averaging $2,929 per year), 36 teaching assistantships with full tuition reimbursements (averaging $3,283 per year) were awarded; career-related internships or fieldwork, Federal Work-Study, institutionally sponsored loans, unspecified assistantships, and laboratory assistantships also available. Support available to part-time students. Financial award application deadline: 4/1; financial award applicants required to submit FAFSA. In 2008, 35 master's awarded. *Degree program information:* Part-time and evening/weekend programs available. Offers arts and sciences (MA, MM, MS, CGS); biology (MS); communication (MA); criminal justice (MA); English (MA); gerontology (MA, CGS); history (MA); music (MM); visual and performing arts (MM). *Application deadline:* For fall admission, 8/22 priority date for domestic students, 7/1 for international students; for winter admission, 12/12 priority date for domestic students; for spring admission, 1/17 priority date for domestic students, 11/1 for international students. Applications are processed on a rolling basis. *Application fee:* $20 ($30 for international students). Electronic applications accepted. *Application Contact:* Paul Karlowitz, Assistant Dean, 318-342-1758, Fax: 318-342-1755, E-mail: karlowitz@ulm.edu. *Dean,* Dr. Jeffrey D. Cass, 318-342-1750, Fax: 318-342-1755, E-mail: jcass@ulm.edu.

College of Business Administration Students: 32 full-time (15 women), 36 part-time (19 women); includes 25 minority (13 African Americans, 1 American Indian/Alaska Native, 7 Asian Americans or Pacific Islanders, 4 Hispanic Americans). Average age 29. *Faculty:* 14 full-time (4 women). Expenses: Contact institution. *Financial support:* In 2008–09, 11 research assistantships with full tuition reimbursements (averaging $2,500 per year) were awarded; career-related internships or fieldwork, Federal Work-Study, and unspecified assistantships also available. Financial award application deadline: 4/1; financial award applicants required to submit FAFSA. In 2008, 18 master's awarded. *Degree program information:* Part-time and evening/weekend programs available. Offers business administration (MBA). *Application deadline:* For fall admission, 8/22 for domestic students, 7/1 for international students; for winter admission, 12/12 for domestic students; for spring admission, 1/17 for domestic students, 11/1 for international students. Applications are processed on a rolling basis. *Application fee:* $20 ($30 for international students). Electronic applications accepted. *Application Contact:* Dr. Donna Walton Luse, Program Chair, 318-342-1106, Fax: 318-342-1101, E-mail: luse@ulm.edu. *Dean,* Dr. Ronald Berry, 318-342-1100, Fax: 318-342-1101, E-mail: rberry@ulm.edu.

College of Education and Human Development Students: 161 full-time (109 women), 220 part-time (177 women); includes 122 minority (113 African Americans, 1 Asian American or Pacific Islander, 8 Hispanic Americans), 5 international. Average age 33. *Faculty:* 29 full-time (17 women), 10 part-time/adjunct (7 women). Expenses: Contact institution. *Financial support:* In 2008–09, 30 research assistantships (averaging $2,896 per year), 9 teaching assistantships (averaging $2,708 per year) were awarded; career-related internships or fieldwork, Federal Work-Study, institutionally sponsored loans, and unspecified assistantships also available. Financial award application deadline: 4/1; financial award applicants

University of Louisiana at Monroe (continued)

required to submit FAFSA. In 2008, 167 master's, 6 doctorates, 7 other advanced degrees awarded. *Degree program information:* Part-time and evening/weekend programs available. Postbaccalaureate distance learning degree programs offered. Offers administration and supervision (M Ed); applied exercise physiology (MS); clinical exercise physiology (MS); counseling (M Ed); curriculum and instruction (M Ed, Ed D); education (M Ed, MA, MAT, MS, Ed D, PhD, SSP); educational leadership (M Ed, Ed D); elementary education (M Ed, MAT); elementary education (1-5) (M Ed); general psychology (MS); grades 1-5 (M Ed); marriage and family therapy (MA, PhD); multiple levels grades K-12 (MAT); reading education (K-12) (M Ed); school psychology (MS, SSP); secondary education 6-12 (M Ed, MAT); SPED-academically gifted education (K-12) (M Ed); SPED-early intervention education (birth-3) (M Ed); SPED-educational diagnostics education (PreK-12) (M Ed); substance abuse counseling (MA). *Application deadline:* For fall admission, 8/22 priority date for domestic students, 7/1 for international students; for winter admission, 12/12 priority date for domestic students; for spring admission, 1/17 priority date for domestic students, 11/1 for international students. Applications are processed on a rolling basis. *Application fee:* $20 ($30 for international students). Electronic applications accepted. *Application Contact:* Dr. Jack Palmer, Director of Graduate Studies, 318-342-1250, Fax: 318-342-1240, E-mail: palmer@ulm.edu. *Dean*, Dr. Sandra M. Lemoine, 318-342-1235, Fax: 318-342-1240, E-mail: slemoine@ulm.edu.

College of Health Sciences Students: 24 full-time (23 women), 6 part-time (5 women); includes 2 African Americans, 1 American Indian/Alaska Native, 1 Asian American or Pacific Islander. Average age 26. *Faculty:* 6 full-time (all women). Expenses: Contact institution. *Financial support:* In 2008–09, 1 research assistantship with full tuition reimbursement (averaging $2,500 per year), 3 teaching assistantships with full tuition reimbursements (averaging $2,500 per year) were awarded; career-related internships or fieldwork, Federal Work-Study, and unspecified assistantships also available. Financial award application deadline: 4/1; financial award applicants required to submit FAFSA. In 2008, 16 master's awarded. Offers health sciences (MS); speech-language pathology (MS). *Application deadline:* For fall admission, 8/22 priority date for domestic students, 7/1 for international students; for winter admission, 12/12 priority date for domestic students; for spring admission, 1/17 for domestic students, 11/1 for international students. Applications are processed on a rolling basis. *Application fee:* $20 ($30 for international students). Electronic applications accepted. *Application Contact:* Dr. Paxton E Oliver, Associate Dean, 318-342-1622, Fax: 318-342-1606, E-mail: poliver@ulm.edu. *Dean*, Dr. Denny Ryman, 318-342-1622, Fax: 318-342-1606, E-mail: ryman@ulm.edu.

UNIVERSITY OF LOUISVILLE, Louisville, KY 40292-0001

General Information State-supported, coed, university. CGS member. *Enrollment:* 20,834 graduate, professional, and undergraduate students; 3,105 full-time matriculated graduate/professional students (1,624 women), 1,720 part-time matriculated graduate/professional students (1,052 women). *Enrollment by degree level:* 907 first professional, 2,845 master's, 1,073 doctoral. *Graduate faculty:* 1,552 full-time (554 women), 572 part-time/adjunct (286 women). *Graduate housing:* Rooms and/or apartments available to single and married students. *Student services:* Campus employment opportunities, campus safety program, career counseling, child daycare facilities, exercise/wellness program, free psychological counseling, grant writing training, international student services, low-cost health insurance, multicultural affairs office, services for students with disabilities. *Library facilities:* William F. Ekstrom Library plus 4 others. *Online resources:* library catalog, web page. *Collection:* 2.2 million titles, 47,062 serial subscriptions, 43,551 audiovisual materials. *Research affiliation:* Argonne National Laboratory, Oak Ridge National Laboratory.

Computer facilities: Computer purchase and lease plans are available. 425 computers available on campus for general student use. A campuswide network can be accessed from student residence rooms and from off campus. Online class registration is available. *Web address:* http://www.louisville.edu/.

General Application Contact: Libby Leggett, Information Contact, 502-852-3108, E-mail: gradadm@louisville.edu.

GRADUATE UNITS

Graduate School Students: 2,270 full-time (1,216 women), 1,758 part-time (1,064 women); includes 497 minority (351 African Americans, 9 American Indian/Alaska Native, 82 Asian Americans or Pacific Islanders, 55 Hispanic Americans), 410 international. Average age 32. Expenses: Contact institution. *Financial support:* Fellowships with full tuition reimbursements, research assistantships with full tuition reimbursements, teaching assistantships with full and partial tuition reimbursements, career-related internships or fieldwork, Federal Work-Study, institutionally sponsored loans, scholarships/grants, traineeships, tuition waivers (partial), and unspecified assistantships available. Financial award applicants required to submit FAFSA. *Degree program information:* Part-time and evening/weekend programs available. *Application deadline:* Applications are processed on a rolling basis. *Application fee:* $50. Electronic applications accepted. *Application Contact:* Libby Leggett, Director, Graduate Admissions, 502-852-3101, Fax: 502-852-6536, E-mail: gradadm@louisville.edu. *Interim Dean*, Dr. William M. Pierce, 502-852-6495, Fax: 502-852-6616, E-mail: wmpier01@louisville.edu.

College of Arts and Sciences Students: 504 full-time (277 women), 308 part-time (183 women); includes 95 minority (72 African Americans, 3 American Indian/Alaska Native, 10 Asian Americans or Pacific Islanders, 10 Hispanic Americans), 114 international. Average age 32. *Faculty:* 385 full-time (159 women), 177 part-time/adjunct (87 women). Expenses: Contact institution. *Financial support:* Fellowships with full tuition reimbursements, research assistantships with full tuition reimbursements, teaching assistantships with full tuition reimbursements, career-related internships or fieldwork, institutionally sponsored loans, scholarships/grants, tuition waivers (partial), and unspecified assistantships available. In 2008, 182 master's, 37 doctorates awarded. *Degree program information:* Part-time and evening/weekend programs available. Offers administration of planning organizations (MUP); African and Diaspora studies (MA); African-American studies (MA); analytical chemistry (MS, PhD); applied and industrial mathematics (PhD); art history (MA, PhD); arts and sciences (MA, MFA, MPA, MS, MUP, PhD, Certificate); biochemistry (MS, PhD); biology (MS, PhD); chemical physics (PhD); clinical psychology (MA, PhD); communication (MA); creative art (MA); creative writing (MA); curatorial studies (MA); English (MA); English rhetoric and composition (PhD); environmental biology (PhD); experimental psychology (PhD); French (MA); history (MA); housing and community development (MUP); human resources management (MPA); humanities (MA, PhD); inorganic chemistry (MS, PhD); justice administration (MS); land use and environmental planning (MUP); literature (MA); mathematics (MA); non-profit management (MPA); organic chemistry (MS, PhD); performance (MFA); philosophy (MA); physical chemistry (MS, PhD); physics (MS, PhD); political science (MA); psychology (MA); public administration (MPA); public policy and administration (MPA); rhetoric and composition (MA, PhD); sociology (MA); Spanish (MA); spatial analysis (MUP); urban and public affairs (PhD); urban planning (MUP); urban planning and development (PhD); urban policy and administration (PhD); women's and gender studies (MA, Certificate). *Application deadline:* Applications are processed on a rolling basis. *Application fee:* $50. *Application Contact:* Libby Leggett, Director, Graduate Admissions, 502-852-3101, Fax: 502-852-6536, E-mail: gradadm@louisville.edu. *Dean*, Dr. J. Blaine Hudson, 502-852-2234, Fax: 502-852-6888, E-mail: jbhuds01@louisville.edu.

College of Business Students: 106 full-time (30 women), 232 part-time (79 women); includes 11 African Americans, 14 Asian Americans or Pacific Islanders, 5 Hispanic Americans, 48 international. Average age 31. 340 applicants, 52% accepted, 147 enrolled. *Faculty:* 45 full-time (10 women), 9 part-time/adjunct (2 women). Expenses: Contact institution. *Financial support:* In 2008–09, 3 fellowships with full tuition reimbursements (averaging $21,000 per year), 10 research assistantships with full tuition reimbursements (averaging $12,000 per year), 10 teaching assistantships with full tuition reimbursements (averaging $21,000 per year) were awarded; scholarships/grants, health care benefits, and unspecified assistantships also available. Financial award application deadline: 3/15; financial award applicants required to submit FAFSA. In 2008, 193 master's awarded. *Degree program information:* Part-time programs available. Offers accountancy (MAC); business (MAC, MBA, PhD); business administration (MBA); entrepreneurship (PhD). *Application deadline:* For fall admission, 7/15 for domestic students; for winter admission, 4/15 for domestic students; for spring admission, 11/15 for domestic students. Applications are processed on a rolling basis. *Application fee:* $50. Electronic applications accepted. *Application Contact:* Kevin J Kane, Director, Master's Programs, 502-852-3969, Fax: 502-852-4901, E-mail: kevin.kane@louisville.edu. *Dean*, Dr. Charles Moyer, 502-852-6443, Fax: 502-852-7557, E-mail: charlie.moyer@louisville.edu.

College of Education and Human Development Students: 486 full-time (333 women), 789 part-time (587 women); includes 155 minority (124 African Americans, 3 American Indian/Alaska Native, 15 Asian Americans or Pacific Islanders, 13 Hispanic Americans), 32 international. Average age 34. 720 applicants, 68% accepted, 343 enrolled. *Faculty:* 89 full-time (54 women), 75 part-time/adjunct (59 women). Expenses: Contact institution. *Financial support:* In 2008–09, 206 students received support, including 7 fellowships with full tuition reimbursements available (averaging $18,000 per year), 28 research assistantships with full tuition reimbursements available (averaging $18,000 per year), 9 teaching assistantships with full tuition reimbursements available (averaging $18,000 per year); career-related internships or fieldwork, Federal Work-Study, and scholarships/grants also available. Financial award application deadline: 6/1. In 2008, 182 master's, 37 doctorates awarded. *Degree program information:* Part-time and evening/weekend programs available. Postbaccalaureate distance learning degree programs offered. Offers art education (MAT); counseling and personnel services (M Ed, PhD); curriculum and instruction (PhD); early elementary education (M Ed, MAT); education and human development (M Ed, MA, MAT, MS, Ed D, PhD, Ed S); educational and counseling psychology (M Ed, PhD); educational leadership and organizational development (Ed D, PhD); exercise physiology (MS); health education (M Ed); higher education (MA); human resource education (MS); instructional technology (M Ed); interdisciplinary early childhood education (M Ed, MAT); middle school education (M Ed, MAT); music education (MAT); p-12 educational administration (M Ed, Ed S); physical education (MAT); reading education (M Ed); secondary education (M Ed, MAT); special education (M Ed, MAT); sport administration (MS). *Application fee:* $50. Electronic applications accepted. *Application Contact:* Libby Leggett, Director, Graduate Admissions, 502-852-3101, Fax: 502-852-6536, E-mail: gradadm@louisville.edu. *Interim Dean*, Dr. Blake Haselton, 502-852-6411, Fax: 502-852-1464, E-mail: blake.haselton@louisville.edu.

Interdisciplinary Studies Students: 11 full-time (8 women), 7 part-time (3 women); includes 3 African Americans, 2 Asian Americans or Pacific Islanders. Average age 33. Expenses: Contact institution. Offers interdisciplinary studies (MA, MS). *Application deadline:* Applications are processed on a rolling basis. *Application fee:* $50.

J.B. Speed School of Engineering Students: 337 full-time (72 women), 153 part-time (29 women); includes 34 minority (12 African Americans, 1 American Indian/Alaska Native, 15 Asian Americans or Pacific Islanders, 6 Hispanic Americans), 177 international. Average age 28. 298 applicants, 53% accepted, 107 enrolled. *Faculty:* 78 full-time (11 women), 12 part-time/adjunct (4 women). Expenses: Contact institution. *Financial support:* In 2008–09, 97 students received support, including 23 fellowships with full tuition reimbursements available (averaging $20,000 per year), 79 research assistantships with full tuition reimbursements available (averaging $19,296 per year), 45 teaching assistantships with full tuition reimbursements available (averaging $19,556 per year); Federal Work-Study and scholarships/grants also available. Financial award application deadline: 6/30; financial award applicants required to submit FAFSA. In 2008, 200 master's, 24 doctorates awarded. *Degree program information:* Part-time programs available. Offers chemical engineering (M Eng, MS, PhD); civil and environmental engineering (M Eng, MS, PhD); computer engineering and computer science (M Eng, MS); computer science (MS); computer science and engineering (PhD); electrical and computer engineering (M Eng, MS, PhD); engineering (M Eng, MS, PhD); engineering management (M Eng); industrial engineering (M Eng, MS, PhD); mechanical engineering (M Eng, MS). *Application deadline:* For fall admission, 5/1 for domestic and international students; for spring admission, 10/1 for domestic students, 11/1 for international students. Applications are processed on a rolling basis. *Application fee:* $50. Electronic applications accepted. *Application Contact:* Dr. Mike Day, Associate Dean, 502-852-6100, Fax: 502-852-0392, E-mail: day@louisville.edu. *Dean*, Dr. Mickey R. Wilhelm, 502-852-6281, Fax: 502-852-7033, E-mail: wilhelm@louisville.edu.

Raymond A. Kent School of Social Work Students: 282 full-time (229 women), 67 part-time (54 women); includes 93 minority (84 African Americans, 2 American Indian/Alaska Native, 2 Asian Americans or Pacific Islanders, 5 Hispanic Americans), 7 international. Average age 32. 314 applicants, 78% accepted, 142 enrolled. *Faculty:* 23 full-time (15 women), 38 part-time/adjunct (21 women). Expenses: Contact institution. *Financial support:* In 2008–09, 80 students received support, including 2 fellowships with full tuition reimbursements available (averaging $19,000 per year), 8 research assistantships with full tuition reimbursements available (averaging $19,000 per year); Federal Work-Study, institutionally sponsored loans, scholarships/grants, health care benefits, tuition waivers (full), and unspecified assistantships also available. Support available to part-time students. Financial award application deadline: 6/1; financial award applicants required to submit FAFSA. In 2008, 156 master's, 5 doctorates awarded. *Degree program information:* Part-time and evening/weekend programs available. Offers marriage and family therapy (PMC); social work (MSSW, PhD). *Application deadline:* For fall admission, 7/31 for domestic and international students. Applications are processed on a rolling basis. *Application fee:* $50. Electronic applications accepted. *Application Contact:* Libby Leggett, Director, Graduate Admissions, 502-852-3101, Fax: 502-852-6536, E-mail: gradadm@louisville.edu. *Dean*, Dr. Terry Singer, 502-852-6402, Fax: 502-852-0422, E-mail: terry.singer@louisville.edu.

School of Music Students: 48 full-time (18 women), 12 part-time (6 women); includes 3 African Americans, 1 Asian American or Pacific Islander, 4 Hispanic Americans, 6 international. Average age 28. *Faculty:* 33 full-time (10 women), 38 part-time/adjunct (10 women). Expenses: Contact institution. *Financial support:* In 2008–09, 3 fellowships with full tuition reimbursements (averaging $12,000 per year), 20 teaching assistantships with full tuition reimbursements (averaging $12,000 per year) were awarded; scholarships/grants, health care benefits, tuition waivers (full and partial), and unspecified assistantships also available. In 2008, 26 master's awarded. *Degree program information:* Part-time programs available. Offers music education (MME); music history (MM, PhD); music history and literature (MM); music literature (PhD); music performance (MM); music theory and composition (MM); musicology (PhD); performance (MM); theory and composition (MM). *Application deadline:* For fall admission, 3/15 priority date for domestic students. Applications are processed on a rolling basis. *Application fee:* $50. *Application Contact:* Amanda Boyd, Admissions Counselor, 502-852-1623, Fax: 502-852-1874, E-mail: gomusic@louisville.edu. *Dean*, Dr. Christopher Doane, 502-852-6907, Fax: 502-852-1874, E-mail: doane@louisville.edu.

School of Nursing Students: 48 full-time (41 women), 57 part-time (53 women); includes 5 African Americans, 1 Asian American or Pacific Islander, 2 international. Average age 34. 63 applicants, 97% accepted, 45 enrolled. *Faculty:* 28 full-time (25 women), 4 part-time/adjunct (3 women). Expenses: Contact institution. *Financial support:* In 2008–09, 45 students received support, including 2 fellowships with full tuition reimbursements available (averaging $20,000 per year), 5 research assistantships with full tuition reimbursements available (averaging $18,000 per year), 5 teaching assistantships with full tuition reimbursements available (averaging $18,000 per year); institutionally sponsored loans, scholarships/grants, traineeships, health care benefits, and unspecified assistantships also available. Support available to part-time students. Financial award application deadline: 4/15; financial award applicants required to submit FAFSA. In 2008, 18 master's awarded. *Degree program information:* Part-time programs available. Offers adult nurse practitioner (MSN); family nurse practitioner (MSN); health professions education (MSN); neonatal nurse practitioner (MSN); nursing research (PhD); psychiatric mental health nurse practitioner (MSN). *Application deadline:* For fall admission, 4/1 priority date for domestic and international students; for spring admission, 10/1 priority date for domestic students, 10/1 for international students. Applications are processed on a rolling basis. *Application fee:* $50 ($0 for international students). *Application Contact:* Dr. Rosalie O'Dell Mainous, Associate Dean for Graduate Academic Affairs, 502-852-8387, Fax: 502-852-8783, E-mail: romain01@louisville.edu. *Dean*, Dr. Marcia J. Hern, 502-852-8300, Fax: 502-852-5044, E-mail: m.hern@gwise.louisville.edu.

School of Public Health and Information Sciences Students: 97 full-time (53 women), 65 part-time (41 women); includes 14 African Americans, 13 Asian Americans or Pacific Islanders, 3 Hispanic Americans, 24 international. Average age 33. 160 applicants, 61% accepted, 70 enrolled. *Faculty:* 30 full-time (11 women), 2 part-time/adjunct (0 women). Expenses: Contact institution. *Financial support:* In 2008–09, 24 students received support, including 18 research assistantships with full tuition reimbursements available (averaging $20,000 per year); unspecified assistantships also available. Financial award application deadline: 5/1; financial award applicants required to submit FAFSA. In 2008, 34 master's, 4 doctorates, 1 other advanced degree awarded. *Degree program information:* Part-time and evening/weekend programs available. Offers biostatistics (PhD); biostatistics-decision science (MS); clinical research, epidemiology and statistics (MS, Certificate); epidemiology (MS); public health (MPH); public health and information sciences (MPH, MS, PhD, Certificate); public health sciences (PhD). *Application deadline:* For fall admission, 2/1 for domestic and international students. Applications are processed on a rolling basis. *Application fee:* $50. Electronic applications accepted. *Application Contact:* Tammi Alvey Thomas, Assistant Director of Academic and Student Affairs, 502-852-3289, Fax: 502-852-3294, E-mail: tammi.thomas@louisville.edu. *Dean,* Dr. Richard D. Clover, 502-852-3297, Fax: 502-852-3291, E-mail: rdclov01@gwise.louisville.edu.

Louis D. Brandeis School of Law Students: 351 full-time (155 women), 68 part-time (29 women); includes 41 minority (23 African Americans, 9 Asian Americans or Pacific Islanders, 9 Hispanic Americans). Average age 24. 1,152 applicants, 42% accepted, 148 enrolled. *Faculty:* 33 full-time (12 women), 11 part-time/adjunct (4 women). Expenses: Contact institution. *Financial support:* In 2008–09, 197 students received support; fellowships, research assistantships, teaching assistantships, career-related internships or fieldwork, Federal Work-Study, scholarships/grants, and tuition waivers (partial) available. Support available to part-time students. Financial award application deadline: 6/1; financial award applicants required to submit FAFSA. In 2008, 127 JDs awarded. *Degree program information:* Part-time and evening/weekend programs available. Offers law (JD). *Application deadline:* For fall admission, 3/1 priority date for domestic students, 3/1 for international students. Applications are processed on a rolling basis. *Application fee:* $50. Electronic applications accepted. *Application Contact:* Brandon L Hamilton, Assistant Dean for Admission and Financial Aid, 502-852-6365, Fax: 502-852-8971, E-mail: lawadmissions@louisville.edu. *Dean,* James Ming Chen, 502-852-6879, Fax: 502-852-0862, E-mail: jim.chen@louisville.edu.

School of Dentistry Students: 346 full-time (154 women), 7 part-time (2 women); includes 59 minority (30 African Americans, 6 American Indian/Alaska Native, 18 Asian Americans or Pacific Islanders, 5 Hispanic Americans), 13 international. Average age 27. *Faculty:* 69 full-time (20 women), 80 part-time/adjunct (23 women). Expenses: Contact institution. *Financial support:* In 2008–09, 1 fellowship with tuition reimbursement, 10 research assistantships (averaging $3,000 per year) were awarded. In 2008, 71 first professional degrees, 10 master's awarded. Offers dentistry (DMD, MS); oral biology (MS). *Application deadline:* For fall admission, 1/1 for domestic and international students. Applications are processed on a rolling basis. *Application fee:* $50. Electronic applications accepted. *Application Contact:* Robin Benningfield, Admissions Counselor, 502-852-5081, Fax: 502-852-1210, E-mail: dmdadms@louisville.edu. *Dean,* Dr. John J Sauk, 502-852-1304, Fax: 502-852-3364, E-mail: jjsauk01@louisville.edu.

School of Medicine Students: 840 full-time (409 women), 23 part-time (15 women); includes 138 minority (60 African Americans, 2 American Indian/Alaska Native, 66 Asian Americans or Pacific Islanders, 10 Hispanic Americans), 62 international. Average age 26. *Faculty:* 689 full-time (206 women), 74 part-time/adjunct (24 women). Expenses: Contact institution. *Financial support:* In 2008–09, 30 fellowships with full tuition reimbursements (averaging $22,000 per year) were awarded; career-related internships or fieldwork, institutionally sponsored loans, scholarships/grants, traineeships, tuition waivers (full and partial), and unspecified assistantships also available. In 2008, 146 first professional degrees, 61 master's, 40 doctorates awarded. Offers anatomical sciences and neurobiology (MS, PhD); audiology (Au D); biochemistry and molecular biology (MS, PhD); communicative disorders (MS); medicine (MD, MS, Au D, PhD); microbiology and immunology (MS, PhD); pharmacology and toxicology (MS, PhD); physiology and biophysics (MS, PhD). *Application deadline:* For fall admission, 1/15 for domestic students. Applications are processed on a rolling basis. *Application fee:* $50. *Application Contact:* Director of Admissions, 502-852-5793, Fax: 502-852-6849. *Dean,* Dr. Edward C. Halperin, 502-852-1499, Fax: 502-852-1484, E-mail: edward.halperin@louisville.edu.

See Close-Up on page 1021.

UNIVERSITY OF MAINE, Orono, ME 04469

General Information State-supported, coed, university. CGS member. *Graduate housing:* Rooms and/or apartments available on a first-come, first-served basis to single and married students. Housing application deadline: 8/1. *Research affiliation:* Jackson Laboratory (medical genetics), Bigelow Laboratories for Ocean Sciences (marine science), Mount Desert Island Biological Laboratory (marine molecular biology), Sensor Research Development Corporation (electrical sensors), Maine Medical Center Research Institute (clinical medicine).

GRADUATE UNITS

Graduate School *Degree program information:* Part-time and evening/weekend programs available. Offers biomedical sciences (PhD); information systems (MS); interdisciplinary studies (PhD); liberal studies (MA); teaching (MST). Electronic applications accepted.

Climate Change Institute *Degree program information:* Part-time programs available. Offers climate change (MS). Electronic applications accepted.

College of Business, Public Policy and Health *Degree program information:* Part-time and evening/weekend programs available. Offers accounting (MS); business administration (MBA); business and sustainability (MBA); business, public policy and health (MA, MBA, MPA, MS, MSW, PhD, CAS); economics (MA); financial economics (MA); nursing (MS, CAS); public administration (MPA, PhD); social work (MSW). Electronic applications accepted.

College of Education and Human Development *Degree program information:* Part-time and evening/weekend programs available. Offers counselor education (M Ed, MA, MS, Ed D, CAS); curriculum, assessment, and instruction (M Ed); educational leadership (M Ed, Ed D, CAS); elementary and secondary education (M Ed); elementary education (M Ed, MAT, MS, CAS); higher education (M Ed, MA, MS, Ed D, CAS); human development (MS); human development and family relations (MS); instructional technology (M Ed); kinesiology and physical education (M Ed, MS); literacy education (M Ed, MA, MS, Ed D, CAS); science education (M Ed, MS, CAS); secondary education (M Ed, MA, MAT, MS, CAS); social studies education (M Ed, MA, MS, CAS); special education (M Ed, CAS). Electronic applications accepted.

College of Engineering *Degree program information:* Part-time programs available. Offers biological engineering (MS); chemical engineering (MS, PhD); civil engineering (MS, PhD); computer engineering (MS); electrical engineering (MS, PhD); engineering (MS, PhD); mechanical engineering (MS, PhD); spatial information science and engineering (MS, PhD). Electronic applications accepted.

College of Liberal Arts and Sciences *Degree program information:* Part-time and evening/weekend programs available. Offers chemistry (MS, PhD); clinical psychology (PhD); communication (MA); communication sciences and disorders (MA); computer science (MS, PhD); developmental psychology (MA); engineering physics (M Eng); English (MA); experimental psychology (MA, PhD); French (MA, MAT); history (MA, PhD); liberal arts and sciences (M Eng, MA, MAT, MM, MS, PhD); mathematics (MA); music (MM); physics (MS, PhD); social psychology (MA). Electronic applications accepted.

College of Natural Sciences, Forestry, and Agriculture *Degree program information:* Part-time and evening/weekend programs available. Offers animal sciences (MPS, MS); biochemistry (MPS, MS); biochemistry and molecular biology (PhD); biological sciences (PhD); botany and plant pathology (MS); earth sciences (MS, PhD); ecology and environmental science (MS, PhD); ecology and environmental sciences (MS, PhD); entomology (MS); food and nutritional sciences (PhD); food science and human nutrition (MS); forest resources (PhD); forestry (MF, MS); horticulture (MS); marine biology (MS, PhD); marine policy (MS); microbiology (MPS, MS, PhD); natural sciences, forestry, and agriculture (MF, MPS, MS, MWC, PhD); oceanography (MS, PhD); plant science (PhD); plant, soil, and environmental sciences (MS); resource economics and policy (MS); resource utilization (MS); wildlife conservation (MWC); wildlife ecology (MS, PhD); zoology (MS, PhD). Electronic applications accepted.

UNIVERSITY OF MAINE AT FARMINGTON, Farmington, ME 04938-1990

General Information State-supported, coed, comprehensive institution.

GRADUATE UNITS

Program in Education Offers administration (MS Ed); educational technology (MS Ed); studies in literature and literacy (MS Ed).

UNIVERSITY OF MANAGEMENT AND TECHNOLOGY, Arlington, VA 22209

General Information Proprietary, coed, comprehensive institution. *Graduate housing:* On-campus housing not available.

GRADUATE UNITS

Program in Business Administration *Degree program information:* Part-time and evening/weekend programs available. Postbaccalaureate distance learning degree programs offered (no on-campus study). Offers acquisition management (DBA); general management (MBA, DBA); project management (MBA, DBA). Electronic applications accepted.

Program in Computer Science and Information Technology *Degree program information:* Part-time and evening/weekend programs available. Postbaccalaureate distance learning degree programs offered (no on-campus study). Offers computer science (MS); information technology (AC); information technology project management (MS); management information systems (MS); project management (AC); software engineering (MS). Electronic applications accepted.

Program in Criminal Justice Offers criminal justice (MS).

Program in Management *Degree program information:* Part-time and evening/weekend programs available. Postbaccalaureate distance learning degree programs offered (no on-campus study). Offers acquisition management (MS, AC); general management (MS); project management (MS, AC); public administration (MPA, MS, AC). Electronic applications accepted.

UNIVERSITY OF MANITOBA, Winnipeg, MB R3T 2N2, Canada

General Information Province-supported, coed, university. *Graduate housing:* Rooms and/or apartments available to single and married students. *Research affiliation:* Canada Department of Agriculture Research Station, Freshwater Institute, Atomic Energy of Canada, Manitoba Department of Mines, Resources, and Environmental Management, Northern Scientific Training Program (Northern studies), Taiga Biological Research Trust.

GRADUATE UNITS

Faculty of Dentistry Offers dental diagnostic and surgical sciences (M Dent); dentistry (DMD, M Dent, M Sc, PhD); oral and maxillofacial surgery (M Dent); oral biology (M Sc, PhD); orthodontics (M Sc); periodontology (M Dent); preventive dental science (M Sc); restorative dentistry (M Dent).

Faculty of Graduate Studies *Degree program information:* Part-time programs available.

Asper School of Business Offers business (M Sc, MBA, PhD).

Clayton H. Riddell Faculty of Environment, Earth, and Resources Offers environment (M Env); environment and geography (M Sc); environment, earth, and resources (M Env, M Sc, MA, MNRM, PhD); geography (MA, PhD); geology (M Sc, PhD); geophysics (M Sc, PhD); natural resources and environmental management (PhD); natural resources management (MNRM).

College Universitaire de Saint Boniface Offers Canadian studies (MA); education (M Ed).

Faculty of Agricultural and Food Sciences Offers agribusiness (M Sc, PhD); agricultural and food sciences (M Sc, PhD); agronomy and plant protection (M Sc, PhD); animal science (M Sc, PhD); entomology (M Sc, PhD); food and nutritional sciences (PhD); food science (M Sc); foods and nutrition (M Sc); horticulture (M Sc, PhD); plant breeding and genetics (M Sc, PhD); plant physiology-biochemistry (M Sc, PhD); soil science (M Sc, PhD).

Faculty of Architecture Offers architecture (M Arch, M Land Arch, MCP, MID); city planning (MCP); interior design (MID); landscape architecture (M Land Arch).

Faculty of Arts Offers anthropology (MA, PhD); archival studies (MA); arts (MA, MPA, PhD); classics (MA); clinical psychology (PhD); economics (MA, PhD); English (MA, PhD); French (MA, PhD); German language and literature (MA); history (MA, PhD); Icelandic language and literature (MA); linguistics (MA, PhD); native studies (MA); philosophy (MA); political studies (MA); psychology (MA, PhD); public administration (MPA); religion (MA, PhD); school psychology (MA); Slavic languages and literatures (MA); sociology (MA, PhD).

Faculty of Education Offers adult and post-secondary education (M Ed); education (M Ed, PhD); educational administration (M Ed); guidance and counseling (M Ed); inclusive special education (M Ed); language and literacy (M Ed); second language education (M Ed); social foundations of education (M Ed); studies in curriculum, teaching and learning (M Ed).

Faculty of Engineering Offers biosystems engineering (M Eng, M Sc, PhD); civil engineering (M Eng, M Sc, PhD); electrical and computer engineering (M Eng, M Sc, PhD); engineering (M Eng, M Sc, PhD); mechanical and manufacturing engineering (M Eng, M Sc, PhD).

Faculty of Human Ecology Offers family social sciences (M Sc); human ecology (M Sc); human nutritional sciences (M Sc); textile sciences (M Sc).

Faculty of Kinesiology and Recreation Management Offers kinesiology and recreation management (M Sc); recreation studies (MA).

Faculty of Law Offers law (LL M). Electronic applications accepted.

Faculty of Nursing Offers cancer nursing (MN); nursing (MN).

Faculty of Pharmacy Offers pharmacy (M Sc, PhD).

Faculty of Science Offers botany (M Sc, PhD); chemistry (M Sc, PhD); computer science (M Sc, PhD); ecology (M Sc, PhD); mathematical, computational and statistical sciences (MMCSS); mathematics (M Sc, PhD); microbiology (M Sc, PhD); physics and astronomy (M Sc, PhD); science (M Sc, MMCSS, PhD); statistics (M Sc, PhD); zoology (M Sc, PhD).

Faculty of Social Work Offers social work (MSW, PhD).

Interdisciplinary Programs Offers disability studies (M Sc, MA); individual interdisciplinary studies (M Sc, MA, PhD); interdisciplinary studies (M Sc, MA, PhD).

Marcel A. Desautels Faculty of Music Offers music (M Mus).

School of Medical Rehabilitation Offers applied health sciences (PhD); occupational therapy (MOT); physical therapy (MPT); rehabilitation (M Sc).

Faculty of Medicine *Degree program information:* Part-time programs available. Offers medicine (M Sc, PhD). Electronic applications accepted.

Graduate Programs in Medicine *Degree program information:* Part-time programs available. Offers biochemistry and medical genetics (M Sc, PhD); community health sciences (M Sc, MPH, PhD, G Dip); human anatomy and cell science (M Sc, PhD); immunology (M Sc, PhD); medical microbiology (M Sc, PhD); medicine (M Sc, MPH, PhD, G Dip); pathology (M Sc); pediatrics and child health (M Sc); pharmacology and therapeutics (M Sc, PhD); physiology (M Sc, PhD); psychiatry (M Sc); rehabilitation (M Sc); surgery (M Sc).

UNIVERSITY OF MARY, Bismarck, ND 58504-9652

General Information Independent-religious, coed, comprehensive institution. *Enrollment:* 2,863 graduate, professional, and undergraduate students; 464 full-time matriculated graduate/professional students (316 women), 400 part-time matriculated graduate/professional students (240 women). *Enrollment by degree level:* 762 master's, 59 doctoral. *Graduate faculty:* 41 full-time (21 women), 34 part-time/adjunct (13 women). *Tuition:* Full-time $6700; part-time $430 per credit hour. *Required fees:* $430 per credit hour. One-time fee: $40 full-time. Tuition and fees vary according to course load and program. *Graduate housing:* Room and/or

University of Mary (continued)

apartments available on a first-come, first-served basis to single students; on-campus housing not available to married students. Typical cost: $3000 per year ($5700 including board). Room and board charges vary according to board plan, campus/location and housing facility selected. Housing application deadline: 7/15. *Student services:* Campus employment opportunities, campus safety program, career counseling, exercise/wellness program, free psychological counseling, services for students with disabilities. *Library facilities:* University of Mary Library. *Online resources:* library catalog, access to other libraries' catalogs. *Collection:* 63,259 titles, 222 serial subscriptions, 6,708 audiovisual materials.

Computer facilities: 235 computers available on campus for general student use. A campuswide network can be accessed from student residence rooms and from off campus. Online class registration is available. *Web address:* http://www.umary.edu/.

General Application Contact: Dr. Kathy Perrin, Director of Graduate Studies, 701-355-8119, Fax: 701-255-7687, E-mail: kperrin@umary.edu.

GRADUATE UNITS

Department of Occupational Therapy Students: 40 full-time (37 women), 20 part-time (17 women); includes 1 minority (Asian American or Pacific Islander), 1 international. *Faculty:* 6 full-time (5 women). Expenses: Contact institution. *Financial support:* In 2008–09, 2 teaching assistantships with full tuition reimbursements (averaging $2,500 per year) were awarded; career-related internships or fieldwork, Federal Work-Study, institutionally sponsored loans, scholarships/grants, and unspecified assistantships also available. Support available to part-time students. Financial award applicants required to submit FAFSA. In 2008, 22 master's awarded. *Degree program information:* Part-time programs available. Postbaccalaureate distance learning degree programs offered (minimal on-campus study). Offers entry level (MSOT); post professional (MSOT). *Application deadline:* For spring admission, 3/15 priority date for domestic and international students. Applications are processed on a rolling basis. *Application fee:* $40. Electronic applications accepted. *Application Contact:* Dr. Wanda Berg, OT Admissions Director, 701-355-8022, E-mail: wberg@umary.edu. *Program Director,* Dr. Janeene Sibla, 701-255-7500, Fax: 701-255-7687.

Department of Physical Therapy Students: 64 full-time (41 women), 1 part-time (0 women). Average age 25. 40 applicants, 75% accepted, 28 enrolled. *Faculty:* 6 full-time (3 women), 3 part-time/adjunct (1 woman). Expenses: Contact institution. *Financial support:* In 2008–09, teaching assistantships with partial tuition reimbursements (averaging $2,500 per year); career-related internships or fieldwork also available. Financial award applicants required to submit FAFSA. Offers physical therapy (DPT). *Application deadline:* For fall admission, 1/1 priority date for domestic students; for spring admission, 3/1 priority date for domestic students. Applications are processed on a rolling basis. *Application fee:* $40. Electronic applications accepted. *Application Contact:* Dr. Joellen Marie Roller, Program Director, 701-355-8053, Fax: 701-255-7687, E-mail: rollerj@umary.edu. *Program Director,* Dr. Joellen Marie Roller, 701-355-8053, Fax: 701-255-7687, E-mail: rollerj@umary.edu.

Division of Nursing Students: 80 full-time (74 women), 46 part-time (43 women); includes 6 minority (4 African Americans, 1 American Indian/Alaska Native, 1 Asian American or Pacific Islander), 2 international. Average age 39. *Faculty:* 2 full-time (both women), 8 part-time/adjunct (5 women). Expenses: Contact institution. *Financial support:* In 2008–09, 14 fellowships with partial tuition reimbursements, 3 teaching assistantships with partial tuition reimbursements were awarded; institutionally sponsored loans also available. Support available to part-time students. Financial award application deadline: 7/1. In 2008, 65 master's awarded. *Degree program information:* Part-time and evening/weekend programs available. Postbaccalaureate distance learning degree programs offered (minimal on-campus study). Offers family nurse practitioner (MSN); nurse administrator (MSN); nursing educator (MSN). *Application deadline:* For fall admission, 4/15 priority date for domestic students. Applications are processed on a rolling basis. *Application fee:* $40. Electronic applications accepted. *Application Contact:* Joanne Lassiter, Advisor, 701-355-8379, Fax: 701-255-7687, E-mail: jllassiter@umary.edu. *Director,* Glenda Reemts, 701-255-7500 Ext. 8041, Fax: 701-255-7687, E-mail: greemts@umary.edu.

Divison of Social and Behavioral Sciences Students: 26 full-time (25 women), 5 part-time (3 women); includes 1 minority (American Indian/Alaska Native). *Faculty:* 4 full-time (2 women), 12 part-time/adjunct (8 women). Expenses: Contact institution. *Financial support:* Applicants required to submit FAFSA. In 2008, 16 master's awarded. *Degree program information:* Part-time programs available. Postbaccalaureate distance learning degree programs offered (minimal on-campus study). Offers addiction counseling (MSC); community counseling (MSC); school counseling (MSC). *Application deadline:* For fall admission, 8/1 priority date for domestic students. *Application fee:* $40. *Application Contact:* Jeanette Shaeffer, Accelerated and Distance Education Administrative Assistant, 701-355-8128, Fax: 701-255-7687, E-mail: jgschae@umary.edu. *Program Director for Counseling Graduate Studies,* James Renner, 701-355-8177, Fax: 701-255-7687, E-mail: jrenner@umary.edu.

Gary Tharaldson School of Business Students: 244 full-time (131 women), 240 part-time (113 women); includes 63 minority (12 African Americans, 35 American Indian/Alaska Native, 8 Asian Americans or Pacific Islanders, 8 Hispanic Americans), 23 international. Average age 37. *Faculty:* 200 part-time/adjunct (64 women). Expenses: Contact institution. *Financial support:* Career-related internships or fieldwork available. Support available to part-time students. Financial award applicants required to submit FAFSA. In 2008, 261 master's awarded. *Degree program information:* Part-time and evening/weekend programs available. Offers health care (MBA); human resource management (MBA); management (MBA); project management (MPM); strategic leadership (MSSL). *Application deadline:* Applications are processed on a rolling basis. *Application fee:* $40. *Application Contact:* Wayne G. Maruska, Graduate Program Advisor, 701-355-8134, Fax: 701-255-7687, E-mail: wmaruska@umary.edu. *Director of the School of Accelerated and Distance Education,* Dr. Shanda Traiser, 701-355-8160, Fax: 701-255-7687, E-mail: straiser@umary.edu.

Gary Tharaldson School of Business Offers business (MBA, MPM, MSSL).

Program in Education Students: 3 full-time (2 women), 55 part-time (37 women); includes 6 minority (all American Indian/Alaska Native). Average age 33. *Faculty:* 5 full-time (4 women), 12 part-time/adjunct (7 women). Expenses: Contact institution. *Financial support:* In 2008–09, 1 teaching assistantship with full tuition reimbursement was awarded; career-related internships or fieldwork also available. Support available to part-time students. Financial award application deadline: 8/1; financial award applicants required to submit FAFSA. In 2008, 10 master's awarded. *Degree program information:* Part-time programs available. Offers college teaching (M Ed); curriculum, instruction and assessment (M Ed); early childhood education (M Ed); early childhood special education (M Ed); elementary education administration (M Ed); emotional disorders (M Ed); learning disabilities (M Ed); reading (M Ed); secondary education administration (M Ed); special education (M Ed); special education strategist (M Ed). *Application deadline:* Applications are processed on a rolling basis. *Application fee:* $40. *Application Contact:* Leona Friedig, Administrative Secretary, 701-355-8058, E-mail: lfriedig@umary.edu. *Director,* Dr. Rebecca Yunker Salveson, 701-355-8186, E-mail: rysalves@umary.edu.

UNIVERSITY OF MARY HARDIN-BAYLOR, Belton, TX 76513

General Information Independent-religious, coed, comprehensive institution. *Enrollment:* 2,696 graduate, professional, and undergraduate students; 95 full-time matriculated graduate/professional students (62 women), 104 part-time matriculated graduate/professional students (73 women). *Enrollment by degree level:* 164 master's, 35 doctoral. *Graduate faculty:* 30 full-time (18 women), 10 part-time/adjunct (2 women). *Tuition:* Full-time $11,340; part-time $630 per credit hour. *Required fees:* $1350; $75 per credit hour. $50 per semester. Tuition and fees vary according to degree level. *Graduate housing:* On-campus housing not available. *Student services:* Campus employment opportunities, career counseling, exercise/wellness program, free psychological counseling, international student services, multicultural affairs office, services for students with disabilities, teacher training. *Library facilities:* Townsend Memorial Library. *Online resources:* library catalog.

Computer facilities: Computer purchase and lease plans are available. 275 computers available on campus for general student use. A campuswide network can be accessed from student residence rooms and from off campus. Online class registration is available. *Web address:* http://www.umhb.edu/.

General Application Contact: Sherry Rosenblad, Director of Graduate Admissions, 254-295-4020, Fax: 254-295-5301, E-mail: srosenblad@umhb.edu.

GRADUATE UNITS

Graduate Studies in Business Administration Students: 17 full-time (9 women), 5 part-time (all women); includes 2 minority (1 Asian American or Pacific Islander, 1 Hispanic American), 5 international. Average age 29. *Faculty:* 3 full-time (2 women), 5 part-time/adjunct (1 woman). Expenses: Contact institution. *Financial support:* Federal Work-Study and scholarships (for some active duty military personnel only) available. Financial award applicants required to submit FAFSA. In 2008, 7 master's awarded. *Degree program information:* Part-time and evening/weekend programs available. Offers accounting (MBA); management (MBA). *Application deadline:* For fall admission, 6/1 priority date for domestic students; for spring admission, 11/1 for domestic students. Applications are processed on a rolling basis. *Application fee:* $35 ($135 for international students). Electronic applications accepted. *Application Contact:* Dr. Chrisann Merriman, Graduate Program Director, MBA Program, 254-295-4647, E-mail: chrisann.merriman@umhb.edu. *Graduate Program Director, MBA Program,* Dr. Chrisann Merriman, 254-295-4647, E-mail: chrisann.merriman@umhb.edu.

Graduate Studies in Counseling and Psychology Students: 46 full-time (29 women), 26 part-time (24 women); includes 14 minority (6 African Americans, 3 Asian Americans or Pacific Islanders, 5 Hispanic Americans), 2 international. Average age 32. *Faculty:* 7 full-time (5 women), 3 part-time/adjunct (1 woman). Expenses: Contact institution. *Financial support:* Research assistantships with full tuition reimbursements, Federal Work-Study and scholarships (for some active duty military personnel only) available. Support available to part-time students. Financial award applicants required to submit FAFSA. In 2008, 44 master's awarded. *Degree program information:* Part-time and evening/weekend programs available. Offers community counseling (MA); marriage and family Christian counseling (MA); psychology and counseling (MA); school counseling and psychology (MA). *Application deadline:* For fall admission, 6/1 priority date for domestic students; for spring admission, 11/1 for domestic students. Applications are processed on a rolling basis. *Application fee:* $35 ($135 for international students). Electronic applications accepted. *Application Contact:* Dr. Raylene B. Statz, Graduate Program Director, 254-295-4548, E-mail: rstatz@umhb.edu. *Graduate Program Director,* Dr. Raylene B. Statz, 254-295-4548, E-mail: rstatz@umhb.edu.

Graduate Studies in Education Students: 33 full-time (23 women), 59 part-time (36 women); includes 20 minority (12 African Americans, 8 Hispanic Americans), 1 international. Average age 37. *Faculty:* 14 full-time (7 women), 2 part-time/adjunct (0 women). Expenses: Contact institution. *Financial support:* Federal Work-Study, scholarships/grants, and scholarships (for some active duty military personnel only) available. Support available to part-time students. Financial award application deadline: 6/1; financial award applicants required to submit FAFSA. In 2008, 25 master's awarded. *Degree program information:* Part-time and evening/weekend programs available. Offers educational administration (M Ed, Ed D); educational psychology (M Ed); exercise and sport science (M Ed); general studies (M Ed); reading education (M Ed). *Application deadline:* For fall admission, 6/1 priority date for domestic students; for spring admission, 11/1 for domestic students. Applications are processed on a rolling basis. *Application fee:* $35 ($135 for international students). Electronic applications accepted. *Application Contact:* Dr. Austin Vasek, Graduate Program Director, 254-295-4185, Fax: 254-295-4480, E-mail: austin.vasek@umhb.edu. *Graduate Program Director,* Dr. Austin Vasek, 254-295-4185, Fax: 254-295-4480, E-mail: austin.vasek@umhb.edu.

Graduate Studies in Information Systems Students: 3 full-time (1 woman), 2 part-time (0 women); includes 1 minority (African American), 2 international. Average age 32. *Faculty:* 2 full-time (0 women). Expenses: Contact institution. *Financial support:* Federal Work-Study and scholarships (for some active duty military personnel only) available. Support available to part-time students. Financial award applicants required to submit FAFSA. In 2008, 2 master's awarded. *Degree program information:* Part-time and evening/weekend programs available. Offers information systems (MS). *Application deadline:* For fall admission, 6/1 priority date for domestic students; for spring admission, 11/1 for domestic students. Applications are processed on a rolling basis. *Application fee:* $35 ($135 for international students). Electronic applications accepted. *Application Contact:* Dr. Patrick Jaska, Graduate Program Director, 254-295-4654, E-mail: pjaska@umhb.edu. *Graduate Program Director,* Dr. Patrick Jaska, 254-295-4654, E-mail: pjaska@umhb.edu.

Graduate Studies in Nursing Students: 8 part-time (all women); includes 1 minority (African American). Average age 40. *Faculty:* 4 full-time (all women). Expenses: Contact institution. *Financial support:* Applicants required to submit FAFSA. *Degree program information:* Part-time and evening/weekend programs available. Offers nursing (MSN). *Application deadline:* For fall admission, 6/1 priority date for domestic students; for spring admission, 11/1 priority date for domestic students. Applications are processed on a rolling basis. *Application fee:* $35 ($135 for international students). Electronic applications accepted. *Application Contact:* Dr. Margaret Prydun, Program Director, 254-295-4674, E-mail: margaret.prydun@umhb.edu. *Program Director,* Dr. Margaret Prydun, 254-295-4674, E-mail: margaret.prydun@umhb.edu.

UNIVERSITY OF MARYLAND, BALTIMORE, Baltimore, MD 21201

General Information State-supported, coed, graduate-only institution. CGS member. *Enrollment by degree level:* 2,588 first professional, 1,813 master's, 710 doctoral, 75 other advanced degrees. *Graduate faculty:* 1,610 full-time (675 women), 748 part-time/adjunct (426 women). Tuition, state resident: full-time $7038; part-time $391 per credit hour. Tuition, nonresident: full-time $12,330; part-time $685 per credit hour. *Required fees:* $727; $10 per credit hour. $273.50 per semester. Tuition and fees vary according to course load, degree level and program. *Graduate housing:* Rooms and/or apartments available on a first-come, first-served basis to single and married students. *Student services:* Campus employment opportunities, campus safety program, career counseling, exercise/wellness program, free psychological counseling, grant writing training, international student services, low-cost health insurance, multicultural affairs office, services for students with disabilities, writing training. *Library facilities:* Health Sciences and Human Services Library plus 1 other. *Collection:* 322,581 titles, 2,609 serial subscriptions. *Research affiliation:* University of Maryland Medical System (Medical), University of Maryland BioPark (Biology), University of Maryland Biotechnology Institute (Biology).

Computer facilities: A campuswide network can be accessed from student residence rooms and from off campus. Online class registration is available. *Web address:* http://www.umaryland.edu/.

General Application Contact: Keith T. Brooks, Director, Graduate Enrollment Affairs, 410-706-7131, Fax: 410-706-3473, E-mail: kbrooks@umaryland.edu.

GRADUATE UNITS

Graduate School *Degree program information:* Part-time and evening/weekend programs available. Offers biochemistry (MS, PhD); biochemistry and molecular biology (MS, PhD); biomedical sciences—dental (MS, PhD); cancer biology (PhD); cell and molecular physiology (PhD); dental hygiene (MS); epidemiology (MS, PhD); gerontology (PhD); human genetics and genomic medicine (PhD); marine-estuarine-environmental sciences (MS, PhD); medical and research technology (MS); molecular medicine (MS, PhD); molecular microbiology and immunology (PhD); molecular toxicology and pharmacology (PhD); neuroscience (PhD); oral biology (MS); oral pathology (MS, PhD); pharmaceutical health service research (MS, PhD); pharmaceutical sciences (PhD); pharmacy administration (PhD); physical rehabilitation science (PhD); toxicology (MS, PhD). Electronic applications accepted.

School of Nursing *Degree program information:* Part-time programs available. Offers community health nursing (MS); direct nursing (PhD); gerontological nursing (MS); indirect nursing (PhD); maternal-child nursing (MS); medical-surgical nursing (MS); nurse-midwifery education (MS); nursing (MS, PhD); nursing administration (MS); nursing education (MS); nursing health policy (MS); primary care nursing (MS); psychiatric nursing (MS). Electronic applications accepted.

School of Social Work Students: 653 full-time (581 women), 193 part-time (172 women); includes 335 minority (256 African Americans, 2 American Indian/Alaska Native, 27 Asian

Americans or Pacific Islanders, 50 Hispanic Americans), 25 international. Average age 29. 778 applicants, 71% accepted, 384 enrolled. *Faculty:* 53 full-time (30 women), 20 part-time/adjunct (13 women). Expenses: Contact institution. *Financial support:* Fellowships with full tuition reimbursements, research assistantships with full tuition reimbursements, teaching assistantships with partial tuition reimbursements, career-related internships or fieldwork and Federal Work-Study available. Support available to part-time students. Financial award applicants required to submit FAFSA. In 2008, 411 master's, 9 doctorates awarded. Offers social work (MSW, PhD). *Application deadline:* For fall admission, 2/28 priority date for domestic and international students; for spring admission, 11/15 priority date for domestic and international students. Applications are processed on a rolling basis. *Application fee:* $55. Electronic applications accepted. *Application Contact:* Marianne Wood, Assistant Dean for Admissions, 410-706-7922, Fax: 410-706-6046, E-mail: mwood@ssw.umaryland.edu. *Dean and Professor*, Dr. Richard P. Barth, 410-706-7794, Fax: 410-706-0273, E-mail: rbarth@ssw.umaryland.edu.

Professional and Advanced Education Programs in Dentistry Offers advanced general dentistry (Certificate); dentistry (DDS); endodontics (Certificate); oral and experimental pathology (Certificate); oral biology (MS); oral-maxillofacial surgery (Certificate); orthodontics (Certificate); pediatric dentistry (Certificate); periodontics (Certificate); prosthodontics (Certificate).

Professional Program in Pharmacy Offers pharmacy (Pharm D). Electronic applications accepted.

School of Law Students: 714 full-time (379 women), 183 part-time (97 women); includes 281 minority (114 African Americans, 6 American Indian/Alaska Native, 97 Asian Americans or Pacific Islanders, 64 Hispanic Americans), 15 international. Average age 26. 3,735 applicants, 15% accepted, 306 enrolled. *Faculty:* 62 full-time (33 women), 43 part-time/adjunct (13 women). Expenses: Contact institution. *Financial support:* In 2008–09, 733 students received support. Federal Work-Study, institutionally sponsored loans, and scholarships/grants available. Support available to part-time students. Financial award application deadline: 3/1; financial award applicants required to submit FAFSA. In 2008, 268 JDs awarded. *Degree program information:* Part-time and evening/weekend programs available. Offers law (JD). *Application deadline:* For fall admission, 4/1 priority date for domestic and international students. Applications are processed on a rolling basis. *Application fee:* $65. Electronic applications accepted. *Application Contact:* Connie Beals, Executive Director of Admissions and Student Recruiting, 410-706-3492, Fax: 410-706-1793, E-mail: admissions@law.umaryland.edu. *Dean/Professor of Law*, Phoebe A. Haddon, 410-706-7214, Fax: 410-706-4045, E-mail: phaddon@law.umaryland.edu.

School of Medicine Students: 1,024 full-time (631 women), 157 part-time (114 women); includes 343 minority (122 African Americans, 1 American Indian/Alaska Native, 184 Asian Americans or Pacific Islanders, 36 Hispanic Americans), 59 international. Average age 27. 5,543 applicants, 13% accepted, 375 enrolled. *Faculty:* 1,182 full-time (424 women), 190 part-time/adjunct (102 women). Expenses: Contact institution. *Financial support:* In 2008–09, 210 research assistantships with partial tuition reimbursements (averaging $25,000 per year) were awarded; fellowships also available. Financial award application deadline: 3/1. In 2008, 146 first professional degrees, 50 master's, 105 doctorates awarded. *Degree program information:* Part-time and evening/weekend programs available. Offers biostatistics (MS); clinical research (MS); epidemiology (PhD); epidemiology and preventive medicine (MPH, MS); gerontology (PhD); human genetics (MS, PhD); medicine (MD, MPH, MS, DPT, DScPT, PhD); molecular epidemiology (PhD); pathology (MS); physical rehabilitation science (PhD); physical therapy and rehabilitation science (DPT); toxicology (MS, PhD). *Application fee:* $50. *Application Contact:* Dr. E. Albert Reece, Dean and Vice President for Medical Affairs, 410-706-7410, Fax: 410-706-0235, E-mail: deanmed@som.umaryland.edu. *Dean and Vice President for Medical Affairs*, Dr. E. Albert Reece, 410-706-7410, Fax: 410-706-0235, E-mail: deanmed@som.umaryland.edu.

UNIVERSITY OF MARYLAND, BALTIMORE COUNTY, Baltimore, MD 21250

General Information State-supported, coed, university. CGS member. *Enrollment:* 12,268 graduate, professional, and undergraduate students; 1,092 full-time matriculated graduate/professional students (597 women), 1,338 part-time matriculated graduate/professional students (731 women). *Enrollment by degree level:* 1,473 master's, 746 doctoral, 211 other advanced degrees. *Graduate faculty:* 432 full-time, 168 part-time/adjunct. *Graduate housing:* Room and/or apartments available on a first-come, first-served basis to single students; on-campus housing not available to married students. Housing application deadline: 6/1. *Student services:* Campus employment opportunities, campus safety program, career counseling, child daycare facilities, exercise/wellness program, free psychological counseling, grant writing training, international student services, low-cost health insurance, multicultural affairs office, services for students with disabilities, teacher training, writing training. *Library facilities:* Albin O. Kuhn Library and Gallery plus 1 other. *Online resources:* library catalog, web page, access to other libraries' catalogs. *Collection:* 1 million titles, 4,204 serial subscriptions, 7,500 audiovisual materials. *Research affiliation:* Sciences Applications International Corp. (information systems and technology), Halliburton Energy Services (provider of products and services to oil and gas industries), IBM (computers and information technology), BouMatic (dairy industry), Pfizer Incorporated (pharmaceuticals), Fujitsu Laboratories of America (information technology and communications).

Computer facilities: 875 computers available on campus for general student use. A campuswide network can be accessed from student residence rooms and from off campus. Online class registration, student account information are available. *Web address:* http://www.umbc.edu/.

General Application Contact: Kathryn Nee, Coordinator of Domestic Admissions, 410-455-2944, E-mail: nee@umbc.edu.

GRADUATE UNITS

Graduate School Students: 1,092 full-time (597 women), 1,338 part-time (731 women); includes 497 minority (270 African Americans, 7 American Indian/Alaska Native, 157 Asian Americans or Pacific Islanders, 63 Hispanic Americans), 418 international. Average age 33. 2,128 applicants, 58% accepted, 737 enrolled. *Faculty:* 215 full-time, 79 part-time/adjunct. Expenses: Contact institution. *Financial support:* In 2008–09, 561 students received support, including 79 fellowships with tuition reimbursements available (averaging $16,186 per year), 254 research assistantships with tuition reimbursements available (averaging $16,186 per year), 228 teaching assistantships with tuition reimbursements available (averaging $16,186 per year); career-related internships or fieldwork, Federal Work-Study, scholarships/grants, traineeships, health care benefits, and unspecified assistantships also available. Support available to part-time students. Financial award applicants required to submit FAFSA. In 2008, 449 master's, 93 doctorates, 63 other advanced degrees awarded. *Degree program information:* Part-time and evening/weekend programs available. Postbaccalaureate distance learning degree programs offered (no on-campus study). Offers aging policy for the elderly (PhD); epidemiology of aging (PhD); marine-estuarine-environmental sciences (MS, PhD); social, cultural, and behavioral sciences (PhD). *Application deadline:* For fall admission, 1/1 for international students; for spring admission, 5/1 for international students. Applications are processed on a rolling basis. *Application fee:* $50. Electronic applications accepted. *Application Contact:* Kathryn Nee, Coordinator of Domestic Admissions, 410-455-2944, E-mail: nee@umbc.edu. *Interim Vice Provost for Graduate Education*, Dr. Janet c. Rutledge, 410-455-2199.

College of Arts, Humanities and Social Sciences Students: 462 full-time (338 women), 740 part-time (555 women); includes 230 minority (135 African Americans, 7 American Indian/Alaska Native, 51 Asian Americans or Pacific Islanders, 37 Hispanic Americans), 83 international. Average age 34. 721 applicants, 63% accepted, 382 enrolled. *Faculty:* 405 full-time, 148 part-time/adjunct. Expenses: Contact institution. *Financial support:* Fellowships, research assistantships, teaching assistantships, career-related internships or fieldwork, scholarships/grants, health care benefits, and unspecified assistantships available. Financial award applicants required to submit FAFSA. In 2008, 258 master's, 27 doctorates, 52 other advanced degrees awarded. Offers administration, planning, and policy (MS); American contemporary music (Postbaccalaureate Certificate); applied behavioral analysis (MA); applied developmental psychology (PhD); applied sociology (MA, Post-baccalaureate Certificate); arts, humanities and social science (MA, MAT, MFA, MPP, MPS, MS, PhD, Certificate, Postbaccalaureate Certificate); computer/web-based instruction (Post-baccalaureate Certificate); distance education (Postbaccalaureate Certificate); early childhood education (MAT); economic policy analysis (MA); education (MA, MAT, Post-baccalaureate Certificate); elementary education (MAT); elementary/middle science education (Postbaccalaureate Certificate); emergency health services (MS); emergency management (Postbaccalaureate Certificate); gender and women's studies (Postbaccalaureate Certificate); geographic information systems (MPS, Certificate); geography and environmental systems (MPS, MS, PhD, Certificate); historical studies (MA); human services psychology (MA, PhD); human services psychology/clinical (PhD); imaging and digital arts (MFA); industrial organizational psychology (MPS); intercultural communication (MA); language, literacy, and culture (PhD); math education (Postbaccalaureate Certificate); nonprofit sector (Postbaccalaureate Certificate); preventive medicine and epidemiology (MS); psychology (MPS); public policy (MPP, PhD); secondary education (MAT); STEM education (Postbaccalaureate Certificate); teaching (MAT); teaching English as a second language (MA). *Application deadline:* For fall admission, 1/1 for international students; for spring admission, 5/1 for international students. Applications are processed on a rolling basis. *Application fee:* $50. Electronic applications accepted. *Application Contact:* Kathryn Nee, Coordinator of Domestic Admissions, 410-455-2944, E-mail: nee@umbc.edu. *Dean*, Dr. John Jeffries, 410-455-2312, Fax: 410-455-1045, E-mail: jeffries@umbc.edu.

College of Engineering and Information Technology Students: 324 full-time (92 women), 526 part-time (142 women); includes 204 minority (101 African Americans, 85 Asian Americans or Pacific Islanders, 18 Hispanic Americans), 224 international. Average age 31. 635 applicants, 64% accepted, 227 enrolled. *Faculty:* 77 full-time (19 women), 20 part-time/adjunct (5 women). Expenses: Contact institution. *Financial support:* In 2008–09, 12 fellowships with full tuition reimbursements (averaging $21,250 per year), 85 research assistantships with full tuition reimbursements (averaging $18,900 per year), 89 teaching assistantships with full tuition reimbursements (averaging $18,625 per year) were awarded; career-related internships or fieldwork, Federal Work-Study, scholarships/grants, health care benefits, tuition waivers (partial), and unspecified assistantships also available. Support available to part-time students. Financial award application deadline: 6/30; financial award applicants required to submit FAFSA. In 2008, 161 master's, 36 doctorates, 11 other advanced degrees awarded. *Degree program information:* Part-time and evening/weekend programs available. Postbaccalaureate distance learning degree programs offered (no on-campus study). Offers biochemical regulatory engineering (Postbaccalaureate Certificate); chemical and biochemical engineering (MS, PhD); civil and environmental engineering (MS, PhD); civil engineering (MS, PhD); computer engineering (MS, PhD); computer science (MS, PhD); electrical engineering (MS, PhD); engineering and information technology (MS, PhD, Postbaccalaureate Certificate); engineering management (MS, Post-baccalaureate Certificate); human-centered computing (MS, PhD); information systems (MS, PhD); mechanical engineering (MS, PhD, Postbaccalaureate Certificate); mechatronics (Postbaccalaureate Certificate); systems engineering (MS, Postbaccalaureate Certificate). *Application deadline:* For fall admission, 6/1 for domestic students, 1/1 for international students; for spring admission, 11/1 for domestic students, 6/1 for international students. Applications are processed on a rolling basis. *Application fee:* $50. Electronic applications accepted. *Application Contact:* Graduate School, 410-455-2537, E-mail: umbcgrad@umbc.edu. *Dean*, Dr. Warren DeVries, 410-455-3270, Fax: 410-455-3559, E-mail: wdevries@umbc.edu.

College of Natural and Mathematical Sciences Students: 255 full-time (131 women), 70 part-time (34 women); includes 55 minority (28 African Americans, 21 Asian Americans or Pacific Islanders, 6 Hispanic Americans), 111 international. Average age 29. 367 applicants, 44% accepted, 98 enrolled. *Faculty:* 84 full-time (17 women), 29 part-time/adjunct (2 women). Expenses: Contact institution. *Financial support:* In 2008–09, 12 fellowships with full tuition reimbursements, 70 research assistantships with full tuition reimbursements, 114 teaching assistantships with full tuition reimbursements were awarded. In 2008, 30 master's, 30 doctorates awarded. *Degree program information:* Part-time programs available. Offers applied mathematics (MS, PhD); applied molecular biology (MS); applied physics (MS, PhD); astrophysics (PhD); atmospheric physics (MS, PhD); biochemistry (MS, PhD); biological sciences (MS, PhD); biostatistics (PhD); chemistry (MS, PhD); environmental statistics (MS); molecular and cell biology (PhD); natural and mathematical sciences (MS, PhD); neurosciences and cognitive sciences (PhD); optics (MS, PhD); quantum optics (PhD); solid state physics (MS, PhD); statistics (MS, PhD). *Application deadline:* Applications are processed on a rolling basis. Electronic applications accepted. *Application Contact:* Kathryn Nee, Coordinator of Domestic Admissions, 410-455-2944, E-mail: nee@umbc.edu. *Dean*, Dr. Philip J. Rous, 410-455-5827, Fax: 410-455-5831, E-mail: rous@umbc.edu.

Continuing and Professional Studies Offers biotechnology management (Graduate Certificate).

UNIVERSITY OF MARYLAND, COLLEGE PARK, College Park, MD 20742

General Information State-supported, coed, university. CGS member. *Enrollment:* 36,956 graduate, professional, and undergraduate students; 6,922 full-time matriculated graduate/professional students (3,463 women), 3,414 part-time matriculated graduate/professional students (1,494 women). *Enrollment by degree level:* 115 first professional, 4,939 master's, 4,677 doctoral, 605 other advanced degrees. *Graduate faculty:* 2,967 full-time (1,055 women), 900 part-time/adjunct (397 women). Tuition, state resident: full-time $9129; part-time $471 per credit hour. Tuition, nonresident: full-time $18,381; part-time $1016 per credit hour. *Required fees:* $1137; $374 per year. Tuition and fees vary according to course level, course load and program. *Graduate housing:* Rooms and/or apartments available on a first-come, first-served basis to single and married students. *Student services:* Campus employment opportunities, campus safety program, career counseling, child daycare facilities, exercise/wellness program, free psychological counseling, international student services, low-cost health insurance, multicultural affairs office, services for students with disabilities. *Library facilities:* McKeldin Library plus 6 others. *Online resources:* library catalog, web page, access to other libraries' catalogs. *Collection:* 3.7 million titles, 42,393 serial subscriptions, 389,267 audiovisual materials. *Research affiliation:* Bae Systems (Microsystem mechanics), Fraunhaufer USA (Computer sciences), General Dynamics (Robotics), JBS International (Substance abuse research), Science Applications International (Nanosensors), Telcordia Technologies (Communications and networking).

Computer facilities: Computer purchase and lease plans are available. 11,097 computers available on campus for general student use. A campuswide network can be accessed from student residence rooms and from off campus. Online class registration, student account information, financial aid summary are available. *Web address:* http://www.maryland.edu/.

General Application Contact: Dr. Charles Caramello, Dean of Graduate School, 301-405-0376, Fax: 301-314-9305.

GRADUATE UNITS

Academic Affairs Students: 84 full-time (48 women), 627 part-time (300 women); includes 168 minority (88 African Americans, 1 American Indian/Alaska Native, 47 Asian Americans or Pacific Islanders, 32 Hispanic Americans), 46 international. Average age 30. 723 applicants, 79% accepted, 389 enrolled. Expenses: Contact institution. *Financial support:* In 2008–09, 5,755 students received support, including 11 fellowships with full and partial tuition reimbursements available (averaging $12,297 per year), 3 research assistantships with tuition reimbursements available (averaging $19,658 per year), 8 teaching assistantships with tuition reimbursements available (averaging $15,920 per year); career-related internships or fieldwork, Federal Work-Study, institutionally sponsored loans, and scholarships/grants also available. Support available to part-time students. Financial award applicants required to submit FAFSA. In 2008, 26 first professional degrees, 1,968 master's, 653 doctorates awarded. *Degree program information:* Part-time and evening/weekend programs available. Postbaccalaureate distance learning degree programs offered (no on-campus study). Offers history, library, and information services. *Application deadline:* For fall admission, 2/1 for domestic and international students; for spring admission, 6/1 for domestic and international students. Applications are processed on a rolling basis. *Application fee:* $60. Electronic applications accepted. *Applica-*

University of Maryland, College Park (continued)

tion Contact: Dean of Graduate School, 301-405-0376, Fax: 301-314-9305. *Dean of the Graduate School,* Dr. Charles Caramello, 301-405-0376, Fax: 301-314-9305, E-mail: ccaramel@umd.edu.

A. James Clark School of Engineering Students: 1,116 full-time (266 women), 583 part-time (112 women); includes 278 minority (84 African Americans, 4 American Indian/Alaska Native, 143 Asian Americans or Pacific Islanders, 47 Hispanic Americans), 750 international. 3,168 applicants, 28% accepted, 448 enrolled. *Faculty:* 457 full-time (56 women), 93 part-time/adjunct (11 women). Expenses: Contact institution. *Financial support:* In 2008–09, 65 fellowships (averaging $15,094 per year), 549 research assistantships (averaging $21,412 per year), 207 teaching assistantships (averaging $18,539 per year) were awarded; career-related internships or fieldwork, Federal Work-Study, institutionally sponsored loans, and scholarships/grants also available. Support available to part-time students. Financial award applicants required to submit FAFSA. In 2008, 350 master's, 133 doctorates awarded. *Degree program information:* Part-time and evening/weekend programs available. Postbaccalaureate distance learning degree programs offered. Offers aerospace engineering (M Eng); bioengineering (MS, PhD); chemical engineering (M Eng, MS, PhD); civil and environmental engineering (M Eng, MS, PhD); civil engineering (M Eng); electrical and computer engineering (M Eng, MS, PhD); electrical engineering (M Eng, MS, PhD); electronic packaging and reliability (MS, PhD); engineering (Certificate); engineering and public policy (MS); fire protection engineering (M Eng); manufacturing and design (MS, PhD); materials science and engineering (M Eng, MS, PhD); mechanical engineering (M Eng); mechanics and materials (MS, PhD); nuclear engineering (ME, MS, PhD); reliability engineering (M Eng, MS, PhD); systems engineering (M Eng); telecommunications (MS); thermal and fluid sciences (MS, PhD). *Application deadline:* For fall admission, 2/1 for domestic and international students; for spring admission, 6/1 for domestic and international students. Applications are processed on a rolling basis. *Application fee:* $60. Electronic applications accepted. *Application Contact:* Dr. Charles Caramello, Dean of the Graduate School, 301-405-0376, Fax: 301-314-9305, E-mail: ccaramel@umd.edu. *Dean,* Dr. Darryll Pines, 301-405-3576, Fax: 301-314-5908, E-mail: pines@umd.edu.

College of Agriculture and Natural Resources Students: 317 full-time (191 women), 32 part-time (20 women); includes 8 African Americans, 10 Asian Americans or Pacific Islanders, 6 Hispanic Americans, 102 international. 365 applicants, 31% accepted, 84 enrolled. *Faculty:* 320 full-time (133 women), 45 part-time/adjunct (28 women). Expenses: Contact institution. *Financial support:* In 2008–09, 5 fellowships with full and partial tuition reimbursements (averaging $13,815 per year), 82 research assistantships with tuition reimbursements (averaging $17,550 per year), 76 teaching assistantships with tuition reimbursements (averaging $16,631 per year) were awarded; career-related internships or fieldwork, Federal Work-Study, and scholarships/grants also available. Support available to part-time students. Financial award applicants required to submit FAFSA. In 2008, 28 first professional degrees, 21 master's, 27 doctorates awarded. *Degree program information:* Part-time and evening/weekend programs available. Offers agriculture and natural resources (DVM, MS, PhD); agriculture economics (MS, PhD); agronomy (MS, PhD); animal sciences (MS, PhD); environmental science and technology (MS, PhD); food science (MS, PhD); horticulture (PhD); natural resource sciences (MS, PhD); nutrition (MS, PhD); resource economics (MS, PhD); veterinary medical sciences (MS, PhD); veterinary medicine (DVM, MS, PhD). *Application deadline:* For fall admission, 5/15 for domestic students, 2/1 for international students; for spring admission, 6/1 for international students. Applications are processed on a rolling basis. *Application fee:* $60. Electronic applications accepted. *Application Contact:* Dean of Graduate School, 301-405-0376, Fax: 301-314-9305. *Dean,* Dr. Cheng-i Wei, 301-405-2072, Fax: 301-314-9146, E-mail: wei@umd.edu.

College of Arts and Humanities Students: 932 full-time (587 women), 169 part-time (89 women); includes 177 minority (75 African Americans, 3 American Indian/Alaska Native, 62 Asian Americans or Pacific Islanders, 37 Hispanic Americans), 194 international. 2,212 applicants, 24% accepted, 264 enrolled. *Faculty:* 437 full-time (220 women), 212 part-time/adjunct (112 women). Expenses: Contact institution. *Financial support:* In 2008–09, 77 fellowships with full and partial tuition reimbursements (averaging $13,910 per year), 37 research assistantships with tuition reimbursements (averaging $19,233 per year), 563 teaching assistantships with tuition reimbursements (averaging $16,662 per year) were awarded; career-related internships or fieldwork, Federal Work-Study, and scholarships/grants also available. Support available to part-time students. Financial award applicants required to submit FAFSA. In 2008, 1,146 master's, 92 doctorates awarded. *Degree program information:* Part-time and evening/weekend programs available. Offers American studies (MA, PhD); Arabic (Graduate Certificate); art (MFA); art history (MA, PhD); arts and humanities (M Ed, MA, MFA, MM, MPS, DMA, Ed D, PhD, Graduate Certificate); classics (MA); communication (MA, PhD); comparative literature (MA, PhD); creative writing (MA, MFA, PhD); dance (MFA); English language and literature (MA, PhD); ethnomusicology (MA); French (MA); French language and literature (MA); German (MA); Germanic language and literature (MA, PhD); history (MA, PhD); Japanese (MA); Jewish studies (MA); languages, literature, and cultures (MA, PhD); linguistics (MA, PhD); modern French studies (PhD); music (M Ed, MA, MM, DMA, Ed D, PhD); Persian (MPS, Graduate Certificate); philosophy (MA, PhD); Russian (MA); second language instruction (PhD); second language learning (PhD); second language measurement and assessment (PhD); second language use (PhD); Spanish (MA); Spanish and Portuguese (MA, PhD); theatre (MA, MFA, PhD); women's studies (MA, PhD). *Application deadline:* For fall admission, 5/1 for domestic students, 2/1 for international students; for spring admission, 10/1 for domestic students, 6/1 for international students. Applications are processed on a rolling basis. *Application fee:* $60. Electronic applications accepted. *Application Contact:* Dean of Graduate School, 301-405-0376, Fax: 301-314-9305. *Dean,* Dr. James F. Harris, 301-405-0949, Fax: 301-314-9148, E-mail: jfharris@umd.edu.

College of Behavioral and Social Sciences Students: 727 full-time (433 women), 133 part-time (79 women); includes 125 minority (42 African Americans, 2 American Indian/Alaska Native, 47 Asian Americans or Pacific Islanders, 34 Hispanic Americans), 214 international. 2,293 applicants, 20% accepted, 181 enrolled. *Faculty:* 372 full-time (165 women), 111 part-time/adjunct (48 women). Expenses: Contact institution. *Financial support:* In 2008–09, 69 fellowships with full and partial tuition reimbursements (averaging $16,489 per year), 91 research assistantships with tuition reimbursements (averaging $16,583 per year), 404 teaching assistantships with tuition reimbursements (averaging $16,488 per year) were awarded; career-related internships or fieldwork, Federal Work-Study, and scholarships/grants also available. Support available to part-time students. Financial award applicants required to submit FAFSA. In 2008, 116 master's, 88 doctorates awarded. *Degree program information:* Part-time and evening/weekend programs available. Offers American politics (PhD); applied anthropology (MAA); audiology (MA, PhD); behavioral and social sciences (MA, MAA, MS, Au D, PhD); clinical psychology (PhD); comparative politics (PhD); criminology and criminal justice (MA, PhD); developmental psychology (PhD); economics (MA, PhD); experimental psychology (PhD); geography (MA, PhD); hearing and speech sciences (Au D); industrial psychology (MA, MS, PhD); international relations (PhD); language pathology (MA, PhD); neuroscience (PhD); neurosciences and cognitive sciences (PhD); political economy (PhD); political theory (PhD); social psychology (PhD); sociology (MA, PhD); speech (MA, PhD); survey methodology (MS, PhD). *Application deadline:* For fall admission, 5/1 for domestic students, 2/1 for international students; for spring admission, 10/1 for domestic students, 6/1 for international students. Applications are processed on a rolling basis. *Application fee:* $60. Electronic applications accepted. *Application Contact:* Dean of Graduate School, 301-405-0376, Fax: 301-314-9305. *Dean,* Dr. Edward Montgomery, 301-405-1691, Fax: 301-314-9086, E-mail: montgome@umd.edu.

College of Chemical and Life Sciences Students: 531 full-time (314 women), 168 part-time (117 women); includes 75 minority (28 African Americans, 29 Asian Americans or Pacific Islanders, 18 Hispanic Americans), 185 international. 1,177 applicants, 26% accepted, 173 enrolled. *Faculty:* 272 full-time (103 women), 24 part-time/adjunct (11 women). Expenses: Contact institution. *Financial support:* In 2008–09, 42 fellowships with full and partial tuition reimbursements (averaging $16,773 per year), 101 research assistantships with tuition reimbursements (averaging $19,567 per year), 290 teaching assistantships with tuition reimbursements (averaging $19,019 per year) were awarded; career-related internships or fieldwork, Federal Work-Study, and scholarships/grants also available. Support available to part-time students. Financial award applicants required to submit FAFSA. In 2008, 77 master's, 54 doctorates awarded. *Degree program information:* Part-time and evening/weekend programs available. Offers analytical chemistry (MS, PhD); behavior, ecology, and systematics (PhD); behavior, ecology, evolution, and systematics (MS, PhD); biochemistry (MS, PhD); biology (MS, PhD); cell biology and molecular genetics (MS, PhD); chemical and life sciences (MLS, MS, PhD); chemistry (MS, PhD); entomology (MS, PhD); inorganic chemistry (MS, PhD); life sciences (MLS); marine-estuarine-environmental sciences (MS, PhD); molecular and cellular biology (PhD); organic chemistry (MS, PhD); physical chemistry (MS, PhD); plant biology (MS, PhD); sustainable development and conservation biology (MS). *Application deadline:* For fall admission, 2/1 for domestic and international students. Applications are processed on a rolling basis. *Application fee:* $60. Electronic applications accepted. *Application Contact:* Dean of Graduate School, 301-405-0376, Fax: 301-314-9305. *Dean,* Dr. Norma M. Allewell, 301-405-2071, Fax: 301-314-9949, E-mail: allewell@umd.edu.

College of Computer, Mathematical and Physical Sciences Students: 774 full-time (182 women), 77 part-time (18 women); includes 75 minority (18 African Americans, 1 American Indian/Alaska Native, 46 Asian Americans or Pacific Islanders, 10 Hispanic Americans), 338 international. 2,351 applicants, 19% accepted, 169 enrolled. *Faculty:* 625 full-time (112 women), 100 part-time/adjunct (18 women). Expenses: Contact institution. *Financial support:* In 2008–09, 43 fellowships with full and partial tuition reimbursements (averaging $16,754 per year), 389 research assistantships with tuition reimbursements (averaging $19,639 per year), 300 teaching assistantships with tuition reimbursements (averaging $18,012 per year) were awarded; career-related internships or fieldwork, Federal Work-Study, and scholarships/grants also available. Support available to part-time students. Financial award applicants required to submit FAFSA. In 2008, 78 master's, 117 doctorates awarded. *Degree program information:* Part-time and evening/weekend programs available. Postbaccalaureate distance learning degree programs offered. Offers applied mathematics (MS, PhD); astronomy (MS, PhD); atmospheric and oceanic science (MS, PhD); chemical physics (MS, PhD); computer science (MS, PhD); computer, mathematical and physical sciences (MA, MS, PhD); geology (MS, PhD); mathematical statistics (MA, PhD); mathematics (MA, PhD); physics (MS, PhD). *Application deadline:* For fall admission, 12/1 for domestic students, 2/1 for international students; for spring admission, 10/1 for domestic students, 6/1 for international students. Applications are processed on a rolling basis. *Application fee:* $60. Electronic applications accepted. *Application Contact:* Dean of Graduate School, 301-405-0376, Fax: 301-314-9305. *Dean,* Dr. Stephen Halperin, 301-405-4906, Fax: 301-405-9377, E-mail: shalper@umd.edu.

College of Education Students: 822 full-time (650 women), 520 part-time (399 women); includes 395 minority (241 African Americans, 7 American Indian/Alaska Native, 85 Asian Americans or Pacific Islanders, 62 Hispanic Americans), 128 international. 1,261 applicants, 37% accepted, 307 enrolled. *Faculty:* 194 full-time (134 women), 83 part-time/adjunct (66 women). Expenses: Contact institution. *Financial support:* In 2008–09, 111 fellowships with full and partial tuition reimbursements (averaging $14,834 per year), 40 research assistantships with tuition reimbursements (averaging $17,389 per year), 299 teaching assistantships with tuition reimbursements (averaging $16,365 per year) were awarded; career-related internships or fieldwork, Federal Work-Study, and scholarships/grants also available. Support available to part-time students. Financial award applicants required to submit FAFSA. In 2008, 278 master's, 93 doctorates, 5 other advanced degrees awarded. *Degree program information:* Part-time and evening/weekend programs available. Postbaccalaureate distance learning degree programs offered. Offers college student personnel (M Ed, MA); college student personnel administration (PhD); community counseling (CAGS); community/career counseling (M Ed, MA); counseling and personnel services (M Ed, MA, PhD); counseling psychology (PhD); counselor education (PhD); curriculum and educational communications (M Ed, MA, Ed D, PhD); early childhood/elementary education (M Ed, MA, Ed D, PhD); education (M Ed, MA, Ed D, PhD, AGSC, CAGS); education leadership, higher education and international education (MA, Ed D, PhD); education policy studies (M Ed, MA, PhD); human development (M Ed, MA, Ed D, PhD); measurement (MA, PhD); program evaluation (MA, PhD); reading (M Ed, MA, PhD, CAGS); rehabilitation counseling (M Ed, MA, AGSC); school counseling (M Ed, MA); school psychology (M Ed, MA, PhD); secondary education (M Ed, MA, Ed D, PhD, CAGS); social foundations of education (M Ed, MA, Ed D, PhD, CAGS); special education (M Ed, MA, PhD, CAGS); statistics (MA, PhD); teaching English to speakers of other languages (M Ed). *Application deadline:* For fall admission, 5/1 for domestic students, 2/1 for international students; for spring admission, 10/1 for domestic students, 6/1 for international students. Applications are processed on a rolling basis. *Application fee:* $60. Electronic applications accepted. *Application Contact:* Dean of Graduate School, 301-405-0376, Fax: 301-314-9305. *Dean,* Donna L. Wiseman, 301-405-2336, Fax: 301-314-9890, E-mail: dlwise@umd.edu.

College of Information Studies Students: 260 full-time (190 women), 180 part-time (116 women); includes 48 minority (19 African Americans, 20 Asian Americans or Pacific Islanders, 9 Hispanic Americans), 89 international. 631 applicants, 55% accepted, 152 enrolled. *Faculty:* 21 full-time (11 women), 17 part-time/adjunct (12 women). Expenses: Contact institution. *Financial support:* In 2008–09, 2 fellowships with full and partial tuition reimbursements (averaging $12,900 per year), 3 research assistantships (averaging $19,209 per year), 87 teaching assistantships with tuition reimbursements (averaging $15,738 per year) were awarded; career-related internships or fieldwork, Federal Work-Study, scholarships/grants, and tuition waivers (full and partial) also available. Support available to part-time students. Financial award application deadline: 2/1; financial award applicants required to submit FAFSA. In 2008, 161 master's, 3 doctorates awarded. *Degree program information:* Part-time and evening/weekend programs available. Offers information studies (MIM, MLS, PhD). *Application deadline:* For fall admission, 2/1 for domestic and international students; for spring admission, 10/1 for domestic students, 6/1 for international students. Applications are processed on a rolling basis. *Application fee:* $60. Electronic applications accepted. *Application Contact:* Dean of Graduate School, 301-405-0376, Fax: 301-314-9305. *Dean,* Dr. Jennifer Preece, 301-405-2036, Fax: 301-314-9145, E-mail: preece@umd.edu.

Phillip Merrill College of Journalism Students: 59 full-time (37 women), 20 part-time (10 women); includes 17 minority (11 African Americans, 3 Asian Americans or Pacific Islanders, 3 Hispanic Americans), 13 international. 182 applicants, 42% accepted, 24 enrolled. *Faculty:* 22 full-time (10 women), 36 part-time/adjunct (12 women). Expenses: Contact institution. *Financial support:* In 2008–09, 7 fellowships with full and partial tuition reimbursements (averaging $14,919 per year), 22 teaching assistantships with tuition reimbursements (averaging $17,514 per year) were awarded; research assistantships with tuition reimbursements, career-related internships or fieldwork, Federal Work-Study, and scholarships/grants also available. Support available to part-time students. Financial award applicants required to submit FAFSA. In 2008, 32 master's, 7 doctorates awarded. *Degree program information:* Part-time and evening/weekend programs available. Offers broadcast journalism (MA); journalism (MA); journalism and media studies (PhD); online news (MA); public affairs reporting (MA). *Application deadline:* For fall admission, 2/1 for domestic and international students. Applications are processed on a rolling basis. *Application fee:* $60. Electronic applications accepted. *Application Contact:* Dean of Graduate School, 301-405-0376, Fax: 301-314-9305. *Acting Dean,* Lee Thornton, 301-405-2393, E-mail: lthornto@umd.edu.

Robert H. Smith School of Business Students: 802 full-time (292 women), 872 part-time (240 women); includes 464 minority (129 African Americans, 4 American Indian/Alaska Native, 282 Asian Americans or Pacific Islanders, 49 Hispanic Americans), 339 international. 2,430 applicants, 39% accepted, 608 enrolled. *Faculty:* 142 full-time (33 women), 47 part-time/adjunct (11 women). Expenses: Contact institution. *Financial support:* In 2008–09, 48 fellowships with full and partial tuition reimbursements (averaging $24,927 per year), 186 teaching assistantships with tuition reimbursements (averaging $16,499 per year) were awarded; research assistantships with tuition reimbursements, Federal Work-Study and scholarships/grants also available. Support available to part-time students. Financial award applicants required to submit FAFSA. In 2008, 594 master's, 13 doctorates awarded. *Degree program information:* Part-time and evening/weekend programs available. Postbaccalaureate distance learning degree programs offered. Offers business (EMBA, MBA, MS, PhD); business administration (EMBA, MBA); business and management (MS, PhD).

Application deadline: For fall admission, 5/1 for domestic students, 2/1 for international students. Applications are processed on a rolling basis. *Application fee:* $60. Electronic applications accepted. *Application Contact:* Dean of Graduate School, 301-405-0376, Fax: 301-314-9305. *Dean,* Dr. Anand Anandalingam, 301-405-2308, E-mail: ganand@umd.edu.

School of Architecture, Planning and Preservation Students: 182 full-time (90 women), 76 part-time (26 women); includes 58 minority (29 African Americans, 2 American Indian/Alaska Native, 15 Asian Americans or Pacific Islanders, 12 Hispanic Americans), 27 international. 490 applicants, 41% accepted, 100 enrolled. *Faculty:* 35 full-time (10 women), 26 part-time/adjunct (7 women). Expenses: Contact institution. *Financial support:* In 2008–09, 8 fellowships with full and partial tuition reimbursements (averaging $15,687 per year), 1 research assistantship with tuition reimbursement (averaging $19,089 per year), 112 teaching assistantships with tuition reimbursements (averaging $14,934 per year) were awarded; career-related internships or fieldwork, Federal Work-Study, and scholarships/grants also available. Support available to part-time students. Financial award applicants required to submit FAFSA. In 2008, 40 master's, 2 doctorates awarded. *Degree program information:* Part-time and evening/weekend programs available. Offers architecture (M Arch); architecture, planning and preservation (M Arch, MCP, MHP, MRED, PhD, Certificate); historic preservation (MHP, Certificate); real estate development (MRED); urban and regional planning/design (PhD); urban studies and planning (MCP). *Application deadline:* For fall admission, 1/1 for domestic and international students; for spring admission, 10/15 for domestic students, 6/1 for international students. Applications are processed on a rolling basis. *Application fee:* $60. Electronic applications accepted. *Application Contact:* Dean of Graduate School, 301-405-0376, Fax: 301-314-9305. *Dean,* Garth Rockcastle, 301-405-5755, Fax: 301-314-9583, E-mail: gcr@umd.edu.

School of Public Health Students: 177 full-time (134 women), 35 part-time (30 women); includes 58 minority (39 African Americans, 1 American Indian/Alaska Native, 14 Asian Americans or Pacific Islanders, 4 Hispanic Americans), 32 international. 420 applicants, 22% accepted, 59 enrolled. *Faculty:* 94 full-time (52 women), 38 part-time/adjunct (25 women). Expenses: Contact institution. *Financial support:* In 2008–09, 23 fellowships with full and partial tuition reimbursements (averaging $13,304 per year), 20 research assistantships with tuition reimbursements (averaging $15,861 per year), 75 teaching assistantships with tuition reimbursements (averaging $15,851 per year) were awarded; career-related internships or fieldwork, Federal Work-Study, and scholarships/grants also available. Support available to part-time students. Financial award applicants required to submit FAFSA. In 2008, 37 master's, 17 doctorates awarded. *Degree program information:* Part-time and evening/weekend programs available. Offers biostatistics (MPH); community health education (MPH); environmental health sciences (MPH); epidemiology (MPH, PhD); family studies (PhD); health services administration (MHA, PhD); kinesiology (MA, PhD); marriage and family therapy (MS); maternal and child health (PhD); public health (MA, MHA, MPH, MS, PhD); public/community health (PhD). *Application deadline:* For fall admission, 5/1 for domestic students, 2/1 for international students; for spring admission, 10/1 for domestic students, 6/1 for international students. Applications are processed on a rolling basis. *Application fee:* $60. Electronic applications accepted. *Application Contact:* Dean of Graduate School, 301-405-0376, Fax: 301-314-9305. *Dean,* Dr. Robert Gold, 301-405-2437, Fax: 301-314-9167, E-mail: rsgold@umd.edu.

School of Public Policy Students: 173 full-time (82 women), 57 part-time (26 women); includes 36 minority (15 African Americans, 12 Asian Americans or Pacific Islanders, 9 Hispanic Americans), 54 international. 593 applicants, 47% accepted, 94 enrolled. *Faculty:* 37 full-time (16 women), 23 part-time/adjunct (9 women). Expenses: Contact institution. *Financial support:* In 2008–09, 16 fellowships with full and partial tuition reimbursements (averaging $12,455 per year), 3 research assistantships with tuition reimbursements (averaging $16,754 per year), 90 teaching assistantships with tuition reimbursements (averaging $14,587 per year) were awarded; Federal Work-Study and scholarships/grants also available. Support available to part-time students. Financial award applicants required to submit FAFSA. In 2008, 88 master's, 9 doctorates awarded. *Degree program information:* Part-time and evening/weekend programs available. Postbaccalaureate distance learning degree programs offered. Offers policy studies (PhD); public management (MPM); public policy (MPM, MPP, PhD). *Application deadline:* For fall admission, 12/15 for domestic students, 2/1 for international students; for spring admission, 10/15 for domestic students, 6/1 for international students. Applications are processed on a rolling basis. *Application fee:* $60. Electronic applications accepted. *Application Contact:* Dean of Graduate School, 301-405-0376, Fax: 301-314-9305. *Dean,* Dr. Donald Kettl, 301-405-6355, E-mail: sfetter@umd.edu.

UNIVERSITY OF MARYLAND EASTERN SHORE, Princess Anne, MD 21853-1299

General Information State-supported, coed, university. CGS member. *Graduate housing:* On-campus housing not available.

GRADUATE UNITS

Graduate Programs *Degree program information:* Part-time and evening/weekend programs available. Offers applied computer science (MS); career and technology education (M Ed); criminology and criminal justice (MS); education leadership (Ed D); food and agricultural sciences (MS); food science and technology (PhD); guidance and counseling (M Ed); marine-estuarine-environmental sciences (MS, PhD); organizational leadership (PhD); physical therapy (DPT); rehabilitation counseling (MS); special education (M Ed); teaching (MAT); toxicology (MS, PhD). Electronic applications accepted.

See Close-Up on page 1023.

UNIVERSITY OF MARYLAND UNIVERSITY COLLEGE, Adelphi, MD 20783

General Information State-supported, coed, comprehensive institution. CGS member. *Enrollment:* 34,172 graduate, professional, and undergraduate students; 248 full-time matriculated graduate/professional students (151 women), 11,616 part-time matriculated graduate/professional students (6,472 women). *Enrollment by degree level:* 10,610 master's, 208 doctoral, 1,046 other advanced degrees. *Graduate faculty:* 175 full-time (64 women), 451 part-time/adjunct (158 women). Tuition, state resident: full-time $7416; part-time $412 per credit hour. Tuition, nonresident: full-time $11,862; part-time $659 per credit hour. *Required fees:* $180; $10 per credit hour. *Graduate housing:* On-campus housing not available. *Student services:* Campus employment opportunities, career counseling, international student services, services for students with disabilities, writing training.

Computer facilities: 375 computers available on campus for general student use. A campuswide network can be accessed from off campus. Online class registration is available. *Web address:* http://www.umuc.edu/.

General Application Contact: Coordinator, Graduate Admissions, 301-985-7155, Fax: 301-985-7072, E-mail: newgrad@umuc.edu.

GRADUATE UNITS

Graduate School of Management and Technology Students: 248 full-time (151 women), 11,616 part-time (6,472 women); includes 5,605 minority (4,250 African Americans, 53 American Indian/Alaska Native, 800 Asian Americans or Pacific Islanders, 502 Hispanic Americans), 417 international. Average age 35. 4,859 applicants, 100% accepted, 2494 enrolled. *Faculty:* 175 full-time (64 women), 451 part-time/adjunct (158 women). Expenses: Contact institution. *Financial support:* Federal Work-Study and scholarships/grants available. Support available to part-time students. Financial award application deadline: 6/1; financial award applicants required to submit FAFSA. In 2008, 2,089 master's, 14 doctorates, 386 other advanced degrees awarded. *Degree program information:* Part-time and evening/weekend programs available. Postbaccalaureate distance learning degree programs offered (no on-campus study). Offers accounting and financial management (MS, Certificate); accounting and information technology (MS, Certificate); biotechnology studies (MS, Certificate); business administration (Exec MBA, MBA, Certificate); distance education (MDE, Certificate); education (M Ed); environmental management (MS, Certificate); financial management and information systems (MS, Certificate); health administration informatics (MS, Certificate); health care administration (MS, Certificate); information technology (Exec MS, MS, Certificate); international management (MIM, Certificate); management (MS, Certificate); management and technology (Exec MBA, Exec MS, M Ed, MBA, MDE, MIM, MS, DM, Certificate); technology management (Exec MS, MS, Certificate). *Application deadline:* Applications are processed on a rolling basis. *Application fee:* $50. Electronic applications accepted. *Application Contact:* Coordinator, Graduate Admissions, 301-985-7155, Fax: 301-985-7072, E-mail: newgrad@umuc.edu. *Vice President and Dean of Graduate Studies,* Dr. Michael S. Frank, 301-985-7040, Fax: 301-985-4611.

UNIVERSITY OF MARY WASHINGTON, Fredericksburg, VA 22401-5358

General Information State-supported, coed, comprehensive institution. *Graduate housing:* On-campus housing not available.

GRADUATE UNITS

College of Graduate and Professional Studies *Degree program information:* Part-time and evening/weekend programs available. Offers business administration (MBA); education (M Ed); management information systems (MSMIS).

UNIVERSITY OF MASSACHUSETTS AMHERST, Amherst, MA 01003

General Information State-supported, coed, university. CGS member. *Enrollment:* 26,359 graduate, professional, and undergraduate students; 2,956 full-time matriculated graduate/professional students (1,530 women), 2,194 part-time matriculated graduate/professional students (1,064 women). *Enrollment by degree level:* 2,761 master's, 2,344 doctoral, 45 other advanced degrees. *Graduate faculty:* 1,247 full-time (410 women). Tuition, state resident: full-time $2640. Tuition, nonresident: full-time $9936. One-time fee: $332 full-time. Tuition and fees vary according to course load. *Graduate housing:* Rooms and/or apartments available on a first-come, first-served basis to single and married students. Typical cost: $6700 per year ($12,000 including board) for single students; $9372 per year for married students. Room and board charges vary according to board plan and housing facility selected. Housing application deadline: 8/15. *Student services:* Campus employment opportunities, campus safety program, career counseling, child daycare facilities, exercise/wellness program, free psychological counseling, grant writing training, international student services, low-cost health insurance, multicultural affairs office, services for students with disabilities, teacher training. *Library facilities:* W. E. B. Du Bois Library plus 1 other. *Online resources:* library catalog, web page, access to other libraries' catalogs. *Collection:* 3.3 million titles, 57,233 serial subscriptions, 25,230 audiovisual materials.

Computer facilities: 450 computers available on campus for general student use. A campuswide network can be accessed from student residence rooms and from off campus. Online class registration, online housing assignments, bill payment, Learning Management System, file storage, web hosting, blogs are available. *Web address:* http://www.umass.edu/.

General Application Contact: Jean M. Ames, Supervisor of Admissions, 413-545-0722, Fax: 413-577-0010, E-mail: gradadm@grad.umass.edu.

GRADUATE UNITS

Graduate School Students: 2,956 full-time (1,530 women), 2,194 part-time (1,064 women); includes 634 minority (223 African Americans, 19 American Indian/Alaska Native, 213 Asian Americans or Pacific Islanders, 179 Hispanic Americans), 1,196 international. Average age 32. 9,163 applicants, 32% accepted, 1438 enrolled. *Faculty:* 1,247 full-time (410 women). Expenses: Contact institution. *Financial support:* In 2008–09, 236 fellowships with full tuition reimbursements (averaging $6,806 per year), 1,432 research assistantships with full tuition reimbursements (averaging $9,009 per year), 1,255 teaching assistantships with full tuition reimbursements (averaging $9,091 per year) were awarded; career-related internships or fieldwork, Federal Work-Study, scholarships/grants, traineeships, tuition waivers (full), and unspecified assistantships also available. Support available to part-time students. Financial award application deadline: 2/1. In 2008, 1,223 master's, 292 doctorates awarded. *Degree program information:* Part-time and evening/weekend programs available. Postbaccalaureate distance learning degree programs offered (minimal on-campus study). Offers biological chemistry and molecular biophysics (PhD); biomedicine (PhD); cellular and developmental biology (PhD); civil engineering and business administrationenvironmental engineering and business administrationinterdisciplinary studies (MS, PhD); marine science and technology (MS); mechanical engineering and business administrationneuroscience and behavior (MS, PhD); organismic and evolutionary biology (MS, PhD); plant biology (MS, PhD); sports management and business administration. *Application deadline:* For fall admission, 2/1 for domestic and international students; for spring admission, 10/1 for domestic and international students. Applications are processed on a rolling basis. *Application fee:* $50 ($65 for international students). Electronic applications accepted. *Application Contact:* Jean M. Ames, Supervisor of Admissions, 413-545-0721, Fax: 413-577-0100, E-mail: gradadm@grad.umass.edu. *Dean,* Dr. John R. Mullin, 413-545-5271, Fax: 413-545-3754.

College of Engineering Students: 308 full-time (75 women), 41 part-time (5 women); includes 20 minority (4 African Americans, 10 Asian Americans or Pacific Islanders, 6 Hispanic Americans), 208 international. Average age 27. 1,264 applicants, 24% accepted, 91 enrolled. *Faculty:* 108 full-time (12 women). Expenses: Contact institution. *Financial support:* In 2008–09, 19 fellowships with full tuition reimbursements (averaging $6,609 per year), 344 research assistantships with full tuition reimbursements (averaging $13,045 per year), 74 teaching assistantships with full tuition reimbursements (averaging $5,558 per year) were awarded; career-related internships or fieldwork, Federal Work-Study, scholarships/grants, traineeships, and unspecified assistantships also available. Support available to part-time students. Financial award application deadline: 2/1. In 2008, 101 master's, 38 doctorates awarded. *Degree program information:* Part-time programs available. Offers chemical engineering (MS, PhD); civil engineering (MS, PhD); electrical and computer engineering (MS, PhD); engineering (MS, PhD); environmental engineering (MS); industrial engineering and operations research (MS, PhD); mechanical engineering (MS, PhD). *Application deadline:* Applications are processed on a rolling basis. *Application fee:* $50 ($65 for international students). Electronic applications accepted. *Application Contact:* Jean M. Ames, Supervisor of Admissions, 413-545-0722, Fax: 413-577-0010, E-mail: gradadm@grad.umass.edu. *Dean,* Dr. Michael Malone, 413-545-6388, Fax: 413-545-6388.

College of Humanities and Fine Arts Students: 476 full-time (272 women), 237 part-time (139 women); includes 100 minority (40 African Americans, 4 American Indian/Alaska Native, 19 Asian Americans or Pacific Islanders, 37 Hispanic Americans), 112 international. Average age 31. 1,841 applicants, 26% accepted, 204 enrolled. *Faculty:* 246 full-time (99 women). Expenses: Contact institution. *Financial support:* In 2008–09, 34 fellowships with full tuition reimbursements (averaging $4,672 per year), 40 research assistantships with full tuition reimbursements (averaging $8,131 per year), 368 teaching assistantships with full tuition reimbursements (averaging $10,005 per year) were awarded; career-related internships or fieldwork, Federal Work-Study, scholarships/grants, traineeships, and unspecified assistantships also available. Support available to part-time students. In 2008, 141 master's, 18 doctorates awarded. *Degree program information:* Part-time programs available. Offers Afro-American studies (MA, PhD); ancient history (MA); architecture (M Arch, MS); architecture and design (M Arch); art (M Arch, MA, MFA, MS); art history (MA); Asian languages and literatures (MA); British Empire history (MA); Chinese (MA); comparative literature (MA, PhD); creative writing (MFA); English and American literature (MA, PhD); European (medieval and modern) history (MA, PhD); French (MA, MAT); French and Francophone studies (MA, MAT); German and Scandinavian studies (MA, PhD); Hispanic literatures, cultures and linguistics (MA, MAT, PhD); humanities and fine arts (M Arch, MA, MAT, MFA, MM, MS, PhD); interior design (MS); Islamic history (MA); Italian studies (MAT); Japanese (MA); Latin American history (MA, PhD); Latin and classical humanities (MAT); linguistics (MA, PhD); modern global history (MA); music (MM, PhD); philosophy (MA, PhD); public history (MA); science and technology history (MA); teaching Spanish (MAT); theater (MFA); U.S. history (MA, PhD). *Application deadline:* Applications are processed on a rolling basis. *Application fee:* $50 ($65 for international students). Electronic applications accepted. *Application Contact:* Jean M. Ames, Supervisor of Admissions, 413-545-0722,

University of Massachusetts Amherst (continued)

Fax: 413-577-0010, E-mail: gradadm@grad.umass.edu. *Dean*, Dr. Joel W. Martin, 413-545-4169, Fax: 413-545-4171.

College of Natural Resources and the Environment Students: 236 full-time (120 women), 77 part-time (39 women); includes 23 minority (8 African Americans, 1 American Indian/Alaska Native, 8 Asian Americans or Pacific Islanders, 6 Hispanic Americans), 78 international. Average age 31. 441 applicants, 44% accepted, 96 enrolled. *Faculty:* 170 full-time (37 women). Expenses: Contact institution. *Financial support:* In 2008–09, 19 fellowships with full tuition reimbursements (averaging $11,686 per year), 220 research assistantships with full tuition reimbursements (averaging $9,873 per year), 136 teaching assistantships with full tuition reimbursements (averaging $7,139 per year) were awarded; career-related internships or fieldwork, Federal Work-Study, scholarships/grants, traineeships, and unspecified assistantships also available. Support available to part-time students. Financial award application deadline: 2/1. In 2008, 72 master's, 27 doctorates awarded. *Degree program information:* Part-time programs available. Postbaccalaureate distance learning degree programs offered (minimal on-campus study). Offers entomology (MS, PhD); food science (MS, PhD); forest resources (MS, PhD); landscape architecture (MLA); mammalian and avian biology (MS, PhD); microbiology (MS, PhD); natural resources and the environment (MLA, MRP, MS, PhD); plant and soil sciences (MS, PhD); regional planning (MRP, PhD); resource economics (MS, PhD); soil science (MS); wildlife and fisheries conservation (MS, PhD). *Application deadline:* Applications are processed on a rolling basis. *Application fee:* $50 ($65 for international students). Electronic applications accepted. *Application Contact:* Jean M. Ames, Supervisor of Admissions, 413-545-0722, Fax: 413-577-0010, E-mail: gradadm@grad.umass.edu. *Dean*, Dr. Steven D. Goodwin, 413-545-2766, Fax: 413-545-5853.

College of Natural Sciences and Mathematics Students: 612 full-time (219 women), 101 part-time (29 women); includes 42 minority (8 African Americans, 2 American Indian/Alaska Native, 13 Asian Americans or Pacific Islanders, 19 Hispanic Americans), 342 international. Average age 28. 1,993 applicants, 20% accepted, 161 enrolled. *Faculty:* 264 full-time (48 women). Expenses: Contact institution. *Financial support:* In 2008–09, 43 fellowships with full tuition reimbursements (averaging $7,743 per year), 590 research assistantships with full tuition reimbursements (averaging $14,294 per year), 334 teaching assistantships with full tuition reimbursements (averaging $9,517 per year) were awarded; career-related internships or fieldwork, Federal Work-Study, scholarships/grants, traineeships, and unspecified assistantships also available. Support available to part-time students. In 2008, 114 master's, 94 doctorates awarded. *Degree program information:* Part-time programs available. Offers applied mathematics (MS); astronomy (MS, PhD); biochemistry (MS); chemistry (MS, PhD); computer science (MS, PhD); geography (MS); geosciences (MS, PhD); mathematics and statistics (MS, PhD); natural sciences and mathematics (MS, PhD); physics (MS, PhD); polymer science and engineering (MS, PhD). *Application deadline:* Applications are processed on a rolling basis. *Application fee:* $50 ($65 for international students). Electronic applications accepted. *Application Contact:* Jean M. Ames, Supervisor of Admissions, 413-545-0722, Fax: 413-577-0010, E-mail: gradadm@grad.umass.edu. *Dean*, Dr. James F. Kurose, 413-545-1785, Fax: 413-545-9784.

College of Social and Behavioral Sciences Students: 380 full-time (234 women), 181 part-time (97 women); includes 90 minority (32 African Americans, 4 American Indian/Alaska Native, 17 Asian Americans or Pacific Islanders, 37 Hispanic Americans), 133 international. Average age 33. 1,196 applicants, 20% accepted, 110 enrolled. *Faculty:* 195 full-time (81 women). Expenses: Contact institution. *Financial support:* In 2008–09, 34 fellowships with full tuition reimbursements (averaging $8,305 per year), 156 research assistantships with full tuition reimbursements (averaging $7,696 per year), 308 teaching assistantships with full tuition reimbursements (averaging $9,724 per year) were awarded; career-related internships or fieldwork, Federal Work-Study, scholarships/grants, traineeships, and unspecified assistantships also available. Support available to part-time students. In 2008, 70 master's, 39 doctorates awarded. *Degree program information:* Part-time programs available. Postbaccalaureate distance learning degree programs offered (minimal on-campus study). Offers anthropology (MA, PhD); clinical psychology (MS, PhD); cognitive psychology (MS, PhD); communication (MA, PhD); developmental science (MS, PhD); economics (MA, PhD); labor studies (MS); political science (MA, PhD); psychology of peace and violence (MS, PhD); public policy and administration (MPPA); social and behavioral sciences (MA, MPPA, MS, PhD); social psychology (MS, PhD); sociology (MA, PhD); union leadership and administration (MS). *Application deadline:* Applications are processed on a rolling basis. *Application fee:* $50 ($65 for international students). Electronic applications accepted. *Application Contact:* Jean M. Ames, Supervisor of Admissions, 413-545-0722, Fax: 413-577-0010, E-mail: gradadm@grad.umass.edu. *Dean*, Dr. Janet Rifkin, 413-545-4173, Fax: 413-577-0905.

Isenberg School of Management Students: 216 full-time (93 women), 866 part-time (265 women); includes 153 minority (29 African Americans, 5 American Indian/Alaska Native, 98 Asian Americans or Pacific Islanders, 21 Hispanic Americans), 115 international. Average age 34. 778 applicants, 63% accepted, 358 enrolled. *Faculty:* 78 full-time (18 women). Expenses: Contact institution. *Financial support:* In 2008–09, 13 fellowships with full tuition reimbursements (averaging $8,445 per year), 90 research assistantships with full tuition reimbursements (averaging $9,175 per year), 72 teaching assistantships with full tuition reimbursements (averaging $8,424 per year) were awarded; career-related internships or fieldwork, Federal Work-Study, scholarships/grants, traineeships, and unspecified assistantships also available. Support available to part-time students. Financial award application deadline: 2/1. In 2008, 337 master's, 11 doctorates awarded. *Degree program information:* Part-time and evening/weekend programs available. Postbaccalaureate distance learning degree programs offered (no on-campus study). Offers accounting (MS); business administration (MBA); hospitality and tourism management (MS); management (MBA, MS, PMBA, PhD); sport management (MS, PhD). *Application deadline:* For fall admission, 2/1 for domestic and international students. Applications are processed on a rolling basis. *Application fee:* $50 ($65 for international students). Electronic applications accepted. *Application Contact:* Jean M. Ames, Supervisor of Admissions, 413-545-0722, Fax: 413-577-0010, E-mail: gradadm@grad.umass.edu. *Dean*, Dr. D. Anthony Butterfield, 415-545-5583, Fax: 413-577-2234.

School of Education Students: 383 full-time (265 women), 345 part-time (238 women); includes 122 minority (63 African Americans, 3 American Indian/Alaska Native, 21 Asian Americans or Pacific Islanders, 35 Hispanic Americans), 102 international. Average age 36. 633 applicants, 62% accepted, 229 enrolled. *Faculty:* 75 full-time (41 women). Expenses: Contact institution. *Financial support:* In 2008–09, 5 fellowships with full tuition reimbursements (averaging $3,167 per year), 97 research assistantships with full tuition reimbursements (averaging $9,362 per year), 74 teaching assistantships with full tuition reimbursements (averaging $5,800 per year) were awarded; career-related internships or fieldwork, Federal Work-Study, scholarships/grants, traineeships, and unspecified assistantships also available. Support available to part-time students. Financial award application deadline: 1/15. In 2008, 245 master's, 46 doctorates awarded. *Degree program information:* Part-time programs available. Postbaccalaureate distance learning degree programs offered (minimal on-campus study). Offers bilingual, English as a second language, and multicultural education (M Ed, CAGS); child and family studies (Ed D, CAGS); child study and early education (M Ed); education (M Ed, Ed D, PhD, CAGS); educational administration (M Ed, CAGS); educational policy and leadership (Ed D); elementary teacher education (M Ed, CAGS); higher education (M Ed, CAGS); international education (M Ed); language, literacy and culture (Ed D); learning, media and technology (CAGS); mathematics, science, and learning technologies (Ed D); policy studies in education (CAGS); reading and writing (M Ed); research and evaluation methods (Ed D); school counselor education (M Ed, CAGS); school psychology (CAGS); secondary teacher education (M Ed, CAGS); social justice education (M Ed, Ed D, CAGS); special education (M Ed, Ed D, CAGS); teacher education and school improvement (Ed D). *Application deadline:* For fall admission, 1/15 for domestic and international students. Applications are processed on a rolling basis. *Application fee:* $50 ($65 for international students). Electronic applications accepted. *Application Contact:* Jean M. Ames, Supervisor of Admissions, 413-545-0722, Fax: 413-577-0010, E-mail: gradadm@grad.umass.edu. *Dean*, Dr. Christine B. McCormick, 413-545-6984, Fax: 413-545-4240.

School of Nursing Students: 32 full-time (31 women), 84 part-time (79 women); includes 15 minority (10 African Americans, 2 Asian Americans or Pacific Islanders, 3 Hispanic Americans), 5 international. Average age 44. 107 applicants, 53% accepted, 35 enrolled. *Faculty:* 18 full-time (all women). Expenses: Contact institution. *Financial support:* In 2008–09, 33 fellowships with full tuition reimbursements (averaging $4,428 per year), 2 research assistantships with full tuition reimbursements (averaging $4,290 per year), 20 teaching assistantships with full tuition reimbursements (averaging $9,155 per year) were awarded; career-related internships or fieldwork, Federal Work-Study, scholarships/grants, traineeships, tuition waivers (full), and unspecified assistantships also available. Support available to part-time students. Financial award application deadline: 2/1. In 2008, 6 master's, 3 doctorates awarded. *Degree program information:* Part-time programs available. Postbaccalaureate distance learning degree programs offered (minimal on-campus study). Offers nursing (MS, DNP, PhD). *Application deadline:* For fall admission, 2/1 for domestic and international students. Applications are processed on a rolling basis. *Application fee:* $50 ($65 for international students). Electronic applications accepted. *Application Contact:* Jean M. Ames, Supervisor of Admissions, 413-545-0722, Fax: 413-577-0010, E-mail: gradadm@grad.umass.edu. *Graduate Program Director*, Dr. M. Christine King, 413-577-2322, Fax: 413-577-2550.

School of Public Health and Health Sciences Students: 206 full-time (162 women), 241 part-time (154 women); includes 54 minority (24 African Americans, 19 Asian Americans or Pacific Islanders, 11 Hispanic Americans), 82 international. Average age 34. 660 applicants, 50% accepted, 158 enrolled. *Faculty:* 78 full-time (47 women). Expenses: Contact institution. *Financial support:* In 2008–09, 4 fellowships with full tuition reimbursements (averaging $8,560 per year), 101 research assistantships with full tuition reimbursements (averaging $8,022 per year), 76 teaching assistantships with full tuition reimbursements (averaging $6,811 per year) were awarded; career-related internships or fieldwork, Federal Work-Study, scholarships/grants, traineeships, tuition waivers (full), and unspecified assistantships also available. Support available to part-time students. Financial award application deadline: 2/1. In 2008, 129 master's, 6 doctorates awarded. *Degree program information:* Part-time programs available. Postbaccalaureate distance learning degree programs offered (no on-campus study). Offers communication disorders (MA, Au D, PhD); kinesiology (MS, PhD); nutrition (MPH, MS); public health (PhD); public health and health sciences (MA, MPH, MS, Au D, PhD). *Application deadline:* For fall admission, 2/1 for domestic and international students. Applications are processed on a rolling basis. *Application fee:* $50 ($65 for international students). Electronic applications accepted. *Application Contact:* Jean M. Ames, Supervisor of Admissions, 413-545-0722, Fax: 413-577-0010, E-mail: gradadm@grad.umass.edu. *Dean*, Dr. C. Marjorie Aelion, 413-545-2526, Fax: 413-545-0501.

UNIVERSITY OF MASSACHUSETTS BOSTON, Boston, MA 02125-3393

General Information State-supported, coed, university. CGS member. *Graduate housing:* On-campus housing not available. *Research affiliation:* John F. Kennedy Presidential Library (twentieth century history and politics).

GRADUATE UNITS

Office of Graduate Studies *Degree program information:* Part-time and evening/weekend programs available. Postbaccalaureate distance learning degree programs offered.

College of Liberal Arts *Degree program information:* Part-time and evening/weekend programs available. Offers American studies (MA); applied sociology (MA); archival methods (MA); bilingual education (MA); clinical psychology (PhD); English (MA); English as a second language (MA); foreign language pedagogy (MA); historical archaeology (MA); history (MA); liberal arts (MA, PhD).

College of Management *Degree program information:* Part-time and evening/weekend programs available. Offers business administration (MBA); management (MBA).

College of Nursing and Health Sciences *Degree program information:* Part-time and evening/weekend programs available. Offers nursing (MS, PhD).

College of Public and Community Service *Degree program information:* Part-time and evening/weekend programs available. Offers dispute resolution (MA, Certificate); human services (MS); public and community service (MA, MS, Certificate).

College of Science and Mathematics *Degree program information:* Part-time and evening/weekend programs available. Offers applied physics (MS); biology (MS); biotechnology and biomedical science (MS); chemistry (MS); computer science (MS, PhD); environmental biology (PhD); environmental sciences (MS); environmental, earth and ocean sciences (PhD); molecular, cellular and organismal biology (PhD); science and mathematics (MS, PhD).

Division of Continuing Education *Degree program information:* Part-time and evening/weekend programs available. Offers continuing education (Certificate); women in politics and government (Certificate).

Graduate College of Education *Degree program information:* Part-time and evening/weekend programs available. Offers critical and creative thinking (MA, Certificate); education (M Ed, Ed D); educational administration (M Ed, CAGS); elementary and secondary education/certification (M Ed); family therapy (M Ed, CAGS); forensic counseling (M Ed, CAGS); higher education administration (Ed D); instructional design (M Ed); mental health counseling (M Ed, CAGS); rehabilitation counseling (M Ed, CAGS); school guidance counseling (M Ed, CAGS); school psychology (M Ed, CAGS); special education (M Ed); teacher certification (M Ed); urban school leadership (Ed D).

John W. McCormack Graduate School of Policy Studies *Degree program information:* Part-time and evening/weekend programs available. Offers gerontology (MA, MS, PhD, Certificate); gerontology research (MA); management in aging services (MA); public affairs (MS); public policy (PhD); women in politics and government (Certificate). Certificate program in women in politics and government offered jointly with Division of Continuing Education.

UNIVERSITY OF MASSACHUSETTS DARTMOUTH, North Dartmouth, MA 02747-2300

General Information State-supported, coed, university. *Enrollment:* 9,155 graduate, professional, and undergraduate students; 315 full-time matriculated graduate/professional students (136 women), 625 part-time matriculated graduate/professional students (352 women). *Enrollment by degree level:* 735 master's, 63 doctoral, 142 other advanced degrees. *Graduate faculty:* 279 full-time (104 women), 156 part-time/adjunct (80 women). Tuition, state resident: full-time $2071; part-time $86.29 per credit. Tuition, nonresident: full-time $8099; part-time $337.46 per credit. *Required fees:* $7946. Tuition and fees vary according to class time, course load and reciprocity agreements. *Graduate housing:* Room and/or apartments available on a first-come, first-served basis to single students; on-campus housing not available to married students. Typical cost: $6693 per year. Housing application deadline: 3/14. *Student services:* Campus employment opportunities, campus safety program, career counseling, child daycare facilities, exercise/wellness program, free psychological counseling, grant writing training, international student services, low-cost health insurance, multicultural affairs office, services for students with disabilities, teacher training, writing training. *Library facilities:* University of Massachusetts Dartmouth Library. *Online resources:* library catalog, web page, access to other libraries' catalogs. *Collection:* 463,000 titles, 2,783 serial subscriptions, 8,200 audiovisual materials. *Research affiliation:* National Aeronautics and Space Administration (NASA) (SMAST), National Oceanic and Atmospheric Administration (NOAA) (marine sciences), Cape Cod Cranberry Growers Association (agriculture), Woods Hole Oceanographic Institution (marine sciences), Office of Naval Research (ONR) (mechanical), National Textile Center (materials).

Computer facilities: 368 computers available on campus for general student use. A campuswide network can be accessed from student residence rooms and from off campus. Online class registration is available. *Web address:* http://www.umassd.edu/.

General Application Contact: Elan Turcotte-Shamski, Graduate Admissions Officer, 508-999-8604, Fax: 508-999-8183, E-mail: graduate@umassd.edu.

GRADUATE UNITS

Graduate School Students: 315 full-time (136 women), 625 part-time (352 women); includes 60 minority (23 African Americans, 2 American Indian/Alaska Native, 15 Asian Americans or Pacific Islanders, 20 Hispanic Americans), 223 international. Average age 32. 795 applicants, 75% accepted, 304 enrolled. *Faculty:* 279 full-time (104 women), 156 part-time/adjunct (80 women). Expenses: Contact institution. *Financial support:* In 2008–09, 1 fellowship with full tuition reimbursement (averaging $16,614 per year), 133 research assistantships with full tuition reimbursements (averaging $11,484 per year), 152 teaching assistantships with full tuition reimbursements (averaging $6,858 per year) were awarded; career-related internships or fieldwork, Federal Work-Study, scholarships/grants, and unspecified assistantships also available. Support available to part-time students. Financial award application deadline: 3/1; financial award applicants required to submit FAFSA. In 2008, 295 master's, 2 doctorates, 24 other advanced degrees awarded. *Degree program information:* Part-time programs available. Offers biomedical engineering and biotechnology (PhD). *Application deadline:* Applications are processed on a rolling basis. *Application fee:* $40 ($60 for international students). Electronic applications accepted. *Application Contact:* Elan Turcotte-Shamski, Graduate Admissions Officer, 508-999-8604, Fax: 508-999-8183, E-mail: graduate@umassd.edu. *Director for Graduate Studies and Admissions*, Scott Webster, 508-999-8202, Fax: 508-999-8183, E-mail: swebster@umassd.edu.

Charlton College of Business Students: 56 full-time (26 women), 123 part-time (52 women); includes 15 minority (6 African Americans, 1 American Indian/Alaska Native, 4 Asian Americans or Pacific Islanders, 4 Hispanic Americans), 26 international. Average age 32. 153 applicants, 75% accepted, 71 enrolled. *Faculty:* 43 full-time (10 women), 36 part-time/adjunct (7 women). Expenses: Contact institution. *Financial support:* In 2008–09, 6 research assistantships with full tuition reimbursements (averaging $4,500 per year), 3 teaching assistantships with full tuition reimbursements (averaging $3,778 per year) were awarded; Federal Work-Study and unspecified assistantships also available. Support available to part-time students. Financial award application deadline: 3/1; financial award applicants required to submit FAFSA. In 2008, 89 master's, 17 other advanced degrees awarded. *Degree program information:* Part-time programs available. Offers accounting (Postbaccalaureate Certificate); business (MBA, PMC, Postbaccalaureate Certificate); business administration (MBA); e-commerce (PMC); finance (PMC); general management (PMC); leadership (PMC); management (Postbaccalaureate Certificate); marketing (PMC); supply chain management (PMC). *Application deadline:* For fall admission, 6/1 for domestic students, 4/1 for international students; for spring admission, 10/1 for domestic students, 8/1 for international students. *Application fee:* $40 ($60 for international students). Electronic applications accepted. *Application Contact:* Elan Turcotte-Shamski, Graduate Admissions Officer, 508-999-8604, Fax: 508-999-8183, E-mail: graduate@umassd.edu. *Assistant Dean*, Dr. Dan Braha, 508-910-6961, Fax: 508-999-8779, E-mail: dbraha@umassd.edu.

College of Arts and Sciences Students: 55 full-time (31 women), 76 part-time (51 women); includes 16 minority (6 African Americans, 4 Asian Americans or Pacific Islanders, 6 Hispanic Americans), 18 international. Average age 31. 94 applicants, 60% accepted, 35 enrolled. *Faculty:* 80 full-time (30 women), 53 part-time/adjunct (32 women). Expenses: Contact institution. *Financial support:* In 2008–09, 18 research assistantships with full tuition reimbursements (averaging $8,826 per year), 45 teaching assistantships with full tuition reimbursements (averaging $10,707 per year) were awarded; career-related internships or fieldwork, Federal Work-Study, and unspecified assistantships also available. Support available to part-time students. Financial award application deadline: 3/1; financial award applicants required to submit FAFSA. In 2008, 36 master's awarded. *Degree program information:* Part-time programs available. Offers arts and sciences (MA, MS, PhD, PMC, Postbaccalaureate Certificate); behavior analyst (PMC); biology (MS); chemistry (MS, PhD); clinical psychology (MA); general psychology (MA); Luso-Afro-Brazilian studies (PhD); marine biology (MS); Portuguese (MA); professional writing (MA, Postbaccalaureate Certificate). *Application fee:* $40 ($60 for international students). *Application Contact:* Elan Turcotte-Shamski, Graduate Admissions Officer, 508-999-8604, Fax: 508-999-8183, E-mail: graduate@umassd.edu. *Dean*, Dr. William Hogan, 508-999-8200, Fax: 508-999-8183, E-mail: whogan@umassd.edu.

College of Engineering Students: 105 full-time (26 women), 128 part-time (28 women); includes 6 minority (2 African Americans, 3 Asian Americans or Pacific Islanders, 1 Hispanic American), 157 international. Average age 27. 282 applicants, 77% accepted, 62 enrolled. *Faculty:* 62 full-time (8 women), 22 part-time/adjunct (5 women). Expenses: Contact institution. *Financial support:* In 2008–09, 1 fellowship with full tuition reimbursement (averaging $16,614 per year), 59 research assistantships with full tuition reimbursements (averaging $9,854 per year), 65 teaching assistantships with full tuition reimbursements (averaging $6,384 per year) were awarded; Federal Work-Study and unspecified assistantships also available. Support available to part-time students. Financial award application deadline: 3/1; financial award applicants required to submit FAFSA. In 2008, 81 master's, 2 doctorates awarded. *Degree program information:* Part-time programs available. Offers acoustics (Postbaccalaureate Certificate); civil and environmental engineering (MS); communications (Postbaccalaureate Certificate); computer engineering (MS, PhD); computer networks and distributed systems (Postbaccalaureate Certificate); computer science (MS); computer systems (Postbaccalaureate Certificate); computer systems engineering (Postbaccalaureate Certificate); digital signal processing (Postbaccalaureate Certificate); electrical engineering (MS, PhD); electrical engineering systems (Postbaccalaureate Certificate); engineering (MS, PhD, Postbaccalaureate Certificate); mechanical engineering (MS); physics (MS); software development and design (Postbaccalaureate Certificate); textile chemistry (MS); textile technology (MS). *Application deadline:* For fall admission, 4/20 for domestic students, 2/20 for international students; for spring admission, 11/15 for domestic students, 9/15 for international students. Applications are processed on a rolling basis. *Application fee:* $40 ($60 for international students). Electronic applications accepted. *Application Contact:* Elan Turcotte-Shamski, Graduate Admissions Officer, 508-999-8604, Fax: 508-999-8183, E-mail: graduate@umassd.edu. *Dean*, Dr. Robert Peck, 508-999-8539, Fax: 508-999-9137, E-mail: rpeck@umassd.edu.

College of Nursing Students: 1 (woman) full-time, 70 part-time (66 women); includes 3 minority (2 African Americans, 1 American Indian/Alaska Native). Average age 42. 28 applicants, 93% accepted, 19 enrolled. *Faculty:* 30 full-time (all women), 25 part-time/adjunct (all women). Expenses: Contact institution. *Financial support:* In 2008–09, 8 teaching assistantships with full tuition reimbursements (averaging $2,375 per year) were awarded; Federal Work-Study and scholarships/grants also available. Support available to part-time students. Financial award application deadline: 3/1; financial award applicants required to submit FAFSA. In 2008, 19 master's, 1 other advanced degree awarded. *Degree program information:* Part-time programs available. Offers adult health/adult nurse practitioner (MS); adult health/advanced practice (MS); adult nurse practitioner (PMC); community nursing/advanced practice (MS); individualized nursing (PMC); nursing (PhD). *Application deadline:* For fall admission, 4/20 for domestic students, 2/20 for international students; for spring admission, 11/15 for domestic students, 9/15 for international students. *Application fee:* $40 ($60 for international students). Electronic applications accepted. *Application Contact:* Elan Turcotte-Shamski, Graduate Admissions Officer, 508-999-8604, Fax: 508-999-8183, E-mail: graduate@umassd.edu. *Director*, Dr. Gail Russell, 508-999-8251, Fax: 508-999-9127, E-mail: grussell@umassd.edu.

College of Visual and Performing Arts Students: 38 full-time (28 women), 44 part-time (27 women); includes 5 minority (3 Asian Americans or Pacific Islanders, 2 Hispanic Americans), 6 international. Average age 33. 84 applicants, 54% accepted, 20 enrolled. *Faculty:* 38 full-time (17 women), 15 part-time/adjunct (8 women). Expenses: Contact institution. *Financial support:* In 2008–09, 4 research assistantships with full tuition reimbursements (averaging $3,950 per year), 30 teaching assistantships with full tuition reimbursements (averaging $3,500 per year) were awarded; Federal Work-Study and unspecified assistantships also available. Support available to part-time students. Financial award application deadline: 3/1; financial award applicants required to submit FAFSA. In 2008, 28 master's awarded. *Degree program information:* Part-time programs available. Offers art education (MAE); ceramics (MFA, Postbaccalaureate Certificate); digital media (MFA); drawing (MFA); fibers (MFA); fibers/textiles (Postbaccalaureate Certificate); graphic design (MFA); illustration (MFA); jewelry/metals (MFA, Postbaccalaureate Certificate); painting (MFA); photography (MFA); printmaking (MFA); sculpture (MFA); typography (MFA); visual and performing arts (MAE, MFA, Postbaccalaureate Certificate); wood/furniture design (MFA, Postbaccalaureate Certificate). *Application deadline:* Applications are processed on a rolling basis. *Application fee:* $40 ($60 for international students). Electronic applications accepted. *Application Contact:* Elan Turcotte-Shamski, Graduate Admissions Officer, 508-999-8604, Fax: 508-999-8183, E-mail: graduate@umassd.edu. *Dean*, Adrian Tio, 508-999-9295, Fax: 508-999-9126, E-mail: atio@umassd.edu.

School of Education, Public Policy, and Civic Engagement Students: 24 full-time (13 women), 167 part-time (116 women); includes 12 minority (6 African Americans, 6 Hispanic Americans). Average age 36. 119 applicants, 93% accepted, 79 enrolled. *Faculty:* 14 full-time (8 women), 5 part-time/adjunct (3 women). Expenses: Contact institution. *Financial support:* In 2008–09, 1 research assistantship with full tuition reimbursement (averaging $9,000 per year) was awarded; Federal Work-Study, scholarships/grants, and unspecified assistantships also available. Support available to part-time students. Financial award application deadline: 3/1; financial award applicants required to submit FAFSA. In 2008, 39 master's, 6 other advanced degrees awarded. *Degree program information:* Part-time programs available. Offers education, public policy, and civic engagement (MAT, MPP, Postbaccalaureate Certificate); elementary education (MAT, Postbaccalaureate Certificate); environmental policy (Postbaccalaureate Certificate); middle school education (MAT); principal initial licensure (Postbaccalaureate Certificate); public policy (MPP); secondary school education (MAT). *Application deadline:* For fall admission, 4/20 for domestic students, 2/20 for international students; for spring admission, 11/15 for domestic students, 9/15 for international students. *Application fee:* $40 ($60 for international students). Electronic applications accepted. *Application Contact:* Elan Turcotte-Shamski, Graduate Admissions Officer, 508-999-8604, Fax: 508-999-8183, E-mail: graduate@umassd.edu. *Interim Dean*, Dr. Ismael Ramirez-Soto, 508-999-9051, E-mail: iramirezsoto@umassd.edu.

School of Marine Science and Technology Students: 36 full-time (11 women), 17 part-time (12 women); includes 3 minority (1 African American, 1 Asian American or Pacific Islander, 1 Hispanic American), 16 international. Average age 30. 35 applicants, 66% accepted, 18 enrolled. *Faculty:* 12 full-time (1 woman). Expenses: Contact institution. *Financial support:* In 2008–09, 45 research assistantships with full tuition reimbursements (averaging $16,340 per year), 1 teaching assistantship with full tuition reimbursement (averaging $10,340 per year) were awarded. Financial award application deadline: 3/1; financial award applicants required to submit FAFSA. In 2008, 3 master's awarded. Offers marine science and technology (MS, PhD). *Application deadline:* For fall admission, 4/20 priority date for domestic students, 2/20 for international students. Applications are processed on a rolling basis. *Application fee:* $40 ($60 for international students). Electronic applications accepted. *Application Contact:* Elan Turcotte-Shamski, Graduate Admissions Officer, 508-999-8604, Fax: 508-999-8183, E-mail: graduate@umassd.edu. *Associate Dean*, Dr. Avijit Gangopadhyay, 508-910-6330, Fax: 508-999-8197, E-mail: agangopadhya@umassd.edu.

UNIVERSITY OF MASSACHUSETTS LOWELL, Lowell, MA 01854-2881

General Information State-supported, coed, university. *Graduate housing:* Rooms and/or apartments available on a first-come, first-served basis to single students and available to married students. Housing application deadline: 4/1.

GRADUATE UNITS

College of Arts and Sciences *Degree program information:* Part-time and evening/weekend programs available. Offers analytical chemistry (PhD); applied mathematics (MS); applied mechanics (PhD); applied physics (MS, PhD); arts and sciences (MA, MM, MS, PhD, Sc D, Graduate Certificate); atmospheric science (MS, PhD); biochemistry (PhD); biological sciences (MS); biotechnology (MS); chemistry (MS, PhD); community social psychology (MA); computational mathematics (PhD); computer science (MS, PhD, Sc D); criminal justice and criminology (MA); environmental studies (PhD); green chemistry (PhD); inorganic chemistry (PhD); mathematics (MS); music education (MM); organic chemistry (PhD); physics (MS, PhD); polymer science (MS); radiological science and protection (MS); regional economic and social development (MA, Graduate Certificate); sound recording technology (MM).

College of Management *Degree program information:* Part-time and evening/weekend programs available. Offers business administration (MBA); foundations of business (Graduate Certificate); new venture creation (Graduate Certificate).

Graduate School of Education *Degree program information:* Part-time and evening/weekend programs available. Postbaccalaureate distance learning degree programs offered (no on-campus study). Offers administration, planning, and policy (CAGS); curriculum and instruction (M Ed, CAGS); educational administration (M Ed); language arts and literacy (Ed D); leadership in schooling (Ed D); math and science education (Ed D); reading and language (M Ed, CAGS). Electronic applications accepted.

James B. Francis College of Engineering *Degree program information:* Part-time and evening/weekend programs available. Offers chemical engineering (MS Eng, D Eng, PhD); civil and environmental engineering (MS Eng, Certificate); computer engineering (MS Eng); elastomers (Graduate Certificate); electrical engineering (MS Eng, D Eng); energy engineering (MS Eng, D Eng, PhD); engineering (MS Eng, MSES, D Eng, PhD, Certificate, Graduate Certificate); environmental engineering (MSES, D Eng); environmental studies (MSES, PhD, Certificate); mechanical engineering (MS Eng, D Eng, PhD); medical plastics design and manufacturing (Graduate Certificate); plastics design (Graduate Certificate); plastics engineering (MS Eng, D Eng, PhD); plastics engineering fundamentals (Graduate Certificate); plastics materials (Graduate Certificate); plastics processing (Graduate Certificate); polymer science/plastics engineering (PhD); sustainable infrastructure for developing nations (Certificate).

School of Health and Environment *Degree program information:* Part-time programs available. Offers adult psychiatric and mental health nursing (MS, Graduate Certificate); cleaner production and pollution prevention (MS, Sc D); clinical laboratory sciences (MS); clinical pathology (Graduate Certificate); environmental risk assessment (Certificate); epidemiology (MS, Sc D); ergonomics and safety (MS, Sc D); family health nursing (MS); gerontological nursing (MS, Graduate Certificate); geropsychiatric nursing (Graduate Certificate); health and environment (MS, DPT, PhD, Sc D, Certificate, Graduate Certificate); health management and policy (MS, Graduate Certificate); identification and control of ergonomic hazards (Certificate); job stress and healthy job redesign (Certificate); nursing (PhD); nursing education (Graduate Certificate); nutritional sciences (Graduate Certificate); occupational and environmental hygiene (MS, Sc D); palliative and end-of-life nursing care (Graduate Certificate); physical therapy (DPT); public health laboratory sciences (Graduate Certificate); radiological health physics and general work environment protection (Certificate); work environment policy (MS, Sc D).

See Close-Up on page 1025.

UNIVERSITY OF MASSACHUSETTS WORCESTER, Worcester, MA 01655-0115

General Information State-supported, coed, graduate-only institution. CGS member. *Enrollment by degree level:* 445 first professional, 135 master's, 415 doctoral. *Graduate faculty:* 993 full-time (321 women), 131 part-time/adjunct (95 women). Tuition, state resident: full-time $2640. Tuition, nonresident: full-time $9856. Full-time tuition and fees vary according to course load, degree level, program, reciprocity agreements and student level. *Graduate housing:* On-campus housing not available. *Student services:* Campus employment opportunities, campus safety program, career counseling, child daycare facilities, free psychological counseling, grant writing training, international student services, low-cost health insurance, multicultural affairs office, services for students with disabilities, writing training. *Library facilities:* Lamar Soutter Library. *Online resources:* library catalog, web page, access to other libraries' catalogs. *Collection:* 209,411 titles, 4,961 serial subscriptions, 1,530 audiovisual materials. *Research affiliation:* Worcester Polytechnic Institute (biomedical engineering).

Computer facilities: 117 computers available on campus for general student use. A campuswide network can be accessed from off campus. Online class registration, Student account (Bursar) & Blackboard Vista Web management s are available. *Web address:* http://www.umass.edu/.

University of Massachusetts Worcester (continued)

General Application Contact: Karen Lawton, Director of Admissions, 508-856-2303, E-mail: karen.lawton@umassmed.edu.

GRADUATE UNITS

Graduate School of Biomedical Sciences Students: 394 full-time (216 women); includes 29 minority (6 African Americans, 1 American Indian/Alaska Native, 20 Asian Americans or Pacific Islanders, 2 Hispanic Americans), 156 international. Average age 28. 574 applicants, 35% accepted, 84 enrolled. *Faculty:* 239 full-time (61 women), 98 part-time/adjunct (21 women). Expenses: Contact institution. *Financial support:* In 2008–09, 394 students received support, including 394 research assistantships with full tuition reimbursements available (averaging $28,000 per year); scholarships/grants, health care benefits, tuition waivers (full), and unspecified assistantships also available. In 2008, 42 doctorates awarded. Offers biochemistry and molecular pharmacology (PhD); biomedical engineering and medical physics (PhD); biomedical sciences (PhD); cancer biology (PhD); cell biology (PhD); cellular and molecular physiology (PhD); clinical and population health research (PhD); clinical investigation (MS); medical sciences (PhD); molecular genetics and microbiology (PhD); neuroscience (PhD). *Application deadline:* For fall admission, 12/15 for domestic and international students. *Application fee:* $25 ($50 for international students). Electronic applications accepted. *Application Contact:* Michael Cole, Director of Admissions and Recruitment, 508-856-4135, Fax: 508-856-3659, E-mail: michael.cole@umassmed.edu. *Dean,* Dr. Anthony Carruthers, 508-856-4135.

Graduate School of Nursing Students: 147 full-time (128 women), 9 part-time (all women); includes 15 minority (8 African Americans, 1 American Indian/Alaska Native, 6 Asian Americans or Pacific Islanders). Average age 37. 241 applicants, 35% accepted, 52 enrolled. *Faculty:* 15 full-time (13 women), 31 part-time/adjunct (29 women). Expenses: Contact institution. *Financial support:* In 2008–09, 80 students received support. Scholarships/grants and traineeships available. Support available to part-time students. Financial award application deadline: 5/18; financial award applicants required to submit FAFSA. In 2008, 62 master's, 3 doctorates awarded. Offers adult acute/critical care nurse practitioner (MS, Post Master's Certificate); adult acute/critical care nurse practitioner and gerontological nurse practitioner (MS, Post Master's Certificate); adult primary care nurse practitioner (MS, Post Master's Certificate); adult primary care nurse practitioner and gerontological nurse practitioner (Post Master's Certificate); family nurse practitioner (MS); gerontological nurse practitioner (Post Master's Certificate); nurse educator (MS); nursing (PhD). *Application deadline:* For fall admission, 3/15 for domestic students. Applications are processed on a rolling basis. *Application fee:* $40 ($60 for international students). *Application Contact:* Diane Brescia, Admissions Coordinator, 508-856-3488, Fax: 508-856-5851, E-mail: diane.brescia@umassmed.edu. *Dean,* Dr. Paulette Seymour-Route, 508-856-5801, Fax: 508-856-5851, E-mail: Paulette.Seymour-Route@umassmed.edu.

School of Medicine Students: 445 full-time (245 women); includes 93 minority (24 African Americans, 1 American Indian/Alaska Native, 58 Asian Americans or Pacific Islanders, 10 Hispanic Americans). Average age 26. 814 applicants, 24% accepted, 115 enrolled. *Faculty:* 978 full-time (308 women), 100 part-time/adjunct (66 women). Expenses: Contact institution. *Financial support:* In 2008–09, 395 students received support. Institutionally sponsored loans, scholarships/grants, health care benefits, tuition waivers (partial), and unspecified assistantships available. Financial award application deadline: 4/15; financial award applicants required to submit FAFSA. In 2008, 102 MDs awarded. Offers medicine (MD). *Application deadline:* For fall admission, 12/15 for domestic students. *Application fee:* $75. Electronic applications accepted. *Application Contact:* Karen Lawton, Director of Admissions, 508-856-2303, E-mail: karen.lawton@umassmed.edu. *Dean/Provost/Executive Deputy Chancellor,* Dr. Terence R. Plotte, 508-856-8000.

UNIVERSITY OF MEDICINE AND DENTISTRY OF NEW JERSEY, Newark, NJ 07107-1709

General Information State-supported, coed, graduate-only institution. CGS member. *Enrollment:* 3,730 full-time matriculated graduate/professional students (2,094 women), 1,209 part-time matriculated graduate/professional students (908 women). *Enrollment by degree level:* 2,206 first professional, 1,448 master's, 1,153 doctoral, 132 other advanced degrees. *Graduate housing:* Room and/or apartments available on a first-come, first-served basis to single students; on-campus housing not available to married students. Typical cost: $9180 per year. *Student services:* Campus employment opportunities, campus safety program, career counseling, child daycare facilities, exercise/wellness program, free psychological counseling, international student services, low-cost health insurance, multicultural affairs office, services for students with disabilities. *Library facilities:* George F. Smith Library of the Health Sciences plus 3 others. *Online resources:* library catalog, web page. *Collection:* 265,623 titles, 9,545 serial subscriptions, 3,683 audiovisual materials. *Research affiliation:* Robert Wood Johnson University Hospital (adult care hospitalization), Public Health Research Institute (public health), Kessler Institute for Rehabilitation (physical rehabilitation), Coriell Institute for Medical Research (cancer and human development).

Computer facilities: Distance learning, continuing education available. *Web address:* http://www.umdnj.edu/.

General Application Contact: University Registrar, 973-972-5338.

GRADUATE UNITS

Graduate School of Biomedical Sciences Offers biochemistry and molecular biology (MS, PhD); biomedical engineering (MS, PhD, Certificate); biomedical sciences (MBS, MS, PhD, Certificate); biomedical sciences (interdisciplinary) (PhD); cell and molecular biology (MS, PhD); cell biology and molecular medicine (PhD); cellular and molecular pharmacology (MS, PhD); environmental sciences/exposure assessment (PhD); integrative neuroscience (PhD); microbiology and molecular genetics (PhD); molecular biosciences (PhD); molecular genetics, microbiology and immunology (MS, PhD); molecular pathology and immunology (PhD); neuroscience (MS, PhD); pharmacology and physiology (PhD); physiology and integrative biology (MS, PhD). Electronic applications accepted.

New Jersey Dental School Students: 451 full-time (252 women), 2 part-time (1 woman); includes 177 minority (27 African Americans, 1 American Indian/Alaska Native, 125 Asian Americans or Pacific Islanders, 24 Hispanic Americans), 38 international. Average age 26. 2,181 applicants, 8% accepted, 88 enrolled. *Faculty:* 81 full-time (24 women), 122 part-time/adjunct (23 women). Expenses: Contact institution. *Financial support:* Federal Work-Study and scholarships/grants available. Financial award applicants required to submit FAFSA. In 2008, 67 first professional degrees, 11 master's, 14 other advanced degrees awarded. Offers dental science (MS); dentistry (DMD); endodontics (Certificate); oral medicine (Certificate); orthodontics (Certificate); pediatric dentistry (Certificate); periodontics (Certificate); prosthodontics (Certificate). *Application deadline:* For fall admission, 2/1 for domestic students. Applications are processed on a rolling basis. *Application fee:* $75. Electronic applications accepted. *Application Contact:* Dr. Jeffrey Linfante, Director of Admissions and Student Recruitment, 973-972-5362, Fax: 973-972-0309, E-mail: linfante@umdnj.edu. *Dean,* Dr. Cecile A. Feldman, 973-972-4633, Fax: 973-972-3689, E-mail: feldman@umdnj.edu.

New Jersey Medical School Students: 746 full-time (337 women); includes 451 minority (85 African Americans, 268 Asian Americans or Pacific Islanders, 98 Hispanic Americans). Average age 25. 4,244 applicants, 9% accepted, 194 enrolled. *Faculty:* 684 full-time (246 women), 106 part-time/adjunct (42 women). Expenses: Contact institution. *Financial support:* Federal Work-Study, scholarships/grants, and tuition reimbursements available. In 2008, 143 MDs awarded. Offers medicine (MD). *Application deadline:* For fall admission, 12/1 for domestic students. Applications are processed on a rolling basis. *Application fee:* $75. Electronic applications accepted. *Application Contact:* Dr. George F. Heinrich, Assistant Dean for Admissions, 973-972-4631, Fax: 973-972-7986, E-mail: heinrich@umdnj.edu. *Interim Dean,* Dr. Robert L Johnson, 973-972-4538, Fax: 973-972-7104, E-mail: rjohnson@umdnj.edu.

Robert Wood Johnson Medical School Students: 681 full-time (374 women); includes 309 minority (65 African Americans, 1 American Indian/Alaska Native, 214 Asian Americans or Pacific Islanders, 29 Hispanic Americans). Average age 25. 3,368 applicants, 10% accepted, 156 enrolled. *Faculty:* 915 full-time (350 women), 181 part-time/adjunct (104 women). Expenses: Contact institution. *Financial support:* Federal Work-Study and scholarships/grants available. Financial award applicants required to submit FAFSA. In 2008, 152 MDs awarded. Offers medicine (MD). *Application deadline:* For fall admission, 12/1 for domestic students. Applications are processed on a rolling basis. *Application fee:* $75. Electronic applications accepted. *Application Contact:* Dr. David Seiden, Associate Dean for Student Affairs, 732-235-4690, Fax: 732-235-5078, E-mail: seiden@umdnj.edu. *Dean,* Dr. Peter Amenta, 732-235-6300, Fax: 732-235-6315, E-mail: amenta@umdnj.edu.

School of Health Related Professions *Degree program information:* Part-time programs available. Offers biomedical informatics (MS, PhD); cardiopulmonary sciences (PhD); clinical laboratory sciences (PhD); clinical nutrition (MS, DCN); dietetic internship (Certificate); health care informatics (Certificate); health related professions (MPT, MS, DCN, DPT, PhD, Certificate); health sciences (MS, PhD); health systems (MS); interdisciplinary studies (PhD); nurse midwifery (Certificate); nutrition (PhD); physical therapy (MPT); physical therapy (entry level) (DPT); physical therapy (post-professional level) (DPT); physical therapy/movement science (PhD); physician assistant (MS); professional counseling (Certificate); psychiatric rehabilitation (MS, PhD); radiologist assistant (MS); rehabilitation counseling (MS); vocational rehabilitation (MS). Electronic applications accepted.

School of Nursing *Degree program information:* Part-time programs available. Offers adult health (MSN); adult occupational health (MSN); advanced practice nursing (MSN, Post Master's Certificate); family nurse practitioner (MSN); nurse anesthesia (MSN); nursing (MSN); nursing informatics (MSN); urban health (PhD); women's health practitioner (MSN). Electronic applications accepted.

School of Osteopathic Medicine Students: 428 full-time (240 women); includes 198 minority (80 African Americans, 88 Asian Americans or Pacific Islanders, 30 Hispanic Americans). Average age 26. 3,284 applicants, 5% accepted, 108 enrolled. *Faculty:* 182 full-time (67 women), 33 part-time/adjunct (24 women). Expenses: Contact institution. *Financial support:* Federal Work-Study and scholarships/grants available. Financial award applicants required to submit FAFSA. In 2008, 85 DOs awarded. Offers osteopathic medicine (DO). *Application deadline:* For fall admission, 2/1 for domestic students. Applications are processed on a rolling basis. *Application fee:* $90. Electronic applications accepted. *Application Contact:* Dr. Thomas A. Cavalieri, Dean, 856-566-6996, Fax: 856-566-6865, E-mail: cavalita@umdnj.edu. *Dean,* Dr. Thomas A. Cavalieri, 856-566-6996, Fax: 856-566-6865, E-mail: cavalita@umdnj.edu.

UMDNJ–School of Public Health (UMDNJ, Rutgers, NJIT) Newark Campus Offers public health (MPH, Dr PH, PhD, Certificate). Electronic applications accepted.

UMDNJ–School of Public Health (UMDNJ, Rutgers, NJIT) Piscataway/New Brunswick Campus Offers biostatistics (MS); epidemiology (Certificate); general public health (Certificate); public health (MPH, Dr PH, PhD). Electronic applications accepted.

UMDNJ–School of Public Health (UMDNJ, Rutgers, NJIT) Stratford/Camden Campus Offers general public health (Certificate); public health (MPH). Electronic applications accepted.

UNIVERSITY OF MEMPHIS, Memphis, TN 38152

General Information State-supported, coed, university. CGS member. *Enrollment:* 20,214 graduate, professional, and undergraduate students; 1,987 full-time matriculated graduate/professional students (1,089 women), 2,414 part-time matriculated graduate/professional students (1,635 women). *Enrollment by degree level:* 411 first professional, 3,115 master's, 875 doctoral. *Graduate faculty:* 574 full-time (205 women), 70 part-time/adjunct (38 women). Tuition, state resident: full-time $6242; part-time $330 per credit hour. Tuition, nonresident: full-time $17,828; part-time $815 per credit hour. *Required fees:* $1156; $70 per credit hour. *Graduate housing:* Rooms and/or apartments available on a first-come, first-served basis to single students and available to married students. Typical cost: $3480 per year ($5580 including board) for single students. Room and board charges vary according to board plan and housing facility selected. Housing application deadline: 7/1. *Student services:* Campus employment opportunities, campus safety program, career counseling, child daycare facilities, exercise/wellness program, free psychological counseling, grant writing training, international student services, low-cost health insurance, multicultural affairs office, services for students with disabilities, teacher training, writing training. *Library facilities:* McWherter Library plus 4 others. *Online resources:* library catalog, web page, access to other libraries' catalogs. *Collection:* 1.8 million titles, 9,500 serial subscriptions, 30,773 audiovisual materials. *Research affiliation:* Memphis Biotech Foundation, Campbell Clinic Orthopaedics, Federal Express, Oak Ridge National Laboratory, St. Jude Children's Research Hospital, Gulf Coast Research Laboratory.

Computer facilities: 2,000 computers available on campus for general student use. A campuswide network can be accessed from off campus. Online class registration is available. *Web address:* http://www.memphis.edu/.

General Application Contact: Information Contact, 901-678-2531, Fax: 901-678-5023, E-mail: gradsch@memphis.edu.

GRADUATE UNITS

Cecil C. Humphreys School of Law Students: 395 full-time (169 women), 19 part-time (13 women); includes 58 minority (41 African Americans, 3 American Indian/Alaska Native, 10 Asian Americans or Pacific Islanders, 4 Hispanic Americans), 1 international. Average age 26. 1,026 applicants, 30% accepted, 148 enrolled. *Faculty:* 24 full-time (8 women), 22 part-time/adjunct (8 women). Expenses: Contact institution. *Financial support:* In 2008–09, 329 students received support, including 26 research assistantships with full and partial tuition reimbursements available (averaging $3,000 per year), 3 teaching assistantships (averaging $3,000 per year); career-related internships or fieldwork, Federal Work-Study, scholarships/grants, and unspecified assistantships also available. Support available to part-time students. Financial award application deadline: 4/1; financial award applicants required to submit FAFSA. In 2008, 130 JDs awarded. *Degree program information:* Part-time programs available. Offers law (JD). *Application deadline:* For fall admission, 3/1 priority date for domestic and international students. Applications are processed on a rolling basis. *Application fee:* $25 ($40 for international students). Electronic applications accepted. *Application Contact:* Dr. Sue Ann McClellan, Assistant Dean for Law Admissions, Recruiting and Scholarships, 901-678-5403, Fax: 901-678-5210, E-mail: smcclell@memphis.edu. *Dean,* Dr. Kevin H. Smith, 901-678-2421, Fax: 901-678-5210, E-mail: ksmith@memphis.edu.

Graduate School Students: 1,586 full-time (915 women), 2,398 part-time (1,626 women); includes 1,151 minority (1,038 African Americans, 13 American Indian/Alaska Native, 62 Asian Americans or Pacific Islanders, 38 Hispanic Americans), 484 international. Average age 33. 2,666 applicants, 74% accepted, 604 enrolled. *Faculty:* 574 full-time (205 women), 70 part-time/adjunct (38 women). Expenses: Contact institution. *Financial support:* In 2008–09, 127 research assistantships with full tuition reimbursements (averaging $5,200 per year), 234 teaching assistantships with full tuition reimbursements (averaging $5,300 per year) were awarded; fellowships with full tuition reimbursements, career-related internships or fieldwork, Federal Work-Study, institutionally sponsored loans, scholarships/grants, and unspecified assistantships also available. Support available to part-time students. Financial award applicants required to submit CSS PROFILE. In 2008, 861 master's, 126 doctorates, 38 other advanced degrees awarded. *Degree program information:* Part-time and evening/weekend programs available. Postbaccalaureate distance learning degree programs offered. *Application deadline:* For fall admission, 7/1 for domestic students, 5/1 for international students; for spring admission, 12/1 for domestic students, 9/15 for international students. Applications are processed on a rolling basis. *Application fee:* $35 ($60 for international students). Electronic applications accepted. *Application Contact:* Dr. Karen D. Weddle-West, Vice Provost for Graduate Studies, 901-678-4653, Fax: 901-678-0378, E-mail: gradsch@memphis.edu. *Vice Provost for Graduate Studies,* Dr. Karen D. Weddle-West, 901-678-4653, Fax: 901-678-0378, E-mail: gradsch@memphis.edu.

College of Arts and Sciences Students: 647 full-time (343 women), 395 part-time (242 women); includes 199 minority (169 African Americans, 2 American Indian/Alaska Native, 15 Asian Americans or Pacific Islanders, 13 Hispanic Americans), 184 international. Average age 32. 774 applicants, 60% accepted, 237 enrolled. *Faculty:* 242 full-time (78 women), 14 part-time/adjunct (3 women). Expenses: Contact institution. *Financial support:* In 2008–09, 488 students received support; fellowships with full tuition reimbursements available, research assistantships with full tuition reimbursements available, teaching assistantships with full tuition reimbursements available, career-related internships or fieldwork, Federal Work-Study, institutionally sponsored loans, scholarships/grants, and tuition waivers (full and partial) available. Financial award application deadline: 6/1; financial award applicants required to submit FAFSA. In 2008, 210 master's, 47 doctorates, 14 other advanced degrees awarded. *Degree program information:* Part-time and evening/weekend programs available. Offers anthropology (MA); applied computer science (MS); applied mathematics (MS); applied statistics (PhD); arts and sciences (MA, MCRP, MFA, MHA, MPA, MPH, MS, PhD, Graduate Certificate); bioinformatics (MS); biology (MS, PhD); chemistry (MS, PhD); city and regional planning (MCRP); clinical psychology (PhD); computer science (MS, PhD); computer sciences (MS); creative writing (MFA); criminology and criminal justice (MA); earth sciences (MA, MS, PhD, Graduate Certificate); English (MA, Graduate Certificate); experimental psychology (PhD); French (MA); general psychology (MS); health administration (MHA); history (MA, PhD); interdisciplinary studies (MA, MS, Graduate Certificate); mathematics (MS, PhD); nonprofit administration (MPA); philosophy (MA, PhD); physics (MS); political science (MA); public health (MPH); public management and policy (MPA); school psychology (MA, PhD); sociology (MA); Spanish (MA); statistics (MS, PhD); urban management and planning (MPA); writing and language studies (PhD). *Application deadline:* Applications are processed on a rolling basis. *Application fee:* $35 ($60 for international students). *Application Contact:* Dr. Linda Bennett, Associate Dean for Graduate Studies and Research, 901-678-2253, Fax: 901-678-4831, E-mail: lbennett@memphis.edu. *Dean,* Dr. Henry A. Kurtz, 901-678-3067, Fax: 901-678-4831, E-mail: hkurtz@memphis.edu.

College of Communication and Fine Arts Students: 172 full-time (97 women), 90 part-time (45 women); includes 41 minority (34 African Americans, 2 American Indian/Alaska Native, 3 Asian Americans or Pacific Islanders, 2 Hispanic Americans), 32 international. Average age 32. 158 applicants, 73% accepted, 66 enrolled. *Faculty:* 84 full-time (27 women), 8 part-time/adjunct (5 women). Expenses: Contact institution. *Financial support:* In 2008–09, 32 students received support; research assistantships with full tuition reimbursements available, teaching assistantships with full tuition reimbursements available, career-related internships or fieldwork, Federal Work-Study, institutionally sponsored loans, and PhD assistantships available. Financial award application deadline: 6/1; financial award applicants required to submit FAFSA. In 2008, 69 master's, 20 doctorates, 3 other advanced degrees awarded. *Degree program information:* Part-time programs available. Postbaccalaureate distance learning degree programs offered (no on-campus study). Offers applied music (M Mu, DMA); architecture (M Arch); art (Graduate Certificate); art history (MA); ceramics (MFA); communication (MA); communication and fine arts (M Arch, M Mu, MA, MFA, DMA, PhD, Graduate Certificate); communication arts (PhD); composition (M Mu, DMA); conducting (M Mu, DMA); film and video production (MA); general journalism (MA); graphic design (MFA); historical musicology (PhD); interior design (MFA); jazz and studio performance (M Mu); journalism administration (MA); music education (M Mu, DMA); musicology (M Mu); painting (MFA); printmaking/photography (MFA); sculpture (MFA); theatre (MFA). *Application deadline:* For fall admission, 8/1 for domestic students; for spring admission, 12/1 for domestic students. Applications are processed on a rolling basis. *Application fee:* $35 ($60 for international students). *Application Contact:* Moira J. Logan, Associate Dean/Director of Research and Graduate Studies, 901-678-2350, Fax: 901-678-5118, E-mail: mlogan1@memphis.edu. *Dean,* Dr. Richard R. Ranta, 901-678-2350, Fax: 901-678-5118, E-mail: rranta@memphis.edu.

College of Education Students: 262 full-time (205 women), 819 part-time (616 women); includes 475 minority (452 African Americans, 6 American Indian/Alaska Native, 8 Asian Americans or Pacific Islanders, 9 Hispanic Americans), 30 international. Average age 34. 335 applicants, 70% accepted, 100 enrolled. *Faculty:* 104 full-time (55 women), 38 part-time/adjunct (28 women). Expenses: Contact institution. *Financial support:* In 2008–09, 889 students received support; research assistantships with tuition reimbursements available, teaching assistantships with tuition reimbursements available, career-related internships or fieldwork, scholarships/grants, tuition waivers (partial), and community assistantships available. Financial award application deadline: 6/1; financial award applicants required to submit FAFSA. In 2008, 268 master's, 42 doctorates, 1 other advanced degree awarded. *Degree program information:* Part-time and evening/weekend programs available. Offers adult education (Ed D); clinical nutrition (MS); community education (Ed D); counseling (MS, Ed D); counseling psychology (PhD); early childhood education (MAT, MS, Ed D); education (M Ed, MAT, MS, Ed D, PhD, Ed S, Graduate Certificate); educational leadership (Ed D); educational psychology and research (MS, PhD); elementary education (MAT); exercise and sport science (MS); health promotion (MS); higher education (Ed D); instruction and curriculum (MS, Ed D); instruction design and technology (MS, Ed D); leadership (MS); middle grades education (MAT); physical education teacher education (MS); policy studies (Ed D); reading (MS, Ed D); school administration and supervision (MS); secondary education (MAT); special education (MAT, MS, Ed D); sport and leisure commerce (MS); student personnel (MS). *Application deadline:* Applications are processed on a rolling basis. *Application fee:* $35 ($60 for international students). *Application Contact:* Dr. Ernest A. Rakow, Associate Dean of Administration and Graduate Programs, 901-678-2363, Fax: 901-678-4778, E-mail: erakow@memphis.edu. *Dean,* Dr. Donald J. Wagner, 901-678-4265, Fax: 901-678-4778, E-mail: djwagner@memphis.edu.

Fogelman College of Business and Economics Students: 237 full-time (108 women), 203 part-time (65 women); includes 64 minority (43 African Americans, 2 American Indian/Alaska Native, 15 Asian Americans or Pacific Islanders, 4 Hispanic Americans), 129 international. Average age 30. 265 applicants, 68% accepted, 94 enrolled. *Faculty:* 60 full-time (9 women), 4 part-time/adjunct (0 women). Expenses: Contact institution. *Financial support:* In 2008–09, 160 students received support; research assistantships with tuition reimbursements available, teaching assistantships with tuition reimbursements available, career-related internships or fieldwork, scholarships/grants, and unspecified assistantships available. Financial award application deadline: 6/1; financial award applicants required to submit FAFSA. In 2008, 170 master's, 8 doctorates awarded. *Degree program information:* Part-time programs available. Offers accounting (MBA, MS, PhD); accounting systems (MS); business and economics (IMBA, MA, MBA, MS, PhD); economics (MA, PhD); executive business administration (MBA); finance (PhD); finance, insurance, and real estate (MBA, MS); international business administration (IMBA); management (MBA, MS, PhD); management information systems (MBA, MS, PhD); management science (MBA); marketing (MBA, MS); marketing and supply chain management (PhD); real estate development (MS); taxation (MS). *Application deadline:* For fall admission, 8/1 for domestic students; for spring admission, 12/1 for domestic students. *Application fee:* $35 ($60 for international students). *Application Contact:* Dr. Carol V. Danehower, Associate Dean for Programs, 901-678-3721, Fax: 901-678-4705, E-mail: fcbegp@memphis.edu. *Dean,* Rajiv Grover, 901-678-2940, Fax: 901-678-3759, E-mail: rgrover@memphis.edu.

Herff College of Engineering Students: 109 full-time (30 women), 38 part-time (12 women); includes 11 African Americans, 3 Asian Americans or Pacific Islanders, 67 international. Average age 29. 86 applicants, 76% accepted, 33 enrolled. *Faculty:* 36 full-time (4 women), 3 part-time/adjunct (0 women). Expenses: Contact institution. *Financial support:* In 2008–09, 31 students received support; fellowships with full tuition reimbursements available, research assistantships with full tuition reimbursements available, teaching assistantships with full tuition reimbursements available, career-related internships or fieldwork, tuition waivers (full and partial), and unspecified assistantships available. Financial award application deadline: 6/1. In 2008, 30 master's, 2 doctorates awarded. *Degree program information:* Part-time programs available. Offers automatic control systems (MS); biomedical engineering (MS, PhD); biomedical systems (MS); civil engineering (PhD); communications and propagation systems (MS); computer engineering technology (MS); design and mechanical engineering (MS); electrical engineering (PhD); electronics engineering technology (MS); energy systems (MS); engineering (MS, PhD); engineering computer systems (MS); environmental engineering (MS); foundation engineering (MS); industrial engineering (MS); manufacturing engineering technology (MS); mechanical engineering (PhD); mechanical systems (MS); power systems (MS); structural engineering (MS); transportation engineering (MS); water resources engineering (MS). *Application deadline:* For fall admission, 8/1 for domestic students; for spring admission, 12/1 for domestic students. *Application fee:* $35 ($60 for international students). Electronic applications accepted. *Application Contact:* Dr. Steven M. Slack, Associate Dean, 901-678-4791, Fax: 901-678-4180, E-mail: sslack@memphis.edu. *Dean,* Dr. Richard C. Warder, 901-678-4306, Fax: 901-678-4180, E-mail: rcwarder@memphis.edu.

School of Audiology and Speech-Language Pathology Students: 78 full-time (74 women), 6 part-time (all women); includes 6 minority (3 African Americans, 3 Asian Americans or Pacific Islanders), 5 international. Average age 26. 167 applicants, 40% accepted, 26 enrolled. *Faculty:* 15 full-time (7 women). Expenses: Contact institution. *Financial support:* In 2008–09, 56 students received support; research assistantships with full tuition reimbursements available. Financial award application deadline: 6/1; financial award applicants required to submit FAFSA. In 2008, 21 master's, 7 doctorates awarded. *Degree program information:* Part-time programs available. Offers audiology and speech-language pathology (MA, Au D, PhD). *Application deadline:* For fall admission, 2/1 for domestic students. *Application fee:* $35 ($60 for international students). *Application Contact:* Dr. David J. Wark, Coordinator of Graduate Studies, 901-678-5891, E-mail: dwark@memphis.edu. *Dean,* Dr. Maurice Mendel, 901-678-5800, Fax: 901-525-1282, E-mail: dlluna@memphis.edu.

University College Students: 19 full-time (14 women), 83 part-time (59 women); includes 46 African Americans, 1 Asian American or Pacific Islander. Average age 41. 52 applicants, 85% accepted, 6 enrolled. *Faculty:* 8 full-time (4 women). Expenses: Contact institution. *Financial support:* In 2008–09, 98 students received support; research assistantships with full tuition reimbursements available, teaching assistantships, unspecified assistantships available. Financial award application deadline: 6/1; financial award applicants required to submit FAFSA. In 2008, 43 master's awarded. *Degree program information:* Part-time and evening/weekend programs available. Offers liberal studies (MALS); merchandising and consumer science (MS); strategic leadership (MPS). *Application deadline:* For fall admission, 7/1 for domestic students, 5/1 for international students; for spring admission, 11/1 for domestic students, 9/15 for international students. Applications are processed on a rolling basis. *Application fee:* $35 ($60 for international students). Electronic applications accepted. *Application Contact:* Dr. Herbert McCree, Coordinator of Graduate Studies, 901-678-4171, Fax: 901-678-3363, E-mail: hmccree@memphis.edu. *Dean,* Dr. Dan Lattimore, 901-678-2991.

Loewenberg School of Nursing Students: 21 full-time (20 women), 175 part-time (164 women); includes 60 minority (56 African Americans, 4 Asian Americans or Pacific Islanders), 1 international. Average age 35. 140 applicants, 76% accepted, 37 enrolled. *Faculty:* 18 full-time (17 women), 1 (woman) part-time/adjunct. Expenses: Contact institution. *Financial support:* In 2008–09, 141 students received support. Application deadline: 6/1. In 2008, 51 master's, 1 other advanced degree awarded. Offers nursing (MSN, Graduate Certificate). *Application fee:* $35 ($60 for international students). *Application Contact:* Dr. Robert Koch, Associate Dean/Director of Graduate Studies, 901-678-2003, Fax: 901-678-4906, E-mail: rkoch@memphis.edu. *Dean,* Dr. Marjorie Luttrell, 901-678-2003, Fax: 901-678-4906, E-mail: mluttrel@memphis.edu.

See Close-Up on page 1027.

UNIVERSITY OF MIAMI, Coral Gables, FL 33124

General Information Independent, coed, university. CGS member. *Enrollment:* 15,323 graduate, professional, and undergraduate students; 4,377 full-time matriculated graduate/professional students (2,060 women), 406 part-time matriculated graduate/professional students (257 women). *Enrollment by degree level:* 2,100 first professional, 1,597 master's, 1,073 doctoral, 13 other advanced degrees. *Graduate faculty:* 917 full-time (256 women), 13 part-time/adjunct (5 women). *Tuition:* Full-time $25,632; part-time $1424 per credit. *Required fees:* $274; $102 per semester. Tuition and fees vary according to course load, campus/location and program. *Graduate housing:* On-campus housing not available. *Student services:* Campus employment opportunities, campus safety program, career counseling, child daycare facilities, exercise/wellness program, free psychological counseling, grant writing training, international student services, low-cost health insurance, multicultural affairs office, services for students with disabilities, teacher training, writing training. *Library facilities:* Otto G. Richter Library plus 7 others. *Online resources:* library catalog, web page, access to other libraries' catalogs. *Collection:* 3.2 million titles, 62,621 serial subscriptions, 140,145 audiovisual materials. *Research affiliation:* Howard Hughes Medical Institute (Biology), The Buoniconti Fund: Miami Project to Cure Paralysis (Paralysis research), Organization for Tropical Studies, National Center for Atmospheric Research (Atmospheric Science).

Computer facilities: Computer purchase and lease plans are available. 1,800 computers available on campus for general student use. A campuswide network can be accessed from student residence rooms and from off campus. Online class registration, online student account information are available. *Web address:* http://www.miami.edu/.

General Application Contact: Office of Graduate Studies, 305-284-4154.

GRADUATE UNITS

Graduate School Students: 2,248 full-time (1,075 women), 338 part-time (218 women); includes 697 minority (134 African Americans, 2 American Indian/Alaska Native, 86 Asian Americans or Pacific Islanders, 475 Hispanic Americans), 594 international. Average age 30. 3,874 applicants, 39% accepted, 663 enrolled. *Faculty:* 917 full-time (256 women), 13 part-time/adjunct (5 women). Expenses: Contact institution. *Financial support:* In 2008–09, 1,742 students received support, including 91 fellowships with full and partial tuition reimbursements available (averaging $20,708 per year), 232 research assistantships with full and partial tuition reimbursements available (averaging $20,376 per year), 499 teaching assistantships with full and partial tuition reimbursements available (averaging $16,360 per year); career-related internships or fieldwork, Federal Work-Study, institutionally sponsored loans, scholarships/grants, traineeships, health care benefits, tuition waivers (full and partial), and unspecified assistantships also available. Support available to part-time students. Financial award application deadline: 3/1; financial award applicants required to submit FAFSA. In 2008, 910 master's, 173 doctorates, 23 other advanced degrees awarded. *Degree program information:* Part-time and evening/weekend programs available. Postbaccalaureate distance learning degree programs offered. Offers advanced professional studies (MS Ed, Ed S); bilingual and bicultural counseling (Certificate); biochemistry and molecular biology (PhD); cancer biology (PhD); counseling (MS Ed, Certificate); counseling and research (MS Ed); counseling psychology (PhD); early childhood special education (Ed S); education (MS Ed, PhD, Certificate, Ed S); elementary education-initial certification/TESOL (MS Ed); epidemiology (PhD); exceptional student education, pre–K disabilities and ESOL (MS Ed, Ed S); exceptional student education, pre-k disabilities and ESOL (MS Ed, Ed S); exceptional student education, reading and ESOL (MS Ed, Ed S); exercise physiology (MS Ed, PhD); higher education administration (MS Ed, Ed D, Certificate); higher education administration/enrollment management (Certificate); higher education leadership (Ed D); international administration (MAIA); language and literacy learning in multilingual settings (PhD); marriage and family therapy (MS Ed); mathematics and science education (PhD); medicine (MD, MPH, MSPH, DPT, PhD); mental health counseling (MS Ed); microbiology and immunology (PhD); molecular and cellular pharmacology (PhD); molecular cell and developmental biology (PhD); neuroscience (PhD); physical therapy (DPT, PhD); physiology and biophysics (PhD); public health (MPH, MSPH); reading (MS Ed, Ed S); research, measurement, and evaluation (MS Ed, PhD); special education (PhD); sport administration (MS Ed); sports medicine (MS Ed); teaching and learning (PhD, Certificate). *Application fee:* $50. Electronic applications accepted. *Application Contact:* Sandra Abraham, Assistant Dean, 305-284-4154, E-mail: graduateschool@miami.edu. *Dean,* Dr. Terri A. Scandura, 305-284-4154, Fax: 305-284-5441, E-mail: graduateschool@miami.edu.

College of Arts and Sciences Students: 471 full-time (263 women), 83 part-time (61 women); includes 150 minority (31 African Americans, 20 Asian Americans or Pacific Islanders, 99 Hispanic Americans), 139 international. Average age 30. 1,041 applicants, 28% accepted, 128 enrolled. *Faculty:* 271 full-time (81 women), 1 part-time/adjunct (0 women). Expenses: Contact institution. *Financial support:* In 2008–09, 489 students received support, including 44 fellowships with full tuition reimbursements available (averaging $18,800 per year), 48 research assistantships with full tuition reimbursements available (averaging $18,800 per year), 238 teaching assistantships with full tuition reimbursements available (averaging $18,800 per year); scholarships/grants, traineeships, health care benefits, and unspecified assistantships also available. Financial award application deadline:

University of Miami (continued)

3/1; financial award applicants required to submit FAFSA. In 2008, 98 master's, 42 doctorates awarded. *Degree program information:* Part-time and evening/weekend programs available. Offers adult clinical (PhD); art history (MA); arts and sciences (MA, MAIA, MALS, MFA, MPA, MS, PhD); behavioral neuroscience (PhD); biology (MS, PhD); ceramics/glass (MFA); chemistry (MS); child clinical (PhD); computer science (MS, PhD); creative writing (MFA); developmental psychology (PhD); English (MA, PhD); genetics and evolution (MS, PhD); geography (MA); graphic design/multimedia (MFA); health clinical (PhD); history (MA, PhD); inorganic chemistry (PhD); international studies (MA, PhD); Latin American studies (MA); liberal studies (MALS); mathematics (MA, MS, PhD); organic chemistry (PhD); painting (MFA); philosophy (MA, PhD); photography/digital imaging (MFA); physical chemistry (PhD); physics (MS, PhD); political science (MPA); printmaking (MFA); psychology (MS); romance studies (PhD); sculpture (MFA); sociology (MA, PhD). *Application deadline:* For fall admission, 1/15 for domestic students. Applications are processed on a rolling basis. *Application fee:* $65. Electronic applications accepted. *Application Contact:* Dr. Charles Mallery, Associate Dean, 305-284-3188, Fax: 305-284-5673, E-mail: gradadmin@mail.as.miami.edu. *Dean,* Dr. Michael R. Halleran, 305-284-4117, Fax: 305-284-5673, E-mail: gradadmin@mail.as.miami.edu.

College of Engineering Students: 168 full-time (46 women), 33 part-time (9 women); includes 61 minority (15 African Americans, 16 Asian Americans or Pacific Islanders, 30 Hispanic Americans), 88 international. Average age 30. 250 applicants, 50% accepted, 38 enrolled. *Faculty:* 59 full-time (6 women), 1 (woman) part-time/adjunct. Expenses: Contact institution. *Financial support:* In 2008–09, 127 students received support, including 6 fellowships with full tuition reimbursements available (averaging $20,400 per year), 47 research assistantships with full tuition reimbursements available (averaging $20,400 per year), 37 teaching assistantships with full tuition reimbursements available (averaging $20,400 per year); career-related internships or fieldwork, institutionally sponsored loans, scholarships/grants, health care benefits, tuition waivers (partial), and unspecified assistantships also available. Support available to part-time students. Financial award application deadline: 12/1; financial award applicants required to submit FAFSA. In 2008, 73 master's, 17 doctorates awarded. *Degree program information:* Part-time and evening/weekend programs available. Offers architectural engineering (MSAE); biomedical engineering (MSBE, PhD); civil engineering (MSCE, PhD); electrical and computer engineering (MSECE, PhD); engineering (MS, MSAE, MSBE, MSCE, MSECE, MSEVH, MSIE, MSME, MSOES, PhD); environmental health and safety (MS); ergonomics (PhD); industrial engineering (MSIE, PhD); management of technology (MS); mechanical and aerospace engineering (MSME, PhD); occupational ergonomics and safety (MS, MSOES). *Application deadline:* For fall admission, 12/1 priority date for domestic and international students; for spring admission, 11/1 priority date for domestic and international students. Applications are processed on a rolling basis. *Application fee:* $65. Electronic applications accepted. *Application Contact:* Sharon D. Manjarres, Staff Associate, 305-284-2942, Fax: 305-284-2885, E-mail: s.manjarres@miami.edu. *Dean,* Dr. James M Tien, 305-284-2404, Fax: 305-284-4792, E-mail: gradadm.eng@miami.edu.

Frost School of Music Students: 181 full-time (74 women), 4 part-time (2 women); includes 26 minority (4 African Americans, 1 American Indian/Alaska Native, 5 Asian Americans or Pacific Islanders, 16 Hispanic Americans), 42 international. Average age 28. 323 applicants, 47% accepted, 75 enrolled. *Faculty:* 48 full-time (12 women). Expenses: Contact institution. *Financial support:* In 2008–09, 145 students received support, including 1 fellowship with full tuition reimbursement available (averaging $22,000 per year), 89 teaching assistantships with full tuition reimbursements available (averaging $12,000 per year); career-related internships or fieldwork, Federal Work-Study, and tuition waivers (full and partial) also available. Financial award application deadline: 2/1. In 2008, 41 master's, 21 doctorates awarded. Offers accompanying and chamber music (MM, DMA); choral conducting (MM, DMA); composition (MM, DMA); electronic music (MM); instrumental conducting (MM, DMA); instrumental performance (MM, DMA, AD); jazz composition (DMA); jazz pedagogy (MM); jazz performance (MM, DMA); keyboard performance and pedagogy (MM, DMA); media writing and production (MM); multiple woodwinds (MM, DMA); music (MM, MS, DMA, PhD, AD, Spec M); music business and entertainment industries (MM); music education (MM, PhD, Spec M); music engineering (MS); music theory (MM); music therapy (MM); musicology (MM); piano performance (MM, DMA, AD); studio jazz writing (MM); vocal pedagogy (DMA); vocal performance (MM, DMA, AD). *Application deadline:* For fall admission, 2/1 priority date for domestic and international students; for spring admission, 11/1 priority date for domestic and international students. Applications are processed on a rolling basis. *Application fee:* $65. Electronic applications accepted. *Application Contact:* Dr. Edward Paul Asmus, Associate Dean for Graduate Studies, 305-284-2241, Fax: 305-284-6475, E-mail: ed.asmus@miami.edu. *Dean,* Shelton Berg, 305-284-2241, Fax: 305-284-6475, E-mail: sberg@miami.edu.

Rosenstiel School of Marine and Atmospheric Science Students: 191 full-time (90 women), 9 part-time (4 women); includes 16 minority (7 African Americans, 1 Asian American or Pacific Islander, 8 Hispanic Americans), 58 international. Average age 28. 230 applicants, 38% accepted, 48 enrolled. *Faculty:* 99 full-time (19 women), 95 part-time/adjunct (21 women). Expenses: Contact institution. *Financial support:* In 2008–09, 177 students received support, including 35 fellowships with full tuition reimbursements available (averaging $25,287 per year), 74 research assistantships with full tuition reimbursements available (averaging $25,287 per year), 49 teaching assistantships with full tuition reimbursements available (averaging $25,287 per year); career-related internships or fieldwork, Federal Work-Study, institutionally sponsored loans, scholarships/grants, and unspecified assistantships also available. Financial award application deadline: 1/1; financial award applicants required to submit FAFSA. In 2008, 24 master's, 17 doctorates awarded. *Degree program information:* Part-time programs available. Offers applied marine physics (MS, PhD); marine affairs and policy (MA, MS); marine and atmospheric chemistry (MS, PhD); marine and atmospheric science (MA, MS, PhD); marine biology and fisheries (MA, MS, PhD); marine geology and geophysics (MS, PhD); meteorology (MS, PhD); physical oceanography (MS, PhD). *Application deadline:* For fall admission, 1/1 priority date for domestic and international students. Applications are processed on a rolling basis. *Application fee:* $65. Electronic applications accepted. *Application Contact:* Dr. Larry Peterson, Associate Dean, 305-421-4155, Fax: 305-421-4771, E-mail: gso@rsmas.miami.edu. *Dean,* Dr. Roni Avissar, 305-421-4000, Fax: 305-421-4711, E-mail: gso@rsmas.miami.edu.

School of Architecture Students: 58 full-time (25 women), 9 part-time (4 women); includes 18 minority (4 African Americans, 1 Asian American or Pacific Islander, 13 Hispanic Americans), 5 international. Average age 28. 111 applicants, 68% accepted, 26 enrolled. *Faculty:* 27 full-time (4 women), 1 part-time/adjunct (0 women). Expenses: Contact institution. *Financial support:* In 2008–09, 60 students received support, including 13 research assistantships (averaging $2,000 per year), 16 teaching assistantships (averaging $2,000 per year); career-related internships or fieldwork, Federal Work-Study, institutionally sponsored loans, scholarships/grants, tuition waivers (partial), and unspecified assistantships also available. Support available to part-time students. Financial award application deadline: 2/1; financial award applicants required to submit FAFSA. In 2008, 19 master's awarded. Offers architecture (M Arch); suburb and town design (M Arch). *Application deadline:* For fall admission, 2/1 priority date for domestic students, 2/1 for international students. Applications are processed on a rolling basis. *Application fee:* $65. Electronic applications accepted. *Application Contact:* Jude Alexander, Coordinator, 305-284-3060, Fax: 305-284-6879, E-mail: jude@miami.edu. *Director of Graduate Studies,* Teofilo Victoria, 305-284-3060, Fax: 305-284-6879, E-mail: tvictoria@miami.edu.

School of Business Administration Students: 557 full-time (197 women), 26 part-time (11 women); includes 163 minority (16 African Americans, 18 Asian Americans or Pacific Islanders, 129 Hispanic Americans), 114 international. Average age 30. 608 applicants, 43% accepted, 92 enrolled. *Faculty:* 105 full-time (25 women). Expenses: Contact institution. *Financial support:* In 2008–09, 184 students received support, including 2 fellowships with full tuition reimbursements available (averaging $20,000 per year), 10 research assistantships with full and partial tuition reimbursements available (averaging $20,000 per year), 5 teaching assistantships with full and partial tuition reimbursements available (averaging $20,000 per year); career-related internships or fieldwork, Federal Work-Study, institutionally sponsored loans, scholarships/grants, and unspecified assistantships also available. Support available to part-time students. Financial award application deadline: 3/1; financial award applicants required to submit FAFSA. In 2008, 411 master's, 1 doctorate awarded. *Degree program information:* Part-time and evening/weekend programs available. Offers accounting (MBA); business administration (MA, MBA, MP Acc, MS, MS Tax, MSPM, PhD); computer information systems (MBA); economic development (MA, PhD); environmental economics (PhD); executive and professional (MBA); finance (MBA); human resource economics (MA, PhD); international business (MBA); international economics (MA, PhD); macroeconomics (PhD); management (MBA); management science (MBA); marketing (MBA); professional accounting (MP Acc); professional management (MSPM); taxation (MS Tax). *Application deadline:* For fall admission, 6/30 priority date for domestic and international students; for spring admission, 10/31 priority date for domestic and international students. Applications are processed on a rolling basis. *Application fee:* $65. Electronic applications accepted. *Application Contact:* Christina Raecke, Director of Graduate Business Recruiting and Admissions, 305-284-4607, Fax: 305-284-1878, E-mail: mba@miami.edu. *Vice Dean,* Dr. Anuj Mehrotra, 305-284-2510, Fax: 305-284-5905, E-mail: mba@miami.edu.

School of Communication Students: 98 full-time (54 women), 10 part-time (3 women); includes 33 minority (7 African Americans, 2 Asian Americans or Pacific Islanders, 24 Hispanic Americans), 18 international. Average age 26. 320 applicants, 48% accepted, 50 enrolled. *Faculty:* 39 full-time (12 women). Expenses: Contact institution. *Financial support:* In 2008–09, 70 students received support, including 1 fellowship with full tuition reimbursement available (averaging $15,700 per year), 43 teaching assistantships with full tuition reimbursements available (averaging $15,700 per year); Federal Work-Study, institutionally sponsored loans, scholarships/grants, tuition waivers (partial), and unspecified assistantships also available. Financial award application deadline: 3/1; financial award applicants required to submit FAFSA. In 2008, 48 master's awarded. *Degree program information:* Part-time programs available. Offers communication (PhD); communication studies (MA); film studies (MA, PhD); motion pictures (MFA); print journalism (MA); public relations (MA); Spanish language journalism (MA); television broadcast journalism (MA). *Application deadline:* For fall admission, 12/15 priority date for domestic and international students. Applications are processed on a rolling basis. *Application fee:* $65. Electronic applications accepted. *Application Contact:* Dr. Leonardo C. Ferreira, Director of Graduate Studies, 305-284-3180, Fax: 305-284-8701, E-mail: lferreira@miami.edu. *Dean,* Dr. Sam L. Grogg, 305-284-3420, Fax: 305-284-2454, E-mail: sgrogg@miami.edu.

School of Nursing and Health Studies Students: 80 full-time (61 women), 37 part-time (34 women); includes 58 minority (16 African Americans, 5 Asian Americans or Pacific Islanders, 37 Hispanic Americans), 5 international. Average age 35. 224 applicants, 44% accepted, 69 enrolled. *Faculty:* 15 full-time (11 women). Expenses: Contact institution. *Financial support:* In 2008–09, 67 students received support, including 1 fellowship (averaging $36,000 per year), 6 research assistantships with tuition reimbursements available (averaging $36,000 per year), 4 teaching assistantships with tuition reimbursements available (averaging $36,000 per year); Federal Work-Study, institutionally sponsored loans, scholarships/grants, and unspecified assistantships also available. Support available to part-time students. Financial award application deadline: 3/1; financial award applicants required to submit FAFSA. In 2008, 23 master's, 2 doctorates awarded. *Degree program information:* Part-time programs available. Offers acute care (MSN); nursing (PhD); primary care (MSN). *Application deadline:* For fall admission, 4/30 priority date for domestic students; for spring admission, 11/1 priority date for domestic students. Applications are processed on a rolling basis. *Application fee:* $65. Electronic applications accepted. *Application Contact:* Anne Stabb, Graduate Advisor, 305-284-2533, Fax: 305-284-4827, E-mail: astabb@miami.edu. *Dean,* Dr. Nilda Peragallo, 305-284-2107, Fax: 305-667-3787, E-mail: nperagallo@miami.edu.

UNIVERSITY OF MICHIGAN, Ann Arbor, MI 48109

General Information State-supported, coed, university. CGS member. *Enrollment:* 41,028 graduate, professional, and undergraduate students; 13,110 full-time matriculated graduate/professional students (6,032 women), 1,924 part-time matriculated graduate/professional students (717 women). *Enrollment by degree level:* 3,727 first professional, 6,212 master's, 5,091 doctoral, 15,034 other advanced degrees. *Graduate faculty:* 5,290 full-time (1,851 women), 1,230 part-time/adjunct (606 women). Tuition, state resident: full-time $16,162. Tuition, nonresident: full-time $32,876. Tuition and fees vary according to course level, course load, degree level, program and student level. *Graduate housing:* Rooms and/or apartments available to single and married students. Typical cost: $11,320 (including board) for single students; $11,320 (including board) for married students. Room and board charges vary according to board plan, campus/location and housing facility selected. *Student services:* Campus employment opportunities, campus safety program, career counseling, child daycare facilities, exercise/wellness program, free psychological counseling, grant writing training, international student services, low-cost health insurance, multicultural affairs office, services for students with disabilities, teacher training, writing training. *Library facilities:* University Library plus 24 others. *Online resources:* library catalog, web page, access to other libraries' catalogs. *Collection:* 8.2 million titles, 74,022 serial subscriptions, 102,217 audiovisual materials.

Computer facilities: Computer purchase and lease plans are available. 2,254 computers available on campus for general student use. A campuswide network can be accessed from student residence rooms and from off campus. Online class registration, personal webpages are available. *Web address:* http://www.umich.edu/.

General Application Contact: Admissions Office, 734-764-8129, Fax: 734-647-7740, E-mail: rackadmis@umich.edu.

GRADUATE UNITS

College of Pharmacy Offers medicinal chemistry (PhD); pharmaceutical sciences (PhD); pharmacy (Pharm D, PhD); social and administrative sciences (PhD).

Horace H. Rackham School of Graduate Studies Students: 6,431 full-time (2,865 women), 1,054 part-time (505 women); includes 1,110 minority (327 African Americans, 24 American Indian/Alaska Native, 506 Asian Americans or Pacific Islanders, 253 Hispanic Americans), 2,523 international. Average age 28. 17,725 applicants, 33% accepted, 2303 enrolled. Expenses: Contact institution. *Financial support:* Fellowships with full and partial tuition reimbursements, research assistantships with full and partial tuition reimbursements, teaching assistantships with full and partial tuition reimbursements, career-related internships or fieldwork, Federal Work-Study, scholarships/grants, traineeships, health care benefits, and unspecified assistantships available. Support available to part-time students. In 2008, 1,688 master's, 745 doctorates, 2 other advanced degrees awarded. Offers biological chemistry (PhD); biomedical sciences (PhD); biophysics (PhD); cell and developmental biology (PhD); cellular and molecular biology (PhD); education and psychology (PhD); English and education (PhD); human genetics (MS, PhD); immunology (PhD); microbiology and immunology (PhD); modern Middle Eastern and North African studies (AM); molecular and cellular pathology (PhD); molecular and integrative physiology (PhD); neuroscience (PhD); pharmacology (PhD); survey methodology (MS, PhD, Certificate). *Application deadline:* Applications are processed on a rolling basis. *Application fee:* $60 ($75 for international students). Electronic applications accepted. *Application Contact:* Admissions Office, 734-764-8129, E-mail: rackadmis@umich.edu. *Dean of the Graduate School and Vice President for Academic Affairs,* Dr. Janet A. Weiss, 734-764-4400.

College of Engineering Students: 2,218 full-time (467 women), 300 part-time (50 women); includes 318 minority (71 African Americans, 1 American Indian/Alaska Native, 182 Asian Americans or Pacific Islanders, 64 Hispanic Americans), 1,293 international. Average age 27. 5,388 applicants, 36% accepted, 734 enrolled. *Faculty:* 331 full-time (50 women). Expenses: Contact institution. *Financial support:* In 2008–09, fellowships with full tuition reimbursements (averaging $15,000 per year), research assistantships with full tuition reimbursements (averaging $15,000 per year), teaching assistantships with full tuition reimbursements (averaging $15,000 per year) were awarded; career-related internships or fieldwork, Federal Work-Study, institutionally sponsored loans, scholarships/grants, traineeships, health care benefits, tuition waivers (full and partial), and unspecified assistantships also available. Support available to part-time students. Financial award applicants required to submit FAFSA. In 2008, 782 master's, 240 doctorates awarded. *Degree program information:* Part-time programs available. Postbaccalaureate distance learning degree programs offered (no on-campus study). Offers aerospace engineering (M Eng, MS, MSE,

PhD); atmospheric (MS); atmospheric and space sciences (PhD); automotive engineering (M Eng); biomedical engineering (MS, MSE, PhD); chemical engineering (MSE, PhD, Ch E); civil engineering (MSE, PhD, CE); computer science and engineering (MS, MSE, PhD); concurrent marine design (M Eng); construction engineering and management (M Eng, MSE); electrical engineering (MS, MSE, PhD); electrical engineering systems (MS, MSE, PhD); energy systems engineering (MESE); engineering (M Eng, MESE, MS, MSE, D Eng, PhD, CE, Certificate, Ch E, Mar Eng, Nav Arch, Nuc E); environmental engineering (MSE, PhD); financial engineering (MS); geoscience and remote sensing (PhD); global automotive and manufacturing engineering (M Eng); industrial and operations engineering (MS, MSE, PhD); integrated microsystems (M Eng); macromolecular science and engineering (MS, MSE, PhD); manufacturing (M Eng, D Eng); materials science and engineering (MS, PhD); mechanical engineering (MSE, PhD); naval architecture and marine engineering (MS, MSE, PhD, Mar Eng, Nav Arch); nuclear engineering (Nuc E); nuclear engineering and radiological sciences (MSE, PhD); nuclear science (MS, PhD); pharmaceutical engineering (M Eng); space and planetary sciences (PhD); space engineering (M Eng); space sciences (MS); structural engineering (M Eng). *Application deadline:* Applications are processed on a rolling basis. *Application fee:* $60 ($75 for international students). Electronic applications accepted. *Application Contact:* Prof. S. Jack Hu, Associate Dean, Research and Graduate Education, 734-647-7030, Fax: 734-647-7045, E-mail: jackhu@umich.edu. *Chair*, Prof. David C. Munson, 734-647-7010, Fax: 734-647-7009, E-mail: munson@umich.edu.

College of Literature, Science, and the Arts Students: 1,977 full-time (968 women). Expenses: Contact institution. *Financial support:* Fellowships with full and partial tuition reimbursements, research assistantships with full and partial tuition reimbursements, teaching assistantships with full and partial tuition reimbursements, career-related internships or fieldwork, Federal Work-Study, institutionally sponsored loans, scholarships/grants, traineeships, health care benefits, tuition waivers (full and partial), and unspecified assistantships available. Support available to part-time students. In 2008, 353 master's, 281 doctorates awarded. Offers American culture (AM, PhD); analytical chemistry (PhD); ancient Israel/Hebrew Bible (AM, PhD); anthropology (PhD); anthropology and history (PhD); applied and interdisciplinary mathematics (AM, MS, PhD); applied economics (AM); applied physics (PhD); applied statistics (AM); Arabic (AM, PhD); Armenian (AM, PhD); Asian languages and cultures (MA, PhD); Asian studies: China (AM, Graduate Certificate); astronomy and astrophysics (PhD); biopsychology (PhD); chemical biology (PhD); Christianity in late antiquity (PhD); classical art and archaeology (PhD); classical studies (PhD); clinical psychology (PhD); cognition and perception (PhD); communication studies (PhD); comparative literature (PhD); creative writing (MFA); developmental psychology (PhD); early Christian studies (AM, PhD); ecology and evolutionary biology (MS, PhD); ecology and evolutionary biology-Frontiers (MS); economics (AM, PhD); Egyptology (AM, PhD); English and education (PhD); English and women's studies (PhD); English language and literature (PhD); French (PhD); general linguistics (PhD); geology (MS, PhD); German (AM, PhD); Greek (AM); Greek and Roman history (PhD, Certificate); Hebrew (AM); Hebrew literature (PhD); history (PhD); history and women's studies (PhD); history of art (PhD); inorganic chemistry (PhD); Islamic studies (AM, PhD); Japanese studies (AM); Latin (AM); lesbian, gay, bisexual, transgender, queer (LGBTQ) studies (Certificate); linguistics and Germanic languages and literatures (PhD); literature, science, and the arts (AM, MA, MAT, MFA, MS, PhD, Certificate, Graduate Certificate); material chemistry (PhD); mathematics (AM, MS, PhD); medieval and early modern studies (Certificate); Mesopotamian and ancient Near Eastern studies (AM, PhD); molecular, cellular, and developmental biology (MS, PhD); oceanography: marine geology and geochemistry (MS, PhD); organic chemistry (PhD); Persian (AM, PhD); personality and social contexts (PhD); philosophy (AM, PhD); physical chemistry (PhD); physics (MS, PhD); political science (AM, PhD); psychology and women's studies (PhD); public policy and economics (PhD); public policy and sociology (PhD); Rabbinic literature (PhD); Romance linguistics (PhD); Russian (AM); Russian and East European studies (AM, Certificate); screen arts and cultures (PhD, Certificate); Slavic languages and literatures (PhD); social psychology (PhD); social work and economics (PhD); social work and political science (PhD); social work and sociology (PhD); sociology (PhD); sociology and women's studies (PhD); South Asian studies (MA, Certificate); Southeast Asian studies (MA, Graduate Certificate); Spanish (PhD); statistics (AM, PhD); teaching Latin (MAT); teaching of Arabic as a foreign language (AM); Turkish (AM, PhD); women's studies (Certificate); women's studies and sociology (PhD). *Application fee:* $60 ($75 for international students). Electronic applications accepted. *Application Contact:* Rackham Graduate School Admissions Office, 734-764-8129, E-mail: rackadmis@umich.edu. *Dean*, Dr. Terrence J. McDonald, 734-764-1817.

Gerald R. Ford School of Public Policy *Degree program information:* Part-time programs available. Offers public policy (MPA, MPP, PhD). Electronic applications accepted.

School of Art and Design Students: 26 full-time (18 women); includes 2 minority (1 African American, 1 Hispanic American), 2 international. Average age 30. 68 applicants, 21% accepted, 9 enrolled. *Faculty:* 44 full-time, 20 part-time/adjunct. Expenses: Contact institution. *Financial support:* In 2008–09, 26 students received support, including 30 fellowships with full and partial tuition reimbursements available, 50 teaching assistantships with full and partial tuition reimbursements available; research assistantships with full and partial tuition reimbursements available, Federal Work-Study, scholarships/grants, health care benefits, tuition waivers (partial), and unspecified assistantships also available. Support available to part-time students. Financial award application deadline: 3/15; financial award applicants required to submit FAFSA. In 2008, 10 master's awarded. Offers art and design (MFA). *Application deadline:* For fall admission, 1/1 for domestic and international students. *Application fee:* $55. Electronic applications accepted. *Application Contact:* Dr. Bradley R. Smith, Associate Dean for Graduate Studies, 734-647-3504, Fax: 734-936-0469, E-mail: brdsmith@umich.edu. *Dean*, Bryan Rogers, 734-763-4093, Fax: 734-615-9753, E-mail: blrogers@umich.edu.

School of Education Students: 431 full-time (312 women), 69 part-time (52 women); includes 91 minority (41 African Americans, 29 Asian Americans or Pacific Islanders, 21 Hispanic Americans), 26 international. 667 applicants, 45% accepted, 180 enrolled. *Faculty:* 52 full-time (30 women). Expenses: Contact institution. *Financial support:* In 2008–09, 429 fellowships (averaging $3,696 per year), 196 research assistantships with full tuition reimbursements (averaging $16,070 per year), 71 teaching assistantships with full tuition reimbursements (averaging $16,135 per year) were awarded; career-related internships or fieldwork, Federal Work-Study, institutionally sponsored loans, scholarships/grants, health care benefits, tuition waivers, and unspecified assistantships also available. Support available to part-time students. Financial award applicants required to submit FAFSA. In 2008, 139 master's, 34 doctorates awarded. Offers academic affairs and student development (PhD); cross specialization (PhD); curriculum development (MA); development (AM); early childhood education (MA, PhD); education (AM, MA, MS, PhD); educational administration and policy (MA, PhD); educational foundations and policy (MA, PhD); English education (MA); English language learning in school settings (MA); higher education (AM); individually designed concentration (PhD); learning technologies (MA, PhD); literacy, language, and culture (MA, PhD); mathematics education (MA, PhD); medical and professional education (AM); organizational behavior and management (PhD); postsecondary science education (MS); public policy (PhD); research methods (MA); research, evaluation, and assessment (PhD); science education (MA, PhD); social studies education (MA); teaching and teacher education (PhD). *Application deadline:* For fall admission, 12/1 priority date for domestic students, 12/1 for international students. *Application fee:* $60 ($75 for international students). Electronic applications accepted. *Application Contact:* Roberta Perry, Office of Student Services, 734-764-7563, Fax: 734-763-1495, E-mail: ed.grad.admit@umich.edu. *Dean*, Deborah Loewenberg Ball, 734-615-4415, Fax: 734-764-3473, E-mail: dball@umich.edu.

School of Information *Degree program information:* Part-time programs available. Offers archives and records management (MS); human-computer interaction (MS); information (MS, PhD); information economics, management and policy (MS); library and information services (MS). Electronic applications accepted.

School of Kinesiology Students: 67 full-time (32 women); includes 15 minority (2 African Americans, 1 American Indian/Alaska Native, 7 Asian Americans or Pacific Islanders, 5 Hispanic Americans), 7 international. 93 applicants, 43% accepted, 24 enrolled. *Faculty:* 25 full-time (10 women). Expenses: Contact institution. *Financial support:* In 2008–09, 11 fellowships, 10 research assistantships, 12 teaching assistantships were awarded; Federal Work-Study, scholarships/grants, health care benefits, and unspecified assistantships also available. Financial award application deadline: 1/15. In 2008, 19 master's, 5 doctorates awarded. Offers kinesiology (MS, PhD); sport management (AM). *Application deadline:* For fall admission, 1/15 priority date for domestic students, 1/15 for international students. Applications are processed on a rolling basis. *Application fee:* $60 ($75 for international students). Electronic applications accepted. *Application Contact:* Charlene F. Ruloff, Graduate Program Coordinator, 734-764-1343, Fax: 734-647-2808, E-mail: cruloff@umich.edu. *Interim Dean*, Dr. Gregory D. Cartee, PhD, 734-764-5210.

The School of Music, Theatre, and Dance Students: 280 full-time (145 women); includes 42 minority (18 African Americans, 2 American Indian/Alaska Native, 16 Asian Americans or Pacific Islanders, 6 Hispanic Americans), 57 international. 978 applicants, 32% accepted. *Faculty:* 84 full-time (25 women), 34 part-time/adjunct (10 women). Expenses: Contact institution. *Financial support:* Fellowships, teaching assistantships, career-related internships or fieldwork, Federal Work-Study, institutionally sponsored loans, and scholarships/grants available. Financial award application deadline: 2/1; financial award applicants required to submit FAFSA. In 2008, 76 master's, 29 doctorates awarded. Offers composition (MA, MM, A Mus D); composition and theory (PhD); conducting (MM, A Mus D); design (MFA); media arts (MA); modern dance performance and choreography (MFA); music education (MM, PhD, Spec M); music, theatre, and dance (MA, MFA, MM, A Mus D, PhD, Spec M); musicology (MA, PhD); performance (MM, A Mus D, Spec M); theatre (PhD); theory (MA, PhD). *Application deadline:* For fall admission, 12/1 for domestic and international students; for winter admission, 9/15 for domestic and international students. Applications are processed on a rolling basis. *Application fee:* $60 ($75 for international students). Electronic applications accepted. *Application Contact:* Laura Hoffman, Assistant Dean for Enrollment Management and Student Services, 734-734/764-0593, Fax: 734-763-5097, E-mail: lauras@umich.edu. *Dean*, Christopher Kendall, 734-764-0584, Fax: 734-763-5097, E-mail: ckndll@umich.edu.

School of Nursing *Degree program information:* Part-time programs available. Post-baccalaureate distance learning degree programs offered (minimal on-campus study). Offers adult acute care nurse practitioner (MS); adult nurse practitioner (Post Master's Certificate); adult primary care/adult nurse practitioner (MS); community care (Post Master's Certificate); community care/home care (MS); community health nursing (MS, Post Master's Certificate); family nurse practitioner (MS, Post Master's Certificate); gerontology nurse practitioner (MS); gerontology nursing (MS); gerontology-clinical nurse specialist (MS); infant, child, adolescent health nurse practitioner (MS); medical-surgical clinical nurse specialist (MS); nurse midwifery (MS, Post Master's Certificate); nursing (MS, PhD, Post Master's Certificate); nursing business and health systems (MS); occupational health nursing (MS); parent-child nursing (MS, Post Master's Certificate); psychiatric mental health nurse practitioner (MS); psychiatric mental health nursing (MS); psychiatric mental health nursing- clinical nurse specialist (MS). Electronic applications accepted.

Jean and Samuel Frankel Center for Judaic Studies Students: 7 full-time (5 women), 1 (woman) part-time. Average age 26. 6 applicants, 50% accepted, 1 enrolled. *Faculty:* 27 full-time (12 women). Expenses: Contact institution. *Financial support:* In 2008–09, 14 fellowships were awarded; summer research fellowships also available. In 2008, 1 master's awarded. *Degree program information:* Part-time programs available. Offers Judaic studies (MA, Graduate Certificate). *Application deadline:* For fall admission, 1/10 for domestic and international students; for winter admission, 9/1 for domestic and international students. *Application fee:* $60 ($75 for international students). Electronic applications accepted. *Application Contact:* Tracy Ann Darnell, Student/Fellow Coordinator, 734-615-6097, Fax: 734-936-2186, E-mail: tdarnell@umich.edu. *Director*, Prof. Deborah Dash Moore, 734-763-9047, Fax: 734-936-2186, E-mail: ddmoore@umich.edu.

Law School Students: 1,151 (491 women); includes 276 minority (61 African Americans, 20 American Indian/Alaska Native, 142 Asian Americans or Pacific Islanders, 53 Hispanic Americans), 40 international. 5,577 applicants, 21% accepted, 361 enrolled. *Faculty:* 92 full-time (30 women), 29 part-time/adjunct (12 women). Expenses: Contact institution. *Financial support:* In 2008–09, 1,024 students received support. Career-related internships or fieldwork, Federal Work-Study, institutionally sponsored loans, and scholarships/grants available. Financial award applicants required to submit FAFSA. In 2008, 387 first professional degrees, 43 master's, 5 doctorates awarded. Offers comparative law (MCL); international tax (LL M); law (JD, LL M, SJD). *Application deadline:* For fall admission, 2/15 for domestic students. Applications are processed on a rolling basis. *Application fee:* $60. Electronic applications accepted. *Application Contact:* Sarah C. Zearfoss, Assistant Dean and Director of Admissions, 734-764-0537, Fax: 734-647-3218, E-mail: law.jd.admissions@umich.edu. *Dean*, Evan H. Caminker, 734-764-1358.

Medical School *Degree program information:* Part-time programs available. Offers bioinformatics (MS, PhD); medicine (MD, MS, PhD). Electronic applications accepted.

Ross School of Business at the University of Michigan Students: 1,186 full-time (373 women), 682 part-time (131 women); includes 416 minority (74 African Americans, 8 American Indian/Alaska Native, 280 Asian Americans or Pacific Islanders, 54 Hispanic Americans), 492 international. Average age 28. 3,229 applicants, 23% accepted, 582 enrolled. *Faculty:* 78 full-time (12 women), 47 part-time/adjunct (14 women). Expenses: Contact institution. *Financial support:* In 2008–09, 123 students received support; fellowships, scholarships/grants available. Financial award application deadline: 3/1; financial award applicants required to submit FAFSA. In 2008, 839 master's, 15 doctorates awarded. *Degree program information:* Part-time and evening/weekend programs available. Offers business (M Acc, MBA); business administration (PhD); supply chain management (MSCM). *Application deadline:* For fall admission, 11/1 for domestic and international students; for winter admission, 1/5 for domestic and international students; for spring admission, 3/1 for domestic and international students. *Application fee:* $200. Electronic applications accepted. *Application Contact:* Soojin Kwon Koh, Director of Admissions, 734-763-5796, Fax: 734-763-7804, E-mail: rossmba@umich.edu. *Dean*, Dr. Robert J Dolan, 734-764-1361, Fax: 734-763-0671, E-mail: rjdolan@umich.edu.

School of Dentistry *Degree program information:* Part-time programs available. Offers biomaterials (MS); dental hygiene (MS); dentistry (DDS, MS, PhD, Certificate); endodontics (MS); oral health sciences (PhD); orthodontics (MS); pediatric dentistry (MS); periodontics (MS); prosthodontics (MS); restorative dentistry (MS). Electronic applications accepted.

School of Natural Resources and Environment Students: 283 (148 women); includes 28 minority (8 African Americans, 13 Asian Americans or Pacific Islanders, 7 Hispanic Americans), 24 international. Average age 27. 498 applicants, 65% accepted. *Faculty:* 39 full-time, 23 part-time/adjunct. Expenses: Contact institution. *Financial support:* Fellowships with tuition reimbursements, research assistantships with tuition reimbursements, teaching assistantships with tuition reimbursements, career-related internships or fieldwork, Federal Work-Study, institutionally sponsored loans, scholarships/grants, health care benefits, unspecified assistantships, and Peace Corps Fellows available. Support available to part-time students. Financial award application deadline: 1/5; financial award applicants required to submit FAFSA. In 2008, 76 master's, 10 doctorates awarded. Offers aquatic sciences: research and management (MS); behavior, education and communication (MS); conservation biology (MS); environmental informatics (MS); environmental justice (MS); environmental policy and planning (MS); industrial ecology (Certificate); landscape architecture (MLA, PhD); natural resources and environment (MS, PhD); spatial analysis (Certificate); sustainable systems (MS); terrestrial ecosystems (MS). *Application deadline:* For fall admission, 1/5 priority date for domestic and international students. Applications are processed on a rolling basis. *Application fee:* $60 ($75 for international students). Electronic applications accepted. *Application Contact:* Adam D Ancira, Recruiting and Admissions Coordinator, 734-764-6453, Fax: 734-936-2195, E-mail: snre.gradteam@umich.edu. *Dean*, Dr. Rosina Bierbaum, 734-764-2550, Fax: 734-763-8965, E-mail: rbierbau@umich.edu.

School of Public Health Students: 755 full-time, 111 part-time; includes 206 minority (69 African Americans, 3 American Indian/Alaska Native, 105 Asian Americans or Pacific Islanders, 29 Hispanic Americans), 153 international. Average age 27. 1,659 applicants, 62% accepted, 370 enrolled. *Faculty:* 109 full-time (42 women), 74 part-time/adjunct (43 women).

University of Michigan (continued)

Expenses: Contact institution. *Financial support:* In 2008–09, 121 research assistantships with full and partial tuition reimbursements (averaging $15,199 per year), 27 teaching assistantships with full and partial tuition reimbursements (averaging $15,199 per year) were awarded; fellowships, career-related internships or fieldwork, Federal Work-Study, institutionally sponsored loans, scholarships/grants, traineeships, health care benefits, and unspecified assistantships also available. Support available to part-time students. In 2008, 311 master's, 19 doctorates awarded. *Degree program information:* Part-time and evening/weekend programs available. Offers biostatistics (MPH, MS, PhD); clinical research design and statistical analysis (MS); dental public health (MPH); environmental health sciences (MS, PhD); environmental quality and health (MPH); epidemiological science (PhD); epidemiology (MPH); health behavior and health education (MPH, PhD); health management and policy (MHSA, MPH, MS); health services organization and policy (PhD); hospital and molecular epidemiology (MPH); human nutrition (MPH); industrial hygiene (MPH, MS); international health (MPH); nutritional sciences (MS); occupational and environmental epidemiology (MPH); public health (MHSA, MPH, MS, PhD); toxicology (MPH, MS, PhD). MS and PhD offered through the Horace H. Rackham School of Graduate Studies. *Application deadline:* For fall admission, 12/1 priority date for domestic students, 1/15 priority date for international students. Applications are processed on a rolling basis. *Application fee:* $60 ($75 for international students). Electronic applications accepted. *Application Contact:* Kiran Dhiman, Admissions Coordinator, 734-764-5425, Fax: 734-763-5455, E-mail: sph.inquiries@umich.edu. *Dean,* Kenneth E. Warner, 734-764-5425, Fax: 734-763-5455, E-mail: kwarner@umich.edu.

School of Social Work Offers social work (MSW, PhD); social work and social science (PhD). PhD offered through the Horace H. Rackham School of Graduate Studies. Electronic applications accepted.

Taubman College of Architecture and Urban Planning Students: 402 full-time (194 women), 24 part-time (13 women); includes 69 minority (13 African Americans, 43 Asian Americans or Pacific Islanders, 13 Hispanic Americans), 92 international. Average age 0. 957 applicants, 51% accepted, 187 enrolled. *Faculty:* 138 full-time (59 women), 15 part-time/adjunct (5 women). Expenses: Contact institution. *Financial support:* In 2008–09, 182 students received support; fellowships with full and partial tuition reimbursements available, research assistantships with full and partial tuition reimbursements available, teaching assistantships with full and partial tuition reimbursements available, career-related internships or fieldwork, Federal Work-Study, institutionally sponsored loans, scholarships/grants, and unspecified assistantships available. Support available to part-time students. Financial award application deadline: 1/15; financial award applicants required to submit FAFSA. In 2008, 125 master's, 12 doctorates awarded. *Degree program information:* Part-time programs available. Offers architecture (M Arch, M Sc, PhD); architecture and urban planning (M Arch, M Sc, MUD, MUP, PhD, Certificate); real estate development (Certificate); urban and regional planning (MUP, PhD, Certificate); urban design (MUD); urban planning (MUP). *Application deadline:* For fall admission, 1/15 for domestic and international students; for winter admission, 11/15 for domestic students, 10/15 for international students. *Application fee:* $60 ($75 for international students). Electronic applications accepted. *Application Contact:* Meghan Lee, Admissions Counselor, 734-764-1649, Fax: 734-763-2322, E-mail: meglee@umich.edu. *Dean,* Monica Ponce de Leon, 734-764-1315, Fax: 734-763-2322, E-mail: mpdl@umich.edu.

UNIVERSITY OF MICHIGAN–DEARBORN, Dearborn, MI 48128-1491

General Information State-supported, coed, comprehensive institution. *Enrollment:* 8,311 graduate, professional, and undergraduate students; 244 full-time matriculated graduate/professional students (125 women), 1,547 part-time matriculated graduate/professional students (694 women). *Enrollment by degree level:* 1,791 master's. *Graduate faculty:* 294 full-time (104 women), 191 part-time/adjunct (75 women). *Graduate housing:* On-campus housing not available. *Student services:* Campus employment opportunities, campus safety program, career counseling, child daycare facilities, exercise/wellness program, free psychological counseling, grant writing training, international student services, low-cost health insurance, multicultural affairs office, services for students with disabilities, teacher training, writing training. *Library facilities:* Mardigian Library. *Online resources:* library catalog, web page, access to other libraries' catalogs. *Collection:* 366,577 titles, 589 serial subscriptions, 5,737 audiovisual materials.

Computer facilities: Computer purchase and lease plans are available. 350 computers available on campus for general student use. A campuswide network can be accessed from off campus. Online class registration, Tuition and application payments accepted online are available. *Web address:* http://www.umd.umich.edu/.

General Application Contact: Kimberly Lewandowski, Graduate Programs Coordinator, 313-593-1494, Fax: 313-436-9156, E-mail: umdgrad@umd.umich.edu.

GRADUATE UNITS

College of Arts, Sciences, and Letters Students: 48 full-time (28 women), 153 part-time (71 women); includes 36 minority (19 African Americans, 2 American Indian/Alaska Native, 9 Asian Americans or Pacific Islanders, 6 Hispanic Americans). Average age 36. 84 applicants, 50% accepted, 31 enrolled. *Faculty:* 169 full-time (65 women), 113 part-time/adjunct (41 women). Expenses: Contact institution. *Financial support:* In 2008–09, 1 fellowship (averaging $2,500 per year), 2 research assistantships (averaging $2,500 per year) were awarded; Federal Work-Study and scholarships/grants also available. Support available to part-time students. Financial award application deadline: 4/1; financial award applicants required to submit FAFSA. In 2008, 38 master's awarded. *Degree program information:* Part-time and evening/weekend programs available. Offers applied and computational mathematics (MS); arts, sciences, and letters (MA, MPA, MPP, MS, Certificate); assessment and evaluation (Certificate); clinical health psychology (MS); environmental science (MS); health psychology (MS); liberal studies (MA); nonprofit leadership (Certificate); public administration (MPA); public policy (MPP). *Application deadline:* For fall admission, 8/1 priority date for domestic students, 4/1 for international students; for winter admission, 12/1 priority date for domestic students, 11/1 for international students; for spring admission, 4/1 for domestic students, 3/1 for international students. Applications are processed on a rolling basis. *Application fee:* $60 ($75 for international students). Electronic applications accepted. *Application Contact:* Carol Ligienza, Graduate Program Coordinator, CASL Graduate Programs, 313-593-1183, Fax: 313-583-6498, E-mail: caslgrad@umd.umich.edu. *Dean,* Dr. Kathryn Anderson-Levitt, 313-593-5490, Fax: 313-593-5552, E-mail: katieal@umd.umich.edu.

College of Business Students: 68 full-time (32 women), 470 part-time (131 women); includes 128 minority (16 African Americans, 107 Asian Americans or Pacific Islanders, 5 Hispanic Americans). Average age 30. 188 applicants, 58% accepted, 55 enrolled. *Faculty:* 32 full-time (12 women), 7 part-time/adjunct (0 women). Expenses: Contact institution. *Financial support:* Career-related internships or fieldwork, Federal Work-Study, and scholarships/grants available. Support available to part-time students. Financial award application deadline: 4/1; financial award applicants required to submit FAFSA. In 2008, 164 master's awarded. *Degree program information:* Part-time and evening/weekend programs available. Postbaccalaureate distance learning degree programs offered (no on-campus study). Offers accounting (MS); finance (MS); management (MBA). *Application deadline:* For fall admission, 8/1 priority date for domestic students, 6/1 for international students; for winter admission, 12/1 priority date for domestic students, 10/1 for international students; for spring admission, 4/1 priority date for domestic students, 2/1 for international students. Applications are processed on a rolling basis. *Application fee:* $60. Electronic applications accepted. *Application Contact:* Julie Tigani, Academic Advisor/Counselor, 313-593-5460, Fax: 313-271-9838, E-mail: tigani@umd.umich.edu. *Dean,* Dr. Kim Schatzel, 313-593-5106, Fax: 313-271-9836, E-mail: schatzel@umd.umich.edu.

College of Engineering and Computer Science Students: 65 full-time (13 women), 476 part-time (93 women); includes 141 minority (16 African Americans, 94 Asian Americans or Pacific Islanders, 31 Hispanic Americans), 57 international. Average age 31. 258 applicants, 72% accepted, 106 enrolled. *Faculty:* 60 full-time (2 women), 20 part-time/adjunct (1 woman). Expenses: Contact institution. *Financial support:* In 2008–09, 19 students received support, including 31 research assistantships with full tuition reimbursements available (averaging $15,722 per year); fellowships, teaching assistantships, career-related internships or fieldwork and Federal Work-Study also available. Financial award application deadline: 4/1; financial award applicants required to submit FAFSA. In 2008, 183 master's awarded. *Degree program information:* Part-time and evening/weekend programs available. Offers automotive systems engineering (MSE, PhD); computer and information science (MS); computer engineering (MSE); electrical engineering (MSE); engineering and computer science (MS, MSE, D Eng, PhD); engineering management (MS); industrial and systems engineering (MSE); information systems and technology (MS); information systems engineering (PhD); manufacturing systems engineering (MSE, D Eng); mechanical engineering (MSE); software engineering (MS). *Application deadline:* For fall admission, 6/15 for domestic students, 4/1 for international students; for winter admission, 12/1 for domestic students, 10/15 for international students; for spring admission, 2/15 for domestic and international students. Applications are processed on a rolling basis. *Application fee:* $60 ($75 for international students). Electronic applications accepted. *Application Contact:* Dr. Kashev Varde, Associate Dean, 313-593-5117, Fax: 313-593-9967, E-mail: varde@engin.umd.umich.edu. *Dean,* Dr. Subrata Sengupta, 313-593-5290, Fax: 313-593-9967, E-mail: razal@engin.umd.umich.edu.

School of Education Students: 57 full-time (48 women), 512 part-time (420 women); includes 78 minority (51 African Americans, 4 American Indian/Alaska Native, 5 Asian Americans or Pacific Islanders, 18 Hispanic Americans), 1 international. Average age 33. 162 applicants, 96% accepted, 140 enrolled. *Faculty:* 34 full-time (20 women), 83 part-time/adjunct (73 women). Expenses: Contact institution. *Financial support:* Career-related internships or fieldwork and Federal Work-Study available. Support available to part-time students. Financial award application deadline: 4/1; financial award applicants required to submit FAFSA. In 2008, 194 master's awarded. *Degree program information:* Part-time and evening/weekend programs available. Offers education (M Ed, MA, MAT, MPA, MS, Certificate); emotional impairments endorsement (M Ed); inclusion specialist (M Ed); learning disabilities endorsement (M Ed); science education (MS); teaching (MAT). *Application deadline:* For fall admission, 8/1 priority date for domestic students, 8/3 for international students; for winter admission, 12/1 for domestic students, 1/4 for international students; for spring admission, 4/1 for domestic students, 3/4 for international students. Applications are processed on a rolling basis. *Application fee:* $60 ($75 for international students). Electronic applications accepted. *Application Contact:* Graduate Secretary, 313-593-5091. *Dean,* Dr. Paul Zionts, 313-593-5435, E-mail: pzionts@umich.edu.

See Close-Up on page 1029.

UNIVERSITY OF MICHIGAN–FLINT, Flint, MI 48502-1950

General Information State-supported, coed, comprehensive institution. CGS member. *Enrollment:* 7,260 graduate, professional, and undergraduate students; 261 full-time matriculated graduate/professional students (191 women), 844 part-time matriculated graduate/professional students (555 women). *Enrollment by degree level:* 962 master's, 143 doctoral. *Graduate faculty:* 81 full-time (44 women), 42 part-time/adjunct (21 women). Tuition, state resident: full-time $9973; part-time $415.50 per credit. Tuition, nonresident: full-time $14,960; part-time $623.30 per credit. *Required fees:* $368; $141 per term. Tuition and fees vary according to course level, course load, degree level and student level. *Graduate housing:* Room and/or apartments available on a first-come, first-served basis to single students; on-campus housing not available to married students. Typical cost: $7900 (including board). Room and board charges vary according to board plan and housing facility selected. *Student services:* Campus employment opportunities, campus safety program, career counseling, child daycare facilities, exercise/wellness program, free psychological counseling, international student services, low-cost health insurance, services for students with disabilities, teacher training, writing training. *Library facilities:* Frances Willson Thompson Library. *Online resources:* library catalog, web page, access to other libraries' catalogs. *Collection:* 266,696 titles, 907 serial subscriptions, 23,039 audiovisual materials.

Computer facilities: Computer purchase and lease plans are available. 251 computers available on campus for general student use. A campuswide network can be accessed from student residence rooms and from off campus. Online class registration is available. *Web address:* http://www.umflint.edu/.

General Application Contact: Bradley T. Maki, Director of Graduate Admissions, 810-762-3171, Fax: 810-766-6789, E-mail: bmaki@umflint.edu.

GRADUATE UNITS

College of Arts and Sciences Students: 37 full-time (22 women), 143 part-time (72 women); includes 25 minority (15 African Americans, 8 Asian Americans or Pacific Islanders, 2 Hispanic Americans), 24 international. Average age 33. 168 applicants, 72% accepted, 65 enrolled. *Faculty:* 16 full-time (3 women), 3 part-time/adjunct (1 woman). Expenses: Contact institution. *Financial support:* Federal Work-Study, scholarships/grants, and unspecified assistantships available. Support available to part-time students. Financial award application deadline: 6/1; financial award applicants required to submit FAFSA. In 2008, 18 master's awarded. *Degree program information:* Part-time programs available. Offers arts and sciences (MA, MS); biology (MS); computer science and information systems (MS); English (MA); social sciences (MA). *Application deadline:* For fall admission, 8/1 priority date for domestic students, 5/1 priority date for international students; for winter admission, 11/15 priority date for domestic students, 9/1 priority date for international students; for spring admission, 3/15 priority date for domestic students, 1/1 priority date for international students. Applications are processed on a rolling basis. *Application fee:* $55. Electronic applications accepted. *Application Contact:* Bradley T. Maki, Director of Graduate Admissions, 810-762-3171, Fax: 810-766-6789, E-mail: bmaki@umflint.edu. *Dean,* Dr. D. J. Trela, 810-762-3234, Fax: 810-762-3006, E-mail: djtrela@umflint.edu.

Graduate Programs Students: 27 full-time (19 women), 176 part-time (115 women); includes 36 minority (34 African Americans, 2 Hispanic Americans), 9 international. Average age 38. 150 applicants, 67% accepted, 79 enrolled. *Faculty:* 13 full-time (5 women), 7 part-time/adjunct (1 woman). Expenses: Contact institution. *Financial support:* Career-related internships or fieldwork, Federal Work-Study, scholarships/grants, and unspecified assistantships available. Support available to part-time students. Financial award application deadline: 6/1; financial award applicants required to submit FAFSA. In 2008, 89 master's awarded. *Degree program information:* Part-time and evening/weekend programs available. Postbaccalaureate distance learning degree programs offered (minimal on-campus study). Offers American culture (MLS); public administration (MPA). *Application deadline:* For fall admission, 8/1 for domestic students, 5/1 for international students; for winter admission, 11/15 for domestic students, 9/1 for international students; for spring admission, 3/15 for domestic students, 1/1 for international students. *Application fee:* $55. Electronic applications accepted. *Application Contact:* Bradley T. Maki, Director of Graduate Admissions, 810-762-3171, Fax: 810-766-6789, E-mail: bmaki@umflint.edu. *Associate Provost and Dean of Graduate Programs,* Dr. Vahid Lotfi, 810-762-3171, Fax: 810-766-6789.

School of Education and Human Services Students: 21 full-time (16 women), 208 part-time (184 women); includes 23 minority (18 African Americans, 3 American Indian/Alaska Native, 2 Hispanic Americans). Average age 35. 76 applicants, 78% accepted, 45 enrolled. *Faculty:* 12 full-time (10 women), 13 part-time/adjunct (8 women). Expenses: Contact institution. *Financial support:* Federal Work-Study, scholarships/grants, and unspecified assistantships available. Support available to part-time students. Financial award application deadline: 6/1; financial award applicants required to submit FAFSA. In 2008, 68 master's awarded. *Degree program information:* Part-time programs available. Offers early childhood education (MA); education (MA); education and human services (MA); elementary education with teaching certification (MA); literacy (K-12) (MA); special education (MA); technology in education (MA). *Application deadline:* For fall admission, 8/1 priority date for domestic students, 5/1 priority date for international students; for winter admission, 11/15 priority date for domestic students, 9/15 priority date for international students; for spring admission, 3/15 priority date for domestic students, 1/15 priority date for international students. Applications are processed on a rolling basis. *Application fee:* $55. *Application Contact:* Beulah Alexander, Executive Secretary, 810-766-6879, Fax: 810-766-6891, E-mail: beulaha@umflint.edu. *Dean,* Dr. Susanne Chandler, 810-766-6878, Fax: 810-766-6891, E-mail: chandes@umflint.edu.

School of Health Professions and Studies Students: 158 full-time (124 women), 114 part-time (98 women); includes 31 minority (17 African Americans, 7 Asian Americans or Pacific Islanders, 7 Hispanic Americans), 4 international. Average age 32. 399 applicants,

35% accepted, 101 enrolled. *Faculty:* 27 full-time (20 women), 17 part-time/adjunct (11 women). Expenses: Contact institution. *Financial support:* Career-related internships or fieldwork, Federal Work-Study, scholarships/grants, and traineeships available. Support available to part-time students. Financial award application deadline: 6/1; financial award applicants required to submit FAFSA. In 2008, 30 master's, 33 doctorates awarded. *Degree program information:* Part-time programs available. Offers anesthesia (MSA); health education (MS); health professions and studies (MS, MSA, DNP, DPT); nursing (DNP); online transitional (DPT); traditional entry-level (DPT). *Application deadline:* For fall admission, 8/1 priority date for domestic students, 5/1 priority date for international students; for winter admission, 11/15 priority date for domestic students, 9/1 priority date for international students; for spring admission, 3/15 priority date for domestic students, 1/1 priority date for international students. Applications are processed on a rolling basis. *Application fee:* $55. Electronic applications accepted. *Application Contact:* Brad T Maki, Executive Secretary, 810-762-3171, Fax: 810-766-6789, E-mail: bmaki@umflint.edu. *Interim Dean,* Dr. Betty Velthouse, 810-237-6503, Fax: 810-237-6532, E-mail: bavhouse@umflint.edu.

School of Management Students: 23 full-time (9 women), 157 part-time (61 women); includes 27 minority (15 African Americans, 2 American Indian/Alaska Native, 8 Asian Americans or Pacific Islanders, 2 Hispanic Americans), 15 international. Average age 32. 150 applicants, 57% accepted, 63 enrolled. *Faculty:* 8 full-time (0 women), 6 part-time/adjunct (1 woman). Expenses: Contact institution. *Financial support:* Federal Work-Study, scholarships/grants, and unspecified assistantships available. Support available to part-time students. Financial award application deadline: 6/1; financial award applicants required to submit FAFSA. In 2008, 86 master's awarded. *Degree program information:* Part-time programs available. Postbaccalaureate distance learning degree programs offered (minimal on-campus study). Offers management (MBA). *Application deadline:* For fall admission, 8/1 priority date for domestic students, 5/1 priority date for international students; for winter admission, 12/1 priority date for domestic students, 9/1 priority date for international students; for spring admission, 2/15 priority date for domestic students, 1/15 priority date for international students. Applications are processed on a rolling basis. *Application fee:* $55. Electronic applications accepted. *Application Contact:* D. Nicol Taylor-Vargo, MBA Program Coordinator, 810-237-6591, Fax: 810-237-6685, E-mail: dntaylor@umflint.edu. *Dean,* Dr. Jack A. Helmuth, 810-237-6589, Fax: 810-237-6685, E-mail: jhelmuth@umflint.edu.

UNIVERSITY OF MINNESOTA, DULUTH, Duluth, MN 55812-2496

General Information State-supported, coed, comprehensive institution. *Graduate housing:* Room and/or apartments available to single students; on-campus housing not available to married students. Housing application deadline: 3/1. *Research affiliation:* Environmental Protection Agency Environmental Research Laboratory (aquatic biology), Minnesota Geological Survey, Northeastern Minnesota National Historical Center (local history), U.S. Forest Service, Northcentral Forest Experiment Station.

GRADUATE UNITS

Graduate School *Degree program information:* Part-time and evening/weekend programs available. Postbaccalaureate distance learning degree programs offered (minimal on-campus study). Offers toxicology (MS, PhD).

College of Education and Human Service Professions *Degree program information:* Part-time and evening/weekend programs available. Postbaccalaureate distance learning degree programs offered (minimal on-campus study). Offers communication sciences and disorders (MA); education (Ed D); education and human service professions (MA, MSW, Ed D); social work (MSW).

College of Liberal Arts *Degree program information:* Part-time programs available. Offers criminology (MA); English (MA); liberal arts (MA, MLS); liberal studies (MLS).

College of Science and Engineering *Degree program information:* Part-time and evening/weekend programs available. Postbaccalaureate distance learning degree programs offered (minimal on-campus study). Offers applied and computational mathematics (MS); chemistry and biochemistry (MS); computer science (MS); electrical and computer engineering (MSECE); engineering management (MSEM); environmental health and safety (MEHS); geological sciences (MS, PhD); integrated biosciences (MS, PhD); physics (MS); science and engineering (MEHS, MS, MSECE, MSEM, PhD).

Labovitz School of Business and Economics *Degree program information:* Part-time and evening/weekend programs available. Offers business administration (MBA); business and economics (MBA).

School of Fine Arts *Degree program information:* Part-time programs available. Offers fine arts (MFA, MM); graphic design (MFA); music education (MM); performance (MM).

Medical School *Degree program information:* Part-time programs available. Offers biochemistry, molecular biology and biophysics (MS, PhD); medicine (MD, MS, PhD); microbiology, immunology and molecular pathobiology (MS, PhD); pharmacology (MS, PhD); physiology (MS, PhD).

UNIVERSITY OF MINNESOTA, TWIN CITIES CAMPUS, Minneapolis, MN 55455-0213

General Information State-supported, coed, university. CGS member. *Graduate housing:* Rooms and/or apartments available on a first-come, first-served basis to single and married students. Housing application deadline: 5/1.

GRADUATE UNITS

Carlson School of Management Average age 28. *Faculty:* 135 full-time (36 women), 122 part-time/adjunct (42 women). Expenses: Contact institution. *Financial support:* Fellowships with full and partial tuition reimbursements, research assistantships with full tuition reimbursements, teaching assistantships with full and partial tuition reimbursements, career-related internships or fieldwork, Federal Work-Study, institutionally sponsored loans, scholarships/grants, health care benefits, tuition waivers (full and partial), and unspecified assistantships available. Support available to part-time students. Financial award application deadline: 4/1; financial award applicants required to submit FAFSA. *Degree program information:* Part-time and evening/weekend programs available. Offers accountancy (M Acc); accounting (MBA, PhD); business administration (MBA, PhD); business taxation (MBT); entrepreneurship (MBA); finance (MBA, PhD); healthcare management (MBA); human resources and industrial relations (MA, PhD); information and decision sciences (MBA, PhD); international business (MBA); management (EMBA, M Acc, MA, MBA, MBT, MS, MSMOT, PhD); marketing and logistics management (MBA, PhD); operations and management science (MBA, PhD); strategic management and organization (MBA, PhD); supply chain management (MBA). Electronic applications accepted. *Application Contact:* Information Contact, 612-625-3014, Fax: 612-625-6002, E-mail: gsquest@umn.edu. *Dean,* Dr. Alison Davis-Blake, 612-624-7876, Fax: 612-624-6374, E-mail: davi1273@umn.edu.

College of Pharmacy *Degree program information:* Part-time programs available. Offers experimental and clinical pharmacology (MS, PhD); medicinal chemistry (MS, PhD); pharmaceutics (PhD); pharmacy (Pharm D, MS, PhD); social and administrative pharmacy (MS, PhD); social, administrative and clinical pharmacy (MS, PhD).

College of Veterinary Medicine Students: 444 full-time (338 women); includes 36 minority (5 African Americans, 2 American Indian/Alaska Native, 20 Asian Americans or Pacific Islanders, 9 Hispanic Americans), 36 international. 1,208 applicants, 13% accepted, 113 enrolled. *Faculty:* 137 full-time (54 women). Expenses: Contact institution. *Financial support:* In 2008–09, 312 students received support, including 47 research assistantships with full tuition reimbursements available (averaging $20,772 per year), 19 teaching assistantships with full tuition reimbursements available (averaging $26,500 per year); fellowships with full tuition reimbursements available, career-related internships or fieldwork, Federal Work-Study, traineeships, health care benefits, and unspecified assistantships also available. Support available to part-time students. Financial award applicants required to submit FAFSA. In 2008, 92 first professional degrees, 11 master's, 13 doctorates awarded. *Degree program information:* Part-time programs available. Offers comparative and molecular bioscience (MS, PhD); veterinary medicine (MS, PhD). *Application deadline:* For fall admission, 10/1 for domestic and international students. Electronic applications accepted. *Application Contact:* Dr. Trevor Ames, Dean, 612-624-6244, Fax: 612-624-8753. *Dean,* Dr. Trevor Ames, 612-624-6244, Fax: 612-624-8753.

Graduate School *Degree program information:* Part-time and evening/weekend programs available. Postbaccalaureate distance learning degree programs offered (minimal on-campus study). Offers biophysical sciences and medical physics (MS, PhD); genetic counseling (MS); health informatics (MHI, MS, PhD); history of science, technology and medicine (MA, PhD); integrative biology and physiology (PhD); microbial engineering (MS); microbiology, immunology and cancer biology (PhD); molecular, cellular, developmental biology and genetics (PhD); neuroscience (MS, PhD); scientific computation (MS, PhD); stem cell biology (MS, PhD). Electronic applications accepted.

College of Biological Sciences *Degree program information:* Part-time programs available. Offers biochemistry, molecular biology and biophysics (PhD); biological science (MBS); biological sciences (MBS, MS, PhD); ecology, evolution, and behavior (MS, PhD); plant biological sciences (MS, PhD). Electronic applications accepted.

College of Design Offers apparel (MA, MS, PhD); architecture (M Arch); design (M Arch, MA, MFA, MLA, MS, PhD, Postbaccalaureate Certificate); design communication (MA, MS, PhD); housing studies (MA, MS, PhD, Postbaccalaureate Certificate); interactive design (MFA); interior design (MA, MS, PhD); landscape architecture (MLA, MS); sustainable design (MS). Electronic applications accepted.

College of Education and Human Development Students: 1,569 full-time (1,148 women), 1,088 part-time (751 women); includes 349 minority (143 African Americans, 27 American Indian/Alaska Native, 112 Asian Americans or Pacific Islanders, 67 Hispanic Americans), 237 international. Average age 34. 2,100 applicants, 61% accepted, 1003 enrolled. *Faculty:* 164 full-time (81 women). Expenses: Contact institution. *Financial support:* In 2008–09, 71 fellowships (averaging $24,994 per year), 319 research assistantships with full tuition reimbursements (averaging $26,302 per year), 213 teaching assistantships with full tuition reimbursements (averaging $27,600 per year) were awarded; scholarships/grants and tuition waivers (partial) also available. Financial award applicants required to submit FAFSA. In 2008, 1,143 master's, 133 doctorates, 213 other advanced degrees awarded. *Degree program information:* Part-time programs available. Offers adapted physical education (MA, PhD); adult education (M Ed, MA, Ed D, PhD, Certificate); agricultural, food and environmental education (M Ed, MA, Ed D, PhD); art education (M Ed, MA, PhD); biomechanics (MA); biomechanics and neural control (PhD); business and industry education (M Ed, MA, Ed D, PhD); business education (M Ed); child psychology (MA, PhD); children's literature (M Ed, MA, PhD); Chinese (M Ed); coaching (Certificate); comparative and international development education (MA, PhD); counseling and student personnel psychology (MA, PhD, Ed S); curriculum and instruction (M Ed, MA, Ed D, PhD, Certificate); developmental adapted physical education (M Ed); disability policy and services (Certificate); early childhood education (M Ed, MA, PhD); earth science (M Ed); education and human development (M Ed, MA, MSW, Ed D, PhD, Certificate, Ed S); educational administration (MA, Ed D, PhD); educational psychology (PhD); elementary education (M Ed, MA, PhD); elementary special education (M Ed); English (M Ed); English as a second language (M Ed); English education (MA, PhD); environmental education (M Ed); evaluation studies (MA, PhD); exercise physiology (MA, PhD); family education (M Ed, MA, Ed D, PhD); French (M Ed); German (M Ed); Hebrew (M Ed); higher education (MA, PhD); human factors/ergonomics (MA, PhD); human resource development (M Ed, MA, Ed D, PhD, Certificate); instructional systems and technology (M Ed, MA, PhD); international/comparative sport (MA, PhD); Japanese (M Ed); kinesiology (M Ed, MA, PhD, Certificate); language arts (MA, PhD); language immersion education (Certificate); leisure services/management (MA, PhD); life sciences (M Ed); literacy education (MA); marketing education (M Ed); marriage and family therapy (MA, PhD); mathematics (M Ed); mathematics education (MA, PhD); middle school science (M Ed); motor development (MA, PhD); motor learning/control (MA, PhD); outdoor education/recreation (MA, PhD); physical education (M Ed); postsecondary administration (Ed D); program evaluation (Certificate); psychological foundations of education (MA, PhD, Ed S); reading education (MA, PhD); recreation, park, and leisure studies (M Ed, MA, PhD); school psychology (MA, PhD, Ed S); school-to-work (Certificate); science (M Ed); science education (MA, PhD); second languages and cultures (M Ed); second languages and cultures education (MA, PhD); social studies (M Ed); social studies education (MA, PhD); social work (MSW, PhD); Spanish (M Ed); special education (M Ed, MA, PhD, Ed S); sport and exercise science (M Ed); sport management (M Ed, MA, PhD); sport psychology (MA, PhD); sport sociology (MA, PhD); staff development (Certificate); talent development and gifted education (Certificate); teacher leadership (M Ed); teaching (M Ed); technical education (Certificate); technology education (M Ed, MA); technology enhanced learning (Certificate); therapeutic recreation (MA, PhD); work and human resource education (M Ed, MA, Ed D, PhD); writing education (M Ed, MA, PhD); youth development leadership (M Ed). *Application fee:* $55. *Application Contact:* Dr. Mary Bents, Associate Dean, 612-625-6501, Fax: 612-626-1580, E-mail: mbents@tc.umn.edu. *Dean,* Dr. Jean K. Quam, 612-626-9252, Fax: 612-626-7496, E-mail: jquam@umn.edu.

College of Food, Agricultural and Natural Resource Sciences *Degree program information:* Part-time and evening/weekend programs available. Offers animal science (MS, PhD); applied economics (MS, PhD); applied plant sciences (MS, PhD); bioproducts and biosystems science engineering and management (MS, PhD); conservation biology (MS, PhD); entomology (MS, PhD); food science (MS, PhD); food, agricultural and natural resource sciences (MS, PhD); natural resources science and management (MS, PhD); nutrition (MS, PhD); plant pathology (MS, PhD); soil science (MS, PhD); water resources science (MS, PhD). Electronic applications accepted.

College of Liberal Arts *Degree program information:* Part-time and evening/weekend programs available. Offers American studies (PhD); ancient and medieval art and archaeology (MA, PhD); anthropology (MA, PhD); art (MFA); art history (MA, PhD); Asian literatures, cultures, and media (PhD); audiology (Au D); biological psychopathology (PhD); classics (MA, PhD); clinical psychology (PhD); cognitive and biological psychology (PhD); communication studies (MA, PhD); comparative literature (PhD); comparative studies in discourse and society (PhD); counseling psychology (PhD); design technology (MFA); economics (PhD); English (MA, MFA, PhD); English as a second language (MA); feminist studies (PhD); French (MA, PhD); geographic information science (MGIS); geography (MA, MGIS, PhD); Germanic studies: German and Scandinavian studies track (PhD); Germanic studies: German track (MA, PhD); Germanic studies: Germanic medieval studies track (MA, PhD); Germanic studies: Scandinavian studies track (MA); Germanic studies: teaching track (MA); Greek (MA, PhD); health journalism (professional program) (MA); Hispanic and Luso-Brazilian literatures and linguistics (PhD); Hispanic linguistics (MA); Hispanic literature (MA); history (MA, PhD); industrial/organizational psychology (PhD); Latin (MA, PhD); liberal arts (MA, MFA, MGIS, MM, MS, Au D, DMA, PhD); linguistics (MA, PhD); Lusophone literature (MA); mass communication (MA, PhD); music (MA, MM, DMA, PhD); personality, individual differences, and behavior genetics (PhD); philosophy (MA, PhD); political science (PhD); quantitative/psychometric methods (PhD); religions in antiquity (MA); school psychology (PhD); social psychology (PhD); sociology (MA, PhD); speech-language pathology (MA); speech-language-hearing sciences (PhD); statistics (MS, PhD); strategic communication (professional program) (MA); theatre arts and dance (MA, PhD). Electronic applications accepted.

Hubert H. Humphrey Institute of Public Affairs *Degree program information:* Part-time and evening/weekend programs available. Offers advanced policy analysis methods (MPP); economic and community development (MPP); environmental planning (MURP); foreign policy (MPP); housing and community development (MURP); land use and urban design (MURP); public affairs (MPA, MPP, MS, MURP); public and nonprofit leadership and management (MPP); regional, economic and workforce development (MURP); science technology and environmental policy (MPP); science, technology, and environmental policy (MS); social policy (MPP); transportation planning (MURP); women and public policy (MPP). Electronic applications accepted.

School of Nursing *Degree program information:* Part-time programs available. Postbaccalaureate distance learning degree programs offered (minimal on-campus study). Offers adolescent nursing (MS); adult health clinical nurse specialist (MS); advanced clinical specialist in gerontology (MS); children with special health care needs (MS); family nurse practitioner (MS); gerontological nurse practitioner (MS); nurse anesthetist (MS);

University of Minnesota, Twin Cities Campus (continued)

nurse midwifery (MS); nursing (MN, MS, DNP, PhD); nursing and health care systems administration (MS); pediatric clinical nurse specialist (MS); pediatric nurse practitioner (MS); psychiatric mental health clinical nurse specialist (MS); public health nursing (MS); women's health nurse practitioner (MS).

Institute of Technology *Degree program information:* Part-time and evening/weekend programs available. Postbaccalaureate distance learning degree programs offered (minimal on-campus study). Offers aerospace engineering (M Aero E); aerospace engineering and mechanics (MS, PhD); biomedical engineering (MS, PhD); chemical engineering (M Ch E, MS Ch E, PhD); chemistry (MS, PhD); civil engineering (MCE, MS, PhD); computer and information sciences (MCIS, MS, PhD); computer engineering (M Comp E, MS); electrical engineering (MEE, MSEE, PhD); geological engineering (M Geo E, MS, PhD); geology (MS, PhD); geophysics (MS, PhD); history of science and technology (MA, PhD); industrial engineering (MSIE, PhD); materials science and engineering (M Mat SE, MS Mat SE, PhD); mechanical engineering (MSME, PhD); technology (M Aero E, M Ch E, M Comp E, M Geo E, M Mat SE, MA, MCE, MCIS, MCS, MEE, MS, MS Ch E, MS Mat SE, MSEE, MSIE, MSISE, MSME, MSMOT, MSST, PhD). Electronic applications accepted.

School of Mathematics *Degree program information:* Part-time programs available. Offers mathematics (MS, PhD).

School of Physics and Astronomy *Degree program information:* Part-time programs available. Offers astronomy (MS, PhD); astrophysics (MS, PhD); physics (MS, PhD).

Technological Leadership Institute Students: 77 full-time (14 women); includes 6 African Americans, 13 Asian Americans or Pacific Islanders. 58 applicants, 71% accepted, 30 enrolled. *Faculty:* 16 full-time (1 woman), 11 part-time/adjunct (0 women). Expenses: Contact institution. *Financial support:* In 2008–09, 3 students received support, including 3 fellowships with tuition reimbursements available (averaging $2,500 per year); institutionally sponsored loans and scholarships/grants also available. Support available to part-time students. Financial award application deadline: 7/15; financial award applicants required to submit FAFSA. In 2008, 38 master's awarded. *Degree program information:* Evening/weekend programs available. Offers infrastructure systems engineering (MSISE); management of technology (MSMOT); security technologies (MS, MSST). *Application deadline:* For fall admission, 6/15 priority date for domestic students; for spring admission, 10/15 for domestic students. Applications are processed on a rolling basis. *Application fee:* $55 ($75 for international students). Electronic applications accepted. *Application Contact:* Ann Bechtell, Admission Associate, 612-624-8826, Fax: 612-624-7510, E-mail: mot-cdtl@umn.edu. *Director*, Dr. Massoud Amin, 612-624-5747, Fax: 612-624-7510.

Law School Students: 809 full-time (339 women); includes 114 minority (13 African Americans, 11 American Indian/Alaska Native, 67 Asian Americans or Pacific Islanders, 23 Hispanic Americans), 48 international. Average age 25. 2,783 applicants, 30% accepted, 233 enrolled. *Faculty:* 67 full-time (28 women), 177 part-time/adjunct (80 women). Expenses: Contact institution. *Financial support:* In 2008–09, 491 students received support; fellowships, research assistantships, teaching assistantships, career-related internships or fieldwork, Federal Work-Study, institutionally sponsored loans, scholarships/grants, and tuition waivers (partial) available. Financial award application deadline: 5/1; financial award applicants required to submit FAFSA. In 2008, 253 JDs, 22 master's awarded. Offers law (JD, LL M). *Application deadline:* For fall admission, 4/1 for domestic students. Applications are processed on a rolling basis. *Application fee:* $75. Electronic applications accepted. *Application Contact:* Julie Tigges, Director of Admissions, 612-625-3487, Fax: 612-625-2011, E-mail: umnlsadm@umn.edu. *Dean*, David Wippman, 612-625-4841.

Medical School *Degree program information:* Part-time and evening/weekend programs available. Offers medicine (MD, MA, MS, DPT, PhD); pharmacology (MS, PhD); physical therapy (DPT).

Graduate Programs in Medicine *Degree program information:* Part-time and evening/weekend programs available. Offers medicine (MA).

School of Dentistry Offers dentistry (DDS, MS, PhD, Certificate); endodontics (MS, Certificate); oral biology (MS, PhD); oral health services for older adults (geriatrics) (MS, Certificate); orthodontics (MS); pediatric dentistry (MS); periodontology (MS); prosthodontics (MS); temporomandibular joint disorders (MS).

School of Public Health *Degree program information:* Part-time programs available. Postbaccalaureate distance learning degree programs offered (minimal on-campus study). Offers biostatistics (MPH, MS, PhD); clinical research (MS); community health education (MPH); core concepts (Certificate); environmental and occupational epidemiology (MPH, MS, PhD); environmental chemistry (MS, PhD); environmental health policy (MPH, MS, PhD); environmental infectious diseases (MPH, MS, PhD); environmental toxicology (MPH, MS, PhD); epidemiology (MPH, PhD); exposure sciences (MS); food safety and biosecurity (Certificate); general environmental health (MPH, MS); global environmental health (MPH, MS, PhD); health services research, policy, and administration (MS, PhD); healthcare administration (MHA); industrial hygiene (MPH, MS, PhD); maternal and child health (MPH); occupational health and safety (Certificate); occupational health nursing (MPH, MS, PhD); occupational medicine (MPH); preparedness, response and recovery (Certificate); public health (MHA, MPH, MS, PhD, Certificate); public health administration and policy (MPH); public health nutrition (MPH); public health practice (MPH). Electronic applications accepted.

UNIVERSITY OF MISSISSIPPI, Oxford, University, MS 38677

General Information State-supported, coed, university. CGS member. *Enrollment:* 15,289 graduate, professional, and undergraduate students; 1,684 full-time matriculated graduate/professional students (856 women), 738 part-time matriculated graduate/professional students (496 women). *Enrollment by degree level:* 662 first professional, 1,111 master's, 590 doctoral, 59 other advanced degrees. *Graduate housing:* Rooms and/or apartments available to single and married students. *Student services:* Campus employment opportunities, campus safety program, career counseling, free psychological counseling, international student services, low-cost health insurance, teacher training. *Library facilities:* J. D. Williams Library plus 3 others. *Online resources:* library catalog, web page, access to other libraries' catalogs. *Collection:* 1.9 million titles, 31,104 serial subscriptions, 52,752 audiovisual materials. *Research affiliation:* ElSohly Laboratories (national products research), Greenstone Industries (engineering), Combustion Research and Flow Technology, Inc. (fluid dynamics), Research Corporation (advancement of science), Cumberland Emerging Technologies (pharmaceutics).

Computer facilities: 1,200 computers available on campus for general student use. A campuswide network can be accessed from student residence rooms and from off campus. Online class registration, application for admission, registration for orientation are available. *Web address:* http://www.olemiss.edu/.

General Application Contact: Dr. Christy M. Wyandt, Associate Dean of Graduate School, 662-915-7474, Fax: 662-915-7577, E-mail: cwyandt@olemiss.edu.

UNIVERSITY OF MISSISSIPPI MEDICAL CENTER, Jackson, MS 39216-4505

General Information State-supported, coed, upper-level institution. *Enrollment:* 1,495 full-time matriculated graduate/professional students (749 women), 95 part-time matriculated graduate/professional students (82 women). *Enrollment by degree level:* 567 first professional, 249 master's, 281 doctoral, 493 other advanced degrees. *Graduate faculty:* 726 full-time (304 women), 125 part-time/adjunct (62 women). *Graduate housing:* On-campus housing not available. *Student services:* Campus employment opportunities, campus safety program, career counseling, exercise/wellness program, free psychological counseling, international student services, low-cost health insurance, multicultural affairs office, services for students with disabilities. *Library facilities:* Rowland Medical Library. *Online resources:* library catalog, web page, access to other libraries' catalogs. *Collection:* 310,016 titles, 2,732 serial subscriptions. *Research affiliation:* NASA–Stennis Space Center (imaging technology), Catfish Genetics Research Unit (immunology), Oak Ridge National Laboratory (physiology, biomedical engineering), Gulf Coast Research Laboratory (microbiology).

Computer facilities: Computer purchase and lease plans are available. 90 computers available on campus for general student use. A campuswide network can be accessed from off campus. *Web address:* http://www.umc.edu/.

General Application Contact: Barbara Westerfield, Director, Student Records and Registrar, 601-984-1080, Fax: 601-984-1079, E-mail: bwesterfield@registrar.umsmed.edu.

GRADUATE UNITS

School of Dentistry Students: 138 full-time (62 women), 1 part-time (0 women); includes 26 minority (18 African Americans, 3 Asian Americans or Pacific Islanders, 5 Hispanic Americans). Average age 25. 97 applicants, 32% accepted, 30 enrolled. *Faculty:* 28 full-time (6 women), 36 part-time/adjunct (7 women). Expenses: Contact institution. *Financial support:* Institutionally sponsored loans and scholarships/grants available. Financial award application deadline: 4/1; financial award applicants required to submit FAFSA. In 2008, 28 first professional degrees awarded. Offers craniofacial and dental research (MS, PhD); dentistry (DMD, MS, PhD). *Application deadline:* For fall admission, 12/1 for domestic students. Applications are processed on a rolling basis. *Application fee:* $10. *Application Contact:* Barbara Westerfield, Director, Student Records and Registrar, 601-984-1080, Fax: 601-984-1079, E-mail: bwesterfield@registrar.umsmed.edu. *Dean*, Dr. James Hupp, 601-984-6000, Fax: 601-984-6014, E-mail: dentistry@sod.umsmed.edu.

School of Graduate Studies in the Health Sciences Students: 196 full-time (140 women), 71 part-time (64 women); includes 72 minority (33 African Americans, 37 Asian Americans or Pacific Islanders, 2 Hispanic Americans). Average age 28. 172 applicants, 54% accepted, 68 enrolled. *Faculty:* 101 full-time (28 women), 6 part-time/adjunct (3 women). Expenses: Contact institution. *Financial support:* In 2008–09, 71 students received support, including 71 research assistantships (averaging $16,234 per year). Financial award application deadline: 3/15; financial award applicants required to submit FAFSA. In 2008, 31 master's, 15 doctorates awarded. Offers anatomy (MS, PhD); biochemistry (MS, PhD); clinical health sciences (MS, PhD); health sciences (MS, MSN, PhD); maternal-fetal medicine (MS); microbiology (MS, PhD); nursing (MSN, PhD); pathology (MS, PhD); pharmacology (MS, PhD); physiology and biophysics (MS, PhD); toxicology (MS, PhD). *Application deadline:* Applications are processed on a rolling basis. *Application fee:* $10. *Application Contact:* Barbara Westerfield, Director, Student Records and Registrar, 601-984-1080, Fax: 601-984-1079, E-mail: bwesterfield@registrar.umsmed.edu. *Dean*, Dr. Joey Granger, 601-984-1600, Fax: 601-984-1637, E-mail: jgranger@pharmacology.umsmed.edu.

School of Health Related Professions Students: 240 full-time (187 women), 23 part-time (18 women); includes 26 minority (25 African Americans, 1 Asian American or Pacific Islander). 67 applicants, 57% accepted, 36 enrolled. *Faculty:* 26 full-time (21 women). Expenses: Contact institution. *Financial support:* Institutionally sponsored loans and scholarships/grants available. Support available to part-time students. Financial award application deadline: 4/1; financial award applicants required to submit FAFSA. In 2008, 25 master's awarded. *Degree program information:* Part-time programs available. Offers health related professions (MOT, MPT); occupational therapy (MOT); physical therapy (MPT). *Application deadline:* Applications are processed on a rolling basis. *Application fee:* $10. *Application Contact:* Dr. Ben L. Mitchell, Dean, 601-984-6300, Fax: 601-984-6344, E-mail: bmitchell@shrp.umsmed.edu. *Dean*, Dr. Ben L. Mitchell, 601-984-6300, Fax: 601-984-6344, E-mail: bmitchell@shrp.umsmed.edu.

School of Medicine Students: 922 full-time (360 women); includes 213 minority (109 African Americans, 3 American Indian/Alaska Native, 89 Asian Americans or Pacific Islanders, 12 Hispanic Americans). Average age 24. *Faculty:* 409 full-time (155 women), 74 part-time/adjunct (35 women). Expenses: Contact institution. *Financial support:* In 2008–09, 374 students received support. Institutionally sponsored loans and scholarships/grants available. Financial award application deadline: 4/1. In 2008, 103 MDs awarded. Offers medicine (MD). *Application deadline:* For fall admission, 9/15 for domestic students; for winter admission, 12/1 for domestic students. Applications are processed on a rolling basis. *Application fee:* $10. *Application Contact:* Dr. Steven T. Case, Associate Dean for Medical School Admissions, 601-984-5010, Fax: 601-984-5008, E-mail: admitmd@som.umsmed.edu. *Dean*, Dr. Daniel W. Jones, 601-984-1010.

UNIVERSITY OF MISSOURI–COLUMBIA, Columbia, MO 65211

General Information State-supported, coed, university. CGS member. *Enrollment:* 30,200 graduate, professional, and undergraduate students; 3,897 full-time matriculated graduate/professional students (2,120 women), 3,261 part-time matriculated graduate/professional students (2,120 women). *Enrollment by degree level:* 1,130 first professional, 3,786 master's, 2,132 doctoral, 110 other advanced degrees. *Graduate faculty:* 1,678 full-time (520 women), 70 part-time/adjunct (32 women). *Graduate housing:* Rooms and/or apartments available on a first-come, first-served basis to single and married students. Housing application deadline: 10/1. *Student services:* Campus employment opportunities, campus safety program, career counseling, child daycare facilities, exercise/wellness program, free psychological counseling, grant writing training, international student services, low-cost health insurance, multicultural affairs office, services for students with disabilities, teacher training, writing training. *Library facilities:* Ellis Library plus 10 others. *Online resources:* library catalog, web page, access to other libraries' catalogs. *Collection:* 3.3 million titles, 54,347 serial subscriptions, 29,522 audiovisual materials.

Computer facilities: 1,080 computers available on campus for general student use. A campuswide network can be accessed from student residence rooms and from off campus. Online class registration, telephone registration are available. *Web address:* http://www.missouri.edu/.

General Application Contact: Terrence Grus, Director of Graduate Admissions and Academic Records, 573-882-6312, E-mail: GradAdmissions@missouri.edu.

GRADUATE UNITS

College of Veterinary Medicine Students: 310 full-time (228 women), 56 part-time (28 women); includes 23 minority (4 African Americans, 2 American Indian/Alaska Native, 5 Asian Americans or Pacific Islanders, 12 Hispanic Americans), 13 international. Average age 25. *Faculty:* 112 full-time (36 women), 8 part-time/adjunct (3 women). Expenses: Contact institution. *Financial support:* Fellowships, research assistantships, teaching assistantships, career-related internships or fieldwork, institutionally sponsored loans, and tuition waivers (full and partial) available. Support available to part-time students. In 2008, 66 first professional degrees, 11 master's, 11 doctorates awarded. Offers laboratory animal medicine (MS); pathobiology (MS, PhD); veterinary biomedical sciences (MS); veterinary clinical sciences (MS); veterinary medicine (DVM); veterinary medicine and surgery (MS); veterinary pathobiology (MS, PhD). *Application Contact:* Dr. Neil Olson, Dean, E-mail: olsonne@missouri.edu. *Dean*, Dr. Neil Olson, E-mail: olsonne@missouri.edu.

Graduate School Students: 2,783 full-time (1,541 women), 3,245 part-time (2,112 women); includes 443 minority (198 African Americans, 29 American Indian/Alaska Native, 97 Asian Americans or Pacific Islanders, 119 Hispanic Americans), 1,138 international. Average age 31. 5,932 applicants, 48% accepted, 1855 enrolled. *Faculty:* 1,678 full-time (520 women), 70 part-time/adjunct (32 women). Expenses: Contact institution. *Financial support:* Fellowships with full and partial tuition reimbursements, research assistantships with full and partial tuition reimbursements, teaching assistantships with full and partial tuition reimbursements, career-related internships or fieldwork, institutionally sponsored loans, scholarships/grants, traineeships, and tuition waivers (full and partial) available. Support available to part-time students. In 2008, 1,455 master's, 326 doctorates, 69 other advanced degrees awarded. *Degree program information:* Part-time and evening/weekend programs available. Offers dispute resolution (LL M); genetics (PhD); health administration (MHA); health informatics (MHA); health services management (MHA); neuroscience (MS, PhD); public health (MPH). *Application deadline:* Applications are processed on a rolling basis. *Application fee:* $45 ($60 for international students). *Application Contact:* Terrence Grus, Director of Graduate Admissions and Academic Records, E-mail: GradAdmissions@missouri.edu. *Vice-Provost for Advanced Studies and Dean of the Graduate School*, Dr. Pamela Benoit, 573-884-4178, E-mail: benoitp@missouri.edu.

College of Agriculture, Food and Natural Resources Students: 130 full-time (73 women), 111 part-time (50 women); includes 10 minority (5 African Americans, 3 American Indian/

Alaska Native, 2 Asian Americans or Pacific Islanders), 82 international. Average age 30. 204 applicants, 41% accepted, 61 enrolled. *Faculty:* 126 full-time (26 women), 7 part-time/adjunct (1 woman). Expenses: Contact institution. *Financial support:* Fellowships, research assistantships, teaching assistantships, institutionally sponsored loans available. In 2008, 43 master's, 20 doctorates awarded. *Degree program information:* Part-time programs available. Offers agricultural economics (MS, PhD); agricultural education (MS, PhD); agriculture, food and natural resources (MS, PhD); animal sciences (MS, PhD); biochemistry (MS, PhD); entomology (MS, PhD); food science (MS, PhD); foods and food systems management (MS); horticulture (MS, PhD); human nutrition (MS); plant microbiology and pathology (MS, PhD); plant sciences (MS, PhD); rural sociology (MS, PhD). *Application deadline:* Applications are processed on a rolling basis. *Application fee:* $45 ($60 for international students). *Application Contact:* Dr. Bryan L. Garton, Associate Dean, E-mail: gartonb@missouri.edu. *Dean,* Dr. Thomas L. Payne, 573-882-3846, E-mail: paynet@missouri.edu.

College of Arts and Sciences Students: 694 full-time (316 women), 428 part-time (190 women); includes 78 minority (24 African Americans, 4 American Indian/Alaska Native, 22 Asian Americans or Pacific Islanders, 28 Hispanic Americans), 317 international. Average age 30. 1,588 applicants, 22% accepted, 239 enrolled. *Faculty:* 534 full-time (186 women), 36 part-time/adjunct (15 women). Expenses: Contact institution. *Financial support:* Fellowships, research assistantships, teaching assistantships, career-related internships or fieldwork, institutionally sponsored loans, and tuition waivers (full and partial) available. In 2008, 161 master's, 113 doctorates awarded. *Degree program information:* Part-time programs available. Offers analytical chemistry (MS, PhD); anthropology (MA, PhD); applied mathematics (MS); art (MFA); art history and archaeology (MA, PhD); arts and sciences (MA, MFA, MM, MS, MST, PhD); classical studies (MA, PhD); communication (MA, PhD); economics (MA, PhD); English (MA, PhD); evolutionary biology and ecology (MA, PhD); French (MA, PhD); genetic, cellular and developmental biology (MA, PhD); geography (MA); geological sciences (MS, PhD); German (MA); history (MA, PhD); inorganic chemistry (MS, PhD); literature (MA); mathematics (MA, MST, PhD); music (MA, MM); neurobiology and behavior (MA, PhD); organic chemistry (MS, PhD); philosophy (MA, PhD); physical chemistry (MS, PhD); physics and astronomy (MS, PhD); political science (MA, PhD); psychological sciences (MA, MS, PhD); religious studies (MA); sociology (MA, PhD); Spanish (MA, PhD); statistics (MA, PhD); teaching (MA); theatre (MA, PhD). *Application deadline:* Applications are processed on a rolling basis. *Application fee:* $45 ($60 for international students). *Application Contact:* Dr. Michael J. O'Brien, Dean, 573-882-4422, E-mail: obrienm@missouri.edu. *Dean,* Dr. Michael J. O'Brien, 573-882-4422, E-mail: obrienm@missouri.edu.

College of Education Students: 510 full-time (390 women), 1,079 part-time (822 women); includes 126 minority (59 African Americans, 10 American Indian/Alaska Native, 23 Asian Americans or Pacific Islanders, 34 Hispanic Americans), 106 international. Average age 34. 894 applicants, 59% accepted, 451 enrolled. *Faculty:* 94 full-time (55 women), 9 part-time/adjunct (6 women). Expenses: Contact institution. *Financial support:* Fellowships, research assistantships, teaching assistantships, institutionally sponsored loans and scholarships/grants available. In 2008, 450 master's, 45 doctorates, 34 other advanced degrees awarded. *Degree program information:* Part-time and evening/weekend programs available. Offers administration and supervision of special education (PhD); agricultural education (M Ed, PhD, Ed S); art education (M Ed, PhD, Ed S); behavior disorders (M Ed, PhD); business and office education (M Ed, PhD, Ed S); counseling psychology (M Ed, MA, PhD, Ed S); curriculum development of exceptional students (M Ed, PhD); early childhood education (M Ed, PhD, Ed S); early childhood special education (M Ed, PhD); education (M Ed, MA, Ed D, PhD, Ed S); education administration (M Ed, MA, Ed D, PhD, Ed S); educational psychology (M Ed, MA, PhD, Ed S); educational technology (M Ed, Ed S); elementary education (M Ed, PhD, Ed S); English education (M Ed, PhD, Ed S); foreign language education (M Ed, PhD, Ed S); general special education (M Ed, MA, PhD); health education and promotion (M Ed, PhD); higher and adult education (M Ed, MA, Ed D, PhD, Ed S); information science and learning technology (PhD); learning and instruction (M Ed); learning disabilities (M Ed, PhD); library science (MA); marketing education (M Ed, PhD, Ed S); mathematics education (M Ed, PhD, Ed S); mental retardation (M Ed, PhD); music education (M Ed, PhD, Ed S); reading education (M Ed, PhD, Ed S); school psychology (M Ed, MA, PhD, Ed S); science education (M Ed, PhD, Ed S); social studies education (M Ed, PhD, Ed S); vocational education (M Ed, PhD, Ed S). *Application deadline:* Applications are processed on a rolling basis. *Application fee:* $45 ($60 for international students). *Application Contact:* Adrienne Vaughn, Recruitment Coordinator, E-mail: alvhcd@mizzou.edu. *Interim Dean,* Dr. Rose Porter, 573-882-8524, E-mail: porterr@missouri.edu.

College of Engineering Students: 206 full-time (51 women), 226 part-time (42 women); includes 23 minority (6 African Americans, 8 Asian Americans or Pacific Islanders, 9 Hispanic Americans), 281 international. Average age 27. 682 applicants, 36% accepted, 111 enrolled. *Faculty:* 111 full-time (10 women), 10 part-time/adjunct (0 women). Expenses: Contact institution. *Financial support:* Fellowships, research assistantships, teaching assistantships, institutionally sponsored loans available. In 2008, 89 master's, 39 doctorates awarded. *Degree program information:* Part-time programs available. Offers agricultural engineering (MS); biological engineering (MS, PhD); chemical engineering (MS, PhD); civil engineering (MS, PhD); computer science (MS, PhD); electrical and computer engineering (MS, PhD); engineering (ME, MS, PhD); environmental engineering (MS, PhD); geotechnical engineering (MS, PhD); industrial and manufacturing systems engineering (MS, PhD); mechanical and aerospace engineering (MS, PhD); structural engineering (MS, PhD); transportation and highway engineering (MS); water resources (MS, PhD). *Application deadline:* Applications are processed on a rolling basis. *Application fee:* $45 ($60 for international students). *Application Contact:* Dr. Lex Akers, Associate Dean for Academic Programs and James D. Dowell Professor of Electrical and Computer Engineering, 573-882-4765, E-mail: akersl@missouri.edu. *Dean,* Dr. James E. Thompson, 573-882-4378, E-mail: thompsonje@missouri.edu.

College of Human Environmental Science Students: 71 full-time (53 women), 61 part-time (39 women); includes 15 minority (11 African Americans, 3 Asian Americans or Pacific Islanders, 1 Hispanic American), 24 international. Average age 32. 119 applicants, 43% accepted, 29 enrolled. *Faculty:* 33 full-time (19 women), 1 (woman) part-time/adjunct. Expenses: Contact institution. *Financial support:* Fellowships, research assistantships, teaching assistantships, institutionally sponsored loans available. In 2008, 18 master's, 6 doctorates awarded. *Degree program information:* Part-time programs available. Offers design with digital media (MA, MS); environmental design (MS); exercise physiology (MA, PhD); human development and family studies (MA, MS, PhD); human environmental science (MA, MS, PhD); nutritional sciences (MS, PhD); personal financial planning (MS); textile and apparel management (MA, MS). *Application deadline:* Applications are processed on a rolling basis. *Application fee:* $45 ($60 for international students). *Application Contact:* Carla J. Beckmann, Academic Advisor, 573-882-6423, E-mail: jeromebeckmannc@missouri.edu. *Dean,* Dr. Stephen R. Jorgensen, 573-882-6227, E-mail: jorgens@missouri.edu.

Harry S Truman School of Public Affairs Students: 51 full-time (21 women), 31 part-time (15 women); includes 8 minority (3 African Americans, 1 American Indian/Alaska Native, 3 Asian Americans or Pacific Islanders, 1 Hispanic American), 24 international. Average age 31. 77 applicants, 61% accepted, 22 enrolled. *Faculty:* 13 full-time (3 women). Expenses: Contact institution. *Financial support:* Fellowships, research assistantships, teaching assistantships, institutionally sponsored loans available. In 2008, 50 master's awarded. Offers public affairs (MPA). *Application deadline:* For fall admission, 2/15 priority date for domestic students. Applications are processed on a rolling basis. *Application fee:* $45 ($60 for international students). *Application Contact:* Jessica Hosey, 573-882-3471, E-mail: hoseyj@missouri.edu. *Director,* Dr. Bart Wechsler, E-mail: wechslerb@missouri.edu.

Informatics Institute Students: 18 full-time (6 women), 19 part-time (4 women); includes 6 minority (5 African Americans, 1 Hispanic American), 14 international. Average age 38. 24 applicants, 38% accepted, 6 enrolled. Expenses: Contact institution. Offers informatics (PhD). *Application Contact:* Brenda Montague, 573-882-9007, E-mail: muiiadmissions@missouri.edu. *Director,* Dr. Chi-Ren Shyu, 573-882-3884, E-mail: shyuc@missouri.edu.

Nuclear Science and Engineering Institute Students: 34 full-time (5 women), 12 part-time (6 women); includes 9 minority (2 Asian Americans or Pacific Islanders, 7 Hispanic Americans), 9 international. Average age 29. 44 applicants, 48% accepted, 8 enrolled. *Faculty:* 5 full-time (0 women). Expenses: Contact institution. *Financial support:* Fellowships, research assistantships, teaching assistantships, institutionally sponsored loans available. In 2008, 19 master's, 4 doctorates awarded. Offers nuclear power engineering (MS, PhD). *Application deadline:* For fall admission, 3/15 priority date for domestic students. *Application fee:* $45 ($60 for international students). *Application Contact:* Latricia Vaughn, 573-882-8201, E-mail: vaughnlj@missouri.edu. *Department Chair,* Dr. Wynn Volkert, E-mail: volkertw@missouri.edu.

Robert J. Trulaske, Sr. College of Business Students: 307 full-time (111 women), 33 part-time (14 women); includes 20 minority (8 African Americans, 4 American Indian/Alaska Native, 4 Asian Americans or Pacific Islanders, 4 Hispanic Americans), 68 international. Average age 25. 506 applicants, 39% accepted, 146 enrolled. *Faculty:* 58 full-time (14 women), 5 part-time/adjunct (3 women). Expenses: Contact institution. *Financial support:* Fellowships, research assistantships, teaching assistantships, institutionally sponsored loans available. In 2008, 214 master's, 6 doctorates awarded. *Degree program information:* Part-time programs available. Offers accountancy (M Acc, PhD); business (M Acc, MBA, PhD); business administration (MBA, PhD). *Application deadline:* Applications are processed on a rolling basis. *Application fee:* $45 ($60 for international students). *Application Contact:* Dr. Bruce Walker, Dean, 573-882-6688. *Dean,* Dr. Bruce Walker, 573-882-6688.

School of Journalism Students: 174 full-time (115 women), 119 part-time (78 women); includes 26 minority (6 African Americans, 2 American Indian/Alaska Native, 5 Asian Americans or Pacific Islanders, 13 Hispanic Americans), 62 international. Average age 30. 283 applicants, 42% accepted, 96 enrolled. *Faculty:* 68 full-time (32 women), 6 part-time/adjunct (1 woman). Expenses: Contact institution. *Financial support:* Fellowships, research assistantships, teaching assistantships, career-related internships or fieldwork and institutionally sponsored loans available. In 2008, 91 master's, 10 doctorates awarded. *Degree program information:* Part-time programs available. Offers journalism (MA, PhD). *Application deadline:* For fall admission, 2/1 priority date for domestic students; for winter admission, 9/1 priority date for domestic students. Applications are processed on a rolling basis. *Application fee:* $45 ($60 for international students). *Application Contact:* Ginny Cowell, 573-882-4852, E-mail: cowellvj@missouri.edu. *Associate Dean,* Dr. Esther Thorson, 573-882-9590, E-mail: thorsone@missouri.edu.

School of Natural Resources Students: 47 full-time (21 women), 57 part-time (20 women); includes 6 minority (all African Americans), 26 international. Average age 32. 65 applicants, 48% accepted, 28 enrolled. *Faculty:* 38 full-time (4 women), 2 part-time/adjunct (0 women). Expenses: Contact institution. *Financial support:* Fellowships, research assistantships, teaching assistantships, institutionally sponsored loans and scholarships/grants available. In 2008, 6 master's, 2 doctorates awarded. *Degree program information:* Part-time programs available. Offers atmospheric science (MS, PhD); fisheries and wildlife (MS, PhD); forestry (MS, PhD); natural resources (MNR, MS, PhD); parks, recreation and tourism (MS); soil science (MS, PhD). *Application deadline:* Applications are processed on a rolling basis. *Application fee:* $45 ($60 for international students). *Application Contact:* Dr. Mark Ryan, Director, E-mail: ryanmr@missouri.edu. *Director,* Dr. Mark Ryan, E-mail: ryanmr@missouri.edu.

School of Social Work Students: 94 full-time (82 women), 122 part-time (110 women); includes 20 minority (13 African Americans, 3 Asian Americans or Pacific Islanders, 4 Hispanic Americans), 3 international. Average age 32. 98 applicants, 72% accepted, 57 enrolled. *Faculty:* 15 full-time (10 women), 1 part-time/adjunct (0 women). Expenses: Contact institution. *Financial support:* Fellowships, research assistantships, teaching assistantships, institutionally sponsored loans available. In 2008, 58 master's awarded. *Degree program information:* Part-time programs available. Offers social work (MSW). *Application deadline:* For fall admission, 1/15 priority date for domestic students. Applications are processed on a rolling basis. *Application fee:* $45 ($60 for international students). *Application Contact:* Crystal Null, 573-884-9385, E-mail: nullc@missouri.edu. *Director,* Dr. Marjorie Sable, E-mail: sablem@missouri.edu.

Sinclair School of Nursing Students: 25 full-time (24 women), 200 part-time (191 women); includes 11 minority (6 African Americans, 3 Asian Americans or Pacific Islanders, 2 Hispanic Americans), 3 international. Average age 39. 107 applicants, 54% accepted, 44 enrolled. *Faculty:* 23 full-time (21 women), 4 part-time/adjunct (3 women). Expenses: Contact institution. *Financial support:* Fellowships, research assistantships, teaching assistantships, career-related internships or fieldwork, institutionally sponsored loans, traineeships, and tuition waivers (full) available. In 2008, 40 master's, 4 doctorates awarded. *Degree program information:* Part-time programs available. Offers nursing (MS, PhD). *Application deadline:* For fall admission, 2/1 priority date for domestic students. Applications are processed on a rolling basis. *Application fee:* $45 ($60 for international students). *Application Contact:* Amie Orth, 573-882-0200, E-mail: ortha@missouri.edu. *Department Chair,* Dr. Roxanne W. McDaniel, E-mail: mcdanielr@missouri.edu.

School of Health Professions Students: 153 full-time (129 women), 5 part-time (all women); includes 5 minority (1 American Indian/Alaska Native, 4 Asian Americans or Pacific Islanders). Average age 24. 183 applicants, 41% accepted, 66 enrolled. *Faculty:* 32 full-time (25 women), 5 part-time/adjunct (4 women). Expenses: Contact institution. *Financial support:* Fellowships, research assistantships, teaching assistantships, institutionally sponsored loans available. In 2008, 96 master's awarded. Offers communication science and disorders (MHS); diagnostic medical ultrasound (MHS); health professions (MHS, MOT, MPT); occupational therapy (MOT); physical therapy (MPT). *Application deadline:* For fall admission, 3/1 priority date for domestic students. Applications are processed on a rolling basis. *Application fee:* $45 ($60 for international students). *Application Contact:* Ruth Crozier, Director, Student Affairs, E-mail: CrozierR@health.missouri.edu. *Dean,* Dr. Richard E. Oliver, 573-884-6705, E-mail: oliverr@health.missouri.edu.

School of Law Students: 445 full-time (176 women), 22 part-time (10 women); includes 70 minority (28 African Americans, 7 American Indian/Alaska Native, 22 Asian Americans or Pacific Islanders, 13 Hispanic Americans), 4 international. Average age 26. *Faculty:* 35 full-time (13 women), 14 part-time/adjunct (7 women). Expenses: Contact institution. *Financial support:* Fellowships, Federal Work-Study and institutionally sponsored loans available. Financial award application deadline: 3/1; financial award applicants required to submit FAFSA. In 2008, 148 JDs, 15 master's awarded. Offers law (JD, LL M). *Application deadline:* For fall admission, 3/1 priority date for domestic students. Applications are processed on a rolling basis. *Application Contact:* Tracy Gonzalez, Assistant Dean for Admissions, Career Development and Student Services, 573-884-2979, E-mail: gonzalezt@missouri.edu. *Dean,* Dr. R. Lawrence Dessem, 573-882-3246, E-mail: dessemrl@law.missouri.edu.

School of Medicine Students: 492 full-time (238 women), 39 part-time (25 women); includes 74 minority (31 African Americans, 5 American Indian/Alaska Native, 36 Asian Americans or Pacific Islanders, 2 Hispanic Americans), 37 international. Average age 26. *Faculty:* 375 full-time (96 women), 51 part-time/adjunct (20 women). Expenses: Contact institution. *Financial support:* Fellowships, research assistantships, teaching assistantships, career-related internships or fieldwork, institutionally sponsored loans, and scholarships/grants available. Support available to part-time students. Financial award applicants required to submit FAFSA. In 2008, 89 first professional degrees, 32 master's, 8 doctorates awarded. *Degree program information:* Part-time programs available. Offers medicine (MD, MS, PhD); public health (MS). *Application deadline:* Applications are processed on a rolling basis. *Application Contact:* Marivern Easton, Enrollment Specialist, Admissions, Recruitment and Records, 573-882-8047, E-mail: eastonm@missouri.edu. *Interim Dean,* Dr. Robert Churchill, 573-884-8733, E-mail: churchillr@missouri.edu.

Graduate Programs in Medicine Students: 41 full-time (19 women), 28 part-time (18 women); includes 7 minority (all African Americans), 19 international. Average age 28. 50 applicants, 46% accepted, 22 enrolled. *Faculty:* 72 full-time (19 women), 6 part-time/adjunct (2 women). Expenses: Contact institution. *Financial support:* Fellowships, research assistantships, teaching assistantships, career-related internships or fieldwork and institutionally sponsored loans available. In 2008, 1 master's, 14 doctorates awarded. *Degree program information:* Part-time programs available. Offers medicine (MS, PhD); molecular microbiology and immunology (MS, PhD); pathology and anatomical sciences (MS); pharmacology (MS, PhD); physiology (MS, PhD). *Application deadline:* Applications are processed on a rolling basis. *Application fee:* $45 ($60 for international students). *Application Contact:* Dr. John Gay, Associate Dean for Graduate Medical Education, 573-882-4637, E-mail:

University of Missouri–Columbia (continued)

gayj@health.missouri.edu. *Interim Dean*, Dr. Roberta Churchill, 573-884-8733, E-mail: churchillr@missouri.edu.

UNIVERSITY OF MISSOURI–KANSAS CITY, Kansas City, MO 64110-2499

General Information State-supported, coed, university. CGS member. *Enrollment:* 14,499 graduate, professional, and undergraduate students; 2,777 full-time matriculated graduate/professional students (1,365 women), 2,144 part-time matriculated graduate/professional students (1,243 women). *Enrollment by degree level:* 1,566 first professional, 2,600 master's, 632 doctoral, 123 other advanced degrees. *Graduate faculty:* 698 full-time (297 women), 467 part-time/adjunct (234 women). Tuition, state resident: full-time $5376; part-time $298.70 per credit hour. Tuition, nonresident: full-time $13,882; part-time $771.20 per credit hour. *Required fees:* $640.28; $34.65 per contact hour. $30 per semester. Tuition and fees vary according to course load and program. *Graduate housing:* Room and/or apartments available on a first-come, first-served basis to single students; on-campus housing not available to married students. Typical cost: $9560 (including board). *Student services:* Campus employment opportunities, campus safety program, career counseling, child daycare facilities, exercise/wellness program, free psychological counseling, international student services, multicultural affairs office, services for students with disabilities, writing training. *Library facilities:* Miller-Nichols Library plus 3 others. *Online resources:* library catalog, web page, access to other libraries' catalogs. *Collection:* 1.8 million titles, 30,976 serial subscriptions, 444,679 audiovisual materials. *Research affiliation:* St. Luke's Hospital (health sciences), Children's Mercy Hospital (health sciences), Truman Medical Center (health sciences), Veterans Administration Hospital (health sciences), Midwest Research Institute (health sciences).

Computer facilities: Computer purchase and lease plans are available. 728 computers available on campus for general student use. A campuswide network can be accessed from student residence rooms and from off campus. Online class registration is available. *Web address:* http://www.umkc.edu/.

General Application Contact: Jennifer DeHaemeas, Director of Admissions, 816-235-1111, Fax: 816-235-5544, E-mail: admit@umkc.edu.

GRADUATE UNITS

College of Arts and Sciences Students: 264 full-time (176 women), 385 part-time (245 women); includes 41 minority (2 African Americans, 2 American Indian/Alaska Native, 10 Asian Americans or Pacific Islanders, 27 Hispanic Americans), 31 international. Average age 32. 420 applicants, 66% accepted, 236 enrolled. *Faculty:* 222 full-time (93 women), 176 part-time/adjunct (85 women). Expenses: Contact institution. *Financial support:* In 2008–09, 1 fellowship with partial tuition reimbursement (averaging $18,000 per year), 40 research assistantships with full and partial tuition reimbursements (averaging $13,565 per year), 181 teaching assistantships with full and partial tuition reimbursements (averaging $12,763 per year) were awarded; career-related internships or fieldwork, Federal Work-Study, institutionally sponsored loans, scholarships/grants, and tuition waivers (full and partial) also available. Support available to part-time students. Financial award application deadline: 3/1; financial award applicants required to submit FAFSA. In 2008, 198 master's, 2 doctorates awarded. *Degree program information:* Part-time and evening/weekend programs available. Offers acting (MFA); analytical chemistry (MS, PhD); art history (MA, PhD); arts and sciences (MA, MFA, MS, MSW, PhD); criminal justice and criminology (MS); design technology (MFA); economics (MA, PhD); English (MA, PhD); environmental and urban geosciences (MS); geosciences (PhD); history (MA, PhD); inorganic chemistry (MS, PhD); mathematics and statistics (MA, MS, PhD); organic chemistry (MS, PhD); physical chemistry (MS, PhD); physics (MS, PhD); political science (MA, PhD); polymer chemistry (MS, PhD); psychology (MA, PhD); Romance languages and literatures (MA); sociology (MA, PhD); studio art (MA); theatre (MA). *Application deadline:* Applications are processed on a rolling basis. *Application fee:* $45 ($50 for international students). Electronic applications accepted. *Application Contact:* Jennifer DeHaemeas, Director of Admissions, 816-235-1111, Fax: 816-235-5544, E-mail: admit@umkc.edu. *Dean*, Dr. Karen Vorst, 816-235-1307, Fax: 816-235-1308.

School of Social Work Students: 115 full-time (97 women), 69 part-time (59 women); includes 44 minority (37 African Americans, 1 Asian American or Pacific Islander, 6 Hispanic Americans), 1 international. Average age 33. 102 applicants, 93% accepted, 84 enrolled. *Faculty:* 11 full-time (8 women), 12 part-time/adjunct (9 women). Expenses: Contact institution. *Financial support:* In 2008–09, 3 research assistantships with partial tuition reimbursements (averaging $11,280 per year) were awarded; career-related internships or fieldwork and institutionally sponsored loans also available. Financial award application deadline: 3/1; financial award applicants required to submit FAFSA. In 2008, 74 master's awarded. *Degree program information:* Part-time and evening/weekend programs available. Offers social work (MSW). *Application deadline:* For fall admission, 4/30 for domestic and international students; for spring admission, 12/1 for domestic and international students. Applications are processed on a rolling basis. *Application fee:* $45 ($50 for international students). *Application Contact:* Jennifer DeHaemeas, Director of Admissions, 816-235-1111, Fax: 816-235-5544, E-mail: admit@umkc.edu. *Program Director*, Dr. Michael Smith, 816-235-1025, E-mail: soc-wk@umkc.edu.

Conservatory of Music Students: 151 full-time (73 women), 110 part-time (59 women); includes 17 minority (9 African Americans, 2 American Indian/Alaska Native, 3 Asian Americans or Pacific Islanders, 3 Hispanic Americans), 64 international. Average age 29. 146 applicants, 59% accepted, 80 enrolled. *Faculty:* 52 full-time (20 women), 34 part-time/adjunct (19 women). Expenses: Contact institution. *Financial support:* In 2008–09, 51 teaching assistantships with partial tuition reimbursements (averaging $8,217 per year) were awarded; fellowships with partial tuition reimbursements, career-related internships or fieldwork, Federal Work-Study, institutionally sponsored loans, scholarships/grants, tuition waivers (partial), and unspecified assistantships also available. Support available to part-time students. Financial award application deadline: 3/1; financial award applicants required to submit FAFSA. In 2008, 47 master's, 12 doctorates awarded. *Degree program information:* Part-time programs available. Offers composition (MM, DMA); conducting (MM, DMA); music (MA); music education (MME, PhD); music history and literature (MM); music theory (MM); performance (MM, DMA). PhD is offered as an interdisciplinary degree through the School of Graduate Studies. *Application deadline:* For fall admission, 1/15 priority date for domestic students, 1/15 for international students. *Application fee:* $45 ($50 for international students). *Application Contact:* James Elswick, Associate Director, 816-235-2932, Fax: 816-235-5264, E-mail: cadmissions@umkc.edu. *Dean*, Peter Witte, 816-235-2731, Fax: 816-235-5265, E-mail: wittep@umkc.edu.

Henry W. Bloch School of Business and Public Administration Students: 203 full-time (99 women), 433 part-time (188 women); includes 73 minority (33 African Americans, 3 American Indian/Alaska Native, 24 Asian Americans or Pacific Islanders, 13 Hispanic Americans), 47 international. Average age 30. 284 applicants, 79% accepted, 203 enrolled. *Faculty:* 42 full-time (13 women), 24 part-time/adjunct (6 women). Expenses: Contact institution. *Financial support:* In 2008–09, 20 research assistantships with partial tuition reimbursements (averaging $7,809 per year), 4 teaching assistantships with partial tuition reimbursements (averaging $9,900 per year) were awarded; fellowships, career-related internships or fieldwork, Federal Work-Study, institutionally sponsored loans, scholarships/grants, tuition waivers (full and partial), and unspecified assistantships also available. Support available to part-time students. Financial award application deadline: 3/1; financial award applicants required to submit FAFSA. In 2008, 228 master's awarded. *Degree program information:* Part-time and evening/weekend programs available. Offers accounting (MS); business administration (MBA); entrepreneurship and innovation (PhD); public affairs (MPA, PhD). PhD is an interdisciplinary degree offered by the School of Graduate Studies. *Application deadline:* For fall admission, 5/1 priority date for domestic and international students; for spring admission, 10/1 priority date for domestic and international students. Applications are processed on a rolling basis. *Application fee:* $45 ($50 for international students). Electronic applications accepted. *Application Contact:* 816-235-1111, E-mail: admit@umkc.edu. *Dean*, Dr. Teng-Kee Tan, 816-235-2215, Fax: 816-235-2206.

School of Biological Sciences Students: 24 full-time (11 women), 29 part-time (22 women); includes 4 minority (3 Asian Americans or Pacific Islanders, 1 Hispanic American), 2 international. Average age 32. 34 applicants, 62% accepted, 19 enrolled. *Faculty:* 40 full-time (9 women), 5 part-time/adjunct (2 women). Expenses: Contact institution. *Financial support:* In 2008–09, 18 research assistantships with full tuition reimbursements (averaging $20,852 per year), 13 teaching assistantships with full tuition reimbursements (averaging $21,488 per year) were awarded; Federal Work-Study, institutionally sponsored loans, scholarships/grants, tuition waivers (full and partial), and unspecified assistantships also available. Support available to part-time students. Financial award application deadline: 3/1; financial award applicants required to submit FAFSA. In 2008, 18 master's awarded. *Degree program information:* Part-time and evening/weekend programs available. Offers biology (MA); cell biology and biophysics (PhD); cellular and molecular biology (MS); molecular biology and biochemistry (PhD). PhD is an interdisciplinary degree offered by the School of Graduate Studies. *Application deadline:* For fall admission, 2/15 priority date for domestic and international students. Applications are processed on a rolling basis. *Application fee:* $45 ($50 for international students). *Application Contact:* Laura Batenic, Information Contact, 816-235-2352, Fax: 816-235-5158, E-mail: batenicl@umkc.edu. *Dean*, Dr. Lawrence A. Dreyfus, 816-235-5246, Fax: 816-235-5158, E-mail: dreyfusl@umkc.edu.

School of Computing and Engineering Students: 252 full-time (66 women), 131 part-time (25 women); includes 17 minority (2 African Americans, 12 Asian Americans or Pacific Islanders, 3 Hispanic Americans), 317 international. Average age 24. 447 applicants, 53% accepted, 172 enrolled. *Faculty:* 41 full-time (6 women), 16 part-time/adjunct (1 woman). Expenses: Contact institution. *Financial support:* In 2008–09, 20 research assistantships with partial tuition reimbursements (averaging $15,169 per year), 11 teaching assistantships with partial tuition reimbursements (averaging $10,408 per year) were awarded; fellowships, career-related internships or fieldwork, Federal Work-Study, scholarships/grants, tuition waivers (partial), and unspecified assistantships also available. Support available to part-time students. Financial award application deadline: 3/1; financial award applicants required to submit FAFSA. In 2008, 112 master's awarded. *Degree program information:* Part-time programs available. Offers civil engineering (MS); computer and electrical engineering (PhD); computer science (MS); computer science and informatics (PhD); computing (PhD); electrical engineering (MS); engineering (PhD); mechanical engineering (MS); telecommunications (PhD). PhD (interdisciplinary) offered through the School of Graduate Studies. *Application deadline:* For fall admission, 1/15 priority date for domestic students, 1/15 for international students. Applications are processed on a rolling basis. *Application fee:* $45 ($50 for international students). *Application Contact:* Dr. Kevin Z. Truman, Dean, 816-235-2399, Fax: 816-235-5159. *Dean*, Dr. Kevin Z. Truman, 816-235-2399, Fax: 816-235-5159.

School of Dentistry Students: 408 full-time (163 women), 48 part-time (27 women); includes 50 minority (7 African Americans, 4 American Indian/Alaska Native, 26 Asian Americans or Pacific Islanders, 13 Hispanic Americans), 5 international. Average age 27. 213 applicants, 58% accepted, 123 enrolled. *Faculty:* 101 full-time (41 women), 88 part-time/adjunct (26 women). Expenses: Contact institution. *Financial support:* In 2008–09, 5 fellowships (averaging $60,795 per year), 9 research assistantships (averaging $16,270 per year) were awarded; career-related internships or fieldwork, Federal Work-Study, institutionally sponsored loans, and tuition waivers (full and partial) also available. Support available to part-time students. Financial award application deadline: 3/1; financial award applicants required to submit FAFSA. In 2008, 100 first professional degrees, 4 other advanced degrees awarded. Offers advanced education in dentistry (Graduate Dental Certificate); dental hygiene education (MS); dental specialties (Graduate Dental Certificate); dentistry (DDS); diagnostic sciences (Graduate Dental Certificate); oral and maxillofacial surgery (Graduate Dental Certificate); oral biology (MS, PhD); orthodontics and dentofacial orthopedics (Graduate Dental Certificate); pediatric dentistry (Graduate Dental Certificate); periodontics (Graduate Dental Certificate); prosthodontics (Graduate Dental Certificate). PhD is interdisciplinary and offered through the School of Graduate Studies. *Application deadline:* For fall admission, 2/1 for domestic and international students. *Application fee:* $45 ($50 for international students). *Application Contact:* 816-235-2080. *Dean*, Dr. Marsha Pyle, 816-235-2010.

School of Education Students: 178 full-time (136 women), 428 part-time (302 women); includes 145 minority (110 African Americans, 4 American Indian/Alaska Native, 11 Asian Americans or Pacific Islanders, 20 Hispanic Americans), 16 international. Average age 33. 204 applicants, 76% accepted, 137 enrolled. *Faculty:* 60 full-time (47 women), 62 part-time/adjunct (48 women). Expenses: Contact institution. *Financial support:* In 2008–09, 16 research assistantships with partial tuition reimbursements (averaging $11,325 per year) were awarded; fellowships with full tuition reimbursements, teaching assistantships, career-related internships or fieldwork, Federal Work-Study, institutionally sponsored loans, and tuition waivers (full and partial) also available. Support available to part-time students. Financial award application deadline: 3/1; financial award applicants required to submit FAFSA. In 2008, 147 master's, 10 doctorates, 38 other advanced degrees awarded. *Degree program information:* Part-time and evening/weekend programs available. Offers administration (Ed D); counseling and guidance (MA, Ed S); counseling psychology (PhD); curriculum and instruction (MA, Ed S); education (PhD); educational administration (Ed S); reading education (MA, Ed S); special education (MA). PhD with concentration in 'education" is an interdisciplinary degree offered by the School of Graduate Studies. *Application deadline:* For fall admission, 4/1 priority date for domestic and international students; for spring admission, 11/1 priority date for domestic and international students. Applications are processed on a rolling basis. *Application fee:* $45 ($50 for international students). *Application Contact:* Student Services Office, 816-235-2234, Fax: 816-235-6544, E-mail: education@umkc.edu. *Dean*, Dr. Linda Edwards, 816-235-2236, Fax: 816-235-5270, E-mail: education@umkc.edu.

School of Graduate Studies Students: 112 full-time (45 women), 251 part-time (97 women); includes 17 minority (7 African Americans, 6 Asian Americans or Pacific Islanders, 4 Hispanic Americans), 163 international. Average age 35. 172 applicants, 40% accepted, 58 enrolled. Expenses: Contact institution. *Financial support:* Fellowships with partial tuition reimbursements, research assistantships with partial tuition reimbursements, teaching assistantships with partial tuition reimbursements, career-related internships or fieldwork, Federal Work-Study, tuition waivers (partial), and unspecified assistantships available. Support available to part-time students. Financial award application deadline: 3/1; financial award applicants required to submit FAFSA. In 2008, 32 doctorates awarded. Offers interdisciplinary studies (PhD). Students select two or more subjects. *Application deadline:* For fall admission, 1/15 priority date for domestic and international students. Applications are processed on a rolling basis. *Application fee:* $45 ($50 for international students). Electronic applications accepted. *Application Contact:* Qunicy Bennett Johnson, Administrative Assistant, 816-235-1559, Fax: 816-235-1310, E-mail: bennettq@umkc.edu. *Dean*, Dr. Ronald MacQuarrie, 816-235-1301, Fax: 816-235-1310, E-mail: macquarrier@umkc.edu.

School of Law Students: 479 full-time (180 women), 50 part-time (23 women); includes 58 minority (25 African Americans, 4 American Indian/Alaska Native, 15 Asian Americans or Pacific Islanders, 14 Hispanic Americans), 21 international. Average age 27. *Faculty:* 32 full-time (13 women), 1 part-time/adjunct (0 women). Expenses: Contact institution. *Financial support:* In 2008–09, 22 teaching assistantships with partial tuition reimbursements (averaging $2,537 per year) were awarded; fellowships with partial tuition reimbursements, research assistantships, career-related internships or fieldwork, Federal Work-Study, institutionally sponsored loans, scholarships/grants, and tuition waivers (full and partial) also available. Support available to part-time students. Financial award application deadline: 3/1; financial award applicants required to submit FAFSA. In 2008, 150 JDs, 22 master's awarded. *Degree program information:* Part-time programs available. Offers law (JD, LL M). *Application deadline:* For fall admission, 3/1 priority date for domestic and international students. Applications are processed on a rolling basis. *Application fee:* $50. Electronic applications accepted. *Application Contact:* Debbie Brooks, Director of Admissions, 816-325-1644, Fax: 816-235-5276, E-mail: brooksdv@umkc.edu. *Dean*, Ellen Y. Suni, 816-235-1677, Fax: 816-235-5276, E-mail: sunie@umkc.edu.

School of Medicine Students: 384 full-time (214 women), 1 part-time (0 women); includes 164 minority (17 African Americans, 1 American Indian/Alaska Native, 134 Asian Americans or Pacific Islanders, 12 Hispanic Americans). Average age 22. 598 applicants, 16% accepted, 93 enrolled. *Faculty:* 30 full-time (6 women), 10 part-time/adjunct (4 women). Expenses: Contact institution. *Financial support:* In 2008–09, 2 research assistantships (averaging $16,385 per year) were awarded; fellowships, career-related internships or fieldwork, Federal Work-Study, institutionally sponsored loans, scholarships/grants, and tuition waivers (partial) also available. Financial award application deadline: 3/1; financial award applicants required to submit FAFSA. In 2008, 86 MDs awarded. Offers medicine (MD). *Application deadline:* For fall admission, 11/15 for domestic and international students. *Application fee:* $50. *Application Contact:* MaryAnne Morgenegg, Selection Administrative Assistant, 816-235-1870, Fax: 816-235-6579, E-mail: morgeneggm@umkc.edu. *Dean*, Dr. Betty Drees, 816-235-1808, E-mail: dreesb@umkc.edu.

School of Nursing Students: 23 full-time (19 women), 274 part-time (251 women); includes 28 minority (11 African Americans, 2 American Indian/Alaska Native, 9 Asian Americans or Pacific Islanders, 6 Hispanic Americans). Average age 35. 113 applicants, 81% accepted, 84 enrolled. *Faculty:* 33 full-time (27 women), 39 part-time/adjunct (37 women). Expenses: Contact institution. *Financial support:* In 2008–09, 10 teaching assistantships with partial tuition reimbursements (averaging $5,160 per year) were awarded; fellowships, research assistantships, career-related internships or fieldwork, Federal Work-Study, institutionally sponsored loans, and tuition waivers (full and partial) also available. Support available to part-time students. Financial award application deadline: 3/1; financial award applicants required to submit FAFSA. In 2008, 75 master's, 3 doctorates awarded. *Degree program information:* Part-time programs available. Postbaccalaureate distance learning degree programs offered (minimal on-campus study). Offers adult clinical nurse specialist (MSN); family nurse practitioner (MSN); neonatal nurse practitioner (MSN); nurse educator (MSN); nurse executive (MSN); nursing (PhD); pediatric nurse practitioner (MSN). *Application deadline:* For fall admission, 2/1 priority date for domestic and international students; for spring admission, 9/1 priority date for domestic and international students. *Application fee:* $45 ($50 for international students). *Application Contact:* Leah Wilder, Coordinator for Admissions and Recruitment, 816-235-5768, Fax: 816-235-1701, E-mail: wilderl@umkc.edu. *Dean*, Dr. Lora Lacey-Haun, 816-235-1700, Fax: 816-235-1701, E-mail: lacey-haunc@umkc.edu.

School of Pharmacy Students: 299 full-time (183 women), 4 part-time (3 women); includes 45 minority (9 African Americans, 34 Asian Americans or Pacific Islanders, 2 Hispanic Americans), 11 international. Average age 25. 471 applicants, 31% accepted, 127 enrolled. *Faculty:* 45 full-time (22 women), 11 part-time/adjunct (5 women). Expenses: Contact institution. *Financial support:* In 2008–09, 25 research assistantships with full and partial tuition reimbursements (averaging $9,758 per year), 19 teaching assistantships with full tuition reimbursements (averaging $11,622 per year) were awarded; fellowships, career-related internships or fieldwork, Federal Work-Study, institutionally sponsored loans, tuition waivers (full and partial), and unspecified assistantships also available. Financial award application deadline: 3/1; financial award applicants required to submit FAFSA. In 2008, 72 first professional degrees, 1 master's awarded. Postbaccalaureate distance learning degree programs offered (minimal on-campus study). Offers pharmaceutical sciences (MS, PhD); pharmacy (Pharm D). *Application deadline:* For fall admission, 12/5 for domestic students, 12/15 for international students; for spring admission, 10/1 for domestic students. Applications are processed on a rolling basis. *Application fee:* $45 ($50 for international students). Electronic applications accepted. *Application Contact:* Shelly M. Janasz, Director, Student Services, 816-235-2400, Fax: 816-235-5190, E-mail: janaszs@umkc.edu. *Dean*, Dr. Robert W. Piepho, 816-235-1609, Fax: 816-235-5190, E-mail: piephor@umkc.edu.

UNIVERSITY OF MISSOURI–ST. LOUIS, St. Louis, MO 63121

General Information State-supported, coed, university. CGS member. *Enrollment:* 15,617 graduate, professional, and undergraduate students; 795 full-time matriculated graduate/professional students (496 women), 2,180 part-time matriculated graduate/professional students (1,510 women). *Enrollment by degree level:* 2,337 master's, 583 doctoral, 52 other advanced degrees. *Graduate faculty:* 423 full-time (163 women). Tuition, state resident: full-time $5377; part-time $298.70 per credit hour. Tuition, nonresident: full-time $13,381; part-time $472.50 per credit hour. *Required fees:* $4078; $52 per credit hour. *Graduate housing:* Rooms and/or apartments available on a first-come, first-served basis to single and married students. Typical cost: $4490 per year ($5576 including board) for single students. Room and board charges vary according to board plan and housing facility selected. Housing application deadline: 7/1. *Student services:* Campus employment opportunities, campus safety program, career counseling, child daycare facilities, exercise/wellness program, free psychological counseling, grant writing training, international student services, low-cost health insurance, multicultural affairs office, services for students with disabilities. *Library facilities:* Thomas Jefferson Library plus 2 others. *Online resources:* library catalog, web page, access to other libraries' catalogs. *Collection:* 1.2 million titles, 3,181 serial subscriptions, 3,905 audiovisual materials. *Research affiliation:* St. Louis Zoo (biology), Missouri Botanical Garden (biology), Donald Danforth Plant Science Center (biology).

Computer facilities: Computer purchase and lease plans are available. 1,280 computers available on campus for general student use. A campuswide network can be accessed from student residence rooms and from off campus. Online class registration is available. *Web address:* http://www.umsl.edu/.

General Application Contact: Graduate Admissions, 314-516-5458, Fax: 314-516-6996, E-mail: gradadm@umsl.edu.

GRADUATE UNITS

College of Arts and Sciences Students: 356 full-time (208 women), 437 part-time (264 women); includes 77 minority (45 African Americans, 4 American Indian/Alaska Native, 18 Asian Americans or Pacific Islanders, 10 Hispanic Americans), 128 international. Average age 31. *Faculty:* 250 full-time (92 women). Expenses: Contact institution. *Financial support:* In 2008–09, 79 research assistantships with full and partial tuition reimbursements (averaging $11,502 per year), 120 teaching assistantships with full and partial tuition reimbursements (averaging $11,822 per year) were awarded; fellowships with full and partial tuition reimbursements, career-related internships or fieldwork, Federal Work-Study, health care benefits, and unspecified assistantships also available. Support available to part-time students. Financial award applicants required to submit FAFSA. In 2008, 234 master's, 36 doctorates awarded. *Degree program information:* Part-time and evening/weekend programs available. Offers advanced social perspective (MA); American literature (MA); American politics (MA); applied mathematics (MA, PhD); applied physics (MS); arts and sciences (MA, MFA, MS, MSW, PhD, Certificate, Graduate Certificate); astrophysics (MS); behavioral neuroscience (PhD); biology (MS, PhD); biotechnology (Certificate); chemistry (MS, PhD); clinical psychology respecialization (Certificate); community conflict intervention (MA); community psychology (PhD); comparative politics (MA); computer science (MS, PhD); creative writing (MFA); criminology and criminal justice (MA, PhD); English (MA); English literature (MA); general economics (MA); general psychology (MA); gerontology (MS, Certificate); industrial/organizational psychology (PhD); international politics (MA); linguistics (MA); long term care administration (Certificate); managerial economics (Certificate); mathematics (PhD); museum studies (MA, Certificate); philosophy (MA); physics (PhD); political process and behavior (MA); political science (PhD); program design and evaluation research (MA); public administration and public policy (MA); social policy planning and administration (MA); teaching of writing (Graduate Certificate); tropical biology and conservation (Certificate); urban and regional politics (MA). *Application deadline:* Applications are processed on a rolling basis. *Application fee:* $35 ($40 for international students). Electronic applications accepted. *Application Contact:* Graduate Admissions, 314-516-5458, Fax: 314-516-6996, E-mail: gradadm@umsl.edu. *Interim Dean*, Dr. Tereas Thiel, 314-516-5501.

School of Social Work Students: 53 full-time (48 women), 62 part-time (56 women); includes 14 minority (11 African Americans, 1 Asian American or Pacific Islander, 2 Hispanic Americans), 3 international. Average age 32. *Faculty:* 10 full-time (8 women). Expenses: Contact institution. *Financial support:* In 2008–09, 2 research assistantships with full and partial tuition reimbursements (averaging $8,550 per year), 6 teaching assistantships with full and partial tuition reimbursements (averaging $8,100 per year) were awarded. Financial award applicants required to submit FAFSA. In 2008, 47 master's awarded. Offers social work (MS, MSW, Certificate). *Application deadline:* For fall admission, 2/15 for domestic and international students. *Application fee:* $35 ($40 for international students). Electronic applications accepted. *Application Contact:* 314-516-5458, Fax: 314-516-6996, E-mail: gradadm@umsl.edu. *Graduate Program Director*, Dr. Margaret Sherraden, 314-516-6364, Fax: 314-516-5816, E-mail: socialwork@umsl.edu.

College of Business Administration Students: 167 full-time (79 women), 322 part-time (40 women); includes 60 minority (25 African Americans, 28 Asian Americans or Pacific Islanders, 7 Hispanic Americans), 78 international. Average age 34. *Faculty:* 48 full-time (11 women). Expenses: Contact institution. *Financial support:* In 2008–09, 29 research assistantships with full and partial tuition reimbursements (averaging $7,052 per year), 6 teaching assistantships with full and partial tuition reimbursements (averaging $13,950 per year) were awarded; career-related internships or fieldwork, Federal Work-Study, and institutionally sponsored loans also available. Support available to part-time students. Financial award application deadline: 4/1; financial award applicants required to submit FAFSA. In 2008, 200 master's awarded. *Degree program information:* Part-time and evening/weekend programs available. Offers accounting (MBA); business administration (M Acc, MBA, MSIS, PhD, Certificate); finance (MBA); human resource management (Certificate); information systems (MSIS, PhD); logistics and supply chain management (MBA, PhD, Certificate); management (MBA); marketing (MBA); marketing management (Certificate); operations (MBA); quantitative management science (MBA). *Application deadline:* For fall admission, 7/1 priority date for domestic and international students; for spring admission, 12/1 priority date for domestic and international students. Applications are processed on a rolling basis. *Application fee:* $35 ($40 for international students). Electronic applications accepted. *Application Contact:* 314-516-5458, Fax: 314-516-6996, E-mail: gradadm@umsl.edu. *Assistant Director*, Karl Kottemann, 314-516-5885, Fax: 314-516-6420, E-mail: mba@umsl.edu.

College of Education Students: 215 full-time (166 women), 1,098 part-time (841 women); includes 325 minority (282 African Americans, 7 American Indian/Alaska Native, 17 Asian Americans or Pacific Islanders, 19 Hispanic Americans), 26 international. Average age 34. *Faculty:* 72 full-time (39 women). Expenses: Contact institution. *Financial support:* In 2008–09, 45 research assistantships with full and partial tuition reimbursements (averaging $9,198 per year), 10 teaching assistantships with full and partial tuition reimbursements (averaging $11,563 per year) were awarded. Financial award application deadline: 4/1; financial award applicants required to submit FAFSA. In 2008, 255 master's, 18 doctorates, 21 other advanced degrees awarded. *Degree program information:* Part-time and evening/weekend programs available. Offers adult and higher education (Ed D); counseling (PhD); counselor education (Ed D); education (M Ed, Ed D, PhD, Certificate, Ed S); educational administration (Ed D); educational leadership and policy studies (PhD); educational psychology (PhD). *Application deadline:* For fall admission, 7/1 priority date for domestic and international students; for spring admission, 12/1 priority date for domestic and international students. Applications are processed on a rolling basis. *Application fee:* $35 ($40 for international students). Electronic applications accepted. *Application Contact:* 314-516-5458, Fax: 314-516-6996, E-mail: gradadm@umsl.edu. *Director of Graduate Studies*, Dr. Kathleen Haywood, 314-516-5483, Fax: 314-516-5227, E-mail: kathleen_haywood@umsl.edu.

Division of Counseling Students: 57 full-time (51 women), 148 part-time (125 women); includes 33 minority (28 African Americans, 1 American Indian/Alaska Native, 2 Asian Americans or Pacific Islanders, 2 Hispanic Americans), 8 international. Average age 31. *Faculty:* 7 full-time (3 women). Expenses: Contact institution. *Financial support:* In 2008–09, 4 research assistantships with full and partial tuition reimbursements (averaging $6,000 per year) were awarded. Financial award application deadline: 4/1; financial award applicants required to submit FAFSA. In 2008, 58 master's awarded. *Degree program information:* Part-time and evening/weekend programs available. Offers community counseling (M Ed); elementary school counseling (M Ed); secondary school counseling (M Ed). *Application deadline:* For fall admission, 6/1 for domestic and international students; for spring admission, 10/1 for domestic and international students. *Application fee:* $35 ($40 for international students). Electronic applications accepted. *Application Contact:* 314-516-5458, Fax: 314-516-6996, E-mail: gradadm@umsl.edu. *Chair*, Dr. Mark Pope, 314-516-5782.

Division of Educational Leadership and Policy Studies Students: 30 full-time (19 women), 211 part-time (156 women); includes 102 minority (95 African Americans, 1 American Indian/Alaska Native, 1 Asian American or Pacific Islander, 5 Hispanic Americans), 4 international. Average age 35. *Faculty:* 19 full-time (8 women), 6 part-time/adjunct (4 women). Expenses: Contact institution. *Financial support:* In 2008–09, 8 research assistantships (averaging $5,983 per year) were awarded. Financial award application deadline: 4/1; financial award applicants required to submit FAFSA. In 2008, 60 master's, 23 Certificates awarded. *Degree program information:* Part-time and evening/weekend programs available. Offers adult and higher education (M Ed); educational administration (M Ed, Ed S); institutional research (Certificate). *Application deadline:* For fall admission, 7/1 priority date for domestic and international students; for spring admission, 12/1 priority date for domestic and international students. Applications are processed on a rolling basis. *Application fee:* $35 ($40 for international students). Electronic applications accepted. *Application Contact:* 314-516-5458, Fax: 314-516-6996, E-mail: gradadm@umsl.edu. *Chair*, Dr. E. Paulette Savage, 514-516-5944.

Division of Educational Psychology, Research, and Evaluation Students: 14 full-time (13 women), 18 part-time (5 women); includes 1 minority (Asian American or Pacific Islander). Average age 29. *Faculty:* 13 full-time (4 women). Expenses: Contact institution. *Financial support:* In 2008–09, 2 research assistantships (averaging $12,118 per year), 1 teaching assistantship (averaging $13,842 per year) were awarded. Financial award application deadline: 4/1; financial award applicants required to submit FAFSA. In 2008, 9 other advanced degrees awarded. Offers education (Ed D); educational psychology (PhD); program evaluation and assessment (Certificate); school psychology (Ed S). *Application deadline:* For fall admission, 3/1 for domestic and international students. *Application fee:* $35 ($40 for international students). Electronic applications accepted. *Application Contact:* 314-516-5458, Fax: 314-516-6996, E-mail: gradadm@umsl.edu. *Chairperson*, Dr. Matthew Keefer, 314-516-5783, Fax: 314-516-5784, E-mail: keefer@umsl.edu.

Division of Teaching and Learning Students: 81 full-time (57 women), 505 part-time (400 women); includes 123 minority (107 African Americans, 2 American Indian/Alaska Native, 6 Asian Americans or Pacific Islanders, 8 Hispanic Americans), 6 international. Average age 32. *Faculty:* 32 full-time (16 women). Expenses: Contact institution. *Financial support:* In 2008–09, 3 teaching assistantships (averaging $9,600 per year) were awarded; research assistantships. Financial award application deadline: 4/1; financial award applicants required to submit FAFSA. In 2008, 140 master's awarded. *Degree program information:* Part-time and evening/weekend programs available. Offers elementary education (M Ed); secondary education (M Ed); secondary school teaching (Certificate); special education (M Ed); teaching English to speakers of other languages (Certificate). *Application deadline:* For fall admission, 7/1 priority date for international students; for spring admission, 12/1 priority date for domestic and international students. *Application fee:* $35 ($40 for international students). Electronic applications accepted. *Application Contact:* 314-516-5458, Fax: 314-516-6996, E-mail: gadadm@umsl.edu. *Chair*, Dr. Joseph Polman, 314-516-5791.

College of Fine Arts and Communication Students: 10 full-time (8 women), 32 part-time (22 women); includes 4 minority (3 African Americans, 1 Hispanic American), 4 international. Average age 30. *Faculty:* 24 full-time (10 women). Expenses: Contact institution. *Financial support:* In 2008–09, 5 teaching assistantships (averaging $12,000 per year) were awarded. In 2008, 31 master's awarded. Offers communication (MA); fine arts and communication (MA, MME); music education (MME). *Application deadline:* For fall admission, 7/15 priority date for domestic and international students; for spring admission, 12/1 priority date for domestic and international students. Applications are processed on a rolling basis. *Application fee:* $35 ($40 for international students). Electronic applications accepted. *Application Contact:* 314-516-5458, Fax: 314-516-6996, E-mail: gradadm@umsl.edu. *Dean*, Dr. John Hylton, 314-516-5911, Fax: 314-516-5910.

College of Nursing Students: 17 full-time (16 women), 195 part-time (186 women); includes 23 minority (21 African Americans, 1 Asian American or Pacific Islander, 1 Hispanic American), 1 international. Average age 36. *Faculty:* 14 full-time (all women), 19 part-time/adjunct (all women). Expenses: Contact institution. *Financial support:* In 2008–09, 1 research assistantship with full and partial tuition reimbursement (averaging $12,341 per year), 4 teaching assistantships with full and partial tuition reimbursements (averaging $6,170 per year) were awarded. Financial award application deadline: 4/1; financial award applicants required to submit FAFSA. In 2008, 43 master's, 4 doctorates awarded. Offers family nurse practitioner (MSN); nurse practitioner (Post Master's Certificate); nursing (DNP, PhD). *Application deadline:* For fall admission, 4/1 for domestic and international students; for spring admission, 10/4 for domestic and international students. *Application fee:* $35 ($40 for international students). Electronic applications accepted. *Application Contact:* 314-516-5458, Fax: 314-516-6996, E-mail: gradadm@umsl.edu. *Dean*, Dean Juliann Sebastian, 314-516-6066.

University of Missouri–St. Louis (continued)

College of Optometry Students: 180 full-time (99 women), 2 part-time (1 woman); includes 24 minority (10 African Americans, 1 American Indian/Alaska Native, 11 Asian Americans or Pacific Islanders, 2 Hispanic Americans), 5 international. Average age 23. 364 applicants, 24% accepted, 48 enrolled. *Faculty:* 23 full-time (6 women), 14 part-time/adjunct (4 women). Expenses: Contact institution. *Financial support:* In 2008–09, 142 students received support, including 6 research assistantships with full and partial tuition reimbursements available (averaging $500 per year), 4 teaching assistantships with full and partial tuition reimbursements available (averaging $16,000 per year); fellowships with full tuition reimbursements available, Federal Work-Study, institutionally sponsored loans, scholarships/grants, tuition waivers (partial), and unspecified assistantships also available. Financial award applicants required to submit FAFSA. In 2008, 38 first professional degrees, 1 doctorate awarded. Offers optometry (OD, MS, PhD); vision science (MS, PhD). *Application deadline:* For fall admission, 2/15 for domestic and international students. Applications are processed on a rolling basis. *Application fee:* $50. Electronic applications accepted. *Application Contact:* Dr. Edward S. Bennett, Director, Student Services, 314-516-6263, Fax: 314-516-6708, E-mail: optstuaff@umsl.edu. *Dean,* Dr. Larry J. Davis, 314-516-5606, Fax: 314-516-6708, E-mail: optometry@umsl.edu.

Graduate School Students: 20 full-time (12 women), 58 part-time (35 women); includes 18 minority (17 African Americans, 1 Hispanic American), 4 international. Average age 34. *Faculty:* 8 full-time (4 women), 7 part-time/adjunct (1 woman). Expenses: Contact institution. *Financial support:* In 2008–09, 1 research assistantship with full tuition reimbursement (averaging $12,000 per year) was awarded. Financial award application deadline: 4/1; financial award applicants required to submit FAFSA. In 2008, 22 master's awarded. *Degree program information:* Part-time and evening/weekend programs available. Offers health policy (MPPA); local government management (MPPA); managing human resources and organization (MPPA); nonprofit organization management (MPPA); nonprofit organization management and leadership (Certificate); policy research and analysis (MPPA). *Application deadline:* For fall admission, 7/1 priority date for domestic and international students; for spring admission, 12/1 priority date for domestic and international students. Applications are processed on a rolling basis. *Application fee:* $35 ($40 for international students). Electronic applications accepted. *Application Contact:* Graduate Admissions, 314-516-5458, Fax: 314-516-6996, E-mail: gradadm@umsl.edu. *Dean,* Dr. Judith Walker de Felix, 314-516-5898, Fax: 314-516-7017, E-mail: graduate@umsl.edu.

See Close-Up on page 1031.

UNIVERSITY OF MOBILE, Mobile, AL 36613

General Information Independent-religious, coed, comprehensive institution. *Enrollment:* 1,597 graduate, professional, and undergraduate students; 51 full-time matriculated graduate/professional students (46 women), 124 part-time matriculated graduate/professional students (98 women). *Enrollment by degree level:* 175 master's. *Graduate faculty:* 16 full-time (6 women), 6 part-time/adjunct (3 women). *Tuition:* Full-time $7560; part-time $420 per credit hour. *Required fees:* $240; $120 per semester. *Graduate housing:* Room and/or apartments available on a first-come, first-served basis to single students; on-campus housing not available to married students. Typical cost: $4320 per year ($7320 including board). Housing application deadline: 8/15. *Student services:* Campus employment opportunities, career counseling, free psychological counseling, international student services, low-cost health insurance. *Library facilities:* J. L. Bedsole Library. *Online resources:* library catalog, web page. *Collection:* 107,563 titles, 325 serial subscriptions, 1,717 audiovisual materials.

Computer facilities: 110 computers available on campus for general student use. A campuswide network can be accessed from student residence rooms and from off campus. Online class registration is available. *Web address:* http://www.umobile.edu/.

General Application Contact: Dr. Anne B. Lowery, Dean, School of Business, 251-442-2332, Fax: 251-442-2523, E-mail: alowery@umobile.edu.

GRADUATE UNITS

Graduate Programs Students: 51 full-time (46 women), 124 part-time (98 women); includes 84 minority (81 African Americans, 3 American Indian/Alaska Native), 4 international. Average age 33. *Faculty:* 16 full-time (6 women), 6 part-time/adjunct (3 women). Expenses: Contact institution. In 2008, 64 master's awarded. *Degree program information:* Part-time and evening/weekend programs available. Offers biblical/theological studies (MA); business administration (MBA); education (MA); marriage and family counseling (MA); nursing (MSN); religious studies (MA). *Application deadline:* For fall admission, 8/3 priority date for domestic students. Applications are processed on a rolling basis. *Application fee:* $40 ($50 for international students). *Application Contact:* Dr. Anne B. Lowery, Dean, Graduate Programs, 251-442-2332, Fax: 251-442-2523, E-mail: alowery@umobile.edu. *Dean,* Dr. Anne B. Lowery.

THE UNIVERSITY OF MONTANA, Missoula, MT 59812-0002

General Information State-supported, coed, university. CGS member. *Graduate housing:* Rooms and/or apartments available on a first-come, first-served basis to single and married students. *Research affiliation:* Arthur Carhart National Wilderness Training Center (environmental), Nature Center at Ft. Missoula Museum (environmental), World Trade Center (business), Rocky Mountain National Laboratories (medical), Community Hospital Medical Center (medical), Aldo Leopold Wilderness Institute (forestry).

GRADUATE UNITS

Graduate School *Degree program information:* Part-time programs available. Offers individual interdisciplinary programs (IIP) (PhD); interdisciplinary studies (MIS).

College of Arts and Sciences *Degree program information:* Part-time programs available. Offers anthropology (MA); applied geoscience (PhD); arts and sciences (MA, MFA, MPA, MS, PhD, Ed S); biochemistry (MS); biochemistry and microbiology (MS, PhD); chemistry (MS, PhD); clinical psychology (PhD); communication studies (MA); computer science (MS); creative writing (MFA); criminology (MA); cultural heritage (MA); cultural heritage studies (PhD); ecology of infectious disease (PhD); economics (MA); environmental studies (MS); experimental psychology (PhD); fiction (MFA); forensic anthropology (MA); French (MA); geography (MA); geology (MS, PhD); German (MA); historical anthropology (PhD); history (MA, PhD); integrative microbiology and biochemistry (PhD); linguistics (MA); literature (MA); mathematics (MA, PhD); mathematics education (MA); microbial ecology (MS, PhD); microbiology (MS); non-fiction (MFA); organismal biology and ecology (MS, PhD); philosophy (MA); poetry (MFA); political science (MA, MPA); public administration (MPA); rural and environmental change (MA); school psychology (MA, PhD, Ed S); sociology (MA); Spanish (MA); teaching (MA).

College of Forestry and Conservation Offers ecosystem management (MEM, MS); fish and wildlife biology (PhD); forestry (MS, PhD); recreation management (MS); resource conservation (MS); wildlife biology (MS).

College of Health Professions and Biomedical Sciences Offers biomedical and pharmaceutical sciences (MS, PhD); biomedical sciences (PhD); health professions and biomedical sciences (Pharm D, MPH, MS, MSW, DPT, PhD, CPH); neuroscience (MS, PhD); pharmaceutical sciences (MS); pharmacy (Pharm D); physical therapy (DPT); public health (MPH, CPH); social work (MSW); toxicology (MS, PhD).

School of Business Administration *Degree program information:* Part-time and evening/weekend programs available. Postbaccalaureate distance learning degree programs offered (minimal on-campus study). Offers accounting (M Acct); business administration (M Acct, MBA).

School of Education *Degree program information:* Part-time programs available. Offers counselor education (MA, Ed D, Ed S); counselor education and supervision (Ed D); curriculum and instruction (M Ed, Ed D); education (M Ed, MA, MS, Ed D, Ed S); educational leadership (M Ed, Ed D, Ed S); exercise science (MS); health and human performance (MS); health promotion (MS); mental health counseling (MA); school counseling (MA).

School of Fine Arts Offers fine arts (MA, MFA); music (MM).

School of Journalism Offers journalism (MA). Electronic applications accepted.

School of Law Offers law (JD).

UNIVERSITY OF MONTEVALLO, Montevallo, AL 35115

General Information State-supported, coed, comprehensive institution. *Enrollment:* 3,025 graduate, professional, and undergraduate students; 192 full-time matriculated graduate/professional students (161 women), 222 part-time matriculated graduate/professional students (175 women). *Enrollment by degree level:* 361 master's, 53 other advanced degrees. Tuition, state resident: full-time $5280; part-time $220 per credit hour. Tuition, nonresident: full-time $10,560; part-time $440 per credit hour. *Required fees:* $482; $113 per semester. One-time fee: $25 part-time. *Graduate housing:* Room and/or apartments guaranteed to single students; on-campus housing not available to married students. Typical cost: $4356 (including board). *Student services:* Campus employment opportunities, campus safety program, career counseling, free psychological counseling, international student services, low-cost health insurance, writing training. *Library facilities:* Carmichael Library. *Online resources:* library catalog, web page, access to other libraries' catalogs. *Collection:* 264,123 titles, 35,402 serial subscriptions, 4,810 audiovisual materials.

Computer facilities: 340 computers available on campus for general student use. A campuswide network can be accessed from student residence rooms and from off campus. Online class registration is available. *Web address:* http://www.montevallo.edu/.

General Application Contact: Rebecca Hartley, Coordinator for Graduate Studies, 205-665-6350, Fax: 205-665-6353, E-mail: hartleyrs@montevallo.edu.

GRADUATE UNITS

College of Arts and Sciences Students: 35 full-time (34 women), 6 part-time (all women); includes 3 minority (1 African American, 1 American Indian/Alaska Native, 1 Asian American or Pacific Islander). Expenses: Contact institution. *Financial support:* Federal Work-Study, scholarships/grants, and unspecified assistantships available. In 2008, 19 master's awarded. *Degree program information:* Part-time and evening/weekend programs available. Offers arts and sciences (MA, MS); English literature (MA); speech-language pathology (MS). *Application deadline:* For fall admission, 7/15 for domestic students; for spring admission, 11/15 for domestic students. *Application fee:* $25. *Application Contact:* Rebecca Hartley, Coordinator for Graduate Studies, 205-665-6350, Fax: 205-665-6353, E-mail: hartleyrs@montevallo.edu. *Dean,* Dr. Mary Beth Armstrong, 205-665-6508.

College of Education Students: 157 full-time (127 women), 216 part-time (169 women); includes 72 minority (64 African Americans, 6 Asian Americans or Pacific Islanders, 2 Hispanic Americans), 2 international. Expenses: Contact institution. *Financial support:* Federal Work-Study, scholarships/grants, and unspecified assistantships available. In 2008, 67 master's, 8 Ed Ss awarded. *Degree program information:* Part-time and evening/weekend programs available. Offers community counseling (M Ed); education (M Ed, Ed S); elementary education (M Ed); instructional leadership (M Ed, Ed S); marriage and family (M Ed); school counseling (M Ed); secondary/high school education (M Ed). *Application deadline:* For fall admission, 7/15 for domestic students; for spring admission, 11/15 for domestic students. *Application fee:* $25. *Application Contact:* Rebecca Hartley, Assistant Director, 205-665-6350, E-mail: hartleyrs@montevallo.edu. *Dean,* Dr. Jack Riley, 205-665-6350, E-mail: rileyj@montevallo.edu.

UNIVERSITY OF NEBRASKA AT KEARNEY, Kearney, NE 68849-0001

General Information State-supported, coed, comprehensive institution. CGS member. *Graduate housing:* Rooms and/or apartments available on a first-come, first-served basis to single and married students.

GRADUATE UNITS

College of Graduate Study *Degree program information:* Part-time and evening/weekend programs available.

College of Business and Technology *Degree program information:* Part-time and evening/weekend programs available. Offers business administration (MBA); business and technology (MBA). Electronic applications accepted.

College of Education *Degree program information:* Part-time and evening/weekend programs available. Offers adapted physical education (MA Ed); counseling (MS Ed, Ed S); curriculum and instruction (MS Ed); education (MA Ed, MS Ed, Ed S); educational administration (MA Ed, Ed S); exercise science (MA Ed); instructional technology (MS Ed); master teacher (MA Ed); reading education (MA Ed); school psychology (Ed S); special education (MA Ed); speech pathology (MS Ed); supervisor (MA Ed). Electronic applications accepted.

College of Fine Arts and Humanities *Degree program information:* Part-time and evening/weekend programs available. Offers art education (MA Ed); creative writing (MA); fine arts and humanities (MA, MA Ed); French (MA Ed); German (MA Ed); literature (MA); music education (MA Ed); Spanish (MA Ed). Electronic applications accepted.

College of Natural and Social Sciences *Degree program information:* Part-time and evening/weekend programs available. Offers biology (MS); history (MA); natural and social sciences (MA, MS, MS Ed); science education (MS Ed). Electronic applications accepted.

UNIVERSITY OF NEBRASKA AT OMAHA, Omaha, NE 68182

General Information State-supported, coed, university. CGS member. *Graduate housing:* Room and/or apartments available on a first-come, first-served basis to single students; on-campus housing not available to married students.

GRADUATE UNITS

Graduate Studies and Research *Degree program information:* Part-time programs available. Postbaccalaureate distance learning degree programs offered (no on-campus study). Offers public health (MPH); writing (MFA). Electronic applications accepted.

College of Arts and Sciences *Degree program information:* Part-time and evening/weekend programs available. Offers advanced writing (Certificate); arts and sciences (MA, MAT, MS, PhD, Certificate, Ed S); biology (MS); developmental psychology (PhD); English (MA); geographic information science (Certificate); geography (MA); history (MA); industrial/organizational psychology (MS, PhD); language teaching (MA); mathematics (MA, MAT, MS); political science (MS); psychobiology (PhD); psychology (MA); school psychology (MS, Ed S); teaching English to speakers of other languages (Certificate); technical communication (Certificate). Electronic applications accepted.

College of Business Administration *Degree program information:* Part-time and evening/weekend programs available. Offers accounting (M Acc); business administration (EMBA, M Acc, MA, MBA, MS); economics (MA, MS). Electronic applications accepted.

College of Communication, Fine Arts and Media *Degree program information:* Part-time and evening/weekend programs available. Offers communication (MA); communication, fine arts and media (MA, MM); music (MM); theatre (MA). Electronic applications accepted.

College of Education *Degree program information:* Part-time and evening/weekend programs available. Offers community counseling (MA, MS); counseling gerontology (MA, MS); education (MA, MS, Ed D, Certificate, Ed S); educational administration and supervision (MS, Ed D, Ed S); elementary education (MA, MS); health, physical education, and recreation (MA, MS); instruction in urban schools (Certificate); instructional technology (Certificate); reading education (MS); school counseling (MA, MS); secondary education (MA, MS); special education (MS); speech-language pathology (MA, MS); student affairs practice in higher education (MA, MS).

College of Information Science and Technology *Degree program information:* Part-time and evening/weekend programs available. Offers computer science (MA, MS); information science and technology (MA, MS, PhD, Certificate); information technology (PhD); management information systems (MS). Electronic applications accepted.

College of Public Affairs and Community Service *Degree program information:* Part-time and evening/weekend programs available. Postbaccalaureate distance learning degree programs offered (no on-campus study). Offers criminal justice (MA, MS, PhD); gerontology (Certificate); public administration (MPA, PhD); public affairs and community service (MA, MPA, MS, MSW, PhD, Certificate); public management (Certificate); social gerontology (MA); social work (MSW); urban studies (MS). Electronic applications accepted.

UNIVERSITY OF NEBRASKA–LINCOLN, Lincoln, NE 68588

General Information State-supported, coed, university. CGS member. *Enrollment:* 23,537 graduate, professional, and undergraduate students; 2,663 full-time matriculated graduate/professional students (1,255 women), 1,621 part-time matriculated graduate/professional students (832 women). *Enrollment by degree level:* 547 first professional, 1,932 master's, 1,782 doctoral, 23 other advanced degrees. *Graduate faculty:* 1,070 full-time (306 women), 11 part-time/adjunct (3 women). Tuition, state resident: full-time $4275; part-time $237.50 per credit hour. Tuition, nonresident: full-time $11,525; part-time $640.25 per credit hour. *Required fees:* $1068; $10.35 per credit hour. $440.70 per semester. Tuition and fees vary according to course load and program. *Graduate housing:* Rooms and/or apartments available on a first-come, first-served basis to single and married students. Typical cost: $7020 (including board) for single students. Room and board charges vary according to board plan, campus/location and housing facility selected. Housing application deadline: 7/1. *Student services:* Campus employment opportunities, campus safety program, career counseling, child daycare facilities, exercise/wellness program, free psychological counseling, grant writing training, international student services, low-cost health insurance, multicultural affairs office, services for students with disabilities, teacher training, writing training. *Library facilities:* Love Memorial Library plus 7 others. *Online resources:* library catalog, web page, access to other libraries' catalogs. *Collection:* 3.5 million titles, 29,245 serial subscriptions, 37,036 audiovisual materials. *Research affiliation:* U.S. Meat Animal Research Center.

Computer facilities: 600 computers available on campus for general student use. A campuswide network can be accessed from student residence rooms and from off campus. Online class registration is available. *Web address:* http://www.unl.edu/.

General Application Contact: Dr. Ellen Weissinger, Dean of Graduate Studies, 402-472-2875, Fax: 402-472-0589, E-mail: graduate@unl.edu.

GRADUATE UNITS

College of Law Students: 412 full-time (172 women), 5 part-time (3 women); includes 45 minority (16 African Americans, 5 American Indian/Alaska Native, 11 Asian Americans or Pacific Islanders, 13 Hispanic Americans). *Faculty:* 28 full-time (8 women), 1 part-time/adjunct (0 women). Expenses: Contact institution. *Financial support:* Fellowships, research assistantships, teaching assistantships, career-related internships or fieldwork, Federal Work-Study, institutionally sponsored loans, health care benefits, and tuition waivers (full) available. In 2008, 124 JDs, 5 master's awarded. Offers law (JD); legal studies (MLS); space and telecommunications law (LL M). *Application deadline:* For fall admission, 3/1 for domestic students. *Application fee:* $25. Electronic applications accepted. *Application Contact:* Glenda Pierce, Assistant Dean, 402-472-2161, Fax: 402-472-5185. *Dean,* Steven Willborn, 402-472-2161.

Graduate College Students: 2,251 full-time (1,083 women), 1,616 part-time (829 women); includes 251 minority (80 African Americans, 19 American Indian/Alaska Native, 81 Asian Americans or Pacific Islanders, 71 Hispanic Americans), 850 international. Average age 33. *Faculty:* 1,042 full-time (298 women), 10 part-time/adjunct (3 women). Expenses: Contact institution. *Financial support:* Fellowships with full tuition reimbursements, research assistantships with full tuition reimbursements, teaching assistantships, career-related internships or fieldwork, Federal Work-Study, health care benefits, and unspecified assistantships available. Support available to part-time students. In 2008, 781 master's, 258 doctorates, 6 other advanced degrees awarded. *Degree program information:* Part-time and evening/weekend programs available. Postbaccalaureate distance learning degree programs offered. Offers administration, curriculum and instruction (Ed D, PhD); environmental health, occupational health and toxicology (MS, PhD); survey research and methodology (MS, PhD). *Application fee:* $40. Electronic applications accepted. *Application Contact:* Ginny Gross, Director of Graduate Admissions, 402-472-2878, Fax: 402-472-0589, E-mail: grad_admissions@unl.edu. *Vice Chancellor for Research and Dean of Graduate Studies,* Dr. Prem Paul, 402-472-3123, Fax: 402-472-0589, E-mail: grad_admissions@unl.edu.

College of Agricultural Sciences and Natural Resources Students: 368 full-time (181 women), 193 part-time (97 women); includes 6 African Americans, 11 Asian Americans or Pacific Islanders, 5 Hispanic Americans, 182 international. Average age 31. *Faculty:* 235 full-time (36 women), 1 part-time/adjunct (0 women). Expenses: Contact institution. *Financial support:* Fellowships, research assistantships, teaching assistantships, career-related internships or fieldwork, Federal Work-Study, health care benefits, and unspecified assistantships available. Support available to part-time students. Financial award application deadline: 2/15. In 2008, 96 master's, 46 doctorates awarded. Offers agribusiness (MBA); agricultural economics (MS, PhD); agricultural sciences and natural resources (M Ag, MA, MBA, MS, PhD); agronomy (MS, PhD); animal science (MS, PhD); biochemistry (MS, PhD); community development (M Ag); distance education specialization (MS); entomology (MS, PhD); food science and technology (MS, PhD); geography (PhD); horticulture (MS, PhD); leadership development (MS); leadership education (MS); mechanized systems management (MS); natural resources (MS, PhD); nutrition (MS, PhD); nutrition outreach education specialization (MS); statistics (MS, PhD); teaching and extension education specialization (MS); veterinary science (MS). *Application fee:* $40. Electronic applications accepted. *Application Contact:* Ginny Gross, Director of Graduate Admissions, 402-472-2878, Fax: 402-472-0589, E-mail: grad_admissions@unl.edu. *Dean,* Dr. Steven S. Waller, 402-472-2201.

College of Architecture Students: 82 full-time (30 women), 22 part-time (11 women); includes 5 minority (1 African American, 1 American Indian/Alaska Native, 2 Asian Americans or Pacific Islanders, 1 Hispanic American), 3 international. Average age 29. *Faculty:* 25 full-time (6 women). Expenses: Contact institution. *Financial support:* Fellowships, research assistantships, teaching assistantships, Federal Work-Study and health care benefits available. Support available to part-time students. Financial award application deadline: 2/15. In 2008, 5 master's awarded. Offers architecture (M Arch, MCRP, MS, PhD); community and regional planning (MCRP); interior design (MS). *Application deadline:* For fall admission, 2/1 for domestic and international students. *Application fee:* $40. Electronic applications accepted. *Application Contact:* Ginny Gross, Director of Graduate Admissions, 402-472-2878, Fax: 402-472-0589, E-mail: grad_admissions@unl.edu. *Dean,* Wayne Drummond, 402-472-3592, Fax: 402-472-3806.

College of Arts and Sciences Students: 703 full-time (337 women), 312 part-time (172 women); includes 74 minority (22 African Americans, 3 American Indian/Alaska Native, 19 Asian Americans or Pacific Islanders, 30 Hispanic Americans), 240 international. Average age 32. *Faculty:* 345 full-time (109 women). Expenses: Contact institution. *Financial support:* Fellowships, research assistantships, teaching assistantships, Federal Work-Study, health care benefits, and unspecified assistantships available. Support available to part-time students. In 2008, 147 master's, 85 doctorates awarded. Offers analytical chemistry (PhD); anthropology (MA); arts and sciences (M Sc T, MA, MAT, MS, PhD, Graduate Certificate); astronomy (MS, PhD); biochemistry (PhD); bioinformatics (MS, PhD); biological sciences (MA, MS, PhD); biopsychology (PhD); chemistry (MS); classics and religious studies (MA); clinical psychology (PhD); cognitive psychology (PhD); composition and rhetoric (MA, PhD); computer engineering (MS, PhD); computer science (MS, PhD); creative writing (MA, PhD); developmental psychology (PhD); French (MA, PhD); geography (MA, PhD); geosciences (MS, PhD); German (MA, PhD); history (MA, PhD); information technology (PhD); inorganic chemistry (PhD); instructional communication (MA, PhD); interpersonal communication (MA, PhD); literature studies (MA, PhD); marketing, communication studies, and advertising (MA, PhD); materials chemistry (PhD); mathematics (MA, MAT, MS, PhD); mathematics and computer science (PhD); organic chemistry (PhD); organizational communication (MA, PhD); philosophy (MA, PhD); physical chemistry (PhD); physics (MS, PhD); political science (MA, PhD); professional archaeology (MA); psychology (MA); public policy analysis (Graduate Certificate); rhetoric and culture (MA, PhD); social/personality psychology (PhD); sociology (MA, PhD); Spanish (MA, PhD). *Application fee:* $40. Electronic applications accepted. *Application Contact:* Ginny Gross, Director of Graduate Admissions, 402-472-2878, Fax: 402-472-0589, E-mail: grad_admissions@unl.edu. *Dean,* Dr. Richard Hoffmann, 402-472-2891, Fax: 402-472-1123.

College of Business Administration Students: 243 full-time (91 women), 197 part-time (49 women); includes 35 minority (8 African Americans, 4 American Indian/Alaska Native, 19 Asian Americans or Pacific Islanders, 4 Hispanic Americans), 80 international. Average age 32. *Faculty:* 56 full-time (15 women), 1 part-time/adjunct. Expenses: Contact institution. *Financial support:* Fellowships, research assistantships, teaching assistantships, Federal Work-Study and health care benefits available. Support available to part-time students. Financial award application deadline: 2/15. In 2008, 150 master's, 14 doctorates awarded. *Degree program information:* Part-time and evening/weekend programs available. Offers accountancy (MPA, PhD); actuarial science (MS); business (MA, MBA, PhD); business administration (MA, MBA, MPA, MS, PhD); economics (MA, PhD); finance (MA, PhD); management (MA, PhD); marketing (MA, PhD). *Application fee:* $40. Electronic applications accepted. *Application Contact:* Ginny Gross, Director of Graduate Admissions, 402-472-2878, Fax: 402-472-0589, E-mail: grad_admissions@unl.edu. *Dean,* Cynthia H. Milligan, 402-472-9500, Fax: 402-472-5180.

College of Education and Human Sciences Students: 380 full-time (295 women), 657 part-time (436 women); includes 81 minority (31 African Americans, 8 American Indian/Alaska Native, 18 Asian Americans or Pacific Islanders, 24 Hispanic Americans), 59 international. Average age 34. *Faculty:* 113 full-time (56 women), 1 part-time/adjunct. Expenses: Contact institution. *Financial support:* Fellowships, research assistantships, teaching assistantships, Federal Work-Study, health care benefits, and unspecified assistantships available. Financial award application deadline: 2/15. In 2008, 214 master's, 75 doctorates, 6 other advanced degrees awarded. Offers adult and continuing education (MA); audiology and hearing science (Au D); audiology research (PhD); child development/early childhood education (MS, PhD); child, youth and family studies (MS); clinical audiology (Au D); cognition, learning and development (MA); community nutrition and health promotion (MS); counseling psychology (MA); education and human sciences (M Ed, MA, MS, MST, Au D, Ed D, PhD, Certificate, Ed S); educational administration (M Ed, MA, Ed D, Certificate); educational psychology (MA, Ed S); educational studies (Ed D, PhD); family and consumer sciences education (MS, PhD); family financial planning (MS); family science (MS, PhD); gerontology (PhD); human sciences (PhD); marriage and family therapy (MS); medical family therapy (PhD); merchandising (MS); nutrition (MS, PhD); nutrition and exercise (MS); nutrition and health sciences (MS, PhD); psychological studies in education (PhD); quantitative, qualitative, and psychometric methods (MA); school psychology (MA, Ed S); special education (M Ed, MA, Ed S); speech-language pathology and audiology (MS, Au D); teaching, learning and teacher education (M Ed, MA, MST, Ed D, PhD); textile history/quilt studies (MA); textile science (MS); textile-apparel (MA); textiles, clothing and design (MA, MS); vocational and adult education (M Ed, MA); youth development (MS). *Application fee:* $40. Electronic applications accepted. *Application Contact:* Dr. Marjorie J. Kostelnik, Dean, 402-472-2911. *Dean,* Dr. Marjorie J. Kostelnik, 402-472-2911.

College of Engineering Students: 314 full-time (70 women), 155 part-time (28 women); includes 21 minority (7 African Americans, 1 American Indian/Alaska Native, 9 Asian Americans or Pacific Islanders, 4 Hispanic Americans), 251 international. Average age 30. *Faculty:* 147 full-time (14 women), 4 part-time/adjunct (1 woman). Expenses: Contact institution. *Financial support:* Fellowships with full tuition reimbursements, research assistantships with full tuition reimbursements, teaching assistantships, Federal Work-Study and health care benefits available. Support available to part-time students. Financial award application deadline: 2/15. In 2008, 101 master's, 26 doctorates awarded. Offers agricultural and biological systems engineering (MS, PhD); architectural engineering (M Eng, MAE, MS, PhD); chemical and biomolecular engineering (MS, PhD); chemical and materials engineering (PhD); civil engineering (MS, PhD); electrical engineering (MS, PhD); engineering (M Eng, MAE, MEE, MS, PhD); engineering management (M Eng); engineering mechanics (MS, PhD); environmental engineering (MS, PhD); industrial and management systems engineering (MS, PhD); manufacturing systems engineering (MS); mechanical engineering (MS, PhD); mechanized systems management (MS). *Application fee:* $40. Electronic applications accepted. *Application Contact:* Ginny Gross, Director of Graduate Admissions, 402-472-2878, Fax: 402-472-0589, E-mail: grad_admissions@unl.edu. *Dean,* Dr. David H. Allen, 402-472-3181, Fax: 402-472-7792.

College of Fine and Performing Arts Students: 118 full-time (51 women), 64 part-time (11 women); includes 4 African Americans, 1 Asian American or Pacific Islander, 2 Hispanic Americans, 17 international. Average age 30. *Faculty:* 64 full-time (25 women), 2 part-time/adjunct (1 woman). Expenses: Contact institution. *Financial support:* Fellowships, research assistantships, teaching assistantships, Federal Work-Study and health care benefits available. Support available to part-time students. Financial award application deadline: 2/15. In 2008, 41 master's, 12 doctorates awarded. Offers acting (MFA); art and art history (MA, MFA); art history (MA); composition (MM, DMA); conducting (MM, DMA); costume (MFA); directing (MFA); fine and performing arts (MA, MFA, MM, DMA, PhD); music education (MM, PhD); music history (MM); music theory (MM); performance (MM, DMA); piano pedagogy (MM); stage design (MFA); studio art (MFA); woodwind specialties (MM). *Application fee:* $40. Electronic applications accepted. *Application Contact:* Ginny Gross, Director of Graduate Admissions, 402-472-2878, Fax: 402-472-0589, E-mail: grad_admissions@unl.edu. *Dean,* Dr. Giacomo Oliva, 402-472-9339, Fax: 402-472-9353.

College of Journalism and Mass Communications Students: 22 full-time (12 women), 48 part-time (21 women); includes 4 minority (2 American Indian/Alaska Native, 1 Asian American or Pacific Islander, 1 Hispanic American), 4 international. Average age 33. *Faculty:* 17 full-time (7 women). Expenses: Contact institution. *Financial support:* Fellowships, research assistantships, teaching assistantships, Federal Work-Study, health care benefits, and unspecified assistantships available. Financial award application deadline: 2/15. In 2008, 23 master's awarded. Postbaccalaureate distance learning degree programs offered (no on-campus study). Offers marketing, communication and advertising (MA); professional journalism (MA). *Application deadline:* For fall admission, 3/15 for domestic students, 3/1 for international students; for spring admission, 10/15 for domestic students. Applications are processed on a rolling basis. *Application fee:* $40. Electronic applications accepted. *Application Contact:* Ginny Gross, Director of Graduate Admissions, 402-472-2878, Fax: 402-472-0589, E-mail: grad_admissions@unl.edu. *Dean,* Dr. Will Norton, 402-472-3041.

UNIVERSITY OF NEBRASKA MEDICAL CENTER, Omaha, NE 68198

General Information State-supported, coed, upper-level institution. CGS member. *Graduate housing:* On-campus housing not available. *Research affiliation:* UNeMed Corporation (biotechnology).

GRADUATE UNITS

College of Dentistry Offers dentistry (DDS, MS, PhD, Certificate).

College of Medicine Students: 481 full-time (200 women); includes 43 minority (14 African Americans, 5 American Indian/Alaska Native, 13 Asian Americans or Pacific Islanders, 11 Hispanic Americans). Average age 22. 1,415 applicants, 12% accepted, 126 enrolled. *Faculty:* 583 full-time, 100 part-time/adjunct. Expenses: Contact institution. *Financial support:* Career-related internships or fieldwork, Federal Work-Study, institutionally sponsored loans, and tuition waivers (full) available. Support available to part-time students. Financial award application deadline: 2/1; financial award applicants required to submit FAFSA. In 2008, 115 first professional degrees awarded. Offers medicine (MD, Certificate). *Application deadline:* For fall admission, 11/1 for domestic students. Applications are processed on a rolling basis. *Application fee:* $70. Electronic applications accepted. *Application Contact:* Gigi R. Rogers, Administrative Coordinator, 402-559-2259, Fax: 402-559-6840, E-mail: grrogers@unmc.edu. *Dean,* Dr. John L. Gollan, 402-559-4146, Fax: 402-559-4148.

College of Pharmacy Students: 258 full-time (178 women); includes 25 minority (6 African Americans, 14 Asian Americans or Pacific Islanders, 5 Hispanic Americans). Average age 23. 174 applicants, 37% accepted, 65 enrolled. *Faculty:* 28 full-time (4 women), 2 part-time/adjunct (0 women). Expenses: Contact institution. *Financial support:* Career-related internships or fieldwork, Federal Work-Study, institutionally sponsored loans, and scholarships/grants available. Support available to part-time students. Financial award application deadline: 4/1; financial award applicants required to submit FAFSA. In 2008, 61 Pharm Ds awarded. Offers pharmacy (Pharm D). *Application deadline:* For fall admission, 1/1 for domestic students. *Application fee:* $45. Electronic applications accepted. *Application Contact:* Dr. Charles H. Krobot, Associate Dean for Academic Affairs, 402-559-4333, Fax: 402-559-5060, E-mail:

University of Nebraska Medical Center (continued)

ckrobot@unmc.edu. *Dean,* Dr. Courtney V. Fletcher, 402-559-4333, Fax: 402-559-5060, E-mail: cfletcher@unmc.edu.

Graduate Studies *Degree program information:* Part-time programs available. Post-baccalaureate distance learning degree programs offered. Offers biochemistry and molecular biology (MS, PhD); cancer research (PhD); environmental health, occupational health and toxicology (MS, PhD); genetics, cell biology and anatomy (MS, PhD); medical sciences (MS, PhD); neuroscience (MS, PhD); nursing (MSN, PhD); pathology and microbiology (MS, PhD); pharmaceutical sciences (MS, PhD); pharmacology (MS, PhD); physiology (MS, PhD); public health (MPH). Electronic applications accepted.

School of Allied Health Professions Offers allied health professions (MPAS, MPS, DPT, Certificate); cytotechnology (Certificate); dietetic internship (Certificate); distance education perfusion education (MPS); perfusion science (MPS); physical therapy education (DPT); physician assistant education (MPAS).

UNIVERSITY OF NEVADA, LAS VEGAS, Las Vegas, NV 89154-9900

General Information State-supported, coed, university. CGS member. *Enrollment:* 28,617 graduate, professional, and undergraduate students; 1,967 full-time matriculated graduate/professional students (1,143 women), 1,961 part-time matriculated graduate/professional students (1,218 women). *Enrollment by degree level:* 2,981 master's, 840 doctoral, 107 other advanced degrees. *Graduate faculty:* 706 full-time (242 women), 143 part-time/adjunct (65 women). Tuition, state resident: part-time $198 per credit. Tuition, nonresident: part-time $415.75 per credit. *Required fees:* $4 per credit. $252 per semester. Tuition and fees vary according to course load. *Graduate housing:* Room and/or apartments available on a first-come, first-served basis to single students; on-campus housing not available to married students. Typical cost: $11,000 (including board). Room and board charges vary according to board plan. Housing application deadline: 5/1. *Student services:* Campus employment opportunities, campus safety program, career counseling, child daycare facilities, exercise/wellness program, free psychological counseling, grant writing training, international student services, low-cost health insurance, multicultural affairs office, services for students with disabilities, teacher training, writing training. *Library facilities:* Lied Library. *Online resources:* library catalog, web page, access to other libraries' catalogs. *Collection:* 1.3 million titles, 18,568 serial subscriptions, 82,459 audiovisual materials.

Computer facilities: 2,100 computers available on campus for general student use. A campuswide network can be accessed from student residence rooms and from off campus. Online class registration is available. *Web address:* http://www.unlv.edu/.

General Application Contact: Frederick Krauss, Director of Graduate Outreach, 702-895-5773, Fax: 702-895-4180, E-mail: frederick.krauss@unlv.edu.

GRADUATE UNITS

Graduate College Students: 1,954 full-time (1,106 women), 1,980 part-time (1,255 women); includes 680 minority (206 African Americans, 22 American Indian/Alaska Native, 214 Asian Americans or Pacific Islanders, 238 Hispanic Americans), 342 international. Average age 33. 3,130 applicants, 58% accepted, 1188 enrolled. *Faculty:* 706 full-time (242 women), 143 part-time/adjunct (65 women). Expenses: Contact institution. *Financial support:* In 2008–09, 905 students received support, including 6 fellowships with full and partial tuition reimbursements available (averaging $55,000 per year), 352 research assistantships with partial tuition reimbursements available (averaging $122,609 per year), 547 teaching assistantships with partial tuition reimbursements available (averaging $125,211 per year); institutionally sponsored loans, scholarships/grants, health care benefits, and unspecified assistantships also available. Financial award application deadline: 3/1. In 2008, 1,252 master's, 115 doctorates, 48 other advanced degrees awarded. *Degree program information:* Part-time and evening/weekend programs available. *Application deadline:* For fall admission, 8/1 for domestic students, 5/1 for international students; for spring admission, 12/1 for domestic students, 10/1 for international students. *Application fee:* $60 ($75 for international students). Electronic applications accepted. *Application Contact:* Graduate College Admissions Evaluator, 702-895-3320, Fax: 702-895-4180, E-mail: gradcollege@unlv.edu. *Vice President for Research and Dean of the Graduate College,* Dr. Ronald Smith, 702-895-4070, Fax: 702-895-4180, E-mail: ron.smith@unlv.edu.

College of Business Students: 256 full-time (110 women), 174 part-time (73 women); includes 64 minority (11 African Americans, 1 American Indian/Alaska Native, 35 Asian Americans or Pacific Islanders, 17 Hispanic Americans), 46 international. Average age 31. 423 applicants, 57% accepted, 146 enrolled. *Faculty:* 48 full-time (6 women), 5 part-time/adjunct (2 women). Expenses: Contact institution. *Financial support:* In 2008–09, 34 students received support, including 13 research assistantships with partial tuition reimbursements available (averaging $10,167 per year), 21 teaching assistantships with partial tuition reimbursements available (averaging $10,000 per year); institutionally sponsored loans, scholarships/grants, health care benefits, and unspecified assistantships also available. Financial award application deadline: 3/1. In 2008, 168 master's awarded. *Degree program information:* Part-time and evening/weekend programs available. Offers accounting (MS); business (EMBA, MA, MBA, MS); business administration (EMBA, MBA); economics (MA); management information systems (MS). *Application deadline:* For fall admission, 8/1 for domestic students, 5/1 for international students; for spring admission, 12/1 for domestic students, 10/1 for international students. Applications are processed on a rolling basis. *Application fee:* $60 ($75 for international students). Electronic applications accepted. *Application Contact:* Graduate College Admissions Evaluator, 702-895-3320, Fax: 702-895-4180, E-mail: gradcollege@unlv.edu. *Dean,* Dr. Paul Jarley, 702-895-3362, Fax: 702-895-4090, E-mail: paul.jarley@unlv.edu.

College of Education Students: 524 full-time (392 women), 855 part-time (615 women); includes 275 minority (87 African Americans, 9 American Indian/Alaska Native, 69 Asian Americans or Pacific Islanders, 110 Hispanic Americans), 29 international. Average age 35. 668 applicants, 79% accepted, 413 enrolled. *Faculty:* 108 full-time (58 women), 55 part-time/adjunct (40 women). Expenses: Contact institution. *Financial support:* In 2008–09, 133 students received support, including 102 research assistantships with partial tuition reimbursements available (averaging $10,313 per year), 31 teaching assistantships with partial tuition reimbursements available (averaging $11,000 per year); institutionally sponsored loans, scholarships/grants, health care benefits, and unspecified assistantships also available. Financial award application deadline: 3/1. In 2008, 574 master's, 28 doctorates, 10 other advanced degrees awarded. *Degree program information:* Part-time and evening/weekend programs available. Offers addiction studies (Advanced Certificate); community mental health (MS); curriculum and instruction (M Ed, Ed D, PhD); early childhood education (M Ed); education (M Ed, MS, Ed D, Exec Ed D, PhD, Advanced Certificate, Ed S); educational leadership (M Ed, MS, Ed D, Exec Ed D, PhD); educational psychology (MS, PhD); learning and technology (PhD); physical education (M Ed, MS); rehabilitation counseling (Advanced Certificate); school counseling (M Ed); school psychology (Ed S); special education (MS, Ed D, PhD, Ed S); sports education leadership (PhD); teacher education (PhD). *Application deadline:* For fall admission, 8/1 for domestic students, 5/1 for international students; for spring admission, 12/1 for domestic and international students. Applications are processed on a rolling basis. *Application fee:* $60 ($75 for international students). Electronic applications accepted. *Application Contact:* Graduate College Admissions Evaluator, 702-895-3320, Fax: 702-895-4180, E-mail: gradcollege@unlv.edu. *Interim Dean,* Dr. William Speer, 702-895-3375, Fax: 702-895-4068, E-mail: william.speer@unlv.edu.

College of Fine Arts Students: 139 full-time (63 women), 53 part-time (23 women); includes 21 minority (2 African Americans, 2 American Indian/Alaska Native, 4 Asian Americans or Pacific Islanders, 13 Hispanic Americans), 19 international. Average age 31. 205 applicants, 53% accepted, 67 enrolled. *Faculty:* 58 full-time (11 women), 33 part-time/adjunct (7 women). Expenses: Contact institution. *Financial support:* In 2008–09, 98 students received support, including 22 research assistantships with partial tuition reimbursements available (averaging $10,833 per year), 76 teaching assistantships with partial tuition reimbursements available (averaging $10,586 per year); institutionally sponsored loans, scholarships/grants, health care benefits, and unspecified assistantships also available. Financial award application deadline: 3/1. In 2008, 55 master's, 2 doctorates awarded. *Degree program information:* Part-time programs available. Offers architecture (M Arch); art (MFA); fine arts (M Arch, MA, MFA, MM, DMA); music (MM); musical arts (DMA); screenwriting (MFA); theatre arts (MA, MFA). *Application deadline:* For fall admission, 8/1 for domestic students, 5/1 for international students; for spring admission, 12/1 for domestic students, 10/1 for international students. Applications are processed on a rolling basis. *Application fee:* $60 ($75 for international students). Electronic applications accepted. *Application Contact:* Graduate College Admissions Evaluator, 702-895-3320, Fax: 702-895-4180, E-mail: gradcollege@unlv.edu. *Dean,* Dr. Jeffrey Koep, 702-895-4210, Fax: 702-895-4194, E-mail: jeffrey.koep@unlv.edu.

College of Liberal Arts Students: 215 full-time (129 women), 152 part-time (84 women); includes 47 minority (13 African Americans, 2 American Indian/Alaska Native, 12 Asian Americans or Pacific Islanders, 20 Hispanic Americans), 11 international. Average age 35. 424 applicants, 33% accepted, 93 enrolled. *Faculty:* 130 full-time (51 women), 11 part-time/adjunct (4 women). Expenses: Contact institution. *Financial support:* In 2008–09, 203 students received support, including 2 fellowships with full tuition reimbursements available (averaging $17,000 per year), 24 research assistantships with partial tuition reimbursements available (averaging $12,263 per year), 177 teaching assistantships with partial tuition reimbursements available (averaging $11,684 per year); institutionally sponsored loans, scholarships/grants, health care benefits, and unspecified assistantships also available. Financial award application deadline: 3/1. In 2008, 52 master's, 18 doctorates, 2 other advanced degrees awarded. *Degree program information:* Part-time programs available. Offers anthropology (MA, PhD); creative writing (MFA); English (MA, PhD); ethics and policy studies (MA); Hispanic studies (MA); history (MA, PhD); liberal arts (MA, MFA, PhD, Certificate); political science (PhD); psychology (PhD); sociology (MA, PhD); Spanish translation (Certificate); women's studies (Certificate). *Application deadline:* For fall admission, 8/1 for domestic students, 5/1 for international students; for spring admission, 12/1 for domestic students, 10/1 for international students. Applications are processed on a rolling basis. *Application fee:* $60 ($75 for international students). Electronic applications accepted. *Application Contact:* Graduate College Admissions Evaluator, 702-895-3320, Fax: 702-895-4180, E-mail: gradcollege@unlv.edu. *Dean,* Dr. Chris Hudgins, 702-895-3401, Fax: 702-895-4097, E-mail: chris.hudgins@unlv.edu.

College of Science Students: 170 full-time (65 women), 78 part-time (33 women); includes 26 minority (7 African Americans, 1 American Indian/Alaska Native, 15 Asian Americans or Pacific Islanders, 3 Hispanic Americans), 54 international. Average age 32. 168 applicants, 63% accepted, 63 enrolled. *Faculty:* 110 full-time (17 women), 5 part-time/adjunct (1 woman). Expenses: Contact institution. *Financial support:* In 2008–09, 165 students received support, including 3 fellowships with full tuition reimbursements available (averaging $18,000 per year), 43 research assistantships with partial tuition reimbursements available (averaging $14,303 per year), 119 teaching assistantships with partial tuition reimbursements available (averaging $12,420 per year); institutionally sponsored loans, scholarships/grants, health care benefits, and unspecified assistantships also available. Financial award application deadline: 3/1. In 2008, 39 master's, 11 doctorates awarded. *Degree program information:* Part-time programs available. Offers astronomy (MS); biochemistry (MS); chemistry (MS, PhD); geoscience (MS, PhD); life sciences (MS, PhD); mathematical sciences (MS, PhD); physics (MS, PhD); radiochemistry (PhD); science (MA, MS, PhD); water resources management (MS). *Application deadline:* For fall admission, 8/1 for domestic students, 5/1 for international students; for spring admission, 12/1 for domestic students, 10/1 for international students. Applications are processed on a rolling basis. *Application fee:* $60 ($75 for international students). Electronic applications accepted. *Application Contact:* Graduate College Admissions Evaluator, 702-895-3320, Fax: 702-895-4180, E-mail: gradcollege@unlv.edu. *Interim Dean,* Dr. Wanda Taylor, 702-895-3487, Fax: 702-895-4159, E-mail: wanda.taylor@unlv.edu.

Greenspun College of Urban Affairs Students: 218 full-time (163 women), 260 part-time (164 women); includes 116 minority (54 African Americans, 1 American Indian/Alaska Native, 14 Asian Americans or Pacific Islanders, 47 Hispanic Americans), 10 international. Average age 35. 447 applicants, 60% accepted, 173 enrolled. *Faculty:* 61 full-time (30 women), 2 part-time/adjunct (1 woman). Expenses: Contact institution. *Financial support:* In 2008–09, 54 students received support, including 17 research assistantships with partial tuition reimbursements available (averaging $10,000 per year), 37 teaching assistantships with partial tuition reimbursements available (averaging $10,933 per year); institutionally sponsored loans, scholarships/grants, health care benefits, and unspecified assistantships also available. Financial award application deadline: 3/1. In 2008, 152 master's, 4 doctorates, 32 other advanced degrees awarded. *Degree program information:* Part-time and evening/weekend programs available. Offers communication studies (MA); criminal justice (MA); crisis and emergency management (MS); environmental studies (MS, PhD); forensic social work (Advanced Certificate); journalism and media studies (MA); marriage and family therapy (MS, Advanced Certificate); non-profit management (Certificate); public administration (MPA); public affairs (PhD); public management (Certificate); social work (MSW); urban affairs (MA, MPA, MS, MSW, PhD, Advanced Certificate, Certificate). *Application deadline:* For fall admission, 8/1 for domestic students, 5/1 for international students; for spring admission, 12/1 for domestic students, 10/1 for international students. Applications are processed on a rolling basis. *Application fee:* $60 ($75 for international students). Electronic applications accepted. *Application Contact:* Graduate College Admissions Evaluator, 702-895-3320, Fax: 702-895-4180, E-mail: gradcollege@unlv.edu. *Dean,* Dr. E. Lee Bernick, 702-895-3291, Fax: 702-895-4231, E-mail: lee.burnick@unlv.edu.

Howard R. Hughes College of Engineering Students: 131 full-time (23 women), 100 part-time (23 women); includes 32 minority (7 African Americans, 1 American Indian/Alaska Native, 17 Asian Americans or Pacific Islanders, 7 Hispanic Americans), 105 international. Average age 31. 270 applicants, 59% accepted, 56 enrolled. *Faculty:* 70 full-time (8 women), 17 part-time/adjunct (0 women). Expenses: Contact institution. *Financial support:* In 2008–09, 127 students received support, including 1 fellowship with full tuition reimbursement available (averaging $20,000 per year), 57 research assistantships with partial tuition reimbursements available (averaging $11,723 per year), 69 teaching assistantships with partial tuition reimbursements available (averaging $10,624 per year); institutionally sponsored loans, scholarships/grants, health care benefits, and unspecified assistantships also available. Financial award application deadline: 3/1. In 2008, 62 master's, 10 doctorates awarded. *Degree program information:* Part-time programs available. Offers aerospace engineering (MS); biomedical engineering (MS); civil and environmental engineering (MS, PhD); computer science (MS, PhD); construction management (MS); electrical and computer engineering (MSE, PhD); engineering (MS, MSE, PhD); informatics (MS, PhD); materials and nuclear engineering (MS); mechanical engineering (MS); transportation (MS). *Application deadline:* For fall admission, 8/1 for domestic students, 5/1 for international students; for spring admission, 12/1 for domestic students, 10/1 for international students. Applications are processed on a rolling basis. *Application fee:* $60 ($75 for international students). Electronic applications accepted. *Application Contact:* Graduate College Admissions Evaluator, 702-895-3320, Fax: 702-895-4180, E-mail: gradcollege@unlv.edu. *Dean,* Dr. Eric Sandgren, 702-895-3699, Fax: 702-895-4059, E-mail: eric.sandgren@unlv.edu.

School of Allied Health Sciences Students: 114 full-time (60 women), 34 part-time (10 women); includes 11 minority (1 African American, 1 American Indian/Alaska Native, 7 Asian Americans or Pacific Islanders, 2 Hispanic Americans), 7 international. Average age 28. 128 applicants, 32% accepted, 23 enrolled. *Faculty:* 29 full-time (10 women), 3 part-time/adjunct (2 women). Expenses: Contact institution. *Financial support:* In 2008–09, 37 students received support, including 27 research assistantships with partial tuition reimbursements available (averaging $10,816 per year), 10 teaching assistantships with partial tuition reimbursements available (averaging $11,000 per year); institutionally sponsored loans, scholarships/grants, health care benefits, and unspecified assistantships also available. Financial award application deadline: 3/1. In 2008, 16 master's, 33 doctorates awarded. *Degree program information:* Part-time programs available. Offers exercise physiology (MS); health physics (MS); health sciences (MS, DPT); kinesiology (MS); physical therapy (DPT). *Application deadline:* For fall admission, 8/1 for domestic students, 5/1 for international students; for spring admission, 12/1 for domestic students, 10/1 for international students. Applications are processed on a rolling basis. *Application fee:* $60 ($75 for international students). Electronic applications accepted. *Application Contact:* Graduate

College Admissions Evaluator, 702-895-3320, Fax: 702-895-4180, E-mail: gradcollege@unlv.edu. *Interim Dean*, Dr. Carolyn Yucha, 702-895-3906, Fax: 702-895-5050, E-mail: carolyn.yucha@unlv.edu.

School of Community Health Sciences Students: 70 full-time (50 women), 95 part-time (73 women); includes 38 minority (15 African Americans, 1 American Indian/Alaska Native, 14 Asian Americans or Pacific Islanders, 8 Hispanic Americans), 12 international. Average age 34. 118 applicants, 74% accepted, 63 enrolled. *Faculty:* 15 full-time (5 women). Expenses: Contact institution. *Financial support:* In 2008–09, 14 students received support, including 12 research assistantships with partial tuition reimbursements available (averaging $10,364 per year), 2 teaching assistantships with partial tuition reimbursements available (averaging $10,000 per year); institutionally sponsored loans, scholarships/grants, health care benefits, and unspecified assistantships also available. Financial award application deadline: 3/1. In 2008, 39 master's awarded. Offers community health sciences (M Ed, MHA, MPH); health care administration (MHA); health care promotion (M Ed); public health (MPH). *Application deadline:* For fall admission, 6/1 priority date for domestic students, 5/1 for international students; for spring admission, 11/1 priority date for domestic students, 10/1 for international students. Applications are processed on a rolling basis. *Application fee:* $60 ($75 for international students). Electronic applications accepted. *Application Contact:* Dr. Mary Guinan, Dean, 702-895-5090, Fax: 702-895-5184, E-mail: mary.guinan@unlv.edu. *Dean*, Dr. Mary Guinan, 702-895-5090, Fax: 702-895-5184, E-mail: mary.guinan@unlv.edu.

School of Nursing Students: 68 full-time (56 women), 94 part-time (83 women); includes 33 minority (4 African Americans, 1 American Indian/Alaska Native, 20 Asian Americans or Pacific Islanders, 8 Hispanic Americans), 20 international. Average age 40. 128 applicants, 59% accepted, 54 enrolled. *Faculty:* 35 full-time (30 women), 5 part-time/adjunct (all women). Expenses: Contact institution. *Financial support:* In 2008–09, 7 students received support, including 5 research assistantships with partial tuition reimbursements available (averaging $11,750 per year), 2 teaching assistantships (averaging $15,000 per year); institutionally sponsored loans, scholarships/grants, health care benefits, and unspecified assistantships also available. Financial award application deadline: 3/1. In 2008, 40 master's, 3 doctorates, 4 other advanced degrees awarded. *Degree program information:* Part-time programs available. Postbaccalaureate distance learning degree programs offered (minimal on-campus study). Offers family nurse practitioner (Advanced Certificate); nursing (MS, PhD); nursing education (Advanced Certificate). *Application deadline:* For fall admission, 3/1 priority date for domestic and international students. Applications are processed on a rolling basis. *Application fee:* $60 ($75 for international students). Electronic applications accepted. *Application Contact:* Graduate College Admissions Evaluator, 702-895-3320, Fax: 702-895-4180, E-mail: gradcollege@unlv.edu. *Interim Dean*, Dr. Carolyn Yucha, 702-895-3906, Fax: 702-895-5050, E-mail: carolyn.yucha@unlv.edu.

William F. Harrah College of Hotel Administration Students: 62 full-time (32 women), 66 part-time (37 women); includes 17 minority (5 African Americans, 2 American Indian/Alaska Native, 7 Asian Americans or Pacific Islanders, 3 Hispanic Americans), 29 international. Average age 33. 151 applicants, 45% accepted, 37 enrolled. *Faculty:* 42 full-time (16 women), 7 part-time/adjunct (3 women). Expenses: Contact institution. *Financial support:* In 2008–09, 33 students received support, including 30 research assistantships with partial tuition reimbursements available (averaging $10,077 per year), 3 teaching assistantships with partial tuition reimbursements available (averaging $12,000 per year); institutionally sponsored loans, scholarships/grants, health care benefits, and unspecified assistantships also available. Financial award application deadline: 3/1. In 2008, 55 master's, 6 doctorates awarded. *Degree program information:* Part-time programs available. Offers food and beverage management (Certificate); hospitality administration (MHA, PhD); hotel administration (MS); sport and leisure services management (MS). *Application deadline:* For fall admission, 8/1 for domestic students, 5/1 for international students; for spring admission, 12/1 for domestic students, 10/1 for international students. Applications are processed on a rolling basis. *Application fee:* $60 ($75 for international students). Electronic applications accepted. *Application Contact:* Graduate College Admissions Evaluator, 702-895-3320, Fax: 702-895-4180, E-mail: gradcollege@unlv.edu. *Dean*, Dr. Stuart Mann, 702-895-3308, Fax: 702-895-4109, E-mail: stuart.mann@unlv.edu.

William S. Boyd School of Law Students: 110 full-time (48 women), 47 part-time (21 women); includes 48 minority (8 African Americans, 5 American Indian/Alaska Native, 20 Asian Americans or Pacific Islanders, 15 Hispanic Americans). 1,755 applicants, 23% accepted, 157 enrolled. *Faculty:* 42 full-time (20 women), 15 part-time/adjunct (4 women). Expenses: Contact institution. *Financial support:* In 2008–09, 360 students received support. Career-related internships or fieldwork and scholarships/grants available. Support available to part-time students. Financial award application deadline: 2/1; financial award applicants required to submit FAFSA. In 2008, 141 JDs awarded. *Degree program information:* Part-time and evening/weekend programs available. Offers law (JD). *Application deadline:* For fall admission, 3/15 priority date for domestic and international students. Applications are processed on a rolling basis. *Application fee:* $50. Electronic applications accepted. *Application Contact:* Elizabeth M Karl, Admissions and Records Assistant, 702-895-2440, Fax: 702-895-2414, E-mail: elizabeth.karl@unlv.edu. *Dean*, John V. White, 702-895-3671, Fax: 702-895-1095.

See Close-Up on page 1033.

UNIVERSITY OF NEVADA, RENO, Reno, NV 89557

General Information State-supported, coed, university. CGS member. *Enrollment:* 16,867 graduate, professional, and undergraduate students; 998 full-time matriculated graduate/professional students (583 women), 1,618 part-time matriculated graduate/professional students (906 women). *Enrollment by degree level:* 53 first professional, 1,699 master's, 836 doctoral, 28 other advanced degrees. *Graduate faculty:* 1,035 full-time (321 women). Tuition, state resident: full-time $1710; part-time $1140 per semester. Tuition, nonresident: full-time $7115. *Required fees:* $158 per semester. *Graduate housing:* Rooms and/or apartments available on a first-come, first-served basis to single and married students. Typical cost: $5425 per year ($9285 including board) for single students. Room and board charges vary according to board plan. Housing application deadline: 5/16. *Student services:* Campus employment opportunities, campus safety program, child daycare facilities, exercise/wellness program, free psychological counseling, international student services, low-cost health insurance, multicultural affairs office, services for students with disabilities, teacher training. *Library facilities:* Mathewson-IGT Knowledge Center plus 2 others. *Online resources:* library catalog, web page, access to other libraries' catalogs. *Collection:* 1.1 million titles, 24,527 serial subscriptions, 23,345 audiovisual materials. *Research affiliation:* Desert Research Institute (natural resource sciences/environmental sciences).

Computer facilities: Computer purchase and lease plans are available. 500 computers available on campus for general student use. A campuswide network can be accessed from student residence rooms and from off campus. Online class registration is available. *Web address:* http://www.unr.edu/.

General Application Contact: Lisa Oliveto, Recruitment Coordinator, 775-327-2361, Fax: 775-784-6064, E-mail: loliveto@unr.edu.

GRADUATE UNITS

Graduate School Students: 998 full-time (583 women), 1,618 part-time (906 women); includes 447 minority (57 African Americans, 23 American Indian/Alaska Native, 200 Asian Americans or Pacific Islanders, 167 Hispanic Americans), 359 international. Average age 33. 1,986 applicants, 51% accepted, 709 enrolled. *Faculty:* 1,035 full-time (321 women). Expenses: Contact institution. *Financial support:* In 2008–09, 4 fellowships with partial tuition reimbursements (averaging $26,328 per year), 423 research assistantships with partial tuition reimbursements (averaging $14,000 per year), 485 teaching assistantships with partial tuition reimbursements (averaging $14,000 per year) were awarded; career-related internships or fieldwork, Federal Work-Study, institutionally sponsored loans, scholarships/grants, health care benefits, and unspecified assistantships also available. Support available to part-time students. Financial award application deadline: 3/1; financial award applicants required to submit FAFSA. In 2008, 626 master's, 112 doctorates, 4 other advanced degrees awarded. *Degree program information:* Part-time and evening/weekend programs available. Postbaccalaureate distance learning degree programs offered (no on-campus study). Offers atmospheric sciences (MS, PhD); Basque studies (PhD); biomedical engineering (MS, PhD); cell and molecular biology (MS, PhD); cellular and molecular pharmacology and physiology (PhD); chemical physics (PhD); ecology, evolution, and conservation biology (PhD); environmental sciences and health (MS, PhD); hydrogeology (MS, PhD); hydrology (MS, PhD); social psychology (PhD). *Application deadline:* Applications are processed on a rolling basis. *Application fee:* $60 ($95 for international students). Electronic applications accepted. *Application Contact:* Michele Sandberg, Application Contact, 775-784-7026, Fax: 775-784-6064, E-mail: gradschool@unr.edu. *Interim Dean*, Dr. Marsha Read, 775-784-6869, Fax: 775-784-6064, E-mail: read@unr.nevada.edu.

College of Agriculture, Biotechnology and Natural Resources Students: 53 full-time (30 women), 43 part-time (26 women); includes 6 minority (1 African American, 2 Asian Americans or Pacific Islanders, 3 Hispanic Americans), 14 international. Average age 33. 86 applicants, 55% accepted, 36 enrolled. *Faculty:* 87 full-time (29 women). Expenses: Contact institution. *Financial support:* In 2008–09, 54 research assistantships with partial tuition reimbursements (averaging $20,000 per year), 11 teaching assistantships with partial tuition reimbursements (averaging $20,000 per year) were awarded; Federal Work-Study, institutionally sponsored loans, scholarships/grants, health care benefits, and unspecified assistantships also available. Financial award application deadline: 3/1; financial award applicants required to submit FAFSA. In 2008, 23 master's, 2 doctorates awarded. Offers agriculture, biotechnology and natural resources (MS, PhD); animal science (MS); biochemistry (MS, PhD); biotechnology (MS); natural resources and environmental sciences (MS); nutrition (MS); resource economics (MS, PhD). *Application deadline:* For fall admission, 3/1 priority date for domestic and international students; for spring admission, 11/1 priority date for domestic and international students. Applications are processed on a rolling basis. *Application fee:* $60 ($95 for international students). Electronic applications accepted. *Application Contact:* Michele Sandberg, Application Contact, 775-784-7026, Fax: 775-784-6064, E-mail: gradschool@unr.edu. *Dean*, Dr. David Thawley, 775-784-1610.

College of Business Administration Students: 97 full-time (33 women), 163 part-time (64 women); includes 32 minority (4 African Americans, 1 American Indian/Alaska Native, 15 Asian Americans or Pacific Islanders, 12 Hispanic Americans), 20 international. Average age 31. 170 applicants, 68% accepted, 87 enrolled. *Faculty:* 58 full-time (18 women). Expenses: Contact institution. *Financial support:* In 2008–09, 22 research assistantships with partial tuition reimbursements, 1 teaching assistantship with partial tuition reimbursement were awarded; career-related internships or fieldwork, Federal Work-Study, institutionally sponsored loans, scholarships/grants, health care benefits, and unspecified assistantships also available. Financial award application deadline: 3/1; financial award applicants required to submit FAFSA. In 2008, 95 master's awarded. *Degree program information:* Part-time programs available. Postbaccalaureate distance learning degree programs offered. Offers accounting and information systems (M Acc); business administration (M Acc, MA, MBA, MS); economics (MA, MS); finance (MS); information systems (MS). *Application deadline:* Applications are processed on a rolling basis. *Application fee:* $60 ($95 for international students). Electronic applications accepted. *Application Contact:* Dr. Greg Mosier, Dean, 775-784-4912. *Dean*, Dr. Greg Mosier, 775-784-4912.

College of Education Students: 224 full-time (174 women), 473 part-time (378 women); includes 78 minority (13 African Americans, 3 American Indian/Alaska Native, 21 Asian Americans or Pacific Islanders, 41 Hispanic Americans), 22 international. Average age 37. 334 applicants, 55% accepted, 144 enrolled. *Faculty:* 75 full-time (45 women). Expenses: Contact institution. *Financial support:* In 2008–09, 63 research assistantships with partial tuition reimbursements, 10 teaching assistantships with partial tuition reimbursements were awarded; Federal Work-Study, institutionally sponsored loans, scholarships/grants, health care benefits, and unspecified assistantships also available. Financial award application deadline: 3/1; financial award applicants required to submit FAFSA. In 2008, 188 master's, 12 doctorates, 4 other advanced degrees awarded. Offers counseling and educational psychology (M Ed, MA, MS, Ed D, PhD, Ed S); curriculum and instruction (PhD); curriculum, teaching and learning (Ed D, PhD); education (M Ed, MA, MS, Ed D, PhD, Ed S); educational leadership (M Ed, MA, MS, Ed D, PhD, Ed S); educational specialties (M Ed, MA, MS, Ed D, PhD); elementary education (M Ed, MA, MS); human development and family studies (MS); literacy studies (M Ed, MA, Ed D, PhD); secondary education (M Ed, MA, MS); special education (M Ed, MA, MS, Ed D, PhD); special education and disability studies (PhD); teaching English to speakers of other languages (MA). *Application deadline:* Applications are processed on a rolling basis. *Application fee:* $60 ($95 for international students). Electronic applications accepted. *Application Contact:* Michele Sandberg, Application Contact, 775-784-7026, Fax: 775-784-6064, E-mail: gradschool@unr.edu. *Dean*, Dr. William E. Sparkman, 775-784-4345.

College of Engineering Students: 98 full-time (26 women), 130 part-time (21 women); includes 30 minority (3 African Americans, 1 American Indian/Alaska Native, 21 Asian Americans or Pacific Islanders, 5 Hispanic Americans), 113 international. Average age 30. 290 applicants, 57% accepted, 64 enrolled. *Faculty:* 76 full-time (6 women). Expenses: Contact institution. *Financial support:* In 2008–09, 50 research assistantships with partial tuition reimbursements (averaging $18,000 per year), 32 teaching assistantships with partial tuition reimbursements (averaging $14,000 per year) were awarded; fellowships, Federal Work-Study, institutionally sponsored loans, scholarships/grants, health care benefits, and tuition waivers (full) also available. Financial award application deadline: 3/1; financial award applicants required to submit FAFSA. In 2008, 68 master's, 4 doctorates awarded. Offers chemical engineering (MS, PhD); civil and environmental engineering (MS, PhD); computer engineering (MS); computer science (MS); computer science and engineering (MS, PhD); electrical engineering (MS, PhD); engineering (MS, PhD); materials science and engineering (MS, PhD); mechanical engineering (MS, PhD). *Application deadline:* For fall admission, 3/1 priority date for domestic and international students. Applications are processed on a rolling basis. *Application fee:* $60 ($95 for international students). Electronic applications accepted. *Application Contact:* Michele Sandberg, Application Contact, 775-784-7026, Fax: 775-784-6064, E-mail: gradschool@unr.edu. *Dean*, Dr. Emmanuel 'Manos" Maragakis, 775-784-6925, E-mail: maragaki@unr.edu.

College of Liberal Arts Students: 187 full-time (107 women), 271 part-time (15 women); includes 44 minority (11 African Americans, 3 American Indian/Alaska Native, 9 Asian Americans or Pacific Islanders, 21 Hispanic Americans), 19 international. Average age 35. 428 applicants, 41% accepted, 120 enrolled. *Faculty:* 194 full-time (76 women). Expenses: Contact institution. *Financial support:* In 2008–09, 112 research assistantships with partial tuition reimbursements (averaging $14,000 per year), 182 teaching assistantships with partial tuition reimbursements (averaging $14,000 per year) were awarded; fellowships, Federal Work-Study, institutionally sponsored loans, scholarships/grants, health care benefits, tuition waivers (full), and unspecified assistantships also available. Financial award application deadline: 3/1; financial award applicants required to submit FAFSA. In 2008, 113 master's, 36 doctorates awarded. *Degree program information:* Part-time and evening/weekend programs available. Postbaccalaureate distance learning degree programs offered (no on-campus study). Offers anthropology (MA, PhD); behavior analysis (MA, PhD); clinical psychology (MA, PhD); cognitive brain science (MA, PhD); criminal justice (MA); English (MA, MATE, PhD); fine arts (MFA); French (MA); German (MA); history (MA, PhD); judicial studies (MJS, PhD); justice management (MJM); liberal arts (MA, MATE, MFA, MJM, MJS, MM, MPA, PhD); music (MA, MM); philosophy (MA); political science (MA, PhD); public administration (MPA); public administration and policy (MPA); social research and justice studies (MA, MJM, MJS, PhD); sociology (MA); Spanish (MA); speech communications (MA). *Application deadline:* Applications are processed on a rolling basis. *Application fee:* $60 ($95 for international students). Electronic applications accepted. *Application Contact:* Michele Sandberg, Application Contact, 775-784-7026, Fax: 775-784-6064, E-mail: gradschool@unr.edu. *Dean*, Dr. Heather Hardy, 775-784-6155.

College of Science Students: 75 full-time (33 women), 140 part-time (45 women); includes 17 minority (4 African Americans, 7 Asian Americans or Pacific Islanders, 6 Hispanic Americans), 74 international. Average age 38. 176 applicants, 49% accepted, 63 enrolled. *Faculty:* 147 full-time (25 women). Expenses: Contact institution. *Financial support:* In 2008–09, 94 research assistantships with partial tuition reimbursements (averaging $16,000 per year), 46 teaching assistantships with partial tuition reimbursements (averaging $16,000 per year) were awarded; Federal Work-Study, institutionally sponsored loans, scholarships/grants, health care benefits, and unspecified assistantships also available. Financial award

University of Nevada, Reno (continued)

application deadline: 3/1; financial award applicants required to submit FAFSA. In 2008, 51 master's, 13 doctorates awarded. Offers biology (MS); chemistry (MS, PhD); earth sciences and engineering (MS, PhD); geochemistry (MS, PhD); geography (MS, PhD); geological engineering (MS, PhD); geology (MS, PhD); geophysics (MS, PhD); land use planning (MS); mathematics (MS); mining engineering (MS); physics (MS, PhD); science (MATM, MS, PhD); teaching mathematics (MATM). *Application deadline:* Applications are processed on a rolling basis. *Application fee:* $60 ($95 for international students). Electronic applications accepted. *Application Contact:* Michele Sandberg, Application Contact, 775-784-7026, Fax: 775-784-6064, E-mail: gradschool@unr.edu. *Acting Dean*, Dr. Jeff Thompson, 775-784-4591, Fax: 775-784-4592, E-mail: thompsonj@unr.edu.

Division of Health Sciences Students: 113 full-time (91 women), 66 part-time (59 women); includes 28 minority (5 African Americans, 11 Asian Americans or Pacific Islanders, 12 Hispanic Americans), 9 international. Average age 35. 179 applicants, 65% accepted, 94 enrolled. *Faculty:* 67 full-time (50 women). Expenses: Contact institution. *Financial support:* In 2008–09, 29 research assistantships with partial tuition reimbursements (averaging $14,000 per year), 2 teaching assistantships with partial tuition reimbursements (averaging $14,000 per year) were awarded; Federal Work-Study, institutionally sponsored loans, scholarships/grants, health care benefits, and unspecified assistantships also available. Financial award application deadline: 3/1; financial award applicants required to submit FAFSA. In 2008, 50 master's awarded. Offers health and human sciences (MPH, MS, MSN, MSW, PhD); nursing (MSN); public health (MPH, PhD); social work (MSW); speech pathology (PhD); speech pathology and audiology (MS). *Application deadline:* Applications are processed on a rolling basis. *Application fee:* $60 ($95 for international students). Electronic applications accepted. *Application Contact:* Michele Sandberg, Application Contact, 775-784-7026, Fax: 775-784-6064, E-mail: gradschool@unr.edu. *Vice President*, Dr. John McDonald, 775-784-6976, E-mail: jam@unr.edu.

Donald W. Reynolds School of Journalism Students: 8 full-time (5 women), 2 part-time (both women); includes 2 minority (1 Asian American or Pacific Islander, 1 Hispanic American), 1 international. Average age 36. 16 applicants, 69% accepted, 11 enrolled. *Faculty:* 5 full-time (1 woman). Expenses: Contact institution. *Financial support:* In 2008–09, 4 research assistantships with partial tuition reimbursements (averaging $14,000 per year), 2 teaching assistantships with partial tuition reimbursements (averaging $14,000 per year) were awarded; Federal Work-Study, institutionally sponsored loans, scholarships/grants, health care benefits, and unspecified assistantships also available. Financial award application deadline: 3/1; financial award applicants required to submit FAFSA. In 2008, 8 master's awarded. Offers journalism (MA). *Application deadline:* For fall admission, 3/15 priority date for domestic and international students; for spring admission, 12/1 priority date for domestic and international students. Applications are processed on a rolling basis. *Application fee:* $60 ($95 for international students). Electronic applications accepted. *Application Contact:* Michele Sandberg, Application Contact, 775-784-7026, Fax: 775-784-6064, E-mail: gradschool@unr.edu. *Graduate Program Director*, Dr. Donica Mensing, 775-784-4187, E-mail: dmensing@unr.edu.

School of Medicine Expenses: Contact institution. *Financial support:* Fellowships, research assistantships, teaching assistantships, Federal Work-Study, institutionally sponsored loans, and health care benefits available. Support available to part-time students. Financial award application deadline: 3/1; financial award applicants required to submit FAFSA. In 2008, 51 MDs awarded. Offers medicine (MD). *Application deadline:* Applications are processed on a rolling basis. *Application Contact:* Peggy Dupey, PhD, Interim Associate Dean for Admissions and Student Affairs, 775-784-6063, E-mail: asa@med.unr.edu. *Dean*, Dr. OLE THIENHAUS, 775-784-6001, Fax: 775-784-8251, E-mail: othienhaus@unr.edu.

UNIVERSITY OF NEW BRUNSWICK FREDERICTON, Fredericton, NB E3B 5A3, Canada

General Information Province-supported, coed, university. *Enrollment:* 11,017 graduate, professional, and undergraduate students; 896 full-time matriculated graduate/professional students (398 women), 446 part-time matriculated graduate/professional students (299 women). *Graduate faculty:* 446 full-time (159 women), 99 part-time/adjunct (32 women). *Graduate tuition:* Tuition and fees charges are reported in Canadian dollars. *Tuition, area resident:* Full-time $5562 Canadian dollars. Tuition, Canadian resident: full-time $9450 Canadian dollars. *Required fees:* $333 Canadian dollars. *Graduate housing:* Rooms and/or apartments available on a first-come, first-served basis to single and married students. Housing application deadline: 5/31. *Student services:* Campus employment opportunities, campus safety program, career counseling, child daycare facilities, exercise/wellness program, free psychological counseling, grant writing training, international student services, low-cost health insurance, multicultural affairs office, services for students with disabilities, teacher training, writing training. *Library facilities:* Harriet Irving Library plus 3 others. *Online resources:* library catalog, web page, access to other libraries' catalogs. *Collection:* 1.3 million titles, 22,564 serial subscriptions. *Research affiliation:* Petroleum Research Atlantic Canada (petroleum), Huntsman Marine Science Centre (marine sciences), Atlantic Associate for Research in the Mathematical Sciences (mathematical sciences), Atlantic Hydrogen Inc. (hydrogen), Pulp and Paper Research Institute of Canada (pulp and paper), National Research Council Institute for Information Technology (informaton technology).

Computer facilities: 592 computers available on campus for general student use. A campuswide network can be accessed from student residence rooms and from off campus. Online class registration is available. *Web address:* http://www.unb.ca/.

General Application Contact: Dr. Edmund Biden, Acting Dean of Graduate Studies, 506-458-7154, Fax: 506-453-4817, E-mail: biden@unb.ca.

GRADUATE UNITS

Faculty of Law Tuition and fees charges are reported in Canadian dollars. Offers law (LL B). Electronic applications accepted.

School of Graduate Studies Students: 896 full-time (398 women), 446 part-time (299 women). *Faculty:* 446 full-time (159 women), 99 part-time/adjunct (32 women). Expenses: Contact institution. *Financial support:* In 2008–09, 97 fellowships, 807 research assistantships, 404 teaching assistantships were awarded; scholarships/grants and tuition waivers also available. Support available to part-time students. In 2008, 358 master's, 42 doctorates awarded. *Degree program information:* Part-time and evening/weekend programs available. Postbaccalaureate distance learning degree programs offered (minimal on-campus study). Offers applied health services (MAHSR); interdisciplinary studies (M IDST, PhD); people, property and alternative dispute resolution (M Phil); philosophy politics and economics (M Phil); sustainable development (M Phil). *Application deadline:* 1/31 for domestic and international students. Applications are processed on a rolling basis. *Application fee:* $50 Canadian dollars. *Application Contact:* Dr. Edmund Biden, Acting Dean of Graduate Studies, 506-458-7150, Fax: 506-453-4817, E-mail: biden@unb.ca. *Acting Dean of Graduate Studies*, Dr. Edmund Biden, 506-458-7150, Fax: 506-453-4817, E-mail: biden@unb.ca.

Faculty of Arts Students: 197 full-time (106 women), 26 part-time (15 women). *Faculty:* 79 full-time (36 women), 27 part-time/adjunct (11 women). Expenses: Contact institution. *Financial support:* In 2008–09, 47 fellowships, 55 research assistantships, 9 teaching assistantships were awarded. In 2008, 44 master's, 11 doctorates awarded. *Degree program information:* Part-time programs available. Offers anthropology (MA); applied economics and finance (M Sc); arts (M Sc, MA, PhD); classics (MA); economics (MA); English (MA, PhD); history (MA, PhD); political science (MA); psychology (MA, PhD); sociology (MA, PhD). *Application deadline:* For fall admission, 1/31 priority date for domestic students; for winter admission, 1/31 priority date for domestic students; for spring admission, 1/31 priority date for domestic students. Applications are processed on a rolling basis. *Application fee:* $50 Canadian dollars. *Application Contact:* Dr. Gwen Davies, Dean of Graduate Studies, 506-458-7150, Fax: 506-453-4817, E-mail: daviesg@unb.ca. *Dean*, Dr. James Murray, 506-458-7485, Fax: 506-453-5102, E-mail: jsm@unb.ca.

Faculty of Business Administration Students: 40 full-time (17 women), 37 part-time (16 women). *Faculty:* 37 full-time (13 women). Expenses: Contact institution. *Financial support:* In 2008–09, 1 fellowship was awarded; research assistantships, teaching assistantships. In 2008, 59 master's awarded. *Degree program information:* Part-time programs available. Offers business administration (MBA). *Application deadline:* For fall admission, 3/1 priority date for domestic students. Applications are processed on a rolling basis. *Application fee:* $50 Canadian dollars. *Application Contact:* Marilyn Davis, Acting Graduate Secretary, 506-453-4766, Fax: 506-453-3561, E-mail: mbacontact@unb.ca. *Director of Graduate Studies*, Judy Roy, 506-458-7307, Fax: 506-453-3561, E-mail: jroy@unb.ca.

Faculty of Computer Science Students: 60 full-time (18 women), 14 part-time (4 women). *Faculty:* 22 full-time (4 women). Expenses: Contact institution. *Financial support:* In 2008–09, 3 fellowships, 76 research assistantships, 40 teaching assistantships were awarded. In 2008, 18 master's, 3 doctorates awarded. *Degree program information:* Part-time programs available. Offers computer science (M Sc CS, PhD). *Application deadline:* For fall admission, 3/1 priority date for domestic students. Applications are processed on a rolling basis. *Application fee:* $50 Canadian dollars. Electronic applications accepted. *Application Contact:* Linda Sales, Graduate Secretary, 506-458-7285, Fax: 506-453-3566, E-mail: lsales@unb.ca. *Director of Graduate Studies*, Dr. Patricia Evans, 506-458-7276, Fax: 506-453-3566, E-mail: pevans@unb.ca.

Faculty of Education Students: 69 full-time (51 women), 260 part-time (202 women). *Faculty:* 34 full-time (21 women), 17 part-time/adjunct (9 women). Expenses: Contact institution. *Financial support:* In 2008–09, 3 fellowships, 25 research assistantships, 13 teaching assistantships were awarded; tuition waivers also available. In 2008, 133 master's, 4 doctorates awarded. *Degree program information:* Part-time programs available. Offers education (M Ed, PhD). *Application deadline:* 1/31 priority date for domestic and international students. Applications are processed on a rolling basis. *Application fee:* $50 Canadian dollars. *Application Contact:* Carolyn King, Graduate Secretary, 506-458-7147, Fax: 506-453-3569, E-mail: kingc@unb.ca. *Director of Graduate Studies*, Dr. Ellen Carusetta, 506-453-3544, Fax: 506-453-3569, E-mail: carusett@unb.ca.

Faculty of Engineering Students: 200 full-time (42 women), 29 part-time (3 women). *Faculty:* 68 full-time (10 women), 17 part-time/adjunct (1 woman). Expenses: Contact institution. *Financial support:* In 2008–09, 14 fellowships, 267 research assistantships, 151 teaching assistantships were awarded; career-related internships or fieldwork also available. In 2008, 49 master's, 12 doctorates awarded. *Degree program information:* Part-time programs available. Offers applied mechanics (M Eng, M Sc E, PhD); chemical engineering (M Eng, M Sc E, PhD); construction engineering and management (M Eng, M Sc E, PhD); electrical and computer engineering (M Eng, M Sc E, PhD); engineering (M Eng, M Sc E, PhD, Certificate, Diploma); environmental engineering (M Eng, M Sc E, PhD); environmental studies (M Eng); geotechnical engineering (M Eng, M Sc E, PhD); groundwater/hydrology (M Eng, M Sc E, PhD); land information management (Diploma); mapping, charting and geodesy (Diploma); materials (M Eng, M Sc E, PhD); mechanical engineering (M Eng, M Sc E, PhD); pavements (M Eng, M Sc E, PhD); structures (M Eng, M Sc E, PhD); surveying engineering (M Eng, M Sc E, PhD); transportation (M Eng, M Sc E, PhD). *Application deadline:* For fall admission, 3/1 priority date for domestic students. Applications are processed on a rolling basis. *Application fee:* $50 Canadian dollars. *Application Contact:* Dr. David Coleman, Dean, 506-453-4570, Fax: 506-453-4569, E-mail: dcoleman@unb.ca. *Dean*, Dr. David Coleman, 506-453-4570, Fax: 506-453-4569, E-mail: dcoleman@unb.ca.

Faculty of Forestry and Environmental Management Students: 69 full-time (34 women), 10 part-time (3 women). *Faculty:* 32 full-time (2 women). Expenses: Contact institution. *Financial support:* In 2008–09, 4 fellowships, 115 research assistantships, 43 teaching assistantships were awarded. In 2008, 10 master's, 2 doctorates awarded. *Degree program information:* Part-time programs available. Offers ecological foundations of forest management (PhD); environmental management (MEM); forest engineering (M Sc FE, MFE); forest products marketing (MBA); forest resources (M Sc F, MF, PhD). *Application deadline:* For fall admission, 3/1 priority date for domestic students. Applications are processed on a rolling basis. *Application fee:* $50 Canadian dollars. *Application Contact:* Faith Sharpe, Graduate Secretary, 506-458-7520, Fax: 506-453-3538, E-mail: fsharpe@unb.ca. *Director of Graduate Studies*, Dr. John Kershaw, 506-453-4933, Fax: 506-453-3538, E-mail: kershaw@unb.ca.

Faculty of Kinesiology Students: 32 full-time (13 women), 7 part-time (6 women). *Faculty:* 17 full-time (7 women). Expenses: Contact institution. *Financial support:* In 2008–09, 2 fellowships with tuition reimbursements were awarded; research assistantships, teaching assistantships, career-related internships or fieldwork and scholarships/grants also available. In 2008, 7 master's awarded. *Degree program information:* Part-time programs available. Offers exercise and sport science (M Sc); sport and recreation administration (MA). *Application deadline:* For winter admission, 1/31 for domestic students; for spring admission, 3/31 for domestic students. Applications are processed on a rolling basis. *Application fee:* $50 Canadian dollars. Electronic applications accepted. *Application Contact:* Linda O'Brien, Graduate Secretary, 506-453-4576, Fax: 506-453-3511, E-mail: lobrien@unb.ca. *Acting Director of Graduate Studies*, Dr. Wayne Albert, 506-447-3254, Fax: 506-453-3511, E-mail: walbert@unb.ca.

Faculty of Nursing Students: 16 full-time (14 women), 38 part-time (all women). *Faculty:* 27 full-time (all women), 5 part-time/adjunct (4 women). Expenses: Contact institution. *Financial support:* In 2008–09, 2 fellowships, 4 research assistantships, 6 teaching assistantships were awarded. In 2008, 8 master's awarded. Offers nurse educator (MN); nurse practitioner (MN); nursing (MN). *Application deadline:* For winter admission, 2/5 for domestic students. *Application fee:* $50 Canadian dollars. *Application Contact:* Francis Perry, Graduate Secretary, 506-451-6844, Fax: 506-447-3057, E-mail: fperry@unb.ca. *Director of Graduate Studies*, Gail Storr, 506-458-7643, Fax: 506-447-3057, E-mail: storr@unb.ca.

Faculty of Science Students: 162 full-time (67 women), 12 part-time (4 women). *Faculty:* 92 full-time (15 women), 15 part-time/adjunct (3 women). Expenses: Contact institution. *Financial support:* In 2008–09, 16 fellowships (averaging $2,975 per year), 248 research assistantships, 140 teaching assistantships were awarded. In 2008, 22 master's, 9 doctorates awarded. *Degree program information:* Part-time programs available. Offers biology (M Sc, PhD); chemistry (M Sc, PhD); geology (M Sc, PhD); mathematics and statistics (M Sc, PhD); physics (M Sc, PhD); science (M Sc, PhD). *Application deadline:* For fall admission, 3/1 priority date for domestic students. Applications are processed on a rolling basis. *Application fee:* $50 Canadian dollars. *Application Contact:* Dean of Graduate Studies. *Dean*, Dr. David MaGee, 506-470-5625, Fax: 506-453-3570, E-mail: dmagee@unb.ca.

UNIVERSITY OF NEW BRUNSWICK SAINT JOHN, Saint John, NB E2L 4L5, Canada

General Information Province-supported, coed, comprehensive institution. *Graduate faculty:* 42 full-time (12 women), 36 part-time/adjunct (10 women). *International tuition:* $9450 full-time. *Tuition, area resident:* Full-time $5562. *Required fees:* $333. *Graduate housing:* Rooms and/or apartments available on a first-come, first-served basis to single and married students. Housing application deadline: 3/31. *Student services:* Campus employment opportunities, campus safety program, career counseling, exercise/wellness program, free psychological counseling, grant writing training, international student services, low-cost health insurance, multicultural affairs office, services for students with disabilities, teacher training, writing training. *Library facilities:* Ward Chipman Library. *Online resources:* library catalog, web page, access to other libraries' catalogs. *Collection:* 155,500 titles, 700 serial subscriptions.

Computer facilities: 100 computers available on campus for general student use. A campuswide network can be accessed from student residence rooms and from off campus. Online class registration is available. *Web address:* http://www.unb.ca/.

General Application Contact: Dr. Don Desserud, Associate Dean of Graduate Studies, 506-648-5727, Fax: 506-648-5528, E-mail: desserud@unbsj.ca.

GRADUATE UNITS

Department of Biology Students: 26 full-time (13 women), 7 part-time (3 women). *Faculty:* 14 full-time (4 women), 22 part-time/adjunct (2 women). Expenses: Contact institution. *Financial support:* In 2008–09, 12 fellowships, 57 research assistantships, 8 teaching assistantships were awarded; scholarships/grants and unspecified assistantships also available. In 2008, 9 master's, 1 doctorate awarded. *Degree program information:* Part-time programs available. Offers biology (M Sc, PhD). *Application deadline:* For fall admission, 2/15 for domestic and international students. *Application fee:* $50 Canadian dollars. *Application Contact:* Kim Banks, Secretary, 506-648-5605, Fax: 506-648-5811, E-mail: kbanks@unbsj.ca. *Director of*

Graduate Studies, Biology, Dr. Kelly Munkittrick, 506-648-5825, Fax: 506-648-5811, E-mail: krm@unbsj.ca.

Department of Psychology Students: 4 full-time (all women). *Faculty:* 9 full-time (4 women). Expenses: Contact institution. *Financial support:* In 2008–09, 1 fellowship, 7 research assistantships, 2 teaching assistantships were awarded; unspecified assistantships also available. Support available to part-time students. Financial award application deadline: 2/1. In 2008, 1 master's awarded. Offers applied and experimental psychology (PhD); clinical psychology (PhD); experimental psychology (MA). *Application deadline:* For fall admission, 2/1 for domestic students. *Application fee:* $50. Electronic applications accepted. *Application Contact:* Frances Stevens, Secretary, 506-648-5640, Fax: 506-648-5780, E-mail: fstevens@unb.ca. *Director of Graduate Studies*, Dr. Lily Both, 506-648-5769, Fax: 506-648-5780, E-mail: lboth@unbsj.ca.

Faculty of Business Students: 31 full-time (12 women), 17 part-time (9 women), 24 international. Average age 26. 93 applicants, 78% accepted, 25 enrolled. *Faculty:* 19 full-time (4 women), 14 part-time/adjunct (8 women). Expenses: Contact institution. *Financial support:* In 2008–09, 4 students received support; fellowships, research assistantships, teaching assistantships, career-related internships or fieldwork and scholarships/grants available. In 2008, 20 master's awarded. *Degree program information:* Part-time programs available. Offers administration (MBA); electronic commerce (MBA); international business (MBA); natural resource management (MBA). *Application deadline:* For fall admission, 5/15 for domestic and international students. *Application fee:* $100. *Application Contact:* Tammy Morin, Secretary, 506-648-5746, Fax: 506-648-5574, E-mail: tmorin@unbsj.ca. *Director of Graduate Studies*, Deborah Armstrong, 506-648-5752, Fax: 506-648-5574, E-mail: armstron@unbsj.ca.

UNIVERSITY OF NEW ENGLAND, Biddeford, ME 04005-9526

General Information Independent, coed, comprehensive institution. *Graduate housing:* On-campus housing not available.

GRADUATE UNITS

College of Arts and Sciences *Degree program information:* Part-time programs available. Postbaccalaureate distance learning degree programs offered (minimal on-campus study). Offers applied biosciences (MS); arts and sciences (MS, MS Ed, CAGS); educational leadership (CAGS); general studies (MS Ed); literacy (MS Ed); marine science (MS); teaching methodologies (MS Ed).

College of Health Professions *Degree program information:* Part-time programs available. Postbaccalaureate distance learning degree programs offered (minimal on-campus study). Offers health professions (MS, MSW, DPT, Certificate); nurse anesthesia (MS); occupational therapy (MS); physical therapy (DPT); physician assistant (MS); post professional occupational therapy (MS); post professional physical therapy (DPT).

School of Social Work *Degree program information:* Part-time programs available. Offers addictions counseling (Certificate); gerontology (Certificate); social work (MSW). Electronic applications accepted.

College of Osteopathic Medicine Offers osteopathic medicine (DO, MPH, Certificate); public health (MPH, Certificate).

UNIVERSITY OF NEW HAMPSHIRE, Durham, NH 03824

General Information State-supported, coed, university. CGS member. *Enrollment:* 14,964 graduate, professional, and undergraduate students; 1,246 full-time matriculated graduate/professional students (752 women), 1,113 part-time matriculated graduate/professional students (650 women). *Enrollment by degree level:* 1,785 master's, 512 doctoral, 62 other advanced degrees. *Graduate faculty:* 607 full-time (199 women). Tuition, state resident: full-time $9720; part-time $540 per credit hour. Tuition, nonresident: full-time $23,200; part-time $954 per credit hour. *Required fees:* $1446; $361.50 per term. *Graduate housing:* Rooms and/or apartments available on a first-come, first-served basis to single and married students. Typical cost: $6000 per year ($9700 including board) for single students. Room and board charges vary according to board plan and housing facility selected. Housing application deadline: 7/15. *Student services:* Campus employment opportunities, campus safety program, career counseling, child daycare facilities, exercise/wellness program, free psychological counseling, grant writing training, international student services, low-cost health insurance, multicultural affairs office, services for students with disabilities, teacher training, writing training. *Library facilities:* Dimond Library plus 4 others. *Online resources:* library catalog, web page, access to other libraries' catalogs. *Collection:* 2.2 million titles, 50,043 serial subscriptions, 39,508 audiovisual materials.

Computer facilities: Computer purchase and lease plans are available. 345 computers available on campus for general student use. A campuswide network can be accessed from student residence rooms and from off campus. Online class registration is available. *Web address:* http://www.unh.edu/.

General Application Contact: Dovev Levine, Graduate Admissions Office, 603-862-3000, Fax: 603-862-0275, E-mail: grad.school@unh.edu.

GRADUATE UNITS

Center for Graduate and Professional Studies Students: 81 full-time (54 women), 154 part-time (92 women); includes 11 minority (2 African Americans, 7 Asian Americans or Pacific Islanders, 2 Hispanic Americans), 5 international. 87 applicants, 80% accepted, 54 enrolled. Expenses: Contact institution. *Financial support:* In 2008–09, 21 students received support, including 1 teaching assistantship; fellowships, research assistantships, Federal Work-Study, scholarships/grants, health care benefits, and unspecified assistantships also available. Support available to part-time students. Financial award application deadline: 3/1; financial award applicants required to submit FAFSA. In 2008, 106 master's, 3 other advanced degrees awarded. *Degree program information:* Part-time and evening/weekend programs available. Offers business administration (MBA); counseling (M Ed); education (M Ed, MAT); educational administration and supervision (M Ed, CAGS); industrial statistics (Certificate); public administration (MPA); public health (MPH, Certificate); social work (MSW). *Application deadline:* For fall admission, 6/1 for domestic students, 4/1 for international students; for spring admission, 12/1 for domestic students. Applications are processed on a rolling basis. *Application fee:* $60. Electronic applications accepted. *Application Contact:* Graduate Admissions Office, 603-862-3000, Fax: 603-862-0275, E-mail: grad.school@unh.edu. *Director*, Kate Ferreira, 603-641-4313, E-mail: unhm.gradcenter@unh.edu.

Graduate School Students: 1,246 full-time (752 women), 1,113 part-time (650 women); includes 103 minority (17 African Americans, 7 American Indian/Alaska Native, 44 Asian Americans or Pacific Islanders, 35 Hispanic Americans), 266 international. 2,184 applicants, 58% accepted, 640 enrolled. *Faculty:* 607 full-time (199 women). Expenses: Contact institution. *Financial support:* In 2008–09, 857 students received support, including 52 fellowships, 205 research assistantships, 429 teaching assistantships; career-related internships or fieldwork, Federal Work-Study, scholarships/grants, traineeships, health care benefits, tuition waivers (full and partial), and unspecified assistantships also available. Support available to part-time students. Financial award application deadline: 2/15; financial award applicants required to submit FAFSA. In 2008, 818 master's, 50 doctorates, 19 other advanced degrees awarded. *Degree program information:* Part-time and evening/weekend programs available. Offers college teaching (MST); earth and environmental science (PhD); environmental education (MA); interdisciplinary studies (Postbaccalaureate Certificate); natural resources and earth system science (PhD); natural resources and environmental studies (PhD). *Application deadline:* For fall admission, 4/1 priority date for domestic and international students; for winter admission, 12/1 priority date for domestic students; for spring admission, 4/1 for domestic students. Applications are processed on a rolling basis. *Application fee:* $60. Electronic applications accepted. *Application Contact:* Dovev L. Levine, Admissions Officer, 603-862-3000, Fax: 603-862-0275, E-mail: grad.school@unh.edu. *Dean*, Dr. Harry J. Richards, 603-862-3005, Fax: 603-862-0275, E-mail: harry.richards@unh.edu.

College of Engineering and Physical Sciences Students: 230 full-time (76 women), 214 part-time (64 women); includes 16 minority (2 African Americans, 8 Asian Americans or Pacific Islanders, 6 Hispanic Americans), 161 international. Average age 30. 529 applicants, 65% accepted, 112 enrolled. *Faculty:* 162 full-time (25 women). Expenses: Contact institution. *Financial support:* In 2008–09, 318 students received support, including 22 fellowships, 127 research assistantships, 144 teaching assistantships; career-related internships or fieldwork, Federal Work-Study, scholarships/grants, and tuition waivers (full and partial) also available. Support available to part-time students. Financial award application deadline: 2/15; financial award applicants required to submit FAFSA. In 2008, 110 master's, 18 doctorates awarded. *Degree program information:* Part-time and evening/weekend programs available. Offers applied mathematics (MS); chemical engineering (MS, PhD); chemistry (MS, MST, PhD); chemistry education (PhD); civil engineering (MS, PhD); computer science (MS, PhD); earth sciences (MS); electrical engineering (MS, PhD); engineering and physical sciences (MS, MST, PhD, Postbaccalaureate Certificate); hydrology (MS); industrial statistics (Postbaccalaureate Certificate); materials science (MS, PhD); mathematics (MS, MST, PhD); mathematics education (PhD); mechanical engineering (MS, PhD); ocean engineering (MS, PhD); ocean mapping (MS, Postbaccalaureate Certificate); physics (MS, PhD); statistics (MS); systems design (PhD). *Application deadline:* For fall admission, 4/1 priority date for domestic students, 4/1 for international students; for winter admission, 12/1 priority date for domestic students. Applications are processed on a rolling basis. *Application fee:* $60. Electronic applications accepted. *Application Contact:* Dr. Joe Klewicki, Dean, 603-862-1781. *Dean*, Dr. Joe Klewicki, 603-862-1781.

College of Liberal Arts Students: 352 full-time (244 women), 492 part-time (334 women); includes 38 minority (5 African Americans, 4 American Indian/Alaska Native, 13 Asian Americans or Pacific Islanders, 16 Hispanic Americans), 18 international. Average age 34. 707 applicants, 49% accepted, 166 enrolled. *Faculty:* 193 full-time (90 women). Expenses: Contact institution. *Financial support:* In 2008–09, 237 students received support, including 11 fellowships, 9 research assistantships, 144 teaching assistantships; career-related internships or fieldwork, Federal Work-Study, scholarships/grants, and tuition waivers (full and partial) also available. Support available to part-time students. Financial award application deadline: 2/15. In 2008, 303 master's, 12 doctorates, 9 other advanced degrees awarded. *Degree program information:* Part-time programs available. Offers counseling (M Ed, MA); early childhood education (M Ed); education (PhD); educational administration (M Ed, CAGS); elementary education (M Ed, MAT); English (MFA, PhD); English education (MST); history (MA, PhD); justice studies (MA); language and linguistics (MA); liberal arts (M Ed, MA, MALS, MAT, MFA, MPA, MST, PhD, CAGS, Postbaccalaureate Certificate); liberal studies (MALS); literature (MA); museum studies (MA); music education (MA); music history (MA); painting (MFA); political science (MA); psychology (PhD); public administration (MPA); reading (M Ed); secondary education (M Ed, MAT); sociology (MA, PhD); Spanish (MA); special education (M Ed, Postbaccalaureate Certificate); special needs (M Ed); teacher leadership (M Ed, Postbaccalaureate Certificate); writing (MA). *Application deadline:* For fall admission, 4/1 for domestic students; for winter admission, 12/1 for domestic students; for spring admission, 4/1 for domestic students. Applications are processed on a rolling basis. *Application fee:* $60. Electronic applications accepted. *Application Contact:* Dr. Marilyn Hoskin, Dean, 603-862-2062. *Dean*, Dr. Marilyn Hoskin, 603-862-2062.

College of Life Sciences and Agriculture Students: 103 full-time (64 women), 94 part-time (62 women); includes 10 minority (2 African Americans, 1 American Indian/Alaska Native, 6 Asian Americans or Pacific Islanders, 1 Hispanic American), 16 international. Average age 34. 192 applicants, 35% accepted, 38 enrolled. *Faculty:* 125 full-time (31 women). Expenses: Contact institution. *Financial support:* In 2008–09, 134 students received support, including 6 fellowships, 44 research assistantships, 82 teaching assistantships; career-related internships or fieldwork, Federal Work-Study, scholarships/grants, and tuition waivers (full and partial) also available. Support available to part-time students. Financial award application deadline: 2/15. In 2008, 28 master's, 10 doctorates awarded. *Degree program information:* Part-time programs available. Offers animal and nutritional sciences (PhD); animal science (MS); biochemistry (MS, PhD); environmental conservation (MS); forestry (MS); genetics (MS, PhD); life sciences and agriculture (MS, PhD); microbiology (MS, PhD); nutritional sciences (MS); plant biology (MS, PhD); resource administration (MS); resource economics (MS); soil science (MS); water resources management (MS); wildlife (MS); zoology (MS, PhD). *Application deadline:* For fall admission, 4/1 for domestic and international students. Applications are processed on a rolling basis. *Application fee:* $60. Electronic applications accepted. *Application Contact:* Tom Brady, Dean, 603-862-1453. *Dean*, Tom Brady, 603-862-1453.

School of Health and Human Services Students: 282 full-time (250 women), 161 part-time (136 women); includes 20 minority (5 African Americans, 2 American Indian/Alaska Native, 8 Asian Americans or Pacific Islanders, 5 Hispanic Americans), 3 international. Average age 31. 423 applicants, 63% accepted, 156 enrolled. *Faculty:* 79 full-time (43 women). Expenses: Contact institution. *Financial support:* In 2008–09, 57 students received support, including 2 research assistantships, 31 teaching assistantships; fellowships, career-related internships or fieldwork, Federal Work-Study, scholarships/grants, and tuition waivers (full and partial) also available. Support available to part-time students. Financial award application deadline: 2/15. In 2008, 208 master's, 1 other advanced degree awarded. *Degree program information:* Part-time and evening/weekend programs available. Offers communication sciences and disorders (Postbaccalaureate Certificate); early childhood intervention (MS); family studies (MS); health and human services (MPH, MS, MSW, Postbaccalaureate Certificate); kinesiology (MS); language and literature disabilities (MS); marriage and family therapy (MS); nursing (MS, Postbaccalaureate Certificate); occupational therapy (MS, Postbaccalaureate Certificate); public health (MPH, Postbaccalaureate Certificate); recreation administration (MS); social work (MSW, Postbaccalaureate Certificate); therapeutic recreation (MS). *Application deadline:* For fall admission, 4/1 priority date for domestic students, 4/1 for international students; for winter admission, 12/1 priority date for domestic students. Applications are processed on a rolling basis. *Application fee:* $60. Electronic applications accepted. *Application Contact:* Dr. Barbara Arrington, Dean, 603-862-1178. *Dean*, Dr. Barbara Arrington, 603-862-1178.

Whittemore School of Business and Economics Students: 218 full-time (80 women), 112 part-time (35 women); includes 14 minority (2 African Americans, 8 Asian Americans or Pacific Islanders, 4 Hispanic Americans), 57 international. Average age 34. 290 applicants, 76% accepted, 156 enrolled. *Faculty:* 47 full-time (10 women). Expenses: Contact institution. *Financial support:* In 2008–09, 64 students received support, including 1 fellowship, 2 research assistantships, 19 teaching assistantships; career-related internships or fieldwork, Federal Work-Study, scholarships/grants, and tuition waivers (full and partial) also available. Support available to part-time students. Financial award application deadline: 2/15. In 2008, 158 master's, 1 doctorate, 7 other advanced degrees awarded. *Degree program information:* Part-time and evening/weekend programs available. Offers accounting (MS); business administration (MBA); business and economics (MA, MBA, MS, PhD, Postbaccalaureate Certificate); economics (MA, PhD); executive business administration (MBA); health management (MBA); management of technology (MS, Postbaccalaureate Certificate). *Application deadline:* For fall admission, 4/1 for domestic and international students; for winter admission, 12/1 for domestic students. Applications are processed on a rolling basis. *Application fee:* $60. Electronic applications accepted. *Application Contact:* Dr. Daniel Innis, Dean, 603-862-1983. *Dean*, Dr. Daniel Innis, 603-862-1983.

UNIVERSITY OF NEW HAVEN, West Haven, CT 06516-1916

General Information Independent, coed, comprehensive institution. CGS member. *Enrollment:* 5,233 graduate, professional, and undergraduate students; 968 full-time matriculated graduate/professional students (503 women), 713 part-time matriculated graduate/professional students (362 women). *Enrollment by degree level:* 1,681 master's. *Graduate faculty:* 103 full-time (21 women), 120 part-time/adjunct (24 women). *Tuition:* Full-time $15,075; part-time $670 per credit. *Required fees:* $240; $45 per trimester. Tuition and fees vary according to course load and program. *Graduate housing:* On-campus housing not available. *Student services:* Campus employment opportunities, campus safety program, career counseling, free psychological counseling, international student services, low-cost health insurance, multicultural affairs office, services for students with disabilities, writing training. *Library facilities:* Marvin K. Peterson Library.

Computer facilities: Computer purchase and lease plans are available. 300 computers available on campus for general student use. A campuswide network can be accessed from student residence rooms and from off campus. Online class registration, computer repair services are available. *Web address:* http://www.newhaven.edu/.

University of New Haven (continued)

General Application Contact: Eloise Gormley, Director of Graduate Admissions, 203-932-7449, Fax: 203-932-7137, E-mail: gradinfo@newhaven.edu.

GRADUATE UNITS

Graduate School Students: 968 full-time (503 women), 713 part-time (362 women); includes 276 minority (149 African Americans, 12 American Indian/Alaska Native, 50 Asian Americans or Pacific Islanders, 65 Hispanic Americans), 340 international. Average age 30. 2,171 applicants, 71% accepted, 683 enrolled. *Faculty:* 103 full-time (21 women), 120 part-time/adjunct (24 women). Expenses: Contact institution. *Financial support:* In 2008–09, 225 students received support, including 28 research assistantships with partial tuition reimbursements available (averaging $5,784 per year), 86 teaching assistantships with partial tuition reimbursements available (averaging $6,287 per year); career-related internships or fieldwork, Federal Work-Study, and unspecified assistantships also available. Support available to part-time students. Financial award applicants required to submit FAFSA. In 2008, 776 master's awarded. *Degree program information:* Part-time and evening/weekend programs available. *Application deadline:* For fall admission, 5/31 for international students; for winter admission, 10/15 for international students; for spring admission, 1/15 for international students. Applications are processed on a rolling basis. *Application fee:* $50. *Application Contact:* Eloise Gormley, Director of Graduate Admissions, 203-932-7449, Fax: 203-932-7137, E-mail: gradinfo@newhaven.edu. *Associate Provost and Dean of Graduate Studies,* Dr. Ira Kleinfeld, 203-932-7063.

College of Arts and Sciences Students: 306 full-time (206 women), 218 part-time (158 women); includes 57 minority (27 African Americans, 3 American Indian/Alaska Native, 7 Asian Americans or Pacific Islanders, 20 Hispanic Americans), 60 international. Average age 28. 554 applicants, 64% accepted, 235 enrolled. Expenses: Contact institution. *Financial support:* Research assistantships with partial tuition reimbursements, teaching assistantships with partial tuition reimbursements, career-related internships or fieldwork, Federal Work-Study, scholarships/grants, tuition waivers, and unspecified assistantships available. Support available to part-time students. Financial award application deadline: 5/1; financial award applicants required to submit FAFSA. In 2008, 244 master's awarded. *Degree program information:* Part-time and evening/weekend programs available. Offers arts and sciences (MA, MS, Certificate); cellular and molecular biology (MS); community psychology (MA, Certificate); education (MS); environmental sciences (MS); human nutrition (MS); industrial and organizational psychology (MA, Certificate). *Application deadline:* For fall admission, 5/31 for international students; for winter admission, 10/15 for international students; for spring admission, 1/15 for international students. Applications are processed on a rolling basis. *Application fee:* $50. *Application Contact:* Eloise Gormley, Director of Graduate Admissions, 203-932-7449, Fax: 203-932-7137, E-mail: gradinfo@newhaven.edu. *Dean,* Dr. Ronald Nowaczyk, 203-932-7257.

College of Business Students: 423 full-time (172 women), 258 part-time (133 women); includes 59 minority (37 African Americans, 1 American Indian/Alaska Native, 13 Asian Americans or Pacific Islanders, 8 Hispanic Americans), 67 international. Average age 32. 611 applicants, 79% accepted, 257 enrolled. *Faculty:* 33 full-time (8 women), 32 part-time/adjunct (4 women). Expenses: Contact institution. *Financial support:* Research assistantships with partial tuition reimbursements, teaching assistantships with partial tuition reimbursements, career-related internships or fieldwork, Federal Work-Study, scholarships/grants, tuition waivers, and unspecified assistantships available. Support available to part-time students. Financial award application deadline: 5/1; financial award applicants required to submit FAFSA. In 2008, 289 master's awarded. *Degree program information:* Part-time and evening/weekend programs available. Offers accounting (MBA); business (EMBA, MBA, MPA, MS); business administration (EMBA, MBA); business policy and strategy (MBA); corporate taxation (MS); finance (MBA); finance and financial services (MS); financial accounting (MS); health care administration (MS); health care management (MBA, MPA); human resources management (MBA); industrial relations (MS); international business (MBA); managerial accounting (MS); marketing (MBA); personnel and labor relations (MPA); public relations (MBA); public taxation (MS); sports management (MBA); taxation (MS); technology management (MBA). *Application deadline:* For fall admission, 5/31 for international students; for winter admission, 10/15 for international students; for spring admission, 1/15 for international students. Applications are processed on a rolling basis. *Application fee:* $50. *Application Contact:* Eloise Gormley, Director of Graduate Admissions, 203-932-7449, Fax: 203-932-7137, E-mail: gradinfo@newhaven.edu. *Dean,* Dr. Richard Highfield, 203-932-7115.

Henry C. Lee College of Criminal Justice and Forensic Sciences Students: 129 full-time (99 women), 99 part-time (46 women); includes 53 minority (28 African Americans, 1 American Indian/Alaska Native, 5 Asian Americans or Pacific Islanders, 19 Hispanic Americans), 5 international. Average age 28. 229 applicants, 75% accepted, 101 enrolled. *Faculty:* 14 full-time (1 woman), 15 part-time/adjunct (1 woman). Expenses: Contact institution. *Financial support:* Research assistantships with partial tuition reimbursements, teaching assistantships with partial tuition reimbursements, career-related internships or fieldwork, Federal Work-Study, scholarships/grants, tuition waivers, and unspecified assistantships available. Support available to part-time students. Financial award applicants required to submit FAFSA. In 2008, 136 master's awarded. *Degree program information:* Part-time and evening/weekend programs available. Offers advanced investigation (MS); correctional counseling (MS); criminal justice and forensic sciences (MS); criminal justice management (MS); criminalistics (MS); fire science (MS); forensic science (MS); industrial hygiene (MS); national security and public safety (MS); occupational safety and health management (MS); security management (MS). *Application deadline:* For fall admission, 5/31 for international students; for winter admission, 10/15 for international students; for spring admission, 1/15 for international students. Applications are processed on a rolling basis. *Application fee:* $50. *Application Contact:* Eloise Gormley, Director of Graduate Admissions, 203-932-7449, Fax: 203-932-7137, E-mail: gradinfo@newhaven.edu. *Dean,* Dr. Richard Ward, 203-932-7260.

Tagliatela College of Engineering Students: 110 full-time (26 women), 123 part-time (18 women); includes 20 minority (7 African Americans, 1 American Indian/Alaska Native, 4 Asian Americans or Pacific Islanders, 8 Hispanic Americans), 119 international. Average age 29. 777 applicants, 69% accepted, 82 enrolled. Expenses: Contact institution. *Financial support:* Research assistantships with partial tuition reimbursements, teaching assistantships with partial tuition reimbursements, career-related internships or fieldwork, Federal Work-Study, scholarships/grants, tuition waivers, and unspecified assistantships available. Support available to part-time students. Financial award applicants required to submit FAFSA. In 2008, 106 master's awarded. *Degree program information:* Part-time and evening/weekend programs available. Offers applications software (MS); civil engineering design (Certificate); electrical engineering (MSEE); engineering (EMS, MS, MSEE, MSIE, MSME, Certificate); engineering management (EMS); environmental engineering (MS); industrial engineering (MSIE); logistics (Certificate); management information systems (MS); mechanical engineering (MSME); systems software (MS). *Application deadline:* For fall admission, 5/30 for international students; for winter admission, 10/15 for international students; for spring admission, 1/15 for international students. Applications are processed on a rolling basis. *Application fee:* $50. *Application Contact:* Eloise Gormley, Director of Graduate Admissions, 203-932-7449, Fax: 203-932-7137, E-mail: gradinfo@newhaven.edu. *Dean,* Dr. Barry Farbrother, 203-932-7167.

See Close-Up on page 1035.

UNIVERSITY OF NEW MEXICO, Albuquerque, NM 87131-2039

General Information State-supported, coed, university. CGS member. *Graduate housing:* Rooms and/or apartments available on a first-come, first-served basis to single and married students. *Research affiliation:* Sandia National Laboratories, Los Alamos National Laboratory, Lovelace Respiratory Research Institute, Phillips Laboratory.

GRADUATE UNITS

Graduate School *Degree program information:* Part-time and evening/weekend programs available. Postbaccalaureate distance learning degree programs offered. Offers computational science and engineering (Graduate Certificate); nanoscience and microsystems (MS, PhD); water resources (MWR). Electronic applications accepted.

College of Arts and Sciences *Degree program information:* Part-time and evening/weekend programs available. Offers American studies (MA, PhD); anthropology (MA, MS, PhD); arts and sciences (MA, MFA, MS, PhD, Graduate Certificate); biology (MS, PhD); biomedical physics (MS, PhD); chemistry (MS, PhD); clinical psychology (MS, PhD); communication (MA, PhD); comparative literature and cultural studies (MA); creative writing (MFA); earth and planetary sciences (MS, PhD); economics (MA, PhD); English (MA, MFA, PhD); French (MA); French studies (PhD); geography (MS); German studies (MA); history (MA, PhD); Latin American studies (MA, PhD); linguistics (MA, PhD); mathematics (MS, PhD); optical science and engineering (MS, PhD); philosophy (MA, PhD); physics (MS, PhD); political science (MA, PhD); Portuguese (MA); psychology (PhD); sociology (MA, PhD); Spanish (MA); Spanish and Portuguese (PhD); speech and hearing sciences (MS); statistics (MS, PhD); women studies (Graduate Certificate). Electronic applications accepted.

College of Education Offers art education (MA); counselor education (MA, PhD); education (MA, MS, Ed D, PhD, EDSPC, Graduate Certificate); educational leadership (MA, Ed D, EDSPC); educational linguistics (Ed D, PhD); educational psychology (MA, PhD); elementary education (MA, EDSPC); family studies (MA, PhD); health education (MS); intensive social, language and behavioral needs (Graduate Certificate); language, literacy and sociocultural studies (MA, Ed D, PhD); multicultural teacher and childhood education (Ed D, PhD, EDSPC); nutrition (MS); organizational learning and instructional technologies (MA, PhD, EDSPC); physical education (MS, Ed D, PhD, EDSPC); physical education, sports and exercise science (PhD); secondary education (MA, EDSPC); special education (MA, Ed D, PhD, EDSPC). Electronic applications accepted.

College of Fine Arts *Degree program information:* Part-time programs available. Offers art history (MA, PhD); dramatic writing (MFA); fine arts (M Mu, MA, MFA, PhD); music (M Mu); studio arts (MFA); theater and dance (MA).

College of Nursing *Degree program information:* Part-time programs available. Postbaccalaureate distance learning degree programs offered (minimal on-campus study). Offers nursing (MSN, PhD). Electronic applications accepted.

College of Pharmacy *Degree program information:* Part-time programs available. Offers pharmaceutical sciences (MS, PhD); pharmacy (Pharm D, MS, PhD). Electronic applications accepted.

School of Architecture and Planning *Degree program information:* Part-time programs available. Offers architecture (M Arch); architecture and planning (M Arch, MCRP, MLA, Graduate Certificate); community and regional planning (MCRP); historic preservation and regionalism (Graduate Certificate); landscape architecture (MLA); town design (Graduate Certificate).

School of Engineering *Degree program information:* Part-time and evening/weekend programs available. Offers chemical engineering (MS, PhD); civil engineering (MS); computer engineering (MS, PhD); computer science (MS, PhD); construction management (MCM); electrical engineering (MS, PhD); engineering (PhD); manufacturing engineering (MEME); mechanical engineering (MS); nuclear engineering (MS, PhD). Electronic applications accepted.

School of Public Administration *Degree program information:* Part-time and evening/weekend programs available. Postbaccalaureate distance learning degree programs offered (no on-campus study). Offers public administration (MPA). Electronic applications accepted.

Robert O. Anderson Graduate School of Management Students: 190 full-time (91 women), 289 part-time (147 women); includes 168 minority (7 African Americans, 10 American Indian/Alaska Native, 28 Asian Americans or Pacific Islanders, 123 Hispanic Americans), 33 international. Average age 33. 196 applicants, 55% accepted, 101 enrolled. *Faculty:* 58 full-time (19 women), 32 part-time/adjunct (10 women). Expenses: Contact institution. *Financial support:* In 2008–09, 87 students received support, including 36 fellowships (averaging $2,000 per year), 50 research assistantships with partial tuition reimbursements available (averaging $6,000 per year), 1 teaching assistantship with partial tuition reimbursement available (averaging $7,500 per year); career-related internships or fieldwork, Federal Work-Study, scholarships/grants, and unspecified assistantships also available. Support available to part-time students. Financial award application deadline: 6/1. In 2008, 215 master's awarded. *Degree program information:* Part-time and evening/weekend programs available. Offers accounting (MBA); advanced accounting (M Acct); finance (MBA); human resources management (MBA); international management (MBA); international management in Latin America (MBA); management (EMBA, M Acct, MBA); management information systems (MBA); management of technology (MBA); marketing management (MBA); operations management (MBA); policy and planning (MBA); professional accounting (M Acct); tax accounting (M Acct). *Application deadline:* For fall admission, 6/1 priority date for domestic students, 5/1 for international students; for spring admission, 11/1 priority date for domestic students, 10/1 for international students. Applications are processed on a rolling basis. *Application fee:* $50. Electronic applications accepted. *Application Contact:* Loyola Chastain, Academic Advisement Manager, 505-277-3290, Fax: 505-277-8436, E-mail: mba@mgt.unm.edu. *Dean,* Douglas M. Brown, 505-277-6148, Fax: 505-277-0344, E-mail: browndm@mgt.unm.edu.

School of Law Students: 346 full-time (185 women); includes 161 minority (12 African Americans, 31 American Indian/Alaska Native, 12 Asian Americans or Pacific Islanders, 106 Hispanic Americans). 1,070 applicants, 25% accepted, 118 enrolled. *Faculty:* 32 full-time (16 women), 26 part-time/adjunct (9 women). Expenses: Contact institution. *Financial support:* Career-related internships or fieldwork, Federal Work-Study, and scholarships/grants available. Financial award application deadline: 3/1; financial award applicants required to submit FAFSA. In 2008, 114 JDs awarded. Offers law (JD). *Application deadline:* For fall admission, 2/15 priority date for domestic and international students. Applications are processed on a rolling basis. *Application fee:* $50. Electronic applications accepted. *Application Contact:* Susan L. Mitchell, Assistant Dean for Admissions and Financial Aid, 505-277-0959, Fax: 505-277-9958, E-mail: mitchell@law.unm.edu. *Dean,* Leo Romero, 505-277-4700, Fax: 505-277-9558, E-mail: romero@law.unm.edu.

School of Medicine Offers biochemistry and molecular biology (MS, PhD); cell biology and physiology (MS, PhD); clinical laboratory science (MS); dental hygiene (MS); medicine (MD, MOT, MPH, MPT, MS, PhD); molecular genetics and microbiology (MS, PhD); neuroscience (MS, PhD); occupational therapy (MOT); pathology (MS, PhD); physical therapy (MPT); public health (MPH); toxicology (MS, PhD). Electronic applications accepted.

UNIVERSITY OF NORTH ALABAMA, Florence, AL 35632-0001

General Information State-supported, coed, comprehensive institution. *Enrollment:* 7,203 graduate, professional, and undergraduate students; 459 full-time matriculated graduate/professional students (222 women), 828 part-time matriculated graduate/professional students (455 women). *Enrollment by degree level:* 1,269 master's, 18 other advanced degrees. *Graduate faculty:* 11 full-time (5 women), 75 part-time/adjunct (27 women). Tuition, state resident: full-time $4704; part-time $196 per credit hour. Tuition, nonresident: full-time $9408; part-time $392 per credit hour. *Required fees:* $882. Tuition and fees vary according to course load and program. *Graduate housing:* Rooms and/or apartments available on a first-come, first-served basis to single and married students. Typical cost: $4658 (including board) for single students. Room and board charges vary according to board plan and housing facility selected. *Student services:* Campus employment opportunities, career counseling, child daycare facilities, exercise/wellness program, grant writing training, international student services, multicultural affairs office, services for students with disabilities. *Library facilities:* Collier Library plus 2 others. *Online resources:* library catalog, web page, access to other libraries' catalogs. *Collection:* 393,457 titles, 3,742 serial subscriptions, 13,155 audiovisual materials.

Computer facilities: 1,000 computers available on campus for general student use. A campuswide network can be accessed from student residence rooms and from off campus. Online class registration is available. *Web address:* http://www.una.edu/.

General Application Contact: Kim Mauldin, Director of Admissions, 256-765-4608, Fax: 256-765-4960, E-mail: komauldin@una.edu.

GRADUATE UNITS

College of Arts and Sciences Students: 17 full-time (11 women), 45 part-time (27 women); includes 5 minority (all African Americans). Average age 32. *Faculty:* 9 part-time/adjunct (3 women). Expenses: Contact institution. In 2008, 20 master's awarded. *Degree program information:* Part-time and evening/weekend programs available. Offers arts and sciences (MA, MAEN, MSCJ); criminal justice (MSCJ); English (MAEN); history and political science (MA). *Application deadline:* For fall admission, 7/1 priority date for domestic students; for spring admission, 12/1 for domestic students. Applications are processed on a rolling basis. *Application fee:* $25. *Application Contact:* Kim Mauldin, Director of Admissions, 256-765-4608, Fax: 256-765-4960, E-mail: komauldin@una.edu. *Dean,* Dr. Vagn Hansen, 256-765-4288, Fax: 256-765-4778, E-mail: vhansen@una.edu.

College of Business Students: 349 full-time (156 women), 473 part-time (204 women); includes 298 minority (39 African Americans, 4 American Indian/Alaska Native, 250 Asian Americans or Pacific Islanders, 5 Hispanic Americans), 232 international. Average age 31. *Faculty:* 7 full-time (3 women), 18 part-time/adjunct (3 women). Expenses: Contact institution. *Financial support:* Federal Work-Study available. Support available to part-time students. Financial award application deadline: 4/1. In 2008, 394 master's awarded. *Degree program information:* Part-time and evening/weekend programs available. Offers business (MBA). *Application deadline:* For fall admission, 7/1 priority date for domestic students; for spring admission, 12/1 for domestic students. Applications are processed on a rolling basis. *Application fee:* $25. Electronic applications accepted. *Application Contact:* Kim Mauldin, Director of Admissions, 256-765-4608, Fax: 256-765-4960, E-mail: komauldin@una.edu. *Dean,* Dr. Kerry Gatlin, 256-765-4261, Fax: 256-765-4170, E-mail: kpgatlin@una.edu.

College of Education Students: 76 full-time (42 women), 204 part-time (156 women); includes 21 minority (17 African Americans, 3 American Indian/Alaska Native, 1 Hispanic American), 8 international. Average age 33. *Faculty:* 4 full-time (2 women), 37 part-time/adjunct (17 women). Expenses: Contact institution. *Financial support:* Federal Work-Study available. Support available to part-time students. Financial award application deadline: 4/1. In 2008, 141 master's, 13 other advanced degrees awarded. *Degree program information:* Part-time and evening/weekend programs available. Offers collaborative teacher special education (MA Ed); counseling (MA Ed); education (MA, MA Ed, Ed S); education leadership (Ed S); elementary education (MA Ed, Ed S); learning disabilities (MA Ed); mentally retarded (MA Ed); mild learning handicapped (MA Ed); non-school-based counseling (MA); non-school-based teaching (MA); secondary education (MA Ed, Ed S). *Application deadline:* For fall admission, 7/1 priority date for domestic students; for spring admission, 12/1 for domestic students. Applications are processed on a rolling basis. *Application fee:* $25. Electronic applications accepted. *Application Contact:* Kim Mauldin, Director of Admissions, 256-765-4608, Fax: 256-765-4960, E-mail: komauldin@una.edu. *Dean,* Dr. Donna Jacobs, 256-765-4252, Fax: 256-765-4664, E-mail: dpjacobs@una.edu.

College of Nursing and Allied Health Students: 3 full-time (all women), 43 part-time (40 women); includes 5 minority (4 African Americans, 1 American Indian/Alaska Native). Average age 32. *Faculty:* 2 full-time (both women). Expenses: Contact institution. In 2008, 17 master's awarded. Offers nursing and allied health (MSN). *Application Contact:* Kim Mauldin, Director of Admissions, 256-465-4608, Fax: 256-765-4960, E-mail: komauldin@una.edu. *Dean,* Dr. Birdie Bailey, 256-765-4984, E-mail: bibailey@una.edu.

THE UNIVERSITY OF NORTH CAROLINA AT ASHEVILLE, Asheville, NC 28804-3299

General Information State-supported, coed, comprehensive institution. *Graduate housing:* On-campus housing not available.

GRADUATE UNITS

Graduate Studies *Degree program information:* Part-time and evening/weekend programs available.

THE UNIVERSITY OF NORTH CAROLINA AT CHAPEL HILL, Chapel Hill, NC 27599

General Information State-supported, coed, university. CGS member. *Graduate housing:* Rooms and/or apartments available on a first-come, first-served basis to single and married students. *Research affiliation:* Centers for Disease Control, Research Triangle Institute, Triangle Universities Nuclear Laboratory.

GRADUATE UNITS

Eshelman School of Pharmacy Students: 103 full-time (52 women); includes 8 African Americans, 7 Asian Americans or Pacific Islanders, 41 international. Average age 26. 165 applicants, 25% accepted, 30 enrolled. *Faculty:* 93 full-time (35 women), 3 part-time/adjunct (1 woman). Expenses: Contact institution. *Financial support:* In 2008–09, 16 students received support, including 16 fellowships with full tuition reimbursements available (averaging $22,500 per year), 49 research assistantships with full tuition reimbursements available (averaging $22,500 per year), 38 teaching assistantships with full tuition reimbursements available (averaging $22,500 per year); career-related internships or fieldwork, Federal Work-Study, institutionally sponsored loans, scholarships/grants, traineeships, health care benefits, and unspecified assistantships also available. Financial award application deadline: 4/1. In 2008, 10 doctorates awarded. *Degree program information:* Part-time programs available. Postbaccalaureate distance learning degree programs offered (minimal on-campus study). Offers pharmacy (MS, PhD). *Application deadline:* For fall admission, 4/1 for domestic and international students. Applications are processed on a rolling basis. *Application fee:* $75. Electronic applications accepted. *Application Contact:* Amber M. Allen, Graduate Services Manager, 919-843-9759, Fax: 919-966-3525, E-mail: amber_allen@unc.edu. *Dean,* Dr. Robert A. Blouin, 919-966-1122, Fax: 919-966-6919, E-mail: bob_blouin@unc.edu.

Graduate School Postbaccalaureate distance learning degree programs offered (minimal on-campus study). Offers materials science (MS, PhD); public policy (PhD); Russian and east European studies (MA). Electronic applications accepted.

College of Arts and Sciences *Degree program information:* Part-time programs available. Offers acting (MFA); anthropology (MA, PhD); art history (MA, PhD); arts and sciences (MA, MCRP, MFA, MPA, MRP, MS, MSRA, PhD, Certificate); athletic training (MA); biological psychology (PhD); botany (MA, MS, PhD); cell biology, development, and physiology (MA, MS, PhD); cell motility and cytoskeleton (PhD); chemistry (MA, MS, PhD); city and regional planning (MCRP); classical archaeology (MA, PhD); classics (MA, PhD); clinical psychology (PhD); cognitive psychology (PhD); communication studies (MA, PhD); comparative literature (MA, PhD); computer science (MS, PhD); costume production (MFA); developmental psychology (PhD); ecology (MA, MS, PhD); ecology and behavior (MA, MS, PhD); economics (MS, PhD); English (MA, PhD); exercise physiology (MA); folklore (MA); French (MA, PhD); genetics and molecular biology (MA, MS, PhD); geography (MA, PhD); geological sciences (MS, PhD); history (MA, PhD); Italian (MA, PhD); Latin American studies (Certificate); linguistics (MA, PhD); literature and linguistics (MA, PhD); marine sciences (MS, PhD); mathematics (MA, MS, PhD); morphology, systematics, and evolution (MA, MS, PhD); music (MA, PhD); operations research (MS, PhD); philosophy (MA, PhD); physics (MS, PhD); planning (PhD); Polish literature (PhD); political science (MA, PhD); Portuguese (MA, PhD); public administration (MPA); public policy analysis (PhD); quantitative psychology (PhD); recreation and leisure studies (MSRA); religious studies (MA, PhD); Romance languages (MA, PhD); Romance philology (MA, PhD); Russian literature (MA, PhD); Serbo-Croatian literature (PhD); Slavic linguistics (MA, PhD); social psychology (PhD); sociology (MA, PhD); Spanish (MA, PhD); sport administration (MA); statistics (MS, PhD); studio art (MFA); technical production (MFA); trans-Atlantic studies (MA). Electronic applications accepted.

School of Education *Faculty:* 59 full-time (32 women), 34 part-time/adjunct (17 women). Expenses: Contact institution. *Financial support:* In 2008–09, 105 students received support, including 13 fellowships with full and partial tuition reimbursements available, 61 research assistantships with full and partial tuition reimbursements available, 26 teaching assistantships with full tuition reimbursements available; Federal Work-Study, traineeships, and unspecified assistantships also available. Support available to part-time students. Financial award application deadline: 3/1; financial award applicants required to submit FAFSA. In 2008, 118 master's, 30 doctorates awarded. *Degree program information:* Part-time programs available. Offers culture, curriculum and change (MA, PhD); early childhood, intervention and literacy (MA, PhD); education (M Ed, MA, MAT, MSA, Ed D, PhD); education for experienced teachers (K-12) (M Ed); education for experienced teachers, early childhood intervention and family support (M Ed); educational leadership (Ed D); educational psychology, measurement and evaluation (MA, PhD); English (Grades 9-12) (MAT); French (Grades K-12) (MAT); German (Grades K-12) (MAT); Japanese (Grades K-12) (MAT); Latin (Grades 9-12) (MAT); mathematics (Grades 9-12) (MAT); music (Grades K-12) (MAT); school administration (MSA); school counseling (M Ed); school psychology (M Ed, MA, PhD); science (Grades 9-12) (MAT); social studies (Grades 9-12) (MAT); Spanish (Grades K-12) (MAT). *Application deadline:* For fall admission, 1/1 priority date for domestic and international students. Applications are processed on a rolling basis. *Application fee:* $60. Electronic applications accepted. *Application Contact:* Janet Carroll, Registrar, 919-962-8690, Fax: 919-962-1533, E-mail: jscarrol@email.unc.edu. *Interim Dean,* Dr. Jill Fitzgerald, 919-966-7000, Fax: 919-962-1533.

School of Information and Library Science *Degree program information:* Part-time programs available. Offers information and library science (MSIS, MSLS, PhD, CAS). Electronic applications accepted.

School of Journalism and Mass Communication Students: 88 full-time (49 women), 1 (woman) part-time; includes 19 minority (4 African Americans, 13 Asian Americans or Pacific Islanders, 2 Hispanic Americans). Average age 30. 219 applicants, 24% accepted, 35 enrolled. *Faculty:* 47 full-time (19 women). Expenses: Contact institution. *Financial support:* In 2008–09, 14 research assistantships with full tuition reimbursements (averaging $14,000 per year), 14 teaching assistantships with full tuition reimbursements (averaging $14,000 per year) were awarded; institutionally sponsored loans and health care benefits also available. Financial award application deadline: 3/1; financial award applicants required to submit FAFSA. In 2008, 20 master's, 5 doctorates awarded. *Degree program information:* Part-time programs available. Offers mass communication (MA, PhD). *Application deadline:* For fall admission, 1/1 for domestic and international students. *Application fee:* $75. Electronic applications accepted. *Application Contact:* Dr. Anne Johnston, Associate Dean for Graduate Studies, 919-962-4286, Fax: 919-962-0620, E-mail: jomcgrad@unc.edu. *Dean,* Dr. Jean Folkerts, 919-962-1204, Fax: 919-962-0620.

School of Public Health *Degree program information:* Part-time programs available. Postbaccalaureate distance learning degree programs offered (minimal on-campus study). Offers air, radiation and industrial hygiene (MPH, MS, MSEE, MSPH, PhD); aquatic and atmospheric sciences (MPH, MS, MSPH, PhD); biostatistics (MPH, MS, Dr PH, PhD); environmental engineering (MPH, MS, MSEE, MSPH, PhD); environmental health sciences (MPH, MS, MSPH, PhD); environmental management and policy (MPH, MS, MSPH, PhD); epidemiology (MPH, PhD); health behavior and health education (MPH, PhD); health care and prevention (MPH); health policy and administration (MHA, MPH, MSPH, Dr PH, PhD); leadership (MPH); maternal and child health (MPH, MSPH, Dr PH, PhD); nutrition (MPH, Dr PH, PhD); nutritional biochemistry (MS); occupational health nursing (MPH); professional practice program (MPH); public health (MHA, MPH, MS, MSEE, MSPH, Dr PH, PhD); public health nursing (MS). Electronic applications accepted.

School of Social Work *Degree program information:* Part-time programs available. Offers social work (MSW, PhD). Electronic applications accepted.

Kenan-Flagler Business School *Degree program information:* Evening/weekend programs available. Postbaccalaureate distance learning degree programs offered (minimal on-campus study). Offers accounting (PhD); business (MAC, MBA, PhD); business administration (MBA, PhD); finance (PhD); marketing (PhD); operations management (PhD); organizational behavior (PhD); strategy (PhD). Electronic applications accepted.

National Institutes of Health Sponsored Programs Offers cell motility and cytoskeleton (PhD).

School of Dentistry Offers dental hygiene (MS); dentistry (DDS, MS, PhD); endodontics (MS); epidemiology (PhD); operative dentistry (MS); oral and maxillofacial pathology (MS); oral and maxillofacial radiology (MS); oral biology (PhD); orthodontics (MS); pediatric dentistry (MS); periodontology (MS); prosthodontics (MS). Electronic applications accepted.

School of Law Offers law (JD). Electronic applications accepted.

School of Medicine Offers allied health sciences (MPT, MS, Au D, DPT, PhD); audiology (Au D); biochemistry and biophysics (MS, PhD); biomedical engineering (MS, PhD); cell and developmental biology (PhD); cell and molecular physiology (PhD); experimental pathology (PhD); genetics and molecular biology (MS, PhD); human movement science (MS, PhD); immunology (MS, PhD); medicine (MD, MPT, MS, Au D, DPT, PhD); microbiology (MS, PhD); microbiology and immunology (MS, PhD); neurobiology (PhD); occupational science (MS, PhD); pathology and laboratory medicine (PhD); pharmacology (PhD); physical therapy (MPT, MS, DPT); physical therapy—off campus (DPT); physical therapy—on campus (DPT); rehabilitation counseling and psychology (MS); speech and hearing sciences (MS, Au D, PhD); toxicology (MS, PhD). Electronic applications accepted.

School of Nursing *Degree program information:* Part-time programs available. Offers nursing (MSN, PhD, PMC).

THE UNIVERSITY OF NORTH CAROLINA AT CHARLOTTE, Charlotte, NC 28223-0001

General Information State-supported, coed, university. CGS member. *Enrollment:* 23,300 graduate, professional, and undergraduate students; 1,628 full-time matriculated graduate/professional students (859 women), 2,094 part-time matriculated graduate/professional students (1,310 women). *Enrollment by degree level:* 1,741 master's, 282 doctoral, 71 other advanced degrees. *Graduate faculty:* 796 full-time (310 women), 81 part-time/adjunct (37 women). Tuition, state resident: full-time $2919; part-time $122 per credit hour. Tuition, nonresident: full-time $13,126; part-time $547 per credit hour. *Required fees:* $1779; $91 per credit hour. Tuition and fees vary according to program. *Graduate housing:* Room and/or apartments available on a first-come, first-served basis to single students; on-campus housing not available to married students. Typical cost: $3286 per year ($6465 including board). Room and board charges vary according to board plan and housing facility selected. Housing application deadline: 5/1. *Student services:* Campus employment opportunities, campus safety program, career counseling, free psychological counseling, grant writing training, international student services, low-cost health insurance, multicultural affairs office, services for students with disabilities, writing training. *Library facilities:* J. Murrey Atkins Library. *Online resources:* library catalog, web page, access to other libraries' catalogs. *Collection:* 1 million titles, 29,174 serial subscriptions, 20,178 audiovisual materials.

Computer facilities: 1,400 computers available on campus for general student use. A campuswide network can be accessed from student residence rooms and from off campus. Online class registration is available. *Web address:* http://www.uncc.edu/.

General Application Contact: Dr. Thomas L. Reynolds, Dean and Associate Provost, 704-687-3372, Fax: 687-547-3279, E-mail: gradadm@.uncc.edu.

GRADUATE UNITS

Graduate School Students: 1,628 full-time (859 women), 1,741 part-time (1,310 women); includes 544 minority (365 African Americans, 8 American Indian/Alaska Native, 90 Asian Americans or Pacific Islanders, 81 Hispanic Americans), 755 international. Average age 30. 3,352 applicants, 65% accepted, 1301 enrolled. *Faculty:* 796 full-time (310 women), 81 part-time/adjunct (37 women). Expenses: Contact institution. *Financial support:* In 2008–09, 2,000 students received support, including 18 fellowships (averaging $15,542 per year), 903 research assistantships (averaging $7,808 per year), 782 teaching assistantships (averaging $9,405 per year); career-related internships or fieldwork, Federal Work-Study, institutionally sponsored loans, scholarships/grants, traineeships, unspecified assistantships, and 124 administrative assistantships ($7,261 average) also available. Support available to part-time students. Financial award application deadline: 4/1; financial award applicants required to submit FAFSA. In 2008, 1,058 master's, 45 doctorates, 52 other advanced degrees awarded. *Degree program information:* Part-time and evening/weekend programs available. Postbaccalaureate distance learning degree programs offered (no on-campus study). *Application deadline:* For fall admission, 7/15 for domestic students, 5/1 for international students; for spring admission, 11/15 for domestic students, 10/1 for international students. Applications are processed on a rolling basis. *Application fee:* $55. Electronic applications accepted. *Application Contact:* Kathy B. Giddings, Director of Graduate Admissions, 704-687-3366,

The University of North Carolina at Charlotte (continued)

Fax: 704-687-3279, E-mail: agidding@uncc.edu. *Dean and Associate Provost*, Dr. Thomas L. Reynolds, 704-687-3372, Fax: 687-547-3279, E-mail: gradadm@email.uncc.edu.

Belk College of Business Students: 310 full-time (142 women), 448 part-time (160 women); includes 82 minority (37 African Americans, 2 American Indian/Alaska Native, 32 Asian Americans or Pacific Islanders, 11 Hispanic Americans), 239 international. Average age 30. 630 applicants, 68% accepted, 290 enrolled. *Faculty:* 76 full-time (19 women), 9 part-time/adjunct (0 women). Expenses: Contact institution. *Financial support:* In 2008–09, 1 fellowship (averaging $25,000 per year), 67 research assistantships (averaging $6,248 per year), 81 teaching assistantships (averaging $9,237 per year) were awarded; career-related internships or fieldwork, Federal Work-Study, institutionally sponsored loans, scholarships/grants, unspecified assistantships, and 19 administrative assistantships ($5,938 average) also available. Support available to part-time students. Financial award application deadline: 4/1; financial award applicants required to submit FAFSA. In 2008, 267 master's awarded. *Degree program information:* Part-time and evening/weekend programs available. Offers accounting (M Acc); business (M Acc, MBA, MS, PhD); business administration (MBA, PhD); economics (MS); mathematical finance (MS); sports marketing management (MBA). *Application deadline:* For fall admission, 7/15 for domestic students, 5/1 for international students; for spring admission, 11/15 for domestic students, 10/1 for international students. Applications are processed on a rolling basis. *Application fee:* $55. Electronic applications accepted. *Application Contact:* Kathy B. Giddings, Director of Graduate Admissions, 704-687-3366, Fax: 704-687-3279, E-mail: agidding@uncc.edu. *Interim Dean*, Dr. Stephen Ott, 704-687-2165, Fax: 704-687-4014.

College of Arts and Architecture Students: 63 full-time (43 women), 4 part-time (3 women); includes 12 minority (6 African Americans, 5 Asian Americans or Pacific Islanders, 1 Hispanic American). Average age 27. 83 applicants, 61% accepted, 26 enrolled. *Faculty:* 46 full-time (16 women), 2 part-time/adjunct (both women). Expenses: Contact institution. *Financial support:* In 2008–09, 10 research assistantships (averaging $7,925 per year), 20 teaching assistantships (averaging $6,620 per year) were awarded; career-related internships or fieldwork, Federal Work-Study, institutionally sponsored loans, scholarships/grants, unspecified assistantships, and 2 administrative assistantships ($9,032 average) also available. Support available to part-time students. Financial award application deadline: 4/1; financial award applicants required to submit FAFSA. In 2008, 17 master's awarded. Offers arts and architecture (M Arch). *Application deadline:* For fall admission, 2/15 for domestic students, 1/31 for international students. *Application fee:* $55. Electronic applications accepted. *Application Contact:* Kathy B. Giddings, Director of Graduate Admissions, 704-687-3366, Fax: 704-687-3279, E-mail: agidding@uncc.edu. *Dean*, Kenneth A. Lambla, 704-687-4841, Fax: 704-687-3353, E-mail: kalambla@email.uncc.edu.

College of Arts and Sciences Students: 343 full-time (194 women), 418 part-time (246 women); includes 98 minority (60 African Americans, 1 American Indian/Alaska Native, 11 Asian Americans or Pacific Islanders, 26 Hispanic Americans), 114 international. Average age 29. 826 applicants, 47% accepted, 240 enrolled. *Faculty:* 351 full-time (132 women), 21 part-time/adjunct (6 women). Expenses: Contact institution. *Financial support:* In 2008–09, 10 fellowships (averaging $17,484 per year), 337 research assistantships (averaging $8,020 per year), 339 teaching assistantships (averaging $10,095 per year) were awarded; career-related internships or fieldwork, Federal Work-Study, institutionally sponsored loans, scholarships/grants, unspecified assistantships, and 41 administrative assistantships ($7,699 average) also available. Support available to part-time students. Financial award application deadline: 4/1; financial award applicants required to submit FAFSA. In 2008, 147 master's, 8 doctorates awarded. *Degree program information:* Part-time and evening/weekend programs available. Offers applied mathematics (MS, PhD); applied physics (MS); arts and sciences (MA, MPA, MS, PhD); biology (MA, MS, PhD); chemistry (MS); communication studies (MA); community/clinical psychology (MA); criminal justice (MS); earth sciences (MS); English (MA); English education (MA); geography (MA); geography and urban and regional analysis (PhD); gerontology (MA); health psychology (PhD); history (MA); industrial/organizational psychology (MA); Latin American studies (MA); liberal studies (MA); mathematics (MS); mathematics education (MA); optical science and engineering (MS, PhD); organizational science (PhD); public administration (MPA); public policy (PhD); religious studies (MA); sociology (MA); Spanish (MA). *Application deadline:* For fall admission, 7/15 for domestic students, 5/1 for international students; for spring admission, 11/15 for domestic students, 10/1 for international students. Applications are processed on a rolling basis. *Application fee:* $55. Electronic applications accepted. *Application Contact:* Kathy B. Giddings, Director of Graduate Admissions, 704-687-3366, Fax: 704-687-3279, E-mail: agidding@uncc.edu. *Dean*, Dr. Nancy A Gutierrez, 704-687-4303, Fax: 704-687-3228, E-mail: ngutierr@email.uncc.edu.

College of Computing and Informatics Students: 225 full-time (54 women), 91 part-time (33 women); includes 23 minority (12 African Americans, 9 Asian Americans or Pacific Islanders, 2 Hispanic Americans), 171 international. Average age 27. 443 applicants, 75% accepted, 110 enrolled. *Faculty:* 47 full-time (14 women), 5 part-time/adjunct (0 women). Expenses: Contact institution. *Financial support:* In 2008–09, 3 fellowships (averaging $11,000 per year), 153 research assistantships (averaging $8,207 per year), 105 teaching assistantships (averaging $11,353 per year) were awarded; career-related internships or fieldwork, Federal Work-Study, institutionally sponsored loans, scholarships/grants, unspecified assistantships, and 8 administrative assistantships ($7,571 average) also available. Support available to part-time students. Financial award application deadline: 4/1; financial award applicants required to submit FAFSA. In 2008, 94 master's, 11 doctorates awarded. *Degree program information:* Part-time and evening/weekend programs available. Offers computer science (MS); computing and informatics (MS, PhD); information technology (MS, PhD). *Application deadline:* For fall admission, 7/1 for domestic students, 5/1 for international students; for spring admission, 11/1 for domestic students, 10/1 for international students. Applications are processed on a rolling basis. *Application fee:* $55. Electronic applications accepted. *Application Contact:* Kathy B. Giddings, Director of Graduate Admissions, 704-687-3366, Fax: 704-687-3279, E-mail: agidding@uncc.edu. *Dean*, Dr. Mirsad Hadzikadic, 704-687-3119, Fax: 704-687-6979, E-mail: mirsad@email.uncc.edu.

College of Education Students: 192 full-time (146 women), 805 part-time (675 women); includes 205 minority (166 African Americans, 5 American Indian/Alaska Native, 14 Asian Americans or Pacific Islanders, 20 Hispanic Americans), 7 international. Average age 34. 483 applicants, 83% accepted, 342 enrolled. *Faculty:* 116 full-time (69 women), 26 part-time/adjunct (18 women). Expenses: Contact institution. *Financial support:* In 2008–09, 2 fellowships (averaging $19,460 per year), 48 research assistantships (averaging $11,865 per year), 65 teaching assistantships (averaging $6,899 per year) were awarded; career-related internships or fieldwork, Federal Work-Study, institutionally sponsored loans, scholarships/grants, unspecified assistantships, and 36 administrative assistantships ($8,222 average) also available. Support available to part-time students. Financial award application deadline: 4/1; financial award applicants required to submit FAFSA. In 2008, 269 master's, 16 doctorates, 49 other advanced degrees awarded. *Degree program information:* Part-time and evening/weekend programs available. Postbaccalaureate distance learning degree programs offered (no on-campus study). Offers art education (K-12) (MAT); counseling (MA, PhD); curriculum and supervision (M Ed); dance education (K-12) (MAT); education (M Ed, MA, MAT, MSA, Ed D, PhD, CAS); educational administration (CAS); educational leadership (Ed D); elementary education (M Ed); elementary education (K-6) (MAT); English as a second language (K-12) (MAT); foreign language education (K-12) (MAT); general teacher education (MAT); instructional systems technology (M Ed); middle grades and secondary education (M Ed); middle grades education (6-9) (MAT); music education (K-12) (MAT); reading, language and literacy (M Ed); school administration (MSA); secondary education (9-12) (MAT); special education (M Ed, PhD); special education (K-12) (MAT); teaching English as a second language (M Ed); theatre education (K-12) (MAT); urban education (PhD); urban literacy (PhD); urban math (PhD). *Application deadline:* For fall admission, 7/1 for domestic students, 5/1 for international students; for spring admission, 11/1 for domestic students, 10/1 for international students. Applications are processed on a rolling basis. *Application fee:* $55. Electronic applications accepted. *Application Contact:* Kathy B. Giddings, Director of Graduate Admissions, 704-687-3366, Fax: 704-687-3279, E-mail: agidding@uncc.edu. *Dean*, Dr. Mary Lynne Calhoun, 704-687-8722, Fax: 704-687-4705, E-mail: mlcalhou@email.uncc.edu.

College of Health and Human Services Students: 274 full-time (225 women), 194 part-time (172 women); includes 99 minority (68 African Americans, 17 Asian Americans or Pacific Islanders, 14 Hispanic Americans), 22 international. Average age 32. 355 applicants, 102% accepted, 192 enrolled. *Faculty:* 66 full-time (48 women), 16 part-time/adjunct (9 women). Expenses: Contact institution. *Financial support:* In 2008–09, 1 fellowship (averaging $4,000 per year), 41 research assistantships (averaging $11,635 per year), 6 teaching assistantships (averaging $10,833 per year) were awarded; career-related internships or fieldwork, Federal Work-Study, institutionally sponsored loans, scholarships/grants, traineeships, unspecified assistantships, and 13 administrative assistantships ($5,575 average) also available. Support available to part-time students. Financial award application deadline: 4/1; financial award applicants required to submit FAFSA. In 2008, 165 master's awarded. *Degree program information:* Part-time and evening/weekend programs available. Postbaccalaureate distance learning degree programs offered (no on-campus study). Offers clinical exercise physiology (MS); health and human services (MHA, MS, MSN, MSPH, MSW, PhD); health care administration (MHA); health services research (PhD); nursing advanced clinical (MSN); nursing anesthesia (MSN); nursing systems population (MSN); public health (MSPH); social work (MSW). *Application deadline:* For fall admission, 7/1 for domestic students, 5/1 for international students; for spring admission, 11/1 for domestic students, 10/1 for international students. Applications are processed on a rolling basis. *Application fee:* $55. Electronic applications accepted. *Application Contact:* Kathy B. Giddings, Director of Graduate Admissions, 704-687-3366, Fax: 704-687-3279, E-mail: agidding@uncc.edu. *Dean*, Dr. Karen Schmaling, 704-687-4651, Fax: 704-687-3180.

The William States Lee College of Engineering Students: 215 full-time (55 women), 134 part-time (21 women); includes 16 African Americans, 2 Asian Americans or Pacific Islanders, 7 Hispanic Americans, 202 international. Average age 27. 532 applicants, 63% accepted, 101 enrolled. *Faculty:* 94 full-time (12 women), 2 part-time/adjunct (both women). Expenses: Contact institution. *Financial support:* In 2008–09, 1 fellowship (averaging $4,000 per year), 237 research assistantships (averaging $6,305 per year), 166 teaching assistantships (averaging $8,111 per year) were awarded; career-related internships or fieldwork, Federal Work-Study, institutionally sponsored loans, scholarships/grants, unspecified assistantships, and 4 administrative assistantships ($6,182 average) also available. Support available to part-time students. Financial award application deadline: 4/1; financial award applicants required to submit FAFSA. In 2008, 99 master's, 10 doctorates awarded. *Degree program information:* Part-time and evening/weekend programs available. Offers civil engineering (MSCE); electrical engineering (MSEE, PhD); engineering (MS, MSCE, MSE, MSEE, MSME, PhD); engineering management (MS); infrastructure and environmental systems (PhD); infrastructure and environmental systems design (PhD); infrastructure and environmental systems management (PhD); infrastructure and environmental systems science (PhD); mechanical engineering (MSME, PhD). *Application deadline:* For fall admission, 7/1 for domestic students, 5/1 for international students; for spring admission, 11/1 for domestic students, 10/1 for international students. Applications are processed on a rolling basis. *Application fee:* $55. Electronic applications accepted. *Application Contact:* Kathy B. Giddings, Director of Graduate Admissions, 704-687-3366, Fax: 704-687-3279, E-mail: agidding@uncc.edu. *Dean*, Dr. Robert E. Johnson, 704-687-2301, Fax: 704-687-2352, E-mail: robejohn@email.uncc.edu.

THE UNIVERSITY OF NORTH CAROLINA AT GREENSBORO, Greensboro, NC 27412-5001

General Information State-supported, coed, university. CGS member. *Graduate housing:* Room and/or apartments available to single students; on-campus housing not available to married students. Housing application deadline: 5/15. *Research affiliation:* Moses Cone Memorial Hospital, North Carolina Zoological Park, North Carolina Baptist Hospital.

GRADUATE UNITS

Graduate School *Degree program information:* Part-time and evening/weekend programs available. Postbaccalaureate distance learning degree programs offered (minimal on-campus study). Offers conflict resolution (MA, Certificate); genetic counseling (MS); gerontology (MS, Certificate); liberal studies (MALS). Electronic applications accepted.

Bryan School of Business and Economics *Degree program information:* Part-time programs available. Offers accounting (MS); accounting systems (MS); applied economics (MA); business administration (MBA, PMC, Postbaccalaureate Certificate); business and economics (MA, MBA, MS, PhD, Certificate, PMC, Postbaccalaureate Certificate); economics (PhD); financial accounting and reporting (MS); financial analysis (PMC); financial economics (MA); information systems (PhD); information technology (Certificate); information technology and management (MS); supply chain management (Certificate); tax concentration (MS). Electronic applications accepted.

College of Arts and Sciences *Degree program information:* Part-time programs available. Offers acting (MFA); advanced Spanish language and Hispanic cultural studies (Certificate); American literature (PhD); applied geography (MA); arts and sciences (M Ed, MA, MFA, MPA, MS, PhD, Certificate); biochemistry (MS); biology (MS); chemistry (MS); clinical psychology (MA, PhD); cognitive psychology (MA, PhD); communication studies (MA); computer science (MS); creative writing (MFA); criminology (MA); design (MFA); developmental psychology (MA, PhD); directing (MFA); English (M Ed, MA, PhD, Certificate); English literature (PhD); film and video production (MFA); French (MA); geographic information science (Certificate); geography (PhD); historic preservation (Certificate); history (MA); Latin (M Ed); mathematics (MA, PhD); museum studies (Certificate); nonprofit management (Certificate); public affairs (MPA); rhetoric and composition (PhD); social psychology (MA, PhD); sociology (MA); Spanish (MA, Certificate); studio arts (MFA); theater education (M Ed); theater for youth (MFA); U.S. history (PhD); urban and economic development (Certificate); women's and gender studies (MA, Certificate). Electronic applications accepted.

School of Education *Degree program information:* Part-time and evening/weekend programs available. Offers advanced school counseling (PMC); college teaching and adult learning (Certificate); counseling and counselor education (PhD); counseling and educational development (MS); couple and family counseling (PMC); cross-categorical special education (M Ed); curriculum and instruction (M Ed); curriculum and teaching (PhD); education (M Ed, MLIS, MS, MSA, Ed D, PhD, Certificate, Ed S, PMC); educational leadership (Ed D, Ed S); educational research, measurement and evaluation (PhD); English as a second language (Certificate); higher education (M Ed, PhD); interdisciplinary studies in special education (M Ed); leadership early care and education (Certificate); library and information studies (MLIS); school administration (MSA); school counseling (PMC); special education (M Ed, PhD); supervision (M Ed); teacher education and development (PhD). Electronic applications accepted.

School of Health and Human Performance Offers community health education (MPH, Dr PH); dance (MA, MFA); exercise and sports science (M Ed, MS, Ed D, PhD); health and human performance (M Ed, MA, MFA, MPH, MS, Dr PH, Ed D, PhD); parks and recreation management (MS); speech language pathology (PhD); speech pathology and audiology (MA). Electronic applications accepted.

School of Human Environmental Sciences Offers consumer, apparel, and retail studies (MS, PhD); historic preservation (Certificate); human development and family studies (M Ed, MS, PhD); human environmental sciences (M Ed, MS, MSW, PhD, Certificate); interior architecture (MS); museum studies (Certificate); nutrition (MS, PhD); social work (MSW). Electronic applications accepted.

School of Music Offers composition (MM); education (MM); music education (PhD); performance (MM, DMA). Electronic applications accepted.

School of Nursing Offers adult clinical nurse specialist (MSN, PMC); adult/gerontological nurse practitioner (MSN, PMC); nurse anesthesia (MSN, PMC); nursing (PhD); nursing administration (MSN); nursing education (MSN). Electronic applications accepted.

THE UNIVERSITY OF NORTH CAROLINA AT PEMBROKE, Pembroke, NC 28372-1510

General Information State-supported, coed, comprehensive institution. CGS member. *Graduate housing:* Room and/or apartments available on a first-come, first-served basis to single students; on-campus housing not available to married students. Housing application deadline: 4/15.

GRADUATE UNITS

Graduate Studies *Degree program information:* Part-time and evening/weekend programs available. Offers art education (MA, MAT); English education (MA, MAT); mathematics education (MA, MAT); music education (MA, MAT); physical education (MA, MAT); public administration (MPA); science education (MA); service agency counseling (MA); social studies education (MA, MAT).

School of Business *Degree program information:* Part-time and evening/weekend programs available. Offers business (MBA); business administration (MBA).

School of Education *Degree program information:* Part-time and evening/weekend programs available. Offers elementary education (MA Ed); middle grades education (MA Ed, MAT); reading education (MA Ed); school administration (MSA); school counseling (MA Ed).

UNIVERSITY OF NORTH CAROLINA SCHOOL OF THE ARTS, Winston-Salem, NC 27127-2188

General Information State-supported, coed, comprehensive institution. *Enrollment:* 879 graduate, professional, and undergraduate students; 112 full-time matriculated graduate/professional students (62 women), 2 part-time matriculated graduate/professional students (1 woman). *Enrollment by degree level:* 114 master's. *Graduate faculty:* 76. Tuition, state resident: full-time $3797. Tuition, nonresident: full-time $15,670. *Required fees:* $1791. *Graduate housing:* Room and/or apartments available on a first-come, first-served basis to single students. Housing application deadline: 5/16. *Student services:* Campus employment opportunities, campus safety program, career counseling, exercise/wellness program, free psychological counseling, grant writing training, international student services, low-cost health insurance, services for students with disabilities, writing training. *Library facilities:* Semans Library plus 1 other. *Online resources:* library catalog, access to other libraries' catalogs. *Collection:* 87,917 titles, 490 serial subscriptions.

Computer facilities: 60 computers available on campus for general student use. A campuswide network can be accessed from student residence rooms and from off campus. *Web address:* http://www.ncarts.edu/.

General Application Contact: Sheeler Lawson, Director of Admissions, 336-770-3290, Fax: 336-770-3370, E-mail: admissions@uncsa.edu.

GRADUATE UNITS

School of Design and Production Students: 66 full-time (39 women); includes 5 minority (1 African American, 4 Hispanic Americans), 2 international. Average age 25. 86 applicants, 77% accepted, 48 enrolled. *Faculty:* 19 full-time (4 women), 16 part-time/adjunct (6 women). Expenses: Contact institution. *Financial support:* In 2008–09, 53 teaching assistantships with partial tuition reimbursements (averaging $1,500 per year) were awarded; career-related internships or fieldwork, Federal Work-Study, and unspecified assistantships also available. Support available to part-time students. Financial award application deadline: 3/15; financial award applicants required to submit FAFSA. In 2008, 11 master's awarded. Offers costume design (MFA); costume technology (MFA); scene design (MFA); scene painting/properties (MFA); sound design (MFA); stage automation (MFA); technical direction (MFA); wig and make-up design (MFA). *Application deadline:* For fall admission, 4/1 priority date for domestic students. Applications are processed on a rolling basis. *Application fee:* $60 ($100 for international students). Electronic applications accepted. *Application Contact:* Sheeler Lawson, Director of Admissions, 336-770-3290, Fax: 336-770-3370, E-mail: admissions@uncsa.edu. *Dean,* Joseph A. Tilford, 336-770-3214 Ext. 103, Fax: 336-770-3213.

School of Filmmaking Students: 7 full-time (0 women); includes 1 minority (Asian American or Pacific Islander). Average age 25. 6 applicants, 33% accepted, 2 enrolled. *Faculty:* 3 full-time (0 women). Expenses: Contact institution. *Financial support:* In 2008–09, fellowships (averaging $2,000 per year); career-related internships or fieldwork and Federal Work-Study also available. Support available to part-time students. Financial award application deadline: 3/15; financial award applicants required to submit FAFSA. In 2008, 3 master's awarded. Offers film music composition (MFA). *Application deadline:* For fall admission, 4/1 priority date for domestic students. Applications are processed on a rolling basis. *Application fee:* $60 ($100 for international students). *Application Contact:* Sheeler Lawson, Director of Admissions, 336-770-3290, Fax: 336-770-3370, E-mail: admissions@uncsa.edu. *Dean,* Jordan Kerner, 336-770-1330, Fax: 336-770-1339, E-mail: kernerj@uncsa.edu.

School of Music Students: 60 full-time (19 women); includes 5 minority (3 African Americans, 1 American Indian/Alaska Native, 1 Hispanic American), 26 international. Average age 25. *Faculty:* 30 full-time (9 women), 11 part-time/adjunct (3 women). Expenses: Contact institution. *Financial support:* In 2008–09, 8 fellowships with partial tuition reimbursements (averaging $2,000 per year), 10 teaching assistantships with partial tuition reimbursements (averaging $3,000 per year) were awarded; career-related internships or fieldwork and Federal Work-Study also available. Support available to part-time students. Financial award application deadline: 3/15; financial award applicants required to submit FAFSA. In 2008, 12 master's awarded. Offers music performance (MM); orchestral conducting (MM). *Application deadline:* For fall admission, 4/1 priority date for domestic students. Applications are processed on a rolling basis. *Application fee:* $60 ($100 for international students). *Application Contact:* Sheeler Lawson, Director of Admissions, 336-770-3290, Fax: 336-770-3370, E-mail: admissions@uncsa.edu. *Dean,* Dr. Michael Rothkopf, 336-770-3251, Fax: 336-770-3248, E-mail: rothk@uncsa.edu.

THE UNIVERSITY OF NORTH CAROLINA WILMINGTON, Wilmington, NC 28403-3297

General Information State-supported, coed, comprehensive institution. CGS member. *Enrollment:* 12,195 graduate, professional, and undergraduate students; 501 full-time matriculated graduate/professional students (329 women), 831 part-time matriculated graduate/professional students (526 women). *Enrollment by degree level:* 1,289 master's, 43 doctoral. *Graduate faculty:* 285 full-time (107 women), 29 part-time/adjunct (12 women). Tuition, state resident: full-time $4838. Tuition, nonresident: full-time $14,898. Tuition and fees vary according to course load, campus/location and program. *Graduate housing:* Room and/or apartments available on a first-come, first-served basis to single students; on-campus housing not available to married students. Typical cost: $5004 per year ($8154 including board). Room and board charges vary according to board plan and housing facility selected. Housing application deadline: 3/31. *Student services:* Campus employment opportunities, campus safety program, career counseling, exercise/wellness program, free psychological counseling, international student services, low-cost health insurance, services for students with disabilities. *Library facilities:* William Madison Randall Library. *Online resources:* library catalog, web page, access to other libraries' catalogs. *Collection:* 1 million titles, 30,000 serial subscriptions, 116,241 audiovisual materials.

Computer facilities: Computer purchase and lease plans are available. 1,170 computers available on campus for general student use. A campuswide network can be accessed from student residence rooms and from off campus. Online class registration is available. *Web address:* http://www.uncw.edu/.

General Application Contact: Dr. Robert D. Roer, Dean, Graduate School and Research, 910-962-4117, Fax: 910-962-3787, E-mail: roer@uncw.edu.

GRADUATE UNITS

Center for Marine Science Students: 4 full-time (3 women), 34 part-time (19 women); includes 2 minority (both Hispanic Americans). 28 applicants, 46% accepted, 7 enrolled. *Faculty:* 66 full-time (16 women). Expenses: Contact institution. *Financial support:* In 2008–09, research assistantships with full and partial tuition reimbursements (averaging $10,000 per year), 11 teaching assistantships with full and partial tuition reimbursements (averaging $10,000 per year) were awarded; scholarships/grants and unspecified assistantships also available. Support available to part-time students. In 2008, 9 master's awarded. *Degree program information:* Part-time programs available. Offers marine science (MS). *Application deadline:* For fall admission, 3/15 for domestic students. *Application fee:* $60. *Application Contact:* Dr. Joan Willey, Graduate Coordinator, 910-962-3459, E-mail: willeyj@uncw.edu. *Director,* Dr. Daniel Baden, 910-962-2301, E-mail: badend@uncw.edu.

College of Arts and Sciences Students: 208 full-time (133 women), 370 part-time (219 women); includes 66 minority (27 African Americans, 2 American Indian/Alaska Native, 15 Asian Americans or Pacific Islanders, 22 Hispanic Americans), 24 international. Average age 30. 812 applicants, 44% accepted, 218 enrolled. *Faculty:* 207 full-time (63 women), 20 part-time/adjunct (9 women). Expenses: Contact institution. *Financial support:* In 2008–09, research assistantships with full and partial tuition reimbursements (averaging $10,000 per year), 207 teaching assistantships with full and partial tuition reimbursements (averaging $10,000 per year) were awarded; career-related internships or fieldwork and Federal Work-Study also available. Support available to part-time students. Financial award application deadline: 3/15. In 2008, 176 master's, 1 doctorate awarded. *Degree program information:* Part-time programs available. Offers applied gerontology (MS); arts and sciences (MA, MALS, MFA, MPA, MS, MSW, PhD, Graduate Certificate); biology (MS); chemistry and biochemistry (MS); coastal management (MA); computer science and information systems (MS); creative writing (MFA); criminology (MA); English (MA); environmental education and interpretation (MA); environmental management (MA); geology (MS); Hispanic studies (Graduate Certificate); history (MA); individualized study (MA); liberal studies (MALS); marine biology (MS, PhD); marine science (MS); mathematical sciences (MS); psychology (MA); public and international affairs (MPA); public sociology (MA); social work (MSW). *Application deadline:* Applications are processed on a rolling basis. *Application fee:* $45. *Application Contact:* Dr. Robert D. Roer, Dean, Graduate School and Research, 910-962-4117, Fax: 910-962-3787, E-mail: roer@uncw.edu. *Dean,* Dr. David Cordle, 910-962-3111, Fax: 910-962-3114, E-mail: cordled@uncw.edu.

School of Business Students: 68 full-time (35 women), 102 part-time (34 women); includes 12 minority (5 African Americans, 4 Asian Americans or Pacific Islanders, 3 Hispanic Americans), 5 international. Average age 28. 186 applicants, 62% accepted, 100 enrolled. Expenses: Contact institution. *Financial support:* In 2008–09, 13 teaching assistantships with full and partial tuition reimbursements (averaging $9,000 per year) were awarded; career-related internships or fieldwork, Federal Work-Study, and unspecified assistantships also available. Support available to part-time students. Financial award application deadline: 3/15. In 2008, 103 master's awarded. *Degree program information:* Part-time and evening/weekend programs available. Offers accountancy (MSA); business (MBA, MSA); business administration (MBA). *Application deadline:* Applications are processed on a rolling basis. *Application fee:* $60. *Application Contact:* Dr. Karen Barnhill, Graduate Coordinator, 910-962-3903, E-mail: barnhillk@uncw.edu. *Dean,* Dr. Lawrence Clark, 910-962-7672, E-mail: clarkl@uncw.edu.

School of Education Students: 84 full-time (62 women), 148 part-time (130 women); includes 16 minority (11 African Americans, 1 American Indian/Alaska Native, 1 Asian American or Pacific Islander, 3 Hispanic Americans), 1 international. Average age 33. 145 applicants, 69% accepted, 90 enrolled. Expenses: Contact institution. *Financial support:* In 2008–09, 19 teaching assistantships with full and partial tuition reimbursements (averaging $14,000 per year) were awarded; career-related internships or fieldwork, Federal Work-Study, and unspecified assistantships also available. Support available to part-time students. Financial award application deadline: 3/15. In 2008, 93 master's awarded. *Degree program information:* Part-time and evening/weekend programs available. Offers curriculum, instruction and supervision (M Ed); education (M Ed, MAT, MS, MSA, Ed D); educational leadership (M Ed, MSA, Ed D); elementary education (M Ed); instructional technology (MS); language and literacy education (M Ed); middle grades education (M Ed). *Application deadline:* For fall admission, 6/1 for domestic students. Applications are processed on a rolling basis. *Application fee:* $60. *Application Contact:* Dr. Hank Weddington, Associate Dean, 910-962-3361, E-mail: weddingtonh@uncw.edu. *Interim Dean,* Dr. Karen Wetherill, 910-962-3354, E-mail: wetherillk@uncw.edu.

School of Nursing Students: 24 full-time (22 women), 28 part-time (27 women); includes 7 minority (3 African Americans, 3 American Indian/Alaska Native, 1 Hispanic American), 1 international. Average age 36. 30 applicants, 83% accepted, 23 enrolled. *Faculty:* 9 full-time (all women), 1 (woman) part-time/adjunct. Expenses: Contact institution. *Financial support:* In 2008–09, 2 teaching assistantships with full and partial tuition reimbursements (averaging $9,500 per year) were awarded. Financial award application deadline: 3/15. In 2008, 8 master's awarded. Offers family nurse practitioner (MSN); nurse educator (MSN). *Application deadline:* For fall admission, 3/1 for domestic students. Applications are processed on a rolling basis. *Application fee:* $60. Electronic applications accepted. *Application Contact:* Dr. Julie Taylor, Graduate Coordinator, 910-962-7927, E-mail: taylorjs@uncw.edu. *Graduate Program Coordinator,* Dr. Julie S Taylor, 910-962-7927, E-mail: taylorjs@uncw.edu.

UNIVERSITY OF NORTH DAKOTA, Grand Forks, ND 58202

General Information State-supported, coed, university. CGS member. *Graduate housing:* Rooms and/or apartments guaranteed to single students and available on a first-come, first-served basis to married students. *Research affiliation:* Environmental Energy Research Center, North Dakota Geological Survey, U.S. Department of Agriculture–Human Nutrition Laboratory, Neuropsychiatric Research Institute (neurosciences).

GRADUATE UNITS

Graduate School *Degree program information:* Part-time and evening/weekend programs available. Postbaccalaureate distance learning degree programs offered (minimal on-campus study). Offers earth system science and policy (MEM, MS, PhD). Electronic applications accepted.

College of Arts and Sciences *Degree program information:* Part-time programs available. Postbaccalaureate distance learning degree programs offered. Offers arts and sciences (M Ed, M Mus, MA, MFA, MS, DA, DMEd, PhD); botany (MS, PhD); chemistry (MS, PhD); clinical psychology (PhD); communication (MA, PhD); communication sciences and disorders (PhD); counseling psychology (PhD); criminal justice (PhD); ecology (MS, PhD); English (MA, PhD); entomology (MS, PhD); environmental biology (MS, PhD); experimental psychology (PhD); fisheries/wildlife (MS, PhD); forensic psychology (MA, MS); genetics (MS, PhD); geography (MA, MS); history (MA, DA, PhD); linguistics (MA); mathematics (M Ed, MS); music (M Mus); music education (M Mus, DMEd); physics (MS, PhD); psychology (MA); sociology (MA); speech-language pathology (MS); theatre arts (MA); visual arts (MFA); zoology (MS, PhD). Electronic applications accepted.

College of Business and Public Administration *Degree program information:* Part-time and evening/weekend programs available. Postbaccalaureate distance learning degree programs offered. Offers accountancy (M Acc); applied economics (MSAE); business administration (MBA); business and public administration (M Acc, MBA, MPA, MSAE); public administration (MPA). Electronic applications accepted.

College of Education and Human Development *Degree program information:* Part-time and evening/weekend programs available. Postbaccalaureate distance learning degree programs offered (minimal on-campus study). Offers counseling (MA); early childhood education (MS); education and human development (M Ed, MA, MS, MSW, Ed D, PhD, Specialist); education/general studies (MS); educational leadership (M Ed, MS, Ed D, PhD, Specialist); elementary education (M Ed, MS); instructional design and technology (M Ed, MS); kinesiology (MS); measurement and statistics (Ed D, PhD); reading education (M Ed, MS); secondary education (Ed D, PhD); social work (MSW); special education (Ed D, PhD). Electronic applications accepted.

College of Nursing *Degree program information:* Part-time and evening/weekend programs available. Postbaccalaureate distance learning degree programs offered (minimal on-campus study). Offers nursing (MS, PhD). Electronic applications accepted.

John D. Odegard School of Aerospace Sciences *Degree program information:* Part-time and evening/weekend programs available. Postbaccalaureate distance learning degree programs offered (minimal on-campus study). Offers aerospace sciences (MS, PhD); atmospheric sciences (MS, PhD); aviation (MS); computer science (MS); space studies (MS). Electronic applications accepted.

University of North Dakota (continued)

School of Engineering and Mines *Degree program information:* Part-time programs available. Offers chemical engineering (M Engr, MS); civil engineering (M Engr); electrical engineering (M Engr, MS); engineering (PhD); engineering and mines (M Engr, MA, MS, PhD); environmental engineering (M Engr, MS); geological engineering (M Engr, MS); geology (MA, MS, PhD); mechanical engineering (M Engr, MS); sanitary engineering (M Engr). Electronic applications accepted.

School of Law Offers law (JD).

School of Medicine and Health Sciences Postbaccalaureate distance learning degree programs offered (minimal on-campus study). Offers anatomy (MS, PhD); biochemistry (MS, PhD); clinical laboratory science (MS); medicine (MD, MOT, MPAS, MPT, MS, DPT, PhD); medicine and health sciences (MD, MOT, MPAS, MPT, MS, DPT, PhD); microbiology and immunology (MS, PhD); occupational therapy (MOT); pharmacology (MS, PhD); physical therapy (MPT, DPT); physician assistant (MPAS); physiology (MS, PhD).

UNIVERSITY OF NORTHERN BRITISH COLUMBIA, Prince George, BC V2N 4Z9, Canada

General Information Province-supported, coed, university. *Graduate housing:* Room and/or apartments available on a first-come, first-served basis to single students; on-campus housing not available to married students. Housing application deadline: 2/15. *Research affiliation:* Houston Forest Products (forestry—wood debris management), TRC Cedar Ltd. (forestry—cyanolicen growth rate study), Remote Law Online Systems Corp. (computer science), Canadian Natural Oils Ltd. (chemistry—oil fractionation), Stella Jones Inc. (forestry—douglas fir cores), Insurance Corporation of BC (moose involved in highway traffic accidents).

GRADUATE UNITS

Office of Graduate Studies *Degree program information:* Part-time and evening/weekend programs available. Postbaccalaureate distance learning degree programs offered (no on-campus study).

UNIVERSITY OF NORTHERN COLORADO, Greeley, CO 80639

General Information State-supported, coed, university. CGS member. *Enrollment:* 11,925 graduate, professional, and undergraduate students; 633 full-time matriculated graduate/professional students (430 women), 743 part-time matriculated graduate/professional students (546 women). *Enrollment by degree level:* 800 master's, 388 doctoral, 188 other advanced degrees. *Graduate faculty:* 293 full-time (130 women). Tuition, state resident: full-time $4370; part-time $242.75 per credit hour. Tuition, nonresident: full-time $12,366; part-time $687 per credit hour. *Required fees:* $664.20; $36.90 per credit hour. *Graduate housing:* Rooms and/or apartments available on a first-come, first-served basis to single and married students. Typical cost: $3664 per year ($7784 including board) for single students; $3664 per year ($7784 including board) for married students. Housing application deadline: 5/30. *Student services:* Campus employment opportunities, campus safety program, career counseling, exercise/wellness program, free psychological counseling, international student services, low-cost health insurance, multicultural affairs office, services for students with disabilities, teacher training. *Library facilities:* James A. Michener Library plus 2 others. *Online resources:* library catalog, web page, access to other libraries' catalogs. *Collection:* 1 million titles, 3,417 serial subscriptions.

Computer facilities: Computer purchase and lease plans are available. 1,169 computers available on campus for general student use. A campuswide network can be accessed from student residence rooms and from off campus. Online class registration is available. *Web address:* http://www.unco.edu/.

General Application Contact: Linda Sisson, Graduate Student Admission Coordinator, 970-351-1807, Fax: 970-351-2371, E-mail: linda.sisson@unco.edu.

GRADUATE UNITS

Graduate School Students: 633 full-time (430 women), 743 part-time (546 women); includes 125 minority (28 African Americans, 14 American Indian/Alaska Native, 14 Asian Americans or Pacific Islanders, 69 Hispanic Americans), 110 international. Average age 32. 1,162 applicants, 73% accepted, 389 enrolled. *Faculty:* 293 full-time (130 women). Expenses: Contact institution. *Financial support:* In 2008–09, 146 research assistantships (averaging $6,815 per year), 133 teaching assistantships (averaging $8,374 per year) were awarded; fellowships, career-related internships or fieldwork, Federal Work-Study, institutionally sponsored loans, scholarships/grants, traineeships, tuition waivers (partial), and unspecified assistantships also available. Support available to part-time students. Financial award application deadline: 3/1; financial award applicants required to submit FAFSA. In 2008, 565 master's, 81 doctorates, 27 other advanced degrees awarded. *Degree program information:* Part-time and evening/weekend programs available. Postbaccalaureate distance learning degree programs offered (minimal on-campus study). *Application deadline:* Applications are processed on a rolling basis. *Application fee:* $50 ($60 for international students). Electronic applications accepted. *Application Contact:* Linda Sisson, Graduate Student Admission Coordinator, 970-351-1807, Fax: 970-351-2371, E-mail: linda.sisson@unco.edu. *Assistant Vice President, Research and Extended Studies/Dean of Graduate School,* Dr. Robbyn Wacker, 970-351-2817, Fax: 970-351-2371.

College of Education and Behavioral Sciences Students: 269 full-time (204 women), 443 part-time (349 women); includes 59 minority (8 African Americans, 4 American Indian/Alaska Native, 15 Asian Americans or Pacific Islanders, 32 Hispanic Americans), 33 international. Average age 35. 398 applicants, 75% accepted, 174 enrolled. *Faculty:* 80 full-time (42 women). Expenses: Contact institution. *Financial support:* In 2008–09, 32 research assistantships (averaging $5,527 per year), 23 teaching assistantships (averaging $5,951 per year) were awarded; fellowships, unspecified assistantships also available. Financial award application deadline: 3/1; financial award applicants required to submit FAFSA. In 2008, 260 master's, 41 doctorates, 27 other advanced degrees awarded. *Degree program information:* Part-time programs available. Postbaccalaureate distance learning degree programs offered. Offers applied psychology and counselor education (MA, PhD, Psy D, Ed S); applied statistics and research methods (MS, PhD); clinical counseling (MA); counseling psychology (Psy D); counselor education and supervision (PhD); early childhood education (MA); education and behavioral sciences (MA, MAT, MS, Ed D, PhD, Psy D, Ed S); educational leadership (MA, Ed D, Ed S); educational media (MA); educational psychology (MA, PhD); educational research, leadership and technology (MA, MS, Ed D, PhD, Ed S); educational studies (MAT, Ed D); educational technology (MA, PhD); higher education and student affairs leadership (PhD); interdisciplinary studies (MA); psychological sciences (MA, PhD); reading (MA); school counseling (MA); school library education (MA); school psychology (PhD, Ed S); special education (MA, Ed D); teacher education (MA, MAT, Ed D). *Application deadline:* Applications are processed on a rolling basis. *Application fee:* $50 ($60 for international students). *Application Contact:* Linda Sisson, Graduate Student Admission Coordinator, 970-351-1807, Fax: 970-351-2371, E-mail: linda.sisson@unco.edu. *Dean,* Dr. Eugene P. Sheehan, 970-351-2817, Fax: 970-351-2312, E-mail: coeinfo@unco.edu.

College of Humanities and Social Sciences Students: 45 full-time (30 women), 29 part-time (15 women); includes 9 minority (2 African Americans, 1 American Indian/Alaska Native, 1 Asian American or Pacific Islander, 5 Hispanic Americans), 2 international. Average age 32. 52 applicants, 92% accepted, 26 enrolled. *Faculty:* 59 full-time (23 women). Expenses: Contact institution. *Financial support:* In 2008–09, 6 research assistantships (averaging $5,009 per year), 28 teaching assistantships (averaging $8,272 per year) were awarded; fellowships, unspecified assistantships also available. Financial award application deadline: 3/1; financial award applicants required to submit FAFSA. In 2008, 41 master's awarded. *Degree program information:* Part-time programs available. Offers clinical sociology (MA); communication (MA); communication studies (MA); English (MA); history (MA); humanities and social sciences (MA); modern languages and cultural studies (MA); social sciences (MA); Spanish/teaching (MA). *Application deadline:* Applications are processed on a rolling basis. *Application fee:* $50 ($60 for international students). Electronic applications accepted. *Application Contact:* Linda Sisson, Graduate Student Admission Coordinator, 970-351-1807, Fax: 970-351-2371, E-mail: linda.sisson@unco.edu. *Dean,* Dr. David Caldwell, 970-351-2707, Fax: 970-351-1571.

College of Natural and Health Sciences Students: 233 full-time (157 women), 141 part-time (105 women); includes 32 minority (3 African Americans, 3 American Indian/Alaska Native, 4 Asian Americans or Pacific Islanders, 22 Hispanic Americans), 28 international. Average age 32. 500 applicants, 62% accepted, 132 enrolled. *Faculty:* 90 full-time (46 women). Expenses: Contact institution. *Financial support:* In 2008–09, 37 research assistantships (averaging $5,649 per year), 57 teaching assistantships (averaging $10,439 per year) were awarded; fellowships, unspecified assistantships also available. Financial award application deadline: 3/1; financial award applicants required to submit FAFSA. In 2008, 160 master's, 32 doctorates awarded. Offers audiology (Au D); biological education (PhD); biological sciences (MS); chemistry education (PhD); chemistry, earth sciences and physics (MA, MS, PhD); chemistry: education (MS); chemistry: research (MS); clinical nurse specialist in chronic illness (MS); earth sciences (MA); exercise science (MS, PhD); family nurse practitioner (MS); gerontology (MA); human rehabilitation (PhD); human sciences (MA, MPH, Au D, PhD); mathematical teaching (MA); mathematics (MA, PhD); mathematics education (PhD); mathematics: liberal arts (MA); natural and health sciences (MA, MPH, MS, Au D, PhD); nursing education (MS, PhD); public health education (MPH); rehabilitation counseling (MA); speech language pathology (MA); sport administration (MS, PhD); sport pedagogy (MS, PhD). *Application deadline:* Applications are processed on a rolling basis. *Application fee:* $50 ($60 for international students). Electronic applications accepted. *Application Contact:* Linda Sisson, Graduate Student Admission Coordinator, 970-351-1807, Fax: 970-351-2371, E-mail: linda.sisson@unco.edu. *Dean,* Dr. Denise A. Battles, 970-351-2877, Fax: 970-351-2176.

College of Performing and Visual Arts Students: 70 full-time (28 women), 32 part-time (18 women); includes 6 minority (2 African Americans, 2 Asian Americans or Pacific Islanders, 2 Hispanic Americans), 13 international. Average age 33. 98 applicants, 87% accepted, 41 enrolled. *Faculty:* 36 full-time (12 women). Expenses: Contact institution. *Financial support:* In 2008–09, 32 research assistantships (averaging $4,062 per year), 18 teaching assistantships (averaging $6,099 per year) were awarded; fellowships, unspecified assistantships also available. Financial award application deadline: 3/1; financial award applicants required to submit FAFSA. In 2008, 30 master's, 8 doctorates awarded. *Degree program information:* Part-time programs available. Offers collaborative keyboard (MM); conducting (MM); instrumental performance (MM); jazz studies (MM); music conducting (DA); music education (MM, DA); music history and literature (MM, DA); music performance (DA); music theory and composition (MM, DA); performing and visual arts (MA, MM, DA); visual arts (MA); vocal performance (MM). *Application deadline:* Applications are processed on a rolling basis. *Application fee:* $50 ($60 for international students). Electronic applications accepted. *Application Contact:* Linda Sisson, Graduate Student Admission Coordinator, 970-351-1807, Fax: 970-351-2371, E-mail: linda.sisson@unco.edu. *Dean,* Dr. Andrew J. Svedlow, 970-351-2515, Fax: 970-351-2699.

UNIVERSITY OF NORTHERN IOWA, Cedar Falls, IA 50614

General Information State-supported, coed, comprehensive institution. CGS member. *Enrollment:* 12,998 graduate, professional, and undergraduate students; 639 full-time matriculated graduate/professional students (428 women), 699 part-time matriculated graduate/professional students (458 women). *Enrollment by degree level:* 1,215 master's, 107 doctoral, 16 other advanced degrees. Tuition, state resident: full-time $6446. Tuition, nonresident: full-time $14,874. *Required fees:* $852. *Graduate housing:* Rooms and/or apartments available on a first-come, first-served basis to single students and available to married students. Typical cost: $3230 per year ($6790 including board) for single students. Room and board charges vary according to board plan. *Student services:* Campus employment opportunities, campus safety program, career counseling, child daycare facilities, exercise/wellness program, free psychological counseling, grant writing training, international student services, low-cost health insurance, multicultural affairs office, services for students with disabilities. *Library facilities:* Rod Library. *Online resources:* library catalog, web page, access to other libraries' catalogs. *Collection:* 1.2 million titles, 6,841 serial subscriptions, 29,730 audiovisual materials.

Computer facilities: Computer purchase and lease plans are available. 1,900 computers available on campus for general student use. A campuswide network can be accessed from student residence rooms and from off campus. Online class registration, course registration, student account, degree audit, program of study are available. *Web address:* http://www.uni.edu/.

General Application Contact: Laurie S. Russell, Record Analyst, 319-273-2623, Fax: 319-273-6792, E-mail: laurie.russell@uni.edu.

GRADUATE UNITS

Graduate College Students: 639 full-time (428 women), 699 part-time (458 women); includes 95 minority (61 African Americans, 2 American Indian/Alaska Native, 13 Asian Americans or Pacific Islanders, 19 Hispanic Americans), 174 international. Average age 33. 1,116 applicants, 49% accepted, 322 enrolled. Expenses: Contact institution. *Financial support:* In 2008–09, 1,084 students received support; fellowships, research assistantships, teaching assistantships, career-related internships or fieldwork, Federal Work-Study, institutionally sponsored loans, scholarships/grants, tuition waivers (full and partial), and unspecified assistantships available. Support available to part-time students. Financial award application deadline: 2/1; financial award applicants required to submit FAFSA. In 2008, 478 master's, 15 doctorates, 9 other advanced degrees awarded. *Degree program information:* Part-time and evening/weekend programs available. Offers philanthropy and nonprofit development (MA); public policy (MPP); women's and gender studies (MA). *Application deadline:* For fall admission, 8/1 for domestic students, 2/1 for international students; for winter admission, 12/1 for domestic students. Applications are processed on a rolling basis. *Application fee:* $30 ($50 for international students). Electronic applications accepted. *Application Contact:* Laurie S. Russell, Record Analyst, 319-273-2623, Fax: 319-273-6792, E-mail: laurie.russell@uni.edu. *Interim Dean,* Dr. Sue Joseph, 319-273-2748, Fax: 319-273-2243, E-mail: sue.joseph@uni.edu.

College of Business Administration Students: 70 full-time (36 women), 38 part-time (9 women); includes 5 minority (2 African Americans, 3 Asian Americans or Pacific Islanders), 42 international. 97 applicants, 44% accepted, 34 enrolled. Expenses: Contact institution. *Financial support:* Career-related internships or fieldwork, Federal Work-Study, scholarships/grants, and tuition waivers (full and partial) available. Support available to part-time students. Financial award application deadline: 2/1. In 2008, 63 master's awarded. *Degree program information:* Part-time and evening/weekend programs available. Offers accounting (M Acc); business administration (M Acc, MBA). *Application deadline:* For fall admission, 8/1 priority date for domestic students. Applications are processed on a rolling basis. *Application fee:* $30 ($50 for international students). *Application Contact:* Laurie S. Russell, Record Analyst, 319-273-2623, Fax: 319-273-6792, E-mail: laurie.russell@uni.edu. *Dean,* Dr. Farzad Moussavi, 319-273-6240, Fax: 319-273-2922, E-mail: farzad.moussavi@uni.edu.

College of Education Students: 188 full-time (133 women), 435 part-time (315 women); includes 42 minority (33 African Americans, 4 Asian Americans or Pacific Islanders, 5 Hispanic Americans), 33 international. 386 applicants, 54% accepted, 114 enrolled. Expenses: Contact institution. *Financial support:* Career-related internships or fieldwork, Federal Work-Study, institutionally sponsored loans, scholarships/grants, and tuition waivers (full and partial) available. Support available to part-time students. Financial award application deadline: 2/1. In 2008, 191 master's, 15 doctorates, 9 other advanced degrees awarded. *Degree program information:* Part-time and evening/weekend programs available. Offers communication and training technology (MA); community health education (Ed D); counseling (MA, MAE, Ed D); curriculum and instruction (MAE, Ed D); early childhood education (MAE); education (MA, MAE, Ed D, Ed S); educational administration (Ed D); educational leadership (MAE, Ed D); educational media (MA); educational psychology (MAE); educational technology (MA); elementary education (MAE); elementary principal (MAE); elementary reading and language arts (MAE); health education (MA, Ed D); leisure services (MA, Ed D); middle school/junior high education (MAE); physical education (MA); postsecondary education (MAE); professional development for teachers (MAE); program administration (MA); reading (MAE); reading education (MAE); rehabilitation studies (Ed D); school counseling (MAE); school library media studies (MA); school psychology (Ed S); scientific basis of physical education (MA); secondary principal (MAE); secondary reading (MAE); special education (MAE, Ed D); student affairs (MAE); teaching/coaching (MA); youth/human services administration (MA). *Application deadline:* For fall admission, 8/1 priority date for domestic students. Applications are processed on a rolling basis. *Application fee:* $30 ($50 for international students). Electronic applications accepted. *Application Contact:* Laurie S. Russell, Record Analyst, 319-273-2623, Fax: 319-273-6792, E-mail: laurie.russell@uni.edu. *Dean,* Dr. William Callahan, 319-273-2167, Fax: 319-273-5886, E-mail: bill.callahan@uni.edu.

College of Humanities and Fine Arts Students: 170 full-time (131 women), 76 part-time (58 women); includes 27 minority (15 African Americans, 2 Asian Americans or Pacific Islanders, 10 Hispanic Americans), 38 international. 227 applicants, 52% accepted, 74 enrolled. Expenses: Contact institution. *Financial support:* Career-related internships or fieldwork, Federal Work-Study, scholarships/grants, and tuition waivers (full and partial) available. Support available to part-time students. Financial award application deadline: 2/1. In 2008, 105 master's awarded. *Degree program information:* Part-time and evening/weekend programs available. Offers art (MA); art education (MA); audiology (MA); communication studies (MA); composition (MM); conducting (MM); English (MA); French (MA); German (MA); humanities and fine arts (MA, MM); jazz pedagogy (MM); music (MA, MM); music education (MA, MM); music history (MM); performance (MM); piano performance and pedagogy (MM); Spanish (MA); speech pathology (MA); teaching English to speakers of other languages (MA); teaching English to speakers of other languages/French (MA); teaching English to speakers of other languages/German (MA); teaching English to speakers of other languages/Spanish (MA); two languages (MA). *Application deadline:* For fall admission, 8/1 priority date for domestic students. Applications are processed on a rolling basis. *Application fee:* $30 ($50 for international students). Electronic applications accepted. *Application Contact:* Laurie S. Russell, Record Analyst, 319-273-2623, Fax: 319-273-6792, E-mail: laurie.russell@uni.edu. *Dean,* Dr. Reinhold Bubser, 319-273-2725, Fax: 319-273-2731, E-mail: reinhold.bubser@uni.edu.

College of Natural Sciences Students: 74 full-time (34 women), 90 part-time (44 women); includes 3 minority (2 African Americans, 1 Hispanic American), 46 international. 171 applicants, 43% accepted, 45 enrolled. Expenses: Contact institution. *Financial support:* Teaching assistantships, career-related internships or fieldwork, Federal Work-Study, scholarships/grants, and tuition waivers (full and partial) available. Support available to part-time students. Financial award application deadline: 2/1. In 2008, 41 master's awarded. *Degree program information:* Part-time and evening/weekend programs available. Offers biology (MA, MS, PSM); chemistry (MA, MS, PSM); computer science (MA, MS); environmental health (MS); environmental science (MS); environmental technology (MS); industrial technology (MA, PSM, DIT); mathematics (MA); mathematics for middle grades (MA); natural sciences (MA, MS, PSM, DIT); physics (MA, PSM); science education (MA). *Application deadline:* For fall admission, 8/1 priority date for domestic students. Applications are processed on a rolling basis. *Application fee:* $30 ($50 for international students). Electronic applications accepted. *Application Contact:* Laurie S. Russell, Record Analyst, 319-273-2623, Fax: 319-273-6792, E-mail: laurie.russell@uni.edu. *Dean,* Dr. Joel Haack, 319-273-2585, Fax: 319-273-2893, E-mail: joel.haack@uni.edu.

College of Social and Behavioral Sciences Students: 116 full-time (81 women), 47 part-time (22 women); includes 13 minority (6 African Americans, 1 American Indian/Alaska Native, 4 Asian Americans or Pacific Islanders, 2 Hispanic Americans), 11 international. 199 applicants, 40% accepted, 47 enrolled. Expenses: Contact institution. *Financial support:* Career-related internships or fieldwork, Federal Work-Study, scholarships/grants, and tuition waivers (full and partial) available. Support available to part-time students. Financial award application deadline: 2/1. In 2008, 53 master's awarded. *Degree program information:* Part-time and evening/weekend programs available. Offers criminology (MA); geography (MA); history (MA); political science (MA); psychology (MA); social and behavioral sciences (MA, MSW); social science (MA); social work (MSW); sociology (MA). *Application deadline:* For fall admission, 8/1 priority date for domestic students. Applications are processed on a rolling basis. *Application fee:* $30 ($50 for international students). Electronic applications accepted. *Application Contact:* Laurie S. Russell, Record Analyst, 319-273-2623, Fax: 319-273-6792, E-mail: laurie.russell@uni.edu. *Interim Dean,* Dr. John Johnson, 319-273-2585, Fax: 319-273-2222.

UNIVERSITY OF NORTH FLORIDA, Jacksonville, FL 32224-2645

General Information State-supported, coed, comprehensive institution. *Enrollment:* 15,280 graduate, professional, and undergraduate students; 745 full-time matriculated graduate/professional students (479 women), 1,056 part-time matriculated graduate/professional students (682 women). *Enrollment by degree level:* 1,605 master's, 196 doctoral. *Graduate faculty:* 405 full-time (162 women). Tuition, state resident: full-time $5782.08; part-time $240.92 per credit hour. Tuition, nonresident: full-time $19,974; part-time $832.26 per credit hour. *Required fees:* $952.80; $39.70 per credit hour. *Graduate housing:* Rooms and/or apartments available on a first-come, first-served basis to single and married students. Typical cost: $4273 per year ($7366 including board) for single students; $4273 per year ($7366 including board) for married students. Room and board charges vary according to board plan and housing facility selected. Housing application deadline: 7/15. *Student services:* Campus employment opportunities, campus safety program, career counseling, child daycare facilities, exercise/wellness program, free psychological counseling, international student services, low-cost health insurance, multicultural affairs office, services for students with disabilities, teacher training, writing training. *Library facilities:* Thomas G. Carpenter Library. *Online resources:* library catalog, web page, access to other libraries' catalogs. *Collection:* 957,625 titles, 3,979 serial subscriptions, 27,447 audiovisual materials.

Computer facilities: Computer purchase and lease plans are available. 750 computers available on campus for general student use. A campuswide network can be accessed from student residence rooms and from off campus. Online class registration, applications software are available. *Web address:* http://www.unf.edu/.

General Application Contact: Kiersten Jarvis, Graduate Coordinator, The Graduate School, 904-620-1360, Fax: 904-620-1362, E-mail: kiersten.jarvis@unf.edu.

GRADUATE UNITS

Brooks College of Health Students: 246 full-time (179 women), 135 part-time (112 women); includes 80 minority (43 African Americans, 3 American Indian/Alaska Native, 20 Asian Americans or Pacific Islanders, 14 Hispanic Americans), 16 international. Average age 33. 589 applicants, 30% accepted, 111 enrolled. *Faculty:* 62 full-time (42 women). Expenses: Contact institution. *Financial support:* In 2008–09, 163 students received support; research assistantships, teaching assistantships, career-related internships or fieldwork, Federal Work-Study, scholarships/grants, and tuition waivers (partial) available. Support available to part-time students. Financial award application deadline: 4/1; financial award applicants required to submit FAFSA. In 2008, 76 master's awarded. *Degree program information:* Part-time and evening/weekend programs available. Offers community health (MPH); geriatric management (MSH); health (MHA, MPH, MPT, MS, MSH, MSN, Certificate); health administration (MHA); health behavior research and evaluation (Certificate); nutrition (MSH); physical therapy (MPT); rehabilitation counseling (MS). *Application deadline:* For fall admission, 7/1 priority date for domestic students, 5/1 for international students; for spring admission, 11/1 priority date for domestic students, 10/1 for international students. Applications are processed on a rolling basis. *Application fee:* $30. Electronic applications accepted. *Application Contact:* Heather Kenney, Director of Advising, 904-620-2810, Fax: 904-620-1030, E-mail: heather.kenney@unf.edu. *Dean,* Dr. Pamela Chally, 904-620-2810, Fax: 904-620-1030, E-mail: pchally@unf.edu.

School of Nursing Students: 79 full-time (56 women), 67 part-time (59 women); includes 31 minority (13 African Americans, 3 American Indian/Alaska Native, 9 Asian Americans or Pacific Islanders, 6 Hispanic Americans), 1 international. Average age 37. 173 applicants, 31% accepted, 46 enrolled. *Faculty:* 22 full-time (16 women). Expenses: Contact institution. *Financial support:* In 2008–09, 33 students received support, including 1 research assistantship (averaging $405 per year). Financial award application deadline: 4/1; financial award applicants required to submit FAFSA. In 2008, 30 master's awarded. Offers advanced practice nursing (MSN); primary care nurse practitioner (Certificate). *Application deadline:* For fall admission, 5/1 for domestic and international students. Applications are processed on a rolling basis. *Application fee:* $30. Electronic applications accepted. *Application Contact:* Beth Dibble, 904-620-2684, E-mail: bdibble@unf.edu. *Chair,* Dr. Lillia Loriz, 904-620-2684, E-mail: lloriz@unf.edu.

Coggin College of Business Students: 214 full-time (104 women), 361 part-time (172 women); includes 101 minority (37 African Americans, 2 American Indian/Alaska Native, 35 Asian Americans or Pacific Islanders, 27 Hispanic Americans), 40 international. Average age 29. 364 applicants, 54% accepted, 132 enrolled. *Faculty:* 56 full-time (13 women). Expenses: Contact institution. *Financial support:* In 2008–09, 112 students received support; research assistantships, teaching assistantships, career-related internships or fieldwork, Federal Work-Study, scholarships/grants, and tuition waivers (partial) available. Support available to part-time students. Financial award application deadline: 4/1; financial award applicants required to submit FAFSA. In 2008, 204 master's awarded. *Degree program information:* Part-time and evening/weekend programs available. Offers accounting (M Acct); business (M Acct, MBA); business administration (MBA). *Application deadline:* For fall admission, 7/1 priority date for domestic students, 5/1 for international students; for spring admission, 11/1 priority date for domestic students, 10/1 for international students. Applications are processed on a rolling basis. *Application fee:* $30. Electronic applications accepted. *Application Contact:* Cheryl Campbell, Graduate Advisor, 904-620-2575, Fax: 904-620-2832, E-mail: ccampbell@unf.edu. *Dean,* Dr. John P McAllister, 904-620-2590, Fax: 904-620-3861, E-mail: jmcallis@unf.edu.

College of Arts and Sciences Students: 149 full-time (96 women), 164 part-time (112 women); includes 49 minority (21 African Americans, 1 American Indian/Alaska Native, 8 Asian Americans or Pacific Islanders, 19 Hispanic Americans), 12 international. Average age 30. 322 applicants, 48% accepted, 105 enrolled. *Faculty:* 199 full-time (73 women). Expenses: Contact institution. *Financial support:* In 2008–09, 147 students received support, including 9 research assistantships (averaging $1,885 per year), 33 teaching assistantships (averaging $4,788 per year); career-related internships or fieldwork, Federal Work-Study, scholarships/grants, and tuition waivers (partial) also available. Support available to part-time students. Financial award application deadline: 4/1; financial award applicants required to submit FAFSA. In 2008, 100 master's awarded. *Degree program information:* Part-time and evening/weekend programs available. Offers applied ethics (Graduate Certificate); applied sociology (MS); arts and sciences (MA, MAC, MPA, MS, MSCJ, Graduate Certificate); biology (MA, MS); counseling psychology (MAC); criminal justice (MSCJ); English (MA); European history (MA); general psychology (MA); mathematical sciences (MS); practical philosophy and applied ethics (MA); public administration (MPA); statistics (MS); US history (MA). *Application deadline:* For fall admission, 7/1 priority date for domestic students, 5/1 for international students; for spring admission, 11/1 priority date for domestic students, 10/1 for international students. Applications are processed on a rolling basis. *Application fee:* $30. Electronic applications accepted. *Application Contact:* Kiersten Jarvis, Graduate Coordinator, The Graduate School, 904-620-1360, Fax: 904-620-1362, E-mail: kiersten.jarvis@unf.edu. *Dean,* Dr. Barbara Hetrick, 904-620-2560, Fax: 904-620-2929, E-mail: barbara.hetrick@unf.edu.

College of Computing, Engineering, and Construction Students: 19 full-time (3 women), 52 part-time (10 women); includes 16 minority (5 African Americans, 9 Asian Americans or Pacific Islanders, 2 Hispanic Americans), 14 international. Average age 32. 116 applicants, 59% accepted, 19 enrolled. *Faculty:* 35 full-time (6 women). Expenses: Contact institution. *Financial support:* In 2008–09, 22 students received support, including 4 research assistantships (averaging $1,903 per year), 2 teaching assistantships (averaging $1,497 per year); Federal Work-Study and tuition waivers (partial) also available. Support available to part-time students. Financial award application deadline: 4/1; financial award applicants required to submit FAFSA. In 2008, 15 master's awarded. *Degree program information:* Part-time programs available. Offers computer and information sciences (MS). *Application deadline:* For fall admission, 7/1 priority date for domestic students, 5/1 for international students; for spring admission, 11/1 priority date for domestic students, 10/1 for international students. Applications are processed on a rolling basis. *Application fee:* $30. Electronic applications accepted. *Application Contact:* Dr. Roger Eggen, Director of Graduate Studies for Computer Science, 904-320-2985, Fax: 904-620-2988, E-mail: ree@unf.edu. *Dean,* Dr. Neal Coulter, 904-620-1350, E-mail: ncoulter@unf.edu.

College of Education and Human Services Students: 117 full-time (97 women), 344 part-time (276 women); includes 84 minority (56 African Americans, 1 American Indian/Alaska Native, 7 Asian Americans or Pacific Islanders, 20 Hispanic Americans), 11 international. Average age 35. 209 applicants, 48% accepted, 84 enrolled. *Faculty:* 53 full-time (28 women). Expenses: Contact institution. *Financial support:* In 2008–09, 245 students received support, including 4 research assistantships (averaging $3,725 per year), 1 teaching assistantship (averaging $2,640 per year); career-related internships or fieldwork, Federal Work-Study, scholarships/grants, and tuition waivers (partial) also available. Support available to part-time students. Financial award application deadline: 4/1; financial award applicants required to submit FAFSA. In 2008, 154 master's, 10 doctorates awarded. *Degree program information:* Part-time and evening/weekend programs available. Offers counselor education (M Ed); deaf education (M Ed); disability services (M Ed); education and human services (M Ed, Ed D); educational leadership (M Ed, Ed D); exceptional student education (M Ed); instructional leadership (M Ed); mental health counseling (M Ed); school counseling (M Ed). *Application deadline:* For fall admission, 7/1 priority date for domestic students, 5/1 for international students; for spring admission, 11/1 priority date for domestic students, 10/1 for international students. Applications are processed on a rolling basis. *Application fee:* $30. Electronic applications accepted. *Application Contact:* Dr. John Kemppainen, Director, Office of Student Services, 904-620-2530, Fax: 904-620-1135, E-mail: jkemppai@unf.edu. *Dean,* Dr. Larry Daniel, 904-620-2520, E-mail: ldaniel@unf.edu.

Division of Curriculum and Instruction Students: 22 full-time (18 women), 70 part-time (59 women); includes 17 minority (10 African Americans, 2 Asian Americans or Pacific Islanders, 5 Hispanic Americans), 2 international. Average age 31. 47 applicants, 53% accepted, 18 enrolled. *Faculty:* 23 full-time (11 women). Expenses: Contact institution. *Financial support:* In 2008–09, 21 students received support; teaching assistantships, career-related internships or fieldwork, Federal Work-Study, and tuition waivers (partial) available. Support available to part-time students. Financial award application deadline: 4/1; financial award applicants required to submit FAFSA. In 2008, 44 master's awarded. *Degree program information:* Part-time and evening/weekend programs available. Offers elementary education (M Ed); secondary education (M Ed). *Application deadline:* For fall admission, 7/1 priority date for domestic students, 5/1 for international students; for spring admission, 11/1 priority date for domestic students, 10/1 for international students. Applications are processed on a rolling basis. *Application fee:* $30. Electronic applications accepted. *Application Contact:* Dr. John Kemppainen, Director, Office of Student Services, 904-620-2530, Fax: 904-620-1135, E-mail: jkemppai@unf.edu. *Chair,* Dr. Ronghua Ouyang, 904-620-2610, E-mail: sgupton@unf.edu.

UNIVERSITY OF NORTH TEXAS, Denton, TX 76203

General Information State-supported, coed, university. CGS member. *Enrollment:* 34,698 graduate, professional, and undergraduate students; 2,516 full-time matriculated graduate/professional students (1,378 women), 4,378 part-time matriculated graduate/professional students (2,912 women). *Graduate faculty:* 886 full-time (0 women), 264 part-time/adjunct (0 women). *Graduate housing:* Rooms and/or apartments available on a first-come, first-served basis to single and married students. *Student services:* Campus employment opportunities, campus safety program, career counseling, child daycare facilities, exercise/wellness program, free psychological counseling, international student services, low-cost health insurance, multicultural affairs office, services for students with disabilities, teacher training. *Library facilities:* Willis Library plus 4 others. *Online resources:* library catalog, web page, access to other libraries' catalogs. *Collection:* 2.5 million titles, 29,688 serial subscriptions, 152,579 audiovisual materials. *Research affiliation:* Texas Instruments, Inc. (physics and material science), Cotton Incorporated (natural science), Delta and Pine Land Company (natural science), Semiconductor Research Corporation (materials science), Sematech (physical science), Texas Utilities (physical science).

Computer facilities: 725 computers available on campus for general student use. A campuswide network can be accessed from student residence rooms and from off campus. Online class registration is available. *Web address:* http://www.unt.edu/.

University of North Texas (continued)

General Application Contact: Dr. Donna Hughes, Director of Admissions, 940-565-2383, Fax: 940-565-2141, E-mail: gradsch@unt.edu.

GRADUATE UNITS

College of Information Offers computer education and cognitive systems (MS); information (M Ed, MS, Ed D, PhD); information science (MS, PhD); library science (MS).

Robert B. Toulouse School of Graduate Studies Students: 2,516 full-time (1,378 women), 4,378 part-time (2,912 women); includes 1,590 minority (673 African Americans, 45 American Indian/Alaska Native, 260 Asian Americans or Pacific Islanders, 612 Hispanic Americans), 917 international. Average age 31. 6,127 applicants, 48% accepted, 1562 enrolled. *Faculty:* 943 full-time (348 women). Expenses: Contact institution. *Financial support:* Fellowships with partial tuition reimbursements, research assistantships with partial tuition reimbursements, teaching assistantships, career-related internships or fieldwork, Federal Work-Study, institutionally sponsored loans, scholarships/grants, unspecified assistantships, and library assistantships available. Support available to part-time students. Financial award applicants required to submit FAFSA. In 2008, 1,522 master's, 214 doctorates awarded. *Degree program information:* Part-time and evening/weekend programs available. Postbaccalaureate distance learning degree programs offered. *Application deadline:* For fall admission, 7/15 for domestic students; for spring admission, 11/15 for domestic students. Applications are processed on a rolling basis. *Application fee:* $50 ($75 for international students). Electronic applications accepted. *Application Contact:* Dr. Lawrence J. Schneider, Associate Dean, 940-565-2383, Fax: 940-565-2141. *Dean,* Dr. Michael Monticino, 940-565-2383, Fax: 940-565-2141, E-mail: terrell@unt.edu.

College of Arts and Sciences Students: 767 full-time (418 women), 518 part-time (282 women); includes 244 minority (68 African Americans, 8 American Indian/Alaska Native, 53 Asian Americans or Pacific Islanders, 115 Hispanic Americans), 177 international. Average age 30. 1,584 applicants, 35% accepted, 349 enrolled. *Faculty:* 384 full-time (140 women). Expenses: Contact institution. *Financial support:* In 2008–09, 25 research assistantships (averaging $11,510 per year), 300 teaching assistantships (averaging $11,510 per year) were awarded; fellowships, career-related internships or fieldwork, Federal Work-Study, institutionally sponsored loans, tuition waivers (partial), and unspecified assistantships also available. Support available to part-time students. Financial award applicants required to submit FAFSA. In 2008, 207 master's, 68 doctorates awarded. *Degree program information:* Part-time and evening/weekend programs available. Offers arts and sciences (MA, MFA, MJ, MS, Au D, PhD, Graduate Certificate); audiology (Au D); biochemistry (MS, PhD); biology (MA, MS, PhD); chemistry (MS, PhD); clinical psychology (PhD); communication studies (MA, MS); counseling psychology (MA, MS, PhD); creative writing (MA); economic research (MS); economics (MA, MS); English (MA, PhD); environmental science (MS, PhD); experimental psychology (MA, MS, PhD); French (MA); geography (MS); health psychology and behavioral medicine (PhD); history (MA, MS, PhD); journalism (MA, MJ); labor and industrial relations (MS); mathematics (MA, MS, PhD); molecular biology (MA, MS, PhD); narrative journalism (Graduate Certificate); philosophy (MA, PhD); physics (MA, MS, PhD); political science (MA, MS, PhD); radio, television and film (MA, MFA, MS); Spanish (MA); speech-language pathology (MA, MS). *Application deadline:* For fall admission, 7/15 for international students; for spring admission, 11/15 for international students. *Application fee:* $50 ($75 for international students). *Application Contact:* Dr. Lawrence J. Schneider, Associate Dean, 940-565-2383, Fax: 940-565-2141. *Dean,* Dr. Warren Burggren, 940-565-2497, Fax: 940-565-4517, E-mail: burggren@unt.edu.

College of Business Administration Students: 288 full-time (143 women), 377 part-time (152 women); includes 167 minority (76 African Americans, 5 American Indian/Alaska Native, 35 Asian Americans or Pacific Islanders, 51 Hispanic Americans), 132 international. Average age 29. 274 applicants, 55% accepted, 124 enrolled. *Faculty:* 107 full-time (27 women). Expenses: Contact institution. *Financial support:* Fellowships, research assistantships, teaching assistantships, career-related internships or fieldwork, Federal Work-Study, and institutionally sponsored loans available. Financial award applicants required to submit FAFSA. In 2008, 182 master's, 15 doctorates awarded. *Degree program information:* Part-time and evening/weekend programs available. Offers accounting (MS, PhD); business administration (MBA, MS, PhD); business computer information systems (PhD); decision technologies (MS); finance (PhD); finance, insurance, real estate, and law (MS); information technology (MS); managementmanagement science (PhD); marketing and logistics (PhD); real estate (MS); taxation (MS). *Application deadline:* For fall admission, 7/15 for domestic students; for spring admission, 11/15 for domestic students. Applications are processed on a rolling basis. *Application fee:* $50 ($75 for international students). *Application Contact:* Dr. Randall S. Guttery, Associate Dean for Graduate Programs, 940-565-8977, Fax: 940-369-8978, E-mail: mbacoba@unt.edu. *Dean,* Dr. O. Finley Graves, 940-565-3037, Fax: 940-565-4930, E-mail: gravey@unt.edu.

College of Education Students: 342 full-time (260 women), 1,253 part-time (923 women); includes 435 minority (250 African Americans, 12 American Indian/Alaska Native, 40 Asian Americans or Pacific Islanders, 133 Hispanic Americans), 79 international. Average age 35. 586 applicants, 52% accepted, 282 enrolled. *Faculty:* 117 full-time (67 women). Expenses: Contact institution. *Financial support:* In 2008–09, 5 fellowships (averaging $16,750 per year), 12 research assistantships (averaging $5,000 per year) were awarded; teaching assistantships, career-related internships or fieldwork, Federal Work-Study, institutionally sponsored loans, and tuition waivers (partial) also available. Support available to part-time students. Financial award application deadline: 4/15; financial award applicants required to submit FAFSA. In 2008, 383 master's, 55 doctorates awarded. *Degree program information:* Part-time and evening/weekend programs available. Offers adolescent (Certificate); adult (Certificate); alternative initial certification (Certificate); applied technology, training and development (M Ed, MS, Ed D, PhD); autism intervention (M Ed); behavioral specialist (Certificate); child/play therapy (Certificate); college/university (Certificate); community (Certificate); community college (MS); computer education and cognitive systems (MS); counseling (M Ed, MS, PhD, Certificate); couple and family (Certificate); curriculum and instruction (M Ed, Ed D, PhD); development and family studies (MS, Certificate); early childhood education (MS, Ed D); EC-12 certification (M Ed); education (M Ed, MS, Ed D, PhD, Certificate); educational administration (M Ed, Ed D, PhD); educational computing (PhD); educational psychology (M Ed, MS, PhD, Certificate); educational research (PhD); elementary school (M Ed, MS); emotional disorders/behavioral disorders (M Ed); group (Certificate); higher education (M Ed, MS, Ed D, PhD); higher education (Certificate); inclusion specialist (Certificate); kinesiology (MS); mild/moderate disability (Certificate); re-integration-traumatic brain injury (Certificate); reading education (M Ed, MS, Ed D, PhD); recreation and leisure studies (MS, Certificate); recreation management (Certificate); school psychology (MS); secondary education (M Ed, Certificate); secondary school (M Ed); special education (M Ed, MS, PhD, Certificate); transition (M Ed); transition emotional disorders/behavioral disorders (Certificate); traumatic brain injury (M Ed); university (M Ed). *Application deadline:* For fall admission, 7/15 for domestic students; for spring admission, 11/15 for domestic students. *Application fee:* $50 ($75 for international students). *Application Contact:* Dr. Lawrence J. Schneider, Associate Dean, 940-565-2383, Fax: 940-565-2141. *Dean,* Dr. Jean Keller, 940-565-2233, Fax: 940-565-4415, E-mail: jkeller@unt.edu.

College of Engineering Students: 211 full-time (48 women), 92 part-time (16 women); includes 31 minority (11 African Americans, 1 American Indian/Alaska Native, 12 Asian Americans or Pacific Islanders, 7 Hispanic Americans), 224 international. Average age 27. 164 applicants, 52% accepted, 78 enrolled. *Faculty:* 62 full-time (9 women). Expenses: Contact institution. *Financial support:* In 2008–09, 19 students received support, including 2 fellowships with full tuition reimbursements available (averaging $20,000 per year), 34 research assistantships with full tuition reimbursements available (averaging $17,500 per year), 23 teaching assistantships with full tuition reimbursements available (averaging $14,700 per year). Financial award application deadline: 2/8; financial award applicants required to submit FAFSA. In 2008, 94 master's, 8 doctorates awarded. Offers computer science (MS); computer science and engineering (PhD); electrical engineering (MS); engineering (MS, PhD); engineering technology (MS); materials science and engineering (MS, PhD). *Application deadline:* For fall admission, 7/15 for domestic students; for spring admission, 11/15 for domestic students. Applications are processed on a rolling basis. *Application fee:* $50 ($75 for international students). Electronic applications accepted. *Application Contact:* Dr. Lawrence J. Schneider, Associate Dean, 940-565-2383, Fax: 940-565-2141. *Associate Dean,* Dr. Reza Mirshams, 940-565-4300, Fax: 940-369-8570, E-mail: mirshams@egw.unt.edu.

College of Music Students: 392 full-time (179 women), 180 part-time (75 women); includes 74 minority (17 African Americans, 3 American Indian/Alaska Native, 20 Asian Americans or Pacific Islanders, 34 Hispanic Americans), 167 international. Average age 30. 486 applicants, 45% accepted, 137 enrolled. *Faculty:* 94 full-time (22 women), 15 part-time/adjunct (7 women). Expenses: Contact institution. *Financial support:* In 2008–09, 272 students received support, including 96 fellowships with partial tuition reimbursements available (averaging $8,515 per year), 86 teaching assistantships with partial tuition reimbursements available (averaging $6,174 per year); research assistantships, career-related internships or fieldwork, Federal Work-Study, institutionally sponsored loans, and scholarships/grants also available. Financial award application deadline: 4/1. In 2008, 82 master's, 34 doctorates awarded. Offers composition (MM, DMA); jazz studies (MM); music (MA); music education (MM, MME, PhD); music theory (MM, PhD); musicology (MM, PhD); performance (MM, DMA). *Application deadline:* For fall admission, 7/15 for domestic students; for spring admission, 11/15 for domestic students. *Application fee:* $50 ($75 for international students). *Application Contact:* Becky Hughes, Admissions and Scholarship Services, 940-367-7771, Fax: 940-565-2002, E-mail: becky.hughes@unt.edu. *Dean,* Dr. James C. Scott, 940-565-3704, Fax: 940-565-2002, E-mail: james.scott@unt.edu.

College of Public Affairs and Community Service Students: 209 full-time (119 women), 309 part-time (198 women); includes 140 minority (93 African Americans, 3 American Indian/Alaska Native, 13 Asian Americans or Pacific Islanders, 31 Hispanic Americans), 47 international. Average age 34. 271 applicants, 51% accepted, 133 enrolled. *Faculty:* 80 full-time (33 women). Expenses: Contact institution. *Financial support:* In 2008–09, 6 students received support; fellowships, research assistantships, teaching assistantships, career-related internships or fieldwork, Federal Work-Study, institutionally sponsored loans, scholarships/grants, and tuition waivers (full and partial) available. Support available to part-time students. Financial award applicants required to submit FAFSA. In 2008, 156 master's, 8 doctorates awarded. *Degree program information:* Part-time and evening/weekend programs available. Offers aging (Certificate); applied anthropology (MA, MS); applied economics (MS); applied gerontology (PhD); behavior analysis (MS); criminal justice (MS); general studies in aging (MA, MS); global and comparative (PhD); health and illness (PhD); long term care, senior housing, and aging services (MA, MS); public administration (MPA); public administration and management (PhD); public affairs and community service (MA, MPA, MS, PhD, Certificate); rehabilitation counseling (MS); social stratification and inequality (PhD); sociology (MA, MS). *Application deadline:* For fall admission, 7/15 for domestic students; for spring admission, 11/15 for domestic students. Applications are processed on a rolling basis. *Application fee:* $50 ($75 for international students). *Application Contact:* Dr. Lawrence J. Schneider, Associate Dean, 940-565-2383, Fax: 940-565-2141. *Dean,* Dr. Tom Evenson, 940-565-2239, Fax: 940-565-4663, E-mail: evenson@pacs.unt.edu.

College of Visual Arts and Design Students: 84 full-time (62 women), 75 part-time (51 women); includes 34 minority (7 African Americans, 1 American Indian/Alaska Native, 8 Asian Americans or Pacific Islanders, 18 Hispanic Americans), 10 international. Average age 32. 59 applicants, 58% accepted, 25 enrolled. *Faculty:* 53 full-time (27 women). Expenses: Contact institution. *Financial support:* In 2008–09, 12 fellowships (averaging $8,250 per year), 40 teaching assistantships (averaging $7,200 per year) were awarded; career-related internships or fieldwork, Federal Work-Study, institutionally sponsored loans, and unspecified assistantships also available. Support available to part-time students. Financial award application deadline: 4/1. In 2008, 32 master's, 1 doctorate awarded. *Degree program information:* Part-time programs available. Offers art education (MA, PhD); art history (MA); art museum education (Certificate); arts leadership (Certificate); design (MFA); metalsmithing and jewelry (MFA); visual arts and design (MA, MFA, MS, PhD, Certificate). *Application deadline:* For fall admission, 7/15 priority date for domestic students; for spring admission, 11/15 for domestic students. Applications are processed on a rolling basis. *Application fee:* $50 ($75 for international students). *Application Contact:* Dr. Lawrence J. Schneider, Associate Dean, 940-565-2383, Fax: 940-565-2141. *Dean,* Dr. Robert Milnes, 940-565-4003, Fax: 940-565-4717, E-mail: milnes@unt.edu.

Interdisciplinary Studies Students: 3 full-time (2 women), 8 part-time (3 women); includes 4 minority (3 African Americans, 1 Hispanic American). Average age 31. 8 applicants, 38% accepted, 1 enrolled. Expenses: Contact institution. *Financial support:* In 2008–09, 1 student received support, including 1 fellowship (averaging $2,000 per year); career-related internships or fieldwork, Federal Work-Study, and institutionally sponsored loans also available. Financial award application deadline: 4/1; financial award applicants required to submit FAFSA. In 2008, 4 master's awarded. *Degree program information:* Part-time programs available. Offers interdisciplinary studies (MA, MS). *Application deadline:* For fall admission, 7/15 for domestic students; for winter admission, 11/15 for domestic students. *Application fee:* $50 ($75 for international students). *Application Contact:* Dr. Lawrence J. Schneider, Associate Dean, 940-565-2383, Fax: 940-565-2141. *Head,* Donna Hughes, 940-565-2383, Fax: 940-565-2141, E-mail: hughesd@unt.edu.

School of Merchandising and Hospitality Management Students: 26 full-time (24 women), 27 part-time (26 women); includes 13 minority (6 African Americans, 2 Asian Americans or Pacific Islanders, 5 Hispanic Americans), 14 international. Average age 28. 432 applicants, 4% accepted, 16 enrolled. *Faculty:* 22 full-time (15 women). Expenses: Contact institution. *Financial support:* In 2008–09, 1 fellowship (averaging $10,000 per year), 5 teaching assistantships (averaging $6,300 per year) were awarded; research assistantships, career-related internships or fieldwork, Federal Work-Study, and institutionally sponsored loans also available. Financial award application deadline: 4/1; financial award applicants required to submit FAFSA. In 2008, 10 master's awarded. *Degree program information:* Part-time programs available. Postbaccalaureate distance learning degree programs offered (no on-campus study). Offers hospitality management (MS); merchandising (MS). *Application deadline:* For fall admission, 7/15 for domestic students; for spring admission, 11/15 for domestic students. *Application fee:* $50 ($75 for international students). *Application Contact:* Dr. Lisa Kennon, Coordinator, 940-565-4757, Fax: 940-565-4348, E-mail: kennon@smhm.unt.edu. *Dean,* Dr. Judith C. Forney, 940-565-2436, Fax: 940-565-4348, E-mail: jforney@smhm.unt.edu.

See Close-Up on page 1037.

UNIVERSITY OF NORTH TEXAS HEALTH SCIENCE CENTER AT FORT WORTH, Fort Worth, TX 76107-2699

General Information State-supported, coed, graduate-only institution. CGS member. *Graduate faculty:* 304 full-time, 36 part-time/adjunct. Tuition, state resident: full-time $11,153. Tuition, nonresident: full-time $26,803. *Required fees:* $1800. *Graduate housing:* On-campus housing not available. *Student services:* Campus employment opportunities, campus safety program, career counseling, exercise/wellness program, free psychological counseling, grant writing training, international student services, low-cost health insurance, multicultural affairs office, services for students with disabilities. *Library facilities:* Gibson D. Lewis Health Sciences Library. *Online resources:* library catalog, web page. *Collection:* 144,303 titles, 2,141 serial subscriptions, 12,868 audiovisual materials. *Research affiliation:* Myogen, Inc. (cardiac research), My-tech, Inc. (cardiovascular research), Novopharm, Inc. (gene control), Ethnobotanical Product Investigation Consortium (natural plant products), Genelink (familial DNA depository), Botanical Research Institutions of Texas.

Computer facilities: A campuswide network can be accessed from off campus. *Web address:* http://www.hsc.unt.edu/.

General Application Contact: Information Contact, 817-735-2000.

GRADUATE UNITS

Graduate School of Biomedical Sciences Offers anatomy and cell biology (MS, PhD); biochemistry and molecular biology (MS, PhD); biomedical sciences (MS, PhD); biotechnology (MS); forensic genetics (MS); integrative physiology (MS, PhD); medical science (MS); microbiology and immunology (MS, PhD); pharmacology (MS, PhD); science education (MS).

School of Public Health *Degree program information:* Part-time and evening/weekend programs available. Offers biostatistics (MPH); community health (MPH); disease control and prevention (Dr PH); environmental health (MPH); epidemiology (MPH); health behavior (MPH); health policy and management (MPH, Dr PH). Electronic applications accepted.

Texas College of Osteopathic Medicine Offers health professions (MPAS); osteopathic medicine (DO); physician assistant studies (MPAS). Electronic applications accepted.

UNIVERSITY OF NOTRE DAME, Notre Dame, IN 46556

General Information Independent-religious, coed, university. CGS member. *Graduate housing:* Rooms and/or apartments available on a first-come, first-served basis to single and married students. Housing application deadline: 5/1. *Student services:* Campus employment opportunities, campus safety program, career counseling, child daycare facilities, exercise/wellness program, free psychological counseling, grant writing training, international student services, low-cost health insurance, multicultural affairs office, services for students with disabilities, teacher training, writing training. *Library facilities:* Hesburgh Library plus 8 others. *Online resources:* library catalog. *Collection:* 3 million titles, 42,029 serial subscriptions, 62,296 audiovisual materials. *Research affiliation:* Space Telescope Science Institute, Brookhaven National Laboratory, Fermi National Accelerator Laboratory, Argonne National Laboratory.

Computer facilities: 261 computers available on campus for general student use. A campuswide network can be accessed from student residence rooms and from off campus. Online class registration is available. *Web address:* http://www.nd.edu/.

General Application Contact: Dr. Barbara Turpin, Director of Graduate Admissions, 574-631-7706, Fax: 574-631-4183.

GRADUATE UNITS

Graduate School Expenses: Contact institution. *Financial support:* Fellowships with full tuition reimbursements, research assistantships with full tuition reimbursements, teaching assistantships with full tuition reimbursements, career-related internships or fieldwork, institutionally sponsored loans, scholarships/grants, traineeships, tuition waivers (full and partial), and unspecified assistantships available. Support available to part-time students. *Degree program information:* Part-time programs available. *Application fee:* $50. Electronic applications accepted. *Application Contact:* Dr. Barbara Turpin, Director of Graduate Admissions, 574-631-7706, Fax: 574-631-4183. *Dean of the Graduate School,* Dr. Gregory Sterling, 574-631-6291, Fax: 574-631-4183, E-mail: gradsch@nd.edu.

College of Arts and Letters Expenses: Contact institution. *Financial support:* Fellowships with full tuition reimbursements, research assistantships with full tuition reimbursements, teaching assistantships with full tuition reimbursements, career-related internships or fieldwork, scholarships/grants, and tuition waivers (full and partial) available. Support available to part-time students. *Degree program information:* Part-time programs available. Offers art history (MA); arts and letters (M Div, M Ed, MA, MFA, MMS, MSM, MTS, PhD); cognitive psychology (PhD); counseling psychology (PhD); creative writing (MFA); design (MFA); developmental psychology (PhD); early Christian studies (MA); economics and econometrics (MA, PhD); educational initiatives (M Ed, MA); English (MA, PhD); French and Francophone studies (MA); history (MA, PhD); history and philosophy of science (MA, PhD); humanities (M Div, MA, MFA, MMS, MSM, MTS, PhD); Iberian and Latin American studies (MA); international peace studies (MA, PhD); Italian studies (MA); literature (PhD); medieval studies (MMS, PhD); philosophy (PhD); political science (PhD); quantitative psychology (PhD); Romance literatures (MA); social science (M Ed, MA, PhD); sociology (PhD); studio art (MFA); theology (M Div, MA, MSM, MTS, PhD). *Application fee:* $50. Electronic applications accepted. *Application Contact:* Dr. Barbar Turpin, Director of Graduate Admissions, 574-631-7706, Fax: 574-631-4183. *Dean,* Dr. John T. McGreevy, 574-631-6642.

College of Engineering Expenses: Contact institution. *Financial support:* Fellowships with full tuition reimbursements, research assistantships with full tuition reimbursements, teaching assistantships with full tuition reimbursements, scholarships/grants, tuition waivers (full), and unspecified assistantships available. Financial award application deadline: 2/1. Offers aerospace and mechanical engineering (M Eng, PhD); aerospace engineering (MS Aero E); bioengineering (MS Bio E); chemical and biomolecular engineering (MS Ch E, PhD); civil engineering (MSCE); civil engineering and geological sciences (PhD); computer science and engineering (MSCSE, PhD); electrical engineering (MSEE, PhD); engineering (M Eng, MEME, MS, MS Aero E, MS Bio E, MS Ch E, MS Env E, MSCE, MSCSE, MSEE, MSME, PhD); environmental engineering (MS Env E); geological sciences (MS); mechanical engineering (MEME, MSME). *Application deadline:* For fall admission, 2/1 priority date for domestic students. *Application fee:* $50. Electronic applications accepted. *Application Contact:* Dr. Barbara Turpin, Director of Graduate Admissions, 574-631-7706, Fax: 574-631-4183, E-mail: gradad@nd.edu. *Dean,* Dr. Peter Kilpatrick, 574-631-5534.

College of Science Expenses: Contact institution. *Financial support:* Fellowships with full tuition reimbursements, research assistantships with full tuition reimbursements, teaching assistantships with full tuition reimbursements, traineeships and tuition waivers (full) available. Financial award application deadline: 2/1. Offers algebra (PhD); algebraic geometry (PhD); applied mathematics (MSAM); aquatic ecology, evolution and environmental biology (MS, PhD); biochemistry (MS, PhD); cellular and molecular biology (MS, PhD); complex analysis (PhD); differential geometry (PhD); genetics (MS, PhD); inorganic chemistry (MS, PhD); logic (PhD); organic chemistry (MS, PhD); partial differential equations (PhD); physical chemistry (MS, PhD); physics (MS, PhD); physiology (MS, PhD); science (MS, MSAM, PhD); topology (PhD); vector biology and parasitology (MS, PhD). *Application deadline:* For fall admission, 2/1 priority date for domestic students. *Application fee:* $50. Electronic applications accepted. *Application Contact:* Dr. Barbara Turpin, Director of Graduate Admissions, 574-631-7706, Fax: 574-631-4183. *Dean,* Dr. Gregory Crawford, 574-631-6456.

School of Architecture Students: 46 full-time (17 women); includes 3 minority (1 African American, 2 Asian Americans or Pacific Islanders), 4 international. 84 applicants, 30% accepted, 16 enrolled. *Faculty:* 20 full-time (2 women), 1 part-time/adjunct (0 women). Expenses: Contact institution. *Financial support:* Fellowships with full tuition reimbursements, research assistantships, teaching assistantships, institutionally sponsored loans and tuition waivers (full) available. Financial award application deadline: 2/1. In 2008, 9 master's awarded. Offers architectural design and urbanism (M ADU); architecture (M Arch). *Application deadline:* For fall admission, 2/1 priority date for domestic and international students. *Application fee:* $50. Electronic applications accepted. *Application Contact:* Dr. Barbara Turpin, Director of Graduate Admissions, 574-631-7706, Fax: 574-631-4183. *Director of Graduate Studies,* Prof. Philip Bess, 574-631-2312.

Law School Students: 584 full-time (233 women); includes 120 minority (26 African Americans, 8 American Indian/Alaska Native, 36 Asian Americans or Pacific Islanders, 50 Hispanic Americans), 24 international. Average age 24. 3,319 applicants, 23% accepted, 179 enrolled. *Faculty:* 50 full-time (15 women), 39 part-time/adjunct (16 women). Expenses: Contact institution. *Financial support:* In 2008–09, 455 students received support, including 455 fellowships with tuition reimbursements available (averaging $14,401 per year); research assistantships, teaching assistantships, career-related internships or fieldwork, Federal Work-Study, institutionally sponsored loans, scholarships/grants, health care benefits, unspecified assistantships, and university dormitory rector assistants also available. Financial award application deadline: 2/15; financial award applicants required to submit FAFSA. In 2008, 186 JDs, 17 master's, 2 doctorates awarded. Offers human rights (LL M, JSD); international and comparative law (LL M); law (JD). *Application deadline:* For fall admission, 11/1 priority date for domestic students; for winter admission, 3/15 for domestic students. Applications are processed on a rolling basis. *Application fee:* $60. Electronic applications accepted. *Application Contact:* Melissa Ann Fruscione, Acting Director of Admissions and Financial Aid, 574-631-6626, Fax: 574-631-5474, E-mail: lawadmit@nd.edu. *Dean,* Patricia A. O'Hara, 574-631-6789, Fax: 574-631-8400, E-mail: o'hara.3@nd.edu.

Mendoza College of Business *Degree program information:* Part-time and evening/weekend programs available. Postbaccalaureate distance learning degree programs offered (minimal on-campus study). Offers accountancy (MS); administration (MNA); business (MBA, MNA, MS); business administration (MBA); executive business administration (MBA). Electronic applications accepted.

UNIVERSITY OF OKLAHOMA, Norman, OK 73019-0390

General Information State-supported, coed, university. CGS member. *Enrollment:* 26,185 graduate, professional, and undergraduate students; 3,424 full-time matriculated graduate/professional students (1,692 women), 3,163 part-time matriculated graduate/professional students (1,658 women). *Enrollment by degree level:* 521 first professional, 4,488 master's, 1,520 doctoral, 58 other advanced degrees. *Graduate faculty:* 1,101 full-time (334 women), 173 part-time/adjunct (70 women). Tuition, state resident: full-time $3744; part-time $156 per credit hour. Tuition, nonresident: full-time $13,577; part-time $565.70 per credit hour. *Required fees:* $2415.40; $90.10 per credit hour. *Graduate housing:* Rooms and/or apartments available on a first-come, first-served basis to single and married students. Typical cost: $5992 per year ($9330 including board) for single students; $5992 per year ($9330 including board) for married students. *Student services:* Campus employment opportunities, campus safety program, career counseling, child daycare facilities, exercise/wellness program, free psychological counseling, grant writing training, international student services, low-cost health insurance, services for students with disabilities, writing training. *Library facilities:* Bizzell Memorial Library plus 8 others. *Online resources:* library catalog, web page, access to other libraries' catalogs. *Collection:* 4.7 million titles, 51,585 serial subscriptions, 6,695 audiovisual materials. *Research affiliation:* Federal Aviation Administration Aeronautical Center, Oklahoma Geological Survey, National Severe Storms Laboratory, Oklahoma Climatological Survey.

Computer facilities: Computer purchase and lease plans are available. 3,600 computers available on campus for general student use. A campuswide network can be accessed from student residence rooms and from off campus. Online class registration is available. *Web address:* http://www.ou.edu/.

General Application Contact: Patricia Lynch, Director of Admissions, 405-325-2251, Fax: 405-325-7124, E-mail: plynch@ou.edu.

GRADUATE UNITS

College of Law Students: 517 full-time (233 women); includes 113 minority (28 African Americans, 45 American Indian/Alaska Native, 22 Asian Americans or Pacific Islanders, 18 Hispanic Americans), 2 international. Average age 23. 1,137 applicants, 29% accepted, 178 enrolled. *Faculty:* 41 full-time (17 women), 12 part-time/adjunct (2 women). Expenses: Contact institution. *Financial support:* In 2008–09, 401 students received support. Career-related internships or fieldwork, Federal Work-Study, institutionally sponsored loans, scholarships/grants, and tuition waivers (full and partial) available. Financial award application deadline: 3/1; financial award applicants required to submit FAFSA. In 2008, 167 JDs awarded. Offers law (JD). *Application deadline:* For fall admission, 3/15 for domestic students. Applications are processed on a rolling basis. *Application fee:* $50. Electronic applications accepted. *Application Contact:* Kathie Madden, Admissions Coordinator, 405-325-4728, Fax: 405-325-0502, E-mail: kmadden@ou.edu. *Dean,* Dr. Andrew M. Coats, 405-325-4699, Fax: 405-325-7712, E-mail: acoats@ou.edu.

Graduate College Students: 3,458 full-time (1,716 women), 3,374 part-time (1,776 women); includes 1,385 minority (557 African Americans, 339 American Indian/Alaska Native, 230 Asian Americans or Pacific Islanders, 259 Hispanic Americans), 852 international. Average age 30. 2,716 applicants, 71% accepted, 1508 enrolled. *Faculty:* 1,101 full-time (334 women), 173 part-time/adjunct (70 women). Expenses: Contact institution. *Financial support:* In 2008–09, 119 fellowships with full tuition reimbursements (averaging $3,769 per year), 883 research assistantships with full and partial tuition reimbursements (averaging $13,049 per year), 917 teaching assistantships with full and partial tuition reimbursements (averaging $13,252 per year) were awarded; career-related internships or fieldwork, Federal Work-Study, institutionally sponsored loans, scholarships/grants, traineeships, health care benefits, tuition waivers (full and partial), and unspecified assistantships also available. Support available to part-time students. Financial award applicants required to submit FAFSA. In 2008, 1,543 master's, 179 doctorates awarded. *Degree program information:* Part-time and evening/weekend programs available. Postbaccalaureate distance learning degree programs offered (no on-campus study). Offers interdisciplinary studies (MA, MS, PhD). *Application deadline:* For fall admission, 4/1 for domestic and international students; for spring admission, 11/1 for domestic students, 9/1 for international students. Applications are processed on a rolling basis. *Application fee:* $40 ($90 for international students). Electronic applications accepted. *Application Contact:* Miranda Sowell, Coordinator of Graduate Admissions, 405-325-3811, Fax: 405-325-5346, E-mail: mgsowell@ou.edu. *Dean/Vice President of Research,* Lee Williams, 405-325-3811, Fax: 405-325-5346, E-mail: lwilliams@ou.edu.

College of Architecture Students: 61 full-time (31 women), 38 part-time (9 women); includes 13 minority (6 African Americans, 3 American Indian/Alaska Native, 2 Asian Americans or Pacific Islanders, 2 Hispanic Americans), 25 international. 71 applicants, 82% accepted, 34 enrolled. *Faculty:* 34 full-time (7 women), 1 (woman) part-time/adjunct. Expenses: Contact institution. *Financial support:* In 2008–09, 44 students received support, including 7 research assistantships with partial tuition reimbursements available (averaging $10,145 per year), 12 teaching assistantships with partial tuition reimbursements available (averaging $9,586 per year); career-related internships or fieldwork, Federal Work-Study, institutionally sponsored loans, scholarships/grants, health care benefits, tuition waivers (full and partial), and unspecified assistantships also available. Support available to part-time students. Financial award applicants required to submit FAFSA. In 2008, 39 master's awarded. *Degree program information:* Part-time programs available. Offers architecture (M Arch, MLA, MRCP, MS, MSAUS, MSCA); construction science (MS); landscape architecture (MLA); regional and city planning (MRCP). *Application deadline:* For fall admission, 4/1 for domestic and international students; for spring admission, 11/1 for domestic students, 9/1 for international students. Applications are processed on a rolling basis. *Application fee:* $40 ($90 for international students). Electronic applications accepted. *Application Contact:* Terry Patterson, Professor/Graduate Liaison, 405-325-3869, Fax: 405-325-7558, E-mail: tpatterson@ou.edu. *Dean,* Charles W Graham, 405-325-2444, Fax: 405-325-7558, E-mail: cwgraham@ou.edu.

College of Arts and Sciences Students: 1,358 full-time (762 women), 1,446 part-time (837 women); includes 702 minority (316 African Americans, 152 American Indian/Alaska Native, 110 Asian Americans or Pacific Islanders, 124 Hispanic Americans), 251 international. 1,055 applicants, 74% accepted, 575 enrolled. *Faculty:* 516 full-time (181 women), 105 part-time/adjunct (47 women). Expenses: Contact institution. *Financial support:* In 2008–09, 999 students received support, including 60 fellowships with full tuition reimbursements available (averaging $4,455 per year), 193 research assistantships with full and partial tuition reimbursements available (averaging $13,026 per year), 588 teaching assistantships with full and partial tuition reimbursements available (averaging $13,941 per year); career-related internships or fieldwork, Federal Work-Study, institutionally sponsored loans, scholarships/grants, traineeships, health care benefits, tuition waivers (full and partial), and unspecified assistantships also available. Support available to part-time students. Financial award applicants required to submit FAFSA. In 2008, 853 master's, 69 doctorates awarded. Offers anthropology (MA, PhD); arts and sciences (M Nat Sci, MA, MHR, MLIS, MPA, MS, MSKM, MSW, PhD, Certificate); astrophysics (MS, PhD); botany (MS, PhD); cellular and behavioral neurobiology (PhD); chemistry and biochemistry (MS, PhD); communication (MA, PhD); ecology and evolutionary biology (PhD); economics (MA, PhD); English (MA, PhD); French (MA, PhD); German (MA); health and exercise science (MS, PhD); history (MA, PhD); history of science (MA, PhD); human relations (MHR); knowledge management (MSKM); library and information studies (MLIS); mathematics (MA, MS, PhD); microbiology (MS, PhD); Native American studies (MA); organizational dynamics (MS); philosophy (MA, PhD); physics (MS, PhD); political science (MA, MPA, PhD); psychology (MS, PhD); public administration (MPA); school library media specialist (Certificate); social work (MSW); sociology (MA, PhD); Spanish (MA, PhD); zoology (M Nat Sci, MS, PhD). *Application deadline:* For fall admission, 4/1 for domestic and international students; for spring admission, 11/1 for domestic students, 9/1 for international students. Applications are processed on a rolling basis. *Application fee:* $40 ($90 for international students). Electronic applications accepted. *Application Contact:* Paul B. Bell, JR, Dean and Vice Provost, 405-325-2077, Fax: 405-325-7709, E-mail: pbell@ou.edu. *Dean and Vice Provost,* Paul B. Bell, JR, 405-325-2077, Fax: 405-325-7709, E-mail: pbell@ou.edu.

College of Atmospheric and Geographic Sciences Students: 97 full-time (35 women), 34 part-time (10 women); includes 8 minority (1 African American, 2 American Indian/Alaska Native, 4 Asian Americans or Pacific Islanders, 1 Hispanic American), 27 international. 76

University of Oklahoma (continued)

applicants, 41% accepted, 25 enrolled. *Faculty:* 59 full-time (9 women), 8 part-time/adjunct (2 women). Expenses: Contact institution. *Financial support:* In 2008–09, 33 students received support, including 14 fellowships with full tuition reimbursements available (averaging $5,000 per year), 82 research assistantships with partial tuition reimbursements available (averaging $16,680 per year), 32 teaching assistantships with partial tuition reimbursements available (averaging $14,461 per year); career-related internships or fieldwork, scholarships/grants, health care benefits, tuition waivers (partial), and unspecified assistantships also available. Financial award application deadline: 2/1; financial award applicants required to submit FAFSA. In 2008, 31 master's, 9 doctorates awarded. *Degree program information:* Part-time programs available. Offers atmospheric and geographic sciences (M Pr Met, MA, MS Metr, PhD); geography (MA, PhD); meteorology (M Pr Met, MS Metr, PhD). *Application deadline:* For fall admission, 2/1 priority date for domestic students, 4/1 for international students; for spring admission, 11/1 for domestic students, 9/1 for international students. Applications are processed on a rolling basis. *Application fee:* $40 ($90 for international students). Electronic applications accepted. *Application Contact:* Miranda Sowell, Coordinator of Graduate Admissions, 405-325-3811, Fax: 405-325-5346, E-mail: mgsowell@ou.edu. *Dean,* Dr. John T. Snow, 405-325-3095, Fax: 405-325-1180, E-mail: jsnow@ou.edu.

College of Earth and Energy Students: 135 full-time (35 women), 32 part-time (9 women); includes 10 minority (2 African Americans, 1 American Indian/Alaska Native, 3 Asian Americans or Pacific Islanders, 4 Hispanic Americans), 107 international. 178 applicants, 49% accepted, 46 enrolled. *Faculty:* 47 full-time (3 women), 3 part-time/adjunct (0 women). Expenses: Contact institution. *Financial support:* In 2008–09, 10 students received support, including 80 research assistantships (averaging $14,209 per year), 42 teaching assistantships (averaging $14,463 per year); career-related internships or fieldwork, scholarships/grants, tuition waivers (partial), and unspecified assistantships also available. Financial award applicants required to submit FAFSA. In 2008, 31 master's, 8 doctorates awarded. Offers earth and energy (MS, PhD); geological engineering (MS, PhD); geology (MS, PhD); geophysics (MS); natural gas engineering (MS); petroleum engineering (MS, PhD). *Application deadline:* For fall admission, 2/1 priority date for domestic students, 4/1 for international students; for spring admission, 9/1 for domestic and international students. Applications are processed on a rolling basis. *Application fee:* $40 ($90 for international students). Electronic applications accepted. *Application Contact:* Linda Goeringer, Academic Counselor, 405-325-3821, Fax: 405-325-3180, E-mail: lgoeringer@ou.edu. *Associate Provost/Director,* Doug Elmore, 405-325-3253, Fax: 405-325-3140, E-mail: delmore@ou.edu.

College of Education Students: 318 full-time (217 women), 455 part-time (325 women); includes 186 minority (78 African Americans, 64 American Indian/Alaska Native, 17 Asian Americans or Pacific Islanders, 27 Hispanic Americans), 33 international. 278 applicants, 71% accepted, 161 enrolled. *Faculty:* 78 full-time (45 women), 9 part-time/adjunct (3 women). Expenses: Contact institution. *Financial support:* In 2008–09, 305 students received support, including 8 fellowships with full tuition reimbursements available (averaging $4,221 per year), 110 research assistantships with partial tuition reimbursements available (averaging $11,776 per year), 28 teaching assistantships with partial tuition reimbursements available (averaging $10,970 per year); career-related internships or fieldwork, Federal Work-Study, institutionally sponsored loans, scholarships/grants, tuition waivers (full and partial), and unspecified assistantships also available. Support available to part-time students. Financial award applicants required to submit FAFSA. In 2008, 109 master's, 37 doctorates awarded. *Degree program information:* Evening/weekend programs available. Postbaccalaureate distance learning degree programs offered (no on-campus study). Offers adult and higher education (M Ed, PhD); community counseling (M Ed); counseling psychology (PhD); education (Certificate); educational administration, curriculum and supervision (M Ed, Ed D, PhD); educational studies (M Ed, PhD); historical, philosophical, and social foundations of education (M Ed, PhD); instructional leadership and academic curriculum (M Ed, PhD); instructional psychology (M Ed, PhD); school counseling (M Ed); special education (M Ed, PhD). *Application deadline:* For fall admission, 6/1 for domestic students, 4/1 for international students; for spring admission, 11/1 for domestic students, 9/1 for international students. Applications are processed on a rolling basis. *Application fee:* $40 ($90 for international students). Electronic applications accepted. *Application Contact:* Dr. Joan Karen Smith, Dean, 405-325-1081, Fax: 405-325-7390, E-mail: jksmith@ou.edu. *Dean,* Dr. Joan Karen Smith, 405-325-1081, Fax: 405-325-7390, E-mail: jksmith@ou.edu.

College of Engineering Students: 382 full-time (98 women), 137 part-time (20 women); includes 53 minority (7 African Americans, 13 American Indian/Alaska Native, 19 Asian Americans or Pacific Islanders, 14 Hispanic Americans), 269 international. 393 applicants, 80% accepted, 121 enrolled. *Faculty:* 138 full-time (16 women), 8 part-time/adjunct (0 women). Expenses: Contact institution. *Financial support:* In 2008–09, 90 students received support, including 5 fellowships with full tuition reimbursements available (averaging $4,409 per year), 228 research assistantships with partial tuition reimbursements available (averaging $13,421 per year), 76 teaching assistantships with partial tuition reimbursements available (averaging $11,694 per year); career-related internships or fieldwork, Federal Work-Study, institutionally sponsored loans, scholarships/grants, traineeships, tuition waivers (full and partial), and unspecified assistantships also available. Support available to part-time students. Financial award applicants required to submit FAFSA. In 2008, 92 master's, 29 doctorates awarded. Offers aerospace engineering (MS, PhD); air (M Env Sc); bioengineering (MS, PhD); chemical engineering (MS, PhD); civil engineering (MS, PhD); computer science (MS, PhD); electrical and computer engineering (MS, PhD); engineering (M Env Sc, MS, D Engr, PhD); engineering physics (MS, PhD); environmental engineering (MS); environmental science (M Env Sc, PhD); geotechnical engineering (MS); groundwater management (M Env Sc); hazardous solid waste (M Env Sc); industrial engineering (MS, PhD); mechanical engineering (MS, PhD); occupational safety and health (M Env Sc); process design (M Env Sc); structures (MS); telecommunication systems engineering (MS); water quality resources (M Env Sc). *Application deadline:* For fall admission, 6/1 for domestic students, 4/1 for international students; for spring admission, 11/1 for domestic students, 9/1 for international students. Applications are processed on a rolling basis. *Application fee:* $40 ($90 for international students). Electronic applications accepted. *Application Contact:* Miranda Sowell, Coordinator of Graduate Admissions, 405-325-3811, Fax: 405-325-5346, E-mail: mgsowell@ou.edu. *Dean,* Dr. Thomas Landers, 405-325-2621, Fax: 405-325-7508, E-mail: landers@ou.edu.

College of Fine Arts Students: 139 full-time (83 women), 80 part-time (47 women); includes 25 minority (5 African Americans, 7 American Indian/Alaska Native, 7 Asian Americans or Pacific Islanders, 6 Hispanic Americans), 24 international. 122 applicants, 61% accepted, 45 enrolled. *Faculty:* 94 full-time (32 women), 4 part-time/adjunct (1 woman). Expenses: Contact institution. *Financial support:* In 2008–09, 90 students received support, including 13 fellowships (averaging $5,308 per year), 45 research assistantships with partial tuition reimbursements available (averaging $10,400 per year), 87 teaching assistantships with partial tuition reimbursements available (averaging $10,273 per year); scholarships/grants, health care benefits, tuition waivers (partial), and unspecified assistantships also available. Financial award application deadline: 4/7; financial award applicants required to submit FAFSA. In 2008, 47 master's, 12 doctorates awarded. *Degree program information:* Part-time programs available. Offers acting (MFA); art (MA, MFA); art history (MA, MFA); ceramics (MFA); choral conducting (M Mus); conducting (M Mus Ed, DMA); dance (MFA); design (MFA); directing (MFA); drama (MA); film and video (MFA); fine arts (M Mus, M Mus Ed, MA, MFA, DMA, PhD); general (M Mus Ed); instrumental (M Mus Ed); instrumental conducting (M Mus); music composition (M Mus, DMA); music education (M Mus Ed, PhD); music theory (M Mus); musicology (M Mus); organ (M Mus, DMA); painting (MFA); photography (MFA); piano (M Mus, DMA); printmaking (MFA); visual communications (MFA); voice (M Mus, DMA); wind/percussion/string (M Mus, DMA). *Application deadline:* For fall admission, 6/1 for domestic students, 4/1 for international students; for spring admission, 11/1 for domestic students, 9/1 for international students. Applications are processed on a rolling basis. *Application fee:* $40 ($90 for international students). Electronic applications accepted. *Application Contact:* Jonathan Hils, Graduate Liaison, 405-325-2691, Fax: 405-325-1668, E-mail: hils@ou.edu. *Dean,* Dr. Rich Taylor, 405-325-7370, Fax: 405-325-1667, E-mail: rich.taylor@ou.edu.

College of Liberal Studies Students: 15 full-time (10 women), 328 part-time (178 women); includes 64 minority (39 African Americans, 15 American Indian/Alaska Native, 3 Asian Americans or Pacific Islanders, 7 Hispanic Americans). 96 applicants, 98% accepted, 81 enrolled. *Faculty:* 9 full-time (7 women), 24 part-time/adjunct (15 women). Expenses: Contact institution. *Financial support:* In 2008–09, 144 students received support. Career-related internships or fieldwork, scholarships/grants, and tuition waivers (partial) available. Support available to part-time students. Financial award applicants required to submit FAFSA. In 2008, 71 master's awarded. *Degree program information:* Part-time programs available. Postbaccalaureate distance learning degree programs offered (no on-campus study). Offers administrative leadership (MLS); integrated studies (MLS); interprofessional human and health services (MLS); museum studies (MLS). *Application deadline:* For fall admission, 7/15 priority date for domestic students, 4/1 for international students; for spring admission, 12/1 for domestic students, 9/1 for international students. Applications are processed on a rolling basis. *Application fee:* $40 ($90 for international students). Electronic applications accepted. *Application Contact:* Dr. Julie Raadschelders, MA Program Coordinator, 405-325-1061, Fax: 405-325-9632, E-mail: jraadschelders@ou.edu. *Dean and Vice President for University Outreach,* Dr. James Pappas, 405-325-6361, Fax: 405-325-7196, E-mail: jpappas@ou.edu.

Gaylord College of Journalism and Mass Communication Students: 47 full-time (25 women), 43 part-time (24 women); includes 15 minority (5 African Americans, 5 American Indian/Alaska Native, 2 Asian Americans or Pacific Islanders, 3 Hispanic Americans), 10 international. 38 applicants, 68% accepted, 19 enrolled. *Faculty:* 32 full-time (11 women), 3 part-time/adjunct (1 woman). Expenses: Contact institution. *Financial support:* In 2008–09, 31 students received support, including 2 fellowships (averaging $4,500 per year), 13 research assistantships (averaging $12,751 per year), 20 teaching assistantships (averaging $12,341 per year); Federal Work-Study, scholarships/grants, health care benefits, tuition waivers (full and partial), and unspecified assistantships also available. Support available to part-time students. Financial award application deadline: 2/1; financial award applicants required to submit FAFSA. In 2008, 23 master's awarded. *Degree program information:* Part-time programs available. Offers advertising and public relations (MA); information gathering and distribution (MA); journalism and mass communication (MA); mass communication management and policy (MA); professional writing (MPW); telecommunication and new technology (MA). *Application deadline:* For fall admission, 7/1 for domestic students, 4/1 for international students; for spring admission, 11/1 for domestic students, 9/1 for international students. *Application fee:* $40 ($90 for international students). Electronic applications accepted. *Application Contact:* David Craig, Director of Graduate Studies, 405-325-5206, Fax: 405-325-7565, E-mail: dcraig@ou.edu. *Dean,* Joe Foote, 405-325-2721, Fax: 405-325-7565, E-mail: jfoote@ou.edu.

Michael F. Price College of Business Students: 193 full-time (82 women), 150 part-time (40 women); includes 45 minority (7 African Americans, 12 American Indian/Alaska Native, 20 Asian Americans or Pacific Islanders, 6 Hispanic Americans), 57 international. 232 applicants, 53% accepted, 95 enrolled. *Faculty:* 59 full-time (13 women), 6 part-time/adjunct (0 women). Expenses: Contact institution. *Financial support:* In 2008–09, 63 students received support, including 55 research assistantships with partial tuition reimbursements available (averaging $11,795 per year), 20 teaching assistantships with partial tuition reimbursements available (averaging $14,097 per year); career-related internships or fieldwork, Federal Work-Study, scholarships/grants, tuition waivers (full and partial), and unspecified assistantships also available. Support available to part-time students. Financial award applicants required to submit FAFSA. In 2008, 113 master's, 11 doctorates awarded. Offers accounting (M Acc); business administration (MBA, PhD); management (MS); management information systems (MS). *Application deadline:* For fall admission, 4/1 for domestic and international students; for spring admission, 11/1 for domestic students, 9/1 for international students. Applications are processed on a rolling basis. *Application fee:* $40 ($90 for international students). Electronic applications accepted. *Application Contact:* Gina Amundson, Director of Graduate Programs, 405-325-4107, Fax: 405-325-7753, E-mail: gamundson@ou.edu. *Dean,* Dr. Kenneth Evans, 405-325-2070, Fax: 405-325-3421, E-mail: evansk@ou.edu.

School of International and Area Studies Students: 6 full-time (5 women), 3 part-time (1 woman); includes 1 minority (Hispanic American). 7 applicants, 57% accepted, 2 enrolled. *Faculty:* 16 full-time (3 women), 1 part-time/adjunct (0 women). Expenses: Contact institution. *Financial support:* In 2008–09, 8 students received support, including 4 research assistantships (averaging $10,564 per year), 6 teaching assistantships with partial tuition reimbursements available (averaging $13,170 per year); tuition waivers (full) and unspecified assistantships also available. Financial award applicants required to submit FAFSA. In 2008, 2 master's awarded. Offers international studies (MA). *Application deadline:* For fall admission, 2/15 for domestic students, 4/1 for international students; for spring admission, 10/15 for domestic students, 9/1 for international students. Applications are processed on a rolling basis. *Application fee:* $40 ($90 for international students). Electronic applications accepted. *Application Contact:* Mitchell Smith, Associate Professor, 405-325-8893, Fax: 405-325-0718, E-mail: mps@ou.edu. *Director,* Dr. Millie C Audas, 405-325-1606, Fax: 405-325-7387, E-mail: maudas@ou.edu.

See Close-Up on page 1039.

UNIVERSITY OF OKLAHOMA HEALTH SCIENCES CENTER, Oklahoma City, OK 73190

General Information State-supported, coed, upper-level institution. CGS member. *Enrollment:* 3,913 graduate, professional, and undergraduate students; 1,922 full-time matriculated graduate/professional students (1,147 women), 524 part-time matriculated graduate/professional students (398 women). *Enrollment by degree level:* 1,155 first professional, 1,021 master's, 195 doctoral, 12 other advanced degrees. *Graduate faculty:* 276 full-time (106 women), 14 part-time/adjunct (3 women). Tuition, state resident: full-time $3120; part-time $156 per credit hour. Tuition, nonresident: full-time $11,314; part-time $565.70 per credit hour. *Required fees:* $1470.50; $51.20 per credit hour. $223.25 per term. Tuition and fees vary according to course load and campus/location. *Graduate housing:* Rooms and/or apartments available on a first-come, first-served basis to single and married students. Typical cost: $4085 per year for single students; $8170 per year for married students. *Student services:* Campus employment opportunities, campus safety program, career counseling, exercise/wellness program, free psychological counseling, grant writing training, international student services, low-cost health insurance, multicultural affairs office, teacher training, writing training. *Library facilities:* Robert M. Bird Health Sciences Library plus 3 others. *Online resources:* library catalog, web page, access to other libraries' catalogs. *Collection:* 300,260 titles, 4,028 serial subscriptions. *Research affiliation:* Oklahoma Children's Memorial Hospital (pediatrics), Veterans Administration Medical Center (clinical and applied medicine), University of Oklahoma Medical Center, Oklahoma Medical Research Foundation, Dean A. McGee Eye Institute (ophthalmology).

Computer facilities: Computer purchase and lease plans are available. 120 computers available on campus for general student use. A campuswide network can be accessed from off campus. Online class registration is available. *Web address:* http://www.ouhsc.edu/.

General Application Contact: Dr. James J. Tomasek, Dean of the Graduate College, 405-271-2085, Fax: 405-271-1155, E-mail: james-tomasek@ouhsc.edu.

GRADUATE UNITS

College of Dentistry Offers dentistry (DDS, MS, Certificate); general dentistry (Certificate); orthodontics (MS); periodontics (MS). Electronic applications accepted.

College of Medicine Students: 841 full-time (395 women), 110 part-time (53 women); includes 164 minority (13 African Americans, 59 American Indian/Alaska Native, 87 Asian Americans or Pacific Islanders, 5 Hispanic Americans), 47 international. Average age 26. 1,931 applicants, 16% accepted, 242 enrolled. *Faculty:* 117 full-time (25 women), 47 part-time/adjunct (11 women). Expenses: Contact institution. *Financial support:* In 2008–09, 74 research assistantships with full and partial tuition reimbursements (averaging $22,000 per year) were awarded; fellowships, teaching assistantships, career-related internships or fieldwork, Federal Work-Study, institutionally sponsored loans, and tuition waivers (full and partial) also available. Support available to part-time students. In 2008, 140 first professional degrees, 58 master's, 14 doctorates awarded. Offers biochemistry (MS, PhD); biochemistry and molecular biology (MS, PhD); biological psychology (MS, PhD); cell biology (MS, PhD); genetic counseling (MS); immunology (MS, PhD); medical radiation physics (MS, PhD); medical sciences (MS); medicine (MD, MHS, MS, PhD); microbiology (MS, PhD); microbiology and immunology (MS, PhD); molecular biology (MS, PhD); neuroscience (MS, PhD); pathology (PhD); physician associate (MHS); physiology (MS, PhD); psychiatry and behavioral sciences (MS, PhD); radiological sciences (MS, PhD). *Application fee:* $25 ($50 for international students). Electronic applications accepted. *Application Contact:* Dr. James J. Tomasek, PhD, Dean of the Graduate College, 405-271-2085, Fax: 405-271-1155, E-mail: james-tomasek@ouhsc.edu. *Executive Dean,* Dr. Dewayne Andrews, MD, 405-271-2265.

College of Pharmacy Students: 519 full-time (309 women), 12 part-time (4 women); includes 164 minority (11 African Americans, 48 American Indian/Alaska Native, 90 Asian Americans or Pacific Islanders, 15 Hispanic Americans), 12 international. Average age 26. 314 applicants, 48% accepted, 120 enrolled. *Faculty:* 23 full-time (3 women), 4 part-time/adjunct (2 women). Expenses: Contact institution. *Financial support:* In 2008–09, 6 research assistantships (averaging $17,000 per year) were awarded; fellowships, teaching assistantships, career-related internships or fieldwork and institutionally sponsored loans also available. In 2008, 120 first professional degrees, 1 master's, 2 doctorates awarded. Offers pharmacy (Pharm D, MS, PhD). *Application fee:* $50. *Application Contact:* Dr. Keith Swanson, Director of Student Services, 405-271-6598, E-mail: keith-swanson@ouhsc.edu. *Dean,* Dr. Douglas Voth, 405-271-6484.

Graduate College Students: 767 full-time (594 women), 509 part-time (384 women); includes 212 minority (48 African Americans, 100 American Indian/Alaska Native, 47 Asian Americans or Pacific Islanders, 17 Hispanic Americans), 96 international. Average age 30. 1,214 applicants, 40% accepted, 353 enrolled. *Faculty:* 239 full-time (87 women), 111 part-time/adjunct (50 women). Expenses: Contact institution. *Financial support:* Fellowships, research assistantships, teaching assistantships, career-related internships or fieldwork, Federal Work-Study, institutionally sponsored loans, scholarships/grants, traineeships, and tuition waivers (full and partial) available. Support available to part-time students. In 2008, 373 master's, 33 doctorates, 79 other advanced degrees awarded. *Degree program information:* Part-time and evening/weekend programs available. *Application fee:* $50. *Application Contact:* Karolyn Ruffin, Graduate Program Coordinator, 405-271-2085 Ext. 48823, Fax: 405-271-1155, E-mail: karolyn-ruffin@ouhsc.edu. *Dean of the Graduate College,* Dr. James J. Tomasek, 405-271-2085, Fax: 405-271-1155, E-mail: james-tomasek@ouhsc.edu.

College of Allied Health Students: 353 full-time (290 women), 58 part-time (57 women); includes 53 minority (9 African Americans, 28 American Indian/Alaska Native, 11 Asian Americans or Pacific Islanders, 5 Hispanic Americans), 1 international. Average age 26. 401 applicants, 48% accepted, 153 enrolled. *Faculty:* 28 full-time (19 women), 17 part-time/adjunct (16 women). Expenses: Contact institution. *Financial support:* Fellowships, career-related internships or fieldwork, Federal Work-Study, institutionally sponsored loans, and traineeships available. Support available to part-time students. In 2008, 116 master's, 13 doctorates, 21 other advanced degrees awarded. *Degree program information:* Part-time programs available. Offers allied health (MOT, MPT, MS, Au D, PhD, Certificate); allied health sciences (PhD); audiology (MS, Au D, PhD); communication sciences and disorders (Certificate); education of the deaf (MS); nutritional sciences (MS); occupational therapy (MOT); physical therapy (MPT); rehabilitation sciences (MS); speech-language pathology (MS, PhD). *Application deadline:* For fall admission, 7/1 priority date for domestic students; for winter admission, 5/1 for domestic students; for spring admission, 12/1 for domestic students. *Application fee:* $50. *Application Contact:* Dr. Jan Womack, Associate Dean, Academic and Student Affairs, 405-271-6588, Fax: 405-271-3120, E-mail: jan-womack@ouhsc.edu. *Dean,* Dr. Carole Sullivan, 405-271-2288, Fax: 405-271-1190, E-mail: carole-sullivan@ouhsc.edu.

College of Nursing Students: 41 full-time (36 women), 129 part-time (122 women); includes 41 minority (8 African Americans, 22 American Indian/Alaska Native, 8 Asian Americans or Pacific Islanders, 3 Hispanic Americans), 2 international. Average age 38. 110 applicants, 28% accepted, 26 enrolled. *Faculty:* 27 full-time (25 women), 9 part-time/adjunct (8 women). Expenses: Contact institution. *Financial support:* In 2008–09, 6 research assistantships (averaging $6,000 per year) were awarded; teaching assistantships, institutionally sponsored loans, scholarships/grants, and traineeships also available. Support available to part-time students. Financial award application deadline: 8/1. In 2008, 41 master's awarded. *Degree program information:* Part-time programs available. Offers nursing (MS). *Application deadline:* For fall admission, 6/1 for domestic students; for winter admission, 4/1 for domestic students; for spring admission, 11/1 for domestic students. Applications are processed on a rolling basis. *Application fee:* $50. *Application Contact:* Dr. Francene Weatherby, Information Contact, 405-271-2420, Fax: 405-271-3443, E-mail: francene-weatherby@ouhsc.edu. *Dean,* Dr. Carol Kenner, 405-271-2420, E-mail: carol-kenner@ouhsc.edu.

College of Public Health Students: 130 full-time (80 women), 144 part-time (95 women); includes 58 minority (18 African Americans, 23 American Indian/Alaska Native, 13 Asian Americans or Pacific Islanders, 4 Hispanic Americans), 40 international. Average age 32. 209 applicants, 64% accepted, 72 enrolled. *Faculty:* 37 full-time (14 women), 33 part-time/adjunct (12 women). Expenses: Contact institution. *Financial support:* In 2008–09, 26 research assistantships (averaging $13,000 per year) were awarded; fellowships, career-related internships or fieldwork, Federal Work-Study, institutionally sponsored loans, traineeships, and tuition waivers (partial) also available. Support available to part-time students. Financial award application deadline: 5/1. In 2008, 80 master's, 4 doctorates awarded. *Degree program information:* Part-time programs available. Offers biostatistics (MPH, MS, Dr PH, PhD); epidemiology (MPH, MS, Dr PH, PhD); general public health (MPH, Dr PH); health administration and policy (MHA, MPH, MS, Dr PH, PhD); health promotion sciences (MPH, MS, Dr PH, PhD); occupational and environmental health (MPH, MS, Dr PH, PhD); preparedness and terrorism (MPH); public health (MHA, MPH, MS, Dr PH, PhD). *Application deadline:* For fall admission, 7/1 for domestic students; for winter admission, 4/1 for domestic students; for spring admission, 12/1 for domestic students. Applications are processed on a rolling basis. *Application fee:* $50. *Application Contact:* Robin Howell, Information Contact, 405-271-2308, E-mail: robin_howell@ouhsc.edu. *Dean,* Dr. Gary Raskob, 405-271-2232.

UNIVERSITY OF OREGON, Eugene, OR 97403

General Information State-supported, coed, university. CGS member. *Graduate housing:* Rooms and/or apartments available to single and married students. *Research affiliation:* Oregon Research Institute, Decision Research, Battelle Pacific Northwest Laboratories, National Renewable Energy Laboratory, Stanford Linear Accelerator Center, Naval Research Laboratories.

GRADUATE UNITS

Graduate School *Degree program information:* Part-time and evening/weekend programs available. Offers applied information management (MS).

Charles H. Lundquist College of Business *Degree program information:* Part-time and evening/weekend programs available. Offers accounting (M Actg, PhD); business (M Actg, MA, MBA, MS, PhD); decision sciences (MA, MS); finance (PhD); management (PhD); management: general business (MBA); marketing (PhD).

College of Arts and Sciences *Degree program information:* Part-time and evening/weekend programs available. Offers anthropology (MA, MS, PhD); arts and sciences (MA, MFA, MS, PhD); Asian studies (MA); biochemistry (MA, MS, PhD); chemistry (MA, MS, PhD); Chinese (MA, PhD); classical civilization (MA); classics (MA); clinical psychology (PhD); cognitive psychology (MA, MS, PhD); comparative literature (MA, PhD); computer and information science (MA, MS, PhD); creative writing (MFA); developmental psychology (MA, MS, PhD); ecology and evolution (MA, MS, PhD); economics (MA, MS, PhD); English (MA, PhD); environmental science, studies, and policy (PhD); environmental studies (MA, MS); French (MA); geography (MA, MS, PhD); geological sciences (MA, MS, PhD); Germanic languages and literatures (MA, PhD); Greek (MA); history (MA, PhD); human physiology (MS, PhD); independent study: folklore (MA, MS); international studies (MA); Italian (MA); Japanese (MA, PhD); Latin (MA); linguistics (MA, PhD); marine biology (MA, MS, PhD); mathematics (MA, MS, PhD); molecular, cellular and genetic biology (PhD); neuroscience and development (PhD); philosophy (MA, PhD); physics (MA, MS, PhD); physiological psychology (MA, MS, PhD); political science (MA, MS, PhD); psychology (MA, MS, PhD); Romance languages (MA, PhD); Russian and East European Studies (MA); social/personality psychology (MA, MS, PhD); sociology (MA, MS, PhD); Spanish (MA); theater arts (MA, MFA, MS, PhD).

College of Education *Degree program information:* Part-time programs available. Offers education (M Ed, MA, MS, D Ed, PhD).

School of Architecture and Allied Arts *Degree program information:* Part-time and evening/weekend programs available. Offers architecture (M Arch); architecture and allied arts (M Arch, MA, MCRP, MFA, MI Arch, MLA, MPA, MS, PhD); art (MFA); art history (MA, PhD); arts management (MA, MS); community and regional planning (MCRP); historic preservation (MS); interior architecture (MI Arch); landscape architecture (MLA); public policy and management (MA, MPA, MS).

School of Journalism and Communication *Degree program information:* Part-time programs available. Offers journalism and communication (MA, MS, PhD).

School of Music *Degree program information:* Part-time programs available. Offers composition (M Mus, DMA, PhD); conducting (M Mus); dance (MA, MS); jazz studies (M Mus); music (M Mus, MA, MS, DMA, PhD); music education (M Mus, DMA, PhD); music history (PhD); music theory (PhD); performance (M Mus, DMA); piano pedagogy (M Mus).

School of Law Offers law (JD, MA, MS).

UNIVERSITY OF OTTAWA, Ottawa, ON K1N 6N5, Canada

General Information Province-supported, coed, university. CGS member. *Graduate housing:* Rooms and/or apartments available on a first-come, first-served basis to single and married students. *Research affiliation:* Bell Canada (telecommunications, data security), Virox Technologies (disinfectants), Shipley (advanced materials), EnPharma Pharmaceuticals (medical drug development), Communications and Information Technology Ontario (CITO) (telecommunications), Oncology, Inc. (cancer, neuromuscular diseases, genetics).

GRADUATE UNITS

Faculty of Graduate and Postdoctoral Studies *Degree program information:* Part-time and evening/weekend programs available. Offers biomedical engineering (MA Sc); e-business technologies (M Sc, MEBT); globalization and international development (MA); population health (PhD); systems science (M Sc, M Sys Sc, Certificate). Electronic applications accepted.

Faculty of Arts *Degree program information:* Part-time and evening/weekend programs available. Offers arts (M Geog, M Mus, M Sc, MA, PhD, Certificate); classical studies (MA); communication (MA); directing for theatre (MA); economics (PhD); English (PhD); geography (PhD); history (MA, PhD); interpreting (MA); lettres Françaises (MA, PhD); linguistics (MA, PhD); music (M Mus, MA); orchestral studies (Certificate); philosophy (MA, PhD); piano pedagogy research (Certificate); political science (PhD); psychology (PhD); religious studies (PhD); Spanish (MA, PhD); Spanish translation (MA); translation (MA); translation studies (PhD). Electronic applications accepted.

Faculty of Education Postbaccalaureate distance learning degree programs offered (minimal on-campus study). Offers education (M Ed, MA Ed, PhD, Certificate). Electronic applications accepted.

Faculty of Engineering Offers chemical engineering (M Eng, MA Sc, PhD); civil engineering (M Eng, MA Sc, PhD); computer science (MCS, PhD); electrical and computer engineering (M Eng, MA Sc, PhD); engineering (M Eng, MA Sc, MCS, PhD, Certificate); engineering management (M Eng); information technology (Certificate); mechanical and aerospace engineering (M Eng, MA Sc, PhD); project management (Certificate). Electronic applications accepted.

Faculty of Health Sciences *Degree program information:* Part-time and evening/weekend programs available. Offers audiology (M Sc); health sciences (M Sc, MA, PhD, Certificate); human kinetics (MA); nurse practitioner (Certificate); nursing (M Sc, PhD); nursing/primary health care (M Sc); orthophony (M Sc). Electronic applications accepted.

Faculty of Law *Degree program information:* Part-time and evening/weekend programs available. Offers law (LL M, LL D). Electronic applications accepted.

Faculty of Medicine Offers biochemistry (M Sc, PhD); cellular and molecular medicine (M Sc, PhD); epidemiology (M Sc); medicine (MD, M Sc, PhD); microbiology and immunology (M Sc, PhD). Electronic applications accepted.

Faculty of Science *Degree program information:* Part-time and evening/weekend programs available. Offers biology (M Sc, PhD); chemistry (M Sc, PhD); earth sciences (M Sc, PhD); mathematics and statistics (M Sc, PhD); physics (M Sc, PhD); science (M Sc, PhD). Electronic applications accepted.

Faculty of Social Sciences *Degree program information:* Part-time and evening/weekend programs available. Offers criminology (MA, MCA); economics (MA, PhD); education (MA); English (MA); history (MA); human kinetics (MA); law (LL M); lettres Françaises (MA); nursing (M Sc); pastoral studies (MA); political science (MA); political studies (MA, PhD); psychology (PhD); religious studies (MA); social sciences (LL M, M Sc, MA, MCA, MSS, PhD); social work (MSS); sociology (MA); sociology and anthropology (MA). Electronic applications accepted.

Telfer School of Management *Degree program information:* Part-time and evening/weekend programs available. Offers business administration (MBA); executive business administration (EMBA); health administration (MHA); management (EMBA, MBA, MHA). Electronic applications accepted.

UNIVERSITY OF PENNSYLVANIA, Philadelphia, PA 19104

General Information Independent, coed, university. CGS member. *Enrollment:* 19,018 graduate, professional, and undergraduate students; 9,728 full-time matriculated graduate/professional students (4,812 women), 2,062 part-time matriculated graduate/professional students (1,260 women). *Enrollment by degree level:* 2,389 first professional, 5,739 master's, 3,459 doctoral, 203 other advanced degrees. *Graduate faculty:* 2,524 full-time (730 women), 1,639 part-time/adjunct (589 women). *Tuition:* Full-time $24,720; part-time $4583 per course. *Required fees:* $2074; $338 per course. Tuition and fees vary according to course load, degree level, campus/location and program. *Graduate housing:* Rooms and/or apartments available on a first-come, first-served basis to single and married students. Typical cost: $10,755 per year ($14,400 including board) for single students; $10,755 per year ($14,400 including board) for married students. Room and board charges vary according to board plan, campus/location and housing facility selected. Housing application deadline: 4/1. *Student services:* Campus employment opportunities, campus safety program, career counseling, child daycare facilities, exercise/wellness program, free psychological counseling, international student services, low-cost health insurance, multicultural affairs office, services for students with disabilities, writing training. *Library facilities:* University of Pennsylvania Libraries plus 15 others. *Online resources:* library catalog, web page, access to other libraries' catalogs. *Collection:* 5.8 million titles, 50,252 serial subscriptions, 91,180 audiovisual materials. *Research affiliation:* Children's Hospital of Philadelphia, Wistar Institute of Anatomy and Biology, BioAdvance, Regional Nanotechnology Center.

Computer facilities: Computer purchase and lease plans are available. 1,295 computers available on campus for general student use. A campuswide network can be accessed from student residence rooms and from off campus. Online class registration, billing information, financial aid application, status, academic records, student services are available. *Web address:* http://www.upenn.edu/.

General Application Contact: Karen Lawrence, Assistant Vice Provost for Graduate Education, 215-898-1842, Fax: 215-898-6567, E-mail: graded@pobox.upenn.edu.

GRADUATE UNITS

Annenberg School for Communication Students: 83 full-time (49 women), 5 part-time (4 women); includes 11 minority (9 African Americans, 2 Hispanic Americans), 21 international. 376 applicants, 5% accepted, 16 enrolled. *Faculty:* 19 full-time (7 women), 5 part-time/adjunct (1 woman). Expenses: Contact institution. *Financial support:* In 2008–09, 86 students received support; fellowships, research assistantships, teaching assistantships, institutionally sponsored loans, scholarships/grants, traineeships, health care benefits, and unspecified assistantships available. Financial award application deadline: 12/15. In 2008, 8 doctorates awarded. Offers communication (PhD). *Application deadline:* For fall admission, 1/2 for domestic students.

University of Pennsylvania (continued)

Application fee: $70. Electronic applications accepted. *Application Contact:* Beverly Henry, Graduate Studies Coordinator, 215-573-1091, Fax: 215-898-2024, E-mail: bhenry@asc.upenn.edu. *Dean,* Michael X Delli Carpini, PhD.

Graduate School of Education Students: 841 full-time (601 women), 383 part-time (280 women); includes 179 minority (101 African Americans, 3 American Indian/Alaska Native, 54 Asian Americans or Pacific Islanders, 21 Hispanic Americans), 136 international. 1,548 applicants, 59% accepted, 518 enrolled. *Faculty:* 47 full-time (23 women), 35 part-time/adjunct (16 women). Expenses: Contact institution. *Financial support:* In 2008–09, 104 students received support; fellowships, research assistantships, teaching assistantships, institutionally sponsored loans, scholarships/grants, traineeships, health care benefits, and unspecified assistantships available. Financial award application deadline: 12/15. In 2008, 388 master's, 85 doctorates awarded. *Degree program information:* Part-time programs available. Offers applied psychology and human development (M Phil, MS Ed, PhD); counseling and psychological services (PhD); counseling psychology (M Phil); education (M Phil, MS Ed, Ed D, PhD); education, culture and society (MS Ed, PhD); educational leadership (MS Ed, Ed D, PhD); educational linguistics (PhD); elementary and secondary education (MS Ed); foundations and practices in education (MS Ed, Ed D, PhD); human development (MS Ed, PhD); intercultural communication (MS Ed, Ed D, PhD); learning science and technologies (MS Ed); policy, management and evaluation (M Phil, MS Ed, Ed D, PhD); reading, writing, and literacy (MS Ed, Ed D, PhD); teaching English to speakers of other languages (MS Ed); teaching English to speakers of other languages and intercultural communication (MS Ed, PhD). *Application deadline:* For fall admission, 12/15 priority date for domestic students. Applications are processed on a rolling basis. *Application fee:* $70. Electronic applications accepted. *Application Contact:* Alyssa D'Alconzo, Associate Director, Admissions, 215-898-6415, Fax: 215-746-6884, E-mail: admissions@gse.upenn.edu. *Graduate Dean,* Dr. Andrew Porter, 215-898-7014.

Law School Students: 787 full-time (367 women); includes 218 minority (57 African Americans, 3 American Indian/Alaska Native, 101 Asian Americans or Pacific Islanders, 57 Hispanic Americans), 25 international. Average age 24. 5,811 applicants, 16% accepted, 250 enrolled. *Faculty:* 58 full-time (13 women), 34 part-time/adjunct (10 women). Expenses: Contact institution. *Financial support:* In 2008–09, 621 students received support, including 2 research assistantships with tuition reimbursements available (averaging $21,000 per year), 21 teaching assistantships (averaging $2,500 per year); fellowships, career-related internships or fieldwork, Federal Work-Study, institutionally sponsored loans, and scholarships/grants also available. Financial award application deadline: 3/1; financial award applicants required to submit FAFSA. In 2008, 257 JDs, 91 master's, 4 doctorates awarded. Offers law (JD, LL CM, LL M, SJD). *Application deadline:* For fall admission, 2/15 for domestic students. Applications are processed on a rolling basis. *Application fee:* $75. Electronic applications accepted. *Application Contact:* Renee Post, Associate Dean of Admissions and Financial Aid, 215-898-7400, Fax: 215-898-9606, E-mail: admissions@law.upenn.edu. *Dean,* Michael A. Fitts, 215-898-7400, Fax: 215-573-2025.

School of Arts and Sciences Students: 1,604 full-time (793 women), 690 part-time (392 women); includes 178 minority (68 African Americans, 5 American Indian/Alaska Native, 72 Asian Americans or Pacific Islanders, 33 Hispanic Americans), 519 international. 5,849 applicants, 18% accepted, 552 enrolled. *Faculty:* 489 full-time (143 women), 33 part-time/adjunct (12 women). Expenses: Contact institution. *Financial support:* In 2008–09, 1,733 students received support; fellowships, research assistantships, teaching assistantships, institutionally sponsored loans, scholarships/grants, traineeships, health care benefits, and unspecified assistantships available. Financial award application deadline: 12/15. In 2008, 392 master's, 185 doctorates awarded. *Degree program information:* Part-time and evening/weekend programs available. Offers ancient history (AM, PhD); anthropology (AM, MS, PhD); applied mathematics and computational science (PhD); art and archaeology of the Mediterranean world (AM, PhD); arts and sciences (AM, MA, MBA, MES, MGA, MLA, MS, PhD); biology (PhD); chemistry (MS, PhD); classical studies (AM, PhD); comparative literature (AM, PhD); criminology (MA, MS, PhD); demography (AM, PhD); earth and environmental science (MS, PhD); East Asian languages and civilization (AM, PhD); economics (AM, PhD); English (AM, PhD); French (AM, PhD); Germanic languages (AM, PhD); history (AM, PhD); history and sociology of science (AM, PhD); history of art (AM, PhD); international studies (AM); Italian (AM, PhD); linguistics (AM, PhD); literary theory (AM, PhD); mathematics (AM, PhD); medical physics (MS); music (AM, PhD); near eastern languages and civilization (AM, PhD); organizational dynamics (MS); philosophy (AM, PhD); physics (PhD); political science (AM, PhD); psychology (PhD); religious studies (PhD); sociology (AM, PhD); South Asian regional studies (AM, PhD); Spanish (AM, PhD). *Application deadline:* For fall admission, 12/15 priority date for domestic students. Applications are processed on a rolling basis. *Application fee:* $70. Electronic applications accepted. *Application Contact:* Patricia Rea, Associate Director for Admissions, 215-573-5816, Fax: 215-573-8068, E-mail: gdasadmis@sas.upenn.edu. *Associate Dean for Graduate Studies,* Dr. Ralph M Rosen, 215-898-7156, Fax: 215-573-8068, E-mail: gdasdmis@sas.upenn.edu.

College of Liberal and Professional Studies Students: 94 full-time (52 women), 313 part-time (177 women); includes 26 minority (12 African Americans, 1 American Indian/Alaska Native, 9 Asian Americans or Pacific Islanders, 4 Hispanic Americans), 29 international. 387 applicants, 47% accepted, 118 enrolled. Expenses: Contact institution. In 2008, 86 master's awarded. Offers environmental studies (MES); individualized study (MLA). *Application deadline:* For fall admission, 12/1 priority date for domestic students. *Application fee:* $70. Electronic applications accepted. *Application Contact:* Patricia Rea, Coordinator for Admissions, 215-573-5816, Fax: 215-573-8068, E-mail: gdasadmis@sas.upenn.edu. *Associate Dean/Director,* Dr. Kristine Billmyer, 215-898-8681, E-mail: gdasdmis@sas.upenn.edu.

Fels Institute of Government Students: 38 full-time (22 women), 86 part-time (48 women); includes 22 minority (18 African Americans, 1 Asian American or Pacific Islander, 3 Hispanic Americans), 6 international. 199 applicants, 38% accepted, 32 enrolled. Expenses: Contact institution. *Financial support:* Fellowships, institutionally sponsored loans and scholarships/grants available. Financial award application deadline: 1/15; financial award applicants required to submit FAFSA. In 2008, 63 master's awarded. *Degree program information:* Part-time and evening/weekend programs available. Offers government (MGA). *Application deadline:* For fall admission, 1/15 for domestic students. Applications are processed on a rolling basis. *Application fee:* $70. *Application Contact:* Patricia Rea, Coordinator for Admissions, 215-746-6684, Fax: 215-898-6238, E-mail: gdasadmis@sas.upenn.edu. *Director,* David B. Thornburgh, 215-898-2600.

Joseph H. Lauder Institute of Management and International Studies Students: 123 full-time (45 women). Average age 27. Expenses: Contact institution. *Financial support:* Fellowships with tuition reimbursements, career-related internships or fieldwork and scholarships/grants available. In 2008, 57 master's awarded. Offers international studies (MA); management and international studies (MBA). Applications made concurrently and separately to Lauder Institute and Wharton MBA program. *Application deadline:* For fall admission, 10/12 for domestic students; for winter admission, 1/4 for domestic students. Electronic applications accepted. *Application Contact:* Marcy R. Bevan, Director of Admissions, 215-898-1215, Fax: 215-898-2067, E-mail: lauderinfo@wharton.upenn.edu. *Director,* Mauro Guillen, 215-898-1215.

School of Dental Medicine Students: 516 full-time (287 women); includes 231 minority (23 African Americans, 2 American Indian/Alaska Native, 182 Asian Americans or Pacific Islanders, 24 Hispanic Americans). Average age 24. 2,445 applicants, 12% accepted, 115 enrolled. *Faculty:* 70 full-time (22 women), 306 part-time/adjunct (73 women). Expenses: Contact institution. *Financial support:* In 2008–09, 270 students received support. Federal Work-Study and scholarships/grants available. Financial award application deadline: 6/15; financial award applicants required to submit FAFSA. In 2008, 128 DMDs awarded. Offers dental medicine (DMD). *Application deadline:* For fall admission, 1/1 for domestic and international students. Applications are processed on a rolling basis. *Application fee:* $50. *Application Contact:* Corky Cacas, Director of Admissions, 215-898-8943, Fax: 215-573-9648, E-mail: dental-admissions@dental.upenn.edu. *Dean,* Dr. Denis Kinane, 215-898-8941, Fax: 215-573-4075.

School of Design Students: 569 full-time (305 women), 16 part-time (10 women); includes 110 minority (27 African Americans, 4 American Indian/Alaska Native, 55 Asian Americans or Pacific Islanders, 24 Hispanic Americans), 115 international. 1,605 applicants, 43% accepted, 259 enrolled. *Faculty:* 33 full-time (14 women), 22 part-time/adjunct (7 women). Expenses: Contact institution. *Financial support:* In 2008–09, 19 students received support; fellowships, research assistantships, teaching assistantships, institutionally sponsored loans, scholarships/grants, traineeships, health care benefits, and unspecified assistantships available. Financial award application deadline: 12/15. In 2008, 227 master's, 5 doctorates, 76 other advanced degrees awarded. *Degree program information:* Part-time programs available. Offers architecture (M Arch, PhD); city and regional planning (MCP, PhD, Certificate); conservation and heritage management (Certificate); design (M Arch, MCP, MFA, MLA, MS, PhD, Certificate); fine arts (MFA); historic conservation (Certificate); historic preservation (MS); landscape architecture and regional planning (MLA); landscape studies (Certificate); real estate design and development (PhD, Certificate); urban design (PhD, Certificate). *Application deadline:* For fall admission, 1/2 priority date for domestic students. *Application fee:* $70. *Application Contact:* Joan Weston, Director of Admissions and Financial Aid, 215-898-6520, Fax: 215-573-6809, E-mail: admissions@design.upenn.edu. *Associate Dean,* Patricia Woldar, 215-898-3425, Fax: 215-573-6654, E-mail: admissions@design.upenn.edu.

School of Engineering and Applied Science Students: 790 full-time (219 women), 318 part-time (68 women); includes 120 minority (21 African Americans, 1 American Indian/Alaska Native, 84 Asian Americans or Pacific Islanders, 14 Hispanic Americans), 504 international. 3,159 applicants, 32% accepted, 401 enrolled. *Faculty:* 105 full-time (14 women), 30 part-time/adjunct (1 woman). Expenses: Contact institution. *Financial support:* In 2008–09, 384 students received support; fellowships, research assistantships, teaching assistantships, institutionally sponsored loans, scholarships/grants, traineeships, health care benefits, and unspecified assistantships available. Financial award application deadline: 12/15. In 2008, 341 master's, 69 doctorates awarded. *Degree program information:* Part-time and evening/weekend programs available. Offers applied mechanics (MSE, PhD); bioengineering (MSE, PhD); biotechnology (MS); chemical engineering (MSE, PhD); computer and information science (MCIT, MSE, PhD); computer graphics and game technology (MSE); electrical and systems engineering (MSE, PhD); engineering and applied science (EMBA, MCIT, MS, MSE, PhD, AC); materials science and engineering (MSE, PhD); mechanical engineering (MSE, PhD); technology management (EMBA); telecommunications and networking (MSE). *Application deadline:* For fall admission, 6/1 priority date for domestic students, 5/1 priority date for international students; for spring admission, 11/1 priority date for domestic students, 10/1 priority date for international students. Applications are processed on a rolling basis. *Application fee:* $70. Electronic applications accepted. *Application Contact:* Academic Programs Office, 215-898-4542, Fax: 215-573-5577, E-mail: engstats@seas.upenn.edu. *Dean,* Eduardo D. Glandt, 215-898-7244, Fax: 215-573-2018, E-mail: seasdean@seas.upenn.edu.

School of Medicine Students: 1,509 full-time (756 women), 35 part-time (23 women); includes 457 minority (83 African Americans, 12 American Indian/Alaska Native, 266 Asian Americans or Pacific Islanders, 96 Hispanic Americans), 81 international. Average age 24. *Faculty:* 2,332 full-time (807 women), 1,271 part-time/adjunct (561 women). Expenses: Contact institution. *Financial support:* Fellowships, research assistantships, teaching assistantships, career-related internships or fieldwork, Federal Work-Study, institutionally sponsored loans, scholarships/grants, and unspecified assistantships available. Financial award application deadline: 1/2; financial award applicants required to submit FAFSA. In 2008, 148 first professional degrees, 28 master's, 86 doctorates awarded. *Degree program information:* Part-time programs available. Offers medicine (MD, MS, MSCE, PhD). *Application deadline:* Applications are processed on a rolling basis. Electronic applications accepted. *Application Contact:* Gaye Sheffler, Director, Admissions, 215-898-8001, Fax: 215-898-0833, E-mail: sheffler@mail.med.upenn.edu. *Dean,* Dr. Arthur M. Rubenstein, 215-898-6796, Fax: 215-573-2030, E-mail: amrdean@mail.med.upenn.edu.

Biomedical Graduate Studies Students: 688 full-time (350 women); includes 167 minority (27 African Americans, 6 American Indian/Alaska Native, 96 Asian Americans or Pacific Islanders, 38 Hispanic Americans), 68 international. 1,082 applicants, 22% accepted, 97 enrolled. *Faculty:* 636. Expenses: Contact institution. *Financial support:* Fellowships, research assistantships, scholarships/grants, traineeships, and unspecified assistantships available. In 2008, 13 master's, 108 doctorates awarded. Offers biochemistry and molecular biophysics (PhD); biomedical studies (MS, PhD); biostatistics (MS, PhD); cancer biology (PhD); cell biology and physiology (PhD); developmental biology (PhD); developmental stem cell regenerative biology (PhD); gene therapy and vaccines (PhD); genetics and gene regulation (PhD); genomics and computational biology (PhD); immunology (PhD); microbiology, virology, and parasitology (PhD); neuroscience (PhD); pharmacology (PhD). *Application deadline:* For fall admission, 12/8 priority date for domestic and international students. Applications are processed on a rolling basis. *Application fee:* $70. Electronic applications accepted. *Application Contact:* Sarah Gormley, Admissions Coordinator, 215-898-1030, Fax: 215-898-2671, E-mail: gormley@mail.med.upenn.edu. *Director,* Dr. Susan R. Ross, 215-898-1030.

Center for Clinical Epidemiology and Biostatistics Students: 68 full-time (40 women), 28 part-time (19 women); includes 25 minority (5 African Americans, 18 Asian Americans or Pacific Islanders, 2 Hispanic Americans). Average age 30. 52 applicants, 71% accepted, 33 enrolled. *Faculty:* 72 full-time (27 women), 119 part-time/adjunct (40 women). Expenses: Contact institution. *Financial support:* In 2008–09, 65 students received support, including 60 fellowships with full and partial tuition reimbursements available (averaging $42,000 per year); career-related internships or fieldwork, scholarships/grants, health care benefits, unspecified assistantships, and faculty/staff benefits for partial tuition coverage also available. Financial award application deadline: 1/15. In 2008, 21 master's awarded. *Degree program information:* Part-time programs available. Offers clinical epidemiology (MSCE); epidemiology (PhD). PhD offered through the School of Arts and Sciences. *Application deadline:* For fall admission, 1/15 priority date for domestic and international students. Applications are processed on a rolling basis. *Application fee:* $0. Electronic applications accepted. *Application Contact:* Shanta C. Layton, Associate Director for Graduate Training in Epidemiology, 215-573-2382, Fax: 215-573-5315, E-mail: shanta2@mail.med.upenn.edu. *Director,* Dr. Harold I. Feldman, 215-573-0901, Fax: 215-573-2265, E-mail: hfeldman@mail.med.upenn.edu.

School of Nursing Students: 178 full-time (154 women), 283 part-time (266 women); includes 67 minority (25 African Americans, 34 Asian Americans or Pacific Islanders, 8 Hispanic Americans), 15 international. 383 applicants, 55% accepted, 173 enrolled. *Faculty:* 54 full-time (49 women), 58 part-time/adjunct (53 women). Expenses: Contact institution. *Financial support:* In 2008–09, 54 students received support; fellowships, research assistantships, teaching assistantships, institutionally sponsored loans, scholarships/grants, traineeships, health care benefits, and unspecified assistantships available. Financial award application deadline: 12/15. In 2008, 166 master's, 12 doctorates, 2 other advanced degrees awarded. *Degree program information:* Part-time programs available. Postbaccalaureate distance learning degree programs offered. Offers acute care nurse practitioner (MSN); administration/consulting (MSN); adult and special populations (MSN); adult health nurse practitioner (MSN); adult oncology nurse practitioner (MSN); child and family (MSN); family health nurse practitioner (MSN, Certificate); geropsychiatrics (MSN); health leadership (MSN); neonatal nurse practitioner (MSN); nurse anesthetist (MSN); nurse midwifery (MSN); nursing (MSN, PhD, Certificate); nursing and health care administration (MSN, PhD); pediatric acute/chronic care nurse practitioner (MSN); pediatric critical care nurse practitioner (MSN); pediatric nurse practitioner (MSN); pediatric oncology nurse practitioner (MSN); perinatal advanced practice nurse specialist (MSN); primary care (MSN); women's healthcare nurse practitioner (MSN). *Application deadline:* For fall admission, 2/15 priority date for domestic students. Applications are processed on a rolling basis. *Application fee:* $70. *Application Contact:* Sylvia VJ English, Enrollment Management Coordinator, 866-867-6877, Fax: 215-573-8439, E-mail: admissions@nursing.upenn.edu. *Assistant Dean of Admissions and Financial Aid,* 866-867-6877, Fax: 215-573-8439, E-mail: admissions@nursing.upenn.edu.

School of Social Policy and Practice Offers social policy and practice (MSW, PhD); social welfare (PhD); social work (MSW). Electronic applications accepted.

School of Veterinary Medicine Offers veterinary medicine (VMD).

Wharton School *Degree program information:* Evening/weekend programs available. Offers accounting (PhD); applied economics (PhD); business (MBA, PhD); business administration (MBA); business and public policy (MBA, PhD); ethics and legal studies (PhD); finance (MBA, PhD); health care management (MBA, PhD); health care management and economics (PhD); insurance and risk management (MBA, PhD); legal studies and business ethics (MBA, PhD); management (MBA, PhD); marketing (PhD); operations and information management (PhD); real estate (MBA, PhD); statistics (MBA, PhD). Electronic applications accepted.

The Wharton MBA Program for Executives *Degree program information:* Evening/weekend programs available. Offers executive business administration (MBA).

UNIVERSITY OF PHOENIX, Phoenix, AZ 85034-7209

General Information Proprietary, coed, comprehensive institution. *Graduate housing:* On-campus housing not available.

GRADUATE UNITS

The Artemis School *Degree program information:* Evening/weekend programs available. Postbaccalaureate distance learning degree programs offered. Electronic applications accepted.

College of Education *Degree program information:* Evening/weekend programs available. Postbaccalaureate distance learning degree programs offered (no on-campus study). Offers administration and supervision (MAEd); adult education and training (MAEd); curriculum and instruction (MAEd); curriculum and instruction-adult education (MAEd); curriculum and instruction-computer education (MAEd); curriculum and instruction-English and language arts education (MAEd); curriculum and instruction-English as a second language (MAEd); curriculum and instruction-mathematics education (MAEd); curriculum education (MAEd); early childhood (MAEd); elementary teacher education (MAEd); secondary teacher education (MAEd); special education (MAEd). Electronic applications accepted.

College of Health and Human Services *Degree program information:* Evening/weekend programs available. Postbaccalaureate distance learning degree programs offered. Offers administration of justice and security (MS); community counseling (MSC); education (MHA); family nurse practitioner (MSN); gerontology (MHA); health administration (MHA); health care education (MSN); health care management (MBA, MSN); informatics (MHA); marriage, family, and child therapy (MSC); nursing (MSN); nursing for nurse practitioners (MSN); psychology (MS). Electronic applications accepted.

John Sperling School of Business *Degree program information:* Evening/weekend programs available. Offers business (MBA, MIS, MM, MSA). Electronic applications accepted.

College of Graduate Business and Management *Degree program information:* Evening/weekend programs available. Postbaccalaureate distance learning degree programs offered. Offers accountancy (MSA); accounting (MBA); business administration (MBA); global management (MBA); human resources management (MBA, MM); management (MM); marketing (MBA); public administration (MBA, MM). Electronic applications accepted.

College of Information Systems and Technology *Degree program information:* Evening/weekend programs available. Offers e-business (MBA); management (MIS); technology management (MBA). Electronic applications accepted.

School of Advanced Studies *Degree program information:* Evening/weekend programs available. Offers business administration (DBA); education (Ed D); health administration (DHA); organizational management (DM). Electronic applications accepted.

UNIVERSITY OF PHOENIX–ATLANTA CAMPUS, Sandy Springs, GA 30350-4153

General Information Proprietary, coed, comprehensive institution. *Graduate housing:* On-campus housing not available.

GRADUATE UNITS

The Artemis School *Degree program information:* Evening/weekend programs available. Electronic applications accepted.

College of Health and Human Services *Degree program information:* Evening/weekend programs available. Postbaccalaureate distance learning degree programs offered. Offers administration of justice and security (MS); health administration (MHA); health care management (MBA); nursing (MSN); nursing/health care education (MSN). Electronic applications accepted.

John Sperling School of Business *Degree program information:* Evening/weekend programs available. Offers business (MBA, MIS, MM). Electronic applications accepted.

College of Graduate Business and Management *Degree program information:* Evening/weekend programs available. Postbaccalaureate distance learning degree programs offered. Offers accounting (MBA); business administration (MBA); global management (MBA); human resources management (MBA, MM); management (MM); marketing (MBA); public administration (MM).

College of Information Systems and Technology *Degree program information:* Evening/weekend programs available. Offers information systems (MIS); technology management (MBA). Electronic applications accepted.

UNIVERSITY OF PHOENIX–AUGUSTA CAMPUS, Augusta, GA 30909-4583

General Information Proprietary, comprehensive institution.

GRADUATE UNITS

College of Graduate Business and Management Postbaccalaureate distance learning degree programs offered. Offers accounting (MBA); business administration (MBA); business and management (MBA, MM); global management (MBA); human resources management (MBA, MM); management (MM); marketing (MBA); public administration (MBA, MM).

College of Health and Human Services Postbaccalaureate distance learning degree programs offered. Offers health administration (MHA); health care management (MBA); nursing (MSN); nursing/health care education (MSN).

College of Information Systems and Technology Offers information systems (MIS); technology management (MBA).

College of Social and Behavioral Science Offers administration of justice and security (MS).

UNIVERSITY OF PHOENIX–AUSTIN CAMPUS, Austin, TX 78759

General Information Proprietary, comprehensive institution.

GRADUATE UNITS

College of Education Offers curriculum and instruction (MA Ed).

College of Graduate Business and Management Postbaccalaureate distance learning degree programs offered. Offers accounting (MBA); business administration (MBA); business and management (MBA); e-business (MBA); global management (MBA); human resources management (MBA, MM); management (MM); marketing (MBA); public administration (MBA).

College of Health and Human Services Postbaccalaureate distance learning degree programs offered. Offers health administration (MHA); health care management (MBA).

College of Information Systems and Technology Offers information systems (MIS); technology management (MBA).

College of Social and Behavioral Science Postbaccalaureate distance learning degree programs offered. Offers administration of justice and security (MS); psychology (MS).

UNIVERSITY OF PHOENIX–BAY AREA CAMPUS, Pleasanton, CA 94588-3677

General Information Proprietary, coed, comprehensive institution. *Graduate housing:* On-campus housing not available.

GRADUATE UNITS

The Artemis School *Degree program information:* Evening/weekend programs available. Postbaccalaureate distance learning degree programs offered. Electronic applications accepted.

College of Education *Degree program information:* Evening/weekend programs available. Postbaccalaureate distance learning degree programs offered (no on-campus study). Offers curriculum instruction (MA Ed); curriculum instruction—adult education (MA Ed); elementary teacher education (MA Ed); secondary teacher education (MA Ed). Electronic applications accepted.

College of Health and Human Services *Degree program information:* Evening/weekend programs available. Postbaccalaureate distance learning degree programs offered (no on-campus study). Offers administration of justice and security (MS); family nurse practitioner (MSN); health care management (MBA); marriage, family and child therapy (MSC); nursing (MSN); nursing/health care education (MSN). Electronic applications accepted.

John Sperling School of Business *Degree program information:* Evening/weekend programs available. Postbaccalaureate distance learning degree programs offered. Offers business (MBA, MIS, MM). Electronic applications accepted.

College of Graduate Business and Management *Degree program information:* Evening/weekend programs available. Postbaccalaureate distance learning degree programs offered (no on-campus study). Offers accounting (MBA); business administration (MBA); global management (MBA); human resources management (MBA, MM); marketing (MBA); public administration (MBA, MM). Electronic applications accepted.

College of Information Systems and Technology *Degree program information:* Evening/weekend programs available. Offers e-business (MBA); information systems (MIS); technology management (MBA). Electronic applications accepted.

UNIVERSITY OF PHOENIX–BIRMINGHAM CAMPUS, Birmingham, AL 35244.

General Information Proprietary, coed, comprehensive institution.

GRADUATE UNITS

College of Graduate Business and Management Offers accounting (MBA); business administration (MBA); global management (MBA); human resources management (MBA, MM); management (MM); marketing (MBA); public administration (MM).

College of Health and Human Services Offers education (MHA); gerontology (MHA); health administration (MHA); health care management (MBA); informatics (MHA); nursing (MSN); nursing/health care education (MSN).

College of Information Systems and Technology Offers information systems (MIS); technology management (MBA).

College of Social and Behavioral Science Offers administration of justice and security (MS); psychology (MS).

UNIVERSITY OF PHOENIX–BOSTON CAMPUS, Braintree, MA 02184-4949

General Information Proprietary, coed, comprehensive institution. *Graduate housing:* On-campus housing not available.

GRADUATE UNITS

John Sperling School of Business *Degree program information:* Evening/weekend programs available. Offers business (MBA). Electronic applications accepted.

College of Graduate Business and Management *Degree program information:* Evening/weekend programs available. Offers administration (MBA); global management (MBA).

College of Information Systems and Technology *Degree program information:* Evening/weekend programs available. Offers technology management (MBA). Electronic applications accepted.

UNIVERSITY OF PHOENIX–CENTRAL FLORIDA CAMPUS, Maitland, FL 32751-7057

General Information Proprietary, coed, comprehensive institution. *Graduate housing:* On-campus housing not available.

GRADUATE UNITS

The Artemis School *Degree program information:* Evening/weekend programs available. Electronic applications accepted.

College of Education *Degree program information:* Evening/weekend programs available. Offers administration and supervision (MA Ed); curriculum and instruction (MA Ed); curriculum and instruction-computer education (MA Ed); curriculum and instruction-mathematics education (MA Ed); early childhood education (MA Ed); elementary teacher education (MA Ed); secondary teacher education (MA Ed). Electronic applications accepted.

College of Health and Human Services *Degree program information:* Evening/weekend programs available. Offers health administration (MHA); health and human services (MSN); health care management (MBA); nursing (MSN); nursing/health care education (MSN). Electronic applications accepted.

John Sperling School of Business *Degree program information:* Evening/weekend programs available. Offers business (MBA, MIS, MM). Electronic applications accepted.

College of Graduate Business and Management *Degree program information:* Evening/weekend programs available. Offers accounting (MBA); business administration (MBA); business and management (MM); global management (MBA); human resources management (MBA, MM); management (MM); marketing (MBA); public administration (MBA, MM). Electronic applications accepted.

College of Information Systems and Technology *Degree program information:* Evening/weekend programs available. Offers management (MIS); technology management (MBA). Electronic applications accepted.

UNIVERSITY OF PHOENIX–CENTRAL MASSACHUSETTS CAMPUS, Westborough, MA 01581-3906

General Information Proprietary, coed, comprehensive institution. *Graduate housing:* On-campus housing not available.

GRADUATE UNITS

The Artemis School *Degree program information:* Evening/weekend programs available. Electronic applications accepted.

College of Education *Degree program information:* Evening/weekend programs available. Offers education (MA Ed). Electronic applications accepted.

John Sperling School of Business *Degree program information:* Evening/weekend programs available. Offers business (MBA). Electronic applications accepted.

College of Graduate Business and Management *Degree program information:* Evening/weekend programs available. Offers business administration (MBA); global management (MBA). Electronic applications accepted.

College of Information Systems and Technology *Degree program information:* Evening/weekend programs available. Offers technology management (MBA). Electronic applications accepted.

UNIVERSITY OF PHOENIX–CENTRAL VALLEY CAMPUS, Fresno, CA 93720-1562

General Information Proprietary, coed, comprehensive institution.

GRADUATE UNITS

College of Education Offers curriculum and instruction (MA Ed); curriculum and instruction-computer education (MA Ed); elementary teacher education (MA Ed); secondary teacher education (MA Ed).

University of Phoenix–Central Valley Campus (continued)

College of Graduate Business and Management Offers accounting (MBA); business administration (MBA); global management (MBA); human resources management (MBA, MM); management (MM); marketing (MBA); public administration (MBA, MM).

College of Health and Human Services Offers education (MHA); gerontology (MHA); health administration (MHA); health care management (MBA); nursing (MSN).

College of Information Systems and Technology Offers information systems (MIS); technology management (MBA).

College of Social and Behavioral Science Offers marriage, family and child therapy (MSC).

UNIVERSITY OF PHOENIX–CHARLOTTE CAMPUS, Charlotte, NC 28273-3409

General Information Proprietary, coed, comprehensive institution. *Graduate housing:* On-campus housing not available.

GRADUATE UNITS

The Artemis School *Degree program information:* Evening/weekend programs available. Electronic applications accepted.

College of Health and Human Services *Degree program information:* Evening/weekend programs available. Offers health care management (MBA). Electronic applications accepted.

John Sperling School of Business *Degree program information:* Evening/weekend programs available. Offers business (MBA, MIS, MISM). Electronic applications accepted.

College of Graduate Business and Management *Degree program information:* Evening/weekend programs available. Offers accounting (MBA); business administration (MBA); global management (MBA). Electronic applications accepted.

College of Information Systems and Technology *Degree program information:* Evening/weekend programs available. Offers information systems (MIS); information systems management (MISM); technology management (MBA). Electronic applications accepted.

UNIVERSITY OF PHOENIX–CHATTANOOGA CAMPUS, Chattanooga, TN 37421-3707

General Information Proprietary, comprehensive institution.

GRADUATE UNITS

College of Education Offers administration and supervision (MA Ed); curriculum and instruction (MA Ed); elementary teacher education (MA Ed); secondary teacher education (MA Ed).

College of Graduate Business and Management Postbaccalaureate distance learning degree programs offered. Offers accounting (MBA); business administration (MBA); business and management (MBA); global management (MBA); human resources management (MBA, MM); management (MM); marketing (MBA); public administration (MBA, MM).

College of Health and Human Services Offers education (MHA); gerontology (MHA); health administration (MHA); health care management (MBA).

College of Information Systems and Technology Postbaccalaureate distance learning degree programs offered. Offers information systems (MIS); technology management (MBA).

College of Social and Behavioral Science Postbaccalaureate distance learning degree programs offered. Offers administration of justice and security (MS); psychology (MSP).

UNIVERSITY OF PHOENIX–CHEYENNE CAMPUS, Cheyenne, WY 82009

General Information Proprietary, comprehensive institution.

GRADUATE UNITS

College of Graduate Business and Management Postbaccalaureate distance learning degree programs offered. Offers global management (MBA); human resources management (MBA, MM); management (MM); marketing (MBA); public administration (MBA, MM).

College of Health and Human Services Postbaccalaureate distance learning degree programs offered. Offers health administration (MHA); health care management (MBA); nursing (MSN); nursing/health care education (MSN).

College of Information Systems and Technology Offers information systems (MIS); technology management (MBA).

College of Social and Behavioral Science Postbaccalaureate distance learning degree programs offered. Offers administration of justice and security (MS); psychology (MS).

UNIVERSITY OF PHOENIX–CHICAGO CAMPUS, Schaumburg, IL 60173-4399

General Information Proprietary, coed, comprehensive institution. *Graduate housing:* On-campus housing not available.

GRADUATE UNITS

John Sperling School of Business *Degree program information:* Evening/weekend programs available. Offers business (MBA, MIS, MM).

College of Graduate Business and Management *Degree program information:* Evening/weekend programs available. Offers business administration (MBA); global management (MBA); human resources management (MBA); information systems (MIS); management (MM). Electronic applications accepted.

College of Information Systems and Technology *Degree program information:* Evening/weekend programs available. Offers e-business (MBA); information systems (MIS); management (MM); technology management (MBA). Electronic applications accepted.

UNIVERSITY OF PHOENIX–CINCINNATI CAMPUS, West Chester, OH 45069-4875

General Information Proprietary, coed, comprehensive institution. *Graduate housing:* On-campus housing not available.

GRADUATE UNITS

The Artemis School *Degree program information:* Evening/weekend programs available. Electronic applications accepted.

College of Health and Human Services *Degree program information:* Evening/weekend programs available. Postbaccalaureate distance learning degree programs offered. Offers administration of justice and security (MS); health care management (MBA); nursing (MSN); psychology (MS). Electronic applications accepted.

John Sperling School of Business *Degree program information:* Evening/weekend programs available. Postbaccalaureate distance learning degree programs offered. Offers business (MBA, MIS, MM). Electronic applications accepted.

College of Graduate Business and Management *Degree program information:* Evening/weekend programs available. Offers accounting (MBA); business administration (MBA); global management (MBA); human resources management (MBA, MM); management (MM); marketing (MBA); public administration (MM). Electronic applications accepted.

College of Information Systems and Technology *Degree program information:* Evening/weekend programs available. Postbaccalaureate distance learning degree programs offered. Offers electronic business (MBA); information systems (MIS); technology management (MBA). Electronic applications accepted.

UNIVERSITY OF PHOENIX–CLEVELAND CAMPUS, Independence, OH 44131-2194

General Information Proprietary, coed, comprehensive institution. *Graduate housing:* On-campus housing not available.

GRADUATE UNITS

The Artemis School *Degree program information:* Evening/weekend programs available. Electronic applications accepted.

College of Health and Human Services *Degree program information:* Evening/weekend programs available. Postbaccalaureate distance learning degree programs offered. Offers administration of justice and security (MS); health care management (MBA); nursing (MSN); psychology (MS). Electronic applications accepted.

John Sperling School of Business *Degree program information:* Evening/weekend programs available. Offers business (MBA, MIS, MM). Electronic applications accepted.

College of Graduate Business and Management *Degree program information:* Evening/weekend programs available. Postbaccalaureate distance learning degree programs offered (no on-campus study). Offers accounting (MBA); business administration (MBA); global management (MBA); human resources management (MBA, MM); management (MM); marketing (MBA); public administration (MBA, MM). Electronic applications accepted.

College of Information Systems and Technology *Degree program information:* Evening/weekend programs available. Postbaccalaureate distance learning degree programs offered (no on-campus study). Offers information management (MIS); technology management (MBA). Electronic applications accepted.

UNIVERSITY OF PHOENIX–COLUMBIA CAMPUS, Columbia, SC 29223

General Information Proprietary, comprehensive institution.

GRADUATE UNITS

College of Graduate Business and Management Postbaccalaureate distance learning degree programs offered. Offers business administration (MBA).

College of Information Systems and Technology Offers technology management (MBA).

UNIVERSITY OF PHOENIX–COLUMBUS GEORGIA CAMPUS, Columbus, GA 31904-6321

General Information Proprietary, coed, comprehensive institution. *Graduate housing:* On-campus housing not available.

GRADUATE UNITS

The Artemis School *Degree program information:* Evening/weekend programs available. Electronic applications accepted.

College of Health and Human Services Postbaccalaureate distance learning degree programs offered. Offers administration of justice and security (MS); health administration (MHA); health care management (MBA); nursing (MSN). Electronic applications accepted.

John Sperling School of Business *Degree program information:* Evening/weekend programs available. Postbaccalaureate distance learning degree programs offered. Offers business (MBA, MIS, MM). Electronic applications accepted.

College of Graduate Business and Management *Degree program information:* Evening/weekend programs available. Offers accounting (MBA); business administration (MBA); global management (MBA); human resources management (MBA, MM); management (MM); marketing (MBA); public administration (MBA). Electronic applications accepted.

College of Information Systems and Technology *Degree program information:* Evening/weekend programs available. Postbaccalaureate distance learning degree programs offered. Offers e-business (MBA); information systems (MIS); technology management (MBA). Electronic applications accepted.

UNIVERSITY OF PHOENIX–COLUMBUS OHIO CAMPUS, Columbus, OH 43240-4032

General Information Proprietary, coed, comprehensive institution. *Graduate housing:* On-campus housing not available.

GRADUATE UNITS

The Artemis School *Degree program information:* Evening/weekend programs available. Postbaccalaureate distance learning degree programs offered. Electronic applications accepted.

College of Health and Human Services *Degree program information:* Evening/weekend programs available. Postbaccalaureate distance learning degree programs offered. Offers administration of justice and security (MS); health care management (MBA); nursing (MSN); psychology (MS). Electronic applications accepted.

John Sperling School of Business *Degree program information:* Evening/weekend programs available. Postbaccalaureate distance learning degree programs offered. Offers business (MBA, MIS, MM). Electronic applications accepted.

College of Graduate Business and Management *Degree program information:* Evening/weekend programs available. Postbaccalaureate distance learning degree programs offered. Offers accounting (MBA); business administration (MBA); global management (MBA); human resources management (MBA, MM); management (MM); marketing (MBA); public administration (MM). Electronic applications accepted.

College of Information Systems and Technology Postbaccalaureate distance learning degree programs offered. Offers information systems (MIS); technology management (MBA).

UNIVERSITY OF PHOENIX–DALLAS CAMPUS, Dallas, TX 75251-2009

General Information Proprietary, coed, comprehensive institution. *Graduate housing:* On-campus housing not available.

GRADUATE UNITS

The Artemis School *Degree program information:* Evening/weekend programs available. Postbaccalaureate distance learning degree programs offered. Electronic applications accepted.

College of Education Offers curriculum and instruction (MA Ed).

College of Health and Human Services Postbaccalaureate distance learning degree programs offered. Offers administration of justice and security (MS); health administration (MHA); health care management (MBA); psychology (MS). Electronic applications accepted.

John Sperling School of Business *Degree program information:* Evening/weekend programs available. Postbaccalaureate distance learning degree programs offered. Offers business (MBA, MIS, MM).

College of Graduate Business and Management *Degree program information:* Evening/weekend programs available. Postbaccalaureate distance learning degree programs offered. Offers accounting (MBA); business administration (MBA); global management (MBA); human resources management (MBA, MM); management (MM); marketing (MBA); public administration (MBA, MM). Electronic applications accepted.

College of Information Systems and Technology *Degree program information:* Evening/weekend programs available. Offers e-business (MBA); information systems (MIS); technology management (MBA). Electronic applications accepted.

UNIVERSITY OF PHOENIX–DENVER CAMPUS, Lone Tree, CO 80124-5453

General Information Proprietary, coed, comprehensive institution. *Graduate housing:* On-campus housing not available.

GRADUATE UNITS

The Artemis School *Degree program information:* Evening/weekend programs available. Postbaccalaureate distance learning degree programs offered. Electronic applications accepted.

College of Education *Degree program information:* Evening/weekend programs available. Offers administration and supervision (MAEd); curriculum instruction (MAEd); elementary teacher education (MAEd); school counseling (MSC); secondary teacher education (MAEd). Electronic applications accepted.

College of Health and Human Services *Degree program information:* Evening/weekend programs available. Postbaccalaureate distance learning degree programs offered. Offers administration of justice and security (MS); community counseling (MSC); health administration (MHA); health care management (MBA); marriage, family and child therapy (MSC); nursing (MSN); psychology (MS). Electronic applications accepted.

John Sperling School of Business *Degree program information:* Evening/weekend programs available. Postbaccalaureate distance learning degree programs offered. Offers business (MBA, MIS, MM, MSA). Electronic applications accepted.

College of Graduate Business and Management *Degree program information:* Evening/weekend programs available. Postbaccalaureate distance learning degree programs offered. Offers accountancy (MSA); accounting (MBA); business administration (MBA); e-business (MBA); global management (MBA); human resources management (MBA, MM); management (MM); marketing (MBA); public administration (MBA, MM). Electronic applications accepted.

College of Information Systems and Technology *Degree program information:* Evening/weekend programs available. Postbaccalaureate distance learning degree programs offered. Offers e-business (MBA); management (MIS); technology management (MBA). Electronic applications accepted.

UNIVERSITY OF PHOENIX–DES MOINES CAMPUS, Des Moines, IA 50266

General Information Proprietary, comprehensive institution.

GRADUATE UNITS

College of Graduate Business and Management Postbaccalaureate distance learning degree programs offered. Offers accounting (MBA); business administration (MBA); global management (MBA); human resources management (MBA, MM); management (MM); marketing (MBA); public administration (MBA, MM).

College of Health and Human Services Offers health care management (MBA).

College of Information Systems and Technology Postbaccalaureate distance learning degree programs offered. Offers information systems (MIS); technology management (MBA).

College of Social and Behavioral Science Postbaccalaureate distance learning degree programs offered. Offers administration of justice and security (MS).

UNIVERSITY OF PHOENIX–EASTERN WASHINGTON CAMPUS, Spokane Valley, WA 99212-2531

General Information Proprietary, coed, comprehensive institution. *Graduate housing:* On-campus housing not available.

GRADUATE UNITS

The Artemis School *Degree program information:* Evening/weekend programs available. Electronic applications accepted.

College of Health and Human Services *Degree program information:* Evening/weekend programs available. Offers health care management (MBA). Electronic applications accepted.

John Sperling School of Business *Degree program information:* Evening/weekend programs available. Offers business (MBA). Electronic applications accepted.

College of Graduate Business and Management *Degree program information:* Evening/weekend programs available. Offers accounting (MBA); business administration (MBA); human resources management (MBA); marketing (MBA); public administration (MBA). Electronic applications accepted.

College of Information Systems and Technology Offers technology management (MBA).

UNIVERSITY OF PHOENIX–FAIRFIELD COUNTY, Norwalk, CT 06854-1799

General Information Proprietary, comprehensive institution.

GRADUATE UNITS

College of Graduate Business and Management Offers business and management (MBA).

UNIVERSITY OF PHOENIX–HARRISBURG CAMPUS, Harrisburg, PA 17112

General Information Proprietary, comprehensive institution.

GRADUATE UNITS

College of Graduate Business and Management Postbaccalaureate distance learning degree programs offered. Offers accounting (MBA); business administration (MBA); business and management (MBA); global management (MBA); human resources management (MBA, MM); management (MM); marketing (MBA); public administration (MBA, MM).

College of Health and Human Services Postbaccalaureate distance learning degree programs offered. Offers health administration (MHA); health care management (MBA); nursing (MSN); nursing/health care education (MSN).

College of Information Systems and Technology Postbaccalaureate distance learning degree programs offered. Offers information systems (MIS); technology management (MBA).

College of Social and Behavioral Science Postbaccalaureate distance learning degree programs offered. Offers administration of justice and security (MS); psychology (MS).

UNIVERSITY OF PHOENIX–HAWAII CAMPUS, Honolulu, HI 96813-4317

General Information Proprietary, coed, comprehensive institution. *Graduate housing:* On-campus housing not available.

GRADUATE UNITS

The Artemis School *Degree program information:* Evening/weekend programs available. Electronic applications accepted.

College of Education *Degree program information:* Evening/weekend programs available. Offers administration and supervision (MA Ed); curriculum and instruction (MA Ed); elementary education (MA Ed); secondary education (MA Ed); special education (MA Ed); teacher education for elementary licensure (MA Ed). Electronic applications accepted.

College of Health and Human Services *Degree program information:* Evening/weekend programs available. Offers administration of justice and security (MS); community counseling (MSC); education (MHA); family nurse practitioner (MSN); gerontology (MHA); health administration (MHA); health care management (MBA); marriage, family and child therapy (MSC); nursing (MSN); nursing/health care education (MSN); psychology (MS). Electronic applications accepted.

John Sperling School of Business *Degree program information:* Evening/weekend programs available. Offers business (MBA, MIS, MM). Electronic applications accepted.

College of Graduate Business and Management *Degree program information:* Evening/weekend programs available. Offers accounting (MBA); business administration (MBA); global management (MBA); human resources management (MBA, MM); management (MM); marketing (MBA); public administration (MBA, MM). Electronic applications accepted.

College of Information Systems and Technology *Degree program information:* Evening/weekend programs available. Offers information systems (MIS); technology management (MBA). Electronic applications accepted.

UNIVERSITY OF PHOENIX–HOUSTON CAMPUS, Houston, TX 77079-2004

General Information Proprietary, coed, comprehensive institution. *Graduate housing:* On-campus housing not available.

GRADUATE UNITS

The Artemis School *Degree program information:* Evening/weekend programs available. Postbaccalaureate distance learning degree programs offered. Electronic applications accepted.

College of Education Offers curriculum and instruction (MA Ed).

College of Health and Human Services Postbaccalaureate distance learning degree programs offered. Offers administration of justice and security (MS); health administration (MHA); health care management (MBA); psychology (MS). Electronic applications accepted.

John Sperling School of Business *Degree program information:* Evening/weekend programs available. Postbaccalaureate distance learning degree programs offered. Offers business (MBA, MIS, MM). Electronic applications accepted.

College of Graduate Business and Management *Degree program information:* Evening/weekend programs available. Postbaccalaureate distance learning degree programs offered. Offers accounting (MBA); business administration (MBA); global management (MBA); human resources management (MBA, MM); management (MM); marketing (MBA); public administration (MBA, MM). Electronic applications accepted.

College of Information Systems and Technology *Degree program information:* Evening/weekend programs available. Postbaccalaureate distance learning degree programs offered. Offers e-business (MBA); information systems (MIS); technology management (MBA). Electronic applications accepted.

UNIVERSITY OF PHOENIX–IDAHO CAMPUS, Meridian, ID 83642-3014

General Information Proprietary, coed, comprehensive institution. *Graduate housing:* On-campus housing not available.

GRADUATE UNITS

The Artemis School *Degree program information:* Evening/weekend programs available. Postbaccalaureate distance learning degree programs offered. Electronic applications accepted.

College of Education *Degree program information:* Evening/weekend programs available. Offers administration and supervision (MA Ed); curriculum and instruction (MA Ed); elementary teacher education (MA Ed); secondary teacher education (MA Ed). Electronic applications accepted.

College of Health and Human Services *Degree program information:* Evening/weekend programs available. Postbaccalaureate distance learning degree programs offered. Offers administration of justice and security (MS); health administration (MHA); health care management (MBA); nursing (MSN); nursing/health care education (MSN); psychology (MS). Electronic applications accepted.

John Sperling School of Business *Degree program information:* Evening/weekend programs available. Postbaccalaureate distance learning degree programs offered. Offers business (MBA, MIS, MM). Electronic applications accepted.

College of Graduate Business and Management *Degree program information:* Evening/weekend programs available. Postbaccalaureate distance learning degree programs offered. Offers accounting (MBA); administration (MBA); global management (MBA); human resources management (MBA, MM); management (MM); marketing (MBA); public administration (MM). Electronic applications accepted.

College of Information Systems and Technology *Degree program information:* Evening/weekend programs available. Offers information systems (MIS); technology management (MBA). Electronic applications accepted.

UNIVERSITY OF PHOENIX–INDIANAPOLIS CAMPUS, Indianapolis, IN 46250-932

General Information Proprietary, coed, comprehensive institution. *Graduate housing:* On-campus housing not available.

GRADUATE UNITS

The Artemis School *Degree program information:* Evening/weekend programs available. Postbaccalaureate distance learning degree programs offered. Electronic applications accepted.

College of Education Offers elementary teacher education (MA Ed); secondary teacher education (MA Ed).

College of Health and Human Services *Degree program information:* Evening/weekend programs available. Postbaccalaureate distance learning degree programs offered. Offers administration of justice and security (MS); health administration (MHA); health care management (MBA); nursing (MSN); nursing/health care education (MSN); psychology (MS). Electronic applications accepted.

John Sperling School of Business *Degree program information:* Evening/weekend programs available. Offers business (MBA, MIS, MM). Electronic applications accepted.

College of Graduate Business and Management *Degree program information:* Evening/weekend programs available. Offers accounting (MBA); business administration (MBA); global management (MBA); human resources management (MBA, MM); management (MM); marketing (MBA); public administration (MM). Electronic applications accepted.

College of Information Systems and Technology *Degree program information:* Evening/weekend programs available. Offers information systems (MIS); technology management (MBA). Electronic applications accepted.

UNIVERSITY OF PHOENIX–JERSEY CITY CAMPUS, Jersey City, NJ 07310

General Information Proprietary, comprehensive institution.

GRADUATE UNITS

College of Graduate Business and Management Offers accounting (MBA); business administration (MBA); global management (MBA); human resources management (MBA, MM); management (MM); marketing (MBA); public administration (MBA, MM).

College of Health and Human Services Postbaccalaureate distance learning degree programs offered. Offers health care management (MBA).

College of Information Systems and Technology Postbaccalaureate distance learning degree programs offered. Offers information systems (MIS); technology management (MBA).

College of Social and Behavioral Science Postbaccalaureate distance learning degree programs offered. Offers administration of justice and security (MS); psychology (MS).

UNIVERSITY OF PHOENIX–KANSAS CITY CAMPUS, Kansas City, MO 64131-4517

General Information Proprietary, coed, comprehensive institution. *Graduate housing:* On-campus housing not available.

GRADUATE UNITS

The Artemis School *Degree program information:* Evening/weekend programs available. Postbaccalaureate distance learning degree programs offered. Electronic applications accepted.

College of Education Postbaccalaureate distance learning degree programs offered. Offers administration and supervision (MA Ed).

College of Health and Human Services *Degree program information:* Evening/weekend programs available. Postbaccalaureate distance learning degree programs offered. Offers administration of justice and security (MS); community counseling (MSC); health administration (MHA); health care management (MBA); nursing (MSN).

John Sperling School of Business *Degree program information:* Evening/weekend programs available. Offers business (MBA, MIS, MM). Electronic applications accepted.

College of Graduate Business and Management *Degree program information:* Evening/weekend programs available. Offers accounting (MBA); business administration (MBA); global management (MBA); human resources management (MBA, MM); management (MM); marketing (MBA); public administration (MBA). Electronic applications accepted.

University of Phoenix–Kansas City Campus (continued)

College of Information Systems and Technology *Degree program information:* Evening/weekend programs available. Offers management (MIS); technology management (MBA). Electronic applications accepted.

UNIVERSITY OF PHOENIX–LAS VEGAS CAMPUS, Las Vegas, NV 89128

General Information Proprietary, coed, comprehensive institution. *Graduate housing:* On-campus housing not available.

GRADUATE UNITS

The Artemis School *Degree program information:* Evening/weekend programs available. Postbaccalaureate distance learning degree programs offered. Electronic applications accepted.

College of Education *Degree program information:* Evening/weekend programs available. Offers administration and supervision (MA Ed); curriculum and instruction (MA Ed); school counseling (MSC); teacher education-elementary licensure (MA Ed). Electronic applications accepted.

College of Health and Human Services Postbaccalaureate distance learning degree programs offered. Offers administration of justice and security (MS); health administration (MHA); health care management (MBA); marriage, family, and child therapy (MSC); mental health counseling (MSC); nursing (MSN); nursing/health care education (MSN); psychology (MS). Electronic applications accepted.

John Sperling School of Business *Degree program information:* Evening/weekend programs available. Postbaccalaureate distance learning degree programs offered. Offers business (MBA, MIS, MM). Electronic applications accepted.

College of Graduate Business and Management *Degree program information:* Evening/weekend programs available. Postbaccalaureate distance learning degree programs offered (no on-campus study). Offers accounting (MBA); business administration (MBA); global management (MBA); human resources management (MBA, MM); management (MM); marketing (MBA); public administration (MM). Electronic applications accepted.

College of Information Systems and Technology *Degree program information:* Evening/weekend programs available. Offers information systems (MIS); technology management (MBA). Electronic applications accepted.

UNIVERSITY OF PHOENIX–LITTLE ROCK CAMPUS, Little Rock, AR 72211-3500

General Information Proprietary, coed, comprehensive institution. *Graduate housing:* On-campus housing not available.

GRADUATE UNITS

John Sperling School of Business *Degree program information:* Evening/weekend programs available. Offers business (MBA, MM). Electronic applications accepted.

College of Graduate Business and Management *Degree program information:* Evening/weekend programs available. Offers business and management (MBA, MM). Electronic applications accepted.

UNIVERSITY OF PHOENIX–LOUISIANA CAMPUS, Metairie, LA 70001-2082

General Information Proprietary, coed, comprehensive institution. *Graduate housing:* On-campus housing not available.

GRADUATE UNITS

The Artemis School *Degree program information:* Evening/weekend programs available. Postbaccalaureate distance learning degree programs offered. Electronic applications accepted.

College of Education Postbaccalaureate distance learning degree programs offered. Offers curriculum and instruction (MA Ed); early childhood education (MA Ed).

College of Health and Human Services *Degree program information:* Evening/weekend programs available. Postbaccalaureate distance learning degree programs offered (no on-campus study). Offers administration of justice and security (MS); health administration (MHA); health care management (MBA); nursing (MSN); psychology (MS). Electronic applications accepted.

John Sperling School of Business *Degree program information:* Evening/weekend programs available. Offers business (MBA, MIS, MM). Electronic applications accepted.

College of Graduate Business and Management *Degree program information:* Evening/weekend programs available. Offers accounting (MBA); business administration (MBA); global management (MBA); human resources management (MBA, MM); management (MM); marketing (MBA); public administration (MBA). Electronic applications accepted.

College of Information Systems and Technology *Degree program information:* Evening/weekend programs available. Offers information systems/management (MIS); technology management (MBA). Electronic applications accepted.

UNIVERSITY OF PHOENIX–LOUISVILLE CAMPUS, Louisville, KY 40223-3839

General Information Proprietary, comprehensive institution.

GRADUATE UNITS

College of Graduate Business and Management Postbaccalaureate distance learning degree programs offered. Offers business administration (MBA); e-business (MBA); management (MM).

College of Health and Human Services Postbaccalaureate distance learning degree programs offered. Offers health care management (MBA).

College of Information Systems and Technology Postbaccalaureate distance learning degree programs offered. Offers technology management (MBA).

UNIVERSITY OF PHOENIX–MADISON CAMPUS, Madison, WI 53718-2416

General Information Proprietary, comprehensive institution.

GRADUATE UNITS

College of Graduate Business and Management Offers accounting (MBA); business and management (MBA); e-business (MBA); global management (MBA); human resources management (MBA, MM); management (MM); marketing (MBA); public administration (MBA).

College of Health and Human Services Offers health care management (MBA).

College of Information Systems and Technology Offers information systems (MIS); management (MIS); technology management (MBA).

UNIVERSITY OF PHOENIX–MARYLAND CAMPUS, Columbia, MD 21045-5424

General Information Proprietary, coed, comprehensive institution. *Graduate housing:* On-campus housing not available.

GRADUATE UNITS

The Artemis School Electronic applications accepted.

College of Health and Human Services *Degree program information:* Evening/weekend programs available. Offers administration of justice and security (MS); health administration (MHA); health care education (MSN); health care management (MBA); nursing (MSN); psychology (MS). Electronic applications accepted.

John Sperling School of Business *Degree program information:* Evening/weekend programs available. Offers business (MBA, MIS, MM). Electronic applications accepted.

College of Graduate Business and Management *Degree program information:* Evening/weekend programs available. Offers accounting (MBA); business administration (MBA); e-business (MBA); global management (MBA); human resources management (MBA, MM); management (MM); marketing (MBA); public administration (MBA, MM). Electronic applications accepted.

College of Information Systems and Technology *Degree program information:* Evening/weekend programs available. Offers information systems (MIS); technology management (MBA). Electronic applications accepted.

UNIVERSITY OF PHOENIX–MEMPHIS CAMPUS, Cordova, TN 38018

General Information Proprietary, comprehensive institution.

GRADUATE UNITS

College of Education Offers administration and supervision (MA Ed); curriculum and instruction (MA Ed); elementary teacher education (MA Ed); secondary teacher education (MA Ed).

College of Graduate Business and Management Offers acounting (MBA); business and management (MBA); e-business (MBA); global management (MBA); human resources management (MBA, MM); management (MM); marketing (MBA); public administration (MBA, MM).

College of Health and Human Services Offers health administration (MHA); health care management (MBA).

College of Information Systems and Technology Offers information systems (MIS); technology management (MBA).

College of Social and Behavioral Science Offers administration of justice and security (MS).

UNIVERSITY OF PHOENIX–METRO DETROIT CAMPUS, Troy, MI 48098-2623

General Information Proprietary, coed, comprehensive institution. *Graduate housing:* On-campus housing not available.

GRADUATE UNITS

The Artemis School *Degree program information:* Evening/weekend programs available. Electronic applications accepted.

College of Education *Degree program information:* Evening/weekend programs available. Offers administration and supervision (MA Ed); adult education and training (MA Ed); curriculum and instruction (MA Ed); special education (MA Ed); teacher education elementary (MA Ed). Electronic applications accepted.

College of Health and Human Services *Degree program information:* Evening/weekend programs available. Offers administration of justice and security (MS); health administration (MHA); health care education (MSN); health care management (MBA); nursing (MSN). Electronic applications accepted.

John Sperling School of Business *Degree program information:* Evening/weekend programs available. Offers business (MBA, MIS, MM, MS). Electronic applications accepted.

College of Graduate Business and Management *Degree program information:* Evening/weekend programs available. Offers accountancy (MS); accounting (MBA); business administration (MBA); global management (MBA); human resources management (MBA, MM); management (MM); marketing (MBA). Electronic applications accepted.

College of Information Systems and Technology *Degree program information:* Evening/weekend programs available. Offers management (MIS); technology management (MBA). Electronic applications accepted.

UNIVERSITY OF PHOENIX–MINNEAPOLIS/ST. LOUIS PARK CAMPUS, St. Louis Park, MN 55426

General Information Proprietary, comprehensive institution.

GRADUATE UNITS

College of Graduate Business and Management Offers accounting (MBA); business administration (MBA); global management (MBA); human resources management (MBA); management (MM); marketing (MBA); public administration (MBA).

College of Health and Human Services Offers community counseling (MSC); family nurse practitioner (MSN); health care education (MSN); health care managerment (MBA); nursing (MSN).

College of Information Systems and Technology Offers technology management (MBA).

UNIVERSITY OF PHOENIX–NASHVILLE CAMPUS, Nashville, TN 37214-5048

General Information Proprietary, coed, comprehensive institution. *Graduate housing:* On-campus housing not available.

GRADUATE UNITS

The Artemis School *Degree program information:* Evening/weekend programs available. Electronic applications accepted.

College of Education *Degree program information:* Evening/weekend programs available. Offers administration and supervision (MA Ed); curriculum and instruction (MA Ed); elementary teacher education (MA Ed); secondary teacher education (MA Ed). Electronic applications accepted.

College of Health and Human Services *Degree program information:* Evening/weekend programs available. Offers health administration (MHA); health care management (MBA). Electronic applications accepted.

John Sperling School of Business *Degree program information:* Evening/weekend programs available. Offers business (MBA, MM). Electronic applications accepted.

College of Graduate Business and Management *Degree program information:* Evening/weekend programs available. Offers business administration (MBA); human resources management (MBA); management (MM). Electronic applications accepted.

College of Information Systems and Technology *Degree program information:* Evening/weekend programs available. Offers technology management (MBA). Electronic applications accepted.

UNIVERSITY OF PHOENIX–NEW MEXICO CAMPUS, Albuquerque, NM 87109-4645

General Information Proprietary, coed, comprehensive institution. *Graduate housing:* On-campus housing not available.

GRADUATE UNITS

The Artemis School *Degree program information:* Evening/weekend programs available. Electronic applications accepted.

College of Education *Degree program information:* Evening/weekend programs available. Offers administration and supervision (MAEd); curriculum and instruction (MAEd); elementary teacher education (MAEd); school counseling (MSC); secondary teacher education (MAEd). Electronic applications accepted.

College of Health and Human Services *Degree program information:* Evening/weekend programs available. Offers administration of justice and security (MS); health administration (MHA); health care education (MSN); health care management (MBA); marriage and family therapy (MSC); nursing (MSN); psychology (MS). Electronic applications accepted.

John Sperling School of Business *Degree program information:* Evening/weekend programs available. Offers business (MBA, MIS, MM, MS). Electronic applications accepted.

College of Graduate Business and Management *Degree program information:* Evening/weekend programs available. Offers accounting (MBA); business administration (MBA);

global management (MBA); human resource management (MBA); human resources managemetn (MM); management (MM); marketing (MBA). Electronic applications accepted.

College of Information Systems and Technology *Degree program information:* Evening/weekend programs available. Offers e-business (MBA); information systems (MS); technology management (MBA). Electronic applications accepted.

UNIVERSITY OF PHOENIX–NORTHERN NEVADA CAMPUS, Reno, NV 89511

General Information Proprietary, coed, comprehensive institution.

GRADUATE UNITS

College of Education Offers administration and supervision (MA Ed); curriculum and instruction (MA Ed); elementary teacher education (MA Ed); secondary teacher education (MA Ed).

College of Graduate Business and Management Offers accounting (MBA); business administration (MBA); global management (MBA); human resources management (MBA, MM); management (MM); marketing (MBA); public administration (MBA, MM).

College of Health and Human Services Offers health administration (MHA); health care education (MSN); health care management (MBA); nursing (MSN).

College of Information Systems and Technology Offers information systems (MIS); technology management (MBA).

College of Social and Behavioral Science Offers administration of justice and security (MS); marriage, family and child therapy (MSC); psychology (MS); school counseling (MSC).

UNIVERSITY OF PHOENIX–NORTHERN VIRGINIA CAMPUS, Reston, VA 20190

General Information Proprietary, coed, comprehensive institution.

GRADUATE UNITS

College of Education Offers administration and supervision (MA Ed).

College of Graduate Business and Management Offers accounting (MBA); business administration (MBA); e-business (MBA); global management (MBA); human resources management (MBA, MM); management (MM); marketing (MBA); public administration (MBA).

College of Health and Human Services Offers health administration (MHA); health care management (MBA); nursing (MSN).

College of Information Systems and Technology Offers information systems and technology (MIS); management (MIS); technology management (MBA).

College of Social and Behavioral Science Offers administration of justice and security (MS).

UNIVERSITY OF PHOENIX–NORTH FLORIDA CAMPUS, Jacksonville, FL 32216-0959

General Information Proprietary, coed, comprehensive institution. *Graduate housing:* On-campus housing not available.

GRADUATE UNITS

The Artemis School *Degree program information:* Evening/weekend programs available. Electronic applications accepted.

College of Education *Degree program information:* Evening/weekend programs available. Offers administration and supervision (MA Ed); curriculum and instruction (MA Ed); early childhood education (MA Ed); elementary teacher education (MA Ed); secondary teacher education (MA Ed). Electronic applications accepted.

College of Health and Human Services *Degree program information:* Evening/weekend programs available. Offers health administration (MHA); health care education (MSN); health care management (MBA); nursing (MSN). Electronic applications accepted.

John Sperling School of Business *Degree program information:* Evening/weekend programs available. Offers business (MBA, MIS, MM). Electronic applications accepted.

College of Graduate Business and Management *Degree program information:* Evening/weekend programs available. Offers accounting (MBA); business administration (MBA); global management (MBA); human resources management (MBA, MM); management (MM); marketing (MBA); public administration (MBA, MM). Electronic applications accepted.

College of Information Systems and Technology *Degree program information:* Evening/weekend programs available. Offers information systems (MIS); management (MIS). Electronic applications accepted.

UNIVERSITY OF PHOENIX–NORTHWEST ARKANSAS CAMPUS, Rogers, AR 72756-9615

General Information Proprietary, comprehensive institution.

GRADUATE UNITS

College of Graduate Business and Management Offers accounting (MBA); business and management (MBA); global management (MBA); human resources management (MBA, MM); management (MM); marketing (MBA); public administration (MBA, MM).

College of Health and Human Services Offers health administration (MHA); health care education (MSN); health care management (MBA); nursing (MSN).

College of Information Systems and Technology Offers information systems (MIS); technology management (MBA).

College of Social and Behavioral Science Offers administration of justice and security (MS).

UNIVERSITY OF PHOENIX–OKLAHOMA CITY CAMPUS, Oklahoma City, OK 73116-8244

General Information Proprietary, coed, comprehensive institution. *Graduate housing:* On-campus housing not available.

GRADUATE UNITS

College of Health and Human Services Offers administration of justice and security (MS); health care management (MBA); nursing (MSN); psychology (MS).

John Sperling School of Business *Degree program information:* Evening/weekend programs available. Offers business (MBA). Electronic applications accepted.

College of Graduate Business and Management *Degree program information:* Evening/weekend programs available. Offers accounting (MBA); business administration (MBA); global management (MBA); human resource management (MBA); management (MM); marketing (MBA). Electronic applications accepted.

College of Information Systems and Technology *Degree program information:* Evening/weekend programs available. Offers e-business (MBA); technology management (MBA). Electronic applications accepted.

UNIVERSITY OF PHOENIX–OMAHA CAMPUS, Omaha, NE 68154-5240

General Information Proprietary, comprehensive institution.

GRADUATE UNITS

College of Education Offers administration and supervision (MA Ed); curriculum and instruction (MA Ed); elementary teacher education (MA Ed); secondary teacher education (MA Ed); special education (MA Ed).

College of Graduate Business and Management Offers accounting (MBA); business and management (MBA); global management (MBA); human resources management (MBA, MM); management (MM); marketing (MBA); public administration (MM); public adminstration (MBA).

College of Health and Human Services Offers health administration (MHA); health care management (MBA).

College of Information Systems and Technology Offers information systems (MIS); technology management (MBA).

College of Social and Behavioral Science Offers administration of justice and security (MS).

UNIVERSITY OF PHOENIX–OREGON CAMPUS, Tigard, OR 97223

General Information Proprietary, coed, comprehensive institution. *Graduate housing:* On-campus housing not available.

GRADUATE UNITS

The Artemis School *Degree program information:* Evening/weekend programs available. Electronic applications accepted.

College of Education *Degree program information:* Evening/weekend programs available. Offers curriculum and instruction (MA Ed); early childhood education (MA Ed); elementary education (MA Ed); secondary education (MA Ed). Electronic applications accepted.

College of Health and Human Services *Degree program information:* Evening/weekend programs available. Offers administration of justice and security (MS); health administration (MHA); health care management (MBA); nursing (MSN); psychology (MS). Electronic applications accepted.

The John Sperling School of Business *Degree program information:* Evening/weekend programs available. Offers business (MBA, MIS, MM). Electronic applications accepted.

College of Graduate Business and Management *Degree program information:* Evening/weekend programs available. Offers accounting (MBA); business administration (MBA); global management (MBA); human resource management (MM); human resources management (MBA); management (MM); marketing (MBA); public administration (MM). Electronic applications accepted.

College of Information Systems and Technology *Degree program information:* Evening/weekend programs available. Offers information systems (MIS); technology management (MBA). Electronic applications accepted.

UNIVERSITY OF PHOENIX–PHILADELPHIA CAMPUS, Wayne, PA 19087-2121

General Information Proprietary, coed, comprehensive institution. *Graduate housing:* On-campus housing not available.

GRADUATE UNITS

The Artemis School *Degree program information:* Evening/weekend programs available. Electronic applications accepted.

College of Health and Human Services *Degree program information:* Evening/weekend programs available. Offers administration of justice and security (MS); health administration (MHA); health care education (MSN); health care management (MBA); nursing (MSN); psychology (MS). Electronic applications accepted.

The John Sperling School of Business *Degree program information:* Evening/weekend programs available. Offers business (MBA, MIS, MM). Electronic applications accepted.

College of Graduate Business and Management *Degree program information:* Evening/weekend programs available. Offers accounting (MBA); business administration (MBA); global management (MBA); human resources management (MBA, MM); management (MM); marketing (MBA); public administration (MM). Electronic applications accepted.

College of Information Systems and Technology *Degree program information:* Evening/weekend programs available. Offers information systems (MIS); technology management (MBA). Electronic applications accepted.

UNIVERSITY OF PHOENIX–PHOENIX CAMPUS, Phoenix, AZ 85040-1958

General Information Proprietary, coed, comprehensive institution. CGS member. *Graduate housing:* On-campus housing not available.

GRADUATE UNITS

The Artemis School *Degree program information:* Evening/weekend programs available. Electronic applications accepted.

College of Education *Degree program information:* Evening/weekend programs available. Offers administration and supervision (MA Ed); adult education and training (MA Ed); curriculum and instruction (MA Ed); early childhood education (MA Ed); elementary teacher education (MA Ed); secondary teacher education (MA Ed); special education (MA Ed). Electronic applications accepted.

College of Health and Human Services *Degree program information:* Evening/weekend programs available. Offers community counseling (MSC); education (MHA); family nurse practitioner (MSN); gerontology (MHA); health administration (MHA); health care education (MSN); health care management (MBA); informatics (MHA); marriage, family, and child therapy (MSC); nurse practitioner (Certificate); nursing (MSN); nursing health care education (Certificate); psychology (MS). Electronic applications accepted.

The John Sperling School of Business *Degree program information:* Evening/weekend programs available. Offers business (MBA, MIS, MM, MS). Electronic applications accepted.

College of Graduate Business and Management *Degree program information:* Evening/weekend programs available. Offers accountancy (MS); accounting (MBA); business administration (MBA); global management (MBA); human resources management (MBA, MM); management (MM); marketing (MBA). Electronic applications accepted.

College of Information Systems and Technology *Degree program information:* Evening/weekend programs available. Offers management (MIS); technology management (MBA). Electronic applications accepted.

UNIVERSITY OF PHOENIX–PITTSBURGH CAMPUS, Pittsburgh, PA 15276

General Information Proprietary, coed, comprehensive institution. *Graduate housing:* On-campus housing not available.

GRADUATE UNITS

The Artemis School *Degree program information:* Evening/weekend programs available. Electronic applications accepted.

College of Health and Human Services *Degree program information:* Evening/weekend programs available. Offers administration of justice and security (MS); health administration (MHA); health care education (MSN); health care management (MBA); nursing (MSN); psychology (MS). Electronic applications accepted.

John Sperling School of Business *Degree program information:* Evening/weekend programs available. Offers business (MBA, MIS, MM). Electronic applications accepted.

College of Graduate Business and Management *Degree program information:* Evening/weekend programs available. Offers accounting (MBA); business administration (MBA); global management (MBA); human resources management (MBA, MM); management (MM); marketing (MBA); public administration (MBA, MM). Electronic applications accepted.

College of Information Systems and Technology *Degree program information:* Evening/weekend programs available. Offers e-business (MBA); information systems (MIS); technology management (MBA). Electronic applications accepted.

UNIVERSITY OF PHOENIX–PUERTO RICO CAMPUS, Guaynabo, PR 00968

General Information Proprietary, coed, comprehensive institution. *Graduate housing:* On-campus housing not available.

GRADUATE UNITS

The Artemis School *Degree program information:* Evening/weekend programs available. Electronic applications accepted.

College of Education *Degree program information:* Evening/weekend programs available. Offers administration and supervision (MA Ed); early childhood education (MA Ed); school counselor (MSC). Electronic applications accepted.

College of Health and Human Services *Degree program information:* Evening/weekend programs available. Offers marriage and family counseling (MSC); mental health counseling (MSC). Electronic applications accepted.

John Sperling School of Business *Degree program information:* Evening/weekend programs available. Offers business (MBA). Electronic applications accepted.

College of Graduate Business and Management *Degree program information:* Evening/weekend programs available. Offers accounting (MBA); business administration (MBA); global management (MBA); human resource management (MBA); marketing (MBA). Electronic applications accepted.

College of Information Systems and Technology *Degree program information:* Evening/weekend programs available. Offers technology management (MBA). Electronic applications accepted.

UNIVERSITY OF PHOENIX–RALEIGH CAMPUS, Raleigh, NC 27606

General Information Proprietary, coed, comprehensive institution.

GRADUATE UNITS

College of Graduate Business and Management Offers accounting (MBA); business administration (MBA); e-business (MBA); global management (MBA); human resources management (MBA); marketing (MBA).

College of Health and Human Services Offers health care management (MBA).

College of Information Systems and Technology Offers information systems and technology (MIS); management (MIS); technology management (MBA).

UNIVERSITY OF PHOENIX–RENTON LEARNING CENTER, Renton, WA 98005

General Information Proprietary, comprehensive institution. *Graduate housing:* On-campus housing not available.

GRADUATE UNITS

College of Graduate Business and Management *Degree program information:* Evening/weekend programs available. Offers accounting (MBA); business and management (MBA, MM); global management (MBA); human resources management (MBA, MM); marketing (MBA); public administration (MBA, MM). Electronic applications accepted.

College of Health and Human Services *Degree program information:* Evening/weekend programs available. Offers health administration (MHA); health care education (MSN); health care management (MBA); nursing (MSN). Electronic applications accepted.

College of Information Systems and Technology *Degree program information:* Evening/weekend programs available. Offers information systems (MIS); technology management (MBA). Electronic applications accepted.

College of Social and Behavioral Science Offers administration of justice and security (MS).

UNIVERSITY OF PHOENIX–RICHMOND CAMPUS, Richmond, VA 23230

General Information Proprietary, coed, comprehensive institution. *Graduate housing:* On-campus housing not available.

GRADUATE UNITS

The Artemis School *Degree program information:* Evening/weekend programs available. Electronic applications accepted.

College of Education Offers administration and supervision (MA Ed); curriculum and instruction (MA Ed).

College of Health and Human Services *Degree program information:* Evening/weekend programs available. Offers administration of justice and security (MS); health administration (MHA); health care education (MSN); health care management (MBA); nursing (MSN); psychology (MS). Electronic applications accepted.

John Sperling School of Business *Degree program information:* Evening/weekend programs available. Offers business (MBA, MIS, MM). Electronic applications accepted.

College of Graduate Business and Management *Degree program information:* Evening/weekend programs available. Offers accounting (MBA); business administration (MBA); global management (MBA); human resources management (MBA, MM); management (MM); marketing (MBA); public administration (MBA, MM). Electronic applications accepted.

College of Information Systems and Technology *Degree program information:* Evening/weekend programs available. Offers information systems (MIS); technology management (MBA). Electronic applications accepted.

UNIVERSITY OF PHOENIX–SACRAMENTO VALLEY CAMPUS, Sacramento, CA 95833-3632

General Information Proprietary, coed, comprehensive institution. *Graduate housing:* On-campus housing not available.

GRADUATE UNITS

The Artemis School *Degree program information:* Evening/weekend programs available. Electronic applications accepted.

College of Education *Degree program information:* Evening/weekend programs available. Offers adult education (MA Ed); curriculum instruction (MA Ed); elementary teacher education (MA Ed); secondary teacher education (MA Ed); teacher education (Certificate). Electronic applications accepted.

College of Health and Human Services *Degree program information:* Evening/weekend programs available. Offers administration of justice and security (MS); community counseling (MSC); family nurse practitioner (MSN); health administration (MHA); health care education (MSN); health care management (MBA); marriage, family and child counseling (MSC); nursing (MSN); psychology (MS). Electronic applications accepted.

John Sperling School of Business *Degree program information:* Evening/weekend programs available. Offers business (MBA, MIS, MM). Electronic applications accepted.

College of Graduate Business and Management *Degree program information:* Evening/weekend programs available. Offers accounting (MBA); business administration (MBA); global management (MBA); human resources management (MBA, MM); management (MM); marketing (MBA); public administration (MBA, MM). Electronic applications accepted.

College of Information Systems and Technology *Degree program information:* Evening/weekend programs available. Offers management (MIS); technology management (MBA). Electronic applications accepted.

UNIVERSITY OF PHOENIX–ST. LOUIS CAMPUS, St. Louis, MO 63043-4828

General Information Proprietary, coed, comprehensive institution. *Graduate housing:* On-campus housing not available.

GRADUATE UNITS

The Artemis School *Degree program information:* Evening/weekend programs available. Electronic applications accepted.

College of Health and Human Services *Degree program information:* Evening/weekend programs available. Offers administration of justice and security (MS); health administration (MHA); health care management (MBA); nursing (MSN). Electronic applications accepted.

John Sperling School of Business *Degree program information:* Evening/weekend programs available. Offers business (MBA, MIS, MM). Electronic applications accepted.

College of Graduate Business and Management *Degree program information:* Evening/weekend programs available. Offers accounting (MBA); business administration (MBA); global management (MBA); human resources management (MBA, MM); management (MM); marketing (MBA); public administration (MM). Electronic applications accepted.

College of Information Systems and Technology *Degree program information:* Evening/weekend programs available. Offers information systems (MIS); technology management (MBA). Electronic applications accepted.

UNIVERSITY OF PHOENIX–SAN ANTONIO CAMPUS, San Antonio, TX 78230

General Information Proprietary, comprehensive institution.

GRADUATE UNITS

College of Education Offers curriculum and instruction (MA Ed).

College of Graduate Business and Management Offers accounting (MBA); business administration (MBA); e-business (MBA); global management (MBA); human resources management (MBA, MM); management (MM); marketing (MBA); public administration (MBA, MM).

College of Health and Human Services Offers health administration (MHA); health care management (MBA).

College of Information Systems and Technology Offers information systems (MIS); technology management (MBA).

College of Social and Behavioral Science Offers administration of justice and security (MS); psychology (MS).

UNIVERSITY OF PHOENIX–SAN DIEGO CAMPUS, San Diego, CA 92123

General Information Proprietary, coed, comprehensive institution. *Graduate housing:* On-campus housing not available.

GRADUATE UNITS

The Artemis School *Degree program information:* Evening/weekend programs available. Electronic applications accepted.

College of Education *Degree program information:* Evening/weekend programs available. Offers curriculum and instruction (MA Ed); elementary teacher education (MA Ed); secondary teacher education (MA Ed). Electronic applications accepted.

College of Health and Human Services *Degree program information:* Evening/weekend programs available. Offers administration of justice and security (MS); health care education (MSN); health care management (MBA); marriage, family and child counseling (MSC); marriage, family and child therapy (MSC); nursing (MSN). Electronic applications accepted.

John Sperling School of Business *Degree program information:* Evening/weekend programs available. Offers business (MBA, MIS, MM). Electronic applications accepted.

College of Graduate Business and Management *Degree program information:* Evening/weekend programs available. Offers accounting (MBA); business administration (MBA); global management (MBA); human resources management (MBA, MM); management (MM); marketing (MBA); public administration (MBA). Electronic applications accepted.

College of Information Systems and Technology *Degree program information:* Evening/weekend programs available. Offers management (MIS); technology management (MBA). Electronic applications accepted.

UNIVERSITY OF PHOENIX–SAVANNAH CAMPUS, Savannah, GA 31405-7400

General Information Proprietary, comprehensive institution.

GRADUATE UNITS

College of Graduate Business and Management Offers accounting (MBA); business administration (MBA); global management (MBA); human resources management (MBA, MM); management (MM); marketing (MBA); public administration (MBA, MM).

College of Health and Human Services Offers health administration (MHA); health care management (MBA); nursing (MSN); nursing/health care education (MSN).

College of Information Systems and Technology Offers information systems and technology (MIS); technology management (MBA).

College of Social and Behavioral Science Offers administration of justice and security (MS).

UNIVERSITY OF PHOENIX–SOUTHERN ARIZONA CAMPUS, Tucson, AZ 85711

General Information Proprietary, coed, comprehensive institution. *Graduate housing:* On-campus housing not available.

GRADUATE UNITS

The Artemis School *Degree program information:* Evening/weekend programs available. Electronic applications accepted.

College of Education *Degree program information:* Evening/weekend programs available. Offers administration and supervision (MA Ed); adult education and training (MA Ed); curriculum instruction (MA Ed); educational counseling (MA Ed); elementary teacher education (MA Ed); school counseling (MSC); secondary teacher education (MA Ed); special education (MA Ed, Certificate). Electronic applications accepted.

College of Health and Human Services *Degree program information:* Evening/weekend programs available. Offers administration of justice and security (MS); family nurse practitioner (MSN, Certificate); health administration (MHA); health care management (MBA); marriage, family and child therapy (MSC); nursing (MSN); psychology (MS). Electronic applications accepted.

John Sperling School of Business *Degree program information:* Evening/weekend programs available. Offers business (MBA, MIS, MM, MS). Electronic applications accepted.

College of Graduate Business and Management *Degree program information:* Evening/weekend programs available. Offers accountancy (MS); accounting (MBA); business administration (MBA); global management (MBA); human resources management (MBA); management (MM); marketing (MBA). Electronic applications accepted.

College of Information Systems and Technology *Degree program information:* Evening/weekend programs available. Offers information systems (MIS); technology management (MBA). Electronic applications accepted.

UNIVERSITY OF PHOENIX–SOUTHERN CALIFORNIA CAMPUS, Costa Mesa, CA 92626

General Information Proprietary, coed, comprehensive institution. *Graduate housing:* On-campus housing not available.

GRADUATE UNITS

The Artemis School *Degree program information:* Evening/weekend programs available. Electronic applications accepted.

College of Education *Degree program information:* Evening/weekend programs available. Offers adult education and training (MA Ed); curriculum and instruction (MA Ed); elementary teacher education (MA Ed); secondary teacher education (MA Ed). Electronic applications accepted.

College of Health and Human Services *Degree program information:* Evening/weekend programs available. Offers administration of justice and security (MS); family nurse practitioner (MSN, Certificate); health administration (MHA); health care education (MSN); health care management (MBA); marriage, family and child therapy (MSC); nursing (MSN); psychology (MS). Electronic applications accepted.

John Sperling School of Business *Degree program information:* Evening/weekend programs available. Offers business (MBA, MIS, MM). Electronic applications accepted.

College of Graduate Business and Management *Degree program information:* Evening/weekend programs available. Offers accounting (MBA); business administration (MBA); global managment (MBA); human resources management (MBA, MM); management (MM); marketing (MBA); public administration (MBA, MM). Electronic applications accepted.

College of Information Systems and Technology *Degree program information:* Evening/weekend programs available. Offers information systems (MIS); technology management (MBA). Electronic applications accepted.

UNIVERSITY OF PHOENIX–SOUTHERN COLORADO CAMPUS, Colorado Springs, CO 80919-2335

General Information Proprietary, coed, comprehensive institution. *Graduate housing:* On-campus housing not available.

GRADUATE UNITS

The Artemis School *Degree program information:* Evening/weekend programs available. Electronic applications accepted.

College of Education *Degree program information:* Evening/weekend programs available. Offers administration and supervision (MA Ed); curriculum and instruction (MA Ed); elemenary teacher education (MA Ed); principal licensure certification (Certificate); school counseling (MSC); secondary teacher education (MA Ed). Electronic applications accepted.

College of Health and Human Services *Degree program information:* Evening/weekend programs available. Offers administration of justice and security (MS); community counseling (MSC); education (MHA); gerontology (MHA); health administration (MHA); health care management (MBA); marriage, family and child therapy (MSC); nursing (MSN); psychology (MS). Electronic applications accepted.

John Sperling School of Business *Degree program information:* Evening/weekend programs available. Offers business (MBA, MM). Electronic applications accepted.

College of Graduate Business and Management *Degree program information:* Evening/weekend programs available. Offers accounting (MBA); business administration (MBA); global management (MBA); human resources management (MBA, MM); management (MM); marketing (MBA); public administration (MM). Electronic applications accepted.

College of Information Systems and Technology *Degree program information:* Evening/weekend programs available. Offers technology management (MBA). Electronic applications accepted.

UNIVERSITY OF PHOENIX–SOUTH FLORIDA CAMPUS, Fort Lauderdale, FL 33309

General Information Proprietary, coed, comprehensive institution. *Graduate housing:* On-campus housing not available.

GRADUATE UNITS

The Artemis School *Degree program information:* Evening/weekend programs available. Electronic applications accepted.

College of Education *Degree program information:* Evening/weekend programs available. Offers administration and supervision (MA Ed); curriculum and instruction (MA Ed); early childhood education (MA Ed); elementary teacher education (MA Ed); secondary teacher education (MA Ed). Electronic applications accepted.

College of Health and Human Services *Degree program information:* Evening/weekend programs available. Offers health administration (MHA); health care education (MSN); health care management (MBA); nursing (MSN). Electronic applications accepted.

John Sperling School of Business *Degree program information:* Evening/weekend programs available. Offers business (MBA, MIS, MM). Electronic applications accepted.

College of Graduate Business and Management *Degree program information:* Evening/weekend programs available. Offers accounting (MBA); business administration (MBA); global management (MBA); human resource management (MBA); human resources management (MM); management (MM); marketing (MBA); public administration (MBA, MM). Electronic applications accepted.

College of Information Systems and Technology *Degree program information:* Evening/weekend programs available. Offers management (MIS); technology management (MBA). Electronic applications accepted.

UNIVERSITY OF PHOENIX–SPRINGFIELD CAMPUS, Springfield, MO 65804-7211

General Information Proprietary, coed, comprehensive institution.

GRADUATE UNITS

College of Education Offers administration and supervision (MA Ed); curriculum and instruction (MA Ed); English and language arts education (MA Ed).

College of Graduate Business and Management Offers accounting (MBA); business administration (MBA); global management (MBA); human resources management (MBA, MM); management (MM); marketing (MBA); public administration (MBA, MM).

College of Health and Human Services Offers health administration (MHA); health care management (MBA); nursing (MSN).

College of Information Systems and Technology Offers information systems (MIS); technology management (MBA).

College of Social and Behavioral Science Offers administration of justice and security (MS).

UNIVERSITY OF PHOENIX–TULSA CAMPUS, Tulsa, OK 74146-3801

General Information Proprietary, coed, comprehensive institution. *Graduate housing:* On-campus housing not available.

GRADUATE UNITS

College of Health and Human Services Offers administration of justice and security (MS); health care management (MBA); nursing (MSN); psychology (MS).

John Sperling School of Business *Degree program information:* Evening/weekend programs available. Offers business (MBA, MIS, MM, MS).

College of Graduate Business and Management *Degree program information:* Evening/weekend programs available. Offers accounting (MBA); business (MM); business administration (MBA); global management (MBA); human resources management (MBA); marketing (MBA).

College of Information Systems and Technology Offers information systems and technology (MIS); technology management (MBA).

UNIVERSITY OF PHOENIX–UTAH CAMPUS, Salt Lake City, UT 84123-4617

General Information Proprietary, coed, comprehensive institution. *Graduate housing:* On-campus housing not available.

GRADUATE UNITS

The Artemis School *Degree program information:* Evening/weekend programs available. Electronic applications accepted.

College of Education *Degree program information:* Evening/weekend programs available. Offers administration and supervision (MA Ed); curriculum and instruction (MA Ed); elementary teacher education (MA Ed); school counseling (MSC); secondary teacher education (MA Ed); special education (MA Ed). Electronic applications accepted.

College of Health and Human Services *Degree program information:* Evening/weekend programs available. Offers health care management (MBA); healthcare education (MSN); mental health counseling (MSC); nursing (MSN). Electronic applications accepted.

John Sperling School of Business *Degree program information:* Evening/weekend programs available. Offers business (MBA, MIS, MM). Electronic applications accepted.

College of Graduate Business and Management *Degree program information:* Evening/weekend programs available. Offers accounting (MBA); business administration (MBA); global management (MBA); human resource management (MBA, MM); management (MM); marketing (MBA); technology management (MBA). Electronic applications accepted.

College of Information Systems and Technology *Degree program information:* Evening/weekend programs available. Offers information systems and technology (MIS). Electronic applications accepted.

UNIVERSITY OF PHOENIX–VANCOUVER CAMPUS, Burnaby, BC V5C 6G9, Canada

General Information Proprietary, coed, comprehensive institution. *Graduate housing:* On-campus housing not available.

GRADUATE UNITS

The Artemis School *Degree program information:* Evening/weekend programs available. Electronic applications accepted.

College of Education *Degree program information:* Evening/weekend programs available. Offers administration and supervision (MA Ed); curriculum and instruction (MA Ed). Electronic applications accepted.

College of Health and Human Services *Degree program information:* Evening/weekend programs available. Offers health care management (MBA). Electronic applications accepted.

John Sperling School of Business *Degree program information:* Evening/weekend programs available. Offers business (MBA, MM). Electronic applications accepted.

College of Graduate Business and Management *Degree program information:* Evening/weekend programs available. Offers accounting (MBA); business administration (MBA); global management (MBA); human resources management (MBA, MM); marketing (MBA). Electronic applications accepted.

College of Information Systems and Technology *Degree program information:* Evening/weekend programs available. Offers technology management (MBA). Electronic applications accepted.

UNIVERSITY OF PHOENIX–WEST FLORIDA CAMPUS, Temple Terrace, FL 33637

General Information Proprietary, coed, comprehensive institution. *Graduate housing:* On-campus housing not available.

GRADUATE UNITS

The Artemis School *Degree program information:* Evening/weekend programs available. Electronic applications accepted.

College of Education *Degree program information:* Evening/weekend programs available. Offers administration and supervision (MA Ed); curriculum and instruction (MA Ed); curriculum and technology (MA Ed); early childhood education (MA Ed); elementary teacher education (MA Ed); secondary teacher education (MA Ed).

College of Health and Human Services *Degree program information:* Evening/weekend programs available. Postbaccalaureate distance learning degree programs offered. Offers health administration (MHA); health care education (MSN); health care management (MBA); nursing (MSN). Electronic applications accepted.

The John Sperling School of Business *Degree program information:* Evening/weekend programs available. Offers business (MBA, MIS, MM). Electronic applications accepted.

College of Graduate Business and Management *Degree program information:* Evening/weekend programs available. Offers accounting (MBA); business administration (MBA); global management (MBA); human resources management (MBA, MM); management (MM); marketing (MBA); public administration (MBA, MM). Electronic applications accepted.

College of Information Systems and Technology *Degree program information:* Evening/weekend programs available. Offers information systems (MIS); technology management (MBA). Electronic applications accepted.

UNIVERSITY OF PHOENIX–WEST MICHIGAN CAMPUS, Walker, MI 49544

General Information Proprietary, coed, comprehensive institution. *Graduate housing:* On-campus housing not available.

GRADUATE UNITS

The Artemis School *Degree program information:* Evening/weekend programs available. Electronic applications accepted.

College of Education *Degree program information:* Evening/weekend programs available. Offers administration and supervision (MA Ed); curriculum and instruction (MA Ed). Electronic applications accepted.

College of Health and Human Services *Degree program information:* Evening/weekend programs available. Offers health care management (MBA); nursing (MSN). Electronic applications accepted.

The John Sperling School of Business *Degree program information:* Evening/weekend programs available. Offers business (MBA). Electronic applications accepted.

College of Graduate Business and Management *Degree program information:* Evening/weekend programs available. Offers accounting (MBA); business administration (MBA); global management (MBA); human resource management (MBA). Electronic applications accepted.

College of Information Systems and Technology *Degree program information:* Evening/weekend programs available. Offers e-business (MBA); technology management (MBA). Electronic applications accepted.

UNIVERSITY OF PHOENIX–WICHITA CAMPUS, Wichita, KS 67226-4011

General Information Proprietary, coed, comprehensive institution. *Graduate housing:* On-campus housing not available.

University of Phoenix–Wichita Campus (continued)

GRADUATE UNITS

John Sperling School of Business *Degree program information:* Evening/weekend programs available. Offers business and management (MBA). Electronic applications accepted.

College of Graduate Business and Management *Degree program information:* Evening/weekend programs available. Offers business and management (MBA). Electronic applications accepted.

UNIVERSITY OF PHOENIX–WISCONSIN CAMPUS, Brookfield, WI 53045-6608

General Information Proprietary, coed, comprehensive institution. *Graduate housing:* On-campus housing not available.

GRADUATE UNITS

The Artemis School *Degree program information:* Evening/weekend programs available. Electronic applications accepted.

College of Health and Human Services *Degree program information:* Evening/weekend programs available. Offers healthcare management (MBA). Electronic applications accepted.

John Sperling School of Business *Degree program information:* Evening/weekend programs available. Offers business (MBA, MIS, MM). Electronic applications accepted.

College of Graduate Business and Management *Degree program information:* Evening/weekend programs available. Offers accounting (MBA); administration (MBA); global management (MBA); human resources management (MBA); management (MM); marketing (MBA); public administration (MBA). Electronic applications accepted.

College of Information Systems and Technology *Degree program information:* Evening/weekend programs available. Offers information systems (MIS); technology management (MBA). Electronic applications accepted.

UNIVERSITY OF PITTSBURGH, Pittsburgh, PA 15260

General Information State-related, coed, university. CGS member. *Enrollment:* 27,562 graduate, professional, and undergraduate students; 7,174 full-time matriculated graduate/professional students (3,839 women), 2,961 part-time matriculated graduate/professional students (1,813 women). *Enrollment by degree level:* 1,841 first professional, 4,596 master's, 2,944 doctoral, 754 other advanced degrees. *Graduate faculty:* 3,898 full-time (1,462 women), 771 part-time/adjunct (379 women). Tuition, state resident: full-time $15,772; part-time $640 per credit. Tuition, nonresident: full-time $27,996; part-time $1147 per credit. *Required fees:* $690; $175 per term. *Student services:* Campus employment opportunities, campus safety program, career counseling, exercise/wellness program, free psychological counseling, international student services, low-cost health insurance, services for students with disabilities, writing training. *Library facilities:* Hillman Library plus 24 others. *Online resources:* library catalog, web page, access to other libraries' catalogs. *Collection:* 5.1 million titles, 48,637 serial subscriptions, 194,311 audiovisual materials. *Research affiliation:* Technology Collaboration (formerly Pittsburgh Digital Greenhouse), Innovation Works (formerly Ben Franklin Technology Center of Western Pennsylvania), Pittsburgh Life Sciences Greenhouse.

Computer facilities: Computer purchase and lease plans are available. 1,150 computers available on campus for general student use. A campuswide network can be accessed from student residence rooms and from off campus. Online class listings, online tuition payment available. *Web address:* http://www.pitt.edu/.

General Application Contact: Information Contact, 412-624-4141, E-mail: graduate@pitt.edu.

GRADUATE UNITS

Graduate School of Public and International Affairs Students: 269 full-time (144 women), 98 part-time (56 women); includes 43 minority (26 African Americans, 8 Asian Americans or Pacific Islanders, 9 Hispanic Americans), 19 international. Average age 25. 635 applicants, 72% accepted, 178 enrolled. *Faculty:* 27 full-time (7 women), 54 part-time/adjunct (18 women). Expenses: Contact institution. *Financial support:* In 2008–09, 139 students received support, including 31 fellowships (averaging $14,360 per year); career-related internships or fieldwork, scholarships/grants, tuition waivers (full and partial), and unspecified assistantships also available. Support available to part-time students. Financial award application deadline: 2/1. In 2008, 160 master's, 8 doctorates awarded. *Degree program information:* Part-time and evening/weekend programs available. Offers development planning (MPPM); development policy (PhD); foreign and security policy (PhD); international development (MPPM); international political economy (MPPM, PhD); international security studies (MPPM); management of non profit organizations (MPPM); metropolitan management and regional development (MPPM); policy analysis and evaluation (MPPM); public administration (PhD); public and international affairs (MID, MPA, MPIA, MPPM, PhD, MPA/MID); public policy (PhD). *Application deadline:* For fall admission, 2/1 for domestic students, 1/15 for international students; for spring admission, 11/1 for domestic students, 8/1 for international students. *Application fee:* $50. Electronic applications accepted. *Application Contact:* Michael T. Rizzi, Senior Graduate Enrollment Counselor, 412-648-7640, Fax: 412-648-7641, E-mail: rizzim@pitt.edu. *Dean and Professor*, Dr. John T.S. Keeler, 412-648-7636, Fax: 412-648-2605, E-mail: keeler@pitt.edu.

Division of International Development Students: 51 full-time (37 women), 4 part-time (all women); includes 7 minority (2 African Americans, 2 Asian Americans or Pacific Islanders, 3 Hispanic Americans), 4 international. Average age 25. 141 applicants, 72% accepted, 30 enrolled. *Faculty:* 27 full-time (7 women), 54 part-time/adjunct (18 women). Expenses: Contact institution. *Financial support:* In 2008–09, 32 students received support, including 5 fellowships (averaging $19,662 per year); scholarships/grants, tuition waivers (full and partial), and unspecified assistantships also available. Financial award application deadline: 2/1. In 2008, 37 master's awarded. *Degree program information:* Part-time programs available. Offers development planning and environmental sustainability (MID); human security (MID); nongovernmental organizations and civil society (MID). *Application deadline:* For fall admission, 2/1 for domestic students, 1/5 for international students; for spring admission, 11/1 for domestic students, 8/1 for international students. *Application fee:* $50. Electronic applications accepted. *Application Contact:* Elizabeth Hruby, Graduate Enrollment Counselor, 412-648-7640, Fax: 412-648-7641, E-mail: eah44@pitt.edu. *Director, International Development Divisions*, Dr. Louis Picard, 412-648-7659, Fax: 412-648-2605, E-mail: picard@pitt.edu.

Division of Public and Urban Affairs Students: 45 full-time (29 women), 23 part-time (16 women); includes 10 minority (8 African Americans, 1 Asian American or Pacific Islander, 1 Hispanic American), 2 international. Average age 25. 123 applicants, 84% accepted, 37 enrolled. *Faculty:* 27 full-time (7 women), 54 part-time/adjunct (18 women). Expenses: Contact institution. *Financial support:* In 2008–09, 18 students received support, including 2 fellowships (averaging $8,000 per year); scholarships/grants, tuition waivers (full and partial), and unspecified assistantships also available. Financial award application deadline: 2/1. In 2008, 37 master's awarded. *Degree program information:* Part-time and evening/weekend programs available. Offers policy research and analysis (MPA); public and nonprofit management (MPA, MPA/MID); urban and regional affairs (MPA). *Application deadline:* For fall admission, 2/1 for domestic students, 1/15 for international students; for spring admission, 11/1 for domestic students, 8/1 for international students. *Application fee:* $50. *Application Contact:* Denene K Hefflin, Graduate Enrollment Counselor, 412-648-7640, Fax: 412-648-7641, E-mail: dkh7@pitt.edu. *Director, Public and Urban Affairs Division*, Dr. David Y. Miller, 412-648-7606, Fax: 412-648-2605, E-mail: dymiller@pitt.edu.

International Affairs Division Students: 133 full-time (60 women), 20 part-time (7 women); includes 18 minority (10 African Americans, 4 Asian Americans or Pacific Islanders, 4 Hispanic Americans), 6 international. Average age 25. 263 applicants, 81% accepted, 85 enrolled. *Faculty:* 27 full-time (7 women), 54 part-time/adjunct (18 women). Expenses: Contact institution. *Financial support:* In 2008–09, 66 students received support, including 28 fellowships (averaging $13,166 per year); career-related internships or fieldwork, scholarships/grants, tuition waivers (full and partial), and unspecified assistantships also available. Financial award application deadline: 2/1. In 2008, 71 master's awarded. *Degree program information:* Part-time and evening/weekend programs available. Offers global political economy (MPIA); human security (MPIA); security and intelligence studies (MPIA). *Application deadline:* For fall admission, 3/1 for domestic students, 1/15 for international students; for spring admission, 11/1 for domestic students, 8/1 for international students. *Application fee:* $50. Electronic applications accepted. *Application Contact:* Michael T Rizzi, Senior Graduate Enrollment Counselor, 412-648-7640, Fax: 412-648-7641, E-mail: rizzim@pitt.edu. *Director, International Affairs and International Development Divisions*, Dr. Martin Staniland, 412-648-7656, Fax: 412-648-2605, E-mail: mstan@pitt.edu.

Graduate School of Public Health Students: 404 full-time (294 women), 197 part-time (125 women); includes 105 minority (53 African Americans, 40 Asian Americans or Pacific Islanders, 12 Hispanic Americans), 154 international. Average age 31. 1,213 applicants, 56% accepted, 189 enrolled. *Faculty:* 153 full-time (68 women), 115 part-time/adjunct (37 women). Expenses: Contact institution. *Financial support:* In 2008–09, 170 students received support, including 5 fellowships with full tuition reimbursements available (averaging $25,105 per year), 165 research assistantships with full tuition reimbursements available (averaging $21,391 per year), 13 teaching assistantships with full tuition reimbursements available (averaging $29,963 per year); career-related internships or fieldwork, scholarships/grants, traineeships, health care benefits, and unspecified assistantships also available. Support available to part-time students. In 2008, 120 master's, 34 doctorates awarded. *Degree program information:* Part-time programs available. Offers behavioral and community health sciences (MPH, Dr PH); bioscience of infectious diseases (MPH); biostatistics (MPH, MS, Dr PH, PhD); community and behavioral intervention of infectious diseases (MPH); environmental and occupational health (MPH, MS, PhD); epidemiology (MPH, MS, Dr PH, PhD); genetic counseling (MS); health policy and management (MHA, MPH); human genetics (MS, PhD); infectious diseases and microbiology (MS, Dr PH, PhD); lesbian, gay, bisexual and transgender health and wellness (Certificate); LGBT health and wellness (Certificate); minority health and health disparities (Certificate); occupational medicine (MPH); program evaluation (Certificate); public health (MHA, MPH, MS, Dr PH, PhD, Certificate); public health and aging (Certificate); public health awareness and disaster response (Certificate); public health genetics (MPH, Certificate); public health preparedness (Certificate); risk assessment (Certificate). *Application deadline:* For fall admission, 1/4 for domestic students, 4/1 priority date for international students; for winter admission, 9/1 priority date for international students; for spring admission, 2/1 priority date for international students. Applications are processed on a rolling basis. *Application fee:* $50 ($60 for international students). Electronic applications accepted. *Application Contact:* 412-624-5200, Fax: 412-624-3755, E-mail: stuaff@pitt.edu. *Dean*, Dr. Donald S. Burke, 412-624-3001, Fax: 412-624-3309, E-mail: donburke@pitt.edu.

Joint CMU-Pitt PhD Program in Computational Biology Students: 40 full-time (8 women); includes 4 minority (all Asian Americans or Pacific Islanders), 23 international. Average age 25. 129 applicants, 15% accepted, 7 enrolled. *Faculty:* 67 full-time (13 women). Expenses: Contact institution. *Financial support:* In 2008–09, 22 students received support, including 27 research assistantships with full tuition reimbursements available (averaging $24,650 per year). Support available to part-time students. Offers computational biology (PhD). *Application deadline:* For fall admission, 1/15 priority date for domestic and international students. *Application fee:* $50. Electronic applications accepted. *Application Contact:* Maureen Hernandez, Assistant Programs Coordinator, 412-648-8107, Fax: 412-648-3163, E-mail: mhdez@pitt.edu. *Director*, Dr. Ivet Bahar, 412-648-3332, Fax: 412-648-3163, E-mail: bahar@pitt.edu.

Katz Graduate School of Business Students: 423 full-time (116 women), 462 part-time (164 women); includes 56 minority (23 African Americans, 26 Asian Americans or Pacific Islanders, 7 Hispanic Americans), 252 international. Average age 27. 1,184 applicants, 40% accepted, 318 enrolled. *Faculty:* 81 full-time (19 women), 23 part-time/adjunct (7 women). Expenses: Contact institution. *Financial support:* In 2008–09, 137 students received support, including 13 fellowships with full tuition reimbursements available (averaging $18,450 per year), 30 research assistantships with full tuition reimbursements available (averaging $18,450 per year), 3 teaching assistantships with full tuition reimbursements available (averaging $23,330 per year); career-related internships or fieldwork, Federal Work-Study, scholarships/grants, health care benefits, and unspecified assistantships also available. Financial award application deadline: 1/15; financial award applicants required to submit FAFSA. In 2008, 257 master's, 14 doctorates awarded. *Degree program information:* Part-time and evening/weekend programs available. Offers accounting (MAC, PhD); business (EMBA, MAC, MBA, MS, MSIS, PhD); business administration (MBA); finance (MBA, PhD); information science (PhD); information systems (MBA, MSIS); international business (MBA); international business administration (MBA); management of information systems (MS); marketing (MBA, PhD); operations/decision sciences/artificial intelligence (PhD); organizational behavior and human resource management (MBA, PhD); strategic planning (PhD); strategy, environment and organizations (MBA). *Application deadline:* For fall admission, 3/1 for domestic students; for winter admission, 12/1 for domestic and international students; for spring admission, 1/15 for domestic and international students. Applications are processed on a rolling basis. *Application fee:* $50. Electronic applications accepted. *Application Contact:* Cliff McCormick, Director, Office of Enrollment Management, 412-648-1700, Fax: 412-648-1659, E-mail: mba@katz.pitt.edu. *Dean*, Dr. John T. Delaney, 412-648-1556, Fax: 412-648-1552, E-mail: jtdelaney@katz.pitt.edu.

School of Arts and Sciences Students: 1,710 full-time (844 women), 101 part-time (68 women); includes 221 minority (47 African Americans, 1 American Indian/Alaska Native, 105 Asian Americans or Pacific Islanders, 68 Hispanic Americans), 453 international. 4,241 applicants, 22% accepted, 360 enrolled. *Faculty:* 747 full-time (254 women), 127 part-time/adjunct (42 women). Expenses: Contact institution. *Financial support:* In 2008–09, 2,106 students received support, including 357 fellowships with full tuition reimbursements available, 1,080 research assistantships with full tuition reimbursements available, 669 teaching assistantships with full and partial tuition reimbursements available; career-related internships or fieldwork, Federal Work-Study, institutionally sponsored loans, scholarships/grants, traineeships, health care benefits, tuition waivers (full and partial), and unspecified assistantships also available. Support available to part-time students. Financial award applicants required to submit FAFSA. In 2008, 159 master's, 183 doctorates, 17 other advanced degrees awarded. *Degree program information:* Part-time programs available. Offers anthropology (MA, PhD); applied linguistics (PhD); applied mathematics (MA, MS); applied statistics (MA, MS); arts and sciences (MA, MFA, MS, PM Sc, PMS, PhD, Certificate, Doctoral Certificate, Master's Certificate); chemistry (MS, PhD); classics (MA, PhD); communication (MA, PhD); composition and theory (MA, PhD); computer science (MS, PhD); cultural and critical studies (PhD); East Asian studies (MA); ecology and evolution (PhD); economics (PhD); English (MA); ethnomusicology (MA, PhD); financial mathematics (PMS); French (MA, PhD); geographical information systems (PM Sc); geology and planetary science (MS, PhD); German studies (MA, PhD); Hispanic languages and literatures (MA, PhD); Hispanic linguistics (MA, PhD); historical musicology (MA, PhD); history (MA, PhD); history and philosophy of science (MA, PhD); history of art and architecture (MA, PhD); intelligent systems (MS, PhD); Italian (MA); linguistics (MA); mathematics (MA, MS, PhD); molecular, cellular, and developmental biology (PhD); performance pedagogy (MFA); philosophy (MA, PhD); physics (MS, PhD); political science (MA, PhD); psychology (MS, PhD); religion (PhD); religious studies (MA); Slavic languages and literatures (MA, PhD); sociolinguistics (PhD); sociology (MA, PhD); statistics (MA, MS, PhD); TESOL—teaching English to speakers of other languages (Certificate); theatre and performance studies (MA, PhD); women's studies (Doctoral Certificate, Master's Certificate); writing (MFA). *Application deadline:* Applications are processed on a rolling basis. *Application fee:* $50. Electronic applications accepted. *Application Contact:* Dave R. Carmen, Administrative Secretary, 412-624-6094, Fax: 412-624-6855, E-mail: drc41@pitt.edu. *Associate Dean, Graduate Studies and Research*, Dr. Nicole Constable, 412-624-6094, Fax: 412-624-6855, E-mail: constable@fcas.pitt.edu.

Center for Bioethics and Health Law Students: 9 full-time (4 women), 9 part-time (5 women); includes 1 minority (Asian American or Pacific Islander). 10 applicants, 70% accepted, 4 enrolled. *Faculty:* 4 full-time (1 woman), 3 part-time/adjunct (1 woman). Expenses: Contact institution. *Financial support:* Tuition waivers (partial) available. In 2008, 1 master's awarded. *Degree program information:* Part-time programs available. Offers bioethics (MA). *Application deadline:* For fall admission, 2/1 priority date for domestic students, 6/30 for international students. Applications are processed on a rolling basis.

Application fee: $50. Electronic applications accepted. *Application Contact:* Janet E. Malis, Administrative Assistant, 412-647-5785, Fax: 412-647-5877, E-mail: bioethic@pitt.edu. *Director of Graduate Education,* Dr. Lisa S. Parker, 412-647-5780, Fax: 412-647-5877, E-mail: lisap@pitt.edu.

Center for Neuroscience Students: 81 full-time (39 women); includes 15 minority (4 African Americans, 1 American Indian/Alaska Native, 7 Asian Americans or Pacific Islanders, 3 Hispanic Americans), 11 international. Average age 25. 150 applicants, 15% accepted, 12 enrolled. *Faculty:* 85 full-time (20 women). Expenses: Contact institution. *Financial support:* In 2008–09, 36 fellowships with full tuition reimbursements (averaging $24,000 per year), 42 research assistantships with full tuition reimbursements (averaging $24,000 per year), 3 teaching assistantships with full tuition reimbursements (averaging $24,000 per year) were awarded. Financial award application deadline: 1/2. In 2008, 11 doctorates awarded. Offers neurobiology (PhD); neuroscience (PhD). *Application deadline:* For fall admission, 1/2 priority date for domestic and international students. *Application fee:* $50. Electronic applications accepted. *Application Contact:* Joan M. Blaney, Administrator, 412-624-5043, Fax: 412-624-9198, E-mail: jblaney@pitt.edu. *Co-Director, Graduate Program,* Dr. Alan Sved, 412-624-6996, Fax: 412-624-9188.

School of Dental Medicine Students: 375 full-time (128 women); includes 97 minority (4 African Americans, 3 American Indian/Alaska Native, 64 Asian Americans or Pacific Islanders, 26 Hispanic Americans), 18 international. Average age 28. 2,748 applicants, 11% accepted, 104 enrolled. *Faculty:* 117 full-time (39 women), 122 part-time/adjunct (24 women). Expenses: Contact institution. *Financial support:* In 2008–09, 315 students received support. Scholarships/grants and stipends available. Financial award application deadline: 4/30; financial award applicants required to submit FAFSA. In 2008, 87 first professional degrees, 18 Certificates awarded. Offers craniofacial and maxillofacial surgery (Certificate); dental anesthesia (Certificate); dental medicine (DMD, MDS, Certificate); endodontics (MDS, Certificate); general dentistry (Certificate); general practice residency (Certificate); oral and maxillofacial pathology (Certificate); oral and maxillofacial surgery (Certificate); orthodontics and dentofacial orthopedics (MDS, Certificate); pediatric dentistry (MDS, Certificate); periodontics (MDS, Certificate); prosthodontics (MDS, Certificate). *Application deadline:* Applications are processed on a rolling basis. Electronic applications accepted. *Application Contact:* Rosemary Mangold, Recruitment/Financial Aid Officer, 412-648-8437, Fax: 412-648-9571, E-mail: mangold@pitt.edu. *Dean,* Dr. Thomas W. Braun, 412-648-8900, Fax: 412-648-8219, E-mail: twb3@pitt.edu.

School of Education Students: 580 full-time (433 women), 663 part-time (493 women); includes 196 minority (107 African Americans, 3 American Indian/Alaska Native, 64 Asian Americans or Pacific Islanders, 22 Hispanic Americans), 21 international. 905 applicants, 75% accepted, 535 enrolled. *Faculty:* 98 full-time (55 women), 115 part-time/adjunct (74 women). Expenses: Contact institution. *Financial support:* In 2008–09, 26 fellowships (averaging $14,485 per year), 44 research assistantships with full and partial tuition reimbursements (averaging $10,832 per year), 67 teaching assistantships with full and partial tuition reimbursements (averaging $10,251 per year) were awarded; career-related internships or fieldwork, Federal Work-Study, institutionally sponsored loans, scholarships/grants, traineeships, tuition waivers (partial), and unspecified assistantships also available. Support available to part-time students. Financial award applicants required to submit FAFSA. In 2008, 340 master's, 60 doctorates awarded. *Degree program information:* Part-time and evening/weekend programs available. Postbaccalaureate distance learning degree programs offered (minimal on-campus study). Offers applied developmental psychology (M Ed, MS, PhD); cognitive studies (PhD); developmental movement (MS); early childhood education (M Ed); early education of disabled students (M Ed); education (M Ed, MA, MAT, MS, Ed D, PhD); education of students with mental and physical disabilities (M Ed); elementary education (M Ed, MAT); English/communications education (M Ed, MAT); exercise physiology (MS, PhD); foreign languages education (M Ed, MAT); general special education (M Ed); higher education (M Ed, Ed D); higher education management (M Ed, Ed D); mathematics education (M Ed, MAT, Ed D); reading education (M Ed, Ed D); research methodology (M Ed, MA, PhD); school leadership (M Ed, Ed D); science education (M Ed, MAT, MS, Ed D); secondary education (M Ed, MAT, MS, Ed D, PhD); social and comparative analysis in education (M Ed, MA, Ed D, PhD); social studies education (M Ed, MAT); special education (M Ed, Ed D, PhD); vision studies (M Ed). *Application deadline:* For fall admission, 2/1 priority date for domestic students, 2/1 for international students; for spring admission, 11/15 priority date for domestic students, 7/1 for international students. Applications are processed on a rolling basis. *Application fee:* $50. Electronic applications accepted. *Application Contact:* Marianne L. Budziszewski, Director of Admissions and Enrollment Services, 412-648-7056, Fax: 412-648-1899, E-mail: soeinfo@pitt.edu. *Dean,* Dr. Alan Lesgold, 412-648-1773, Fax: 412-648-1825, E-mail: al@pitt.edu.

School of Engineering Students: 418 full-time (120 women), 217 part-time (40 women); includes 58 minority (16 African Americans, 2 American Indian/Alaska Native, 25 Asian Americans or Pacific Islanders, 15 Hispanic Americans), 218 international. 1,727 applicants, 36% accepted, 214 enrolled. *Faculty:* 108 full-time (15 women), 208 part-time/adjunct (17 women). Expenses: Contact institution. *Financial support:* In 2008–09, 353 students received support, including 60 fellowships with full tuition reimbursements available (averaging $20,772 per year), 184 research assistantships with full tuition reimbursements available (averaging $22,000 per year), 109 teaching assistantships with full tuition reimbursements available (averaging $21,000 per year); scholarships/grants, traineeships, and tuition waivers (full and partial) also available. Financial award application deadline: 4/15. In 2008, 105 master's, 41 doctorates awarded. *Degree program information:* Part-time programs available. Offers bioengineering (MSBENG, PhD); chemical engineering (MS Ch E, PhD); civil and environmental engineering (MSCEE, PhD); electrical engineering (MSEE, PhD); engineering (MS Ch E, MSBENG, MSCEE, MSEE, MSIE, MSME, MSPE, PhD); industrial engineering (MSIE, PhD); mechanical engineering and materials science (MSME, PhD); petroleum engineering (MSPE). *Application deadline:* For fall admission, 3/1 priority date for domestic students; for spring admission, 7/1 priority date for domestic students. Applications are processed on a rolling basis. *Application fee:* $50. Electronic applications accepted. *Application Contact:* 412-624-9800, Fax: 412-624-9808, E-mail: admin@engrng.pitt.edu. *Dean,* Dr. Gerald D. Holder, 412-624-9811, Fax: 412-624-0412, E-mail: holder@engrng.pitt.edu.

School of Health and Rehabilitation Sciences Students: 548 full-time (424 women), 77 part-time (47 women); includes 39 minority (24 African Americans, 11 Asian Americans or Pacific Islanders, 4 Hispanic Americans), 111 international. Average age 28. 805 applicants, 64% accepted, 293 enrolled. *Faculty:* 90 full-time (50 women), 11 part-time/adjunct (8 women). Expenses: Contact institution. *Financial support:* In 2008–09, 43 research assistantships with full and partial tuition reimbursements (averaging $20,293 per year), 23 teaching assistantships with full tuition reimbursements (averaging $15,532 per year) were awarded; fellowships with full tuition reimbursements, career-related internships or fieldwork, Federal Work-Study, scholarships/grants, traineeships, and unspecified assistantships also available. Financial award applicants required to submit FAFSA. In 2008, 118 master's, 67 doctorates awarded. *Degree program information:* Part-time programs available. Offers assistive rehabilitation technology (Certificate); communication science and disorders (MA, MS, Au D, CScD, PhD); dietetics (MS); disability studies (Certificate); health and rehabilitation sciences (MA, MOT, MS, Au D, CScD, DPT, PhD, Certificate); occupational therapy (MOT); physical therapy (DPT); rehabilitation science (PhD). *Application deadline:* For fall admission, 1/31 for international students. Applications are processed on a rolling basis. *Application fee:* $50. Electronic applications accepted. *Application Contact:* Shameem Gangjee, Director of Admissions, 412-383-6558, Fax: 412-383-6535, E-mail: admissions@shrs.pitt.edu. *Dean,* Dr. Clifford E. Brubaker, 412-383-6560, Fax: 412-383-6535, E-mail: cliffb@pitt.edu.

School of Information Sciences Students: 326 full-time (177 women), 357 part-time (267 women); includes 83 minority (47 African Americans, 2 American Indian/Alaska Native, 17 Asian Americans or Pacific Islanders, 17 Hispanic Americans), 142 international. 732 applicants, 85% accepted, 285 enrolled. *Faculty:* 29 full-time (8 women), 9 part-time/adjunct (5 women). Expenses: Contact institution. *Financial support:* Fellowships with partial tuition reimbursements, research assistantships with full and partial tuition reimbursements, teaching assistantships with full and partial tuition reimbursements, career-related internships or fieldwork, scholarships/grants, health care benefits, tuition waivers (full and partial), and unspecified assistantships available. Financial award application deadline: 1/15; financial award applicants required to submit FAFSA. In 2008, 258 master's, 14 doctorates, 2 other advanced degrees awarded. *Degree program information:* Part-time and evening/weekend programs available. Postbaccalaureate distance learning degree programs offered (minimal on-campus study). Offers information science (MSIS, PhD, Certificate); information sciences (MLIS, MSIS, MST, PhD, Certificate); library and information science (MLIS, PhD, Certificate); telecommunications and networking (MST, PhD, Certificate). *Application deadline:* For fall admission, 1/15 priority date for domestic and international students; for winter admission, 9/15 priority date for domestic students, 6/15 for international students; for spring admission, 1/15 priority date for domestic students, 12/15 priority date for international students. Applications are processed on a rolling basis. *Application fee:* $50. Electronic applications accepted. *Application Contact:* Shabana Reza, Student Recruiting Coordinator, 412-624-3988, Fax: 412-624-5231, E-mail: sreza@sis.pitt.edu. *Dean and Professor,* Dr. Ronald L. Larsen, 412-624-5139, Fax: 412-624-5231, E-mail: rlarsen@sis.pitt.edu.

School of Law Students: 717 full-time (326 women), 17 part-time (13 women); includes 112 minority (44 African Americans, 1 American Indian/Alaska Native, 48 Asian Americans or Pacific Islanders, 19 Hispanic Americans), 19 international. 2,113 applicants, 37% accepted, 242 enrolled. *Faculty:* 47 full-time (18 women), 47 part-time/adjunct (13 women). Expenses: Contact institution. *Financial support:* In 2008–09, 388 students received support, including 3 fellowships (averaging $6,667 per year), 36 research assistantships (averaging $5,440 per year); teaching assistantships, career-related internships or fieldwork, Federal Work-Study, scholarships/grants, and unspecified assistantships also available. Financial award application deadline: 3/1; financial award applicants required to submit FAFSA. In 2008, 255 first professional degrees, 12 master's awarded. Offers business law (MSL); civil litigation (Certificate); constitutional law (MSL); criminal law and justice (MSL); disabilities law (MSL); dispute resolution (MSL); education law (MSL); elder and estate planning law (MSL); employment and labor law (MSL); environment and real estate law (MSL); environmental law, science and policy (Certificate); family law (MSL); general law and jurisprudence (MSL); health law (Certificate); intellectual property and technology (MSL); intellectual property and technology law (Certificate); international and comparative law (LL M, MSL); international law (Certificate); law (JD, LL M, MSL, Certificate); personal injury and civil litigation (MSL); regulatory law (MSL); self-designed (MSL); sports and entertainment law (MSL). *Application deadline:* For fall admission, 3/1 for domestic students. Applications are processed on a rolling basis. *Application fee:* $55. Electronic applications accepted. *Application Contact:* Charmaine McCall, Assistant Dean of Admissions and Financial Aid, 412-648-1413, Fax: 412-648-1318, E-mail: cmccall@pitt.edu. *Dean,* Mary Crossley, 412-648-1401, Fax: 412-648-2647, E-mail: crossley@pitt.edu.

School of Medicine Students: 863 full-time (424 women), 64 part-time (36 women); includes 323 minority (63 African Americans, 3 American Indian/Alaska Native, 224 Asian Americans or Pacific Islanders, 33 Hispanic Americans), 110 international. 6,192 applicants, 10% accepted, 216 enrolled. *Faculty:* 1,985 full-time (614 women), 68 part-time/adjunct (42 women). Expenses: Contact institution. *Financial support:* In 2008–09, 359 students received support, including fellowships with full tuition reimbursements available (averaging $24,650 per year), research assistantships with full tuition reimbursements available (averaging $24,650 per year); teaching assistantships, institutionally sponsored loans, scholarships/grants, traineeships, health care benefits, and unspecified assistantships also available. Financial award application deadline: 4/16; financial award applicants required to submit FAFSA. In 2008, 148 first professional degrees, 29 master's, 34 doctorates, 12 other advanced degrees awarded. Offers biochemistry and molecular genetics (MS, PhD); biomedical informatics (MS, PhD, Certificate); cell biology and molecular physiology (MS, PhD); cellular and molecular pathology (MS, PhD); clinical and translational science (PhD); clinical research (MS, Certificate); immunology (MS, PhD); integrative molecular biology (PhD); interdisciplinary biomedical sciences (PhD); medical education (MS, Certificate); medicine (MD, MS, PhD, Certificate); molecular biophysics and structural biology (PhD); molecular pharmacology (PhD); molecular virology and microbiology (MS, PhD); neurobiology (PhD). *Application deadline:* For fall admission, 11/15 for domestic students; for winter admission, 1/15 priority date for domestic students. Applications are processed on a rolling basis. *Application fee:* $75. Electronic applications accepted. *Application Contact:* Dr. Arthur S. Levine, MD, Dean and Senior Vice Chancellor, Health Sciences, 412-648-8975, Fax: 412-648-1236, E-mail: alevine@hs.pitt.edu. *Dean and Senior Vice Chancellor, Health Sciences,* Dr. Arthur S. Levine, MD, 412-648-8975, Fax: 412-648-1236, E-mail: alevine@hs.pitt.edu.

School of Nursing *Degree program information:* Part-time programs available. Offers acute care nurse practitioner (MSN); adult nurse practitioner (MSN); anesthesia nursing (MSN); family nurse practitioner (MSN); medical/surgical clinical nurse specialist (MSN); nursing (MSN, DNP, PhD); nursing administration (MSN); nursing education (MSN); nursing informatics (MSN); nursing practice (DNP); nursing research (MSN); pediatric nurse practitioner (MSN); psychiatric and mental health clinical nurse specialist (MSN); psychiatric primary care nurse practitioner (MSN). Electronic applications accepted.

School of Pharmacy Students: 454 full-time (276 women), 2 part-time (0 women); includes 48 minority (12 African Americans, 2 American Indian/Alaska Native, 31 Asian Americans or Pacific Islanders, 3 Hispanic Americans), 21 international. Average age 23. 932 applicants, 17% accepted, 116 enrolled. *Faculty:* 80 full-time (34 women), 135 part-time/adjunct (64 women). Expenses: Contact institution. *Financial support:* In 2008–09, 146 students received support, including 1 fellowship (averaging $40,000 per year), 14 teaching assistantships with full tuition reimbursements available (averaging $15,675 per year); career-related internships or fieldwork, Federal Work-Study, institutionally sponsored loans, scholarships/grants, and health care benefits also available. Financial award application deadline: 10/1. In 2008, 107 first professional degrees, 1 master's, 7 doctorates awarded. Offers pharmaceutical sciences (MS, PhD); pharmacy (Pharm D, MS, PhD). Electronic applications accepted. *Application Contact:* Marcia L. Borrelli, Director of Student Services, 412-383-9000, Fax: 412-383-9996, E-mail: borrelli@pitt.edu. *Dean,* Dr. Patricia Dowley Kroboth, 412-624-2400, Fax: 412-648-1086.

School of Social Work Students: 363 full-time (297 women), 236 part-time (190 women); includes 98 minority (80 African Americans, 9 Asian Americans or Pacific Islanders, 9 Hispanic Americans). Average age 28. 418 applicants, 61% accepted, 247 enrolled. *Faculty:* 22 full-time (13 women), 38 part-time/adjunct (32 women). Expenses: Contact institution. *Financial support:* In 2008–09, 225 students received support, including 1 research assistantship with full tuition reimbursement available (averaging $11,830 per year), 6 teaching assistantships with full tuition reimbursements available (averaging $14,014 per year); fellowships, career-related internships or fieldwork, institutionally sponsored loans, scholarships/grants, traineeships, tuition waivers (full), and unspecified assistantships also available. Financial award application deadline: 3/31; financial award applicants required to submit FAFSA. In 2008, 207 master's, 11 doctorates awarded. *Degree program information:* Part-time programs available. Postbaccalaureate distance learning degree programs offered (no on-campus study). Offers gerontology (Certificate); social work (MSW, PhD). *Application deadline:* For fall admission, 5/1 for domestic and international students. Applications are processed on a rolling basis. *Application fee:* $40 ($50 for international students). Electronic applications accepted. *Application Contact:* Philip Mack, Director of Admissions, 412-624-6346, Fax: 412-624-6323, E-mail: psm8@pitt.edu. *Dean,* Dr. Larry E. Davis, 412-624-6304, Fax: 412-624-6323, E-mail: ledavis@pitt.edu.

University Center for International Studies Expenses: Contact institution. Offers African studies (Certificate); Asian studies (Certificate); European Union studies (Certificate); global studies (Certificate); Latin American studies (Certificate); Russian and East European studies (Certificate); West European studies (Certificate). *Application Contact:* Information Contact, 412-624-4141, E-mail: graduate@pitt.edu. *Director, University Center for International Studies,* Lawrence F. Feick, 412-648-7374, Fax: 412-624-4672, E-mail: feick@pitt.edu.

UNIVERSITY OF PORTLAND, Portland, OR 97203-5798

General Information Independent-religious, coed, comprehensive institution. *Enrollment:* 3,661 graduate, professional, and undergraduate students; 157 full-time matriculated graduate/professional students (102 women), 383 part-time matriculated graduate/professional students (265 women). *Enrollment by degree level:* 525 master's, 15 doctoral. *Graduate faculty:* 84 full-time (26 women), 11 part-time/adjunct (5 women). *Tuition:* Full-time $7380; part-time $8.20 per credit hour. *Graduate housing:* On-campus housing not available. *Student services:* Campus employment opportunities, campus safety program, career counseling, exercise/wellness program, free psychological counseling, international student services, low-cost

University of Portland (continued)

health insurance, multicultural affairs office, services for students with disabilities, teacher training, writing training. *Library facilities:* Wilson M. Clark Library plus 1 other. *Online resources:* library catalog, web page, access to other libraries' catalogs. *Collection:* 350,000 titles, 1,400 serial subscriptions, 11,044 audiovisual materials. *Research affiliation:* Portland Area Nursing Consortium, Kaiser Center Health Resources, Oregon Graduate Institute of Science and Technology (applied engineering, applied physics).

Computer facilities: 575 computers available on campus for general student use. A campuswide network can be accessed from student residence rooms and from off campus. Online class registration is available. *Web address:* http://www.up.edu/.

General Application Contact: Dr. Thomas G. Greene, Assistant to the Provost and Dean of the Graduate School, 503-943-7107, Fax: 503-943-7315, E-mail: greene@up.edu.

GRADUATE UNITS

Graduate School Students: 157 full-time (102 women), 383 part-time (265 women); includes 69 minority (4 African Americans, 2 American Indian/Alaska Native, 48 Asian Americans or Pacific Islanders, 15 Hispanic Americans), 113 international. Average age 33. *Faculty:* 84 full-time (26 women), 11 part-time/adjunct (5 women). Expenses: Contact institution. *Financial support:* Career-related internships or fieldwork and Federal Work-Study available. Support available to part-time students. Financial award application deadline: 3/1; financial award applicants required to submit FAFSA. In 2008, 204 master's awarded. *Degree program information:* Part-time and evening/weekend programs available. Postbaccalaureate distance learning degree programs offered (minimal on-campus study). *Application deadline:* For fall admission, 7/15 priority date for domestic and international students; for spring admission, 12/15 priority date for domestic and international students. Applications are processed on a rolling basis. *Application fee:* $50. *Application Contact:* Chris James Olinger, Administrative Assistant, 503-943-7107, Fax: 503-943-7315, E-mail: olingerc@up.edu. *Assistant to the Provost and Dean of the Graduate School,* Dr. Thomas G. Greene, 503-943-7107, Fax: 503-943-7315, E-mail: greene@up.edu.

College of Arts and Sciences Students: 8 full-time (4 women), 33 part-time (23 women); includes 1 American Indian/Alaska Native, 5 Asian Americans or Pacific Islanders, 2 Hispanic Americans, 2 international. Average age 40. 27 applicants, 63% accepted, 12 enrolled. *Faculty:* 14 full-time (3 women), 1 part-time/adjunct (0 women). Expenses: Contact institution. *Financial support:* Teaching assistantships, career-related internships or fieldwork, Federal Work-Study, scholarships/grants, and tuition waivers (partial) available. Support available to part-time students. Financial award application deadline: 3/1; financial award applicants required to submit FAFSA. *Degree program information:* Part-time and evening/weekend programs available. Offers arts and sciences (MA, MFA, MS); communication (MA); directing (MFA); drama (MFA); management communication (MS); music (MA); pastoral ministry (MA). *Application deadline:* For fall admission, 7/15 priority date for domestic and international students; for spring admission, 12/15 priority date for domestic and international students. Applications are processed on a rolling basis. *Application fee:* $50. *Application Contact:* Chris James Olinger, Administrative Assistant, 503-943-7107, Fax: 503-943-7315, E-mail: olingerc@up.edu. *Dean,* Rev. Stephen Rowan, 503-943-7221, E-mail: rowan@up.edu.

Dr. Robert B. Pamplin, Jr. School of Business Students: 65 full-time (33 women), 58 part-time (25 women); includes 12 minority (1 African American, 1 American Indian/Alaska Native, 6 Asian Americans or Pacific Islanders, 4 Hispanic Americans), 23 international. Average age 30. *Faculty:* 24 full-time (5 women). Expenses: Contact institution. *Financial support:* Federal Work-Study, scholarships/grants, and tuition waivers (partial) available. Support available to part-time students. Financial award application deadline: 3/1; financial award applicants required to submit FAFSA. In 2008, 56 master's awarded. *Degree program information:* Part-time and evening/weekend programs available. Offers business (MBA). *Application deadline:* For fall admission, 7/15 priority date for domestic and international students; for spring admission, 12/15 priority date for domestic and international students. Applications are processed on a rolling basis. *Application fee:* $50. *Application Contact:* Melissa McCarthy, Academic Specialist, 503-943-7225, E-mail: mccarthy@up.edu. *Associate Dean,* Dr. Howard Feldman, 503-943-7224, E-mail: feldman@up.edu.

School of Education Students: 45 full-time (32 women), 177 part-time (127 women); includes 1 African American, 35 Asian Americans or Pacific Islanders, 3 Hispanic Americans, 85 international. Average age 35. *Faculty:* 19 full-time (8 women), 10 part-time/adjunct (5 women). Expenses: Contact institution. *Financial support:* Federal Work-Study and scholarships/grants available. Support available to part-time students. Financial award application deadline: 3/1; financial award applicants required to submit FAFSA. In 2008, 144 master's awarded. *Degree program information:* Part-time and evening/weekend programs available. Offers education (M Ed, MA, MAT). M Ed also available through the Graduate Outreach Program for teachers residing in the Oregon and Washington State areas. *Application deadline:* For fall admission, 7/15 priority date for domestic and international students; for spring admission, 12/15 priority date for domestic and international students. Applications are processed on a rolling basis. *Application fee:* $50. *Application Contact:* Dr. Bruce Weitzel, Associate Dean, 503-943-7135, E-mail: weitzel@up.edu. *Dean,* Dr. Maria Ciriello, OP, 503-943-7135, Fax: 503-943-8042, E-mail: ciriello@up.edu.

School of Engineering Students: 2 full-time (0 women), 1 part-time (0 women); includes 1 Asian American or Pacific Islander, 2 international. Average age 28. *Faculty:* 16 full-time (0 women). Expenses: Contact institution. *Financial support:* Teaching assistantships, career-related internships or fieldwork, Federal Work-Study, and scholarships/grants available. Support available to part-time students. Financial award application deadline: 3/1; financial award applicants required to submit FAFSA. In 2008, 1 master's awarded. *Degree program information:* Part-time and evening/weekend programs available. Offers engineering (ME). *Application deadline:* For fall admission, 7/15 priority date for domestic and international students; for spring admission, 12/15 priority date for domestic and international students. Applications are processed on a rolling basis. *Application fee:* $50. *Application Contact:* Dr. Khalid Khan, Director, 503-943-7276, E-mail: khan@up.edu. *Dean,* Dr. Zia Yamayee, 503-943-7314.

School of Nursing Students: 37 full-time (33 women), 43 part-time (39 women); includes 1 African American, 1 Asian American or Pacific Islander, 1 Hispanic American, 1 international. Average age 34. *Faculty:* 11 full-time (10 women). Expenses: Contact institution. *Financial support:* Fellowships, research assistantships, Federal Work-Study and scholarships/grants available. Support available to part-time students. Financial award application deadline: 3/1; financial award applicants required to submit FAFSA. In 2008, 8 master's awarded. *Degree program information:* Part-time and evening/weekend programs available. Postbaccalaureate distance learning degree programs offered (minimal on-campus study). Offers clinical nurse leader (MS); nursing (DNP). *Application deadline:* For fall admission, 11/2 priority date for domestic and international students; for spring admission, 1/7 priority date for domestic and international students. Applications are processed on a rolling basis. *Application fee:* $50. *Application Contact:* Dr. Susan Mascato, Associate Dean, 503-943-7211, E-mail: mascato@up.edu. Dr. Joanne Warner, Fax: 503-943-7729, E-mail: warner@up.edu.

UNIVERSITY OF PRINCE EDWARD ISLAND, Charlottetown, PE C1A 4P3, Canada

General Information Province-supported, coed, comprehensive institution. *Graduate housing:* Room and/or apartments available on a first-come, first-served basis to single students; on-campus housing not available to married students. *Research affiliation:* Agriculture Canada Research Station, Diagnostic Chemicals, Ltd., Canadian Food Inspection Agency, AquaHealth, NRC Institute for Nutrisciences and Health, PEI Food Technology Centre.

GRADUATE UNITS

Atlantic Veterinary College *Degree program information:* Part-time programs available. Offers anatomy (M Sc, PhD); bacteriology (M Sc, PhD); clinical pharmacology (M Sc, PhD); clinical sciences (M Sc, PhD); epidemiology (M Sc, PhD); fish health (M Sc, PhD); food animal nutrition (M Sc, PhD); immunology (M Sc, PhD); microanatomy (M Sc, PhD); parasitology (M Sc, PhD); pathology (M Sc, PhD); pharmacology (M Sc, PhD); physiology (M Sc, PhD); toxicology (M Sc, PhD); veterinary medicine (DVM, M Sc, M Vet Sc, PhD); veterinary science (M Vet Sc); virology (M Sc, PhD).

Faculty of Arts *Degree program information:* Part-time programs available. Offers island studies (MA).

Faculty of Education *Degree program information:* Part-time programs available. Offers leadership and learning (M Ed).

Faculty of Science Offers biology (M Sc); chemistry (M Sc).

UNIVERSITY OF PUERTO RICO, MAYAGÜEZ CAMPUS, Mayagüez, PR 00681-9000

General Information Commonwealth-supported, coed, university. CGS member. *Graduate housing:* On-campus housing not available. *Research affiliation:* Tropical Agriculture Research Station, Corporation for the Development and Administration of Marine Resources of Puerto Rico.

GRADUATE UNITS

Graduate Studies *Degree program information:* Part-time and evening/weekend programs available. Electronic applications accepted.

College of Agricultural Sciences *Degree program information:* Part-time programs available. Offers agricultural economics (MS); agricultural education (MS); agricultural extension (MS); agricultural sciences (MS); agronomy (MS); animal industry (MS); crop protection (MS); food science and technology (MS); horticulture (MS); soils (MS).

College of Arts and Sciences *Degree program information:* Part-time programs available. Offers applied chemistry (PhD); applied mathematics (MS); arts and sciences (MA, MS, PhD); biology (MS); chemistry (MS); computational sciences (MS); English education (MA); geology (MS); Hispanic studies (MA); marine sciences (MS, PhD); physics (MS); pure mathematics (MS); statistics (MS).

College of Business Administration *Degree program information:* Part-time and evening/weekend programs available. Offers business administration (MBA); finance (MBA); human resources (MBA); industrial management (MBA).

College of Engineering *Degree program information:* Part-time programs available. Offers chemical engineering (ME, MS, PhD); civil engineering (ME, MS, PhD); computer engineering (ME, MS); computing information science and engineering (PhD); electrical engineering (ME, MS); engineering (ME, MS, PhD); industrial engineering (ME); management systems (MS); mechanical engineering (ME, MS).

UNIVERSITY OF PUERTO RICO, MEDICAL SCIENCES CAMPUS, San Juan, PR 00936-5067

General Information Commonwealth-supported, coed, primarily women, upper-level institution. *Graduate housing:* On-campus housing not available.

GRADUATE UNITS

Graduate School of Public Health *Degree program information:* Part-time programs available. Offers biostatistics (MPH); demography (MS); developmental disabilities-early intervention (Certificate); environmental health (MS, Dr PH); epidemiology (MPH, MS); evaluation research of health systems (MS); gerontology (MPH, Certificate); health services administration (MHSA); industrial hygiene (MS); maternal and child health (MPH); nurse midwifery (MPH, Certificate); nutrition (MS); public health (MHSA, MPH, MPHE, MS, Dr PH, Certificate); public health education (MPHE).

School of Dental Medicine Offers dental medicine (DMD, MSD, Certificate); dentistry (DMD, MSD, Certificate); general dentistry (Certificate); oral and maxillofacial surgery (MSD, Certificate); orthodontics (MSD, Certificate); pediatric dentistry (MSD, Certificate); prosthodontics (MSD, Certificate). Electronic applications accepted.

School of Health Professions Offers audiology (Au D); clinical laboratory science (MS); clinical research (MS, Certificate, Graduate Certificate); cytotechnology (Certificate); dietetics (Certificate); health information administration (MS); health professions (MS, Au D, Certificate); medical technology (Certificate); occupational therapy (MS); physical therapy (MS); speech-language pathology (MS). Electronic applications accepted.

School of Medicine Offers medicine (MD, MS, PhD). Electronic applications accepted.

Division of Graduate Studies Offers anatomy (MS, PhD); biochemistry (MS, PhD); biomedical sciences (MS, PhD); microbiology (MS, PhD); pharmacology and toxicology (MS, PhD); physiology (MS, PhD). Electronic applications accepted.

School of Nursing Offers anesthesia (MSN); critical care nursing (MSN); family and community nursing (MSN); family nurse practitioner (MSN); mental health and psychiatric nursing (MSN); nursing (MSN). Electronic applications accepted.

School of Pharmacy *Degree program information:* Part-time and evening/weekend programs available. Offers industrial pharmacy (MS); pharmaceutical sciences (MS); pharmacy (Pharm D). Electronic applications accepted.

UNIVERSITY OF PUERTO RICO, RÍO PIEDRAS, San Juan, PR 00931-3300

General Information Commonwealth-supported, coed, university. CGS member. *Graduate housing:* Room and/or apartments available to single students; on-campus housing not available to married students. Housing application deadline: 6/15. *Research affiliation:* U.S. Department of Education (social sciences, general studies), U.S. Department of Health and Human Services (social sciences, biology), National Science Foundation (ecology, biology), Ocean Concervancy (ecology, biology), Ford International (ecology), U.S. Department of Defense (physics, biology).

GRADUATE UNITS

College of Business Administration *Degree program information:* Part-time programs available. Offers accounting (MBA); economics management (MBA); finance (MBA, PhD); general business (MBA); human resources management (MBA); international trade (PhD); marketing (MBA); production management (MBA); quantitative methods (MBA); trade and international business (MBA).

College of Education *Degree program information:* Part-time programs available. Offers biology education (M Ed); chemistry education (M Ed); child education (M Ed); curriculum and teaching (Ed D); education (M Ed, MS, Ed D); educational research and evaluation (M Ed); English education (M Ed); exercise sciences (MS); family ecology and nutrition (M Ed); guidance and counseling (M Ed, Ed D); history education (M Ed); mathematics education (M Ed); physics education (M Ed); school administration and supervision (M Ed, Ed D); secondary education (M Ed); Spanish education (M Ed); special education (M Ed); teaching English as a second language (M Ed).

College of Humanities *Degree program information:* Part-time programs available. Offers comparative literature (MA); English (MA, PhD); Hispanic studies (MA, PhD); history (MA, PhD); humanities (MA, PhD, Certificate); linguistics (MA); philosophy (MA); translation (MA, Certificate).

College of Natural Sciences *Degree program information:* Part-time programs available. Offers biology (MS, PhD); chemical physics (PhD); chemistry (MS); mathematics (MS, PhD); natural sciences (MS, PhD); physical chemistry (PhD); physics (MS).

College of Social Sciences *Degree program information:* Part-time programs available. Offers clinical psychology (MA); economics (MA); industrial organizational psychology (MA); investigative academic psychology (MA); psychology (PhD); social sciences (MA, MPA, MRC, MSW, PhD); sociology (MA).

Graduate School of Rehabilitation Counseling *Degree program information:* Part-time programs available. Offers rehabilitation counseling (MRC).

Graduate School of Social Work *Degree program information:* Part-time programs available. Offers social work (MSW, PhD).

School of Public Administration *Degree program information:* Part-time programs available. Offers public administration (MPA).

Graduate School of Information Sciences and Technologies *Degree program information:* Part-time programs available. Offers administration of academic libraries (PMC); administration of public libraries (PMC); administration of special libraries (PMC); consultant in information services (PMC); documents and files administration (Post-Graduate Certificate); electronic information resources analyst (Post-Graduate Certificate); librarianship (Post-Graduate Certificate); librarianship and information services (MLS); master librarian (Post-Graduate Certificate); specialist in legal information (PMC).

Graduate School of Planning *Degree program information:* Part-time programs available. Offers planning (MP).

School of Architecture *Degree program information:* Part-time programs available. Offers architecture (M Arch).

School of Communication *Degree program information:* Part-time programs available. Offers communication (MA).

School of Law *Degree program information:* Part-time and evening/weekend programs available. Offers law (JD, LL M).

UNIVERSITY OF PUGET SOUND, Tacoma, WA 98416

General Information Independent, coed, comprehensive institution. *Enrollment:* 2,858 graduate, professional, and undergraduate students; 234 full-time matriculated graduate/professional students (183 women), 29 part-time matriculated graduate/professional students (22 women). *Enrollment by degree level:* 158 master's, 105 doctoral. *Graduate faculty:* 24 full-time (16 women), 9 part-time/adjunct (7 women). *Tuition:* Full-time $29,820; part-time $4260 per unit. Tuition and fees vary according to program. *Graduate housing:* Room and/or apartments available on a first-come, first-served basis to single students; on-campus housing not available to married students. Typical cost: $4890 per year ($8760 including board). Housing application deadline: 5/1. *Student services:* Campus employment opportunities, campus safety program, career counseling, exercise/wellness program, free psychological counseling, international student services, low-cost health insurance, multicultural affairs office, services for students with disabilities, teacher training, writing training. *Library facilities:* Collins Memorial Library. *Online resources:* library catalog, web page, access to other libraries' catalogs. *Collection:* 423,352 titles, 99,500 serial subscriptions, 12,862 audiovisual materials.

Computer facilities: 320 computers available on campus for general student use. A campuswide network can be accessed from student residence rooms and from off campus. Online class registration, financial aid, admission, student employment are available. *Web address:* http://www.ups.edu/.

General Application Contact: Dr. George H. Mills, Vice President for Enrollment, 253-879-3211, Fax: 253-879-3993, E-mail: admission@pugetsound.edu.

GRADUATE UNITS

Graduate Studies Students: 234 full-time (183 women), 29 part-time (22 women); includes 41 minority (4 African Americans, 4 American Indian/Alaska Native, 26 Asian Americans or Pacific Islanders, 7 Hispanic Americans), 4 international. Average age 28. 512 applicants, 53% accepted, 121 enrolled. *Faculty:* 24 full-time (16 women), 9 part-time/adjunct (7 women). Expenses: Contact institution. *Financial support:* In 2008–09, 64 students received support, including 39 fellowships (averaging $8,350 per year), 1 teaching assistantship with tuition reimbursement available (averaging $14,204 per year); career-related internships or fieldwork, scholarships/grants, and tuition waivers (full) also available. Support available to part-time students. Financial award application deadline: 3/31; financial award applicants required to submit FAFSA. In 2008, 73 master's, 27 doctorates awarded. *Application deadline:* For fall admission, 1/15 for domestic and international students. Applications are processed on a rolling basis. *Application fee:* $75. Electronic applications accepted. *Application Contact:* Dr. George H. Mills, Vice President for Enrollment, 253-879-3211, Fax: 253-879-3993, E-mail: admission@pugetsound.edu. *Associate Dean*, Dr. Sarah Y. Moore, 253-879-3207.

School of Education Students: 44 full-time (31 women), 23 part-time (17 women); includes 6 minority (3 African Americans, 2 Asian Americans or Pacific Islanders, 1 Hispanic American). Average age 27. 105 applicants, 80% accepted, 54 enrolled. *Faculty:* 11 full-time (7 women), 1 (woman) part-time/adjunct. Expenses: Contact institution. *Financial support:* In 2008–09, 14 students received support, including 1 teaching assistantship with tuition reimbursement available (averaging $14,204 per year); fellowships, career-related internships or fieldwork, scholarships/grants, and tuition waivers (full) also available. Support available to part-time students. Financial award application deadline: 3/31; financial award applicants required to submit FAFSA. In 2008, 42 master's awarded. Offers education (M Ed, MAT); elementary education (MAT); mental health counseling (M Ed); pastoral counseling (M Ed); school counseling (M Ed); secondary education (MAT). *Application deadline:* For fall admission, 3/1 priority date for domestic and international students. Applications are processed on a rolling basis. *Application fee:* $75. Electronic applications accepted. *Application Contact:* Dr. George H. Mills, Vice President for Enrollment, 253-879-3211, Fax: 253-879-3993, E-mail: admission@pugetsound.edu. *Dean*, Dr. John Woodward, 253-879-3375, E-mail: woodward@pugetsound.edu.

School of Occupational Therapy and Physical Therapy Students: 190 full-time (152 women), 6 part-time (5 women); includes 35 minority (1 African American, 4 American Indian/Alaska Native, 24 Asian Americans or Pacific Islanders, 6 Hispanic Americans), 4 international. Average age 28. 407 applicants, 46% accepted, 67 enrolled. *Faculty:* 13 full-time (9 women), 8 part-time/adjunct (6 women). Expenses: Contact institution. *Financial support:* In 2008–09, 50 students received support, including 39 fellowships (averaging $8,350 per year); career-related internships or fieldwork and scholarships/grants also available. Support available to part-time students. Financial award application deadline: 3/31; financial award applicants required to submit FAFSA. In 2008, 31 master's, 27 doctorates awarded. Offers occupational therapy (MOT, MSOT); occupational therapy and physical therapy (MOT, MSOT, DPT); physical therapy (DPT). *Application deadline:* For fall admission, 12/15 priority date for domestic and international students. *Application fee:* $75. Electronic applications accepted. *Application Contact:* Dr. George H. Mills, Vice President for Enrollment, 253-879-3211, Fax: 253-879-3993, E-mail: admission@pugetsound.edu. *Head*, 253-879-3281.

UNIVERSITY OF REDLANDS, Redlands, CA 92373-0999

General Information Independent, coed, comprehensive institution. *Graduate housing:* Rooms and/or apartments available on a first-come, first-served basis to single students and available to married students. Housing application deadline: 8/19. *Research affiliation:* Environmental Systems Research Institute (geographic information systems).

GRADUATE UNITS

College of Arts and Sciences Offers arts and sciences (MM, MS); communicative disorders (MS); geographic information systems (MS). Electronic applications accepted.

School of Music *Degree program information:* Part-time programs available. Offers music (MM).

School of Business *Degree program information:* Evening/weekend programs available. Offers business (MBA); information technology (MS); management (MA).

School of Education *Degree program information:* Part-time and evening/weekend programs available. Offers education (MA, Ed D, Certificate).

UNIVERSITY OF REGINA, Regina, SK S4S 0A2, Canada

General Information Province-supported, coed, university. *Enrollment:* 11,363 graduate, professional, and undergraduate students; 654 full-time matriculated graduate/professional students (336 women), 772 part-time matriculated graduate/professional students (473 women). *Enrollment by degree level:* 1,099 master's, 214 doctoral. *Graduate faculty:* 355 full-time (105 women), 62 part-time/adjunct (18 women). *Graduate housing:* Room and/or apartments available on a first-come, first-served basis to single students; on-campus housing not available to married students. *Student services:* Campus employment opportunities, campus safety program, career counseling, child daycare facilities, exercise/wellness program, free psychological counseling, international student services, low-cost health insurance, multicultural affairs office, services for students with disabilities, teacher training, writing training. *Library facilities:* Dr. John Archer Library plus 3 others. *Online resources:* library catalog, web page, access to other libraries' catalogs. *Collection:* 1.1 million titles, 16,592 serial subscriptions, 12,358 audiovisual materials. *Research affiliation:* AUTO 21-The Automobile of the 21st Century (development of automobile and impact on society/environment), Petroleum Technology Research Center (greenhouse gas remediation), Communities of Tomorrow (community sustainability), Jefferson Laboratory/Southeastern Universities Research Association, Inc. (electromagnetic physics), TR Labs (telecommunications), Institute for Robotics and Intelligent Systems (knowledge-based systems, artificial intelligence).

Computer facilities: 300 computers available on campus for general student use. A campuswide network can be accessed from student residence rooms. Online class registration is available. *Web address:* http://www.uregina.ca/.

General Application Contact: Dr. Dongyan Blachford, Associate Dean, 306-585-5186, Fax: 306-337-2444, E-mail: grad.studies@uregina.ca.

GRADUATE UNITS

Faculty of Graduate Studies and Research Students: 654 full-time (336 women), 772 part-time (473 women). 901 applicants, 64% accepted. *Faculty:* 355 full-time (105 women), 62 part-time/adjunct (18 women). Expenses: Contact institution. *Financial support:* In 2008–09, 164 fellowships (averaging $15,930 per year), 41 research assistantships (averaging $13,720 per year), 132 teaching assistantships (averaging $6,650 per year) were awarded; career-related internships or fieldwork, institutionally sponsored loans, and scholarships/grants also available. Financial award application deadline: 6/15. In 2008, 324 master's, 19 doctorates awarded. *Degree program information:* Part-time and evening/weekend programs available. *Application deadline:* For fall admission, 3/15 priority date for domestic students; for winter admission, 7/15 priority date for domestic students; for spring admission, 9/15 priority date for domestic students. Applications are processed on a rolling basis. *Application fee:* $85 ($100 for international students). Electronic applications accepted. *Application Contact:* Dr. Dongyan Blachford, Associate Dean, 306-585-5186, Fax: 306-337-2444, E-mail: dongyan.blachford@uregina.ca. *Dean*, Dr. Rod Kelln, 306-585-5185, Fax: 306-337-2444, E-mail: rod.kelln@uregina.ca.

Faculty of Arts Students: 140 full-time (94 women), 99 part-time (58 women). 140 applicants, 52% accepted. *Faculty:* 152 full-time (50 women), 11 part-time/adjunct (5 women). Expenses: Contact institution. *Financial support:* In 2008–09, 49 fellowships (averaging $15,930 per year), 13 research assistantships (averaging $13,720 per year), 24 teaching assistantships (averaging $6,650 per year) were awarded; career-related internships or fieldwork and scholarships/grants also available. Financial award application deadline: 6/15. In 2008, 32 master's, 2 doctorates awarded. *Degree program information:* Part-time programs available. Offers anthropology (MA); arts (M Sc, MA, PhD); Canadian plains studies (MA, PhD); clinical psychology (MA, PhD); English (MA, PhD); experimental and applied psychology (MA, PhD); French (MA); geography (M Sc, MA, PhD); gerontology (M Sc, MA); history (MA, PhD); human justice (MA); indigenous studies (MA); justice studies (MA); linguistics (MA); philosophy (MA); police studies (MA); political science (MA); religious studies (MA, PhD); social and political thought (MA); social studies (MA, PhD); sociology (MA, PhD); women's studies (MA). *Application deadline:* Applications are processed on a rolling basis. *Application fee:* $85 ($100 for international students). Electronic applications accepted. *Application Contact:* Dr. Dongyan Blachford, Associate Dean, 306-585-5186, Fax: 306-337-2444, E-mail: dongyan.blachford@uregina.ca. *Dean*, Dr. Thomas Chase, 306-585-4895, Fax: 306-585-5368, E-mail: thomas.chase@uregina.ca.

Faculty of Education Students: 89 full-time (72 women), 314 part-time (230 women). 142 applicants, 80% accepted. *Faculty:* 42 full-time (20 women), 4 part-time/adjunct (3 women). Expenses: Contact institution. *Financial support:* In 2008–09, 11 fellowships (averaging $15,550 per year), 3 research assistantships (averaging $13,500 per year), 14 teaching assistantships (averaging $6,720 per year) were awarded; career-related internships or fieldwork and scholarships/grants also available. Financial award application deadline: 6/15. In 2008, 77 master's awarded. *Degree program information:* Part-time programs available. Offers adult education (M Ad Ed); curriculum and instruction (M Ed); education (M Ad Ed, M Ed, MHRD, PhD); educational administration (M Ed); educational psychology (M Ed); human resources development (MHRD). *Application deadline:* For fall admission, 2/15 for domestic students; for winter admission, 2/15 for domestic students; for spring admission, 2/15 for domestic students. *Application fee:* $85 ($100 for international students). Electronic applications accepted. *Application Contact:* Tania Gates, Graduate Program Coordinator, 306-585-4506, Fax: 306-585-5387, E-mail: edgrad@uregina.ca. *Associate Dean, Graduate Program and Research*, Dr. Warren Wessel, 306-585-4555, Fax: 306-585-5387, E-mail: warren.wessel@uregina.ca.

Faculty of Engineering and Applied Science Students: 152 full-time (40 women), 53 part-time (10 women). 196 applicants, 47% accepted. *Faculty:* 39 full-time (7 women), 37 part-time/adjunct (10 women). Expenses: Contact institution. *Financial support:* In 2008–09, 43 fellowships (averaging $15,800 per year), 9 research assistantships (averaging $12,500 per year), 41 teaching assistantships (averaging $6,720 per year) were awarded; career-related internships or fieldwork and scholarships/grants also available. Financial award application deadline: 6/15. In 2008, 34 master's, 3 doctorates awarded. Offers advanced manufacturing and processing (MA Sc); electronic systems engineering (M Eng, MA Sc, PhD); engineering and applied science (M Eng, MA Sc, PhD); environmental systems engineering (M Eng, MA Sc, PhD); industrial systems engineering (M Eng, MA Sc, PhD); petroleum systems engineering (M Eng, MA Sc, PhD); process systems engineering (M Eng, MA Sc). *Application deadline:* Applications are processed on a rolling basis. *Application fee:* $85 ($100 for international students). Electronic applications accepted. *Application Contact:* Crystal Pick, Information Contact, 306-337-2603, E-mail: crystal.pick@uregina.ca. *Dean*, Dr. Paitoon Tontiwachwuthikul, 306-585-4160, Fax: 306-585-4855, E-mail: paitoon.tontiwachwuthikul@uregina.ca.

Faculty of Fine Arts Students: 19 full-time (12 women), 8 part-time (6 women). 28 applicants, 68% accepted. *Faculty:* 21 full-time (12 women). Expenses: Contact institution. *Financial support:* In 2008–09, 13 students received support, including 6 fellowships (averaging $15,930 per year), 1 research assistantship (averaging $13,720 per year), 2 teaching assistantships (averaging $6,650 per year); scholarships/grants also available. Financial award application deadline: 6/15. In 2008, 2 master's awarded. *Degree program information:* Part-time programs available. Offers fine arts (M Mus, MA, MFA, PhD); music (M Mus); music theory (MA); musicology (MA, PhD); visual arts (MA, MFA). *Application deadline:* For fall admission, 3/15 for domestic students. *Application fee:* $85 ($100 for international students). *Application Contact:* Randal Rogers, Graduate Program Coordinator, 306-585-4746, Fax: 306-585-5544, E-mail: randal.rogers@uregina.ca. *Dean*, Dr. Ruth Chambers, 306-585-5575, Fax: 306-585-5544, E-mail: ruth.chambers@uregina.ca.

Faculty of Kinesiology and Health Studies Students: 18 full-time (10 women), 19 part-time (14 women). 14 applicants, 71% accepted. *Faculty:* 15 full-time (5 women), 3 part-time/adjunct (0 women). Expenses: Contact institution. *Financial support:* In 2008–09, 3 fellowships (averaging $15,930 per year), 1 research assistantship (averaging $13,720 per year), 3 teaching assistantships (averaging $6,650 per year) were awarded; scholarships/grants also available. Offers kinesiology and health studies (PhD); physical activity studies (M Sc). *Application deadline:* Applications are processed on a rolling basis. *Application fee:* $85 ($100 for international students). *Application Contact:* Shannon Morrison, Graduate Program Coordinator, 306-585-5005, E-mail: shannon.morrison@uregina.ca. *Dean*, Dr. Shanthi Johnson, 306-585-3180, Fax: 306-585-4854, E-mail: shanthi.johnson@uregina.ca.

Faculty of Science Students: 98 full-time (43 women), 66 part-time (24 women). 113 applicants, 54% accepted. *Faculty:* 80 full-time (13 women), 25 part-time/adjunct (1 woman). Expenses: Contact institution. *Financial support:* In 2008–09, 32 fellowships (averaging $15,930 per year), 4 research assistantships (averaging $13,720 per year), 22 teaching assistantships (averaging $6,650 per year) were awarded; career-related internships or fieldwork and scholarships/grants also available. Financial award application deadline: 6/15. In 2008, 27 master's, 4 doctorates awarded. *Degree program information:* Part-time programs available. Offers analytical chemistry (M Sc, PhD); biochemistry (M Sc, PhD); biology (M Sc, PhD); computer science (M Sc, PhD); geology (M Sc, PhD); inorganic

University of Regina (continued)

chemistry (M Sc, PhD); mathematics (M Sc, MA, PhD); organic chemistry (M Sc, PhD); physical chemistry (M Sc, PhD); physics (M Sc, PhD); science (M Sc, MA, PhD); statistics (M Sc, MA). *Application deadline:* Applications are processed on a rolling basis. *Application fee:* $85 ($100 for international students). *Application Contact:* Dr. R. Brien Maguire, Information Contact, 306-585-4756, Fax: 306-585-4745, E-mail: brien.maguire@uregina.ca. *Dean*, Dr. Katherine Bergman, 306-585-4143, Fax: 306-585-4894.

Faculty of Social Work Students: 13 full-time (12 women), 57 part-time (46 women). 35 applicants, 46% accepted. *Faculty:* 13 full-time (6 women), 3 part-time/adjunct (2 women). Expenses: Contact institution. *Financial support:* In 2008–09, 3 fellowships (averaging $15,930 per year), 1 research assistantship (averaging $13,720 per year), 1 teaching assistantship (averaging $6,650 per year) were awarded; career-related internships or fieldwork and scholarships/grants also available. Financial award application deadline: 6/15. In 2008, 14 master's, 1 doctorate awarded. *Degree program information:* Part-time programs available. Offers social work (MASW, MSW, PhD). *Application deadline:* For fall admission, 2/15 for domestic students. *Application fee:* $85 ($100 for international students). *Application Contact:* Dr. Miguel Sanchez, Graduate Program Coordinator, 306-585-4848, Fax: 306-585-4872, E-mail: miguel.sanchez@uregina.ca. *Dean*, Dr. David Broad, 306-585-4588, E-mail: david.broad@uregina.ca.

Johnson-Shoyama Graduate School of Public Policy Students: 53 full-time (25 women), 63 part-time (38 women). 100 applicants, 82% accepted. *Faculty:* 6 full-time (3 women). Expenses: Contact institution. *Financial support:* In 2008–09, 8 fellowships (averaging $15,930 per year), 2 research assistantships (averaging $13,720 per year), 5 teaching assistantships (averaging $6,650 per year) were awarded. Financial award application deadline: 6/15. In 2008, 40 master's awarded. *Degree program information:* Part-time and evening/weekend programs available. Offers economic analysis for public policy (Master's Certificate); non-profit management (Master's Certificate); public management (MPA, Master's Certificate); public policy (MPA, PhD, Master's Certificate). *Application deadline:* Applications are processed on a rolling basis. *Application fee:* $85 ($100 for international students). Electronic applications accepted. *Application Contact:* Devon Anderson, Information Contact, 306-585-5462, E-mail: devon.anderson@uregina.ca. *Associate Dean*, Dr. Ken Rasmussen, 306-585-5463, E-mail: ken.rasmussen@uregina.ca.

Kenneth Levene Graduate School of Business Students: 62 full-time (18 women), 80 part-time (52 women). 133 applicants, 89% accepted. *Faculty:* 25 full-time (5 women), 3 part-time/adjunct (0 women). Expenses: Contact institution. *Financial support:* In 2008–09, 7 fellowships (averaging $15,930 per year), 2 research assistantships (averaging $13,720 per year), 6 teaching assistantships (averaging $6,650 per year) were awarded; scholarships/grants also available. Financial award application deadline: 6/15. In 2008, 79 master's awarded. *Degree program information:* Part-time and evening/weekend programs available. Offers business (MBA, MHRM, Master's Certificate); business administration (MBA); business fundamentals (Master's Certificate); general management (Master's Certificate); human resources management (MHRM, Master's Certificate); international business (Master's Certificate). *Application deadline:* Applications are processed on a rolling basis. *Application fee:* $85 ($100 for international students). Electronic applications accepted. *Application Contact:* Information Contact. *Associate Dean*, Dr. Sylvain Charlebois, 306-585-4716, Fax: 306-585-4805, E-mail: sylvain.charlebois@uregina.ca.

UNIVERSITY OF RHODE ISLAND, Kingston, RI 02881

General Information State-supported, coed, university. CGS member. *Enrollment:* 15,904 graduate, professional, and undergraduate students; 1,530 full-time matriculated graduate/professional students (902 women), 916 part-time matriculated graduate/professional students (569 women). *Enrollment by degree level:* 576 first professional. Tuition, state resident: full-time $8024; part-time $446 per credit. Tuition, nonresident: full-time $21,046; part-time $1169 per credit. *Required fees:* $1056; $26 per credit. $30 per semester. One-time fee: $95 part-time. *Graduate housing:* Rooms and/or apartments available on a first-come, first-served basis to single and married students. *Student services:* Campus employment opportunities, campus safety program, career counseling, free psychological counseling, international student services, low-cost health insurance, multicultural affairs office, services for students with disabilities. *Library facilities:* University Library plus 1 other. *Online resources:* library catalog, web page. *Collection:* 1.2 million titles, 7,926 serial subscriptions, 11,671 audiovisual materials. *Research affiliation:* USDA URI Food Stamp Nutrition Education Project, Sustainable Coastal Communities and Ecosystems (SUCCESS)—Leader With Associates, Rhode Island Network for Molecular Toxicology, RI Sea Grant Omnibus FY 2008-2010, Rhode Island Teacher Education Renewal (RITER), Toward the First Census of Marine Life—Education and Outreach Strategies.

Computer facilities: Computer purchase and lease plans are available. 552 computers available on campus for general student use. A campuswide network can be accessed from student residence rooms and from off campus. Online class registration is available. *Web address:* http://www.uri.edu.

General Application Contact: Harold D. Bibb, Associate Dean of the Graduate School, 401-874-2262, Fax: 401-874-5491.

GRADUATE UNITS

Graduate School Students: 1,530 full-time (902 women), 916 part-time (569 women); includes 199 minority (56 African Americans, 3 American Indian/Alaska Native, 89 Asian Americans or Pacific Islanders, 51 Hispanic Americans), 230 international. Expenses: Contact institution. *Financial support:* Career-related internships or fieldwork, Federal Work-Study, institutionally sponsored loans, health care benefits, tuition waivers (full and partial), and unspecified assistantships available. Support available to part-time students. *Degree program information:* Part-time and evening/weekend programs available. *Application Contact:* Harold D. Bibb, Associate Dean of the Graduate School, 401-874-2262, Fax: 401-874-5491, E-mail: urigrad@etal.uri.edu. *Associate Dean of the Graduate School*, Harold Bibb, 401-874-2262, Fax: 401-874-5491, E-mail: urigrad@etal.uri.edu.

College of Arts and Sciences Expenses: Contact institution. *Financial support:* Fellowships, research assistantships, teaching assistantships available. Offers applied mathematical sciences (MS, PhD); applied mathematics (PhD); arts and sciences (MA, MLIS, MM, MPA, MS, PhD, Certificate, Graduate Certificate); behavioral science (PhD); chemistry (MS, PhD); clinical psychology (MA, PhD); communication studies (MA); computer science (MS, PhD); digital forensics (Graduate Certificate); English (MA, PhD); history (MA); library and information studies (MLIS); mathematics (MS, PhD); music (MM); physics (MS, PhD); political science (MA); public policy and administration (MA, MPA, Certificate); school psychology (MS, PhD); Spanish (MA); statistics (MS). *Application deadline:* Applications are processed on a rolling basis. *Application Contact:* Harold D. Bibb, Associate Dean of the Graduate School, 401-874-2262, Fax: 401-874-5491. *Dean*, Winifed Brownell, 401-874-4101.

College of Business Administration Expenses: Contact institution. Postbaccalaureate distance learning degree programs offered. Offers accounting (MS); business administration (PhD); finance (MBA); finance and insurance (PhD); international business (MBA); international sports management (MBA); management (MBA); management science (MBA); management science and information systems (PhD); marketing (MBA, PhD). *Application Contact:* Lisa Lancellotta, MBA Coordinator, 401-874-4241. *Dean*, Mark Higgins, 401-874-4244, E-mail: markhiggins@uri.edu.

College of Engineering Expenses: Contact institution. *Financial support:* Research assistantships, teaching assistantships, tuition waivers (full) available. *Degree program information:* Part-time programs available. Offers biomedical engineering (MS, PhD); chemical engineering (MS, PhD); computer engineering (MS, PhD); design/systems (MS, PhD); electrical engineering (MS, PhD); engineering (MS, MSCE, PhD); environmental engineering (MSCE); fluid mechanics (MS, PhD); geotechnical engineering (MSCE, PhD); industrial and manufacturing engineering (PhD); manufacturing systems engineering (MS); ocean engineering (MS, PhD); solid mechanics (MS, PhD); structural engineering (MS, PhD); thermal sciences (MS, PhD); transportation engineering (MSCE). *Application deadline:* Applications are processed on a rolling basis. *Application fee:* $35. *Application Contact:* George Veyera, Interim Associate Dean, 401-874-5985, E-mail: veyera@egr.uri.edu. *Interim Dean*, Dr. Raymond Wright, 401-874-2186, Fax: 401-874-2786, E-mail: wrightr@uri.edu.

College of Human Science and Services Expenses: Contact institution. *Degree program information:* Evening/weekend programs available. Offers adapted physical education (MS); adult education (MA); audiology (Au D); college student personnel (MS); cultural studies of sport and physical culture (MS); education (PhD); elementary education (MA); exercise science (MS); human development and family studies (MS); human science and services (MA, MM, MS, Au D, DPT, PhD); marriage and family therapy (MS); music education (MM); physical education pedagogy (MS); physical therapy (DPT); psychosocial/behavioral aspects of physical activity (MS); reading education (MA); secondary education (MA); speech-language pathology (MS); textiles, fashion merchandising and design (MS). *Application Contact:* Harold D. Bibb, Associate Dean of the Graduate School, 401-874-2262, Fax: 401-874-5491. *Dean*, Dr. W. Lynn McKinney, 401-874-4047, E-mail: lynnm@uri.ed.

College of Nursing Expenses: Contact institution. Offers administration (MS); clinical nurse leader (MS); clinical specialist in gerontology (MS); clinical specialist in psychiatric/mental health (MS); family nurse practitioner (MS); gerontological nurse practitioner (MS); nursing (PhD); nursing education (MS). *Application Contact:* Harold D. Bibb, Associate Dean of the Graduate School, 401-874-2262, Fax: 401-874-5491. *Dean*, Dr. Dayle Joseph, 401-874-2766, E-mail: dayle@uri.edu.

College of Pharmacy Expenses: Contact institution. Offers biomedical and pharmaceutical sciences (MS, PhD); medicinal chemistry and pharmacognosy (MS, PhD); pharmaceutical sciences (MS, PhD); pharmaceutics and pharmacokinetics (MS, PhD); pharmacology and toxicology (MS, PhD); pharmacy (Pharm D, MS, PhD); pharmacy practice (MS, PhD). *Application Contact:* Harold D. Bibb, Associate Dean of the Graduate School, 401-874-2262, Fax: 401-874-5491. *Interim Dean*, Dr. Ronald Jordan, 401-874-2761, E-mail: ronjordan@uri.edu.

College of the Environment and Life Sciences Expenses: Contact institution. *Financial support:* Tuition waivers (full and partial) available. *Degree program information:* Part-time programs available. Offers animal health and disease (MS); animal science (MS); aquaculture (MS); aquatic pathology (MS); biochemistry (MS, PhD); biological sciences (MS, PhD); biotechnology (MS); clinical laboratory science (MS); clinical laboratory sciences (MS); cytopathology (MS); entomology (MS, PhD); environment and life sciences (MA, MESM, MMA, MS, PhD); environmental and natural resource economics (MS, PhD); environmental science and management (MESM); environmental sciences (MS, PhD); fisheries (MS); food science (MS, PhD); marine affairs (MA, MMA, PhD); microbiology (MS, PhD); molecular genetics (MS, PhD); nutrition (MS, PhD); plant sciences (MS, PhD). *Application fee:* $35. *Application Contact:* Harold D. Bibb, Associate Dean of the Graduate School, 401-874-2262, Fax: 401-874-5491. *Dean*, Dr. Jeffrey Seemann, 401-874-2957, E-mail: jseemann@uri.edu.

Graduate School of Oceanography Expenses: Contact institution. Offers oceanography (MO, MS, PhD). *Application Contact:* Harold D. Bibb, Associate Dean of the Graduate School, 401-874-2262, Fax: 401-874-5491. *Dean*, Dr. David Farmer, 401-874-6222, E-mail: thedean@gso.uri.edu.

Labor Research Center Average age 32. Expenses: Contact institution. *Financial support:* Fellowships, research assistantships, teaching assistantships, career-related internships or fieldwork, Federal Work-Study, institutionally sponsored loans, and tuition waivers (full and partial) available. Support available to part-time students. *Degree program information:* Part-time and evening/weekend programs available. Offers labor relations and human resources (MS). *Application fee:* $35. *Application Contact:* Harold D. Bibb, Associate Dean of the Graduate School, 401-874-2262, Fax: 401-874-5491. *Director*, Dr. Richard Scholl, 401-874-2239, E-mail: rscholl@uri.edu.

UNIVERSITY OF RICHMOND, Richmond, University of Richmond, VA 23173

General Information Independent, coed, comprehensive institution. *Graduate housing:* On-campus housing not available.

GRADUATE UNITS

Robins School of Business *Degree program information:* Part-time and evening/weekend programs available. Offers business (MBA).

School of Law Offers law (JD). Electronic applications accepted.

UNIVERSITY OF RIO GRANDE, Rio Grande, OH 45674

General Information Independent, coed, comprehensive institution. *Enrollment:* 2,070 graduate, professional, and undergraduate students; 23 full-time matriculated graduate/professional students (13 women), 154 part-time matriculated graduate/professional students (106 women). *Enrollment by degree level:* 177 master's. *Graduate faculty:* 4 full-time (1 woman), 17 part-time/adjunct (8 women). *Tuition:* Full-time $8096; part-time $508 per credit hour. *Graduate housing:* Room and/or apartments guaranteed to single students; on-campus housing not available to married students. Typical cost: $7000 (including board). *Student services:* Campus employment opportunities, campus safety program, career counseling, child daycare facilities, free psychological counseling, grant writing training, international student services, low-cost health insurance, multicultural affairs office, services for students with disabilities, teacher training. *Library facilities:* Jeanette Albiez Davis Library plus 2 others. *Online resources:* library catalog, web page, access to other libraries' catalogs. *Collection:* 96,731 titles, 850 serial subscriptions.

Computer facilities: 300 computers available on campus for general student use. A campuswide network can be accessed from student residence rooms and from off campus. Online class registration is available. *Web address:* http://www.rio.edu/.

General Application Contact: Dreama Hudson, Graduate Secretary, 740-245-7167, Fax: 740-245-7175, E-mail: dhudson@rio.edu.

GRADUATE UNITS

Graduate School Students: 23 full-time (13 women), 154 part-time (106 women), 2 international. Average age 35. *Faculty:* 9 full-time (3 women), 6 part-time/adjunct (2 women). Expenses: Contact institution. *Financial support:* Career-related internships or fieldwork available. Support available to part-time students. Financial award application deadline: 7/1; financial award applicants required to submit FAFSA. In 2008, 128 master's awarded. *Degree program information:* Part-time and evening/weekend programs available. Offers classroom teaching (M Ed). *Application deadline:* Applications are processed on a rolling basis. *Application fee:* $20. *Application Contact:* Dreama Hudson, Graduate Secretary, 740-245-7167, Fax: 740-245-7175, E-mail: dhudson@rio.edu. *Coordinator*, Dr. Greg Miller, 740-245-7364, E-mail: gmiller@rio.edu.

UNIVERSITY OF ROCHESTER, Rochester, NY 14627-0250

General Information Independent, coed, university. CGS member. *Graduate housing:* Rooms and/or apartments available on a first-come, first-served basis to single and married students. Housing application deadline: 5/15. *Research affiliation:* Brookhaven National Laboratory, Fermi National Accelerator Laboratory, Argonne National Laboratory, Lawrence Livermore National Laboratory, Los Alamos National Laboratory, Numerous corporations (Biomedical).

GRADUATE UNITS

The College, Arts and Sciences *Degree program information:* Part-time programs available. Offers arts and sciences (MA, MS, PhD); biology (MS, PhD); brain and cognitive sciences (MS, PhD); chemistry (MS, PhD); clinical psychology (PhD); computer science (MS, PhD); developmental psychology (PhD); economics (MA, PhD); English (MA, PhD); geological sciences (MS, PhD); history (MA, PhD); mathematics (MA, MS, PhD); philosophy (MA, PhD); physics (MA, MS, PhD); physics and astronomy (PhD); political science (MA, PhD); psychology (MA); social-personality psychology (PhD); visual and cultural studies (MA, PhD). Electronic applications accepted.

The College, School of Engineering and Applied Sciences *Degree program information:* Part-time programs available. Offers biomedical engineering (MS, PhD); chemical engineering (MS, PhD); electrical and computer engineering (MS, PhD); engineering and applied sciences (MS, PhD); materials science (MS, PhD); mechanical engineering (MS, PhD).

Institute of Optics Offers optics (MS, PhD).

Eastman School of Music *Degree program information:* Part-time programs available. Offers composition (MA, MM, DMA, PhD); conducting (MM, DMA); education (MA, PhD); jazz studies/contemporary media (MM); music education (MM, DMA); musicology (MA, PhD); pedagogy of music theory (MA); performance and literature (MM, DMA); piano accompanying and chamber music (MM, DMA); theory (MA, PhD).

Margaret Warner Graduate School of Education and Human Development *Degree program information:* Part-time and evening/weekend programs available. Offers education and human development (MAT, MS, Ed D, PhD).

School of Medicine and Dentistry *Degree program information:* Part-time programs available. Offers medicine (MD); medicine and dentistry (MD, MA, MPH, MS, PhD, Certificate). Electronic applications accepted.

Graduate Programs in Medicine and Dentistry *Degree program information:* Part-time programs available. Offers biochemistry (MS, PhD); biomedical genetics (MS, PhD); biophysics (MS, PhD); epidemiology (MS, PhD); health services research and policy (PhD); marriage and family therapy (MS); medical statistics (MS); medicine and dentistry (MA, MPH, MS, PhD); microbiology (MS, PhD); neurobiology and anatomy (MS, PhD); neuroscience (MS, PhD); oral biology (MS); pathology (MS, PhD); pharmacology (MS, PhD); physiology (MS, PhD); public health (MPH); statistics (MA, PhD); toxicology (MS, PhD). Electronic applications accepted.

School of Nursing Students: 47 full-time (42 women), 176 part-time (167 women); includes 25 minority (15 African Americans, 5 Asian Americans or Pacific Islanders, 5 Hispanic Americans), 7 international. Average age 36. 67 applicants, 76% accepted, 47 enrolled. *Faculty:* 37 full-time (30 women), 16 part-time/adjunct (15 women). Expenses: Contact institution. *Financial support:* In 2008–09, 48 students received support, including 13 fellowships with full and partial tuition reimbursements available (averaging $14,988 per year); scholarships/grants, traineeships, health care benefits, tuition waivers (partial), and unspecified assistantships also available. Support available to part-time students. Financial award application deadline: 6/30. In 2008, 69 master's, 4 doctorates awarded. *Degree program information:* Part-time programs available. Offers acute care nurse practitioner (MS); adult nurse practitioner (MS); adult psychiatric mental health nurse practitioner (MS); care of children and families/pediatric nurse practitioner (MS); care of children and families/pediatric nurse practitioner with pediatric behavioral health (MS); care of children and families/pediatric nurse practitioner/neonatal nurse practitioner (MS); child and adolescent psychiatric mental health nurse practitioner (MS); clinical nurse leader (MS); disaster response and emergency preparedness (MS); family nurse practitioner (MS); health practice research (PhD); health promotion, education and technology (MS); nursing (Certificate). *Application deadline:* For fall admission, 11/1 priority date for domestic and international students. *Application fee:* $50. *Application Contact:* Elaine Andolina, Director of Admissions, 585-275-2375, Fax: 585-756-8299, E-mail: elaine_andolina@urmc.rochester.edu. *Dean,* Dr. Kathy P. Parker, 585-273-5639, Fax: 585-273-1268, E-mail: kathy_parker@urmc.rochester.edu.

William E. Simon Graduate School of Business Administration *Degree program information:* Part-time and evening/weekend programs available. Offers business administration (MBA, MS, PhD).

UNIVERSITY OF ST. AUGUSTINE FOR HEALTH SCIENCES, St. Augustine, FL 32086

General Information Proprietary, coed, graduate-only institution. *Enrollment by degree level:* 91 master's, 412 doctoral. *Graduate faculty:* 23 full-time (15 women), 24 part-time/adjunct (3 women). *Tuition:* Full-time $27,600; part-time $525 per hour. *Required fees:* $500. *Graduate housing:* On-campus housing not available. *Student services:* Campus employment opportunities, exercise/wellness program, free psychological counseling, international student services, low-cost health insurance, services for students with disabilities, teacher training, writing training. *Library facilities:* Main library plus 1 other. *Online resources:* library catalog, web page. *Collection:* 2,200 titles.

Computer facilities: 20 computers available on campus for general student use. A campuswide network can be accessed. *Web address:* http://www.usa.edu/.

General Application Contact: Dian Hartley, Director of Admissions, 904-826-0084 Ext. 207, Fax: 904-826-0085, E-mail: dhartley@usa.edu.

GRADUATE UNITS

Division of Advanced Studies *Degree program information:* Part-time programs available. Postbaccalaureate distance learning degree programs offered (minimal on-campus study). Offers advanced studies (MH Sc, DH Sc, TDPT).

Division of Entry-Level Physical Therapy Offers entry-level physical therapy (DPT).

Division of Occupational Therapy Offers occupational therapy (MOT, OTD).

Division of Physical Therapy Offers physical therapy (DPT, Certificate).

UNIVERSITY OF ST. FRANCIS, Joliet, IL 60435-6169

General Information Independent-religious, coed, comprehensive institution. *Enrollment:* 2,146 graduate, professional, and undergraduate students; 268 full-time matriculated graduate/professional students (196 women), 1,156 part-time matriculated graduate/professional students (918 women). *Enrollment by degree level:* 1,410 master's, 14 other advanced degrees. *Graduate faculty:* 37 full-time (25 women), 90 part-time/adjunct (46 women). *Tuition:* Part-time $560 per credit hour. Part-time tuition and fees vary according to program. *Student services:* Campus employment opportunities, campus safety program, career counseling, exercise/wellness program, free psychological counseling, multicultural affairs office, services for students with disabilities, teacher training, writing training. *Library facilities:* University of St. Francis Library. *Online resources:* library catalog, web page, access to other libraries' catalogs. *Collection:* 117,111 titles, 13,500 serial subscriptions, 4,500 audiovisual materials.

Computer facilities: 365 computers available on campus for general student use. A campuswide network can be accessed from student residence rooms and from off campus. Online class registration, billing/payment are available. *Web address:* http://www.stfrancis.edu/.

General Application Contact: Sandra Sloka, Director of Admissions for Graduate and Degree Completion Programs, 800-735-7500, Fax: 815-740-5032, E-mail: ssloka@stfrancis.edu.

GRADUATE UNITS

College of Arts and Sciences Students: 28 full-time (25 women), 5 part-time (4 women); includes 16 minority (all African Americans). Average age 33. 37 applicants, 62% accepted, 15 enrolled. *Faculty:* 6 full-time (4 women). Expenses: Contact institution. *Financial support:* In 2008–09, 32 students received support. Tuition waivers (partial) available. Support available to part-time students. Financial award applicants required to submit FAFSA. In 2008, 18 master's awarded. *Degree program information:* Part-time and evening/weekend programs available. Offers social work (MSW). *Application deadline:* Applications are processed on a rolling basis. *Application fee:* $30. Electronic applications accepted. *Application Contact:* Sandra Sloka, Director of Admissions for Graduate and Degree Completion Programs, 800-735-7500, Fax: 815-740-5032, E-mail: ssloka@stfrancis.edu. *Dean,* Dr. Robert Kase, 815-740-3367, Fax: 815-740-6366.

College of Business and Health Administration Students: 35 full-time (19 women), 128 part-time (68 women); includes 25 minority (13 African Americans, 3 Asian Americans or Pacific Islanders, 9 Hispanic Americans). Average age 38. 98 applicants, 80% accepted, 49 enrolled. *Faculty:* 7 full-time (2 women), 9 part-time/adjunct (3 women). Expenses: Contact institution. *Financial support:* In 2008–09, 67 students received support. Tuition waivers (partial) available. Support available to part-time students. Financial award applicants required to submit FAFSA. In 2008, 62 master's awarded. *Degree program information:* Part-time and evening/weekend programs available. Postbaccalaureate distance learning degree programs offered (no on-campus study). Offers business (MBA, MSM). *Application deadline:* Applications are processed on a rolling basis. *Application fee:* $30. Electronic applications accepted. *Application Contact:* Sandra Sloka, Director of Admissions for Graduate and Degree Completion Programs, 800-735-7500, Fax: 815-740-5032, E-mail: ssloka@stfrancis.edu. *Dean,* Dr. Michael LaRocco, 815-740-3395, Fax: 815-774-2920, E-mail: mlarocco@stfrancis.edu.

School of Business Expenses: Contact institution. *Financial support:* Applicants required to submit FAFSA. *Degree program information:* Part-time and evening/weekend programs available. Postbaccalaureate distance learning degree programs offered (no on-campus study). Offers business (MBA, MSM).

School of Professional Studies Students: 74 full-time (64 women), 469 part-time (384 women); includes 69 minority (36 African Americans, 1 American Indian/Alaska Native, 12 Asian Americans or Pacific Islanders, 20 Hispanic Americans). Average age 44. 177 applicants, 85% accepted, 115 enrolled. *Faculty:* 3 full-time (0 women), 37 part-time/adjunct (18 women). Expenses: Contact institution. *Financial support:* In 2008–09, 148 students received support. Tuition waivers (partial) available. Support available to part-time students. Financial award applicants required to submit FAFSA. In 2008, 207 master's awarded. *Degree program information:* Part-time and evening/weekend programs available. Postbaccalaureate distance learning degree programs offered (no on-campus study). Offers health administration (MS); training and development (MS). *Application deadline:* Applications are processed on a rolling basis. *Application fee:* $30. Electronic applications accepted. *Application Contact:* Sandra Sloka, Director of Admissions for Graduate and Degree Completion Programs, 800-735-7500, Fax: 815-740-5032, E-mail: ssloka@stfrancis.edu. *Dean,* Dr. Michael LaRocco, 815-740-5025, Fax: 815-774-2920, E-mail: mlarocco@stfrancis.edu.

College of Education Students: 51 full-time (32 women), 395 part-time (322 women); includes 37 minority (13 African Americans, 4 Asian Americans or Pacific Islanders, 20 Hispanic Americans). Average age 33. 198 applicants, 89% accepted, 129 enrolled. *Faculty:* 8 full-time (6 women), 32 part-time/adjunct (18 women). Expenses: Contact institution. *Financial support:* In 2008–09, 240 students received support. Scholarships/grants, tuition waivers (partial), and unspecified assistantships available. Support available to part-time students. Financial award applicants required to submit FAFSA. In 2008, 181 master's awarded. *Degree program information:* Part-time and evening/weekend programs available. Offers educational leadership (MS); elementary education certification (M Ed); reading (MS); secondary education certification (M Ed); special education (M Ed); teaching and learning (MS). *Application deadline:* Applications are processed on a rolling basis. *Application fee:* $30. Electronic applications accepted. *Application Contact:* Sandra Sloka, Director of Admissions for Graduate and Degree Completion Programs, 800-735-7500, Fax: 815-740-5032, E-mail: ssloka@stfrancis.edu. *Dean,* Dr. John Gambro, 815-740-3332, Fax: 815-740-2264, E-mail: jgambro@stfrancis.edu.

College of Nursing and Allied Health Students: 70 full-time (46 women), 104 part-time (95 women); includes 42 minority (14 African Americans, 5 American Indian/Alaska Native, 5 Asian Americans or Pacific Islanders, 18 Hispanic Americans). Average age 38. 65 applicants, 60% accepted, 29 enrolled. *Faculty:* 12 full-time (all women), 7 part-time/adjunct (5 women). Expenses: Contact institution. *Financial support:* In 2008–09, 68 students received support. Scholarships/grants, traineeships, tuition waivers (partial), and unspecified assistantships available. Support available to part-time students. Financial award applicants required to submit FAFSA. In 2008, 34 master's awarded. *Degree program information:* Part-time and evening/weekend programs available. Offers nursing (MSN); nursing practice (DNP); physician assistant studies (MS). *Application deadline:* Applications are processed on a rolling basis. *Application fee:* $30. Electronic applications accepted. *Application Contact:* Sandra Sloka, Director of Admissions for Graduate and Degree Completion Programs, 800-735-7500, Fax: 815-740-5032, E-mail: ssloka@stfrancis.edu. *Dean,* Dr. Maria Connolly, 815-740-3840, Fax: 815-740-4243, E-mail: mconnolly@stfrancis.edu.

UNIVERSITY OF SAINT FRANCIS, Fort Wayne, IN 46808-3994

General Information Independent-religious, coed, comprehensive institution. *Graduate housing:* Room and/or apartments available on a first-come, first-served basis to single students; on-campus housing not available to married students.

GRADUATE UNITS

Graduate School *Degree program information:* Part-time and evening/weekend programs available. Offers business administration (MBA); fine art (MA); general psychology (MS); mental health counseling (MS); nursing (MSN); pastoral counseling (MS); physician assistant studies (MS); school counseling (MS Ed); special education (MS Ed).

UNIVERSITY OF SAINT MARY, Leavenworth, KS 66048-5082

General Information Independent-religious, coed, comprehensive institution. *Graduate housing:* On-campus housing not available.

GRADUATE UNITS

Graduate Programs *Degree program information:* Part-time and evening/weekend programs available. Postbaccalaureate distance learning degree programs offered (no on-campus study). Offers business administration (MBA); curriculum and instruction (MAT); education (MA, MAT); management (MS); psychology (MA); special education (MA); teaching (MA). Electronic applications accepted.

UNIVERSITY OF SAINT MARY OF THE LAKE–MUNDELEIN SEMINARY, Mundelein, IL 60060

General Information Independent-religious, men only, graduate-only institution. *Enrollment by degree level:* 167 first professional, 7 master's, 13 doctoral, 35 other advanced degrees. *Graduate faculty:* 45 full-time (5 women), 11 part-time/adjunct (1 woman). *Tuition:* Full-time $18,087; part-time $480 per credit hour. *Required fees:* $250; $250. One-time fee: $50 full-time. *Graduate housing:* Room and/or apartments guaranteed to single students; on-campus housing not available to married students. Housing application deadline: 8/1. *Student services:* Campus employment opportunities, campus safety program, free psychological counseling, international student services, low-cost health insurance, multicultural affairs office. *Library facilities:* Feehan Memorial Library. *Online resources:* library catalog, web page. *Collection:* 192,000 titles, 432 serial subscriptions, 611 audiovisual materials.

Computer facilities: 20 computers available on campus for general student use. A campuswide network can be accessed from student residence rooms. *Web address:* http://www.usml.edu/.

General Application Contact: Very Rev. Dennis J. Lyle, Rector-President, 847-566-6401, Fax: 847-566-7330.

GRADUATE UNITS

School of Theology Students: 222 full-time (4 women); includes 10 minority (2 African Americans, 3 Asian Americans or Pacific Islanders, 5 Hispanic Americans), 78 international. Average age 30. 95 applicants, 75% accepted, 71 enrolled. *Faculty:* 45 full-time (5 women), 11 part-time/adjunct (1 woman). Expenses: Contact institution. *Financial support:* Career-related internships or fieldwork available. In 2008, 38 first professional degrees, 1 master's, 1 doctorate, 10 other advanced degrees awarded. Offers theology (M Div, STB, MA, D Min, Certificate, STL). *Application deadline:* Applications are processed on a rolling basis. *Application fee:* $0. Electronic applications accepted. *Application Contact:* Rev. Raymond J. Webb, Academic Dean, 847-566-6401. *Academic Dean,* Rev. Raymond J. Webb, 847-566-6401.

UNIVERSITY OF ST. MICHAEL'S COLLEGE, Toronto, ON M5S 1J4, Canada

General Information Independent-religious, coed, graduate-only institution. *Enrollment by degree level:* 31 first professional, 94 master's, 72 doctoral, 36 other advanced degrees. *Graduate faculty:* 11 full-time (3 women), 18 part-time/adjunct (8 women). *Graduate housing:* Room and/or apartments available on a first-come, first-served basis to single students; on-campus housing not available to married students. Typical cost: $9355 Canadian dollars (including board). Housing application deadline: 8/15. *Student services:* Campus employment opportunities, campus safety program, career counseling, international student services, low-cost health insurance, services for students with disabilities, writing training. *Library*

University of St. Michael's College (continued)

facilities: John Kelly Library plus 8 others. *Online resources:* library catalog, web page, access to other libraries' catalogs. *Collection:* 357,000 titles, 10,500 serial subscriptions, 42 audiovisual materials.

Computer facilities: 96 computers available on campus for general student use. A campuswide network can be accessed from student residence rooms and from off campus. Online class registration is available. *Web address:* http://www.utoronto.ca/stmikes/theology/.

General Application Contact: Emil Iruthayathas, Student Services Officer, 416-926-7140, Fax: 416-926-7294, E-mail: usmctheology.registrar@utoronto.ca.

GRADUATE UNITS

Faculty of Theology Students: 113 full-time (41 women), 120 part-time (70 women); includes 26 minority (7 African Americans, 19 Asian Americans or Pacific Islanders), 21 international. Average age 40. *Faculty:* 11 full-time (3 women), 18 part-time/adjunct (8 women). Expenses: Contact institution. *Financial support:* Fellowships with partial tuition reimbursements, research assistantships with partial tuition reimbursements, teaching assistantships with partial tuition reimbursements, scholarships/grants, tuition waivers (partial), and bursaries available. Financial award application deadline: 2/1. *Degree program information:* Part-time programs available. Offers Catholic leadership (MA); eastern Christian studies (Diploma); religious education (Diploma); theological studies (Diploma); theology (M Div, MA, MRE, MTS, D Min, PhD, Th D); theology and Jewish studies (MA). *Application deadline:* For fall admission, 1/15 for domestic and international students. Applications are processed on a rolling basis. *Application fee:* $25 Canadian dollars. Electronic applications accepted. *Application Contact:* Fr. Mario O. D'Souza, Dean, 416-926-7140, Fax: 416-926-7294, E-mail: mario.dsouza@utoronto.ca. *Dean,* Fr. Mario O. D'Souza, 416-926-7140, Fax: 416-926-7294, E-mail: mario.dsouza@utoronto.ca.

UNIVERSITY OF ST. THOMAS, St. Paul, MN 55105-1096

General Information Independent-religious, coed, university. *Enrollment:* 1,162 full-time matriculated graduate/professional students (611 women), 3,470 part-time matriculated graduate/professional students (1,856 women). *Enrollment by degree level:* 522 first professional, 3,641 master's, 235 doctoral, 234 other advanced degrees. *Graduate housing:* On-campus housing not available. *Student services:* Campus employment opportunities, campus safety program, career counseling, child daycare facilities, exercise/wellness program, free psychological counseling, international student services, low-cost health insurance, multicultural affairs office, services for students with disabilities. *Library facilities:* O'Shaughnessy-Frey Library plus 3 others. *Online resources:* library catalog, web page, access to other libraries' catalogs. *Collection:* 510,355 titles, 2,743 serial subscriptions, 7,824 audiovisual materials.

Computer facilities: 1,549 computers available on campus for general student use. A campuswide network can be accessed from student residence rooms and from off campus. Online class registration is available. *Web address:* http://www.stthomas.edu/.

General Application Contact: Dr. Angeline Barretta-Herman, Associate Vice President for Academic Affairs, 651-962-6033, Fax: 651-962-6702, E-mail: a9barrettahe@stthomas.edu.

GRADUATE UNITS

Graduate Studies Students: 1,162 full-time (611 women), 3,470 part-time (1,856 women); includes 480 minority (193 African Americans, 12 American Indian/Alaska Native, 200 Asian Americans or Pacific Islanders, 75 Hispanic Americans), 211 international. Average age 28. Expenses: Contact institution. *Financial support:* Fellowships, research assistantships, teaching assistantships, career-related internships or fieldwork, institutionally sponsored loans, and scholarships/grants available. Support available to part-time students. In 2008, 152 first professional degrees, 1,064 master's, 26 doctorates, 153 other advanced degrees awarded. *Degree program information:* Part-time and evening/weekend programs available. Postbaccalaureate distance learning degree programs offered (no on-campus study). Offers advanced studies in software engineering (Certificate); computer security (Certificate); information systems (MSDD, Certificate); software design and development (Certificate); software engineering (MS); software management (MS); software systems (MSS). *Application Contact:* Dr. Angeline Barretta-Herman, Associate Vice President for Academic Affairs, 651-962-6033, Fax: 651-962-6702, E-mail: a9barrettahe@stthomas.edu. *Executive Vice President for Academic Affairs,* Dr. Susan J. Huber, 651-962-6720, Fax: 651-962-6702, E-mail: sjhuber@stthomas.edu.

College of Arts and Sciences *Degree program information:* Part-time and evening/weekend programs available. Offers art history (MA); arts and sciences (MA); Catholic studies (MA); English (MA); music education (MA).

Graduate School of Professional Psychology Students: 60 full-time (48 women), 122 part-time (96 women); includes 12 minority (4 African Americans, 7 Asian Americans or Pacific Islanders, 1 Hispanic American), 6 international. Average age 34. 179 applicants, 55% accepted, 73 enrolled. *Faculty:* 9 full-time (4 women), 9 part-time/adjunct (2 women). Expenses: Contact institution. *Financial support:* Fellowships, research assistantships, institutionally sponsored loans and scholarships/grants available. Support available to part-time students. Financial award application deadline: 8/1; financial award applicants required to submit FAFSA. In 2008, 39 master's, 17 doctorates awarded. *Degree program information:* Part-time and evening/weekend programs available. Offers counseling psychology (MA, Psy D); marriage and family psychology (Certificate). *Application deadline:* For fall admission, 3/1 priority date for domestic students; for winter admission, 2/1 priority date for domestic students; for spring admission, 9/15 priority date for domestic students, 3/1 for international students. *Application fee:* $50. *Application Contact:* Laurie Dupont, Administrative Assistant, 651-962-4669, Fax: 651-962-4651, E-mail: LDupont@stthomas.edu. *Associate Dean,* Dr. Burton (Skip) Nolan, 651-962-4655, Fax: 651-962-4651, E-mail: bnolan@stthomas.edu.

Opus College of Business Students: 156 full-time (51 women), 1,475 part-time (617 women); includes 91 minority (17 African Americans, 2 American Indian/Alaska Native, 54 Asian Americans or Pacific Islanders, 18 Hispanic Americans), 68 international. Average age 31. 515 applicants, 88% accepted, 331 enrolled. *Faculty:* 89 full-time (25 women), 125 part-time/adjunct (40 women). Expenses: Contact institution. *Financial support:* Fellowships, research assistantships, career-related internships or fieldwork, institutionally sponsored loans, and scholarships/grants available. Support available to part-time students. Financial award application deadline: 7/1; financial award applicants required to submit FAFSA. In 2008, 484 master's awarded. *Degree program information:* Part-time and evening/weekend programs available. Postbaccalaureate distance learning degree programs offered (minimal on-campus study). Offers accountancy (MS); business (MBA, MBC, MS); business administration (MBA); business communication (MBC); health care business administration (MBA); real estate (MS). *Application deadline:* For fall admission, 6/1 for domestic students, 4/15 for international students; for spring admission, 11/1 for domestic students. Applications are processed on a rolling basis. *Application fee:* $60. Electronic applications accepted. *Application Contact:* William Woodson, Assistant Dean and Director, 651-962-4200, Fax: 651-962-4129, E-mail: ustmba@stthomas.edu. *Dean,* Dr. Christopher Puto, 651-962-4200, Fax: 651-962-4129, E-mail: cob@stthomas.edu.

Saint Paul Seminary School of Divinity *Degree program information:* Part-time and evening/weekend programs available. Offers divinity (M Div, MA, MARE); religious education (MARE); theology (MA). Electronic applications accepted.

School of Education Students: 114 full-time (86 women), 998 part-time (721 women); includes 110 minority (56 African Americans, 1 American Indian/Alaska Native, 32 Asian Americans or Pacific Islanders, 21 Hispanic Americans), 14 international. Average age 35. 404 applicants, 81% accepted, 251 enrolled. *Faculty:* 32 full-time (21 women), 68 part-time/adjunct (44 women). Expenses: Contact institution. *Financial support:* Fellowships, research assistantships, career-related internships or fieldwork, institutionally sponsored loans, and scholarships/grants available. Support available to part-time students. Financial award applicants required to submit FAFSA. In 2008, 267 master's, 19 doctorates, 1 other advanced degree awarded. *Degree program information:* Part-time and evening/weekend programs available. Offers athletics and activities administration (MA); autism spectrum disorders (Certificate); community education administration (MA); critical pedagogy (Ed D); curriculum and instruction (MA, Ed S); director of special education (Ed S); e-learning (Certificate); education (MA, MAT, Ed D, Certificate, Ed S); educational leadership (Ed S); educational leadership and administration (MA); elementary (MAT); gifted, creative, and talented education (MA, Certificate); human resource management (Certificate); human resources and change leadership (MA); international leadership (Certificate); leadership (Ed D); leadership in student affairs (MA, Certificate); learning technologies (Certificate); learning technology (MA, Certificate); multicultural education (Certificate); organization development (Certificate); Orton-Gillingham reading (Certificate); police leadership (MA); public policy and leadership (MA, Certificate); reading (MA, Certificate); special education (MA). *Application deadline:* For fall admission, 6/1 priority date for domestic students; for spring admission, 11/1 priority date for domestic students. Applications are processed on a rolling basis. *Application fee:* $50. *Application Contact:* Vicky L. Rasmusson, Admissions Coordinator, 651-962-4430, Fax: 651-962-4169, E-mail: VLRasmusson@stthomas.edu. *Interim Dean,* Dr. Bruce H. Kramer, 651-962-4435, Fax: 651-962-4169, E-mail: BHKramer@stthomas.edu.

School of Engineering Offers engineering and technology management (Certificate); manufacturing systems (MS); manufacturing systems engineering (MMSE); systems engineering (MS); technology management (MS). Electronic applications accepted.

School of Law Students: 451 full-time (201 women); includes 60 minority (20 African Americans, 2 American Indian/Alaska Native, 21 Asian Americans or Pacific Islanders, 17 Hispanic Americans). Average age 27. 1,713 applicants, 48% accepted, 151 enrolled. *Faculty:* 30 full-time (13 women), 51 part-time/adjunct (20 women). Expenses: Contact institution. *Financial support:* In 2008–09, 261 students received support. Scholarships/grants available. Financial award application deadline: 7/1; financial award applicants required to submit FAFSA. In 2008, 144 JDs awarded. Offers law (JD). *Application deadline:* For fall admission, 7/1 priority date for domestic and international students. Applications are processed on a rolling basis. *Application fee:* $50. Electronic applications accepted. *Application Contact:* Cari Haaland, Director of Admissions, 651-962-4895, Fax: 651-962-4876, E-mail: lawschool@stthomas.edu. *Dean,* Thomas M. Mengler, 651-962-4880, Fax: 651-962-4881, E-mail: tmmengler@stthomas.edu.

School of Social Work Students: 174 full-time (159 women), 186 part-time (167 women); includes 37 minority (17 African Americans, 2 American Indian/Alaska Native, 10 Asian Americans or Pacific Islanders, 8 Hispanic Americans), 2 international. Average age 31. 212 applicants, 86% accepted, 109 enrolled. *Faculty:* 14 full-time (10 women), 29 part-time/adjunct (20 women). Expenses: Contact institution. *Financial support:* In 2008–09, 178 students received support, including 14 research assistantships (averaging $1,000 per year); fellowships, career-related internships or fieldwork, institutionally sponsored loans, scholarships/grants, and unspecified assistantships also available. Support available to part-time students. Financial award application deadline: 7/1; financial award applicants required to submit FAFSA. In 2008, 90 master's awarded. *Degree program information:* Part-time and evening/weekend programs available. Postbaccalaureate distance learning degree programs offered (minimal on-campus study). Offers social work (MSW). *Application deadline:* For fall admission, 1/10 for domestic students. *Application fee:* $35. Electronic applications accepted. *Application Contact:* Lisa Dalsin, Program Manager, 651-962-5810, Fax: 651-962-5819, E-mail: msw@stthomas.edu. *Dean and Professor,* Dr. Barbara W. Shank, 651-962-5801, Fax: 651-962-5819, E-mail: bwshank@stthomas.edu.

UNIVERSITY OF ST. THOMAS, Houston, TX 77006-4696

General Information Independent-religious, coed, comprehensive institution. CGS member. *Enrollment:* 3,246 graduate, professional, and undergraduate students; 283 full-time matriculated graduate/professional students (115 women), 768 part-time matriculated graduate/professional students (462 women). *Enrollment by degree level:* 90 first professional, 922 master's, 17 doctoral, 22 other advanced degrees. *Graduate faculty:* 83 full-time (32 women), 30 part-time/adjunct (14 women). *Tuition:* Full-time $13,554; part-time $753 per credit. *Required fees:* $224; $224 per year. *Graduate housing:* Room and/or apartments available on a first-come, first-served basis to single students; on-campus housing not available to married students. Typical cost: $4700 per year ($7700 including board). *Student services:* Campus employment opportunities, campus safety program, career counseling, free psychological counseling, international student services, services for students with disabilities. *Library facilities:* Doherty Library plus 1 other. *Online resources:* library catalog, web page, access to other libraries' catalogs. *Collection:* 223,898 titles, 19,351 serial subscriptions, 1,474 audiovisual materials.

Computer facilities: A campuswide network can be accessed from student residence rooms and from off campus. Online class registration is available. *Web address:* http://www.stthom.edu/.

General Application Contact: Dr. Dominic Aquila, Dean, Arts and Sciences, 713-942-5049, Fax: 713-525-3849, E-mail: aquilad@stthom.edu.

GRADUATE UNITS

Cameron School of Business Students: 149 full-time (79 women), 297 part-time (157 women); includes 158 minority (42 African Americans, 1 American Indian/Alaska Native, 39 Asian Americans or Pacific Islanders, 76 Hispanic Americans), 101 international. Average age 31. 151 applicants, 89% accepted, 125 enrolled. *Faculty:* 21 full-time (7 women), 5 part-time/adjunct (1 woman). Expenses: Contact institution. *Financial support:* In 2008–09, 19 students received support. Federal Work-Study, scholarships/grants, and unspecified assistantships available. Support available to part-time students. Financial award application deadline: 3/1; financial award applicants required to submit FAFSA. In 2008, 253 master's awarded. *Degree program information:* Part-time and evening/weekend programs available. Offers business (MBA, MSA). *Application deadline:* Applications are processed on a rolling basis. *Application fee:* $35. Electronic applications accepted. *Application Contact:* Sandra Flanagan, Enrollment Coordinator, 713-525-2115, Fax: 713-525-2110, E-mail: flanags@stthom.edu. *Dean,* Dr. Bahman Mirshab, 713-525-2100, Fax: 713-525-2110, E-mail: mirshab@stthom.edu.

Center for Thomistic Studies Students: 14 full-time (2 women), 12 part-time (1 woman); includes 5 minority (2 African Americans, 3 Asian Americans or Pacific Islanders), 3 international. Average age 32. 21 applicants, 43% accepted, 7 enrolled. *Faculty:* 6 full-time (1 woman). Expenses: Contact institution. *Financial support:* In 2008–09, 13 students received support. Federal Work-Study, scholarships/grants, and unspecified assistantships available. Support available to part-time students. Financial award application deadline: 3/1; financial award applicants required to submit FAFSA. In 2008, 1 master's, 2 doctorates awarded. *Degree program information:* Part-time programs available. Offers philosophy (MA, PhD). *Application deadline:* For fall admission, 2/1 priority date for domestic students. Applications are processed on a rolling basis. *Application fee:* $35. Electronic applications accepted. *Application Contact:* Pamela Butler, Administrative Assistant II, 713-525-3591, Fax: 713-942-3464, E-mail: butlerp@stthom.edu. *Director,* Dr. Mary Catherine Sommers, 713-525-3591, Fax: 713-942-3464, E-mail: sommers@stthom.edu.

Program in Liberal Arts Students: 35 full-time (27 women), 99 part-time (72 women); includes 38 minority (16 African Americans, 2 Asian Americans or Pacific Islanders, 20 Hispanic Americans), 8 international. Average age 36. 51 applicants, 73% accepted, 31 enrolled. *Faculty:* 32 full-time (13 women), 8 part-time/adjunct (6 women). Expenses: Contact institution. *Financial support:* In 2008–09, 11 students received support. Federal Work-Study and scholarships/grants available. Support available to part-time students. Financial award application deadline: 3/1; financial award applicants required to submit FAFSA. In 2008, 38 master's awarded. *Degree program information:* Part-time and evening/weekend programs available. Offers liberal arts (MLA). *Application deadline:* Applications are processed on a rolling basis. *Application fee:* $35. Electronic applications accepted. *Application Contact:* Kate Henderson, MLA Program Assistant, 713-525-3556, Fax: 713-525-6924, E-mail: henderlk@stthom.edu. *Dean,* Dr. Ravi Srinivas, 713-525-6924, Fax: 713-525-6924, E-mail: srinivas@stthom.edu.

School of Education Students: 9 full-time (7 women), 255 part-time (189 women); includes 92 minority (27 African Americans, 8 Asian Americans or Pacific Islanders, 57 Hispanic Americans), 17 international. Average age 37. 266 applicants, 86% accepted, 217 enrolled. *Faculty:* 14 full-time (8 women), 10 part-time/adjunct (6 women). Expenses: Contact institution.

Financial support: In 2008–09, 44 students received support. Federal Work-Study and scholarships/grants available. Support available to part-time students. Financial award application deadline: 3/1; financial award applicants required to submit FAFSA. In 2008, 91 master's awarded. *Degree program information:* Part-time and evening/weekend programs available. Offers education (M Ed). *Application deadline:* Applications are processed on a rolling basis. *Application fee:* $35. Electronic applications accepted. *Application Contact:* Paula C. Hollis, Administrative Assistant, 713-525-3541, Fax: 713-525-3871, E-mail: hollisp@stthom.edu. *Dean,* Dr. Robert M. LeBlanc, 713-525-3548, Fax: 713-525-3871, E-mail: leblancr@stthom.edu.

School of Theology Students: 85 full-time (9 women), 105 part-time (43 women); includes 41 minority (5 African Americans, 11 Asian Americans or Pacific Islanders, 25 Hispanic Americans), 20 international. Average age 40. 44 applicants, 86% accepted, 30 enrolled. *Faculty:* 10 full-time (3 women), 7 part-time/adjunct (1 woman). Expenses: Contact institution. *Financial support:* In 2008–09, 14 students received support. Federal Work-Study and scholarships/grants available. Support available to part-time students. Financial award application deadline: 3/1; financial award applicants required to submit FAFSA. In 2008, 19 M Divs, 29 master's awarded. *Degree program information:* Part-time programs available. Offers theology (M Div, MAPS, MAT). *Application deadline:* Applications are processed on a rolling basis. *Application fee:* $35. Electronic applications accepted. *Application Contact:* Connie Henry, Office Manager, 713-686-4345 Ext. 231, Fax: 713-683-8673, E-mail: henryc@stthom.edu. *Dean,* Dr. Sandra C. Magie, 713-686-4345 Ext. 242, Fax: 713-683-8673, E-mail: smagie@stthom.edu.

UNIVERSITY OF SAN DIEGO, San Diego, CA 92110-2492

General Information Independent-religious, coed, university. CGS member. *Enrollment:* 7,882 graduate, professional, and undergraduate students; 1,420 full-time matriculated graduate/professional students (724 women), 1,034 part-time matriculated graduate/professional students (608 women). *Enrollment by degree level:* 1,025 first professional, 1,195 master's, 199 doctoral, 35 other advanced degrees. *Graduate faculty:* 141 full-time (73 women), 156 part-time/adjunct (83 women). *Tuition:* Full-time $19,710; part-time $1129 per unit. *Required fees:* $154. Full-time tuition and fees vary according to course load and degree level. *Graduate housing:* Room and/or apartments available on a first-come, first-served basis to single students; on-campus housing not available to married students. Typical cost: $11,870 (including board). Room and board charges vary according to board plan and housing facility selected. Housing application deadline: 5/1. *Student services:* Campus employment opportunities, career counseling, child daycare facilities, free psychological counseling, international student services, low-cost health insurance, multicultural affairs office, services for students with disabilities, teacher training. *Library facilities:* Helen K. and James S. Copley Library plus 1 other. *Online resources:* library catalog, access to other libraries' catalogs. *Collection:* 704,887 titles, 38,488 serial subscriptions, 23,392 audiovisual materials. *Research affiliation:* Leon R. Hubbard Hatchery (marine science, ocean studies), Community College Leadership Development Initiative (education), Old Globe Theater (dramatic arts), Hubbs Seaworld Research Institute (marine science, ocean studies), Southwest Fisheries Science Center (marine science, ocean studies).

Computer facilities: Computer purchase and lease plans are available. 765 computers available on campus for general student use. A campuswide network can be accessed from student residence rooms and from off campus. Online class registration is available. *Web address:* http://www.sandiego.edu/.

General Application Contact: Dr. John Mosby, Associate Director of Graduate Admissions, 619-260-4524, Fax: 619-260-4158, E-mail: grads@sandiego.edu.

GRADUATE UNITS

College of Arts and Sciences Students: 40 full-time (20 women), 54 part-time (30 women); includes 18 minority (1 African American, 1 Asian American or Pacific Islander, 16 Hispanic Americans), 3 international. Average age 30. 450 applicants, 14% accepted, 28 enrolled. *Faculty:* 20 full-time (11 women), 5 part-time/adjunct (1 woman). Expenses: Contact institution. *Financial support:* In 2008–09, 58 students received support, including 14 fellowships; career-related internships or fieldwork, Federal Work-Study, institutionally sponsored loans, scholarships/grants, and unspecified assistantships also available. Support available to part-time students. Financial award application deadline: 4/1; financial award applicants required to submit FAFSA. In 2008, 39 master's awarded. *Degree program information:* Part-time and evening/weekend programs available. Offers arts and sciences (MA, MFA, MS); dramatic arts (MFA); history (MA); international relations (MA); marine science (MS). *Application deadline:* Applications are processed on a rolling basis. *Application fee:* $45. Electronic applications accepted. *Application Contact:* Dr. John Mosby, Associate Director of Graduate Admissions, 619-260-4524, Fax: 619-260-4158, E-mail: grads@sandiego.edu. *Dean,* Dr. Mary K. Boyd, 619-260-4545, E-mail: deanboyd@sandiego.edu.

Hahn School of Nursing and Health Science Students: 128 full-time (109 women), 167 part-time (146 women); includes 73 minority (14 African Americans, 5 American Indian/Alaska Native, 36 Asian Americans or Pacific Islanders, 18 Hispanic Americans), 5 international. Average age 37. 204 applicants, 85% accepted, 105 enrolled. *Faculty:* 14 full-time (13 women), 30 part-time/adjunct (25 women). Expenses: Contact institution. *Financial support:* In 2008–09, 249 students received support. Scholarships/grants and traineeships available. Support available to part-time students. Financial award application deadline: 4/1; financial award applicants required to submit FAFSA. In 2008, 70 master's, 9 doctorates awarded. *Degree program information:* Part-time and evening/weekend programs available. Offers accelerated nursing (for RNs) (MSN); adult clinical nurse specialist (MSN); adult nurse practitioner (MSN); clinical nursing (MSN); entry-level nursing (for non-RNs) (MSN); executive nurse leader (MSN); family nurse practitioner (MSN); nursing (PhD); nursing practice (DNP); pediatric nurse practitioner (MSN). *Application deadline:* For fall admission, 3/1 priority date for domestic students, 3/1 for international students; for spring admission, 11/1 priority date for domestic students, 11/1 for international students. Applications are processed on a rolling basis. *Application fee:* $45. Electronic applications accepted. *Application Contact:* Dr. John Mosby, Associate Director of Graduate Admissions, 619-260-4524, Fax: 619-260-4158, E-mail: grads@sandiego.edu. *Dean,* Dr. Sally Hardin, 619-260-4550, Fax: 619-260-6814.

Joan B. Kroc School of Peace Studies Students: 14 full-time (11 women), 4 international. Average age 27. 49 applicants, 59% accepted, 14 enrolled. *Faculty:* 1 (woman) full-time. Expenses: Contact institution. *Financial support:* In 2008–09, 14 students received support, including 9 fellowships; career-related internships or fieldwork, Federal Work-Study, institutionally sponsored loans, scholarships/grants, and unspecified assistantships also available. Support available to part-time students. Financial award application deadline: 4/1; financial award applicants required to submit FAFSA. In 2008, 10 master's awarded. Offers peace and justice studies (MA). *Application deadline:* For fall admission, 2/15 for domestic and international students. *Application fee:* $45. Electronic applications accepted. *Application Contact:* Dr. John Mosby, Associate Director of Graduate Admissions, 619-260-4524, Fax: 619-260-4158, E-mail: grads@sandiego.edu. *Dean,* Fr. William Headley, E-mail: wheadley@sandiego.edu.

School of Business Administration Students: 184 full-time (70 women), 238 part-time (76 women); includes 52 minority (3 African Americans, 1 American Indian/Alaska Native, 25 Asian Americans or Pacific Islanders, 23 Hispanic Americans), 38 international. Average age 32. 509 applicants, 62% accepted, 174 enrolled. *Faculty:* 35 full-time (10 women), 16 part-time/adjunct (5 women). Expenses: Contact institution. *Financial support:* In 2008–09, 284 students received support. Career-related internships or fieldwork, Federal Work-Study, institutionally sponsored loans, scholarships/grants, and unspecified assistantships available. Support available to part-time students. Financial award application deadline: 4/1; financial award applicants required to submit FAFSA. In 2008, 257 master's awarded. *Degree program information:* Part-time and evening/weekend programs available. Offers accountancy (MS); business administration (MBA); executive leadership (MSEL); global leadership (MSGL); international business administration (IMBA); real estate (MSRE); supply chain management (MS, Certificate); taxation (MS). *Application fee:* $80. Electronic applications accepted. *Application Contact:* Dr. John Mosby, Associate Director of Graduate Admissions, 619-260-4524, Fax: 619-260-4158, E-mail: grads@sandiego.edu. *Interim Dean,* Dr. David Pyke, 619-260-4886, E-mail: sbadean@sandiego.edu.

School of Law Students: 846 full-time (341 women), 262 part-time (120 women); includes 297 minority (23 African Americans, 11 American Indian/Alaska Native, 177 Asian Americans or Pacific Islanders, 86 Hispanic Americans), 21 international. Average age 26. 4,329 applicants, 35% accepted, 345 enrolled. *Faculty:* 43 full-time (18 women), 50 part-time/adjunct (11 women). Expenses: Contact institution. *Financial support:* In 2008–09, 972 students received support. Career-related internships or fieldwork, Federal Work-Study, institutionally sponsored loans, and scholarships/grants available. Support available to part-time students. Financial award application deadline: 3/1; financial award applicants required to submit FAFSA. In 2008, 324 first professional degrees, 72 master's awarded. *Degree program information:* Part-time and evening/weekend programs available. Offers business and corporate law (LL M); comparative law (LL M); general studies (LL M); international law (LL M); law (JD); taxation (LL M, Diploma). *Application deadline:* For fall admission, 2/1 priority date for domestic students. Applications are processed on a rolling basis. *Application fee:* $50. Electronic applications accepted. *Application Contact:* Carl J. Eging, Director of Admissions and Financial Aid, 619-260-4528, Fax: 619-260-2218, E-mail: eging@sandiego.edu. *Dean,* Kevin Cole, 619-260-2330, Fax: 619-260-2218.

School of Leadership and Education Sciences Students: 208 full-time (173 women), 313 part-time (236 women); includes 139 minority (28 African Americans, 2 American Indian/Alaska Native, 37 Asian Americans or Pacific Islanders, 72 Hispanic Americans), 12 international. Average age 32. 476 applicants, 66% accepted, 207 enrolled. *Faculty:* 28 full-time (20 women), 55 part-time/adjunct (41 women). Expenses: Contact institution. *Financial support:* In 2008–09, 387 students received support. Career-related internships or fieldwork, Federal Work-Study, institutionally sponsored loans, unspecified assistantships, and stipends available. Support available to part-time students. Financial award application deadline: 4/1; financial award applicants required to submit FAFSA. In 2008, 178 master's, 13 doctorates awarded. *Degree program information:* Part-time and evening/weekend programs available. Offers clinical mental health counseling (MA); curriculum and teaching (M Ed); higher education leadership (MA); leadership and education sciences (M Ed, MA, MAT, PhD, Certificate); leadership studies (MA, PhD); literacy, culture and teaching English to speakers of other languages (M Ed); marital and family therapy (MA); mathematics, science and technology education (M Ed); nonprofit leadership and management (MA, Certificate); school counseling (MA); special education (M Ed); teaching (MAT). *Application fee:* $45. *Application Contact:* Dr. John Mosby, Associate Director of Graduate Admissions, 619-260-4524, Fax: 619-260-4158, E-mail: grads@sandiego.edu. *Dean,* Dr. Paula A. Cordeiro, 619-260-4540, Fax: 619-260-6835, E-mail: cordeiro@sandiego.edu.

See Close-Up on page 1041.

UNIVERSITY OF SAN FRANCISCO, San Francisco, CA 94117-1080

General Information Independent-religious, coed, university. *Enrollment:* 8,750 graduate, professional, and undergraduate students; 2,781 full-time matriculated graduate/professional students (1,679 women), 489 part-time matriculated graduate/professional students (287 women). *Enrollment by degree level:* 703 first professional, 2,258 master's, 309 doctoral. *Graduate faculty:* 111 full-time (48 women), 271 part-time/adjunct (143 women). *Tuition:* Full-time $19,350; part-time $1075 per credit hour. Tuition and fees vary according to course load, degree level, campus/location and program. *Graduate housing:* Room and/or apartments available on a first-come, first-served basis to single students; on-campus housing not available to married students. Typical cost: $7730 per year ($11,540 including board). Room and board charges vary according to campus/location and housing facility selected. *Student services:* Campus employment opportunities, career counseling, free psychological counseling, international student services, low-cost health insurance, multicultural affairs office, services for students with disabilities, teacher training. *Library facilities:* Gleeson Library plus 2 others. *Online resources:* library catalog, web page, access to other libraries' catalogs. *Collection:* 1.1 million titles, 5,560 serial subscriptions. *Research affiliation:* NASA–Ames Research Center.

Computer facilities: Computer purchase and lease plans are available. 350 computers available on campus for general student use. A campuswide network can be accessed from student residence rooms and from off campus. Online class registration is available. *Web address:* http://www.usfca.edu/.

General Application Contact: Information Contact, 415-422-4723, Fax: 415-422-2217, E-mail: graduate@usfca.edu.

GRADUATE UNITS

College of Arts and Sciences Students: 592 full-time (282 women), 61 part-time (23 women); includes 127 minority (25 African Americans, 68 Asian Americans or Pacific Islanders, 34 Hispanic Americans), 155 international. Average age 29. 1,367 applicants, 79% accepted, 286 enrolled. *Faculty:* 35 full-time (10 women), 42 part-time/adjunct (11 women). Expenses: Contact institution. *Financial support:* In 2008–09, 395 students received support; fellowships, research assistantships, teaching assistantships, career-related internships or fieldwork, Federal Work-Study, institutionally sponsored loans, and tuition waivers (partial) available. Support available to part-time students. Financial award application deadline: 3/2; financial award applicants required to submit FAFSA. In 2008, 306 master's awarded. *Degree program information:* Part-time and evening/weekend programs available. Offers arts and sciences (MA, MFA, MS); Asia Pacific studies (MA); biology (MS); chemistry (MS); computer science (MS); economics (MA); environmental management (MS); financial analysis (MS); international and development economics (MA); international studies (MA); investor relations (MA); risk management (MS); sport management (MA); theology (MA); Web science (MS); writing (MFA). *Application deadline:* Applications are processed on a rolling basis. *Application fee:* $55 ($65 for international students). *Application Contact:* Information Contact, 415-422-5135, Fax: 415-422-2217, E-mail: asgraduate@usfca.edu. *Dean,* Dr. Jennifer Turpin, 415-422-6373.

College of Professional Studies Students: 425 full-time (250 women), 17 part-time (12 women); includes 164 minority (32 African Americans, 3 American Indian/Alaska Native, 69 Asian Americans or Pacific Islanders, 60 Hispanic Americans), 22 international. Average age 36. 268 applicants, 71% accepted, 131 enrolled. *Faculty:* 10 full-time (3 women), 48 part-time/adjunct (21 women). Expenses: Contact institution. *Financial support:* In 2008–09, 243 students received support. Available to part-time students. Application deadline: 3/2. In 2008, 163 master's awarded. *Degree program information:* Part-time and evening/weekend programs available. Offers health services administration (MPA); information systems (MS); nonprofit administration (MNA); organization development (MS); project management (MS); public administration (MPA). *Application fee:* $55 ($65 for international students). *Application Contact:* 415-422-6000, E-mail: graduate@usfca.edu. *Dean,* Dr. John Fitzgibbons, SJ, 415-422-2592.

Masagung Graduate School of Management Students: 335 full-time (153 women), 16 part-time (7 women); includes 88 minority (6 African Americans, 63 Asian Americans or Pacific Islanders, 19 Hispanic Americans), 51 international. Average age 30. 527 applicants, 67% accepted, 155 enrolled. *Faculty:* 23 full-time (5 women), 16 part-time/adjunct (8 women). Expenses: Contact institution. *Financial support:* In 2008–09, 194 students received support; fellowships, research assistantships, teaching assistantships, career-related internships or fieldwork, Federal Work-Study, and institutionally sponsored loans available. Support available to part-time students. Financial award application deadline: 3/2; financial award applicants required to submit FAFSA. In 2008, 113 master's awarded. *Degree program information:* Part-time and evening/weekend programs available. Offers business administration (MBA); business economics (MBA); e-business (MBA); entrepreneurship (MBA); finance (MBA); international business (MBA); management (MBA); marketing (MBA); telecommunications management and policy (MBA). *Application deadline:* For fall admission, 7/1 priority date for domestic students; for spring admission, 11/30 for domestic students. Applications are processed on a rolling basis. *Application Contact:* Kelly Brookes, Director, MBA Program, 415-422-2221, Fax: 415-422-6315, E-mail: mba@usfca.edu. *Dean,* Dr. Michael Duffy, 415-422-6771, Fax: 415-422-2502.

University of San Francisco (continued)

School of Education Students: 677 full-time (519 women), 206 part-time (143 women); includes 262 minority (63 African Americans, 3 American Indian/Alaska Native, 90 Asian Americans or Pacific Islanders, 106 Hispanic Americans), 49 international. Average age 35. 765 applicants, 66% accepted, 296 enrolled. *Faculty:* 21 full-time (16 women), 87 part-time/adjunct (57 women). Expenses: Contact institution. *Financial support:* In 2008–09, 519 students received support; fellowships, research assistantships, teaching assistantships available. Financial award application deadline: 3/2; financial award applicants required to submit FAFSA. In 2008, 261 master's, 49 doctorates awarded. *Degree program information:* Part-time and evening/weekend programs available. Offers Catholic school leadership (MA, Ed D); Catholic school teaching (MA); counseling (MA); counseling psychology (Ed D); digital media and learning (MA); education (MA, Ed D); international and multicultural education (MA, Ed D); learning and instruction (MA, Ed D); multicultural literature for children and young adults (MA); organization and leadership (MA, Ed D); teaching (MA); teaching English as a second language (MA); teaching reading (MA). *Application fee:* $55 ($65 for international students). *Application Contact:* Beth Teabue, Associate Director of Graduate Outreach, 415-422-5467, E-mail: schoolofeducation@usfca.edu. *Dean*, Dr. Walter Gmelch, 415-422-6525.

School of Law Students: 547 full-time (288 women), 156 part-time (72 women); includes 205 minority (44 African Americans, 3 American Indian/Alaska Native, 97 Asian Americans or Pacific Islanders, 61 Hispanic Americans), 33 international. Average age 28. 4,305 applicants, 37% accepted, 267 enrolled. *Faculty:* 15 full-time (7 women), 49 part-time/adjunct (18 women). Expenses: Contact institution. *Financial support:* In 2008–09, 613 students received support. Career-related internships or fieldwork, Federal Work-Study, and institutionally sponsored loans available. Support available to part-time students. Financial award application deadline: 3/2; financial award applicants required to submit FAFSA. In 2008, 224 JDs, 15 master's awarded. *Degree program information:* Part-time and evening/weekend programs available. Offers intellectual property and technology law (LL M); international transactions and comparative law (LL M); law (JD, LL M). *Application deadline:* For fall admission, 4/1 for domestic students. Applications are processed on a rolling basis. *Application Contact:* Alan P. Guerrero, Director of Admissions, 415-422-6586, E-mail: lawadmissions@usfca.edu. *Dean*, Jeffrey Brand, 415-422-6304.

School of Nursing Students: 205 full-time (187 women), 33 part-time (30 women); includes 80 minority (12 African Americans, 1 American Indian/Alaska Native, 51 Asian Americans or Pacific Islanders, 16 Hispanic Americans), 1 international. Average age 36. 216 applicants, 47% accepted, 78 enrolled. *Faculty:* 7 full-time (all women), 32 part-time/adjunct (30 women). Expenses: Contact institution. *Financial support:* In 2008–09, 177 students received support. Institutionally sponsored loans available. Financial award application deadline: 3/2. In 2008, 79 master's, 6 doctorates awarded. *Degree program information:* Part-time programs available. Offers clinical nurse leader (MSN); family nurse practitioner (DNP); healthcare systems leadership (MSN, DNP); nursing practice (DNP). *Application deadline:* Applications are processed on a rolling basis. *Application fee:* $40. *Application Contact:* Information Contact, 415-422-4723, Fax: 415-422-2217. *Dean*, Dr. Judith Karshmer, 415-422-6681, Fax: 415-422-6877, E-mail: nursing@usfca.edu.

UNIVERSITY OF SASKATCHEWAN, Saskatoon, SK S7N 5A2, Canada

General Information Province-supported, coed, university. *Graduate housing:* Rooms and/or apartments available on a first-come, first-served basis to single and married students. *Research affiliation:* Canada Agriculture, Saskatchewan Research Council, University Hospital, Innovation Place.

GRADUATE UNITS

College of Dentistry Offers dentistry (DMD). Electronic applications accepted.

College of Graduate Studies and Research *Degree program information:* Part-time programs available.

College of Agriculture *Degree program information:* Part-time programs available. Offers agricultural economics (M Ag, M Sc, MA, PhD); agriculture (M Ag, M Sc, MA, PhD); animal and poultry science (M Ag, M Sc, PhD); applied microbiology and food science (M Ag, M Sc, PhD); plant sciences (M Ag, M Sc, PhD); soil science (M Ag, M Sc, PhD).

College of Arts and Sciences *Degree program information:* Part-time programs available. Offers archaeology (MA, PhD); art and art history (MFA); arts and sciences (M Math, M Sc, MA, MFA, PhD, Diploma); biology (M Sc, PhD, Diploma); chemistry (M Sc, PhD); computer science (M Sc, PhD); drama (MA); economics (MA); English (MA, PhD); geography (M Sc, MA, PhD); geological sciences (M Sc, PhD, Diploma); history (MA, PhD); languages and linguistics (MA); mathematics and statistics (M Math, MA, PhD); music (MA); native studies (MA, PhD); philosophy (MA); physics ad engineering physics (M Sc, PhD); political studies (MA); psychology (MA, PhD); religious studies and anthropology (MA); sociology (MA, PhD); women's and gender studies (MA, PhD).

College of Education *Degree program information:* Part-time programs available. Offers curriculum studies (M Ed, PhD, Diploma); education (M Ed, MC Ed, PhD, Diploma); educational administration (M Ed, PhD, Diploma); educational foundations (M Ed, MC Ed, PhD, Diploma); educational psychology and special education (M Ed, PhD, Diploma).

College of Engineering Offers agricultural and bioresource engineering (M Eng, M Sc, PhD); biomedical engineering (M Eng, M Sc, PhD); chemical engineering (M Eng, M Sc, PhD); civil and geological engineering (M Eng, M Sc, PhD); electrical engineering (M Eng, M Sc, PhD); engineering (M Eng, M Sc, PhD, Diploma); environmental engineering (M Eng, M Sc, PhD, Diploma); mechanical engineering (M Sc, PhD).

College of Kinesiology Offers kinesiology (M Sc, PhD, Diploma).

College of Law *Degree program information:* Part-time programs available. Offers law (LL B, LL M).

College of Nursing *Degree program information:* Part-time programs available. Offers nursing (MN).

College of Pharmacy and Nutrition Offers pharmacy and nutrition (M Sc, PhD).

Edwards School of Business *Degree program information:* Part-time programs available. Offers accounting (M Sc, MP Acc); agribusiness management (MBA); biotechnology management (MBA); commerce (M Sc, MBA, MP Acc); finance (M Sc); health services management (MBA); indigenous management (MBA); industrial relations and organizational behavior (M Sc); international business management (MBA); marketing (M Sc).

Toxicology Centre Offers toxicology (M Sc, PhD, Diploma).

College of Medicine Offers anatomy and cell biology (M Sc, PhD); biochemistry (M Sc, PhD); community health and epidemiology (M Sc, PhD); medicine (MD, M Sc, PhD); microbiology and immunology (M Sc, PhD); obstetrics, gynecology and reproductive services (M Sc, PhD); pathology (M Sc, PhD); pharmacology (M Sc, PhD); physiology (M Sc, PhD); psychiatry (M Sc, PhD); surgery (M Sc).

Western College of Veterinary Medicine Students: 130 full-time (68 women); includes 9 minority (all African Americans). *Faculty:* 49 full-time (17 women), 16 part-time/adjunct. Expenses: Contact institution. *Financial support:* Fellowships, teaching assistantships available. Financial award application deadline: 1/31. In 2008, 14 master's, 6 doctorates awarded. Offers herd medicine and theriogenology (M Sc, M Vet Sc, PhD); large animal clinical sciences (M Sc, M Vet Sc, PhD); small animal clinical sciences (M Sc, M Vet Sc, PhD); veterinary anatomy (M Sc); veterinary anesthesiology, radiology and surgery (M Vet Sc); veterinary biomedical sciences (M Sc, M Vet Sc, PhD); veterinary internal medicine (M Vet Sc); veterinary medicine (DVM, M Sc, M Vet Sc, PhD); veterinary microbiology (M Sc, M Vet Sc, PhD); veterinary pathology (M Sc, M Vet Sc, PhD); veterinary physiological sciences (M Sc, PhD). *Application deadline:* For fall admission, 7/1 priority date for domestic students. *Application fee:* $50. *Application Contact:* Dr. Norman C. Rawlings, Associate Dean, Research, 306-966-7068, Fax: 306-966-8747, E-mail: norman.rawlings@usask.ca. *Dean*, Dr. C. S. Rhodes, 306-966-7447, Fax: 306-966-8747, E-mail: charles.rhodes@usask.ca.

THE UNIVERSITY OF SCRANTON, Scranton, PA 18510

General Information Independent-religious, coed, comprehensive institution. CGS member. *Enrollment:* 5,651 graduate, professional, and undergraduate students; 696 full-time matriculated graduate/professional students (444 women), 757 part-time matriculated graduate/professional students (528 women). *Enrollment by degree level:* 1,351 master's, 102 doctoral. *Graduate faculty:* 135 full-time (57 women), 68 part-time/adjunct (29 women). *Graduate housing:* Room and/or apartments available to single students; on-campus housing not available to married students. *Student services:* Campus employment opportunities, career counseling, exercise/wellness program, free psychological counseling, international student services, multicultural affairs office, services for students with disabilities, writing training. *Library facilities:* Harry and Jeanette Weinberg Memorial Library plus 1 other. *Online resources:* library catalog, web page, access to other libraries' catalogs. *Collection:* 383,984 titles, 23,572 serial subscriptions. *Research affiliation:* Wyoming Valley Health Care System (nursing), Community Medical Center (health services), National Health Management Center (health care management), Allied Services (rehabilitation), Lackawanna River Corridor Association (environment), Universidad Iberoamericana (counseling and human services).

Computer facilities: Computer purchase and lease plans are available. 927 computers available on campus for general student use. A campuswide network can be accessed from student residence rooms and from off campus. Online class registration is available. *Web address:* http://www.scranton.edu/.

General Application Contact: Joseph M. Roback, Director of Admissions, 570-941-4385, Fax: 570-941-5928, E-mail: roback j2@scranton.edu.

GRADUATE UNITS

College of Graduate and Continuing Education Students: 696 full-time (444 women), 757 part-time (528 women); includes 133 minority (74 African Americans, 4 American Indian/Alaska Native, 18 Asian Americans or Pacific Islanders, 37 Hispanic Americans), 88 international. Average age 32. 827 applicants, 88% accepted. *Faculty:* 135 full-time (57 women), 68 part-time/adjunct (29 women). Expenses: Contact institution. *Financial support:* In 2008–09, 98 students received support, including 98 teaching assistantships with full and partial tuition reimbursements available (averaging $6,645 per year); fellowships, career-related internships or fieldwork, Federal Work-Study, and unspecified assistantships also available. Support available to part-time students. Financial award application deadline: 3/1. In 2008, 619 master's, 36 doctorates awarded. *Degree program information:* Part-time and evening/weekend programs available. Postbaccalaureate distance learning degree programs offered (no on-campus study). Offers accounting (MBA); adult health nursing (MSN); biochemistry (MA, MS); chemistry (MA, MS); clinical chemistry (MA, MS); community counseling (MS); curriculum and instruction (MA, MS); early childhood education (MA, MS); educational administration (MS); elementary education (MS); English as a second language (MS); family nurse practitioner (MSN, PMC); finance (MBA); general business administration (MBA); health administration (MHA); history (MA); human resources (MS); human resources administration (MS); human resources development (MS); international business (MBA); management information systems (MBA); marketing (MBA); nurse anesthesia (MSN, PMC); occupational therapy (MS); operations management (MBA); organizational leadership (MS); physical therapy (MPT, DPT); professional counseling (CAGS); reading education (MS); rehabilitation counseling (MS); school counseling (MS); secondary education (MS); software engineering (MS); special education (MS); theology (MA). *Application deadline:* Applications are processed on a rolling basis. *Application fee:* $50. *Application Contact:* Joseph M. Roback, Director of Admissions, 570-941-4385, Fax: 570-941-5928, E-mail: roback j2@scranton.edu. *Dean*, Dr. W. Jeffrey Welsh, 570-941-6300, Fax: 570-941-5995, E-mail: welshw2@scranton.edu.

UNIVERSITY OF SIOUX FALLS, Sioux Falls, SD 57105-1699

General Information Independent-religious, coed, comprehensive institution. *Enrollment:* 1,564 graduate, professional, and undergraduate students; 367 part-time matriculated graduate/professional students (226 women). *Enrollment by degree level:* 353 master's, 14 other advanced degrees. *Graduate faculty:* 19 full-time (11 women), 17 part-time/adjunct (9 women). *Graduate housing:* Rooms and/or apartments available on a first-come, first-served basis to single and married students. *Student services:* Campus employment opportunities, campus safety program, career counseling, exercise/wellness program, low-cost health insurance, services for students with disabilities, writing training. *Library facilities:* Norman B. Mears Library. *Online resources:* library catalog, web page, access to other libraries' catalogs. *Collection:* 85,713 titles, 378 serial subscriptions.

Computer facilities: 150 computers available on campus for general student use. A campuswide network can be accessed from student residence rooms and from off campus. Online class registration is available. *Web address:* http://www.usiouxfalls.edu/.

General Application Contact: Student Contact, 605-331-5000.

GRADUATE UNITS

Fredrikson School of Education Students: 235 part-time (179 women); includes 2 minority (1 African American, 1 American Indian/Alaska Native). 55 applicants, 100% accepted, 47 enrolled. *Faculty:* 9 full-time (8 women), 10 part-time/adjunct (7 women). Expenses: Contact institution. *Financial support:* In 2008–09, 58 students received support. Available to part-time students. Applicants required to submit FAFSA. In 2008, 84 master's, 11 Ed Ss awarded. *Degree program information:* Part-time and evening/weekend programs available. Offers leadership (M Ed); reading (M Ed); superintendent (Ed S); teaching (M Ed); technology (M Ed). Summer admission only. *Application deadline:* Applications are processed on a rolling basis. *Application fee:* $25. *Application Contact:* Dawn Olson, Director of Graduate Programs in Education, 605-575-2083, Fax: 605-575-2079, E-mail: dawn.olson@usiouxfalls.edu. *Director of Graduate Programs in Education*, Dawn Olson, 605-575-2083, Fax: 605-575-2079, E-mail: dawn.olson@usiouxfalls.edu.

John T. Vucurevich School of Business Students: 138 part-time (74 women); includes 2 minority (1 African American, 1 Asian American or Pacific Islander). 50 applicants, 90% accepted, 45 enrolled. *Faculty:* 8 full-time (3 women), 7 part-time/adjunct (2 women). Expenses: Contact institution. *Financial support:* In 2008–09, 47 students received support. Institutionally sponsored loans, scholarships/grants, and tuition waivers (full) available. Financial award applicants required to submit FAFSA. In 2008, 32 master's awarded. *Degree program information:* Part-time and evening/weekend programs available. Offers business (MBA). *Application fee:* $25. *Application Contact:* Student Contact, 605-331-6680. *Director*, Rebecca T. Murdock, 605-575-2068, E-mail: mba@usiouxfalls.edu.

UNIVERSITY OF SOUTH AFRICA, Pretoria 0003, South Africa

General Information Private, coed, university.

GRADUATE UNITS

College of Agriculture and Environmental Sciences Offers agriculture (MS); consumer science (MCS); environmental management (MA, MS, PhD); environmental science (MA, MS, PhD); geography (MA, MS, PhD); horticulture (M Tech); human ecology (MHE); life sciences (MS); nature conservation (M Tech).

College of Economic and Management Sciences Offers accounting (D Admin, D Com); accounting science (DA); auditing (D Admin, D Com); business administration (M Tech); business economics (D Admin); business leadership (DBL); business management (D Admin, D Com); economic management analysis (M Tech); economics (D Admin, D Com, PhD); human resource development (M Tech); industrial psychology (D Admin, D Com, PhD); logistics (D Com); marketing (M Tech); public administration (D Admin, D Com, DPA, PhD); public management (M Tech); quantitative management (D Admin, D Com); real estate (M Tech); statistics (D Admin, PhD); tourism management (D Admin, D Com); transport economics (D Admin, D Com).

College of Human Sciences Offers adult education (M Ed); African languages (MA, PhD); African politics (MA, PhD); Afrikaans (MA, PhD); ancient history (MA, PhD); ancient Near Eastern studies (MA, PhD); anthropology (MA, PhD); applied linguistics (MA); Arabic (MA, PhD); archaeology (MA); art history (MA); Biblical archaeology (MA); Biblical studies (M Th, D Th, PhD); Christian spirituality (M Th, D Th); church history (M Th, D Th); classical studies (MA, PhD); clinical psychology (MA); communication (MA, PhD); comparative education

(M Ed, Ed D); consulting psychology (D Admin, D Com, PhD); curriculum studies (M Ed, Ed D); development studies (M Admin, MA, D Admin, PhD); didactics (M Ed, Ed D); education (M Tech); education management (M Ed, Ed D); educational psychology (M Ed); English (MA); environmental education (M Ed); French (MA, PhD); German (MA, PhD); Greek (MA); guidance and counseling (M Ed); health studies (MA, PhD); history (MA, PhD); history of education (Ed D); inclusive education (M Ed, Ed D); information and communications technology policy and regulation (MA); information science (MA, MIS, PhD); international politics (MA, PhD); Islamic studies (MA, PhD); Italian (MA, PhD); Judaica (MA, PhD); linguistics (MA, PhD); mathematical education (M Ed); mathematics education (MA); missiology (M Th, D Th); modern Hebrew (MA, PhD); musicology (MA, MMus, D Mus, PhD); natural science education (M Ed); New Testament (M Th, D Th); Old Testament (D Th); pastoral therapy (M Th, D Th); philosophy (MA); philosophy of education (M Ed, Ed D); politics (MA, PhD); Portuguese (MA, PhD); practical theology (M Th, D Th); psychology (MA, MS, PhD); psychology of education (M Ed, Ed D); public health (MA); religious studies (MA, D Th, PhD); Romance languages (MA); Russian (MA, PhD); Semitic languages (MA, PhD); social behavior studies in HIV/AIDS (MA); social science (mental health) (MA); social science in development studies (MA); social science in psychology (MA); social science in social work (MA); social science in sociology (MA); social work (MSW, DSW, PhD); socio-education (M Ed, Ed D); sociolinguistics (MA); sociology (MA, PhD); Spanish (MA, PhD); systematic theology (M Th, D Th); TESOL (teaching English to speakers of other languages) (MA); theological ethics (M Th, D Th); theory of literature (MA, PhD); urban ministries (D Th); urban ministry (M Th).

College of Law Offers correctional services management (M Tech); criminology (MA, PhD); law (LL M, LL D); penology (MA, PhD); police science (MA, PhD); policing (M Tech); security risk management (M Tech); social science in criminology (MA).

College of Science, Engineering and Technology Offers chemical engineering (M Tech); information technology (M Tech).

Graduate School of Business Leadership Offers business leadership (MBA, MBL, DBL).

Institute for Science and Technology Education Offers mathematics, science and technology education (M Sc, PhD).

UNIVERSITY OF SOUTH ALABAMA, Mobile, AL 36688-0002

General Information State-supported, coed, university. CGS member. *Enrollment:* 14,064 graduate, professional, and undergraduate students; 2,328 full-time matriculated graduate/professional students (1,624 women), 688 part-time matriculated graduate/professional students (526 women). *Enrollment by degree level:* 282 first professional, 2,256 master's, 415 doctoral, 63 other advanced degrees. *Graduate faculty:* 355 full-time (119 women), 5 part-time/adjunct (2 women). Tuition, state resident: full-time $4656. Tuition, nonresident: full-time $9312. *Graduate housing:* Rooms and/or apartments available to single and married students. Typical cost: $5344 (including board) for single students. *Student services:* Campus employment opportunities, campus safety program, career counseling, exercise/wellness program, free psychological counseling, grant writing training, international student services, low-cost health insurance, multicultural affairs office, services for students with disabilities, writing training. *Library facilities:* University Library plus 1 other. *Online resources:* library catalog, web page, access to other libraries' catalogs. *Collection:* 1.1 million titles, 7,344 serial subscriptions. *Research affiliation:* Gulf Coast Universities Consortium, Alabama EPSCoR Programs, Von Braun Center for Science and Innovation, Oak Ridge Associated Universities, Rand Gulf State Policy Institute, Dauphin Island Marine Laboratory.

Computer facilities: 500 computers available on campus for general student use. A campuswide network can be accessed from student residence rooms and from off campus. Online class registration is available. *Web address:* http://www.southalabama.edu/.

General Application Contact: Dr. B. Keith Harrison, Dean, Graduate School, 251-460-6310, Fax: 251-461-1513, E-mail: kharriso@usouthal.edu.

GRADUATE UNITS

College of Medicine Students: 330 full-time (165 women), 3 part-time (1 woman); includes 57 minority (25 African Americans, 3 American Indian/Alaska Native, 26 Asian Americans or Pacific Islanders, 3 Hispanic Americans), 12 international. Average age 33. 1,899 applicants, 53% accepted, 658 enrolled. *Faculty:* 51 full-time (7 women), 1 part-time/adjunct (0 women). Expenses: Contact institution. *Financial support:* Fellowships, research assistantships, institutionally sponsored loans available. In 2008, 65 first professional degrees, 3 doctorates awarded. Offers biochemistry and molecular biology (PhD); cell biology and neuroscience (PhD); medicine (MD, PhD); microbiology and immunology (PhD); pharmacology (PhD); physiology (PhD). *Application deadline:* For fall admission, 6/1 for domestic and international students. *Application fee:* $35. Electronic applications accepted. *Application Contact:* Dean of the Graduate School, E-mail: kharriso@usouthal.edu. *Director of Graduate Studies*, Dr. Ronald Balczon, 251-460-6101.

Graduate School Students: 1,998 full-time (1,459 women), 685 part-time (525 women); includes 448 minority (355 African Americans, 22 American Indian/Alaska Native, 35 Asian Americans or Pacific Islanders, 36 Hispanic Americans), 319 international. 1,839 applicants, 54% accepted, 647 enrolled. *Faculty:* 293 full-time (108 women), 4 part-time/adjunct (2 women). Expenses: Contact institution. *Financial support:* Fellowships, research assistantships, teaching assistantships, career-related internships or fieldwork, institutionally sponsored loans, and traineeships available. Support available to part-time students. Financial award application deadline: 4/1. In 2008, 719 master's, 69 doctorates, 10 other advanced degrees awarded. *Degree program information:* Part-time and evening/weekend programs available. Offers environmental toxicology (MS). *Application deadline:* For fall admission, 7/15 priority date for domestic students, 6/15 for international students; for spring admission, 12/1 for domestic students, 11/1 for international students. Applications are processed on a rolling basis. *Application fee:* $35. *Application Contact:* Dr. B. Keith Harrison, Dean of the Graduate School, 251-460-6310, Fax: 251-461-1513, E-mail: kharriso@usouthal.edu. *Dean of the Graduate School*, Dr. B. Keith Harrison, 251-460-6310, Fax: 251-461-1513, E-mail: kharriso@usouthal.edu.

College of Allied Health Professions Students: 298 full-time (236 women), 65 part-time (46 women); includes 26 minority (15 African Americans, 2 American Indian/Alaska Native, 6 Asian Americans or Pacific Islanders, 3 Hispanic Americans), 1 international. 119 applicants, 98% accepted, 70 enrolled. *Faculty:* 28 full-time (17 women). Expenses: Contact institution. *Financial support:* Fellowships, research assistantships, career-related internships or fieldwork available. Support available to part-time students. Financial award application deadline: 4/1. In 2008, 72 master's, 43 doctorates awarded. Offers allied health professions (MHS, MS, Au D, DPT, PhD); audiology (Au D); communication sciences and disorders (PhD); occupational therapy (MS); physical therapy (DPT); physician assistant studies (MHS); speech and hearing sciences (MS). *Application deadline:* For fall admission, 7/15 priority date for domestic students, 6/15 for international students; for spring admission, 12/1 for domestic students, 11/1 for international students. Applications are processed on a rolling basis. *Application fee:* $35. *Application Contact:* Dr. Julio F. Turrens, Director of Graduate Studies, 251-380-2785. *Director of Graduate Studies*, Dr. Julio F. Turrens, 251-380-2785.

College of Arts and Sciences Students: 156 full-time (94 women), 98 part-time (58 women); includes 37 minority (28 African Americans, 4 American Indian/Alaska Native, 5 Asian Americans or Pacific Islanders), 13 international. 198 applicants, 54% accepted, 82 enrolled. *Faculty:* 139 full-time (39 women), 2 part-time/adjunct (1 woman). Expenses: Contact institution. *Financial support:* Fellowships, research assistantships, teaching assistantships, career-related internships or fieldwork available. Support available to part-time students. Financial award application deadline: 4/1. In 2008, 44 master's, 5 doctorates, 1 other advanced degree awarded. *Degree program information:* Part-time and evening/weekend programs available. Offers arts and sciences (MA, MPA, MS, PhD, Certificate); biological sciences (MS); communication (MA); English (MA); gerontology (Certificate); history (MA); marine sciences (MS, PhD); mathematics (MS); psychology (MS); public administration (MPA); sociology (MA). *Application deadline:* For fall admission, 7/15 priority date for domestic students, 6/15 for international students; for spring admission, 12/1 for domestic students, 11/1 for international students. Applications are processed on a rolling basis. *Application fee:* $35. *Application Contact:* Dr. S. L. Varghese, Director of Graduate Studies, 251-460-6280. *Director of Graduate Studies*, Dr. S. L. Varghese, 251-460-6280.

College of Education Students: 334 full-time (282 women), 307 part-time (258 women); includes 171 minority (154 African Americans, 6 American Indian/Alaska Native, 4 Asian Americans or Pacific Islanders, 7 Hispanic Americans), 23 international. 243 applicants, 44% accepted, 89 enrolled. *Faculty:* 51 full-time (28 women). Expenses: Contact institution. *Financial support:* In 2008–09, 23 research assistantships, 10 teaching assistantships were awarded; career-related internships or fieldwork also available. Support available to part-time students. Financial award application deadline: 4/1. In 2008, 188 master's, 9 doctorates, 9 other advanced degrees awarded. *Degree program information:* Part-time programs available. Offers community counseling (MS); early childhood education (M Ed); education (M Ed, MS, PhD, Ed S); educational administration (Ed S); educational leadership (M Ed); educational media (M Ed, MS); elementary education (M Ed); exercise science (MS); health education (M Ed); instructional design and development (MS, PhD); physical education (M Ed); reading education (M Ed); rehabilitation counseling (MS); school counseling (M Ed); school psychometry (M Ed); science education (M Ed); secondary education (M Ed); special education (M Ed, Ed S); therapeutic recreation (MS). *Application deadline:* For fall admission, 7/15 priority date for domestic students, 6/15 priority date for international students; for spring admission, 12/1 priority date for domestic students, 11/1 priority date for international students. Applications are processed on a rolling basis. *Application fee:* $35. *Application Contact:* Dr. B. Keith Harrison, Dean of the Graduate School, 251-460-6310, Fax: 251-461-1513, E-mail: kharriso@usouthal.edu. *Director of Graduate Studies*, Dr. Abigail Baxter, 251-380-2738.

College of Engineering Students: 190 full-time (33 women), 30 part-time (4 women); includes 7 minority (2 African Americans, 2 Asian Americans or Pacific Islanders, 3 Hispanic Americans), 191 international. 310 applicants, 50% accepted, 59 enrolled. *Faculty:* 29 full-time (1 woman). Expenses: Contact institution. *Financial support:* Research assistantships, career-related internships or fieldwork and institutionally sponsored loans available. Support available to part-time students. Financial award application deadline: 4/1. In 2008, 117 master's awarded. *Degree program information:* Part-time programs available. Offers chemical engineering (MS Ch E); civil engineering (MSCE); electrical engineering (MSEE); engineering (MS Ch E, MSCE, MSEE, MSME); mechanical engineering (MSME). *Application deadline:* For fall admission, 7/15 priority date for domestic students, 6/15 for international students; for spring admission, 12/1 for domestic students, 11/1 for international students. Applications are processed on a rolling basis. *Application fee:* $35. *Application Contact:* Dr. B. Keith Harrison, Director of Graduate Studies, 251-460-6160. *Director of Graduate Studies*, Dr. Thomas G. Thomas, 251-460-6140.

College of Nursing Students: 821 full-time (745 women), 168 part-time (149 women); includes 180 minority (141 African Americans, 6 American Indian/Alaska Native, 15 Asian Americans or Pacific Islanders, 18 Hispanic Americans), 11 international. 674 applicants, 50% accepted, 251 enrolled. *Faculty:* 20 full-time (18 women), 1 (woman) part-time/adjunct. Expenses: Contact institution. In 2008, 226 master's, 12 doctorates awarded. Offers adult health nursing (MSN); community/mental health nursing (MSN); maternal/child nursing (MSN); nursing (DNP). *Application deadline:* For fall admission, 7/15 for domestic students; for spring admission, 12/1 for domestic students. *Application fee:* $35. *Application Contact:* Dr. B. Keith Harrison, Dean of the Graduate School, 251-460-6310, Fax: 251-461-1513, E-mail: kharriso@usouthal.edu. *Director of Graduate Education*, Dr. Rosemary Rhodes, 251-434-3414.

Mitchell College of Business Students: 121 full-time (48 women), 11 part-time (9 women); includes 13 minority (4 African Americans, 5 American Indian/Alaska Native, 1 Asian American or Pacific Islander, 3 Hispanic Americans), 17 international. 137 applicants, 55% accepted, 58 enrolled. *Faculty:* 23 full-time (7 women). Expenses: Contact institution. *Financial support:* Research assistantships available. Support available to part-time students. Financial award application deadline: 4/1. In 2008, 31 master's awarded. *Degree program information:* Part-time and evening/weekend programs available. Offers accounting (M Acct); business (M Acct, MBA); general management (MBA). *Application deadline:* For fall admission, 7/1 priority date for domestic students, 6/15 priority date for international students; for spring admission, 12/1 priority date for domestic students, 11/1 priority date for international students. Applications are processed on a rolling basis. *Application fee:* $35. *Application Contact:* Dr. B. Keith Harrison, Dean of the Graduate School, 251-460-6310, Fax: 251-461-1513, E-mail: kharriso@usouthal.edu. *Director of Graduate Studies*, Dr. John Gamble, 251-460-6419.

School of Computer and Information Sciences Students: 73 full-time (18 women), 6 part-time (1 woman); includes 5 minority (3 African Americans, 2 Asian Americans or Pacific Islanders), 59 international. 146 applicants, 62% accepted, 32 enrolled. *Faculty:* 12 full-time (1 woman). Expenses: Contact institution. *Financial support:* Research assistantships, career-related internships or fieldwork and institutionally sponsored loans available. Support available to part-time students. Financial award application deadline: 4/1. In 2008, 36 master's awarded. *Degree program information:* Part-time and evening/weekend programs available. Offers computer science (MS); information systems (MS). *Application deadline:* For fall admission, 7/15 priority date for domestic students, 6/15 priority date for international students; for spring admission, 12/1 for domestic students, 11/1 priority date for international students. Applications are processed on a rolling basis. *Application fee:* $35. *Application Contact:* Dr. B. Keith Harrison, Dean of the Graduate School, 251-460-6310, Fax: 251-461-1513, E-mail: kharriso@usouthal.edu. *Director of Graduate Studies*, Dr. Roy Daigle, 251-460-6390.

See Close-Up on page 1043.

UNIVERSITY OF SOUTH CAROLINA, Columbia, SC 29208

General Information State-supported, coed, university. CGS member. *Graduate housing:* Rooms and/or apartments available to single and married students. *Research affiliation:* E. I. du Pont de Nemours and Company (engineering, chemical engineering), Westinghouse/Savannah River Corporation (environmental restoration, hazardous waste remediation), Motorola Corporation–Energy Production Division (electrochemical engineering), Glaxo-Wellcome, Inc. (pharmaceuticals), NCR Corporation (electrical and computer engineering).

GRADUATE UNITS

The Graduate School *Degree program information:* Part-time and evening/weekend programs available. Postbaccalaureate distance learning degree programs offered. Offers gerontology (Certificate). Electronic applications accepted.

Arnold School of Public Health *Degree program information:* Part-time programs available. Postbaccalaureate distance learning degree programs offered (minimal on-campus study). Offers biostatistics (MPH, MSPH, Dr PH, PhD); communication sciences and disorders (MCD, MSP, PhD); environmental health science (MS); environmental quality (MPH, MS, MSPH, PhD); epidemiology (MPH, MSPH, Dr PH, PhD); exercise science (MS, DPT, PhD); general public health (MPH); hazardous materials management (MPH, MSPH, PhD); health education (MAT); health promotion, education, and behavior (MPH, MS, MSPH, Dr PH, PhD); health services policy and management (MHA, MPH, Dr PH, PhD); industrial hygiene (MPH, MSPH, PhD); physical activity and public health (MPH); public health (MAT, MCD, MHA, MPH, MS, MSP, MSPH, DPT, Dr PH, PhD, Certificate); school health education (Certificate). Electronic applications accepted.

College of Arts and Sciences *Degree program information:* Part-time and evening/weekend programs available. Offers anthropology (MA, PhD); applied statistics (CAS); archives (MA); art education (IMA, MA, MAT); art history (MA); art studio (MA); arts and sciences (IMA, M Math, MA, MAT, MFA, MIS, MMA, MPA, MS, PSM, PhD, CAS, Certificate); biology (MS, PhD); biology education (IMA, MAT); chemistry and biochemistry (IMA, MAT, MS, PhD); clinical/community psychology (MA, PhD); comparative literature (MA, PhD); creative writing (MFA); criminology and criminal justice (MA, PhD); ecology, evolution and organismal biology (MS, PhD); English (MA, PhD); English education (MAT); experimental psychology (MA, PhD); foreign languages (MAT); French (MA); general psychology (MA); geography (MA, MS, PhD); geography education (IMA); geological sciences (MS, PhD); German (MA); historic preservation (MA); history (MA, PhD); industrial statistics (MIS); international studies (MA, PhD); linguistics (MA, PhD); marine science (MS, PhD); mathematics (MA, MS, PhD); mathematics education (M Math, MAT); media arts (MMA); molecular, cellular, and developmental biology (MS, PhD); museum (MA); museum management (Certificate); philosophy (MA, PhD); physics and astronomy (IMA, MAT, MS, PSM, PhD);

University of South Carolina (continued)

political science (MA, MPA, PhD); public administration (MPA); public history (MA, Certificate); religious studies (MA); school psychology (PhD); sociology (MA, PhD); Spanish (MA); statistics (MS, PhD); studio art (MFA); teaching English to speakers of other languages (Certificate); theater (MA, MAT, MFA); women's studies (Certificate). Electronic applications accepted.

College of Education *Degree program information:* Part-time and evening/weekend programs available. Postbaccalaureate distance learning degree programs offered (minimal on-campus study). Offers art education (IMA, MAT); business education (IMA, MAT); counseling education (PhD, Ed S); curriculum and instruction (Ed D); early childhood education (M Ed, Ed D, PhD); education (IMA, M Ed, MAT, MS, MT, Ed D, PhD, Certificate, Ed S); educational administration (M Ed, PhD, Ed S); educational psychology, research (M Ed, PhD); educational technology (M Ed); elementary education (MAT, Ed D, PhD); English (MAT); foreign language (MAT); foundations in education (PhD); health education (MAT); higher education and student affairs (M Ed); higher education leadership (Certificate); language and literacy (M Ed, PhD); mathematics (MAT); physical education (IMA, MAT, MS, PhD); science (IMA, MAT); secondary (Ed D); secondary education (IMA, MAT, MT, Ed D, PhD); social studies (MAT); special education (M Ed, MAT, PhD); teaching (M Ed, Ed S); theatre and speech (MAT). Electronic applications accepted.

College of Engineering and Computing *Degree program information:* Part-time and evening/weekend programs available. Postbaccalaureate distance learning degree programs offered (minimal on-campus study). Offers chemical engineering (ME, MS, PhD); civil engineering (ME, MS, PhD); computer science and engineering (ME, MS, PhD); electrical engineering (ME, MS, PhD); engineering and computing (ME, MS, PhD); mechanical engineering (ME, MS, PhD); nuclear engineering (ME, MS, PhD); software engineering (MS). Electronic applications accepted.

College of Hospitality, Retail, and Sport Management *Degree program information:* Part-time programs available. Postbaccalaureate distance learning degree programs offered (minimal on-campus study). Offers hospitality, retail, and sport management (MIHTM, MR, MS); hotel, restaurant and tourism management (MIHTM); live sport and entertainment events (MS); public assembly facilities management (MS); retailing (MR). Electronic applications accepted.

College of Mass Communications and Information Studies Offers journalism and mass communications (MA, MMC, PhD); library and information science (MLIS, PhD, Certificate, Specialist); mass communications and information studies (MA, MLIS, MMC, PhD, Certificate, Specialist).

College of Nursing *Degree program information:* Part-time programs available. Postbaccalaureate distance learning degree programs offered (minimal on-campus study). Offers acute care clinical specialist (MSN); acute care nurse practitioner (MSN, Certificate); adult nurse practitioner (MSN); advanced practice clinical nursing (MSN, Certificate); advanced practice nursing in primary care (MSN, Certificate); advanced practice nursing in psychiatric mental health (MSN, Certificate); clinical nursing (MSN); community mental health and psychiatric health nursing (MSN); community/public health clinical nurse specialist (MSN); family nurse practitioner (MSN); health nursing (MSN); nursing administration (MSN); nursing practice (DNP); nursing science (PhD); pediatric nurse practitioner (MSN); psychiatric/mental health nurse practitioner (MSN); psychiatric/mental health specialist (MSN); women's health nurse practitioner (MSN). Electronic applications accepted.

College of Social Work *Degree program information:* Part-time programs available. Offers social work (MSW, PhD). Electronic applications accepted.

Moore School of Business *Degree program information:* Part-time and evening/weekend programs available. Postbaccalaureate distance learning degree programs offered (minimal on-campus study). Offers accountancy (M Acc); business administration (MBA, PhD); business measurement and assurance (M Acc); economics (MA, PhD); human resources (MHR); international business administration (IMBA). Electronic applications accepted.

School of Music *Degree program information:* Part-time programs available. Offers composition (MM, DMA); conducting (MM, DMA); jazz studies (MM); music education (MM Ed, PhD); music history (MM); music performance (Certificate); music theory (MM); opera theater (MM); performance (MM, DMA); piano pedagogy (MM, DMA). Electronic applications accepted.

School of the Environment *Degree program information:* Part-time programs available. Postbaccalaureate distance learning degree programs offered (no on-campus study). Offers earth and environmental resources management (MEERM); environment (MEERM). Electronic applications accepted.

School of Law Offers law (JD).

School of Medicine Offers biomedical science (MBS, PhD); genetic counseling (MS); medicine (MD, MBS, MNA, MRC, MS, PhD, Certificate); nurse anesthesia (MNA); psychiatric rehabilitation (Certificate); rehabilitation counseling (MRC, Certificate). Electronic applications accepted.

South Carolina College of Pharmacy *Degree program information:* Part-time programs available. Offers pharmaceutical sciences (MS, PhD); pharmacy (Pharm D, MS, PhD). Electronic applications accepted.

See Close-Up on page 1045.

UNIVERSITY OF SOUTH CAROLINA AIKEN, Aiken, SC 29801-6309

General Information State-supported, coed, comprehensive institution. *Graduate housing:* Room and/or apartments available on a first-come, first-served basis to single students; on-campus housing not available to married students.

GRADUATE UNITS

Program in Applied Clinical Psychology *Degree program information:* Part-time and evening/weekend programs available. Offers applied clinical psychology (MS). Electronic applications accepted.

School of Education *Degree program information:* Part-time and evening/weekend programs available. Offers education (M Ed); educational technology (M Ed); elementary education (M Ed). Electronic applications accepted.

UNIVERSITY OF SOUTH CAROLINA UPSTATE, Spartanburg, SC 29303-4999

General Information State-supported, coed, comprehensive institution. *Enrollment:* 5,063 graduate, professional, and undergraduate students; 3 full-time matriculated graduate/professional students (all women), 61 part-time matriculated graduate/professional students (57 women). *Enrollment by degree level:* 64 master's. *Graduate faculty:* 8 full-time (6 women), 2 part-time/adjunct (1 woman). Tuition, state resident: full-time $9436; part-time $467 per semester hour. Tuition, nonresident: full-time $20,336; part-time $992 per semester hour. *Graduate housing:* On-campus housing not available. *Student services:* Campus employment opportunities, campus safety program, career counseling, child daycare facilities, exercise/wellness program, free psychological counseling, grant writing training, international student services, low-cost health insurance, multicultural affairs office, services for students with disabilities, teacher training. *Library facilities:* University of South Carolina Upstate Library. *Online resources:* library catalog, web page, access to other libraries' catalogs. *Collection:* 201,237 titles, 27,405 serial subscriptions, 6,886 audiovisual materials.

Computer facilities: 400 computers available on campus for general student use. A campuswide network can be accessed from student residence rooms. Online class registration is available. *Web address:* http://www.uscupstate.edu/.

General Application Contact: Dr. Rebecca L. Stevens, Director of Graduate Programs, 864-503-5521, Fax: 864-503-5574, E-mail: rstevens@uscupstate.edu.

GRADUATE UNITS

Graduate Programs Students: 3 full-time (all women), 61 part-time (57 women); includes 9 minority (6 African Americans, 3 Asian Americans or Pacific Islanders), 2 international. Average age 34. 43 applicants, 91% accepted, 36 enrolled. *Faculty:* 8 full-time (6 women), 2 part-time/adjunct (1 woman). Expenses: Contact institution. *Financial support:* Institutionally sponsored loans and institutional work-study available. Financial award application deadline: 7/15; financial award applicants required to submit FAFSA. In 2008, 12 master's awarded. *Degree program information:* Part-time and evening/weekend programs available. Offers early childhood education (M Ed); elementary education (M Ed); special education: visual impairment (M Ed). *Application deadline:* Applications are processed on a rolling basis. *Application fee:* $40. *Application Contact:* Donette Stewart, Associate Vice Chancellor for Enrollment Services, 864-503-5280, E-mail: dstewart@uscupstate.edu. Dr. Rebecca L. Stevens, 864-503-5521, Fax: 864-503-5574, E-mail: ystevens@uscupstate.edu.

THE UNIVERSITY OF SOUTH DAKOTA, Vermillion, SD 57069-2390

General Information State-supported, coed, university. *Graduate housing:* Rooms and/or apartments available to single students and available on a first-come, first-served basis to married students.

GRADUATE UNITS

Graduate School *Degree program information:* Part-time and evening/weekend programs available. Postbaccalaureate distance learning degree programs offered (no on-campus study). Offers administrative studies (MS); interdisciplinary studies (MA). Electronic applications accepted.

College of Arts and Sciences *Degree program information:* Part-time programs available. Postbaccalaureate distance learning degree programs offered. Offers American political institutions (PhD); arts and sciences (MA, MNS, MPA, MS, Au D, PhD); audiology (Au D); biology (MA, MNS, MS, PhD); chemistry (MNS, MS, PhD); clinical psychology (MA, PhD); communication studies (MA); communications disorders (MA); computational sciences and statistics (PhD); computer science (MS); English (MA, PhD); history (MA); human factors (MA, PhD); mathematics (MA, MNS, MS); political science (MA, PhD); public administration (MPA, PhD); public policy (PhD); speech-language pathology (MA). Electronic applications accepted.

College of Fine Arts Offers art (MFA); fine arts (MA, MFA, MM); music (MM); theatre (MA, MFA). Electronic applications accepted.

School of Business *Degree program information:* Part-time and evening/weekend programs available. Postbaccalaureate distance learning degree programs offered (no on-campus study). Offers business (MBA, MP Acc); business administration (MBA); professional accountancy (MP Acc). Electronic applications accepted.

School of Education *Degree program information:* Part-time and evening/weekend programs available. Postbaccalaureate distance learning degree programs offered (no on-campus study). Offers counseling and psychology in education (MA, PhD, Ed S); curriculum and instruction (Ed D, Ed S); education (MA, MS, Ed D, PhD, Ed S); educational administration (MA, Ed D, Ed S); elementary education (MA); health, physical education and recreation (MA); secondary education (MA); special education (MA); technology for education and training (MS, Ed S). Electronic applications accepted.

School of Law *Degree program information:* Part-time programs available. Offers law (JD). Electronic applications accepted.

School of Medicine and Health Sciences *Degree program information:* Part-time programs available. Offers cardiovascular research (MS, PhD); cellular and molecular biology (MS, PhD); medicine (MD); medicine and health science (MD, MS, DPT, PhD); molecular microbiology and immunology (MS, PhD); neuroscience (MS, PhD); occupational therapy (MS); physical therapy (DPT); physician assistant studies (MS); physiology and pharmacology (MS, PhD).

UNIVERSITY OF SOUTHERN CALIFORNIA, Los Angeles, CA 90089

General Information Independent, coed, university. CGS member. *Enrollment:* 33,747 graduate, professional, and undergraduate students; 13,589 full-time matriculated graduate/professional students (6,663 women), 3,550 part-time matriculated graduate/professional students (1,264 women). *Enrollment by degree level:* 2,682 first professional, 9,288 master's, 4,243 doctoral, 176 other advanced degrees. *Graduate faculty:* 2,031 full-time (655 women), 1,101 part-time/adjunct (398 women). *Tuition:* Full-time $19,285; part-time $1299 per unit. *Required fees:* $554; $283 per semester. Tuition and fees vary according to course load and program. *Graduate housing:* Rooms and/or apartments available on a first-come, first-served basis to single and married students. Typical cost: $10,800 per year ($15,842 including board) for single students; $10,800 per year ($15,842 including board) for married students. *Student services:* Campus employment opportunities, campus safety program, career counseling, child daycare facilities, exercise/wellness program, free psychological counseling, grant writing training, international student services, low-cost health insurance, multicultural affairs office, services for students with disabilities, teacher training, writing training. *Library facilities:* Doheny Memorial Library plus 17 others. *Online resources:* library catalog, web page, access to other libraries' catalogs. *Collection:* 4.4 million titles, 60,852 serial subscriptions, 82,957 audiovisual materials. *Research affiliation:* City of Hope Cancer Center (medicine), Rancho Los Amigos Medical Center (medicine), Children's Hospital Los Angeles (medicine), Doheny Eye Institute (medicine), Norris Cancer Hospital (medicine).

Computer facilities: Computer purchase and lease plans are available. 2,700 computers available on campus for general student use. A campuswide network can be accessed from student residence rooms and from off campus. Online class registration, online degree progress, financial aid applications, document sharing, calendars, personal Web space, customizable Web portal, course management systems (including data and video) are available. *Web address:* http://www.usc.edu/.

General Application Contact: Joseph Sanosa, Associate Director of Graduate Admission, 213-740-1111, Fax: 213-821-0200, E-mail: gradadm@usc.edu.

GRADUATE UNITS

Graduate School Students: 11,495 full-time (5,421 women), 2,835 part-time (939 women); includes 4,621 minority (595 African Americans, 62 American Indian/Alaska Native, 2,860 Asian Americans or Pacific Islanders, 1,104 Hispanic Americans), 4,062 international. Expenses: Contact institution. *Financial support:* Fellowships, research assistantships, teaching assistantships available. In 2008, 565 first professional degrees, 3,888 master's, 691 doctorates, 135 other advanced degrees awarded. *Application fee:* $85. Electronic applications accepted. *Application Contact:* Jean Morrison, Vice Provost for Academic Affairs/Graduate Program Director, Women in Science and Engineering, 213-740-9033. *Vice Provost for Academic Affairs/Graduate Program Director, Women in Science and Engineering,* Jean Morrison, 213-740-9033.

Annenberg School for Communication *Degree program information:* Part-time and evening/weekend programs available. Offers broadcast journalism (MA); communication (MA, MCM, MPD, PhD); communication management (MCM); global communicationonline journalism (MA); print journalism (MA); public diplomacy (MPD); specialized journalism (MA); strategic public relations (MA). Electronic applications accepted.

College of Letters, Arts and Sciences Students: 1,498 full-time (773 women), 93 part-time (45 women); includes 299 minority (48 African Americans, 10 American Indian/Alaska Native, 149 Asian Americans or Pacific Islanders, 92 Hispanic Americans), 593 international. Expenses: Contact institution. In 2008, 240 master's, 171 doctorates, 10 other advanced degrees awarded. Offers American studies and ethnicity (PhD); applied mathematics (MS, PhD); art history (MA, PhD); biology (MS); brain and cognitive science (PhD); chemical physics (PhD); chemistry (MA, MS, PhD); classics (MA, PhD); clinical science (PhD); comparative literature (MA, PhD); computational molecular biology (MS); developmental psychology (PhD); East Asian languages and cultures (MA, PhD); East Asian linguistics (PhD); East Asian studies (MA); economic development programming (MA); economics (MA, PhD); English (MA, PhD); fiction (MPW); geographic information science and technology (MS, Graduate Certificate); geological sciences (MS, PhD); Hispanic linguistics (MA, PhD); history (PhD); history of collecting and display (Graduate Certificate); human behavior (MHB); integrative and evolutionary biology (PhD); Internet (MPW); letters, arts and sciences (MA, MHB, MPW, MS, PhD, Graduate Certificate); linguistics (MA, PhD); literature and creative writing (PhD); marine environmental biology (MS); mathematics (PhD); molecular biology (PhD); neurobiology (PhD); neuroscience (MS, PhD); non-fiction (MPW); philosophy (MA, PhD); physics (MA, MS, PhD); playwriting (MPW); poetry (MPW); politics and international relations (PhD); professional writing (MPW); psychology (MA); quantitative methods (PhD); screenwriting (MPW); Slavic languages and literatures (MA, PhD); social psychology (PhD); sociology (PhD); statistics (MS); visual studies (Graduate Certificate). *Application fee:* $85. Electronic applications accepted. *Application Contact:* Howard Gillman, Dean. *Dean,* Howard Gillman.

Davis School of Gerontology Students: 59 full-time (45 women), 25 part-time (18 women); includes 27 minority (5 African Americans, 1 American Indian/Alaska Native, 15 Asian Americans or Pacific Islanders, 6 Hispanic Americans), 5 international. 81 applicants, 60% accepted, 33 enrolled. *Faculty:* 16 full-time (5 women), 9 part-time/adjunct (6 women). Expenses: Contact institution. *Financial support:* In 2008–09, 33 students received support, including 4 fellowships with full and partial tuition reimbursements available (averaging $20,000 per year), 16 research assistantships with full and partial tuition reimbursements available (averaging $16,000 per year); Federal Work-Study, scholarships/grants, traineeships, and unspecified assistantships also available. Financial award application deadline: 2/1. In 2008, 14 master's, 5 doctorates awarded. *Degree program information:* Part-time and evening/weekend programs available. Postbaccalaureate distance learning degree programs offered (no on-campus study). Offers gerontology (MA, MS, PhD, Graduate Certificate). *Application deadline:* For fall admission, 2/1 priority date for domestic and international students; for spring admission, 10/1 priority date for domestic and international students. Applications are processed on a rolling basis. *Application fee:* $85. Electronic applications accepted. *Application Contact:* Jim deVera, Student Advisor, 213-740-1729, E-mail: edevera@usc.edu. *Assistant Dean,* Maria Henke, 213-740-1363, E-mail: mhenke@usc.edu.

Gould School of Law Students: 701 full-time (323 women); includes 241 minority (46 African Americans, 4 American Indian/Alaska Native, 107 Asian Americans or Pacific Islanders, 84 Hispanic Americans), 90 international. 5,595 applicants, 21% accepted, 204 enrolled. *Faculty:* 55 full-time (20 women), 38 part-time/adjunct (7 women). Expenses: Contact institution. *Financial support:* In 2008–09, 400 students received support. Application deadline: 3/2. In 2008, 202 first professional degrees, 86 master's awarded. Offers comparative law for foreign attorneys (MCL); law (JD); law for foreign-educated attorneys (LL M). *Application deadline:* For fall admission, 2/1 priority date for domestic students, 2/1 for international students. Applications are processed on a rolling basis. *Application fee:* $75. *Application Contact:* Chloe Reid, Associate Dean for Admissions, 213-740-2523. *Dean,* Dean Robert Rasmussen, 213-740-2523, E-mail: dean@law.usc.edu.

Marshall School of Business Students: 1,436 full-time (423 women), 515 part-time (157 women); includes 752 minority (36 African Americans, 6 American Indian/Alaska Native, 626 Asian Americans or Pacific Islanders, 84 Hispanic Americans), 359 international. 3,631 applicants, 42% accepted, 947 enrolled. *Faculty:* 214 full-time (57 women), 14 part-time/adjunct (0 women). Expenses: Contact institution. *Financial support:* In 2008–09, 63 students received support; fellowships, research assistantships, teaching assistantships, career-related internships or fieldwork, Federal Work-Study, scholarships/grants, health care benefits, and unspecified assistantships available. In 2008, 765 master's, 9 doctorates awarded. *Degree program information:* Part-time and evening/weekend programs available. Offers accounting (M Acc); business (M Acc, MBA, MBT, MS, PhD); business administration (MBA, MM, MS, PhD); business taxation (MBT). *Application fee:* $85. Electronic applications accepted. *Application Contact:* James Ellis, Dean, 213-740-6422, E-mail: dean@marshall.usc.edu. *Dean,* James Ellis, 213-740-6422, E-mail: dean@marshall.usc.edu.

Roski School of Fine Arts Students: 45 full-time (31 women), 2 part-time (both women); includes 17 minority (5 African Americans, 1 American Indian/Alaska Native, 5 Asian Americans or Pacific Islanders, 6 Hispanic Americans). 301 applicants, 14% accepted. *Faculty:* 6 full-time (3 women), 7 part-time/adjunct (4 women). Expenses: Contact institution. *Financial support:* In 2008–09, 23 students received support; fellowships, research assistantships, teaching assistantships, career-related internships or fieldwork, Federal Work-Study, and scholarships/grants available. Financial award application deadline: 2/1; financial award applicants required to submit FAFSA. In 2008, 25 master's awarded. Offers fine arts (MFA, MPAS); public art studies (MPAS). *Application deadline:* For fall admission, 2/1 for domestic students. *Application fee:* $85. *Application Contact:* Penelope Jones, Director of Admissions, 213-740-9153, Fax: 213-740-8938, E-mail: penelope@usc.edu. *Dean,* Ruth Weisberg, 213-740-2787, Fax: 213-740-8938, E-mail: finearts@usc.edu.

Rossier School of Education Students: 924 full-time (638 women), 94 part-time (66 women); includes 517 minority (113 African Americans, 12 American Indian/Alaska Native, 192 Asian Americans or Pacific Islanders, 200 Hispanic Americans), 69 international. 950 applicants, 70% accepted, 407 enrolled. *Faculty:* 96 full-time (51 women), 27 part-time/adjunct (15 women). Expenses: Contact institution. *Financial support:* In 2008–09, 385 students received support; research assistantships with full and partial tuition reimbursements available, teaching assistantships with tuition reimbursements available, career-related internships or fieldwork, Federal Work-Study, scholarships/grants, health care benefits, and unspecified assistantships available. Support available to part-time students. Financial award applicants required to submit FAFSA. In 2008, 250 master's, 150 doctorates awarded. Offers education (MAT, ME, MMFT, MS, Ed D, PhD); educational psychology (Ed D, PhD); educational psychology/instructional technology (ME); higher education administration (Ed D); higher education administration and policy (PhD); K-12 leadership in urban school settings (Ed D); K-12 policy and practice (PhD); marriage, family and child counseling (MMFT); postsecondary administration and student affairs ERROR!!!PASAERROR!!! (ME); school counseling (ME); teacher education in multicultural societies (Ed D); teaching and teaching credential (MAT); teaching English as a foreign language (ME); teaching English to speakers of other languages (MS). *Application fee:* $85. Electronic applications accepted. *Application Contact:* Karen Gallagher. Karen Gallagher.

School of Architecture Students: 148 full-time (71 women), 6 part-time (3 women); includes 26 minority (2 African Americans, 14 Asian Americans or Pacific Islanders, 10 Hispanic Americans), 70 international. 305 applicants, 73% accepted, 109 enrolled. *Faculty:* 16 full-time, 30 part-time/adjunct. Expenses: Contact institution. *Financial support:* Application deadline: 5/5. In 2008, 47 master's awarded. Offers architecture (M Arch, MBS, MHP, ML Arch, MLA, PhD). *Application deadline:* For fall admission, 1/15 priority date for domestic and international students. Applications are processed on a rolling basis. *Application fee:* $85. Electronic applications accepted. *Application Contact:* Julette Sanders, Director of Graduate Admissions, 213-821-2168, E-mail: archgrad@usc.edu. *Dean,* Qingyun Ma, 213-740-2723, E-mail: archdean@usc.edu.

School of Cinematic Arts Students: 621 full-time (248 women), 32 part-time (14 women); includes 168 minority (54 African Americans, 5 American Indian/Alaska Native, 68 Asian Americans or Pacific Islanders, 41 Hispanic Americans), 94 international. 951 applicants, 18% accepted, 150 enrolled. *Faculty:* 78 full-time (25 women), 198 part-time/adjunct (41 women). Expenses: Contact institution. *Financial support:* In 2008–09, 246 students received support; fellowships with tuition reimbursements available, research assistantships with tuition reimbursements available, teaching assistantships with tuition reimbursements available, career-related internships or fieldwork, Federal Work-Study, scholarships/grants, and unspecified assistantships available. Support available to part-time students. Financial award applicants required to submit FAFSA. In 2008, 206 master's, 13 doctorates awarded. Offers cinema-television (MA); cinema-television (critical studies) (PhD); cinematic arts (MA, MFA, PhD, Graduate Certificate); cinematic arts (media arts and practice) (PhD); film and video production (MFA); film, video, and computer animation (MFA); interactive media (MFA); motion picture producing (MFA); writing in screen and television (Graduate Certificate). *Application fee:* $85. Electronic applications accepted. *Application Contact:* L. Katherine Harrington, Associate Dean and Executive Director of Admissions. *Dean,* Elizabeth Daley.

School of Dentistry Students: 1,350 full-time (777 women), 24 part-time (20 women); includes 553 minority (41 African Americans, 4 American Indian/Alaska Native, 431 Asian Americans or Pacific Islanders, 77 Hispanic Americans), 121 international. 675 applicants, 62% accepted, 270 enrolled. *Faculty:* 104 full-time (63 women), 66 part-time/adjunct (45 women). Expenses: Contact institution. *Financial support:* In 2008–09, 391 students received support. In 2008, 189 first professional degrees, 126 master's, 117 doctorates, 7 other advanced degrees awarded. Offers biokinesiology (MS, PhD); craniofacial biology (MS, PhD, Graduate Certificate); dentistry (DDS, MA, MS, DPT, OTD, PhD, Graduate Certificate); occupational science (PhD); occupational therapy (MA, OTD); physical therapy (DPT). *Application Contact:* Harold Slavkin, Dean. *Dean,* Harold Slavkin.

School of Pharmacy Students: 813 full-time (577 women), 47 part-time (39 women); includes 533 minority (18 African Americans, 3 American Indian/Alaska Native, 477 Asian Americans or Pacific Islanders, 35 Hispanic Americans), 71 international. Expenses: Contact institution. In 2008, 174 first professional degrees, 44 master's, 13 doctorates, 4 other advanced degrees awarded. Offers clinical research design and management (Graduate Certificate); food safety (Graduate Certificate); molecular pharmacology and toxicology (MS, PhD); patient and product safety (Graduate Certificate); pharmaceutical economics and policy (MS, PhD); pharmaceutical sciences (MS, PhD); pharmacy (Pharm D, MS, D Sc, PhD, Graduate Certificate); preclinical drug development (Graduate Certificate); regulatory science (MS, D Sc). *Application fee:* $85. *Application Contact:* Pete Vanderveen, Dean. *Dean,* Pete Vanderveen.

School of Policy, Planning, and Development Students: 585 full-time (307 women), 220 part-time (124 women); includes 287 minority (56 African Americans, 6 American Indian/Alaska Native, 123 Asian Americans or Pacific Islanders, 102 Hispanic Americans), 164 international. 1,071 applicants, 67% accepted, 355 enrolled. *Faculty:* 30 full-time (7 women), 46 part-time/adjunct (11 women). Expenses: Contact institution. *Financial support:* In 2008–09, 251 students received support, including 4 fellowships with full tuition reimbursements available (averaging $29,527 per year), 62 research assistantships with full and partial tuition reimbursements available (averaging $33,895 per year), 6 teaching assistantships with full tuition reimbursements available (averaging $11,093 per year); scholarships/grants, traineeships, and tuition waivers (full and partial) also available. Financial award applicants required to submit FAFSA. In 2008, 285 master's, 17 doctorates, 13 other advanced degrees awarded. Offers health administration (EMHA, MHA); international public policy and management (MPPM); leadership (EML); policy, planning, and development (EMHA, EML, M Pl, MHA, MPA, MPP, MPPM, MRED, MS, DPPD, PhD, Graduate Certificate); public administration (MPA); public policy (MPP); real estate development (MRED). *Application fee:* $85. Electronic applications accepted. *Application Contact:* Marisol Gonzalez, Director of Recruitment and Admission, 213-740-0550, Fax: 213-740-7573, E-mail: marisolr@usc.edu. *Head,* Dr. Jack H Knott, 213-740-0350, Fax: 213-740-5379, E-mail: jhknott@usc.edu.

School of Social Work Students: 646 full-time (573 women), 121 part-time (104 women); includes 451 minority (100 African Americans, 3 American Indian/Alaska Native, 98 Asian Americans or Pacific Islanders, 250 Hispanic Americans), 23 international. 858 applicants, 71% accepted, 342 enrolled. *Faculty:* 58 full-time (34 women), 46 part-time/adjunct (30 women). Expenses: Contact institution. *Financial support:* In 2008–09, 90 students received support. Career-related internships or fieldwork, Federal Work-Study, institutionally sponsored loans, scholarships/grants, and health care benefits available. Support available to part-time students. Financial award application deadline: 5/1; financial award applicants required to submit FAFSA. In 2008, 279 master's, 5 doctorates awarded. Offers community organization, planning and administration (MSW); families and children (MSW); health (MSW); military social work and veterans services (MSW); older adults (MSW); public child welfare (MSW); school settings (MSW); social work (MSW, PhD); systems of mental illness recovery (MSW); work and life (MSW). *Application deadline:* For fall admission, 4/1 priority date for domestic students, 2/1 for international students. *Application fee:* $85. Electronic applications accepted. *Application Contact:* Janine Luzano, Director of Admissions and Financial Aid, 213-740-2013, E-mail: sswadm@usc.edu. *Dean,* Marilyn Flynn, 213-740-8311.

School of Theatre Students: 40 full-time (16 women); includes 19 minority (10 African Americans, 3 Asian Americans or Pacific Islanders, 6 Hispanic Americans), 4 international. *Faculty:* 10 full-time (3 women), 7 part-time/adjunct (3 women). Expenses: Contact institution. *Financial support:* In 2008–09, 40 students received support, including 40 fellowships with partial tuition reimbursements available (averaging $15,000 per year); Federal Work-Study, scholarships/grants, health care benefits, and unspecified assistantships also available. Financial award applicants required to submit FAFSA. In 2008, 3 master's awarded. Offers acting (MFA); applied theatre arts (MA); dramatic writing (MFA). *Application Contact:* Sergio Ramierez, Director, Academic and Student Services, E-mail: sergio.ramirez@usc.edu. *Director, Academic and Student Services,* Sergio Ramierez, 213-821-4163, E-mail: sergio.ramirez@usc.edu.

Thornton School of Music Students: 363 full-time (168 women), 40 part-time (28 women); includes 81 minority (8 African Americans, 2 American Indian/Alaska Native, 53 Asian Americans or Pacific Islanders, 18 Hispanic Americans), 110 international. 734 applicants, 31% accepted, 145 enrolled. *Faculty:* 83 full-time (17 women), 112 part-time/adjunct (36 women). Expenses: Contact institution. *Financial support:* In 2008–09, 65 teaching assistantships with full tuition reimbursements (averaging $9,500 per year) were awarded; Federal Work-Study, scholarships/grants, health care benefits, and unspecified assistantships also available. Support available to part-time students. Financial award application deadline: 5/5; financial award applicants required to submit FAFSA. In 2008, 81 master's, 39 doctorates awarded. *Degree program information:* Part-time programs available. Offers choral music (MM); composition (MM); historical musicology (PhD); jazz studies (MM); music education (MM); performance (MM, DMA). *Application deadline:* For fall admission, 12/1 for domestic and international students; for spring admission, 10/1 for domestic and international students. *Application fee:* $85. Electronic applications accepted. *Application Contact:* PJ Woolston, Director of Admission, 213-740-8986, Fax: 213-740-8995, E-mail: woolston@thornton.usc.edu. *Dean,* Dr. Robert A Cutietta, 213-740-2311, Fax: 213-740-3217, E-mail: musdean@usc.edu.

Viterbi School of Engineering Students: 2,266 full-time (451 women), 1,616 part-time (319 women); includes 650 minority (53 African Americans, 5 American Indian/Alaska Native, 499 Asian Americans or Pacific Islanders, 93 Hispanic Americans), 2,289 international. 6,123 applicants, 46% accepted, 1221 enrolled. *Faculty:* 164 full-time (15 women), 66 part-time/adjunct (12 women). Expenses: Contact institution. *Financial support:* In 2008–09, 858 students received support, including 103 fellowships with full tuition reimbursements available (averaging $30,000 per year), 492 research assistantships with full tuition reimbursements available (averaging $18,800 per year), 263 teaching assistantships with full tuition reimbursements available (averaging $18,800 per year); institutionally sponsored loans and scholarships/grants also available. Financial award application deadline: 12/1. In 2008, 1,437 master's, 152 doctorates, 13 other advanced degrees awarded. *Degree program information:* Part-time programs available. Postbaccalaureate distance learning degree programs offered (no on-campus study). Offers aerospace and mechanical engineering: computational fluid and solid mechanics (MS); aerospace and mechanical engineering: dynamics and control (MS); aerospace engineering (MS, PhD, Engr); applied mechanics (MS); astronautical engineering (Engr, Graduate Certificate); biomedical engineering (MS, PhD); chemical engineering (MS, PhD, Engr); civil engineering (MS, PhD); computer engineering (MS, PhD); computer networks (MS); computer science (MS, PhD); computer security (MS); computer-aided engineering (ME, Graduate Certificate); construction management (MCM); digital supply chain management (MS); electrical engineering (MS, PhD, Engr); engineering (MCM, ME, MS, PhD, Engr, Graduate Certificate); engineering management (MS); engineering technology commercialization (Graduate Certificate); engineering technology communication (Graduate Certificate); environmental engineering (MS, PhD); environmental quality management (ME); game development (MS); health systems operations (Graduate Certificate); high performance computing and simulations (MS); industrial and systems engineering (MS, PhD, Engr); intelligent robotics (MS); manufacturing engineering (MS); materials science and engineering (MS, PhD, Engr); mechanical engineering (MS, PhD, Engr); medical device and diagnostic engineering (MS); multimedia and creative technologies (MS); operations research engineering (MS); optimization and supply chain management (Graduate Certificate); petroleum engineering (MS, PhD, Engr, Graduate Certificate); product development engineering (MS); safety systems and security (MS); software engineering (MS); structural design (ME); sustainable cities (Graduate Certificate); systems architecting and engineering (MS, Graduate Certificate); systems safety and security (Graduate Certificate); transportation systems (Graduate Certificate). *Application deadline:* For fall admission, 4/1 priority date for domestic and international students; for spring admission, 10/1 priority date for domestic and international students. Applications

University of Southern California (continued)
are processed on a rolling basis. *Application fee:* $85. Electronic applications accepted. *Application Contact:* Margery Berti, Associate Dean, 213-740-6241, Fax: 213-740-2367, E-mail: berti@usc.edu. *Dean,* Dr. Yannis C. Yortsos, 213-740-0617, Fax: 213-740-8493, E-mail: engrdean@usc.edu.

Keck School of Medicine Students: 1,408 full-time (795 women); includes 543 minority (54 African Americans, 9 American Indian/Alaska Native, 307 Asian Americans or Pacific Islanders, 173 Hispanic Americans), 228 international. Average age 25. 8,446 applicants, 8% accepted, 371 enrolled. *Faculty:* 1,208 full-time (380 women), 54 part-time/adjunct (23 women). Expenses: Contact institution. *Financial support:* In 2008–09, 829 students received support, including 50 fellowships with full and partial tuition reimbursements available, 209 research assistantships with full and partial tuition reimbursements available, 50 teaching assistantships with full and partial tuition reimbursements available; career-related internships or fieldwork, Federal Work-Study, institutionally sponsored loans, scholarships/grants, traineeships, and unspecified assistantships also available. Support available to part-time students. Financial award application deadline: 2/1. In 2008, 169 first professional degrees, 127 master's, 31 doctorates awarded. Offers genetic, molecular and cellular biology (PhD); medicine (MD, MPAP, MPH, MS, PhD); systems biology and disease (PhD). *Application fee:* $85. Electronic applications accepted. *Application Contact:* Marisela Zuniga, Administrative Coordinator, Graduate Affairs, 323-442-1607, Fax: 323-442-1199, E-mail: mzuniga@usc.edu. *Dean,* Dr. Carmen A. Puliafito, 323-442-1900.

Graduate Programs in Medicine Students: 729 full-time (473 women); includes 269 minority (27 African Americans, 5 American Indian/Alaska Native, 146 Asian Americans or Pacific Islanders, 91 Hispanic Americans), 210 international. Average age 26. 1,828 applicants, 17% accepted, 210 enrolled. *Faculty:* 243 full-time (79 women), 14 part-time/adjunct (5 women). Expenses: Contact institution. *Financial support:* In 2008–09, 50 fellowships, 242 research assistantships, 35 teaching assistantships were awarded; career-related internships or fieldwork, Federal Work-Study, institutionally sponsored loans, scholarships/grants, traineeships, health care benefits, and unspecified assistantships also available. Support available to part-time students. Financial award application deadline: 5/5. In 2008, 127 master's, 31 doctorates awarded. Offers applied biostatistics/epidemiology (MS); biochemistry and molecular biology (MS, PhD); biometry/epidemiology (MPH); biostatistics (MS, PhD); cell and neurobiology (MS, PhD); child and family health (MPH); epidemiology (PhD); experimental and molecular pathology (MS); genetic epidemiology and statistical genetics (PhD); global health leadership (MPH); health behavior research (PhD); health communication (MPH); health promotion (MPH); medicine (MPAP, MPH, MS, PhD); molecular epidemiology (MS, PhD); molecular microbiology and immunology (MS, PhD); pathobiology (PhD); physiology and biophysics (MS, PhD); primary care physician assistant (MPAP); public health (MPH). *Application fee:* $85. Electronic applications accepted. *Application Contact:* Marisela Zuniga, Administrative Coordinator, 323-442-1607, Fax: 323-442-1199, E-mail: mzuniga@usc.edu. *Associate Dean for Graduate Affairs,* Dr. Debbie Johnson, 323-442-1446, Fax: 323-442-1199, E-mail: johnsond@usc.edu.

UNIVERSITY OF SOUTHERN INDIANA, Evansville, IN 47712-3590

General Information State-supported, coed, comprehensive institution. CGS member. *Enrollment:* 10,126 graduate, professional, and undergraduate students; 123 full-time matriculated graduate/professional students (92 women), 600 part-time matriculated graduate/professional students (456 women). *Enrollment by degree level:* 704 master's, 19 doctoral. *Graduate faculty:* 64 full-time (27 women), 10 part-time/adjunct (8 women). Tuition, state resident: full-time $4374; part-time $243 per credit hour. Tuition, nonresident: full-time $8622; part-time $479 per credit hour. *Required fees:* $220; $22.75 per term. Tuition and fees vary according to course load and reciprocity agreements. *Graduate housing:* Rooms and/or apartments available on a first-come, first-served basis to single and married students. Typical cost: $3350 per year ($6648 including board) for single students; $3350 per year ($6648 including board) for married students. Room and board charges vary according to board plan. Housing application deadline: 3/1. *Student services:* Campus employment opportunities, campus safety program, career counseling, child daycare facilities, exercise/wellness program, free psychological counseling, international student services, low-cost health insurance, multicultural affairs office, services for students with disabilities. *Library facilities:* David L. Rice Library. *Online resources:* library catalog, web page, access to other libraries' catalogs. *Collection:* 336,457 titles, 22,135 serial subscriptions, 5,744 audiovisual materials.

Computer facilities: 306 computers available on campus for general student use. A campuswide network can be accessed from student residence rooms and from off campus. Online class registration is available. *Web address:* http://www.usi.edu/.

General Application Contact: Dr. Peggy F. Harrel, Director, Graduate Studies, 812-465-7015, Fax: 812-464-1956, E-mail: pharrel@usi.edu.

GRADUATE UNITS

Graduate Studies Students: 123 full-time (92 women), 600 part-time (456 women); includes 39 minority (28 African Americans, 1 American Indian/Alaska Native, 5 Asian Americans or Pacific Islanders, 5 Hispanic Americans), 22 international. Average age 33. 311 applicants, 98% accepted, 252 enrolled. *Faculty:* 64 full-time (27 women), 10 part-time/adjunct (8 women). Expenses: Contact institution. *Financial support:* In 2008–09, 299 students received support. Federal Work-Study, scholarships/grants, tuition waivers (full and partial), and unspecified assistantships available. Financial award application deadline: 3/1; financial award applicants required to submit FAFSA. In 2008, 229 master's awarded. *Degree program information:* Part-time and evening/weekend programs available. *Application deadline:* Applications are processed on a rolling basis. *Application fee:* $25. Electronic applications accepted. *Application Contact:* Dr. Peggy F. Harrel, Director, Graduate Studies, 812-465-7015, Fax: 812-464-1956, E-mail: pharrel@usi.edu. *Director,* Dr. Peggy F. Harrel, 812-465-7015, Fax: 812-464-1956, E-mail: pharrel@usi.edu.

College of Business Students: 10 full-time (3 women), 96 part-time (38 women); includes 2 minority (1 African American, 1 Hispanic American), 17 international. Average age 30. 28 applicants, 93% accepted, 21 enrolled. *Faculty:* 18 full-time (3 women). Expenses: Contact institution. *Financial support:* In 2008–09, 16 students received support. Federal Work-Study, scholarships/grants, tuition waivers (full and partial), and unspecified assistantships available. Financial award application deadline: 3/1; financial award applicants required to submit FAFSA. In 2008, 35 master's awarded. *Degree program information:* Part-time and evening/weekend programs available. Offers accountancy (MSA); business (MBA, MSA); business administration (MBA). *Application deadline:* For fall admission, 8/15 for domestic students, 3/1 priority date for international students. Applications are processed on a rolling basis. *Application fee:* $25. Electronic applications accepted. *Application Contact:* Information Contact, 812-464-1803. *Dean,* Dr. Mohammed F. Khayum, 812-465-1926, E-mail: mkhayum@usi.edu.

College of Education and Human Services Students: 67 full-time (56 women), 156 part-time (129 women); includes 15 minority (11 African Americans, 1 American Indian/Alaska Native, 2 Asian Americans or Pacific Islanders, 1 Hispanic American), 3 international. Average age 32. 111 applicants, 99% accepted, 88 enrolled. *Faculty:* 21 full-time (13 women), 1 part-time/adjunct (0 women). Expenses: Contact institution. *Financial support:* In 2008–09, 115 students received support. Federal Work-Study, scholarships/grants, tuition waivers (full and partial), and unspecified assistantships available. Financial award application deadline: 3/1; financial award applicants required to submit FAFSA. In 2008, 64 master's awarded. *Degree program information:* Part-time and evening/weekend programs available. Offers education and human services (MS, MSW); elementary education (MS); secondary education (MS); social work (MSW). *Application deadline:* Applications are processed on a rolling basis. *Application fee:* $25. *Application Contact:* Dr. Vella L. Goebel, Director, 812-461-5306, E-mail: vgoebel@usi.edu. *Dean,* Dr. Julie Edmister, 812-464-1811, E-mail: jhedmister@usi.edu.

College of Liberal Arts Students: 5 full-time (1 woman), 59 part-time (38 women); includes 4 minority (all African Americans), 1 international. Average age 35. 19 applicants, 84% accepted, 13 enrolled. *Faculty:* 12 full-time (8 women). Expenses: Contact institution. *Financial support:* In 2008–09, 43 students received support. Federal Work-Study, scholarships/grants, tuition waivers (full and partial), and unspecified assistantships available. Financial award application deadline: 3/1; financial award applicants required to submit FAFSA. In 2008, 23 master's awarded. *Degree program information:* Part-time and evening/weekend programs available. Offers liberal arts (MA, MPA); liberal studies (MA); public administration (MPA). *Application deadline:* For fall admission, 8/15 priority date for domestic students, 3/1 priority date for international students. Applications are processed on a rolling basis. *Application fee:* $25. *Application Contact:* Dr. Thomas M. Rivers, Director, 812-464-1753, E-mail: trivers@usi.edu. *Dean,* Dr. David L. Glassman, 812-464-1855.

College of Nursing and Health Professions Students: 41 full-time (32 women), 273 part-time (246 women); includes 18 minority (12 African Americans, 3 Asian Americans or Pacific Islanders, 3 Hispanic Americans). Average age 35. 149 applicants, 99% accepted, 128 enrolled. *Faculty:* 6 full-time (5 women), 8 part-time/adjunct (7 women). Expenses: Contact institution. *Financial support:* In 2008–09, 124 students received support. Federal Work-Study, scholarships/grants, tuition waivers (full and partial), and unspecified assistantships available. Financial award application deadline: 3/1; financial award applicants required to submit FAFSA. In 2008, 107 master's awarded. *Degree program information:* Part-time programs available. Postbaccalaureate distance learning degree programs offered (minimal on-campus study). Offers health administration (MHA); nursing (MSN, DNP); nursing and health professions (MHA, MSN, MSOT, DNP); occupational therapy (MSOT). *Application deadline:* Applications are processed on a rolling basis. *Application fee:* $25. *Application Contact:* Dr. Peggy F. Harrel, Director, Graduate Studies, 812-465-7015, Fax: 812-464-1956, E-mail: pharrel@usi.edu. *Dean,* Dr. Nadine Coudret, 812-465-1151, E-mail: ncoudret@usi.edu.

College of Science and Engineering Students: 16 part-time (5 women), 1 international. Average age 34. 4 applicants, 100% accepted, 2 enrolled. *Faculty:* 7 full-time (4 women), 1 (woman) part-time/adjunct. Expenses: Contact institution. *Financial support:* In 2008–09, 1 student received support. Federal Work-Study, scholarships/grants, tuition waivers (full and partial), and unspecified assistantships available. Financial award application deadline: 3/1; financial award applicants required to submit FAFSA. *Degree program information:* Part-time and evening/weekend programs available. Offers industrial management (MS); science and engineering (MS). *Application deadline:* For fall admission, 8/15 priority date for domestic students, 3/1 priority date for international students. Applications are processed on a rolling basis. *Application fee:* $25. *Application Contact:* Dr. Peggy F. Harrel, Director, Graduate Studies, 812-465-7015, Fax: 812-464-1956, E-mail: pharrel@usi.edu. *Dean,* Dr. Scott A. Gordon, 812-465-7137, E-mail: sgordon@usi.edu.

UNIVERSITY OF SOUTHERN MAINE, Portland, ME 04104-9300

General Information State-supported, coed, comprehensive institution. CGS member. *Graduate housing:* Rooms and/or apartments available on a first-come, first-served basis to single and married students.

GRADUATE UNITS

College of Arts and Sciences *Degree program information:* Part-time and evening/weekend programs available. Postbaccalaureate distance learning degree programs offered (minimal on-campus study). Offers American and New England studies (MA); arts and sciences (MA, MFA, MM, MS, MSW); biology (MS); creative writing (MFA); music (MM); social work (MSW); statistics (MS). Electronic applications accepted.

College of Education and Human Development Students: 157 full-time (118 women), 374 part-time (294 women); includes 10 minority (2 African Americans, 5 American Indian/Alaska Native, 1 Asian American or Pacific Islander, 2 Hispanic Americans). 377 applicants, 69% accepted, 214 enrolled. *Faculty:* 38 full-time (18 women), 38 part-time/adjunct (20 women). Expenses: Contact institution. *Financial support:* In 2008–09, 82 students received support, including 16 research assistantships (averaging $4,500 per year), 3 teaching assistantships with partial tuition reimbursements available (averaging $5,000 per year); career-related internships or fieldwork, Federal Work-Study, institutionally sponsored loans, scholarships/grants, and unspecified assistantships also available. Support available to part-time students. Financial award application deadline: 3/1; financial award applicants required to submit FAFSA. In 2008, 221 master's, 2 doctorates, 14 other advanced degrees awarded. *Degree program information:* Part-time and evening/weekend programs available. Postbaccalaureate distance learning degree programs offered (minimal on-campus study). Offers adult education (MS); adult learning (CAS); applied behavior analysis (Certificate); applied literacy (MS Ed); assistant principal (Certificate); athletic administration (Certificate); counseling (MS, CAS); early language and literacy (Certificate); education and human development (MS, MS Ed, Psy D, CAS, Certificate); educational leadership (MS Ed, CAS); English as a second language (MS Ed, CAS); literacy education (MS Ed, CAS, Certificate); mental health rehabilitation technician/community (Certificate); middle-level education (Certificate); professional educator (MS Ed); school psychology (MS, Psy D); self-design in special education (MS); teaching all students (MS); teaching and learning (MS Ed). *Application fee:* $50. Electronic applications accepted. *Application Contact:* Robin Audesse, Associate Director of Graduate Admissions, 207-780-5306, Fax: 207-780-5193, E-mail: raudesse@usm.maine.edu. *Dean,* Betty Lou Whitford, 207-780-5371, Fax: 207-780-5315.

College of Nursing and Health Professions *Degree program information:* Part-time programs available. Offers adult health nursing (PMC); clinical nurse leader (MS); clinical nurse specialist psychiatric-mental health nursing (MS); family nursing (PMC); medical/surgical nursing (MS); nurse practitioner adult health nursing (MS); nurse practitioner family nursing (MS); nurse practitioner psychiatric/mental health nursing (MS); psychiatric-mental health nursing (PMC). Electronic applications accepted.

Edmund S. Muskie School of Public Service *Degree program information:* Part-time and evening/weekend programs available. Postbaccalaureate distance learning degree programs offered (minimal on-campus study). Offers child and family policy (Certificate); community planning and development (MCPD, Certificate); health policy and management (MS, Certificate); non-profit management (Certificate); public policy (PhD); public policy and management (MPPM); public service (MCPD, MPPM, MS, PhD, Certificate). Electronic applications accepted.

Lewiston-Auburn College Offers leadership studies (MLS).

Program in Occupational Therapy *Degree program information:* Part-time programs available. Offers occupational therapy (MOT). Electronic applications accepted.

School of Applied Science, Engineering, and Technology *Degree program information:* Part-time and evening/weekend programs available. Offers applied medical sciences (MS); applied science, engineering, and technology (MS); computer science (MS); manufacturing systems (MS). Electronic applications accepted.

School of Business *Degree program information:* Part-time and evening/weekend programs available. Offers accounting (MSA); business administration (MBA). Electronic applications accepted.

University of Maine School of Law Students: 269 full-time (122 women); includes 12 minority (2 African Americans, 1 American Indian/Alaska Native, 6 Asian Americans or Pacific Islanders, 3 Hispanic Americans), 1 international. Average age 26. 697 applicants, 49% accepted, 92 enrolled. *Faculty:* 16 full-time (6 women), 14 part-time/adjunct (4 women). Expenses: Contact institution. *Financial support:* In 2008–09, 128 students received support, including 20 fellowships (averaging $3,000 per year), 6 research assistantships (averaging $2,400 per year), 5 teaching assistantships (averaging $2,400 per year); career-related internships or fieldwork, Federal Work-Study, scholarships/grants, and tuition waivers (full and partial) also available. Support available to part-time students. Financial award application deadline: 2/1; financial award applicants required to submit FAFSA. In 2008, 71 JDs awarded. *Degree program information:* Part-time programs available. Offers law (JD). *Application deadline:* For fall admission, 3/1 for domestic and international students. Applications are processed on a rolling basis. *Application fee:* $50. Electronic applications accepted. *Application Contact:* David Pallozzi, Assistant Dean for Admissions, 207-780-4341, Fax: 207-780-4239, E-mail: mainelaw@usm.maine.edu. *Dean,* Peter R. Pitegoff, 207-780-4344, Fax: 207-780-4239.

UNIVERSITY OF SOUTHERN MISSISSIPPI, Hattiesburg, MS 39406-0001

General Information State-supported, coed, university. CGS member. *Enrollment:* 14,793 graduate, professional, and undergraduate students; 1,413 full-time matriculated graduate/professional students (861 women), 1,318 part-time matriculated graduate/professional students (891 women). *Enrollment by degree level:* 1,831 master's, 970 doctoral. *Graduate faculty:* 572 full-time (221 women), 12 part-time/adjunct (4 women). *Graduate housing:* Rooms and/or apartments available on a first-come, first-served basis to single students and available to married students. Typical cost: $3244 per year ($5544 including board) for single students. Housing application deadline: 3/1. *Student services:* Campus employment opportunities, career counseling, child daycare facilities, exercise/wellness program, free psychological counseling, grant writing training, international student services, low-cost health insurance, services for students with disabilities, teacher training. *Library facilities:* Cook Memorial Library plus 5 others. *Online resources:* library catalog, web page. *Collection:* 1.2 million titles, 4,570 serial subscriptions, 31,469 audiovisual materials. *Research affiliation:* Oak Ridge Associated Universities (U.S. Department of Energy BSC, CHE), Geological Sciences, Coastal Sciences (physics).

Computer facilities: Computer purchase and lease plans are available. 600 computers available on campus for general student use. A campuswide network can be accessed from student residence rooms and from off campus. Online class registration is available. *Web address:* http://www.usm.edu/.

General Application Contact: Dr. Susan Siltanen, University Director, 601-266-4369, Fax: 601-266-5138, E-mail: susan.siltanen@usm.edu.

GRADUATE UNITS

Graduate School Students: 1,413 full-time (861 women), 1,318 part-time (891 women); includes 531 minority (448 African Americans, 9 American Indian/Alaska Native, 23 Asian Americans or Pacific Islanders, 51 Hispanic Americans), 241 international. Average age 34. 1,715 applicants, 49% accepted, 643 enrolled. *Faculty:* 475 full-time (184 women), 55 part-time/adjunct (21 women). Expenses: Contact institution. *Financial support:* In 2008–09, 13 fellowships with full and partial tuition reimbursements (averaging $15,000 per year), 364 research assistantships with full and partial tuition reimbursements (averaging $9,970 per year), 374 teaching assistantships with full and partial tuition reimbursements (averaging $9,970 per year) were awarded; career-related internships or fieldwork, Federal Work-Study, institutionally sponsored loans, scholarships/grants, traineeships, and unspecified assistantships also available. Support available to part-time students. Financial award application deadline: 3/15; financial award applicants required to submit FAFSA. In 2008, 757 master's, 121 doctorates awarded. *Degree program information:* Part-time and evening/weekend programs available. *Application deadline:* For fall admission, 2/1 priority date for domestic and international students. Applications are processed on a rolling basis. *Application fee:* $35. Electronic applications accepted. *Application Contact:* Shonna Breland, Manager of Graduate Admissions, 601-266-5994, Fax: 601-266-5138, E-mail: shonna.breland@usm.edu. *University Director,* Dr. Susan Siltanen, 601-266-4369, Fax: 601-266-5138, E-mail: susan.siltanen@usm.edu.

College of Arts and Letters Students: 283 full-time (134 women), 233 part-time (139 women); includes 67 minority (43 African Americans, 3 American Indian/Alaska Native, 4 Asian Americans or Pacific Islanders, 17 Hispanic Americans), 39 international. Average age 34. 296 applicants, 65% accepted, 137 enrolled. *Faculty:* 136 full-time (51 women), 11 part-time/adjunct (3 women). Expenses: Contact institution. *Financial support:* In 2008–09, 14 fellowships with full tuition reimbursements (averaging $12,500 per year), 16 research assistantships with full tuition reimbursements (averaging $9,300 per year), 186 teaching assistantships with full tuition reimbursements (averaging $8,252 per year) were awarded; career-related internships or fieldwork, Federal Work-Study, institutionally sponsored loans, scholarships/grants, tuition waivers, and unspecified assistantships also available. Financial award application deadline: 3/15; financial award applicants required to submit FAFSA. In 2008, 123 master's, 32 doctorates awarded. *Degree program information:* Part-time and evening/weekend programs available. Postbaccalaureate distance learning degree programs offered. Offers anthropology (MA); art education (MAE); arts and letters (MA, MAE, MATL, MFA, MM, MME, MS, DMA, PhD); conducting (MM); English (MA, PhD); French (MATL); history (MA, MS, PhD); history and literature (MM); international development (PhD); mass communication (MA, MS, PhD); music education (MME, PhD); performance (MM); performance and pedagogy (DMA); philosophy (MA); political science (MA, MS); public relations (MS); Spanish (MATL); speech communication (MA, MS, PhD); teaching English to speakers of other languages (TESOL) (MATL); theatre (MFA); theory and composition (MM); woodwind performance (MM). *Application deadline:* For fall admission, 5/1 for domestic students, 3/1 for international students. Applications are processed on a rolling basis. *Application fee:* $30. Electronic applications accepted. *Application Contact:* Dr. Shonna Breland, Manager of Graduate Admissions, 601-266-4369, Fax: 601-266-5138, E-mail: graduatestudies@usm.edu. *Dean,* Dr. Denise Von Hermann, 601-266-4315, Fax: 601-266-6541, E-mail: denise.vonhermann@usm.edu.

College of Business Students: 74 full-time (40 women), 48 part-time (21 women); includes 18 minority (16 African Americans, 1 American Indian/Alaska Native, 1 Hispanic American), 13 international. Average age 28. 101 applicants, 61% accepted, 55 enrolled. *Faculty:* 12 full-time (4 women), 1 (woman) part-time/adjunct. Expenses: Contact institution. *Financial support:* In 2008–09, 21 research assistantships with full tuition reimbursements (averaging $6,000 per year), 1 teaching assistantship with full tuition reimbursement (averaging $6,000 per year) were awarded; Federal Work-Study and institutionally sponsored loans also available. Support available to part-time students. Financial award application deadline: 3/15; financial award applicants required to submit FAFSA. In 2008, 56 master's awarded. *Degree program information:* Part-time and evening/weekend programs available. Offers accountancy (MPA); business (MBA, MPA); business administration (MBA). *Application deadline:* For fall admission, 7/15 priority date for domestic students, 3/1 for international students; for spring admission, 11/15 priority date for domestic students, 11/5 for international students. Applications are processed on a rolling basis. *Application fee:* $30. Electronic applications accepted. *Application Contact:* Dr. Francis Daniel, Graduate Coordinator, 601-266-4664, Fax: 601-266-5814. *Dean,* Dr. Harold Doty, 601-266-4659, Fax: 601-266-5814.

College of Education and Psychology Students: 275 full-time (210 women), 576 part-time (458 women); includes 191 minority (170 African Americans, 1 American Indian/Alaska Native, 6 Asian Americans or Pacific Islanders, 14 Hispanic Americans), 18 international. Average age 36. 438 applicants, 41% accepted, 158 enrolled. *Faculty:* 87 full-time (48 women), 12 part-time/adjunct (6 women). Expenses: Contact institution. *Financial support:* In 2008–09, 80 research assistantships with full tuition reimbursements (averaging $9,586 per year), 53 teaching assistantships with full tuition reimbursements (averaging $7,775 per year) were awarded; career-related internships or fieldwork, Federal Work-Study, and institutionally sponsored loans also available. Financial award application deadline: 3/15; financial award applicants required to submit FAFSA. In 2008, 268 master's, 56 doctorates, 61 other advanced degrees awarded. *Degree program information:* Part-time programs available. Offers adult education (M Ed, Ed D, PhD, Ed S); alternative secondary teacher education (MAT); business technology education (MS); child and family studies (MS); clinical psychology (MA, PhD); counseling psychology (PhD); early childhood education (M Ed, Ed S); early intervention (MS); education and psychology (M Ed, MA, MAT, MLIS, MS, Ed D, PhD, Ed S, SLS); education of the gifted (M Ed, Ed D, PhD, Ed S); educational administration (M Ed, Ed D, PhD, Ed S); elementary education (M Ed, Ed D, PhD, Ed S); experimental psychology (MA, PhD); higher education (PhD); instructional technology (MS); library and information science (MLIS, SLS); marriage and family therapy (MS); psychology (MS); reading (M Ed, MS, Ed S); school psychology (MA, PhD); secondary education (M Ed, MS, Ed D, PhD, Ed S); special education (M Ed, Ed D, PhD, Ed S); technical occupational education (MS). *Application deadline:* For fall admission, 3/1 for domestic and international students; for spring admission, 11/1 for domestic and international students. Applications are processed on a rolling basis. *Application fee:* $30. Electronic applications accepted. *Application Contact:* Shonna Breland, Manager of Graduate Admissions, 601-266-6563, Fax: 601-266-5138. *Interim Chair,* Dr. Wanda Maulding, 601-266-4568, Fax: 601-266-4175.

College of Health Students: 388 full-time (302 women), 162 part-time (109 women); includes 155 minority (144 African Americans, 1 American Indian/Alaska Native, 7 Asian Americans or Pacific Islanders, 3 Hispanic Americans), 25 international. Average age 32. 385 applicants, 57% accepted, 165 enrolled. *Faculty:* 76 full-time (50 women), 18 part-time/adjunct (10 women). Expenses: Contact institution. *Financial support:* In 2008–09, 1 fellowship with full tuition reimbursement (averaging $16,000 per year), 45 research assistantships with full tuition reimbursements (averaging $8,397 per year), 12 teaching assistantships with full tuition reimbursements (averaging $7,756 per year) were awarded; career-related internships or fieldwork, Federal Work-Study, institutionally sponsored loans, scholarships/grants, and tuition waivers (partial) also available. Financial award application deadline: 3/15; financial award applicants required to submit FAFSA. In 2008, 201 master's, 5 doctorates awarded. *Degree program information:* Part-time and evening/weekend programs available. Offers adult health nursing (MSN); community health nursing (MSN); epidemiology and biostatistics (MPH); ethics (PhD); family nurse practitioner (MSN); health (MA, MPH, MS, MSN, MSW, Au D, Ed D, PhD); health education (MPH); health policy/administration (MPH); human performance (MS, Ed D, PhD); interscholastic athletic administration (MS); leadership (PhD); medical technology (MS); nursing service administration (MSN); nutrition and food systems (MS, PhD); occupational/environmental health (MPH); policy analysis (PhD); psychiatric nursing (MSN); public health nutrition (MPH); recreation and leisure management (MS); social work (MSW); speech and hearing sciences (MA, MS, Au D); sport administration (MS); sport and coaching education (MS); sport management (MS); sports and high performance materials (MS). *Application deadline:* For fall admission, 3/1 for domestic and international students. Applications are processed on a rolling basis. *Application fee:* $30. Electronic applications accepted. *Application Contact:* Shonna Breland, Manager of Graduate Admissions, 601-266-6563, Fax: 601-266-5138. *Dean,* Dr. Michael Forster, 601-266-4866.

College of Science and Technology Students: 376 full-time (164 women), 182 part-time (91 women); includes 69 minority (53 African Americans, 3 American Indian/Alaska Native, 3 Asian Americans or Pacific Islanders, 10 Hispanic Americans), 141 international. Average age 32. 418 applicants, 45% accepted, 127 enrolled. *Faculty:* 164 full-time (31 women), 13 part-time/adjunct (1 woman). Expenses: Contact institution. *Financial support:* In 2008–09, 4 fellowships with full tuition reimbursements (averaging $16,250 per year), 189 research assistantships with full tuition reimbursements (averaging $14,464 per year), 137 teaching assistantships with full tuition reimbursements (averaging $10,259 per year) were awarded; career-related internships or fieldwork, Federal Work-Study, institutionally sponsored loans, and tuition waivers (full) also available. Support available to part-time students. Financial award application deadline: 3/15; financial award applicants required to submit FAFSA. In 2008, 109 master's, 28 doctorates awarded. *Degree program information:* Part-time and evening/weekend programs available. Offers administration of justice (PhD); analytical chemistry (MS, PhD); architecture and construction visualization (MS); biochemistry (MS, PhD); coastal sciences (MS, PhD); computational science (MS, PhD); computational science: mathematics (PhD); computer science (MS, PhD); construction management and technology (MS); corrections (MA, MS); economic development (MS); engineering technology (MS); environmental biology (MS, PhD); geography (MS, PhD); geology (MS); human capital development (PhD); hydrographic science (MS); inorganic chemistry (MS, PhD); juvenile justice (MA, MS); law enforcement (MA, MS); logistics management and technology (MS); marine biology (MS, PhD); marine science (MS, PhD); mathematics (MS); microbiology (MS, PhD); molecular biology (MS, PhD); organic chemistry (MS, PhD); physical chemistry (MS, PhD); physics (MS); polymer science (MS); polymer science and engineering (PhD); science and mathematics education (MS, PhD); science and technology (MA, MS, PhD); workforce training and development (MS). *Application deadline:* For fall admission, 3/1 priority date for domestic students, 3/1 for international students. Applications are processed on a rolling basis. *Application fee:* $25 ($30 for international students). *Application Contact:* Shonna Breland, Manager of Graduate Admissions, 601-266-6563, Fax: 601-266-5138. *Dean,* Dr. Rex Gandy, 601-266-4883, Fax: 601-266-5829.

UNIVERSITY OF SOUTHERN NEVADA, Henderson, NV 89014

General Information Private, coed, graduate-only institution. *Enrollment by degree level:* 628 first professional, 10 master's. *Graduate faculty:* 51 full-time (25 women), 26 part-time/adjunct (9 women). *Tuition:* Full-time $36,200. *Required fees:* $2533. Full-time tuition and fees vary according to program. *Graduate housing:* On-campus housing not available. *Student services:* Campus safety program, international student services, low-cost health insurance, services for students with disabilities. *Library facilities:* University of Southern Nevada Library Learning Resource Center plus 1 other. *Online resources:* library catalog, web page. *Collection:* 4,250 titles, 124 serial subscriptions, 667 audiovisual materials.

Computer facilities: 20 computers available on campus for general student use. A campuswide network can be accessed from off campus. *Web address:* http://www.usn.edu/.

General Application Contact: Dr. Okeleke Nzeogwu, Director, MBA Program, 702-968-1659, E-mail: onzeogwu@usn.edu.

GRADUATE UNITS

College of Pharmacy Students: 628 full-time (347 women); includes 306 minority (45 African Americans, 3 American Indian/Alaska Native, 242 Asian Americans or Pacific Islanders, 16 Hispanic Americans), 14 international. Average age 27. 1,593 applicants, 17% accepted, 227 enrolled. *Faculty:* 48 full-time (25 women), 20 part-time/adjunct (7 women). Expenses: Contact institution. *Financial support:* In 2008–09, 596 students received support. GSL available. Financial award application deadline: 3/2; financial award applicants required to submit FAFSA. In 2008, 132 Pharm Ds awarded. Offers pharmacy (Pharm D). *Application deadline:* For fall admission, 12/8 for domestic and international students. Applications are processed on a rolling basis. *Application fee:* $150. *Application Contact:* Dr. Michael DeYoung, Associate Dean for Admissions, 702-990-4433 Ext. 2006, Fax: 702-990-4435, E-mail: mdeyoung@usn.edu. *Dean, College of Pharmacy,* Dr. Renee Coffman, 702-990-4433 Ext. 2017, Fax: 702-990-4435, E-mail: rcoffman@usn.edu.

MBA Program Students: 10 full-time (4 women); includes 8 minority (4 African Americans, 3 Asian Americans or Pacific Islanders, 1 Hispanic American), 1 international. Average age 34. 11 applicants, 100% accepted, 7 enrolled. *Faculty:* 3 full-time (0 women), 6 part-time/adjunct (2 women). Expenses: Contact institution. *Financial support:* In 2008–09, 6 students received support. GSL available. Financial award application deadline: 3/2; financial award applicants required to submit FAFSA. In 2008, 8 master's awarded. *Degree program information:* Evening/weekend programs available. Offers business administration (MBA). *Application deadline:* Applications are processed on a rolling basis. *Application fee:* $100. *Application Contact:* Dr. Okeleke Nzeogwu, Program Director, 702-990-4433 Ext. 1659, Fax: 702-990-4435, E-mail: onzeogwu@usn.edu. *Program Director,* Dr. Okeleke Nzeogwu, 702-990-4433 Ext. 1659, Fax: 702-990-4435, E-mail: onzeogwu@usn.edu.

UNIVERSITY OF SOUTH FLORIDA, Tampa, FL 33620-9951

General Information State-supported, coed, university. CGS member. *Enrollment:* 46,189 graduate, professional, and undergraduate students; 4,028 full-time matriculated graduate/professional students (2,503 women), 4,641 part-time matriculated graduate/professional students (3,112 women). *Enrollment by degree level:* 6,520 master's, 2,149 doctoral. *Graduate faculty:* 1,094 full-time (426 women), 135 part-time/adjunct (75 women). Tuition, state resident: full-time $2624.40; part-time $291.60 per credit hour. Tuition, nonresident: full-time $7822; part-time $869.13 per credit hour. *Graduate housing:* Rooms and/or apartments available on a first-come, first-served basis to single students and available to married students. Housing application deadline: 7/1. *Student services:* Campus employment opportunities, campus safety program, career counseling, child daycare facilities, exercise/wellness program, free psychological counseling, grant writing training, international student services, low-cost health insurance, multicultural affairs office, services for students with disabilities, writing training. *Library facilities:* Tampa Campus Library plus 5 others. *Online resources:* library catalog, web page. *Collection:* 2.2 million titles, 42,049 serial subscriptions, 50,422 audiovisual materials. *Research affiliation:* Veterans Administration Medical Center, All Children's Hospital, Harris Corporation (electronics), Tampa General Hospital, Shriners Hospitals, H. L. Moffitt Cancer Center.

University of South Florida (continued)

Computer facilities: Computer purchase and lease plans are available. 825 computers available on campus for general student use. A campuswide network can be accessed from student residence rooms and from off campus. Online class registration is available. *Web address:* http://www.usf.edu/.

General Application Contact: Dr. Karen Liller, Interim Dean, Graduate School/Associate Vice President for Research and Innovation, 813-974-2846, Fax: 813-974-5762, E-mail: kliller@grad.usf.edu.

GRADUATE UNITS

Center for Entrepreneurship *Faculty:* 11 full-time (3 women). Expenses: Contact institution. *Financial support:* Applicants required to submit FAFSA. *Degree program information:* Part-time and evening/weekend programs available. Offers entrepreneurship (MS, Graduate Certificate). *Application deadline:* For fall admission, 2/15 for domestic students, 7/2 for international students; for spring admission, 10/15 for domestic students. *Application fee:* $30. *Application Contact:* Dr. Michael W. Fountain, Director, 813-974-7900, Fax: 813-974-7663, E-mail: fountain@coba.usf.edu. *Director,* Dr. Michael W. Fountain, 813-974-7900, Fax: 813-974-7663, E-mail: fountain@coba.usf.edu.

College of Medicine Students: 390 full-time (246 women), 62 part-time (36 women); includes 170 minority (65 African Americans, 2 American Indian/Alaska Native, 47 Asian Americans or Pacific Islanders, 56 Hispanic Americans), 28 international. Average age 27. 123 applicants, 100% accepted, 123 enrolled. *Faculty:* 189 full-time (57 women), 5 part-time/adjunct (4 women). Expenses: Contact institution. In 2008, 65 master's, 32 doctorates awarded. *Degree program information:* Part-time programs available. Offers aging and neuroscience (MSMS); allergy, immunology and infectious disease (PhD); anatomy (PhD); biochemistry and molecular biology (MS, PhD); clinical and translational research (MSMS, PhD); health sciences (MSMS); medical microbiology and immunology (PhD); medical science (MSMS); medicine (MD, MS, MSMS, DPT, PhD); molecular medicine (PhD); molecular pharmacology and physiology (PhD); neuroscience (PhD); pathology (PhD); pharmacology and therapeutics (PhD); physiology and biophysics (PhD); women';s health (MSMS). *Application deadline:* For fall admission, 2/15 for domestic students, 1/2 for international students. *Application fee:* $30. Electronic applications accepted. *Application Contact:* Stephen K. Klasko, Dean, 813-974-0533, Fax: 813-974-3886, E-mail: sklasko@hsc.usf.edu. *Dean,* Stephen K. Klasko, 813-974-0533, Fax: 813-974-3886, E-mail: sklasko@hsc.usf.edu.

School of Physical Therapy Students: 104 full-time (84 women); includes 23 minority (6 African Americans, 1 American Indian/Alaska Native, 10 Asian Americans or Pacific Islanders, 6 Hispanic Americans). 36 applicants, 100% accepted, 36 enrolled. Expenses: Contact institution. *Financial support:* Applicants required to submit FAFSA. In 2008, 20 master's awarded. Offers physical therapy (MS, DPT). *Application deadline:* For fall admission, 9/1 for domestic students, 2/1 for international students. *Application fee:* $30. *Application Contact:* David Newman, Coordinator, 813-974-1326, Fax: 813-974-8614, E-mail: dnewman1@health.usf.edu. *Coordinator,* David Newman, 813-974-1326, Fax: 813-974-8614, E-mail: dnewman1@health.usf.edu.

Graduate School Students: 32 full-time (22 women), 1 (woman) part-time; includes 4 minority (1 African American, 1 American Indian/Alaska Native, 1 Asian American or Pacific Islander, 1 Hispanic American), 5 international. 136 applicants, 13% accepted, 6 enrolled. *Faculty:* 1 full-time (0 women). Expenses: Contact institution. *Financial support:* Applicants required to submit FAFSA. In 2008, 41 master's, 7 doctorates awarded. *Degree program information:* Part-time and evening/weekend programs available. Postbaccalaureate distance learning degree programs offered. Offers applied behavior analysis (MA); cancer biology (PhD). *Application deadline:* For fall admission, 2/15 priority date for domestic students, 1/2 priority date for international students; for spring admission, 10/1 priority date for domestic students, 6/1 priority date for international students. Applications are processed on a rolling basis. *Application fee:* $30. Electronic applications accepted. *Application Contact:* Dr. Karen D. Liller, Interim Dean, 813-974-7359, Fax: 813-974-5762, E-mail: kliller@grad.usf.edu. *Interim Dean,* Dr. Karen D. Liller, 813-974-7359, Fax: 813-974-5762, E-mail: kliller@grad.usf.edu.

College of Arts and Sciences Students: 969 full-time (543 women), 851 part-time (553 women); includes 307 minority (120 African Americans, 8 American Indian/Alaska Native, 40 Asian Americans or Pacific Islanders, 139 Hispanic Americans), 196 international. Average age 24. 1,675 applicants, 64% accepted, 389 enrolled. *Faculty:* 364 full-time (229 women), 28 part-time/adjunct (14 women). Expenses: Contact institution. *Financial support:* Career-related internships or fieldwork, Federal Work-Study, institutionally sponsored loans, scholarships/grants, tuition waivers (full and partial), and unspecified assistantships available. Support available to part-time students. Financial award applicants required to submit FAFSA. In 2008, 581 master's, 82 doctorates awarded. *Degree program information:* Part-time and evening/weekend programs available. Postbaccalaureate distance learning degree programs offered (minimal on-campus study). Offers Africana studies (MLA); aging studies (PhD); American studies (MA); analytical chemistry (MS, PhD); applied anthropology (MA, PhD); applied physics (PhD); arts and sciences (MA, MFA, MLA, MPA, MS, MSW, MURP, Au D, PhD, Graduate Certificate); biochemistry (MS, PhD); cell biology and molecular biology (MS); classics: latin/greek (MA); clinical psychology (MA, PhD); coastal marine biology (MS); coastal marine biology and ecology (PhD); cognitive and neural sciences (MA, PhD); communication (MA, PhD); communication sciences and disorders (MA, MS, Au D, PhD); computational chemistry (MS, PhD); conservation biology (MS, PhD); criminal justice administration (MA); criminology (MA, PhD); Cuban studies (Graduate Certificate); English (MA, MFA, PhD); environmental chemistry (MS, PhD); environmental science and policy (MS); French (MA); geography (MA, MURP, PhD); geology (MS, PhD); gerontology (MA); history (MA, PhD); industrial-organizational psychology (MA, PhD); inorganic chemistry (MS, PhD); Latin American and Caribbean studies (Graduate Certificate); Latin American Caribbean and Latino Studies (MA); Latin American, Caribbean and Latino studies (MA); liberal arts (MLA); library and information science (MA); linguistics (MA); linguistics: ESL (MA); mass communications (MA); mathematics (MA, PhD, Graduate Certificate); molecular and cell biology (PhD); organic chemistry (MS); philosophy (MA, PhD); physical chemistry (MS, PhD); physics (MS); political science (MA); polymer chemistry (MS, PhD); public administration (MPA); rehabilitation and mental health counseling (MA); religious studies (MA); social work (MSW, PhD); sociology (MA, PhD); Spanish (MA); statistics (MA, Graduate Certificate); women's studies (MA). *Application deadline:* For fall admission, 2/15 priority date for domestic students, 1/2 priority date for international students; for spring admission, 10/15 priority date for domestic students, 6/2 priority date for international students. *Application fee:* $30. *Application Contact:* Sylvia Gardner, Administrative Assistant, 813-974-0853, Fax: 813-974-5911, E-mail: gardner@cas.usf.edu. *Interim Dean,* Dr. Eric Eisenberg, 813-974-2503, Fax: 813-974-5911, E-mail: Eisenber@cas.usf.edu.

College of Business Administration Students: 352 full-time (141 women), 462 part-time (183 women); includes 180 minority (42 African Americans, 3 American Indian/Alaska Native, 68 Asian Americans or Pacific Islanders, 67 Hispanic Americans), 115 international. Average age 25. 831 applicants, 59% accepted, 278 enrolled. *Faculty:* 70 full-time (19 women), 3 part-time/adjunct (2 women). Expenses: Contact institution. *Financial support:* Career-related internships or fieldwork, scholarships/grants, health care benefits, and unspecified assistantships available. Financial award applicants required to submit FAFSA. In 2008, 344 master's, 9 doctorates awarded. *Degree program information:* Part-time and evening/weekend programs available. Offers accounting (M Acc); business administration (M Acc, MA, MBA, MS, MSM, PhD); economics (MA, PhD); finance (MS); management information systems (MS). *Application deadline:* For fall admission, 6/1 for domestic students, 1/2 for international students; for spring admission, 10/15 for domestic students, 6/1 for international students. *Application fee:* $30. *Application Contact:* Irene Hurst, Program Director, 813-974-3335, Fax: 813-974-4518, E-mail: Hurst@coba.usf.edu. *Dean,* Dr. Robert Forsythe, 813-974-3229, Fax: 813-974-3030, E-mail: rforsyth@coba.usf.edu.

College of Education Students: 617 full-time (470 women), 1,397 part-time (1,061 women); includes 458 minority (241 African Americans, 6 American Indian/Alaska Native, 42 Asian Americans or Pacific Islanders, 169 Hispanic Americans), 45 international. Average age 30. 1,185 applicants, 58% accepted, 490 enrolled. *Faculty:* 134 full-time (82 women), 36 part-time/adjunct (21 women). Expenses: Contact institution. *Financial support:* Career-related internships or fieldwork, Federal Work-Study, institutionally sponsored loans, and scholarships/grants available. Support available to part-time students. Financial award applicants required to submit FAFSA. In 2008, 569 master's, 44 doctorates awarded. *Degree program information:* Part-time and evening/weekend programs available. Offers adult education (MA, Ed D, PhD, Ed S); career and technical education (MA); college student affairs (M Ed); counselor education (MA, PhD, Ed S); early childhood education (M Ed, MAT, PhD, Ed S); education (M Ed, MA, MAT, Ed D, PhD, Ed S); education of the mentally handicapped (MA); educational leadership (M Ed, Ed D, Ed S); educational measurement and research (M Ed, PhD, Ed S); elementary education (M Ed, MA, Ed D, PhD, Ed S); English education (M Ed, MA, MAT, PhD); ese (MA, MAT); foreign language education (M Ed, MA, MAT); gifted education (M Ed); gifted education (online) (MA); higher education/community college teaching (MA, PhD, Ed S); instructional technology (M Ed, Ed S); interdisciplinary education (PhD, Ed S); learning disabilities (M Ed, MA); mathematics education (M Ed, MA, PhD, Ed S); mathematics education 5-9 (MAT); mathematics education 6-12 (MAT); mental retardation (M Ed); middle school education (M Ed); motor disabilities (M Ed); physical education (MA); reading education (M Ed, MA, PhD, Ed S); reading education and language arts (PhD); school psychology (MA, PhD, Ed S); science education (MA, MAT, PhD, Ed S); second language acquisition/instructional technology (PhD); secondary education (PhD); social science education (M Ed, MA, MAT); special education (PhD, Ed S); student affairs administration (PhD); vocational education (Ed D, Ed S). *Application deadline:* For fall admission, 2/15 for domestic students, 1/2 for international students; for spring admission, 10/15 for domestic students, 6/1 for international students. *Application fee:* $30. Electronic applications accepted. *Application Contact:* Colleen S. Kennedy, Dean, 813-974-3400, Fax: 813-974-3826, E-mail: kennedy@coedu.usf.edu. *Dean,* Colleen S. Kennedy, 813-974-3400, Fax: 813-974-3826, E-mail: kennedy@coedu.usf.edu.

College of Engineering Students: 416 full-time (118 women), 311 part-time (70 women); includes 164 minority (58 African Americans, 1 American Indian/Alaska Native, 51 Asian Americans or Pacific Islanders, 54 Hispanic Americans), 293 international. Average age 25. 722 applicants, 67% accepted, 167 enrolled. *Faculty:* 84 full-time (9 women), 10 part-time/adjunct (2 women). Expenses: Contact institution. *Financial support:* Career-related internships or fieldwork, Federal Work-Study, scholarships/grants, health care benefits, and unspecified assistantships available. Financial award application deadline: 3/1; financial award applicants required to submit FAFSA. In 2008, 226 master's, 52 doctorates awarded. *Degree program information:* Part-time and evening/weekend programs available. Offers biomedical engineering (MSBE, MSES, PhD); chemical engineering (MCHE, ME, MSCH, MSES, PhD); civil and environmental engineering (MEVE, MSES, MSEV); civil engineering (MCE, MSCE, PhD); computer science (MSCP, MSCS); computer science and engineering (ME, MSES, PhD); electrical engineering (ME, MSEE, MSES, PhD); engineering (ME); engineering management (MSEM); engineering science (PhD); industrial engineering (MIE, MSIE, PhD); materials science and engineering (MSE); mechanical engineering (ME, MME, MSES, MSME, PhD). *Application deadline:* For fall admission, 2/15 for domestic students, 1/2 priority date for international students; for spring admission, 10/15 for domestic students, 6/1 priority date for international students. Applications are processed on a rolling basis. *Application fee:* $30. Electronic applications accepted. *Application Contact:* Marsha L. Brett, Administrative Assistant, 813-974-3782, Fax: 813-974-5094, E-mail: brett@eng.usf.edu. *Dean,* Dr. John Wieneck, 813-974-2530, Fax: 813-974-5094, E-mail: wieneck@eng.usf.edu.

College of Marine Science Students: 60 full-time (42 women), 35 part-time (23 women); includes 13 minority (5 African Americans, 8 Hispanic Americans), 7 international. Average age 31. 72 applicants, 32% accepted, 14 enrolled. *Faculty:* 20 full-time (4 women). Expenses: Contact institution. In 2008, 9 master's, 5 doctorates awarded. *Degree program information:* Part-time and evening/weekend programs available. Offers marine science (MS, PhD). *Application deadline:* For fall admission, 1/15 for domestic students, 1/2 for international students; for spring admission, 10/1 for domestic students, 7/1 for international students. Applications are processed on a rolling basis. *Application fee:* $30. *Application Contact:* Ted VanVleet, Program Director, 727-553-1165, Fax: 727-553-1189, E-mail: vanleet@marine.usf.edu. *Dean,* Dr. William T Hogarth, 727-553-1130, Fax: 727-553-1189, E-mail: pbetzer@marine.usf.edu.

College of Nursing Students: 186 full-time (167 women), 523 part-time (469 women); includes 167 minority (86 African Americans, 2 American Indian/Alaska Native, 26 Asian Americans or Pacific Islanders, 53 Hispanic Americans), 4 international. Average age 33. 356 applicants, 44% accepted, 152 enrolled. *Faculty:* 33 full-time (29 women), 9 part-time/adjunct (7 women). Expenses: Contact institution. *Financial support:* Federal Work-Study, institutionally sponsored loans, scholarships/grants, traineeships, tuition waivers (partial), and unspecified assistantships available. Financial award application deadline: 2/1; financial award applicants required to submit FAFSA. In 2008, 78 master's, 16 doctorates awarded. *Degree program information:* Part-time programs available. Offers nursing (MS, DNP, PhD). *Application deadline:* For fall admission, 6/1 for domestic students, 1/2 for international students; for spring admission, 10/15 for domestic students, 6/15 for international students. Applications are processed on a rolling basis. *Application fee:* $30. *Application Contact:* Mary Webb, Director of Student Affairs, 813-974-3442, Fax: 813-974-3118, E-mail: mwebb@health.usf.edu. *Dean,* Dr. Patricia A. Burns, 813-974-9091, Fax: 813-974-5418, E-mail: pburns@hsc.usf.edu.

College of Public Health Students: 323 full-time (240 women), 366 part-time (264 women); includes 188 minority (96 African Americans, 1 American Indian/Alaska Native, 32 Asian Americans or Pacific Islanders, 59 Hispanic Americans), 96 international. Average age 33. 597 applicants, 75% accepted, 194 enrolled. *Faculty:* 64 full-time (30 women), 26 part-time/adjunct (11 women). Expenses: Contact institution. *Financial support:* In 2008–09, 18 fellowships with full tuition reimbursements (averaging $32,033 per year), 91 research assistantships with full and partial tuition reimbursements (averaging $55,103 per year), 41 teaching assistantships (averaging $57,460 per year) were awarded; career-related internships or fieldwork, Federal Work-Study, institutionally sponsored loans, scholarships/grants, traineeships, and unspecified assistantships also available. Support available to part-time students. Financial award applicants required to submit FAFSA. In 2008, 126 master's, 14 doctorates awarded. *Degree program information:* Part-time and evening/weekend programs available. Postbaccalaureate distance learning degree programs offered (minimal on-campus study). Offers community and family health (MPH, MSPH, DPH, PhD); environmental and occupational health (MPH, MSPH, PhD); epidemiology and biostatistics (MPH, MSPH, PhD); global health (MPH, MSPH, DPH, PhD); health policy and management (MHA, MPH, MSPH, PhD); public health (MHA, MPH, MSPH, DPH, PhD); public health practice (MPH). *Application deadline:* For fall admission, 6/1 for domestic students, 1/2 for international students; for spring admission, 10/15 for domestic students, 7/1 for international students. Applications are processed on a rolling basis. *Application fee:* $30. Electronic applications accepted. *Application Contact:* Michelle Hodge, Academic Advisor, 813-974-6665, Fax: 813-974-8121, E-mail: mrobinso@health.usf.edu. *Dean,* Dr. Donna J. Petersen, 813-974-3623, Fax: 813-974-7390.

College of The Arts Students: 172 full-time (81 women), 83 part-time (40 women); includes 57 minority (11 African Americans, 3 American Indian/Alaska Native, 11 Asian Americans or Pacific Islanders, 32 Hispanic Americans), 17 international. 236 applicants, 44% accepted, 70 enrolled. *Faculty:* 48 full-time (14 women), 18 part-time/adjunct (9 women). Expenses: Contact institution. *Financial support:* Fellowships with partial tuition reimbursements, research assistantships with partial tuition reimbursements, teaching assistantships with partial tuition reimbursements, scholarships/grants and unspecified assistantships available. Financial award applicants required to submit FAFSA. In 2008, 48 master's, 1 doctorate awarded. *Degree program information:* Part-time and evening/weekend programs available. Offers architecture and community design (M Arch); art history (MA); chamber music (MM); composition (MM); conducting (MM); electro-acoustic music (MM); jazz studies (MM); music (MA); performance (MM); piano pedagogy (MM); studio art (MFA); theory (MM); visual and performing arts (M Arch, MA, MFA, MM, PhD). *Application deadline:* For fall admission, 1/15 for domestic students, 1/2 for international students. *Application fee:* $30. *Application Contact:* Barton Lee, Coordinator, 813-974-2301, Fax: 813-974-2091, E-mail: blee@arts.usf.edu. *Dean,* Ron Jones, 813-974-2301.

THE UNIVERSITY OF TAMPA, Tampa, FL 33606-1490

General Information Independent, coed, comprehensive institution. CGS member. *Enrollment:* 5,800 graduate, professional, and undergraduate students; 195 full-time matriculated graduate/professional students (85 women), 477 part-time matriculated graduate/professional students (256 women). *Enrollment by degree level:* 672 master's. *Graduate faculty:* 57 full-time (27 women), 28 part-time/adjunct (15 women). *Tuition:* Full-time $7552; part-time $472 per credit hour. *Required fees:* $70; $70 per year. *Graduate housing:* Room and/or apartments available on a first-come, first-served basis to single students; on-campus housing not available to married students. Typical cost: $7978 (including board). Housing application deadline: 5/1. *Student services:* Campus employment opportunities, campus safety program, career counseling, exercise/wellness program, international student services, services for students with disabilities, writing training. *Library facilities:* Macdonald Kelce Library. *Online resources:* library catalog, web page. *Collection:* 286,521 titles, 27,666 serial subscriptions, 7,066 audiovisual materials. *Research affiliation:* Tampa General Hospital (nursing).

Computer facilities: Computer purchase and lease plans are available. 528 computers available on campus for general student use. A campuswide network can be accessed from student residence rooms and from off campus. Online class registration is available. *Web address:* http://www.ut.edu/.

General Application Contact: Karen Full, Director of Admissions, Graduate and Continuing Studies, 813-257-3642, E-mail: kfull@ut.edu.

GRADUATE UNITS

John H. Sykes College of Business Students: 190 full-time (80 women), 343 part-time (141 women); includes 92 minority (17 African Americans, 3 American Indian/Alaska Native, 20 Asian Americans or Pacific Islanders, 52 Hispanic Americans), 89 international. Average age 31. 496 applicants, 51% accepted, 186 enrolled. *Faculty:* 42 full-time (14 women), 13 part-time/adjunct (3 women). Expenses: Contact institution. *Financial support:* In 2008–09, 90 students received support, including 60 research assistantships with tuition reimbursements available (averaging $6,000 per year); career-related internships or fieldwork and unspecified assistantships also available. Support available to part-time students. Financial award applicants required to submit FAFSA. In 2008, 203 master's awarded. *Degree program information:* Part-time and evening/weekend programs available. Offers accounting (MBA, MS); economics (MBA); entrepreneurship and innovation (MBA); finance (MBA, MS); information systems management (MBA); international business (MBA); management (MBA); marketing (MBA, MS); nonprofit management (MBA). *Application deadline:* For fall admission, 7/15 for domestic students, 6/1 for international students; for spring admission, 12/15 for domestic students, 11/1 for international students. Applications are processed on a rolling basis. *Application fee:* $40. Electronic applications accepted. *Application Contact:* Karen Full, Director of Admissions, Graduate and Continuing Studies, 813-257-3642, E-mail: kfull@ut.edu. *Associate Dean, Graduate and Continuing Studies*, Dr. Don Morrill, 813-253-6100, E-mail: dmorrill@ut.edu.

Nursing Program Students: 5 full-time (all women), 94 part-time (86 women); includes 16 minority (8 African Americans, 1 American Indian/Alaska Native, 7 Hispanic Americans), 2 international. Average age 40. 62 applicants, 60% accepted, 29 enrolled. *Faculty:* 9 full-time (all women), 2 part-time/adjunct (both women). Expenses: Contact institution. *Financial support:* In 2008–09, 2 students received support, including 2 research assistantships with tuition reimbursements available (averaging $4,248 per year); career-related internships or fieldwork and unspecified assistantships also available. Support available to part-time students. Financial award applicants required to submit FAFSA. In 2008, 18 master's awarded. *Degree program information:* Part-time and evening/weekend programs available. Offers adult nurse practitioner (MSN); family nurse practitioner (MSN). *Application deadline:* For fall admission, 7/15 for domestic students, 6/1 for international students. Applications are processed on a rolling basis. *Application fee:* $40. Electronic applications accepted. *Application Contact:* Paige James, Graduate Advisor and Recruiter, 813-258-7409, Fax: 813-259-5403, E-mail: pjames@ut.edu. *Director*, Dr. Maria Warda, 813-253-6223, Fax: 813-258-7214, E-mail: mwarda@ut.edu.

Program in Teaching Students: 40 part-time (29 women); includes 6 minority (3 African Americans, 1 Asian American or Pacific Islander, 2 Hispanic Americans). Average age 30. 96 applicants, 58% accepted, 42 enrolled. *Faculty:* 6 full-time (4 women), 13 part-time/adjunct (10 women). Expenses: Contact institution. *Financial support:* In 2008–09, 2 students received support. Faculty/staff grants available. Financial award applicants required to submit FAFSA. In 2008, 36 master's awarded. *Degree program information:* Part-time and evening/weekend programs available. Offers curriculum and instruction (M Ed); math education (MAT); science education (MAT); social science education (MAT). *Application deadline:* For fall admission, 5/1 for domestic students. *Application fee:* $40. *Application Contact:* Paige James, Graduate Advisor and Recruiter, 813-258-7409, Fax: 813-259-5403, E-mail: pjames@ut.edu. *Associate Professor of Education*, Dr. Martha Harrison, 813-253-3333 Ext. 3373, E-mail: mharrison@ut.edu.

THE UNIVERSITY OF TENNESSEE, Knoxville, TN 37996

General Information State-supported, coed, university. CGS member. *Enrollment:* 30,410 graduate, professional, and undergraduate students; 4,148 full-time matriculated graduate/professional students (2,330 women), 2,116 part-time matriculated graduate/professional students (1,126 women). *Enrollment by degree level:* 759 first professional, 3,688 master's, 1,817 doctoral. *Graduate faculty:* 1,172 full-time (390 women), 16 part-time/adjunct (6 women). *Tuition, area resident:* Part-time $348 per credit hour. Tuition, state resident: full-time $6262. Tuition, nonresident: full-time $18,920; part-time $1052 per credit hour. *Required fees:* $812; $36 per credit hour. Tuition and fees vary according to program. *Graduate housing:* Rooms and/or apartments available on a first-come, first-served basis to single and married students. Typical cost: $3160 per year ($3728 including board) for single students. Room and board charges vary according to board plan. Housing application deadline: 2/1. *Student services:* Campus employment opportunities, campus safety program, career counseling, exercise/wellness program, free psychological counseling, grant writing training, international student services, low-cost health insurance, multicultural affairs office, services for students with disabilities, teacher training, writing training. *Library facilities:* John C. Hodges Library plus 6 others. *Online resources:* library catalog, web page, access to other libraries' catalogs. *Collection:* 3 million titles, 27,000 serial subscriptions, 41,431 audiovisual materials. *Research affiliation:* Electric Power Research Institute (energy systems), Exxon Corporation (materials Science), Eastman Chemical Co. (chemical engineering), Siemens Medical Solutions USA (medical imaging), Lockheed Martin Corporation (engineering), Oak Ridge National Laboratory & Biology Division (engineering, science).

Computer facilities: Computer purchase and lease plans are available. 600 computers available on campus for general student use. A campuswide network can be accessed from student residence rooms and from off campus. Online class registration, Blackboard Course Management System are available. *Web address:* http://www.tennessee.edu/.

General Application Contact: Michael Ickowitz, Associate Director of Graduate and International Admissions, 865-974-3251, Fax: 865-974-6541, E-mail: graduateadmissions@utk.edu.

GRADUATE UNITS

College of Law Students: 468 full-time (218 women); includes 91 minority (57 African Americans, 5 American Indian/Alaska Native, 15 Asian Americans or Pacific Islanders, 14 Hispanic Americans), 4 international. Average age 24. 1,411 applicants, 29% accepted, 153 enrolled. *Faculty:* 45 full-time (20 women), 39 part-time/adjunct (14 women). Expenses: Contact institution. *Financial support:* In 2008–09, 356 students received support, including 7 research assistantships with full tuition reimbursements available (averaging $4,400 per year); career-related internships or fieldwork, Federal Work-Study, institutionally sponsored loans, scholarships/grants, and unspecified assistantships also available. Support available to part-time students. Financial award application deadline: 3/1; financial award applicants required to submit FAFSA. In 2008, 143 JDs awarded. Offers business transactions (JD); law (JD). *Application deadline:* For fall admission, 3/1 priority date for domestic and international students. Applications are processed on a rolling basis. *Application fee:* $15. Electronic applications accepted. *Application Contact:* Janet S. Hatcher, Admissions and Financial Aid Advisor, 865-974-4131, Fax: 865-974-1572, E-mail: hatcher@utk.edu. *Director of Admissions, Financial Aid and Career Services*, Dr. Karen R. Britton, 865-974-4131, Fax: 865-974-1572, E-mail: lawadmit@utk.edu.

Graduate School *Degree program information:* Part-time and evening/weekend programs available. Postbaccalaureate distance learning degree programs offered (minimal on-campus study). Offers aviation systems (MS); comparative and experimental medicine (MS, PhD). Electronic applications accepted.

College of Agricultural Sciences and Natural Resources *Degree program information:* Part-time programs available. Postbaccalaureate distance learning degree programs offered (minimal on-campus study). Offers agricultural education (MS); agricultural extension education (MS); agricultural sciences and natural resources (MS, PhD); animal anatomy (PhD); biosystems engineering (MS, PhD); biosystems engineering technology (MS); breeding (MS, PhD); entomology (MS, PhD); floriculture (MS); food science and technology (MS, PhD); forestry (MS); integrated pest management and bioactive natural products (PhD); landscape design (MS); management (MS, PhD); nutrition (MS, PhD); physiology (MS, PhD); plant pathology (MS, PhD); public horticulture (MS); turfgrass (MS); wildlife and fisheries science (MS); woody ornamentals (MS). Electronic applications accepted.

College of Architecture and Design Offers architecture (professional) (M Arch); architecture (research) (M Arch); architecture and design (M Arch, MA, MLA, MS); landscape architecture (MLA); landscape architecture (research) (MA, MS). Electronic applications accepted.

College of Arts and Sciences *Degree program information:* Part-time and evening/weekend programs available. Offers accompanying (MM); American history (PhD); analytical chemistry (MS, PhD); applied linguistics (PhD); applied mathematics (MS); archaeology (MA, PhD); arts and sciences (M Math, MA, MFA, MM, MPA, MS, PhD); audiology (MA); behavior (MS, PhD); biochemistry, cellular and molecular biology (MS, PhD); biological anthropology (MA, PhD); ceramics (MFA); chemical physics (PhD); choral conducting (MM); clinical psychology (PhD); composition (MM); computer science (MS, PhD); costume design (MFA); criminology (MA, PhD); cultural anthropology (MA, PhD); drawing (MFA); ecology (MS, PhD); energy, environment, and resource policy (MA, PhD); English (MA, PhD); environmental chemistry (MS, PhD); European history (PhD); evolutionary biology (MS, PhD); experimental psychology (MA, PhD); French (MA, PhD); genome science and technology (MS, PhD); geography (MS, PhD); geology (MS, PhD); German (MA, PhD); graphic design (MFA); hearing science (PhD); history (MA); inorganic chemistry (MS, PhD); instrumental conducting (MM); inter-area studies (MFA); Italian (PhD); jazz (MM); lighting design (MFA); mathematical ecology (PhD); mathematics (M Math, MS, PhD); media arts (MFA); medical ethics (MA, PhD); microbiology (MS, PhD); modern foreign languages (PhD); music education (MM); music theory (MM); musicology (MM); organic chemistry (MS, PhD); painting (MFA); performance (MFA, MM); philosophy (MA, PhD); physical chemistry (MS, PhD); physics (MS, PhD); piano pedagogy and literature (MM); plant physiology and genetics (MS, PhD); political economy (MA, PhD); political science (MA, MPA, PhD); polymer chemistry (MS, PhD); Portuguese (PhD); printmaking (MFA); psychology (MA); public administration (MPA); religious studies (MA); Russian (PhD); scene design (MFA); sculpture (MFA); Spanish (MA); speech and hearing science (PhD); speech and language pathology (PhD); speech and language science (PhD); speech pathology (MA); theatre technology (MFA); theoretical chemistry (PhD); watercolor (MFA); zoo-archaeology (MA, PhD). Electronic applications accepted.

College of Business Administration *Degree program information:* Part-time programs available. Postbaccalaureate distance learning degree programs offered (minimal on-campus study). Offers accounting (M Acc, PhD); business administration (M Acc, MA, MBA, MS, PhD); economics (MA, PhD); finance (MBA, PhD); industrial and organizational psychology (PhD); industrial statistics (MS); logistics and transportation (MBA, PhD); management (PhD); management science (MS, PhD); marketing (MBA, PhD); operations management (MBA); professional business administration (MBA); statistics (MS, PhD); systems (M Acc); taxation (M Acc); teacher licensure (MS); training and development (MS). Electronic applications accepted.

College of Communication and Information *Degree program information:* Part-time and evening/weekend programs available. Postbaccalaureate distance learning degree programs offered (no on-campus study). Offers advertising (MS, PhD); broadcasting (MS, PhD); communications (MS, PhD); information sciences (MS, PhD); journalism (MS, PhD); public relations (MS, PhD); speech communication (MS, PhD). Electronic applications accepted.

College of Education, Health and Human Sciences *Degree program information:* Part-time and evening/weekend programs available. Postbaccalaureate distance learning degree programs offered (no on-campus study). Offers adult education (MS); applied educational psychology (MS); art education (MS); biomechanics/sports medicine (MS, PhD); child and family studies (MS, PhD); collaborative learning (Ed D); college student personnel (MS); community health (PhD); community health education (MPH); consumer services management (MS); counseling education (PhD); cultural studies in education (PhD); curriculum (MS, Ed S); curriculum, educational research and evaluation (Ed D, PhD); early childhood education (MS, PhD); early childhood special education (MS); education of deaf and hard of hearing (MS); education, health and human sciences (MPH, MS, Ed D, PhD, Ed S); educational administration and policy studies (Ed D, PhD); educational administration and supervision (MS, Ed S); educational psychology (Ed D, PhD); elementary education (MS, Ed S); elementary teaching (MS); English education (MS, Ed S); exercise physiology (MS, PhD); exercise science (MS, PhD); foreign language/ESL education (MS, Ed S); gerontology (MPH); health planning/administration (MPH); health promotion and health education (MS); hospitality management (MS); hotel, restaurant, and tourism management (MS); instructional technology (MS, Ed D, PhD, Ed S); literacy, language and ESL education (PhD); literacy, language education, and ESL education (Ed D); mathematics education (MS, Ed S); mental health counseling (MS); modified and comprehensive special education (MS); nutrition (MS); nutrition science (PhD); reading education (MS, Ed S); recreation and leisure studies (MS); rehabilitation counseling (MS); retail and consumer sciences (MS); retailing and consumer sciences (PhD); safety (MS); school counseling (MS, Ed S); school psychology (PhD, Ed S); science education (MS, Ed S); secondary teaching (MS); social foundations (MS); social science education (MS, Ed S); socio-cultural foundations of sports and education (PhD); special education (Ed S); sport management (MS); sport studies (MS, PhD); teacher education (Ed D, PhD); textile science (MS, PhD); therapeutic recreation (MS); tourism (MS). Electronic applications accepted.

College of Engineering Students: 547 full-time (106 women), 229 part-time (28 women); includes 62 minority (34 African Americans, 2 American Indian/Alaska Native, 16 Asian Americans or Pacific Islanders, 10 Hispanic Americans), 290 international. 1,267 applicants, 39% accepted, 139 enrolled. *Faculty:* 142 full-time (11 women), 87 part-time/adjunct (2 women). Expenses: Contact institution. *Financial support:* In 2008–09, 2 fellowships with full tuition reimbursements (averaging $19,932 per year), 272 research assistantships with full tuition reimbursements (averaging $17,486 per year), 107 teaching assistantships with full tuition reimbursements (averaging $14,710 per year) were awarded; career-related internships or fieldwork, Federal Work-Study, institutionally sponsored loans, health care benefits, and unspecified assistantships also available. Financial award application deadline: 2/1; financial award applicants required to submit FAFSA. In 2008, 229 master's, 65 doctorates awarded. *Degree program information:* Part-time and evening/weekend programs available. Postbaccalaureate distance learning degree programs offered. Offers aerospace engineering (MS, PhD); applied artificial intelligence (MS); biomedical engineering (MS, PhD); chemical engineering (MS, PhD); civil engineering (MS, PhD); composite materials (MS, PhD); computational mechanics (MS, PhD); computer engineering (MS, PhD); computer science (MS, PhD); electrical engineering (MS, PhD); engineering (MS, PhD); engineering management (MS); engineering science (MS, PhD); environmental engineering (MS); fluid mechanics (MS, PhD); human factors engineering (MS); industrial engineering (MS, PhD); information engineering (MS); manufacturing systems engineering (MS); materials science and engineering (MS, PhD); mechanical engineering (MS, PhD); optical engineering (MS, PhD); polymer engineering (MS, PhD); radiological engineering (MS, PhD); solid mechanics (MS, PhD). *Application deadline:* For fall admission, 2/1 priority date for domestic and international students; for spring admission, 6/15 priority date for international students. Applications are processed on a rolling basis. *Application fee:* $35. Electronic applications accepted. *Application Contact:* Dr. Masood Parang, Associate Dean of Student Affairs,

The University of Tennessee (continued)

865-974-2454, Fax: 865-974-9871, E-mail: mparang@utk.edu. *Dean,* Dr. Way Kuo, 865-974-5321, Fax: 865-974-8890, E-mail: way@utk.edu.

College of Nursing *Degree program information:* Part-time programs available. Offers nursing (MSN, PhD). Electronic applications accepted.

College of Social Work *Degree program information:* Part-time programs available. Offers clinical social work practice (MSSW); social welfare management and community practice (MSSW); social work (PhD). Electronic applications accepted.

College of Veterinary Medicine Offers veterinary medicine (DVM).

THE UNIVERSITY OF TENNESSEE AT CHATTANOOGA, Chattanooga, TN 37403-2598

General Information State-supported, coed, comprehensive institution. CGS member. *Enrollment:* 9,807 graduate, professional, and undergraduate students; 583 full-time matriculated graduate/professional students (359 women), 819 part-time matriculated graduate/professional students (472 women). *Enrollment by degree level:* 1,104 master's, 152 doctoral, 84 other advanced degrees. *Graduate faculty:* 150 full-time (60 women), 19 part-time/adjunct (9 women). Tuition, state resident: full-time $6150; part-time $281 per credit hour. Tuition, nonresident: full-time $16,710; part-time $867 per credit hour. *Required fees:* $1100; $128 per credit hour. $550 per semester. *Graduate housing:* Rooms and/or apartments available on a first-come, first-served basis to single and married students. Typical cost: $5416 per year ($8216 including board) for single students. Housing application deadline: 8/1. *Student services:* Campus employment opportunities, campus safety program, career counseling, child daycare facilities, exercise/wellness program, free psychological counseling, international student services, low-cost health insurance, services for students with disabilities, teacher training, writing training. *Library facilities:* Lupton Library. *Online resources:* library catalog, web page, access to other libraries' catalogs. *Collection:* 586,633 titles, 1,822 serial subscriptions, 18,888 audiovisual materials. *Research affiliation:* Highland Biological Field Station (NC), Tennessee Valley Authority, Gulf Coast Research Laboratory.

Computer facilities: 300 computers available on campus for general student use. A campuswide network can be accessed from student residence rooms and from off campus. Online class registration is available. *Web address:* http://www.utc.edu/.

General Application Contact: Dr. Stephanie Bellar, Interim Dean of Graduate Studies, 423-425-4666, Fax: 423-425-5223, E-mail: stephanie-bellar@utc.edu.

GRADUATE UNITS

Graduate School Students: 579 full-time (356 women), 761 part-time (435 women); includes 158 minority (101 African Americans, 8 American Indian/Alaska Native, 31 Asian Americans or Pacific Islanders, 18 Hispanic Americans), 42 international. Average age 31. 854 applicants, 59% accepted, 316 enrolled. *Faculty:* 140 full-time (50 women), 19 part-time/adjunct (9 women). Expenses: Contact institution. *Financial support:* In 2008–09, 100 fellowships with full and partial tuition reimbursements (averaging $4,231 per year), 17 research assistantships with full and partial tuition reimbursements (averaging $5,712 per year), 4 teaching assistantships with full and partial tuition reimbursements (averaging $4,263 per year) were awarded; career-related internships or fieldwork, Federal Work-Study, institutionally sponsored loans, scholarships/grants, tuition waivers (partial), and unspecified assistantships also available. Support available to part-time students. Financial award application deadline: 4/1; financial award applicants required to submit FAFSA. *Degree program information:* Part-time and evening/weekend programs available. *Application deadline:* For fall admission, 8/1 priority date for domestic students, 6/1 for international students; for spring admission, 12/1 priority date for domestic students, 10/1 for international students. Applications are processed on a rolling basis. *Application fee:* $30 ($35 for international students). Electronic applications accepted. *Application Contact:* Dr. Stephanie Bellar, Dean of Graduate Studies, 423-425-4666, Fax: 423-425-5223, E-mail: stephanie-bellar@utc.edu. *Dean of Graduate Studies,* Dr. Stephanie Bellar, 423-425-4666, Fax: 423-425-5223, E-mail: stephanie-bellar@utc.edu.

College of Arts and Sciences Students: 118 full-time (65 women), 118 part-time (76 women); includes 31 minority (22 African Americans, 6 Asian Americans or Pacific Islanders, 3 Hispanic Americans), 7 international. Average age 30. 163 applicants, 77% accepted, 68 enrolled. *Faculty:* 48 full-time (13 women), 5 part-time/adjunct (3 women). Expenses: Contact institution. *Financial support:* In 2008–09, 32 fellowships with full and partial tuition reimbursements (averaging $4,300 per year), 1 research assistantship with full and partial tuition reimbursement (averaging $6,720 per year), 4 teaching assistantships with full and partial tuition reimbursements (averaging $4,263 per year) were awarded; career-related internships or fieldwork, Federal Work-Study, institutionally sponsored loans, scholarships/grants, tuition waivers (partial), and unspecified assistantships also available. Support available to part-time students. Financial award application deadline: 4/1; financial award applicants required to submit FAFSA. In 2008, 73 master's awarded. *Degree program information:* Part-time and evening/weekend programs available. Offers arts and sciences (MA, MM, MPA, MS, MSCJ, Postbaccalaureate Certificate); criminal justice (MSCJ); English (MA); environmental sciences (MS); industrial/organizational psychology (MS); music (MM); public administration (MPA, Postbaccalaureate Certificate); research psychology (MS). *Application deadline:* For fall admission, 8/1 priority date for domestic students, 6/1 for international students; for spring admission, 12/1 priority date for domestic students, 10/1 for international students. Applications are processed on a rolling basis. *Application fee:* $30 ($35 for international students). Electronic applications accepted. *Application Contact:* Dr. Stephanie Bellar, Dean of Graduate Studies, 423-425-4666, Fax: 423-425-5223, E-mail: stephanie-bellar@utc.edu. *Dean,* Dr. Herb Burhenn, 423-425-4635, Fax: 423-425-4279, E-mail: herbert-burhenn@utc.edu.

College of Business Students: 97 full-time (44 women), 148 part-time (50 women); includes 26 minority (13 African Americans, 4 American Indian/Alaska Native, 6 Asian Americans or Pacific Islanders, 3 Hispanic Americans), 4 international. Average age 30. 130 applicants, 75% accepted, 54 enrolled. *Faculty:* 28 full-time (9 women), 3 part-time/adjunct (1 woman). Expenses: Contact institution. *Financial support:* In 2008–09, 10 fellowships with full and partial tuition reimbursements (averaging $5,304 per year) were awarded; career-related internships or fieldwork, Federal Work-Study, institutionally sponsored loans, scholarships/grants, tuition waivers (partial), and unspecified assistantships also available. Support available to part-time students. Financial award application deadline: 4/1; financial award applicants required to submit FAFSA. In 2008, 105 master's awarded. *Degree program information:* Part-time and evening/weekend programs available. Offers accountancy (M Acc); business (M Acc, MBA); business administration (MBA). *Application deadline:* For fall admission, 8/1 priority date for domestic students, 6/1 for international students; for spring admission, 12/1 priority date for domestic students, 10/1 for international students. Applications are processed on a rolling basis. *Application fee:* $30 ($35 for international students). Electronic applications accepted. *Application Contact:* Dr. Stephanie Bellar, Dean of Graduate Studies, 423-425-4666, Fax: 423-425-5223, E-mail: stephanie-bellar@utc.edu. *Dean,* Dr. Richard P. Casavant, 423-425-4313, Fax: 423-425-5255, E-mail: richard-casavant@utc.edu.

College of Engineering and Computer Science Students: 51 full-time (17 women), 105 part-time (20 women); includes 26 minority (13 African Americans, 12 Asian Americans or Pacific Islanders, 1 Hispanic American), 27 international. Average age 32. 163 applicants, 40% accepted, 41 enrolled. *Faculty:* 20 full-time (2 women), 1 part-time/adjunct (0 women). Expenses: Contact institution. *Financial support:* In 2008–09, 8 fellowships with full and partial tuition reimbursements (averaging $4,792 per year), 17 research assistantships with full and partial tuition reimbursements (averaging $9,375 per year) were awarded; career-related internships or fieldwork, Federal Work-Study, institutionally sponsored loans, scholarships/grants, tuition waivers (partial), and unspecified assistantships also available. Support available to part-time students. Financial award application deadline: 4/1; financial award applicants required to submit FAFSA. In 2008, 26 master's, 4 doctorates, 6 other advanced degrees awarded. *Degree program information:* Part-time and evening/weekend programs available. Offers chemical engineering (MS); civil engineering (MS); computational engineering (MS, PhD); computer science (MS, Graduate Certificate); electrical engineering (MS); engineering and computer science (MS, PhD, Graduate Certificate); engineering management (MS, Graduate Certificate); industrial engineering (MS); mechanical engineering (MS). *Application deadline:* For fall admission, 8/1 priority date for domestic students, 6/1 for international students; for spring admission, 12/1 priority date for domestic students, 10/1 for international students. Applications are processed on a rolling basis. *Application fee:* $30 ($35 for international students). Electronic applications accepted. *Application Contact:* Dr. Stephanie Bellar, Dean of Graduate Studies, 423-425-4666, Fax: 423-425-5223, E-mail: stephanie-bellar@utc.edu. *Dean,* Dr. William Sutton, 423-425-2256, Fax: 423-425-5229, E-mail: will-sutton@utc.edu.

College of Health, Education and Professional Studies Students: 314 full-time (230 women), 389 part-time (289 women); includes 75 minority (53 African Americans, 4 American Indian/Alaska Native, 7 Asian Americans or Pacific Islanders, 11 Hispanic Americans), 4 international. Average age 33. 398 applicants, 54% accepted, 153 enrolled. *Faculty:* 44 full-time (26 women), 10 part-time/adjunct (5 women). Expenses: Contact institution. *Financial support:* In 2008–09, 40 fellowships with full and partial tuition reimbursements (averaging $4,123 per year) were awarded; career-related internships or fieldwork, Federal Work-Study, institutionally sponsored loans, scholarships/grants, tuition waivers (partial), and unspecified assistantships also available. Support available to part-time students. Financial award application deadline: 4/1; financial award applicants required to submit FAFSA. In 2008, 181 master's, 51 doctorates, 12 other advanced degrees awarded. *Degree program information:* Part-time and evening/weekend programs available. Offers administration (MSN); adult health (MSN); certified nurse anesthetist (Post-Master's Certificate); counseling (M Ed); education (M Ed, MSN, Post-Master's Certificate); educational leadership (Ed D); educational specialist (Ed S); educational technology (Ed S); elementary education (M Ed); family nurse practitioner (MSN, Post-Master's Certificate); health and human performance (MS); health, education and professional studies (M Ed, MS, MSN, DPT, Ed D, Ed S, Post-Master's Certificate); learning and leadership (Ed D); nurse anesthesia (MSN); physical therapy (DPT); school leadership (M Ed, Post-Master's Certificate); school psychology (Ed S); secondary education (M Ed); special education (M Ed). *Application deadline:* For fall admission, 8/1 priority date for domestic students, 6/1 for international students; for spring admission, 12/1 priority date for domestic students, 10/1 for international students. Applications are processed on a rolling basis. *Application fee:* $30 ($35 for international students). Electronic applications accepted. *Application Contact:* Dr. Stephanie Bellar, Dean of Graduate Studies, 423-425-4666, Fax: 423-425-5223, E-mail: stephanie-bellar@utc.edu. *Dean,* Dr. Mary Tanner, 423-425-4249, Fax: 423-425-4044, E-mail: mary-tanner@utc.edu.

THE UNIVERSITY OF TENNESSEE AT MARTIN, Martin, TN 38238-1000

General Information State-supported, coed, comprehensive institution. *Enrollment:* 7,578 graduate, professional, and undergraduate students; 369 matriculated graduate/professional students (243 women). *Enrollment by degree level:* 369 master's. *Graduate faculty:* 146. Tuition, state resident: full-time $6084; part-time $340 per semester hour. Tuition, nonresident: full-time $16,726; part-time $932 per semester hour. *Graduate housing:* Rooms and/or apartments guaranteed to single students and available to married students. Typical cost: $2300 per year ($4600 including board) for single students; $4300 per year for married students. Room and board charges vary according to board plan, campus/location and housing facility selected. Housing application deadline: 3/1. *Student services:* Campus employment opportunities, campus safety program, career counseling, child daycare facilities, exercise/wellness program, free psychological counseling, international student services, low-cost health insurance, multicultural affairs office, services for students with disabilities, teacher training, writing training. *Library facilities:* Paul Meek Library. *Online resources:* library catalog, web page, access to other libraries' catalogs. *Collection:* 533,854 titles, 1,203 serial subscriptions, 13,734 audiovisual materials. *Research affiliation:* Department of Education (academic extensions), National Writing Project (humanities), University of Tennessee Research Foundation (science and technology).

Computer facilities: 725 computers available on campus for general student use. A campuswide network can be accessed from student residence rooms and from off campus. Online class registration, online fee payments, degree progress, financial aid data, housing applications, transcripts are available. *Web address:* http://www.utm.edu/.

General Application Contact: Linda S. Arant, Student Services Specialist, 731-881-7012, Fax: 731-881-7499, E-mail: larant@utm.edu.

GRADUATE UNITS

Graduate Programs Students: 369 (243 women). 167 applicants, 96% accepted, 107 enrolled. *Faculty:* 146. Expenses: Contact institution. *Financial support:* In 2008–09, 32 research assistantships with full tuition reimbursements available (averaging $5,664 per year), 6 teaching assistantships with full tuition reimbursements (averaging $5,030 per year) were awarded; career-related internships or fieldwork, scholarships/grants, tuition waivers (partial), and unspecified assistantships also available. Support available to part-time students. Financial award application deadline: 3/1. In 2008, 125 master's awarded. *Degree program information:* Part-time programs available. Postbaccalaureate distance learning degree programs offered (minimal on-campus study). *Application deadline:* For fall admission, 8/1 priority date for domestic students, 8/1 for international students; for spring admission, 1/1 priority date for domestic students, 1/1 for international students. Applications are processed on a rolling basis. *Application fee:* $30 ($50 for international students). Electronic applications accepted. *Application Contact:* Linda S. Arant, Student Services Specialist, 731-881-7012, Fax: 731-881-7499, E-mail: larant@utm.edu. *Assistant Vice Chancellor and Dean of Graduate Studies,* Dr. Victoria S. Seng, 731-881-7012, Fax: 731-881-7499, E-mail: vseng@utm.edu.

College of Agriculture and Applied Sciences Students: 59 (41 women). 40 applicants, 100% accepted, 23 enrolled. *Faculty:* 28. Expenses: Contact institution. *Financial support:* In 2008–09, 7 students received support, including 7 research assistantships with full tuition reimbursements available (averaging $6,649 per year); scholarships/grants, tuition waivers (partial), and unspecified assistantships also available. Support available to part-time students. Financial award application deadline: 3/1. In 2008, 9 master's awarded. *Degree program information:* Part-time programs available. Postbaccalaureate distance learning degree programs offered (no on-campus study). Offers agricultural and natural resources management (MSANR); agriculture and applied sciences (MSANR, MSFCS); dietetics (MSFCS); general family and consumer sciences (MSFCS). *Application deadline:* For fall admission, 8/1 priority date for domestic students, 8/1 for international students; for spring admission, 1/1 for domestic and international students. Applications are processed on a rolling basis. *Application fee:* $30 ($50 for international students). Electronic applications accepted. *Application Contact:* Linda S. Arant, Student Services Specialist, 731-881-7012, Fax: 731-881-7499, E-mail: larant@utm.edu. *Dean,* Dr. James Byford, 731-881-7250, E-mail: jbyford@utm.edu.

College of Business and Public Affairs Students: 52 (20 women). 16 applicants, 94% accepted, 13 enrolled. *Faculty:* 28. Expenses: Contact institution. *Financial support:* In 2008–09, 11 students received support, including 11 research assistantships with full tuition reimbursements available (averaging $5,674 per year); career-related internships or fieldwork and unspecified assistantships also available. Support available to part-time students. Financial award application deadline: 3/1. In 2008, 26 master's awarded. *Degree program information:* Part-time programs available. Postbaccalaureate distance learning degree programs offered (no on-campus study). Offers business (MBA); business and public affairs (MBA). *Application deadline:* For fall admission, 8/1 priority date for domestic students, 8/1 for international students; for spring admission, 1/1 priority date for domestic students, 8/1 for international students. Applications are processed on a rolling basis. *Application fee:* $30 ($50 for international students). Electronic applications accepted. *Application Contact:* Linda Arant, Student Services Specialist, 731-881-7012, Fax: 731-881-7499, E-mail: larant@utm.edu. *Dean,* Dr. Ernest Moser, 731-881-7227, Fax: 731-881-7241, E-mail: emoser@utm.edu.

College of Education and Behavioral Sciences Students: 258 (182 women). 111 applicants, 95% accepted, 71 enrolled. *Faculty:* 47. Expenses: Contact institution. *Financial support:* In 2008–09, 20 students received support, including 15 research assistantships with full tuition reimbursements available (averaging $5,269 per year), 5 teaching assistantships with full tuition reimbursements available (averaging $5,274 per year); career-related internships or fieldwork, scholarships/grants, and unspecified assistantships also available. Support available to part-time students. Financial award application deadline: 3/1. In 2008, 89 master's awarded. *Degree program information:* Part-time programs available. Postbaccalaureate distance learning degree programs offered (minimal on-campus study). Offers advanced elementary (MS Ed); advanced secondary (MS Ed); community counseling (MS Ed); education and behavioral sciences (MS Ed); educational administration and supervision (MS Ed); initial licensure comprehensive (MS Ed); initial licensure elementary (MS Ed); initial licensure secondary (MS Ed); school counseling (MS Ed). *Application deadline:* For fall admission, 8/1 priority date for domestic students, 8/1 for international students; for spring admission, 1/1 priority date for domestic students, 1/1 for international students. Applications are processed on a rolling basis. *Application fee:* $30 ($50 for international students). Electronic applications accepted. *Application Contact:* Linda Arant, Student Services Specialist, 731-881-7012, Fax: 731-881-7499, E-mail: larant@utm.edu. *Dean,* Dr. Mary Lee Hall, 731-881-7127, Fax: 731-881-7975, E-mail: mlhall@utm.edu.

THE UNIVERSITY OF TENNESSEE HEALTH SCIENCE CENTER, Memphis, TN 38163-0002

General Information State-supported, coed, upper-level institution. CGS member. *Graduate housing:* Room and/or apartments available on a first-come, first-served basis to single students; on-campus housing not available to married students. Housing application deadline: 2/28. *Research affiliation:* Saint Jude's Children's Research Hospital, Veterans Administration Medical Center, LePasses Rehabilitation Center, LeBonheur Children's Medical Center.

GRADUATE UNITS

College of Allied Health Sciences *Degree program information:* Part-time and evening/weekend programs available. Postbaccalaureate distance learning degree programs offered (minimal on-campus study). Offers allied health sciences (MCP, MDH, MHIIM, MOT, MSCLS, MSPT, DPT, ScDPT, TDPT). Electronic applications accepted.

College of Dentistry Offers dentistry (DDS); oral and maxillofacial surgery (Certificate); orthodontics (MS); pediatric dentistry (MS, Certificate); periodontics (MS); prosthodontics (Certificate). Electronic applications accepted.

College of Graduate Health Sciences *Degree program information:* Part-time programs available. Offers anatomy and neurobiology (PhD); health sciences (MS, PhD); integrated program in biomedical sciences (MS, PhD); nursing (PhD); pharmaceutical sciences (MS, PhD). Electronic applications accepted.

College of Medicine Offers biomedical engineering (MS, PhD); medicine (MD, MS, PhD). Electronic applications accepted.

College of Nursing Postbaccalaureate distance learning degree programs offered (minimal on-campus study). Offers nursing (MSN, DNP, PhD). Electronic applications accepted.

College of Pharmacy Offers pharmacy (Pharm D, MS, PhD). Electronic applications accepted.

THE UNIVERSITY OF TENNESSEE–OAK RIDGE NATIONAL LABORATORY GRADUATE SCHOOL OF GENOME SCIENCE AND TECHNOLOGY, Oak Ridge, TN 37830-8026

General Information State-supported, coed, graduate-only institution. *Graduate housing:* Rooms and/or apartments available on a first-come, first-served basis to single and married students. *Research affiliation:* Oak Ridge National Laboratory.

GRADUATE UNITS

Graduate Program Offers life sciences (MS, PhD). Electronic applications accepted.

THE UNIVERSITY OF TENNESSEE SPACE INSTITUTE, Tullahoma, TN 37388-9700

General Information State-supported, coed, primarily men, graduate-only institution. *Enrollment by degree level:* 152 master's, 41 doctoral. *Graduate faculty:* 27 full-time (3 women), 38 part-time/adjunct (2 women). Tuition, state resident: full-time $6262; part-time $348 per hour. Tuition, nonresident: full-time $18,920; part-time $1052 per hour. *Required fees:* $180; $10 per hour. *Graduate housing:* Room and/or apartments available on a first-come, first-served basis to single students; on-campus housing not available to married students. Typical cost: $1620 per year. *Student services:* Campus employment opportunities, career counseling, free psychological counseling, international student services, low-cost health insurance, writing training. *Library facilities:* Art & Helen Mason Library. *Online resources:* web page. *Collection:* 25,000 titles, 125 serial subscriptions, 80 audiovisual materials. *Research affiliation:* International Space University (space engineering), Air Force Institute of Technology (aerospace engineering), RWTH Technical University (Aachen, Germany) (aerospace engineering), U.S. Air Force—Arnold Engineering Development Center (aerospace engineering).

Computer facilities: 100 computers available on campus for general student use. A campuswide network can be accessed from student residence rooms and from off campus. Online class registration is available. *Web address:* http://www.utsi.edu/.

General Application Contact: Dee Merriman, Coordinator III, 931-393-7293, Fax: 931-393-7201, E-mail: dmerrima@utsi.edu.

GRADUATE UNITS

Graduate Programs Students: 64 full-time (13 women), 129 part-time (18 women); includes 20 minority (12 African Americans, 5 Asian Americans or Pacific Islanders, 3 Hispanic Americans), 21 international. 59 applicants, 88% accepted, 28 enrolled. *Faculty:* 27 full-time (3 women), 38 part-time/adjunct (2 women). Expenses: Contact institution. *Financial support:* In 2008–09, 3 fellowships with full and partial tuition reimbursements (averaging $2,000 per year), 44 research assistantships with full tuition reimbursements (averaging $17,791 per year) were awarded; career-related internships or fieldwork, Federal Work-Study, institutionally sponsored loans, health care benefits, tuition waivers (full and partial), and unspecified assistantships also available. In 2008, 28 master's, 3 doctorates awarded. *Degree program information:* Part-time programs available. Postbaccalaureate distance learning degree programs offered. Offers aerospace engineering (MS, PhD); applied mathematics (MS); aviation systems (MS); electrical engineering and computer science (MS, PhD); engineering and applied science (MS, PhD); engineering management (MS, PhD); engineering sciences (MS, PhD); materials science and engineering (MS); mechanical engineering (MS, PhD); mechanics (MS, PhD); physics (MS, PhD). *Application deadline:* For fall admission, 2/1 for international students; for spring admission, 6/15 for international students. Applications are processed on a rolling basis. *Application fee:* $35. Electronic applications accepted. *Application Contact:* Dee Merriman, Coordinator III, 931-393-7293, Fax: 931-393-7201, E-mail: dmerrima@utsi.edu. *Dean and Professor,* Dr. Greg Sedrick, 931-393-7318, Fax: 931-393-7201, E-mail: gsedrick@utsi.edu.

THE UNIVERSITY OF TEXAS AT ARLINGTON, Arlington, TX 76019

General Information State-supported, coed, university. CGS member. *Enrollment:* 25,084 graduate, professional, and undergraduate students; 2,961 full-time matriculated graduate/professional students (1,283 women), 3,132 part-time matriculated graduate/professional students (1,736 women). *Enrollment by degree level:* 5,195 master's, 898 doctoral. *Graduate faculty:* 527 full-time (156 women), 128 part-time/adjunct (57 women). Tuition, state resident: full-time $6500. Tuition, nonresident: full-time $11,558. *Graduate housing:* Rooms and/or apartments available on a first-come, first-served basis to single and married students. Typical cost: $3398 per year ($6412 including board) for single students; $3398 per year ($6412 including board) for married students. Room and board charges vary according to board plan. *Student services:* Campus employment opportunities, campus safety program, career counseling, child daycare facilities, exercise/wellness program, free psychological counseling, international student services, multicultural affairs office, services for students with disabilities, teacher training, writing training. *Library facilities:* Central Library plus 2 others. *Online resources:* library catalog, web page, access to other libraries' catalogs. *Collection:* 1.2 million titles, 58,417 serial subscriptions, 11,601 audiovisual materials. *Research affiliation:* Administration for Children & Family (Social Work), Texas Department of Protective and Regulatory Services (social work), National Institute of Standards and Technology (ARRI), Columbia University (physics), Department of Energy (bioengineering), National Science Foundation (materials science and engineering).

Computer facilities: 1,000 computers available on campus for general student use. A campuswide network can be accessed from student residence rooms and from off campus. Online class registration is available. *Web address:* http://www.uta.edu/.

General Application Contact: Dr. Phil Cohen, Dean of Graduate Studies, 817-272-3186, Fax: 817-272-2625, E-mail: graduate.school@uta.edu.

GRADUATE UNITS

Graduate School Students: 2,961 full-time (1,283 women), 3,132 part-time (1,735 women); includes 1,348 minority (583 African Americans, 22 American Indian/Alaska Native, 306 Asian Americans or Pacific Islanders, 437 Hispanic Americans), 1,910 international. Average age 36. 5,630 applicants, 77% accepted, 2378 enrolled. *Faculty:* 527 full-time (156 women), 128 part-time/adjunct (57 women). Expenses: Contact institution. *Financial support:* Fellowships, research assistantships, teaching assistantships, career-related internships or fieldwork, Federal Work-Study, institutionally sponsored loans, scholarships/grants, traineeships, and tuition waivers (partial) available. Financial award application deadline: 6/1; financial award applicants required to submit FAFSA. In 2008, 1,694 master's, 153 doctorates awarded. *Degree program information:* Part-time and evening/weekend programs available. Postbaccalaureate distance learning degree programs offered (no on-campus study). *Application deadline:* For fall admission, 6/16 for domestic students. Applications are processed on a rolling basis. *Application fee:* $35 ($50 for international students). *Application Contact:* Dr. Phil Cohen, Dean of Graduate Studies, 817-272-3186, Fax: 817-272-2625, E-mail: graduate.school@uta.edu. *Dean of Graduate Studies,* Dr. Phil Cohen, 817-272-3186, Fax: 817-272-2625, E-mail: graduate.school@uta.edu.

College of Business Students: 817 full-time (328 women), 757 part-time (316 women); includes 351 minority (122 African Americans, 3 American Indian/Alaska Native, 125 Asian Americans or Pacific Islanders, 101 Hispanic Americans), 489 international. Average age 32. 1,164 applicants, 91% accepted, 720 enrolled. *Faculty:* 67 full-time (15 women), 13 part-time/adjunct (3 women). Expenses: Contact institution. *Financial support:* In 2008–09, 100 students received support, including 5 fellowships (averaging $1,000 per year), 30 research assistantships (averaging $6,000 per year), 45 teaching assistantships (averaging $13,000 per year); career-related internships or fieldwork, Federal Work-Study, institutionally sponsored loans, and scholarships/grants also available. Financial award application deadline: 6/1; financial award applicants required to submit FAFSA. In 2008, 552 master's, 12 doctorates awarded. *Degree program information:* Part-time and evening/weekend programs available. Postbaccalaureate distance learning degree programs offered (no on-campus study). Offers accounting (MP Acc, MS, PhD); business (MA, MBA, MP Acc, MS, MSHRM, PhD); business statistics (PhD); economics (MA); finance (MBA, PhD); health care administration (MS); human resources (MSHRM); information systems (MBA, MS, PhD); management (MBA, PhD); management sciences (MBA); marketing (MBA, PhD); marketing research (MS); operations management (PhD); quantitative finance (MS); real estate (MBA, MS); taxation (MS). *Application deadline:* For fall admission, 6/5 for domestic students, 4/1 for international students; for spring admission, 10/15 for domestic students, 9/1 for international students. Applications are processed on a rolling basis. *Application fee:* $35 ($50 for international students). *Application Contact:* Rebecca Neilson, Director of Graduate Business Services, 817-272-3649, Fax: 817-272-5799, E-mail: rneilson@uta.edu. *Dean,* Dr. Daniel Himarios, 817-272-2881, Fax: 817-272-2073, E-mail: himarios@uta.edu.

College of Education Students: 114 full-time (70 women), 413 part-time (331 women); includes 200 minority (112 African Americans, 3 American Indian/Alaska Native, 12 Asian Americans or Pacific Islanders, 73 Hispanic Americans), 9 international. Average age 35. 415 applicants, 86% accepted, 215 enrolled. *Faculty:* 29 full-time (15 women), 8 part-time/adjunct (3 women). Expenses: Contact institution. *Financial support:* In 2008–09, 9 fellowships (averaging $1,000 per year), 6 research assistantships (averaging $6,250 per year), 10 teaching assistantships with full tuition reimbursements (averaging $5,200 per year) were awarded; career-related internships or fieldwork, Federal Work-Study, scholarships/grants, and unspecified assistantships also available. Financial award application deadline: 6/1; financial award applicants required to submit FAFSA. In 2008, 159 master's awarded. *Degree program information:* Part-time and evening/weekend programs available. Offers curriculum and instruction (M Ed); educational leadership and policy studies (M Ed); K-16 educational, leadership and policy studies (PhD); physiology of exercise (MS); teaching (M Ed T). *Application deadline:* For fall admission, 6/5 priority date for domestic students, 4/3 priority date for international students; for spring admission, 10/17 priority date for domestic students, 9/5 priority date for international students. Applications are processed on a rolling basis. *Application fee:* $35 ($50 for international students). Electronic applications accepted. *Application Contact:* Kas McConnell, Graduate Advisor, 817-272-7489, Fax: 817-272-7624, E-mail: coedadvising@uta.edu. *Dean,* Dr. Jeanne M. Gerlach, 817-272-2591, Fax: 817-272-2530, E-mail: coeadvising@uta.edu.

College of Engineering Students: 983 full-time (226 women), 595 part-time (121 women); includes 135 minority (22 African Americans, 72 Asian Americans or Pacific Islanders, 41 Hispanic Americans), 1,182 international. Average age 27. 2,421 applicants, 67% accepted, 513 enrolled. *Faculty:* 124 full-time (12 women), 23 part-time/adjunct (1 woman). Expenses: Contact institution. *Financial support:* Fellowships, research assistantships, teaching assistantships, career-related internships or fieldwork, Federal Work-Study, institutionally sponsored loans, scholarships/grants, and tuition waivers (partial) available. Financial award application deadline: 6/1; financial award applicants required to submit FAFSA. In 2008, 382 master's, 65 doctorates awarded. *Degree program information:* Part-time and evening/weekend programs available. Postbaccalaureate distance learning degree programs offered (minimal on-campus study). Offers aerospace engineering (M Engr, MS, PhD); bioengineering (MS, PhD); civil engineering (M Engr, MS, PhD); computer science and engineering (M Engr, M Sw En, MS, PhD); electrical engineering (M Engr, MS, PhD); engineering (M Engr, M Sw En, MS, PhD); engineering management (MS); industrial engineering (MS, PhD); logistics (MS); materials science and engineering (M Engr, MS, PhD); mechanical engineering (M Engr, MS, PhD); systems engineering (MS). *Application deadline:* For fall admission, 6/6 for domestic students, 4/4 for international students; for spring admission, 10/17 for domestic students, 9/5 for international students. Applications are processed on a rolling basis. *Application fee:* $35 ($50 for international students). *Application Contact:* Dr. Lynn L. Peterson, Associate Dean for Academic Affairs, 817-272-2571, Fax: 817-272-2548, E-mail: peterson@uta.edu. *Dean,* Dr. Bill D. Carroll, 817-272-2571, Fax: 817-272-5110, E-mail: carroll@uta.edu.

College of Liberal Arts Students: 106 full-time (41 women), 8 part-time (4 women); includes 108 minority (42 African Americans, 4 American Indian/Alaska Native, 15 Asian Americans or Pacific Islanders, 47 Hispanic Americans), 41 international. Average age 34. 356 applicants, 78% accepted, 180 enrolled. *Faculty:* 237 full-time (92 women), 18 part-time/adjunct (10 women). Expenses: Contact institution. *Financial support:* Fellowships, research assistantships, teaching assistantships, career-related internships or fieldwork, Federal Work-Study, institutionally sponsored loans, and scholarships/grants available. Financial award application deadline: 3/1; financial award applicants required to submit FAFSA. In 2008, 99 master's, 20 doctorates awarded. Offers anthropology (MA); art and art history (MFA); communication (MA); criminology and criminal justice (MA); education (MM); English (MA); French (MA); history (MA); humanities (MA); liberal arts (MA, MFA, MM, PhD); linguistics (MA, PhD); literature (PhD); performance (MM); political science (MA); sociology (MA); Spanish (MA); teaching English to speakers of other languages (MA); transatlantic history (PhD). *Application deadline:* For fall admission, 6/16 for domestic students. Applications are processed on a rolling basis. *Application fee:* $35 ($50 for international students). *Application Contact:* Dr. Kimberly Van Noort, Associate Dean, 817-272-3291, E-mail: vannoort@uta.edu. *Dean,* Dr. Beth S. Wright, 817-272-3291, Fax: 817-272-3255, E-mail: bwright@uta.edu.

College of Science Students: 295 full-time (141 women), 134 part-time (71 women); includes 75 minority (22 African Americans, 4 American Indian/Alaska Native, 17 Asian Americans or Pacific Islanders, 32 Hispanic Americans), 129 international. Average age 31. 350 applicants, 64% accepted, 157 enrolled. *Faculty:* 111 full-time (22 women), 9 part-time/adjunct (2 women). Expenses: Contact institution. *Financial support:* In 2008–09, 22 fellowships

The University of Texas at Arlington (continued)

(averaging $1,000 per year), 61 research assistantships (averaging $14,000 per year), 102 teaching assistantships (averaging $15,500 per year) were awarded; career-related internships or fieldwork, Federal Work-Study, institutionally sponsored loans, scholarships/grants, tuition waivers (partial), and unspecified assistantships also available. Financial award application deadline: 6/1; financial award applicants required to submit FAFSA. In 2008, 75 master's, 27 doctorates awarded. *Degree program information:* Part-time and evening/weekend programs available. Offers biology (MS); chemistry (MS, PhD); environmental and earth sciences (MS, PhD); environmental science (MS, PhD); experimental psychology (PhD); geology (MS, PhD); health psychology (PhD); industrial organizational psychology (MS); mathematics (MA, MS, PhD); physics (MS); physics and applied physics (PhD); psychology (MS); quantitative biology (PhD); science (MA, MS, PhD). *Application deadline:* For fall admission, 6/16 for domestic students. Applications are processed on a rolling basis. *Application fee:* $35 ($50 for international students). *Application Contact:* Dr. Robert F. McMahon, Director, 817-272-3492, Fax: 817-272-3511, E-mail: r.mcmahon@uta.edu. *Interim Dean,* Dr. Paul B. Paulus, 817-272-3491, Fax: 817-272-3511, E-mail: paulus@uta.edu.

School of Architecture Students: 133 full-time (53 women), 40 part-time (17 women); includes 40 minority (6 African Americans, 11 Asian Americans or Pacific Islanders, 23 Hispanic Americans), 18 international. Average age 30. 165 applicants, 68% accepted, 71 enrolled. *Faculty:* 24 full-time (2 women), 13 part-time/adjunct (5 women). Expenses: Contact institution. *Financial support:* In 2008–09, 5 fellowships with partial tuition reimbursements (averaging $1,000 per year), 2 research assistantships with partial tuition reimbursements (averaging $5,700 per year), 8 teaching assistantships with partial tuition reimbursements (averaging $5,700 per year) were awarded; career-related internships or fieldwork, Federal Work-Study, scholarships/grants, health care benefits, tuition waivers (partial), and unspecified assistantships also available. Support available to part-time students. Financial award application deadline: 6/1; financial award applicants required to submit FAFSA. In 2008, 57 master's awarded. *Degree program information:* Part-time and evening/weekend programs available. Offers architecture (M Arch, MLA); landscape architecture (MLA). *Application deadline:* For fall admission, 6/16 for domestic students, 4/1 for international students; for spring admission, 10/15 for domestic students, 9/5 for international students. Applications are processed on a rolling basis. *Application fee:* $35 ($50 for international students). Electronic applications accepted. *Application Contact:* David Jones, Associate Dean, 817-272-2801, Fax: 817-272-5098, E-mail: djonesarch@uta.edu. *Dean,* Donald Gatzke, 817-272-2801, Fax: 817-272-5098, E-mail: gatzke@uta.edu.

School of Nursing Students: 67 full-time (59 women), 368 part-time (333 women); includes 112 minority (60 African Americans, 4 American Indian/Alaska Native, 28 Asian Americans or Pacific Islanders, 20 Hispanic Americans), 3 international. Average age 37. 273 applicants, 90% accepted, 171 enrolled. *Faculty:* 26 full-time (all women), 20 part-time/adjunct (17 women). Expenses: Contact institution. *Financial support:* In 2008–09, 27 students received support, including 24 fellowships with partial tuition reimbursements available (averaging $3,000 per year), 6 research assistantships (averaging $7,992 per year), 7 teaching assistantships (averaging $10,080 per year); career-related internships or fieldwork and traineeships also available. Financial award application deadline: 6/1; financial award applicants required to submit FAFSA. In 2008, 80 master's, 3 doctorates awarded. *Degree program information:* Part-time and evening/weekend programs available. Offers administration/supervision of nursing (MSN); nurse practitioner (MSN); nursing science (PhD); teaching of nursing (MSN). *Application deadline:* For fall admission, 6/5 for domestic students, 4/3 for international students; for spring admission, 10/7 for domestic students, 9/5 for international students. Applications are processed on a rolling basis. *Application fee:* $40 ($70 for international students). *Application Contact:* Dr. Mary Schira, Graduate Advisor and Associate Dean, 817-272-2329, Fax: 817-272-2065, E-mail: schira@uta.edu. *Dean,* Dr. Elizabeth C. Poster, 817-272-2776, Fax: 817-272-5006, E-mail: poster@uta.edu.

School of Social Work Students: 321 full-time (283 women), 226 part-time (200 women); includes 225 minority (134 African Americans, 4 American Indian/Alaska Native, 16 Asian Americans or Pacific Islanders, 71 Hispanic Americans), 21 international. Average age 32. 297 applicants, 91% accepted, 208 enrolled. *Faculty:* 26 full-time (17 women), 27 part-time/adjunct (9 women). Expenses: Contact institution. *Financial support:* In 2008–09, 355 students received support, including 40 fellowships (averaging $2,000 per year), 10 research assistantships (averaging $6,000 per year), 10 teaching assistantships (averaging $6,000 per year); career-related internships or fieldwork, Federal Work-Study, institutionally sponsored loans, scholarships/grants, and unspecified assistantships also available. Support available to part-time students. Financial award application deadline: 6/1; financial award applicants required to submit FAFSA. In 2008, 243 master's, 18 doctorates awarded. *Degree program information:* Part-time and evening/weekend programs available. Postbaccalaureate distance learning degree programs offered (no on-campus study). Offers social work (MSSW, PhD). *Application deadline:* For fall admission, 6/5 for domestic students; for winter admission, 10/17 for domestic students. Applications are processed on a rolling basis. *Application fee:* $35 ($50 for international students). Electronic applications accepted. *Application Contact:* Darlene Santee, Director of Admissions, 817-272-3613, Fax: 817-272-5229. *Interim Dean,* Dr. Phillip Popple, 817-272-3181, Fax: 817-272-5229, E-mail: popplepr@uta.edu.

School of Urban and Public Affairs Students: 81 full-time (37 women), 207 part-time (111 women); includes 102 minority (63 African Americans, 10 Asian Americans or Pacific Islanders, 29 Hispanic Americans), 18 international. Average age 34. 189 applicants, 91% accepted, 112 enrolled. *Faculty:* 15 full-time (7 women), 7 part-time/adjunct (4 women). Expenses: Contact institution. *Financial support:* In 2008–09, 8 students received support, including 10 fellowships (averaging $1,500 per year), 5 research assistantships (averaging $4,000 per year); teaching assistantships, career-related internships or fieldwork and Federal Work-Study also available. Financial award application deadline: 6/1; financial award applicants required to submit FAFSA. In 2008, 47 master's, 8 doctorates awarded. *Degree program information:* Part-time and evening/weekend programs available. Postbaccalaureate distance learning degree programs offered. Offers city and regional planning (MCRP); interdisciplinary science (MA); public administration (MPA); urban and public affairs (MA, MCRP, MPA, PhD). *Application deadline:* For fall admission, 6/5 for domestic students, 4/3 for international students; for spring admission, 10/16 for domestic students, 9/11 for international students. Applications are processed on a rolling basis. *Application fee:* $35 ($50 for international students). Electronic applications accepted. *Application Contact:* Linda Slaughter, Administrative Clerk, 817-272-3071, Fax: 817-272-5008, E-mail: slaughter@uta.edu. *Dean,* Dr. Barbara Becker, 817-272-3071, Fax: 817-272-3255, E-mail: bbecker@uta.edu.

THE UNIVERSITY OF TEXAS AT AUSTIN, Austin, TX 78712-1111

General Information State-supported, coed, university. CGS member. *Graduate housing:* Rooms and/or apartments available to single students and available on a first-come, first-served basis to married students.

GRADUATE UNITS

Graduate School *Degree program information:* Part-time and evening/weekend programs available. Offers computational and applied mathematics (MA, PhD); technology commercialization (MS); writing (MFA). Electronic applications accepted.

Cockrell School of Engineering *Degree program information:* Part-time and evening/weekend programs available. Offers aerospace engineering (MSE, PhD); architectural engineering (MSE); biomedical engineering (MS, PhD); chemical engineering (MSE, PhD); civil engineering (MS, PhD); electrical and computer engineering (MSE, PhD); energy and earth resources (MA); engineering (MA, MS, MSE, PhD); engineering mechanics (MS, PhD); environmental and water resources engineering (MS, PhD); materials science and engineering (MS, PhD); mechanical engineering (MS, PhD); operations research and industrial engineering (MS, PhD); petroleum engineering (MS, PhD). Electronic applications accepted.

College of Communication *Degree program information:* Part-time programs available. Offers advertising (MA, PhD); audiology (Au D, PhD); communication (MA, MFA, Au D, PhD); communication studies (MA, PhD); film and video production (MFA); journalism (MA, PhD); radio-television-film (MA, PhD); screenwriting (MFA); speech language pathology (MA, PhD). Electronic applications accepted.

College of Education *Degree program information:* Part-time programs available. Offers academic educational psychology (M Ed, MA); behavioral health (PhD); counseling psychology (PhD); counselor education (M Ed); curriculum and instruction (M Ed, MA, Ed D, PhD); education (M Ed, MA, Ed D, PhD); educational administration (M Ed, Ed D, PhD); exercise and sport psychology (M Ed, MA); foreign language education (MA, PhD); health education (M Ed, MA, Ed D, PhD); human development and culture (PhD); kinesiology (M Ed, MA); learning, cognition and instruction (PhD); quantitative methods (PhD); school psychology (PhD); science and mathematics education (M Ed, MA, PhD); special education (M Ed, MA, Ed D, PhD). Electronic applications accepted.

College of Fine Arts *Degree program information:* Part-time programs available. Offers acting (MFA); art education (MA); art history (MA, PhD); dance (MFA); design (MFA); directing (MFA); drama and theatre for youth (MFA); fine arts (M Music, MA, MFA, DMA, PhD); music (M Music, DMA, PhD); performance as public practice (MA, MFA, PhD); playwriting (MFA); studio art (MFA); theatre technology (MFA); theatrical design (MFA). Electronic applications accepted.

College of Liberal Arts *Degree program information:* Part-time programs available. Offers African Diaspora studies (MA, PhD); American studies (MA, PhD); Arabic (MA, PhD); archaeology (MA, PhD); Asian cultures and languages (MA, PhD); Asian studies (MA); classics (MA, PhD); comparative literature (MA, PhD); creative writing (MA); economics (MA, MS Econ, PhD); English (MA, PhD); folklore and public culture (MA, PhD); French (MA, PhD); French linguistics (MA, PhD); geography and the environment (MA, PhD); Germanic studies (MA, PhD); government (PhD); Hebrew (MA); Hispanic linguistics (MA, PhD); Hispanic literature (MA, PhD); history (MA, PhD); Italian studies (MA, PhD); Latin American studies (MA, PhD); liberal arts (MA, MS Econ, PhD); linguistic anthropology (MA, PhD); linguistics (MA, PhD); Luso-Brazilian literature (MA, PhD); Mexican American studies (MA); Middle Eastern studies (MA, PhD); philosophy (PhD); physical anthropology (MA, PhD); psychology (PhD); Romance linguistics (MA, PhD); Russian, East European, and Eurasian studies (MA); Slavic languages (MA, PhD); social anthropology (MA, PhD); sociology (MA, PhD). Electronic applications accepted.

College of Natural Sciences *Degree program information:* Part-time programs available. Offers analytical chemistry (MA, PhD); astronomy (MA, PhD); biochemistry (MA, PhD); biological sciences (MA, PhD); computer sciences (MA, MSCS, PhD); ecology, evolution and behavior (MA, PhD); human development and family sciences (MA, PhD); inorganic chemistry (MA, PhD); marine science (MS, PhD); mathematics (MA, PhD); microbiology (PhD); natural sciences (MA, MS, MS Stat, MSCS, PhD); nutrition (MA); nutritional sciences (MA, PhD); organic chemistry (MA, PhD); physical chemistry (MA, PhD); physics (MA, MS, PhD); plant biology (MA, PhD); statistics (MS Stat); textile and apparel technology (MS). Electronic applications accepted.

College of Pharmacy Offers pharmacy (Pharm D, MS, PhD). Electronic applications accepted.

Institute for Cellular and Molecular Biology Offers cellular and molecular biology (PhD).

The Institute for Neuroscience Offers neuroscience (PhD). Electronic applications accepted.

Jackson School of Geosciences *Degree program information:* Part-time programs available. Offers geosciences (MA, MS, PhD). Electronic applications accepted.

Lyndon B. Johnson School of Public Affairs *Degree program information:* Part-time programs available. Offers global policy studies (MGPS); public affairs (MP Aff); public policy (PhD). Electronic applications accepted.

McCombs School of Business Offers accounting (MPA, PhD); business (MBA, MPA, PhD); business administration (MBA); finance (PhD); information systems (PhD); management (PhD); marketing (PhD); risk analysis and decision making (PhD); supply chain and operations management (PhD). Electronic applications accepted.

School of Architecture Offers architecture (M Arch); community and regional planning (MSCRP, PhD); historic preservation (MS); history of architecture (MA, PhD); landscape architecture (MLA); urban design (MSUD). Electronic applications accepted.

School of Information *Degree program information:* Part-time programs available. Offers information (MS, PhD). Electronic applications accepted.

School of Nursing *Degree program information:* Part-time programs available. Offers nursing (MSN, PhD). Electronic applications accepted.

School of Social Work *Degree program information:* Part-time programs available. Offers social work (MSSW, PhD).

School of Law Students: 1,233 full-time (532 women); includes 367 minority (76 African Americans, 5 American Indian/Alaska Native, 89 Asian Americans or Pacific Islanders, 197 Hispanic Americans). Average age 24. 4,850 applicants, 25% accepted, 388 enrolled. *Faculty:* 126 full-time (45 women), 113 part-time/adjunct (29 women). Expenses: Contact institution. *Financial support:* In 2008–09, 1,107 students received support, including 100 research assistantships, 32 teaching assistantships (averaging $3,900 per year); career-related internships or fieldwork, scholarships/grants, and tuition waivers (full) also available. Financial award application deadline: 3/31; financial award applicants required to submit FAFSA. In 2008, 441 JDs, 37 master's awarded. Offers law (JD, LL M). *Application deadline:* For fall admission, 2/1 for domestic students. *Application fee:* $70. Electronic applications accepted. *Application Contact:* 512-232-1200, Fax: 512-471-2765, E-mail: admissions@law.utexas.edu. *Dean,* Lawrence Sager, 512-232-1120, Fax: 512-471-6987, E-mail: lsager@law.utexas.edu.

THE UNIVERSITY OF TEXAS AT BROWNSVILLE, Brownsville, TX 78520-4991

General Information State-supported, coed, comprehensive institution. CGS member. *Graduate housing:* Room and/or apartments available to single students; on-campus housing not available to married students.

GRADUATE UNITS

Graduate Studies *Degree program information:* Part-time and evening/weekend programs available. Postbaccalaureate distance learning degree programs offered (no on-campus study).

College of Liberal Arts *Degree program information:* Part-time and evening/weekend programs available. Offers behavioral sciences (MAIS); English (MA); government (MAIS); history (MAIS); interdisciplinary studies (MAIS); liberal arts (MA, MAIS, MPPM); public policy and management (MPPM); Spanish (MA).

College of Science, Mathematics and Technology *Degree program information:* Part-time and evening/weekend programs available. Offers biological sciences (MS, MSIS); mathematics (MS); physics (MS).

School of Business *Degree program information:* Part-time and evening/weekend programs available. Postbaccalaureate distance learning degree programs offered (minimal on-campus study). Offers business (MBA).

School of Education *Degree program information:* Part-time and evening/weekend programs available. Postbaccalaureate distance learning degree programs offered (minimal on-campus study). Offers bilingual education (M Ed); counseling and guidance (M Ed); curriculum and instruction (M Ed); early childhood education (M Ed); educational administration (M Ed); educational technology (M Ed); English as a second language (M Ed); reading specialist (M Ed); special education/educational diagnostician (M Ed).

School of Health Sciences Offers health sciences (MSN).

THE UNIVERSITY OF TEXAS AT DALLAS, Richardson, TX 75083-0688

General Information State-supported, coed, university. CGS member. *Enrollment:* 14,944 graduate, professional, and undergraduate students; 2,581 full-time matriculated graduate/professional students (1,136 women), 2,434 part-time matriculated graduate/professional students (998 women). *Enrollment by degree level:* 30 first professional, 3,978 master's, 1,007 doctoral. *Graduate faculty:* 393 full-time (81 women), 60 part-time/adjunct (20 women). Tuition, state resident: full-time $8320. Tuition, nonresident: full-time $15,054. Part-time tuition and fees vary according to course load. *Graduate housing:* Rooms and/or apartments available on a first-come, first-served basis to single and married students. Typical cost: $6828 (including board) for single students; $6828 (including board) for married students. Room and board charges vary according to board plan and housing facility selected. Housing application deadline: 5/31. *Student services:* Campus employment opportunities, campus safety program, career counseling, child daycare facilities, exercise/wellness program, free psychological counseling, grant writing training, international student services, low-cost health insurance, multicultural affairs office, services for students with disabilities, teacher training, writing training. *Library facilities:* Eugene McDermott Library plus 1 other. *Online resources:* library catalog, web page, access to other libraries' catalogs. *Collection:* 1.9 million titles, 5,054 audiovisual materials.

Computer facilities: Computer purchase and lease plans are available. 630 computers available on campus for general student use. A campuswide network can be accessed from student residence rooms and from off campus. Online class registration is available. *Web address:* http://www.utdallas.edu/.

General Application Contact: Dr. Austin Cunningham, Dean for Graduate Studies, 972-883-2234, E-mail: cunning@utdallas.edu.

GRADUATE UNITS

Erik Jonsson School of Engineering and Computer Science Students: 832 full-time (187 women), 368 part-time (92 women); includes 120 minority (15 African Americans, 82 Asian Americans or Pacific Islanders, 23 Hispanic Americans), 885 international. Average age 28. 2,385 applicants, 56% accepted, 395 enrolled. *Faculty:* 90 full-time (8 women), 6 part-time/adjunct (1 woman). Expenses: Contact institution. *Financial support:* In 2008–09, 227 research assistantships with full tuition reimbursements (averaging $20,124 per year), 83 teaching assistantships with full tuition reimbursements (averaging $17,796 per year) were awarded; fellowships with full tuition reimbursements, career-related internships or fieldwork, Federal Work-Study, institutionally sponsored loans, scholarships/grants, and unspecified assistantships also available. Support available to part-time students. Financial award application deadline: 4/30; financial award applicants required to submit FAFSA. In 2008, 228 master's, 38 doctorates awarded. *Degree program information:* Part-time and evening/weekend programs available. Offers computer engineering (MS, PhD); computer science (MS, PhD); electrical engineering (MSEE, PhD); engineering and computer science (MS, MSEE, MSME, MSTE, PhD); materials science and engineering (MS, PhD); materials science engineering (PhD); mechanical engineering (MSME); microelectronics (MSEE, PhD); software engineering (MS, PhD); telecommunications (MSEE, MSTE, PhD). *Application deadline:* For fall admission, 7/15 for domestic students, 5/1 priority date for international students; for spring admission, 11/15 for domestic students, 9/1 priority date for international students. Applications are processed on a rolling basis. *Application fee:* $50 ($100 for international students). Electronic applications accepted. *Application Contact:* Dr. Cy Cantrell, Associate Dean, 972-883-6234, Fax: 972-883-2813, E-mail: gradecs@utdallas.edu. *Dean,* Dr. Mark Spong, 972-883-2974, Fax: 972-883-2813, E-mail: ecsdean@utdallas.edu.

School of Arts and Humanities Students: 201 full-time (107 women), 194 part-time (105 women); includes 82 minority (30 African Americans, 3 American Indian/Alaska Native, 23 Asian Americans or Pacific Islanders, 26 Hispanic Americans), 31 international. Average age 38. 173 applicants, 80% accepted, 83 enrolled. *Faculty:* 52 full-time (15 women), 6 part-time/adjunct (2 women). Expenses: Contact institution. *Financial support:* In 2008–09, 10 research assistantships with tuition reimbursements (averaging $10,339 per year), 74 teaching assistantships with tuition reimbursements (averaging $10,152 per year) were awarded; fellowships, Federal Work-Study, institutionally sponsored loans, scholarships/grants, and unspecified assistantships also available. Support available to part-time students. Financial award application deadline: 4/30; financial award applicants required to submit FAFSA. In 2008, 88 master's, 11 doctorates awarded. *Degree program information:* Part-time and evening/weekend programs available. Offers arts and technology (MFA); emerging media and communications (MA); humanities (MA, MAT, PhD). *Application deadline:* For fall admission, 7/15 for domestic students, 5/1 priority date for international students; for spring admission, 11/15 for domestic students, 9/1 priority date for international students. Applications are processed on a rolling basis. *Application fee:* $50 ($100 for international students). Electronic applications accepted. *Application Contact:* Dr. Michael Wilson, Associate Dean of Graduate Studies, 972-883-2756, Fax: 972-883-2989, E-mail: mwilson@utdallas.edu. *Dean,* Dr. Dennis M. Kratz, 972-883-2984, Fax: 972-883-2989, E-mail: dkratz@utdallas.edu.

School of Behavioral and Brain Sciences Students: 346 full-time (287 women), 62 part-time (45 women); includes 69 minority (12 African Americans, 1 American Indian/Alaska Native, 29 Asian Americans or Pacific Islanders, 27 Hispanic Americans), 36 international. Average age 28. 457 applicants, 50% accepted, 146 enrolled. *Faculty:* 41 full-time (18 women), 12 part-time/adjunct (10 women). Expenses: Contact institution. *Financial support:* In 2008–09, 14 research assistantships with tuition reimbursements (averaging $15,006 per year), 51 teaching assistantships with tuition reimbursements (averaging $10,700 per year) were awarded; fellowships, career-related internships or fieldwork, Federal Work-Study, institutionally sponsored loans, scholarships/grants, and unspecified assistantships also available. Support available to part-time students. Financial award application deadline: 4/30; financial award applicants required to submit FAFSA. In 2008, 145 master's, 14 doctorates awarded. *Degree program information:* Part-time and evening/weekend programs available. Offers applied cognition and neuroscience (MS); audiology (Au D); behavioral and brain sciences (MS, Au D, PhD); cognition and neuroscience (PhD); communication disorders (MS); communication sciences (PhD); early childhood disorders (MS); psychological sciences (MS, PhD). *Application deadline:* For fall admission, 7/15 for domestic students, 5/1 priority date for international students; for spring admission, 11/15 for domestic students, 9/1 priority date for international students. Applications are processed on a rolling basis. *Application fee:* $50 ($100 for international students). Electronic applications accepted. *Application Contact:* Dr. Robert D. Stillman, Program Head, 972-883-3106, Fax: 972-883-3022, E-mail: stillman@utdallas.edu. *Dean,* Dr. Bert Moore, 972-883-2355, Fax: 972-883-2491, E-mail: bmoore@utdallas.edu.

School of Economic, Political and Policy Sciences Students: 200 full-time (86 women), 266 part-time (126 women); includes 128 minority (59 African Americans, 2 American Indian/Alaska Native, 26 Asian Americans or Pacific Islanders, 41 Hispanic Americans), 88 international. Average age 36. 265 applicants, 73% accepted, 104 enrolled. *Faculty:* 57 full-time (16 women), 6 part-time/adjunct (1 woman). Expenses: Contact institution. *Financial support:* In 2008–09, 16 research assistantships with tuition reimbursements (averaging $14,687 per year), 68 teaching assistantships with tuition reimbursements (averaging $12,078 per year) were awarded; fellowships, career-related internships or fieldwork, Federal Work-Study, institutionally sponsored loans, scholarships/grants, and unspecified assistantships also available. Support available to part-time students. Financial award application deadline: 4/30; financial award applicants required to submit FAFSA. In 2008, 64 master's, 18 doctorates awarded. *Degree program information:* Part-time and evening/weekend programs available. Offers applied sociology (MS); criminology (MS, PhD); economic, political and policy sciences (MA, MPA, MPP, MS, PhD); economics (MS, PhD); geospatial sciences (MS, PhD); international political economy (MS); legislative studies (MA); political science (PhD); public affairs (MPA, PhD); public policy (MPP); public policy and political economy (PhD). *Application deadline:* For fall admission, 7/15 for domestic students, 5/1 priority date for international students; for spring admission, 11/15 for domestic students, 9/1 priority date for international students. Applications are processed on a rolling basis. *Application fee:* $50 ($100 for international students). Electronic applications accepted. *Application Contact:* Dr. Euel Elliot, Director of Graduate Studies, 972-883-2066, Fax: 972-883-6297, E-mail: eelliott@utdallas.edu. *Dean,* Dr. Brian Berry, 972-883-2395, Fax: 972-883-6297, E-mail: brian.berry@utdallas.edu.

School of Interdisciplinary Studies Students: 13 full-time (10 women), 27 part-time (17 women); includes 15 minority (8 African Americans, 4 Asian Americans or Pacific Islanders, 3 Hispanic Americans). Average age 39. 24 applicants, 83% accepted, 15 enrolled. *Faculty:* 3 full-time (2 women). Expenses: Contact institution. *Financial support:* Fellowships, research assistantships, teaching assistantships with tuition reimbursements, career-related internships or fieldwork, Federal Work-Study, institutionally sponsored loans, and scholarships/grants available. Support available to part-time students. Financial award application deadline: 4/30; financial award applicants required to submit FAFSA. In 2008, 22 master's awarded. *Degree program information:* Part-time and evening/weekend programs available. Offers interdisciplinary studies (MA). *Application deadline:* For fall admission, 7/15 for domestic students, 5/1 priority date for international students; for spring admission, 11/15 for domestic students, 9/1 priority date for international students. Applications are processed on a rolling basis. *Application fee:* $50 ($100 for international students). Electronic applications accepted. *Application Contact:* Dr. Elizabeth Salter, Associate Dean, 972-883-2323, Fax: 972-883-2440, E-mail: emsalter@utdallas.edu. *Dean,* Dr. George Fair, 972-883-2350, Fax: 972-883-2440, E-mail: gwfair@utdallas.edu.

School of Management Students: 752 full-time (349 women), 1,377 part-time (545 women); includes 621 minority (95 African Americans, 7 American Indian/Alaska Native, 389 Asian Americans or Pacific Islanders, 130 Hispanic Americans), 665 international. Average age 31. 1,766 applicants, 74% accepted, 617 enrolled. *Faculty:* 77 full-time (13 women), 28 part-time/adjunct (6 women). Expenses: Contact institution. *Financial support:* In 2008–09, 9 research assistantships with tuition reimbursements (averaging $13,103 per year), 104 teaching assistantships with tuition reimbursements (averaging $13,020 per year) were awarded; fellowships, career-related internships or fieldwork, Federal Work-Study, institutionally sponsored loans, scholarships/grants, and unspecified assistantships also available. Support available to part-time students. Financial award application deadline: 4/30; financial award applicants required to submit FAFSA. In 2008, 765 master's, 10 doctorates awarded. *Degree program information:* Part-time and evening/weekend programs available. Postbaccalaureate distance learning degree programs offered. Offers accounting (PhD); audit and professional (MS); cohort (MBA); electronic commerce (MS); executive business administration (EMBA); finance (MS, PhD); financial analysis (MS); global leadership (EMBA); global online (MBA); health care systems (MS); healthcare management (EMBA, MS); information management (MS); information security and assurance (MS); information systems (PhD); innovation and entrepreneurship (MS); internal audit (MS); international management (MA, PhD); international services (MS); management (EMBA, MA, MBA, MS, PhD); managerial (MS); marketing (PhD); organizations and strategy (MS); professional business admininstration (MBA); project management (EMBA); supply chain management (MS); taxation (MS). *Application deadline:* For fall admission, 7/15 for domestic students, 5/1 priority date for international students; for spring admission, 11/15 for domestic students, 9/1 priority date for international students. Applications are processed on a rolling basis. *Application fee:* $50 ($100 for international students). Electronic applications accepted. *Application Contact:* David B. Ritchey, Director of Advising, 972-883-2750, Fax: 972-883-6425, E-mail: davidr@utdallas.edu. *Dean,* Dr. Hasan Pirkul, 972-883-2705, Fax: 972-883-2799, E-mail: hpirkul@utdallas.edu.

School of Natural Sciences and Mathematics Students: 237 full-time (110 women), 140 part-time (68 women); includes 66 minority (13 African Americans, 37 Asian Americans or Pacific Islanders, 16 Hispanic Americans), 166 international. Average age 32. 589 applicants, 46% accepted, 101 enrolled. *Faculty:* 75 full-time (9 women), 2 part-time/adjunct (0 women). Expenses: Contact institution. *Financial support:* In 2008–09, 55 research assistantships with tuition reimbursements (averaging $18,615 per year), 102 teaching assistantships with tuition reimbursements (averaging $13,500 per year) were awarded; fellowships, career-related internships or fieldwork, Federal Work-Study, institutionally sponsored loans, scholarships/grants, and unspecified assistantships also available. Support available to part-time students. Financial award application deadline: 4/30. In 2008, 84 master's, 22 doctorates awarded. *Degree program information:* Part-time and evening/weekend programs available. Offers applied mathematics (MS, PhD); applied physics (MS); bioinformatics and computational biology (MS); biotechnology (MS); chemistry (MS, PhD); engineering mathematics (MS); geochemistry (MS, PhD); geophysics (MS); geospatial information sciences (MS, PhD); hydrogeology (MS, PhD); mathematical science (MS); mathematics education (MAT); molecular and cell biology (MS, PhD); natural sciences and mathematics (MAT, MS, PhD); physics (MS, PhD); science education (MAT); sedimentary, stratigraphy, paleontology (PhD); statistics (MS, PhD); stratigraphy, paleontology (MS); structural geology and tectonics (MS, PhD). *Application deadline:* For fall admission, 7/15 for domestic students, 5/1 priority date for international students; for spring admission, 11/15 for domestic students, 9/1 priority date for international students. Applications are processed on a rolling basis. *Application fee:* $50 ($100 for international students). Electronic applications accepted. *Application Contact:* Dr. Juan E. Gonzalez, Associate Dean, 972-883-2526, Fax: 972-883-6371, E-mail: jgonzal@utdallas.edu. *Dean,* Dr. Myron B. Salamon, 972-883-2416, Fax: 972-883-6371, E-mail: salamon@utdallas.edu.

THE UNIVERSITY OF TEXAS AT EL PASO, El Paso, TX 79968-0001

General Information State-supported, coed, university. CGS member. *Graduate housing:* Room and/or apartments available on a first-come, first-served basis to single students; on-campus housing not available to married students. Housing application deadline: 5/1.

GRADUATE UNITS

Graduate School *Degree program information:* Part-time and evening/weekend programs available. Postbaccalaureate distance learning degree programs offered. Offers environmental science and engineering (PhD); materials science and engineering (PhD). Electronic applications accepted.

College of Business Administration *Degree program information:* Part-time and evening/weekend programs available. Postbaccalaureate distance learning degree programs offered. Offers accounting (M Acc); business administration (M Acc, MBA, MS); economics (MS). Electronic applications accepted.

College of Education *Degree program information:* Part-time and evening/weekend programs available. Offers education (M Ed, MA, Ed D, PhD); educational administration (M Ed); educational diagnostics (M Ed); educational leadership and administration (Ed D); guidance and counseling (M Ed); instruction (M Ed); reading education (M Ed); special education (M Ed); teaching, learning, and culture (PhD). Electronic applications accepted.

College of Engineering *Degree program information:* Part-time and evening/weekend programs available. Offers civil engineering (MS, PhD); computer engineering (MS); computer science (MS, PhD); electrical and computer engineering (PhD); electrical engineering (MS); engineering (MEENE, MIT, MS, MSENE, PhD); environmental engineering (MEENE, MSENE); industrial engineering (MS); information technology (MIT); manufacturing engineering (MS); mechanical engineering (MS); metallurgical and materials engineering (MS). Electronic applications accepted.

College of Health Sciences *Degree program information:* Part-time and evening/weekend programs available. Postbaccalaureate distance learning degree programs offered. Offers health education (MS); health sciences (MOT, MPH, MPT, MS, PhD); interdisciplinary health sciences (PhD); kinesiology (MS); occupational therapy (MOT); physical therapy (MPT); public health (MPH); speech-language pathology (MS). Electronic applications accepted.

College of Liberal Arts *Degree program information:* Part-time and evening/weekend programs available. Offers art education (MA); border history (MA); clinical psychology (MA); communication (MA); creative writing in English (MFA); creative writing in Spanish (MFA); English and American literature (MA); experimental psychology (MA); history (MA, PhD); liberal arts (MA, MAIS, MAT, MFA, MM, PhD); linguistics (MA); music education (MM); music performance (MM); political science (MA); psychology (PhD); rhetoric and composition (PhD); rhetoric and writing studies (MA); sociology (MA); studio art (MA); teaching English (MAT). Electronic applications accepted.

College of Science *Degree program information:* Part-time and evening/weekend programs available. Offers applied mathematics (MS); bioinformatics (MS); biological sciences (MS, PhD); chemistry (MS, PhD); geological sciences (MS, PhD); geophysics (MS, PhD); interdisciplinary studies (MSIS); mathematics (MAT, MS); physics (MS); science (MAT, MS, MSIS, PhD); statistics (MS). Electronic applications accepted.

Institute for Policy and Economic Development Offers intelligence and national security studies (MS); leadership studies (MLS); public administration (MPA).

School of Nursing Offers evidence-based practice (Certificate); family nurse practitioner (MSN, Certificate); health care leadership and management (Certificate); nurse clinician

The University of Texas at El Paso (continued)

educator (MSN); nurse educator (Certificate); nursing systems management (MSN); women's health care nurse practitioner (MSN). Electronic applications accepted.

THE UNIVERSITY OF TEXAS AT SAN ANTONIO, San Antonio, TX 78249-0617

General Information State-supported, coed, university. CGS member. *Graduate housing:* Rooms and/or apartments available on a first-come, first-served basis to single and married students. *Research affiliation:* Texas Data Center (population studies), Southwest Research Center (engineering).

GRADUATE UNITS

College of Business *Degree program information:* Part-time and evening/weekend programs available. Offers accountancy (M Accy); applied statistics (PhD); business (Exec MBA, M Accy, MA, MBA, MS, MSIT, MSMOT, PhD); business administration-accounting (PhD); business administration-finance (PhD); business administration-information technology (PhD); business administration-marketing (PhD); business administration-organizational management (PhD); business economics (MBA); business finance (MBA); economics (MA); executive business administration (Exec MBA); finance (MS); information systems (MBA); information technology (MSIT); international business (MBA); management accounting (MBA); management science (MBA); management technology (MSMOT); marketing management (MBA); statistics (MS); taxation (MBA). Electronic applications accepted.

College of Education and Human Development *Degree program information:* Part-time and evening/weekend programs available. Offers adult education and college teaching (MA); bicultural-bilingual studies (MA); counseling (MA); counselor education and supervision (PhD); culture, literacy, and language (PhD); curriculum and instruction (MA); early childhood education (MA); education and human development (M Ed, MA, MA Ed, MS, Ed D, PhD, Graduate Certificate); educational leadership (M Ed, Ed D); health and kinesiology (MS); higher education administration (Graduate Certificate); instructional technology (MA); kinesiology and health promotion (MA Ed); reading (MA); special education (MA); teaching English as a second language (MA). Electronic applications accepted.

College of Engineering *Degree program information:* Part-time and evening/weekend programs available. Offers biomedical engineering (MS, PhD); civil engineering (MSCE); computer engineering (MS); electrical engineering (MSEE, PhD); engineering (MS, MSCE, MSEE, MSME, PhD); environmental science and engineering (PhD); mechanical engineering (MSME). Electronic applications accepted.

College of Liberal and Fine Arts *Degree program information:* Part-time and evening/weekend programs available. Offers anthropology (MA, PhD); art history (MA); communication (MA); creative writing (Graduate Certificate); English (MA, PhD); history (MA); keyboard pedagogy (Graduate Certificate); keyboard performance (Graduate Certificate); liberal and fine arts (MA, MFA, MM, MS, PhD, Graduate Certificate); music (MM); political science (MA); psychology (MS); sociology (MS); Spanish (MA); Spanish translation studies (Graduate Certificate); studio art (MFA). Electronic applications accepted.

College of Public Policy *Degree program information:* Part-time and evening/weekend programs available. Offers applied demography (PhD); justice policy (MS); public administration (MPA); public policy (MPA, MS, MSW, PhD); social work (MSW). Electronic applications accepted.

College of Sciences *Degree program information:* Part-time and evening/weekend programs available. Offers applied/industrial mathematics (MS); biology (MS, PhD); biotechnology (MS); chemistry (MS, PhD); computer science (MS, PhD); environmental sciences (MS); geology (MS); mathematics (MS); physics (MS, PhD); sciences (MS, PhD). Electronic applications accepted.

THE UNIVERSITY OF TEXAS AT TYLER, Tyler, TX 75799-0001

General Information State-supported, coed, comprehensive institution. CGS member. *Enrollment:* 6,117 graduate, professional, and undergraduate students; 224 full-time matriculated graduate/professional students (138 women), 611 part-time matriculated graduate/professional students (407 women). *Enrollment by degree level:* 1 first professional, 827 master's, 17 doctoral. *Graduate faculty:* 173 full-time (64 women). *Graduate housing:* Rooms and/or apartments available on a first-come, first-served basis to single and married students. *Student services:* Campus employment opportunities, campus safety program, career counseling, exercise/wellness program, free psychological counseling, grant writing training, services for students with disabilities, teacher training, writing training. *Library facilities:* Robert Muntz Library. *Online resources:* library catalog, web page. *Collection:* 486,895 titles, 525 serial subscriptions, 5,522 audiovisual materials. *Research affiliation:* Embassy of Arab Republic of Egypt Cultural and Education Bureau (electrical engineering), TransAtlantic Lines, Inc (civil engineering), American Society of Civil Engineers (civil engineering), Mcgraw-Hill Co. (civil engineering), Renaissance Society of America (art history), American Lung Association of the Central States (biology).

Computer facilities: 139 computers available on campus for general student use. A campuswide network can be accessed from student residence rooms and from off campus. Online class registration is available. *Web address:* http://www.uttyler.edu/.

General Application Contact: Dr. Alecia Wolf, Graduate Services Coordinator, 903-566-7457, Fax: 903-566-7007, E-mail: awolf@uttyler.edu.

GRADUATE UNITS

College of Arts and Sciences *Degree program information:* Part-time and evening/weekend programs available. Postbaccalaureate distance learning degree programs offered. Offers art and art history (MA, MAIS, MFA); arts and sciences (MA, MAIS, MAT, MFA, MPA, MS, MSIS); biology (MS); communication (MA); criminal justice (MS); English (MA); history (MA); interdisciplinary studies (MAIS, MSIS); mathematics (MS, MSIS); political science (MA); public administration (MPA); sociology (MS). Electronic applications accepted.

College of Business and Technology *Degree program information:* Part-time and evening/weekend programs available. Postbaccalaureate distance learning degree programs offered (no on-campus study). Offers business and technology (MBA, MS, PhD). Electronic applications accepted.

School of Business Administration Students: 15 full-time (6 women), 152 part-time (60 women); includes 34 minority (16 African Americans, 1 American Indian/Alaska Native, 5 Asian Americans or Pacific Islanders, 12 Hispanic Americans), 1 international. 45 applicants, 100% accepted, 13 enrolled. *Faculty:* 14 full-time (9 women). Expenses: Contact institution. In 2008, 35 master's awarded. *Degree program information:* Part-time programs available. Postbaccalaureate distance learning degree programs offered (no on-campus study). Offers business administration (MBA); general management (MBA); health care (MBA). *Application deadline:* For fall admission, 8/17 priority date for domestic students, 7/1 priority date for international students; for spring admission, 12/21 priority date for domestic students, 11/1 priority date for international students. *Application fee:* $25 ($50 for international students). *Application Contact:* Dr. Mary Fischer. *Interim Dean and Professor of Accounting*, Dr. Mary Fischer, 903-566-7433, Fax: 903-566-7372.

School of Human Resource Development and Technology Students: 14 full-time (8 women), 46 part-time (27 women); includes 17 minority (9 African Americans, 8 Hispanic Americans), 5 international. Average age 36. 18 applicants, 100% accepted, 9 enrolled. *Faculty:* 8 full-time (1 woman). Expenses: Contact institution. *Financial support:* Career-related internships or fieldwork, institutionally sponsored loans, scholarships/grants, and health care benefits available. Support available to part-time students. Financial award application deadline: 7/1. In 2008, 12 master's awarded. *Degree program information:* Part-time and evening/weekend programs available. Postbaccalaureate distance learning degree programs offered (no on-campus study). Offers human resource development (MS, PhD); industrial management (MS); industrial safety (MS). *Application deadline:* For fall admission, 8/17 priority date for domestic students, 5/30 for international students; for spring admission, 12/21 priority date for domestic students, 10/30 for international students. *Application fee:* $25 ($50 for international students). Electronic applications accepted. *Application Contact:* Dr. Rita Dobbs, Director of Graduate Studies, 903-566-7260, Fax: 903-566-7068, E-mail: rdobbs@uttyler.edu. *Chair*, Dr. W. Clayton Allen, 903-566-7328, Fax: 903-565-5650, E-mail: callen@mail.uttyl.edu.

College of Education and Psychology *Degree program information:* Part-time and evening/weekend programs available. Offers clinical psychology (MS); counseling psychology (MA); education and psychology (M Ed, MA, MS, MSIS); educational leadership (M Ed); interdisciplinary studies (MSIS); school counseling (MA).

School of Education Students: 11 full-time (all women), 44 part-time (41 women); includes 10 minority (6 African Americans, 1 American Indian/Alaska Native, 3 Hispanic Americans), 1 international. Average age 36. 14 applicants, 100% accepted, 9 enrolled. *Faculty:* 17 full-time (7 women). Expenses: Contact institution. *Financial support:* In 2008–09, 2 research assistantships (averaging $12,000 per year) were awarded; scholarships/grants also available. Financial award application deadline: 7/1. In 2008, 29 master's awarded. *Degree program information:* Part-time and evening/weekend programs available. Offers early childhood education (M Ed, MA); reading (M Ed, MA); special education (M Ed, MA). *Application deadline:* For fall admission, 8/17 priority date for domestic students, 7/1 priority date for international students; for spring admission, 12/21 priority date for domestic students, 11/1 priority date for international students. Applications are processed on a rolling basis. *Application fee:* $25 ($50 for international students). Electronic applications accepted. *Application Contact:* Dr. Kathy Morrison, Program Director for Curriculum and Instruction and Early Childhood, 903-566-7016, Fax: 903-565-5560, E-mail: kmorrison@uttyler.edu. *Interim Director*, Dr. Michael Odell, 903-566-7133, Fax: 903-565-5648, E-mail: modell@uttyler.edu.

College of Engineering and Computer Science Students: 4 full-time (2 women), 5 part-time (1 woman); includes 3 Asian Americans or Pacific Islanders, 1 Hispanic American, 2 international. Average age 31. 1 applicant, 100% accepted, 1 enrolled. Expenses: Contact institution. *Financial support:* In 2008–09, 5 research assistantships with tuition reimbursements (averaging $2,333 per year), 1 teaching assistantship (averaging $2,333 per year) were awarded. Financial award application deadline: 7/1; financial award applicants required to submit FAFSA. In 2008, 7 master's awarded. *Degree program information:* Part-time programs available. Offers civil engineering (MS); computer science (MS); electrical engineering (MS); engineering and computer science (MS, MSIS); interdisciplinary studies (MSIS); mechanical engineering (MS). *Application deadline:* Applications are processed on a rolling basis. *Application fee:* $25 ($50 for international students). Electronic applications accepted. *Application Contact:* Dr. Jim Nelson, Dean, 903-566-7267, Fax: 903-566-7148, E-mail: jnelson@uttyler.edu. *Dean*, Dr. Jim Nelson, 903-566-7267, Fax: 903-566-7148, E-mail: jnelson@uttyler.edu.

College of Nursing and Health Sciences *Degree program information:* Part-time and evening/weekend programs available. Postbaccalaureate distance learning degree programs offered. Offers health and kinesiology (M Ed, MA); kinesiology (MS); nurse practitioner (MSN); nursing (PhD); nursing administration (MSN); nursing and health sciences (M Ed, MA, MS, MSN, PhD); nursing education (MSN). Electronic applications accepted.

THE UNIVERSITY OF TEXAS HEALTH SCIENCE CENTER AT HOUSTON, Houston, TX 77225-0036

General Information State-supported, coed, upper-level institution. *Graduate housing:* On-campus housing not available.

GRADUATE UNITS

Graduate School of Biomedical Sciences Students: 372 full-time (194 women); includes 73 minority (11 African Americans, 25 Asian Americans or Pacific Islanders, 37 Hispanic Americans), 139 international. Average age 26. 587 applicants, 33% accepted, 111 enrolled. *Faculty:* 582 full-time (154 women). Expenses: Contact institution. *Financial support:* Fellowships with full tuition reimbursements, research assistantships with full tuition reimbursements, teaching assistantships, institutionally sponsored loans, scholarships/grants, and health care benefits available. Financial award application deadline: 12/15. In 2008, 17 master's, 53 doctorates awarded. Offers biochemistry and molecular biology (MS, PhD); biomathematics and biostatistics (MS, PhD); biomedical sciences (MS, PhD); cancer biology (MS, PhD); cell and regulatory biology (MS, PhD); genes and development (MS, PhD); genetic counseling (MS); human and molecular genetics (MS, PhD); immunology (MS, PhD); medical physics (MS, PhD); microbiology and molecular genetics (MS, PhD); molecular carcinogenesis (MS, PhD); molecular pathology (MS, PhD); neuroscience (MS, PhD); virology and gene therapy (MS, PhD). *Application deadline:* For fall admission, 12/15 priority date for domestic students, 12/15 for international students; for spring admission, 11/1 for domestic students. Applications are processed on a rolling basis. *Application fee:* $10. Electronic applications accepted. *Application Contact:* Dr. Victoria P. Knutson, Associate Dean of Admissions, 713-500-9860, Fax: 713-500-9877, E-mail: victoria.p.knutson@uth.tmc.edu. *Dean*, Dr. George M. Stancel, 713-500-9880, Fax: 713-500-9877, E-mail: george.m.stancel@uth.tmc.edu.

Medical School Offers medicine (MD). Electronic applications accepted.

School of Health Information Sciences *Degree program information:* Part-time programs available. Postbaccalaureate distance learning degree programs offered (no on-campus study). Offers health informatics (MS, PhD, Certificate). Electronic applications accepted.

School of Nursing *Degree program information:* Part-time programs available. Offers nursing (MSN, DNP, PhD). Electronic applications accepted.

School of Public Health *Degree program information:* Part-time programs available. Offers public health (MPH, MS, Dr PH, PhD, Certificate). Electronic applications accepted.

The University of Texas Dental Branch at Houston Offers dentistry (DDS, MS). Electronic applications accepted.

THE UNIVERSITY OF TEXAS HEALTH SCIENCE CENTER AT SAN ANTONIO, San Antonio, TX 78229-3900

General Information State-supported, coed, upper-level institution. CGS member. *Enrollment:* 1,834 full-time matriculated graduate/professional students (988 women), 335 part-time matriculated graduate/professional students (238 women). *Enrollment by degree level:* 1,273 first professional, 519 master's, 294 doctoral, 83 other advanced degrees. *Graduate faculty:* 224 full-time (83 women), 54 part-time/adjunct (9 women). Tuition, state resident: full-time $2016; part-time $112 per credit hour. Tuition, nonresident: full-time $7848; part-time $436 per credit hour. *Required fees:* $425 per term. One-time fee: $70. *Graduate housing:* On-campus housing not available. *Student services:* Campus safety program, exercise/wellness program, free psychological counseling, international student services, low-cost health insurance. *Library facilities:* Dolph Briso Library. *Collection:* 192,576 titles, 2,501 serial subscriptions. *Research affiliation:* University Hospital, Southwest Research Institute, Southwest Foundation for Biomedical Research, Veterans Administration Hospital.

Computer facilities: 1,000 computers available on campus for general student use. A campuswide network can be accessed from off campus. *Web address:* http://www.uthscsa.edu/.

General Application Contact: Ralph M. Flanigan, Assistant Registrar, 210-567-2620, Fax: 210-567-2685, E-mail: flanigan@uthscsa.edu.

GRADUATE UNITS

Dental School Offers dentistry (DDS, MS, Certificate). Electronic applications accepted.

Graduate School of Biomedical Sciences Students: 1,834 full-time (988 women), 335 part-time (238 women); includes 80 minority (7 African Americans, 40 Asian Americans or Pacific Islanders, 33 Hispanic Americans), 87 international. Average age 29. *Faculty:* 224 full-time (83 women), 54 part-time/adjunct (9 women). Expenses: Contact institution. *Financial support:* In 2008–09, 212 teaching assistantships (averaging $26,000 per year) were awarded; fellowships, research assistantships, career-related internships or fieldwork, Federal Work-Study, institutionally sponsored loans, and tuition waivers (full) also available. Support available to part-time students. Financial award application deadline: 4/1; financial award applicants required to submit FAFSA. In 2008, 5 master's, 27 doctorates awarded. *Degree program information:* Part-time and evening/weekend programs available. Offers biochemistry (MS, PhD); biomedical sciences (MS, MSN, PhD); cellular and structural biology (MS, PhD);

microbiology and immunology (PhD); molecular medicine (MS, PhD); pharmacology (PhD); physiology (MS, PhD); radiological sciences (MS, PhD). *Application deadline:* For fall admission, 4/1 for domestic and international students; for spring admission, 10/1 for domestic and international students. Applications are processed on a rolling basis. *Application fee:* $0. Electronic applications accepted. *Application Contact:* Nicquet Blake, PhD, Assistant Dean for Graduate Student Recruitment, 210-567-3709, Fax: 210-567-3719, E-mail: blaken@uthscsa.edu. *Interim Dean*, Robert L. Reddick, MD, 210-567-3709, Fax: 210-567-3719, E-mail: reddick@uthscsa.edu.

School of Nursing Students: 31 full-time (24 women), 186 part-time (166 women); includes 101 minority (17 African Americans, 1 American Indian/Alaska Native, 7 Asian Americans or Pacific Islanders, 76 Hispanic Americans). Average age 39. 123 applicants, 46% accepted, 39 enrolled. *Faculty:* 37 full-time (all women), 2 part-time/adjunct (0 women). Expenses: Contact institution. *Financial support:* In 2008–09, 42 students received support; research assistantships, teaching assistantships, institutionally sponsored loans and scholarships/grants available. Financial award application deadline: 4/1; financial award applicants required to submit FAFSA. In 2008, 68 master's, 4 doctorates awarded. *Degree program information:* Part-time programs available. Offers nursing (MSN, PhD). *Application deadline:* For fall admission, 2/1 for domestic students; for spring admission, 9/1 for domestic students. *Application fee:* $45. *Application Contact:* Dr. Beverly Robinson, Associate Dean for Graduate Nursing Program and Director of Doctoral Studies, 210-567-5815, Fax: 210-567-3813, E-mail: robinsonb@uthscsa.edu. *Dean*, Dr. Eileen T. Breslin, 210-567-5800, Fax: 210-567-5929, E-mail: breslin@uthscsa.edu.

School of Allied Health Sciences Offers clinical laboratory sciences (MS); deaf education and hearing science (MED); dental hygiene (MS); occupational therapy (MOT); physical therapy (MPT); physician assistant studies (MS).

School of Medicine Offers medicine (MD, MPH).

THE UNIVERSITY OF TEXAS MEDICAL BRANCH, Galveston, TX 77555

General Information State-supported, coed, comprehensive institution. CGS member. *Enrollment:* 2,338 graduate, professional, and undergraduate students; 1,595 full-time matriculated graduate/professional students (930 women), 273 part-time matriculated graduate/professional students (232 women). *Enrollment by degree level:* 903 first professional, 647 master's, 318 doctoral. *Graduate housing:* Rooms and/or apartments available on a first-come, first-served basis to single and married students. *Student services:* Campus employment opportunities, campus safety program, career counseling, exercise/wellness program, free psychological counseling, international student services, low-cost health insurance, multicultural affairs office, services for students with disabilities. *Library facilities:* Moody Medical Library. *Online resources:* library catalog, web page, access to other libraries' catalogs. *Research affiliation:* Shriners Hospitals (burns and wound healing).

Computer facilities: Computer purchase and lease plans are available. A campuswide network can be accessed from student residence rooms and from off campus. Online class registration is available. *Web address:* http://www.utmb.edu/.

General Application Contact: Vicki Brewer, University Registrar/Director of Enrollment Services, 409-772-1215, Fax: 409-772-4466, E-mail: enrollment.services@utmb.edu.

GRADUATE UNITS

Graduate School of Biomedical Sciences Students: 238 full-time (126 women), 51 part-time (30 women); includes 59 minority (14 African Americans, 14 Asian Americans or Pacific Islanders, 31 Hispanic Americans), 78 international. Average age 31. 319 applicants, 37% accepted, 63 enrolled. Expenses: Contact institution. *Financial support:* In 2008–09, research assistantships with full tuition reimbursements (averaging $25,000 per year); career-related internships or fieldwork, Federal Work-Study, institutionally sponsored loans, scholarships/grants, traineeships, health care benefits, and unspecified assistantships also available. Support available to part-time students. Financial award applicants required to submit FAFSA. In 2008, 27 master's, 41 doctorates awarded. Offers biochemistry (PhD); bioinformatics (PhD); biomedical sciences (MA, MMS, MPH, MS, PhD); biophysics (PhD); cell biology (PhD); cellular physiology and molecular biophysics (MS, PhD); clinical science (MS, PhD); computational biology (PhD); emerging and tropical infectious diseases (PhD); experimental pathology (PhD); medical humanities (MA, PhD); medical science (MMS); microbiology and immunology (MS, PhD); neuroscience (PhD); nursing (PhD); pharmacology (MS); pharmacology and toxicology (PhD); preventive medicine and community health (MPH, MS, PhD); public health (MPH); structural biology (PhD). *Application deadline:* Applications are processed on a rolling basis. *Application fee:* $30 ($75 for international students). Electronic applications accepted. *Application Contact:* Dr. Dorian H. Coppenhaver, Associate Dean for Student Affairs, 409-772-2665, Fax: 409-747-0772, E-mail: dcoppenh@utmb.edu. *Dean*, Dr. Cary W. Cooper, 409-772-2665, Fax: 409-747-0772, E-mail: ccooper@utmb.edu.

Center for Biodefense and Emerging Infectious Diseases Expenses: Contact institution. *Financial support:* Tuition waivers and unspecified assistantships available. Offers biodefense training (PhD). *Application Contact:* Dr. Dorian H. Coppenhaver, Associate Dean for Student Affairs, 409-772-2665, Fax: 409-747-0772, E-mail: dcoppenh@utmb.edu. *Executive Director*, Dr. Clarence J. Peters, 409-772-0090, Fax: 409-747-0762, E-mail: cjpeters@utmb.edu.

School of Health Professions Students: 405 full-time (334 women), 4 part-time (3 women); includes 120 minority (25 African Americans, 3 American Indian/Alaska Native, 42 Asian Americans or Pacific Islanders, 50 Hispanic Americans), 2 international. Average age 26. 943 applicants, 22% accepted, 148 enrolled. Expenses: Contact institution. *Financial support:* Career-related internships or fieldwork, Federal Work-Study, institutionally sponsored loans, and scholarships/grants available. Financial award applicants required to submit FAFSA. In 2008, 62 master's awarded. Offers health professions (MOT, MPAS, MPT, DPT); occupational therapy (MOT); physical therapy (MPT, DPT); physician assistant studies (MPAS). *Application deadline:* For fall admission, 11/1 for domestic students. Applications are processed on a rolling basis. *Application fee:* $30. Electronic applications accepted. *Application Contact:* Dr. Henry Cavazos, Associate Dean for Academic and Student Affairs, 409-772-3004, E-mail: hcavazos@utmb.edu. *Dean*, Dr. Elizabeth J. Protas, 409-772-3001, Fax: 409-747-1623, E-mail: ejprotas@utmb.edu.

School of Medicine Students: 903 full-time (426 women); includes 387 minority (89 African Americans, 6 American Indian/Alaska Native, 143 Asian Americans or Pacific Islanders, 149 Hispanic Americans), 3 international. Average age 25. Expenses: Contact institution. *Financial support:* Federal Work-Study, institutionally sponsored loans, scholarships/grants, and tuition waivers (full and partial) available. Financial award applicants required to submit FAFSA. In 2008, 194 MDs awarded. Offers medicine (MD). *Application deadline:* For fall admission, 10/1 for domestic students. *Application fee:* $75 ($120 for international students). *Application Contact:* Dr. Lauree Thomas, Associate Dean for Admissions and Student Affairs, 409-772-1442, Fax: 409-772-5148, E-mail: lauthoma@utmb.edu. *Dean*, Dr. Garland D. Anderson, 409-772-4793, Fax: 409-772-9598, E-mail: ganderso@utmb.edu.

School of Nursing Students: 49 full-time (44 women), 214 part-time (195 women); includes 76 minority (28 African Americans, 4 American Indian/Alaska Native, 17 Asian Americans or Pacific Islanders, 27 Hispanic Americans). Average age 40. 956 applicants, 19% accepted, 153 enrolled. Expenses: Contact institution. *Financial support:* Research assistantships, teaching assistantships, Federal Work-Study, institutionally sponsored loans, scholarships/grants, and traineeships available. Support available to part-time students. Financial award applicants required to submit FAFSA. In 2008, 55 master's awarded. *Degree program information:* Part-time programs available. Postbaccalaureate distance learning degree programs offered (minimal on-campus study). Offers nursing (MSN, PhD). *Application deadline:* For fall admission, 1/15 for domestic students. Applications are processed on a rolling basis. *Application fee:* $30. Electronic applications accepted. *Application Contact:* Dr. Ernestine H. Cuellar, Associate Dean for Student Affairs/Admissions, 409-772-8205, E-mail: ehcuella@utmb.edu. *Dean*, Dr. Pamela G. Watson, 409-772-1510, Fax: 409-772-5118, E-mail: pgwatson@utmb.edu.

THE UNIVERSITY OF TEXAS OF THE PERMIAN BASIN, Odessa, TX 79762-0001

General Information State-supported, coed, comprehensive institution. *Graduate housing:* Rooms and/or apartments available on a first-come, first-served basis to single and married students. Housing application deadline: 6/15.

GRADUATE UNITS

Office of Graduate Studies *Degree program information:* Part-time and evening/weekend programs available.

College of Arts and Sciences *Degree program information:* Part-time and evening/weekend programs available. Offers applied research psychology (MA); arts and sciences (MA, MS); biology (MS); clinical psychology (MA); computer science (MS); criminal justice administration (MS); English (MA); geology (MS); history (MA); kinesiology (MS); political science (MPA); Spanish (MA).

School of Business *Degree program information:* Part-time and evening/weekend programs available. Offers accountancy (MPA); business (MBA, MPA); management (MBA).

School of Education Offers bilingual/English as a second language education (MA); counseling (MA); early childhood education (MA); education (MA); educational leadership (MA); professional education (MA); reading (MA); special education (MA).

THE UNIVERSITY OF TEXAS–PAN AMERICAN, Edinburg, TX 78541-2999

General Information State-supported, coed, comprehensive institution. CGS member. *Graduate housing:* Room and/or apartments available on a first-come, first-served basis to single students; on-campus housing not available to married students. *Research affiliation:* Howard Hughes Medical Institute (medical science), Boeing (engineering), Robert Wood Johnson (health science), Lockheed Martin (manufacturing engineering), Texas Instruments (curriculum and instruction), Pfizer (health disparities).

GRADUATE UNITS

College of Arts and Humanities *Degree program information:* Part-time and evening/weekend programs available. Offers art (MFA); arts and humanities (M Mus, MA, MAIS, MFA, MSIS); communication (MA); English (MA, MAIS); English as a second language (MA); ethnomusicology (M Mus); history (MA, MAIS); interdisciplinary studies (MAIS); music education (M Mus); performance (M Mus); Spanish (MA); theatre (MA).

College of Business Administration *Degree program information:* Part-time and evening/weekend programs available. Offers accounting (M Acc, MS); business administration (M Acc, MBA, MS, PhD); computer information systems (PhD); economics (PhD); finance (PhD); management (PhD); marketing (PhD).

College of Education *Degree program information:* Part-time and evening/weekend programs available. Offers bilingual education (M Ed); counseling (M Ed); early childhood education (M Ed); education (M Ed, MA, MS, Ed D); educational diagnostician (M Ed); educational leadership (M Ed, Ed D); elementary education (M Ed); gifted education (M Ed); kinesiology (MS); reading (M Ed); school psychology (MA); secondary education (M Ed); special education (M Ed).

College of Health Sciences and Human Services *Degree program information:* Part-time and evening/weekend programs available. Offers adult health nursing (MSN); communication sciences and disorders (MS); family nurse practitioner (MSN); health sciences and human services (MS, MSN, MSSW); occupational therapy (MS); pediatric nurse practitioner (MSN); rehabilitation counseling (MS); social work (MSSW).

College of Science and Engineering *Degree program information:* Part-time and evening/weekend programs available. Offers biology (MS); chemistry (MS); computer science (MS); electrical engineering (MS); manufacturing engineering (MS); mathematical science (MS); mathematics teaching (MS); mechanical engineering (MS); science and engineering (MS).

College of Social and Behavioral Sciences *Degree program information:* Part-time and evening/weekend programs available. Postbaccalaureate distance learning degree programs offered (minimal on-campus study). Offers criminal justice (MS); psychology (MA); public administration (MPA); social and behavioral sciences (MA, MPA, MS); sociology (MS).

THE UNIVERSITY OF TEXAS SOUTHWESTERN MEDICAL CENTER AT DALLAS, Dallas, TX 75390

General Information State-supported, coed, upper-level institution. *Enrollment:* 2,461 graduate, professional, and undergraduate students; 1,699 full-time matriculated graduate/professional students (889 women), 634 part-time matriculated graduate/professional students (270 women). *Enrollment by degree level:* 923 first professional, 202 master's, 646 doctoral, 562 other advanced degrees. *Graduate faculty:* 1,539 full-time, 425 part-time/adjunct. Tuition, state resident: full-time $3600. Tuition, nonresident: full-time $10,344. *Required fees:* $763. *Graduate housing:* Rooms and/or apartments available on a first-come, first-served basis to single and married students. *Student services:* Campus employment opportunities, campus safety program, exercise/wellness program, free psychological counseling, grant writing training, international student services, low-cost health insurance, multicultural affairs office, services for students with disabilities, writing training. *Library facilities:* University of Texas Southwestern Library plus 1 other. *Online resources:* library catalog, web page, access to other libraries' catalogs. *Collection:* 257,782 titles, 2,865 serial subscriptions.

Computer facilities: 150 computers available on campus for general student use. A campuswide network can be accessed from off campus. *Web address:* http://www.utsouthwestern.edu/.

General Application Contact: Anne Mclane, Associate Director of Admissions, 214-648-5617, Fax: 214-648-3289, E-mail: admissions@utsouthwestern.edu.

GRADUATE UNITS

Southwestern Allied Health Sciences School Students: 177 full-time (143 women); includes 45 minority (6 African Americans, 1 American Indian/Alaska Native, 18 Asian Americans or Pacific Islanders, 20 Hispanic Americans), 1 international. Average age 26. 1,016 applicants, 9% accepted, 76 enrolled. *Faculty:* 85 full-time (58 women). Expenses: Contact institution. *Financial support:* Application deadline: 3/1. In 2008, 38 master's awarded. Offers allied health sciences (MPAS, MPT, DPT); physical therapy (DPT); physician assistant studies (MPAS). *Application Contact:* Anne Mclane, Associate Director of Admissions, 214-648-6708, Fax: 214-648-2102, E-mail: admissions@utsouthwestern.edu. *Dean*, Dr. Raul Caetano, 214-648-1500.

Southwestern Graduate School of Biomedical Sciences Students: 599 full-time (309 women), 128 part-time (64 women); includes 209 minority (25 African Americans, 9 American Indian/Alaska Native, 110 Asian Americans or Pacific Islanders, 65 Hispanic Americans), 122 international. Average age 26. 1,308 applicants, 17% accepted, 136 enrolled. *Faculty:* 345 full-time (80 women), 89 part-time/adjunct (18 women). Expenses: Contact institution. *Financial support:* Fellowships, research assistantships, teaching assistantships, career-related internships or fieldwork, Federal Work-Study, institutionally sponsored loans, scholarships/grants, traineeships, and tuition waivers (full and partial) available. Financial award application deadline: 3/1; financial award applicants required to submit FAFSA. In 2008, 28 master's, 112 doctorates awarded. Offers biological chemistry (PhD); biomedical sciences (MA, MS, MSCS, PhD); cell regulation (PhD); genetics and development (PhD); immunology (PhD); integrative biology (PhD); medical scientist training (PhD); molecular biophysics (PhD); molecular microbiology (PhD); neuroscience (PhD). *Application deadline:* For fall admission, 12/15 priority date for domestic students. Applications are processed on a rolling basis. *Application fee:* $0. Electronic applications accepted. *Application Contact:* 214-648-5617, Fax: 214-648-3289, E-mail: admissions@utsouthwestern.edu. *Dean*, Dr. Melanie H. Cobb, 214-645-6122, Fax: 214-648-2102, E-mail: melanie.cobb@utsouthwestern.edu.

Division of Applied Science Students: 34 full-time (12 women), 23 part-time (11 women); includes 14 minority (9 Asian Americans or Pacific Islanders, 5 Hispanic Americans), 26 international. Average age 26. 102 applicants, 14% accepted, 10 enrolled. *Faculty:* 1,872 full-time (688 women). Expenses: Contact institution. In 2008, 6 master's, 5 doctorates

The University of Texas Southwestern Medical Center at Dallas (continued)

awarded. Offers biomedical communications (MA); biomedical engineering (MS, PhD). *Application fee:* $0. *Application Contact:* Dr. Melanie H. Cobb, Dean, 214-645-6122, Fax: 214-648-2102, E-mail: melanie.cobb@utsouthwestern.edu. *Dean,* Dr. Melanie H. Cobb, 214-645-6122, Fax: 214-648-2102, E-mail: melanie.cobb@utsouthwestern.edu.

Division of Clinical Science Students: 86 full-time (57 women), 86 part-time (47 women); includes 49 minority (9 African Americans, 1 American Indian/Alaska Native, 22 Asian Americans or Pacific Islanders, 17 Hispanic Americans), 5 international. Average age 26. 211 applicants, 17% accepted, 36 enrolled. Expenses: Contact institution. *Financial support:* Applicants required to submit FAFSA. In 2008, 17 master's, 9 doctorates awarded. Offers clinical psychology (PhD); clinical science (MSCS); radiological sciences (MS, PhD); rehabilitation counseling psychology (MS). *Application Contact:* Dr. Melanie H. Cobb, Dean, 214-645-6122, Fax: 214-648-2102, E-mail: melanie.cobb@utsouthwestern.edu. *Dean,* Dr. Melanie H. Cobb, 214-645-6122, Fax: 214-648-2102, E-mail: melanie.cobb@utsouthwestern.edu.

Southwestern Medical School Students: 923 full-time (437 women); includes 467 minority (54 African Americans, 2 American Indian/Alaska Native, 288 Asian Americans or Pacific Islanders, 123 Hispanic Americans), 7 international. Average age 25. 3,268 applicants, 13% accepted, 229 enrolled. *Faculty:* 1,464 full-time, 402 part-time/adjunct. Expenses: Contact institution. *Financial support:* In 2008–09, 700 students received support. Federal Work-Study and institutionally sponsored loans available. Financial award application deadline: 3/15; financial award applicants required to submit FAFSA. In 2008, 233 MDs awarded. Offers medicine (MD). *Application deadline:* For fall admission, 10/15 for domestic students. Applications are processed on a rolling basis. *Application fee:* $65. Electronic applications accepted. *Application Contact:* Anne Mclane, Associate Director of Admissions, 214-648-5617, Fax: 214-648-3289, E-mail: admissions@utsouthwestern.edu. *Dean,* Dr. Alfred Gilman, 214-648-2509.

THE UNIVERSITY OF THE ARTS, Philadelphia, PA 19102-4944

General Information Independent, coed, comprehensive institution. *Graduate housing:* Room and/or apartments available to single students; on-campus housing not available to married students. Housing application deadline: 6/1. *Research affiliation:* The Franklin Institute (general science education), Philadelphia Museum of Art (arts and culture), School District of Philadelphia (education), Ben Franklin Technology Partners (high tech department and creative/cultural production in Philadelphia).

GRADUATE UNITS

College of Art and Design *Degree program information:* Part-time programs available. Offers art and design (MA, MAT, MFA, MID); art education (MA); book arts/printmaking (MFA); ceramics (MFA); industrial design (MID); museum communication (MA); museum education (MA); museum exhibition planning and design (MFA); painting (MFA); sculpture (MFA); visual arts (MAT). Electronic applications accepted.

College of Performing Arts *Degree program information:* Part-time programs available. Offers performing arts (MAT, MM).

School of Music *Degree program information:* Part-time programs available. Offers jazz studies (MM); music education (MAT). Electronic applications accepted.

UNIVERSITY OF THE CUMBERLANDS, Williamsburg, KY 40769-1372

General Information Independent-religious, coed, comprehensive institution. *Graduate housing:* Room and/or apartments available to single students; on-campus housing not available to married students.

GRADUATE UNITS

Graduate Programs in Education *Degree program information:* Part-time and evening/weekend programs available. Offers early childhood education (MA Ed); elementary (P-5) (MA Ed, MAT); elementary education (MA Ed, MAT); elementary/secondary principalship (MA Ed, Certificate); middle school (5-9) (MA Ed, MAT); middle school education (MA Ed, MAT); principalship (Ed S); reading and writing specialist (MA Ed); secondary education (MA Ed, MAT); special education (MA Ed, MAT); specialization in supervision of instruction/superintendency (Ed S).

UNIVERSITY OF THE DISTRICT OF COLUMBIA, Washington, DC 20008-1175

General Information District-supported, coed, comprehensive institution. CGS member. *Graduate housing:* On-campus housing not available.

GRADUATE UNITS

College of Arts and Sciences *Degree program information:* Part-time and evening/weekend programs available. Offers arts and sciences (MA, MS, MST); clinical psychology (MS); counseling (MS); early childhood education (MA); English composition and rhetoric (MA); mathematics (MST); special education (MA); speech and language pathology (MS).

David A. Clarke School of Law Offers law (JD). Electronic applications accepted.

School of Business and Public Administration *Degree program information:* Part-time and evening/weekend programs available. Offers business administration (MBA); business and public administration (MBA, MPA); public administration (MPA).

UNIVERSITY OF THE FRASER VALLEY, Abbotsford, BC V2S 7M8, Canada

General Information Province-supported, coed, comprehensive institution. *Graduate housing:* Room and/or apartments available on a first-come, first-served basis to single students. Housing application deadline: 5/15.

GRADUATE UNITS

Graduate Studies *Degree program information:* Evening/weekend programs available. Offers criminal justice (MA). Electronic applications accepted.

UNIVERSITY OF THE INCARNATE WORD, San Antonio, TX 78209-6397

General Information Independent-religious, coed, comprehensive institution. *Enrollment:* 6,361 graduate, professional, and undergraduate students; 432 full-time matriculated graduate/professional students (282 women), 819 part-time matriculated graduate/professional students (542 women). *Enrollment by degree level:* 264 first professional, 825 master's, 162 doctoral. *Graduate faculty:* 76 full-time (40 women), 49 part-time/adjunct (26 women). *Tuition:* Full-time $11,520; part-time $640 per credit hour. *Required fees:* $1494; $83 per credit hour. One-time fee: $50. Tuition and fees vary according to degree level and program. *Graduate housing:* Room and/or apartments available on a first-come, first-served basis to single students; on-campus housing not available to married students. Typical cost: $4250 per year ($7380 including board). Room and board charges vary according to board plan and housing facility selected. Housing application deadline: 5/1. *Student services:* Campus employment opportunities, career counseling, exercise/wellness program, free psychological counseling, international student services, low-cost health insurance, services for students with disabilities. *Library facilities:* J.E. and M.E. Mabee Library. *Online resources:* library catalog, web page. *Collection:* 260,111 titles, 42,574 serial subscriptions, 14,484 audiovisual materials.

Computer facilities: Computer purchase and lease plans are available. 175 computers available on campus for general student use. A campuswide network can be accessed from student residence rooms. Online class registration is available. *Web address:* http://www.uiw.edu/.

General Application Contact: Janet Kaufman, Graduate Admissions Counselor, 210-829-6005, Fax: 210-829-3921, E-mail: admis@uiwtx.edu.

GRADUATE UNITS

Feik School of Pharmacy Students: 256 full-time (187 women), 8 part-time (4 women); includes 162 minority (16 African Americans, 2 American Indian/Alaska Native, 60 Asian Americans or Pacific Islanders, 84 Hispanic Americans), 5 international. Average age 26. *Faculty:* 21 full-time (11 women). Expenses: Contact institution. *Financial support:* Federal Work-Study and scholarships/grants available. Financial award applicants required to submit FAFSA. Offers pharmacy (Pharm D). *Application deadline:* For fall admission, 1/5 for domestic students. *Application fee:* $100. *Application Contact:* Dr. Carmita A. Coleman, Assistant Dean of Student Affairs, 210-883-1000, Fax: 210-883-1013, E-mail: rxadmissions@uiwtx.edu. *Founding Dean,* Dr. Arcelia Johnson-Fannin, 210-883-1015, Fax: 210-822-1516, E-mail: johnsonf@uiwtx.edu.

School of Graduate Studies and Research Students: 176 full-time (95 women), 811 part-time (538 women); includes 519 minority (88 African Americans, 3 American Indian/Alaska Native, 14 Asian Americans or Pacific Islanders, 414 Hispanic Americans), 129 international. Average age 35. *Faculty:* 55 full-time (29 women), 49 part-time/adjunct (26 women). Expenses: Contact institution. *Financial support:* In 2008–09, 1 fellowship, 10 research assistantships were awarded; Federal Work-Study, scholarships/grants, and tuition waivers (partial) also available. Financial award applicants required to submit FAFSA. In 2008, 294 master's, 20 doctorates awarded. *Degree program information:* Part-time and evening/weekend programs available. Postbaccalaureate distance learning degree programs offered (no on-campus study). *Application deadline:* Applications are processed on a rolling basis. *Application fee:* $20. Electronic applications accepted. *Application Contact:* Andrea Cyterski-Acosta, Dean of Enrollment, 210-829-6005, Fax: 210-829-3921, E-mail: admis@uiwtx.edu. *Dean,* Dr. Kevin Vichcales, 210-829-3157, Fax: 210-805-3559, E-mail: vichcale@uiwtx.edu.

College of Humanities, Arts, and Social Sciences Students: 25 part-time (14 women); includes 13 minority (2 African Americans, 11 Hispanic Americans), 1 international. Average age 40. *Faculty:* 1 (woman) full-time, 1 part-time/adjunct (0 women). Expenses: Contact institution. *Financial support:* In 2008–09, 2 research assistantships were awarded; Federal Work-Study, scholarships/grants, and tuition waivers (partial) also available. Financial award applicants required to submit FAFSA. In 2008, 6 master's awarded. *Degree program information:* Part-time and evening/weekend programs available. Offers humanities, arts, and social sciences (MA); multidisciplinary studies (MA); religious studies (MA). *Application deadline:* Applications are processed on a rolling basis. *Application fee:* $20. Electronic applications accepted. *Application Contact:* Andrea Cyterski-Acosta, Dean of Enrollment, 210-829-6005, Fax: 210-829-3921, E-mail: admis@uiwtx.edu. *Dean,* Dr. Bob Connelly, 210-829-6022, Fax: 210-829-3880, E-mail: bobc@uiwtx.edu.

Dreeben School of Education Students: 28 full-time (19 women), 251 part-time (173 women); includes 144 minority (36 African Americans, 2 American Indian/Alaska Native, 2 Asian Americans or Pacific Islanders, 104 Hispanic Americans), 36 international. Average age 39. *Faculty:* 14 full-time (5 women), 12 part-time/adjunct (9 women). Expenses: Contact institution. *Financial support:* In 2008–09, 4 research assistantships were awarded; Federal Work-Study, scholarships/grants, and tuition waivers (partial) also available. Financial award applicants required to submit FAFSA. In 2008, 57 master's, 20 doctorates awarded. *Degree program information:* Part-time and evening/weekend programs available. Postbaccalaureate distance learning degree programs offered. Offers adult education (M Ed, MA); all-level teaching (MAT); cross-cultural education (M Ed, MA); early childhood literacy (M Ed, MA); education (M Ed, MA, MAT, PhD); elementary teaching (MAT); general education (M Ed, MA); Higher Education (PhD); instructional technology (M Ed, MA); international education and entrepreneurship (PhD); kinesiology (M Ed, MA); literacy (M Ed, MA); mathematics education (PhD); organizational leadership (PhD); organizational learning and learning (M Ed, MA); reading (M Ed, MA); secondary teaching (MAT); special education (M Ed, MA); teacher leadership (M Ed, MA). *Application deadline:* Applications are processed on a rolling basis. *Application fee:* $20. Electronic applications accepted. *Application Contact:* Andrea Cyterski-Acosta, Dean of Enrollment, 210-829-6005, Fax: 210-829-3921, E-mail: admis@uiwtx.edu. *Dean,* Dr. Denise Staudt, 210-829-2761, Fax: 210-829-2765, E-mail: staudt@uiwtx.edu.

H-E-B School of Business and Administration Students: 102 full-time (48 women), 396 part-time (250 women); includes 275 minority (35 African Americans, 7 Asian Americans or Pacific Islanders, 233 Hispanic Americans), 49 international. Average age 32. *Faculty:* 17 full-time (8 women), 27 part-time/adjunct (12 women). Expenses: Contact institution. *Financial support:* In 2008–09, 2 research assistantships were awarded; Federal Work-Study, scholarships/grants, and tuition waivers (partial) also available. Financial award applicants required to submit FAFSA. In 2008, 190 master's awarded. *Degree program information:* Part-time and evening/weekend programs available. Postbaccalaureate distance learning degree programs offered (no on-campus study). Offers accounting (MS); adult education (MAA); applied administration (MAA); business and administration (MAA, MBA, MS, Certificate); communication arts (MAA); general business (MBA); healthcare administration (MAA); instructional technology (MAA); international business (MBA, Certificate); international business strategy (MBA); nutrition (MAA); organizational development (MAA, Certificate); project management (Certificate); sports management (MAA, MBA). *Application deadline:* Applications are processed on a rolling basis. *Application fee:* $20. Electronic applications accepted. *Application Contact:* Andrea Cyterski-Acosta, Dean of Enrollment, 210-829-6005, Fax: 210-829-3921, E-mail: admis@uiwtx.edu. *Dean,* Dr. Shawn Daly, 210-829-3924, Fax: 210-805-3564, E-mail: sdaly@uiwtx.edu.

School of Interactive Media and Design Students: 8 full-time (6 women), 27 part-time (11 women); includes 23 minority (2 African Americans, 21 Hispanic Americans), 4 international. Average age 32. *Faculty:* 3 full-time (1 woman), 2 part-time/adjunct (0 women). Expenses: Contact institution. *Financial support:* Federal Work-Study, scholarships/grants, and tuition waivers (partial) available. Financial award applicants required to submit FAFSA. In 2008, 5 master's awarded. *Degree program information:* Part-time and evening/weekend programs available. Offers communication arts (MA); instructional technology (MA); interactive media and design (MA). *Application deadline:* Applications are processed on a rolling basis. *Application fee:* $20. Electronic applications accepted. *Application Contact:* Andrea Cyterski-Acosta, Dean of Enrollment, 210-829-6005, Fax: 210-829-3921, E-mail: admis@uiwtx.edu. *Dean,* Dr. Cheryl Anderson, 210-829-6091, Fax: 210-829-3196, E-mail: cheryl.anderson@uiwtx.edu.

School of Mathematics, Science, and Engineering Students: 17 full-time (12 women), 44 part-time (36 women); includes 31 minority (3 African Americans, 1 American Indian/Alaska Native, 4 Asian Americans or Pacific Islanders, 23 Hispanic Americans), 5 international. Average age 33. *Faculty:* 11 full-time (7 women), 4 part-time/adjunct (3 women). Expenses: Contact institution. *Financial support:* In 2008–09, 2 research assistantships were awarded; Federal Work-Study and scholarships/grants also available. Financial award applicants required to submit FAFSA. In 2008, 19 master's awarded. *Degree program information:* Part-time and evening/weekend programs available. Offers administration (MS); biology (MA, MS); mathematics teaching (MA); mathematics, science, and engineering (MA, MS); medical nutrition therapy (MS); multidisciplinary sciences (MA); nutrition education and health promotion (MS); nutrition services administration (MS); research statistics (MS). *Application deadline:* Applications are processed on a rolling basis. *Application fee:* $20. Electronic applications accepted. *Application Contact:* Andrea Cyterski-Acosta, Dean of Enrollment, 210-829-6005, Fax: 210-829-3921, E-mail: admis@uiwtx.edu. *Dean,* Dr. Glen Edward James, 210-829-3152, Fax: 210-829-3153, E-mail: gjames@uiwtx.edu.

School of Nursing and Health Professions Students: 22 full-time (11 women), 71 part-time (56 women); includes 34 minority (10 African Americans, 1 Asian American or Pacific Islander, 23 Hispanic Americans), 34 international. Average age 37. *Faculty:* 9 full-time (7 women), 3 part-time/adjunct (2 women). Expenses: Contact institution. *Financial support:* Research assistantships, Federal Work-Study, scholarships/grants, and tuition waivers (partial) available. Financial award applicants required to submit FAFSA. In 2008, 17 master's awarded. *Degree program information:* Part-time and evening/weekend programs available. Offers kinesiology (MS); nursing (MSN); nursing and health professions (MS, MSN, Certificate); sport management (MS, Certificate); sport pedagogy (Certificate). *Application deadline:* Applications are processed on a rolling basis. *Application fee:* $20. Electronic applications accepted. *Application Contact:* Andrea Cyterski-Acosta, Dean of Enrollment,

210-829-6005, Fax: 210-829-3921, E-mail: admis@uiwtx.edu. *Dean*, Dr. Kathleen Light, 210-829-3982, Fax: 210-829-3174, E-mail: light@uiwtx.edu.

School of Optometry Expenses: Contact institution. *Financial support:* Federal Work-Study and scholarships/grants available. Financial award applicants required to submit FAFSA. Offers optometry (OD). *Application deadline:* For fall admission, 7/15 for domestic students. Applications are processed on a rolling basis. *Application fee:* $50. Electronic applications accepted. *Application Contact:* Henry Cantu, Director of Admissions and Student Services, 210-883-1193, Fax: 210-883-1191, E-mail: hmcantu@uiwtx.edu. *Founding Dean*, Dr. Hani Ghazi-Birry, 210-883-1190, Fax: 210-883-1191, E-mail: optometry@uiwtx.edu.

UNIVERSITY OF THE PACIFIC, Stockton, CA 95211-0197

General Information Independent, coed, university. CGS member. *Enrollment:* 6,251 graduate, professional, and undergraduate students; 2,087 full-time matriculated graduate/professional students (1,135 women), 707 part-time matriculated graduate/professional students (412 women). *Enrollment by degree level:* 2,155 first professional, 408 master's, 207 doctoral, 24 other advanced degrees. *Graduate faculty:* 276 full-time (112 women), 278 part-time/adjunct (125 women). *Tuition:* Full-time $30,380; part-time $950 per unit. *Required fees:* $300. *Graduate housing:* Rooms and/or apartments available on a first-come, first-served basis to single and married students. Housing application deadline: 7/1. *Student services:* Campus employment opportunities, campus safety program, career counseling, free psychological counseling, international student services, low-cost health insurance, multicultural affairs office, services for students with disabilities, teacher training. *Online resources:* library catalog, web page. *Research affiliation:* Lawrence Hall of Science.

Computer facilities: 350 computers available on campus for general student use. A campuswide network can be accessed from student residence rooms and from off campus. Online class registration is available. *Web address:* http://www.pacific.edu/.

General Application Contact: Office of Graduate Admissions, 209-946-2344.

GRADUATE UNITS

Arthur A. Dugoni School of Dentistry Expenses: Contact institution. *Financial support:* In 2008–09, 374 students received support. Institutionally sponsored loans, scholarships/grants, and stipends available. Support available to part-time students. Financial award application deadline: 3/2; financial award applicants required to submit FAFSA. Offers advanced education in general dentistry (Certificate); dentistry (DDS, MSD, Certificate); international dental studies (DDS); oral and maxillofacial surgery (Certificate). *Application deadline:* For fall admission, 9/15 priority date for international students. Applications are processed on a rolling basis. Electronic applications accepted. *Application Contact:* Dr. Craig S. Yarborough, Associate Dean for Institutional Advancement and Student Services, 415-929-6491. *Dean*, Dr. Arthur A. Dugoni, 415-929-6424.

College of the Pacific Students: 6 full-time (3 women), 77 part-time (52 women); includes 21 minority (3 African Americans, 1 American Indian/Alaska Native, 11 Asian Americans or Pacific Islanders, 6 Hispanic Americans), 3 international. Average age 26. 103 applicants, 53% accepted, 39 enrolled. *Faculty:* 38 full-time (13 women), 5 part-time/adjunct (3 women). Expenses: Contact institution. *Financial support:* Teaching assistantships, institutionally sponsored loans available. Support available to part-time students. Financial award application deadline: 3/1; financial award applicants required to submit FAFSA. In 2008, 15 master's awarded. Offers biological sciences (MS); communication (MA); psychology (MA); sport sciences (MA). *Application fee:* $75. *Application Contact:* Information Contact, 209-946-2261. *Dean*, Dr. Robert Cox, 209-946-2023.

Conservatory of Music Students: 8 full-time (6 women), 10 part-time (8 women); includes 4 minority (2 African Americans or Pacific Islanders, 2 Hispanic Americans), 1 international. Average age 28. 16 applicants, 63% accepted, 6 enrolled. *Faculty:* 4 full-time (3 women), 3 part-time/adjunct (2 women). Expenses: Contact institution. *Financial support:* Teaching assistantships, institutionally sponsored loans available. Support available to part-time students. Financial award application deadline: 3/1; financial award applicants required to submit FAFSA. In 2008, 1 master's awarded. Offers music (MA, MM); music education (MM); music therapy (MA). *Application deadline:* For fall admission, 3/1 priority date for domestic students; for spring admission, 10/1 priority date for domestic students. Applications are processed on a rolling basis. *Application fee:* $75. *Application Contact:* Dr. Therese West, Chairperson, 209-946-3194. *Dean*, Dr. Steven Anderson, 209-946-2417.

Eberhardt School of Business Students: 38 full-time (23 women), 3 part-time (all women); includes 10 minority (1 African American, 9 Asian Americans or Pacific Islanders), 8 international. Average age 25. 65 applicants, 49% accepted, 21 enrolled. *Faculty:* 24 full-time (9 women). Expenses: Contact institution. *Financial support:* Fellowships, research assistantships, Federal Work-Study and institutionally sponsored loans available. Support available to part-time students. Financial award application deadline: 3/1; financial award applicants required to submit FAFSA. In 2008, 33 master's awarded. *Degree program information:* Part-time programs available. Offers business (MBA). *Application deadline:* For fall admission, 7/31 priority date for domestic students; for spring admission, 11/30 for domestic students. Applications are processed on a rolling basis. *Application fee:* $75. *Application Contact:* Dr. Chris Lozano, MBA Recruiting Director, 209-946-2597, Fax: 209-946-2586, E-mail: clozano@pacific.edu. *Dean*, Dr. Richard Flaherty, 209-946-2466, Fax: 209-946-2586.

McGeorge School of Law Students: 620 full-time (304 women), 396 part-time (194 women); includes 271 minority (33 African Americans, 14 American Indian/Alaska Native, 134 Asian Americans or Pacific Islanders, 90 Hispanic Americans). Average age 24. 2,627 applicants, 41% accepted. *Faculty:* 55 full-time (22 women), 73 part-time/adjunct (34 women). Expenses: Contact institution. *Financial support:* In 2008–09, 925 students received support, including 9 fellowships, 76 research assistantships (averaging $1,961 per year); career-related internships or fieldwork, Federal Work-Study, institutionally sponsored loans, and scholarships/grants also available. Support available to part-time students. Financial award applicants required to submit FAFSA. In 2008, 301 JDs, 49 master's awarded. *Degree program information:* Part-time and evening/weekend programs available. Offers advocacy (JD); advocacy practice and teaching (LL M); criminal justice (JD); intellectual property (JD); international legal studies (JD); international water resources law (LL M, JSD); law (JD); public law and policy (JD); public policy and law (LL M); tax (JD); transnational business practice (LL M). *Application deadline:* For fall admission, 3/15 priority date for domestic students. Applications are processed on a rolling basis. *Application fee:* $50. Electronic applications accepted. *Application Contact:* 916-739-7105, Fax: 916-739-7134, E-mail: admissionsmcgeorge@uop.edu. *Dean*, Elizabeth Rindskopf Parker, 916-739-7151, E-mail: elizabeth@uop.edu.

School of Education Students: 80 full-time (59 women), 123 part-time (80 women); includes 69 minority (17 African Americans, 16 Asian Americans or Pacific Islanders, 36 Hispanic Americans), 3 international. Average age 35. 116 applicants, 80% accepted, 62 enrolled. *Faculty:* 20 full-time (12 women), 5 part-time/adjunct (all women). Expenses: Contact institution. *Financial support:* In 2008–09, 13 teaching assistantships were awarded; institutionally sponsored loans also available. Support available to part-time students. Financial award application deadline: 3/1; financial award applicants required to submit FAFSA. In 2008, 57 master's, 24 doctorates awarded. Offers curriculum and instruction (M Ed, MA, Ed D); education (M Ed); educational administration (MA, Ed D); educational psychology (MA, Ed D); school psychology (Ed S); special education (MA). *Application deadline:* For fall admission, 3/1 priority date for domestic students; for spring admission, 10/15 for domestic students. Applications are processed on a rolling basis. *Application fee:* $75. *Application Contact:* Office of Graduate Admissions, 209-946-2344. *Dean*, Dr. Lynn Beck, 209-946-2683, E-mail: lbeck@pacific.edu.

School of International Studies *Faculty:* 7 full-time (4 women). Expenses: Contact institution. *Financial support:* Application deadline: 3/1. Offers intercultural relations (MA); international studies (MA). *Application fee:* $75. *Application Contact:* Office of Graduate Admissions, 209-946-2344. *Dean*, Dr. Margee Ensign, 209-946-2650, E-mail: mensign@pacific.edu.

School of Pharmacy and Health Sciences Students: 756 full-time (478 women), 80 part-time (49 women); includes 464 minority (10 African Americans, 1 American Indian/Alaska Native, 419 Asian Americans or Pacific Islanders, 34 Hispanic Americans), 47 international. Average age 27. 411 applicants, 34% accepted, 76 enrolled. *Faculty:* 59 full-time (29 women), 25 part-time/adjunct (17 women). Expenses: Contact institution. *Financial support:* In 2008–09, 33 teaching assistantships were awarded; career-related internships or fieldwork, Federal Work-Study, and institutionally sponsored loans also available. Support available to part-time students. Financial award application deadline: 3/1; financial award applicants required to submit FAFSA. In 2008, 189 first professional degrees, 29 master's, 42 doctorates awarded. Offers pharmaceutical sciences (MS, PhD); pharmacy (Pharm D); pharmacy and health sciences (Pharm D, MS, DPT, PhD); physical therapy (MS, DPT); speech-language pathology (MS). *Application fee:* $75. *Application Contact:* Cyndi Porter, Outreach Officer, 209-946-3957, Fax: 209-946-2410, E-mail: cporter@pacific.edu. *Dean*, Dr. Philip Oppenheimer, 209-946-2561, Fax: 209-946-2410.

UNIVERSITY OF THE ROCKIES, Colorado Springs, CO 80903

General Information Independent, coed, graduate-only institution.

GRADUATE UNITS

Graduate Programs

UNIVERSITY OF THE SACRED HEART, San Juan, PR 00914-0383

General Information Independent-religious, coed, comprehensive institution. *Graduate housing:* Room and/or apartments available on a first-come, first-served basis to single students; on-campus housing not available to married students. Housing application deadline: 5/31.

GRADUATE UNITS

Graduate Programs *Degree program information:* Part-time and evening/weekend programs available. Offers contemporary culture and media (MA); creative writing (MA); early childhood education (M Ed); editing for media (MA); human resource management (MBA); human rights and anti-discriminatory processes (MASJ); information systems auditing (MS); information systems management (MBA); instruction systems and education technology (M Ed); International marketing (MBA); management information systems (MBA); marketing (MBA); mediation and transformation of conflicts (MASJ); non-profit organization (MS); occupational health and safety (MS); occupational nursing (MSN); public relations (MA); publicity (MA); scriptwriting (MA); taxation (MBA).

UNIVERSITY OF THE SCIENCES IN PHILADELPHIA, Philadelphia, PA 19104-4495

General Information Independent, coed, university. CGS member. *Enrollment:* 3,000 graduate, professional, and undergraduate students; 119 full-time matriculated graduate/professional students (73 women), 174 part-time matriculated graduate/professional students (105 women). *Enrollment by degree level:* 3 first professional, 189 master's, 91 doctoral, 10 other advanced degrees. *Graduate faculty:* 50 full-time (13 women), 31 part-time/adjunct (11 women). *Tuition:* Full-time $21,402; part-time $1189 per credit. Tuition and fees vary according to program. *Graduate housing:* On-campus housing not available. *Student services:* Campus employment opportunities, campus safety program, career counseling, free psychological counseling, international student services, low-cost health insurance, services for students with disabilities, writing training. *Library facilities:* Joseph W. England Library plus 1 other. *Online resources:* library catalog, web page, access to other libraries' catalogs. *Collection:* 87,125 titles, 9,817 serial subscriptions. *Research affiliation:* Progenra (Molecular Biology), Biotech, Pharma & Device (Drug Delivery), Encapsulation Systems (analytical chemistry), Johnson and Johnson (cell biology), Ortho-McNeil (Pharmacy), Polymedix (computational chemistry).

Computer facilities: Computer purchase and lease plans are available. 190 computers available on campus for general student use. A campuswide network can be accessed from student residence rooms and from off campus. Online class registration is available. *Web address:* http://www.usip.edu/.

General Application Contact: Dr. Rodney J. Wigent, Dean, College of Graduate Studies, 215-596-8886, Fax: 215-895-1185, E-mail: graduate@usp.edu.

GRADUATE UNITS

College of Graduate Studies Students: 119 full-time (73 women), 174 part-time (105 women); includes 38 minority (11 African Americans, 24 Asian Americans or Pacific Islanders, 3 Hispanic Americans), 48 international. Average age 32. 865 applicants, 26% accepted, 69 enrolled. *Faculty:* 50 full-time (13 women), 31 part-time/adjunct (11 women). Expenses: Contact institution. *Financial support:* In 2008–09, 2 fellowships with full tuition reimbursements (averaging $21,999 per year), 5 research assistantships with full tuition reimbursements (averaging $13,840 per year), 33 teaching assistantships with full and partial tuition reimbursements (averaging $19,455 per year) were awarded; institutionally sponsored loans, scholarships/grants, traineeships, tuition waivers (full and partial), and unspecified assistantships also available. Support available to part-time students. Financial award application deadline: 5/1. In 2008, 1 first professional degree, 75 master's, 12 doctorates, 7 other advanced degrees awarded. *Degree program information:* Part-time and evening/weekend programs available. Offers biochemistry (MS, PhD); bioinformatics (MS); biomedical writing (MS); cell and molecular biology (PhD); cell biology (MS); chemistry (MS, PhD); health policy (MPH, MS); health psychology (MS); medical marketing writing (Certificate); pharmaceutical business (MBA); pharmaceutics (MS, PhD); pharmacognosy (MS, PhD); pharmacology (MS, PhD); pharmacy administration (MS); public health (MPH); regulatory affairs writing (Certificate); toxicology (MS, PhD). *Application deadline:* For fall admission, 5/1 for international students; for winter admission, 10/1 for international students; for spring admission, 3/1 for international students. Applications are processed on a rolling basis. *Application fee:* $50. Electronic applications accepted. *Application Contact:* Joyce D'Angelo, Administrative Assistant, 215-596-8937, E-mail: j.dangel@usp.edu. *Dean*, Dr. Rodney J. Wigent, 215-596-8886, Fax: 215-895-1185, E-mail: graduate@usp.edu.

Mayes College of Healthcare Business and Policy Students: 37 full-time (22 women), 108 part-time (66 women); includes 5 African Americans, 12 Asian Americans or Pacific Islanders, 4 international. 95 applicants, 72% accepted, 30 enrolled. *Faculty:* 17 full-time (7 women), 25 part-time/adjunct (8 women). Expenses: Contact institution. Offers healthcare business and policy (MBA, MPH, MS, PhD, Certificate). *Application Contact:* Joyce D'Angelo, Administrative Assistant, 215-596-8937, E-mail: j.dangel@usp.edu. *Dean*, Dr. Rodney J. Wigent, 215-596-8886, Fax: 215-895-1185, E-mail: graduate@usp.edu.

Misher College of Arts and Sciences Students: 54 full-time (33 women), 38 part-time (24 women); includes 6 African Americans, 5 Asian Americans or Pacific Islanders, 28 international. Average age 27. 164 applicants, 48% accepted, 22 enrolled. *Faculty:* 24 full-time (6 women), 6 part-time/adjunct (3 women). Expenses: Contact institution. *Financial support:* In 2008–09, 1 fellowship, 3 research assistantships (averaging $11,371 per year), 16 teaching assistantships (averaging $18,595 per year) were awarded. In 2008, 25 master's, 3 doctorates awarded. Offers arts and sciences (MS, PhD). *Application Contact:* Joyce D'Angelo, Administrative Assistant, 215-596-8937, E-mail: j.dangel@usp.edu. *Dean*, Dr. Rodney J. Wigent, 215-596-8886, Fax: 215-895-1185, E-mail: graduate@usp.edu.

Philadelphia College of Pharmacy Students: 28 full-time (18 women), 28 part-time (15 women); includes 7 Asian Americans or Pacific Islanders, 16 international. Average age 31. 556 applicants, 6% accepted, 16 enrolled. *Faculty:* 9 full-time (0 women). Expenses: Contact institution. *Financial support:* In 2008–09, 3 students received support, including 1 fellowship (averaging $22,000 per year), 2 research assistantships (averaging $17,550 per year), 17 teaching assistantships (averaging $20,265 per year); career-related internships or fieldwork also available. Support available to part-time students. Financial award application deadline: 4/15; financial award applicants required to submit FAFSA. In 2008, 2 first professional degrees, 9 master's, 6 doctorates awarded. Offers pharmacy (Pharm D, MS, PhD). *Application deadline:* For fall admission, 4/15 for domestic students; for spring admission, 10/24 for domestic students. *Application fee:* $50. *Application Contact:* Andrea Bagden, Secretary, 215-596-8492, Fax: 215-895-1185, E-mail: flex@usip.edu. *Dean*, Dr. George E. Downs, 215-596-8939, Fax: 215-596-8977.

UNIVERSITY OF THE SOUTHWEST, Hobbs, NM 88240-9129

General Information Independent, coed, comprehensive institution. *Enrollment:* 588 graduate, professional, and undergraduate students; 116 full-time matriculated graduate/professional

University of the Southwest (continued)

students (82 women), 74 part-time matriculated graduate/professional students (49 women). *Enrollment by degree level:* 190 master's. *Graduate faculty:* 6 full-time (5 women), 3 part-time/adjunct (1 woman). *Tuition:* Full-time $5400; part-time $425 per credit hour. *Graduate housing:* Room and/or apartments available to single students; on-campus housing not available to married students. Typical cost: $4200 per year ($6810 including board). *Student services:* Campus employment opportunities, teacher training.

Computer facilities: 35 computers available on campus for general student use. A campuswide network can be accessed from student residence rooms. Online class registration is available. *Web address:* http://www.usw.edu/.

General Application Contact: Dr. Steve Hill, Dean/Recruiting, 505-392-6561 Ext. 1010, Fax: 575-392-6006, E-mail: shill@usw.edu.

GRADUATE UNITS

Graduate Programs Students: 116 full-time (82 women), 74 part-time (49 women); includes 70 minority (5 African Americans, 65 Hispanic Americans). Average age 37. 97 applicants, 94% accepted, 87 enrolled. *Faculty:* 6 full-time (5 women), 3 part-time/adjunct (1 woman). Expenses: Contact institution. *Financial support:* In 2008–09, 83 students received support, including 1 research assistantship with partial tuition reimbursement available; Federal Work-Study, scholarships/grants, and tuition waivers (partial) also available. Support available to part-time students. Financial award application deadline: 4/1; financial award applicants required to submit FAFSA. In 2008, 34 master's awarded. *Degree program information:* Part-time and evening/weekend programs available. Postbaccalaureate distance learning degree programs offered. Offers business administration (MBA); curriculum and instruction (MSE); early childhood education (MSE); educational administration (MSE); educational counseling (MSE); educational diagnostician (MSE); school business administration (MSE); special education (MSE). *Application deadline:* For fall admission, 3/1 priority date for domestic students; for spring admission, 10/1 for domestic students. Applications are processed on a rolling basis. *Application fee:* $50. Electronic applications accepted. *Application Contact:* Kerrie Mitchell, Coordinator of Financial Aid, 575-392-6561 Ext. 1075, Fax: 575-392-6006, E-mail: kmitchell@usw.edu. *Provost,* Dr. Dennis G. Atherton, 505-392-6561 Ext. 1069, Fax: 505-392-6006, E-mail: datherton@usw.edu.

UNIVERSITY OF THE VIRGIN ISLANDS, Saint Thomas, VI 00802-9990

General Information Territory-supported, coed, comprehensive institution. *Enrollment:* 2,393 graduate, professional, and undergraduate students; 45 full-time matriculated graduate/professional students (34 women), 116 part-time matriculated graduate/professional students (103 women). *Enrollment by degree level:* 161 master's. *Graduate faculty:* 29 full-time (14 women), 9 part-time/adjunct (4 women). Tuition, territory resident: full-time $4950; part-time $275 per credit. Tuition, nonresident: full-time $9900; part-time $550 per credit. *Graduate housing:* On-campus housing not available. *Student services:* Campus employment opportunities, career counseling. *Library facilities:* Ralph M. Paiewonsky Library. *Online resources:* library catalog, web page. *Collection:* 106,361 titles, 113,623 serial subscriptions, 3,000 audiovisual materials.

Computer facilities: A campuswide network can be accessed from student residence rooms and from off campus. Online class registration is available. *Web address:* http://www.uvi.edu/.

General Application Contact: Edward L. Alexander, Director of Admissions, 340-693-1224, Fax: 340-693-1167, E-mail: ealexan@uvi.edu.

GRADUATE UNITS

Graduate Programs Students: 45 full-time (34 women), 116 part-time (103 women); includes 124 minority (115 African Americans, 3 Asian Americans or Pacific Islanders, 6 Hispanic Americans), 13 international. Average age 37. 141 applicants, 60% accepted, 49 enrolled. *Faculty:* 24 full-time (8 women), 9 part-time/adjunct (5 women). Expenses: Contact institution. *Financial support:* Career-related internships or fieldwork and scholarships/grants available. Financial award application deadline: 4/15; financial award applicants required to submit FAFSA. In 2008, 454 master's awarded. *Degree program information:* Part-time and evening/weekend programs available. *Application deadline:* For fall admission, 4/30 for domestic and international students; for spring admission, 10/30 for domestic and international students. Applications are processed on a rolling basis. *Application fee:* $30. *Application Contact:* Edward L. Alexander, Director of Admissions/Registrar, Fax: 340-693-1167, E-mail: ealexan@uvi.edu.

Division of Business Administration Students: 8 full-time (5 women), 16 part-time (13 women); includes 19 minority (all African Americans), 2 international. Average age 34. 24 applicants, 58% accepted, 8 enrolled. *Faculty:* 7 full-time (1 woman). Expenses: Contact institution. *Financial support:* Application deadline: 4/15. In 2008, 3 master's awarded. *Degree program information:* Part-time and evening/weekend programs available. Offers business administration (MBA). *Application deadline:* For fall admission, 4/30 for domestic and international students; for spring admission, 10/30 for domestic and international students. *Application fee:* $30. *Application Contact:* Edward L. Alexander, Director of Admissions, 340-693-1224, Fax: 340-693-1167, E-mail: ealexan@uvi.edu. *Dean,* Dr. Micheal Vineyard, 340-693-1301, Fax: 340-693-1305, E-mail: mvineyar@uvi.edu.

Division of Education Students: 16 full-time (all women), 83 part-time (77 women); includes 79 minority (71 African Americans, 3 Asian Americans or Pacific Islanders, 5 Hispanic Americans), 10 international. Average age 36. 62 applicants, 74% accepted, 24 enrolled. *Faculty:* 8 full-time (5 women), 6 part-time/adjunct (4 women). Expenses: Contact institution. *Financial support:* Scholarships/grants available. Financial award application deadline: 4/15. In 2008, 42 master's awarded. *Degree program information:* Part-time and evening/weekend programs available. Offers education (MAE). *Application deadline:* For fall admission, 4/30 for domestic and international students; for spring admission, 11/30 for domestic and international students. *Application fee:* $25. *Application Contact:* Edward L. Alexander, Director of Admissions, 340-693-1224, Fax: 340-693-1167, E-mail: ealexan@uvi.edu. *Interim Dean,* Dr. Joane McKay, 340-693-1321, Fax: 340-693-1335, E-mail: jmckay@uvi.edu.

Division of Humanities and Social Sciences Students: 5 full-time (all women), 16 part-time (12 women); includes 20 minority (18 African Americans, 2 Hispanic Americans), 1 international. Average age 37. 15 applicants, 67% accepted, 9 enrolled. *Faculty:* 1 full-time (0 women), 2 part-time/adjunct (0 women). Expenses: Contact institution. *Financial support:* Career-related internships or fieldwork and scholarships/grants available. Financial award application deadline: 4/15; financial award applicants required to submit FAFSA. In 2008, 2 master's awarded. *Degree program information:* Part-time and evening/weekend programs available. Offers humanities and social sciences (MPA). *Application deadline:* For fall admission, 4/30 for domestic and international students; for spring admission, 10/30 for domestic and international students. *Application fee:* $30. *Application Contact:* Edward L. Alexander, Director of Admissions, 340-693-1224, Fax: 340-693-1167, E-mail: ealexan@uvi.edu. *Dean,* Dr. George Lord, 340-693-1261, Fax: 340-693-1265, E-mail: glord@uvi.edu.

Division of Science and Mathematics Students: 16 full-time (8 women), 1 (woman) part-time; includes 8 minority (7 African Americans, 1 Hispanic American). Average age 31. 37 applicants, 76% accepted, 8 enrolled. *Faculty:* 8 full-time (2 women), 1 (woman) part-time/adjunct. Expenses: Contact institution. *Financial support:* Career-related internships or fieldwork and scholarships/grants available. Financial award application deadline: 4/15; financial award applicants required to submit FAFSA. In 2008, 7 master's awarded. *Degree program information:* Part-time programs available. Postbaccalaureate distance learning degree programs offered. Offers environmental and marine science (MS); mathematics for secondary teachers (MA); science and mathematics (MA, MS). *Application deadline:* For fall admission, 4/30 for domestic and international students; for spring admission, 10/30 for domestic and international students. *Application fee:* $30. *Application Contact:* Edward L. Alexander, Director of Admissions, 340-693-1224, Fax: 340-693-1167, E-mail: ealexan@uvi.edu. *Dean,* Dr. Camille McKayle, 340-693-1230, Fax: 340-693-1245, E-mail: cmkayl@uvi.edu.

UNIVERSITY OF THE WEST, Rosemead, CA 91770

General Information Independent, coed, comprehensive institution. *Graduate housing:* Room and/or apartments guaranteed to single students; on-campus housing not available to married students.

GRADUATE UNITS

Department of Business Administration *Degree program information:* Part-time and evening/weekend programs available. Offers business administration (EMBA); finance (MBA); information technology and management (MBA); international business (MBA); nonprofit organization management (MBA).

Department of Religious Studies *Degree program information:* Part-time and evening/weekend programs available. Offers Buddhist studies (MA, DBS); comparative religions (MA); religious studies (PhD).

THE UNIVERSITY OF TOLEDO, Toledo, OH 43606-3390

General Information State-supported, coed, university. CGS member. *Graduate housing:* Room and/or apartments available to single students; on-campus housing not available to married students. *Research affiliation:* NASA–Glen Research Center at Lewis Field (aerospace engineering), Merck and Company (pharmaceutical research), Midwest Astronomical Data Reduction and Analysis Facility (astronomy), Edison Industrial Systems Center (systems integration, quality control, mathematical modeling), Ohio Aerospace Institute (aerospace research), National Renewable Energy Laboratory (thin films, photovoltaics).

GRADUATE UNITS

College of Graduate Studies *Degree program information:* Part-time and evening/weekend programs available. Postbaccalaureate distance learning degree programs offered. Electronic applications accepted.

College of Arts and Sciences *Degree program information:* Part-time and evening/weekend programs available. Offers analytical chemistry (MS, PhD); applied mathematics (MS, PhD); arts and sciences (MA, MLS, MMP, MPA, MS, PhD, Certificate); behavioral (PhD); biological chemistry (MS, PhD); biology (MS, PhD); biology (ecology track) (MS, PhD); clinical psychology (PhD); communication studies (Certificate); economics (MA); English as a second language (MA); experimental psychology (MA); French (MA); geographic information systems and applied geographics (Certificate); geography (MA); geology (MS); German (MA); health care policy (MPA); healthcare policy (Certificate); history (MA, PhD); inorganic chemistry (MS, PhD); liberal studies (MLS); literature (MA); mathematics (MA, PhD); municipal administration (MPA, Certificate); organic chemistry (MS, PhD); performance (MMP); philosophy (MA); physical chemistry (MS, PhD); physics (MS, PhD); planning (MA); political science (MA); public administration (MPA, Certificate); sociology (MA); Spanish (MA); statistics (MS, PhD); teaching of writing (Certificate). Electronic applications accepted.

College of Business Administration *Degree program information:* Part-time and evening/weekend programs available. Offers accounting (MBA, MSA); business administration (EMBA, MBA, MSA, DME); business administration-general (MBA); finance and business economics (MBA); human resource management (MBA); information systems (MBA); international business (MBA); management (MBA); manufacturing management (MBA, DME); marketing (MBA); operations management (MBA). Electronic applications accepted.

College of Education *Degree program information:* Part-time and evening/weekend programs available. Offers art education (ME); career and technical education (Ed S); career and technical training (ME); curriculum and instruction (ME, DE, PhD, Ed S); early childhood education (ME, Ed S); education (MAE, ME, MES, MME, DE, PhD, Ed S); education and biology (MES); education and chemistry (MES); education and economics (MAE); education and English (MAE); education and French (MAE); education and geology (MES); education and German (MAE); education and history (MAE); education and mathematics (MAE, MES); education and physics (MES); education and political science (MAE); education and sociology (MAE); education and Spanish (MAE); educational administration and supervision (ME, DE, Ed S); educational media (DE, PhD, Ed S); educational psychology (ME, DE, PhD); educational research and measurement (ME, PhD); educational sociology (DE, PhD); educational technology (ME); educational theory and social foundations (ME); elementary education (DE, PhD, Ed S); English as a second language (MAE); foundations of education (DE, PhD); gifted and talented (PhD, Ed S); health education (ME); higher education (ME, PhD); history of education (DE, PhD); middle childhood education (ME); music education (MME); philosophy of education (DE, PhD); physical education (ME); secondary education (ME, DE, PhD, Ed S); special education (ME, DE, PhD, Ed S). Electronic applications accepted.

College of Engineering Students: 177 full-time (38 women), 156 part-time (30 women); includes 5 minority (4 African Americans, 1 Hispanic American), 239 international. Average age 28. 446 applicants, 58% accepted, 126 enrolled. *Faculty:* 68 full-time (11 women). Expenses: Contact institution. *Financial support:* In 2008–09, 76 research assistantships with full tuition reimbursements (averaging $14,262 per year), 122 teaching assistantships with full tuition reimbursements (averaging $13,615 per year) were awarded; Federal Work-Study, scholarships/grants, tuition waivers (full and partial), and unspecified assistantships also available. Support available to part-time students. Financial award application deadline: 4/1. In 2008, 73 master's, 13 doctorates awarded. *Degree program information:* Part-time and evening/weekend programs available. Postbaccalaureate distance learning degree programs offered (minimal on-campus study). Offers bioengineering (MS, PhD); biomedical engineering (PhD); chemical engineering (MS, PhD); civil engineering (MS, PhD); computer science (MS, PhD); electrical engineering (MS, PhD); engineering (MS, PhD); general engineering (MS); industrial engineering (MS, PhD); mechanical engineering (MS, PhD). *Application deadline:* For fall admission, 5/31 priority date for domestic students. Applications are processed on a rolling basis. *Application fee:* $45. Electronic applications accepted. *Application Contact:* Dr. Mohamed Samir Hefzy, PhD, Professor and Associate Dean, Graduate Studies and Research Administration, 419-530-7391, Fax: 419-530-7392, E-mail: mhefzy@eng.utoledo.edu. *Professor and Dean,* Dr. Nagi Naganathan, PhD, 419-530-8000, Fax: 419-530-8006, E-mail: nagi.naganathan@utoledo.edu.

College of Health Science and Human Service Offers community counseling (MA); counselor education (MA, PhD, Ed S); counselor education and school psychology (MA, PhD, Ed S); counselor education and supervision (PhD); criminal justice (MA, Certificate); exercise science (MSX, PhD); guidance/counselor education (PhD); health and rehabilitative services (MA); health education (PhD); health science and human service (MA, MS, MSBS, MSW, MSX, DPT, OTD, PhD, Certificate, Ed S); human donation science (MS, Certificate); juvenile justice (Certificate); kinesiology (MSX, PhD); occupational therapy (OTD); physical therapy (DPT); physician assistant studies (MSBS); recreation and leisure (MA); school counseling (MA); school psychology (MA, Ed S); severe behavioral spectrum (Certificate); social work (MSW); speech-language pathology (MA).

College of Medicine Offers anatomic pathology (Certificate); biochemistry and molecular biology (MSBS); bioinformatics and proteomics/genomics (MSBS, Certificate); biostatistics and epidemiology (Certificate); cancer biology (MSBS, PhD); cardiovascular and metabolic diseases (MSBS, PhD); contemporary gerontological practice (Certificate); diagnostic radiology (MSBS); emergency response (Certificate); gerontology (Certificate); global health (Certificate); infection, immunity and transplantation (MSBS); infection, immunology and transplantation (PhD); medical physics (MSBS); medical physics-clinical radiation oncology (MSBS); medical sciences (MSBS); medicine (MPH, MS, MSBS, MSOH, PhD, Certificate, PhD/MSBS); neurosciences and neurological disorders (MS, PhD); occupational health (MSOH, Certificate); oral biology (MSBS); orthopedic science (MSBS); pathology (Certificate); public health (MPH, Certificate); radiation oncology (MSBS); surgery (MSBS); urology (MSBS). Electronic applications accepted.

College of Nursing *Degree program information:* Part-time programs available. Offers adult health practitioner/clinical nurse specialist (MSN); adult nurse practitioner (Certificate); entry-level nursing initiative (GEMINI) (MSN); family nurse practitioner (MSN, Certificate); nursing education (Certificate); pediatric nurse practitioner (Certificate); pediatric nurse practitioner/clinical nurse specialist (MSN); RN to MSN (MSN).

College of Pharmacy Offers administrative pharmacy (MSPS); industrial pharmacy (MSPS); medicinal and biological chemistry (MS, PhD); pharmacology toxicology (MSPS); pharmacy (MS, MSPS, PhD). Electronic applications accepted.

College of Law Students: 342 full-time (135 women), 152 part-time (57 women); includes 42 minority (15 African Americans, 1 American Indian/Alaska Native, 9 Asian Americans or Pacific Islanders, 17 Hispanic Americans), 10 international. Average age 27. 1,023 applicants, 32% accepted, 137 enrolled. *Faculty:* 31 full-time (12 women), 16 part-time/adjunct (5 women). Expenses: Contact institution. *Financial support:* In 2008–09, 496 students received support, including 17 research assistantships (averaging $516 per year), 33 teaching assistantships; career-related internships or fieldwork, Federal Work-Study, and scholarships/grants also available. Support available to part-time students. Financial award application deadline: 8/1; financial award applicants required to submit FAFSA. In 2008, 141 JDs awarded. *Degree program information:* Part-time and evening/weekend programs available. Offers law (JD). *Application deadline:* For fall admission, 7/31 priority date for domestic students, 7/31 for international students. Applications are processed on a rolling basis. *Application fee:* $0. Electronic applications accepted. *Application Contact:* Carol E. Frendt, Assistant Dean of Law Admissions, 419-530-4131, Fax: 419-530-4345, E-mail: law.admissions@utoledo.edu. *Dean,* Douglas E. Ray, 419-530-2379, Fax: 419-530-4526, E-mail: douglas.ray@utoledo.edu.

UNIVERSITY OF TORONTO, Toronto, ON M5S 1A1, Canada

General Information Province-supported, coed, university. CGS member. *Graduate housing:* Rooms and/or apartments available on a first-come, first-served basis to single students and available to married students. *Student services:* Campus employment opportunities, campus safety program, career counseling, child daycare facilities, exercise/wellness program, free psychological counseling, international student services, services for students with disabilities, writing training. *Library facilities:* Robart's Library plus 43 others. *Online resources:* library catalog, web page. *Collection:* 13.4 million titles, 77,145 serial subscriptions. *Research affiliation:* Fields Institute for Research in Mathematical Sciences, Canadian Institute for Theoretical Astrophysics, Royal Ontario Museum, Pontifical Institute of Medieval Studies, Hospital for Sick Children, Center for Addiction and Mental Health.

Computer facilities: 2,000 computers available on campus for general student use. A campuswide network can be accessed from student residence rooms and from off campus. *Web address:* http://www.utoronto.ca/uoft.html.

General Application Contact: Information Contact, 416-978-7756, Fax: 416-978-4367, E-mail: gradschool@utoronto.ca.

GRADUATE UNITS

Faculty of Dentistry Offers dental anesthesia (M Sc); dental public health (M Sc); dentistry (DDS, M Sc, PhD); endodontics (M Sc); oral and maxillofacial surgery and anesthesia (M Sc); oral pathology (M Sc); oral radiology (M Sc); orthodontics (M Sc); pediatric dentistry (M Sc); periodontology (M Sc); prosthodontics (M Sc).

Faculty of Law *Degree program information:* Part-time programs available. Offers law (JD, LL M, MSL, SJD).

Faculty of Medicine Offers medicine (MD, M Sc, M Sc BMC, M Sc OT, M Sc PT, MH Sc, PhD).

School of Graduate Studies Students: 12,039 full-time (6,677 women), 1,847 part-time (1,263 women). 22,012 applicants, 38% accepted, 4938 enrolled. *Faculty:* 4,049. Expenses: Contact institution. *Financial support:* In 2008–09, 6,466 fellowships (averaging $6,774 per year), 320 research assistantships (averaging $5,572 per year), 4,300 teaching assistantships (averaging $3,294 per year) were awarded; career-related internships or fieldwork and institutionally sponsored loans also available. In 2008, 3,164 master's, 728 doctorates, 10 other advanced degrees awarded. *Degree program information:* Part-time and evening/weekend programs available. *Application fee:* $100 Canadian dollars. Electronic applications accepted. *Application Contact:* Prof. Susan Pfeiffer, Dean, 416-978-2390, Fax: 416-946-7021, E-mail: sgs.dean@utoronto.ca. *Dean,* Prof. Susan Pfeiffer, 416-978-2390, Fax: 416-946-7021, E-mail: sgs.dean@utoronto.ca.

Humanities Division *Degree program information:* Part-time programs available. Offers art history (MA, PhD); classics (MA, PhD); comparative literature (MA, PhD); composition (M Mus, DMA); drama (MA, PhD); East Asian studies (MA, PhD); English (MA, PhD); French language and literature (MA, PhD); Germanic languages and literatures (MA, PhD); history (MA, PhD); history and philosophy of science and technology (MA, PhD); humanities (M Mus, MA, MM St, MVS, DMA, PhD); Italian studies (MA, PhD); linguistics (MA, PhD); medieval studies (MA, PhD); museum studies (MM St); music education (MA, PhD); musicology/theory (MA, PhD); Near and Middle Eastern civilizations (MA, PhD); performance (M Mus, DMA); philosophy (MA, PhD); religion (MA, PhD); Slavic languages and literatures (MA, PhD); South Asian studies (MA, PhD); Spanish and Portuguese (MA, PhD); visual studies (MVS).

Life Sciences Division *Degree program information:* Part-time programs available. Offers biochemistry (M Sc, PhD); bioethics (MH Sc); biomedical communications (M Sc BMC); cell and systems biology (M Sc, PhD); ecology and evolutionary biology (M Sc, PhD); forestry (M Sc F, MFC, PhD); genetic counseling (M Sc); immunology (M Sc, PhD); laboratory medicine and pathobiology (M Sc, PhD); life sciences (M Sc, M Sc BMC, M Sc F, MA, MFC, MH Sc, MN, PhD); medical biophysics (M Sc, PhD); medical science (M Sc, PhD); molecular and medical genetics (M Sc, PhD); nursing science (MN, PhD); nutritional sciences (M Sc, PhD); pharmaceutical sciences (M Sc, PhD); pharmacology and toxicology (M Sc, PhD); physical education and health (M Sc, PhD); physiology (M Sc, PhD); psychology (MA, PhD); public health sciences (M Sc, MH Sc, PhD); rehabilitation science (M Sc, PhD); speech-language pathology (M Sc, MH Sc, PhD).

Physical Sciences Division *Degree program information:* Part-time programs available. Offers aerospace science and engineering (M Eng, MA Sc, PhD); applied science and engineering (M Eng, MA Sc, MH Sc, PhD); astronomy and astrophysics (M Sc, PhD); biomedical engineering (MA Sc, PhD); chemical engineering and applied chemistry (M Eng, MA Sc, PhD); chemistry (M Sc, PhD); civil engineering (M Eng, MA Sc, PhD); clinical biomedical engineering (MH Sc); computer science (M Sc, PhD); electrical and computer engineering (M Eng, MA Sc, PhD); geology (M Sc, MA Sc, PhD); materials science and engineering (M Eng, MA Sc, PhD); mathematics (M Sc, MMF, PhD); mechanical and industrial engineering (M Eng, MA Sc, PhD); physical sciences (M Eng, M Sc, MA Sc, MH Sc, MMF, PhD); physics (M Sc, PhD); statistics (M Sc, PhD).

Social Sciences Division *Degree program information:* Part-time and evening/weekend programs available. Offers anthropology (M Sc, MA, PhD); architecture, landscape and design (M Arch, MLA, MUD); criminology (MA, PhD); economics (MA, MFE, PhD); education (M Ed, MA, MT, Ed D, PhD); European, Russian and Eurasian studies (MA); geography (M Sc, MA, PhD); industrial relations and human resources (MHRIR, PhD); information studies (MI St, PhD, G Dip); management (MBA, MMPA, PhD); planning (M Sc Pl); political science (MA, PhD); social sciences (M Arch, M Ed, M Sc, M Sc Pl, MA, MBA, MFE, MHRIR, MI St, MLA, MMPA, MSW, MT, MUD, Ed D, PhD, G Dip); social work (MSW, PhD); sociology (M Ed, MA, Ed D, PhD); urban design studies (MUD).

UNIVERSITY OF TRINITY COLLEGE, Toronto, ON M5S 1H8, Canada

General Information Independent-religious, coed, graduate-only institution. *Enrollment by degree level:* 36 first professional, 30 master's, 28 doctoral, 29 other advanced degrees. *Graduate faculty:* 4 full-time (1 woman), 34 part-time/adjunct (7 women). *Graduate tuition:* Tuition and fees charges are reported in Canadian dollars. *Tuition:* Part-time $1889 Canadian dollars per course. *Required fees:* $50 Canadian dollars per semester. Tuition and fees vary according to degree level. *Graduate housing:* Room and/or apartments available on a first-come, first-served basis to single students; on-campus housing not available to married students. Typical cost: $5487 Canadian dollars (including board). Room and board charges vary according to board plan. Housing application deadline: 7/15. *Student services:* Campus employment opportunities, campus safety program, career counseling, child daycare facilities, exercise/wellness program, free psychological counseling, international student services, low-cost health insurance, services for students with disabilities. *Library facilities:* The John W. Graham Library. *Online resources:* library catalog, web page, access to other libraries' catalogs. *Collection:* 200,000 titles, 400 serial subscriptions, 1,500 audiovisual materials.

Computer facilities: 5 computers available on campus for general student use. A campuswide network can be accessed from student residence rooms and from off campus. Online class registration, Anti virus software are available. *Web address:* http://www.trinity.utoronto.ca/.

General Application Contact: Rachel Richards, Administrative Assistant to the Dean, Faculty of Divinity, 416-978-2133, Fax: 416-978-4949, E-mail: divinity@trinity.utoronto.ca.

GRADUATE UNITS

Faculty of Divinity Students: 51 full-time (19 women), 72 part-time (35 women). Average age 45. *Faculty:* 4 full-time (1 woman), 34 part-time/adjunct (7 women). Expenses: Contact institution. *Financial support:* Fellowships, teaching assistantships, career-related internships or fieldwork, institutionally sponsored loans, and bursaries available. Support available to part-time students. Financial award application deadline: 5/15. *Degree program information:* Part-time programs available. Offers ministry (Diploma); ministry for church musicians (Diploma); theology (M Div, MTS, Th M, D Min, PhD, Th D, Diploma, L Th). *Application deadline:* For fall admission, 3/31 priority date for domestic and international students; for winter admission, 12/31 for domestic and international students; for spring admission, 4/30 priority date for domestic and international students. Applications are processed on a rolling basis. *Application fee:* $0. *Application Contact:* Rachel Richards, Administrative Assistant to the Dean, 416-978-2133, Fax: 416-978-4949, E-mail: divinity@trinity.utoronto.ca. *Dean,* Dr. David Neelands, 416-978-7750, Fax: 416-978-4949, E-mail: divdean@trinity.utoronto.ca.

UNIVERSITY OF TULSA, Tulsa, OK 74104-3189

General Information Independent-religious, coed, university. CGS member. *Enrollment:* 4,192 graduate, professional, and undergraduate students; 951 full-time matriculated graduate/professional students (401 women), 247 part-time matriculated graduate/professional students (107 women). *Enrollment by degree level:* 514 master's, 148 doctoral. *Graduate faculty:* 184 full-time (49 women), 21 part-time/adjunct (8 women). *Tuition:* Full-time $15,408; part-time $899 per credit hour. *Required fees:* $3.33 per credit hour. One-time fee: $200 full-time. Tuition and fees vary according to course load and program. *Graduate housing:* Rooms and/or apartments available on a first-come, first-served basis to single and married students. Typical cost: $4368 per year ($7850 including board) for single students; $4368 per year ($11,850 including board) for married students. Room and board charges vary according to board plan and housing facility selected. Housing application deadline: 2/1. *Student services:* Campus employment opportunities, campus safety program, career counseling, child daycare facilities, exercise/wellness program, free psychological counseling, international student services, low-cost health insurance, multicultural affairs office, services for students with disabilities, teacher training, writing training. *Library facilities:* McFarlin Library plus 1 other. *Online resources:* library catalog, web page, access to other libraries' catalogs. *Collection:* 1.1 million titles, 27,905 serial subscriptions, 20,362 audiovisual materials. *Research affiliation:* NEXT (Network of Excellence in Training) (petrophysics), Chevron Texaco (petroleum engineering).

Computer facilities: Computer purchase and lease plans are available. 900 computers available on campus for general student use. A campuswide network can be accessed from student residence rooms and from off campus. Online class registration is available. *Web address:* http://www.utulsa.edu/.

General Application Contact: Dr. Janet A. Haggerty, Associate Vice President of Research and Dean of the Graduate School, 918-631-2336, Fax: 918-631-2156, E-mail: grad@utulsa.edu.

GRADUATE UNITS

College of Law Students: 391 full-time (159 women), 33 part-time (14 women); includes 64 minority (5 African Americans, 41 American Indian/Alaska Native, 8 Asian Americans or Pacific Islanders, 10 Hispanic Americans), 3 international. Average age 27. 1,293 applicants, 44% accepted, 139 enrolled. *Faculty:* 35 full-time (17 women), 32 part-time/adjunct (12 women). Expenses: Contact institution. *Financial support:* In 2008–09, 215 students received support. Federal Work-Study and scholarships/grants available. Support available to part-time students. Financial award applicants required to submit FAFSA. In 2008, 166 first professional degrees, 2 master's awarded. *Degree program information:* Part-time programs available. Offers American Indian and indigenous law (LL M); American law for foreign lawyers (LL M); comparative and international law (Certificate); entrepreneurial law (Certificate); health law (Certificate); law (JD); lawyering skills (Certificate); Native American law (Certificate); public policy and regulation (Certificate); resources, energy, and environmental law (Certificate). *Application deadline:* For fall admission, 2/1 priority date for domestic and international students. Applications are processed on a rolling basis. *Application fee:* $30. Electronic applications accepted. *Application Contact:* April M. Fox, Assistant Dean of Admissions and Financial Aid, 918-631-2406, Fax: 918-631-3630, E-mail: april-fox@utulsa.edu. *Dean,* Janet Levit, 918-631-2400, Fax: 918-631-3126, E-mail: janet-levit@utulsa.edu.

Graduate School Students: 417 full-time (182 women), 245 part-time (116 women); includes 50 minority (8 African Americans, 23 American Indian/Alaska Native, 10 Asian Americans or Pacific Islanders, 9 Hispanic Americans), 186 international. Average age 28. 885 applicants, 52% accepted, 208 enrolled. *Faculty:* 184 full-time (49 women), 21 part-time/adjunct (8 women). Expenses: Contact institution. *Financial support:* In 2008–09, 231 students received support, including 27 fellowships with full and partial tuition reimbursements available (averaging $7,604 per year), 23 research assistantships with full and partial tuition reimbursements available (averaging $9,889 per year), 181 teaching assistantships with full and partial tuition reimbursements available (averaging $9,764 per year); career-related internships or fieldwork, Federal Work-Study, institutionally sponsored loans, scholarships/grants, traineeships, tuition waivers (partial), and unspecified assistantships also available. Support available to part-time students. Financial award application deadline: 2/1; financial award applicants required to submit FAFSA. In 2008, 197 master's, 25 doctorates awarded. *Degree program information:* Part-time and evening/weekend programs available. *Application deadline:* Applications are processed on a rolling basis. *Application fee:* $40. Electronic applications accepted. *Application Contact:* Graduate School, 918-631-2336, Fax: 918-631-2156, E-mail: grad@utulsa.edu. *Associate Vice President of Research and Dean of the Graduate School,* Dr. Janet A. Haggerty, 918-631-2336, Fax: 918-631-2156, E-mail: grad@utulsa.edu.

College of Arts and Sciences Students: 137 full-time (97 women), 67 part-time (49 women); includes 21 minority (7 African Americans, 9 American Indian/Alaska Native, 1 Asian American or Pacific Islander, 4 Hispanic Americans), 8 international. Average age 30. 260 applicants, 48% accepted, 63 enrolled. *Faculty:* 65 full-time (27 women), 8 part-time/adjunct (4 women). Expenses: Contact institution. *Financial support:* In 2008–09, 129 students received support, including 25 fellowships with full and partial tuition reimbursements available (averaging $10,290 per year), 19 research assistantships with full and partial tuition reimbursements available (averaging $12,096 per year), 85 teaching assistantships with full and partial tuition reimbursements available (averaging $8,869 per year); career-related internships or fieldwork, Federal Work-Study, scholarships/grants, traineeships, tuition waivers (full and partial), and unspecified assistantships also available. Support available to part-time students. Financial award application deadline: 2/1; financial award applicants required to submit FAFSA. In 2008, 46 master's, 14 doctorates awarded. *Degree program information:* Part-time and evening/weekend programs available. Offers anthropology (MA); art (MA, MFA, MTA); arts and sciences (MA, MFA, MS, MSMSE, MTA, PhD); clinical psychology (MA, PhD); education (MA); English language and literature (MA, MTA, PhD); history (MA, MTA); industrial/organizational psychology (MA, PhD); mathematics and science education (MSMSE); speech-language pathology (MS); teaching arts (MTA). *Application deadline:* Applications are processed on a rolling basis. *Application fee:* $40. Electronic applications accepted. *Application Contact:* Graduate School, 918-631-2336, Fax: 918-631-2156, E-mail: grad@utulsa.edu. *Dean,* Dr. Dale Thomas Benediktson, 918-631-2222, Fax: 918-631-3721, E-mail: dale-benediktson@utulsa.edu.

College of Engineering and Natural Sciences Students: 125 full-time (38 women), 56 part-time (21 women); includes 14 minority (5 American Indian/Alaska Native, 6 Asian Americans or Pacific Islanders, 3 Hispanic Americans), 77 international. Average age 27. 271 applicants, 50% accepted, 58 enrolled. *Faculty:* 90 full-time (13 women), 13 part-time/adjunct (3 women). Expenses: Contact institution. *Financial support:* In 2008–09, 110

University of Tulsa (continued)

students received support, including 18 fellowships with full and partial tuition reimbursements available (averaging $3,522 per year), 47 research assistantships with full and partial tuition reimbursements available (averaging $8,877 per year), 66 teaching assistantships with full and partial tuition reimbursements available (averaging $10,648 per year); career-related internships or fieldwork, Federal Work-Study, scholarships/grants, tuition waivers (full and partial), and unspecified assistantships also available. Support available to part-time students. Financial award application deadline: 2/1; financial award applicants required to submit FAFSA. In 2008, 65 master's, 6 doctorates awarded. *Degree program information:* Part-time programs available. Offers biochemistry (MS); biological sciences (MS, MTA, PhD); chemical engineering (ME, MSE, PhD); chemistry (MS, PhD); computer science (MS, PhD); electrical engineering (ME, MSE); engineering and natural sciences (ME, MS, MSE, MTA, PhD); engineering physics (MS); geosciences (MS, PhD); mathematical sciences (MS, MTA); mechanical engineering (ME, MSE, PhD); petroleum engineering (ME, MSE, PhD); physics (MS). *Application deadline:* Applications are processed on a rolling basis. *Application fee:* $40. Electronic applications accepted. *Application Contact:* Graduate School, 918-631-2336, Fax: 918-631-2156, E-mail: grad@utulsa.edu. *Dean,* Dr. Steve J. Bellovich, 918-631-2288, E-mail: steven-bellovich@utulsa.edu.

Collins College of Business Students: 85 full-time (34 women), 96 part-time (37 women); includes 12 minority (1 African American, 7 American Indian/Alaska Native, 2 Asian Americans or Pacific Islanders, 2 Hispanic Americans), 21 international. Average age 28. 185 applicants, 63% accepted, 60 enrolled. *Faculty:* 28 full-time (24 women), 1 part-time/adjunct (0 women). Expenses: Contact institution. *Financial support:* In 2008–09, 51 students received support, including 1 fellowship with full and partial tuition reimbursement available (averaging $9,000 per year), 2 research assistantships with full and partial tuition reimbursements available (averaging $8,695 per year), 48 teaching assistantships with full and partial tuition reimbursements available (averaging $10,574 per year); career-related internships or fieldwork, Federal Work-Study, institutionally sponsored loans, scholarships/grants, tuition waivers (full and partial), and unspecified assistantships also available. Support available to part-time students. Financial award application deadline: 2/1; financial award applicants required to submit FAFSA. In 2008, 70 master's awarded. *Degree program information:* Part-time and evening/weekend programs available. Postbaccalaureate distance learning degree programs offered (minimal on-campus study). Offers accounting (MBA); business (M Tax, MBA, MS); business administration (MBA); corporate finance (MS); energy management (MBA); finance (MS); finance/applied mathematicsinternational business (MBA); investments and portfolio management (MS); management information systems (MBA); risk management (MS); taxation (MBA). *Application deadline:* Applications are processed on a rolling basis. *Application fee:* $40. Electronic applications accepted. *Application Contact:* Information Contact, E-mail: graduate-business@utulsa.edu. *Dean,* Dr. W. Gale Sullenburger, 918-631-2213, E-mail: gale-sullenberger@utulsa.edu.

See Close-Up on page 1047.

UNIVERSITY OF UTAH, Salt Lake City, UT 84112-1107

General Information State-supported, coed, university. CGS member. *Graduate housing:* Rooms and/or apartments available on a first-come, first-served basis to single and married students. Housing application deadline: 4/1. *Research affiliation:* Hunter Cancer Institute (cancer treatment and research), Myriad Genetics (pharmaceutical research/manufacturing), Evans and Sutherland (technology development), ARUP, John A. Moran Eye Center (vision treatment and research institute).

GRADUATE UNITS

The Graduate School Expenses: Contact institution. *Financial support:* In 2008–09, 383 fellowships with full and partial tuition reimbursements (averaging $12,500 per year), 738 research assistantships with full and partial tuition reimbursements (averaging $12,500 per year), 712 teaching assistantships with full and partial tuition reimbursements (averaging $12,500 per year) were awarded; career-related internships or fieldwork, Federal Work-Study, institutionally sponsored loans, scholarships/grants, traineeships, health care benefits, tuition waivers (full), unspecified assistantships, and graduate assistantships also available. Support available to part-time students. Financial award applicants required to submit FAFSA. *Degree program information:* Part-time and evening/weekend programs available. Offers biological chemistry (PhD); biostatistics (MST); biotechnology (PSM); business (MST); computational science (PSM); econometrics (MST); economics (MST); educational psychology (MST); environmental engineering (ME, MS, PhD); environmental science (PSM); mathematics (MST); molecular biology (PhD); science instrumentation (PSM); sociology (MST); statistics (M Stat). *Application deadline:* For fall admission, 4/1 priority date for domestic students, 4/1 for international students; for winter admission, 4/1 for international students; for spring admission, 11/1 priority date for domestic students, 11/1 for international students. Applications are processed on a rolling basis. Electronic applications accepted. *Application Contact:* Dr. David S. Chapman, Dean, 801-581-7642, Fax: 801-585-6749, E-mail: dchapman@admin.utah.edu. *Dean,* Dr. David S. Chapman, 801-581-7642, Fax: 801-585-6749, E-mail: dchapman@admin.utah.edu.

College of Architecture and Planning Students: 126 full-time (39 women), 10 part-time (2 women); includes 6 minority (2 Asian Americans or Pacific Islanders, 4 Hispanic Americans), 12 international. Average age 30. 120 applicants, 64% accepted, 56 enrolled. *Faculty:* 17 full-time (5 women). Expenses: Contact institution. *Financial support:* In 2008–09, 29 fellowships with partial tuition reimbursements, 3 research assistantships with partial tuition reimbursements, 29 teaching assistantships with partial tuition reimbursements were awarded; career-related internships or fieldwork, Federal Work-Study, and scholarships/grants also available. Financial award application deadline: 2/1; financial award applicants required to submit FAFSA. In 2008, 33 master's awarded. *Degree program information:* Part-time programs available. Offers architectural studies (MS); architecture (M Arch); architecture and planning (M Arch, MCMP, MS, PhD); city and metropolitan planning (MCMP); metropolitan planning, policy and design (PhD). *Application fee:* $45 ($65 for international students). Electronic applications accepted. *Application Contact:* Mayra Focht, Admissions Advisor, 801-581-8254, Fax: 801-581-8217, E-mail: focht@arch.utah.edu. *Director,* Prof. Brenda Scheer, 801-581-8254, Fax: 801-581-8217, E-mail: scheer@arch.utah.edu.

College of Education Students: 239 full-time (170 women), 267 part-time (182 women); includes 87 minority (10 African Americans, 8 American Indian/Alaska Native, 25 Asian Americans or Pacific Islanders, 44 Hispanic Americans), 14 international. Average age 36. 398 applicants, 47% accepted, 167 enrolled. *Faculty:* 56 full-time (33 women), 15 part-time/adjunct (11 women). Expenses: Contact institution. *Financial support:* Fellowships with full tuition reimbursements, research assistantships with full tuition reimbursements, teaching assistantships with full and partial tuition reimbursements, career-related internships or fieldwork, Federal Work-Study, institutionally sponsored loans, scholarships/grants, tuition waivers (full and partial), and unspecified assistantships also available. Support available to part-time students. Financial award application deadline: 2/1; financial award applicants required to submit FAFSA. In 2008, 244 master's, 29 doctorates awarded. *Degree program information:* Part-time and evening/weekend programs available. Offers counseling psychology (PhD); early childhood hearing impairments (M Ed, MS); early childhood special education (M Ed, PhD); early childhood vision impairments (M Ed, MS); education (M Ed, M Phil, M Stat, MA, MAT, MS, Ed D, PhD); education, culture, and society (M Ed, MA, MS, PhD); educational leadership and policy (M Ed, M Phil, Ed D, PhD); educational psychology (MA); elementary education (MAT); hearing impairments (M Ed, MS); mild/moderate disabilities (MS, PhD); professional counseling (MS); professional practice (M Ed); professional psychology (M Ed); research in special education (MS); school counseling (M Ed, MS); school psychology (MS, PhD); secondary education (MAT); severe disabilities (MS); statistics (M Stat); teaching and learning (M Ed, M Phil, MA, MS, PhD); vision impairments (M Ed). *Application deadline:* For fall admission, 4/1 for domestic and international students; for spring admission, 11/1 for domestic and international students. Applications are processed on a rolling basis. *Application fee:* $45 ($65 for international students). Electronic applications accepted. *Application Contact:* Mindy Jones, Executive Secretary, 801-581-8222, Fax: 801-581-5223, E-mail: mindy.jones@utah.edu. *Dean,* Michael Hardman, 801-581-8121, Fax: 801-585-6476, E-mail: michael.hardman@utah.edu.

College of Engineering Students: 580 full-time (104 women), 259 part-time (28 women); includes 43 minority (4 African Americans, 2 American Indian/Alaska Native, 23 Asian Americans or Pacific Islanders, 14 Hispanic Americans), 336 international. Average age 29. 1,253 applicants, 44% accepted, 226 enrolled. *Faculty:* 141 full-time (14 women), 10 part-time/adjunct (2 women). Expenses: Contact institution. *Financial support:* Fellowships, research assistantships, teaching assistantships, career-related internships or fieldwork, Federal Work-Study, institutionally sponsored loans, and traineeships available. Support available to part-time students. Financial award application deadline: 2/1; financial award applicants required to submit FAFSA. In 2008, 208 master's, 46 doctorates awarded. *Degree program information:* Part-time programs available. Offers bioengineering (ME, MS, PhD); chemical engineering (ME, MS, PhD); civil engineering (MS, PhD); computational engineering and science (MS); computational science (MS); computer science (M Phil, MS, PhD); computing (MS, PhD); electrical engineering (M Phil, ME, MS, PhD, EE); engineering (M Phil, ME, MS, PhD, EE); environmental engineering (ME, MS, PhD); materials science and engineering (MS, PhD); mechanical engineering (M Phil, ME, MS, PhD); nuclear engineering (ME, MS, PhD). *Application deadline:* For fall admission, 4/1 for domestic and international students; for spring admission, 11/1 for domestic and international students. Applications are processed on a rolling basis. *Application fee:* $45 ($65 for international students). *Application Contact:* Dianne Leonard, Coordinator, Administrative Program, 801-585-7769, Fax: 801-581-8692, E-mail: dleonard@coe.utah.edu. *Dean,* Dr. Richard B. Brown, 801-581-6912, E-mail: brown@coe.utah.edu.

College of Fine Arts Students: 117 full-time (82 women), 54 part-time (34 women); includes 14 minority (2 American Indian/Alaska Native, 8 Asian Americans or Pacific Islanders, 4 Hispanic Americans), 20 international. Average age 32. 235 applicants, 47% accepted, 60 enrolled. *Faculty:* 85 full-time (38 women), 25 part-time/adjunct (7 women). Expenses: Contact institution. *Financial support:* Fellowships with full tuition reimbursements, research assistantships, teaching assistantships with full and partial tuition reimbursements, career-related internships or fieldwork, Federal Work-Study, institutionally sponsored loans, and scholarships/grants available. Financial award application deadline: 2/1; financial award applicants required to submit FAFSA. In 2008, 55 master's, 2 doctorates awarded. *Degree program information:* Part-time programs available. Offers art history (MA); ballet (MFA); ceramics (MFA); community-based art education (MFA); drawing (MFA); film studies (MFA); fine arts (M Mus, MA, MFA, DMA, PhD); graphic design (MFA); modern dance (MA, MFA); music (M Mus, MA, DMA, PhD); painting (MFA); photography/digital imaging (MFA); printmaking (MFA); sculpture/intermedia (MFA). *Application deadline:* For fall admission, 4/1 for domestic and international students; for spring admission, 11/1 for domestic and international students. *Application fee:* $45 ($65 for international students). *Application Contact:* Brent Lee Schneider, Associate Dean, 801-587-9811, Fax: 801-585-3066, E-mail: brent.schneider@utah.edu. *Dean and Associate Vice-President for the Arts,* Dr. Raymond Tymas Jones, 801-581-6764, Fax: 801-581-3066.

College of Health Students: 421 full-time (257 women), 79 part-time (35 women); includes 17 minority (1 African American, 3 American Indian/Alaska Native, 2 Asian Americans or Pacific Islanders, 11 Hispanic Americans), 30 international. Average age 30. 594 applicants, 48% accepted, 187 enrolled. *Faculty:* 70 full-time (39 women), 6 part-time/adjunct (4 women). Expenses: Contact institution. *Financial support:* Fellowships, research assistantships with tuition reimbursements, teaching assistantships with tuition reimbursements, career-related internships or fieldwork, Federal Work-Study, institutionally sponsored loans, scholarships/grants, health care benefits, and unspecified assistantships available. Financial award application deadline: 2/1; financial award applicants required to submit FAFSA. In 2008, 109 master's, 119 doctorates awarded. *Degree program information:* Part-time and evening/weekend programs available. Offers audiology (Au D, PhD); exercise and sport science (MS, PhD); health (M Phil, MA, MOT, MS, Au D, DPT, Ed D, PhD, PPDPT); health promotion and education (M Phil, MS, Ed D, PhD); nutrition (MS); occupational therapy (MOT); parks, recreation, and tourism (M Phil, MS, Ed D, PhD); physical therapy (DPT, PPDPT); speech-language pathology (MA, MS, PhD). *Application deadline:* For fall admission, 1/15 for domestic students, 4/1 for international students; for spring admission, 11/15 for domestic students, 11/1 for international students. Applications are processed on a rolling basis. *Application fee:* $45 ($65 for international students). *Application Contact:* Dr. James E. Graves, Dean, 801-581-8537, Fax: 801-581-5580, E-mail: james.graves@health.utah.edu. *Dean,* Dr. James E. Graves, 801-581-8537, Fax: 801-581-5580, E-mail: james.graves@health.utah.edu.

College of Humanities Students: 267 full-time (135 women), 135 part-time (70 women); includes 36 minority (5 African Americans, 1 American Indian/Alaska Native, 14 Asian Americans or Pacific Islanders, 16 Hispanic Americans), 40 international. Average age 35. 519 applicants, 40% accepted, 118 enrolled. *Faculty:* 163 full-time (73 women), 1 part-time/adjunct (0 women). Expenses: Contact institution. *Financial support:* In 2008–09, 157 students received support, including 2 fellowships with full and partial tuition reimbursements available (averaging $12,600 per year), 8 research assistantships with full and partial tuition reimbursements available (averaging $10,000 per year), 127 teaching assistantships with full and partial tuition reimbursements available (averaging $11,500 per year); career-related internships or fieldwork, Federal Work-Study, institutionally sponsored loans, scholarships/grants, and health care benefits also available. Financial award application deadline: 2/1; financial award applicants required to submit FAFSA. In 2008, 42 master's, 23 doctorates awarded. *Degree program information:* Part-time programs available. Offers American studies (MA, PhD); anthropology (MA); applied linguistics (MA, PhD); Arabic (MA, PhD); Arabic and linguistics (MA, PhD); Asian studies (MA); British American literature (MA, PhD); communication (M Phil, MA, MS, PhD); comparative literary and cultural studies (MA, PhD); creative writing (MA, MFA, PhD); French (MA, MALP); German (MA, MALP, PhD); Hebrew (MA); history (MA, PhD); humanities (M Phil, MA, MALP, MAT, MFA, MS, PhD); language pedagogy (MALP); linguistics (MA, PhD); literature (PhD); Persian (MA, PhD); philosophy (MA, MS, PhD); political science (MA, PhD); rhetoric and composition (PhD); rhetoric/composition (MA, PhD); Spanish (MA, MALP, PhD); Turkish (MA); world languages with secondary teaching licensure (MA). *Application deadline:* For fall admission, 4/1 for domestic and international students; for spring admission, 11/1 for domestic and international students. Applications are processed on a rolling basis. *Application fee:* $45 ($65 for international students). *Application Contact:* Mark Bergstrom, Associate Dean, 801-581-6214, Fax: 801-585-5190, E-mail: mark.bergstrom@utah.edu. *Dean and Associate Vice President of Interdisciplinary Studies,* Dr. Robert D. Newman, 801-581-6214, Fax: 801-585-5190, E-mail: robert.newman@utah.edu.

College of Mines and Earth Sciences Students: 107 full-time (27 women), 53 part-time (18 women); includes 5 minority (3 Asian Americans or Pacific Islanders, 2 Hispanic Americans), 64 international. Average age 31. 140 applicants, 44% accepted, 29 enrolled. *Faculty:* 43 full-time (5 women), 5 part-time/adjunct (0 women). Expenses: Contact institution. *Financial support:* In 2008–09, 8 fellowships (averaging $15,000 per year) were awarded; research assistantships, teaching assistantships, career-related internships or fieldwork and institutionally sponsored loans also available. Support available to part-time students. Financial award application deadline: 2/15; financial award applicants required to submit FAFSA. In 2008, 23 master's, 9 doctorates awarded. *Degree program information:* Part-time programs available. Offers atmospheric sciences (MS, PhD); environmental engineering (ME, MS, PhD); geological engineering (ME, MS, PhD); geology (MS, PhD); geophysics (MS, PhD); metallurgical engineering (ME, MS, PhD); mines and earth sciences (ME, MS, PhD); mining engineering (ME, MS, PhD). *Application deadline:* For fall admission, 4/1 for domestic and international students; for spring admission, 11/1 for domestic and international students. *Application fee:* $45 ($65 for international students). Electronic applications accepted. *Application Contact:* Sharon P. Christenson, Executive Assistant to the Dean, 801-581-8767, Fax: 801-581-5560, E-mail: sharon.christenson@utah.edu. *Dean,* Dr. Francis H. Brown, 801-581-8767, Fax: 801-581-5560, E-mail: frank.brown@utah.edu.

College of Nursing Students: 163 full-time (135 women), 118 part-time (97 women); includes 24 minority (3 American Indian/Alaska Native, 10 Asian Americans or Pacific Islanders, 11 Hispanic Americans), 4 international. Average age 40. 196 applicants, 71% accepted, 116 enrolled. *Faculty:* 52 full-time (43 women), 9 part-time/adjunct (8 women). Expenses: Contact institution. *Financial support:* In 2008–09, 29 students received support; fellowships with partial tuition reimbursements available, research assistantships with partial tuition reimbursements available, teaching assistantships with partial tuition reimbursements available, scholarships/grants available. Financial award application deadline: 2/1; financial award applicants required to submit FAFSA. In 2008, 74 master's, 11 doctorates awarded. *Degree program information:* Part-time programs available. Postbaccalaureate distance learning degree programs offered (minimal on-campus study). Offers gerontology (MS, Certificate); nursing (MS, DNP, PhD, Certificate). *Application deadline:* For fall admission, 4/1 for domestic and international students; for spring admission, 11/1 for domestic and international students. Applications are processed on a rolling basis. *Application fee:* $45 ($65 for international students). *Application Contact:* Lara Randolin, Graduate Adviser, 801-585-6658, Fax: 801-585-9705, E-mail: lara.randolin@nurs.utah.edu. *Dean,* Dr. Maureen Keefe, 801-581-8262, Fax: 801-581-4642, E-mail: maureen.keefe@nurs.utah.edu.

College of Pharmacy Students: 236 full-time (188 women), 25 part-time (12 women); includes 23 minority (2 African Americans, 14 Asian Americans or Pacific Islanders, 7 Hispanic Americans), 23 international. Average age 28. 339 applicants, 20% accepted, 59 enrolled. *Faculty:* 52 full-time (14 women), 30 part-time/adjunct (15 women). Expenses: Contact institution. *Financial support:* In 2008–09, 58 students received support, including 3 fellowships (averaging $15,000 per year), 43 research assistantships (averaging $25,000 per year); teaching assistantships, Federal Work-Study, institutionally sponsored loans, and tuition waivers (full) also available. Support available to part-time students. In 2008, 40 first professional degrees, 3 master's, 15 doctorates awarded. *Degree program information:* Part-time programs available. Offers medicinal chemistry (MS, PhD); pharmaceutics and pharmaceutical chemistry (MS, PhD); pharmacology and toxicology (PhD); pharmacotherapy (MS); pharmacy (Pharm D, MS, PhD). *Application deadline:* For fall admission, 1/15 for domestic students. Applications are processed on a rolling basis. *Application fee:* $35 ($55 for international students). *Application Contact:* Office of Admissions, 801-581-7281, Fax: 801-585-3034, E-mail: admissionweb_grad@saff.utah.edu. *Dean,* Dr. John W. Mauger, 801-581-6731.

College of Science Students: 360 full-time (118 women), 73 part-time (20 women); includes 22 minority (3 African Americans, 1 American Indian/Alaska Native, 7 Asian Americans or Pacific Islanders, 11 Hispanic Americans), 164 international. Average age 29. 774 applicants, 23% accepted, 87 enrolled. *Faculty:* 149 full-time (14 women), 9 part-time/adjunct (1 woman). Expenses: Contact institution. *Financial support:* Fellowships with full tuition reimbursements, research assistantships with full and partial tuition reimbursements, teaching assistantships with full and partial tuition reimbursements, career-related internships or fieldwork, scholarships/grants, and traineeships available. Financial award application deadline: 2/15; financial award applicants required to submit FAFSA. In 2008, 52 master's, 55 doctorates awarded. *Degree program information:* Part-time programs available. Offers biology (MS, PhD); chemical physics (PhD); chemistry (M Phil, MA, MS, PhD); mathematics (M Phil, M Stat, MA, MS, PhD); medical physics (PhD); molecular biology (PhD); physics (MA, MS, PhD); science (M Phil, M Stat, MA, MS, PhD); science teacher education (MS). *Application deadline:* For fall admission, 4/1 for domestic and international students; for spring admission, 11/1 for domestic and international students. Applications are processed on a rolling basis. *Application fee:* $45 ($65 for international students). *Application Contact:* Shelly DeWitt, Administrative Assistant, 801-581-6958, E-mail: office@science.utah.edu. *Dean,* Pierre V. Sokolsky, 801-581-6958, Fax: 801-585-3169, E-mail: sokolsky@science.utah.edu.

College of Social and Behavioral Science Students: 267 full-time (123 women), 221 part-time (89 women); includes 40 minority (3 African Americans, 1 American Indian/Alaska Native, 14 Asian Americans or Pacific Islanders, 22 Hispanic Americans), 97 international. Average age 29. 637 applicants, 38% accepted, 137 enrolled. *Faculty:* 143 full-time (50 women), 14 part-time/adjunct (4 women). Expenses: Contact institution. *Financial support:* Fellowships, research assistantships, teaching assistantships, career-related internships or fieldwork, Federal Work-Study, and institutionally sponsored loans available. Support available to part-time students. Financial award application deadline: 2/1; financial award applicants required to submit FAFSA. In 2008, 93 master's, 25 doctorates awarded. *Degree program information:* Part-time programs available. Offers anthropology (M Phil, MA, MS, PhD); clinical psychology (PhD); econometrics (M Stat); economics (M Phil, MA, MS); geography (MA, MS, PhD); human development and social policy (MS); international affairs and global enterprises (MS); political science (MA, MS, PhD); psychology (PhD); public administration (Exec MPA, MPA); public policy (MPP); social and behavioral science (Exec MPA, M Phil, M Stat, MA, MPA, MPP, MS, PhD, Certificate); sociology (M Stat, MA, MS, PhD). *Application deadline:* Applications are processed on a rolling basis. *Application fee:* $45 ($65 for international students). *Application Contact:* Stephen E. Reynolds, Associate Dean, 801-581-8620, Fax: 801-585-5081, E-mail: stephen.reynolds@csbs.utah.edu. *Dean,* J. Steven Ott, 801-581-6781, Fax: 801-585-5081, E-mail: jsott@csbs.utah.edu.

College of Social Work Students: 322 full-time (246 women), 51 part-time (29 women); includes 45 minority (2 African Americans, 8 American Indian/Alaska Native, 12 Asian Americans or Pacific Islanders, 23 Hispanic Americans), 13 international. Average age 33. 306 applicants, 48% accepted, 111 enrolled. *Faculty:* 30 full-time (16 women), 8 part-time/adjunct (4 women). Expenses: Contact institution. *Financial support:* In 2008–09, 158 fellowships with full and partial tuition reimbursements (averaging $3,500 per year), 34 research assistantships with full and partial tuition reimbursements (averaging $7,000 per year), 6 teaching assistantships with full and partial tuition reimbursements (averaging $5,000 per year) were awarded; Federal Work-Study and institutionally sponsored loans also available. Support available to part-time students. Financial award application deadline: 3/15; financial award applicants required to submit FAFSA. In 2008, 148 master's, 4 doctorates awarded. *Degree program information:* Part-time programs available. Postbaccalaureate distance learning degree programs offered (minimal on-campus study). Offers social work (MSW, PhD). *Application deadline:* For fall and spring admission, 11/1 for domestic and international students. Applications are processed on a rolling basis. *Application fee:* $50. *Application Contact:* Dr. Mary Jane Taylor, Associate Dean, 801-581-8828, Fax: 801-585-3219, E-mail: maryjane.taylor@socwk.utah.edu. *Dean,* Dr. Jannah H. Mather, 801-581-6194, Fax: 801-585-3219, E-mail: jannah.mather@socwk.utah.edu.

David Eccles School of Business Students: 679 full-time (152 women), 65 part-time (20 women); includes 46 minority (2 African Americans, 2 American Indian/Alaska Native, 32 Asian Americans or Pacific Islanders, 10 Hispanic Americans), 78 international. Average age 32. 792 applicants, 64% accepted, 370 enrolled. *Faculty:* 64 full-time (20 women), 2 part-time/adjunct (0 women). Expenses: Contact institution. *Financial support:* In 2008–09, 28 students received support, including 8 fellowships with partial tuition reimbursements available, 13 teaching assistantships with partial tuition reimbursements available; career-related internships or fieldwork, health care benefits, and unspecified assistantships also available. Financial award application deadline: 2/1; financial award applicants required to submit FAFSA. In 2008, 416 master's, 10 doctorates awarded. *Degree program information:* Part-time and evening/weekend programs available. Offers accounting (M Acc, PhD); business (EMBA, M Acc, M Stat, MBA, MS, PhD); business administration (EMBA, M Stat, MBA, PhD); finance (MS, PhD). *Application fee:* $45 ($65 for international students). Electronic applications accepted. *Application Contact:* Lori Frandsden, Academic Coordinator, 801-581-8625, Fax: 801-587-3380, E-mail: lori.frandsen@business.utah.edu. *Dean,* Dr. Jack Brittain, 801-587-3860, Fax: 801-587-3380, E-mail: jack.brittain@business.utah.edu.

School of Medicine Offers biochemistry (MS, PhD); biostatistics (M Stat); experimental pathology (PhD); human genetics (MS, PhD); laboratory medicine and biomedical science (MS); medical informatics (MS, PhD, Certificate); medicine (MD, M Phil, M Stat, MPAS, MPH, MS, MSPH, PhD, Certificate); neurobiology and anatomy (PhD); neuroscience (PhD); oncological sciences (M Phil, MS, PhD); physician assistant (MPAS); physiology (PhD); public health (MPH, MSPH, PhD).

S.J. Quinney College of Law Offers law (JD, LL M).

UNIVERSITY OF VERMONT, Burlington, VT 05405

General Information State-supported, coed, university. CGS member. *Enrollment:* 12,800 graduate, professional, and undergraduate students; 1,842 matriculated graduate/professional students (1,099 women). *Enrollment by degree level:* 458 first professional. *Graduate faculty:* 702 full-time, 604 part-time/adjunct. Tuition, state resident: part-time $488 per credit. Tuition, nonresident: part-time $1232 per credit. *Graduate housing:* Rooms and/or apartments available on a first-come, first-served basis to single and married students. *Student services:* Career counseling, free psychological counseling, low-cost health insurance. *Library facilities:* Bailey-Howe Library plus 2 others. *Online resources:* library catalog, web page. *Collection:* 2.6 million titles, 18,891 serial subscriptions, 44,095 audiovisual materials. *Research affiliation:* Miner Institute (animal sciences).

Computer facilities: Computer purchase and lease plans are available. 475 computers available on campus for general student use. A campuswide network can be accessed from student residence rooms and from off campus. Online class registration, Web pages, online course support are available. *Web address:* http://www.uvm.edu/.

General Application Contact: Dr. Patricia Stokowski, Interim Dean, 802-656-3160, Fax: 802-656-0519, E-mail: graduate.admissions@uvm.edu.

GRADUATE UNITS

College of Medicine Students: 507 (292 women); includes 73 minority (7 African Americans, 1 American Indian/Alaska Native, 57 Asian Americans or Pacific Islanders, 8 Hispanic Americans), 30 international. 6,252 applicants, 4% accepted, 126 enrolled. *Faculty:* 284 full-time (59 women), 608 part-time/adjunct. Expenses: Contact institution. *Financial support:* Fellowships, research assistantships, teaching assistantships, Federal Work-Study available. In 2008, 97 first professional degrees, 1 master's, 10 doctorates awarded. Offers biochemistry (MS, PhD); clinical and translational science (MS, PhD); medicine (MD, MS, PhD); microbiology and molecular genetics (MS, PhD); molecular physiology and biophysics (MS, PhD); neuroscience (PhD); pathology (MS); pharmacology (MS, PhD). *Application deadline:* Applications are processed on a rolling basis. *Application Contact:* Dr. Frederick Moria, Dean, 802-656-2156. *Dean,* Dr. Frederick Moria, 802-656-2156.

Graduate College Students: 1,384 (852 women); includes 99 minority (24 African Americans, 5 American Indian/Alaska Native, 39 Asian Americans or Pacific Islanders, 31 Hispanic Americans), 146 international. 2,100 applicants, 47% accepted, 386 enrolled. *Faculty:* 361. Expenses: Contact institution. *Financial support:* Fellowships, research assistantships, teaching assistantships, career-related internships or fieldwork, Federal Work-Study, traineeships, tuition waivers (full and partial), and analytical assistantships available. Support available to part-time students. In 2008, 359 master's, 84 doctorates awarded. *Degree program information:* Part-time programs available. Offers cell and molecular biology (MS, PhD). *Application deadline:* For fall admission, 4/1 priority date for domestic and international students; for spring admission, 11/15 priority date for domestic and international students. Applications are processed on a rolling basis. *Application fee:* $40. Electronic applications accepted. *Application Contact:* Dr. Patricia Stokowski, Interim Dean, 802-656-3160, Fax: 802-656-0519, E-mail: graduate.admissions@uvm.edu. *Interim Dean,* Dr. Patricia Stokowski, 802-656-3160, Fax: 802-656-0519, E-mail: graduate.admissions@uvm.edu.

College of Agriculture and Life Sciences Students: 141 (86 women); includes 4 minority (all Asian Americans or Pacific Islanders), 19 international. 183 applicants, 53% accepted, 40 enrolled. Expenses: Contact institution. *Financial support:* Fellowships, research assistantships, teaching assistantships, career-related internships or fieldwork, Federal Work-Study, and tuition waivers (full and partial) available. Financial award application deadline: 3/1. In 2008, 32 master's, 4 doctorates awarded. *Degree program information:* Part-time programs available. Offers agriculture and life sciences (MPA, MS, MSD, PhD); animal sciences (MS, PhD); animal, nutrition and food sciences (PhD); community development and applied economics (MS); dietetics (MSD); field naturalist (MS); microbiology and molecular genetics (MS, PhD); nutritional sciences (MS); plant and soil science (MS, PhD); plant biology (MS, PhD); public administration (MPA). *Application fee:* $40. Electronic applications accepted. *Application Contact:* Dr. Thomas C. Vogelmann, Dean, 802-656-2980. *Dean,* Dr. Thomas C. Vogelmann, 802-656-2980.

College of Arts and Sciences Students: 255 (162 women); includes 17 minority (6 African Americans, 4 Asian Americans or Pacific Islanders, 7 Hispanic Americans), 33 international. 541 applicants, 41% accepted, 81 enrolled. Expenses: Contact institution. *Financial support:* Fellowships, research assistantships, teaching assistantships, career-related internships or fieldwork and Federal Work-Study available. In 2008, 60 master's, 14 doctorates awarded. *Degree program information:* Part-time programs available. Offers arts and sciences (MA, MAT, MS, MST, PhD); biology (MS, PhD); biology education (MST); chemistry (MS, PhD); clinical psychology (PhD); communication sciences (MS); English (MA); French (MA); geology (MS); German (MA); Greek (MA); Greek and Latin (MAT); historic preservation (MS); history (MA); Latin (MA); physics (MS); psychology (PhD). *Application fee:* $40. Electronic applications accepted. *Application Contact:* Dr. Eleanor Miller, Dean, 802-656-3166. *Dean,* Dr. Eleanor Miller, 802-656-3166.

College of Education and Social Services Students: 391 (301 women); includes 29 minority (11 African Americans, 6 Asian Americans or Pacific Islanders, 12 Hispanic Americans), 3 international. 461 applicants, 58% accepted, 132 enrolled. Expenses: Contact institution. *Financial support:* Fellowships, research assistantships, teaching assistantships, career-related internships or fieldwork and Federal Work-Study available. In 2008, 166 master's, 24 doctorates awarded. *Degree program information:* Part-time programs available. Offers counseling (MS); curriculum and instruction (M Ed, MAT); curriculum of instruction (MAT); education and social services (M Ed, MAT, MS, MSW, Ed D); educational leadership (M Ed); educational leadership & policy studies (Ed D); educational leadership and policy studies (Ed D); educational studies (M Ed); higher education and student affairs administration (M Ed); interdisciplinary studies (M Ed); reading and language arts (M Ed); social work (MSW); special education (M Ed). *Application fee:* $40. Electronic applications accepted. *Application Contact:* Dr. Fayneese Miller, Dean, 802-656-3424. *Dean,* Dr. Fayneese Miller, 802-656-3424.

College of Engineering and Mathematics Students: 171 (47 women); includes 9 minority (1 African American, 7 Asian Americans or Pacific Islanders, 1 Hispanic American), 51 international. 289 applicants, 52% accepted, 49 enrolled. Expenses: Contact institution. *Financial support:* Fellowships, research assistantships, teaching assistantships, Federal Work-Study available. Financial award application deadline: 3/1. In 2008, 32 master's, 11 doctorates awarded. *Degree program information:* Part-time programs available. Offers biomedical engineering (MS); biostatistics (MS); civil and environmental engineering (MS, PhD); computer science (MS, PhD); electrical engineering (MS, PhD); engineering and mathematics (MS, MST, PhD); materials science (MS, PhD); mathematics (MS, MST, PhD); mathematics education (MST); mechanical engineering (MS, PhD); statistics (MS). *Application deadline:* For fall admission, 4/1 priority date for domestic students. Applications are processed on a rolling basis. *Application fee:* $40. Electronic applications accepted. *Application Contact:* Dr. Domenico Grasso, Dean, 802-656-3390. *Dean,* Dr. Domenico Grasso, 802-656-3390.

College of Nursing and Health Sciences Students: 149 (122 women); includes 14 minority (3 African Americans, 2 American Indian/Alaska Native, 8 Asian Americans or Pacific Islanders, 1 Hispanic American), 3 international. 221 applicants, 53% accepted, 19 enrolled. Expenses: Contact institution. *Financial support:* Fellowships, research assistantships, teaching assistantships, Federal Work-Study available. Financial award application deadline: 3/1. In 2008, 7 master's, 10 doctorates awarded. *Degree program information:* Part-time programs available. Offers nursing (MS); nursing and health sciences (MS, DPT); physical therapy (DPT). *Application deadline:* For fall admission, 4/1 priority date for domestic students. Applications are processed on a rolling basis. *Application fee:* $40. Electronic applications accepted. *Application Contact:* Dr. Betty Rambur, Dean, 802-656-3830. *Dean,* Dr. Betty Rambur, 802-656-3830.

The Rubenstein School of Environment and Natural Resources Students: 99 (47 women); includes 11 minority (2 African Americans, 6 Asian Americans or Pacific Islanders, 3 Hispanic Americans), 7 international. 125 applicants, 38% accepted, 23 enrolled. Expenses: Contact institution. *Financial support:* Fellowships, research assistantships, teaching assistantships, Federal Work-Study available. Financial award application deadline: 3/1. In 2008, 32 master's, 5 doctorates awarded. *Degree program information:* Part-time programs available. Offers environment and natural resources (MS, PhD); natural resources (MS, PhD). *Application deadline:* For fall admission, 3/1 priority date for domestic students. Applications are processed on a rolling basis. *Application fee:* $40. Electronic applications accepted. *Application Contact:* Mary Watzin, Director/Coordinator, 802-656-2620. *Director/Coordinator,* Mary Watzin, 802-656-2620.

University of Vermont (continued)

School of Business Administration Students: 58 (23 women); includes 4 minority (1 African American, 2 Asian Americans or Pacific Islanders, 1 Hispanic American), 4 international. 50 applicants, 74% accepted, 17 enrolled. *Faculty:* 25. Expenses: Contact institution. *Financial support:* Fellowships, teaching assistantships, Federal Work-Study available. Financial award application deadline: 3/1. In 2008, 20 master's awarded. *Degree program information:* Part-time programs available. Offers accounting (M Acc); business administration (M Acc, MBA). *Application deadline:* For fall admission, 4/1 priority date for domestic students. Applications are processed on a rolling basis. *Application fee:* $40. Electronic applications accepted. *Application Contact:* Dr. M. Gurdon, Coordinator, 802-656-0513. *Dean,* Dr. R. DeWitt, 802-656-0513.

UNIVERSITY OF VICTORIA, Victoria, BC V8W 2Y2, Canada

General Information Province-supported, coed, university. *Graduate housing:* Rooms and/or apartments available on a first-come, first-served basis to single and married students. Housing application deadline: 2/1. *Research affiliation:* Dominion Astrophysical Observatory, Bamfield Marine Research Station (marine biology), Tri-University Meson Facility, Canada/France/Hawaii Telescope Observatory, Institute of Ocean Sciences (geography, oceanography).

GRADUATE UNITS

Faculty of Graduate Studies *Degree program information:* Part-time programs available. Postbaccalaureate distance learning degree programs offered (no on-campus study). Electronic applications accepted.

Faculty of Business *Degree program information:* Part-time programs available. Offers business (MBA). Electronic applications accepted.

Faculty of Education Offers aboriginal communities counseling (M Ed); art education (M Ed, PhD); coaching studies (co-operative education) (M Ed); counseling (M Ed, MA); curriculum studies (M Ed, MA, PhD); early childhood education (M Ed, PhD); education (M Ed, M Sc, MA, PhD); educational psychology (M Ed, MA, PhD); educational studies (PhD); kinesiology (M Sc, MA); language and literacy (M Ed, MA, PhD); leadership studies (M Ed, MA); leisure service administration (MA); mathematics (M Ed, MA, PhD); music education (M Ed, MA, PhD); physical education (MA); science (M Ed, MA, PhD); social studies (M Ed, MA); social, cultural and foundational studies (MA, PhD); technology and environmental education (PhD).

Faculty of Engineering Offers computer science (M Sc, PhD); electrical and computer engineering (M Eng, MA Sc, PhD); engineering (M Eng, M Sc, MA Sc, PhD); mechanical engineering (M Eng, MA Sc, PhD).

Faculty of Fine Arts Offers composition (M Mus); design (MFA); digital multimedia (MFA); directing (MFA); drawing (MFA); fine arts (M Mus, MA, MFA, PhD); history in art (MA, PhD); musicology (MA, PhD); musicology with performance (MA); painting (MFA); performance (M Mus); photography (MFA); sculpture (MFA); theatre history (MA); video (MFA); writing (MFA).

Faculty of Human and Social Development Offers advanced nursing practice (advanced practice leadership option) (MN); advanced nursing practice (nurse educator option) (MN); advanced nursing practice (nurse practitioner option) (MN); child and youth care (MA, PhD); dispute resolution (MADR); health information science (M Sc); human and social development (M Sc, MA, MADR, MN, MPA, MSW, PhD); indigenous governance (MA); nursing (PhD); public administration (MPA, PhD); social work (MSW); studies in policy and practice (MA).

Faculty of Humanities Offers applied linguistics (MA); English (MA, PhD); German studies (MA); Greek and Roman studies (MA, PhD); Hispanic and Italian studies (MA); Hispanic studies (MA); history (MA, PhD); humanities (MA, PhD); linguistics (MA, PhD); literature (MA); Pacific and Asian studies (MA); philosophy (MA); teaching emphasis (MA).

Faculty of Science Offers astronomy and astrophysics (M Sc, PhD); biochemistry (M Sc, PhD); biology (M Sc, PhD); chemistry (M Sc, PhD); condensed matter physics (M Sc, PhD); earth and ocean sciences (M Sc, PhD); experimental particle physics (M Sc, PhD); mathematics and statistics (M Sc, MA, PhD); medical physics (M Sc, PhD); microbiology (M Sc, PhD); ocean physics (M Sc, PhD); science (M Sc, MA, PhD); theoretical physics (M Sc, PhD). Electronic applications accepted.

Faculty of Social Sciences Offers anthropology (MA); clinical psychology (PhD); clinical psychology (neuropsychology) (M Sc); cognition and brain science (M Sc, PhD); economics (MA, PhD); experimental neuropsychology (M Sc, PhD); geography (M Sc, MA, PhD); individualized study (M Sc, PhD); life span development psychology (PhD); life span developmental psychology (M Sc); political science (MA, PhD); social psychology (M Sc, PhD); social sciences (M Sc, MA, PhD); sociology (MA, PhD).

Faculty of Law *Degree program information:* Part-time programs available. Offers law (LL B, LL M, PhD). Electronic applications accepted.

UNIVERSITY OF VIRGINIA, Charlottesville, VA 22903

General Information State-supported, coed, university. CGS member. *Enrollment:* 24,541 graduate, professional, and undergraduate students; 6,041 full-time matriculated graduate/professional students (2,787 women), 355 part-time matriculated graduate/professional students (212 women). *Enrollment by degree level:* 1,720 first professional, 2,322 master's, 2,352 doctoral, 2 other advanced degrees. *Graduate faculty:* 2,171 full-time (688 women), 197 part-time/adjunct (94 women). Tuition, state resident: full-time $10,452. Tuition, nonresident: full-time $20,010. *Required fees:* $2176. Part-time tuition and fees vary according to course load and program. *Graduate housing:* Rooms and/or apartments available on a first-come, first-served basis to single and married students. Housing application deadline: 6/1. *Student services:* Campus employment opportunities, campus safety program, career counseling, child daycare facilities, exercise/wellness program, free psychological counseling, grant writing training, international student services, low-cost health insurance, multicultural affairs office, services for students with disabilities, teacher training, writing training. *Library facilities:* Alderman Library plus 14 others. *Online resources:* library catalog, web page. *Collection:* 5.5 million titles, 131,854 audiovisual materials. *Research affiliation:* The Judge Advocate General's School, U.S. Army, Federal Executive Institute, National Radio Astronomy Observatory.

Computer facilities: Computer purchase and lease plans are available. A campuswide network can be accessed from student residence rooms and from off campus. Online class registration, online course management tool are available. *Web address:* http://www.virginia.edu/.

General Application Contact: Dean, 434-924-0311.

GRADUATE UNITS

College and Graduate School of Arts and Sciences Students: 1,597 full-time (812 women), 70 part-time (64 women); includes 98 minority (34 African Americans, 2 American Indian/Alaska Native, 43 Asian Americans or Pacific Islanders, 19 Hispanic Americans), 306 international. Average age 29. 4,115 applicants, 22% accepted, 378 enrolled. *Faculty:* 631 full-time (197 women), 49 part-time/adjunct (19 women). Expenses: Contact institution. *Financial support:* Fellowships with partial tuition reimbursements, research assistantships, teaching assistantships with tuition reimbursements, career-related internships or fieldwork, Federal Work-Study, institutionally sponsored loans, traineeships, tuition waivers (full and partial), and unspecified assistantships available. Financial award applicants required to submit FAFSA. In 2008, 306 master's, 149 doctorates awarded. *Degree program information:* Part-time programs available. Offers anthropology (MA, PhD); art and architectural history (MA, PhD); arts and sciences (MA, MFA, MS, PhD); astronomy (MS, PhD); biology (MA, MS, PhD); chemistry (MA, MS, PhD); classical art and archaeology (MA, PhD); classics (MA, PhD); creative writing (MFA); drama (MFA); East Asian studies (MA); economics (MA, PhD); English (MA, PhD); environmental sciences (MA, MS, PhD); foreign affairs (MA, PhD); French (MA, PhD); German (MA, PhD); government (MA, PhD); history (MA, PhD); history of art and architecture (MA, PhD); immunology (PhD); Italian (MA); linguistics (MA); math education (MA); mathematics (MA, PhD); music (MA, PhD); philosophy (MA, PhD); physics (MA, MS, PhD); physics education (MA); psychology (MA, PhD); religious studies (MA, PhD); Slavic languages and literatures (MA, PhD); sociology (MA, PhD); Spanish (MA, PhD); statistics (MS, PhD). *Application deadline:* Applications are processed on a rolling basis. *Application fee:* $60. Electronic applications accepted. *Application Contact:* Aaron Mills, Associate Dean of Graduate Academic Programs and Research, 434-924-6739, Fax: 434-924-6737, E-mail: grad-a-s@virginia.edu. *Dean,* Meredith Jung-En Woo.

Center for Biomedical Ethics 5 applicants, 20% accepted, 0 enrolled. Expenses: Contact institution. *Financial support:* Applicants required to submit FAFSA. Offers bioethics (MA). *Application deadline:* Applications are processed on a rolling basis. *Application fee:* $60. Electronic applications accepted. *Application Contact:* Margaret Mohrmann, Director, 434-924-5974, E-mail: mem7e@virginia.edu. *Director,* Margaret Mohrmann, 434-924-5974, E-mail: mem7e@virginia.edu.

Curry School of Education Students: 630 full-time (471 women), 163 part-time (104 women); includes 75 minority (36 African Americans, 1 American Indian/Alaska Native, 19 Asian Americans or Pacific Islanders, 19 Hispanic Americans), 35 international. Average age 30. 907 applicants, 61% accepted, 163 enrolled. *Faculty:* 91 full-time (50 women), 9 part-time/adjunct (7 women). Expenses: Contact institution. *Financial support:* Fellowships, research assistantships, teaching assistantships, Federal Work-Study available. Financial award application deadline: 1/5; financial award applicants required to submit FAFSA. In 2008, 437 master's, 79 doctorates, 46 other advanced degrees awarded. Offers administration and supervision (M Ed, Ed D, PhD, Ed S); applied developmental science (M Ed, PhD); clinical and school psychology (PhD); communication disorders (M Ed); counselor education (M Ed, Ed D, PhD, Ed S); curriculum and instruction (M Ed, Ed D, PhD, Ed S); early childhood-developmental risk (MT); education (M Ed, MT, Ed D, PhD, Ed S); education evaluation (PhD); educational evaluation (M Ed); educational policy studies (M Ed, Ed D); educational psychology (M Ed, Ed D, PhD, Ed S); educational research (Ed D, PhD); elementary (M Ed, MT, Ed D, PhD); English (M Ed, Ed D); English education (MT, PhD); foreign language (M Ed); foreign language education (MT); gifted education (M Ed); health and physical education (M Ed, Ed D); higher education (M Ed, Ed D, PhD, Ed S); instructional technology (M Ed, PhD, Ed S); kinesiology (M Ed, MT, Ed D, PhD); math education (PhD); mathematics (M Ed, Ed D); reading (M Ed, Ed D, Ed S); reading education (PhD); research statistics and evaluation (Ed D, PhD); school psychology (Ed D, PhD); science (Ed D); science education (PhD); social foundations (PhD); social studies (M Ed); social studies education (MT, PhD); special education (M Ed, Ed D, PhD, Ed S); student affairs practice (M Ed); world languages education (MT). *Application deadline:* Applications are processed on a rolling basis. *Application fee:* $60. Electronic applications accepted. *Application Contact:* Joanne McNergney, Assistant Dean for Admissions and Student Affairs, E-mail: curry-admissions@virginia.edu. *Dean,* Robert C. Pianta, 434-924-3334.

Darden Graduate School of Business Administration Students: 718 full-time (208 women), 61 part-time (8 women); includes 105 minority (30 African Americans, 50 Asian Americans or Pacific Islanders, 25 Hispanic Americans), 216 international. Average age 30. 2,758 applicants, 23% accepted, 329 enrolled. *Faculty:* 63 full-time (12 women), 5 part-time/adjunct (2 women). Expenses: Contact institution. *Financial support:* Career-related internships or fieldwork available. Financial award applicants required to submit FAFSA. In 2008, 380 master's awarded. Offers business administration (MBA, PhD). *Application deadline:* For fall admission, 3/4 for domestic and international students. Applications are processed on a rolling basis. *Application fee:* $200. Electronic applications accepted. *Application Contact:* Sara Neher, Director of Admissions, 434-924-3900, E-mail: darden@virginia.edu. *Dean,* Robert F. Bruner, 434-924-3900, E-mail: darden@virginia.edu.

Frank Batten Sr. School of Leadership and Public Policy Students: 52 full-time (32 women); includes 6 minority (2 African Americans, 4 Asian Americans or Pacific Islanders). Average age 23. 2 applicants, 0% accepted. Expenses: Contact institution. Offers leadership and public policy (MPP); public policy (MPP). *Application deadline:* For fall admission, 2/20 for domestic and international students. Applications are processed on a rolling basis. Electronic applications accepted. *Application Contact:* Edith Simms, Director of Admissions and Student Affairs, 434-243-4383, E-mail: els8a@virginia.edu. *Dean,* Harry Harding.

McIntire School of Commerce Students: 221 full-time (87 women), 1 part-time (0 women); includes 53 minority (12 African Americans, 2 American Indian/Alaska Native, 30 Asian Americans or Pacific Islanders, 9 Hispanic Americans), 26 international. Average age 27. 177 applicants, 77% accepted, 86 enrolled. *Faculty:* 63 full-time (20 women), 2 part-time/adjunct (1 woman). Expenses: Contact institution. *Financial support:* Fellowships, research assistantships, teaching assistantships, career-related internships or fieldwork and Federal Work-Study available. Financial award applicants required to submit FAFSA. In 2008, 177 master's awarded. Offers accounting (MS); commerce (MSC); financial services (MSC); management of information technology (MS); marketing and management (MSC). *Application deadline:* Applications are processed on a rolling basis. *Application fee:* $75. Electronic applications accepted.

School of Architecture Students: 166 full-time (108 women), 2 part-time (1 woman); includes 11 minority (3 African Americans, 6 Asian Americans or Pacific Islanders, 2 Hispanic Americans), 8 international. Average age 28. 693 applicants, 31% accepted, 61 enrolled. *Faculty:* 37 full-time (15 women), 2 part-time/adjunct (1 woman). Expenses: Contact institution. *Financial support:* Fellowships, career-related internships or fieldwork, Federal Work-Study, and institutionally sponsored loans available. Financial award applicants required to submit FAFSA. In 2008, 79 master's awarded. Offers architectural history (M Arch H, PhD); architecture (M Arch); landscape architecture (M Land Arch); urban and environmental planning (MUEP, JD/MUEP). *Application deadline:* Applications are processed on a rolling basis. *Application fee:* $60. Electronic applications accepted. *Application Contact:* Graduate Admissions Officer, 434-924-6442, Fax: 434-982-2678, E-mail: arch-admissions@virginia.edu. *Dean,* Karen Van Lengen, 434-924-3715.

School of Engineering and Applied Science Students: 648 full-time (161 women), 19 part-time (1 woman); includes 70 minority (22 African Americans, 38 Asian Americans or Pacific Islanders, 10 Hispanic Americans), 253 international. Average age 26. 1,606 applicants, 19% accepted, 146 enrolled. *Faculty:* 179 full-time (24 women), 4 part-time/adjunct (1 woman). Expenses: Contact institution. *Financial support:* Fellowships with full tuition reimbursements, research assistantships with full tuition reimbursements, teaching assistantships with full tuition reimbursements, career-related internships or fieldwork available. Financial award application deadline: 1/15; financial award applicants required to submit FAFSA. In 2008, 171 master's, 81 doctorates awarded. *Degree program information:* Part-time programs available. Postbaccalaureate distance learning degree programs offered (no on-campus study). Offers biomedical engineering (ME, MS, PhD); chemical engineering (ME, MS, PhD); civil engineering (ME, MS, PhD); computer engineering (ME, MS, PhD); computer science (MCS, MS, PhD); electrical engineering (ME, MS, PhD); engineering and applied science (MCS, ME, MEP, MMSE, MS, PhD); engineering physics (MEP, MS, PhD); materials science (MMSE, MS, PhD); mechanical and aerospace engineering (ME, MS, PhD); systems and information engineering (ME, MS, PhD). *Application deadline:* For fall admission, 8/1 for domestic students, 4/1 for international students; for winter admission, 12/1 for domestic students, 8/1 for international students; for spring admission, 5/1 for domestic students, 1/1 for international students. Applications are processed on a rolling basis. *Application fee:* $60. Electronic applications accepted. *Application Contact:* Kathryn C. Thornton, Associate Dean for Graduate Programs, 434-924-3897, Fax: 434-982-3044, E-mail: seas-grad-admission@virginia.edu. *Dean,* James H. Aylor.

School of Law Students: 1,188 full-time (489 women); includes 183 minority (71 African Americans, 12 American Indian/Alaska Native, 73 Asian Americans or Pacific Islanders, 27 Hispanic Americans), 42 international. Average age 25. 6,933 applicants, 21% accepted, 424 enrolled. *Faculty:* 76 full-time (20 women), 6 part-time/adjunct (3 women). Expenses: Contact institution. *Financial support:* Fellowships, career-related internships or fieldwork, Federal Work-Study, and institutionally sponsored loans available. Financial award application deadline: 3/1; financial award applicants required to submit FAFSA. In 2008, 398 JDs, 38 master's awarded. Offers law (JD, LL M, SJD, JD/MUEP). *Application deadline:* For fall admission, 3/2 priority date for domestic students, 3/2 for international students. Applications are processed on a rolling basis. *Application fee:* $75. Electronic applications accepted. *Application Contact:* Jason Wu Trujillo, Senior Assistant Dean for Admissions and Financial Aid, 434-924-7351, Fax: 434-982-2128, E-mail: lawadmit@virginia.edu. *Dean,* Paul G. Mahoney, 434- 924-7351, E-mail: lawadmit@virginia.edu.

School of Medicine Students: 822 full-time (405 women), 12 part-time (7 women); includes 221 minority (49 African Americans, 1 American Indian/Alaska Native, 125 Asian Americans or Pacific Islanders, 46 Hispanic Americans), 46 international. Average age 26. 4,894 applicants, 9% accepted, 176 enrolled. *Faculty:* 934 full-time (279 women), 111 part-time/adjunct (55 women). Expenses: Contact institution. *Financial support:* Institutionally sponsored loans and scholarships/grants available. Financial award applicants required to submit FAFSA. In 2008, 42 master's, 46 doctorates awarded. Offers biochemistry (PhD); biological and physical sciences (MS); biophysics (PhD); cell biology (PhD); clinical investigation and patient-oriented research (MS); clinical research (MS); experimental pathology (PhD); informatics in medicine (MS); medicine (MD, MPH, MS, PhD); microbiology (PhD); neuroscience (PhD); pharmacology (PhD); physiology (PhD); public health (MPH); surgery (MS). *Application deadline:* Applications are processed on a rolling basis. *Application fee:* $80. Electronic applications accepted. *Application Contact:* Lesley Thomas, Director, Admissions Office, 434-924-5571, Fax: 434-982-2586. *Vice President and Dean,* Steven T. DeKosky, 434-924-5118, E-mail: slh2m@virginia.edu.

School of Nursing Students: 51 full-time (46 women), 27 part-time (all women); includes 15 minority (8 African Americans, 2 Asian Americans or Pacific Islanders, 5 Hispanic Americans), 1 international. Average age 43. 90 applicants, 32% accepted, 22 enrolled. *Faculty:* 50 full-time (47 women), 4 part-time/adjunct (3 women). Expenses: Contact institution. *Financial support:* Fellowships, research assistantships, teaching assistantships, Federal Work-Study and scholarships/grants available. Financial award applicants required to submit FAFSA. In 2008, 6 doctorates awarded. *Degree program information:* Part-time programs available. Offers acute and specialty care (MSN); acute care nurse practitioner (MSN); clinical nurse leadership (MSN); community-public health leadership (MSN); nursing (DNP, PhD); psychiatric mental health counseling (MSN). *Application deadline:* Applications are processed on a rolling basis. *Application fee:* $60. Electronic applications accepted. *Application Contact:* Clay Hysell, Assistant Dean for Graduate Student Services, 434-924-0141, E-mail: nur-osa@virginia.edu. *Dean,* Dorrie K. Fontaine, 434-924-0141.

UNIVERSITY OF WASHINGTON, Seattle, WA 98195

General Information State-supported, coed, university. CGS member. *Graduate housing:* Rooms and/or apartments available on a first-come, first-served basis to single and married students. Housing application deadline: 5/1. *Research affiliation:* Fred Hutchinson Cancer Research Center, Children's Hospital and Regional Medical Center (pediatric research).

GRADUATE UNITS

Graduate School *Degree program information:* Part-time and evening/weekend programs available. Postbaccalaureate distance learning degree programs offered (minimal on-campus study). Offers biology for teachers (MS); education (M Ed, Professional Certificate); global trade, transportation and logistics studies (Certificate); museology (MA); Near and Middle Eastern studies (PhD); quantitative ecology and resource management (MS, PhD). Electronic applications accepted.

College of Architecture and Urban Planning *Degree program information:* Part-time and evening/weekend programs available. Offers architecture (M Arch, MS); architecture and urban planning (M Arch, MLA, MS, MSCM, MSCPI, MUP, PhD, Certificate); built environment (PhD); construction management (MSCM); design computing (Certificate); design firm leadership and management (Certificate); historic preservation (Certificate); landscape architecture (MLA); lighting (Certificate); strategic planning for critical infrastructures (MSCPI); urban design (Certificate); urban design and planning (PhD); urban planning (MUP). Electronic applications accepted.

College of Arts and Sciences *Degree program information:* Part-time and evening/weekend programs available. Offers acting (MFA); animal behavior (PhD); anthropology (MA, PhD); applied mathematics (MS, PhD); art (MFA); art history (MA, PhD); arts and sciences (MA, MAIS, MAT, MC, MFA, MM, MS, Au D, DMA, PhD); astronomy (MS, PhD); atmospheric sciences (MS, PhD); audiology (Au D); biology (PhD); Buddhist studies (MA, PhD); Central Asian studies (MAIS); chemistry (MS, PhD); child psychology (PhD); China studies (MAIS); Chinese language and literature (MA, PhD); choral conducting (MM, DMA); classics (MA, PhD); classics and philosophy (PhD); clinical psychology (PhD); cognition and perception (PhD); communication (MA, MC, PhD); comparative literature (MA, PhD); comparative religion (MAIS); computational linguistics (MA); costume design (MFA); creative writing (MFA); dance (MFA); design (MFA); developmental psychology (PhD); directing (MFA); dramatic theory (PhD); East European studies (MAIS); economics (PhD); English as a second language (MAT); English literature and language (MA, MAT, PhD); ethnomusicology (MA); French (MA, PhD); French and Italian studies (MA, PhD); geography (MA, PhD); geology (MS, PhD); geophysics (MS, PhD); Germanics (MA, PhD); Hispanic literary and cultural studies (MA); history (MA, PhD); industrial design (MFA); international studies (MAIS); Italian (MA); Japan studies (MAIS); Japanese language and literature (MA, PhD); Korea studies (MAIS); Korean language and literature (MA, PhD); lighting design (MFA); linguistics (MA, PhD); mathematics (MA, MS, PhD); Middle Eastern studies (MAIS); music (MA, MM, DMA, PhD); music education (MA, PhD); music history (MA, PhD); Near Eastern languages and civilization (MA); numerical analysis (MS); optimization (MS); painting and drawing (MFA); philosophy (MA, PhD); photography (MFA); physics (MS, PhD); political science (MA, PhD); quantitative psychology (PhD); Romance linguistics (MA, PhD); Russian literature (MA, PhD); Russian studies (MAIS); Russian, East European and Central Asian studies (MAIS); Scandinavian studies (MA, PhD); scenic design (MFA); Slavic linguistics (MA, PhD); social psychology and personality (PhD); sociology (MA, PhD); South Asian language and literature (MA, PhD); South Asian studies (MAIS); Spanish and Portuguese (MA); speech and hearing sciences (PhD); speech-language pathology (MS); statistics (MS, PhD); theatre and performance history (PhD); visual communication design (MFA); women studies (PhD). Electronic applications accepted.

College of Education *Degree program information:* Part-time and evening/weekend programs available. Offers curriculum and instruction (M Ed, Ed D, PhD); early childhood special education (M Ed); educational leadership and policy studies (M Ed, Ed D, PhD); educational psychology (M Ed, PhD); emotional and behavioral disabilities (M Ed); human development and cognition (M Ed); instructional leadership (M Ed); intercollegiate athletic leadership (M Ed); learning disabilities (M Ed); learning sciences (M Ed, PhD); low-incidence disabilities (M Ed); measurement, statistics and research design (M Ed); school psychology (M Ed); severe disabilities (M Ed); special education (M Ed, Ed D, PhD); teacher education (MIT). Electronic applications accepted.

College of Engineering Students: 1,076 full-time (286 women), 395 part-time (85 women); includes 242 minority (24 African Americans, 5 American Indian/Alaska Native, 176 Asian Americans or Pacific Islanders, 37 Hispanic Americans), 423 international. Average age 28. 3,217 applicants, 29% accepted, 357 enrolled. *Faculty:* 215 full-time (41 women), 176 part-time/adjunct (32 women). Expenses: Contact institution. *Financial support:* In 2008–09, 900 students received support, including 151 fellowships with full tuition reimbursements available (averaging $18,774 per year), 560 research assistantships with full tuition reimbursements available (averaging $23,887 per year), 172 teaching assistantships with full tuition reimbursements available (averaging $21,807 per year); career-related internships or fieldwork, Federal Work-Study, institutionally sponsored loans, scholarships/grants, traineeships, health care benefits, tuition waivers (full), unspecified assistantships, and stipend supplements also available. Financial award application deadline: 2/28; financial award applicants required to submit FAFSA. In 2008, 332 master's, 108 doctorates awarded. *Degree program information:* Part-time programs available. Postbaccalaureate distance learning degree programs offered (minimal on-campus study). Offers aeronautics and astronautics (MSAA); bioengineering (MME, MS, PhD); chemical engineering (MS Ch E, MSE, PhD); composite materials and structures (MAE); computer science (MS, PhD); construction engineering (MSCE); electrical engineering (MSEE, PhD); engineering (MAE, MME, MS, MS Ch E, MSAA, MSCE, MSE, MSEE, MSHCDE, MSIE, MSMSE, MSTC, PhD); environmental engineering (MS, MSCE, MSE, PhD); hydrology, water resources, and environmental fluid mechanics (MS, MSCE, MSE, PhD); industrial and systems engineering (MSIE, PhD); interdisciplinary Japanese (MSTC); materials science and engineering (MS, MSE, MSMSE, PhD); materials science and engineering nanotechnology (PhD); mechanical engineering (MS, MSE, PhD); structural and geotechnical engineering and mechanics (MS, MSCE, MSE, PhD); transportation and construction engineering (MS, MSE, PhD); transportation engineering (MSCE); user-centered design (MSHCDE, PhD). *Application deadline:* For fall admission, 12/15 for domestic students, 11/1 priority date for international students. Applications are processed on a rolling basis. *Application fee:* $50. Electronic applications accepted. *Application Contact:* Dr. Eve Riskin, Associate Dean, Academic Affairs, 206-543-8590, Fax: 206-685-0666, E-mail: riskin@u.washington.edu. *Dean,* Dr. Matthew O'Donnell, 206-543-0340, Fax: 206-685-0666, E-mail: odonnel@u.washington.edu.

College of Forest Resources Offers bioresource science and engineering (MS, PhD); environmental horticulture (MEH); environmental horticulture and urban forestry (MS, PhD); forest ecology (MS, PhD); forest management (MFR); forest soils (MS, PhD); forest systems and bioenergy (MS, PhD); restoration ecology (MS, PhD); social sciences (MS, PhD); sustainable resource management (MS, PhD); wildlife science (MS, PhD). Electronic applications accepted.

College of Ocean and Fishery Sciences Offers aquatic and fishery sciences (MS, PhD); biological oceanography (MS, PhD); chemical oceanography (MS, PhD); marine affairs (MMA, Graduate Certificate); marine geology and geophysics (MS, PhD); ocean and fishery sciences (MMA, MS, PhD, Graduate Certificate); physical oceanography (MS, PhD). Electronic applications accepted.

Daniel J. Evans School of Public Affairs *Degree program information:* Part-time and evening/weekend programs available. Offers public administration (MPA); public policy and management (PhD). Electronic applications accepted.

The Information School Students: 321 full-time (197 women), 212 part-time (165 women); includes 84 minority (10 African Americans, 5 American Indian/Alaska Native, 41 Asian Americans or Pacific Islanders, 28 Hispanic Americans), 56 international. Average age 32. 613 applicants, 56% accepted, 223 enrolled. *Faculty:* 38 full-time (16 women), 18 part-time/adjunct (11 women). Expenses: Contact institution. *Financial support:* In 2008–09, 54 students received support, including 1 fellowship with full tuition reimbursement available (averaging $15,360 per year), 23 research assistantships with full and partial tuition reimbursements available (averaging $15,360 per year), 16 teaching assistantships with full tuition reimbursements available (averaging $15,360 per year); career-related internships or fieldwork, Federal Work-Study, institutionally sponsored loans, scholarships/grants, health care benefits, tuition waivers (full and partial), and unspecified assistantships also available. Support available to part-time students. Financial award application deadline: 2/28; financial award applicants required to submit FAFSA. In 2008, 162 master's, 3 doctorates awarded. *Degree program information:* Part-time and evening/weekend programs available. Postbaccalaureate distance learning degree programs offered (minimal on-campus study). Offers information management (MSIM); information science (PhD); library and information science (MLIS). *Application deadline:* For fall admission, 12/15 for domestic students, 11/1 for international students. *Application fee:* $50. Electronic applications accepted. *Application Contact:* Jennifer Veltri, Admissions Counselor, 206-616-5541, Fax: 206-616-3152, E-mail: jveltri@u.washington.edu. *Dean,* Dr. Harry Bruce.

Michael G. Foster School of Business Students: 381 full-time, 497 part-time; includes 147 minority (9 African Americans, 2 American Indian/Alaska Native, 117 Asian Americans or Pacific Islanders, 19 Hispanic Americans), 190 international. Average age 32. 1,545 applicants, 45% accepted, 524 enrolled. *Faculty:* 110 full-time (33 women), 55 part-time/adjunct (29 women). Expenses: Contact institution. *Financial support:* Fellowships with partial tuition reimbursements, research assistantships with partial tuition reimbursements, teaching assistantships with partial tuition reimbursements, Federal Work-Study, institutionally sponsored loans, and scholarships/grants available. Financial award application deadline: 2/28; financial award applicants required to submit FAFSA. In 2008, 474 master's, 12 doctorates awarded. *Degree program information:* Part-time and evening/weekend programs available. Offers auditing and assurance (MP Acc); business (PhD); business administration (evening) (MBA); business administration (full-time) (MBA); executive business administration (MBA); global business administration (MBA); global executive business administration (MBA); taxation (MP Acc); technology management (MBA). *Application deadline:* For fall admission, 3/15 for domestic students, 1/15 for international students. *Application fee:* $75. Electronic applications accepted. *Application Contact:* Erin Ernst, Assistant Director of Admissions, 206-543-4661, Fax: 206-616-7351, E-mail: mba@u.washington.edu. *Dean,* James Jiambalvo, 206-543-4750.

School of Dentistry Offers dental surgery (DDS); dentistry (DDS, MS, MSD, PhD, Certificate); endodontics (MSD, Certificate); oral biology (MS, MSD, PhD); oral medicine (MSD); orthodontics (MSD, Certificate); pediatric dentistry (MSD, Certificate); periodontics (MSD, PhD, Certificate); prosthodontics (MSD, Certificate).

School of Law Offers Asian law (LL M, PhD); intellectual property law and policy (LL M); law (JD); law of sustainable international development (LL M); taxation (LL M).

School of Medicine *Degree program information:* Part-time programs available. Offers biochemistry (PhD); bioethics (MA); biological structure (PhD); biomedical and health informatics (MS, PhD); comparative medicine (MS); experimental and molecular pathology (PhD); genome sciences (PhD); immunology (MS, PhD); laboratory medicine (MS); medicine (MD, MA, MOT, MS, DPT, PhD); microbiology (PhD); molecular and cellular biology (PhD); neurobiology and behavior (PhD); occupational therapy (MOT); pharmacology (PhD); physical therapy (DPT); physiology and biophysics (PhD); rehabilitation science (PhD). Electronic applications accepted.

School of Nursing *Degree program information:* Part-time programs available. Offers nursing (MN, MS, DNP, PhD, Graduate Certificate).

School of Public Health Students: 490 full-time (335 women), 239 part-time (169 women); includes 151 minority (30 African Americans, 6 American Indian/Alaska Native, 90 Asian Americans or Pacific Islanders, 25 Hispanic Americans), 74 international. Average age 33. 1,186 applicants, 43% accepted, 282 enrolled. *Faculty:* 175 full-time (81 women), 197 part-time/adjunct (75 women). Expenses: Contact institution. *Financial support:* In 2008–09, 451 students received support, including 55 fellowships with full and partial tuition reimbursements available (averaging $12,188 per year), 130 research assistantships with full and partial tuition reimbursements available (averaging $18,597 per year), 29 teaching assistantships with full and partial tuition reimbursements available (averaging $13,411 per year); career-related internships or fieldwork, Federal Work-Study, institutionally sponsored loans, scholarships/grants, traineeships, health care benefits, tuition waivers (full and partial), and unspecified assistantships also available. Support available to part-time students. In 2008, 217 master's, 52 doctorates awarded. *Degree program information:* Part-time and evening/weekend programs available. Postbaccalaureate distance learning degree programs offered (minimal on-campus study). Offers bioinformatics (PhD); biostatistics (MPH, MS, PhD); cancer prevention and control (PhD); clinical research (MS); community oriented public health practice (MPH); economics or finance (PhD); environmental and occupational health (MPH); environmental and occupational hygiene (PhD); environmental health (MS); epidemiology (MPH, MS, PhD); evaluation sciences (PhD); executive program (MHA); genetic epidemiology (MS); global health (MPH); global health—peace corps international (MPH); health behavior and health promotion (PhD); health care and population health research (MPH); health policy analysis and process (PhD); health policy and analysis and process (MPH); health services (MS, PhD); health services administration (EMHA, MHA); in residence program (MHA); maternal/child health (MPH); nutritional sciences (MPH, MS, PhD); occupational and environmental exposure sciences (MS); occupational and environmental medicine (MPH); occupational health (PhD); pathobiology (PhD); population health and social determinants (PhD); public health (EMHA, MHA, MPH, MS, PhD); public health genetics (MPH, MS, PhD); social and behavioral sciences (MPH); sociology and demography (PhD); statistical genetics (PhD); toxicology (MS, PhD). *Application fee:* $50. Electronic applications accepted. *Application Contact:* Marcia Syverson, Manager, Student Services, 206-543-1144, Fax: 206-543-3813, E-mail: sphoss@u.washington.edu. *Dean,* Dr. Patricia Wahl, 206-543-1144.

School of Social Work *Degree program information:* Evening/weekend programs available. Postbaccalaureate distance learning degree programs offered (minimal on-campus study). Offers social work (MSW, PhD).

School of Social Work, Tacoma Campus *Degree program information:* Part-time and evening/weekend programs available. Offers social work (MSW). Electronic applications accepted.

University of Washington (continued)

School of Pharmacy *Degree program information:* Part-time and evening/weekend programs available. Postbaccalaureate distance learning degree programs offered. Offers medicinal chemistry (PhD); pharmaceutics (MS, PhD); pharmacy (Pharm D, MS, PhD).

UNIVERSITY OF WASHINGTON, BOTHELL, Bothell, WA 98011-8246

General Information State-supported, coed, comprehensive institution. *Enrollment:* 2,261 graduate, professional, and undergraduate students; 135 full-time matriculated graduate/professional students (64 women), 207 part-time matriculated graduate/professional students (175 women). *Enrollment by degree level:* 342 master's. *Graduate housing:* On-campus housing not available. *Student services:* Campus employment opportunities, campus safety program, career counseling, exercise/wellness program, international student services, low-cost health insurance, services for students with disabilities, writing training.

Computer facilities: 315 computers available on campus for general student use. A campuswide network can be accessed from off campus. Online class registration, online course management system are available. *Web address:* http://www.uwb.edu.

General Application Contact: Jill Orcutt, Director of Admissions, E-mail: jorcutt@uwb.edu.

GRADUATE UNITS

Program in Business Administration Students: 78 full-time (20 women); includes 1 African American, 23 Asian Americans or Pacific Islanders. Average age 32. 102 applicants, 48% accepted, 48 enrolled. *Faculty:* 20 full-time (3 women), 6 part-time/adjunct (4 women). Expenses: Contact institution. *Financial support:* Career-related internships or fieldwork and Federal Work-Study available. In 2008, 40 master's awarded. *Degree program information:* Part-time and evening/weekend programs available. Offers business administration (MA). *Application deadline:* For fall admission, 4/16 priority date for domestic and international students. Applications are processed on a rolling basis. *Application fee:* $50. Electronic applications accepted. *Application Contact:* Don Whitney, MBA Manager, 425-352-5434, Fax: 425-352-5277. *Director of Business Program,* Prof. Steven Holland, 425-352-5232, Fax: 425-352-5277, E-mail: sholland@uwb.edu.

Program in Education Students: 11 full-time (9 women), 114 part-time (90 women); includes 3 African Americans, 3 Asian Americans or Pacific Islanders, 2 Hispanic Americans. Average age 34. 117 applicants, 74% accepted, 41 enrolled. *Faculty:* 9 full-time (7 women), 1 (woman) part-time/adjunct. Expenses: Contact institution. *Financial support:* Federal Work-Study and unspecified assistantships available. In 2008, 28 master's awarded. Offers education (MA). *Application deadline:* For fall admission, 8/14 priority date for domestic and international students; for spring admission, 2/12 priority date for domestic and international students. Applications are processed on a rolling basis. *Application fee:* $50. Electronic applications accepted. *Application Contact:* Amelia Bowers, Education Program Advisor, 425-352-5274, Fax: 425-352-5455, E-mail: abowers@uwb.edu. *Interim Director,* Prof. Linda Watts, 425-352-3399, Fax: 425-352-5234, E-mail: camb@uwb.edu.

Program in Nursing Students: 1 full-time (0 women), 73 part-time (70 women); includes 9 minority (3 African Americans, 3 Asian Americans or Pacific Islanders, 3 Hispanic Americans). Average age 46. 105 applicants, 55% accepted, 45 enrolled. *Faculty:* 8 full-time (all women). Expenses: Contact institution. *Financial support:* Federal Work-Study and unspecified assistantships available. In 2008, 19 master's awarded. *Degree program information:* Part-time programs available. Offers nursing (MA). *Application deadline:* For fall admission, 3/1 priority date for domestic and international students. Applications are processed on a rolling basis. *Application fee:* $50. Electronic applications accepted. *Application Contact:* Judy Lynn, Administrative Coordinator, 425-352-5376, Fax: 425-352-3237, E-mail: jlynn@uwb.edu. *Nursing Program Director,* Prof. Mary Baroni, 425-352-3543, Fax: 425-352-3237, E-mail: mbaroni@uwb.edu.

Program in Policy Studies Students: 27 full-time (21 women), 19 part-time (14 women); includes 12 minority (1 African American, 2 American Indian/Alaska Native, 7 Asian Americans or Pacific Islanders, 2 Hispanic Americans). Average age 32. 63 applicants, 51% accepted, 27 enrolled. *Faculty:* 9 full-time (4 women), 2 part-time/adjunct (both women). Expenses: Contact institution. *Financial support:* In 2008–09, 9 students received support, including 5 fellowships (averaging $15,000 per year), 1 research assistantship (averaging $2,000 per year); Federal Work-Study, tuition waivers (full), and unspecified assistantships also available. Financial award applicants required to submit FAFSA. In 2008, 15 master's awarded. *Degree program information:* Evening/weekend programs available. Offers policy studies (MA). *Application deadline:* For fall admission, 3/1 priority date for domestic and international students. Applications are processed on a rolling basis. *Application fee:* $50. Electronic applications accepted. *Application Contact:* Andrew Brusletten, Program Manager, 425-352-5427, Fax: 425-352-3462, E-mail: abrusletten@uwb.edu. *Interim Director, Interdisciplinary Studies Program,* Prof. Bruce Burgett, 425-352-5403, E-mail: bburgett@uwb.edu.

UNIVERSITY OF WASHINGTON, TACOMA, Tacoma, WA 98402-3100

General Information State-supported, coed, comprehensive institution. *Enrollment:* 2,965 graduate, professional, and undergraduate students; 192 full-time matriculated graduate/professional students (127 women), 329 part-time matriculated graduate/professional students (260 women). *Enrollment by degree level:* 521 master's. *Graduate faculty:* 98 full-time (54 women), 6 part-time/adjunct (1 woman). Tuition, state resident: full-time $10,476; part-time $498 per credit. Tuition, nonresident: full-time $22,947; part-time $1092 per credit. Tuition and fees vary according to course load, degree level and program. *Graduate housing:* Room and/or apartments available on a first-come, first-served basis to single students; on-campus housing not available to married students. Typical cost: $7140 per year. Room charges vary according to housing facility selected. Housing application deadline: 5/15. *Student services:* Campus employment opportunities, campus safety program, career counseling, exercise/wellness program, grant writing training, services for students with disabilities, teacher training, writing training. *Library facilities:* University of Washington Library. *Online resources:* library catalog, web page, access to other libraries' catalogs. *Collection:* 7.4 million titles, 61,979 serial subscriptions, 129,644 audiovisual materials. *Research affiliation:* City of Tacoma/Port of Tacoma (Water quality and sustainablility studies), South Sound Public and Private Schools (Internships and Educational Research).

Computer facilities: 138 computers available on campus for general student use. A campuswide network can be accessed from student residence rooms and from off campus. Online class registration, (online courseware-Blackboard) are available. *Web address:* http://www.tacoma.washington.edu/.

General Application Contact: Joan Abe, Director of Admissions, 206-543-5929, E-mail: uwgrad@u.washington.edu.

GRADUATE UNITS

Graduate Programs Students: 192 full-time (127 women), 329 part-time (260 women); includes 99 minority (22 African Americans, 6 American Indian/Alaska Native, 38 Asian Americans or Pacific Islanders, 33 Hispanic Americans). Average age 35. 324 applicants, 55% accepted, 132 enrolled. *Faculty:* 98 full-time (54 women), 6 part-time/adjunct (1 woman). Expenses: Contact institution. *Financial support:* Federal Work-Study, institutionally sponsored loans, and scholarships/grants available. Support available to part-time students. In 2008, 156 master's awarded. *Degree program information:* Part-time and evening/weekend programs available. Offers accounting (MBA); certified financial analyst (MBA); computing and software systems (MS); educational administrator (M Ed); interdisciplinary studies (MA); K-8 teacher education (M Ed); nursing (MN); professional certification (M Ed); secondary science education (M Ed); social work (MSW); special education (M Ed). *Application deadline:* For fall admission, 4/15 priority date for domestic and international students; for winter admission, 10/15 priority date for domestic and international students; for spring admission, 1/15 priority date for domestic and international students. Applications are processed on a rolling basis. *Application fee:* $65 ($75 for international students). Electronic applications accepted. *Application Contact:* Joan Abe, Director, Graduate School, 253-543-5929, E-mail: uwgrad@u.washington.edu. *Chancellor,* Dr. Patricia Spakes, 253-692-5646, E-mail: pspakes@u.washington.edu.

UNIVERSITY OF WATERLOO, Waterloo, ON N2L 3G1, Canada

General Information Province-supported, coed, university. CGS member. *Graduate housing:* Rooms and/or apartments available on a first-come, first-served basis to single and married students. *Research affiliation:* Waterloo Maple Inc. (symbolic computation research), Bell Canada (bell university labs), GM Canada (basic research), IBM (basic research), Com Dev International (telecommunications), Nortel (telecommunications).

GRADUATE UNITS

Graduate Studies *Degree program information:* Part-time and evening/weekend programs available. Postbaccalaureate distance learning degree programs offered (no on-campus study). Electronic applications accepted.

Centre for Business, Entrepreneurship and Technology Offers business, entrepreneurship and technology (MBET). Electronic applications accepted.

Faculty of Applied Health Sciences *Degree program information:* Part-time programs available. Offers applied health sciences (M Sc, MA, MPH, PhD); health studies and gerontology (M Sc, PhD); kinesiology (M Sc, PhD); public health (MPH); recreation and leisure studies (MA, PhD). Electronic applications accepted.

Faculty of Arts *Degree program information:* Part-time and evening/weekend programs available. Offers accounting (M Acc, PhD); ancient Mediterranean cultures (MA); anthropology (MA); arts (M Acc, M Tax, MA, MA Sc, MFA, PhD); economics (MA, PhD); English language and literature (PhD); finance (M Acc); French (MA, PhD); German (MA, PhD); global governance (MA, PhD); history (MA, PhD); literary studies (MA); philosophy (MA, PhD); psychology (MA, MA Sc, PhD); public issues (MA); religious diversity in North America (PhD); rhetoric and communication design (MA); Russian (MA); sociology (MA, PhD); studio art (MFA); taxation (M Tax). Electronic applications accepted.

Faculty of Engineering *Degree program information:* Part-time and evening/weekend programs available. Postbaccalaureate distance learning degree programs offered (no on-campus study). Offers applied operations research (MA Sc, MMS, PhD); architecture (M Arch); chemical engineering (M Eng, MA Sc, PhD); civil and environmental engineering (M Eng, MA Sc, PhD); electrical and computer engineering (M Eng, MA Sc, PhD); electrical and computer engineering (software engineering) (MA Sc); engineering (M Arch, M Eng, MA Sc, MBET, MMS, PhD); information systems (MA Sc, MMS, PhD); management of technology (MA Sc, MMS, PhD); mechanical engineering (M Eng, MA Sc, PhD); mechanical engineering design and manufacturing (M Eng); systems design engineering (M Eng, MA Sc, PhD). Electronic applications accepted.

Faculty of Environmental Studies *Degree program information:* Part-time programs available. Offers environment and resource studies (MES); environmental studies (MA, MAES, MES, PhD); geography (MA, PhD); local economic development (MAES); planning (MA, MAES, MES, PhD); tourism policy and planning (MAES). Electronic applications accepted.

Faculty of Mathematics Offers actuarial science (M Math, PhD); applied mathematics (M Math, PhD); biostatistics (PhD); combinatorics and optimization (M Math, PhD); computer science (M Math, PhD); mathematics (M Math, PhD); pure mathematics (M Math, PhD); software engineering (M Math); statistics (M Math, PhD); statistics and computing (M Math); statistics-biostatistics (M Math); statistics-computing (M Math); statistics-finance (M Math). Electronic applications accepted.

Faculty of Science *Degree program information:* Part-time programs available. Offers biology (M Sc, PhD); chemistry and biochemistry (M Sc, PhD); earth sciences (M Sc, PhD); physics (M Sc, PhD); science (M Sc, PhD); vision science (M Sc, PhD). Electronic applications accepted.

THE UNIVERSITY OF WEST ALABAMA, Livingston, AL 35470

General Information State-supported, coed, comprehensive institution. *Graduate housing:* Rooms and/or apartments available on a first-come, first-served basis to single students and available to married students.

GRADUATE UNITS

School of Graduate Studies *Degree program information:* Part-time and evening/weekend programs available.

College of Education *Degree program information:* Part-time and evening/weekend programs available. Offers continuing education (MSCE); early childhood education (M Ed); education (M Ed, MAT, MSCE); elementary education (M Ed); guidance and counseling (M Ed, MSCE); library media (M Ed); physical education (M Ed, MAT); school administration (M Ed); secondary education (MAT); special education (M Ed).

College of Liberal Arts Offers history (MAT); language arts (MAT); liberal arts (MAT); social science (MAT).

College of Natural Sciences and Mathematics Offers biological sciences (MAT); mathematics (MAT); natural sciences and mathematics (MAT).

THE UNIVERSITY OF WESTERN ONTARIO, London, ON N6A 5B8, Canada

General Information Province-supported, coed, university. *Enrollment:* 32,334 graduate, professional, and undergraduate students; 4,105 full-time matriculated graduate/professional students (2,042 women), 504 part-time matriculated graduate/professional students (304 women). *Enrollment by degree level:* 3,028 master's, 1,581 doctoral. *Graduate faculty:* 1,821. *Graduate housing:* Rooms and/or apartments available on a first-come, first-served basis to single and married students. *Student services:* Campus employment opportunities, campus safety program, career counseling, child daycare facilities, exercise/wellness program, free psychological counseling, grant writing training, international student services, low-cost health insurance, multicultural affairs office, services for students with disabilities, teacher training, writing training. *Library facilities:* The University of Western Ontario Libraries plus 7 others. *Online resources:* library catalog, web page, access to other libraries' catalogs. *Collection:* 3.5 million titles, 54,546 serial subscriptions, 1.8 million audiovisual materials.

Computer facilities: Computer purchase and lease plans are available. 351 computers available on campus for general student use. A campuswide network can be accessed from student residence rooms and from off campus. Online class registration is available. *Web address:* http://www.uwo.ca/.

General Application Contact: Andrea Legato, Coordinator, Graduate Student Recruitment and Retention, 519-661-2111 Ext. 81130, Fax: 519-661-3730, E-mail: alegato2@uwo.ca.

GRADUATE UNITS

Faculty of Graduate Studies *Degree program information:* Part-time and evening/weekend programs available. Postbaccalaureate distance learning degree programs offered. Electronic applications accepted.

Biosciences Division *Degree program information:* Part-time programs available. Postbaccalaureate distance learning degree programs offered. Offers biochemistry (M Sc, PhD); biology (M Sc, PhD); biosciences (M Cl Sc, M Sc, MA, MPT, PhD, CAS); clinical neurological sciences (M Sc, PhD); epidemiology and biostatistics (M Sc, PhD); family medicine (M Cl Sc); manipulative therapy (CAS); medical biophysics (M Sc, PhD); microbiology and immunology (M Sc, PhD); pathology (M Sc, PhD); physical therapy (MPT); physiology (M Sc, PhD); plant and environmental sciences (M Sc); plant sciences (M Sc, PhD); plant sciences and environmental sciences (PhD); plant sciences and molecular biology (M Sc, PhD); psychology (MA, PhD); wound healing (CAS); zoology (M Sc, PhD).

Center for the Study of Theory and Criticism Offers theory and criticism (MA, PhD).

Faculty of Arts and Humanities *Degree program information:* Part-time programs available. Offers arts and humanities (M Mus, MA, PhD); Canadian literature (MA); classical studies (MA); comparative literature (MA, PhD); English (PhD); English literature (MA); French (MA, PhD); music (M Mus, PhD); philosophy (MA, PhD); popular music and culture (MA); Spanish (MA).

Faculty of Information and Media Studies Offers journalism (MA); library and information science (MLIS, PhD); media studies (MA, PhD).

Health Sciences Division Offers audiology (M Cl Sc, M Sc); health sciences (M Cl Sc, M Sc, M Sc N, MA, MCTS, MN NP, PhD); kinesiology (M Sc, MA, PhD); nurse practitioner

(MN NP); nursing (M Sc N, MN NP, PhD); occupational therapy (M Sc); speech-language pathology (M Cl Sc, M Sc).

Physical Sciences Division *Degree program information:* Part-time programs available. Offers applied mathematics (M Sc, PhD); astronomy (M Sc, PhD); chemical and biochemical engineering (ME Sc, PhD); chemistry (M Sc, PhD); civil and environmental engineering (M Eng, ME Sc, PhD); computer science (M Sc, PhD); electrical and computer engineering (M Eng, ME Sc, PhD); environment and sustainability (MES); geology (M Sc, PhD); geology and environmental science (M Sc, PhD); geophysics (M Sc, PhD); geophysics and environmental science (M Sc, PhD); mathematics (M Sc, PhD); mechanical and materials engineering (M Eng, ME Sc, PhD); physical sciences (M Eng, M Sc, ME Sc, MES, PhD); physics (M Sc, PhD); statistical and actuarial sciences (M Sc, PhD); theoretical physics (PhD). Electronic applications accepted.

Social Sciences Division *Degree program information:* Part-time and evening/weekend programs available. Offers anthropology (MA, PhD); counseling psychology (M Ed); curriculum studies (M Ed); economics (MA, PhD); education (M Ed); educational policy studies (M Ed); educational psychology/special education (M Ed); geography (M Sc, MA, PhD); history (MA, PhD); political science (MA, MPA, PhD); social sciences (M Ed, M Sc, MA, MPA, PhD); sociology (MA, PhD).

Faculty of Law Offers law (LL B, LL M, Diploma).

Richard Ivey School of Business Offers business (EMBA, PhD); corporate strategy and leadership elective (MBA); entrepreneurship elective (MBA); finance elective (MBA); health sector stream (MBA); international management elective (MBA); marketing elective (MBA). Electronic applications accepted.

Schulich School of Medicine and Dentistry Offers medicine (MD); medicine and dentistry (DDS, MD, M Cl D, M Cl Sc, M Sc, MA, PhD).

School of Dentistry Offers dentistry (DDS, M Cl D); orthodontics (M Cl D).

UNIVERSITY OF WEST FLORIDA, Pensacola, FL 32514-5750

General Information State-supported, coed, comprehensive institution. CGS member. *Enrollment:* 10,491 graduate, professional, and undergraduate students; 344 full-time matriculated graduate/professional students (224 women), 1,051 part-time matriculated graduate/professional students (672 women). *Enrollment by degree level:* 1,169 master's, 169 doctoral, 57 other advanced degrees. *Graduate faculty:* 126 full-time (44 women), 31 part-time/adjunct (14 women). Tuition, state resident: full-time $6095; part-time $253.97 per credit hour. Tuition, nonresident: full-time $21,919; part-time $913.31 per credit hour. *Graduate housing:* Room and/or apartments available on a first-come, first-served basis to single students; on-campus housing not available to married students. Typical cost: $6900 (including board). Room and board charges vary according to housing facility selected. *Student services:* Campus employment opportunities, campus safety program, career counseling, child daycare facilities, exercise/wellness program, free psychological counseling, international student services, low-cost health insurance, multicultural affairs office, services for students with disabilities, teacher training. *Library facilities:* John C. Pace Library plus 2 others. *Online resources:* library catalog, web page, access to other libraries' catalogs. *Collection:* 996,243 titles, 5,019 serial subscriptions, 8,830 audiovisual materials. *Research affiliation:* Pensacola Bay Area Convention and Visitors Bureau (Pensacola Tourism study), Software Engineering Research Consortium (Motorola, Northrup Grumman through Ball State University) (software engineering), University of Southern Mississippi Consortium on Coastal Estaurine Research (microbial biofilms and coastal estaurine research).

Computer facilities: Computer purchase and lease plans are available. 1,100 computers available on campus for general student use. A campuswide network can be accessed from student residence rooms and from off campus. Online class registration is available. *Web address:* http://www.uwf.edu/.

General Application Contact: Terry McCray, Assistant Director of Graduate Admissions, 850-473-7718, Fax: 850-473-7714, E-mail: gradadmissions@uwf.edu.

GRADUATE UNITS

College of Arts and Sciences: Arts Students: 116 full-time (77 women), 155 part-time (104 women); includes 45 minority (20 African Americans, 2 American Indian/Alaska Native, 7 Asian Americans or Pacific Islanders, 16 Hispanic Americans), 3 international. Average age 30. 247 applicants, 65% accepted, 95 enrolled. *Faculty:* 37 full-time (11 women), 3 part-time/adjunct (1 woman). Expenses: Contact institution. *Financial support:* In 2008–09, 14 research assistantships with partial tuition reimbursements (averaging $3,086 per year), 19 teaching assistantships with partial tuition reimbursements (averaging $3,545 per year) were awarded; career-related internships or fieldwork, Federal Work-Study, institutionally sponsored loans, scholarships/grants, tuition waivers (full and partial), and unspecified assistantships also available. Support available to part-time students. Financial award application deadline: 4/15; financial award applicants required to submit FAFSA. In 2008, 51 master's awarded. *Degree program information:* Part-time and evening/weekend programs available. Offers arts and sciences: arts (MA); communication arts (MA); counseling (MA); counseling-licensed mental health counselor (MA); creative writing (MA); general (MA); historic preservation (MA); history (MA); industrial-organizational (MA); interdisciplinary humanities (MA); literature (MA); political science (MA); public history (MA). *Application deadline:* For fall admission, 6/1 for domestic students, 5/15 for international students; for spring admission, 11/1 for domestic students, 10/1 for international students. Applications are processed on a rolling basis. *Application fee:* $30. *Application Contact:* Terry McCray, Assistant Director of Graduate Admissions, 850-473-7718, Fax: 850-473-7714, E-mail: gradadmissions@uwf.edu. *Dean,* Dr. Jane Halonen, 850-474-2688.

Division of Anthropology and Archaeology Students: 24 full-time (16 women), 23 part-time (14 women); includes 9 minority (1 African American, 1 American Indian/Alaska Native, 3 Asian Americans or Pacific Islanders, 4 Hispanic Americans). Average age 29. 49 applicants, 57% accepted, 17 enrolled. *Faculty:* 9 full-time (3 women). Expenses: Contact institution. *Financial support:* In 2008–09, 5 research assistantships (averaging $3,760 per year), 4 teaching assistantships (averaging $3,760 per year) were awarded; career-related internships or fieldwork, scholarships/grants, tuition waivers (partial), and unspecified assistantships also available. Financial award application deadline: 4/15; financial award applicants required to submit FAFSA. In 2008, 7 master's awarded. Offers anthropology (MA); historical archaeology (MA). *Application deadline:* For fall admission, 6/1 for domestic students, 5/15 for international students; for spring admission, 11/1 for domestic students, 10/1 for international students. *Application fee:* $30. *Application Contact:* Terry McCray, Assistant Director of Graduate Admissions, 850-473-7718, Fax: 850-473-7714, E-mail: gradadmissions@uwf.edu. *Interim Chair,* Dr. John Bratten, 850-857-6278, E-mail: anthropology@uwf.edu.

College of Arts and Sciences: Sciences Students: 44 full-time (21 women), 119 part-time (55 women); includes 32 minority (14 African Americans, 1 American Indian/Alaska Native, 12 Asian Americans or Pacific Islanders, 5 Hispanic Americans), 11 international. Average age 31. 97 applicants, 66% accepted, 46 enrolled. *Faculty:* 32 full-time (9 women), 8 part-time/adjunct (3 women). Expenses: Contact institution. *Financial support:* In 2008–09, 22 research assistantships with partial tuition reimbursements (averaging $2,506 per year), 58 teaching assistantships with partial tuition reimbursements (averaging $4,583 per year) were awarded; career-related internships or fieldwork, Federal Work-Study, institutionally sponsored loans, scholarships/grants, and tuition waivers (full and partial) also available. Support available to part-time students. Financial award application deadline: 4/15; financial award applicants required to submit FAFSA. In 2008, 45 master's awarded. *Degree program information:* Part-time and evening/weekend programs available. Offers arts and sciences: sciences (MA, MPH, MS, MST); computer science (MS); environmental science (MS); mathematical sciences (MS); software engineering (MS). *Application deadline:* For fall admission, 6/1 for domestic students, 5/15 for international students; for spring admission, 11/1 for domestic students, 10/1 for international students. Applications are processed on a rolling basis. *Application fee:* $30. *Application Contact:* Terry McCray, Assistant Director of Graduate Admissions, 850-473-7715, Fax: 850-473-7714, E-mail: gradadmissions@uwf.edu. *Dean,* Dr. Jane Halonen, 850-474-2688.

School of Allied Health and Life Sciences Students: 10 full-time (5 women), 47 part-time (33 women); includes 12 minority (7 African Americans, 1 American Indian/Alaska Native, 3 Asian Americans or Pacific Islanders, 1 Hispanic American), 4 international. Average age 31. 41 applicants, 51% accepted, 15 enrolled. *Faculty:* 10 full-time (2 women), 6 part-time/adjunct (3 women). Expenses: Contact institution. *Financial support:* In 2008–09, 9 research assistantships with partial tuition reimbursements (averaging $2,064 per year), 43 teaching assistantships with partial tuition reimbursements (averaging $4,733 per year) were awarded; scholarships/grants and tuition waivers (partial) also available. Financial award application deadline: 4/15; financial award applicants required to submit FAFSA. In 2008, 18 master's awarded. *Degree program information:* Part-time programs available. Offers allied health and life sciences (MA, MPH, MS, MST); biological chemistry (MS); biology (MS); biology education (MST); biotechnology (MS); coastal zone studies (MS); environmental biology (MS); public health (MPH). *Application deadline:* For fall admission, 6/1 for domestic students, 5/15 for international students; for spring admission, 11/1 for domestic students, 10/1 for international students. Applications are processed on a rolling basis. *Application fee:* $30. *Application Contact:* Terry McCray, Assistant Director of Graduate Admissions, 850-473-7718, Fax: 850-473-7714, E-mail: gradadmissions@uwf.edu. *Chairperson,* Dr. George L. Stewart, 850-474-2748.

College of Business Students: 41 full-time (25 women), 122 part-time (53 women); includes 25 minority (8 African Americans, 1 American Indian/Alaska Native, 7 Asian Americans or Pacific Islanders, 9 Hispanic Americans), 23 international. Average age 29. 85 applicants, 54% accepted, 39 enrolled. *Faculty:* 19 full-time (3 women), 6 part-time/adjunct (3 women). Expenses: Contact institution. *Financial support:* In 2008–09, 96 fellowships (averaging $800 per year), 19 research assistantships with partial tuition reimbursements (averaging $4,900 per year) were awarded; career-related internships or fieldwork, scholarships/grants, and unspecified assistantships also available. Support available to part-time students. Financial award application deadline: 4/15; financial award applicants required to submit FAFSA. In 2008, 69 master's awarded. *Degree program information:* Part-time and evening/weekend programs available. Offers accounting (M Acc, MA); business (M Acc, MA, MBA); business administration (MBA). *Application deadline:* For fall admission, 6/30 for domestic students, 5/15 for international students; for spring admission, 11/1 for domestic students, 10/1 for international students. Applications are processed on a rolling basis. *Application fee:* $30. *Application Contact:* Dr. W Timothy O'Keefe, Associate Dean/Director, 850-474-2348. *Dean,* Dr. F. Edward Ranelli, 850-474-2348.

College of Professional Studies Students: 143 full-time (101 women), 655 part-time (460 women); includes 172 minority (109 African Americans, 12 American Indian/Alaska Native, 21 Asian Americans or Pacific Islanders, 30 Hispanic Americans), 8 international. Average age 36. 407 applicants, 62% accepted, 183 enrolled. *Faculty:* 38 full-time (21 women), 14 part-time/adjunct (7 women). Expenses: Contact institution. *Financial support:* In 2008–09, 142 fellowships (averaging $677 per year) were awarded; career-related internships or fieldwork, Federal Work-Study, scholarships/grants, tuition waivers (partial), and unspecified assistantships also available. Support available to part-time students. Financial award application deadline: 4/15; financial award applicants required to submit FAFSA. In 2008, 257 master's, 39 doctorates, 27 other advanced degrees awarded. *Degree program information:* Part-time and evening/weekend programs available. Offers acquisition and contract administration (MSA); biomedical/pharmaceutical (MSA); career and technical studies (M Ed); clinical teaching (MA); college student personnel administration (M Ed); criminal justice administration (MSA); curriculum and instruction (Ed D, Ed S); curriculum and instruction: special education (M Ed); education (M Ed, MA); education leadership (MSA); educational leadership (M Ed, Ed S); elementary education (M Ed); guidance and counseling (M Ed); habilitative science (MA); healthcare administration (MSA); instructional technology (M Ed); middle and secondary level education and ESOL (M Ed); nursing administration (MSA); primary education (M Ed); public administration (MSA); reading education (M Ed); special education (M Ed). *Application deadline:* For fall admission, 6/1 for domestic students, 5/15 for international students; for spring admission, 11/1 for domestic students, 10/1 for international students. Applications are processed on a rolling basis. *Application fee:* $30. *Application Contact:* Terry McCray, Assistant Director of Graduate Admissions, 850-473-7718, Fax: 850-473-7714, E-mail: gradadmissions@uwf.edu. *Dean,* Dr. Donald Chu, 850-474-2769, Fax: 850-474-3205.

Division of Health, Leisure, and Exercise Science Students: 23 full-time (12 women), 47 part-time (31 women); includes 13 minority (7 African Americans, 1 American Indian/Alaska Native, 2 Asian Americans or Pacific Islanders, 3 Hispanic Americans), 4 international. Average age 30. 30 applicants, 87% accepted, 17 enrolled. *Faculty:* 5 full-time (2 women), 2 part-time/adjunct (1 woman). Expenses: Contact institution. *Financial support:* In 2008–09, 12 fellowships (averaging $970 per year) were awarded; teaching assistantships with partial tuition reimbursements, career-related internships or fieldwork, Federal Work-Study, scholarships/grants, and tuition waivers (partial) also available. Support available to part-time students. Financial award application deadline: 4/15; financial award applicants required to submit FAFSA. In 2008, 40 master's awarded. *Degree program information:* Part-time and evening/weekend programs available. Offers exercise science (MS); health education (MS); health, leisure, and exercise science (MS); physical education (MS). *Application deadline:* For fall admission, 6/1 for domestic students, 5/15 for international students; for spring admission, 11/1 for domestic students, 10/1 for international students. Applications are processed on a rolling basis. *Application fee:* $30. *Application Contact:* Terry McCray, Assistant Director of Graduate Admissions, 850-473-7718, Fax: 850-473-7714, E-mail: gradadmissions@uwf.edu. *Chairperson,* Dr. John Todorovich, 850-473-7248, Fax: 850-474-2106.

School of Justice Studies and Social Work Offers social work (MSW).

UNIVERSITY OF WEST GEORGIA, Carrollton, GA 30118

General Information State-supported, coed, comprehensive institution. CGS member. *Enrollment:* 11,252 graduate, professional, and undergraduate students; 468 full-time matriculated graduate/professional students (340 women), 1,554 part-time matriculated graduate/professional students (1,200 women). *Enrollment by degree level:* 1,089 master's, 85 doctoral, 848 other advanced degrees. *Graduate faculty:* 241 full-time (137 women), 16 part-time/adjunct (8 women). Tuition, state resident: full-time $2844; part-time $158 per semester hour. Tuition, nonresident: full-time $11,340; part-time $630 per semester hour. *Required fees:* $1120; $41.56 per semester hour. $186 per semester. Tuition and fees vary according to course load. *Graduate housing:* Room and/or apartments available on a first-come, first-served basis to single students; on-campus housing not available to married students. Typical cost: $3042 per year ($5874 including board). Room and board charges vary according to board plan and housing facility selected. Housing application deadline: 6/1. *Student services:* Campus employment opportunities, campus safety program, career counseling, child daycare facilities, exercise/wellness program, free psychological counseling, international student services, low-cost health insurance, multicultural affairs office, services for students with disabilities, teacher training, writing training. *Library facilities:* Irvine Sullivan Ingram Library. *Online resources:* library catalog, web page, access to other libraries' catalogs. *Collection:* 536,446 titles, 16,131 serial subscriptions, 11,634 audiovisual materials.

Computer facilities: 1,000 computers available on campus for general student use. A campuswide network can be accessed from student residence rooms and from off campus. Online class registration is available. *Web address:* http://www.westga.edu/.

General Application Contact: Dr. Charles W. Clark, Dean, 678-839-6508, E-mail: cclark@westga.edu.

GRADUATE UNITS

Graduate School Students: 468 full-time (340 women), 1,554 part-time (1,200 women); includes 569 minority (513 African Americans, 6 American Indian/Alaska Native, 18 Asian Americans or Pacific Islanders, 32 Hispanic Americans), 31 international. Average age 35. 710 applicants, 78% accepted, 207 enrolled. *Faculty:* 241 full-time (137 women), 16 part-time/adjunct (8 women). Expenses: Contact institution. *Financial support:* In 2008–09, 120 research assistantships with partial tuition reimbursements (averaging $5,000 per year) were awarded; career-related internships or fieldwork, tuition waivers (partial), and unspecified assistantships also available. Support available to part-time students. Financial award applicants required to submit FAFSA. In 2008, 346 master's, 8 doctorates, 141 other advanced degrees awarded. *Degree program information:* Part-time and evening/weekend programs available. Postbaccalaureate distance learning degree programs offered (no on-campus study). *Applica-*

University of West Georgia (continued)

tion deadline: For fall admission, 7/18 priority date for domestic students; for spring admission, 11/27 for domestic students. *Application fee:* $30. Electronic applications accepted. *Application Contact:* Cheryl Lynn Thomas Hill, Director of Graduate Admissions, 678-839-6419, Fax: 678-839-5949, E-mail: gradsch@westga.edu. *Interim Dean*, Dr. Charles W. Clark, 678-839-6508, E-mail: cclark@westga.edu.

College of Arts and Sciences Students: 106 full-time (61 women), 115 part-time (65 women); includes 35 minority (27 African Americans, 2 Asian Americans or Pacific Islanders, 6 Hispanic Americans), 7 international. Average age 32. 112 applicants, 77% accepted, 32 enrolled. *Faculty:* 142 full-time (49 women), 4 part-time/adjunct (2 women). Expenses: Contact institution. *Financial support:* In 2008–09, 40 research assistantships with full tuition reimbursements (averaging $6,000 per year) were awarded; career-related internships or fieldwork and unspecified assistantships also available. Support available to part-time students. Financial award applicants required to submit FAFSA. In 2008, 69 master's, 8 other advanced degrees awarded. *Degree program information:* Part-time programs available. Offers applied computer science (MS); arts and sciences (M Mus, MA, MPA, MS, MSN, Psy D, Certificate); biology (MS); criminology (MA); English (MA); geographic information systems (Certificate); geosciences (Certificate); history (MA, Certificate); human centered computing (Certificate); individual, organizational, and community transformation: consciousness and society (Psy D); museum studies (Certificate); music education (M Mus); nursing (MSN); performance (M Mus); psychology (MA, Psy D); public administration (MPA); public management (Certificate); rural and small town planning (MS); sociology (MA); software development (Certificate); system and network administration (Certificate); teaching and applied mathematics (MS); Web technologies (Certificate). *Application deadline:* For fall admission, 7/18 priority date for domestic students; for spring admission, 11/27 for domestic students. *Application fee:* $30. Electronic applications accepted. *Application Contact:* Dr. Charles W. Clark, Dean, 678-839-6508, E-mail: cclark@westga.edu. *Interim Dean*, Dr. Donadrian Rice, 678-839-6405, Fax: 678-839-4898.

College of Education Students: 289 full-time (238 women), 1,295 part-time (1,055 women); includes 476 minority (439 African Americans, 5 American Indian/Alaska Native, 9 Asian Americans or Pacific Islanders, 23 Hispanic Americans), 4 international. Average age 36. 494 applicants, 79% accepted, 135 enrolled. *Faculty:* 60 full-time (21 women), 10 part-time/adjunct (4 women). Expenses: Contact institution. *Financial support:* In 2008–09, 46 research assistantships with partial tuition reimbursements (averaging $6,000 per year) were awarded; career-related internships or fieldwork and unspecified assistantships also available. Support available to part-time students. Financial award applicants required to submit FAFSA. In 2008, 242 master's, 8 doctorates, 133 other advanced degrees awarded. *Degree program information:* Part-time and evening/weekend programs available. Offers administration and supervision (M Ed, Ed S); art education (M Ed); art teacher education (Ed S); biology/secondary education (Ed S); business education (M Ed, Ed S); early childhood education (M Ed, Ed S); economics/secondary teacher education (Ed S); education (M Ed, Ed D, Ed S); education-French (M Ed); education-Spanish (M Ed); English teacher education (Ed S); French language teacher education (Ed S); guidance and counseling (M Ed, Ed S); history teacher education (Ed S); mathematics teacher education (Ed S); media (M Ed, Ed S); middle grades education (M Ed, Ed S); physical education (M Ed); reading education (M Ed); school improvement (Ed D); science teacher education (Ed S); secondary education (M Ed, Ed S); social science teacher education (Ed S); Spanish language teacher education (Ed S); special education-general (M Ed, Ed S); speech-language pathology (M Ed). *Application deadline:* Applications are processed on a rolling basis. *Application fee:* $30. *Application Contact:* Dr. Charles W. Clark, Dean, 678-839-6508, E-mail: cclark@westga.edu. *Dean*, Dr. Kim Metcalf, 678-839-6570, Fax: 678-839-6098, E-mail: kmetcalf@westga.edu.

Richards College of Business Students: 60 full-time (28 women), 114 part-time (54 women); includes 48 minority (39 African Americans, 7 Asian Americans or Pacific Islanders, 2 Hispanic Americans), 20 international. Average age 29. 94 applicants, 76% accepted, 29 enrolled. *Faculty:* 32 full-time (9 women), 2 part-time/adjunct (0 women). Expenses: Contact institution. *Financial support:* In 2008–09, 10 students received support; research assistantships with full tuition reimbursements available, career-related internships or fieldwork, tuition waivers (partial), and unspecified assistantships available. Financial award application deadline: 7/1; financial award applicants required to submit FAFSA. In 2008, 25 master's awarded. *Degree program information:* Part-time and evening/weekend programs available. Offers accounting and finance (MP Acc); business (MBA, MP Acc); business administration (MBA). *Application deadline:* For fall admission, 7/18 priority date for domestic students; for spring admission, 11/27 for domestic students. *Application fee:* $30. Electronic applications accepted. *Application Contact:* Dr. Charles W. Clark, Dean, 678-839-6508, E-mail: cclark@westga.edu. *Dean*, Dr. Faye S. McIntyre, 678-839-6467, E-mail: fmcintyr@westga.edu.

UNIVERSITY OF WINDSOR, Windsor, ON N9B 3P4, Canada

General Information Province-supported, coed, university. *Graduate housing:* Rooms and/or apartments available on a first-come, first-served basis to single and married students. Housing application deadline: 6/7. *Research affiliation:* DaimlerChrysler Automotive Research and Development Centre.

GRADUATE UNITS

Faculty of Graduate Studies *Degree program information:* Part-time and evening/weekend programs available. Electronic applications accepted.

Faculty of Arts and Social Sciences *Degree program information:* Part-time programs available. Offers adult clinical (MA, PhD); applied social psychology (MA, PhD); arts and social sciences (MA, MFA, MSW, PhD); child clinical (MA, PhD); clinical neuropsychology (MA, PhD); communication and social justice (MA); criminology (MA); English: creative writing and language and literature (MA); English: language and literature (MA); history (MA); philosophy (MA); political science (MA); social work (MSW); sociology (MA); sociology-social justice (PhD); visual arts (MFA). Electronic applications accepted.

Faculty of Education *Degree program information:* Part-time and evening/weekend programs available. Offers education (M Ed); educational studies (PhD). Electronic applications accepted.

Faculty of Engineering *Degree program information:* Part-time programs available. Offers civil engineering (M Eng, MA Sc, PhD); electrical engineering (M Eng, MA Sc, PhD); engineering (M Eng, MA Sc, PhD); engineering materials (M Eng, MA Sc, PhD); environmental engineering (M Eng, MA Sc, PhD); industrial engineering (M Eng, MA Sc); manufacturing systems engineering (PhD); mechanical engineering (M Eng, MA Sc, PhD). Electronic applications accepted.

Faculty of Human Kinetics *Degree program information:* Part-time programs available. Offers human kinetics (MHK). Electronic applications accepted.

Faculty of Nursing Offers nursing (M Sc, MN). Electronic applications accepted.

Faculty of Science *Degree program information:* Part-time programs available. Offers biological sciences (M Sc, PhD); chemistry and biochemistry (M Sc, PhD); computer science (M Sc, PhD); earth sciences (M Sc, PhD); economics (MA); mathematics (M Sc); physics (M Sc, PhD); science (M Sc, MA, PhD); statistics (M Sc, PhD). Electronic applications accepted.

GLIER-Great Lakes Institute for Environmental Research Offers environmental science (M Sc, PhD). Electronic applications accepted.

Odette School of Business *Degree program information:* Evening/weekend programs available. Offers business (MBA, MM). Electronic applications accepted.

THE UNIVERSITY OF WINNIPEG, Winnipeg, MB R3B 2E9, Canada

General Information Province-supported, coed, comprehensive institution. *Graduate housing:* On-campus housing not available.

GRADUATE UNITS

Faculty of Theology *Degree program information:* Part-time programs available. Offers marriage and family therapy (MMFT, Certificate); sacred theology (STM); theology (M Div).

Graduate Studies *Degree program information:* Part-time and evening/weekend programs available. Offers history (MA); public administration (MPA); religious studies (MA).

UNIVERSITY OF WISCONSIN–EAU CLAIRE, Eau Claire, WI 54702-4004

General Information State-supported, coed, comprehensive institution. CGS member. *Enrollment:* 10,889 graduate, professional, and undergraduate students; 114 full-time matriculated graduate/professional students (85 women), 333 part-time matriculated graduate/professional students (204 women). *Enrollment by degree level:* 432 master's, 15 other advanced degrees. *Graduate faculty:* 334 full-time (126 women), 11 part-time/adjunct (5 women). Tuition, state resident: full-time $6426; part-time $400.60 per credit. Tuition, nonresident: full-time $17,560; part-time $975.32 per credit. One-time fee: $56 full-time. *Graduate housing:* Room and/or apartments guaranteed to single students; on-campus housing not available to married students. Typical cost: $2730 per year ($5210 including board). Room and board charges vary according to board plan and housing facility selected. *Student services:* Campus employment opportunities, campus safety program, career counseling, child daycare facilities, exercise/wellness program, free psychological counseling, grant writing training, international student services, low-cost health insurance, multicultural affairs office, services for students with disabilities, teacher training, writing training. *Library facilities:* William D. McIntyre Library plus 1 other. *Online resources:* library catalog, web page, access to other libraries' catalogs. *Collection:* 744,695 titles, 24,360 serial subscriptions, 10,297 audiovisual materials. *Research affiliation:* Research Corporation (chemistry, geology, physics/astronomy), Camille and Henry Dreyfus Foundation, Inc. (chemistry), Chevron Phillips Chemical Company (chemistry), SRI International (chemistry), American Chemical Society Petroleum Research Fund (chemistry, geology), Xcel Energy (biology, geography).

Computer facilities: 1,150 computers available on campus for general student use. A campuswide network can be accessed from student residence rooms and from off campus. Online class registration is available. *Web address:* http://www.uwec.edu/.

General Application Contact: Kristina Anderson, Director of Admissions, 715-836-5415, Fax: 715-836-2409, E-mail: admissions@uwec.edu.

GRADUATE UNITS

College of Arts and Sciences Students: 34 full-time (17 women), 42 part-time (25 women); includes 6 minority (4 American Indian/Alaska Native, 1 Asian American or Pacific Islander, 1 Hispanic American), 1 international. Average age 29. 77 applicants, 48% accepted, 37 enrolled. *Faculty:* 237 full-time (81 women), 8 part-time/adjunct (4 women). Expenses: Contact institution. *Financial support:* In 2008–09, 49 students received support. Application deadline: 3/1. In 2008, 27 master's awarded. Offers arts and sciences (MA, MSE, Ed S); English (MA); history (MA); school psychology (MSE, Ed S). *Application deadline:* For fall admission, 7/1 for domestic students, 6/1 priority date for international students; for spring admission, 12/1 for domestic students, 11/1 priority date for international students. Applications are processed on a rolling basis. *Application fee:* $56. Electronic applications accepted. *Application Contact:* Kristina Anderson, Director of Admissions, 715-836-5415, Fax: 715-836-2409, E-mail: admissions@uwec.edu. *Dean*, Dr. Donald Christian, 715-836-2542, Fax: 715-836-3292, E-mail: christdp@uwec.edu.

College of Business Students: 8 full-time (5 women), 184 part-time (84 women); includes 15 minority (4 African Americans, 4 American Indian/Alaska Native, 7 Asian Americans or Pacific Islanders), 2 international. Average age 31. 150 applicants, 61% accepted, 47 enrolled. *Faculty:* 32 full-time (8 women), 1 part-time/adjunct (0 women). Expenses: Contact institution. *Financial support:* In 2008–09, 33 students received support. Application deadline: 3/1. In 2008, 35 master's awarded. Offers business (MBA); business administration (MBA). *Application deadline:* For fall admission, 7/1 priority date for domestic students, 6/1 priority date for international students; for spring admission, 12/1 priority date for domestic students, 11/1 priority date for international students. Applications are processed on a rolling basis. *Application fee:* $56. Electronic applications accepted. *Application Contact:* Kristina Anderson, Director of Admissions, 715-836-5415, Fax: 715-836-2409, E-mail: admissions@uwec.edu. *Dean*, Dr. V. Thomas Dock, 715-836-5509, Fax: 715-836-4014, E-mail: dockv@uwec.edu.

College of Education and Human Sciences Students: 12 full-time (5 women), 62 part-time (21 women); includes 4 minority (3 Asian Americans or Pacific Islanders, 1 Hispanic American), 2 international. Average age 30. 173 applicants, 32% accepted, 23 enrolled. *Faculty:* 36 full-time (19 women), 2 part-time/adjunct (1 woman). Expenses: Contact institution. *Financial support:* In 2008–09, 50 students received support. Application deadline: 3/1. In 2008, 53 master's awarded. Offers communication sciences and disorders (MS); education and human sciences (MAT, MEPD, MS, MSE, MST); education and professional development (MEPD); elementary education (MST); English (MST); history/social science (MAT, MST); mathematics (MAT, MST); reading (MST); special education (MSE). *Application deadline:* For fall admission, 7/1 priority date for domestic students, 6/1 priority date for international students; for spring admission, 12/1 priority date for domestic students, 11/1 priority date for international students. Applications are processed on a rolling basis. *Application fee:* $56. Electronic applications accepted. *Application Contact:* Kristina Anderson, Director of Admissions, 715-836-5415, Fax: 715-836-2409, E-mail: admissions@uwec.edu. *Dean*, Dr. Gail Scukanec, 715-836-3264, Fax: 715-836-3245, E-mail: scukangp@uwec.edu.

College of Nursing and Health Sciences Students: 31 full-time (28 women), 65 part-time (60 women); includes 1 minority (American Indian/Alaska Native). Average age 36. 54 applicants, 72% accepted, 5 enrolled. *Faculty:* 16 full-time (15 women). Expenses: Contact institution. *Financial support:* In 2008–09, 53 students received support. Application deadline: 3/1. In 2008, 14 master's awarded. Offers nursing (MSN); nursing and health sciences (MSN). *Application deadline:* For fall admission, 2/1 priority date for domestic students, 6/1 priority date for international students; for spring admission, 11/1 priority date for international students. Applications are processed on a rolling basis. *Application fee:* $56. Electronic applications accepted. *Application Contact:* Kristina Anderson, Director of Admissions, 715-836-5415, Fax: 715-836-2409, E-mail: admissions@uwec.edu. *Associate Dean*, Dr. Mary Zwygart-Stauffacher, 715-836-4977, Fax: 715-836-5925, E-mail: zwygarmc@uwec.edu.

UNIVERSITY OF WISCONSIN–GREEN BAY, Green Bay, WI 54311-7001

General Information State-supported, coed, comprehensive institution. *Enrollment:* 6,275 graduate, professional, and undergraduate students; 39 full-time matriculated graduate/professional students (32 women), 123 part-time matriculated graduate/professional students (75 women). *Enrollment by degree level:* 162 master's. *Graduate faculty:* 22 full-time (10 women), 14 part-time/adjunct (10 women). Tuition, state resident: full-time $6426; part-time $357 per credit. Tuition, nonresident: full-time $16,771; part-time $932 per credit. *Required fees:* $1224; $68 per credit. Full-time tuition and fees vary according to course load and reciprocity agreements. *Graduate housing:* Room and/or apartments available on a first-come, first-served basis to single students; on-campus housing not available to married students. Typical cost: $3300 per year. Room charges vary according to housing facility selected. Housing application deadline: 5/1. *Student services:* Campus employment opportunities, campus safety program, career counseling, free psychological counseling, international student services, low-cost health insurance, multicultural affairs office, services for students with disabilities. *Library facilities:* Cofrin Library. *Online resources:* library catalog, web page, access to other libraries' catalogs. *Collection:* 360,795 titles, 4,452 serial subscriptions, 48,563 audiovisual materials. *Research affiliation:* R. W. Beck (Brown County waste-to-energy study), Robert E. Lee & Associates (endangered species survey for Brown County landfill site selection), Kimberly Clark (sludge recovery), Research Corporation (examination of the function structure, gene of Fetuin), Abbott Laboratories (anaerobic digestion systems).

Computer facilities: Computer purchase and lease plans are available. 550 computers available on campus for general student use. A campuswide network can be accessed from student residence rooms and from off campus. Online class registration, online degree progress, online financial records and bill paying are available. *Web address:* http://www.uwgb.edu/.

General Application Contact: Pam Harvey-Jacobs, Director of Admissions, 920-465-2111, Fax: 920-465-5754, E-mail: uwgb@uwgb.edu.

GRADUATE UNITS

Graduate Studies Students: 39 full-time (32 women), 123 part-time (75 women); includes 13 minority (10 American Indian/Alaska Native, 3 Asian Americans or Pacific Islanders), 2 international. Average age 32. 79 applicants, 92% accepted, 47 enrolled. *Faculty:* 22 full-time (10 women), 14 part-time/adjunct (10 women). Expenses: Contact institution. *Financial support:* In 2008–09, 1 research assistantship, 4 teaching assistantships were awarded; career-related internships or fieldwork, Federal Work-Study, institutionally sponsored loans, and aid for veterans and their family members also available. Financial award application deadline: 7/15; financial award applicants required to submit FAFSA. In 2008, 41 master's awarded. *Degree program information:* Part-time and evening/weekend programs available. Offers applied leadership for teaching and learning (MS Ed); environmental science and policy (MS); management (MS); social work (MSW). *Application deadline:* For fall admission, 8/1 for domestic students; for spring admission, 11/1 for domestic students. Applications are processed on a rolling basis. *Application fee:* $56. Electronic applications accepted. *Application Contact:* Pam Harvey-Jacobs, Director of Admissions, 920-465-2111, Fax: 920-465-5754, E-mail: uwgb@uwgb.edu. *Dean of Professional Studies and Outreach,* Fritz Erickson, 920-465-2123, Fax: 920-465-2728, E-mail: ericksof@uwgb.edu.

UNIVERSITY OF WISCONSIN–LA CROSSE, La Crosse, WI 54601-3742

General Information State-supported, coed, comprehensive institution. CGS member. *Enrollment:* 9,900 graduate, professional, and undergraduate students; 441 full-time matriculated graduate/professional students (262 women), 809 part-time matriculated graduate/professional students (564 women). *Enrollment by degree level:* 1,168 master's, 82 doctoral. *Graduate faculty:* 169 full-time (76 women), 18 part-time/adjunct (13 women). Tuition, state resident: full-time $6485; part-time $360 per credit hour. Tuition, nonresident: full-time $16,830; part-time $935 per credit hour. *Required fees:* $846. Tuition and fees vary according to program and reciprocity agreements. *Graduate housing:* Room and/or apartments available on a first-come, first-served basis to single students; on-campus housing not available to married students. Typical cost: $3130 per year ($5420 including board). Room and board charges vary according to housing facility selected. Housing application deadline: 5/1. *Student services:* Campus employment opportunities, campus safety program, career counseling, child daycare facilities, exercise/wellness program, free psychological counseling, grant writing training, international student services, low-cost health insurance, multicultural affairs office, services for students with disabilities, teacher training, writing training. *Library facilities:* Murphy Library. *Online resources:* library catalog, web page, access to other libraries' catalogs. *Collection:* 695,925 titles, 1,052 serial subscriptions.

Computer facilities: 600 computers available on campus for general student use. A campuswide network can be accessed from student residence rooms and from off campus. Online class registration is available. *Web address:* http://www.uwlax.edu/.

General Application Contact: Kathryn Kiefer, Associate Director of Admissions, 608-785-8939, E-mail: admissions@uwlax.edu.

GRADUATE UNITS

Office of University Graduate Studies Students: 441 full-time (262 women), 809 part-time (564 women); includes 36 minority (6 African Americans, 6 American Indian/Alaska Native, 13 Asian Americans or Pacific Islanders, 11 Hispanic Americans), 88 international. Average age 29. 511 applicants, 100% accepted, 336 enrolled. *Faculty:* 169 full-time (76 women), 18 part-time/adjunct (13 women). Expenses: Contact institution. *Financial support:* In 2008–09, 112 research assistantships with partial tuition reimbursements (averaging $7,500 per year) were awarded; career-related internships or fieldwork, Federal Work-Study, institutionally sponsored loans, scholarships/grants, traineeships, health care benefits, tuition waivers (full and partial), unspecified assistantships, and grant-funded positions, contract-funded assistantships also available. Support available to part-time students. Financial award application deadline: 3/15; financial award applicants required to submit FAFSA. In 2008, 593 master's awarded. *Degree program information:* Part-time and evening/weekend programs available. Postbaccalaureate distance learning degree programs offered (minimal on-campus study). *Application deadline:* For fall admission, 6/15 for international students. *Application fee:* $45. Electronic applications accepted. *Application Contact:* Kathryn Kiefer, Associate Director of Admissions, 608-785-8939, E-mail: admissions@uwlax.edu. *Director,* Dr. Vijendra Agarwal, 608-785-8124, Fax: 608-785-8179, E-mail: agarwal.vije@uwlax.edu.

College of Business Administration Students: 21 full-time (11 women), 33 part-time (13 women); includes 2 minority (1 Asian American or Pacific Islander, 1 Hispanic American), 14 international. Average age 30. 24 applicants, 100% accepted, 11 enrolled. *Faculty:* 30 full-time (8 women). Expenses: Contact institution. *Financial support:* In 2008–09, 4 research assistantships with partial tuition reimbursements (averaging $6,014 per year) were awarded; Federal Work-Study, health care benefits, tuition waivers (partial), and unspecified assistantships also available. Support available to part-time students. Financial award application deadline: 3/15; financial award applicants required to submit FAFSA. In 2008, 18 master's awarded. *Degree program information:* Part-time and evening/weekend programs available. Offers business administration (MBA). *Application deadline:* For fall admission, 5/1 priority date for domestic students; for spring admission, 10/1 priority date for domestic students. Applications are processed on a rolling basis. *Application fee:* $45. *Application Contact:* Amelia Dittman, Assistant to the Dean, 608-785-8092, Fax: 608-785-6700, E-mail: dittman.amel@uwlax.edu. *Associate Dean,* Dr. Bruce May, 608-785-8095, Fax: 608-785-6700, E-mail: may.bruce@uwlax.edu.

College of Liberal Studies Students: 128 full-time (74 women), 563 part-time (424 women); includes 23 minority (3 African Americans, 3 American Indian/Alaska Native, 9 Asian Americans or Pacific Islanders, 8 Hispanic Americans), 36 international. Average age 30. 170 applicants, 100% accepted, 127 enrolled. *Faculty:* 46 full-time (31 women), 18 part-time/adjunct (13 women). Expenses: Contact institution. *Financial support:* In 2008–09, 39 research assistantships with partial tuition reimbursements (averaging $7,500 per year) were awarded; career-related internships or fieldwork, Federal Work-Study, institutionally sponsored loans, scholarships/grants, health care benefits, and unspecified assistantships also available. Support available to part-time students. In 2008, 358 master's awarded. Offers college student development and administration (MS Ed); elementary education (MEPD); emotional disturbance (MS Ed); K–12 (MEPD); learning disabilities (MS Ed); liberal studies (MEPD, MS Ed, Ed S); professional development (MEPD); reading (MS Ed); school psychology (MS Ed, Ed S); secondary education (MEPD); special education (MS Ed); student affairs administration (MS Ed). *Application deadline:* For fall admission, 2/15 for domestic students. *Application fee:* $45. Electronic applications accepted. *Application Contact:* Kathryn Kiefer, Associate Director of Admissions, 608-785-8939, E-mail: admissions@uwlax.edu. *Dean,* Dr. Ruthann Benson, 608-785-8113, Fax: 608-785-8119, E-mail: benson.ruth@uwlax.edu.

College of Science and Health Students: 302 full-time (187 women), 213 part-time (127 women); includes 11 minority (3 African Americans, 3 American Indian/Alaska Native, 3 Asian Americans or Pacific Islanders, 2 Hispanic Americans), 38 international. Average age 27. 317 applicants, 100% accepted, 198 enrolled. *Faculty:* 93 full-time (37 women). Expenses: Contact institution. *Financial support:* In 2008–09, 69 research assistantships with partial tuition reimbursements (averaging $7,300 per year) were awarded; career-related internships or fieldwork, Federal Work-Study, scholarships/grants, traineeships, health care benefits, tuition waivers (partial), unspecified assistantships, and grant-funded positions, contract-funded assistantships also available. Support available to part-time students. Financial award application deadline: 3/15; financial award applicants required to submit FAFSA. In 2008, 217 master's awarded. *Degree program information:* Part-time programs available. Offers aquatic sciences (MS); athletic training (MS); biology (MS); cellular and molecular biology (MS); clinical exercise physiology (MS); clinical microbiology (MS); community health education (MPH, MS); human performance (MS); microbiology (MS); nurse anesthesia (MS); occupational therapy (MS); physical education teaching (MS); physical therapy (MSPT, DPT); physician assistant studies (MS); physiology (MS); recreation (MS); school health education (MS); science and health (MPH, MS, MSE, MSPT, DPT); software engineering (MSE); special/adapted physical education (MS); sport administration (MS). Electronic applications accepted. *Application Contact:* Kathryn Kiefer, Associate Director of Admissions, 608-785-8939, E-mail: admissions@uwlax.edu. *Interim Dean,* Dr. Bruce Riley, 608-785-8218, Fax: 608-785-8221, E-mail: riley.bruc@uwlax.edu.

UNIVERSITY OF WISCONSIN–MADISON, Madison, WI 53706-1380

General Information State-supported, coed, university. CGS member. *Enrollment:* 42,030 graduate, professional, and undergraduate students; 7,203 full-time matriculated graduate/professional students (3,556 women), 1,644 part-time matriculated graduate/professional students (854 women). *Enrollment by degree level:* 3,518 master's, 5,329 doctoral. *Graduate faculty:* 4,057. *Graduate housing:* Rooms and/or apartments available on a first-come, first-served basis to single and married students. *Student services:* Campus employment opportunities, campus safety program, career counseling, child daycare facilities, exercise/wellness program, free psychological counseling, grant writing training, international student services, low-cost health insurance, multicultural affairs office, services for students with disabilities, teacher training, writing training. *Library facilities:* Memorial Library plus 40 others. *Online resources:* library catalog, web page, access to other libraries' catalogs. *Research affiliation:* U.S. Department of Agriculture–Forest Products Laboratory, University Research Association, Institute on Tropical Studies, U.S. Department of Agriculture–Dairy Forage Research Center.

Computer facilities: A campuswide network can be accessed from student residence rooms and from off campus. Online class registration is available. *Web address:* http://www.wisc.edu/.

General Application Contact: Information Contact, 608-262-2433, Fax: 608-262-5134, E-mail: gradadmiss@mail.bascom.wisc.edu.

GRADUATE UNITS

Development Studies Program Offers development studies (PhD). Electronic applications accepted.

Graduate School Students: 7,203 full-time (3,556 women), 1,644 part-time (854 women); includes 898 minority (242 African Americans, 73 American Indian/Alaska Native, 330 Asian Americans or Pacific Islanders, 253 Hispanic Americans), 2,079 international. Average age 29. 18,546 applicants, 22% accepted, 2356 enrolled. Expenses: Contact institution. *Financial support:* In 2008–09, 5,442 students received support, including 522 fellowships with full and partial tuition reimbursements available (averaging $15,280 per year), 198 research assistantships with full and partial tuition reimbursements available (averaging $13,155 per year), 1,743 teaching assistantships with full and partial tuition reimbursements available (averaging $10,500 per year); career-related internships or fieldwork, Federal Work-Study, institutionally sponsored loans, scholarships/grants, traineeships, health care benefits, tuition waivers (full and partial), and unspecified assistantships also available. Support available to part-time students. Financial award applicants required to submit FAFSA. In 2008, 2,127 master's, 982 doctorates awarded. *Degree program information:* Part-time and evening/weekend programs available. Postbaccalaureate distance learning degree programs offered (minimal on-campus study). Offers biophysics (PhD); cellular and molecular biology (PhD); engine systems (ME); neuroscience (PhD); professional practice (ME). *Application deadline:* Applications are processed on a rolling basis. *Application fee:* $45. Electronic applications accepted. *Application Contact:* 608-262-2433, Fax: 608-262-5134, E-mail: gradadmiss@mail.bascom.wisc.edu. *Dean,* Dr. Martin Cadwallader, 608-262-1044.

College of Agricultural and Life Sciences *Degree program information:* Part-time programs available. Offers agricultural and applied economics (MA, MS, PhD); agricultural and life sciences (MA, MPS, MS, PhD); agroecology (MS); agronomy (MS, PhD); animal sciences (MS, PhD); bacteriology (MS); biochemistry (PhD); biological systems engineering (MS, PhD); dairy science (MS, PhD); entomology (MS, PhD); food science (MS, PhD); forest and wildlife ecology (MS, PhD); genetic counseling (MS); genetics (PhD); horticulture (MS, PhD); landscape architecture (MA, MS); life sciences communication (MPS, MS); mass communication (PhD); nutritional sciences (MS, PhD); plant breeding and plant genetics (MS, PhD); plant pathology (MS, PhD); soil science (MS, PhD). Electronic applications accepted.

College of Engineering *Degree program information:* Part-time programs available. Postbaccalaureate distance learning degree programs offered (minimal on-campus study). Offers biomedical engineering (MS, PhD); chemical engineering (MS, PhD); civil and environmental engineering (MS, PhD); electrical engineering (MS, PhD); energy systems (ME); engineering (ME, MS, PhD, PDD); engineering mechanics (MS, PhD); environmental chemistry and technology (MS, PhD); geological engineering (MS, PhD); industrial and systems engineering (MS, PhD); limnology and marine science (MS, PhD); manufacturing systems engineering (MS); materials engineering (MS, PhD); materials science (MS, PhD); mechanical engineering (MS, PhD); nuclear engineering and engineering physics (MS, PhD); polymers (ME). Electronic applications accepted.

College of Letters and Science *Degree program information:* Part-time and evening/weekend programs available. Postbaccalaureate distance learning degree programs offered (minimal on-campus study). Offers African history (MA, PhD); African languages and literature (MA, PhD); Afro-American studies (MA); applied English linguistics (MA); archaeology (PhD); area studies (MA); art history (MA, PhD); astronomy (PhD); atmospheric and oceanic sciences (MS, PhD); biological anthropology (PhD); biology of brain and behavior (PhD); biometry (MS); botany (MS, PhD); cartography and geographic information systems (MS); Central Asian history (MA, PhD); chemistry (MS, PhD); Chinese literature (MA, PhD); Chinese thought (MA, PhD); choral (MM, DMA); civilizations and cultures (PhD); classics (MA, PhD); clinical psychology (PhD); cognitive neurosciences (PhD); communication science (MA, PhD); comparative literature (MA, PhD); comparative world history (MA, PhD); composition (MM, DMA); composition and rhetoric (PhD); computer sciences (MS, PhD); creative writing (MFA); cultural anthropology (PhD); curriculum and instruction (MS, PhD); developmental psychology (PhD); East Asian history (MA, PhD); economics (PhD); English language and linguistics (PhD); ethnomusicology (MA, PhD); European history (MA, PhD); family and consumer journalism (PhD); film (MA, PhD); folklore (PhD); French (MA, PhD); French studies (MFS, Certificate); gender and women's history (MA, PhD); geographic information systems (Certificate); geography (MS, PhD); geology (MS, PhD); geophysics (MS, PhD); German (MA, PhD); Greek (MA); Hebrew and Semitic studies (MA, PhD); historical musicology (PhD); history of medicine (MA); history of science (MA, PhD); instrumental (MM, DMA); international public affairs (MPIA); Italian (MA, PhD); Japanese linguistics (MA, PhD); Japanese literature (MA, PhD); journalism and mass communication (MA); languages and cultures of Asia (MA); languages and literatures (PhD); Latin (MA); Latin American and Caribbean history (MA, PhD); Latin American, Caribbean and Iberian studies (MA); letters and science (MA, MFA, MFS, MM, MPA, MPIA, MS, MSW, DMA, PhD, Certificate); library and information studies (MA, PhD); linguistics (MA, PhD); literary studies (MA, PhD); literature (MA, PhD); mass communication (PhD); mathematics (PhD); media and cultural studies (MA, PhD); Middle Eastern history (MA, PhD); music (MA, MM, DMA, PhD); music education (MM); music history (MA); music performance (MM, DMA); music theory (MA, PhD); normal aspects of speech, language and hearing (MS, PhD); orchestral (MM, DMA); perception (PhD); philology (PhD); philosophy (MA, PhD); physics (MA, MS, PhD); political science (PhD); Portuguese (MA, PhD); psychology (PhD); public affairs (MPA, MPIA); religions of Asia (PhD); rhetoric (MA, PhD); rural sociology (MS); Slavic languages and literature (MA, PhD); social and personality psychology (PhD); social welfare (PhD); social work (MSW); sociology (MS, PhD); South Asian history (MA, PhD); Southeast Asian history (MA, PhD); Southeast Asian studies (MA); Spanish (MA, PhD); speech-language pathology (MS, PhD); statistics (MS, PhD); theatre and drama (MA, MFA, PhD); United States history (MA, PhD); urban and regional planning (MS, PhD); zoology (MA, MS, PhD). Electronic applications accepted.

Gaylord Nelson Institute for Environmental Studies Students: 150 (94 women); includes 11 minority (3 African Americans, 2 American Indian/Alaska Native, 4 Asian Americans or Pacific Islanders, 2 Hispanic Americans), 11 international. Average age 31. 225 applicants,

University of Wisconsin–Madison (continued)

55% accepted, 40 enrolled. *Faculty:* 6 full-time (3 women), 149 part-time/adjunct (29 women). Expenses: Contact institution. *Financial support:* In 2008–09, 103 students received support, including 16 fellowships with full tuition reimbursements available (averaging $16,605 per year), 19 research assistantships with full tuition reimbursements available (averaging $19,032 per year), 32 teaching assistantships with full tuition reimbursements available (averaging $12,894 per year); career-related internships or fieldwork, Federal Work-Study, scholarships/grants, traineeships, health care benefits, unspecified assistantships, and project assistantships also available. Financial award application deadline: 1/2. In 2008, 40 master's, 7 doctorates awarded. *Degree program information:* Part-time programs available. Offers conservation biology and sustainable development (MS); environment and resources (MS, PhD); environmental monitoring (MS, PhD); environmental studies (MS, PhD); water resources management (MS). *Application deadline:* For fall admission, 1/15 for domestic students, 1/5 for international students; for spring admission, 10/15 for domestic and international students. *Application fee:* $56. Electronic applications accepted. *Application Contact:* Jim Miller, Student Services Coordinator, 608-263-4373, Fax: 608-262-2273, E-mail: jemiller@wisc.edu. *Chair,* William Bland, 608-262-5518, Fax: 608-262-2273, E-mail: wlbland@wisc.edu.

School of Education Offers administration (Certificate); art (MA, MFA); art education (MA); counseling (MS); counseling psychology (MS, PhD); curriculum and instruction (MS, PhD); education (MA, MFA, MS, PhD, Certificate); education and mathematics (MA); educational policy (MS, PhD); educational policy studies (MA, PhD); educational psychology (MS, PhD); French education (MA); German education (MA); kinesiology (MS, PhD); music education (MS); occupational therapy (MS, PhD); rehabilitation psychology (MA, MS, PhD); science education (MS); Spanish education (MA); special education (MA, MS, PhD); therapeutic science (MS).

School of Human Ecology Offers consumer behavior and family economics (MS, PhD); design studies (MFA, MS, PhD); human development and family studies (MS, PhD). Electronic applications accepted.

Wisconsin School of Business Students: 375 full-time (138 women), 242 part-time (66 women); includes 58 minority (23 African Americans, 4 American Indian/Alaska Native, 22 Asian Americans or Pacific Islanders, 9 Hispanic Americans), 109 international. Average age 30. 1,237 applicants, 34% accepted, 317 enrolled. *Faculty:* 75 full-time (17 women). Expenses: Contact institution. *Financial support:* In 2008–09, 243 students received support, including 18 fellowships with partial tuition reimbursements available (averaging $15,583 per year), 54 research assistantships with full tuition reimbursements available (averaging $8,149 per year), 86 teaching assistantships with full tuition reimbursements available (averaging $12,300 per year); career-related internships or fieldwork, Federal Work-Study, institutionally sponsored loans, scholarships/grants, health care benefits, and unspecified assistantships also available. Support available to part-time students. In 2008, 265 master's, 14 doctorates awarded. *Degree program information:* Part-time and evening/weekend programs available. Offers accountancy (M Acc); accounting and information systems (PhD); actuarial science (MS); actuarial science, risk management and insurance (PhD); applied corporate finance (MBA); applied security analysis (MBA); arts administration (MBA); brand and product management (MBA); business (M Acc, MBA, MS, PhD); business administration (MBA); entrepreneurial management (MBA); finance, investment, and banking (PhD); information systems (PhD); management and human resources (PhD); marketing (PhD); marketing research (MBA); operations and information management (PhD); operations and technology management (MBA); quantitative finance (MS); real estate (MBA); real estate and urban land economics (PhD); risk management and insurance (MBA); strategic human resource management (MBA); strategic management in the life and engineering sciences (MBA); supply chain management (MBA). *Application deadline:* Applications are processed on a rolling basis. *Application fee:* $56. Electronic applications accepted. *Application Contact:* Seann Sweeney, Assistant Director of MBA Marketing and Recruiting, 608-262-4000, Fax: 608-265-4192, E-mail: ssweeney@bus.wisc.edu. *Dean,* Dr. Michael M. Knetter, 608-262-1758, E-mail: dean@bus.wisc.edu.

Law School Expenses: Contact institution. *Financial support:* Fellowships with partial tuition reimbursements, research assistantships with full tuition reimbursements, teaching assistantships with full tuition reimbursements, career-related internships or fieldwork, Federal Work-Study, institutionally sponsored loans, scholarships/grants, tuition waivers (partial), and unspecified assistantships available. Support available to part-time students. Financial award application deadline: 3/1; financial award applicants required to submit FAFSA. In 2008, 292 JDs, 22 master's, 10 doctorates awarded. *Degree program information:* Part-time programs available. Offers law (JD, LL M, SJD). *Application deadline:* Applications are processed on a rolling basis. Electronic applications accepted.

School of Medicine and Public Health Expenses: Contact institution. *Financial support:* Fellowships with full tuition reimbursements, research assistantships with full tuition reimbursements, teaching assistantships with full tuition reimbursements, scholarships/grants, traineeships, and tuition waivers (full) available. *Degree program information:* Part-time programs available. Postbaccalaureate distance learning degree programs offered (minimal on-campus study). Offers biomolecular chemistry (MS, PhD); cancer biology (PhD); clinical research (PhD); endocrinology-reproductive physiology (MS, PhD); epidemiology (MS); genetics and medical genetics (MS, PhD); health physics (MS); health services research (MS, PhD); medical physics (MS, PhD); medicine (MD, MPH, MS, PhD); medicine and public health (MD, MPH, MS, PhD); microbiology (PhD); molecular and cellular pharmacology (PhD); pathology and laboratory medicine (PhD); physiology (PhD); population health sciences (MPH, MS, PhD); social and behavioral health sciences (MS, PhD). Electronic applications accepted. *Application Contact:* Information Contact, 608-262-2433, Fax: 608-262-5134, E-mail: gradadmiss@mail.bascom.wisc.edu. *Dean,* Dr. Robert N. Golden, 608-263-4910, Fax: 608-265-3286, E-mail: rngolden@wisc.edu.

Molecular and Environmental Toxicology Center Students: 38 full-time (24 women); includes 3 minority (1 American Indian/Alaska Native, 2 Asian Americans or Pacific Islanders), 9 international. Average age 29. 40 applicants, 33% accepted, 10 enrolled. *Faculty:* 66 full-time (18 women). Expenses: Contact institution. *Financial support:* In 2008–09, 6 research assistantships with tuition reimbursements (averaging $22,500 per year) were awarded; fellowships with tuition reimbursements, traineeships, health care benefits, and unspecified assistantships also available. In 2008, 1 master's, 6 doctorates awarded. Offers molecular and environmental toxicology (MS, PhD). *Application deadline:* For fall admission, 12/15 priority date for domestic and international students. *Application fee:* $45. Electronic applications accepted. *Application Contact:* Eileen M. Stevens, Program Administrator, 608-263-4580, Fax: 608-262-5245, E-mail: emstevens@wisc.edu. *Director,* Dr. Christopher Bradfield, 608-262-2024, E-mail: bradfield@oncology.wisc.edu.

School of Nursing Students: 64 full-time (63 women), 157 part-time (150 women); includes 11 minority (3 African Americans, 2 American Indian/Alaska Native, 4 Asian Americans or Pacific Islanders, 2 Hispanic Americans), 3 international. Average age 37. 92 applicants, 58% accepted, 46 enrolled. *Faculty:* 20 full-time (19 women), 1 part-time/adjunct (0 women). Expenses: Contact institution. *Financial support:* In 2008–09, 70 students received support, including 11 fellowships with full tuition reimbursements available (averaging $22,000 per year), 9 research assistantships with full tuition reimbursements available (averaging $20,000 per year), 8 teaching assistantships with full tuition reimbursements available (averaging $14,000 per year); career-related internships or fieldwork, Federal Work-Study, institutionally sponsored loans, scholarships/grants, traineeships, health care benefits, and unspecified assistantships also available. Support available to part-time students. Financial award application deadline: 6/1. In 2008, 6 doctorates awarded. *Degree program information:* Part-time programs available. Offers nursing (PhD). *Application deadline:* For fall admission, 3/1 priority date for domestic students; for spring admission, 10/1 priority date for domestic students. *Application fee:* $45. Electronic applications accepted. *Application Contact:* Marcia L. Voss, Graduate Program Coordinator, 608-263-5258, Fax: 608-263-5332, E-mail: mlvoss@wisc.edu. *Dean,* Dr. Katharyn A. May, 608-263-5155, Fax: 608-263-5323, E-mail: kamay@wisc.edu.

School of Pharmacy Offers pharmaceutical sciences (PhD); pharmacy (Pharm D, MS, PhD); social and administrative sciences in pharmacy (MS, PhD). Electronic applications accepted.

School of Veterinary Medicine Students: 360 full-time (268 women); includes 43 minority (6 African Americans, 6 American Indian/Alaska Native, 18 Asian Americans or Pacific Islanders, 13 Hispanic Americans), 13 international. Average age 26. *Faculty:* 75 full-time. Expenses: Contact institution. *Financial support:* Fellowships, research assistantships, teaching assistantships, career-related internships or fieldwork, Federal Work-Study, institutionally sponsored loans, and scholarships/grants available. Support available to part-time students. Financial award application deadline: 3/1. In 2008, 69 first professional degrees awarded. Offers comparative biomedical sciences (MS, PhD); veterinary medicine (DVM, MS, PhD). *Application Contact:* Dr. Daryl D. Buss, Dean, 608-263-6716, E-mail: bussd@svm.vetmed.wisc.edu. *Dean,* Dr. Daryl D. Buss, 608-263-6716, E-mail: bussd@svm.vetmed.wisc.edu.

UNIVERSITY OF WISCONSIN–MILWAUKEE, Milwaukee, WI 53201-0413

General Information State-supported, coed, university. CGS member. *Enrollment:* 29,215 graduate, professional, and undergraduate students; 2,318 full-time matriculated graduate/professional students (1,354 women), 2,215 part-time matriculated graduate/professional students (1,413 women). *Enrollment by degree level:* 3,392 master's, 1,070 doctoral, 71 other advanced degrees. *Graduate faculty:* 848 full-time (340 women). Tuition, state resident: full-time $7320; part-time $165 per credit. Tuition, nonresident: full-time $17,840; part-time $714 per credit. Tuition and fees vary according to campus/location, program and reciprocity agreements. *Graduate housing:* Room and/or apartments available on a first-come, first-served basis to single students; on-campus housing not available to married students. Typical cost: $5700 per year ($7900 including board). Room and board charges vary according to board plan, campus/location and housing facility selected. Housing application deadline: 4/7. *Student services:* Campus employment opportunities, campus safety program, career counseling, child daycare facilities, free psychological counseling, international student services, low-cost health insurance, multicultural affairs office, services for students with disabilities. *Library facilities:* Golda Meir Library. *Online resources:* library catalog, web page, access to other libraries' catalogs. *Collection:* 1.4 million titles, 8,240 serial subscriptions. *Research affiliation:* We Energies (environment, wind turbine technology), Veolia Water SA (water research), Rockwell Automation (informatics, sensors and devices, materials), Johnson Controls (environment, advanced automation), GE Healthcare (informatics, biomedical/imaging).

Computer facilities: 1,000 computers available on campus for general student use. A campuswide network can be accessed from student residence rooms and from off campus. Online class registration is available. *Web address:* http://www.uwm.edu/.

General Application Contact: General Information Contact, 414-229-4982, Fax: 414-229-6967, E-mail: gradschool@uwm.edu.

GRADUATE UNITS

Graduate School Students: 2,318 full-time (1,354 women), 2,215 part-time (1,413 women); includes 533 minority (238 African Americans, 28 American Indian/Alaska Native, 141 Asian Americans or Pacific Islanders, 126 Hispanic Americans), 508 international. Average age 32. 3,910 applicants, 49% accepted, 1111 enrolled. *Faculty:* 848 full-time (340 women). Expenses: Contact institution. *Financial support:* In 2008–09, 103 fellowships with partial tuition reimbursements (averaging $15,000 per year), 89 research assistantships with partial tuition reimbursements (averaging $17,200 per year), 769 teaching assistantships with full tuition reimbursements (averaging $18,100 per year) were awarded; career-related internships or fieldwork, Federal Work-Study, tuition waivers (partial), and unspecified assistantships also available. Support available to part-time students. Financial award application deadline: 4/15; financial award applicants required to submit FAFSA. In 2008, 1,191 master's, 129 doctorates awarded. *Degree program information:* Part-time and evening/weekend programs available. Offers multidisciplinary studies (PhD). *Application deadline:* For fall admission, 1/1 priority date for domestic students; for spring admission, 9/1 for domestic students. Applications are processed on a rolling basis. *Application fee:* $45 ($75 for international students). *Application Contact:* General Information Contact, 414-229-4982, Fax: 414-229-6967, E-mail: gradschool@uwm.edu. *Dean of Graduate School/Vice Chancellor for Research and Economic Development,* Colin Scanes, 414-229-2591, Fax: 414-229-2348, E-mail: scanes@uwm.edu.

College of Engineering and Applied Science Students: 119 full-time (26 women), 151 part-time (22 women); includes 25 minority (5 African Americans, 11 Asian Americans or Pacific Islanders, 9 Hispanic Americans), 125 international. Average age 32. 292 applicants, 57% accepted, 73 enrolled. *Faculty:* 61 full-time (6 women). Expenses: Contact institution. *Financial support:* In 2008–09, 12 research assistantships, 56 teaching assistantships were awarded; fellowships, career-related internships or fieldwork, Federal Work-Study, and unspecified assistantships also available. Support available to part-time students. Financial award application deadline: 4/15. In 2008, 41 master's, 13 doctorates awarded. *Degree program information:* Part-time programs available. Offers civil engineering (MS); computer science (MS, PhD); electrical and computer engineering (MS); engineering (PhD); engineering and applied science (MS, PhD, Certificate); engineering management (MS); engineering mechanics (MS); industrial and management engineering (MS); manufacturing engineering (MS); materials engineering (MS); mechanical engineering (MS); medical informatics (PhD). *Application deadline:* For fall admission, 1/1 priority date for domestic students; for spring admission, 9/1 for domestic students. Applications are processed on a rolling basis. *Application fee:* $45 ($75 for international students). *Application Contact:* David Yu, General Information Contact, 414-229-4982, Fax: 414-229-6169, E-mail: yu@uwm.edu. *Dean,* Dr. Michael R Lovell, 414-229-4126, E-mail: mlovell@uwm.edu.

College of Health Sciences Students: 149 full-time (121 women), 34 part-time (21 women); includes 13 minority (8 African Americans, 2 American Indian/Alaska Native, 3 Hispanic Americans), 11 international. Average age 27. 257 applicants, 30% accepted, 42 enrolled. *Faculty:* 50 full-time (26 women). Expenses: Contact institution. *Financial support:* In 2008–09, 9 research assistantships, 10 teaching assistantships were awarded; career-related internships or fieldwork, Federal Work-Study, and unspecified assistantships also available. Support available to part-time students. Financial award application deadline: 4/15. In 2008, 68 master's awarded. *Degree program information:* Part-time programs available. Offers clinical laboratory science (MS); communication sciences and disorders (MS); ergonomics (Certificate); health sciences (MS, DPT, PhD, Certificate); healthcare informatics (MS, Certificate); kinesiology/human movement sciences (MS); occupational therapy (MS); physical therapy (DPT); therapeutic recreation (Certificate). *Application deadline:* For fall admission, 1/1 priority date for domestic students; for spring admission, 9/1 for domestic students. Applications are processed on a rolling basis. *Application fee:* $45 ($75 for international students). *Application Contact:* Roger O Smith, General Information Contact, 414-229-6697, Fax: 414-229-6697, E-mail: smithro@uwm.edu. *Acting Dean,* Johannes Britz, 414-229-4709, E-mail: britz@uwm.edu.

College of Letters and Sciences Students: 764 full-time (389 women), 541 part-time (339 women); includes 130 minority (45 African Americans, 12 American Indian/Alaska Native, 31 Asian Americans or Pacific Islanders, 42 Hispanic Americans), 247 international. Average age 32. 1,416 applicants, 43% accepted, 343 enrolled. *Faculty:* 404 full-time (136 women). Expenses: Contact institution. *Financial support:* In 2008–09, 6 fellowships, 62 research assistantships, 577 teaching assistantships were awarded; career-related internships or fieldwork, Federal Work-Study, and unspecified assistantships also available. Support available to part-time students. Financial award application deadline: 4/15. In 2008, 275 master's, 65 doctorates awarded. *Degree program information:* Part-time programs available. Offers Africology (PhD); anthropology (PhD); art history (MA); art museum studies (Certificate); biogeochemistry (PhD); biological sciences (MS, PhD); chemistry (MS, PhD); classics and Hebrew studies (MAFLL); clinical psychology (MS, PhD); communication (MA, PhD); comparative literature (MAFLL); creative writing (PhD); economics (MA, PhD); English (MA); French and Italian (MAFLL); geography (MA, MS, PhD); geological sciences (MS, PhD); German (MAFLL); global history (PhD); history (MA); human resources and labor relations (MHRLR); international human resources and labor relations (Certificate); letters and sciences (MA, MAFLL, MHRLR, MLS, MPA, MS, PhD, Certificate); liberal studies (MLS); linguistics (PhD); mathematics (MS, PhD); media studies (MA); mediation and negotiation (Certificate); modern studies (PhD); museum studies (Certificate); philosophy (MA); physics (MS, PhD); political science (MA, PhD); professional writing (PhD); professional writing and communication (Certificate); psychology (MS, PhD); public administration (MPA); rhetoric and composition (PhD); rhetorical leadership (Certificate);

Slavic studies (MAFLL); sociology (MA); Spanish (MA); translation (Certificate); urban history (PhD); urban studies (MS, PhD). *Application deadline:* For fall admission, 1/1 priority date for domestic students; for spring admission, 9/1 for domestic students. Applications are processed on a rolling basis. *Application fee:* $45 ($75 for international students). *Application Contact:* General Information Contact, 414-229-4982, Fax: 414-229-6967, E-mail: gradschool@uwm.edu. *Dean,* G. Richard Meadows, 414-229-5895, E-mail: meadows@uwm.edu.

College of Nursing Students: 159 full-time (148 women), 118 part-time (100 women); includes 32 minority (15 African Americans, 1 American Indian/Alaska Native, 11 Asian Americans or Pacific Islanders, 5 Hispanic Americans), 6 international. Average age 39. 113 applicants, 54% accepted, 44 enrolled. *Faculty:* 33 full-time (32 women). Expenses: Contact institution. *Financial support:* In 2008–09, 10 teaching assistantships were awarded; career-related internships or fieldwork, Federal Work-Study, and unspecified assistantships also available. Support available to part-time students. Financial award application deadline: 4/15. In 2008, 68 master's, 9 doctorates awarded. *Degree program information:* Part-time programs available. Offers family nursing practitioner (Post Master's Certificate); health professional education (Certificate); nursing (MS, PhD); public health (Certificate). *Application deadline:* For fall admission, 1/1 priority date for domestic students; for spring admission, 9/1 for domestic students. Applications are processed on a rolling basis. *Application fee:* $45 ($75 for international students). *Application Contact:* Ellen K. Murphy, Representative, 414-229-5468. *Representative,* Karen Morin, 414-229-5503, Fax: 414-229-6474, E-mail: morin@uwm.edu.

Peck School of the Arts Students: 76 full-time (43 women), 33 part-time (18 women); includes 8 minority (2 African Americans, 4 Asian Americans or Pacific Islanders, 2 Hispanic Americans), 9 international. Average age 32. 143 applicants, 40% accepted, 45 enrolled. *Faculty:* 81 full-time (41 women). Expenses: Contact institution. *Financial support:* In 2008–09, 33 teaching assistantships were awarded; career-related internships or fieldwork, Federal Work-Study, and unspecified assistantships also available. Support available to part-time students. Financial award application deadline: 4/15. In 2008, 52 master's awarded. *Degree program information:* Part-time programs available. Offers art (MA, MFA); art education (MA, MFA, MS); arts (MA, MFA, MM, MS, Certificate); chamber music performance (Certificate); dance (MFA); film (MFA); music composition (MM); music education (MM); music history and literature (MM); opera and vocal arts (Certificate); string pedagogy (MM); theatre (MFA). *Application deadline:* For fall admission, 1/1 priority date for domestic students; for spring admission, 9/1 for domestic students. Applications are processed on a rolling basis. *Application fee:* $45 ($75 for international students). *Application Contact:* Denis Sargent, General Information Contact, 414-229-6053, Fax: 414-229-6967, E-mail: artgrado@uwm.edu. *Dean,* Wade Hobgood, 414-229-4762, E-mail: whobgood@uwm.edu.

School of Architecture and Urban Planning Students: 185 full-time (61 women), 25 part-time (15 women); includes 17 minority (4 African Americans, 1 American Indian/Alaska Native, 6 Asian Americans or Pacific Islanders, 6 Hispanic Americans), 15 international. Average age 28. 187 applicants, 63% accepted, 50 enrolled. *Faculty:* 32 full-time (6 women). Expenses: Contact institution. *Financial support:* In 2008–09, 23 teaching assistantships were awarded; career-related internships or fieldwork, Federal Work-Study, and unspecified assistantships also available. Support available to part-time students. Financial award application deadline: 4/15. In 2008, 39 master's, 3 doctorates awarded. *Degree program information:* Part-time programs available. Offers architecture (PhD); architecture and urban planning (M Arch, MUP, PhD, Certificate); geographic information systems (Certificate); preservation studies (Certificate); urban planning (MUP). *Application deadline:* For fall admission, 1/1 priority date for domestic students; for spring admission, 9/1 for domestic students. Applications are processed on a rolling basis. *Application fee:* $45 ($75 for international students). *Application Contact:* Joan Simuncak, Senior Administrative Program Specialist, 414-229-4015, Fax: 414-229-6967, E-mail: joanarch@uwm.edu. *Dean,* Robert Greenstreet, 414-229-4016, E-mail: bobg@uwm.edu.

School of Education Students: 281 full-time (218 women), 344 part-time (269 women); includes 152 minority (91 African Americans, 6 American Indian/Alaska Native, 23 Asian Americans or Pacific Islanders, 32 Hispanic Americans), 16 international. Average age 34. 427 applicants, 51% accepted, 117 enrolled. *Faculty:* 74 full-time (50 women). Expenses: Contact institution. *Financial support:* In 2008–09, 12 teaching assistantships were awarded; career-related internships or fieldwork, Federal Work-Study, and unspecified assistantships also available. Support available to part-time students. Financial award application deadline: 4/15. In 2008, 213 master's, 18 doctorates awarded. *Degree program information:* Part-time programs available. Offers administrative leadership (Certificate); administrative leadership and supervision in education (MS); adult and continuing education (PhD); assistive technology and accessible design (Certificate); counseling (school, community) (MS); counseling psychology (PhD); cultural foundations of education (MS); curriculum and instruction (PhD); curriculum planning and instruction improvement (MS); early childhood education (MS); education (MS, PhD, Certificate, Ed S); educational administration (PhD); educational and media technology (PhD); educational psychology (PhD); elementary education (MS); exceptional education (MS); junior high/middle school education (MS); learning and development (MS); multicultural studies (PhD); reading education (MS); research methodology (MS, PhD); school psychology (PhD); secondary education (MS); social foundations of education (PhD); teaching in an urban setting (MS). *Application deadline:* For fall admission, 1/1 priority date for domestic students; for spring admission, 9/1 for domestic students. Applications are processed on a rolling basis. *Application fee:* $45 ($75 for international students). *Application Contact:* General Information Contact, 414-229-4982, Fax: 414-229-6967, E-mail: gradschool@uwm.edu. *Dean,* Alfonzo Thurman, 414-229-4181, E-mail: athurman@uwm.edu.

School of Information Studies Students: 106 full-time (77 women), 423 part-time (351 women); includes 32 minority (8 African Americans, 13 Asian Americans or Pacific Islanders, 11 Hispanic Americans), 17 international. Average age 36. 287 applicants, 74% accepted, 110 enrolled. *Faculty:* 20 full-time (8 women). Expenses: Contact institution. *Financial support:* In 2008–09, 2 teaching assistantships were awarded; career-related internships or fieldwork, Federal Work-Study, and unspecified assistantships also available. Support available to part-time students. Financial award application deadline: 4/15. In 2008, 174 master's awarded. *Degree program information:* Part-time programs available. Offers advanced studies in library and information science (CAS); archives and records administration (CAS); information studies (MLIS, PhD). *Application deadline:* For fall admission, 1/1 priority date for domestic students; for spring admission, 9/1 for domestic students. Applications are processed on a rolling basis. *Application fee:* $45 ($75 for international students). *Application Contact:* Dietmar Wolfram, 414-229-6836, E-mail: dwolfram@uwm.edu. *Dean,* Johannes Britz, 414-229-4709, Fax: 414-229-4848.

School of Social Welfare Students: 189 full-time (165 women), 117 part-time (102 women); includes 61 minority (42 African Americans, 3 American Indian/Alaska Native, 7 Asian Americans or Pacific Islanders, 9 Hispanic Americans). Average age 31. 329 applicants, 57% accepted, 126 enrolled. *Faculty:* 28 full-time (14 women). Expenses: Contact institution. *Financial support:* In 2008–09, 5 fellowships, 8 teaching assistantships were awarded; career-related internships or fieldwork, Federal Work-Study, and unspecified assistantships also available. Support available to part-time students. Financial award application deadline: 4/15. In 2008, 144 master's awarded. *Degree program information:* Part-time programs available. Offers administration (MS); applied gerontology (Certificate); corrections (MS); law enforcement (MS); marriage and family therapy (Certificate); non-profit management (Certificate); social welfare (MS, MSW, PhD, Certificate); social work (MSW, PhD). *Application deadline:* For fall admission, 1/1 priority date for domestic students; for spring admission, 9/1 for domestic students. Applications are processed on a rolling basis. *Application fee:* $45 ($75 for international students). *Application Contact:* Steven Brandl, General Information Contact, 414-229-5443, Fax: 414-229-6967, E-mail: sgb@uwm.edu. *Dean,* Stan Stojkovic, 414-229-4400, E-mail: stojkovi@uwm.edu.

Sheldon B. Lubar School of Business Students: 290 full-time (111 women), 429 part-time (177 women); includes 63 minority (18 African Americans, 3 American Indian/Alaska Native, 35 Asian Americans or Pacific Islanders, 7 Hispanic Americans), 62 international. Average age 32. 462 applicants, 51% accepted, 161 enrolled. *Faculty:* 56 full-time (17 women). Expenses: Contact institution. *Financial support:* In 2008–09, 2 fellowships, 38 teaching assistantships were awarded; career-related internships or fieldwork, Federal Work-Study, and unspecified assistantships also available. Support available to part-time students. Financial award application deadline: 4/15. In 2008, 265 master's, 9 doctorates awarded. *Degree program information:* Part-time and evening/weekend programs available. Offers business (MBA, PhD, Certificate); executive business administration (Exec MBA); management science (MS, PhD); nonprofit management and leadership (Certificate). *Application deadline:* For fall admission, 1/1 priority date for domestic students; for spring admission, 9/1 for domestic students. Applications are processed on a rolling basis. *Application fee:* $45 ($75 for international students). *Application Contact:* Sara Sandin, 414-229-5403, E-mail: mba-ms@uwm.edu. *Dean,* V. Kanti Prasad, 414-229-6256, Fax: 414-229-2372, E-mail: vkp@uwm.edu.

UNIVERSITY OF WISCONSIN–OSHKOSH, Oshkosh, WI 54901

General Information State-supported, coed, comprehensive institution. *Graduate housing:* Room and/or apartments available on a first-come, first-served basis to single students; on-campus housing not available to married students.

GRADUATE UNITS

The Office of Graduate Studies *Degree program information:* Part-time and evening/weekend programs available. Offers social work (MSW). Electronic applications accepted.

College of Business *Degree program information:* Part-time programs available. Offers business (GMBA, MBA); business administration (MBA); global business administration (GMBA). Electronic applications accepted.

College of Education and Human Services *Degree program information:* Part-time and evening/weekend programs available. Offers counseling (MSE); cross-categorical (MSE); curriculum and instruction (MSE); early childhood: exceptional education needs (MSE); education and human services (MS, MSE); educational leadership (MS); non-licensure (MSE); reading education (MSE). Electronic applications accepted.

College of Letters and Science *Degree program information:* Part-time and evening/weekend programs available. Offers biology (MS); English (MA); experimental psychology (MS); general agency (MPA); health care (MPA); industrial/organizational psychology (MS); letters and science (MA, MPA, MS, MSW); mathematics education (MS). Electronic applications accepted.

College of Nursing *Degree program information:* Part-time programs available. Offers adult health and illness (MSN); family nurse practitioner (MSN). Electronic applications accepted.

UNIVERSITY OF WISCONSIN–PARKSIDE, Kenosha, WI 53141-2000

General Information State-supported, coed, comprehensive institution. *Graduate housing:* Room and/or apartments available on a first-come, first-served basis to single students; on-campus housing not available to married students.

GRADUATE UNITS

College of Arts and Sciences *Degree program information:* Part-time programs available. Offers applied molecular biology (MAMB); arts and sciences (MAMB). Electronic applications accepted.

School of Business and Technology *Degree program information:* Part-time and evening/weekend programs available. Offers business administration (MBA); business and technology (MBA, MSCIS); computer and information systems (MSCIS). Electronic applications accepted.

UNIVERSITY OF WISCONSIN–PLATTEVILLE, Platteville, WI 53818-3099

General Information State-supported, coed, comprehensive institution. *Enrollment:* 7,379 graduate, professional, and undergraduate students; 79 full-time matriculated graduate/professional students (55 women), 533 part-time matriculated graduate/professional students (255 women). *Enrollment by degree level:* 612 master's. *Graduate faculty:* 5 full-time (2 women), 90 part-time/adjunct (16 women). *Graduate housing:* On-campus housing not available. *Student services:* Campus employment opportunities, campus safety program, career counseling, child daycare facilities, exercise/wellness program, free psychological counseling, grant writing training, international student services, low-cost health insurance, multicultural affairs office, services for students with disabilities, teacher training, writing training. *Library facilities:* Karrmann Library. *Online resources:* library catalog, web page, access to other libraries' catalogs. *Collection:* 362,247 titles, 2,116 serial subscriptions.

Computer facilities: 1,200 computers available on campus for general student use. A campuswide network can be accessed from student residence rooms and from off campus. Online class registration is available. *Web address:* http://www.uwplatt.edu/.

General Application Contact: Lisa Popp, School of Graduate Studies, 608-342-1322, Fax: 608-342-1389, E-mail: poppl@uwplatt.edu.

GRADUATE UNITS

School of Graduate Studies Students: 79 full-time (55 women), 533 part-time (255 women); includes 62 minority (38 African Americans, 3 American Indian/Alaska Native, 7 Asian Americans or Pacific Islanders, 14 Hispanic Americans), 102 international. 190 applicants, 59% accepted. *Faculty:* 5 full-time (2 women), 90 part-time/adjunct (16 women). Expenses: Contact institution. *Financial support:* Research assistantships with partial tuition reimbursements, career-related internships or fieldwork, Federal Work-Study, institutionally sponsored loans, scholarships/grants, and unspecified assistantships available. Support available to part-time students. In 2008, 160 master's awarded. *Degree program information:* Part-time and evening/weekend programs available. Postbaccalaureate distance learning degree programs offered (no on-campus study). *Application deadline:* For fall admission, 7/1 priority date for domestic students; for spring admission, 11/1 for domestic students. Applications are processed on a rolling basis. *Application fee:* $56. Electronic applications accepted. *Application Contact:* Lisa Popp, School of Graduate Studies, 608-342-1322, Fax: 608-342-1389, E-mail: poppl@uwplatt.edu. *Dean,* Dr. David P. Van Buren, 608-342-1262, Fax: 608-342-1270, E-mail: vanburen@uwplatt.edu.

College of Engineering, Mathematics and Science Students: 1 full-time (0 women), 96 part-time (16 women); includes 9 minority (6 African Americans, 2 Asian Americans or Pacific Islanders, 1 Hispanic American). 2 applicants, 50% accepted. Expenses: Contact institution. *Financial support:* Research assistantships with partial tuition reimbursements available. *Degree program information:* Part-time programs available. Offers computer science (MS); engineering, mathematics and science (MS). *Application deadline:* For fall admission, 7/1 priority date for domestic students; for spring admission, 11/1 for domestic students. *Application fee:* $56. *Application Contact:* Lisa Popp, School of Graduate Studies, 608-342-1322, Fax: 608-342-1389, E-mail: poppl@uwplatt.edu. *Dean,* Dr. Rich Shultz, 608-342-1561, Fax: 608-342-1566, E-mail: masoom@uwplatt.edu.

College of Liberal Arts and Education Students: 67 full-time (51 women), 185 part-time (140 women); includes 31 minority (23 African Americans, 1 American Indian/Alaska Native, 1 Asian American or Pacific Islander, 6 Hispanic Americans), 79 international. 81 applicants, 56% accepted. *Faculty:* 4 full-time (1 woman), 54 part-time/adjunct (14 women). Expenses: Contact institution. *Financial support:* Research assistantships with partial tuition reimbursements, career-related internships or fieldwork, Federal Work-Study, institutionally sponsored loans, scholarships/grants, and unspecified assistantships available. Support available to part-time students. In 2008, 82 master's awarded. *Degree program information:* Part-time programs available. Offers adult education (MSE); counselor education (MSE); elementary education (MSE); liberal arts and education (MSE); middle school education (MSE); secondary education (MSE); vocational and technical education (MSE). *Application deadline:* For fall admission, 7/1 priority date for domestic students; for spring admission, 11/1 for domestic students. Applications are processed on a rolling basis. *Application fee:* $56. Electronic applications accepted. *Application Contact:* Lisa Popp, School of Graduate Studies, 608-342-1322, Fax: 608-342-1389, E-mail: poppl@uwplatt.edu. *Dean,* Dr. Mittie Nimocks, 608-342-1151, Fax: 608-342-1409, E-mail: nimocksm@uwplatt.edu.

Distance Learning Center Students: 10 full-time (4 women), 347 part-time (115 women); includes 31 minority (15 African Americans, 2 American Indian/Alaska Native, 6 Asian

University of Wisconsin–Platteville (continued)

Americans or Pacific Islanders, 8 Hispanic Americans), 23 international. 107 applicants, 62% accepted. *Faculty:* 15 part-time/adjunct. Expenses: Contact institution. *Financial support:* Scholarships/grants available. Support available to part-time students. In 2008, 78 master's awarded. *Degree program information:* Part-time and evening/weekend programs available. Postbaccalaureate distance learning degree programs offered (no on-campus study). Offers criminal justice (MS); engineering (MS); project management (MS). *Application deadline:* For fall admission, 7/1 priority date for domestic students; for spring admission, 11/1 priority date for domestic students. Applications are processed on a rolling basis. *Application fee:* $56. Electronic applications accepted. *Application Contact:* Chris Jentz, 800-362-5460, Fax: 608-342-1071, E-mail: disted@uwplatt.edu. *Executive Director*, Dawn Drake, 800-362-5460, Fax: 608-342-1071, E-mail: disted@uwplatt.edu.

UNIVERSITY OF WISCONSIN–RIVER FALLS, River Falls, WI 54022-5001

General Information State-supported, coed, comprehensive institution. CGS member. *Graduate housing:* Room and/or apartments available on a first-come, first-served basis to single students; on-campus housing not available to married students.

GRADUATE UNITS

Outreach and Graduate Studies *Degree program information:* Part-time programs available. Electronic applications accepted.

College of Agriculture, Food, and Environmental Sciences *Degree program information:* Part-time programs available. Offers agricultural education (MS); agriculture, food, and environmental sciences (MS). Electronic applications accepted.

College of Arts and Science *Degree program information:* Part-time programs available. Offers arts and science (MA, MSE); fine arts (MSE); mathematics education (MSE); science education (MSE); social science education (MSE); teaching English to speakers of other languages (MA). Electronic applications accepted.

College of Business and Economics Offers business and economics (MBA, MM). Electronic applications accepted.

College of Education and Professional Studies *Degree program information:* Part-time programs available. Offers communicative disorders (MS); counseling (MSE); education and professional studies (MS, MSE, Ed S); elementary education (MSE); professional development shared inquiry communities (MSE); reading (MSE); school psychology (MSE, Ed S); secondary education-communicative disorders (MSE).

UNIVERSITY OF WISCONSIN–STEVENS POINT, Stevens Point, WI 54481-3897

General Information State-supported, coed, comprehensive institution. *Enrollment:* 9,155 graduate, professional, and undergraduate students; 112 full-time matriculated graduate/professional students (85 women), 150 part-time matriculated graduate/professional students (105 women). *Enrollment by degree level:* 262 master's. *Graduate faculty:* 259 full-time (93 women), 4 part-time/adjunct (1 woman). Full-time tuition and fees vary according to reciprocity agreements. *Graduate housing:* Room and/or apartments available on a first-come, first-served basis to single students; on-campus housing not available to married students. Typical cost: $3148 per year ($5180 including board). *Student services:* Campus employment opportunities, campus safety program, career counseling, child daycare facilities, exercise/wellness program, free psychological counseling, grant writing training, international student services, multicultural affairs office, services for students with disabilities, teacher training, writing training. *Library facilities:* Learning Resources Center. *Online resources:* library catalog, web page, access to other libraries' catalogs. *Collection:* 1.1 million titles, 18,428 serial subscriptions, 8,850 audiovisual materials.

Computer facilities: 634 computers available on campus for general student use. A campuswide network can be accessed from student residence rooms and from off campus. Online class registration is available. *Web address:* http://www.uwsp.edu/.

General Application Contact: Catherine Glennon, Director of Admissions, 715-346-2441, E-mail: admiss@uwsp.edu.

GRADUATE UNITS

College of Fine Arts and Communication Students: 3 full-time (2 women), 1 international. Expenses: Contact institution. *Financial support:* Teaching assistantships, career-related internships or fieldwork, Federal Work-Study, institutionally sponsored loans, and unspecified assistantships available. Support available to part-time students. Financial award application deadline: 5/1; financial award applicants required to submit FAFSA. *Degree program information:* Part-time programs available. Offers fine arts and communication (MA, MM Ed); interpersonal communication (MA); mass communication (MA); music (MM Ed); organizational communication (MA); public relations (MA). *Application deadline:* For fall admission, 5/1 priority date for domestic students. Applications are processed on a rolling basis. *Application fee:* $45. *Application Contact:* Catherine Glennon, Director of Admissions, 715-346-2441, E-mail: admiss@uwsp.edu. *Dean*, Jeff Morin, 715-346-4920, Fax: 715-346-2718, E-mail: jmorin@uwse.edu.

College of Letters and Science Expenses: Contact institution. *Financial support:* Research assistantships, teaching assistantships, Federal Work-Study and unspecified assistantships available. Support available to part-time students. Financial award application deadline: 5/1; financial award applicants required to submit FAFSA. Offers biology (MST); business and economics (MBA); English (MST); history (MST); letters and science (MBA, MST). *Application deadline:* For fall admission, 5/1 priority date for domestic students. Applications are processed on a rolling basis. *Application fee:* $45. *Application Contact:* Catherine Glennon, Director of Admissions, 715-346-2441, E-mail: admiss@uwsp.edu. *Interim Dean*, Dr. Charles Clark, 715-346-4224.

College of Natural Resources Students: 37 full-time (19 women), 29 part-time (19 women); includes 2 American Indian/Alaska Native, 1 international. Expenses: Contact institution. *Financial support:* Research assistantships, teaching assistantships, career-related internships or fieldwork, Federal Work-Study, and unspecified assistantships available. Support available to part-time students. Financial award application deadline: 5/1; financial award applicants required to submit FAFSA. In 2008, 33 master's awarded. *Degree program information:* Part-time programs available. Offers natural resources (MS). *Application deadline:* For fall admission, 3/15 priority date for domestic students; for spring admission, 11/15 for domestic students. Applications are processed on a rolling basis. *Application fee:* $45. *Application Contact:* Catherine Glennon, Director of Admissions, 715-346-2441, E-mail: admiss@uwsp.edu. *Dean*, Dr. Christine Thomas, 715-346-4617, Fax: 715-346-3624.

College of Professional Studies *Degree program information:* Part-time programs available.

School of Communicative Disorders Students: 46 full-time (all women); includes 1 American Indian/Alaska Native. Expenses: Contact institution. *Financial support:* Research assistantships, teaching assistantships, Federal Work-Study and unspecified assistantships available. Financial award application deadline: 5/1; financial award applicants required to submit FAFSA. Offers communicative disorders (MS, Au D). *Application deadline:* For fall admission, 1/10 for domestic students. *Application fee:* $45. *Application Contact:* Leslie Plonsker, Information Contact, 715-346-2328, Fax: 715-346-2157, E-mail: lplonske@uwsp.edu. *Head*, Dr. Gary Cumley, 715-346-4699, Fax: 715-346-2157, E-mail: gcumley@uwsp.edu.

School of Education *Degree program information:* Part-time programs available. Offers education—general/reading (MSE); education—general/special (MSE); educational administration (MSE); elementary education (MSE); guidance and counseling (MSE).

School of Health Promotion and Human Development Students: 2 part-time (both women). Expenses: Contact institution. *Financial support:* Research assistantships, teaching assistantships, career-related internships or fieldwork, Federal Work-Study, and unspecified assistantships available. Support available to part-time students. Financial award application deadline: 5/1; financial award applicants required to submit FAFSA. *Degree program information:* Part-time programs available. Offers human and community resources (MS); nutritional sciences (MS). *Application deadline:* For fall admission, 5/1 priority date for domestic students. Applications are processed on a rolling basis. *Application fee:* $45. *Application Contact:* Dr. Jasia Steinmetz, Information Contact, 715-346-2830, Fax: 715-346-2720, E-mail: jsteinme@uwsp.edu. *Head*, Dr. Marty Loy, 715-346-2830, Fax: 715-346-2720.

UNIVERSITY OF WISCONSIN–STOUT, Menomonie, WI 54751

General Information State-supported, coed, comprehensive institution. *Enrollment:* 8,811 graduate, professional, and undergraduate students; 305 full-time matriculated graduate/professional students (208 women), 503 part-time matriculated graduate/professional students (321 women). *Enrollment by degree level:* 713 master's, 18 other advanced degrees. *Graduate faculty:* 146 full-time (60 women), 36 part-time/adjunct (25 women). *International tuition:* $10,512 full-time. Tuition, state resident: full-time $6227; part-time $345.93 per credit. Tuition, nonresident: full-time $9998; part-time $555.42 per credit. Tuition and fees vary according to course load, program and reciprocity agreements. *Graduate housing:* Room and/or apartments available on a first-come, first-served basis to single students; on-campus housing not available to married students. *Student services:* Campus employment opportunities, career counseling, child daycare facilities, exercise/wellness program, free psychological counseling, grant writing training, international student services, low-cost health insurance, multicultural affairs office, services for students with disabilities, teacher training, writing training. *Library facilities:* Library Learning Center. *Online resources:* library catalog, web page, access to other libraries' catalogs. *Collection:* 229,986 titles, 1,784 serial subscriptions, 16,142 audiovisual materials.

Computer facilities: Computer purchase and lease plans are available. 590 computers available on campus for general student use. A campuswide network can be accessed from student residence rooms and from off campus. Online class registration, all undergraduates receive a laptop computer are available. *Web address:* http://www.uwstout.edu/.

General Application Contact: Anne E. Johnson, Graduate Student Evaluator (Admissions and Assistantship Coordinator), 715-232-1322, Fax: 715-232-2413, E-mail: johnsona@uwstout.edu.

GRADUATE UNITS

Graduate School Students: 305 full-time (208 women), 503 part-time (321 women); includes 48 minority (15 African Americans, 3 American Indian/Alaska Native, 17 Asian Americans or Pacific Islanders, 13 Hispanic Americans), 67 international. Average age 32. 588 applicants, 63% accepted, 294 enrolled. *Faculty:* 146 full-time (60 women), 36 part-time/adjunct (25 women). Expenses: Contact institution. *Financial support:* In 2008–09, 90 research assistantships with partial tuition reimbursements (averaging $4,759 per year), 34 teaching assistantships with partial tuition reimbursements (averaging $5,436 per year) were awarded; Federal Work-Study, scholarships/grants, traineeships, tuition waivers (partial), and unspecified assistantships also available. Support available to part-time students. Financial award application deadline: 5/1; financial award applicants required to submit FAFSA. In 2008, 256 master's, 20 other advanced degrees awarded. *Degree program information:* Part-time programs available. Postbaccalaureate distance learning degree programs offered (minimal on-campus study). *Application deadline:* Applications are processed on a rolling basis. *Application fee:* $45. Electronic applications accepted. *Application Contact:* Anne E. Johnson, Graduate Student Evaluator (Admissions and Assistantship Coordinator), 715-232-1322, Fax: 715-232-2413, E-mail: johnsona@uwstout.edu. *Director, Office of Graduate Studies*, Dr. Claudia Johnston, 715-232-1666, Fax: 715-232-2413, E-mail: johnstoncl@uwstout.edu.

College of Human Development Students: 175 full-time (130 women), 87 part-time (76 women); includes 15 minority (7 African Americans, 1 American Indian/Alaska Native, 3 Asian Americans or Pacific Islanders, 4 Hispanic Americans), 38 international. Average age 30. 290 applicants, 48% accepted, 99 enrolled. Expenses: Contact institution. *Financial support:* In 2008–09, 42 research assistantships with partial tuition reimbursements (averaging $4,516 per year), 24 teaching assistantships with partial tuition reimbursements (averaging $4,092 per year) were awarded; Federal Work-Study, scholarships/grants, tuition waivers (partial), and unspecified assistantships also available. Support available to part-time students. Financial award application deadline: 5/1; financial award applicants required to submit FAFSA. In 2008, 97 master's awarded. *Degree program information:* Part-time programs available. Postbaccalaureate distance learning degree programs offered (no on-campus study). Offers applied psychology (MS); family studies and human development (MS); food and nutritional sciences (MS); human development (MS); marriage and family therapy (MS); mental health counseling (MS); vocational rehabilitation (MS). *Application fee:* $45. Electronic applications accepted. *Application Contact:* Anne E. Johnson, Graduate Student Evaluator (Admissions and Assistantship Coordinator), 715-232-1322, Fax: 715-232-2413, E-mail: johnsona@uwstout.edu. *Dean*, Dr. John Wesolek, 715-232-2687, Fax: 715-232-2366, E-mail: wesolekj@uwstout.edu.

College of Technology, Engineering, and Management Students: 41 full-time (6 women), 146 part-time (52 women); includes 14 minority (4 African Americans, 1 American Indian/Alaska Native, 5 Asian Americans or Pacific Islanders, 4 Hispanic Americans), 27 international. Average age 32. 114 applicants, 80% accepted, 76 enrolled. Expenses: Contact institution. *Financial support:* In 2008–09, 2 research assistantships with partial tuition reimbursements (averaging $3,792 per year) were awarded; teaching assistantships, Federal Work-Study, scholarships/grants, tuition waivers (full and partial), and unspecified assistantships also available. Support available to part-time students. Financial award application deadline: 5/1; financial award applicants required to submit FAFSA. In 2008, 51 master's awarded. *Degree program information:* Part-time programs available. Postbaccalaureate distance learning degree programs offered (minimal on-campus study). Offers information and communication technologies (MS); manufacturing engineering (MS); risk control (MS); technology management (MS); technology, engineering, and management (MS); training and development (MS). *Application fee:* $45. Electronic applications accepted. *Application Contact:* Anne E. Johnson, Graduate Student Evaluator (Admissions and Assistantship Coordinator), 715-232-1322, Fax: 715-232-2413, E-mail: johnsona@uwstout.edu. *Interim Dean*, Dr. Carol Mooney, 715-232-1444, Fax: 715-232-1274, E-mail: mooneyc@uwstout.edu.

School of Education Students: 91 full-time (72 women), 212 part-time (144 women); includes 18 minority (4 African Americans, 1 American Indian/Alaska Native, 8 Asian Americans or Pacific Islanders, 5 Hispanic Americans), 2 international. Average age 32. 152 applicants, 71% accepted, 92 enrolled. Expenses: Contact institution. *Financial support:* In 2008–09, 22 research assistantships with partial tuition reimbursements (averaging $6,368 per year), 10 teaching assistantships with partial tuition reimbursements (averaging $8,661 per year) were awarded; Federal Work-Study, scholarships/grants, tuition waivers (partial), and unspecified assistantships also available. Support available to part-time students. Financial award application deadline: 5/1; financial award applicants required to submit FAFSA. In 2008, 104 master's, 20 other advanced degrees awarded. *Degree program information:* Part-time programs available. Postbaccalaureate distance learning degree programs offered (no on-campus study). Offers career and technical education (MS, Ed S); education (MS, MS Ed, Ed S); industrial/technology education (MS); school counseling (MS); school psychology (MS Ed, Ed S). *Application deadline:* Applications are processed on a rolling basis. *Application fee:* $45. Electronic applications accepted. *Application Contact:* Anne E. Johnson, Graduate Student Evaluator (Admissions and Assistantship Coordinator), 715-232-1322, Fax: 715-232-2413, E-mail: johnsona@wwstout.edu. *Interim Dean*, Dr. Mary Hopkins-Best, 715-232-2687, Fax: 715-232-1244, E-mail: hopkinsbestm@uwstout.edu.

UNIVERSITY OF WISCONSIN–SUPERIOR, Superior, WI 54880-4500

General Information State-supported, coed, comprehensive institution. *Graduate housing:* Rooms and/or apartments available on a first-come, first-served basis to single students and available to married students. Housing application deadline: 7/1. *Research affiliation:* Great Lakes Indian Fish and Wildlife Commission, Wisconsin Department of Natural Resources (biology), Environmental Protection Agency (biology), The Mexican National Institute for Ecology (biology), The Mexican Marine National Park Service (biology), Coastal Zone Management Institute and Authority of Belize (biology), Fisheries Department, Government of Belize (biology).

GRADUATE UNITS

Graduate Division *Degree program information:* Part-time and evening/weekend programs available. Postbaccalaureate distance learning degree programs offered (minimal on-campus study). Offers art education (MA); art history (MA); art therapy (MA); arts administration (MA); community counseling (MSE); educational administration (MSE, Ed S); educational psychology (MSE); elementary school counseling (MSE); emotional/behavior disabilities (MSE); human relations (MSE); instruction (MSE); learning disabilities (MSE); mass communication (MA); secondary school counseling (MSE); special education (MSE); speech communication (MA); studio arts (MA); teaching reading (MSE); theater (MA).

UNIVERSITY OF WISCONSIN–WHITEWATER, Whitewater, WI 53190-1790

General Information State-supported, coed, comprehensive institution. *Graduate housing:* Rooms and/or apartments available on a first-come, first-served basis to single students and available to married students. Housing application deadline: 9/1. *Research affiliation:* Generac Power Systems (manufacturing), American Ag-Tec International (international marketing), American Family Insurance (insurance), R.A Smith and Associates (civil engineering), Sho-Deen (property management and development), WEBCO (lightning radioactive transfer).

GRADUATE UNITS

School of Graduate Studies *Degree program information:* Part-time and evening/weekend programs available. Postbaccalaureate distance learning degree programs offered (no on-campus study). Electronic applications accepted.

College of Arts and Communications *Degree program information:* Part-time and evening/weekend programs available. Postbaccalaureate distance learning degree programs offered (no on-campus study). Offers arts and communications (MS); corporate communication (MS); mass communication (MS). Electronic applications accepted.

College of Business and Economics *Degree program information:* Part-time and evening/weekend programs available. Postbaccalaureate distance learning degree programs offered (no on-campus study). Offers accounting (MPA); business and economics (MBA, MPA, MS, MS Ed); finance (MBA); general business education (MS); human resource management (MBA); information technology management (MBA); international business (MBA); management (MBA); marketing (MBA); operations and supply chain management (MBA); post-secondary business education (MS); school business management (MS Ed); secondary business education (MS); technology and training (MBA). Electronic applications accepted.

College of Education *Degree program information:* Part-time and evening/weekend programs available. Postbaccalaureate distance learning degree programs offered (no on-campus study). Offers communicative disorders (MS); community counseling (MS Ed); curriculum and instruction (MS); education (MS, MS Ed); higher education (MS Ed); reading (MS Ed); safety (MS); school counseling (MS Ed); special education (MS Ed). Electronic applications accepted.

College of Letters and Sciences *Degree program information:* Part-time and evening/weekend programs available. Offers letters and sciences (MS Ed, Ed S); school psychology (Ed S). Electronic applications accepted.

UNIVERSITY OF WYOMING, Laramie, WY 82070

General Information State-supported, coed, university. CGS member. *Enrollment:* 12,067 graduate, professional, and undergraduate students; 1,326 full-time matriculated graduate/professional students (679 women), 1,197 part-time matriculated graduate/professional students (745 women). *Enrollment by degree level:* 118 first professional, 430 master's, 80 doctoral, 14 other advanced degrees. *Graduate faculty:* 684 full-time (223 women), 29 part-time/adjunct (19 women). *Graduate housing:* Rooms and/or apartments available on a first-come, first-served basis to single and married students. Typical cost: $3418 per year ($5014 including board) for single students. *Student services:* Campus employment opportunities, campus safety program, career counseling, child daycare facilities, exercise/wellness program, free psychological counseling, international student services, low-cost health insurance, multicultural affairs office, services for students with disabilities, teacher training, writing training. *Library facilities:* William Robertson Coe Library plus 6 others. *Online resources:* library catalog, web page, access to other libraries' catalogs. *Collection:* 1.4 million titles, 65,337 serial subscriptions, 8,161 audiovisual materials.

Computer facilities: Computer purchase and lease plans are available. 1,269 computers available on campus for general student use. A campuswide network can be accessed from student residence rooms and from off campus. Online class registration is available. *Web address:* http://www.uwyo.edu/.

General Application Contact: Michell Anderson, Graduate Admissions Coordinator, 307-766-3802, Fax: 307-766-2374, E-mail: manders2@uwyo.edu.

GRADUATE UNITS

College of Law Students: 221 full-time (101 women), 1 part-time (0 women); includes 14 minority (1 African American, 5 Asian Americans or Pacific Islanders, 8 Hispanic Americans), 1 international. Average age 28. 229 applicants, 100% accepted, 74 enrolled. *Faculty:* 15 full-time (6 women), 2 part-time/adjunct (1 woman). Expenses: Contact institution. *Financial support:* In 2008–09, 180 fellowships (averaging $2,242 per year), 18 research assistantships (averaging $1,610 per year), 7 teaching assistantships with full and partial tuition reimbursements (averaging $2,337 per year) were awarded; career-related internships or fieldwork, Federal Work-Study, institutionally sponsored loans, and scholarships/grants also available. Financial award application deadline: 5/1; financial award applicants required to submit FAFSA. In 2008, 72 JDs awarded. Offers law (JD). *Application deadline:* For fall admission, 3/7 for domestic students. Applications are processed on a rolling basis. *Application fee:* $50. Electronic applications accepted. *Application Contact:* Anthony D. Pledger, JD, Admissions and Student Services Coordinator, 307-766-3359, E-mail: apledger@uwyo.edu. *Assistant Dean*, Denise Burke, 307-766-6416, E-mail: dburke@uwyo.edu.

Graduate School Students: 1,326 full-time (679 women), 1,197 part-time (745 women); includes 127 minority (15 African Americans, 27 American Indian/Alaska Native, 28 Asian Americans or Pacific Islanders, 57 Hispanic Americans), 284 international. Average age 33. 2,522 applicants, 75% accepted, 1105 enrolled. *Faculty:* 684 full-time (223 women), 19 part-time/adjunct (9 women). Expenses: Contact institution. *Financial support:* In 2008–09, research assistantships with full tuition reimbursements (averaging $11,349 per year), teaching assistantships with full tuition reimbursements (averaging $15,795 per year) were awarded; fellowships, career-related internships or fieldwork, Federal Work-Study, institutionally sponsored loans, scholarships/grants, traineeships, health care benefits, tuition waivers (full and partial), and unspecified assistantships also available. Support available to part-time students. Financial award applicants required to submit FAFSA. In 2008, 118 first professional degrees, 430 master's, 80 doctorates, 14 other advanced degrees awarded. *Degree program information:* Part-time and evening/weekend programs available. Postbaccalaureate distance learning degree programs offered. Offers ecology (MS, PhD); molecular and cellular life sciences (PhD). *Application deadline:* Applications are processed on a rolling basis. *Application fee:* $50. Electronic applications accepted. *Application Contact:* Michell Anderson, Credentials Analyst/Advising Assistant, 307-766-2287, Fax: 307-766-2374, E-mail: manders2@uwyo.edu. *Dean*, Dr. Don A. Roth, 307-766-2287, Fax: 307-766-2374, E-mail: rothdon@uwyo.edu.

College of Agriculture Students: 77 full-time (37 women), 40 part-time (26 women), 29 international. Average age 27. 88 applicants, 51% accepted, 38 enrolled. *Faculty:* 101 full-time (22 women), 2 part-time/adjunct (1 woman). Expenses: Contact institution. *Financial support:* In 2008–09, 3 fellowships, 15 research assistantships, 32 teaching assistantships were awarded; career-related internships or fieldwork, Federal Work-Study, institutionally sponsored loans, scholarships/grants, tuition waivers (partial), and unspecified assistantships also available. Financial award application deadline: 3/1. In 2008, 21 master's, 12 doctorates awarded. *Degree program information:* Part-time programs available. Offers agricultural and applied economics (MS); agriculture (MS, PhD); agroecology (MS); agronomy (MS, PhD); animal sciences (MS, PhD); early childhood development (MS); entomology (MS, PhD); entomology/water resources (MS, PhD); family and consumer sciences (MS); food science and human nutrition (MS); molecular biology (MS, PhD); pathobiology (MS); rangeland ecology and watershed management (MS, PhD); rangeland ecology and watershed management/water resources (MS, PhD); reproductive biology (MS, PhD); soil science (MS); soil science/water resources (PhD). *Application deadline:* Applications are processed on a rolling basis. *Application fee:* $50. Electronic applications accepted. *Application Contact:* Michell Anderson, Credentials Analyst/Advising Assistant, 307-766-2287, Fax: 307-766-2374, E-mail: manders2@uwyo.edu. *Dean*, Dr. Frank D. Galey, 307-766-4133.

College of Arts and Sciences Students: 334 full-time (165 women), 205 part-time (104 women); includes 23 minority (7 American Indian/Alaska Native, 7 Asian Americans or Pacific Islanders, 9 Hispanic Americans), 80 international. Average age 30. 436 applicants, 51% accepted, 157 enrolled. *Faculty:* 298 full-time (101 women), 16 part-time/adjunct (8 women). Expenses: Contact institution. *Financial support:* Fellowships, research assistantships with full and partial tuition reimbursements, teaching assistantships with full and partial tuition reimbursements, career-related internships or fieldwork, Federal Work-Study, institutionally sponsored loans, scholarships/grants, traineeships, tuition waivers (full and partial), and unspecified assistantships available. Financial award application deadline: 3/1. In 2008, 120 master's, 21 doctorates awarded. *Degree program information:* Part-time programs available. Offers American studies (MA); anthropology (MA, PhD); arts and sciences (MA, MAT, MFA, MM, MME, MP, MPA, MS, MST, PhD); botany (MS, PhD); botany/water resources (MS); chemistry (MS, PhD); communication (MA); community and regional planning and natural resources (MP); creative writing (MFA); English (MA); French (MA); geography (MA, MP, MST); geography/water resources (MA); geology (MS, PhD); geophysics (MS, PhD); German (MA); history (MA, MAT); international peace corps (MA); international studies (MA); mathematics (MA, MAT, MS, MST, PhD); mathematics/computer science (PhD); music education (MME); performance (MM); philosophy (MA); political science (MA); psychology (MA, MS, PhD); public administration (MPA); rural planning and natural resources (MP); sociology (MA); Spanish (MA); statistics (MS, PhD); zoology and physiology (MS, PhD). *Application deadline:* Applications are processed on a rolling basis. *Application fee:* $50. Electronic applications accepted. *Application Contact:* Audrey C. Shalinsky, Associate Dean, 307-766-4106, Fax: 307-766-2697, E-mail: asdean@uwyo.edu. *Dean*, B. Oliver Walter, 307-766-4106, Fax: 307-766-2697, E-mail: asdean@uwyo.edu.

College of Business Students: 62 full-time (28 women), 85 part-time (31 women); includes 7 minority (3 African Americans, 1 American Indian/Alaska Native, 3 Hispanic Americans), 23 international. Average age 36. 181 applicants, 56% accepted, 64 enrolled. *Faculty:* 46 full-time (10 women). Expenses: Contact institution. *Financial support:* In 2008–09, 72 research assistantships with partial tuition reimbursements (averaging $5,348 per year), 25 teaching assistantships with partial tuition reimbursements (averaging $5,348 per year) were awarded; fellowships, career-related internships or fieldwork, Federal Work-Study, institutionally sponsored loans, and tuition waivers (partial) also available. Financial award application deadline: 3/1; financial award applicants required to submit FAFSA. In 2008, 53 master's, 7 doctorates awarded. *Degree program information:* Part-time and evening/weekend programs available. Postbaccalaureate distance learning degree programs offered (minimal on-campus study). Offers accounting (MS); business (MBA, MS, PhD); business administration (MBA); economics (MS, PhD); economics and finance (MS, PhD); finance (MS). *Application deadline:* For fall admission, 2/1 for domestic and international students. Applications are processed on a rolling basis. *Application fee:* $50. *Application Contact:* Lori Lewis, Office Associate, 307-766-2449, Fax: 307-766-4028, E-mail: mba@uwyo.edu. *Dean*, Dr. Brent A. Hathaway, 307-766-4194.

College of Education Students: 78 full-time (62 women), 343 part-time (224 women); includes 35 minority (6 African Americans, 10 American Indian/Alaska Native, 2 Asian Americans or Pacific Islanders, 17 Hispanic Americans), 13 international. Average age 41. 141 applicants, 57% accepted, 65 enrolled. *Faculty:* 61 full-time (33 women). Expenses: Contact institution. *Financial support:* In 2008–09, 18 teaching assistantships with full tuition reimbursements were awarded; fellowships, research assistantships, career-related internships or fieldwork, Federal Work-Study, scholarships/grants, and unspecified assistantships also available. Financial award application deadline: 1/31. In 2008, 119 master's, 20 doctorates, 13 other advanced degrees awarded. Postbaccalaureate distance learning degree programs offered. Offers adult and postsecondary education (MA, Ed D, PhD, Ed S); community mental health (MS); counselor education and supervision (PhD); curriculum and instruction (MA, Ed D, PhD); distance education (Ed D, PhD); education (MA, MS, MST, Ed D, PhD, Certificate, Ed S); educational leadership (MA, Ed D, Certificate); instructional technology (MS, Ed D, PhD); school counseling (MS); science and mathematics teaching (MS, MST); special education (MA, PhD, Ed S); student affairs (MS). *Application deadline:* For fall admission, 12/1 for domestic students; for spring admission, 12/1 for domestic students. Applications are processed on a rolling basis. *Application fee:* $50. Electronic applications accepted. *Application Contact:* Dr. Suzanne Young, Associate Dean, 307-766-3145, Fax: 307-766-6668, E-mail: mikeday@uwyo.edu. *Dean*, Dr. Kay Persichitte, 307-766-3145, Fax: 307-766-6668, E-mail: patmc@uwyo.edu.

College of Engineering and Applied Sciences Students: 144 full-time (34 women), 55 part-time (16 women); includes 4 minority (1 Asian American or Pacific Islander, 3 Hispanic Americans), 88 international. Average age 28. 135 applicants, 59% accepted, 41 enrolled. *Faculty:* 83 full-time (7 women), 2 part-time/adjunct (1 woman). Expenses: Contact institution. *Financial support:* Fellowships, research assistantships, teaching assistantships, career-related internships or fieldwork, Federal Work-Study, and institutionally sponsored loans available. Support available to part-time students. In 2008, 36 master's, 16 doctorates awarded. *Degree program information:* Part-time programs available. Offers atmospheric science (MS, PhD); chemical engineering (MS, PhD); civil engineering (MS, PhD); computer science (MS, PhD); electrical engineering (MS, PhD); engineering and applied sciences (MS, PhD); environmental engineering (MS); mechanical engineering (MS, PhD); petroleum engineering (MS, PhD). *Application deadline:* Applications are processed on a rolling basis. *Application fee:* $50. Electronic applications accepted. *Application Contact:* Michell Anderson, Coordinator for Graduate Admissions, 307-766-2287, Fax: 307-766-2374, E-mail: manders2@uwyo.edu. *Dean*, Dr. Robert Ettema, 307-766-4257, Fax: 307-766-4444, E-mail: gplumb@uwyo.edu.

College of Health Sciences Students: 322 full-time (205 women), 128 part-time (110 women); includes 24 minority (3 African Americans, 2 American Indian/Alaska Native, 9 Asian Americans or Pacific Islanders, 10 Hispanic Americans), 12 international. Average age 32. 235 applicants, 65% accepted, 105 enrolled. *Faculty:* 66 full-time (38 women). Expenses: Contact institution. *Financial support:* In 2008–09, teaching assistantships with tuition reimbursements (averaging $10,062 per year); fellowships, research assistantships, career-related internships or fieldwork, Federal Work-Study, institutionally sponsored loans, scholarships/grants, traineeships, tuition waivers (full), and unspecified assistantships also available. Support available to part-time students. Financial award application deadline: 3/1. In 2008, 46 first professional degrees, 70 master's awarded. *Degree program information:* Part-time programs available. Postbaccalaureate distance learning degree programs offered (minimal on-campus study). Offers health sciences (Pharm D, MS, MSW); kinesiology and health (MS); nursing (MS); pharmacy (Pharm D); social work (MSW); speech-language pathology (MS). *Application fee:* $50. Electronic applications accepted. *Application Contact:* Lisa Shipley, Manager, Student Advising, 307-766-6706, E-mail: lshipley@uwyo.edu. *Interim Dean*, Dr. Beverky O. Sullivan, 307-766-6556, Fax: 307-766-6608, E-mail: admin.hs@uwyo.edu.

UPPER IOWA UNIVERSITY, Fayette, IA 52142-1857

General Information Independent, coed, comprehensive institution. *Graduate housing:* On-campus housing not available.

GRADUATE UNITS

Online Master's Programs *Degree program information:* Part-time programs available. Postbaccalaureate distance learning degree programs offered (no on-campus study). Offers accounting (MBA); corporate financial management (MBA); global business (MBA); health and human services (MPA); homeland security (MPA); human resources management (MBA); justice administration (MPA); organizational development (MBA); public personnel management (MPA); quality management (MBA). MBA also available at Madison, Wisconsin campus. Electronic applications accepted.

URBANA UNIVERSITY, Urbana, OH 43078-2091

General Information Independent, coed, comprehensive institution. *Graduate housing:* On-campus housing not available.

GRADUATE UNITS

Division of Business Administration *Degree program information:* Part-time and evening/weekend programs available. Offers business administration (MBA).

Division of Education and Allied Professions *Degree program information:* Part-time and evening/weekend programs available. Offers classroom education (M Ed).

URSULINE COLLEGE, Pepper Pike, OH 44124-4398

General Information Independent-religious, Undergraduate: women only; graduate: coed, comprehensive institution. *Enrollment:* 1,426 graduate, professional, and undergraduate students; 44 full-time matriculated graduate/professional students (37 women), 282 part-time matriculated graduate/professional students (244 women). *Enrollment by degree level:* 326 master's. *Graduate faculty:* 12 full-time (11 women), 27 part-time/adjunct (19 women). *Tuition:* Full-time $13,590; part-time $775 per credit hour. *Required fees:* $220; $70 per semester. *Graduate housing:* Room and/or apartments available on a first-come, first-served basis to single students; on-campus housing not available to married students. Typical cost: $9530 (including board). Room and board charges vary according to board plan. Housing application deadline: 8/20. *Student services:* Career counseling, exercise/wellness program, free psychological counseling, multicultural affairs office, services for students with disabilities, teacher training. *Library facilities:* Ralph M. Besse Library. *Online resources:* library catalog, web page, access to other libraries' catalogs. *Collection:* 163,617 titles, 7,806 serial subscriptions, 10,518 audiovisual materials.

Computer facilities: 72 computers available on campus for general student use. A campuswide network can be accessed from student residence rooms. *Web address:* http://www.ursuline.edu/.

General Application Contact: Brandi Rizzo, Graduate Recruiter, 440-646-8146, Fax: 440-684-6088, E-mail: gradsch@ursuline.edu.

GRADUATE UNITS

School of Graduate Studies Students: 44 full-time (37 women), 282 part-time (244 women); includes 51 minority (43 African Americans, 3 Asian Americans or Pacific Islanders, 5 Hispanic Americans), 1 international. Average age 37. 118 applicants, 97% accepted, 77 enrolled. *Faculty:* 12 full-time (11 women), 27 part-time/adjunct (19 women). Expenses: Contact institution. *Financial support:* In 2008–09, 289 students received support. Federal Work-Study available. Financial award application deadline: 3/1; financial award applicants required to submit FAFSA. In 2008, 157 master's awarded. *Degree program information:* Part-time programs available. Offers art education (MA); art therapy counseling (MA); care management (MSN); early childhood education (MA); education (MA); educational administration (MA); historic preservation (MA); language arts education (MA); liberal studies (MALS); life science education (MA); management (MM, MMT); math education (MA); middle school education (MA); ministry (MA); nurse practitioner (MSN); nursing education (MSN); palliative care (MSN); social studies education (MA); special education (MA). *Application deadline:* For fall admission, 8/1 priority date for domestic students. Applications are processed on a rolling basis. *Application fee:* $25. Electronic applications accepted. *Application Contact:* Lauren Anderson, Admission Specialist, 440-646-8119, Fax: 440-684-6088, E-mail: gradsch@ursuline.edu. *Dean of Graduate Studies,* Dr. Alison Benders, 440-646-8119, Fax: 440-684-6088, E-mail: gradsch@ursuline.edu.

UTAH STATE UNIVERSITY, Logan, UT 84322

General Information State-supported, coed, university. CGS member. *Graduate housing:* Rooms and/or apartments available on a first-come, first-served basis to single and married students. *Research affiliation:* Boeing Aerospace and Engineering (science and engineering), Duke Energy Corporation (engineering), Kennecott Copper Corporation (natural resources), Kraft, Inc. (agriculture), National Endowment for Financial Education (education).

GRADUATE UNITS

School of Graduate Studies *Degree program information:* Part-time and evening/weekend programs available. Postbaccalaureate distance learning degree programs offered (minimal on-campus study).

College of Agriculture *Degree program information:* Part-time programs available. Postbaccalaureate distance learning degree programs offered (minimal on-campus study). Offers agricultural systems technology (MS); agriculture (MDA, MFMS, MS, PhD); animal science (MS, PhD); biometeorology (MS, PhD); bioveterinary science (MS, PhD); dairy science (MS); dietetic administration (MDA); ecology (MS, PhD); family and consumer sciences education (MS); food microbiology and safety (MFMS); nutrition and food sciences (MS, PhD); nutrition science (MS, PhD); plant science (MS, PhD); soil science (MS, PhD); toxicology (MS, PhD).

College of Business *Degree program information:* Part-time and evening/weekend programs available. Postbaccalaureate distance learning degree programs offered (no on-campus study). Offers accountancy (M Acc); applied economics (MS); business (M Acc, MA, MBA, MS, Ed D, PhD); business administration (MBA); business education (MS); business information systems (MS); business information systems and education (Ed D); economics (MA, MS, PhD); education (PhD); human resource management (MS).

College of Education and Human Services *Degree program information:* Part-time and evening/weekend programs available. Postbaccalaureate distance learning degree programs offered (no on-campus study). Offers audiology (Au D, Ed S); business information systems (Ed D, PhD); clinical/counseling/school psychology (PhD); communication disorders and deaf education (M Ed); communicative disorders and deaf education (MA, MS); curriculum and instruction (Ed D, PhD); disability disciplines (PhD); education and human services (M Ed, MA, MFHD, MRC, MS, Au D, Ed D, PhD, Ed S); elementary education (M Ed, MA, MS); family and human development (MFHD); family, consumer, and human development (MS, PhD); health, physical education and recreation (M Ed, MS); instructional technology (M Ed, MS, PhD, Ed S); rehabilitation counselor education (MRC); research and evaluation (PhD); research and evaluation methodology (PhD); school counseling (MS); school psychology (MS); secondary education (M Ed, MA, MS); special education (M Ed, MS, Ed S).

College of Engineering *Degree program information:* Part-time and evening/weekend programs available. Offers aerospace engineering (MS, PhD); biological and agricultural engineering (MS, PhD); civil and environmental engineering (ME, MS, PhD, CE); electrical engineering (ME, MS, PhD); engineering (ME, MS, PhD, CE); industrial technology (MS); irrigation engineering (MS, PhD); mechanical engineering (ME, MS, PhD). Electronic applications accepted.

College of Humanities, Arts and Social Sciences *Degree program information:* Part-time and evening/weekend programs available. Postbaccalaureate distance learning degree programs offered (minimal on-campus study). Offers advanced technical practice (MFA); American studies (MA, MS); art (MA, MFA); bioregional planning (MS); design (MFA); English (MA, MS); folklore (MA, MS); history (MA, MS); humanities, arts and social sciences (MA, MFA, MLA, MS, MSLT, MSS, PhD); interior design (MS); journalism and communication (MA, MS); landscape architecture (MLA); political science (MA, MS); second language teaching (MSLT); sociology (MA, MS, MSS, PhD); theatre arts (MA, MFA); western American literature and culture (MA, MS).

College of Natural Resources *Degree program information:* Part-time programs available. Offers bioregional planning (MS); ecology (MS, PhD); fisheries biology (MS, PhD); forestry (MS, PhD); geography (MA, MS); human dimensions of ecosystem science and management (MS, PhD); natural resources (MA, MNR, MS, PhD); range science (MS, PhD); recreation resource management (MS, PhD); watershed science (MS, PhD); wildlife biology (MS, PhD).

College of Science *Degree program information:* Part-time and evening/weekend programs available. Offers biochemistry (MS, PhD); biology (MS, PhD); chemistry (MS, PhD); computer science (MCS, MS, PhD); ecology (MS, PhD); geology (MS); industrial mathematics (MS); mathematical sciences (PhD); mathematics (M Math, MS); physics (MS, PhD); science (M Math, MCS, MS, PhD); statistics (MS).

UTAH VALLEY UNIVERSITY, Orem, UT 84058-5999

General Information State-supported, coed, comprehensive institution.

GRADUATE UNITS

Program in Education Offers education (M Ed).

Program in Nursing Offers nursing (MSN). Electronic applications accepted.

UTICA COLLEGE, Utica, NY 13502-4892

General Information Independent, coed, comprehensive institution. *Enrollment:* 3,101 graduate, professional, and undergraduate students; 165 full-time matriculated graduate/professional students (124 women), 434 part-time matriculated graduate/professional students (267 women). *Enrollment by degree level:* 108 first professional, 491 master's. *Graduate faculty:* 65 full-time (28 women). *Tuition:* Full-time $22,611; part-time $840 per credit hour. *Required fees:* $50 per semester. Tuition and fees vary according to class time, course load, degree level and program. *Graduate housing:* Room and/or apartments available on a first-come, first-served basis to single students; on-campus housing not available to married students. Housing application deadline: 3/1. *Student services:* Campus employment opportunities, campus safety program, career counseling, international student services, low-cost health insurance, services for students with disabilities. *Library facilities:* Frank E. Gannett Memorial Library. *Online resources:* library catalog, web page. *Collection:* 185,292 titles, 1,093 serial subscriptions, 10,033 audiovisual materials.

Computer facilities: 179 computers available on campus for general student use. A campuswide network can be accessed from student residence rooms. Online class registration is available. *Web address:* http://www.utica.edu/.

General Application Contact: John D. Rowe, Director of Graduate Admissions, 315-792-3824, Fax: 315-792-3003, E-mail: jrowe@utica.edu.

GRADUATE UNITS

Department of Physical Therapy Students: 72 full-time (47 women), 36 part-time (22 women); includes 15 minority (8 African Americans, 1 American Indian/Alaska Native, 6 Asian Americans or Pacific Islanders), 2 international. Average age 28. *Faculty:* 8 full-time (4 women). Expenses: Contact institution. *Financial support:* Career-related internships or fieldwork, scholarships/grants, tuition waivers (partial), and unspecified assistantships available. Support available to part-time students. Financial award application deadline: 3/15; financial award applicants required to submit FAFSA. Offers physical therapy (DPT, TDPT). *Application deadline:* Applications are processed on a rolling basis. *Application fee:* $50. Electronic applications accepted. *Application Contact:* John D. Rowe, Director of Graduate Admissions, 315-792-3824, Fax: 315-792-3003, E-mail: jrowe@utica.edu. *Director of Physical Therapy,* Dr. Shauna Malta, 315-792-3313, E-mail: smalta@utica.edu.

Liberal Studies Program Students: 4 full-time (3 women), 33 part-time (26 women); includes 2 minority (1 African American, 1 Asian American or Pacific Islander), 1 international. Average age 33. *Faculty:* 19 full-time (8 women). Expenses: Contact institution. *Financial support:* Career-related internships or fieldwork, scholarships/grants, tuition waivers (partial), and unspecified assistantships available. Support available to part-time students. Financial award application deadline: 3/15; financial award applicants required to submit FAFSA. In 2008, 3 master's awarded. *Degree program information:* Part-time and evening/weekend programs available. Offers liberal studies (MS). *Application deadline:* Applications are processed on a rolling basis. *Application fee:* $50. Electronic applications accepted. *Application Contact:* John D. Rowe, Director of Graduate Admissions, 315-792-3824, Fax: 315-792-3003, E-mail: jrowe@utica.edu. *Coordinator, Liberal Studies,* Dr. Lawrence Aaronson, 315-792-3092, E-mail: laaronson@utica.edu.

Program in Accountancy Students: 2 full-time (1 woman), 21 part-time (12 women); includes 7 minority (5 African Americans, 1 American Indian/Alaska Native, 1 Hispanic American), 1 international. Average age 34. *Faculty:* 7 full-time (0 women). Expenses: Contact institution. *Financial support:* Career-related internships or fieldwork, scholarships/grants, tuition waivers (partial), and unspecified assistantships available. Support available to part-time students. Financial award application deadline: 3/15; financial award applicants required to submit FAFSA. In 2008, 3 master's awarded. *Degree program information:* Part-time and evening/weekend programs available. Postbaccalaureate distance learning degree programs offered. Offers accountancy (MBA). *Application deadline:* Applications are processed on a rolling basis. *Application fee:* $50. Electronic applications accepted. *Application Contact:* John D. Rowe, Director of Graduate Admissions, 315-792-3824, Fax: 315-792-3003, E-mail: jrowe@utica.edu. *MBA Director,* Dr. Hartwell Herring, 315-792-3335, E-mail: hherring@utica.edu.

Program in Economic Crime and Fraud Management Students: 1 (woman) full-time, 85 part-time (44 women); includes 9 minority (5 African Americans, 1 Asian American or Pacific Islander, 3 Hispanic Americans), 4 international. Average age 40. *Faculty:* 7 full-time (0 women). Expenses: Contact institution. *Financial support:* Career-related internships or fieldwork, scholarships/grants, tuition waivers (partial), and unspecified assistantships available. Support available to part-time students. Financial award application deadline: 3/15; financial award applicants required to submit FAFSA. In 2008, 47 master's awarded. *Degree program information:* Part-time and evening/weekend programs available. Postbaccalaureate distance learning degree programs offered (minimal on-campus study). Offers economic crime and fraud management (MBA). *Application deadline:* Applications are processed on a rolling basis. *Application fee:* $50. Electronic applications accepted. *Application Contact:* John D. Rowe, Director of Graduate Admissions, 315-792-3824, Fax: 315-792-3003, E-mail: jrowe@utica.edu. *Director of Economic Crime Graduate Programs,* Dr. R. Bruce McBride, 315-792-3808, E-mail: rmcbride@utica.edu.

Program in Economic Crime Management Students: 1 (woman) full-time, 122 part-time (74 women); includes 20 minority (8 African Americans, 5 American Indian/Alaska Native, 1 Asian American or Pacific Islander, 6 Hispanic Americans), 2 international. Average age 37. *Faculty:* 4 full-time (0 women). Expenses: Contact institution. *Financial support:* Career-related internships or fieldwork, scholarships/grants, tuition waivers (partial), and unspecified assistantships available. Support available to part-time students. Financial award application deadline: 3/15; financial award applicants required to submit FAFSA. In 2008, 17 master's awarded. *Degree program information:* Part-time programs available. Postbaccalaureate distance learning degree programs offered (minimal on-campus study). Offers economic crime management (MS). *Application deadline:* Applications are processed on a rolling basis. *Application fee:* $50. Electronic applications accepted. *Application Contact:* John D. Rowe, Director of Graduate Admissions, 315-792-3824, Fax: 315-792-3003, E-mail: jrowe@utica.edu. *Director of Economic Crime Graduate Programs,* Dr. R. Bruce McBride, 315-792-3808, E-mail: rmcbride@utica.edu.

Program in Health Care Administration Average age 23. Expenses: Contact institution. Offers health care administration (MS). *Application Contact:* John D. Rowe, Director of Graduate Admissions, 315-792-3824, Fax: 315-792-3003, E-mail: jrowe@utica.edu. *Head,* Dr. Dana Hart, 315-792-3375, E-mail: dhart@utica.edu.

Program in Occupational Therapy Students: 46 full-time (40 women), 2 part-time (1 woman); includes 3 minority (1 African American, 2 Hispanic Americans), 1 international. Average age 29. *Faculty:* 7 full-time (all women). Expenses: Contact institution. *Financial support:* Career-related internships or fieldwork, scholarships/grants, tuition waivers (partial), and unspecified assistantships available. Support available to part-time students. Financial award application deadline: 3/15; financial award applicants required to submit FAFSA. In 2008, 32 master's awarded. *Degree program information:* Part-time and evening/weekend programs available. Offers occupational therapy (MS). *Application deadline:* Applications are processed on a rolling basis. *Application fee:* $50. Electronic applications accepted. *Application Contact:* John D. Rowe, Director of Graduate Admissions, 315-792-3824, Fax: 315-792-3003, E-mail: jrowe@utica.edu. *Director, Occupational Therapy Program,* Sally Townsend, 315-792-3239, E-mail: stownsend@utica.edu.

Teacher Education Programs Students: 39 full-time (31 women), 112 part-time (75 women); includes 3 minority (2 African Americans, 1 Hispanic American). Average age 29. *Faculty:* 10

full-time (7 women). Expenses: Contact institution. *Financial support:* Career-related internships or fieldwork, scholarships/grants, tuition waivers (partial), and unspecified assistantships available. Support available to part-time students. Financial award application deadline: 3/15; financial award applicants required to submit FAFSA. In 2008, 43 master's awarded. Offers teacher education (MS, MS Ed, CAS). *Application deadline:* Applications are processed on a rolling basis. *Application fee:* $50. Electronic applications accepted. *Application Contact:* John D. Rowe, Director of Graduate Admissions, 315-792-3824, Fax: 315-792-3003, E-mail: jrowe@utica.edu. *Director, Institute for Excellence in Education,* Dr. Lois Fisch, 315-792-3815, E-mail: lfisch@utica.edu.

VALDOSTA STATE UNIVERSITY, Valdosta, GA 31698

General Information State-supported, coed, university. CGS member. *Enrollment:* 11,490 graduate, professional, and undergraduate students; 596 full-time matriculated graduate/professional students (448 women), 940 part-time matriculated graduate/professional students (701 women). *Graduate faculty:* 211 full-time (92 women). *Graduate housing:* Rooms and/or apartments available on a first-come, first-served basis to single and married students. Housing application deadline: 7/1. *Student services:* Campus employment opportunities, campus safety program, career counseling, exercise/wellness program, free psychological counseling, grant writing training, international student services, low-cost health insurance, multicultural affairs office, services for students with disabilities, teacher training, writing training. *Library facilities:* Odum Library. *Online resources:* library catalog, web page, access to other libraries' catalogs. *Collection:* 626,173 titles, 2,788 serial subscriptions, 23,938 audiovisual materials.

Computer facilities: Computer purchase and lease plans are available. 1,550 computers available on campus for general student use. A campuswide network can be accessed from student residence rooms. Online class registration, online classes are available. *Web address:* http://www.valdosta.edu/.

General Application Contact: Dr. Karla Hull, E-mail: khull@valdosta.edu.

GRADUATE UNITS

Graduate School Students: 596 full-time (448 women), 940 part-time (701 women); includes 280 minority (241 African Americans, 9 American Indian/Alaska Native, 14 Asian Americans or Pacific Islanders, 16 Hispanic Americans). Average age 28. 1,105 applicants, 50% accepted, 470 enrolled. *Faculty:* 211 full-time (92 women). Expenses: Contact institution. *Financial support:* In 2008–09, 53 students received support, including 47 research assistantships with full tuition reimbursements available (averaging $2,452 per year), 3 teaching assistantships with full tuition reimbursements available (averaging $2,800 per year); career-related internships or fieldwork, institutionally sponsored loans, scholarships/grants, traineeships, tuition waivers (partial), and unspecified assistantships also available. Support available to part-time students. Financial award application deadline: 7/1; financial award applicants required to submit FAFSA. In 2008, 476 master's, 9 doctorates, 5 other advanced degrees awarded. *Degree program information:* Part-time and evening/weekend programs available. Post-baccalaureate distance learning degree programs offered (minimal on-campus study). Offers business administration (MBA); clinical/counseling psychology (MS); criminal justice (MS); early childhood education (M Ed, Ed S); educational leadership (M Ed, Ed D, Ed S); English (MA); history (MA); industrial/organizational psychology (MS); library and information science (MLIS); marriage and family therapy (MS); middle grades education (M Ed, Ed S); reading education (M Ed); school counseling (M Ed, Ed S); school psychology (Ed S); secondary education (M Ed, Ed S); sociology (MS); special education (M Ed, Ed S). *Application deadline:* For fall admission, 7/1 for domestic and international students; for spring admission, 11/1 for domestic and international students. Applications are processed on a rolling basis. *Application fee:* $40. Electronic applications accepted. *Application Contact:* Rebecca Waters, Coordinator of Graduate Admissions, 229-333-5694, Fax: 229-245-3853, E-mail: rlwaters@valdost.edu. Dr. Karla Hull, E-mail: khull@valdosta.edu.

Division of Social Work Students: 46 full-time (42 women), 57 part-time (53 women); includes 42 minority (38 African Americans, 4 American Indian/Alaska Native). Average age 29. 86 applicants, 56% accepted, 28 enrolled. *Faculty:* 7 full-time (4 women). Expenses: Contact institution. *Financial support:* In 2008–09, 4 students received support, including 2 research assistantships with full tuition reimbursements available (averaging $2,452 per year); career-related internships or fieldwork, institutionally sponsored loans, scholarships/grants, and unspecified assistantships also available. Financial award application deadline: 7/1; financial award applicants required to submit FAFSA. In 2008, 39 master's awarded. *Degree program information:* Part-time and evening/weekend programs available. Offers social work (MSW). *Application deadline:* For fall admission, 3/15 for domestic and international students. Applications are processed on a rolling basis. *Application fee:* $40. *Application Contact:* Rebecca Waters, Coordinator of Graduate Admissions, 229-333-5694, Fax: 229-245-3853, E-mail: rlwaters@valdosta.edu. *Director,* Dr. Martha Giddings, 229-249-4864, Fax: 229-245-4341, E-mail: mgidding@valdosta.edu.

VALPARAISO UNIVERSITY, Valparaiso, IN 46383

General Information Independent-religious, coed, comprehensive institution. *Enrollment:* 3,976 graduate, professional, and undergraduate students; 805 full-time matriculated graduate/professional students (389 women), 247 part-time matriculated graduate/professional students (148 women). *Enrollment by degree level:* 575 first professional, 423 master's, 17 doctoral, 37 other advanced degrees. *Graduate faculty:* 30 full-time (10 women), 130 part-time/adjunct (60 women). *Graduate housing:* On-campus housing not available. *Student services:* Campus employment opportunities, campus safety program, career counseling, exercise/wellness program, free psychological counseling, international student services, low-cost health insurance, multicultural affairs office, services for students with disabilities, teacher training, writing training. *Library facilities:* Christopher Center for Library and Information Resources plus 1 other. *Online resources:* library catalog, web page. *Collection:* 506,437 titles, 50,199 serial subscriptions, 6,594 audiovisual materials.

Computer facilities: 901 computers available on campus for general student use. A campuswide network can be accessed from student residence rooms and from off campus. Online class registration, Web academic information, degree audit are available. *Web address:* http://www.valpo.edu/.

General Application Contact: Dr. David L. Rowland, Dean, Graduate Studies and Continuing Education, 219-464-5313, Fax: 219-464-5381, E-mail: David.Rowland@valpo.edu.

GRADUATE UNITS

Graduate Division Students: 269 full-time (152 women), 187 part-time (124 women); includes 32 minority (14 African Americans, 7 Asian Americans or Pacific Islanders, 11 Hispanic Americans), 111 international. Average age 30. *Faculty:* 91 part-time/adjunct (43 women). Expenses: Contact institution. *Financial support:* Career-related internships or fieldwork, traineeships, and unspecified assistantships available. Support available to part-time students. Financial award applicants required to submit FAFSA. In 2008, 188 master's, 23 other advanced degrees awarded. *Degree program information:* Part-time and evening/weekend programs available. Offers business management (for counseling students) (Certificate); Chinese studies (MA); clinical mental health counseling (MA); community counseling (MA); English (MALS, Post-Master's Certificate); English studies and communication (MA); ethics and values (MALS, Post-Master's Certificate); gerontology (MALS, Post-Master's Certificate); history (MALS, Post-Master's Certificate); human behavior and society (MALS, Post-Master's Certificate); information technology (MS); initial licensure (M Ed); international commerce and policy (MS); liberal studies (MALS, Post-Master's Certificate); school psychologysports administration (MS); teaching and learning (M Ed); teaching of English to speakers of other languages (TESOL) (Certificate); theology (MALS, Post-Master's Certificate); theology and ministry (MALS, Post-Master's Certificate). *Application deadline:* Applications are processed on a rolling basis. *Application fee:* $30 ($50 for international students). Electronic applications accepted. *Application Contact:* Jamie Haney, Coordinator of Recruitment Activities, 219-464-5313, Fax: 219-464-5381, E-mail: Jamie.Haney@valpo.edu. *Dean, Graduate Studies and Continuing Education,* Dr. David L. Rowland, 219-464-5313, Fax: 219-464-5381, E-mail: David.Rowland@valpo.edu.

College of Business Administration Students: 23 full-time (8 women), 28 part-time (14 women); includes 1 minority (African American), 6 international. Average age 28. *Faculty:* 12 part-time/adjunct (4 women). Expenses: Contact institution. *Financial support:* Available to part-time students. Applicants required to submit FAFSA. In 2008, 35 master's awarded. *Degree program information:* Part-time and evening/weekend programs available. Offers business administration (MBA); engineering management (MEM); management (Certificate). *Application deadline:* Applications are processed on a rolling basis. *Application fee:* $30 ($50 for international students). Electronic applications accepted. *Application Contact:* Cindy Tuholski, Assistant Director of Graduate Programs in Management, 219-465-7952, Fax: 219-464-5789, E-mail: Cindy.Tuholski@valpo.edu. *Director of Graduate Programs in Management,* Bruce MacLean, 219-465-7952, Fax: 219-464-5789, E-mail: Bruce.MacLean@valpo.edu.

College of Nursing Students: 20 full-time (19 women), 38 part-time (33 women); includes 6 minority (2 African Americans, 2 Asian Americans or Pacific Islanders, 2 Hispanic Americans). Average age 40. *Faculty:* 7 part-time/adjunct (all women). Expenses: Contact institution. *Financial support:* Available to part-time students. Applicants required to submit FAFSA. In 2008, 13 master's, 8 other advanced degrees awarded. *Degree program information:* Part-time and evening/weekend programs available. Offers management (Certificate); nursing (MSN, Post-Master's Certificate); nursing education (MSN). *Application deadline:* Applications are processed on a rolling basis. *Application fee:* $30 ($50 for international students). Electronic applications accepted. *Application Contact:* Jamie Haney, Coordinator of Recruitment Activities, 219-464-5313, Fax: 219-464-5381, E-mail: Jamie.Haney@valpo.edu. *Dean,* Dr. Janet Brown, 219-464-5289, Fax: 219-464-5425, E-mail: janet.brown@valpo.edu.

School of Law *Degree program information:* Part-time programs available. Offers law (JD, LL M). Electronic applications accepted.

VANCOUVER ISLAND UNIVERSITY, Nanaimo, BC V9R 5S5, Canada

General Information Province-supported, coed, comprehensive institution. *Graduate housing:* Room and/or apartments available on a first-come, first-served basis to single students; on-campus housing not available to married students. Housing application deadline: 3/5.

GRADUATE UNITS

Program in Business Administration *Degree program information:* Part-time and evening/weekend programs available. Offers business administration (EMBA, IMBA, MBA). Program offered jointly with University of Hertfordshire. Electronic applications accepted.

VANCOUVER SCHOOL OF THEOLOGY, Vancouver, BC V6T 1L4, Canada

General Information Independent-religious, coed, graduate-only institution. *Graduate housing:* Rooms and/or apartments guaranteed to single students and available to married students. Housing application deadline: 4/7.

GRADUATE UNITS

Graduate and Professional Programs *Degree program information:* Part-time programs available. Offers spiritual direction (Graduate Diploma); theological studies (MATS); theology (M Div, Th M, Dip CS). Electronic applications accepted.

VANDERBILT UNIVERSITY, Nashville, TN 37240-1001

General Information Independent, coed, university. CGS member. *Enrollment:* 12,093 graduate, professional, and undergraduate students; 5,402 matriculated graduate/professional students. *Enrollment by degree level:* 5,402 other advanced degrees. *Graduate housing:* On-campus housing not available. *Student services:* Campus employment opportunities, campus safety program, career counseling, child daycare facilities, exercise/wellness program, free psychological counseling, grant writing training, international student services, low-cost health insurance, multicultural affairs office, services for students with disabilities, teacher training, writing training. *Library facilities:* Jean and Alexander Heard Library plus 7 others. *Collection:* 1.8 million titles, 26,885 serial subscriptions, 153,450 audiovisual materials. *Research affiliation:* AstraZeneca (Medicine), Amgen (Medicine), SAIC Frederick (Engineering & Computer Science), Chevron Phillips (Chemical Engineering), Boeing Aerospace Corporation (Engineering & Computer Science), BAE Systems (Engineering & Computer Science).

Computer facilities: 400 computers available on campus for general student use. A campuswide network can be accessed from student residence rooms and from off campus. Productivity and educational software available. *Web address:* http://www.vanderbilt.edu/.

General Application Contact: Walter B. Bieschke, Program Coordinator for Graduate Admissions, 615-343-6321, Fax: 615-343-6687, E-mail: vandygrad@vanderbilt.edu.

GRADUATE UNITS

Divinity School *Degree program information:* Part-time programs available. Offers divinity (M Div, MTS). Electronic applications accepted.

Graduate School Students: 2,108; includes 248 minority (118 African Americans, 12 American Indian/Alaska Native, 62 Asian Americans or Pacific Islanders, 56 Hispanic Americans), 497 international. Average age 29. 5,968 applicants, 16% accepted, 455 enrolled. Expenses: Contact institution. *Financial support:* Fellowships with full and partial tuition reimbursements, research assistantships with full tuition reimbursements, teaching assistantships with full tuition reimbursements, career-related internships or fieldwork, Federal Work-Study, institutionally sponsored loans, scholarships/grants, traineeships, health care benefits, tuition waivers (full and partial), and unspecified assistantships available. Support available to part-time students. Financial award application deadline: 1/15; financial award applicants required to submit CSS PROFILE or FAFSA. In 2008, 226 master's, 284 doctorates awarded. *Degree program information:* Part-time programs available. Offers analytical chemistry (MAT, MS, PhD); anthropology (MA, PhD); astronomy (MS); biochemistry (MS, PhD); biological sciences (MS, PhD); biomedical informatics (MS, PhD); cancer biology (MS, PhD); cell and developmental biology (MS, PhD); classics (MA); community research and action (MS, PhD); creative writing (MFA); earth and environmental sciences (MS); economic development (MA); economics (MA, MAT, PhD); English (MA, MAT, PhD); French (MA, MAT, PhD); German (MA, MAT, PhD); history (MA, MAT, PhD); human genetics (PhD); inorganic chemistry (MAT, MS, PhD); Latin (MAT); Latin American studies (MA); leadership and policy studies (PhD); learning, teaching and diversity (MS, PhD); liberal arts and science (MLAS); mathematics (MA, MAT, MS, PhD); microbiology and immunology (MS, PhD); molecular physiology and biophysics (MS, PhD); neuroscience (PhD); nursing science (PhD); organic chemistry (MAT, MS, PhD); pathology (PhD); pharmacology (PhD); philosophy (MA, PhD); physical chemistry (MAT, MS, PhD); physics (MA, MAT, MS, PhD); political science (MA, MAT, PhD); Portuguese (MA); psychological sciences (MA, PhD); religion (MA, PhD); sociology (MA, PhD); Spanish (MA, MAT, PhD); Spanish and Portuguese (PhD); theoretical chemistry (MAT, MS, PhD). *Application deadline:* For fall admission, 1/15 for domestic and international students. *Application fee:* $0. Electronic applications accepted. *Application Contact:* Walter B. Bieschke, Program Coordinator for Graduate Admissions, 615-343-6321, Fax: 615-343-6687, E-mail: vandygrad@vanderbilt.edu. *Associate Provost for Research and Dean of the Graduate School,* Dennis G. Hall, PhD, 615-322-2809, Fax: 615-343-9936, E-mail: dennis.g.hall@vanderbilt.edu.

Center for Medicine, Health, and Society Students: 1 full-time (0 women), 1 (woman) part-time. Average age 28. 3 applicants, 67% accepted, 2 enrolled. Expenses: Contact institution. *Financial support:* Federal Work-Study, scholarships/grants, and health care benefits available. Financial award application deadline: 1/15; financial award applicants required to submit CSS PROFILE or FAFSA. Offers medicine, health, and society (MA). *Application deadline:* For fall admission, 1/15 for domestic and international students. *Application fee:* $0. Electronic applications accepted. *Application Contact:* Walter B. Bieschke, Program Coordinator for Graduate Admissions, 615-343-6321, Fax: 615-343-6687, E-mail: vandygrad@vanderbilt.edu. *Director,* Dr. Arlene Tuchman, E-mail: arleen.m.tuchman@vanderbilt.edu.

Owen Graduate School of Management *Degree program information:* Evening/weekend programs available. Offers business administration (MBA); executive business administration (MBA); finance (PhD); management (MBA, MSF, PhD); marketing (PhD); operations manage-

Vanderbilt University (continued)

ment (PhD); organization studies (PhD). Students in the 5-year MBA program enter as undergraduate freshman. Electronic applications accepted.

Peabody College Students: 337 full-time (281 women), 152 part-time (96 women); includes 56 minority (37 African Americans, 9 Asian Americans or Pacific Islanders, 10 Hispanic Americans), 22 international. Average age 27. 638 applicants, 58% accepted, 196 enrolled. *Faculty:* 143 full-time (75 women), 78 part-time/adjunct (58 women). Expenses: Contact institution. *Financial support:* In 2008–09, 388 students received support, including 3 fellowships with full and partial tuition reimbursements available, 167 research assistantships with full and partial tuition reimbursements available, 33 teaching assistantships with full and partial tuition reimbursements available; career-related internships or fieldwork, Federal Work-Study, institutionally sponsored loans, scholarships/grants, traineeships, tuition waivers (partial), and unspecified assistantships also available. Support available to part-time students. Financial award application deadline: 2/1; financial award applicants required to submit FAFSA. In 2008, 188 master's, 31 doctorates awarded. *Degree program information:* Part-time programs available. Offers child studies (M Ed); community development and action (M Ed); education (M Ed, MPP, Ed D); education policy (MPP); educational leadership and policy (Ed D); elementary education (M Ed); English language learners (M Ed); higher education (M Ed); higher education, leadership and policy (Ed D); human development counseling (M Ed); human resource development (M Ed); international education policy and management (M Ed); learning and instruction (M Ed); learning, diversity, and urban studies (M Ed); organizational leadership (M Ed); reading education (M Ed); secondary education (M Ed); special education (M Ed). *Application deadline:* For fall admission, 12/31 priority date for domestic and international students; for spring admission, 11/1 priority date for domestic and international students. Applications are processed on a rolling basis. *Application fee:* $0. Electronic applications accepted. *Application Contact:* Kimberly Brazil-Tanner, Recruitment Coordinator, 615-332-8410, Fax: 615-322-8401, E-mail: kim.brazil@vanderbilt.edu. *Dean,* Dr. Camilla P. Benbow, 615-322-8407, Fax: 615-322-8501, E-mail: camilla.benbow@vanderbilt.edu.

School of Engineering Students: 383 full-time (102 women), 14 part-time (2 women); includes 37 minority (17 African Americans, 2 American Indian/Alaska Native, 13 Asian Americans or Pacific Islanders, 5 Hispanic Americans), 149 international. Average age 26. 1,796 applicants, 10% accepted, 103 enrolled. *Faculty:* 124 full-time (22 women), 17 part-time/adjunct (2 women). Expenses: Contact institution. *Financial support:* Fellowships with full tuition reimbursements, research assistantships with full tuition reimbursements, teaching assistantships with full tuition reimbursements, career-related internships or fieldwork, Federal Work-Study, institutionally sponsored loans, scholarships/grants, traineeships, health care benefits, and tuition waivers (full and partial) available. Support available to part-time students. Financial award application deadline: 1/15; financial award applicants required to submit CSS PROFILE or FAFSA. In 2008, 76 master's, 51 doctorates awarded. *Degree program information:* Part-time programs available. Offers biomedical engineering (M Eng, MS, PhD); chemical and biomolecular engineering (M Eng, MS, PhD); civil engineering (M Eng, MS, PhD); computer science (M Eng, MS, PhD); electrical engineering (M Eng, MS, PhD); engineering (M Eng, MS, PhD); environmental engineering (M Eng, MS, PhD); environmental management (MS, PhD); materials science (M Eng, MS, PhD); mechanical engineering (M Eng, MS, PhD). MS and PhD offered through the Graduate School. *Application deadline:* For fall admission, 1/15 for domestic and international students; for spring admission, 11/1 for domestic and international students. *Application fee:* $0. Electronic applications accepted. *Application Contact:* Dolores A. Black, Coordinator, Graduate Student Recruiting, 615-343-3308, Fax: 615-343-8006, E-mail: dolores.black@vanderbilt.edu. *Dean,* Dr. Kenneth F. Galloway, 615-322-0720, Fax: 615-343-8006, E-mail: kenneth.f.galloway@vanderbilt.edu.

School of Medicine Offers audiology (Au D, PhD); biomedical and biological sciences (PhD); chemical and physical biology (PhD); clinical investigation (MS); education of the deaf (MED); hearing and speech sciences (MS); medical physics (MS); medicine (MED, MPH, MS, Au D, PhD); public health (MPH); speech-language-pathology (MS). Electronic applications accepted.

School of Nursing Students: 374 full-time (343 women), 301 part-time (277 women); includes 69 minority (43 African Americans, 3 American Indian/Alaska Native, 12 Asian Americans or Pacific Islanders, 11 Hispanic Americans). Average age 29. 704 applicants, 64% accepted, 348 enrolled. *Faculty:* 118 full-time (102 women), 429 part-time/adjunct (309 women). Expenses: Contact institution. *Financial support:* In 2008–09, 380 students received support, including 1 research assistantship (averaging $5,000 per year); teaching assistantships, scholarships/grants, health care benefits, and tuition waivers also available. Support available to part-time students. Financial award application deadline: 3/15; financial award applicants required to submit FAFSA. In 2008, 287 master's, 4 doctorates awarded. *Degree program information:* Part-time programs available. Postbaccalaureate distance learning degree programs offered (minimal on-campus study). Offers adult acute care nurse practitioner (MSN); adult health nurse practitioner/forensic (MSN); adult nurse practitioner/cardiovascular disease management and prevention (MSN); adult nurse practitioner/palliative care (MSN); clinical management (clinical nurse leader/specialist) (MSN); family nurse practitioner (MSN); gerontology nurse practitioner (MSN); health systems management (MSN); neonatal nurse practitioner (MSN); nurse midwifery (MSN); nursing informatics (MSN); nursing practice (DNP); nursing science (PhD); nutrition (MS); pediatric acute care nurse practitioner (MSN); pediatric primary care nurse practitioner (MSN); psychiatric-mental health nurse practitioner (MSN); women's health nurse practitioner (MSN). *Application deadline:* For fall admission, 12/1 priority date for domestic and international students. Applications are processed on a rolling basis. *Application fee:* $50. *Application Contact:* Cheryl Feldner, Assistant Director of Admissions, 615-322-3800, Fax: 615-343-0333, E-mail: cheryl.feldner@vanderbilt.edu. *Dean,* Dr. Colleen Conway-Welch, 615-343-8776, Fax: 615-343-7711, E-mail: colleen.conway-welch@vanderbilt.edu.

Vanderbilt University Law School Students: 608 full-time (296 women); includes 100 minority (54 African Americans, 3 American Indian/Alaska Native, 19 Asian Americans or Pacific Islanders, 24 Hispanic Americans), 48 international. Average age 24. 4,336 applicants, 25% accepted, 191 enrolled. *Faculty:* 51 full-time (19 women), 69 part-time/adjunct (28 women). Expenses: Contact institution. *Financial support:* In 2008–09, 413 students received support. Career-related internships or fieldwork, Federal Work-Study, institutionally sponsored loans, scholarships/grants, and health care benefits available. Financial award application deadline: 2/15; financial award applicants required to submit FAFSA. In 2008, 222 first professional degrees, 24 master's awarded. Offers law (JD, LL M); law and economics (PhD). *Application deadline:* For fall admission, 9/15 for domestic and international students; for spring admission, 3/15 for domestic and international students. Applications are processed on a rolling basis. *Application fee:* $50. Electronic applications accepted. *Application Contact:* Admissions Office, 615-322-6452, Fax: 615-322-1531. *Assistant Dean for Admissions,* G. Todd Morton, 615-322-6452, Fax: 615-322-1531.

VANDERCOOK COLLEGE OF MUSIC, Chicago, IL 60616-3731

General Information Independent, coed, comprehensive institution. *Graduate housing:* Rooms and/or apartments available on a first-come, first-served basis to single and married students. Housing application deadline: 6/1.

GRADUATE UNITS

Program in Music Education *Degree program information:* Part-time programs available. Offers music education (MM Ed). Offered during summer only.

VANGUARD UNIVERSITY OF SOUTHERN CALIFORNIA, Costa Mesa, CA 92626-9601

General Information Independent-religious, coed, comprehensive institution. *Enrollment:* 2,149 graduate, professional, and undergraduate students; 133 full-time matriculated graduate/professional students (83 women), 157 part-time matriculated graduate/professional students (88 women). *Enrollment by degree level:* 290 master's. *Graduate faculty:* 15 full-time (7 women), 15 part-time/adjunct (9 women). *Graduate housing:* Rooms and/or apartments available on a first-come, first-served basis to single and married students. Typical cost: $4212 per year ($6926 including board) for single students; $8424 per year ($13,852 including board) for married students. Room and board charges vary according to board plan. Housing application deadline: 5/1. *Student services:* Campus employment opportunities, career counseling, free psychological counseling, international student services, low-cost health insurance, teacher training. *Library facilities:* O. Cope Budge Library. *Online resources:* library catalog, web page. *Collection:* 164,333 titles, 17,342 serial subscriptions, 6,023 audiovisual materials.

Computer facilities: 150 computers available on campus for general student use. A campuswide network can be accessed from student residence rooms and from off campus. Online class registration is available. *Web address:* http://www.vanguard.edu/.

General Application Contact: Drake Levasheff, Director of Graduate Admissions, 714-966-5499, Fax: 714-966-5471, E-mail: dlevasheff@vanguard.edu.

GRADUATE UNITS

Graduate Program in Business Students: 18 full-time (8 women), 10 part-time (4 women); includes 10 minority (1 American Indian/Alaska Native, 2 Asian Americans or Pacific Islanders, 7 Hispanic Americans), 1 international. Average age 35. 16 applicants, 50% accepted, 7 enrolled. *Faculty:* 2 full-time (0 women), 2 part-time/adjunct (0 women). Expenses: Contact institution. *Financial support:* Scholarships/grants available. Financial award applicants required to submit FAFSA. In 2008, 9 master's awarded. *Degree program information:* Part-time and evening/weekend programs available. Offers business (MBA). *Application deadline:* For fall admission, 4/1 priority date for domestic and international students; for spring admission, 10/1 priority date for domestic and international students. Applications are processed on a rolling basis. *Application fee:* $45. Electronic applications accepted. *Application Contact:* Joy Petrie, Graduate Coordinator, 714-556-3610 Ext. 3704, Fax: 714-662-5228, E-mail: jzeiger@vanguard.edu. *Dean,* Dr. David Alford, 714-556-3610 Ext. 3701, Fax: 714-662-5228, E-mail: dalford@vanguard.edu.

Graduate Program in Clinical Psychology Students: 41 full-time (34 women), 27 part-time (24 women); includes 19 minority (1 African American, 2 American Indian/Alaska Native, 3 Asian Americans or Pacific Islanders, 13 Hispanic Americans). Average age 30. 93 applicants, 49% accepted, 26 enrolled. *Faculty:* 3 full-time (all women), 5 part-time/adjunct (2 women). Expenses: Contact institution. *Financial support:* In 2008–09, 62 students received support. Scholarships/grants and unspecified assistantships available. Financial award application deadline: 3/2; financial award applicants required to submit FAFSA. *Degree program information:* Part-time and evening/weekend programs available. Offers clinical psychology (MS). *Application deadline:* For fall admission, 4/1 priority date for domestic and international students; for winter admission, 11/1 for domestic and international students. Applications are processed on a rolling basis. *Application fee:* $45. Electronic applications accepted. *Application Contact:* Asha Harrington, Graduate Psychology Coordinator, 714-556-3610 Ext. 3550, Fax: 714-662-5226, E-mail: gradpsych@vanguard.edu. *Director,* Dr. Jerre White, 714-556-3610 Ext. 3550, Fax: 714-662-5226, E-mail: jwhite@vanguard.edu.

Graduate Programs in Education Students: 53 full-time (36 women), 66 part-time (43 women); includes 19 minority (4 Asian Americans or Pacific Islanders, 15 Hispanic Americans). Average age 31. 67 applicants, 90% accepted, 53 enrolled. *Faculty:* 5 full-time (4 women), 7 part-time/adjunct (all women). Expenses: Contact institution. *Financial support:* In 2008–09, 103 students received support, including 3 teaching assistantships (averaging $417 per year); scholarships/grants and unspecified assistantships also available. Financial award application deadline: 3/2; financial award applicants required to submit FAFSA. In 2008, 27 master's awarded. *Degree program information:* Evening/weekend programs available. Offers education (MA). *Application deadline:* For fall admission, 4/1 priority date for domestic and international students; for spring admission, 10/1 priority date for domestic and international students. Applications are processed on a rolling basis. *Application fee:* $45. Electronic applications accepted. *Application Contact:* Michelle Romo, Graduate Education Coordinator, 714-556-3610 Ext. 3302, Fax: 714-966-5495, E-mail: mromo@vanguard.edu. *Dean,* Dr. Jerry Ternes, 714-556-3610 Ext. 3303, Fax: 714-966-5495, E-mail: jternes@vanguard.edu.

Graduate Programs in Religion Students: 21 full-time (5 women), 54 part-time (17 women); includes 13 minority (1 African American, 1 American Indian/Alaska Native, 3 Asian Americans or Pacific Islanders, 8 Hispanic Americans), 2 international. Average age 38. 21 applicants, 57% accepted, 9 enrolled. *Faculty:* 5 full-time (0 women), 1 part-time/adjunct (0 women). Expenses: Contact institution. *Financial support:* In 2008–09, 3 teaching assistantships (averaging $3,333 per year) were awarded; scholarships/grants, tuition waivers (partial), and unspecified assistantships also available. Financial award application deadline: 3/2. *Degree program information:* Part-time and evening/weekend programs available. Offers leadership studies (MA); theological studies (MTS). *Application deadline:* For fall admission, 4/1 priority date for domestic and international students; for spring admission, 10/1 priority date for domestic and international students. Applications are processed on a rolling basis. *Application fee:* $45. Electronic applications accepted. *Application Contact:* Angel McGee, Secretary, Graduate Program in Religion, 714-556-3610 Ext. 3237, Fax: 714-957-9317, E-mail: angel.mcgee@vanguard.edu. *Associate Dean,* Dr. Richard Israel, 714-556-3610 Ext. 3223, Fax: 714-957-9317.

VASSAR COLLEGE, Poughkeepsie, NY 12604

General Information Independent, coed. *Enrollment:* 2,389 graduate, professional, and undergraduate students. *Tuition:* Part-time $1335 per term. *Graduate housing:* On-campus housing not available. *Student services:* Campus employment opportunities, campus safety program, career counseling, child daycare facilities, exercise/wellness program, free psychological counseling, international student services, low-cost health insurance, multicultural affairs office, services for students with disabilities. *Library facilities:* Vassar College Libraries plus 4 others. *Online resources:* library catalog, web page, access to other libraries' catalogs. *Collection:* 948,415 titles, 10,417 serial subscriptions, 28,749 audiovisual materials. *Research affiliation:* Ford Program, Alfred P. Sloan Foundation (humanities, social sciences).

Computer facilities: Computer purchase and lease plans are available. 300 computers available on campus for general student use. A campuswide network can be accessed from student residence rooms and from off campus. Online class registration, Ethernet are available. *Web address:* http://www.vassar.edu/.

General Application Contact: Jannay Morrow, Dean of Studies, 914-437-5257.

GRADUATE UNITS

Graduate Programs Expenses: Contact institution. *Financial support:* Career-related internships or fieldwork available. *Degree program information:* Part-time programs available. Offers biology (MA, MS); chemistry (MA, MS). Applicants accepted only if enrolled in undergraduate programs at Vassar College. *Application fee:* $60. *Application Contact:* Jannay Morrow, Dean of Studies, 914-437-5257. *Dean of Studies,* Jannay Morrow, 914-437-5257.

VAUGHN COLLEGE OF AERONAUTICS AND TECHNOLOGY, Flushing, NY 11369-1037

General Information Independent, coed, primarily men, comprehensive institution.

GRADUATE UNITS

Graduate Programs Offers airport management (MS).

VERMONT LAW SCHOOL, South Royalton, VT 05068-0096

General Information Independent, coed, graduate-only institution. *Graduate housing:* On-campus housing not available.

GRADUATE UNITS

Law School *Degree program information:* Part-time programs available. Offers law (JD, LL M, MSEL). Electronic applications accepted.

Environmental Law Center *Degree program information:* Part-time programs available. Offers environmental law (LL M, MSEL).

VICTORIA UNIVERSITY, Toronto, ON M5S 1K7, Canada

General Information Independent-religious, coed, graduate-only institution. *Enrollment by degree level:* 73 first professional, 29 master's, 44 doctoral, 3 other advanced degrees.

Graduate faculty: 11 full-time (5 women), 9 part-time/adjunct (3 women). *Graduate tuition:* Tuition and fees charges are reported in Canadian dollars. *Tuition:* Full-time $5670 Canadian dollars. *Required fees:* $325 Canadian dollars. One-time fee: $35 Canadian dollars full-time. *Graduate housing:* Rooms and/or apartments available on a first-come, first-served basis to single and married students. Typical cost: $6900 Canadian dollars per year ($10,000 Canadian dollars including board) for single students; $10,140 Canadian dollars per year for married students. Room and board charges vary according to board plan and campus/location. Housing application deadline: 6/30. *Student services:* Campus employment opportunities, campus safety program, career counseling, free psychological counseling, international student services, low-cost health insurance, services for students with disabilities, writing training. *Library facilities:* Emmanuel Library plus 2 others. *Online resources:* library catalog, web page, access to other libraries' catalogs. *Collection:* 70,000 titles, 144 serial subscriptions, 883 audiovisual materials.

Computer facilities: 110 computers available on campus for general student use. A campuswide network can be accessed from student residence rooms and from off campus. Online class registration is available. *Web address:* http://www.vicu.utoronto.ca/.

General Application Contact: Dr. Brian Clarke, Director for Advanced Degree Studies, 416-585-4547, Fax: 416-585-4516, E-mail: b.clarke@utoronto.ca.

GRADUATE UNITS

Emmanuel College Students: 97 full-time (54 women), 52 part-time (34 women); includes 18 minority (2 African Americans, 1 American Indian/Alaska Native, 11 Asian Americans or Pacific Islanders, 4 Hispanic Americans), 7 international. Average age 42. 56 applicants, 88% accepted, 34 enrolled. *Faculty:* 11 full-time (5 women), 9 part-time/adjunct (3 women). Expenses: Contact institution. *Financial support:* In 2008–09, 78 students received support, including 2 fellowships (averaging $11,000 per year), 13 teaching assistantships (averaging $11,000 per year); career-related internships or fieldwork and scholarships/grants also available. Support available to part-time students. Financial award application deadline: 5/30. In 2008, 18 first professional degrees, 2 master's, 3 doctorates, 3 other advanced degrees awarded. *Degree program information:* Part-time programs available. Offers theology (M Div, MA, MPS, MRE, MTS, Th M, D Min, PhD, Th D, Certificate, Diploma, L Th). *Application deadline:* For fall admission, 6/30 for domestic students, 1/15 for international students; for winter admission, 11/30 for domestic students; for spring admission, 3/30 for domestic students. *Application fee:* $0. Electronic applications accepted. *Application Contact:* Wanda Chin, Registrar, 416-585-4538, Fax: 416-585-4516, E-mail: wanda.chin@utoronto.ca. *Principal,* Dr. Mark G. Toulouse, 416-585-4540, Fax: 416-585-4516, E-mail: m.toulouse@utoronto.ca.

VILLANOVA UNIVERSITY, Villanova, PA 19085-1699

General Information Independent-religious, coed, comprehensive institution. CGS member. *Enrollment:* 10,275 graduate, professional, and undergraduate students; 1,345 full-time matriculated graduate/professional students (604 women), 1,734 part-time matriculated graduate/professional students (814 women). *Enrollment by degree level:* 742 first professional, 2,144 master's, 99 doctoral, 94 other advanced degrees. *Graduate faculty:* 274. *Graduate housing:* On-campus housing not available. *Student services:* Career counseling, exercise/wellness program, free psychological counseling, international student services, low-cost health insurance, multicultural affairs office, services for students with disabilities. *Library facilities:* Falvey Library plus 2 others. *Online resources:* library catalog, web page, access to other libraries' catalogs. *Collection:* 720,500 titles, 12,000 serial subscriptions, 8,200 audiovisual materials.

Computer facilities: Computer purchase and lease plans are available. 6,609 computers available on campus for general student use. A campuswide network can be accessed from student residence rooms and from off campus. Online class registration, learning management system, Web-based laundry reservation, electronic portfolios, data vaulting, calendar system, basketball ticket lottery, printing are available. *Web address:* http://www.villanova.edu/.

General Application Contact: Dr. Gerald Long, Dean, Graduate School of Liberal Arts and Sciences, 610-519-7093, Fax: 610-519-7096.

GRADUATE UNITS

College of Engineering Students: 57 full-time (14 women), 248 part-time (60 women); includes 23 minority (5 African Americans, 1 American Indian/Alaska Native, 11 Asian Americans or Pacific Islanders, 6 Hispanic Americans), 89 international. *Faculty:* 66 full-time (7 women), 25 part-time/adjunct (2 women). Expenses: Contact institution. *Financial support:* In 2008–09, research assistantships with full and partial tuition reimbursements (averaging $13,100 per year); Federal Work-Study, scholarships/grants, tuition waivers (full and partial), and unspecified assistantships also available. Support available to part-time students. Financial award application deadline: 1/15. In 2008, 91 master's, 2 doctorates awarded. *Degree program information:* Part-time and evening/weekend programs available. Postbaccalaureate distance learning degree programs offered (minimal on-campus study). Offers chemical engineering (MSChE); civil engineering (MSCE); communication systems engineering (Certificate); computer architectures (Certificate); computer engineering (MSCPE, Certificate); electric power systems (Certificate); electrical engineering (MSEE, Certificate); electro mechanical systems (Certificate); electro-mechanical systems (Certificate); engineering (MSCPE, MSChE, MSEE, MSME, MSTE, MSWREE, PhD, Certificate); high frequency systems (Certificate); intelligent systems (Certificate); machinery dynamics (Certificate); mechanical engineering (MSME); thermofluid systems (Certificate); transportation engineering (MSTE); water resources and environmental engineering (MSWREE); wireless and digital communications (Certificate). *Application deadline:* For fall admission, 8/1 priority date for domestic students, 4/1 priority date for international students; for spring admission, 12/1 for domestic students, 10/1 for international students. Applications are processed on a rolling basis. *Application fee:* $50. Electronic applications accepted. *Application Contact:* College of Engineering, Graduate Programs Office, 610-519-5840, Fax: 610-519-5859, E-mail: engineering.grad@villanova.edu. *Dean,* Dr. Gary A. Gabriele, 610-519-4960, Fax: 610-519-5859, E-mail: gary.gabriele@villanova.edu.

College of Nursing Students: 27 full-time (24 women), 204 part-time (178 women); includes 20 minority (9 African Americans, 10 Asian Americans or Pacific Islanders, 1 Hispanic American), 2 international. Average age 33. 128 applicants, 60% accepted, 58 enrolled. *Faculty:* 15 full-time (all women), 3 part-time/adjunct (2 women). Expenses: Contact institution. *Financial support:* In 2008–09, 53 students received support, including 5 teaching assistantships with full tuition reimbursements available (averaging $12,165 per year); institutionally sponsored loans, scholarships/grants, traineeships, tuition waivers (full), and unspecified assistantships also available. Financial award application deadline: 3/1; financial award applicants required to submit FAFSA. In 2008, 52 master's, 5 doctorates awarded. *Degree program information:* Part-time programs available. Postbaccalaureate distance learning degree programs offered (minimal on-campus study). Offers adult nurse practitioner (MSN, Post Master's Certificate); geriatric nurse practitioner (MSN, Post Master's Certificate); health care administration (MSN); nurse anesthetist (MSN, Post Master's Certificate); nursing (PhD); nursing education (MSN, Post Master's Certificate); pediatric nurse practitioner (MSN, Post Master's Certificate). *Application deadline:* For fall admission, 7/1 priority date for domestic students, 7/1 for international students; for spring admission, 11/1 priority date for domestic students, 11/1 for international students. Applications are processed on a rolling basis. *Application fee:* $50. *Application Contact:* Dean, Graduate School of Liberal Arts and Sciences. *Assistant Dean and Director, Graduate Program,* Dr. Marguerite K. Schlag, 610-519-4907, Fax: 610-519-7650, E-mail: marguerite.schlag@villanova.edu.

Graduate School of Liberal Arts and Sciences Students: 413 full-time (233 women), 549 part-time (326 women); includes 103 minority (35 African Americans, 38 Asian Americans or Pacific Islanders, 30 Hispanic Americans), 83 international. Average age 29. 738 applicants, 66% accepted, 266 enrolled. *Faculty:* 128 full-time (47 women), 47 part-time/adjunct (14 women). Expenses: Contact institution. *Financial support:* Research assistantships, teaching assistantships, career-related internships or fieldwork, Federal Work-Study, scholarships/grants, and unspecified assistantships available. Support available to part-time students. Financial award applicants required to submit FAFSA. In 2008, 383 master's, 3 doctorates awarded. *Degree program information:* Part-time and evening/weekend programs available. Offers applied statistics (MS); biology (MA, MS); chemistry (MS); communication (MA); community counseling (MS); computer science (MS); counseling and human relations (MS); criminology, law and society (MA); educational leadership (MA); elementary school counseling (MS); elementary teacher education (MA); English (MA); higher education (MA); Hispanic studies (MA); history (MA); human resource development (MS); humanities and Augustinian tradition (MA); liberal arts and sciences (MA, MPA, MS, PhD); liberal studies (MA); mathematical sciences (MA); philosophy (PhD); political science (MA, MPA); psychology (MS); public administration (MPA); secondary school counseling (MS); secondary teacher education (MA); software engineering (MS); theatre (MA); theology (MA). *Application deadline:* For fall admission, 8/1 for domestic and international students; for spring admission, 12/1 for domestic and international students. Applications are processed on a rolling basis. *Application fee:* $50. Electronic applications accepted. *Application Contact:* Dr. Gerald Long, Dean, Graduate School of Liberal Arts and Sciences, 610-519-7093, Fax: 610-519-7096. *Dean,* Dr. Gerald Long, 610-519-7090, Fax: 610-519-7096.

School of Law Students: 765 full-time (326 women), 82 part-time (37 women); includes 140 minority (26 African Americans, 4 American Indian/Alaska Native, 73 Asian Americans or Pacific Islanders, 37 Hispanic Americans). Average age 26. 3,168 applicants, 39% accepted, 276 enrolled. *Faculty:* 79 full-time (34 women), 107 part-time/adjunct (24 women). Expenses: Contact institution. *Financial support:* In 2008–09, 237 students received support, including 91 research assistantships, 13 teaching assistantships; career-related internships or fieldwork, Federal Work-Study, institutionally sponsored loans, and scholarships/grants also available. Support available to part-time students. Financial award application deadline: 3/15; financial award applicants required to submit FAFSA. In 2008, 226 JDs, 24 master's awarded. Offers law (JD, LL M); tax (LL M). *Application deadline:* For fall admission, 3/1 for domestic and international students. Applications are processed on a rolling basis. *Application fee:* $75. Electronic applications accepted. *Application Contact:* Noe Bernal, Assistant Dean for Admissions, 610-519-7007, Fax: 610-519-6291, E-mail: admissions@law.villanova.edu. *Dean,* Mark A. Sargent, 610-519-7007, Fax: 610-519-6472.

Villanova School of Business Students: 140 full-time, 507 part-time. Average age 30. *Faculty:* 79 full-time, 18 part-time/adjunct. Expenses: Contact institution. *Financial support:* In 2008–09, 19 research assistantships with full and partial tuition reimbursements (averaging $13,100 per year) were awarded. Support available to part-time students. Financial award application deadline: 3/31. *Degree program information:* Part-time and evening/weekend programs available. Offers accountancy (MAC); business (EMBA, MAC, MBA, MSF); corporate management (general) (MBA); executive business administration (EMBA); finance (MBA); international business (MBA); management information systems (MBA); marketing (MBA). *Application deadline:* Applications are processed on a rolling basis. *Application fee:* $50. Electronic applications accepted. *Application Contact:* Meredith L. Kwiatek, Assistant Director, 610-519-7016, Fax: 610-519-6273, E-mail: meredith.kwiatek@villanova.edu. *Assistant Dean of Graduate Business Programs,* Simone L. Pollard, 610-519-4336, Fax: 610-519-6273, E-mail: simone.pollard@villanova.edu.

See Close-Up on page 1049.

VIRGINIA COLLEGE AT BIRMINGHAM, Birmingham, AL 35209

General Information Proprietary, coed, comprehensive institution. *Graduate faculty:* 200. *Student services:* Campus employment opportunities, campus safety program, career counseling, teacher training, writing training. *Library facilities:* Elma Bell Library plus 2 others. *Online resources:* library catalog. *Collection:* 3,900 titles, 120 serial subscriptions, 40 audiovisual materials.

Computer facilities: A campuswide network can be accessed. *Web address:* http://www.vc.edu/.

General Application Contact: Vincent Femia, Director of Admissions, 205-802-1200, E-mail: admissions@vc.edu.

GRADUATE UNITS

Program in Business Administration Expenses: Contact institution. *Financial support:* Career-related internships or fieldwork, Federal Work-Study, institutionally sponsored loans, and scholarships/grants available. Support available to part-time students. Financial award applicants required to submit FAFSA. *Degree program information:* Part-time and evening/weekend programs available. Postbaccalaureate distance learning degree programs offered (no on-campus study). Offers business administration (MBA). *Application Contact:* Vincent Femia, Director of Admissions, 205-802-1200, E-mail: admissions@vc.edu. *Unit Head,* Joann Wilson, 877-812-8428, E-mail: admissions@vc.edu.

Virginia College Online Expenses: Contact institution. *Financial support:* Applicants required to submit FAFSA. *Degree program information:* Part-time and evening/weekend programs available. Postbaccalaureate distance learning degree programs offered (no on-campus study). Offers business administration (MBA); criminal justice (MCJ); cybersecurity (MC). *Application Contact:* Hugh Jensen, Director of Admissions, 877-207-1933, E-mail: vcoadm@vc.edu. *President, Virginia College Online,* Stan Banks, 877-207-1933, E-mail: vcoadm@vc.edu.

VIRGINIA COMMONWEALTH UNIVERSITY, Richmond, VA 23284-9005

General Information State-supported, coed, university. CGS member. *Graduate housing:* Room and/or apartments available on a first-come, first-served basis to single students; on-campus housing not available to married students. *Research affiliation:* Center for Innovative Technology (biotechnology), Virginia Biotechnology Research Park.

GRADUATE UNITS

Graduate School *Degree program information:* Part-time and evening/weekend programs available. Offers interdisciplinary studies (MIS). Electronic applications accepted.

College of Humanities and Sciences *Degree program information:* Part-time and evening/weekend programs available. Offers account management (MS); account planning (MS); analytical chemistry (MS, PhD); applied mathematics (MS); applied social research (CASR); art direction (MS); biology (MS); chemical physics (PhD); clinical psychology (PhD); copywriting (MS); counseling psychology (PhD); creative brand management (MS); creative media planning (MS); creative writing (MFA); criminal justice (MS, CCJA); English (MA); fiction (MFA); fictional poetry (MFA); forensic science (MS); gender violence intervention (Certificate); general psychology (PhD); geographic information systems (Certificate); government and public affairs (MA, MPA, MS, MURP, PhD, CASR, CCJA, CPM, CURP, Certificate, Graduate Certificate); historic preservation planning (Certificate); history (MA); homeland security and emergency preparedness (MA, Graduate Certificate); humanities and sciences (MA, MFA, MPA, MS, MURP, PhD, CASR, CCJA, CPM, CURP, Certificate, Graduate Certificate); inorganic chemistry (MS, PhD); literature (MA); mass communications (MS, PhD); mathematics (MS); media, art, and text (PhD); medical physics (MS, PhD); nonprofit management (Graduate Certificate); operations research (MS); organic chemistry (MS, PhD); physical chemistry (MS, PhD); physics and applied physics (MS); planning information systems (Certificate); poetry (MFA); political science and public administration (MPA); public management (CPM); public policy and administration (PhD); scholastic journalism (MS); sociology (MS); statistical sciences and operations research (MS, Certificate); strategic public relations (MS); urban and regional planning (MURP); urban revitalization (CURP); writing and rhetoric (MA).

School of Allied Health Professions *Degree program information:* Part-time programs available. Offers advanced physical therapy (MS); aging studies (CAS); allied health professions (MHA, MS, MSHA, MSNA, MSOT, PhD, CAS, CPC); clinical laboratory sciences (MS); entry-level physical therapy (MS); gerontology (MS, PhD); health administration (MHA, MSHA, PhD); health related sciences (PhD); health services organization and research (PhD); nurse anesthesia (MSNA); occupational therapy (MS, MSOT); patient counseling (MS, CPC); physical therapy (PhD); physiology (PhD); radiation sciences (PhD); rehabilitation counseling (MS, CPC); rehabilitation leadership (PhD).

School of Business *Degree program information:* Part-time and evening/weekend programs available. Offers accounting (M Acc, MBA, PhD); business (M Acc, M Tax, MA, MBA, MS, PhD, Certificate, Postbaccalaureate Certificate); business administration (MBA, Postbaccalaureate Certificate); decision sciences (MBA); economics (MA, MBA, MS); finance,

Virginia Commonwealth University (continued)

insurance, and real estate (MS); information systems (MS, PhD); management (Certificate); marketing and business law (Certificate); real estate and urban land development (Certificate); taxation (M Tax).

School of Education *Degree program information:* Part-time programs available. Offers adult literacy (M Ed); adults with disabilities (MS Ed); athletic training (MSAT); counselor education (M Ed); curriculum and instruction (M Ed); early childhood (M Ed); early education (MT); education (M Ed, MS, MSAT, MT, PhD, Certificate); educational leadership (PhD); educational psychology (PhD); emotionally disturbed (M Ed, MT); health and movement sciences (MS); human resource development (M Ed); instructional leadership (PhD); learning disabilities (M Ed); mentally retarded (M Ed, MT); middle education (MT); reading (M Ed); recreation, parks and sports leadership (MS); rehabilitation and movement science (PhD); research and evaluation (PhD); secondary education (MT, Certificate); severely/profoundly handicapped (M Ed); special education (MT); special education and disability leadership (PhD); urban services leadership (PhD).

School of Engineering Offers biomedical engineering (MS, PhD); chemical and life science engineering (MS, PhD); computer science (MS, PhD, Certificate); electrical engineering (MS, PhD); engineering (PhD); mechanical engineering (MS, PhD); nuclear engineering (MS).

School of Life Sciences Offers bioinformatics (MS); environmental communication (MIS); environmental health (MIS); environmental policy (MIS); environmental sciences (MIS); integrative life sciences (PhD); life sciences (MIS, MS, PhD).

School of Nursing *Degree program information:* Part-time and evening/weekend programs available. Offers adult health nursing (MS); child health nursing (MS); family health nursing (MS); health system (PhD); immunocompetence (PhD); nurse practitioner (MS, Certificate); nursing administration (MS); psychiatric-mental health nursing (MS); risk and resilience (PhD); women's health nursing (MS).

School of Social Work Offers social work (MSW, PhD).

School of the Arts *Degree program information:* Part-time programs available. Offers acting (MFA); architectural history (MA); art education (MAE); art history (MA, PhD); ceramics (MFA); costume design (MFA); design/visual communications (MFA); directing (MFA); education (MM); fibers (MFA); furniture design (MFA); glassworking (MFA); graphic design (MFA); historical studies (MA); interior environment (MFA); jewelry/metalworking (MFA); kinetic imaging (MFA); museum studies (MA); music (MM); painting (MFA); pedagogy (MFA); photography and film (MFA); printmaking (MFA); scene design/technical theater (MFA); sculpture (MFA); theatre (MFA).

Medical College of Virginia-Professional Programs *Degree program information:* Part-time programs available. Offers medicine (DDS, MD, Pharm D, MPH, MS, PhD). Electronic applications accepted.

School of Dentistry Offers dentistry (DDS, MS). Electronic applications accepted.

School of Medicine Offers anatomy (MS, PhD); anatomy and neurobiology (MS, PhD); anatomy and physical therapy (PhD); biochemistry (MS, PhD); biostatistics (MS, PhD); epidemiology and community health (PhD); genetic counseling (MS); human genetics (PhD); medicine (MD, MPH, MS, PhD); microbiology and immunology (MS, PhD); molecular biology and genetics (MS, PhD); neuroscience (MS, PhD); pathology (MS, PhD); pharmacology (PhD); pharmacology and toxicology (MS); physiology (MS, PhD). Electronic applications accepted.

School of Pharmacy *Degree program information:* Part-time programs available. Offers pharmaceutics (Pharm D, MS, PhD); pharmacy (Pharm D, MS, PhD).

Program in Pre-Medical Basic Health Sciences Offers anatomy (CBHS); biochemistry (CBHS); human genetics (CBHS); microbiology (CBHS); pharmacology (CBHS); physiology (CBHS).

VIRGINIA INTERNATIONAL UNIVERSITY, Fairfax, VA 22030

General Information Proprietary, coed, comprehensive institution. *Tuition:* Full-time $9126; part-time $517 per credit hour. *Required fees:* $100. One-time fee: $100 full-time. *Graduate housing:* Room and/or apartments available on a first-come, first-served basis to single students; on-campus housing not available to married students. Typical cost: $5000 per year. *Student services:* Campus employment opportunities, career counseling, free psychological counseling, grant writing training, international student services, low-cost health insurance, writing training. *Research affiliation:* Apple Federal Credit Union (Financial Management). *Web address:* http://www.viu.edu/.

General Application Contact: Yoko Uchida, Director of Admissions and Records, 703-591-7042, E-mail: yuchida@viu.edu.

GRADUATE UNITS

Graduate Programs Students: 378 full-time (182 women). Expenses: Contact institution. Offers business (MBA); computer science (MS); information systems (MSIS). *Application deadline:* For fall admission, 7/31 for domestic students, 7/3 for international students; for spring admission, 12/18 for domestic students, 11/20 for international students. *Application fee:* $100. *Application Contact:* Yoko Uchida, Director of Admissions and Records, 703-591-7042, E-mail: yuchida@viu.edu.

VIRGINIA POLYTECHNIC INSTITUTE AND STATE UNIVERSITY, Blacksburg, VA 24061

General Information State-supported, coed, university. CGS member. *Graduate housing:* Room and/or apartments available on a first-come, first-served basis to single students; on-campus housing not available to married students. Housing application deadline: 5/16. *Research affiliation:* VCOM-Virginia College of Osteopathic Medicine (biomedical engineering and sciences), Carillion Biomedical (biomedical engineering and sciences).

GRADUATE UNITS

Graduate School Electronic applications accepted.

College of Agriculture and Life Sciences Offers agribusiness (MS); agricultural economics (MS, PhD); agricultural extension education (MS, PhD); agriculture and life sciences (MS, PhD); animal science (MS, PhD); applied economics (MS); crop and soil environmental sciences (MS, PhD); developmental and international economics (PhD); econometrics (PhD); entomology (MS, PhD); food science and technology (MS, PhD); horticulture (MS, PhD); human nutrition, foods and exercise (MS, PhD); life sciences (MS, PhD); macro and micro economics (PhD); markets and industrial organizations (PhD); plant pathology (MS, PhD); plant physiology and weed science (MS, PhD); plant protection (MS); poultry science (MS, PhD); public and regional/urban economics (PhD); resource and environmental economics (PhD). Electronic applications accepted.

College of Architecture and Urban Studies Offers architecture (M Arch, MS); architecture and urban studies (M Arch, MLA, MPA, MPIA, MS, MURP, PhD, CAGS); architecture design research (PhD); building construction (MS); environmental design and planning (PhD); environmental planning and policy (MURP); government and international affairs (MPIA); housing, community and economic development (MURP); international development planning (MURP); land use and physical planning (MURP); landscape architecture (MLA); planning, governance and globalization (PhD); public administration and policy (MPA, PhD, CAGS); urban and regional planning (MURP). Electronic applications accepted.

College of Engineering Offers aerospace engineering (M Eng, MS, PhD); biological systems engineering (M Eng, MS, PhD); chemical engineering (M Eng, MS, PhD); civil engineering (M Eng, MS, PhD); computer engineering (M Eng, MS, PhD); computer science (MS, PhD); electrical engineering (M Eng, MS, PhD); engineering (M Eng, MEA, MIS, MS, PhD); engineering administration (MEA); engineering education (PhD); engineering mechanics (MS, PhD); environmental engineering (M Eng, MS); environmental sciences and engineering (MS); industrial engineering (M Eng, MS, PhD); information systems (MIS); materials science and engineering (M Eng, MS, PhD); mechanical engineering (M Eng, MS, PhD); mining and minerals engineering (M Eng, MS, PhD); ocean engineering (MS); operations research (M Eng, MS, PhD); systems engineering (M Eng, MS). Electronic applications accepted.

College of Liberal Arts and Human Sciences *Degree program information:* Part-time programs available. Offers administration and supervision of special education (Ed D, PhD, Ed S); adult development and aging (MS, PhD); adult learning and human resource development (MS, PhD); apparel business and economics (MS, PhD); apparel product design and analysis (MS, PhD); apparel quality analysis (MS, PhD); arts administration (MFA); career and technical education (MS Ed, Ed D, PhD, Ed S); child development (MS, PhD); communication (MA); consumer studies (MS, PhD); costume design (MFA); counselor education (MA Ed, Ed D, PhD, Ed S); creative writing (MFA); curriculum and instruction (MA Ed, Ed D, PhD, Ed S); education (MA Ed, MS Ed, Ed D, PhD, Ed S); educational leadership (MA Ed, Ed D, PhD); educational psychology (PhD); educational research and evaluation (PhD); English (MA); family financial management (MS, PhD); family studies (MS, PhD); foreign languages and literatures (MA); health and physical education (MS Ed); health promotion (MS); higher education (MA Ed, PhD); history (MA); household equipment (MS, PhD); housing (MS, PhD); instructional design and technology (MA, Ed D, PhD, Ed S); interior design (MS, PhD); liberal arts and human sciences (MA, MA Ed, MFA, MS, MS Ed, Ed D, PhD, Ed S); lighting design (MFA); marriage and family therapy (MS, PhD); mathematics education (MA Ed, PhD); philosophy (MA); political science (MA); property management (MFA); resource management (MS, PhD); rhetoric and writing (PhD); scenic design (MFA); science and technology studies (MS, PhD); secondary English education (MA Ed); social, political, ethical and cultural thought (PhD, Graduate Certificate); sociology (MS, PhD); stage management (MFA); technical theatre (MFA). Electronic applications accepted.

College of Natural Resources Offers fisheries and wildlife sciences (MS, PhD); forest biology (MF, MS, PhD); forest biometry (MF, MS, PhD); forest management/economics (MF, MS, PhD); forest products marketing (MF, MS, PhD); geography (MS, PhD); industrial forestry operations (MF, MS, PhD); natural resources (MF, MNR, MS, PhD); outdoor recreation (MF, MS, PhD); wood science and engineering (MF, MS, PhD). Electronic applications accepted.

College of Science Offers applied mathematics (MS, PhD); applied physics (MS, PhD); bio-behavioral sciences (PhD); botany (MS, PhD); chemistry (MS, PhD); clinical psychology (PhD); developmental psychology (PhD); ecology and evolutionary biology (MS, PhD); economics (MA, PhD); genetics and developmental biology (MS, PhD); geological sciences (MS, PhD); geophysics (MS, PhD); industrial/organizational psychology (PhD); mathematical physics (MS, PhD); microbiology (MS, PhD); physics (MS, PhD); psychology (MS); pure mathematics (MS, PhD); science (MA, MS, PhD); statistics (MS, PhD); zoology (MS, PhD). Electronic applications accepted.

Intercollege Offers biomedical engineering and sciences (MS, PhD); genetics, bioinformatics and computational biology (PhD); information technology (MIT); interdisciplinary studies (MIT, MS, PhD); macromolecular science and engineering (MS, PhD). Electronic applications accepted.

Pamplin College of Business Offers accounting and information systems (MACIS, PhD); business (MACIS, MBA, MS, PhD); business administration (MBA); business information technology (MS, PhD); finance (PhD); hospitality and tourism management (MS, PhD); management (PhD); marketing (PhD). Electronic applications accepted.

Virginia-Maryland Regional College of Veterinary Medicine Offers biomedical and veterinary sciences (MS, PhD); veterinary medicine (DVM, MS, PhD).

VIRGINIA STATE UNIVERSITY, Petersburg, VA 23806-0001

General Information State-supported, coed, comprehensive institution. *Graduate housing:* Room and/or apartments available on a first-come, first-served basis to single students; on-campus housing not available to married students. Housing application deadline: 5/1. *Research affiliation:* Swiss Institute Nuclear Research Laboratory (physics), NASA–Langley Research Center (physics), Brookhaven National Laboratory (physics), Los Alamos National Laboratory–Continuous Electron Beam Accelerator Facility (physics).

GRADUATE UNITS

School of Graduate Studies, Research, and Outreach *Degree program information:* Part-time and evening/weekend programs available. Offers interdisciplinary studies (MIS).

School of Agriculture Offers agriculture (MS); plant science (MS).

School of Engineering, Science and Technology Offers behavioral and community health sciences (PhD); biology (MS); clinical health psychology (PhD); clinical psychology (MS); computer science (MS); engineering, science and technology (M Ed, MS); general psychology (MS); mathematics (MS); mathematics education (M Ed); physics (MS).

School of Liberal Arts and Education *Degree program information:* Part-time and evening/weekend programs available. Offers career and technical studies (M Ed, MS, CAGS); economics (MA); education (M Ed, MS); educational administration and supervision (M Ed, MS); English (MA); history (MA); liberal arts and education (M Ed, MA, MS, CAGS).

VIRGINIA UNION UNIVERSITY, Richmond, VA 23220-1170

General Information Independent-religious, coed, comprehensive institution. *Graduate housing:* Room and/or apartments available on a first-come, first-served basis to single students; on-campus housing not available to married students.

GRADUATE UNITS

School of Theology *Degree program information:* Part-time and evening/weekend programs available. Offers theology (M Div, D Min).

VIRGINIA UNIVERSITY OF LYNCHBURG, Lynchburg, VA 24501-6417

General Information Independent-religious, coed, comprehensive institution.

GRADUATE UNITS

Graduate Programs

VITERBO UNIVERSITY, La Crosse, WI 54601-4797

General Information Independent-religious, coed, primarily women, comprehensive institution. *Graduate housing:* Rooms and/or apartments available to single and married students. Housing application deadline: 4/2.

GRADUATE UNITS

Graduate Program in Business Offers business (MBA).

Graduate Program in Education *Degree program information:* Part-time and evening/weekend programs available. Offers education (MA). Courses held on weekends and during summer.

Graduate Program in Nursing Students: 28 full-time (26 women), 32 part-time (all women); includes 3 minority (1 African American, 1 Asian American or Pacific Islander, 1 Hispanic American). Average age 37. *Faculty:* 5 full-time, 5 part-time/adjunct. Expenses: Contact institution. *Financial support:* In 2008–09, 9 students received support. Institutionally sponsored loans, scholarships/grants, and traineeships available. Financial award application deadline: 6/1; financial award applicants required to submit FAFSA. *Degree program information:* Part-time programs available. Postbaccalaureate distance learning degree programs offered (minimal on-campus study). Offers nursing (MSN). *Application deadline:* For spring admission, 2/1 priority date for domestic students. Applications are processed on a rolling basis. *Application fee:* $50. *Application Contact:* 608-796-3671. *Director,* Dr. Bonnie Nesbitt, 608-796-3688, Fax: 608-796-3668, E-mail: bjnesbitt@viterbo.edu.

WAGNER COLLEGE, Staten Island, NY 10301-4495

General Information Independent, coed, comprehensive institution. *Graduate housing:* Room and/or apartments available on a first-come, first-served basis to single students; on-campus housing not available to married students. Housing application deadline: 4/1. *Research affiliation:* Staten Island University Hospital.

GRADUATE UNITS

Division of Graduate Studies *Degree program information:* Part-time and evening/weekend programs available. Offers accelerated business administration (MBA); accounting (MS); adolescent education (MS Ed); advanced physician assistant studies (MS); childhood education (MS Ed); early childhood education (birth-grade 2) (MS Ed); educational leadership (Certificate); family nurse practitioner (Certificate); finance (MBA); health care administration (MBA); international business (MBA); literacy (B-6) (MS Ed); management (Exec MBA, MBA); marketing (MBA); microbiology (MS); middle level education (5-9) (MS Ed); nursing (MS); school building leader (Certificate); school district leader (Certificate).

WAKE FOREST UNIVERSITY, Winston-Salem, NC 27109

General Information Independent, coed, university. CGS member. *Enrollment:* 6,862 graduate, professional, and undergraduate students; 2,418 matriculated graduate/professional students. *Graduate faculty:* 1,900. *Graduate housing:* On-campus housing not available. *Student services:* Career counseling, free psychological counseling, grant writing training, international student services, low-cost health insurance, multicultural affairs office, services for students with disabilities, teacher training, writing training. *Library facilities:* Z. Smith Reynolds Library plus 3 others. *Online resources:* library catalog, web page, access to other libraries' catalogs. *Collection:* 923,123 titles, 16,448 serial subscriptions.

Computer facilities: 150 computers available on campus for general student use. A campuswide network can be accessed from student residence rooms and from off campus. Online class registration, financial information online, drop-add, transcript requests are available. *Web address:* http://www.wfu.edu/.

GRADUATE UNITS

Babcock Graduate School of Management Students: 517 full-time (164 women); includes 88 minority (45 African Americans, 1 American Indian/Alaska Native, 33 Asian Americans or Pacific Islanders, 9 Hispanic Americans), 35 international. *Faculty:* 40 full-time (7 women), 16 part-time/adjunct (8 women). Expenses: Contact institution. *Financial support:* In 2008–09, 222 students received support. Scholarships/grants available. Financial award applicants required to submit FAFSA. In 2008, 281 master's awarded. *Degree program information:* Evening/weekend programs available. Offers accountancy (MSA); assurance services (MSA); business administration (MA, MBA); entrepreneurship (MBA); finance (MBA); health care (MBA); management (MA, MBA, MSA); marketing (MBA); operations management (MBA); tax consulting (MSA); transaction services (MSA). *Application deadline:* Applications are processed on a rolling basis. *Application fee:* $75. Electronic applications accepted. *Application Contact:* Ginny Kerlin, Administrative Assistant, 336-758-5422, Fax: 336-758-5830, E-mail: admissions@mba.wfu.edu. *Dean,* Steve Reinemund, 336-758-5422, Fax: 336-758-5830, E-mail: admissions@mba.wfu.edu.

Graduate School of Arts and Sciences Students: 388 full-time (199 women), 47 part-time (32 women); includes 44 minority (29 African Americans, 9 Asian Americans or Pacific Islanders, 6 Hispanic Americans), 48 international. Average age 28. 767 applicants, 35% accepted, 215 enrolled. *Faculty:* 204 full-time (71 women), 49 part-time/adjunct (32 women). Expenses: Contact institution. *Financial support:* In 2008–09, 347 students received support, including 38 fellowships with full tuition reimbursements available, 35 research assistantships with full tuition reimbursements available, 146 teaching assistantships with full tuition reimbursements available; scholarships/grants, tuition waivers (full and partial), and unspecified assistantships also available. Support available to part-time students. Financial award application deadline: 1/15; financial award applicants required to submit FAFSA. In 2008, 185 master's, 9 doctorates awarded. *Degree program information:* Part-time programs available. Offers accountancy (MSA); analytical chemistry (MS, PhD); arts and sciences (MA, MA Ed, MALS, MS, MSA, PhD); biology (MS, PhD); computer science (MS); counseling (MA); English (MA); health and exercise science (MS); inorganic chemistry (MS, PhD); liberal studies (MALS); mathematics (MA); organic chemistry (MS, PhD); physical chemistry (MS, PhD); physics (MS, PhD); psychology (MA); religion (MA); secondary education (MA Ed); speech communication (MA). *Application deadline:* For fall admission, 1/15 for domestic and international students. *Application fee:* $60. Electronic applications accepted. *Application Contact:* Carol DiGiantommaso, Admissions Coordinator, 336-758-5301, Fax: 336-758-4230, E-mail: gradschl@wfu.edu. *Dean,* Dr. Lorna G. Moore, 336-758-5808, Fax: 336-758-4230, E-mail: moore@wfu.edu.

School of Law Offers law (JD, LL M, SJD). LL M for foreign law graduates in American law. Electronic applications accepted.

School of Medicine Offers medicine (MD, MS, PhD). Electronic applications accepted.

Graduate Programs in Medicine Offers biochemistry (PhD); cancer biology (PhD); comparative medicine (MS); health sciences research (MS); medicine (MS, PhD); microbiology and immunology (PhD); molecular and cellular pathobiology (MS, PhD); molecular genetics and genomics (PhD); molecular medicine (MS, PhD); neurobiology and anatomy (PhD); neuroscience (PhD); pharmacology (PhD); physiology (PhD). Electronic applications accepted.

Virginia Tech-Wake Forest University School of Biomedical Engineering and Sciences Offers biomedical engineering (MS, PhD). Electronic applications accepted.

WALDEN UNIVERSITY, Minneapolis, MN 55401

General Information Proprietary, coed, upper-level institution. CGS member. *Enrollment:* 26,585 full-time matriculated graduate/professional students (20,802 women), 5,350 part-time matriculated graduate/professional students (4,288 women). *Enrollment by degree level:* 19,435 master's, 12,491 doctoral, 9 other advanced degrees. *Graduate faculty:* 72 full-time, 1,422 part-time/adjunct. *Tuition:* Full-time $12,877; part-time $520 per credit. *Required fees:* $1230. Tuition and fees vary according to course load, degree level and program. *Graduate housing:* On-campus housing not available. *Student services:* Career counseling, free psychological counseling, services for students with disabilities, writing training. *Web address:* http://www.waldenu.edu/.

General Application Contact: Jennifer Hall, Director of Enrollment, 866-4-WALDEN, E-mail: info@walden.edu.

GRADUATE UNITS

Graduate Programs Students: 26,585 full-time (20,802 women), 5,350 part-time (4,288 women); includes 9,925 minority (7,973 African Americans, 272 American Indian/Alaska Native, 574 Asian Americans or Pacific Islanders, 1,106 Hispanic Americans), 438 international. Average age 39. 13,564 applicants, 60% accepted, 6004 enrolled. *Faculty:* 72 full-time, 1,422 part-time/adjunct. Expenses: Contact institution. *Financial support:* In 2008–09, 782 students received support, including 2 fellowships; Federal Work-Study, scholarships/grants, unspecified assistantships, and family tuition reduction; active duty/veteran tuition reduction; group tuition reduction; interest-free payment plans also available. Support available to part-time students. Financial award applicants required to submit FAFSA. In 2008, 6,488 master's, 219 doctorates, 1 other advanced degree awarded. *Degree program information:* Part-time and evening/weekend programs available. Postbaccalaureate distance learning degree programs offered (minimal on-campus study). *Application deadline:* Applications are processed on a rolling basis. *Application fee:* $50. Electronic applications accepted. *Application Contact:* Jennifer Hall, Director of Student Enrollment, 866-4-WALDEN, E-mail: info@walden.edu. *President,* Jonathan A. Kaplan, 800-925-3368.

NTU School of Engineering and Applied Science Students: 17 full-time (3 women), 110 part-time (13 women); includes 28 minority (11 African Americans, 11 Asian Americans or Pacific Islanders, 6 Hispanic Americans), 9 international. Average age 35. 106 applicants, 19% accepted, 10 enrolled. *Faculty:* 27 part-time/adjunct. Expenses: Contact institution. *Financial support:* Fellowships, Federal Work-Study, scholarships/grants, unspecified assistantships, and family tuition reduction; active duty/veteran tuition reduction; group tuition reduction; interest-free payment plans available. Support available to part-time students. Financial award applicants required to submit FAFSA. In 2008, 29 master's, 1 other advanced degree awarded. *Degree program information:* Part-time and evening/weekend programs available. Postbaccalaureate distance learning degree programs offered (no on-campus study). Offers competitive product management (Certificate); engineering management (Certificate); software engineering (MS); software project management (Certificate); software testing (Certificate); systems engineering (MS, Certificate); technical project management (Certificate). *Application deadline:* Applications are processed on a rolling basis. *Application fee:* $50. Electronic applications accepted. *Application Contact:* Jennifer Hall, Director of Enrollment, 866-4-WALDEN, E-mail: info@walden.edu. *Interim Associate Dean,* Colin Wightman, 800-925-3368.

Richard W. Riley College of Education and Leadership Students: 13,895 full-time (11,411 women), 2,143 part-time (1,793 women); includes 4,215 minority (3,388 African Americans, 117 American Indian/Alaska Native, 194 Asian Americans or Pacific Islanders, 516 Hispanic Americans), 126 international. Average age 37. 5,433 applicants, 70% accepted, 3031 enrolled. *Faculty:* 26 full-time, 661 part-time/adjunct. Expenses: Contact institution. *Financial support:* In 2008–09, 639 students received support, including 1 fellowship; Federal Work-Study, scholarships/grants, unspecified assistantships, and family tuition reduction; active duty/veteran tuition reduction; group tuition reduction; interest-free payment plans also available. Support available to part-time students. Financial award applicants required to submit FAFSA. In 2008, 5,007 master's, 111 doctorates awarded. *Degree program information:* Part-time and evening/weekend programs available. Postbaccalaureate distance learning degree programs offered (minimal on-campus study). Offers administrator leadership for teaching and learning (Ed D, Ed S); early childhood education (birth-grade 3) (MAT); education (MS, PhD); educational technology (Ed S); higher education and adult learning (Ed D); special education: emotional/behavioral disorders (K-12) (MAT); special education: learning disabilities (K-12) (MAT); teacher leadership (Ed D, Ed S). *Application deadline:* Applications are processed on a rolling basis. *Application fee:* $50. Electronic applications accepted. *Application Contact:* Jennifer Hall, Director of Enrollment, 866-4-WALDEN, E-mail: info@waldenu.edu. *Vice President,* Victoria Reid, 800-925-3368.

School of Counseling and Social Service Students: 1,235 full-time (1,026 women), 129 part-time (111 women); includes 595 minority (505 African Americans, 21 American Indian/Alaska Native, 16 Asian Americans or Pacific Islanders, 53 Hispanic Americans), 18 international. Average age 39. 724 applicants, 50% accepted, 250 enrolled. *Faculty:* 6 full-time, 76 part-time/adjunct. Expenses: Contact institution. *Financial support:* Fellowships, Federal Work-Study, scholarships/grants, unspecified assistantships, and family tuition reduction; active duty/veteran tuition reduction; group tuition reduction; interest-free payment plans available. Support available to part-time students. Financial award applicants required to submit FAFSA. In 2008, 12 master's, 5 doctorates awarded. *Degree program information:* Part-time and evening/weekend programs available. Postbaccalaureate distance learning degree programs offered (minimal on-campus study). Offers human services (PhD); mental health counseling (MS). *Application deadline:* Applications are processed on a rolling basis. *Application fee:* $50. Electronic applications accepted. *Application Contact:* Jennifer Hall, Director of Enrollment, 866-4-WALDEN, E-mail: info@waldenu.edu. *Associate Dean,* Dr. Savitri Dixon-Saxon, 800-925-3368.

School of Health Sciences Students: 1,658 full-time (1,303 women), 635 part-time (503 women); includes 1,099 minority (905 African Americans, 20 American Indian/Alaska Native, 94 Asian Americans or Pacific Islanders, 80 Hispanic Americans), 61 international. Average age 39. 1,396 applicants, 55% accepted, 529 enrolled. *Faculty:* 6 full-time, 134 part-time/adjunct. Expenses: Contact institution. *Financial support:* In 2008–09, 5 students received support; fellowships, Federal Work-Study, scholarships/grants, unspecified assistantships, and family tuition reduction; active duty/veteran tuition reduction; group tuition reduction; interest-free payment plans available. Support available to part-time students. Financial award applicants required to submit FAFSA. In 2008, 165 master's, 10 doctorates awarded. *Degree program information:* Part-time and evening/weekend programs available. Postbaccalaureate distance learning degree programs offered (minimal on-campus study). Offers clinical research administration (MS); health services (PhD); healthcare administration (MHA); public health (MPH, PhD). *Application deadline:* Applications are processed on a rolling basis. *Application fee:* $50. Electronic applications accepted. *Application Contact:* Jennifer Hall, Director of Enrollment, 866-4-WALDEN, E-mail: info@waldenu.edu. *Associate Dean,* Dr. Joanne Flowers, 800-925-3368.

School of Management Students: 3,077 full-time (1,691 women), 593 part-time (365 women); includes 1,521 minority (1,256 African Americans, 33 American Indian/Alaska Native, 94 Asian Americans or Pacific Islanders, 138 Hispanic Americans), 107 international. Average age 40. 2,056 applicants, 47% accepted, 690 enrolled. *Faculty:* 13 full-time, 205 part-time/adjunct. Expenses: Contact institution. *Financial support:* Fellowships, Federal Work-Study, scholarships/grants, unspecified assistantships, and family tuition reduction; active duty/veteran tuition reduction; group tuition reduction; interest-free payment plans available. Support available to part-time students. Financial award applicants required to submit FAFSA. In 2008, 480 master's, 50 doctorates awarded. *Degree program information:* Part-time and evening/weekend programs available. Postbaccalaureate distance learning degree programs offered (minimal on-campus study). Offers applied management and decision sciences (PhD); business information management (MISM); enterprise information security (MISM); entrepreneurship (MBA, DBA); finance (MBA, DBA); global supply chain management (DBA); human resource management (MBA); information systems management (DBA); international business (DBA); IT strategy and governance (MISM); leadership (MBA, DBA); managing global software and service supply chains (MISM); marketing (MBA, DBA); project management (MBA); risk management (MBA); self-designed (MBA, DBA); social impact management (DBA); sustainable futures (MBA); technology (MBA); technology entrepreneurship (DBA). *Application deadline:* Applications are processed on a rolling basis. *Application fee:* $50. Electronic applications accepted. *Application Contact:* Jennifer Hall, Director of Enrollment, 866-4-WALDEN, E-mail: info@waldenu.edu. *Associate Dean,* Dr. Wanda Gravett, 800-925-3368.

School of Nursing Students: 2,220 full-time (2,083 women), 786 part-time (744 women); includes 491 minority (304 African Americans, 22 American Indian/Alaska Native, 80 Asian Americans or Pacific Islanders, 85 Hispanic Americans), 25 international. Average age 43. 1,634 applicants, 57% accepted, 598 enrolled. *Faculty:* 3 full-time, 74 part-time/adjunct. Expenses: Contact institution. *Financial support:* In 2008–09, 135 students received support; fellowships, Federal Work-Study, scholarships/grants, unspecified assistantships, and family tuition reduction; active duty/veteran tuition reduction; group tuition reduction; interest-free payment plans available. Support available to part-time students. Financial award applicants required to submit FAFSA. In 2008, 491 master's awarded. *Degree program information:* Part-time and evening/weekend programs available. Postbaccalaureate distance learning degree programs offered (no on-campus study). Offers nursing (Post-Master's Certificate); nursing education (MS); nursing informatics (MS); nursing leadership and management (MS). *Application deadline:* Applications are processed on a rolling basis. *Application fee:* $50. Electronic applications accepted. *Application Contact:* Jennifer Hall, Director of Enrollment, 866-4-WALDEN, E-mail: info@walden.edu. *Associate Dean,* Dr. Sara Torres, 800-925-3368.

School of Psychology Students: 3,198 full-time (2,489 women), 810 part-time (664 women); includes 1,319 minority (1,013 African Americans, 51 American Indian/Alaska Native, 68 Asian Americans or Pacific Islanders, 187 Hispanic Americans), 72 international. Average age 40. 1,468 applicants, 60% accepted, 612 enrolled. *Faculty:* 16 full-time, 190 part-time/adjunct. Expenses: Contact institution. *Financial support:* In 2008–09, 1 fellowship was awarded; Federal Work-Study, scholarships/grants, unspecified assistantships, and family tuition reduction; active duty/veteran tuition reduction; group tuition reduction; interest-free payment plans also available. Support available to part-time students. Financial award applicants required to submit FAFSA. In 2008, 203 master's, 37 doctorates awarded. *Degree program information:* Part-time and evening/weekend programs available. Postbaccalaureate distance learning degree programs offered (minimal on-campus study). Offers clinical assessment (Post-Doctoral Certificate); clinical child psychology (Post-Doctoral Certificate); clinical psychology (Post-Doctoral Certificate); counseling psychology (Post-Doctoral Certificate); forensic psychology (MS); general psychology (Post-Doctoral Certificate); health psychology (Post-Doctoral Certificate); organizational psychology (Post-Doctoral Certificate); organizational psychology and development (Certificate); psychology (MS, PhD); school psychology (Post-Doctoral Certificate); teaching online (Post-Master's Certificate). *Application deadline:* Applications are processed on a rolling basis. *Application fee:* $50. Electronic applications accepted. *Application Contact:* Jennifer Hall, 866-4-WALDEN, E-mail: info@waldenu.edu. *Associate Dean,* Dr. Nina Nabors, 800-925-3368.

School of Public Policy and Administration Students: 1,285 full-time (794 women), 144 part-time (96 women); includes 657 minority (591 African Americans, 8 American Indian/

Walden University (continued)

Alaska Native, 17 Asian Americans or Pacific Islanders, 41 Hispanic Americans), 20 international. Average age 39. 727 applicants, 54% accepted, 284 enrolled. *Faculty:* 2 full-time, 55 part-time/adjunct. Expenses: Contact institution. *Financial support:* In 2008–09, 3 students received support; fellowships with tuition reimbursements available, Federal Work-Study, scholarships/grants, unspecified assistantships, and family tuition reduction; active duty/veteran tuition reduction; group tuition reduction; interest-free payment plans available. Support available to part-time students. Financial award applicants required to submit FAFSA. In 2008, 101 master's, 6 doctorates awarded. *Degree program information:* Part-time and evening/weekend programs available. Postbaccalaureate distance learning degree programs offered (minimal on-campus study). Offers general public policy and administration (MPA); government management (Certificate); health policy (MPA); homeland security policy (MPA); interdisciplinary policy studies (MPA); law and public policy (MPA); local government management for sustainable communities (MPA); nonprofit management (Certificate); nonprofit management and leadership (MPA, MS); policy analysis (MPA); public management and leadership (MPA); public policy and administration (PhD); terrorism, mediation, and peace (MPA). *Application deadline:* Applications are processed on a rolling basis. *Application fee:* $50. Electronic applications accepted. *Application Contact:* Jennifer Hall, 866-4-WALDEN, E-mail: info@waldenu.edu. *Interim Associate Dean,* Dr. Mark Gordon, 800-925-3368.

WALLA WALLA UNIVERSITY, College Place, WA 99324-1198

General Information Independent-religious, coed, comprehensive institution. *Enrollment:* 1,800 graduate, professional, and undergraduate students; 215 full-time matriculated graduate/professional students (160 women), 22 part-time matriculated graduate/professional students (13 women). *Enrollment by degree level:* 237 master's. *Graduate faculty:* 29 full-time (16 women), 22 part-time/adjunct (15 women). *Tuition:* Full-time $25,584; part-time $492 per credit. Tuition and fees vary according to course load. *Graduate housing:* Rooms and/or apartments available on a first-come, first-served basis to single and married students. *Student services:* Campus employment opportunities, career counseling, free psychological counseling, international student services, low-cost health insurance, multicultural affairs office, services for students with disabilities. *Library facilities:* Peterson Memorial Library plus 3 others. *Online resources:* library catalog, web page, access to other libraries' catalogs. *Collection:* 273,266 titles, 3,727 serial subscriptions, 3,451 audiovisual materials.

Computer facilities: Computer purchase and lease plans are available. 118 computers available on campus for general student use. A campuswide network can be accessed from student residence rooms and from off campus. Online class registration, online forum, online classifieds, online student directory are available. *Web address:* http://www.wallawalla.edu/.

General Application Contact: Dr. Joe G. Galusha, Dean of Graduate Studies, 509-527-2421, Fax: 509-527-2237, E-mail: joe.galusha@wallawalla.edu.

GRADUATE UNITS

Graduate School Students: 215 full-time (160 women), 22 part-time (13 women); includes 39 minority (1 African American, 16 American Indian/Alaska Native, 7 Asian Americans or Pacific Islanders, 15 Hispanic Americans), 4 international. Average age 36. 230 applicants, 69% accepted, 133 enrolled. *Faculty:* 29 full-time (17 women), 28 part-time/adjunct (20 women). Expenses: Contact institution. *Financial support:* In 2008–09, 200 students received support, including 10 teaching assistantships (averaging $11,109 per year); research assistantships, career-related internships or fieldwork, Federal Work-Study, scholarships/grants, tuition waivers (partial), and unspecified assistantships also available. Support available to part-time students. Financial award application deadline: 4/1; financial award applicants required to submit FAFSA. In 2008, 156 master's awarded. *Degree program information:* Part-time and evening/weekend programs available. Offers biology (MS). *Application deadline:* Applications are processed on a rolling basis. *Application fee:* $50. Electronic applications accepted. *Application Contact:* Suzan Logan, Administrative Assistant to Graduate Dean, 509-527-2421, Fax: 509-527-2237, E-mail: donna.fisher@wallawalla.edu. *Dean of Graduate Studies,* Dr. Joe G. Galusha, 509-527-2421, Fax: 509-527-2237, E-mail: joe.galusha@wallawalla.edu.

School of Education and Psychology Students: 32 full-time (18 women), 5 part-time (3 women); includes 3 minority (all Asian Americans or Pacific Islanders), 1 international. Average age 30. 64 applicants, 55% accepted, 34 enrolled. *Faculty:* 7 full-time (3 women), 5 part-time/adjunct (3 women). Expenses: Contact institution. *Financial support:* In 2008–09, 29 students received support; research assistantships, teaching assistantships, Federal Work-Study and tuition waivers (partial) available. Support available to part-time students. Financial award application deadline: 4/1; financial award applicants required to submit FAFSA. In 2008, 16 master's awarded. *Degree program information:* Part-time programs available. Offers counseling psychology (MA); curriculum and instruction (M Ed, MA, MAT); educational leadership (M Ed, MA, MAT); literacy instruction (M Ed, MA, MAT); students at risk (M Ed, MA, MAT); teaching (MAT). *Application deadline:* For fall admission, 4/1 priority date for domestic students. Applications are processed on a rolling basis. *Application fee:* $50. Electronic applications accepted. *Application Contact:* Dr. Joe G. Galusha, Dean of Graduate Studies, 509-527-2421, Fax: 509-527-2237, E-mail: joe.galusha@wallawalla.edu. *Dean,* Dr. Julian Melgosa, 509-527-2272, Fax: 509-527-2248, E-mail: julian.melgosa@wallawalla.edu.

School of Social Work Students: 180 full-time (140 women), 11 part-time (8 women); includes 35 minority (1 African American, 16 American Indian/Alaska Native, 4 Asian Americans or Pacific Islanders, 14 Hispanic Americans), 3 international. Average age 37. 167 applicants, 84% accepted, 105 enrolled. *Faculty:* 17 full-time (13 women), 22 part-time/adjunct (17 women). Expenses: Contact institution. *Financial support:* In 2008–09, 150 students received support. Career-related internships or fieldwork, Federal Work-Study, and scholarships/grants available. Support available to part-time students. Financial award application deadline: 4/1; financial award applicants required to submit FAFSA. In 2008, 100 master's awarded. *Degree program information:* Part-time programs available. Offers social work (MSW). *Application deadline:* For fall admission, 7/15 priority date for domestic students. Applications are processed on a rolling basis. *Application fee:* $50. Electronic applications accepted. *Application Contact:* Dr. Joe G. Galusha, Dean of Graduate Studies, 509-527-2421, Fax: 509-527-2237, E-mail: joe.galusha@wallawalla.edu. *Dean, Wilma Hepker School of Sociology and Social Work,* Dr. Pamela Cress, 509-527-2273, Fax: 509-527-2270, E-mail: pam.cress@wallawalla.edu.

WALSH COLLEGE OF ACCOUNTANCY AND BUSINESS ADMINISTRATION, Troy, MI 48007-7006

General Information Independent, coed, upper-level institution. *Graduate housing:* On-campus housing not available.

GRADUATE UNITS

Graduate Programs *Degree program information:* Part-time and evening/weekend programs available. Offers accountancy (MSPA); business administration (MBA); business information technology (MSBIT); economics (MAE); finance (MSF); management (MSM); taxation (MST). Electronic applications accepted.

WALSH UNIVERSITY, North Canton, OH 44720-3396

General Information Independent-religious, coed, comprehensive institution. CGS member. *Enrollment:* 2,738 graduate, professional, and undergraduate students; 139 full-time matriculated graduate/professional students (101 women), 308 part-time matriculated graduate/professional students (211 women). *Enrollment by degree level:* 376 master's, 71 doctoral. *Graduate faculty:* 22 full-time (13 women), 31 part-time/adjunct (16 women). *Tuition:* Full-time $9450; part-time $525 per credit. Part-time tuition and fees vary according to course load and program. *Graduate housing:* Room and/or apartments available on a first-come, first-served basis to single students; on-campus housing not available to married students. Typical cost: $5100 per year ($7400 including board). Housing application deadline: 7/15. *Student services:* Campus employment opportunities, campus safety program, career counseling, exercise/wellness program, free psychological counseling, international student services, low-cost health insurance, multicultural affairs office, services for students with disabilities, teacher training, writing training. *Library facilities:* Brother Edmond Drouin Library. *Online resources:* library catalog, web page, access to other libraries' catalogs. *Collection:* 241,075 titles, 6,257 serial subscriptions, 2,530 audiovisual materials. *Research affiliation:* McKinley Freshman Academy, Battelle for Kids.

Computer facilities: 357 computers available on campus for general student use. A campuswide network can be accessed from student residence rooms and from off campus. Online class registration is available. *Web address:* http://www.walsh.edu/.

General Application Contact: Brett Freshour, Vice President of Enrollment Management, 330-490-7286, Fax: 330-490-7165, E-mail: bfreshour@walsh.edu.

GRADUATE UNITS

Graduate Studies Students: 139 full-time (101 women), 308 part-time (211 women); includes 20 minority (9 African Americans, 3 American Indian/Alaska Native, 5 Asian Americans or Pacific Islanders, 3 Hispanic Americans), 3 international. Average age 33. 226 applicants, 42% accepted, 91 enrolled. *Faculty:* 22 full-time (13 women), 31 part-time/adjunct (16 women). Expenses: Contact institution. *Financial support:* In 2008–09, 320 students received support, including 32 research assistantships with partial tuition reimbursements available (averaging $5,500 per year); tuition waivers (partial) and unspecified assistantships also available. Support available to part-time students. Financial award application deadline: 12/31. In 2008, 123 master's, 5 doctorates awarded. *Degree program information:* Part-time and evening/weekend programs available. Offers business administration (MBA); education (MA); mental health counseling (MA); physical therapy (DPT); school counseling (MA); theology (MA). *Application deadline:* Applications are processed on a rolling basis. *Application fee:* $25. Electronic applications accepted. *Application Contact:* Angela Piverotto, Director of Graduate and Transfer Admissions, 330-490-7174, Fax: 330-490-7165, E-mail: apiverotto@walsh.edu. *Provost,* Dr. Laurence Bove, 330-490-7122, Fax: 330-490-7165, E-mail: lbove@walsh.edu.

WARNER PACIFIC COLLEGE, Portland, OR 97215-4099

General Information Independent-religious, coed, comprehensive institution. *Graduate housing:* Rooms and/or apartments available on a first-come, first-served basis to single and married students. Housing application deadline: 7/1.

GRADUATE UNITS

Graduate Programs *Degree program information:* Part-time programs available. Offers biblical and theological studies (MA); biblical studies (M Rel); education (M Ed); management/organizational leadership (MS); pastoral ministries (M Rel); religion and ethics (M Rel); teaching (MA); theology (M Rel).

WARNER UNIVERSITY, Lake Wales, FL 33859

General Information Independent-religious, coed, comprehensive institution. *Enrollment:* 112 full-time matriculated graduate/professional students (74 women), 19 part-time matriculated graduate/professional students (12 women). *Enrollment by degree level:* 131 master's. *Graduate faculty:* 11 full-time (4 women), 6 part-time/adjunct (3 women). *Tuition:* Part-time $437 per credit hour. *Graduate housing:* Room and/or apartments available on a first-come, first-served basis to single students; on-campus housing not available to married students. Typical cost: $3220 per year ($6080 including board). *Student services:* Career counseling, services for students with disabilities. *Library facilities:* Pontious Learning Resource Center. *Online resources:* library catalog, web page. *Collection:* 56,419 titles, 224 serial subscriptions, 14,935 audiovisual materials.

Computer facilities: 75 computers available on campus for general student use. A campuswide network can be accessed. *Web address:* http://www.warner.edu/.

General Application Contact: Dr. Ed Jump, MBA Admissions Director, 863-638-7693, Fax: 863-638-7290, E-mail: james.jump@warner.edu.

GRADUATE UNITS

School of Business Students: 34 full-time (18 women), 7 part-time (3 women); includes 20 minority (13 African Americans, 1 Asian American or Pacific Islander, 6 Hispanic Americans), 1 international. Average age 30. 8 applicants, 100% accepted, 6 enrolled. *Faculty:* 5 full-time (1 woman), 2 part-time/adjunct (1 woman). Expenses: Contact institution. *Financial support:* In 2008–09, 18 students received support. Scholarships/grants available. In 2008, 23 master's awarded. *Degree program information:* Part-time and evening/weekend programs available. Offers business (MBA). *Application deadline:* Applications are processed on a rolling basis. *Application fee:* $50. Electronic applications accepted. *Application Contact:* Dr. Cynthia Robinson, Dean, 800-309-9563, Fax: 863-638-4907, E-mail: admissions@warner.edu. *Dean,* Dr. Cynthia Robinson, 863-638-7120.

School of Professional Studies Students: 56 full-time (40 women), 7 part-time (5 women); includes 23 minority (21 African Americans, 2 Hispanic Americans). Average age 39. 20 applicants, 100% accepted, 20 enrolled. *Faculty:* 2 full-time (1 woman), 4 part-time/adjunct (2 women). Expenses: Contact institution. *Financial support:* In 2008–09, 5 students received support. Scholarships/grants available. Financial award applicants required to submit FAFSA. In 2008, 27 master's awarded. *Degree program information:* Part-time and evening/weekend programs available. Postbaccalaureate distance learning degree programs offered. Offers management (MSM). *Application deadline:* Applications are processed on a rolling basis. *Application fee:* $50. Electronic applications accepted. *Application Contact:* Dr. Ed Jump, MBA Admissions Director, 863-638-7693, Fax: 863-638-7290, E-mail: james.jump@warner.edu. *Master of Science in Management Coordinator,* Dr. Ed Jump, 863-638-1426.

Teacher Education Department Students: 22 full-time (16 women), 5 part-time (4 women); includes 5 minority (all African Americans), 1 international. Average age 35. 12 applicants, 100% accepted, 11 enrolled. *Faculty:* 4 full-time (2 women). Expenses: Contact institution. *Financial support:* In 2008–09, 11 students received support. Scholarships/grants available. Financial award applicants required to submit FAFSA. In 2008, 17 master's awarded. *Degree program information:* Part-time and evening/weekend programs available. Offers teacher education (MAEd). *Application deadline:* Applications are processed on a rolling basis. *Application fee:* $50. Electronic applications accepted. *Application Contact:* Dr. Terry Fasel, Dean, 863-309-9563, Fax: 863-638-7125, E-mail: admissons@warner.edu. *Dean,* Dr. Terry Fasel, 800-309-9563, Fax: 863-638-7125, E-mail: admissions@warner.edu.

WARREN WILSON COLLEGE, Swannanoa, Asheville, NC 28815-9000

General Information Independent-religious, coed, comprehensive institution. *Graduate housing:* Room and/or apartments guaranteed to single students; on-campus housing not available to married students.

GRADUATE UNITS

MFA Program for Writers Postbaccalaureate distance learning degree programs offered (minimal on-campus study). Offers creative writing (MFA).

WARTBURG THEOLOGICAL SEMINARY, Dubuque, IA 52004-5004

General Information Independent-religious, coed, graduate-only institution. *Graduate housing:* Rooms and/or apartments available on a first-come, first-served basis to single and married students. Housing application deadline: 4/30. *Research affiliation:* Menighetsfakultet (Oslo, Norway), Augustana Theologische Hochschule (Neuendettelsau, Germany).

GRADUATE UNITS

Graduate and Professional Programs Offers diaconal ministry (MA); theology (M Div, MA, MATDE, STM). Electronic applications accepted.

WASHBURN UNIVERSITY, Topeka, KS 66621

General Information City-supported, coed, comprehensive institution. CGS member. *Graduate housing:* Room and/or apartments available on a first-come, first-served basis to single students; on-campus housing not available to married students.

GRADUATE UNITS

College of Arts and Sciences *Degree program information:* Part-time and evening/weekend programs available. Offers arts and sciences (M Ed, MA, MLS); clinical psychology (MA); curriculum and instruction (M Ed); educational leadership (M Ed); liberal studies (MLS); reading (M Ed); special education (M Ed).

School of Applied Studies *Degree program information:* Part-time and evening/weekend programs available. Postbaccalaureate distance learning degree programs offered. Offers applied studies (MCJ, MSW); clinical social work (MSW); criminal justice (MCJ). Electronic applications accepted.

School of Business Students: 16 full-time (7 women), 61 part-time (28 women); includes 12 minority (3 African Americans, 6 Asian Americans or Pacific Islanders, 3 Hispanic Americans), 3 international. Average age 29. 32 applicants, 100% accepted, 31 enrolled. *Faculty:* 17 full-time (4 women), 4 part-time/adjunct (1 woman). Expenses: Contact institution. *Financial support:* In 2008–09, 21 students received support. Available to part-time students. Application deadline: 2/15. In 2008, 22 master's awarded. *Degree program information:* Part-time and evening/weekend programs available. Offers business (MBA). *Application deadline:* For fall admission, 7/1 priority date for domestic and international students; for spring admission, 11/15 priority date for domestic and international students. Applications are processed on a rolling basis. *Application fee:* $40 ($70 for international students). Electronic applications accepted. *Application Contact:* Dr. Robert J. Boncella, MBA Program Director, 785-670-2047, Fax: 785-670-1063, E-mail: mba.advisor@washburn.edu. *Dean,* Dr. David L. Sollars, 785-670-1308, Fax: 785-670-1063, E-mail: david.sollars@washburn.edu.

School of Law Students: 429 full-time (176 women); includes 55 minority (15 African Americans, 9 American Indian/Alaska Native, 11 Asian Americans or Pacific Islanders, 20 Hispanic Americans). Average age 26. 722 applicants, 60% accepted, 153 enrolled. *Faculty:* 28 full-time (11 women), 31 part-time/adjunct (12 women). Expenses: Contact institution. *Financial support:* In 2008–09, 200 students received support. Career-related internships or fieldwork, Federal Work-Study, and scholarships/grants available. Support available to part-time students. Financial award applicants required to submit FAFSA. Offers law (JD). *Application deadline:* For fall admission, 4/1 priority date for domestic and international students; for spring admission, 11/1 priority date for domestic and international students. Applications are processed on a rolling basis. *Application fee:* $40. Electronic applications accepted. *Application Contact:* Karla Whitaker, Director of Admissions, 785-670-1185, Fax: 785-670-1120, E-mail: karla.whitaker@washburn.edu. *Dean,* Thomas J. Romig, 785-670-1662, Fax: 785-670-3249, E-mail: thomas.romig@washburn.edu.

WASHINGTON AND LEE UNIVERSITY, Lexington, VA 24450-0303

General Information Independent, coed, comprehensive institution. *Graduate housing:* Room and/or apartments available to single students. Housing application deadline: 4/15.

GRADUATE UNITS

School of Law Offers law (JD); U.S. law (LL M). Electronic applications accepted.

WASHINGTON COLLEGE, Chestertown, MD 21620-1197

General Information Independent, coed, comprehensive institution. *Graduate housing:* On-campus housing not available.

GRADUATE UNITS

Graduate Programs *Degree program information:* Part-time and evening/weekend programs available. Offers English (MA); history (MA); psychology (MA).

WASHINGTON STATE UNIVERSITY, Pullman, WA 99164

General Information State-supported, coed, university. CGS member. *Graduate housing:* Rooms and/or apartments available on a first-come, first-served basis to single and married students. Housing application deadline: 3/1. *Research affiliation:* Battelle Pacific Northwest Laboratories (biochemistry, engineering).

GRADUATE UNITS

College of Veterinary Medicine Students: 388 full-time (321 women); includes 31 minority (3 African Americans, 4 American Indian/Alaska Native, 15 Asian Americans or Pacific Islanders, 9 Hispanic Americans), 2 international. Average age 24. 949 applicants, 11% accepted, 103 enrolled. *Faculty:* 82 full-time (17 women), 2 part-time/adjunct (both women). Expenses: Contact institution. *Financial support:* Fellowships, research assistantships with partial tuition reimbursements, teaching assistantships with partial tuition reimbursements, career-related internships or fieldwork, Federal Work-Study, institutionally sponsored loans, scholarships/grants, traineeships, and tuition waivers (partial) available. Support available to part-time students. Financial award application deadline: 3/1; financial award applicants required to submit FAFSA. In 2008, 93 first professional degrees awarded. *Degree program information:* Part-time programs available. Offers neuroscience (MS, PhD); veterinary and comparative anatomy, pharmacology, and physiology (MS, PhD); veterinary clinical sciences (MS); veterinary medicine (DVM, MS, PhD); veterinary microbiology and pathology (MS, PhD); veterinary science (MS, PhD). *Application deadline:* For fall admission, 10/1 for domestic and international students. Applications are processed on a rolling basis. *Application fee:* $60. Electronic applications accepted. *Application Contact:* Julie K. Smith, Principal Assistant, 509-335-3164, E-mail: jksmith@vetmed.wsu.edu. *Dean,* Dr. Bryan K. Slinker, PhD, 509-335-9515, Fax: 509-335-0160, E-mail: vetmed-dean@vetmed.wsu.edu.

Graduate School *Degree program information:* Part-time programs available. Offers interdisciplinary studies (PhD). Campuses also located at Spokane, Tri-Cities, and Vancouver. Electronic applications accepted.

College of Agricultural, Human, and Natural Resource Sciences *Degree program information:* Part-time programs available. Offers agribusiness (MA, Certificate); agricultural economics (MA, PhD); agricultural, human, and natural resource sciences (MA, MS, MSLA, PhD, Certificate); agriculture (MS); animal sciences (MS, PhD); apparel, merchandising, design and textiles (MA); applied economics (MA); applied statistics (MS); crop sciences (MS, PhD); economics (MA, PhD, Certificate); entomology (MS, PhD); food science (MS, PhD); horticulture (MS, PhD); human development (MA); interdisciplinary (PhD); interior design (MA); international business economics (Certificate); landscape architecture (MSLA); molecular plant sciences (MS, PhD); plant pathology (MS, PhD); soil sciences (MS, PhD); theoretical statistics (MS). Electronic applications accepted.

College of Business Offers accounting and business law (M Acc); accounting and information systems (M Acc); accounting and taxation (M Acc); business (M Acc, MBA, PhD); business administration (MBA, PhD); finance, insurance and real estate (PhD).

College of Education Offers counseling psychology (Ed M, MA, PhD, Certificate); curriculum and instruction (Ed D, PhD); diverse languages (M Ed, MA); education (Ed M, M Ed, MA, MIT, MS, Ed D, PhD, Certificate); educational leadership (M Ed, MA, Ed D, PhD); educational psychology (Ed M, MA, PhD); elementary education (M Ed, MA, MIT); exercise science (MS); higher education (Ed M, MA, Ed D, PhD); higher education with sport management (Ed M); literacy education (M Ed, MA, PhD); math education (PhD); school psychologist (Certificate); secondary education (M Ed, MA). Electronic applications accepted.

College of Engineering and Architecture Offers architecture (M Arch); architecture design theory (MS); biological and agricultural engineering (MS, PhD); chemical engineering (MS, PhD); chemical engineering and bioengineering (MS, PhD); civil engineering (MS, PhD); computer engineering (MS, PhD); computer science (MS, PhD); electrical engineering (MS, PhD); electrical engineering and computer science (MS, PhD); engineering and architecture (M Arch, MS, PhD); environmental engineering (MS); material science engineering (MS); mechanical and materials engineering (MS, PhD); mechanical engineering (MS, PhD).

College of Liberal Arts Offers archaeology (MA, PhD); ceramics (MFA); clinical psychology (PhD); composition (MA); crime and deviance (MA, PhD); criminal justice (MA, PhD); cultural anthropology (MA, PhD); digital media (MFA); drawing (MFA); early and modern European history (MA, PhD); English (MA, PhD); environmental history (MA, PhD); environments, community and demographics (MA, PhD); ethnic studies (MA, PhD); evolutionary anthropology (MA, PhD); experimental psychology (PhD); feminist studies (MA, PhD); foreign languages with emphasis in Spanish (MA); health communications (MA, PhD); history (MA, PhD); institutions and social organizations (MA, PhD); intercultural and international communications (MA, PhD); jazz (MA); Latin American history (MA, PhD); liberal arts (MA, MFA, MS, PhD); literature (MA, PhD); media and society (MA, PhD); media process and effects (MA, PhD); modern East Asia history (MA, PhD); music (MA); music education (MA); organizational communications (MA, PhD); painting (MFA); performance (MA); philosophy (MA); photography (MFA); political science (MA, PhD); political sociology (MA, PhD); print making (MFA); psychology (MS); public history (MA, PhD); sculpture (MFA); social inequality (MA, PhD); social psychology and life course (MA, PhD); teaching of English (MA); US history (MA, PhD); women's history (MA, PhD); world history (MA, PhD). Electronic applications accepted.

College of Pharmacy Offers health policy and administration (MHPA); human nutrition (MS); nutrition (PhD); pharmaceutical science (Pharm D); pharmacology and toxicology (MS, PhD); pharmacy (Pharm D, MHPA, MS, PhD).

College of Sciences Offers applied mathematics (MS, PhD); biochemistry and biophysics (MS, PhD); biological sciences (MS, PhD); biology (MS); botany (MS, PhD); chemistry (MS, PhD); earth and environmental sciences (MS, PhD); environmental and natural resource sciences (PhD); environmental science (MS, PhD); genetics and cell biology (MS, PhD); geology (MS, PhD); materials science (PhD); mathematics teaching (MS, PhD); microbiology (MS, PhD); molecular biosciences (MS, PhD); natural resource sciences (MS); physics (MS, PhD); sciences (MS, PhD); zoology (MS, PhD).

WASHINGTON STATE UNIVERSITY SPOKANE, Spokane, WA 99210-1495

General Information State-supported, coed, graduate-only institution.

GRADUATE UNITS

Graduate Programs Offers cellular physiology (MS); clinical exercise physiology (MS); clinical physiology (MS); criminal justice (MA, PhD); educational leadership (Ed M, MA); engineering management (METM); health policy and administration (MHPA); principal (Certificate); professional certification for teachers (Certificate); program administrator (Certificate); school psychologist (Certificate); speech and hearing sciences (MA); superintendent (Certificate); teaching (MIT).

Intercollegiate College of Nursing Offers nursing (MN).

Interdisciplinary Design Institute *Degree program information:* Part-time programs available. Offers architecture (M Arch, MS); design (Dr DES); interior design (MA); landscape architecture (MS).

Program in Pharmacy Offers pharmacy (Pharm D).

WASHINGTON STATE UNIVERSITY TRI-CITIES, Richland, WA 99352-1671

General Information State-supported, coed, graduate-only institution. *Graduate housing:* On-campus housing not available.

GRADUATE UNITS

Graduate Programs *Degree program information:* Part-time programs available. Offers applied environmental science (MS); atmospheric science (MS); biology (MS); chemistry (MS); counseling (Ed M); earth science (MS); educational leadership (Ed M, Ed D); environmental and occupational health science (MS); environmental regulatory compliance (MS); environmental science (PhD); environmental toxicology and risk assessment (MS); literacy (Ed M); secondary certification (Ed M); teaching (MIT); water resource science (MS). Electronic applications accepted.

College of Business *Degree program information:* Part-time and evening/weekend programs available. Offers business management (MBA).

College of Engineering and Computer Science *Degree program information:* Part-time programs available. Offers computer science (MS, PhD); electrical and computer engineering (PhD); electrical engineering (MS); mechanical engineering (MS, PhD).

Intercollegiate College of Nursing *Degree program information:* Part-time programs available. Postbaccalaureate distance learning degree programs offered (minimal on-campus study). Offers nursing (MN).

WASHINGTON STATE UNIVERSITY VANCOUVER, Vancouver, WA 98686

General Information State-supported, coed, graduate-only institution. *Graduate housing:* On-campus housing not available.

GRADUATE UNITS

Graduate Programs *Degree program information:* Part-time programs available. Offers business administration (MBA); education (Ed M, MIT, Ed D); environmental science (MS); history (MA); public affairs (MPA).

Intercollegiate College of Nursing Offers nursing (MN). Electronic applications accepted.

School of Engineering and Computer Science *Degree program information:* Part-time programs available. Offers computer science (MS); mechanical engineering (MS).

WASHINGTON THEOLOGICAL UNION, Washington, DC 20012

General Information Independent-religious, coed, graduate-only institution. *Graduate housing:* Room and/or apartments available on a first-come, first-served basis to single students; on-campus housing not available to married students.

GRADUATE UNITS

Graduate and Professional Programs *Degree program information:* Part-time programs available. Postbaccalaureate distance learning degree programs offered. Offers theology (M Div, MA, MAPS, MTS, D Min).

WASHINGTON UNIVERSITY IN ST. LOUIS, St. Louis, MO 63130-4899

General Information Independent, coed, university. CGS member. *Graduate housing:* Rooms and/or apartments available on a first-come, first-served basis to single and married students.

GRADUATE UNITS

George Warren Brown School of Social Work *Degree program information:* Part-time programs available. Offers public health (MPH); social work (MSW, PhD). Electronic applications accepted.

Graduate School of Arts and Sciences Offers American history (MA, PhD); anthropology (PhD); art history (MA, PhD); arts and sciences (MA, MA Ed, MAT, MFAW, MM, PhD); Asian history (MA, PhD); British history (MA, PhD); chemistry (PhD); Chinese (MA); Chinese and comparative literature (PhD); classical archaeology (MA, PhD); classics (MA); clinical psychology (PhD); comparative literature (MA, PhD); earth and planetary sciences (MA); East Asian studies (MA); economics (PhD); educational research (PhD); elementary education (MA Ed); English and American literature (MA, PhD); European history (MA, PhD); French (MA, PhD); general experimental psychology (PhD); Germanic languages and literature (MA, PhD); Japanese (MA); Japanese and comparative literature (PhD); Latin American history (MA, PhD); mathematics (MA, PhD); Middle Eastern history (MA, PhD); movement science (PhD); music (MM, PhD); philosophy (MA, PhD); philosophy/neuroscience/psychology (PhD); physics (PhD); planetary sciences (PhD); political economy and public policy (MA); political science (PhD); secondary education (MA Ed, MAT); social psychology (PhD); social work (PhD); Spanish (MA, PhD); statistics (MA); writing (MFAW). Electronic applications accepted.

Division of Biology and Biomedical Sciences Offers biochemistry (PhD); chemical biology (PhD); computational biology (PhD); developmental biology (PhD); ecology (PhD); environ-

Washington University in St. Louis (continued)

mental biology (PhD); evolution, ecology and population biology (PhD); evolutionary biology (PhD); genetics (PhD); immunology (PhD); molecular biophysics (PhD); molecular cell biology (PhD); molecular genetics (PhD); molecular microbiology and microbial pathogenesis (PhD); neurosciences (PhD); plant biology (PhD). Electronic applications accepted.

Henry Edwin Sever Graduate School of Engineering and Applied Science *Degree program information:* Part-time and evening/weekend programs available. Offers biomedical engineering (MS, D Sc, PhD); chemical engineering (MS, D Sc); computer engineering (MS, PhD); computer science (MS, PhD); electrical engineering (MS, D Sc, PhD); engineering and applied science (MCE, MCM, MEM, MIM, MS, MSCE, MSE, MSEE, MSEE, MTM, D Sc, PhD); environmental engineering (MS, D Sc); mechanical, aerospace and structural engineering (MS, D Sc, PhD); systems science and mathematics (MS, D Sc, PhD). Electronic applications accepted.

Olin Business School Offers accounting (MS); business (EMBA, M Acc, MBA, MS, PhD); business administration (EMBA, MBA); finance (MS). Electronic applications accepted.

Sam Fox School of Design and Visual Arts Offers architecture (M Arch); design and visual arts (M Arch, MFA, MUD); urban design (MUD).

Graduate School of Art Students: 46 full-time (27 women); includes 2 minority (1 Asian American or Pacific Islander, 1 Hispanic American), 3 international. Average age 28. 84 applicants, 48% accepted, 19 enrolled. *Faculty:* 23 full-time (10 women). Expenses: Contact institution. *Financial support:* In 2008–09, 45 students received support, including research assistantships with partial tuition reimbursements available (averaging $4,000 per year), teaching assistantships with partial tuition reimbursements available (averaging $4,000 per year); fellowships with partial tuition reimbursements available, Federal Work-Study, institutionally sponsored loans, scholarships/grants, health care benefits, and unspecified assistantships also available. Financial award application deadline: 1/5; financial award applicants required to submit FAFSA. In 2008, 13 master's awarded. Offers art (MFA). *Application deadline:* For fall admission, 1/5 for domestic and international students. *Application fee:* $75. Electronic applications accepted. *Application Contact:* Prof. Patricia Olynyk, Director, 314-935-5884, Fax: 314-935-8413, E-mail: olynyk@samfox.wustl.edu. *Dean,* Dean Franklin 'Buzz" Spector, 314-935-6500, Fax: 314-935-4862, E-mail: spector@samfox.wustl.edu.

School of Law Offers law (JD, LL M, MJS, JSD). Electronic applications accepted.

School of Medicine Students: 1,084; includes 290 minority (47 African Americans, 5 American Indian/Alaska Native, 211 Asian Americans or Pacific Islanders, 27 Hispanic Americans), 25 international. Average age 23. Expenses: Contact institution. *Financial support:* Fellowships, research assistantships, career-related internships or fieldwork, Federal Work-Study, and institutionally sponsored loans available. Support available to part-time students. Financial award applicants required to submit FAFSA. In 2008, 125 first professional degrees, 209 master's awarded. Offers audiology (Au D); clinical (MS); clinical investigation (MS); computational (MS); deaf education (MS); genetic epidemiology (Certificate); medicine (MD, MS, MSOT, Au D, DPT, OTD, PhD, Certificate, PPDPT); movement science (PhD); occupational therapy (MSOT, OTD); physical therapy (DPT, PhD, PPDPT); speech and hearing sciences (PhD). *Application Contact:* Dr. W. Edwin Dodson, Associate Dean, 314-362-6848, Fax: 314-362-4658, E-mail: wumscoa@msnotes.wustl.edu. *Dean,* Dr. Larry Shapiro, 314-362-6827.

See Close-Up on page 1051.

WAYLAND BAPTIST UNIVERSITY, Plainview, TX 79072-6998

General Information Independent-religious, coed, comprehensive institution. *Enrollment:* 1,234 graduate, professional, and undergraduate students; 7 full-time matriculated graduate/professional students (6 women), 214 part-time matriculated graduate/professional students (144 women). *Enrollment by degree level:* 221 master's. *Graduate faculty:* 40 full-time (13 women), 5 part-time/adjunct (0 women). *Tuition:* Part-time $310 per credit hour. *Required fees:* $9 per credit hour. $60 per semester. *Graduate housing:* Rooms and/or apartments available on a first-come, first-served basis to single and married students. Typical cost: $3600 per year for single students; $3600 per year for married students. Room charges vary according to board plan and housing facility selected. *Student services:* Campus employment opportunities, career counseling, free psychological counseling, international student services, teacher training. *Library facilities:* J.E. and L.E. Mabee Learning Resource Center. *Online resources:* library catalog, web page, access to other libraries' catalogs. *Collection:* 128,786 titles, 497 serial subscriptions, 12,138 audiovisual materials.

Computer facilities: Computer purchase and lease plans are available. 241 computers available on campus for general student use. A campuswide network can be accessed from student residence rooms and from off campus. Online class registration is available. *Web address:* http://www.wbu.edu/.

General Application Contact: Dr. Bobby Hall, Vice President of Academic Services, 806-291-3410, Fax: 806-291-1953, E-mail: hallb@wbu.edu.

GRADUATE UNITS

Graduate Programs Students: 7 full-time (6 women), 214 part-time (144 women); includes 57 minority (19 African Americans, 3 American Indian/Alaska Native, 5 Asian Americans or Pacific Islanders, 30 Hispanic Americans), 2 international. Average age 35. 96 applicants, 94% accepted. *Faculty:* 40 full-time (13 women), 5 part-time/adjunct (0 women). Expenses: Contact institution. *Financial support:* Federal Work-Study, institutionally sponsored loans, and scholarships/grants available. Support available to part-time students. Financial award application deadline: 5/1; financial award applicants required to submit FAFSA. In 2008, 46 master's awarded. *Degree program information:* Part-time and evening/weekend programs available. Postbaccalaureate distance learning degree programs offered (no on-campus study). Offers Christian ministry (MCM); counseling (MA); education (M Ed); general business (MBA); government administration (MPA); health care administration (MBA); homeland security (MPA); human resource management (MBA); international management (MBA); justice administration (MPA); management (MA, MBA); management information systems (MBA); multidisciplinary science (MS); religion (MA). *Application deadline:* Applications are processed on a rolling basis. *Application fee:* $50. *Application Contact:* Amanda Stanton, Graduate Studies, 806-291-3414, Fax: 806-291-1950, E-mail: stanton@wbu.edu. *Vice President of Academic Services,* Dr. Bobby Hall, 806-291-3410, Fax: 806-291-1953, E-mail: hallb@wbu.edu.

WAYNESBURG UNIVERSITY, Waynesburg, PA 15370-1222

General Information Independent-religious, coed, comprehensive institution. *Graduate housing:* Room and/or apartments available on a first-come, first-served basis to single students; on-campus housing not available to married students. Housing application deadline: 8/1.

GRADUATE UNITS

Graduate and Professional Studies *Degree program information:* Part-time and evening/weekend programs available. Offers business (MBA); counseling psychology (MA); education (MAT); nursing (MSN); nursing practice (DNP); special education (M Ed); technology (M Ed). Electronic applications accepted.

WAYNE STATE COLLEGE, Wayne, NE 68787

General Information State-supported, coed, comprehensive institution. CGS member. *Graduate housing:* Room and/or apartments available on a first-come, first-served basis to single students; on-campus housing not available to married students. *Research affiliation:* Nebraska Business Development Center, Social Sciences Research Center.

GRADUATE UNITS

Department of Health, Human Performance and Sport *Degree program information:* Part-time and evening/weekend programs available. Offers exercise science (MSE); organizational management (MS). Electronic applications accepted.

School of Business and Technology *Degree program information:* Part-time and evening/weekend programs available. Postbaccalaureate distance learning degree programs offered (minimal on-campus study). Offers business and technology (MBA).

School of Education and Counseling *Degree program information:* Part-time and evening/weekend programs available. Offers alternative education (MSE); business and information technology education (MSE); communication arts education (MSE); counseling (MSE); counselor education (MSE); curriculum and instruction (MSE); early childhood education (MSE); education and counseling (MSE, Ed S); educational administration (MSE, Ed S); elementary administration (MSE); elementary and secondary administration (MSE); elementary education (MSE); English as a second language (MSE); English education (MSE); family and consumer sciences education (MSE); guidance and counseling (MSE); industrial technology and vocational education (MSE); learning communities (MSE); mathematics education (MSE); music education (MSE); school counseling (MSE); science education (MSE); secondary administration (MSE); social science education (MSE); special education (MSE).

WAYNE STATE UNIVERSITY, Detroit, MI 48202

General Information State-supported, coed, university. CGS member. *Graduate housing:* Rooms and/or apartments available on a first-come, first-served basis to single and married students. *Research affiliation:* Henry Ford Health Systems, Detroit Medical Center, Southeastern Michigan Health Association, Michigan State University, University of Michigan, Van Andel Research Institute.

GRADUATE UNITS

College of Education *Degree program information:* Evening/weekend programs available. Offers education (M Ed, MA, MAT, Ed D, PhD, Certificate, Ed S). Electronic applications accepted.

Division of Administrative and Organizational Studies Offers administration and supervision-secondary (Ed S); college and university teaching (Certificate); curriculum and instruction (PhD); educational leadership (M Ed, Ed S); educational leadership and policy studies (Ed D, PhD); elementary education curriculum and instruction (MA, Ed S); general administration and supervision (Ed D, PhD, Ed S); higher education (Ed D, PhD); instructional technology (M Ed, Ed D, PhD, Ed S); secondary curriculum and instruction (M Ed, Ed S). Electronic applications accepted.

Division of Kinesiology, Health and Sports Studies Offers health education (M Ed); kinesiology (M Ed); physical education (M Ed); recreation and park services (MA); sports administration (MA). Electronic applications accepted.

Division of Teacher Education Offers adult and continuing education (M Ed); art education (M Ed); bilingual/bicultural education (M Ed, MAT); business education (M Ed, MAT); career and technical education (M Ed, Ed D, PhD, Ed S); curriculum and instruction (Ed D, PhD, Ed S); distributive education (M Ed, MAT); early childhood education (M Ed); elementary education (M Ed, MAT, Ed D, PhD, Ed S); elementary education curriculum and instruction (M Ed); English education (M Ed); English education-secondary (M Ed, Ed S); foreign language education (M Ed); general education (Ed D, Ed S); health occupations education (M Ed); industrial education (M Ed); mathematics education (M Ed, Ed S); pre-school and parent education (M Ed); reading (M Ed, Ed D, Ed S); reading, languages and literature (Ed D); school music-vocal (M Ed); science education (M Ed, MAT, Ed S); secondary education (MAT); secondary school reading (M Ed); social studies education (M Ed, Ed S); special education (M Ed, Ed D, PhD, Ed S); teacher education (MAT, Ed D, PhD). Electronic applications accepted.

Division of Theoretical and Behavioral Foundations *Degree program information:* Evening/weekend programs available. Offers counseling (M Ed, MA, Ed D, PhD, Ed S); education evaluation and research (M Ed, Ed D, PhD); educational psychology (M Ed, Ed D, PhD, Ed S); educational sociology (M Ed, Ed D, PhD, Ed S); history and philosophy of education (M Ed, Ed D, PhD); rehabilitation counseling and community inclusion (MA, Ed S); school and community psychology (MA, Ed S); school clinical psychology (Ed S). Electronic applications accepted.

College of Engineering *Degree program information:* Part-time programs available. Offers biomedical engineering (MS, PhD); chemical engineering (MS, PhD); civil engineering (MS, PhD); computer engineering (MS, PhD); electrical engineering (MS, PhD); electronics and computer control systems (MS); engineering (MS, PhD, Certificate); engineering management (MS); environmental auditing (Certificate); hazardous materials management on public lands (Certificate); hazardous waste (MS, Certificate); hazardous waste control (Certificate); hazardous waste management (MS); industrial engineering (MS, PhD); manufacturing engineering (MS); materials science and engineering (MS, PhD, Certificate); mechanical engineering (MS, PhD); metallurgical engineering (MS, PhD); polymer engineering (Certificate).

Division of Engineering Technology Offers engineering technology (MS). Electronic applications accepted.

College of Fine, Performing and Communication Arts Offers art (MA, MFA); art history (MA); choral conducting (MM); communication studies (MA, PhD); composition (MM); design and merchandising (MA); dispute resolution (MADR, Certificate); fine, performing and communication arts (MA, MADR, MFA, MM, PhD, Certificate); music (MA, MM); music education (MM); orchestral studies (Certificate); performance (MM); public relations and organizational communication (MA); radio-TV-film (MA, PhD); speech communication (MA, PhD); theatre (MA, MFA, PhD); theory (MM). Electronic applications accepted.

College of Liberal Arts and Sciences *Degree program information:* Evening/weekend programs available. Offers anthropology (MA, PhD); applied mathematics (MA, PhD); audiology (MA, MS, Au D, PhD); behavioral and cognitive neuroscience (PhD); biological sciences (MA, MS, PhD); chemistry (MA, MS, PhD); classics (MA); classics, Greek, and Latin (MA); clinical psychology (PhD); cognitive and social psychology (PhD); communication disorders and science (MA, PhD); comparative literature (MA); computer science (MA, MS, PhD); criminal justice (MPA); economic development (Certificate); economics (MA, PhD); English (MA, PhD); French (MA); geography (MA); geology (MA, MS); German (MA); German and Slavic studies (MA, PhD); history (MA, PhD); human development (MA); industrial relations (MAIR); industrial/organizational psychology (PhD); Italian (MA); language learning (MA); Latin (MA); liberal arts and sciences (MA, MAIR, MPA, MS, MUP, Au D, PhD, Certificate); linguistics (MA); mathematical statistics (MA, PhD); mathematics (MA, MS, PhD); modern languages (PhD); molecular biotechnology (MS); Near Eastern and Asian studies (MA); Near Eastern studies (MA); nutrition and food science (MA, MS, PhD); philosophy (MA, PhD); physics (MA, MS, PhD); political science (MA, MPA, PhD); psychology (MA, MS, PhD); public administration (MPA); Russian (MA); scientific computing (Certificate); sociology (MA, PhD); Spanish (MA); speech-language pathology (MA, PhD); urban planning (MUP).

College of Nursing *Degree program information:* Part-time programs available. Offers adult acute care nursing (MSN); adult primary care nursing (MSN); advanced practice nursing with women, neonates and children (MSN); community health nursing (MSN); neonatal nurse practitioner (Certificate); nursing (MSN, PhD, Certificate); nursing education (Certificate); psychiatric mental health nurse practitioner (MSN, Certificate); transcultural nursing (MSN, Certificate). Electronic applications accepted.

Eugene Applebaum College of Pharmacy and Health Sciences *Degree program information:* Part-time and evening/weekend programs available. Offers clinical laboratory science (MS); clinical laboratory sciences (MS, Certificate); experimental technology in pharmaceutical sciences (Certificate); health systems pharmacy management (MS); hospital pharmacy (MS); medical technology (Certificate); medicinal chemistry (MS, PhD); nurse anesthesia (MS); nursing anesthesia (MS, Certificate); occupational and environmental health sciences (MPH, MS, Certificate, Post-Master's Certificate); occupational therapy (MOT, MS); pediatric nurse anesthesia (Certificate); pharmaceutical administration (MS, PhD); pharmaceutical sciences (MS, PhD); pharmaceutics (MS, PhD); pharmacology (MS, PhD); pharmacy (Pharm D); pharmacy and health sciences (Pharm D, MOT, MPH, MPT, MS, PhD, Certificate, Post-Master's Certificate); physical therapy (MPT); physician assistant studies (MS). Electronic applications accepted.

Graduate School *Degree program information:* Part-time and evening/weekend programs available. Offers alcohol and drug abuse studies (Certificate); archival administration (Certificate); developmental disabilities (Certificate); gerontology (Certificate); infant mental health (Certificate); library and information science (MLIS, Spec); library science (MS, Spec); molecular and cellular toxicology (MS, PhD); molecular biology and genetics (MS, PhD). Electronic applications accepted.

Law School *Degree program information:* Part-time and evening/weekend programs available. Offers law (JD, LL M, PhD). Electronic applications accepted.

School of Business Administration *Degree program information:* Part-time and evening/weekend programs available. Offers accounting (MS); business administration (MBA, PhD); interdisciplinary studies (PhD); taxation (MS). Electronic applications accepted.

School of Medicine *Degree program information:* Part-time and evening/weekend programs available. Offers medicine (MD, MPH, MS, PhD, Certificate). Electronic applications accepted.

Graduate Programs in Medicine *Degree program information:* Part-time and evening/weekend programs available. Offers anatomy (MS, PhD); basic medical science (MS); biochemistry and molecular biology (MS, PhD); cancer biology (MS, PhD); cellular and clinical neurobiology (PhD); community health (MS); community health services (Certificate); immunology and microbiology (MS, PhD); medical physics (PhD); medical research (MS); medicine (MPH, MS, PhD, Certificate); pathology (MS, PhD); pharmacology (MS, PhD); physiology (MS, PhD); psychiatry and behavioral neurosciences (MS); public health (MPH); public health practice (Certificate); radiological physics (MS); rehabilitation science administration (Certificate); rehabilitation sciences (MS). Electronic applications accepted.

School of Social Work *Degree program information:* Part-time and evening/weekend programs available. Offers interdisciplinary studies (PhD); social work (MSW); social work practice with families and couples (Certificate). Electronic applications accepted.

WEBBER INTERNATIONAL UNIVERSITY, Babson Park, FL 33827-0096

General Information Independent, coed, comprehensive institution.

GRADUATE UNITS

Graduate School of Business *Degree program information:* Part-time and evening/weekend programs available. Offers accounting (MBA); management (MBA); security management (MBA); sports management (MBA).

WEBER STATE UNIVERSITY, Ogden, UT 84408-1001

General Information State-supported, coed, comprehensive institution. *Graduate housing:* Rooms and/or apartments available on a first-come, first-served basis to single and married students. *Research affiliation:* Raytheon Training Corporation (education).

GRADUATE UNITS

College of Arts and Humanities *Degree program information:* Part-time and evening/weekend programs available. Offers arts and humanities (MENG); English (MENG).

College of Health Professions *Degree program information:* Part-time and evening/weekend programs available. Offers health administration (MHA); health professions (MHA).

College of Social and Behavioral Sciences *Degree program information:* Part-time and evening/weekend programs available. Offers criminal justice (MCJ); social and behavioral sciences (MCJ).

Jerry and Vickie Moyes College of Education *Degree program information:* Part-time and evening/weekend programs available. Offers athletic training (MSAT); curriculum and instruction (M Ed); education (M Ed, MSAT).

John B. Goddard School of Business and Economics *Degree program information:* Part-time and evening/weekend programs available. Postbaccalaureate distance learning degree programs offered. Offers accountancy (M Acc); business administration (MBA); business and economics (M Acc, MBA). Electronic applications accepted.

WEBSTER UNIVERSITY, St. Louis, MO 63119-3194

General Information Independent, coed, comprehensive institution. *Enrollment:* 3,940 full-time matriculated graduate/professional students (2,386 women), 11,885 part-time matriculated graduate/professional students (7,139 women). *Enrollment by degree level:* 15,423 master's, 37 doctoral, 365 other advanced degrees. *Graduate faculty:* 82 full-time, 1,513 part-time/adjunct. *Tuition:* Part-time $550 per credit hour. Tuition and fees vary according to degree level, campus/location and program. *Graduate housing:* Room and/or apartments available on a first-come, first-served basis to single students; on-campus housing not available to married students. Typical cost: $6720 per year. Housing application deadline: 7/1. *Student services:* Campus employment opportunities, campus safety program, career counseling, exercise/wellness program, free psychological counseling, international student services, multicultural affairs office, services for students with disabilities, teacher training, writing training. *Library facilities:* Emerson Library. *Online resources:* library catalog, web page, access to other libraries' catalogs. *Collection:* 286,655 titles, 1,821 serial subscriptions, 19,135 audiovisual materials. *Research affiliation:* Literacy Investment for Tomorrow.

Computer facilities: 450 computers available on campus for general student use. A campuswide network can be accessed from student residence rooms. Online class registration is available. *Web address:* http://www.webster.edu/.

General Application Contact: Matt Nolan, Director of Graduate and Evening Student Admissions, 314-968-7089, Fax: 314-968-7462, E-mail: gadmit@webster.edu.

GRADUATE UNITS

College of Arts and Sciences Students: 1,230 full-time (971 women), 1,578 part-time (1,236 women); includes 1,428 minority (1,140 African Americans, 14 American Indian/Alaska Native, 43 Asian Americans or Pacific Islanders, 231 Hispanic Americans), 81 international. Average age 35. *Faculty:* 18 full-time (11 women), 354 part-time/adjunct. Expenses: Contact institution. *Financial support:* Career-related internships or fieldwork and Federal Work-Study available. Support available to part-time students. Financial award application deadline: 4/1; financial award applicants required to submit FAFSA. In 2008, 786 master's awarded. *Degree program information:* Part-time and evening/weekend programs available. Postbaccalaureate distance learning degree programs offered. Offers arts and sciences (MA, MS, MSN); counseling (MA); environmental management (MS); gerontology (MA); international nongovernmental organizations (MA); international relations (MA); legal analysis (MA); legal studies (MA); nurse anesthesia (MS); nursing (MSN); patent agency (MA); professional science management and leadership (MA). *Application deadline:* Applications are processed on a rolling basis. *Application fee:* $35 ($50 for international students). *Application Contact:* Matt Nolan, Director of Graduate and Evening Student Admissions, 314-968-7089, Fax: 314-968-7462, E-mail: gadmit@webster.edu. *Dean*, Dr. David Carl Wilson, 314-968-7160, Fax: 314-963-6043, E-mail: wilson@webster.edu.

Leigh Gerdine College of Fine Arts Students: 11 full-time (9 women), 26 part-time (16 women); includes 4 minority (1 African American, 3 Asian Americans or Pacific Islanders). Average age 30. 12 applicants, 92% accepted, 10 enrolled. *Faculty:* 13 full-time (3 women), 12 part-time/adjunct. Expenses: Contact institution. *Financial support:* Fellowships, teaching assistantships, career-related internships or fieldwork and Federal Work-Study available. Support available to part-time students. Financial award application deadline: 4/1; financial award applicants required to submit FAFSA. In 2008, 18 master's awarded. *Degree program information:* Part-time and evening/weekend programs available. Offers art (MA); arts management and leadership (MFA); church music (MM); composition (MM); conducting (MM); fine arts (MA, MFA, MM); jazz studies (MM); music (MA); music education (MM); performance (MM); piano (MM). *Application deadline:* Applications are processed on a rolling basis. *Application fee:* $35 ($50 for international students). *Application Contact:* Director of Graduate and Evening Student Admissions, Fax: 314-968-7116, E-mail: gadmit@webster.edu. *Dean*, Peter Sargent, 314-968-7006, Fax: 314-963-6048, E-mail: sargenpe@webster.edu.

School of Business and Technology Students: 2,504 full-time (1,251 women), 9,129 part-time (4,964 women); includes 5,205 minority (3,971 African Americans, 61 American Indian/Alaska Native, 406 Asian Americans or Pacific Islanders, 767 Hispanic Americans), 385 international. Average age 35. 2,112 applicants, 99% accepted, 1818 enrolled. *Faculty:* 25 full-time (5 women), 1,077 part-time/adjunct. Expenses: Contact institution. *Financial support:* Career-related internships or fieldwork and Federal Work-Study available. Support available to part-time students. Financial award application deadline: 4/1; financial award applicants required to submit FAFSA. In 2008, 4,357 master's, 7 doctorates, 29 other advanced degrees awarded. *Degree program information:* Part-time and evening/weekend programs available. Postbaccalaureate distance learning degree programs offered (no on-campus study). Offers business (MA); business and organizational security management (MA, MBA); business and technology (MA, MBA, MHA, MPA, MS, DM, Certificate); computer resources and information management (MA, MBA); computer science/distributed systems (MS, Certificate); environmental management (MBA, MS); finance (MA, MBA); health care management (MA); health services management (MA, MBA); human resources development (MA, MBA); human resources management (MA, MBA); international business (MA, MBA); management (DM); management and leadership (MA, MBA); marketing (MA, MBA); procurement and acquisitions management (MA, MBA); public administration (MA); quality management (MA); space systems operations management (MS); telecommunications management (MA, MBA). *Application deadline:* Applications are processed on a rolling basis. *Application fee:* $35 ($50 for international students). *Application Contact:* Director of Graduate and Evening Student Admissions, Fax: 314-968-7116, E-mail: gadmit@webster.edu. *Dean*, Dr. Benjamin Ola Akande, 314-968-5951, Fax: 314-968-7077, E-mail: akandeb@webster.edu.

School of Communications Students: 41 full-time (30 women), 289 part-time (208 women); includes 126 minority (113 African Americans, 3 American Indian/Alaska Native, 2 Asian Americans or Pacific Islanders, 8 Hispanic Americans), 9 international. Average age 31. 58 applicants, 95% accepted, 47 enrolled. *Faculty:* 6 full-time (3 women), 28 part-time/adjunct. Expenses: Contact institution. *Financial support:* Career-related internships or fieldwork and Federal Work-Study available. Support available to part-time students. Financial award application deadline: 4/1; financial award applicants required to submit FAFSA. In 2008, 70 master's awarded. *Degree program information:* Part-time and evening/weekend programs available. Postbaccalaureate distance learning degree programs offered. Offers advertising and marketing communications (MA); communications (MA); communications management (MA); media communications (MA); media literacy (MA); public relations (MA). *Application deadline:* Applications are processed on a rolling basis. *Application fee:* $35 ($50 for international students). *Application Contact:* Director of Graduate and Evening Student Admissions, Fax: 314-968-7116, E-mail: gadmit@webster.edu. *Dean*, Debra Carpenter, 314-968-7154, Fax: 314-963-6106, E-mail: carpenda@webster.edu.

School of Education Students: 153 full-time (125 women), 731 part-time (614 women); includes 206 minority (182 African Americans, 1 American Indian/Alaska Native, 7 Asian Americans or Pacific Islanders, 16 Hispanic Americans), 5 international. Average age 34. 237 applicants, 99% accepted, 210 enrolled. *Faculty:* 22 full-time (14 women), 86 part-time/adjunct. Expenses: Contact institution. *Financial support:* Career-related internships or fieldwork and Federal Work-Study available. Support available to part-time students. Financial award application deadline: 4/1; financial award applicants required to submit FAFSA. In 2008, 305 master's, 15 other advanced degrees awarded. *Degree program information:* Part-time programs available. Postbaccalaureate distance learning degree programs offered. Offers administrative leadership (Ed S); communications (MAT); early childhood education (MAT); education (MAT, Ed S); education leadership (Ed S); educational technology (MAT); mathematics (MAT); multidisciplinary studies (MAT); school systems, superintendency and leadership (Ed S); social science (MAT); special education (MAT). *Application deadline:* Applications are processed on a rolling basis. *Application fee:* $35 ($50 for international students). *Application Contact:* Director of Graduate and Evening Student Admissions, Fax: 314-968-7116, E-mail: gadmit@webster.edu. *Dean*, Dr. Brenda Fyfe, 314-968-6913, Fax: 314-968-7118, E-mail: fyfebv@webster.edu.

WESLEYAN COLLEGE, Macon, GA 31210-4462

General Information Independent-religious, Undergraduate: women only; graduate: coed, comprehensive institution. *Graduate housing:* Room and/or apartments available on a first-come, first-served basis to single students; on-campus housing not available to married students. Housing application deadline: 5/1.

GRADUATE UNITS

Department of Business and Economics Offers business administration (EMBA); business and economics (EMBA).

Department of Education *Degree program information:* Part-time programs available. Offers early childhood education (MA); middle-level mathematics and middle-level science education (MA).

WESLEYAN UNIVERSITY, Middletown, CT 06459-0260

General Information Independent, coed, university. CGS member. *Enrollment:* 3,149 graduate, professional, and undergraduate students; 145 full-time matriculated graduate/professional students (62 women). *Enrollment by degree level:* 45 master's, 100 doctoral. *Graduate faculty:* 79 full-time (15 women), 7 part-time/adjunct (0 women). *Graduate housing:* Rooms and/or apartments available on a first-come, first-served basis to single and married students. Housing application deadline: 6/15. *Student services:* Campus employment opportunities, campus safety program, career counseling, child daycare facilities, exercise/wellness program, free psychological counseling, international student services, low-cost health insurance, multicultural affairs office, writing training. *Library facilities:* Olin Memorial Library plus 2 others. *Online resources:* library catalog, web page, access to other libraries' catalogs. *Collection:* 1.7 million titles, 9,812 serial subscriptions. *Research affiliation:* Woods Hole Oceanographic Institution, Cold Springs Marine Laboratory.

Computer facilities: Computer purchase and lease plans are available. 190 computers available on campus for general student use. A campuswide network can be accessed from student residence rooms and from off campus. Online class registration, electronic portfolio, online course drop/add, Blackboard course management system are available. *Web address:* http://www.wesleyan.edu/.

General Application Contact: Information Contact, 860-685-2000.

GRADUATE UNITS

Graduate Liberal Studies Program *Degree program information:* Part-time and evening/weekend programs available. Offers liberal studies (MALS, CAS).

Graduate Programs Students: 145 full-time (62 women); includes 8 minority (1 African American, 1 American Indian/Alaska Native, 2 Asian Americans or Pacific Islanders, 4 Hispanic Americans), 52 international. Average age 27. 326 applicants, 16% accepted, 31 enrolled. *Faculty:* 79 full-time (15 women), 7 part-time/adjunct (0 women). Expenses: Contact institution. *Financial support:* In 2008–09, 48 research assistantships with tuition reimbursements, 86 teaching assistantships with tuition reimbursements were awarded; fellowships with tuition reimbursements, institutionally sponsored loans and tuition waivers (full and partial) also available. Financial award application deadline: 4/15; financial award applicants required to submit FAFSA. In 2008, 29 master's, 12 doctorates awarded. Offers astronomy (MA); biochemistry (MA, PhD); cell biology (PhD); chemical physics (MA, PhD); comparative physiology (PhD); developmental biology (PhD); earth and environmental sciences (MA); ethnomusicology (PhD); genetics (PhD); inorganic chemistry (MA, PhD); mathematics (MA, PhD); molecular biology (PhD); music (MA); neurophysiology (PhD); organic chemistry (MA, PhD); physical chemistry (MA, PhD); physics (MA, PhD); population biology (PhD); psychology (MA); theoretical chemistry (MA, PhD). *Application deadline:* Applications are processed on a rolling basis. Electronic applications accepted. *Application Contact:* Dr. John R Kirn, Director of Graduate Studies, 860-685-3494, E-mail: jbruno@wesleyan.edu. *Director of Graduate Studies*, Dr. John R Kirn, 860-685-3494, E-mail: jbruno@wesleyan.edu.

WESLEY BIBLICAL SEMINARY, Jackson, MS 39206

General Information Independent-religious, coed, graduate-only institution. *Graduate housing:* Room and/or apartments available on a first-come, first-served basis to single students; on-campus housing not available to married students.

GRADUATE UNITS

Graduate Programs *Degree program information:* Part-time programs available. Offers Biblical literature (MA); Christian studies (MA); evangelism (M Div); family life ministry (M Div);

Wesley Biblical Seminary (continued)
honors research (M Div); missions (M Div); pastoral ministry (M Div); teaching (M Div); theology (MA). Electronic applications accepted.

WESLEY COLLEGE, Dover, DE 19901-3875

General Information Independent-religious, coed, comprehensive institution. *Graduate housing:* On-campus housing not available.

GRADUATE UNITS

Business Program *Degree program information:* Part-time and evening/weekend programs available. Offers environmental management (MBA); executive leadership (MBA); management (MBA). Executive leadership concentration also offered at New Castle, DE location.

Education Program *Degree program information:* Part-time and evening/weekend programs available. Offers education (M Ed, MA Ed, MAT).

Environmental Studies Program *Degree program information:* Part-time and evening/weekend programs available. Offers environmental studies (MS).

Nursing Program *Degree program information:* Part-time and evening/weekend programs available. Offers nursing (MSN). Electronic applications accepted.

WESLEY THEOLOGICAL SEMINARY, Washington, DC 20016-5690

General Information Independent-religious, coed, graduate-only institution. *Graduate housing:* Rooms and/or apartments available to single and married students. Housing application deadline: 7/1.

GRADUATE UNITS

Graduate and Professional Programs *Degree program information:* Part-time programs available. Offers theology (M Div, MA, MTS, D Min).

WEST CHESTER UNIVERSITY OF PENNSYLVANIA, West Chester, PA 19383

General Information State-supported, coed, comprehensive institution. CGS member. *Enrollment:* 13,619 graduate, professional, and undergraduate students; 602 full-time matriculated graduate/professional students (431 women), 1,215 part-time matriculated graduate/professional students (907 women). *Enrollment by degree level:* 1,579 master's, 238 other advanced degrees. Tuition, state resident: full-time $6430; part-time $357 per credit. Tuition, nonresident: full-time $10,288; part-time $572 per credit. *Required fees:* $652.50; $50 per credit. $67 per semester. *Graduate housing:* Room and/or apartments available on a first-come, first-served basis to single students; on-campus housing not available to married students. Typical cost: $5978 per year ($8376 including board). Room and board charges vary according to board plan, campus/location and housing facility selected. Housing application deadline: 5/1. *Student services:* Campus employment opportunities, campus safety program, career counseling, child daycare facilities, exercise/wellness program, free psychological counseling, grant writing training, international student services, low-cost health insurance, multicultural affairs office, services for students with disabilities, teacher training, writing training. *Library facilities:* Francis Harvey Green Library plus 1 other. *Online resources:* library catalog, web page, access to other libraries' catalogs. *Collection:* 1.3 million titles, 8,493 serial subscriptions, 74,002 audiovisual materials. *Research affiliation:* Turner Biosystems (biology), University Corporation for Atmospheric Research (geology and astronomy), Texas Instruments (mathematics).

Computer facilities: Computer purchase and lease plans are available. 1,200 computers available on campus for general student use. A campuswide network can be accessed from student residence rooms and from off campus. Online class registration is available. *Web address:* http://www.wcupa.edu/.

General Application Contact: Office of Graduate Studies, 610-436-2943, Fax: 610-436-2763, E-mail: gradstudy@wcupa.edu.

GRADUATE UNITS

Office of Graduate Studies Students: 602 full-time (431 women), 1,215 part-time (907 women); includes 198 minority (126 African Americans, 1 American Indian/Alaska Native, 39 Asian Americans or Pacific Islanders, 32 Hispanic Americans), 51 international. Average age 33. 1,404 applicants, 86% accepted, 599 enrolled. Expenses: Contact institution. *Financial support:* In 2008–09, 159 research assistantships with full and partial tuition reimbursements (averaging $5,000 per year) were awarded; unspecified assistantships also available. Support available to part-time students. Financial award application deadline: 2/15; financial award applicants required to submit FAFSA. In 2008, 572 master's, 35 other advanced degrees awarded. *Degree program information:* Part-time and evening/weekend programs available. Postbaccalaureate distance learning degree programs offered (minimal on-campus study). *Application deadline:* For fall admission, 4/15 priority date for domestic students, 3/15 for international students; for spring admission, 10/15 for domestic students, 9/1 for international students. Applications are processed on a rolling basis. *Application fee:* $35. Electronic applications accepted. *Application Contact:* Office of Graduate Studies, 610-436-2943, Fax: 610-436-2763, E-mail: gradstudy@wcupa.edu. *Interim Dean,* Dr. Janet Hickman, 610-436-2943, Fax: 610-436-2763, E-mail: jhickman@wcupa.edu.

College of Arts and Sciences Students: 175 full-time (105 women), 289 part-time (165 women); includes 50 minority (26 African Americans, 19 Asian Americans or Pacific Islanders, 5 Hispanic Americans), 20 international. Average age 33. 438 applicants, 88% accepted, 175 enrolled. Expenses: Contact institution. *Financial support:* In 2008–09, 61 research assistantships with full and partial tuition reimbursements (averaging $5,000 per year) were awarded; unspecified assistantships also available. Support available to part-time students. Financial award application deadline: 2/15; financial award applicants required to submit FAFSA. In 2008, 149 master's, 4 other advanced degrees awarded. *Degree program information:* Part-time and evening/weekend programs available. Offers applied statistics (MS, Certificate); arts and sciences (M Ed, MA, MS, MSA, Certificate, Teaching Certificate); biology (MS, Teaching Certificate); biology—thesis (MS); business ethics (Certificate); clinical chemistry (MS); clinical mental health (Certificate); clinical psychology (MA); communication studies (MA); computer science (MS, Certificate); computer security (Certificate); earth-space science (Teaching Certificate); English (MA, Teaching Certificate); English—non-thesis option (MA); French (M Ed, MA, Teaching Certificate); general psychology (MA); general science (Teaching Certificate); German (Teaching Certificate); gerontology (Certificate); healthcare ethics (Certificate); history (M Ed, MA); holocaust and genocide studies (MA, Certificate); industrial psychology (MA); information systems (Certificate); Latin (Teaching Certificate); leadership for women (MSA, Certificate); long term health care (MSA); mathematics (MA, Teaching Certificate); philosophy (MA); physical science: earth science (MA); social studies/history (Teaching Certificate); Spanish (M Ed, MA, Teaching Certificate); TESL (MA, Certificate); Web technology (Certificate). *Application deadline:* For fall admission, 4/15 priority date for domestic students, 3/15 for international students; for spring admission, 10/15 for domestic students, 9/1 for international students. Applications are processed on a rolling basis. *Application fee:* $35. Electronic applications accepted. *Application Contact:* Office of Graduate Studies, 610-436-2943, Fax: 610-436-2763, E-mail: gradstudy@wcupa.edu. *Dean,* Dr. Lori Vermeulen, 610-436-3521, Fax: 610-436-3150, E-mail: lvermeulen@wcupa.edu.

College of Business and Public Affairs Students: 98 full-time (72 women), 140 part-time (72 women); includes 40 minority (25 African Americans, 8 Asian Americans or Pacific Islanders, 7 Hispanic Americans). Average age 34. 250 applicants, 86% accepted, 121 enrolled. Expenses: Contact institution. *Financial support:* In 2008–09, 17 research assistantships with full and partial tuition reimbursements (averaging $5,000 per year) were awarded; career-related internships or fieldwork and unspecified assistantships also available. Support available to part-time students. Financial award application deadline: 2/15; financial award applicants required to submit FAFSA. In 2008, 106 master's, 12 other advanced degrees awarded. *Degree program information:* Part-time and evening/weekend programs available. Offers administration (Certificate); business (Certificate); business administration: economics-finance (MBA); business administration: tech-electronic (MBA); business and public affairs (MA, MBA, MS, MSA, MSW, Certificate); criminal justice (MS); executive (MBA); general business (MBA); geographic technology (Certificate); geography (MA); human resource management (MSA, Certificate); individualized (MSA); management (MBA); non profit administration (Certificate); nonprofit administration (MSA); public administration (MSA); regional planning (MSA); social work (MSW); training and development (MSA). *Application deadline:* For fall admission, 4/15 priority date for domestic students, 3/15 for international students; for spring admission, 10/15 for domestic students, 9/1 for international students. Applications are processed on a rolling basis. *Application fee:* $35. Electronic applications accepted. *Application Contact:* Office of Graduate Studies, 610-436-2943, Fax: 610-436-2763, E-mail: gradstudy@wcupa.edu. *Dean,* Dr. Christopher Fiorentino, 610-436-2824, E-mail: cfiorentino@wcupa.edu.

College of Education Students: 192 full-time (150 women), 559 part-time (511 women); includes 67 minority (46 African Americans, 1 American Indian/Alaska Native, 6 Asian Americans or Pacific Islanders, 14 Hispanic Americans), 1 international. Average age 33. 379 applicants, 92% accepted, 195 enrolled. Expenses: Contact institution. *Financial support:* In 2008–09, 38 research assistantships with full and partial tuition reimbursements (averaging $5,000 per year) were awarded; unspecified assistantships also available. Support available to part-time students. Financial award application deadline: 2/15; financial award applicants required to submit FAFSA. In 2008, 206 master's, 1 other advanced degree awarded. *Degree program information:* Part-time and evening/weekend programs available. Offers autism (Certificate); counseling (Teaching Certificate); counseling and educational psychology (M Ed, MS, Certificate, Teaching Certificate); early childhood and special education (M Ed, Certificate, Teaching Certificate); early childhood education (M Ed, Teaching Certificate); educational research (MS); elementary education (M Ed, Teaching Certificate); elementary school counseling (M Ed); entrepreneurial education (Certificate); higher education counseling (MS); literacy (M Ed, Certificate, Teaching Certificate); professional and secondary education (M Ed, MS, Certificate, Teaching Certificate); professional counselor license preparation (Certificate); reading (M Ed, Teaching Certificate); secondary education (M Ed); secondary school counseling (M Ed); special education (M Ed, Teaching Certificate); teaching and learning with technology (Certificate). *Application deadline:* For fall admission, 4/15 priority date for domestic students, 3/15 for international students; for spring admission, 10/15 for domestic students, 9/1 for international students. Applications are processed on a rolling basis. *Application fee:* $35. Electronic applications accepted. *Application Contact:* Office of Graduate Studies, 610-436-2943, Fax: 610-436-2763, E-mail: gradstudy@wcupa.edu. *Dean,* Dr. Joseph Malak, 610-436-2428, E-mail: jmalak@wcupa.edu.

College of Health Sciences Students: 124 full-time (96 women), 172 part-time (126 women); includes 36 minority (27 African Americans, 4 Asian Americans or Pacific Islanders, 5 Hispanic Americans), 29 international. Average age 35. 279 applicants, 71% accepted, 84 enrolled. Expenses: Contact institution. *Financial support:* In 2008–09, 39 research assistantships with full and partial tuition reimbursements (averaging $5,000 per year) were awarded; unspecified assistantships also available. Support available to part-time students. Financial award application deadline: 2/15; financial award applicants required to submit FAFSA. In 2008, 92 master's, 12 other advanced degrees awarded. *Degree program information:* Part-time and evening/weekend programs available. Postbaccalaureate distance learning degree programs offered (minimal on-campus study). Offers adapted physical education (Certificate); communicative disorders (MA); emergency preparedness (Certificate); exercise physiology (MS); health and physical education (Teaching Certificate); health care administration (Certificate); health sciences (M Ed, MA, MPH, MS, MSA, MSN, Certificate, Teaching Certificate); integrative health (Certificate); nursing (MSN); nursing education (MSN, Certificate); parish nursing (Certificate); physical education (MS); public health (MPH); school health (M Ed); school nursing (Teaching Certificate); speech correction (Teaching Certificate); sport and athletic administration (MSA). *Application deadline:* For fall admission, 4/15 priority date for domestic students, 3/15 for international students; for spring admission, 10/15 for domestic students, 9/1 for international students. Applications are processed on a rolling basis. *Application fee:* $35. Electronic applications accepted. *Application Contact:* Office of Graduate Studies, 610-436-2943, Fax: 610-436-2763, E-mail: gradstudy@wcupa.edu. *Dean,* Dr. Donald E. Barr, 610-436-2938, Fax: 610-436-2860, E-mail: dbarr@wcupa.edu.

College of Visual and Performing Arts Students: 13 full-time (8 women), 55 part-time (33 women); includes 5 minority (2 African Americans, 2 Asian Americans or Pacific Islanders, 1 Hispanic American), 1 international. Average age 34. 58 applicants, 95% accepted, 24 enrolled. Expenses: Contact institution. *Financial support:* In 2008–09, 4 research assistantships with full and partial tuition reimbursements (averaging $5,000 per year) were awarded; unspecified assistantships also available. Support available to part-time students. Financial award application deadline: 2/15; financial award applicants required to submit FAFSA. In 2008, 19 master's awarded. *Degree program information:* Part-time and evening/weekend programs available. Offers 21st Century music education (Certificate); accompanying (MM); Kodaly methodology (Certificate); music education (MM, Teaching Certificate); music education-technology (MM); music history (MA); music technology (Certificate); music: theory and composition (MM); Orff-Schulwerk (Certificate); performance (MM); piano pedagogy (MM, Certificate); visual and performing arts (MA, MM, Certificate, Teaching Certificate). *Application deadline:* For fall admission, 4/15 priority date for domestic students, 3/15 for international students; for spring admission, 10/15 for domestic students, 9/1 for international students. Applications are processed on a rolling basis. *Application fee:* $35. Electronic applications accepted. *Application Contact:* Dr. J. Bryan Burton, Graduate Coordinator, 610-436-2222, E-mail: jburton@wcupa.edu. *Dean,* Dr. Timothy Blair, 610-436-2489, Fax: 610-436-2873, E-mail: tblair@wcupa.edu.

See Close-Up on page 1053.

WESTERN CAROLINA UNIVERSITY, Cullowhee, NC 28723

General Information State-supported, coed, comprehensive institution. CGS member. *Graduate housing:* Rooms and/or apartments available to single students and guaranteed to married students. *Research affiliation:* North Carolina Center for the Advancement of Teaching.

GRADUATE UNITS

Graduate School *Degree program information:* Part-time and evening/weekend programs available. Postbaccalaureate distance learning degree programs offered.

College of Arts and Sciences *Degree program information:* Part-time and evening/weekend programs available. Offers applied mathematics (MS); arts and sciences (MA, MPA, MS); biology (MS); chemistry (MS); English (MA); history (MA); political science and public affairs (MPA); science and entrepreneurship (MS); teaching English as a second language or foreign language (MA).

College of Business *Degree program information:* Part-time and evening/weekend programs available. Postbaccalaureate distance learning degree programs offered. Offers accountancy (M Ac); business administration (MBA); entrepreneurship (ME); project management (MPM); sport management (MS).

College of Education and Allied Professions *Degree program information:* Part-time and evening/weekend programs available. Postbaccalaureate distance learning degree programs offered. Offers biology, two-year college teaching (MA Ed); community college administration (MA Ed); community college and higher education (MA Ed); community college teaching (MA Ed); community counseling (M Ed, MS); comprehensive education (MA Ed); counseling (M Ed, MA Ed, MS); education and allied professions (M Ed, MA, MA Ed, MAT, MS, MSA, Ed D, Ed S); educational leadership (MA Ed, MSA, Ed D, Ed S); educational supervision (MA Ed); English, two-year college teaching (MA Ed); general psychology (MA); human resources (MS); mathematics, two-year college teaching (MA Ed); physical education, two-year college teaching (MA Ed); school counseling (MA Ed); school psychology (MA); teaching (MAT); teaching degrees (MA Ed, MAT).

College of Fine and Performing Arts *Degree program information:* Part-time programs available. Offers art and design (MFA); fine and performing arts (MFA, MM); music (MM).

College of Health and Human Sciences *Degree program information:* Part-time and evening/weekend programs available. Offers communication sciences and disorders (MS); health and human sciences (MHS, MPT, MS, MSN, MSW); health sciences (MHS); nursing (MSN); physical therapy (MPT); social work (MSW).

Kimmel School of Construction Management and Technology *Degree program information:* Part-time and evening/weekend programs available. Postbaccalaureate distance learning degree programs offered. Offers construction management (MCM); construction management and technology (MCM, MS); engineering and technology (MS).

WESTERN CONNECTICUT STATE UNIVERSITY, Danbury, CT 06810-6885

General Information State-supported, coed, comprehensive institution. CGS member. *Enrollment:* 6,462 graduate, professional, and undergraduate students; 85 full-time matriculated graduate/professional students (52 women), 499 part-time matriculated graduate/professional students (353 women). *Enrollment by degree level:* 540 master's, 44 doctoral. *Graduate faculty:* 53 full-time (21 women), 43 part-time/adjunct (21 women). Tuition, state resident: full-time $4377; part-time $363 per credit. Tuition, nonresident: full-time $12,195; part-time $363 per credit. *Required fees:* $3574; $60 per credit. Part-time tuition and fees vary according to degree level and program. *Graduate housing:* Rooms and/or apartments available on a first-come, first-served basis to single and married students. Typical cost: $5384 per year ($9158 including board) for single students; $10,768 per year ($18,316 including board) for married students. Room and board charges vary according to board plan. Housing application deadline: 4/1. *Student services:* Campus employment opportunities, career counseling, child daycare facilities, free psychological counseling, international student services, low-cost health insurance, multicultural affairs office, services for students with disabilities. *Library facilities:* Ruth Haas Library plus 1 other. *Online resources:* library catalog, web page, access to other libraries' catalogs. *Collection:* 216,284 titles, 1,010 serial subscriptions. *Research affiliation:* Smithsonian Institution Affiliations Program, The Jane Goodall Institute, Center for Financial Forensics and Informational Security, New England Educational Assessment Network, American Society for Microbiology, National Undergraduate Research Center.

Computer facilities: 928 computers available on campus for general student use. A campuswide network can be accessed from student residence rooms and from off campus. Online class registration is available. *Web address:* http://www.wcsu.edu/.

General Application Contact: Chris Shankle, Associate Director of Graduate Studies, 203-837-9005, Fax: 203-837-8326, E-mail: shanklec@wcsu.edu.

GRADUATE UNITS

Division of Graduate Studies Students: 85 full-time (52 women), 499 part-time (353 women); includes 45 minority (15 African Americans, 3 American Indian/Alaska Native, 11 Asian Americans or Pacific Islanders, 16 Hispanic Americans), 4 international. Average age 35. 298 applicants, 60% accepted, 137 enrolled. *Faculty:* 53 full-time (21 women), 43 part-time/adjunct (21 women). Expenses: Contact institution. *Financial support:* Fellowships, teaching assistantships, career-related internships or fieldwork available. Support available to part-time students. Financial award application deadline: 5/1; financial award applicants required to submit FAFSA. In 2008, 207 master's, 14 doctorates awarded. *Degree program information:* Part-time programs available. *Application deadline:* For fall admission, 8/5 priority date for domestic students; for spring admission, 1/5 priority date for domestic students. Applications are processed on a rolling basis. *Application fee:* $50. *Application Contact:* Chris Shankle, Associate Director of Graduate Studies, 203-837-9005, Fax: 203-837-8326, E-mail: shanklec@wcsu.edu. *Dean, Division of Graduate Studies,* Dr. Ellen D. Durnin, 203-837-8386, Fax: 203-837-8326, E-mail: durnine@wcsu.edu.

Ancell School of Business Students: 5 full-time (4 women), 80 part-time (45 women); includes 7 minority (3 African Americans, 2 Asian Americans or Pacific Islanders, 2 Hispanic Americans), 1 international. Average age 34. 57 applicants, 30% accepted, 17 enrolled. *Faculty:* 8 full-time (1 woman), 1 part-time/adjunct (0 women). Expenses: Contact institution. *Financial support:* Fellowships, career-related internships or fieldwork available. Support available to part-time students. Financial award application deadline: 5/1; financial award applicants required to submit FAFSA. In 2008, 32 master's awarded. *Degree program information:* Part-time programs available. Offers accounting (MBA); business (MBA, MHA, MS); business administration (MBA); health administration (MHA); justice administration (MS). *Application deadline:* For fall admission, 8/5 priority date for domestic students; for spring admission, 1/5 priority date for domestic students. Applications are processed on a rolling basis. *Application fee:* $50. *Application Contact:* Chris Shankle, Associate Director of Graduate Studies, 203-837-9005, Fax: 203-837-8326, E-mail: shanklec@wcsu.edu. *Dean,* Dr. Allen Morton, 203-837-9600, Fax: 203-837-8527, E-mail: mortona@wcsu.edu.

School of Arts and Sciences Students: 38 full-time (17 women), 111 part-time (65 women); includes 17 minority (7 African Americans, 2 American Indian/Alaska Native, 3 Asian Americans or Pacific Islanders, 5 Hispanic Americans), 2 international. Average age 37. 118 applicants, 64% accepted, 39 enrolled. *Faculty:* 19 full-time (4 women), 35 part-time/adjunct (16 women). Expenses: Contact institution. *Financial support:* Fellowships, teaching assistantships, career-related internships or fieldwork available. Support available to part-time students. Financial award application deadline: 5/1; financial award applicants required to submit FAFSA. In 2008, 40 master's awarded. *Degree program information:* Part-time programs available. Offers arts and sciences (MA, MFA); biological and environmental sciences (MA); earth and planetary sciences (MA); English (MA); history (MA); literature option (MA); mathematics (MA); professional writing (MFA); TESOL option (MA); theoretical mathematics (MA); writing option (MA). *Application deadline:* For fall admission, 8/5 priority date for domestic students; for spring admission, 1/5 priority date for domestic students. Applications are processed on a rolling basis. *Application fee:* $50. *Application Contact:* Chris Shankle, Associate Director of Graduate Studies, 203-837-9005, Fax: 203-837-8326, E-mail: shanklec@wcsu.edu. *Dean,* Dr. Linda Vaden-Goad, 203-837-9400, Fax: 203-837-8525.

School of Professional Studies Students: 20 full-time (17 women), 281 part-time (225 women); includes 16 minority (4 African Americans, 1 American Indian/Alaska Native, 5 Asian Americans or Pacific Islanders, 6 Hispanic Americans), 1 international. Average age 34. 97 applicants, 68% accepted, 65 enrolled. *Faculty:* 20 full-time (14 women), 6 part-time/adjunct (4 women). Expenses: Contact institution. *Financial support:* Fellowships, career-related internships or fieldwork available. Support available to part-time students. Financial award application deadline: 5/1. In 2008, 116 master's, 14 doctorates awarded. *Degree program information:* Part-time programs available. Offers adult nurse practitioner (MSN); clinical nurse specialist (MSN); community counseling (MS); curriculum (MS); English education (MS); instructional leadership (Ed D); instructional technology (MS); mathematics education (MS); reading (MS); school counseling (MS); special education (MS). *Application deadline:* For fall admission, 8/5 priority date for domestic students; for spring admission, 1/5 priority date for domestic students. Applications are processed on a rolling basis. *Application fee:* $50. *Application Contact:* Chris Shankle, Associate Director of Graduate Admissions, 203-837-9005, Fax: 203-837-8326, E-mail: shanklec@wcsu.edu. *Dean,* Dr. Lynne Clark, 203-837-9500, Fax: 203-837-8526, E-mail: clarkl@wcsu.edu.

School of Visual and Performing Arts Students: 22 full-time (14 women), 27 part-time (18 women); includes 1 African American, 1 Asian American or Pacific Islander, 3 Hispanic Americans. Average age 32. 26 applicants, 73% accepted, 16 enrolled. *Faculty:* 6 full-time (2 women). Expenses: Contact institution. In 2008, 19 master's awarded. *Degree program information:* Part-time programs available. Offers illustration (MFA); music education (MS); painting (MFA); visual and performing arts (MFA, MS). *Application deadline:* For fall admission, 8/5 priority date for domestic students; for spring admission, 1/5 priority date for domestic students. *Application fee:* $50. *Application Contact:* Chris Shankle, Associate Director of Graduate Studies, 203-837-9005, Fax: 203-837-8326, E-mail: shanklec@wcsu.edu. *Dean,* Dr. Carol A. Hawkes, 203-837-8851, Fax: 203-837-3223, E-mail: hawkesc@wcsu.edu.

WESTERN GOVERNORS UNIVERSITY, Salt Lake City, UT 84107

General Information Independent, coed, comprehensive institution. *Graduate housing:* On-campus housing not available.

GRADUATE UNITS

Program in Information Security and Assurance Postbaccalaureate distance learning degree programs offered. Offers information security and assurance (MS).

Programs in Business Postbaccalaureate distance learning degree programs offered. Offers information technology management (MBA); management and strategy (MBA); strategic leadership (MBA). Electronic applications accepted.

Teachers College *Degree program information:* Part-time and evening/weekend programs available. Postbaccalaureate distance learning degree programs offered (no on-campus study). Offers English language learning (K-12) (MA); learning and technology (M Ed, MA); management and innovation (M Ed); mathematics education (5-12) (MA); mathematics education (5-9) (MA); mathematics education (K-6) (MA); measurement and evaluation (M Ed); science (5-12) (MA); science education (5-9) (MA); teaching (MAT); technology for principals (Post-Graduate Certificate). Electronic applications accepted.

WESTERN ILLINOIS UNIVERSITY, Macomb, IL 61455-1390

General Information State-supported, coed, comprehensive institution. CGS member. *Enrollment:* 13,175 graduate, professional, and undergraduate students; 835 full-time matriculated graduate/professional students (403 women), 1,074 part-time matriculated graduate/professional students (726 women). *Enrollment by degree level:* 1,756 master's, 46 doctoral, 107 other advanced degrees. Tuition, state resident: full-time $5696; part-time $237.34 per credit hour. Tuition, nonresident: full-time $11,392; part-time $474.68 per credit hour. *Required fees:* $1453; $60.55 per credit hour. *Graduate housing:* Rooms and/or apartments available on a first-come, first-served basis to single and married students. Typical cost: $4350 per year ($7210 including board) for single students; $5360 per year for married students. *Student services:* Campus employment opportunities, campus safety program, career counseling, exercise/wellness program, free psychological counseling, international student services, low-cost health insurance, multicultural affairs office, services for students with disabilities, writing training. *Library facilities:* Leslie Malpass Library plus 4 others. *Online resources:* library catalog, web page. *Collection:* 998,041 titles, 3,200 serial subscriptions. *Research affiliation:* Clean Energy Community Foundation (wind energy), Huron Mountain Foundation (biology), The Nature Conservancy (biology), McDonalds Corporation (education), Earthwatch Institute (biology), Finzelburg Inc. (kinesiology).

Computer facilities: 1,000 computers available on campus for general student use. A campuswide network can be accessed from student residence rooms and from off campus. Online class registration is available. *Web address:* http://www.wiu.edu/.

General Application Contact: Evelyn A. Hoing, Assistant Director of Graduate Studies, 309-298-1806, Fax: 309-298-2345, E-mail: grad-office@wiu.edu.

GRADUATE UNITS

School of Graduate Studies Students: 835 full-time (403 women), 1,074 part-time (726 women); includes 120 minority (70 African Americans, 3 American Indian/Alaska Native, 15 Asian Americans or Pacific Islanders, 32 Hispanic Americans), 221 international. Average age 29. 1,114 applicants, 59% accepted. Expenses: Contact institution. *Financial support:* In 2008–09, 479 students received support, including 421 research assistantships with full tuition reimbursements available (averaging $7,040 per year), 58 teaching assistantships with full tuition reimbursements available (averaging $8,120 per year). Financial award applicants required to submit FAFSA. In 2008, 618 master's, 9 doctorates, 56 other advanced degrees awarded. *Degree program information:* Part-time programs available. Postbaccalaureate distance learning degree programs offered (no on-campus study). *Application deadline:* Applications are processed on a rolling basis. *Application fee:* $30. Electronic applications accepted. *Application Contact:* Evelyn A. Hoing, Assistant Director of Graduate Studies, 309-298-1806, Fax: 309-298-2345, E-mail: ea-hoing@wiu.edu. *Director of Graduate Studies/Associate Provost,* Dr. Judith Dallinger, 309-298-1806, Fax: 309-298-2345, E-mail: grad-office@wiu.edu.

College of Arts and Sciences Students: 250 full-time (112 women), 87 part-time (56 women); includes 19 minority (13 African Americans, 3 Asian Americans or Pacific Islanders, 3 Hispanic Americans), 61 international. Average age 29. 299 applicants, 62% accepted. Expenses: Contact institution. *Financial support:* In 2008–09, 156 students received support, including 130 research assistantships with full tuition reimbursements available (averaging $7,040 per year), 26 teaching assistantships with full tuition reimbursements available (averaging $8,120 per year). Financial award applicants required to submit FAFSA. In 2008, 93 master's, 27 other advanced degrees awarded. *Degree program information:* Part-time programs available. Offers applied math (Certificate); arts and sciences (MA, MLAS, MS, Certificate, SSP); biological sciences (MS); chemistry (MS); clinical/community mental health (MS); community development (Certificate); English (MA, Certificate); environmental geographic information systems (Certificate); general psychology (MS); geography (MA); history (MA); liberal arts and sciences (MLAS); mathematics (MS); physics (MS); political science (MA); psychology (MS, SSP); public and non-profit management (Certificate); school psychology (SSP); sociology (MA); zoo and aquarium studies (Certificate). *Application deadline:* Applications are processed on a rolling basis. *Application fee:* $30. Electronic applications accepted. *Application Contact:* Evelyn Hoing, Assistant Director of Graduate Studies, 309-298-1806, Fax: 309-298-2345, E-mail: grad-office@wiu.edu. *Interim Dean,* Dr. Susan Martinelli-Fernandez, 309-298-1828.

College of Business and Technology Students: 172 full-time (57 women), 85 part-time (36 women); includes 11 minority (7 African Americans, 3 Asian Americans or Pacific Islanders, 1 Hispanic American), 120 international. Average age 27. 220 applicants, 64% accepted. Expenses: Contact institution. *Financial support:* In 2008–09, 74 students received support, including 64 research assistantships with full tuition reimbursements available (averaging $7,040 per year), 10 teaching assistantships with full tuition reimbursements available (averaging $8,120 per year). Financial award applicants required to submit FAFSA. In 2008, 118 master's awarded. *Degree program information:* Part-time programs available. Offers accountancy (M Acct); business administration (MBA); business and technology (M Acct, MA, MBA, MS, Certificate); computer science (MS); economics (MA, Certificate); manufacturing engineering systems (MS). *Application deadline:* Applications are processed on a rolling basis. *Application fee:* $30. Electronic applications accepted. *Application Contact:* Evelyn Hoing, Assistant Director of Graduate Studies, 309-298-1806, Fax: 309-298-2345, E-mail: grad-office@wiu.edu. *Dean,* Dr. Tom Erekson, 309-298-2442.

College of Education and Human Services Students: 306 full-time (162 women), 879 part-time (620 women); includes 82 minority (47 African Americans, 3 American Indian/Alaska Native, 6 Asian Americans or Pacific Islanders, 26 Hispanic Americans), 26 international. Average age 32. 415 applicants, 67% accepted. Expenses: Contact institution. *Financial support:* In 2008–09, 169 students received support, including 157 research assistantships with full tuition reimbursements available (averaging $7,040 per year), 12 teaching assistantships (averaging $8,120 per year). Financial award applicants required to submit FAFSA. In 2008, 355 master's, 9 doctorates, 29 other advanced degrees awarded. *Degree program information:* Part-time and evening/weekend programs available. Postbaccalaureate distance learning degree programs offered (no on-campus study). Offers college student personnel (MS); counseling (MS Ed); distance learning (Certificate); education and human services (MA, MS, MS Ed, Ed D, Certificate, Ed S); educational and interdisciplinary studies (MS Ed); educational leadership (MS Ed, Ed D, Ed S); elementary education (MS Ed); graphic applications (Certificate); health education (MS); health services administration (Certificate); instructional design and technology (MS); kinesiology (MS); law enforcement and justice administration (MA); multimedia (Certificate); police executive administration (Certificate); reading (MS Ed); recreation, park, and tourism administration (MS); special education (MS Ed); sport management (MS); technology integration in education (Certificate); training development (Certificate). *Application deadline:* Applications are processed on a rolling basis. *Application fee:* $30. Electronic applications accepted. *Application Contact:* Evelyn Hoing, Assistant Director of Graduate Studies, 309-298-1806, Fax: 309-298-2345, E-mail: grad-office@wiu.edu. *Interim Dean,* Dr. Bernard N DiGrino, 309-298-1690.

College of Fine Arts and Communication Students: 107 full-time (72 women), 23 part-time (14 women); includes 8 minority (3 African Americans, 3 Asian Americans or Pacific Islanders, 2 Hispanic Americans), 14 international. Average age 29. 180 applicants, 32%

Western Illinois University (continued)

accepted. Expenses: Contact institution. *Financial support:* In 2008–09, 80 students received support, including 70 research assistantships with full tuition reimbursements available (averaging $7,040 per year), 10 teaching assistantships with full tuition reimbursements available (averaging $8,120 per year). Financial award applicants required to submit FAFSA. In 2008, 52 master's awarded. *Degree program information:* Part-time programs available. Offers acting (MFA); communication (MA); communication sciences and disorders (MS); costume design (MFA); directing (MFA); fine arts and communication (MA, MFA, MM, MS); lighting design/theatre technology (MFA); museum studies (MA); music (MM); scenic design (MFA). *Application deadline:* Applications are processed on a rolling basis. *Application fee:* $30. Electronic applications accepted. *Application Contact:* Evelyn Hoing, Assistant Director of Graduate Studies, 309-298-1806, Fax: 309-298-2345, E-mail: grad-office@wiu.edu. *Dean,* Dr. Paul K. Kreider, 309-298-1552.

WESTERN INTERNATIONAL UNIVERSITY, Phoenix, AZ 85021-2718

General Information Proprietary, coed, comprehensive institution. *Enrollment:* 2,651 graduate, professional, and undergraduate students; 730 full-time matriculated graduate/professional students (375 women). *Enrollment by degree level:* 730 master's. *Graduate faculty:* 149 part-time/adjunct (49 women). *Graduate housing:* On-campus housing not available. *Student services:* International student services, services for students with disabilities, writing training. *Library facilities:* Learning Resource Center. *Online resources:* web page. *Collection:* 7,500 titles, 125 serial subscriptions.

Computer facilities: Computer purchase and lease plans are available. 50 computers available on campus for general student use. A campuswide network can be accessed from off campus. Online class registration is available. *Web address:* http://www.wintu.edu/.

General Application Contact: Karen Janitell, Director of Enrollment, 602-943-2311 Ext. 1063, Fax: 602-371-8637, E-mail: karen_janitell@apollogrp.edu.

GRADUATE UNITS

Graduate Programs in Business Students: 730 full-time (375 women); includes 189 minority (60 African Americans, 13 American Indian/Alaska Native, 52 Asian Americans or Pacific Islanders, 64 Hispanic Americans), 105 international. Average age 35. *Faculty:* 149 part-time/adjunct (49 women). Expenses: Contact institution. *Financial support:* In 2008–09, 103 students received support. Career-related internships or fieldwork and scholarships/grants available. Support available to part-time students. Financial award applicants required to submit FAFSA. In 2008, 150 master's awarded. *Degree program information:* Evening/weekend programs available. Postbaccalaureate distance learning degree programs offered (no on-campus study). Offers business (MA, MBA, MPA, MS); business administration (MBA); finance (MBA); information system engineering (MS); information technology (MBA); innovative leadership (MA); international business (MBA); management (MBA); marketing (MBA); organization development (MBA); public administration (MPA). *Application deadline:* Applications are processed on a rolling basis. *Application fee:* $85 ($100 for international students). *Application Contact:* Karen Janitell, Director of Enrollment, 602-943-2311 Ext. 1063, Fax: 602-371-8637, E-mail: karen_janitell@apollogrp.edu. *Chief Academic Officer,* Dr. Deborah DeSimone, 602-943-2311 Ext. 1135, Fax: 602-749-0752, E-mail: deborah.desimone@apollogrp.edu.

WESTERN KENTUCKY UNIVERSITY, Bowling Green, KY 42101

General Information State-supported, coed, comprehensive institution. CGS member. *Graduate housing:* Room and/or apartments guaranteed to single students; on-campus housing not available to married students. Housing application deadline: 4/1. *Research affiliation:* Bowling Green Field Station for Animal Studies (U.S. Fish and Wildlife Service), Roybal Center (gerontology).

GRADUATE UNITS

Graduate Studies *Degree program information:* Part-time and evening/weekend programs available. Postbaccalaureate distance learning degree programs offered (minimal on-campus study).

College of Education and Behavioral Sciences *Degree program information:* Part-time and evening/weekend programs available. Postbaccalaureate distance learning degree programs offered (no on-campus study). Offers business and marketing education (MA Ed, MAE); counseling (MA Ed); counselor education (Ed S); education and behavioral science (MA Ed); education and behavioral sciences (MA, MAE, MS, Ed S); educational administration (MAE); elementary education (MA Ed, MAE, Ed S); exceptional child education (MAE); interdisciplinary early child education (MAE); library media education (MS); literacy (MAE); middle grades education (MAE); middle years education (MA Ed); psychology (MA); school administration (Ed S); school psychology (Ed S); secondary education (MA Ed, MAE, Ed S); student affairs (MA Ed).

College of Health and Human Services *Degree program information:* Part-time and evening/weekend programs available. Offers communication disorders (MS); health and human services (MHA, MPH, MS, MSN, MSW); healthcare administration (MHA); nursing (MSN); physical education (MS); public health (MPH); recreation (MS); social work (MSW).

Gordon Ford College of Business *Degree program information:* Part-time and evening/weekend programs available. Offers business (MBA); business administration (MBA).

Ogden College of Science and Engineering *Degree program information:* Part-time and evening/weekend programs available. Offers agriculture (MA Ed, MS); biology (MA Ed, MS); chemistry (MA Ed, MS); computer science (MS); geography and geology (MAE, MS); mathematics (MA Ed, MS); science and engineering (MA Ed, MAE, MS).

Potter College of Arts and Letters *Degree program information:* Part-time and evening/weekend programs available. Postbaccalaureate distance learning degree programs offered. Offers art education (MA Ed); arts and letter (MA, MA Ed, MPA); communication (MA); education (MA); English (MA Ed); folk studies (MA); history (MA, MA Ed); literature (MA); music (MA Ed); political science (MPA); sociology (MA); teaching English as a second language (MA); writing (MA).

WESTERN MICHIGAN UNIVERSITY, Kalamazoo, MI 49008-5202

General Information State-supported, coed, university. CGS member. *Graduate housing:* Rooms and/or apartments available on a first-come, first-served basis to single and married students. Housing application deadline: 7/1. *Research affiliation:* Argonne National Laboratory (particle physics), Central States Universities, Inc., Ames Research Center (manufacturing education), Copper Development Association, Inc. (plastics extrusion), Pharmacia and Upjohn Company (electron microscopy), Flowserve Corporation (mechanical pumps and seals).

GRADUATE UNITS

Graduate College *Degree program information:* Part-time and evening/weekend programs available.

College of Arts and Sciences *Degree program information:* Part-time programs available. Offers anthropology (MA); applied and computational mathematics (MS); applied economics (MA, PhD); applied statistics (MS); arts and sciences (MA, MDA, MFA, MPA, MS, PhD, Graduate Certificate); behavior analysis (MA, PhD); biological sciences (MS, PhD); chemistry (MA, PhD); clinical psychology (MA, PhD); communication (MA); comparative religion (MA); creative writing (MFA); development administration (MDA); earth science (MA, MS); electron microscopy (MS); English (MA, PhD); English education (MA, PhD); experimental psychology (MA, PhD); geography (MA); geosciences (MA, MS, PhD); health care administration (Graduate Certificate); history (MA, PhD); industrial/organizational psychology (MA); mathematics (MA, PhD); mathematics education (MA, PhD); medieval studies (MA); molecular biotechnology (MS); nonprofit leadership and administration (Graduate Certificate); philosophy (MA); physics (MA, PhD); political science (MA, PhD); professional writing (MA); public administration (PhD); public affairs and administration (MPA); science education (PhD); sociology (MA, PhD); Spanish (MA, PhD); statistics (MS, PhD).

College of Education *Degree program information:* Part-time programs available. Offers career and technical education (MA); counselin psychology (MA); counseling psychology (PhD); counselor education (MA, Ed D, PhD, Ed S, Graduate Certificate); educational leadership (MA, Ed D, PhD, Ed S); educational technology (MA); evaluation, measurement and research (MA, PhD, Graduate Certificate); exercise and sports medicine (MS); family and consumer sciences (MA); human resources development (MA); marriage and family therapy (MA); physical education (MA); socio-cultural foundations and educational thought (MA).

College of Engineering and Applied Sciences *Degree program information:* Part-time programs available. Offers civil engineering (MS); computer engineering (MSE, PhD); computer science (MS, PhD); electrical and computer engineering (PhD); electrical engineering (MSE); engineering and applied sciences (MS, MSE, PhD); engineering management (MS); industrial engineering (MSE); manufacturing engineering (MS); mechanical engineering (MSE, PhD); paper and imaging science and engineering (MS, PhD).

College of Fine Arts *Degree program information:* Part-time programs available. Offers art education (MA); composition (MM); conducting (MM); fine arts (MA, MFA, MM); music education (MM); music therapy (MM); performance (MM); studio design (MFA).

College of Health and Human Services *Degree program information:* Part-time programs available. Offers audiology (Au D); blind rehabilitation (MA); health and human services (MA, MS, MSW, Au D); occupational therapy (MS); physician assistant (MS); social work (MSW); speech-language pathology (MA).

Haworth College of Business *Degree program information:* Part-time programs available. Offers accountancy (MSA); business (MBA, MSA); finance (MBA).

WESTERN NEW ENGLAND COLLEGE, Springfield, MA 01119

General Information Independent, coed, comprehensive institution. *Enrollment:* 3,722 graduate, professional, and undergraduate students; 437 full-time matriculated graduate/professional students (218 women), 520 part-time matriculated graduate/professional students (289 women). *Enrollment by degree level:* 139 first professional, 112 master's. *Graduate faculty:* 61 full-time (16 women), 80 part-time/adjunct (23 women). Tuition and fees vary according to course load, campus/location and program. *Graduate housing:* On-campus housing not available. *Student services:* Campus safety program, career counseling, exercise/wellness program, free psychological counseling, services for students with disabilities, writing training. *Library facilities:* D'Amour Library plus 1 other. *Online resources:* library catalog, web page, access to other libraries' catalogs. *Collection:* 131,350 titles, 155 serial subscriptions, 4,220 audiovisual materials.

Computer facilities: Computer purchase and lease plans are available. 460 computers available on campus for general student use. A campuswide network can be accessed from student residence rooms and from off campus. Online class registration is available. *Web address:* http://www.wnec.edu/.

General Application Contact: Assistant Vice President, Graduate Studies and Continuing Education, 413-782-1517, Fax: 413-782-1777, E-mail: study@wnec.edu.

GRADUATE UNITS

School of Arts and Sciences Students: 281 part-time (162 women). Expenses: Contact institution. *Financial support:* Available to part-time students. Application deadline: 4/1. In 2008, 18 master's awarded. *Degree program information:* Part-time and evening/weekend programs available. Offers arts and sciences (M Ed, MAET, MAMT, PhD); behavior analysis (PhD); elementary education (M Ed); English for teachers (MAET); mathematics for teachers (MAMT). *Application deadline:* Applications are processed on a rolling basis. *Application fee:* $30. *Application Contact:* Assistant Vice President, Graduate Studies and Continuing Education, 413-782-1517, Fax: 413-782-1777, E-mail: study@wnec.edu. *Dean,* Dr. Saeed Ghahramani, 413-782-1218, Fax: 413-796-2118, E-mail: sghahram@wnec.edu.

School of Business Students: 145 part-time (80 women). Average age 29. *Faculty:* 33 full-time (13 women), 17 part-time/adjunct (0 women). Expenses: Contact institution. *Financial support:* Available to part-time students. Application deadline: 4/1. In 2008, 39 master's awarded. *Degree program information:* Part-time and evening/weekend programs available. Offers accounting (MSA); business (MBA, MSA); general business (MBA); sport management (MBA). *Application deadline:* Applications are processed on a rolling basis. *Application fee:* $30. *Application Contact:* Assistant Vice President, Graduate Studies and Continuing Education, 413-782-1517, Fax: 413-782-1777, E-mail: study@wnec.edu. *Dean,* Dr. Julie Siciliano, 413-782-1231.

School of Engineering Students: 28 part-time (3 women). *Faculty:* 19 full-time (3 women), 2 part-time/adjunct (0 women). Expenses: Contact institution. *Financial support:* Available to part-time students. Application deadline: 4/1. In 2008, 12 master's awarded. *Degree program information:* Part-time and evening/weekend programs available. Offers electrical engineering (MSE); engineering (MSE, MSEM); mechanical engineering (MSE); production management (MSEM). *Application deadline:* Applications are processed on a rolling basis. *Application fee:* $30. *Application Contact:* Assistant Vice President, Graduate Studies and Continuing Education, 413-782-1517, Fax: 413-782-1777, E-mail: ce@wnec.edu. *Dean,* Dr. S. Hossein Cheraghi, 413-782-1272, E-mail: cheraghi@wnec.edu.

School of Law *Degree program information:* Part-time and evening/weekend programs available. Offers estate planning/elder law (LL M); law (JD). Electronic applications accepted.

WESTERN NEW MEXICO UNIVERSITY, Silver City, NM 88062-0680

General Information State-supported, coed, comprehensive institution. *Graduate housing:* Rooms and/or apartments available on a first-come, first-served basis to single and married students. Housing application deadline: 6/30.

GRADUATE UNITS

Graduate Division *Degree program information:* Part-time programs available. Postbaccalaureate distance learning degree programs offered (minimal on-campus study). Offers business administration (MBA); interdisciplinary studies (MA). Electronic applications accepted.

School of Education Offers bilingual education (MAT); counseling (MA); educational leadership (MA); elementary education (MAT); reading (MAT); school psychology (MA); secondary education (MAT); special education (MAT); TESOL (teaching English to speakers of other languages) (MAT). Electronic applications accepted.

WESTERN OREGON UNIVERSITY, Monmouth, OR 97361-1394

General Information State-supported, coed, comprehensive institution. *Graduate housing:* Room and/or apartments available on a first-come, first-served basis to single students; on-campus housing not available to married students. *Research affiliation:* Teaching Research Institute (education).

GRADUATE UNITS

Graduate Programs *Degree program information:* Part-time and evening/weekend programs available. Postbaccalaureate distance learning degree programs offered (minimal on-campus study).

College of Education *Degree program information:* Part-time and evening/weekend programs available. Postbaccalaureate distance learning degree programs offered (minimal on-campus study). Offers bilingual education (MS Ed); deaf education (MS Ed); early childhood special education (MS Ed); education (MAT, MS, MS Ed); health (MS Ed); humanities (MAT, MS Ed); information technology (MS Ed); initial licensure (MAT); mathematics (MAT, MS Ed); rehabilitation counseling (MS); science (MAT, MS Ed); secondary education (MAT, MS Ed); social science (MAT, MS Ed); special education (MS Ed).

College of Liberal Arts and Sciences *Degree program information:* Part-time and evening/weekend programs available. Offers contemporary music (MM); criminal justice (MA, MS); liberal arts and sciences (MA, MM, MS).

WESTERN SEMINARY, Portland, OR 97215-3367

General Information Independent-religious, coed, graduate-only institution. *Graduate housing:* On-campus housing not available.

GRADUATE UNITS

Graduate Programs *Degree program information:* Part-time and evening/weekend programs available. Offers biblical and theological studies (MA, G Dip); biblical studies (Certificate); children / youth at risk (MA); coaching (MA); counseling (MA, Certificate); evangelism and equipping (MA); intercultural studies (MA, D Miss, Certificate, G Dip); pastoral care to women (MA); pastoral counseling (M Div); pastoral leadership (D Min); theology (Th M); youth and family ministry (MA); youth ministry (MA).

WESTERN SEMINARY–SACRAMENTO CAMPUS, Sacramento, CA 95821

General Information Independent-religious, coed, graduate-only institution.

GRADUATE UNITS

Graduate Programs Postbaccalaureate distance learning degree programs offered. Offers exegetical theology (MA); marital and family therapy (MA); ministry (M Div); specialized ministry (MA).

WESTERN SEMINARY–SAN JOSE CAMPUS, Los Gatos, CA 95032-4520

General Information Independent-religious, coed, graduate-only institution.

GRADUATE UNITS

Graduate Programs Postbaccalaureate distance learning degree programs offered. Offers exegetical theology (MA); expositional ministry (M Div); marital and family therapy (MA); ministry (M Div); pastoral ministry (M Div); specialized ministry (MA).

WESTERN STATES CHIROPRACTIC COLLEGE, Portland, OR 97230-3099

General Information Independent, coed, graduate-only institution. *Graduate housing:* On-campus housing not available. *Research affiliation:* Oregon Center for Complimentary and Alternative Medicine in Craniofacial Disorders (complimentary and alternative medicine), Oregon Center for Complimentary and Alternative Medicine (complimentary and alternative medicine), Consortial Center for Chiropractic Research (Palmer Chiropractic College, Davenport, IA) (chiropractic).

GRADUATE UNITS

Professional Program Offers chiropractic (DC).

WESTERN STATE UNIVERSITY COLLEGE OF LAW, Fullerton, CA 92831-3000

General Information Proprietary, coed, graduate-only institution. *Enrollment by degree level:* 377 first professional. *Graduate faculty:* 25 full-time (9 women), 19 part-time/adjunct (6 women). *Tuition:* Full-time $31,000; part-time $10,400 per semester. *Graduate housing:* On-campus housing not available. *Student services:* Campus employment opportunities, campus safety program, career counseling, free psychological counseling, international student services, low-cost health insurance, services for students with disabilities. *Library facilities:* Law Library. *Online resources:* library catalog, web page, access to other libraries' catalogs. *Collection:* 206,941 titles, 3,151 serial subscriptions, 84 audiovisual materials.

Computer facilities: 45 computers available on campus for general student use. A campuswide network can be accessed. Lexis, Westlaw, Dialog, Nexis, Cali, Authority, Hein Online available. *Web address:* http://www.wsulaw.edu/.

General Application Contact: Gloria Switzer, Assistant Dean of Admission, 714-459-1101, Fax: 714-441-1748, E-mail: adm@wsulaw.edu.

GRADUATE UNITS

Professional Program Students: 250 full-time (128 women), 127 part-time (64 women); includes 120 minority (18 African Americans, 3 American Indian/Alaska Native, 63 Asian Americans or Pacific Islanders, 36 Hispanic Americans), 5 international. Average age 28. 1,426 applicants, 48% accepted, 162 enrolled. *Faculty:* 25 full-time (9 women), 19 part-time/adjunct (6 women). Expenses: Contact institution. *Financial support:* In 2008–09, 5 fellowships (averaging $3,960 per year) were awarded; career-related internships or fieldwork, Federal Work-Study, and scholarships/grants also available. Support available to part-time students. Financial award application deadline: 9/15; financial award applicants required to submit FAFSA. In 2008, 93 JDs awarded. *Degree program information:* Part-time and evening/weekend programs available. Offers law (JD). *Application deadline:* For fall admission, 5/1 priority date for domestic and international students; for spring admission, 10/1 priority date for domestic and international students. Applications are processed on a rolling basis. *Application fee:* $50. Electronic applications accepted. *Application Contact:* Gloria Switzer, Assistant Dean of Admission, 714-459-1101, Fax: 714-441-1748, E-mail: adm@wsulaw.edu.

WESTERN THEOLOGICAL SEMINARY, Holland, MI 49423-3622

General Information Independent-religious, coed, graduate-only institution. *Graduate housing:* Rooms and/or apartments available on a first-come, first-served basis to single and married students.

GRADUATE UNITS

Graduate and Professional Programs *Degree program information:* Part-time programs available. Postbaccalaureate distance learning degree programs offered (minimal on-campus study). Offers theology (M Div, M Th, D Min).

WESTERN UNIVERSITY OF HEALTH SCIENCES, Pomona, CA 91766-1854

General Information Independent, coed, graduate-only institution. *Enrollment by degree level:* 1,979 first professional, 414 master's. *Graduate faculty:* 131 full-time (61 women), 13 part-time/adjunct (10 women). *Graduate housing:* On-campus housing not available. *Student services:* Campus safety program, career counseling, exercise/wellness program, free psychological counseling, international student services, low-cost health insurance, services for students with disabilities, teacher training. *Collection:* 18,000 titles, 350 serial subscriptions. *Research affiliation:* Watson Pharmaceuticals Inc. (pharmaceutical sciences).

Computer facilities: 27 computers available on campus for general student use. A campuswide network can be accessed from off campus. Online class registration is available. *Web address:* http://www.westernu.edu/.

General Application Contact: Information Contact, 909-469-5335, Fax: 909-469-5570, E-mail: admissions@westernu.edu.

GRADUATE UNITS

College of Allied Health Professions Students: 344 full-time (242 women), 55 part-time (35 women); includes 194 minority (18 African Americans, 121 Asian Americans or Pacific Islanders, 55 Hispanic Americans). Average age 29. 1,030 applicants, 23% accepted, 145 enrolled. *Faculty:* 15 full-time (8 women), 3 part-time/adjunct (all women). Expenses: Contact institution. *Financial support:* Institutionally sponsored loans and scholarships/grants available. Financial award application deadline: 3/2; financial award applicants required to submit FAFSA. In 2008, 102 master's, 33 doctorates awarded. Offers allied health professions (MS, DPT); health sciences (MS); physical therapy (DPT); physician assistant studies (MS). *Application Contact:* Karen Hutton-Lopez, Director of Admissions, 909-469-5650, Fax: 909-469-5570, E-mail: admissions@westernu.edu. *Dean,* Dr. Stephanie Bowlin, 909-469-5383.

College of Dental Medicine Expenses: Contact institution. Offers dental medicine (DMD). *Application Contact:* Marie Anderson, Director of Admissions, 909-469-5485, Fax: 909-469-5570, E-mail: admissions@westernu.edu. *Dean,* Dr. James J. Koelbl, 909-706-3504, E-mail: jkoelbl@westernu.edu.

College of Graduate Nursing Students: 198 full-time (170 women), 9 part-time (7 women); includes 96 minority (11 African Americans, 61 Asian Americans or Pacific Islanders, 24 Hispanic Americans), 1 international. Average age 33. 236 applicants, 62% accepted, 92 enrolled. *Faculty:* 8 full-time (all women), 2 part-time/adjunct (both women). Expenses: Contact institution. *Financial support:* Institutionally sponsored loans, scholarships/grants, and veterans educational benefits available. Financial award application deadline: 3/2; financial award applicants required to submit FAFSA. In 2008, 25 master's awarded. *Degree program information:* Part-time and evening/weekend programs available. Postbaccalaureate distance learning degree programs offered. Offers family nurse practitioner (MSN). *Application deadline:* For fall admission, 3/1 priority date for domestic students. Applications are processed on a rolling basis. *Application fee:* $60. *Application Contact:* Jeanene White, Information Contact, 909-469-5541, Fax: 909-469-5570, E-mail: admissions@westernu.edu. *Dean,* Karen J. Hanford, 909-469-5243, Fax: 909-469-5521, E-mail: khanford@westernu.edu.

College of Optometry Expenses: Contact institution. Offers optometry (OD). *Application Contact:* Marie Anderson, Director of Admissions, 909-469-5485, Fax: 909-469-5570, E-mail: admissions@westernu.edu. *Dean,* Dr. Elizabeth Hoppe, 909-706-3497, E-mail: ehoppe@westernu.edu.

College of Osteopathic Medicine of the Pacific Students: 847 full-time (412 women); includes 391 minority (9 African Americans, 3 American Indian/Alaska Native, 344 Asian Americans or Pacific Islanders, 35 Hispanic Americans), 1 international. Average age 27. 3,222 applicants, 16% accepted, 221 enrolled. *Faculty:* 39 full-time (10 women), 4 part-time/adjunct (1 woman). Expenses: Contact institution. *Financial support:* Fellowships, research assistantships, teaching assistantships, institutionally sponsored loans, scholarships/grants, tuition waivers (full), unspecified assistantships, and veterans educational benefits available. Financial award application deadline: 3/2; financial award applicants required to submit FAFSA. In 2008, 195 DOs awarded. Offers osteopathic medicine (DO). *Application deadline:* For fall admission, 4/15 for domestic students. Applications are processed on a rolling basis. *Application fee:* $65. *Application Contact:* Susan Hanson, Director of Admissions, 909-469-5329, Fax: 909-469-5570, E-mail: admissions@westernu.edu. *Dean,* Dr. Clinton Adams, 909-469-5423, Fax: 909-469-5535, E-mail: aclinton@westernu.edu.

College of Pharmacy Students: 543 full-time (397 women), 1 part-time (0 women); includes 407 minority (11 African Americans, 381 Asian Americans or Pacific Islanders, 15 Hispanic Americans), 10 international. Average age 27. 1,810 applicants, 11% accepted, 120 enrolled. *Faculty:* 30 full-time (13 women), 1 (woman) part-time/adjunct. Expenses: Contact institution. *Financial support:* Institutionally sponsored loans, scholarships/grants, and veterans educational benefits available. Financial award application deadline: 3/2; financial award applicants required to submit FAFSA. In 2008, 124 first professional degrees, 3 master's awarded. Offers pharmaceutical sciences (MS); pharmacy (Pharm D, MS). *Application deadline:* For fall admission, 11/1 for domestic and international students. *Application fee:* $65. *Application Contact:* Kathryn Ford, Director of Admissions, 909-469-5542, Fax: 909-469-5570, E-mail: admissions@westernu.edu. *Dean,* Dr. Daniel Robinson, 909-469-5581, Fax: 909-469-5539.

College of Podiatric Medicine Expenses: Contact institution. Offers podiatric medicine (DPM). *Application Contact:* Marie Anderson, Director of Admissions, 909-469-5485, Fax: 909-469-5570, E-mail: admissions@westernu.edu. *Dean,* Dr. Lawrence B. Harkless, 909-706-3498, E-mail: lharkless@westernu.edu.

College of Veterinary Medicine Students: 396 full-time (303 women); includes 106 minority (3 African Americans, 6 American Indian/Alaska Native, 68 Asian Americans or Pacific Islanders, 29 Hispanic Americans). Average age 28. 755 applicants, 25% accepted, 97 enrolled. *Faculty:* 39 full-time (22 women), 3 part-time/adjunct (all women). Expenses: Contact institution. *Financial support:* Institutionally sponsored loans, scholarships/grants, and veterans educational benefits available. Financial award application deadline: 3/2; financial award applicants required to submit FAFSA. In 2008, 69 DVMs awarded. Offers veterinary medicine (DVM). *Application deadline:* For fall admission, 10/1 for domestic students. *Application fee:* $75. *Application Contact:* Karen Hutton-Lopez, Director of Admissions, 909-469-5650, Fax: 909-469-5570, E-mail: admissions@westernu.edu. *Dean,* Dr. Phil Nelson, 909-469-5637, Fax: 909-469-5635.

WESTERN WASHINGTON UNIVERSITY, Bellingham, WA 98225-5996

General Information State-supported, coed, comprehensive institution. CGS member. *Graduate housing:* Rooms and/or apartments available on a first-come, first-served basis to single and married students. Housing application deadline: 5/1. *Research affiliation:* NARSAD (mental health), Teck Cominco Ltd., Research Corporation, Dreyfus Foundation, Golden Associates, American Metals Technology.

GRADUATE UNITS

Graduate School *Degree program information:* Part-time programs available. Electronic applications accepted.

College of Business and Economics *Degree program information:* Part-time and evening/weekend programs available. Offers business and economics (MBA, MP Acc). Electronic applications accepted.

College of Fine and Performing Arts *Degree program information:* Part-time programs available. Offers fine and performing arts (M Mus, MA); music (M Mus). Electronic applications accepted.

College of Humanities and Social Sciences *Degree program information:* Part-time programs available. Offers anthropology (MA); communication sciences and disorders (MA); English (MA); exercise science (MS); experimental psychology (MS); history (MA); humanities and social sciences (M Ed, MA, MS); mental health counseling (MS); political science (MA); school counseling (M Ed); sport psychology (MS). Electronic applications accepted.

College of Sciences and Technology Offers biology (MS); chemistry (MS); computer science (MS); geology (MS); mathematics (MS); natural science/science education (M Ed); sciences and technology (M Ed, MS). Electronic applications accepted.

Huxley College of the Environment *Degree program information:* Part-time programs available. Offers environment (M Ed, MS); environmental education (M Ed); environmental science (MS); geography (MS); marine and estuarine science (MS). Electronic applications accepted.

Woodring College of Education *Degree program information:* Part-time programs available. Postbaccalaureate distance learning degree programs offered (minimal on-campus study). Offers continuing and college education (M Ed); education (M Ed, MA, MIT); educational administration (M Ed); elementary education (M Ed); rehabilitation counseling (MA); secondary education (MIT); special education (M Ed); student affairs administration (M Ed). Electronic applications accepted.

WESTFIELD STATE COLLEGE, Westfield, MA 01086

General Information State-supported, coed, comprehensive institution. *Enrollment:* 5,548 graduate, professional, and undergraduate students; 37 full-time matriculated graduate/professional students (29 women), 239 part-time matriculated graduate/professional students (159 women). *Enrollment by degree level:* 245 master's, 31 other advanced degrees. *Graduate faculty:* 21 full-time (9 women), 29 part-time/adjunct (10 women). *Graduate housing:* On-campus housing not available. *Student services:* Career counseling, exercise/wellness program, free psychological counseling, low-cost health insurance, multicultural affairs office. *Library facilities:* Governor Joseph B. Ely Library. *Online resources:* library catalog, web page. *Collection:* 150,121 titles, 4,426 audiovisual materials.

Computer facilities: Computer purchase and lease plans are available. 275 computers available on campus for general student use. A campuswide network can be accessed from student residence rooms and from off campus. Online class registration, online transcripts and billing information are available. *Web address:* http://www.wsc.ma.edu/.

General Application Contact: Michelle Janke, Admissions Coordinator, 413-572-8022, Fax: 413-572-5227, E-mail: mjanke@wsc.ma.edu.

GRADUATE UNITS

Division of Graduate and Continuing Education Students: 37 full-time (29 women), 239 part-time (159 women); includes 3 minority (all African Americans). Average age 32. *Faculty:* 21 full-time (9 women), 29 part-time/adjunct (10 women). Expenses: Contact institution. *Financial support:* In 2008–09, 11 research assistantships with full and partial tuition reimburse-

Westfield State College (continued)

ments (averaging $1,600 per year) were awarded; teaching assistantships, career-related internships or fieldwork, Federal Work-Study, and tuition waivers (full and partial) also available. Support available to part-time students. Financial award application deadline: 4/1; financial award applicants required to submit CSS PROFILE. In 2008, 94 master's, 3 other advanced degrees awarded. *Degree program information:* Part-time and evening/weekend programs available. Offers applied behavior analysis (MA); criminal justice (MS); early childhood education (M Ed); elementary education (M Ed); English (MA); history (M Ed); mental health counseling (MA); occupational education (M Ed, CAGS); physical education (M Ed); reading (M Ed); school administration (M Ed, CAGS); school guidance (MA); secondary education (M Ed); special education (M Ed); technology for educators (M Ed). *Application deadline:* Applications are processed on a rolling basis. *Application fee:* $30. *Application Contact:* Michelle Janke, Admissions Coordinator, 413-572-8022, Fax: 413-572-5227, E-mail: mjanke@wsc.ma.edu. *Dean of Graduate and Continuing Education,* Dr. Kimberly Tobin, 413-572-8805, Fax: 413-572-5227, E-mail: ktobin@wsc.ma.edu.

WEST LIBERTY STATE UNIVERSITY, West Liberty, WV 26074

General Information State-supported, coed, comprehensive institution.

GRADUATE UNITS

School of Education Offers education (MA Ed). Electronic applications accepted.

WESTMINSTER CHOIR COLLEGE OF RIDER UNIVERSITY, Princeton, NJ 08540-3899

General Information Independent, coed, comprehensive institution. *Graduate housing:* On-campus housing not available.

GRADUATE UNITS

Graduate Programs in Music *Degree program information:* Part-time programs available. Offers choral conducting (MM); composition (MM); music education (MM, MME); organ performance (MM); piano accompanying and coaching (MM); piano pedagogy and performance (MM); piano performance (MM); sacred music (MM); vocal pedagogy and performance (MM); vocal training (MVP). Electronic applications accepted.

WESTMINSTER COLLEGE, New Wilmington, PA 16172-0001

General Information Independent-religious, coed, comprehensive institution. *Graduate housing:* On-campus housing not available.

GRADUATE UNITS

Programs in Education *Degree program information:* Part-time and evening/weekend programs available. Offers administration (M Ed, Certificate); general education (M Ed); guidance and counseling (M Ed, Certificate); reading (M Ed, Certificate).

WESTMINSTER COLLEGE, Salt Lake City, UT 84105-3697

General Information Independent, coed, comprehensive institution. *Enrollment:* 2,863 graduate, professional, and undergraduate students; 355 full-time matriculated graduate/professional students (164 women), 373 part-time matriculated graduate/professional students (147 women). *Enrollment by degree level:* 713 master's, 15 other advanced degrees. *Graduate faculty:* 51 full-time (33 women), 14 part-time/adjunct (5 women). *Tuition:* Part-time $840 per credit hour. Tuition and fees vary according to course load and program. *Graduate housing:* Room and/or apartments available on a first-come, first-served basis to single students; on-campus housing not available to married students. Typical cost: $3706 per year ($6672 including board). Room and board charges vary according to board plan and housing facility selected. *Student services:* Campus employment opportunities, campus safety program, career counseling, exercise/wellness program, free psychological counseling, grant writing training, international student services, low-cost health insurance, multicultural affairs office, services for students with disabilities, teacher training, writing training. *Library facilities:* Giovale Library plus 1 other. *Online resources:* library catalog, web page, access to other libraries' catalogs. *Collection:* 181,319 titles, 9,857 serial subscriptions, 6,154 audiovisual materials. *Research affiliation:* Key Bank (Entrepreneurship), Zions Bank (Entrepreneurship).

Computer facilities: 403 computers available on campus for general student use. A campuswide network can be accessed from student residence rooms and from off campus. Online class registration is available. *Web address:* http://www.westminstercollege.edu/.

General Application Contact: Joel Bauman, Vice President of Enrollment Services, 801-832-2200, Fax: 801-832-3101, E-mail: admission@westminstercollege.edu.

GRADUATE UNITS

The Bill and Vieve Gore School of Business Students: 203 full-time (49 women), 238 part-time (56 women); includes 35 minority (3 African Americans, 1 American Indian/Alaska Native, 15 Asian Americans or Pacific Islanders, 16 Hispanic Americans), 12 international. Average age 31. 324 applicants, 50% accepted, 134 enrolled. *Faculty:* 30 full-time (11 women), 15 part-time/adjunct (5 women). Expenses: Contact institution. *Financial support:* In 2008–09, 236 students received support. Career-related internships or fieldwork and tuition reimbursement available. Support available to part-time students. Financial award applicants required to submit FAFSA. In 2008, 141 master's, 24 other advanced degrees awarded. *Degree program information:* Part-time and evening/weekend programs available. Offers business administration (MBA, Certificate); technology management (MBATM). *Application deadline:* Applications are processed on a rolling basis. *Application fee:* $40. Electronic applications accepted. *Application Contact:* Joel Bauman, Vice President of Enrollment Services, 801-832-2200, Fax: 801-832-3101, E-mail: admission@westminstercollege.edu. *Dean,* John Groesbeck, 801-832-2600, Fax: 801-832-3106, E-mail: jgroesbeck@westminstercollege.edu.

Program in Counseling Psychology Students: 23 full-time (18 women); includes 4 minority (1 American Indian/Alaska Native, 1 Asian American or Pacific Islander, 2 Hispanic Americans). Average age 30. 35 applicants, 66% accepted, 11 enrolled. *Faculty:* 5 full-time (all women), 4 part-time/adjunct (3 women). Expenses: Contact institution. *Financial support:* In 2008–09, 18 students received support. Career-related internships or fieldwork available. Support available to part-time students. Financial award applicants required to submit FAFSA. *Degree program information:* Part-time and evening/weekend programs available. Offers counseling psychology (MSPC). *Application deadline:* For fall admission, 2/6 priority date for domestic and international students. Applications are processed on a rolling basis. *Application fee:* $40. Electronic applications accepted. *Application Contact:* Joel Bauman, Vice President of Enrollment Services, 801-832-2200, Fax: 801-832-3101, E-mail: admission@westminstercollege.edu. *Director,* Janine Wanlass, 801-832-2428, E-mail: jwanlass@westminstercollege.edu.

Program in Professional Communication Students: 16 full-time (13 women), 53 part-time (40 women); includes 4 minority (1 American Indian/Alaska Native, 2 Asian Americans or Pacific Islanders, 1 Hispanic American), 2 international. Average age 33. 36 applicants, 83% accepted, 24 enrolled. *Faculty:* 7 full-time (3 women), 4 part-time/adjunct (2 women). Expenses: Contact institution. *Financial support:* In 2008–09, 32 students received support. Career-related internships or fieldwork and tuition reimbursement available. Support available to part-time students. Financial award applicants required to submit FAFSA. In 2008, 15 master's awarded. *Degree program information:* Part-time and evening/weekend programs available. Offers professional communication (MPC). *Application deadline:* For fall admission, 8/1 priority date for domestic students. Applications are processed on a rolling basis. *Application fee:* $40. Electronic applications accepted. *Application Contact:* Joel Bauman, Vice President of Enrollment Services, 801-832-2200, Fax: 801-832-3101, E-mail: admission@westminstercollege.edu. *Director,* Dr. Helen Hodgson, 801-832-2821, Fax: 801-832-3102, E-mail: hhodgson@westminstercollege.edu.

School of Education Students: 59 full-time (45 women), 31 part-time (20 women); includes 8 minority (2 African Americans, 3 Asian Americans or Pacific Islanders, 3 Hispanic Americans), 2 international. Average age 32. 97 applicants, 87% accepted, 59 enrolled. *Faculty:* 13 full-time (11 women), 26 part-time/adjunct (22 women). Expenses: Contact institution. *Financial support:* In 2008–09, 55 students received support. Career-related internships or fieldwork and tuition reimbursement available. Support available to part-time students. Financial award applicants required to submit FAFSA. In 2008, 32 master's awarded. *Degree program information:* Part-time and evening/weekend programs available. Offers education (M Ed, MAT). *Application deadline:* Applications are processed on a rolling basis. *Application fee:* $40. Electronic applications accepted. *Application Contact:* Joel Bauman, Vice President of Enrollment Services, 801-832-2200, Fax: 801-832-3101, E-mail: admission@westminstercollege.edu. *Interim Dean,* Robert Shaw, 801-832-2470, Fax: 801-832-3105.

School of Nursing and Health Sciences Students: 51 full-time (37 women), 39 part-time (23 women); includes 3 minority (all Asian Americans or Pacific Islanders), 1 international. Average age 34. 138 applicants, 54% accepted, 59 enrolled. *Faculty:* 12 full-time (7 women). Expenses: Contact institution. *Financial support:* In 2008–09, 69 students received support. Career-related internships or fieldwork and tuition reimbursement available. Support available to part-time students. Financial award applicants required to submit FAFSA. In 2008, 14 master's awarded. *Degree program information:* Part-time and evening/weekend programs available. Offers family nurse practitioner (MSN); nurse anesthesia (MSNA); nurse education (MSNED); nursing (MSN); nursing education (MSN); public health (MPH). *Application deadline:* Applications are processed on a rolling basis. *Application fee:* $40. Electronic applications accepted. *Application Contact:* Joel Bauman, Vice President of Enrollment Services, 801-832-2200, Fax: 801-832-3101, E-mail: admission@westminstercollege.edu. *Dean,* Dr. Sheryl Steadman, 801-832-2164, Fax: 801-832-3110, E-mail: ssteadman@westminstercollege.edu.

WESTMINSTER SEMINARY CALIFORNIA, Escondido, CA 92027-4128

General Information Independent-religious, coed, primarily men, graduate-only institution. *Graduate housing:* On-campus housing not available.

GRADUATE UNITS

Programs in Theology *Degree program information:* Part-time and evening/weekend programs available. Offers Biblical studies (MA); historical theology (MA); theological studies (M Div, MA).

WESTMINSTER THEOLOGICAL SEMINARY, Philadelphia, PA 19118

General Information Independent-religious, coed, primarily men, graduate-only institution. *Graduate housing:* Room and/or apartments available on a first-come, first-served basis to single students; on-campus housing not available to married students.

GRADUATE UNITS

Graduate and Professional Programs *Degree program information:* Part-time programs available. Offers apologetics (Th M); Biblical and urban studies (Certificate); Biblical counseling (MA); biblical studies (MAR); Christian studies (Certificate); church history (Th M); counseling (M Div); general studies (M Div, MAR); hermeneutics and Bible interpretations (PhD); historical and theological studies (PhD); historical theology (Th M); New Testament (Th M); Old Testament (Th M); pastoral counseling (D Min); pastoral ministry (M Div, D Min); systematic theology (Th M); theological studies (MAR); urban missions (M Div, MA, MAR, D Min).

WEST TEXAS A&M UNIVERSITY, Canyon, TX 79016-0001

General Information State-supported, coed, comprehensive institution. *Graduate housing:* Room and/or apartments available on a first-come, first-served basis to single students; on-campus housing not available to married students. *Research affiliation:* Pantex (chemistry), Agricultural Research (agricultural), Owens Corning (sports exercise), Agriculture Experiment Station (agriculture), Engineering Experiment Station (math/science).

GRADUATE UNITS

College of Agriculture, Nursing, and Natural Sciences *Degree program information:* Part-time and evening/weekend programs available. Offers agricultural business and economics (MS); agriculture (PhD); agriculture, nursing, and natural sciences (MS, MSN, PhD); animal science (MS); biology (MS); chemistry (MS); engineering technology (MS); environmental science (MS); mathematics (MS); nursing (MSN); plant science (MS). Electronic applications accepted.

College of Business *Degree program information:* Part-time and evening/weekend programs available. Postbaccalaureate distance learning degree programs offered (minimal on-campus study). Offers accounting (MP Acc); accounting/business administration (MPA); business (MBA, MP Acc, MPA, MS); business administration (MBA); finance and economics (MS); professional accounting (MPA). Electronic applications accepted.

College of Education and Social Sciences *Degree program information:* Part-time and evening/weekend programs available. Postbaccalaureate distance learning degree programs offered (minimal on-campus study). Offers administration (M Ed); counseling education (M Ed); criminal justice (MA); curriculum and instruction (M Ed); education and social sciences (M Ed, MA, MS); educational diagnostician (M Ed); educational technology (M Ed); history (MA); political science (MA); professional counseling (MA); psychology (MA); reading (M Ed); special education (M Ed); sports and exercise science (MS). Electronic applications accepted.

College of Fine Arts and Humanities *Degree program information:* Part-time and evening/weekend programs available. Offers art (MA); communication (MA); communication disorders (MS); English (MA); fine arts and humanities (MA, MFA, MM, MS); music (MA); performance (MM); studio art (MFA). Electronic applications accepted.

Program in Interdisciplinary Studies *Degree program information:* Part-time and evening/weekend programs available. Postbaccalaureate distance learning degree programs offered (minimal on-campus study). Offers interdisciplinary studies (MA, MS). Electronic applications accepted.

WEST VIRGINIA SCHOOL OF OSTEOPATHIC MEDICINE, Lewisburg, WV 24901-1196

General Information State-supported, coed, graduate-only institution. *Enrollment by degree level:* 598 first professional. *Graduate faculty:* 57 full-time (23 women), 93 part-time/adjunct (48 women). *Graduate housing:* On-campus housing not available. *Student services:* Campus employment opportunities, campus safety program, career counseling, exercise/wellness program, multicultural affairs office, services for students with disabilities. *Library facilities:* WVSOM Library. *Online resources:* library catalog, web page. *Collection:* 26,132 titles, 468 serial subscriptions, 1,912 audiovisual materials.

Computer facilities: 13 computers available on campus for general student use. A campuswide network can be accessed from off campus. *Web address:* http://www.wvsom.edu.

General Application Contact: Donna S. Varney, Director of Admissions, 304-647-6373, Fax: 304-647-6384, E-mail: dvarney@wvsom.edu.

GRADUATE UNITS

Professional Program Students: 598 full-time (294 women); includes 99 minority (7 African Americans, 3 American Indian/Alaska Native, 76 Asian Americans or Pacific Islanders, 13 Hispanic Americans). Average age 27. *Faculty:* 57 full-time (23 women), 93 part-time/adjunct (48 women). Expenses: Contact institution. *Financial support:* Teaching assistantships with full and partial tuition reimbursements, Federal Work-Study, scholarships/grants, tuition waivers (full), and unspecified assistantships available. Financial award application deadline: 4/1; financial award applicants required to submit FAFSA. Offers osteopathic medicine (DO). *Application deadline:* For fall admission, 2/15 for domestic students. Applications are processed on a rolling basis. *Application fee:* $155. Electronic applications accepted. *Application Contact:* Donna S. Varney, Director of Admissions, 304-647-6373, Fax: 304-647-6384, E-mail: dvarney@wvsom.edu. *President,* Dr. Richard Rafes, JD, 304-645-6270 Ext. 200, Fax: 304-645-4859.

WEST VIRGINIA STATE UNIVERSITY, Institute, WV 25112-1000

General Information State-supported, coed, comprehensive institution. *Graduate housing:* Rooms and/or apartments available on a first-come, first-served basis to single and married students.

GRADUATE UNITS

Graduate Programs Offers biotechnology (MA, MS); media studies (MA).

WEST VIRGINIA UNIVERSITY, Morgantown, WV 26506

General Information State-supported, coed, university. CGS member. *Graduate housing:* Rooms and/or apartments available on a first-come, first-served basis to single and married students. Housing application deadline: 1/22. *Research affiliation:* Federal Bureau of Investigation (FBI) (biometrics research), NASA IV and V Center (GOCO addressing software verification/validation), Research Partnership for an Energy Secure America (energy research), Florida A & M (plasma physics), University of Pittsburgh and Carnegie Mellon University (energy research), National Energy Technology Laboratory (fossil energy and environmental research).

GRADUATE UNITS

College of Business and Economics *Degree program information:* Part-time programs available. Postbaccalaureate distance learning degree programs offered. Offers business administration (MBA); business and economics (MA, MBA, MPA, MSIR, PhD); industrial relations (MSIR). Electronic applications accepted.

Division of Accounting *Degree program information:* Part-time and evening/weekend programs available. Offers accounting (MPA). Electronic applications accepted.

Division of Economics and Finance Offers business analysis (MA); developmental financial economics (PhD); environmental and resource economics (PhD); international economics (PhD); mathematical economics (MA); monetary economics (PhD); public finance (PhD); public policy (MA); regional and urban economics (PhD); statistics and economics (MA). Electronic applications accepted.

College of Creative Arts *Degree program information:* Part-time programs available. Offers acting (MFA); art education (MA); art history (MA); ceramics (MFA); creative arts (MA, MFA, MM, DMA, PhD); graphic design (MFA); music composition (MM, DMA); music education (MM, PhD); music history (MM); music performance (MM, DMA); music theory (MM); painting (MFA); printmaking (MFA); sculpture (MFA); studio art (MA); theatre design/technology (MFA).

College of Engineering and Mineral Resources *Degree program information:* Part-time programs available. Offers aerospace engineering (MSAE, PhD); chemical engineering (MS Ch E, PhD); civil engineering (MSCE, MSE, PhD); computer engineering (PhD); computer science (MSCS, PhD); electrical engineering (MSEE, PhD); engineering (MSE); engineering and mineral resources (MS, MS Ch E, MS Min E, MSAE, MSCE, MSCS, MSE, MSEE, MSIE, MSME, MSPNGE, MSSE, PhD); industrial engineering (MSE, MSIE, PhD); industrial hygiene (MS); mechanical engineering (MSME, PhD); mining engineering (MS Min E, PhD); occupational safety and health (PhD); petroleum and natural gas engineering (MSPNGE, PhD); safety management (MS); software engineering (MSSE).

College of Human Resources and Education *Degree program information:* Part-time and evening/weekend programs available. Postbaccalaureate distance learning degree programs offered (no on-campus study). Offers audiology (Au D); autism spectrum disorder (5-adult) (MA); autism spectrum disorder (K-6) (MA); child development and family studies (MA); counseling (MA); counseling psychology (PhD); curriculum and instruction (Ed D); early intervention/early childhood special education (MA); educational leadership (Ed D); educational psychology (MA); elementary education (MA); gifted education (1-12) (MA); higher education administration (MA); higher education curriculum and teaching (MA); human resources and education (MA, MS, Au D, Ed D, PhD); instructional design and technology (MA, Ed D); low vision (PreK-adult) (MA); multicategorical special education (5-adult) (MA); multicategorical special education (K-6) (MA); public school administration (MA); reading (MA); rehabilitation counseling (MS); secondary education (MA); severe/multiple disabilities (K-adult) (MA); special education (MA, Ed D); speech-language pathology (MS); vision impairments (PreK-adult) (MA). Electronic applications accepted.

College of Law *Degree program information:* Part-time programs available. Offers law (JD). Electronic applications accepted.

Davis College of Agriculture, Forestry and Consumer Sciences *Degree program information:* Part-time programs available. Offers agricultural and extension education (MS, PhD); agricultural and resource economics (MS); agricultural sciences (PhD); agriculture, forestry and consumer sciences (M Agr, MS, MSF, PhD); agronomy (MS); animal and food sciences (PhD); animal and nutritional sciences (MS); animal breeding (MS, PhD); biochemical and molecular genetics (MS, PhD); breeding (MS); cytogenetics (MS, PhD); descriptive embryology (MS, PhD); developmental genetics (MS); entomology (MS); environmental microbiology (MS); experimental morphogenesis/teratology (MS); food sciences (MS); forest resource science (PhD); forestry (MSF); horticulture (MS); human and community development (PhD); human genetics (MS, PhD); immunogenetics (MS, PhD); life cycles of animals and plants (MS, PhD); molecular aspects of development (MS, PhD); mutagenesis (MS, PhD); natural resource economics (PhD); nutrition (MS); oncology (MS, PhD); physiology (MS); plant and soil sciences (PhD); plant genetics (MS, PhD); plant pathology (MS); population and quantitative genetics (MS, PhD); production management (MS); recreation, parks and tourism resources (MS); regeneration (MS, PhD); reproduction (MS); reproductive physiology (MS, PhD); resource management (PhD); resource management and sustainable development (PhD); teaching vocational-agriculture (MS); teratology (PhD); toxicology (MS, PhD); wildlife and fisheries resources (MS). Electronic applications accepted.

Eberly College of Arts and Sciences *Degree program information:* Part-time and evening/weekend programs available. Postbaccalaureate distance learning degree programs offered (minimal on-campus study). Offers African history (MA, PhD); African-American history (MA, PhD); American history (MA, PhD); American public policy and politics (MA); analytical chemistry (MS, PhD); Appalachian/regional history (MA, PhD); applied mathematics (MS, PhD); applied physics (MS, PhD); arts and sciences (MA, MALS, MFA, MLS, MPA, MS, MSW, PhD); astrophysics (MS, PhD); behavior analysis (PhD); cell and molecular biology (MS, PhD); chemical physics (MS, PhD); clinical psychology (MA, PhD); communication in instruction (MA); communication studies (PhD); communication theory and research (MA); condensed matter physics (MS, PhD); corporate and organizational communication (MA); creative writing (MFA); development psychology (PhD); discrete mathematics (PhD); East Asian history (MA, PhD); elementary particle physics (MS, PhD); energy and environmental resources (MA); English (MA, PhD); environmental and evolutionary biology (MS, PhD); European history (MA, PhD); forensic biology (MS, PhD); French (MA); genomic biology (MS, PhD); geographic information systems (PhD); geography (MA, PhD); geography-regional development (PhD); geology (MS, PhD); geomorphology (MS, PhD); geophysics (MS, PhD); GIS/cartographic analysis (MA); history of science and technology (MA, PhD); hydrogeology (MS, PhD); inorganic chemistry (MS, PhD); interdisciplinary mathematics (MS); international and comparative public policy and politics (MA); Latin American history (MA); liberal studies (MALS); linguistics (MA); literary/cultural studies (MA, PhD); materials physics (MS, PhD); mathematics for secondary education (MS); neurobiology (MS, PhD); organic chemistry (MS, PhD); paleontology (MS, PhD); petroleum geology (PhD); petrology (MS, PhD); physical chemistry (MS, PhD); plasma physics (MS, PhD); political science (PhD); psychology (MS); public policy analysis (PhD); pure mathematics (MS); regional development (MA); solid state physics (MS, PhD); Spanish (MA); statistical physics (MS, PhD); statistics (MS); stratigraphy (MS, PhD); structure (MS, PhD); teaching English to speakers of other languages (MA); theoretical chemistry (MS, PhD); theoretical physics (MS, PhD); writing (MA). Electronic applications accepted.

School of Applied Social Sciences *Degree program information:* Part-time programs available. Offers aging and health care (MSW); applied social research (MA); applied social sciences (MA, MLS, MPA, MSW); children and families (MSW); community mental health (MSW); community organization and social administration (MSW); direct (clinical) social work practice (MSW); legal studies (MLS); public administration (MPA).

Perley Isaac Reed School of Journalism *Degree program information:* Part-time programs available. Postbaccalaureate distance learning degree programs offered (no on-campus study). Offers integrated marketing communications (MS); journalism (MSJ). MS program taught exclusively online. Electronic applications accepted.

School of Dentistry Offers dentistry (DDS, MS); endodontics (MS); orthodontics (MS); prosthodontics (MS).

Division of Dental Hygiene *Degree program information:* Part-time programs available. Offers dental hygiene (MS).

School of Medicine *Degree program information:* Part-time and evening/weekend programs available. Offers community health/preventative medicine (MPH); medicine (MD, MOT, MPH, MS, DPT, PhD); occupational therapy (MOT); physical therapy (DPT); public health (MPH); public health sciences (PhD).

Graduate Programs at the Health Sciences Center *Degree program information:* Part-time and evening/weekend programs available. Postbaccalaureate distance learning degree programs offered (minimal on-campus study). Offers biochemistry and molecular biology (MS, PhD); cancer cell biology (PhD); cellular and integrative physiology (MS, PhD); exercise physiology (MS, PhD); health sciences (MS, PhD); immunology and microbial pathogenesis (MS, PhD); neuroscience (PhD); pharmaceutical and pharmacological sciences (MS, PhD).

School of Nursing *Degree program information:* Part-time programs available. Postbaccalaureate distance learning degree programs offered (minimal on-campus study). Offers nurse practitioner (Certificate); nursing (MSN, DNP, PhD). Electronic applications accepted.

School of Pharmacy Offers administrative pharmacy (PhD); behavioral pharmacy (MS, PhD); biopharmaceutics/pharmacokinetics (MS, PhD); clinical pharmacy (Pharm D); industrial pharmacy (MS); medicinal chemistry (MS, PhD); pharmaceutical chemistry (MS, PhD); pharmaceutics (MS, PhD); pharmacology and toxicology (MS); pharmacy (MS); pharmacy administration (MS).

School of Physical Education Offers athletic coaching education (MS); athletic training (MS); physical education/teacher education (MS, PhD); sport and exercise psychology (PhD); sport management (MS). Electronic applications accepted.

WEST VIRGINIA UNIVERSITY INSTITUTE OF TECHNOLOGY, Montgomery, WV 25136

General Information State-supported, coed, comprehensive institution. *Graduate housing:* Room and/or apartments available to single students; on-campus housing not available to married students.

GRADUATE UNITS

College of Engineering *Degree program information:* Part-time programs available. Offers control systems engineering (MS); engineering (MS).

WEST VIRGINIA WESLEYAN COLLEGE, Buckhannon, WV 26201

General Information Independent-religious, coed, comprehensive institution. *Graduate housing:* Room and/or apartments available to single students; on-campus housing not available to married students.

GRADUATE UNITS

Department of Business and Economics *Degree program information:* Part-time and evening/weekend programs available. Offers business and economics (MBA).

WHEATON COLLEGE, Wheaton, IL 60187-5593

General Information Independent-religious, coed, comprehensive institution. CGS member. *Graduate housing:* Rooms and/or apartments available on a first-come, first-served basis to single and married students. Housing application deadline: 4/1.

GRADUATE UNITS

Graduate School Offers biblical and theological studies (MA, PhD); biblical archaeology (MA); biblical exegesis (MA); biblical studies (MA); Christian formation and ministry (MA); clinical psychology (MA, Psy D); counseling ministries (MA); elementary level (MAT); evangelism (MA); general history of Christianity (MA); historical and systematic theology (MA); intercultural studies (MA); intercultural studies/teaching English as a second language (MA); missions (MA); religion in American life (MA); secondary level (MAT); teaching English as a second language (Certificate).

WHEELING JESUIT UNIVERSITY, Wheeling, WV 26003-6295

General Information Independent-religious, coed, comprehensive institution. *Graduate housing:* Rooms and/or apartments available on a first-come, first-served basis to single and married students.

GRADUATE UNITS

Center for Professional and Graduate Studies *Degree program information:* Part-time and evening/weekend programs available. Offers organizational leadership (MSOL).

Department of Business *Degree program information:* Part-time and evening/weekend programs available. Offers accounting (MS); business administration (MBA). Electronic applications accepted.

Department of Nursing *Degree program information:* Part-time and evening/weekend programs available. Postbaccalaureate distance learning degree programs offered (minimal on-campus study). Offers nursing (MSN). Electronic applications accepted.

Department of Physical Therapy Postbaccalaureate distance learning degree programs offered (no on-campus study). Offers physical therapy (DPT). Electronic applications accepted.

WHEELOCK COLLEGE, Boston, MA 02215-4176

General Information Independent, coed, primarily women, comprehensive institution. *Graduate housing:* Room and/or apartments available on a first-come, first-served basis to single students; on-campus housing not available to married students. Housing application deadline: 5/1.

GRADUATE UNITS

Graduate Programs *Degree program information:* Part-time and evening/weekend programs available. Postbaccalaureate distance learning degree programs offered (minimal on-campus study). Offers education (MS, MSW).

Division of Arts and Sciences Offers human development (MS). Electronic applications accepted.

Division of Child and Family Studies *Degree program information:* Part-time programs available. Postbaccalaureate distance learning degree programs offered (minimal on-campus study). Offers family studies (MS); family support and parent education (MS); family, culture, and society (MS). Electronic applications accepted.

Division of Education Postbaccalaureate distance learning degree programs offered (minimal on-campus study). Offers early childhood education (MS); education leadership (MS); elementary education (MS); language, literacy, and reading (MS); teaching students with moderate disabilities (MS). Electronic applications accepted.

Division of Social Work Offers social work (MSW). Electronic applications accepted.

WHITTIER COLLEGE, Whittier, CA 90608-0634

General Information Independent, coed, comprehensive institution. *Graduate housing:* On-campus housing not available.

GRADUATE UNITS

Graduate Programs *Degree program information:* Part-time and evening/weekend programs available. Offers educational administration (MA Ed); elementary education (MA Ed); secondary education (MA Ed).

Whittier Law School *Degree program information:* Part-time and evening/weekend programs available. Offers foreign legal studies (LL M); law (JD). Electronic applications accepted.

WHITWORTH UNIVERSITY, Spokane, WA 99251-0001

General Information Independent-religious, coed, comprehensive institution. *Graduate housing:* Room and/or apartments available on a first-come, first-served basis to single students; on-campus housing not available to married students. Housing application deadline: 5/1.

GRADUATE UNITS

School of Education *Degree program information:* Part-time and evening/weekend programs available. Postbaccalaureate distance learning degree programs offered (minimal on-campus study). Offers education (M Ed, MAT, MIT).

Graduate Studies in Education *Degree program information:* Part-time and evening/weekend programs available. Offers administration (M Ed); counseling (M Ed); elementary education (M Ed); gifted and talented (MAT); school counselors (M Ed); secondary education (M Ed); social agency/church setting (M Ed); special education (MAT); teaching (MIT).

School of Global Commerce and Management Students: 38 full-time (17 women), 5 part-time (3 women); includes 8 minority (7 Asian Americans or Pacific Islanders, 1 Hispanic American), 7 international. Average age 30. 43 applicants, 58% accepted, 20 enrolled. *Faculty:* 6 full-time (2 women), 13 part-time/adjunct (3 women). Expenses: Contact institution. *Financial support:* In 2008–09, 9 students received support; fellowships with tuition reimbursements available, career-related internships or fieldwork, Federal Work-Study, institutionally sponsored loans, and scholarships/grants available. Support available to part-time students. Financial award application deadline: 3/1. In 2008, 16 master's awarded. *Degree program information:* Part-time and evening/weekend programs available. Offers business administration (MBA); global commerce and management (MBA, MIM); international management (MIM). *Application deadline:* For fall admission, 8/20 priority date for domestic students; for spring admission, 1/8 priority date for domestic students. Applications are processed on a rolling basis. *Application fee:* $35. Electronic applications accepted. *Application Contact:* Bonnie Wakefield, Assistant Director, Graduate Studies in Business, 509-777-4606, Fax: 509-777-3723, E-mail: bwakefield@whitworth.edu. *Director, Graduate Studies in Business,* Mary Alberts, 509-777-4280, Fax: 509-777-3723, E-mail: malberts@whitworth.edu.

WICHITA STATE UNIVERSITY, Wichita, KS 67260

General Information State-supported, coed, university. CGS member. *Graduate housing:* Rooms and/or apartments available on a first-come, first-served basis to single and married students. *Research affiliation:* Boeing Aircraft Company (aeronautical engineering), Raytheon Aircraft Company (aeronautical engineering), Cessna Aircraft Company (aeronautical engineering), Bombardier (aeronautical engineering), Cisco Systems (computer engineering), Sikorsky Aircraft Corporation (aeronautical engineering).

GRADUATE UNITS

Graduate School *Degree program information:* Part-time and evening/weekend programs available. Electronic applications accepted.

College of Education *Degree program information:* Part-time and evening/weekend programs available. Offers communications sciences (MA, PhD); counseling (M Ed); curriculum and instruction (M Ed); education (M Ed, MA, Ed D, PhD, Ed S); education administration (M Ed, Ed D); educational psychology (M Ed); physical education (M Ed); school psychology (Ed S); special education (M Ed); sports administration (M Ed). Electronic applications accepted.

College of Engineering *Degree program information:* Part-time and evening/weekend programs available. Offers aerospace engineering (MS, PhD); electrical engineering (MS, PhD); engineering (MEM, MS, PhD); industrial and manufacturing engineering (MEM, MS, PhD); mechanical engineering (MS, PhD). Electronic applications accepted.

College of Fine Arts *Degree program information:* Part-time programs available. Offers art education (MA); fine arts (MA, MFA, MM, MME); music (MM); music education (MME); studio arts (MFA). Electronic applications accepted.

College of Health Professions *Degree program information:* Part-time programs available. Offers clinical nurse specialist (MSN); health professions (MPH, MPT, MSN); nurse midwifery (MSN); nurse practitioner (MSN); nursing and health care systems administration (MSN); physical therapy (MPT); public health (MPH). Electronic applications accepted.

Fairmount College of Liberal Arts and Sciences *Degree program information:* Part-time and evening/weekend programs available. Offers anthropology (MA); applied mathematics (PhD); biological sciences (MS); chemistry (MS, PhD); communication (MA); community/clinical psychology (PhD); computer science (MS); creative writing (MA, MFA); criminal justice (MA); English (MA, MFA); environmental science (MS); geology (MS); gerontology (MA); history (MA); human factors (PhD); liberal arts and sciences (MA, MFA, MPA, MS, MSW, PhD); mathematics (MS); physics (MS); political science (MA); psychology (MA); public administration (MPA); social work (MSW); sociology (MA); Spanish (MA); statistics (MS). Electronic applications accepted.

W. Frank Barton School of Business *Degree program information:* Part-time and evening/weekend programs available. Offers accountancy (MPA); business (EMBA, MBA, MS); business economics (MA); economic analysis (MA); economics (MA); professional accountancy (MPA). Electronic applications accepted.

WIDENER UNIVERSITY, Chester, PA 19013-5792

General Information Independent, coed, comprehensive institution. CGS member. *Enrollment:* 6,601 graduate, professional, and undergraduate students; 2,040 full-time matriculated graduate/professional students (1,074 women), 1,133 part-time matriculated graduate/professional students (772 women). *Enrollment by degree level:* 1,406 first professional, 927 master's, 732 doctoral, 108 other advanced degrees. *Graduate faculty:* 194 full-time (97 women), 152 part-time/adjunct (61 women). *Graduate housing:* Rooms and/or apartments available on a first-come, first-served basis to single students and available to married students. Housing application deadline: 5/30. *Student services:* Campus employment opportunities, career counseling, child daycare facilities, exercise/wellness program, free psychological counseling, international student services, multicultural affairs office, teacher training, writing training. *Library facilities:* Wolfgram Memorial Library. *Online resources:* library catalog, web page, access to other libraries' catalogs. *Collection:* 218,284 titles, 2,335 serial subscriptions. *Research affiliation:* Small Business Administration, Riverfront Development Corporation (engineering, management), Advanced Technology Center (engineering).

Computer facilities: 345 computers available on campus for general student use. A campuswide network can be accessed from student residence rooms and from off campus. Online class registration is available. *Web address:* http://www.widener.edu/.

General Application Contact: Dr. Roberta Nolan, Assistant to Associate Provost for Graduate Studies, 610-499-4125, Fax: 610-499-4676, E-mail: gradmc@mail.widener.edu.

GRADUATE UNITS

College of Arts and Sciences Students: 4 full-time (2 women), 56 part-time (38 women); includes 14 minority (12 African Americans, 2 Asian Americans or Pacific Islanders). Average age 31. 45 applicants, 89% accepted. *Faculty:* 9 full-time (2 women), 8 part-time/adjunct (1 woman). Expenses: Contact institution. *Financial support:* Career-related internships or fieldwork and institutionally sponsored loans available. Support available to part-time students. Financial award application deadline: 4/1. In 2008, 12 master's awarded. *Degree program information:* Part-time and evening/weekend programs available. Offers arts and sciences (MA, MPA); criminal justice (MA); liberal studies (MA); public administration (MPA). *Application deadline:* Applications are processed on a rolling basis. *Application fee:* $25 ($300 for international students). *Application Contact:* Dr. Roberta Nolan, Assistant to Associate Provost for Graduate Studies, 610-499-4125, Fax: 610-499-4676, E-mail: gradmc@mail.widener.edu. *Dean,* Dr. Matthew Poslusny, 610-499-4007, E-mail: mposlusny@widener.edu.

Graduate Programs in Engineering Students: 22 full-time (3 women), 33 part-time (1 woman); includes 1 minority (American Indian/Alaska Native), 26 international. Average age 29. 439 applicants, 46% accepted, 23 enrolled. *Faculty:* 10 full-time (1 woman), 4 part-time/adjunct (0 women). Expenses: Contact institution. *Financial support:* In 2008–09, 5 teaching assistantships with partial tuition reimbursements (averaging $8,000 per year) were awarded; research assistantships, unspecified assistantships also available. Financial award application deadline: 3/15. In 2008, 22 master's awarded. *Degree program information:* Part-time and evening/weekend programs available. Offers chemical engineering (M Eng); civil engineering (M Eng); computer and software engineering (M Eng); engineering management (M Eng); management and technology (MSMT); mechanical engineering (M Eng); telecommunications engineering (M Eng). *Application deadline:* For fall admission, 8/1 priority date for domestic students, 4/1 priority date for international students; for winter admission, 2/1 priority date for international students; for spring admission, 12/1 priority date for domestic students, 9/1 priority date for international students. Applications are processed on a rolling basis. *Application fee:* $25 ($300 for international students). *Application Contact:* Christine M. Weist, Assistant to Associate Provost for Graduate Studies, 610-499-4351, Fax: 610-499-4277, E-mail: christine.m.weist@widener.edu. *Assistant Dean,* Nora J. Kogut, 610-499-4037, Fax: 610-499-4059, E-mail: njkogut@widener.edu.

School of Business Administration Students: 24 full-time (7 women), 195 part-time (80 women); includes 22 minority (12 African Americans, 1 American Indian/Alaska Native, 8 Asian Americans or Pacific Islanders, 1 Hispanic American), 12 international. Average age 34. 254 applicants, 91% accepted. *Faculty:* 14 full-time (6 women), 6 part-time/adjunct (2 women). Expenses: Contact institution. *Financial support:* In 2008–09, 11 research assistantships with full tuition reimbursements were awarded; career-related internships or fieldwork, Federal Work-Study, and traineeships also available. Support available to part-time students. Financial award application deadline: 5/1. In 2008, 85 master's awarded. *Degree program information:* Part-time and evening/weekend programs available. Offers accounting information systems (MS); business administration (MBA, MHA, MHR, MS); health and medical services administration (MBA, MHA); human resource management (MHR, MS); taxation (MS). *Application deadline:* For fall admission, 8/1 priority date for domestic students; for spring admission, 12/1 for domestic students. Applications are processed on a rolling basis. *Application fee:* $25 ($300 for international students). Electronic applications accepted. *Application Contact:* Ann Seltzer, Graduate Enrollment Administrator, 610-499-4305, E-mail: apseltzer@widener.edu. *Dean,* Dr. Savas Ozatalay, 610-499-4300, Fax: 610-499-4615.

School of Human Service Professions Students: 531 full-time (394 women), 660 part-time (501 women); includes 152 minority (115 African Americans, 1 American Indian/Alaska Native, 18 Asian Americans or Pacific Islanders, 18 Hispanic Americans), 9 international. Average age 34. 592 applicants, 71% accepted. *Faculty:* 64 full-time (39 women), 70 part-time/adjunct (34 women). Expenses: Contact institution. *Financial support:* Fellowships, research assistantships, teaching assistantships, career-related internships or fieldwork, Federal Work-Study, institutionally sponsored loans, tuition waivers (partial), unspecified assistantships, and stipends available. Support available to part-time students. Financial award applicants required to submit FAFSA. In 2008, 285 master's, 110 doctorates awarded. *Degree program information:* Part-time and evening/weekend programs available. Offers human service professions (M Ed, MS, MSW, DPT, Ed D, PhD, Psy D). *Application Contact:* Dr. Stephen C. Wilhite, Dean, 610-499-4351, Fax: 610-499-4277, E-mail: stephen.c.wilhite@widener.edu. *Dean,* Dr. Stephen C. Wilhite, 610-499-4351, Fax: 610-499-4277, E-mail: stephen.c.wilhite@widener.edu.

Center for Education Students: 203 full-time (154 women), 415 part-time (298 women); includes 50 minority (34 African Americans, 1 American Indian/Alaska Native, 5 Asian Americans or Pacific Islanders, 10 Hispanic Americans), 3 international. Average age 39. 139 applicants, 88% accepted. *Faculty:* 34 full-time (22 women), 37 part-time/adjunct (14 women). Expenses: Contact institution. *Financial support:* Career-related internships or fieldwork, tuition waivers (full and partial), and unspecified assistantships available. Support available to part-time students. Financial award application deadline: 5/1. In 2008, 168 master's, 31 doctorates awarded. *Degree program information:* Part-time and evening/weekend programs available. Offers adult education (M Ed); counseling in higher education (M Ed); counselor education (M Ed); early childhood education (M Ed); educational foundations (M Ed); educational leadership (M Ed); educational psychology (M Ed); elementary education (M Ed); English and language arts (M Ed); health education (M Ed); higher education leadership (Ed D); home and school visitor (M Ed); human sexuality (M Ed); mathematics education (M Ed); middle school education (M Ed); principalship (M Ed); reading and language arts (Ed D); reading education (M Ed); school administration (Ed D); science education (M Ed); social studies education (M Ed); special education (M Ed); technology education (M Ed). *Application deadline:* Applications are processed on a rolling basis. *Application fee:* $25 ($300 for international students). Electronic applications accepted. *Application Contact:* Dr. Roberta D. Nolan, Director of Graduate Admissions, 610-499-4125, E-mail: rdnolan@widener.edu. *Associate Dean,* Dr. Michael W. LeDoux, 610-499-4294, Fax: 610-499-4623, E-mail: mwledoux@widener.edu.

Center for Social Work Education Students: 54 full-time (49 women), 226 part-time (199 women); includes 78 minority (71 African Americans, 2 Asian Americans or Pacific Islanders, 5 Hispanic Americans), 1 international. Average age 33. 184 applicants, 95% accepted. *Faculty:* 15 full-time (9 women), 16 part-time/adjunct (9 women). Expenses: Contact institution. *Financial support:* In 2008–09, 11 students received support, including 6 fellowships; career-related internships or fieldwork, Federal Work-Study, institutionally sponsored loans, and unspecified assistantships also available. Support available to part-time students. Financial award applicants required to submit FAFSA. In 2008, 117 master's awarded. *Degree program information:* Part-time programs available. Offers social work education (MSW, PhD). *Application deadline:* For fall admission, 3/1 for domestic students. Applications are processed on a rolling basis. *Application fee:* $25 ($300 for international students). Electronic applications accepted. *Application Contact:* Jill L. Brinker, Secretary, 610-499-1513, Fax: 610-499-4617, E-mail: socialwork@widener.edu. *Associate Dean and Director,* Dr. Paula T. Silver, 610-499-1150, Fax: 610-499-4617, E-mail: socialwork@widener.edu.

Institute for Graduate Clinical Psychology Students: 165 full-time (124 women), 4 part-time (1 woman); includes 19 minority (9 African Americans, 7 Asian Americans or Pacific Islanders, 3 Hispanic Americans), 4 international. Average age 25. 208 applicants, 31% accepted. *Faculty:* 15 full-time (6 women), 18 part-time/adjunct (10 women). Expenses: Contact institution. *Financial support:* Research assistantships, teaching assistantships, career-related internships or fieldwork, Federal Work-Study, institutionally sponsored loans, scholarships/grants, and stipends available. In 2008, 26 doctorates awarded. Offers clinical psychology (Psy D). *Application deadline:* For fall admission, 12/31 for domestic students. *Application fee:* $75. Electronic applications accepted. *Application Contact:* Ellen Madison, Admissions Coordinator, 611-499-1206, Fax: 610-499-4625, E-mail: ellen.t.madison@widener.edu. *Associate Dean/Director,* Dr. Virginia Brabender, 610-499-1208, Fax: 610-499-4625, E-mail: graduate.psychology@widener.edu.

Institute for Physical Therapy Education Students: 109 full-time (67 women), 14 part-time (3 women); includes 5 minority (1 African American, 4 Asian Americans or Pacific Islanders), 1 international. Average age 25. 82 applicants, 93% accepted. *Faculty:* 8 full-time (5 women), 1 (woman) part-time/adjunct. Expenses: Contact institution. *Financial support:* Teaching assistantships, Federal Work-Study, institutionally sponsored loans, and scholarships/grants available. Financial award application deadline: 5/1; financial award applicants required to submit FAFSA. In 2008, 53 doctorates awarded. Offers physical therapy education (MS, DPT). *Application deadline:* For fall admission, 1/30 for domestic students. Applications are processed on a rolling basis. *Application fee:* $40. *Application Contact:* Dr. Robin L. Dole, Associate Dean and Director, 610-499-1159, Fax: 610-499-1231, E-mail: robin.l.dole@widener.edu. *Associate Dean and Director,* Dr. Robin L. Dole, 610-499-1159, Fax: 610-499-1231, E-mail: robin.l.dole@widener.edu.

School of Law at Harrisburg Students: 451 full-time (199 women), 8 part-time (5 women); includes 34 minority (12 African Americans, 2 American Indian/Alaska Native, 11 Asian Americans or Pacific Islanders, 9 Hispanic Americans). Average age 26. *Faculty:* 26 full-time (12 women), 18 part-time/adjunct (6 women). Expenses: Contact institution. *Financial support:* Fellowships, research assistantships, career-related internships or fieldwork, Federal Work-Study, institutionally sponsored loans, and scholarships/grants available. Support available to part-time students. Financial award application deadline: 2/15; financial award applicants required to submit FAFSA. In 2008, 120 JDs awarded. *Degree program information:* Part-time programs available. Offers law (JD). *Application deadline:* For fall admission, 5/15 for domestic students. Applications are processed on a rolling basis. *Application fee:* $60. Electronic applications accepted. *Application Contact:* Barbara L. Ayars, Assistant Dean of Admissions, 302-477-2210, Fax: 302-477-2224, E-mail: barbara.l.ayars@law.widener.edu. *Dean,* Linda L. Ammons, 302-477-2100, Fax: 302-477-2282, E-mail: llammons@widener.edu.

School of Law at Wilmington Students: 945 full-time (416 women), 13 part-time (5 women); includes 118 minority (49 African Americans, 2 American Indian/Alaska Native, 53 Asian Americans or Pacific Islanders, 14 Hispanic Americans), 2 international. Average age 27. 2,376 applicants, 39% accepted, 351 enrolled. *Faculty:* 58 full-time (23 women), 42 part-time/adjunct (15 women). Expenses: Contact institution. *Financial support:* Career-related internships or fieldwork, Federal Work-Study, institutionally sponsored loans, and scholarships/grants available. Support available to part-time students. Financial award application deadline: 2/15; financial award applicants required to submit FAFSA. In 2008, 266 first professional degrees, 28 master's, 3 doctorates awarded. *Degree program information:* Part-time programs available. Offers corporate law and finance (LL M); health law (LL M, MJ, D Law); juridical science (SJD); law (JD). *Application deadline:* For fall admission, 5/15 for domestic students; for spring admission, 12/1 for domestic students. Applications are processed on a rolling basis. *Application fee:* $60. *Application Contact:* Barbara L. Ayars, Assistant Dean of Admissions, 302-477-2210, Fax: 302-477-2224, E-mail: barbara.l.ayars@law.widener.edu. *Dean,* Linda L. Ammons, 302-477-2100, Fax: 302-477-2282, E-mail: llammons@widener.edu.

School of Nursing Students: 12 full-time (11 women), 129 part-time (103 women); includes 13 minority (8 African Americans, 2 American Indian/Alaska Native, 1 Asian American or Pacific Islander, 2 Hispanic Americans), 1 international. Average age 33. 77 applicants, 79% accepted. *Faculty:* 12 full-time (all women), 4 part-time/adjunct (3 women). Expenses: Contact institution. *Financial support:* Career-related internships or fieldwork, Federal Work-Study, and traineeships available. Support available to part-time students. Financial award application deadline: 4/1. In 2008, 34 master's, 11 doctorates awarded. *Degree program information:* Part-time and evening/weekend programs available. Offers nursing (MSN, DN Sc, PhD, PMC). *Application deadline:* For fall admission, 7/1 for domestic students; for winter admission, 3/1 for domestic students; for spring admission, 11/1 for domestic students. Applications are processed on a rolling basis. *Application fee:* $25 ($300 for international students). Electronic applications accepted. *Application Contact:* Betty A. Boyles, Information Contact, 610-499-4207, Fax: 610-499-4216, E-mail: betty.a.boyles@widener.edu. *Assistant Dean for Graduate Studies,* Dr. Mary B. Walker, 610-499-4208, Fax: 610-499-4216, E-mail: mary.b.walker@widener.edu.

See Close-Up on page 1055.

WILFRID LAURIER UNIVERSITY, Waterloo, ON N2L 3C5, Canada

General Information Province-supported, coed, comprehensive institution. *Graduate housing:* Rooms and/or apartments available on a first-come, first-served basis to single students and available to married students. Housing application deadline: 4/1.

GRADUATE UNITS

Faculty of Graduate Studies Electronic applications accepted.

Faculty of Arts Offers archaeology and classical studies (MA); arts (M Sc, MA, MES, MIPP, PhD); communication studies (MA); cultural analysis and social theory (MA); English and film studies (MA, PhD); geography and environmental studies (M Sc, MA, MES, PhD); global governance (PhD); history (MA, PhD); international public policy (MIPP); philosophy (MA); political science (MA); religion and culture (MA, PhD); sociology (MA). Electronic applications accepted.

Faculty of Music Offers music (MMT). Electronic applications accepted.

Faculty of Science Offers biology (M Sc); brain and cognition (M Sc, PhD); chemistry (M Sc); community psychology (MA, PhD); kinesiology and physical education (M Sc); mathematics (M Sc); science (M Sc, MA, PhD); social and developmental psychology (MA, PhD). Electronic applications accepted.

Faculty of Social Work *Degree program information:* Part-time programs available. Offers social work (MSW, PhD). Electronic applications accepted.

School of Business and Economics *Degree program information:* Part-time and evening/weekend programs available. Offers business (M Fin, M Sc, PhD); business administration (MBA); business and economics (M Fin, M Sc, MA, MBA, PhD); economics (MA). Electronic applications accepted.

Waterloo Lutheran Seminary *Degree program information:* Part-time programs available. Offers Christian ethics (M Th); divinity (M Div); homiletics (M Th); ministry (D Min); pastoral counseling (M Th); spirituality in a health care setting (Diploma); theological studies (MTS); theology (Diploma). Electronic applications accepted.

WILKES UNIVERSITY, Wilkes-Barre, PA 18766-0002

General Information Independent, coed, comprehensive institution. CGS member. *Enrollment:* 5,901 graduate, professional, and undergraduate students; 545 full-time matriculated graduate/professional students (313 women), 3,047 part-time matriculated graduate/professional students (2,080 women). *Enrollment by degree level:* 269 first professional, 3,230 master's, 93 doctoral. Tuition and fees vary according to degree level and program. *Graduate housing:* On-campus housing not available. *Student services:* Campus employment opportunities, career counseling, free psychological counseling, international student services, low-cost health insurance, multicultural affairs office, services for students with disabilities. *Library facilities:* Eugene S. Farley Library. *Online resources:* library catalog, access to other libraries' catalogs.

Computer facilities: Computer purchase and lease plans are available. 570 computers available on campus for general student use. A campuswide network can be accessed from student residence rooms and from off campus. Online class registration is available. *Web address:* http://www.wilkes.edu/.

General Application Contact: Kathleen Houlihan, Director of Graduate Studies, 570-408-3235, Fax: 570-408-7846, E-mail: kathleen.houlihan@wilkes.edu.

GRADUATE UNITS

College of Graduate and Professional Studies Students: 545 full-time (313 women), 3,047 part-time (2,080 women); includes 79 minority (20 African Americans, 3 American Indian/Alaska Native, 30 Asian Americans or Pacific Islanders, 26 Hispanic Americans), 69 international. Average age 33. Expenses: Contact institution. *Financial support:* Federal Work-Study and unspecified assistantships available. Financial award application deadline: 3/1; financial award applicants required to submit FAFSA. In 2008, 71 first professional degrees, 986 master's awarded. *Degree program information:* Part-time and evening/weekend programs available. Postbaccalaureate distance learning degree programs offered (minimal on-campus study). *Application deadline:* Applications are processed on a rolling basis. *Application fee:* $45. *Application Contact:* Kathleen Houlihan, Director of Graduate Studies, 570-408-3235, Fax: 570-408-7846, E-mail: kathleen.houlihan@wilkes.edu. *Dean,* Dr. Michael Speziale, 570-408-4679, Fax: 570-408-7846, E-mail: michael.speziale@wilkes.edu.

College of Arts, Humanities and Social Sciences Students: 123 full-time (66 women), 2,060 part-time (1,437 women); includes 39 minority (8 African Americans, 3 American Indian/Alaska Native, 9 Asian Americans or Pacific Islanders, 19 Hispanic Americans), 3 international. Average age 34. Expenses: Contact institution. *Financial support:* Federal Work-Study and unspecified assistantships available. Financial award application deadline: 3/1. In 2008, 854 master's awarded. *Degree program information:* Part-time and evening/weekend programs available. Postbaccalaureate distance learning degree programs offered (minimal on-campus study). Offers arts, humanities and social sciences (MA, MFA); creative writing (MA, MFA). *Application fee:* $40. *Application Contact:* Kathleen Houlihan, Director of Graduate Studies, 570-408-3235, Fax: 570-408-7846, E-mail: kathleen.houlihan@wilkes.edu. *Dean,* Dr. Darin Fields, 570-408-4600, Fax: 570-408-7860, E-mail: darin.fields@wilkes.edu.

College of Science and Engineering Students: 21 full-time (5 women), 35 part-time (10 women); includes 3 minority (all Asian Americans or Pacific Islanders), 34 international. Average age 26. Expenses: Contact institution. In 2008, 6 master's awarded. *Degree program information:* Part-time programs available. Offers electrical engineering (MSEE); engineering operations and strategy (MS); mathematics (MS, MS Ed); science and engineering (MS, MS Ed, MSEE). *Application fee:* $45. *Application Contact:* Kathleen Houlihan, Director of Graduate Studies, 570-408-3235, Fax: 570-408-7846, E-mail: kathleen.houlihan@wilkes.edu. *Dean,* Dr. Dale Bruns, 570-408-4600, Fax: 570-408-7860, E-mail: dale.bruns@wilkes.edu.

Jay S. Sidhu School of Business and Leadership Students: 52 full-time (20 women), 111 part-time (56 women); includes 6 minority (2 African Americans, 3 Asian Americans or Pacific Islanders, 1 Hispanic American), 18 international. Average age 29. Expenses: Contact institution. *Financial support:* Federal Work-Study and unspecified assistantships available. Financial award application deadline: 3/1; financial award applicants required to submit FAFSA. In 2008, 61 master's awarded. *Degree program information:* Part-time and evening/weekend programs available. Offers accounting (MBA); entrepreneurship (MBA); finance (MBA); human resource management (MBA); international business (MBA); management (MBA); marketing (MBA). *Application deadline:* Applications are processed on a rolling basis. *Application fee:* $45. *Application Contact:* Kathleen Houlihan, Director of Graduate Studies, 570-408-3235, Fax: 570-408-7846, E-mail: kathleen.houlihan@wilkes.edu. *Dean,* Dr. Paul Browne, 570-408-4701, Fax: 570-408-7846, E-mail: paul.browne@wilkes.edu.

Nesbitt College of Pharmacy and Nursing Students: 302 full-time (191 women), 34 part-time (all women); includes 23 minority (7 African Americans, 1 American Indian/Alaska Native, 14 Asian Americans or Pacific Islanders, 1 Hispanic American), 2 international. Average age 25. Expenses: Contact institution. *Financial support:* Federal Work-Study and unspecified assistantships available. Financial award application deadline: 3/1. In 2008, 63 first professional degrees, 21 master's awarded. *Degree program information:* Part-time and evening/weekend programs available. Offers nursing (MSN); pharmacy (Pharm D); pharmacy and nursing (Pharm D, MSN). *Application deadline:* Applications are processed on a rolling basis. *Application Contact:* Kathleen Houlihan, Director of Graduate Studies, 570-408-3235, Fax: 570-408-7846, E-mail: kathleen.houlihan@wilkes.edu. *Dean,* Dr. Bernard Graham, 570-408-4280, Fax: 570-408-7828, E-mail: bernard.graham@wilkes.edu.

School of Education Students: 76 full-time (55 women), 2,332 part-time (1,609 women); includes 42 minority (11 African Americans, 1 American Indian/Alaska Native, 11 Asian Americans or Pacific Islanders, 19 Hispanic Americans), 12 international. Average age 33. Expenses: Contact institution. *Financial support:* Federal Work-Study and unspecified assistantships available. Financial award application deadline: 3/1; financial award applicants required to submit FAFSA. In 2008, 861 master's awarded. *Degree program information:* Part-time and evening/weekend programs available. Postbaccalaureate distance learning degree programs offered (minimal on-campus study). Offers classroom technology (MS Ed); educational computing (MS Ed); educational development and strategies (MS Ed); educational leadership (MS Ed); educational technology (Ed D); elementary education (MS Ed); higher education administration (Ed D); instructional technology (MS Ed); K-12 administration (Ed D); school business leadership (MS Ed); secondary education (MS Ed); special education (MS Ed). *Application deadline:* Applications are processed on a rolling basis. *Application fee:* $45. *Application Contact:* Kathleen Houlihan, Director of Graduate Studies, 570-408-3235, Fax: 570-408-7846, E-mail: kathleen.houlihan@wilkes.edu. *Dean,* Dr. Michael Speziale, 570-408-4679, Fax: 570-408-4905, E-mail: michael.speziale@wilkes.edu.

WILLAMETTE UNIVERSITY, Salem, OR 97301-3931

General Information Independent-religious, coed, comprehensive institution. *Enrollment:* 2,716 graduate, professional, and undergraduate students; 655 full-time matriculated graduate/professional students (278 women), 160 part-time matriculated graduate/professional students (85 women). *Enrollment by degree level:* 433 first professional, 382 master's. *Graduate faculty:* 47 full-time (14 women), 52 part-time/adjunct (20 women). *Graduate housing:* Room and/or apartments available on a first-come, first-served basis to single students; on-campus housing not available to married students. Housing application deadline: 6/1. *Student services:* Campus employment opportunities, campus safety program, career counseling, free psychological counseling, international student services, low-cost health insurance, services for students with disabilities. *Library facilities:* Mark O. Hatfield Library plus 1 other. *Online resources:* library catalog, web page, access to other libraries' catalogs. *Collection:* 317,000 titles, 1,400 serial subscriptions.

Computer facilities: 400 computers available on campus for general student use. A campuswide network can be accessed from student residence rooms and from off campus. Online class registration is available. *Web address:* http://www.willamette.edu/.

General Application Contact: Office of Graduate Admissions, 503-370-6300.

GRADUATE UNITS

College of Law Students: 423 full-time (175 women), 5 part-time (1 woman); includes 66 minority (6 African Americans, 6 American Indian/Alaska Native, 29 Asian Americans or Pacific Islanders, 25 Hispanic Americans), 1 international. Average age 27. 1,094 applicants, 47% accepted, 159 enrolled. *Faculty:* 37 full-time (13 women), 20 part-time/adjunct (4 women). Expenses: Contact institution. *Financial support:* In 2008–09, 361 students received support; fellowships with partial tuition reimbursements available, research assistantships with partial tuition reimbursements available, Federal Work-Study, scholarships/grants, and tuition waivers (full and partial) available. Financial award application deadline: 3/1; financial award applicants required to submit FAFSA. In 2008, 106 JDs awarded. Offers law (JD, LL M). *Application deadline:* For fall admission, 3/1 priority date for domestic students, 3/1 for international students. Applications are processed on a rolling basis. *Application fee:* $50. Electronic applications accepted. *Application Contact:* Carolyn Dennis, Director of Admission, 503-370-6282, Fax: 503-370-6087, E-mail: law-admission@willamette.edu. *Dean,* Symeon C. Symeonides, 503-370-6402, Fax: 503-370-6828, E-mail: symeon@willamette.edu.

George H. Atkinson Graduate School of Management Students: 157 full-time (61 women), 108 part-time (48 women); includes 30 minority (2 American Indian/Alaska Native, 16 Asian Americans or Pacific Islanders, 12 Hispanic Americans), 54 international. Average age 25. 248 applicants, 86% accepted, 111 enrolled. *Faculty:* 18 full-time (4 women), 18 part-time/adjunct (4 women). Expenses: Contact institution. *Financial support:* In 2008–09, 180 students received support, including 12 research assistantships (averaging $1,500 per year); career-related internships or fieldwork, Federal Work-Study, scholarships/grants, and unspecified assistantships also available. Financial award application deadline: 5/1; financial award applicants required to submit FAFSA. In 2008, 43 master's awarded. *Degree program information:* Part-time and evening/weekend programs available. Offers early career MBA (full-time) (MBA); MBA for career change (full-time) (MBA); MBA for professionals (part-time) (MBA). *Application deadline:* For fall admission, 1/9 priority date for domestic and international students; for winter admission, 3/1 priority date for domestic and international students; for spring admission, 5/1 priority date for domestic and international students. Applications are processed on a rolling basis. Electronic applications accepted. *Application Contact:* Judy O'Neill, Assistant Dean and Director of Admission, 503-370-6167, Fax: 503-370-3011, E-mail: joneill@willamette.edu. *Dean,* Debra J. Ringold, 503-370-6440, Fax: 503-370-3011, E-mail: dringold@willamette.edu.

School of Education *Degree program information:* Evening/weekend programs available. Offers teaching (MAT). Electronic applications accepted.

WILLIAM CAREY UNIVERSITY, Hattiesburg, MS 39401-5499

General Information Independent-religious, coed, comprehensive institution. *Graduate housing:* Room and/or apartments available on a first-come, first-served basis to single students; on-campus housing not available to married students. Housing application deadline: 8/15.

GRADUATE UNITS

School of Business *Degree program information:* Part-time programs available. Offers business (MBA).

School of Education *Degree program information:* Part-time programs available. Offers art education (M Ed); art of teaching (M Ed); elementary education (M Ed, Ed S); English education (M Ed); gifted education (M Ed); history and social science (M Ed); mild/moderate disabilities (M Ed); secondary education (M Ed).

William Carey University (continued)

School of Nursing *Degree program information:* Part-time programs available. Offers nursing (MSN).

School of Psychology and Counseling *Degree program information:* Part-time programs available. Offers counseling psychology (MS).

WILLIAM HOWARD TAFT UNIVERSITY, Santa Ana, CA 92704

General Information Proprietary, coed, graduate-only institution.

GRADUATE UNITS

Graduate Programs

Bernard E. Witkin School of Law Offers American jurisprudence (LL M); law (JD); taxation (LL M).

The Boyer Graduate School of Education Offers education (M Ed).

W. Edwards Deming School of Business Offers taxation (MS).

WILLIAM MITCHELL COLLEGE OF LAW, St. Paul, MN 55105-3076

General Information Independent, coed, graduate-only institution. *Graduate housing:* On-campus housing not available.

GRADUATE UNITS

Professional Program *Degree program information:* Part-time and evening/weekend programs available. Offers law (JD). Electronic applications accepted.

WILLIAM PATERSON UNIVERSITY OF NEW JERSEY, Wayne, NJ 07470-8420

General Information State-supported, coed, comprehensive institution. CGS member. *Graduate housing:* Room and/or apartments available on a first-come, first-served basis to single students; on-campus housing not available to married students.

GRADUATE UNITS

Christos M. Cotsakos College of Business *Degree program information:* Part-time and evening/weekend programs available. Offers business (MBA). Electronic applications accepted.

College of Education Offers counseling services (M Ed); education (M Ed, MAT); educational leadership (M Ed); elementary education (M Ed, MAT); reading (M Ed); special education (M Ed). Electronic applications accepted.

College of Science and Health *Degree program information:* Part-time and evening/weekend programs available. Offers biotechnology (MS); general biology (MA); limnology and terrestrial ecology (MA); molecular biology (MA); nursing (MSN); physiology (MA); science and health (MA, MS, MSN); speech pathology (MS). Electronic applications accepted.

College of the Arts and Communication *Degree program information:* Part-time and evening/weekend programs available. Offers art (MFA); arts and communication (MA, MFA, MM); communication and media studies (MA); music (MM); visual arts (MA). Electronic applications accepted.

College of the Humanities and Social Sciences *Degree program information:* Part-time and evening/weekend programs available. Offers clinical and counseling psychology (MA); English (MA); history (MA); humanities and social sciences (MA); public policy and international affairs (MA); sociology (MA). Electronic applications accepted.

See Close-Up on page 1057.

WILLIAMS COLLEGE, Williamstown, MA 01267

General Information Independent, coed, comprehensive institution. *Graduate housing:* Room and/or apartments available on a first-come, first-served basis to single students; on-campus housing not available to married students. *Research affiliation:* Clark Art Institute.

GRADUATE UNITS

Program in the History of Art *Degree program information:* Part-time programs available. Offers history of art (MA). Offered jointly with Sterling and Francine Clark Art Institute. Electronic applications accepted.

WILLIAM WOODS UNIVERSITY, Fulton, MO 65251-1098

General Information Independent-religious, coed, comprehensive institution. *Graduate housing:* On-campus housing not available.

GRADUATE UNITS

Graduate and Adult Studies *Degree program information:* Evening/weekend programs available. Offers administration (Ed S); agriculture (MBA); athletic/activities administration (M Ed); curriculum and instruction (M Ed); curriculum leadership (Ed S); elementary administration (M Ed); health management (MBA); human resources (MBA); principalship (Ed S); secondary administration (M Ed); special education director (M Ed). Electronic applications accepted.

WILMINGTON COLLEGE, Wilmington, OH 45177

General Information Independent-religious, coed, comprehensive institution. *Graduate housing:* On-campus housing not available.

GRADUATE UNITS

Department of Education *Degree program information:* Part-time programs available. Offers reading (M Ed); special education (M Ed).

WILMINGTON UNIVERSITY, New Castle, DE 19720-6491

General Information Independent, coed, comprehensive institution. *Graduate housing:* On-campus housing not available.

GRADUATE UNITS

Division of Behavioral Science *Degree program information:* Part-time and evening/weekend programs available. Offers administration of human services (MS); administration of justice (MS); community counseling (MS). Electronic applications accepted.

Division of Business *Degree program information:* Part-time and evening/weekend programs available. Offers business administration (MBA); finance (MBA); health care administration (MBA, MS); homeland security (MBA, MS); human resource management (MS); management (MS); management information systems (MBA); organizational leadership (MS); public administration (MS); transportation and logistics (MBA, MS). Electronic applications accepted.

Division of Education *Degree program information:* Part-time and evening/weekend programs available. Offers applied education technology (M Ed); career and technical education (M Ed); elementary and secondary school counseling (M Ed); elementary special education (M Ed); elementary studies (M Ed); instruction: gifted and talented (M Ed); instruction: teaching and learning (M Ed); literacy (M Ed); reading (M Ed); school leadership (M Ed); secondary teaching (MAT). Electronic applications accepted.

Division of Information Technology and Advanced Communications *Degree program information:* Part-time and evening/weekend programs available. Offers corporate training (MS); information assurance (MS); information systems technologies (MS); Internet web design (MS); management information systems (MS). Electronic applications accepted.

Division of Nursing and Allied Health *Degree program information:* Part-time programs available. Offers adult nurse practitioner (MSN); family nurse practitioner (MSN); gerontology (MSN); leadership (MSN); nursing (MSN); women's nurse practitioner (MSN). Electronic applications accepted.

Program in Innovation and Leadership *Degree program information:* Part-time programs available. Offers education innovation (Ed D); organizational leadership (Ed D). Electronic applications accepted.

WINEBRENNER THEOLOGICAL SEMINARY, Findlay, OH 45840

General Information Independent-religious, coed, graduate-only institution. *Enrollment by degree level:* 49 first professional, 40 master's, 10 doctoral. *Graduate faculty:* 6 full-time (1 woman), 5 part-time/adjunct (2 women). *Tuition:* Full-time $10,500; part-time $410 per credit hour. *Required fees:* $110 per trimester. *Graduate housing:* On-campus housing not available. *Student services:* Campus employment opportunities, career counseling, free psychological counseling, international student services. *Library facilities:* Winebrenner Seminary Library. *Online resources:* library catalog, access to other libraries' catalogs. *Collection:* 44,400 titles, 105 serial subscriptions, 720 audiovisual materials.

Computer facilities: A campuswide network can be accessed from off campus. *Web address:* http://www.winebrenner.edu/.

General Application Contact: Jim Wilder, Regional Coordinator, 419-434-4220, Fax: 419-434-4267, E-mail: admissions@winebrenner.edu.

GRADUATE UNITS

Graduate Programs Students: 50 full-time (14 women), 49 part-time (20 women); includes 9 minority (all African Americans), 3 international. Average age 38. 16 applicants, 94% accepted, 13 enrolled. *Faculty:* 6 full-time (1 woman), 5 part-time/adjunct (2 women). Expenses: Contact institution. *Financial support:* In 2008–09, 32 students received support. Institutionally sponsored loans, scholarships/grants, and tuition waivers (partial) available. Support available to part-time students. Financial award application deadline: 7/1; financial award applicants required to submit FAFSA. In 2008, 10 first professional degrees, 10 master's awarded. *Degree program information:* Part-time and evening/weekend programs available. Offers church development (MA); family ministry (MA); theological study (MA); theological/ministerial studies (D Min); theology/ministerial studies (M Div). *Application deadline:* For fall admission, 8/15 priority date for domestic students; for winter admission, 12/15 priority date for domestic students; for spring admission, 4/15 priority date for domestic students. Applications are processed on a rolling basis. *Application fee:* $25. Electronic applications accepted. *Application Contact:* Jim Wilder, Regional Coordinator, 419-434-4220, Fax: 419-434-4267, E-mail: admissions@winebrenner.edu. *Vice President for Academic Advancement*, Dr. M. John Nissley, 419-434-4247, Fax: 419-434-4267, E-mail: jnissley@winebrenner.edu.

WINGATE UNIVERSITY, Wingate, NC 28174-0159

General Information Independent-religious, coed, comprehensive institution. *Graduate housing:* Rooms and/or apartments available on a first-come, first-served basis to single and married students. Housing application deadline: 8/15.

GRADUATE UNITS

Program in Business Administration *Degree program information:* Part-time and evening/weekend programs available. Offers business administration (MBA). Electronic applications accepted.

Program in Education *Degree program information:* Part-time and evening/weekend programs available. Offers educational leadership (MA Ed); elementary education (MA Ed, MAT); physical education (MA Ed); sport administration (MA Ed).

School of Pharmacy Offers pharmacy (Pharm D). Electronic applications accepted.

WINONA STATE UNIVERSITY, Winona, MN 55987-5838

General Information State-supported, coed, comprehensive institution. *Enrollment:* 8,220 graduate, professional, and undergraduate students; 291 full-time matriculated graduate/professional students (212 women), 139 part-time matriculated graduate/professional students (105 women). *Enrollment by degree level:* 372 master's, 12 doctoral, 46 other advanced degrees. *Graduate faculty:* 57 full-time (38 women). Tuition, state resident: full-time $5280. Tuition, nonresident: full-time $7940. *Required fees:* $540. *Graduate housing:* Room and/or apartments available to single students; on-campus housing not available to married students. Typical cost: $6720 (including board). Housing application deadline: 3/2. *Student services:* Campus employment opportunities, campus safety program, career counseling, child daycare facilities, exercise/wellness program, free psychological counseling, international student services, low-cost health insurance, services for students with disabilities. *Library facilities:* Darrel W. Krueger. *Online resources:* library catalog, web page, access to other libraries' catalogs. *Collection:* 350,000 titles, 1,000 serial subscriptions, 8,000 audiovisual materials.

Computer facilities: Computer purchase and lease plans are available. 1,400 computers available on campus for general student use. A campuswide network can be accessed from student residence rooms and from off campus. Online class registration is available. *Web address:* http://www.winona.edu/.

General Application Contact: Dr. Nancy Jannik, Director of Graduate Studies, 507-457-5010, E-mail: njannik@winona.edu.

GRADUATE UNITS

College of Education Students: 196 full-time (133 women), 89 part-time (58 women); includes 12 minority (3 African Americans, 3 American Indian/Alaska Native, 5 Asian Americans or Pacific Islanders, 1 Hispanic American). Average age 32. 117 applicants, 83% accepted, 81 enrolled. *Faculty:* 28 full-time (17 women). Expenses: Contact institution. *Financial support:* Fellowships, career-related internships or fieldwork, Federal Work-Study, and unspecified assistantships available. Support available to part-time students. In 2008, 102 master's, 11 other advanced degrees awarded. *Degree program information:* Part-time and evening/weekend programs available. Offers community counseling (MS); education (MS, Ed S); educational leadership (Ed S); general school leadership (MS); K-12 principalship (MS); outdoor education/adventure based leadership (MS); professional development (MS); school counseling (MS); special education (MS); sports management (MS); teacher leadership (MS). *Application deadline:* For fall admission, 8/8 priority date for domestic students; for spring admission, 2/17 for domestic students. Applications are processed on a rolling basis. *Application fee:* $20. *Application Contact:* Sally Standiford, Dean, 507-457-2570, E-mail: sstandiford@winona.edu. *Dean*, Sally Standiford, 507-457-2570, E-mail: sstandiford@winona.edu.

College of Liberal Arts Students: 19 full-time (14 women), 5 part-time (4 women); includes 9 minority (all Asian Americans or Pacific Islanders). Average age 28. 21 applicants, 67% accepted, 8 enrolled. *Faculty:* 14 full-time (7 women). Expenses: Contact institution. *Financial support:* Career-related internships or fieldwork, Federal Work-Study, and unspecified assistantships available. Support available to part-time students. Financial award applicants required to submit FAFSA. In 2008, 7 master's awarded. *Degree program information:* Part-time programs available. Offers English (MA, MS); liberal arts (MA, MS). *Application deadline:* For fall admission, 7/26 priority date for domestic students; for spring admission, 12/8 for domestic students. Applications are processed on a rolling basis. *Application fee:* $20. *Application Contact:* Dr. Lee Gray, Director of Graduate Studies, 507-457-5346, E-mail: lgray@winona.edu. *Dean*, Dr. Troy Paino, 507-457-5017, E-mail: tpaino@winona.edu.

College of Nursing and Health Sciences Students: 76 full-time (65 women), 45 part-time (43 women); includes 6 minority (2 African Americans, 3 Asian Americans or Pacific Islanders, 1 Hispanic American). Average age 36. 98 applicants, 53% accepted, 48 enrolled. *Faculty:* 9 full-time (8 women), 12 part-time/adjunct (11 women). Expenses: Contact institution. *Financial support:* In 2008–09, 17 students received support, including 3 research assistantships with partial tuition reimbursements available (averaging $6,000 per year); Federal Work-Study, traineeships, and unspecified assistantships also available. Support available to part-time students. Financial award application deadline: 8/15; financial award applicants required to submit FAFSA. In 2008, 26 master's, 5 other advanced degrees awarded. *Degree program information:* Part-time programs available. Postbaccalaureate distance learning degree programs offered (no on-campus study). Offers adult nurse practitioner (MS, Post Master's Certificate); clinical nurse specialist (MS, Post Master's Certificate); family nurse practitioner (MS, Post Master's Certificate); nurse administrator (MS); nurse educator (MS, Post Master's Certificate); nursing (DNP). *Application deadline:* For fall admission, 12/1 for domestic and international students. *Application fee:* $20. *Application Contact:* Dr. Nancy Jannik, Director of Graduate Studies, 507-457-5010, E-mail: njannik@winona.edu. *Dean*, Dr. William J. McBreen, 507-457-5122, E-mail: wmcbreen@winona.edu.

WINSTON-SALEM STATE UNIVERSITY, Winston-Salem, NC 27110-0003

General Information State-supported, coed, comprehensive institution. CGS member. *Enrollment:* 6,422 graduate, professional, and undergraduate students; 249 full-time matriculated graduate/professional students (197 women), 218 part-time matriculated graduate/professional students (172 women). *Enrollment by degree level:* 467 master's. *Graduate faculty:* 50 full-time (20 women), 12 part-time/adjunct (9 women). Tuition, state resident: full-time $2139; part-time $1664.28 per semester. Tuition, nonresident: full-time $6555; part-time $4977.67 per semester. *Required fees:* $1067.50; $862.03. *Graduate housing:* On-campus housing not available. *Student services:* Campus employment opportunities, campus safety program, career counseling, exercise/wellness program, free psychological counseling, international student services, teacher training. *Library facilities:* O'Kelly Library. *Online resources:* library catalog.

Computer facilities: 600 computers available on campus for general student use. A campuswide network can be accessed from student residence rooms and from off campus. Online class registration is available. *Web address:* http://www.wssu.edu/.

General Application Contact: Monica Elliot, Data Enrollment Communication Specialist, 336-750-3045, Fax: 336-750-3042, E-mail: elliottm@wssu.edu.

GRADUATE UNITS

Department of Occupational Therapy Students: 46 full-time (40 women); includes 24 minority (22 African Americans, 2 Asian Americans or Pacific Islanders). Average age 22. 35 applicants, 77% accepted, 27 enrolled. *Faculty:* 5 full-time (all women). Expenses: Contact institution. *Financial support:* In 2008–09, 15 students received support; research assistantships, teaching assistantships, career-related internships or fieldwork, institutionally sponsored loans, scholarships/grants, and tuition waivers (partial) also available. Offers occupational therapy (MS). *Application deadline:* For fall admission, 3/15 for domestic and international students. Applications are processed on a rolling basis. *Application fee:* $40. Electronic applications accepted. *Application Contact:* 336-750-2102, Fax: 336-750-3042, E-mail: graduate@wssu.edu. *Chair and Associate Professor*, Dr. Dorothy P. Bethea, 336-750-3172, Fax: 336-750-3173, E-mail: betheadp@wssu.edu.

Department of Physical Therapy Students: 46 full-time (13 women), 1 (woman) part-time; includes 20 minority (18 African Americans, 1 Asian American or Pacific Islander, 1 Hispanic American). *Faculty:* 7 full-time (5 women), 7 part-time/adjunct (2 women). Expenses: Contact institution. *Financial support:* In 2008–09, 26 students received support, including 7 teaching assistantships (averaging $2,500 per year); career-related internships or fieldwork, institutionally sponsored loans, scholarships/grants, and tuition waivers (partial) also available. In 2008, 17 master's awarded. Offers physical therapy (MPT). *Application deadline:* For fall admission, 1/31 for domestic and international students. Applications are processed on a rolling basis. *Application fee:* $40. Electronic applications accepted. *Application Contact:* School of Graduate Studies and Research, 336-750-2102, Fax: 336-750-3042, E-mail: graduate@wssu.edu. *Chair and Professor*, Dr. Teresa Conner-Kerr, 336-750-2193, Fax: 336-750-2192, E-mail: connerkerrt@wssu.edu.

Program in Business Administration Students: 43 full-time (22 women), 3 part-time (1 woman); includes 28 minority (26 African Americans, 1 Asian American or Pacific Islander, 1 Hispanic American). Average age 40. *Faculty:* 17 full-time (5 women). Expenses: Contact institution. *Financial support:* In 2008–09, 10 students received support, including 4 research assistantships (averaging $5,000 per year), 4 teaching assistantships (averaging $5,000 per year); career-related internships or fieldwork, institutionally sponsored loans, and tuition waivers (partial) also available. In 2008, 10 master's awarded. *Degree program information:* Part-time and evening/weekend programs available. Postbaccalaureate distance learning degree programs offered (minimal on-campus study). Offers business administration (MBA). *Application deadline:* For fall admission, 7/15 for domestic and international students; for spring admission, 11/15 for domestic and international students. Applications are processed on a rolling basis. *Application fee:* $40. Electronic applications accepted. *Application Contact:* Graduate Studies and Research, 336-750-2102, Fax: 336-750-3042, E-mail: graduate@wssu.edu. *Unit Head*, Dr. Suresh Gopalan, 336-750-2344, Fax: 336-750-2335, E-mail: gopalans@wssu.edu.

Program in Computer Science and Information Technology Students: 6 full-time (4 women), 11 part-time (4 women); includes 10 minority (all African Americans). *Faculty:* 9 full-time (4 women). Expenses: Contact institution. *Financial support:* In 2008–09, 7 students received support, including 2 research assistantships (averaging $5,000 per year), 5 teaching assistantships (averaging $3,958 per year); career-related internships or fieldwork, institutionally sponsored loans, scholarships/grants, tuition waivers (partial), and unspecified assistantships also available. In 2008, 10 master's awarded. *Degree program information:* Part-time programs available. Offers computer science and information technology (MS). *Application deadline:* For fall admission, 7/1 for domestic and international students; for spring admission, 11/1 for domestic and international students. Applications are processed on a rolling basis. *Application fee:* $40. Electronic applications accepted. *Application Contact:* Graduate Studies and Research, 336-750-2102, Fax: 336-750-3042, E-mail: graduate@wssu.edu. *Chair*, Dr. Elva Jones, 336-750-2485, Fax: 336-750-2499, E-mail: jonese@wssu.edu.

Program in Elementary Education Students: 2 full-time (1 woman), 81 part-time (80 women); includes 13 minority (all African Americans). Average age 32. 35 applicants, 100% accepted, 35 enrolled. *Faculty:* 4 full-time (1 woman). Expenses: Contact institution. *Financial support:* Research assistantships, teaching assistantships, career-related internships or fieldwork and institutionally sponsored loans available. In 2008, 5 master's awarded. *Degree program information:* Part-time and evening/weekend programs available. Postbaccalaureate distance learning degree programs offered (minimal on-campus study). Offers elementary education (M Ed). *Application deadline:* For fall admission, 7/15 for domestic and international students. Applications are processed on a rolling basis. *Application fee:* $40. Electronic applications accepted. *Application Contact:* Graduate Studies and Research, 336-750-2102, Fax: 336-750-3042, E-mail: graduate@wssu.edu. *Chair, Education*, Dr. Cathy Griffin-Famble, 336-750-2550, Fax: 336-750-2335, E-mail: famblecg@wssu.edu.

Program in Nursing Students: 88 full-time (82 women), 31 part-time (30 women); includes 65 minority (64 African Americans, 1 Hispanic American). Average age 38. 50 applicants, 100% accepted, 46 enrolled. *Faculty:* 8 full-time (6 women). Expenses: Contact institution. *Financial support:* In 2008–09, 24 students received support, including 2 research assistantships (averaging $5,000 per year), 1 teaching assistantship (averaging $2,500 per year); career-related internships or fieldwork, institutionally sponsored loans, scholarships/grants, traineeships, and tuition waivers (partial) also available. In 2008, 37 master's awarded. *Degree program information:* Part-time and evening/weekend programs available. Postbaccalaureate distance learning degree programs offered. Offers nursing (MSN). *Application deadline:* For fall admission, 7/15 for domestic and international students; for spring admission, 11/15 for domestic and international students. Applications are processed on a rolling basis. *Application fee:* $40. Electronic applications accepted. *Application Contact:* Graduate Studies and Research, 336-750-2102, Fax: 336-750-3042, E-mail: graduate@wssu.edu. *Chair*, Dr. Gohar Karami, 336-750-3278, Fax: 336-750-2568, E-mail: karamig@wssu.edu.

Program in Rehabilitation Counseling *Degree program information:* Part-time programs available. Postbaccalaureate distance learning degree programs offered (minimal on-campus study). Offers rehabilitation counseling (MRC). Electronic applications accepted.

WINTHROP UNIVERSITY, Rock Hill, SC 29733

General Information State-supported, coed, comprehensive institution. *Graduate housing:* Rooms and/or apartments available to single and married students. Housing application deadline: 3/1.

GRADUATE UNITS

College of Arts and Sciences *Degree program information:* Part-time programs available. Offers arts and sciences (MA, MLA, MS, SSP); biology (MS); English (MA); history (MA); human nutrition (MS); liberal arts (MLA); psychology (MS, SSP); social work (MA); Spanish (MA). Electronic applications accepted.

College of Business Administration *Degree program information:* Part-time and evening/weekend programs available. Postbaccalaureate distance learning degree programs offered (no on-campus study). Offers business administration (MBA, MS, Certificate); software development (MS); software project management (Certificate). Electronic applications accepted.

College of Education *Degree program information:* Part-time programs available. Offers agency counseling (M Ed); education (M Ed, MAT, MS); educational leadership (M Ed); middle level education (M Ed); physical education (MS); reading education (M Ed); school counseling (M Ed); secondary education (M Ed, MAT); special education (M Ed). Electronic applications accepted.

College of Visual and Performing Arts *Degree program information:* Part-time programs available. Offers art (MFA); art administration (MA); art education (MA); conducting (MM); music education (MME); performance (MM); visual and performing arts (MA, MFA, MM, MME). Electronic applications accepted.

WISCONSIN SCHOOL OF PROFESSIONAL PSYCHOLOGY, Milwaukee, WI 53225-4960

General Information Independent, coed, graduate-only institution. *Graduate housing:* On-campus housing not available.

GRADUATE UNITS

Program in Clinical Psychology *Degree program information:* Part-time and evening/weekend programs available. Offers clinical psychology (MA, Psy D).

WITTENBERG UNIVERSITY, Springfield, OH 45501-0720

General Information Independent-religious, coed, comprehensive institution.

GRADUATE UNITS

Graduate Program

WOODBURY UNIVERSITY, Burbank, CA 91504-1099

General Information Independent, coed, comprehensive institution. *Graduate housing:* Room and/or apartments available on a first-come, first-served basis to single students; on-campus housing not available to married students. Housing application deadline: 5/1.

GRADUATE UNITS

School of Architecture Offers real estate development (M Arch).

School of Business and Management *Degree program information:* Part-time and evening/weekend programs available. Offers business administration (MBA); organizational leadership (MA).

WOODS HOLE OCEANOGRAPHIC INSTITUTION, Woods Hole, MA 02543-1541

General Information Independent, coed, graduate-only institution. CGS member. *Graduate housing:* Rooms and/or apartments guaranteed to single students and available on a first-come, first-served basis to married students.

GRADUATE UNITS

MIT/WHOI Joint Program in Oceanography/Applied Ocean Science and Engineering Offers applied ocean sciences (PhD); biological oceanography (PhD, Sc D); chemical oceanography (PhD, Sc D); civil and environmental and oceanographic engineering (PhD); electrical and oceanographic engineering (PhD); geochemistry (PhD); geophysics (PhD); marine biology (PhD); marine geochemistry (PhD, Sc D); marine geology (PhD, Sc D); marine geophysics (PhD); mechanical and oceanographic engineering (PhD); ocean engineering (PhD); oceanographic engineering (M Eng, MS, PhD, Sc D, Eng); paleoceanography (PhD); physical oceanography (PhD, Sc D). Electronic applications accepted.

WORCESTER POLYTECHNIC INSTITUTE, Worcester, MA 01609-2280

General Information Independent, coed, university. CGS member. *Enrollment:* 4,561 graduate, professional, and undergraduate students; 533 full-time matriculated graduate/professional students (164 women), 455 part-time matriculated graduate/professional students (108 women). *Enrollment by degree level:* 699 master's, 205 doctoral, 84 other advanced degrees. *Graduate faculty:* 134 full-time (27 women), 50 part-time/adjunct (8 women). *Graduate housing:* On-campus housing not available. *Student services:* Campus employment opportunities, campus safety program, career counseling, exercise/wellness program, free psychological counseling, grant writing training, international student services, low-cost health insurance, multicultural affairs office, services for students with disabilities, teacher training, writing training. *Library facilities:* George C. Gordon Library. *Online resources:* library catalog, web page, access to other libraries' catalogs. *Collection:* 272,022 titles, 56,300 serial subscriptions, 1,941 audiovisual materials. *Research affiliation:* Manufacturing Advancement Center, Massachusetts Extension Partnership, Massachusetts Biomedical Initiatives, Alden Research Laboratory (hydraulics), University of Massachusetts Medical School at Worcester (basic, transitional and clinical medical research), Tufts University (veterinary medicine).

Computer facilities: Computer purchase and lease plans are available. 500 computers available on campus for general student use. A campuswide network can be accessed from student residence rooms and from off campus. Online class registration, online course content are available. *Web address:* http://www.wpi.edu/.

General Application Contact: Lynne Dougherty, Administrative Assistant, 508-831-5301, Fax: 508-831-5717, E-mail: grad@wpi.edu.

GRADUATE UNITS

Graduate Studies and Research Students: 533 full-time (164 women), 455 part-time (108 women); includes 57 minority (24 African Americans, 1 American Indian/Alaska Native, 16 Asian Americans or Pacific Islanders, 16 Hispanic Americans), 338 international. Average age 32. 1,810 applicants, 60% accepted, 358 enrolled. *Faculty:* 134 full-time (27 women), 50 part-time/adjunct (8 women). Expenses: Contact institution. *Financial support:* In 2008–09, 222 students received support, including 24 fellowships with full tuition reimbursements available (averaging $22,152 per year), 73 research assistantships with full and partial tuition reimbursements available (averaging $22,488 per year), 125 teaching assistantships with full and partial tuition reimbursements available (averaging $21,288 per year); career-related internships or fieldwork, institutionally sponsored loans, scholarships/grants, tuition waivers (partial), and unspecified assistantships also available. Financial award application deadline: 1/15. In 2008, 323 master's, 18 doctorates awarded. *Degree program information:* Part-time and evening/weekend programs available. Postbaccalaureate distance learning degree programs offered (no on-campus study). Offers advanced computer science (Advanced Certificate); advanced computer systems (Advanced Certificate); applied mathematics (MS); applied statistics (MS); artificial intelligence (Graduate Certificate); artificial intelligence data and knowledge (Advanced Certificate); biochemistry (MS, PhD); biology and biotechnology (MS); biomedical engineering (M Eng, MS, PhD, Graduate Certificate); bioscience administration (MS); biotechnology (PhD); building regulatory integration in construction management (Advanced Certificate); chemical engineering (MS, PhD); chemistry (MS, PhD); civil engineering (MS, PhD); clinical engineering (M Eng); compilers and languages (Advanced Certificate); computational fields (Advanced Certificate, Graduate Certificate); computational mechanics (Advanced Certificate); computer and communication networks (Advanced Certificate, Graduate Certificate); computer and communications networks (MS, Graduate Certificate); computer based support systems for construction management (Advanced Certificate); computer science (PhD); computer systems database design graphics (Graduate Certificate); construction project management (MS, Graduate Certificate); customized management (Graduate Certificate); data and knowledge based systems (Advanced Certificate); electrical engineering (MS, PhD); environmental engineering (MS, Graduate Certificate); financial mathematics (MS); fire protection engineering (MS, PhD); geotechnical engineering (Graduate Certificate); image processing (Graduate Certificate); image science (Advanced Certificate); impact engineering (MS); industrial mathematics (MS, Graduate Certificate); industrial statistics

Worcester Polytechnic Institute (continued)

(Graduate Certificate); information security (Graduate Certificate); information security management (Graduate Certificate); information technology (MS); interdisciplinary social science (PhD); management of technology (Graduate Certificate); manufacturing engineering (MS, PhD, Graduate Certificate); manufacturing engineering management (MS); marketing and technological innovation (MS); master builder (Graduate Certificate); master builder environmental engineering (M Eng); materials process engineering (MS); materials science and engineering (MS, PhD, Advanced Certificate); materials/transportation (Graduate Certificate); mathematical sciences (PhD); mathematics (MME); mechanical engineering (MS, PhD, Advanced Certificate); operations design and leadership (MS); physics (MS, PhD); power systems management (MS); robotics (MS); social science (PhD); software engineering (Graduate Certificate); structural engineering (Graduate Certificate); system dynamics (MS, Graduate Certificate); systems engineering (MS); systems modeling (MS); technology (MBA); technology marketing (Graduate Certificate); visualization programming languages (Graduate Certificate); waste minimization and management (Advanced Certificate). *Application deadline:* For fall admission, 1/15 priority date for domestic and international students; for spring admission, 10/15 priority date for domestic and international students. Applications are processed on a rolling basis. *Application fee:* $70. Electronic applications accepted. *Application Contact:* Lynne Dougherty, Administrative Assistant, 508-831-5301, Fax: 508-831-5717, E-mail: grad@wpi.edu.

See Close-Up on page 1059.

WORCESTER STATE COLLEGE, Worcester, MA 01602-2597

General Information State-supported, coed, comprehensive institution. *Enrollment:* 5,378 graduate, professional, and undergraduate students; 101 full-time matriculated graduate/professional students (93 women), 251 part-time matriculated graduate/professional students (195 women). *Enrollment by degree level:* 346 master's, 6 other advanced degrees. *Graduate faculty:* 30 full-time (20 women), 19 part-time/adjunct (10 women). Tuition, state resident: full-time $2700; part-time $150 per credit. Tuition, nonresident: full-time $2700; part-time $150 per credit. *Required fees:* $1530; $85 per credit. *Graduate housing:* On-campus housing not available. *Student services:* Campus safety program, career counseling, free psychological counseling, international student services, low-cost health insurance, multicultural affairs office, services for students with disabilities, teacher training, writing training. *Library facilities:* Worcester State College Library. *Online resources:* library catalog, web page, access to other libraries' catalogs. *Collection:* 174,299 titles, 523 serial subscriptions, 13,008 audiovisual materials.

Computer facilities: Computer purchase and lease plans are available. 500 computers available on campus for general student use. A campuswide network can be accessed from student residence rooms and from off campus. Online class registration is available. *Web address:* http://www.worcester.edu/.

General Application Contact: Nicole Brown, Assistant Dean of Graduate and Continuing Education, 508-929-8787, Fax: 508-929-8100, E-mail: nbrown@worcester.edu.

GRADUATE UNITS

Graduate Studies Students: 101 full-time (93 women), 251 part-time (195 women); includes 25 minority (4 African Americans, 2 American Indian/Alaska Native, 5 Asian Americans or Pacific Islanders, 14 Hispanic Americans), 10 international. Average age 33. 425 applicants, 51% accepted, 96 enrolled. *Faculty:* 30 full-time (20 women), 19 part-time/adjunct (10 women). Expenses: Contact institution. *Financial support:* In 2008–09, 36 students received support, including 36 research assistantships with full tuition reimbursements available (averaging $4,800 per year); career-related internships or fieldwork, scholarships/grants, and unspecified assistantships also available. Financial award application deadline: 3/1; financial award applicants required to submit FAFSA. In 2008, 183 master's awarded. *Degree program information:* Part-time and evening/weekend programs available. Offers accounting (MS); biotechnology (MS); community health nursing (MS); early childhood education (M Ed); elementary education (M Ed); English (M Ed); health care administration (MS); health education (M Ed); history (M Ed); leadership and administration (M Ed, CAGS); middle school education (M Ed); moderate special needs (M Ed); non-profit management (MS); occupational therapy (MOT); organizational leadership (MS); reading (M Ed, CAGS); school psychology (M Ed, CAGS); secondary education (M Ed); Spanish (M Ed); speech-language pathology (MS). *Application deadline:* Applications are processed on a rolling basis. *Application fee:* $30. *Application Contact:* Nicole Brown, Assistant Dean of Continuing Education, 508-929-8787, Fax: 508-929-8100, E-mail: nbrown@worcester.edu. *Associate Vice President for Continuing Education and Outreach/Dean of the Graduate School,* Dr. William H. White, 508-929-8111, Fax: 508-929-8100, E-mail: wwhite@worcester.edu.

WORLD MEDICINE INSTITUTE: COLLEGE OF ACUPUNCTURE AND HERBAL MEDICINE, Honolulu, HI 96828

General Information Independent, coed, graduate-only institution. *Graduate housing:* On-campus housing not available.

GRADUATE UNITS

Program in Acupuncture and Oriental Medicine *Degree program information:* Part-time and evening/weekend programs available. Offers acupuncture and Oriental medicine (M Ac OM).

WRIGHT INSTITUTE, Berkeley, CA 94704-1796

General Information Independent, coed, graduate-only institution. *Graduate housing:* On-campus housing not available.

GRADUATE UNITS

Program in Clinical Psychology Students: 328 full-time (234 women); includes 61 minority (9 African Americans, 1 American Indian/Alaska Native, 23 Asian Americans or Pacific Islanders, 28 Hispanic Americans), 5 international. Average age 34. 333 applicants, 35% accepted, 61 enrolled. *Faculty:* 10 full-time (7 women), 35 part-time/adjunct (16 women). Expenses: Contact institution. *Financial support:* In 2008–09, 78 students received support, including 42 teaching assistantships (averaging $1,600 per year); fellowships, research assistantships, career-related internships or fieldwork and Federal Work-Study also available. Financial award application deadline: 7/1. In 2008, 48 doctorates awarded. Offers clinical psychology (Psy D). *Application deadline:* For fall admission, 1/15 priority date for domestic students, 1/15 for international students. *Application fee:* $50. Electronic applications accepted. *Application Contact:* Liz Hertz, Director of Admissions, 510-841-9230 Ext. 111, Fax: 510-841-0167, E-mail: lhertz@wrightinst.edu. *Dean,* Dr. Charles Alexander, 510-841-9230 Ext. 101, E-mail: calexander@wi.edu.

Program in Counseling Psychology Offers counseling psychology (MA).

WRIGHT STATE UNIVERSITY, Dayton, OH 45435

General Information State-supported, coed, university. CGS member. *Graduate housing:* Rooms and/or apartments available on a first-come, first-served basis to single students and available to married students. *Research affiliation:* Wright-Patterson Air Force Base (research and development, systems and logistics), Wright-Patterson Air Force Base Medical Center, Veterans Administration Medical Center, Scott-Kettering Magnetic Resonance Research Laboratory (medical science), Edison Biotechnology Center, Edison Materials Technology Center (processing).

GRADUATE UNITS

School of Graduate Studies *Degree program information:* Part-time and evening/weekend programs available. Offers interdisciplinary studies (MA, MS). Electronic applications accepted.

College of Education and Human Services *Degree program information:* Part-time and evening/weekend programs available. Offers adolescent young adult (M Ed, MA); advanced curriculum and instruction (Ed S); advanced educational leadership (Ed S); career, technology and vocational education (M Ed, MA); chemical dependency (MRC); classroom teacher education (M Ed, MA); computer/technology education (M Ed, MA); counseling (M Ed, MA, MS); curriculum and instruction: teacher leader (MA); early childhood education (M Ed, MA); education and human services (M Ed, MA, MRC, MS, MST, Ed S); educational administrative specialist: teacher leader (M Ed); educational administrative specialist: vocational education administration (M Ed, MA); educational leadership (M Ed, MA); gifted educational needs (M Ed, MA); health, physical education, and recreation (M Ed, MA); higher education-adult education (Ed S); intervention specialist (M Ed, MA); library/media (M Ed, MA); middle childhood education (M Ed, MA); mild to moderate educational needs (M Ed, MA); moderate to intensive educational needs (M Ed, MA); multi-age (M Ed, MA); pupil personnel services (M Ed, MA); rehabilitation counseling (MRC); severe disabilities (MRC); student affairs in higher education-administration (M Ed, MA); superintendent (Ed S); vocational education (M Ed, MA); workforce education (M Ed, MA).

College of Engineering and Computer Science *Degree program information:* Part-time and evening/weekend programs available. Offers biomedical and human factors engineering (MSE); biomedical engineering (MSE); computer engineering (MSCE); computer science (MS); computer science and engineering (MS, MSCE, PhD); electrical engineering (MSE); engineering (PhD); engineering and computer science (MS, MSCE, MSE, PhD); human factors engineering (MSE); materials science and engineering (MSE); mechanical and materials engineering (MSE); mechanical engineering (MSE).

College of Liberal Arts *Degree program information:* Part-time programs available. Offers composition and rhetoric (MA); criminal justice and social problems (MA); English (MA); history (MA); humanities (M Hum); international and comparative politics (MA); liberal arts (M Hum, M Mus, MA, MPA); literature (MA); music education (M Mus); performance (M Mus); public administration (MPA); teaching English to speakers of other languages (MA).

College of Nursing and Health *Degree program information:* Part-time and evening/weekend programs available. Offers acute care nurse practitioner (MS); administration of nursing and health care systems (MS); adult health (MS); child and adolescent health (MS); community health (MS); family nurse practitioner (MS); nurse practitioner (MS); nursing and health (MS); school nurse (MS).

College of Science and Mathematics *Degree program information:* Part-time and evening/weekend programs available. Offers anatomy (MS); applied mathematics (MS); applied statistics (MS); biochemistry and molecular biology (MS); biological sciences (MS); biomedical sciences (PhD); chemistry (MS); earth science education (MST); environmental sciences (PhD); geological sciences (MS); geophysics (MS); human factors and industrial/organizational psychology (MS, PhD); mathematics (MS); medical physics (MS); microbiology and immunology (MS); physics (MS); physics education (MST); physiology and biophysics (MS); science and mathematics (MS, MST, PhD).

Raj Soin College of Business *Degree program information:* Part-time and evening/weekend programs available. Offers accountancy (M Acc, MBA); accounting (MBA); business (M Acc, MBA, MIS, MS); business administration (MBA); business economics (MBA); finance (MBA); flexible business (MBA); health care management (MBA); information systems (MIS); international business (MBA); logistics and supply chain management (MS); management information technology (MBA); management, innovation and change (MBA); marketing (MBA); project management (MBA); social and applied economics (MS); supply chain management (MBA).

School of Medicine Offers aerospace medicine (MS); health promotion and education (MPH); medicine (MD, MPH, MS, PhD); pharmacology and toxicology (MS); public health management (MPH); public health nursing (MPH).

School of Professional Psychology Offers clinical psychology (Psy D).

WYCLIFFE COLLEGE, Toronto, ON M5S 1H7, Canada

General Information Independent-religious, coed, graduate-only institution. *Graduate housing:* Rooms and/or apartments guaranteed to single students and available on a first-come, first-served basis to married students. Housing application deadline: 5/1.

GRADUATE UNITS

Division of Advanced Degree Studies *Degree program information:* Part-time programs available. Offers theology (MA, Th M, D Min, PhD, Th D).

Division of Basic Degree Studies *Degree program information:* Part-time programs available. Offers Christian Studies (Diploma); theology (M Div, M Rel, MTS).

XAVIER UNIVERSITY, Cincinnati, OH 45207

General Information Independent-religious, coed, comprehensive institution. *Enrollment:* 6,584 graduate, professional, and undergraduate students; 779 full-time matriculated graduate/professional students (437 women), 1,650 part-time matriculated graduate/professional students (968 women). *Enrollment by degree level:* 2,336 master's, 93 doctoral. *Graduate faculty:* 161 full-time (72 women), 136 part-time/adjunct (70 women). Tuition and fees vary according to course load, degree level and program. *Graduate housing:* Room and/or apartments available on a first-come, first-served basis to single students; on-campus housing not available to married students. Housing application deadline: 5/1. *Student services:* Campus employment opportunities, campus safety program, career counseling, exercise/wellness program, international student services, low-cost health insurance, multicultural affairs office, services for students with disabilities, teacher training, writing training. *Library facilities:* McDonald Memorial Library at Xavier University. *Online resources:* library catalog, web page, access to other libraries' catalogs. *Collection:* 363,140 titles, 55,934 serial subscriptions, 11,029 audiovisual materials.

Computer facilities: Computer purchase and lease plans are available. 250 computers available on campus for general student use. A campuswide network can be accessed from student residence rooms and from off campus. Online class registration is available. *Web address:* http://www.xu.edu/.

General Application Contact: Roger Bosse, Interim Director of Graduate Studies, 513-745-3357, Fax: 513-745-1048, E-mail: bosse@xavier.edu.

GRADUATE UNITS

College of Arts and Sciences Students: 11 full-time (6 women), 35 part-time (20 women). Average age 33. 29 applicants, 66% accepted, 14 enrolled. *Faculty:* 25 full-time (9 women). Expenses: Contact institution. *Financial support:* Scholarships/grants and unspecified assistantships available. Support available to part-time students. Financial award applicants required to submit FAFSA. In 2008, 11 master's awarded. *Degree program information:* Part-time programs available. Offers arts and sciences (MA); English (MA); theology (MA). *Application deadline:* Applications are processed on a rolling basis. *Application fee:* $35. Electronic applications accepted. *Application Contact:* Dr. Janice B. Walker, Dean, 513-745-3101, Fax: 513-745-1099, E-mail: walker@xavier.edu. *Dean,* Dr. Janice B. Walker, 513-745-3101, Fax: 513-745-1099, E-mail: walker@xavier.edu.

College of Social Sciences, Health and Education Students: 493 full-time (354 women), 859 part-time (687 women); includes 136 minority (97 African Americans, 6 American Indian/Alaska Native, 21 Asian Americans or Pacific Islanders, 12 Hispanic Americans), 12 international. Average age 32. *Faculty:* 77 full-time (44 women), 115 part-time/adjunct (61 women). Expenses: Contact institution. *Financial support:* Career-related internships or fieldwork, scholarships/grants, traineeships, unspecified assistantships, and residency stipends available. Support available to part-time students. Financial award applicants required to submit FAFSA. In 2008, 565 master's, 12 doctorates awarded. *Degree program information:* Part-time and evening/weekend programs available. Offers clinical nurse leader (MSN); clinical psychology (Psy D); criminal justice (MS); forensic nursing (MSN); health services administration (MHSA); healthcare law (MSN); nursing administration (MSN); occupational therapy (MOT); psychology (MA); school nursing (MSN); social sciences, health and education (M Ed, MA, MHSA, MOT, MS, MSN, Psy D); sport administration (M Ed). *Application fee:* $35. *Application Contact:* Roger Bosse, Interim Director of Graduate Studies, 513-745-3357, Fax: 513-745-1048, E-mail: bosse@xavier.edu. *Dean,* Dr. Mark Meyers, 513-745-3119, Fax: 513-745-1058, E-mail: meyersd3@xavier.edu.

School of Education Students: 251 full-time (192 women), 615 part-time (497 women); includes 80 minority (61 African Americans, 4 American Indian/Alaska Native, 7 Asian Americans or Pacific Islanders, 8 Hispanic Americans), 4 international. Average age 32. *Faculty:* 33 full-time (17 women), 79 part-time/adjunct (43 women). Expenses: Contact institution. *Financial support:* Applicants required to submit FAFSA. In 2008, 371 master's awarded. Offers community counseling (MA); education (M Ed, MA); educational administration (M Ed); elementary education (M Ed); human resource development (M Ed); Montessori (M Ed); multicultural literature for children (M Ed); reading (M Ed); school counseling (MA); secondary education (M Ed); special education (M Ed). *Application deadline:* Applications are processed on a rolling basis. *Application fee:* $35. Electronic applications accepted. *Application Contact:* Dr. Jennifer Fager, Associate Dean, 513-745-3495, Fax: 513-745-1052, E-mail: fagerj@xavier.edu. *Associate Dean*, Dr. Jennifer Fager, 513-745-3495, Fax: 513-745-1052, E-mail: fagerj@xavier.edu.

Williams College of Business Students: 275 full-time (77 women), 756 part-time (261 women); includes 140 minority (42 African Americans, 72 Asian Americans or Pacific Islanders, 26 Hispanic Americans), 20 international. Average age 31. 431 applicants, 74% accepted, 294 enrolled. *Faculty:* 47 full-time (14 women), 18 part-time/adjunct (6 women). Expenses: Contact institution. *Financial support:* In 2008–09, 252 students received support. Scholarships/grants and tuition waivers (partial) available. Financial award application deadline: 3/1; financial award applicants required to submit FAFSA. In 2008, 326 master's awarded. *Degree program information:* Part-time and evening/weekend programs available. Offers business (Exec MBA, MBA); business administration (Exec MBA, MBA); e-commerce (MBA); finance (MBA); international business (MBA); management information systems (MBA); marketing (MBA). *Application deadline:* For fall admission, 8/1 priority date for domestic students, 5/1 for international students; for spring admission, 12/1 priority date for domestic students, 9/1 for international students. Applications are processed on a rolling basis. *Application fee:* $35. Electronic applications accepted. *Application Contact:* Jennifer Bush, Executive Director, MBA Programs, 513-745-3525, Fax: 513-745-2929, E-mail: bush@xavier.edu. *Dean*, Dr. Ali Malekzadeh, 513-745-3528, Fax: 513-745-2929, E-mail: malekzadeh@xavier.edu.

XAVIER UNIVERSITY OF LOUISIANA, New Orleans, LA 70125-1098

General Information Independent-religious, coed, comprehensive institution. CGS member. *Graduate housing:* On-campus housing not available.

GRADUATE UNITS

College of Pharmacy Offers pharmacy (Pharm D). Electronic applications accepted.

Graduate School *Degree program information:* Part-time and evening/weekend programs available. Offers curriculum and instruction (MA); education administration and supervision (MA); guidance and counseling (MA).

Institute for Black Catholic Studies *Degree program information:* Part-time programs available. Offers pastoral theology (Th M).

YALE UNIVERSITY, New Haven, CT 06520

General Information Independent, coed, university. CGS member. *Graduate housing:* Rooms and/or apartments available on a first-come, first-served basis to single and married students. Housing application deadline: 6/1. *Research affiliation:* Howard Hughes Medical Institute, J. B. Pierce Foundation (environmental physiology), Haskins Laboratories (speech, hearing, reading).

GRADUATE UNITS

Divinity School Students: 327 full-time (158 women), 35 part-time (20 women); includes 55 minority (36 African Americans, 11 Asian Americans or Pacific Islanders, 8 Hispanic Americans), 34 international. Average age 32. 558 applicants, 50% accepted, 159 enrolled. *Faculty:* 35 full-time (12 women), 14 part-time/adjunct (2 women). Expenses: Contact institution. *Financial support:* In 2008–09, 300 fellowships (averaging $14,260 per year) were awarded; career-related internships or fieldwork, Federal Work-Study, and scholarships/grants also available. Support available to part-time students. Financial award application deadline: 3/1; financial award applicants required to submit FAFSA. In 2008, 74 first professional degrees, 68 master's awarded. *Degree program information:* Part-time programs available. Offers divinity (M Div, MAR, STM). *Application deadline:* For fall admission, 1/15 for domestic and international students. *Application fee:* $75. Electronic applications accepted. *Application Contact:* Anna T. Ramirez, Associate Dean of Admissions and Financial Aid, 203-432-9802, Fax: 203-432-7475, E-mail: anna.ramirez@yale.edu. *Dean*, Dr. Harold W. Attridge, 203-432-5306, Fax: 203-432-9712, E-mail: harold.attridge@yale.edu.

Graduate School of Arts and Sciences *Degree program information:* Part-time programs available. Offers African studies (MA); African-American studies (PhD); American studies (PhD); anthropology (M Phil, MA, PhD); applied mathematics (M Phil, MS, PhD); Arabic and Islamic studies (MA, PhD); archaeological studies (MA); archaeology of the ancient Near East (MA, PhD); arts and sciences (M Phil, MA, MS, PhD, M E Sc/MA); Assyriology (MA, PhD); astronomy (PhD); behavioral neuroscience (PhD); biochemistry, molecular biology and chemical biology (PhD); biogeochemistry (PhD); biophysical chemistry (PhD); cell biology (PhD); cellular and developmental biology (PhD); cellular and molecular physiology (PhD); classics (M Phil, MA, PhD); climate dynamics (PhD); clinical psychology (PhD); cognitive psychology (PhD); comparative and historical sociology (PhD); comparative literature (PhD); computer science (MS, PhD); cultural sociology and social theory (PhD); developmental psychology (PhD); East Asian languages and literatures (PhD); East Asian languages and literatures and film studies (PhD); East Asian studies (MA); ecology and evolutionary biology (PhD); economics (PhD); Egyptology (MA, PhD); English language and literature (MA, PhD); environmental sciences (PhD); experimental pathology (MS, PhD); film studies (PhD); forestry (PhD); French (M Phil, MA, PhD); genetics (PhD); geochemistry (PhD); geophysics (PhD); German (PhD); Graeco-Arabic studies (MA, PhD); history (M Phil, MA, PhD); history of art (PhD); history of science and medicine (MS, PhD); immunobiology (PhD); inorganic chemistry (PhD); international and development economics (MA); international relations (MA, M E Sc/MA); Italian language and literature (PhD); Latin American literature (PhD); linguistics (PhD); Luso-Brazilian and Spanish/Spanish American literatures (PhD); mathematics (M Phil, MS, PhD); medieval Slavic literature and philology (PhD); medieval studies (M Phil, PhD); meteorology (PhD); molecular biophysics and biochemistry (PhD); music history (MA); music theory (MA); neurobiology (PhD); neuroscience (PhD); Northwest Semitic, Bible, comparative Semitics (MA, PhD); oceanography (PhD); organic chemistry (PhD); paleontology (PhD); paleooceanography (PhD); petrology (PhD); philosophy (PhD); physical and theoretical chemistry (PhD); physics (PhD); plant sciences (PhD); Polish literature (PhD); political science (PhD); religious studies (PhD); Renaissance studies (PhD); Russian and East European studies (MA); Russian literature (PhD); Slavic languages and literatures and film studies (PhD); social stratification and the life course (PhD); social/personality psychology (PhD); solar and terrestrial physics (PhD); Spanish peninsular literature (PhD); statistics (MA, PhD); tectonics (PhD).

School of Engineering and Applied Science *Degree program information:* Part-time programs available. Offers applied physics (MS, PhD); biomedical engineering (MS, PhD); chemical engineering (MS, PhD); electrical engineering (MS, PhD); engineering and applied science (MS, PhD); environmental engineering (MS, PhD); mechanical engineering (MS, PhD).

School of Architecture Offers architecture (M Arch, M Env Des, MEM).

School of Art Students: 119 full-time (59 women); includes 26 minority (6 African Americans, 9 Asian Americans or Pacific Islanders, 11 Hispanic Americans), 18 international. Average age 27. 1,151 applicants, 6% accepted, 56 enrolled. *Faculty:* 7 full-time (3 women), 36 part-time/adjunct (12 women). Expenses: Contact institution. *Financial support:* In 2008–09, 90 students received support, including 56 teaching assistantships (averaging $1,650 per year); Federal Work-Study and scholarships/grants also available. Financial award application deadline: 3/1; financial award applicants required to submit FAFSA. In 2008, 56 master's awarded. Offers graphic design (MFA); painting/printmaking (MFA); photography (MFA); sculpture (MFA). *Application deadline:* For fall admission, 1/6 for domestic and international students. *Application fee:* $90. *Application Contact:* Patricia Ann DeChiara, Director of Academic Affairs, 203-432-2600, E-mail: artschool.info@yale.edu. *Dean*, Robert Storr, 203-432-2606.

School of Drama Offers drama (MFA, DFA, Certificate). Electronic applications accepted.

School of Forestry and Environmental Studies *Degree program information:* Part-time programs available. Offers forestry and environmental studies (MEM, MES, MF, MFS, PhD). Electronic applications accepted.

School of Medicine *Degree program information:* Part-time programs available. Offers biological and biomedical sciences (PhD); computational biology and bioinformatics (PhD); immunology (PhD); medicine (MD, MM Sc, MPH, MS, PhD, MM Sc/MPH); microbiology (PhD); molecular biophysics and biochemistry (PhD); molecular cell biology, genetics, and development (PhD); neurobiology (PhD); neuroscience (PhD); pharmacological sciences and molecular medicine (PhD); pharmacology (PhD); physician associate (MM Sc, MM Sc/MPH); physiology and integrative medical biology (PhD). Electronic applications accepted.

School of Public Health *Degree program information:* Part-time programs available. Offers biostatistics (MPH, MS, PhD); chronic disease epidemiology (MPH, PhD); environmental health sciences (MPH, PhD); epidemiology of microbial diseases (MPH, PhD); global health (MPH); health management (MPH); health policy and administration (MPH, PhD); parasitology (PhD); social and behavioral sciences (MPH). MS and PhD offered through the Graduate School. Electronic applications accepted.

School of Music Students: 222 full-time (100 women); includes 31 minority (5 African Americans, 23 Asian Americans or Pacific Islanders, 3 Hispanic Americans), 83 international. Average age 24. 1,207 applicants, 12% accepted, 109 enrolled. *Faculty:* 27 full-time (7 women), 31 part-time/adjunct (6 women). Expenses: Contact institution. *Financial support:* In 2008–09, 221 students received support, including 221 fellowships (averaging $30,000 per year); Federal Work-Study, institutionally sponsored loans, and scholarships/grants also available. Financial award application deadline: 5/30; financial award applicants required to submit FAFSA. In 2008, 82 master's, 7 doctorates, 27 ADs awarded. Offers music (MM, MMA, DMA, AD, Certificate). *Application deadline:* For fall admission, 12/1 for domestic and international students. *Application fee:* $100. Electronic applications accepted. *Application Contact:* Suzanne M. Stringer, Registrar and Financial Aid Administrator, 203-432-1962, Fax: 203-432-7448, E-mail: suzanne.stringer@yale.edu. *Dean*, Robert Blocker, 203-432-4160, Fax: 203-432-7542.

School of Nursing Students: 279 full-time (261 women), 50 part-time (45 women); includes 53 minority (17 African Americans, 3 American Indian/Alaska Native, 22 Asian Americans or Pacific Islanders, 11 Hispanic Americans), 13 international. Average age 28. 537 applicants, 38% accepted, 115 enrolled. *Faculty:* 54 full-time (51 women), 95 part-time/adjunct (90 women). Expenses: Contact institution. *Financial support:* In 2008–09, 197 fellowships (averaging $5,650 per year), 18 research assistantships with tuition reimbursements (averaging $25,333 per year) were awarded; Federal Work-Study, institutionally sponsored loans, scholarships/grants, traineeships, and health care benefits also available. Support available to part-time students. Financial award application deadline: 2/1; financial award applicants required to submit FAFSA. In 2008, 80 master's, 3 doctorates, 2 other advanced degrees awarded. *Degree program information:* Part-time programs available. Postbaccalaureate distance learning degree programs offered (minimal on-campus study). Offers nursing (MSN, PhD, Post Master's Certificate). *Application deadline:* For fall admission, 11/1 priority date for domestic students. *Application fee:* $65. Electronic applications accepted. *Application Contact:* Angela Kuhne, Director, Admissions, 203-737-1793, Fax: 203-737-5409, E-mail: angela.kunhe@yale.edu. *Dean*, Dr. Margaret Grey, 203-785-2393, Fax: 203-785-6455, E-mail: margaret.grey@yale.edu.

Yale Law School Students: 588 full-time (286 women). Average age 25. 3,109 applicants, 8% accepted, 189 enrolled. *Faculty:* 65 full-time, 25 part-time/adjunct. Expenses: Contact institution. *Financial support:* Application deadline: 3/15. In 2008, 196 JDs, 16 master's, 2 doctorates awarded. Offers law (JD, LL M, MSL, JSD). *Application deadline:* For fall admission, 2/15 for domestic students. Applications are processed on a rolling basis. *Application fee:* $75. Electronic applications accepted. *Application Contact:* Asha Rangappa, Associate Dean, 203-432-4995, E-mail: admissions.law@yale.edu. *Dean*, Harold Hongju Koh, 203-432-1660.

Yale School of Management Offers accounting (PhD); business administration (MBA, PhD); financial economics (PhD); management (MBA, PhD); marketing (PhD). Electronic applications accepted.

YESHIVA BETH MOSHE, Scranton, PA 18505-2124

General Information Independent-religious, men only, comprehensive institution.

GRADUATE UNITS

Graduate Programs

YESHIVA DERECH CHAIM, Brooklyn, NY 11218

General Information Independent-religious, men only, comprehensive institution.

GRADUATE UNITS

Graduate Program

YESHIVA KARLIN STOLIN RABBINICAL INSTITUTE, Brooklyn, NY 11204

General Information Independent-religious, men only, comprehensive institution. *Graduate housing:* On-campus housing not available.

GRADUATE UNITS

Graduate Programs

YESHIVA OF NITRA RABBINICAL COLLEGE, Mount Kisco, NY 10549

General Information Independent-religious, men only, comprehensive institution.

GRADUATE UNITS

Graduate Programs

YESHIVA SHAAR HATORAH TALMUDIC RESEARCH INSTITUTE, Kew Gardens, NY 11418-1469

General Information Independent-religious, men only, comprehensive institution.

GRADUATE UNITS

Graduate Programs

YESHIVATH VIZNITZ, Monsey, NY 10952

General Information Independent-religious, men only, comprehensive institution.

GRADUATE UNITS

Graduate Programs

YESHIVATH ZICHRON MOSHE, South Fallsburg, NY 12779

General Information Independent-religious, men only, comprehensive institution.

GRADUATE UNITS

Graduate Programs *Degree program information:* Part-time programs available.

YESHIVA TORAS CHAIM TALMUDICAL SEMINARY, Denver, CO 80204-1415

General Information Independent-religious, men only, comprehensive institution.

GRADUATE UNITS

Graduate Programs

YESHIVA UNIVERSITY, New York, NY 10033-3201

General Information Independent, coed, university. CGS member. *Graduate housing:* On-campus housing not available.

GRADUATE UNITS

Azrieli Graduate School of Jewish Education and Administration *Degree program information:* Part-time and evening/weekend programs available. Offers Jewish education and administration (MS, Ed D, Specialist).

Benjamin N. Cardozo School of Law Students: 1,038 full-time (523 women), 144 part-time (80 women); includes 234 minority (51 African Americans, 3 American Indian/Alaska Native, 111 Asian Americans or Pacific Islanders, 69 Hispanic Americans), 71 international. Average age 25. 4,790 applicants, 27% accepted, 371 enrolled. *Faculty:* 57 full-time (20 women), 75 part-time/adjunct (24 women). Expenses: Contact institution. *Financial support:* In 2008–09, 944 students received support, including 65 research assistantships; career-related internships or fieldwork, Federal Work-Study, institutionally sponsored loans, scholarships/grants, health care benefits, and tuition waivers (full and partial) also available. Support available to part-time students. Financial award application deadline: 4/15; financial award applicants required to submit FAFSA. In 2008, 362 JDs, 68 master's awarded. *Degree program information:* Part-time programs available. Offers comparative legal thought (LL M); general studies (LL M); intellectual property law (LL M); law (JD). *Application deadline:* For fall admission, 4/1 priority date for domestic students; for spring admission, 12/1 priority date for domestic students. Applications are processed on a rolling basis. *Application fee:* $70. Electronic applications accepted. *Application Contact:* David G. Martinidez, Dean of Admissions, 212-790-0274, Fax: 212-790-0482, E-mail: lawinfo@yu.edu. *Dean of Admissions*, David G. Martinidez, 212-790-0274, Fax: 212-790-0482, E-mail: lawinfo@yu.edu.

Bernard Revel Graduate School of Jewish Studies *Degree program information:* Part-time programs available. Offers Jewish studies (MA, PhD).

Ferkauf Graduate School of Psychology *Degree program information:* Part-time programs available. Offers clinical psychology (Psy D); health psychology (PhD); mental health counseling psychology (MA); psychology (MA, PhD, Psy D); school/clinical-child psychology (Psy D).

Sy Syms School of Business *Degree program information:* Part-time programs available. Offers accounting (MS).

Wurzweiler School of Social Work Students: 207 full-time (164 women), 204 part-time (149 women); includes 162 minority (95 African Americans, 7 American Indian/Alaska Native, 5 Asian Americans or Pacific Islanders, 55 Hispanic Americans). Average age 41. 390 applicants, 69% accepted, 177 enrolled. *Faculty:* 26 full-time (14 women), 64 part-time/adjunct (44 women). Expenses: Contact institution. *Financial support:* In 2008–09, 167 students received support, including 2 teaching assistantships (averaging $5,000 per year); career-related internships or fieldwork, Federal Work-Study, institutionally sponsored loans, and scholarships/grants also available. Financial award application deadline: 4/15; financial award applicants required to submit FAFSA. In 2008, 163 master's, 7 doctorates awarded. *Degree program information:* Part-time and evening/weekend programs available. Offers social work (MSW, PhD). *Application deadline:* For fall admission, 5/1 priority date for domestic students; for spring admission, 10/31 for domestic students. Applications are processed on a rolling basis. *Application fee:* $50. *Application Contact:* Ruth Bigman, Director of Admissions, 212-960-0811, Fax: 212-960-0822, E-mail: rbigman@yu.edu. *Dean*, Dr. Sheldon R. Gelman, 212-960-0820, Fax: 212-960-0822, E-mail: srgelman@yu.edu.

YORK COLLEGE OF PENNSYLVANIA, York, PA 17405-7199

General Information Independent, coed, comprehensive institution. *Enrollment:* 5,627 graduate, professional, and undergraduate students; 46 full-time matriculated graduate/professional students (27 women), 250 part-time matriculated graduate/professional students (154 women). *Enrollment by degree level:* 296 master's. *Graduate faculty:* 27 full-time (13 women), 13 part-time/adjunct (8 women). *Tuition:* Full-time $10,404; part-time $578 per credit. *Required fees:* $1360; $320 per semester. *Graduate housing:* On-campus housing not available. *Student services:* Campus employment opportunities, campus safety program, career counseling, free psychological counseling, international student services, low-cost health insurance, multicultural affairs office, services for students with disabilities. *Library facilities:* Schmidt Library. *Online resources:* library catalog, web page, access to other libraries' catalogs. *Collection:* 250,642 titles, 31,713 serial subscriptions, 12,515 audiovisual materials.

Computer facilities: 650 computers available on campus for general student use. A campuswide network can be accessed from student residence rooms and from off campus. Online class registration is available. *Web address:* http://www.ycp.edu/.

General Application Contact: Nancy Spataro, Director of Admissions, 717-815-1600, Fax: 717-849-1607, E-mail: admissions@ycp.edu.

GRADUATE UNITS

Department of Business Administration Students: 22 full-time (9 women), 128 part-time (50 women); includes 7 minority (4 African Americans, 2 Asian Americans or Pacific Islanders, 1 Hispanic American), 3 international. Average age 29. 55 applicants, 85% accepted, 37 enrolled. *Faculty:* 17 full-time (4 women), 1 (woman) part-time/adjunct. Expenses: Contact institution. *Financial support:* Federal Work-Study and scholarships/grants available. Financial award application deadline: 4/15; financial award applicants required to submit FAFSA. In 2008, 52 master's awarded. *Degree program information:* Part-time and evening/weekend programs available. Offers business administration (MBA). *Application deadline:* For fall admission, 7/15 priority date for domestic students; for spring admission, 12/15 priority date for domestic students. Applications are processed on a rolling basis. *Application fee:* $60. Electronic applications accepted. *Application Contact:* Brenda Adams, 717-815-1491, Fax: 717-600-3999, E-mail: badams@ycp.edu. *MBA Director*, Eric Hostler, 717-815-1947, E-mail: ehostler@ycp.edu.

Department of Education Students: 93 part-time (76 women). Average age 30. 17 applicants, 76% accepted, 9 enrolled. *Faculty:* 3 full-time (2 women), 7 part-time/adjunct (5 women). Expenses: Contact institution. *Financial support:* Federal Work-Study available. In 2008, 20 master's awarded. *Degree program information:* Part-time and evening/weekend programs available. Offers education (M Ed). *Application deadline:* For fall admission, 7/15 priority date for domestic students, 4/1 priority date for international students; for spring admission, 11/15 priority date for domestic students, 10/1 priority date for international students. Applications are processed on a rolling basis. *Application fee:* $60. Electronic applications accepted. *Application Contact:* Nancy Spataro, Director of Admissions, 717-815-1600, Fax: 717-849-1607, E-mail: admissions@ycp.edu. *Director*, Dr. Stacey Dammann, 717-815-6476, E-mail: sdammann@ycp.edu.

Department of Nursing Students: 24 full-time (18 women), 29 part-time (28 women); includes 3 minority (1 African American, 2 Asian Americans or Pacific Islanders). Average age 40. 34 applicants, 68% accepted, 15 enrolled. *Faculty:* 7 full-time (all women), 5 part-time/adjunct (2 women). Expenses: Contact institution. *Financial support:* Federal Work-Study available. In 2008, 8 master's awarded. *Degree program information:* Part-time and evening/weekend programs available. Offers nursing (MS). *Application deadline:* For fall admission, 7/15 priority date for domestic students; for spring admission, 11/15 priority date for domestic students. Applications are processed on a rolling basis. *Application fee:* $60. Electronic applications accepted. *Application Contact:* Nancy Spataro, Director of Admissions, 717-815-1600, Fax: 717-849-1607, E-mail: admissions@ycp.edu. *Coordinator*, Lynn Warner, 717-815-1212, E-mail: lwarner@ycp.edu.

YORK UNIVERSITY, Toronto, ON M3J 1P3, Canada

General Information Province-supported, coed, university. *Graduate housing:* Rooms and/or apartments available on a first-come, first-served basis to single and married students. *Research affiliation:* Imperial Oil LMT, National Palace Museum (Taiwan), Unicorn Children's Foundation (developmental and learning disorders), Smithsonian Institution (astronomy, physics, space), Beijing Municipality (management training), German Academic Exchange (German studies).

GRADUATE UNITS

Faculty of Graduate Studies *Degree program information:* Part-time and evening/weekend programs available. Offers communication and culture (MA, PhD); environmental studies (MES, PhD); interdisciplinary studies (MA); law (LL B, LL M, PhD). Electronic applications accepted.

Atkinson Faculty of Liberal and Professional Studies Offers disaster and emergency management (MA); human resources management (MHRM, PhD); liberal and professional studies (MA, MHRM, MPPAL, MSW, PhD); public policy, administration and law (MPPAL); social work (MSW, PhD).

Faculty of Arts *Degree program information:* Part-time programs available. Offers arts (M Sc, MA, PhD); economics (MA, PhD); English (MA, PhD); geography (M Sc, MA, PhD); history (MA, PhD); humanities (MA, PhD); international development studies (MA); philosophy (MA, PhD); political science (MA, PhD); social and political thought (MA, PhD); social anthropology (MA, PhD); sociology (MA, PhD); theoretical and applied linguistics (MA, PhD); women's studies (MA, PhD). Electronic applications accepted.

Faculty of Education *Degree program information:* Part-time programs available. Offers education (M Ed, PhD). Electronic applications accepted.

Faculty of Fine Arts *Degree program information:* Part-time programs available. Offers art history (MA, PhD); composition (MA); dance (MA, MFA); design (M Des); film (MA, MFA, PhD); fine arts (M Des, MA, MFA, PhD); musicology and ethnomusicology (MA, PhD); theatre (MFA); theatre studies (MA, PhD); visual arts (MFA, PhD). Electronic applications accepted.

Faculty of Health Offers critical disability studies (MA, PhD); health (M Sc, M Sc N, MA, PhD); kinesiology and health science (M Sc, MA, PhD); nursing (M Sc N); psychology (MA, PhD).

Faculty of Science and Engineering *Degree program information:* Part-time and evening/weekend programs available. Offers biology (M Sc, PhD); chemistry (M Sc, PhD); computer science (M Sc, PhD); earth and space science (M Sc, PhD); industrial and applied mathematics (M Sc); mathematics and statistics (MA, PhD); physics and astronomy (M Sc, PhD); science and engineering (M Sc, MA, PhD).

Glendon College Offers French studies (MA); public and international affairs (MA); translation (MA).

Schulich School of Business *Degree program information:* Part-time and evening/weekend programs available. Offers accounting (PhD); business (EMBA, MBA); finance (PhD); international business (IMBA); marketing (PhD); operations management and information systems (PhD); organizational behaviour and industrial relations (PhD); policy/strategic management (PhD); public administration (MPA). Electronic applications accepted.

YO SAN UNIVERSITY OF TRADITIONAL CHINESE MEDICINE, Los Angeles, CA 90066

General Information Private, coed, graduate-only institution. *Graduate housing:* On-campus housing not available.

GRADUATE UNITS

Program in Acupuncture and Traditional Chinese Medicine *Degree program information:* Part-time programs available. Postbaccalaureate distance learning degree programs offered (no on-campus study). Offers acupuncture and traditional Chinese medicine (MATCM).

YOUNGSTOWN STATE UNIVERSITY, Youngstown, OH 44555-0001

General Information State-supported, coed, comprehensive institution. CGS member. *Graduate housing:* Room and/or apartments available on a first-come, first-served basis to single students; on-campus housing not available to married students. *Research affiliation:* Ohio Supercomputer Center (computational chemistry and physics), Northeast Ohio Universities College of Medicine (medicine), Parker-Hannifin Corporation (engineering technology), Ohio Mass Spectrometry Consortium (chemistry and biology), BioRemedial Technologies Inc. (environmental bioremediation).

GRADUATE UNITS

Graduate School *Degree program information:* Part-time and evening/weekend programs available.

Beeghly College of Education *Degree program information:* Part-time and evening/weekend programs available. Offers adolescent/young adult education (MS Ed); community counseling (MS Ed); content area concentration (MS Ed); early childhood education (MS Ed); education (MS Ed, Ed D); educational administration (MS Ed); educational leadership (Ed D); educational technology (MS Ed); gifted and talented education (MS Ed); literacy (MS Ed); middle childhood education (MS Ed); school counseling (MS Ed); special education (MS Ed).

Bitonte College of Health and Human Services *Degree program information:* Part-time and evening/weekend programs available. Offers criminal justice (MS); health and human services (MHHS, MPH, MS, MSN, DPT); nursing (MSN); physical therapy (DPT); public health (MPH).

College of Fine and Performing Arts *Degree program information:* Part-time and evening/weekend programs available. Offers fine and performing arts (MM); jazz studies (MM); music education (MM); music history and literature (MM); music theory and composition (MM); performance (MM).

College of Liberal Arts and Social Sciences *Degree program information:* Part-time programs available. Offers applied behavior analysis (MS); economics (MA); English (MA); environmental studies (MS); financial economics (MA); history (MA); industrial/institutional management (Certificate); liberal arts and social sciences (MA, MS, Certificate); risk management (Certificate).

College of Science, Technology, Engineering and Mathematics *Degree program information:* Part-time and evening/weekend programs available. Offers analytical chemistry (MS); applied mathematics (MS); biochemistry (MS); chemistry education (MS); civil and environmental engineering (MSE); computer engineering (MSE); computer science (MS); computing and information systems (MCIS); electrical engineering (MSE); environmental biology (MS); industrial and systems engineering (MSE); inorganic chemistry (MS); mechanical engineering (MSE); molecular biology, microbiology, and genetic (MS); organic chemistry (MS); physical chemistry (MS); physiology and anatomy (MS); science, technology, engineering and mathematics (MCIS, MSE); secondary mathematics (MS); statistics (MS).

Williamson College of Business Administration *Degree program information:* Part-time and evening/weekend programs available. Offers accounting (MBA); business administration (MBA, Certificate); enterprise resource planning (Certificate); marketing (MBA).

CLOSE-UPS
OF INSTITUTIONS OFFERING
GRADUATE AND PROFESSIONAL WORK

ANGELO STATE UNIVERSITY

College of Graduate Studies

Programs of Study

Angelo State University offers programs in twenty-two areas of study, leading to Master of Arts, Master of Business Administration (M.B.A.), Master of Education, Master of Professional Accountancy, Master of Public Administration, Doctor of Physical Therapy (D.P.T.), Master of Science, and Master of Science in Nursing (M.S.N.) degrees as well as integrated B.B.A./M.B.A. (accounting), B.B.A./Master of Professional Accountancy, and RN-to-M.S.N. degrees.

Major areas of study include accounting, animal science, biology, business administration, communication, counseling psychology (with course work leading to Texas state licensure as a Licensed Professional Counselor or a psychological associate), curriculum and instruction, educational diagnostics, educational guidance and counseling, English, applied psychology, history, industrial/organizational psychology, interdisciplinary studies, kinesiology, nursing, physical therapy, public administration, reading specialization, school administration, and student development and leadership in higher education. Those programs in education that have Texas State professional certification meet the academic requirements to sit for the certification exam. The M.S.N. program is an online program.

Research Facilities

The Porter Henderson Library has comprehensive electronic resources, including an online catalog and a campuswide fiber-optic computer network with Internet connectivity. The total library holdings surpass 1.5 million items in a variety of formats. Resources include a partial depository for federal documents, a depository for Texas state documents, and the West Texas collection, which contains numerous primary sources in the forms of diaries, journals, and memoirs of early settlers and pioneers from Texas.

The 6,000-acre Management, Instruction, and Research Center is a multipurpose agricultural production and wildlife management area. This multimillion-dollar complex includes four instructional and research laboratories for animal science, animal anatomy and physiology, animal reproduction, animal nutrition, wildlife management, wool and mohair technology, and plant and range sciences.

The graduate programs are supported by seven state-of-the-art microcomputer labs, more than 100 software packages, and a 20:1 student-computer ratio. Additional special facilities include the Small Business Development Center, International Trade Office, Language Learning Center, and school-based clinics.

Financial Aid

Academic Excellence Graduate Scholarships (AEGS), covering tuition and fees, are awarded on a competitive basis to full-time or part-time graduate students. Carr Research Scholarships in the amount of $3000 plus itemized expenses up to $500 are available to support research projects.

Teaching assistantships paying $11,095 per academic year are available in some departments. Students must have completed 18 hours of graduate work in the field in which they teach and meet other criteria. Most graduate assistantships pay a maximum of $7490 per academic year, and they are available in most departments. Summer assistantships, residence hall assistantships, and student loans are also available.

Cost of Study

For the 2008–09 regular fall and spring semesters, tuition for students taking 9 semester credit hours per year was $4212.40 for Texas residents and $9271.20 for nonresidents. Additional expenses include the cost of books and supplies, parking fees, and special course fees. Tuition and fees are subject to change without notice.

Living and Housing Costs

Limited dormitory housing is available. Information about on-campus housing may be obtained from the Residential Program Office at 325-942-2035.

Student Group

Graduate student enrollment is approximately 450, and the total student population is 6,200. The graduate group is composed of 66 percent women, with approximately two thirds of all students attending part-time.

Location

Angelo State University is located in San Angelo, Texas (population 100,000). San Angelo, county seat of Tom Green County, is located in the heart of West Texas at the juncture of the Middle and North Concho Rivers. The city is a trading and shopping center for those in the ranching, farming, and oil industries and is an important medical and retirement center. Three lakes, a symphony orchestra, theaters, art galleries, museums, good shopping districts, proximity to the Texas Hill Country, and its famous friendly attitude make San Angelo an attractive place to live and study.

The University and The College

Angelo State University, which was established in 1965, is a regional comprehensive institution of higher learning offering programs in the liberal and fine arts, sciences, teacher education, education for the health professions, and business administration. The purpose of the College of Graduate Studies is to provide advanced specialized training that strengthens the academic and professional competence of its students. The graduate programs are designed to develop students' capacities for independent study, train students in the techniques of research, and acquaint them with research in their fields of study. Angelo State University is a member of the Texas Tech University system.

Applying

All students seeking admission to the College of Graduate Studies must complete and file an application and residency form, available on the Web. An official copy of all transcripts of credits from all colleges and universities attended must be received directly from the institution(s). M.B.A. applicants must submit GMAT scores; applicants to all other programs must submit GRE scores. A $40 application fee is required of domestic students and $50 of international students. Students may apply for fall, spring, or summer admission, with the exception of Doctor of Physical Therapy and Master of Science in industrial/organizational psychology applicants. Applications for the D.P.T. program are accepted in the fall and spring preceding the summer when classes begin. Applications for the M.S. in industrial/organizational psychology program have a February 1 deadline for classes beginning the following fall.

Correspondence and Information

College of Graduate Studies
Angelo State University
ASU Station #11025
San Angelo, Texas 76909-1025

Phone: 325-942-2169
Fax: 325-942-2194
E-mail: graduate.school@angelo.edu
Web site: http://www.angelo.edu/gradschool

DEPARTMENT HEADS AND GRADUATE PROGRAM ADVISERS

Accounting, Economics, Finance: Dr. Tom Bankston, Department Head; Dr. Norman Sunderman, Program Advisor (telephone: 325-942-2046).
Animal Science: Dr. Gil Engdahl, Department Head; Dr. Cody Scott, Program Advisor (telephone: 325-942-2027).
Biology: Dr. J. Kelly McCoy, Department Head; Dr. Bonnie Amos, Program Advisor (telephone: 325-942-2189).
Business Administration: Dr. Tom Badgett, Department Head; Dr. Carol Diminnie, Program Advisor (telephone: 325-942-2383).
Communications: Dr. Shawn Wahl, Department Head; Dr. Lana Marlow, Program Advisor (telephone: 325-942-2031).
Curriculum and Instruction: Dr. Jim Summerlin, Department Head.
Guidance and Counseling: Dr. Mary McGlamery, Program Advisor (telephone: 325-942-2647).
School Administration: Dr. Jim Summerlin, Program Advisor (telephone: 325-942-2647).
Student Development and Leadership in Higher Education: Dr. Alaric Williams, Program Advisor (telephone: 325-942-2647).
Superintendent Certificate: Dr. Jim Summerlin, Program Advisor (telephone: 325-942-2647).
Teacher Education: Dr. Linda Lucksinger, Department Head.
Educational Diagnostics: Dr. Mary Sanders and Dr. Richard Evans, Program Advisors (telephone: 325-942-2052).
Reading Specialist: Dr. Ann Bullion-Mears, Program Advisor (telephone: 325-942-2052).
English: Dr. John Wegner, Department Head; Dr. Mary Ellen. Hartje, Program Advisor (telephone: 325-942-2273).
Government: Dr. Ed C. Olson, Department Head (telephone: 325-942-2262).
Public Administration: Dr. Jack Barbour, Program Advisor (telephone: 325-942-2262 Ext. 282).
History: Dr. Kenneth Heineman, Department Head; Dr. Shirley Eoff, Program Advisor (telephone: 325-942-2203).
Interdisciplinary Studies: Dr. Brian May, Program Advisor (telephone: 325-942-2169).
Kinesiology: Dr. Doyle Carter, Department Head; Dr. Warren Simpson, Program Advisor (telephone: 325-942-2173).
Nursing: Dr. Susan Wilkinson, Department Head; Dr. Molly Walker, Program Advisor (telephone: 325-942-2060).
Physical Therapy: Dr. Scott Hasson, Department Head; Mark Pape, Program Advisor (telephone: 325-942-2545).
Psychology: Dr. William Davidson, Department Head.
Counseling Psychology: Dr. Sangeeta Singg, Program Advisor (telephone: 325-942-2219 Ext. 251).
Applied Psychology: Dr. James Forbes, Program Advisor (telephone: 325-942-2219 Ext. 249).
Industrial/Organizational Psychology: Dr. Kraig Schell, Program Advisor (telephone: 325-942-2219 Ext. 243).

ANTIOCH UNIVERSITY LOS ANGELES

Graduate Programs

Programs of Study

Antioch University Los Angeles (AULA) is a small graduate school with a grand vision. Its five master's programs are regarded as among the best in the nation. Because the world needs women and men who are committed to serving society's most critical needs in education, business, psychology, and creative writing, Antioch's programs prepare students to be agents of change. Long an educational innovator, Antioch University Los Angeles offers graduate programs that reflect a dedication to social justice and activism. The University's programs empower people who know that one person can make a difference—people who can educate a generation of children who possess real knowledge and competence, not just test-taking skills; lead and manage businesses with an eye on success beyond the bottom line; counsel, support, and guide people through the conflicts and stresses of contemporary life; and develop an awareness of and appreciation for culturally diverse writers and traditions.

The University offers teacher credentialing and a Master of Arts in education(TC/MAE); a Master of Arts in education, leadership, and change (MAEx); a Master of Arts in organizational management (MAOM) program; a Master of Arts in clinical psychology, a Master of Arts in psychology (MAP); and a Master of Fine Arts (M.F.A.) in creative writing program. It also offers certificate programs in three areas: applied community psychology, teaching of creative writing, and publishing arts. The teacher credentialing program is approved by the California Commission on Teacher Credentialing; currently a multiple subject credential and a specialist credential (mild-moderate) are offered.

Research Facilities

Antioch's library includes limited collections of books and journals as well as a math and writing center. Students can study, conduct research, and access databases online. Through Antioch University in Yellow Springs, Ohio, Antioch Los Angeles students have access to the resources of OhioLINK, a consortium of Ohio's college and university libraries and the State Library of Ohio. Serving more than 500,000 students and faculty and staff members at eighty institutions, OhioLINK's membership includes seventeen public universities, twenty-three community/technical colleges, thirty-nine private colleges, and the State Library of Ohio. Through OhioLINK, Antioch Los Angeles students can conduct research using a very wide selection of academic books and journals.

In the computer center, students have access to Mac and IBM-compatible computers Monday through Saturday. Printers are available for student use at no additional cost. Assistance is available during many hours to assist with routine matters, the FirstClass e-mail system, and OhioLINK library resources.

Financial Aid

Antioch University has several scholarship opportunities for new and returning students each quarter; a list is available at http://www.antiochla.edu/scholarships. The University offers a comprehensive financial aid program, with students receiving assistance in the form of grants, scholarships, student loans, and part-time employment. Funds are available from federal and state governments, private sponsors, and University resources. More than 65 percent of Antioch students receive some form of financial assistance. The Financial Aid Office can design an aid package based on each student's eligibility and personal level of need. For questions about applying for financial aid, students should contact Trofina Pacleb (telephone: 310-578-1080 Ext. 410; e-mail: trofina_pacleb@antiochla.edu).

Cost of Study

Tuition for 2008–09 varied by program. The Teacher Credentialing and Master of Arts in Education (TC/MAE) program tuition was $5475 for full-time (13–23 units) and $3290 for half-time (6–12 units). Tuition for the Master of Arts in Education, Leadership, and Change (MAEx) program was $548 per unit for full-time (more than 9 units) and $3290 for half-time (5–9 units). The Master of Arts in Psychology (MAP) program tuition rates were $590 per unit for full-time (17–18 units), $5900 for full-time (8–16 units), $4130 for 7 units, $3540 for half-time (4–6 units), and $590 per unit for less than full-time. The Master of Arts in Organizational Management (MAOM) program tuition was $688 per unit for 8 or more units, $688 per unit for 5–7 units, and $699 per unit for 1–4 units; full-time is considered 8 or more units, half-time is 4–7 units. Tuition for the Master of Fine Arts in creative writing (M.F.A.) was $6610 for the winter/spring session, $9845 for the fourth semester, $5938 per semester for the post-M.F.A. certificate in the teaching of creative writing, and $6000 for the publishing arts certificate.

Additional fees may include (but are not necessarily limited to) charges for materials, late registration, enrollment maintenance, parking, graduation, transcripts, tuition payment plan, late payments, late registration, and returned checks.

Living Costs

On-campus housing is not available.

Student Group

There are 553 full-time and 222 part-time students, 534 of whom are women. Students enjoy the intimacy and interchange of small classes and usually undertake service-learning projects that engage them in valuable work within their communities.

Location

The campus is centrally located within Los Angeles, at the intersection of I-405 and California State Route 90. AULA is nestled among small, sleepy communities like Marina del Rey and Venice as well as the larger, more vibrant cities of Culver City and Palms. Just 10 minutes from Los Angeles International Airport and 20 minutes from Hollywood, the campus is ideal for working adults commuting to campus for classes.

The University

Antioch University Los Angeles (AULA) is a private, higher education institution that serves students who desire to complete an undergraduate degree, secure a graduate degree for professional or personal advancement, or seek the education necessary for a career change. The institution is committed to providing high quality educational opportunities and stresses the cultivation of analytic and critical skills in a supportive environment devoted to individual student development, interactive education, experiential learning, and social justice. AULA strives to educate students who have the vision and the skills to work creatively as change agents locally and globally.

AULA has grown from a handful of students in 1972 to an active campus that serves approximately 700 students each quarter.

Applying

In general, students must submit the completed application, a nonrefundable application fee, official transcripts from all regionally accredited institutions attended for all undergraduate and postgraduate work, a resume, and two letters of recommendation. An interview may be required. M.F.A. candidates must also submit samples of their work. Application requirements and deadlines vary by program; students should check online for more information.

Correspondence and Information

Admissions
Antioch University Los Angeles
400 Corporate Pointe
Culver City, California 90230

Phone: 310-578-1090 Ext. 411
Fax: 310-822-4824
E-mail: admissions@antiochla.edu
Web site: http://www.antiochla.edu

THE FACULTY AND THEIR RESEARCH

M.A. in Education

Fred Chapel, Core Faculty; Ed.D., Fielding Graduate Institute. Science education, student motivation, qualitative research methods, grounded theory, action research, conceptual change theory, systems thinking, classroom discourse, inquiry-based instruction.

J. Cynthia McDermott, Program Chair; Ed.D., Temple. Pedagogy and democratic teaching, classroom community, literature for K–12, history and philosophy of education.

Terry Smith, Ph.D. candidate, Pepperdine. Advanced use of educational technology, Web pages, Second Life, creating multiple-class Internet projects, blogging, wikis, and video in the classroom.

M.F.A. in Creative Writing

Jenny Factor, Core Faculty; M.F.A., Bennington. Poetry, English language and literature.

Steve Heller, Core Faculty and Program Chair; M.F.A., Bowling Green State; Ed.D., Oklahoma State. Fiction.

Tara Ison, Core Faculty; M.F.A., Bennington. Creative writing.

Emily Rapp, Core Faculty; M.F.A., Texas at Austin. Literary memoirs, historical fiction, literary fiction (novellas, short fiction, novels), children's literature.

Dorothy Allison, Guest Artist/Lecturer. Creative nonfiction.

Betsy Amster, Guest Artist/Lecturer. Publishing arts.

Dodie Bellamy, Mentor Faculty; M.S., Indiana.

Gayle Brandeis, Mentor Faculty; M.F.A., Antioch Los Angeles. Fiction.

Leonard Chang, Mentor Faculty; M.F.A., California, Irvine. Creative writing.

Susan Taylor Chehak, Mentor Faculty; M.F.A., Iowa. Creative writing.

Mark Cull, Guest Artist/Lecturer. Publishing arts.

Jim Daniels, Mentor Faculty; M.F.A., Bowling Green State. Creative writing.

Ben Doller, Mentor Faculty; M.F.A., Iowa. Poetry.

Mark Doty, Guest Artist/Lecturer. Poetry.

Tananarive Due, Guest Artist/Lecturer; M.A., Leeds (England). Fiction.

Charles Flowers, Guest Artist/Lecturer; M.F.A., Oregon. Publishing arts.

Ed Frankel, Guest Artist/Lecturer; M.A., UCLA. Critical paper seminar, teaching academic writing.

Kate Gale, Mentor Faculty; Ph.D., Claremont. Publishing arts.

Richard Garcia, Mentor Faculty; M.F.A., Warren Wilson. Poetry.

Alistair McCartney, Mentor Faculty; M.F.A., Antioch Los Angeles. Fiction.

Bernadette Murphy, Mentor Faculty; M.F.A., Antioch Los Angeles. Creative nonfiction.

Aino Paasonen, Mentor Faculty; Ph.D., UCLA. Translation + adaptation.

Carol Potter, Mentor Faculty; M.F.A., Massachussetts Amherst. Poetry.

Rob Roberge, Mentor Faculty; M.F.A., Norwich. Fiction.

Sharman Apt Russell, Mentor Faculty; M.F.A., Montana. Creative nonfiction.

Cheryl Strayed, Mentor Faculty; M.F.A., Syracuse. Fiction.

Alma Luz Vilanueva, Mentor Faculty; M.F.A., Norwich. Fiction.

Marcos Villatoro, Mentor Faculty. Creative nonfiction.

Amy Sage Webb, Associate Faculty; M.F.A., Arizona State. Pedagogy specialist.

Terry Wolverton, Mentor Faculty; Ph.D., UCLA. Fiction.

M.A. in Organizational Management

Robert Aholt, Adjunct Faculty; M.B.A., USC.

Ruth Ellen Curran, Faculty; M.S.B.A., California State, Northridge. Recruitment and retention strategy, performance management, direct and variable pay.

Michele DeRosa, Faculty; M.A., Caltech. Career development and management, performance improvement, change management, personnel selection methods, group-process facilitation, executive coaching, values discovery and alignment.

John Dupre, Faculty; M.B.A., UCLA. Organizational development (assessment and intervention), workforce morale and productivity, human relations in the workplace.

Ken Goldstein, Faculty; M.S., William Paterson. Management development, organizational development, organizational assessment and intervention.

Jeanne Hartley, Faculty; M.S.O.D., Pepperdine. Organizational behavior, team-building and process dynamics, small-group dynamics, interpersonal communication skills in the workplace, management principles.

Bob Lazzarini, Faculty and Program Chair; M.B.A., Washington (Seattle). For-profit and not-for-profit organizations, management education.

Freddy J. Nager, Adjunct Faculty; M.B.A., USC. Marketing strategy and communications, particularly in relation to the arts, other non-profit ventures, and social entrepreneurship.

Susan Nero, Faculty and Interim Dean of Academic Affairs; Ph.D., UCLA. Applications of social sciences to people in organizational settings.

David Nicoll, Adjunct Faculty; Ph.D., USC. Obtaining competitive advantage by linking strategy formation with the development of an organization's core competencies.

Susan Wyatt, Faculty; Ph.D., Fielding Graduate Institute. Paradoxes in the relationship between individuals, organizations and society.

M.A. in Psychology

George Bermudez, Core Faculty; Ph.D., CUNY, City College. Community and clinical psychology, with focus on bilingual/bicultural services; psychodynamic psychotherapy; organizational and group studies.

Daniel Bruzzone, Faculty; Psy.D. Phillips Graduate Institute. Clinical psychology; forensic psychology; cognitive, behavioral, psychodynamic, family, and postmodern theories; evaluation and treatment of children, adolescents and adults; couple therapy; family therapy; gerontology; treatment of childhood trauma.

Lynda Chassler, Associate Faculty; M.S.W., Adelphi.

Lauren Costine, Associate Faculty; Ph.D., Antioch Los Angeles. Humanistic psychotherapy, behavioral counseling, mental health counseling.

Steven David, Associate Faculty; Ph.D., USC.

Mario Desalvo, Associate Faculty; Ph.D., Pacifica Graduate. Family systems theory, object relation's theory, self-psychology, analytic psychology and cognitive behavioral therapy.

Grant Elliott, Associate Faculty and Director of Weekend and Satellite Programs; M.A., Antioch Los Angeles. Marriage and family therapy.

Andrew Jen, Core Faculty; Ph.D., California School of Professional Psychology. Multicultural community clinical psychology.

Gregor V. Sarkisian, Core Faculty; Ph.D., Missouri–Kansas City. Child protection and family services, community psychology.

Douglas Sadownick, Core Faculty; Ph.D., Pacifica Graduate. Gay liberation ideas.

Claudia Owens Shields, Core Faculty; Ph.D., California School of Professional Psychology. Human diversity and multicultural competence.

Matthew D. Silverstein, Associate Faculty; Ph.D., Pacifica Graduate. Investigation into gay men's dreams as a window into indigenously gay psychological life.

Sylvie Taylor, Core Faculty; Ph.D., UCLA. Community psychology; child advocacy and social policy impacting children, youth, and families; multicultural mental health; stress resilience among poor African American children.

Joy Turek, Program Chair; Ph.D., U.S. International. Psychology of humor.

ARCADIA UNIVERSITY

Graduate and Professional Studies

Programs of Study

The Master of Arts (M.A.) degree is offered in counseling psychology, English, and humanities. The M.A. in Counseling Psychology program prepares students for work in schools (elementary and/or secondary), hospitals, businesses, industries, or community settings. The M.A. in English offers the following specializations: professional writing and teaching writing, writing and communications, and literary and critical studies. The M.A. in Humanities program provides an interdisciplinary study of one of the following areas: literature and modern language; fine arts, theater, and music; or history, philosophy, and religion. The Master of Arts in Education (M.A.Ed.) offers areas of concentrations in art, computer education, English, environmental education, history, mathematics, music, psychology, theater arts, and written communication. The environmental education program offered in cooperation with the Schuylkill Center for Environmental Education can also lead to Pennsylvania certification.

The Master of Education (M.Ed.) includes areas of concentration in art, early childhood education, educational leadership, elementary education, Instructional Technology, language arts, mathematics education, reading, school library science, science education, secondary education, and special education. Pennsylvania certification is available in all of the above areas except Instructional Technology. Secondary certification includes biology, chemistry, English, general science, mathematics, and social studies. Principal K–12, ESL, superintendent's letter of eligibility, and supervisory certification are also available. The Doctor of Education (Ed.D.) is offered in special education. This three-year, part-time program is designed to increase the level of professional expertise among practitioners in the field and find ways to effectively implement best-practices programs in school settings.

The Master of Science in Forensic Science (M.S.F.S.) is earned through a two-year, full-time program operated in partnership with the Fredric Rieders Family Renaissance Foundation (FRFRF) and in collaboration NMS Labs, one of the nation's premier forensic science laboratories. The program is fully accredited by the Forensic Science Education Program Accreditation Commission (FEPAC). Arcadia's M.S.F.S. program focuses primarily on criminalistics, forensic toxicology, and forensic biology and, secondarily, on technical investigation. The Master of Science in Genetic Counseling (M.S.G.C.) is earned through a two-year, full-time program that includes a combination of scientific, medical, psychological, and clinical courses and practical experiences. The program, which is accredited by the American Board of Genetic Counseling, prepares counselors to deal with the new medical technologies related to human genetics and reproduction and to apply knowledge from the natural sciences and psychology in order to address the needs of patients, community lay groups, and health and human services professionals.

The Master of Public Health (M.P.H.) is an entry-level degree in the field of public health. It trains graduates to work effectively as public-health professionals in a wide array of health-related organizations. Both the Master of Science (M.S.) in Health Education program and the Master of Arts (M.A.) in Health Education program are designed for school health and physical education teachers and community health educators. Both degree programs provide a breadth of knowledge in health education and train health educators to assess needs and plan and implement programs within the school and community settings. The Doctor of Physical Therapy (D.P.T.) is earned through a full-time, entry-level program that provides the academic study and clinical experience required by the American Physical Therapy Association (APTA) for work as a professional physical therapist. The program consists of 2½ academic years of formal course work integrated with clinical internships. The program is accredited by the APTA. The Transitional Doctor of Physical Therapy (T.D.P.T.) is a transitional pathway for practicing clinicians intending to make their final education congruent with students graduating from entry-level D.P.T. programs.

The Master of Arts in International Peace and Conflict Resolution (M.A.I.P.C.R.) features a year of study and fieldwork experience abroad and prepares students for career positions in nongovernmental organizations (NGOs) and intergovernmental organizations (IGOs). The Master of Medical Science (M.M.S.) Physician Assistant Studies program consists of a two-year educational program, divided into didactic course work, clinical instruction, and clinical rotations. Dual-degree programs combine the M.M.S. degree with either the M.P.H. or M.S. degree in health education. The Certificate of Advanced Study (C.A.S.) program is a post-master's program that allows specialization and research in an area of education but does not lead to a graduate degree. The Master of Business Administration (M.B.A.) with an international perspective is a part-time, accelerated program that is completed in twenty-two months. The program couples academic course work with leading industry technology and a focus on international business, which includes two separate one-week study-abroad sessions—one studying business in a developed economy and one in a developing economy.

Research Facilities

The Landman Library has 139,203 volumes, more than 57,000 units of microfilm, and 798 print periodical subscriptions. Students have access to several online bibliographical databases, and materials are made available through interlibrary loan and through membership in a cooperative group of academic libraries. For students of science and psychology, there are excellent laboratory facilities in Boyer Hall. Internet services for students include a campuswide wireless network, Telnet, file transfer protocol (ftp), and e-mail. Student laboratories are located in Boyer Hall, which houses three PC labs and one Macintosh lab; Landman Library; Brubaker Hall; and the Educational Enhancement Center in Taylor Hall. In addition, some academic departments (such as fine arts, biology, and psychology) maintain computer equipment for their specific disciplines. All instructional buildings house PC-equipped teaching classrooms. Specialized library material is available in different programs' resource centers as well as an online medical library.

Financial Aid

Arcadia offers several partial-tuition scholarships to its top applicants in each of the full-time graduate programs. A limited number of graduate assistantships are available to full-time students, and all students enrolled in one of the full-time programs or those matriculating in any graduate program and taking at least 6 credits per semester may apply for a Federal Stafford Student Loan. Several alternative loans are also available, as is a ten-month interest-free payment plan through Key Education Resources.

Cost of Study

Tuition for 2008–09 for part-time graduate programs was $590 per credit. Tuition for the physical therapy, genetic counseling, physician assistant, forensic science, and international peace and conflict resolution programs ranged from $21,840 to $28,500 per year.

Living and Housing Costs

There are a variety of housing options in proximity to the University.

Student Group

Graduate enrollment at Arcadia University consists of approximately 1,750 students. The majority of students study part-time. The genetic counseling, forensic science, international peace and conflict resolution, and physician assistant programs require a two-year, full-time commitment. The Doctor of Physical Therapy requires a 2½-year, full-time commitment.

Location

The University is located in Glenside, Pennsylvania, a suburb of Philadelphia, 14 miles from the center of the city. Theaters, museums, and the Philadelphia Orchestra are half an hour away by train or car. On campus, there are always a variety of lectures, concerts, and plays.

The University

Arcadia University, founded in 1853, is a comprehensive university committed to providing an education that integrates liberal learning with career preparation. The University operates one of the country's largest campus-based centers for study abroad and supports a wide array of cultural, intellectual, and recreational activities.

Applying

Admission to graduate programs is based on an overall evaluation of credentials, including the applicant's undergraduate record, which should show a B average or better in the major field. Applicants to the Physician Assistant Studies or DPT programs should apply through the Physical Therapist Centralized Application Service (PTCAS) before January 15. Applications for the Physical Therapy program are processed by the PTCAS at http://www.ptcas.org. Applications for the Physician Assistant Studies program are processed by the Centralized Application Service for Physician Assistants (CASPA) at http://www.caspaonline.org. Applications are not accepted by CASPA after January 15. The deadline for the doctorate in special education and the forensic science program is February 15, and the deadline for the international peace and conflict resolution program is April 1. Applicants who do not fulfill admission requirements or who have undergraduate deficiencies may be admitted conditionally.

Correspondence and Information

Office of Enrollment Management
Arcadia University
450 S. Easton Road
Glenside, Pennsylvania 19038-3295

Phone: 215-572-2910
877-272-2342 (toll-free)
Fax: 215-572-4049
E-mail: admiss@arcadia.edu
Web site: http://www.arcadia.edu

FACULTY HEADS AND PROGRAM COORDINATORS

Michael L. Berger, Vice President for Academic Affairs and Provost; Ed.D., Columbia.
Mark P. Curchack, Dean of Graduate and Professional Studies; Ph.D., Berkeley.
Maureen Guim, Associate Dean of Graduate and Professional Studies; M.Ed., Arcadia.

Chairpersons

Business: Annette Halpin, Associate Professor; Ph.D., La Salle.
Counseling: Eleonora Bartoli, Assistant Professor; Ph.D., Chicago.
Education: Steve Gulkus, Associate Professor; Ph.D., West Virginia.
English: Richard Wertime, Professor; Ph.D., Pennsylvania.
Forensic Science: Lawrence Presley, Director; M.S., Pittsburgh.
Genetic Counseling: Kathleen D. Valverde, Assistant Professor; M.S., C.G.C., Sarah Lawrence.
Health Education: Andrea Crivelli-Kovach, Associate Professor; Ph.D., Temple.
Humanities: Richard Wertime, Professor; Ph.D., Pennsylvania.
International Peace and Conflict Resolution: Warren Haffar, Assistant Professor; Ph.D., Pennsylvania.
Physical Therapy: Rebecca Craik, Professor; Ph.D., Temple.
Physician Assistant: Michael Dryer, Assistant Professor; Dr.P.H., George Washington.
Public Health: Andrea Crivelli-Kovach, Associate Professor; Ph.D., Temple.

Programs of Study Barry University offers more than fifty high-quality graduate degree programs that prepare students for career change and advancement. Classes are offered on evenings or Saturdays for many programs to meet the needs of the working professional. The faculty provides personal attention and is well attuned to the learning styles of adult students. The experience at Barry is academically rewarding and challenging, with interaction with dedicated professors and diverse peers who bring real-world experience to the classroom.

The School of Adult and Continuing Education offers the M.A. in administration and Master of Public Administration (M.P.A.) at sites across the state of Florida.

The College of Arts and Sciences offers the M.A. in broadcast communication, liberal studies, pastoral ministry for Hispanics, practical theology, and public relations and corporate communications; the M.A. and M.F.A. in photography; and the M.S. in clinical psychology. The M.A. in pastoral theology is offered in Arcadia, Florida. The Doctor of Ministry (D.Min.) is offered at the main campus in Miami Shores.

The Andreas School of Business offers the Master of Business Administration (M.B.A.), with concentrations in accounting, finance, health-services administration, international business, management, and marketing. The School of Business also offers the M.S. in accounting and management.

The Adrian Dominican School of Education offers programs in Miami Shores and Orlando. Counseling programs (M.S. and Ed.S.) are available, with specializations in marital, couple, and family counseling/therapy; mental health counseling; rehabilitation counseling; school counseling; and dual specializations in marital, couple, and family counseling/therapy and mental health counseling and mental health counseling and rehabilitation counseling. The Ph.D. in counseling is also offered. The M.S. is available in educational computing and technology, educational leadership, exceptional student education (with endorsements in autism and gifted), Montessori education, reading, and teaching English to speakers of other languages (TESOL). The M.S. is also offered in organizational learning and leadership, with a specialization in higher education administration. The Ed.S. is available in educational computing and technology, educational leadership, Montessori education, and reading. Barry also offers a Specialist in School Psychology (S.S.P.) degree. The Ph.D. program in leadership and education has specializations in educational computing and technology, exceptional student education, higher education administration, human resource development, and leadership. The Ph.D. is available in curriculum and instruction, with specializations in culture, language, and literacy (TESOL); curriculum evaluation and research; early childhood education; elementary education; and reading.

The College of Health Sciences offers the M.S. in anesthesiology, biology, biomedical science, health services administration, and occupational therapy. Students can also earn a Master of Public Health (M.P.H.). Also available are a Master of Science in Nursing (M.S.N.), with specializations in nursing administration, nursing education, and nurse practitioner (family and acute care); an M.S.N./M.B.A. dual degree; a nursing Ph.D.; and Doctor of Nursing Practice (D.N.P.). There are also transitional and accelerated programs for qualified RNs to move seamlessly to the M.S.N.

The School of Human Performance and Leisure Sciences offers the Master of Science in sport management and an M.S./M.B.A. dual-degree program. The M.S. in movement science is also available, with a general M.S. option or specializations in exercise science, injury and sport biomechanics, and sport and exercise psychology.

The Dwayne O. Andreas School of Law offers the Juris Doctor (J.D.) degree.

The School of Podiatric Medicine offers programs leading to the Doctor of Podiatric Medicine and Surgery (D.P.M.) and D.P.M./M.B.A. and D.P.M./M.P.H. dual degrees. Also available are the M.S. in anatomy and a physician assistant program leading to certification and the Master of Clinical Medical Science (M.C.M.Sc.).

The School of Social Work offers the M.S.W. The Advanced Standing M.S.W. program is available to students with a recent B.S.W. from a school whose program is accredited by the Council on Social Work Education.

None of the graduate programs requires a foreign language for admission or graduation.

Research Facilities Campus facilities include the Monsignor William Barry Library, photography and digital imaging labs, a human performance lab, an athletics training room, a biomechanics lab, a complete television production studio, an academic computing center, an education lab, multimedia business classrooms, art studios, a performing arts center, a nursing lab, and several other well-equipped science labs.

Financial Aid Financial aid is available. Professional scholarships are available for full-time social work students, educators, nurses, and members of a religious community. Some schools offer scholarships and other forms of financial assistance. Barry University also participates in the full array of federal and state financial aid programs. Prospective students should contact their intended program for details. Additional information is also available from the Office of Financial Aid (phone: 305-899-3673; e-mail: finaid@mail.barry.edu).

Cost of Study Tuition for 2008–09 was $815 per credit for master's programs and $930 per credit for doctoral programs. Tuition for adult and continuing education, law, public health, physician assistant, and podiatric medicine programs vary.

Living and Housing Costs Campus housing is available for full-time graduate students, space permitting. Barry University provides assistance in locating off-campus housing.

Student Group The total University enrollment for 2008–09 was 8,581, with 3,531 students registered in graduate and professional programs. The majority of graduate students are studying part-time in evening and weekend classes.

Location The University's 122-acre campus is located in Miami Shores, which is between the cities of Miami and Fort Lauderdale. This ideal location provides students with access to one of the nation's most dynamic multicultural environments and all of its business, cultural, and recreational opportunities.

The University Barry University is an independent, coeducational university, with a history of distinguished graduate programs. Founded in 1940, the University has grown steadily in size and diversity, while maintaining a low student-faculty ratio, thus providing for the individual needs of its academic community. The University's various partnerships with local businesses, schools, hospitals, and community organizations ensure that students gain professional experience and hone their skills.

Applying Applicants are expected to have earned a 3.0 cumulative GPA or above in undergraduate work and 3.25 or higher in graduate work for Ph.D. applicants. They are usually required to submit scores on standardized tests (such as the GRE, MAT, MCAT, or GMAT); the specific test requirement depends on the program. Applicants who do not give evidence of being native English speakers are required to submit a TOEFL score of at least 550 (paper-based) or 213 (computer-based); the minimum acceptable score is 600 for the School of Podiatric Medicine. The student's application and credentials (transcripts, recommendations, and test scores) should be sent to the university and should be received at least thirty days prior to the beginning of the term for which admission is desired. Students applying to the podiatric medicine and the physician assistant programs are required to apply via the national application process. Application deadlines, admission requirements, and start terms vary among programs. Prospective students should contact their intended program for details.

Correspondence and Information

Office of Admission
Barry University
11300 Northeast Second Avenue
Miami Shores, Florida 33161-6695

Phone: 305-899-3100
800-695-2279 (toll-free)
Fax: 305-899-2971
E-mail: gradadmissions@mail.barry.edu
Web site: http://www.barry.edu

FACULTY HEADS

School of Adult and Continuing Education
Carol-Rae Sodano, Ed.D., Widener; Dean.
Administration: Robert Scully, D.B.A., Nova; Program Coordinator.
Public Administration: Richard Orman, Ph.D., Maxwell; Program Coordinator.

College of Arts and Sciences
Karen A. Callaghan, Ph.D., Ohio State; Dean.
Clinical Psychology: Frank Muscarella, Ph.D., Louisville; Program Director.
Communication: Denis E. Vogel, Ph.D., Florida State; Chair.
Liberal Studies: Aphrodite Alexandrakis, Ph.D., Miami (Florida); Program Director.
Pastoral Ministry for Hispanics: Rev. Mario B. Vizcaino, Ph.D., Gregorian (Rome); Director, Southeast Pastoral Institute.
Photography: Silvia Lizama, M.F.A., RIT; Chair.
Theology: Mark Wedig, O.P., Ph.D., Catholic University; Chair.

School of Business
Jeffrey Mello, Ph.D., Northeastern; Interim Dean.
Manuel Tejeda, Ph.D., Miami (Florida); Interim Associate Dean.
Michael Broihahn, M.B.A., M.S., Wisconsin; Director of Graduate Programs.

Adrian Dominican School of Education
Terry Piper, Ph.D., Alberta; Dean.
John Dezek, Ed.D., Western Michigan; Associate Dean.
Catheryn Weitman, Ph.D., Texas A&M; Associate Dean.
Counseling: M. Sylvia Fernandez, Ph.D., Southern Illinois Carbondale; Chair.
Curriculum and Instruction: Jill Farrell, Ed.D., Florida International; Chair.
Educational Computing and Technology: Joel Levine, Ed.D., Florida International; Chair.
Educational Leadership: Carmen L. McCrink, Ph.D., Miami (Florida); Chair.
Exceptional Student Education: Judith Harris-Looby, Ph.D., Miami (Florida); Chair.
Leadership and Education: Carmen L. McCrink, Ph.D., Miami (Florida); Director.
Montessori Education: Ijya Tulloss, Ed.D., Nova Southeastern; Program Director.
Organizational Learning and Leadership: David Kopp, Ph.D., Barry; Chair.
Reading: Joyce Warner, Ph.D., Pennsylvania; Program Director.
School Psychology: M. Sylvia Fernandez, Ph.D., Southern Illinois Carbondale; Program Coordinator.
Teaching English to Speakers of Other Languages (TESOL): Sam Perkins, Ph.D., Georgia State; Program Coordinator.

College of Health Sciences
Pegge Bell, Ph.D., Virginia; Dean.
Anesthesiology: John McFadden, M.S.N., Tennessee; Associate Dean and Program Administrator.
Biology: Ralph Laudan, Ph.D., Rutgers; Associate Dean and Program Director.
Biomedical Sciences: Ralph Laudan, Ph.D., Rutgers; Associate Dean and Program Director.
Health Services Administration: Alan S. Whiteman, Ph.D., Walden; Associate Dean and Program Director.
Nursing: Claudette Spalding, Ph.D., Barry; Associate Dean and Chair.
Occupational Therapy: Belkis Landa-Gonzalez, Ed.D., Florida International; Program Director.
Public Health: Richard T. Patton, M.P.H., North Carolina at Chapel Hill; Program Director.

School of Human Performance and Leisure Sciences
Stephen Anderson, Ph.D., Maryland; Interim Dean and Chair.
Maritza Ryder, M.S., Barry; Assistant Dean.
Leta Hicks, Ed.D., Oklahoma State; Director of Graduate Programs.
Athletic Training: Carl Cramer, Ed.D., Kansas State; Program Director.
Exercise Science: Connie Mier, Ph.D., Texas; Program Coordinator.
Injury and Sport Biomechanics: Kathy Ludwig, Ph.D., Texas Woman's; Program Coordinator.
Sport and Exercise Psychology: Gualberto Cremades, Ph.D., Houston; Program Coordinator.
Sport Management: Daniel Rosenberg, Ph.D., North Carolina; Program Coordinator.

School of Law
Leticia M. Diaz, J.D., Ph.D., Rutgers; Dean.
Glen-Peter Ahlers Sr., J.D., Washburn; Associate Dean for Information Services.
Frank L. Schiavo, J.D., Villanova; Interim Assistant Dean for Academic Affairs.

School of Podiatric Medicine and Surgery
John P. Nelson, D.P.M., Ohio College of Podiatric Medicine; Interim Dean.
Michael Siegel, Ph.D., Florida; Associate Academic Dean.
Physician Assistant Program: Doreen Parkhurst, M.D., Boston University; Assistant Dean and Program Director.

School of Social Work
Debra McPhee, Ph.D., Toronto; Dean.
Phyllis Scott, Ph.D., Barry; Associate Dean.
Social Work: Preeti Charania, M.S.W., Nirmala Niketan College of Social Work (India); Program Director.

Barry's south Florida location gives students access to one of the nation's most dynamic multicultural environments.

Barry University's faculty is well attuned to the learning styles of adult students.

BOSTON UNIVERSITY

BOSTON UNIVERSITY

Graduate School of Arts and Sciences

Programs of Study

The Graduate School of Arts and Sciences at Boston University offers forty-two master's programs and thirty-two Ph.D. programs in the humanities, social sciences, and natural sciences. There is, in addition, one division within the Graduate School that provides formal linkage to other professional graduate opportunities at Boston University: the Division of Religious and Theological Studies.

Freestanding master's programs within the Graduate School are offered through some research centers and institutes.

Additional academic options may be pursued through cross-registration in any of the University's other schools and colleges. Through an area consortium arrangement, students may also register for courses at many other graduate schools in the Boston area.

Research Facilities

The Boston University library system holds more than 4.5 million volumes in books and microform. Central service is provided by the Mugar Memorial Library. Among the units contained within this central facility are a music library, an African Studies library, and a Department of Special Collections, containing rare books and manuscripts. Numerous departmental libraries are located throughout the campus. An interlibrary loan system further extends the available resources, and a consortium arrangement enables graduate students to use the facilities of many Boston-area academic and research libraries.

The University provides laboratories for research and training in disciplines ranging from the physical sciences to the dramatic arts. The recently constructed Metcalf Center for Science and Engineering, for example, houses state-of-the-art facilities for science and engineering students. The University's Academic Computing Center, the Center for Computational Science, and individual departments provide computing resources, from parallel supercomputers to personal workstations, interconnected on a campuswide broadband network.

Financial Aid

Highly qualified graduate students are eligible for Presidential Fellowships and Dean's Fellowships, which include full-tuition scholarships and a stipend of $18,900 for the 2009–10 academic year. Teaching fellowships provide stipends of $18,400 for 2009–10, plus a tuition scholarship. The Martin Luther King Jr. Fellowships are available to students beginning graduate studies in any department who are committed to the principles espoused by Dr. King. Nominations are accepted from the department of application. A wide variety of grants and awards (e.g., graduate scholarships and research assistantships) are made annually by individual departments and centers. In addition, graduate students at Boston University are eligible to participate in a variety of federally funded programs.

Cost of Study

For 2009–10, full-time tuition is $37,910 for the academic year. Part-time tuition is $1184 per credit hour. The part-time registration fee is $40 per semester, and the George Sherman Union fee is $95 per semester (charged to full-time students). Graduate students enrolled for continuing study pay $2368 per semester. The estimated cost of books and supplies is $1188 per year.

Living and Housing Costs

A limited number of rooms and apartments in University residences are available for graduate students. Information may be obtained from the Housing Office, 25 Buick Street. The Office of Rental Property Management, 19 Deerfield Street, has information about off-campus housing.

Costs of living in Boston are comparable to those in any large metropolitan city. Average housing costs range from $850 to $1200 per month.

Student Group

The Graduate School has 1,985 students, of whom approximately 49 percent are women and 35 percent come from abroad.

Location

The character of Boston results from a rich blend of its historical heritage, active cultural life, and contemporary growth in business, technology, and medicine. Some sixty colleges and universities are located in greater Boston. Within Boston's compact central area are a host of galleries, the Public Garden, an active theater district, and the Freedom Trail, along which are located some of the most important landmarks in U.S. history. The Museum of Fine Arts, open without charge to Boston University students, has notable Oriental, Egyptian, American portrait, and French Impressionist collections. The Boston Symphony Orchestra, the Opera Company of Boston, and many fine chamber and jazz groups offer annual seasons; the Boston Pops season includes free outdoor summer concerts. Boston is the home of the Red Sox, the New England Patriots, the Celtics, the Bruins, and the New England Revolution.

The University

Boston University is an independent, coeducational, nonsectarian university. Founded by the Methodist Episcopal Church for the improvement of theological training, it has since its incorporation in 1869 been fully open to women and to all minorities. Its more than 31,000 students and more than 3,800 faculty members contribute to its ranking as one of the world's largest independent universities. The main campus, on the south bank of the Charles River just west of downtown Boston, houses the Graduate School of Arts and Sciences, the College of Arts and Sciences, the School of Law, the School of Management, Metropolitan College, the College of Communication, Sargent College of Allied Health Professions, the School of Social Work, and the School of Theology. On the medical campus are the School of Medicine, the School of Public Health, the Goldman School of Dental Medicine, and the Graduate School of Medical Sciences.

Applying

Applications for admission with financial aid consideration for the fall semester must be received by January 15 for most programs; students should refer to the *Graduate School Bulletin* for exceptions. Some departments accept students in the spring semester, for which applications must be received by October 15 for financial aid consideration. Applications must include official transcripts from all colleges and universities attended, letters of recommendation from at least 2 faculty members in the proposed field of graduate study, and official results of the Graduate Record Examinations (General and Subject Tests) and/or the Miller Analogies Test, as required by the department to which the student is applying. Students from abroad must also submit the International Student Data Form and official English translations of all academic records. Students whose native language is not English must submit results of the Test of English as a Foreign Language (TOEFL). A nonrefundable application fee of $70 is required of all applicants. This fee cannot be waived.

Although financial aid competitions within individual programs begin in early January, students who wish to be considered for special Graduate School fellowships are urged to submit their application with all supporting documents by December 1.

Correspondence and Information

Graduate School of Arts and Sciences
Boston University
705 Commonwealth Avenue
Boston, Massachusetts 02215

Phone: 617-353-2696
E-mail: grartsci@bu.edu
Web site: http://www.bu.edu/cas/admissions/graduate/

FACULTY HEADS

Departments, Divisions, and Programs
African American Studies Program: Linda Heywood, Professor; Ph.D., Columbia.
American and New England Studies Program: Anita Patterson, Associate Professor; Ph.D., Harvard.
Anthropology Department: Robert Weller, Professor; Ph.D., Johns Hopkins.
Applied Linguistics Program: Mary Catherine O'Connor, Associate Professor; Ph.D., Berkeley.
Archaeology Department: Ricardo Elia, Associate Professor; Ph.D., Boston University.
Art History Department: Fred Kleiner, Professor; Ph.D., Columbia.
Astronomy Department: James Jackson, Professor; Ph.D., MIT.
Bioinformatics Program (Interdisciplinary): Charles DeLisi, Professor; Ph.D., NYU.
Biology Department: Geoffrey Cooper, Professor; Ph.D., Miami (Florida).
Biostatistics Program: Lisa Sullivan, Professor; Ph.D., Boston University.
Cellular Biophysics Program: M. Carter Cornwall, Professor; Ph.D., Utah.
Chemistry Department: John Straub, Professor; Ph.D., Columbia.
Classical Studies Department: Loren J. Samons II, Professor; Ph.D., Brown.
Cognitive and Neural Systems Program: Ennio Mingolla, Professor; Ph.D., Connecticut.
Computer Science Department: Stan Sclaroff, Professor; Ph.D., MIT.
Creative Writing: Leslie Epstein, Professor; D.F.A., Yale.
Earth Sciences Department: Guido Salvucci, Professor; Ph.D., MIT.
Economics Department: Kevin Lang, Professor; Ph.D., MIT.
English Department: Laurence Breiner, Professor; Ph.D., Yale.
Geography and Environment Department: Mark Friedl, Professor; Ph.D., California, Santa Barbara.
History Department: Charles Dellheim, Professor; Ph.D., Yale.
International Relations Department: Erik Goldstein, Professor; Ph.D., Cambridge.
Boston University Marine Program: Richard Murray, Professor; Ph.D., Berkeley.
Mathematics and Statistics Department: Ralph D'Agostino, Professor; Ph.D., Harvard.
Molecular Biology, Cell Biology, and Biochemistry: Kimberly McCall, Associate Professor and Director; Ph.D., Harvard.
Music Department: Victor Coelho, Professor; Ph.D., UCLA.
Neuroscience Program: William Eldred III, Professor; Ph.D., Colorado Health Science Center.
Philosophy Department: Daniel Dahlstrom, Professor; Ph.D., Saint Louis.
Physics Department: Bennett Goldberg, Professor; Ph.D., Brown.
Political Science Department: Walter Connor, Professor; Ph.D., Princeton.
Preservation Studies Program: Claire Dempsey, Associate Professor and Director; M.A., Boston University.
Psychology Department: Michael Lyons, Professor; Ph.D., Louisville.
Religious and Theological Studies Division: Jonathan Klawans, Associate Professor and Director; Ph.D., Columbia.
Romance Studies Department: Christopher Maurer, Professor; Ph.D., Pennsylvania.
Sociology Department: Nancy Ammerman, Professor; Ph.D., Yale.
Sociology/Social Work (Interdisciplinary): Mary Elizabeth Collins, Professor; M.S.W., Ph.D., Chicago.
Women's Studies: Shahla Haeri, Assistant Professor and Director; Ph.D., UCLA.

Centers and Institutes
Center for Adaptive Systems: Stephen Grossberg, Professor; Ph.D., Rockefeller.
African Studies Center: James McCann, Professor; Ph.D., Michigan State.
Institute for American Political History: Bruce Schulman, Professor; Ph.D., Stanford.
Center for Anxiety and Related Disorders: Michael Otto, Professor; Ph.D., Mexico.
Center for Archaeological Studies: James Wiseman, Professor; Ph.D., Chicago.
Center for the Study of Asia: William Grimes, Associate Professor; Ph.D., Princeton.
Institute for Astrophysical Research: James Jackson, Professor; Ph.D., MIT.
Boston University Humanities Foundation: James Winn, Professor; Ph.D., Yale.
Center for Chemical Methodology and Library Development: John Porco, Professor; Ph.D., Harvard.
Institute for Classical Traditions: Wolfgang Haase, Professor; Ph.D., Tübingen (Germany).
Center for Computational Science: Claudio Rebbi, Professor; Ph.D., Torino.
Institute for the Study of Conflict, Ideology, and Policy: Uri Ra'anan, Professor; Ph.D., Oxford.
International Center for East Asian Archaeology and Cultural History: Robert Murowchick, Research Associate Professor; Ph.D., Harvard.
Center for Ecology and Conservation Biology: Thomas Kunz, Professor; Ph.D., Kansas.
Institute for Economic Development: Dilip Mookherjee, Professor; Ph.D., London School of Economics.
Editorial Institute: Christopher Ricks, Professor; D.Litt. (hon.), Oxford; Archie Burnett, Professor; D.Phil., Oxford.
Center for Energy and Environmental Studies: Robert Kaufmann, Professor; Ph.D., Pennsylvania.
Center for Integrated Space Weather Modeling: W. Jeffrey Hughes, Professor; Ph.D., London (England).
International History Institute: William Keylor, Professor; Ph.D., Columbia.
Center for International Relations: Andrew Bacevich, Professor; Ph.D., Princeton.
Elie Weisel Center for Judaic Studies: Steven Katz, Professor; Ph.D., Cambridge.
Center for Memory and Brain: Howard Eichenbaum, Professor; Ph.D., Michigan.
Institute for the Study of Muslim Societies and Civilizations: Thomas Barfield, Professor; Ph.D., Harvard.
Center for Nanoscience and Nanobiotechnology: Bennett Goldberg, Professor; Ph.D., Brown.
Neuromuscular Research Center: Carlo De Luca, Professor; Ph.D., Queen's at Kingston.
Center for the Philosophy and History of Science: Alfred Tauber, Professor; M.D., Tufts.
Institute for Philosophy and Religion: Allen Speight, Professor; Ph.D., Chicago.
Center for Polymer Studies: H. Eugene Stanley, Professor; Ph.D., Harvard.
Center for Remote Sensing: Farouk El-Baz, Research Professor; Ph.D., Missouri–Rolla.
Science and Mathematics Education Center: Kenneth Brecher, Professor; Ph.D., MIT.
Center for Space Physics: Supriya Chakrabarti, Professor; Ph.D., Berkeley.
Center for Transportation Studies: T. R. Lakshmanan, Professor; Ph.D., Ohio State.

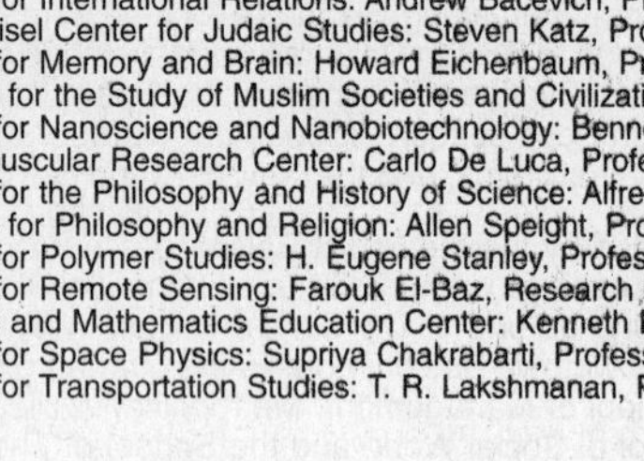
Boston University along the Charles River.

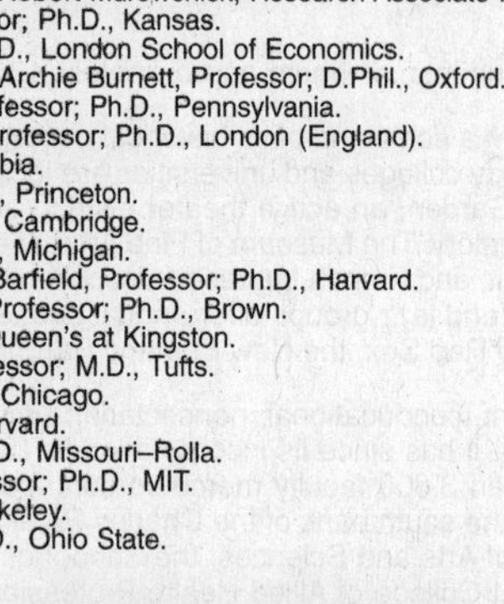
Marsh Chapel.

The campus along Commonwealth Avenue.

Graduate College
BGSU.

BOWLING GREEN STATE UNIVERSITY

Graduate College

Programs of Study

Bowling Green State University (BGSU) offers Doctor of Philosophy (Ph.D.) programs in American culture studies (communication, English (rhetoric), history, popular culture, and sociology), applied philosophy, biological sciences, communication disorders, communication studies, English (rhetoric and composition), higher education administration, history, interdisciplinary studies, leadership studies, mathematics, photochemical sciences, psychology (clinical, developmental, experimental, industrial-organizational, and quantitative), sociology, and theater and film. A Doctor of Education (Ed.D.) degree is offered in leadership studies, along with a Doctoral of Musical Arts (D.M.A.). Other graduate and specialist programs include technology management (consortium degree), education specialist (administration and supervision, mathematics supervision, reading, and school psychology), and specialist in applied biology (immunohematology).

Graduate certificates are offered in bioinformatics, ethnic studies, food and nutrition, geospatial technology, international scientific and technical communication, organizational change, public history, proteomics/genomics, quality systems, and women's studies.

BGSU offers the Master of Accountancy (M.Acc.) degree. The Master of Arts (M.A.) degree is offered in American culture studies, art, art education, college student personnel, communication studies, cross-cultural and international education, economics, English (English literature and technical writing), French, German, guidance and counseling, history, mathematics, philosophy, political science (dual degree with German only), popular culture, psychology (clinical, developmental, experimental, industrial/organizational, and quantitative), sociology, Spanish, and theater and film. The Master of Arts in Teaching (M.A.T.) degree is offered in American culture studies, biological sciences, chemistry, French, geology, German, history, mathematics, physics, Spanish, and theater and film. The Master of Arts/Science is offered in interdisciplinary studies. The Master of Business Administration (M.B.A.) degree is offered in finance, management information systems, marketing, and supply chain management. The Master of Education (M.Ed.) degree is offered in business education; career and technology education; classroom technology; curriculum and teaching; educational administration and supervision; guidance and counseling; human movement, sport, and leisure studies (developmental kinesiology, recreation and leisure, and sport administration); interdisciplinary studies; reading; school psychology; and special education. BGSU also offers the Master of Family and Consumer Sciences (M.F.C.S.) degree. The Master of Fine Arts (M.F.A.) degree is offered in fine art and creative writing. The Master of Industrial Technology (M.I.T.) is offered in construction management and technology and manufacturing technology. BGSU also offers the Master of Music (M.M.) in composition, education, ethnomusicology, history, performance, and theory; Master of Organization Development (M.O.D.); Master of Public Administration (M.P.A.); Master of Public Health (M.P.H.); and Master of Rehabilitation Counseling (M.R.C.) degrees. The Master of Science (M.S.) degree is offered in applied statistics, biological sciences, chemistry, communication disorders, computer science, criminal justice, geology, and physics.

Ph.D. requirements include a minimum of 90 semester hours of graduate work beyond the baccalaureate. A minimum of 30 semester hours of graduate work beyond the baccalaureate is required for the master's degree; the choice of Plan I (thesis option) or Plan II (comprehensive examination option) is available in most programs. The Graduate College at BGSU is committed to helping students identify personal and professional goals. Through a comprehensive set of facilities and programs, opportunities are provided to pursue high-quality graduate education in an environment conducive to advanced study and research.

Research Facilities

The University libraries have approximately 2 million volumes and approximately 1.6 million microforms, including subscriptions to 6,000 periodicals and 600,000 government documents. In addition to providing a range of regular and specialized research facilities, the University supports a number of research centers and institutes. These include the Center for Archival Collections; the Center for Biomolecular Sciences; the Center for Family and Demographic Research; the Center for Neuroscience, Mind and Behavior; the Center for Photochemical Sciences; the Center for Regional Development; the Institute for the Study of Culture and Society; the Center for Microscopy and Microanalysis; the Institute for Great Lakes Research; the Institute for Psychological Research and Application; the Reading Center; the Social Philosophy and Policy Center; the National Institute for the Study of Digital Media; and the Statistical Consulting Center.

Financial Aid

Departmental assistantships in 2009–10 provide tuition scholarships and stipend payments totaling as much as $45,804 for master's assistantships and $50,960 for doctoral assistantships. About 80 percent of the University's full-time graduate students are awarded assistantship or fellowship support. Student employment and loans are available as sources of graduate student support.

Cost of Study

Tuition in 2009–10 is $477 per credit hour for Ohio residents and $782 per credit hour for nonresidents.

Living and Housing Costs

On-campus housing is not available for graduate students. Numerous apartments and other housing are available near the campus. For more information, those interested should contact Off-Campus Housing at 419-372-2458 or visit the Web site at http://www.bgsu.edu/offices/sa/offcampus/page42263.html.

Student Group

The University maintains an enrollment of about 14,000 undergraduates and approximately 3,000 graduate students on the main campus. Students represent all fifty states and fifty countries. The opportunities to meet people and exchange ideas at Bowling Green are greatly enhanced by the residential nature of the campus.

Location

Bowling Green is a northwestern Ohio community, located 23 miles south of Toledo and within a 100-mile radius of Ann Arbor, Detroit, Cleveland, and Columbus. The community offers numerous recreational and cultural programs that supplement the activities offered by the University.

The University

Bowling Green, a state-assisted university, was founded in 1910. The University has a 1,250-acre campus. Graduate programs are offered in six academic colleges—Arts and Sciences, Business Administration, Education and Human Development, Health and Human Services, Musical Arts, and Technology—within the Graduate College. Each year, the University invites visiting scholars, guest artists, and celebrities to lecture, perform, and meet informally with students to exchange ideas and information.

Applying

Applicants must have graduated with a baccalaureate degree from a regionally accredited college or university. Assistantships are awarded for the academic year beginning in the fall semester. Applicants for financial aid are encouraged to complete the admission process by January 15. The application for admission to the Graduate College should be submitted with a $30 nonrefundable application fee. Students should apply six months in advance for admission to a Ph.D. program and three months in advance for a master's program. International students should allow more time for the application process. Two official transcripts from all colleges attended are required. GRE General Test or GMAT scores must be submitted. TOEFL scores must be submitted by all applicants whose first language is not English. Three letters of recommendation must be forwarded to the department to which admission is requested.

Correspondence and Information

Office of Graduate Admissions
120 McFall Center
Bowling Green State University
Bowling Green, Ohio 43403-0180

Phone: 419-372-2791
Fax: 419-372-8569
E-mail: prospct@bgsu.edu
Web site: http://www.bgsu.edu/colleges/gradcol

FACULTY HEADS

All telephone numbers are preceded by the area code 419.

GRADUATE COLLEGE

Deanne Snavely, Ph.D., Interim Vice Provost for Research and Dean of the Graduate College, 372-0433.
Martha Gaustad, Ph.D., Associate Dean, 372-7710.
Lisa Chavers, Ph.D., Assistant Dean for Graduate Studies and Director of Project Search, 372-0343.
Terry Lawrence, Ph.D., Assistant Dean for Graduate Admissions, 372-7710.

ACADEMIC DEANS

Simon Morgan-Russell, Ph.D., Dean, College of Arts and Sciences, 372-2340.
Rodney Rogers, Ph.D., College of Business Administration, 372-3411.
Rosalind Hammond, Ph.D., Interim Dean, College of Education and Human Development, 372-7403.
Linda Petrosino, Ph.D., College of Health and Human Services, 372-8243.
Richard Kennell, Ph.D., College of Musical Arts, 372-2188.
C. Wayne Unsell, Ph.D., College of Technology, 372-2438.
Sara Bushong, Interim Dean, College of University Libraries, 372-2106.
Marcia Salazar-Valentine, Ph.D., Interim Dean, Continuing and Extended Education, 372-8183.

DEGREE PROGRAM GRADUATE COORDINATORS

College of Arts and Sciences
American Culture Studies: Don McQuarie, Ph.D., 372-0586 (dmcquar@bgsu.edu).
Art (School of): Mille Guldbeck, M.F.A., 372-9319 (guld@bgsu.edu).
Biology: Karen Root, Ph.D., 372-8559 (kvroot@bgsu.edu).
Chemistry: Tom Kinstle, Ph.D., 372-2658 (tkinstl@bgsu.edu).
Communication Studies: Joshua Atkinson, Ph.D., 372-3403 (jatkins@bgsu.edu).
Computer Science: Ron Lancaster, Ph.D., 372-8697 (rlancast@bgsu.edu).
English/Creative Writing: Lawrence Coates, Ph.D., 372-2111 (coatesl@bgsu.edu).
Ethnic Studies: Timothy Messer-Kruse, Ph.D., 372-6056 (tmesser@bgsu.edu).
Geology: Jeff Snyder, Ph.D., 372-0533 (jasnyd@bgsu.edu).
German, Russian, and East Asian Languages: Edgar Landgraf, Ph.D., 372-9517 (elandgr@bgsu.edu).
History: Stephen Ortiz, Ph.D., 372-2030 (sortiz@bgsu.edu).
Mathematics and Statistics: John Chen, Ph.D., 372-7461 (jchen@bgsu.edu).
Philosophy: Sara Worley, Ph.D., 372-2899 (sworley@bgsu.edu).
Photochemical Sciences: Phil Castellano, Ph.D., 372-2033 (castell@bgsu.edu).
Physics and Astronomy: Lewis Fulcher, Ph.D., 372-2635 (fulcher@bgsu.edu).
Political Science/Public Administration: Shannon Orr, Ph.D., 372-7593 (skorr@bgsu.edu).
Popular Culture: Jeffrey Brown, Ph.D., 372-2982 (jabrown@bgsu.edu).
Psychology: Rob Carels, Ph.D., 372-9405 (rcarels@bgsu.edu).
Romance & Classical Studies/French: Robert Berg, Ph.D., 372-7148 (rberg@bgsu.edu).
Romance & Classical Studies/Spanish: Ernesto Delgrado, Ph.D., 372-7150 (eedelg@bgsu.edu).
Sociology: Steve Cernkovich, Ph.D., 372-2743 (scernko@bgsu.edu).
Technical Writing: Gary Heba, Ph.D., 372-7545 (gheba@bgsu.edu).
Theater and Film: Lesa Lockford, Ph.D., 372-9381 (lockflo@bgsu.edu).
Women's Studies: Radhika Gajjala, Ph.D., 372-0528 (radhik@bgsu.edu).

College of Business Administration
Accounting/MIS: David Stott, Ph.D., 372-2709 (dstott@bgsu.edu).
Applied Statistics/Operations Research: Richard McGrath, Ph.D., 372-8451 (rnmcgra@bgsu.edu).
Economics: Peter VanderHart, Ph.D., 372-8070 (pvander@bgsu.edu).
Graduate Studies in Business (M.B.A.): Toby Swick, Ph.D., 372-2488 (tswick@bgsu.edu).
Organization Development: Brian Childs, Ph.D., 372-8823 (bchilds@bgsu.edu).

College of Education and Human Development
DIS/School and Mental Health Counseling: Gregory Garske, Ph.D., 372-7319 (ggarske@bgsu.edu).
DIS/Rehabilitation Counseling: Jay Stewart, Ph.D., 372-7301 (jstewar@bgsu.edu).
DIS/School Psychology: Audrey Ellenwood, Ph.D., 372-9848 (aellenw@bgsu.edu).
DIS/Special Education: Lessie Cochran, Ph.D., 372-7298 (llcochr@bgsu.edu).
DTL/Business Education: Bob Berns, Ph.D., 372-2904 (rberns@bgsu.edu).
DTL/Classroom Technology: Allison Goedde, Ph.D., 372-7394 (agoedde@bgnet.bgsu.edu).
DTL/Curriculum and Teaching: Larry Grasser, Ph.D., 372-9619 (larrygr@bgsu.edu).
DTL/Reading: Cindy Hendricks, Ph.D., 372-7341 (cindyg@bgsu.edu).
Family and Consumer Sciences: Dawn Anderson, Ph.D., 372-8090 (dawna@bgsu.edu).
Human Movement/Sport/Leisure Studies: Dawn Anderson, Ph.D., 372-8090 (dawna@bgsu.edu).
LPS/College Student Personnel: Michael Coomes, Ph.D., 372-7157 (mcoomes@bgsu.edu).
LPS/Ed Foundations and Inquiry Program: Rachel Vannatta, Ph.D., 372-7350 (rvanna@bgsu.edu).
LPS/Ed Administration and Leadership Studies: Patrick Pauken, Ph.D., 372-2550 (paukenp@bgsu.edu).
LPS/Higher Education Administration: Michael Coomes, Ph.D., 372-7157 (mcoomes@bgsu.edu).
LPS/MACIE: Peggy Booth, Ph.D., 372-9950 (boothmz@bgsu.edu).

College of Health and Human Services
Communication Disorders: Tim Brackenbury, Ph.D., 372-2515 (tbracke@bgsu.edu).
Criminal Justice: Melissa Burek, Ph.D., 372-2326 (mwburek@bgsu.edu).
Gerontology: Nancy Orel, Ph.D., 372-7768 (norel@bgsu.edu).
Public Health: Fleming Fallon, Ph.D., 372-8316 (ffallon@bgsu.edu).

College of Musical Arts
Robert Satterlee, Ph.D., 372-2360 (rsatter@bgsu.edu).

College of Technology
Career & Technology Education: Terry Herman, Ph.D., 372-7265 (hermant@bgsu.edu).
Construction Management: Will Roudebush, Ph.D., 372-8275 (wroudeb@bgsu.edu).
Industrial Technology: Alan Atalah, Ph.D., 372-8354 (aatalah@bgsu.edu).

"Electric Falcon," the electric automobile developed by the College of Technology.

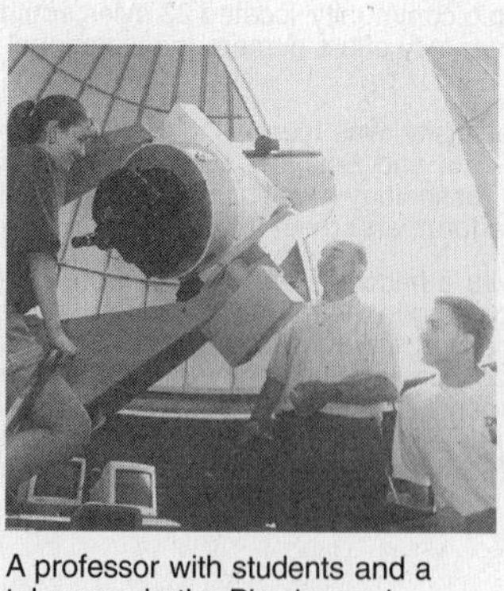
A professor with students and a telescope in the Physics and Astronomy Observatory.

Theater production of "The Good Times Are Killing Me."

BROOKLYN COLLEGE OF THE CITY UNIVERSITY OF NEW YORK

Division of Graduate Studies

Programs of Study

The Brooklyn College Division of Graduate Studies, founded in 1935, offers more than sixty full- and part-time master's degrees and advanced certificate programs. These include programs leading to the Master of Arts, Master of Arts in Teaching, Master of Fine Arts, Master of Music, Master of Professional Studies, Master of Public Health, Master of Science, and Master of Science in Education degrees as well as to a combined Bachelor of Science/Master of Professional Studies degree (in business information systems). In addition, on the Brooklyn College campus doctoral students can pursue courses in biology, chemistry, computer and information science, earth and environmental sciences, physics, and psychology. The City University of New York Graduate Center (CUNY Grad Center) administers doctoral programs in more than thirty disciplines but, depending on the field, some courses are offered only at the senior colleges of CUNY.

The following Master of Arts programs are offered in the liberal arts and sciences: art history, biology, chemistry, community health (community health education, thanatology), computer science, economics, English, French, geology, history, Judaic studies, liberal studies, mathematics, music (musicology, performance practice), physics, political science (urban policy and administration), psychology (experimental, industrial and organizational, and mental health counseling), sociology, Spanish, speech (public communication), and theater (history and criticism).

Programs leading to the Master of Fine Arts degree are offered in: art (digital art, drawing and painting, photography, printmaking, sculpture), creative writing (fiction, playwriting, poetry), performance and interactive media arts (PIMA), television production, and theater (acting, design and technical production, directing, dramaturgy, and performing arts management). An interdisciplinary Advanced Certificate is also offered in performance and interactive media arts.

Programs leading to the Master of Music degree are offered in composition and in performance.

A program leading to the Master of Public Health degree is offered in community health (health-care management, health-care policy and administration).

Programs leading to the Master of Science degree are offered in accounting, computer science and health science, exercise science and rehabilitation, information systems, media studies, nutrition, physical education (sports management), and speech-language pathology.

The teacher education program offers Master of Arts programs in art and music (all grades); biology, chemistry, English, French, middle childhood education (general science), mathematics, physics, social studies, and Spanish (grades 7–12). The teacher education program also offers a Master of Arts in Teaching program in Adolescence Science Education (7–12).

The Master of Science in Education degree is offered with specializations in: childhood education (bilingual teaching, liberal arts, mathematics, and science and environmental education, grades 1–6); early childhood education (birth–grade 2); educational leadership (school building leader, school district leader); health education (all grades); literacy education; middle childhood specialist studies (mathematics, grades 5–9); physical education (all grades); school counseling (bilingual extension may also be earned); school psychologist (bilingual extension may also be earned); and teaching students with disabilities in early childhood education, childhood education, and middle childhood education. Advanced certificate programs are offered in autism spectrum disorders, bilingual education, gifted education, grief counseling, music education, parallel and distributed computing, school counseling, and school psychology.

(For a full listing of current course programs, visit http://depthome.brooklyn.cuny.edu/schooled/.

Research Facilities

Outside of the classroom, students are supported by the most technologically advanced library in CUNY, which houses more than 1.3 million volumes; by more than 1,300 public-access computers; by widespread Wi-Fi access; and by a Web portal that provides a wide variety of personalized services. Brooklyn College also maintains state-of-the-art facilities to support instruction: technology-enhanced classrooms and lecture halls; large-scale, comfortable computer labs with college-wide access open from 16 to 24 hours each day, with free printing and more than a thousand Dell, Apple, and Sun workstations; more than fifty discipline-specific computer labs; and video-conferencing facilities. Additional special libraries are available for art, music, classics, and speech communication arts and sciences.

A number of campus research centers are available, and many of them publish their own scholarly research. These include the Africana Research Center, the Applied Sciences Institute, the Archaeological Research Center, the Center for Health Promotion, the Center for Italian-American Studies, the Center for Latino Studies, the Center for the Study of World Television, the Children's Studies Center, the Ethyle R. Wolfe Institute for the Humanities, and the H. Wiley Hitchcock Institute for Studies in American Music. Other special facilities include solid-state and solar-energy laboratories, nuclear physics laboratories, an astronomical observatory, the Early Childhood Center, the Infant Study Center, a greenhouse, an electronic music studio and the Center for Computer Music, and the Diana Rogovin Davidow Speech and Hearing Center (and affiliated Center for Assistive Technology).

Financial Aid

Scholarships, tuition waivers, loans, college work-study, graduate assistantships, fellowships, and internships may be available to qualified students. A monthly payment plan is also available. Graduate students are encouraged to apply for scholarship funding. Applications are available beginning in September for the following fall semester. They may be found online at http://scholarships.brooklyn.cuny.edu. Federal and state aid programs available to eligible students include Federal Perkins Loans, Federal Work-Study, Ford Federal Direct Student Loans, and the New York State Tuition Assistance Program (TAP). Fellowships, lectureships, and research assistantships are available from College funds, research grants, and outside agencies. Students may also apply through their departments for Fulbright scholarships and other international fellowships.

Cost of Study

The Division of Graduate Studies at Brooklyn College provides advanced education of superior quality at a comparatively modest tuition. For 2009–10, full-time graduate tuition for New York State residents is $3680 per semester, and $310 per credit for part-time studies. Tuition for nonresidents and international students is $575 per credit, full- or part-time. Tuition and fees are subject to change without notice.

Living and Housing Costs

Brooklyn College does not provide on-campus housing but is associated with a residence hall that will start occupancy in fall 2010, and the neighborhood around the College has a variety of affordable housing options.

Student Group

Students from all over the world attend the Division of Graduate Studies. About 69 percent are women and more than 86 percent attend part time. The average age of students is 32.

Location

Situated on one of the loveliest urban campuses in the country, the College encompasses 26 acres of broad lawns and tree-lined walkways and features a classic quadrangle surrounded by red brick Georgian-style buildings. A second green quadrangle will extend the campus when a state-of-the-art student services and physical education building, currently under construction, is completed in 2009. The many different cultures of Brooklyn contribute to the wide ethnic diversity of the College's student and teacher population. Easy accessibility to a wide variety of New York City cultural events and institutions enriches students' educational experience. Subway and bus transportation to all points inside and outside the borough is easily accessible from the College. On-campus parking for students is available on a limited basis.

The College

Brooklyn College, founded in 1930, was the first four-year, coeducational liberal arts college in New York City. In 1961 the College became part of the City University of New York. In fall 2008, 13,012 undergraduate and 3,678 graduate students were enrolled in more than 135 degree and certificate programs. Brooklyn College is accredited by the Middle States Commission on Higher Education, the Council on Education for Public Health, the American Dietetic Association, the Education Standards Board of American Speech-Language-Hearing Association, and the National Council for Accreditation of Teacher Education. The College's academic programs are registered by the New York State Department of Education.

Applying

Admission to the Division of Graduate Studies is determined by graduate faculty, departmental, and/or program committees. All applicants are advised to review special admissions and matriculation requirements for each program as stated in the Brooklyn College Graduate Bulletin. Applicants must have a baccalaureate degree from an accredited institution and have completed an approved program with a minimum average of B in the major and B- overall. Some programs require specialized tests such as the GRE. Applications and supporting credentials, including official transcripts, must be received by either February 1 or March 1 for most programs for priority consideration for admission, but each program has special requirements, and deadlines vary. For a complete listing of graduate program admission requirements and deadlines, see the Brooklyn College Web site page for Graduate Admissions, Application Requirements. Students educated outside the United States must file applications by February 1 for the summer and fall terms and by October 1 for the spring term. Late applicants may also submit their applications on a rolling basis; acceptance is determined solely by the department. Students must apply online at the College Web site, at http://www.brooklyn.edu/pg.

Correspondence and Information

Office of Admissions
Brooklyn College of the City University of New York
2900 Bedford Avenue
Brooklyn, New York 11210-2889

Phone: 718-951-5001
Web site: http://www.brooklyn.edu/pg

THE FACULTY

Karen L. Gould, President; Ph.D., Oregon.
Louise Hainline, Dean of Research and Graduate Studies; Ph.D., Harvard.
Geraldine Faria, Assistant Dean of Research and Graduate Studies; Ph.D., Denver.
Deborah A. Shanley, Dean of the School of Education; Ed.D., Columbia.
Kathleen McSorley, Assistant Dean of the School of Education; Ed.D., Syracuse.

DEPARTMENT AND PROGRAM HEADS

Art
Michael Mallory, Chairperson and Counselor for the Graduate M.A. Program in Art History; Ph.D., Columbia.
Jennifer McCoy, Graduate Deputy (Art); M.F.A., Rensselaer.
Mona Hadler, Graduate Deputy (Art History); Ph.D., Columbia.

Biology
Peter Lipke, Chairperson; Ph.D., California, Berkeley.
Charlene Forest, Graduate Deputy; Ph.D., Indiana.

Chemistry
James Howell, Chairperson; Ph.D., Cornell; Ph.D., Caltech.
Richard Magliozzo, Graduate Deputy; Ph.D., CUNY Graduate Center.

Computer and Information Science
Yedidyah Langsam, Chairperson; Ph.D., Polytechnic of NYU.
Keith Harrow, Graduate Deputy (Administrative); Ph.D., NYU.
Daniel Kopec, Graduate Deputy (Counseling); Ph.D., Edinburgh.

Conservatory of Music
Bruce MacIntyre, Director; Ph.D., CUNY Graduate Center.
Stephanie Jensen-Moulton, Graduate Deputy; Ph.D., CUNY Graduate Center.

Economics
Robert Bell, Chairperson; Ph.D., Brunel (England).
Hershey Friedman, Director of Business Programs, Ph.D., CUNY Graduate Center.
Hervé J. Queneau, Assistant Graduate Deputy (Economics); Ph.D., Paris.
Stanley Sauber, Assistant Graduate Deputy (Accounting); CPA.
Emanuel Thorne, Graduate Deputy (Economics); Ph.D., Yale.
Moishe Zelcer, Graduate Deputy (Accounting); Ph.D., CUNY Graduate Center.

School of Education
Deborah A. Shanley, Dean; Ed.D., Columbia Teachers College.
Kathleen McSorley, Assistant Dean; Ed.D., Syracuse.
Adolescence Education: Stephen Phillips; M.A., Stanford.
Childhood Bilingual Education: Alma Rubal-Lopez; Ph.D., Yeshiva.
Childhood Education: Sharon O'Connor-Petruso; P.D., Ed.D., St. John's (New York).
Childhood Middle School: Mary Chiusano; M.A., NYU.
Coordinator of Teaching Fellows: Stephen Phillips; M.A. Stanford.
Early Childhood Education: Mary DeBey, Ph.D., SUNY at Albany.
Educational Leadership: David Bloomfield, J.D., Columbia.
Middle Childhood Mathematics Education: Mary Chiusano; M.A., NYU.
School Counseling (Advanced Certificate and M.S. in Education): Lynda Sarnoff, M.S.Ed., Hofstra.
School Psychology (Advanced Certificate and M.S. in Education): Florence Rubinson, Ph.D., Fordham.
Teacher of Students with Disabilities in Early Childhood, Childhood, and Middle Childhood Education: Pauline Bynoe; Ed.D., Columbia Teachers College.

English
Ellen Tremper, Chairperson; Ph.D., Harvard.
Mark Patkowski, Graduate Deputy; Ph.D., NYU.

General Science
Eleanor Miele, Interdepartmental Coordinator; Ph.D., Columbia.

Geology
Wayne G. Powell, Chairperson; Ph.D., Queen's University (Canada).
John Chamberlain Jr., Graduate Deputy; Ph.D., Rochester.

Health and Nutrition Sciences
Janet K. Grommet, Chairperson; Ph.D., Michigan State.
Kathleen Axen, Graduate Deputy (Nutrition); Ph.D., Columbia.
Jean Grassman, Graduate Deputy (Health); Ph.D., California, Berkeley.

History
David G. Troyansky, Chairperson; Ph.D., Brandeis.
Steven Remy, Graduate Deputy; Ph.D., Ohio.

Judaic Studies
Sara Reguer, Chairperson; Ph.D., Columbia.
Sharon Flatto, Graduate Deputy; Ph.D., Yale.

Liberal Studies
Philip Gallagher, Co-director; Ph.D., Notre Dame.
Mark Patkowski, Co-director; Ph.D., NYU.

Mathematics
George Shapiro, Chairperson; Ph.D., Harvard.
Laurel Cooley, Graduate Deputy; Ph.D., NYU

Modern Languages and Literatures
William Childers, Chairperson and Graduate Adviser; Ph.D., Columbia.
Margarite Fernández Olmos, Graduate Deputy; Ph.D., NYU.

Performance and Interactive Media Arts
John Jannone, Director; M.F.A., Rensselaer.

Physical Education and Exercise Science
Charles Tobey, Chairperson; Ed.D., Columbia.
Michael Hipscher, Graduate Deputy; M.A., NYU.

Physics
Peter Lesser, Acting Chairperson; Ph.D., Rochester.
Ming-Kung Liou, Graduate Deputy; Ph.D., Manitoba (Canada).

Political Science
Sally Bermanzohn, Chairperson; Ph.D., CUNY Graduate Center.
Mark Ungar, Graduate Deputy; Ph.D., Columbia.
Joseph F. Wilson, Graduate Deputy (Worker Education Program); Ph.D., Columbia.

Psychology
R. Glen Hass, Chairperson; Ph.D., Duke.
Elisabeth Brauner, Subprogram Head (Mind, Brain, and Behavior); Ph.D., Göttingen (Germany).
Benzion Chanowitz, Graduate Deputy; Ph.D., CUNY Graduate Center.

Sociology
Kenneth A. Gould, Chairperson; Ph.D., Northwestern.
Alex Vitale, Graduate Deputy; Ph.D., CUNY Graduate Center.

Speech Communication Arts and Sciences
Michele Emmer, Chairperson; Ph.D., CUNY Graduate Center.
Gail Gurland, Graduate Deputy (Teacher of Students with Speech and Language Disabilities); Ph.D., CUNY Graduate Center.

Television and Radio
George R. Rodman, Chairperson; Ph.D., USC.
Stuart MacLelland, Graduate Deputy; M.F.A., CUNY, Brooklyn.

Theater
Thomas Bullard, Chairperson; M.F.A., Yale.
Tobie Stein, Graduate Deputy; Ph.D., CUNY Graduate Center.

DISTINGUISHED PROFESSORS

Eric Alterman (English); Ph.D., Stanford.
Edwin Burrows (History); Ph.D., Columbia.
Jack Flam (Art); Ph.D., NYU.
Tania León (Music); M.A., NYU.
Ursula Oppens (Music); M.S., Juilliard.
Rohit Parikh (Computer and Information Science); Ph.D., Harvard.
Theodore Raphan (Computer and Information Science); Ph.D., CUNY Graduate Center.
Anthony Sclafani (Psychology), Ph.D., Chicago.

BRYN MAWR COLLEGE

Graduate School of Arts and Sciences

Programs of Study

Bryn Mawr's Ph.D. programs prepare graduates for teaching, research, and curatorial careers in academic institutions, museums, government and nongovernment agencies, and private enterprise. Options for graduates of the program in clinical developmental psychology also include counseling and school and hospital administration. The Ph.D. is offered in chemistry; classical and Near Eastern archaeology; clinical developmental psychology; Greek, Latin, and classical studies; history of art; mathematics; and physics. The M.A. program in French prepares students for the best American Ph.D. programs as well as for teaching and other professions. A full-time course load is 3 units (courses) per semester; 6 units are required for the M.A. and 12 for the Ph.D. The M.A. can be earned in one or two years. Ph.D. preliminary examinations are normally taken in the fourth or fifth year, followed by two to three years on the dissertation. The program in clinical developmental psychology follows a somewhat different schedule and requires 18 units for completion.

Bryn Mawr is both teaching and research intensive. The Ph.D. programs in the sciences offer particularly close mentoring in teaching and research and are well suited to students who aim for an academic career. Bryn Mawr's small scale and informality guarantee easy access to faculty mentors and facilitate participation in the academic offerings of other departments. Students typically take an active role in the design of their program of courses and their research. Good writing skills, independence, and originality are prized in all programs.

Research Facilities

Collectively, the Mariam Coffin Canaday Library, the Lois and Reginald Collier Science Library, and the Rhys Carpenter Library contain more than 1 million volumes. Rhys Carpenter Library at Bryn Mawr is a specialized library for archaeology, classics, and the history of art and architecture, and it has more than 140,000 volumes, a Visual Resources Center, 103 networked carrels for students, five classrooms, and a computer lab. Bryn Mawr's library consortium with Haverford and Swarthmore Colleges makes over 1 million additional volumes readily accessible.

The Park Science complex includes state-of-the-art laboratories that house major equipment. For use in the Chemistry Department are a 300 MHz high-resolution NMR spectrometer, a high pressure liquid chromatograph-mass spectrometer (LC-MS), a gas chromatograph–mass spectrometer, (GC-MS), an FT-IR spectrophotometer, an atomic force microscope (AFM), fluorescence diode array UV-Vis spectrometers, centrifuges, radioisotope facilities, a cold room, and a computational modeling workstation. In addition, faculty members' research laboratories contain the appropriate instrumentation to perform experiments in biological, organic, inorganic, and physical chemistry.

The Physics Department has three well-established research laboratories with a fourth beginning development September 2009. The Photo-Physics Laboratory houses three optical tables; three Nd:YAG pump lasers; two commercial, tunable dye lasers; two auto-tracking harmonic crystal systems; a differentially pumped vacuum chamber with a supersonic pulsed valve to produce molecular beams and time-of-flight mass and fluorescence detection capabilities. The Ultracold Rydberg Atom Laboratory houses three optical tables, a rubidium magneto-optical trap, a pulsed Nd:YAG laser pumping several dye lasers, a mode-locked and q-switched Nd:YAG laser, and a high-vacuum atomic beam system. The Solid State NMR Laboratory houses three fixed-frequency solid state NMR spectrometers for relaxation rate measurements and two complete variable-temperature (77–400 K) experimental stations. A new materials science lab is being developed which will involve equipment needed to make and spectroscopically analyze various types of nanostructures.

Financial Aid

Bryn Mawr offers numerous fellowships and teaching and research assistantships for full-time study, as well as grants, tuition awards, and summer stipends. Nine-month fellowship stipends begin at $15,000. Fellowships can be guaranteed for multiple years, after which alternative forms of aid may be available. Assistantship stipends range from $14,000 to $23,150, depending on the field. Summer stipends range from $2500 to $4000. Health insurance subsidies may also be awarded and vary from year to year. The Marguerite N. Farley Fellowship is reserved for students who come from outside the U.S., and carries a stipend of $16,000. The Graduate Group in Archaeology, Classics, and History of Art offers to beginning students fellowships for multidisciplinary study with a twelve-month stipend of $20,000, and the Areté (Excellence) fellowships with a stipend of $20,000. In the Graduate Group in Science and Mathematics, members of under-represented minority groups are eligible for a Dean's Fellowship with a stipend of $20,000.

Cost of Study

Full-time tuition, consisting of six courses per year, is $31,340; part-time tuition is $5290 per course. Units of supervised work cost $845, and the fee for maintaining matriculation (continuing enrollment) is $430 per semester.

Living and Housing Costs

Students live locally or in Philadelphia. Shared apartments can be rented for $600 to $900 per month, studio apartments begin at $800 per month, and food costs are about $200 per month. Other expenses include transportation (about $165 per month if commuting from Philadelphia) and health insurance (approximately $2500 per year for domestic students and approximately $1500 for international students).

Student Group

Total enrollment in the Graduate School of Arts and Sciences is approximately 155, of which women form 75 percent; typically, 5–10 percent are international students. Twenty-five percent of students are full-time, and 85 percent receive some form of financial aid. Programs range in size from 3 to 30 students; the largest enrollments are in clinical developmental psychology and history of art.

Student Outcomes

Of Ph.D. graduates in the past five years, nearly 85 percent are employed in the field of their degree. Occupations include college and university faculty members, research scientists, museum curators, clinicians and counselors, editors, and academic and foundation administrators.

Location

Bryn Mawr is a suburb of Philadelphia, the fifth-largest city in the U.S. It is well served by rail lines (the Main Line) and by bus. Philadelphia is renowned for music, museums, and sports, and it is also a culinary mecca with restaurants serving many cuisines. The metropolitan area has more than 100 museums and fifty colleges and universities, with a total population of 220,000 students.

The College and The School

Bryn Mawr is a liberal arts college for women with two coeducational graduate schools: the Graduate School of Arts and Sciences and the Graduate School of Social Work and Social Research. Founded in 1885, Bryn Mawr was the first institution in the U.S. to offer the Ph.D. to women, and graduate education continues to be a significant part of its mission. Graduates number approximately 400, out of a total enrollment of approximately 1,750 including undergraduates.

Applying

The deadline for application for admission with financial aid is January 4, 2010. Applications for admission without aid are accepted up to June 30, 2010, in all programs except clinical developmental psychology. GRE scores, a writing sample, and three letters of recommendation are required. Nonnative speakers of English must submit a TOEFL score (minimum 600, paper-based; 250, computer-based). Additional requirements vary by department. Please visit the Web site for detailed information.

Correspondence and Information

Lea Miller, Program Assistant
Graduate School of Arts and Sciences
Bryn Mawr College
101 North Merion Avenue
Bryn Mawr, Pennsylvania 19010-2899

Phone: 610-526-5072
E-mail: lrmiller@brynmawr.edu
Web site: http://www.brynmawr.edu/gsa

THE FACULTY AND THEIR RESEARCH

Chemistry

Sharon J. Nieter Burgmayer, Professor; Ph.D., North Carolina, 1984. Inorganic and bioinorganic chemistry: the role of transition metals in enzymes.
Michelle M. Francl, Professor; Ph.D., California, Irvine, 1983. Physical chemistry, computational chemistry and molecular architecture.
Jonas Goldsmith, Assistant Professor; Ph.D., Cornell, 2002. Electrochemistry, development and characterization of functional nanomaterials.
William Malachowski, Associate Professor; Ph.D., Michigan, 1993. Synthetic organic chemistry, peptidomimetic synthesis, development of new asymmetric synthetic methods.
Frank B. Mallory, Professor; Ph.D., Caltech, 1958. Organic chemistry, photochemistry and clear magnetic resonance spectroscopy.
Susan A. White, Professor and Chair; Ph.D., Johns Hopkins, 1988. Biochemistry, biochemical studies of RNA and RNA-protein interactions.

Classical and Near Eastern Archaeology

Mehmet-Ali Ataç, Assistant Professor; Ph.D., Harvard, 2003. Visual and intellectual traditions of the ancient Near East; Neo-Assyrian iconography, Near Eastern and Egyptian kingship.
A. A. Donohue, Professor; Ph.D., NYU, 1984. History and historiography of classical art.
Astrid Lindenlauf, Assistant Professor; Ph.D., University College (London), 2001. Greek art and archaeology, fortifications and warfare, urbanism, disposal and recycling practices.
Peter Magee, Associate Professor; Ph.D., Sydney, 1996. Archaeology of south Asia, Iran, and Arabia; field methods; materials analysis.
James C. Wright, Professor and Chair; Ph.D., Bryn Mawr, 1978. Prehistory of the Aegean basin, settlement forms and architecture of classical Greece, theory and method.

Clinical Developmental Psychology

Kimberly Wright Cassidy, Associate Professor; Ph.D., Pennsylvania, 1993. Cognition and education, children's theory of mind, pheriological/prosodic aspects of language, children's understanding of literature.
Clark R. McCauley, Professor; Ph.D., Pennsylvania, 1970. Intergroup conflict, terrorism and extremism, social cognition, individual differences, health psychology, stereotype.
Leslie Rescorla, Professor; Ph.D., Yale, 1976. Empirically based assessment of children's problems and competencies, preschool language development and language delay, child psychiatric disorders, ability and achievement in school children.
Marc Schulz, Associate Professor; Ph.D., Berkeley, 1994. Emotions and close relationships, emotion regulation, marital relationships and their effects on children, family child-rearing environments, work stress and its impact on family life.
Anjali Thapar, Associate Professor; Ph.D., Case Western Reserve, 1994. Cognitive psychology, memory processes, aging.
Earl Thomas, Professor and Chair; Ph.D., Yale, 1967. Neurobiology and psychopharmacology, anxiety, animal models of psychopathology.
Robert H. Wozniak, Professor; Ph.D., Michigan, 1971. Developmental theory, history of psychology, speech regulation of action, early identification of autism, gesture and language development, family belief systems.

French

Koffi Anyinéfa, Associate Professor (Haverford College); Ph.D., Bayreuth (Germany), 1989. Francophone African and Caribbean literature.
Grace M. Armstrong, Professor and Chair; Ph.D., Princeton, 1973. Medieval French literature, feminist studies, narrative techniques.
Francis Higginson, Associate Professor; Ph.D., Berkeley, 1997. Twentieth-century French and Francophone literature, critical theory.
Brigitte Mahuzier, Associate Professor; Ph.D., Cornell, 1988. Narrative and poetry of the nineteenth and twentieth centuries; feminist, gender, and queer theory; visual arts and aesthetic theory.
David Sedley, Associate Professor (Haverford College); Ph.D., Princeton, 1999. Sixteenth- and seventeenth-century literature, critical theory.

Greek, Latin, and Classical Studies

Annette Baertschi, Assistant Professor; Ph.D., Humboldt, 2006. Post-Augustan poetry, ancient magic, Latin meter, reception.
Catherine Conybeare, Associate Professor; Ph.D., Toronto, 1997. Late antique and early medieval Latin prose, cultural history, critical theory.
Radcliffe Edmonds, Associate Professor; Ph.D., Chicago, 1999. Greek myth, Greco-Roman religion and magic, Greek philosophy.
Richard Hamilton, Professor and Chair; Ph.D., Michigan, 1971. Greek lyric poetry, Greek drama, Greek religion.
Russell T. Scott, Professor; Ph.D., Yale, 1964. Roman history and historiography, Latin literature, Roman archaeology.

History of Art

David J. Cast, Professor; Ph.D., Columbia, 1970. Renaissance art and criticism, architecture post-1400, twentieth-century British art.
Christiane Hertel, Professor; Ph.D., Tübingen (Germany), 1985. German, Austrian, and Netherlandish art and architecture; German intellectual history; aesthetics and art theory.
Homay King, Associate Professor; Ph.D., Berkeley, 2003. American film history; film, feminist, psychoanalytic, and rhetorical theory.
Dale Kinney, Professor; Ph.D., NYU, 1975. Late antique and medieval Italian art, medieval architecture, spolia.
Steven Z. Levine, Professor; Ph.D., Harvard, 1974. Sixteenth-to-twentieth-century French painting, psychoanalysis, self-portraiture, visual theory.
Gridley McKim-Smith, Professor; Ph.D., Harvard, 1974. Seventeenth-century Spanish painting and sculpture, scientific analysis of works of art, costume.
Lisa Saltzman, Professor and Chair; Ph.D., Harvard, 1994. Post–World War II art and theory, gender and identity, memory and trauma.

Mathematics

Leslie C. Cheng, Associate Professor; Ph.D., Pittsburgh, 1998. Fourier analysis on Euclidean spaces, oscillatory integrals, singular integrals, Hardy spaces.
Victor J. Donnay, Professor; Ph.D., NYU, 1986. Dynamical systems, ergodic theory, differential geometry.
Helen G. Grundman, Professor; Ph.D., Berkeley, 1989. Algebra, algebraic number theory, analytic number theory.
Rhonda Hughes, Professor; Ph.D., Illinois, 1975. Functional analysis, harmonic and wavelet analysis, operator theory.
Paul M. Melvin, Professor; Ph.D., Berkeley, 1977. Algebraic and differential topology, low-dimensional manifolds, quantum topology.
Lisa Traynor, Professor and Chair; Ph.D., SUNY at Stony Brook, 1992. Symplectic topology, contact geometry, differential geometry and topology.

Physics

Peter A. Beckmann, Professor; Ph.D., British Columbia, 1985. Chemical physics, condensed-matter physics.
Elizabeth F. McCormack, Professor; Ph.D., Yale, 1989. Atomic, molecular, and optical physics.
Michael W. Noel, Associate Professor and Chair; Ph.D., Rochester, 1996. Atomic, molecular, and optical physics.
Michael B. Schulz, Assistant Professor; Ph.D. Stanford, 2002. Theoretical physics with a focus on string theory and its applications to quantum field theory.
Xuemei May Cheng, Assistant Professor; Ph.D., Johns Hopkins, 2006. Condensed matter physics, magnetic materials.

CALDWELL COLLEGE

Graduate Programs

Programs of Study

Caldwell College offers a Ph.D. in applied behavior analysis (ABA), master's degree programs (Master of Business Administration and Master of Arts) and postbaccalaureate and post-master's certificate programs in the areas of applied behavioral analysis, business, education, pastoral ministry, and psychology. All programs are designed to meet the scheduling needs of adult students and the accepted professional standards for each discipline.

The 90-credit doctoral program in ABA is designed to prepare students for high-level employment within areas where there are growing demands for competent professionals with expertise in applied behavior analysis, namely developmental services, special education, mental health, and academia. Students are required to show proficiency in coursework, practicum, and dissertation research and must possess an M.A. in ABA or a closely related field, in addition to other requirements, to be admitted to the Ph.D. program.

The 39-credit-hour M.B.A. degree program is offered as a generalist degree or with an optional concentration in accounting or nonprofit management. This program is designed to prepare students to meet the demands of the twenty-first century business world. Courses are offered evenings, Saturdays, and via distance learning.

The Master of Arts (M.A.) degree is offered in several areas, including four in education. The M.A. in curriculum and instruction comprises 36 credit hours, and students may elect to complete one of three optional specializations—educational technology, special education, or supervisor's certification. An M.A. in educational administration is offered for students who seek certification as a school administrator, supervisor, or business administrator. Students can pursue this 36-credit-hour degree program on campus in a traditional program or in the innovative, dynamic one-year Off-Campus Leadership Development (OCLD) fast-track program. An M.A. in special education prepares students to teach in an inclusive or self-contained classroom or to work in a related field in special education. In this program, students may also choose an option to earn a certification in learning disabilities teacher consultant (LDTC). The M.A. in literacy instruction is a 30-credit program designed for K–12 certificated classroom teachers who seek to improve and/or enhance their knowledge and skills in literacy instruction. Through the structure of the course offerings, this graduate literacy program is designed to balance the requirement of successful K–12 reading and writing development. Through a selection of appropriate courses, a reading specialist certification may also be acquired.

In psychology, the M.A. is offered in counseling psychology in a 60-credit-hour degree program, with optional specializations available in school counseling and in New Jersey's only graduate art therapy curriculum, which is accredited by the American Art Therapy Association. The M.A. in applied behavior analysis is a 45-credit-hour program that trains students to meet the educational needs of children with autism-spectrum disorders and cognitive delays. The ABA core is approved by the Behavior Analyst Certification Board, Inc.®

A 36-credit-hour M.A. in pastoral ministry prepares individuals to support the pastoral mission of the Roman Catholic or other churches. Its nontraditional format, with classes offered on Saturdays and optional weekend nights, meets the personal and professional scheduling needs of students. It also offers an optional concentration in church administration, a growing need in today's church. The College also has added an 18 credit postbaccalaureate certificate program in pastoral ministry.

Postbaccalaureate certificate programs are also offered in education. The Post-Baccalaureate Teacher Certification Program enables individuals who have bachelor's degrees to earn their elementary (K–8 or K–8 with P–3) teacher certification or K–12 subject-specific certification. The Post-Baccalaureate Special Education Certification Program prepares current teachers to earn additional certification as a Teacher of Students with Disabilities.

The College also offers seven post-master's programs. The Professional Counselor Licensing Program is intended for those who hold a master's degree in counseling or a closely related field and who need additional credits to qualify as a Licensed Professional Counselor in New Jersey. The School Counseling Specialization is intended for those who hold a master's degree in education, psychology, or a related field and need additional credits to qualify for a New Jersey school counselor credential. A post-master's program for Director of School Counseling certification has received state approval. The Supervisor's Certificate Program meets New Jersey certification requirements for the Supervisor's Certificate for educators and those in educational support services. The College also offers a post-master's non-degree program in applied behavior analysis designed to introduce students to the field of behavior analysis and to prepare them for employment within the fields where there are growing demands for competent professionals in ABA, namely developmental services, special education, and mental health. In addition, the College offers a post-master's master's degree in art therapy. The 36-credit Post-Master's Art Therapy Master's program is especially designed for persons who already possess a master's degree in counseling or a related mental health field (social work, psychology, psychiatric nursing, marriage and family therapy) and would like to become registered as an art therapist with the American Art Therapy Association or integrate the practice of art therapy into their clinical work.

In education, post-master's programs are offered in principal's certification, supervisor's certification, and LDTC certification. The Principal's Certification Program is designed to meet New Jersey certification requirements for the principal's certificate for applicants who have a master's degree in educational leadership, curriculum and instruction, or a recognized field of leadership or management. The Supervisor's Certification Program is designed to meet New Jersey certification requirements for the supervisor's certificate for applicants who have a master's degree and three years experience under New Jersey certification for teaching or support services. The LDTC Certification Program is designed to meet the New Jersey Department of Education requirements for Learning Disabilities Teacher Consultant (LDTC) certification for applicants who have a master's degree and general education teaching certification.

Research Facilities

Caldwell College's Jennings Library offers students approximately 145,000 volumes, more than 3,000 bound periodicals, and more than 5,000 microfilm reels. It also provides access to more than 9,000 journal and newspaper titles in a variety of formats: electronic, paper, and microform. The audiovisual collection numbers almost 2,000 items and contains videotapes and audiotapes, compact discs, filmstrips, etc. There is full Internet access through various workstation clusters and remote access 24 hours a day, seven days a week, which allows for continuous access to most online databases. Online access to the collection is available through the Dynix Automated System (CALCAT), which is available on and off campus via the Internet. The collections are developed continuously to support the curricular needs of students and the faculty. As a member of the OCLC (Online Computer Library Center) and the New Jersey Library Network, the library provides access to more than 30 million titles in more than 5,000 national and international libraries. A curriculum laboratory has texts for grades K–12, visual aids, and other resources.

Computer labs, which include up-to-date personal computers installed with current software and multimedia equipment, offer free scanning and laser printing. Other computer labs dedicated to specific areas of study include the Education, Business, Psychology, and Writing labs. Technology-enhanced classrooms are equipped with digital audio and video and computer equipment. All offices, classrooms, and labs are connected to the campus network and the Internet. Wide-screen video and computer graphic capability and satellite reception are available. Through an agreement with Microsoft Corporation, certain software is available for sale to registered students at greatly reduced prices.

Through an almost $2-million federal government grant to establish the Center for Excellence in Teaching on campus, Caldwell College recently renovated its biology, physics, and chemistry laboratories in order to implement innovative teacher preparation programs that emphasize the effective use of technology in classrooms, the refinement of math and science training, special education teacher training, and the development of programs for disadvantaged students. The Center for Educational Technology, which is supported by Caldwell College and AT&T, offers local teachers a variety of services to assist them in implementing technology into the teaching and learning experience.

Financial Aid

Financial aid in the form of federal aid, tuition discounts, and graduate assistantships is available to matriculated graduate students who are taking at least 6 credits; some aid requires full-time status (9 credits).

Cost of Study

For the 2009–10 academic year, graduate tuition is $735 per credit hour.

Living and Housing Costs

Limited on-campus housing is available to graduate students.

Student Group

Caldwell College enrolls approximately 650 graduate students.

Location

Wooded areas surround Caldwell College's campus, which is located in suburban Caldwell, New Jersey. The College is near major highways and public transportation and is only 20 miles from New York City. Within walking distance is the town center, which has a variety of shops and restaurants. Area and regional attractions include theaters, museums, parks, ski resorts, malls, the Meadowlands Sports Complex, and the New Jersey shore. Many corporate headquarters are easily accessible and provide a variety of internship opportunities.

The College

Founded in 1939 by the Sisters of Saint Dominic, Caldwell College is committed to serving a diverse student population of all ages. The College offers high-quality career-related programs that prepare graduates to take advantage of opportunities in an increasingly complex society. The integration of the arts, humanities, and sciences with the deepest expression of the contemplative and creative spirit of men and women forms the basis of the educational philosophy of Caldwell College. The hallmark of a Caldwell College education is small classes, quality, professional relevance, and scheduling that accommodates working adults.

Applying

Students should begin the application process by submitting the online application. Specific application requirements vary by program. Students should consult the College's Web site to determine the requirements for the program in which they are interested, or they should contact the Center for Graduate and Continuing Studies for more information.

Correspondence and Information

Dr. Dennis R. DeLong, Dean
Center for Graduate and Continuing Studies
Caldwell College
120 Bloomfield Avenue
Caldwell, New Jersey 07006

Phone: 973-618-3544
Fax: 973-618-3690
E-mail: graduate@caldwell.edu
Web site: http://www.caldwell.edu/graduate

THE CORE FACULTY

In addition to the following core graduate faculty members—all of whom are full-time members of the Caldwell College faculty—the graduate faculty also includes talented and accomplished adjuncts who bring both academic and professional experience into the classrooms.

Rosann Bar, Associate Professor of Sociology; M.A., M.Phil., Ph.D., Columbia.
Ann Marie Callahan, Associate Professor of Business; M.S., Seton Hall; M.B.A., Saint Peter's; CPA.
Walter Cmielewski, Associate Professor of Education; Ed.D., Seton Hall.
Lori Harris-Ransom, Professor of Business; M.A., J.D., Saint Louis.
Joanne Jasmine, Assistant Professor of Education; Ed.D., Columbia.
Anatoly Kandel, Associate Professor of Business and Toohey Chair in Economics; Ph.D., Institute of World Economy (Moscow); Ph.D., Columbia.
Thomas R. Keen, Professor of Business; M.B.A., Fairleigh Dickinson; Ph.D., Walden.
Stephen Maret, Professor of Psychology; M.Phil., Ph.D., Drew.
John McIntyre, Professor of Education; Ed.D., Rutgers.
Sr. Barbara Moore, O.P., Assistant Professor of Theology and Pastoral Ministry; D.Min., Drew.
Joan Moriarty, Assistant Professor of Education; Ed.D., Seton Hall.
Alvin Neiman, Professor of Business; M.B.A., Seton Hall; CPA.
Donald Noone, Professor of Business; Ph.L., Fordham; Ph.D., Rutgers.
Bernard C. O'Rourke, Associate Professor of Business; M.B.A., Fordham; J.D., King's Inns Law School (Dublin).
Joseph Pedoto, Associate Professor of Psychology; Ph.D., Seton Hall.
Luciane Pereira-Pasarin, Assistant Professor of Psychology, Ph.D., Stony Brook.
Patrick Progar, Associate Professor of Psychology; Ph.D., Wisconsin–Milwaukee; BCBA.
Kenneth F. Reeve, Associate Professor of Psychology; Ph.D., CUNY Graduate Center.
Sharon A. Reeve, Assistant Professor of Education and Psychology; Ph.D., CUNY Graduate Center; BCBA.
Edith Dunfee Ries, Associate Professor of Education; Ed.D., Rutgers.
Anthony Romano, Assistant Professor of Business; M.B.A., Adelphi; Ph.D., Capella.
Edward J. Schons, Professor of Business; M.B.A., Boston University; M.B.A., Ph.D., Rutgers.
Joanne Seelaus, Associate Professor of Education; Ed.D., Fordham.
Tina Sidener, Assistant Professor of Psychology; Ph.D., Western Michigan; BCBA.
Stacey M. Solomon, Assistant Professor of Psychology; Ph.D., Virginia.
Janice Stewart, Professor of Education; Ph.D., Illinois.
James Vivinetto, Assistant Professor of Education; Ed.D., Seton Hall.
Sr. Catherine Waters, O.P., Professor of Psychology; Ph.D., Fordham; LPC.
Marie Wilson, Associate Professor of Art Therapy; M.A., Norwich; ATR-BC, LPC.
Rita Wolpert, Professor of Psychology; Ed.D., Columbia.

CENTRAL WASHINGTON UNIVERSITY

Graduate Studies and Research

Programs of Study

Central Washington University (CWU) offers programs that lead to the following degrees: Master of Arts, Master of Arts for Teachers, Master of Education, Master of Fine Arts, Master of Music, Master of Professional Accountancy, and Master of Science.

Master of Arts programs include art (M.A. and M.F.A.), English (literature, TESOL), history, and theater production (summers only), and theater studies. Master of Science degree programs are available in biological sciences, chemistry, engineering technology, exercise science, experimental psychology, family and consumer sciences, geology, health and physical education, mental health counseling, resource management, and primate behavior. There is a Master of Professional Accountancy in accounting. A Master of Arts in Teaching mathematics is available, in the summer only. Master of Education programs include master teacher, reading specialist, school counseling, instructional leadership, school psychology, and special education.

A minimum of 45 quarter credits is needed for a master's degree, though some programs require more credits. As the capstone project, programs may require a thesis, a project, or a comprehensive examination in lieu of the thesis. A final oral examination is standard for most programs.

CWU encourages collaborative research among graduate students and faculty members. It is committed to ensuring that graduate students gain as much hands-on experience as possible in their programs. A measure of CWU's success is that graduate students regularly give conference presentations, exhibitions, and performances. Music students have performed with nationally recognized orchestras and at the Metropolitan Opera. Graduate students typically conduct research as part of federally sponsored grants in such areas as biological sciences, geographic information systems, geology, and resource management, and others have won awards for art.

Research Facilities

In addition to its library, CWU's massive science facility and the completely renovated education building augment CWU's instructional and research facilities. The Chimpanzee and Human Communications Institute is the home of world-famous, sign language–using chimpanzees. The Geographic Information Systems Laboratory, Applied Social Data Center, and Community Psychology Services Clinic provide students with exceptional research opportunities. Computing services include access to the Internet, an online public catalog, and online bibliographic retrieval services. The James E. Brooks Library makes CWU the largest repository of state documents in central Washington.

Financial Aid

Graduate assistantships are available in each of CWU's departments offering graduate degrees. Approximately 44 percent of all full-time enrolled graduate students received appointments in 2009–10. About two thirds of the graduate assistants teach; the remainder serve as research assistants and a few perform service functions. The stipend package for a Washington State resident for the 2009–10 academic year is $16,102. Other financial support can be obtained through the Office of Financial Aid from federal and state sources for students demonstrating financial need. There are also employment opportunities on and off campus. Furthermore, graduate students may apply for travel and research funds on a competitive basis through the Office of Graduate Studies and Research.

Cost of Study

Graduate tuition for 2009–10 is $2319 per quarter for full-time (10–18 quarter credit hours) Washington State residents and $5185 per quarter for nonresidents. For resident part-time students, tuition was $231.94 per credit hour; $518.50 per credit hour for nonresidents. There is a $72 per quarter health service fee, a $42 per quarter athletic fee, a $25 per quarter technology fee, a $3 Central transit fee, and, for Ellensburg campus-based students, a $64 Student Union Building fee and a $95 recreation center fee. The cost of tuition for summer school 2009 was $208 per credit hour for both in-state and out-of-state graduate students.

Living and Housing Costs

University Housing Services offers a variety of apartments starting at $515 per month for a studio and running up to $869 for a three-bedroom apartment. Rents off campus range from $600 to $900 per month depending on the size and extras. The University also makes available rooms in residence halls for graduate students. Assistance with locating off-campus housing is available as well. Dining Services offers reasonably priced, quarterly contracts in its four dining halls. Meals vary at each location, and there are several meal plan options from which to choose.

Student Group

As of the fall quarter 2008, there were 421 graduate students at CWU enrolled in twenty-seven programs across nineteen departments; they make up just over 4 percent of the University's 10,300 students. Graduate classes are small and there are regular opportunities to work closely with professors and fellow students. The largest graduate programs are in education, psychology, and resource management. Other departments average between 12 and 30 enrolled graduate students.

Location

CWU's main campus is in Ellensburg, Washington. The community prides itself on quality living, and students experience a friendly and safe small-town atmosphere. This is complemented by diverse cultural and social fare offered by the University's proximity to the Cascade Mountains, Seattle, Puget Sound, Yakima, the Yakima River Valley, Spokane, and the Columbia River recreational areas. The Kittitas Valley boasts four distinct seasons and abundant sunshine.

The University

CWU is one of six state-assisted universities in the state. It was founded in 1890 as the Washington State Normal School and became a comprehensive university in 1977. Graduate programs were first offered in fall 1947. Fully accredited, CWU provides graduate programming at its instructional centers in Lynnwood, Moses Lake, Pierce County, Des Moines, Wenatchee, and Yakima, as well as Ellensburg. The campus is a mixture of traditional and modern architecture stretching across 380 acres of shaded lawns framed by evergreens and landscaped walkways. A nationally renowned Japanese garden in the center of the grounds offers a serene place to think, reflect, and relax. CWU is four blocks from historic downtown Ellensburg. Most shops and restaurants are within walking distance. The city and campus are accessible by wheelchairs, bicycles, and strollers. Other points of interest include an arts complex housing the Sarah Spurgeon Gallery, the contemporary music education building, a theater, a massive science facility, Nicholson Athletic Pavilion, and the new recreation center.

Applying

Application materials may be obtained from the University. The application fee is $50. Applicants should have earned at least a 3.0 GPA over the last 60 semester hours (90 quarter hours) of graded course work. Some programs require scores on the General Test of the GRE. The M.P.A. program requires GMAT scores. Students whose native language is not English must score at least 550 (paper-based), 213 (computer-based), or 79 (Internet-based) on the TOEFL. Students should contact the relevant department as they may need to supply other materials when submitting the application. Priority consideration is given to applications received by February 1 for fall quarter admissions. Assistantship applications should be submitted by March 1 for the following summer and academic year. Financial aid applications should be made directly to the Office of Financial Aid by March 1.

Correspondence and Information

Graduate Studies and Research
Central Washington University
400 East University Way
Ellensburg, Washington 98926-7510

Phone: 509-963-3103
Fax: 509-963-1799
E-mail: masters@cwu.edu
Web site: http://www.cwu.edu/~masters

GRADUATE AFFAIRS

The area code is 509 for all phone and fax numbers.

Graduate Studies and Research
(Phone: 963-3103; fax: 963-1799; e-mail: masters@cwu.edu)
Roger S. Fouts, Interim Dean of Graduate Studies and Research; Ph.D., Nevada Reno.
Vacant: Director of University Research.

Graduate Programs and Contacts

Accounting (M.P.A.): Professional accountancy. Ronald Tidd, Graduate Coordinator; Ph.D., Minnesota. (phone: 963-3340; fax: 963-2875; e-mail: mpa@cwu.edu)

Art (M.A., M.F.A.): Ceramics, computer art, drawing, jewelry and metalsmithing, painting, photography, sculpture, wood design. Liahna Armstrong, Graduate Coordinator; Ph.D., UCLA. (phone: 963-2265; fax: 963-1918; e-mail: lotus@cwu.edu)

Biological Sciences (M.S.): Botany, microbiology-parasitology, stream ecology and fisheries, terrestrial ecology. Lixing Sun, Graduate Coordinator; Ph.D., SUNY. (phone: 963-2780; fax: 963-2730; e-mail: lixing@cwu.edu)

Chemistry (M.S.): Analytical, biological, inorganic, medicinal, organic, physical. Anthony Diaz, Graduate Coordinator; Ph.D., Oregan State. (phone: 963-2811; fax: 963-1050; e-mail: diaza@cwu.edu)

Education (M.Ed.): Master teacher, Cathy Bertelson, Graduate Coordinator; Ph.D., Minnesota. (phone: 963-2155; e-mail: bertelso@cwu.edu). School administration and instructional leadership, Henry Williams, Graduate Coordinator; Ed.D., East Tennessee State. (phone: 963-3816; e-mail: williamh@cwu.edu). Reading specialist, Carol Butterfield, Graduate Coordinator; Ph.D., Arizona. (phone: 963-1480; e-mail: butterfc@cwu.edu. Special education, David Majsterek, Graduate Coordinator; Ed.D., New Mexico State. (phone: 963-1473; e-mail: majstere@cwu.edu)

English (M.A.): Literature, TESOL. Laila Abdalla, Graduate Coordinator; Ph.D., McGill. (phone: 963-1546; fax: 963-1561; e-mail: abadallal@cwu.edu)

Family and Consumer Sciences (M.S.): Family and consumer sciences education and family studies. Jan Bowers, Department Chair and Graduate Coordinator; Ph.D., Kansas State. (phone: 963-2766; fax: 963-2787; e-mail: bowersj@cwu.edu)

Geology (M.S.): Climate change, geomorphology, neotectonics, tectonics. Beth Pratt-Sitaula, Graduate Coordinator; Ph.D., California, Santa Barbara. (phone: 963-2702; fax: 963-2821; e-mail: psitaula@geology.cwu.edu)

History (M.A.): American women's history, Colonial America, East Africa, Latin America, modern Europe, modern Japan, Russia, Western America, Dan Herman, Graduate Coordinator; Ph.D., Berkeley. (phone: 963-1655; fax: 963-1654; e-mail: hermand@cwu.edu)

Industrial and Engineering Technology (M.S.): Engineering technology. Darren Olson, Graduate Coordinator; Ph.D., Indiana State. (phone: 206-963-1756; fax: 206-963-1795; e-mail: olsondar@cwu.edu)

Mathematics (M.A.T.): Teaching mathematics (summer only). Mark Oursland, Graduate Coordinator; Ed.D., Montana State. (phone: 963-2103; fax: 963-3226; e-mail: oursland@cwu.edu)

Music (M.M.): Composition, conducting, music education, performance, performance pedagogy. Larry Gookin, Graduate Coordinator; M.M., Oregon (phone: 963-1216; fax: 963-1239; e-mail: gookinl@cwu.edu)

Nutrition, Exercise, and Health Sciences (M.S.): Exercise science and nutrition. Leo D'Aquisto, Graduate Coordinator; Ed.D., Northern Colorado. (phone: 963-1911; fax: 963-1848; e-mail: acquisto@cwu.edu)

Physical Education, School and Public Health (M.S): Health and physical education, Stephen Jefferies, Graduate Coordinator; Ph.D., Oregon. (phone: 963-2241; e-mail: jefferis@cwu.edu)

Psychology (M.S., M.Ed.): Experimental psychology, mental health counseling psychology (M.S.), school counseling, school psychology (M.Ed.). Robert Brammer, School Counseling and Mental Health Counseling Director; Ph.D., USC. (phone: 963-2381; fax: 963-2307; e-mail: brammerr@cwu.edu); Eugene Johnson, School Psychology Director; Ph.D., South Dakota. (phone: 963-2381, fax: 963-2307; e-mail: johnsong@cwu.edu); Wendy Williams, Experimental Psychology (general or applied behavior analysis) Director; Ph.D., Washington State. (phone: 963-2381; fax 963-2307; e-mail: williamsw@cwu.edu)

Resource Management (M.S.): Stream flow, water quality and riparian management, natural resources policy, wildlife and fisheries economics, resource systems, cultural resource management, geographic information systems, linkages between cultural and natural resource management. Steven Hackenberger, Co-Director; Ph.D., Washington State. (phone: 963-3224; fax: 963-2315; e-mail: hackenbe@cwu.edu); Karl Lillquist, Program Co-Director; Ph.D., Utah. (phone: 963-1184; fax: 963-1047; e-mail: lilliquis@cwu.edu)

Theatre Arts (M.A.): Theater production (summer only) or Theater Studies. Nadine Pederson, Graduate Coordinator; Ph.D., CUNY. (phone: 963-1766; fax: 963-1767; e-mail: pederson@cwu.edu)

CHAPMAN UNIVERSITY

Graduate Studies

Programs of Study Chapman offers the Juris Doctor (law); the Ph.D. in education; the Doctor of Physical Therapy (D.P.T.); the Master of Arts (M.A.) in education, educational psychology, English, marriage and family therapy, international studies, school counseling, special education, teaching (elementary), or teaching (secondary); the Master of Fine Arts (M.F.A.) in creative writing, film production, film and television producing, production design, or screenwriting; and the Master of Science (M.S.) in food science, economic systems design, communication sciences and disorders, and health communication. Also offered are the Master of Business Administration; the Executive M.B.A.; the J.D./M.B.A.; the M.B.A./M.F.A. in film and television producing; and the M.B.A./M.S. in food science. Many of the degree programs offer specializations.

Public school credential programs include multiple subjects with bilingual emphasis, single subject, pupil personnel school counseling (PPS), special education credentials mild moderate and moderate severe Level 1, special education credentials mild moderate and moderate severe Level II, and preliminary administrative services credentials (Tier 1). Credential programs can be combined with one of the degree programs in education.

Required units vary with each degree; however, each program comprises courses that best prepare students to continue a career or enter a new profession. Program requirements include advancement to degree candidacy after the completion of 12 units. Some programs require a comprehensive examination, taken at the end of or during the final semester of course work. Some programs offer a thesis project option in place of the comprehensive examination. One or two internship courses that provide practical experience in the student's field are required for some programs. Course work from other accredited institutions may be transferred; a maximum of 6 credits may be applied to a program. At least 24 credits must be taken in residence.

Research projects are essential to many degree programs and are undertaken in research courses or through cooperative education. Because class sizes are kept small, students can readily communicate with faculty members about research projects and general academic work.

Research Facilities Academic and research centers and institutes include the nationally recognized A. Gary Anderson Center for Economic Research, the Economic Science Institute, the Science of Teaching and Research Institute, Albert Schweitzer Institute, Ludie and David C. Henley Social Science Research Laboratory, Walter Schmid Center for International Business, Center for Global Trade and Development, Ralph W. Leatherby Center for Entrepreneurship Business Ethics, Roger C. Hobbs Institute for Real Estate, Law, and Environmental Studies, Institute for the Study of Media and the Public Interest, John Fowles Center for Creative Writing, Center for Educational and Social Equity, Barry and Phyllis Rodgers Center for Holocaust Education, a state-of-the-art human performance laboratory and research vivarium, food science and nutrition food-tasting and research laboratories, and a community clinic for psychological counseling and research. The computer lab has DEC MicroVAX and NCR Tower facilities, and there are also IBM PC and Apple Macintosh laboratories. The Chapman University Leatherby Libraries contain more than 220,000 volumes, more than 30,000 full text electronic journals, more than 8,000 electronic books, and 2,500 journal titles as well as DVDs, videos, CDs, and other media. Chapman has the largest collection of Albert Schweitzer memorabilia in the western United States; a permanent exhibit is on display in the Argyros Forum.

Financial Aid Many financial aid opportunities are available for qualified students, including Chapman University Fellowships and loans, which are based on need and academic achievement; graduate assistantships; residence life positions; employment; California State Graduate Fellowships; Federal Stafford Student Loans; Benefits for Veterans and Dependents; and an employer-paid tuition plan. Students interested in any of these opportunities should contact the Financial Aid Office (714-997-6741).

Cost of Study Tuition for 2008–09 varied by program. Part-time and full-time students, as well as California and non-California residents, were charged the same tuition rate. Tuition for a full-time student (9 credits per semester) was approximately $10,000 to $34,500 per academic year, depending on the student's program. Books and personal expenses add to annual costs.

Living and Housing Costs Chapman offers limited housing for graduate students. Off-campus housing is available.

Student Group Graduate study programs enroll more than 1,820 students each year on the Orange campus. Courses are scheduled so that both full- and part-time students can attend. Many students have been working in their field and bring practical experience to the classroom; they come from many states and countries, and about 50 percent of them are women. Students who choose to enroll at Chapman want a small-campus atmosphere, personalized attention, a superior faculty, and the education that will enable them to succeed in a highly competitive professional world. Opportunities for graduates are plentiful due to the concentration of business and industry in Orange County and throughout southern California. People for whom graduates may eventually work sit on many College advisory boards.

Location The beautiful tree-lined campus in Orange, California, is 35 miles southeast of Los Angeles. Ocean breezes are less than 10 miles away; mountains and deserts are within an hour's drive. Just minutes from the University are major recreation and entertainment venues, including the Orange County Performing Arts Center, Disneyland, Disney's California Adventure, Knott's Berry Farm, Angel Stadium, and Honda Center.

The University Chapman is an independent, private institution and has provided liberal and professional education of distinction since it was founded in 1861 by the Christian Church (Disciples of Christ). It has continued to meet the needs of its students with fine academic programs and individualized attention. Undergraduate and graduate degree programs are offered. The graduate curricula are designed to offer advanced study in specific disciplines to broaden and deepen a student's knowledge. Faculty members include distinguished academicians, and noted professional practitioners. Chapman is accredited by and is a member of the Western Association of Schools and Colleges. It is also a member of the Independent Colleges of Southern California, the College Entrance Examination Board, the Western College Association, the Association of Independent California Colleges and Universities, the American Council on Education, the American Association of Colleges for Teacher Education, the Division of Higher Education of the Christian Church (Disciples of Christ), and the American Assembly of Collegiate Schools of Business. Its teacher training and credential programs are approved by the California State Department of Education. The school psychology program is approved by the National Association of School Psychologists. The physical therapy program is accredited by the Commission on Accreditation in the Physical Therapy Education of the American Physical Therapy Association and by the Physical Therapy Examining Committee of the Board of Medical Quality Assurance of the State of California. The M.B.A. program is fully accredited by AACSB International–The Association to Advance Collegiate Schools of Business. The School of Law is fully approved by the American Bar Association. The marriage and family therapy program is accredited by COAMFTE, the Commission on Accreditation for Marriage and Family Therapy Education of AAMFT, the American Association for Marriage and Family Therapy. The communication sciences and disorders program is accredited by the Council of Academic Accreditation of ASHA, the American Speech-Language-Hearing Association. The program is in candidacy status.

Applying Students are admitted in the fall, spring, and summer for most programs. Applicants should submit $60 and a completed Application for Graduate Studies; official transcripts of all postsecondary work, showing the completion of a bachelor's degree; scores on the GMAT, GRE (General or Subject test), MAT, or CSET; TOEFL or IELTS scores, for international students; two letters of recommendation; and a statement of intent. Departments, however, should be consulted for specific program requirements.

Correspondence and Information

Office of Graduate Admission
Argyros Forum, Room 304
Chapman University
Orange, California 92866

Phone: 714-997-6786
Fax: 714-997-6713
E-mail: gradadmit@chapman.edu
Web site: http://www.chapman.edu

PROGRAM DIRECTORS

Business Administration: Jon Kaplan, Assistant Dean for Graduate and Executive Programs, Argyros School of Business and Economics; M.B.A., UCLA.
Creative Writing: Patrick Fuery, Chair, Department of English; Ph.D., Murdock (Australia).
Communication Sciences and Disorders: Judy K. Montgomery, Professor of Education; Ph.D. Claremont.
Economic Systems Design: Stephen Rassenti, Director, Economic Science Institute, Professor of Economics and Mathematics; Ph.D., Arizona.
Education: Mary McNeil, Associate Dean of Education; Ed.D., Boston University.
Educational Psychology: Michael Hass, Associate Professor and Coordinator of Educational Psychology Programs; Ph.D., California, Irvine.
English: Patrick Fuery, Chair, Department of English; Ph.D., Murdock (Australia).
Film Production, Film and Television Producing, Screenwriting, Production Design, M.B.A./M.F.A., Film and Television Producing, and JD/M.F.A., Film and Television Producing: Alexandra Rose, Professor of Film and Media Arts, Chair of the Graduate Conservatory; B.A., Wisconsin–Madison.
Food Science: Anuradha Prakash, Associate Professor of Food Science and Program Director, Department of Physical Sciences; Ph.D., Ohio State.
Health Communication: Lisa Sparks, Director, Health Communication program, Professor of Communication Studies; Ph.D., Oklahoma.
International Studies: James Coyle, Director, Center for Global Education, Director International Studies Program; Ph.D., George Washington.
Law: John Eastman, Dean, School of Law; Ph.D., Claremont, J.D., Chicago.
Physical Therapy: Jaclyn Brechter, Chair, Department of Physical Therapy; Ph.D., USC.
Psychology: Georg Eifert, Professor of Psychology and Chair, Department of Psychology; Ph.D., Frankfurt (Germany).
School Counseling: John Brady, Associate Professor and Coordinator of Counselor Education Programs; Ph.D., US International.
Special Education: Dawn Hunter, Associate Professor of Education; Ph.D., Maryland, College Park.

Argyros Forum.

CHESTNUT HILL COLLEGE

Graduate Programs

Programs of Study

The School of Graduate Studies of Chestnut Hill College (CHC) offers the following master's degree and certificate programs: Clinical and Counseling Psychology, Education, Educational Leadership, Instructional Technology, Holistic Spirituality, and Administration of Human Services. The School also offers an APA-accredited Doctor of Psychology (Psy.D.) degree in clinical psychology, state certification programs, and a variety of post-master's programs.

The Clinical and Counseling Psychology program (M.A. and M.S. degrees) includes concentrations in child and adolescent therapy, marriage and family therapy, trauma studies, and addictions treatment, and a new concentration in forensic treatment. Students may also opt for a generalist curriculum. A post-master's certificate for licensure preparation prepares students for the licensure exam to become a LPC or LMFT in Pennsylvania and other states. Post-master's certificates are available in all areas of specialization. The APA-accredited Doctor of Psychology program is open to applicants who have a master's degree in counseling psychology or a closely related field. For applicants who have a bachelor's degree in psychology or the required four prerequisite courses, the combined M.S./Psy.D. track is available. All programs offered by the Department of Professional Psychology are practitioner based, and classes are taught by faculty members who are actively working in the field. Master's-level courses are also offered on the DeSales University campus in Center Valley, Pennsylvania.

The Education Department offers the M.Ed. in early childhood education, elementary education, secondary education, and educational leadership (accelerated/intensive format) with optional principal certification. Students may also opt for the following state certification programs: Instructional I and II, Special Education, Reading Specialist, and various secondary education areas. A Montessori Certificate (AMS) is also offered.

The Instructional Technology program offers M.S. degrees and various certificates in education and technology, instructional design in e-learning, and instructional design specialist. CHC also offers Pennsylvania Department of Education (P.D.E.) Instructional Technology Specialist Certification. The Education and Technology program helps teachers develop new leadership skills and expertise in the use of technology in the achievement of curricular goals and applications of constructivist principles to today's changing classroom. The Instructional Design program was created for students involved in technology who are challenged by cultural and technological changes. The e-learning track presents cutting-edge technology as the next wave in professional training, education, and design. The goal of the specializations is the preparation of professionals to assume leadership roles in the transformation of their work environments. The majority of course work for these programs is offered through a distance/on-site format.

The Holistic Spirituality program (M.A. degree) includes concentrations in spiritual direction and health care. Several certificate programs are also available, including a new certificate in bereavement care. Each of the programs combine academic rigor with experiential learning in ways that promote the integration of theory and practice. The Holistic Spirituality program presents an annual summer Festival of Spirituality featuring nationally known theologians in public lectures, extended conversations, and intensive course formats. Each summer's festival is designed to advance the relationships between spirituality and the Bible, justice issues, and/or ecological concerns.

The Administration of Human Services program (M.S. degree) combines courses in management, public policy, and social issues to prepare students for supervisory and leadership positions in health and human-service organizations. With an emphasis on social change and diversity, this degree provides a comprehensive knowledge base about organizations, their philosophy and structure, and the specialized services that are provided. This program is offered in an accelerated format. Certificates are also available.

Research Facilities

Chestnut Hill College provides access to state-of-the-art hardware and software in five computer labs and a new building offering computer access from every workstation. The Logue Library offers an electronic research center, an online catalog, and nearly 140,000 volumes on three floors of open stacks. Among the electronic resources are ERIC, PsychINFO, LexisNexis, ProQuestReligion, JSTOR, EBSCOhost Elite, and Wilson OmniFile Mega, MLA. Specialized psychology demonstration rooms are available for live observation and taping of clinical sessions. Studio TV labs are used by the applied technology program; video editing and specialized multimedia development labs are used by other graduate programs.

Financial Aid

Chestnut Hill College offers a number of graduate assistantships for students at the master's and doctoral levels. The majority of students finance their education through student loans. The Financial Aid Office is available to assist students with the loan application process. Some graduate programs (Education and Holistic Spirituality) offer a discounted tuition to teachers and those in church-affiliated ministry.

Cost of Study

Tuition for 2009–10 is $515 per credit for the Administration of Human Services and Holistic Spirituality programs, $530 per credit for the Clinical and Counseling Psychology programs, $510 per credit for the Education programs, and $787 per credit for the doctoral program.

Living and Housing Costs

A variety of urban and suburban housing options are available within an easy commute to the campus.

Student Group

With classes primarily in the evening and on weekends, the School of Graduate Studies at Chestnut Hill College caters to the needs of the working professional. Degree programs should be completed within six years of matriculation. Within that time frame, students can choose their own pace for most programs; some opt to study full-time, while others take one or two courses per semester. Small classes and a welcoming atmosphere make Chestnut Hill College an excellent choice for traditional students as well as working professionals and those who wish to change careers.

Location

Chestnut Hill College is located in the northwestern corner of Philadelphia, easily accessible to all of the Philadelphia neighborhoods, outlying areas, and adjoining states. It is also near numerous cultural, athletic, and recreational activities in the region. The campus has a suburban feel, while remaining accessible via public transportation and major routes.

The College

Chestnut Hill College, founded by the Sisters of St. Joseph in 1924, is an independent Catholic institution that fosters equality through education and welcomes women and men of all backgrounds. The School of Graduate Studies provides a quality education that takes into equal account the academic, professional, and personal needs of both women and men. The aim of the graduate programs is to graduate professionals who are skilled, ethical, knowledgeable, and confident practitioners in their respective fields.

Applying

Applications for all master's-level programs are considered on a rolling admissions basis. Master's degree students may begin in any semester: fall, spring, or summer. Current application deadlines and requirements for the Psy.D. program are available online, with cohorts beginning each fall. All applicants are evaluated on the basis of the entire application packet, which includes the application, transcripts of all previous college study, three letters of recommendation, MAT or GRE General Test scores (PPST scores for education), and a 400- to 600-word statement of professional goals. Applicants with graduate degrees may be exempt from one or more requirements. Special admission requirements apply to the Holistic Spirituality and Psy.D. programs. Interviews with department chairs are required for qualified applicants. Tours and/or interviews with the Director of Graduate Admissions or a graduate admissions counselor are available.

Correspondence and Information

For master's program information and all applications:
Jayne Mashett
Director of Graduate Admissions
Chestnut Hill College
9601 Germantown Avenue
Philadelphia, Pennsylvania 19118-2693
Phone: 215-248-7170 (graduate office)
Fax: 215-248-7161
E-mail: gradadmissions@chc.edu
Web site: http://www.chc.edu

For Psy.D. program information:
Mary Steinmetz
Director of Psy.D. Admissions
Chestnut Hill College
9601 Germantown Avenue
Philadelphia, Pennsylvania 19118-2693
Phone: 215-248-7077
Fax: 215-248-7155
E-mail: profpsyc@chc.edu
Web site: http://www.chc.edu

THE FACULTY

Note: Research interests of the Psy.D. faculty members are available on the Web at http://www.chc.edu/graduate/psydfac.htm. Information on the entire faculty can be found at http://www.chc.edu/faculty/.

David Arena, Assistant Professor of Psychology; Psy.D., Widener.
Stephen Berk, Assistant Professor of Education; Ph.D., Temple.
Richard W. Black, Assistant Professor of Education; Ed.D., Temple.
David Borsos, Assistant Professor of Psychology; Ph.D., Temple.
Scott W. Browning, Professor of Psychology; Ph.D., Berkeley.
Melanie Cohen-Goodman, Assistant Professor of Education; Ph.D., Temple.
Dominic Cotugno, Associate Professor of Education; Ed.D., Temple.
Margery Covello, Assistant Professor of Education; Ed.D., Immaculata.
Carolynne Ervin, Coordinator of Spiritual Direction Program; M.A., Creighton.
Mary Kay Flannery, S.S.J., Associate Professor of Religious Studies; D.Min., Catholic Theological Union.
Elaine R. Green, Associate Professor of Sociology; Dean, School of Continuing Studies; and Chair, Administration of Human Services; Ed.D., Temple.
Barbara Hogan, Associate Professor of Human Services; Ph.D., Temple.
Jessica Kahn, Associate Professor of Education; Ph.D., Pennsylvania.
Thomas E. Klee, Associate Professor of Psychology; Ph.D., Temple.
Mary M. Lindsay, S.S.J., Assistant Professor of Psychology; Ph.D., Temple.
Susan McGroarty, Assistant Professor of Psychology; Ph.D., Pennsylvania.
Joseph A. Micucci, Professor and Chair of Psychology; Ph.D., Minnesota.
Catherine Nerney, S.S.J., Associate Professor of Religious Studies; Ph.D., Catholic University.
Carol M. Pate, Assistant Professor and Chair, Education Department; Ed.D., Indiana.
Cheryll Rothery-Jackson, Director of Clinical Training; Psy.D., Rutgers.
Ralph E. Swan, Assistant Professor and Coordinator of Instructional Technology; Ph.D., Pennsylvania.
Margaret H. Vogelson, Professor of Education; Ph.D., Temple.

CITY COLLEGE OF THE CITY UNIVERSITY OF NEW YORK

Graduate Programs

Programs of Study

The City College of New York (CCNY) is similar to a small university offering a rich program of graduate study through the College of Liberal Arts and Science and the Schools of Architecture, Education, and Engineering. The College of Liberal Arts and Science offers the Master of Arts (M.A.) in art history, biochemistry, biology, chemistry, earth and atmospheric sciences, economics, English (English literature and language and literacy), history, international relations, mathematics (operations research, probability, pure mathematics, and statistics), museum studies, music, physics, psychology (general and mental health counseling), sociology, Spanish, and study of the Americas; the Master of Fine Arts (M.F.A.) in creative writing, fine art, and media arts production (film and video); and the Master of Public Administration (M.P.A.) in public service management. The Bernard and Ann Spitzer School of Architecture offers the Master of Architecture (M.Arch.), the Master of Landscape Architecture (M.L.A.), and the Master of Urban Planning (M.U.P.) in urban design. The School of Education offers the Master of Science in Education (M.S.Ed.) degree in administration and supervision, bilingual education K–12 (Chinese, Haitian-Creole, and Spanish), developmental and remedial reading, early childhood education, elementary education (curriculum and teaching), special education, special education–bilingual, and TESOL-bilingual. In addition, the Master of Arts in Education (M.A.Ed.) degree is offered in art education, English education, mathematics education, science education, and social studies. A bilingual component may be added to each of these programs. Advanced certificate programs are offered in administration and supervision and developmental and remedial reading. The Grove School of Engineering offers both the Master of Engineering (M.E.) and the Master of Science (M.S.) in biomedical, chemical, civil, electrical, and mechanical engineering; computer science; and information systems. The Doctor of Philosophy (Ph.D.) degree is offered for all programs excluding computer science and information systems. Interdepartmental programs are offered in air pollution control, engineering mechanics, and environmental engineering.

Research Facilities

The Morris Raphael Cohen Library in the North Academic Center houses more than 1 million volumes and is the largest in the CUNY system. Besides its general collection, it contains facilities for architecture, engineering, music, and science. Many library processes are computerized for rapid and efficient access to information. The University-wide Integrated Library System (CUNY Plus) provides online access to most holdings at both City College and all the libraries in the CUNY system. The Marshak Science Building houses more than 200 teaching and research laboratories, a planetarium, a weather station, an electron microscope, laser research facilities, a science and engineering library, and a physical education complex. The Grove School of Engineering houses the Benjamin Levich Institute for Physiochemical Hydrodynamics, the Center for Biomedical Engineering, the Clean Fuels Institute, the Center for Water Resources and Environmental Research, the Institute for Municipal Waste Research, the Earthquake Research Center, and the Institute for Ultrafast Spectroscopy and Lasers. The Grove School of Engineering also provides a wide range of networked computer facilities for both teaching and research.

Financial Aid

Graduate study at CCNY is supported by a combination of student fees, state funds, private and foundation contributions, and federal research grants. The Office of Financial Aid administers federal and state grants, loans, and work-study programs. The College offers a number of nonteaching assistantships and part-time teaching lectureships. These programs are administered by the Financial Aid Office. For more information, students should contact the Financial Aid Office at 212-650-5819 Ext. 6656.

Cost of Study

In the College of Liberal Arts and Science and the School of Education, tuition for in-state students is $310 per credit; in the Schools of Engineering and Architecture, it is $360 per credit. For out-of-state and international students, tuition is $575 per credit in the College of Liberal Arts and Science and the School of Education; in the Schools of Engineering and Architecture, it is $640 per credit.

Living and Housing Costs

Campus housing is available in "The Towers." For information, students should phone 917-507-0070 or visit http://www.ccnytowers.com. Apartments and studios can also be found independently throughout the five boroughs of New York City. Estimated living expenses for one year is between $8500 and $10,000. For assistance, students can call 212-650-5370.

Student Group

The student body reflects a wide range of ethnic and cultural diversity. Students come from more than 100 different countries and speak more than ninety languages. Most are from Africa, Asia, the Caribbean, Latin America, and Europe. The students lend an international flavor to the campus and reflect the ethnic diversity of New York City. This has led City College to develop extensive international linkages. There are student and faculty exchanges with universities in Africa, Asia, Israel, and the Dominican Republic. The total student enrollment is approximately 14,392; of these, 3,211 are graduate students.

Location

The campus occupies 35 acres in upper Manhattan along Convent Avenue in an area known as Hamilton Heights in Harlem. It is an urban campus within easy commuting distance of midtown Manhattan.

The College

The City College of New York is the oldest institution in the City University of New York system. Founded in 1847 as the Free Academy, it was first housed at 23rd Street and Lexington Avenue. The name was changed in 1866 to the College of the City of New York; now it is called "City" or "CCNY." Although it originally granted only the bachelor's degree, CCNY began to expand its program offerings to advanced levels more than sixty years ago. Since 1961, it has offered a wide range of master's programs, and through the City University of New York offers doctoral study on campus in the sciences, all branches of engineering, computer science, and psychology. CCNY is known for its commitment to academic excellence combined with access to higher education. Immigrants and their children have historically used the College as a vehicle for upward mobility.

Applying

Graduate study is open to well-qualified students who possess a bachelor's degree from an accredited U.S. institution or the equivalent from an international institution and have an adequate background in the field of study they wish to pursue. Students are evaluated based on their previous academic record, generally with a minimum B average (3.0) required; letters of recommendation from scholars with whom they have studied; and writing samples, portfolios, Graduate Record Exams (GRE) test scores, and auditions (required by some programs only). International students whose native language is not English and who do not have a resident alien card must take the TOEFL (Test of English as a Foreign Language).

Correspondence and Information

Office of Graduate Admissions
Administration Building, Room 101
City College of the City University of New York
138th Street and Convent Avenue
New York, New York 10031

Phone: 212-650-6977
Fax: 212-650-6417
E-mail: gradadm@ccny.cuny.edu
Web site: http://www.ccny.cuny.edu

THE FACULTY

City College's faculty represents a broad range of disciplines, and many of its members have earned the nation's highest forms of recognition—Guggenheim and Fulbright awards—as well as grants amounting to millions of dollars in support of their research and scholarship. The faculty is internationally known for its research activities.

CLARION
UNIVERSITY

CLARION UNIVERSITY OF PENNSYLVANIA

Division of Graduate Studies

Programs of Study

Clarion University awards the degrees of Master of Arts, Master of Business Administration, Master of Education, Master of Science, and Master of Science in Library Science. The Master of Education is offered in education, reading, and science education; and the Master of Science in biology, mass media arts and journalism, nursing, rehabilitative sciences, special education, and speech-language pathology. The M.S. in Nursing is a joint program offered by Clarion and Edinboro University of Pennsylvania. In addition, the Division offers a Certificate of Advanced Studies in Library Science, school library media certification, and secondary teacher certification and an Instructional Technology Specialist Certificate.

Clarion University is accredited by the Middle States Association of Colleges and Schools. The graduate program in business administration is accredited by AACSB International–The Association to Advance Collegiate Schools of Business. The graduate program in speech-language pathology is accredited by the Council on Academic Accreditation of the American Speech-Language-Hearing Association. The graduate program in library science is accredited by the American Library Association. The graduate program in nursing is accredited by the National League for Nursing Accrediting Commission. Clarion University of Pennsylvania is a member of the American Association of State Colleges and Universities and the American Association of Colleges for Teacher Education.

Research Facilities

Facilities supporting graduate programs at Clarion University include modern science laboratories supplied with excellent instrumentation, well-equipped clinical support areas for special education and communication sciences and disorders, a modern business administration building, technologically equipped classrooms for library science, radio and television studios and experimental audiovisual facilities in communication, and a fully equipped word processing lab.

The University libraries offer graduate students a broad collection of resources and services to support classwork and research. In addition to more than 400,000 print volumes, the University libraries provide electronic indexing and full-text access to thousands of periodicals, newspapers, and reference sources in a range of subject areas. The library offers access to a broad range of electronic databases, periodicals, and other services to distance education students through the library's Web site at http://www.clarion.edu/library. Interlibrary loan service further enables users to expand their research.

The Center for Computing Services is responsible for all telephone, data network, and central computing services. The center houses the University telephone system as well as various servers that support central technical services, such as the iClarion student portal, e-mail, Internet and Web access, Clarion's Web site, and Blackboard courseware for online course work. Computing Services also supports sixteen general access labs and smart classrooms located across the Clarion and Venango campuses.

Registered students automatically receive an e-mail account, the ability to create their own Web pages, and access to the Internet. Other academic services for instruction and research include support of the following computer languages and packages: COBOL, FORTRAN, BASIC, Pascal, SAS, C, C++, SPSS, and business simulations.

Financial Aid

Graduate assistantships are awarded on a competitive basis for the nine-month academic year and are renewable. In 2009–10, compensation for a graduate assistant is either $2355 for 10 hours per week and a waiver of one-half tuition or $4710 for 20 hours per week and a waiver of full tuition. Interested students should apply to the appropriate academic office or to the Division of Graduate Studies. Additional information regarding financial aid is available through the Office of Financial Aid.

Cost of Study

In 2009–10, graduate tuition and fees for Pennsylvania residents are $4390 per semester for full-time study (9 to 15 hours) or $566 per hour part-time. Out-of-state students will pay $6442 for full-time study or $812 per hour part-time. Tuition and fees are subject to change without notice. The cost of books is estimated at $600 per semester.

Living and Housing Costs

University-owned housing is available to graduate students for $3950 per semester. Housing throughout the town of Clarion, though at a premium, is available at costs ranging from $500 to $700 per month. The Office of Residence Life has information regarding private housing. In 2009–10, food service can be obtained in the University Dining Hall for $1268 per semester.

Student Group

The total enrollment at Clarion University is more than 7,200 students, of whom more than 1,000 are graduate students. The graduate enrollment represents many states and several other countries.

Location

Clarion is located high on the Allegheny Plateau overlooking the Clarion River. The rural setting is one of Pennsylvania's most scenic resort areas. The rolling, wooded countryside, interspersed with small farms, offers some of the best outdoor recreational opportunities to be found anywhere in northwestern Pennsylvania, with the Clarion River and its tributaries providing an ideal setting for boating, swimming, and other aquatic sports.

The University

Founded in 1867 as Carrier Seminary, the institution has evolved to a state normal school, to Clarion State Teachers College, to Clarion State College, and finally to Clarion University of Pennsylvania of the State System of Higher Education. Clarion's 99-acre main campus has thirty-eight buildings. It is within the borough of Clarion, some 2 miles north of Interstate 80 at Exits 62 and 64, and is approximately 2 hours' driving time from the urban centers of Pittsburgh, Erie, and Youngstown. Clarion's 64-acre Venango Campus, located in Oil City, has four buildings, including the modern Suhr Library. The McKeever Environmental Education Center is located in Mercer County.

Applying

Admission materials may be obtained from the Division of Graduate Studies. The application for admission should be received at least thirty days prior to the semester for which the student seeks entrance. Assistantships are generally awarded in the spring for the following fall semester. Application for an assistantship should be made before March 1.

Correspondence and Information

Division of Graduate Studies
Clarion University of Pennsylvania
Clarion, Pennsylvania 16214
Phone: 814-393-2337
Fax: 814-393-2722
Web site: http://www.clarion.edu/graduatestudies

DEPARTMENT AND PROGRAM HEADS

Brenda Sanders Dédé, Assistant Vice President for Academic Affairs; Ed.D., Texas Southern.
Biology: Andrew Keth, Ph.D., Penn State.
Business: Brenda J. Ponsford, Ph.D., Virginia Tech.
Education: Patricia L. Kolencik, Ed.D., Pittsburgh.
English: Janet K. Kneppper, Ph.D., Pennsylvania.
Library Science: Andrea Miller, Ph.D., Pittsburgh.
Mass Media Arts and Journalism: Myrna Kuehn, Ph.D., Penn State.
Nursing: Debbie J. Ciesielka, D.Ed., Indiana of Pennsylvania.
Rehabilitative Sciences: Mark Kilwein, Ph.D., Ohio State.
Science Education: Bruce Smith, Ph.D., Penn State.
Special Education: Richard A. Sabousky, Ph.D., Kent State.
Speech-Language Pathology: Janis Jarecki-Liu, Ph.D., Kent State.

CLARK UNIVERSITY

CLARK UNIVERSITY

Graduate School

Programs of Study

The Graduate School of Clark University offers the following degrees: Doctor of Philosophy, Master of Arts, Master of Arts in Teaching, Master of Business Administration, Master of Public Administration, Master of Science in Finance, Master of Science in Professional Communication, and Master of Science in Information Technology.

The Doctor of Philosophy is conferred in biology, chemistry, economics, geography, history, physics, and psychology. Postdoctoral training is conducted in geography, psychology, and the sciences.

The Master of Arts is awarded in community development and planning; education; English; environmental science and policy; geographic information science, development, and environment (GISDE); information technology; international development; and communications. The Master of Business Administration and the Master of Science in Finance are offered in the Graduate School of Management. The Graduate School also offers accelerated B.A./M.A. programs (to qualifying Clark undergraduates) in biology, chemistry, communications, community development and planning, education, environmental science and policy, finance, geographic information science (GIS), history, international development, management, and physics.

An academic year of study in residence, which is eight courses, is a minimum requirement for a master's degree. One year of full-time study in residence—not less than eight courses beyond the master's—is required for the doctorate. Study in residence is broadly defined as graduate work done at Clark University under the immediate personal supervision of at least one member of the University faculty.

Research Facilities

The Arthur B. Sackler Science Center and Lasry Center for Bioscience emphasize the interdisciplinary nature of the sciences at Clark and provide teaching amphitheaters and seminar rooms, research laboratories, computer facilities, and a science library. The psychology department is also equipped with laboratory and computer facilities. The Graduate School of Geography maintains several GIS and remote-sensing laboratories and the Guy H. Burnham Map and Aerial Photography Library. The George Perkins Marsh Institute provides research space and the J. X. Kasperson Library, a first-rate collection on human environment themes. Clark Labs provides specialized GIS research space for the production of IDRISI and related GIS software. Clark's newest research institute, the Mosakowski Institute for Public Enterprise, aims to improve the effectiveness of governments and other institutions through the successful mobilization of university research. At the core of the institute's mission is the attempt to make academic research more useful to those who have responsibility for addressing important public problems.

The Robert Hutchings Goddard Library provides fine quarters for large collections in all graduate fields. Most graduate departments provide study space for graduate students and maintain equipment necessary for study and research.

Financial Aid

Graduate fellowships and scholarships are provided by the University for well-qualified graduate students. Financial aid is also available through grants from special funds and sponsored research grants. Several departments participate in national fellowship programs.

Cost of Study

Tuition for the academic year 2008–09 was $33,900. Special fees included health insurance, a diploma fee of $150 for the doctorate and $100 for the master's degree, a $30 activity fee, and a fee of $200 per semester for students who have completed all formal University and departmental residence requirements. Tuition waivers and stipends are offered to students in Ph.D. programs and many master's programs.

Living and Housing Costs

Living accommodations for both married and single graduate students are available a short distance from the campus at various costs. The University has a limited number of on-campus rooms available for single graduate students.

Student Group

During 2008–09, there were 626 full-time and 295 part-time graduate students in residence, of whom 422 were men and 499 were women. Approximately two thirds of the graduate students receive financial assistance in the form of remission of tuition and/or stipends in amounts that vary depending upon the field of study.

Location

Worcester, a city of diversified industry, is a rapidly emerging educational and cultural center. It has ten schools of higher learning with more than 10,000 students, as well as a modern medical school. Major cultural attractions include the Worcester Art Museum, Higgins Armory Museum, Worcester Historical Society, Worcester Public Library, and American Antiquarian Society. Worcester's Civic Center, the DCU Center, offers a wide variety of popular performing artists and athletic events. The Worcester Music Festival presents an annual series of concerts. The Hanover Theatre for the Performing Arts offers Broadway tours, nationally recognized performers, and family shows. Other theatrical productions, symphonic concerts, light operas, folk festivals, and lecture series are offered regularly at venues around the city. Boston and Cambridge are less than an hour's drive away.

The University

Clark University was founded as a graduate institution in 1887 and awarded its first doctorate in 1891. Undergraduate liberal arts education was established in 1902. The University has twenty-eight major buildings situated on a 35-acre campus. The Robert Hutchings Goddard Library was opened in 1969 and is nationally known for its design as well as its holdings. It was named in honor of the father of the Space Age, who was a Clark alumnus and professor of physics at Clark from 1914 until 1942.

Applying

Applicants from American and other institutions should contact the department in which they expect to do their major work. Application deadlines for admission and financial aid vary by department. Students should contact the department or program of interest for the date. An application fee of $50 is charged. Further information can be obtained from the University's Web site.

Correspondence and Information

Chair, Department of (specify)
Clark University
950 Main Street
Worcester, Massachusetts 01610
Web site: http://www.clarku.edu/graduate

THE FACULTY

The chairpersons of departments and the directors of interdepartmental programs offering graduate work at Clark are listed below.

Biology: Dr. Susan Foster.
Chemistry: Dr. Frederick Greenaway.
Community Development: Dr. William F. Fisher.
Economics: Dr. Wayne Gray.
Education: Dr. Thomas Del Prete.
English: Dr. Virginia Vaughan.
Environmental Science and Policy: Dr. William F. Fisher.
Finance: Dr. Edward J. Ottensmeyer.
Geographic Information Science (GISDE): Dr. William F. Fisher.
Geography: Dr. Jody Emel.
History: Dr. Amy Richter.
Information Technology: Dr. Dennis Wadsworth.
International Development: Dr. William F. Fisher.
Management: Dr. Edward J. Ottensmeyer.
Physics: Dr. Charles Agosta.
Professional Communication: Dr. Max Hess.
Psychology: Dr. Marianne Wiser.
Public Administration: Dr. Alice E. Smith.

THE COLLEGE AT BROCKPORT, STATE UNIVERSITY OF NEW YORK

Graduate Studies

Programs of Study

The College at Brockport, State University of New York, is accredited by the Middle States Association of Colleges and Schools and the Board of Regents of the University of the State of New York. The College offers forty graduate programs, including M.A. degrees in communication, dance, English, history, liberal studies, mathematics, and psychology; M.S. degrees in accounting (including forensic accounting), biological sciences (including a professional science master's), computational science, environmental science and biology, mental health counseling, and recreation and leisure; M.F.A. degrees in dance and visual studies; an M.P.A. in public administration; M.S.Ed. degrees in counseling (including school counseling), education (including graduate teacher certification programs), educational administration, health education, and physical education; a Master of Science in Social Work (M.S.W., offered jointly with Nazareth College of Rochester); Certificates of Advanced Study (C.A.S.) in school building leader, school business administration, school counseling, and school district leader; two advanced certificate programs offered by the Department of Public Administration in arts administration (in conjunction with the M.F.A. in visual studies) and nonprofit management; and one teacher certification only program in bilingual education.

Graduate teacher certification programs include bilingual education, biology and general science 5–12, chemistry and general science 5–12, childhood education 1–6, childhood literacy birth to grade 6, dance pre-K–12, earth sciences and general science 5–12, English 5–12, health education pre-K–12, mathematics 5–12, physical education pre-K–12, physics and general science 5–12, school building leader, school business leader, school counselor, school district leader, and social studies 5–12.

Research Facilities

The College at Brockport's Drake Memorial Library offers a full range of services and houses a collection of more than 450,000 books, 800 print serial subscriptions, 101,000 bound periodicals, 25,000 online serial subscriptions, 2 million microforms, and 10,000 media items. Students can access electronic reserves, conduct online searches, and download publications from remote sites or from PCs in the library. The library's extended hours are particularly helpful for students whose classes meet in the evenings. The College's two-story computing center is augmented by satellite computing labs, providing more than 700 public-access workstations to students and offering standard and specialized software as well as Internet access. Students studying primarily at The College at Brockport's MetroCenter in downtown Rochester can use the MetroCenter's three computer labs, which provide PCs that are linked to the Internet and Drake Memorial Library.

The College at Brockport is home to several centers, institutes, and unique academic endeavors that enrich the academic enterprise, including the Center for Philosophic Exchange, sponsoring programs of philosophic inquiry on academic and public issues; the Child and Adolescent Stress Management Institute, offering preventive health programming to campus and public audiences; the Congress on Research in Dance, providing opportunities for dance scholars, professionals, and graduate students to exchange ideas and methodologies through publication, conferences, and workshops; the Hunter Institute on Young Children, supporting educational and scholarly activities of the College's faculty and staff, focusing on the early childhood years, which benefits the academic endeavors of Brockport's education and human development students; the Visual Studies Workshop, an affiliate of The College at Brockport, offering courses and the M.F.A. program for Brockport graduate art students; and the Writers Forum and Videotape Library, advancing the appreciation for and practice of the art of writing through sponsored public readings by writers of local, national, and international reputation.

Financial Aid

Of the 1,123 matriculated graduate students enrolled for fall 2008, 495 full- and part-time students (44 percent) received financial aid. Some graduate students hold teaching, graduate, and research assistantships. A competitive fellowship program provides opportunities for students who have been admitted to graduate study and who will contribute to the diversity of the student body in the graduate program in which enrollment is sought. Full- or partial-tuition scholarships accompany most assistantships and fellowships. Graduate Opportunity Tuition Scholarships are available to students who participated in undergraduate EOP, HEOP, or SEEK programs, as funding permits.

Cost of Study

Full-time tuition is $8370 per academic year for New York State residents and $13,250 per academic year for nonresidents. Part-time tuition was $349 per credit for residents and $552 per credit for nonresidents. All tuition rates are subject to adjustment by the Board of Trustees. College fees totaled $777 per academic year for full-time graduate students and $32.18 per credit for part-time students. Because the M.S.W. program operates as a bi-institutional joint-degree program, the tuition structure for this program varies from the tuition of The College at Brockport. For current tuition rates, applicants may contact the program directly by phone at 585-395-8450 or by e-mail at grcmsw@brockport.edu.

Living and Housing Costs

On-campus housing is offered to graduate students on a limited, first-come, space-available basis. On-campus housing offers easy access to computing facilities, the library, recreational and dining facilities, and cultural events. All standard services are provided, including Internet and cable TV access and free laundry facilities. A double-occupancy room is $5700 per person per academic year. Meal plans vary in cost, with a current average of $3590 per academic year.

Off-campus housing is available in private homes in the community or through College Suites and is within walking distance to the campus.

Student Group

The College at Brockport's total enrollment for fall 2008 was 8,275 (3,479 men and 4,796 women), with a graduate student population of 1,305 (462 men and 843 women), of whom 327 (121 men and 206 women) were engaged in full-time study.

Location

The College at Brockport is located in the village of Brockport, 16 miles west of Rochester, New York. Brockport combines the familiarity and friendliness of a charming college town with easy access to the opportunities of a metropolitan city. The College's 435-acre campus is only 10 miles from the southern shores of Lake Ontario, with its many parks and beaches; within short driving distance of New York State's renowned Finger Lakes; and within easy reach of area ski resorts. The College is 20 minutes by car from the Monroe County International Airport, 1 hour from Niagara Falls, and 3 hours from Toronto.

The College

Student success is at the heart of the College's mission statement: "Brockport has the success of its students as its highest priority, emphasizing student learning and committed to advancing teaching, scholarship, creative endeavors, and service." The foundation for today's comprehensive institution was laid in 1841 with the opening of the Brockport Collegiate Institute. Over the years, the College has expanded beyond its sole focus on teacher education to become a comprehensive institution offering both baccalaureate and master's programs. Since the College began sponsoring graduate education over half a century ago, the graduate alumni now number more than 13,000.

The campus includes sixty-eight buildings, professional-quality athletic fields, and open and wooded land. Recent renovations include Hartwell Hall ($10 million), which houses several departments, including the Department of Dance, with theater and performance spaces; Lennon Hall Science Complex ($20 million); and the Seymour College Union, with expanded dining facilities, 24-hour computer lab, and enhanced student activity space.

Applying

Applications for admission are submitted online directly to the Office of Graduate Studies. Deadlines for filing applications vary by department. Application forms and instructions describing the credentials required for admission to The College at Brockport's graduate programs are available at http://www.brockport.edu/graduate/apps/ or from the Office of Graduate Studies Web site at http://www.brockport.edu/graduate/.

Correspondence and Information

Office of Graduate Studies
The College at Brockport, State University of New York
350 New Campus Drive
Brockport, New York 14420

Phone: 585-395-5465 or 2525
E-mail: gradadmit@brockport.edu
Web site: http://www.brockport.edu/graduate

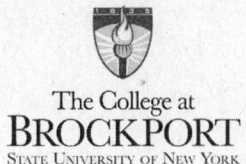

GRADUATE PROGRAM ADMINISTRATORS AND DIRECTORS

The area code for all numbers is 585.

ADMINISTRATORS

Dean of Graduate Studies: Susan Stites-Doe, Ph.D., 395-2525, sstites@brockport.edu.
Director of Graduate Studies: Julian Ortiz, M.A., 395-5465, jortiz@brockport.edu.
Graduate Admission Counselor: Danielle A. Welch, B.A., 395-5465, dwelch@brockport.edu.
School of the Arts, Humanities and Social Science: Virginia M. Bacheler, M.S., Associate Dean, 395-2349, vbachele@brockport.edu.
School of Education and Human Services: Eileen L. Daniel, D.Ed., Associate Dean, 395-2510, edaniel@brockport.edu.
School of Health and Human Performance: Francis X. Short, P.E.D., Dean, 395-2350, fshort@brockport.edu.
School of Science and Mathematics: Stuart Appelle, Ph.D., Dean, 395-2394, sappelle@brockport.edu.
Other Administrative Unit: P. Michael Fox, Ph.D., Assistant Vice Provost, 395-2504, mfox@brockport.edu.

GRADUATE PROGRAM DIRECTORS/CONTACTS

School of the Arts, Humanities and Social Science
Communication (M.A.): Alexander Lyon, Ph.D., 395-5772, alyon@brockport.edu.
Dance (M.A./M.F.A.): Maura Keefe, Ph.D., 395-5302, mkeefe@brockport.edu.
English (M.A.): Miriam E. Burstein, Ph.D., 395-5827, mburstei@brockport.edu or Stefan Jurasinski, Ph.D., 395-5714, sjurasin@brockport.edu.
History (M.A.): Morag S. Martin, Ph.D., 395-5690, mmartin@brockport.edu.
Visual Studies Workshop (M.F.A.): Kristen Merola, M.F.A., 442-8676, kmerola@brockport.edu.

School of Education and Human Services
Counselor Education (M.S./M.S.Ed./C.A.S.): Susan Rachel Seem, Ph.D., 395-2258, sseem@brockport.edu.
Education and Human Development (M.S.Ed.): Barbara Smithgall, M.S., 395-2326, bsmithga@brockport.edu.
Educational Administration (M.S.Ed./C.A.S.): Donald R. Covell, C.A.S., 395-5804, dcovell@brockport.edu.
Public Administration (M.P.A.): James E. Fatula, Ph.D., 395-2375, jfatula@brockport.edu.
Social Work (M.S.W.): Carol Brownstein-Evans, Ph.D., 395-8450, grcmsw@brockport.edu.

School of Health and Human Performance
Health Science (M.S.Ed.): Patti Follansbee, Ph.D., 395-5483, pfollans@brockport.edu.
Physical Education (M.S.Ed.): Alisa James, Ed.D., 395-5330, ajames@brockport.edu.
Recreation and Leisure (M.S.): Lynda J. Sperazza, Ph.D., 395-5490, lsperazza@brockport.edu.

School of Science and Mathematics
Biological Sciences (M.S.): Adam Rich, Ph.D., 395-5740, arich@brockport.edu.
Computational Sciences (M.S.): Robert E. Tuzun, Ph.D., 395-5368, rtuzun@brockport.edu.
Environmental Science and Biology (M.S.): Christopher J. Norment, Ph.D., 395-5748, cnorment@brockport.edu.
Mathematics (M.A.): Sanford S. Miller, Ph.D., 395-2046, smiller@brockport.edu.
Psychology (M.A.): Janet F. Gillespie, Ph.D., 395-2433, jgillesp@brockport.edu.

Other Administrative Unit
Business Administration and Economics: Accounting (M.S.): Donald Kent Jr., Ph.D., 395-5521, dkent@brockport.edu.
Liberal Studies (M.A.): Kulathur S. Rajasethupathy, Ph.D., 395-2262, kraja@brockport.edu.

COLLEGE OF MOUNT ST. JOSEPH

Graduate Studies

Programs of Study

The advanced degree programs offered by the College of Mount St. Joseph (the Mount) specialize in the cultivation of ethical leadership skills in business, depth in ministry, and expertise in the teaching and health professions. Graduate degree programs include: a Master of Arts (M.A.) in education, a Master of Arts (M.A.) in religious studies, a Master of Science in Organizational Leadership (M.S.O.L.), a Master of Nursing (M.N.), and a Doctor of Physical Therapy (D.P.T.).

The M.A. degree programs in education meet the needs of college graduates who are prospective or experienced teachers. The major in teaching is offered to students who hold a bachelor's degree and are interested in seeking initial teacher licensure and a Master of Arts degree. The professional advancement programs are ideal for practicing teachers who wish to enhance their skills in the classroom or advance to positions of leadership while obtaining a Master of Arts degree. An intensive course of study integrates theory and field work in diverse educational settings. Classes meet during late afternoon and evening hours, in the summer months, and occasionally on weekends.

The TEAM (Teacher Education Accelerated Master's) programs prepare adults to enter the teaching profession through an intense learning and apprentice format. Three programs are offered: TEAM–IEC (Inclusive Early Childhood), TEAM–AYA (Adolescent/Young Adult), and TEAM–MSE (Multicultural/Special Education). The Mount's TEAM programs lead to a Master of Arts in education with a major in teaching, and can be completed in seventeen months. The programs are open to qualified students who have a bachelor's degree.

The Master of Arts in religious studies program, which concentrates on spiritual and pastoral care, is designed to enhance and integrate the interpersonal skills and theological knowledge of health-care professionals, educators, and ministers who serve in diverse populations and social contexts. Small classes, academic advising, and personal attention provide an environment conducive to the development of pastoral competence. Core courses are offered on weekends, enabling adult students to continue working while completing degree requirements in two years.

The Master of Science in Organizational Leadership program takes a multidisciplinary approach and emphasizes values, spirituality, and ethics while focusing on the development of effective leadership skills that can be used in any type of organization. Areas of study include leadership, people and organizations, organizational decision making, and technology. The M.S.O.L. degree can be completed in fewer than two years. All courses are offered on Saturdays.

The Master of Nursing program is a full-time, accelerated graduate-level program for individuals who have earned an undergraduate degree in a discipline other than nursing and would like to pursue a nursing career. The program includes advanced course work and can be completed with clinical experience in as little as fifteen months. The M.N. is accredited by the Commission on Collegiate Nursing Education and is supported by the Ohio Board of Nursing.

The Doctor of Physical Therapy program is designed to prepare clinicians who can think critically and solve problems; apply scientifically validated therapeutic skills and techniques effectively; respect the dignity of individuals; and understand the responsibilities of the health-care provider in the twenty-first century. This program is fully accredited by the Commission on Accreditation in Physical Therapy Education. Upon completion, a graduate must apply for and successfully pass the National Physical Therapy Examination conducted by each state's licensing board.

Research Facilities

The Mount's Archbishop Alter Library owns more than 96,000 volumes and provides access to more than 140 databases, online reference sources, and research assistance. Document delivery and interlibrary loan facilitate the prompt acquisition of materials available anywhere in the country. With FOCUS, the library's online public access catalog, patrons may search for materials available at the College library and other area libraries. OHIOLINK, a statewide network of public universities and private colleges, provides quick access to materials and full access to the Internet.

Financial Aid

Financial aid is available to all students enrolled at the Mount, with priority given to those in need of financial assistance. Students must complete a financial aid application. Five scholarships, each in the amount of $1000, are awarded annually to women who are graduate students in education and/or religious studies. To qualify, applicants must take at least 12 credit hours during the academic year.

A special grant is available to any individual enrolled in the religious studies graduate program who is a paid or volunteer minister serving in a congregation, hospital, health-care facility, social service agency, diocese, or educational institution. This grant reduces tuition during all semesters. Verification of employment/volunteer service and submission of a FAFSA form are required.

Cost of Study

Tuition for graduate programs is as follows: education (M.A.), $500 per hour; religious studies (M.A.), $500 per hour; organizational leadership (M.S.O.L.), $550 per hour; nursing (M.N.), $37,300 for the program; and physical therapy (D.P.T.), $79,650 for the program or $8850 per semester. The tuition rates for TEAM programs in education are: Inclusive Early Childhood (TEAM-IEC), $500 per hour; Adolescent/Young Adult (TEAM-AYA), $500 per hour; and Multicultural/Special Education (TEAM-MSE), $500 per hour.

Living and Housing Costs

Apartments are for rent at reasonable rates in the immediate area.

Student Group

Total enrollment at the Mount exceeds 2,100. There are more than 300 graduate students, with 43 percent attending full time.

Location

Located 15 minutes from downtown Cincinnati, the College of Mount St. Joseph is situated on a 92-acre suburban campus overlooking the Ohio River. The College is easily accessible from the airport, bus terminal, railway station, and interstate. Well known for its scenic and rolling hills, greater Cincinnati offers numerous parks, cultural and arts events, museums, theaters, professional athletics, shopping areas, and a wide assortment of fine restaurants.

The College

The College of Mount St. Joseph is a private, Catholic, coeducational college of 2,100 students that provides a professional and liberal arts education. Founded in 1920 by the Sisters of Charity, the Mount is dedicated to preparing the ethical leaders of tomorrow and equipping them with values, integrity, and social responsibility.

Small class sizes encourage individualized learning, and students have opportunities for career experience, leadership development, service learning, and participation in a wide variety of activities. In addition to its graduate programs, the Mount offers more than thirty-five undergraduate academic programs and nine associate degrees.

The Mount is fully accredited by the Higher Learning Commission of the North Central Association of Colleges and Schools and is consistently ranked among the top Midwest regional universities for quality and value, by *U.S. News & World Report* in its guide to America's Best Colleges. The College also received above-peer student ratings in more than 70 areas according to the 2008 Noel-Levitz Student Satisfaction Inventory (SSI).

Applying

Students interested in applying should contact the Office of Graduate Admission to obtain application forms and other program materials.

Correspondence and Information

Office of Graduate Admission
College of Mount St. Joseph
5701 Delhi Road
Cincinnati, Ohio 45233

Phone: 513-244-GRAD
800-654-9314 (toll-free)
E-mail: admission@mail.msj.edu
Web site: http://www.msj.edu

THE FACULTY

Education: Mary West, Associate Professor and Chair; Ph.D., Ohio State; phone: 513-244-4935; fax: 513-244-4867; e-mail: mary_west@mail.msj.edu..
Nancy Cavanaugh, Instructor; M.Ed., Cincinnati.
Anneka Clay, Instructor; M.Ed., Cincinnati.
Tsila Evers, Assistant Professor; Ph.D., Michigan.
James Green, Assistant Professor; Ph.D., Ohio State.
Kathleen Hulgin, Assistant Professor; Ph.D., Syracuse.
Angela Miller, Assistant Professor; M.Ed., Xavier.
Mifrando Obach, Associate Professor; Ph.D., Tulane.
Jay Parks, TEAM-IEC Coordinator; M.Ed., Cincinnati.
Deborah Ranz-Smith, Assistant Professor; Ed.D., Cincinnati.
Clarissa Rosas, Associate Professor; Ph.D., New Mexico.
Paul Sallada, Director of Clinical Experiences; M.Ed., Cincinnati.
Rick Santoro, Instructor, M.Ed., Cincinnati.
Linda Schoenstedt, Assistant Professor; Ed.D., Montana State.
Kim Shibinski, Assistant Professor; Ed.D., South Carolina.
Richard Sparks, Professor of Education; Ed.D., Cincinnati.
Nursing: Mary Kishman, Associate Professor and Graduate Nursing Chair; Ph.D., Cincinnati; RN; phone: 513-244-4726; fax: 513-451-2547; e-mail: mary_kishman@mail.msj.edu.
Joe Barone, Assistant Professor; M.S.N., Washington; RN.
Gail Burns, Assistant Professor; M.S.N., D.N.P., Alabama; RN.
Donna Glankler, Assistant Professor; M.S.N., Cincinnati; RN.
Nancy Hinzman, Associate Professor; M.S.N., Indiana; RNC.
Susan Johnson, Professor and Division Dean; Ph.D., Cincinnati; RN.
Bill Lonneman, Assistant Professor; M.A., M.S.N., Indiana; RN.
Nancy Rowley, Assistant Professor; M.S.N., Cincinnati; RN.
Darla Vale, Professor; Ph.D., Rush; RN, CRRN.
Organizational Leadership: Daryl Smith, Assistant Professor and Chair; Ph.D., Washington (Seattle); phone: 513-244-4920; fax: 513-244-4270; e-mail: daryl_smith@mail.msj.edu.
John Ballard, Associate Professor; Ph.D., Purdue.
Elizabeth Bartley, Professor; Ph.D., Cincinnati.
Mark Bell, Instructor; M.B.A., Maryland; CPA.
Mary Ann Edwards, Associate Professor; D.B.A., Argosy University.
Missy Houlette, Assistant Professor; Ph.D., Delaware.
David Kroger, Instructor; M.S., Dayton.
Charles Kroncke, Associate Professor; Ph.D., Auburn.
Judy Singleton, Assistant Professor; Ph.D., Cincinnati.
Georgana Taggart, Associate Professor; J.D., Northern Kentucky.
Ron White, Professor; Ph.D., Kentucky.
Physical Therapy: Karen Holtgrefe, Assistant Professor and Chair; D.H.S., Indianapolis; PT; phone: 513-244-3299; fax: 513-451-2547; e-mail: karen_holtgrefe@mail.msj.edu.
Lisa Dehner, Associate Professor; Ph.D., Virginia; PT.
Marsha Eifert Mangine, Assistant Professor; Ed.D., Cincinnati; PT.
Adrick Harrison, Assistant Professor; M.P.T., Medical University of South Carolina; CSCS.
Susan Johnson, Associate Professor and Program Director; Ph.D., Cincinnati; RN.
Kevin Lawrence, Assistant Professor; D.H.S., Indianapolis; OCS.
Renee Loftspring, Assistant Professor; Ed.D., Cincinnati; PT.
Ann McCormick, Assistant Professor; Ph.D. candidate, Virginia; PT.
Peter Mosher, Assistant Professor; D.P.T., St. Louis; PT.
Religious Studies: John Trokan, Associate Professor and Chair; D.Min., Saint Mary of the Lake–Muldelein Seminary; phone: 513-244-4496; fax: 513-244-4788; e-mail: john_trokan@mail.msj.edu.
Sister Marge Kloos, Associate Professor; D.Min., United Theological Seminary (Ohio); SC.
Harriet Luckman, Associate Professor; Ph.D., Marquette.
Jozef D. Zalot, Assistant Professor; Ph.D., Marquette.

Adjunct Faculty
Georgiana Abplanalp, M.Ed., Xavier.
R. Casey Barach, M.B.A., J.D., Cincinnati.
Marina Branch, B.H.S., Kentucky; PT.
John Berrens, Ph.D., Cincinnati.
Sister Mary Bookser, Ph.D., United Theological Seminary (Ohio).
Lisa Campbell, Ed.D., Cincinnati.
Debby Combs, M.S.O.L., Mount St. Joseph.
Elaine Crable, Ph.D., Georgia.
Cynthia Dillard, M.Ed., Cincinnati.
Megan Douglas, D.P.T., University of St. Augustine for Health Sciences.
Matt Ernst, M.P.T., Mount St. Joseph.
Tom Ernst, M.P.T., Mount St. Joseph.
Ann Fershtman, M.S.P.T., Virginia.
Beth Flanigan, M.S.N., Cincinnati; RN.
C. Edward Green, J.D., Northern Kentucky.
Jeanine Gunn, D.P.T., USC.
Annie Hawkins, Ed.D., Cincinnati.
Erin Hofmeyer, D.P.T., Mount St. Joseph.
Jennifer Hosler, M.N., Mount St. Joseph; RN.
Kim Hunter, M.B.A., Toledo.
John Miriam Jones, Ph.D., Notre Dame; SC.
Erin Kelley, M.P.T., Washington (St. Louis).
Jenny Kilgore, Ph.D., Miami (Ohio).
Miriam Kinard, M.Ed., Cincinnati.
Marina Krivonos, M.B.A., Daemen; PT.
Christina Montecalvo, M.Ed., Xavier (Cincinnati).
Gwendolyn T. Olmstead, Ph.D., Arkansas.
Jeffrey Osborne, M.N., Mount St. Joseph; RN.
Peggy Riegel, M.Ed., Miami.
Karen Rutz, B.S., Evansville; PT.
Susan Scherrer, M.Ed., Cincinnati.
Eric Schneider, M.P.T., Mount St. Joseph.
Carolyn Shisler, B.S., Marquette; PT.
Jennifer Sirotak, D.P.T., Saint Louis.
Jane Shulman, M.Ed., Xavier.
Julie Slewitzke, M.P.T., Ohio State.
Jeff Taylor-Hass, M.P.T., Saint Louis.
Joyce Williams, D.Min., United Theological Seminary (Ohio).
Molly Woosley, D.P.T., Mount St. Joseph.

THE COLLEGE OF NEW JERSEY

The College of New Jersey

Graduate Programs

Programs of Study

The College of New Jersey (TCNJ) offers the following advanced degrees: Master of Arts (M.A.) in counselor education or English; Master of Arts in Teaching (M.A.T.) in deaf and hard of hearing/elementary education (five-year program for TCNJ undergraduate students only), early childhood education, elementary education, health and physical education, secondary education, special education, or technology education; Master of Education (M.Ed.) in educational leadership–principal certification, educational leadership–instruction (a collaborative program in conjunction with the Regional Training Center), elementary and secondary education (Global Program only), health or physical education, reading K–12, special education, special education/teacher of students who are blind or visually impaired, or teaching English as a second language; Master of Science (M.S.) in educational technology; Master of Science in Nursing (M.S.N.) in adult nurse practitioner studies, clinical nurse leader studies, family nurse practitioner studies, or neonatal nurse practitioner studies; and Educational Specialist (Ed.S.) in marriage and family therapy.

Graduate certificate programs and/or post-master's programs are offered in adult nurse practitioner studies; bilingual education (main campus and Global Program); educational leadership–principal certification; family nurse practitioner studies; instructional licensure-teacher of preschool–grade 3; learning disabilities teacher/consultant studies, reading specialist studies; substance awareness coordinator studies; teacher certification for international schools (Global Program only); teacher of students with disabilities; or teaching English as a second language.

Global opportunities in education are also available for graduate students. Graduate global programs at TCNJ have been in existence for more than twenty-five years and provide course work leading toward a master's degree in education and state of New Jersey certification in teaching and administration. Courses are taught by TCNJ faculty members and other internationally recognized professors. Courses are offered June through July at TCNJ sites in Mallorca, Spain; Bangkok, Thailand; and Johannesburg, South Africa. During the academic year, courses are available in La Paz, Bolivia; Cairo, Egypt; and Hsinchu, Taiwan.

For the convenience of the majority of graduate students who pursue degrees while being employed full-time, graduate courses held on the Ewing campus are offered during the day and in the evening.

Research Facilities

TCNJ offers a state-of-the-art library that serves as an exciting intellectual, cultural, and social center for the College community. The five-story, 135,000-square-foot facility will provide cutting-edge services to the TCNJ community well into the twenty-first century. In addition to housing traditional library collections and services in an atmosphere that is both friendly and elegant, a key feature of the new library is its wide array of carefully considered and thoughtful amenities, which make using the facility both a pleasure and a convenience. The library provides twenty-four group-study rooms (one reserved for graduate students), ample and comfortable seating, tables and carrels, and both WiFi and LAN Internet access throughout, with power connections at every carrel and study table. Special design features include a café, a secure, late night/24-hour study area, and a 105-seat multipurpose auditorium. The library also houses the Instructional Technology Services facility, creating ideal one-stop shopping for students working on projects.

Library collections include more than 560,000 volumes and 200,000 microforms as well as subscriptions to more than 1,400 periodicals. The library also subscribes to more than seventy-five electronic indexes covering more than 14,000 scholarly journals, including full-text resources. A media facility offers viewing and listening equipment as well as sound recordings, videos, and interactive computer software. PCs are available for public access to electronic resources. Collections are constantly augmented by new acquisitions, and interlibrary loan and document delivery services are available as well. The library is also an active participant in a number of library networks and maintains cooperative arrangements with many regional academic libraries, from which students may borrow directly. TCNJ librarians are an important resource in and of themselves. In addition to advanced studies in library and information science, each subject-librarian has additional graduate degrees in one of the major academic areas, and students are encouraged to consult them in person and online.

In addition to providing new library facilities for the College community, TCNJ has met the challenge of the computer field's phenomenal growth with installations of computer facilities in each of its seven schools. The School of Education also houses a speech, language, and hearing center.

Financial Aid

The College of New Jersey offers financial aid to qualified matriculated students through a combination of loans, grants, and/or employment. To be considered for all financial aid programs, students must submit the Free Application for Federal Student Aid (FAFSA) to the College Financial Assistance Office. Graduate assistantships are available to qualified full-time students on a competitive basis.

Cost of Study

Tuition for graduate courses for 2008–09 was $557 per semester hour of credit for New Jersey residents and $845.50 per semester hour of credit for out-of-state residents. Additional fees include ID, student center, library, and health insurance (for full-time students). Tuition and fees are subject to change by action of the New Jersey State Legislature.

Living and Housing Costs

As the majority of TCNJ's graduate students attend classes part-time in the evenings, the College does not offer on-campus housing for graduate students. Graduate students who seek housing in the area can get assistance from the Office of Residence Life.

Student Group

The College of New Jersey had an enrollment of approximately 6,200 undergraduate students and 800 graduate students in 2007–08.

Student Outcomes

The College of New Jersey's excellent reputation has afforded graduates outstanding opportunities when entering their professional fields. Many TCNJ graduates receive job placements through various on-campus recruitment programs sponsored by the Office of Career Services.

Location

The College of New Jersey is located on 289 tree-lined acres in suburban Ewing, New Jersey, 7 miles from the state capital in Trenton. Woodlands and two lakes surround the academic and residential buildings. More than thirty-five buildings make up the physical plant, most of which are built in the classic Georgian Colonial architecture. The campus is 30 miles from Philadelphia and 60 miles from New York's theaters, museums, and other attractions. The nearby towns of Princeton and New Hope offer additional cultural activities.

The College

Founded in 1855, the College has grown from its early years as a teachers' college to a multipurpose institution comprising seven schools: Art, Media, and Music; Business; Culture and Society; Education; Engineering; Nursing, Health, and Exercise Science; and Science. Graduate study is available in the Schools of Culture and Society, Education, and Nursing, Health, and Exercise Science.

TCNJ introduced its first advanced degree program, a Master of Science in elementary education, in 1947. Over the years, the number of graduate programs has steadily increased. At present there are more than fifty specialized graduate degree and certificate programs.

TCNJ's academic programs are accredited by the Middle States Association of Colleges and Schools, the National Council for Accreditation of Teacher Education (NCATE), the Council for the Accreditation of Counseling and Related Educational Programs (CACREP), and other appropriate professional associations.

Applying

Students of proven ability with undergraduate degrees in appropriate fields are eligible to apply for graduate study. Applications should be submitted online (http://www.tcnj.edu/~graduate) along with the $70 nonrefundable application fee. Transcripts of all previous college or university work and other supporting documentation as noted on the Web should be forwarded to the Office of Graduate Studies. Acceptable scores on the appropriate national standardized tests are required for all degree programs.

Application deadlines for matriculation are April 15 for the fall semester and October 15 for the spring semester, with the following exceptions. The deadline for all M.A.T. programs is March 1 (summer start). The deadline for the M.Ed. in educational leadership-principal immersion is March 1 (summer start). The deadlines for the M.Ed. in educational leadership-instruction are August 1 for fall, October 15 for spring, and March 1 for summer. The deadlines for the M.A. and Ed.S. programs in counselor education are March 1 for fall and October 1 for spring. The nonmatriculation application deadlines are August 1 for fall and December 1 for spring. Prospective students should note that there is no nonmatriculation for the M.Ed. in educational leadership–instruction program.

Correspondence and Information

Office of Graduate Studies
Paul Loser Hall, Room 109
The College of New Jersey
P.O. Box 7718
Ewing, New Jersey 08628

Phone: 609-771-2300
Fax: 609-637-5105
E-mail: graduate@tcnj.edu
Web site: http://www.tcnj.edu/~graduate

DEANS AND PROGRAM COORDINATORS

SCHOOL OF CULTURE AND SOCIETY
Deborah Compte, Interim Dean; Ph.D., Princeton.

Graduate Program Coordinator
English: Michele Tarter, Associate Professor; Ph.D., Colorado.

SCHOOL OF EDUCATION
William Behre, Dean; Ph.D., Michigan.

Graduate Program Coordinators
Counselor Education: Mark Woodford, Assistant Professor and Chair; Ph.D., Virginia. Mark Kiselica, Professor; Ph.D., Penn State. Mary Lou Ramsey, Professor; Ed.D., Fairleigh Dickinson. Atsuko Seto, Assistant Professor; Ph.D., Wyoming. Charlene Alderfer, Associate Professor; Ed.D., Massachusetts Amherst.
Deaf and Hard of Hearing/Elementary Education Five-Year Program: Barbara Strassman, Professor; Ed.D., Columbia Teachers College.
Early Childhood Education: Arti Joshi, Assistant Professor; M.S., Bombay (India).
Educational Leadership-Instruction: Alan Amtzis, Director; Ph.D., Boston College.
Educational Leadership-Principal: Donald Leake, Associate Professor; Ph.D., Ohio State.
Educational Technology: Amy G. Dell, Professor; Ph.D., Rochester.
Elementary Education: Brenda Leake, Associate Professor; Ph.D., Ohio State.
Health and Physical Education: Aristomen Chilakos, Professor; Ph.D., Temple.
Instructional Licensure-Teacher of Preschool–Grade 3: Joby Eberly, Assistant Professor; Ph.D., Rutgers.
Reading K–12: Kathryne Speaker, Assistant Professor; Ed.D., Temple.
School Personnel Licensure: Joby Eberly, Assistant Professor; Ph.D., Rutgers.
Secondary Education: Ruth Palmer, Associate Professor; Ph.D., Howard. John Karsnitz, Professor; Ph.D., Ohio State.
Special Education: Shridevi Rao, Assistant Professor; Ph.D., Syracuse.
TESOL/Bilingual Education: Yiqiang Wu, Associate Professor; Ph.D., Texas A&M.

SCHOOL OF NURSING, HEALTH, AND EXERCISE SCIENCE
Susan Bakewell-Sachs, Dean; M.S.N., Ph.D., Pennsylvania; CRNP.
Jay Hoffman, Professor and Chair, Health and Exercise Science; Ph.D., Connecticut.

Graduate Program Coordinators
Nursing: Leslie Rice, Assistant Professor; M.S.N., Pennsylvania; Ph.D., New York.
Health and Exercise Science: Aristomen Chilakos, Professor; Ph.D., Temple.

MAJOR RESEARCH PROJECTS

Grant Awards
Adaptive technology center; Dr. Amy G. Dell, School of Education.
Advanced education nursing traineeship program; Dr. Claire Lindberg, School of Nursing.
Infant functional status and discharge management; Dr. Susan Bakewell-Sachs, School of Nursing.
Preparing special and elementary educators to use inquiry and design-based learning; Dr. Amy Dell, School of Education.
Provisional teacher program; Dr. Anthony Evangelisto, School of Education.
TECH-NJ (Technology, Educators, and Children with Disabilities–New Jersey); Dr. Amy G. Dell, School of Education.
The New Jersey Teacher Quality Enhancement Recruitment Project; Dr. Sharon Sherman, School of Education and Dr. Cathy Liebars, School of Science.
Deaf/Blind Family and Community Educational Support; Dr. Jerry Petroff, School of Education.
Institute of Educational Design, Evaluation, and Assessment; Dr. Debra Frank, School of Education.

Support of Scholarly Activity Awards (SOSA)
Conversation analysis of native/nonnative speakers; Dr. Jean Wong, School of Education.
Facilitating transition from school to employment for individuals with challenging behavior; Dr. Shridevi Rao, School of Education.
HIV symptom distress project; Dr. Claire Lindberg, School of Nursing.
Issues of literacy and teaching elementary students of color; Dr. Deborah Thompson, School of Education.
The reception of Dante and Chaucer within the work of their literary successors; Dr. Glenn Steinberg, School of Culture and Society.
When boys become parents: understanding and helping teen fathers; Dr. Mark Kiselica, School of Education.
Writing the republic; Dr. David Blake, School of Culture and Society.

The clock tower above Green Hall, the main administrative building on campus, is a well-known symbol of TCNJ tradition.

The College is made up of more than thirty-eight Georgian-style buildings all situated on a 289-acre suburban campus.

The College of New Jersey's tree-lined campus, which provides spectacular foliage, offers a beautiful setting for students all year long.

THE COLLEGE OF SAINT ROSE

Programs of Study

The College of Saint Rose offers graduate programs leading to the degrees of Master of Arts, Master of Science, Master of Science in Education, and Master of Business Administration as well as graduate certificates of advanced study. Graduate programs meet the needs of both part-time and full-time students. Courses are scheduled in the late afternoon and evening to accommodate the large number of students whose days are filled with other activities. Part-time students usually finish in two to three years, full-time students in 1½ years.

Fields of study include accounting, adolescence education, art education, business administration, business and marketing education, childhood education, college student services administration, communication sciences and disorders, communications, computer information systems, early childhood education, educational computing, educational leadership and administration, educational psychology, educational technology specialist studies, English, history and political science, literacy, mental health counseling, music education, school counseling, school psychology, special education, and technology education. The College of Saint Rose also offers a joint J.D./M.B.A. degree with Albany Law School and a full-time, one-year M.B.A., in addition to the part-time evening M.B.A. program. The College also offers graduate certificates of advanced study in numerous fields, including computer information systems, educational computing, financial planning, not-for-profit management, school building leadership, and school district leadership.

The objectives of Saint Rose graduate study are to encourage intellectual curiosity, foster creative thought, and promote careful research and professional competence. To these ends, programs are designed to provide essential core materials and to allow options for electives. The programs in adolescence education, childhood education, early childhood education, educational technology specialist studies, school counseling, and special education also lead to professional education certification. In addition to a master's degree, certification-only programs are available for adolescence education, applied technology, art education, business and marketing education, educational leadership and administration, and literacy.

Small classes, opportunities for independent study, research assistantships, and, in many programs, internships or various practicum or fieldwork experiences facilitate the learning process. Through the College's membership in the Hudson-Mohawk Association of Colleges and Universities, full-time students may cross-register for graduate courses at other institutions in the Capital Region.

The College operates on an academic year of two 15-week semesters, fall and spring; two 6-week summer sessions; and a 3-week summer immersion program. The accounting and M.B.A. programs offer three 11-week sessions annually.

Research Facilities

The Neil Hellman Library houses 233,627 volumes, 643 periodical subscriptions, 313,339 titles on microform, and 3,180 DVD/VHS items and audio CDs, 35,000 e-books, 50 database subscriptions, and a collection of rare books and provides access to 30,000 full-text periodical titles. Students requiring additional information can borrow books and articles through the College's membership in a nationwide interlibrary loan cooperative. Graduate students have access to computer labs featuring IBM and Macintosh computers with Internet access. The Patricia Standish Education and Curriculum Library, in the Thelma P. Lally School of Education, serves the educational and professional needs of preservice and practicing educators throughout the region and provides ready access to extensive research and curriculum materials. The Music Building provides state-of-the-art facilities for music majors at Saint Rose, including the Saints and Sinners Sound Studio, a sixteen-track professional recording studio, and the Henry and Alice Cooper Finks Music Library. In addition, the Thelma P. Lally School of Education's multidisciplinary Joy Emery Educational and Clinical Services Center includes ten treatment/assessment rooms, an audiology laboratory with sound booth, and a play area that allows clinicians to assess the cognitive and psychosocial development of children. The College's new $14-million Massry Center for the Arts will house an art gallery and a 400-seat recital hall, becoming the hub of musical and visual arts activity; a gathering space for students, performers, composers, scholars, and teachers; and a place for the community to celebrate those Saint Rose programs, which are increasing both in popularity and prominence.

Financial Aid

Saint Rose serves graduate students through a variety of federal, state, and institutional programs, which include loans, grants, and employment opportunities. Graduate assistantships and merit, diversity, international, and second-chance scholarships are available to matriculated students. Matriculating graduate students may apply for campus-based assistance (assistantships and Federal Perkins Loans) by completing the Free Application for Federal Student Aid (FAFSA).

Cost of Study

The cost of graduate tuition in 2009–10 is $626 per credit hour. A technology fee of $22 per credit and a student records fee of $60 per semester are also charged.

Living and Housing Costs

The College's Office of Residence Life assists graduate students in locating suitable off-campus housing.

Student Group

Saint Rose has a total enrollment of more than 5,000 students, of whom approximately 2,000 are graduate students. Approximately 60 percent of the graduate students attend part-time. Students come from colleges and universities throughout the United States and other countries, with the largest number from New York and neighboring states. In addition to students who are pursuing a degree, Saint Rose welcomes individuals who are taking courses toward teaching certification and students who seek personal or professional enrichment.

Location

The Albany area, which is known as Tech Valley, offers extensive cultural and recreational opportunities. In addition to the many extracurricular activities offered by Saint Rose and several other colleges in the area, students may enjoy the Albany Symphony Orchestra, the Capital Repertory Theatre, the Albany Institute of History and Art, the New York State Museum, and other theater groups, museums, galleries, and historic sites. The College's location in the capital of New York State provides a special opportunity for students to seek involvement with the State Legislature and a large variety of government agencies. New York City, Boston, and Montreal are all less than a 4-hour drive from Saint Rose.

The College

The College of Saint Rose, which was founded in 1920, is a private, independent, coeducational liberal arts and sciences college with a strong tradition of academic excellence and service to the community. Located in Albany's Pine Hills residential neighborhood, the College enjoys all the advantages of a major metropolitan area. Its 25-acre campus, which is made up of a combination of more than eighty modern buildings and historic Victorian homes, creates an informal environment that is conducive to personal, as well as professional, growth and enrichment. Saint Rose supports educational innovation and faculty-student interaction. Faculty members and students often are engaged in joint research projects. The College is fully accredited by the Middle States Association of Colleges and Schools, the Board of Regents of the University of the State of New York, the National Association of Schools of Art and Design, the Council on Academic Accreditation of the American Speech-Language-Hearing Association, the Association of Collegiate Business Schools and Programs, the National Association of Schools of Music, the National Council for the Accreditation of Teacher Education, and the Council of Social Work Education.

Applying

Applicants must file a graduate application, official transcripts of all postsecondary course work, a statement of purpose, two letters of recommendation for graduate study, and any other forms of evidence to support their credentials by the application deadline before the beginning of the semester in which they wish to begin study. The preferred application deadline for the fall semester is June 1; for the spring semester, it is October 15; and for the summer semesters, it is March 15. Candidates applying to the master's degree program in communication sciences and disorders must submit their applications by February 1 for fall and summer admission and by October 1 for spring admission. Candidates applying to the master's degree program in school psychology must submit their applications by March 1 for consideration for the fall semester. Applicants to the master's degree program in counseling or college student services administration must submit their applications by April 15 for the fall semester or by October 15 for the spring semester. Some applicants for the M.B.A. or the M.S. in accounting program are required to submit Graduate Management Admission Test scores. The nonrefundable application fee is $35. An online application is available at http://www.strose.edu/gradapply.

Correspondence and Information

Graduate and Continuing Education Admissions
The College of Saint Rose
432 Western Avenue
Albany, New York 12203-1490

Phone: 518-454-5143
800-637-8556 Ext. 2 (toll-free)
Fax: 518-458-5479
E-mail: grad@strose.edu
Web site: http://www.strose.edu/gradapply

DEANS OF SCHOOLS, PROGRAM CHAIRS, AND DESCRIPTIONS

SCHOOL OF ARTS AND HUMANITIES
Lorna Shaw, Dean; Ph.D., Howard.

Art Education (Master of Science)
Karene Faul, Chair; M.F.A., Notre Dame.

Provides permanent certification for those who are provisionally certified in art education as well as those who have a background in fine arts but no teaching experience. Curriculum emphasizes studio work.

Communications (Master of Arts)
Karen McGrath, Graduate Coordinator; Ph.D., Southern Illinois.

Offers concentrations in journalism and public relations for communications professionals who want to build on skills that they use in the workplace.

English (Master of Arts)
Hollis Seamon, Graduate Coordinator; D.A., SUNY at Albany.

With concentrations in literature and writing, this program can be tailored to meet students' personal and professional needs. Fulfills the academic requirement for permanent certification for those who are provisionally certified to teach English at the secondary level.

History/Political Science (Master of Arts)
Benjamin Clansy, Graduate Coordinator; Ph.D., Colorado.

Focuses on the historical, political, and international dimensions of the American experience. Fulfills the academic requirement for permanent certification for those who are provisionally certified to teach social studies at the secondary level.

Music Education (Master of Science)
Bruce Roter, Graduate Coordinator; Ph.D., Rutgers.

Prepares students to teach music in grades K–12 by providing a specialized, in-depth study of learning and teaching music. Meets the needs of current teachers pursuing permanent certification, as well as those who have undergraduate degrees in music but no teaching experience.

SCHOOL OF BUSINESS
Severin C. Carlson, Dean; D.B.A., Indiana.

Accounting (Master of Science)
Barry Hughes, Chair; M.S., Saint Rose.

Qualifies students in New York State to take the CPA exam, provided they have 60 credits of liberal arts courses and 45 credits of undergraduate business courses. Also geared toward students who already work in accounting but want to advance in their field and those who want to enter the field of accounting for the first time.

Business/Economics (Master of Business Administration)
K. Michael Mathews, Chair; D.B.A., Louisiana Tech.

Provides students with the skills and knowledge to become effective managers in today's rapidly changing and competitive business environment. Offers an accelerated part-time option for working professionals and a one-year, full-time intensive option with an internship component.

SCHOOL OF EDUCATION
Margaret M. Kirwin, Dean; Ed.D., SUNY at Albany.

Adolescence Education (Master of Science in Education)
Designed for anyone who wants to teach at the middle or high school level. Fulfills all the education course work requirements for provisional certification to teach biology, business/marketing, chemistry, earth science, English, mathematics, social studies, or Spanish in grades 7–12.

Childhood Education (Master of Science in Education)
Designed for students who want to teach at the elementary school level (grades 1–6) and who are not yet provisionally certified.

College Student Services Administration (Master of Science in Education)
Michael Bologna, Chair; Ph.D., SUNY at Albany.

Prepares students for careers on college and university campuses, working in the offices of the registrar, financial aid, admissions, residence life, and student affairs.

Communication Sciences and Disorders (Master of Science in Education)
David DeBonis, Chair; Ph.D., SUNY at Albany.

Accredited by the American Speech-Language-Hearing Association and approved by New York State to license speech-language pathologists and to certify teachers of the speech and hearing handicapped.

Counseling (Master of Science in Education)
Michael Bologna, Chair; Ph.D., SUNY at Albany.

Offers concentrations in school counseling, community mental health counseling, and college mental health counseling.

Early Childhood Education (Master of Science in Education)
Designed for those who want to work with children in nursery schools, early childhood centers, Head Start programs, or elementary schools. Leads to initial New York State certification to teach through grade 2.

Educational Leadership and Administration (Master of Science in Education, Certificates of Advanced Study in School Building Leadership and School District Leadership)
Perry Berkowitz, Graduate Coordinator; Ed.D., Massachusetts.

Designed for educators who wish to become certified as administrators, principals, or superintendents at the school and/or school district levels.

Educational Psychology (Master of Science in Education)
Richard Brody, Chair; Ph.D., SUNY at Albany.

Designed for those with no prior experience in education and for those who have a background in education and want to expand their skills and expertise. Also fulfills the academic requirement for permanent certification for those who are provisionally certified in childhood, adolescence, or special education.

Literacy (Master of Science in Education)
Theresa Ward, Assistant Professor; Ed.D., Central Florida.

Designed for teachers who have provisional teaching certification in elementary education, secondary education, or special education and want additional certification in reading.

School Psychology (Master of Science in Education)
Maria Fast, Cochair; Ph.D., SUNY at Albany. Steven Hoff, Cochair; Ph.D., NYU.

Prepares students for careers as certified school psychologists.

Special Education (Master of Science in Education)
Theresa Ward, Assistant Professor; Ed.D., Central Florida.

Prepares teachers to address the variety of needs among students with disabilities and is designed for those with and without provisional certification in special education.

Teacher Education (Master of Science in Education)
Patricia Baldwin, M.S.Ed., SUNY at New Paltz.

Designed to provide a master's degree leading to professional teaching certification in grades K–12, under New York State requirements.

SCHOOL OF MATHEMATICS AND SCIENCES
Richard J. Thompson, Dean; Ph.D., Penn State.

Computer Information Systems (Master of Science)
Ian MacDonald, Chair; Ph.D., SUNY at Albany.

A part-time or full-time evening program designed for students with some experience in computer technology and programming who wish to advance their skills and knowledge in areas such as software design and programming, computer architecture, and database theory.

COLLEGE OF STATEN ISLAND OF THE CITY UNIVERSITY OF NEW YORK

Graduate Degree Programs

Programs of Study

The College of Staten Island offers master's degrees in biology (M.S.); business management (M.S.); cinema and media studies (M.A.); computer science (M.S.); education: childhood (elementary) education (M.S.Ed.), adolescence (secondary) education (M.S.Ed.), middle childhood generalist (grades 5–9) (M.S.Ed.), special education (M.S.Ed.); English (M.A.); environmental science (M.S.); history (M.A.); liberal studies (M.A.); mental health counseling (M.A.); neuroscience, mental retardation, and developmental disabilities (M.S.); and nursing: adult health nursing (M.S.) and gerontological nursing (M.S.). Post-master's advanced certificates are awarded in leadership in education, adult health nursing, cultural competence, gerontological nursing, and nursing education.

The doctoral program in nursing and physical therapy is offered jointly with the City University Graduate School and University Center. The College also participates in the City University's doctoral programs in biology, chemistry, computer science, and physics.

Research Facilities

The academic buildings house approximately 200 modern laboratories and classrooms. Academic and research programs are served by a computer network that allows students and faculty members full access to specialized software, the Internet, online library resources, and e-mail. All major computer languages and software packages are supported. The library holds up to 300,000 volumes, computer facilities for database searching, periodical subscriptions, and media services. The College library is a member of the City University of New York (CUNY) integrated library system. Students and faculty members have free access to ERIC as well as various databases on CD-ROM or via the Internet. The College's devotion to research is evident in its maintenance of the Center for Developmental Neuroscience and Developmental Disabilities, the Center for Environmental Science, the Center for the Study of Staten Island, and the CUNY High Performance Computing Facility. In addition, the Center for the Arts, complete with a 900-seat concert hall, a 450-seat fully equipped theater, a recital hall, an experimental theater, an art gallery, a conference center, a lecture hall, and studios, provides facilities for teaching and public assembly.

Financial Aid

The Office of Student Financial Assistance administers federal and state grant, loan, and work-study programs to assist students with financial need to attend the College of Staten Island. Students should contact the Office of Student Financial Assistance early in the admission process to discuss eligibility requirements and responsibilities. The College offers a limited number of tuition waivers for matriculated graduate students who demonstrate need. In some departments, graduate assistant positions are available for full-time graduate students, and information about these positions may be obtained from the individual program departments.

Cost of Study

In 2009–10, tuition for New York State residents was $310 per credit, or $3680 per semester for 12 or more credits. Tuition for nonresidents was $575 per credit.

Living and Housing Costs

For the 2009–10 academic year, dependent students budgeted a minimum of $1070 for books and supplies, $850 for local transportation, $2754 for meals and personal expenses, and $1500 for housing. Independent students budgeted the same amounts for books, supplies, and transportation, plus $14,128 for food, housing, and personal expenses for a nine-month academic year.

Student Group

Nearly 1,000 graduate students enrolled at the College of Staten Island in the 2009 fall semester. The graduate population reflects a wide range of ethnicity, social and economic backgrounds, educational and professional experiences, and aspirations.

Location

The College of Staten Island is located in New York City in the Borough of Staten Island. Completed in 1994, the 204-acre campus of the College of Staten Island is the largest one for a college in New York City. Set in a parklike landscape, the campus is centrally located on Staten Island and is accessible by automobile and public transportation.

The College

The College of Staten Island, is a four-year senior college of the City University of New York that offers exceptional opportunities to all its students. Programs in the liberal arts and sciences and professional studies lead to bachelor's and associate degrees. The master's degree is awarded in fourteen professional and liberal arts and sciences fields of study. The College participates in doctoral programs of the City University Graduate School and University Center in biology, chemistry, computer science, physics, and psychology.

Applying

Requirements for admission and application deadlines vary by program and department. Students should contact the Office of Recruitment and Admissions for additional information or to arrange an admissions interview or campus tour.

Correspondence and Information

Emmanuel Esperance, Jr., Interim Director for Recruitment and Admissions
Office of Recruitment and Admissions
North Administration Building (2A), Room 103
College of Staten Island
2800 Victory Boulevard
Staten Island, New York 10314

Phone: 718-982-2010
Fax: 718-982-2500
E-mail: admissions@mail.csi.cuny.edu
Web site: http://www.csi.cuny.edu

GRADUATE PROGRAM FACULTY HEADS

Adolescence Education: Eileen Donoghue, Ed.D., Associate Professor, Department of Education; David Kritt, Ph.D., Assistant Professor, Department of Education.

Biology: Frank T. Burbrink, Ph.D., Assistant Professor, Department of Biology.

Business: John Sandler, Ph.D., Assistant Professor, Department of Business.

Childhood Education: Gregory Seals, Ph.D., Assistant Professor, Department of Education; Vivian Shulman, Ph.D., Assistant Professor, Department of Education.

Cinema Studies: Matthew Solomon, Ph.D., Assistant Professor, Department of Media Culture.

Computer Science: Anatoliy Gordonov, Ph.D., Assistant Professor, Department of Computer Science.

Educational Leadership: Ruth Silverberg, Ed.D., Professor, Department of Education; Susan Sullivan, Ed.D., Assistant Professor, Department of Education.

English: Maryann Feola, Ph.D., Professor, Department of English.

Environmental Science: Alfred Levine, Ph.D., Professor, Department of Engineering Science and Physics; Center for Environmental Science.

History: Sandra Gambetti, Ph.D., Assistant Professor, Department of History.

Liberal Studies: David Traboulay, Ph.D., Professor, Department of History.

Mental Health Counseling: Judith Kuppersmith, Ph.D., Associate Professor, Department of Psychology.

Neuroscience, Mental Retardation and Developmental Disabilities: Probal Banerjee, Ph.D., Associate Professor, Department of Chemistry; Andrzej Wieraszko, Ph.D., Professor, Department of Biology.

Nursing (Adult Health and Gerontology): Margaret Lunney, Ph.D., Professor, Department of Nursing.

Special Education: Eleni Tournaki, Ph.D., Assistant Professor, Department of Education.

THE COLLEGE OF WILLIAM AND MARY

Graduate Studies

Programs of Study

The Faculty of Arts and Sciences offers M.A., M.S., and Ph.D. programs in a number of disciplines and the Master of Public Policy (M.P.P.). Joint or concurrent degree programs leading to the M.P.P./M.B.A., M.P.P/J.D., M.P.P./M.S. in marine science, M.P.P./M.S. in computational operations research, and M.A. in American studies/J.D. are also offered. The Mason School of Business offers a full-time M.B.A., a part-time (Flex) M.B.A., an Executive M.B.A., and a Master of Accounting (M.Acc.). Joint-degree programs in law (M.B.A./J.D.) and public policy (M.B.A./M.P.P.) are also offered. A joint degree program leading to the M.B.A./Master of Global Management (M.G.M.) is offered in collaboration with the Thunderbird School of Global Management. The School of Education offers an M.A.Ed. in elementary school teaching (with an emphasis in reading, language, and literacy), gifted education, and secondary school teaching; an M.Ed. in counseling, educational leadership (with emphases in general K–12 administration and higher education administration), school psychology, and special education; an Ed.S. in school psychology; and an Ed.D. and Ph.D. in counselor education and educational policy planning and leadership (with emphases in general K–12 administration, gifted education administration, higher education, and special education administration). *U.S. News & World Report* ranks William and Mary among the top fifty in a national survey of 191 doctoral degree–granting schools of education. The College was also ranked sixth in the country in terms of the quality of its teaching. The William and Mary School of Law offers the J.D. and LL.M. degrees as well as three joint degrees: J.D./M.A. in American studies, J.D./M.B.A., and J.D./M.P.P. The School of Marine Science offers M.S. and Ph.D. programs in marine science. Examples of areas of specialization available to marine science students include the biology, chemistry, geology, and physics of oceanic, coastal, and estuarine systems; marine fisheries science; environmental toxicology; microbiology; and pathology.

Research Facilities

The libraries of the College are the central Earl Gregg Swem Library; the chemistry, physics, geology, biology, and music libraries; the William and Mary School of Law Library; the School of Marine Science Library; the Professional Resource Center in the Mason School of Business; and the Learning Resource Center/Curriculum Library in the School of Education. Specialized laboratories, equipment, publication organizations, collections, and other facilities are available in a variety of departments and institutes, including the Applied Research Center, which houses the Jefferson Lab library; the Omohundro Institute of Early American History and Culture; the Virginia Institute of Marine Science; the Center for Archaeological Research; the Archaeological Conservation Center; the Institute of Bill of Rights Law; the Integrated Science Center; Muscarelle Museum; the Center for Public Policy Research; and the William Small Physical Laboratory. Research opportunities are extended in conjunction with neighboring organizations that include the Colonial Williamsburg Foundation, the Thomas Jefferson National Accelerator Facility, the Eastern State Hospital, the National Center for State Courts, and the Langley Research Center of the National Aeronautics and Space Administration (NASA). Graduate students and faculty members are working at national laboratories and accelerator installations throughout the world.

Financial Aid

Fellowships, scholarships, institutional and grant-funded assistantships, internships, apprenticeships, work-study arrangements, and loans are available. Duties are limited so that assistants can progress toward their degrees at the normal pace. Most of the funds are assigned through the departments and schools. While there is often some flexibility, early application is recommended.

Most Arts and Sciences graduate students receive experience and financial support provided by research or teaching assistantships, internships, or apprenticeships. Students in the School of Marine Science (SMS) are generally funded throughout their graduate programs by grant-supported stipends.

Cost of Study

Specific information regarding tuition and fees can be found at http://www.wm.edu/admission/financialaid/tuition/index.php.

Living and Housing Costs

Conveniently located College housing for graduate and professional students is available, but many graduate and professional students elect to live off campus. Details regarding on-campus living and housing costs and options can be found at http://www.wm.edu/offices/residencelife/index.php.

Student Group

The total enrollment of 7,892 in fall 2008 included 5,811 undergraduates and 1,958 graduate and professional students. Most are full-time students who live on or in the vicinity of the campus. In each graduate school, there is an active graduate student association.

Location

Williamsburg is on a Chesapeake Bay peninsula between the York and James Rivers, on Interstate 64, 50 miles from Richmond, 45 miles from Norfolk, and 150 miles from Washington, D.C. The College is the center of a historic and popular tourist area that includes Colonial Williamsburg, Yorktown, Jamestown, a major water-sports region, and an exceptional concentration of cultural activities. Williamsburg has direct limousine service to the Newport News, Norfolk, and Richmond airports, and bus and railway service is also available.

The College

Offering thirty-six undergraduate programs, fourteen master's and Ph.D. programs in arts and sciences and marine science, and business, education, and law degrees, the College of William and Mary (W&M) provides the expertise and opportunities of a major research university along with the faculty mentoring and dedication to teaching found at a small liberal arts college. The College of William and Mary was chartered in 1693 by King William III and Queen Mary II as the second college in the American colonies. In 1779, the College established the first chair of law in the United States. With a student-faculty ratio of 11:1, W&M is one of the nation's premier "Public Ivies". Indeed, *U.S. News & World Report* ranked W&M sixth among all public universities and thirty-third overall among all public and private universities in 2009. The 1,200-acre main campus in Williamsburg encompasses most of the activities of the university and includes buildings ranging in age from those built around the time of the granting of the royal charter to recent construction. The School of Marine Science campus is located at Gloucester Point.

Applying

There are substantial variations in deadlines and procedures among the departments and schools, and applicants should request information from those in their areas of interest as soon as possible. Most programs are designed for students who wish to begin their studies in the fall semester.

Correspondence and Information

For more information about the College of William and Mary, students can access its Web site at http://www.wm.edu/.

Office of Graduate Studies and Research
Faculty of Arts and Sciences
The College of William and Mary
P.O. Box 8795
Williamsburg, Virginia 23187-8795
Phone: 757-221-2467
Fax: 757-221-4874

Director of M.B.A. Admissions or M.Acc. Admissions
School of Business
The College of William and Mary
P.O. Box 8795
Williamsburg, Virginia 23187-8795
Phone: 757-221-2900 (M.B.A.)
757-221-2875 (M.Acc.)
Fax: 757-221-2958 (M.B.A.)
757-221-2958 (M.Acc.)

Dean of Graduate Studies
School of Marine Science
The College of William and Mary
P.O. Box 1346
Gloucester Point, Virginia 23062
Phone: 804-684-7106

Dean of Admissions
William and Mary School of Law
The College of William and Mary
P.O. Box 8795
Williamsburg, Virginia 23187-8795
Phone: 757-221-3785

Associate Dean of Academic Programs
School of Education
The College of William and Mary
P.O. Box 8795
Williamsburg, Virginia 23187-8795
Phone: 757-221-2317

DEPARTMENT CONTACTS AND RESEARCH AREAS

FACULTY OF ARTS AND SCIENCES

American Studies (M.A., M.A./Ph.D., Ph.D., J.D./M.A. with law): Jean Brown, Program Administrator (jxbrow@wm.edu). Program encourages students to use interdisciplinary approaches to explore the diverse past and present cultures of the peoples of the United States. The program has special strengths in African American studies, cultural studies, popular and material cultures, cultural and intellectual history, American history and literature, and women's history.

Anthropology (M.A., Ph.D.): Dr. Martin Gallivan, Graduate Director (mdgall@wm.edu or http://www.wm.edu/as/graduate/). The M.A. in historical archaeology is designed as a terminal degree to prepare students for careers in cultural resource management and related professions. The M.A./Ph.D. program prepares students for long-term research and teaching in anthropology and strives to integrate social and cultural theory within historical studies in archaeology and anthropology. Faculty interests include comparative colonialism, the African diaspora, Native America, the Caribbean, and the archaeology of Colonial America. Students have access to rich historical, archaeological, and museum resources, as well as opportunities to participate in a wide variety of ongoing projects in the mid-Atlantic region and the Caribbean.

Applied Science (M.S., Ph.D.): Dr. Christopher Del Negro, Graduate Director (info@as.wm.edu). An interdisciplinary graduate program in the physical and natural sciences is offered by the core faculty of Applied Science in cooperation with affiliate faculty from the Departments of Biology, Chemistry, Computer Science, Mathematics, and Physics and the Virginia Institute of Marine Science (VIMS), as well as from NASA-Langley Research Center (LaRC), and the Thomas Jefferson National Accelerator Facility (JLab). Faculty research interests include nondestructive evaluation, robotics, medical imaging, epidemic modeling, nanotechnology, surface science, electronic and magnetic materials, physical and chemical properties and characterization of polymers, laser spectroscopy, solid-state nuclear magnetic resonance, neurophysiology, and computational neuroscience and cell biology.

Biology (M.A., M.S.): Dr. Patty Zwollo, Graduate Director (pxzwol@wm.edu). Program is designed for students who desire an intensive, closely mentored research experience and advanced biology training. Graduates go on to doctoral programs, including medicine and law as well as traditional Ph.D. programs in biology, or find employment in environmental analysis or pharmaceuticals/biotechnology.

Chemistry (M.A., M.S., joint M.S./Ph.D. program with Applied Science): Dr. Deborah Bebout, Graduate Director (dcbebo@wm.edu). Program offers a thesis-based degree in areas of biochemistry and organic, inorganic, physical, polymer, and analytical chemistry. The program is designed for students who desire additional academic experience before pursuing an industrial career, a professional degree, or a Ph.D. degree.

Computer Science (M.S., Ph.D.): Dr. Evgenia Smirni, Graduate Director (esmirni@cs.wm.edu or http://www.wm.edu/computerscience). Research areas include computer systems and architecture, parallel and distributed processing, high-performance computing, performance modeling and simulation, software engineering, networked and embedded computer systems, numerical linear algebra and optimization, parallel mesh generation, cryptography, security, and algorithms. Interdisciplinary research opportunities can be found nearby at NASA-Langley, Jefferson Lab, VIMS, and the Applied Science Department. In addition to the traditional M.S. degree in computer science the department offers an M.S. degree specialization in computational operations research. Detailed information is available at http://www.math.wm.edu/~leemis/or.html.

History (M.A., Ph.D.): Dr. Leisa Meyer, Graduate Director (gradap@wm.edu). Ph.D. students specialize in American history; M.A.-level students specialize in American or comparative history. In cooperation with the Omohundro Institute of Early American History and Culture, Colonial Williamsburg, and Swem Library, the department offers students practical work experience through apprenticeships in archives and manuscripts, scholarly publishing, humanities computing, historical archaeology, architectural history, and teaching.

Physics (M.S., Ph.D.): Dr. Marc Sher, Graduate Admissions (grad@physics.wm.edu). Research specialties include accelerator physics; atomic, molecular, and optical physics; nuclear and particle physics; plasma theory and nonlinear dynamics; condensed matter physics; and computational physics. Collaborative research efforts and the proximity of NASA-Langley and Jefferson Lab bring graduate students into contact with the international community.

Psychology (M.A.): Dr. Joshua Burk, Graduate Director (jabur2@wm.edu). M.A. program includes core courses in all major subfields, a yearlong statistics sequence, a professional development seminar, and opportunities to conduct research with faculty members whose publications are on a par with faculties in the top quarter of Ph.D.-granting institutions.

Public Policy (M.P.P., J.D./M.P.P. with law, M.B.A./M.P.P. with business, M.S./M.P.P. with marine science): Professor Elaine McBeth, Admissions Director (mcbeth@wm.edu). Two-year interdisciplinary program prepares students for careers in public service by combining training in quantitative techniques and economic analysis with political analysis and law.

SCHOOL OF BUSINESS

M.B.A., M.B.A./J.D., M.B.A./M.P.P., M.B.A./M.G.M.: Kathy Pattison, Director of M.B.A. Admissions (admissions@mason.wm.edu or http://mba.wm.edu). Led by a faculty who have been ranked third among the nation's best, William and Mary M.B.A. students transform their careers through the distinctive Career Acceleration Modules, which integrate advanced academic training in business with ongoing direct contact with companies and business experts. Career Acceleration Modules in Business to Business Marketing, Consumer Brand Management, Corporate Finance, Enterprise Engineering, Entrepreneurship, and Investments and Financial Services are offered. M.B.A. students receive individualized leadership and career coaching from a corps of executive partners who have worked at senior levels within business and represent a broad set of industries and experiences. In summer 2009 the Mason School of Business moved into Alan B. Miller Hall, its state-of-the-art, 160,000-square-foot new home.

M.Acc.: Martha Howard, Assistant Director, Master of Accounting Program (macc@mason.wm.edu or http://mason.wm.edu/macc). A full-time, two-semester residential program, the M.Acc. program offers a cutting-edge curriculum that includes valuation, a financial instruments module, and a trip to visit the regulators (SEC, FASB, PCAOB). Students may draw from accounting courses and M.B.A. electives to tailor the program according to their professional goals. The program accepts applications from accounting and non-accounting majors alike. The following prerequisites are required prior to admission: Principles of Accounting, Statistics, Financial Management, Introduction to Information Technology, Intermediate Accounting, and Auditing. Intermediate Accounting and Auditing are offered as intensive courses prior to the start of fall classes.

SCHOOL OF EDUCATION

M.Ed., M.A.Ed., Ed.D., Ed.S., Ph.D.: Thomas Ward, Associate Dean of Academic Programs (tjward@wm.edu or http://education.wm.edu). Nationally certified programs prepare teachers for elementary, middle, and secondary education; prepare specialists in counseling, gifted education, and school psychology; and prepare students for educational policy, planning, and leadership roles for K–12 and higher education. Programs are organized into three divisions: curriculum and instruction; educational policy, planning, and leadership; and school psychology and counseling education.

WILLIAM AND MARY SCHOOL OF LAW

J.D., LL.M., J.D./M.A. in American Studies, J.D./M.B.A., J.D./M.P.P.: Faye F. Shealy, Associate Dean of Admission (lawadm@wm.edu or http://www.wm.edu/law/). Established in 1779, William and Mary School of Law is the nation's oldest, located near Colonial Williamsburg and within easy driving distance of Norfolk, Richmond, and Washington, D.C. A nationally recognized law school, William and Mary is well-known for the innovative Legal Skills Program—a nationally recognized model for teaching professional skills and ethics. The technologically advanced McGlothlin Courtroom is home of the Center for Legal and Court Technology. The Institute of Bill of Rights Law sponsors programs on emerging constitutional issues. The Supreme Court Preview, held each fall, includes nationally known journalists and academic commentators. The faculty members include nationally and internationally recognized experts in a wide range of subjects. Students, faculty members, administrators, and staff members maintain an exceptionally collegial learning and scholarly community.

SCHOOL OF MARINE SCIENCE

M.S., M.S./M.P.P., Ph.D.: Iris Anderson, Dean of Graduate Studies (iris@vims.edu or http://www.vims.edu). The School of Marine Science (SMS), the educational program of the Virginia Institute of Marine Sciences (VIMS), offers both M.S. and Ph.D. degrees in marine sciences. Although emphasis is on the study of estuarine and coastal ecosystems, research is performed in marine ecosystems worldwide. The school is organized into four departments: biological sciences, environmental and aquatic animal health, fisheries sciences, and physical science (including physical, chemical, and geological oceanography). In addition, SMS/VIMS offers a joint program in marine and environmental policy with the Thomas Jefferson program in public policy. SMS/VIMS also contributes to the College-wide environmental science and policy curriculum. Considerable attention is also paid to advisory services and outreach in response to both policy and private needs and interests.

COLORADO SCHOOL OF MINES

Graduate School

Programs of Study

The Colorado School of Mines (CSM) offers graduate education and research in areas related to the environment, energy, minerals, and materials. Advanced degrees are offered in chemical engineering, chemistry, engineering and technology management, engineering systems, environmental science and engineering, geochemistry, geology and geological engineering, geophysics and geophysical engineering, hydrology, international political economy of resources, materials science, mathematical and computer sciences, metallurgical and materials engineering, mineral economics, mining and earth systems engineering, nuclear engineering, petroleum engineering, and applied physics.

The master's degree requirements vary across major departments, although a minimum of 30 credit hours must be met for both thesis and nonthesis master's. The School accepts a maximum of 9 semester hours of transfer credit for thesis degree programs and 15 semester hours for non-thesis degrees. Course work requirements for master's degree programs are established by the major departments.

Like master's degree programs, course work requirements for Ph.D. degrees are established by the major department. The minimum credit hour requirement for the Ph.D. degree is 72 hours beyond the bachelor's degree. At least 24 semester hours must be research credits earned under the supervision of a CSM faculty adviser, and at least 18 credit hours of course work must be applied to the degree program. Students with an earned master's degree may receive credit toward their Ph.D. requirements.

Professional master's degree programs emphasizing graduate-level work require a minimum of 30 hours of course work. These programs focus on emerging multidisciplinary fields of study and are designed to provide career-oriented skills and knowledge. Professional master's programs are offered in environmental geochemistry, mineral exploration and mining geosciences, and petroleum reservoir systems.

Graduate certificate programs are offered in international political economy through the Liberal Arts and International Studies Division. The program consists of two 15-hour certificates. Course work focuses in four areas: area studies; international political risk assessment and mitigation; geopolitics and economic geography; and global environmental politics and policies.

Research Facilities

CSM maintains twenty-five research centers and institutes dedicated to various aspects of research in the fields of environment, minerals, energy, and materials. Major areas include energy, exploration, mineral and petroleum production, environmental sciences and engineering, fuels science and engineering, materials science and engineering, automated and expert systems, and bioengineering (including bioenergy, biomaterials, and intelligent biomedical devices). Central Colorado is the home of numerous companies and high-tech industries working in these fields, and the nearby Rocky Mountains provide an excellent laboratory for educational fieldwork in the earth science disciplines. Located within a short distance of the CSM campus are valuable research facilities, including those of the U.S. Geological Survey, the National Park Service, the National Renewable Energy Laboratory, the U.S. Bureau of Reclamation, and the National Institute of Standards and Technology. CSM's proximity to the University of Colorado and Colorado State University provides opportunities for collaborative research and study in a wide variety of fields.

Financial Aid

Financial aid in the form of graduate research and teaching assistantships, as well as industrial, state, and federal fellowships, is available to full-time graduate students on a competitive basis. Financial assistance is provided to approximately 72 percent of all full-time graduate students.

Cost of Study

Tuition for the 2007–08 academic year was $4482 per semester for full-time state residents and $10,872 for full-time nonresidents. Part-time rates (between 4 and 9 credits) were $498 per credit for state residents and $1208 per credit for nonresidents. Student fees for all students are $643.50 per semester, and health insurance costs approximately $690 per semester.

Living and Housing Costs

Numerous options are available both on and off the campus. On-campus housing is available in the Mines Park complex. This apartment-style housing offers one-, two-, and three-bedroom apartments ranging from $650 to $1170 per month. Family housing is also available in this complex from $650 to $750 per month. There is a wide variety of private housing in the Golden and West Denver areas.

Student Group

The graduate enrollment of approximately 850 is composed of full- and part-time students. The latter are mainly practicing professionals working in the Denver area. Approximately 23 percent are international students, representing sixty-seven different nations. Approximately 27 percent of the graduate students are women.

Location

The School is located in Golden, a community of 15,000 people in the eastern foothills of the Rocky Mountains, about 15 minutes west of Denver. Colorado's world-famous ski resorts are a short drive from the campus, and the Rocky Mountains offer a variety of year-round outdoor activities. Hiking, backpacking, camping, fishing, hunting, bicycling, rock climbing, rafting, kayaking, and white-water canoeing are popular activities in Colorado. Golden's mild and dry climate has more than 300 sunny days a year.

The School

CSM offers engineering and applied science programs with a special focus on resource production and utilization. Founded in 1874 to support a growing mining industry in the Colorado territory, the school became the Colorado School of Mines when Colorado became a state in 1876. As the School grew, its mission widened from a focus on nonfuel minerals to encompass a broad range of engineering and science disciplines dealing with energy, minerals, materials, and the environment.

Applying

Interested individuals wishing to apply for graduate studies at the Colorado School of Mines should provide a duplicate set of transcripts from previous colleges, GRE scores, and three letters of recommendation along with the admissions application. Applications can be accessed online at the Web address listed in this In-Depth Description.

Correspondence and Information

Office of Graduate Studies
Colorado School of Mines
Golden, Colorado 80401

Phone: 303-273-3247
800-446-9488 (toll-free)
Fax: 303-273-3244
E-mail: grad-school@mines.edu
Web site: http://www.mines.edu/Admiss/grad

PROGRAMS, FACULTY HEADS, AND AREAS OF SPECIALIZATION

Chemical Engineering: Dr. James F. Ely, Head (303-273-3885). Advanced materials (nanocomposites, directed colloidal assemblies, microelectronics, photovoltaics, biobased materials), separation science and technologies (membranes for hydrogen separation, biorefining), theoretical and applied thermodynamics (molecular simulations, thermophysical properties), fuel cells (kinetic modeling, catalysts, membranes), computational chemistry, computer-aided process simulation, combustion science and engineering, mathematical modeling of transport processes, methane hydrates, microfluidics, microgravity combustion. Center for Hydrates, Center for Environmental Risk Assessment, Colorado Institute for Fuels and Energy Research, Colorado Institute for Macromolecular Science and Engineering, Center for Commercial Applications of Combustion in Space.

Chemistry and Geochemistry: Dr. Daniel M. Knauss, Head (303-273-3625). Environmental chemistry, exploration geochemistry, biogeochemistry, inorganic/organometallic chemistry, fuel chemistry, catalysis and surface chemistry, polymer chemistry, materials chemistry, NMR, separation science, mass spectrometry, computational chemistry, laser spectroscopy.

Economics and Business: Dr. Roderick G. Eggert, Director (303-273-3981). Applied microeconomics; energy, mineral, and environmental economics; engineering and technology management; quantitative business methods; project management; international trade and economic development; technology entrepreneurship; business and investment decision making, including operations research/operations management; decision making under uncertainty; discounted cash flow analysis; managing new product development; simulation; financial risk management; corporate finance. International joint-degree program in petroleum economics and management with Institut Français du Pétrole.

Engineering: Dr. Terry Parker, Director (303-273-3657). Chemically reacting flow as applied to combustion and material processing; geotechnical engineering; earthquake and structural engineering; intelligent signal processing and control as applied to manufacturing, robotics, biomechanics, and telecommunications; static and dynamic behavior of solid-state and granular materials; analysis, design, and control of electric power systems. Power Systems Engineering Research Center; Center for Automation, Robotics and Distributed Intelligence; Center for Combustion and Environmental Research; Center for Intelligent Biomedical Devices and Musculoskeletal Systems. Web site: http://egweb.mines.edu

Environmental Science and Engineering: Dr. Robert L. Siegrist, Director (303-384-2158). Water and waste reclamation and reuse; environmental biotechnology; environmental chemistry and radiochemistry; site characterization and remediation; environmental systems modeling. Center for Experimental Study of Subsurface Environmental Processes, Environmental Engineering Pilot Laboratory, Laboratory for Applied and Environmental Radiochemistry, Environmental Biotechnology Lab, CSM/Golden Water Treatment Pilot Plant, Mines Park Water Reclamation Test Site, Integrated Environmental Teaching Lab. Web site: http://www.mines.edu/academic/envsci/

Geology and Geological Engineering: Dr. John D. Humphrey, Head (303-273-3819). Predictive sediment modeling, aquifer-contaminant flow modeling, waste management, water-rock interactions, petroleum geology, mineral deposits, economic geology, geotechnical engineering, environmental geology, groundwater engineering, petrology, structural geology. International Groundwater Modeling Center.

Geophysics and Geophysical Engineering: Dr. Terence K. Young, Head (303-273-3454). Applied geophysics, including seismic exploration, seismic data processing, gravity and geomagnetic fields, electrical and electromagnetic mapping and sounding, ground-penetrating radar, petrophysics, borehole geophysics, well logging, satellite remote sensing, groundwater exploration and exploitation, geohazard mitigation, mathematical geophysics, environmental and geotechnical geophysics. Center for Wave Phenomena, Reservoir Characterization Project, Center for Petrophysics, Center for Rock Abuse, Gravity and Magnetics Research Consortium, Near-Surface Seismology Group. Web site: http://www.mines.edu/Academic/geophysics

Liberal Arts and International Studies: Dr. Laura Pang, Director (303-273-3595). Program offers a master's degree program in international political economy of resources and graduate certificate programs in international political economy. International political economy of area studies, international political economy of resources and the environment, theories of globalization, case studies of global corporations, international political risk assessment and mitigation, theories of international political economy, comparative development theories of regions, political economy of ethnicity, theories and empirical case studies of comparative regimes, global political geography, comparative political cultures.

Materials Science: Dr. John J. Moore, Program Director (303-273-3660). Bonding theory, ceramics, coatings, composites, surface engineering, thin-films and advanced coatings, electronic materials, joining science, materials chemistry, mechanics of materials, metal and alloy systems, phase transformations, photovoltaic materials, polymeric materials, biomaterials, nuclear materials, solid-state physics, solid-state thermodynamics, structural and structured defects, surfaces/interfaces, transport and kinetics. Center for Computation and Simulation for Materials and Engineering, Center for Solar and Electronic Materials.

Mathematical and Computer Sciences: Dr. Graeme Fairweather, Head (303-273-3860). Applied mathematics: direct and inverse scattering, inverse problems, micro-local analysis, numerical analysis, scientific computing, symbolic computing, wave propagation. Computer science: algorithms, computational geometry, computer networks, databases, graphics, machine learning, mobile computing, sensor networks, visualization. Statistics: biostatistics, epidemiological methods, statistical seismic data processing, statistical regularization of inverse problems. Actively participates in Center for Wave Phenomena; Center for Automation, Robotics and Distributed Intelligence.

Metallurgical and Materials Engineering: Dr. John J. Moore, Head (303-273-3770); Dr. Gerard P. Martins, Graduate Affairs (303-273-3798); Physical and Mechanical Metallurgy: Dr. Stephen Liu (303-273-3796), Dr. David Matlock (303-273-3775); Physicochemical Processing of Materials: Dr. Patrick Taylor (303-384-2130); Ceramic Engineering: Dr. Dennis Readey (303-273-3437). Ceramics glasses and thin films; castings; coatings; composites, intermetallics, and smart materials; corrosion; electronic materials; extractive metallurgy, waste processing, and recycling; forming; advanced NDE methods; nuclear materials; photovoltaics; process modeling and control; surface engineering; synthesis and processing of materials; welding and joining. Five Research Centers: Advanced Coatings and Surface Engineering Laboratory; Advanced Steel Processing and Products Research Center; Center for Welding, Joining, and Coatings Research; Colorado Center for Advanced Ceramics; W. J. Kroll Institute for Extractive Metallurgy.

Mining Engineering: Dr. Tibor G. Rozgonyi, Head (303-273-3653). Mine evaluation, planning and design, mine productivity analysis, mine automation and robotics, underground excavation, tunneling and geotechnical engineering, rock fragmentation and explosive engineering, rock mechanics, bulk material handling, mineral processing and mine environmental remediation and sustainable development. Earth Mechanics Research Institute, Edgar Experimental Mine and Western Mining Resource Center.

Petroleum Engineering: Dr. Ramona M. Graves, Head (303-273-3746). Reservoir management; field development; computer simulation; geostatistics; interdisciplinary integration of petroleum engineering, geology, and geophysics; petroleum economics; enhanced oil and gas production; subsidence; drilling in space and laser drilling; well completion design; sand control; dynamic rock mechanics; petrophysics; geochemistry; hydrocarbon hydrates; multiphase flow in pipelines; fluid flow in porous media; and environmental issues.

Physics: Dr. James A. McNeil, Head (303-273-3844). Applied optics: lasers, ultrafast optics and X-ray generation, spectroscopy, near-field and multiphoton microscopy, nonlinear optics. Nuclear: low-energy reactions, nuclear astrophysics, nuclear theory, fusion plasma diagnostics. Electronic materials: photovoltaics, nanostructures and quantum dots, thin-film semiconductors, transparent conductors, amorphous materials, magnetic materials. Solid state: X-ray diffraction, Raman spectroscopy, electron microscopy, self-assembled systems, condensed-matter theory. Surface and interfaces: X-ray photoelectron and Auger spectroscopy, scanning probe microscopy. Center for Commercial Applications of Combustion in Space.

Environmental science class being held in the foothills outside campus.

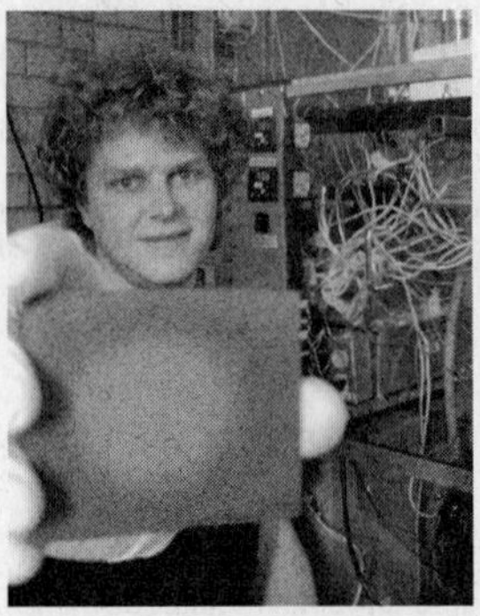

Materials science and physics students work on solar cell research.

CONCORDIA UNIVERSITY

School of Graduate Studies

Programs of Study

Concordia University offers programs leading to doctoral and master's degrees, graduate diplomas, and graduate certificates. Ph.D.'s are awarded in art education, art history, biology, building engineering, business administration, chemistry, civil engineering, communication, computer science, economics, education, electrical and computer engineering, film and moving image studies, history, mathematics, mechanical engineering, political science, psychology, and religion. There are also interdisciplinary programs that lead to the Ph.D. in humanities and the Ph.D. in a special individualized program. The minimum residence requirement is two years of full-time study or the equivalent in part-time study. All Ph.D. programs are a minimum of 90 credits. Students entering without having completed a master's degree normally require more time. It is rare to complete a Ph.D. in less than three years. All Ph.D. programs require a thesis.

Master's degrees (M.A., M.A.Sc., M.Sc., M.Eng., M.Comp.Sc., M.Ap.Comp.Sc., M.B.A., M.I.M., M.T.M., or M.F.A.) are available in applied linguistics, art education, art history, biology, business administration (executive option and professional), chemistry, child study, computer science, creative arts therapies, economics, educational studies, educational technology, engineering (aerospace, building, civil, electrical, and mechanical), English, environmental impact assessment, exercise science, film studies, geography, planning and environment, history, history and philosophy of religion, human systems intervention, industrial engineering, information systems security, investment management, journalism studies, Judaic studies, littératures francophones et résonances médiatiques, mathematics, media studies, philosophy, psychology, public policy and public administration, quality systems engineering, religion, social and cultural anthropology, sociology, software engineering, studio arts, teaching of mathematics, theological studies, and traductologie. Most master's programs require 45 credits and have a one year's minimum residence. Programs in business administration, creative arts therapies, studio arts, and educational technology require more than 45 credits and take proportionately longer. Many master's programs have a nonthesis option.

Graduate diplomas are offered in adult education, advanced music performance, biotechnology and genomics, business administration, chartered accountancy, communication studies, community economic development, computer science, economics, environmental impact assessment, instructional technology, investment management, journalism, and traduction. Diploma programs are 30 or more credits, normally take one year of full-time study, and do not require a thesis.

Graduate certificates are offered in anglais-français en langue et techniques de localisation, building engineering, business administration, digital technologies in design art practice, environmental engineering, management accounting, mechanical engineering, music therapy, service engineering and network management, and 3-D graphics and game development. Graduate certificates are normally 15 credits, can be completed in one year, and do not require a thesis.

One credit is deemed the equivalent of 45 hours of work by the student, which includes lectures, laboratory sessions, seminars, research, and preparation of assignments. The minimum full-time credit load for an individual graduate student is 24 credits over twelve months.

Research Facilities

The University's libraries have a rapidly expanding collection of reference and research materials and an extensive collection of government documents and newspapers on microfilm, microfiche, and microcard. The expanded Vanier Library houses unusual special collections. The main library has been designated a full depository library for Canadian federal government documents. Various cooperative arrangements exist with other research libraries in the Montreal area. Modern buildings house the well-equipped engineering and science laboratories, used for both teaching and research.

Financial Aid

Scholarships and fellowships are available on a competitive basis; Concordia fellowships are currently valued at $2900 per term (master's level) and $3600 per term (doctoral level). All dollar amounts are in Canadian funds. Certain fellowships have a higher value. Work at the University in the form of part-time lecturer contracts, teaching assistantships, and research assistantships is limited. Information about the possibility of this kind of work is available from the graduate program in which the applicant hopes to enroll. The Graduate Awards Directory, available on the School of Graduate Studies Web site listed in the Correspondence and Information section, gives details about many awards tenable at Concordia and elsewhere. International students are strongly advised to apply for awards available to them from their own country or through agencies in their own country.

Cost of Study

For 2009–10, tuition for Québec residents is $1155 per term (second- and third-cycle programs) and for non-Québec residents, $2033 per term (second-cycle programs) and $1155 per term (third-cycle programs); tuition for international students is $4025 (JMSB) and $4351 (all other students) per term. Students pay a number of miscellaneous fees, which are assessed at the time of registration. International students must also pay approximately $865 for health insurance per year.

Living and Housing Costs

The expenses for a single student for an eight-month stay total approximately $21,000 (lodging, food, and transportation, $18,000; books and supplies, $1000; clothing, $500; and miscellaneous, $1500).

Student Group

There are approximately 6,500 graduate students enrolled in the University. A significant number are bilingual and/or come from multicultural backgrounds.

Location

Montreal is the second-largest city in Canada, with a population of nearly 3 million. Roughly three quarters of the population is French speaking. Montreal has all the attractions one would expect of a large cosmopolitan area: many theatres and museums, a rich musical life, numerous places of historic interest, and beautiful parks, including the famous Mount Royal Park. The climate is variable, with temperatures ranging from 30°C in summer to -20°C in winter.

The University

Concordia University is one of four universities in the Montreal area. It was formed in 1974, when Sir George Williams University and Loyola College of Montreal merged the green spaces of the Loyola Campus and the urban downtown campus of Sir George Williams to complement each other. There are approximately 30,000 students enrolled in graduate and undergraduate programs. An interuniversity agreement makes it possible for graduate students to elect a certain number of their courses from any one of Montreal's four universities regardless of where they are enrolled.

Applying

Applicants can apply online at http://connect2.concordia.ca. There is a $100 application fee. Along with the application form, applicants must provide three academic assessments and arrange for official transcripts of university-level work to be sent directly by the registrar of the institution attended. Application deadlines vary for each program. While most students begin their degrees in the fall term, some programs accept students in the summer or the winter term. The deadline for financial aid applications is December 15.

Correspondence and Information

School of Graduate Studies
Concordia University
1455 de Maisonneuve Boulevard, West
Montreal, Québec H3G 1M8
Canada

Phone: 514-848-2424 Ext. 3800
Fax: 514-842-2812
Web site: http://graduatestudies.concordia.ca

FACULTY RESEARCH AREAS

Accountancy: financial and management accountancy, behavioural accountancy, accountancy education, auditing, management control in nonprofit organizations.
Administration: international financing consortia, efficiency of capital markets, financing of small and medium-sized businesses, corporate finance, capital markets, business economics.
Aerospace: aeronautics and propulsion, avionics and control, structures and materials, space engineering.
Applied Human Sciences: applications of group development and small-group leadership, organizational development and change interventions, cross-cultural perspectives of management and leadership, coaching and mentoring relationships, community intervention.
Applied Linguistics: teaching English as a second/foreign language, second language learning, evaluation of language programs, teacher education for second/foreign language learning.
Art Education: development of symbolization and aesthetic response in children; the early development of artists; history of art education; museum education; adult education; multicultural and aboriginal issues; women in art and art education; built environment education; response to art; postmodernism; digital technologies and art education, ethnography; life history; oral history; action research; descriptive research; feminist research; video and photographic documentation; community-based video; studio-based inquiry; studio theory and practice.
Art History: Amerindian and Inuit art and architecture; North American architecture, craft, painting, photography, and sculpture, as well as other media, from the seventeenth to the twenty-first centuries; European art and theory from the Middle Ages to the present; art criticism; cultural studies; feminist and gender studies; industrial archaeology and museum studies.
Biology: animal biology and behaviour, cell biology/biochemistry, ecology and conservation, microbiology/molecular biology, plant biochemistry, biotechnology and genomics.
Building Engineering: computer-aided design, performance of building envelope and materials, building environment (HVAC, acoustics, illumination, air quality), building and energy, wind effects on buildings, building structures and construction management.
Business Administration: Ph.D., professional M.B.A., Executive M.B.A.
Chemistry and Biochemistry: analytical and bioanalytical chemistry, biochemistry and biophysical chemistry, bioinorganic and physical inorganic chemistry, organic and physical organic chemistry, computational chemistry, materials and solid-state chemistry, synthetic inorganic chemistry.
Child Study: children's social behaviour in day-care settings, children and technology, historical perspectives on child care, early childhood curriculum, popular culture of youth and children, health and well-being, gender issues, teaching and teacher education, family and children, international issues in early childhood education, learning and cognition and educational psychology.
Civil Engineering: structural engineering, bridge engineering, structural mechanics, earthquake engineering, water resources, fluids engineering, geotechnical engineering, transportation.
Communication: information and communication technologies and society, media and cultural studies, discourse studies, organizational communication and networks of communication, international communication and development, media creation, design and practices.
Computer Science and Software Engineering: computer systems and VLSI architecture, database and information systems, parallel and distributed computing, mathematics of computation, pattern recognition, artificial intelligence, image processing, programming languages and methodology, software engineering, theoretical computer science.
Creative Arts Therapies: art psychotherapy, rehabilitation through art and drama, sand-play therapy, guided imagery in music, development and creative art therapy assessments, narrative therapy, storytelling as therapeutic process, art and psychoanalysis (postmodern theory French School of Thought).
Economics: economic theory, economic development and planning, financial economics, public economics, international economics, industrial economics, labour economics, econometrics, mathematical economics.
Educational Studies: adult education, education of immigrants and minorities, sociology of education and issues of difference in the classroom, political education, philosophy and history of education, women and development, curricular debate, various aspects of adult learning and professional development, literacy and education, education in developing countries.
Educational Technology: human performance technology, human resources development, educational cybernetics, systems analysis and design, media research and development, distance education.
Electrical and Computer Engineering: systems, control, and robotics; circuits and systems; communications; computer communications and protocols; signal processing; high-performance architecture; software engineering; VLSI systems; microelectronics; microwaves and optoelectronics; antennas and electromagnetic compatibility; power electronics and adjustable speed drives.
English: English literature from the Middle Ages to the present; European, Canadian, American, and postcolonial literature; genres; creative writing; composition; women's literature.
Environmental Impact Assessment: river management, climate change, urban design, immigration, sustainable forestry, landscape ecology, indigenous resource management, political ecology, sustainable transportation, population and environment, economic development, and metropolitan government.
Études françaises: littératures francophones, writing, translation, court interpretation.
Exercise Science: athletic therapy, clinical exercise physiology.
Film Studies: Canadian film, experimental film, gay and lesbian filmmaking, experimental documentary and ethnography, Third World cinemas and auteur studies, film acting, film and philosophy, Japanese cinema, Indian cinema, documentary film, feminist theory, film theory and American cinema.
Geography, Planning, and Environment: policy-oriented studies, with an emphasis on urban, environmental, and social issues, including watershed management, port development and planning, urban design, immigration, sustainable forestry, indigenous resource management, and metropolitan government.
History: Histories of the Americas and of Europe, India, East Asia, the Middle East, and Africa; subfields and genres cluster around five main themes: culture; gender and sexuality; public history and memory; international and transnational history; and genocide and human rights.
Humanities: interdisciplinary doctoral studies in the humanities, social sciences, and fine arts.
Information Systems Engineering: information systems security, service engineering and network management, 3-D graphics and game development.
Journalism: ethics, Québec media, broadcast public affairs.
Mathematics: number theory–computational algebra, mathematical physics–differential geometry, dynamical systems, statistics–actuarial mathematics, mathematics education.
Mechanical and Industrial Engineering: computational fluid dynamics, industrial control systems and robotics, composites, mechanical systems and manufacturing, microfabrication and micromechatronics, thermofluid and propulsion, biomedical and human factor engineering, vehicle systems engineering, industrial engineering.
Music: advanced music performance, music therapy.
Philosophy: epistemology and metaphysics; logic, semantics and philosophy of science; ethics and political theory; history of philosophy.
Physics: quantum and high-energy physics, condensed-matter physics, theoretical physics, applied physics.
Political Science: public policy and public administration, Canadian and Québec politics, international politics, comparative politics, political theory.
Psychology: behavioural neuroscience, clinical and health research, human development and developmental processes, cognitive science.
Quality Systems Engineering: quality systems engineering, service engineering and network management, 3-D graphics and game development.
Religion: comparative religious ethics; ancient, medieval, and modern Judaism; women and religion; Christianity; Islam; Hinduism; Buddhism; sociology and philosophy of religion; new religious movements.
Social and Cultural Anthropology: gender from a cross-cultural perspective, economic anthropology, legal anthropology, anthropological linguistics, development, urban anthropology, community, ethnic studies, ethnographic writing, visual anthropology, information technologies, popular culture, youth culture, race, the politics of identity, globalization and transnationalism.
Sociology: research interests range from new rural economy and development to race and ethnic relations, comparative social history, social theory, and cultural sociology.
Specialized Individualized Programs: innovative studies that cross more than one recognized field.
Studio Arts: film production, open media, painting, photography, print media, sculpture, ceramics and fibres.
Theological Studies: Biblical periods, patristic age, fundamental and applied ethics, spirituality and contemporary theology.

DARTMOUTH COLLEGE

DARTMOUTH COLLEGE

Graduate School

Programs of Study

Dartmouth awards the A.M. degree in comparative literature and digital music and the M.S. degree in computer science; earth sciences; health policy and clinical practice sciences; and physics. The Ph.D. degree is awarded in biochemistry, biology, chemistry, cognitive neuroscience, computer science, earth sciences, engineering sciences, evaluative clinical sciences, experimental and molecular medicine, genetics, mathematics, microbiology and immunology, pharmacology and toxicology, physics and astronomy, physiology, and psychological and brain sciences. A special program leading to the degree of Master of Arts in Liberal Studies (M.A.L.S.) is also offered. Cross-disciplinary training programs are offered in environmental sciences, molecular and cellular biology, and nanomaterials.

Graduate degrees are also offered by the professional Schools of Medicine (M.D.), Engineering (M.E.M., M.S., Ph.D.), and Business Administration (M.B.A.).

Dartmouth's graduate programs are small and selective and are designed to provide more flexibility than the traditional Ph.D. program usually allows. Breadth within the discipline, significant teaching experience, and a broadly conceived research-thesis project are the basic elements in each of the graduate programs. Research achievement is naturally the most fundamental aspect of the Ph.D. program, and the limited enrollment in each program ensures the student a close apprentice/colleague relationship with his or her research supervisor. Most students are expected to teach during part of their graduate career, and considerable emphasis is placed on carefully supervised teaching experience of increasing responsibility.

Research Facilities

Several significant research and teaching facilities at Dartmouth have been designed to encourage contact and intellectual exchange among scholars in related disciplines. The Sherman Fairchild Physical Sciences Center and the Burke Chemistry Laboratory building house programs in earth sciences, chemistry, and physics and provide a common library, service shops, and computing facilities. Similarly, the Gilman-Remsen-Vail cluster provides overlapping facilities and space for training in biochemistry, biology, molecular cell biology, genetics, microbiology and immunology, pharmacology, and physiology. Moore Hall provides modern facilities for training in psychological and brain sciences, including the first MRI in the country dedicated to basic research. Kemeny Hall (mathematics program) and MacLean Engineering Sciences Center (engineering sciences) embody Dartmouth's integrative approach to research and learning. Finally, state-of-the-art research facilities at the Dartmouth-Hitchcock Medical Complex provide a rich training environment for programs in experimental and molecular medicine, microbiology and immunology, pharmacology and toxicology, and physiology.

All residence halls, classrooms, laboratories, and offices are networked at Dartmouth. Innovative ways are used to integrate personal computers into the curriculum, administration, and operation as well as the daily life of all members of the Dartmouth community. More than 12,000 network ports, a campuswide wireless network, and a variety of utilities make access to central computers and the Internet easy. The computing services group also maintains several clusters of personal computers and workstations throughout the campus for faculty student use. Berry Library, at the geographic and intellectual hub of the campus, houses the central machine room with a wide variety of computers for academic and administrative needs and general-purpose use. The center is open 24 hours a day, seven days a week and is a centrally located hub of information technology activity.

Financial Aid

Most students in the Ph.D. programs receive financial assistance through a program of scholarships, fellowships, and loans. These are made possible by Dartmouth funds and by federal and private fellowships and traineeships. Dartmouth is an authorized lender under the Federal Stafford Student Loan program. In 2007–08, fellowships for first-year students carried stipends of $1872 per month plus a scholarship covering full tuition. Insofar as is consistent with the duration of individual awards, each student's program of course work, teaching, and research is designed to promote most effectively his or her academic progress without reference to the source of financial support.

Cost of Study

Tuition for the academic year 2008–09 was $36,690. Full tuition scholarships are generally awarded to all admitted students.

Living and Housing Costs

The College assists graduate students in arranging for appropriate housing, either in College facilities or in private accommodations in the Hanover area. College-owned apartments are available at various rents for graduate students.

Student Group

Dartmouth is coeducational. The undergraduate student body numbers approximately 4,100. The graduate and professional school enrollment is about 1,670; approximately 600 of these students are enrolled in the graduate programs of arts and sciences.

Location

Dartmouth College is located in Hanover, New Hampshire, a town of about 6,000 on the border of New Hampshire and Vermont. Hanover is less than 3 hours' driving distance from Boston and Albany and about 4 hours from Montreal. The Hanover area provides excellent opportunities for hiking, canoeing, climbing, and skiing and is near many of northern New England's lake and skiing resorts.

The College

The Hopkins Center for the Performing Arts serves as the cultural focus of the College. The center sponsors an active film society, two full concert series, and a very active drama program. In addition, all students and faculty members have access to workshops for sculpture, painting, and various craft forms as well as to membership in various choral and instrumental music groups. Dartmouth also makes available to its graduate students the extensive facilities of the Dartmouth Outing Club and the Dartmouth College Athletic Council.

Applying

Applications may be submitted online through Dartmouth's Graduate Studies Web site or through individual graduate programs. In general, applications require a completed application form, undergraduate transcripts, three letters of recommendation, and scores from the General Test of the Graduate Record Examinations. Particular details and additional application information can be obtained from each graduate program. Dartmouth College is committed to its policy of nondiscrimination. A statement of this policy and the mechanism for redress of grievances can be found in the College's *Affirmative Action Plan*. For a copy, interested students should call 603-646-3197.

Correspondence and Information

Department of (specify intended major)
Dartmouth College
Hanover, New Hampshire 03755-3526
Phone: 603-646-6578
E-mail: sandra.j.spiegel@dartmouth.edu
Web site: http://www.dartmouth.edu/~gradstdy/

DEANS AND DEPARTMENTAL CHAIRS

Brian Pogue, Dean of Graduate Studies.
Gary L. Hutchins, Assistant Dean of Graduate Studies.

Biochemistry
Professor Charles Barlowe, Dartmouth Medical School, 7200 Remsen Building, Room 407 (telephone: 603-650-6516).

Biological Sciences
Professor Thomas Jack, 6044 Gilman Hall (telephone: 603-646-3367).

Chemistry
Professor David Glueck, 6128 Burke Hall (telephone: 603-646-1568).

Comparative Literature
Professor Silvia Spitta, 6051 Reed Hall (telephone: 603-646-6498).

Computer Science
Professor Prasad Jayanti, 6211 Sudikoff Laboratory (telephone: 603-646-1292).

Earth Sciences
Professor Carl Renshaw, 6105 Fairchild Hall (telephone: 603-646-3365).

The Dartmouth Institute for Health Policy and Clinical Practice
Professor Ann Flood, Dartmouth Medical School (telephone: 603-653-0854).

Experimental and Molecular Medicine
Professor Murray Korc, Dartmouth-Hitchcock Medical Complex, One Medical Center Drive (telephone: 603-650-7936).

Genetics
Professor Jay Dunlap, Dartmouth Medical School, 7400 Remsen Hall, Room 701 (telephone: 603-650-1108).

Master of Arts in Liberal Studies
Professor Don Pease, 6092 Wentworth Hall, Room 116 (telephone: 603-646-3592).

Mathematics
Professor Dan Rockmore, 6188 Bradley Hall (telephone: 603-646-3260).

Microbiology and Immunology
Professor Randolph Noelle, Dartmouth Medical School, 7556 Borwell, Room 603W (telephone: 603-650-8607).

Molecular and Cellular Biology
Professor Dean Madden, Dartmouth Medical School, 406C Vail, (telephone: 603-650-1164).

Music
Professor Larry Polansky, 6187 Hopkins Center (telephone: 603-646-2139).

Pharmacology and Toxicology
Professor Ethan Dmitrovsky, Dartmouth Medical School, 7650 Remsen Hall, Room 523 (telephone: 603-650-1667).

Physics and Astronomy
Professor Jay Lawrence, 6127 Wilder Laboratory (telephone: 603-646-2963).

Physiology
Professor Hermes Yeh, Dartmouth Medical School, 7700 Borwell (telephone: 603-660-7717).

Psychological and Brain Sciences
Professor Ann Clark, 353 Moore Hall (telephone: 603-646-3036).

Thayer School of Engineering
Professor Brian Pogue, 8000 Cummings Hall (telephone: 603-646-3861).

The Sherman Fairchild Physical Sciences Center.

Research lab in Sherman Fairchild Physical Sciences Center.

The Burke Chemistry Laboratory building.

DOMINICAN COLLEGE

Graduate Programs

Programs of Study

Dominican College offers a doctoral program in physical therapy (PT) as well as master's degree programs in business administration, childhood education, nursing (family nurse practitioner), occupational therapy (OT), and special education. These programs are offered in formats that take into consideration the professional and personal commitments of working adults. The business administration program is offered in the evening in an accelerated format. The nursing program is offered in an evening format, with each class meeting once a week. The occupational therapy, physical therapy, childhood education, and special education programs are offered on weekends; classes are offered approximately every third weekend.

The Doctor of Physical Therapy (D.P.T.) degree program, introduced in summer 2005, offers three options to accommodate students from a variety of educational backgrounds. Students who possess bachelor's degrees may apply directly to the entry-level D.P.T. program without first completing a master's degree program. Freshmen undergraduate students may enroll in a dual-degree option in biology and physical therapy (B.A./D.P.T. degree), which enables them to overlap their fourth year of undergraduate studies with the first year of doctoral studies. Licensed physical therapists can pursue the transitional doctoral degree (tD.P.T.) in two trimesters. Both the entry-level D.P.T. and the tD.P.T. are offered in a weekend format and are combined with online learning, allowing students to pursue other responsibilities during the week. The Doctor of Physical Therapy program at Dominican College is accredited by the National Commission on Physical Therapy Education and is registered by the New York State Education Department.

The M.S. in nursing, the family nurse practitioner program, is designed to prepare an advanced-practice family nurse practitioner. The curriculum for the master's degree program integrates current trends in nurse practitioner research, practice, and education. Emphasis is placed on integration of practice and theory across diverse settings where primary care is delivered within the context of family-centered care. Students engage in classroom instruction and experiential teaching and learning opportunities that prepare them in assessment, role development, and in-depth clinical practice. Students are encouraged to take electives that strengthen teaching, clinical practice, and/or research interests. The program is accredited by the Commission on Collegiate Nursing Education (CCNE).

The College offers an entry-level B.S./M.S. degree in occupational therapy for new college students, transfers, COTAs, and students holding other degrees. The program prepares its graduates for entry-level practice and provides graduates with the skills necessary to respond to societal trends and changes in human services. Its problem-solving approach develops the student's clinical reasoning and critical-thinking skills. The program is fully accredited by the Accreditation Council for Occupational Therapy Education (ACOTE) of the American Occupational Therapy Association (AOTA).

The College offers three M.S.Ed. degree programs. One program leads to certification as a teacher of students with disabilities, including those with multiple and severe disabilities. The second program focuses on certifying teachers of the blind and visually impaired, and the third is designed for aspiring teachers who majored in a field other than education and leads to certification in childhood education.

The primary goal of the Master of Business Administration program is to prepare adults for obtaining professional opportunities in any of the functional areas of business by providing them with sound theoretical and practical knowledge in all of those areas. The program is tailored for students interested in broad-based study in the area of business administration. In addition, students who elect to do so may select courses that will allow them to specialize in the area of human resource management.

Research Facilities

All the graduate programs require research by way of projects or papers. Dominican College has an Institutional Review Board that adheres to federal policy on all research activities involving human subjects. The College supports research activities by providing online databases that can be accessed in the library, computer laboratories, and the residence halls as well as from off-campus locations. These online databases include First Search, Proquest Direct, Country Watch, Ebscohest, Mergent Online, Inotrac, Serial Solution, and PubMedical. In addition, the new Center for Health and Science Education opened in 2005 and provides state-of-the-art labs.

Financial Aid

The Financial Aid Office assists graduate students with obtaining various kinds of loans. Some students may be eligible for federal/state aid.

Cost of Study

For the academic year 2009–10, the tuition for the master's-level courses was $670 per credit.

Living and Housing Costs

Since the graduate programs meet in a weekend or evening format and the participants are active professionals, students choose to commute from their homes.

Student Group

The College has a total student body of over 1,900 graduate and undergraduate students.

Student Outcomes

The programs are intended to prepare professionals in their respective fields. They provide significant enhancement of skills for those students who are already working in their field and allow for professional development and career enhancement.

Location

The College is located in Rockland County, New York. The beautiful Hudson Valley campus is located 17 miles north of New York City and 3 miles north of Bergen County, New Jersey. The College is easily reached by car or public transportation and from the major airports of New York and New Jersey.

The College

Dominican College, founded by the sisters of St. Dominic of Blauvelt, New York, in 1952, is chartered by the University of the State of New York and accredited by the Middle States Association of Colleges and Schools. Dominican College is an independent four-year liberal arts college offering undergraduate degrees in more than thirty disciplines, with graduate programs in five areas of study. The College does not discriminate on the basis of sex, race, color, religion, disability, or national or ethnic origin.

Applying

Applicants for master's degree programs must have a bachelor's degree from an accredited college or university. They should submit a completed application along with the application fee, three letters of recommendation, and transcripts from all institutions attended. Each program has specific additional admissions requirements.

Correspondence and Information

Joyce Elbe
Director of Admissions
Dominican College
470 Western Highway
Orangeburg, New York 10962

Phone: 866-4DC-INFO (toll-free)
Fax: 845-365-3150
E-mail: admissions@dc.edu
Web site: http://www.dc.edu

THE FACULTY

Sandra Countee, Associate Professor of Occupational Therapy and Program Director, Occupational Therapy Program; Ph.D., NYU.
Michael Galuchi, Associate Professor and Program Director, Physical Therapy Program; Ed.D., Columbia Teachers College.
Sr. Beryl Herdt, Professor of Allied Health and Coordinator of Graduate Studies; Ph.D., St. John's (New York).
Ken Mias, Assistant Professor of Business Administration and Director, M.B.A. Program; M.B.A., LIU.
Rona Shaw, Professor of Special Education and Coordinator of Graduate Education Programs; Ed.D., Columbia Teachers College.
Lynne Weissman, Assistant Professor of Nursing and Coordinator of the Graduate Family Nurse Practitioner Program; M.S., Columbia; PNP.

The fully equipped 25,000-square-foot Hennessy Center is available to all students and features a 1,000-seat gymnasium, physical fitness center, suspended track, locker rooms, athletic department offices, and a multipurpose room for student gatherings.

The Granito Center gives students access to a student health center, a video conferencing center and satellite downlink facility, a bookstore, and dining services.

Commencement.

DRAKE UNIVERSITY

Graduate Programs

Programs of Study

Drake University offers top-quality programs leading to master's, specialist, and doctoral degrees. The College of Business and Public Administration offers the Master of Business Administration (M.B.A.), the Master of Public Administration (M.P.A.), the Master of Accounting (M.Acc.), and the Master of Financial Management (M.F.M.). All programs are fully accredited by AACSB International–The Association to Advance Collegiate Schools of Business. The M.B.A. and M.P.A. may be combined with a degree in law or pharmacy. Although the joint programs require full-time enrollment, students seeking graduate programs within the College of Business and Public Administration alone may enroll on either a full-time or part-time basis, since most courses are offered as evening classes. Drake also offers a Master of Communication Leadership (M.C.L.) program. This is a unique and specialized master's-level program designed to prepare professionals working in communication-related jobs with the skill set to excel as leaders and decision makers in the communication profession. The program's curriculum blends course work from both the College of Business and Public Administration and the School of Journalism and Mass Communication.

The School of Education offers a variety of degree programs and numerous endorsements. A limited number of endorsements are offered online. Degrees include the Master of Arts in Teaching (M.A.T.) and Master of Science in Teaching (M.S.T.), which are designed to help individuals become certified elementary or secondary school teachers while earning a master's degree. Additional degrees include the Master of Science (M.S.) in adult learning and organizational performance, rehabilitation administration, and rehabilitation placement. Also offered is a Master of Science in counseling with concentrations in elementary and secondary school counseling, mental health counseling, and rehabilitation counseling. The Master of Science in Education (M.S.E.) is offered in educational leadership, effective teaching and learning, and special education. The Educational Specialist (Ed.S.) and Doctor of Education (Ed.D.) are offered in education leadership.

The College of Pharmacy and Health Sciences offers the Doctor of Pharmacy (Pharm.D.) degree and joint programs. Through joint degree programs, students may obtain a Pharm.D. degree combined with advanced degrees in business, law, and public administration.

Drake Law School, one of the twenty-five oldest law schools in the country, offers the J.D. and joint programs. Through joint degree programs, students may obtain a degree in law combined with advanced degrees in business, public administration, political science, social work, or agricultural economics.

Research Facilities

State-of-the-art physical facilities are available in many disciplines. The Morgan E. Cline Hall of Pharmacy and Health Sciences provides students with technologically advanced research resources. Cowles Library collections include more than 600,000 books and journals, 100,000 federal and state government documents, 777,000 microform records, 118 electronic databases, and approximately 22,000 scholarly online journals. Computer labs are available in both the Cowles and Law Libraries and around campus. The Dwight D. Opperman Hall and Law Library is a wireless environment containing extensive computer and Web resources, numerous study areas and rooms, and more than 330,000 volumes.

Financial Aid

The Office of Student Financial Planning offers financial information and services to graduate students. Graduate assistantships are available in a limited number of areas and are administered and awarded through application to specific departments. Student loans (for U.S. citizens only) and part-time employment, both on- and off-campus, are also available. The Office of Student Financial Planning also has information about other scholarship possibilities. Students working for companies that offer tuition assistance may enroll in the Employer Tuition Deferment Plan. This plan provides the option of a delayed payment based on the anticipated tuition reimbursement provided by the student's employer.

Cost of Study

Tuition within the College of Business and Public Administration, the School of Journalism and Mass Communication, and the School of Education is charged on a per-credit-hour basis. The M.B.A., M.Acc., and M.F.M. programs are currently $495 per credit hour; the M.P.A. is $445; and programs within the School of Education are $380 per credit hour. Students attending the Pharm.D. and law degree programs are generally full-time students and are charged the current full-time tuition rates of $27,320 and $28,850, respectively.

Living and Housing Costs

The cost of living in the Des Moines area is low compared to many metropolitan areas, particularly in housing expenses. Numerous housing options are available within the Drake neighborhood and are within walking distance of the campus. On-campus adult student housing is quite limited. Off-campus rent varies but generally ranges from $450 to $700 per month.

Student Group

Approximately 2,400 students are enrolled in Drake's graduate, law, and pharmacy programs. Of those, more than 950 are full-time law and pharmacy students. Graduate programs other than law and pharmacy offer the majority of courses either in the evening or on weekends, which allows many adults who are working full-time to pursue their degree while continuing to work. Students find that attendance with other professionals in the area brings an added dimension to their experience, as does attending class with 300 international students representing more than fifty countries. Faculty members are available to assist and advise students and to supervise their research. Classes are small enough to allow for maximum interaction.

Student Outcomes

Drake alumni live in all fifty states and many countries and hold positions as corporate CEOs, teachers, journalists, and state Supreme Court justices. Drake graduates are leaders in their fields, including education, business, journalism, pharmacy, and law. Upon graduation, students who are currently working and attending classes on a part-time basis are prepared to advance within their companies or to seek other opportunities. Those not yet in the work world are not only prepared for their first employment opportunity, but also for advancement beyond their first position. Drake is known for educating students for the variety of careers they may have throughout their lifetimes and for teaching students to be flexible and manage and create positive change. The graduating class of 2007 had an overall placement rate of 99.1 percent.

Location

Drake University's scenic campus is located in a residential neighborhood in Des Moines, a city of 450,000 people. As Iowa's capital and largest city, Des Moines is a metropolitan center for business (especially insurance), government, publishing, broadcasting, advertising, and the arts. The quality of life is enriched by the people of Iowa, who are noted for their friendliness, honesty, strong work ethic, and educational values. The Des Moines International Airport, which is served by major airlines, is just 15 minutes by car from the safe campus, and the University's 150-acre community is within 10 minutes of downtown Des Moines. Des Moines was named by *Kiplinger's Personal Finance* as one of the country's fifteen "super cities" where "people are moving and opportunity is knocking." Because of its central U.S. location, the climate in Iowa has a cycle of four distinct seasons.

The University

Founded in 1881, Drake University is a highly ranked private, independent university that is nationally recognized for teaching excellence and academic reputation within a student-centered learning environment. The University is accredited by the North Central Association of Colleges and Schools, and professional programs are accredited by their corresponding professional associations. Drake's faculty members are very accessible for advising and mentoring, and the overall student-faculty ratio is 15:1. More than 95 percent of the faculty members hold the highest degree in their fields.

Applying

Applications may be obtained from the Office of Graduate Admission, or students may link to an online application or download the form at http://www.drake.edu/graduate/applying/. Most programs offer rolling admission; however, applications to the doctoral programs and certain other programs do have specific deadlines. Some programs also offer admission for the fall term only; most consider students for fall, spring, and summer admission. Students must submit the application for admission, application fee, official transcripts from each college or university previously attended, and appropriate entrance examination official score reports (when required), two letters of recommendation, an essay indicating why the applicant wishes to pursue the program, and a copy of a current resume, as well as any additional information specified by the department to which the student is applying.

Correspondence and Information

Ann J. Martin, Graduate Coordinator
Office of Graduate Admission
Drake University
2507 University Avenue
Des Moines, Iowa 50311

Phone: 515-271-3871
800-443-7253 Ext. 3871 (toll-free in the U.S.)
Fax: 515-271-2831
E-mail: gradadmission@drake.edu
ann.martin@drake.edu
Web site: http://www.drake.edu

Drake University

FACULTY HEADS

David Maxwell, President; Ph.D., Brown.
Ronald J. Troyer, Provost; Ph.D., Western Michigan.

Web Sites by School or College
College of Business and Public Administration: http://www.cbpa.drake.edu
College of Pharmacy and Health Sciences: http://www.drake.edu/cphs
Law School: http://www.law.drake.edu
School of Education: http://www.drake.edu/soe
School of Journalism and Mass Communication: http://www.drake.edu/journalism/sjmcsite/

DREW UNIVERSITY

The Caspersen School of Graduate Studies

Programs of Study

The Caspersen School of Graduate Studies offers students an opportunity to pursue graduate studies in a setting that emphasizes small class size, individual attention from faculty members, and the ability to explore a wide range of scholarly interests.

The globally focused Master of Arts in Teaching (M.A.T.) program offers a one-year full-time track and a two-year part-time track. M.A.T. students learn leading-edge pedagogies while studying deeply in one of six content areas (biology, chemistry, English, math, social studies, or Spanish).

The low-residency Master of Fine Arts in Poetry and Poetry in Translation program offers some of America's most talented poets as faculty mentors who work one-on-one with students. The program is divided into two 10-day on-campus residencies and two mentorship semesters each year.

Drew also offers an interdisciplinary Arts and Letters program (M.Litt., D.Litt.), emphasizing broad competence in the liberal arts, and an innovative Medical Humanities program (M.M.H.; D.M.H.), conducted jointly by Drew and Raritan Bay Medical Center. Medical Humanities addresses topics such as biomedical ethics, medical narrative, and the history of medicine. Full- or part-time study is available in both the Arts and Letters and Medical Humanities programs.

Research Facilities

The Rose Memorial Library houses 499,417 volumes plus a large collection of manuscripts, journals, and other primary source material. It also has an unusually large collection of periodicals with special strengths in the basic areas of graduate study offered at Drew. The library is a depository for the publications of the federal government and the state of New Jersey. It also collects the official documents of the United Nations. The Center for Holocaust Studies is located on campus, and the United Methodist Archive and History Center, adjacent to the library, houses one of the most extensive collections of American religious history and Methodistica in the world.

Financial Aid

Financial aid may take the form of scholarships, loans, employment, or any combination of these. Both need and achievement are taken into account in determining the amount of assistance to be made available. Merit-based awards range from 20 percent of tuition to 100 percent of tuition. Applicants must file financial aid forms.

Cost of Study

In 2008–09, tuition for the Master of Arts in Teaching program was $790 per credit. Tuition for the M.F.A. in Poetry program was $421 per credit, plus an $850 residency fee. Arts and Letters and Medical Humanities tuition was $849 per credit, with reduced rates for senior citizens and full-time educators.

Living and Housing Costs

Drew offers a variety of housing options in dormitories or apartments for both single and married students. For 2008–09, the cost was approximately $6400 to $13,000 for the academic year, depending on size requirements. Meal plans can be provided for an additional charge. Commuter rooms are also available.

Student Group

The total University enrollment is 2,630 students; of this number, 404 are in the Graduate School. Of the total number of graduate students, 63 percent are women and 10 percent are self-identified members of minority groups.

Location

Drew is located on a beautiful, 186-acre campus in Madison, New Jersey (population 18,000), 25 miles west of Manhattan. Commuter rail and bus lines provide easy access to New York City and all its educational, cultural, and entertainment opportunities.

The University

One of the major characteristics of the Graduate School is the emphasis on interdisciplinary studies. Its size allows for graduate education on a personal level with many small seminars, one-to-one tutorials, and classes that encourage discussion and lively interaction. Faculty members excel in teaching as well as in scholarship and research.

Applying

Evaluation of an applicant's qualifications for admission is based on previous course work and grade point average, letters of recommendation, personal statement, and writing sample. GRE General Test scores are required of U.S. and Canadian citizens who apply for the M.A.T. program. International students who are not native English speakers are required to submit recent TOEFL and TWE scores. Arts and Letters and Medical Humanities candidates may be admitted for the fall, spring, or summer semester. M.F.A. in Poetry candidates may begin the program in January or June. Master of Arts in Teaching candidates are admitted for the June start term only. The deadline for receipt of admissions and financial aid forms varies by program; students should contact the Office of Graduate Admissions for more information.

Prospective students are encouraged to attend the Graduate Open House held each fall and spring.

Correspondence and Information

Director of Graduate Admissions
Drew University
Madison, New Jersey 07940
Phone: 973-408-3110
Fax: 973-408-3040
E-mail: gradm@drew.edu
Web site: http://www.drew.edu/grad

THE FACULTY

Fran Bernstein, Assistant Professor of History; Ph.D., Columbia.
William Campbell, Adjunct Professor of Parasitology and Fellow, Charles A. Dana Research Institute; Ph.D., Wisconsin.
Luis Campos, Assistant Professor of History; Ph.D., Harvard.
Robert Carnevale, Adjunct Assistant Professor of English; M.F.A., Columbia.
James Carter, Assistant Professor of History; Ph.D., Houston.
Philip E. Chase, Adjunct Assistant Professor of English; Ph.D., Drew.
Gabriel M. Coless, Affiliate Professor of Church History; S.Th.D., Pontificio Instituto Liturgico (Rome).
David A. Cowell, Professor of Political Science; Ph.D., Georgetown.
Paolo Cucchi, Professor of French and Italian and Dean; Ph.D., Princeton.
Phyllis D. DeJesse, Adjunct Assistant Professor of Medical Humanities; D.M.H., Drew.
Sloane Drason-Knigge, Adjunct Assistant Professor of Holocaust Studies; Ph.D., Drew.
Lillie Edwards, Associate Professor of History and African American Studies; Ph.D., Chicago.
C. Wyatt Evans, Assistant Professor of History; Ph.D., Drew.
Roxanne Friedenfels, Professor of Sociology; Ph.D., Michigan.
Jonathan Golden, Assistant Professor of Religious Studies, Associate Director of Caspersen Centers; Ph.D., Pennsylvania.
David Graybeal, Professor of Church and Society; Ph.D., Yale.
Richard Greenwald, Dean, Caspersen School of Graduate Studies, Associate Professor of History; Ph.D., NYU.
Yasuko Grosjean, Associate Professor of Japanese Literature and Culture; Ph.D., Drew.
James Paul Hala, Professor of English; Ph.D., Michigan.
Herbert Huffmon, Professor of Old Testament; Ph.D., Michigan.
Sandra Jamieson, Associate Professor of English; Ph.D., SUNY at Binghamton.
Donald F. Kent, Adjunct Associate Professor of Medical History; M.D., Pennsylvania, Ph.D., Drew.
Christine A. Kinealy, Professor of Irish History; Ph.D. Trinity College (Dublin).
Wendy Kolmar, Professor of English; Ph.D., Indiana.
Cassandra Laity, Associate Professor of English; Ph.D., Michigan.
Edwina Lawler, Associate Professor of German and Russian; Ph.D., Drew.
Perry Leavell Jr., Professor of History; Ph.D., Tulane.
John Lenz, Associate Professor of Classics; Ph.D., Columbia.
Neal Levi, Assistant Professor of English; Ph.D. Columbia.
Thomas Magnell, Professor of Philosophy; D.Phil., Oxford.
Richard A. Marfuggi, Adjunct Assistant Professor of Medical Humanities; D.M.H., Drew.
Rosemary McLaughlin, Associate Professor of Theater Arts; M.F.A., Rutgers.
Karen H. McNamara, Adjunct Assistant Professor of Children's Literature; D.Litt., Drew.
Margaret Micchelli, Adjunct Professor; Ph.D., Rutgers.
Jo Ann Middleton, Director of Medical Humanities; Ph.D., Drew.
John R. Middleton, Affiliate Associate Professor of Clinical Ethics; M.D., University of Medicine and Dentistry of New Jersey.
A. Johan Noordsij, Affiliate Professor of Psychiatry; M.D., Leiden (Netherlands).
Frank Occhiogrosso, Professor of English; Ph.D., Johns Hopkins.
Nadine Ollman, Professor of English; Ph.D., Pennsylvania.
Glen A. Olsen, Adjunct Assistant Professor of Music History; D.Litt., Drew.
Roberto Osti, Adjunct Assistant Professor of Medical Illustration; M.F.A., New York Academy of Art.
James H. Pain, Henry and Annie M. Pfeiffer Professor of Religion and Dean; D.Phil., Oxford.
Dale Patterson, Adjunct Assistant Professor of Religious History; Ph.D., Drew.
Philip Peek, Professor of Anthropology; Ph.D., Indiana.
Virginia Phelan, Affiliate Associate Professor of Comparative Literature; Ph.D., Rutgers.
Jonathan W. Reader, Associate Professor of Sociology; Ph.D., Cornell.
Robert Ready, Professor of English; Ph.D., Columbia.
William B. Rogers, Affiliate Professor of History and Associate Dean; Ph.D., Drew.
Joseph Romance, Associate Professor of Political Science; Ph.D., Rutgers.
Jonathan Rose, Assistant Professor of History; Ph.D., Pennsylvania.
Ann Saltzman, Associate Professor of Psychology; Ph.D., CUNY Graduate Center.
Peggy Samuels, Associate Professor of English; Ph.D., CUNY Graduate Center.
Philip C. Scibilia, Adjunct Assistant Professor of Medical Humanities; D.M.H., Drew.
Merrill M. Skaggs, Professor of English; Ph.D., Duke.
Geraldine Smith-Wright, Professor of English; Ph.D., Rutgers.
Sharon Sundue, Assistant Professor of History; Ph.D., Harvard.
Linda Swerdlow, Assistant Professor of Education, Director of M.A.T. Program; Ph.D., NYU.
Jerome A. Travers, Adjunct Assistant Professor of Family Studies; Ph.D., Fordham.
Linda Van Blerkom, Associate Professor of Anthropology; Ph.D., Colorado.
Jeremy Varon, Associate Professor of History; Ph.D., Cornell.
Jennifer Holly Wells, Adjunct Lecturer of English; M.Phil., Drew.
Laura Winters, Adjunct Associate Professor of English; Ph.D., Drew.
Carol A. Wipf, Adjunct Associate Professor of English; Ph.D., Illinois at Champaign–Urbana.
Eugene Zins, Adjunct Associate Professor of Medical Humanities; M.D., Pennsylvania.

D'YOUVILLE COLLEGE

Graduate Studies

Programs of Study

D'Youville College offers the Doctor of Education (Ed.D.) degree in educational leadership and health policy and health education. Doctor of Chiropractic (D.C.) and Doctor of Physical Therapy (D.P.T.) programs are also offered. Master of Science (M.S.) degrees are offered in business administration, clinical nurse specialist studies in community health nursing, education (childhood, adolescence, special education, and TESOL), health services administration, international business, nurse practitioner studies (master's degree and post-master's certificate), nursing (with choice of clinical focus), occupational therapy, and physical therapy. Advanced certificate programs in clinical research associate studies, health services administration, long-term-care administration, and nursing and health-related professions education are also available. Five-year B.S./M.S. degrees are offered in dietetics, international business, nursing, and occupational therapy.

Research Facilities

D'Youville's Library Resources Center contains 154,000 volumes, including microtext and software, and subscribes to 630 periodicals and newspapers. The library also has access to 18,624 full-text journals via the Internet.

Financial Aid

In order to apply for federal aid, the Free Application for Federal Student Aid (FAFSA) must be completed. Graduate students must be matriculated for 6 or more credit hours in a degree program. Sources of federal aid include Federal Perkins Loans, the Federal Work-Study Program, Veterans' Benefits, Federal Stafford Student Loans, and Graduate Nursing Loans. The New York State Tuition Assistance Program (TAP) is available to full-time (at least 12 credit hours), matriculated graduate students who are residents of New York State. D'Youville College offers three forms of scholarships for graduate students matriculated in a master's degree program, including the Program Merit Scholarship, the Disadvantaged Student Scholarship, and the Retention Award. Nurse traineeship assistance is available to students enrolled for a minimum of 9 credit hours per semester in the Graduate Nursing Program. Canadian students (citizens and landed immigrants) are offered a 20 percent tuition reduction and may also apply for the Ontario Student Assistance Program (OSAP). Private education loans are also available to both U.S. and Canadian citizens.

Cost of Study

Graduate tuition for 2008–09 was $675 (M.S.) and $725 (Ed.D. and D.P.T.) per credit hour. The Doctor of Chiropractic was $9400 per semester. A general fee of between $37 and $75 was required, based on credit hours taken. A Student Association fee of $2 per credit hour was applied toward concerts, yearbooks, activities, and guest lectures.

Living and Housing Costs

Marquerite Hall, the residence facility, houses men and women students on separate floors, with the exception of the designated coed floors. For 2008–09, room and board cost $4650 per semester. Overnight accommodation is available, space permitting. A new residence-apartment complex opened in 2005 and houses 175 junior, senior, and graduate students in one- and four-bedroom apartments. Rates for 2008–09 were around $3800 per semester, based on the type of apartment reserved.

Student Group

Graduate degree programs are enhanced by a 13:1 student-faculty ratio. The graduate enrollment is more than 800 full-time and 550 part-time students. Seventy-three percent of the student population are women, 14 percent are from minority groups, and 62 percent are international students. D'Youville's proximity to the Canadian border accounts for the majority of the international student population.

Location

D'Youville's location is ideally set in a residential community of Buffalo, New York. D'Youville College is minutes from the Peace Bridge to Canada and is approximately 90 minutes from Toronto and 25 minutes from Niagara Falls, making it a gateway to recreation areas in western New York and Ontario.

The College

D'Youville College is a private, coeducational liberal arts and professional college located in residential Buffalo, New York, approximately 1 mile from the Peace Bridge. The Grey Nuns founded D'Youville College in 1908. With a student population of just over 2,900, D'Youville offers its students the diversity and resources of a much larger college and the attention and accessibility that are usually attributed to a small college. The College's 7-acre campus offers students comprehensive facilities, modern computer labs, state-of-the-art medical labs, and modern classrooms.

Applying

Completed application files are reviewed on a rolling admissions basis for most programs. The Doctor of Physical Therapy program has a November 30 application deadline for entry the following fall. The Doctor of Chiropractic program requires a minimum of 90 credit hours of undergraduate course work for application to the professional phase of the program. All other program candidates must have earned a baccalaureate degree from an accredited college or university. Candidates for the Ed.D. programs must have earned a master's degree from an accredited college or university. A baccalaureate degree in nursing from an approved or accredited college or university and RN licensure are required for admission to the graduate nursing programs. Licensure as a registered nurse in New York State and a minimum of one year of experience as a registered nurse are required of candidates applying to the nurse practitioner studies programs. Admission to graduate programs is based on an overall evaluation of credentials, including the applicant's undergraduate record, which should show approximately a B average or better in the major field. Applicants who do not fulfill admission requirements may be admitted provisionally. Applicants to the Ed.D. programs should show a 3.25 GPA or better in their master's course work. Admission to Ed.D. programs is competitive. Applicants whose native language is not English must submit a minimum TOEFL score of 500. The College does not require Graduate Record Examinations (GRE) or Miller Analogies Test (MAT) scores. Applicants for the M.B.A. program are required to take the GMAT.

Correspondence and Information

Linda E. Fisher
Director of Graduate Admissions
D'Youville College
One D'Youville Square
320 Porter Avenue
Buffalo, New York 14201-9985
Phone: 716-829-8400
800-777-3921 (toll-free)
Fax: 716-829-7900
E-mail: fisherl@dyc.edu
Web site: http://www.dyc.edu

THE FACULTY

Chiropractic
Steven Zajac, Coordinator of Clinical Services; D.C., National University of Health Sciences; DACBO.
Peter Diakow, Director of Chiropractic Program; D.C., Canadian Memorial Chiropractic.

Education
Jamie DeWaters, Professor; Ph.D., SUNY at Buffalo.
Sheila G. Dunn, Associate Professor; Ed.D., SUNY at Buffalo.
Robert J. Gamble, Associate Professor; Ph.D., SUNY at Buffalo.
Nancy M. Kaczmarek, GNSH, Associate Professor and Department Chair; Ph.D., SUNY at Buffalo.
James Lalley, Assistant Professor; Ph.D., SUNY at Buffalo.
Cathleen March, Assistant Professor; Ph.D., SUNY at Buffalo.
Robert Miller, Assistant Professor; Ph.D., SUNY at Buffalo.
Thomas Traverse, Assistant Professor; M.A., SUNY at Buffalo.
Stephen E. Williams, Assistant Professor; Ed.D., Clark.

Educational Leadership
Mark Garrison, Associate Professor and Director of Doctoral Programs; Ph.D., SUNY at Buffalo.

Health Policy and Health Education
Mark Garrison, Associate Professor and Director of Doctoral Programs; Ph.D., SUNY at Buffalo.

Health Services Administration
Walter Iwanenko, Assistant Professor and Department Chair; Ph.D., SUNY at Buffalo.
Elizabeth Miranda, Assistant Professor; J.D., SUNY at Buffalo.
James Notaro, Assistant Professor; Ph.D., North Carolina at Chapel Hill.
Judith H. Schiffert, Assistant Professor; Ed.D., SUNY at Buffalo.

International Business
Peter Eimer, Assistant Professor; M.B.A., Pittsburgh.
Joseph Fennell, Associate Professor; M.B.A., Columbia.
Bonnie Fox-Garrity, Assistant Professor; M.A., North Carolina at Chapel Hill.
Amable Pauline, Assistant Professor and Department Chair; Ph.D., Wisconsin–Madison.
Arup Sen, Assistant Professor; Ph.D. candidate, SUNY at Buffalo.

Nursing
Carol A. Gutt, Associate Professor; Ed.D., SUNY at Buffalo. Wellness, child health, curriculum, women's health, women's issues, stress management, leadership roles.
Dorothy Hoehne, Associate Professor; Ph.D., SUNY at Buffalo. Pediatrics, hospice with adults and children, instruction, experimental/qualitative research, spouse and child abuse, wellness, rehabilitation, curriculum.
Verna Kieffer, Associate Professor and Department Chair; D.N.S., SUNY at Buffalo. Adult health, critical care, qualitative research, quality-of-life issues, professional-practice issues.
Edith Malizia, Associate Professor and Assistant to the Chair; Ed.D., SUNY at Buffalo. Adult health, professional issues, professional socialization, leadership and management.
Pam Miller, Clinical Coordinator; M.S., SUNY at Buffalo; RN, Women's health NP.

Occupational Therapy
Merlene Gingher, Associate Professor and Department Chair; Ed.D., SUNY at Buffalo. Grerontic occupational therapy, range of motion in the elderly.
April Rockwood, Assistant Professor; M.S., SUNY at Buffalo. Pediatric practice, school-based OT, learning styles.
Elizabeth Stanton, Associate Professor; Ph.D., SUNY at Buffalo. Mental health issues, hospice care, culture and health.

Physical Therapy
James Karnes, Associate Professor; Ph.D., SUNY at Buffalo. Neuroanatomy/enruophysiology, gross anatomy, functional morphology.
Penelope Klein, Associate Professor; Ed.D., Syracuse. Tai chi, health-care systems and cost analysis.
Lynn Rivers, Associate Professor and Department Chair; Ph.D., SUNY at Buffalo. Health-care policy; physical activity; health promotion for individuals with chronic disabilities, with emphasis on African Americans.
John Rouselle, Associate Professor; Ed.D., SUNY at Buffalo. Exercise physiology, psychophysiology, wellness, health education.

EAST TENNESSEE STATE UNIVERSITY

School of Graduate Studies

Programs of Study

The East Tennessee State University (ETSU) School of Graduate Studies offers almost 100 different program choices, including over thirty master's degree programs (with many concentrations), fourteen certificate programs, and nine doctoral programs. Graduate certificates are offered in archival studies, biostatistics, business administration, economic development, emerging technologies, entrepreneurial leadership, epidemiology, family nurse practitioner, gerontology, health-care management, nursing, rural health care, teaching English as a second language, and urban planning. Doctoral programs include the Au.D. in audiology, the Ph.D. in biomedical sciences, the Ed.D. in educational leadership and policy analysis, the Ph.D. in environmental health, the Ph.D. in nursing, the D.P.T. in physical therapy, the Ph.D. in clinical psychology, the Ph.D. in early childhood education, and the D.P.H. in public health. In addition, ETSU's College of Pharmacy offers the Pharm.D, and the M.D. is offered through the James H. Quillen College of Medicine, which is recognized by national publications for its programs in rural, family, and primary-care medicine.

Research Facilities

The wireless Sherrod Library, which opened in spring 1999, has 192,000 square feet, can hold 800,000 volumes, seats 1,800 students, has multiple computer stations, and houses 420 individual study carrels, including a limited number of private rooms for students who are working on theses or dissertations. Twenty-five laptop computers are available for in-library use and 4-hour checkout. Three public microcomputer labs contain 170 PCs and sixteen Macs, all of which provide access to the campus e-mail server, the Internet, and the library online catalog system. There are forty-one departmental computer labs totaling approximately 1200 computers with access restricted to students of that department. The Archives of Appalachia and the law collection in Sherrod Library provide access to political, social, historical, and cultural records of the southern Appalachian Mountains.

Financial Aid

In addition to the wide range of private and federal aid offerings, ETSU has approximately 600 graduate assistantships and tuition scholarships. Graduate assistants are required to work 20 hours weekly in teaching, research, or administrative roles. Their stipends, which are set by individual programs, begin at $6000 (for a nine-month contract), and there is also in-state and out-of-state tuition remission. Tuition scholars are required to work 8 hours weekly for full-tuition remission, both in state and out of state. In addition to departmental assignments, assistantships and tuition scholarships are also available in nonacademic departments across the campus, such as University Housing, Sherrod Library, and various administrative offices. For information regarding all types of financial aid, students should visit the ETSU Web site at http://www.etsu.edu/gradstud/gasch/gasch_faq.asp.

Cost of Study

For 2008–09, residential graduate students paid $305 per semester hour, which did not exceed $2886 per semester. Nonresident graduate students paid out-of-state tuition of $473 per semester hour, which did not exceed $5446 per semester. Graduate assistants and tuition scholars receive remission of graduate tuition. Additional fees, such as student activity and general access fees are not included in the tuition rates listed. Prospective students can find a schedule of tuition and fees at http://www.etsu.edu/comptrol/bursar.htm.

Living and Housing Costs

For single students, residence halls (double occupancy) were available at costs ranging from $1340 to $2225 per semester and residence halls (single occupancy) were available at costs ranging from $2680 to $4450 in 2008–09; a furnished efficiency for single graduate students was $1750 per semester; a furnished one-bedroom for married graduate students was $1905; a furnished two-bedroom for married graduate students was $2135. BucRidge Apartments, Phase I, is a 300-bed apartment complex that offers 25 four-bedroom, two-bath units and 100 two-bedroom, two-bath apartments. BucRidge Apartments, Phase II, is a 112-bed apartment complex that offers 56 two-bedroom, two-bath apartments; all rooms are fully furnished with kitchens and washers and dryers, have common living rooms and balconies or patios, and have telephone, TV, and data jacks in each bedroom. A clubhouse and recreational facilities are available to all occupants. Rent is variable, depending on occupancy and terms of lease.

Student Group

In fall 2006, more than 12,000 students were enrolled. Graduate students accounted for about 2,400 of that total.

Location

The main campus is located in Johnson City, 100 miles northeast of Knoxville, near the state lines of Virginia, Kentucky, West Virginia, North Carolina, and South Carolina. The University has locations in Kingsport, Bristol, Elizabethton, and Greeneville. With a population of more than 482,930, the Tri-Cities Tennessee/Virginia area is the nation's only region to be designated an All America City. Conveniently situated just a few miles off Interstates 81 and 26, ETSU is easily accessible by automobile and is served by Tri-Cities Regional Airport. The campus has more than 350 tree-shaded acres and more than seventy buildings. Recreational opportunities include biking, boating, climbing, fishing, golf, hiking, jogging, skiing (snow and water), tennis, and white-water rafting. This region provides tenancy to six major area hospitals affiliated with the University in various capacities, including the adjacent James H. Quillen Veterans Affairs Medical Center. The University's Division of Health Sciences (Medicine, Nursing, and Public and Allied Health) and the regional med-tech community make up the only center for health sciences between Knoxville and Roanoke, Virginia.

The University

Founded in 1911, ETSU is one of six state universities governed by the Tennessee Board of Regents (TBR) system, the largest higher-education system in Tennessee and the sixth-largest in the nation, providing programs to more than 180,000 students in ninety of Tennessee's ninety-five counties. Accredited by the Commission on Colleges of the Southern Association of Colleges and Schools, ETSU has nine colleges and two schools: the Colleges of Arts and Sciences, Business and Technology, Clinical and Rehabilitative Science, Education, Honors, Medicine, Nursing, Pharmacy, and Public Health and the Schools of Continuing Studies and Graduate Studies. ETSU leads all TBR schools in the number of interactive television courses and leads the senior TBR institutions in Web-based instruction and in overall distance education course. ETSU offers a wide range of evening and online courses that support students who work full-time. Unique offerings include ETSU's internationally acclaimed advanced visualization computer animation, a 3-D design program housed in the Scott M. Niswonger Digital Media Center. ETSU is large enough to offer many choices in programs and activities but small enough to avoid the intimidation and anonymity of a larger university.

Applying

Application for admission to graduate study is open to any person with a bachelor's degree from a regionally accredited institution. All domestic application materials should be filed with the School of Graduate Studies at least six weeks prior to the semester in which the applicant plans to enroll. International applications must be received twelve weeks prior to the expected date of enrollment. Application forms are available online at http://www.etsu.edu/gradstud/forms/admission_forms.asp. Students can request a paper application by e-mail or by writing to the University's address. The current application fee is $25 for U.S. residents and $35 for international students.

Correspondence and Information

School of Graduate Studies
Box 70720
East Tennessee State University
Johnson City, Tennessee 37614-1710

Phone: 423-439-4221
E-mail: gradsch@etsu.edu
Web site: http://www.etsu.edu/gradstud

PROGRAM CONTACTS

Listed below are the graduate school administration and the graduate coordinators of the various programs with the graduate degree(s) available in each area.

Graduate School Administration
Cecilia McIntosh, Dean (423-439-6147)
Jeffrey Beck, Associate Dean (423-439-8638)
Wayne Gillespie, Assistant Dean (423-439-4704)
Queen Brown, Office Manager (423-439-6146)
David Moore, Admissions Counselor/Recruiter (423-439-6149)

College of Arts and Sciences
Gordon Anderson, Dean

Art (M.A., M.F.A.): Don Davis (423-439-7864)
Biological Sciences:
Biology (M.S.): Mike Zavada (423-439-6919)
Microbiology (M.S.): Bert Lampson (423-439-4572)
Paleontology (M.S.): Blaine Schubert (423-439-8419)
Chemistry (M.S.): Chu-Ngi Ho (423-439-6914)
Communication, Professional (M.A.): Jack Mooney (423-439-4168)
Criminal Justice and Criminology (M.A.): Steven Ellwanger (423-439-4671)
English (M.A.): Shawna Lictenwalner (423-439-5993)
History (M.A.): Mel Page (423-439-6802)
Mathematical Sciences (M.A.): Robert Gardner (423-439-6977)
Psychology (M.A. and Ph.D.):
Clinical: Peggy Cantrell (423-439-6660)
General: Russell Brown (423-439-5863)
Social Work (M.S.W.): Barbara Grissett (423-439-6015)
Sociology and Anthropology (M.A.): Leslie McCallister (423-439-4370)
Teaching English as a Second Language Certificate: Theresa McGarry (423-439-5995)

College of Business and Technology
Linda R. Garceau, Dean

Accountancy (M.Acc.): Gary Burkette (423-439-5314)
Business Administration Certificate: Martha Pointer (423-439-5314)
Clinical Nutrition (M.S.): Beth Lowe (423-439-7537)
Computer and Information Sciences (M.S): Martin Barrett (423-439-7409); Phil Pfeiffer (423-439-5355)
Economic Development Certificate: David Briley (423-439-6697)
Entrepreneurial Leadership Certificate: Andrew Czuchry (423-439-5314)
Master of Business Administration (M.B.A.) Certificate: Martha Pointer (423-439-5314)
Master of Business Administration (M.B.A.) Accelerated: Pete Cornett (423-439-4622)
Public Administration (M.P.M. and M.C.M.): David Briley (423-439-6697)
Urban Planning Certificate: David Briley (423-439-6697)

College of Clinical and Rehabilitative Sciences
Nancy Scherer, Dean

Allied Health (M.S.): Ester Verhovsek (423-547-0235)
Audiology (Au.D.): Patricia Chase (423-439-5252)
Physical Therapy (D.P.T.): Susan Epps (423-439-8275)
Speech Pathology (M.S.): Vijay Guntupalli (423-439-4261)

College of Education
Hal Knight, Dean

Counseling (M.A.): Janna Scarborough (423-439-7688)
Early Childhood Education (M.A., M.Ed.): Amy Malkus (423-439-7656)
Early Childhood Education (Ph.D.): Pamela Evanshen (423-439-7694)
Educational Leadership and Policy Analysis (M.Ed., Ed.S., Ed.D): Jim Lampley (423-439-7619); Pam Scott (423-439-7618); Virginia Foley (423-439-4430); Janna Scarborough (423-439-7688); Eric Glover (423-439-4430)
Educational Media and Educational Technology (M.Ed.): Lee Daniels (423-439-7843); Linda Steele (423-439-7851)
Elementary Education (M.Ed.): Leslie Perry (423-439-7602)
Exercise Physiology and Performance: Mike Stone (423-439-5796)
K–12 Physical Education: Diana Mozen (423-439-6157)
Reading Education (M.A., M.Ed.): Jane Melendez (423-439-7910)
Secondary Education (M.Ed.): Tammy Barnes (423-439-4155)
Special Education (M.Ed.): James Fox (423-439-7556)
Sports Management: Keunsu Han (423-439-4382)
Storytelling (M.A., M.Ed.): Joseph Sobol (423-439-7863)
Teacher Education with multiple levels (M.A.T.): Aimee Govett (423-439-7678); Tammy Barnes (423-439-4155)

College of Nursing
Patricia Smith, Dean

Nursing Graduate Programs: Kathleen Raymond (423-439-4589)
Nursing (M.S.N.):
Nurse Practitioner: Linda Garrett (423-439-4084)
Nursing Administration: Janne Dunham-Taylor (423-439-4494)
Nursing (Ph.D.): Sadie Hutson (423-439-6362)
RODP (Regents Online Degree Program): Nancy Granberry (423-439-4611)

College of Pharmacy
Dr. Larry D. Calhoun, Dean

Pharmacology (Pharm.D.): Alok Agrawal (423-439-6336)

College of Public Health
Randolph Wykoff, Dean

Environmental Health (M.S.E.H.): Kurt Maier (423-439-7635)
Epidemiology Certificate: James Anderson (423-439-4332)
Gerontology Certificate: James Florence (423-439-6720)
Health Care Management Certificate: Brian Martin (423-439-4429)
Public Health (M.P.H.): Brian C. Martin (423-439-4429)
Public Health (Dr.P.H): Robert Pack (423-439-4540)

James H. Quillen College of Medicine
Philip Bagnell, Dean of Medicine

Biomedical Sciences (Ph.D.):
Mitchell Robinson, Associate Dean (423-439-2028)
Anatomy and Cell Biology: Dennis DeFoe (423-439-2010)
Biochemistry: Yue Zou (423-439-2124)
Microbiology: Robert Schoborg (423-439-6295)
Pharmacology: Alok Agrawal (423-439-6336)
Physiology: Tom Ecay (423-439-2046)

School of Continuing Studies
Norma McRae, Dean

Archival Studies Graduate Certificate: Marie Tedesco (423-439-5792)
Liberal Studies (M.A.L.S.): Marie Tedesco (423-439-5792)
Professional Studies (M.A.P.S.): Jo Lobertini (423-439-4223)

EMORY
GRADUATE SCHOOL

EMORY UNIVERSITY

Graduate School

Programs of Study

The Graduate School at Emory University offers the Master of Arts (M.A.) in educational studies, film studies, music, and sacred music; the Master of Science (M.S.) in biostatistics, computer science, and mathematics; and the Master of Science in Clinical Research (MSCR) for physicians or Ph.D.'s in health-related sciences. Professional degrees awarded are the Master of Education (M.Ed.) and Master of Arts in Teaching (M.A.T.). A Diploma for Advanced Study in Teaching is also available.

The Doctor of Philosophy (Ph.D.) is offered in anthropology, art history, behavioral sciences and health education, biological and biomedical sciences, biomedical engineering, biostatistics, business, chemistry, comparative literature, computer science and informatics, economics, educational studies, English, epidemiology, French, health sciences research and health policy, history, liberal arts, mathematics, nursing, philosophy, physics, political science, psychology, religion, sociology, Spanish, and women's studies.

Programs within the Graduate Division of Biological and Biomedical Sciences include biochemistry, cell and developmental biology, genetics and molecular biology, immunology and molecular pathogenesis, microbiology and molecular genetics, molecular and systems pharmacology, neuroscience, nutrition and health sciences, and population biology, ecology, and evolution. A six-year Medical Scientist Program leads to a combined M.D./Ph.D. Programs in psychology include clinical psychology, cognitive and developmental psychology, and neuroscience and animal behavior. Courses of study within the Graduate Division of Religion include ethics and society; Hebrew Bible; historical studies in theology and religion; New Testament; person, community, and religious practices; theological studies; West and South Asian religion; and the J.D./Ph.D. program. The program in biomedical engineering is offered jointly with the Georgia Institute of Technology.

M.A. and M.S. degrees require a minimum of two semesters of residence; M.Ed. and M.A.T. degrees and the diploma require at least three semesters of residence; and the Ph.D. degree requires a minimum of four semesters of residence.

Research Facilities

Holdings of the five Emory libraries (Health Sciences Library, Law Library, Oxford College Library, Theology Library, and the General Libraries, made up of the Woodruff, Candler, Chemistry, and Math and Science Libraries) total approximately 2.7 million volumes. The libraries also offer access to thousands of electronic information resources. The Center for Library and Information Resources provides an integrated service environment that brings together technology and media specialists with librarians in a facility that includes an information commons, electronic classrooms, a distance learning classroom, the Center for Interactive Teaching, a state-of-the-art language lab and classrooms, the new high-tech Heilbrun Music and Media Library, the Electronic Services Data Center, group study rooms, and comfortable study spaces with data connections as well as wireless access throughout the building. The Special Collections and Archives Division of Woodruff Library contains modern literary manuscript archives, notable African American collections, and other major archival and manuscript holdings.

Facilities in the biomedical sciences include a large number of specialized laboratories as well as the opportunities associated with a number of affiliated or adjacent research institutions: the Robert W. Woodruff Health Sciences Center, the Winship Cancer Institute, the Yerkes National Primate Research Center, the Emory Vaccine Center, the U.S. Centers for Disease Control and Prevention, and the American Cancer Society.

Additional facilities include the Information Technology Division and the Michael C. Carlos Museum. The Carter Center of Emory University provides resources for the study of national and international policy issues.

Financial Aid

All Emory University graduate fellowships are based on academic merit. They provide stipend and tuition scholarships for five years. All applications are due by January 3. Some programs have earlier deadlines; prospective students should check with the program. Tuition assistance grants are awarded to some teachers who are admitted to master's programs in the Division of Educational Studies. Information regarding extra-University financial aid (loans, work-study, or veterans' benefits) may be obtained from the Financial Aid Office.

Cost of Study

In 2009–10, full-time tuition is $16,400 (12 semester hours or more); the computing fee is $50 per semester; and the student activity and recreation fee is $188 per semester. Students must either join the Emory student health insurance plan, which costs $2158 per year, or demonstrate equivalent coverage under another policy. Many scholarships include a health insurance subsidy.

Living and Housing Costs

A variety of on- and off-campus housing is available. On-campus housing includes the Graduate Residential Center, which is located in a five-story complex, with one-, two-, and three-bedroom furnished and unfurnished (except three-bedroom) apartments. The apartments have central heat and air-conditioning and are equipped with a full kitchen, washer and dryer units, and full bathrooms (one per bedroom). All utilities are included in the rental price.

Student Group

Total University enrollment is more than 12,000. In fall 2008, total enrollment in degree programs in the Graduate School was 1,793: 701 men and 1,092 women. Twenty-one percent were international students, and 96 percent of the students received merit awards.

Location

Emory University's wooded campus is located in an attractive residential section of Atlanta. Easily accessible by bus and metro from Emory, downtown Atlanta provides an exciting, progressive atmosphere with many recreational and cultural activities, often with reduced rates for students. Increased attention is being paid to the city's past and its historical development and the revitalization of the downtown area. With a population of 3 million, Atlanta is relatively close to the Appalachian Mountains, the Atlantic coast, and the Gulf coast.

The University

Founded by the Methodist Church in 1836, Emory received its university charter in 1915 and moved from Oxford, Georgia, to the northeast Atlanta campus. The University comprises the Graduate School, Emory College, Oxford College, and the schools of business, law, medicine, nursing, public health, and theology. The Graduate School was organized as a division of the University in 1919. Extracurricular activities are plentiful.

Applying

Minimum requirements for admission include a baccalaureate degree from an accredited four-year college, an undergraduate academic average of C, an academic average of B for the last two undergraduate years, and satisfactory scores on the General Test of the GRE. Applicants are considered without regard to race, color, national origin, religion, sex, sexual orientation, age, handicap, or veteran status. Applicants may apply online at http://www.emory.edu/GSOAS/. Applications are due by January 3. Some programs have earlier deadlines; students should check with the program.

Correspondence and Information

Emory University Graduate School
209 Administration Building
201 Dowman Drive
Atlanta, Georgia 30322

Phone: 404-727-6028
E-mail: gradschool-l@listserv.cc.emory.edu
Web site: http://www.graduateschool.emory.edu

DIRECTORS OF GRADUATE STUDY AND THEIR RESEARCH

Anthropology: John Kingston, Director of Graduate Studies; Ph.D., Harvard, 1992. Biological anthropology, ecology of human evolution, paleoecology, paleontology; East Africa.

Art History: Eric R. Varner, Director of Graduate Studies; Ph.D., Yale, 1993. Roman portrait sculpture, Imperial iconography, Roman women, monuments and topography of ancient Rome.

Behavioral Sciences and Health Education: Michelle Kegler, Director of Graduate Studies and Deputy Director of Emory Prevention Research Center; Dr.P.H., North Carolina, 1995. Cancer prevention, community-based research, evaluation, faith-based health, health promotion, obesity prevention, rural health, smoking prevention/cessation.

Biochemistry, Cell and Developmental Biology: Anita Corbett, Director; Ph.D., Vanderbilt, 1992. Interplay between nucleocytoplasmic transport and cell-cycle progression in yeast.

Biological/Biomedical Sciences: Keith D. Wilkinson, Director; Ph.D., Michigan, 1977. Mechanism and regulation of protein synthesis and degradation.

Biomedical Engineering: Gilda Barbarino, Associate Chair and Director of Graduate Studies; Ph.D., Rice, 1986. Sickle cell adhesion, cellular engineering, tissue engineering and bioreactors.

Biostatistics: Robert H. Lyles, Director of Graduate Studies; Ph.D., North Carolina, 1996. Adjustment methods for multiplicative measurement error in multiple linear regression, with applications in occupational epidemiology.

Business: Grace Pownall, Director of Doctoral Studies; Ph.D., Chicago, 1985. Information and global capital markets, voluntary disclosure incentives and practices, international accounting.

Chemistry: James Kindt, Director of Graduate Studies; Ph.D., Yale, 1999. Theoretical/computational chemistry.

Clinical Research: Henry Blumberg, Principal Investigator and Director; M.D., Vanderbilt. Hospital and molecular epidemiology, nosocomial and community control of tuberculosis, clinical research training.

Comparative Literature: Deborah Elise White, Director of Graduate Studies; Ph.D., Yale, 1993. Romanticism and literary theory.

Economics: Maria Arbatskaya, Director of Graduate Studies; Ph.D., Indiana, 1999. Industrial organization, applied game theory.

Educational Studies: Yuk Fai Cheong, Quantitative Research Methodology and Director of Graduate Studies; Ph.D., Michigan State. Research design and statistics; multilevel, Bayesian, and Rasch analyses as applied to the study and measurement of human development and learning.

English: Benjamin Reiss, Director of Graduate Studies; Ph.D., Berkeley, 1997. Ninteenth-century American literature and culture, with strong interests in popular culture, medicine, race, disability, and environmental issues.

Epidemiology: Michele Marcus, Director of Graduate Studies; Ph.D., Columbia, 1986.

Film Studies: Matthew Bernstein, Director of Graduate Studies; Ph.D., Wisconsin, 1987. American film industry, classical and contemporary Hollywood cinema, nonfiction film, film comedy, the social problem film, African-Americans in film, Japanese cinema, post-war European cinema, historiography.

French: Claire Nouvet, Director of Graduate Studies; Ph.D., Princeton, 1981. Medieval French literature and culture.

Genetics and Molecular Biology: Andreas Fritz, Director; Ph.D., Basel (Switzerland), 1988. Molecular and genetic mechanisms of the early patterning of the nervous system and segmentation of the mesoderm.

Graduate Institute of the Liberal Arts: Michael Moon, Director of Graduate Studies; Ph.D., Johns Hopkins, 1989. Late-nineteenth and early-twentieth century American literature and culture, including film, especially in relation to the history and theory of sexuality and of mass culture.

Health Services Research and Health Policy: David H. Howard, Director of Graduate Studies; Ph.D., Harvard, 2000. Differences in chronic disease rate between the U.S. and Europe, impact of poor health on receipt of cancer screening tests, waiting time as a price for deceased donor transplants.

History: Jonathan Prude, Director of Graduate Studies; Ph.D., Harvard, 1976. Nineteenth-century American social, labor, and cultural history; relations between culture and class during the "long" nineteenth century stretching from the founding of the United States to the early 1900s.

Immunology and Molecular Pathogenesis: Brian D. Evavold, Director; Ph.D., Chicago, 1989. T-cell activation, antigen recognition, EAE autoimmunity model, role of SHP-1 phosphatase in T-cell responses.

Mathematics and Computer Science: James Nagy, Director of Graduate Studies; Ph.D., North Carolina State, 1991. Numerical linear algebra, scientific computation, numerical solution to ill-posed problems, image restoration and reconstruction.

M.D./Ph.D. Program: Charles Parkos, Director of Graduate Studies; Ph.D., M.D., 1987, California, San Diego. Pathophysiology of musosal inflammation, broadly applicable to many inflammatory diseases.

Microbiology and Molecular Genetics: Samuel Speck, Director; Ph.D., Northwestern. Pathogenesis of gamma-herpesviruses, development of lymphoma and other cancers.

Molecular and Systems Pharmacology: Eddie Morgan, Director; Ph.D., Glasgow, 1979. Regulation of drug metabolizing enzymes, cytochrome P-450, inflammation, biological effects of nitric oxide.

Music: Lynn Wood Bertrand, Director of Graduate Studies; Ph.D., Cincinnati, 1978. Contemporary Passion music.

Neuroscience: Yoland Smith, Director; Ph.D., Laval, 1987. The pathophysiology of Parkinson's disease, changes in the synaptic plasticity of the basal ganglia in normal and pathological conditions.

Nursing: Kenneth Hepburn, Director of Graduate Studies; Ph.D., Washington (Seattle), 1968. Aging and geriatric medicine, family practice and community health.

Nutrition and Health Sciences: Usha Ramakrishnan, Director; Ph.D., Cornell, 1993. Maternal and child nutrition, micronutrient malnutrition, nutrition assessment.

Philosophy: Steven K. Strange, Director of Graduate Studies; Ph.D., Texas at Austin, 1981. Ancient philosophy, especially Platonism and Hellenistic philosophy, the history of Platonism, and the history of ethics.

Physics: Laura Finzi, Director of Graduate Studies; Ph.D., New Mexico, 1990. The thermodynamics and kinetics of protein-induced conformational changes in DNA, the structures of nucleo-protein assemblies relevant to transcriptional regulation.

Political Science: Clifford J. Carrubba, Director of Graduate Studies; Ph.D., Stanford, 1998. Legislative behavior and roll call vote analysis, the design and change of judicial institutions (with application to the European Court of Justice), statistical tests of game theoretic models.

Population Biology, Ecology, and Evolution: Bruce Levin, Director; Ph.D., Michigan, 1967. Population biology and evolution of bacteria, evolution and control of infectious disease.

Psychology: Lynne Nygaard, Director of Graduate Studies; Ph.D., Brown, 1991. Auditory imagery during reading, perceptual learning of voice and accent, emotional prosody and meaning.

Religion: Michael Joseph Brown, Director of Graduate Studies; Ph.D., Chicago, 1998. Christian origins, especially in the Greco-Roman context; Christianity in Roman Egypt; the Gospel according to Matthew; receptions of the Bible in modern culture.

Sociology: Cathryn Johnson, Director of Graduate Studies; Ph.D., Iowa, 1990. Social psychology, status and power, work and formal organizations, emotions.

Spanish: Hernán Feldman, Director of Graduate Studies; Ph.D., Indiana. Nineteenth and twentieth century Río de la Plata literature; critical legal studies; deconstruction and political theory; comics and film; tango, blues, and heavy metal music.

Women's Studies: Rosemarie Garland-Thomson, Director of Graduate Studies; Ph.D., Brandeis, 1993. Feminist theory, American literature, disability studies.

EMPORIA STATE UNIVERSITY

Graduate Studies

Programs of Study

Emporia State University (ESU) offers courses leading to the Master of Arts (M.A.) in biology, English, history, and teaching of English as a second language (TESOL).

The Master of Science is offered in art therapy; biology; business education (available totally online); clinical psychology; curriculum and instruction (pre-K–12 curriculum leadership, pre-K–12 effective practitioner, pre-K–12 national board certification); early childhood education; educational administration; health, physical education, and recreation; instructional design and technology; master teacher studies (elementary subject matter, reading specialist); mathematics; mental health counseling; physical sciences (chemistry, earth science, physical sciences, physics); psychology; rehabilitation counseling; school counseling; school psychology; and special education.

The Master of Arts in Teaching is offered in social sciences. The University also offers Master of Business Administration (accounting, general, information systems), Master of Library Science, and Master of Music degree programs.

The Specialist in Education (Ed.S.) degree is offered in school psychology, and the Ph.D. is offered in library and information management.

Courses for the M.A. in TESOL are offered both online and in traditional face-to-face formats.

The University conducts an academic year of two semesters plus a nine-week summer session in which graduate courses are offered in every field.

The University is accredited by the North Central Association of Colleges and Schools and is a member of the Council of Graduate Schools in the United States. Its programs are recognized by the American Chemical Society, National Association of Schools of Music, AACSB International–The Association to Advance Collegiate Schools of Business, National Council for Accreditation of Teacher Education, American Library Association, American Art Therapy Association, Council on Rehabilitative Education, Kansas State Department of Education, and Council for Accreditation of Counseling and Related Educational Programs (CACREP).

Research Facilities

The William Allen White Library contains more than 1 million books, government documents, periodicals, theses, and nonprint materials. The library provides online access to a large number of bibliographic, full-text, and full-image databases. Other resources are available via the Internet at public access computers located in the library, via Web access through the home page, or through a proxy service for distance education students. Materials not available at ESU can be requested from other libraries throughout the world by utilizing the interlibrary loans service. Other key library resources are the Special Collections Department, located in White Library, and the University Archives, located in Anderson Library on the west campus.

The Departments of Biological Sciences and Physical Sciences have the Jones Biotechnology Laboratories and the Jones Environmental Chemistry Laboratories, with state-of-the-art equipment. The University operates four natural areas for biological research in tall grass prairie, upland and deciduous forest, and marshland. The Department of Psychology and Special Education has a state-of-the-art research laboratory for students and faculty members. The Department of Counselor Education and Rehabilitation Programs supports a state-of-the-art counseling clinic for training students and providing service to the community.

Financial Aid

Most departments offering graduate work, as well as numerous other units within the University, award graduate assistantships. During the academic year, the University employs at least 185 graduate assistants. To qualify for an assistantship, an applicant must have a minimum overall grade point average of 2.5 for four years or 2.75 for the last two years of undergraduate study, based on a 4.0 scale. Students may be eligible for tuition reductions during each term in which they hold an assistantship appointment. Nonresident full-time graduate assistants are assessed fees at the same rate as residents of Kansas.

Cost of Study

In 2008–09, fees for a full graduate course load were $2409 per semester for state residents and $6435 per semester for nonresidents. For the summer session, resident fees were $217 per credit hour, and nonresident fees were $552 per credit hour. Fees are subject to change by action of the Board of Regents.

Living and Housing Costs

The Department of Residential Life offers graduate students a number of cost-effective living arrangements. Residence Hall rates range from $1513 to $1756 per semester. Emporia State Apartments rent for $231 to $378 per month (utilities not included). Students can contact the department by telephone at 620-341-5264 or by e-mail (reslife@emporia.edu) for more information.

Student Group

The total on-campus enrollment is 6,354, with 291 full-time and 1,743 part-time graduate students. About 30 percent of the full-time graduate students receive financial assistance of some kind; 6 percent are international students. In 2008, six Ed.S. degrees, 513 master's degrees, and one Ph.D. degree were conferred.

Student Outcomes

Approximately 60 percent of the graduates find employment in their major fields of study within the state of Kansas, 29 percent of the graduates are employed in their major field of study outside the state of Kansas, 2 percent find employment outside their major field of study, 5 percent continue their education, and 4 percent are unemployed.

Location

Emporia, with a population of more than 26,000, is an educational, industrial, trade, and medical center serving 60,000 people in east-central Kansas. It is situated on the eastern edge of the famous Bluestem region of the Flint Hills and is surrounded by numerous lakes and recreational facilities. The city is located on the Kansas Turnpike, Interstate Highway 35. Three major metropolitan areas of the state—Topeka, Kansas City, and Wichita—are within 100 miles.

The University

The University, founded in 1863, has a long, diverse, and exciting history, which is reflected in its twenty-three different graduate programs in education, library science and information management, business, and liberal arts and sciences. Although all programs are of high quality, the University is particularly well known for its teacher education and library and information management programs. At ESU, small class sizes are the norm.

Applying

Applications for admission to the Graduate School should be made thirty days before the first day of an enrollment period. Some academic departments have earlier deadlines. For admission as a master's degree student, an applicant must have a minimum grade point average of 2.5 in the last 60 hours of undergraduate study. Applicants for the M.A. in English and the M.S. in special education must have at least a 2.75 grade point average or at least a 3.0 in the major. Applicants for the Specialist in Education degree must hold a master's degree from an accredited college or university with grades of B or better in three fourths of the credit hours taken for the degree. Applicants for the M.S. in psychology, school psychology, or art therapy must have a cumulative grade point average of at least 3.0 or at least 3.25 for the last 60 hours of an undergraduate program. Applicants for the M.A. in history must have a 3.0 GPA in 12 hours of history.

Correspondence and Information

Graduate Studies
Campus Box 4003
Emporia State University
Emporia, Kansas 66801-5087

Phone: 620-341-5403
800-950-GRAD (toll-free)
Fax: 620-341-5909
E-mail: gradinfo@emporia.edu
Web site: http://www.emporia.edu/grad

FACULTY HEADS

The following list shows specializations, research, and/or exhibits of the faculty within each graduate program and the chair or graduate adviser of each department.

Biological Sciences (M.S., M.A.): Scott Crupper, Ph.D., Coordinator of Graduate Studies. Animal and plant ecology, animal behavior, cellular and molecular biology, ecology and physiology of grassland plants, endocrinology, entomology, environmental biochemistry and physiology, evolutionary biology, fisheries and wildlife management, ichthyology, immunology, invertebrate and vertebrate zoology, mammalogy, microbiology, ornithology, population and molecular genetics, plant and animal anatomy/physiology, plant and animal taxonomy/systematics, biology education, soil science.

Business (M.B.A., M.S. in business education): Joseph Wen, Ph.D., Dean. Accounting, information systems, finance, economics, international business, management, and marketing. Faculty specializations include business teacher education and vocational education.

Counselor Education and Rehabilitation Programs (M.S.): Patricia Neufeld, Ph.D., Chair. Special education (adaptive concentration and gifted, talented, and creative concentration) and school counseling. Faculty specializations include assessment, inclusion, collaboration with teachers and parents, curriculum integration, special education attrition, mental retardation and autism, and implementation and management of school counseling program.

Early Childhood/Elementary Teacher Education (M.S.): Jean Morrow, Ed.D., Chair. Master teacher (elementary subject matter, reading specialist), early childhood education, postbaccalaureate teacher certification. Faculty specializations include authentic assessment, cooperative learning, curriculum integration, reading recovery, inclusion, and multicultural education. Distance learning is available for many courses in all programs.

English (M.A.): Mel Storm, Ph.D., Director of Graduate Studies. Rhetoric and composition, creative writing, and English and American literatures. Courses for in-service teachers and for those who wish to pursue careers in community college teaching are also available. Dual master's degrees are offered with the School of Library and Information Management. Faculty specializations include medieval literature and language, Renaissance literature, eighteenth- and nineteenth-century British literature, nineteenth-century American literature, twentieth-century American literature, contemporary literature, world literature, women's studies, American studies, young adult fiction, English education, creative writing, folklore, popular culture, gender and ethnic studies, critical theory, rhetoric and composition, linguistics, and journalism.

Health, Physical Education, and Recreation (M.S.): Kathy Ermler, Ed.D., Chair. Pedagogy, exercise physiology, technology in health and physical education, sports ethics, administration, psychology of sport and physical education, motor behavior, health promotion and health education. The entire Master of Science in physical education may be completed through the online delivery.

History (M.A.): Deborah Gerish, Ph.D., Coordinator. Faculty specialties include Colonial U.S., nineteenth-century U.S., political history of the South, women's history, twentieth-century political history in U.S. and Europe, Kansas history, Native American cultures, and public history. A dual master's degree is offered with the School of Library and Information Management.

Instructional Design and Technology (M.S.): Marcus Childress, Ph.D., Chair. Instructional design and technology. Faculty specializations include distance and online learning, online games/virtual reality, multimedia, instructional and curricular design, cooperative learning, integrating technology into teaching and learning, study skills, digital learning strategies (high-tech study skills), learning styles, digital storytelling, vocabulary acquisition methodologies, universal design, assistive technology, and heutagogy in distance learning. All courses in the M.S. program are offered via the Internet (http://idt.emporia.edu).

Library and Information Management (M.L.S., Ph.D.): Gwen Alexander, Ph.D., Dean. Analysis of information services and delivery systems, community analysis, economics of information, information brokering, information management, information transfer, library and information science education, management of library and information systems, organization and retrieval of information, psychology of information use, sociology of information, technology applications to information storage and retrieval. Dual master's degrees are offered with the Departments of Music, History, Social Sciences, and English and the School of Business. School library media and information management certification is also available. Regional programs are offered in various locations in the western half of the country.

Mathematics (M.S.): Larry Scott, Ph.D., Chair. Applied mathematics, combinatorics, commutative algebra and field theory, computer science, functional analysis, mathematics education, numerical solutions of differential equations, optimization, probability and statistics, real and complex analysis, topology.

Modern Languages and Literatures (M.A. in TESOL): Abdelilah Sehlaoui, Ed.D., and Manjula Shinge, Ph.D., Program Coordinators. Applied linguistics, sociolinguistics, second language acquisition, cross-/intercultural communication, CALL.

Music (M.M.): Allan Comstock, D.M.A., Chair. Concentrations in music education and performance. Areas of study and research include elementary and secondary music education; choral and instrumental conducting; vocal and instrumental methods and performance; jazz performance and instruction; applied studies in voice, keyboard, woodwinds, brass, strings, and percussion; music computer applications; digital audio recordings.

Physical Sciences (M.S.): DeWayne Backhus, Ph.D., Chair. Concentrations in chemistry, earth science (with an online option), physical science, and physics. All programs are designed to prepare students for additional degree work at the doctoral level, industrial or government employment, or teaching. Research opportunities are available in a number of areas within each discipline; NASA-funded research exists in each discipline concentration.

Psychology and Special Education (M.S., Ed.S.): Brian Schrader, Ph.D., Interim Chair. Clinical psychology, general and industrial/organizational psychology, mental health counseling, rehabilitation counseling, art therapy, and school psychology. Faculty specializations include teaching psychology at the secondary level, psychometrics, neuropsychology, cognition, behavioral toxicology, clinical applications of art, child and adolescent development, statistics, learning, performance appraisal, adolescent art therapy, human resources practices in organizations, autism, social skills training, at-risk youth, evaluation of intervention programs, bullying, study-abroad programs, refugee and immigrant populations, job/career satisfaction, school safety, and assessment and interventions in schools.

School Leadership/Middle and Secondary Teacher Education (M.S.): Jerry Will, Ph.D., Chair. Degree and certification programs in elementary and secondary school leadership (i.e., building, program, and district levels), curriculum and instruction (effective practitioner studies, national board certification, curriculum leadership), master's program, postbaccalaureate teacher certification, and driver education. Varied courses are offered online and via ITV.

Social Sciences (M.A.T., M.A.): Darla Mallein, Ph.D., Coordinator. The multidisciplinary M.A.T. degree in social sciences, designed specifically for licensed secondary social studies teachers, allows candidates to concentrate their focus in the areas of American history, world history, geography, and political science. It emphasizes mastery of the methods of teaching the social sciences within the professional educational context, with the aim of developing each candidate's skills as critical thinkers, creative planners, and effective practitioners.

Relaxing campus environment.

Interactive classes.

Technology in the classroom.

FAIRLEIGH DICKINSON UNIVERSITY

Graduate Studies

Programs of Study

Nearly fifty full- and part-time graduate programs are offered through Fairleigh Dickinson University's (FDU) four degree-granting colleges on its two northern New Jersey campuses. Graduate study is offered at the Maxwell Becton College of Arts and Sciences at the College at Florham; University College: Arts, Sciences, and Professional Studies and the Petrocelli College of Continuing Studies on the Metropolitan Campus (both offer a number of programs on the College at Florham campus); and the Silberman College of Business (offers programs accredited by AACSB International on both campuses). The majority of the University's graduate classes are scheduled during the evenings and on weekends for the convenience of working professionals. Not all programs are offered on both campuses.

Master of Science (M.S.) programs are offered in biology, chemistry (with a concentration in pharmaceutical chemistry), computer engineering, computer science, electrical engineering, electronic commerce, hospitality management studies, management information systems, medical technology, nursing (adult nurse practitioner studies with a concentration in administration or education), and systems sciences (with a concentration in environmental studies).

Master of Arts (M.A.) programs are offered in corporate and organizational communication, education for certified teachers, educational leadership, English and comparative literature, history, international studies, learning disabilities, mathematical foundations, media and professional communications, multilingual education, political science, psychology (clinical counseling, forensic, general-theoretical, industrial/organizational, organizational behavior, and school psychology), and science (with concentrations in cosmetic science, elementary science specialist studies, and science teaching specialist studies).

A Master of Fine Arts (M.F.A.) in creative writing is offered as a low-residency program, with concentrations in poetry, fiction, and creative nonfiction.

Master of Arts in Teaching (M.A.T.) programs are available in elementary education (with certification in grades K–5), English as a second language (with certification in grades K–12), and subject area certification grades K–12 in biological science, chemistry, earth science, English, mathematics, physical science, physics, social studies, and world languages.

Master of Business Administration (M.B.A.) programs are offered in entrepreneurial studies, finance, human resource management, international business, management (with concentrations in corporate communication, global business management, information systems, and management for executives and health-care and life sciences professionals), marketing, and pharmaceutical management. In addition, an M.S. in accounting and an M.S. in taxation are offered.

Students may earn a joint M.A./M.B.A. degree in corporate and organizational communication and management and industrial psychology and human resource management.

Professional degree programs are available, such as the Master of Administrative Sciences (M.A.S.), featuring new online specializations in global security and terrorism studies, emergency management administration, and forensic administration, and a Master of Public Administration (M.P.A.), with specializations in health services administration, Jewish communal service, nursing management, public management, and global transportation studies

The University offers a nationally recognized, five-year, full-time Ph.D. program in clinical psychology that is fully accredited by the American Psychological Association. The program adheres to the scientist/practitioner model, requiring a number of clinical and research practicums in addition to an extensive classroom curriculum. A doctoral dissertation and a one-year clinical internship are required of all students. Program faculty interests include work in adult, child, and family therapy; childhood anxiety disorders; gerontology; quantitative methods; personality assessment; addictive behaviors; adult attachment processes; and gender bias. A doctoral program in school psychology leading to the Psy.D. is also available for the practicing professional.

A Doctor of Nursing Practice (D.N.P.) was launched in the spring of 2007. The 40-credit executive model prepares nursing professionals to be clinically expert as providers and educators. A joint-degree program leading to the Doctor of Physical Therapy (D.P.T.) is also offered in conjunction with the University of Medicine and Dentistry of New Jersey (UMDNJ).

Silberman College has educational partnerships with a growing network of international universities in Belize, Brazil, China, Costa Rica, France, Germany, Greece, India, and Monaco. Many programs offer the opportunity for students to participate in classes that incorporate a short-term study-abroad experience. Students may also opt to enroll for a semester-abroad experience at select partner schools. International seminars are held at FDU's Wroxton College in England in many areas of study, including the M.F.A. and M.A. programs in English and comparative literature and corporate and organizational communications and the M.A.S. with a specialization in global leadership.

Research Facilities

FDU offers a wide range of library, computer, health-care skills, and scientific laboratory equipment on both campuses to support student and faculty member research in virtually all graduate disciplines. A new, state-of-the-art cybercrime research laboratory, funded by the U.S. Department of Justice, is located on FDU's Metropolitan Campus. In addition, the University supports the dissemination of research activities through special departmental centers and research institutes.

Financial Aid

A limited number of research, honors research, teaching, and graduate administrative fellowships are available at FDU. Some programs, such as the Master of Arts in Teaching, the Master of Arts in corporate and organizational communication, and the Master of Public Administration, offer paid internships. Eligible domestic graduate students enrolled at least half-time may borrow up to a maximum of $20,500 annually in subsidized and unsubsidized loans under the Federal Stafford Student Loan program. In addition, FDU offers students a number of attractive flexible financing programs.

Cost of Study

Tuition for most nonbusiness graduate programs in 2008–09 was $921 per credit; most graduate business programs were $947 per credit. Fees include an annual technology fee of $308 for part-time students or $648 for full-time students. Several programs, such as the M.B.A programs for executives and health-care and life sciences professionals, the M.B.A. in global management, the M.A. in psychology (with a concentration in organizational behavior for managers), and doctoral-level programs, carry an inclusive full-program fee.

Living and Housing Costs

The University currently offers only limited on-campus housing for graduate students, offered on a first-come, first-served basis. The annual costs at the Metropolitan Campus are $6900 for a standard double room and $3614 for the standard eleven-meal plan, which includes $300 in flex dollars. International students should contact the University's international student organizations for assistance in locating housing.

Student Group

There are a total of 3,589 graduate students enrolled at Fairleigh Dickinson University. The College at Florham enrolls a total of 927 graduate students, and the Metropolitan Campus enrolls 2,642 graduate students.

Location

FDU has two major campus locations in northern New Jersey. The Metropolitan Campus is located less than 10 miles from New York City among seventy-three buildings on a modern, 88-acre site in Teaneck. The College at Florham is situated in the heart of New Jersey's growing corporate center. The campus's Georgian-style buildings span 166 acres of wooded grounds on what was once a private estate. Wroxton College, the University's British campus, is located near Banbury, between Oxford and Stratford-upon-Avon, which is 75 miles from London. In fall 2007, the University began offering select undergraduate degree programs at its FDU-Vancouver location in British Columbia, Canada.

The University

Founded in 1942, FDU is New Jersey's largest private university, with more than 11,000 students. In addition to its two major northern New Jersey campuses, FDU also offers graduate studies to residents of central New Jersey through its Fort Monmouth extension center in Eatontown, and the M.A.S. program is offered at more than fifty off-site locations throughout New Jersey.

Applying

Students can apply for graduate admission for the fall, spring, or summer semester. Requirements vary from program to program, but all require a baccalaureate degree from an accredited institution. To be considered for admission, an FDU application for graduate admission and official transcripts of previous college work must be filed. In some cases, letters of recommendation may be required. Depending on the college in which admission is sought, test scores on the Graduate Record Examinations, Graduate Management Admission Test, or Praxis must be submitted.

Correspondence and Information

Metropolitan Campus
Office of Graduate Admissions
Fairleigh Dickinson University
1000 River Road, T-KB1-01
Teaneck, New Jersey 07666

Phone: 201-692-2554
Fax: 201-692-2560
E-mail: grad@fdu.edu
Web site: http://www.fdu.edu

College at Florham
Office of Graduate Admissions
Fairleigh Dickinson University
285 Madison Avenue, M-MS1-01
Madison, New Jersey 07940

Phone: 973-443-8905
Fax: 973-443-8088
E-mail: grad@fdu.edu
Web site: http://www.fdu.edu

RESEARCH AREAS

COLLEGE OF ARTS AND SCIENCES, COLLEGE AT FLORHAM

The faculty of the Maxwell Becton College of Arts and Sciences offers master's degree programs that emphasize applied research in a variety of disciplinary and interdisciplinary areas. Becton faculty members also serve as the directors or editors of a journal of student research in psychology, two professional journals (*Literary Review* and the *Atlantic Journal of Communication),* and the Fairleigh Dickinson University Press.

Arts and Humanities: digital image processing, animation, and video; literary studies, including Shakespeare, nineteenth- and twentieth-century American authors, and world literature in English; history and theory of communications; corporate and organizational communication (language and social interaction, corporate relations, and quality management); and creative writing.

Biology, Chemistry, Computer Science, and Mathematics: pharmaceutical chemistry; biomedical sciences; ecology; implementation of programming languages, computational complexity, analysis, watermarking techniques, statistics, and actuarial science; quadratic and Hermitian forms.

Psychology: gambling, risk-taking behavior, and drive reduction theory; reduction of reinforcement frequency and increases in response-force requirements as aversive unconditioned stimuli; interpersonal power as an approach to conceptualizing psychopathology; bioenergetic techniques in treating psychopathology; neuropsychology of perception and cognitive processes; the effect of mass media on interpersonal awareness; organizational psychology, including managers' perceptions of problematic employee behavior and techniques for behavioral change; problems of the visibly handicapped.

Social Sciences and History: peaceful transitions to democracy, Japanese defense policy, campaign finance reform, campaign strategies and electoral behavior, race and gender in the antebellum South, the portrayal of sexual norms in women's magazines, anthropology of law, twentieth-century intellectual history, constitutional law and American politics, child soldiers, self-society relationships in the U.S. and the Middle East, concepts of culture in the U.S. in the Middle East, globalization and culture.

PETROCELLI COLLEGE OF CONTINUING STUDIES, METROPOLITAN CAMPUS AND COLLEGE AT FLORHAM

International School of Hospitality and Tourism Management: applied research in hospitality management, including internships with the Greater Atlantic City Hotel-Motel Association and numerous research opportunities with the properties in the New York/New Jersey area.

Public Administration Institute: applied research on problems in state and local government, administrative justice, emergency planning and management, administrative science, health services management, performance evaluation, and comparative health systems.

School of Administrative Science: degree and certificate programs for working professionals in government agencies and not-for-profit organizations; new online specializations in global security and terrorism studies, emergency management studies, and computer security and forensic administration.

SILBERMAN COLLEGE OF BUSINESS, METROPOLITAN CAMPUS AND COLLEGE AT FLORHAM

The faculty of the Silberman College of Business is committed to exemplary teaching and scholarship. Research activities are an integral part of accomplishing the mission of the college. Research work, which includes textbooks, journal articles, conference papers, and presentations before professional organizations, keeps the faculty current in its fields. The college also coordinates a number of applied research projects that are conducted for major corporations, manufacturing and industrial firms, and related organizations. The knowledge and experience gained through their research activities is adopted into lecture material and shared with students. Key research areas include entrepreneurship, both corporate and small ventures; enterprise resource planning; information systems management issues; integrated marketing communications; strategic pricing; and human resource management and development.

UNIVERSITY COLLEGE: ARTS, SCIENCES, AND PROFESSIONAL STUDIES, METROPOLITAN CAMPUS

There has been a growing emphasis on original research and scholarship by the faculty members and graduate students of the University College. The faculty of the School of History, Political and International Studies are involved in research in African political and economic programs, the Middle East and its impact on global affairs, American constitutional law in transition, comparative government, the impact of technology in America, and the child citizen in America. Seasonal affective disorder, eating problems, personality development and psychological testing are among the research projects of the clinical psychology doctoral program. American writers of the nineteenth and twentieth centuries are the focus of the English and comparative literature department, while the Peter Sammartino School of Education conducts innovative research in learning disabilities and bilingual education. Science and engineering faculty members receive research funding for work in such diverse areas as high-temperature superconductivity, underwater digital imaging enhancement, digital image transmission, and ADA computer programming language. The campus's Wiener Library contains nearly 250,000 volumes and 1,600 periodicals and includes diverse special collections. The college also offers graduate students access to a wide range of computer resources and outstanding science research equipment in its biology, chemistry, and engineering laboratories.

Arts and Humanities: origins of civilization; the Middle East and its problems; constitutional law and the Supreme Court; world regions and international relations; international law and organizations; study of American playwright Lanford Wilson; the star-spangled screen; American World War II films; popular culture in twentieth-century America; handling of time in William Faulkner; film history; media effects; advertising outcomes and effects; role of culture and language education at the school level; development of bicultural instructional materials for teaching; adult development as it concerns change agents, self-esteem; leadership related to learning by children with educational handicaps; use of ESL strategies in developing standard English among black English speakers; educational and research programs in cooperation with state and local agencies and school systems, as well as with the federal Department of Education.

Behavioral and Social Sciences: clinical psychology, personality assessment, psychological consequences of exposure to toxics, obesity, factors of sexual harassment, program evaluation, quantitative methods, jury selection, politics and the global economy, international problems and conflict resolution, politics and processes in government.

Nursing and Allied Health: critical thinking; educational technology and pedagogy; obesity and stressful life events; parenting behaviors and perceived competence, perceived health status; ethnography of community health nursing.

Science and Engineering: aquatic ecology; prokaryotic and eukaryotic metabolism; protozoan genetics and ecology; industrial applications of bacterial enzymes; biofouling of reverse osmosis membranes; hormone function, using monoclonal antibodies; multimedia applications in histology and parasitology; enzyme inhibitors; cell culture media (growth factors); natural product antimicrobial testing; development of text systems to access environmental toxicity; physical and colloid chemistry (membranes); geochemistry (carbonate chemistry of water); theoretical organic chemistry (computational methods); consumer-provided cooperation in the transit-planning process; high-resolution, far-infrared spectroscopy; infrared optics (optical properties of solids and powders); computer simulation (sociological theory in pattern evasions); computer methods in engineering and statistical applications; software reuse; management information systems; operation systems; organizational memory; optics (light-wave technology); optical communications; parallel and fault-tolerant systems; electronic commerce; pattern recognition; computer engineering; wireless and digital communications; digital signal and image processing; computer networks.

FLORIDA INSTITUTE OF TECHNOLOGY

Graduate School

Programs of Study

The Graduate School offers master's, education specialist's (Ed.S.), and doctoral degree programs. The College of Business offers the M.B.A. degree. The College of Engineering offers Ph.D. and M.S. degrees in aerospace engineering, chemical engineering, civil engineering, computer engineering, computer science, electrical engineering, environmental science, mechanical engineering, ocean engineering, and oceanography. Master's programs are also offered in computer information systems, engineering management, environmental resources management, software engineering, and systems engineering. The College of Science offers master's and doctoral degrees in applied mathematics, biological sciences, chemistry, elementary science education, mathematics education, physics, science education, and space sciences. Master's degrees are offered in applied mathematics, computer education, environmental education, math education, operations research, and teaching. The Ed.S. degree in science education is also awarded. In the College of Psychology and Liberal Arts, the School of Psychology offers the Psy.D. degree in clinical psychology, the M.S. in applied behavior analysis, and the M.S. and Ph.D. in industrial/organizational psychology. A master's degree in technical and professional communication is offered through Liberal Arts Studies. The School of Aeronautics offers a Master of Science degree in aeronautics with specializations in airport development and management and aviation safety and a Master of Science degree in aviation human factors.

Research Facilities

Laboratories on campus are equipped for research in the various programs of study. These are supplemented by the Life Science Research Complex, Applied Research Laboratories, Claude Pepper Institute for Aging and Therapeutic Research, Reproductive Biology Laboratory, Center for Energy Alternatives, and aquaculture and marine research facilities at Oceanside in Vero Beach. Additional facilities include a solar energy research laboratory and laboratories for optical and solid-state physics, environmental and water pollution analysis, electromagnetics, materials testing and research, electron microscopy, and cytogenetics, as well as in numerous other areas.

The Academic and Research Computing Services (ARCS) provides graduate students with a wide range of computing resources for course work and research. These resources include a Sun Enterprise 3000 and Harris Lab 5227 with several Sun SPARC and GSI Workstations. These machines are connected internally as part of the campus network and externally to the Internet. Many programs and departments have their own computing resources that are also connected to the campus network. Access to these computing resources is available in computer labs and academic units and through dial-up lines. Programming languages supported include C, Pascal, ADA, Fortran, and C++. A staff of professionals is available to assist users with consultation and documentation. In addition to these resources, ARCS maintains a large microcomputer center in the Library Pavilion.

Financial Aid

Graduate student assistantships for instruction and research are available to well-qualified master's and doctoral degree students. Assistantships carry stipends plus a tuition waiver. In some cases, a tuition waiver alone may be awarded for a limited amount of service. Assistantships for master's degree students are normally for an academic year; assistantships for doctoral students are renewable on a yearly basis.

Graduate students may apply for a Florida Tech Graduate Scholarship when submitting an application for admission. Scholarships are only awarded at the time of admission. The average award is $5000 and is renewable annually. Students may not have both an assistantship and a scholarship.

Cost of Study

Tuition for graduate study is $1015 per semester hour in 2009–10. A tuition deposit of $300 (deducted from the first semester's tuition charge) is required of all new students. Books are estimated to cost $800 per year.

Living and Housing Costs

Room and board on campus cost approximately $4500 per semester in 2009–10. On-campus housing (dormitories and apartments) is available for full-time graduate students, but priority for dormitory rooms is given to undergraduate students. Many apartment complexes and rental houses are available near the campus.

Student Group

Graduate students constitute more than one fourth of the students attending Florida Tech's Melbourne campus. Enrolled graduate and undergraduate students represent forty-nine states and more than 101 countries.

Location

Melbourne is located on the central east coast of Florida. The area offers a delightful year-round subtropical climate and is 10 minutes from the ocean beaches. Kennedy Space Center and the massive NASA complex are just 45 minutes north of Melbourne. The city of Orlando, Walt Disney World, and EPCOT are 1 hour west of the Florida Tech main campus.

The Institute

Florida Institute of Technology is a distinctive, independent university, founded in 1958 by a group of scientists and engineers to fulfill a need for specialized, advanced educational opportunities on the Space Coast of Florida. Florida Tech is the only comprehensive, independent scientific and technological university in the southeast. Supported by both industry and the community, Florida Tech is the recipient of many research grants and contracts, a number of which provide financial support for graduate students.

Applying

Forms for applying to the Graduate School and for assistantships are sent on request. Applications for assistantships must be submitted by January 15. Department of Biology students must complete the application process by March 1. Doctor of Psychology applicants must complete the application process by January 15 and begin their program of study in the fall. Applied behavior analysis applicants must apply by March 1. Industrial/organizational psychology applicants must complete the application process by February 1. An online application and related forms are available on the graduate admissions page of the Florida Tech Web site at http://www.fit.edu/grad.

Correspondence and Information

Graduate Admissions Office
Florida Institute of Technology
150 West University Boulevard
Melbourne, Florida 32901-6975

Phone: 321-674-8027
800-944-4348 (toll-free in the U.S.)
Fax: 321-723-9468
E-mail: grad-admissions@fit.edu
Web site: http://www.fit.edu/grad

DEPARTMENT HEADS AND PROGRAM CHAIRS

The faculty members listed below will be pleased to answer inquiries concerning programs and degrees or to provide general university information.

COLLEGE OF AERONAUTICS
W. E. Scott, Ph.D., Dean.
J. Cain, Ph.D., Associate Dean.
Airport Development and Management (M.S.): J. Cain, Ph.D., Program Chairman.
Aviation Human Factors (M.S.): J. Cain, Ph.D., Program Chairman.
Aviation Safety (M.S.): J. Cain, Ph.D., Program Chairman.

COLLEGE OF BUSINESS
R. E. Niebuhr, Ph.D., Dean.
A. Vamosi, Ph.D., Associate Dean.
Business Administration (M.B.A.)

COLLEGE OF ENGINEERING
T. D. Waite, Ph.D., Dean.
E. H. Kalajian, Ph.D., Associate Dean.
Chemical Engineering (M.S., Ph.D.): P. A. Jennings, Ph.D., Department Head.
Civil Engineering (M.S., Ph.D.): A. Pandit, Ph.D., Department Head.
Computer Sciences (M.S., Ph.D.): W. Shoaff, Ph.D., Department Head.
Electrical and Computer Engineering (M.S., Ph.D.): S. Kozaitis, Ph.D., Department Head.
Engineering Systems (M.S.): M. Shaikh, Ph.D., Department Head.
Marine and Environmental Systems (M.S., Ph.D.): G. Maul, Ph.D., Department Head.
Mechanical and Aerospace Engineering (M.S., Ph.D.): P. Hsu, Ph.D., Department Head.

COLLEGE OF PSYCHOLOGY AND LIBERAL ARTS
School of Psychology
M. B. Kenkel, Psy.D., Dean.
Applied Behavior Analysis (M.S.): J. Martinez-Diaz, Ph.D., Department Head.
Clinical Psychology (Psy.D.): K. Mulligan, Ph.D., Director Clinical Training.
Industrial/Organizational Psychology (M.S., Ph.D.): L. Steelman, Ph.D., Department Head.
Organizational Behavior Management (M.S.): J. Martinez-Diaz, Ph.D., Department Head.
Liberal Arts Studies
Humanities and Communications (M.S.): R. Taylor, Ph.D., Department Head.

COLLEGE OF SCIENCE
G. Nelson, Ph.D., Dean.
H. K. Rassoul, Ph.D., Associate Dean.
Biological Sciences (M.S., Ph.D.): R. Aronson, Ph.D., Department Head.
Chemistry (M.S., Ph.D.): M. W. Babich, Ph.D., Department Head.
Mathematics Sciences (M.S., Ph.D.): V. Lakshmikatham, Ph.D., Department Head.
Physics and Space Sciences (M.S., Ph.D.): T. Oswald, Ph.D., Department Head.
Science and Mathematics Education (M.S., Ed.S., Ph.D.): D. Cook, Ph.D., Department Head.

FLORIDA INTERNATIONAL UNIVERSITY

University Graduate School

Programs of Study Graduate programs are offered at Florida International University (FIU) in the following fields (asterisks denote fields in which only a master's degree is offered): *accounting, adult education, *advertising and public relations, *African and African diaspora studies, *architecture, *art education, *Asian studies, biology, biomedical engineering, business administration, chemistry, civil engineering, comparative sociology, *computer engineering, computer science, *construction management, *counselor education, *creative writing, *criminal justice, curriculum and instruction, dietetics and nutrition, *early childhood education, *earth sciences (educational), *educational leadership and policy studies, economics, educational administration and supervision, educational leadership, electrical engineering, *elementary education, *engineering management, *English, *English for non-English speakers (TESOL), *environmental engineering, *environmental studies, exceptional student education, *finance, *foreign language education: TESOL, *forensic science, *French education, geosciences, higher education administration, history, hospitality management, human resource development, *human resource management, *interior design, *international business, *international development education, international real estate, *international relations, international studies, *international and intercultural education, *landscape architecture, *Latin American and Caribbean studies, *liberal studies, *linguistics, management information systems, *mass communication, *materials science engineering, *mathematical sciences, mechanical engineering, *modern language education, *music, *music education, nursing, *occupational therapy, *physical education, physical therapy, physics, political science, psychology, *public administration, public health, public management, *reading education, *religious studies, school psychology, social welfare, *social work, *sociology, Spanish, *Spanish education, *special education, speech-language pathology, statistics, *taxation, *telecommunications and networking engineering, *urban education, and *visual arts.

Research Facilities The libraries at University Park and the Biscayne Bay Campus house more than 1 million volumes, along with numerous periodicals, maps, microfilms, institutional archives, curriculum materials, and government documents. Access to 9,300 periodicals and serials is available. Interlibrary loan services offer access to holdings at major libraries throughout the country, and the online catalog gives information about the collections of all the libraries in the State University System of Florida. Special research centers and institutes include the following: the Academy for the Art of Teaching, the High-Performance Database Research Center, the Hemispheric Center for Environmental Technology, the International Hurricane Center, the Latin American and Caribbean Center, and the Southeast Florida Center on Aging.

Financial Aid Graduate students may qualify for assistantships and fellowships and other awards that are offered through FIU's schools, colleges, and departments. To apply, students should contact the departmental dean's office. A limited number of awards are available for students who demonstrate need through the Free Application for Federal Student Aid (FAFSA; http://www.fafsa.ed.gov). The form is available at all U.S. colleges and universities.

Cost of Study For the 2008–09 academic year, per-credit-hour fees for new graduate students were $299 for Florida residents and $803 for non-Florida residents. Fees include a $10 athletic fee, a $67 student health fee, and a transportation access fee of $82 per semester (fall and spring; $76 in the summer term).

Living and Housing Costs Graduate student housing is available at University Park (phone: 305-348-4190) and the Biscayne Bay Campus (phone: 305-919-5587).

Student Group The graduate student community includes 6,500 students from all fifty states and more than 110 nations.

Student Outcomes Graduates of the University proceed to a wide variety of academic and professional careers in academic institutions, government agencies, nonprofit organizations, private industry, and entrepreneurial enterprises.

Location Located in suburban west Miami-Dade County, the 342-acre University Park campus is notable for its distinctive architecture, lush tropical landscape, and impressive outdoor sculpture park. The Biscayne Bay Campus is situated on 200 acres on Biscayne Bay in North Miami, which encompasses a natural mangrove preserve. FIU also operates Broward-Pines Center in Pembroke Pines. A major research facility, the 40-acre Engineering Center is located near the University Park campus. The Downtown Center, located in downtown Miami, offers graduate-level business courses for busy professionals.

The University FIU is a public, multicampus research university and a member of the State University System of Florida. The University is ranked as a Research University in the High Research Activity category of the Carnegie Foundation's prestigious classification system. FIU offers more than 100 graduate and advanced academic and professional degrees.

Applying Applicants who have earned a bachelor or master's degree or the equivalent from a regionally accredited institution or a recognized institution of higher learning are welcome to apply. The Graduate Admissions Office must receive official transcripts, diplomas, and/or certificates directly from all previously attended institutions. Documents in a language other than English must be translated by an official translation agency. Applicants must submit GRE or GMAT scores, depending on program requirements. Students whose native language is not English must also submit TOEFL scores.

Correspondence and Information

Graduate Admissions Office
Florida International University
P.O. Box 659004
Miami, Florida 33265
Phone: 305-348-7442
Fax: 305-348-7441
E-mail: gradadm@fiu.edu
Web site: http://gradschool.fiu.edu

GRADUATE PROGRAMS

COLLEGE OF ARCHITECTURE AND THE ARTS
Architecture: http://www.fiu.edu/~soa
Landscape Architecture: http://www.fiu.edu/~soa

COLLEGE OF ARTS AND SCIENCES
African and African Diaspora Studies: http://www.fiu.edu/~africana
Asian Studies: http://asian.fiu.edu/
Biology: http://www.fiu.edu/~biology
Chemistry: http://www.fiu.edu/orgs/chemistry
Creative Writing: http://w3.fiu.edu/CRWRITING
Criminal Justice: http://swjpa.fiu.edu/cj/
Economics: http://www.fiu.edu/orgs/economics
English: http://www.fiu.edu/~english
Environmental Studies: http://www.fiu.edu/~envstud
Forensic Science: http://www.fiu.edu/~ifri
Geology: http://www.fiu.edu/orgs/geology
History: http://www.fiu.edu/~history
International Relations: http://www.fiu.edu/~intlrel
Latin American and Caribbean Studies: http://lacc.fiu.edu/
Liberal Studies: http://www.fiu.edu/~liberal
Linguistics: http://linguistics.fiu.edu/
Mathematics: http://w3.fiu.edu/math
Modern Languages: http://www.fiu.edu/orgs/modlang
Music: http://www.fiu.edu/~music
Physics: http://www.fiu.edu/physics
Political Science: http://www.fiu.edu/~polsci
Public Administration: http://swjpa.fiu.edu/pa/MPA.htm
Public Management: http://swjpa.fiu.edu/pa/PHDPM.htm
Psychology: http://w3.fiu.edu/psych
Religious Studies: http://www.fiu.edu/~religion
Sociology: http://www.fiu.edu/orgs/socant
Statistics: http://www.fiu.edu/~statdept
Visual Arts: http://www.fiu.edu/~visart

COLLEGE OF BUSINESS ADMINISTRATION
Accounting: http://business.fiu.edu/chapman/master_of_accounting.cfm
Business Administration: http://business.fiu.edu/chapman/phd_programs.cfm
Finance: http://business.fiu.edu/chapman/master_of_science_in_finance.cfm
Human Resource Management: http://business.fiu.edu/chapman/master_of_science_in_hrm.cfm
International Business: http://business.fiu.edu/chapman/master_of_intl_business.cfm
International Real Estate: http://business.fiu.edu/chapman/master_of_science_in_intl_real_estate.cfm
Management Information Systems: http://business.fiu.edu/chapman/master_of_science_in_mis.cfm

COLLEGE OF EDUCATION
Adult Education and Human Resource Development: http://www.fiu.edu/~elps/aehrd.htm
Art Education: http://www.fiu.edu/~curricul/programs_ms_arted.html
Community Mental Health: http://fiu.edu/~edpsy/mentalhealth.htm
Counselor Education: http://www.fiu.edu/~edpsy/counseloredhome.htm
Curriculum and Instruction: http://www.fiu.edu/~curricul/
Early Childhood Education: http://education.fiu.edu/graduate_programs/ms_earlychilded.htm
Educational Administration/Supervision: http://education.fiu.edu/graduate_programs/phd_adminandsuper.htm
Elementary Education: http://www.fiu.edu/~curricul/admissionprocessEDS.htm
English for Non-English Speakers (TESOL): http://education.fiu.edu/graduate_programs/ms_foreignlaned.htm
Exceptional Student Education: http://www.fiu.edu/%7Eedpsy/sped_graduate.htm
Higher Education/Community College Teaching: http://education.fiu.edu/graduate_programs/ms_highered.htm
Human Resource Development: http://education.fiu.edu/graduate_programs/ms_humanresource.htm
International Development Education: http://education.fiu.edu/graduate_programs/ms_intern_interculted.htm
Mathematics Education: http://education.fiu.edu/graduate_programs/ms_mathed.htm
Modern Languages: http://education.fiu.edu/graduate_programs/ms_modlanged.htm
Physical Education: http://www.fiu.edu/~hper/physicalEducationMS.htm
Reading Education: http://education.fiu.edu/graduate_programs/ms_readinged.htm
School Psychology: http://www.fiu.edu/~edpsy
Special Education: http://www.fiu.edu/~edpsy/sped_graduate.htm
Technology Education: http://education.fiu.edu/graduate_programs/ms_urbaned.htm
Urban Education: http://education.fiu.edu/graduate_programs/ms_urbaned.htm

COLLEGE OF ENGINEERING AND COMPUTING
Biomedical Engineering: http://www.eng.fiu.edu/bmei
Civil Engineering: http://www.eng.fiu.edu/ce
Computer Science: http://www.cs.fiu.edu
Construction Management: http://www.cm.fiu.edu/
Electrical and Computer Engineering: http://www.eng.fiu.edu/ece
Engineering Management: http://www.eng.fiu.edu/ie
Environmental Engineering: http://www.eng.fiu.edu/ce
Materials Science Engineering: http://www.eng.fiu.edu/cec/CEC_MS_Material.htm
Mechanical Engineering: http://www.eng.fiu.edu/me

COLLEGE OF NURSING AND HEALTH SCIENCES
Nursing: http://chua2.fiu.edu/nursing
Occupational Therapy: http://chua2.fiu.edu/ot
Physical Therapy: http://chua2.fiu.edu/physicaltherapy
Speech-Language Pathology: http://csd.fiu.edu

STEMPEL SCHOOL OF PUBLIC HEALTH
Dietetics and Nutrition: http://chua2.fiu.edu/dietetics-nutrition/
Public Health: http://chua2.fiu.edu/publichealth
Social Welfare: http://swjpa.fiu.edu/socialwork/PHDSW.htm
Social Work: http://swjpa.fiu.edu/socialwork

SCHOOL OF HOSPITALITY AND TOURISM MANAGEMENT
Hospitality Management: http://hospitality.fiu.edu/

SCHOOL OF JOURNALISM AND MASS COMMUNICATION
Advertising/Public Relations: http://jmc.fiu.edu/sjmc
Journalism/Broadcasting: http://jmc.fiu.edu/sjmc
College of Law: http://law.fiu.edu
College of Medicine: http://medicine.fiu.edu

FLORIDA STATE UNIVERSITY

The Graduate School

Programs of Study Florida State University (FSU), a Carnegie Doctoral/Research University with very high research activities, offers doctoral programs in seventy-three areas and master's programs in 114 areas. Advanced master's and specialist degrees are offered in twenty-eight programs. The University is comprised of fifteen colleges: Arts and Sciences; Business; Communication and Information; Criminology and Criminal Justice; Education; Engineering; Human Sciences; Law; Medicine; Motion Picture, Television, and Recording Arts; Music; Nursing; Social Sciences; Social Work; and Visual Arts, Theatre, and Dance. Students may pursue a number of interdisciplinary degrees, and several joint-degree programs are available.

FSU ranks among the top fifty public research universities in the country in the number of doctoral degrees awarded annually.

Research Facilities Florida State University libraries contain approximately 3.4 million volumes, more than 107,000 serials, more than 9 million microfilms, and approximately 451,000 e-books. The libraries are committed to innovative use of new electronic technologies to enhance the research capabilities of students and faculty members. The University has more than ninety research centers, institutes, and special laboratories. Prominent among these are the National High Magnetic Field Laboratory, which is dedicated to research in supermagnetic fields and has application in the life sciences, transportation, and materials research. Among other research facilities are the Super FN Tandem Van de Graff Accelerator in Nuclear Research; the Institute for Molecular Biophysics; the Learning Systems Institute, which focuses on instructional systems design technology; the Institute for Science and Public Affairs, which focuses on assisting state and private agencies and the related units on aging, populations studies, family studies, and policy studies; the Marine Laboratory, which is located on the northern Gulf; the Geophysical Fluid Dynamics Institute; several centers devoted to atmospheric, oceanic, and climatic studies; the Center for Materials Research and Technology; and the Center for Music Research.

Financial Aid Graduate students may compete for many forms of financial assistance for graduate study. There is an annual competition for nonduty University fellowships with stipends ranging from $18,000 to $23,000, plus tuition waivers with some departments supplementing this amount. In addition, a health insurance subsidy of up to $1250 per student per academic year is offered toward the purchase of the single coverage, University-sponsored comprehensive student health insurance plan. All graduate programs offer teaching or research assistantships, with some programs funding many of their enrolled graduate students. Assistantship stipends vary from program to program, but in combination with tuition waivers they are competitive with other universities. Graduate assistants are eligible for a health insurance subsidy of $200 to $400 per student per academic year toward the University-sponsored student health insurance plan (single coverage). Student loans are available through the Office of Financial Aid, 4474 UCT, Florida State University, Tallahassee, Florida 32306 (Web site: http://www.ais.fsu.edu/finaid).

Cost of Study Tuition and fees for an in-state resident for 2008–09 were $6738 for the academic year; this is based on 12 hours of graduate enrollment each term. The comparable amount for out-of-state graduate students was $21,891.60. Most students who receive a fellowship or an assistantship have both in-state and out-of-state tuition waived.

Living and Housing Costs The University provides some housing for graduate students, but the majority of graduate students secure private housing, much of it within walking distance or free bus service of the University. There are many apartment complexes in Tallahassee and private dormitories near the University. For more information about housing, students can contact Housing, 108 CAW, Florida State University, Tallahassee, Florida 32306 (Web site: http://www.housing.fsu.edu). Generally, the cost of living in Tallahassee is moderate.

Student Group Florida State enrolled more than 39,136 students in 2008–09, including more than 7,100 graduate students, of whom 62 percent were full-time. The overall student body is 55.7 percent women, and members of minority groups constitute 25.3 percent of all students. All fifty states and a large number of other countries are represented in the student body.

Student Outcomes FSU awards more than 2,079 master's degrees and approximately 337 doctoral degrees each year. Students find many rewarding opportunities, ranging from faculty positions in colleges and universities to postdoctoral appointments in other leading universities. The University has a Career Center to assist graduate students, and departments actively assist graduates in their search for employment.

Location FSU is located in Tallahassee, the capital of Florida and the home of two other educational institutions, Florida A&M University, a historically black university, and Tallahassee Community College. Tallahassee is situated about 40 miles from the Gulf of Mexico, with some of the world's most beautiful beaches within an easy drive. The climate permits year-round outdoor activity. Recreation and sports activities abound for both participants and observers. Cultural activities are very rich as well. The outstanding College of Music and College of Visual Arts, Theatre, and Dance are the catalysts for several series of plays, musical performances, and operas, and the University operates both public television and radio stations. A new culture and science center is slated to open soon in downtown Tallahassee.

The University FSU is a fully accredited public university and functions as a component of the eleven-member State University System of Florida. While the University provides an extensive and high-quality undergraduate program, it has a central mission in graduate education and research. Its mission statement recounts that "the University's primary role is to serve as a center for advanced graduate and professional studies while emphasizing research and providing excellence in undergraduate programs." It has a distinguished faculty that has regularly included Nobel laureates and members of prestigious national academic societies. Its expenditures in sponsored research exceed $206.5 million per year. For more information about Florida State University, prospective students should visit the University Web site at http://www.fsu.edu.

Applying All domestic and international students may apply or seek information about a program online at http://www.admissions.fsu.edu; they should contact the academic department to which they are applying if they wish to be considered for financial assistance. While there are University-wide requirements for admission, the requirements for each program are set by the faculty members in that program and may be higher than the University-wide requirements. The GRE General Test is required of all students (GMAT for business). Applications are carefully reviewed, with due consideration to the academic record, test scores, letters of recommendation, and expressions of interest. An Internet-based TOEFL score of 80 or better is required for applicants whose native language is not English. While admission deadlines vary by department, students should submit all materials by early January to be considered for all forms of financial assistance.

Correspondence and Information

For admissions:
Graduate Admissions
A2500 UCA
Florida State University
282 Champion Way
P.O. Box 3062400
Tallahassee, Florida 32306-2400
Phone: 850-644-3420
Fax: 850-644-0197
E-mail: admissions@admin.fsu.edu
Web site: http://www.fsu.edu

For specific programs:
(Department or Program)
Florida State University
Tallahassee, Florida 32306

The Graduate School
408 Westcott
Florida State University
222 South Copeland Avenue
P.O. Box 3061410
Tallahassee, Florida 32306-1410
Phone: 850-644-3501
Fax: 850-644-2969
E-mail: gradschool@www.fsu.edu
Web site: http://www.gradschool.fsu.edu

DIRECTORS OF GRADUATE PROGRAMS

COLLEGE OF ARTS AND SCIENCES

American and Florida Studies (M.A.): Dr. Kathleen Erndl (850-644-0207; kerndl@fsu.edu). **Anthropology (Ph.D./M.S.):** Dr. Lynn Schepartz (850-645-7844; lschepartz@fsu.edu). **Biological Science (Ph.D./M.S.):** Dr. George Bates (850-644-3023; bates@bio.fsu.edu). **Chemistry and Biochemistry (Ph.D.):** Dr. Geoffrey Strouse (850-645-1898; strouse@chem.fsu.edu). **Classics (Ph.D./M.A.):** Dr. Laurel Fulkerson (850-644-0305; lfulkerson@fsu.edu). **Computer Science (Ph.D./M.S.):** Dr. Michael Mascagni (850-644-3290; admissions@cs.fsu.edu). **English (Ph.D./M.A.):** Dr. Stan Gontarski (850-644-6038; sgontarski@fsu.edu). **Geology (Ph.D./M.S.):** Dr. Vincent Salters (850-644-1934; salters@magnet.fsu.edu). **Geophysical Fluid Dynamics (Ph.D.):** Dr. Carol Clayson (850-645-5625; cclayson@fsu.edu). **History (Ph.D./M.A.):** Dr. Michael Creswell (850-644-9532; mcreswell@fsu.edu). **Interdisciplinary Humanities (Ph.D.):** Dr. Nancy Warren (850-644-5077; nwarren@fsu.edu). **Mathematics (Ph.D./M.S.):** Dr. Betty Anne Case (850-644-1586; case@math.fsu.edu). **Meteorology (Ph.D./M.S.):** Dr. Philip Cunningham (850-644-4334; pcunningham@fsu.edu). **Modern Languages (Ph.D./M.A.):** Dr. Reinier Leushuis (850-644-8179; rleushuis@fsu.edu). **Molecular Biophysics (Ph.D.):** Dr. Geoffrey Strouse (850-645-1898; strouse@chem.fsu.edu). **Neuroscience (Ph.D.):** Dr. Rick Hyson (850-644-5824; hyson@psy.fsu.edu). **Oceanography (Ph.D./M.S.):** Ms. Michaela Lupiani (850-644-6700; lupiani@ocean.fsu.edu). **Philosophy (Ph.D./M.S.):** Dr. Randy Clarke (850-645-7473; rkclarke@fsu.edu). **Physics (Ph.D./M.S.):** Dr. Simon Capstick (850-644-1724; scapstick@fsu.edu). **Psychology (Ph.D.):** Dr. Ashby Plant (850-644-5533; plant@psy.fsu.edu). **Psychology (Applied Behavioral Analysis) (M.S.):** Dr. Ellen Berler (850-644-2040; berler@psy.fsu.edu). **Religion (Ph.D.):** Dr. Bryan Cuevas (850-644-9879; bcuevas@fsu.edu). **Statistics (Ph.D.):** Dr. Eric Chicken (850-644-9841; chicken@stat.fsu.edu).

COLLEGE OF BUSINESS

Accounting (Ph.D.): Dr. Richard Morton (850-644-7877; rmorton@cob.fsu.edu). **(M.Acc.):** Dr. Gregory Gerard (850-644-9115; ggerard@cob.fsu.edu). **Business Administration (Ph.D./M.B.A./M.S.):** Dr. Bruce Lamont (850-644-9846; blamont@fsu.edu). (M.B.A./M.S.): Dr. Victor Ranft (850-644-7837; vranft@cob.fsu.edu). **Finance (Ph.D.):** Dr. David Peterson (850-644-8200; dpeters@cob.fsu.edu). (M.S.): Dr. Gary Benesh (850-644-8209; gbenesh@cob.fsu.edu). **Management (Ph.D.):** Dr. Chad Van Iddekinge (850-644-7867; cvanidde@fsu.edu). **Management Information Systems (Ph.D.):** Dr. Ashley Bush (850-644-2779; abush@cob.fsu.edu). **(M.S.):** Dr. Molly Wasko (850-644-0916; mwasko@fsu.edu). **Marketing (Ph.D.):** Dr. Mike Brady (850-644-7853; mbrady@cob.fsu.edu). **(M.S.):** Dr. Larry Giunipero (850-644-8224; lgiunipero@cob.fsu.edu). **Risk Management and Insurance (Ph.D.):** Dr. James Carson (850-644-5858; jcarson@fsu.edu). **(M.S.):** Dr. Kathleen McCullough (850-644-8358; kmccullough@cob.fsu.edu).

COLLEGE OF COMMUNICATION AND INFORMATION

Communications (Ph.D.): Dr. Arthur Raney (850-644-5034; araney@fsu.edu). **Communication Disorders (Ph.D.):** Dr. Juliann Woods (850-645-4972; juliann.woods@comm.fsu.edu). **Library and Information Studies (Ph.D./M.A./M.S.):** Dr. Corinne Jorgensen (850-644-8116; corinne.jorgensen@cci.fsu.edu).

COLLEGE OF CRIMINOLOGY AND CRIMINAL JUSTICE

Ph.D./M.S.: Ms. Margarita Frankeberger (850-644-7373; mfrankeberger@fsu.edu).

COLLEGE OF EDUCATION

Career Counseling (Specialist/M.S.): Dr. Janet Lenz (850-644-9547; jlenz@admin.fsu.edu). **Counseling Psychology and School Psychology (combined Ph.D.):** Dr. Steven Pfeiffer (850-644-8796; pfeiffer@coe.fsu.edu). **Early Childhood Education (Ph.D./Specialist/M.S.):** Dr. Ithel Jones (850-644-8468; ijones@coe.fsu.edu). **Educational Leadership and Policy (Ph.D.):** Dr. Jeffrey Milligan (850-644-8171; milligan@coe.fsu.edu). **Educational Leadership Administration (Ph.D./Ed.D./Specialist/M.S.):** Dr. Judith Irvin (850-644-6447; irvin@coe.fsu.edu). **Educational Policy Studies and Evaluation (Ph.D./M.S.):** Dr. Lora Cohen-Vogel (850-644-8164; lcohenvogel@fsu.edu). **Elementary Education (Ph.D./Specialist/M.S.):** Dr. Diana Rice (850-644-4685; rice@coe.fsu.edu). **English Education (Ph.D./Specialist/M.S.):** Dr. Susan Wood (850-644-1909; swood@fsu.edu). **Foreign and Second Language Teaching (M.S./M.A.):** Dr. Rebecca Galeano (850-644-2129; galeano@coe.fsu.edu). **Higher Education (Ph.D./M.S.):** Dr. Shouping Hu (850-644-6777; shu@fsu.edu). **History and Philosophy of Education (M.S.):** Dr. Jeffrey Milligan (850-644-8171; milligan@coe.fsu.edu). **Instructional Systems (Ph.D./M.S.):** Dr. Vanessa Dennen (850-644-8783; vdennen@fsu.edu). **Learning and Cognition (Ph.D./M.S.):** Dr. Alysia Roehrig (850-644-8781; aroehrig@fcrr.org). **Math Education (Ph.D./M.S.):** Dr. Leslie Aspinwall (850-644-8427; laspinwall@fsu.edu). **Measurement and Statistics (Ph.D./M.S.):** Dr. Betsy Becker (850-645-2371; bbecker@fsu.edu). **Mental Health Counseling (Specialist/M.S.):** Dr. Georgios Lampropoulos (850-645-1293; glampropoulos@fsu.edu). **Open and Distance Learning (M.S.):** Dr. Vanessa Dennen (850-644-8783; vdennen@fsu.edu). **Performance Improvement and Human Resource Development (M.S.):** Dr. Robert Reiser (850-644-4592; rreiser@fsu.edu). **Physical Education (M.S./Specialist):** Dr. Tom Ratliffe (850-644-7588; ratliffe@coe.fsu.edu). **Reading Education (Ph.D./Specialist/M.S.):** Dr. Carolyn Piazza (850-644-8476; cpiazza@fsu.edu). **School Psychology (Specialist/M.S.):** Dr. Angela Canto (850-644-9440; acanto@fsu.edu). **Science Education (Ph.D./Specialist/M.S.):** Dr. Victor Sampson (850-644-1286; vsampson@fsu.edu). **(M.S.):** Dr. Alejandro Gallard (850-644-7813; agallard@fsu.edu). **(M.S. Distance):** Dr. Nancy Davis (850-644-7804; ndavis@fsu.edu). **Socio-Cultural Development (M.S.):** Dr. Jeffrey Milligan (850-644-8171; milligan@coe.fsu.edu). **Social Science Education (Ph.D./Specialist/M.S.):** Dr. Toni Kirkwood-Tucker (850-644-6553; kirkwoodtf@aol.com). **Special Education (Ph.D./Specialist/M.S.):** Dr. Stephanie Al Otaiba (850-644-0717; salotaiba@fcrr.org). **Special Education Studies (M.S. Distance):** Dr. Mary Francis Hanline (850-644-8417; mhanline@fsu.edu). **Sport Management (Ph.D.):** Dr. Jeff James (850-644-9214; jdjames@fsu.edu). **(M.S.):** Dr. Cecile Reynaud (850-644-4298; reynaud@fsu.edu). **Sport Psychology (Ph.D./M.S.):** Dr. Robert Eklund (850-645-2909; eklund@coe.fsu.edu). **Visual Disabilities (M.S.):** Dr. Sandra Lewis (850-644-8409; slewis@fsu.edu).

COLLEGE OF ENGINEERING

Chemical and Biomedical Engineering (Ph.D./M.S.): Dr. Teng Ma (850-410-6558; teng@eng.fsu.edu). **Civil Engineering (Ph.D./M.S.):** Dr. Ren Moses (850-410-6191; moses@eng.fsu.edu). **Electrical Engineering (Ph.D.):** Dr. Thomas Baldwin (850-410-6584; tbaldwin@eng.fsu.edu). **Industrial Engineering (Ph.D.):** Dr. Okenwa Okoli (850-410-6352; okoli@eng.fsu.edu). **Mechanical Engineering (Ph.D.):** Dr. Emmanuel Collins (850-410-6373; ecollins@eng.fsu.edu).

COLLEGE OF HUMAN SCIENCES

Family and Child Sciences (Ph.D./M.S.): Dr. Robert Lee (850-644-1412; relee@fsu.edu). **Marriage and the Family (Ph.D./M.S.):** Dr. Robert Lee (850-644-1412; relee@fsu.edu). **Nutrition, Food, and Exercise Sciences (Ph.D./M.S.):** Dr. Bahram Arjmandi (850-644-1928; barjmandi@fsu.edu). **Textiles and Consumer Sciences (Ph.D./M.S.):** Dr. Jeanne Heitmeyer (850-644-5578; jheitmey@mailer.fsu.edu).

COLLEGE OF LAW

J.D./LL.M.: Ms. Jennifer Kessinger (850-644-3787; jkessinger@fsu.edu) or Ms. Deborah Hood (850-644-3787; dhood@law.fsu.edu).

COLLEGE OF MEDICINE

Biomedical Sciences (Ph.D.): Dr. Mohamed Kabbaj (850-644-4930; mohamed.kabbaj@med.fsu.edu). **(M.D.):** Dr. Randolph Rill (850-644-3661; randolph.rill@med.fsu.edu).

COLLEGE OF MOTION PICTURE, TELEVISION, AND RECORDING ARTS

M.F.A.: Mr. Reb Braddock (850-644-8524; rbraddock@admin.fsu.edu).

COLLEGE OF MUSIC

Ph.D./D.M./Ed.D./M.M./M.A.: Dr. Seth Beckman (850-644-5848; sbeckman@admin.fsu.edu).

COLLEGE OF NURSING

D.N.P./M.S.N.: Dr. Dianne Speake (850-644-6846; dspeake@nursing.fsu.edu).

COLLEGE OF SOCIAL SCIENCES

Asian Studies (M.A./M.S.): Dr. Lee Metcalf (850-644-4418; lmetcalf@fsu.edu). **Demography/Population Center (M.S.):** Dr. Isaac Eberstein (850-644-7108; ieberstn@fsu.edu). **Economics (Ph.D./M.S.):** Dr. Thomas Zuehlke (850-644-7206; tzuehlke@fsu.edu). **Geography (Ph.D./M.S.):** Dr. Mark Horner (850-644-8377; mhorner@fsu.edu). **International Affairs (M.A./M.S.):** Dr. Lee Metcalf (850-644-4418; lmetcalf@fsu.edu). **Political Science (Ph.D./M.A./M.S.):** Dr. Charles Barrilleaux (850-644-7643; cbarrilleaux@fsu.edu). **Public Administration and Policy (Ph.D.):** Dr. Robert Eger (850-645-1914; reger@fsu.edu). **(M.P.A.):** Dr. Earle Klay (850-644-3525; eklay@fsu.edu). **Russian and East European Studies (M.A./M.S.):** Dr. Lee Metcalf (850-644-4418; lmetcalf@fsu.edu). **Sociology (Ph.D.):** Dr. John Reynolds (850-644-4321; john.reynolds@fsu.edu). **Urban and Regional Planning (Ph.D.):** Dr. Ivonne Audirac (850-644-9801; iaudirac@fsu.edu). **(M.S.P.):** Dr. Jeffrey Brown (850-644-8519; jrbrown3@fsu.edu).

COLLEGE OF SOCIAL WORK

Ph.D.: Dr. Jim Hinterlong (850-644-3577; jhinterlong@fsu.edu). **M.S.W.:** Mr. Craig Stanley (850-644-9741; cstanley@fsu.edu).

COLLEGE OF VISUAL ARTS, THEATRE, AND DANCE

Acting (M.F.A.): Mr. GregLearning (941-351-9010; greg.learning@conservatory.fsu.edu). **American Dance Studies (M.A.):** Ms. Tricia Young (850-644-1023; young@dance.fsu.edu). **Art (M.F.A.):** Ms. Holly Hanessian (850-590-8097; haha_works@yahoo.com).**Art Education (Ph.D./M.S.):** Dr. Patricia Villeneuve (pvilleneuve@fsu.edu). **Art History (Ph.D./M.A.):** Dr. Kathy Braun (850-644-8207; kbraun@fsu.edu. **Arts Administration (M.A.):** Dr. Patricia Villeneuve (pvilleneuve@fsu.edu). **Art Therapy (M.S.):** Dr. Marcia Rosal (850-644-2926; mrosal@fsu.edu). **Dance (M.F.A./M.A.):** Ms. Patricia Phillips (850-644-1023; pphillip@fsu.edu). **Costume Design (M.F.A.):** Ms. Colleen Muscha (850-644-7514; cmuscha@mailer.fsu.edu). **Directing (M.F.A.):** Mr. Fred Chappell (850-644-7237; fchappell@fsu.edu). **Interior Design (M.F.A./M.A./M.S.):** Dr. Lisa Waxman (850-644-8326; lwaxman@fsu.edu). **Lighting Design (M.F.A.):** Ms. Sarah Maines (850-644-7251; smaines@fsu.edu).**Scene Design (M.F.A.):** Mr. Dale Jordan (850-644-4537; dfjordan@fsu.edu). **Technical Direction (M.F.A.):** Mr. Robert Coleman (850-644-4305; rcoleman@fsu.edu). **Theater (Ph.D./M.F.A./M.S.):** Dr. Mary Dahl (850-644-7238; mkdahl@admin.fsu.edu). **Theater Management (M.F.A.):** Mr. David Rowell (850-645-1958; drowell@admin.fsu.edu).

GRAND VALLEY STATE UNIVERSITY

Graduate Studies

Programs of Study

Grand Valley State University (GVSU) offers 26 graduate programs. Graduate programs include the Educational Specialist in Leadership (Ed.S.); Master of Arts (M.A.) in English; Master of Business Administration (M.B.A.); Master of Science (M.S.) in biology, biostatistics, cell and molecular biology, communications, computer information systems, criminal justice, health sciences, medical and bioinformatics, occupational therapy; Master of Education (M.Ed.) in adult and higher education, college student affairs leadership, early childhood education, educational differentiation, educational leadership, educational technology integration, elementary education, graduate teacher certification, middle level education, reading/language arts, school counseling, school library/media services, secondary level education, special education, and teaching English to speakers of other languages/TESOL); Master of Health Administration (M.H.A.); Master of Public Administration (M.P.A.); Master of Physician Assistant Studies (M.P.A.S.); Master of Science in Accounting (M.S.A.); Master of Science in Engineering (M.S.E.); Master of Science in Nursing (M.S.N.); Master of Science in Taxation (M.S.T.); Master of Social Work (M.S.W.); and Doctor of Physical Therapy (D.P.T.).

Research Facilities

The Steelcase Library, which is located in the Richard M. DeVos Center, has a computer-operated robotic retrieval system that holds the library's circulating collection and can accommodate 250,000 volumes. The 10,400-square-foot library also includes a circulation desk, a traditional reference desk, microfilm/fiche reader/printers, computers, a reading room, a photocopy room, a library instruction center with computers for database access, staff offices, and workspaces. Librarians staff the reference desk. The tables and carrels are wired for laptop computer use. The reading room holds the expanded reference collection and the current issue of 700 journal titles. This library also houses the Grand Rapids Bar Association's law collection. The entire GVSU library system houses more than 777,000 volumes, 3,690 periodical subscriptions, 523,000 electronic journals, and 22,318 reels of microfilm. Computer facilities are available throughout the campus, and all labs run on MS Office Suite, SPSS, SAS, SAP, and departmental-specific applications for course instruction. In addition to having wireless access in the main plaza, there are multiple network connections throughout the DeVos Center and wireless connectivity in all academic buildings. DeVos also has forty kiosk stations for access to e-mail, student records, and library resources.

Financial Aid

Grand Valley State University offers graduate assistantships through various departments to help students finance their education. Many assistantships cover tuition and include a stipend for hours worked in conjunction with faculty members. Domestic students may also apply for federal student aid. Tuition reimbursement options are available through some local employers.

Cost of Study

Tuition for 2008–09 was $425 per credit hour for in-state students and $600 per credit hour for out-of-state and international students. There are no additional fees charged to students for tuition or academic programs. Students who qualify for a graduate assistantship are considered Michigan residents for tuition purposes.

Living and Housing Costs

Grand Valley State University offers housing for graduate students at the Robert C. Pew Campus, in downtown Grand Rapids. Housing 180 students, Peter F. Secchia Hall has one-, two-, three-, and four-bedroom units and is located directly across the street from the academic facilities. Winter Hall features fully furnished one- and two-bedroom efficiencies. The most recent costs range from $2316 to $3430 per semester. Off-campus housing within walking distance of the campus is readily available in the Grand Rapids community.

Student Group

Grand Valley State University enrolls approximately 3,476 graduate students each year. The graduate student population at GVSU ranges from full-time students directly out of an undergraduate program to part-time students with many years of professional experience. Approximately 65 percent of the students are women, and a small percentage are international students who represent more than thirty countries.

Location

Grand Valley State University's main campus is located in Allendale, Michigan. The Pew Campus, which is located in downtown Grand Rapids, comprises the majority of Grand Valley's graduate programs. Located on a 15-acre site just west of the Grand River, Grand Valley is in the heart of the city. Grand Rapids is the second-largest city in Michigan, with a vibrant economy and a revitalized downtown that provides students numerous social and professional opportunities. As the University continues to grow, regional sites offer graduate programs at locations such as Muskegon, Holland, and Traverse City, Michigan.

The University

Grand Valley State University was established in 1963 in Allendale, Michigan. Grand Valley enrolls approximately 23,892 students, approximately 3,476 of whom are graduate students. The Pew Campus in downtown Grand Rapids is the only full-service campus in the city and houses the majority of Grand Valley's graduate programs. The DeVos Center is a 250,000-square-foot facility that includes a state-of-the-art library, more than sixty classrooms and laboratories, faculty and staff offices, and more than 320 computers for student use.

Correspondence and Information

Graduate Admissions
117B DeVos Center
Grand Valley State University
401 Fulton Street West
Grand Rapids, Michigan 49504

Phone: 616-331-2025
800-748-0246 (toll-free)
Fax: 616-331-6476
E-mail: admissions@gvsu.edu
Web site: http://www.gvsu.edu/grad

GRADUATE PROGRAM DIRECTORS

Priscilla Kimboko, Ph.D., Dean of Graduate Studies and Grants Administration.
John Stevenson, Ph.D., Associate Dean of Graduate Studies and Grants Administration.
Accounting: Claudia Bajema, M.B.A.
Biology: Mark Luttenton, Ph.D.
Biomedical Sciences: Debra Burg, Ph.D.
Biostatistics: Robert Downer, Ph.D.
Business: Claudia Bajema, M.B.A.
Cell and Molecular Biology: Mark Staves, Ph.D.
Communication: Michael Pritchard, Ed.D.
Computer Information Systems: D. Robert Adams, Ph.D.
Criminal Justice: Debra Ross, Ph.D.
Education: Stephen Worst, M.A.
Engineering: Charlie Standridge, Ph.D.
English: Benjamin Lockerd, Ph.D.
Health Administration: Stephen Borders, Ph.D.
Medical and Bioinformatics: Paul Leidig, Ph.D.
Nursing: Andrea Bostrom, Ph.D.
Occupational Therapy: Cynthia Grapczynski, Ed.D.
Physical Therapy: John Peck, Ph.D.
Physician Assistant Studies: Wallace Boeve, Ed.D.
Public Administration: Mark Hoffman, Ph.D.
Social Work: Elaine Schott, Ph.D.
Taxation: Claudia Bajema, M.B.A.

HARVARD UNIVERSITY

Graduate School of Arts and Sciences

Programs of Study The Graduate School of Arts and Sciences offers master's and Ph.D. degrees under fifty-four departments, committees, and divisions within the Harvard Faculty of Arts and Sciences (FAS). It also offers a joint M.D./Ph.D. program in cooperation with the Harvard Medical School , a joint J.D./Ph.D. program the Harvard Law School, and a special program in health science and technology with the Medical School and the Massachusetts Institute of Technology. In many departments, the master's degree is awarded only in progress to the doctorate, and applications for the master's degree only are not accepted. Common to all programs are a residence requirement, a tuition requirement, and a requirement of continuous registration from admission until completion of the degree program. Candidates for a master's degree must complete a minimum of one year of full-time study in residence at full tuition (see below). The requirements for the Ph.D. vary considerably from subject to subject, but in all departments a minimum of two years of full-time study in residence at full tuition is required. Candidates for the Ph.D. are normally expected to demonstrate language proficiency, pass general or qualifying examinations, and write a thesis based on original research.

Research Facilities The University offers outstanding resources for study and research. The University library system has holdings of more than 11 million volumes and is composed of three main libraries—Widener Memorial, Lamont, and Hilles—and more than ninety other collections. These include special libraries in rare books and manuscripts, art, science, geology, Asian studies, government, music, and anthropology and separate libraries in many departments and research institutes. Several computing facilities with DEC and IBM mainframes and microcomputers are available for research, computing, thesis work, and word processing. Special research facilities in the sciences include the Harvard Stem Cell Institute; the Broad Institute; the Center for Astrophysics, which combines the Harvard Observatory and the Smithsonian Astrophysical Observatory; the Center for Earth and Planetary Sciences; the Harvard Forest; the University Herbaria; and laboratories in chemistry, biology, biochemistry, physics, applied sciences, anthropology, and medical sciences. Facilities and institutes in the social sciences and humanities include the Harvard-Yenching Institute, the Fairbank Center for East Asian Research, the Edwin O. Reischauer Institute for Japanese Studies, the Center for Middle Eastern Studies, the Center for Jewish Studies, the Center for the Study of World Religions, the Center for European Studies, the Ukrainian Research Institute, the Russian Research Center, the Committee on Latin American and Iberian Studies, the Committee on African Studies, the Harvard Institute for International Development, the Center for International Affairs, the Center for American Political Studies, the W. E. B. DuBois Institute for Afro-American Studies, the Center for Urban Studies, the Carpenter Center for the Visual Arts, and the Loeb Drama Center. The University museums are also available for research and study; these include the Fogg and Arthur M. Sackler art museums, the Peabody Museum of Archaeology and Ethnology, the Semitic Museum, the Museum of Comparative Zoology, the Botanical Museum, and the Mineralogical Museum. Research affiliations are maintained with a variety of other institutions, including the Woods Hole Oceanographic Institute, the Arnold Arboretum, Dumbarton Oaks Library, the Center for Hellenic Studies, and Villa i Tatti.

Financial Aid Assistance is available through Harvard and outside fellowships, assistantships, federal work-study, and loans. Financial aid is awarded based on both merit and need, as determined by the Office of Admissions and Financial Aid. Most admitted students are guaranteed full support for two or more years of study. In the third and following years, most students can support themselves through teaching and research. If necessary, loan funds are usually available to supplement these sources.

Cost of Study All students must register for full-time study. For the academic year 2009–10, tuition and fees were $36,836 for those in the first two years of study. Reduced tuition of $11,900 was charged to students in the third and fourth years. Those in later years pay a facilities fee of $2230 per year if they are in residence. A health insurance fee of $1126 per year is included in the cost for students in residence. Students on leave to conduct research and advanced students living outside the Cambridge area pay an active file fee of $300 per year.

Living and Housing Costs The standard student budget reflects the cost of living in the Boston area. For 2009–10, the average ten-month budget for a single student was approximately $22,140. Dormitory rooms rent for $5432 to $8608 per year; board is available at an additional cost in some cases. Rents for University-owned apartments range from $1000 to $4132 per month.

Student Group The Graduate School of Arts and Sciences has an enrollment of nearly 3,700. The student body is extremely diverse. Approximately 28 percent of the students are international; 45 percent are women. The underrepresented minority community is nearly 6 percent. Approximately 24 percent are in humanities programs, while some 45 percent are in natural sciences and 31 percent in social sciences. The wide range of interests of the students is reflected in a variety of organizations and activities.

Location Most facilities of the University are located in Cambridge and Boston. The two cities and their environs offer wide cultural and recreational opportunities. The University itself has excellent athletic facilities and sponsors numerous arts and public affairs activities. Within the area are many opportunities for public service. Other resources include museums, music, drama, dance, and sports. Recreational areas on the Atlantic coast and in the mountains and forests of New England are easily accessible.

The University Harvard University is a complex of the Faculty of Arts and Sciences and nine other professional and graduate faculties. The FAS comprises Harvard College and the Graduate School of Arts and Sciences. Founded in 1636, Harvard College is the oldest college in the United States. Founded in 1872, the Graduate School of Arts and Sciences is the largest graduate institution in the University.

Applying Students are admitted to graduate study only at the beginning of the academic year; there are no admissions for the spring term. The application deadlines are December 3, December 7, December 14, or January 2. Students should check http://www.gsas.harvard.edu for the appropriate program deadline. The application fee is $90.

Correspondence and Information

Office of Admissions and Financial Aid
Graduate School of Arts and Sciences
Harvard University
1350 Massachusetts Avenue, 350
Cambridge, Massachusetts 02138

Phone: 617-495-5315
E-mail: admiss@fas.harvard.edu
Web site: http://www.gsas.harvard.edu

OFFICERS AND PROGRAMS IN THE GRADUATE SCHOOL OF ARTS AND SCIENCES

Allan M. Brandt, Dean of the Graduate School of Arts and Sciences and Amalie Moses Kass Professor of the History of Medicine.
Margot N. Gill, Administrative Dean of the Graduate School of Arts and Sciences.

DEPARTMENTS AND COMMITTEES AND GRADUATE DEGREES AWARDED FOR 2008–09

Humanities
Department of African and African American Studies (Ph.D.).
Department of Celtic Languages and Literatures (A.M., Ph.D.).
Department of the Classics (Ph.D.).
Department of Comparative Literature (Ph.D.).
Department of East Asian Languages and Civilizations (Ph.D.).
Department of English and American Literature and Language (Ph.D.).
Department of Germanic Languages and Literatures (A.M., Ph.D.).
Committee on Inner Asian and Altaic Studies (Ph.D.).
Department of Linguistics (Ph.D.).
Department of Music (A.M., Ph.D.).
Department of Near Eastern Languages and Civilizations (A.M., Ph.D.).
Department of Philosophy (Ph.D.).
Committee on Regional Studies—East Asia (A.M.).
Committee on the Study of Religion (Ph.D.).
Department of Romance Languages and Literatures (A.M., Ph.D.).
Department of Sanskrit and Indian Studies (A.M., Ph.D.).
Department of Slavic Languages and Literatures (Ph.D.).

Natural Sciences
Department of Astronomy (Ph.D.).
Committee on Biological Sciences in Dental Medicine (Ph.D.).
Committee on Biological Sciences in Public Health (Ph.D.).
*Committee on Biophysics (Ph.D.).
Committee on Biostatistics (Ph.D.).
*Committee on Chemical Biology.
Committee on Chemical Physics (Ph.D.).
*Committee on Systems Biology.
*Department of Chemistry and Chemical Biology (Ph.D.).
Department of Earth and Planetary Sciences (Ph.D.).
School of Engineering and Applied Sciences (S.M., M.E., Ph.D.).
The Harvard Forest (M.F.S.).
Division of Health Science and Technology (M.D./Ph.D., Ph.D.).
Department of Mathematics (Ph.D.).
*Division of Medical Sciences (Ph.D.).
*Department of Molecular and Cellular Biology (Ph.D.).
*Department of Organismic and Evolutionary Biology (Ph.D.).
Department of Physics (Ph.D.).
Department of Statistics (A.M., Ph.D.).

*Participating program in Harvard Integrated Life Sciences

Social Sciences
Department of Anthropology (A.M., Ph.D.).
Committee on Architecture, Landscape Architecture, and Urban Planning (Ph.D.).
Committee on Business Economics (Ph.D.).
Department of Economics (Ph.D.).
Program in Film and Visual Studies (Ph.D.).
Department of Government (Ph.D.).
Committee on Health Policy (Ph.D.).
Department of History (Ph.D.).
Committee on the History of American Civilization (Ph.D.).
Department of History of Science (A.M., Ph.D.).
Committee on Science, Technology, and Management (Ph.D.).
Committee on Middle Eastern Studies (A.M., Ph.D.).
Committee on Organizational Behavior (Ph.D.).
Committee on Political Economy and Government (Ph.D.).
Department of Psychology (Ph.D.).
Committee on Public Policy (Ph.D.).
Committee on Regional Studies—Russia, Eastern Europe, and Central Asia (A.M.).
Committee on Social Policy (Ph.D.).
Department of Sociology (Ph.D.).

HAWAI'I PACIFIC UNIVERSITY

Graduate Studies

Programs of Study

Hawai'i Pacific University offers leading master's degree programs in business administration, communication, diplomacy and military studies, economics, global leadership and sustainable development, information systems, nursing, marine science, organizational change, teaching English as a second language, social work, and secondary education. The Master of Business Administration (M.B.A.) program offers concentrations in accounting, e-business, economics, finance, human resource management, information systems, international business, management, marketing, organizational change, and travel industry management. The M.B.A. program requires 42 semester hours of graduate work. Prerequisite study in business subjects may be required.

The Master of Science in Information Systems (M.S.I.S.) is designed to create a generation of decision-makers and experts in information technology, systems design, and problem solving with automated resources. Students can individualize their program with elective courses or concentrations in knowledge management, decision science, telecommunications security, and software engineering. Students lacking a background in the technical, scientific, and analytical realms are required to complete selected prerequisites to fully prepare for the program. Thirty-six semester hours of graduate work are required to complete the program.

The Master of Arts in human resource management (M.A./HRM) emphasizes the study and practices of human relations and managing personnel. These include human resource planning, recruitment and selection, compensation management and benefits, human resource development, labor-management relations, employment law, safety and health, and global perspective on human resources. Some undergraduate prerequisites may be required. The program requires completion of 36 semester hours of graduate work.

The Master of Arts in global leadership and sustainable development (M.A./GLSD) is designed to prepare students to become leaders in all types of organizations that include multinational, governmental, and not-for-profit organizations. Courses include Comparative Management Systems, Global Markets in Transition, International Business Management, and Systems Management. Some prerequisites may be required. Forty-two semester hours of graduate work are required to complete the program.

The Master of Arts in organizational change (M.A./OC) emphasizes the management, design, implementation, and application of organizational change. Courses include Organizational Change and Development, National and Community Change and Development, Culture and Human Organization, and Organizational Behavior. Some prerequisite courses may be required. Forty-two semester hours of graduate work are required to complete the program.

The Master of Science in Nursing (M.S.N.) offers concentrations for those interested in becoming family nurse practitioners or community-based health clinical nurse specialists. Students who have an RN but lack a Bachelor of Science in nursing may enter the RN to M.S.N. Pathway. Forty-two semester hours are required to complete the M.S.N. with a clinical nurse specialist concentration, and 48 semester hours are required to complete the M.S.N. with a nurse educator or a family nurse practitioner concentration.

The Master of Science in Marine Science (M.S.M.S.) is designed to provide students with the knowledge and skills necessary to place them in marine-related technical positions in industry, government, and education or for entry into a doctoral marine science program. Courses include Cell and Molecular Biology, Aquatic Chemistry, Marine Ecology, and Toxicology. Some prerequisite courses may be required. The M.S.M.S. program requires 34 hours of graduate work.

The Master of Arts in communication (M.A./COM) is designed to prepare students for careers in business communication, marketing, advertising, mass media, public relations, entertainment, broadcast or print journalism, sales, the Internet, writing, or education. Some prerequisite courses may be required. Thirty-nine semester hours of graduate work are required to complete the program.

The Master of Arts in Teaching English as a Second Language (M.A.T.E.S.L.) requires 37 semester hours of graduate work. Courses include English Phonology and the Teaching of Pronunciation, English Syntax and the Teaching of Grammar, and Methods of Teaching Oral/Aural English. Some prerequisite courses may be required.

The Master of Arts in diplomacy and military studies (M.A./DMS) explores the complex relationships of politics, society, and the military. The M.A./DMS degree is useful for those who are professional military officers or work in government positions. Some prerequisites may be required. The M.A./DMS program requires 42 hours of graduate work.

The Master of Arts in Social Work (M.S.W.) program is built on a foundation of liberal arts and is committed to the preparation of professional social work practitioners who take pride in their careers. The program prepares social workers to become effective cross-cultural practitioners by focusing on direct planning, administration, and community practice. The M.S.W. program requires 61 semester hours of graduate work.

The Master of Education (M.Ed.) in secondary education program develops professional educators who are reflective practitioners dedicated to the scholarship of teaching and school renewal. The program is based on an innovative, standards-driven, field-based curriculum that employs cutting-edge educational technology to integrate content and pedagogy. The M.Ed. program requires 41 semester hours of graduate work.

Research Facilities

To support graduate studies, HPU's Meader and Atherton libraries offer over 110,000 bound volumes, 350,000 microfiche items, and periodical subscriptions to 1,500 print titles and 30,000 electronic journals. Databases of public and state university libraries, legislative information, and business-oriented statistical data are also available in the libraries or online. Students can access HPU's library databases, course information, their academic information and an e-mail account through Pipeline, the university's internal Web site for students. The University's accessible on-campus computer center houses more than 100 computers with specialized software to support graduate academic programs. HPU also provides free Wi-Fi so students can have wireless access to Pipeline resources anywhere on campus using laptops. A significant number of online courses are available as well.

Financial Aid

The University participates in all federal financial aid programs designated for graduate students. These programs provide aid in the form of subsidized (need-based) and unsubsidized (non-need-based) Federal Stafford Student Loans. Through these loans, funds may be available to cover a student's entire cost of education. To apply for aid, students must submit the Free Application for Federal Student Aid (FAFSA) beginning January 1. Mailing of student award letters usually begins by the end of March. The University also offers several types of institutional graduate scholarships and assistantships to new full-time, degree-seeking students. The Trustees' Scholar Program provides a 50 percent tuition waiver for two semesters; the Deans' Scholarship Program, a 20 percent tuition waiver for one semester; and the International Scholar Program, a 20 to 50 percent tuition waiver. Graduate assistantships, which give students a 50 percent tuition waiver for one semester, are also available. Priority consideration is given to those students who apply by the deadline.

Cost of Study

Tuition for graduate students enrolled in fall and spring semesters is determined on a per-credit basis; full-time status for a graduate student is 9 credits. Tuition for the optional winter and summer sessions is also determined on a per-credit basis. The estimated minimum funds needed for a nine-month academic year (September to May), based on 2009–10 school-year expenses, is $25,739. For the 2009–10 academic year, full-time tuition is $11,880 for most graduate degree programs while books, supplies, and transportation cost $1885, and health insurance costs $880.

Living and Housing Costs

Most graduate students live in off-campus housing. The cost to live in off-campus apartments is approximately $11,094 for a double occupancy room.

Student Group

University enrollment currently stands at more than 8,200. HPU is one of the most culturally diverse universities in America with students from all 50 U.S. states and more than 100 countries.

Location

Hawai'i Pacific combines the excitement of an urban, downtown campus with the serenity of a residential campus and a pristine marine institute. The main campus is ideally located in downtown Honolulu, the business and financial center of the Pacific. Eight miles away, situated on 135 acres in Kaneohe, the windward Hawai'i Loa campus is the site of environmental sciences, marine biology, nursing, oceanography, and several liberal arts programs. The third campus, The Oceanic Institute, an affiliate of HPU, is an applied aquaculture research facility located on a 56-acre site at Makapu'u Point on the windward coast of Oahu, Hawaii. Students can travel between the three sites using the convenient HPU shuttle service. There are also eight military campus programs located at Pearl Harbor, Barbers Point, Hickam Air Force Base, Schofield Barracks, Fort Shafter, Tripler Army Medical Center, Kaneohe Marine Corps Air Station, and Camp Smith.

The University

Hawai'i Pacific University (HPU) is a private, nonprofit university with approximately 8,200 students. Founded in 1965, HPU prides itself on maintaining strong academic programs, small class sizes, individual attention to students, and a diverse faculty and student population. HPU is recognized as a "Best in the West" college by the *Princeton Review* and a "Best Buy" by *Barron's* business magazine. HPU offers more than 50 acclaimed undergraduate programs and 12 distinguished graduate programs. The University has a faculty of more than 500, a student-faculty ratio of 18:1, and an average class size of less than 25. A wide range of counseling and other student support services are available. There are more than seventy student organizations on campus, including the Graduate Student Organization.

Applying

Students must have a baccalaureate degree from an accredited college or university in the United States or an equivalent degree from another country. Applicants should complete and forward a graduate admissions application, send in the $50 nonrefundable application fee, have official transcripts sent from all colleges or universities previously attended, and forward two letters of recommendation. A personal statement about the applicant's academic and career goals is required; submitting a resume is optional. Applicants who have taken the Graduate Management Admission Test (GMAT) should have their scores sent directly to the Graduate Admissions Office. International students should submit scores of a recognized English proficiency test such as TOEFL. Admissions decisions are made on a rolling basis, and applicants are notified between one and two weeks after all documents have been submitted. Applicants are encouraged to submit their applications online.

Correspondence and Information

Graduate Admissions
Hawai'i Pacific University
1164 Bishop Street, Suite 911
Honolulu, Hawaii 96813

Phone: 808-544-1135
866-GRAD-HPU (toll-free)
Fax: 808-544-0280
E-mail: graduate@hpu.edu
Web site: http://www.hpu.edu/hpugrad

THE FACULTY

Valentina M. Abordonado, Professor of English, Education; Ph.D., Arizona.
Leina'ala Ahu Isa, Assistant Professor of Management; Ed.D., Hawaii at Manoa.
Michelle Alarcon-Catt, Assistant Professor of Management; M.B.A., Pepperdine.
Dale Allison, Professor of Nursing; Ph.D., Pennsylvania.
Margaret Anderson, Associate Professor of Nursing; Ed.D., San Francisco.
Pierre Asselin, Associate Professor of History; Ph.D., Hawaii at Manoa.
Margo Bare, Instructor in Social Work; M.S.W., Pennsylvania.
John Barnum, Associate Professor of Communication; Ph.D., Texas at Austin.
Patrick Bratton, Assistant Professor of Political Science; Ph.D., Catholic University.
Peter Britos, Associate Professor of Communication; Ph.D., USC.
Dale Burke, Instructor of Communication; D.Min., Ancilla Domini College, Graduate Theological Foundation.
Patricia Burrell, Professor of Nursing; Ph.D., Utah.
Randy Caine, Professor of Nursing; Ed.D, Pepperdine.
Brian Cannon, Assistant Professor of Communication; Ph.D., Regent University (Virginia).
Kathleen Cassity, Assistant Professor of English; Ph.D., Hawaii at Manoa.
Randall Chang, Assistant Professor of Economics; Ph.D., Claremont.
Grace Cheng, Associate Professor of Political Science; Ph.D., Hawaii at Manoa.
Richard Chepkevich, Instructor in Computer Science/Information Systems; M.S.S.M., USC.
Justin Gukhyun Cho, Associate Professor of Management; Ph.D., MIT.
Bee-Leng Chua, Associate Professor of Management; Ph.D., Ohio.
Katherine Clarke, Instructor of Communication; M.A., Denver.
Steven Combs, Professor of Communication; Ph.D., USC.
Kenneth Cook, Professor of Linguistics; Ph.D., California, San Diego.
Catherine Critz, Associate Professor of Nursing; Ph.D, Syracuse.
Cheryl Crozier-Garcia, Associate Professor of Human Resource Management; Ph.D., Walden.
ReNel Davis, Professor of Nursing; Ph.D., Colorado.
Thomas Dowd, Instructor of Communication; M.A., California State, Northridge.
Erik Drabkin, Affiliate Associate Professor of Economics; Ph.D., UCLA.
Jiason Fang, Associate Professor of Chemistry; Ph.D., Texas A&M.
Hobie Feagai, Associate Professor of Nursing; Ed.D., Argosy/okina: Hawai'i.
Mark Fox, Instructor of Social Work; M.S.W., Arizona State.
Susan Fox-Wolfgramm, Professor of Management; Ph.D., Texas Tech.
Matthew George, Assistant Professor of Communication; Ph.D., Berkeley.
Gerald Glover, Professor of Organizational Change; Ph.D., Florida.
Allison Gough, Associate Professor of Political Science, Ph.D., Hawaii.
John Gutrich, Associate Professor of Environmental Sciences; Ph.D., Ohio State.
Joseph Ha, Associate Professor of Marketing; Ph.D., Rutgers.
Barbara Hannum, Assistant Professor of English (ESL); M.A., Hawai'i at Manoa.
John P.Hart, Professor of Communication; Ph.D., Kansas.
Russell Hart, Associate Professor of History; Ph.D., Ohio State.
David Horgen, Associate Professor of Chemistry; Ph.D., Illinois at Chicago.
William Hummel, Instructor of Social Work; M.S.W., CUNY, Hunter.
Karl Hyrenbach, Assistant Professor of Oceanography; Ph.D., California, San Diego (Scripps).
Lowell Ing, Assistant Professor of Communication; M.F.A., CUNY, City College.
Brenda Jensen, Assistant Professor of Biology; Ph.D., California, San Diego (Scripps).
Gordon Jones, Professor of Computer Science and Information Systems; Ph.D., New Mexico.
Carlos Juarez, Professor of Political Science; Ph.D., UCLA.
Samuel Kahng, Assistant Professor of Oceanography; Ph.D., Hawaii at Manoa.
Anne Kennedy, Assistant Professor of Communication; Ph.D., Bowling Green State.
Jean Kirschenmann, Assistant Professor of English (ESL); M.A., Hawaii at Manoa.
Margo Kitts, Associate Professor of Humanities/Rel. Studies; Ph.D., Berkeley.
Edward Klein, Professor of Applied Linguistics; Ph.D., Hawaii at Manoa.
Mark Lane, Associate Professor of Finance; Ph.D., Missouri.
Leroy Laney, Professor of Finance and Economics; Ph.D., Colorado.
Patricia Lange-Otsuka, Professor of Nursing; Ed.D., Nova Southeastern.
Laurence LeDoux, Assistant Professor of Communication; D.A., Oregon.
Candis Lee, Assistant Professor of English (ESL); Ed.D., USC.
Cathrine Linnes, Assistant Professor of Information Systems; Ph.D., Nova Southeastern.
Ernesto Lucas, Associate Professor of Economics; Ph.D., Hawaii at Manoa.
Marianne Luken, Instructor of Communication; M.I.A., School for International Training.
Lorraine Marais, Associate Professor of Social Work; Ed.D., Western Michigan.
Howard Markowitz, Assistant Professor of Psychology; Ph.D., Union (Ohio).
Sandra McKay, Professor of Linguistics; Ph.D., Minnesota.
Daniel Morgan, Instructor of Sociology; M.A., Miami (Florida).
Hanh Nguyen, Assistant Professor of Applied Linguistics; Ph.D., Wisconsin–Madison.
Patricia Nishimoto, Assistant Professor of Social Work; Ph.D., University of Hawaii, Manoa.
Scott Okamoto, Associate Professor of Social Work; Ph.D., Hawaii at Manoa.
Regina Ostergaard-Klem, Adjunct Professor of Mathematics; Ph.D., Johns Hopkins.
Aytun Ozturk, Associate Professor of Quantitative Methods; Ph.D., Pittsburgh.
Edgar Palafox, Instructor of Human Resource Management; M.S., Hawai'i Pacific.
Joseph Patoskie, Associate Professor of Travel Industry Management; Ph.D., Texas Tech.
Penny Pence Smith, Assistant Professor of Communication; Ph.D., North Carolina at Chapel Hill.
James Primm, Associate Professor of Political Science; Ph.D., Hawaii at Manoa.
Kenneth Rossi, Assistant Professor of Information Systems; Ed.D., USC.
Lawrence Rowland, Assistant Professor of Information Systems; Ed.D., USC.
Catherine Sajna, Assistant Professor of English; M.A., Hawaii at Manoa.
George Satterfield, Associate Professor of History, Ph.D., Illinois at Urbana-Champaign.
Mary Sheridan, Professor of Social Work; Ph.D., Hawaii at Manoa.
Malia Smith, Instructor of Communication; M.A., Hawai'i Pacific.
William Soderman, Associate Professor of Information Systems; Ph.D., Georgia.
Edward Souza, Instructor of Information Systems; M.S., Hawai'i Pacific.
Lisa Steinmueller, Assistant Professor of Nursing; MSN/MBA, Hawai'i Pacific.
Min Min Thaw, Assistant Professor of Economics; M.A., Hawaii at Manoa.
Paul Tran, Instructor of Social Work; M.S.W., San Francisco State.
Lewis Trusty, Instructor of Communication; M.A., USC.
Catherine Unabia, Assistant Professor of Biology; Ph.D., Hawaii at Manoa.
Edwin Van Gorder, Associate Professor of Mathematics; Ph.D., Stanford.
Eric Vetter, Associate Professor of Biology; Ph.D., California, San Diego (Scripps).
Niti Villinger, Associate Professor of Management; Ph.D., Cambridge.
Richard Ward, Associate Professor of Organizational Change; Ed.D., USC.
Warren Wee, Associate Professor of Accounting; Ph.D., Hawaii at Manoa.
Kristi West, Assistant Professor of Biology; Ph.D., L'Universite de la Polynesie Francaise, Hawaii at Manoa.
Arthur Whatley, Professor of Management; Ph.D., North Texas State.
Linda Wheeler, Assistant Professor of Education; Ed.D., Hawaii at Manoa.
James D. Whitfield, Professor of Communication; Ph.D., Texas Tech.
John Windrow, Instructor of Journalism; M.A., Missouri–Columbia.
Christopher Winn, Associate Professor of Oceanography; Ph.D., Hawaii at Manoa.
Yanjun Zhao; Ph.D., Southern Illinois Carbondale.
Larry Zimmerman, Assistant Professor of Organizational Change; Ph.D., Nebraska–Lincoln.

IMMACULATA UNIVERSITY

College of Graduate Studies

Programs of Study

Immaculata University offers programs of study leading to the Master of Arts in applied communication, counseling psychology, cultural and linguistic diversity (bilingual studies and teaching English to speakers of other languages), educational leadership, music therapy (accredited by National Association of Schools of Music), nutrition education (with an ADA Dietetic Internship), and organization leadership (with concentrations in health-care services and organizational effectiveness). Also available are curricula leading to the Master of Science in Nursing (M.S.N.), the Doctor of Education (Ed.D.) in educational leadership and administration, and the Doctor of Psychology (Psy.D.) in clinical psychology. The Doctor of Psychology in clinical psychology is accredited by the American Psychological Association. Pennsylvania certification for school nurses, school superintendents, elementary and secondary school teachers, school psychologists, elementary and secondary school guidance counselors, principals, special education, and supervisor for curriculum and instruction, special education, and specialty areas is also offered. Certificates are available in teaching English to speakers of other languages (TESOL), organizational effectiveness, health care, and existential humanistic psychotherapy.

The total semester hours required in each master's program vary from 36 to 60, depending on the program of study.

A unique feature of the master's programs is the required 9-credit integrative core curriculum. The core, along with course work in the area of specific concentration, provides an integrative, holistic, and humanistic approach to graduate education. Through close, ongoing advisement as well as the curriculum and career counseling, each student's personal development is assisted and monitored while he or she acquires the strong theoretical and practical preparation necessary for responsible professional practice.

The College of Graduate Studies is sensitive to the needs of the adult learner. Classes are offered in the late afternoon, evenings, and weekends to accommodate both part-time and full-time students. Innovative accelerated courses covering special topics are offered in intensive time blocks for elective credit or seminar experience.

Research Facilities

Gabriele Library is a freestanding 52,000-square-foot library offering a quiet place to study with the latest advances in Internet and electronic access. With subscriptions to Sage Premiere, PsycArticles, PsycBooks, Academic Search, CINAHL, Proquest Nursing, Business Source, JSTOR, and LexisNexis, the Gabriele Library serves the needs of students researching in the areas of education, psychology, business, science, humanities, health, and other fields by providing access to over 19,000 journals. These resources are in addition to the fully integrated online book catalog. The library provides students with wireless connectivity, an AV/computer room, fifty-five desktop PCs, notebook computers, photocopiers, printers, a fully equipped media classroom and closed-circuit TV room, group study rooms, and a digitized microfilm/fiche reader/printer.

Financial Aid

Thirty percent of the students receive financial aid. Federal Stafford Student Loans (subsidized and unsubsidized) and Federal Perkins Loans are available to students enrolled at least half-time in any discipline. Merit scholarships are awarded annually in a competitive process. A limited number of graduate assistantships are also available.

Cost of Study

Estimated tuition for 2008–09 was $540 per credit for 500- and 600-level courses and $750 per credit for 700-level courses. The practicum fee varies with the program. The graduation fee is approximately $100.

Living and Housing Costs

Limited on-campus housing is available. Most students commute to the campus. The University is located in a rapidly growing suburban area offering many off-campus housing options, the cost of which varies widely.

Student Group

Total enrollment at Immaculata University is approximately 3,200. The graduate student body of 1,200 women and men comprises recent college graduates, professionals with several years of experience in their field, and those returning to study after a number of years.

Student Outcomes

Students leaving Immaculata University's graduate programs typically are quickly engaged in positions with the helping professions. Many students come to Immaculata University's graduate programs to study part-time, while continuing their full-time employment with an eye toward advancement as a result of their studies. Other graduates report that their degree at Immaculata University has allowed them to make a complete career change and that they have generally found employment within a few months of graduation in fields that are closely allied to their studies. Employers frequently report their satisfaction with the quality and depth of preparation they find in the Immaculata graduates they hire.

Location

Immaculata's 390-acre campus overlooks the rapidly growing Chester Valley and is located in Frazer, Pennsylvania, on the Main Line, about 20 miles west of Philadelphia. Proximity to Philadelphia provides access to a great many cultural, academic, and recreational facilities. The University's close working relationships with the surrounding community offer excellent resources for internships, practicums, and professional experiences.

The University and The College

Immaculata University is fully accredited by the Middle States Association of Colleges and Schools Commission on Higher Education. Founded in 1920 by the Sisters, Servants of the Immaculate Heart of Mary, the University began the College of Graduate Studies in 1983; it is now celebrating its twenty-fifth year.

The expansion of program offerings in the College of Graduate Studies is yet another example of Immaculata's continuing commitment to meeting the needs of a rapidly changing, highly complex, and diversified society. Immaculata's tradition of excellence and creative, responsive innovation is exemplified in its College of Graduate Studies.

Applying

The deadlines for those seeking admission to the Psy.D. programs in clinical psychology are January 15 for a May start or February 1 for a September start. Application deadlines for the Ed.D. program are November 1, March 1, and June 1. The application fee is $50. The Psy.D. programs in clinical offers admission to students with B.A./B.S.- and M.A.-level degrees. Applications to the master's and certification/certificate programs are welcomed throughout the year and should be accompanied by a $40 application fee.

Applicants should forward official transcripts of all completed undergraduate and graduate work, two recommendations from academic and professional sources, and a writing sample. Application materials, interview appointments, and campus visit information are available by writing, calling, or e-mailing the College of Graduate Studies at Immaculata University. Open houses are held three times per year, usually in October, March, and July.

Additional requirements may include acceptable scores on either the Miller Analogies Test or the Graduate Record Examinations. Music therapy applicants are required to participate in an entrance audition and interview. M.S.N. applicants must have a bachelor's degree in nursing and be registered nurses. Educational leadership and administration program candidates must provide a copy of their teaching certificate. Applicants to the dietetic internship must provide a copy of their verification statement and complete a separate application packet. Applicants should contact the graduate office for more specific program requirements and information.

Correspondence and Information

College of Graduate Studies
1145 King Road, Campus Box 500
Immaculata University
Immaculata, Pennsylvania 19345-0500

Phone: 610-647-4400 Ext. 3211 or 3212
Fax: 610-993-8550
E-mail: graduate@immaculata.edu
Web site: http://www.immaculata.edu

THE FACULTY

Faculty members are listed below according to department. Those who also teach in the core are indicated by an asterisk.

Sr. Ann M. Heath, Dean of the College of Graduate Studies; Ph.D., Bryn Mawr.

Core
Pamela Lunardi, Psy.D., Immaculata.
Sr. Jane Anne Molinaro, Ph.D., Ohio State.
Anne Reinsmith, D.Min., Eastern Baptist Theological Seminary.
Kathleen Soeder, Ed.D., Immaculata.
Suzann Steadman, Psy.D., Immaculata.

Cultural and Linguistic Diversity
Margaret van Naerssen, Coordinator; Ph.D., USC.
Diane Colom, Turabo (Puerto Rico).
Deborah Falk, M.A., Cabrini.
Joseph Leap, M.A., West Chester.
David Cassells Johnson, M.A., Northern Iowa.
Kalala Kabongo-Mianda, Ph.D., Pennsylvania.
Marcia Vega, M.S., Wilkes.

Educational Leadership
Sr. Carol Anne Couchara, Chair; Ed.D., Lehigh.
David Brennan, Ed.D., Immaculata.
Valerie Burnett, Ed.D., Immaculata.
Sr. Anne Marie Burton, Ed.D., Temple.
Mary Calderone, Ed.D., Immaculata.
Sr. Joseph Marie Carter, Ed.D., Immaculata.
*Christina Charnitski, Ph.D., Drexel.
Joseph J. Corabi, Ed.D., Widener.
Joyce Jeuell, Ed.D., Immaculata.
Michael Kelly, Ed.D., Immaculata.
David Morgan, Ed.D., Pennsylvania.
Kathleen Nolan, Ph.D., Saint Louis.
Joseph O'Brien, Ed.D., Immaculata.
Thomas O'Brien, Ed.D., Immaculata.
Mary Rounds, Ed.D., Pennsylvania.
Thomas Scholvin, Ed.D., Nova Southeastern.
Charles F. Stefanski, Ed.D., Temple.
Robert Urzillo, Ed.D., West Virginia.

Music Therapy
Anthony Meadows, Chair; Ph.D., Temple.
*William Carr, D.M.A., Catholic University.
Kelly Meashey, M.M.T., Temple.
Bryan Muller, M.M.T., Temple
Kathleen Murphy, M.M.T., Temple.

Nursing
Janice Cranmer, Chair; Ed.D., Temple.
Jane Tang, Graduate Director; Ph.D., Iowa.
Marguerite Ambrose, D.N.Sc., Widener.
Susan Burke, Ph.D., Catholic University.
Sr. Paula Jameson, M.S.N., Widener.
Jean Klein, D.N.Sc., Widener.
Margaret Lacey, Ph.D., Temple.
Kathleen Lawler, M.S.N., Temple.
Gail Lehner, M.S.N., Neumann.
Stephanie Trinkl, D.N.Sc., Widener.

Nutrition Education
*Laura B. Frank, Chair; Ph.D., Temple; RD.
Elizabeth Gasho, M.Ed., Temple; RD, LDN, CNSD.
Sr. M. Carroll Isselmann, Ed.D., Rutgers; RD.
Susan W. Johnston, M.S., West Chester; RD, LDN.
Rena K. Quinton, Ph.D., Florida International; RD, LDN.

Organization Studies
*Janice Jacobs, Chair; Ph.D., Temple.
Eric Anderson, Ph.D., Fuller Theological Seminary.
Johanna Bishop, M.S.Ed., Wilmington (Delaware).
Charlene Fitzwater, M.B.A., Kansas.
Glenn Forte, M.A., Villanova.
Donna Hammacher, J.D., Temple.
M. E. Jones, Ph.D., Drexel.
Valerie Martin, M.A.T., Hartford.
Rod Napier, Ph.D., Chicago.
Julie Roberts, Ph.D., Temple.
Julie Ryan, Ph.D., Capella.
Ed Travis, Ed.D., Massachusetts.

Psychology
Jed A. Yalof, Chair; Psy.D., ABPP, ABSNP, Illinois School of Professional Psychology.
Pamela Abraham, Psy.D., Baylor.
Donna Alberici, M.S., Villanova.
*Janet Belitsky, Psy.D., Immaculata.
Cris Chambers, Psy.D., Immaculata.
Maria Cuddy-Casey, Ph.D., Nova Southeastern.
Craig Cunningham, M.Ed., Villanova.
Barbara W. Domingos, Ph.D., Bryn Mawr.
Francien Dorliae, Psy.D., Immaculata.
Janet L. Etzi, Psy.D., Widener.
Julie Guay, Psy.D., Argosy (Chicago).
David Harman, Ph.D., Chicago.
Paul Haughton, Psy.D., Hahnemann.
Edward Jenny, Psy.D., Immaculata.
Angela Jones, Ph.D., Temple.
Sr. Donna Kelley, Psy.D., Loyola Maryland.
Thomas Legere, Ph.D., Union (New York).
Todd Lewis, Ph.D., Drexel.
Marijo Lucas, Ph.D., Auburn.
Nancy Mahoney, M.A., West Chester.
Lynn Malara, Ph.D., Temple.
Marie McGrath, Ph.D., Temple.
Edward Moon, Psy.D., Illinois School of Professional Psychology.
*Sr. Jeannine Marie O'Kane, Ph.D., Fordham.
Roger Osmun, Ph.D., Temple.
Michael Overtorf, M.A., Dayton.
Louise Shuman, Psy.D., Immaculata.
Jenn Zivertnik, Ph.D., Temple.

RESEARCH

Cultural and Linguistic Diversity (M.A.): Second-language acquisition, sociolinguistics, phonology, ESL, TESOL, forensic linguistics.
Counseling Psychology (M.A.) and **Clinical Psychology (Psy.D.):** Supervision, ethics, psychology of teaching, gender, spirituality, gerontology, sexuality, cultural diversity, women's issues, psychoanalytic psychotherapy, existentialism, personality testing, learning disabilities.
Educational Leadership/Administration (M.A., Ed.D.): Assessment, character education, special education, educational theory and policy, school leadership trends, instructional practices, school accountability.
Music Therapy (M.A.): Music psychotherapy, behavioral music therapy, cultural music therapy, music healing.
Nutrition Education (M.A.): Obesity and weight control, nutrition counseling, mentoring of students in dietetics, multicultural nutrition, sports nutrition, school health and nutrition.

Immaculata University is committed to the principle of equal educational opportunity without discrimination by race, color, religion, gender, age, national origin, or condition of handicap.

INDIANA STATE UNIVERSITY

College of Graduate and Professional Studies

Programs of Study

Indiana State University (ISU) offers more than 100 graduate courses of study leading to a graduate certificate or a master's, education specialist's, or doctoral degree in the Colleges of Arts and Sciences, Business, Education, Health and Human Performance, Nursing, and Technology. The College of Arts and Sciences offers the Psy.D. in clinical psychology and the Ph.D. in ecology and organismal biology, geography, and life sciences. The Department of Art offers the M.F.A. The Department of Music offers the M.M. degree. The Department of Political Science offers the M.P.A. Both the M.A. and the M.S. are available in communication, criminology, ecology and organismal biology, English, history, life science, mathematics, political science, and psychology. The M.A. degree is offered in art; languages, literatures, and linguistics; and geography. The M.S. degree is offered in family and consumer sciences, geology, life sciences, and science education. The College of Business offers the M.B.A. degree. The College of Education offers the Ph.D. in counseling psychology, counselor education, curriculum and instruction, educational administration, and school psychology. The Ed.S. degree is offered in school administration and school psychology. The M.Ed. is offered in curriculum and instruction, early childhood education, elementary education, reading education, school administration, school counseling, and school psychology. The M.A. and M.S. are offered in communication disorders and special education. The M.S. is offered in educational technology, mental health counseling, and student affairs and higher education. The College of Health and Human Performance offers the M.A. and M.S. in health, safety, and environmental health sciences; physical education; and recreation and sport management. The M.S. is offered in athletic training. The College of Nursing offers the M.S. in nursing. The College of Technology offers the Ph.D. in technology management. The M.S. is offered in career and technical education teaching, electronics and computer technology, human resource development, industrial technology, and technology education.

Research Facilities

Indiana State University Cunningham Memorial Library houses more than 2.5 million items, subscribes to more than 5,000 periodicals, and provides access to more than 20,000 full-text electronic periodicals. These can be accessed through an online system that also connects with other college libraries in Terre Haute and Indiana. The ISU library provides collaborative workstations to facilitate group and collaborative research. All students enrolled at ISU have access to a wireless network that allows them to access the Internet from most locations on the campus. Several departments offer specialized research facilities. The Instructional and Research Technology Services offers services (at no cost to students) that include statistical design consultation, research design consultation, design and analysis of sample research surveys, and presentation of statistical graphs and tables. The Psychology Clinic serves as a training facility for clinical psychology doctoral students. The Porter School Psychology Center provides research opportunities for students in counseling and school psychology. The ISU Remote Sensing Laboratory specializes in earth resources analysis using computer-aided processing of satellite data. The Technology Services Center engages in cooperative research with industry using CAD/CAM and other related technologies. A radiation laboratory provides students experience with the latest technology. The Center for Research and Management Services utilizes students to provide research for local area and statewide businesses in fields of economic development and targeted industry studies.

Financial Aid

Eligible graduate students may apply for institutional graduate assistantships through the respective academic departments. ISU graduate assistantships include a stipend and a tuition fee waiver. The tuition fee waivers are exclusive of building and student services fees, for up to 18 hours per academic year. For policies regarding graduate assistantships and fee waivers, students should visit the College of Graduate and Professional Studies Web site.

There are also opportunities for graduates to apply for scholarships and fellowships at ISU, some of which include the Paul A. Witty Fellowships, which are available for eligible students specializing in educating gifted and creative children and the Gertrude and Theodore Debs Memorial Fellowships, available for eligible students specializing in American labor and reform movements. There are also the Kweku Bentil Awards, which recognize full-time students who have shown exceptional scholarship and leadership skills. The Noyce Scholarship Program provides an assistantship and fee waiver for students in the College of Arts and Sciences. Detailed information regarding the application process for these fellowships can be found online at the College of Graduate and Professional Studies Web site. Applications received prior to March 1 are given preference.

The Office of Student Financial Aid assists ISU graduate students in obtaining further educational funding opportunities through the Federal Perkins Loan (National Direct Student Loans) and Federal Stafford Student Loan programs, PLUS loans, or the College Work-Study Program. The office can be contacted at 812-237-2215 or at http://www.indstate.edu/finaid/.

Cost of Study

Tuition and fees for the 2008–09 academic year were $309 per semester hour for in-state students and $614 per semester hour for out-of-state students. The maximum load for fall and spring semesters is 12 semester hours. Summer Session I runs eight weeks, with three-, five-, and eight-week class options. A maximum of 9 credit hours may be earned during Session I. Summer Session II runs five weeks, and a maximum of 6 credit hours may be earned.

Living and Housing Costs

In addition to traditional residence halls, Indiana State University offers furnished and unfurnished apartment-style housing for graduate students at its University Apartments at reasonable and competitive rental rates. Each apartment is self-contained with its own bedroom(s), bathroom, living/dining area, and kitchen with an electric range, refrigerator, and garbage disposal. Utilities and free local telephone service are also included. Furnished apartments have one- or two-bedroom options and range from $562 to $630 per month. Unfurnished apartments have one-, two-, or three-bedroom options and range from $518 to $704 per month. Low-cost housing is also available in the surrounding community.

Student Group

Since 1927, ISU's graduate programs have prepared students for careers in a wide range of teaching, research, and service professions. The campus has the highest diversity of students among four-year institutions in Indiana. Both the areas of study and the student population are diverse. Graduate programs attract applicants from all over the United States and from forty-three countries around the world. Approximately 15 percent of the graduate students are international, 33 percent are out-of-state students, 13 percent are members of minority groups, and 58 percent are women. The average graduate student age is 33.

Location

The campus is located adjacent to the central business district of Terre Haute, Indiana, which is an industrial and commercial city of approximately 61,000 located in west-central Indiana. Cultural activities include amateur and professional theatrical productions, symphonies, and art exhibits. Excellent county and state parks are within easy driving distance. The city is convenient to the four major metropolitan areas of Indianapolis, St. Louis, Chicago, and Cincinnati.

The University and The School

Indiana State University is listed as one of the nation's best-value colleges by *The Princeton Review* in its 2008 edition of "America's Best Value Colleges." Indiana State University has grown during its 140-year history from Indiana State Normal School to Indiana State Teachers College and Indiana State College to full university status. With a graduate student population of approximately 2,000, students can be assured of a close mentoring experience and significant research opportunities within their academic program.

Applying

Applications to the College of Graduate and Professional Studies can be submitted online, by mail, or in person.

Prospective applicants should visit the College of Graduate and Professional Studies Web site at http://www.graduate.indstate.edu and check with their respective departments for specific deadlines and additional required admissions materials, such as test scores, letters of recommendation, and other documents. Students generally receive a response acknowledging receipt of the application and other communication from the College of Graduate and Professional Studies within one to two weeks. Once admitted, students receive instructions regarding academic advisement and registration.

International students must submit a TOEFL score of 550 or better and an Affidavit of Financial Support. For additional requirements and documentation, students should visit the Graduate School Web site or the International Affairs Center at http://www.indstate.edu/IAC/.

Correspondence and Information

Dr. Jay D. Gatrell, Dean
College of Graduate and Professional Studies
Indiana State University
Terre Haute, Indiana 47809-1904
Phone: 812-237-3005
800-444-GRAD (4723) (toll-free)
Fax: 812-237-8060
E-mail: grdstudy@isugw.indstate.edu
Web site: http://graduate.indstate.edu

For U.S. applicants, mail to:
Graduate Admissions
Indiana State University
Erickson Hall 218 North Sixth Street
Terre Haute, Indiana 47809-1904
Phone: 812-237-3005
800-444-GRAD (4723) (toll-free)
Fax: 812-237-8060
E-mail: grdstudy@isugw.indstate.edu

For international applicants, mail to:
Graduate Admissions
Indiana State University
Erickson Hall 218 North Sixth Street
Terre Haute, Indiana 47809-1904
Phone: 812-237-3005
800-444-GRAD (4723) toll-free)
Fax: 812-237-8060
E-mail: grdstudy@isugw.indstate.edu
Web site: http://graduate.indstate.edu

THE FACULTY

Deans

Jay D. Gatrell, Ph.D.; Dean, College of Graduate and Professional Studies.
Thomas Sauer, Ph.D.; Dean, College of Arts and Sciences.
Nancy J. Merritt, Ph.D.; Dean, College of Business.
Bradley Balch, Ph.D.; Dean, College of Education.
Richard B. Williams, Ph.D.; Dean, College of Nursing, Health, and Human Services.
W. Tad Foster, Ph.D.; Dean, College of Technology.

Department Chairpersons and Directors of Graduate Degree Programs

Art: Alden Cavanaugh, Ph.D., Professor and Interim Chairperson.
Athletic Training: Jeffrey Edwards, Ph.D., Professor and Interim Chairperson.
Biology: Arthur Halpern, Ph.D., Provisional Chairperson.
Business Administration: Dale Varble, Ph.D., Associate Dean and M.B.A. Director.
Center for Science Education: Elizabeth Brown, Ph.D., Interim Program Director.
Clinical Psychology: Virgil Sheets, Ph.D., Professor and Interim Chairperson.
Communication: David Worley, Ph.D., Professor and Interim Chairperson.
Communication Disorders and School Counseling, School, and Educational Psychology: Michele Boyer, Ph.D., Department Chairperson.
Counseling Education: Debra Leggett, Ph.D., Program Director.
Counseling Psychology: James L. Campbell, Ph.D., Program Director.
Criminology and Criminal Justice: David Skelton, Ed.D., J.D., Professor and Chairperson.
Curriculum, Instruction, and Media Technology: Susan Kiger, Ph.D., Interim Department Chairperson.
Educational and School Psychology: Eric Hampton, Ph.D., Professor.
Educational Leadership, Administration, and Foundations: Josh Powers, Ph.D., Professor and Chairperson.
Electronics, Computer, and Mechanical Engineering Technology: Ming Zhou, Ph.D., Professor and Chairperson.
Elementary, Early, and Special Education: Diana Quatroche, Ph.D., Professor and Chairperson.
English: Robert Perrin, Ph.D., Professor and Chairperson; Graduate Program Contact Person: Dr. Matthew C. Brennan.
Family and Consumer Sciences: Frederica Kramer, Ph.D., Professor and Chairperson.
Geography, Geology, and Anthropology: Russ Stafford, Ph.D., Chairperson and Program Coordinator; Graduate Program Contact Persons: Dr. Greg Bierly (Geography), Dr. James Speer (Geology).
Health, Safety, and Environmental Health Sciences: Y. Peterson, Ph.D., Professor and Interim Department Chairperson.
History: Christopher Olsen, Ph.D., Professor and Acting Chairperson; Graduate Program Contact Person: Dr. Richard Schneirov.
Human Resource Development: James Smallwood, Ph.D., Professor and Chairperson.
Industrial Technology: Marion Schafer, Ph.D., Program Coordinator.
Languages, Literatures, and Linguistics: Ronald Dunbar, Ph.D., Professor and Chairperson.
Mathematics and Computer Science: B. Rao Kopparty, Ph.D., Professor and Chairperson.
Mental Health Counseling: Matthew Draper, Ph.D., Program Director.
Music: Randall Mitchell, Ph.D., Professor and Interim Chairperson.
Nursing: Esther Acree, M.S.N., RN, Sp.Cl.Nsg., FNP; Professor and Interim Dean.
Physical Education: Jeffrey E. Edwards, Ph.D., Professor and Acting Department Chairperson.
Political Science: Michael Chambers, Ph.D., Professor and Chairperson.
Psychology: Virgil Sheets, Ph.D., Professor and Chairperson; M.A./M.S. Program Contact Person: Dr. Liz O'Laughlin.
Public Administration: Stan Buchanan, Ph.D., Assistant Professor and Program Coordinator.
Recreation and Sport Management: Steve Smidley, Ph.D., Department Chairperson; Graduate Program Contact Person: Dr. Thomas H. Sawyer.
School Administration and Supervision: Joshua Powers, Ph.D., Professor and Chairperson.
School Counseling, M.Ed., and Licensure Programs: Tonya Balch, Ph.D., Program Director.
School Psychology: Eric Hampton, Ph.D., Professor and Interim Chairperson.
Science Education: Susan Berta, Ph.D., Professor and Interim Coordinator.
Social Science Education: Daniel Clark, Ph.D., Interim Program Director.
Student Affairs and Higher Education: Denise Collins, Ph.D., Professor and Program Coordinator.
Technology Education: James Smallwood, Ph.D., Professor and Chairperson.
Technology Management: James Smallwood, Ph.D., Program Director.

INDIANA UNIVERSITY OF PENNSYLVANIA

School of Graduate Studies and Research

Programs of Study

The School of Graduate Studies and Research at IUP offers programs of study leading to the Doctor of Education, Doctor of Psychology, and Doctor of Philosophy degrees in the areas of administration and leadership studies (educational administration track or human services track), clinical psychology, communications media, criminology, curriculum and instruction, English, nursing, and school psychology.

Master of Arts, Master of Science, Master of Business Administration, Master of Education, and Master of Fine Arts degrees are available in adult and community education, adult education and communications technology, applied archaeology, applied mathematics, art, biology, business administration, business and workforce development, chemistry, community counseling, criminology, education, educational psychology, education of exceptional persons, elementary and middle school mathematics education, secondary school mathematics education, elementary or secondary school counseling, employment and labor relations, English (English education, English generalist, literature, or teaching English to speakers of other languages), food and nutrition, geography, health and physical education, health services administration, history, literacy, music, nursing, physics, public affairs, safety sciences, science for disaster response, sociology, speech-language pathology, sport science, and student affairs in higher education. IUP also offers graduate programs in the Pittsburgh area.

The School of Graduate Studies and Research offers specialization or certification in elementary/secondary principal, geographic information science and geospatial techniques, reading specialist, safety sciences, school counseling, school psychology, elementary/secondary principal, special education, and supervisor of pupil services.

Residency requirements are established at the program level; thus, doctoral and M.F.A. students will find that residency requirements may vary from program to program. Students should check with their departments, the graduate coordinator, or the program handbook to determine the residency requirement for a particular program.

The University operates on an academic year of two semesters, plus summer and winter sessions.

Research Facilities

The University library contains more than 878,000 book volumes, 1,700 periodical subscriptions, 19,649 electronic serials subscriptions, and 2.4 million units of microform materials and other documents and is a select federal depository. The computer center is available to members of the University community at all times. Specialized laboratories and research equipment are available for advanced master's, post-master's, and doctoral students. There are numerous research centers on campus.

Financial Aid

IUP offers a limited number of assistantships to degree-seeking graduate students. Full 20-hour assistantships currently pay a stipend plus a waiver of tuition for graduate course work. Various loan opportunities are available. Funds exist to support student research and attendance at professional meetings to present papers.

Cost of Study

In 2008–09, full-time graduate tuition was $3215 per semester for in-state students and $5144 per semester for out-of-state students. Tuition for part-time study is $357 per semester credit for in-state students and $572 per credit for out-of-state students. Visit http://www.iup.edu/bursar/tuitionfees/ for the most current tuition and fee information.

Living and Housing Costs

University residence halls and off-campus rooms and apartments are available. Costs vary depending upon room size, proximity, and whether or not meals are included in the arrangement. Visit http://www.iup.edu/housing for specific information.

Student Group

Approximately 2,382 students are enrolled in programs leading to the various graduate degrees. The total University enrollment is approximately 14,310. Students represent American minority groups, most states, and a number of countries.

Location

Indiana, Pennsylvania, a community of 28,000, is 59 miles northeast of Pittsburgh. A wide variety of cultural and recreational activities in urban, suburban, and rural settings are available in and near the town of Indiana and in Pittsburgh.

The University

Founded as a higher education institution in 1875 and designated a university in 1965, IUP is classified as a Doctoral/Research University. It has three campuses and more than 700 faculty members.

Applying

An admissions packet is available by request from the School of Graduate Studies and Research or online at the School's Web site (http://www.iup.edu/graduatestudies). Information describing individual programs is available directly from departmental graduate coordinators, or online at http://www.iup.edu/graduatestudies/programs/.

Correspondence and Information

School of Graduate Studies and Research
Stright Hall, Room 101
210 South Tenth Street
Indiana University of Pennsylvania
Indiana, Pennsylvania 15705-1048

Phone: 724-357-2222
Fax: 724-357-4862
E-mail: graduate-admissions@iup.edu
Web site: http://www.iup.edu/graduatestudies

THE FACULTY

Listed below are IUP's graduate degree program areas. Each is followed by the name of the corresponding graduate coordinator and campus e-mail address.

PROGRAM AREAS
Administration and Leadership Studies, Education Track: Dr. Robert Millward (millward@iup.edu).
Administration and Leadership Studies, Human Services Track: Dr. John Anderson (jaa@iup.edu).
Adult and Community Education: Dr. Gary Dean (gjdean@iup.edu).
Adult Education and Communications Technology: Dr. Jeffrey Ritchey (jeffrey.ritchey@iup.edu).
Applied Archaeology: Dr. Phillip Neusius (phillip.neusius@iup.edu).
Art: Ms. Susan Palmisano (palmisan@iup.edu).
Biology: Dr. Robert Gendron (rgendron@iup.edu).
Business Administration: Dr. Krish Krishnan (krishnan@iup.edu).
Business and Workforce Development: Dr. Dawn Woodland (woodland@iup.edu).
Chemistry: Dr. Keith Kyler (keith.kyler@iup.edu).
Clinical Psychology: Dr. Beverly Goodwin (goodwin@iup.edu).
Communications Media: Dr. Mark Piwinsky (mark.piwinsky@iup.edu).
Community Counseling: Dr. Claire Dandeneau (cdanden@iup.edu).
Counselor Education: Dr. Claire Dandeneau (cdanden@iup.edu).
Criminology, M.A.: Dr. Shannon Phaneuf (s.phaneuf1@iup.edu).
Criminology, Ph.D.: Dr. Jennifer Roberts (jroberts@iup.edu).
Curriculum and Instruction: Dr. Mary Jalongo (mjalongo@iup.edu).
Education of Exceptional Persons: Dr. Becky Knickelbein (becky.knickelbein@iup.edu).
Educational Psychology: Dr. Joseph Kovaleski (jkov@iup.edu).
Employment and Labor Relations: Dr. Jennie Bullard (jbullard@iup.edu).
English, Generalist, Literature, and Literature and Criticism: Dr. David Downing (david.downing@iup.edu).
English, M.A.T.E., TESOL, and Composition: Dr. Ben Rafoth (bennett.rafoth@iup.edu).
Food and Nutrition: Dr. Stephanie Taylor-Davis (stdavis@iup.edu).
Geography: Dr. Kevin Patrick (kpatrick@iup.edu).
Health and Physical Education: Dr. Linda Klingaman (lrklinga@iup.edu).
Health Services Administration: Dr. Jennie Bullard (jbullard@iup.edu).
History: Dr. Alan Baumler (alan.baumler@iup.edu).
Literacy: Dr. Anne Creany (acreany@iup.edu).
Math, Applied: Dr. Yu-Ju Kuo (yu-ju-kuo@iup.edu).
Math Education, Elementary and Middle School: Dr. Larry Feldman (lmfeldmn@iup.edu).
Math Education, Secondary: Dr. Margaret Stempien (mmstemp@iup.edu).
Music, Performance, Education, Theory/Composition, History: Dr. Stephanie Caulder (scaulder@iup.edu).
Nursing, Education, Administration: Dr. Nashat Zuraikat (zuraikat@iup.edu).
Nursing, Ph.D.: Dr. Teresa Shellenbarger (tshell@iup.edu).
Physics: Dr. Gregory Kenning (ccpm@iup.edu).
Principal Certification: Dr. Cathy Kaufman (ckaufman@iup.edu).
Professional Studies, Master of Education: Dr. Valeri Helterbran (vhelter@iup.edu).
Public Affairs: Dr. Susan Martin (susan.martin@iup.edu).
Safety Sciences, Technical Track and Certificate of Recognition: Dr. Christopher Janicak (cjanicak@iup.edu).
School Psychology: Dr. Joseph Kovaleski (jkov@iup.edu).
Science for Disaster Response: Dr. Roberta Eddy (roberta.eddy@iup.edu).
Sociology: Dr. Valerie Gunter (val.gunter@iup.edu).
Speech-Language Pathology: Dr. Shari Robertson (srobert@iup.edu).
Sport Science: Dr. Mark Sloniger (mark.sloniger@iup.edu) and Dr. Robert Kostelnik (bkostel@iup.edu).
Student Affairs in Higher Education: Dr. Linda Hall (linda.hall@iup.edu).

IONA COLLEGE

School of Arts and Science and Hagan Business School Graduate Programs

Programs of Study

Iona College offers graduate programs leading to the degree of Master of Arts, Master of Science, Master of Science in Education, Master of Science in Teaching, or Master of Business Administration. Fields of study in the School of Arts & Science include computer science, criminal justice, education/teaching, educational leadership, educational technology, English, history, Italian, marriage and family therapy, mental health counseling, psychology (experimental, industrial/organizational, school), public relations, Spanish, and telecommunications. Certificate programs are available in educational technology, marriage and family therapy, public relations, and telecommunications. Offered through the Hagan School of Business, the M.B.A. degree is available with specializations in accounting, financial management, health-care management, human resource management, information systems, management, and marketing. Certificates are available in business continuity and risk management, e-commerce, international business, and more.

Graduate programs at Iona College are offered at the main campus in New Rochelle and at the Rockland Graduate Center (the College's branch campus in Pearl River, New York). These programs are specially designed to meet the needs of part-time students, although many programs serve the student who would like to attend full-time. Classes are conveniently scheduled in the late afternoon and early evening to accommodate students' workdays. Depending on the number of credits required of a graduate program, a dedicated part-time student can expect to complete his or her degree in as little as two years. Each program is designed with a core requirement and elective courses. Internships and practicum experiences are built into many programs so students may gain hands-on experience.

Research Facilities

In recent years, the College underwent an ambitious $83-million building campaign that transformed the campus. The new Hynes Athletics Center provides students with access to cardio machines and free weights, an aerobic/dance studio and classes, a pool, a rowing tank, and more. New residence halls, an arts center, and a student union offer students impressive facilities for classes and extracurricular activities. With its TV and radio stations, extensive room for clubs, comfortable lounges, bookstore, food court, and café, the Robert V. LaPenta Student Union is the hub of campus life. In fall 2009, the main library reopened after an extensive expansion and renovation. New features include a multimedia seminar room and group study facilities equipped for students to collaborate on podcasts and digital projects—all while enjoying the services of the library's café (one of two outlets on campus). The library has installed fifty-two dual-boot iMacs, which can run both Microsoft Windows and the latest Mac OS, making Iona one of a handful of colleges to invest in this cutting-edge technology. Iona College features fully wireless facilities offering students high-speed access to the Internet and possesses more than 700 networked computers and two fully networked computer labs located at Iona's graduate center in Rockland County. Computer lab assistants are available to help students with their questions, and one lab stays open 24 hours a day, seven days a week. All students have e-mail accounts and access to the Internet.

Financial Aid

Iona College serves graduate students through a variety of state, federal, and institutional programs that include loans, scholarships, and assistantships. Scholarships are available based on undergraduate GPA or GRE or GMAT scores. To be eligible for federal loans, students must complete the FAFSA and the Iona College loan application.

Cost of Study

The cost of graduate tuition for the 2009–10 academic year is $850 per credit hour.

Living and Housing Costs

On-campus housing is not available for graduate students.

Student Group

There are approximately 900 students enrolled in graduate programs at Iona College. Most of these students are employed full-time and attend classes on a part-time basis in the evenings.

Student Outcomes

Some organizations that employ Iona graduates include American Express, Avon, Bristol-Meyers, Gannett Co., IBM, Lenox Hill and Sound Shore Hospitals, MasterCard, NBC, Sports Illustrated, top school districts, Verizon, Wyeth Pharmaceuticals, and Xerox.

Location

Iona's main campus is located on 35 acres in New Rochelle, New York, 20 minutes north of Manhattan. New Rochelle is a beautiful suburb of 70,000 located on Long Island Sound and is well served by mass transportation and highways. Iona's Rockland Graduate Center is 3 miles from the Palisades Parkway in Pearl River. Both campuses offer plentiful parking for evening students. The location of both campuses in the NYC metropolitan area allows students to take advantage of the many cultural, internship, and employment opportunities available.

The College

Iona College is a comprehensive, coed Catholic college, founded in 1940 by the Congregation of Christian Brothers. The overall enrollment is about 4,200 students, of whom 900 study at the graduate level.

Iona offers study in more than twenty graduate areas and is accredited by the Middle States Association of Colleges and Schools. In the School of Arts & Science, specialized recognitions are held by the following programs: education programs are accredited by NCATE: National Council for Accreditation of Teacher Education, public relations and journalism are accredited by ACEJMC: Accrediting Council of Education in Journalism and Mass Communication, and marriage and family therapy is accredited by COAMFTE: Commission on Accreditation for Marriage and Family Therapy Education. Graduates of mental health counseling and school psychology are licensure eligible. The Hagan School is accredited by AACSB International–The Association to Advance Collegiate Schools of Business.

Applying

Applications for Iona's School of Arts & Science graduate programs are available by mail or can be completed online at http://www.iona.edu/ionagrad/admission.html. To be considered, an applicant must submit the application and required application fee, official transcripts from all colleges attended, and two letters of recommendation. Interviews (in person or by phone) and other application materials may be required by some programs. Applications should be submitted at least a month before the intended start term. Applicants to mental health counseling, psychology, and marriage and family therapy are strongly encouraged to apply by February 1, as enrollments in those programs are limited.

Candidates for the Hagan School of Business may enter the graduate program in the fall (September), winter (November), or spring (March) trimester or in the summer session. The completed application, with fee, must be accompanied by two letters of recommendation, official transcripts from all postsecondary schools, and GMAT scores. All documents must be received no later than two weeks prior to the start of the session for which the candidate is applying.

Correspondence and Information

Office of Graduate Admissions
School of Arts & Science
Iona College
715 North Avenue
New Rochelle, New York 10801
Phone: 914-633-2502
800-231-IONA (toll-free)
Fax: 914-633-2277
E-mail: admissions@iona.edu
Web site: http://www.iona.edu

Director of M.B.A. Admissions
Hagan School of Business
Iona College
715 North Avenue
New Rochelle, New York 10801
Phone: 914-633-2288
Fax: 914-633-2012
E-mail: hagan@iona.edu
Web site: http://www.iona.edu/hagan

Graduate Admissions Office
Rockland Graduate Center
Concourse Level
Two Blue Hill Plaza
P.O. Box 1522
Pearl River, New York 10965
Phone: 845-620-1350
Fax: 845-620-1260
E-mail: rockland@iona.edu
Web site: http://www.iona.edu/rockland

DEPARTMENT AND PROGRAM HEADS

Computer Science: Robert Schiaffino, Associate Professor and Chair; Ph.D., Polytechnic Institute of NYU.
Criminal Justice: Paul O'Connell, Associate Professor and Chair; Ph.D., St. John's (New York).
Education: Catherine M. O'Callaghan, Professor and Chair; Ph.D.; Fordham.
Education Technology: Robert Schiaffino, Associate Professor and Chair; Ph.D., Polytechnic Institute of NYU.
English: Laura Shea, Professor and Chair; Ph.D.; Boston University.
History: Br. James Carroll, Associate Professor and Chair; Ph.D., Notre Dame.
Italian and Spanish: Thomas Mussio, Associate Professor and Chair; Ph.D., Michigan.
Marriage and Family Therapy: Robert A. Burns, Associate Professor and Chair; Ph.D., St. John's (New York).
Psychology: Pauline Jirik-Babb, Associate Professor and Chair; Ph.D., NYU.
Public Relations: Br. Raymond Smith, Associate Professor and Chair; Ph.D., NYU.
Telecommunications: Robert Schiaffino, Associate Professor and Chair; Ph.D., Polytechnic Institute of NYU.

ITHACA COLLEGE

Division of Graduate Studies

Programs of Study

All of Ithaca College's graduate degree programs promise an intellectual environment in which a close-knit group of similarly directed colleagues, both fellow students and nationally recognized faculty members, will work and walk alongside new students to help clarify their vision, guide their study, nurture their talent, and creatively and broadly help shape their future.

Perhaps most importantly, all of the College's graduate degrees feature one common and crucial component: students get the opportunity to experiment, practice, and hone real life and work skills in practical, hands-on, experiential learning, teaching, and working situations. Students who are at Ithaca College to perform will be on stage. Those there to gain credentials as a speech pathologist are responsible for real clients with real problems to solve. Students studying human performance work alongside real athletes. In research, internships, clinical placements, performance opportunities, and real-world applications, a student's journey and time at Ithaca is predicated on practice as well as on theory.

Since 1943, when Ithaca College offered its first master's degrees, it has awarded nearly 6,000 graduate diplomas to dedicated and talented professionals. The College offers master's degrees in adolescence education, business administration, childhood education, communications, exercise and sport sciences, health and physical education, music, physical and occupational therapy, speech-language pathology, and sport management. Its graduates are recognized leaders in their fields, enriching their professions and the world around them.

Ithaca College also offers a variety of professional development opportunities. Some offerings provide undergraduate or graduate credit and can be pathways toward degree programs. Others are noncredit programs offering continuing education units (CEUs). All offerings are designed to meet the needs of professionals in a variety of fields; some of these programs lead to a certificate from Ithaca College. For more information about current offerings, students should visit http://www.ithaca.edu/profdev or contact the Office of Certificate and Professional Programs in the Division of Graduate and Professional Studies at 607-274-3527.

Research Facilities

The library is open more than 100 hours a week to provide a complete range of information services and resources in both electronic and print formats. Information Technology Services (ITS) maintains an extensive collection of programming languages, data-analysis packages, and business programs to support the curriculum. Networked computers, both Macintosh and PCs, are available in thirty facilities across campus. One lab is open 24 hours a day and the rest are open from early morning to late at night throughout the fall and spring semesters. Laboratories are staffed by student consultants skilled at helping people use the computers.

Financial Aid

A limited number of assistantships are available in each of the master's degree programs on a competitive basis. Assistantships supplement tuition and offer a small salary in exchange for on-campus responsibilities.

Cost of Study

The 2008–09 graduate tuition rate varied by program: $679 per credit for business, $527 per credit for adolescence education and health and physical education, and $603 per credit for all other programs.

Living and Housing Costs

The College maintains no housing facilities for graduate students. Off-campus housing is available at various rates. Several meal plans are available in the College dining halls. Prices per semester were as follows: $1067 with $110 bonus dollars for seven meals per week, $2398.50 for ten meals per week, and $2639 for ten, fourteen, or twenty meals per week with bonus dollars.

Student Group

Approximately 500 students are enrolled in graduate programs.

Location

Ithaca, New York, is also the site of Cornell University. A majority of the city's 29,000 permanent residents are academically oriented, while a transient population of some 23,000 students, artists, scientists, and scholars enriches its unique academic atmosphere. Many visitors are drawn to Ithaca by the striking beauty of the scenery, the opportunities for outdoor life, and the cultural activity of a cosmopolitan community where there is extensive interest in the humanities, sciences, music, and drama. Students have frequent occasions to share in and contribute to these interests and opportunities.

The College

Constructed on a naturally terraced hillside, the unobstructed view of the surrounding countryside provides one of the finest vistas in the Finger Lakes region. The facilities were designed to take advantage of that view and to blend with the natural beauty of the terrain. Residence halls, dining halls, and academic buildings are located in spacious, closely knit units at the center of the site. Classrooms, laboratories, lecture halls, and specialized facilities have been designed to utilize modern teaching technology. The campus is surrounded by an abundance of recreational facilities, including an outdoor Olympic-size swimming pool, fitness trail, playing fields, and tennis courts. Recent construction includes additions to the Schools of Music and Health Sciences and Human Performance. A new fitness center has also recently been completed.

Applying

Applications for admission are available online at http://www.ithaca.edu/gradstudies. The deadlines for application, with the necessary transcripts and recommendations vary by program. The General Test of the Graduate Record Examinations is required by exercise and sport sciences, speech-language pathology, sport management, and teaching students with speech and language disabilities. The Graduate Management Admission Test (GMAT) is required for business administration.

Admission requirements include a bachelor's degree from an accredited college, a minimum 3.0 undergraduate GPA, and typically an undergraduate major or the equivalent in the proposed field. Online applications and catalogs can be found at http://www.ithaca.edu/gradstudies.

Correspondence and Information

Division of Graduate and Professional Studies
Ithaca College
Peggy Ryan Williams Hall
Ithaca, New York 14850-7142

Phone: 607-274-3527
Fax: 607-274-1263
E-mail: gradstudies@ithaca.edu
Web site: http://www.ithaca.edu/gradstudies

THE FACULTY

Business Administration
Donald Eckrich, Professor and Chair; D.B.A., Kentucky.
Alka Bramhandkar, Associate Professor; Ph.D., SUNY at Binghamton.
Joanne Burress, Associate Professor; Ph.D., SUNY at Buffalo.
Joseph Cheng, Associate Professor; Ph.D., SUNY at Binghamton.
Mark Cordano, Assistant Professor; Ph.D., Pittsburgh.
G. Scott Erickson, Associate Professor; Ph.D., Lehigh.
Eileen Kelly, Professor; Ph.D., Cincinnati.
Eric Lewis, Associate Professor; Ph.D., Union (New York).
Patricia Libby, Associate Professor; Ph.D., Michigan.
Donald Lifton, Associate Professor; Ph.D., Cornell.
Jeffrey Lippitt, Associate Professor; Ph.D., Penn State.
Granger Macy, Associate Professor; Ph.D., Indiana.
Michael McCall, Professor; Ph.D., Arizona State.
Abraham Mulugetta, Professor; Ph.D., Wisconsin.
Gwen Seaquist, Associate Professor; J.D., Mississippi.
Donald Simmons, Assistant Professor; Ph.D., SUNY at Binghamton.
Joseph Sprangel, Instructor; M.B.A., Spring Arbor.
William Tastle, Associate Professor; Ph.D., SUNY at Binghamton.
Fahri Unsal, Professor; Ph.D., Cornell.
M. Raquibuz Zaman, Professor; Ph.D., Cornell.

Communications
Howard Kalman, Assistant Professor and Chair; Ph.D., Indiana.
Dennis Charsky, Assistant Professor; Ph.D., Northern Colorado.
Diane M. Gayeski, Professor; Ph.D., Maryland.
Ari Kissiloff, Assistant Professor; M.S., Ithaca.
Gordon Rowland, Professor; Ph.D., Indiana.
Steven A. Seidman, Associate Professor; Ph.D., Indiana.
Cory Lynn Young, Assistant Professor; Ph.D., Bowling Green

Exercise and Sport Sciences
Jeff Ives, Associate Professor and Chair; Ph.D., Massachusetts.
Mary DePalma, Professor; Ph.D., Cornell.
Noah Gentner, Associate Professor; Ph.D., Tennessee.
Betsy A. Keller, Professor; Ph.D., Massachusetts.
Deborah King, Associate Professor; Ph.D., Pennsylvania.
Tom Pfaff, Associate Professor; Ph.D., Syracuse.
Kent Scribner, Professor; Ed.D., Syracuse.
Gary A. Sforzo, Professor; Ph.D., Maryland.
Greg Shelley, Associate Professor; Ph.D., Utah.
John Sigg, Associate Professor; Ph.D., Toledo.
Tom Swensen, Associate Professor; Ph.D., Tennessee.
Kent D. Wagoner, Assistant Professor; Ph.D., Georgia.

Health Promotion and Physical Education
Deborah A. Wuest, Professor and Chair; Ed.D., Boston University.
Stewart Auyash, Associate Professor; Ph.D., Penn State.
Srijana M. Bajracharya, Associate Professor; Ph.D., Auburn.
Mary K. Bentley, Associate Professor; Ph.D., Maryland.
Phoebe Constantinou, Assistant Professor; Ed.D., Columbia.
Ann Kolodji, Assistant Professor; Ph.D., Pennsylvania.
Prithwi Raj Subramaniam, Associate Professor; Ph.D., Illinois.

School of Humanities and Sciences
Linda Hanrahan, Associate Professor and Chair; Ed.D., Rutgers.
Ellen Cohen-Rosenthal, Instructor; Ph.D., Alfred.
M. Cathrene Connery, Assistant Professor; Ph.D., New Mexico.
Elizabeth Bleicher, Assistant Professor; Ph.D., USC.
Vicki Cameron, Professor; Ph.D., Colorado.
Edward Cluett, Associate Professor; Ph.D. Cornell.
Ellen Cohen-Rosenthal, Instructor; Ph.D., Alfred.
Vivian Bruce Conger, Associate Professor; Ph.D., Cornell.
James Conklin, Associate Professor; Ph.D., Rochester.
Maria Di Francesco, Assistant Professor; Ph.D., SUNY at Buffalo.
Louise Donohue, Assistant Professor; M.A., SUNY at Binghamton.
Jason Freitag, Assistant Professor; Ph.D., Columbia.
Marian MacCurdy, Professor; Ph.D., Syracuse.
Thomas J. Pfaff, Associate Professor; Ph.D., Syracuse.
Eric Robinson, Professor; Ph.D., SUNY at Binghamton.
Margaret Robinson, Assistant Professor; M.S., SUNY at Binghamton.
Martin Sternstein, Professor; Ph.D., Cornell.
James Swafford, Associate Professor; Ph.D. Duke.
Michael Trotti, Associate Professor; Ph.D., North Carolina at Chapel Hill.
Michael Twomey, Professor; Ph.D., Cornell.
Kirsten Wasson, Assistant Professor; Ph.D., Wisconsin.
Zenon Wasyliw, Associate Professor; Ph.D., SUNY at Binghamton.
Aaron Weinberg, Assistant Professor; Ph.D., Wisconsin–Madison.

Music
Timothy A. Johnson, Assistant Professor (Music Therapy, History, and Composition) and Chair; Ph.D., SUNY at Buffalo.
Rebecca Ansel, Assistant Professor (Violin); D.M.A., Michigan.
Susan Avery, Assistant Professor (Music Education); Ph.D., Rochester (Eastman).
Diane Birr, Associate Professor (Piano); M.M., Indiana.
Leslie Black, Assistant Professor (Theory); Ph.D., Yale.
Randie Blooding, Associate Professor (Voice); D.M.A., Ohio State.
Frank Campos, Professor (Trumpet and Music Education); M.M., North Texas State.
Pablo Cohen, Adjunct Assistant Professor (Classical Guitar); M.M., Temple.
Craig Cummings, Associate Professor (Music History); Ph.D., Indiana.
Charis Dimaras, Associate Professor (Performance); D.M.A., Manhattan School of Music.
Lawrence A. Doebler, Professor and Director of Chorale Music; M.M., Washington (St. Louis).
D. Kim Dunnick, Professor (Trumpet); D.M., Indiana.
Richard Edwards, Assistant Professor (Music Education); M.M., North Carolina at Greensboro.
Richard Faria, Associate Professor (Clarinet); M.M., Michigan State.
Mark Fonder, Professor (Music Education); Ed.D., Illinois.
Janet Galvan, Professor (Music Education); Ed.D., North Carolina.
Michael Galvan, Professor (Clarinet and Music Education); M.M., Illinois.
Lee Goodhew-Romm, Professor (Bassoon); M.M., SMU.
Jennifer Hayghe, Assistant Professor (Piano); D.M.A., Juilliard.
Jennifer Haywood, Assistant Professor (Music Education); Ph.D., Toronto.
Bradley Hougham, Assistant Professor (Voice); M.A., CUNY, Queens.
Daniel Isbell, Assistant Professor (Music Education); Ph.D., Colorado at Boulder.
Rebecca Jemian, Assistant Professor (Theory); Ph.D., Indiana.
Keith A. Kaiser, Associate Professor (Music Education); M.M., Redlands.
Jennifer Kay, Assistant Professor (Voice); D.M.A., Boston University.
Sally Lamb, Assistant Professor (Composition); D.M.A., Cornell.
Deborah Lifton, Adjunct Assistant Professor (Voice); M.M., Manhattan School of Music.
Deborah Martin, Associate Professor (Piano); D.M., Indiana.
Steven Mauk, Professor (Saxophone); D.M.A., Michigan.
Carol McAmis, Professor (Voice); M.M., Kansas.
Wendy Herbener Mehne, Professor (Flute); D.M.A., Wisconsin.
Phiroze Mehta, Professor (Piano); M.M., Massachusetts.
Jeffery Meyer, Assistant Professor and Director of Orchestras; D.M.A., SUNY at Stony Brook.
Deborah Montgomery, Professor (Voice); M.M., Illinois.
Debra Moree, Associate Professor (Viola and Violin); M.M., Indiana.
Paige Morgan, Associate Professor (Music Performance); D.M.A., Rochester (Eastman).
Timothy A. Nord, Associate Professor (Music Technology); Ph.D., Wisconsin.
David Pacun, Assistant Professor (Theory); Ph.D., Chicago.
David Parks, Professor (Voice); D.M.A., Arizona.
Patrice Pastore, Professor (Voice); M.M., New England Conservatory.
Alex Perialas, Assistant Professor (Recording); B.S., Ithaca.
Elizabeth Peterson, Assistant Professor (Music Education); M.M., Northwestern.
Stephen G. Peterson, Professor (Music Performance); Ph.D., Northwestern.
Mark Radice, Professor (Music History); Ph.D., Rochester (Eastman).
Sanford Reuning, Adjunct Assistant Professor (Suzuki Strings); B.M., Illinois.
Harold Reynolds, Professor (Trombone); D.M.A., Rochester (Eastman).
Deborah Rifkin, Assistant Professor (Theory); Ph.D., Rochester (Eastman).
Peter Rothbart, Professor (Electroacoustic); D.M.A., Cleveland Institute of Music.
Alex Shuhan, Associate Professor (French Horn); B.M., Rochester (Eastman).
Peter Siberman, Assistant Professor (Theory); Ph.D., Rochester (Eastman).
Elizabeth P. Simkin, Associate Professor (Cello); M.M., Rochester (Eastman).
Gordon Stout, Professor (Percussion) and Chair of Performance Studies; M.M., Rochester (Eastman).
Edward Swenson, Professor; Ph.D., Cornell.
David Unland, Associate Professor (Baritone and Tuba); M.S., Illinois at Urbana-Champaign.
Nicholas Walker, Assistant Professor (Double Bass); D.M.A., Stony Brook, SUNY.
Susan Waterbury, Associate Professor; M.M., Rochester (Eastman).
John White, Assistant Professor; Ph.D., Indiana.
Baruch Whitehead, Assistant Professor (Music Education); Ph.D., Capella.
Dana Wilson, Professor (Composition); Ph.D., Rochester (Eastman).

Occupational Therapy
Melinda A. Cozzolino, Associate Professor (Associate Member) and Chair of Graduate Program; O.T.D., Creighton; OTR/L.
Carole W. Dennis, Associate Professor and Chair of Occupational Therapy; M.A., Connecticut; Sc.D., Boston University.
Rita Daly, Adjunct Instructor; M.S., D'Youville; OTR/L.
Julie Dorsey, Assistant Professor; M.S., Ithaca.
Judy Gonyea, Assistant Professor; O.T.D., Creighton.
Catherine Y. Gordon, Associate Professor; Ed.D., SUNY at Buffalo; OTR.
Diane M. Long, Associate Professor and Curriculum Director; M.S., SUNY at Buffalo; OTR/L.
Meghan McNally, Lecturer (Adjunct Member); M.P.A., SUNY at Binghampton.
Sunny Winstead, Lecturer (Adjunct Member); M.S., Virginia Commonwealth; OTR/L.

Physical Therapy
Ernest Nalette, Associate Professor, Chair of the Graduate Program, and Director of the Rochester Unit; Ed.D., Vermont.
Katherine L. Beissner, Professor; Ph.D., Syracuse.
Christine Burns, Adjunct Professor; Ed.M., M.B.A., Rochester.
Lynda J. Dimitroff, Associate Professor; Ph.D., Southern Illinois, Carbondale.
Jeffrey Houck, Assistant Professor; Ph.D., Iowa; PT.
Helene Marie Larin, Associate Professor; Ph.D., Toronto.
Deborah A. Nawoczenski, Professor; Ph.D., Iowa; PT.
Karen W. Nolan, Assistant Professor; M.S., Rochester; PT.
Angela Rosenberg, Adjunct Professor; Dr.P.H., North Carolina at Chapel Hill.

Speech-Language Pathology/Audiology
Luanne Andersson, Assistant Professor and Chair; Ph.D., Connecticut.
Elizabeth Begley, Clinical Assistant Professor; M.A., California.
Christine M. P. Cecconi, Clinical Associate Professor; M.A., Bowling Green State.
Douglas E. Cross, Associate Professor; Ph.D., Tennessee.
Barbara Ann Johnson, Professor; Ph.D., Florida.
Mary Pitti, Clinical Assistant Professor; M.S., Ithaca.
Marie Sanford, Clinical Associate Professor; M.S., Ithaca.
Richard J. Schissel, Associate Professor; Ph.D., Penn State.
John C. Stephens, Clinical Assistant Professor; M.S., Ithaca.
Kal M. Telage, Professor; Ph.D., Ohio.

Sport Management
Ellen J. Staurowsky, Professor and Chair; Ed.D., Temple.
F. Wayne Blann, Professor; Ed.D., Boston University.
Annemarie Farrell, Assistant Professor; Ph.D., Ohio.
Stephen D. Mosher, Professor; Ph.D., Massachusetts Amherst.
John T. Wolohan, Associate Professor; J.D., Western New England.

KANSAS STATE UNIVERSITY

The Graduate School

K-STATE Kansas State University

Programs of Study

Kansas State University's (KSU) Graduate School offers advanced study in sixty-seven master's degree programs, forty-four doctoral programs, and twenty-nine certificate programs, with more than 4,700 graduate students enrolled. There is an increasing emphasis on innovative interdisciplinary programs.

Opportunities exist for research and scholarly activities in the areas of agriculture, architecture and design, biochemistry, business administration, education, engineering, food science, genetics, human ecology, humanities and fine arts, natural sciences, social sciences, and veterinary medicine. Examples of areas for graduate study and research include atomic physics, automated manufacturing, software engineering, space biology, infectious disease research, prairie ecology, rural sociology, wheat genetics, molecular biology, nutrition and public health, theater, cancer biology, materials science, industrial and organizational psychology, military history, high-energy physics, milling science, functional foods, food service, and human development.

The Graduate School requires 30 semester hours beyond the bachelor's degree to obtain the master's degree, although some programs require more than 30 semester hours. Many programs require a substantial research project, although a nonthesis option is available in some programs. In the professional programs, that option predominates.

Doctoral programs require 90 semester hours beyond the bachelor's degree to obtain a Ph.D. and 94 semester hours beyond to obtain an Ed.D. Both programs include original research and a dissertation. Admission to candidacy requires the successful completion of the preliminary examinations.

The Division of Continuing Education offers many courses and degree programs through distance education, using a variety of delivery methods, including the World Wide Web, DVDs, videotapes, audiotapes, Telenet 2, and other technologies. KSU offers the following through distance learning: the Adult and Continuing Education Master's Program (Kansas City, Fort Leavenworth, or Wichita), an Agribusiness Master's Degree, the Classroom Technology Specialty, the Educational Administration and Leadership Master's Program, Engineering Degree Programs, English as a Second Language Specialty in Elementary/Secondary Education Program, Food Science, Gerontology, Industrial/Organization Psychology, Personal Financial Planning, and Youth Development. Several graduate certificate programs are also offered through the Division of Continuing Education.

Postbaccalaureate certificates provide a means to recognize mastery in a specialized area or to supplement a graduate degree. KSU currently offers twenty-nine certificate programs in a variety of areas.

Research Facilities

KSU ranks among the nation's top seventy public research universities, with a growing foundation of research infrastructure to support rigorous training in scholarly research. Most recently, in 2008, KSU was selected as the location for the National Bio and Agro Defense Facility. The campus contains numerous specialized centers of interdisciplinary focused research, and these provide graduate students with dynamic training in their disciplines. Students should consult the KSU Research Facilities and Centers Web page at http://www.ksu.edu/Directories/research-facilities.html for a partial listing of these centers.

Financial Aid

Nearly half of KSU graduate students receive some type of financial assistance, including University graduate fellowships, teaching and research assistantships, or other forms of University employment and loans. Full-tuition waivers are given to graduate teaching assistants who receive at least a half-time appointment, and tuition reductions are available for graduate research assistants.

The KSU Office of Student Financial Assistance administers the federal assistance programs, work-study programs, and loans for which graduate students are eligible.

Cost of Study

For 2008–09, tuition for Kansas residents ranged from $269.40 for 1 graduate credit hour per semester to $3232.80 for 12 credit hours. Nonresident tuition ranged from $619.75 for 1 graduate credit hour per semester to $7437 for 12 credit hours. Fees in addition to tuition include campus privilege fees that range from $79.20 to $336.60. Some colleges have additional tuition surcharges and equipment fees.

Overall annual expenses, including living expenses, for a full-time student who completes 24 hours and is paying nonresident tuition are about $29,850.

Living and Housing Costs

KSU has over 700 apartment units for graduate students. Married couples with children and single parents have priority. One-bedroom apartments on a semester basis range from $360 to $520 per month for traditional and newly constructed units, respectively, and two-bedroom apartments range from $425 to $980 per month for traditional and newly constructed units. On a yearly basis in Manhattan, a typical one-bedroom apartment ranges from $490 to $535 per month, and two-bedroom apartments range from $540 to $650 per month.

Student Group

The KSU graduate student population of more than 4,700 is made up of approximately 40 percent men and 60 percent women. Approximately one fourth of the population is made up of international students from more than 70 countries. About two thirds of all graduate students are nontraditional (age 25 or older or married).

Student Outcomes

KSU graduates are highly sought after. They often receive multiple job offers, and many find employment well before graduation. They are leaders in public and private sectors, at government agencies, and at all levels of business and the private sector.

A sample of employers includes the National Institutes of Health, Argonne and Sandia National Labs, Nintendo, Merck, Pfizer, Cargill, Kellogg's, Hershey Foods, Anheuser-Busch, Motorola, AT&T Bell Labs, Texas Instruments, Rockwell International, and Sprint.

Location

KSU's picturesque 668-acre campus features many buildings of native limestone. KSU is centrally located in Manhattan (population 50,000), about 125 miles west of Kansas City. Manhattan has a new municipal airport, excellent schools, a daily newspaper, and numerous recreational facilities and cultural offerings. International festivals, Cinco de Mayo, Juneteenth, and Native American observances are held annually.

The University

Founded in 1863 as the first land-grant college, KSU is an internationally recognized, comprehensive research university with excellent academic programs carried out in a lively intellectual and cultural atmosphere.

In 1996, the University received the National Science Foundation's Recognition Award for the Integration of Research and Education. KSU was one of only ten universities selected.

Since 1974, KSU has ranked in the top 1 percent of all U.S. universities in the number of its graduates selected as Rhodes scholars.

Applying

Students should request admission applications and supplementary program information directly from the department or program coordinator. The Graduate School forwards correspondence to the appropriate program.

U.S. citizens should have all application materials on file by February 1 to receive priority consideration for full admission and for consideration for fellowships or graduate assistantships for the following fall semester. International students should apply no later than nine months prior to the term in which they wish to enroll.

Correspondence and Information

The Graduate School
103 Fairchild Hall
Kansas State University
Manhattan, Kansas 66506-1103

Phone: 785-532-6191
800-651-1816 (toll-free in the U.S.)
Fax: 785-532-2983
E-mail: grad@ksu.edu
Web site: http://www.k-state.edu/grad

PROGRAMS AND COORDINATORS

Students should contact the program coordinators listed below for more information.

COLLEGE OF AGRICULTURE
Agricultural Economics (M.S., Ph.D.): John Crespi.
Agricultural Economics–Agribusiness (M.A.B.): Allen Featherstone.
Agronomy (M.S., Ph.D.): Bill Schapaugh.
Animal Sciences and Industry (M.S., Ph.D.): Evan Titgmeyer.
Entomology (M.S., Ph.D.): Tom Phillips.
Grain Science and Industry (M.S., Ph.D.): David Wetzel.
Horticulture (M.S., Ph.D.): Channa Rajashekar.
Plant Pathology (M.S., Ph.D.): Bill Bockus.

COLLEGE OF ARCHITECTURE PLANNING AND DESIGN
Postprofessional Master's Program in Architecture (M.S.Arch.): Carol Martin Watts.
Professional Master's Programs. Architecture (M.Arch.): Carol Martin Watts.
Landscape Architecture (M.L.A.): Stephanie Rolley.
Regional and Community Planning (M.R.C.P.): Al Keithley.
Community Development (M.S.): Al Keithley.
Interior Architecture and Product Design (M.I.A.P.D.): Neal Hubbell.

COLLEGE OF ARTS AND SCIENCES

Sciences and Mathematics
Biology (M.S., Ph.D.): S. Keith Chapes.
Chemistry (M.S., Ph.D.): Christer Aakeroy.
Geology (M.S., cooperative Ph.D. with the University of Kansas): C. G. (Jack) Oviatt.
Mathematics (M.S., Ph.D.): David Yetter.
Microbiology (Ph.D.): S. Keith Chapes.
Physics (M.S., Ph.D.): Brett Esry.
Statistics (M.S., Ph.D.): Weixing Song.

Humanities and Fine Arts
English (M.A.): Greg Eiselein.
Fine Arts (M.F.A.): Elliott Pujol.
History (M.A., Ph.D.): Louise Breen.
Modern Languages (M.A.): Claire Dehon.
Music (M.M.): Frederick Burrack.
Communication Studies, Theater, and Dance (M.A.). Speech: Bill Schenk-Hamlin. Theater: Sally Bailey.

Social Sciences
Economics (M.A., Ph.D.): James Ragan.
Geography (M.A., Ph.D.): Kevin Blake.
Kinesiology (M.S.): Tom Barstow.
Journalism and Mass Communication (M.S.): Hyun-Seung Jin.
Political Science (M.A.): James Franke.
Psychology (M.S., Ph.D.): Clive Fullagar.
Public Administration (M.P.A.): Krishna Tummala.
Sociology (M.A., Ph.D.): Gerad Middendorf.

COLLEGE OF BUSINESS ADMINISTRATION
Accountancy (M.Acc.): Jeffrey Katz.
Business Administration (M.B.A.): Jeffrey Katz.

COLLEGE OF EDUCATION
Students should contact Marjorie Hancock for information related to the following programs.

Academic Advising (M.S.).
Adult and Continuing Education (M.S., Ed.D., Ph.D.).
Counseling and Student Development (M.S., Ed.D., Ph.D.).
Curriculum and Instruction (M.S., Ed.D., Ph.D.).
Educational Administration and Leadership (M.S., Ed.D.).
Special Education (M.S., Ed.D.).

COLLEGE OF ENGINEERING
Architectural Engineering (M.S.): Kimberly Kramer.
Biological and Agricultural Engineering (M.S., Ph.D.): Naiqian Zhang.
Chemical Engineering (M.S., Ph.D.): James Edgar.
Civil Engineering (M.S., Ph.D.): Hayder Rasheed.
Computer Science (M.S., Ph.D.): Gurdip Singh.
Electrical Engineering (M.S., Ph.D.): Andrew Rys.
Engineering Management (M.E.M.): E. Stanley Lee.
Industrial Engineering (M.S., Ph.D.): E. Stanley Lee.
Mechanical Engineering (M.S., Ph.D.): Steve Eckels.
Nuclear Engineering (M.S., Ph.D.): Steve Eckels.
Operations Research (M.S.): E. Stanley Lee.
Software Engineering (M.S.E.): Gurdip Singh.

COLLEGE OF HUMAN ECOLOGY
Apparel and Textiles (M.S.): Jana Hawley.
Dietetics (M.S.): Deborah Canter.
Family Studies and Human Services (M.S.): Maurice MacDonald.
Gerontology (M.S.): Gayle Doyle.
Food Service Hospitality Management and Dietetics Administration (M.S.): Deborah Canter.
Human Ecology (Ph.D.).
Apparel and Textiles: Jana Hawley.
Family Life Education and Consultation: Maurice MacDonald.
Food Service and Hospitality Management: Deborah Canter.
Life Span Human Development: Maurice MacDonald.
Marriage and Family Therapy: Maurice MacDonald.
Personal Financial Planning: John Grable.
Human Nutrition (M.S., Ph.D.). Food Science: Edgar Chambers IV. Nutrition: Mark Haub.

COLLEGE OF VETERINARY MEDICINE
Biomedical Sciences (M.S.): Michael Kenney.
Pathobiology (Ph.D.): T. G. Nagaraja.
Physiology (Ph.D.): Mark Weiss.

GRADUATE CERTIFICATE PROGRAMS
Academic Advising: Stephen Benton.
Air Quality: Larry Erickson and Mo Hosni.
Applied Statistics: John Boyer.
Business Administration: Jeffrey Katz.
Community Planning and Development: Al Keithley.
Complex Fluid Flows: Steve Eckels.
Conflict Resolution: Terrie McCants.
Digital Teaching and Learning: Rosemary Talab.
Entomology: Tom Phillips.
Feedlot Production Management: Dan Thomson.
Food Safety and Defense: Scott Smith.
Food Science: Scott Smith.
Geoenvironmental: David Steward.
Geographic Information Science: J. M. Shawn Hutchinson.
Gerontology: Pam Evans.
International Service: Jeffrey Pickering.
Occupational Health Psychology: Ron Downey.
Organizational Leadership: Jeffrey Katz.
Personal Financial Planning: John Grable.
Public Administration: Krishna Tummala.
Public Health Core Concepts: Michael Cates.
Real-Time Embedded System Design: Mitchell Neilsen.
Stem Cell Biotechnology: Duane Davis.
Teaching and Learning: Lawrence Scharmann.
Teaching Students with Autism Spectrum Disorders: Marilyn Kaff.
Technical Writing and Professional Communications: Gregory Eiselein.
Women's Studies: Torry Dickinson.
Youth Development Administration: Elaine Johannes.
Youth Development Professional: Elaine Johannes.

INTERDISCIPLINARY PROGRAMS
Biochemistry: (M.S., Ph.D.): Michal Zolkiewski.
Environmental Design and Planning (Ph.D.): Wendy Ornelas.
Food Science (M.S., Ph.D.): J. Scott Smith.
Genetics (M.S., Ph.D.): Barbara Valent.
Public Health (M.P.H.): Michael Cates.
Security Studies (M.A., Ph.D.): Mark Parillo.

LMU|LA

Loyola Marymount University

LOYOLA MARYMOUNT UNIVERSITY

Programs of Study

The mission of the Graduate Division at Loyola Marymount University (LMU) is to provide high-quality postbaccalaureate degree programs that serve to expand knowledge and foster professional development. Consistent with the Jesuit and Marymount traditions, LMU's rigorous graduate programs share the common goal of educating the whole person and offer unparalleled opportunities to its students in order to prepare them for life and leadership in the twenty-first century.

Graduate students are taught by dedicated and talented faculty members, most of whom hold doctoral degrees. Although they are well-regarded academicians and researchers, the faculty's primary objective is teaching. Classes are small—the average graduate class size is 14 students—and faculty members are accessible. Furthermore, most of the graduate programs are planned with working individuals in mind; therefore, a majority of the graduate courses are held in the late afternoon or evening.

The Graduate Division offers curricula leading to the Doctor of Education (Ed.D.), Master of Arts (M.A.), Master of Arts in Teaching (M.A.T., in mathematics), Master of Business Administration (M.B.A.), Master of Fine Arts (M.F.A.), Master of Science (M.S.), and Master of Science in Engineering (M.S.E.). In addition, the School of Education offers a variety of credential and certificate programs. Certificate programs are also offered through the Seaver College of Science and Engineering.

The Ed.D. is awarded in educational leadership for social justice. The M.A. is offered in administration; bilingual elementary education; bilingual secondary education; biliteracy, leadership, and intercultural education; bioethics; Catholic inclusive education; Catholic school administration; child and adolescent literacy; early childhood education; educational psychology; elementary education; English (literature, creative writing, and rhetoric and composition); general education; literacy and language arts; literacy education; marital and family therapy; pastoral theology; philosophy; school counseling (guidance and counseling, and Catholic school counseling); secondary education; special education; teaching English as a Second Language; and theology. The M.A.T. degree is conferred in mathematics. The M.B.A. degree is offered with emphases in accounting decision systems, entrepreneurial organizations, financial decision systems, human resource management, information and decision sciences, international business systems, management and organizational behavior, and marketing management; the Executive M.B.A. is also offered. The M.F.A. is awarded in film production, screenwriting, and television production. The M.S. is conferred in computer science, environmental science, and systems engineering. The M.S.E. is available in civil engineering, electrical engineering, and mechanical engineering. Dual-degree programs include the M.B.A./J.D. in business administration and law and the M.S./M.B.A. in systems engineering and leadership.

Research Facilities

Loyola Marymount University is proud of its Von der Ahe Library, which contains approximately 500,000 volumes of books and journals, 15,000 video recordings, 3,050 current periodical subscriptions, and more than 16,000 electronic periodical subscriptions and provides network access to various online index databases. The William H. Hannon Library, scheduled to open in fall 2009, will house 88,000 square feet of space in an LEED-certified building. The University is also the home of a variety of centers and institutes dedicated to specialized research, including the Bioethics Institute; Center for Accounting Ethics, Governance and the Public Interest; Center for Asian Business; Center for Equity and Excellence in English Learner Education and Research; Center for Ethics and Business; Center for Executive Learning; Center for Ignatian Spirituality; Center for Religion and Spirituality; Center for Service and Action; Leavey Center for the Study of Los Angeles; Center for Teaching Excellence; Leadership in Equity, Advocacy, and Diversity Center (LEAD); Marymount Institute for Faith, Culture, and Arts.

Financial Aid

In addition to the availability of a wide variety of federal and state financial aid programs, Loyola Marymount students may also benefit from several scholarship offerings, graduate assistantships, and other graduate student employment opportunities.

Cost of Study

Tuition for the 2008–09 academic year for most programs was $849 per unit (most classes are 3 units). All programs in the School of Education cost $872 per unit, except the doctoral program, which cost $1100 per unit. Tuition for the College of Science and Engineering, Department of Marital Family Therapy, and School of Film and Television was approximately $887 per unit. Tuition was $1031 per unit for the M.B.A. and the Systems Engineering Leadership Program.

Living and Housing Costs

Limited on-campus graduate student housing is available on a first-come, first-served basis. Room and board in the surrounding residential area averages around $11,000 for the academic year.

Student Group

Loyola Marymount University is the home of more than 5,500 undergraduate and 1,900 graduate students. LMU graduate students represent a diverse mixture of religions, geographical origins, ethnicities, and interests. In keeping with these values, LMU oversees over 140 student clubs and organizations that provide a forum—and social events—for the wide variety of student interests.

Location

The Graduate Division at Loyola Marymount University is located in the Westchester area: a friendly, peaceful, residential neighborhood with easy access to the cultural richness of southern California. One mile from the Pacific Ocean, LMU's students enjoy ocean and mountain vistas as well as the moderate climate and crisp breezes characteristic of a coastal location. Loyola Marymount is situated in an ideal location for living and learning.

The University

Founded in 1911, Loyola Marymount University is one of the premiere Jesuit universities in the country. The strength of LMU is in its commitment to providing excellent academic programs in an environment that supports the development of the whole person. Proof of Loyola Marymount's success can be found in its more than 70,000 alumni, each a living representative of the academic excellence, moral and ethical standards, and spirit of high achievement that personify the Loyola Marymount experience.

Applying

Loyola Marymount University welcomes applications from students without regard to race, color, gender, creed, national origin, disability, marital status, or religion. All prospective graduate students are expected to provide evidence of suitable preparation for graduate-level work. Individual programs have specific deadlines, prerequisites, or additional requirements. Interested students should visit LMU's Web site (http://graduate.lmu.edu) for more information.

The application for graduate admission to LMU can be completed in one of two ways. It is recommended that applicants apply using the online application at http://apply.embark.com/grad/lmu. However, hard copies of applications are also accepted. Students should contact Graduate Admissions for a paper application.

Correspondence and Information

Graduate Admissions
University Hall, Suite 2500
Loyola Marymount University
One LMU Drive
Los Angeles, California 90045-2659

Phone: 310-338-2721
888-946-5681 (toll-free)
Fax: 310-338-6086
E-mail: graduate@lmu.edu
Web site: http://graduate.lmu.edu

PROGRAM DIRECTORS

Bioethics Program: Dr. James Walter. (jwalter@lmu.edu; 310-258-8621)
Civil Engineering and Environmental Science Program: Professor Joseph Reichenberger. (jreichenberger@lmu.edu; 310-338-2830)
Electrical Engineering and Computer Science Program: Dr. Stephanie August. (saugust@lmu.edu; 310-338-5973)
Marital and Family Therapy Program: Dr. Debra Linesch. (dlinesch@lmu.edu; 310-338-4562)
M.B.A. Program: Dr. Rachelle Katz. (rkatz@lmu.edu; 310-338-2848)
Mechanical Engineering Program: Dr. Bo Oppenheim. (boppenheim@lmu.edu; 310-338-2825)
Systems Engineering: Dr. Fred Brown. (fbrown@lmu.edu; 310-338-7878)
Teaching Mathematics Program (M.A.T.): Dr. Edward Mosteig. (emosteig@lmu.edu; 310-338-2381)
English Department: Dr. Stephen Shepherd. (sshephe1@lmu.edu; 310-568-6225)
Philosophy Department: Dr. Mark Morelli. (mmorelli@lmu.edu; 310-338-7384)
School of Education (Clinical Education): Dr. Marta Sanchez. (soeinfo@lmu.edu; 310-338-2863)
School of Education (Educational Leadership: School Administration and Leadership, Doctoral Program–Leadership for Social Justice): Dr. Elizabeth Reilly. (soeinfo@lmu.edu; 310-338-2863)
School of Education (Educational Support Services: Catholic Inclusion, School Counseling, School Psychology/Educational Psychology, Special Education): Dr. Tom Batsis, O.Carm. (soeinfo@lmu.edu; 310-338-2863)
School of Education (Elementary and Secondary Education: Child and Adolescent Literacy, Elementary Education, General Education, Literacy Education, Literacy and Language Arts, Secondary Education, 2042 Professional Clear Credential): Dr. Irene Oliver. (soeinfo@lmu.edu; 310-338-2863)
School of Education (Language and Culture in Education: Bilingual Elementary Education, Bilingual Secondary Education, Biliteracy, Leadership, and Intercultural Education): Dr. Yvette Lapayese. (soeinfo@lmu.edu; 310-338-2863)
School of Education (Specialized Programs in Urban Education: Catholic School Administration, LMU/LA CAST, Non-Cohort University Interns, PLACE, TFA): Dr. Edmundo Litton. (soeinfo@lmu.edu; 310-338-2863)
School of Film and Television: Prof. Glenn Gebhard. (ggebhard@lmu.edu; 310-338-3025)
Theology and Pastoral Theology Department: Dr. Michael Horan. (mhoran@lmu.edu; 310-338-2755)

Loyola Marymount University campus.

LOYOLA UNIVERSITY CHICAGO

The Graduate School

Programs of Study

The Graduate School oversees a variety of academic programs leading to doctoral (Ph.D.) and master's (M.A., M.S.) degrees. The School fosters graduate education and advanced research across traditionally defined disciplines as well as interdisciplinary environments. The students and faculty together strive to fulfill the University's mission of pursuing knowledge in the service of humanity.

Research Facilities

The combined libraries of the University contain more than 1 million volumes, with standing orders for more than 7,800 serials, 650,000 microforms, and 21,000 pieces of audiovisual material. The library subscribes to several computerized online services, data search networks, and interlibrary access and loan programs.

Loyola's campuses are interconnected by a high-speed fiber-optics network. Each campus has computing centers equipped with extensive software options and standard programming environments. Loyola's WiFi wireless network allows students to access the University's network and the Internet from several locations on both campuses.

The Department of Computer Science provides a Linux-based laboratory with thirty-two new computing systems running the latest open source software. Students have access to experimental systems, including computational clusters and embedded systems, through its Emerging Technologies Laboratory.

Specialized laboratory facilities are maintained in the basic medical science, science, and social science departments.

Financial Aid

To learn about graduate financial aid at Loyola, students should visit http://luc.edu/finaid, e-mail gradfinaid@luc.edu, or call 773-508-2984. Awards are offered on a competitive basis to Loyola's most talented Graduate School students and normally range from $14,000 to $25,000. Most awards are announced in the spring preceding enrollment, and most are renewable, based on academic performance, and can be held for up to four or five years.

Cost of Study

Students should visit http://luc.edu/bursar to learn the latest tuition rates for nursing, social work, medical sciences, pastoral studies, and all other graduate programs. Tuition for courses offered by the Graduate School for the 2008–09 academic year was approximately $750 per credit hour.

Living and Housing Costs

Housing costs in the Chicago area vary considerably. Information is available through the Graduate School.

Student Group

Of the approximately 14,000 students attending Loyola University Chicago, more than 1,500 are enrolled in the various departments and programs of the Graduate School. Students come from all areas of the United States and many other countries.

Student Outcomes

More than 100,000 Loyola alumni are spread throughout every state of the nation and in at least 121 countries throughout the world. Among their ranks are hundreds of CEOs of major corporations and health-care institutions, dozens of state and national legislators, scores of circuit court and federal judges, and a number of presidents of nationally recognized universities.

Location

Graduate-level classes are held at Loyola's two Chicago campuses and at the Loyola University Medical Center in suburban Maywood. The Lake Shore Campus is located on Chicago's North Side, right along Lake Michigan, in a diverse and dynamic residential area. The Water Tower Campus in downtown Chicago is situated in the midst of the city's cultural and commercial center on the Magnificent Mile. The Loyola University Medical Center is one of the leading medical research and teaching institutions in the nation. Graduate programs also offer study-abroad options at Loyola's John Felice Rome Center in Italy and at other locations around the globe.

Loyola students have access to the world-renowned Newberry Center for Renaissance Studies, as well as such leading institutions as the Art Institute of Chicago, the Chicago Historical Society, and the Library of International Relations. In the social sciences, Loyola participates in the Inter-University Consortium for Political and Social Research.

The University

Founded in 1870, Loyola is a Jesuit, Catholic university dedicated to excellence in teaching, research, health care, and community service. Programs in the University's nine schools and colleges focus not only on intellectual growth but also on the social, cultural, and spiritual development of the students they serve.

Applying

All applicants must submit a completed application form and official transcripts. Most departments and programs also require the results of the Graduate Record Examinations. Additional material is required by some departments. Students should consult the *Graduate School Bulletin* for details. Applicants may apply online at http://luc.edu/gpem.

Applications are accepted throughout the year by most departments. Students who wish to be considered for need-based financial aid and merit awards must have their completed applications on file by February 1. Because there are some exceptions to this deadline, students should consult the *Graduate School Bulletin* for details.

Students from abroad must have proficiency in written and spoken English. Students for whom English is not the native language are required to submit scores from the TOEFL. Students from other countries are tested for competence in the English language and may have to take ESL courses.

Detailed descriptions of programs and procedures are found in the *Graduate School Bulletin.*

Correspondence and Information

Requests for additional information and applications should be directed to:

Loyola University Chicago
820 North Michigan Avenue, Suite 800
Chicago, Illinois 60611
Phone: 312-915-8900
Web site: http://luc.edu/gpem

GRADUATE PROGRAMS

Arts and Sciences
Applied Statistics (M.S.)
Biology (M.S.)
Chemistry (Ph.D., M.S.)
Child Development (Ph.D.)
Computer Science (M.S.)
Computer Science: Information Technology (M.S.)
Computer Science: Software Technology (M.S.)
Criminal Justice (M.A.)
Criminal Justice: Chicago Police Department Cohort (M.A.)
English (Ph.D., M.A.)
History (Ph.D., M.A.)
History: Public History (M.A.)
Mathematics and Statistics (M.S.)
Medical Sciences (M.A.)
Philosophy (Ph.D., M.A.)
Philosophy: Applied (M.A.)
Political Science (Ph.D., M.A.)
Public Policy (M.P.P.)
Psychology: Applied Social (Ph.D., M.A.)
Psychology: Clinical (Ph.D.)
Psychology: Developmental (Ph.D.)
Sociology (Ph.D., M.A.)
Sociology: Applied (M.A.)
Spanish (M.A.)
Theology (Ph.D., M.A.)
Urban Affairs (M.A.)
Women's Studies and Gender Studies (M.A. and certificate)

Biomedical Sciences
Biochemistry, Molecular and Cellular (Ph.D., M.S.)
Bioethics and Health Policy (online M.A., online certificate)
Cell and Molecular Physiology (Ph.D., M.S.)
Cellular Biology, Neurobiology, and Anatomy (Ph.D., M.S.)
Clinical Research Methods (M.S.)
Integrated Program in the Biomedical Sciences (Ph.D.)
M.D./Ph.D. Program with Stritch School of Medicine
Microbiology and Immunology (Ph.D., M.S.)
Molecular Biology (Ph.D., M.S.)
Neuroscience (Ph.D., M.S.)
Pharmacology and Experimental Therapeutics (Ph.D., M.S.)
Public Health (M.P.P.)

Business
Accountancy (M.S.)
Business Administration (M.B.A.)
Business Administration: Health Care Management (M.B.A.)
Business Ethics (certificate)
Data Warehousing (certificate)
Finance (M.S.)
Human Resources (M.S.)
Information Systems Management (M.S.)
Integrated Marketing Communications (M.S.)

Education
Administration and Supervision (Ed.D.)
Behavior Intervention Specialist (M.Ed.)
Community Counseling (M.A., M.Ed.)
Counseling Psychology (Ph.D.)
Cultural and Educational Policy Studies (Ph.D., M.A., M.Ed.)
Curriculum and Instruction (Ed.D., M.Ed.)
Educational Psychology (M.Ed.)
Elementary Education (M.Ed.)
Higher Education (M.Ed., Ph.D.)
Middle School Mathematics (M.Ed.)
Reading (M.Ed.)
Reading Teacher Endorsement (certificate)
Research Methodology (Ph.D., M.A., M.Ed.)
School Counseling (M.Ed., Type 73 certificate)
School Psychology (Ph.D., Ed.S., M.Ed./Ed.S.)
School Technology (M.Ed.)
Science Education (M.Ed.)
Secondary Education (M.Ed.)
Special Education (M.Ed.)
Type 75 Superintendent (certificate)

Law: Master of Jurisprudence
Business Law (M.J.)
Child and Family Law (M.J.)
Health Law (M.J. and online M.J.)

Nursing
Doctor of Nursing Practice (D.N.P.)
Nursing (Ph.D.)
Nursing, summer (Ph.D.)
Acute Care CNS (M.S.N.)
Acute Care NP (M.S.N.)
Adult CNS (M.S.N.)
Adult NP (M.S.N.)
Cardiovascular Advance Practice Nursing (CNS and NP subspecialty and online certificate)
Dietetics (M.S.)
Family NP (M.S.N.)
Health Care Informatics (online certificate)
Health Systems Management (M.S.N.)
Oncology CNS (M.S.N. and online certificate)
Outcomes Performance Management (online certificate)
PICES: Population-based Infection Control and Environmental Safety (M.S.N. and online certificate)
Post-Master's Nurse Practitioner (certificate)
Women's Health NP (M.S.N.).

Pastoral Studies
Divinity (M.Div.)
Pastoral Counseling (M.A., certificate)
Pastoral Studies (M.A., online M.A.)
Religious Education (M.A., certificate)
Spiritual Direction (certificate)
Spirituality (M.A.)

Social Work
Social Work (Ph.D., M.S.W.)
Advanced Domestic Violence Counseling with Diverse Populations (certificate)
Family and School Partnerships–Advanced Practice in Schools (certificate)
Non-Profit Management and Philanthropy (certificate)
Type 73 (certificate)

MANHATTANVILLE COLLEGE

School of Graduate and Professional Studies

Programs of Study

Manhattanville's School of Graduate and Professional Studies offers career-oriented individuals the opportunity to acquire the skills they need to become effective leaders and advance their career tracks. The School offers part-time and accelerated programs at both the undergraduate and graduate levels. Manhattanville offers six business programs of study. The six Master of Science (M.S.) programs (Leadership and Strategic Management, Organizational Management and Human Resource Development, Integrated Marketing Communications, International Management, Finance, and Sport Business Management) are offered in convenient one-weekend-per-month, weekday, and evening class schedules. A Certificate in Nonprofit Leadership program is also offered. The curriculum is designed and taught by executives presently employed in their field of expertise. Two Master of Arts (M.A.) programs are also offered (Liberal Studies and Writing). All master's programs have been developed to be completed within two years.

The Master of Science in Leadership and Strategic Management program is a 39-credit program providing advanced training in strategic management and planning and fostering the development of effective leadership skills. The learning is current, streamlined, and designed to allow managers and executives to excel in a rapidly changing and increasingly global work environment. Degree requirements include twelve courses and a final integrative project.

The Master of Science in Organizational Management and Human Resource Development program is a 36-credit program that provides training in human resources skills and organizational management for professionals who want to enter or already work in the human resources field. Emphasis is on a strong theoretical background as well as development of practical, administrative, and management skills for individuals in corporations, small businesses, government, education, and the not-for-profit sector. Degree requirements include eleven courses and a thesis or final project option.

The Master of Science in Integrated Marketing Communications program is a 36-credit program. It provides advanced training in developing a communications strategy that is integrated with an organization's marketing and financial objectives. Students learn the principles of effective communications in global settings and the communication issues involved in marketing brand management and public relations. Degree requirements include eleven courses and a final integrative project.

The Master of Science in International Management program is a 36-credit program designed to prepare business leaders to meet the evolving challenges of international management and to seize opportunities for business success in both mature and expanding markets. Courses are designed to emphasize the development of practical management skills against a strong background of theory and values-based leadership principles. The learning environment promotes a high level of interaction between faculty members and students and among students themselves. Degree requirements include eleven courses and a final integrative project.

The Master of Science in Finance degree is a 36-credit program designed for working professionals who seek a career in finance or for experienced finance professionals who seek to enhance their knowledge of the field. Graduates of the program will be equipped for a variety of career opportunities including positions in multinational industrial corporations and financial institutions. The curriculum combines four elective courses with eight core courses to provide a broad management view of the world of finance and to address trends in the globally competitive financial marketplace. The program provides students a strong foundation in the principles and analytical techniques of finance upon which they will explore practical business applications.

The Master of Science in Sport Business Management degree is a 36-credit program which provides individuals with the necessary knowledge and business skills to assume a leadership role in sports management. The course work provides an interdisciplinary approach to the study of sport management intended to provide a thorough foundation in sport and business while allowing flexibility for students to explore a wide variety of opportunities within the field. The program includes an internship to assist students in preparing for middle and upper level positions within a variety of markets including, but not limited to, professional sports, intercollegiate athletics, and amateur and youth athletic organizations.

The Master of Arts in Liberal Studies (M.A.L.S.), a 30-credit program, has been aptly described as a "time for your mind." This unique master's degree program cuts across many disciplines—art, literature, music, psychology, religion, sociology, philosophy, history, and politics. The M.A.L.S., designed for adult and part-time students, is self-paced and flexibly scheduled.

The Master of Arts in Writing program is a 32-credit program designed for writers and aspiring writers. The program enables students to develop skills in writing while deepening their knowledge of the humanities. All required courses are scheduled in the evening, with the exception of the intensive Summer Writers' Week and Writers' Weekend. A final project of an original piece of writing is required.

The Certificate in Nonprofit Leadership requires 18 credits and may be completed in nine months. Under the guidance of executives and consultants currently working in the nonprofit and private sectors, the program targets key topics of concern to the leaders of nonprofit organizations with a focus on its application to day-to-day decisions. The curriculum is also well suited to accelerate the understanding of the challenges facing leaders in the nonprofit sector for those aspiring to leadership positions.

For individuals who have not yet completed their undergraduate degrees, Manhattanville offers three accelerated programs for part-time students: Bachelor of Science (B.S.) in Behavioral Studies program, the B.S. in Communications Management program, and the B.S. in Organizational Management program. Students may pursue a dual degree in Creative Writing. Eligible students may take up to 8 credits in graduate-level courses, which can be applied toward both the undergraduate degree and the Master of Arts in Writing. This program is designed for students with a grade point average of 3.4 or better. Students may also pursue a dual-degree program with the School of Education. Eligible students may take up to five graduate-level education courses, which can be applied toward both the undergraduate degree and the Master of Arts in Teaching. These accelerated programs are designed for students who have earned an Associate of Arts degree or those who have accumulated 60–75 undergraduate credits with a grade point average of 2.5 or better and now want the personal and professional benefits of earning a degree. To enroll, students must have at least two years of work experience. Most of these programs may be completed within eighteen months.

Research Facilities

Manhattanville has been named one of the Top 100 Wired Colleges in the U.S. The Manhattanville Library capitalizes on the power of the Internet to connect students with information and analysis found in powerful subscription databases, electronic journals, and electronic books. Manhattanville is one of the first colleges in the U.S. to outsource a service that enables students to interact online with experienced reference librarians at any time of the day or night from anywhere in the world. The virtual research service, "Ask a Librarian 24/7," uses co-browsing to connect students with professional librarians who can answer questions about research and help students navigate the College's extensive array of subscription databases and other library resources. Manhattanville's teaching library, which supports the School of Education, ranks among the foremost undergraduate teaching libraries in the country. The Menendez Language Laboratory includes tapes and record libraries that provide materials for class instruction and individual practice in French, Spanish, Russian, Italian, German, Chinese, Japanese, Hindi, Marathi, modern Hebrew, and English as a second language. The College provides a writing clinic, a reading clinic, audiovisual facilities, and a bibliographic instruction program. The library building is open 24 hours a day, seven days a week through most of the fall and spring semesters, and it has computer labs, quiet study areas, group-study rooms, and a café, where students and faculty members can meet informally.

Financial Aid

Federal Stafford Student Loans, as well as a deferred payment plan, are available for graduate students. For further information, prospective students can contact the Office of Financial Aid, Reid Hall, Purchase, New York, 10577 (telephone: 914-323-5357).

Cost of Study

For 2009–10, tuition is $730 per credit for Master of Science degrees, $700 per credit for Master of Arts degrees, and $590 for the adult accelerated undergraduate degree completion programs. There is a semester registration fee of $50.

Living and Housing Costs

Most School of Graduate and Professional Studies students live off campus and work in communities throughout Westchester and the surrounding counties. For campus housing information, students should call Residence Life at 914-323-5217.

Location

Manhattanville's 100-acre suburban campus is located in New York's Westchester County, just minutes from White Plains to the west and Greenwich, Connecticut, to the east. It is 30 miles from Manhattan. Many prominent corporate offices—IBM, MasterCard, Morgan Stanley, and PepsiCo—are headquartered nearby. The campus is accessible by public transportation.

The College

Manhattanville College is a coeducational, independent liberal arts college whose mission is to educate ethically and socially responsible leaders for the global community. Founded in 1841, the College has 1,700 undergraduate students and 1,100 graduate students. Manhattanville offers bachelor's and master's degrees in more than fifty academic concentrations in the arts and sciences. Its curriculum nurtures intellectual curiosity and independent thinking.

Applying

Applications to the School of Graduate and Professional Studies are reviewed on a continuing basis. Application requirements for the B.S. and M.S. programs include a completed application form, a resume, an autobiographical essay, an admissions interview, two recommendations, and official transcripts of all previous undergraduate and graduate college work.

For the Master of Arts in Writing program, submission of a 10- to 12-page creative writing sample, including at least five pages of prose, is substituted for the resume and letters of recommendation.

Correspondence and Information

Admissions Office
Graduate and Professional Studies
Manhattanville College
2900 Purchase Street
Purchase, New York 10277

Phone: 914-694-3425
Fax: 914-323-1988
E-mail: gps@mville.edu
Web site: http://www.mville.edu

THE FACULTY

School of Graduate and Professional Studies Administration

Donald J. Richards, Acting Dean; Ph.D., Notre Dame; M.B.A., LIU.
Andrea J. Covell, Assistant Dean; Ph.D., USC.
Karen Sirabian, Director, M.A. in Writing Program; M.A., Manhattanville.
Dave Torromeo, Director, M.S. Sport Business Management; M.S., Iona.
John Fontana, Interim Director, M.S. Finance; M.B.A., Fordham.

MICHIGAN STATE UNIVERSITY

Graduate School

Programs of Study

Michigan State University has thirteen graduate degree granting colleges with more than 100 departments offering approximately 300 programs of study leading to a master's and/or doctoral degree. Doctoral degree offerings are: accounting; African American and African studies; agricultural, food, and resource economics; American studies; animal science; anthropology; applied mathematics; astrophysics and astronomy; biochemistry and molecular biology; biosystems engineering; business information systems; cell and molecular biology; chemical engineering; chemical physics; chemistry; Chicano/Latino studies; civil engineering; communication; communicative sciences and disorders; community, agriculture, recreation, and resource studies; comparative medicine and integrative biology; computer science; construction management; criminal justice; crop and soil sciences; curriculum, instruction and teacher education; curriculum, teaching, and educational policy; economics; educational policy; educational psychology and educational technology; electrical engineering; engineering mechanics; English; entomology; environmental engineering; environmental geosciences; epidemiology; family and child ecology; finance; fisheries and wildlife; food science; forestry; French language and literature; genetics; geography; geological sciences; German studies; higher, adult, and lifelong education; Hispanic cultural studies; history; horticulture; human nutrition; industrial relations and human resources; K–12 educational administration; kinesiology; large animal clinical sciences; linguistics; logistics; marketing; materials science and engineering; mathematics; mathematics education; measurement and quantitative methods; mechanical engineering; media and information studies; microbiology; microbiology and molecular genetics; music (composition, conducting, education, and performance); neuroscience; nursing; operations and sourcing management; organizational behavior–human resource management; packaging; pathobiology; pharmacology and toxicology; philosophy; physics; physiology; plant biology; plant breeding and genetics; plant pathology; political science; psychology; public health; rehabilitation counselor education; retailing; rhetoric and writing; school psychology; second language studies; social work; sociology; special education; statistics; strategic management; and zoology. Interdepartmental doctoral degree programs that link environmental toxicology or plant breeding and genetics with a traditional academic discipline are also available. Interdisciplinary graduate specializations include ecology, evolutionary biology and behavior; environmental science and policy program; ethics and development; and gender studies. Professional Science Masters (PSM) programs include: biomedical laboratory operations, computational chemistry, food safety and toxicology, industrial mathematics, industrial microbiology, integrative pharmacology, and zoo and aquarium science. Fully online programs include: criminal justice–master of science; education–master of arts; packaging–master of science; public health–graduate specialization; and youth development–master of arts.

Research Facilities

With a rapidly growing collection of more than 4.8 million volumes and tens of thousands of online resources, the University's libraries are well designed to serve educational and research programs. Fiber and broadband cable support a campuswide data and video network. Vector and parallel processing, geographic visualization, and database systems are available to all students and faculty members for both instruction and research. Shared facilities exist for electron and laser confocal microscopy, mass spectrometry, magnetic resonance, protein and nucleic acid sequencing, and materials fabrication.

A more complete listing of research facilities is found in the Academic Programs catalog.

Financial Aid

More than 3,000 assistantships are available in the various departments. In 2009–10, half-time assistantship stipends range from $1332 to $3396 per month. In addition to the stipend, substantial tuition waivers and health insurance are included for all assistants. During 2008–09, in addition to the above grants, more than 3,000 fellowships were held by graduate students. These included NSF fellowships, NIH and NIMH traineeships, Ford Foundation fellowships, and numerous other grants sponsored by industry, foundations, and government agencies as well as University graduate fellowships. Many of the fellowships pay tuition and fees in addition to stipends.

MSU Distinguished Fellowships and University Enrichment Fellowships are awarded each year in a University-wide competition. The stipend, beginning in fall 2009, is $24,000 per year plus tuition, fees, and health insurance.

MSU Student Aid Grants, Federal Perkins Loans, Supplemental Loans for Students (SLS), and Federal Stafford Student Loans are also available to graduate and professional students.

Cost of Study

The University operates on the semester system. In 2009–10, the tuition for out-of-state graduate students is $966.50 per credit, and the tuition for in-state graduate students is $478.25 per credit.

Living and Housing Costs

Housing for 872 graduate students is provided in Owen Hall, the graduate residence center. Charges are $3272 per semester for a single-occupancy room, $2802 per semester for a double-occupancy room, and $3687 per semester for a designated single (single in a double-occupancy room) for 2009–10. These charges include a $300 credit toward Owen Hall food purchases, plus 75 residence hall meal accesses.

The University also operates 1,846 one- and two-bedroom apartments for graduate students and their families. These apartments start at $663 per month for one bedroom. Two-bedroom apartments start at $774. These rates include heat, water, electric, cable, local phone service including caller ID and voicemail, Ethernet, and trash removal.

Off-campus housing costs vary widely.

Student Group

The University had a fall 2008 enrollment of 46,648 students on the East Lansing campus; 10,311 of these are graduate and graduate professional students.

Student Outcomes

During the last five years, on average, 91 percent of the doctoral degree recipients and 91.5 percent of the master's degree recipients have secured job placement. Graduates have chosen the following career paths over the last five years: 36 percent of the doctoral graduates and 6.5 percent of the master's graduates are with hospital or medical services; 36 percent of the doctoral graduates and 7 percent of the master's graduates are employed by colleges or universities; 3.5 percent of the doctoral graduates and 12 percent of the master's graduates are attending graduate school or postdoctoral assignments; 2 percent of the doctoral graduates and 14 percent of the master's graduates are employed in elementary or secondary schools; 9 percent of the doctoral graduates and 8 percent of the master's graduates are with governmental agencies; plus other exciting career directions too numerous to mention.

Location

East Lansing offers the advantages of a small university town, with entertainment, sports, and cultural events provided by outstanding University programs. Contiguous with Lansing, the capital of Michigan, and within 2 hours driving time of Detroit, East Lansing also provides the advantages of a larger metropolitan area.

The University

Founded in 1855, Michigan State University brought a new concept of higher education into being in the United States, combining education and research with public service as well as broad access to the citizenry. This approach set the pattern for the nation's land-grant institutions. The 5,200-acre campus, with 2,100 acres in existing or planned development, is essentially an arboretum park, providing a dynamic environment and an excellent atmosphere for study and research.

Applying

Applications for admission and supporting documents should be received by the graduate programs in time to meet appropriate departmental deadlines. Since these vary, students should correspond with a specific department prior to the date of desired enrollment. If a student is also applying for a graduate assistantship or fellowship, application materials should be received by December 31 prior to the fall semester of first enrollment.

Correspondence and Information

Department of (specify)
Michigan State University
East Lansing, Michigan 48824
Web site: http://grad.msu.edu/

Office of Admissions
Michigan State University
East Lansing, Michigan 48824
Phone: 517-355-8332

FACULTY CHAIRS AND DIRECTORS

Graduate School
J. Ian Gray, Ph.D., Vice President for Research and Graduate Studies.
Karen L. Klomparens, Ph.D., Dean of the Graduate School and Associate Provost for Graduate Education.

Department of Accounting and Information Systems: Dr. Sanjay Gupta, Chairperson.
Department of Advertising, Public Relations, and Retailing: Dr. Richard T. Cole Chairperson.
Department of Agricultural, Food, and Resource Economics: Dr. Steven D. Hanson, Chairperson.
Department of Animal Science: Dr. Karen I. Plaut, Chairperson.
Department of Anthropology: To be announced.
Department of Art and Art History: Thomas G. Berding, Chairperson.
Department of Biochemistry and Molecular Biology: Dr. Thomas Sharkey, Chairperson.
Program in Biomedical Laboratory Diagnostics: Dr. John Gerlach, Director.
Department of Biosystems and Agricultural Engineering: Dr. Ajit Srivastava, Chairperson.
Program in Cell and Molecular Biology: Dr. Susan Conrad, Director.
Department of Chemical Engineering and Materials Science: Dr. Martin Hawley, Chairperson.
Department of Chemistry: Dr. John L. McCracken, Chairperson.
Program in Chicano/Latino Studies: Dr. Sheila Contreras, Director.
Department of Civil and Environmental Engineering: Dr. R. S. Harichandran, Chairperson.
Department of Communication: Dr. Charles Atkin, Chairperson.
Department of Communicative Sciences and Disorders: Dr. E. James Potchen, Chairperson.
Department of Community, Agriculture, Recreation, and Resource Studies: Dr. David Wright, Chairperson.
Program in Comparative Medicine and Integrative Biology: Dr. Vilma Yuzbasiyan-Gurkan, Director.
Department of Computer Science and Engineering: Dr. Matt Mutka, Chairperson.
Department of Counseling, Educational Psychology, and Special Education: Dr. Richard Prawat, Chairperson.
School of Criminal Justice: Dr. Edmund F. McGarrell, Director.
Department of Crop and Soil Sciences: Dr. James J. Kells, Chairperson.
Interdepartmental Program in Ecology, Evolutionary Biology, and Behavior: Dr. Kay Holekamp, Director.
Department of Economics: Dr. Carl Davidson, Chairperson.
Department of Educational Administration: Dr. Marilyn J. Amey, Chairperson.
Department of Electrical and Computer Engineering: Dr. Timothy Grotjohn, Chairperson.
Department of English: Dr. Stephen Arch, Chairperson.
Department of Entomology: Dr. Ernest Delfosse, Chairperson.
Doctoral Specialization in Environmental Science and Policy Program: Dr. George Leroi, Acting Director.
Department of Epidemiology: Dr. Joseph Gardiner, Chairperson.
Department of Family and Child Ecology: Dr. Karen Wampler, Chairperson.
Department of Finance: Dr. G. Geoffrey Booth, Chairperson.
Department of Fisheries and Wildlife: Dr. Michael Jones, Chairperson.
Department of Food Science and Human Nutrition: Dr. Gale M. Strasburg, Chairperson.
Department of Forestry: Dr. Daniel E. Keathley, Chairperson.
Department of French, Classics, and Italian: Dr. Anna Norris, Chairperson.
Program in Genetics: Dr. Barbara Sears, Director.
Department of Geography: Dr. Richard E. Groop, Chairperson.
Department of Geological Sciences: Dr. Ralph E. Taggart, Chairperson.
Department of History: To be announced.
Department of Horticulture: Dr. Randolph Beaudry, Acting Chairperson.
School of Hospitality Business: Dr. Ronald F. Cichy, Director.
School of Journalism: Dr. Jane Briggs-Bunting, Director.
Department of Kinesiology: Dr. Deborah L. Feltz, Chairperson.
School of Labor and Industrial Relations: Dr. William Cooke, Director.
Department of Large Animal and Clinical Sciences: Dr. Raymond Geor, Chairperson.
Center for Latin American and Caribbean Studies: Dr. Robert Blake, Director.
Department of Linguistics and Germanic, Slavic, Asian, and African Languages: Dr. David K. Prestel, Chairperson.
Department of Management: Dr. Donald E. Conlon, Chairperson.
Department of Marketing: Dr. Roger Calantone, Chairperson.
Department of Mathematics: Dr. Yang Wang, Chairperson.
Department of Mechanical Engineering: Dr. Eann Patterson, Chairperson.
Department of Microbiology and Molecular Genetics: Dr. Walter Esselman, Chairperson.
College of Music: Professor James B. Forger, Dean.
College of Nursing: Dr. Mary Mundt, Dean.
School of Packaging: Dr. Susan Selke, Director.
Department of Pathobiology and Diagnostic Investigation: Dr. Jennifer Thomas, Acting Chairperson.
Department of Pharmacology and Toxicology: Dr. Joseph R. Haywood II, Chairperson.
Department of Philosophy: Dr. Richard Peterson, Chairperson.
Department of Physics and Astronomy: Dr. Wolfgang W. Bauer, Chairperson.
Department of Physiology: Dr. William S. Spielman, Chairperson.
School of Planning, Design, and Construction: Dr. Mark Wilson, Director.
Department of Plant Biology: Dr. Richard E. Triemer, Chairperson.
Department of Plant Pathology: Dr. R. Hammerschmidt, Chairperson.
Department of Political Science: Dr. Richard C. Hula, Chairperson.
Department.of Psychology: Dr. Neal Schmitt, Chairperson.
Program in Second Language Studies: Dr. Susan Gass, Director.
Department of Small Animal Clinical Sciences: Dr. Charles E. DeCamp, Chairperson.
School of Social Work: Dr. Gary R. Anderson, Director.
Department of Sociology: Dr. Janet L. Bokemeier, Chairperson.
Department of Spanish and Portuguese: Dr. Douglas Noverr, Chairperson.
Department of Statistics and Probability: Prof. Hira L. Koul, Chairperson.
Department of Supply Chain Management: Prof. David Closs, Chairperson.
Department of Teacher Education: Dr. Suzanne Wilson, Chairperson.
Department of Telecommunication, Information Studies, and Media: Dr. Charles Steinfield, Chairperson.
Department of Theatre: Dr. George F. Peters, Chairperson.
Program in Urban and Regional Planning: Dr. Mark Wilson, Director.
Department of Writing, Rhetoric, and American Cultures: Dr. Kathleen Geissler, Chairperson.
Department of Zoology: Dr. Fred C. Dyer, Chairperson.

Michigan Tech
Michigan Technological University

MICHIGAN TECHNOLOGICAL UNIVERSITY

Graduate School

Programs of Study Doctoral degree programs include atmospheric sciences, biological sciences, biomedical engineering, chemical engineering, chemistry, civil engineering, computational science and engineering, computer science, electrical engineering, engineering, engineering physics, environmental engineering, forest molecular genetics and biotechnology, forest science, geological engineering, geology, industrial heritage and archaeology, materials science and engineering, mathematical sciences, mechanical engineering–engineering mechanics, physics, and rhetoric and technical communication.

Master's programs include applied ecology, applied natural resource economics, applied science education, biological sciences, chemical engineering, chemistry, civil engineering, computer engineering, computer science, electrical engineering, engineering, engineering mechanics, environmental engineering, environmental engineering science, environmental policy, forest ecology and management, forest molecular genetics and biotechnology, forestry, geological engineering, geology, geophysics, industrial archaeology, materials science and engineering, mathematical sciences, M.B.A., mechanical engineering, physics, and rhetoric and technical communication.

Michigan Tech is the nation's number 1 Peace Corps Master's International (PCMI) program school. Michigan Tech offers seven PCMI programs, the most of any university in the country. PCMI programs are available in applied science education, civil engineering, environmental engineering, forestry, mechanical engineering, mitigation of natural geological hazards, and rhetoric and technical communication.

Michigan Tech offers graduate certificates in advanced electric power engineering, nanotechnology, and sustainability.

Research concentrations include biotechnology, composites, remote sensing, and transportation.

For more program information, students should visit http://www.mtu.edu/gradschool.

Research Facilities Michigan Tech ranks among the top twenty universities nationwide in terms of the percentage of research funded by industry. The University's faculty and graduate students received over $60 million in external research funding during the 2007–08 academic year. Tech averages almost seventeen inventions and four licenses per $10 million in research. Unique to the University are research centers and institutes that allow researchers and graduate students from across campus and industry to collaborate on interdisciplinary projects, including the Biotechnology Research Center (BRC); Center for Integrated Systems in Sensing, Imaging, and Communication (CISSIC); Center for Technological Innovation, Leadership, and Entrepreneurship (CenTILE); Computational Science and Engineering Research Institute (CSERI); Ecosystem Science Center (ESC); National Institute for Climatic Change Research (NICCR); Institute for Engineering Materials (IEM); Institute of Materials Processing (IMP); Isle Royale Institute (IRI); Keweenaw Research Center (KRC); Michigan Tech Transportation Institute (MTTI); University Transportation Center for Materials in Sustainable Transportation Infrastructure (MiSTI); Multi-Scale Technologies Institute (MuSTI); Power and Energy Research Center (PERC); Remote Sensing Institute (RSI); Lake Superior Ecosystem Research Center (LaSER); Sustainable Futures Institute (SFI); Center for Environmentally Benign Functional Materials (CEBFM); Michigan Tech Center for Water and Society (MTCWS); and Product and Process Architecture Alignment Consortium (P2A2 Consortium).

For more information about Michigan Tech's research centers and institutes, students should visit http://www.mtu.edu/gradschool.

Financial Aid Approximately 55 percent of Michigan Tech's graduate students receive financial support. To find out more about financial support visit http://www.mtu.edu/gradschool.

Cost of Study On average, tuition is around $567 per credit. Information about estimated expenses is available at http://www.mtu.edu/gradschool.

Living and Housing Costs Michigan Tech has furnished apartments that accommodate single and married students. More information about University apartments can be obtained at http://www.mtu.edu/gradschool.

Student Group The University has a total enrollment of 7018 students; 984 are graduate students. Michigan Tech is large enough to be rich in resources, but small enough to provide a highly personalized graduate education.

Student Outcomes Michigan Tech graduates "Create the future and change the world." Among their many accomplishments, Michigan Tech graduates have invented new nanosensor technologies, designed integrated hydrologic-economic-institutional water models, initiated and developed three Lake Superior coastal peatlands, and invented a hydrogel system to mitigate secondary injury following spinal cord damage.

Location Houghton is ranked by *Men's Journal* magazine as one of the top 10 places to live in the country. Michigan Tech's campus overlooks the Keweenaw waterway, a long, winding ribbon of water that connects the campus to the world's largest lake, Lake Superior. For those who like adventure, the University operates its own downhill ski and snowboard area, eighteen-hole golf course, and 600-acre recreational forest that has some of the best-groomed cross-country ski, snowshoe, and mountain bike trails in the country.

The University *U. S. News & World Report's* 2010 rankings rate three of Michigan Tech's graduate engineering programs in the top 50 nationwide. The annual rankings evaluated 198 graduate schools of engineering and Michigan Tech's programs ranked as follows: environmental engineering (33), mechanical engineering (48), and materials science and engineering (49). Two other graduate programs at Michigan Tech ranked in the top 100 nationwide, as did the College of Engineering overall. Those rankings include: civil engineering (58), geological and mining engineering and sciences (77), and the College of Engineering (82). Academic Analytics ranks the Geological and Mining Engineering number 6 in the U.S. and the Forestry program number 1 in the nation. Michigan Tech's Master of Business Administration program ranked in the top 100 M.B.A. programs around the world for its emphasis on sustainability and social/environmental issues. The National Science Foundation's annual report on research expenditures ranks Michigan Tech nineteenth in the nation in the proportion of research supported by industry.

Michigan Tech's first-of-its-kind, transatlantic graduate program allows students on both sides of the Atlantic Ocean to earn dual forest resources master's degrees from Michigan Tech and a Finnish or Swedish university.

The Michigan Tech Writing Center is the only writing center to receive the National Writing Program of Excellence Award in 2007, and the second writing center to be recognized in the history of the award.

The M.S. in Industrial Archaeology program at Michigan Technological University is unique in the United States, and one of the few in the world to explicitly study industrial archaeology.

The University has an English as a second language program and the International Graduate Teaching Assistants Assistance Program.

According to *Reader's Digest,* the University is ranked third in the nation among forty-five campuses that received an "A" rating, based on its readiness to handle on-campus threats to safety and security.

Applying Students may apply online, for free, to Michigan Technological University. The application form can be downloaded from http://www.mtu.edu/gradschool. Applications should be submitted at least six weeks before the start of the applicant's desired semester of entrance. Applicants can request letters of recommendation and track their status online.

Correspondence and Information

Graduate School
Michigan Technological University
1400 Townsend Drive
Houghton, Michigan 49931-1295

Phone: 906-487-2327
Fax: 906-487-2284
E-mail: gradadms@mtu.edu
Web site: http://www.mtu.edu/gradschool

THE FACULTY

The University places a premium on matching the professional and personal interests of graduate students with those of faculty mentors who are experts in their fields. On average, faculty members and graduate students receive over $60.3 million in external research funding. Michigan Tech currently holds seventy-three patents in the U.S. and abroad. Nearly 30 percent of the invention disclosures processed by Michigan Tech's Office of Technology and Economic Development include graduate students as inventors. Michigan Tech has licensed intellectual property developed on campus to eighty-two companies from twelve countries.

More information about Michigan Tech's outstanding faculty, innovative research, and world-class, cutting-edge facilities can be found at http://www.mtu.edu/gradschool.

Michigan Tech is committed to international, discovery-based learning experiences.

Michigan Tech graduates "Create the future and change the world."

Michigan Tech's campus overlooks the Keweenaw waterway.

MISSOURI STATE UNIVERSITY

Graduate College

Programs of Study

Missouri State University (MSU) offers forty-eight graduate programs leading to the Master of Accountancy (M.Acc.), Master of Arts (M.A.), Master of Arts in Teaching (M.A.T.), Master of Business Administration (M.B.A.), Master of Health Administration (M.H.A.), Master of Global Studies (M.G.S.), Master of Music (M.M.), Master of Natural and Applied Science (M.N.A.S.), Doctor of Physical Therapy (D.P.T.), Master of Public Administration (M.P.A.), Master of Public Health (M.P.H.), Master of Science (M.S.), Master of Science in Education (M.S.Ed.), Master of Science in Nursing (M.S.N.), Master of Social Work (M.S.W.), Specialist in Education (Ed.S.), and Doctorate in Educational Leadership (Ed.D.), and Doctor of Audiology (Au.D.) degrees. Programs of study are available in accounting, administrative studies, applied anthropology, audiology, biology, business administration, cell and molecular biology, chemistry, communication, communication sciences and disorders, computer information systems, counseling, criminology, defense and strategic studies, early childhood and family development, educational administration, educational leadership, elementary education, English, geospatial sciences, global studies, health administration, health promotion and wellness management, history, instructional media technology, materials science, mathematics, music, natural and applied science, nurse anesthesia, nursing, physical therapy, physician assistant studies, plant science, project management, psychology, public administration, public health, reading, religious studies, secondary education, social work, special education, student affairs, teaching, theater, and writing. All programs are accredited by the North Central Association of Colleges and Schools, and many programs are professionally accredited.

Missouri State University also offers seventeen accelerated master's programs and eighteen for-credit graduate certificate programs. Accelerated master's programs enable outstanding MSU undergraduate students to begin graduate work while completing their undergraduate program. Accelerated master's programs are in the areas of accountancy, biology, business administration, cell and molecular biology, chemistry, communication, geospatial sciences, global studies, materials science, mathematics, natural and applied science, nursing, plant science, project management, public administration, religious studies, and theater. Graduate certificate programs include autism spectrum disorders, conflict and dispute resolution, defense and strategic studies, forensic accounting, forensic child psychology, geospatial information sciences, homeland security and defense, instructional technology specialist, orientation and mobility, Ozarks studies, post-master's nurse educator, post-master's family nurse practitioner, project management, public management, religious studies for the professions, sports management, technology management, and teaching English to speakers of other languages.

Research Facilities

Missouri State University libraries have comprehensive electronic resources, including an online catalog, electronic indexes and full-text resources, and Internet accessibility. The University is a member of the Center for Research Libraries and is both a U.S. and United Nations document depository. Other facilities include a K–12 laboratory school and numerous research centers, including the Bull Shoals Field Station, the Center for Archaeological Research, the Jordan Valley Innovation Center, the Center for Applied Science and Engineering, the Missouri State Fruit Experiment Station, and the Ozarks Environmental and Water Resources Institute.

Financial Aid

Financial assistance is available through a variety of scholarships, graduate assistantships, grants, loans, and work-study programs. Graduate assistantship stipends range from $7340 to $9730 for the nine-month academic year (2009–10) and include a full tuition scholarship (resident or nonresident) for up to 15 hours a semester. Students on academic-year assistantships also receive a 6-hour tuition scholarship for the summer term. To be eligible for an assistantship, a student must be admitted to a graduate program and have a minimum GPA of 3.0 (cumulative or in the last 60 hours of undergraduate course work). The Missouri Outreach Graduate Opportunity (MOGO) Scholarship provides a partial remission of out-of-state fees for full-time students in eligible graduate programs who are not Missouri residents. The MOGO Scholarship has a value of three-fourths of the nonresident graduate student fees for 9 credit hours (5 credits hours in the summer).

Cost of Study

For the 2009–10 academic year, graduate-level course fees are $214 per credit hour for Missouri residents and $418 per credit hour for nonresidents. Internet courses in the administrative studies program are $235 per credit hour. Internet courses in computer information systems are $410 per credit hour. An additional student services fee is assessed per semester based on enrolled credit hours (courses taught via Internet excluded). This fee is $348 for full-time students (9 credit hours).

Living and Housing Costs

The average cost per year for room and board in residence halls is $6190 in 2009–10. Exact rates depend on room style and meal plan. Furnished apartments are available for graduate, married, and nontraditional students for $6090 to $8100 per year (twelve-month lease). University and privately owned apartments are within a reasonable distance of the campus.

Student Group

The total student population is approximately 20,000, of which 16 percent are graduate students. Students come from across the United States and from approximately eighty countries.

Location

Missouri State University is located in Springfield, the third-largest city in Missouri with a metropolitan service region of more than 400,000. Located in the heart of the Ozarks recreational area, the University is within easy driving distance of numerous recreational lakes, streams, and parks. The community of Springfield is supported by an industrial/manufacturing base and an expanding service industry in tourism, with people drawn by the natural beauty and recreation of the Ozarks and the musical attractions in nearby Branson. Springfield has an extensive health and medical economy serving southwest Missouri, northwest Arkansas, southeast Kansas, and northeast Oklahoma.

The University

Missouri State University founded in 1905 is a multicampus metropolitan university system with a statewide mission in public affairs. The University offers more than 150 undergraduate majors and forty-eight graduate programs, many of which are the strongest of their kind in the state. The students experience college life at its best, with NCAA Division I athletics and more than 250 student organizations.

Applying

Missouri State University invites applications from students with strong records of undergraduate performance. To apply to a program, prospective students must complete the Graduate College application as well as submit a $35 application fee. To complete the application, the Graduate College also requires students to submit two official copies of their transcripts, showing all prior academic work. Students should also contact the department or program to which they are applying to determine what additional materials (i.e., GRE, GMAT, letters of recommendation, resume, and/or other materials) are needed to complete their application. The application deadline to avoid a late fee is three weeks prior to the beginning of the desired semester of entrance; however, students are strongly encouraged to submit required paperwork before this date to allow for appropriate processing time. Many programs admit students only once a year and have specific deadlines. Prospective students should refer to program admission requirements. The graduate catalog and admission application can be accessed via the Web site listed in this description.

Correspondence and Information

Frank Einhellig, Dean
Graduate College
Missouri State University
901 South National Avenue
Springfield, Missouri 65897

Phone: 417-836-5335
417-836-4770 (MO Relay TDD)
866-767-4723 (toll-free)
Fax: 417-836-6888
E-mail: graduatecollege@missouristate.edu
Web site: http://graduate.missouristate.edu

FIELDS OF STUDY AND FACULTY ADVISERS

E-mail addresses of faculty members are in parentheses. All phone numbers are in area code 417.

Graduate College: Frank Einhellig, Dean (frankeinhellig@missouristate.edu); Thomas Tomasi, Associate Dean (tomtomasi@missouristate.edu); 836-5335.
Administrative Studies (M.S.): John Bourhis, Program Director (johnbouris@missouristate.edu); 836-6390. This program is available on campus and as an Internet program. Options in applied communication, criminal justice, environmental management, project management, and sports management.
College of Arts and Letters: Carey Adams, Dean (careyadams@missouristate.edu); 836-5247.
Communication (M.A.): Dr. Isabelle Bauman, Program Director (isabellebauman@missouristate.edu); 836-4830. Graduate certificate program in conflict and dispute resolution.
English (M.A.): Dr. Linda Moser, Program Director (lmoser@missouristate.edu); 836-6606. Tracks in literature, creative writing, and TESOL, and graduate certificate programs in TESOL and Ozarks Studies.
Music (M.M.): Robert Quebbeman, Program Director (robertquebbeman@missouristate.edu); 836-5648. Program accredited by the National Association of Schools of Music (NASM). Options in conducting, theory and composition, pedagogy, performance, and education.
Theater (M.A.): Dr. Christopher Herr, Program Director (jherr@missouristate.edu); 836-4400. Program accredited by the National Association of Schools of Theater.
Writing (M.A.): Dr. Linda Moser, Program Director (lmoser@missouristate.edu); 836-6606. Tracks in rhetoric and composition and technical and professional writing.
College of Business Administration: Danny Arnold, Dean (darnold@missouristate.edu); 836-5646. Programs accredited by AACSB International–The Association to Advance Collegiate Schools of Business.
Accounting (M.Acc.): School of Accountancy; Dr. David Byrd, Program Director (davidbyrd@missouristate.edu); 836-4183. Graduate certificate program in forensic accounting.
Business Administration (M.B.A.): James Simmerman, Program Director (jamessimmerman@missouristate.edu); 836-5646. Concentrations in accounting, computer information systems, finance, international management, management, and marketing.
Computer Information Systems (M.S.): David Meinert, Program Director (davidmeinert@missouristate.edu); 836-4131.
Health Administration (M.H.A.): Robert Lunn, Program Director (robertlunn@missouristate.edu); 836-5647.
Project Management (M.S.): Dr. Neal Callahan, Program Director (nelacallahan@missouristate.edu); 836-5160. Graduate certificate programs in project management and technology management.
College of Education: Dennis J. Kear, Dean (denniskear@missouristate.edu); 836-5254. Programs accredited by the Department of Elementary and Secondary Education (DESE) and the National Council for Accreditation of Teacher Education (NCATE).
Counseling (M.S.): Dr. Leslie Anderson, Community Agency Program Coordinator (alanderson@missouristate.edu); 836-5449; Dr. Paul Blisard, Elementary and Secondary Program Coordinator(pblisard@missouristate.edu); 836-5449.
Early Childhood and Family Development (M.S.): Joanna Cemore, Program Coordinator (joannacemore@missouristate.edu); 836-8403.
Educational Administration (Ed.S. and M.S.Ed.): Gerald Moseman, M.S.Ed. Program Coordinator (geraldmoseman@missouristate.edu), 836-5490; Robert Watson, Ed.S. Program Coordinator (robertwatson@missouristate.edu); 836-6951. Options in elementary principal, secondary principal, and superintendent.
Educational Leadership (Ed.D.): Cynthia MacGregor, Program Coordinator (cmacgregor@missouristate.edu); 836-6046. Cooperative program with the University of Missouri–Columbia (UMC). Degree conferred by UMC.
Elementary Education (M.S.Ed.): Dale Range, Program Coordinator (dalerange@missouristate.edu); 836-6099.
Instructional Media Technology (M.S.Ed.): School of Teacher Education, Fred H. Groves, Program Coordinator (fredgroves@missouristate.edu); 836-6769. Program accredited by the Association for Educational and Communications Technology (AECT). Instructional Technology Specialist graduate certificate program.
Reading (M.S.Ed.): Deanne Camp, Program Director (deannecamp@missouristate.edu); 836-6983. Program accredited by the International Reading Association (IRA).
Secondary Education (M.S.Ed.): For information, students should contact the area of emphasis department or Eric Eckert, Coordinator of Graduate Admissions and Recruitment (ericeckert@missouristate.edu); 836-5331. Areas of emphasis include agriculture, art, biology, business, chemistry, earth science, English, family and consumer sciences, geography, history, mathematics, modern and classical languages, music, natural science, physical education, physics, social science, and speech and theater.
Special Education (M.S.Ed.): Paris DePaepe, Program Coordinator (parisdepaepe@missouristate.edu); 836-4761. Program accredited by the Council for Exceptional Children (CEC). Graduate certificate programs in autism spectrum disorders and orientation/mobility.
Teaching (M.A.T.): Emmett Sawyer, Program Coordinator (emmettsawyer@missouristate.edu); 836-3170.
College of Health and Human Services: Helen Reid, Dean (helenreid@missouristate.edu); 836-4176.
Cell and Molecular Biology (M.S.): Christopher Field, Program Director (chrisfield@missouristate.edu); 836-5478.
Communication Sciences and Disorders (M.S.): Neil DiSarno, Department Head, Program Director (neildisarno@missouristate.edu); 836-5368. Program options in audiology, education of the deaf/hard of hearing, and speech-language pathology. Audiology and speech-language pathology programs accredited by the American Speech-Language-Hearing Association. Education-of-the-deaf/hard-of-hearing program accredited by the Council of Education of the Deaf.
Health Promotion and Wellness Management (M.S.): Sarah McCallister, Department Head, Program Director (sarahmccallister@missouristate.edu); 836-5370. Graduate certificate program in sports management.
Nurse Anesthesia (M.S.): Ben Timson, Program Director (bentimson@missouristate.edu; 836-4145. Program accredited by the Council on Accreditation of Nurse Anesthesia Education Programs.
Nursing (M.S.N.): Kathryn Hope, Department Head, Program Director (kathrynhope@missouristate.edu); 836-5310. Program accredited by the National League for Nursing Accrediting Commission (NLNAC). Post-master's graduate certificate programs for nurse educator and family nurse practitioner.
Physical Therapy (M.P.T.): Scott Wallentine, Program Admissions Coordinator (swallentine@missouristate.edu); 836-4514. Program accredited by the Commission on Accreditation in Physical Therapy Education (CAPTE).
Physician Assistant Studies (M.S.): Roberto Canales, Program Director (robertocanales@missouristate.edu); 836-615. Program accredited by the Accreditation Review Commission on Education for the Physician Assistant (ARC-PA).
Psychology (M.S.): Dr. David Lutz, Clinical Program Director (davidlutz@missouristate.edu); 836-5830. Dr. D. Wayne Mitchell, Experimental Program Director (waynemitchell@missouristate.edu); 836-6941. Dr. Carol Shoptaugh, Industrial Organizational Program Director (carolshoptaugh@missouristate.edu); 836-5788. Options in industrial/organizational, clinical, and experimental psychology. Graduate certificate program in forensic child psychology.
Public Health (M.P.H.): Vickie Sanchez, Program Director (vickiesanche@missouristate.edu); 836-5310.
Social Work (M.S.W.): Dr. Darry R. Haslam, Program Director (dhaslam@missouristate.edu); 836-4259. Program accredited by the Council on Social Work Education.
College of Humanities and Public Affairs: Victor H. Matthews, Dean (victormatthews@missouristate.edu); 836-5529. Graduate certificate program in homeland security and defense.
Applied Anthropology (M.S.): William Wedenoja, Program Director (billwedenoja@missouristate.edu); 836-5641.
Criminology (M.S.): Karl Kunkel, Department Head and Program Director (karlkunkel@missouristate.edu); 836-5640.
Defense and Strategic Studies (M.S.): Keith B. Payne, Department Head, Program Director (kbpayne@missouristate.edu); 703-218-3565. Graduate certificate program in defense and strategic studies. Located in Fairfax, Virginia.
History (M.A.): F. Thornton Miller, Program Director (ftmiller@missouristate.edu); 836-5511.
Global Studies (M.G.S.); Beat Kernen, Department Head (beatkernen@missouristate.edu), 836-5630.
Public Administration (M.P.A.): Dr. Kant Patel, Program Director (kantpatel@missouristate.edu); 836-5825. Program accredited by the National Association of Schools for Public Affairs and Administration. Graduate certificate program in public management.
Religious Studies (M.A.): Mark Given, Department Head, Program Director (markgiven@missouristate.edu); 836-6681. Graduate certificate program in religious studies for the professions.
College of Natural and Applied Sciences: Tamera Jahnke, Dean (tamerajahnke@missouristate.edu); 836-5249.
Biology (M.S.): Dr. Alexander Wait, Program Director (alexanderwait@missouristate.edu); 836-5802.
Chemistry (M.S.): Dr. Erich D. Steinle, Program Director (esteinle@missouristate.edu); 836-5319.
Geospacial Sciences in Geography and Geology (M.S.): Bob Pavlowsky, Program Director (bobpavlowsky@missouristate.edu); 836-8473. Graduate certificate program in geospatial information sciences.
Materials Science (M.S.): Kartik Ghosh, Program Director (kartikghosh@missouristate.edu); 836-6025.
Mathematics (M.S.): Yungchen Cheng, Department Head and Program Director (yungchencheng@missouristate.edu); 836-5112.
Natural and Applied Science (M.N.A.S.): Dr. Arbindra Rimal, Program Director (arbindrarimal@missouristate.edu); 836-5094. An interdisciplinary program in which students select from of the following primary emphasis areas: agriculture, biology, chemistry, computer science, geography, geology and planning, mathematics, physics, astronomy, and materials science.
Plant Science (M.S.): Dr. Arbindra Rimal, Program Director (arbindrarimal@missouristate.edu); 836-5094.

MONMOUTH UNIVERSITY

Graduate School

Programs of Study

The Graduate School offers programs in several areas designed for students who wish to acquire advanced knowledge and skills in their chosen fields of study and engage in research and other scholarly activities. The programs are administered through the Wayne D. McMurray School of Humanities and Social Sciences; the Marjorie K. Unterberg School of Nursing and Health Studies; the Leon Hess Business School; the School of Science; the School of Education; and the School of Social Work.

The School of Humanities and Social Sciences awards the Master of Arts (M.A.) in criminal justice, corporate and public communication, English, history, mental health counseling, public policy, and psychological counseling and a Master of Arts in Liberal Arts (M.A.L.A.). This school also offers a post-master's certificate in professional counseling and graduate certificates in criminal justice administration, public relations specialist, public service communication, and human resources communication.

The School of Nursing and Health Studies offers a Master of Science in Nursing (M.S.N.) as well as advanced practice nursing post-master's certificates in adult nurse practitioner, adult psychiatric and mental health practitioner, and family nurse practitioner; post-master's certificates in nursing education and nursing administration; and graduate certificates in forensic nursing, school nursing, and school nursing–noninstructional. An RN to M.S.N. direct program is offered that allows nurses to more quickly attain an M.S.N. degree.

The School of Science awards Master of Science (M.S.) degrees in computer science and software engineering. Certificates are available in computer science, software design and development, software development, and software engineering.

The School of Education offers three programs leading to master's degrees: the Master of Arts in Teaching (M.A.T.), the Master of Education (M.Ed.), and the Master of Science in Education (M.S.Ed.). The M.S.Ed. program offers concentrations in principal, principal–school administrator, special education, reading specialist, and school counseling. Education endorsement certification programs are available in early childhood, ESL, substance awareness coordinator, and teacher of students with disabilities. Post-master's certification endorsement programs are offered in learning disabilities teacher-consultant, reading specialist, principal, supervisor, counseling, and director of school counseling services. An accelerated twelve-month M.A.T. program is offered, as are accelerated ESL endorsement programs.

The School of Business Administration offers the Master of Business Administration (M.B.A.) program with optional tracks in accounting, finance, and real estate and the M.B.A. with a concentration in health-care management. The school also offers post-master's certificate programs in accounting and health-care management. In addition, there is a full-time accelerated M.B.A. program that can be completed in one year.

The School of Social Work awards a Master of Social Work (M.S.W.) degree and a post-master's certificate in play therapy.

Research Facilities

The Monmouth University Library holds approximately 260,000 volumes and nearly 31,000 electronic journal subscriptions. Academic programs are amply supported by state-of-the-art computer hardware and software and classroom/laboratory facilities. Computer workstations that are specifically dedicated to student use are distributed among forty-five instructional and open-use laboratories and include both PC and Macintosh workstations. Wireless connectivity is available throughout most of the campus. All students receive a computer account that provides them with e-mail, World Wide Web browsing and authoring tools, and electronic access to the Monmouth University Library catalog.

Financial Aid

Financial aid is available in the form of fellowships, assistantships, and loans. Fellowships are awarded to qualified students on the basis of outstanding undergraduate cumulative grade point average. A limited number of assistantships are available to continuing students, with preference given to those maintaining a high grade point average. To determine eligibility for all other forms of aid, applicants must file the FAFSA form, which is available online at http://www.fafsa.ed.gov or at the Financial Aid Office. Monmouth University participates in the Federal Direct Student Loan Program, which makes both need- and non-need-based loans available to students who file the FAFSA. Alternative loan funding sources are available to those students who might not otherwise qualify for federal funding.

Cost of Study

Tuition for study in 2009–10 is $773 per credit. A University fee is assessed each semester.

Living and Housing Costs

Due to Monmouth's proximity to the beach, there are ample off-campus housing opportunities that are conveniently located near the University. These accommodations are relatively inexpensive since the academic year is also the off-season for tourism. A file of off-campus residences for rent is maintained by the Office of Off-Campus and Commuter Services.

Student Group

Monmouth University enrolls approximately 6,000 students, approximately 1,700 of whom are enrolled in the Graduate School. The diverse student body includes many international students representing twenty-eight different countries.

Location

Monmouth University is located less than a mile from the Atlantic Ocean on a 156-acre campus in the quiet, suburban town of West Long Branch, New Jersey. The campus is only 1 hour from both New York City and Philadelphia. Both can be easily accessed by train. Commuter bus service is also available. The surrounding area has numerous activities, restaurants, and cultural events. Its proximity to high-technology firms, financial institutions, and a thriving business-industrial sector provides Monmouth students and graduates with a wide variety of employment possibilities.

The University

Monmouth University is a private, moderate-sized coeducational teaching university committed to providing a learning environment that enables men and women to pursue their educational goals and realize their full potential for making significant contributions to their community and society. Small classes that allow for individual attention and student-faculty dialogue, together with careful academic advising and career counseling, are hallmarks of a Monmouth education. The Rebecca Stafford Student Center houses the Office of Student Services, the Center for Student Success, placement services, computer laboratories, study lounges, a full-service cafeteria, and student activities meeting rooms and offices. The University's NCAA Division I intercollegiate athletics program includes nine men's and ten women's teams.

Applying

An application for admission to the Graduate School includes a completed application form with application fee, official transcript of the undergraduate record, score reports from the appropriate entrance examination, transcripts of any graduate work done elsewhere, and two letters of recommendation covering the candidate's personal and professional qualifications to pursue graduate work. Additional requirements may apply, based on the program. Students should contact the Office of Graduate Admission for details. International students must also provide evidence of English proficiency.

The application deadlines are July 15 for the fall term, November 15 for the spring term, and May 1 for the summer sessions. The deadline for applications to the M.S.W. program is March 15. An initial review of the complete application for admission is conducted by the Office of Graduate Admission. The file is then forwarded to the faculty director of the program for an admission decision. All correspondence should be conducted with the Office of Graduate Admission.

Correspondence and Information

Kevin L. Roane
Director of Graduate Admission
Monmouth University
West Long Branch, New Jersey 07764-1898
Phone: 732-571-3452
800-320-7754 (toll-free)
Fax: 732-263-5123
E-mail: gradadm@monmouth.edu
Web site: http://www.monmouth.edu/admission

FACULTY HEADS AND PROGRAMS

Master of Arts in History (M.A.): Chris DeRosa, Program Director and Assistant Professor of History; Ph.D., Temple.

The program accommodates students who wish to specialize in European, United States, or world history. The program is designed not only for recent college graduates but also for secondary school teachers of history and social studies and professionals in government, the military, and business. Thesis and nonthesis options are available.

Master of Arts in Psychological Counseling (M.A.): Frances K. Trotman, Program Director, Professor of Psychology, and Chair of the Department of Psychological Counseling; Ph.D., Columbia.

The program offers practical and theoretical courses in quantitative methods, intervention skills, and assessment methods. The program equips students with proficiencies in the traditional counseling field as well as in emerging areas. Upon completion of the program, students may pursue an advanced degree or enter the post-master's certification program.

Master of Science in Mental Health Counseling (M.S.): Frances K. Trotman, Program Director, Professor of Psychology, and Chair of the Department of Psychological Counseling; Ph.D., Columbia.

The program, which is accredited by the Council for Accreditation of Counseling and Related Educational Programs (CACREP), prepares students for the Professional Counselor Licensure Examination. Courses satisfy criteria prescribed by the New Jersey State Board of Professional Counselor Examiners. The curriculum concentrates on developing the basic course areas, specialty areas, research and evaluation skills, and practical experiences.

Master of Arts in Liberal Arts (M.A.L.A.): Aaron Ansell, Program Director and Assistant Professor of History and Anthropology; Ph.D., Chicago.

This program is an interdisciplinary approach to the graduate study of the humanities, the natural and applied sciences, and the social and behavioral sciences. Students are encouraged to cross disciplinary boundaries and to combine various areas into a degree program that satisfies personal curiosity and contributes to the achievement of professional objectives.

Master of Science in Software Engineering (M.S.): Daniela Rosca, Program Director and Associate Professor of Software Engineering; Ph.D., Old Dominion.

The software engineering program is ABET accredited. Students learn to develop, validate, implement, and maintain high-quality software products. Specialization tracks are offered in embedded software, information management, organizational management, software technology, and telecommunications.

Master of Science in Computer Science (M.S.): Cui Yu, Program Director and Assistant Professor of Computer Science; Ph.D., National University of Singapore.

The program includes concentrations in computer networks, intelligent information systems, and security of information systems and networks. The computer networks concentration includes study in analysis/modeling and simulation. The program is open to students with undergraduate degrees other than computer science (some preparatory work may be required).

Master of Science in Nursing (M.S.N.): Janet Mahoney, Dean, Program Director, and Associate Professor of Nursing; Ph.D., NYU.

The nursing program is designed to prepare the professional nurse for advanced practice nursing. Tracks are offered in adult or family nurse practitioner, nursing administration, adult psychiatric and mental health, school nursing, nursing education, and forensic nursing.

Master of Education (M.Ed.): Laurel Chehayl, M.Ed. Program Representative and Assistant Professor of Education; Ph.D., Kent State.

The Master of Education program is designed for fully certified teachers and other experienced education professionals to increase their knowledge and skills in specific content areas and earn additional credentials in the field of education. Graduates of the program master educational research and curriculum design as well as progressive theory and approaches to teaching.

Master of Science in Education (M.S.Ed.): Terri Rothman, Chair, Program Director, and Associate Professor of Educational Leadership and Special Education; Ph.D., SUNY at Albany.

The Department of Educational Leadership, School Counseling, and Special Education provides research-based master's and endorsement programs that are linked to national, state, and local standards and effectively prepare individuals to serve as support specialists, leaders, literacy coaches, and master teachers in educational settings. Toward this end, faculty and staff members and students within the department value diversity; pursue reflective inquiry; apply problem-solving strategies; promote innovative, interdisciplinary educational practice; effectively integrate technology; and collaboratively support and assist colleagues within the professional areas of special education, reading, educational counseling, supervision, and educational administration. The School of Education is accredited by the Council for Accreditation of Counseling and Related Educational Programs (CACREP).

Master of Arts in Teaching (M.A.T.): Shelia Baldwin, M.A.T. Program Representative and Associate Professor of Education; Ph.D., Texas A&M. Sarah Moore, Program Coordinator; M.A.Ed., Georgian Court.

The Master of Arts in Teaching (M.A.T.) provides initial certification in five program areas: early childhood (P–3), elementary education (K–5), elementary education and middle school specialization (K–8), secondary content certification (9–12), and elementary and secondary education (K–12). Programs have been designed to emphasize state and national curriculum standards and research-based best practices. The M.A.T. program ensures that its candidates are well prepared with appropriate knowledge, skills, and understanding in order to improve learning in educational systems through a commitment to lifelong learning and responsiveness to communities that represent diverse viewpoints, cultures, and learning styles. The M.A.T. program is offered in part-time, full-time, and accelerated formats. The School of Education is provisionally accredited by the National Council for Accreditation of Teacher Education (NCATE).

Master of Business Administration (M.B.A.): Donald R. Smith, Program Director of the M.B.A. Program and Associate Professor; Ph.D., Berkeley.

The comprehensive M.B.A. program provides a balance of theory and practice. Students learn the business disciplines as well as specific organizational functions. Current issues and realistic applications of skill and knowledge are discussed with prominent business executives who serve as visiting lecturers and adjunct professors. The program requires between 30 and 48 credit hours of study, depending on the student's background. The M.B.A. program is offered in part-time, full-time, and accelerated formats.

Master of Arts in Criminal Justice (M.A.): Gregory J. Coram, Program Director and Associate Professor; Psy.D., Indiana State.

The program offers a broad perspective on the criminal justice system and its various institutions and processes. The curriculum offers concentrations in administration and in homeland security. The administration concentration prepares criminal justice professionals or precareer students for supervisory and administrative roles. The concentration in homeland security prepares individuals to assist in preventing, anticipating, and preparing for natural and man-made catastrophic events. This concentration will also provide opportunities for criminal justice professionals to work with federal, state, and local governmental agencies. In addition, trained professionals are finding many new opportunities in the private sector, protecting large multi-national companies and organizations.

Master of Arts in Corporate and Public Communication (M.A.): Eleanor Novek, Program Director and Associate Professor of Communication; Ph.D., Pennsylvania.

The program prepares students to become effective communication specialists in a number of fields, from interpersonal communication to mass media. Specialist certificates are available in human resources communication, public relations, and public service communication.

Master of Social Work (M.S.W.): Nora Smith, Program Director and Associate Professor of Social Work; Ph.D., SUNY at Albany.

The program prepares students for professional practice aimed at improving the quality of life for vulnerable individuals, families, and communities, both locally and internationally. Social workers with master's degrees gain access to a new world of career opportunities, including licensing (either the License of Social Work or the License of Clinical Social Work) and specialized practice. The program offers two concentrations—one in services to families and children and one in international and community development.

Master of Arts in English (M.A.): Heide Estes, Program Director and Associate Professor of English; Ph.D., NYU.

The courses at Monmouth provide a broad education in English literature and a sound foundation for further graduate study. Secondary school teachers can fulfill their continuing education requirements and accrue credits toward salary increases by taking courses in the program. Those interested in personal enrichment or career advancement find that the course work improves critical-thinking abilities along with reading, speaking, and writing skills. To broaden the options for students in the program, four concentrations are offered: literature, creative writing, rhetoric and writing, and New Jersey studies.

Master of Arts in Public Policy (M.A.): Joseph Patten, Program Director and Associate Professor of Political Science; Ph.D., West Virginia.

The Master of Arts in public policy is a 30-credit program that appeals to those who wish to work in the public interest. The program focuses on the role of ethics in public policy and provides opportunities for experiential learning internships. Students can learn about the public policy process and policy analysis, improve critical thinking, increase oral and written communication skills, and develop research skills.

MONTCLAIR STATE UNIVERSITY

MONTCLAIR STATE UNIVERSITY

Graduate Programs

Programs of Study

Montclair State University is a major source of cultural, economic, and educational life in northern New Jersey. The University has developed doctoral programs in pedagogy (Ed.D.), math pedagogy (Ed.D.), audiology (Sc.D.), environmental management (Ph.D.), and counselor education (Ph.D.). Students have the opportunity to choose from more than eighty-five graduate programs, which include a variety of master's degree programs as well as teaching certifications and other certificate programs. For a complete listing of available programs, students should visit http://www.montclair.edu/graduate.

Nationally accredited by all four arts accreditation agencies, the College of the Arts offers conservatory-style and professional training through its more than fifty majors, minors, and concentrations, including an M.F.A., as well as fifteen other graduate programs in areas such as studio art, public and organizational relations, theater, music, art, music education, and arts and museum management.

The College of Education and Human Services is committed to advancing knowledge and educating professionals in a diverse array of fields, including teaching, nutrition and food science, counseling, health education, educational leadership, and literacy education. In addition to its more than fifty graduate programs that lead to a master's degree, certificate, or certification, the University offers doctoral programs, which include the Ed.D. in pedagogy and the Ph.D. in counselor education.

The College of Humanities and Social Sciences offers a doctoral degree in audiology and twenty other graduate programs that lead to a master's degree, certification, or certificate in areas such as applied linguistics, child advocacy, communication sciences and disorders, educational psychology, English, French, history, law and governance, psychology, and Spanish.

The College of Science and Mathematics offers more than thirty-five graduate programs, including one of the nation's few doctoral programs in environmental management, a doctorate in mathematics pedagogy, and a combined chemistry/M.B.A. program to prepare students for careers in the region's large pharmaceutical industry. The University also offers master's degrees in biology and molecular biology, chemistry and biochemistry, computer science, environmental science, geoscience, mathematics, statistics, and teaching middle grades mathematics.

The School of Business offers the Master of Business Administration (M.B.A.) with concentrations in accounting, finance, international business, management, management information systems, and marketing. An executive-style Saturday M.B.A. program is offered at the Brookdale Community College campus in Lincroft. The School of Business also offers master's degrees in accounting and chemical business.

Research Facilities

Montclair State's on-campus microcomputer laboratories offer Internet access, individual e-mail accounts for students in good standing, and specialized software in numerous fields. A comprehensive multimedia environment provides for the most sophisticated technological classes and conferences.

The Harry A. Sprague Library houses a superior collection of 1.5 million items, with more than 3,000 periodical subscriptions, 32,000 government documents, 430,000 books, and 1 million media items, which include government and reference reports on microfilm, corporate annual reports, spoken-word and music recordings, and classical and award-winning productions on videotape. Electronic databases provide access to many resources. The library is a designated government documents depository. For further information, students should visit the library Web site at http://library.montclair.edu/.

Financial Aid

In addition to the Federal Stafford Student Loan Program, a limited number of students may be eligible for graduate assistantships or graduate scholarships. The graduate assistantships cover University-wide tuition and fees, and provide students with a master's-level stipend in exchange for working 20 hours per week during the ten-month academic year. Students wishing to be considered for a graduate assistantship should indicate this preference on the admission application. A small number of graduate scholarships are also available. Information about graduate scholarships can be found online at http://www.montclair.edu/graduate. Prospective students should visit the University's Web site or contact the Graduate School for additional information. For information on other assistance that may be available, prospective students should contact the Office of Student Financial Aid (phone: 973-655-4461).

Cost of Study

In 2009–10, tuition and fees begin at $619.44 per credit for New Jersey residents and $884.04 per credit for nonresidents and international students. Tuition and fees vary depending on the program and are subject to change.

Living and Housing Costs

At Montclair State University, on-campus housing is available for a limited number of graduate students. For up-to-date housing costs and information, students should visit the Office of Residential Housing and Education Web site at http://www.montclair.edu/resed/. Meal plans are available in flexible package and cost options, depending on individual needs.

Student Group

Montclair State University's enrollment is approximately 17,000 students; close to 4,000 are graduate students, with approximately 4 percent of the graduate population being international students. The majority of the graduate students are working professionals, who enhance the programs by bringing a wealth of knowledge into the classrooms. Most graduate courses are offered in the evening hours to accommodate working students.

Location

The University is conveniently located on a beautiful 200-acre hilltop campus in Montclair, New Jersey. This suburban town is surrounded by a rich diversity of cultural and recreational opportunities in northern New Jersey and in New York City, which is located 14 miles from the campus. Train and bus service to New York City are available from the campus.

The University

Since its establishment in 1908, Montclair State has been recognized for its high academic standards, outstanding faculty members, and vital academic programs. With approximately 17,000 students and 492 full-time faculty members, Montclair State University is New Jersey's second-largest university, combining the breadth and scope of a large university with the small class size and individual attention of a small college. Montclair State began offering master's degrees in 1932, and two doctoral programs were recently added. The University has been designated a Center of Excellence for the Fine and Performing Arts and is the only institution in New Jersey to receive two Governor's Challenge for Excellence grants. The University is the home of the renowned Center of Pedagogy, which epitomizes the University's belief in the scholarship of application—the practical application of knowledge.

Applying

Admission credentials are processed as soon as they are received. Most programs do not have specific deadlines and utilize rolling admissions. For those programs without a specific deadline, the University recommends that students submit their credentials as far in advance as possible from the semester they plan to begin their studies to ensure a timely review of their application. Some programs have fixed deadlines (as early as February 15 for the fall semester and October 15 for the spring semester); students should refer to the school's Web site for the most up-to-date information on admissions deadlines. The admission decision is based on a number of criteria, including the undergraduate grade point average, standardized test scores, letters of recommendation, and statement of objectives. Some fine arts programs may also require a satisfactory portfolio review or a successful audition. Please visit the University's Web site for detailed information about application requirements.

Correspondence and Information

The Graduate School
Montclair State University
One Normal Ave
Montclair, New Jersey 07043

Phone: 973-655-5147
800-955-GRAD (toll-free)
Fax: 973-655-7869
E-mail: graduate.school@montclair.edu
Web site: http://www.montclair.edu/graduate

GRADUATE PROGRAM COORDINATORS

DOCTORAL DEGREES

Audiology (Sc.D.)
Department of Communication Sciences and Disorders: 973-655-7752.

Counselor Education (Ph.D.)
Department of Counseling and Educational Leadership: 973-655-7216.

Pedagogy (Ed.D.)
Specialization in Philosophy for Children: 973-655-7332.

Mathematics Pedagogy (Ed.D)
Department of Mathematics Sciences: 973-655-7275.

Environmental Management (Ph.D.)
Department of Environmental Science: 973-655-5423.

MASTER'S DEGREES

Master of Arts (M.A.)
Applied Linguistics: 973-655-4286.
Child Advocacy: 973-655-3290.
Child Advocacy/Public Child Welfare: 973-655-4188.
Communication Sciences and Disorders: 973-655-7946.
Communication Studies/Speech Pathology: 973-655-7471.
Counseling: 973-655-5211.
Counseling/Addictions Counseling: 973-655-7216.
Counseling/Community Counseling: 973-655-7216.
Counseling/School Counseling: 973-655-7216.
Counseling/Student Affairs/Counseling in Higher Education: 973-655-7216.
Educational Leadership: 973-655-7216.
Educational Psychology: 973-655-5201.
Educational Psychology/Child/Adolescent Clinical Psychology: 973-655-5201.
Educational Psychology/Clinical Psychology for Spanish-English Bilinguals: 973-655-5201.
English: 973-655-4274.
Environmental Studies/Environmental Education: 973-655-4448.
Environmental Studies/Environmental Management: 973-655-4448.
Environmental Studies/Environmental Science: 973-655-4448.
Exercise Science and Physical Education/Exercise Sciences: 973-655-5253.
Exercise Science and Physical Education/Sports Administration and Coaching: 973-655-5253.
Exercise Science and Physical Education/Teaching and Supervision of Physical Education: 973-655-5253.
Family and Child Studies: 973-655-4171.
Fine Arts: 973-655-4210.
Fine Arts/Museum Management: 973-655-4210.
Fine Arts/Studio: 973-655-4210.
French/French Literature: 973-655-5143.
French/French Studies: 973-655-5143.
Health Education: 973-655-5253.
Law and Governance: 973-655-4152.
Law and Governance/Conflict Management and Peace Studies: 973-655-4152.
Law and Governance/Governance, Compliance, and Regulation: 973-655-4152.
Law and Governance/Intellectual Property: 973-655-4152.
Law and Governance/Legal Management, Information, and Technology: 973-655-4152.
Music/Music Education: 973-655-7212.
Music/Music Performance: 973-655-7212.
Music/Music Theory and Composition: 973-655-7212.
Music/Music Therapy: 973-655-7212.
Physical Education: 973-655-5253.
Psychology: 973-655-5201.
Psychology/Industrial and Organizational Psychology: 973-655-5201.
Public and Organizational Relations: 973-655-4232.
Reading: 973-655-5407.
Social Sciences–History: 973-655-4228.
Spanish: 973-655-4285.
Teaching Middle Grades Mathematics: 973-655-5132.
Theater/Arts Management: 973-655-4217.
Theater/Production/Stage Management: 973-655-4217.
Theater/Theater Studies: 973-655-4217.

Master of Arts in Teaching (M.A.T.)
Master of Arts in Teaching (Content Areas): 973-655-5187.
Master of Arts in Teaching (Early Childhood Education): 973-655-5407.
Master of Arts in Teaching (Elementary Education): 973-655-5407.
Early Childhood Education and Teacher of Students with Disabilities: 973-655-5187.
Elementary Education and Teacher of Students with Disabilities: 973-655-5187.

Master of Business Administration (M.B.A.)
M.B.A. Program Office: 973-655-4306.
M.B.A./Accounting Program Office: 973-655-4174.
M.B.A./Finance Program Office: 973-655-5255.
M.B.A./International Business Program Office: 973-655-4280.
M.B.A./Management Program Office: 973-655-4306.
M.B.A./Management Information Systems Program Office: 973-655-5444.
M.B.A./Marketing Program Office: 973-655-4254.

Master of Education (M.Ed.)
Early Childhood and Elementary Education: 973-655-5407.
Early Childhood Special Education: 973-655-5407.
Learning Disabilities: 973-655-5187.
Special Education: 973-655-5187.
Teacher Leadership: 973-655-5187.

Master of Fine Arts (M.F.A.)
Department of Art and Design: 973-655-7295.

Master of Science (M.S.)
Biology: 973-655-4397.
Biology/Biology Science Education: 973-655-4397.
Biology/Ecology and Evolution: 973-655-4397.
Biology/Physiology: 973-655-4397.
Chemistry: 973-655-5140.
Chemistry/Biochemistry: 973-655-5140.
Computer Science: 973-655-4166.
Computer Science/Informatics: 973-655-4166.
Geoscience: 973-655-4448.
Mathematics: 973-655-5108.
Mathematics/Mathematics Education: 973-655-5108.
Mathematics/Pure and Applied Mathematics: 973-655-5132.
Molecular Biology: 973-655-4397.
Nutrition and Food Science: 973-655-4154.
Statistics: 973-655-5132.

CERTIFICATE PROGRAMS

Accounting: 973-655-4147.
Advanced Counseling: 973-655-7216.
American Dietetics Association (ADA): 973-655-5253.
Artist Diploma: 973-655-7212.
Child Advocacy: 973-655-3290.
CISCO: 973-655-4166.
Conflict Management in the Workplace: 973-655-4157.
Food Safety Instructor: 973-655-5253.
Geographic Information Science: 973-655-7558.
Gifted and Talented Education: 973-655-4104.
Health Education: 973-655-5253.
Human Sexuality Education: 973-655-5254.
International Business: 973-655-4208.
Management: 973-655-3306.
Molecular Biology: 973-655-4397.
Music Therapy: 973-655-7212.
Nutrition and Exercise Science: 973-655-5253.
Object Oriented Computing: 973-655-4166.
Paralegal Studies: 973-655-4152.
Performer's Certificate: 973-655-7212.
Philosophy for Children: 973-655-4063.
Teaching English to Speakers of Other Languages (TESOL): 973-655-4286.
Teaching Middle Grades Mathematics: 973-655-5132.
Translation and Interpretation in Spanish: 973-655-4285.
Water Resource Management: 973-655-4448.

Educational Services Certification
Associate School Library Media Specialist: 973-655-5187.
Certified Drug and Alcohol Counselor (CADC) Eligibility: 973-655-7216.
Learning Disabilities Teacher-Consultant: 973-655-7361.
Principal: 973-655-5170.
Reading Specialist: 973-655-5407.
Speech-Language Specialist: 973-655-7946.
Substance Awareness Coordinator: 973-655-6996.
Supervisor: 973-655-5170.

NEW MEXICO INSTITUTE OF MINING AND TECHNOLOGY

Graduate Studies

Programs of Study

New Mexico Institute of Mining and Technology offers graduate courses and research opportunities leading to the M.S. degree in biology, chemistry, computer science, electrical engineering, mechanical engineering, civil and environmental engineering, geochemistry, geology, geophysics, hydrology, materials engineering, mathematics, mineral engineering, petroleum engineering, and physics. A Master of Engineering Management is also offered, as is a Master of Science for teachers for certified teachers of high school mathematics and science.

The Institute offers programs of study and research leading to the Ph.D. degree in chemistry, computer science, geochemistry, geology, geophysics, hydrology, materials engineering, mathematics, petroleum engineering, and physics.

The Institute is strongly research oriented in fields of study dealing with natural physical resources, such as the atmosphere and water. Some research topics are hydrology, geochemistry, volcanology (the Southwest and Antarctic), economic geology, stratigraphy and sedimentation, mineral exploration and recovery (including the biology and chemistry of leaching), fuel and energy research (production, use, and environmental considerations), nuclear and hazardous-waste hydrology, enhanced oil recovery, explosives (including the effect of high energized and strain rates on materials), mine ventilation and fire control, cave studies, seismological crustal studies, geotechnical and soil mechanics, environmental engineering, thunderstorm electrification and cloud physics, stellar and extragalactic processes, radio astronomy, and atmospheric chemistry.

Research Facilities

Graduate research opportunities are supported by a number of on-campus research groups, such as the Bureau of Geology, the Petroleum Recovery Research Center, and the Research and Development Office, including the Geophysical Research Center for geophysics, hydrology, and climatology and a Center for Explosives Technology Research. Special facilities include the Langmuir Laboratory for Atmospheric Research (for studies of lightning, atmospheric physics, chemistry, and air quality), the Magdalena Ridge Observatory, Waldo Experimental Mines, and the EMRTC Field Laboratory for explosives research. There are also materials characterization laboratories for structure/property correlation (TEM, SEM, EPMA, FIM, AFM, and mechanical testing). The Very Large Array Radio Telescope and the Very Large Baseline Array, both facilities of the National Radio Astronomy Observatory, are headquartered on the campus. Cooperative research opportunities are available with the Sandia National Laboratories and Kirtland Air Force Base in Albuquerque and with Los Alamos National Laboratories. Modern computer and library facilities and a wide range of analytical equipment are available, including a liquid scintillation spectrometer, a stable isotope mass spectrometer, automated XRF and XRD spectrometers, a microprobe, a geochronology Ar/Ar laboratory, NMR spectrometers, a quadruple mass spectrometer, FT-IR UV/vis, fluorescence and GC/M spectrometers, GCs, HPLCs, DSC, seismological equipment, a thunderstorm-penetrating airplane, instrumented balloons and rockets, cloud physics radar, and the space plasma laboratory, including a helicon plasma generator, a fluid inclusion laboratory, and a quantitative mineralogy laboratory.

Financial Aid

In 2009, minimum stipends vary from $16,427 for nine months for beginning M.S. assistants to $39,000 for doctoral students who were on twelve-month appointments and had completed candidacy requirements.

Cost of Study

Tuition (based on a 12-credit-hour load) per semester for 2009–10 is $2384 for residents and $7182 for nonresidents. Those with teaching/research appointments qualify for resident tuition.

Living and Housing Costs

The cost of room and board for single students living in residence halls in 2009–10 is approximately $6000 per semester. Housing for married students started at approximately $600 per month for unfurnished one- or two-bedroom efficiency apartments. Housing in Socorro is also available.

Student Group

Tech has approximately 2,500 students, of whom about 600 are graduate students. About 51 percent of graduate students are women. International students from thirty-five countries constitute 10 percent of the student body.

Location

Socorro (population 9,000) is located in the Rio Grande Valley, in central New Mexico, 75 miles south of Albuquerque on Interstate 25. The campus is at an elevation of 1,400 meters. Nearby mountains reach 3,280 meters in elevation. The principal sources of income in New Mexico are scientific research, agriculture, minerals (including petroleum, copper, potash, and coal), lumbering, and tourism. New Mexico's cultural diversity provides an unusual political and social environment. Historic sites, ghost towns, and ancient Indian ruins are all within a short driving distance of the campus.

The Institute

New Mexico Tech, which started as the New Mexico School of Mines in 1889, has achieved international recognition in petroleum engineering, materials engineering, atmospheric physics, geosciences, mineral-resource engineering, and explosives technology. Its faculty is outstanding in such diverse areas as astrophysics, atmospheric physics, biomedical research, seismology, geochemistry, economic geology, mineral exploration, groundwater hydrology, bacteria leaching of ores, laser and ion surface modification, intermetallics, ceramic and metal matrix composites, solid oxide fuel cells, capacitor dielectrics and high-temperature superconductors, and all areas of chemistry and petroleum recovery.

Applying

Tech encourages interested people who have a bachelor's or master's degree from an accredited college and a record indicating potential for advanced study and research in science or engineering to apply for admission. Transcripts of previous college work, references from 3 professors and/or professionals, and GRE General Test and Subject Test scores are required. International students must also submit TOEFL scores.

Correspondence and Information

Dr. David B. Johnson
Dean of Graduate Studies
New Mexico Institute of Mining and Technology
801 Leroy Place
Socorro, New Mexico 87801
Phone: 505-835-5513
800-428-TECH (8324; toll-free)
E-mail: graduate@nmt.edu
Web site: http://www.nmt.edu

THE FACULTY AND THEIR RESEARCH

Biology. T. Kieft, Chairman: environmental biology, microbiology. K. Kirk: evolutionary ecology. J. Naik: vascular physiology, blood-flow control. R. Reiss: molecular biology and evolution. S. Rogelj: cell, cell adhesion, molecular biology, biosensors, nanoparticles, biofilms, antimicrobial materials, pathogen detection. S. Shors: viral immunology.

Chemistry. W. Steelant, Chairman: biochemistry, biomembrane structures, signal transduction. J. Altig: physical chemistry, computational chemistry, chemical education. M. Heagy: organic chemistry, fluorescence, physical organic chemistry. I. Janser: organic chemistry, chemistry in aqueous media. A Kornienko: organic chemistry, medicinal chemistry. T. Pietrass: inorganic chemistry, physical chemistry, magnetic resonance spectroscopy. M. Pullin: environmental chemistry, geochemistry. W. Steelant: biochemistry, biomembrane structures, signal transduction. L. Werbelow: theoretical chemistry, chemical physics, spectroscopy. O. Wingenter: atmospheric chemistry. P. Zhang: bioanalytical chemistry, nanomaterials, fluorescence spectroscopy.

Civil and Environmental Engineering. M. P. Cal, Chairman: air pollution engineering, fate and transport of pollutants, pavement engineering. P. V. Brady: aquatic chemistry, global change, groundwater remediation. A. Budek: structural engineering. F. Y. C. Huang: hazardous waste management, biological and chemical waste treatment, environmental systems modeling, risk assessment. C. P. Richardson: biological wastewater treatment, groundwater contamination, site remediation. C. Wilson: structural control, structural dynamics, earthquake engineering.

Computer Science. L. Liebrock, Chairman: parallel processing, high-performance computing, well-posedness analysis, software security testing, graphics and visualization, information security. H. Clausen: operating systems and systems programming, broadband Internet, secure software construction. J.-L. Lassez: bioinformatics, search engines. S. Mazumdar: database systems, massive storage systems, computational logic. D. Shin: access control, digital identity management, online privacy, pervasive computing security, applied cryptography. H. Soliman: computer networks, Internet protocols and security, image compression using neural wireless networks, wireless sensor networks, fiber optics routing. A. Sung: computational intelligence and its applications, information assurance, modeling and simulation, algorithms.

Earth and Environmental Science. A. R. Campbell, Chairman: metallic ore deposits, stable isotope geochemistry. R. C. Aster: earthquake and volcanic seismology and seismic structure. G. Axen: continental tectonics and fault mechanics; extensional, convergent, and wrench settings. S. Bilek: earthquake rupture processes, tsunami generation, fault-zone material properties. P. Boston: cave and karst studies, geomicrobiology. K. Condie: trace element and isotope geochemistry, Precambrian studies. B. Harrison: soil properties, recurrence intervals of earthquakes, soil salinization in arid environments, soil stability. J. Hendrickx: soil water physics, vadose zone hydrology, soil contamination. D. B. Johnson: biostratigraphy, pleozoic depositional environments. J. B. Johnson: volcano geophysics, infrasound, volcanic monitoring. P. R. Kyle: igneous geochemistry, antarctic geology, volcanology. W. C. McIntosh: argon geochronology, cenozoic volcanism in southwestern united states, Antarctic volcanism. P. S. Mozley: environmental geology, sedimentary petrology, low-temperature geochemistry. F. M. Phillips: groundwater chemistry, isotope hydrology, groundwater dating, quaternary studies. C. M. Snelson: neotecotnics, exploration seismology, lithospheric structure. G. Spinelli: hydrogeology of oceanic lithosphere, groundwater–surface water interactions, sediment physical properties, sedimentology. E. Vivoni: surface water hydrology. J. L. Wilson: groundwater hydrology, numerical and analytic modeling, stochastic hydrology, colloid and bacterial transport.

Electrical Engineering. S. W. Teare, Chairman: experimental adaptive optics, radiation effects on semiconductors, directed energy. R. Arechiga: speech recognition. A. Jorgensen: optical interferometry techniques and instrumentation. R. Bond: design for test/manufacturability, teaching effectiveness. E. Calloni (adjunct): gravitational wave interferometry. A. El-Osery: wireless communications, control systems, soft computing. H. Erives: integration and calibration of hyperspectral and multispectral space sensors, airborne and space-borne image analysis. P. Krehbiel (adjunct): lightning, thunderstorms, radar. G. Mansfield (adjunct): radar systems. J. Meason (adjunct): nuclear, electromagnetic, and space radiation effects and directed energy. D. Reicher (adjunct): physics and simulation of thin films. S. R. Restaino (adjunct): adaptive optics, novel optical systems. W. Rison: atmospheric electricity, instrumentation, lightning protection. R. Thomas: lightning, thunderstorms, and instrumentation. K. Wedeward: control and power systems. D. Wick (adjunct): experimental adaptive and active optics. H. Xiao (adjunct): photonic/fiber sensors, intelligent sensor networks, optical communications, computer vision.

Mechanical Engineering. S. Bakhtiyarov, Chairman: non-Newtonian fluid mechanics, heat and mass transfer, oil recovery, rheology, metalcasting, materials processing, multiphase flows, instrumentation, fluidized beds, porous medium flows, nanotechnology, self-healing materials, tribology, turbulence, microgravity. A. Belyaev: membranes technology, water purification, gases separation, chemical engineering. P. Cooper: explosives engineering. H. Dinwiddie: dynamic antenna modeling. P. Gerity: robotics, system integration, technology turnkey and licensing. A. Ghosh: macrobehavior of composites, biomechanics, finite element analysis experimental mechanics and instrumentation, structural health monitoring and restoration construction materials and project management. J. Kennedy: science and applications of explosives. S. Lim: energetic materials, explosives science and technology, linear and conical shaped charges, active protection system, shockwave mechanics, detonation theory, explosives characterization. W. Marcy: aerodynamics, flight dynamics, wind tunnel. J. Meason: electromagnetic directed energy, nuclear engineering. J. Meason: electromagnetic directed energy, nuclear, engineering. B. Melof: pyrotechnics, improvised explosives, fuel air explosions, explosive diagnostics. A. R. Miller: finite element analysis, explosive synthesis of materials, high-temperature system and simulation, actuators and actuator controls. K. Miller: system dynamics, system modeling and simulation, nonlinear reduced order models, distributed turbulent pressure loads. K. Morris: test measurement, process control systems. W. Ostergren: mechanics of materials, structural anlaysis, machine design, propulsion and power systems. K. Salehpoor: biomedical engineering (artificial organs, design of biomedical devices and implants, blood flow, prevention of hemolysis and blood coagulation in biomedical devices, materials biocompatibility, physiological systems, mechanisms of alterations in human health conditions), energy (alternative energy and alternative fuel). J. Scarbrough: machine design, metalworking. W. Shuter: failure analysis of geo-structures. J. Stofleth: instrumentation techniques for explosives testing, experimentation and explosives. A. Watts: design and performance analysis of inertial navigation systems, integrated GPS inertial navigation and guidance and control systems design for ballistic missiles and maneuvering reentry vehicles. N. Yilmaz: computational fluid dynamics, reactive flow, combustion and chemical kinetics, fire modeling, internal combustion engines. A. Zagrai: intelligent systems, structures and mechanisms, structural monitoring and infrastructure security.

Master of Engineering Management. Designed for engineers and applied scientists with work experience; offered both on campus and via Internet streaming.

Materials Engineering. J. McCoy, Chairman: polymer blends, phase transitions, interfaces. T. D. Burleigh: corrosion mechanisms and mechanisms of corrosion protection. P. Fuierer: electronic ceramics, magnetic ceramics, sol-gel thin films. D. Hirschfeld: engineering ceramics and advanced composites, processing, protective coatings, thermal spray, solid free-form fabrication. O. T. Inal: plasma-assisted (HCD and DC) CVD; design/modification of reactive solder/braze alloys; radiation-, shock-, and laser-induced defects; explosive ceramic and metal working; laser and plasma surface modification; enhancement of low-temperature ductility in ordered intermetallics; plasma spray deposition of oxide coatings. N. Kalugin: optoelectronics and nonlinear optics, nanostructures and nanotechnology, TeraHz lasers and photodetectors, solid-state physics of nanostructures, semiconductor materials and devices. P. Lu: electron microscopy and high-resolution electron microscopy, electronic thin film, chemical vapor deposition. B. Majumdar: mechanisms and mechanics of deformation and fracture, thin films and interfaces, composites, advanced alloys. J. McCoy: polymer blends, phase transitions, interfaces. Adjunct faculty: Browning, Curro, Hockensmith, Jacobson, Lowe, Ravi, Romig, Sickafus, Smith.

Mathematics. A. Hossain, Chairman: theory and applications of statistics, estimation, reliability and regression diagnostics. R. Aitbayev: numerical partial differential equations, numerical analysis. I. Avramidi: geometric analysis, mathematical physics, quantum field theory, differential geometry. B. Borchers: optimization, inverse problems. R. Ibragimov: fluid mechanics, geophysical fluid dynamics, multiphase flows, atmosphere-ocean dynamics, lie group analysis of differential equations, mathematical modeling. G. Kerr: thermoelasticity, integral equations. O. Makhnin: stochastic processes, spatial statistics, computational statistics, time series. S. Schaffer: applied mathematics, numerical analysis, control theory. J. Starrett: dynamical systems, physics models, knot theory. W. D. Stone: differential equations, mathematical biology, industrial mathematics. B. Wang: partial differential equations, dynamical systems, applied mathematics.

Mineral Engineering. N. Mojtabai, Chairman: rock blasting and fragmentation, ground vibration, geomechanics, mining applications. C. Aimone-Martin: rock blasting, ground vibration, soil mechanics, instrumentation, geostatistics. J. Barker: industrial minerals. W. S. Chavez Jr.: ore deposit genesis and natural resources utilization, mine waste assessment and remediation. A. Fakhimi: geomechanics, numerical modeling. I. Gundiler: hydrometallurgy, mineral processing. V. McLemore: economic geology. K. Oravescz: rock mechanics, surveying, instrumentation. I. Walder: geochemistry, mine waste assessment and remediation.

Petroleum and Chemical Engineering. T. Engler, Chairman, Petroleum Engineering: formation evaluation, petrophysics, unconventionial gas recovery. D. Weinkauf, Chairman, Chemical Engineering: polymer engineering, plasma polymerication, membrane separations, microsensors. R. Balch: geophysics, artificial intelligence, reservoir characterization. R. Bretz: transport phenomena, phase behavior, natural gas processing. J. Buckley: petrophysics and surface chemistry, reservoir wettability. H. Y. Chen: well testing, reservoir mechanics. R. Grigg: gas flooding processes, phase behavior. R. Lee: natural gas storage, applied numerical methods, phase behavior. R. Seright: profile control, polymer, water and chemical flooding. J. Taber: oil recovery processes, mechanisms. M. Tartis: biomedical engineering. L. Teufel: rock mechanics, naturally fractured reservoir characterization in situ stresses, reservoir simulation including stress distribution, subsidence mechanisms.

Physics. D. Westpfahl, Chairman: dynamics of spiral and dwarf galaxies. I. Avramidi: mathematical physics, analysis on manifolds, quantum field theory. K. Balasubramanian: spectroscopy and polarized radiative transfer dynamics for solar active regions, vector magnetometry. D. Buscher: optical/IR interferometry, atmospheric seeing measurement, adaptive optics, early and late stages of stellar evolution. S. Colgate: astrophysics, plasma physics, atmospheric physics. M. Creech-Eakman: stellar astrophysics, mass loss, optical/IR interferometry, IR instrumentation. K. Eack: production of energetic particles and gamma rays in thunderstorms. J. Eilek: plasma astrophysics, quasars, radio galaxies, pulsars. M. Goss: radio astronomy, interstellar medium. C. Haniff: spatial interferometry at optical and near-infrared wavelengths, atmospheric turbulence, imaging theory, evolved stars. T. Hankins: radio astronomy of pulsars, instrumentation, signal processing. P. Hofner: star formation, interstellar medium, X-ray astronomy. R. M. Juberias: outer planets observations and atmospheric dynamics. D. Klinglesmith: asteroids, robotic telescope operations. P. Krehbiel: lightning studies, radar meteorology, thunderstorm electrification, remote sensing. G. Manney: atmospheric science, stratospheric dynamics/transport, stratospheric polar processes and ozone loss. J. Meason: nuclear physics, nuclear and space radiation effects, electromagnetic radiation effects and directed energy. K. Minschwaner: radiative transfer and climate, physics of the middle and upper atmosphere. S. Myers: cosmology, extragalactic radio astronomy, interferometric imaging algorithms. T. Pietrass: organic chemistry, organic synthesis, physical organic chemistry. D. Raymond: geophysical fluid dynamics, cloud physics, clouds and climate. W. Rison: atmospheric electricity, radar meteorology, instrumentation. V. Romereo: energetic materials, shock phenomena, high-energy physics. M. Rupen: gas and dust in galaxies, radio transients. E. Ryan: asteroid collisional physics, observational and theoretical studies. W. Ryan: asteroid astronomy, high-energy physics. S. Sessions: field theoretic approaches to atmospheric physics. R. Sonnenfeld: charge transport by lightning, embedded systems and instrumentation, tribocharging of ice. G. Taylor: very long baseline radio astronomy, active galactic nuclei. S. Teare: adaptive optics, instrumentation, astrophysics. R. Thomas: atmospheric physics, instrumentation. J. Ulvestad: compact radio sources, Seyfert galaxies, AGNs, space, VLBI techniques and future missions. W. Winn: thunderstorm electrification, electric discharges in gases, instrumentation. L. Young: star formation and the interstellar medium, dwarf and elliptical galaxies.

Macey Conference Center and Turtle Bay.

THE NEW SCHOOL: A UNIVERSITY

Graduate Overview

Programs of Study

The New School was founded in New York City in 1919 as a bastion of intellectual and artistic freedom. Today, it is a leading urban university comprising eight schools that offer some of the nation's most respected programs in design, liberal arts, the performing arts, and social and political science. Students from across the country and around the world attend The New School's diverse programs, enjoying small class sizes, superior resources, and the renowned faculty of artists, scholars, and professionals who practice what they teach.

The New School for General Studies was the first university in the United States for adults. The graduate programs offered are the M.A. and M.S. in international affairs, the M.A. in media studies (online and on campus), the M.A. in teaching English to speakers of other languages (MATESOL) (offered entirely online or coupled with a summer residency), the M.F.A. in creative writing, and graduate certificates in media management (online only) and documentary media studies. Students can attend most programs on a part-time or full-time basis.

The New School for Social Research is the University's graduate center for the core social sciences and philosophy. It began in 1933 as the University in Exile, a haven for refugee European scholars; today it maintains that progressive tradition by viewing world peace and global justice not as abstract ideals but as central and practical goals of every course of study. The school offers the M.A. and Ph.D. in anthropology, economics, historical studies, philosophy, political science, psychology, and sociology; the M.A. in global political economy and finance and liberal studies; and the M.S. in economics.

Milano The New School for Management and Urban Policy trains students for leadership in the nonprofit, public, and private sectors. The superb faculty of scholars and professionals blends theory with practice and progressive analysis with hands-on activism. Milano students work on local and global issues affecting organizations and urban communities in New York City and around the world. The school offers the M.S. in nonprofit management, organizational change management, and urban policy analysis management; the Ph.D. in public and urban policy; and graduate certificates.

At Parsons The New School for Design, students do not just learn about art and design—they redefine it. Successful alumni have paved the way for future graduates for a century, and the school remains committed to finding innovative design solutions to real-world problems. Parsons offers the M.A. in the history of decorative arts and fashion studies; the M.Arch.; the M.F.A. in design and technology, fine arts, lighting design, photography, and interior design; and a dual-degree M.Arch./M.F.A. in architecture and lighting design.

New graduate programs in fashion design and society, transdisciplinary design, and design management are in development.

Mannes College The New School for Music is an internationally renowned conservatory of classical music that provides a solid foundation for the serious student of music to pursue a career in music. The instructors are top professionals in their fields and include scholars, composers, conductors, and performing artists from some of the world's most highly regarded orchestras, ensembles, and opera companies. Mannes offers the M.M. and professional diplomas in music and performance or composition and arranging (for classical musicians).

The New School for Drama trains students for careers in the theater as actors, directors, and playwrights. Students work on full-scale productions with peers, faculty members, and guest artists, and classes and rehearsals often involve collaboration between students from all three concentrations. Over the course of three years, students are challenged by their classmates, mentored by a faculty of professional artists, and inspired to find their own voice. The school offers the M.F.A. in acting, directing, and playwriting.

Research Facilities

In addition to University-wide computer labs and a vast library system, each school offers its students unique resources. Students at The New School have access to a wide range of materials and resources from state-of-the-art practice rooms, multimedia labs, studios, and performance spaces to collections, archives, and institutes.

The New School is also a member of the Research Library Association of South Manhattan, one of the largest interuniversity library consortia in the country. Members of the consortium include The New School's Raymond Fogelman Library, which houses 173,000 volumes on the social sciences and philosophy; New York University's Elmer Holmes Bobst Library; and the Cooper Union Library. The total holdings of these libraries exceed 4.1 million volumes and 25,000 journals. Beyond the consortium are the rich resources of New York City, including 250 METRO-member libraries and the public library systems of the five New York boroughs.

Financial Aid

Many students in degree programs at The New School take advantage of financial aid programs. The University uses applications such as the FAFSA or Undergraduate International Student Scholarship Application to assess student eligibility for federal, state, and institutional financial aid. Graduate students should contact their academic department for separate applications for institutional awards, such as assistantships.

Cost of Study

The cost of attending The New School varies from program to program. For the cost of each program of study and information about on-campus housing charges, prospective students should visit http://www.newschool.edu/tuition/.

Living and Housing Costs

The University offers on-campus housing, University-run apartments, and assistance finding housing off campus. The cost of housing, food, transportation, books, and living expenses in New York City averages $17,000 annually. For more information, students should visit http://www.newschool.edu/studentservices.

Student Group

Students at The New School are talented, driven, and eager to effect change in their chosen fields. Students come from a variety of backgrounds and include undergraduates just out of high school; working professionals earning their bachelor's, master's, or doctoral degrees; and continuing education students and retired professionals eager to take advantage of the University's extensive and varied body of course offerings. Together they represent 101 countries and most of the fifty states. The New School is dedicated to maintaining an environment that promotes diversity and tolerance and that ensures equal opportunity without discrimination in all areas of education and employment, regardless of race, color, sex, sexual preference, religion, physical handicap, and national or ethnic origin.

Location

The New School's location in New York City gives students access to an abundance of resources. Students are encouraged to take advantage of the city's many museums, performance venues, and other cultural institutions, which are only a walk or a subway ride away. An extension of the classroom, the city also offers excellent professional and networking opportunities, and some classes require that students work with outside businesses to complete assignments—giving them unparalleled real-world experience. Internships and apprenticeships with leading New York City companies and organizations in every field are also available, and many students have moved on from internships to successful careers with those companies and organizations upon graduation.

The University

Rooted in New York City but active around the world, The New School is renowned for its pioneering educational programs. The New School's divisions offered the first university-level courses on race and black culture, urban housing, film history, and women's studies, and the first college programs in fashion design, interior design, advertising, and graphic design. Today, New School students participate in programs that strive for academic excellence, technical mastery, innovation, and engaged world citizenship. In addition to offering seventy graduate and undergraduate degrees, the University offers certificate programs and hundreds of continuing education courses. Classes and degree programs are offered online and on campus.

Applying

The New School is looking for talented and dedicated students who demand serious study, whatever their field. Because of the large number of programs offered at The New School, each school has its own application requirements. Students should visit the Web sites for detailed information.

Correspondence and Information

For general information, contact:

The New School
72 Fifth Avenue
New York, NY 10003
Phone: 212-229-5600
E-mail: Webmaster@newschool.edu
Web site: www.newschool.edu

For admissions, contact:

The New School for General Studies
Phone: 212-229-5630
E-mail: nsadmissions@newschool.edu

The New School for Social Research
Phone: 212-229-5710
E-mail: socialresearchadmit@newschool.edu

Milano The New School for Management and Urban Policy
Phone: 212-229-5462
E-mail: milanoadmissions@newschool.edu

Parsons The New School for Design
Phone: 212-229-8910
E-mail: inquiry@newschool.edu

Eugene Lang College The New School for Liberal Arts
Phone: 212-229-5665
E-mail: lang@newschool.edu

Mannes College The New School for Music
Phone: 212-580-0210 Ext. 4862
E-mail: mannesadmissions@newschool.edu

The New School for Drama
Phone: 212-229-5859
E-mail: inquiry@newschool.edu

The New School for Jazz and Contemporary Music
Phone: 212-229-5896 Ext. 4589
E-mail: jazzadm@newschool.edu

GRADUATE PROGRAM FACULTY

The New School prides itself on its exceptional faculty. The University's strong academic programs and dedication to the arts attract leading professionals in their fields. Students should visit each school's Web site for faculty members' biographies and more information.

NEW YORK UNIVERSITY

Graduate School of Arts and Science

Programs of Study

The Graduate School of Arts and Science offers master's and doctoral degrees in fifty-three departments and programs within the Faculty of Arts and Science, including a wide range of interdisciplinary programs. The Graduate School also offers dual degrees with the faculties of the NYU School of Business, the School of Public Service, the School of Law, the School of Medicine, the School of Dentistry, the Steinhardt School, and Long Island University's Palmer School of Library and Information Science. The NYU Institutes for Advanced Study allow distinguished visiting faculty members from throughout the world to join specialists and graduate students at NYU in research activities. Graduate students may also study at La Pietra, NYU's Italian research center on the outskirts of Florence, as well as participate in other global exchange programs.

Departmental requirements for the Ph.D. degree vary among disciplines, but all candidates for the doctoral degree are expected to demonstrate language proficiency and complete a thesis that makes an original contribution to their field of study. Students must also pass departmental qualifying or comprehensive examinations.

Research Facilities

The Elmer Holmes Bobst Library and Study Center houses 2.7 million volumes while providing seating for 3,500 students. The library integrates into one enormous collection more than 2.2 million books, journals, microfilms, and other materials from various libraries of the University. It is one of the world's largest open-stack libraries. With the introduction of BOBCAT (for BOBst Library CATalog), the first online catalog in a New York City library, students may search the library's collections using computer terminals. Among the noteworthy resources of the Bobst Library are special collections in education, science, music, Near Eastern and Ibero-American languages and literatures, and Judaica and Hebraica; the Tamiment Institute Library on the history of the U.S. labor movement; the Fales Library of English and American Literature since 1750; the Robert Frost Library; and numerous rare books and manuscripts. The Avery Fisher Electronics and Media Center, also in Bobst, is a center for research in music and film, with extensive holdings of videos, scores, and recordings. The Courant Institute of Mathematical Sciences has a highly specialized research collection consisting of more than 60,000 volumes in mathematics, computer science, and physics. CDC CYBER, IBM 4341, DEC, and other nonspecialized computer systems are also available in the Courant Institute of Mathematical Sciences.

The NYU art collection and the Grey Art Gallery and Study Center emphasize interdisciplinary study for students, instructors, artists, and scholars, and their exhibits also serve the community at large.

Financial Aid

The financial aid program of the Graduate School of Arts and Science seeks to ensure that outstanding, academically qualified students have financial support while they work toward their degrees. The Graduate School offers an extensive program of support. Awards for fully-funded students include support for tuition, fees, NYU health insurance, and a stipend. The Henry Mitchell MacCracken Program provides up to five years of full support for most entering doctoral students. This includes a one-time, $1000 Dean's Supplementary Fellowship grant for start-up research and educational expenses. New York University offers a full range of loan programs for students who require additional funding.

Cost of Study

In 2008–09, the cost of tuition was $1206 per credit, plus a registration fee of $58 per credit.

Living and Housing

University housing is available to some full-time students. Most students live off campus.

Student Group

The total enrollment at New York University is more than 50,000, with approximately 1,100 Ph.D. students and 1,800 master's students enrolled in the Graduate School of Arts and Science. Students come to NYU from more than 200 undergraduate institutions, all fifty states, and from more than 100 other countries.

Location

New York University is an integral part of the metropolis of New York City—a global city that is also arguably the cultural, artistic, intellectual, and financial center of the nation. The University's chief center for study is at Washington Square in Greenwich Village, which has long been famous for its contributions to the fine arts, literature, and drama and for its personalized, independent style of living. New York University makes a significant contribution to the creative activity of the Greenwich Village area through the high concentration of its faculty members and students residing within a few blocks of the University.

The University

New York University is a private, metropolitan university. Founded in 1831, the University now comprises twelve schools, colleges, and divisions at four centers in Manhattan, seven international campuses, and a 500-acre site at Sterling Forest near Tuxedo, New York, where certain of the University's facilities—notably the Institute of Environmental Medicine—are located. Courses for the Graduate School of Arts and Science are offered primarily at Washington Square; however, courses are also held at the University's Medical Center, the David B. Kriser Dental Center, Sterling Forest, the Institute of Fine Arts, and in the cities of Prague, Florence, London, Paris, Cracow, and Salamanca. Special arrangements have also been made to enable students to use the facilities of such nearby institutions as the Metropolitan Museum of Art, the New York Botanical Garden, the Museum of Modern Art, the Osborn Laboratories for Marine Science, the New York Zoological Society, and the Strang Clinic for Preventive Medicine.

NYU is a member of the distinguished Association of American Universities. The University is accredited by the Middle States Association of Colleges and Schools. Graduate and professional accrediting agencies recognize its degrees in many categories.

Applying

The Graduate School of Arts and Science prefers that applicants file the application online at http://www.nyu.edu/gsas/online. A complete application includes an application fee ($85 for the online application and $95 for paper; some programs may charge a higher fee), three letters of academic reference, GRE scores, and official college transcripts. Many departments also require a writing sample. Applications must be received by Graduate Enrollment Services before the published deadline date. Prospective students should consult the Graduate School of Arts and Science or Web site to read about department deadline dates and program-specific application requirements.

Correspondence and Information

Graduate School of Arts and Science
New York University
P.O. Box 907
New York, New York 10276-0907

Phone: 212-998-8050
E-mail: gsas.admissions@nyu.edu
Web site: http://gsas.nyu.edu

FACULTY HEADS

Catharine R. Stimpson, Dean, Graduate School of Arts and Science; Ph.D., Columbia.
Malcolm N. Semple, Vice Dean, Graduate School of Arts and Science; Ph.D., Monash.
Roberta S. Popik, Associate Dean, Graduate Enrollment Services and GSAS Administration, Graduate School of Arts and Science; Ph.D., Northwestern.
Kathleen T. Talvacchia, Assistant Dean, Academic and Student Life, Graduate School of Arts and Science; Ed.D., Columbia.
Vielka Holness, Director, Master's College, Graduate School of Arts and Science; M.P.A., Columbia.
David P. Giovanella, Director, Graduate Enrollment Services, Graduate School of Arts and Science; M.A., NYU.
Africana Studies: Awam Amkpa, Ph.D., Bristol.
American Studies: Andrew Ross, Ph.D., Kent.
Ancient Near Eastern and Egyptian Studies: Ann Macy Roth, Ph.D., Chicago.
Anthropology: Fred R. Myers, Ph.D., Bryn Mawr.
Atmosphere Ocean Science: David Holland, Ph.D., McGill.
Basic Medical Sciences/Sackler Institute of Biomedical Sciences: Joel D. Oppenheim, Associate Dean; Ph.D., Loyola Chicago.
Bioethics: Life, Health, and Environment: William Ruddick, Ph.D., Harvard.
Biology: Gloria Coruzzi, Ph.D., NYU.
Biomaterials: Van P. Thompson, D.D.S., Maryland.
Biomedical Sciences/Mount Sinai School of Medicine: Diomedes Logothetis, Dean; Ph.D., Harvard.
Chemistry: Nicholas Geacintov, Ph.D., Syracuse.
Cinema Studies: Richard Allen, Ph.D., UCLA.
Classics: Phillip Mitsis, Ph.D., Cornell.
Comparative Literature: Nancy Ruttenburg, Ph.D., Stanford.
Computational Biology: Michael Shelley, Ph.D., Arizona.
Computer Science: Margaret Wright, Ph.D., Stanford.
Creative Writing: Deborah Landau, Ph.D., Brown.
East Asian Studies: Xudong Zhang, Ph.D., Duke.
Economics: David Pearce, Ph.D., Princeton.
English: Phillip Harper, Ph.D., Cornell.
Environmental Health Sciences: Max Costa, Ph.D., Arizona.
Ergonomics and Biomechanics: Margareta Nordin, Med.Dr.Sci., Göteborg (Sweden).
European and Mediterranean Studies: Larry Wolf, Ph.D., Stanford.
Fine Arts: Michele Marincola, M.A., NYU.
French: Judith Graves Miller, Ph.D., Rochester.
German: Eckart Goebel, Ph.D., Free University of Berlin.
Hebrew and Judaic Studies: Lawrence Schiffman, Ph.D., Brandeis.
History: Lauren Benton, Ph.D., Johns Hopkins.
Humanities and Social Thought: Robin Nagle, Ph.D., Columbia.
Institute of French Studies: Edward Berenson, Ph.D., Rochester.
Irish Studies: John Waters, Ph.D., Duke.
Italian Studies: Ruth Ben-Ghiat, Ph.D., Brandeis.
Journalism: Brooke Kroeger, M.S., Columbia.
Latin American and Caribbean Studies: Thomas Abercrombie, Ph.D., Chicago.
Law and Society: Sally Merry, Ph.D., Brandeis.
Linguistics: Richard Kayne, Ph.D., MIT.
Mathematics: Yuri Tschinkel, Ph.D., MIT.
Middle Eastern and Islamic Studies: Zachary Lockman, Ph.D., Harvard.
Museum Studies: Bruce Altshuler, Ph.D., Harvard.
Music: Michael Beckerman, Ph.D., Columbia.
Near Eastern Studies: Michael Gilsenan, Ph.D., Oxford.
Neural Science: J. Anthony Movshon, Ph.D., Cambridge.
Performance Studies: José Esteban Muñoz, Ph.D., Duke.
Philosophy: Stephen Schiffer, Ph.D., Oxford.
Physics: David Grier, Ph.D., Michigan.
Politics: Nathaniel Beck, Ph.D., Yale.
Psychology: Tom Tyler, Ph.D., UCLA.
Religious Studies: Angela Zito, Ph.D., Chicago.
Russian and Slavic Studies: Eliot Borenstein, Ph.D., Wisconsin.
Sociology: Dalton Conley, Ph.D., Columbia.
Spanish and Portuguese: Gerard Aching, Ph.D., Berkeley.
Trauma and Violence Transdisciplinary Studies: Avital Ronell, Ph.D., Princeton.

The view north along Fifth Avenue seen from the center of New York University's Washington Square campus.

The entrance to the administrative offices of the Graduate School of Arts and Science, located at 6 Washington Square North.

NORTH DAKOTA STATE UNIVERSITY

Graduate School

Programs of Study

North Dakota State University (NDSU) offers the Doctor of Philosophy (Ph.D.), Doctor of Nursing Practice (D.N.P.), Doctor of Education (Ed.D.), Doctor of Musical Arts (D.M.A.), Master of Arts (M.A.), Master of Business Administration (M.B.A.), Master of Education, Master of Music, Master of Science (M.S.), Master of Software Engineering (M.S.E.), Master of Transportation and Urban Systems (MTUS), Master of Athletic Training (M.A.Tr.), Master of Accountancy (M. Acct.) and Educational Specialist (Ed.S.) degrees.

The College of Agriculture, Food Systems, and Natural Resources offers the M.S. in agricultural and biosystems engineering, agricultural economics, animal and range sciences, cereal science, entomology, horticulture, international agribusiness, microbiology, plant pathology, plant sciences, and soil science and the Ph.D. in animal sciences, range sciences, cereal science, entomology, molecular pathogenesis, plant pathology, plant sciences, and soil science.

The College of Arts, Humanities, and Social Sciences offers the master's degree in community development, criminal justice, emergency management, English, English practical writing, history, mass communication, music, social science–political science anthropology, sociology, and speech communication; the Ph.D. is offered in communication, criminal justice, emergency management, and history; and the D.M.A. is offered in music.

The College of Business Administration offers the Master of Business Administration and the Master of Accountancy degrees.

The College of Engineering and Architecture offers the M.S. in agricultural and biosystems engineering, civil engineering, construction management and engineering, electrical engineering, environmental engineering, industrial engineering and management, manufacturing engineering, and mechanical engineering and the Ph.D. in agricultural and biosystems engineering, civil engineering, electrical and computer engineering, industrial and manufacturing engineering, and mechanical engineering.

The College of Human Development and Education offers the master's degree in agricultural education, child development and family science, counseling and guidance, education, educational leadership, family and consumer sciences education, merchandising, nutrition and exercise sciences, and secondary education; the Ph.D. in human development and in education; and the Ed.D. in education. Certificates may be earned in family financial planning, gerontology, and merchandising. The Educational Specialist degree may be earned in education leadership.

The College of Pharmacy offers both the M.S. and Ph.D. in pharmaceutical sciences, the M.S. in nursing, and the D.N.P. in nursing practice.

The College of Science and Mathematics offers the M.S. in biochemistry, biology, botany, coatings and polymeric materials, chemistry, computer science, mathematics, physics, psychology, software engineering, statistics, and zoology and the Ph.D. in biochemistry, botany, chemistry, coatings and polymeric materials, computer science, mathematics, physics, psychology, software engineering, statistics, and zoology. Certificate programs are available in software engineering, statistics, and digital enterprise.

The following programs are offered as interdisciplinary degrees: M.S. in emergency management, environmental and conservation sciences, genomics and bioinformatics, and transportation and urban systems. The Master of Managerial Logistics and Master of Transportation and Urban Systems are also offered. The Ph.D. is available in cellular and molecular biology; environmental and conservation sciences; food safety; genomics and bioinformatics; materials and nanotechnology; natural resources management; science, technology, engineering, mathematics (STEM); and transportation and logistics. Certificates are available in college teaching, food protection, transportation and leadership, and transportation and urban systems.

In addition, some graduate degrees (listed below) are available by distance coursework. Students enrolled in an on-campus degree program may choose to take a few distance and continuing education graduate-level online courses to minimize the number of classes they need to take on campus. Students need to check with their adviser to ensure the class will apply to their degree program.

The Great Plains Interactive Distance Education Alliance (Great Plains IDEA) is a consortium of human sciences colleges at eleven universities that can help students reach their goals. Each university brings a unique strength to the multi-institution academic programs. In a multi-institution degree program, students apply and are admitted at one university, enroll in all courses at that university, and graduate or receive a certificate from that university.

All graduate degrees offered through NDSU distance and continuing education or Great Plains IDEA degrees taken through NDSU are awarded an NDSU degree upon successful completion of coursework.

The following degree programs are available online: Master of Software Engineering (M.S.E.); M.S. or M.A. in mass communication; M.S. or M.A. in speech communication; M.S. in construction management; M.S. or M.A. in community development (Great Plains IDEA); M.S. in health, nutrition, and exercise science: dietetics option (Great Plains IDEA); M.S. in child development and family science: family financial planning option (Great Plains IDEA); M.S. in family and consumer sciences education (Great Plains IDEA); M.S. in child development and family science: gerontology option (Great Plains IDEA); M.S. in merchandising (Great Plains IDEA); and M.S. in child development and family science: youth development option (Great Plains IDEA).

The following graduate certificates are available through NDSU online: family financial planning certificate (Great Plains IDEA), food protection certificate, gerontology certificate (Great Plains IDEA), merchandising certificate (Great Plains IDEA), software engineering certificate, and transportation leadership graduate certificate.

Research Facilities

NDSU possesses state-of-the-art facilities in magnetic resonance imaging, high-performance computing, electron microscopy, and computer chip assembly. Located on campus, a Research and Technology Park houses both academic research units and industrial partners, strengthening links between the University and technology-based companies. Research specializations in a wide variety of disciplines have resulted in the establishment of centers, some of which are the Center of Nanoscale Science and Engineering, NSF Coatings Cooperative Research Center, the Bio-imaging and Sensing Center, the Center for Protease Research, the Quentin Burdick Center for Cooperatives, the Center for Agricultural Policy and Trade Studies, the Great Plains Institute of Food Safety, the Upper Great Plains Transportation Institute, and the Institute for Regional Studies. As the state's land-grant institution, NDSU houses the North Dakota Agricultural Experiment Station and Extension Service, with eight research and extension centers located across the state. An Internet2 institution, NDSU provides high-speed network access to classrooms and desktops, an Access Grid facility for global virtual conferencing, and high-speed connections to other universities and federal agencies for research and distance education. Library resources include current electronic and print subscriptions, and an extensive array of specialized, full-text electronic databases, as well as an online catalog that interfaces with other regional, national, and international library catalogs.

Financial Aid

Graduate teaching and research assistantships are awarded to qualified students upon recommendations from individual departments and include tuition waivers for all graduate credits. Approximately half of the graduate students are awarded graduate assistantships. Student activity fees are not waived. Stipend amounts vary widely by discipline. North Dakota's very successful National Science Foundation EPSCoR program is centered at NDSU; it provides generous funding for graduate education through dissertation fellowships and stipends. For more information, students should contact the Financial Aid Office (phone: 701-231-7533).

Cost of Study

In 2009–10, tuition per credit, through 12 credits, is $243.45 for North Dakota residents; $295.25 for Minnesota residents; $365.16 for residents of Saskatchewan, Manitoba, Indiana, Kansas, Michigan, Missouri, Nebraska, Wisconsin, South Dakota, and Montana; and $650 for other students. Student fees per credit, through 12 credits, are $40.09 in 2009–10.

Living and Housing Costs

Apartments for families, as well as single-occupancy units, are located near the University campus in University Village. For residence hall life, the combined room and meal plan cost approximately $6568 per academic year. Housing, utility, and food expenses for 2 people are estimated at $8800 on campus and $8900 off campus.

Student Group

Current enrollment at NDSU is more than 12,000 students on the central campus in Fargo. NDSU also serves several thousand people throughout the state in continuing education and extension programs. Graduate student enrollment is approximately 1,900 students. International students make up approximately 25 percent of the graduate student population, providing a wealth of diversity within both the academic and local communities.

Student Outcomes

North Dakota State University graduates more than 350 master's students and 70 Ph.D. students each year.

Location

With more than 190,000 people, Fargo-Moorhead is the largest metropolitan center between Minneapolis and Seattle and is nestled in the Red River Valley, which is rich in fertile farmlands. In Fargo-Moorhead, three universities and the technical colleges provide a wide variety of educational opportunities, while the community offers access to part-time jobs, internships, parks and other recreational facilities, entertainment, and cultural amenities.

The University

NDSU, the state's land-grant institution, was established in 1890. It is one of the two research institutions within North Dakota's university system of five 2-year schools, three 4-year schools, and three graduate institutions. NDSU is a comprehensive university that offers nationally recognized programs of study within a student-friendly community. Fifty-nine master's programs, forty-four doctoral programs, ten certificate programs, and an Educational Administration (Ed.S.) Specialist program are offered. Over 100 undergraduate majors are offered.

Applying

All application materials are due one month before registration for U.S. students; some departments have earlier deadlines. For international students, the completed application packet (application form, application fee, transcript evaluation fee if international transcripts are included in the application, official transcripts, three letters of reference, and personal statement) and required test scores should be received by the Graduate School by May 1 for the fall semester and August 1 for the spring semester.

Correspondence and Information

The Graduate School
North Dakota State University
P.O. Box 5790
Fargo, North Dakota 58105-5790

Phone: 701-231-7033
Fax: 701-231-6524
E-mail: ndsu.grad.school@ndsu.edu
Web site: http://www.ndsu.edu/gradschool
http://www.ndsu.edu

THE FACULTY

Listed below are North Dakota State University's deans, graduate degree programs, and corresponding phone numbers and e-mail addresses.

College of Agriculture, Food Systems, and Natural Resources: Ken Grafton, Ph.D.
Agribusiness and Applied Economics: 701-231-7466. (E-mail: tom.wahl@ndsu.edu)
Agricultural and Biosystems Engineering: 701-231-7274. (E-mail: janelle.quam@ndsu.edu)
Animal and Range Sciences: 701-231-8386. (E-mail: donald.kirby@ndsu.nodak.edu)
Cereal and Food Sciences: 701-231-7712. (E-mail: deland.myers@ndsu.edu)
Entomology: 701-231-7902. (E-mail: david.rider@ndsu.edu)
Horticulture: 701-231-7971. (E-mail: rod.lym@ndsu.edu)
International Agribusiness: 701-231-7466. (E-mail: tom.wahl@ndsuext.nodak.edu)
Microbiology: 701-231-7511. (E-mail: douglas.freeman@nsdu.edu)
Molecular Pathogenesis: 701-231-7511. (E-mail: douglas.freeman@ndsu.edu)
Plant Pathology: 701-231-8362. (E-mail: jack.rasmussen@ndsu.edu)
Plant Sciences: 701-231-7971. (E-mail: rod.lym@ndsu.edu)
Soil Science: 701-231-8903. (E-mail: donald.kirby@ndsu.edu)

College of Arts, Humanities, and Social Sciences: Thomas Riley, Ph.D.
Communication: 701-231-7705. (E-mail for Ph.D.: judy.pearson@ndsu.edu; e-mail for master's: ross.collins@ndsu.edu)
Community Development: 701-231-7637. (E-mail: gary.goreham@ndsu.edu)
Criminal Justice: 701-231-8938. (E-mail: kevin.thompson@ndsu.edu)
Emergency Management: 701-231-8925. (E-mail: daniel.klenow@ndsu.edu)
English: 701-231-7144. (E-mail: dale.sullivan@ndsu.edu)
History: 701-231-8654. (E-mail: john.cox.1@ndsu.edu)
Mass Communication: 701-231-7705. (E-mail: ross.collins@ndsu.edu)
Musical Arts: 701-231-7932. (E-mail: ej.miller@ndsu.edu)
Political Science: 701-231-8938. (E-mail: kevin.thompson@ndsu.edu)
Sociology/Anthropology: 701-231-8925. (E-mail: daniel.klenow@ndsu.edu)
Speech Communication: 701-231-7705. (E-mail: ross.collins@ndsu.edu)

College of Business Administration: Ronald D. Johnson, Ph.D.
Business Administration: 701-231-7681. (E-mail: paul.brown@ndsu.edu)

College of Engineering and Architecture: Gary Smith, Ph.D.
Agricultural and Biosystems Engineering: 701-231-7261. (E-mail: leslie.backer@ndsu.edu)
Civil Engineering and Construction: 701-231-7245. (E-mail: kalpana.katti@ndsu.edu)
Construction Management and Engineering: 701-231-7879. (E-mail: charles.mcintyre@ndsu.edu)
Electrical and Computer Engineering: 701-231-7019. (E-mail: jacob.glower@ndsu.edu)
Engineering: 701-231-7494. (E-mail: sheri.tomaszewski@ndsu.edu)
Environmental Engineering: 701-231-7245. (E-mail: kalpana.katti@ndsu.edu)
Industrial and Manufacturing Engineering: 701-231-7287. (E-mail: susan.l.peterson.2@ndsu.edu)
Manufacturing Engineering: 701-231-7287. (E-mail: susan.l.peterson.2@ndsu.edu)
Mechanical Engineering: 701-231-8835. (E-mail: alan.kallmeyer@ndsu.edu)

College of Graduate and Interdisciplinary Programs: David Wittrock, Ph.D.
Cellular and Molecular Biology: 701-231-8110. (E-mail: mark.sheridan@ndsu.edu)
College Teaching: 701-231-8221. (E-mail for certificate: lisa.montplaisire@ndsu.edu)
Environmental and Conservation Sciences: 701-231-8449. (E-mail: wei.lin@ndsu.edu)
Food Protection: 701-231-6359. (E-mail for certificate: charlene.hall@ndsu.edu)
Food Safety: 701-231-6359. (E-mail for certificate: charlene.kuss@ndsu.edu)
Genomics: 701-231-8443. (E-mail: phillip.mcclean@ndsu.edu)
Materials and Nontechnology: 701-231-7033. (E-mail: daniel.kroll@ndsu.edu)
Natural Resources Management: 701-231-8180. (E-mail: carolyn.grygiel@ndsu.edu)
Transportation and Logistics: 701-231-7190. (E-mail: denver.tolliver@ndsu.edu)

College of Human Development and Education: Virginia Clark Johnson, Ph.D.
Child Development and Family Science: 701-231-8268. (E-mail: jim.deal@ndsu.edu)
Education Ph.D.: 701-231-7210. (E-mail: ronald.stammen@ndsu.edu)
Family Financial Planning: 701-231-8268. (E-mail for certificate: jim.deal@ndsu.edu)
Gerontology: 701-231-8268. (E-mail for certificate: jim.deal@ndsu.edu)
Health, Nutrition, and Exercise Sciences: 701-231-7474. (E-mail: holly.bastow-shoop@ndsu.edu or jim.deal@ndsu.edu)
Human Development: 701-231-8211. (E-mail: greg.sanders@ndsu.edu)
Merchandising: 701-231-8223. (E-mail for master's and certificate: holly.bastow-shoop@ndsu.edu)
School of Education: 701-231-7202. (E-mail: william.martin@ndsu.edu)
- Agricultural Education: 701-231-7439. (E-mail: brent.young@ndsu.edu)
- Counseling and Guidance (Counseling Education): 701-231-7676. (E-mail: robert.nielsen@ndsu.edu)
- Educational Leadership: 701-231-9732. (E-mail: vicki.ihry@ndsu.edu)
- Family and Consumer Sciences Education: 701-231-7968. (E-mail: mari.borr@ndsu.edu)
- Secondary Education: 701-231-7108. (E-mail: justin.wageman@ndsu.edu)

College of Pharmacy: Charles Peterson, Ph.D.
Nursing: 701-231-7772. (E-mail: mary.mooney@ndsu.edu)
Pharmaceutical Sciences: 701-231-7943. (E-mail: jagdish.singh@ndsu.edu)

College of Science and Mathematics: Kevin McCaul, Ph.D.
Biochemistry: 701-231-8225. (E-mail: john.hershberger@ndsu.edu)
Botany/Biology: 701-231-7087. (E-mail: william.bleier@ndsu.edu)
Chemistry: 701-231-8225. (E-mail: john.hershberger@ndsu.edu)
Coatings and Polymeric Materials: 701-231-7633. (E-mail: stuart.croll@ndsu.edu)
Computer Science: 701-231-8562. (E-mail: carole.huber@ndsu.edu)
Digital Enterprise: 701-231-8562. (E-mail for certificate: carole.huber@ndsu.edu)
Mathematics: 701-231-8561. (E-mail: ndsu.math@ndsu.edu)
Physics: 701-231-7049. (E-mail: dan.kroll@ndsu.edu)
Psychology: 701-231-8622. (E-mail: paul.rokke@ndsu.edu)
Software Engineering: 701-231-8562. (E-mail for Ph.D., master's, and certificate: kenneth.magel@ndsu.edu)
Statistics: 701-231-7532. (E-mail for Ph.D., master's, and certificate: rhonda.magel@ndsu.edu)
Zoology: 701-231-7087. (E-mail: william.bleier@ndsu.edu)

OAKLAND UNIVERSITY

Graduate Study

Programs of Study

Oakland University (OU) offers over 115 graduate degree and certificate programs at the master's, doctoral, and specialist levels. Graduate programs are linked closely to research, scholarship, and public service activities. Students are assumed to be partners in the implementation of programs. In the process, they are educated in the methods of intellectual inquiry and critical analysis and trained in the skills needed for their chosen fields. Through this partnership, the goals and purposes of graduate education are fulfilled.

Doctoral degrees may be earned in applied mathematical sciences (Ph.D.), biological communication (Ph.D.), health and environmental chemistry (Ph.D.), medical physics (Ph.D.), computer science and informatics (Ph.D.), counseling (Ph.D.), early childhood education (Ph.D.), educational leadership (Ph.D.), electrical and computer engineering (Ph.D.), mechanical engineering (Ph.D.), music education (Ph.D.), nursing practice (D.N.P.), physical therapy (D.P.T. and D.Sc.P.T.), reading education (Ph.D.), and systems engineering (Ph.D.). The post-master's degree of Education Specialist (Ed.S.) in leadership is also available.

Post-master's certificates are available in accounting; adult gerontological nurse practitioner; advanced reading and language arts; anesthesia; business economics; conducting; education administration; entrepreneurship; family nurse practitioner; finance; general management; higher education; human resources management; instrumental performance; international business; local government management; management information systems; marketing; music education; nonprofit organization and management; nurse anesthesia; nursing education; piano pedagogy; piano performance; production/operations management; reading, language arts, and literature; vocal pedagogy; and vocal performance.

Master's degrees are offered in accounting (M.Acc.), adult gerontological nurse practitioner studies (M.S.N.), applied statistics (M.S.), biology (M.A. and M.S.), business administration (M.B.A.), chemistry (M.S.), computer science (M.S.), conducting (M.M.), counseling (M.A.), early childhood education (M.Ed.), educational leadership (M.Ed.), educational studies (M.Ed.), electrical and computer engineering (M.S.), embedded systems (M.S.), engineering management (M.S.), English (M.A.), exercise science (M.S.), family nurse practitioner studies (M.S.N.), history (M.A.), industrial applied mathematics (M.S.), industrial and systems engineering (M.S.), information technology management (M.S.), instrumental pedagogy (M.M.), instrumental performance (M.M.), liberal studies (M.A.L.S.), linguistics (M.A.), mathematics (M.A.), mechanical engineering (M.S.), music (M.M.), music education (M.M.), nurse anesthesia (M.S.N.), nursing education (M.S.N.), physical therapy (M.S.), physics (M.S.), piano pedagogy (M.M.), piano performance (M.M.), public administration (M.P.A.), reading and language arts (M.A.T.), reading and language arts with endorsement in early childhood education (M.A.T.), safety management (M.S.), software engineering and information technology (M.S.), special education (M.Ed.), systems engineering (M.S.), teacher leadership (M.Ed.), training and development (M.T.D.), vocal pedagogy (M.M.), and vocal performance (M.M.).

Graduate certificates are available in advanced microcomputer applications, clinical exercise science, complementary medicine and wellness, conducting, corporate and worksite wellness, exercise science, instrumental performance, microcomputer applications, music education, neurological rehabilitation, nursing education, orthopedic manual physical therapy, orthopedics, pediatric rehabilitation, piano pedagogy, piano performance, statistical methods, teaching and learning for rehabilitation professionals, teaching English as a second language, vocal pedagogy, and vocal performance. A teaching endorsement in autism spectrum disorders, early childhood education, English as a second language, and reading is also offered.

Research Facilities

Most University library materials and services are housed in Kresge Library. The library's automated catalog allows patrons to identify resources held not only in the Kresge Library but also in the collections of Wayne State University, the University of Detroit Mercy, Detroit Public Library, and numerous other libraries in the area. Research centers include the Center for Applied Research in Musical Understanding, the Center for Biomedical Research, the Center for Creative and Collaborative Computing, the Center for Integrated Business Research and Education (CIBRE), the Center for Robotics and Advanced Automation, the Eye Research Institute, the Fastening and Joining Research Institute (FAJRI), the Human Systems Initiative, the Lowry Early Childhood Center, Oakland University Center for Autism Research, Education and Support (OUCARES), the Pawley Learning Institute, the Prevention Research Center at Oakland University, the Product Development and Manufacturing Center, and the Public Affairs Research Laboratory. During 2007–08, Oakland's internationally renowned School of Nursing earned almost $1.4 million in external research funds, the Eye Research Institute was awarded more than $1.9 million, the Physics Department was awarded $2.9 million, and the Chemistry Department received more than $1.1 million. The total awarded was more than $7.3 million.

Financial Aid

In order to assist eligible graduate students in financing their education, the University participates in the following programs: King/Chavez/Parks Fellowships, a limited number of which are available for qualified members of minority groups; the Federal Perkins Loan program; the Federal Work-Study Program; and the William Ford Federal Direct Loan Program. Graduate assistants are appointed by departments offering graduate degree programs. Stipends vary by discipline.

Cost of Study

The University operates on the semester system. For 2008–09, the tuition for in-state graduate students was $496 per credit hour. The tuition for out-of-state graduate students was $855.75 per credit hour. Oakland University does not charge additional fees. Full-time graduate students normally carry 8 credits per semester.

Living and Housing Costs

The 2009–10 rate for room and board is $7350 for the academic year. Facilities with a selected number of single rooms are available to graduate students. For students with families, a limited number of two-bedroom town houses and two- to four-bedroom student apartments are available.

Student Group

Total enrollment for fall 2008 was 18,169. Twenty percent of the total enrollment is graduate students. Within the graduate enrollment, 66 percent are women and 14.2 percent are members of ethnic minority groups. The diverse student body includes international students representing many different countries.

Location

Oakland University is located 25 miles north of Detroit in suburban Oakland County. OU is situated on 1,500 rolling acres near parks, recreational areas, and a large concentration of high-technology industries. Many Fortune 500 companies are located in proximity to the campus, which facilitates student research and internship opportunities.

The University

Oakland University, founded in 1957, is a comprehensive state-supported institution of higher education. The University is organized into the College of Arts and Sciences and the Schools of Business Administration, Education and Human Services, Engineering and Computer Science, Health Sciences, and Nursing.

Applying

Application for admission and supporting documents must be submitted to the Graduate Admissions Office in time to meet appropriate program deadlines for each semester. All application materials and deadline information may be obtained from the Graduate Admissions Office. International applicants should submit both a University application and an international student application at least one year before the date they wish to enter the University.

Correspondence and Information

Graduate Admissions
Oakland University
Rochester, Michigan 48309-4401

Phone: 248-370-3167
Fax: 248-370-4114
E-mail: gradmail@oakland.edu
Web site: http://www.oakland.edu/gograd

FACULTY/PROGRAM COORDINATORS

Accounting (M.Acc., post-master's certificate): Donna Free, M.Acc., CPA (phone: 248-370-3287).
Applied Mathematical Sciences (Ph.D.): Fiki Shillor, Ph.D. (phone: 248-370-3439).
Biology (M.S., M.A.): Xiangqun Zeng, Ph.D. (phone: 248-370-2881).
Business Administration (M.B.A.; Executive M.B.A.; M.S. in information technology management; post-master's certificates in business economics, finance, human resources management, international business, management information services, marketing, and production/operations management): Paul Trumbull, B.A. (phone: 248-370-3287).
Chemistry (M.S., Ph.D.): Kathleen Moore, Ph.D. (phone: 248-370-2320).
Counseling (Ph.D. in education): Lisa Hawley, Ph.D. (phone: 248-370-2841).
Counseling (M.A.; post-master's specializations in advanced career counseling, child and adolescent counseling, marriage and family counseling, mental health counseling, and substance-abuse counseling): Lisa Hawley, Ph.D. (phone: 248-370-4179).
Early Childhood Education (Ph.D. in education): Sherri Oden, Ph.D. (phone: 248-370-3027).
Early Childhood Education (M.Ed.): Ambika Bhargava, Ph.D. (phone: 248-370-3026).
Educational Leadership (Ph.D. in education): Julia Smith, Ph.D. (phone: 248-370-3082).
Educational Leadership (M.Ed.): Thomas Tattan, Ph.D. (phone: 248-370-3070).
Leadership (Ed.S.): Brian Clark, Ph.D. (phone: 248-370-3070).
Educational Studies (M.Ed.): Michael MacDonald, Ph.D. (phone: 248-370-2613).
Elementary Education (M.A.T.): Sandra Deng, M.A. (phone: 248-370-4182).
Engineering (Ph.D. in systems engineering, Ph.D. in mechanical engineering, Ph.D. in computer science and informatics, Ph.D. in electrical and computer engineering): Bhushan Bhatt, Ph.D. (phone: 248-370-2233).
Engineering (M.S. in computer science, M.S. in embedded systems, M.S. in software engineering and information technology): Ishwar Sethi, Ph.D. (phone: 248-370-2200).
Engineering (M.S. in engineering management): Sankar Sengupta, Ph.D. (phone: 248-370-2218).
Engineering (M.S. in industrial and systems engineering): Mike Polis, Ph.D. (phone: 248-370-2743).
Engineering (M.S. in mechanical engineering): Gary Barber; Ph.D. (phone: 248-370-2184).
Engineering (M.S. in systems engineering, M.S. in electrical engineering and computer science): Manohar Das, Ph.D. (phone: 248-370-2237).
English (M.A.): Kevin Grimm, Ph.D. (phone: 248-370-2267).
Exercise Science (Graduate certificates in clinical exercise science, complementary medicine and wellness, corporate and worksite wellness, and exercise science): Brian Goslin, Ph.D. (phone: 248-370-4038).
Higher Education (Post-master's certificate): Sandra Packard, Ed.D. (phone: 248-370-3070).
History (M.A.): Don Matthews, Ph.D. (phone: 248-370-3525).
Liberal Studies (M.A.): Linda Benson, Ph.D. (phone: 248-370-3531).
Linguistics (M.A.; graduate certificates in teaching English as a second language and English as a second language teaching (ESL) endorsement): Peter Binkert, Ph.D. (phone: 248-370-2174).
Mathematics (M.S. in applied statistics, M.S. in industrial applied mathematics, M.A. in mathematics, graduate certificate in statistical methods, Ph.D. in applied mathematical science): Rob Kushler, Ph.D. (phone: 248-370-3445).
Music (M.M. in piano performance, piano pedagogy, vocal performance, vocal pedagogy, instrumental performance, instrumental pedagogy, music education, and conducting): Joseph Shively, Ph.D. (phone: 248-370-2287).
Nursing (M.S.N. in adult gerontological nurse practitioner studies, family nurse practitioner studies, nurse anesthesia, and nursing education; post-master's specialization in adult gerontological nurse practitioner studies, family nurse practitioner studies, and nurse anesthesia): Patrina Carper (phone: 248-370-4068).
Physical Therapy (D.P.T.): Susan Saliga, Ph.D. (phone: 248-370-4041).
Physical Therapy (D.Sc.P.T., M.S.): Kristine Thompson, Ph.D. (phone: 248-370-4096).
Physical Therapy (Graduate certificate in neurological rehabilitation): Cathy Larson, M.S. (phone: 248-370-4392).
Physical Therapy (Graduate certificate in orthopedic manual physical therapy): John Krauss, M.S.P.T.; OCS; FAAOMPT (phone: 248-370-4041).
Physical Therapy (Graduate certificate in pediatric rehabilitation): Chris Stiller Sermo, M.A.P.T. (phone: 248-370-4047).
Physical Therapy (Graduate certificate in teaching and learning for rehabilitation professionals): Kristine Thompson, Ph.D. (phone: 248-370-4096).
Physics (Ph.D.): Brad Roth, Ph.D. (phone: 248-370-4871).
Physics (M.S.): Gopalan Srinivasan, Ph.D. (phone: 248-370-3419).
Public Administration (Post-master's certificates in local government management and nonprofit organization and management; M.P.A.): Diane Hartmus, Ph.D. (phone: 248-370-2352).
Reading (Ph.D.): Robert Schwartz, Ph.D. (phone: 248-370-3057).
Reading (M.A.T.): Jim Cipielewski, Ph.D. (phone: 248-370-3054).
Reading (Graduate certificate in microcomputer applications): Ledong Li, Ph.D. (phone: 248-370-4373).
Secondary Education (M.A.T.): Sandra Deng, M.A. (phone: 248-370-4182).
Special Education (M.Ed. in special education; teacher endorsements in autistic impairment, emotional impairment, and learning disability): Carol Swift, Ph.D. (phone: 248-370-3077).
Teacher Certification Sandra Deng, M.A. (phone: 248-370-4182).
Teacher Leadership Bob Maxfield, Ph.D. (phone: 248-370-3070).
Training and Development (M.T.D.): Chaunda Scott, Ph.D. (phone: 248-370-3063).

PACIFIC LUTHERAN UNIVERSITY

Graduate Studies

Programs of Study

Pacific Lutheran University (PLU) offers master's-level graduate degrees in five fields: business (M.B.A.), education (M.A.), nursing (M.S.N.), social sciences (M.A.), and creative writing (M.F.A.). Areas of specialization in education include classroom teaching, educational administration, and initial certification. The social sciences master's program offers a concentration in the area of marriage and family therapy. In nursing, concentrations include care and outcomes management, nurse practitioner studies, and entry-level nursing. The M.B.A. program offers a concentration in technology and innovative management. The M.F.A. in creative writing is a low-residency program.

Specific objectives for the University's graduate programs include increasing the breadth and depth of understanding of graduate students in their chosen disciplines, increasing students' knowledge of ongoing research in their fields of study, immersing students in research processes, developing students' abilities to do independent study and research, and preparing students to enter professional vocations or pursue advanced study leading to doctoral degrees.

The University offers a 4-1-4 calendar that consists of two 14-week semesters bridged by a 4-week January term. A minimum of 32 semester hours is required for each program. Individual programs may require more, depending upon prior preparation and specific degree requirements. Students must complete at least 24 of the required semester hours at PLU. Full-time students may complete most graduate programs in two years; however, some programs are designed to be completed in as little as fourteen months. Graduate students at PLU enjoy small classes and a high level of individual attention from the faculty.

Research Facilities

The Robert A. L. Mortvedt Library is the central multimedia learning resource center serving the entire University community. It contains more than 500,000 books and periodicals, microfilms, and audiovisual materials and receives more than 2,000 current magazines, journals, and newspapers. Computer access to other large libraries in the area combined with e-mail service allows students and faculty members rapid access to many other sources for research. A large computer lab, located in the library, provides PCs, Macintosh computers, and access to the University's DEC Alpha 3400 computer.

Financial Aid

Financial assistance for graduate students is available in the form of Federal Perkins and Federal Stafford Student Loans, graduate assistantships, and scholarships. In addition, students may be eligible for a PLUS loan to a maximum of $3000. A limited number of graduate assistantships are awarded to full-time students in amounts up to $5000 per year.

Cost of Study

Graduate tuition is charged at the rate of $888 per semester credit hour in 2009–10. Some programs have special rates.

Living and Housing Costs

The University has a selection of residence halls that provide comfortable living arrangements. Although these are primarily undergraduate residences, any full-time student is welcome to apply for housing. One hall is designed to accommodate graduate students. An application may be completed through the Residential Life Office. In the surrounding area, there are numerous housing options available for off-campus living.

Student Group

The graduate student population for all programs totals approximately 250. Full-time students comprise about one half of the graduate population. Students come from throughout the United States and from several other countries.

Student Outcomes

More than 96 percent of recent M.B.A. graduates are employed and work in such diverse industries as manufacturing, aerospace, financial services, health care, accounting, and forest products. Graduates with the M.A. in education. have accepted instructional and educational administrative positions across the state and region. Several graduates have been named Washington State Teacher of the Year. Graduates with the M.A. in social sciences (marriage and family therapy concentration) are employed, on average, one month after graduation as licensed/certified marriage and family therapists in mental health centers, social service organizations, group practices, and educational institutions. All students in the M.S.N. program who complete the care and outcomes management concentration have consistently been employed as managed-care coordinators and case managers. Graduates who complete the nurse practitioner studies concentration have been offered positions in ambulatory-care settings.

Location

Pacific Lutheran University is located on a 126-acre campus immediately adjacent to the city of Tacoma (population 193,556). The campus is 40 miles south of Seattle and 20 miles south of Seattle-Tacoma International Airport. Located in the midst of the Puget Sound region, the campus is in the heart of a wide variety of natural attractions, including Mt. Rainier, the Olympic and Cascade mountain ranges, and the Puget Sound.

The University

Pacific Lutheran University is an independent, comprehensive university affiliated with the Evangelical Lutheran Church in America. Total University enrollment is approximately 3,600. The faculty numbers approximately 260 and includes outstanding scholars known nationally and internationally for work in their fields. PLU has become a leader in global education through numerous study-away opportunities and a curriculum that integrates an international focus throughout academics and student life.

The University academic structure consists of five professional schools: Business, Education, Nursing, and Social Work and a College of Arts and Sciences, which has three divisions: Humanities, Social Sciences, and Natural Sciences. The curriculum also offers preprofessional advising in both health professions and law. Graduate students have the opportunity to work closely with faculty members and have access to superb academic facilities.

Applying

Further information and applications for graduate admission may be obtained from the Office of Admission or online at http://www.plu.edu. All application evaluations are based on scholastic qualifications, letters of recommendation, a statement of goals, and preparation in the proposed field of study. Certain programs require scores on standardized examinations and personal interviews. Applications for admission to most programs are acted upon throughout the year. However, all application documents should be received six weeks prior to the semester in which enrollment is sought.

Correspondence and Information

Office of Admission
Pacific Lutheran University
Tacoma, Washington 98447

Phone: 253-535-7151
800-274-6758 (toll-free)
Fax: 253-536-5136
E-mail: admission@plu.edu
Web site: http://www.plu.edu

PROGRAM ADMINISTRATION

Loren J. Anderson, President.
Steven P. Starkovich, Acting Provost and Dean of Graduate Studies.

Graduate Studies
Laura J. Polcyn, Associate Dean of Graduate Studies and Special Academic Programs.

Division of Social Sciences (M.A.)
David Ward, Chair of Marriage and Family Therapy.

School of Business (M.B.A.)
Theresa Ramos, Director of Graduate Programs.

School of Education (M.A.)
Mike Hillis, Co-Interim Dean and Director of Graduate Programs.

School of Nursing (M.S.N.)
Amy Manoso, Graduate Admissions Coordinator.

Department of English (M.F.A.)
Stan Rubin, Director of the M.F.A. program.

PENN STATE HARRISBURG

Graduate Programs

Programs of Study

Penn State Harrisburg offers the following master's, doctoral, and dual-degree programs:

Master of Arts (M.A.) degree programs include the M.A. in American studies, which explores American civilization through history, philosophy, folklore, and the arts and their relationships to economic, political, and social institutions; the M.A. in humanities, an interdisciplinary program; the M.A. in criminal justice, which provides academic leadership for those working in corrections, victims' services, policing and law enforcement, human services, and courts; the M.A. in applied clinical psychology, which prepares students to work as mental health professionals in a variety of settings and provides the academic training necessary for graduates to apply for master's-level licensing as mental-health professionals in the Commonwealth of Pennsylvania; the M.A. in applied behavior analysis, which is designed to teach graduate-level students to become proficient in the clinical practice of applied behavior analysis and to meet certification standards set by the Association for Behavior Analysis and the Behavior Analyst Certification Board (BACB); and the Master of Arts in community psychology and social change, which emphasizes the use of psychology and sociology to meet social needs in the community.

The Doctor of Philosophy (Ph.D.) in American Studies emphasizes critical cultural inquiry and the application of American studies to public heritage, public policy, and cultural resource management.

The Master of Business Administration (M.B.A.) is a professionally oriented program for those seeking or holding management positions in business, engineering, scientific, technical, or health-care organizations.

The Master of Education (M.Ed.), with a major in teaching and curriculum, is designed for school teachers. The M.Ed., with a major in training and development, focuses on the special skills needed by training and development professionals in business, industry, health care, government, and human services. The M.Ed., with a major in health education, provides a broad background in health areas, the skills required to assess and deal with health educational needs, the theoretical basis for understanding health education research, and the knowledge to design, implement, and evaluate health education programs. And the M.Ed. in literacy education is designed to provide full-time and part-time graduate students with a focused program of study in the field of reading education.

The Doctor of Education (D.Ed.) in adult education is a program in which adult education is merged with such areas as counseling and the behavioral sciences, business and organizational development, science and engineering, public affairs, the humanities, and health education.

The Master of Engineering (M.Eng.), with a major in engineering science, provides broad education in advanced aspects of engineering sciences and the opportunity for specialization. The M.Eng. in environmental engineering, offers opportunities for engineers to specialize in solving various environmental problems. The M.Eng. in electrical engineering, offers concentrations in electronic communications systems, control systems, VLSI and computer engineering, and power systems.

The Master of Environmental Pollution Control (M.E.P.C.) or the M.S. in environmental pollution control focus on aspects of air and water pollution control and solid-waste disposal.

The Master of Professional Studies (M.P.S.) in engineering management provides engineers with business perspectives to enhance their ability to manage major projects, participate in business initiatives, develop policies, and other activities in the public and private sectors.

The Master of Public Administration (M.P.A.) is designed for those in or seeking professional careers in government, health care, human service, or public service organizations.

The Ph.D. in public administration combines the traditions of the doctoral degree with flexible class schedules for part-time students and scholar/practitioners.

The Master of Science (M.S.) in applied psychological research focuses on the development of research skills within the context of scientific training in psychology.

The M.S. in computer science offers practical and theoretical applications.

The Master of Science in Information Systems (M.S.I.S.) is offered within the School of Business Administration for technically grounded, upper-level information-resource managers with business organizations.

The Master of Health Administration (M.H.A.) is designed for those in careers in a variety of health-care organizations.

Penn State Harrisburg and the Dickinson School of Law of the Pennsylvania State University offer cooperative, joint programs leading to J.D./M.B.A., J.D./M.P.A., J.D./E.P.C., and J.D./M.S.I.S. degrees, as well as programs with the Penn State College of Medicine at Hershey leading to the Ph.D. degree in pharmacology and an M.B.A. and a Ph.D. in pharmacology and M.S.I.S.

Research Facilities

The campus library contains more than 275,000 volumes (growing by 6,000 a year) and subscribes to 1,300 periodicals. Microform holdings total 1 million units, including complete sets of ERIC, HRAF, Envirofiche, and Library of American Civilization. Wireless networking is available throughout the library. The resources of other libraries of Penn State University are available through LIAS, an online integrated library system of the University libraries. Students also have access to the resources of the Associated College Libraries of Central Pennsylvania, a consortium of area college libraries.

The Computer Center provides support for instruction and research. Facilities include a nineteen-terminal microcomputer lab, a thirty-terminal microcomputer LAN, and a forty-terminal microcomputer LAN that accesses the library's online database search system and an IBM mainframe processing system located at Penn State's University Park campus. Programming support is available through the center's staff. Penn State Harrisburg is also home to the Pennsylvania State Data Center.

Financial Aid

Internships, fellowships, graduate assistantships, graduate work-study awards, grants-in-aid programs, Guaranteed Student Loans, and a minority graduate student assistantship are available.

Cost of Study

In 2008–09, resident tuition was $7388 per semester for full-time study (12 or more credits) and $616 per credit for part-time study (1 to 11 credits). Pennsylvania nonresident full-time tuition was $10,490 per semester, and part-time tuition was $874 per credit. Pennsylvania resident M.B.A. tuition was $682 per credit. Pennsylvania nonresident M.B.A. tuition was $1057 per credit. For business, science, IST, and engineering programs, resident tuition was $651 per credit. Pennsylvania nonresident tuition for business, science, IST, and engineering programs was $915 per credit.

Living and Housing Costs

Seventy-two apartment-style units accommodate a minimum of 300 occupants. Each unit contains four bedrooms, two full bathrooms, a kitchen, living area, and washers and dryers. A second phase of new-student apartment-style housing accommodates 32 freshmen in four units housing 8 students each. Housing is close to classrooms, the library, recreation activities, and food and support services.

Student Group

The college is a major graduate center with approximately 1,400 graduate students, most of whom are employed full-time and attend classes on a part-time basis. The average age of graduate students is 32.

Location

The college is 8 miles from Harrisburg, the state capital. The resources of local, state, and federal agencies; museums; archives; and the state library are nearby. Within 30 miles are the urban centers of York and Lancaster, small towns such as Hershey, and rural settings in Lancaster and Lebanon counties. Business, cultural, industrial, agricultural, residential, and service opportunities abound. Three interstate highways converge in Harrisburg and provide access to Philadelphia, Baltimore, New York City, and Washington, D.C., which also are accessible via nearby rail and air service.

The University

Penn State Harrisburg has a small-college atmosphere, with a student body of about 3,900, yet it has the resources, academic standards, and assets of the state's comprehensive land-grant research university. Graduate programs are designed primarily for persons employed full-time in area businesses, schools, government agencies, and industries, and most courses are held in the evening. A variety of programs and services are also offered through the Eastgate Center in Harrisburg.

Applying

Candidates must have a bachelor's degree from an accredited institution. Applicants generally are expected to have earned a GPA of at least 3.0 (4.0 scale). The GRE is required by some programs. The M.B.A. and M.S.I.S. programs require the GMAT. The M.P.A. program accepts scores from the GRE General Test, GMAT, LSAT, or MAT. The Adult Education Program accepts the GRE or MAT. Candidates from countries in which English is not the primary language must earn at least 550 (paper-based test) or 213 (computer-based test) on the TOEFL. International transcripts must be evaluated by the Educational Credential Evaluators (ECE). ECE evaluations should accompany the application and transcripts. Prospective students must submit an online application at http://www.hbg.psu.edu/admissions/gradapp.php.

Correspondence and Information

Admissions Office
Penn State Harrisburg
777 West Harrisburg Pike
Middletown, Pennsylvania 17057

Phone: 717-948-6250
E-mail: hbgadmit@psu.edu
Web site: http://www.hbg.psu.edu

DEAN AND PROGRAM COORDINATORS

Marian R. Walters, Professor (physiology) and Associate Dean for Research and Graduate Studies; Ph.D., Houston.

Coordinators of Graduate Programs
Adult Education (D.Ed.): Elizabeth Tisdell, Associate Professor (adult education); Ed.D., Georgia.
Applied Behavior Analysis (M.A.): Kimberly Schreck, Associate Professor (psychology); Ph.D., Ohio State.
Applied Clinical Psychology (M.A.): Thomas G. Bowers, Associate Professor (psychology); Ph.D., Penn State.
Applied Psychological Research (M.A.): Thomas G. Bowers, Associate Professor (psychology); Ph.D., Penn State.
American Studies (M.A.): Simon J. Bronner, Distinguished Professor (American studies and folklore); Ph.D., Indiana.American Studies (Ph.D.): Simon J. Bonner, Distinguished Professor (American studies and folklore); Ph.D., Indiana.
Business Administration (M.B.A.): Richard Young, Professor (supply chain management); Ph.D., Penn State.
Community Psychology and Social Change (M.A.): Holly Angelique, Associate Professor (community psychology); Ph.D., Michigan State.
Computer Science (M.S.): Linda M. Null, Associate Professor (computer science); Ph.D., Iowa State.
Criminal Justice (M.A.): Barbara Sims, Professor (criminal justice); Ph.D., Sam Houston State.
Electrical Engineering (M.Eng.): Peter B. Idowu, Associate Professor (engineering); Ph.D., Toledo.
Engineering Management (M.P.S.): Peter B. Idowu, Associate Professor (engineering); Ph.D., Toledo.
Engineering Science (M.Eng.): Peter B. Idowu, Associate Professor (engineering); Ph.D., Toledo.
Environmental Engineering (M.Eng.): Thomas Eberlein, Associate Professor (chemistry); Ph.D., Wisconsin.
Environmental Pollution Control (M.E.P.C. and M.S.): Thomas Eberlein, Associate Professor (chemistry); Ph.D., Wisconsin.
Health Administration (M.H.A.): James T. Ziegenfuss Jr., Professor (management and health care systems); Ph.D., Pennsylvania–Wharton.
Health Education (M.Ed.): Samuel W. Monismith, Associate Professor (health education); D.Ed., Penn State.
Humanities (M.A.): Troy Thomas, Associate Professor (humanities and art); Ph.D., California.
Information Systems (M.S.I.S.): Girish H. Subramanian, Professor (information systems); Ph.D., Temple.Literacy Education (M.Ed.): Barbara Marinak, Assistant Professor (reading); Ph.D., Maryland.
Public Administration (M.P.A.): Jeremy Plant, Professor (public administration and public policy); Ph.D., Virginia.
Public Administration (Ph.D.): Jeremy Plant, Professor (public administration and public policy); Ph.D., Virginia.
Teaching and Curriculum (M.Ed.): Denise G. Meister, Associate Professor (education); Ph.D., Penn State.
Training and Development (M.Ed.): Margaret C. Lohman, Associate Professor (education); Ph.D., Ohio State.

Vartan Plaza, with the college bookstore (left) and the Science and Technology Building (right).

The state-of-the-art library at Penn State Harrisburg.

PENN STATE UNIVERSITY PARK

Graduate School

Programs of Study

Programs of graduate study are offered in the following fields (asterisks precede fields in which only a master's degree is offered; all other fields offer both master's and doctoral programs, except where noted): *accounting, acoustics; adult education; aerospace engineering; agricultural, environmental, and regional economics; agricultural and extension education; agricultural and biological engineering; agronomy; American studies; anatomy; animal science; anthropology; *applied behavior analysis; *applied clinical psychology; applied linguistics (Ph.D. only); *applied psychological research; *applied statistics; architectural engineering; *architecture; *art; *art education; art history; astrobiology (dual-title); astronomy and astrophysics; biobehavioral health; biochemistry and molecular biology; biochemistry, microbiology, and molecular biology; bioengineering; biogeochemistry (dual-title); biology; *biotechnology; business administration; cell and developmental biology; cell and molecular biology; chemical engineering; chemistry; civil engineering; classics and ancient Mediterranean studies (dual-title);*college student affairs; communication arts and sciences; communication sciences and disorders; *community psychology and social change; *community and economic development; comparative and international education (dual-title); comparative literature; *composition/theory; computer science and engineering; *conducting; counseling psychology (Ph.D. only); counselor education; *criminal justice; crime, law, and justice; curriculum and instruction; demography (dual-title); *earth sciences; ecology; economics; educational leadership; educational psychology; educational theory and policy; electrical engineering; energy and mineral engineering; *engineering management; *engineering mechanics; *engineering science; engineering science and mechanics; English; entomology; *environmental engineering; *environmental pollution control; food science; *forensic science; forest resources; French; genetics; *geographic information systems; geography; geosciences; German; *health administration; health education; health policy and administration; higher education; history; horticulture; hotel, restaurant, and institutional management; human development and family studies; human dimensions of natural resources and the environment (dual-title); *human resources and employment relations; *humanities; immunology and infectious diseases; industrial engineering; *information science; information sciences and technology; *information systems; instructional systems; integrative biosciences; *international affairs; kinesiology; *laboratory animal medicine; *landscape architecture; *leadership development; leisure studies; *literacy education; *manufacturing systems engineering; mass communications (Ph.D. only); materials science and engineering; mathematics; mechanical engineering; *media studies; meteorology; microbiology and immunology; molecular medicine; molecular toxicology; music and music education; *music theory; *music theory and history; neuroscience; nuclear engineering; nursing; nutrition; *oil and gas engineering management; operations research (dual-title); pathobiology; *performance; pharmacology; philosophy; physics; physiology; *piano pedagogy and performance; piano performance (D.M.A. only); plant biology; plant pathology; political science; *project management; psychology; public administration; *public health preparedness; *public health sciences; *quality and manufacturing management; rural sociology; *Russian and comparative literature; school psychology; sociology; software engineering; soil science; Spanish; special education; statistics; systems engineering; *teaching and curriculum; *teaching English as a second language; *telecommunications studies; *theater; *training and development; *voice performance and pedagogy; wildlife and fisheries science; women's studies (dual-title); workforce education and development; and *youth and family education. Level I Instructional, Supervisory, Educational Specialist, and Administrative certificates are offered.

Research Facilities

The University Libraries System has more than 5 million cataloged volumes, over 68,000 current serials, and 5.2 million microforms. Automated services are provided through the Library Information Access System developed at Penn State. The Center for Academic Computing (CAC) is the principal provider of central academic computing services. The center operates computers capable of providing not only numerically intensive computing but also electronic access to higher education facilities and research centers worldwide. Penn State and Internet resources include electronic bulletin boards, news and conferencing systems, publications, library catalogs, research databases, discussion groups, and much more. Public laboratories with terminals and desktop computers provide facilities for those without their own equipment.

Financial Aid

Fellowships, traineeships, or assistantships are held by approximately 70 percent of all University Park students. These awards involve remission of tuition and payment of stipends averaging $1610 per month. Awards are usually made by the student's department or on recommendation to another administrative unit. Student loans and work-study funds are available through the Office of Student Aid.

Cost of Study

In 2008–09, tuition for full-time study (except for medical students) was $7388 per semester for residents and $13,196 per semester for nonresidents at all campuses except Penn State Great Valley and business, information sciences and technology, science, and engineering programs. Further information is available on the Web at http://www.bursar.psu.edu.

Living and Housing Costs

Residence hall accommodations and University-owned apartments are available through the Assignment Office for Campus Residences (phone: 814-865-7501).

Student Group

In fall 2008, 12,241 graduate students were enrolled. The University conferred 1,880 advanced degrees, including 620 doctorates, during the 2007–08 year.

Student Outcomes

Graduates of the University typically proceed to a wide variety of academic and nonacademic professional careers in colleges and universities, private industry, government, and nonprofit organizations.

Location

The main campus, University Park, is located in the center of the state in the borough of State College. Pittsburgh, Philadelphia, New York City, and Washington, D.C., are each within a few hours' travel by car and are readily accessible by bus or air. The beautiful mountain country surrounding the community offers seasonal recreation, including boating, camping, fishing, hiking, hunting, skiing, and swimming. Although Penn State is a major graduate and research institution, the community retains a collegiate atmosphere.

The Graduate School

Graduate study is offered in more than 150 major programs, and twenty-eight types of advanced academic and professional degrees are conferred. The faculty of the Graduate School numbers about 3,000. In addition to the University Park campus, Penn State Great Valley near Philadelphia; Penn State Harrisburg; the College of Medicine at Hershey; and Penn State Erie, the Behrend College, offer graduate degree programs.

Applying

Admission is granted jointly by the Graduate School and the department to which the student is applying. Applicants interested in programs at Penn State Erie, the Behrend College; Penn State Great Valley; and Penn State Harrisburg should apply directly to these campuses. Students should contact the Office of Certification and Educational Services, 181 Chambers Building, for information on Level I Instructional, Supervisory, Educational Specialist, or Administrative certificates. Students whose native language is not English or who have not received baccalaureate or master's degrees from an institution in which the language of instruction is English must submit TOEFL or IELTS scores (at the discretion of the program). Application materials and detailed information about specific graduate programs and GRE requirements are available from the individual graduate programs. Because the admission process is time consuming, applications should be submitted as early as possible.

Correspondence and Information

Graduate School
Penn State University
University Park Campus
114 Kern Graduate Building
University Park, Pennsylvania 16802

Phone: 814-865-1795 (Graduate Enrollment Services)
E-mail: gadm@psu.edu
Web site: http://www.gradsch.psu.edu

COLLEGES/CENTERS AND HEADS OF PROGRAMS

Unless otherwise indicated, the mailing address is The Pennsylvania State University, University Park, Pennsylvania 16802. (Penn State Harrisburg is in Middletown, Pennsylvania 17057; the Milton S. Hershey Medical Center, College of Medicine, is in Hershey, Pennsylvania 17033; Penn State Great Valley School of Graduate Professional Studies is in Malvern, Pennsylvania 19355; and Penn State Erie, the Behrend College, is in Erie, Pennsylvania 16563).

Agricultural Sciences
Agricultural and Biological Engineering: Roy Young, 252 Agricultural Engineering. Agricultural and Extension Education: Tracy Hoover, 114 Ferguson. Agricultural, Environmental, and Regional Economics: Stephen Smith, 103C Armsby. Crop and Soil Sciences: David Sylvia, 116 Agricultural Sciences and Industries. Dairy and Animal Science: Terry Etherton, 324L Henning. Entomology: Gary Felton, 501 Agricultural Sciences and Industries. Food Science: John D. Floros, 206 Food Science. Forest Resources: Michael Messina, 319 Forest Resources. Horticulture: Richard Marini, 117 Tyson. Pathobiology: Vivek Kapur, 115 Henning. Plant Pathology: Frederick E. Gildow, 212B Buckhout. Rural Sociology: Stephen Smith, 103C Armsby. Wildlife and Fisheries Science: Michael Messina, 319 Forest Resources. Youth and Family Education: Tracy Hoover, 114 Ferguson.

Arts and Architecture
Architecture: Daniel Willis, 128 Stuckeman. Art: Charles Garoian, 210 Arts Cottage. Art Education: Charles Garoian, 210 Arts Cottage. Art History: Craig Zabel, 240 Borland. Composing: Sue Haug, 233 Music. Composition/Theory: Sue Haug, 233 Music. Conducting: Sue Haug, 233 Music. Landscape Architecture: Brian Orland, 121 Stuckeman Family Building. Music and Music Education: Sue Haug, 233 Music. Music Theory: Sue Haug, 233 Music. Music Theory and History: Sue Haug, 233 Music. Performance: Sue Haug, 233 Music. Piano Pedagogy and Performance: Sue Haug, 233 Music. Piano Performance: Sue Haug, 233 Music. Theater: Dan Carter, 103 Arts. Art: C. Garoian, 210 Patterson. Voice Performance and Pedagogy: Sue Haug, 233 Music.

Business Administration
Business Administration (Ph.D., M.S.): William Ross, 351 Business Building. Business Administration (M.B.A.): Dennis Sheehan, 220 Business Building.

Communications
Mass Communications: John Nichols, 201 Carnegie. Media Studies: John Nichols, 201 Carnegie. Telecommunications Studies: John Nichols, 201 Carnegie.

Earth and Mineral Sciences
Earth Sciences: Katherine Freeman, 2218 EES. Energy and Mineral Engineering: Yaw Yeboah, 103 Hosler. Geographic Information Systems: World Campus: Mark Gahegan, 2217 E.E.S. Geography: Karl Zimmerer, 302 Walker. Geosciences: Timothy Bralower, 507 Dieke. Materials Science and Engineering: Gary Messing, 101 Steidle. Meteorology: William Brune, 503 Walker.

Education
Adult Education: Edgar Farmer, 314 Keller; Elizabeth Tisdell, Penn State Harrisburg. College Student Affairs: Robert Reason, 300 Rackley. Counseling Psychology and Counselor Education: Spencer Niles, 327 Cedar. Curriculum and Instruction: Gregory Kelly, 270 Chambers. Educational Leadership: Gerald LeTendre, 207 Rackley. Educational Psychology: Kathy Ruhl, 125 Cedar. Educational Theory and Policy: Gerald LeTendre, 300 Rackley. Higher Education: Dorothy Evensen, 400 Rackley. Instructional Systems: Edgar Farmer, 314 Keller. School Psychology: Kathy Ruhl, 125 Cedar. Special Education: Kathy Ruhl, 125 Cedar; Roy Clariana, Great Valley. Workforce Education and Development: Edgar Farmer, 301 Keller.

Engineering
Acoustics: Anthony Atchley, 201 Applied Science. Aerospace Engineering: George Lesieutre, 229 Hammond. Agricultural and Biological Engineering: Roy Young, 249 Agricultural Engineering. Architectural Engineering: Chimay Anumba, 104 Engineering A. Chemical Engineering: A. Zydney, 158 Fenske. Civil Engineering: Peggy Johnson, 218 Sackett. Computer Science and Engineering: R. Acharya, 111 IST Building. Electrical Engineering: W. Kenneth Jenkins, 118 Electrical Engineering East. Engineering Mechanics: Judith Todd, 212 EES. Engineering Science: Judith Todd, 212 EES. Environmental Engineering: Peggy Johnson, 218 Sackett. Industrial Engineering: Richard J. Koubek, 310 Leonhard. Mechanical Engineering: Karen Thole, 127 Reber. Nuclear Engineering: Karen Thole, 127 Reber.

Health and Human Development
Biobehavioral Health: Collins Airhihenbuwa, 315 Human Development East. Communication Sciences and Disorders: Gordon Blood, 308 Ford. Health Policy and Administration: Dennis Shea, 604 Ford. Hotel, Restaurant, and Institutional Management: Hubert Van Hoof, 201 Mateer. Human Development and Family Studies: Steven Zarit, 211 South Henderson. Kinesiology: Karl Newell, 276 Recreation Building. Recreation, Parks, and Tourism Management: John Dattilo, 801 Ford. Nursing: Paula Milone-Nuzzo, 210F HHD East. Nutrition: Gordon Jensen, 110F Chandlee Lab.

Hershey Medical Center
Anatomy: Patricia McLaughlin. Biochemistry and Molecular Biology: Judith Bond. Cell and Molecular Biology: Henry Donahue. Laboratory Animal Medicine: Ronald Wilson. Microbiology and Immunology: Richard Courtney. Neuroscience: Robert Milner. Pharmacology: Kent Vrana. Physiology: Leonard S. Jefferson. Public Health Preparedness: Robert Cherry. Public Health Sciences: Vernon Chinchilli.

Intercollege Graduate Degree Programs
Bioengineering: Herbert Lipowsky, 205 Hallowell. Business Administration: John Fizel. Cell and Developmental Biology: Hong Ma, 201 Life Sciences. Demography: Gordon DeJong, 601 Oswald. Ecology: David Eissenstat, 101 Life Sciences. Environmental Pollution Control: Thomas Eberlein, Penn State Harrisburg. Genetics: Richard Ordway, 201 Life Sciences. Immunology and Infectious Diseases: Margherita Cantorna, 201 Life Sciences. Integrative Biosciences: Peter Hudson, 201 Life Sciences, University Park. Molecular Medicine: Charles Lang, Hershey. Molecular Toxicology: Jeffrey Peters, 201 Life Sciences. Operations Research: Richard Koubek, 310 Leonhard. Physiology: Donna Korzick, 101 Life Sciences; Leonard Jefferson, Hershey Medical Center. Plant Biology: Teh-hui Kao, 101 Life Sciences. Quality and Manufacturing Management: Robert Voigt, 344 Leonhard.

Liberal Arts
Anthropology: Nina Jablonski, 413 Carpenter. Applied Linguistics: Joan Kelly Hall, 305 Sparks. Communication Arts and Sciences: James Dillard, 234 Sparks. Comparative Literature: Caroline Eckhardt, 427 Burrowes. Crime, Law, and Justice: John McCarthy, 211 Oswald Tower. Economics: Robert Marshall, 604 Kern. English: Robin Schulze, 107 Burrowes. French: Benedicte Monicat, 233A Burrowes. German: B. R. Page, 427 Burrowes. History: A. G. Roeber, 108 Weaver. Human Resources and Employment Relations: Paul Clark, 133 Willard. Philosophy: John Christman, 240 Sparks. Political Science: Donna Bahry, 202 Pond Lab. Psychology: Melvin Mark, 109 Moore. Sociology: John McCarthy, 211 Oswald Tower. Spanish: William Blue, 237 Burrowes. Teaching English as a Second Language: Joan Kelly Hall, 305 Sparks.

Penn State Erie, Behrend College
Business Administration: John Magenau. Manufacturing Systems Engineering: Ralph Ford. Project Management: John Magenau.

Penn State Great Valley School of Graduate Professional Studies
Business Administration: Daniel Indro. Curriculum and Instruction: Roy Clariana. Engineering Management: James Nemes. Information Science: James Nemes. Leadership Development: Daniel Indro. Software Engineering: James Nemes. Special Education: Roy Clariana. Systems Engineering: John McCool.

Penn State Harrisburg
Adult Education: Elizabeth Tisdell. American Studies: Kathryn Robinson. Applied Behavior Analysis: William Milheim. Applied Clinical Psychology: William Milheim. Applied Psychological Research: B. Bremer. Business Administration: Richard Young. Community Psychology and Social Change: Holly Angelique. Computer Science: Linda Null. Criminal Justice: Barbara Sims. Electrical Engineering: Omid Ansary. Engineering Science: Omid Ansary. Environmental Engineering: Thomas Eberlein. Environmental Pollution Control: Thomas Eberlein. Health Administration: Steven Peterson. Health Education: Samuel Monismith. Humanities: Troy Thomas. Information Systems: Stephen Schappe. Literacy Education: Steven Melnick. Public Administration: Steven Peterson. Teaching and Curriculum: Steven Melnick. Training and Development: Margaret Lohman.

School of Information Sciences and Technology
Information Sciences and Technology: John Yen, 332 IST Building.

School of International Affairs
International Affairs: J. Stewart Combs, 122C Lewis Katz Building.

Science
Applied Statistics: Bruce Lindsay, 326 Thomas. Astronomy and Astrophysics: Eric Feigelson, 525 Davey. Biochemistry, Microbiology, and Molecular Biology: Richard Frisque, 108 Althouse. Biology: Douglas Cavener, 208 Mueller. Biotechnology: Ronald Porter, 201 Life Sciences. Chemistry: Ayusman Sen, 104 Chemistry Building. Forensic Science: Robert Shaler, 107 Whitmore. Mathematics: John Roe, 104 McAllister. Physics: Jayanth Banavar, 104 Davey. Statistics: Bruce Lindsay, 326 Thomas.

QUEENS COLLEGE
OF THE CITY UNIVERSITY OF NEW YORK

Graduate Programs in the Arts and Sciences

Programs of Study

Queens College offers programs of study leading to the Master of Arts in applied linguistics, art history, biology, chemistry, computer science, English literature, French, geology, history, Italian, mathematics, music, physics, psychology, sociology, Spanish, speech-language pathology, and urban affairs. Master of Science degrees are offered in accounting, applied environmental geoscience, and nutrition and exercise science. The interdisciplinary degrees of Master of Arts in Liberal Studies and Master of Arts in Social Sciences are also offered. The Master of Fine Arts degree is offered in English-creative writing and studio art. Master of Science in Education programs are available in bilingual elementary education, counselor education, early childhood education, elementary school education, family and consumer sciences, literacy education, school psychology, secondary school education (art; English; French; general science—biology, chemistry, earth science, and physics; Italian; mathematics; music; physical education; social studies; and Spanish), special education (B–2, 1–6, and 7–12), and teaching English to speakers of other languages. Professional diplomas in applied behavior analysis, education, English language teaching, and school building leader are also offered.

For applicants who seek New York State provisional teacher certification but whose undergraduate programs did not include a background in education, the College offers postbaccalaureate advanced certificate programs in early childhood education, elementary education and secondary education (art–visual arts, biology, chemistry, earth science, English, family and consumer science, French, Italian, mathematics, music, physical education, physics, social studies, and Spanish). Bilingual certification programs are available in counselor education, school psychology, and special education.

The Master of Library Science degree is available for public librarianship and school media specialist. Also offered are advanced certificates in archives and records management preservation and childhood/youth public library and a post-master's advanced certificate in librarianship. All programs are accredited by the American Library Association. Concentrations in various areas also exist in a number of departments. Applicants should contact the Office of Graduate Admissions for more information at 718-997-5200.

Queens College is a major participant in the doctoral programs of the City University of New York (CUNY). Students interested in these programs should contact the CUNY Graduate Center at 212-817-7000, or visit www.gc.cuny.edu.

Research Facilities

The extensive laboratory facilities of the College house state-of-the-art scientific instruments for research in biology, chemistry, computer science, geology, physics, psychology, and health and physical education. There is also a low-temperature physics laboratory. Computing equipment ranges from cutting-edge, high-technology personal computers to highly specialized minicomputers. There are diverse computer laboratories, including a well-equipped social science research laboratory. The Graduate School of Library and Information Studies maintains a fully integrated computer-intensive facility.

Gertz Speech and Hearing Center provides a facility for research and clinical practice experience in communicative disorders. The College is home to an electronic music studio and to one of the best music libraries on the East Coast. It also shares facilities with the American Museum of Natural History, Brookhaven National Laboratory, the Lamont-Doherty Geological Observatory, and leading hospitals. The Benjamin S. Rosenthal Library holds a print collection of over 800,000 volumes, with annual additions of about 10,000 volumes through purchases and gifts. The library subscribes to approximately 1,020 print subscriptions and has online access to over 23,000 journal and periodical titles. The library also has an extensive microform collection.

Financial Aid

A limited number of graduate fellowships, some requiring teaching and/or research, may be available from individual departments through the Office of the Assistant to the Provost for Graduate Admissions. Other kinds of financial aid include New York State Tuition Assistance Program grants, Board of Trustees partial tuition waivers, Federal Perkins Loans, the Federal Direct Student Loan Program, and Federal Work-Study Program awards. Applicants should contact the Financial Aid Office for information. The Cooperative Education Program helps students gain both academic credit and work experience in paid positions.

Cost of Study

Annual tuition is $7360 and $312 per credit for New York State residents and $575 per credit for nonresidents. In addition to tuition, there are various expenses each semester, such as student activity and technology fees.

Living and Housing Costs

In August 2009, the College opened its first residence hall, The Summit, providing students the option of living on campus and enjoying all the latest amenities of residence life. For information, call Terry Walsh, Director of Housing and Residence Life, at 718-997-4881, or visit www.qc.cuny.edu/summit.

Student Group

In fall 2008 4,310 students were registered as graduate students in master's and advanced certificate programs, and many CUNY doctoral students work under the direct supervision of Queens College faculty members. Students come from throughout the United States and from a number of countries. In 2007–08 1,238 master's degrees and 53 advanced certificates were awarded. The Graduate Student Association at Queens College, an elective body representing the interests of all graduate students, offers free help with income tax return preparation and legal counseling.

Location

Queens College is located close to Manhattan, which is easily accessible by public transportation. Students can get reduced-price tickets to many of its cultural attractions. They can also take advantage of the parks and ocean beaches located nearby in Queens and on Long Island.

The College

Established in 1937, Queens College is a coeducational, publicly supported college with an emphasis on the liberal arts and sciences and education. Its attractive, tree-lined campus includes athletic fields, a gymnasium, a pool, tennis courts, fitness center, the soaring Rosenthal Library, and in fall 2009 The Summit, the College's first residence hall. Its Kupferberg Center for the Arts schedules a lively calendar of events, with performances by internationally renowned artists, as part of rich assortment of cultural offerings for the community. Queens College is registered by the New York State Department of Education and accredited by the Middle States Association of Colleges and Schools. The American Association of Colleges for Teacher Education includes the College in its list of member colleges.

Applying

The admission decision is based on the baccalaureate record and evidence of the ability to pursue graduate work. Scores from the General Test of the Graduate Record Examinations (GRE) and Graduate Management Admissions Council (GMAT) are required for admission to certain programs. For fall semester admission, applications should be filed by April 1. For spring semester admission, applications should be filed by November 1 (not all programs admit students in the spring). Applications for school psychology must be filed by March 1 for fall admission (spring applications are not accepted). Applications for Art Studio (M.F.A.) must be filed by March 15 for fall admission and by October 15 for spring admission. Speech-language pathology applications must be filed by February 1 for fall admission (spring applications are not accepted). Counselor education applications must be submitted by March 1. Applications for English-creative writing (M.F.A.) must be filed by February 15 for fall admission (spring applications are not accepted). Applications for the postbaccalaureate advance certificate program in physical education (K–12) must be filed by March 1 for fall admission and by October 1 for spring admission. Financial aid applications should be filed as early as possible. This information is subject to change.

Correspondence and Information

For information about a particular program:
Chair (listed overleaf)
Department of (specify)
Queens College
Flushing, New York 11367

For admission and registration information:
Graduate Admissions Office
Queens College
Flushing, New York 11367
Phone: 718-997-5200
Fax: 718-997-5193
E-mail: graduate_admissions@qc.edu

For other information:
Office of Graduate Studies
Queens College
Flushing, New York 11367
Phone: 718-997-5190
Fax: 718-997-5198
E-mail: steven.schwarz@qc.cuny.edu

THE FACULTY

From its beginnings in 1937, Queens College has made every effort to build a faculty of dedicated teachers and scholars. The list of institutions that have conferred degrees on members of the faculty includes every major university in the United States and several major European universities. Faculty members have received numerous national and international awards and fellowships as well as many sponsored research and training grants through the College's Office of Research and Sponsored Programs.

OFFICE OF GRADUATE STUDIES AND RESEARCH
Rich Bodnar, Ph.D., Acting Dean of Research and Graduate Studies.

OFFICE OF GRADUATE ADMISSIONS
Mario Caruso, M.A., Director of Graduate Admissions.

The following is a list of the heads of departments that offer graduate programs at the College. An asterisk (*) indicates that there is no master's or advanced certificate program in this area, but faculty members participate in the Ph.D. program at the CUNY Graduate Center. A dagger (†) indicates that the program is not currently accepting students.

DIVISION OF THE ARTS AND HUMANITIES
Tamara Evans, Ph.D., Dean of the Faculty for the Arts and Humanities.
Art: William Clark, Ph.D., Chair.
***Classical, Middle Eastern, and Asian Languages and Cultures:** William McClure, Ph.D., Chair.
***Comparative Literature:** Charles Martin, Ph.D., Chair.
***Drama, Dance, and Theatre:** Charles Repole, Ph.D., Chair.
English: Nancy Comley, Ph.D., Chair.
European Languages and Literatures: Royal Brown, Ph.D., Chair.
Hispanic Languages and Literatures: Jose Martinez-Torrejon, Ph.D., Chair.
Linguistics and Communication Disorders: Robert Vago, Ph.D., Chair.
†**Media Studies:** Stuart Liebman, Ph.D., Chair.
Music: Edward Smaldone, Ph.D., Chair and Director, Aaron Copland School of Music.

DIVISION OF MATHEMATICS AND THE NATURAL SCIENCES
Thomas Strekas, Ph.D., Dean of the Faculty for Mathematics and the Natural Sciences.
Biology: Corinne Michels, Ph.D., Chair.
Chemistry: William Hersh, Ph.D., Chair.
Computer Science: Zhigang Xiang, Ph.D., Chair.
Earth and Environmental Sciences: Yan Zheng, Ph.D., Chair.
Family, Nutrition, and Exercise Sciences: Elizabeth Lowe, Ph.D., Chair.
Mathematics: Wallace Goldberg, Ph.D., Chair.
Physics: Alexander Lisyansky, Ph.D., Chair.
Psychology: Ray Johnson, Ph.D., Chair.

DIVISION OF THE SOCIAL SCIENCES
Elizabeth Hendrey, Ph.D., Dean of the Faculty for the Social Sciences.
Accounting and Information Systems: Israel Blumenfrucht, Ph.D., Chair.
***Anthropology:** Sara Stinson, Ph.D., Chair.†
Economics: David Gabel, Ph.D., Chair.
History: Frank Warren, Ph.D., Chair.
Library Science: Virgil Blake, Ph.D., Chair and Director, Graduate School of Library and Information Studies.†
Philosophy: Steven Hicks, Ph.D., Chair.†
Political Science: Patricia Rachal, Ph.D., Chair.
Sociology: Andrew Beveridge, Ph.D., Chair.
Urban Studies: Leonard Rodberg, Ph.D., Chair.

DIVISION OF EDUCATION
Penny Hammrich, Ph.D., Dean of the Faculty for Education.
Educational and Community Programs: Jesse Vazquez, Ph.D., Chair.
Elementary and Early Childhood Education and Services: Elaine Burns, Ph.D., Chair.
Secondary Education and Youth Services: Eleanor Armour-Thomas, Ph.D., Chair.

INTERDISCIPLINARY STUDIES
Liberal Studies: James Jordon, Ph.D., Graduate Adviser.
Social Sciences: Martin Hanlon, Ph.D., Graduate Adviser.

ROBERT MORRIS UNIVERSITY

Programs of Study

Robert Morris University (RMU) offers twenty graduate degree programs. At the master's level, the university offers the Master of Business Administration (M.B.A.) degree and Master of Science (M.S.) degrees in in business education, communications and information systems, competitive intelligence systems, engineering management, human resource management, information security and assurance, information systems management, information technology (IT) project management, instructional leadership, Internet information systems, nonprofit management, nursing, and organizational studies. The University also offers a Doctor of Science (D.Sc.) degree in information systems and communications and a Doctor of Philosophy (Ph.D.) degree in instructional management and leadership. The Doctor of Nursing Practice (D.N.P.) degree is offered in adult nurse practitioner, family nurse practitioner, adult psychiatric and mental health nurse practitioner, and as a completion degree for advanced practice nurses already possessing a master's degree. Postbaccalaureate certification programs are also available for secondary and elementary teachers as well as instructional technology specialists.

The university is accredited by the Middle States Association of Colleges and Schools. RMU schools and programs are also accredited by the Association to Advance Collegiate Schools of Business International, the Teacher Education Accreditation Council, ABET Inc., and the Commission on Collegiate Nursing Education.

Research Facilities

Facilities supporting the graduate programs at Robert Morris University include nine open-access computer laboratories, two physical libraries, and an electronic library offering an array of research databases. Classrooms have been equipped with advanced computer and presentation technology equipment to facilitate teaching and learning.

To support a large number of holdings, the library has a state-of-the-art searchable catalog system. The RMU Electronic Library offers continual off-campus access to more than 100 major research databases. The library is a member of numerous resource-sharing consortia that greatly extend the amount of materials available to support graduate education.

Financial Aid

Graduate loans are available for those who qualify. Students are encouraged to file the Free Application for Federal Student Aid (FAFSA). Robert Morris University participates in the Federal Family Education Loan (FFEL) Program and also offers various interest-free payment plans.

Cost of Study

Tuition for the 2009–10 academic year for the M.B.A. program is $730 per credit. Tuition for the M.S. programs in human resource management and nonprofit management is $710 per credit; tuition for the M.S. programs in communications and information systems, competitive intelligence systems, information security and assurance, information systems management, information technology project management, and Internet information systems is $700 per credit; tuition for the M.S. programs in instructional leadership and business education and the postbaccalaureate teacher certification programs is $675 per credit; tuition for the M.S. in nursing is $740 per credit; tuition for the M.S. in engineering management is $750 per credit; and tuition for the M.S. in organizational studies is $635 per credit. Tuition for the D.Sc. in information systems and communications is $26,445 per year; tuition for the D.N.P. is $21,945 per year for full-time students, $780 per credit for part-time students, and $995 per credit for students in the completion option; and tuition for the Ph.D. in instructional management and leadership is $17,445 per year.

Living and Housing Costs

Students find an abundance of residential living opportunities both on and off campus. There are twelve residence halls on the Moon Township campus that house more than 1,300 students. The D.Sc. program fee includes the cost of the required residencies.

Student Group

RMU enrolls more than 1,000 students in its graduate degree programs. The average age of graduate students is 33, with an age range of 21 to 65. Women make up 54 percent of the graduate student population. Students come from diverse professional and academic backgrounds.

Location

Robert Morris University has three locations. The main campus occupies 230 acres in suburban Moon Township, 17 miles west of downtown Pittsburgh and 15 minutes from Pittsburgh International Airport. RMU also has locations in downtown Pittsburgh and suburban Cranberry Township. Some graduate programs are offered exclusively at one location. Many graduate programs and classes are also offered online.

The University

Robert Morris University, founded in 1921, is a four-year, private, coeducational, independent institution. It has developed a national reputation for its strong business programs and offers sixty undergraduate degrees and twenty master's and doctoral degree programs.

Applying

The graduate programs admit students on a rolling admission basis. However, students are encouraged to submit all required materials at least two months prior to the start of their desired term of entry. Applications can be filed for free through the University's Web site. Students should note that the M.S. in nonprofit management, the M.S. in nursing, the D.Sc. in information systems and communications, the D.N.P., and the Ph.D. in instructional management and leadership programs require an interview as part of the final selection process.

Correspondence and Information

Office of Graduate Admissions
Robert Morris University
6001 University Boulevard
Moon Township, Pennsylvania 15108-1189
Phone: 800-762-0097 (toll-free)
Web site: http://www.rmu.edu

THE FACULTY

SCHOOL OF BUSINESS
Derya A. Jacobs, Dean; Ph.D., Missouri–Rolla.
Lois D. Bryan, Associate Dean; D.Sc., Robert Morris; CPA.
Kurt E. Shimmel, Associate Dean; D.B.A., Cleveland State.

Accounting and Finance Faculty
Robert G. Beaves, Ph.D., Iowa.
Gerald J. Berenbaum, M.B.A., Massachusetts; CPA.
William G. Brucker, M.B.A., J.D., Duquesne; CPA.
Zane Dennick-Ream, M.B.A., Iowa.
Riza Emekter, Ph.D., Nebraska.
Frank Flanegin, Ph.D., Central Florida.
Victoria A. Fratto, M.S., Robert Morris.
Jerry Hanwell, M.B.A., South Carolina; J.D., Duquesne.
David Hess, M.B.A., Ohio State; CPA.
Tanya M. Lee, Ph.D., Arizona State.
Denise C. Letterman, M.B.A., Shippensburg.
Jianyu Ma, Ph.D.
Katie Monroe, J.D., Washington (Seattle); LL.M., Florida.
Stanko Racic, Ph.D., Pittsburgh.
James E. Rebele, Ph.D., Indiana.
Ronald R. Rubenfield, M.B.A., Shippensburg; CPA, CMA.
Zhaoyun Shangguan, Ph.D., Connecticut.

Economics and Legal Studies Faculty
Mark J. Eschenfelder, Ph.D., Missouri.
Adora D. Holstein, Ph.D., Penn State.
Patrick J. Litzinger, Ph.D., Pittsburgh.
Min Lu, Ph.D., British Columbia–Vancouver.
J. Brian O'Roark, Ph.D., George Mason.
Ralph R. Reiland, M.B.A., Duquesne.
Louis B. Swartz, J.D., Duquesne.
Joel A. Waldman, J.D., Miami (Florida).

Management Faculty
Michele T. Cole, J.D., Ph.D., Pittsburgh.
Daria C. Crawley, Ph.D., Michigan.
Qin Geng, Ph.D., Illinois at Urbana-Champaign.
Jeffery K. Guiler, Ph.D., Pittsburgh.
Nell T. Hartley, Ph.D., Vanderbilt.
John Lipinski, Ph.D., Pittsburgh.
Marcel C. Minutolo, M.B.A., Pittsburgh.
Darlene Y. Motley, Ph.D., Pittsburgh.
Edward A. Nicholson, Ph.D., Ohio State.
Jodi A. Potter, Ph.D., Pittsburgh.
Yasmin S. Purohit, Ph.D., Drexel.
William F. Repack, M.S., Loyola.
Alan D. Smith, Ph.D., Akron; CPGS.
Michael A. Yahr, M.B.A., Pittsburgh.
Qin Yang, Ph.D., Temple.

Marketing Faculty
Artemisia Apostolopoulou, Ph.D., Massachusetts.
Scott Branvold, M.A., Mankato State; Ed.D., Utah.
Yun Chu, Ph.D., Texas–Pan American.
John S. Clark, Ph.D., Massachusetts Amherst.
Steven R. Clinton, Ph.D., Michigan State.
Cathleen S. Jones, D.Sc., Robert Morris.
Ersem Karadag, Ph.D., Oklahoma State.
Jill K. Maher, Ph.D., Kent State.
Dean R. Manna, Ph.D., Pittsburgh.
Gayle J. Marco, Ph.D., Pittsburgh.
Richard Mills, Ph.D., Duquesne
Denis P. Rudd, Ed.D., Nevada, Las Vegas; CHA, FMP.
Norman V. Schnurr, M.B.A., Pittsburgh.
David P. Synowka, Ph.D., Pittsburgh.
Yanbin Tu, Ph.D., Connecticut.

SCHOOL OF COMMUNICATIONS AND INFORMATION SYSTEMS
Barbara J. Levine, Dean; Ph.D., Wisconsin–Madison.

Communication Faculty
Barbara Burgess-Lefebvre, M.F.A., Illinois State.
Rex L. Crawley, Ph.D., Ohio.
Michele Reese Edwards, Ph.D., Ohio State.
Seth Finn, Ph.D., Stanford.
Kenneth V. Gargaro, Ph.D., Pittsburgh.
Ann D. Jabro, Ph.D., Penn State.
Marc Seamon, Ph.D., Penn State.

Computer and Information Systems Faculty
Jeanne M. Baugh, Ed.D., West Virginia.
Donald J. Caputo, Ph.D., Pittsburgh.
Gary A. Davis, D.Sc., Robert Morris.
Linda Kavanaugh, Ph.D., Pittsburgh.
Fred G. Kohun, Ph.D., Carnegie Mellon.
Paul J. Kovacs, Ph.D., Pittsburgh.
Joseph Laverty, Ph.D., Pittsburgh.
G. James Leone, Ph.D., Pittsburgh.
Walter Pilof, M.B.A., Xavier (Cincinnati).
Valerie J. Powell, Ph.D., Texas at Austin.
Karen Power, Ph.D., Pittsburgh.
Robert J. Skovira, Ph.D., Pittsburgh.
John Turchek, M.Ed., Duquesne.
David F. Wood, Ph.D., Pittsburgh.
Charles R. Woratschek, Ph.D., Pittsburgh.
Peter Wu, Ph.D., Rensselaer.
John Zeanchock, M.Ed., Indiana of Pennsylvania.

English Studies and Communications Skills Faculty
Diane Todd Bucci, Ph.D., Indiana of Pennsylvania.
Jay S. Carson, D.A., Carnegie Mellon.
Roger Gillan, M.A., Bucknell.
Arthur J. Grant, Ph.D., Wheaton (Illinois).
John Lawson, Ph.D., Northern Illinois.
John D. O'Banion, Ph.D., Northern Illinois.
Sylvia A. Pamboukian, Ph.D., Indiana Bloomington.
Constance M. Ruzich, Ph.D., Pennsylvania.
Jim Vincent, M.A., Indiana.

Media Arts Faculty
Lutz Bacher, Ph.D., Wayne State.
Ferris Crane, M.F.A., Academy of Arts.
Norma E. Gonzalez, M.F.A., LSU.
Timothy J. Hadfield, M.F.A., Chelsea College of Art and Design (London).
Christine Holtz, M.F.A., RIT.
Carolina Loyola-Garcia, M.F.A., Carnegie Mellon.
Jon A. Radermacher, M.F.A., Indiana.
Helena Vanhala, Ph.D., Oregon.
Hyla J. Willis, M.F.A., Carnegie Mellon.

Organizational Studies Faculty
Kathy Davis, Ph.D., South Carolina.
Peter J. Draus, Ed.D., Pittsburgh.
Beatrice Gibbons, Ed.D., University of the Pacific.
Elizabeth M. Stork, Ph.D., Pittsburgh.
Glenn Thiel, Ph.D., Pittsburgh.

SCHOOL OF EDUCATION AND SOCIAL SCIENCES
John E. Graham, Dean; Ed.D., Pittsburgh.
Donna Cellante, Associate Dean; Ed.D., Pittsburgh.

Elementary Education Faculty
Robert DelGreco, Ed.D., Pittsburgh.
Michele N. Hipsky, Ed.D., Duquesne.
Ronald Perry, Ph.D., Pittsburgh.
Daniel J. Shelley, Ph.D., Pittsburgh.

Secondary Education and Graduate Studies Faculty
Richard G. Fuller, D.Ed., Penn State.
Mary A. Hansen, Ph.D., Pittsburgh.
E. Gregory Holdan, Ph.D., Penn State.
George W. Semich, Ed.D., Pittsburgh.
Jon Shank, Ed.D., Pittsburgh.
Lawrence A. Tomei, Ed.D., USC.
John A. Zeanchock, Ed.D., Indiana of Pennsylvania.

Social Sciences Faculty
Daniel P. Barr, Ph.D., Kent State.
William R. Beaver, Ph.D., Carnegie Mellon.
Kathryn Dennick-Brecht, Ed.D., Duquesne.
Philip J. Harold, Ph.D., Catholic University.
William E. Kelly, Ph.D., Louisiana Tech.
John M. McCarthy, Ph.D., Marquette.
Stephen T. Paul, Ph.D., Kansas.
David Wheeler, Ph.D., Washington (Seattle).

SCHOOL OF ENGINEERING, MATHEMATICS, AND SCIENCE
Maria V. Kalevitch, Interim Dean; Ph.D., Academy of Sciences (Lithuania).

Engineering Faculty
Sushil Acharya, D.Eng., Asian Institute of Technology (Thailand).
Zbigniew J. Czajkiewicz, Ph.D., Technical (Poland).
John Hayward, Ph.D., Penn State.
Giuseppe (Joe) Iannelli, Ph.D., Tennessee, Knoxville.
Priyadarshan A. Manohar, Ph.D., Wollongong (Australia).
Yildirim Omurtag, Ph.D., Iowa State.
Arif Sirinterlikci, Ph.D., Ohio State.
Murat Tiryakioglu, Ph.D., Missouri–Rolla; Ph.D., Birmingham (England).

Mathematics Faculty
Kai Chen, Ph.D., Waterloo.
Mark A. Ciancutti, Ph.D., Carnegie Mellon.
Renato Clavijo, Ph.D., Arkansas.
E. Gregory Holdan, Ph.D., Penn State.
David G. Hudak, Ph.D., Carnegie Mellon.
Allen R. Lias, Ph.D., Pittsburgh.
Jeffrey J. Mitchell, Ph.D., Cornell.
Andris Niedra, Ph.D., Pittsburgh.
Monica M. VanDieren, Ph.D., Carnegie Mellon.
Charles W. Zimmerman, Ph.D., Ohio State.

Science Faculty
Paul D. Badger, Ph.D., Pittsburgh.
William J. Dress, Ph.D., Ohio State.
Kenneth A. Lasota, Ph.D., Pittsburgh.
Daniel Short, Ph.D., Liverpool (England).

SCHOOL OF NURSING AND HEALTH SCIENCES
Lynda J. Davidson, Dean; Ph.D., Pittsburgh; RN.
Lynn George, Associate Dean; Ph.D., Duquesne; RN.

Nuclear Medicine Faculty
Angela M. Bires, Ed.D., Duquesne.
Donna L. Mason, M.S., Carlow.

Nursing Faculty
Nadine C. Englert, M.S.N., Pittsburgh; RN.
Patricia D. Fedorka, Ph.D., Pittsburgh; RN.
Stephen Foreman, Ph.D., Berkeley.
Valerie M. Howard, Ed.D., Pittsburgh; RN.
Judith A. Kaufmann, Dr.PH., Pittsburgh.
Kirstyn K. Kameg, M.S.N., Pittsburgh; CRNP, RN.
Lisa W. Locasto, M.S.N., Ohio State; RN.
Katherine Perozzi, M.S.N., Pittsburgh; RN.
Carl A. Ross, Ph.D., Duquesne; RN.

R·I·T

ROCHESTER INSTITUTE OF TECHNOLOGY

Graduate Studies

Programs of Study

The Rochester Institute of Technology (RIT) offers graduate programs of study in many areas.

Business, management, and communication programs are available in business administration (M.B.A., executive M.B.A., fast-track M.B.A.); communication and media technologies (M.S.); elements of health-care leadership (advanced certificate); facilities management (M.S.); finance (M.S.); health information resources (advanced certificate); health systems administration (M.S., advanced certificate); health systems finance (advanced certificate); hospitality-tourism management (M.S.), human resource development (M.S., advanced certificate); innovation management (M.S.); management (M.S.); manufacturing leadership (M.S.); product development (M.S.); project management (advanced certificate); science, technology, and public policy (M.S.), senior-living management (advanced certificate); service leadership and innovation (M.S., advanced certificate); strategic training (advanced certificate); and technical information design (advanced certificate).

Computer science and information technology programs are offered in computer science (M.S.), computer security and information assurance (M.S.), computing and information sciences (Ph.D.), game design and development (M.S.), human-computer interaction (M.S.), information assurance (advanced certificate), information technology (M.S.), interactive multimedia development (advanced certificate), learning and knowledge management systems (M.S., advanced certificate), networking and systems administration (M.S.), software development and management (M.S.), and software engineering (M.S.).

Education programs are available in applied experimental and engineering psychology (M.S.), human resource development (M.S.), school psychology (M.S.), secondary education of students who are deaf and hard of hearing (M.S.), and visual arts education (M.S.T.).

Engineering and technology programs are offered in applied experimental and engineering psychology (M.S.); applied statistics (M.S.); computer engineering (M.S.); electrical engineering (M.S.); engineering management (M.E.); environmental, health, and safety management (M.S.); industrial engineering (M.E., M.S.); manufacturing and mechanical systems integration (M.S.); manufacturing leadership (M.S.); materials science and engineering (M.S., advanced certificate); mechanical engineering (M.E., M.S.); microelectronic engineering (M.S.); microelectronics manufacturing engineering (M.E., M.S.); microsystems engineering (Ph.D.); packaging science (M.S.); product development (M.S.); statistical methods for product and process improvement (advanced certificate); statistical quality (advanced certificate); sustainable engineering (M.E., M.S.); systems engineering (M.E., M.S.); telecommunications engineering technology (M.S.); and vibrations engineering (advanced certificate).

Imaging arts programs are available in arts and design (M.F.A.), ceramics and ceramics sculpture (M.F.A.), computer animation and film (M.F.A.), computer graphics design (M.F.A.), cross-disciplinary professional studies (M.S.), fine arts studio (M.F.A.), glass and glass sculpture (M.F.A.), graphic design (M.F.A.), industrial design (M.F.A.), medical illustration (M.F.A.), metalcrafts and jewelry (M.F.A.), nontoxic intaglio printmaking (advanced certificate), photography (M.F.A.), print media (M.S.), and woodworking and furniture design (M.F.A.).

Science, mathematics, and imaging science programs are offered in astrophysical sciences and technology (Ph.D.), bioinformatics (M.S.), chemistry (M.S.), clinical chemistry (M.S.), color science (M.S.), environmental science (M.S.), imaging science (M.S. and Ph.D.), applied mathematics (M.S.), and materials science and engineering (M.S.).

Programs in medical informatics (M.S.) and sustainability (Ph.D.) are under development.

Research Facilities

State-of-the art technology in campus classrooms and laboratories reflects RIT's emphasis on career education. Six computer centers, a microchip-fabricating clean room, dedicated research laboratories, a student-operated restaurant, design studios, and more than 100 photography darkrooms provide students with the facilities they need to investigate and explore their academic fields. Wallace Library is the primary information source on campus, with full electronic access to research and data worldwide. It houses more than 750,000 items, including 350,000 books, 4,700 journals, 3,100 audio recordings, 6,700 film and video recordings, and 410,000 microforms. The online Infonet menu provides 24-hour access to a wide selection of resources, databases, the Internet, and the library's electronic catalog. Some of the nation's leading companies have supported research and teaching facilities that include the $22-million Center for Integrated Manufacturing Studies, the Sloan Printing Industry Center, and the Chester F. Carlson Center for Imaging Science. RIT's state-of-the-art Center for Excellence in Mathematics, Science and Technology showcases innovative teaching efforts using multimedia instructional technology. RIT offers opportunities to apply advanced technology to many areas of graduate study. Printing, design, and photography students merge these creative disciplines in the Electronic Still Photography Lab. Imaging science students analyze the latest in remote sensing capability from an on-campus remote-controlled observatory. Manufacturing management students evaluate production techniques in the manufacturing bays of the Center for Integrated Manufacturing Studies, and hospitality-tourism management students complete projects on their industry-standard SABRE computer system.

Financial Aid

Graduate scholarships and assistantships are available in most graduate departments. In addition, some departments offer externally funded stipends from corporate or government sources. Students should contact the appropriate department chairperson for additional information. Federal, state, and institutional aid are also available to those who qualify. Applicants seeking financial aid should submit the Free Application for Federal Student Aid (FAFSA) to the Office of Financial Aid by March 15 for consideration for entry for the following September.

Cost of Study

In 2008–09, the cost of full-time study (12–18 credit hours) was $10,058 per quarter. The cost of part-time study (11 credit hours or fewer) was $848 per credit hour.

Living and Housing Costs

Housing Operations handles assignments for University-operated residence halls and more than 1,400 campus apartment units. Apartment rents begin at $803 per month for one-bedroom units for the academic year; reduced summer rates are available. In addition, there are several large local apartment complexes and individual living quarters within a short distance of the campus.

Student Group

The total enrollment at the Institute is 16,000. Enrollment in the graduate degree programs is approximately 2,500.

Location

RIT's campus in suburban Rochester occupies 400 acres on a 1,300-acre site and is located close to the cultural and entertainment districts of Rochester. Gallery and museum exhibits, a philharmonic orchestra, and theaters are located in metropolitan Rochester.

The Institute

RIT is accredited by the Middle States Association of Colleges and Schools and the New York State Board of Regents. It is a privately endowed, nonsectarian institution of higher education. RIT has been a pioneer in professional and career development programs since its founding in 1829. Its principal task is preparing men and women with the knowledge, skills, and attitudes required for technological, managerial, and aesthetic competence. It strives to assist them to mature as perceptive, skilled, and incisive professionals. Each graduate program is built as a freestanding unit and is designed to fill a specific demand in a given field. The thrust of the graduate programs is toward state-of-the-art technology and business, the aesthetic areas of the fine arts, photography, printing, and career-oriented programs in communication, school psychology, and public policy. As one of the pioneers of distance learning, RIT has a well-established and growing online learning division, with more than twenty graduate degrees and certificates available online.

Applying

Applicants should hold a bachelor's degree from a regionally accredited university and demonstrate, in the quality of undergraduate record, experience, and/or creative production, a genuine professional potential. Application deadlines vary by program, and applications must include all postsecondary official transcripts and degree certificates, a personal statement, two letters of recommendation, a $50 application fee, and a slide portfolio where applicable. In addition, some programs require GRE or GMAT scores, and a TOEFL or IELTS score is required for students whose native language is not English.

Correspondence and Information

Office of Graduate Enrollment Services
Bausch & Lomb Center, Building 77, Room 1241
Rochester Institute of Technology
58 Lomb Memorial Drive
Rochester, New York 14623-5604

E-mail: gradinfo@rit.edu
Web site: http://www.rit.edu/grad

GRADUATE PROGRAM CONTACTS

Accounting (M.B.A.)
Ms. Rupa Thind (585-475-6916; gradbus@rit.edu)

Applied and Computational Mathematics
Dr. Hossein Shahmohamad (585-475-7564; hxssma@rit.edu)

Applied Experimental and Engineering Psychology
Dr. Kathleen Chen (585-475-2405; kccgss@rit.edu)

Applied Statistics
Dr. Joseph Voelkel (585-475-6990; cqas@rit.edu)

Astrophysical Sciences and Technology
Dr. Christopher O'Dea (585-475-7493; odea@cis.rit.edu)

Bioinformatics
Dr. Gary Skuse (585-475-2532; grssbi@rit.edu)

Business Administration
Ms. Rupa Thind (585-475-6916; gradbus@rit.edu)

Ceramics
Ms. Julia Galloway (585-475-6114; jmgsac@rit.edu)

Chemistry
Dr. Thomas Smith (585-475-7982; twssch@rit.edu)

Clinical Chemistry
Dr. James Aumer (585-475-2526; jcascl@rit.edu)

Color Science (M.S., Ph.D.)
Mr. Mark Fairchild (585-475-2230; mdf@cis.rit.edu)

Communication and Media Technologies
Dr. Rudy Pugliese (585-475-5925; rrpgsl@rit.edu)

Computer Engineering
Dr. Andreas Savakis (585-475-2987; andreas.savakis@rit.edu)

Computer Graphics Design
Mr. Chris Jackson (585-475-5823; cbjpgd@rit.edu)

Computer Science
Dr. Hans-Peter Bischof (585-475-4994; csgradcoord@cs.rit.edu)

Computer Security and Information Assurance
Dr. Charlie Border (585-475-7946; charles.border@rit.edu)

Computing and Information Sciences
Dr. Pengcheng Shi (585-475-6147; phd@gccis.rit.edu)

Electrical Engineering
Dr. Soheil Dianat (585-475-2165; sadeee@rit.edu)

Engineering Management
Dr. Michael Kuhl (585-475-2134; mekeie@rit.edu)

Environmental Science
Dr. Karl Korfmacher (585-475-5554; kfkscl@rit.edu)

Environmental, Health, and Safety Management
Mr. Joseph Rosenbeck (585-475-6469; jmrcem@rit.edu)

Executive M.B.A.
Ms. Donna Scheid (585-475-7935; djsbbu@rit.edu)

Facility Management
Mr. Scott Wolcott (585-475-6647; sbwite@rit.edu)

Film and Animation
Mr. Howard Lester (585-475-2779; helpph@rit.edu)

Finance
Ms. Rupa Thind (585-475-6916; gradbus@rit.edu)

Fine Arts Studio (M.F.A., M.S.T.)
Mr. Tom Lightfood (585-475-2657; trlfad@rit.edu)

Game Design and Development
Ms. Diane Bills (585-475-6179; itgradcoord@it.rit.edu)

Glass
Ms. Robin Cass (585-475-2650; racsac@rit.edu)

Graphic Design
Ms. Deborah Beardslee (585-475-2664; dabfaa@rit.edu)

Health Information Resources
Dr. Linda Underhill (585-475-7359; lmuism@rit.edu)

Health Systems Administration
Dr. Linda Underhill (585-475-7359; lmuism@rit.edu)

Health Systems Finance
Dr. Linda Underhill (585-475-7359; lmuism@rit.edu)

Hospitality-Tourism Management
Dr. James Jacobs (585-475-6017; jwjism@rit.edu)

Human Resource Development
Dr. Linda Underhill (585-475-7359; lmuism@rit.edu)

Human-Computer Interaction
Ms. Dianne P. Bills (585-475-6179; itgradcoord@rit.edu)

Imaging Science (M.S., Ph.D.)
Dr. Joel Kastner (585-475-7179; kastner@cis.rit.edu)

Industrial Design
Mr. David Morgan (585-475-4769; dcmfaa@rit.edu)

Industrial Engineering (M.E., M.S.)
Dr. Michael Kuhl (585-475-2134; mekeie@rit.edu)

Information Assurance
Dr. Charlie Border (585-475-7946; charlie.border@rit.edu)

Information Technology
Ms. Dianne P. Bills (585-475-6179; itgradcoord@it.rit.edu)

Innovation Management
Ms. Rupa Thind (585-475-6916; gradbus@rit.edu)

Interactive Multimedia Development
Ms. Dianne Bills (585-475-6179; itgradcoord@it.rit.edu)

Learning and Knowledge Management System (M.S., Advanced Certificate)
Ms. Dianne Bills (585-475-6179; itgradcoord@it.rit.edu)

Manufacturing and Mechanical Systems Integration
Mr. Manian Ramkumar (585-475-6081; smrmet@rit.edu)

Manufacturing Leadership
Mr. Mark Smith (585-475-7971; mmlmail@rit.edu)

Materials Science and Engineering (M.S., Advanced Certificate)
Dr. K. S. V. Santhanam (585-475-2920; kserch@rit.edu)

Mechanical Engineering (M.E., M.S.)
Dr. Edward Hensel (585-475-2162; echeme@rit.edu)

Medical Illustration
Mr. Donald Arday (585-475-4985; dkafaa@rit.edu)

Metals
Mr. Len Urso (585-475-2654; laufaa@rit.edu)

Microelectronics Engineering
Dr. Santosh Kurinec (585-475-6065; skkemc@rit.edu)

Microelectronics Manufacturing Engineering
Dr. Santosh Kurinec (585-475-6065; skkemc@rit.edu)

Microsystems Engineering
Dr. Mustafa Abushagur (585-475-2295; maaeen@rit.edu)

Networking and Systems Administration
Dr. Charlie Border (585-475-7946; charles.border@rit.edu)

Non-Toxic Intaglio Print Making
Mr. Keith Howard (585-475-2632; howard@mail.rit.edu)

Packaging Science
Ms. Deanna M. Jacobs (585-475-6801; dmjipk@rit.edu)

Photography
Mr. Richard Gray (585-475-2616; rlgpph@rit.edu)

Print Media
Dr. Twyla Cummings (585-475-5567; tjcppr@rit.edu)

Product Development
Ms. Chris Fisher (585-475-7971; mpdmail@rit.edu)

Professional Studies
Ms. Abby Berner (585-475-7297; abby.berner@rit.edu)

Project Management
Ms. Mary Boyd (585-475-2296; mcbcms@rit.edu)

School Psychology
Dr. Scott Merydith (585-475-7980; spmgsp@rit.edu)

Science, Technology, and Public Policy
Dr. Franz Foltz (585-475-5368; mspolicy@rit.edu)

Secondary Education of Deaf or Hard of Hearing
Dr. Gerald Bateman (585-475-6480; gcbnmp@rit.edu)

Senior Living Management
Dr. Linda Underhill (585-475-7359; lmuism@rit.edu)

Service Leadership and Innovation (M.S., Advanced Certificate, Executive Leader)
Dr. James Jacobs (585-475-6017; jwjism@rit.edu)

Software Development and Management
Ms. Dianne P. Bills (585-475-6179; itgradcoord@it.rit.edu)

Software Engineering
Dr. Mark Ardis (585-475-2949; mark.ardis@se.rit.edu)

Statistical Methods for Product and Process Improvement
Dr. Joseph Voelkel (585-475-6990; cqas@rit.edu)

Statistical Quality
Dr. Joseph Voelkel (585-475-6990; cqas@rit.edu)

Strategic Training
Ms. Abby Berner (585-475-7297; abby.berner@rit.edu)

Sustainable Engineering (M.E., M.S.)
Dr. Jaqueline Mozrall (585-475-7142; jrmeie@rit.edu)

Systems Engineering
Dr. Michael Kuhl (585-475-2134; mekeie@rit.edu)

Technical Information Design
Mr. Thomas Moran (585-475-4936; tfmcad@rit.edu)

Telecommunications Engineering Technology
Dr. Warren Koontz (585-475-5706; telecom@cast-fc.rit.edu)

Vibrations Engineering
Dr. Edward Hensel (585-475-2162; echeme@rit.edu)

Visual Arts
Ms. Carole Woodlock (585-475-7562; cmwfaa@rit.edu)

Woodworking and Furniture Design
Mr. Rich Tannen (585-475-2636; rdtfaa@rit.edu)

ROOSEVELT UNIVERSITY

Graduate Division

Programs of Study

The Graduate Division of Roosevelt University currently offers more than fifty graduate programs.

The College of Arts and Sciences offers the following programs: the Master of Arts (M.A.) in clinical psychology, clinical professional psychology, economics, English, history, industrial/organizational psychology, sociology, Spanish, and women's and gender studies; the Master of Fine Arts (M.F.A.) in creative writing; the Master of Public Administration (M.P.A.); the Master of Science (M.S.) in biotechnology and chemical science, computer science, and mathematics/actuarial science; the Master of Science in Journalism (M.S.J.); and the Master of Science in Integrated Marketing Communications (M.S.I.M.C.).

The Walter E. Heller College of Business Administration offers the following programs: Master of Business Administration (M.B.A.), the Master of Science in Accounting (M.S.A.), the Master of Science in Human Resource Management (M.S.H.R.M.), the Master of Science in Information Systems (M.S.I.S.), the Master of Science in International Business (M.S.I.B.), and the Master of Science in Real Estate (M.S.R.E.).

The College of Education offers the following programs: the Master of Arts (M.A.) in counseling and human services, early childhood education, early childhood professions, educational leadership, elementary education, reading, secondary education, special education, and teacher leadership (MATL).

The Evelyn T. Stone College of Professional Studies offers the following programs: the Master of Arts (M.A.) in training and development and the Master of Science in Hospitality and Tourism Management (M.S.H.T.M.).

The Chicago College of Performing Arts offers the following programs: the Master of Music (M.M.) in composition and performance; the Master of Fine Arts (M.F.A.) in acting; and the Master of Arts (M.A.) in directing. Post-master's diplomas are offered in opera, orchestral instruments, orchestral studies, and piano.

In addition, the Graduate Division offers two doctoral degrees: the Doctor of Education (Ed.D.) in educational leadership and the Doctor of Psychology (Psy.D.) in clinical psychology.

Certificate programs are available in biotechnology; business fraud examination; chemical science; clinical child and family studies; geographic information systems; hospitality and tourism management; hospitality education; information systems; information technology and computer science; instructional design; non-profit management; online teaching; paralegal studies; performance consulting; real estate development; relaxation, meditation, and mindfulness; strategic management; training and development; and women's and gender studies.

Research Facilities

The Murray-Green Library holds more than 225,000 volumes and a variety of research materials including microforms and print and electronic journals and reference subscriptions. A full staff is on duty to assist student researchers at the Chicago Campus. Research services and a smaller collection of books are available at the Schaumburg Campus's McCormick-Tribune Foundation Library. Roosevelt University is a member of the Illinois Library Computer Services Organization (ILCSO), which operates a statewide online circulation system embracing forty-five of the largest libraries in Illinois. It is also backed up by the OCLC international bibliographic network and subscribes to numerous online electronic database services.

Financial Aid

Loans, grants, and scholarships are available for qualified students in all programs of the graduate division. Assistantships that pay stipends and carry tuition waivers are offered in most programs. Graduate students may also apply for college work-study. Partial tuition grants are available to qualified students. Many graduate students finance their education through loans or are reimbursed by their employers. Those interested in financial aid should see the Applying section below for deadlines.

Cost of Study

For the College of Arts and Sciences, College of Business Administration, and College of Professional Studies, the 2008–09 tuition was $737 per graduate-semester hour or $14,730 per year for full-time students. Full-time tuition was $13,640 for the College of Education, and $26,125 for the Chicago College of Performing Arts. Fees include a general student fee of $150 per term and, in some programs, laboratory and other nominal fees.

Living and Housing Costs

The state-of-the-art University Center, an eighteen-floor multiuniversity residence hall, opened in 2004. It houses more than 1,700 students among three urban universities. The cost starts at $7692. Full dining services, a fitness center, and rooftop garden are features of the University Center. Roosevelt on Washington (ROW) in Fornelli Hall offers contemporary apartments with kitchenettes for upperclass undergraduate and graduate students starting at $9400. The cost of living in Chicago is about the same as in most other major cities. Chicago offers many job opportunities, myriad inexpensive services and activities, and a wide choice of living quarters at a variety of rental levels.

Student Group

More than 3,000 full-time and part-time graduate students attend classes at Roosevelt. Students of varied multiracial and ethnic backgrounds and ages from many states and more than twenty-five other countries pursue graduate studies at the University. Most work part-time or full-time and find Roosevelt's flexible class schedules well suited to their schedules. The University's total enrollment of both undergraduate and graduate students is approximately 7,700.

Location

Roosevelt University has two campuses. The Chicago Campus is in the heart of the downtown and is accessible by car or public transportation. Students can take advantage of the many events and activities in the city. The Albert A. Robin Campus is located in northwest suburban Schaumburg, approximately 30 miles from downtown Chicago. The University shuttle service provides daily transport to convenient public transportation so students and faculty and staff members can travel between campuses. In addition to the two campus locations, Roosevelt is continually expanding its course offerings through partnerships with community colleges and corporations and through its Internet-based RU Online program. Currently, the Master of Arts in Teacher Leadership (M.A.T.L.) and the Master of Arts in Training and Development (M.A.T.D.) are available in fully online formats as well as on campus.

The University

Roosevelt University's mission is to educate socially conscious citizens for active and dedicated lives as leaders in their professions and their communities. From its founding as a private university in 1945, Roosevelt pioneered the education of adult and nontraditional students, creating a diverse learning environment for all students, with an emphasis on social justice. Today, its educational programs are recognized nationwide, and students from all races and ethnicities throughout metropolitan Chicago and from around the world pursue degrees at its two campuses. Roosevelt's characteristics provide a number of graduate educational benefits: small classes that encourage an open exchange of ideas, outstanding faculty, excellent academic programs, scheduling flexibility to accommodate working students, and counseling and career planning services.

The Office of Career Services provides opportunities for students to engage in career exploration, career planning, internship experiences, and recruitment programs with major corporations and organizations. Students are able to meet one-on-one with career counselors for individualized sessions in order to clarify their majors; assess their interests, skills, and values; engage in job searches; review resumes and cover letters; participate in mock interviews; and connect with internship and employment opportunities. A number of the office's resources are online, including a job and resume posting system, career education tools, a career resource library, and job development assessments.

Applying

Application for graduate study may be made to the Office of Graduate Admission on either campus or online. Applicants are urged to file their application one semester before the semester in which they plan to enroll; however, the doctoral programs and a few master's programs have earlier deadlines. Most priority deadlines for applications for admission are March 31 for the fall semester, December 1 for the spring semester, and April 15 for the summer terms. The priority application deadline for assistantships is March 31 for the following year, and for some scholarships, the priority deadline is March 31 for fall and October 15 for spring. There is a $25 fee for domestic applications and $35 for international applications. International students must apply at least three months prior to the intended semester, leaving additional time for visas.

Correspondence and Information

Chicago Campus Office of Admission
Roosevelt University
430 S. Michigan Ave.
Chicago, Illinois 60605
Phone: 877-APPLY-RU (877-277-5978) (toll-free)
Fax: 312-341-3523
E-mail: gradadmission@roosevelt.edu
Web site: http://www.roosevelt.edu

Schaumburg Campus Office of Admission
Roosevelt University
1400 N. Roosevelt Blvd.
Schaumburg, Illinois 60173
Phone: 877-APPLY-RU (877-277-5978) (toll-free)
Fax: 847-619-8636
E-mail: gradadmission@roosevelt.edu
Web site: http://www.roosevelt.edu

GRADUATE PROGRAM DIRECTORS

Biotechnology and Chemical Science: Cornelius Watson, Ph.D., Wesleyan. (cwatson@roosevelt.edu)
Business Graduate Programs (Interdepartmental): Connie Wells, Ph.D., Minnesota. (cwells@roosevelt.edu)
Computer Science and Telecommunications: Ken Mihavics, Ph.D., Illinois. (kmihavic@roosevelt.edu)
Counseling and Human Services: Roberto Clemente, Ph.D., Oregon State. (rclemente@roosevelt.edu)
Creative Writing: Scott Blackwood, M.F.A., Texas State. (sblackwood@roosevelt.edu)
Early Childhood Education: Lynne Firsel, Ed.D., Virginia. (lfirsel@roosevelt.edu)
Economics: June Lapidus, Ph.D., Massachusetts Amherst. (jlapidus@roosevelt.edu)
Educational Leadership (M.A.): Susan J. Katz, Ph.D., Indiana State. (skatz@roosevelt.edu)
Educational Leadership (Ed.D.): Susan J. Katz, Ph.D., Indiana State. (skatz@roosevelt.edu)
Education/Teacher Leadership (M.A.T.L.): Daniel White, Ph.D., Syracuse. (dlwhite@roosevelt.edu)
Elementary Education: Ken King, Ed.D., Northern Illinois. (kking@roosevelt.edu)
English: Bonnie Gunzenhauser, Ph.D., Chicago. (bgunzenhauser@roosevelt.edu)
History: Chris Chulos, Ph.D., Chicago. (cchulos@roosevelt.edu)
Hospitality and Tourism Management: Gerald Bober, Ed.D., Northern Illinois. (gbober@roosevelt.edu)
Integrated Marketing Communications: Lee Earle, M.S., Syracuse. (learle@roosevelt.edu)
Journalism: Linda Jones, M.S., Northwestern. (ljones@roosevelt.edu)
Language and Literacy: Margaret Policastro, Ph.D., Northwestern. (mpolicas@roosevelt.edu)
Mathematics: Steve Cohen, Ph.D., Illinois at Chicago. (scohen@roosevelt.edu)
Music Conservatory: Linda Berna, Ph.D., Northwestern. (lberna@roosevelt.edu)
Psychology (M.A.): James Choca, Ph.D., Loyola Chicago. (jchoca@roosevelt.edu)
Psychology (Psy.D): Steven A. Kvaal, Ph.D., Ohio. (skvaal@roosevelt.edu)
Public Administration: Jeff Edwards, Ph.D., Minnesota. (jedwards@roosevelt.edu)
Secondary Education: Linda Pincham, Ed.D., Virginia Tech. (lpincham@roosevelt.edu)
Sociology: Mike Maly, Ph.D., Loyola Chicago. (mmaly@roosevelt.edu)
Spanish: Priscilla Archibald, Ph.D., Stanford. (parchibald@roosevelt.edu)
Special Education: Sharon Grant, Ph.D., Illinois at Chicago. (sgrant@roosevelt.edu)
Theater Conservatory: Joel Fink, D.A., NYU; SEHNAP. (jfink@roosevelt.edu)
Training and Development: George Vukotich, Ph.D., Loyola Chicago. (gvukotich@roosevelt.edu)
Women's and Gender Studies: Ann Brigham, Ph.D., Arizona. (abrigham@roosevelt.edu)

The Murray-Green Library, located at the downtown campus, offers panoramic views of Lake Michigan.

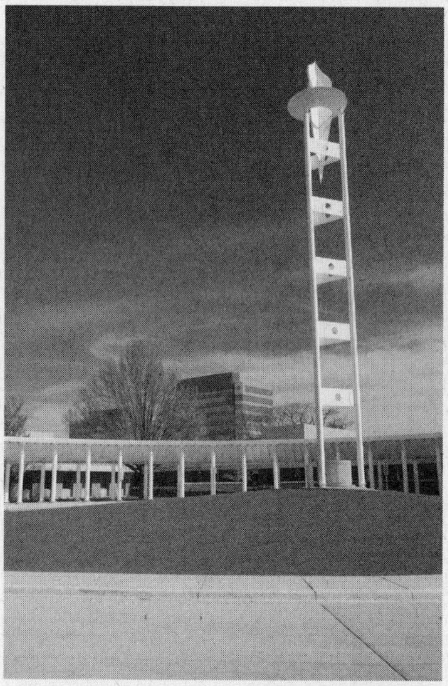

The Albert A. Robin Campus in Schaumburg is architecturally modern with a horizontal profile that encompasses 225,000 square feet and complements the suburban landscape.

The historic Auditorium Building that overlooks Grant Park and Lake Michigan is the center of the Chicago Campus.

ROSEMONT COLLEGE

Schools of Graduate and Professional Studies

Programs of Study

Rosemont College's Schools of Graduate and Professional Studies (SGPS) offer accelerated undergraduate bachelor of science degrees in criminal justice, management, marketing, human resource management, and accounting. Bachelor of arts degrees are available in organizational development and business communication. Graduate degrees are also conferred, including master of arts degrees in counseling psychology, English literature, English and publishing, and curriculum and instruction, as well as a Master of Fine Arts degree in creative writing, a Master of Science in Management, and a Master of Business Administration.

Students may pursue their graduate studies on a full-time or part-time basis. Summer sessions are offered for all programs. Rosemont also offers a fully online Bachelor of Science in Management degree and a fully online Master of Business Administration degree. For more information on all programs, students should visit the College's Web site at http://www.rosemont.edu/gps2.

Research Facilities

The Gertrude Kistler Memorial Library was the first academic building erected on the campus. It houses more than 170,000 volumes, approximately 563 current periodicals, and numerous electronic indexes and databases as well as access to the Internet. The Library also houses a 10,000-volume collection of children's literature. The online catalog, the Rosemont Electronic Learning and Library System (TRELLIS), is the basic index to the library's collections. TRELLIS includes a number of computerized periodical indexes and encyclopedias and provides access to the Internet's World Wide Web.

Financial Aid

Students are eligible to apply for tuition assistance in the form of Federal Stafford Student Loans if they are matriculated in a degree-granting program of study and are enrolled in at least half-time course work (two courses in the fall or spring; one course in each summer session). A limited number of competitive graduate assistantships are also available. Rosemont offers a tuition management option, so students can spread their payments out over the course of their program.

Rosemont College also offers a unique fellowship program that is truly one-of-a-kind in the Philadelphia region. For students beginning a new program in SGPS on or after April, 2009, the Rosemont College Fellowship Program will offer every new student their first course at no cost. Rosemont will also pay for transcripts and for costs of application. In addition, for students who enroll and stay enrolled in at least one course in the fall, one in the spring, and one in the summer per academic year, the comprehensive tuition (which includes all fees and educational charges) will never increase. Rosemont also promises each new student who stays enrolled a fellowship equivalent to 15% of comprehensive tuition on the second third of their degree and a 30% comprehensive tuition fellowship on the last third of their degree.

Cost of Study

Tuition for 2009–10 is $650 per credit hour for all graduate programs and $530 per credit hour for all undergraduate programs.

Living and Housing Costs

On-campus housing is not available for graduate and professional students; however, meal ticket options are available.

Student Group

The Schools of Graduate and Professional Studies serve working professional men and women in their mid-twenties to their mid-fifties. Total enrollment for the Schools is approximately 1,000 students.

Student Outcomes

Students who complete the education programs are employed in public and private schools as teachers, curriculum developers, staff developers, supervisors, counselors, and administrators. English literature and publishing graduates work in publishing houses or in organizations that require professionals who are skilled in publishing. English and creative writing program graduates teach at all levels; they also use their writing skills as entrepreneurs or in businesses that value employees with strong liberal arts backgrounds. Graduates in counseling psychology provide direct client services in schools, mental health centers, hospitals, social service agencies, the criminal justice system, and day treatment centers. Graduates of the business and management programs are employed by various private, public, and nonprofit organizations; corporations; and businesses in the local, regional, national, and international arenas.

Location

Rosemont College is located in Rosemont, Pennsylvania, one of several side-by-side college towns nestled among Philadelphia's historic Main Line suburbs. The College is easily accessible by car, train, or bus. Rosemont is ideally located within a 2-hour radius of New Jersey shore points, Longwood Gardens, the Pocono Mountains, New York City, Baltimore, and Washington, D.C.

The College

Rosemont College is located in suburban Philadelphia and has been educating adult learners for over twenty years. As a community dedicated to educating men and women, SGPS offers students advanced curricula, personalized attention, and practical internship experiences.

Recognizing that graduate students are busy adults, with many commitments in their lives, Rosemont's course scheduling is flexible and adaptable. Classes meet in the evening, on weekends, and online throughout the calendar year. Rosemont's classes are small and the staff's approach is personal—students will never be just a number.

Faculty members are dedicated practitioners who combine real-world expertise with a sincere dedication to teaching and believe that students more readily acquire meaningful skills and knowledge when they are actively involved in the learning process through research, guided discussion, and seminars.

Rosemont academic programs are exceptional and prepare adult learners to meet the demands of today's workplace. Rosemont is accredited by the Middle States Association of Colleges and Schools.

Applying

Applications for admission to all programs are reviewed throughout the year. No standardized test scores are required. The application fee is $50; this fee is waived for online applications.

Correspondence and Information

Schools of Graduate and Professional Studies
Rosemont College
1400 Montgomery Avenue
Rosemont, Pennsylvania 19010

Phone: 610-527-0200 Ext. 2213
888-2ROSEMONT (toll-free)
Fax: 610-526-2964
E-mail: admissions@rosemont.edu
Web site: http://www.rosemont.edu/gps2

FACULTY HEADS AND PROGRAM DIRECTORS

Rosemont College's faculty members are dedicated academicians and practitioners with a genuine commitment to teaching at the graduate level. For more information on the entire faculty, students should visit the College's Web site at http://www.rosemont.edu/gps2.

Liz Corcoran, Director, English Literature and Creative Writing.
Ann S. Hartsock, Director, Curriculum and Instruction.
James Kerns, Director, Criminal Justice.
Kenneth Robinson, Director, Undergraduate Accelerated Business.
Michelle Rosen, Director, English and Publishing.
Leslie Smith, Director, Counseling and Psychology.
Joan Wilder, Director, Graduate Accelerated Business.

RUTGERS, THE STATE UNIVERSITY OF NEW JERSEY, NEWARK

Graduate School

Programs of Study

The Graduate School–Newark offers programs of study leading to a Doctor of Philosophy degree in American studies, biology*, chemistry, criminal justice, environmental science*, global affairs, management*, mathematical sciences*, integrative neuroscience, nursing, physics (applied)*, psychology, public administration, and urban systems. It offers programs leading to a master's degree in American studies, biology*, chemistry, computational biology*, economics, English, environmental geology, environmental science*, fine arts, global affairs, history*, jazz history and research, liberal studies, nursing, physics (applied)*, and political science. The asterisks indicate joint/collaborative programs with NJIT and/or UMDNJ.

Other graduate programs available on the Rutgers–Newark campus are master's programs in criminal justice, public affairs and administration, public health, government accounting, management, professional accounting, and taxation and a J.D. degree through the School of Law. In general, doctoral students must satisfy the course requirements of their area of concentration, pass comprehensive examinations, present their research in an acceptable dissertation, and defend the dissertation in a public examination. Master's students pursue a course of study and must pass a comprehensive examination. While the master's thesis is an option in most programs, in some it is required. Specific requirements for both the doctoral and master's students are determined by the faculty of each program; additional information about these requirements should be obtained from the appropriate program director.

Opportunities for postdoctoral work are available in behavioral and neural sciences, biology, chemistry, and psychology. These programs also offer collaborative research opportunities for visiting scientists.

Research Facilities

Scientific laboratories feature scanning and transmission electron microscopes, a confocal microscope, an automated DNA sequencer, ultracentrifuges, a phosphorimager, scintillation and gamma counters, a solid-phase peptide synthesizer, AVIV circular dichroism spectrophotometer, a time-correlated single photon counting instrument, fluorescence spectrometer, UV-VIS NIR spectrometer, 20-MeV electron accelerator, excimer-isotopic carbon dioxide and semiconductor lasers, Auger spectrometer, quadrupole mass spectrometer, Allegra 3-Tesla functional magnetic resonance imaging instrument, and much more.

Financial Aid

In 2009–10 University teaching assistantships provide a beginning annual salary of $23,112, remission of tuition, and other benefits. Fellowships and internships supported by federal, state, private, and University funds provide annual stipends of up to $18,000 and generally offer tuition remission. Program directors can provide information about support in their respective programs.

Cost of Study

In 2009–10, per-credit tuition (1–11.5 credits) for New Jersey residents is $577 per semester. Twelve credits or more for New Jersey residents is $6924 per semester. Nonresident per-credit tuition (1–11.5 credits) is $886 per semester. Twelve credits or more for nonresidents is $10,632 per semester. The full-time college fee (9 credits or more) is $600 per semester. The part-time college fee (fewer than 9 credits) is $187 per semester. The full-time computer fee is $141.50 per semester, and the part-time computer fee ranges from $59 to $111.50, based on credit hours.

Living and Housing Costs

Housing for graduate students is available in University-operated, furnished single-room apartments. The housing fee for the 2009–10 academic year (September 1 through about May 15) is $7703; for the calendar year (September 1 through about August 15), it is $9209.

Student Group

The University's total enrollment is approximately 47,000 students, of whom 10,785 are in the nine schools and colleges on the Newark campus. The Graduate School–Newark enrolls approximately 1,300 students.

Location

The Rutgers–Newark campus is conveniently located in the center of a diverse and thriving educational, professional, and cultural community in the downtown area of New Jersey's largest city. Located just a few minutes from the Newark campus, the New Jersey Performing Arts Center is a major cultural venue for the greater New York and Newark metropolitan areas and has restored Newark's historic role as the center for arts and culture in New Jersey. Because of its central location, Rutgers–Newark is accessible to a number of major metropolitan areas. New York City can be reached within 20 minutes by train, Philadelphia within an hour by train, and Washington, D.C., within an hour by plane.

The University

Rutgers, The State University of New Jersey, was chartered in 1766 as Queen's College, the eighth institution of higher learning to be founded in the Colonies before the Revolutionary War. Queen's College opened its doors in New Brunswick in 1771 with one instructor and a handful of students. In 1825 the name of the college was changed to Rutgers to honor the former trustee and Revolutionary War veteran Col. Henry Rutgers. Rutgers College became the land-grant institution of New Jersey in 1864 and, almost 100 years later, after a period of phenomenal growth, was designated the State University of New Jersey in 1945. The University's Newark campus was created in 1946 when the University of Newark became part of Rutgers. The Graduate School–Newark was established in 1974. In addition to the Graduate School, Rutgers in Newark includes the College of Arts and Sciences, the College of Nursing, the Rutgers Business School, the School of Criminal Justice, the School of Law, the School of Public Affairs and Administration, and University College.

Applying

Applications may be downloaded from http://www.gradstudy.rutgers.edu or applicants may apply online. The application fee is $65. All programs, except the program in management, require that applicants submit scores on the General Test of the Graduate Record Examinations (GRE); the management program requires scores on the Graduate Management Admission Test (GMAT). Programs in biology, chemistry, and psychology require scores on a GRE Subject Test as well as on the GRE General Test. International students and students whose native language is not English must provide scores on the Test of English as a Foreign Language (TOEFL).

By law and by purpose, Rutgers, The State University of New Jersey, is dedicated to serve all people on an equal and nondiscriminatory basis.

Correspondence and Information

Office of Graduate and Professional Admission
Rutgers, The State University of New Jersey
249 University Avenue
Newark, New Jersey 07102

Phone: 973-353-5205
Web site: http://gradstudy.rutgers.edu

Program Director (specify)
Rutgers, The State University of New Jersey
University Heights
Newark, New Jersey 07102

Web site: http://gsn.newark.rutgers.edu

PROGRAM DIRECTORS

Dr. Gary Roth, Dean of the Graduate School and Vice Chancellor for Academic Programs and Services; Dr. Barry R. Komisaruk, Associate Dean (973-353-5834); Clara G. Bautista, Assistant Dean (973-353-5456); Adriana Afonso, Business Specialist (973-353-5197); and Virgen Reyes, Program Coordinator (973-353-5834; http://gsn.newark.rutgers.edu).

American Studies (M.A., Ph.D.): Dr. Robert Snyder (973-353-5119). Newly established program to train students to become knowledgeable and productive scholars in a wide variety of academic, cultural, and public institutions. The doctoral program's Academic Profession track and Public Scholarship track each require 72 credits of course work and research, including core courses in the theory of American studies, substantial work in at least two of the six interdisciplinary fields of specialization, and the preparation of a dissertation. The master's program requires 24 course credits and 6 thesis credits. (http://americanstudies.newark.rutgers.edu/index.htm)

Biology (M.S., Ph.D.): Dr. Edward Bonder (973-353-1047). Research in neuroimmunology, cytoskeleton, signal transduction in animals and plants, computational neurobiology, molecular evolution, marine biology, environmental toxicology, and the parasitology of AIDS. Facilities are available for sophisticated techniques in molecular biology and biochemistry, microbial ecology, microscopic imaging, electron microscopy, woody plant physiology and development, and cell and tissue culture. (http://newarkbioweb.rutgers.edu/department/index.html)

Chemistry (M.S., Ph.D.): Dr. Frank Jordan (973-353-5470). M.S. and Ph.D. degrees are offered on both a part-time and full-time basis in all major divisions of chemistry, including organic, inorganic, analytical, and physical chemistry and biochemistry. (http://chemistry.rutgers.edu)

Computational Biology (M.S.): Dr. Michael Recce, NJIT (973-596-5535). Joint program offered by NJIT and Rutgers–Newark to address the need for personnel trained in both computer and biological sciences. Applicants with a background in either area gain expertise in the other, as well as take core courses that provide an understanding of computational biology. Areas of specialization are genomics, molecular modeling and drug discovery, computational neuroscience, biostatistics, and physiology. (http://catalog.njit.edu/graduate/programs/computationalbiology.php)

Creative Writing (M.A.): Dr. Jayne Anne Phillips (973-353-1194). Newly established 48-credit studio/research program. The program focuses strongly on 20 credit hours of a writing workshop in a declared genre and requires 7 thesis hours in which students work one-on-one with their mentor professors. Also requires 21 credit hours of graduate courses in literature. (http://mfa.newark.rutgers.edu/abouttheprogram.htm)

Criminal Justice (M.A., Ph.D.): Dr. James Finckenauer (973-353-3301). Research: criminal justice theory, policy, and planning; situational crime prevention; community supervision of offenders; sentencing theory; violence; youth gangs; substance abuse and aggression; juvenile justice; organized crime; law and criminal justice; prosecution and the courts; comparative systems; maritime crime; policing; globalization of crime; business and crime. (http://www.newark.rutgers.edu/rscj/)

Economics (M.A.): Dr. Jason Barr (973-353-5835). Research: transportation safety, financial markets and bubbles, decline of labor unions, household economics, gender differences in the labor market, school choice programs, real estate markets, alcohol and drug use among teenagers, foreign direct investment and the economic transformation of Eastern Europe. (http://andromeda.rutgers.edu/~econnwk/mastersprogram.htm)

English (M.A.): Dr. Janet Larson (973-353-5193). Research: medieval, Renaissance, and eighteenth-century literature; Romanticism; Victorian literature; nineteenth- and twentieth-century American and British literature; modernism; contemporary literature; Marxist, postcolonial, and feminist criticism; literature and technology; African American literature. (http://english-newark.rutgers.edu/)

Environmental Geology (M.S.): Dr. Alec Gates (973-353-5034). A collaborative program with Rutgers–New Brunswick and NJIT. Research: structural geology, radon, aqueous geochemistry, hydrogeology, stratigraphy, applied geophysics, mineralogy, and petrology. (http://geology.newark.rutgers.edu/MSGraduate.php)

Environmental Science (M.S., Ph.D.): Dr. Alexander Gates (973-353-5034). Joint M.S. and Ph.D. program with NJIT. Chemical engineering, coastal processes, ecology, environmental chemistry, environmental engineering, geochemistry, geology, geophysics, and microbiology with emphasis on urban problems. (http://geology.newark.rutgers.edu/MSGraduate.php; http://geology.newark.rutgers.edu/PhDGraduate.php)

Global Affairs (M.S., Ph.D.): Dr. Carlos Seiglie (973-353-5914). Offerings include an M.S. and a Ph.D. in global affairs. Programs are interdisciplinary, drawing on political science, history, economics, law, business, sociology, and anthropology to study the relationship between globalization and emerging forms of global governance. (http://dga.rutgers.edu/academics.html)

History (M.A., M.A.T.): Dr. Gary Farney (973-353-3897). Joint M.A. and M.A.T. degrees offered with NJIT. American social, cultural, political, intellectual, legal, and diplomatic history; African-American history and the history of women; history of technology, the environment, medicine, and public health; European and American political culture; European history and the histories of Asia, Africa, Latin America, and the Near and Middle East; world history and comparative economic development. (http://history.newark.rutgers.edu/)

Integrative Neuroscience (Ph.D.): Dr. Ian Creese, Rutgers–Newark (973-353-3608 or 3380). Joint program with Rutgers–Newark and UMDNJ. The program offers specific research training in behavioral and cognitive neuroscience and molecular, cellular, clinical, and systems neuroscience. Research studies can emphasize either human, animal, or computational approaches. (http://ins.rutgers.edu)

Jazz History and Research (M.A.): Dr. Lewis Porter (973-353-5119). This unique program prepares students to do research, publishing, and teaching by relying on the renowned Institute of Jazz Studies, the largest jazz library in the world. The required twelve courses focus on historiography and research, including transcribing, musical analysis, archival research, and interviewing. Applicants are required to have bachelor's degree in any field and basic competence in playing and reading music. (http://gsn.newark.rutgers.edu/jazz/index.htm)

Liberal Studies (M.A.L.S.): Dr. Barry R. Komisaruk, Acting Director (973-353-5834). Conceptual and historical aspects of ethology; social theory; myth, drama, contemporary fiction, and film; bureaucracy; science and technology policy; poetry and criticism; history of philosophy; women's studies; ethics, philosophy of mind, and philosophy of religion; aesthetics; history of ideas from antiquity to the twenty-first century. (http://gsn.newark.rutgers.edu/liberal/index.htm)

Management (Ph.D.): Dr. Glenn R. Shafer (973-353-1604). Research and doctoral training with majors possible in accounting, information systems, international business, finance, management science, and organization management. There are three majors in information systems: accounting information systems, computer information systems, and information technology. (http://business.rutgers.edu/default.aspx?id=107)

Mathematical Sciences (Ph.D.): Dr. Zhengyu Mao (973-353-3907). Joint program with NJIT. Research: low-dimensional topology, geometric group theory, Riemann surfaces, number theory, algebraic geometry, differential topology, representation theory, automorphic forms, harmonic analysis, Teichmuller theory. (http://andromeda.rutgers.edu/~mathcs/GradProg.html)

M.D./Ph.D.: Graduate School-Newark (973-353-5834). Seven-year program leading to the M.D. from the New Jersey Medical School (NJMS)–University of Medicine and Dentistry of New Jersey (UMDNJ) and the Ph.D. from Rutgers–Newark. Students take two years of biomedical courses at NJMS, then conduct research at Rutgers–Newark for three years, and then return to NJMS for two years of clinical training. Students apply to both institutions simultaneously. Full tuition waiver plus annual salary support. Minority students encouraged to apply. (http://gsn.newark.rutgers.edu/md_phd/index.htm)

Nursing (M.S., Ph.D.): Dr. Mary Ann D. Scoloveno (973-353-3831). Research: care and health promotion of children, adolescents, and adults/aged; symptom management in HIV/AIDS, congestive heart failure, and renal failure; pain control alternatives and exercise in hypertension; quality-of-life issues for women in menopause and with breast cancer and persons with multiple sclerosis and surgeries that change appearance; sleep patterns of hospitalized cardiac patients; patient-care outcomes in vulnerable populations; and high-tech home care. (http://nursing.rutgers.edu/prospective_students/academic_programs)

Physics (Applied; M.S., Ph.D.): Dr. Martin Schaden, Rutgers–Newark (973-353-5091). Joint program offered by Rutgers–Newark and NJIT. Research: applied optics, ultrafast optical phenomena, solid-state physics–microelectronics, molecular beam epitaxy (MBE), materials science, free-electron laser, surface science, biophysics, astrophysics, plasma physics, laser spectroscopy, quantum electronics. (http://andromeda/rutgers.edu/~physics/index.htm)

Political Science (M.A.): Dr. Mara Sidney (973-353-5787). International relations theory, public administration and bureaucracy, environmental politics and policy, policy formation and process evaluation, immigration policy, religion and politics, American human rights policy, generational ethnicity, ethics and international relations, gender and politics, international political economy. (http://politicalscience.newark.rutgers.edu/)

Psychology (Ph.D.): Dr. Kenneth Kressel (973-353-3961). Graduate training and research focusing on basic issues in cognitive and behavioral sciences, with concentrations in the areas of perception, attention, visual cognition, language, cognitive neuroscience, cognitive and perceptual development, social psychology, connectionist modeling, learning and memory, emotion, hormones and behavior, adaptive behavior, and computational neuroimaging. (http://www.psych.rutgers.edu/)

Public Administration (Ph.D.): Dr. Judy Kirchhoff (973-353-1351). The goal of the program is to train and educate public sector leaders, researchers, and educators. Areas of concentration in the doctoral program include productive public management, policy analysis, urban systems, and comparative public management, policy analysis, urban systems, and comparative public management and global governance. (http://spaa.newark.rutgers.edu/)

Public Health (M.P.H.): Dr. Evan Stark (973-353-5253). Joint master's program offered by UMDNJ School of Public Health, NJIT, and Rutgers–Newark, in collaboration with the Public Health Research Institute. The program prepares students to work with communities to identify and assess health needs and problems, plan and implement solutions, monitor progress, and evaluate program outcomes. Specialty tracks are urban and environmental health, quantitative methods: biostatistics and epidemiology, and health policy and administration. All courses are offered in the late afternoon or evening. (http://sph.umdnj.edu/)

Urban Systems (Ph.D.): Dr. Karen A. Franck, NJIT (973-596-3092); Dr. Alan Sadovnik, Rutgers–Newark Urban Education Policy Coordinator (973-353-3532). Joint program offered by NJIT, UMDNJ, and Rutgers–Newark. The program is designed to prepare students to develop research-based knowledge in urban systems and to participate in the development, implementation, and evaluation of policy and services for urban populations. (http://www.umdnj.edu/urbsyweb/)

Women's and Gender Studies (Graduate Concentration): Dr. Laura Lomas (973-353-1027). This four-course concentration can be taken through the programs in English, global affairs, history, liberal studies, political science, or public administration. (http://womenstudies.newark.rutgers.edu/index.html)

SAINT LOUIS UNIVERSITY

Graduate School

Programs of Study

The Graduate School offers more than forty programs of advanced study in a learning environment that fosters critical reflection, intellectual exchange, and personal health and provides the latest learning technologies, including wireless access throughout campus. In addition to the degree programs, certificates may be pursued in anatomical and physiological studies, biosecurity and disaster preparedness, descriptive ethics, higher education administration with emphasis on the community college, rhetorical studies/writing pedagogy, Renaissance studies, women's studies, university teaching skills, geographic information systems, organizational development, and health-care ethics. Post-master's certificates are available in marriage and family therapy and in a variety of nursing specialties. Opportunities for dual-degree programs that facilitate simultaneous training in one of the University's professional schools (e.g., business, law, medicine, nursing, psychology, or social work) also are available.

Research Facilities

Research is a large part of the Saint Louis University (SLU) experience. Per the Carnegie Foundation rankings and listings, SLU is a research-extensive university with high research activity. SLU is one of a handful of Catholic universities in the United States to achieve this designation. In 2008, the Medical Center received grants totaling $57.6 million. This includes funding from numerous governmental sources, such as the National Institutes of Health, National Science Foundation, Centers for Disease Control and Prevention, and private industry associations and foundations. Researchers in areas outside medicine received grants totaling $5.8 million, approximately 80 percent of which support graduate students in a research role. The new Doisy Research Center, at ten stories, 206,000 square feet, and $82 million, stands as a testament to SLU's commitment to use research to combat human suffering caused by disease.

The University's three libraries hold more than 2 million volumes and provide access to more than 40,000 electronic resources including databases, journals, and e-books. Through Saint Louis University's participation in the Online Computer Library Center, users have bibliographic access to more than 45 million titles in sixty-two countries in virtually any language. Special collections include 35 million pages of Vatican manuscripts and extensive theological holdings. The University is a member of the Center for Research Libraries (Chicago), and students also have access to the libraries of the University of Missouri and Washington University in St. Louis. Computer centers and research offices are staffed throughout the campus. The University's urban location has allowed the development of unique research opportunities with numerous public and private agencies and corporations.

Financial Aid

Financial assistance is available to qualified graduate students. Fellowships and teaching, research, and administrative assistantships are awarded in most fields of study; full-tuition scholarships accompany stipends in many instances. Assistantships and fellowships are awarded through individual departments. Federal and state (Missouri) grants and loans and Federal Work-Study Program eligibility may be sought through the University's Office of Student Financial Services; a formal application and the need analysis are mandatory.

Cost of Study

The cost was $885 per Graduate School credit hour for the 2008–09 academic year.

Living and Housing Costs

Multiple options for off-campus living are available. Many apartments directly border SLU or are located within a short distance of the campus. SLU's surrounding neighborhoods offer a wide range of housing options and amenities, including the new downtown loft district. St. Louis County is within 10 miles of the campus and offers alternatives to city living.

Student Group

Of the 12,733 students attending Saint Louis University, 3,210 are students in the Graduate School pursuing advanced degrees. According to a pregraduation survey, students rate their satisfaction with the quality of an SLU education at 4.4 on a 5-point scale.

Location

Located in the heart of Midtown St. Louis, SLU is an ideal urban learning center. The 235-acre campus houses 127 buildings and visitors often say it is one of the most attractive urban campuses in the country. The city of St. Louis and Saint Louis University have a long-standing commitment to each other's vitality and quality of life. The city offers a wide variety of urban entertainment and commerce. Housing, recreation, athletics, and public transportation are all within easy reach of campus.

The University

Saint Louis University is a Jesuit, Catholic university ranked among the top research institutions in the nation. The University fosters the intellectual and leadership development of more than 12,000 students on campuses in St. Louis and Madrid, Spain. Founded in 1818, it is the oldest university west of the Mississippi and the second-oldest Jesuit university in the United States. The University's first graduate degree was awarded in 1834. Through teaching, research, health care, and community service, Saint Louis University is the place where knowledge touches lives. Prospective students can find more information at the University's Web site (http://graduate.slu.edu).

U.S. News & World Report ranks the Ph.D. program in clinical psychology among the top 100 in the country for 2009. Ph.D. programs in biology and history also rank among the nation's best. *Diverse: Issues in Higher Education* ranked SLU twenty-third in the number of doctoral degrees granted to African Americans in psychology.

Applying

Application forms for admission can be obtained from the Graduate School Admissions Office or online at http://graduate.slu.edu. General application deadlines are April 1 for the summer session, July 1 for the fall semester, and November 1 for the spring semester. February 1 is the deadline for applications to be considered for fellowships and is the recommended deadline for assistantship applications. Forms for need-based assistance can be obtained from the Office of Student Financial Services or online at http://www.slu.edu/x21861.xml.

International applicants are required to submit an official TOEFL score or other acceptable proof of English proficiency.

Correspondence and Information

Graduate School Admissions
Saint Louis University
3634 Lindell Boulevard
Verhaegen Hall, Room 117
St. Louis, Missouri 63108
Phone: 314-977-2240
800-SLU-FOR-U (toll-free)
E-mail: gradadm@slu.edu
Web site: http://graduate.slu.edu

Office of Student Financial Services
Saint Louis University
221 North Grand Boulevard
DuBourg Hall, Room 121
St. Louis, Missouri 63103-2907
Phone: 314-977-2350
800-SLU-FOR-U (toll-free)
Web site: http://www.slu.edu/x21861.xml

GRADUATE PROGRAMS BY MAJOR AND CONTACT INFORMATION

American Studies: M.A., M.A.(R), Ph.D.; Dr. Matthew Mancini (heathcje@slu.edu; 314-977-2911).
Anatomy: M.S.(R), Ph.D. certificate; Dr. Daniel Tolbert (anatomy@slu.edu; 314-977-8035).
Biochemistry and Molecular Biology: Ph.D.; Dr. William Sly (biochem@slu.edu; 314-977-9200).
Biology: M.S., M.S.(R), Ph.D.; Dr. Rob Wood (biology@slu.edu; 314-977-3904).
Biomedical Engineering: M.S., M.S.(R); David W. Barnett (biomed@slu.edu; 314-977-8282).
Biosecurity and Disaster Preparedness: M.S., M.P.H., Ph.D., certificate; Dr. Greg Evans (bommarlg@slu.edu; 314-977-8135).
Business Administration (International): Ph.D., B.A.; Dr. Craig R. Van Slyke (cvanslyk@slu.edu; 314-977-2027).
Catholic School Leadership: M.A.; Dr. William Rebore (moorem@slu.edu; 314-977-2508).
Chemistry: M.S., M.S.(R), Ph.D.; Dr. Shelley Minteer (chemdept@slu.edu; 314-977-2850).
Clinical Health Care Ethics: Certificate; Dr. Jill Burkemper (chcecert@slu.edu; 314-977-6662).
Communication: M.A., M.A.(R); Dr. Paaige Turner (commdept@slu.edu; 314-977-3191).
Communication Sciences and Disorders: M.A., M.A.(R); Dr. Travis Threats (commdis@slu.edu; 314-977-2940).
Community Health: M.P.H., M.S.P.H., M.S.; Bernie Backer (sphinfo@slu.edu; 314-977-8144).
Counseling: M.A., M.A.(R); Dr. Craig Smith (cft@slu.edu; 314-977-7108).
Educational Administration: M.A., Ed.S., Ed.D., Ph.D.; Dr. William Rebore (moorem@slu.edu; 314-977-2508).
Educational Leadership: M.A.; Dr. William Rebore (moorem@slu.edu; 314-977-2508).
Educational Studies: M.A., M.A.T., Ed.D., Ph.D.; Dr. Michael Grady (gradymp@slu.edu; 314-977-8178).
Endodontics: M.S.D.(R); Dr. John Hatton (cade@slu.edu; 314-977-8611).
English: M.A., M.A.(R), Ph.D.; Dr. Ruth Benis (benistr@slu.edu; 314-977-3010).
Family Therapy: M.A., M.A.(R), Ph.D.; Dr. Craig Smith (cft@slu.edu; 314-977-7108).
French: M.A.; Dr. Angela Smart (smart@slu.edu; 314-977-2449).
Geographic Information Systems: Certificate; Dr. Robert Cropf (pps@slu.edu; 314-977-3934).
Geophysics: M.S., M.S.(R), Ph.D.; Dr. Keith Koper (wise@eas.slu.edu; 314-977-3116).
Geology: M.S., M.S.(R); Dr. Keith Koper (wise@eas.slu.edu; 314-977-3116).
Health Care Ethics: Ph.D.; Dr. Anna Iltis (chcephd@slu.edu; 314-977-6661).
Health Management and Policy: M.H.A., M.P.H.; Bernie Backer (sphinfo@slu.edu; 314-977-8100).
Higher Education Administration: M.A., Ed.D., Ph.D.; Dr. William Rebore (moorem@slu.edu; 314-977-2508).
Historical Theology: M.A., Ph.D.; Dr. Jay Hammond (theology@slu.edu; 314-977-2986).
History: M.A., M.A.(R), Ph.D.; Dr. Michael Rozbicki (history@slu.edu; 314-977-2910).
Integrated and Applied Science: Ph.D.; Dr. Paul Jelliss (jellissp@slu.edu; 314-977-2834).
Mathematics: M.A., M.A.(R), Ph.D.; Fr. Michael May (mathweb@slu.edu; 314-977-2444).
Marriage and Family Therapy: Certificate; Dr. Craig Smith (cft@slu.edu; 314-977-7108).
Meteorology: M.P.M., M.S.(R), Ph.D.; Dr. Charles Graves (wise@eas.slu.edu; 314-977-3116).
Molecular Microbiology and Immunology: Ph.D.; Dr. William Wold (mmigradprog@slu.edu; 314-977-8853).
Nursing–Doctoral: Ph.D.; Director, Ph.D.; Dr. Andrew Mills (slunurse@slu.edu; 314-977-8909).
Nursing–Master's: M.S.N., M.S.N.(R); Dr. Margie Edel (slunurse@slu.edu; 314-977-8909).
Nursing–Post-Master's Certificate: Dr. Margie Edel (slunurse@slu.edu; 314-977-8909).
Nutrition and Dietetics: M.S.N.D.; Dr. Mildred Mattfeldt-Beman (veggie@slu.edu; 314-977-8663).
Organizational Development Certificate: Dr. Robert Mai (pps@slu.edu; 314-977-1980).
Orthodontics: M.S.D.(R); Dr. Rolf Behrents (cade@slu.edu; 314-977-8611).
Pathology: Ph.D.; Dr. Jacki Kornbluth (kornblut@slu.edu; 314-268-5445).
Periodontics: M.S.D.(R); Dr. D. Douglas Miley (cade@slu.edu; 314-977-8611).
Pharmacological and Physiological Science: Ph.D.; Dr. Thomas Westfall (inquiry@slu.edu; 314-977-6400).
Philosophy: M.A., M.A.(R), Ph.D.; Fr. Theodore Vitali, C.P. (sluphilo@slu.edu; 314-977-3149).
Political Science: M.A., M.A.(R); Dr. Wynne Moskop (moskopww@slu.edu; 314-977-2897).
Psychology–Clinical: M.S.(R), Ph.D.; Dr. Michael Ross (slupsych@slu.edu; 314-977-2300).
Psychology–Experimental: M.S.(R), Ph.D.; Dr. Kimberly Powlishta (psyappex@slu.edu; 314-977-2300).
Psychology–Industrial/Organizational: M.S.(R), Ph.D.; Dr. Edward Sabin (slupsych@slu.edu; 314-977-2300).
Public Administration: M.A.P.A.; Dr. Robert Cropf (pps@slu.edu; 314-977-3934).
Public Health Studies: Ph.D.; Bernie Backer (sphinfo@slu.edu; 314-977-8100).
Public Policy Analysis: Ph.D.; Dr. Robert Cropf (pps@slu.edu; 314-977-3934).
Sociology and Criminology/Criminal Justice: M.A.; Dr. Richard A. Colignon (rcoligno@slu.edu; 314-977-3640).
Spanish: M.A.; Dr. Elsy Cardona (gradsp@slu.edu; 314-977-3670).
Student Personnel Administration: M.A.; Dr. William Rebore (moorem@slu.edu; 314-977-2508).
Theology: M.A.; Dr. James Ginther (theology@slu.edu; 314-977-2881).
Urban Affairs: M.A.U.A.; Dr. Robert Cropf (pps@slu.edu; 314-977-3934).
Urban Planning and Real Estate Development: M.A.U.P.R.D.; Dr. Robert Cropf (pps@slu.edu; 314-977-3934).

Other Programs
M.B.A. Program: (mba@slu.edu; 314-977-MBA1).
School of Allied Health: Athletic Training (atep@slu.edu; 314-977-8561); Occupational Therapy (ot@slu.edu; 314-977-8580); Physical Therapy (ptdept@slu.edu; 314-977-8543); Physician Assistant Studies (majj@slu.edu; 314-977-8648).
School of Law: (admissions@law.slu.edu; 314-977-2800).
School of Medicine: (slumd@slu.edu; 314-977-9870).
School of Social Work: (socserv@slu.edu; 314-977-2722).

The clock tower in John E. Connelly Plaza is a focal point of the St. Louis campus.

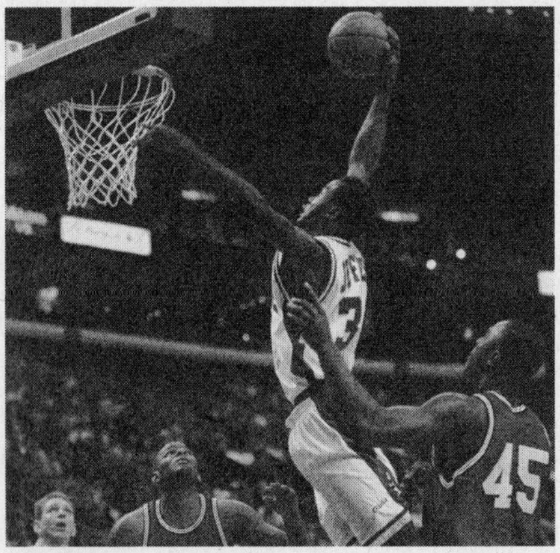

The Billikens began competing as a full member of the Atlantic 10 Conference during the 2005–06 academic year.

St. Louis' rich civic offerings such as the Gateway Arch and the historic Old Courthouse provide students with great options for learning and recreation.

SAINT PETER'S COLLEGE

Graduate Studies

Programs of Study

Saint Peter's College offers selected graduate degrees and certification programs. The Master of Business Administration is a 48-credit program and runs on a trimester calendar. Students can choose from seven areas of concentration: finance, management information systems, marketing, management, international business, human resource management, and risk management. The Master of Science (M.S.) in accountancy is a 30-credit program and also runs on a trimester calendar. Upon graduation, M.S. in accountancy students will have completed the 150 credit hours of education that became a requirement in the year 2000 in the state of New Jersey to sit for the Certified Public Accountant (CPA) examination. The 36-credit Master of Arts in education runs on a semester calendar and offers concentrations in teaching, administration and supervision, reading, special education, and school counseling. For students who earned their undergraduate degrees in an area other than education and want to be certified to teach nursery through eighth grade or ninth through twelfth grade, a 26-credit teacher certification program is offered. Other professional education certifications offered include the supervisor of instruction certificate program and the school business administrator certificate program. The Master of Science in Nursing (M.S.N.) degree program offers two concentrations: a 37-credit concentration in case management and a 39-credit concentration in primary-care adult nurse practitioner studies. For students who already possess a master's degree in nursing and want to earn a certificate as an adult nurse practitioner, a 25-credit post-master's certificate is offered. Saint Peter's also offers an RN to M.S.N. Bridge Program for students who have bachelor's degrees in fields other than nursing and who have an RN license.

Research Facilities

The libraries of Saint Peter's College provide extensive services and research facilities to the College community at both campuses. The Theresa and Edward O'Toole Library in Jersey City is fully automated, and the catalog is accessible via the campus network. The Jersey City and Englewood Cliffs libraries hold more than 300,000 volumes. Every student has a computer ID that permits access to eighteen computer labs, the campus computer network, e-mail, and the Internet. All classrooms are wired for computer access. The Blackboard Classroom System makes class material available 24 hours a day, seven days a week. The College's campus is one of the first in New Jersey to offer students with remote-access-equipped laptops the ability to log onto the College system or the Internet at anytime or anywhere on campus.

Financial Aid

To make financing an education possible, Saint Peter's financial aid advisers help students explore the best means of affording their degree. Options include tuition deferment and installment plans, employer-sponsored tuition reimbursement plans, and student loans. Teachers working full-time at a Catholic school receive a 50 percent discount on tuition when enrolled in a graduate education program. Students may call a financial aid adviser at 201-761-6060 for more information.

Cost of Study

The cost of tuition for graduate study in 2008 was $885 per credit.

Student Group

Saint Peter's College has a total enrollment of more than 3,300 undergraduate and graduate students. The diverse student body includes many international students representing seventy different countries.

Location

Saint Peter's College offers two campuses in convenient locations. The main campus has long been a landmark on Kennedy Boulevard in Jersey City, New Jersey. The College's atmosphere, architecture, and activity reflect a dynamic, vital, urban institution that offers important intellectual resources to the community. The New York City skyline, visible from Jersey City, is a constant reminder of the College's proximity to a major cultural and financial center. The branch campus at Englewood Cliffs in Bergen County, New Jersey, was established as a college for adults. The campus is perched on a bluff overlooking northern Manhattan and the Hudson River, located on the Palisades 1 mile north of the George Washington Bridge.

An off-site location at the Jersey City Waterfront affords graduate students the opportunity to take business courses at a convenient location close to their place of employment in downtown Jersey City. It is also conveniently located close to PATH and ferry transportation. An additional off-site location in South Amboy, New Jersey, offers education and business courses for graduate students.

The College

Saint Peter's College, founded in 1872, is a Jesuit, Catholic, coeducational liberal arts college in an urban setting that seeks to develop the whole person in preparation for a lifetime of learning, leadership, and service in a diverse and global society. Committed to academic excellence and individual attention, Saint Peter's College provides education informed by values.

Applying

To begin the graduate admissions process, students must submit an application, including official undergraduate transcripts. Additional admission requirements (if any) vary with each graduate program and can be requested by the admissions office after the application is received. International applicants must submit the same to begin the application process. An initial review of the complete application for admission is conducted by the Office of Graduate Admissions. The office reserves the right to ask for additional application documentation at any time. All correspondence should be conducted with the Office of Graduate Admissions.

Correspondence and Information

Office of Graduate Admissions
Saint Peter's College
2641 Kennedy Boulevard
Jersey City, New Jersey 07306
Phone: 201-761-6470
Fax: 201-435-5270
E-mail: gradadmit@spc.edu
Web site: http://www.spc.edu

GRADUATE PROGRAMS

Master of Arts in Education (M.A.)
The Master of Arts in education program offers five areas of concentration: administration and supervision, reading, teaching, special education, and counseling. Each concentration prepares teachers for certification by the state of New Jersey. The concentrations have a set of foundation courses which are enhanced by specialized required courses and electives. The M.A. in education runs on a semester calendar.

For persons who earned their undergraduate degrees in an area other than education and want to be certified to teach nursery through eighth grade or ninth through twelfth grade, a 26-credit teacher certification program is offered. The program consists of six courses (18 credits) in addition to 8 credits in student teaching. The teacher certification program can be completed strictly in the evenings or strictly on the weekends. Students can also mix and match their class schedule by taking evening and weekend courses.

Master of Business Administration (M.B.A.)
The M.B.A. program at Saint Peter's has been designed to meet the changing requirements that are occurring in the business workplace. The M.B.A. program offers seven areas of study: finance, management information systems, marketing, international business, management, human resource management, and risk management. The M.B.A. is a 48-credit program. The M.B.A. student may receive credit for prior undergraduate and graduate work, up to 12 credits, with approval from the M.B.A. Coordinator and Adviser. Thus, individuals with undergraduate credit in accounting, statistics, computer science, or economics may complete the M.B.A. program in 36 credits. The program runs on a trimester calendar, with courses offered in the evenings and on weekends.

Master of Science in Accountancy (M.S.)
The 30-credit Master of Science in accountancy runs on a trimester calendar. This program keeps pace with changes in accounting practices and anticipates coming changes in the business environment. Furthermore, graduates of this program will have completed the 150 credit hours of education that became a requirement in the year 2000 by the state of New Jersey to sit for the Certified Public Accountant (CPA) examination. The M.S. in accountancy can be completed strictly in the evenings or strictly on the weekends. Students can also mix and match their class schedule by taking evening and weekend courses.

Master of Science in Nursing (M.S.N.)
The Master of Science in Nursing program offers two areas of specialization: primary-care adult nurse practitioner studies and case management with a functional concentration in nursing administration. Both options consist of core courses that provide a foundation for graduate study and theoretical and clinical practicum courses that prepare graduates for specialization in case management, nursing administration, or in primary care as adult nurse practitioners. The 37-credit M.S.N. in case management curriculum is offered on a trimester basis. The 39-credit M.S.N. adult nurse practitioner studies program is offered on a combined trimester/semester schedule.

For nurses who already possess a master's degree in nursing and want to earn a certificate as an adult nurse practitioner, a 25-credit, post-master's program is offered. Saint Peter's also offers an RN to M.S.N. Bridge Program for students who have bachelor's degrees in fields other than nursing and who have their RN license. Graduate study in nursing is offered exclusively at the Englewood Cliffs campus.

A professor at Saint Peter's College crosses campus on his way to class.

The Englewood Cliffs campus is specifically designed for adult learners and is conveniently located just 5 minutes from the George Washington Bridge.

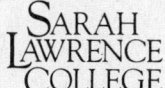

SARAH LAWRENCE COLLEGE

SARAH LAWRENCE COLLEGE

Graduate Programs

Programs of Study

Sarah Lawrence College has been a pioneer in several graduate fields, founding three outstanding programs in human genetics (genetic counseling), health advocacy, and women's history that have served as models nationwide. The College also offers master's degrees in areas where it has particular strength: the art of teaching, child development, creative writing, dance, and theater. The College believes in the importance of close and extensive collaboration with the faculty. Many of the graduate programs combine small seminar classes with individual student-faculty conferences. In all programs, opportunity for fieldwork is extensive and varied. Most graduate programs are for two years of full-time study and require 36 course credits. Part-time study may be arranged in all programs, with the exception of dance and theater.

The Art of Teaching Program leads to a Master of Science degree and recommendation for New York State certification in early childhood (birth–grade 2), childhood (grades 1–6), or dual certification (birth–grade 6). Special features of the program include study of child development, observation, and documentation; empirical courses in curriculum planning, with emphasis on language arts, mathematics, science, and social studies; and integration of theory with fieldwork from the first semester. Field placements and student teaching under master teachers are offered at the Sarah Lawrence Early Childhood Center and public schools in Westchester County and New York City.

The Child Development Program leads to an M.A. and is for students who seek in-depth understanding of childhood functioning in the context of contemporary society. Study of theoretical perspectives and research in developmental psychology is integrated with fieldwork experience. The program is unique in its ongoing combination of theory and fieldwork. Graduates of the program are prepared for direct work with young children in a variety of settings, for teaching child development at an intermediate level, or for pursuing more advanced study in psychology and related fields. In fall 2003, Sarah Lawrence College began offering a dual degree (M.A./M.S.W.) with the New York University School of Social Work and its Child Development Master's Program.

The Dance Program leads to an M.F.A. and is based on the premise that dance is a distinctive art form, calling for the integration of body, mind, and spirit. Daily modern and ballet technique classes are required of all graduate students. Basic physical skills, strength, and control are required for the central focus of the program, the creative use of the dance medium. The student is exposed to vital aspects of the art as a performer, creator, and observer, with music as an integral part. The curriculum centers on choreography, dance improvisation, music improvisation, composition, and the teaching of dance. The dance program offers dancers the opportunity to grow under the guidance of an excellent faculty made up of dancers and dance scholars with professional experience in the New York area and abroad.

The Human Genetics (Genetic Counseling) Program and the Health Advocacy Program, each leading to a master's degree, train health professionals devoted to the health concerns of patients. The interdisciplinary curriculum in each program consists of 40 academic course credits and 600 hours of clinical work or other fieldwork. The location of Sarah Lawrence College in the metropolitan New York area offers a rich network of settings—hospitals, clinics, and community agencies—in which on-site supervised training enables students to integrate theoretical knowledge with practice. The faculty includes professionals and academicians drawn from health and medical disciplines. Small classes and close faculty-student interaction offer a productive and stimulating environment for professional growth. Both programs make use of invited speakers, professional workshops, and community involvement to enrich the learning experience and expose students to new developments in the field. A joint degree in human genetics and health advocacy (M.S./M.A.) is also offered.

The Theatre Program leads to the M.F.A. and is based on the principle that learning comes through practical application, personal experience, and intensive workshops. Working with a faculty of New York City theater professionals, students explore playwriting, acting, directing, design, and technical work in small seminars, tutorials, and collaborative projects.

The Women's History Program leads to the M.A. It was the first in the nation to offer graduate study in the field and emphasizes the combination of scholarship and activism. A joint degree program in women's history and law is offered in cooperation with Pace University Law School.

The Writing Program leads to an M.F.A. This program offers an uncommon opportunity for students to develop as poets or creative nonfiction or fiction writers under the close attention of a nationally renowned faculty. At the center of the course of study are four successive seminars that students take during their two years in the program. In addition to the intensive student-faculty discussions in these seminars, students participate in individual conferences with faculty members every two weeks. This unique aspect of the Sarah Lawrence program provides further intensive scrutiny of students' writing and helps them create the substantial body of work needed to fulfill the program's requirements.

Research Facilities

The College's facilities include classrooms, laboratories, a computer center, and a state-of-the-art sports center; a modern library with 202,265 books and 880 periodicals, which is linked by computer to more than 6,000 other libraries; the Performing Arts Center, which consists of two theaters, a dance studio, and a concert hall; a music building, including a music library; a Science Center; the Early Childhood Center; the Center for Graduate Studies; and the Center for Continuing Education.

Financial Aid

Graduate students are welcome to apply for financial aid. There are two required forms for U.S. citizens (and other federally eligible students) and one form for international students. U.S. citizens should complete the Free Application for Federal Student Aid (FAFSA) and the Financial Aid PROFILE. International students may use the College's International Application for Financial Aid. There are links to all three forms at http://www.sarahlawrence.edu/finaid. March 1 is the College's preferential filing date. It is important that all applicants for financial aid complete either the PROFILE or the international application for aid at the same time as their application for admission. All financial aid is awarded on the basis of need. Students who complete the appropriate forms in a timely manner are automatically considered for all aid resources administered by Sarah Lawrence College. Grants (gift aid) and student loans comprise the two elements of a Sarah Lawrence financial aid package. Every federally eligible aid recipient is offered a student loan. Students are not required to accept the loan in order to receive Sarah Lawrence College gift aid. International students are advised to investigate financing opportunities offered by their government or private institutions. Detailed descriptions and a thorough explanation of financial aid procedures are available in *Financing Your Graduate Education at Sarah Lawrence College,* published and updated by the Office of Graduate Studies. A copy of the booklet is mailed to all students who apply to a graduate studies program.

Cost of Study

Tuition varies according to program. For more information, prospective students should visit http://www.slc.edu/student-accounts/Graduate_Tuition_and_Costs.php.

Living and Housing Costs

Estimated expenses for off-campus housing and food are $16,390 per year.

Student Group

Sarah Lawrence attracts students who seek a creative education and are eager to take responsibility for it. The College draws its approximately 320 graduate students from forty-nine states and thirty-one countries.

Location

The College is situated in the Bronxville/Yonkers community of Bronxville in southern Westchester County, just 15 miles north of midtown Manhattan in New York City. Highways and a commuter railroad make it possible to reach the city in about 30 minutes, enabling students to take advantage of its social, cultural, and intellectual riches and its internship possibilities.

The College

Founded in 1926, Sarah Lawrence is a small liberal arts college for men and women. It is a lively community of students, scholars, and artists, nationally renowned for its unique academic structure, which combines small classes with individual student-faculty conferences.

Applying

Applicants for graduate studies must have received a B.A. or an equivalent degree from an accredited college or university and have at least a 3.0 grade point average. They should request information on the program that interests them at the College address or by calling the College's telephone number. Applicants are asked to complete an application form and to furnish transcripts of all undergraduate work and two letters of recommendation, preferably from former teachers. Personal interviews may be arranged with the program directors and with the Director of Graduate Studies. The creative writing and the performing arts programs require demonstration of the candidate's ability. GRE scores are not required. Application deadlines vary according to program. Prospective students can apply online at https://data.slc.edu/graduate/index.php. Students should visit the Web site at http://www.slc.edu/graduate/index.php.

Correspondence and Information

Susan Guma, Dean of Graduate Studies
Sarah Lawrence College
1 Mead Way
Bronxville, New York 10708

Phone: 914-395-2371
Fax: 914-395-2664
E-mail: grad@sarahlawrence.edu
Web site: http://www.sarahlawrence.edu

THE FACULTY AND GRADUATE PROGRAM DIRECTORS

Art of Teaching
Sara Wilford, Director; M.S.Ed., M.Ed., Bank Street College of Education.
Mary Hebron, Associate Director; M.A., NYU.
Maggie Martinez DeLuca, M.S.Ed., Bank Street College of Education.
Jan Drucker, Ph.D., NYU.
Linwood Lewis, Ph.D., CUNY.
Kathleen Ruen, Ph.D., NYU.

Child Development
Barbara Schecter, Director; Ph.D., Columbia Teachers College.
Carl Barenboim, Ph.D., Rochester.
Charlotte Doyle, Ph.D., Michigan.
Jan Drucker, Ph.D., NYU.
Elizabeth Johnston, D.Phil., Oxford.
Linwood Lewis, Ph.D., CUNY.
Sara Wilford, M.S.Ed., M.Ed., Bank Street College of Education.

Dance
Sara Rudner, Director; M.F.A., Bennington.
Emmy Devine, B.A., Connecticut College.
Dan Hurlin, B.A., Sarah Lawrence.
Rose Anne Thom, B.A., McGill.
John Yannelli, M.F.A., Sarah Lawrence.

Health Advocacy
Laura Weil, Director; M.A., Sarah Lawrence.
Maryann Bailey, Ph.D., Northwestern.
Bruce Berg, Associate Professor and Chair, Department of Political Science, Fordham University; Ph.D., American.
Jennifer Buckley, M.A., Sarah Lawrence.
Sayantani DasGupta, M.D./M.P.H., Johns Hopkins.
Rachel Grob, Ph.D., CUNY Graduate Center.
Catherine M. Handy, Ph.D., NYU.
Alice Herb, J.D., LL.M., NYU.
Christobal J. Jacques, L.M.S.W., M.S.W., CUNY, Hunter.
Rebecca O. Johnson, M.S., Southern New Hampshire; M.F.A., Sarah Lawrence.
Margaret Keller, J.D., M.S., Columbia.
Laura Long, M.S., Sarah Lawrence.
Terry Mizrahi, M.S.W., Columbia; Ph.D., Virginia.
Constance Peterson, M.A., Sarah Lawrence.

Human Genetics
Caroline Lieber, Director; M.S., Sarah Lawrence.
James W. Speer, Associate Director; M.S., Sarah Lawrence.
Jessica Davis, Director of Clinical Training; M.D., Columbia.
Jacob Canick, Ph.D., Brandeis.
Susanne Carter, M.S., Sarah Lawrence.
Peggy Cottrell, M.S., Sarah Lawrence.
Sayantani DasGupta, M.D./M.P.H., Johns Hopkins.
Siobhan Dolan, M.D., Harvard.
Judith Durcan, M.S., Sarah Lawrence.
Marvin Frankel, Ph.D., Chicago.
Eva Bostein Griepp, M.D., NYU.
Susan Gross, M.D., Toronto.
Alice Herb, J.D., LL.M., NYU.
Laura Hercher, M.S., Sarah Lawrence.
Judith Hull, M.S., Sarah Lawrence.
David Kronn, M.D., Trinity College, Dublin.
Sharon LaVigne, M.S., Sarah Lawrence.
Laura Long, M.S., Sarah Lawrence.
Robert Marion, M.D., Yeshiva (Einstein).
Diana Punales Morejon, M.S., Sarah Lawrence.
Sally Nolin, Ph.D., SUNY Health Science Center at Brooklyn.
Elsa Reich, M.S., Sarah Lawrence.
Michael J. Smith, D.S.W., Columbia.
Jennifer Scalia Wilbur, M.S., Sarah Lawrence.

Theater
John Dillon, Director; M.F.A., Columbia (Danforth and Woodrow Wilson Fellow).
William D. McRee, Administrator; M.F.A., Sarah Lawrence.
Ernest Abuba, Member, Ensemble Studio Theatre; Rockefeller Foundation Fellowship.
Edward Allen Baker, B.A., Rhode Island.
Lynn Book, M.F.A., Art Institute of Chicago.
Kevin Confoy, B.A., Rutgers.
Michael Early, M.F.A., Yale.
June Ekman, B.A., Goddard; ACAT, Alexander Technique.
Christine Farrell, M.F.A., Columbia.
Nancy Franklin, Member, Actors Studio and Ensemble Studio Theatre.
Dan Hurlin, B.A., Sarah Lawrence.
Chris Jones, M.F.A., Carnegie Mellon.
Shirley Kaplan, A.A., Briarcliff, Academie de la Grande Chaumiere (Paris).
Doug MacHugh, M.F.A., Sarah Lawrence.
Greg MacPherson, B.A., Vermont.
John McCormack, B.A., Hamilton.
Cassandra Medley, Michigan.
Carol Ann Pelletier, B.A., Brandeis.
Paul Rudd, B.A., Fairfield.
Fanchon Miller Scheier, M.F.A., Sarah Lawrence.
Stuart Spencer, B.A., Sarah Lawrence.
Sterling Swann, B.A., Vassar.
John Yannelli, M.F.A., Sarah Lawrence.

Writing/Creative Nonfiction
Vijay Seshadri, Director; M.F.A., Columbia.
Alexandra Soiseth, Assistant Director; M.F.A., Sarah Lawrence.
Jo Ann Beard, M.A., Iowa.
Rachel Cohen, A.B., Harvard.
Stephen O'Connor, M.A., Berkeley.
Penny Wolfson, M.F.A., Sarah Lawrence.

Writing/Fiction
Brian Morton, Director; B.A., Sarah Lawrence.
Alexandra Soiseth, Assistant Director; M.F.A., Sarah Lawrence.
Jo Ann Beard, M.F.A., Iowa.
Melvin Jules Bukiet, M.F.A., Columbia.
Carolyn Ferrell, M.A., CUNY, City College.
Myra Goldberg, M.A., CUNY Graduate Center.
Joshua Henkin, M.F.A., Michigan.
Kathleen Hill, Ph.D., Wisconsin.
William Melvin Kelley, Writer; Harvard.
Mary La Chapelle, M.F.A., Vermont.
Ernesto Mestre, B.A., Tulane.
Mary Morris, Director; M.Phil., Columbia.
Victoria Redel, M.F.A., Iowa.
Lucy Rosenthal, M.F.A., Yale.
Joan Silber, M.A., NYU.

Writing/Poetry
Kate Knapp Johnson, Director; M.F.A., Sarah Lawrence.
Alexandra Soiseth, Assistant Director; M.F.A., Sarah Lawrence.
Laure-Anne Bosselaar, M.F.A., National Institute for Performing Arts (Belgium).
Kurt Brown, M.A., Colorado.
Tina Chang, M.F.A., Columbia.
Suzanne Gardinier, M.F.A., Columbia.
Matthea Harvey, M.F.A., Iowa.
Cathy Park Hong, M.F.A., Columbia.
Marie Howe, M.F.A., Columbia.
Joan Larkin, M.A., Arizona.
Thomas Lux, B.A., Emerson; University of Iowa Writers Workshop.
Dennis Nurkse, B.A., Harvard.
Kevin Pilkington, M.A., Georgetown.
Victoria Redel, M.F.A., Iowa.
Vijay Seshadri, M.F.A., Columbia.

Women's History
Priscilla Murolo, Director; Ph.D., Yale. U.S. labor history.
Tara James, Associate Director; M.A., Sarah Lawrence.
Eileen Ka-may Cheng, Ph.D., Yale. Nineteenth-century America, with a focus on intellectual and political history.
Rachel Cohen, A.B., Harvard.
Lyde Cullen Sizer, Ph.D., Brown. Women's literary cultures, American popular culture, the American Civil War.
K. Komozi Woodard, Ph.D., Pennsylvania. African American history and culture, with emphasis on the black freedom movement, American urban history, and ghetto formation.

Affiliate Faculty in Women's History
Julie Abraham, Lesbian and Gay Studies.
Bella Brodzki, Literature.
Isabel De Sena, Spanish/Literature.
Mary Dillard, History.
Arnold Krupat, Literature.
Chikwenye Ogunyemi, Literature.
David Peritz, Political Science.
Mary Porter, Anthropology.
Marilyn Power, Economics.
Kasturi Ray, Global Studies.
Sandra Robinson, Asian Studies.
Judith Rodenbeck, Art History.
Shahnaz Rouse, Sociology.
Barbara Schecter, Psychology.
Pauline Watts, History.
Matilde Zimmermann, History.

The College is set on a 35-acre campus reminiscent of a rural English village.

SHIPPENSBURG UNIVERSITY OF PENNSYLVANIA

School of Graduate Studies

Programs of Study

Shippensburg University of Pennsylvania offers programs of study leading to master's degrees (M.A., M.B.A., M.Ed., M.P.A., M.S., and M.S.W.) in administration of justice, applied history, biology, business administration, communication studies, computer science, counseling and college student personnel, curriculum and instruction, educational leadership and policy, geoenvironmental studies, organizational development and leadership, public administration, psychology, reading, social work, and special education. Students may also pursue postgraduate-level supervisory and certification credentials.

Research Facilities

The Ezra Lehman Memorial Library houses more than 2 million items and provides access to electronic resources, including books and articles, which are accessible from students' personal computers 24 hours a day. Via the Keystone Library and Pennsylvania Academic Library networks, students can access the collections of sixty academic libraries. The University maintains two general-purpose microcomputer laboratories (open 24 hours a day) and nineteen labs that have department- or major-specific software. The Center for Applied Research and Policy Analysis, the Center for Education and Human Services, the Center for Interdisciplinary Science, the Frehn-Center for Professional and Organizational Development, the Center for Juvenile Justice Training and Research, and the Center for Local and State Government offer students research opportunities in addition to department research projects.

Financial Aid

Graduate assistantships are awarded on a competitive basis without regard to financial need. They provide a tuition waiver as well as compensation on an hourly scale for work performed. Graduate assistants are required to work 250 hours during the semester and 150 hours during the summer. Applications should be filed by March 1. Residence director (RD) positions are available, with preference given to students enrolled in the counseling and college student personnel program. The RD position is a twelve-month appointment, compensated with a salary and a free apartment and meal plan. RDs also receive a tuition waiver for 6 credits per semester and 3 credits per summer. The University is approved for training veterans and administers a range of loan programs. Funds are available to support student research and attendance at professional meetings to present papers.

Cost of Study

Tuition for 2008–09 was $357 per credit hour for in-state students and $572 per credit hour for out-of-state students. Students also paid an educational services fee of $29 per credit hour. A health services fee of $93 and a technology fee of $90.50 were charged to full-time students. The technology fee for out-of-state students was $136.50. The student union fee was $113 for full-time students and $54 for those attending part-time.

Living and Housing Costs

Off-campus housing is available to graduate students during the fall and spring semesters. For information, students should visit the Web site at http://www.ship.edu/~deanstu/offcampus/. Housing is available on campus during the summer sessions. For summer housing information, students should contact the Dean of Students' office (phone: 717-477-1164; e-mail: deanstu@ship.edu). Various meal plans are available, including Flex Accounts, which can be used like cash in any of the campus dining locations.

Student Group

The University enrolls more than 1,200 graduate students and 6,700 undergraduate students. Most graduate students are part-time (78 percent) and women (69 percent). Graduate students represent various ethnicities, states, and countries. A Graduate Student Association Board represents the academic and social interests of graduate students. Student services include on-site day care, Women's Center, Multicultural Student Affairs, and Counseling Center.

Location

Shippensburg University is located in the Cumberland Valley of south-central Pennsylvania, 40 miles southwest of Harrisburg. It is easily accessible from exits 24 northward and 29 south of Interstate 81 and the Blue Mountain and Carlisle interchanges of the Pennsylvania Turnpike.

The University

Founded in 1871, Shippensburg is consistently rated as one of the best universities in the Northeast. Shippensburg has offered graduate education since 1959 and is one of fourteen universities in the Pennsylvania State System of Higher Education.

Applying

Applicants must present a bachelor's degree from an accredited college or university and an official transcript. In addition, some academic departments may require an interview, additional test scores, goal statements, or letters of recommendation. The application fee is $30. Students may apply and check the status of their application online at http://www.ship.edu/admiss/graduate/index.html.

Correspondence and Information

Office of Graduate Admissions
Shippensburg University
1871 Old Main Drive
Shippensburg, Pennsylvania 17257-2299
Phone: 717-477-1213
800-822-8028 (toll-free)
Fax: 717-477-4016
E-mail: admiss@ship.edu
Web site: http://www.ship.edu/admiss/graduate/index.html

THE FACULTY

Dean of Graduate Studies: Tracy A. Schoolcraft, Ph.D., Penn State.
Dean of Extended Studies: Christina Sax, Ph.D., Virginia Commonwealth.
Dean of Enrollment Services: Thomas W. Speakman, Ed.D., Widener.
Administration of Justice: Kurt L. Kraus, Ph.D., Maine.
Applied History: Susan Rimby, Ph.D., Pittsburgh.
Biology: Gregory Paulson, Ph.D., Washington State.
Business Administration: Patricia Wolf, Ph.D., Maryland.
Communication Studies: Ted Carlin, Ph.D., Bowling Green State.
Computer Science: Carol Wellington, Ph.D., North Carolina State.
Counseling and College Student Personnel: Jan Arminio, Ph.D., Maryland.
Curriculum and Instruction and Reading: Christine A. Royce, Ed.D., Temple.
Educational Leadership and Policy and Special Education: Gerald D. Fowler, Ph.D., Maryland.
Geoenvironmental Studies: Tim Hawkins, Ph.D., Arizona State.
Organizational Development and Leadership: Barbara Denison, Ph.D., Northwestern.
Psychology: Suzanne Morin, Ph.D., Connecticut.
Public Administration: Sara Grove, Ph.D., North Carolina; J.D., Dickinson Law.
Social Work: Deb Jacobs, Ph.D., Brandeis.

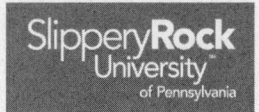

SLIPPERY ROCK UNIVERSITY OF PENNSYLVANIA

Graduate School

Programs of Study

Slippery Rock University offers the Master of Arts degree in community counseling, criminal justice, and student affairs in higher education; the Master of Science degree in adapted physical activity, park and resource management, sport management, and sustainable systems; the Master of Education degree in elementary education/early childhood reading, K–8 math/science (projected to begin summer 2010), physical education, school counseling, secondary education (mathematics/science, social studies/history, English, and educational leadership), and special education (master teacher, mentally and physically handicapped, and school supervision); and the doctorate in physical therapy. While most graduate programs require the successful completion of 30 to 36 credits, the physical therapy program takes 118 hours and requires eight semesters (which includes two summers) for completion. The counseling programs' requirements vary among 48, 51, and 60 credits for completion.

The following programs are offered exclusively online: criminal justice, environmental education, K–8 math/science (projected to begin summer 2010), park and resource management, special education (master teacher and school supervision), and sport management.

Except for the physical therapy program, two semesters compose the academic year; summer sessions are arranged in one 3-week presession, two 5-week sessions, and one 7-week evening term. Up to 12 semester hours of graduate credit from an accredited institution may be transferred into most master's programs.

Research Facilities

Bailey Library houses more than 500,000 volumes of traditional-format materials; hundreds of computers, including laptops for use anywhere in the building; several thousand films for viewing anywhere; a brand-new café; and many amenities that make the library a place for serious study or just relaxing. Through the Pennsylvania State System of Higher Education, more than 30,000 online scholarly journals and thousands of e-books are accessible from any computer. Bailey Library is a great resource for both resident students and commuters.

Slippery Rock University is home to a world-class faculty. With over twenty graduate-level programs, research is available and offered from many different resources. Interested candidates are encouraged to investigate the departmental Web site associated with each program in which they are interested.

Financial Aid

For 2008–09, more than 100 graduate assistantships with waived tuition and stipends of $4000 were offered. Assistantships may be granted for up to two academic years, with full-time recipients working 17.5 hours a week and taking at least 9 graduate credits each semester.

Educational loans are available to graduate students through the Federal Stafford Loan and Graduate Plus Loan Programs. Special Education Graduate Fellowships for special education majors are available through the Bureau of Education for the Handicapped. Information on additional sources of financial aid can be obtained from the Financial Aid Office.

Cost of Study

In 2008–09, Pennsylvania residents who studied full-time paid $4254.54 in tuition and fees per semester; nonresidents paid $6509.89 per semester. The tuition per credit hour for part-time graduate students was $357 for residents and $572 for nonresidents. All fees are subject to change without notice.

Living and Housing Costs

Various housing and living options are available to graduate students, including off-campus independent housing, various on-campus school-sponsored housing options, and optional meal plans. For the 2008–09 year, on-campus rooms started at $1402 per semester. Detailed information can be obtained through the Office of Residence Life.

Student Group

Total graduate enrollment for the fall semester of 2008 was approximately 750. Approximately 1 graduate student in 2 is enrolled on a full-time basis.

Student Outcomes

Recent graduates from Slippery Rock University master's programs have found employment in a variety of professional fields. Overall, 75 percent of graduates have obtained full-time employment in their chosen field within six months of graduation, with health-related disciplines, such as physical education and physical therapy, showing employment rates above 95 percent.

Location

Slippery Rock, a borough of about 3,000 people, adjoins the University. Small shops and restaurants are within two or three blocks of the center of the campus. Pittsburgh, one of the country's largest cities, is about 50 miles to the south, and Erie, located on Lake Erie, is 75 miles to the north. Youngstown, Ohio, is 30 miles to the west. The borough is served by commercial buses from these cities and is located within 10 miles of two major interstate highways, I-80 and I-79. Cultural and recreational activities abound in the area.

The University

In 1889, the citizens of Slippery Rock borough founded the University and gave it their town's picturesque name. The University is one of fourteen state-owned institutions of higher education in Pennsylvania. Its undergraduate academic divisions include the Colleges of Business, Information, and Social Sciences; Education; Health, Environment, and Science; and Humanities, Fine and Performing Arts. The current enrollment of the University is approximately 8,400 undergraduates and 800 graduate students.

Slippery Rock University is fully accredited by the Middle States Association of Colleges and Schools, and appropriate programs are accredited by the National Council for Accreditation of Teacher Education.

Applying

While several graduate-level programs require the submission of supporting credentials, such as letters of recommendation, personal statements, or essays, the general requirement for admission to graduate study includes graduation from an accredited university or college with a major in the area proposed for graduate study, a cumulative grade point average of at least 2.75 (on a 4.0 scale) for most programs, and acceptable scores on either the General Test of the Graduate Record Examinations (GRE) or the Miller Analogies Test (MAT), depending upon the program of study. A nonrefundable fee of $25 must accompany applications for admission to graduate study. A final official transcript must be submitted from the college or university at which the baccalaureate degree was conferred. Generally, applications are accepted on a rolling basis until classes are full. However, it is recommended that applications are submitted two months prior to the opening of the semester for which admission is sought. Application to the doctoral program in physical therapy requires a $35 nonrefundable application fee for both U.S. and non-U.S. citizens. For all other programs, non-U.S. citizens are required to submit a nonrefundable application fee of $30.

Correspondence and Information

Office of Graduate Admissions
124 North Hall
Slippery Rock University
One Morrow Way
Slippery Rock, Pennsylvania 16057

Phone: 724-738-2051
877-SRU-GRAD (toll-free)
Fax: 724-738-2146
E-mail: graduate.admissions@sru.edu
Web site: http://www.sru.edu/graduate

GRADUATE PROGRAM COORDINATORS

Each graduate program has its own primary academic contact, known as a Graduate Program Coordinator, who is a resident faculty member and industry expert who can assist with academic or content questions as well as course registration.

Adapted Physical Activity: Robert Arnhold, Ph.D., Texas Woman's. (Telephone: 724-738-4864; e-mail: robert.arnhold@sru.edu)
Counseling and Development: Michael Ignelzi, Ed.D., Harvard. (Telephone: 724-738-2035; e-mail: michael.ignelzi@sru.edu)
Criminal Justice: David Champion, Ph.D., Indiana of Pennsylvania. (Telephone: 724-738-4462; e-mail: david.champion@sru.edu)
Elementary Education/Early Childhood: Suzanne Rose, Ph.D., Penn State. (Telephone: 724-738-2042; e-mail: suzanne.rose@sru.edu)
Parks and Recreation/Environmental Education: *Park and Resource Management, Environmental Education:* Daniel Dziubek, Ed.D., Pittsburgh. (Telephone: 724-738-2068, e-mail: daniel.dziubek@sru.edu)
Physical Education: Marybeth Miller, Ph.D., Pittsburgh. (Telephone: 724-738-2072; e-mail: marybeth.miller@sru.edu)
Physical Therapy: Carol Martin-Elkins, Ph.D., SUNY Health Science Center at Syracuse. (Telephone: 724-738-2080; e-mail: carol.martin-elkins@sru.edu)
Secondary Education/Foundations of Education: Jeffrey Lehman, Ph.D., Florida. (Telephone: 724-738-2041; e-mail: jeffrey.lehman@sru.edu)
Special Education: Dennis Fair, Ph.D., Pittsburgh. (Telephone: 724-738-2085; e-mail: dennis.fair@sru.edu)
Sport Management: Brian Crow, Ed.D., West Virginia. (Telephone: 724-738-2060; e-mail: brian.crow@sru.edu)

Sustainable energy sources are critical to the planet's future.

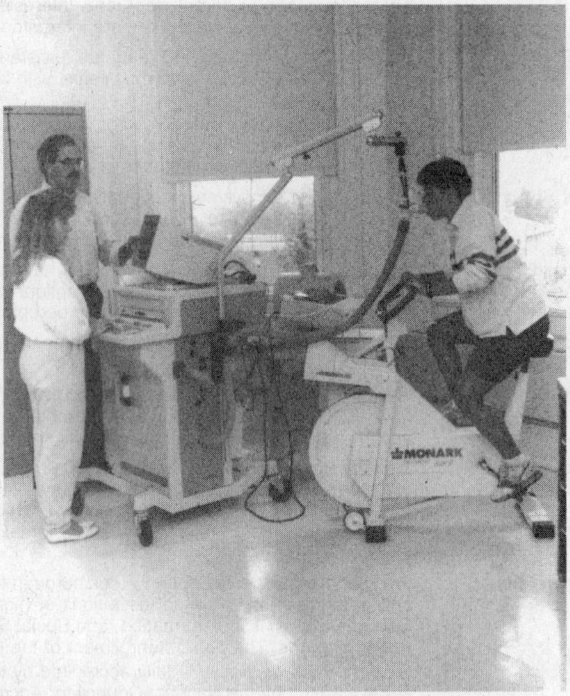

One of Slippery Rock's graduate degrees is the Doctor of Physical Therapy.

Teacher training programs are one of Slippery Rock's strengths.

SOUTHERN CONNECTICUT STATE UNIVERSITY

School of Graduate Studies

Programs of Study

Southern Connecticut State University (SCSU) offers graduate programs leading to the degrees of Master of Arts, Master of Science, Master of Science in Education, Master of Science in Nursing, Master of Library Science, Master of Public Health, Master of Social Work, Master of Marriage and Family Therapy, and Master of Business Administration, as well as an Ed.D. in educational leadership. Graduate programs leading to the Sixth-Year Professional Diploma in special areas of education and library science are also offered.

The Master of Arts degree is awarded in English, history, psychology, and women's studies. The Master of Science degree is offered in biology; chemistry; communications disorders; computer science; instructional technology; recreation and leisure; research, measurement, and evaluation; sociology; and urban studies. The Master of Science in Education degree is awarded in art, bilingual/multicultural education/TESOL, biology, chemistry, counseling, elementary education, English, environmental education, exercise science, history, mathematics, reading, school health education, school psychology, science education, and special education.

The Sixth-Year Professional Diploma is offered in counseling and school psychology, educational leadership, education—classroom teacher specialist studies, educational foundations, library information studies, reading, special education, and science education.

Most graduate programs are offered in the evening for the convenience of students, and some are offered online. Students follow a planned program that includes completing course requirements and taking a comprehensive examination, preparing a thesis, or completing a special project, as appropriate.

Research Facilities

The Hilton C. Buley Library, Southern Connecticut State University's center of education and research, plays an indispensable part in the academic experience of every student. Buley Library provides more than 400,000 monograph volumes, over 60,000 bound periodical volumes, 12,500 nonprint media items, 1,000 electronic books, and 100,000 volume equivalents in micro-format. Current periodical subscriptions include 2,060 individual journal titles; in addition, the library provides access to more than 43,000 full-text electronic journals, 130 Web-based indexes and databases, and over 1,000 e-book titles.

Financial Aid

There are a limited number of teaching and research assistantships available. The chief source of aid is the Federal Stafford Student Loan. Application forms for this loan are available from commercial banks. The School of Graduate Studies also offers competitive research fellowships of approximately $8000.

Cost of Study

Tuition for full-time study for the 2008–09 academic year was $8756 for state residents and $17,852 for out-of-state residents. Part-time study cost $449 per credit hour plus a $55 registration fee and an $8-per-credit-hour information technology fee each semester. Students in some programs are charged differential tuition. Full-time, in-state students in the M.B.A. program and the M.L.S. program were charged $4286 per semester, and out-of-state students in these programs were charged $8814 per semester. Part-time students in these programs were charged $506 per credit. Students enrolled in the doctoral program were charged $580 per credit.

Living and Housing Costs

On-campus housing is available for graduate students. Off-campus accommodations are also readily available close to the campus at a range of prices. Students may choose from a wide range of housing styles and options.

Student Group

Approximately 3,800 graduate students (including approximately 900 full-time) are enrolled in graduate programs in five schools of the University. SCSU has consistently ranked as one of the top ten graduate schools in New England in terms of enrollment.

Location

New Haven, Connecticut's third largest city, is home to three universities, three colleges, and several private schools. New Haven serves as the gateway to New England, where I-95 and I-91 intersect and provide access to New York and Boston.

The University

Southern Connecticut State University is one of four institutions of the Connecticut State University System, which is authorized by the state of Connecticut. It receives its principal financial support from legislative appropriations. It is the policy of Southern Connecticut State University to accept students without regard to race, color, creed, sex, age, national origin, or physical disability.

Applying

Application forms for the School of Graduate Studies are available in the Graduate Office, which is located in Engleman Hall Room B110, or may be obtained by mail or telephone request. An online application is also available at http://www.gradstudies.SouthernCT.edu. Students are advised to send the completed, signed application and official transcripts from every college and graduate school attended, along with a $50 application fee, to the School of Graduate Studies. International students must also send TOEFL scores to the Graduate Studies Office. All other documents, such as requested letters of recommendation or any departmental forms, should be sent directly to the academic department to which application is being made. A personal interview with the appropriate department chairperson or a designated faculty member in the major area of study is a requirement for admission. Requests for appointments must be made to the department. The application and credentials should be submitted well in advance of the semester for which the student seeks admission.

Correspondence and Information

School of Graduate Studies
Southern Connecticut State University
501 Crescent Street
New Haven, Connecticut 06515-1355

Phone: 203-392-5240
800-448-0661 (toll-free)
Web site: http://www.gradstudies.southernct.edu

FACULTY HEADS

Listed below is the chairperson or graduate coordinator of each department.

Art Education: Jesse Whitehead, Coordinator.
Biology: Sean Grace, Coordinator.
Business Administration: Wafeek Abdelsayed, Director.
Chemistry: Robert Snyder, Coordinator.
Communication Disorders: Deborah Weiss, Coordinator.
Computer Science: Lisa Lancor, Coordinator.
Counselor Education: Norris Haynes, Chair.
Education: Maria Diamantis, Chair.
Educational Foundations: Dorothy Vazquez-Levy, Coordinator.
Educational Leadership: Peter Madonia, Chair.
English: Kenneth Florey, Coordinator.
Exercise Science: Robert Axtell, Coordinator.
Foreign Languages: Carlos Arboleda, Chair.
History: Christine Petto, Coordinator.
Library Science and Instructional Technology: Josephine Sche, Chair.
Marriage and Family Therapy: J. Edward Lynch, Chair.
Mathematics: Theresa Bennett, Coordinator.
Nursing: Olive Santavenere, Coordinator.
Psychology: W. Jerome Hauselt, Coordinator.
Public Health: Michael Perlin, Coordinator.
Reading: Nancy Boyles, Coordinator.
Recreation: James McGregor, Coordinator.
Research, Measurement, and Evaluation: William Diffley, Coordinator.
School Health: Doris Marino, Coordinator.
School Psychology: Joy Fopiano, Coordinator.
Science and Environmental Education: Susan Cusato, Chair.
Social Work: Todd Rofuth, Chair.
Sociology: Jessica Kenty-Drane, Coordinator.
Special Education: Pamela Brucker, Chair.
Urban Studies: Peter Sakalowsky, Chair.
Women's Studies: Tricia Lin, Coordinator.

There are many opportunities for graduate students at SCSU to enroll in small classes and work closely with faculty members.

The Hilton C. Buley Library.

SOUTHERN ILLINOIS UNIVERSITY EDWARDSVILLE

SOUTHERN ILLINOIS UNIVERSITY EDWARDSVILLE

The Graduate School

Programs of Study

The Graduate School awards the following degrees: Master of Arts in art therapy counseling, biological sciences, economics and finance, English, history, psychology, sociology, and speech communication; Master of Science in biological sciences, biotechnology management, chemistry, civil engineering, computer management and information systems, computer science, economics and finance, electrical engineering, environmental science management, environmental sciences, family nurse practitioner, geographical studies, health care and nursing administration, industrial engineering, literacy education, mass communications, mathematics, mechanical engineering, nurse anesthesia, nurse educator, physics, psychology, and speech-language pathology; Master of Business Administration; Master of Fine Arts, with studio areas in ceramics, digital art, drawing, metalsmithing, painting, printmaking, sculpture, and textile art or with a specialization in art education; Master of Marketing Research; Master of Music in music education or music performance; Master of Public Administration; Master of Science in Education in curriculum and instruction; educational administration; instructional technology; kinesiology; learning, culture, and society; secondary education with concentrations in nine teaching areas; and special education; Master of Science in Accountancy; Master of Social Work; and Master of Arts in Teaching. The Specialist degree is offered in educational administration and in school psychology. Cooperative doctoral study is offered in some degree programs through special arrangements with Southern Illinois University Carbondale. Post-baccalaureate and post-master's certificates are also offered in several fields. For more information about these programs, students should visit http://www.siue.edu/graduate/.

Final examinations are required of all degree candidates. Projects that must be completed for master's programs include theses, research projects and papers, internships, practicums, exhibitions, or recitals.

Research Facilities

The University has laboratories for the technical sciences, education, human performance, anthropological studies, psychological studies, and urban studies, and it has practice facilities for fine arts, theater, and music. Lovejoy Library has more than 800,000 bound volumes and over 1.3 million microform units, borrowing agreements with libraries locally and throughout the nation, and subscriptions to more than 24,000 journals and periodicals, 18,540 of which are electronic and available to members of the University from their homes or offices. Networked computers are available throughout the campus, including most offices, and numerous academic computing labs are available for use by graduate students. Problem-oriented programs have internship and practicum agreements with government, health, business, welfare, and educational agencies throughout the metropolitan St. Louis area.

Financial Aid

Teaching, research, and general assistantships are available, as are a number of special graduate awards, most of which carry stipends. Application for assistantships is made through department chairs. Application for some special awards is made through the Graduate School. Student employment and various types of loans are available through the Office of Student Financial Aid.

Cost of Study

In 2008–09, tuition and fees for full-time graduate students were $7363 per academic year (fall and spring semesters) for Illinois residents and $16,121 for out-of-state students. Figures were based on 12 semester hours of enrollment each term and are subject to change. St. Louis–area residents taking 6 semester hours or fewer per term pay in-state tuition and fees.

Living and Housing Costs

In 2008–09, rent for on-campus apartments, managed by University Housing, ranged from $3560 for an academic year (fall through spring terms) for a single student sharing a furnished apartment with 3 other students to $1155 a month for a three-bedroom furnished apartment for a family. (Rates are subject to change.) A residence hall room shared with one other person is $4380 per academic year (fall through spring semester). The Housing Office also has lists of available off-campus housing. Reasonably priced meals are served in the University cafeteria, and restaurant and meal plans (mandatory for residence hall residents) are available through the University's dining services. Special housing arrangements can be made for graduate students.

Student Group

More than 13,600 students are enrolled, including about 2,200 full-time and part-time graduate students. Minority groups and other countries are well represented in the enrollment. Evening and weekend classes are offered to accommodate graduate students employed in area schools, businesses, and industries.

Location

The area surrounding the University is rich in cultural advantages. Three other major universities and a number of community colleges share with Southern Illinois University Edwardsville (SIUE) a responsibility for offering advanced educational opportunities to many thousands of people. Live theater, art shows, museums, public parks, Cahokia Mounds, Missouri Botanical Gardens, and the Gateway Arch are some of the attractions of the general area. The St. Louis Symphony Orchestra offers indoor and outdoor concerts. The area has a combination of farmland and urban concentrations. Thriving businesses and large industries offer opportunities for employment. Recreational opportunities for hikers, campers, and canoe enthusiasts exist in the wilderness preserves of the nearby Ozarks and southern Illinois. St. Louis, with its stadium, the Edward Jones Dome, the Scottrade Center, Municipal Opera, and Lambert International Airport, is a 25-minute drive from the University.

The University

The University is situated on 2,660 acres of rolling hills. The main campus consists of large, modern buildings housing classrooms, laboratories, administrative offices, four residence halls, an apartment complex, and a student center with cafeteria, restaurant, recreational facilities, bookstore, bowling alley, and lounge areas. An athletics complex offers a wide range of recreational opportunities, including an indoor pool and student fitness center. Tennis courts, playing fields, and other recreational facilities are located on the periphery of the main campus. Low-cost bus service connects the campus with many nearby Illinois and Missouri centers and the University apartment complex. Ample parking is provided for automobiles. An Art and Design Building opened in 1993, and an outstanding addition to campus music facilities opened in 1995. The School of Nursing has a simulated learning lab; the School of Engineering moved into a state-of-the-art building in 2000; and the School of Pharmacy opened new facilities in 2005.

Applying

Students should file an application for admission with the Office of Graduate Admissions. Admission requirements vary for different programs. Requests for application forms, program information, and financial aid information should be sent to Graduate Admissions, Box 1047. Graduate applications and information are also available on the Web at http://www.siue.edu/graduate/.

Correspondence and Information

Department Chairperson
Southern Illinois University Edwardsville
Edwardsville, Illinois 62026

Phone: 618-650-3160
Fax: 618-650-2081
Web site: http://www.siue.edu/graduate/

FACULTY HEADS

The Graduate School
Dr. Stephen L. Hansen, Associate Provost for Research and Dean.
Dr. Ronald Schaefer, Associate Dean.
Dr. Christa Johnson, Associate Dean.

College of Arts and Sciences
Dr. John Danley, Acting Dean.
Dr. Carl Springer, Associate Dean.
Dr. Wendy Shaw, Associate Dean.
Dr. Kevin Johnson, Assistant Dean.
Art and Design: Thad Duhigg, Chair.
Art Therapy Counseling: Dr. Gussie Klorer, Graduate Program Director.
Biological Sciences: Dr. William Retzlaff, Chair.
Biotechnology Management: Dr. Paul Wanda, Graduate Program Director.
Chemistry: Dr. Robert Dixon, Chair.
English Language and Literature: Dr. Larry LaFond, Chair.
Environmental Sciences: Dr. Zhi-Qing Lin, Graduate Program Director.
Geography: Dr. Randy Pearson, Chair.
Historical Studies: Dr. Anthony Cheeseboro, Chair.
Mass Communications: Dr. Patrick Murphy, Chair.
Mathematics: Dr. Krzysztof Jarosz, Chair.
Music: Dr. Prince Wells, Chair.
Physics: Dr. Abdullatif Hamad, Chair.
Public Administration and Policy Analysis: Dr. T. R. Carr, Chair.
Social Work: Dr. Kathleen Tunney, Chair.
Sociology: Dr. Dave Kauzlarich, Chair.
Speech Communication: Dr. Isaac Blankson, Chair.

School of Business
Dr. Gary Giamartino, Dean
Dr. Janice Joplin, Associate Dean.
Dr. Mary R. Sumner, Associate Dean.
Accounting: Dr. Michael Costigan, Chair.
Computer Management and Information Systems: Dr. Susan Yager, Chair.
Economics and Finance: Dr. Rik Hafer, Chair.
Management/Marketing: Dr. Ralph Giacobbe, Chair.
M.B.A.: Dr. Janice Joplin, Graduate Program Director.

School of Education
Dr. Bette S. Bergeron, Dean.
Dr. Mary Weishaar, Associate Dean.
Dr. Curt Lox, Associate Dean.
Curriculum and Instruction: Dr. Martha Combs, Chair.
Educational Leadership: Dr. Wayne Nelson, Chair.
Kinesiology and Health Education: Dr. William Vogler, Chair.
Psychology: Dr. Paul Rose, Co-Chair, and Dr. Lynn Bartels, Co-Chair.
Special Education and Communication Disorders: Dr. Jean Harrison, Chair.

School of Engineering
Dr. Hasan Sevim, Dean.
Dr. Bradley Noble, Associate Dean.
Dr. Oktay Alkin, Associate Dean.
Civil Engineering: Dr. Susan Morgan, Chair.
Computer Science: Dr. Jerry Weinberg, Chair.
Electrical Engineering: Dr. Oktay Alkin, Chair.
Industrial Engineering: Dr. S. Cem Karacal, Graduate Program Director.
Mechanical and Industrial Engineering: Dr. Keqin Gu, Chair.

School of Nursing
Dr. Marcia Maurer, Dean.
Dr. Mary Ann Boyd, Associate Dean.
Dr. Jackie Clement, Graduate Program Director, Assistant Dean.
Dr. Mary Mulcahy, Assistant Dean.
Family Health and Community Health Nursing: Dr. Patricia Fazzone, Chair.
Primary Care and Health Systems Nursing: Dr. Anne Perry, Chair.

SPRINGFIELD COLLEGE

Graduate Programs

Programs of Study

Graduate study at Springfield College is designed to provide advanced professional preparation for qualified graduates of colleges and universities in the United States and abroad. Fourteen graduate programs, several with a number of subspecialty areas, are coordinated through the Graduate Studies Office. These programs are Art Therapy, Education (administration, early childhood, elementary, secondary, special education), Exercise Science and Sport Studies (athletic training, exercise physiology, health promotion and disease prevention, sport and exercise psychology, strength and conditioning), Health Studies (health education teacher licensure), Human Services, Occupational Therapy, Physical Education (adapted physical education, advanced-level coaching, athletic administration, physical education teacher licensure, sport performance), Physical Therapy, Psychology (athletic counseling, clinical mental health counseling, industrial/organizational psychology, marriage and family therapy, school guidance, student personnel in higher education), Rehabilitation Services (alcohol rehabilitation/substance abuse counseling, developmental disabilities, general counseling and casework, psychiatric rehabilitation/mental health counseling, special services, vocational evaluation/work adjustment), Social Work, and Sport Management and Recreation (recreational management, sport management, therapeutic recreational management). Graduate study is offered on three different levels, leading to the Master of Education, Master of Physical Education, Master of Science, Master of Social Work, Certificate of Advanced Graduate Study, Doctor of Philosophy, Doctor of Physical Therapy, and combined M.S.W./J.D. degrees.

For the Master of Science in Human Services, course work is offered on weekends. The program lasts sixteen months, and students meet one weekend each month. A five-year human services experience (paid or volunteer) is required for admission. Master of Social Work candidates attend classes on a part-time basis, every other weekend, or as full-time students two days a week.

Research Facilities

A well-equipped laboratory for physiology provides an area for student and faculty research. Experiments in the areas of kinesiology and exercise physiology are concerned with oxygen consumption and energy expenditure, strength, electrogoniometry, physical fitness, pulmonary function, and body density. Arrangements can also be made for work in cinematography and somatotyping. The Allied Health Center, the education curriculum laboratory, the College Counseling Center, a counseling laboratory with videotape facilities, a physical education tests and measurements laboratory, a biomechanics laboratory, the Computer Center, the College campgrounds, and the modern Babson Library offer campus opportunities for conducting research related to student interests and areas of study.

Financial Aid

Various types of financial assistance are available. Four All-College Tuition Scholarships are awarded each year. Teaching and research fellowships are offered in administrative and student affairs, art therapy, biology, chemistry, computer science, education, health studies, information and technology services, mathematics, multicultural affairs, occupational therapy, physical education, physical science, physics, psychology, recreation, rehabilitation services, and social sciences. These awards provide tuition waivers for a maximum of 24 semester hours per academic year and a stipend. Graduate assistantships are also available in teaching, coaching, laboratory supervision, research, and administrative areas. A limited number of scholarships, ranging from $200 to the full cost of tuition, are provided for international students. The Financial Aid Office administers federal loan programs.

Cost of Study

For a typical full-time graduate student at Springfield College, tuition and fees for two semesters (nine months) amounted to $17,281 during the 2007–08 academic year. An ample schedule of courses is planned each summer, with the cost based mainly on the number of semester hours carried.

Living and Housing Costs

The College provides three meal plan options for resident students and two options for non-resident students. Both on- and off-campus housing are available. Entertainment costs and other personal expenses vary greatly from student to student. College-owned apartments cost approximately $6410 per academic year.

Student Group

During 2007–08, there were 1,427 graduate students enrolled in the various programs. Sixty-eight percent were women. Students were drawn from twenty-four states and twenty-one countries.

Student Outcomes

Graduates consistently declare themselves well prepared and qualified for employment in the professional fields of art; occupational and physical therapy; education; counseling psychology; sport, wellness, and recreation; and health and human services. The positions include teacher, coach, trainer, counselor, administrator, director, consultant, entrepreneur, and hands-on practitioner. Employers who have recently hired Springfield graduates include the YMCA, Old Sturbridge Village, Veterans Affairs Medical Centers, Baystate Health Systems, Goodwill Industries, Motorola, Harvard University, the National Football League, the American Hockey League, Converse, Advantage Health Corp., the United States Olympic Committee, Disney Wide World of Sports, Hamilton Sundstrand, Merrill Lynch, Morgan Stanley, NBC Sports, Six Flags, United Cerebral Palsy, and Yale New Haven Hospital.

Location

The campus is located on Lake Massasoit, about 3 miles from the downtown area of Springfield, Massachusetts, offering the advantages of a small-town setting within a metropolitan area. The campus site covers 156 acres, including the 56-acre campground fronting on the lake.

The College is within a day's drive of major centers in the northeastern United States. Boston, the largest city in New England, is less than a 2-hour drive away, and New York City is only 3 hours away. The Green Mountains of Vermont and the White Mountains of New Hampshire are easily reached via modern highways going north. The entire area abounds in lakes, mountains, resorts, historic sites, museums, and other attractions.

The College

Springfield College is, and has been since its founding more than 100 years ago, concerned with the preparation of the total person—in spirit, in mind, and in body. Its professional curriculum has been specifically designed to prepare students for careers in what have come to be known as the "human-helping" professions. The College lists more than 30,000 alumni whose professional education at Springfield has enabled them to assume leadership positions in virtually all areas of community service, including recreation, physical education, counseling, psychological services, education, commerce and industry, community leadership and development, rehabilitation services, health promotion, and physical, art, occupational, and recreational therapy.

Applying

Applications for the Physical Therapy and Occupational Therapy Programs are reviewed on a rolling admissions basis beginning December 1 and January 1, respectively. Applications are due by March 1 for the Master of Social Work degree. All other programs follow a rolling admissions process, in which files are reviewed as they become complete. The general application deadline is January 15. The financial aid application deadline is March 1. Notification usually takes a minimum of six weeks from receipt of an application. Candidates lacking undergraduate prerequisites must make up their deficiencies without earning graduate credit for these. Standardized tests and interviews are not a regular part of the admission process for most master's and certificate students. However, the General Test of the GRE is required of exercise science and sport studies, physical education, physical therapy, and sport management and recreation applicants. In some programs, personal interviews are a prerequisite to action on the application. Scores on the General Test of the GRE are also required of doctoral students.

Correspondence and Information

Donald J. Shaw Jr.
Director of Graduate Admissions
Box P.G.
Springfield College
Springfield, Massachusetts 01109

Phone: 413-748-3225
Fax: 413-748-3694
E-mail: graduate@springfieldcollege.edu
Web site: http://www.springfieldcollege.edu

THE FACULTY

There are more than 100 faculty members teaching graduate-level courses. They hold degrees from colleges and universities in the United States and abroad, and approximately two thirds of them have doctorates. Many are authorities in their fields, and all members of the graduate faculty teach. In addition, many engage in research or writing projects as their teaching loads permit.

GRADUATE PROGRAMS
Dean: Betty L. Mann, Associate Professor of Physical Education; D.P.E., Springfield, 1984.
Director of Graduate Admissions: Donald J. Shaw Jr., M.Ed., Springfield, 1970.

Program Coordinators
Art Therapy: Simone Alter-Muri, Professor of Art; Ed.D., Massachusetts, 1994.
Education: Anna Weidhofer, Assistant Professor of Education; Ph.D., USC, 2005.
Exercise Science and Sport Studies: Charles J. Redmond, Associate Professor of Physical Education; M.S.P.T., Boston University, 1981.
Healthcare Management: John J. Doyle Jr., Professor of Economics; Ph.D., Clark, 1976.
Human Services: Ann Marie Frisbe, Coordinator of Admissions, School of Human Services; B.A., St. Michael's, 1993.
Occupational Therapy: Katherine M. Post, Associate Professor of Occupational Therapy; Ph.D., Connecticut, 2004.
Physical Education: Stephen Coulon, Associate Professor of Physical Education; Ph.D., Ohio State, 1987.
Physical Therapy: Linda Tsoumas, Associate Professor of Physical Therapy; Ph.D., Hartford, 2002.
Psychology: Anna Moriarty, Associate Professor of Psychology; Ph.D., US International, 1979.
Rehabilitation Services: Thomas J. Ruscio, Professor of Rehabilitation; C.A.S., Springfield, 1966.
Social Work: Francine Vecchiolla, Dean, School of Social Work; Ph.D., Brandeis, 1987.
Sport Management and Recreation: Donald R. Snyder, Professor of Sport Management and Recreation; Ph.D., Connecticut, 1987.

STATE UNIVERSITY OF NEW YORK INSTITUTE OF TECHNOLOGY

School of Business, School of Information Systems and Engineering Technology, School of Arts and Sciences, and School of Nursing and Health Systems

Programs of Study

Full-time or part-time graduate students at the State University of New York Institute of Technology (SUNYIT) can pursue the Master of Business Administration (M.B.A.) degree or a Master of Science (M.S.) degree in one of fourteen programs, some of which have online options.

In the School of Business, the M.B.A. degree in technology management prepares managers for careers in the high-tech business world. The M.B.A. degree offers both a broad and integrative perspective across business functions as well as a chance to specialize in a field of one's choice. The program, which is available online, offers the following concentrations: accounting and finance, marketing management, health services management, human resource management, and an individually designed concentration. The M.B.A. degree in health services management, also available online, is designed specifically to meet the educational and career goals of students with a desire to apply management techniques in a health-care setting. The School of Business also offers two M.S. degree programs in accountancy and health services administration. The accountancy program, which is also available online, is registered in New York State to satisfy the 150-hour licensure requirement. It prepares students for careers in public, corporate, not-for-profit, and government accounting. Graduates are prepared to sit for professional accounting examinations that lead to credentials such as the CPA and CMA designations. The health services administration program, which is also available online, prepares students for mid- to upper-level management positions in the health-care industry. Graduates may also be qualified to take the national nursing home administrator examination for licensure in the field.

The School of Information Systems and Engineering Technology offers three graduate degrees. The M.S. degree in computer and information science is designed to provide students with a strong theoretical and application-oriented education with course work in systems theory, formal languages, artificial intelligence, computer vision, and information storage and retrieval. Course offerings stress principles of problem-solving methodology that are required of computer professionals working in industry and education or those pursuing advanced degrees. The M.S. degree in advanced technology is an interdisciplinary program with an emphasis on practical applications and is designed for part-time students. The M.S. degree in telecommunications is based on a solid core of telecommunications courses combined with computer science/information systems and business-related components to provide a broad knowledge of network design, management, and maintenance of complex telecommunication systems. The program has gained an international reputation for its industry orientation.

SUNYIT's School of Arts and Sciences offers two Master of Science degree programs. The M.S. in information design and technology (IDT), which is also available online, meets the needs of professionals who use communication technologies to design and manage information. Students use a variety of computer-based tools to create original materials, including Web pages, multimedia presentations, newsletters, and related desktop publishing documents in fields such as education, technical communication, public relations, marketing, instructional design and technology, government service, publications, and corporate communication. The M.S. in applied sociology promotes the application of anthropological and sociological theory and research to design, implement, and evaluate organizationally based interventions. Students learn to integrate various methods of data collection and analysis to use in evaluating social programs.

The School of Nursing and Health Systems offers five M.S. degree programs: adult nurse practitioner, family nurse practitioner, gerontological nurse practitioner, nursing administration, and nursing education. Graduates of the nurse practitioner programs are prepared to focus on health assessments, disease prevention, health promotion, and the monitoring of chronic conditions with appropriate emphasis on the specific patient groups. The nursing administration program is specifically designed to prepare registered nurses to creatively advance the practice of nursing and facilitate the delivery of cost-effective care through the application and testing of administrative knowledge and skills. The nursing education program promotes the core application of theory, research, and health-care policy to the role of the nurse educator within the academic and in-service settings. Graduates of the master's program are qualified to take the American Nurses Association's certification exam. In addition to the M.S. degrees, advanced certificates are offered in all nursing programs.

Research Facilities

Research facilities include the Cayan Library's 192,425 bound volumes, 65,396 microforms, and an extensive collection of professional journals, newspapers, and other national publications. The library serves as a depository for selected state and federal documents. The library participates in SUNYConnect, the State University's virtual library, which offers many online resources. Graduate students also have access to interlibrary loans. SUNYIT's computing facilities include numerous laboratory environments consisting of more than 380 personal computers and workstations in a networked environment that extends to every classroom, office, and dormitory room. Internet access is provided through a fractional T-3 connection. The master's degree program in telecommunications is supported by three voice, data, and network operations laboratories possessing more than $5 million in industry-donated equipment. The IDT program is supported by a networked computer lab and related technologies, including workstations designed for collaborative project work.

Financial Aid

Matriculated graduate students who are enrolled for at least 6 credit hours each semester and are in good academic standing are eligible to apply for aid from the following sources: Federal Work-Study Program, Federal Perkins Loan Program, and Federal Direct Student Loan Program. New York State residents who are enrolled for at least 12 hours are eligible to apply for aid from the Tuition Assistance Program. Graduate assistantships are awarded each academic year to selected students and generally include a state tuition waiver for work performed as a teaching assistant, research assistant, or administrative assistant. Graduate Diversity Fellowships, which include a state tuition waiver and stipend, are available to a limited number of full-time students who demonstrate (in writing) how they will contribute to the diversity of the student body, including having overcome a disadvantage or other impediment to success in higher education.

Cost of Study

Full-time graduate tuition for New York State residents for the 2009–10 academic year is $4185 per semester for all programs except the M.B.A., which is $4305 per semester. The comprehensive student fee is $530 per semester. For non-New York State residents, full-time graduate tuition is $6625 per semester in all programs except the M.B.A., which is $6880 per semester. Part-time graduate tuition costs for the 2009–10 academic year are $349 per credit hour ($359 for the M.B.A.) for residents and $552 per credit hour ($573 for the M.B.A.) for non-New York State residents.

Living and Housing Costs

SUNYIT provides town-house-style residence halls for 584 students at $8810 for room (single rate) and board per academic year. Residence halls are available on a first-come, first-served basis. Assistance in locating off-campus housing is provided. Complete housing rate information is available online at http://www.sunyit.edu/tuition/room_board.inc.

Student Group

SUNYIT offers a small-college atmosphere, enrolling 2,828 undergraduate and graduate students in the fall 2007 semester. There were 149 full-time and 469 part-time graduate students. The ratio of men to women was approximately 1:1. Twelve percent of the students were from minority groups; 3.4 percent were international students. Students work closely with faculty members and receive individual attention with a 19:1 student-faculty ratio. Nearly 100 percent of students who have completed graduate programs at SUNYIT are working full-time in their professional field.

Location

SUNYIT is situated in the geographic center of New York State. The campus is just north of the city of Utica, which is a cultural and recreational center for the Mohawk Valley Region. Museums, theaters, and restaurants are available nearby.

The Institute

SUNYIT was established in 1966 by the SUNY Board of Trustees to provide upper-division and graduate-level education in sciences and technologies and now offers undergraduate and graduate degree programs in technology, professional studies, and selected liberal arts disciplines. The campus includes three major academic, administrative, and student life buildings; two town-house-style residential complexes; a facilities building; and a $14-million library. A new $13.6-million Student Center is under construction, while the $20-million Field House is scheduled to be completed in 2011.

Applying

Applications for graduate admission should be completed by June 1 for the fall semester and November 1 for the spring semester. Although SUNYIT does offer rolling admission in most programs, these application deadlines are required for international students. Students seeking admission to the advanced technology, computer science, and telecommunications programs are required to take the Graduate Record Examinations (GRE) General Test. The Graduate Management Admissions Test (GMAT) is required for those seeking admission to the M.S. degrees in accountancy and health services administration and the M.B.A. degrees in technology management and health services management. Scores from the GMAT follow the recommended guidelines of AACSB International. For complete admissions criteria, students should consult the SUNYIT graduate catalog, available online at http://www.sunyit.edu/catalogs/graduate.inc.

Correspondence and Information

Coordinator of the Graduate Center
State University of New York Institute of Technology
P.O. Box 3050
Utica, New York 13504-3050

Phone: 866-2-SUNYIT (toll-free)
E-mail: gradcenter@sunyit.edu
Web site: http://www.sunyit.edu

THE FACULTY AND THEIR RESEARCH

School of Arts and Sciences (Information Design and Technology, Applied Sociology)
Mona de Vestel, Assistant Professor; M.P.S., NYU. Interactive telecommunications.
Walter Johnston, Associate Professor; Ph.D., Cornell. Technical writing and editing.
Russell Kahn, Associate Professor; Ph.D., SUNY at Albany. Social, political, business, and educational implications of the Web; Web design; computer software documentation.
Kenneth Mazlen, Associate Professor; Ph.D., SUNY at Albany. Social theory, white-collar crime, unemployment and crime.
Kris Paap, Assistant Professor; Ph.D., Wisconsin. White working-class masculinity and construction, women in prison, agricultural safety.
Alphonse Sallett, Associate Professor; Ph.D., Syracuse. Social theory, criminology and the sociology of drug use.
Steven Schneider, Professor; Ph.D., MIT. Computer-mediated communication and computer-mediated instructional systems.
Kathryn Stam, Assistant Professor; Ph.D., Syracuse. Information technology in the workplace, employees' rights and behavior, cross-cultural perspectives on health.
Veronica Tichenor, Assistant Professor; Ph.D., Michigan. Marriages and families, sociology of community, violence and identity construction.
Linda Weber, Associate Professor; Ph.D., North Texas. Social practice, medical sociology, social psychology, health promotion, at-risk youth.

School of Business (M.B.A. in Technology Management; M.S. in Accountancy, Business Management, and Health Services Administration)
John Barnes, Associate Professor; Ph.D., Arizona State. Marketing.
Lisa Berardino, Associate Professor; Ph.D., Virginia Tech. Human resource management in small businesses, adult learning and needs assessment.
Sema Dube, Assistant Professor; Ph.D., George Washington. Firm acquisitions and mergers.
Laura Francis-Gladney, Assistant Professor; Ph.D., Southern Illinois Carbondale. Accounting.
Joseph Gerard, Assistant Professor; Ph.D., Georgia. Technology management.
Stephen Havlovic, Professor and Dean; Ph.D., Ohio State. Human resource management.
Kimberly Jarrell, Assistant Professor; Ph.D., Syracuse. Marketing and technology.
Peter Karl, Associate Professor; J.D., Albany Law; M.B.A., Rensselaer; CPA. Tax, business law, real estate transactions, federal taxation.
Efstathios Kefallonitis, Assistant Professor; Ph.D., Cranfield. Marketing.
Hoseoup Lee, Assistant Professor; Ph.D., Connecticut. Capital markets and accounting information systems.
David McLain, Assistant Professor; Ph.D, Wisconsin-Madison. Technology management.
James Morey, Associate Professor; M.B.A., George Washington. Hospital merger/consolidations, nursing home establishment, expansion and acquisition, operational analysis.
Rafael F. Romero, Associate Professor; Ph.D., West Virginia. Emerging capital markets, international economics.
Gary Scherzer, Associate Professor; M.P.H., Tennessee. Public health, planning, marketing, health policy.
Maureen Smith-Gaffney, Assistant Professor; Ph.D., Ohio State. Accounting.
Janice Welker, Assistant Professor; Ph.D., St. Louis. Managed care, economics.
Robert Yeh, Assistant Professor; Ph.D., Purdue. Quantitative marketing models, statistical applications and mathematical modeling in product designing and product improvement.

School of Information Systems and Engineering Technology (Advanced Technology, Computer Information Science, and Telecommunications)
Bruno Andriamanalimanana, Associate Professor; Ph.D., Lehigh. Combinatorics, coding theory and cryptography.
Daniel Benincasa, Assistant Professor; Ph.D., Rensselaer. Digital signal processing, electrooptic systems, RF systems, communication intelligence systems.
Timothy Busch, Assistant Professor; Ph.D., SUNY at Binghamton. Adversarial modeling, operationally focused simulation, multiresolution modeling, control system reconfigurability.
Roger Cavallo, Professor; Ph.D., SUNY at Binghamton. Systems theory, systems methodology, conceptual modeling, probabilistic database theory.
William Confer, Assistant Professor; Ph.D., Auburn. Real-time systems, embedded systems, computer architecture.
Digendra Kumar Das, Associate Professor; Ph.D., Manchester (England). CAD/CAM/CIM, fluid/prognostics, turbomachinery and thermal sciences and MEMS.
Heather Dussault, Assistant Professor; Ph.D., Rensselaer. Nuclear engineering and science.
Larry Hash, Associate Professor of Telecommunications; Ph.D., North Carolina State. Wireless networks and services, LAN-WAN.
Atlas Hsie, Associate Professor; M.S., Michigan; M.S., Akron; CmfgE, CQE, CRE. Quality and reliability engineering, engineering economics, production management, CAM and robotics.
Raymond G. Jesaitis, Professor; Ph.D., Cornell. Distributed systems, UNIX operating system, numerical methods.
Daniel K. Jones, Assistant Professor; Ph.D., Pittsburgh; PE. Rehabilitation engineering and assistive technology, experimental fluid mechanics and FMS.
Michael J. Medley, Assistant Professor; Ph.D., Rensselaer. Lapped transform domain excision, adaptive nonlinear/linear filtering, RA-OFDM, wireless information assurance, integrated transmission and exploitation.
Rosemary Mullick, Associate Professor; Ph.D., Wayne State. Operating systems, artificial intelligence, computer networks, parallels between human cognition and artificial intelligence and human engineering.
Jorge Novillo, Professor; Ph.D., Lehigh. Combinatorics, complexity, artificial intelligence.
Michael Pittarelli, Professor; Ph.D., SUNY at Binghamton. Systems science, artificial intelligence, statistics, database theory.
Salahuddin Qazi, Associate Professor; Ph.D., Loughborough (England). Fiber optics, optical and wireless communications.
Mohamed Rezk, Associate Professor; D.Eng., Concordia. Circuit theory, computer-aided circuit design, and digital filters.
Ronald Sarner, Distinguished Service Professor; Ph.D., SUNY at Binghamton. Data modeling, statistical inference in the social sciences, instructional computing.
Saumendra Sengupta, Professor; Ph.D., Waterloo. Systems modeling, computer networks and distributed systems, pattern recognition.
Scott Spetka, Associate Professor; Ph.D., UCLA. Distributed database systems and distributed query processing.
Anglo-Kamel Tadros, Associate Professor; Ph.D., Bradford (England). Mechanics of sheet metal forming, computer-aided engineering, finite element analysis.
F. Andrew Wolfe, Associate Professor; Ph.D., Rensselaer; PE. Traffic flow, transportation planning, engineering interaction with society, Erie Canal archeology.

School of Nursing and Health Systems (Nursing Administration, Nursing Education, Gerontological Nurse Practitioner, Family Nurse Practitioner, Adult Nurse Practitioner)
Esther G. Bankert, Dean; Ph.D., SUNY at Albany. Nursing education, curriculum and instruction, research, theory.
Louise Dean-Kelly, Associate Professor; D.N.S., SUNY at Buffalo. Adult and family health, clinical pathophysiology, health promotion and disease prevention.
Darlene Del Prato, Assistant Professor; Ph.D. candidate, Syracuse. Nursing education, theory, curriculum.
Patricia Grust, Instructor; Ph.D. candidate, Walden. Nursing education, legal issues, test and measurement.
Deborah A. Hayes, Clinical Assistant Professor; Ph.D. candidate, Rocky Mountain University of Health Care Professionals. Adult and family health, advanced clinical practice, advanced health assessment.
Jennifer Klimek-Yingling, Instructor; Ph.D. candidate, Rutgers. Adult and family health, pediatric nursing, health assessment.
Gina Myers, Assistant Professor; Ph.D., SUNY at Binghamton. Nursing administration, grant proposal.
Francia Reed, Instructor; M.S., SUNY Technology. Adult and family health, women's health, health assessment.
Kathleen F. Sellers, Associate Professor; Ph.D., Adelphi. Nursing administration, research, health-care systems.
Amy Shaver, Assistant Professor; Ph.D., SUNY at Binghamton. Nursing administration, public health nursing, ethical issues, theory.
Judith Webb, Instructor; M.S., SUNY Technology. Gerontological health, clinical practice, health promotion and disease prevention.
Pat Zawko, Assistant Professor; Ph.D. candidate, Phoenix. Nursing education, public health nursing, instructional design.

TEACHERS COLLEGE, COLUMBIA UNIVERSITY

Programs of Study

Teachers College, Columbia University, is the world's largest and most comprehensive graduate school of education, applied psychology, and health professions. Programs lead to Master of Arts, Master of Science, Master of Education, Doctor of Education, and Doctor of Philosophy degrees. The College comprises the Departments of Arts and Humanities; Biobehavioral Studies; Counseling and Clinical Psychology; Curriculum and Teaching; Health and Behavioral Studies; Human Development; International and Transcultural Studies; Mathematics, Science, and Technology; and Organization and Leadership. These nine departments are augmented by centers, institutes, and projects that reinforce instructional areas with research, service, and experiential initiatives. Teachers College puts strong emphasis on consultation and field research and on close faculty-student relationships. Day and evening classes are available.

Areas of study are administration of special education; adult education; adult learning and leadership; anthropology and education; applied anthropology; applied behavior analysis; applied linguistics; applied physiology; applied physiology and nutrition; art and art education; arts administration; bilingual/bicultural education; blindness and visual impairment; clinical psychology; cognitive studies in education; communication; community nutrition education; comparative and international education; computing and education; conflict resolution; counseling psychology; cross-categorical studies; curriculum and teaching; curriculum and teaching in physical education; deaf and hard of hearing; developmental psychology; early childhood education; early childhood special education; economics and education; educational leadership; educational leadership and management (with Columbia Business School); educational policy; elementary inclusive education; English education; gifted education; guidance and rehabilitation; health-care human resources; health education; higher and postsecondary education; history and education; instructional practice; instructional technology and media; intellectual disabilities/autism; interdisciplinary studies in education; international educational development; kinesiology; learning disabilities; literacy specialist; mathematics education; measurement, evaluation, and statistics; motor learning and control; music and music education; neuroscience and education; nurse executive studies; nursing education; nutrition education; philosophy and education; physical disabilities; physical education; politics and education; psychological counseling; psychology in education; reading and learning disabilities; reading specialist studies; school psychology; science education; social-organizational psychology; social studies; sociology and education; speech and language pathology; supervision of special education; teaching American Sign Language as a foreign language; teaching English to speakers of other languages; and technology specialist.

Research Facilities

The Gottesman Libraries, with more than a million books and materials, is one of the nation's largest and most comprehensive research libraries in education, psychology, and health services. Students also have access to the 9.5 million volumes in the Columbia University library system. Organized research and service activities at Teachers College, in addition to being carried out by individual professors, are conducted through special projects and major institutes.

Financial Aid

Each year, Teachers College awards approximately $5 million of its own funds in scholarship and stipend aid and $2 million of endowed funds to new and continuing students. Most scholarship awards are made on the basis of academic merit. Scholarships are applied to tuition only, and students should expect to provide additional funds for the tuition balance, fees, medical insurance, academic, and living expenses.

Cost of Study

For the 2009–10 academic year, tuition was $1127 per point, with 12 or more points considered full-time. Fees include the Teachers College, $368; Teachers College research, $368; health service, $387; continuous doctoral advisement registration, $3381; and Ph.D. oral defense, $4719. The tuition deposit is $300. Medical insurance ranges from $646 to $1422.

Living and Housing Costs

Teachers College offers a variety of on-campus housing options that are unique to the area and convenient to the campus. Housing for a single student ranges from $3600 to $8800 per semester, depending on the type of setting selected. Family housing ranges from $6700 to $8700 per semester. Teachers College has approximately 705 spaces available for single students and 150 apartments for students with families. The buildings are located in the vibrant and historic urban neighborhood of Morningside Heights. Current residence halls are historic buildings similar to other apartment-style buildings that were in New York City in the early 1900s.

Student Group

There are more than 5,000 students enrolled at Teachers College. About 77 percent are women, 9 percent are African American, 11 percent are Asian American, and 6 percent are Latino/a. The student body is composed of 12 percent international students from eighty different countries and 88 percent domestic students from all fifty states. While about one third of TC students are working toward or developing their teaching career, the balance of the TC student community are pursuing careers in a wide range of fields, including educational policy, educational administration and leadership, arts administration, technology, psychology, social and behavioral sciences, health, communication, and international and comparative education.

Location

The College is located in the Morningside Heights section of Manhattan's Upper West Side, home to such venerable New York landmarks as Lincoln Center, the Cathedral of St. John the Divine, Grant's Tomb, Morningside Park, and the Manhattan School of Music. The Upper West Side is bounded by Central Park on the east and the Hudson River on the west. Because the College is located in New York City, students have access to an outstanding array of learning organizations, including museums, libraries, galleries, corporate learning centers, and K–12 schools.

The College and The University

Teachers College was founded in 1887 to provide a new form of schooling for the teachers of children from low-income families of New York—one that combined a humanitarian concern to help others with a scientific approach to human development. For more than 100 years, Teachers College has conducted research on the central issues facing education, prepared generations of education leaders, and shaped debate and public policy in education. The College provides programs of study in administration, counseling, curriculum development, and school health care and continues its efforts to strengthen teaching skills, prepare leaders to develop and administer psychological and health-care programs, and develop new teaching software. In 1898, Teachers College became affiliated with Columbia University.

Columbia University was founded in 1754 as King's College by royal charter of King George II of England. It is the oldest institution of higher learning in the state of New York and the fifth-oldest in the United States. From its beginnings in a schoolhouse in lower Manhattan, the University has grown to encompass two principal campuses: the historic, neoclassical campus in Morningside Heights and the modern Medical Center in Washington Heights. Today, Columbia is one of the top academic and research institutions in the world, conducting research in medicine, science, the arts, and the humanities. It includes three undergraduate schools, thirteen graduate and professional schools, and a school of continuing education. Sixty-four Nobel laureates have taught or studied at Columbia. Each year, the faculty of approximately 4,000 teaches more than 24,000 students from more than 150 countries.

Applying

Teachers College welcomes applicants who wish to pursue graduate study associated with the education, psychology, and health-related professions. All applicants receive consideration for admission without regard to race, color, creed, religion, sex, national origin, age, or disability. In order to be considered for scholarships, students must meet the early deadline. Admissions applications received after the early deadline may be considered on a space-available basis. Certain programs have special application deadlines. The early deadline for Ph.D. and all psychology doctoral programs is December 15. The early deadline for Ed.D. programs is January 2, with a final deadline of April 1. The early deadline for master's programs is January 15, with a final deadline of April 15. For the spring semester, the early deadline is November 1.

Teachers College requests that applicants collect the required documents for the application process and submit the complete application to the Office of Admission at one time. Admission application deadlines always refer to the date by which the Teachers College Office of Admissions must have received the application components and any other supporting material required by the Department. For more information on applying to Teachers College and for an online application, prospective students may visit the College's Web site at http://www.tc.columbia.edu/admissions.

Correspondence and Information

Teachers College, Columbia University
525 West 120th Street, Box 302
New York, New York 10027

Phone: 212-678-3710
Web site: http://www.tc.columbia.edu

RESEARCH CENTERS AND INSTITUTES

The Center for Adult Education is interested in research on adult and organizational learning and on transformative learning for adults in a variety of settings. The center has conducted award-winning research on literacy and has pioneered an innovative Action Research Professional Development program.

The Center for Arts Education Research is an interdisciplinary arts group that engages in basic and applied research in the arts and human development, art education, and the arts in education. The center calls upon expertise from professionals in visual, music, dance, theater, and media arts and also philosophy, psychology, education, and technology. Studies explore the role of the arts in diverse educational settings.

The Center on Chinese Education is aimed at contributing to a better understanding of education in China and to educational exchange between the United States and China.

The Dean Hope Center for Educational and Psychological Services is both a training and research center for the College and a community resource that provides help to people of all ages with educational and personal problems. Several hundred psychoeducational assessment and evaluation instruments, as well as a growing library of materials for reading remediation, are available for use by the students attending practicums affiliated with the center.

The Center for Health Promotion comprises diverse working groups of faculty members and students who are interested in stimulating research and development efforts responsive to national priorities in health promotion and disease prevention.

The Center for Opportunities and Outcomes for People with Disabilities confronts the challenges facing special education today and broadens the scope of research at Teachers College. The center is committed to producing knowledge and professional expertise that enhances the quality of life for people with disabilities.

The Center for Social Imagination, the Arts, and Education is committed to the development of alternative modes of inventing, creating, and interpreting. Working in the tradition of Dewey, James, and the Existentialists, the center brings schoolchildren, artists, academics, and social activists together in conferences and workshops to explore possibilities of reform and transformation in schools and social communities.

The Center for Technology and School Change helps schools integrate technology into their curricula and daily lives by planning for the use of technology with schools, educating teachers how to use it, planning curriculum projects that include technology, helping teachers to implement projects, and assessing the effect of technology on schools.

The Community College Research Center carries out and promotes research on major issues affecting the development, growth, and changing roles of community colleges in the United States.

The Creative Arts Laboratory prepares teachers of economically disadvantaged and educationally challenged students to change school cultures by integrating the arts into core curricula of public elementary and middle schools.

The Edward D. Mysak Speech-Language and Hearing Center provides advanced students in the Speech and Language Pathology and Audiology Program practical experience in a professional setting. The center offers evaluation and therapy services to individuals who have speech, voice, language, or hearing problems.

The Elbenwood Center for the Study of the Family as Educator pursues various lines of systematic research and inquiry that bring the behavioral sciences to bear in illuminating the educational functions of the family and the relationships between the family and other educative institutions. Recent topics include social networks and educative styles of teenagers, the mediation of television by the family and television in cross-cultural perspective, multigenerational education, grandparents as educators, and immigration.

The Rita Gold Early Childhood Center supports and promotes the growth and development of infants, toddlers, and preschoolers and their families through supportive early care and education; transdisciplinary professional preparation for students; ongoing research to improve practice and inform theory in early development, care, and education for young children and families; and outreach. The center is a resource for students across the College who are engaged in observation, teaching, and research with young children and families.

Hollingworth Center is a service, research, and demonstration site designed to provide internship and training opportunities for the graduate students at Teachers College. The center develops model programs in early childhood education and offers enriching educational services for children and educators in the neighboring communities.

The J. M. Huber Institute for Learning in Organizations conducts research on learning and change in organizations. The institute works through partnerships with organizations, including businesses, not-for-profits, and government agencies, to assist those who want to improve their ability to use learning strategically to address business and organizational challenges.

The Institute for Learning Technologies (ILT) uses digital communications technologies to advance innovation in education and society. Rapid change in information technology is reconfiguring social, cultural, and intellectual possibilities. ILT is a major element of Columbia University's effort to shape these transitions.

The Institute for Urban and Minority Education is committed to better understanding and influencing the educational, psychological, and social development of urban and minority-group students and the schools that serve them.

The Institute of International Studies helps to formulate and coordinate the College's international effort, to serve as both catalyst and repository for grants and gifts in aid of international studies at the College, to strengthen instructional programs with comparative and international thrusts, and to upgrade the quality of research on international or cross-national themes.

The Institute on Education and the Economy (IEE) is an interdisciplinary policy research center that focuses its attention on the interaction between education and the economy. IEE's research agenda includes issues such as the changes in the nature, organization, and skill requirements of work; education reforms designed to address the changing needs of the workplace; work-based learning; employer participation in education; and academic and industry-based skill standards.

The International Center for Cooperation and Conflict Resolution helps individuals as well as institutions better understand the nature of conflict and how to achieve its constructive resolution. The center particularly emphasizes the importance of the social, cultural, organizational, and institutional contexts within which conflicts occur.

The Klingenstein Center for Independent School Education sponsors programs aimed at the professional development of independent school teachers and administrators and research activities that contribute to the advancement of independent school education.

The National Center for Children and Families advances the policy, education, and development of children and their families. The center produces and applies interdisciplinary research to improve practice and raise public awareness of social issues that affect the well-being of America's children and families. This work is accomplished through cutting-edge research and analysis; the systematic training of future leaders, scholars, and policy scientists; and dissemination of information to the media, policy makers, and practitioners on the front lines.

The National Center for Restructuring Education, Schools, and Teaching supports restructuring efforts by documenting successful school improvement initiatives, creating reform networks to share new research findings with practitioners, and linking policy to practice.

The National Center for the Study of Privatization in Education serves as a nonpartisan venue to analyze and disseminate information about the contentious private initiatives in education, including vouchers, charter schools, and educational contracting.

The Research Center for Arts and Culture provides data and ideas for applied research, education, advocacy, policymaking, and action. Collaboration and cooperation with service organizations, trade publishers, and arts institutions strengthen the center's unique position and enable it to translate its findings into useful, practical forms.

The Teachers College Reading and Writing Project is a staff development organization that works in intimate and long-lasting ways with educators in the metropolitan area and provides more limited assistance to educators all over the U.S. to establish reading and writing workshops.

Graduate School
TEMPLE UNIVERSITY®

TEMPLE UNIVERSITY

Graduate School

Programs of Study

Doctor of Philosophy programs are offered in the following fields: African American studies, anthropology, art history, biochemistry, biology, biomedical neuroscience, business administration (accounting, entrepreneurship, finance, international business administration, management information systems, marketing, risk management and insurance, strategic management, tourism and sport), cell biology, chemistry, communication sciences, computer and information science, counseling psychology, criminal justice, dance, economics, educational psychology, engineering, English, geoscience, health ecology, history, kinesiology (athletic training, curriculum and instruction, integrative exercise physiology, psychology of movement), mass media and communication, mathematics, microbiology and immunology, molecular biology and genetics, molecular and cellular physiology, music education, music therapy, pathology, pharmaceutical sciences (medicinal chemistry, pharmaceutics, pharmacodynamics), pharmacology, philosophy, physical therapy, physics, political science, psychology, public health (health policy, social and behavioral health sciences), religion, school psychology, sociology, Spanish, statistics, urban education, and urban studies.

The Doctor of Musical Arts is offered in music composition and music performance (bassoon, cello, clarinet, double bass, flute, French horn, harp, oboe, percussion, piano, trombone, trumpet, tuba, viola, violin, voice). Doctor of Education degrees are offered in curriculum, instruction, and technology in education (language arts, math and science education) and in educational administration. The Doctor of Occupational Therapy and Doctor of Physical Therapy degrees are also offered.

Master's degree programs are offered in accounting and financial management; actuarial science; adult and organizational development; African American studies; architecture; art education; art history; biochemistry; bioengineering; biology; biomedical neuroscience; broadcasting, telecommunications, and mass media; business administration (accounting, business management, financial management, health-care and life sciences innovation, human resource management, information technology management, international business management, marketing management, pharmaceutical management, risk management, strategic management); cell biology; chemistry; choral conducting; civil engineering; clinical research and translational medicine; communication management (media management, government and social policy, strategic and corporate communication management); community and regional planning (sustainable community planning, transportation planning); computer and information science; counseling psychology; creative writing; criminal justice; curriculum, instruction, and technology in education (applied behavioral analysis, career and technical education, early childhood education, elementary education, English education, mathematics education, reading, science education, second and foreign language education, special education, teaching English as a second language); dance; economics; educational administration; educational psychology; electrical engineering; English; environmental engineering; environmental health; epidemiology; finance; financial engineering; geography and urban studies; geology; graduate teacher certification (career and technical education, elementary education, secondary education, special education); health informatics; health-care financial management; health-care management; history; human resource management; information science and technology; information technology management; international business (finance, general and strategic management, human resource management, marketing, risk management and insurance); journalism; kinesiology (athletic training, curriculum and instruction, integrative exercise physiology, psychology of movement); landscape architecture; liberal arts; linguistics; management information systems; marketing; mathematics; mechanical engineering; microbiology and immunology; molecular biology and genetics; molecular and cellular physiology; music composition; music education; music history; music performance (bassoon, cello, clarinet, classical guitar, double bass, flute, French horn, harp, harpsichord, oboe, percussion, piano, saxophone, trombone, trumpet, tuba, viola, violin, voice); music theory; music therapy; nursing; occupational therapy; opera; oral biology; pharmaceutical sciences (medicinal chemistry, pharmaceutics, pharmacodynamics); philosophy; physics; piano accompanying (chamber music, opera coaching); piano pedagogy; political science; public health (environmental health, epidemiology and biostatistics, global health, social and behavioral science); quality assurance and regulatory affairs; religion; school health education; school psychology; social work; sociology; Spanish; speech, language, and hearing science; sport and recreation management; statistics; string pedagogy; therapeutic recreation; tourism and hospitality management; and urban education. Also offered are an executive M.B.A. and an international M.B.A.

Master of Fine Arts degree programs are available in ceramics and glass, dance, fibers and fabric design, film and media arts, graphic and interactive design, metals/jewelry/CAD-CAM, painting, photography, printmaking, sculpture, and theater (acting, design, directing, playwriting).

Research Facilities

The University libraries contain nearly 2.5 million volumes and provide reading space for 2,500 students. Across the main campus, numerous research centers and laboratories offer facilities where faculty members and students engage in collaborative research. In addition, less than 2 miles north of the main academic campus is the Health Sciences Center at Broad and Ontario Streets. This campus houses the Schools of Medicine, Dentistry, and Pharmacy; the College of Health Professions and Social Work; Temple University Hospital; and the Medical Research Building, all of which offer excellent and varied facilities for research in many fields.

Financial Aid

Graduate students are eligible for various kinds of financial assistance from private, University, state, and federal sources. The Office of Student Financial Services (http://www.temple.edu/sfs) administers loans, grants, work-study, and other forms of financial aid. Students should visit the Web site or contact the SFS office directly at 215-204-2244 for additional information about financial assistance.

Cost of Study

Resident tuition for the 2009–10 academic year is $590 per credit hour for most graduate programs, $609 per credit hour for the Tyler School of Art, $630 per credit hour for the College of Engineering, $613 per credit hour for the College of Health Professions and Social Work, $752 per credit hour for the Fox School of Business and Management and the School of Tourism and Hospitality Management, and $854 per credit hour for courses in the School of Pharmacy's Department of Pharmaceutical Sciences. Nonresident tuition is $861 per credit hour for most graduate programs, $897 per credit hour for the Tyler School of Art and the College of Health Professions and Social Work, $902 per credit hour for the College of Engineering, $1116 per credit hour for the Fox School of Business and Management and the School of Tourism and Hospitality Management, and $1133 per credit hour for courses in the School of Pharmacy's Department of Pharmaceutical Sciences.

Living and Housing Costs

On-campus housing is limited. For information on availability, students should contact the Office of University Housing and Residential Life at 215-204-7184 or visit http://www.temple.edu/studentaffairs/housing.

Student Group

With a student body of more than 37,000 students, Temple University is among the fifty largest universities in the country. Since becoming a part of the Commonwealth System of Higher Education, it has placed increased emphasis on upper-division and graduate work. Although the institution has historically served the greater metropolitan area of southeastern Pennsylvania, a significant and growing portion of the student body is from outside Philadelphia.

Location

Philadelphia is the sixth-largest city in the country and has a regional population of more than 6.1 million. It offers a variety of cultural attractions. The city has a world-renowned symphony orchestra, a ballet company, two professional opera companies, and a chamber music society. Besides attracting touring plays, Philadelphia enjoys a professional repertory theater and many amateur productions. All facilities for sports and recreation are easy to reach. The city is world famous for its historic shrines, parks, and eighteenth-century charm, which is carefully maintained in its oldest section. The climate is temperate, with an average winter temperature of 33 degrees and an average summer temperature of 75 degrees.

The University

The development of Temple University has been in line with the ideal of "educational opportunity for the able and deserving student of limited means." With a rich heritage of populist tradition, Temple provides students with an opportunity for education of high quality without regard to race, creed, or station in life. Affiliation with the Commonwealth System of Higher Education undergirds Temple's character as a public institution.

Temple's academic programs are conducted on six campuses in central and north Philadelphia and its nearby suburbs. These locations, as well as numerous extension centers throughout eastern Pennsylvania, give Temple University the distinction of being a fast-growing institution with many superior facilities.

The main campus, located at Broad Street and Montgomery Avenue, is the site of the Colleges of Education, Engineering, Liberal Arts, and Science and Technology; the Esther Boyer College of Music and Dance; the Schools of Communications and Theater, and Tourism and Hospitality Management; the Beasley School of Law; and the Fox School of Business and Management.

Applying

Departmental deadlines for admissions and financial aid vary. Applicants should consult the Graduate Bulletin (http://www.temple.edu/gradbulletin) and the Web site of the program in which they are interested. Notification regarding admission and financial aid is made following the screening of the application.

Correspondence and Information

Richard M. Englert, Ed.D.
Interim Dean of the Graduate School
501 Carnell Hall
Temple University
1803 North Broad Street
Philadelphia, Pennsylvania 19122-6095

Phone: 215-204-1380
Fax: 215-204-8781
Web site: http://www.temple.edu/grad

FACULTY HEADS

Graduate School: Richard M. Englert, Ed.D., Interim Dean.
College of Education: C. Kent McGuire, Ph.D., Dean.
College of Engineering: Keyanoush Sadeghipour, Ph.D., Dean.
College of Health Professions and Social Work: Ronald T. Brown, Ph.D., Dean.
College of Liberal Arts: Teresa Scott Soufas, Ph.D., Dean.
College of Science and Technology: Hai-Lung Dai, Ph.D., Dean.
Esther Boyer College of Music and Dance: Robert T. Stroker, Ph.D., Dean.
James E. Beasley School of Law: JoAnne A. Epps, J.D., Dean.
Maurice H. Kornberg School of Dentistry: Amid I. Ismail, Dr.P.H., Dean.
Richard J. Fox School of Business and Management: M. Moshe Porat, Ph.D., Dean.
School of Communications and Theater: Thomas Jacobson, Ph.D., Interim Dean.
School of Environmental Design: Teresa Scott Soufas, Ph.D., Dean.
School of Medicine: John M. Daly, M.D., Dean.
School of Pharmacy: Peter H. Doukas, Ph.D., Dean.
School of Podiatric Medicine: John A. Mattiacci, D.P.M., Dean.
School of Tourism and Hospitality Management: M. Moshe Porat, Ph.D., Dean.
Tyler School of Art: Robert T. Stroker, Ph.D., Interim Dean.

A time for quiet study in Mitten Hall.

The view from Founder's Garden at Temple's main campus.

TEXAS TECH UNIVERSITY

Graduate School

Programs of Study

Texas Tech University prides itself on being a major comprehensive research university that retains the atmosphere of a smaller liberal arts institution. Although enrollment is over 28,000, Texas Tech students boast of one-on-one interaction with top faculty and an environment that stresses student accomplishment above all else. The University strives to be large enough to provide the best in facilities and academics, but small enough to focus on individual students. Through its Graduate School, School of Law, School of Allied Health, School of Nursing, School of Pharmacy, and School of Medicine, Texas Tech offers a diverse range of graduate studies. The Graduate School offers degrees from ten academic colleges. The College of Agriculture offers the Doctor of Philosophy (Ph.D.), Master of Science (M.S.), Doctor of Education (Ed.D.), and Master of Agriculture (M.Ag.) in a variety of disciplines. In addition, the college offers the Master of Landscape Architecture (M.L.A.). The College of Architecture offers the Master of Architecture (M.Arch.), Master of Science in architecture, and Ph.D. degrees. The College of Arts and Sciences offers many degrees in a vast range of disciplines, including the Ph.D. in eighteen academic disciplines, the Master of Arts (M.A.) in eighteen fields, and the Master of Science in twelve fields. Texas Tech's College of Business Administration offers the Ph.D. in business administration, M.S. in business administration, Master of Science in Accounting (M.S.A.), and Master of Business Administration (M.B.A.) degree programs. Each degree offers concentrations in various areas. An M.B.A. is available as a joint degree with foreign languages, law, nursing, and medicine and also with architecture. The College of Education offers the Master of Education (M.Ed.) in twelve fields, the Doctor of Education, and the Ph.D. The College of Engineering offers the Ph.D. in seven engineering fields, the M.S. in ten fields, the Master of Engineering (M.Eng.), the Master of Science in Environmental Engineering (M.S.Env.E.), and the Master of Science in Environmental Technology Management (M.S.E.T.M.). The College of Human Sciences offers the M.S. as well as the Ph.D. in various fields. The College of Visual and Performing Arts offers Ph.D., M.A., Master of Fine Arts (M.F.A.), Master of Music (M.M.), and Master of Music Education (M.M.Ed.) degrees. In addition, the college offers the Doctor of Musical Arts (D.M.A.). The College of Mass Communication offers the Ph.D. in mass communication and M.S. in mass communication, both designed to prepare students for careers in communications research and academia. The College of Outreach and Distance Education offers a variety of online Master's Degrees and two online doctoral degrees: Doctor of Education in Agricultural Education (a joint program with Texas A&M University) and Doctor of Philosophy in Technical Communication and Rhetoric (TRC). In addition to the online programs several distance degrees are offered through the University's teaching sites in Abilene, Amarillo, Fredericksburg, Marble Falls, and Junction, Texas.

Interdisciplinary degrees housed in the Graduate School include predesigned programs or self-designed programs that are coordinated to meet individual needs. Predesigned programs include applied linguistics, forensic science, heritage management, international affairs, museum science, public administration, sports health, and multidisciplinary science. Self-designed programs may be generated from any of the courses listed in the graduate catalog. Some of the more common minors or areas of interest include comparative literature, environmental evaluation, ethnic studies, fine arts management, land-use planning management and design, Latin American studies, legal studies, neural and behavioral science, risk-taking behavior, and women's studies. The School of Law offers the Doctor of Jurisprudence degree and joint-degree programs with the M.P.A., M.S. in agricultural economics; M.S. in accounting; and M.B.A. The School of Allied Health offers an M.S. in three disciplines: communication disorders (speech-language pathology or audiology), occupational therapy, and physical therapy. The School of Nursing offers a Ph.D. in Nursing, a Master of Science in Nursing, and a joint-degree program with the M.B.A. The School of Pharmacy offers the Doctor of Pharmacy (Pharm.D.). The School of Medicine offers the Doctor of Medicine, medical education in thirty residency programs, Ph.D. and M.S. degrees in six disciplines, and a joint M.B.A./M.D. degree.

Research Facilities

Graduate study is strongly supported by the University and its departments. The library houses more than 4 million volumes and more than 27,000 serials. The high-performance computer center provides students with up-to-date computing facilities. The Advanced Technology Learning Center gives students comprehensive access to the latest computer technology and software. Many departments feature their own library and computer facilities. Consistent dedication to quality and research has earned national and international respect for numerous departments. Every department has its own strengths, and each college possesses its special resources, centers for investigation, and research opportunities. A small sample of the numerous centers and institutes includes the Institute for Ergonomics Research, Institute for Banking and Financial Studies, Child Development Center, Center for Petroleum Mathematics, Southwest Center for German Studies, Institute for Disaster Research, International Center for Arid and Semi-Arid Land Studies, Center for the Study of Addiction, Center for Professional Development, and Institute of Environmental and Human Health. In the new Carnegie classification, Texas Tech was rated as an RU/H: Research University (high research activity), the highest category for graduate degree–granting institutions.

Financial Aid

Graduate students are eligible for an array of scholarships, fellowships, and research or teaching assistantships in many academic disciplines. Part-time employment is readily available both on and off campus. The University participates in most federal and state grant, loan, and work-study programs. Texas Tech University's Gelin Emergency Loan Fund is a special benefit for students in need. Non-Texas residents receiving approved scholarships, fellowships, or assistantships may be eligible to pay Texas resident tuition, which is among the lowest in the nation.

Cost of Study

Graduate School tuition and fees for the 2009–10 academic year for Texas residents are approximately $373 per semester credit hour. Students employed at least half-time as teaching or research assistants pay the same tuition as Texas residents. The graduate nonresident tuition rate for residents of New Mexico and Oklahoma who are legal residents of a county adjacent to Texas is $373 per semester credit hour. Nonresident student tuition is $651 per semester credit hour. Fees may vary but generally include the Texas Tech University identification fee, laboratory fee, informational technology fee, library fee, and general fees. Most fees are waived for half-time teaching and research assistants. Tuition and fees for law and nursing vary and may be confirmed in the course catalog or by contacting the school directly. Texas has no state income tax. Tuition and fees are subject to change.

Living and Housing Costs

Characteristics of Lubbock are low unemployment, low housing costs, and a low cost of living. On-campus living, meals included, in upperclass halls costs $8336 per academic year. Abundant privately owned housing in the city meets most price and amenity demands.

Student Group

More than 50 percent of Texas Tech's 28,000 students have permanent homes more than 300 miles away, making Tech a residential campus. Students come from all parts of Texas, the nation, and more than 100 other countries. Tech's growing graduate and professional student population is about 4,400, most of whom are full-time students.

Location

With a population of approximately 200,000, Lubbock enjoys all the services of a major city. The city has more than sixty parks, numerous cultural and civic events, and a modern and convenient international airport that hosts several major airlines. Lubbock is the principal trade, medical, and financial center in a rich agricultural and petroleum area. Situated on the high plains of west Texas, Lubbock is about an hour's flight from Dallas, Houston, Albuquerque, and Denver. Lubbock enjoys 265 days of sunshine each year, a warm and dry climate, and pleasant weather year-round.

The University

Founded in 1923, Texas Tech is a state-assisted major research university. Texas Tech's campus features expansive lawns and impressive landscaping with unique Spanish Renaissance architecture. The beautiful, spacious campus—one of the largest in the nation—is well-equipped not only for research and study but also for cultural and recreational activities. A fulfilling after-study-hours life can be achieved by participating in the wide array of campus and community activities.

Applying

Application forms for admission can be provided upon request or accessed electronically through the Graduate School Web site. Applications are accepted throughout the year for the fall, spring, and two summer terms. The Graduate School requires a $50 application fee for U.S. citizens and permanent residents and $75 for international applicants.

Correspondence and Information

Shannon Samson
Coordinator for Graduate School Recruitment
Graduate Admissions
Texas Tech University
P.O. Box 41030
Lubbock, Texas 79409-1030

Phone: 806-742-2787 Ext. 239
E-mail: shannon.samson@ttu.edu
Web site: http://www.gradschool.ttu.edu

DEANS AND FACULTY HEADS

Graduate School: Fred Hartmeister, Dean; J.D., Ed.D., Denver (phone: 806-742-2781).

Agricultural Sciences: Marvin Cepica, Dean; Ed.D., Oklahoma State (phone: 806-742-2810).
Agricultural and Applied Economics: Eduardo Segarra, Ph.D., Virginia Tech.
Agricultural Education and Communication: Matt Baker, Ph.D., Ohio State.
Food Science: Kevin Pond, Ph.D., Texas A&M.
Landscape Architecture: Alon Kvashny, Ed.D., West Virginia.
Plant and Soil Science: Thomas Thompson, Ph.D., Iowa State.
Natural Resources Management: Ernest Fish, Ph.D., Arizona.

Architecture: Andrew Vernooy, Dean; M.Arch., Texas at Austin (phone: 806-742-3136).
Associate Dean (Academics): Michael G. Peters, M.Arch., Harvard.
Associate Dean (Research): Glenn Hill, M.Arch., Colorado.

Arts and Sciences: Jane L. Winer, Dean; Ph.D., Ohio State (phone: 806-742-3833).
Biological Sciences: John Zak, Ph.D., Calgary.
Chemistry and Biochemistry: Dominick J. Casadonte Jr., Ph.D., Purdue.
Classical and Modern Languages and Literature: Frederick Suppe, Ph.D., Montana.
Communication Studies: Patrick Hughes, Ph.D., Denver.
Economics and Geography: Joseph E. King, Ph.D., Illinois at Urbana-Champaign.
English: Sam Dragga, Ph.D., Ohio.
Environmental Toxicology: Ronald J. Kendall, Ph.D., Virginia Tech.
Geosciences: Cal Barnes, Ph.D., Oregon.
Health, Exercise, and Sports Sciences: Terry Waldren, Ph.D., Texas Tech.
History: Randy McBee, Ph.D., Columbia.
Mathematics and Statistics: Lawrence Schovanec, Ph.D., Indiana.
Philosophy: Peder G. Christiansen, Ph.D., Wisconsin–Madison.
Physics: Nural Akchurin, Ph.D., Iowa.
Political Science: Phillip D. Marshall, Ph.D., Illinois at Urbana-Champaign.
Psychology: M. David Rudd, Ph.D., Texas.
Sociology, Anthropology, and Social Work: Jeffrey Williams, Ph.D., Texas at Austin.

Business Administration: Allen McInnes, Dean; Ph.D., Texas (phone: 806-742-3188).
Accounting: Robert Ricketts, Ph.D., North Texas.
Finance: Paul Goeble, Ph.D., Georgia.
Information and Quantitative Sciences (MIS): James Hoffman, Ph.D., Nebraska.
Management: William Gardner, Ph.D., Florida State.
Marketing: Debra Laverie, Ph.D., Arizona State.

Education: Sheryl Santos, Dean; Ph.D., Kansas State (phone: 806-742-1837).
Curriculum and Instruction: Doug Simpson, Ph.D., Oklahoma.
Educational Psychology and Leadership: Peggy Johnson, Ph.D., Florida.

Engineering: Pamela Eibeck, Dean; Ph.D., Stanford (phone: 806-742-3451).
Chemical Engineering: M. Nazmul Karim, Ph.D., Manchester.
Civil Engineering: H. Scott Norville, Ph.D., Purdue; PE.
Computer Science: Noé López-Benitez, Ph.D., Purdue.
Electrical Engineering: Jon Bredeson, Ph.D., Northwestern.
Engineering Physics: Jeff Wolstad, Ph.D., Michigan.
Engineering Technology: Randy Burkett, Ph.D., Texas at Austin.
Industrial Engineering: Patrick Patterson, Ph.D., Texas A&M.
Mechanical Engineering: Jharna Chaudhuri, Ph.D., Rutgers.
Petroleum Engineering: Lloyd R. Heinze, Ph.D., Missouri–Rolla; PE.

Human Sciences: Linda Hoover, Dean; Ph.D., Texas Woman's (phone: 806-742-3031).
Applies and Professional Studies: Sterling Shumway, Ph.D., Texas Tech.
Design: Lynn Huffman, Ph.D.,Texas A&M.
Human Development and Family Studies: Anisa Zvonkovic, Ph.D., Penn State.
Nutrition, Hospitality, and Retailing: Lynn Hoffman, Ph.D., Texas A&M.

Mass Communications: Jerry Hudson, Ph.D., North Texas (phone: 806-742-6500).

Honors College: Gary Bell, Dean; Ph.D., UCLA (phone: 806-742-1828).

School of Law: Walter Huffman, Dean; J.D., Texas Tech (phone: 806-742-3793).

Visual and Performing Arts: Carol Edwards, Dean; Ph.D., Florida State (phone: 806-742-0700).
Art: Tina Fuentes, M.F.A., North Texas.
Music: William Ballenger, M.A., Northeast Missouri State.
Theater: Fred Christoffel, M.F.A., Illinois at Urbana-Champaign.

Interdisciplinary Studies: Clifford Fedler, Ph.D., Illinois; Wendell Aycock, Coordinator; Ph.D., South Carolina (phone: 806-742-2787).
Applied Linguistics: Frederick Suppe, Ph.D., Montana.
Forensic Science: Clifford Fedler, Ph.D., Illinois.
Heritage Management: Gary Edson, M.F.A., Tulane.
Multidisciplinary Science: Jeff Lee, Ph.D., Arizona State.
Museum Science: Gary Edson, M.F.A., Tulane.
Public Administration: Thomas Longoria, Ph.D., Texas A&M.

Allied Health: Paul Brooke, Dean; Ph.D., Iowa; FACHE (phone: 806-743-3223).
Communication Disorders: Rajinder Koul, Ph.D., Purdue.
Diagnostic and Primary Care: Hal S. Larsen, Ph.D., Nebraska.
Rehabilitation Services: Steven Sawyer, Ph.D., San Diego.

Graduate School of Biomedical Sciences: Richard Homan, Dean; M.D., SUNY (phone: 806-743-3000).
Cell Biology and Biochemistry: Harry Weitlauf, M.D., Washington (Seattle).
Microbiology and Immunology: Ronald Kennedy, Ph.D., Baylor College of Medicine.
Pharmacology: Reid L. Norman, Ph.D., Kansas.

Nursing: Alexia Green, Dean; Ph.D., Texas Woman's; RN (phone: 806-743-2737).

Medicine: Steven Lee Berk, M.D., Boston University (phone: 806-743-3000).

Pharmacy: Arthur A. Nelson Jr., Dean; R.Ph., Ph.D., Iowa (phone: 806-356-4011).

THOMAS EDISON STATE COLLEGE

Graduate Programs

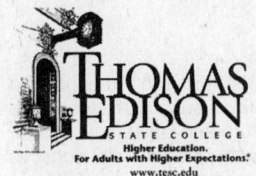

Programs of Study

Thomas Edison State College offers five graduate degree programs that have broad appeal to adult students who desire to build professional expertise by completing high-quality, online degrees.

The Master of Science in Human Resources Management (M.S.H.R.M.) degree serves human resources professionals who wish to become strategic partners in their organizations. This program uses a cohort model and is designed to position human resources professionals as leaders within their organizations. The 36-credit program provides practitioners with technical human resources skills in staffing, providing professional development, managing organizational culture, and measuring and rewarding performance. Skills in assessing and using research and best-practice standards from the human resources field to improve their practice are integrated.

The Master of Science in Management (M.S.M.) degree serves management professionals by integrating management theory and practice as they apply to a wide range of organizations. The program addresses areas critical to managerial success: leadership, organizational understanding, activity management, effective resource use, and managerial self-development. Students may specialize in a selected area by choosing a professional focus area in human resources management, online learning and teaching, public sector auditing, or public service leadership.

The Master of Arts in Liberal Studies (M.A.L.S.) degree provides working professionals an opportunity to study the liberal arts from an applied perspective. Students work from the context of their ongoing professional work. Their study of professionalism, community, and change infuses their professional lives with a deeper understanding of the workplace and their responsibilities as professionals. Students acquire leadership tools as they gain a deeper appreciation of the value and relevance of the arts, sciences, and humanities to the practical concerns of the workplace. The M.A.L.S. program attracts a diverse student body working in positions such as museum curator, college business manager, computer networking specialist, nuclear engineer, and teacher. M.A.L.S. students add depth by designing their own professional focus through the learner-designed area of study.

The Master of Science in Nursing (M.S.N.) degree in nurse education serves registered nurses with a current RN license valid in the United States who have already completed a Bachelor of Science in Nursing degree. Graduates of the 36-credit M.S.N. degree program are awarded a Nurse Educator Certificate in addition to the diploma and are prepared for teaching positions in schools of nursing and health-care settings.

The Master of Arts in Educational Leadership (M.A.Ed.L.) degree is designed to prepare teachers and administrators to become educational leaders serving in the complex environment of elementary and secondary education. The 36-credit M.A.Ed.L. program is designed to present a coherent set of learning experiences that build and deepen students' understanding of educational leadership.

Thomas Edison State College also offers graduate certificates. Graduate certificates are available to students who have earned baccalaureate degrees. Students who successfully complete certificates may apply the credits earned toward a graduate degree at Thomas Edison State College. The College offers graduate certificates in human resources management, online learning and teaching, public service leadership, organizational management and leadership, homeland security, and clinical trials management. The Nurse Educator Certificate is only available to students who have earned a Master of Science in Nursing degree.

Research Facilities

Thomas Edison State College students utilize the rich library research facilities of the New Jersey State Library, which is an affiliate of Thomas Edison State College. Students have access to VALE, the Virtual Academic Libraries Environment, a system that provides access to a network of research libraries.

Financial Aid

Graduate students support their studies with employer tuition aid and loans. Unsubsidized loans are available to all accepted applicants. The Thomas Edison State College Office of Financial Aid & Veterans' Affairs is available to assist students.

Cost of Study

Tuition for the M.S.H.R.M., M.S.M., M.A.Ed.L., and M.A.L.S. was $465 per credit in 2008–09. Fees and tuition are specified in the *Graduate Prospectus*. Books and materials are estimated at $200 to $300 per semester. Tuition for the M.S.N. program was $460 per credit in 2008–09.

Living and Housing Costs

Thomas Edison State College graduate students complete course work through distance education. There are no college-based living and housing costs associated with an education through Thomas Edison State College.

Student Group

Students are working adults who maintain membership in their current professional associations. Graduates are invited to become active in the Thomas Edison State College Alumni Association.

Location

Thomas Edison State College is located in the capital city of Trenton, New Jersey. Students live and study in all fifty states and more than seventy other countries. The College's campus embraces the Kelsey Building at 101 West State Street and the adjacent Townhouse Complex, the Academic Center at 167 West Hanover Street, the Canal Banks Building at 221 West Hanover Street, and the Kuser Mansion at 315 West State Street. The College's state-of-the-art facilities, from electronic classrooms and computer labs to a corporate-style education conference room and other amenities, allow Thomas Edison State College to link students and mentors at dozens of colleges throughout the country and around the world.

The College

Founded in 1972, Thomas Edison State College specializes in providing flexible, high-quality, collegiate learning opportunities for self-directed adults. One of New Jersey's twelve senior public institutions of higher education, the College offers five online graduate degrees as well as fourteen associate and baccalaureate degrees. Thomas Edison State College, a pioneer in the assessment of adult learning and use of educational technologies, enrolls more than 17,300 students. Undergraduate students earn degrees through assessment of their college-level learning, transfer credit, independent study, and online courses. Graduate study is primarily online. Online courses require student interaction and collaboration; intensive communication with mentors is the norm. *Forbes* magazine identified the College as one of the top twenty colleges and universities in the nation in the use of technology to create learning opportunities for adults. The College is home to The John S. Watson Institute for Public Policy, which provides public policy analysis and other assistance to government, community groups, and the private sector.

Applying

Admission is competitive for the M.S.H.R.M., M.S.M., M.A.Ed.L., and M.A.L.S. The programs are open to students with baccalaureate degrees in any field and three to five years' experience appropriate to the program. The application requires a statement of professional goals and analytic essays to demonstrate graduate writing skills, transcripts documenting the earned degree, a resume, and two letters of recommendation. Students are required to have computer access and be proficient in computer use. A minimum TOEFL score of 550 is required for applicants whose primary language in not English. The application fee of $75 is nonrefundable. Applications are accepted throughout the year, and students may apply online.

Admission for the M.S.N., in addition to a current RN license valid in the U.S., requires a baccalaureate degree in nursing. The M.S.N. application requires receipt of an official transcript from the institution where the B.S.N. degree was awarded. Students are required to have computer access and be proficient in computer use. Two years' experience in nursing is recommended. The application fee of $75 is nonrefundable. Applications are accepted throughout the year, and students may obtain a printable application online at the College's Web site.

Correspondence and Information

David Hoftiezer
Director of Admissions
Thomas Edison State College
101 West State Street
Trenton, New Jersey 08608-1176

Phone: 888-442-8372
Fax: 609-984-8447
E-mail: info@tesc.edu
Web site: http://www.tesc.edu

ABOUT THE FACULTY

Thomas Edison State College mentors are selected for their strong academic credentials in the subject area in which they work with students and for their extensive practical experience. Ninety percent of the mentors have earned their doctoral degrees from institutions such as Rutgers, the State University of New Jersey; Temple University; Columbia University; the University of California; and the Union Institute and University. M.S.M. mentors have worked in a variety of industries such as healthcare, telecommunications, manufacturing, market research, and financial services management. M.S.H.R.M. mentors include attorneys, professors, human resources management specialists, and organizational development practitioners. M.A.L.S. mentors have worked in occupations as diverse as corporate consultants, performing artists, librarians, novelists, and public relations executives. M.A.Ed.L. mentors include principals, K–12 school and college administrators, superintendents, and professors of education.

M.S.N. mentors, who are offsite independent contractors, hold a minimum of a master's degree in nursing; approximately 85 percent hold doctoral degrees. Mentors are experienced nurse educators from baccalaureate and higher-degree nursing programs and settings who guide the development, implementation, and evaluation of the programs.

Jefferson

THOMAS JEFFERSON UNIVERSITY

Programs of Study

Thomas Jefferson University (TJU) includes Jefferson School of Health Professions (consisting of Departments of Bioscience Technologies, Couple and Family Therapy, General Studies, Occupational Therapy, Physical Therapy, and Radiologic Sciences), Jefferson School of Nursing, Jefferson School of Population Health, and Jefferson School of Pharmacy, as well as Jefferson Medical College and Jefferson College of Graduate Studies.

The M.D. curriculum at Jefferson Medical College provides opportunities for students to acquire basic knowledge and skills in the biomedical sciences as well as to develop appropriate professional behaviors. Several joint programs are available: M.D./Ph.D., in conjunction with Jefferson College of Graduate Studies; M.D./M.P.H., in conjunction with the Jefferson School of Population Health as well as with the Johns Hopkins Bloomberg School of Public Health; and M.D./M.B.A. in Health Administration, in partnership with Widener University.

Jefferson College of Graduate Studies offers the Master of Science (M.S.) degree in biomedical sciences, cell and developmental biology, microbiology, and pharmacology. The College offers Ph.D. degrees in biochemistry and molecular biology, cell and developmental biology, genetics, immunology and microbial pathogenesis, molecular pharmacology and structural biology, molecular physiology and biophysics, neuroscience, and tissue engineering and regenerative medicine. Graduate certificates are available in informatics for translational and clinical sciences, infectious disease control, clinical research/trials and public health/health systems research.

Jefferson School of Population Health offers degrees and certificates in health policy, public health, healthcare quality, and safety. A J.D./M.P.H. and M.J./M.P.H. are offered in partnership with Widener University.

Jefferson School of Health Professions offers master's degree programs in the bioscience technologies (biotechnology, cytotechnology, and medical technology), couple and family therapy, occupational therapy, and radiologic sciences. Clinical doctorates are available in occupational therapy (O.T.D.) and physical therapy (D.P.T.).

Jefferson School of Nursing offers master's degrees in ten specialties: nurse anesthetist (CRNA), community systems administration, family nurse practitioner, acute care advanced practice nurse, adult advanced practice nurse, oncology advanced practice nurse, pediatric advanced practice nurse, neonatal nurse practitioner, nursing informatics, and women's health nurse practitioner. An M.S.N./M.P.H. is offered in partnership with Jefferson School of Population Health. Post-master's certificates and a Doctor of Nursing Practice (D.N.P.) are also available.

Jefferson School of Pharmacy offers the Doctor of Pharmacy (Pharm.D.).

Research Facilities

The Bluemle Life Sciences Building, with 157,000 square feet of laboratory space, serves as the primary research facility for molecular biology and genetics, molecular virology, microbiology, and immunology. The Farber Institute for Neurosciences is housed in the Jefferson Hospital for Neuroscience building and Jefferson Alumni Hall. Students have access to modern research equipment for molecular analysis of gene expression and functional aspects of the immune system, sophisticated studies of cell physiology, and in-depth studies of embryonic development and all aspects of drug metabolism.

The Center for Translational Medicine is the focal point for research in the Department of Medicine at Thomas Jefferson University. At the forefront of academic health care, the center aims to bridge basic scientific discoveries with physicians' needs for their patients. It focuses on cutting-edge basic molecular biomedical research and its translation into the most efficient and tailored forms of diagnosis and treatment as well as modes of prevention.

The Scott Memorial Library's collection includes approximately 210,000 books and bound print journals, more than 2,600 electronic journal subscriptions, leisure reading materials, the University Archives, and significant holdings of rare books dating to the fifteenth century. JEFFLINE, the University's academic information system, allows 24-hour access to the world's medical literature, including MEDLINE, the premier database for medical literature, and Micromedex CCIS, an extensive drug and chemical resource. Electronic access to full-text articles is available for more than 1,100 journals, electronic textbooks, and other critical knowledge-based resources.

AISR Learning Resources Centers provide access to videos, slides, anatomical models, human skeletons, and a wide variety of education technologies. Computing labs and electronic classrooms include digital-scanning equipment, PDA synchronizing workstations, laptop computers with wireless capabilities, and more than 250 computers.

Financial Aid

The University Office of Student Financial Aid assists students in securing federal, state, institutional, and private funding. A limited number of fellowships are available from the Jefferson College of Graduate Studies on a competitive basis for the support of full-time Ph.D. students with a strong academic background and research potential. The awards provide for the full cost of tuition and a stipend for the student's essential living expenses. The stipend for the 2008–09 academic year was $25,500. More information about general financial aid is available from the financial aid office. Additional information about financial support for Ph.D. students may be obtained from the Jefferson College of Graduate Studies.

Cost of Study

For the 2009–10 academic year, medical school tuition is $44,022 and fees are $525. The comprehensive fee for full-time Ph.D. students is $26,858; however, Ph.D. students are generally awarded fellowship support, which covers tuition and stipend for educational and living expenses. Tuition for M.S. basic science and public health programs and JCGS certificate programs is $879 per credit. Jefferson School of Health Professions' master degree programs have comprehensive fees ranging from $24,103 to $29,943. Per-credit costs for part-time students are $850. Tuition for M.S.N. and D.N.P. programs at Jefferson School of Nursing is $850 per credit. The comprehensive tuition for Jefferson School of Pharmacy is $28,594. Tuition for matriculated students in Jefferson School of Population Health is $880 per credit.

Living and Housing Costs

University apartments are available. Room and board average $15,000 per year. Reasonable alternative housing near the University can also be found.

Location

Thomas Jefferson University's 13-acre campus is centrally located in Philadelphia, within walking distance of many places of cultural interest, including concert halls, theaters, museums, art galleries, and historic sites. Convenient bus and subway lines connect the University with other local universities and several outstanding libraries.

The University

Thomas Jefferson University was founded as Jefferson Medical College in 1824. JMC has awarded more than 26,000 medical degrees and has more living graduates than any other medical school in the nation. Existing basic medical sciences and allied health programs were formally organized within JCGS and JCHP when the two colleges were established in 1969. Public and private funding of Jefferson research exceeds $140 million annually.

Applying

Jefferson Medical College participates in the American Medical College Application Service (AMCAS). After completing this application, prospective students must submit the Jefferson Medical College Secondary Application Form, the nonrefundable $80 application fee, MCAT scores, and letters of recommendation. The deadline for receipt of all supporting materials is January 1.

Admission to all programs in Jefferson College of Graduate Studies requires a bachelor's degree from an accredited institution; strong academic performance, as demonstrated by grade point average; and GRE results. Individual programs have additional or alternate requirements. The application deadline for Ph.D. applications is January 15. Applications received after this date are considered at the discretion of the admissions committee of the desired program. Applications for the M.S., M.P.H., and certificate programs are considered on a rolling basis throughout the year.

Admission to Jefferson School of Health Professions, Jefferson School of Nursing, and Jefferson School of Pharmacy is on a rolling basis and is divided into Admissions Review Periods beginning September 15. The final date to apply to most programs is July 15. Pharmacy applicants apply through the Pharmacy College Application Service (PharmCAS) with a deadline of March 1, and physical therapy applicants apply through the Physical Therapy College Application Service (PTCAS) with a deadline of June 1. Admission is competitive, as the number of seats in each class is limited. Students need not complete all prerequisites before applying, but all course work must be completed before matriculation. In addition to the application, students must submit a nonrefundable $50 fee (reduced to $25 for online application), official transcripts, two letters of recommendation, a personal statement, and GRE or MAT scores, if applicable. English language proficiency is required of all non-U.S. citizens. JCHP interviews all academically eligible students. Applicants should contact the program to which they are applying for specific application guidelines.

Correspondence and Information

Office of Admissions
Jefferson Medical College
1015 Walnut Street, Room 110
Philadelphia, Pennsylvania 19107
Phone: 215-955-6983
E-mail: JMC.admissions@jefferson.edu

Office of Admissions
Jefferson School of Population Health
1015 Walnut Street, Suite 115
Philadelphia, Pennsylvania 19107
Phone: 215-803-5305
E-mail: JSPH@jefferson.edu
Web site: http://www.jefferson.edu/population_health/

Office of Admissions
Jefferson Alumni Hall M-60
Jefferson College of Graduate Studies
1020 Locust Street
Philadelphia, Pennsylvania 19107-6799
Phone: 215-503-4400
E-mail: jcgs-info@jefferson.edu
Web site: http://www.jefferson.edu/jcgs

Office of Admissions
Jefferson School of Health Professions
Jefferson School of Nursing
Jefferson School of Pharmacy
130 South 9th Street, Suite 100
Philadelphia, Pennsylvania 19107
Phone: 215-503-8890
E-mail: JSHPadmissions@jefferson.edu
JSNadmissions@jefferson.edu
JSPadmissions@jefferson.edu
Web site: http://www.jefferson.edu/schools.cfm

THE DEPARTMENTS

Anesthesiology
Zvi Grunwald, James D. Wentzler M.D. Professor and Chair, M.D. (215-955-6161; zvi.grunwald@jefferson.edu)

Biochemistry and Molecular Biology
Jeffrey L. Benovic, Professor and Chair; Ph.D. (215-503-4607; benovic@mail.jci.tju.edu)

Bioscience Technologies
Shirley E. Greening, Professor and Chair; M.S., J.D., CT(ASCP), CFIAC (215-503-8561; shirley.greening@jefferson.edu)

Couple and Family Therapy
Kenneth W. Covelman, Chair; Ph.D. (215-503-8707; kenneth.covelman@jefferson.edu)

Dermatology and Cutaneous Biology
Jouni Uitto, Professor and Chair; M.D., Ph.D. (jouni.uitto@jefferson.edu)

Emergency Medicine
Theodore Arthur Christopher, Associate Professor and Chair; M.D., FACEP (215-955-6844; theodore.christopher@jefferson.edu)

Family Medicine
Richard C. Wender, Chair; M.D. (215-955-2356; richard.wender@jefferson.edu)

Health Policy
JoAnne Reifsnyder, Assistant Professor and Program Director; Ph.D., ACHPN (215-955-4376; joanne.reifsnyder@jefferson.edu)

Healthcare Quality and Safety
Susan DesHarnais, Program Director; Ph.D., M.P.H. (215-955-9306; susan.desharnais@jefferson.edu)

Medicine
Arthur Michael Feldman, Chair; M.D., Ph.D. (arthur.feldman@jefferson.edu)

Microbiology and Immunology
Timothy L. Manser, Professor and Chair; Ph.D. (215-503-4669; manser@mail.jci.tju.edu)

Molecular Physiology and Biophysics
Marion J. Siegman, Chair; Ph.D. (215-503-3975; marion.siegman@jefferson.edu)

Neurology
A. M. Rostami, Professor and Chair; M.D., Ph.D. (a.m.rostami@jefferson.edu)

Neurosurgery
Robert H. Rosenwasser, Professor and Chair; M.D., FACS (215-955-7000; robert.rosenwasser@jefferson.edu)

Nursing
Mary G. Schaal, Professor and Dean of Jefferson School of Nursing; Ed.D., RN (215-503-5090; mary.schaal@jefferson.edu)

Obstetrics and Gynecology
Louis Weinstein, Chair; M.D. (louis.weinstein@jefferson.edu)

Occupational Therapy
Janice P. Burke, Professor, Chair of the Department of Occupational Therapy, and Dean of Jefferson School of Health Professions; Ph.D., OTR/L, FAOTA (215-503-9606; janice.burke@jefferson.edu)

Ophthalmology
Julia A. Haller, Chair; M.D. (215-928-3073; julia.haller@jefferson.edu)

Oral and Maxillofacial Surgery
Robert J. Diecidue, Chair; M.D., D.M.D. (215-955-5131; robert.diecidue@jefferson.edu)

Orthopaedic Surgery
Todd J. Albert, James Edwards Professor and Chairman; M.D. (267-339-3617; tjsurg@aol.com)

Otolaryngology
William Keane, Chair; M.D. (215-955-6760; william.keane@jefferson.edu)

Pathology; Anatomy and Cell Biology
Fred Gorstein, Chair; M.D. (215-955-5110; fred.gorstein@jefferson.edu)

Pediatrics
Jay Greenspan, Chair; M.D. (215-955-0710; jay.greenspan@jefferson.edu)

Pharmacology and Experimental Therapeutics
Scott A. Waldman, Professor and Chair; M.D. (215-955-6086; scott.waldman@jefferson.edu)

Pharmacy
Rebecca S. Finley, Dean of Jefferson School of Pharmacy; Pharm.D., M.S. (215-503-9082; rebecca.finley@jefferson.edu)

Physical Therapy
Ann E. Barr, Professor and Chair; Ph.D., D.P.T. (215-503-8961; ann.barr@jefferson.edu)

Psychiatry and Human Behavior
Michael Vergare, Daniel Lieberman Professor and Chair; M.D. (215-955-6912; mjv002@jefferson.edu)

Public Health
Robert Simmons, Program Director; Dr.P.H., M.P.H., CHES (215-955-7312; robert.simmons@jefferson.edu)

Radiation Oncology
Walter J. Curran Jr., Professor and Chair; M.D. (215-955-6702; walter.curran@jefferson.edu)

Radiologic Sciences
Frances H. Gilman, Assistant Professor and Chair; M.S., RT(R)(CT)(MR)(CV) (215-503-1865; frances.gilman@jefferson.edu)

Radiology
Vijay M. Rao, Professor and Chair; M.D. (215-955-7264; vijay.rao@jefferson.edu)

Rehabilitation Medicine
John Melvin, Chair; M.D. (215-955-7446; john.melvin@jefferson.edu)

Surgery
Charles J. Yeo, Samuel D. Gross Professor and Chair; M.D. (215-955-8643; charles.yeo@jefferson.edu)

Urology
Leonard G. Gomella, Bernard W. Godwin Jr. Professor of Prostate Cancer and Chair; M.D. (215-955-1702; leonard.gomella@jefferson.edu)

TUFTS UNIVERSITY

Graduate School of Arts and Sciences

Programs of Study

The Graduate School of Arts and Sciences offers master's and doctoral programs in selected areas of the natural sciences, social sciences, and the humanities.

The Doctor of Philosophy degree is offered in biology, chemistry, chemistry/biotechnology, child development, drama, education, English, history, mathematics, physics, and psychology. A highly selective interdisciplinary doctorate is available in other areas. Tufts also offers a Doctor of Occupational Therapy.

The Master of Arts degree may be earned in art history, art history and museum studies, child development, classical archaeology, classics, drama, education, English, French, German, history, history and museum studies, mathematics, museum education, music, occupational therapy, philosophy, school psychology, and urban and environmental policy and planning. The Master of Science is offered in biology, chemistry, chemistry/biotechnology, economics, education, mathematics, occupational therapy, physics, and psychology. The Master of Arts in Teaching is available with concentrations in art, early childhood, and secondary education. The Master of Fine Arts degree is awarded in conjunction with the School of the Museum of Fine Arts, Boston. Tufts also offers the Master of Public Policy degree. A Certificate of Advanced Graduate Study may be earned in child development or school psychology.

Full-time students can take one course per semester, for both a grade and credit, through cross-registration agreements with Boston College, Boston University, and Brandeis University.

Research Facilities

The University library system includes the Tisch Library, the Lilly Music Library, and the Edward Ginn Library of the Fletcher School. Through Tufts' membership in the Boston Library Consortium, graduate students also have library privileges at the Massachusetts State Library, the Woods Hole Oceanographic Institute, the Boston Public Library, and the libraries of Amherst College, Boston College, Boston University, Brandeis University, the Massachusetts Institute of Technology, Northeastern University, the University of Connecticut, the University of Massachusetts, the University of New Hampshire, Wellesley College, and Williams College. Drama students have access to the Harvard Theatre Collection.

Special research facilities for science and engineering students include the campus-based Science and Technology Center, which houses selected areas of research in physics and electrical and chemical engineering, as well as laboratory facilities in biology, chemistry, psychology, and electrical and civil engineering. Students are encouraged to pursue collaborative research at off-site facilities, which have included Fermilab, the Woods Hole Oceanographic Institute, and Brookhaven Laboratories. Many researchers carry out collaborative research with colleagues at nearby Boston universities.

Financial Aid

In 2008–09, the School awarded more than $10 million in tuition scholarships. Teaching and research assistantships are available, as are some fellowships. Tufts also awards need-based financial aid through the Federal Perkins Loan, Federal Work-Study, and Federal Direct Student Loan programs.

Cost of Study

Tuition for 2009–10 is $38,096, which covers the full cost of one-year master's programs. Tuition for two-year master's programs is charged for two years. The 2009–10 tuition for two-year programs is as follows: occupational therapy, $38,096; urban and environmental policy and planning, $28,572; school psychology, $33,334; and studio art, $33,368. Part-time tuition is $3810 per course. Ph.D. students are charged tuition for five years. The 2009–10 tuition for Ph.D. programs is $22,858. Other charges include student health insurance, a health service fee, and a student activity fee.

Living and Housing Costs

Living expenses are estimated at about $1200 a month. There is limited on-campus housing for graduate students. Rents for one-bedroom apartments in Medford and Somerville begin at approximately $900 per month. The cost of sharing an apartment averages about $600 per person. A public transportation system serves the greater Boston area and provides easy access to and from the campus.

Student Group

In 2008–09, 1004 students were enrolled in the Graduate School of Arts and Sciences. Of these, 68 percent were women and 13 percent were international students.

Location

The main campus, which spans the Medford-Somerville city line, is 7 miles from downtown Boston, a city where the arts (music, drama, and dance), museums, and sporting events abound. Cape Cod beaches and the mountains and forests of Maine, New Hampshire, and Vermont can be easily reached.

The University

Chartered as a liberal arts college in 1852, today Tufts is a small, selective, private university offering opportunities for undergraduate, graduate, and professional education to more than 7,500 students. The Graduate School of Arts and Sciences, the Fletcher School of Law and Diplomacy, the School of Engineering, the Friedman School of Nutrition Science and Policy, the Sackler School of Graduate Biomedical Sciences, the Cummings School of Veterinary Medicine, and the Schools of Dental Medicine and Medicine offer graduate and/or professional education. The University is accredited by the New England Association of Schools and Colleges.

Applying

Deadlines for applications vary by program. Applicants are required to submit three letters of recommendation, official transcripts from all colleges and universities attended, and a personal statement. Most departments also require the results of the Graduate Record Examinations (GRE). Students whose native language is not English must submit official results of the Test of English as a Foreign Language (TOEFL).

Correspondence and Information

Graduate Studies Office
Tufts University
Ballou Hall, First Floor
Medford, Massachusetts 02155

Phone: 617-627-3395
Fax: 617-627-3016
Web site: http://gradstudy.tufts.edu

FIELDS OF STUDY AND FACULTY ADVISERS

Art and Art History: Ikumi Kaminishi (M.A. program); David Brown (M.F.A. program).
Biology: Juliet Fuhrman.
Chemistry: Arthur Utz.
Child Development: Fred Rothbaum.
Classics: Peter Reid (Classics); Jodi Magness (Classical Archaeology).
Drama: Laurence Senelick.
Economics: Marcelo Bianconi.
Education: Linda Beardsley (Teacher Education); Barbara Brizuela (Educational Studies); Cynthia Robinson (Museum Education); Steven Luz-Alterman (School Psychology); Patty Bode (Art Education).
English: Joseph Litvak.
French: Vincent Pollina.
German: Bernhard Martin.
History: Steven Marrone.
Interdisciplinary Doctorate: Robin Kanarek.
Mathematics: Zbigniew Nitecki.
Music: Jane Bernstein (Musicology); David Locke (Ethnomusicology); John McDonald (Composition); Janet Schmalfeldt (Theory).
Occupational Therapy: Linda Tickle-Degnen.
Philosophy: Avner Baz.
Physics: Krzysztof Sliwa.
Psychology: Holly Taylor.
Urban and Environmental Policy and Planning: Julian Agyeman.

University at Buffalo
The State University of New York

UNIVERSITY AT BUFFALO, THE STATE UNIVERSITY OF NEW YORK

Graduate School

Programs of Study

The Graduate School offers 190 master's degree programs, eighty-three doctoral degree programs, and four professional programs, as well as a number of certificate and dual-degree programs. Interdisciplinary research is available through more than forty centers and graduate groups. The graduate programs and departments fashion individual curricula to meet specific objectives. Each program establishes its own requirements for admission, its own assessment of satisfactory student progress, and its own mandates for satisfactory completion of the degree offered under a broad institutional mandate for excellence. Each department is responsible for admitting its own students. For the master's degree, one year of residence is required, as is a comprehensive test, a thesis based on independent research, or an appropriate special project. For the doctoral degree, the residence requirement is one year; other requirements include an evaluation of the student's work in the doctoral program, an original dissertation, and an oral defense.

Research Facilities

The University at Buffalo (UB) has become a leader in developing and deploying an IT environment that empowers University members to accomplish their goals. Students and faculty members have multimedia e-mail; access to campus high-speed networks in laboratories, classrooms, and University residence halls and apartments; wireless access points on campus; Web access to extensive library resources; easy Web publishing; and extensive technical support and training. Through its digital initiative, the University libraries offer online access to major full-text information products covering journal literature, books, statistical data, worldwide newspapers, and hundreds of databases supporting research in the sciences, social sciences, humanities, and interdisciplinary studies. More than 2,200 personal computers and high-performance workstations are available to students in more than ninety public and departmental computing labs. Students also have access to computing on powerful clusters on UNIX time-sharing machines and to computational resources at one of the leading academic supercomputing sites in the U.S., the Center for Computational Research (CCR).

Many investigative centers and institutes are part of a research enterprise that exceeded $348 million in expenditures in 2008. In addition to governmental and private foundation support for research, UB receives considerable industrial support through research collaborations and affiliations. The University enjoys an international reputation, attracting students from all over the world and maintaining scholarly exchanges with institutions in several nations. Leading-edge interdisciplinary research centers integrating the fields of medicine, engineering, and physical sciences provide students with a unique environment to conduct research at the interfaces of disciplines. Some examples include Center for Single-Molecule Biophysics; Center for Spin Effects and Quantum Information in Nanostructures; Institute for Lasers, Photonics, and Biophotonics; Research Institute on Addictions; Center for Hearing and Deafness; and Toshiba Stroke Research Center. The Center of Excellence in Bioinformatics and Life Sciences, a 129,000-square-foot, state-of-the-art interdisciplinary research facility, opened its doors in 2006 on the Buffalo-Niagara Medical Campus after a commitment of more than $200 million from New York State and private industry. UB is also a founding member of the New York Structural Biology Center, providing investigators access to high-field NMR and cryoelectron microscopy for the elucidation of protein structures. Other specialized centers include the Center for Studies in American Culture, Baldy Center for Law and Social Policy, Center for Rehabilitation Synergy; The Regional Institute, Center for Excellence in Global Enterprise Management, Great Lakes Institute, National Center for Geographic Information and Analysis, The Humanities Institute, Center for Inclusive Design and Environmental Access, MCEER, Institute for Research and Education on Women and Gender, Center for Excellence for Document Analysis and Recognition, Buffalo Protein Therapeutics Consortium, and Center for Unified Biometrics and Sensors.

Financial Aid

Many students hold teaching, graduate, or research assistantships. A number of competitive fellowship programs are also available, including opportunities for students who are members of underrepresented minority groups. Full- or partial-tuition scholarships accompany most assistantships and fellowships. Graduate Opportunity Tuition Scholarships are available to students who participated in undergraduate EOP, HEOP, or SEEK programs. Students should contact the department for information and applications. The most up-to-date contact information for all of UB's graduate and professional programs can be found on the School's Web site.

Cost of Study

Full-time tuition for 2008–09 was $3940 per semester for New York State residents and $6625 per semester for nonresidents. Part-time tuition was $328 per credit hour for residents and $552 per credit hour for nonresidents. Tuition in the professional schools is higher. All tuition rates are subject to adjustment by the Board of Trustees.

Living and Housing Costs

The University at Buffalo has four apartment complexes that house graduate students. Flickinger Court, a two-bedroom townhouse complex, houses only graduate and married students. It is off campus but is part of the University housing system. All its apartments are furnished with appliances, most have bedroom furniture, but utilities are not included. The proposed rate for 2009–10 is $968 per apartment for unfurnished or $988 for furnished. Creekside Village is a two-bedroom townhouse complex on campus that houses only graduate students. These apartments are fully furnished and utilities are included. The proposed rate for 2009–10 is $749 per person. Flint Village and South Lake Village are apartment complexes located on campus and are fully furnished. They house both graduate and undergraduate students in four-bedroom, two-bedroom, single, and studio apartments. The rents include all utilities. For 2009–10, proposed rents for four-bedroom units range from $585 to $720 per student per month, two-bedroom units range from $650 to $720 per student per month, single units range from $740 to $820 per student per month, and studios are $785 per month. Students should visit the Web site at http://www.student-affairs.buffalo.edu/housing for current, detailed information.

Student Group

The total enrollment of 28,192 consists of 14,642 men and 13,550 women. Graduate students number 9,170. The student body includes representatives from more than 100 countries.

Location

Buffalo is a Great Lakes city on an international border with a metropolitan population of more than 1 million. It is a city of friendly neighborhoods with big-city recreation for all tastes: professional sports (football, hockey, lacrosse, and Triple-A baseball), the Buffalo Philharmonic Orchestra, a celebrated theater district, world-class art galleries and museums, and a lively club scene. Buffalo enjoys four distinct seasons in a dramatic setting on Lake Erie and the Niagara River. Skiing, hiking, camping, sailing, boating, and Lake Erie beaches on both the U.S. and Canadian shores and the natural wonder of Niagara Falls are all nearby.

The University

A member of the prestigious Association of American Universities, the University at Buffalo stands in the first rank among the nation's research-intensive public universities. The University's thinking, research, creative activity, and people positively impact and change the world. Like the city it calls home, UB is distinguished by a culture of resilient optimism, resourceful thinking, and pragmatic dreaming that enables it to reach others every day.

The University has three campuses. The South Campus, located in a residential neighborhood in North Buffalo, was designed by E. B. Green, one of America's most respected architects, and has been an important part of the community for generations. It is home to four of the five schools in UB's Academic Health Center and the School of Architecture and Law. The North Campus, developed beginning in the 1970s, is located on 1,200 acres in suburban Amherst and is home to most of the university's non-health sciences divisions. It also is home to apartment-style accommodations for graduate and professional students and their families. UB's growing Downtown Campus includes six properties and is slated to grow significantly in the years ahead.

Applying

Applications should be filed directly with the appropriate department. The quickest and easiest way to apply is online. Deadlines for filing applications vary by department.

Correspondence and Information

Graduate Enrollment Management Services
408 Capen Hall
University at Buffalo, the State University of New York
Buffalo, New York 14260-1606

Phone: 716-645-3482
Fax: 716-645-6998
Web site: http://www.grad.buffalo.edu/admissions

GRADUATE AND PROFESSIONAL PROGRAMS

Interim Vice Provost for Graduate Education and Dean of the Graduate School: Dr. John Ho, 716-645-3786.
Associate Provost and Executive Director of the Graduate School: Dr. Myron A. Thompson, 716-645-6227.

Accounting (M.S.)
Adult/Medical Surgical–Surgical Clinical Nurse Specialist (M.S.)
Adult Health Nursing (M.S., Adv. Cert., post-master's)
Advanced Certificate in Canadian Studies (Adv. Cert.)
Advanced Certificate Program in Professional Science Management (Adv. Cert.)
Aerospace Engineering (M.S., Ph.D.)
American Studies (M.A., Ph.D.)
Anatomical Sciences (M.A., Ph.D.)
Anthropology (M.A., Ph.D.)
Applied Economics: Financial Economics (Adv. Cert.)
Applied Economics: Health Services (Adv. Cert.)
Applied Economics: Information and Internet Economics (Adv. Cert.)
Applied Economics: International Economics (Adv. Cert.)
Applied Economics: Law and Regulation (Adv. Cert.)
Applied Economics: Urban and Regional Economics (Adv. Cert.)
Architecture (M.Arch., M.Arch./M.B.A., M.Arch./M.U.P., M.Arch./M.F.A.)
Art History (M.A.)
Arts Management (M.A.)
Assistive and Rehabilitative Technology (Adv. Cert.)
Audiology (Au.D.)
Behavioral Neuroscience (Ph.D.)
Biochemistry (M.A., Ph.D.)
Biological Sciences (M.A., M.S., Ph.D.)
Biological Sciences (Cellular and Molecular Biology) (Roswell) (Ph.D.)
Biology Education: Adolescence (5–12 or 7–12) (Ed.M., Adv. Cert.)
Biomaterials (M.S.)
Biophysical Sciences (M.S., Ph.D.)
Biophysics (Molecular and Cellular) (Roswell) (M.S., Ph.D.)
Biostatistics (M.A., Ph.D., M.P.H. (Concentration in Biostatistics))
Biotechnology (M.S.)
Business Administration (Concentrations in Accounting, Biotechnology Management, Finance, Information Assurance, Information Systems and E-business, Marketing Management, International Management, Management Consulting, and Supply Chains and Operations Management) (M.B.A., J.D./M.B.A., M.Arch./M.B.A., M.A./M.B.A., M.D./M.B.A., B.S./M.B.A.)
Canadian Studies (Adv. Cert.)
Chemical and Biological Engineering (M.E., M.S., Ph.D.)
Chemistry (M.A., Ph.D.)
Chemistry Education: Adolescence (5–12 or 7–12) (Ed.M., Adv. Cert.)
Child Health Nursing (M.S.)
Childhood Education (1–6) (Ed.M., Adv. Cert.)
Childhood Education with Bilingual Extension (1–6) (Ed.M., Adv. Cert.)
Civil, Structural and Environmental Engineering (M.E., M.S., Ph.D.)
Classics (M.A., Ph.D.)
Clinical Psychology (Ph.D.)
Cognitive Psychology (Ph.D.)
Communication (M.A., Ph.D.)
Communicative Disorders and Sciences (M.A., Ph.D., Au.D.)
Community Health (Ph.D.)
Comparative Literature (M.A., Ph.D.)
Computational Science (Adv. Cert.)
Computer Science and Engineering (M.S., Ph.D.)
Counseling/School and Educational Psychology (Ph.D.)
Counselor Education (Ph.D.)
Criminal Law (LL.M.)
Critical Museum Studies (Adv. Cert.)
Dentistry (D.D.S.)
Early Childhood Education (Birth–grade 2) (Adv. Cert., Ed.M.)
Early Childhood Education with Bilingual Extension (Birth–grade 2) (Ed.M., Adv. Cert.)
Earth Science Education: Adolescence (5–12 or 7–12) (Ed.M., Adv. Cert.)
Evolution, Ecology, and Behavior (M.S., Ph.D.)
Economics (M.A., M.S., Ph.D.)
Educational Administration (Ed.M., Ed.D., Ph.D., Adv. Cert.)
Educational Psychology (M.A., Ph.D.)
Electrical Engineering (M.E., M.S., Ph.D., B.S./M.B.A.)
Elementary Education (Ed.D., Ph.D.)
Endodontics (Adv. Cert.)
English (M.A., Ph.D.)
English Education (Ph.D.)
English Education: Adolescence (5–12 or 7–12) (Ed.M., Adv. Cert.)
English for Speakers of Other Languages (Ed.M., Adv. Cert.)
Epidemiology (M.S.)
Epidemiology and Community Health (Ph.D.)
Executive M.B.A. (M.B.A.)
Exercise Science (M.S., Ph.D., B.S./M.S.)
Family Nurse Practitioner (M.S., Adv. Cert., post-master's)
Finance (M.S.)
Fine Arts (M.F.A.)
Foreign and Second Language Education (Ph.D.)
French Education: Adolescence (5–12 or 7–12) (Adv. Cert., Ed.M.)
French Language and Literature (M.A., Ph.D.)
General Education (Ed.M.)
General Education: Educational Leadership and Policy (Ed.M.)
General Education: Learning and Instruction (Ed.M.)
Geographic Information Science (Adv. Cert.)
Geography (M.A., M.S., Ph.D.)
Geological Sciences (M.A., M.S., Ph.D.)
Geriatric Clinical Nurse Specialist (M.S.)
Geriatric Nurse Practitioner (M.S., Adv. Cert., post-master's)
German Education: Adolescence (5–12 or 7–12) (Ed.M., Adv. Cert.)
Global Gender Studies (M.A., Ph.D.)
Higher Education Administration (Concentration in Student Affairs) (Ph.D., Ed.M.)
History (M.A., Ph.D.)
Humanities: Interdisciplinary with a concentration in African American Studies (M.A.)
Humanities: Interdisciplinary with a concentration in Caribbean Cultural Studies (M.A.)
Humanities: Interdisciplinary with a concentration in Film Studies (M.A.)
Industrial Engineering (M.E., M.S., Ph.D.)
Information Assurance (Adv. Cert.)
Interdisciplinary Graduate Program in Biomedical Sciences (Ph.D.)
Italian Education: Adolescence (5–12 or 7–12) (Adv. Cert., Ed.M.)
Latin Education: Adolescence (5–12 or 7–12) (Adv. Cert., Ed.M.)
Law (J.D., LL.M. General LL.M. program for international students)
Library and Information Science (M.L.S., Adv. Cert.)
Linguistics (M.A., Ph.D.)
Literacy Specialist (Ed.M.)
Management (Ph.D.)
Management Information Systems (M.S.)
Maternal and Women's Health Nurse Practitioner (M.S., Adv. Cert., post-master's)
Mathematics (M.A., Ph.D.)
Mathematics Education (Ph.D.)
Mathematics Education: Adolescence (5–12 or 7–12) (Ed.M., Adv. Cert.)
Maxillofacial Prosthodontics (Adv. Cert.)
Mechanical Engineering (M.S., Ph.D.)
Media Arts Production (M.F.A.)
Medical Scientist Training Program (M.D./Ph.D.)
Medicinal Chemistry (M.S., Ph.D.)
Medicine (M.D.)
Mental Health Counseling (M.S.)
Mentoring Teachers (Adv. Cert.)
Microbiology and Immunology (M.A., Ph.D.)
Microbiology and Immunology (Roswell) (Ph.D.)
Molecular and Cellular Biology (Adv. Cert.)
Music (M.A., Ph.D.)
Music Composition (M.A., Ph.D.)
Music Education (Adv. Cert., Ed.M.)
Music History (M.A.)
Music Performance (M.M.)
Music Theory (M.A., Ph.D.)
Music: Historical Musicology (M.A., Ph.D.)
Natural Sciences Interdisciplinary (Concentration in Computational Linguistics) (M.S.)
Natural Sciences: Interdisciplinary: Natural and Biomedical Sciences (Roswell) (M.S.)
Neonatal Nurse Practitioner (Adv. Cert., M.S.)
Neuroscience (M.S., Ph.D.)
New Media Design (Adv. Cert.)
Nurse Anesthetist (M.S.)
Nursing (Ph.D.)
Nursing Education (Adv. Cert.)
Nutrition (M.S.)
Occupational Therapy/Early Intervention (M.S.)
Occupational Therapy/Physical/Developmental Disabilities (M.S.)
Oral and Maxillofacial Pathology (Adv. Cert.)
Oral and Maxillofacial Surgery (Adv. Cert.)
Oral Biology (Ph.D.)
Oral Sciences (M.S.)
Orthodontics (M.S., Adv. Cert.)
Part-Time Professional M.B.A. (M.B.A.)
Pathology (M.A., Ph.D.)
Pathology (Roswell) (Ph.D.)
Pediatric Dentistry (Adv. Cert.)
Pediatric Nurse Practitioner (Adv. Cert.)
Periodontics (Adv. Cert.)
Pharmaceutical Sciences (M.S., Ph.D.)
Pharmacology and Toxicology (M.A., Ph.D.)
Pharmacology (Molecular Pharmacology and Cancer Therapeutics) (Roswell) (Ph.D.)
Pharmacy Practice (Pharm.D.)
Philosophy (M.A., Ph.D.)
Physical Therapy (D.P.T.)
Physics (M.S., Ph.D.)
Physics Education: Adolescence (5–12 or 7–12) (Ed.M., Adv. Cert.)
Physiology (M.A., Ph.D.)
Political Science (M.A., Ph.D.)
Prosthodontics (Adv. Cert.)
Psychiatric Mental Health Nurse Practitioner (M.S., Adv. Cert., post-master's)
Psychology (M.A., Ph.D.)
Public Health (M.P.H.)
Reading Education (Ph.D.)
Rehabilitation Counseling (M.S.)
Rehabilitation Science (Ph.D.)
Removable Prosthodontics (Adv. Cert.)
School Business and Human Resource Administrator (Adv. Cert.)
School Counseling (Ed.M., Adv. Cert.)
School District Business Leader (Adv. Cert.)
School Media Specialist (M.L.S.)
School Psychology (M.A.)
Science Education (Ph.D.)
Social Foundations (Ph.D.)
Social Studies Education: Adolescence (5–12 or 7–12) (Ed.M., Adv. Cert.)
Social Welfare (Ph.D.)
Social Work (M.S.W., J.D./M.S.W., M.B.A./M.S.W., B.A./M.S.W., M.S.W./M.P.H.)
Social-Personality Psychology (Ph.D.)
Sociology (M.A., Ph.D.)
Spanish Education: Adolescence (5–12 or 7–12) (Adv. Cert., Ed.M.)
Spanish Language and Literature (M.A., Ph.D.)
Special Education (Ph.D.)
Structural Biology (M.S., Ph.D.)
Supply Chains and Operations Management (M.S.)
Teaching and Leading for Diversity (Adv. Cert.)
Teaching English to Speakers of Other Languages (Ed.M.)
Temporomandibular Disorders and Orofacial Pain (Adv. Cert.)
Transportation and Business Geographics (Adv. Cert.)
Urban Planning (M.U.P., M.Arch./M.U.P.)

UNIVERSITY OF CENTRAL MISSOURI

The Graduate School

Programs of Study

The University of Central Missouri (UCM) offers programs leading to the Master of Arts, Master of Arts in Teaching, Master of Business Administration, Master of Science, Master of Science in Education, Education Specialist, and cooperative doctoral degrees. Areas of study include accountancy, aviation safety, biology, business administration, career and technical education leadership, college student personnel administration, counseling, criminal justice, curriculum and instruction, educational technology, English, environmental studies, history, industrial hygiene, industrial management, industrial technology, information technology, library science and information services, literacy education, mass communication, mathematics (applied mathematics), music, occupational safety management, physical education (exercise and sport science), psychology, rural family nursing, school administration, social gerontology, sociology, special education, speech communication, speech-language pathology, teaching English as a second language, and theater. The University also offers Education Specialist degrees in administration (elementary school principalship, secondary school principalship, and superintendency), curriculum and instruction, and human services (professional counseling, learning resources, special education, and technology and occupational education). The two cooperative doctoral programs include the Ph.D. in technology management, with Indiana State University as the degree-granting institution, and the Ed.D. in educational leadership, with the University of Missouri–Columbia as the degree-granting institution.

Research Facilities

The Office of Sponsored Programs in the School of Graduate and Extended Studies provides research support for students and faculty members.

The James C. Kirkpatrick Library houses more than 2.4 million items in print and nonprint formats, CD-ROM databases, a historical children's literature collection, an online public access catalog, and a variety of information networks.

Information Services provides academic computing support using an ATM-based high-speed network with more than 2,000 attached workstations. The network is connected to a Windows NT network domain supported by a cluster of network servers for application, Web, data, and mail services. The networked environment provides high-speed Internet connectivity. Research support is provided through products such as SPSS. Information Services also provides a help desk and basic consulting services.

Financial Aid

Graduate assistantships, providing a competitive stipend and a scholarship covering academic fees, are available to qualified students under the terms of a nine-month contract. Scholarships include the Graduate Student Achievement Award, the State Line Grant Program, the Warren C. Lovinger Graduate Student Scholarship, the President's Diversity Scholarship, and the Graduate Non-Resident Scholarship. The University participates in a full range of federal financial aid programs, including grants, loans, and student employment.

Cost of Study

Graduate tuition and fees for 2009–10 are $270 per credit hour for Missouri residents and $515.80 for nonresident students. Rates for Extended Campus are variable.

Living and Housing Costs

In 2008–09, double rooms cost $1873 per semester and single rooms cost $2660 per semester. One- and two-bedroom apartments and town houses are available at prices ranging from $484 to $653 per month. The University has beautiful accommodations for students with families. Graduate students can select from various meal plan packages. An unlimited-access meal plan is $1100 per semester.

Student Group

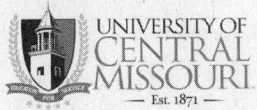

Total enrollment at the University of Central Missouri is about 11,000 students, over 2,000 of whom are doing postgraduate work. The student-faculty ratio is 16:1. International students and ethnic minority students are encouraged to apply. Students attend the University from all fifty states and approximately sixty countries. Enrolled graduate students automatically become members of the Graduate Student Association.

Location

The University of Central Missouri is located 50 miles southeast of Kansas City, in Warrensburg, Missouri. It is easily accessible by highway, bus, and passenger rail service.

The University

Founded in 1871, UCM is a public university with a statewide mission in professional technology that has been fully integrated into a comprehensive liberal arts curriculum. Five colleges offer degree programs encompassing more than 150 areas of study at the undergraduate and graduate levels. Providing top-quality education at affordable cost is one of the institution's top priorities, as is its commitment to rigorous academic standards and thorough career preparation. The campus includes instructional buildings, residence halls, full-service dining, superb athletic facilities, and a spacious University Union. Other facilities on the 1,240-acre campus include a 300-acre recreational and biological research area with fishing lakes and an 18-hole golf course, the Max B. Swisher Skyhaven Airport, 100,000-watt public television and radio stations, and the Prussing University Research Farm.

Applying

A nonrefundable fee of $30 is required for U.S. students and $50 for international students applying for admission to a graduate program.

Correspondence and Information

The School of Graduate and Extended Studies
The University of Central Missouri
Ward Edwards 1800
Warrensburg, Missouri 64093
Phone: 660-543-4621 (admissions information)
660-543-4621 (enrollment information)
877-729-8266 (toll-free)
E-mail: gradinfo@ucmo.edu
Web site: http://www.ucmo.edu/graduate

Master's Degree Programs and Coordinators
Accountancy: Kenneth Stone, Ph.D. (660-543-4816)
Aviation Safety: John Horine, Ed.D. (660-543-4457)
Biology: John Gole, Ph.D. (660-543-8827)
Business Administration: Roger Best, Ph.D. (660-543-8597)
Career and Technical Education Leadership: Barton Washer, Ph.D. (660-543-4580)
College Student Personnel Administration: Robert Bowman, Ph.D. (660-543-8628)
Communication: Shonna Tropf, Ph.D. (660-543-4469)
Counseling: Janelle Cowles, Ed.D. (660-543-8204)
Criminal Justice: Gene Bonham, Ph.D. (660-543-4950)
Curriculum and Instruction: Wayne Williams, Ed.D. (660-543-8701)
Educational Technology: Odin Jurkowski, Ed.D. (660-543-8387)
English: Daniel Schierenbeck, Ph.D. (660-543-8696)
Environmental Studies: Kurt Dean, Ph.D. (660-543-4735)
History: Eric Tenbus, Ph.D. (660-543-8707)
Industrial Hygiene: John Zey, M.S. (660-543-4410)
Industrial Management: Ron Woolsey, Ph.D. (660-543-4340)
Industrial Technology: Ron Woolsey, Ph.D. (660-543-4340)
Information Technology: Sam S. Ramanujan, Ph.D. (660-543-8565)
Library Science and Information Services: Pat Antrim, Ph.D. (660-543-8633)
Literacy Education: Wayne Williams, Ed.D. (660-543-8701)
Master of Arts in Teaching: Wayne Williams, Ed.D. (660-543-8701)
Mathematics: Shing So, Ph.D. (660-543-8839)
Music: J. Franklin Fenley, Ed.D. (660-543-4974)
Occupational Safety Management: Omer Frank, Ph.D. (660-543-4412)
Physical Education, Exercise, and Sport Science: Scott Strohmeyer, Ph.D. (660-543-8191)
Psychology: Jonathan Smith, Ph.D. (660-543-4378)
Rural Family Nursing: Linda Mulligan, Ph.D. (816-802-2226)
School Administration: Doug Thomas, Ed.D. (660-543-8834)
Social Gerontology: Jean Nuernberger, M.S.W. (660-543-8758)
Sociology: Karen Bradley, Ph.D. (660-543-8195)
Special Education: Jerry Neal, Ed.D. (660-543-8797)
Speech-Language Pathology: Carl Harlan, Ph.D. (660-543-4918)
Teaching English as a Second Language: Dennis Muchisky, Ph.D. (660-543-8711)
Theater: Richard Herman, Ph.D. (660-543-4020)

Education Specialist Degree Programs and Coordinators
Administration (Elementary School Principalship, Secondary School Principalship, Superintendency): Doug Thomas, Ed.D. (660-543-8834)
Curriculum and Instruction: Wayne Williams, Ed.D. (660-543-8701)
Human Services
- Guidance and Counseling: Janelle Cowles, Ed.D. (660-543-8204)
- Learning Resources: Pat Antrim, Ph.D. (660-543-8633)
- Special Education: Jerry Neal, Ph.D. (660-543-8497)
- Technology and Occupational Education: Barton Washer, Ph.D. (660-543-4580)

Cooperative Doctoral Degree Programs and Coordinators
Ph.D. in Technology (Indiana State University): John Sutton, Ph.D. (660-543-4439)
Ed.D. in Educational Leadership (University of Missouri–Columbia): Sandy Hutchinson, Ed.D. (660-543-4720)

UNIVERSITY OF CONNECTICUT

Graduate School

UCONN

Programs of Study

The Graduate School of the University of Connecticut offers programs leading to the degrees of Master of Arts, Master of Science, Master of Business Administration, Master of Dental Science, Master of Engineering, Master of Fine Arts (offered in art and dramatic arts), Master of Music, Master of Professional Studies (offered in homeland security leadership, human resources management, and humanitarian services administration), Master of Public Administration, Master of Public Health, and Master of Social Work, as well as to the degrees of Doctor of Audiology, Doctor of Education (educational leadership), Doctor of Musical Arts, Doctor of Nursing Practice, Doctor of Physical Therapy, and Doctor of Philosophy.

Study leading to the degree of Master of Arts or Master of Science is offered in accounting; adult learning; agricultural and resource economics; allied health; animal science; anthropology; applied financial mathematics; applied genomics; applied microbial systems analysis; art history; biochemistry; biodiversity and conservation biology; biomedical engineering; cell biology; chemical engineering; chemistry; civil engineering; clinical and translational research; communication sciences; comparative literary and cultural studies; computer science and engineering; curriculum and instruction; dramatic arts; ecology and evolutionary biology; economics; educational administration; educational psychology; educational technology; electrical engineering; English; environmental engineering; French; genetics and genomics; geography; geological sciences; German; history; human development and family studies; international studies; Italian; Judaic studies; kinesiology; linguistics; materials science; materials science and engineering; mathematics; mechanical engineering; medieval studies; microbiology; music; natural resources—land, water, and air; nursing; nutritional science; oceanography; pathobiology; pharmaceutical science; philosophy; physics; physiology and neurobiology; plant science; political science; polymer science; professional higher education administration; psychology; sociology; Spanish; special education; statistics; structural biology and biophysics; and survey research.

Study leading to the degree of Doctor of Philosophy is offered in adult learning; agricultural and resource economics; animal science; anthropology; biochemistry; biomedical engineering; biomedical science; business administration; cell biology; chemical engineering; chemistry; civil engineering; communication sciences; comparative literary and cultural studies; computer science and engineering; curriculum and instruction; ecology and evolutionary biology; economics; educational administration; educational psychology; educational technology; electrical engineering; English; environmental engineering; French; genetics and genomics; geography; geological sciences; German; history; human development and family studies; Italian; kinesiology; linguistics; materials science; materials science and engineering; mathematics; mechanical engineering; medieval studies; microbiology; music; natural resources–land, water, and air; nursing; nutritional science; oceanography; pathobiology; pharmaceutical science; philosophy; physics; physiology and neurobiology; plant science; political science; polymer science; psychology; public health; social work; sociology; Spanish; special education; statistics; and structural biology and biophysics.

Research Facilities

The Homer Babbidge Library at Storrs seats 2,300 people in a wide variety of study facilities, including individually assigned research studies, group studies, and areas designed for the use of computers, videos, and microtext. The building contains more than 2.7 million volumes of the system's total of more than 4 million volumes, as well as microtext, maps, manuscripts, archives, recordings, and other materials. The library's book and journal holdings as well as many periodical indexes are accessible through HOMER, the online information system. A wide array of electronic resources is available in the reference area of the Babbidge Library. The Thomas J. Dodd Research Center is a fully equipped research facility and a major archive for historic papers. The University has several dozen centers and institutes that promote research in specialized areas of study.

Financial Aid

Available are graduate assistantships for teaching and research, tuition remission awards, Special Graduate Student Fellowships, University predoctoral fellowships, doctoral dissertation fellowships, summer fellowships for doctoral and predoctoral students, and aid in a variety of forms for students in specific programs.

Cost of Study

Course-related fees in 2009–10 for full-time students total $5613 per semester for in-state students and $13,155 per semester for out-of-state students. Fees for part-time study are prorated. Fees are subject to change without notice.

Living and Housing Costs

On-campus housing for graduate students is limited. In 2009–10, students living in the Graduate Residence are charged $3178 per semester. Information about other on-campus housing options is available online at http://www.reslife.uconn.edu. The comprehensive board plan provides three meals a day while classes are in session at a cost of $2362 per semester. Other options are available. Fees are subject to change without notice.

Student Group

Approximately 5,000 students are enrolled in graduate degree programs. About 2,000 are working toward doctoral degrees.

Location

Most graduate degree programs offered by the University are located at the Storrs campus, which is 25 miles northeast of Hartford. Storrs is a scenic, agricultural area. Degree programs in the biomedical sciences and the marine sciences are offered at the University of Connecticut Health Center in Farmington (near Hartford) and at the Marine Sciences Institute at Avery Point (on Long Island Sound), respectively. The School of Social Work is located in West Hartford.

The University

The University of Connecticut grew out of the Storrs Agricultural School, which was founded in 1881 as a direct result of the gift of land, money, and buildings presented to the Connecticut General Assembly by Charles and Augustus Storrs of Mansfield. Master's degree study was offered by 1920. The Graduate School was established officially in 1939, and the University conferred its first Ph.D.'s a decade later.

Applying

Applicants should consult the academic department or program of their choice concerning application deadlines. Applicants are encouraged to apply online. Many programs have early closing dates. Application to some programs may require scores on one or more graduate admission tests, an interview or audition, or demonstrated proof of adequate facility in English for international applicants (the TOEFL is generally required for international applicants whose native language is not English). A complete summary of these requirements is available at http://www.grad.uconn.edu/.

Correspondence and Information

The Graduate School
Unit 1006
University of Connecticut
438 Whitney Road Extension
Storrs, Connecticut 06269-1006

Phone: 860-486-3617
E-mail: gradschool@uconn.edu
Web site: http://www.grad.uconn.edu/

FACULTY HEADS

Accounting: A. J. Rosman, Ph.D.
Adult Learning: B. G. Sheckley, Ph.D.
Agricultural and Resource Economics: R. Lopez, Ph.D.
Allied Health: L. Silbart, Ph.D.
Animal Science: D. Fletcher, Ph.D.
Anthropology: S. O. McBrearty, Ph.D.
Applied Financial Mathematics: J. G. Bridgeman, M.A.
Applied Genomics: L. Strausbaugh, Ph.D.
Applied Microbial Systems Analysis: D. R. Benson, Ph.D.
Art: J. Thorpe, M.F.A.
Art History: J. Thorpe, M.F.A.
Biochemistry: D. R. Benson, Ph.D.
Biodiversity and Conservation Biology: K. Wells, Ph.D.
Biomedical Engineering: D. R. Peterson, Ph.D.
Biomedical Science: L. Klobutcher, Ph.D.
Biophysics, Structural Biology and: D. R. Benson, Ph.D.
Business Administration: C. Earley, Ph.D.
Cell Biology: D. R. Benson, Ph.D.
Chemical Engineering: C. B. Carter, Ph.D.
Chemistry: S. Suib, Ph.D.
Civil Engineering: M. Accorsi, Ph.D.
Communication Science: C. A. Coehlo, Ph.D.
Comparative Literary and Cultural Studies: L. McNeece, Ph.D. and N. Bouchard, Ph.D.
Computer Science and Engineering: R. A. Ammar, Ph.D.
Curriculum and Instruction: M. A. Doyle, Ph.D.
Dental Science: A. R. Hand, D.D.S.
Dramatic Arts: G. M. English, M.F.A.
Ecology and Evolutionary Biology: K. Wells, Ph.D.
Economics: D. R. Heffley, Ph.D.
Educational Administration: B. G. Sheckley, Ph.D.
Educational Psychology: H. Swaminathan, Ph.D.
Educational Technology: M. Young, Ph.D.
Electrical Engineering: P. Luh, Ph.D.
Engineering: M. Choi, Ph.D.
English: A. H. Fairbanks, Ph.D.
Environmental Engineering: A. C. Bagtzoglou, Ph.D.
French: N. Bouchard, Ph.D.
Genetics: D. R. Benson, Ph.D.
Geography: J. P. Osleeb, Ph.D.
Geological Sciences: P. Visscher, Ph.D.
German: N. Bouchard, Ph.D.
History: S. A. Roe, Ph.D.
Human Development and Family Studies: R. M. Sabatelli, Ph.D.
International Studies: E. Mahan, Ph.D.
Italian: N. Bouchard, Ph.D.
Judaic Studies: A. M. Dashefsky, Ph.D.
Kinesiology: C. M. Maresh, Ph.D.
Linguistics: W. Snyder, Ph.D.
Materials Science: H. L. Marcus, Ph.D.
Materials Science and Engineering: C. B. Carter, Ph.D.
Mathematics: M. Neumann, Ph.D.
Mechanical Engineering: B. Cetegen, Ph.D.
Medieval Studies: T. J. Jambeck, Ph.D.
Microbiology: D. R. Benson, Ph.D.
Music: R. W. Bass, Ph.D.
Natural Resources: J. C. Volin, Ph.D.
Nursing: A. R. Bavier, Ed.D.
Nutritional Science: S. Koo, Ph.D.
Oceanography: A. C. Bucklin, Ph.D.
Pathobiology: H. J. Van Kruiningen, D.V.M., Ph.D., M.D.
Pharmaceutical Science: J. B. Morris, Ph.D.
Philosophy: C. L. Elder, Ph.D.
Physical Therapy: C. R. Denegar, Ph.D.
Physics: W. C. Stwalley, Ph.D.
Physiology and Neurobiology: J. L. Renfro, Ph.D.
Plant Science: M. Musgrave, Ph.D.
Political Science: M. A. Boyer, Ph.D.
Polymer Science: T. A. P. Seery, Ph.D.
Professional Higher Education Administration: B. G. Sheckley, Ph.D.
Professional Studies: S. Nesbit, Ph.D.
Psychology: C. A. Lowe, Ph.D.
Public Administration: A. K. Donahue, Ph.D.
Public Health (M.P.H. Program): D. Gregorio, Ph.D.
Public Health (Ph.D. Program): A. M. Ferris, Ph.D.
Social Work: S. Raheim, Ph.D.
Sociology: D. S. Glasberg, Ph.D.
Spanish: N. Bouchard, Ph.D.
Special Education: H. Swaminathan, Ph.D.
Statistics: D. Dey, Ph.D.
Structural Biology and Biophysics: D. R. Benson, Ph.D.
Survey Research: A. K. Donahue, Ph.D.

A study area in the Homer Babbidge Library on the Storrs campus.

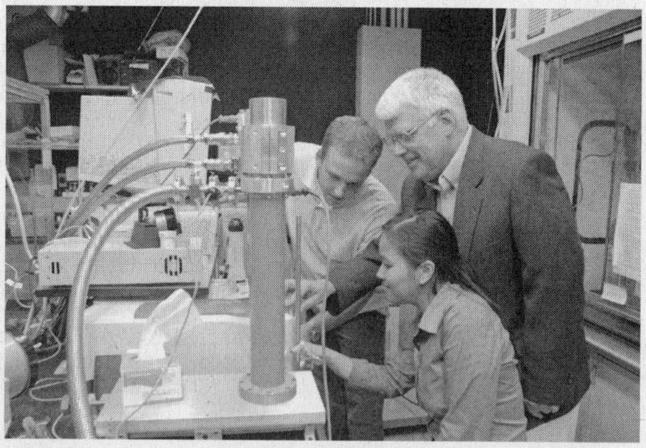

A faculty member works with graduate students in the lab.

Many new buildings on campus have been completed in recent years, including the Chemistry Building shown above.

UNIVERSITY OF DENVER

Graduate Studies

Programs of Study

The University of Denver offers programs of study leading to master's, doctoral, and specialist degrees. The Doctor of Philosophy (Ph.D.) is available from many programs in the Arts and Humanities, Social Sciences, and the Natural Sciences and Mathematics; the School of Engineering and Computer Science; the Morgridge College of Education; the Josef Korbel School of International Studies; and the Graduate School of Social Work. A joint Ph.D. in religious and theological studies is available through the University and the Iliff School of Theology. The Doctor of Psychology (Psy.D.) is available from the Graduate School of Professional Psychology.

An Education Specialist (Ed.S.) degree is available from the Morgridge College of Education. The Juris Doctor (J.D.) is available from the Sturm College of Law.

Master's degrees can be pursued in the Arts and Humanities, Social Sciences, and the Natural Sciences and Mathematics; the School of Engineering and Computer Science; Daniels College of Business; the Morgridge College of Education; the Josef Korbel School of International Studies; University College; the Graduate School of Professional Psychology; the Conflict Resolution Institute; and the Graduate School of Social Work.

Various joint and interdisciplinary degrees, which combine study with two or more programs, are also available.

The Sturm College of Law, Daniels College of Business, the Josef Korbel School of International Studies, the Graduate School of Social Work, the Morgridge College of Education, the Department of Human Communication Studies, and the Department of Psychology offer various dual degrees, which combine study in two programs and award two degrees.

In addition, the University of Denver offers students the opportunity to simultaneously enroll in any two master's degree programs, thus creating flexible dual degrees. These programs must make academic and/or career preparation sense, and no more than 15 credits of each program can be counted toward the other program.

Research Facilities

The University of Denver libraries provide an extensive collection of volumes, periodical subscriptions, and microforms in all subjects covered by University courses and research. Penrose Library has been a U.S. government document depository since 1909. Penrose has numerous online search capabilities that include the Colorado Alliance of Research Libraries (CARL), LexisNexis, Dialog, and other business and humanities indexes. In addition, Penrose has been selected by Higher Education Resource Services to provide scholarly information to the western United States. Students also have access to many other academic and public libraries. The University also possesses excellent media and computer facilities and state-of-the-art research laboratories on campus.

Financial Aid

Two kinds of financial aid are available for graduate students: need-based aid and merit-based aid. Students applying for either kind of aid must be accepted into an eligible graduate program at the University. Need-based financial aid consists of Direct Loans, Federal Perkins Loans, and Federal Work-Study Program awards. Merit-based financial aid consists of graduate tuition scholarships, graduate teaching and research assistantships, and Graduate Studies Doctoral Fellowships. A student who seeks state and federal financial assistance to pursue graduate studies at the University must file the Free Application for Federal Student Aid (FAFSA). For more information, students should contact the graduate school or department in which they wish to enroll.

Cost of Study

For the 2009–10 academic year, tuition is $961 per credit hour. Full-time tuition per quarter (12 to 18 hours) is $11,532. There is an additional technology fee of $4 per credit hour and an activity fee of $50 per quarter. In addition, there is an optional health services fee per quarter and a University insurance fee per six months (which is waived with proof of alternate insurance).

Living and Housing Costs

The yearly rate in 2009–10 for an on-campus, unfurnished one-bedroom apartment is $7650 ($6126 for a studio). The yearly rate for 1 person in an on-campus unfurnished two-bedroom apartment (double occupancy) is $5724. Off-campus apartments are available nearby and range from $650 to $725. A liberal estimate of total monthly living expenses (e.g., rent, board, books, and personal spending) is $1200.

Student Group

Approximately 5,777 graduate students attend the University and compose more than one half of the University's total student enrollment of 10,922 students. Approximately 15 percent of the total graduate student population consists of members of diverse domestic ethnic groups, and an additional 6 percent of the total graduate student population is composed of international students.

Student Outcomes

Students who have received their doctoral degrees from the University have obtained teaching and research positions at universities throughout the U.S. and the world. Master's degree recipients have pursued work in various business sectors and with governments throughout the world. The University has a Career Center that actively works with students and alumni who are seeking employment.

Location

Mile-high Denver, with a population of about 555,000, is the financial, administrative, commercial, and sports center of the Rocky Mountain region. Denver offers many cultural and intellectual attractions, including numerous theater groups, an outstanding symphony orchestra, and fine museums. Denver has a mild climate, with an average of 300 sunny days a year. Excellent outdoor recreation of all kinds, especially skiing, may be enjoyed within an hour's drive of the University.

The University

In 1864, John Evans, second governor of the Colorado Territory, signed the charter establishing Colorado's first private university—the University of Denver. Founded in the spirit of westward expansion, the University is one of the few major private universities between Chicago and the West Coast. The University of Denver is nationally recognized for graduate programming and the quality of the professional schools.

Applying

Each graduate program provides specific information about admission to that school and/or department. Application fees, deadlines, and requirements vary by school and department.

Correspondence and Information

For general information, students should contact:

Graduate Studies, Admissions and Records
University of Denver
2199 South University Boulevard, Room 5
Denver, Colorado 80208

Phone: 303-871-2831
877-871-3119 (toll-free)
Fax: 303-871-4942
E-mail: grad-info@du.edu
Web site: http://www.du.edu

SCHOOLS, PROGRAMS, AND FACULTY

The University of Denver's deans, graduate degree programs, and admissions phone numbers are listed below.

Arts and Humanities: Dean Anne McCall, Ph.D., Strasbourg.
Art and Art History: 303-871-2846 (e-mail: saah-interest@du.edu).
English: 303-871-2266 (e-mail: engl-info@du.edu).
Music: 303-871-6973 (e-mail: Jerrod.Price@du.edu).
Religious Studies: 303-871-2740 (e-mail: rlgs@du.edu).

Natural Sciences and Mathematics: Dean Alayne Parson, Ph.D., Illinois at Chicago.
Biological Sciences: 303-871-3661 (e-mail: rdores@du.edu).
Chemistry and Biochemistry: 303-871-2435 (e-mail: chem-info@du.edu).
Geography: 303-871-2513 (e-mail: geog-info@du.edu).
Mathematics: 303-871-3344 (e-mail: math-info@math.du.edu).
Physics and Astronomy: 303-871-2238 (e-mail: phys-gradinfo@du.edu).

School of Engineering and Computer Science: Dean Rahmat A. Shoureshi, Ph.D., MIT.
Computer Science: 303-871-2453 (e-mail: grad@cs.du.edu).
Electrical and Computer Engineering: 303-871-2102 (e-mail: engrinfo@du.edu).
Mechanical and Materials Engineering: 303-871-2107 (e-mail: engrinfo@du.edu).

Social Sciences: Dean Anne McCall, Ph.D., Strasbourg.
Anthropology: 303-871-2406 (e-mail: anth02@du.edu).
Economics: 303-871-2685 (e-mail: econ04@du.edu).
Psychology: 303-871-3803 (e-mail: phoughta@du.edu).
Public Policy: 303-871-2468 (e-mail: ipps@du.edu)
School of Communication:
- **Digital Media Studies:** 303-871-7716 (e-mail: treddell@du.edu).
- **Human Communication Studies:** 303-871-2385 (e-mail: hcom@du.edu).
- **International and Intercultural Communication:** 303-871-2088 (e-mail: iic@du.edu).
- **Mass Communication and Journalism Studies:** 303-871-2166 (e-mail: mcomadm@du.edu).
- **Public Relations and Advertising:** 303-871-2166 (e-mail: mcomadm@du.edu).

Conflict Resolution Institute: Karen Feste, Director; Ph.D., Minnesota. Contact: 303-871-6477 (e-mail: cri@du.edu).

Daniels College of Business: Dean Christine Riordan, Ph.D., Georgia State. Contact: 303-871-3416; 800-622-4723 (toll-free) (e-mail: daniels@du.edu).

Graduate School of Professional Psychology: Dean Peter Buirski, Ph.D., Adelphi. Contact: 303-871-3873 (e-mail: gsppinfo@du.edu).

Graduate School of Social Work: Dean James Herbert Williams, Ph.D., Washington. Contact: 303-871-2841 (e-mail: gssw-admission@du.edu).

Graduate Tax Program: Mark Vogel, Director; J.D., Notre Dame; CPA. Contact: 303-871-6239 (e-mail: gtp@du.edu).

Iliff School of Theology Joint Ph.D. Program with DU: Theodore Vial, Director; Ph.D., Chicago. Contact: 303-765-3136 (e-mail: jointphd@iliff.edu).

Intermodal Transportation Institute: Cathryne Johnson. Contact: 303-871-4146 (e-mail: du-iti@du.edu).

Josef Korbel Graduate School of International Studies: Dean Tom Farer, J.D., Harvard. Contact: 303-871-2544; 877-474-7236 (toll-free) (e-mail: korbeladm@du.edu).

Morgridge College of Education: Dean Gregory Anderson, Ph.D., City University of New York. Contact: 303-871-2509; 800-835-1607 (toll-free) (e-mail: ed-info@du.edu).

Sturm College of Law: Dean José Roberto Juárez Jr., J.D., Texas. Contact: 303-871-6135 (e-mail: admissions@law.du.edu).

University College: Dean James Davis, Ph.D., Michigan. Contact: 303-871-2291; 800-347-2042 (toll-free) (e-mail: ucolinfo@du.edu).

UNIVERSITY OF FLORIDA

Graduate School

Programs of Study

The University of Florida (UF) Graduate School offers the Ph.D. in eighty-six disciplines, in addition to the Doctor of Audiology, Doctor of Education, and Doctor of Plant Medicine degrees. There are master's programs in 111 disciplines, fourteen Engineer degree programs, and twelve Specialist in Education programs. In addition, a number of interdisciplinary concentrations are available at the doctoral level, and there are many successful joint-degree programs. Professional postbaccalaureate degrees are offered in dentistry, law, medicine, pharmacy, physician assistance, and veterinary medicine.

Research Facilities

UF major research centers include the Archie Carr Center for Sea Turtle Research, the Center for Environmental Systems Commercial Space Technology, the Center for Applied Optimization, the Database Systems Research and Development Center, the Engineering Research Center for Particle Science and Technology, the Florida Museum of Natural History, the Genetics and Cancer Research Center, the McGuire Center for Lepidoptera and Biodiversity, the McKnight Brain Institute, the National High Magnetic Field Laboratory partnership with Florida State University and Los Alamos, the Proton-beam Therapy Center, and the new Public Health and Health Professions, Nursing, and Pharmacy Building.

UF's nine libraries offer more than 4 million catalogued volumes and links to fulltext articles in more than 34,000 journals. Of national significance are the Baldwin Library of Historical Children's Literature, the Latin American Collection, the Map and Imagery Library, the P. K. Yonge Library of Florida History (preeminent Floridiana collection), the Price Library of Judaica, and holdings on architectural preservation and eighteenth-century American architecture, late-nineteenth- and early-twentieth-century German state documents, rural sociology of Florida, and tropical and subtropical agriculture.

Financial Aid

The Graduate Fellowship Initiative (http://www.aa.ufl.edu/fellows) offers Alumni Graduate Fellowships to superior students entering Ph.D. and M.F.A. programs. In addition, qualified graduate students are eligible for other fellowships, assistantships, and awards (http://gradschool.rgp.ufl.edu/students/financial-aid.html). UF also has a substantial number of fellowships targeted specifically for underrepresented students (http://gradschool.rgp.ufl.edu/diversity/introduction.html#ogmp). Applications for these awards should be made to the appropriate department chair on or before February 15 of each year.

Non-Florida tuition payments and in-state tuition payments are available to eligible graduate students who hold assistantships or certain fellowships. These payments cover most tuition charges.

Cost of Study

Tuition and fees for new in-state residents in 2008–09 were $10,238 per year, based on 30 hours of graduate enrollment. The comparable amount for new out-of-state graduate students was $29,144 per year. Near graduation, there are expenses for typing and duplicating a thesis (dissertation) and fees for library processing, microfilming, and publishing the dissertation abstract.

Living and Housing Costs

UF provides some variety in types of accommodations. The double room for 2 students is the most common. Air-conditioned dormitory rooms range from $1893 to $2840 per person per semester. Accommodations for single graduate or professional students in Diamond Apartment Village begin at $500 per person per month. At present, a one-bedroom unfurnished apartment off campus rents for about $650 per month.

Student Group

UF's 50,000 students are from all sixty-seven Florida counties (86 percent), the remaining forty-nine states (9 percent), and 100 other countries (5 percent). The University of Florida is the fifth-largest university in the U.S. and the largest university in the Southeast. UF is the number 1 Florida recruiter and the number 2 U.S. recruiter of National Merit Scholars. Of fall freshmen, 25 percent have GPAs above 4.0 and SAT scores above 1340. UF's student body is made up of 47 percent men. Eighteen percent (9,300) are members of minority groups. Seventy-two percent (36,000) are undergraduate students, 21 percent (10,400) are graduate students, and 8 percent (4,200) are professional students.

Location

An hour from each coast, the Gainesville metropolitan statistical area's population is near 240,000. One of the 100 best U.S. cities, Gainesville's urban forest makes its home in Florida's heart. Highs average 76°F to 82°F in the spring and fall, 89°F to 91°F in the summer, and 69°F in the winter. Alachua County delights nature lovers with its 965 square miles, 65 percent of which are made up of wilderness, lakes, wetlands, and trails.

The University

The University of Florida is a major public, land-grant research university. The state's oldest, largest, and most comprehensive university, UF is among the nation's most academically diverse. One of only seventeen land-grant universities in the Association of American Universities, UF has a long history of established programs in international education, research, and service. UF also has an outstanding intercollegiate sports program.

Applying

First-time UF graduate students need a B average or better for all upper-division undergraduate work, a GRE score acceptable to the program to which they have applied, and a baccalaureate degree from a regionally accredited college, university, or equivalent. Individual departments may have additional requirements. Applicants whose native language is not English need a TOEFL score of at least 550 on the paper-based test, 213 on the computer-based test, or 80 on the Internet-based test; an IELTS score of at least 6 or an MELAB score of 77; or successful completion of the University of Florida English Language Institute program. Deadlines can be found in the graduate catalog and at either http://gradschool.rgp.ufl.edu/catalog/current-catalog/catalog-coverpage.html or at http://www.registrar.ufl.edu.

Correspondence and Information

For general information:
Graduate Admissions Office
201 Criser Hall
University of Florida
P.O. Box 114000
Gainesville, Florida 32611-4000
Phone: 352-392-1365 Ext. 7172
Web site: http://www.admissions.ufl.edu/grad

For program information:
Department of (specify department or program)
College of (specify)
University of Florida
Gainesville, Florida 32611
E-mail: gradschool@rgp.ufl.edu
Web site: http://gradschool.rgp.ufl.edu

COLLEGES AND PROGRAMS

College of Agricultural and Life Sciences (http://www.cals.ufl.edu). Master of Agribusiness: Food and Resource Economics. Master of Agriculture: Agriculture Education and Communication, Animal Sciences, Botany, Food and Resource Economics, Soil and Water Science. Master of Family, Youth, and Community Sciences. Master of Fisheries and Aquatic Sciences. Master of Forest Resources and Conservation. Master of Science: Agricultural and Biological Engineering; Agricultural Education and Communication (Farming Systems); Agronomy; Animal Sciences; Botany; Entomology and Nematology; Family, Youth, and Community Sciences; Fisheries and Aquatic Sciences; Food and Resource Economics; Food Science and Human Nutrition (Nutritional Sciences); Forest Resources and Conservation; Horticultural Science (Environmental Horticulture, Horticultural Sciences); Interdisciplinary Ecology; Microbiology and Cell Science; Plant Molecular and Cellular Biology; Plant Pathology; Soil and Water Science; Wildlife Ecology and Conservation. Doctor of Philosophy: Agricultural and Biological Engineering, Agricultural Education and Communication, Agronomy, Animal Sciences, Botany, Entomology and Nematology, Fisheries and Aquatic Sciences, Food and Resource Economics, Food Science and Human Nutrition (Food Science, Nutritional Sciences), Forest Resources and Conservation, Horticultural Science (Environmental Horticulture, Horticultural Sciences), Interdisciplinary Ecology, Microbiology and Cell Science, Plant Molecular and Cellular Biology, Plant Pathology, Soil and Water Science, Wildlife Ecology and Conservation. Doctor of Plant Medicine.

Warrington College of Business Administration (http://www.cba.ufl.edu). Master of Accounting. Master of Arts: Business Administration (Insurance, Marketing), Economics. Master of Business Administration (M.B.A.): Competitive Strategy, Decision and Information Sciences, Entrepreneurship, Finance, General Business, Global Management, Graham-Buffet Security Analysis, Health Administration, Human Resource Management, International Studies, Latin American Business, Management, Marketing, Real Estate and Urban Analysis, Sports Administration. Master of Science: Business Administration (Entrepreneurship, Insurance, Marketing, Retailing), Finance, Information Systems and Operations Management, Management, Real Estate. Doctor of Philosophy: Business Administration (Accounting, Decision and Information Sciences, Finance, Insurance, Management, Marketing, Real Estate and Urban Analysis), Economics.

College of Dentistry (http://www.dental.ufl.edu). Master of Science: Dental Sciences (Endodontics, Orthodontics, Periodontics, Prosthodontics), Oral Biology.

College of Design, Construction, and Planning (http://www.dcp.ufl.edu). Master of Architecture: Historic Preservation, Sustainable Architecture, Sustainable Design. Master of Arts in Urban and Regional Planning. Master of Building Construction: Building Construction (Sustainable Construction). Master of Interior Design. Master of International Construction Management. Master of Landscape Architecture. Master of Science in Architectural Studies. Master of Science in Building Construction (Sustainable Construction). Doctor of Philosophy: Design, Construction, and Planning (Architecture, Building Construction, Interior Design, Landscape Architecture, Urban and Regional Planning).

College of Education (http://www.coe.ufl.edu). Master of Arts in Education: Curriculum and Instruction, Early Childhood Education, Educational Leadership, Educational Psychology, Elementary Education, English Education, Foundations of Education, Marriage and Family Counseling, Mathematics Education, Mental Health Counseling, Reading Education, Research and Evaluation Methodology, School Counseling and Guidance, School Psychology, Science Education, Social Studies Education, Special Education. Master of Education (majors: same as Master of Arts in Education degree). Specialist in Education (special degree requiring one year of graduate work beyond the master's degree): Curriculum and Instruction, Educational Leadership, Educational Psychology, Foundations of Education, Higher Education Administration, Marriage and Family Counseling, Mental Health Counseling, Research and Evaluation Methodology, School Counseling and Guidance, School Psychology, Special Education. Doctor of Education: Curriculum and Instruction, Educational Leadership, Educational Psychology, Foundations of Education, Higher Education Administration, Marriage and Family Counseling, Mental Health Counseling, Research and Evaluation Methodology, School Counseling and Guidance, School Psychology, Special Education. Doctor of Philosophy: Curriculum and Instruction, Educational Leadership, Educational Psychology, Foundations of Education, Higher Education Administration, Marriage and Family Counseling, Mental Health Counseling, Research and Evaluation Methodology, School Counseling and Guidance, School Psychology, Special Education.

College of Engineering (http://www.eng.ufl.edu). Master of Civil Engineering. Master of Engineering: Aerospace Engineering, Agricultural and Biological Engineering, Biomedical Engineering, Chemical Engineering, Civil Engineering, Coastal and Oceanographic Engineering, Computer Engineering, Electrical and Computer Engineering, Environmental Engineering Sciences, Industrial and Systems Engineering, Materials Science and Engineering, Mechanical Engineering, Nuclear Engineering Sciences. Master of Science: Aerospace Engineering, Biomedical Engineering, Chemical Engineering, Civil Engineering, Coastal and Oceanographic Engineering, Computer Engineering, Digital Arts and Sciences, Electrical and Computer Engineering, Environmental Engineering Sciences, Industrial and Systems Engineering, Materials Science and Engineering, Mechanical Engineering, Nuclear Engineering Sciences. Engineer (special degree requiring one year of graduate work beyond the master's degree: same programs as for Master of Engineering degree, except Biomedical Engineering, Civil Engineering, and Coastal and Oceanographic Engineering). Doctor of Philosophy: Aerospace Engineering, Agricultural and Biological Engineering, Biomedical Engineering, Chemical Engineering, Civil Engineering, Coastal and Oceanographic Engineering, Computer Engineering, Electrical and Computer Engineering, Environmental Engineering Sciences, Industrial and Systems Engineering, Materials Science and Engineering, Mechanical Engineering, Nuclear Engineering Sciences.

College of Fine Arts (http://www.arts.ufl.edu). Master of Arts: Art Education, Art History, Digital Arts and Sciences, Museology (Museum Studies). Master of Fine Arts: Art, Creative Writing, Theater. Master of Music: Music (Choral Conducting, Composition, Instrumental Conducting, Music History and Literature, Music Theory, Performance, Sacred Music), Music Education. Doctor of Philosophy: Art History, Music (Composition, Music History and Literature), Music Education.

College of Health and Human Performance (http://www.hhp.ufl.edu). Master of Science: Applied Physiology and Kinesiology (Athletic Training/Sport Medicine, Biomechanics, Clinical Exercise Physiology, Exercise Physiology, Human Performance, Motor Learning/Control, Sport and Exercise Psychology); Health Education and Behavior; Recreation, Parks, and Tourism; Sport Management. Doctor of Philosophy: Health and Human Performance (Athletic Training/Sport Medicine, Biomechanics, Exercise Physiology, Health Behavior, Motor Learning/Control, Natural Resource Recreation, Sport and Exercise Psychology, Sport Management, Therapeutic Recreation, Tourism).

College of Journalism and Communications (http://www.jou.ufl.edu). Master of Advertising. Master of Arts in Mass Communication. Doctor of Philosophy: Mass Communication.

Levin College of Law (http://www.law.ufl.edu). Master of Laws in Comparative Law. Master of Laws in International Taxation. Master of Laws in Taxation.

College of Liberal Arts and Sciences (http://www.clas.ufl.edu). Master of Arts: Anthropology, Classical Studies, Communication Sciences and Disorders, Criminology and Law, English, French, Geography (Applications of Geographic Technologies), German, History, Latin, Latin American Studies, Linguistics, Mathematics, Museology (Museum Studies), Philosophy, Political Science, Political Science—International Relations, Psychology, Religion, Sociology, Spanish, Women's Studies. Master of Arts in Teaching: Anthropology, French, Geography, Latin, Latin American Studies, Linguistics, Mathematics, Philosophy, Political Science, Political Science—International Relations, Psychology, Spanish. Master of Fine Arts: Creative Writing. Master of Latin. Master of Science: Astronomy, Botany, Chemistry, Computer Science, Geography, Geology, Mathematics, Physics, Psychology, Zoology. Master of Science in Statistics. Master of Science in Teaching: Astronomy, Botany, Chemistry, Geography, Geology, Mathematics, Physics, Zoology. Master of Statistics. Master of Women's Studies. Doctor of Audiology. Doctor of Philosophy: Anthropology, Astronomy, Botany, Chemistry, Classical Studies, Communication Sciences and Disorders, Counseling Psychology, Criminology and Law, English, Geography, Geology, German, History, Linguistics, Mathematics, Philosophy, Physics, Political Science, Psychology, Religious Studies, Romance Languages (French, Spanish), Sociology, Statistics, Zoology.

College of Medicine (http://www.med.ufl.edu). Master of Science: Biochemistry and Molecular Biology, Epidemiology (Biostatistics, Health Management Policy), Medical Sciences (Clinical Investigation). Doctor of Philosophy: Biochemistry and Molecular Biology, Medical Sciences (Biochemistry and Molecular Biology, Genetics, Imaging Science and Technology, Immunology and Microbiology, Molecular Cell Biology, Neuroscience, Physiology, Pharmacology, Toxicology).

College of Nursing (http://con.ufl.edu). Master of Science in Nursing. Doctor of Philosophy: Nursing Practices.

College of Pharmacy (http://www.cop.ufl.edu). Master of Science in Pharmacy: Pharmaceutical Sciences (Forensic Drug Chemistry, Forensic Science, Forensic Serology and DNA, Medicinal Chemistry, Pharmaceutical Outcomes and Policy, Pharmacodynamics, Pharmacy). Doctor of Philosophy: Pharmaceutical Sciences (Medicinal Chemistry, Pharmacodynamics, Pharmacy, Pharmacy Health-Care Administration, Toxicology).

College of Public Health and Health Professions (http://www.phhp.ufl.edu). Master of Health Administration. Master of Health Science: Occupational Therapy, Rehabilitation Counseling. Master of Occupational Therapy. Master of Public Health: Public Health (Biostatistics, Environmental Health, Epidemiology, Public Health Management and Policy, Social and Behavioral Sciences). Doctor of Philosophy: Health Services Research, Psychology (Clinical Psychology), Rehabilitation Science.

College of Veterinary Medicine (http://www.vetmed.ufl.edu). Master of Science: Veterinary Medical Sciences (Forensic Toxicology). Doctor of Philosophy: Veterinary Medical Sciences.

Innovative Program Options (http://www.distancelearning.ufl.edu). UF's Web site for distance education resources and opportunities provides information about the various degrees, certificates, and courses offered.

Interdisciplinary Concentrations and Certificates (http://gradschool.rgp.ufl.edu/students/catalog.html). African Studies, Agroforestry, Animal Molecular and Cellular Biology, Biological Sciences, Chemical Physics, Ecological Engineering, Geographic Information Sciences, Gerontological Studies, Historic Preservation, Hydrologic Sciences, Latin American Studies, Medical Physics, Quantitative Finance, Quantum Theory Project, Toxicology, Translation Studies, Tropical Agriculture, Tropical Conservation and Development, Tropical Studies, Vision Sciences, Wetland Sciences, Women's and Gender Studies.

Combined, Concurrent, and Joint Programs (http://admissions.ufl.edu/ugrad/combdegree.html). Prospective students should check with the major department on the availability of combined (bachelor's/master's), concurrent (simultaneous study toward two graduate degrees), and joint (coupling of graduate and professional degrees) programs.

UNIVERSITY OF LOUISVILLE

School of Interdisciplinary & Graduate School

Programs of Study

The University of Louisville School of Interdisciplinary and Graduate Studies offers graduate degrees in the areas of arts and humanities, biomedical sciences, business, education, engineering, music, natural sciences, nursing, and social work. The University offers doctoral degree programs of study in over thirty different disciplines as well as graduate programs leading to master's degrees, certificates, and specialist's degrees in more than sixty different areas, including interdisciplinary studies.

Research Facilities

The University of Louisville has a number of outstanding on-campus research facilities. With a commitment to doubling doctoral degrees by the year 2020, research opportunities for graduate students are flourishing. New, state-of-the-art research buildings that house numerous centers and institutes have been constructed on the University's three campuses. A complete listing of University institutes for research can be found at http://louisville.edu/provost/centers-and-institutes. In addition, the University of Louisville is a member of a number of prestigious research groups on the state, regional, and national levels.

The University's metropolitan location and mission provide exciting graduate student learning opportunities. The University and the Louisville community are engaged in a number of active partnerships to enhance the quality of life and economic opportunities for residents of Louisville. The goal is to work with various community partners to improve the educational, health, economic, and social status of individuals and families who live in Louisville. The University of Louisville has a number of Distinguished and University Scholars with national and international reputations (http://louisville.edu/research/for-faculty-staff/university-of-louisvilles-scholars.html/) who educate and mentor graduate students on a one-on-one basis.

Translational research and scholarly work is being conducted to prepare graduate students for the ever-changing workforce. Through engagement in both the classroom and the community, graduate students at the University of Louisville are putting theory into practice. They are providing health screenings, teaching underprivileged children in urban schools, and working to find vaccines and cures for terminal diseases. Graduate students at the University of Louisville are provided not only with knowledge but also the tangible skills to succeed in a global society.

The University Libraries, a member of the Association of Research Libraries, has holdings of more than 2.1 million volumes, approximately 16,000 current journal subscriptions, access to more than 20,000 full-text electronic journals, various special collections, media, and microforms. Services offered by the libraries include reference training, including e-reference; state-of-the-art delivery of documents; and intensive information skills training. In addition, the main library has been recently customized with a robotic book retrieval system. Students also have access to the collections of six other area institutions.

Financial Aid

A number of financial awards are available to graduate students. In general, teaching, service, and research assistantships for 2009–10 range from $12,000 to $18,000 in stipend and include full tuition and health insurance. University fellowships are available to doctoral students and carry a stipend of $18,000 to $22,000 plus full tuition and health insurance. Assistantships and fellowships are typically either ten-month or twelve-month renewable positions.

Cost of Study

For the 2009–10 academic year, full-time tuition and fees are $18,504 per year for non-Kentucky residents. For Kentucky residents, full-time tuition and fees are $8622 per year. Student fees are prorated on a credit-hour basis; however, full-time enrollment is considered 9 credit hours each semester.

Living and Housing Costs

Housing is available for single and married students on the University of Louisville's main Belknap Campus and on the downtown Health Sciences Campus. For 2009–10, a small efficiency apartment on campus costs $7776 for twelve months. Partially furnished apartments for married students cost $10,008 for twelve months for two bedrooms, including utilities. The office of housing and residence life is also available to assist graduate students in locating off-campus housing.

Student Group

There are more than 4,500 graduate students at the University, studying in a wide variety of departments. Approximately one fourth of all graduate students are working toward doctoral degrees. University of Louisville students come from all regions of the United States and many other countries. The total University student population is nearly 22,000 students.

Location

Louisville, America's sixteenth-largest city, is a colorful city with a rich history and southern charm. Louisville residents enjoy a stable economic base, low cost of living, close-knit neighborhoods, and wonderful, friendly people. Louisville is home to the famed Kentucky Derby, held the first Saturday in May at Churchill Downs. Resident opera, art, theater, choral, ballet, and orchestral societies provide Louisville with cultural resources beyond those of cities of comparable size. In 2008, Louisville was chosen by the U.S. Conference of Mayors as the "Most Livable City." In August 2008, *Outside* magazine selected Louisville as one of the "20 Best Towns of 2008."

The University

The University traces its history to 1798 with the founding of the Jefferson Seminary. Jefferson Seminary became the University of Louisville in 1846 and in 1970 joined the state university system. Among its twelve schools are the College of Arts and Sciences, College of Business, School of Interdisciplinary and Graduate Studies, Raymond A. Kent School of Social Work, J. B. Speed School of Engineering, Louis D. Brandeis School of Law, School of Music, and College of Education and Human Development, which are located on the main Belknap Campus. The School of Medicine, School of Dentistry, School of Nursing, and School of Public Health and Information Sciences are located in the heart of the growing downtown Health Sciences Center. The University of Louisville strives to be a preeminent research institution.

Applying

For application information, deadline dates, and departmental funding opportunities, students should contact the department to which they wish to apply or the School of Interdisciplinary and Graduate Studies.

Correspondence and Information

School of Interdisciplinary and Graduate Studies
Houchens Suite 105
University of Louisville
Louisville, Kentucky 40292
E-mail: gradadm@louisville.edu
Web site: http://graduate.louisville.edu

FACULTY HEADS

ADMINISTRATION

William M. Pierce, Jr., Ph.D., Vice Provost and Dean.
Beth A. Boehm, Ph.D., Associate Dean.
Paul J. DeMarco, Ph.D., Assistant Dean.

PROGRAMS AND AREAS OF ADVANCED TRAINING

Anatomical Sciences and Neurobiology: http://louisville.edu/medschool/anatomy. Director: Charles Hubscher, Ph.D. (charles.hubscher@louisville.edu)
Anthropology: http://louisville.edu/anthropology. Director: Christopher Tillquist, Ph.D. (crtill01@louisville.edu)
Art Education: http://louisville.edu/education/degrees/mat-edar.html. Director: Barbara Hanger, Ph.D. (barbara.hanger@louisville.edu)
Art History: http://louisville.edu/a-s/finearts/gradprograms.html. Director: Susan Jarosi, Ph.D. (susan.jarosi@louisville.edu)
Art Therapy: http://louisville.edu/education/departments/ecpy/exp-therapy. Director: Eileen Estes, Ph.D. (eoeste01@louisville.edu)
Audiology: http://louisville.edu/medschool/surgery/com-disorders/audiology. Director: David Cunningham, Ph.D. (hearprof@ hotmail.com)
Biochemistry and Molecular Biology: http://biochemistry.louisville.edu. Director: Barbara Clark, Ph.D. (barbara.clark@louisville.edu)
Bioethics and Medical Humanities: http://louisville.edu/bioethicsma. Co-directors: David J. Doukas, M.D. (david.doukas@louisville.edu), and Robert Kimball, Ph.D. (robert.kimball@louisville.edu)
Biology: http://louisville.edu/a-s/biology. Director: Joseph M. Steffen, Ph.D. (joe.steffen@louisville.edu)
Biostatistics–Decision Science: http://louisville.edu/sphis/bb. Master's Director: Steven McCabe, M.D. (steven.mccabe@louisville.edu); Doctoral Director: Somnath Datta, Ph.D. (somnath.datta@louisville.edu)
Chemical Engineering: http://louisville.edu/speed/chemical. Director: Kyung Kang, Ph.D. (kakang01@louisville.edu)
Chemistry: http://louisville.edu/a-s/chemistry. Director: Craig Grapperhaus, Ph.D. (grapperhaus@louisville.edu)
Civil & Environmental Engineering: http://louisville.edu/speed/civil. Director: Mark French, Ph.D. (mark.french@louisville.edu)
Clinical Investigation Sciences: http://louisville.edu/sphis. Director: Susan Muldoon, Ph.D., M.P.H. (susan.muldoon@louisville.edu)
Clinical Psychology: http://louisville.edu/psychology/doctorate/clinical-psychology. Director: Janet Woodruff-Borden, Ph.D. (j.woodruff-borden@louisville.edu)
College Student Personnel: http://louisville.edu/education/departments/ecpy/csp. Director: Amy Hirschy, Ph.D. (ashirs02@louisville.edu)
Communication: http://comm.louisville.edu. Director: Jennifer Gregg, Ph.D. (jlgreg03@louisville.edu)
Communicative Disorders: http://www.louisville.edu/medschool/surgery/com-disorders/slp. Director: Barbara Baker, Ph.D. (barbara.baker@louisville.edu)
Community Health: http://louisville.edu/education/departments/hss/health-education. Director: Carol O'Neal, Ph.D. (ctstin01@louisville.edu)
Computer Engineering and Computer Science: http://louisville.edu/speed/cecs. Director: Mehmed Kantardzic, Ph.D. (mmkant01@louisville.edu)
Counseling Psychology: http://louisville.edu/education/departments/ecpy/counseling-psych. Director: Linda Shapiro, Ph.D. (linda.shapiro@louisville.edu)
Critical and Curatorial Studies: http://louisville.edu/a-s/finearts/gradprograms.html. Director: John Begley, Ph.D. (john.begley@louisville.edu)
Curriculum and Instruction: http://louisville.edu/education/degrees/tl-doctoral-degree.html. Director: Thomas Tretter, Ph.D. (trtret01@louisville.edu)
Early Elementary Education: http://louisville.edu/education/degrees/mat-ered.html. Director: Charles Thompson, Ph.D. (chuck@louisville.edu)
Education Administration: http://louisville.edu/education/degrees/med-edad.html. Director: Phyllis Connelly, Ph.D. (phyllis.connelly@louisville.edu)
Educational Leadership and Organizational Development: http://louisville.edu/education/degrees/elfh-doc-degree.html. Director: Bridgette Pregliasco, Ed.D. (bridgette.pregliasco@louisville.edu)
Electrical and Computer Engineering: http://www.ece.louisville.edu. Director: John Naber, Ph.D. (john.naber@louisville.edu)
Engineering Management: http://louisville.edu/speed/industrial/Eng._Mgmt. Director: Michael Day, Ph.D. (michael.day@louisville.edu)
English: http://louisville.edu/english. Director: Susan Ryan, Ph.D. (sryan@louisville.edu)
Epidemiology: http://sphis.louisville.edu. Director: Richard Baumgartner, Ph.D. (rnbaum01@louisville.edu)
Entrepreneurship: http://business.louisville.edu/entrepreneurshipphd/. Director: David Dubofsky, Ph.D. (d.dubofsky@louisville.edu)
Exercise Physiology: http://louisville.edu/education/departments/hss/exercise_physiology.html. Director: Dean Jacks, Ph.D. (dean.jacks@louisville.edu)
Experimental Psychology: http://louisville.edu/psychology/doctorate/experimental-psychology. Director: Woody Petry, Ph.D. (woody.petry@louisville.edu)
French: http://modernlanguages.louisville.edu/french/ma.php. Director: Wendy Pfeffer, Ph.D. (pfeffer@louisville.edu)
Health and Physical Education: http://louisville.edu/education/degrees/med-hpe.html. Director: William Weinberg, Ph.D. (weinberg@louisville.edu)
Higher Education: http://louisville.edu/education/degrees/ma-hed.html. Director: Bridgette Pregliasco, Ed.D. (bridgette.pregliasco@louisville.edu)
History: http://louisville.edu/a-s/history. Director: Christine Ehrick, Ph.D. (ehrick@louisville.edu)
Human Resource Education: http://louisville.edu/education/degrees/ms-hre.html. Contact: Bridgette Pregliasco, Ed.D. (bridgette.pregliasco@louisville.edu)
Humanities: http://louisville.edu/a-s/humanities. Master's program director: Elaine Wise (elaine.wise@louisville.edu); Doctoral program director: Annette Allen, Ph.D. (acalle01@louisville.edu)
Industrial Engineering: http://louisville.edu/speed/industrial. Director: John Usher, Ph.D. (usher@louisville.edu)
Instructional Technology: http://louisville.edu/education/degrees/med-it.html. Director: Sherri Brown, Ph.D. (slbrow15@louisville.edu)
Interdisciplinary Early Childhood Education: http://louisville.edu/education/degrees/mat-iece.html. Director: Charles Thompson, Ph.D. (chuck@louisville.edu)
Interdisciplinary Studies: http://graduate.louisville.edu. Assistant Dean: Paul J. DeMarco, Ph.D. (paul.demarco@louisville.edu)
Justice Administration: http://www.louisville.edu/justiceadministration. Director: Gennaro Vito, Ph.D. (gf.vito@louisville.edu)
Mathematics: http://math.louisville.edu. Director: Prasanna Sahoo, Ph.D. (sahoo@louisville.edu)
Mechanical Engineering: http://louisville.edu/speed/mechanical. Director: Peter Quesada, Ph.D. (pmques01@louisville.edu)
Mental Health Counseling: http://louisville.edu/education/departments/ecpy/mh-counseling. Director: Nancy Cunningham, Ph.D. (nancy.cunningham@louisville.edu)
Microbiology and Immunology: http://louisville.edu/medschool/microbiology. Director: Uldis Streips, Ph.D. (unstre01@louisville.edu)
Middle School Education: http://louisville.edu/education/degrees/med-msed.html. Director: Marcia Lile, Ph.D. (malile01@louisville.edu)
Music: http://louisville.edu/music. Director: Jean M. Christensen, Ph.D. (jmchri01@louisville.edu)
Music Education: http://louisville.edu/music. Director: Marcia Lile, Ph.D. (malile01@louisville.edu)
Nursing: http://louisville.edu/nursing. Director: Rosalie Mainous (rosalie.mainous@louisville.edu)
Oral Biology: http://louisville.edu/dental/oralbiology. Director: David Scott, Ph.D. (dascot07@louisville.edu)
Pan African Studies: http://louisville.edu/a-s/pas. Director: Denise Martin, Ph.D. (denise.martin@louisville.edu)
Pharmacology and Toxicology: http://louisville.edu/medschool/pharmacology. Director: Gavin Arteel, Ph.D. (gavin.arteel@louisville.edu)
Physics: http://www.physics.louisville.edu. Director: Chris Davis, Ph.D. (c.l.davis@louisville.edu)
Physiology and Biophysics: http://louisville.edu/medschool/physiology. Director: William Wead, Ph.D. (william.wead@louisville.edu)
Political Science: http://louisville.edu/a-s/polsci. Director: Laurie Rhodebeck, Ph.D. (l.rhodebeck@louisville.edu)
Public Administration: http://supa.louisville.edu. Director: Steven Koven, Ph.D. (steven.koven@louisville.edu)
Public Health: http://sphis.louisville.edu. Director: Robert Jacobs, Ph.D. (robert.jacobs@louisville.edu)
Reading Education: http://louisville.edu/education/degrees/med-re.html. Director: Brenda Overturf, Ph.D. (b0over01@louisville.edu)
School Counseling: http://louisville.edu/education/departments/ecpy/sch-counseling. Director: Sandra Duncan, Ph.D. (sandra.duncan@louisville.edu)
Secondary Education: http://louisville.edu/education/degrees/med-se.html. Director: Marcia Lile, Ph.D. (marcia.lile@louisville.edu)
Social Work: http://louisville.edu/kent. Master's Director: Pamela Yankeelov, Ph.D. (pam.yankeelov@louisville.edu); Doctoral Director: Ruth Huber, Ph.D. (ruth.huber@louisville.edu)
Sociology: http://louisville.edu/a-s/soc. Director: Robert Carini, Ph.D. (rmcari01@louisville.edu)
Spanish: http://modernlanguages.louisville.edu/spanish/ma.php. Director: Gregory Hutcheson, Ph.D. (gshutc01@louisville.edu)
Special Education: http://louisville.edu/education/departments/t-l/. Director: Terry Scott, Ph.D. (t.scott@louisville.edu)
Sport Administration: http://louisville.edu/education/departments/hss/spad. Director: Chris Greenwell, Ph.D. (tcgreenwell@louisville.edu)
Studio Art: http://louisville.edu/a-s/finearts/gradprograms.html. Director: John Whitesell, Ph.D. (whitesell@louisville.edu)
Theatre Arts: http://louisville.edu/a-s/ta. Director: Rinda Frye, Ph.D. (r.frye@louisville.edu)
Urban Planning: http://supa.louisville.edu. Master's Director: David Simpson, Ph.D. (dave.simpson@louisville.edu); Doctoral Director: Steven Bourassa, Ph.D. (steven.bourassa@louisville.edu)
Women's and Gender Studies: http://louisville.edu/a-s/ws. Director and Chair: Nancy Theriot, Ph.D. (nmther01@louisville.edu)

UNIVERSITY OF MARYLAND EASTERN SHORE

Graduate School

Programs of Study

The Graduate School of the University of Maryland Eastern Shore (UMES) is featured in *U.S. News & World Report's* A–Z List of Best Graduate School Education for 2009. It offers the following degrees and programs: Master of Arts in Teaching (M.A.T.), secondary teacher initial certification; Master of Education (M.Ed.) in career and technology education, and counselor education and special education; Master of Science (M.S.) in applied computer science, criminology and criminal justice, food and agricultural sciences, marine-estuarine-environmental sciences, rehabilitation counseling, and toxicology. It offers the Doctor of Physical Therapy (D.P.T.) and Doctor of Philosophy (Ph.D.) in food science and technology, marine-estuarine-environmental sciences, toxicology, and organizational leadership. The Doctor of Education (Ed.D.) is limited to students enrolled currently.

For most master's programs, a minimum of 30 semester hours is required in acceptable course work and research credit toward a graduate degree. The M.S. programs in marine-estuarine-environmental sciences and toxicology require a thesis. The master's programs in criminology and criminal justice and food and agricultural sciences offer a thesis or nonthesis option. The D.P.T. program is a three-year program. Two doctoral programs (marine-estuarine-environmental sciences and toxicology) are interdisciplinary and intercampus (within the University System of Maryland). Applicants should consult the individual programs for specific requirements. The three-year organizational and educational leadership programs are offered in a weekend format.

Research Facilities

Students have the opportunity to participate directly in ongoing research, development, and training projects. UMES is an 1890 land-grant and top-tier historically black institution, which conducts research and creative endeavors in several fields including agricultural, environmental, and marine sciences; mathematics and computer applications; and education and allied health. Federal agency support includes the following: U.S. Departments of Agriculture, Commerce, Defense, Education, Energy, Health and Human Services, and the Interior; the National Science Foundation; the National Aeronautics and Space Administration; and the Agency for International Development.

There are a number of research and applications laboratories and facilities on campus and on the University's farm. Students also have access to other University System of Maryland, federal, and state facilities and field sites located throughout the state and region. Library and information resources may be accessed locally through the University System of Maryland's Web site and the Internet.

Financial Aid

Limited financial assistance is available for qualified students, on the basis of merit and/or need from institutional and sponsored funding. Examples of financial assistance are teaching, research and other types of assistantships, fellowships, scholarships, grants, Federal Work-Study, and loan programs.

Cost of Study

In 2008–09, tuition was $234 per semester credit hour for Maryland students and $424 per semester credit hour for out-of-state students.

Living and Housing Costs

Current monthly housing rates range from $200 for a room in a private or group home to $500 for an apartment in the local area. University housing is generally unavailable.

Student Group

UMES has a current graduate enrollment of 465 students, both full- and part-time. More than half the students are women. International students come from Asia, Europe, Africa, Latin America, and the Caribbean.

Student Outcomes

Students find employment in higher education as administrators and faculty; in school systems as special, agriculture, or technology educators and guidance counselors as well as other certified middle and high school teachers; in state agencies and private practice as guidance and rehabilitation counselors; in computer firms and educational settings as computer applications specialists and academic leaders; in private practice as physical therapists; and in federal, state, and local agencies and private businesses as marine, environmental, agricultural, and food scientists. Graduates from the criminology and criminal justice program find employment as specialists and administrative heads.

Location

UMES is reputed to be one of the most beautiful campuses in the United States. It is located in historic Princess Anne, a small town on the eastern shore of Maryland. The town dates back to 1733 and has many buildings and landmarks of historic interest. The area is quiet and ideally suited for a learning environment, yet it is only 2½ hours by car from the abundant cultural and recreational facilities of Washington, D.C., and Baltimore, Maryland. The state's famous seaside resort, Ocean City, is only 45 minutes from the campus. The campus is 13 miles south of the town of Salisbury, which provides shopping and recreational facilities.

The School

The Graduate School at the University of Maryland Eastern Shore has more than 150 graduate faculty members, who, through an elected Graduate Council, determine the policies, procedures, and degree requirements for the various graduate programs. Approved specialists from industry, government, and academia may also serve on student research committees as graduate faculty members.

The University of Maryland Eastern Shore is a public research institution and admits students without regard to sex, race, creed, or ethnic origin.

Applying

Completed application and other pertinent forms, official college/university transcripts, and three letters of evaluation are required. Some graduate programs have additional admission requirements. Admission deadlines vary by graduate program. There is an application fee of $30. International applicants need TOEFL scores or an equivalent and a certification of available finances for study. GRE General Test scores may be required in some cases for the programs in marine-estuarine-environmental sciences, food and agricultural sciences, special education, criminology and criminal justice, food science and technology, and applied computer science. Other programs may use the GRE as a criterion for admission. Education programs may require the PRAXIS examinations. International applicants must have their transcripts evaluated and authenticated by World Education Services.

Correspondence and Information

Jennifer Keane-Dawes, Ph.D.
Interim Dean
School of Graduate Studies
University of Maryland Eastern Shore
Princess Anne, Maryland 21853-1299
Phone: 410-651-6507 or 7966
Fax: 410-651-7571
E-mail: jmkeanedawes@umes.edu
dmprice@umes.edu
Web site: http://www.umes.edu

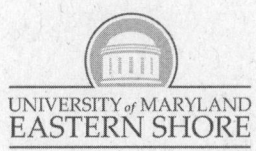

THE FACULTY

Emmanuel Acquah, Professor; Ph.D., Ohio State, 1976.
Mary L. Agnew, Assistant Professor; Ph.D., Georgia, 1994.
Isoken T. Aighewi, Lecturer; Ph.D., Minnesota, 1988.
Ayodele J. Alade, Professor; Ph.D., Utah, 1981.
Arthur L. Allen, Associate Professor; Ph.D., Illinois, 1971.
David Alston Jr., Assistant Professor; Ph.D., North Carolina State, 2001.
Joseph O. Arumula, Professor; Ph.D., Clemson, 1982.
Kathryn Barrett-Gaines, Assistant Professor; Ph.D., Stanford, 2001.
Joseph Beatus, Associate Professor; Ph.D., Maryland College Park, 1996.
Sarah B. Bing, Associate Professor; Ph.D., Georgia, 1976.
Lowell Jay Bishop, Associate Professor; Ph.D., Case Western Reserve, 1988.
Raymond Blakely, Professor; Ph.D., NYU, 1977.
Cheryl Bowers, Assistant Professor; Ph.D., Pennsylvania, 1997.
Eddie Boyd Jr., Assistant Professor; Ph.D., Oklahoma State, 1977.
Ramona Brockett, Associate Professor; Ph.D., Rutgers, 1998.
Henry M. Brooks, Associate Director, Co-op Extension; Ph.D., Ohio State, 1975.
Nicole Buzzetto-More, Assistant Professor; Ed.D., Columbia, 2004.
Albert Casavant, Assistant Professor; Ph.D., Illinois, 1984.
E. William Chapin, Assistant Professor; Ph.D., Princeton, 1969.
Marcos A. Cheney, Associate Professor; Ph.D., California, Davis, 1985.
Leon L. Copeland, Professor; Ed.D., Virginia Tech, 1977.
Leon N. Coursey, Professor; Ph.D., Ohio State, 1971.
I. K. Dabipi, Professor; Ph.D., Louisiana State, 1987.
Robert Dadson, Professor; Ph.D., McGill, 1969.
Gerald F. Day, Associate Professor; Ph.D., Maryland, 1976.
Ejigou Demissie, Professor; Ph.D., Oklahoma State, 1982.
Joseph N. D. Dodoo, Assistant Professor; Ph.D., King's College (London), 1979.
Clayton W. Faubion, Associate Professor; Ph.D., Arkansas, 1998.
Tao Gong, Research Analyst; Ph.D., Tennessee State, 2005.
Thomas Handwerker, Professor; Ph.D., Cornell, 1972.
Jeannine M. Harter-Dennis, Associate Professor; Ph.D., Illinois, 1977.
Fawzy Hashem, Research Associate Professor; Ph.D., Maryland, 1988.
Harry Hoffer, Director, Educational Leadership Program; Ph.D., Union (Ohio), 1991.
Gurdeep Singh Hura, Professor; Ph.D., Roorkee (India), 1984.
C. Dennis Ignasias, Associate Professor; Ph.D., Michigan State, 1967; Ph.D., Wisconsin–Madison, 1973.
Ali Ishaque, Associate Professor; Ph.D., Free University of Brussels, 1998.
Andrea K. Johnson, Assistant Professor; Ph.D., North Carolina State, 2004.
Linda P. Johnson, Associate Professor; Ph.D., Temple, 1995.
Robert Johnson Jr., Associate Professor; Ph.D., St. Louis, 1997.
Teresa Laird, Associate Professor; Ed. D., Texas Southern, 2002.
Wilbert C. Larson, Assistant Professor; Ph.D., Nebraska, 1990.
Kelly Mack, Professor; Ph.D., Howard, 1995.
Malik B. Malik, Associate Professor; Ph.D., Essex, 1985.
Lurline Marsh, Professor; Ph.D., Minnesota, 1984.
Eric B. May, Associate Professor; Ph.D., Oregon State, 1982.
Madhumi Mitra, Assistant Professor; Ph.D., North Carolina State, 2002.
Theodore A. Mollett, Associate Professor; Ph.D., Purdue, 1980.
Thomas S. Mosely, Associate Professor; Ph.D., Howard, 1997.
Abhijit Nagchandhuri, Professor; Ph.D., Duke, 1992.
Anthony K. Nyame, Professor; Ph.D., Georgia, 1987.
Stanley Nyirenda, Director, Institutional Research, Assessment, and Evaluation; Ph.D., Pittsburgh, 1991.
Joseph Okoh, Professor; Ph.D., Howard, 1982.
Emmanuel Onyeozili, Assistant Professor; Ph.D., Florida State, 1998.
Salina Parveen, Assistant Professor; Ph.D., Florida, 1997.
Joseph Pitula, Lecturer; Ph.D., SUNY at Buffalo, 2001.
Kimberly Poole, Assistant Professor; Rh.D., Southern Illinois at Carbondale, 2000.
Michael Rabel, Assistant Professor; D.Sc., Maryland, Baltimore, 2006.
Maryam Rahimi, Associate Professor; Ph.D., Florida State, 1987.
Howard M. Rebach, Professor; Ph.D., Michigan State, 1968.
Douglas E. Ruby, Associate Professor; Ph.D., Michigan, 1976.
Tzachi M. Samocha, Regent's Fellow and Professor; Ph.D., Tel Aviv, 1980.
Jurgen Schwarz, Associate Professor; Ph.D., Cornell, 1993.
Barbara Seabrook, Assistant Professor; Ed.D., Wilmington (Delaware), 1996.
Daniel Seaton, Assistant Professor; Ed.D., Virginia Tech, 1991.
Dinesh Sharma, Professor; Ph.D., Chaudhary Charan Singh (India), 1999.
Anugrah Shaw, Professor; Ph.D., Texas Woman's, 1984.
George S. Shorter, Assistant Professor; Ph.D., Iowa State, 1981.
Bernita Sims-Tucker, Associate Professor; Ph.D., Maryland, 1988.
Gurbax Singh, Professor; Ph.D., Maryland College Park, 1971.
Jeurel Singleton, Lecturer; Ph.D., Ottawa, 1980.
William B. Talley, Associate Professor; Rh.D., Southern Illinois at Carbondale, 1987.
Margarita Treuth, Associate Professor; Ph.D., Maryland College Park, 1992.
Ojiabo Ukoha, Lecturer; Ph.D., Maryland Eastern Shore, 2006.
Karen A. Verbeke, Professor; Ph.D., Maryland College Park, 1982.
Yan Waguespack, Associate Professor; Ph.D., Tulane, 1990.
Allen B. Williams, Assistant Professor; Ph.D., California, Santa Barbara, 1995.
Mark Williams, Assistant Professor; Ph.D., Cincinnati, 1986.
Emin Yilmaz, Professor; Ph.D., Michigan, 1970.
Jianhua Yang, Assistant Professor; Ph.D., Houston, 2006.

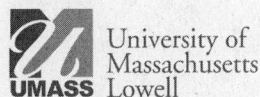

University of Massachusetts
UMASS Lowell

UNIVERSITY OF MASSACHUSETTS LOWELL

Graduate School

Programs of Study

The University of Massachusetts (UMass) Lowell offers more than 100 areas of graduate study in eighteen doctoral degree, over forty master's degree, and more than fifty graduate certificate programs, which are regionally and nationally accredited. Lowell's internationally renowned research faculty members take a deep personal interest in the professional development of their students.

The Doctor of Philosophy (Ph.D.) is offered in biomedical engineering and biotechnology (intercampus), chemistry (with options in biochemistry, environmental studies, polymer science, and polymer science/plastics engineering), computer science (computational mathematics), marine sciences and technology (intercampus), nursing (health promotion–intercampus), physics (with areas of study in atomic physics, elementary particle physics, experimental and theoretical condensed-matter physics, experimental and theoretical nuclear physics, laser physics, optics, and photonics or with options in applied mechanics, atmospheric sciences, energy engineering (nuclear and solar), and radiological sciences), and polymer science (with an option in polymer science/plastics engineering, offered jointly with the chemistry department). Both the Doctor of Engineering (D.Eng.) and the Doctor of Philosophy (Ph.D.) are available, with options in chemical engineering, civil and environmental engineering, computer engineering, electrical engineering, energy engineering, mechanical engineering, and plastics engineering. The Doctor of Science (Sc.D.) is offered in work environment (with options in cleaner production and pollution prevention, epidemiology, occupational and environmental hygiene, occupational ergonomics and safety, and work environment policy). A Doctor of Physical Therapy (D.P.T.) is offered by the School of Health and Environment. The Doctor of Education (Ed.D.) is available in language arts and literacy, leadership in schooling, and mathematics and science education. The Certificate of Advanced Graduate Study (CAGS) is offered in curriculum and instruction, educational administration, planning and policy, and reading and language.

The Master of Arts (M.A.) is offered in community and social psychology, criminal justice, and economic and social development of regions. The Master of Science (M.S.) is available in biological sciences (with an option in biotechnology), biomedical engineering and biotechnology, chemistry, clinical laboratory sciences, computer science (with an option in biochemical informatics), environmental studies (with concentrations in atmospheric science and environmental engineering sciences), health management and policy, marine sciences and technology (intercampus), mathematics (with options in applied mathematics, mathematics for teachers, scientific computing, and statistics and operations research), nursing (with options in adult psychiatric/mental health, family health, and gerontological), physics (with areas of study in atomic physics, elementary particle physics, experimental and theoretical condensed-matter physics, experimental and theoretical nuclear physics, laser physics, optics, and photonics or with an option in optical sciences), radiological sciences and protection, and work environment (with options in cleaner production and pollution prevention, epidemiology, occupational and environmental hygiene, occupational ergonomics and safety, and work environment policy). The Master of Science in Engineering (M.S.Eng.) is offered in chemical engineering, civil engineering (with options in environmental and geoenvironmental, geotechnical, structural, and transportation), computer engineering, electrical engineering (with options in information systems, optoelectronics, and power and energy engineering), energy engineering (nuclear and solar), mechanical engineering, and plastics engineering (with options in elastomeric materials, materials design, medical, and processing materials). The Master of Education (M.Ed.) is offered in curriculum and instruction, educational administration, initial and advanced licensure, reading and language, and science education (online). The Master of Music (M.M.) is available in music education (teaching) and sound recording technology. Also available is the accredited Master of Business Administration (M.B.A.) (with options in accounting, finance, general business, and information technology).

UMass Lowell is among the national leaders in graduate certificate education. Graduate certificates are designed to provide knowledge and expertise vital to today's changing and complex needs in the workplace. In most cases, courses may be applied toward a master's degree program. Most certificates consist of four courses and 12 graduate credits. Graduate certificates are offered in: a wide variety of areas including: biomedical, health, and social sciences; computers, communications, and information systems; engineering and management; education; and environmental studies. A number of programs are also offered online.

Research Facilities

All graduate departments are equipped to support scholarly research through collaboration with twenty-eight campus research centers and institutes. The University of Massachusetts system is ranked fourteenth among all universities in the United States for monies received for intellectual property licensed to the commercial sector. Industrial-community relations are nurtured and enhanced through research collaborations, technology exchange, student internships, and advisory boards. Faculty members routinely interact with industry, business, community groups, and government agencies. Computer and e-mail accounts are issued to all students. The University has hundreds of workstations, PCs, and terminals connected to multiple servers via a state-of-the-art network infrastructure. Multimedia labs, distance learning classrooms, and online programs are available. Lowell's electronic library includes more than 300 databases, more than 28,000 journals, and ninety computer workstations and wireless systems. The library has consortium arrangements with other major libraries, and remote computer access is available.

Financial Aid

Nearly 400 teaching and research assistantships (TAs/RAs) were awarded in 2008–09; interested students should contact the graduate coordinator or chair of the department to which they are applying. Low-interest student loans are also available for citizens of Massachusetts and Canada through the Massachusetts Educational Financing Authority (MEFA). Federal Direct, Stafford, Perkins, and supplemental loans are available.

Cost of Study

In 2009–10, approximate tuition and fees for a 3-credit graduate course are $1678 for Massachusetts residents and $3133 for out-of-state students. New England Regional Tuition is available for some programs of study, in which qualified out-of-state students pay 150 percent of the Massachusetts resident tuition charges.

Living and Housing Costs

Graduate students can find reasonably priced furnished and unfurnished rooms and apartments in the greater Lowell area. The cost of living varies with the type of accommodations desired and the needs and resources of the individual. Apartments commonly require one month's security deposit.

Student Group

The fall 2008 total enrollment was 12,471, of whom 2,765 were graduate students and 9,706 were undergraduates. UMass Lowell enrolled approximately 485 international students.

Student Outcomes

UMass Lowell awards a significant percentage of its total degrees at the graduate level. Response from both graduate student alumni and industry employers reveals high satisfaction with education received and level of preparedness and professional perspective. Graduate students are highly sought by major corporations, both as interns during the course of their studies and as full-time employees upon graduation.

Location

In the heart of the birthplace of America's Industrial Revolution, Lowell, Massachusetts, is 25 miles from Boston and home to the first urban national park in the U.S. The Merrimack River runs through this city of 105,000, which hosts professional baseball and hockey adjacent to the campus. Access to Boston is easy via car or commuter train. New Hampshire, Vermont, and Maine, as well as the shores and beaches of the Atlantic Ocean and Cape Cod, are short driving distances away.

The University

The University of Massachusetts Lowell is one member of the five-campus University of Massachusetts system. Graduate students have access to selected courses at other UMass campuses through the UMass Graduate Studies Consortium. Both the University's Annual Campus Crime and Safety Report and the results and information on the Massachusetts Tests for Educator Licensure are available on the Web site and by request.

Applying

Applications (except for computer science) can be submitted at any time; however, early applications ensure that all materials are processed on time and that due consideration is given to those seeking assistantships. GRE General Test, GMAT (for the M.B.A.), and TOEFL (for international students) scores; official transcripts; a statement of purpose; an application fee ($40 for Massachusetts residents, $60 for all others); and three letters of reference are required. Some departments have deadlines and additional requirements. Complete application packages with step-by-step instructions and course catalogs are available upon request. Online applications (at a reduced fee) are recommended and are available on the Graduate Admissions Web site.

Correspondence and Information

Linda Southworth, Director
Graduate Admissions Office
University of Massachusetts Lowell
883 Broadway Street, Dugan Hall
Lowell, Massachusetts 01854-5130

Phone: 978-934-2390
800-656-GRAD (toll-free)
Fax: 978-934-4058
E-mail: graduate_admissions@uml.edu
Web site: http://www.uml.edu/grad

THE FACULTY

COLLEGE DEANS
E-mail format for faculty members is first name_last name@uml.edu.

Arts and Sciences
Dr. Robert Tamarin (Dean, Sciences Division), Olney 524; 978-934-3847.
Dr. Nina Coppins (Dean [ad interim], Humanities, Fine Arts, and Social Sciences Division), Durgin 112; 978-934-3832.

Continuing Studies and Corporate Education
Dr. Jacqueline Moloney, Southwick 308A; 978-934-2474.

Education
Dr. Anita Greenwood (ad interim), O'Leary Library 510; 978-934-4601.

Engineering
Dr. John Ting, Kitson 311; 978-934-2576.

Health and Environment
Dr. Shorty McKinney, Weed 104; 978-934-4510.

Intercampus Graduate School of Marine Sciences and Technology
Dr. Robert R. Gamache, Olney 302A; 978-934-3904.

Management
Dr. Kathryn Carter, Pasteur 305; 978-934-2741.

GRADUATE PROGRAM COORDINATORS AND DEPARTMENT CHAIRS

Biological Sciences
Dr. Jerome Hojnacki, Coordinator, Olsen 515; 978-934-2870.
Dr. Juliette Rooney-Varga, Coordinator, Olsen 524; 978-934-4715.
Dr. Mark Hines, Chair, Olsen 517; 978-934-2867.

Biomedical Engineering and Biotechnology
Dr. Bryan Buchholz, Director, Kitson 204D; 978-934-3241.

Chemical Engineering
Dr. Francis Bonner, Coordinator, Engineering 306; 978-934-3154.
Dr. Alfred Donatelli, Chair, Engineering 104; 978-934-3171.

Chemistry/Polymer Science
Dr. Eugene Barry, Chair and Coordinator, Olney 313; 978-934-3669.

Civil and Environmental Engineering
Dr. Chronis Stamatiadis, Coordinator, Pasteur 113; 978-934-2283.
Dr. Nathan Gartner, Chair, Falmouth 108; 978-934-2280.

Clinical Laboratory and Nutritional Sciences
Dr. Eugene Rogers, Coordinator, Weed 309A; 978-934-4478.
Dr. Ted Namm, Chair, Weed 314; 978-934-4476.

Computer Science
Dr. Giam Pecelli, Coordinator, Olsen 313; 978-934-3639.
Dr. Jie Wang, Chair, Olsen 313; 978-934-3620.

Criminal Justice
Dr. April Pattavina, Coordinator, Mahoney 203A; 978-934-4145.
Dr. Eve Buzawa, Chair, Mahoney 214; 978-934-4262.

Education
Dr. James Nehring, Coordinator (M.Ed. and CAGS), O'Leary 524; 978-934-4664.
Dr. Michaela Wyman-Colombo, Coordinator (Ed.D.), O'Leary 523; 978-934-4610.
Dr. Vera Ossen, Coordinator (All Licensure Programs), O'Leary 510; 978-934-4604.
Dr. Jay Simmons, Chair, O'Leary 518; 978-934-4615.

Electrical and Computer Engineering
Dr. Anh Tran, Coordinator (M.S.), Ball 317; 978-934-3322.
Dr. Dikshitulu Kalluri, Coordinator (D.Eng.), Ball 421C; 978-934-3318.
Dr. Craig Armiento, Chair, Ball 301; 978-934-3395.

Energy Engineering (M.E.)
Dr. John Duffy, Coordinator (solar), Engineering 330A; 978-934-2968.
Dr. Gilbert Brown, Coordinator (nuclear), Engineering 220; 978-934-3166.

Environmental Studies
Dr. Clifford Bruell, Coordinator, Engineering 105; 978-934-2284.

Health Management and Policy
Dr. James Lee, Coordinator, Weed 300; 978-934-4522.
Dr. Craig Slatin, Chair, Weed 218; 978-934-3291.

Management (M.B.A.)
Dr. Gary Mucica, Coordinator, Pasteur 303; 978-934-2853.
Kathleen Rourke, Pasteur 303; 978-934-2848.

Marine Sciences and Technology
Dr. Frank Colby, Coordinator, Olney 302C; 978-934-3906.

Mathematical Sciences
Dr. Charles Byrne, Coordinator, Olney 428W; 978-934-2447.
Dr. Stephen Pennell, Chair, Olney 428M; 978-934-2710.

Mechanical Engineering
Dr. Majid Charmchi, Coordinator, Ball 224; 978-934-2969.
Dr. John McKelliget, Chair, Engineering 331; 978-934-2974.

Music
Dr. Gena Greher, Coordinator (music education), Durgin 326; 978-934-3893.
Dr. Alex Case, Coordinator (sound recording technology), Durgin 323; 978-934-3878.
Dr. Paula Telesco, Chair, Durgin 107; 978-934-3850.

Nursing
Dr. Susan Houde, Coordinator (M.S.), O'Leary 313Q; 978-934-4426.
Dr. Barbara Mawn, Coordinator (Ph.D.), Weed 218; 978-934-4485.
Dr. Karen Melillo, Chair, O'Leary 312; 978-934-4417.

Physical Therapy
Dr. Keith Hallbourg, Coordinator, Weed 102; 978-934-4402.
Dr. Sean Collins, Chair, Weed 314; 978-934-4375.

Physics
Dr. James Egan, Coordinator, Olney 134; 978-934-3780.
Dr. Robert Giles, Chair, Olney 114; 978-934-1360.

Plastics Engineering
Dr. Stephen McCarthy, Coordinator (M.S.Eng.), Ball 207A; 978-934-3417.
Dr. Jan-Chan Huang, Coordinator (D.Eng.), Ball 213; 978-934-3428.
Dr. Robert Malloy, Chair, Ball 204; 978-934-3435.

Psychology
Dr. Sharon Wasco, Coordinator, Mahoney 6; 978-934-3964.
Dr. Nina Coppens, Chair, Mahoney 110; 978-934-3954.

Radiological Sciences (Physics)
Dr. Clayton French, Coordinator, Pinanski 207; 978-934-3286.

Regional Economic and Social Development
Dr. Philip Moss, Coordinator and Chair, O'Leary 500N; 978-934-2787.

Work Environment
Dr. David Kriebel, Coordinator, Kitson 202D; 978-934-3271.
Dr. Rafael Moure-Eraso, Chair, Kitson 200; 978-934-3250.

Sailing on the Merrimack River.

Riverside walk adjacent to the two campuses.

The University of Massachusetts Lowell is an Equal Opportunity/Affirmative Action, Title IX, H/V, ADA 1990 Employer.

UNIVERSITY OF MEMPHIS

Graduate School

Programs of Study

The Graduate School of the University of Memphis (U of M) awards the Doctor of Philosophy degree in audiology and speech-language pathology, biology, biomedical engineering, business administration, chemistry, communication, computer science, counseling psychology, earth sciences, educational psychology and research, engineering, English, history, mathematical sciences, music, philosophy, and psychology. The degrees of Doctor of Audiology and Doctor of Musical Arts are awarded by the School of Audiology and Speech-Language Pathology and the College of Communication and Fine Arts, respectively. The College of Education offers the Doctor of Education in Counseling, Higher and Adult Education, Instruction and Curriculum Leadership, and Leadership and Policy Studies degrees. The College of Education also offers the interdisciplinary degree of Education Specialist. Master's degrees are offered in fifty-four major areas through six colleges and two schools. The degrees are Master of Science, Master of Arts, Master of Architecture, Master of Fine Arts, Master of Arts in Teaching, Master of Business Administration, International Master of Business Administration, Master of Liberal Arts, Master of Music, Master of City and Regional Planning, Master of Health Administration, Master of Education, Master of Professional Studies, Master of Public Administration, Master of Public Health, and Master of Science in Nursing. Master's degree majors are accounting, advanced studies in teaching and learning, anthropology, applied computer science, architecture, art, art history, bioinformatics, biology, biomedical engineering, business administration, chemistry, city and regional planning, civil engineering, clinical nutrition, communication, computer science, counseling, creative writing, criminal justice, earth sciences, economics, educational psychology and research, electrical and computer engineering, engineering technology, English, health administration, health and sports sciences, history, instruction and curriculum leadership, international business, journalism, leadership and policy studies, liberal studies, mathematical sciences, mechanical engineering, merchandising and consumer sciences, music, nursing, philosophy, physics, political science, professional studies, public administration, public health, psychology, Romance languages, school psychology, sociology, speech-language pathology, theater, and women's and gender studies. Graduate certificates are offered in African American literature, applied lean leadership, artist diploma in music, college teaching, community college teaching and learning, family nurse practitioner (post-master's), geographic information systems, information assurance, instructional computer applications, local government management, museum studies, teaching English as a second language, and women's and gender studies. The Master of Education and Master of Science in Nursing degrees and the family nurse practitioner studies certificate are also offered through the Regents Online Degree Program.

Research Facilities

The University of Memphis Libraries contain more than 1 million bound volumes and 3.4 million microformat items in the Ned R. McWherter Library and five branch libraries (Audiology and Speech-Language Pathology, Chemistry, Earth Sciences, Mathematics, and Music). McWherter Library has a 24-hour learning commons area with numerous computer stations, a cyber café, comfortable reading areas, private research rooms, and small computer labs. The libraries' Web site (http://exlibris.memphis.edu) offers access to the holdings of the libraries and hundreds of electronic databases (some full-text) from all on-campus workstations and via proxy server from all off-campus sites. Reciprocal-use agreements with other academic libraries within the region allow University of Memphis students and faculty members to access additional library collections with the appropriate University of Memphis ID card. The University of Memphis is a full partner and early adopter of Internet2 technology for research and instruction. A network of computer labs provides U of M students with opportunities to tap numerous computing resources: software, utilities, the Internet, PCs, Macintoshes, and laser printers. Consulting, training, and help desk services are available as well.

Among the more than forty specialized research units are the Bureau of Business and Economic Research, Center for Earthquake Research and Information, Center for Humanities, Center for the Study of Higher Education, Institute for Intelligent Systems, Regional Economic Development Center, Center for Research on Women, and, at off-campus sites, the Edward J. Meeman Biological Station (a biological research center), the Chucalissa Indian Village and Museum, and the Center for Community Health. Various service units maintained by the University, such as the Psychological Services Center, the Speech and Hearing Center, and the Integrated Microscopy Center, offer additional facilities. The University is affiliated with the Gulf Coast Research Laboratory, Oak Ridge Associated Universities, the National Center for Toxicological Research, and St. Jude Children's Research Hospital; it maintains joint programs with the University of Tennessee, Memphis. The University receives special funding from the state to support Centers of Excellence in the following areas: audiology and speech pathology, earthquake research, educational policy, Egyptology, and psychology.

Financial Aid

Fellowships, assistantships, and scholarships are available. Stipends for graduate assistants vary among departments and include tuition and fees. Inquiries regarding assistantships and fellowships should be addressed to the department chair or director of graduate studies of the appropriate college. Financial aid is also available through the Federal Perkins Loan program, the Federal Stafford Student Loan program, and the Federal Work-Study Program. Information about student loans and work-study programs should be requested through the Office of Student Financial Aid at http://www.memphis.edu/financialaid.

Cost of Study

The 2008–09 tuition and fees for full-time study on campus were $3699 per semester for Tennessee residents and $9492 per semester for nonresidents. Tuition for part-time students in 2008–09 was $400 per credit hour for Tennessee residents and $885 per credit hour for nonresidents. There are additional fees for Regents Online Degree Program courses. A $20-per-credit-hour surcharge for all art courses, a $25-per-credit-hour surcharge for engineering courses, and a $30-per-credit-hour surcharge for business courses numbered 3000 and higher are also assessed.

Living and Housing Costs

The 2008–09 rates for residence halls on campus ranged from $1530 to $3550 per semester. Single-student apartments and town houses ranged from $2720 to $3855 per semester. The University has 150 apartments on the Park Avenue Campus for student families, with some units specifically built for students with disabilities; the 2008–09 rates ranged from $525 to $715 per month. Utilities are paid by the tenant. Numerous housing facilities also exist off campus in the Memphis community.

Student Group

In the fall of 2008, the University of Memphis had an enrollment of 20,214 students, including 4,401 graduate students. Of the total graduate student population in fall 2008, 2,724 (61 percent) were women and 27 percent were members of minority groups. The majority of students were from Tennessee, but the University attracts students from other states and countries as well.

Location

The Memphis metropolitan area has a population of over 1 million and is one of the South's largest and most attractive cities. As a primary medical, educational, communication, and transportation center, Memphis offers a full range of research opportunities and cultural experiences. The city, known worldwide for its musical heritage, has many fine restaurants, museums, and theaters, as well as one of the nation's largest urban park systems. The Memphis Medical Center is the South's largest and one of the nation's foremost centers of medical research. A public transportation system serves the University and other parts of the city.

The University

The University's modern and beautifully landscaped campus is centrally located in an attractive residential area of Memphis, with shopping, recreation, and entertainment centers nearby. In addition to the facilities on the Main Campus, the University has research and athletic training facilities and housing for student families on the Park Avenue Campus as well as research and clinical facilities in the Medical Center.

Applying

Electronic applications for graduate admission are available at https://spectrumssb2.memphis.edu/pls/PROD/bwskalog.P_DispLoginNon. Applications must include a $35 nonrefundable application fee for domestic applicants or a $60 nonrefundable fee for international students. Domestic application deadlines are: fall semester, July 1; spring semester, December 1; and summer semester, May 1. International application deadlines are: fall semester, May 1; spring semester, September 15; and summer semester, February 1. Individual programs may have earlier deadlines. Consideration for admission requires satisfactory scores on the General Test of the Graduate Record Examinations (GRE) or the Graduate Management Admission Test (GMAT) and an acceptable grade point average. Individual programs may have additional requirements. Students who do not hold degrees from colleges or universities in which English is the classroom language or for whom English is not the native language are also required to provide a satisfactory score on the TOEFL. Applicants whose highest degree is from an international university must have their credentials evaluated by any agency listed on the National Association of Credential Evaluation Services Web site: http://www.naces.org. The course-to-course report is required. Departmental scholarship to cover the cost of the evaluation may be available.

Correspondence and Information

Graduate School
215 Administration Building
University of Memphis
Memphis, Tennessee 38152-3370

Phone: 901-678-2531
Web site: http://www.memphis.edu/gradschool/

FACULTY HEADS

GRADUATE SCHOOL
Karen Weddle-West, Ph.D., Vice Provost for Graduate Studies.

COLLEGE OF ARTS AND SCIENCES
Henry Kurtz, Ph.D., Dean.
Linda Bennett, Ph.D., Associate Dean and Director of Graduate Studies.
Anthropology (M.A.): Ruthbeth Finerman, Ph.D., Chair (901-678-2080).
Bioinformatics (M.S.): Ramin Homayouni, Ph.D., Director (901-678-3550).
Biology (M.S., Ph.D.): Randall Bayer, Ph.D., Chair (901-678-2581).
Chemistry (M.S., Ph.D.): Peter Bridson, Ph.D., Chair (901-678-2622).
City and Regional Planning (M.C.R.P.): Kenneth M. Reardon, Ph.D., Director (901-678-2161).
Computer Science (M.S., Ph.D.): Sajjan G. Shiva, Ph.D., Chair (901-678-5465).
Criminal Justice (M.A.): Randolph Dupont, J.D., Chair (901-678-2737).
Earth Sciences (M.A., M.S., Ph.D.): M. Jerry Bartholomew, Ph.D., Chair (901-678-2177).
English (M.A., M.F.A., Ph.D.): Eric C. Link, Ph.D., Chair (901-678-2651).
Foreign Languages and Literatures (M.A.): Ralph Albanese, Ph.D., Chair (901-678-2506).
Health Administration (M.H.A.): La Don Jones, Ph.D., Interim Director (901-678-5552).
History (M.A., Ph.D.): Janann Sherman, Ph.D., Chair (901-678-2515).
Mathematical Sciences (M.S., Ph.D.): James Jamison, Ph.D., Chair (901-678-2482).
Philosophy (M.A., Ph.D.): Deborah Tollefsen, Ph.D., Chair (901-678-2535).
Physics (M.S.): M. Shah Jahan, Ph.D., Chair (901-678-2410).
Political Science (M.A.): Matthias Kaelberer, Ph.D., Chair (901-678-2395).
Psychology (M.S., Ph.D.): William Zachry, Ph.D., Chair (901-678-2145).
Public and Nonprofit Administration (M.P.A.): Dorothy Norris-Tirrell, Ph.D., Director (901-678-3368).
Public Health (M.P.H.): Lisa M. Klesges, Ph.D., Director (901-678-4514).
Sociology (M.A.): Martin Levin, Ph.D., Chair (901-678-2611).
Women's Studies (M.A.): Wanda Rushing, Ph.D., Director (901-678-3550).

FOGELMAN COLLEGE OF BUSINESS AND ECONOMICS
Rajiv Grover, Ph.D., Dean.
Carol Danehower, D.B.A., Associate Dean for Academic Programs (901-678-3721).
Accountancy (M.S., Ph.D.): Carolyn Callahan, Ph.D., Director (901-678-4022).
Economics (M.A., Ph.D.): William Smith, Ph.D., Chair (901-678-5243).
Finance, Insurance, and Real Estate (M.S., Ph.D.): Ronald H. Spahr, Ph.D., Chair (901-678-5930).
Management (M.S., Ph.D.): Robert Taylor, Ph.D., Chair (901-678-4551).
Management Information Systems (M.S., Ph.D.): Jasbir Dhaliwal, Ph.D., Chair (901-678-4613).
Marketing and Supply Chain Management (M.S., Ph.D.): Marla Stafford, Ph.D., Chair (901-678-2667).

COLLEGE OF COMMUNICATION AND FINE ARTS
Richard Ranta, Ph.D., Dean.
Moira Logan, M.F.A., Associate Dean and Director of Graduate Studies.
Architecture (M.Arch.): **Michael D. Hagge, M.Arch., M.C.R.P., Chair (901-678-2724)**.
Art (M.A., M.F.A.): Richard Lou, M.F.A., Chair (901-678-2216).
Communication (M.A., Ph.D.): Michael Leff, Ph.D., Chair (901-678-2565).
Journalism (M.A.): David Arant, Ph.D., Chair (901-678-2401).
Rudi E. Scheidt School of Music (M.Mu., D.M.A., Ph.D.): Randal Rushing, D.M.A., Interim Director (901-678-3764).
Theater and Dance (M.F.A.): Robert A. Hetherington, M.A., Chair (901-678-2565).

COLLEGE OF EDUCATION
Donald J. Wagner, Ed.D., Dean.
Ernest Rakow, Ph.D., Associate Dean for Administration and Graduate Programs.
Counseling, Educational Psychology and Research (M.S., Ed.D., Ph.D.): Douglas C. Strohmer, Ph.D., Chair (901-678-2841).
Health and Sport Sciences (M.S.): Robin R. Roach, Ed.D., Interim Chair (901-678-2324).
Instruction and Curriculum Leadership (M.S., M.A.T., Ed.D.): Sandra Cooley Nichols, Ph.D., Chair (901-678-2365).
Interdisciplinary (Ed.S.).
Leadership (M.S., Ed.D.): Katrina Meyer, Ph.D., Interim Chair (901-678-2368).

HERFF COLLEGE OF ENGINEERING
Richard C. Warder, Ph.D., Dean.
Steven M. Slack, Ph.D., Associate Dean and Director of Graduate Studies.
Biomedical Engineering (M.S., Ph.D.): Eugene Eckstein, Ph.D., Chair (901-678-3733).
Civil Engineering (M.S., Ph.D.): Shahram Pezeshk, Ph.D., Chair (901-678-2746).
Electrical and Computer Engineering (M.S., Ph.D.): David Russomanno, Ph.D., Chair (901-678-2175).
Engineering Technology (M.S.): Deborah Hochstein, M.S.E., Chair (901-678-2225).
Mechanical Engineering (M.S., Ph.D.): John Hochstein, Ph.D., Chair (901-678-2173).

LOEWENBERG SCHOOL OF NURSING
Marjorie F. Luttrell, Ph.D., Dean.
Robert Koch, Ph.D., Director of Graduate Studies (901-678-2003).
Nursing (M.S.N.).

SCHOOL OF AUDIOLOGY AND SPEECH-LANGUAGE PATHOLOGY
Maurice I. Mendel, Ph.D., Dean.
David Wark, Ph.D., Director of Graduate Studies (901-678-5800).
Audiology and Speech Pathology (M.A., Ph.D., Au.D.).

UNIVERSITY COLLEGE
Dan Lattimore, Ph.D., Dean.
Patricia Stevens, Ed.D., Interim Associate Dean.
Herbert McCree, Ed.D., Interim Director of Graduate Studies (901-678-2716).
Merchandising and Consumer Sciences (M.S.).
Interdisciplinary (M.A.L.S., M.P.S.).

UNIVERSITY OF MICHIGAN–DEARBORN

Graduate Studies

Programs of Study

The University of Michigan–Dearborn (UM–Dearborn) is the campus of choice for more than 8,600 students in southeastern Michigan, including nearly 2,000 graduate students who value accessibility, flexibility, affordability, and preeminence in education. The University is distinguished by its commitment to the provision of exceptional educational opportunities in an interactive, student-centered environment. All of the programs reflect the traditions of excellence, innovation, and leadership that distinguish the University of Michigan.

The University of Michigan–Dearborn offers more than thirty graduate degrees oriented toward working professionals who seek further educational opportunities for career advancement and/or intellectual enrichment. Classes are offered in the late afternoon and evening or on Saturdays for the convenience of those wishing to pursue graduate studies while working full-time.

The College of Arts, Sciences, and Letters offers a Master of Arts in liberal studies; a Master of Science in applied and computational mathematics; a Master of Science in environmental studies; a Master of Science in psychology, with specializations in health psychology and clinical psychology; a Master of Public Policy; and a Master of Public Administration.

The College of Engineering and Computer Science offers Master of Science in Engineering degrees in automotive systems engineering, computer engineering, electrical engineering, industrial and systems engineering, manufacturing systems engineering, and mechanical engineering. Master of Science degrees are offered in computer and information science, engineering management, information systems and technology, and software engineering. The Doctor of Engineering in Manufacturing degree is offered in collaboration with the Program in Manufacturing, College of Engineering, University of Michigan at Ann Arbor. Starting in the fall of 2009, the College will offer two new doctoral degree programs: a Ph.D. in automotive systems engineering and a Ph.D. in information systems engineering. Detailed information is available at http://www.engin.umd.umich.edu/departments/index.php.

The School of Education offers Master of Arts degrees in education and teaching, as well as a Master of Education degree in special education and a Master of Science degree in science education. The School of Education is also planning to offer a doctoral degree in education (Ed.D.) and a master's degree in educational leadership. Additional details will be provided on the School of Education Web site (www.soe.umd.umich.edu).

The School of Management, accredited by AACSB International—The Association to Advance Collegiate Schools of Business—offers a Master of Business Administration (M.B.A.) degree (in both face-to-face and Web-based versions), as well as a Master of Science in accounting, a Master of Science in finance, and an online Master of Science in information systems. The College of Engineering and Computer Science and the School of Management offer a dual-degree M.B.A./M.S.E. in industrial and systems engineering, an M.B.A./M.S. in finance, and an M.B.A./Master of Health Services Administration.

Research Facilities

The University of Michigan–Dearborn's excellent facilities encourage a high level of student-faculty interaction in both the classroom and the laboratory. The Mardigian Library houses a collection of more than 300,000 bound volumes and approximately 1,200 current periodicals. In addition, students have access to the library collections of the University of Michigan at Ann Arbor and both on-campus and off-campus access to many online resources, including full-text periodicals, reference sources, and abstracting and indexing services. The campus maintains two general-purpose computer laboratories with the latest PC workstations. Each school also has dedicated computer laboratories equipped with PCs, Macs, and Sun Workstations, all networked and accessible from remote locations. The College of Engineering and Computer Science operates numerous laboratories, including specialized ones dedicated to manufacturing, machine vision, materials, engines, vehicle electronics, and networks.

Financial Aid

Graduate students may apply for scholarships, loans, internships, and employment. The College of Engineering and Computer Science has a limited number of assistantships available. Many current students obtain support for their graduate education through their employer's educational assistance programs.

Cost of Study

Graduate tuition for 2009–10 can be found on the University of Michigan–Dearborn Web site at http://www.umd.umich.edu/rr_tuition-fees/.

Living and Housing Costs

No on-campus housing is available. A Housing Referral Office is available to assist students in locating housing opportunities in the area.

Student Group

In fall 2008, the University had an approximate enrollment of 8,600, of whom 1,889 were graduate students. Of these graduate students, 45 percent were women, 11 percent were international, and 24 percent were members of minority groups.

Student Outcomes

Graduate students at UM–Dearborn comprise members from virtually all professions. Most have been employed for several years and have gained valuable experience in their particular occupations. The graduate experience enhances their productivity and effectiveness in the workplace. Many report successful promotions within their organizations to higher-paying job offers after graduating. The automotive industry in southeastern Michigan provides worldwide employment opportunities for graduates.

Location

Located in the heart of one of the world's premier manufacturing regions, the University of Michigan–Dearborn campus is approximately 15 miles from downtown Detroit and 15 miles from the Detroit Metropolitan International Airport, and is easily accessible from major area freeways. The Henry Ford Estate–Fair Lane, former home of the automotive pioneer, is a National Historic Landmark and is located on campus.

The University

The Dearborn campus is part of the University of Michigan system. It was established in 1956 through a gift from the Ford Motor Company, and sits on 196 acres of land, including 70 acres of the Henry Ford Estate–Fair Lane. The campus opened its doors in 1959 as a senior college serving the local engineering and business community. In 1971, UM–Dearborn began admitting freshmen and expanded its programs to focus on master's-level education. The campus recently completed a significant infrastructure expansion, opening new buildings for the engineering and science complexes, and acquiring a spacious new facility from the Ford Motor Company to house its Schools of Management and Education.

Applying

Criteria and deadline dates are included in the University's informational materials and can be found on the University's Web site (http://www.umd.umich.edu/graduatestudies/). Applications for admission and supporting documents should be sent directly to the program(s) of interest.

Correspondence and Information

Graduate Studies Office
University of Michigan–Dearborn
4901 Evergreen Road, 1080 AB
Dearborn, Michigan 48128-1491

Phone: 313-593-1494
Fax: 313-436-9156
E-mail: umdgrad@umd.umich.edu
Web site: http://www.umd.umich.edu/graduatestudies/

University of Michigan–Dearborn

THE FACULTY

Teaching is at the core of the University of Michigan–Dearborn's mission. Members of the faculty are dedicated professionals who place great emphasis on their role as teachers. Faculty members carefully train students, mentor them, and interact closely with them both inside and outside the classroom. In addition, faculty members seek to fully engage students in their research, scholarship and creative activities, thereby enriching the students' educational experience, while at the same time advancing the knowledge base of their disciplines. More information about University faculty members may be found on UM–Dearborn's Web site.

UNIVERSITY OF MISSOURI–ST. LOUIS

Graduate School

Programs of Study

The University of Missouri–St. Louis (UM–St. Louis) offers programs of study leading to the Ph.D.: applied mathematics, biology, business administration, chemistry, criminology and criminal justice, education, nursing, physics, political science, psychology, and vision science. The Ed.D. and Ed.S. in education are also administered by the Graduate School. The O.D. in optometry is administered by the School of Optometry.

Master's degrees are offered in the areas of accounting, adult and higher education, biochemistry and biotechnology, biology, business administration, chemistry, communication, computer science, counseling, creative writing, criminology and criminal justice, economics, educational administration, elementary education, English, gerontology, history, information systems, mathematics, museum studies, music education, nursing, philosophy, physics, physiological optics, political science, psychology, public policy administration, secondary education, social work, sociology, and special education. The University also offers numerous graduate certificate programs.

Research Facilities

The three libraries at the University of Missouri–St. Louis (Thomas Jefferson, Ward E. Barnes, and Mercantile) hold more than 20 million volumes and 28,000 full-text, online journals. The Mercantile Library, with collection strengths in Western Americana, holds two distinguished transportation collections, including the Barringer Collection. The Center for Molecular Electronics conducts research at the atomic and molecular levels that are essential for state-of-the-art materials and devices. The International Center for Tropical Ecology promotes research in biodiversity, conservation, and sustainable use of tropical ecosystems. The Center for Neurodynamics conducts research on the effects of stochastic noise on information transfer in natural and artificial neurological systems. Researchers in the Center for Trauma Recovery study the assessment and treatment of post-traumatic stress disorder. The Center for Business and Industrial Studies investigates managerial problems and performs applied research. The Public Policy Research Center conducts research in the areas of public policy and offers experiences for students in urban research. The Center for Transportation Studies studies supply chain management.

Financial Aid

Financial assistance is available to graduate students primarily through assistantships. Departments determine the stipend level for teaching and research assistants. Appointments range from $5000 to $18,000 for master's students and from $7500 to $30,000 for doctoral students.

Cost of Study

Tuition and fees per semester (full-time, 9 credit hours) for 2008–09 were approximately $3150 for residents and $7400 for nonresidents. Estimated annual living and health insurance expenses for international students were $10,003 for the academic year.

Living and Housing Costs

Traditional residence hall or apartment housing is available. Full information is available online at http://www.umsl.edu/services/reslife/.

Student Group

Enrollment in fall 2007 was 12,147 students, of whom 2,803 were graduate students. Sixty-six percent of the graduate students were women, and 13 percent were African American.

Location

The University occupies a suburban campus of more than 300 acres northwest of St. Louis, the major metropolitan area in the state. The campus has easy access to the airport and the downtown area via the MetroLink, which has stops on both the north and south campuses. St. Louis has an abundance of cultural, sports, and entertainment opportunities.

The University

UM–St. Louis is one of four campuses of the University of Missouri System. It was established in 1963 and is the third-largest university in the state. In addition to its role in advancing knowledge as part of a comprehensive research university, UM–St. Louis has a special mission determined by its urban location and its shared land-grant tradition. It works in partnership with other key community institutions to help the St. Louis region progress and prosper.

Applying

Doctoral applications have deadlines as early as January 5 and no later than July 15. Master's degree student applications are generally due July 15 for the fall semester, December 15 for the spring semester, and May 1 for the summer session. Applicants requesting financial aid should submit their applications by March 15. Additional information is available online at the Web address listed in this description.

Correspondence and Information

Graduate Admissions
217 Millennium Student Center
University of Missouri–St. Louis
One University Boulevard
St. Louis, Missouri 63121-4499

Phone: 314-516-5458
Fax: 314-516-6996
E-mail: gradadm@umsl.edu
Web site: http://www.umsl.edu/divisions/graduate

FACULTY RESEARCH

Biology. Animal behavior/behavioral ecology, biochemistry, biogeography, community/evolutionary ecology, conservation biology, evolutionary developmental biology, ecophysiology, evolution of sociality, history of biology, membrane biology and signal transduction, molecular biology, molecular and morphological systematics, microbial genetics, neuroethology of aquatic organisms, plant-animal/insect-microbe interactions, plant biochemical/cellular/molecular biology, plant population genetics/biology, RNA processing and metabolism, studies in tropical and temperate ecosystems, taxonomy.

Business. Accounting, accounting regulation, auditor judgment and decision making, taxation, commercial banking, corporate finance, investments and portfolio management, government regulations, telecommunications, client/server, IS sourcing, decision support systems, international information systems, management of information systems, production/operations management, mathematical programming, transportation routing and scheduling, logistics systems, freight consolidation, simulation, supply chain management, human resources, international management, strategic management, marketing strategy, new product development, advertising, consumer behavior.

Chemistry and Biochemistry. Organometallic chemistry, supramolecular chemistry, transition metal–catalyzed reactions, redox enzymes based on cyclodextrin, serum transferrin chemistry, natural products chemistry, carbohydrate chemistry, organic synthesis, phosphorus chemistry, silicon chemistry, physical organic chemistry, structure-function studies of enzymes, biophysical chemistry, structural studies using NMR spectroscopy and X-ray diffraction, cell model systems, drug discovery and medicinal chemistry, biological polymers, microscopy, chemical education, materials chemistry, nanoscience, nanomaterials and nanocatalysis, elucidation of nanostructures.

Communication. Theory and methodology, intercultural, interpersonal, mass, and organizational.

Computer Science. Computer graphics, scientific computation, CAGD, image processing, computer vision, sensor simulation, knowledge-based information retrieval and classification, artificial intelligence, evolutionary computation, genetic algorithms and genetic programming, fuzzy reasoning, clustering algorithms, machine learning, Bayesian networks, stochastic optimization, software engineering.

Criminology and Criminal Justice. Criminological theory, social control, crime prevention, crime and social institutions, delinquency, violence, gangs, gender, race and ethnicity, victimization, offender decision making, policing, courts, corrections, prisoner re-entry, criminal and juvenile justice policy analysis, evaluation research, qualitative and quantitative methods.

Economics. Applied econometrics; microeconomics; macroeconomics; monetary theory; international trade and comparative systems; urban, state, and local finance; public sector; labor; public policy; law and economics; forensic economics; property rights; industrial organization; telecommunications; health economics; economics of aging; gender; poverty; science and technology.

Education. Instructional strategies; inclusion; ethics and character education; motivation in learning; evaluation of educational programs; counseling (school, community, and marriage/family); remedial and corrective reading; literacy; action research on teacher development; technology and learning; mathematics education (manipulatives); constructivism; behavioral disorder; performance-based assessment; motor development; postmodern thought and deconstruction; higher, adult, and vocational education; methodology, measurement, and assessment; urban education; school-university partnerships and community collaboration; positive behavior support; schoolwide systems of discipline.

English (M.A.) and Creative Writing (M.F.A.). Chaucer, Milton, Shakespeare, medieval, early modern, eighteenth-century, Victorian, American, modern British, and Jewish literature; literary theory; feminist theory; composition theory; creative writing in fiction and poetry; linguistics.

Gerontology. Social security and other pension policies; caregiving and other informal support of the elderly; mental health assessment and treatment; ethnic differences, particularly in health-care behavior; cross-cultural comparisons of retirement patterns and policies; driving assessment and intervention in older adults.

History. United States social and political; nineteenth-century; twentieth-century; African-American; women; slavery and emancipation; urban; environmental; military; St. Louis, Missouri; Native American; German-American ethnic; American West; Roman Empire; European-medieval; eighteenth-century French, German, Spanish, English; economic; women; Renaissance and Reformation; medieval; African; East Asian—Japan, China, Asian-Pacific Rim; Latin American colonial; nineteenth- and twentieth-century sports; museum studies.

Mathematics. Wavelets and computational harmonic analysis, splines and approximation theory, subdivision methods for computer graphics, medical imaging, computational mathematics, string theory, algebraic geometry, differential geometry, transformation groups, statistics, stochastic processes.

Music Education. Psychology of music, application of technology in music education, tests and measurements in music, conducting, choral and instrumental performance, music education curriculum design, affective response to music, music supervision and administration, music software design, urban music education, arts education.

Nursing. Adherence to health treatment, catastrophic stress, exercise and hypertension, informatics and telemetry in health care, psychosocial nursing interventions, quantitative methods in nursing research, injuries and violence as a health problem, women's health.

Philosophy. Ethics (contemporary ethical theory and bioethics), philosophy and history of science (philosophy of medicine and ancient Greek and medieval Arabic traditions), history of philosophy, aesthetics (aesthetic appreciation and environmental aesthetics).

Physics. Astrophysics, observational astronomy, experimental atomic physics, biophysics, theoretical elementary particle physics, experimental and theoretical solid-state physics, nanoscale microscopy.

Physiological Optics (vision science). Aging and Alzheimer's disease, binocular vision in children and adults, contact lenses, control of eye movements, electrophysiology in healthy and diseased visual systems, low vision, mathematical approaches to vision, neurophysiology of visual and oculomotor pathways, public health, theoretical and applied visual optics, theoretical and applied visual psychophysics.

Political Science. American government and politics; political economy; public administration and public policy; urban politics and urban economic development; program evaluation; public law and judicial politics; public opinion and elections; methodology; labor relations; political thought; international law and organization; civil liberties; comparative politics; comparative health policy; environmental politics; interpersonal politics; minority politics; policy implementation and evaluation; political communication; African, Chinese, Japanese, and Latin American politics; Western and Eastern European politics.

Psychology–Behavioral Neuroscience. Neuroendocrinology, neuropharmacology, cognitive processes, cognitive aging, neuropsychology, neuroimaging, psychophysiology, animal cognition.

Psychology–Clinical. Role of culture in mental health, anxiety disorders, post-traumatic stress disorder, relationship between anxiety and physical health, childhood problems, psychology and religion, development of ACT use with children/adolescents, women and sexuality, interventions for family dementia caregiving, issues of aging in place.

Psychology–Industrial/Organizational. Recruitment, interviewing, personality, performance appraisal, compensation and benefits, diversity and discrimination, global issues, work-family conflict, time management, job attitudes, motivation, person by situation fit, competitive climate, mentoring, group processes, leadership, psychometrics, statistics, applied measurement issues, research methodology, social psychology, nonverbal communication.

Public Policy Administration. Managing human resources and organization, policy research and analysis, local government management, health policy, nonprofit organization management and leadership, metropolitan governance, urban and regional planning, welfare policy, social security policy, organization theory, government contracting for services, performance measurement, program evaluation, conflict resolution, defense conversion, labor economics, public-sector microeconomics.

Social Work. Urban-related research issues, family violence, social welfare, gerontology, child abuse and neglect, immigration, substance abuse and minorities, community economic development, international social welfare, addiction, disabilities.

Sociology. Minority groups, stratification, deviance, comparative social organization, health, social psychology, conflict intervention, aging, race and ethnic relations, education, interpersonal violence.

Women's and Gender Studies. Women's and gender issues, feminist and gender theory.

UNIVERSITY OF NEVADA, LAS VEGAS

Graduate College

Programs of Study

The Graduate College at the University of Nevada, Las Vegas (UNLV), strives to advance its mission of becoming a premier metropolitan research university by supporting excellent graduate programs that train graduates in their areas of expertise and contribute to the well-being of the community, state, nation, and the world. With a growing emphasis on interdisciplinary research on urban issues and sustainability, UNLV is a thriving intellectual community of scholars. Graduate education at UNLV is guided by an institutional commitment to the support of students through both the provision of administrative and financial assistance and the creation of enhanced learning opportunities through research, scholarly endeavors, and creative activity. UNLV is classified as a "high research activity" university by the Carnegie Foundation for the Advancement of Teaching. Through its ten schools and colleges, the University offers over 130 graduate degree programs, including more than thirty-six doctoral and professional degree programs.

The College of Business offers the following programs and degrees: accounting, M.S.; business administration, M.B.A.; business administration–full-time day, M.B.A.; executive business administration, Executive M.B.A.; *dual business administration/hotel administration, M.B.A./M.S.; *dual business administration/management information systems. M.B.A./M.S.; *dual business administration/dental medicine, M.B.A./D.M.D.; *dual business administration/law, M.B.A./J.D.; economics, M.A.; and management information systems, M.S.

The College of Education offers the following programs and degrees: counselor education, M.Ed., M.S.; curriculum and instruction, M.Ed., M.S., Ed.S., Ed.D., Ph.D.; educational leadership, M.Ed., M.S., Ed.D., Ph.D., educational leadership–Executive Ed.D.; educational psychology, M.S., Ed.S., Ph.D.; learning and technology, Ph.D.; special education, M.Ed., M.S., Ed.S., Ed.D., Ph.D.; special education–early childhood education, M.Ed.; sports education leadership/physical education, M.Ed., M.S., Ph.D.; and *dual education/law, Ph.D/J.D. The College of Engineering offers the following programs and degrees: civil and environmental engineering, M.S.E., Ph.D.; construction management, M.S.; computer science, M.S., Ph.D.; electrical and computer engineering, M.S., Ph.D.; informatics, M.S., Ph.D.; mechanical engineering, M.S., Ph.D., mechanical engineering–aerospace engineering, M.S.; mechanical engineering–biomedical engineering, M.S.; mechanical engineering–materials and nuclear engineering, M.S.; and transportation, M.S.T. The College of Fine Arts offers the following programs and degrees: architecture, M.Arch.; art, M.F.A.; film/screenwriting, M.F.A.; music, M.M.; musical arts, D.M.A.; and theater, M.A., M.F.A. The Division of Health Sciences offers the following programs and degrees: dental medicine, D.M.D.; *dual dental medicine/business administration, D.M.D./M.B.A.; exercise physiology, M.S.; health-care administration, M.H.A.; health physics, M.S.; health promotion, M.Ed.; kinesiology, M.S.; nursing, M.S.N., Ph.D.; physical therapy, D.P.T.; and public health, M.P.H., Ph.D. The College of Hotel Administration offers the following programs and degrees: hospitality administration, M.H.A., Ph.D.; hotel administration, M.S.; *dual hotel administration/business administration, M.S./M.B.A.; and sports and leisure service management, M.S. The William S. Boyd School of Law offers the following programs and degrees: law, J.D.; *dual law/social work, J.D./M.S.W.; *dual law/business administration, J.D./M.B.A, and *dual law/education, J.D./Ph.D. The College of Liberal Arts offers the following programs and degrees: anthropology, M.A., Ph.D.; creative writing, M.F.A.; English, M.A., Ph.D.; ethics and policy studies, M.A.; foreign languages and literature, M.A.; history, M.A., Ph.D.; political science, M.A., Ph.D.; psychology, M.A., Ph.D.; and sociology, M.A., Ph.D. The College of Sciences offers the following programs and degrees: astronomy, M.S., Ph.D.; biochemistry, M.S.; biological sciences, M.S., Ph.D.; chemistry, M.S., Ph.D.; geoscience, M.S., Ph.D.; mathematical sciences, M.S., Ph.D.; physics, M.S., Ph.D.; radiochemistry, Ph.D.; science, M.A.S.; and water resource management, M.S. The College of Urban Affairs offers the following programs and degrees: communication studies, M.A.; criminal justice, M.A.; environmental studies, M.S., Ph.D.; journalism and media studies, M.A.; marriage and family therapy, M.S.; public administration, M.P.A., public administration–crisis and emergency management, M.S.; public affairs, Ph.D.; and social work, M.S.W. and *dual social work/law, M.S.W./J.D. Graduate certificate programs are offered in a variety of areas, including addiction studies, family nurse practitioner studies, forensic social work, marriage and family therapy, nursing education, public management, rehabilitation counseling, and women's studies.

* These programs are offered jointly with other departments and require full admission into each program.

Research Facilities

The integration of the University's research and graduate program management into the Division of Research and Graduate Studies supports UNLV's commitment to high-quality graduate education. This structure strategically links the ongoing development of UNLV's research infrastructure with the Graduate College directly and enhances research opportunities for graduate students. UNLV has nearly seventy research centers, laboratories, and museums, including, but not limited to, the International Institute of Modern Letters, International Gaming Institute, Harry Reid Center for Environmental Studies, Nevada Institute for Children, Nevada Center for Advanced Computation Methods, Nevada Small Business Development Center, Center for American Indian Research and Education, Center for Energy Research, Center for Business and Economic Research, Center for Health Disparities Research, Center for Urban Horticulture and Water Conservation, and Center for Volcanic and Tectonic Studies.

UNLV also houses the National Supercomputing Center for Energy and the Environment (NSCEE). Funded through the Department of Energy, the NSCEE has national network accessibility. It provides supercomputing training and services to academic and research institutions and government and private industry for research and development related to energy, the environment, medical informatics, and health-care delivery.

The computer facility located on the campus is part of the University of Nevada System Computing Network. UNLV computers are linked through the network to computers at the University of Nevada, Reno, and at Clark County Community College. Time-sharing terminals, remote batch terminals, and local batch terminals give students and faculty members access to the computer network.

UNLV's state-of-the-art Lied Library, one of the most technologically sophisticated in the U.S., contains more than 1 million volumes and occupies more than 300,000 square feet within five stories. UNLV has additional libraries for the disciplines of curriculum and instruction, music, and architecture.

Financial Aid

Financial assistance for graduate students is available in a variety of forms, including competitive graduate teaching and research assistantships that provide partial tuition waivers, generous stipends, optional health insurance, and valuable teaching, administrative, and/or research experience. Generally, assistantships are valued at $10,000 to $12,000 per academic year. In addition, fellowships, scholarships, fee waivers, Federal Work-Study Program awards, Federal Perkins Loans, Federal Stafford Student Loans, Nevada Incentive Grants, and many other opportunities are also available.

Cost of Study

For the 2008–09 academic year, residents and nonresidents paid a $218-per-credit fee for graduate courses. Full-time nonresident tuition (7 or more credits) was $6170 per semester, plus a $218-per-credit fee for graduate courses.

Living and Housing Costs

On-campus housing costs include room and board. Nine dorms are available. Off-campus housing can be found close to the University; the cost of rent averages between $700 and $1200 per month.

Student Group

Graduate and professional students make up more than 6,000 of UNLV's 28,000 students. UNLV has a socially and ethnically diverse student population, as students who are members of minority groups make up more than 30 percent of the student body, and nearly 60 percent of students are women. Graduate students come from all fifty states in the U.S. and fifty-eight other countries. UNLV's programs are designed for traditional and nontraditional, full-time and part-time students. The median age for graduate and professional students is 29 years, and many work full-time while attending UNLV.

Location

Las Vegas is on the southern tip of Nevada in a desert valley surrounded by mountains. The main campus is surrounded by apartments, restaurants, shopping centers, parks, libraries, hospitals, and other facilities of this dynamic city of more than 1.8 million residents.

Within a 30-mile radius lie the shores of Lake Mead, the massive Hoover Dam, the Colorado River recreation area, the snow-skiing and hiking trails of 12,000-foot Mount Charleston, and a panorama of red-rock mountains and eroded sandstone landscapes. In addition, the city is only 4 to 5 hours by car from the beaches of southern California and the national parks of Utah and Arizona.

The University

UNLV's beautiful, modern main campus is located on 340 acres in dynamic southern Nevada. The University has grown dramatically since its founding in 1957. Recently, the University has expanded to include the Shadow Lane Campus and the UNLV Harry Reid Research and Technology Park, both of which are also located in Las Vegas. The University is a member of the American Association of State Colleges and Universities, the Council of Graduate Schools, the Western Association of Graduate Schools, the American Council on Education, and the Western College Association. All programs are fully accredited by the Northwest Association of Schools and Colleges, and many have disciplinary and professional accreditation as well. UNLV's more than 1,000 full-time professors bring degrees and teaching experience from leading universities around the world. Faculty members are involved in important research for government and public service agencies and for scholarly books and journals. Many faculty members have won major awards. UNLV has two semesters (fall and spring) of approximately sixteen weeks each and three summer sessions.

Applying

Minimum requirements for admission include a completed admissions application, official transcripts from all postsecondary institutions attended, a bachelor's degree from an accredited four-year college or university, and a minimum cumulative GPA of 2.75 for the bachelor's degree or 3.0 for the last two years of work. Each academic department has its own additional admissions requirements, such as letters of recommendation, adequate undergraduate prerequisite courses, and/or a writing sample. Many programs require acceptable scores from standardized tests, including scores from the Graduate Record Examinations, Graduate Management Admission Test, or Miller Analogies Test. International students must achieve a minimum score of 80 on the Internet-based Test of English as a Foreign Language.

Correspondence and Information

Graduate College
University of Nevada, Las Vegas
4505 Maryland Parkway, Box 1017
Las Vegas, Nevada 89154-1017

Phone: 702-895-3320
E-mail: gradcollege@unlv.edu
Web site: http://graduatecollege.unlv.edu

FACULTY HEADS AND DEPARTMENT CONTACT NUMBERS

Graduate College
Ron Smith, Ph.D., Vice President for Research and Graduate Dean.
Kate Hausbeck, Ph.D., Senior Associate Dean.
Harriet E. Barlow, Ph.D., Associate Dean for Retention and Professional Development.

College of Business
Paul Jarley, Ph.D., Dean.
Accounting: 702-895-3619.
Business Administration: 702-895-3655.
Economics: 702-895-3776.
Management Information Systems: 702-895-3796.

College of Education
M. Christopher Brown II, Ph.D., Dean.
Counselor Education: 702-895-5994.
Curriculum and Instruction: 702-895-3241 or 702-895-1986.
Educational Leadership: 702-895-3491.
Educational Psychology: 702-895-3253.
Special Education: 702-895-3205.
Sports Education Leadership: 702-895-3491.

College of Engineering
Eric Sandgren, Ph.D., Dean.
Civil and Environmental Engineering: 702-895-3936.
School of Computer Science: 702-895-3681.
Construction Management: 702-895-1461.
Electrical and Computer Engineering: 702-895-4183.
School of Informatics: 702-895-3681.
Mechanical Engineering: 702-895-1331.
Transportation (Civil and Enviromental Engineering): 702-895-3936.

College of Fine Arts
Jeff Koep, Ph.D., Dean.
Architecture: 702-895-3031.
Art: 702-895-3237.
Film: 702-895-3547.
Music: 702-895-3332.
Theater: 702-895-3666.

Division of Health Sciences
Mary Guinan, M.D., Ph.D., Dean, School of Community Health Sciences.
Health Promotion: 702-895-4030.
Health-Care Administration: 702-895-1400.
Environmental and Occupational Health: 702-895-5420.
School of Public Health 702-895-5090.
School of Allied Health Sciences.
Health Physics and Diagnostic Sciences 702-895-4320.
Kinesiology and Nutrition Sciences: 702-895-0996.
Physical Therapy: 702-895-3003.
Karen West, D.M.D., Dean, School of Dental Medicine.
Carolyn Yucha, RN, Ph.D., Dean, School of Nursing.
School of Nursing: 702-895-3360.

College of Hotel Administration
Stuart H. Mann, Ph.D., Dean.
Hospitality Administration: 702-895-3321.
Hotel Administration: 702-895-3321.
Sport and Leisure Service Management: 702-895-1188.

William S. Boyd School of Law
John Valery White, J.D., Dean.
Law: 702-895-3671.

College of Liberal Arts
Christopher Hudgins, Ph.D., Dean
Anthropology: 702-895-3590.
English: 702-895-3533.
Ethics and Policy Studies: 702-895-3307.
Foreign Languages: 702-895-3431.
History: 702-895-3349.
Political Science: 702-895-3307.
Psychology: 702-895-3305.
Sociology: 702-895-3322.

College of Science
Wanda Taylor, Ph.D., Interim Dean.
Chemistry: 702-895-3510.
Geoscience: 702-895-3262.
School of Life Sciences: 702-895-3390.
Mathematical Sciences: 702-895-0386.
Master of Arts in Science: 702-895-3587.
Physics and Astronomy: 702-895-3563.

College of Urban Affairs
Lee Bernick, Ph.D., Interim Dean.
Communication Studies: 702-895-5125.
Criminal Justice: 702-895-0238.
Environmental Studies: 702-895-4440.
Journalism and Media Studies: 702-895-3225.
Marriage and Family Therapy: 702-895-1867.
Public Administration: 702-895-4828.
School of Social Work: 702-895-3311.

The central corridor of the campus contains (from left to right) Grant Hall, Dungan Humanities Building, Dickinson Library, Carlson Education Building, and Ham Hall.

UNIVERSITY OF NEW HAVEN

Graduate Studies

Programs of Study

The University of New Haven (UNH) offers Master of Arts degree programs in community psychology and industrial/organizational psychology. The Master of Business Administration program has eight available areas of concentration, including options in accounting, business policy and strategic leadership, finance, global marketing and e-commerce, human resource management, sports management, a fifth-year CPA exam track, and a track for prospective chartered financial analyst (CFA) candidates. Dual-degree programs allow students to earn both the M.B.A. and the Master of Science in Industrial Engineering and both the M.B.A. and the Master of Public Administration. An Executive M.B.A. degree program is also offered by the University. This program is designed for experienced, upper-level executives and managers.

The Master of Science degree is offered in the areas of cellular and molecular biology, computer science, criminal justice, education, electrical engineering, environmental engineering, environmental science, engineering management, fire science, forensic science, health-care administration, human nutrition, industrial engineering, labor relations, management of sports industries, mechanical engineering, national security and public safety, and taxation. The Master of Public Administration degree is also offered.

Research Facilities

The holdings of the Marvin K. Peterson Library include more than 244,000 volumes and 1,400 print journals and newspaper subscriptions; electronic access to more than 17,940 full-text journal and newspaper titles; U.S. government documents; and numerous corporate annual reports, pamphlet files, and microfilm as well as current and extensive back-issue files of periodicals. Interlibrary loan search and other resources are available through OCLC, First Search, LexisNexis, Dialog, Dow Jones News/Retrieval, and CD-ROM systems.

The UNH Center for Computing Services provides both administrative and academic computing support. Administrators, faculty members, and students have access to the latest in computer technology. Personal computers for student use are spread throughout the campus, with the largest concentration located at the Center for Computing Services. In addition, the Computer-Aided Engineering Center laboratory in the Tagliatela College of Engineering houses workstations plus micros connected by an Ethernet LAN. Graphics, printing and plotting devices, laser printing, and a wide variety of data files, software, and simulation packages are also available.

Financial Aid

Financial aid is available for graduate students through assistantships and loans. The University participates in Federal Stafford Student Loan programs. Teaching, research, or administrative assistantships are available to full-time students. Compensation includes $8 per hour as well as a 50 percent tuition reduction; students typically work 15–20 hours per week.

Cost of Study

Tuition for master's degree students for the 2008–09 academic year was $670 per graduate credit or $2010 per course for most graduate courses. The Graduate Student Council fee is $60 per year, and there is a $25 technology fee each term. All charges and fees are subject to change.

Living and Housing Costs

There is no on-campus housing for graduate students, but the Center for Graduate and Adult Student Services maintains an off-campus housing Web site with listings of apartments in the local area at a variety of costs, a forum for accepted students to find roommates, local maps, and information on local services.

Student Group

Many students are from Connecticut, but each year an increasing number come from other states and many other countries. The graduate student body of more than 1,700 ranges from recent college graduates to professionals with several years of experience in their fields. About 51 percent of the graduate students are women, about 12 percent receive some sort of financial aid, approximately 20 percent are international students, and nearly 16 percent are members of minority groups. Graduates are employed in government service, teaching, private agencies, and business.

Location

The University of New Haven is located in south central Connecticut. Although the campus is located in West Haven, it is less than 3 miles from downtown New Haven and students can easily take advantage of the cultural offerings of the city. New Haven has rail, bus, and air service, and its location at the junction of two major interstate highways places the school within easy driving distance of New York, Boston, and Providence.

The University

The University of New Haven was founded in 1920 and is accredited as a general-purpose institution by the New England Association of Schools and Colleges. A number of graduate classes are held at several off-campus locations across the state as well as New Mexico. The Graduate School follows a trimester schedule with start dates in September, January, and April. Most graduate classes are held in the early evening to accommodate both part-time and full-time students.

Applying

Applicants must hold a baccalaureate degree from an accredited college or university. An applicant for admission to the Graduate School must submit the following before the initial registration: a formal application; a nonrefundable $50 application fee; letters of recommendation; final official transcripts from all previous college work. In addition, a satisfactory TOEFL score (except for students whose native language is English) and certified financial support forms are required for all international students. In some programs, students may be required to take a specific standardized test as part of the application process. All correspondence and requests for materials should be directed to the Graduate Admissions Office. Descriptions of programs and procedures are available in the *Graduate Catalog*. Information about the University of New Haven is available on the Web site at http://www.newhaven.edu.

Correspondence and Information

Graduate Admissions Office
University of New Haven
300 Boston Post Road
West Haven, Connecticut 06516

Phone: 203-932-7440
800-DIAL-UNH (toll-free)
Fax: 203-932-7137
E-mail: gradinfo@newhaven.edu
Web site: http://www.newhaven.edu

FACULTY HEADS

The faculty consists of approximately 470 full- and part-time professors. The coordinators for the various graduate programs and the Associate Provost for Graduate Studies are listed below.

Graduate School: Ira Kleinfeld, Associate Provost for Graduate Studies, Research, and Faculty Development; Eng.Sc.D., Columbia.
Business Administration/Industrial Engineering (dual degree): Alexis N. Sommers, Ph.D., Purdue.
Business Administration/Public Administration (dual degree): Charles N. Coleman, M.P.A., West Virginia.
Cellular and Molecular Biology: Eva Sapi, Ph.D., Eötvös Loránd (Budapest).
Community Psychology: Michael Morris, Ph.D., Boston College.
Computer Science: Tahany Fergany, Ph.D., Connecticut.
Criminal Justice: James Cassidy, Ph.D., Hahnemann.
Education: Paulette Pepin, Ph.D., Fordham.
Electrical Engineering: Bouzid Aliane, Ph.D., Polytechnic.
Engineering Management: Barry J. Farbrother, C.Eng., Hertfordshire (England).
Environmental Engineering: Agamemnon D. Koutsospyros, Ph.D., Polytechnic.
Environmental Science: Roman N. Zajac, Ph.D., Connecticut.
Executive Master of Business Administration: Ben B. Judd, Ph.D., Texas at Arlington.
Fire Science: Sorin Illiescu, M.S., New Haven.
Forensic Science: Virginia M. Maxwell, D.Phil., Oxford.
Health-Care Administration: Charles N. Coleman, M.P.A., West Virginia.
Human Nutrition: Rosa Mo, Ed.D., Columbia.
Industrial Engineering: Alexis Sommers, Ph.D., Purdue.
Industrial/Organizational Psychology: Stuart Sidle, Ph.D., DePaul.
Labor Relations: Charles N. Coleman, M.P.A., West Virginia.
Management of Sports Industries: Gil B. Fried, J.D., Ohio State.
M.B.A./Business Administration: Charles N. Coleman, Coordinator; M.P.A., West Virginia.
Mechanical Engineering: Stephen M. Ross, Ph.D., Johns Hopkins/Konstantine C. Lambrakis, Ph.D., Rensselaer.
National Security and Public Safety: William L. Tayofa, Ph.D., Maryland.
Public Administration: Charles N. Coleman, M.P.A., West Virginia.

Students enjoy easy access to laboratory facilities furnished with modern equipment, data acquisition systems, and software.

UNH engineering students have access to the latest technology in several fully equipped, state-of-the-art learning environments.

The Forensic Science Program, one of the finest in the world, supports extensive well-equipped labs for hands-on work with modern equipment and instruments used in this profession.

UNIVERSITY OF NORTH TEXAS

Toulouse School of Graduate Studies

Programs of Study

The University of North Texas (UNT) offers graduate study in 104 master's degree programs and forty-nine doctoral programs.

Doctoral degrees are offered in accounting, applied gerontology, applied technology and performance improvement, art education, audiology, biological sciences, business computer information science, chemistry, computer science and engineering, counseling, curriculum and instruction, early childhood education, educational administration, educational computing, educational research, higher education, reading education, special education, English, environmental science, finance, history, information science, management, management science, marketing, materials science and engineering, mathematics, molecular biology, music composition, music education, musicology, music performance, music theory, philosophy, physics, political science, psychology (including clinical, counseling, experimental, and health psychology/behavioral medicine), public administration, and sociology.

Master's degrees are offered in most of the above areas plus the following: administration of long-term care and retirement facilities, applied anthropology, applied economics, applied geography, art (including ceramics, communication design, drawing and painting, fashion design, fibers, history, interior design, innovative studies, metalsmithing and jewelry, photography, printmaking, sculpture, and watercolor), behavior analysis, communications studies, computer education and cognitive systems, computer engineering, computer science, creative writing, criminal justice, decision technologies, delivery of community-based services for the aging, economics, educational psychology, electrical engineering, human development and family studies, engineering systems (construction management, electronics technology management, engineering management, mechanical technology management), English, English as a second language, French, hospitality management, information technologies, journalism, kinesiology, labor and industrial relations, library science, linguistics, mechanical and energy engineering, merchandising, music (including jazz studies), philosophy, public administration, radio/television/film, real estate, recreation, rehabilitation counseling, school psychology, secondary education, Spanish, speech/language pathology, taxation, and technical writing.

Master's and doctoral degree programs in several areas are offered in cooperation with the Federation of North Texas Area Universities.

Research Facilities

The University libraries contain more than 5.9 million cataloged holdings and provide diverse, rapidly growing electronic resources. The libraries provide all of the services traditionally associated with academic research libraries, plus services provided by membership in national consortia and electronic access/searching of academic and commercial information resources.

The University's information resources infrastructure includes both central and distributed computing, combining personal computers and several major host computer systems. The campus backbone system combines high-speed fiber optics linking approximately thirty-five buildings, a broadband cable network linking video capabilities at more than 2,000 locations in approximately sixty buildings, and a developing wireless capacity. The campus network is linked to a variety of external networks, including the Internet and World Wide Web, and students and faculty members have access to computer resources both on and off campus through dial-in procedures.

In addition to departmental facilities, specialized or interdisciplinary research facilities are housed in a variety of centers, institutes, and laboratories. Science and technology centers focus on the applied sciences, environmental archaeology, forensic anthropology, ion-beam modification and analysis, nanostructural materials research, network neuroscience, organometallic chemistry, parallel and distributed computing, remote sensing and geographic information systems, and water research. Business research includes centers for information systems research, quality and productivity, and small business. The fine arts include centers for experimental music and intermedia and visual arts education. Humanities, social sciences, and educational research centers focus on inter-American studies, diplomatic and military history, local history, aging, economic development, environmental economic studies, peace studies, sport psychology, public and international affairs, labor and industrial relations, addiction, minority aging, survey research, developmental studies, play therapy, public support of nonprofit agencies, educational reform, educational research, and the school-to-work transition.

Financial Aid

More than 1,000 assistantships are available. The stipends vary according to the amount and level of work required and the background of the student. Half-time appointments and University-awarded scholarships and fellowships of $1000 or more qualify graduate students for in-state tuition rates. The graduate school annually awards a growing number of fellowships to new doctoral and master's students who are departmental nominees. New graduate-support programs have also been developed. Many departments also award scholarships and fellowships.

Loans, including Federal Perkins Loans and Federal Stafford Student Loans, are also available to graduate students.

Cost of Study

For 2008–09, tuition and fees for out-of-state graduate students were estimated at $1833 per 3-credit course, and tuition and fees for in-state graduate students were estimated at $990 per 3-credit course (subject to change).

Living and Housing Costs

Graduate students attending the Toulouse School of Graduate Studies may live in University-owned residence halls for approximately $6600 for two semesters. Nearby off-campus housing is also available at reasonable rates.

Student Group

More than 6,800 of the University's approximately 35,000 students are in the graduate school. UNT serves students from every state in the nation and almost 100 other countries.

Location

The University of North Texas is located in Denton, Texas, about 35 miles north of Dallas–Fort Worth. With a population of approximately 54 million, the metropolitan area is the largest in Texas and the ninth largest in the United States. There is a wide range of employment, cultural, and sports opportunities.

The University

Founded in 1890, the University of North Texas is one of Texas's five major research and graduate institutions and the only comprehensive graduate and research university in the region. The University began offering graduate work at the master's level in 1935 and at the doctoral level in 1950. Approximately 1,200 master's degrees and 150 doctoral degrees are awarded annually. UNT has awarded more than 147,000 degrees at the undergraduate and graduate levels. The Denton campus consists of 140 buildings on 756 acres on the main campus and one building on 200 acres at the Research Park.

Applying

Applications for admission and supporting documents should be received at least six weeks before entrance. For many departments an earlier deadline must be met. Since deadlines vary, students should correspond with a specific department prior to the date of desired enrollment. If a student is also applying for a graduate teaching or research assistantship, fellowship, or scholarship, application materials should be received several months earlier and at least by the deadline established by the award committee.

Correspondence and Information

Toulouse School of Graduate Studies
354 Eagle Student Services Building
University of North Texas
1155 Union Circle #305459
Denton, Texas 76203-5459

Phone: 940-565-2383
Fax: 940-565-2141
E-mail: gradschool@unt.edu
Web site: http://www.tsgs.unt.edu

FACULTY HEADS

GRADUATE SCHOOL

Michael Monticino, Interim Dean.
Lawrence J. Schneider, Associate Dean.
Joseph R. Oppong, Associate Dean.
Donna Hughes, Director of Graduate Services and Admissions.

COLLEGE OF ARTS AND SCIENCES

Warren Burggren, Dean.
Jean B. Schaake, Associate Dean.
Kathryn Gould Cullivan, Associate Dean.

Audiology: Kamakshi Gopal.
Biological Sciences: Art J. Goven, Chair; Beth Chaplek and Thomas LaPoint, Advisers.
Chemistry: Michael Richmond, Chair; Angela Wilson, Adviser.
Communication Studies: Jay Allison, Chair; Brian Richardson, Adviser.
Economics: Steven L. Cobb, Chair; Margie Tieslau and R. Todd Jewel, Advisers.
English: Robert Upchurch, Graduate Chair; Marshall Armintor, Adviser.
Foreign Languages: Marie Christine Koop, Chair; Marijn Kaplan, French Adviser; Cristina Sanchez-Conejero, Spanish Adviser.
Geography: Paul Hudak, Chair; Donald Lyons, Adviser.
History: Richard McCaslin, Chair; Ken Johnson, Adviser.
Journalism: Mitch Land, Interim Chair and Adviser.
Linguistics and Technical Communication: Brenda Sims, Chair and Technical Writing Adviser; Patricia Cukor-Avila, Linguistics Adviser.
Mathematics: Matt Douglass, Chair; Douglas Brozovic, Adviser.
Philosophy: Robert Frodeman, Chair and Adviser.
Physics: Chris Littler, Chair and Adviser.
Political Science: James D. Meernik, Chair; Phillip O. Paolino, Adviser.
Psychology: Linda L. Marshall, Chair; Amy Mayfield, Graduate Coordinator.
Radio/TV/Film: C. Melinda Levin, Chair; Samuel J. Sauls, Adviser.
Speech and Hearing: Earnest J. Moore, Chair; Fang Ling Lu, Adviser.

COLLEGE OF BUSINESS ADMINISTRATION

O. Finley Graves, Dean.
Randall S. Guttery, Associate Dean.

Accounting: Paul D. Hutchison, Interim Chair; Sheila Stratton, Master's Adviser; Carol Ann Frost, Doctoral Adviser.
Business (General): Konni Stubblefield, Master's Adviser; Linda Branson, Doctoral Adviser.
Finance, Insurance, Real Estate, and Law: Marcia Staff, Interim Chair; Kimberly Geideman, M.B.A./M.S.–Finance Adviser and M.S.–Real Estate Adviser; John Kensinger, Doctoral Finance Adviser.
Information Technology and Decision Sciences: Mary C. Jones, Chair; Thomas McGinnis, M.B.A./M.S. Adviser.
Management: Vicki Goodwin, Interim Chair; Christian Lehenbauer, Master's Adviser; Mark Davis, Doctoral Adviser.
Marketing and Logistics: Jeff Sager, Chair; Jeffrey Lewin, Master's Adviser; Audhesh Paswan, Doctoral Adviser.

College of Education
Jerry R. Thomas, Dean.
Judith A. Adkison, Associate Dean.
Michael F. Sayler, Associate Dean.
Mary Harris, Associate Dean.

Counseling, Development and Higher Education: Jan Holden, Chair; Janet Rogers, Counseling Adviser; Kathleen Whitson, Higher Education Adviser.
Kinesiology, Health Promotion, and Recreation: Alan Jackson, Chair; Noreen Goggin, Kinesiology Adviser; Jan Hodges, Recreation and Leisure Studies Adviser.
Teacher Education and Administration: Carol Wickstro, Chair; Frances Van Tassell, Master's Adviser, and Ron Newsom, Doctoral Adviser for Curriculum and Instruction; Donald Easton-Brooks, Master's Adviser, and George Morrison, Doctoral Adviser for Early Childhood Education; Linda Stromberg, Master's Adviser, and Jimmy Byrd, Doctoral Adviser for Educational Administration; Kathleen Mohr, Master's Adviser, and Janelle Mathis, Doctoral Adviser for Reading; Kelly King, Master's Adviser for Secondary Education.
Educational Psychology: Jon Young, Chair and Adviser for Educational Psychology; Becky Glover, Adviser for Development and Family Studies; Dr. Sander Martin, Adviser for School Psychology; Bertina Combes, Adviser for Special Education.

College of Engineering
Costas Tsatsoulis, Dean.
Reza Mirshams, Associate Dean.
Bill Buckles, Associate Dean.

Computer Science and Engineering: Krishna Kavi, Chair; Armin R. Mikler, Adviser.
Electrical Engineering: Murali Varanasi, Chair; Shengli Fu, Adviser.
Engineering Technology: Nourredine Boubekri, Chair; Michael Kozak, Adviser.
Materials Science and Engineering: Rick Reidy, Interim Chair; Nigel Shepherd, Adviser.
Mechanical and Energy Engineering: Nourredine Boubekri, Interim Chair; Sandra Boetcher and Zhi-Gang Feng, Advisers.

COLLEGE OF MUSIC

James C. Scott, Dean.
Warren Henry, Associate Dean
Jon C. Nelson, Associate Dean
John Scott, Associate Dean
Graham Phipps, Adviser.

COLLEGE OF PUBLIC ADMINISTRATION AND COMMUNITY SERVICE

Tom Evenson, Dean.
David McEntire, Associate Dean.

Anthropology: Alicia ReCruz, Chair; Lisa Henry, Adviser.
Applied Economics: Bernard Weinstein, Director; Terry Clower, Adviser.
Behavioral Analysis: Richard G. Smith, Chair; Manish Vaidya, Adviser.
Criminal Justice: Peggy Tobolowsky, Chair; Eric Fritsch, Adviser.
Long-term Care, Senior Housing and Aging Services: Keith Turner, Chair and Master's Adviser; Stan Ingman, Doctoral Adviser for Applied Gerontology.
Public Administration: Bob Bland, Chair; Abraham Benavides, Master's Adviser; Brian Collins, Doctoral Adviser.
Rehabilitation Studies: Linda Holloway, Chair; Eugenia Bodenhamer-Davis, Adviser.
Sociology: Daale Yeatts, Chair; Rudy Seward, Adviser.

COLLEGE OF INFORMATION, LIBRARY SCIENCE AND TECHNOLOGIES

Herman L. Totten, Dean.
Linda Schamber, Associate Dean.
Library and Information Sciences: Toby Faber, Master's Adviser.
Diane Green, Doctoral Adviser.
Learning Technologies: Jeff Allen, Chair; Jerry Wircenski, Adviser for Applied Technology and Performance Improvement; Jim Poirot, Adviser for Computer Education and Cognitive Systems; Cathleen Norris, Adviser for Educational Computing.

SCHOOL OF MERCHANDISING AND HOSPITALITY MANAGEMENT

Judith C. Forney, Dean.
Christy Crutsinger, Associate Dean.
Lisa Kennon, Adviser.

COLLEGE OF VISUAL ARTS AND DESIGN

Robert W. Milnes, Dean.
Marian O'Rourke-Kaplan, Associate Dean.

Art History and Art Education: Kelly Donahue-Wallace, Chair and Adviser.
Design: Cynthia Mohr, Chair and Adviser.
Studio: Jerry Austin, Chair and Adviser.

UNIVERSITY OF OKLAHOMA

Graduate College

Programs of Study

The University of Oklahoma (OU) combines a mixture of academic excellence, varied social cultures, and a blend of scholarly and creative activities that offer exceptional opportunities for graduate study. Graduate education is offered in ninety-seven master's programs and fifty-five doctoral programs on the Norman campus. At the OU Health Sciences Center (OU-HSC), located 19 miles away in Oklahoma City, graduate degrees are offered in twenty-nine master's programs and sixteen doctoral programs. In addition to the Doctor of Philosophy, OU confers the Doctor of Education, Doctor of Engineering, Doctor of Musical Arts, and Doctor of Public Health.

The University of Oklahoma also offers graduate programs at the Tulsa Graduate Research and Education Center, located approximately 120 miles northeast of the main campus in the city of Tulsa. On the Tulsa campus, OU offers graduate programs in architecture, urban studies, human relations, library and information studies, organization dynamics, public administration, social work, and telecomputing. Interdisciplinary degree programs are available at both the master's and doctoral levels on all three campuses.

Master's degree programs require a minimum of 30 semester hours of course work. Doctoral programs require a minimum of 90 semester hours of course work and are awarded for excellence in research scholarship. Doctoral students are also required to complete general written and oral examinations and defend the results of their dissertation research.

Research Facilities

OU is in the process of establishing a new research campus with a center for genomic and biogenetic research, a field in which OU is a national leader. Research and scholarly activity take place on the landscaped 567-acre main campus in Norman, which houses most of the University's academic colleges and research buildings.

OU provides an exceptional networking and computational environment for students, faculty, and staff members. All graduate students at the University have access to e-mail service, digital libraries, the Internet, a central help desk, campus software and licensing, and many other benefits to enhance their graduate experiences. The academic areas of the campus are part of the University intranet system that provides computer access in residence halls, classrooms, student computer labs, and University offices. The $50-million Sarkeys Energy Center has 200 teaching and research laboratories, as well as classrooms, offices, and the Youngblood Energy Library. There are central advanced analytical services, including the Electron Microprobe Library and Samuel Robert Noble Electron Microscopy Laboratory.

The Norman campus is home to Bizzell Memorial Library, the largest research library in the state, with more than 4.9 million volumes and 63,000 print and electronic serials subscriptions. Special collections include the internationally known History of Science Collections, Western History Collections, and Political Commercial Archives. There are also six specialized branch libraries. The Sam Noble Museum of Natural History opened in 2000. The 195,000-square-foot facility is one of the two largest university-based museums in the world. The museum is home to millions of artifacts, ranging from the world's largest apatosaurus to priceless Native American objects. The Fred Jones Jr. Museum of Art, Catlett Music Center, Donald W. Reynolds Performing Arts Center, and the Rupel L. Jones Theatre provide excellent facilities for graduate studies in the Weitenhoffer Family College of Fine Arts. In 2005, the Fred Jones Jr. Museum of Art opened a new addition, designed by acclaimed architect Hugh Newell Jacobsen of Washington, D.C. Named in honor of Mary and Howard Lester of San Francisco, the wing added more than 34,000 square feet to the earlier 27,000-square-foot building and houses the Weitzenhoffer Collection, the single most important collection of French impressionism ever given to an American public university. The University of Oklahoma Press and *World Literature Today* are two internationally recognized agencies for research and scholarship.

Immediately adjacent to the central campus in Norman is the south campus, site of the 271-acre University of Oklahoma Research Campus. Here, the Stephenson Research and Technology Center provides a home for the OU Supercomputing Center for Education and Research, for interdisciplinary programs in biosciences and bioengineering, and for other research initiatives. The National Weather Center houses the University's research programs in meteorology and the National Oceanic and Atmospheric Administration's (NOAA) weather, research and operations programs. One Partners Place fosters collaboration between research and business enterprises. Also located on the south campus are Andrew M. Coats Hall, housing the College of Law; the OU Foundation; Lloyd Noble Center and parking complex; and the Jimmie Austin University of Oklahoma Golf Course.

The University also has a 1,675-acre north campus, which includes the University Research Park, incubator firms, NOAA's National Severe Storms Laboratory, and the National Weather Service's advanced weather forecasting office.

OU's Health Sciences Center includes a 200-acre complex of educational, research, and health-care facilities operated by nineteen public and private entities along with an 11-acre College of Medicine campus in Tulsa. The OU-HSC is the recipient of an $8.7-million grant, which established the Oklahoma Center for Molecular Medicine. Other research and study units associated with the University include the Biological Station at Lake Texoma, the Earth Sciences Observatory at Leonard near Tulsa, the Aquatic Biology and Fisheries Research Center in Noble and Norman, the Oklahoma Climatological Survey, the Oklahoma Biological Survey, the Oklahoma Archeological Survey, and the Center for the Analysis and Prediction of Storms. The Oklahoma Geological Survey, a state agency responsible to the University of Oklahoma Board of Regents, is also housed on the Norman campus.

Financial Aid

Approximately 40 percent of all graduate students attending the University are employed by their departments as either teaching or research assistants. Salaries for these positions vary from unit to unit, but the University's starting rate in 2008–09 was $12,780.76, for a 0.50 FTE graduate assistant on a 12-month appointment. Tuition waivers and health insurance are available for students holding qualified graduate assistant positions. Numerous funding, scholarship, and fellowship opportunities are also available through the university, individual departments and outside programs.

Cost of Study

Tuition for Oklahoma residents was $277.10 per graduate credit hour in 2008–09; nonresident tuition was $686.80 (nonresidents appointed as at least half-time graduate assistants pay the in-state rate). Additional fees are charged in support of academic programs and/or campus activities. These fees vary, depending on a particular student's major, class schedule and campus of enrollment.

Living and Housing Costs

The University offers several on-campus apartment choices. Additionally, there are a large number of privately owned apartments, duplexes, and houses available in Norman, many of which are served by the local mass transit provider, the Cleveland Area Rapid Transit (CART) system, which is free for OU students.

Student Group

There were more than 26,000 students on the Norman campus and almost 4,000 at the Health Sciences Center enrolled in the 2008 fall semester. More than 3,700 of these students were enrolled in the Graduate College in Norman. Approximately one third of the graduate students at OU are enrolled in doctoral programs. One fifth of the overall student body comes from outside Oklahoma, with students from every state. In addition, international students from almost eighty nations make up nearly 20 percent of the graduate student body.

Location

As part of the dynamic Southwest, Oklahoma benefits from both its rich historic heritage and the vital and modern growth of its metropolitan areas. Although by location a suburb of Oklahoma City, Norman is an independent community with a permanent population of more than 95,000. Norman residents enjoy extensive parks and recreation programs and a 10,000-acre lake and park area. *Money* magazine selected Norman as the nation's sixth best place to live in the 2008 edition of its annual rankings.

The College

The Graduate College is the center of advanced study, research, and creative activity for the University. Faculty members and students share an obligation to achieve greater knowledge in their chosen fields and to present their achievements to the scholarly community. Students were first accepted at the University of Oklahoma in 1892. Graduate instruction was offered as early as 1899, and the first master's degree was conferred in 1900. The Graduate School was formally organized in 1909, and the first doctorate was awarded in 1929.

Applying

Application procedures vary depending on the student's academic background. There is a $40 application fee for U.S. citizens and permanent residents and a $75 application fee for international students. Applications for assistantships, fellowships, and other forms of financial aid should be directed to the academic units. Deadlines vary from department to department, but applications should generally be filed no later than January for students desiring admission in the fall term.

Correspondence and Information

Graduate College
University of Oklahoma
731 Elm Avenue, Room 100
Norman, Oklahoma 73019

Phone: 800-522-0772 (toll-free)
E-mail: gradinfo@ou.edu
Web site: http://gradweb.ou.edu/

AREAS OF INSTRUCTION

The graduate faculty consists of more than 600 active scholars in residence on the Norman campus and another 270 at the Health Sciences Center. In addition, the graduate faculty is supplemented by visiting scholars from other institutions and by specialists from government and industry. The names of the programs and the degrees offered are listed along with the telephone number. The area code for all numbers is 405 except for the nursing program, which is a toll-free number.

Norman Campus

Accounting (M.Ac.): telephone: 325-4221; e-mail: fayres@ou.edu.
Accounting (Ph.D.): telephone: 325-4221; e-mail: rlipe@ou.edu.
Aerospace and Mechanical Engineering (M.S., Ph.D.): telephone: 325-1735; e-mail: rparthasarathy@ou.edu.
Anthropology (M.A., Ph.D.): telephone: 325-2490; e-mail: pgilman@ou.edu.
Architecture (M.Arch., M.L.A., M.R.C.P., M.S.C.A.): telephone: 325-2444; e-mail: nharm@ou.edu.
Art (M.A., M.F.A.): telephone: 325-2691; e-mail: hils@ou.edu.
Botany and Microbiology (M.S., Ph.D.): telephone: 325-6281; e-mail: guno@ou.edu.
Business Administration (M.B.A., Ph.D.): telephone: 325-2931; e-mail: rdauffen@ou.edu.
Chemical Engineering (M.S., Ph.D.): telephone: 325-4366; e-mail: nollert@ou.edu.
Chemistry and Biochemistry (M.S., Ph.D.): telephone: 325-2967; e-mail: grichteraddo@ou.edu.
Civil Engineering and Environmental Science (M.S., Ph.D.): telephone: 325-4253; e-mail: gamiller@ou.edu.
Communication (M.A., Ph.D.): telephone: 325-1571; e-mail: amyjj@ou.edu.
Computer Science (M.S., Ph.D.): telephone: 325-0566; e-mail: dtrytten@ou.edu.
Dance (M.F.A.): telephone: 325-4051; e-mail: jlindberg@ou.edu.
Drama (M.A., M.F.A.): telephone: 325-4021; e-mail: torr@ou.edu.
Economics (M.A., Ph.D.): telephone: 325-2861; e-mail: aholmes@ou.edu.
Education (M.Ed., Ph.D., Ed.D.): telephone: 325-5976; e-mail: gnoley@ou.edu.
Electrical and Computer Engineering (M.S., Ph.D.): telephone: 325-4721; e-mail: sluss@ou.edu.
Engineering (M.S., Ph.D.): telephone: 325-2621; e-mail: landers@ou.edu.
Engineering Physics (M.S., Ph.D.): telephone: 325-3961; e-mail: msantos@ou.edu.
English (M.A., Ph.D.): telephone: 325-6219; e-mail: dmair@ou.edu.
Geography (M.A., Ph.D.): telephone: 325-5325; e-mail: fshelley@ou.edu.
Geology and Geophysics (M.S., Ph.D.): telephone: 325-3253; e-mail: delmore@ou.edu.
Health and Exercise Sciences (M.S.): telephone: 325-2717; e-mail: mgbemben@ou.edu.
History (M.A., Ph.D.): telephone: 325-6058; e-mail: rgriswold@ou.edu.
History of Science (M.A., Ph.D.): telephone: 325-2213; e-mail: slivesey@ou.edu.
Human Relations (M.H.R.): telephone: 325-1756; e-mail: smmendoza@ou.edu.
Industrial Engineering (M.S., Ph.D.): telephone: 325-3721; e-mail: rlshehab@ou.edu.
International Studies (M.A.): telephone: 325-8893; e-mail: rhcox@ou.edu.
Journalism and Mass Communication (M.A., Ph.D.): telephone: 325-5206; e-mail: dcraig@ou.edu.
Landscape Architecture (M.L.A.): telephone: 325-2444; e-mail: schurch@ou.edu.
Liberal Studies (M.L.S.): telephone: 325-1061; e-mail: tgabert@ou.edu.
Library and Information Studies (M.L.I.S.): telephone: 325-3921; e-mail: klatrobe@ou.edu.
Mathematics (M.A., M.S., M.S./M.B.A., Ph.D.): telephone: 325-3971; e-mail: pgoodey@ou.edu.
Meteorology (M.S., Ph.D.): telephone: 325-6097; e-mail: fcarr@ou.edu.
Modern Languages (French, German, Spanish for M.A., Ph.D.): telephone: 325-6181; e-mail: genova@ou.edu.
Music (M.Mus., D.M.A.): telephone: 325-5344; e-mail: iwagner@ou.edu.
Music Education (M.Mus.Educ., Ph.D.): telephone: 325-5344; e-mail: iwagner@ou.edu.
Natural Science (M.Nat.Sci.): telephone: 325-1498; e-mail: eamarek@ou.edu.
Petroleum and Geological Engineering (M.S., Ph.D.): telephone: 325-2921; e-mail: crai@ou.edu.
Philosophy (M.A., Ph.D.): telephone: 325-6491; e-mail: wriggs@ou.edu.
Physics and Astronomy (M.S., Ph.D.): telephone: 325-3961; e-mail: doezema@ou.edu.
Political Science (M.A., Ph.D.): telephone: 325-5517; e-mail: mps@ou.edu.
Professional Meteorology (M.S.): telephone: 325-6097; e-mail: fcarr@ou.edu.
Psychology (M.S., Ph.D.): telephone: 325-4599; e-mail: ldeven@ou.edu.
Public Administration (M.P.A.): telephone: 325-5517; e-mail: alfranklin@ou.edu.
Regional and City Planning (M.R.C.P.): telephone: 325-2399; e-mail: rmarshment@ou.edu.
Social Work (M.S.W.): telephone: 325-2821; e-mail: jimar@ou.edu.
Sociology (M.A., Ph.D.): telephone: 325-1571; e-mail: cstjohn@ou.edu.
Zoology (M.S., Ph.D.): telephone: 325-5271; e-mail: wmatthews@ou.edu.

Health Sciences Campus (e-mail: grad-college@ouhsc.edu)

Biochemistry and Molecular Biology (Ph.D.): telephone: 271-2227.
Biological Psychology (M.S., Ph.D.): telephone: 271-2011.
Biostatistics and Epidemiology (M.S., M.P.H., Ph.D., Dr.P.H.): telephone: 271-2229.
Cell Biology (M.S., Ph.D.): telephone: 271-2377.
Communication Sciences and Disorders (M.S., Ph.D.): telephone: 271-4124.
Health Administration and Policy (M.H.A., M.P.H., M.P.A./M.P.H., M.P.H./M.B.A., M.P.H./J.D., M.P.H./M.D., Dr.P.H.): telephone: 271-2114.
Health Promotion Sciences (M.S., M.P.H., Dr.P.H.): telephone: 271-2017.
Microbiology and Immunology (M.S., Ph.D.): telephone: 271-2133.
Neuroscience (M.S., Ph.D.): telephone: 271-2406.
Nursing (M.S., M.S./M.B.A.): telephone: 877-367-OURN (toll-free).
Nutritional Sciences (M.S.): telephone: 271-2113.
Occupational and Environmental Health (M.S., M.P.H., M.S./J.D., Ph.D., Dr.P.H.): telephone: 271-2070.
Orthodontics (M.S.): telephone: 271-6087.
Pathology (Ph.D.): telephone: 271-2693.
Periodontics (M.S.): telephone: 271-6531.
Pharmaceutical Sciences (M.S., M.S./M.B.A., Ph.D.): telephone: 271-3830.
Physiology (M.S., Ph.D.): telephone: 271-2226.
Radiological Sciences (M.S., Ph.D.): telephone: 271-5132.
Rehabilitation Sciences (M.S.): telephone: 271-2131.

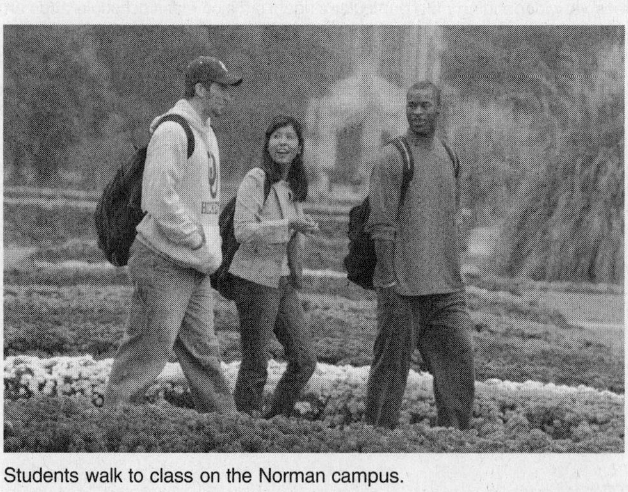

Students walk to class on the Norman campus.

UNIVERSITY OF SAN DIEGO

Graduate Programs

Programs of Study

The University of San Diego (USD) offers programs leading to both doctoral and master's degrees.

The College of Arts and Sciences includes 33 departments and programs with 150 faculty members teaching over 800 graduate and undergraduate classes. Intellectual disciplines within the arts and sciences assist students in developing coherent, integrated and rich world views. The curricula in arts and sciences immerse students in the study of the patterns of human, social, and cultural life. Major concentrations are focused in the humanities, the fine and performing arts, and the social and natural sciences. Graduate degrees offered in the College of Arts and Sciences are: Master of Arts in History, Master of Fine Arts in Dramatic Arts, Master of Arts in International Relations, Master of Science in Marine Science, and Master of Arts in Pastoral Care and Counseling. A Certificate of Advanced Studies in pastoral counseling is offered for licensed health and mental health caregivers. A joint-degree program leading to the J.D./M.A. in international relations is also offered in conjunction with the USD School of Law.

The Joan B. Kroc Institute for Peace and Justice (IPJ) was founded with a generous gift from San Diego philanthropist Joan B. Kroc, who asked that the Institute be a place that not only "talked about peace, but made peace." The 90,000-square-foot building was completed in December of 2001. The Master of Arts in Peace and Justice Studies is an interdisciplinary program emphasizing peace as human development. The goals of the program are: to produce graduates who are capable of relating disciplinary and cross-disciplinary theories of peace and justice to real world problem-solving involving regional and international conflict; to foster scholarly agendas that examine the dynamics of justice and peacebuilding; and to facilitate faculty and student interaction and development across disciplines and academic units at USD, along with outreach to the community and the larger society.

The program takes full advantage of the School of Peace Studies' two institutes: the Joan B. Kroc Institute for Peace and Justice and the Trans-Border Institute.

The School of Business Administration is committed to developing socially responsible leaders and improving global business practice through applied research and innovative, personalized education. As a result, USD School of Business Administration graduates hold professional positions in high technology, new economy corporations, consulting firms, and other entrepreneurial endeavors throughout the Pacific Rim and beyond.

The School of Business Administration offers the M.B.A. and International M.B.A. degrees, with areas of emphasis in corporate social responsibility and sustainable enterprises, finance, international business, management, marketing, new venture management, real estate, and supply chain management. The M.B.A. offers both an evening and full-time option. A dual-degree program is available in conjunction with the Instituto Tecnológico y de Estudios Superiores de Monterrey (ITESM), Mexico. Joint-degree programs leading to the J.D./M.B.A., M.S.N./M.B.A., and J.D./I.M.B.A. are offered in conjunction with the USD School of Law or School of Nursing and Health Science. The School of Business also offers graduate degrees in accountancy, executive leadership, global leadership, real estate, supply chain management, and taxation. The business administration programs are fully accredited by AACSB—The Association to Advance Collegiate Schools of Business—International.

The School of Leadership and Education Sciences has a vision that can be captured in four words: leadership, ethics, reflection, and diversity. Education for human service must have as its foundation a vision for enhancing human dignity and the quality of life. To do so, human service professionals must focus on moral perspectives in their professional and community lives. The faculty members and staff of the School of Leadership and Education Sciences seek to impart this vision to their students. The School of Leadership and Education Sciences offers degrees in the areas of counseling, education, leadership, marital and family therapy, and teaching.

A Doctor of Philosophy (Ph.D.) in leadership studies is also offered by the School of Leadership and Education Sciences.

The Hahn School of Nursing and Health Science is a community of progressive scholars in an intellectually rigorous, research intensive environment. The School educates graduate level nurses to optimize health, promote healing, and alleviate suffering through reflective practice, knowledge generation, service to the community, and leadership at local and global levels. It seeks to deepen our commitment to social justice by influencing health policy and by promoting an ethical approach to nursing characterized by compassion and respect for the dignity of the individual. The Hahn School of Nursing and Health Science offers the following degrees: Accelerated RN to Master's program (post-RN), master's entry program in nursing (for non-RNs), Master of Science in Nursing, Doctor of Philosophy in Nursing, Doctor of Nursing Practice. The School Nurse Health Services Credential, Post-Master's Health Care Systems Certificate, and Post-M.S.N. Nurse Practitioner Certificate are also offered. The M.S.N. program prepares family, pediatric, and adult nurse practitioners and nurse administrators for a variety of health-care settings and prepares nurse case managers for specific client groups in acute, long-term community, and home-health settings.

An outstanding center of legal education with a distinguished faculty, a talented student body, and a dedication to innovation, the University of San Diego School of Law is pursuing and achieving academic excellence and preparing students to practice in the new century. Its 1,100 students share superb credentials, intellectual curiosity and a commitment to learning the law. The demanding but welcoming environment of the law school emphasizes individualized education and services. The USD School of Law is one of only eighty law schools in the country to have a chapter of The Order of the Coif, the most distinguished rank of American law schools. The school is accredited by the American Bar Association and is a member of the Association of American Law Schools. The University of San Diego School of Law offers the degrees of juris doctor (J.D.) and master of laws (LL.M.). Master of laws degrees include specializations in the fields of tax, international law, business and corporate law, and other areas as approved by the law school administration. The law school also offers an LL.M. in comparative law for international lawyers. In addition, there are concurrent degree programs that offer a J.D. degree in conjunction with a master of business administration (M.B.A.), an international master of business administration (I.M.B.A.) or a master of arts in international relations (M.A.).

Research Facilities

Copley Library features more than 714,080 books and 10,450 current journal subscriptions as well as newspapers, government documents, reference books, rare books, and access to many databases. The Media Center has an extensive audiovisual collection. The Legal Research Center in the School of Law maintains a collection in excess of 450,000 volumes.

Financial Aid

For application materials, students should contact the Office of Financial Aid Services, University of San Diego, Hughes Administration Center, 5998 Alcalá Park, San Diego, California 92110-2492 (phone: 619-260-4514 or 800-248-4873 (toll-free); Web site: http://www.sandiego.edu/admissions/financialaid). Students interested in applying for graduate assistantships should contact the graduate schools to which they are applying. Applications for financial aid should be received by April 1 for the fall semester. However, applications are accepted during the year for any portion of the year remaining.

Cost of Study

For the 2008–09 academic year, master's and credential tuition varied between $1120 and $1135 per semester unit, depending upon the program. Doctoral tuition varied between $1135 and $1165 per semester unit.

Living and Housing Costs

Information on graduate housing can be obtained by contacting the Department of Housing and Residence Life, University of San Diego, Mission Crossroads, 5998 Alcalá Park, San Diego, California 92110 (phone: 619-260-4777; Web site: http://www.housing.sandiego.edu).

Student Group

The student population for fall 2008 was approximately 7,832, including 1,593 graduate and 1,120 law students. Students come from all over the U.S., and international students represent about 5 percent of the graduate enrollment.

Student Outcomes

Graduate degree recipients report employment in areas related to their fields of study. For example, in the College of Arts and Sciences, students with international relations degrees secured employment in international business, teaching, and corporate relations; practical theology degrees led to teaching, campus, and catechetical ministries. School of Business graduates were hired in areas such as e-commerce, finance development, project management, and supply chain management. School of Leadership and Education Sciences graduates are employed in teaching at all levels and in counseling, administrative, nonprofit management, and consulting careers. School of Nursing graduates entered clinical, educational, and research settings as well as advanced degree programs.

Location

San Diego, a city of more than 1 million people, is the second-largest city in California and sixth largest in the country. Just 30 minutes north of the border with Mexico, it is situated on a mesa overlooking San Diego bay and offers spectacular views of the Pacific Ocean and surrounding mountains. USD's 180-acre campus provides access to business, cultural, residential, and recreational areas by its proximity to air and rail terminals, city bus stops, and freeways.

The University

USD is an independent, Roman Catholic university that was founded in 1949. The University pursues academic excellence in its teaching, learning, and research to serve the local, national, and international communities. USD possesses the institutional autonomy and integrity necessary to uphold the highest standards of intellectual inquiry and academic freedom. The University comprises six academic schools: the College of Arts and Sciences, the School of Peace Studies, the School of Business, the School of Leadership and Education Sciences, the School of Law, and the School of Nursing and Health Science.

Applying

Application for admission is made to the Office of Graduate Admissions. There are several different applications, depending on the program, which are available online, through the graduate admissions Web site. The Office of Graduate Admissions prefers applications to be submitted online. All applicants must submit the application form, application fee, one official copy of all postsecondary transcripts, three letters of recommendation, and applicable standardized test scores; however, each program has specific requirements for admission. Applicants should consult the programs requirements on the USD Web site for more information. Application deadlines vary. Students should contact Graduate Admissions for program deadlines.

Correspondence and Information

Office of Graduate Admissions
University of San Diego
5998 Alcalá Park
San Diego, California 92110-2492
Phone: 619-260-4524; 800-248-4873 (toll-free)
Fax: 619-260-4158
E-mail: grads@sandiego.edu
Web site: http://www.sandiego.edu/admissions/graduate

Office of Admissions and Financial Aid
School of Law
University of San Diego
Warren Hall, Room 203
5998 Alcalá Park
San Diego, California 92110-2492
Phone: 619-260-4528; 800-248-4873 (toll-free)
E-mail: jdinfo@sandiego.edu
Web site: http://www.sandiego.edu/usdlaw

FACULTY HEADS

DEANS

College of Arts and Sciences: Mary K. Boyd, Ph.D.
School of Business (interim): David Pyke, Ph.D.
School of Law: Kevin Cole, J.D.
School of Leadership and Education Sciences: Paula A. Cordeiro, Ed.D.
School of Nursing and Health Science: Sally Hardin, Ph.D.
School of Peace Studies: Lee Ann Otto, Ph.D.

GRADUATE PROGRAM COORDINATORS

College of Arts and Sciences
Dramatic Arts: Richard Seer, M.F.A.
History: Michael Gonzalez, Ph.D.
International Relations: Emily Edmonds, Ph.D.
Marine Science: Ronald Kaufmann, Ph.D.
Pastoral Care and Counseling: Ellen Colangelo, Ph.D.
Peace and Justice Studies: Lee Ann Otto, Ph.D.

School of Business
Ahler's Center for International Business: Denise Dimon, Ph.D.
Business Administration: Kacy Kilner, M.B.A.

School of Leadership and Education Sciences
American Humanics: Theresa Van Horn, M.A.
Counseling: Susan Zgliczynski, Ph.D.
Leadership Studies: Cheryl Getz, Ed.D.
Learning and Teaching: Judy Mantle, Ph.D.
Marital and Family Therapy: Todd Edwards, Ph.D.
Master of Arts in Teaching: Judy Mantle, Ph.D.
Multiple Subjects Credentials: Judy Mantle, Ph.D.
Single Subject Credentials: Judy Mantle, Ph.D.

School of Nursing and Health Science
Accelerated B.S.N./M.S.N.: Susan Instone, D.N.Sc.
Adult Clinical Nurse Specialist: Susan Instone, D.N.Sc.
Adult Nurse Practitioner: Susan Instone, D.N.Sc.
Doctor of Philosophy (Ph.D.) in Nursing: Patricia Roth, Ph.D.
Family Nurse Practitioner: Susan Instone, D.N.Sc.
Health Care Systems Administration: Susan Instone, D.N.Sc.
Joint M.B.A./M.S.N.: Susan Instone, D.N.Sc.
Master's Entry Program in Nursing: Anita Hunter, Ph.D.
Pediatric Nurse Practitioner: Susan Instone, D.N.Sc.
Post–FNP Urgent/Emergent Care Certificate: Susan Instone, D.N.Sc.
Post–M.S.N. Adult Clinical Nurse Specialist Certificate: Susan Instone, D.N.Sc.
Post–M.S.N. Adult, Family, and Pediatric Nurse Practitioner Certificates: Susan Instone, D.N.Sc.
RN-B.S.N.: Anita Hunter, Ph.D.
Web-Enhanced Family Nurse Practitioner: Susan Instone, D.N.Sc.

UNIVERSITY OF SOUTH ALABAMA

Graduate School

Programs of Study

The Graduate School offers a wide range of graduate degrees, including an interdisciplinary M.S. in environmental toxicology, the M.S. in occupational therapy and in speech and hearing sciences, and an M.H.S. in physician assistant studies (College of Allied Health Professions); the M.A. in communication, English, history, and sociology; the M.S. in biological sciences, mathematics, marine sciences, and psychology; and the Master of Public Administration in the Department of Political Science (College of Arts and Sciences); the Master of Business Administration and the Master of Accounting (Mitchell College of Business); the M.S. in computer and information sciences (School of Computer and Information Sciences); the Master of Education, with concentrations in alternative education, alternative secondary education, early childhood education, educational leadership, educational media, elementary education, health education, physical education, school counseling, school psychometry, and secondary education, as well as a collaborative program; the M.S. in community counseling, exercise technology, instructional design and development, recreation administration, rehabilitation counseling, and therapeutic recreation; and the Educational Specialist degree in counselor education, early childhood education, educational leadership, educational media, elementary education, health education, physical education, secondary education, and special education as well as a collaborative program (College of Education); the M.S. in civil engineering, electrical engineering, chemical engineering, and mechanical engineering (College of Engineering); and the Master of Science in Nursing, with concentrations in adult health nursing, clinical nurse specialist studies, community–mental health nursing, executive and midlevel nursing administration, nursing education, and woman and child health nursing (College of Nursing). The Doctor of Audiology (Au.D.), the Doctor of Nursing Practice (D.N.P.), the Doctor of Physical Therapy, and the Doctor of Pharmacy (collaborative program with Auburn University) are offered. The Ph.D. is offered in communication sciences and disorders, instructional design and development, marine sciences, psychology, and the basic medical sciences, with specializations available in biochemistry, microbiology/immunology, pharmacology, physiology, and structural and cellular biology.

Research Facilities

The graduate program in the basic medical sciences is housed in the College of Medicine, which has the Primate Center, Laboratory of Molecular Biology, Electron Microscopy Center, Mass Spectroscopy Center, Flow Cytometry Center, DNA-Protein Sequencing and Synthesis Center, Sickle-Cell Center, and the Mitchell Cancer Institute.

The graduate program in nursing has access to the clinical facilities of the two University of South Alabama (USA) hospitals, the Mitchell Cancer Institute, and numerous outpatient clinics.

The graduate program in marine sciences is housed in the College of Arts and Sciences, which has the Big Creek Biological Station available during the entire year for field research on reservoirs and streams. The University is a member of the Alabama Marine and Environmental Sciences Consortium and has full access to the consortium's extensive research facilities, which are located on the Gulf of Mexico on Dauphin Island, Alabama. The University is also a member of the Mississippi-Alabama Sea Grant Consortium and the Oak Ridge Associated Universities Consortium.

The Psychological Teaching Clinic is operated in support of the master's and doctoral degree programs in psychology, and the Business Resources Center is available to students in the M.B.A. program. A modern, fully equipped Speech and Hearing Clinic provides research facilities for graduate students in that program.

The University libraries consist of the University (main) Library, USA Archives on the Spring Hill Avenue Campus, the Biomedical Library, two hospital libraries, and library services offered at the Baldwin County campus. The Biomedical Library system serves the information needs of students and faculty members in the Colleges of Medicine, Nursing, and Allied Health Professions, while the main library serves the remaining colleges (Arts and Sciences, Business, Computer and Information Sciences, Continuing Education, Education, and Engineering). Collectively, they provide access to more than 500,000 monographic titles, nearly 3,000 print subscriptions, about 1 million government documents, and an ever-expanding array of Internet-accessible information databases, including full-text article databases that provide electronic access to thousands of additional, unique journal titles or serial publications. The Archives houses one of the largest photographic collections in the region, as well as many important collections, including the papers of Congressmen Jack Edwards and Sonny Callahan, and material from the civil rights era.

Financial Aid

The major University-funded awards are assistantships in master's programs in all fields, with stipends of $6000 to $15,000 for the academic year plus tuition fellowships and remission of out-of-state tuition. Assistants are expected to pay other specific fees. Stipends of $11,000 to $18,000 per year plus tuition fellowships and remission of out-of-state tuition are awarded to students in the Ph.D. programs. Grant-supported awards may offer more generous stipends.

Cost of Study

The basic fees for fall 2008 amounted to $551 per semester plus course fees of $194 per semester hour; a regular student carrying a 9-semester-hour load paid course fees of $1746 per semester, or $3492 for the academic year. Out-of-state rates were $388 per semester hour; a regular student carrying a 9-semester-hour load paid course fees of $3492 per semester, or $6984 for the academic year. There is no tuition fee for Ph.D. students in basic medical sciences.

Living and Housing Costs

The University has extensive housing near the campus for single and married students. Single students may live in dorms, with costs starting at $1372 per semester. A board plan is available with options starting at $1372 per semester. The cost of living in Mobile is slightly below the national average.

Student Group

In 2008–09, the University enrolled 14,279 students, 2,734 of them as graduate students. Fifty-two percent of the graduate students were from Alabama, 36 percent from other states, and 12 percent from other countries.

Student Outcomes

The University of South Alabama awards approximately 650 master's degrees each academic year. Graduates are currently enrolled in Ph.D. programs at Arizona State, Emory, Michigan, Missouri–Columbia, Rutgers, Texas A&M, Washington University in St. Louis, Wisconsin, Yale, and a number of other institutions. Education graduates have found teaching and administrative positions in all fifty states and in Australia, Bahrain, Canada, Germany, Hong Kong, Mexico, Nigeria, Russia, Venezuela, and the Virgin Islands. Others find employment in business and industry, government agencies, and hospitals and clinics throughout the country.

Location

The University is in Mobile, Alabama, a port city and metropolitan area with a population of 476,000. While summers are warm, the overall climate is pleasantly mild. The nearby Gulf of Mexico beaches and extensive water resources of Mobile Bay and its tributaries provide outstanding recreational opportunities.

The University

Founded in 1964, the University comprises the Graduate School; the Colleges of Allied Health Professions, Arts and Sciences, Education, Engineering, Medicine, and Nursing; Mitchell College of Business; the School of Continuing Education and Special Programs; and the School of Computer and Information Sciences. There are three specialized departments: cooperative education, military science, and aerospace studies, and it is the home of the Mitchell Cancer Institute. The University has two major teaching hospitals in Mobile. All facilities are entirely modern.

Applying

The University deadlines for applications and all supporting documents are July 15 for fall, December 1 for spring, and May 1 for summer. Some programs may have earlier deadlines; the requirements for a specific program may be found in the University Bulletin. The admission decision is based on the applicant's previous academic record and on evidence of the ability to pursue work on the graduate level.

Correspondence and Information

For admission information:
Director of Admissions
Meisler Hall 2500
University of South Alabama
Mobile, Alabama 36688-0002
Phone: 800-872-5247 (toll-free)

For the basic medical sciences program:
Graduate Director
Graduate Program in Basic Medical Sciences
College of Medicine (MSB 2366)
University of South Alabama
Mobile, Alabama 36688-0002
Phone: 251-460-6153

For other graduate programs:
Dean of the Graduate School
Mobile Townhouse 222
University of South Alabama
Mobile, Alabama 36688-0002
Phone: 251-460-6310
E-mail: dpatters@usouthal.edu
Web site: http://www.southalabama.edu

DEANS AND DIRECTORS

Graduate School: B. Keith Harrison, Dean; Ph.D., Missouri.
College of Allied Health Professions: Richard E. Talbott, Dean; Ph.D., Oklahoma. Julio Turrens, Director of Graduate Studies; Ph.D., Buenos Aires (Argentina).
College of Arts and Sciences: G. David Johnson, Dean; Ph.D., Southern Illinois at Carbondale. S. L. Varghese, Director of Graduate Studies; Ph.D., Yale.
Mitchell College of Business: Carl Moore, Dean; Ph.D., Alabama. John E. Gamble, Director of Graduate Studies; Ph.D., Alabama.
School of Computer and Information Sciences: Alec F. Yasinsac, Dean; Ph.D., Virginia. Roy Daigle, Director of Graduate Studies; Ph.D., Georgia.
College of Education: Richard L. Hayes, Dean; Ed.D., Boston University. Abigail Baxter, Director of Graduate Studies; Ph.D., Vanderbilt.
College of Engineering: John W. Steadman, Dean; Ph.D., Colorado State. Thomas G. Thomas Jr., Director of Graduate Studies; Ph.D., Alabama in Huntsville.
College of Medicine: Samuel J. Strada, Dean; Ph.D., Vanderbilt. Ronald D. Balczon, Director of Graduate Studies; Ph.D., Baylor.
College of Nursing: Debra C. Davis, Dean; D.S.N., Alabama at Birmingham. Rosemary Rhodes, Director of Graduate Studies; D.N.S., LSU.

A lecture at sea for marine science students at the University of South Alabama.

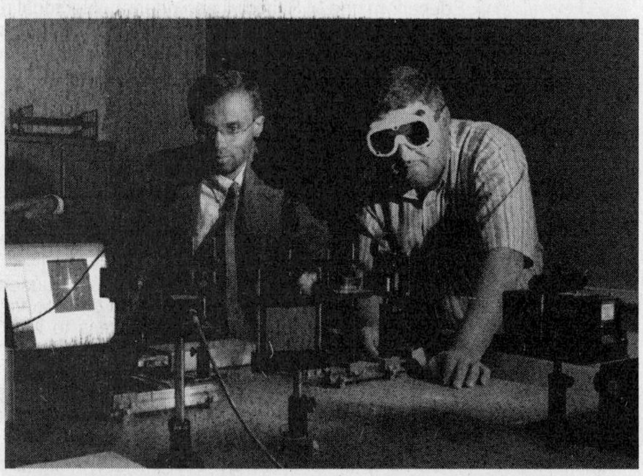

Ultrafast optical processor used for pattern recognition and tracking applications developed in the electrical and computer engineering department at USA.

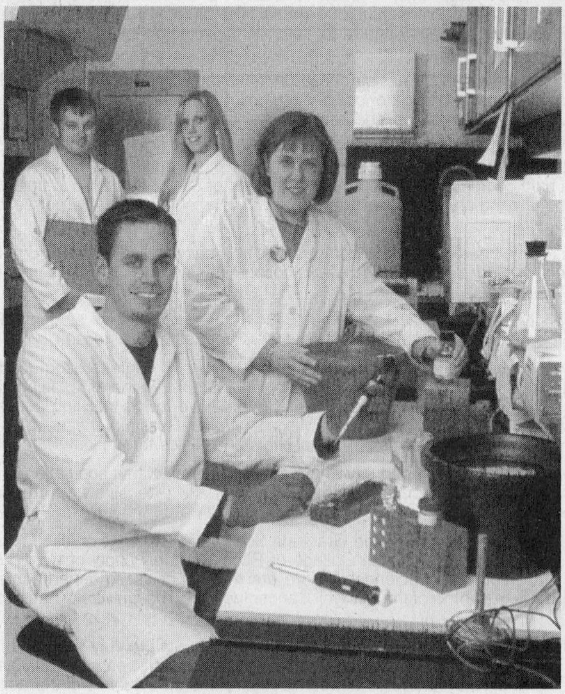

USA basic medical science researchers at work.

UNIVERSITY OF SOUTH CAROLINA

The Graduate School

Programs of Study

The University of South Carolina is the state's flagship university with a comprehensive offering of degree programs including 72 doctoral programs, 134 master's and specialist programs, and 20 certificate programs (a complete list can be found at http://gradschool.sc.edu/graduate_programs.asp). Doctoral degree specializations with significant enrollment are offered in anthropology, biological sciences, biomedical science, business administration, chemistry, communication sciences and disorders, comparative literature, education fields (counselor education, curriculum and instruction, educational administration, education psychology, language and literacy, and physical education), engineering (biomedical, chemical, civil, computer, electrical, mechanical, and nuclear), English, exercise science, geography, geology, history, linguistics, marine science, mass communications, mathematics, several music fields, nursing fields, pharmaceutical science, philosophy, physical therapy, physics, political science, psychology (clinical/community, experimental, and school) public health areas (biostatistics, environmental health sciences, epidemiology, health promotion and education, and health services policy and management), social work, sociology, and statistics.

Master's degrees are offered in all the above fields. Students can also earn master's degrees in accounting, art and theater areas, creative writing, criminology and criminal justice, earth resources management, genetic counseling, hospitality and sport management, human resources, international business, several language areas, library and information science, journalism, nurse anesthesia, professional science master's, public administration, rehabilitation counseling, retailing, and teaching areas.

Research Facilities

The University of South Carolina is one of only twenty-three public universities recognized by the Carnegie Foundation for very high research activity and curricular engagement, outreach, and partnerships. The University's Office of Research and Economic Development provides an extensive Web site to highlight the University of South Carolina's research resources, equipment and facilities (RREF) at http://www.sc.edu/rref/. Active research focus areas include behavioral sciences, bioinfomatics, biomedical sciences, children and families, computing, engineering, environmental sciences, future fuels, health disparities, liberal arts, mathematics and statistics, nanotechnology, physical activity, physical sciences, and social sciences. The University's Thomas Cooper Library provides access to more than 7.5 million volumes, periodicals, microfilm entries, and manuscripts in the University system through the USCAN integrated information system. Significant research centers and institutes include the Baruch Institute for Marine Biology and Coastal Research, the Institute for Biological Research and Technology, the Center for Family in Society, the Southeast Manufacturing Technology Center, the Research Division of the Moore School of Business Administration, the Institute for International Studies, and the Institute for Southern Studies.

Financial Aid

Fellowships are available in many departments. Graduate research and teaching assistantships are available in most departments and provide competitive stipends and full or partial tuition remission. Information about fellowships and assistantships should be obtained from the department of interest.

Cost of Study

Academic fees for full-time study are $4894 per semester for residents and $10,540 per semester for nonresidents. Part-time resident academic fees are $484 per hour; part-time nonresident academic fees are $1028 per hour. Academic fees for students in the health professions and business differ from the above-stated charges. Optional activity, athletic, and health-services fees are based on the student's full- or part-time status.

Living and Housing Costs

Graduate students normally live in off-campus housing, but there are limited housing opportunities on campus for married or single students. The Off-Campus Student Services Office assists students in locating off-campus housing. For complete information see the University's housing Web site at http://www.housing.sc.edu/.

Student Group

Graduate enrollment averages about 6,500. Approximately 32 percent of the graduate students were from out-of-state, representing every state and ninety other countries. The University of South Carolina is the state's flagship university, with the highest percentage of African-American student enrollment in the nation. International students comprise 29 percent of doctoral enrollment; the Office of International Student Services provides support for international students prior to arrival and throughout their study.

Student Outcomes

Research funding at the University of South Carolina reached a record $210.3 million in fiscal year 2009, providing graduate students with increased research opportunities. Doctoral and master's program graduates are nationally competitive for academic, research, and leadership positions in national and multinational corporations, public and private institutions, and government agencies, and are actively recruited on campus.

Location

The University is located in downtown Columbia near the Capitol and the state government complex. Columbia, with a population of 725,000 residents within the metropolitan area, offers a wide range of cultural, sports, and entertainment attractions. Boasting an ideal climate with an average temperature of 65 degrees, the city is geographically located in the center of the state within a 1½ to 3 hours drive to the ocean and the mountains.

The University

The University was founded in 1801, the first state college to be supported by annual public appropriations. Some of the most striking architecture of the region can be found on the campus. In support of its research initiatives, the University has launched the first phase of its research campus, Innovista, a live, learn, and work enterprise that will eventually house 8 million square feet of research buildings, residences, and retail and restaurant space.

Applying

Applications must be submitted online (http://www.gradschool.sc.edu/apply.htm) and require a nonrefundable fee of $50. Application requirements and deadlines vary; please check the appropriate college, school, or department Web site (http://gradschool.sc.edu/graduate_programs.asp). Detailed admission information is given in the *Graduate Studies Bulletin available online at http://bulletin.sc.edu/index.php.*

Correspondence and Information

The Graduate School
University of South Carolina
901 Sumter Street
Byrnes, Suite 304
Columbia, South Carolina 29208

Phone: 803-777-4243
Fax: 803-777-2972
E-mail: gradapp@mailbox.sc.edu
Web site: http://www.gradschool.sc.edu/

DEANS OF COLLEGES AND HEADS OF DEPARTMENTS

Graduate School: Stephen Kresovich, Vice President for Research and Graduate Education.
James Buggy, Interim Dean.
Nancy P. Zimmerman, Associate Dean for Academic Affairs.
Dale Moore, Director of Graduate Admissions.

Moore School of Business: Hildy Teegen, Dean.

College of Education: Les Sternberg, Dean.
Department of Educational Leadership and Policies: Ken Stevenson, Chair.
Department of Educational Studies: Robert Johnson, Chair.
Department of Instruction and Teacher Education: Diane Stephens, Chair.
Department of Physical Education: Karen French, Chair.

College of Engineering and Information Technology: Harry J. Ploehn, Interim Dean.
Department of Chemical Engineering: Mike Matthews, Chair.
Department of Civil and Environmental Engineering: David Waugh, Interim Chair.
Department of Computer Science and Engineering: Duncan Buell, Chair.
Department of Electrical Engineering: Tangali S. Sudarshan, Chair.
Department of Mechanical Engineering: Jamil A. Khan, Interim Chair.

School of the Environment: Madilyn M. Fletcher, Director.

College of Hospitality, Retail, and Sport Management: Brian L. Mihalik, Dean.
School of Hotel, Restaurant, and Tourism Management: Charles Partlow, Chair.
Department of Retailing: Marianne Bickle, Chair.
Department of Sport and Entertainment Management: Tom H. Regan, Chair.

College of Arts and Sciences: Mary Anne Fitzpatrick, Dean.
Department of Anthropology: Ann E. Kingsolver, Chair.
Department of Art: Thorne Compton, Chair.
Department of Biology: Charles R. Lovell, Chair.
Department of Chemistry and Biochemistry: John H. Dawson, Chair.
Program in Comparative Literature: Marja Warehime, Director.
Department of Criminology and Criminal Justice: Shane R. Thye, Chair.
Department of Earth and Ocean Sciences: Venkataraman Lakshmi, Chair.
Department of English Language and Literature: William E. Rivers, Interim Chair.
Department of Geography: Will Graf, Chair.
Department of History: Lacy K. Ford, Chair.
Department of Languages, Literatures, and Cultures: Marja Warehime, Chair.
Program in Linguistics: Robin Morris, Director.
Program in Marine Science: Robert C. Thunell, Director.
Department of Mathematics: Jerrold R. Griggs, Chair.
Department of Philosophy: Anne Bezuidenhout, Chair.
Department of Physics and Astronomy: Chaden Djalali, Chair.
Department of Political Science: Daniel R. Sabia, Chair.
Department of Psychology: John E. Richards, Interim Chair.
Department of Sociology: Lala Carr Steelman, Chair.
Department of Statistics: Don Edwards, Chair.
Department of Theatre, Speech, and Dance: Jim Hunter, Chair.
Program in Women's and Gender Studies: Drucilla K. Barker, Director.

Law School: Walter F. Pratt Jr., Dean.

College of Mass Communications and Information Studies: Charles Bierbauer, Dean.
School of Journalism and Mass Communications: Carol J. Pardun, Director.
School of Library and Information Science: Samantha K. Hastings, Director.

School of Medicine: Richard A. Hoppmann, Dean.

School of Music: Tayloe Harding, Dean

College of Nursing: Peggy Hewlett, Dean.

College of Pharmacy: Randall Rowen, Dean.

Arnold School of Public Health: G. Thomas Chandler, Dean.
Department of Communication Sciences and Disorders: Elaine Frank, Chair.
Department of Environmental Health Science: Dwayne E. Porter, Interim Chair.
Department of Epidemiology and Biostatistics: Robert McKeown, Chair.
Department of Exercise Science: J. Larry Durstine, Chair.
Department of Health Services Policy and Management: Janice C. Probst, Interim Chair.
Department of Health Promotion, Education, and Behavior: Edward Frongillo, Chair.

College of Social Work: Dennis Poole, Dean.

The University of South Carolina is committed to a policy of affirmative action that ensures equal opportunity in education and employment to all qualified persons regardless of race, sex, religion, creed, handicap, disability, veteran status, national origin, or ancestry.

UNIVERSITY OF TULSA

Graduate School

Programs of Study

The Graduate School offers graduate study leading to master's degrees in thirty programs and to Ph.D.'s in nine programs. Interdisciplinary degree programs are also available.

The doctoral degree conferred is the Doctor of Philosophy, with specialization in biological science, chemical engineering, clinical psychology, computer science, English language and literature, geosciences, industrial/organizational psychology, mechanical engineering, and petroleum engineering.

Master's degrees conferred are the Master of Arts (M.A.), Master of Business Administration (M.B.A.), Master of Engineering (M.E.), Master of Fine Arts (M.F.A.), Master of Science (M.S.), Master of Science in Engineering (M.S.E.), Master of Science in Finance (M.S.F.), Master of Science in Math/Science Education (M.S.M.S.E.), Master of Taxation (M.Tax.), and Master of Teaching Arts (M.T.A.).

The master's degree is offered in anthropology, art, biochemistry, biological science, business administration, chemical engineering, chemistry, clinical psychology, computer science, education (with certification in elementary education and secondary education), electrical engineering, engineering physics, English language and literature, finance, fine art, geosciences, history, industrial/organizational psychology, mathematics, math/science education, mechanical engineering, petroleum engineering, physics, speech-language pathology, and taxation (online). Interdisciplinary joint-degree programs include a M.S.F./M.S. in applied mathematics program and an M.B.A./M.S.F. program. Joint master's/Juris Doctor (J.D.) degree programs leading to J.D./M.A. degrees with specialization in anthropology, clinical psychology, English language and literature, history, and industrial/organizational psychology are offered in conjunction with the College of Law; the J.D./M.S. degree in biological science, computer science, and geosciences; a J.D./M.Tax. degree; a J.D./M.S.F. degree; and the J.D./M.B.A. degree are also offered.

Research Facilities

The University libraries house more than 3 million books, bound periodical volumes, microforms, state and federal depository government documents, sound and video recordings, CD-ROM abstracts and indexes, and maps. McFarlin Library, the central facility, orders and catalogs 10,000 new titles each year, subscribes to 2,200 periodicals in paper and fiche formats, and, by way of an online service, provides full-text access to 2,000 more (as well as indexing for a further 10,000). A computerized catalog maintains both bibliographic and circulation records, which currently number more than 650,000. It can be accessed through more than eighty-five terminals in the libraries or remotely by way of campus networks and personal computers. It also acts as a gateway to other databases and, via the Internet, to several hundred library catalogs in this country and abroad. The libraries are also linked electronically to two national utilities (OCLC and RLIN) to facilitate an active interlibrary loan program that borrows about 10,000 items each year from other libraries and loans a slightly smaller number to them.

The College of Law library contains 280,000 volumes, with extensive holdings in natural resources and energy law. Special collections in three areas are recognized internationally for their quality and distinctiveness: twentieth-century American, British, and Irish literature (with holdings that include comprehensive collections for Faulkner, Graves, Joyce, Lawrence, Whitman, and many other writers and 3,500 feet of manuscripts, among them the papers of Richard Ellmann, Richard Murphy, 2001 Nobel laureate V. S. Naipaul, Jean Rhys, and Rebecca West); Native American history and law, with exceptional strength for the Cherokee, Creek, and Osage; and holdings related to petroleum exploration and production in all parts of the world, among them the source documents abstracted for *Petroleum Abstracts,* which has been published at the University since 1960.

The University maintains a robust fiber-optic network that interconnects computing and information resources in all of the University's buildings. The University also offers a ubiquitous wireless network, giving campus community members access to the Internet and campus computing resources while anywhere on campus, either indoors or outside. Centralized and decentralized computing services are provided by numerous servers that are networked to a full complement of peripheral devices. The servers are used for a variety of instructional and research activities, which include accessing the University's library database and other worldwide information resources that are available on the Internet. McFarlin Library reflects the convergence of traditional print and electronic media and provides a cyber café, an open-computing student laboratory, an information/research laboratory, a training laboratory, and a faculty development center. Modern student computing laboratories and high-technology classrooms are located in the College of Arts and Sciences, the College of Business Administration, the College of Engineering and Natural Sciences, and the College of Law. The College of Engineering and Natural Sciences has numerous engineering workstations to support the computer-intensive applications required by scientists and engineers.

Financial Aid

A number of assistantships and fellowships are available for full-time graduate students. The stipends vary according to the amount of work required and the experience of the student. Most appointments provide 9 credit hours of tuition scholarship per semester in addition to the monthly stipend. Other scholarships are available through the sponsorship of corporations, businesses, and individuals. Recipients of these scholarships are often chosen only from applicants who are interested in fields prescribed by the donors. Government-directed student aid is available through the Office of Financial Services.

Cost of Study

All new graduate students at the University of Tulsa graduate school paid tuition at the rate of $856 per credit hour in 2008–09.

Living and Housing Costs

The University offers a variety of housing and dining options, several of which are specifically tailored to the needs of single as well as married graduate students. These options include modern market-quality apartments designated specifically for graduate and law students. Room and board for two semesters in a double-occupancy room averaged $7600 in 2008–09.

Student Group

Approximately 640 of the University's 4,200 students are in the Graduate School; women make up more than 40 percent of that population. More than 10 percent of graduate students are members of minority groups. International students from dozens of nations constitute more than 35 percent of the graduate population.

Location

The University of Tulsa is located in a residential neighborhood just 2 miles from a renovated downtown area. Tulsa has a population of more than 700,000. Symphonies, theater, art galleries, opera, ballet, museums, and outdoor sports are all accessible to students. Guest performers and lecturers regularly visit the campus and the city.

The University

The University was founded in 1894 as Henry Kendall College in Muskogee, Indian Territory. Moving to Tulsa in 1907, the University of Tulsa was chartered in 1921. The University of Tulsa began offering graduate course work in 1933 and was fully accredited through the doctoral level by 1972.

Applying

Applicants for admission to the graduate school must complete a Graduate School application and provide official transcripts, three letters of recommendation, and all appropriate test scores. Admitted students may apply for need-based financial aid by contacting the Financial Services Office. Full-time admitted students who wish to apply for a graduate assistantship must complete a graduate assistantship application.

Correspondence and Information

Dean of the Graduate School
University of Tulsa
800 South Tucker Drive
Tulsa, Oklahoma 74104

Phone: 918-631-2336
800-882-4723 (toll-free)
E-mail: grad@utulsa.edu
Web site: http://www.utulsa.edu/graduate

FACULTY HEADS

GRADUATE SCHOOL
Janet Haggerty, Dean.
Richard Redner, Associate Dean.
John Bury, Assistant Dean.

College of Arts and Sciences
Thomas Benediktson, Dean.
Anthropology: Lamont Lindstrom, Chairperson; George Odell, Adviser.
Art: Susan Dixon, Chairperson; Whitney Forsyth, Adviser.
Clinical Psychology: Judy Berry, Chairperson; Elana Newman, Adviser.
Education: Thomas Benediktson, Chairperson; Tao Wang, Adviser.
English Language and Literature: Lars Engle, Chairperson; Sean Latham, Adviser.
History: Thomas Buoye, Chairperson; Christine Ruane, Adviser.
Industrial/Organizational Psychology: Judy Berry, Chairperson; John McNulty, Adviser.
Speech-Language Pathology: Paula Cadogan, Chairperson; Mary Moody, Adviser.

College of Business Administration
Gale Sullenberger, Dean.
Stephen Rockwell, Director of Graduate Business Programs and Adviser.
Accounting: Karen Cravens, Director.
Finance: Roger P. Bey, Chairperson.
Management: Ralph Jackson, Chairperson.
Management Information Systems: Karen Cravens, Director.
Marketing: Ralph Jackson, Chairperson.
Operations Management: Roger P. Bey, Chairperson.

College of Engineering and Natural Sciences
Steven Bellovich, Dean.
Biochemistry: Dale Teeters, Chairperson; Robert Sheaff, Adviser.
Biological Science: Estelle Levetin, Chairperson; Harrington Wells, Adviser.
Chemical Engineering: Geoffrey Price, Chairperson; Laura Ford, Adviser.
Chemistry: Dale Teeters, Chairperson and Adviser.
Computer Science: Roger Wainwright, Chairperson; Rose Gamble, Adviser.
Electrical Engineering: Gerald Kane, Chairperson; Heng-Ming Tai, Adviser.
Geosciences: Bryan Tapp, Chairperson; Peter Michael, Adviser.
Mathematics: Roger Wainwright, Chairperson; Christian Constanda, Adviser.
Mathematics and Science Education: Robert Howard and Tao Wang, Program Coordinators.
Mechanical Engineering: Edmund Rybicki, Chairperson; Siamack Shirazi, Adviser.
Petroleum Engineering: Mohan Kelkar, Chairperson; Holden Zhang, Adviser.
Physics and Engineering Physics: George Miller, Chairperson and Adviser.

RESEARCH OPPORTUNITIES

Anthropological research projects range from archaeological research investigating Stone Age sites in Jordan to Pithouse and Pueblo sites in the southwestern United States and northwestern Mexico. The department is home to the journal *Lithic Technology.*

Current projects in **biochemistry** address the biochemical basis of human diseases such as cancer and neurodegeneration, new diagnostic tools using nanotechnology, and detecting heavy metals or other toxins in soil and groundwater. There are also active collaborations with chemists to develop and characterize novel antitumor drugs.

Research in **biological science** includes projects in molecular, cell, environmental, and comparative biology. Projects in molecular and cell biology include studies of lymphocyte development, glycobiology, development of the mammalian nervous system, molecular and developmental genetics, and structure-function relationships of microbial light harvesting proteins. Projects in environmental biology include behavioral ecology of colonial birds, population and pollination biology of bees, and microbial population biology. Projects in comparative biology include the evolutionary biology of reptilian viviparity, molecular systematics of algae and fish, aerobiology, and mammalian and invertebrate reproductive biology. The Mervin Bovaird Center for Molecular Biology and Biotechnology augments and promotes graduate training in molecular techniques.

Research in **chemical engineering** is largely experimentally based, involving laboratory and pilot-scale programs. A major focus of activities is in the environmental field. Areas of current research include reaction kinetics and catalysis, supercritical fluids, multiphase chemical reactors and multiphase flows, capillary hydrodynamics, combustion, biological treatment of hazardous wastes and bioremediation of petroleum hydrocarbons, petroleum and natural gas processing, thermodynamics and phase equilibria, fuel-cell technology, and particulate science.

Chemistry research involves synthetic, organic, bioanalytic, environmental, and natural product chemistry; solution kinetics; molecular protective films; and nanotechnology.

Computer science faculty members are involved in research related to network and information systems security, genetic algorithms, medical imaging, parallel and scientific computation, artificial intelligence, distributed artificial intelligence, software engineering, and networking. The Center for Information Security is a National Security Agency "Center of Excellence" and the home of the University's Cyber Corps and Information Assurance programs.

Research opportunities are available in **English language and literature.** The *James Joyce Quarterly, Tulsa Studies in Women's Literature,* and *Nimrod* are published at the University, and the department collaborates with Brown University on the Modernist Journals Project.

Geoscience research is balanced in areas of petroleum exploration/production and environmental science, including clastic sedimentology, petroleum seismology, seismic stratigraphy, structural geology, geochemistry, and biogeoscience. There are also active programs in marine geology, including the petrogenesis of midocean ridge basalts.

Research in **history** concerns early American and Native American history, Russian social and cultural history, late Imperial China, comparative urban history of the Americas, and American diplomacy.

Mechanical engineering research is being conducted in thermal fluid sciences, solid mechanics, erosion/corrosion, composite materials, biologically inspired materials, fatigue, alternative-energy vehicles, manufacturing, thermal spray coatings, and residual stress analysis.

Petroleum engineering research opportunities derive from nine continuing, cooperative industry/University energy-related projects, including artificial lift, drilling, fluid flow, horizontal well completion, reservoir studies and exploitation, hydrates flow, high-viscosity multiphase flow, separation technology, and paraffin deposition. Other petroleum-related projects include research on oil and gas production systems and phase behavior of CO_2 and heavy oils.

Research in **physics** and **engineering physics** draws on active research in fluid dynamics, artificial lift technology, carbon nanotubes, nanotechnology, optics, solid-state physics, and plasma physics theory.

Research in psychology involves issues in theory and measurement of personality and social behavior as applied to problems in clinical and organizational psychology. Active areas of research in **clinical psychology** include trauma studies, randomized control trials of exposure treatments, pain modulation, social-cognitive processing of delusional disorders, psychological assessments, and MMPI studies. **Industrial/organizational psychology** projects currently focus on assessing personality disorders in the workplace, leadership, and managerial performance.

Speech-language pathology research includes neurogenic communication disorders, fluency disorders, aphasia, speech articulation problems, swallowing impairments, and delayed language and literacy development.

VILLANOVA UNIVERSITY

Graduate Studies–Liberal Arts and Sciences

Programs of Study

Master's degrees and certificates are offered in the following areas: biology, communication, computer science, counseling and human relations (community, elementary, and secondary), education (elementary, educational leadership, and secondary), English, Hispanic studies, history, human resource development, liberal studies, mathematics, political science, public administration, theater, and theology. Master's degrees only are offered in the following areas: applied statistics; chemistry; classical studies; criminology, law, and society; psychology; and software engineering. Doctoral degrees are offered in the area of philosophy only.

The academic year consists of two semesters. The first semester begins in mid-August and ends in mid-December. The second semester begins in mid-January and ends in mid-May. In addition, there are three summer sessions—two successive monthlong day sessions and a third evening session that is offered over a two-month period.

Research Facilities

The University library contains more than 780,000 volumes and 5,600 current periodicals. Special library holdings include the collection of the Augustinian Historical Institute and an extensive collection of works in contemporary Continental philosophy.

The Office of University Information Technologies provides data and voice communication, computing services, and access to remote computing and information services over the Internet; offers noncredit seminars and workshops on popular computer software and the use of the Villanova phone system; and maintains state-of-the-art computer labs for students on campus.

Financial Aid

Graduate assistantships are awarded on a competitive basis. The assistantship stipend begins at approximately $13,100 in 2009–10 and carries with it a waiver of all tuition and academic fees. A few research fellowships are also awarded each year. A number of tuition scholarships are available; they provide a waiver of all tuition and academic fees.

In addition, the office of the director of financial aid administers the Federal Stafford Student Loan Program.

Cost of Study

Graduate tuition ranges from approximately $630 to $700 per credit hour in 2009–10. In addition, there is a University fee of $30 each semester.

Living and Housing Costs

The University does not maintain accommodations for graduate students, but second-year students are eligible for positions as resident counselors in the dormitories. The area has a wide selection of living quarters that are convenient to the campus.

Student Group

Approximately 2,200 graduate students were enrolled for the fall 2008 term, of whom 985 were in liberal arts and sciences programs. Total University enrollment is approximately 12,000, including 7,577 full-time undergraduates, 1,000 part-time evening (undergraduate and continuing studies) students, and 1,000 students in the School of Law. There are about equal numbers of men and women graduate students.

Location

Located in the heart of the Delaware Valley's Main Line, the University occupies more than 200 handsomely landscaped acres in the town of Villanova, 12 miles west of Philadelphia. The location combines the advantages of a tranquil suburban setting with proximity to a large metropolitan city that is known for its outstanding contributions in the areas of culture, education, history, recreation, religion, and sport.

The University

Villanova University is a private institution that was founded in 1842 by the Augustinian Fathers. Graduate programs were first administered separately in 1931. Currently, there are six academic units in addition to Graduate Studies—the Colleges of Arts and Sciences, Commerce and Finance, Engineering, and Nursing; the Division of Part-Time Studies; and the School of Law.

Applying

Application forms and the *Graduate Studies Viewbook* may be obtained from the Graduate Studies Office or online at http://www.gradartsci.villanova.edu. Due dates for submission of credentials vary by program. In addition to forwarding the completed application form and official college transcripts, applicants must also arrange to have three letters of recommendation submitted on their behalf. There is an application fee of $50. GRE scores are required by some departments. Descriptions of programs and procedures are found in the *Graduate Studies Viewbook* and on the University's Web site.

Correspondence and Information

Dean, Graduate Studies
College of Liberal Arts and Sciences
Villanova University
800 Lancaster Avenue
Villanova, Pennsylvania 19085-1688

Phone: 610-519-7090
E-mail: gradinformation@villanova.edu
Web site: http://www.gradartsci.villanova.edu/

THE FACULTY

Adele Lindenmeyr, Dean; Ph.D., Princeton.

Listed below are the chairpersons and/or directors for the University's graduate programs.

Master's Programs
Applied Statistics: Douglas Norton, Ph.D., Minnesota.
Biology: Russell M. Gardner, Ph.D., Indiana.
Chemistry: William Scott Kassel, Ph.D., Florida.
Classical Studies (Department of Humanities and Augustinian Traditions): Gary Meltzer, Ph.D., Yale.
Communication: Bryan Crable, Ph.D., Purdue Calumet.
Computer Science: Robert E. Beck, Ph.D., Pennsylvania.
Counseling (Community, Elementary, Secondary): John H. Durnin, Ph.D., Pennsylvania.
Criminology, Law, and Society (Department of Sociology and Criminal Justice): Thomas Arvanites, Ph.D., SUNY at Albany.
Education: John H. Durnin, Ph.D., Pennsylvania.
Educational Leadership: John H. Durnin, Ph.D., Pennsylvania.
Elementary and Secondary Graduate Teacher Education: Connie Titone, Ed.D., Harvard.
English: Evan Radcliffe, Ph.D., Cornell.
Hispanic Studies (Department of Modern Languages and Literature): Mercedes Juliá, Ph.D., Chicago.
History: Marc S. Gallicchio, Ph.D., Temple.
Human Resource Development: David F. Bush, Ph.D., Purdue.
Liberal Studies: Eugene McCarraher, Ph.D., Rutgers.
Mathematics: Douglas Norton, Ph.D., Minnesota.
Political Science: Interim Chair: A. Maria Toyoda, Ph.D., Georgetown.
Psychology: Thomas C. Toppino, Ph.D., New Mexico.
Public Administration: Christine Palus, Ph.D., North Carolina.
Theatre: Rev. Richard G. Cannuli, O.S.A., M.F.A., Pratt.
Theology: Bernard Prusak, Ph.D., Lateran (Rome).

Ph.D. Program
Philosophy: John Carvalho, Ph.D., Duquesne.

WASHINGTON UNIVERSITY IN ST. LOUIS

Graduate School of Arts and Sciences

Programs of Study

The Graduate School of Arts and Sciences offers more than thirty programs leading to the doctorate (Ph.D.) and to the Master of Arts (A.M.). In addition, programs are offered leading to the Master of Arts in Education (M.A.Ed.), Master of Arts in Teaching (M.A.T.), Master of Fine Arts in Writing (M.F.A.W.), Master in Music (M.M.), and Master of Liberal Arts (M.L.A.).

Opportunities for combining a degree available through the Graduate School of Arts and Sciences with a degree from one of the University's professional schools (business, engineering, law, medicine) are also available.

Research Facilities

The Washington University community is served by a network of libraries designed to meet the instructional and research needs of faculty members, students, and staff members. Washington University libraries contain the largest collection of any private academic library system between the Mississippi River and California. John M. Olin Library, the central University library, and twelve school and departmental libraries house many important and unique collections and provide state-of-the-art computerized information retrieval. The combined holdings include more than 3 million books and bound periodicals, 18,000 current serial subscriptions, and access to thousands of electronic journals and databases. For more information, students can visit http://library.wustl.edu.

More than thirty centers and institutes provide a spectrum of research opportunities. They include the Center for Air Pollution Impact and Trend Analysis; Center for the Study of American Business; Center for American Indian Studies; Business, Law, and Economics Center; Arts and Sciences Computing Center; Institutes for Biomedical Computing; McDonnell Center for Cellular and Molecular Neurobiology; Construction Management Center; Carolyne Roehm Electronic Media Center; Center for Engineering Computing; Center for Genetics in Medicine; McDonnell Center for Studies of Higher Brain Function; Center for the History of Freedom; Office of International Studies; International Writers Center; Center for the Study of Islamic Societies and Civilizations; Management Center; Fred Gasche Laboratory for Microstructured Materials Technologies; Markey Center for Research in Molecular Biology of Human Disease; Center for Optimization and Semantic Control; Center for Plant Science and Biotechnology; Center for Political Economy; Center for the Study of Public Affairs; Center for Robotics and Automation; Social Work Research Development Center; McDonnell Center for Space Sciences; Center for the Application of Information Technology; and Urban Research and Design Center.

Financial Aid

The majority of full-time students receive financial support. Financial assistance in the form of scholarships, fellowships, and traineeships is offered annually on a competitive basis through the Graduate School from government, private, or endowed sources. Also available are scholarships, teaching assistantships, research assistantships, and, in applied social sciences, clinical internships; grants and fellowships in national competition; and loans. Specific information may be obtained from the departmental or administrative unit to which the student intends to apply.

Cost of Study

Tuition for the 2009–10 academic year for the Graduate School is $37,800. The cost per credit unit is $1575.

Living and Housing Costs

Many graduate students live in University-owned apartments, some with data connections and shuttle bus service. Listing information for these units as well as non-University housing is available through the University's Apartment Referral Service (http://offcampushousing.wustl.edu/). Rent ranges from $450 to $950 per month for one- to three-bedroom units, respectively.

Student Group

Of the more than 14,000 people attending Washington University, more than 5,000 are graduate students; approximately 2,000 of them are enrolled in the Graduate School of Arts and Sciences. Students come to Washington University from all fifty states and more than eighty international locations.

Location

Washington University has two campuses that lie at opposite ends of Forest Park (one of the largest municipal parks in the nation). The campuses are approximately 5 miles west of downtown St. Louis. The Danforth campus is the location of the Graduate School of Arts and Sciences and all other schools of the University except Medicine. The latter is located on the east, or medical, campus. The Division of Biology and Biomedical Sciences is also located on the medical campus. Free shuttle buses run between the campuses on a regular schedule.

The St. Louis area has nearly 2.4 million residents. The cost of living is affordable. The University's central location provides easy access to the zoo, museums, Science Center, Missouri Botanical Gardens, St. Louis Symphony, Opera Theatre, St. Louis Repertory Theatre, Black Repertory Theatre, Blues hockey, Rams football, and Cardinals baseball. Outdoor adventure beyond the city can be found in the Ozark Mountains and on the rivers of Missouri. Camping, hiking, floating, rock climbing, and spelunking are among the many possibilities within a few hours' drive of St. Louis.

The Graduate School

The Graduate School of Arts and Sciences is a charter member of both the Association of Graduate Schools and the Council of Graduate Schools. The School provides a physical and academic environment in which inquiry, intellectual growth, and discovery can thrive and flourish.

Applying

Prospective students may apply online. Applicants should check with the department or program to which they are applying, as application deadlines vary. Most programs require GRE scores. For international students whose native language is not English, most programs require an official copy of a TOEFL or TSE score.

Correspondence and Information

Graduate School of Arts and Sciences
Campus Box 1187
Washington University in St. Louis
One Brookings Drive
St. Louis, Missouri 63130-4899

Phone: 314-935-6880
Fax: 314-935-4887
E-mail: graduateschool@artsci.wustl.edu
Web site: http://www.artsci.wustl.edu/GSAS/

FACULTY HEADS, DEGREES OFFERED, AND DEPARTMENTAL INTERESTS

Anthropology (Ph.D.): Erik Trinkaus (trinkaus@artsci.wustl.edu). Archaeology, physical anthropology, primate studies, sociocultural anthropology, medical anthropology.
Art History and Archaeology (A.M., Ph.D.): William E. Wallace (wwallace@wustl.edu). Ancient, medieval, Renaissance, Baroque, and modern European and American art history; classical and Chinese archaeology.
Asian and Near Eastern Languages and Literatures (A.M., Ph.D.): Robert Hegel (anell@artsci.wustl.edu). Chinese, Japanese (A.M.); Chinese fiction, theater (joint Ph.D.); Japanese fiction, translation theory (joint Ph.D.).
Division of Biology and Biomedical Sciences (Ph.D.): Rebecca Riney (800-852-9074 (toll-free); e-mail: dbbs-admissions@dbbs.wustl.edu).
- **Biochemistry:** John Cooper (jcooper@wustl.edu). Metabolic regulation, signal transduction, membranes, nucleic acid–protein structure interactions and function, replication, repair, recombination, transcription, translation enzyme kinetics.
- **Computational and Molecular Biophysics:** Nathan Baker (baker@ccb.wustl.edu). Protein and nucleic acid kinetics and thermodynamics, single-molecule enzymology, nanoscience, biomolecular folding, macromolecular structure determination, ion channels and lipid membranes, computational biophysics.
- **Computational and Systems Biology:** Barak Cohen (cohen@genetics.wustl.edu). Systems biology, genomics, sequence analysis, regulatory networks, synthetic biology, metagenomics, metabolomics, proteomics, single cell dynamics, high-throughput technology development, applied math and mathematical models of biological processes, computational biology, comparative genomics, personalized medicine, next generation sequencing and its applications, bioinformatics.
- **Developmental Biology:** Kerry Kornfeld (kornfeld@wustl.edu) and James Skeath (jskeath@genetics.wustl.edu). Development, stem cell biology, regenerative biology, cell biology, genetics, cell signaling, the biology of cancer, epigenetics, circadian rhythms, systems biology.
- **Evolution, Ecology, and Population Biology:** Barbara Schaal (schaal@wustl.edu). Theoretical, experimental population genetics; population, community ecology; phylogenetics, systematics, plant, animal evolution; primate evolution.
- **Human and Statistical Genetics:** Anne Bowcock (bowcock@genetics.wustl.edu) and D. C. Rao (rao@wubios.wustl.edu). Human genetics, statistical genetics, gene mapping, genetics, Mendelian disease, complex disease, mammalian genetics, systems biology, functional genomics.
- **Immunology:** Kenneth Murphy (kmurphy@wustl.edu). Molecular immunology, lineage development, autoimmunity, cancer immunotherapy, transcription factors.
- **Molecular Cell Biology:** Phyllis Hanson (phanson22@wustl.edu) and Jason Weber (jweber@dom.wustl.edu). Cell adhesion, protein trafficking and organelle biogenesis, cell cycle, receptors, signal transduction, gene expression, metabolism, cytoskeleton and motility, membrane excitability, molecular basis of diseases.
- **Molecular Genetics and Genomics:** Tim Schedl (ts@genetics.wustl.edu) and James Skeath (jskeath@genetics.wustl.edu). Genetics, comparative genomics, functional genomics, model organisms, epigenetics, genetics of human disease, development, cell biology, molecular biology, complex traits, bioinformatics, systems biology.
- **Molecular Microbiology and Microbial Pathogenesis:** Tamara Doering (doering@wustl.edu). Molecular microbiology, microbial physiology, infectious disease, microbial pathogenesis, bacteriology, mycology, parasitology, virology, host defense.
- **Neurosciences:** Dora Angelaki (angelaki@wustl.edu) and Paul Taghert (taghertp@pcg.wustl.edu). Neurobiology, neurology, behavior, cognition, computational neuroscience, electrophysiology, sensory systems, motor systems, neuroglia, neuronal development, learning, memory, synaptic plasticity, mind, consciousness, neurodegeneration.
- **Plant Biology:** Tuan-Hua David Ho (ho@wustl.edu). Plant genetics, biochemistry, cell biology, development, molecular evolution, physiology, hormone signaling, response to environment, plant disease.

Business (Ph.D.): Chakravarthi Narasimhan (phdinfo@olin.wustl.edu). Accounting, business economics, finance, marketing, organizational behavior/strategy, operations and manufacturing management.
Chemistry (Ph.D.): Joseph Ackerman (ackerman@ wustl.edu). Bioinorganic, biological, bioorganic, biophysical, materials, nuclear, organic, organometallic, physical, polymer, radiochemistry, theoretical.
Classics (A.M.): Catherine Kean (classics@artsci.wustl.edu). Greek and Latin language; Greek and Roman literature, philosophy, history, and material culture.
Comparative Literature (Ph.D.): Harriet Stone (hastone@wustl.edu). World literature, literary theory, translation studies, global and multicultural theory, comparative drama, comparative arts, East/West comparisons, narrative theory, film.
Earth and Planetary Sciences (Ph.D.): Douglas A. Wiens (epscinfo@levee.wustl.edu). Planetary sciences, geology, geobiology, geochemistry, geodynamics.
East Asian Studies (A.M., A.M./J.D., A.M./M.B.A.): Robert E. Hegel (eas@artsci.wustl.edu). Literature and culture; law; political, economic, and intellectual history; art history and archaeology; anthropology.
Economics (Ph.D.): Michele Boldrin (mboldrin@artsci.wustl.edu). Economic theory, industrial organization, political economy, public economics, macroeconomics, public finance, development economics.
Education (M.A.Ed., M.A.T., Ph.D.): William F. Tate (wtate@wustl.edu). Teacher education, educational studies, urban education, policy studies, science and math education, literacy studies, learning science.
English and American Literature (Ph.D.): Vincent Sherry (vsherry@wustl.edu). African and African-American studies; American; Anglophone Caribbean literatures; British; contemporary literature; eighteenth-century; Irish literature; medieval; modernism; nineteenth-century British; postcolonial literature and theory; Renaissance; seventeenth-century; the long nineteenth-century; theory; women and gender studies, gender and sexuality.
Germanic Languages and Literatures (Ph.D.): Stephan K. Schindler (german@artsci.wustl.edu). Contemporary German literature, German literature and culture prior to 1700, literature and history, film studies, gender studies, German-European literary and cultural relations.
History (Ph.D.): Jean Allman (jallman@wustl.edu). African, American, civil rights history, China, gender, medieval Europe, early modern Britain, central Europe.
Islamic and Near Eastern Studies (A.M.): Pamela Barmash (pbarmash@wustl.edu). Islamic history, Arabic language and literature, Persian language and literature, modern Middle East history.
Jewish and Near Eastern Studies (A.M.): Pamela Barmash (pbarmash@wustl.edu). Hebrew Bible, rabbinic literature, medieval Jewish history, modern Hebrew literature, modern Jewish history.
Mathematics (Ph.D.): David Wright (wright@math.wustl.edu). Algebra, polynomials, polynomial rings and automorphisms, algebraic geometry, geometry of affine space, combinatorics.
Movement Science (Ph.D.): Michael Mueller (muellerm@wustl.edu). Philosophy of human movement function and dysfunction, with special emphasis on bioenergetics, biomechanics, and biocontrol.
Music (M.M., A.M., Ph.D.): Robert Snarrenberg (rsnarren@artsci.wustl.edu). Piano, voice, composition, musicology, ethnomusicology, theory.
Philosophy (A.M., Ph.D.): Mark Rollins (mark@wustl.edu). Ethics, social and political philosophy, history of philosophy, philosophy of law, philosophy of science, philosophy of mind, philosophy of language, theory of knowledge, aesthetics.
Philosophy/Neuroscience/Psychology (Ph.D.): José Bermúdez (bermudez@wustl.edu). Philosophy of mind and language, with a special emphasis on the philosophical dimensions of psychology, neuroscience, and linguistics.
Physics (Ph.D.): Kenneth F. Kelton (kfk@wustl.edu). Experimental and theoretical condensed matter and materials physics, with a focus on structural studies of liquids, glasses, and complex periodic and aperiodic phases; nucleation processes; and the glass transition.
Political Economy (A.M.): Norman Schofield (schofield@wustl.edu). International political economy, public policy.
Political Science (Ph.D.): Andrew Martin (admartin@wustl.edu). American politics, comparative politics, formal theory, international political economy, policy.
Psychology (Ph.D.): Deanna Barch (dbarch@wustl.edu). Behavior/brain/cognition, clinical, development and aging, social/personality.
Romance Languages and Literatures (Ph.D.): Elzbieta Sklodowska (esklodow@wustl.edu). French literature, Spanish and Latin American literature.
Social Work (Ph.D.): Wendy Auslander (phdsw@wustl.edu). Mental health, social and economic development, addictions, aging, child welfare, civic service, disabilities, health, poverty and social policy, youth development and schools.
Speech and Hearing (Ph.D.): William Clark (clarkw@wustl.edu). Speech and hearing sciences, clinical audiology, deaf education, speech and language, sensory neuroscience.
Statistics (A.M.): Steven Krantz (sk@wustl.edu). Mathematical statistics, biostatistics.
The Writing Program (M.F.A.W.): Marshall Klimasewiski (english@wustl.edu). Two-year program: fiction or poetry-writing workshops and academic courses.

WEST CHESTER UNIVERSITY OF PENNSYLVANIA

Graduate Studies

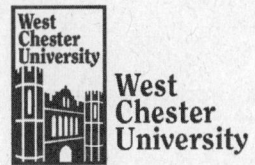

Programs of Study

West Chester University of Pennsylvania offers graduate study leading to the M.A., M.B.A., M.Ed., M.M. (Master of Music), M.P.H., M.S., M.S.W., M.S.N., and M.S.A. (Master of Science in Administration) degrees.

The Master of Arts is offered in communication studies, communicative disorders, English, French, geography, geosciences, history, holocaust and genocide studies, mathematics, music history, philosophy, psychology (general, clinical, and industrial/organizational psychology), Spanish, and teaching English as a second language.

The Master of Business Administration is awarded in general business.

The Master of Education and/or certification is available in autism, early childhood education, elementary and secondary school counseling, elementary education, reading, school health, secondary education, and special education.

The Master of Music is offered in music education, music theory or composition, music performance, and piano pedagogy.

The Master of Science is offered in applied statistics, biology, computer science, criminal justice, higher education counseling, and physical education.

The Master of Science in Administration is awarded in seven concentrations: human resource management, individualized, leadership for women, public administration, sport and athletic administration, training and development, and nonprofit.

West Chester University also offers the Master of Public Health, the Master of Social Work, and the Master of Science in Nursing.

Research Facilities

The Francis Harvey Green Library houses more than 623,000 volumes, 7,700 print and electronic periodical subscriptions, and 72,500 audiovisual items. Its services include interlibrary loans, reference advice, computerized online literature searches, and an instructional materials center. The library's Web site provides continually updated access to a wide array of resources and services including PILOT, the library's catalog, and links to more than 180 specialized databases. The University makes Braille printers, translators, and speech synthesizers available to its visually impaired students. The Library houses a coffee café and a separate study lounge for graduate students.

The Schmucker Science Center houses a fully equipped observatory and planetarium and extensive, well-equipped laboratories. Boucher Hall has state-of-the-art science labs for electronics, mineral spectroscopy, optics, and liquid crystal studies as well as an animal facility and greenhouse.

Financial Aid

A limited number of graduate assistantships are available on a competitive basis. In 2007–08, each carried an annual stipend of $5000 plus remission of tuition. In addition, some summer assistantships are available. Frederick Douglass Graduate Assistantships are also available. Scholarships and awards are offered by individual departments as well. West Chester University also participates in the Federal Perkins Loan and the Federal Stafford Student Loan programs.

Cost of Study

The basic per-semester tuition for full-time in-state residents taking 9 to 15 credits in 2008–09 was $3215 plus a $516 general fee; part-time students were billed at a per-credit rate of $357 for tuition and a $50 general fee for fewer than 9 credits. Out-of-state students paid $5144 for 9 to 15 credits and the general fee; part-time students were billed at the per-credit rate of $572.

Living and Housing Costs

West Chester University offers limited on-campus housing for single graduate students. Choices include designated quiet and honors dormitories, as well as apartment living in a 4- or 5-person fully furnished unit, with each bedroom having either single or double occupancy. Current costs (subject to change) are $2238 (double) in the residence hall or $2599 (single) in the apartments.

Many meal plans are available to students and range in cost from $1020 to $1199 per semester.

The Office of Off-Campus and Commuter Services can provide assistance in identifying available off-campus housing. The office maintains listings and evaluations of apartments and rooms, many within walking distance of the campus.

Student Group

The student body at West Chester University numbers 13,621, of whom 2,200 are graduate students. The Graduate Student Association (GSA) represents graduate students and their interests. The School of Education sponsors an active chapter of Phi Delta Kappa, the international graduate honor society. African-American and Hispanic student unions are active at West Chester. In addition, graduate students are invited to participate in the activities of undergraduate honor societies in which they hold membership. These include Alpha Lambda Delta, Alpha Mu Gamma, Alpha Psi Omega, Gamma Theta Upsilon, Kappa Delta Pi, Pi Gamma Mu, Pi Kappa Delta, Pi Mu Epsilon, Sigma Alpha Iota, Psi Chi, Phi Alpha Theta, Phi Delta Kappa, Phi Epsilon Kappa, Phi Eta Sigma, Phi Kappa Delta, Phi Mu Alpha Sinfonia, and Sigma Delta Pi.

Location

The University is located in West Chester, a community in southeastern Pennsylvania strategically located at the center of the mid-Atlantic corridor. The seat of Chester County government for almost two centuries, West Chester retains much of its historical charm in its buildings and unspoiled countryside while offering the twenty-first-century advantages of a town in the heart of an expanding economic area. West Chester is just 25 miles west of Philadelphia and 17 miles north of Wilmington, Delaware.

The interstate highway system and rail connections make the town accessible from many directions. Philadelphia is just an hour away, and travel to New York or Washington is possible in less than 3 hours.

The University

West Chester University is the largest of the fourteen institutions in the Pennsylvania State System of Higher Education and the fourth-largest in the Philadelphia metropolitan area. Officially founded in 1871, the University traces its heritage to the West Chester Academy, which existed from 1812 to 1869. The University's quadrangle buildings, part of the original campus, are on the National Register of Historic Places, and its 385-acre campus features well-maintained facilities, including eight modern residence halls.

Applying

Applicants are encouraged to apply online at http://www.wcupa.edu/grad—click on apply now. Students should apply by April 15 for fall or October 15 for spring semester of entry. Earlier deadlines exist for some programs and for eligibility for assistantships and financial aid. Students are required to submit official transcripts from all postsecondary institutions they have attended, three letters of recommendation; and scores on either the General Test of the Graduate Record Examination (GRE), Graduate Management Admission Test (GMAT), or Miller Analogies Test (MAT).

Correspondence and Information

Dr. Janet Hickman, Interim Dean of Graduate Studies and Extended Education
West Chester University
Office of Graduate Studies and Extended Education
102 West Rosedale Avenue
West Chester, Pennsylvania 19383

Phone: 610-436-2943
E-mail: gradstudy@wcupa.edu
Web site: http://www.wcupa.edu/grad

GRADUATE PROGRAM INFORMATION AND COORDINATORS

Listed below are West Chester University's graduate degree programs and the program coordinators. For information concerning a specific degree program, students should contact the graduate coordinator listed; for general admission information, they should contact the Office of Graduate Studies at gradstudy@wcupa.edu.

Administration (M.S.A.): Dr. Laurie Bernotsky (lbernotsky@wcupa.edu).
Applied Statistics (M.S.): Dr. Randall Reiger (rreiger@wcupa.edu).
Biology (M.S.): Dr. Judith Greenamyer (jgreenamyer@wcupa.edu).
Business (M.B.A.): Dr. Paul Christ (mba@wcupa.edu).
Communication Studies (M.A.): Dr. Jack Orr (corr@wcupa.edu).
Communicative Disorders (M.A.): Dr. Mareile Koenig (mkoenig@wcupa.edu).
Computer Science (M.S.): Dr. Elaine Milito (emilito@wcupa.edu).
Counselor Education (M.Ed., M.S., Specialist I certificate): Dr. Angelo Gadaleto (agadaleto@wcupa.edu).
Criminal Justice (M.S.): Dr. Mary Brewster (mbrewster@wcupa.edu).
Early Childhood Education: Dr. Catherine Prudhoe (cprudhoe@wcupa.edu).
Elementary Education (M.Ed. and certification): Dr. Connie DiLucchio (cdilucchio@wcupa.edu).
English (M.A.): Dr. Carolyn Sorisio (csorisio@wcupa.edu).
Geography (M.A.): Dr. Joan Welch (jwelch@wcupa.edu).
Geosciences (M.A.): Dr. Steve Good (sgood@wcupa.edu).
Health (M.Ed. in school health and M.P.H.): Dr. Bethann Cinelli (bcinelli@wcupa.edu.)
History (M.A. in history): Dr. William Hewitt (whewitt@wcupa.edu).
History (M.A. in holocaust and genocide studies): Dr. John Friedman (jfriedman@wcupa.edu).
Languages and Cultures (M.A. in French or Spanish): Dr. Rebecca Pauly (rpauly@wcupa.edu).
Mathematics (M.A.): Dr. John Kerrigan (jkerrigan@wcupa.edu).
Music (M.A. in music history and M.M. in music education, instrumental performance, keyboard performance, music theory and composition, and vocal/choral performance): Dr. Bryan Burton (Jburton3@wcupa.edu).
Nursing (M.S.N.): Dr. Ann Stowe (astowe@wcupa.edu).
Philosophy (M.A.): Dr. Helen Schroepfer (hschroepfer@wcupa.edu).
Physical Education (M.S. in physical education): Dr. Sheri Melton (smelton@wcupa.edu).
Psychology (M.A. in clinical, industrial/organizational, and general psychology): Dr. Stefani Yorges (syorges@wcupa.edu).
Reading (M.Ed. and reading specialist certification): Dr. Robert Szabo, (rszabo@wcupa.edu).
Secondary Education (M.Ed.): Dr. Cynthia Haggard (chaggard@wcupa.edu).
Special Education (M.Ed. and certificate programs): Dr. Vicki McGinley, (vmcginley@wcupa.edu).
Social Work (M.S.W.): Dr. Ann Abbott (aabbott@wcupa.edu).
TESL (M.A. in teaching English as a second language): Dr. Charles Grove (cgrove@wcupa.edu).

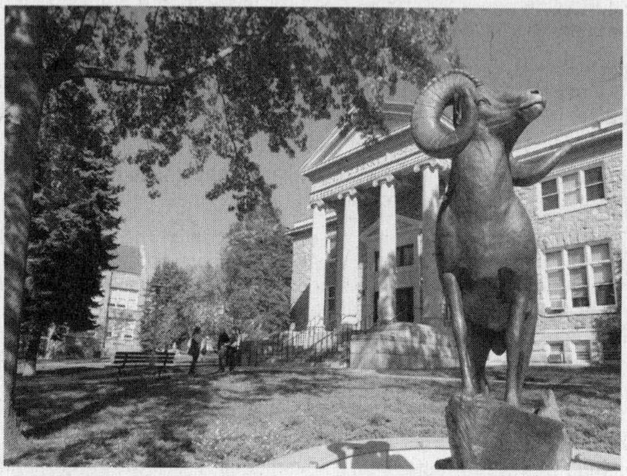

Ram mascot in front of Old Library.

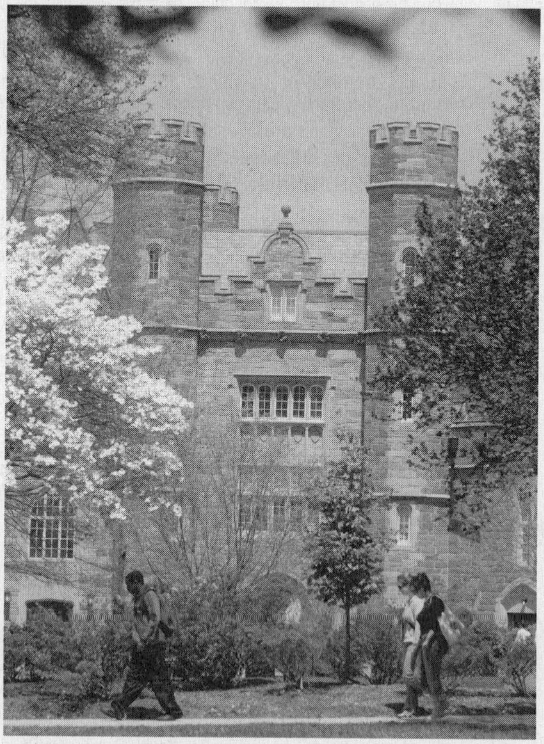

Philips Memorial Hall.

Programs of Study

Widener University awards the degrees of Doctor of Education (Ed.D.), Doctor of Juridical Science (S.J.D.), Doctor of Laws (D.L.), Doctor of Nursing Practice (D.N.P.), Doctor of Philosophy (Ph.D.) in nursing, Doctor of Philosophy (Ph.D.) in social work, Doctor of Physical Therapy (D.P.T.), Doctor of Psychology (Psy.D.), Juris Doctor (J.D.), Master of Arts (M.A.) in criminal justice, Master of Arts in Liberal Studies (M.L.S.), Master of Business Administration (M.B.A.), Master of Business Administration in Health Care Management (M.B.A.-HCM), Master of Education (M.Ed.), Master of Engineering (M.Eng.), Master of Jurisprudence (M.J.), Master of Laws (LL.M.), Master of Public Administration (M.P.A.), Master of Science in Hospitality Management (M.S.H.M.), Master of Science in Nursing (M.S.N.), and Master of Social Work (M.S.W.).

Master of Science degrees are also offered in the following business disciplines: Information Systems (M.S.I.S.), Human Resource/Organizational Leadership (M.S.H.R.O.L.), and Taxation and Financial Planning (M.S.T.F.P.). The M.Ed. program offers more than twenty majors, including counselor education, educational leadership, elementary education, human sexuality education, reading, special education, and supervision. The M.S.N. program offers concentrations in the advanced practice roles of adult health nursing, community-based nursing, emergency/critical care nursing, family nurse practitioner studies, nurse educator studies, and psychiatric/mental health nursing. Post-master's certificates are available in all clinical specialty areas as well as nursing education. The M.Eng. program offers specializations in engineering management and chemical, civil, mechanical, and electrical engineering. An environmental engineering option is also available.

Dual-degree programs include the M.Eng./M.B.A., J.D./M.B.A., J.D./Psy.D., Psy.D./M.B.A., Psy.D./M.B.A.-HCM, Psy.D./M.S.H.R.O.L., Psy.D./M.A. in criminal justice, Psy.D./M.P.A., M.Ed. in human sexuality education/Psy.D., M.S.W./M.Ed. in human sexuality education, M.S.W./Ed.D. in human sexuality, and M.Ed. in adult education/Ed.D. in human sexuality.

Research Facilities

The Wolfgram Memorial Library has a fine collection that includes more than 240,000 volumes, 175,000 microforms, and nearly 2,000 periodical titles. Services include online access to bibliographic information, full-text electronic journals, Web-based databases, audiovisual-media collections and facilities, and access to other libraries' resources through interlibrary loans. Computing facilities are available to meet students' needs.

The Center for Education runs a full-time laboratory preschool and early childhood center. It also has an extensive collection of curriculum materials, a reading laboratory, and a personal computer laboratory for computer-assisted instruction and interactive video.

The School of Law library maintains a collection of more than 600,000 volumes. Contained in the collection are legal publications and journals, treatises, reports, and statutes. Access to a wide range of supporting materials is available through LexisNexis and WESTLAW online legal research services.

Financial Aid

More than 85 percent of the law students receive some form of financial aid. Applicants should complete the Free Application for Federal Student Aid (FAFSA) form at the time of application.

Students in graduate programs other than law can apply for financial aid programs through the Financial Aid Office on the Main Campus. A limited number of graduate assistantships are available to full-time students in graduate programs other than law, and a number of loan programs are available to all eligible students.

Cost of Study

Tuition for Widener's graduate programs is as follows: $784 per credit for Ed.D. courses, $1065 per credit for S.J.D. and LL.M. courses, $763 per credit for Doctor of Philosophy in nursing courses, $747 per credit for social work Ph.D. courses, $25,290 per year for the D.P.T. program, $22,886 per year for the Psy.D. program, $1115 per credit for J.D. students, $576 per credit for graduate criminal justice and M.P.A. courses, $528 per credit for graduate liberal studies courses, $800 per credit for graduate business courses, $617 per credit for M.Ed. courses, $874 per credit for graduate engineering courses, $825 per credit for M.J. and D.L. courses, $659 per credit for graduate hospitality management courses, $669 for M.S.W. courses, and $738 per credit for M.S.N. courses.

Living and Housing Costs

Affordable rental apartments are available within a 3-mile radius of all three campuses.

Student Group

Approximately 3,200 students are pursuing graduate or professional degrees at the University. About 57 percent are women. The student population is largely drawn from the mid-Atlantic region; about 5 percent of the graduate and professional students are from other countries. Students enter with a variety of undergraduate majors, including liberal arts, engineering, business, and nursing.

Location

Widener's Main Campus, occupying more than 100 acres in Chester, Pennsylvania, is easily accessible from Interstate 95. Located in Delaware County, one of the oldest counties in Pennsylvania, the campus is near historic and commercial areas; Philadelphia is just 15 miles north.

The 40-acre Delaware Campus (15 miles southwest of the Main Campus) is located on Route 202 (Concord Pike), north of Wilmington, and is only a short distance from Interstate 95. It houses the School of Law and is also a course site for the School of Business Administration. A branch of the School of Law is located on the 21-acre Harrisburg Campus in central Pennsylvania. Graduate social work, nursing, and education courses are also offered on this campus.

In fall 2004, Widener opened its fourth campus in Exton, Pennsylvania, which houses adult undergraduate education and the Osher Lifelong Learning Institute, a learning cooperative for area retirees. The Institute is the first facility of its kind in the Philadelphia metropolitan region.

The University

Widener University is a multicampus, independent, metropolitan institution located in and accredited by the Commonwealth of Pennsylvania and the state of Delaware. The University distinguishes itself by connecting curricula to societal issues through civic engagement. Flexible course schedules, accessible faculty, and a supportive environment characterize the graduate student experience at Widener.

Applying

Applicants are encouraged to apply for admission online at http://www.widener.edu. The application fee is waived for online applications. Applicants must submit official transcripts of records covering all academic work beyond high school, standardized test scores (e.g., scores on the GMAT, GRE, or LSAT) appropriate to the program they wish to enter, and two to three letters of recommendation. Final selection is based on the quality of the total application, as determined by the student's record of achievement and his or her personal qualification for graduate study and professional practice.

Correspondence and Information

For Widener graduate programs:

Roberta Nolan, Director
Office of Graduate Enrollment Management
Widener University
One University Place
Chester, Delaware 19013

Phone: 610-499-4125
E-mail: gradmc@mail.widener.edu
Web site: http://www.widener.edu

For the Juris Doctor program:

Office of Admissions
Widener University School of Law
4601 Concord Pike
Wilmington, Pennsylvania 19803

Phone: 302-477-2160
E-mail: law.admissions@law.widener.edu
Web site: http://www.law.widener.edu

FACULTY HEADS

Associate Provost for Graduate Studies: Stephen C. Wilhite, D.Phil.

Deans

College of Arts and Sciences: Mathew Poslusny, Ph.D.
School of Business Administration: Savas Ozatalay, Ph.D.
School of Engineering: Fred A. Akl, Ph.D.
School of Hospitality Management: Nicholas J. Hadgis, Ph.D.
School of Human Service Professions: Stephen C. Wilhite, D.Phil.
School of Law: Linda L. Ammons, J.D.
School of Nursing: Deborah Garrison, Ph.D., RN.

WILLIAM PATERSON UNIVERSITY OF NEW JERSEY

Graduate Programs

Programs of Study

William Paterson University offers twenty-one degree programs in the University's five colleges. Eight degrees are awarded: Master of Arts (M.A.), Master of Fine Arts (M.F.A.), Master of Science (M.S.), Master of Education (M.Ed.), Master of Business Administration (M.B.A.), Master of Arts in Teaching (M.A.T.), Master of Music (M.M.), and Master of Science in Nursing (M.S.N.). Degree requirements vary.

The M.A. is offered in clinical and counseling psychology, English (with concentrations in literature and writing), history, media studies, public policy and international affairs, and sociology (with concentrations in crime and justice and diversity studies). The M.F.A. in art offers concentrations in fine arts, media arts, and design arts, with studio courses in ceramics, computer art and animation, textiles, furniture design, graphic design, painting, photography, printmaking, and sculpture. The M.S. is offered in biology, biotechnology, communication disorders (speech-language pathology), and exercise and sport studies. The M.Ed. is offered in professional counseling (with concentrations in agency counseling and school counseling), curriculum and learning (with concentrations in bilingual/English as a second language, early childhood, language arts, learning technologies, school library media, social studies, and teaching children mathematics), educational leadership, reading, and special education (with specializations in developmental disability and learning disability). The M.M. is offered in music, with concentrations in jazz studies, music education, and music management. The M.B.A. is offered with concentrations in accounting, entrepreneurship, finance, general business, marketing, and music management. The M.S.N. is offered in community-based nursing, with tracks in administration, advanced practice, and education. The M.A.T. is offered in elementary education.

The College of Education also offers teacher certification programs for college graduates who wish to obtain initial teaching certification in New Jersey, as well as endorsement programs for certified teachers who wish to obtain additional teaching certification.

Research Facilities

The biological science facilities include animal facilities and rooms for data collection and analysis; the neurobiology facility, including a computerized image processing system and facilities for animal surgery and behavioral and physiological research; electron microscopy facilities, including transmission and scanning electron microscopes and associated specimen preparation equipment, an X-ray analyzer and three darkrooms; biotechnology facilities and tissue culture lab, including an automated DNA sequencer, DNA synthesizer, PCR units, liquid scintillation counter, electrophoresis units, computerized UV spectrophotometers, high-pressure liquid chromatography units and ultracentrifuges; two greenhouses; and a well-equipped ecology laboratory with both stationary and field-oriented aquatic and terrestrial ecological research equipment.

Hobart Hall houses two broadcast-quality TV studios, a multipurpose computer lab, a film studio, an FCC-licensed FM radio station, an uplink and four downlink satellite dishes, a cable system, and a computerized telephone system for voice and data transmission.

The Atrium is a state-of-the-art technology center on campus that holds more than 100 multimedia computers arranged in classrooms with video projection capacity. The media center, which supports multimedia and Internet development, includes scanners, CD-ROM writers, digitizers, and related software tools.

A multiphasic on-site clinic provides practical experience for special education, reading, and communication disorders program participants.

William Paterson University has a fiber-optic ATM backbone interconnecting all faculty offices, classrooms, and laboratories. It is also a member of the VALE Consortium, a nonprofit organization of colleges and universities fostering the growth of video, voice, and data networking in the state.

The David and Lorraine Cheng Library is open seven days a week when classes are in session and includes more than 360,000 volumes and more than 17,000 audiovisual items, with access to more than 23,000 electronic and print periodicals and journals. Approximately 100 databases serve the needs of students. Services include professional reference assistance, online bibliographic searching, an interlibrary loan program, viewing facilities, and the latest in end-use searching. Nonprint resource materials include a microcomputer software collection and an audiovisual collection of film, DVDs, and videocassettes. The library also has added an electronic resource center and a graduate research center connected to the William Paterson network.

Financial Aid

The University is participating in the Federal Direct Loan Program. This program consists of Federal Direct Stafford Student Loans (subsidized and unsubsidized) and the Federal Graduate PLUS program. Students must file the Free Application for Federal Student Aid (FAFSA) to determine their eligibility. The University makes a limited number of graduate assistantships available each year. Assistantships normally carry a stipend of $6000 and a waiver of tuition and fees. Graduate assistants must carry a minimum of 9 credits in each of the fall and spring semesters and work 20 hours per week in an assigned area. Graduate assistantships require a minimum grade point average of 3.0 and are awarded on the basis of availability and applicants' qualifications. Application forms are available in the Office of Graduate Studies. The University also participates in alternative/private loan programs. Information is available via the Alternative Student Loans link on http://www.wpunj.edu/finaid.

Cost of Study

In 2009–10, full-time graduate tuition and fees were $587 per credit for New Jersey residents and $910 per credit for out-of-state students. Other fees apply for books, parking, the Student Center, information technology, and general services. Tuition and fees are subject to change in accordance with policies established by the Board of Trustees.

Living and Housing Costs

On-campus housing is available for single graduate students. Housing options include suite-style, single, and double accommodations or apartment-style living offered in a grouping of 4 students to an apartment. Currently, on-campus housing costs range from $3000 to $4200 per semester, with meal plans available at an additional cost of $1000 to $2185 per semester. The University does not offer family student housing; however, the Office of Residence Life provides an off-campus living listing service. These dwellings are not preapproved by the University and may include listings for shared homes or apartments as well as private rooms. A graduate student selecting such off-campus housing may expect room and board costs of $19,000 for the combined fall and spring semesters. Students are also advised to include $4800 in their budgets for travel as well as an additional $5200 for miscellaneous and personal expenses.

Student Group

The University has 10,256 students, of whom 1,515 (15 percent) are graduate students. Ninety-two percent of the students enrolled in graduate programs pursue their studies on a part-time basis. The traditional service area of the University consists of New Jersey's northernmost counties.

Location

Set on a 370-acre wooded hilltop, the University commands a breathtaking view of the surrounding communities. Located 20 miles west of New York City, the campus is easily accessible from major highways that provide access to the cultural and educational resources available within the metropolitan area.

The University

Founded in the city of Paterson in 1855, William Paterson is one of nine institutions in the New Jersey State Higher Education system. The University moved to the Wayne campus in 1951. In 1966, the University became a comprehensive institution offering undergraduate, graduate, and professional degrees. In 1997, William Paterson was awarded university status by the New Jersey Commission on Higher Education. Governed by a local board of trustees, William Paterson is accredited by the Middle States Association of Colleges and Schools. An on-campus state-certified center provides child care for eligible dependents of full- and part-time students. The Career Development and Advisement Center helps matriculated students and alumni who seek professional advancement or career changes.

Applying

To receive application information and materials, students should contact the Office of Graduate Studies.

Correspondence and Information

Office of Graduate Studies
William Paterson University of New Jersey
300 Pompton Road, R139
Wayne, New Jersey 07470-2103

Phone: 973-720-2237
973-720-3641
E-mail: graduate@wpunj.edu
Web site: http://www.wpunj.edu

GRADUATE PROGRAMS AND DIRECTORS

Art: David Horton (973-720-3284). The M.F.A. program is designed as the professional degree for the fine artist, craftsperson, designer, or media artist or for those wishing to teach at the college or university level. Concentrations are available in fine arts, design arts, or media arts.

Bilingual/English as a Second Language: Dr. Bruce Williams (973-720-3654).

Biology: Dr. Robert Chesney (973-720-3455). Neuroscience, image processing, transmission electron microscopy, protozoology, neuroendocrinology, teratogenic agents and development, animal behavior, behavior genetics, scanning electron microscopy, palynology, muscle physiology, invertebrate zoology, aquatic ecology, ecology and entomology, wetland ecology, and endocrinology.

Biotechnology: Dr. Robert Chesney (973-720-3455). Microbial genetics, molecular biology, protein biochemistry, neurochemistry, algal biochemistry, plant genetic engineering, parasitology, immunochemistry, mycology, molecular biology development, marine biochemistry, and gene activation.

Business Administration: Dr. Francis Cai (973-720-2178). The M.B.A. program is designed to provide students with both the background and perspective necessary for success in today's and tomorrow's business environments. Emphasis is placed on preparing students for the competitive global marketplace. Computer courses are designed to enhance students' skills by providing up-to-date software packages. The major areas of concentration are accounting, entrepreneurship, finance, management, marketing, music, and general business.

Certification Programs: College of Education (973-720-2138). Certification programs are intended for graduates who wish to obtain initial certification or endorsement in the state of New Jersey.

Clinical Health Psychology: Dr. Bruce J. Diamond (973-720-3400). The program prepares students for the professional practice of psychological counseling, assessment, and mental health research in nonschool settings.

Communication Disorders: Dr. Jennifer Hsu (973-720-3352). This ASHA-accredited program provides students the training required to work as speech/language pathologists. The program is affiliated with the ASHA-accredited William Paterson University Speech and Hearing Clinic, which offers clinical services in the diagnosis or treatment of speech, language, and hearing disorders. Students have the opportunity to work with state-of-the-art equipment in audiometric testing, auditory brain stem–evoked responses, and speech and hearing science.

Curriculum and Learning: Dr. Rochelle Goldberg Kaplan (973-720-2598). The M.Ed. program offers concentrations in bilingual/English as a second language, early childhood, language arts, learning technologies, school library media, social studies, and teaching children mathematics.

Education Leadership: Dr. Kevin Walsh (973-720-2130). This graduate program is designed for teachers who aspire to leadership positions in schools.

English: Dr. Andrew Barnes (973-720-2837). Literature concentration: modern English and its background, major authors, early drama, and the novel; seventeenth- and eighteenth-century, romantic, Victorian, and modern British literature; nineteenth- and twentieth-century American literature; and related literature, including women's studies and film. Writing concentration: creative writing, advanced critical writing, writing for the magazine market, fiction writing, poetry writing, book and magazine editing, teaching writing as process, journalism, and script writing for the media.

Exercise and Sport Studies: Dr. Gordon Schmidt (973-720-2790). The graduate program offers two concentrations: exercise physiology and sport pedagogy.

History: Dr. Krista O'Donnell (973-720-2146). Through an innovative curriculum that focuses on historical analysis and the integration of information technology into historical research and teaching, program graduates acquire the skills necessary to communicate historical insights in a diverse and technologically advanced society.

Media Studies: Dr. Casey Lum (973-720-2342). The program encompasses theory, philosophy, and applications in the various areas of communication, including interpersonal communication, mass communication, and telecommunication. Research areas are cable access policy, intercultural communication, legal communication, and film and broadcast theory.

Music: Professor Carol Frierson-Campbell (973-720-3639).

Nursing: Dr. Kem Louie (973-720-3215). The M.S.N. program is designed to provide students the training to work as advanced practitioners, educators, or administrators in nursing. The program combines course work and clinical practice in a variety of settings and includes courses in advanced nursing, health-care systems, health assessment, legislation and social policy, financial management, and labor law.

***Professional Counseling (Agency and School):** Dr. Paula Danzinger (973-720-3085).

Public Policy and International Affairs: Dr. Sheila Collins (973-720-3424). The program provides the foundation for understanding how contemporary public policy crosses and supersedes national boundaries in an increasingly global environment of trade and information.

***Reading:** Dr. Geraldine Mongillo (973-720-3139).

Sociology: Dr. Vincent Parrillo (973-720-3881). The program consists of two interrelated tracks: diversity studies and crime and justice.

***Special Education:** Dr. Christopher Mulrine (Certification) (973-720-3123).

***Teaching:** Dr. Julie Rosenthal (973-720-3087). The Master of Arts in Teaching degree also enables graduates to obtain elementary (N–8) teacher certification.

**Teacher education programs are fully approved by the National Council of Accreditation of Teacher Education and meet the standards of the National Association of State Directors of Teacher Education and Certification.*

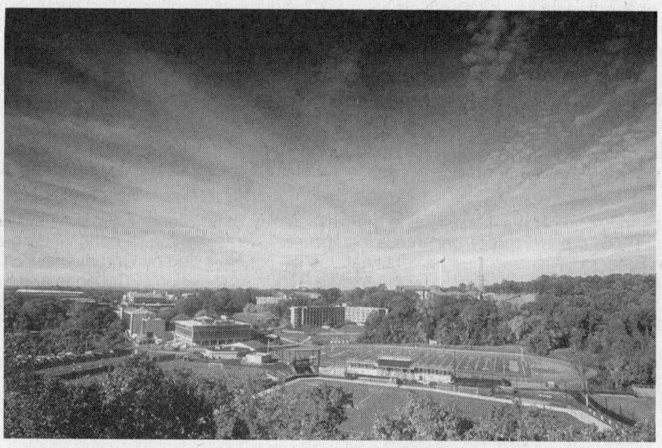

A view of the campus at William Paterson University of New Jersey.

William Paterson University offers abundant study space.

WORCESTER POLYTECHNIC INSTITUTE

Graduate Programs

Programs of Study

Worcester Polytechnic Institute (WPI) offers M.S. and Ph.D. programs in the following sciences: biology and biotechnology, chemistry and biochemistry, computer science, mathematics, and physics. Programs are also offered in the following areas of engineering: biomedical, chemical, civil and environmental, electrical and computer, fire protection, manufacturing, materials science, materials process, and mechanical. The university also offers an M.S. degree in system dynamics, M.S. and Ph.D. degrees in interdisciplinary studies, and M.S. and M.B.A. programs in management.

A biomedical engineering/medical physics joint Ph.D. program is sponsored by WPI and the University of Massachusetts Medical School.

The programs for the M.S. degree require a minimum of 30 credit hours. Although the specific requirements vary, most departments require a thesis of at least 6 semester hours. Arrangements may be made with local industries for thesis research.

The Ph.D. degree requires a minimum of 90 credit hours beyond the bachelor's degree, with a minimum of one year of full-time residence at the Institute.

Research Facilities

In addition to the extensive facilities for research available in all departments, graduate students have the opportunity to conduct research in a number of research institutes, centers, and laboratories, including the Metal Processing Institute, the largest industry-university alliance in North America, and the Bioengineering Institute (BEI), an interdisciplinary life sciences–based research and development organization. BEI and WPI's life sciences–based graduate research programs are located in the new 125,000-square-foot WPI Life Sciences and Bioengineering Center at Gateway Park.

Other research centers include the Aerodynamics Laboratory, Alternative Fuel Economics Laboratory, Analog Research Laboratory, Assistive Technology Resource Center, Atomic Force Microscopy Laboratory, Bacterial Adhesion and Interaction Forces Laboratory, Bioprocess Technology Center, Center for Advanced Integrated Radio Navigation, Center for Holographic Studies and Laser micro-mechaTronics, Center for Industrial Mathematics and Statistics, Center for Inorganic Membrane Studies, Center for Research in Electronic Commerce Technology, Center for Sensory and Physiologic Signal Processing, Center for Wireless Information Network Studies, Collaborative for Entrepreneurship and Innovation, Computer-Aided Manufacturing Laboratory, Convergent Technology Center, Cryptography and Information Security Research Laboratory, Environmental Laboratory, Fire Science and Fire Modeling Laboratories, Fuel Cell Center, Hydrodynamics Laboratory, Integrative Materials Design Center, IPG Photonics Laboratory, Magnetic Resonance Imaging Facility, Materials Testing Laboratory, Microfluidics and Biosensors Laboratory, Nanomaterials and Nanomanufacturing Laboratory, Nondestructive Evaluation and Electromagnetics Research Laboratory, Pavement Research Laboratory, Polymer Laboratory, Robotics Laboratory, Structural Mechanics Impact Laboratory, Surface Metrology Laboratory, Tissue Engineering Laboratory, and Ultrasound Research Laboratory.

WPI is one of only 212 universities nationwide connected to Internet2 (the next generation Internet) and is one of only four institutions in New England with a node on the Access Grid, a worldwide high-speed multimedia conference network.

Central and departmental computation facilities include parallel processing mainframes, a Linux cluster for use in developing massively parallel computation software, a display wall for large-scale tiled visualization, and UNIX-based engineering workstations/minicomputers, all connected by a campuswide 10 gigabit Ethernet backbone. There are several hundred Windows-based personal computers on campus, many in open-access laboratories.

Financial Aid

For the academic year 2009–10, teaching assistantships carry a stipend of $1774 per month, and research assistantship stipends vary between $1774 and $2500 per month. Both assistantships provide remission of tuition for up to 20 credits. A variety of endowed fellowships offer full-time tuition (up to 20 credits) and a stipend of $1774 per month. Additional information may be found online at http://grad.wpi.edu/Prospective/funding.html.

Cost of Study

Graduate tuition for the 2009–10 academic year is $1121 per credit hour. A full-time student must take 18 credits per academic year.

Living and Housing Costs

On-campus graduate student housing is very limited. There is no on-campus housing for married students. Apartments and rooms in private homes near the campus are abundant and available at varying costs. For further information and apartment listings, students should check the Residential Services Office Web site at http://www.wpi.edu/Admin/RSO/Offcampus/.

Student Group

Worcester Polytechnic Institute has a student body of 4,561, of which 1,309 are graduate students. Most states and more than seventy countries are represented.

Location

WPI's 80-acre campus is located in a residential section of Worcester, Massachusetts, New England's second-largest city. Central Massachusetts is home to more than a dozen colleges and universities and is within an hour's drive of cultural and academic centers in Boston, Providence, and Hartford. Worcester forms the western end of a high-technology corridor known for its concentration of companies and research institutions engaged in advanced work in the life sciences and bioengineering. The city's cultural amenities include the Worcester Art Museum (just three blocks from campus) and the new Hanover Theatre for the Performing Arts, which brings touring Broadway shows and prominent performers to the city. The DCU Center offers rock concerts and hosts the American Hockey League's Worcester Sharks. The Tornadoes, of baseball's Can-Am League, play at nearby Fitton Field. Cape Cod and the Berkshires are easily reached for recreation.

The Institute

Founded in 1865, Worcester Polytechnic Institute is one of the leading engineering and technology universities in the United States. The university has offered graduate programs since 1893. Classes are small and provide for close student-faculty relationships. WPI's outstanding research facilities include the new 125,000-square-foot Life Sciences and Bioengineering Center.

Applying

Applicants must submit WPI application forms, official college transcript(s), three letters of recommendation, and a $70 application fee (waived for WPI alumni). Submission of GRE scores or other materials may be required depending on the academic department. International students whose primary language is not English must also submit proof of English language proficiency. WPI accepts either the TOEFL (Test of English as a Foreign Language) or the IELTS (International English Language Testing System). A paper-based TOEFL score of at least 550 (computer-based equivalent: 213, or Internet-based equivalent: 79–80) or an IELTS overall band score of 6.5 with no band score below 6.0 is required for admission. To be considered for funding (assistantships and fellowships), complete applications must be on file by January 15 for fall admission and October 15 for spring admission. Files completed after those deadlines are reviewed on a rolling basis and may not be considered for funding. Some fellowships require an additional application. Students should visit http://grad.wpi.edu/Prospective/funding.html for more information. Inquiries should be directed to the head of the degree program of interest or to the Office of Graduate Admissions.

Correspondence and Information

Office of Graduate Admissions
Worcester Polytechnic Institute
100 Institute Road
Worcester, Massachusetts 01609

Phone: 508-831-5301
Fax: 508-831-5717
E-mail: grad@wpi.edu
Web site: http://www.grad.wpi.edu

FACULTY HEADS AND RESEARCH AREAS

Biology and Biotechnology: Professor Eric W. Overström, Head. The Department offers a full-time research-oriented program for incoming graduate students, leading to either a Doctor of Philosophy (Ph.D.) degree in biotechnology or a Master of Science (M.S.) degree in biology and biotechnology. These programs require students to successfully complete required courses in the field and a thesis project or dissertation that applies the basic principles of biology and biotechnology using hypothesis-driven experimental methods to a specific research problem. Major research strengths in the Department target the following areas: developmental-regenerative biology, plant cell biology and biotechnology, pathogenesis, genetics and molecular biology, molecular ecology and evolution, and bioprocess technology. With their emphasis on both fundamental and applied research, the graduate programs in biology and biotechnology at WPI are designed to support translational studies that have targeted impact in the life and health sciences.

Biomedical Engineering: Professor Yitzhak Mendelson, Interim Head. Major research areas include biomaterials, biomechanics, biofluids, tissue engineering, stem cell and regenerative engineering tissue mechanics, regenerative medicine, nuclear magnetic resonance imaging and spectroscopy, biomedical sensors, biological signal processing, and biomedical instrumentation.

Chemical Engineering: Professor David DiBiasio, Head. The Chemical Engineering Department's research effort is concentrated in the following major areas: nanotechnology/nanomaterials, environmental engineering, energy research, bioengineering, process control, process analysis, chemical process safety, and reaction engineering.

Chemistry and Biochemistry: Professor Kristin K. Wobbe, Head. The three major areas of research in the department are biochemistry and biophysics, including heavy-metal transport and metal homeostasis, enzyme structure and function, computational methods, and others; molecular design and synthesis, encompassing organic synthesis, development of new synthetic methods, medicinal chemistry, supramolecular materials, photovoltaic materials, photophysical properties of cumulenes, host-guest chemistry, and more; and nanotechnology, including photonic and nonlinear optical materials, nanoporous and microporous crystals of organic and coordination compounds, molecular interactions at surfaces, and others.

Civil and Environmental Engineering: Professor Tahar El-Korchi, Department Head. Research areas include impact analysis; vehicle crashworthiness; transportation safety and roadside safety; pavement engineering; construction materials; green and sustainable engineering; fire protection engineering; computer simulation and building information modeling; integration of design and construction of buildings; foundation engineering; materials, biological, chemical, and physical aspects of water and wastewater treatment; water quality and distribution; groundwater flow; contaminant transport and transformation; and hazardous and industrial waste. Graduate courses are offered in structural engineering, construction management, environmental engineering, and transportation engineering. Environmental graduate courses are also offered via distance learning.

Computer Science: Professor Michael A. Gennert, Head. Departmental research includes analysis of algorithms, artificial intelligence, computer graphics, computer vision, database systems, data mining, distributed systems, graph theory, human-computer interaction, intelligent tutoring systems, mobile and wireless communication, multimedia, networks, network and computer security, performance evaluation, programming languages, robotics, software engineering, user interfaces, virtual reality, and visualization. The department is housed in Fuller Laboratories, which was designed specifically for multimedia, high-technology education. The department has numerous general-purpose and specialized computing laboratories, with special devices and printers, a Linux-running cluster, and scores of high-end personal computers and workstations.

Electrical and Computer Engineering: Professor Fred Looft, Head. M.S. and Ph.D. research areas include cognitive- and software-defined radio systems, wireless networking, cryptography and network security, multimedia networks, global positioning systems, cooperative communications, image processing, computational methods for electromagnetics and ultrasonics, analog microelectronics, medical imaging, wireless communications, power quality, and power system state estimation. Approximately $2 million in external research support is received annually. Major facilities include an extensive network of computer workstations and servers, wireless communication systems and networking laboratories, VLSI design and test facilities, RF/microwave laboratories, power electronics/systems laboratories, and embedded systems design laboratories.

Fire Protection Engineering: Professor Kathy Notarianni, Head. Faculty research interests cover a wide range of topics in fire protection engineering and related areas. Research is directed toward fundamental understanding (theoretical and empirical), modeling of phenomena, the development of practical engineering methods, and fire risk and public policy. Research areas include fire-related combustion, flame spread and dust explosions, fire characteristics of materials, fire properties of composite materials, protective clothing, computer fire modeling, building fire safety analysis and design, structural fire behavior, human behavior in fire, fire detection, fire suppression, explosion protection, risk and decision analysis, and building and fire regulatory reform. The combustion and materials research is supported by the Fire Science Laboratory, which contains state-of-the-art bench-scale apparatuses (Cone and 2 FPAs) and a residential-scale fire-test compartment, as well as exhaust hood space for bench- and residential-scale experiments. WPI offers both the master's and doctoral degrees in fire protection engineering as well as a five-year dual-degree program for high school graduates. Graduate courses are offered on campus and via distance learning.

Management: Professor McRae C. Banks, Head. WPI offers innovative management programs integrating business and technology. Concentration areas include entrepreneurship, information security management, information technology, operations management, process design, supply chain management, technological innovation, and technology marketing. Graduate degree programs include the Master of Business Administration (M.B.A.), the Master of Science in marketing and technological innovation, the Master of Science in information technology, and the Master of Science in operations design and leadership. Graduate courses are offered on campus and online via WPI's Advanced Distance Learning Network.

Manufacturing Engineering: Professor Richard D. Sisson, Director, and Professor Yiming Rong, Associate Director. Research areas include fixturing, computer-integrated manufacturing, machining dynamics, tool wear, grinding, and surface metrology. Resources include the Haas Technical Center for computer-controlled machining, with eight CNC tool and UNIX workstations (http://www.me.wpi.edu/MFE/HCCM/index.html). The program also has a dedicated CAM Lab (http://www.me.wpi.edu/Research/CAMLab/) and surface metrology laboratory with conventional profiling, a scanning laser microscope, and software for area-scale fractal analysis (http://www.me.wpi.edu/Research/SurfMet/). The M.S. program includes thesis and nonthesis options. There are no required courses for the Ph.D.; however, residency, a comprehensive exam, and a dissertation are required.

Materials Science and Engineering: Professor Richard D. Sisson Jr., Director, and Professor Yiming Rong, Associate Director. Graduate study ranges over various engineering and science disciplines after focusing on fundamental work in materials science and materials engineering. Close ties with mechanical engineering, manufacturing, and other engineering and science programs are maintained. Facilities and equipment include optical microscopy, X-ray diffraction, casting, welding, mechanical testing, fatigue and fracture mechanics, materials characterization laboratories, and scanning and transmission electron microscopes. There is also the nation's only dedicated Surface Metrology Laboratory, with conventional profiling, scanning laser microscope, and fractal analysis software supporting surface engineering. The Metals Processing Institute, a major university-industry consortium with more than 100 industrial members, is also an integrated part of the program. The Metals Processing Institute is made up of six research centers: the Advanced Casting Research Center, Powder Metallurgy Research Center, Center for Heat Treating Excellence, Center for Imaging and Sensing, Aerospace Materials Education Research Innovation Center, and Sloan Industry Center.

Mathematical Sciences: Professor Bogdan Vernescu, Head. The department offers an M.S. in applied mathematics, which emphasizes analysis, differential equations, numerical methods, mathematical modeling, and discrete mathematics; an M.S. in applied statistics, which emphasizes scientific applications for industry and government; professional M.S. degrees in industrial mathematics and financial mathematics for students interested in industrial careers; a Master of Mathematics for Educators; and a Ph.D. in mathematical sciences, which emphasizes mathematical modeling, scientific computing, and industrial, scientific, and engineering applications. Research interests of the 33 full-time faculty members include Bayesian statistics, biomathematics, biostatistics, composite materials and optimal design, computational fluid dynamics, computational mathematics, cryptography, discrete mathematics, graph theory, mathematical physics, matroid theory, numerical analysis, operations research, optimization, parallel computing, statistical computing, stochastic control, and time-series analysis.

Mechanical Engineering: Professor Gretar Tryggvason, Head. Departmental research includes theoretical, numerical, and experimental work in rarefied gas and plasma dynamics, propulsion, multiphase flows, turbulent flows, fluid-structure interactions, structural analysis, nonlinear dynamics and control, random vibrations, biomechanics and biomaterials, materials processing, mechanics of granular materials, laser holography, MEMS, computer-aided engineering systems, reconfigurable machine design, compliant mechanism design, robotics, and other areas of engineering design. Facilities include the Computational Fluid and Plasma Laboratory, Microflow Laboratory, Rehabilitation Engineering Laboratory, the Center for Holographic Studies and Laser Technology, the Fluid Dynamics Laboratory, the Metal Processing Institute, the Advanced Casting Research Center, the Center for Heat Treating Excellence, the Powder Metallurgy Research Center, the Integrative Materials Design Center, and the Automation and Interventional Medicine Robotics Laboratory.

Physics: Associate Professor Germano Iannacchione, Head. Current research interests include theoretical, computational, and experimental work in soft-condensed-matter physics, quantum physics, biophysics, statistical mechanics, and BEC physics. Specializations include calorimetry and dielectric spectroscopy of complex fluids; thin-film ordering and wetting; microrheology of colloid and granular systems; optical properties of semiconductor superlattices, as measured by inelastic light scattering, luminescence, and excitation spectroscopies; laser spectroscopy of impurity ions in fiber-optic glasses; nonlinear and quantum optics; self-assembly and organization in complex fluids, such as biomaterials, liquid crystals, and proteins; magnetic systems and tunneling states; low-temperature behavior of glassy and amorphous materials; and AFM development.

Social Science and Policy Studies: Associate Professor James K. Doyle, Head. Major research areas include learning sciences, system dynamics, economic dynamics, information economics, sustainable economic development, judgment and decision making, and social psychology.

APPENDIXES

Institutional Changes Since the 2009 Edition

Following is an alphabetical listing of institutions that have recently closed, merged with other institutions, or changed their names or status. In the case of a name change, the former name appears first, followed by the new name.

Albany College of Pharmacy of Union University (Albany, NY): name changed to Albany College of Pharmacy and Health Sciences
Alvernia College (Reading, PA): name changed to Alvernia University
American Academy of Art (Chicago, IL): no longer offers graduate degrees
American InterContinental University (Weston, FL): name changed to American InterContinental University South Florida
Bentley College (Waltham, MA): name changed to Bentley University
College of St. Catherine (St. Paul, MN): name changed to St. Catherine University
The Colorado School of Professional Psychology (Colorado Springs, CO): name changed to University of the Rockies
Myers University (Cleveland, OH): name changed to Chancellor University
Episcopal Theological Seminary of the Southwest (Austin, TX): name changed to Seminary of the Southwest
Five Branches Institute: College of Traditional Chinese Medicine (Santa Cruz, CA): name changed to Five Branches University: Graduate School of Traditional Chinese Medicine
Heidelberg College (Tiffin, OH): name changed to Heidelberg University
Huron University USA in London (London, United Kingdom): closed; now a campus of Hult International Business School (Cambridge, MA)
Husson College (Bangor, ME): name changed to Husson University
Lenoir-Rhyne College (Hickory, NC): name changed to Lenoir-Rhyne University
Loyola College in Maryland (Baltimore, MD): name changed to Loyola University Maryland
Marian College (Indianapolis, IN): name changed to Marian University
Marian College of Fond du Lac (Fond du Lac, WI): name changed to Marian University
Mesivta of Eastern Parkway Rabbinical Seminary (Brooklyn, NY): name changed to Mesivta of Eastern Parkway–Yeshiva Zichron Meilech
Multnomah Bible College and Biblical Seminary (Portland, OR): name changed to Multnomah University
Muskingum College (New Concord, OH): name changed to Muskingum University
Neumann College (Aston, PA): name changed to Neumann University
North Carolina School of the Arts (Winston-Salem, NC): name changed to University of North Carolina School of the Arts
Northwest Christian College (Eugene, OR): name changed to Northwest Christian University
Pacific Graduate School of Psychology (Palo Alto, CA): name changed to Palo Alto University
Pennsylvania College of Optometry (Elkins Park, PA): name changed to Salus University
Psychological Studies Institute (Atlanta, GA): name changed to Richmont Graduate University
Saint Louis University, Madrid (Madrid, Spain): name changed to Saint Louis University–Madrid Campus
Samuel Merritt College (Oakland, CA): name changed to Samuel Merritt University
Schiller International University, American College of Switzerland (Leysin, Switzerland): closed
Sunbridge College (Spring Valley, NY): no longer degree granting
Taylor University College and Seminary (Edmonton, AB, Canada): name changed to Taylor College and Seminary
Taylor University Fort Wayne (Fort Wayne, IN): closed
Touro University College of Osteopathic Medicine (Vallejo, CA): name changed to Touro University
University College of the Fraser Valley (Abbotsford, BC, Canada): name changed to University of the Fraser Valley
University of Northern Virginia (Manassas, VA): no longer accredited by agency recognized by USDE or CHEA
Warner Southern College (Lake Wales, FL): name changed to Warner University

Abbreviations Used in the Guides

The following list includes abbreviations of degree names used in the profiles in the 2010 edition of the guides. Because some degrees (e.g., Doctor of Education) can be abbreviated in more than one way (e.g., D.Ed. or Ed.D.), and because the abbreviations used in the guides reflect the preferences of the individual colleges and universities, the list may include two or more abbreviations for a single degree.

Degrees

Because some degrees (e.g., Doctor of Education) can be abbreviated in more than one way (e.g., D.Ed. or Ed.D.), and because the abbreviations used in the guides reflect the preferences of the individual colleges and universities, the list may include two or more abbreviations for a single degree.

A Mus D	Doctor of Musical Arts
AC	Advanced Certificate
AD	Artist's Diploma Doctor of Arts
ADP	Artist's Diploma
Adv C	Advanced Certificate
Adv M	Advanced Master
AGC	Advanced Graduate Certificate
AGSC	Advanced Graduate Specialist Certificate
ALM	Master of Liberal Arts
AM	Master of Arts
AMRS	Master of Arts in Religious Studies
APC	Advanced Professional Certificate
App Sc	Applied Scientist
App Sc D	Doctor of Applied Science
Au D	Doctor of Audiology
B Th	Bachelor of Theology
CAES	Certificate of Advanced Educational Specialization
CAGS	Certificate of Advanced Graduate Studies
CAL	Certificate in Applied Linguistics
CALS	Certificate of Advanced Liberal Studies
CAMS	Certificate of Advanced Management Studies
CAPS	Certificate of Advanced Professional Studies
CAS	Certificate of Advanced Studies
CASPA	Certificate of Advanced Study in Public Administration
CASR	Certificate in Advanced Social Research
CATS	Certificate of Achievement in Theological Studies
CBHS	Certificate in Basic Health Sciences
CBS	Graduate Certificate in Biblical Studies
CCJA	Certificate in Criminal Justice Administration
CCSA	Certificate in Catholic School Administration
CCTS	Certificate in Clinical and Translational Science
CE	Civil Engineer
CEM	Certificate of Environmental Management
CET	Certificate in Educational Technologies
CGS	Certificate of Graduate Studies
Ch E	Chemical Engineer
CM	Certificate in Management
CMH	Certificate in Medical Humanities
CMM	Master of Church Ministries
CMS	Certificate in Ministerial Studies
CNM	Certificate in Nonprofit Management
CP	Certificate in Performance
CPASF	Certificate Program for Advanced Study in Finance
CPC	Certificate in Professional Counseling Certificate in Publication and Communication
CPH	Certificate in Public Health
CPM	Certificate in Public Management
CPS	Certificate of Professional Studies
CScD	Doctor of Clinical Science
CSD	Certificate in Spiritual Direction
CSS	Certificate of Special Studies
CTS	Certificate of Theological Studies
CURP	Certificate in Urban and Regional Planning
D Admin	Doctor of Administration
D Arch	Doctor of Architecture
D Com	Doctor of Commerce
D Div	Doctor of Divinity
D Ed	Doctor of Education
D Ed Min	Doctor of Educational Ministry
D Eng	Doctor of Engineering
D Engr	Doctor of Engineering
D Env	Doctor of Environment
D Env M	Doctor of Environmental Management
D Law	Doctor of Law
D Litt	Doctor of Letters
D Med Sc	Doctor of Medical Science
D Mgt	Doctor of Management
D Min	Doctor of Ministry
D Min PCC	Doctor of Ministry, Pastoral Care, and Counseling
D Miss	Doctor of Missiology
D Mus	Doctor of Music
D Mus A	Doctor of Musical Arts
D Phil	Doctor of Philosophy
D Ps	Doctor of Psychology
D Sc	Doctor of Science
D Sc D	Doctor of Science in Dentistry
D Sc IS	Doctor of Science in Information Systems
D Sc PA	Doctor of Science in Physician Assistant Studies
D Th	Doctor of Theology
D Th P	Doctor of Practical Theology
DA	Doctor of Accounting Doctor of Arts
DA Ed	Doctor of Arts in Education
DAH	Doctor of Arts in Humanities
DAOM	Doctorate in Acupuncture and Oriental Medicine
DAST	Diploma of Advanced Studies in Teaching
DBA	Doctor of Business Administration
DBL	Doctor of Business Leadership
DBS	Doctor of Buddhist Studies
DC	Doctor of Chiropractic
DCC	Doctor of Computer Science
DCD	Doctor of Communications Design
DCL	Doctor of Civil Law Doctor of Comparative Law
DCM	Doctor of Church Music
DCN	Doctor of Clinical Nutrition
DCS	Doctor of Computer Science
DDN	Diplôme du Droit Notarial
DDS	Doctor of Dental Surgery
DE	Doctor of Education Doctor of Engineering
DED	Doctor of Economic Development
DEIT	Doctor of Educational Innovation and Technology
DEM	Doctor of Educational Ministry
DEPD	Diplôme études Spécialisées
DES	Doctor of Engineering Science
DESS	Diplôme études Supérieures Spécialisées
DFA	Doctor of Fine Arts
DGP	Diploma in Graduate and Professional Studies
DH Ed	Doctor of Health Education
DH Sc	Doctor of Health Sciences
DHA	Doctor of Health Administration
DHCE	Doctor of Health Care Ethics
DHL	Doctor of Hebrew Letters Doctor of Hebrew Literature
DHS	Doctor of Health Science Doctor of Human Services
DHSc	Doctor of Health Science

Dip CS	Diploma in Christian Studies
DIT	Doctor of Industrial Technology
DJ Ed	Doctor of Jewish Education
DJS	Doctor of Jewish Studies
DLS	Doctor of Liberal Studies
DM	Doctor of Management Doctor of Music
DMA	Doctor of Musical Arts
DMD	Doctor of Dental Medicine
DME	Doctor of Manufacturing Management Doctor of Music Education
DMEd	Doctor of Music Education
DMFT	Doctor of Marital and Family Therapy
DMH	Doctor of Medical Humanities
DML	Doctor of Modern Languages
DMM	Doctor of Music Ministry
DMPNA	Doctor of Management Practice in Nurse Anesthesia
DN Sc	Doctor of Nursing Science
DNAP	Doctor of Nurse Anesthesia Practice
DNP	Doctor of Nursing Practice
DNS	Doctor of Nursing Science
DO	Doctor of Osteopathy
DPA	Doctor of Public Administration
DPC	Doctor of Pastoral Counseling
DPDS	Doctor of Planning and Development Studies
DPH	Doctor of Public Health
DPM	Doctor of Plant Medicine Doctor of Podiatric Medicine
DPS	Doctor of Professional Studies
DPT	Doctor of Physical Therapy
DPTSc	Doctor of Physical Therapy Science
Dr DES	Doctor of Design
Dr PH	Doctor of Public Health
Dr Sc PT	Doctor of Science in Physical Therapy
DS	Doctor of Science
DS Sc	Doctor of Social Science
DSJS	Doctor of Science in Jewish Studies
DSL	Doctor of Strategic Leadership
DSM	Doctor of Sport Management
DSN	Doctor of Science in Nursing
DSW	Doctor of Social Work
DTL	Doctor of Talmudic Law
DV Sc	Doctor of Veterinary Science
DVM	Doctor of Veterinary Medicine
EAA	Engineer in Aeronautics and Astronautics
ECS	Engineer in Computer Science
Ed D	Doctor of Education
Ed DCT	Doctor of Education in College Teaching
Ed M	Master of Education
Ed S	Specialist in Education
Ed Sp	Specialist in Education
Ed Sp PTE	Specialist in Education in Professional Technical Education
EDM	Executive Doctorate in Management
EDSPC	Education Specialist
EE	Electrical Engineer
EJD	Executive Juris Doctor
EMBA	Executive Master of Business Administration
EMHA	Executive Master of Health Administration
EMIB	Executive Master of International Business
EMPA	Executive Master of Public Administration Executive Master of Public Affairs
EMS	Executive Master of Science
EMTM	Executive Master of Technology Management
Eng	Engineer
Eng Sc D	Doctor of Engineering Science
Engr	Engineer
Ex Doc	Executive Doctor of Pharmacy
Exec Ed D	Executive Doctor of Education
Exec MBA	Executive Master of Business Administration
Exec MPA	Executive Master of Public Administration
Exec MPH	Executive Master of Public Health
Exec MS	Executive Master of Science
G Dip	Graduate Diploma
GBC	Graduate Business Certificate
GCE	Graduate Certificate in Education
GDM	Graduate Diploma in Management
GDPA	Graduate Diploma in Public Administration
GDRE	Graduate Diploma in Religious Education
GEMBA	Global Executive Master of Business Administration
GMBA	Global Master of Business Administration
GPD	Graduate Performance Diploma
GSS	Graduate Special Certificate for Students in Special Situations
IEMBA	International Executive Master of Business Administration
IMA	Interdisciplinary Master of Arts
IMBA	International Master of Business Administration
IMES	International Masters in Environmental Studies
Ingeniero	Engineer
JCD	Doctor of Canon Law
JCL	Licentiate in Canon Law
JD	Juris Doctor
JD/MUEP	Juris Doctor/Master of Urban and Environmental Planning
JSD	Doctor of Juridical Science Doctor of Jurisprudence Doctor of the Science of Law
JSM	Master of Science of Law
L Th	Licenciate in Theology
LL B	Bachelor of Laws
LL CM	Master of Laws in Comparative Law
LL D	Doctor of Laws
LL M	Master of Laws
LL M in Tax	Master of Laws in Taxation
LL M CL	Master of Laws (Common Law)
M Ac	Master of Accountancy Master of Accounting Master of Acupuncture
M Ac OM	Master of Acupuncture and Oriental Medicine
M Acc	Master of Accountancy Master of Accounting
M Acct	Master of Accountancy Master of Accounting
M Accy	Master of Accountancy
M Actg	Master of Accounting
M Acy	Master of Accountancy
M Ad	Master of Administration
M Ad Ed	Master of Adult Education
M Adm	Master of Administration
M Adm Mgt	Master of Administrative Management
M Admin	Master of Administration
M ADU	Master of Architectural Design and Urbanism
M Adv	Master of Advertising
M Aero E	Master of Aerospace Engineering
M AEST	Master of Applied Environmental Science and Technology
M Ag	Master of Agriculture
M Ag Ed	Master of Agricultural Education
M Agr	Master of Agriculture
M Anesth Ed	Master of Anesthesiology Education
M App Comp Sc	Master of Applied Computer Science
M App St	Master of Applied Statistics
M Appl Stat	Master of Applied Statistics
M Aq	Master of Aquaculture
M Ar	Master of Architecture
M Arc	Master of Architecture
M Arch	Master of Architecture
M Arch I	Master of Architecture I
M Arch II	Master of Architecture II
M Arch E	Master of Architectural Engineering
M Arch H	Master of Architectural History
M Arch Studies	Master of Architectural Studies

M Arch UD	Master of Architecture in Urban Design
M Bioethics	Master in Bioethics
M Biomath	Master of Biomathematics
M Ch	Master of Chemistry
M Ch E	Master of Chemical Engineering
M Chem	Master of Chemistry
M Cl D	Master of Clinical Dentistry
M Cl Sc	Master of Clinical Science
M Comp E	Master of Computer Engineering
M Comp Sc	Master of Computer Science
M Coun	Master of Counseling
M Dent	Master of Dentistry
M Dent Sc	Master of Dental Sciences
M Des	Master of Design
M Des S	Master of Design Studies
M Div	Master of Divinity
M Ec	Master of Economics
M Econ	Master of Economics
M Ed	Master of Education
M Ed T	Master of Education in Teaching
M En	Master of Engineering
M En S	Master of Environmental Sciences
M Eng	Master of Engineering
M Eng Mgt	Master of Engineering Management
M Eng Tel	Master of Engineering in Telecommunications
M Engr	Master of Engineering
M Env	Master of Environment
M Env Des	Master of Environmental Design
M Env E	Master of Environmental Engineering
M Env Sc	Master of Environmental Science
M Fin	Master of Finance
M Geo E	Master of Geological Engineering
M Geoenv E	Master of Geoenvironmental Engineering
M Geog	Master of Geography
M Hum	Master of Humanities
M Hum Svcs	Master of Human Services
M IBD	Master of Integrated Building Delivery
M IDST	Master's in Interdisciplinary Studies
M Kin	Master of Kinesiology
M Land Arch	Master of Landscape Architecture
M Litt	Master of Letters
M Man	Master of Management
M Mat SE	Master of Material Science and Engineering
M Math	Master of Mathematics
M Med Sc	Master of Medical Science
M Mgmt	Master of Management
M Mgt	Master of Management
M Min	Master of Ministries
M Mtl E	Master of Materials Engineering
M Mu	Master of Music
M Mus	Master of Music
M Mus Ed	Master of Music Education
M Music	Master of Music
M Nat Sci	Master of Natural Science
M Oc E	Master of Oceanographic Engineering
M Pharm	Master of Pharmacy
M Phil	Master of Philosophy
M Phil F	Master of Philosophical Foundations
M Pl	Master of Planning
M Plan	Master of Planning
M Pol	Master of Political Science
M Pr Met	Master of Professional Meteorology
M Prob S	Master of Probability and Statistics
M Prof Past	Master of Professional Pastoral
M Psych	Master of Psychology
M Pub	Master of Publishing
M Rel	Master of Religion
M Sc	Master of Science
M Sc A	Master of Science (Applied)
M Sc AHN	Master of Science in Applied Human Nutrition
M Sc BMC	Master of Science in Biomedical Communications
M Sc CS	Master of Science in Computer Science
M Sc E	Master of Science in Engineering
M Sc Eng	Master of Science in Engineering
M Sc Engr	Master of Science in Engineering
M Sc F	Master of Science in Forestry
M Sc FE	Master of Science in Forest Engineering
M Sc Geogr	Master of Science in Geography
M Sc N	Master of Science in Nursing
M Sc OT	Master of Science in Occupational Therapy
M Sc P	Master of Science in Planning
M Sc Pl	Master of Science in Planning
M Sc PT	Master of Science in Physical Therapy
M Sc T	Master of Science in Teaching
M Serv Soc	Master of Social Service
M Soc	Master of Sociology
M Sp Ed	Master of Special Education
M Stat	Master of Statistics
M Sw En	Master of Software Engineering
M Sys Sc	Master of Systems Science
M Tax	Master of Taxation
M Tech	Master of Technology
M Th	Master of Theology
M Th Past	Master of Pastoral Theology
M Tox	Master of Toxicology
M Trans E	Master of Transportation Engineering
M Urb	Master of Urban Planning
M Vet Sc	Master of Veterinary Science
MA	Master of Administration Master of Arts
MA Comm	Master of Arts in Communication
MA Ed	Master of Arts in Education
MA Ed Ad	Master of Arts in Educational Administration
MA Ext	Master of Agricultural Extension
MA Islamic	Master of Arts in Islamic Studies
MA Military Studies	Master of Arts in Military Studies
MA Min	Master of Arts in Ministry
MA Miss	Master of Arts in Missiology
MA Past St	Master of Arts in Pastoral Studies
MA Ph	Master of Arts in Philosophy
MA Psych	Master of Arts in Psychology
MA Sc	Master of Applied Science
MA Sp	Master of Arts (Spirituality)
MA Strategic Intelligence	Master of Arts in Strategic Intelligence
MA Th	Master of Arts in Theology
MA-R	Master of Arts (Research)
MAA	Master of Administrative Arts Master of Applied Anthropology Master of Applied Arts Master of Arts in Administration
MAAAP	Master of Arts Administration and Policy
MAAE	Master of Arts in Art Education
MAAL	Master of Accountancy and Applied Leadership
MAAT	Master of Arts in Applied Theology Master of Arts in Art Therapy
MAB	Master of Agribusiness
MABC	Master of Arts in Biblical Counseling Master of Arts in Business Communication
MABE	Master of Arts in Bible Exposition
MABL	Master of Arts in Biblical Languages
MABM	Master of Agribusiness Management
MABS	Master of Arts in Biblical Studies
MABT	Master of Arts in Bible Teaching
MAC	Master of Accountancy Master of Accounting Master of Arts in Communication Master of Arts in Counseling
MACAT	Master of Arts in Counseling Psychology: Art Therapy
MACC	Master of Arts in Christian Counseling

MACCM	Master of Arts in Church and Community Ministry
MACCT	Master of Accounting
MACE	Master of Arts in Christian Education
MACFM	Master of Arts in Children's and Family Ministry
MACH	Master of Arts in Church History
MACIS	Master of Accounting and Information Systems
MACJ	Master of Arts in Criminal Justice
MACL	Master of Arts in Christian Leadership
MACM	Master of Arts in Christian Ministries Master of Arts in Church Music Master of Arts in Counseling Ministries
MACN	Master of Arts in Counseling
MACO	Master of Arts in Counseling
MAcOM	Master of Acupuncture and Oriental Medicine
MACP	Master of Arts in Counseling Psychology
MACPC	Master of Clinical Pastoral Counseling
MACS	Master of Arts in Catholic Studies
MACSE	Master of Arts in Christian School Education
MACT	Master of Arts in Christian Thought Master of Arts in Communications and Technology
MAD	Master in Educational Institution Administration Master of Art and Design
MADR	Master of Arts in Dispute Resolution
MADS	Master of Animal and Dairy Science Master of Applied Disability Studies
MAE	Master of Aerospace Engineering Master of Agricultural Economics Master of Agricultural Education Master of Architectural Engineering Master of Art Education Master of Arts in Economics Master of Arts in Education Master of Arts in English Master of Automotive Engineering
MAEd	Master of Arts Education
MAEL	Master of Arts in Educational Leadership Master of Arts in Executive Leadership
MAEM	Master of Arts in Educational Ministries
MAEN	Master of Arts in English
MAEP	Master of Arts in Economic Policy
MAES	Master of Arts in Environmental Sciences
MAESL	Master of Arts in English as a Second Language
MAET	Master of Arts in English Teaching
MAF	Master of Arts in Finance
MAFE	Master of Arts in Financial Economics
MAFLL	Master of Arts in Foreign Language and Literature
MAFM	Master of Accounting and Financial Management
MAFS	Master of Arts in Family Studies
MAG	Master of Applied Geography
MAGC	Master of Arts in Global Communication
MAGP	Master of Arts in Gerontological Psychology
MAGU	Master of Urban Analysis and Management
MAH	Master of Arts in Humanities
MAHA	Master of Arts in Humanitarian Assistance Master of Arts in Humanitarian Studies
MAHCM	Master of Arts in Health Care Mission
MAHG	Master of American History and Government
MAHL	Master of Arts in Hebrew Letters
MAHN	Master of Applied Human Nutrition
MAHS	Master of Arts in Human Services
MAHSR	Master of Applied Health Services Research
MAHT	Master of Arts in History Teaching
MAIA	Master of Arts in International Administration
MAIB	Master of Arts in International Business
MAICS	Master of Arts in Intercultural Studies
MAIDM	Master of Arts in Interior Design and Merchandising
MAIH	Master of Arts in Interdisciplinary Humanities
MAIPCR	Master of Arts in International Peace and Conflict Management
MAIR	Master of Arts in Industrial Relations
MAIS	Master of Arts in Intercultural Studies Master of Arts in Interdisciplinary Studies Master of Arts in International Studies
MAIT	Master of Administration in Information Technology Master of Applied Information Technology
MAJ	Master of Arts in Journalism
MAJ Ed	Master of Arts in Jewish Education
MAJCS	Master of Arts in Jewish Communal Service
MAJE	Master of Arts in Jewish Education
MAJS	Master of Arts in Jewish Studies
MAL	Master in Agricultural Leadership
MALA	Master of Arts in Liberal Arts
MALD	Master of Arts in Law and Diplomacy
MALER	Master of Arts in Labor and Employment Relations
MALM	Master of Applied Leadership and Management Master of Arts in Leadership Evangelical Mobilization
MALP	Master of Arts in Language Pedagogy
MALPS	Master of Arts in Liberal and Professional Studies
MALS	Master of Arts in Liberal Studies
MALT	Master of Arts in Learning and Teaching
MAM	Master of Acquisition Management Master of Agriculture and Management Master of Applied Mathematics Master of Arts in Management Master of Arts in Ministry Master of Arts Management Master of Avian Medicine
MAMB	Master of Applied Molecular Biology
MAMC	Master of Arts in Mass Communication Master of Arts in Ministry and Culture Master of Arts in Ministry for a Multicultural Church
MAME	Master of Arts in Missions/Evangelism
MAMFC	Master of Arts in Marriage and Family Counseling
MAMFCC	Master of Arts in Marriage, Family, and Child Counseling
MAMFT	Master of Arts in Marriage and Family Therapy
MAMM	Master of Arts in Ministry Management
MAMS	Master of Applied Mathematical Sciences Master of Arts in Ministerial Studies Master of Arts in Ministry and Spirituality
MAMT	Master of Arts in Mathematics Teaching
MAN	Master of Applied Nutrition
MANM	Master of Arts in Nonprofit Management
MANP	Master of Applied Natural Products
MANT	Master of Arts in New Testament
MAO	Master of Arts in Organizational Psychology
MAOM	Master of Acupuncture and Oriental Medicine Master of Arts in Organizational Management
MAOT	Master of Arts in Old Testament
MAP	Master of Applied Psychology Master of Arts in Planning Master of Public Administration Masters of Psychology
MAP Min	Master of Arts in Pastoral Ministry
MAPA	Master of Arts in Public Administration
MAPC	Master of Arts in Pastoral Counseling
MAPE	Master of Arts in Political Economy
MAPL	Master of Arts in Pastoral Leadership
MAPM	Master of Arts in Pastoral Ministry Master of Arts in Pastoral Music Master of Arts in Practical Ministry
MAPP	Master of Arts in Public Policy
MAPPS	Master of Arts in Asia Pacific Policy Studies
MAPS	Master of Arts in Pastoral Counseling/Spiritual Formation Master of Arts in Pastoral Studies Master of Arts in Public Service
MAPT	Master of Practical Theology
MAPW	Master of Arts in Professional Writing
MAR	Master of Arts in Religion
Mar Eng	Marine Engineer
MARC	Master of Arts in Rehabilitation Counseling
MARE	Master of Arts in Religious Education
MARL	Master of Arts in Religious Leadership
MARS	Master of Arts in Religious Studies

MAS	Master of Accounting Science Master of Actuarial Science Master of Administrative Science Master of Advanced Study Master of Aeronautical Science Master of American Studies Master of Applied Science Master of Applied Statistics Master of Architectural Studies Master of Archival Studies
MASA	Master of Advanced Studies in Architecture
MASAC	Master of Arts in Substance Abuse Counseling
MASD	Master of Arts in Spiritual Direction
MASE	Master of Arts in Special Education
MASF	Master of Arts in Spiritual Formation
MASJ	Master of Arts in Systems of Justice
MASL	Master of Arts in School Leadership
MASLA	Master of Advanced Studies in Landscape Architecture
MASM	Master of Arts in Specialized Ministries
MASP	Master of Applied Social Psychology Master of Arts in School Psychology
MASPAA	Master of Arts in Sports and Athletic Administration
MASS	Master of Applied Social Science Master of Arts in Social Science
MAST	Master of Arts Science Teaching
MASW	Master of Aboriginal Social Work
MAT	Master of Arts in Teaching Master of Arts in Theology Master of Athletic Training Masters in Administration of Telecommunications
Mat E	Materials Engineer
MATCM	Master of Acupuncture and Traditional Chinese Medicine
MATDE	Master of Arts in Theology, Development, and Evangelism
MATDR	Master of Territorial Management and Regional Development
MATE	Master of Arts for the Teaching of English
MATESL	Master of Arts in Teaching English as a Second Language
MATESOL	Master of Arts in Teaching English to Speakers of Other Languages
MATF	Master of Arts in Teaching English as a Foreign Language/Intercultural Studies
MATFL	Master of Arts in Teaching Foreign Language
MATH	Master of Arts in Therapy
MATI	Master of Administration of Information Technology
MATL	Master of Arts in Teaching of Languages Master of Arts in Transformational Leadership
MATM	Master of Arts in Teaching of Mathematics
MATS	Master of Arts in Theological Studies Master of Arts in Transforming Spirituality
MATSL	Master of Arts in Teaching a Second Language
MAUA	Master of Arts in Urban Affairs
MAUD	Master of Arts in Urban Design
MAURP	Master of Arts in Urban and Regional Planning
MAW	Master of Arts in Worship Master of Arts in Writing
MAWL	Master of Arts in Worship Leadership
MAWSHP	Master of Arts in Worship
MAXM	Master of Arts in Christian Ministries
MAYM	Master of Arts in Youth Ministry
MB	Master of Bioinformatics
MBA	Master of Business Administration
MBA-EP	Master of Business Administration–Experienced Professionals
MBAA	Master of Business Administration in Aviation
MBAE	Master of Biological and Agricultural Engineering Master of Biosystems and Agricultural Engineering
MBAH	Master of Business Administration in Health
MBAi	Master of Business Administration–International
MBAICT	Master of Business Administration in Information and Communication Technology
MBAIM	Master of Business Administration in International Management
MBAPA	Master of Business Administration–Physician Assistant
MBATM	Master of Business Administration in Technology Management
MBC	Master of Building Construction
MBE	Master of Bilingual Education Master of Bioengineering Master of Biological Engineering Master of Biomedical Engineering Master of Business and Engineering Master of Business Economics Master of Business Education
MBET	Master of Business, Entrepreneurship and Technology
MBIT	Master of Business Information Technology
MBL	Master of Business Law Master of Business Leadership
MBLE	Master in Business Logistics Engineering
MBMI	Master of Biomedical Imaging and Signals
MBMSE	Master of Business Management and Software Engineering
MBS	Master of Behavioral Science Master of Biblical Studies Master of Biological Science Master of Biomedical Sciences Master of Bioscience Master of Building Science
MBSI	Master of Business Information Science
MBT	Master of Biblical and Theological Studies Master of Biomedical Technology Master of Business Taxation Master's Degree in Biotechnology
MC	Master of Communication Master of Counseling Master of Cybersecurity
MC Ed	Master of Continuing Education
MC Sc	Master of Computer Science
MCA	Master of Arts in Applied Criminology Master of Commercial Aviation
MCAM	Master of Computational and Applied Mathematics
MCC	Master of Computer Science
MCCS	Master of Crop and Soil Sciences
MCD	Master of Communications Disorders Master of Community Development
MCE	Master in Electronic Commerce Master of Christian Education Master of Civil Engineering Master of Control Engineering
MCEM	Master of Construction Engineering Management
MCHE	Master of Chemical Engineering
MCIS	Master of Communication and Information Studies Master of Computer and Information Science Master of Computer Information Systems
MCIT	Master of Computer and Information Technology
MCJ	Master of Criminal Justice
MCJA	Master of Criminal Justice Administration
MCL	Master in Communication Leadership Master of Canon Law Master of Civil Law Master of Comparative Law
MCM	Master of Christian Ministry Master of Church Music Master of City Management Master of Communication Management Master of Community Medicine Master of Construction Management Master of Contract Management Masters of Corporate Media
MCMP	Master of City and Metropolitan Planning
MCMS	Master of Clinical Medical Science
MCP	Master in Science Master of City Planning Master of Community Planning Master of Counseling Psychology Master of Cytopathology Practice
MCPC	Master of Arts in Chaplaincy and Pastoral Care
MCPD	Master of Community Planning and Development
MCRP	Master of City and Regional Planning
MCRS	Master of City and Regional Studies

MCS	Master of Christian Studies Master of Clinical Science Master of Combined Sciences Master of Communication Studies Master of Computer Science Master of Consumer Science
MCSE	Master of Computer Science and Engineering
MCSL	Master of Catholic School Leadership
MCSM	Master of Construction Science/Management
MCST	Master of Science in Computer Science and Information Technology
MCTP	Master of Communication Technology and Policy
MCTS	Master of Clinical and Translational Science
MCVS	Master of Cardiovascular Science
MD	Doctor of Medicine
MDA	Master of Development Administration Master of Dietetic Administration
MDB	Master of Design-Build
MDE	Master of Developmental Economics Master of Distance Education
MDH	Master of Dental Hygiene
MDM	Master of Digital Media
MDR	Master of Dispute Resolution
MDS	Master of Dental Surgery
ME	Master of Education Master of Engineering Master of Entrepreneurship Master of Evangelism
ME Sc	Master of Engineering Science
MEA	Master of Educational Administration Master of Engineering Administration
MEAP	Master of Environmental Administration and Planning
MEBT	Master in Electronic Business Technologies
MEC	Master of Electronic Commerce
MECE	Master of Electrical and Computer Engineering
Mech E	Mechanical Engineer
MED	Master of Education of the Deaf
MEDL	Master of Educational Leadership
MEDS	Master of Environmental Design Studies
MEE	Master in Education Master of Electrical Engineering Master of Energy Engineering Master of Environmental Engineering
MEEM	Master of Environmental Engineering and Management
MEENE	Master of Engineering in Environmental Engineering
MEEP	Master of Environmental and Energy Policy
MEERM	Master of Earth and Environmental Resource Management
MEH	Master in Humanistic Studies Master of Environmental Horticulture
MEHS	Master of Environmental Health and Safety
MEIM	Master of Entertainment Industry Management
MEL	Master of Educational Leadership Master of English Literature
MEM	Master of Ecosystem Management Master of Electricity Markets Master of Engineering Management Master of Environmental Management Master of Marketing
MEME	Master of Engineering in Manufacturing Engineering Master of Engineering in Mechanical Engineering
MEMS	Master of Engineering in Manufacturing Systems
MENG	Master of Arts in English
MENVEGR	Master of Environmental Engineering
MEP	Master of Engineering Physics
MEPC	Master of Environmental Pollution Control
MEPD	Master of Education–Professional Development
MEPM	Master of Environmental Protection Management
MER	Master of Employment Relations
MES	Master of Education and Science Master of Engineering Science Master of Environmental Science Master of Environmental Studies Master of Environmental Systems Master of Special Education
MESM	Master of Environmental Science and Management
MET	Master of Education in Teaching Master of Educational Technology Master of Engineering Technology Master of Entertainment Technology Master of Environmental Toxicology
Met E	Metallurgical Engineer
METM	Master of Engineering and Technology Management
MEVE	Master of Environmental Engineering
MF	Master of Finance Master of Forestry
MFA	Master of Financial Administration Master of Fine Arts
MFAM	Master in Food Animal Medicine
MFAS	Master of Fisheries and Aquatic Science
MFAW	Master of Fine Arts in Writing
MFC	Master of Forest Conservation
MFCS	Master of Family and Consumer Sciences
MFE	Master of Financial Economics Master of Financial Engineering Master of Forest Engineering
MFG	Master of Functional Genomics
MFHD	Master of Family and Human Development
MFM	Master of Financial Mathematics
MFMS	Masters in Food Microbiology and Safety
MFPE	Master of Food Process Engineering
MFR	Master of Forest Resources
MFRC	Master of Forest Resources and Conservation
MFS	Master of Financial Services Master of Food Science Master of Forensic Sciences Master of Forest Science Master of Forest Studies Master of French Studies
MFSA	Master of Forensic Sciences Administration
MFST	Master of Food Safety and Technology
MFT	Master of Family Therapy Master of Food Technology
MFWB	Master of Fishery and Wildlife Biology
MFWCB	Master of Fish, Wildlife and Conservation Biology
MFWS	Master of Fisheries and Wildlife Sciences
MFYCS	Master of Family, Youth and Community Sciences
MG	Master of Genetics
MGA	Master of Governmental Administration
MGD	Master of Graphic Design
MGE	Master of Gas Engineering Master of Geotechnical Engineering
MGH	Master of Geriatric Health
MGIS	Master of Geographic Information Science Master of Geographic Information Systems
MGM	Master of Global Management
MGP	Master of Gestion de Projet
MGPS	Master of Global Policy Studies
MGS	Master of Gerontological Studies Master of Global Studies
MH	Master of Humanities
MH Ed	Master of Health Education
MH Sc	Master of Health Sciences
MHA	Master of Health Administration Master of Healthcare Administration Master of Hospital Administration Master of Hospitality Administration
MHAD	Master of Health Administration
MHCA	Master of Health Care Administration
MHCI	Master of Human-Computer Interaction
MHCL	Master of Health Care Leadership
MHE	Master of Health Education Master of Human Ecology
MHE Ed	Master of Home Economics Education
MHEA	Masters of Higher Education Administration
MHHS	Master of Health and Human Services
MHI	Master of Health Informatics Master of Healthcare Innovation
MHIIM	Master of Health Informatics and Information Management

MHIS	Master of Health Information Systems
MHK	Master of Human Kinetics
MHL	Master of Hebrew Literature
MHM	Master of Hospitality Management
MHMS	Master of Health Management Systems
MHP	Master of Health Physics Master of Heritage Preservation Master of Historic Preservation
MHPA	Master of Heath Policy and Administration
MHPE	Master of Health Professions Education
MHR	Master of Human Resources
MHRD	Master in Human Resource Development
MHRIM	Master of Hotel, Restaurant, and Institutional Management
MHRIR	Master of Human Resources and Industrial Relations
MHRLR	Master of Human Resources and Labor Relations
MHRM	Master of Human Resources Management
MHROD	Master of Human Resources and Organization Development
MHS	Master of Health Science Master of Health Sciences Master of Health Studies Master of Hispanic Studies Master of Human Services Master of Humanistic Studies
MHSA	Master of Health Services Administration
MHSM	Master of Health Sector Management Master of Health Systems Management
MI	Master of Instruction
MI Arch	Master of Interior Architecture
MI St	Master of Information Studies
MIA	Master of Interior Architecture Master of International Affairs
MIAA	Master of International Affairs and Administration
MIAM	Master of International Agribusiness Management
MIB	Master of International Business
MIBA	Master of International Business Administration
MICM	Master of International Construction Management
MID	Master of Industrial Design Master of Industrial Distribution Master of Interior Design Master of International Development
MIE	Master of Industrial Engineering
MIH	Master of Integrative Health
MIHTM	Master of International Hospitality and Tourism Management
MIJ	Master of International Journalism
MILR	Master of Industrial and Labor Relations
MiM	Master in Management
MIM	Master of Industrial Management Master of Information Management Master of International Management
MIMLAE	Master of International Management for Latin American Executives
MIMS	Master of Information Management and Systems Master of Integrated Manufacturing Systems
MIP	Master of Infrastructure Planning Master of Intellectual Property
MIPER	Master of International Political Economy of Resources
MIPP	Master of International Policy and Practice Master of International Public Policy
MIPS	Master of International Planning Studies
MIR	Master of Industrial Relations Master of International Relations
MIS	Master of Industrial Statistics Master of Information Science Master of Information Systems Master of Integrated Science Master of Interdisciplinary Studies Master of International Service Master of International Studies
MISE	Master of Industrial and Systems Engineering
MISKM	Master of Information Sciences and Knowledge Management
MISM	Master of Information Systems Management
MIT	Master in Teaching Master of Industrial Technology Master of Information Technology Master of Initial Teaching Master of International Trade Master of Internet Technology
MITA	Master of Information Technology Administration
MITM	Master of International Technology Management
MITO	Master of Industrial Technology and Operations
MJ	Master of Journalism Master of Jurisprudence
MJ Ed	Master of Jewish Education
MJA	Master of Justice Administration
MJM	Master of Justice Management
MJS	Master of Judicial Studies Master of Juridical Science
MKM	Master of Knowledge Management
ML	Master of Latin
ML Arch	Master of Landscape Architecture
MLA	Master of Landscape Architecture Master of Liberal Arts
MLAS	Master of Laboratory Animal Science Master of Liberal Arts and Sciences
MLAUD	Master of Landscape Architecture in Urban Development
MLD	Master of Leadership Development Master of Leadership Studies
MLE	Master of Applied Linguistics and Exegesis
MLER	Master of Labor and Employment Relations
MLERE	Master of Land Economics and Real Estate
MLHR	Master of Labor and Human Resources
MLI	Master of Legal Institutions
MLI Sc	Master of Library and Information Science
MLIS	Master of Library and Information Science Master of Library and Information Studies
MLM	Master of Library Media
MLOS	Masters in Leadership and Organizational Studies
MLRHR	Master of Labor Relations and Human Resources
MLS	Master of Leadership Studies Master of Legal Studies Master of Liberal Studies Master of Library Science Master of Life Sciences
MLSP	Master of Law and Social Policy
MLT	Master of Language Technologies
MLW	Master of Studies in Law
MM	Master of Management Master of Ministry Master of Missiology Master of Music
MM Ed	Master of Music Education Master of Music Education
MM Sc	Master of Medical Science
MM St	Master of Museum Studies
MM/MLS	Master of Music/Master of Library Science
MMA	Master of Marine Affairs Master of Media Arts Master of Musical Arts
MMAE	Master of Mechanical and Aerospace Engineering
MMAS	Master of Military Art and Science
MMB	Master of Microbial Biotechnology
MMBA	Managerial Master of Business Administration
MMC	Master of Manufacturing Competitiveness Master of Mass Communications Master of Music Conducting
MMCM	Master of Music in Church Music
MMCSS	Masters of Mathematical Computational and Statistical Sciences
MME	Master of Manufacturing Engineering Master of Mathematics Education Master of Mathematics for Educators Master of Mechanical Engineering Master of Medical Engineering Master of Mining Engineering Master of Music Education
MMF	Master of Mathematical Finance

MMFT	Master of Marriage and Family Therapy
MMG	Master of Management
MMH	Master of Management in Hospitality Master of Medical History Master of Medical Humanities
MMIS	Master of Management Information Systems
MMM	Master of Manufacturing Management Master of Marine Management Master of Medical Management
MMME	Master of Metallurgical and Materials Engineering
MMMP	Master of Music in Music Performance
MMP	Master of Management Practice Master of Marine Policy Master of Music Performance
MMPA	Master of Management and Professional Accounting
MMQM	Master of Manufacturing Quality Management
MMR	Master of Marketing Research
MMRM	Master of Marine Resources Management
MMS	Master of Management Science Master of Management Studies Master of Manufacturing Systems Master of Marine Studies Master of Materials Science Master of Medical Science Master of Medieval Studies Master of Modern Studies
MMSE	Master of Manufacturing Systems Engineering
MMSM	Master of Music in Sacred Music
MMT	Master in Marketing Master of Management Master of Music Teaching Master of Music Therapy Masters in Marketing Technology
MMus	Master of Music
MN	Master of Nursing Master of Nutrition
MN NP	Master of Nursing in Nurse Practitioner
MNA	Master of Nonprofit Administration Master of Nurse Anesthesia
MNAL	Master of Nonprofit Administration and Leadership
MNAS	Master of Natural and Applied Science
MNCM	Master of Network and Communications Management
MNE	Master of Network Engineering Master of Nuclear Engineering
MNL	Master in International Business for Latin America
MNM	Master of Nonprofit Management
MNO	Master of Nonprofit Organization
MNPL	Master of Not-for-Profit Leadership
MNPS	Master of New Professional Studies
MNpS	Master of Nonprofit Studies
MNR	Master of Natural Resources
MNRES	Master of Natural Resources and Environmental Studies
MNRM	Master of Natural Resource Management
MNRS	Master of Natural Resource Stewardship
MNS	Master of Natural Science
MO	Master of Oceanography
MOD	Master of Organizational Development
MOGS	Master of Oil and Gas Studies
MOH	Master of Occupational Health
MOL	Master of Organizational Leadership
MOM	Master of Oriental Medicine
MOR	Master of Operations Research
MOT	Master of Occupational Therapy
MP	Master of Physiology Master of Planning
MP Ac	Master of Professional Accountancy
MP Acc	Master of Professional Accountancy Master of Professional Accounting Master of Public Accounting
MP Aff	Master of Public Affairs
MP Th	Master of Pastoral Theology
MPA	Master of Physician Assistant Master of Professional Accountancy Master of Professional Accounting Master of Public Administration Master of Public Affairs
MPAC	Masters in Professional Accounting
MPAID	Master of Public Administration and International Development
MPAP	Master of Physician Assistant Practice Master of Public Affairs and Politics
MPAS	Master of Physician Assistant Science Master of Physician Assistant Studies Master of Public Art Studies
MPC	Master of Pastoral Counseling Master of Professional Communication Master of Professional Counseling
MPD	Master of Product Development Master of Public Diplomacy
MPDS	Master of Planning and Development Studies
MPE	Master of Physical Education Master of Power Engineering
MPEM	Master of Project Engineering and Management
MPH	Master of Public Health
MPHE	Master of Public Health Education
MPHTM	Master of Public Health and Tropical Medicine
MPIA	Master of Public and International Affairs Master Program in International Affairs
MPM	Master of Pastoral Ministry Master of Pest Management Master of Policy Management Master of Practical Ministries Master of Project Management Master of Public Management
MPNA	Master of Public and Nonprofit Administration
MPOD	Master of Positive Organizational Development
MPP	Master of Public Policy
MPPA	Master of Public Policy Administration Master of Public Policy and Administration
MPPAL	Master of Public Policy, Administration and Law
MPPM	Master of Public and Private Management Master of Public Policy and Management
MPPPM	Master of Plant Protection and Pest Management
MPPUP	Master of Public Policy and Urban Planning
MPRTM	Master of Parks, Recreation, and Tourism Management
MPS	Master of Pastoral Studies Master of Perfusion Science Master of Planning Studies Master of Political Science Master of Preservation Studies Master of Professional Studies Master of Public Service
MPSA	Master of Public Service Administration
MPSRE	Master of Professional Studies in Real Estate
MPT	Master of Pastoral Theology Master of Physical Therapy
MPVM	Master of Preventive Veterinary Medicine
MPW	Master of Professional Writing Master of Public Works
MQF	Master of Quantitative Finance
MQM	Master of Quality Management
MQS	Master of Quality Systems
MR	Master of Recreation Master of Retailing
MRA	Master in Research Administration
MRC	Master of Rehabilitation Counseling
MRCP	Master of Regional and City Planning Master of Regional and Community Planning
MRD	Master of Rural Development
MRE	Master of Religious Education
MRED	Master of Real Estate Development
MREM	Master of Resource and Environmental Management
MRLS	Master of Resources Law Studies
MRM	Master of Resources Management
MRP	Master of Regional Planning

MRS	Master of Religious Studies
MRSc	Master of Rehabilitation Science
MS	Master of Science
MS Cmp E	Master of Science in Computer Engineering
MS Kin	Master of Science in Kinesiology
MS Acct	Master of Science in Accounting
MS Aero E	Master of Science in Aerospace Engineering
MS Ag	Master of Science in Agriculture
MS Arch	Master of Science in Architecture
MS Bio E	Master of Science in Bioengineering Master of Science in Biomedical Engineering
MS Bm E	Master of Science in Biomedical Engineering
MS Ch E	Master of Science in Chemical Engineering
MS Chem	Master of Science in Chemistry
MS Cp E	Master of Science in Computer Engineering
MS Eco	Master of Science in Economics
MS Econ	Master of Science in Economics
MS Ed	Master of Science in Education
MS El	Master of Science in Educational Leadership and Administration
MS En E	Master of Science in Environmental Engineering
MS Eng	Master of Science in Engineering
MS Engr	Master of Science in Engineering
MS Env E	Master of Science in Environmental Engineering
MS Exp Surg	Master of Science in Experimental Surgery
MS Int A	Master of Science in International Affairs
MS Mat E	Master of Science in Materials Engineering
MS Mat SE	Master of Science in Material Science and Engineering
MS Met E	Master of Science in Metallurgical Engineering
MS Metr	Master of Science in Meteorology
MS Mgt	Master of Science in Management
MS Min	Master of Science in Mining
MS Min E	Master of Science in Mining Engineering
MS Mt E	Master of Science in Materials Engineering
MS Otal	Master of Science in Otalrynology
MS Pet E	Master of Science in Petroleum Engineering
MS Phys	Master of Science in Physics
MS Phys Op	Master of Science in Physiological Optics
MS Poly	Master of Science in Polymers
MS Psy	Master of Science in Psychology
MS Pub P	Master of Science in Public Policy
MS Sc	Master of Science in Social Science
MS Sp Ed	Master of Science in Special Education
MS Stat	Master of Science in Statistics
MS Surg	Master of Science in Surgery
MS SwE	Master of Science in Software Engineering
MS Tax	Master of Science in Taxation
MS Tc E	Master of Science in Telecommunications Engineering
MS-R	Master of Science (Research)
MSA	Master of School Administration Master of Science Administration Master of Science in Accountancy Master of Science in Accounting Master of Science in Administration Master of Science in Aeronautics Master of Science in Agriculture Master of Science in Anesthesia Master of Science in Architecture Master of Science in Aviation Master of Sports Administration
MSA Phy	Master of Science in Applied Physics
MSAA	Master of Science in Astronautics and Aeronautics
MSAAE	Master of Science in Aeronautical and Astronautical Engineering
MSABE	Master of Science in Agricultural and Biological Engineering
MSAC	Master of Science in Acupuncture
MSACC	Master of Science in Accounting
MSaCS	Master of Science in Applied Computer Science
MSAE	Master of Science in Aeronautical Engineering Master of Science in Aerospace Engineering Master of Science in Applied Economics Master of Science in Architectural Engineering Master of Science in Art Education
MSAL	Master of Sport Administration and Leadership
MSAM	Master of Science in Applied Mathematics
MSANR	Master of Science in Agriculture and Natural Resources Systems Management
MSAPM	Master of Security Analysis and Portfolio Management
MSAS	Master of Science in Applied Statistics Master of Science in Architectural Studies
MSAT	Master of Science in Accounting and Taxation Master of Science in Advanced Technology Master of Science in Athletic Training
MSAUS	Master of Science in Architectural Urban Studies
MSB	Master of Science in Bible Master of Science in Business
MSBA	Master of Science in Business Administration
MSBAE	Master of Science in Biological and Agricultural Engineering Master of Science in Biosystems and Agricultural Engineering
MSBC	Master of Science in Building Construction
MSBE	Master of Science in Biological Engineering Master of Science in Biomedical Engineering Master of Science in Business Education
MSBENG	Master of Science in Bioengineering
MSBIT	Master of Science in Business Information Technology
MSBM	Master of Sport Business Management
MSBME	Master of Science in Biomedical Engineering
MSBMS	Master of Science in Basic Medical Science
MSBS	Master of Science in Biomedical Sciences
MSC	Master of Science in Commerce Master of Science in Communication Master of Science in Computers Master of Science in Counseling Master of Science in Criminology
MSCA	Master of Science in Construction Administration
MSCC	Master of Science in Christian Counseling Master of Science in Community Counseling
MSCD	Master of Science in Communication Disorders Master of Science in Community Development
MSCE	Master of Science in Civil Engineering Master of Science in Clinical Epidemiology Master of Science in Computer Engineering Master of Science in Continuing Education
MSCEE	Master of Science in Civil and Environmental Engineering
MSCF	Master of Science in Computational Finance
MSCH	Master of Science in Chemical Engineering
MSChE	Master of Science in Chemical Engineering
MSCI	Master of Science in Clinical Investigation Master of Science in Curriculum and Instruction
MSCIS	Master of Science in Computer and Information Systems Master of Science in Computer Information Science Master of Science in Computer Information Systems
MSCJ	Master of Science in Criminal Justice
MSCJA	Master of Science in Criminal Justice Administration
MSCJS	Master of Science in Crime and Justice Studies
MSCL	Master of Science in Collaborative Leadership
MSCLS	Master of Science in Clinical Laboratory Studies
MSCM	Master of Science in Conflict Management Master of Science in Construction Management
MScM	Master of Science in Management
MSCP	Master of Science in Clinical Psychology Master of Science in Computer Engineering Master of Science in Counseling Psychology
MSCPE	Master of Science in Computer Engineering
MSCPharm	Master of Science in Pharmacy
MSCPI	Master in Strategic Planning for Critical Infrastructures

MSCRP	Master of Science in City and Regional Planning Master of Science in Community and Regional Planning
MSCS	Master of Science in Clinical Science Master of Science in Computer Science
MSCSD	Master of Science in Communication Sciences and Disorders
MSCSE	Master of Science in Computer Science and Engineering
MSCST	Master of Science in Computer Science Technology
MSCTE	Master of Science in Career and Technical Education
MSD	Master of Science in Dentistry Master of Science in Design Master of Science in Dietetics
MSDD	Master of Software Design and Development
MSDM	Master of Design Methods
MSDR	Master of Dispute Resolution
MSE	Master of Science Education Master of Science in Economics Master of Science in Education Master of Science in Engineering Master of Science in Engineering Management Master of Software Engineering Master of Special Education Master of Structural Engineering
MSE Mgt	Master of Science in Engineering Management
MSECE	Master of Science in Electrical and Computer Engineering
MSED	Master of Sustainable Economic Development
MSEE	Master of Science in Electrical Engineering Master of Science in Environmental Engineering
MSEH	Master of Science in Environmental Health
MSEL	Master of Science in Educational Leadership Master of Science in Executive Leadership Master of Studies in Environmental Law
MSEM	Master of Science in Engineering Management Master of Science in Engineering Mechanics Master of Science in Environmental Management
MSENE	Master of Science in Environmental Engineering
MSEO	Master of Science in Electro-Optics
MSEP	Master of Science in Economic Policy Master of Science in Engineering Physics
MSEPA	Masters of Science in Economics and Policy Analysis
MSES	Master of Science in Embedded Software Engineering Master of Science in Engineering Science Master of Science in Environmental Science Master of Science in Environmental Studies
MSESM	Master of Science in Engineering Science and Mechanics
MSET	Master of Science in Education in Educational Technology Master of Science in Engineering Technology
MSETM	Master of Science in Environmental Technology Management
MSEV	Master of Science in Environmental Engineering
MSEVH	Master of Science in Environmental Health and Safety
MSF	Master of Science in Finance Master of Science in Forestry
MSFA	Master of Science in Financial Analysis
MSFAM	Master of Science in Family Studies
MSFCS	Master of Science in Family and Consumer Science
MSFE	Master of Science in Financial Engineering
MSFOR	Master of Science in Forestry
MSFP	Master of Science in Financial Planning
MSFS	Master of Science in Financial Sciences Master of Science in Forensic Science
MSFSB	Master of Science in Financial Services and Banking
MSFT	Master of Science in Family Therapy
MSGC	Master of Science in Genetic Counseling
MSGL	Master of Science in Global Leadership
MSH	Master of Science in Health Master of Science in Hospice
MSHA	Master of Science in Health Administration
MSHCA	Master of Science in Health Care Administration
MSHCI	Master of Science in Human Computer Interaction
MSHCPM	Master of Science in Health Care Policy and Management
MSHE	Master of Science in Health Education
MSHES	Master of Science in Human Environmental Sciences
MSHFID	Master of Science in Human Factors in Information Design
MSHFS	Master of Science in Human Factors and Systems
MSHP	Master of Science in Health Professions
MSHR	Master of Science in Human Resources
MSHRL	Master of Science in Human Resource Leadership
MSHRM	Master of Science in Human Resource Management
MSHS	Master of Science in Health Science Master of Science in Health Services Master of Science in Health Systems Master of Science in Homeland Security
MSHT	Master of Science in History of Technology
MSI	Master of Science in Instruction
MSIA	Master of Science in Industrial Administration Master of Science in Information Assurance and Computer Security Master of Science in Interior Architecture
MSIB	Master of Science in International Business
MSIDM	Master of Science in Interior Design and Merchandising
MSIDT	Master of Science in Information Design and Technology
MSIE	Master of Science in Industrial Engineering Master of Science in International Economics
MSIEM	Master of Science in Information Engineering and Management
MSIM	Master of Science in Information Management Master of Science in International Management Master of Science in Investment Management
MSIMC	Master of Science in Integrated Marketing Communications
MSIR	Master of Science in Industrial Relations
MSIS	Master of Science in Information Science Master of Science in Information Systems Master of Science in Interdisciplinary Studies
MSISE	Master of Science in Infrastructure Systems Engineering
MSISM	Master of Science in Information Systems Management
MSISPM	Master of Science in Information Security Policy and Management
MSIST	Master of Science in Information Systems Technology
MSIT	Master of Science in Industrial Technology Master of Science in Information Technology Master of Science in Instructional Technology
MSITM	Master of Science in Information Technology Management
MSJ	Master of Science in Journalism Master of Science in Jurisprudence
MSJE	Master of Science in Jewish Education
MSJFP	Master of Science in Juvenile Forensic Psychology
MSJJ	Master of Science in Juvenile Justice
MSJPS	Master of Science in Justice and Public Safety
MSJS	Master of Science in Jewish Studies
MSK	Master of Science in Kinesiology
MSKM	Master of Science in Knowledge Management
MSL	Master of School Leadership Master of Science in Limnology Master of Studies in Law
MSLA	Master of Science in Landscape Architecture Master of Science in Legal Administration
MSLD	Master of Science in Land Development
MSLS	Master of Science in Legal Studies Master of Science in Library Science
MSLT	Master of Second Language Teaching

MSM	Master of Sacred Ministry Master of Sacred Music Master of School Mathematics Master of Science in Management Master of Science in Organization Management Master of Security Management
MSM/MBAA	Master of Science in Management/Master of Business Administration in Aviation
MSMA	Master of Science in Marketing Analysis
MSMAE	Master of Science in Materials Engineering
MSMC	Master of Science in Mass Communications
MSME	Master of Science in Mathematics Education Master of Science in Mechanical Engineering
MSMFE	Master of Science in Manufacturing Engineering
MSMIS	Master of Science in Management Information Systems
MSMIT	Master of Science in Management and Information Technology
MSMM	Master of Science in Manufacturing Management
MSMO	Master of Science in Manufacturing Operations
MSMOT	Master of Science in Management of Technology
MSMS	Master of Science in Management Science Master of Science in Medical Sciences
MSMSE	Master of Science in Manufacturing Systems Engineering Master of Science in Material Science and Engineering Master of Science in Mathematics and Science Education
MSMT	Master of Science in Management and Technology Master of Science in Medical Technology
MSN	Master of Science in Nursing
MSN-R	Master of Science in Nursing (Research)
MSNA	Master of Science in Nurse Anesthesia
MSNE	Master of Science in Nuclear Engineering
MSNED	Master of Science in Nurse Education
MSNM	Master of Science in Nonprofit Management
MSNS	Master of Science in Natural Science Master's of Science in Nutritional Science
MSOD	Master of Science in Organizational Development
MSOEE	Master of Science in Outdoor and Environmental Education
MSOES	Master of Science in Occupational Ergonomics and Safety
MSOH	Master of Science in Occupational Health
MSOL	Master of Science in Organizational Leadership
MSOM	Master of Science in Operations Management Master of Science in Organization and Management Master of Science in Oriental Medicine
MSOR	Master of Science in Operations Research
MSOT	Master of Science in Occupational Technology Master of Science in Occupational Therapy
MSP	Master of Science in Pharmacy Master of Science in Planning Master of Science in Psychology Master of Speech Pathology
MSPA	Master of Science in Physician Assistant Master of Science in Professional Accountancy
MSPAS	Master of Science in Physician Assistant Studies
MSPC	Master of Science in Professional Communications Master of Science in Professional Counseling
MSPE	Master of Science in Petroleum Engineering
MSPG	Master of Science in Psychology
MSPH	Master of Science in Public Health
MSPHR	Master of Science in Pharmacy
MSPM	Master of Science in Professional Management Master of Science in Project Management
MSPNGE	Master of Science in Petroleum and Natural Gas Engineering
MSPS	Master of Science in Pharmaceutical Science Master of Science in Political Science Master of Science in Psychological Services
MSPT	Master of Science in Physical Therapy
MSpVM	Master of Specialized Veterinary Medicine
MSR	Master of Science in Radiology Master of Science in Reading
MSRA	Master of Science in Recreation Administration
MSRC	Master of Science in Resource Conservation
MSRE	Master of Science in Real Estate Master of Science in Religious Education
MSRED	Master of Science in Real Estate Development
MSRLS	Master of Science in Recreation and Leisure Studies
MSRMP	Master of Science in Radiological Medical Physics
MSRS	Master of Science in Rehabilitation Science
MSS	Master of Science in Software Master of Social Science Master of Social Services Master of Software Systems Master of Sports Science Master of Strategic Studies
MSSA	Master of Science in Social Administration
MSSCP	Master of Science in Science Content and Process
MSSE	Master of Science in Software Engineering Master of Science in Space Education Master of Science in Special Education
MSSEM	Master of Science in Systems and Engineering Management
MSSI	Master of Science in Security Informatics Master of Science in Strategic Intelligence
MSSL	Master of Science in Strategic Leadership
MSSLP	Master of Science in Speech-Language Pathology
MSSM	Master of Science in Sports Medicine
MSSPA	Master of Science in Student Personnel Administration
MSSS	Master of Science in Safety Science Master of Science in Systems Science
MSST	Master of Science in Security Technologies
MSSW	Master of Science in Social Work
MSSWE	Master of Science in Software Engineering
MST	Master of Science and Technology Master of Science in Taxation Master of Science in Teaching Master of Science in Technology Master of Science in Telecommunications Master of Science Teaching
MSTC	Master of Science in Technical Communication Master of Science in Telecommunications
MSTCM	Master of Science in Traditional Chinese Medicine
MSTE	Master of Science in Telecommunications Engineering Master of Science in Transportation Engineering
MSTM	Master of Science in Technical Management
MSTM/MBAA	Master of Science in Technical Management/Master of Business Administration in Aviation
MSTOM	Master of Science in Traditional Oriental Medicine
MSUD	Master of Science in Urban Design
MSUESM	Master of Science in Urban Environmental Systems Management
MSW	Master of Social Work
MSWE	Master of Software Engineering
MSWREE	Master of Science in Water Resources and Environmental Engineering
MSX	Master of Science in Exercise Science
MT	Master of Taxation Master of Teaching Master of Technology Master of Textiles
MTA	Master of Tax Accounting Master of Teaching Arts Master of Tourism Administration
MTCM	Master of Traditional Chinese Medicine
MTD	Master of Training and Development
MTE	Master in Educational Technology Master of Teacher Education
MTESOL	Master in Teaching English to Speakers of Other Languages
MTHM	Master of Tourism and Hospitality Management
MTI	Master of Information Technology
MTIM	Masters of Trust and Investment Management
MTL	Master of Talmudic Law
MTLM	Master of Transportation and Logistics Management
MTM	Master of Technology Management Master of Telecommunications Management Master of the Teaching of Mathematics

MTMH	Master of Tropical Medicine and Hygiene
MTOM	Master of Traditional Oriental Medicine
MTP	Master of Transpersonal Psychology
MTPC	Master of Technical and Professional Communication
MTS	Master of Theological Studies
MTSC	Master of Technical and Scientific Communication
MTSE	Master of Telecommunications and Software Engineering
MTT	Master in Technology Management
MTX	Master of Taxation
MUA	Master of Urban Affairs
MUD	Master of Urban Design
MUEP	Master of Urban and Environmental Planning
MUP	Master of Urban Planning
MUPDD	Master of Urban Planning, Design, and Development
MUPP	Master of Urban Planning and Policy
MUPRED	Masters of Urban Planning and Real Estate Development
MURP	Master of Urban and Regional Planning Master of Urban and Rural Planning
MUS	Master of Urban Studies
Mus Doc	Doctor of Music
Mus M	Master of Music
MVM	Master of VLSI and microelectronics
MVP	Master of Voice Pedagogy
MVPH	Master of Veterinary Public Health
MVS	Master of Visual Studies
MWC	Master of Wildlife Conservation
MWE	Master in Welding Engineering
MWPS	Master of Wood and Paper Science
MWR	Master of Water Resources
MWS	Master of Women's Studies
MZS	Master of Zoological Science
Nav Arch	Naval Architecture
Naval E	Naval Engineer
ND	Doctor of Naturopathic Medicine
NE	Nuclear Engineer
NP	Nurse Practitioner
Nuc E	Nuclear Engineer
OD	Doctor of Optometry
OTD	Doctor of Occupational Therapy
PBME	Professional Master of Biomedical Engineering
PD	Professional Diploma
PDD	Professional Development Degree
PGC	Post-Graduate Certificate
Ph L	Licentiate of Philosophy
Pharm D	Doctor of Pharmacy
PhD	Doctor of Philosophy
PhD Otal	Doctor of Philosophy in Otalrynology
Phd Surg	Doctor of Philosophy in Surgery
PhDEE	Doctor of Philosophy in Electrical Engineering
PM Sc	Professional Master of Science
PMBA	Professional Master of Business Administration
PMC	Post Master Certificate
PMD	Post-Master's Diploma
PMS	Professional Master of Science Professional Master's Degree
Post-Doctoral Certificate	Post-Doctoral Certificate
Post-Doctoral MS	Post-Doctoral Master of Science
PPDPT	Postprofessional Doctor of Physical Therapy
PSM	Professional Master of Science
Psy D	Doctor of Psychology
Psy M	Master of Psychology
Psy S	Specialist in Psychology
Psya D	Doctor of Psychoanalysis
Re Dir	Director of Recreation
Rh D	Doctor of Rehabilitation
S Psy S	Specialist in Psychological Services
Sc D	Doctor of Science
Sc M	Master of Science
SCCT	Specialist in Community College Teaching
ScDPT	Doctor of Physical Therapy Science
SD	Doctor of Science Specialist Degree
SJD	Doctor of Juridical Science Doctor of Juridical Science
SLPD	Doctor of Speech-Language Pathology
SLS	Specialist in Library Science
SM	Master of Science
SM Arch S	Master of Science in Architectural Studies
SM Vis S	Master of Science in Visual Studies
SMBT	Master of Science in Building Technology
SP	Specialist Degree
Sp C	Specialist in Counseling
Sp Ed	Specialist in Education
Sp LIS	Specialist in Library and Information Science
SPA	Specialist in Arts
SPCM	Special in Church Music
Spec	Specialist's Certificate
Spec M	Specialist in Music
SPEM	Special in Educational Ministries
SPS	School Psychology Specialist
Spt	Specialist Degree
SPTH	Special in Theology
SSP	Specialist in School Psychology
STB	Bachelor of Sacred Theology
STD	Doctor of Sacred Theology
STL	Licentiate of Sacred Theology
STM	Master of Sacred Theology
TDPT	Transitional Doctor of Physical Therapy
Th D	Doctor of Theology
Th M	Master of Theology
VMD	Doctor of Veterinary Medicine
WEMBA	Weekend Executive Master of Business Administration
XMA	Executive Master of Arts
XMBA	Executive Master of Business Administration

INDEXES

Profiles, Announcements, and Close-Ups

Directories and Subject Areas

Following is an alphabetical listing of directories and subject areas. Also listed are cross-references for subject area names not used in the directory structure of the guides, for example, "Arabic (*see* Near and Middle Eastern Languages)."

Graduate Programs in the Humanities, Arts & Social Sciences

Addictions/Substance Abuse Counseling
Administration (*see* Arts Administration; Public Administration)
African-American Studies
African Languages and Literatures (*see* African Studies)
African Studies
Agribusiness (*see* Agricultural Economics and Agribusiness)
Agricultural Economics and Agribusiness
Alcohol Abuse Counseling (*see* Addictions/Substance Abuse Counseling)
American Indian/Native American Studies
American Studies
Anthropology
Applied Arts and Design—General
Applied Economics
Applied History (*see* Public History)
Applied Social Research
Arabic (*see* Near and Middle Eastern Languages)
Arab Studies (*see* Near and Middle Eastern Studies)
Archaeology
Architectural History
Architecture
Archives Administration (*see* Public History)
Area and Cultural Studies (*see* African-American Studies; African Studies; American Indian/Native American Studies; American Studies; Asian-American Studies; Asian Studies; Canadian Studies; Cultural Studies; East European and Russian Studies; Ethnic Studies; Folklore; Gender Studies; Hispanic Studies; Holocaust Studies; Jewish Studies; Latin American Studies; Near and Middle Eastern Studies; Northern Studies; Pacific Area/Pacific Rim Studies; Western European Studies; Women's Studies)
Art/Fine Arts
Art History
Arts Administration
Arts Journalism
Art Therapy
Asian-American Studies
Asian Languages
Asian Studies
Behavioral Sciences (*see* Psychology)
Bible Studies (*see* Religion; Theology)
Biological Anthropology
Black Studies (*see* African-American Studies)
Broadcasting (*see* Communication; Film, Television, and Video Production)
Broadcast Journalism
Building Science
Canadian Studies
Celtic Languages
Ceramics (*see* Art/Fine Arts)
Child and Family Studies
Child Development
Chinese
Chinese Studies (*see* Asian Languages; Asian Studies)
Christian Studies (*see* Missions and Missiology; Religion; Theology)
Cinema (*see* Film, Television, and Video Production)
City and Regional Planning (*see* Urban and Regional Planning)
Classical Languages and Literatures (*see* Classics)
Classics
Clinical Psychology
Clothing and Textiles
Cognitive Psychology (*see* Psychology—General; Cognitive Sciences)
Cognitive Sciences
Communication—General
Community Affairs (*see* Urban and Regional Planning; Urban Studies)
Community Planning (*see* Architecture; Environmental Design; Urban and Regional Planning; Urban Design; Urban Studies)
Community Psychology (*see* Social Psychology)
Comparative and Interdisciplinary Arts
Comparative Literature
Composition (*see* Music)
Computer Art and Design
Conflict Resolution and Mediation/Peace Studies
Consumer Economics
Corporate and Organizational Communication
Corrections (*see* Criminal Justice and Criminology)
Counseling (*see* Counseling Psychology; Pastoral Ministry and Counseling)
Counseling Psychology
Crafts (*see* Art/Fine Arts)
Creative Arts Therapies (*see* Art Therapy; Therapies—Dance, Drama, and Music)
Criminal Justice and Criminology
Cultural Studies
Dance
Decorative Arts
Demography and Population Studies
Design (*see* Applied Arts and Design; Architecture; Art/Fine Arts; Environmental Design; Graphic Design; Industrial Design; Interior Design; Textile Design; Urban Design)
Developmental Psychology
Diplomacy (*see* International Affairs)
Disability Studies
Drama Therapy (*see* Therapies—Dance, Drama, and Music)
Dramatic Arts (*see* Theater)
Drawing (*see* Art/Fine Arts)
Drug Abuse Counseling (*see* Addictions/Substance Abuse Counseling)
Drug and Alcohol Abuse Counseling (*see* Addictions/Substance Abuse Counseling)
East Asian Studies (*see* Asian Studies)
East European and Russian Studies
Economic Development
Economics
Educational Theater (*see* Theater; Therapies—Dance, Drama, and Music)
Emergency Management
English
Environmental Design
Ethics
Ethnic Studies
Ethnomusicology (*see* Music)
Experimental Psychology
Family and Consumer Sciences—General
Family Studies (*see* Child and Family Studies)
Family Therapy (*see* Child and Family Studies; Clinical Psychology; Counseling Psychology; Marriage and Family Therapy)
Filmmaking (*see* Film, Television, and Video Production)
Film Studies (*see* Film, Television, and Video Production)
Film, Television, and Video Production
Film, Television, and Video Theory and Criticism
Fine Arts (*see* Art/Fine Arts)
Folklore
Foreign Languages (*see* specific language)
Foreign Service (*see* International Affairs; International Development)
Forensic Psychology
Forensic Sciences
Forensics (*see* Speech and Interpersonal Communication)
French
Gender Studies
General Studies (*see* Liberal Studies)
Genetic Counseling
Geographic Information Systems
Geography
German
Gerontology
Graphic Design

Greek (*see* Classics)
Health Communication
Health Psychology
Hebrew (*see* Near and Middle Eastern Languages)
Hebrew Studies (*see* Jewish Studies)
Hispanic Studies
Historic Preservation
History
History of Art (*see* Art History)
History of Medicine
History of Science and Technology
Holocaust Studies
Home Economics (*see* Family and Consumer Sciences—General)
Homeland Security
Household Economics, Sciences, and Management (*see* Family and Consumer Sciences—General)
Human Development
Humanities
Illustration
Industrial and Labor Relations
Industrial and Organizational Psychology
Industrial Design
Interdisciplinary Studies
Interior Design
International Affairs
International Development
International Economics
International Service (*see* International Affairs; International Development)
International Trade Policy
Internet and Interactive Multimedia
Interpersonal Communication (*see* Speech and Interpersonal Communication)
Interpretation (*see* Translation and Interpretation)
Islamic Studies (*see* Near and Middle Eastern Studies; Religion)
Italian
Japanese
Japanese Studies (*see* Asian Languages; Asian Studies; Japanese)
Jewelry (*see* Art/Fine Arts)
Jewish Studies
Journalism
Judaic Studies (*see* Jewish Studies; Religion)
Labor Relations (*see* Industrial and Labor Relations)
Landscape Architecture
Latin American Studies
Latin (*see* Classics)
Law Enforcement (*see* Criminal Justice and Criminology)
Liberal Studies
Lighting Design
Linguistics
Literature (*see* Classics; Comparative Literature; specific language)
Marriage and Family Therapy
Mass Communication
Media Studies
Medical Illustration
Medieval and Renaissance Studies
Metalsmithing (*see* Art/Fine Arts)
Middle Eastern Studies (*see* Near and Middle Eastern Studies)
Military and Defense Studies
Mineral Economics
Ministry (*see* Pastoral Ministry and Counseling; Theology)
Missions and Missiology
Motion Pictures (*see* Film, Television, and Video Production)
Museum Studies
Music
Musicology (*see* Music)
Music Therapy (*see* Therapies—Dance, Drama, and Music)
National Security
Native American Studies (*see* American Indian/Native American Studies)
Near and Middle Eastern Languages
Near and Middle Eastern Studies
Near Environment (*see* Family and Consumer Sciences)
Northern Studies
Organizational Psychology (*see* Industrial and Organizational Psychology)
Oriental Languages (*see* Asian Languages)
Oriental Studies (*see* Asian Studies)
Pacific Area/Pacific Rim Studies
Painting (*see* Art/Fine Arts)
Pastoral Ministry and Counseling
Philanthropic Studies
Philosophy
Photography
Playwriting (*see* Theater; Writing)
Policy Studies (*see* Public Policy)
Political Science
Population Studies (*see* Demography and Population Studies)
Portuguese
Printmaking (*see* Art/Fine Arts)
Product Design (*see* Industrial Design)
Psychoanalysis and Psychotherapy
Psychology—General
Public Administration
Public Affairs
Public History
Public Policy
Public Speaking (*see* Mass Communication; Rhetoric; Speech and Interpersonal Communication)
Publishing
Regional Planning (*see* Architecture; Urban and Regional Planning; Urban Design; Urban Studies)
Rehabilitation Counseling
Religion
Renaissance Studies (*see* Medieval and Renaissance Studies)
Rhetoric
Romance Languages
Romance Literatures (*see* Romance Languages)
Rural Planning and Studies
Rural Sociology
Russian
Scandinavian Languages
School Psychology
Sculpture (*see* Art/Fine Arts)
Security Administration (*see* Criminal Justice and Criminology)
Slavic Languages
Slavic Studies (*see* East European and Russian Studies; Slavic Languages)
Social Psychology
Social Sciences
Sociology
Southeast Asian Studies (*see* Asian Studies)
Soviet Studies (*see* East European and Russian Studies; Russian)
Spanish
Speech and Interpersonal Communication
Sport Psychology
Studio Art (*see* Art/Fine Arts)
Substance Abuse Counseling (*see* Addictions/Substance Abuse Counseling)
Survey Methodology
Sustainable Development
Technical Communication
Technical Writing
Telecommunications (*see* Film, Television, and Video Production)
Television (*see* Film, Television, and Video Production)
Textile Design
Textiles (*see* Clothing and Textiles; Textile Design)
Thanatology
Theater
Theater Arts (*see* Theater)
Theology
Therapies—Dance, Drama, and Music
Translation and Interpretation
Transpersonal and Humanistic Psychology
Urban and Regional Planning
Urban Design
Urban Planning (*see* Architecture; Urban and Regional Planning; Urban Design; Urban Studies)
Urban Studies
Video (*see* Film, Television, and Video Production)
Visual Arts (*see* Applied Arts and Design; Art/Fine Arts; Film, Television, and Video Production; Graphic Design; Illustration; Photography)
Western European Studies
Women's Studies
World Wide Web (*see* Internet and Interactive Multimedia)
Writing

Graduate Programs in the Biological Sciences

Anatomy
Animal Behavior
Bacteriology
Behavioral Sciences (*see* Biopsychology; Neuroscience; Zoology)
Biochemistry
Biological and Biomedical Sciences—General
Biological Chemistry (*see* Biochemistry)
Biological Oceanography (*see* Marine Biology)
Biophysics
Biopsychology
Botany
Breeding (*see* Botany; Plant Biology; Genetics)
Cancer Biology/Oncology
Cardiovascular Sciences
Cell Biology
Cellular Physiology (*see* Cell Biology; Physiology)
Computational Biology
Conservation (*see* Conservation Biology; Environmental Biology)
Conservation Biology
Crop Sciences (*see* Botany; Plant Biology)
Cytology (*see* Cell Biology)
Developmental Biology
Dietetics (*see* Nutrition)
Ecology
Embryology (*see* Developmental Biology)
Endocrinology (*see* Physiology)
Entomology
Environmental Biology
Evolutionary Biology
Foods (*see* Nutrition)
Genetics
Genomic Sciences
Histology (*see* Anatomy; Cell Biology)
Human Genetics
Immunology
Infectious Diseases
Laboratory Medicine (*see* Immunology; Microbiology; Pathology)
Life Sciences (*see* Biological and Biomedical Sciences)
Marine Biology
Medical Microbiology
Medical Sciences (*see* Biological and Biomedical Sciences)
Medical Science Training Programs (*see* Biological and Biomedical Sciences)
Microbiology
Molecular Biology
Molecular Biophysics
Molecular Genetics
Molecular Medicine
Molecular Pathogenesis
Molecular Pathology
Molecular Pharmacology
Molecular Physiology
Molecular Toxicology
Neural Sciences (*see* Biopsychology; Neurobiology; Neuroscience)
Neurobiology
Neuroendocrinology (*see* Biopsychology; Neurobiology; Neuroscience; Physiology)
Neuropharmacology (*see* Biopsychology; Neurobiology; Neuroscience; Pharmacology)
Neurophysiology (*see* Biopsychology; Neurobiology; Neuroscience; Physiology)
Neuroscience
Nutrition
Oncology (*see* Cancer Biology/Oncology)
Organismal Biology (*see* Biological and Biomedical Sciences; Zoology)
Parasitology
Pathobiology
Pathology
Pharmacology
Photobiology of Cells and Organelles (*see* Botany; Cell Biology; Plant Biology)
Physiological Optics (*see* Physiology)
Physiology
Plant Biology
Plant Molecular Biology
Plant Pathology
Plant Physiology
Pomology (*see* Botany; Plant Biology)
Psychobiology (*see* Biopsychology)
Psychopharmacology (*see* Biopsychology; Neuroscience; Pharmacology)
Radiation Biology
Reproductive Biology
Sociobiology (*see* Evolutionary Biology)
Structural Biology
Systems Biology
Teratology
Theoretical Biology (*see* Biological and Biomedical Sciences)
Therapeutics (*see* Pharmacology)
Toxicology
Translational Biology
Tropical Medicine (*see* Parasitology)
Virology
Wildlife Biology (*see* Zoology)
Zoology

Graduate Programs in the Physical Sciences, Mathematics, Agricultural Sciences, the Environment & Natural Resources

Acoustics
Agricultural Sciences
Agronomy and Soil Sciences
Analytical Chemistry
Animal Sciences
Applied Mathematics
Applied Physics
Applied Statistics
Aquaculture
Astronomy
Astrophysical Sciences (*see* Astrophysics; Atmospheric Sciences; Meteorology; Planetary and Space Sciences)
Astrophysics
Atmospheric Sciences
Biological Oceanography (*see* Marine Affairs; Marine Sciences; Oceanography)
Biomathematics
Biometry
Biostatistics
Chemical Physics
Chemistry
Computational Sciences
Condensed Matter Physics
Dairy Science (*see* Animal Sciences)
Earth Sciences (*see* Geosciences)
Environmental Management and Policy
Environmental Sciences
Environmental Studies (*see* Environmental Management and Policy)
Experimental Statistics (*see* Statistics)
Fish, Game, and Wildlife Management
Food Science and Technology
Forestry
General Science (*see* specific topics)
Geochemistry
Geodetic Sciences
Geological Engineering (*see* Geology)
Geological Sciences (*see* Geology)
Geology
Geophysical Fluid Dynamics (*see* Geophysics)
Geophysics
Geosciences
Horticulture
Hydrogeology
Hydrology
Inorganic Chemistry
Limnology
Marine Affairs
Marine Geology

Marine Sciences
Marine Studies (*see* Marine Affairs; Marine Geology; Marine Sciences; Oceanography)
Mathematical and Computational Finance
Mathematical Physics
Mathematical Statistics (*see* Applied Statistics; Statistics)
Mathematics
Meteorology
Mineralogy
Natural Resource Management (*see* Environmental Management and Policy; Natural Resources)
Natural Resources
Nuclear Physics (*see* Physics)
Ocean Engineering (*see* Marine Affairs; Marine Geology; Marine Sciences; Oceanography)
Oceanography
Optical Sciences
Optical Technologies (*see* Optical Sciences)
Optics (*see* Applied Physics; Optical Sciences; Physics)
Organic Chemistry
Paleontology
Paper Chemistry (*see* Chemistry)
Photonics
Physical Chemistry
Physics
Planetary and Space Sciences
Plant Sciences
Plasma Physics
Poultry Science (*see* Animal Sciences)
Radiological Physics (*see* Physics)
Range Management (*see* Range Science)
Range Science
Resource Management (*see* Environmental Management and Policy; Natural Resources)
Solid-Earth Sciences (*see* Geosciences)
Space Sciences (*see* Planetary and Space Sciences)
Statistics
Theoretical Chemistry
Theoretical Physics
Viticulture and Enology
Water Resources

Graduate Programs in Engineering & Applied Sciences

Aeronautical Engineering (*see* Aerospace/Aeronautical Engineering)
Aerospace/Aeronautical Engineering
Aerospace Studies (*see* Aerospace/Aeronautical Engineering)
Agricultural Engineering
Applied Mechanics (*see* Mechanics)
Applied Science and Technology
Architectural Engineering
Artificial Intelligence/Robotics
Astronautical Engineering (*see* Aerospace/Aeronautical Engineering)
Automotive Engineering
Aviation
Biochemical Engineering
Bioengineering
Bioinformatics
Biological Engineering (*see* Bioengineering)
Biomedical Engineering
Biosystems Engineering
Biotechnology
Ceramic Engineering (*see* Ceramic Sciences and Engineering)
Ceramic Sciences and Engineering
Ceramics (*see* Ceramic Sciences and Engineering)
Chemical Engineering
Civil Engineering
Computer and Information Systems Security
Computer Engineering
Computer Science
Computing Technology (*see* Computer Science)
Construction Engineering
Construction Management
Database Systems
Electrical Engineering
Electronic Materials
Electronics Engineering (*see* Electrical Engineering)
Energy and Power Engineering
Energy Management and Policy
Engineering and Applied Sciences
Engineering and Public Affairs (*see* Technology and Public Policy)
Engineering and Public Policy (*see* Energy Management and Policy; Technology and Public Policy)
Engineering Design
Engineering Management
Engineering Mechanics (*see* Mechanics)
Engineering Metallurgy (*see* Metallurgical Engineering and Metallurgy)
Engineering Physics
Environmental Design (*see* Environmental Engineering)
Environmental Engineering
Ergonomics and Human Factors
Financial Engineering
Fire Protection Engineering
Food Engineering (*see* Agricultural Engineering)
Gas Engineering (*see* Petroleum Engineering)
Geological Engineering
Geophysics Engineering (*see* Geological Engineering)
Geotechnical Engineering
Hazardous Materials Management
Health Informatics
Health Systems (*see* Safety Engineering; Systems Engineering)
Highway Engineering (*see* Transportation and Highway Engineering)
Human-Computer Interaction
Human Factors (*see* Ergonomics and Human Factors)
Hydraulics
Hydrology (*see* Water Resources Engineering)
Industrial Engineering (*see* Industrial/Management Engineering)
Industrial/Management Engineering
Information Science
Internet Engineering
Macromolecular Science (*see* Polymer Science and Engineering)
Management Engineering (*see* Engineering Management; Industrial/Management Engineering)
Management of Technology
Manufacturing Engineering
Marine Engineering (*see* Civil Engineering)
Materials Engineering
Materials Sciences
Mechanical Engineering
Mechanics
Medical Informatics
Metallurgical Engineering and Metallurgy
Metallurgy (*see* Metallurgical Engineering and Metallurgy)
Mineral/Mining Engineering
Nanotechnology
Nuclear Engineering
Ocean Engineering
Operations Research
Paper and Pulp Engineering
Petroleum Engineering
Pharmaceutical Engineering
Plastics Engineering (*see* Polymer Science and Engineering)
Polymer Science and Engineering
Public Policy (*see* Energy Management and Policy; Technology and Public Policy)
Reliability Engineering
Robotics (*see* Artificial Intelligence/Robotics)
Safety Engineering
Software Engineering
Solid-State Sciences (*see* Materials Sciences)
Structural Engineering
Surveying Science and Engineering
Systems Analysis (*see* Systems Engineering)
Systems Engineering
Systems Science
Technology and Public Policy
Telecommunications
Telecommunications Management
Textile Sciences and Engineering
Textiles (*see* Textile Sciences and Engineering)
Transportation and Highway Engineering
Urban Systems Engineering (*see* Systems Engineering)

Graduate Programs in Business, Education, Health, Information Studies, Law & Social Work